THE COLLEGE BOARD

College handbook

2007

THE COLLEGE BOARD

College handbook 2007

Forty-Fourth Edition

The College Board, New York

The College Board: Connecting Students to College Success

The College Board is a not-for-profit membership association whose mission is to connect students to college success and opportunity. Founded in 1900, the association is composed of more than 5,000 schools, colleges, universities, and other educational organizations. Each year, the College Board serves seven million students and their parents, 23,000 high schools, and 3,500 colleges through major programs and services in college admissions, guidance, assessment, financial aid, enrollment, and teaching and learning. Among its best-known programs are the SAT®, the PSAT/NMSQT®, and the Advanced Placement Program® (AP®). The College Board is committed to the principles of excellence and equity, and that commitment is embodied in all of its programs, services, activities, and concerns.

Visit the College Board on the Web: www.collegeboard.com.

Editorial inquiries concerning this book should be directed to College Planning Services, College Board, 45 Columbus Avenue, New York, NY 10023-6992; or telephone 212 713-8000.

Copies of this book are available from your local bookseller or may be ordered from College Board Publications, P.O. Box 869010, Plano, TX 75074-0998. The book may also be ordered online through the College Board Store at www.collegeboard.com. The price is $28.95.

Library of Congress Catalog Number: 41-12971

ISBN-13: 978-0-87447-764-1

ISBN-10: 0-87447-764-6

Printed in the United States of America

Contents

Dear Friends,

The College Board is dedicated to connecting students to college success and opportunity. We believe in the principles of excellence and equity in education and try to promote them in all that we do. With the College Board's Handbook series, we hope to put an authoritative source of college information at your fingertips to help connect you to a college education.

College is a dream worth working hard to achieve. I've been a businessman, a governor, and now the president of the College Board, but nothing makes me prouder than to say that I am a college graduate. With perseverance, anyone who desires a college education can attain one. College Board publications can help you get there.

My best wishes on your journey to success.

Gaston Caperton

Gaston Caperton
President
The College Board

Preface

When the *College Board College Handbook* first appeared in 1941, students and parents had little access to college information of any kind. Now, in this Internet age, many find the amount of available information to be overwhelming.

What's needed is a single, trusted source where the key facts about colleges can be compared and contrasted on a consistent basis. From its inception, the *Handbook* has met this need by providing college-bound students and their advisers with the authoritative, reliable, and up-to-date facts necessary to make informed college decisions.

This edition of the *Handbook* presents facts about 3,805 colleges, universities, and technical schools. To be included, an institution must be accredited by a national or regional accrediting association recognized by the U.S. Department of Education and offer some undergraduate degree programs—at least an associate degree.

Throughout the *Handbook*, information is presented in accordance with the Common Data Set initiative, in which the College Board has taken a leading role. The goal of this collaborative effort with other publishers and college administrators is to provide students with the most accurate, consistently comparable data available.

The college descriptions are based on information supplied by the colleges themselves in response to the College Board's Annual Survey of Colleges 2006-07. The survey was completed by participating colleges in the spring of 2006. Several thousand college administrators across the country participated in this effort. Without their continued cooperation, publication of the *Handbook* would not be possible.

A staff of data editors verified the facts to be certain that all descriptions are as complete and accurate as possible. Although the College Board makes every effort to ensure that the information about colleges is correct and up to date, we urge students to confirm facts with the colleges themselves.

The enormous task of data collection, management, and verification was directed by Shauna Morrison, Stan Bernstein, and Cathy Serico with the assistance of Andrew Costello, Renee Gernand, Roger Harris, and Ralph Hockens. Marci Arnold, Mary Anne Blazier, Leah Bledsoe, Doris Chow, Nicole D'Isa, Katrina Kingdon, Lesley McBain, Diana McDermott, and Randy Peery compiled, edited, and verified the data. The Web-based survey tool they used was programmed and maintained by Mike Starinieri, Xuhe Wang, Robert Hargrove, Brenda Levathes, Chuck Johnson, June Ni, and Eugene Xiang.

We thank our readers—you and the millions of students, parents, and counselors whose comments and suggestions over the years have helped to make this the most widely used college directory in the nation. We welcome your suggestions on how the *Handbook* can continue to meet the ever-changing needs of future generations of college-bound students.

Tom Vanderberg
Senior Editor, Guidance Publications
College Planning Services

How to use this book

If you're beginning your college search feeling a bit overwhelmed and intimidated by the sheer number of choices, you're not alone. Just about everyone starts out feeling that way. But even the most daunting job can be easily handled with the right tools and a plan, and the *College Board College Handbook* gives you both.

The *Handbook* is the best place to begin your college search, and you will no doubt find yourself returning to this source as your search progresses and evolves. You should not, however, rely on this book exclusively. Take advantage of the other resources available to you—the Internet, campus visits and interviews, college fairs and viewbooks, your school counselor, family and friends—before you make your final decision. Don't be dismayed if you find that you must change directions more than once as you learn about the colleges. This only means that you are learning more about yourself as well.

Getting started

The *Handbook* is divided into four major sections. The first (where you are now) contains guidance materials to help you plan for college. Four-year college descriptions are in the second section, two-year college descriptions are in the third, and the last section contains tables and indexes. Margin tabs help you to quickly move from section to section.

Although you might be eager to dive right into the college descriptions, it is far better to start your college search with a basic idea of what you want to look for. Take the time to go through the guidance materials in the first section to get on the right track. Read the articles, ranging from college admissions and placement tests to dorm life. The valuable insights you gain will give you confidence as you continue your college search.

Once you can identify your needs and preferences with regard to college size and type and have an idea of what other characteristics are important to you, the indexes at the end of the book will help you locate colleges that fit the bill. For a complete explanation of the various index categories, see "Understanding the college indexes" beginning on page 6.

The heart and soul of the *Handbook*, of course, are the descriptions of four-year and two-year colleges. These follow standard formats to make it easy to find a particular item of information in any description and to compare one college with another. Read "What's in the college descriptions" below to see what the descriptions contain and how the information is presented.

If you are not sure of the meaning of a term found in the *Handbook* descriptions or guidance materials, check the glossary beginning on page 29.

Searching online for colleges

The College Board's Web-based College Search (www.collegeboard.com/collegesearch) is a powerful, fast, and easy tool for creating your list of colleges to investigate. The intuitive interface helps you find colleges that match your requirements, do side-by-side comparisons, and find additional colleges that may also fit the bill. You can also go directly to any college's Web site. With the *College Handbook* as your companion desk reference, you can quickly cut your college search down to size.

What's in the college descriptions

The information in the college descriptions was supplied by the colleges themselves, in response to the College Board's *Annual Survey of Colleges* 2006-07. Every effort was made by the College Board's team of editors to ensure that the information contained herein is completely accurate and up to date, but please be aware that some information may have changed after publication.

Brief descriptions

The 387 colleges that did not return the survey are described in brief with the following information: name, city, state, college type, accreditation, location, and calendar. Annual costs and financial aid information are provided, if available. The addresses to contact for further information are also listed.

Full descriptions

The college. Each description begins with the college's official name—which isn't always the one in popular use. The heading also includes the college's city, state, and Web site address. Most colleges now have Web sites that are invaluable resources in your college search. The designation "CB member" after the college's name indicates that the college is a member of the College Board; the four-digit CB code should be used when requesting that SAT® or Advanced Placement Program® (AP®) scores be sent to the college.

Key facts. The bulleted list highlights information that you may want to compare across colleges and that you'll need if you decide to apply. This information includes:

- Type of institution (e.g., liberal arts college, university) and whether it has a religious affiliation.
- Campus setting and whether it is primarily a residential or a commuter campus.
- Total number of undergraduate students; profile of the undergraduate student body (percent part-time, women, minority breakdown, international); total number of graduate students on campus. *Two-year undergraduate data are included under Student Profile.*
- Percent of applicants admitted to the freshman class, which gives you some idea of how competitive the college is. *Four-year colleges only.*
- Admissions requirements for fall 2007: tests, essay, interview (if required of all applicants).
- Percent of students who graduate within six years (most students take more than four years to earn a bachelor's degree). Caveat: This figure is based on students who enrolled as freshmen and remained to graduate; it does not include students who transferred into or out of the college during that period.

General information. The date the college was founded; what type of institutional accreditation it has; the number and type of degrees awarded in 2004-05, and whether the college has an ROTC program will give you a sense of the academic life on campus. Whether the college organizes its calendar on a semester, trimester, quarter, or some other schedule indicates the way the college structures its courses.

Pay particular attention to the faculty information. The total number of faculty and its makeup are important to your everyday experience at an institution. Class size information, showing percentages of classes with few or many students, is another indication of a college's learning environment. Colleges were also invited to provide a list of special facilities (from arboretums to zoos) or additional unique information about their institution in this section.

For two-year colleges only: This is where you will find total enrollment figures for both degree-seeking and non-degree-seeking students, and information about partnerships with other schools or organizations.

Freshman class profile. (*Four-year colleges*) This provides a snapshot of the college's 2005 freshman class and is presented in tabular format to make it easily accessible. This is the best source of information about whether your own profile fits in with that of students currently attending the college, and whether you'd be comfortable if admitted.

- Number who applied, were admitted, and enrolled.
- Mid-50 percent of enrolled freshmen's SAT/ACT test scores. This is the score range for half the freshman class. (Remember that 25 percent of enrolled freshmen scored below and 25 percent above the reported figures.)
- Information about high school GPA and class rank.
- Percentage who completed the year in good standing and returned as sophomores.
- Percentage who come from out of state, live on campus, are international students, and join fraternities or sororities.

Comparing scores from the SAT

If you took the SAT after March 2005, you won't be able to compare your score on the writing section to last year's freshman class in the college descriptions. You will, however, be able to compare your critical reading score to their verbal score and your math score to theirs. (Although the types of questions used on both of those sections have changed, the difference isn't so great that you can't compare the scores.)

Student profile. (*Two-year colleges*) This is similar to the freshman class profile for four-year colleges, but the data presented covers the entire undergraduate student body.

- Percentage enrolled in transfer or vocational programs. Number admitted and enrolled as first-time, first-year students. Percentage who already have a bachelor's degree or higher. Number who transferred from other institutions.
- Percentage of the total undergraduate student body who are part-time students, live on campus, are women, come from out of state, are minorities, and are international students.

Transfer out. (*Two-year colleges*)

- Percentage of students in transfer programs who go on to four-year colleges.
- Colleges to which most students transferred in 2005.

Basis for selection. This is where you can find the details of a college's admissions policies, including factors the college considers most important in deciding whether or not to offer you admission. Entrance exam policies for returning adult students and special requirements for homeschooled and learning disabled students are also reported here.

High school preparation. Almost all colleges listed in the *Handbook* require a high school diploma or its equivalent. Some colleges have very specific requirements in terms of education background and high school courses taken. The required and recommended number of course units that applicants should have taken in high school is listed here. Where a range is given, the lower number represents the required units; the higher number is a recommendation.

2006–2007 annual costs. You should estimate and anticipate the *total* annual costs for each college you are considering. In doing so, the elements listed below need to be considered. Unless otherwise noted, the reported figures reflect the costs for the 2006-07 academic year.

- *Tuition/fees* include the cost of instruction and mandated fees for all students. For public colleges, both in-state and out-of-state costs are listed. If the college combines tuition, fees, and room and board expenses, that single figure is given as a comprehensive fee.
- *Room/board* figures are for a student living on campus in a double room with a full meal plan. Single rooms or rooms for three or more could cost a lot more or less than the figure reported here. Many colleges have a range of meal plans with fewer meals per week, which would lower your board cost.
- *Books/supplies* expenses can vary depending on the program you take. Some fields, such as art or architecture, may require more expensive supplies.
- *Personal expenses* include items such as clothing, laundry, entertainment, and furnishings. Personal expenses will vary widely depending on your lifestyle. Transportation costs are not included.
- *Per-credit-hour tuition* (*two-year colleges only*) is of particular interest to students planning to attend college part-time.

Financial aid. This information provides a summary of financial aid awarded for the academic year(s) indicated, and describes financial aid award policies for need-based and non-need-based aid. This information will give you an idea of how first-year and undergraduate student assistance has been awarded and will help you compare financial aid policies among the colleges. You should always contact the admissions or financial aid office for complete information and for answers to any questions you might have regarding eligibility and award policies.

Application procedures. This is where you can find out about the college's application procedures and deadlines for both admissions and financial aid.

- *Admissions.* Most colleges require an application fee, noted here, but will waive it for applicants with need. This section also tells you whether or not the college subscribes to the Common Application and if there are other application requirements.
- *Financial aid.* Required forms plus priority, closing, notification, and reply dates are listed for fall term financial aid applications. The Free Application for Federal Student Aid (FAFSA) is required by every college offering federal financial aid. If the college requires the CSS/Financial Aid PROFILE® to determine your eligibility for nonfederal funds, it is noted here. Pay special attention to priority application dates or application deadlines; if the college indicates

"no deadline" for financial aid, it means they will continue to process requests as long as funds are available. You should always apply as early as possible to obtain the best consideration for financial aid awards.

Academics. Many colleges offer a range of special study options that can enrich or enhance your education experience. Special academic programs are listed in this section. Check the Glossary for brief descriptions of each of the programs listed.

College policies on granting credit or advanced standing through the College Board's Advanced Placement Program and College-Level Examination Program® (CLEP®), the International Baccalaureate (IB) program, and/or institutional tests are listed next. Most colleges have a maximum number of credit hours by examination that may be counted toward a degree, which is also listed.

Academic support services list the programs the college provides to assist students in succeeding academically. Preadmission summer programs, special counselors, tutoring, learning disabled programs, and study skills assistance are some of the options offered.

Honors college/program. If a college has a separate undergraduate honors college or a program with different admissions and academic offerings from those available to regular students, this section will tell you what's available and how to apply.

Majors. Only majors leading to a bachelor's degree (for four-year colleges) or an associate degree (for two-year colleges) are included here. They are listed alphabetically by general category. The majors listed here are based on the U.S. Department of Education's Classification of Instructional Programs 2000; colleges were asked to match the majors they offer to this list. Many colleges additionally offer concentrations within a major, which are not reflected here.

Most popular majors. This will give you an idea of whether a substantial number of students are completing a major in an area that is of interest to you. This list is based on the percentage of students who were awarded degrees in each of the general categories listed in the 2004-05 academic year.

Computing on campus. Whether you bring your own computer to campus, or plan on using college-provided workstations, you'll want to know what technological support the college provides for student use, and whether the college requires you to bring your own PC or laptop. This section lists the number of workstations available for student use and where they're located; whether dorms are wired for high-speed Internet access and/or linked to the campus network; if there is a wireless network; if there's online course registration, an online library, or student Web hosting; and whether commuter students can link to the campus network.

Student life. If you attend the college, you will need to know if it requires enrollees to attend freshman orientation, and if it has policies and regulations governing student behavior.

If on-campus housing is available—whether it's in the form of dormitories, apartments, fraternity/sorority housing, or cooperative housing—it will be indicated here. Most dormitories today are coeducational, but many colleges offer single-sex accommodations either in separate buildings or separate floors. Some colleges are now also offering "substance-free" or "wellness" dormitories, whose residents pledge not to use alcohol, tobacco, or any illegal drugs. Finally, you'll want to know whether the college guarantees the availability of on-campus housing for freshmen, or for all four years of study.

Colleges have also provided a selective list of student activities sponsored by the institution. Read the list carefully to see if it reflects the type of student organizations and opportunities of interest to you.

Athletics. Intercollegiate and intramural sports available at the college are listed here, along with the team name. Sports offered for men or women only are indicated by (M) or (W). The athletic association to which the college belongs also is indicated. If you're interested in NCAA division offerings, the indexes starting on page 2083 show, sport by sport, the division level a college offers.

Student services. This section lists the college's basic range of services for students. Among these are health, personal counseling, services for adult students, student employment services, placement service for graduates, veterans' counseling, and on-campus day care. This section also lists special services/facilities for learning disabled students and those with visual, speech, or hearing impairments.

Contact. The last item in each description provides the admissions office's e-mail address, telephone and fax numbers, the name and/or title of the admissions director, and the mailing address of the college office to contact for further information and applications.

Understanding the college indexes

In most of the indexes, colleges are listed alphabetically by state because, for many students, geographic location is a primary requirement. Colleges that are part of a system are listed alphabetically under the system name.

The following explanation of index terms may help you decide whether a certain type of college or a special program or policy interests you.

College type

Liberal arts. Sometimes known as arts and sciences. The study of liberal arts is intended to develop general knowledge and reasoning ability as opposed to specific preparation for a career. Most liberal arts colleges are privately controlled. They generally don't offer as many majors in the technical or scientific disciplines as comprehensive colleges or universities.

Upper-division. Offer the last two years of undergraduate study (junior and senior courses only), usually in specialized programs leading to the bachelor's degree. Students generally transfer to upper-division colleges after completing an associate degree or after finishing their second year of study at a four-year college.

Specialized. Concentrate their offerings in one or two specific areas, such as business or engineering. Students who enroll at specialized colleges generally have a precise idea of what they want to study.

Special characteristics

Colleges for men/women. Some of these colleges may enroll a few women or men, but their student bodies are predominantly of one sex.

Colleges with religious affiliations. Lists each college under the official name of the denomination with which it is affiliated. Student life at some colleges is greatly influenced by the religious affiliation. At other colleges, the affiliation may be historic only, having little influence on college life.

Historically black colleges. Identifies historically or predominantly black colleges that are committed to educating African American students. The information was obtained from the National Association for Equal Opportunity in Higher Education and the U.S. government.

Hispanic-serving colleges. Identifies colleges where Hispanic students comprise at least 25 percent of the total full-time undergraduate enrollment. The information was obtained from the Hispanic Association of Colleges and Universities (HACU).

Tribal colleges. Identifies colleges committed to serving geographically isolated populations of Native Americans. The information was obtained from the Carnegie Classification of Institutions of Higher Education.

Undergraduate enrollment size

The number of students at a college helps determine its environment.

Very small. Fewer than 750 undergraduates.

Small. 750 to 1,999 undergraduates.

Medium to large. 2,000 to 7,499 undergraduates.

Large. 7,500 to 14,999 undergraduates.

Very large. 15,000 or more undergraduates.

Admission selectivity

Admit over 75 percent, 50–75 percent, under 50 percent. Colleges in three categories of selectivity that limit admission to applicants who meet specific requirements.

Open admissions. Colleges that admit virtually all applicants with a high school diploma or its equivalent, as long as space is available.

Many public institutions offer open admissions to state residents but have selective admissions requirements for out-of-state students or to selected programs.

Admissions/placement policies

No closing date. These colleges will accept applications up to the time of registration.

SAT Subject Test required/recommended. These two indexes list colleges that require or recommend that applicants take one or more SAT Subject Tests™ for admission. The college descriptions provide more detailed information.

Colleges that offer ROTC

The U.S. armed forces offer Reserve Officer's Training Corps programs that prepare candidates for commissions in the Air Force, Army, and Navy (Naval ROTC includes the Marine Corps). These programs are offered either at the colleges listed in the index or at cooperating institutions. ROTC programs may take either two or four years to complete. Use this index, organized by branch of service, to find colleges that offer the ROTC program of interest to you.

NCAA sports

Lists National Collegiate Athletic Association (NCAA) sports by division level and the colleges, state by state, that offer them. Also indicates whether each sport is available for men only or for women only. (Crew is an NCAA sport for women only; use the college search on collegeboard.com to find colleges that offer crew for men.) To be an NCAA member, colleges must offer at least four sports and have at least one in each season (fall, winter, and spring).

Alphabetical index of colleges

Lists the name and state abbreviation for every institution in the *Handbook*. If a name has changed, the old name is cross-referenced to the new name.

About accreditation

Every college and university in this book is accredited by an agency recognized by the U.S. Department of Education. That means you can trust that any of them will give you an education that meets basic standards for college-level study, that your studies will qualify for federal need-based financial aid and/or federal education tax breaks, and that the degree you will earn at the end of your studies will be recognized by future employers.

What is accreditation?

Accreditation is a voluntary process of peer review and self-regulation. The standards for each accrediting agency are slightly different but, generally, each agency ensures that its members meet basic standards in their administrative procedures, physical facilities, and the quality of their academic programs.

The agencies listed on the next page are *regional* and *national* agencies that accredit entire institutions. In majors that lead to a professional certification—such as nursing, engineering, or teacher education—there may also be *specialized* agencies that accredit just one program, department, or school at the college. For example, the Accreditation Board for Engineering and Technology (ABET) accredits engineering and engineering technology programs. In addition to guaranteeing the academic quality of programs, these specialized agencies often have a guidance component that helps university students make the transition to professional careers. You can find more information about specialized accrediting agencies in the *College Board Book of Majors*, or at the Council for Higher Education Accreditation's Web site (www.chea.org).

What does accreditation mean to me?

If you attend an accredited college, you can be sure that:

- You will be able to use federal student aid (Title IV money) to help pay for your costs, if you qualify based on financial need.
- Your tuition will qualify for federal income tax deductions and/or credits (if you meet other conditions).
- Academic credits you earn there are eligible to transfer to another accredited college.
- Employers and professional licensing boards will recognize the degree you earn as an academic credential, as will graduate schools and other academic institutions you may apply to.

You should, however, understand what accreditation **doesn't** mean:

- There's no guarantee that you will receive federal need-based financial aid just by attending any college, even if it's accredited.
- Regional and national accreditation ensures that every academic program at the college meets standards, but that doesn't mean that the qualities of every program at the college are equal.
- If you're applying for transfer from one undergraduate institution to another, there's no guarantee that all your credits will count toward the graduation requirements of the college where you plan to finish your degree. If you plan to attend a lower-division college for your first two years of study and then go on to earn a bachelor's degree, be sure to talk to the transfer counselor there before enrolling in courses.
- Similarly, there's no guarantee that graduate schools or employers will see your undergraduate course of study as appropriate preparation for the demands of their program or job requirements.

Regional Accrediting Associations

Middle States Commission on Higher Education
3624 Market Street
Philadelphia, Pennsylvania 19104-2680
www.msche.org

Delaware, District of Columbia, Maryland, New Jersey, New York, Pennsylvania, Puerto Rico, Virgin Islands

New England Association of Schools and Colleges
209 Burlington Road
Bedford, Massachusetts 01730-1433
www.neasc.org

Connecticut, Maine, Massachusetts, New Hampshire, Rhode Island, Vermont

North Central Association of Colleges and Schools
30 North LaSalle Street, Suite 2400
Chicago, Illinois 60602-2504
www.ncacihe.org

Arizona, Arkansas, Colorado, Illinois, Indiana, Iowa, Kansas, Michigan, Minnesota, Missouri, Nebraska, New Mexico, North Dakota, Ohio, Oklahoma, South Dakota, West Virginia, Wisconsin, Wyoming

Northwest Association of Schools and Colleges
8060 165th Avenue NE, Suite 100
Redmond, Washington 98052-3891
www.nwccu.org

Alaska, Idaho, Montana, Nevada, Oregon, Utah, Washington

Southern Association of Colleges and Schools
1866 Southern Lane
Decatur, Georgia 30033-4097
www.sacs.org

Alabama, Florida, Georgia, Kentucky, Louisiana, Mississippi, North Carolina, South Carolina, Tennessee, Texas, Virginia

Western Association of Schools and Colleges
Accrediting Commission for Senior Colleges and Universities
985 Atlantic Avenue, Suite 100
Alameda, California 94501
www.wascweb.org

Accrediting Commission for Community and Junior Colleges
10 Commercial Boulevard
Novato, California 94949
www.accjc.org

American Samoa, California, Guam, Hawaii, Trust Territory of the Pacific

New York Board of Regents
Office of College and University Evaluation
New York State Education Department
Room 110EB
Albany, New York 12234
www.regents.nysed.gov

National Accrediting Associations

ACICS — **Accrediting Council for Independent Colleges and Schools**
750 First Street NE, Suite 980
Washington, D.C. 20002-4241
www.acics.org

ACCSCT — **Accrediting Commission for Career Schools/Colleges of Technology**
2101 Wilson Boulevard, Suite 302
Arlington, Virginia 22201
www.accsct.org

ABHE — **Association for Biblical Higher Education**
5575 S. Semoran Boulevard, Suite 26
Orlando, Florida 32822-1781
www.abhe.org

AARTS — **Association of Advanced Rabbinical and Talmudic Schools**
11 Broadway
New York, New York 10004

ATS — **Association of Theological Schools in the United States and Canada**
10 Summit Park Drive
Pittsburgh, Pennsylvania 15275-1103
www.ats.edu

DETC — **Distance Education and Training Council**
601 18th Street NW
Washington, D.C. 20009
www.detc.org

Selecting a college

There are more than 3,800 accredited colleges in the United States, and each of them is unique in some way. However, they fall into some broad categories—small and large, liberal arts and professionally oriented, academically selective and open admissions. There are also personal criteria you need to consider, such as whether a college is in your hometown or a thousand miles away. You should use this book and other resources at your disposal to get an idea of the types of institutions you're interested in attending and learn more about colleges that fall into those categories. From there, you can create a list of colleges you would like to learn more about, and start requesting information from them, visiting their Web sites, and (if you can) visiting their campuses.

After you've done that, you should narrow your list to colleges to which you plan on applying. This final "short list" may have a dozen colleges, or only one—it all depends on what you want. The application process is explained in detail starting on page 22, but this chapter will help you determine which schools are a "sure bet" for acceptance (often called "safety" schools), which ones will be competitive, and which will be a "reach" for you.

Finding your fit

Everybody has different interests, ambitions, and circumstances. When investigating colleges, you will probably look for different things than your friends, parents, and siblings did when they applied. But there are some "big picture" elements that everyone, including you, should consider.

Type of institution

This will give you a sense of how the college organizes its academic departments. Different types of institutions include:

- **Liberal arts colleges** offer a broad base of courses in the humanities, social sciences, and natural sciences. Most are private and focus mainly on undergraduate students. Classes tend to be small, and personal attention is available. An education at a liberal arts college will prepare you for a broad range of career and graduate school options.
- **Community and junior colleges** offer a degree after the completion of two years of full-time study. They frequently offer technical programs that prepare you for immediate entry into the job market. To learn more about the benefits of attending community college, read "The college next door" on page 14.
- **Agricultural colleges, technical schools, and professional institutes** emphasize preparation for specific careers. Examples include art institutes and music conservatories, Bible colleges, business colleges, schools of health science, seminaries and rabbinical yeshivas, and teacher's colleges.
- **Universities** are generally bigger than colleges and offer more majors and research facilities. Class size often reflects institutional size, and some classes may be taught by graduate students.

  Most universities are subdivided into colleges or schools. For example, a state university might have a large college of liberal arts, a school of engineering and applied sciences, a small school of nursing, a teachers college, and several graduate schools all on the same campus. Different universities have different rules for whether you can, for example, take a computer science course offered by the engineering school while enrolled in the liberal arts college.

Size of the student body and faculty

Size will affect many of your opportunities and experiences, including:

- the range of academic majors offered;
- the possibilities for extracurricular activities and athletics;
- the amount of personal attention you'll receive from faculty, administrators, and other students; and

- the availability and size of academic facilities such as laboratories, libraries, and art studios.

When considering size, be sure to look beyond the raw number of students attending. For example, perhaps you're considering a large university, but you'll be applying to its much smaller school of health sciences.

Also remember to investigate not just the number of faculty, but also how accessible faculty members are to students. You can get a rough sense of this from the "class size" entry in the *Handbook* descriptions, but if you are already interested in a particular major or department, it really helps to visit the campus and talk to students who are enrolled in that program.

Location

Do you want to go home frequently, or do you see this as a time to experience a new part of the country? Perhaps you like an urban environment with access to museums, ethnic food, or major league ball games. Or maybe you hope for easy access to the outdoors or the serenity of a small town.

Academic programs

If you know what you want to study, research the reputations of academic departments by talking to people in the fields that interest you. If you're undecided, relax, pick an academically balanced institution that offers a range of majors and programs, and take courses in subjects you find intriguing. Most colleges offer advising or mentoring to help you find a focus.

Retention and graduation rates

One of the best ways to measure a school's quality and the satisfaction of its students is to learn the percentage of students who return after the first year and the percentage of entering students who remain to graduate. Comparatively good retention and graduation rates are indicators that responsible academic, social, and financial support systems exist for most students. These figures are reported in the *Handbook* descriptions.

Campus life

Consider what your college life will be like beyond the classroom. Aim for a balance between academics, activities, and social life. In your research, try to learn the answers to these questions:

- What extracurricular activities, athletics, and special activities are available?
- Does the community around the college offer interesting outlets for students?
- Are students welcomed by the surrounding community?
- Is there a congregation of my faith on campus? Are there student groups based around my ethnic group or national culture?
- Is the college religiously affiliated? If so, how does that affiliation affect student life—for example, is attendance at services required?
- How do fraternities and sororities influence campus life?
- Is housing guaranteed? How are dorms assigned? (For more about housing options, see page 27.)

Can I afford this college?

Today's college price tags make cost an important consideration for most students. At the same time, most colleges work to ensure that academically qualified students from every economic circumstance can find financial aid. Be sure to look beyond the price tag in considering cost. The *Handbook* descriptions give you a general idea of the college's cost and its financial aid packages. For more detailed "cost profiles" of the colleges, and for general advice about financial aid, see the *College Board Guide to Getting Financial Aid*, which is a companion volume to this book.

Where can I get in?

Of course, finding a college that's the right fit for you is only half of the equation. Unless you're applying to a college with an open admissions policy, you also have to convince the admissions reviewers that you really are a good fit.

What are colleges looking for?

When they review your application, college admissions officers want to see, foremost, "students who have challenged themselves academically," says Martha Pitts, the director of admissions at the University of Oregon. But they don't just want to see good grades; they also want to make sure that candidates will add something positive to the campus community. Mike Sexton, the dean of admissions at Lewis & Clark College, puts it this way: He looks at the applications for "a spark that tells us they'll be good roommates, good lab partners, good to have in class."

One thing you should never do is try to guess what the admissions committee is looking for and try to tailor your application to it. "If students try to force themselves to look like a fit, that's like putting square pegs in round holes—they will be unhappy," says Deren Finks, former dean of admission and financial aid at Harvey Mudd College. Admissions officers read thousands of applications every year, and they can almost instantly tell feigned interest in a college or a false presentation of oneself from the real thing.

The transcript is the most important thing

There it is, in large type, but it bears repeating: Your high school transcript is the most important thing for your application success. Colleges want to see that you've challenged yourself academically throughout high school and that you are willing to put academics first for the next two to four years. But be aware that admissions staff won't just look at "the numbers" on your transcript. "The first thing most colleges and universities will consider will be the high school courses a student chose," says Mary Ellen Anderson, the director of admissions at Indiana University–Bloomington. "Are they challenging? Are they college-prep, honors, or AP courses?"

Anderson adds, "We look at the grade trend over four years." For example, if you barely passed Intro to Biology as a freshman, but then turned around and got a B in AP Biology as a junior, colleges will consider that a plus. On the other hand, if you've been getting steady C's in English for the last three years, colleges may wonder why you haven't improved.

A related factor that admissions officers look for is an upward trend in the difficulty of your course work. Sexton says he becomes concerned when students "start taking a lighter load senior year. I can see why they would do it sometimes, but for some people, it's going to close doors." Don't feel you need to suffocate yourself with too many courses and extracurriculars, but don't try to cruise through your senior year, either.

You can use the college descriptions in this *Handbook* to find out what courses a school requires you to have taken, and what they recommend beyond that requirement. This is your best indication of whether you can get in: Do you have the lab science courses and foreign language study

Where to find more information

Once you've created a list of colleges you'd like to learn more about, you should try to get information from as many sources as possible. Different people will tell you different things about colleges, so the more the merrier!

- **Your school counselor** can tell you about colleges and let you know when college fairs or visits from admissions recruiters are coming to your school. He or she may also have a file of college course catalogs, viewbooks, and other literature.
- **Visiting admissions staff** who come to your school—either by themselves or as part of a large college fair—can tell you more about the college they represent and its application process.
- **College Web sites and guidebooks** offer a wealth of information about majors offered, activities, and life on campus.
- **Returning graduates** who went to your school and come home for breaks will probably be eager to tell you all about their experiences.
- **Campus visits** are a chance to see the campus and its dorms, libraries, and other facilities in person; talk to admissions officers (whether informally or in an interview); observe classes and talk to students; and much more. Try to visit the campus while classes are in session. For tips on planning a visit, read the articles in the "Find a College" section of www.collegeboard.com, or get *Campus Visits & College Interviews* by Zola Dincin Schneider (College Board, 2002).

they require? Have you settled for the required minimum of history and social sciences, or have you taken their full recommendation? You can also learn about the high school GPAs of last year's entering class, and how those students were ranked in their high school.

Test scores are just part of the picture

Your scores on the SAT or the ACT can be important but, generally, they're not as important as your high school transcript. Most often, admissions officers will use your test scores to supplement your transcript or help them interpret it.

Although grades earned in high school courses are very important, they don't always mean the same thing. An A earned in the same course taught by different teachers in your school may not represent exactly the same amount of work, the same teaching, or the same level of learning. Likewise, an A earned in the same course but in different schools and different parts of the country may not really be the same. That's where standardized tests can help.

If you've already taken the SAT or ACT, look at your scores the same way the admissions committee will look at them—objectively. They don't represent all that you've achieved or will achieve. The scores are one indicator of how far along you are right now in developing the skills you need for college and a career. In deciding where to apply to college, it's helpful to compare your scores to those of the mid-50 percent score range of freshmen who enrolled the previous year in the colleges you're considering. You'll find this information in the section titled "freshman class profile" of each four-year college description. If your scores compare favorably, you're on your way to finding the right *match*. But if your scores are higher or lower, it's not necessarily a *mismatch*. Only 50 out of every 100 freshmen had scores in that range, which means 25 had higher scores and 25 had lower scores. You may be well suited for this college in other important ways. You'll be better able to decide after reading the entire college description, visiting the college's Web site, and completing the worksheets in this book.

The college next door

Money in your pocket, close-to-home convenience, a fast track to a career, a chance to build a better academic record, a faculty focused on you—these are some of the advantages of choosing a community or junior college.

Most community colleges deliver two kinds of learning:

- First, applied learning (in fields like physical therapy or computer technology) that can put you in the job market in *two years or less.*
- Second, the first two years of a four-year college program (in areas like business, engineering, or liberal studies), for about *half-price—or less.*

Those two kinds of learning happen in many ways. For example, some students start with training that leads to a job; later, once they're out of school and earning, many return to college for more credits. Others earn a liberal studies degree—equivalent to the first two years of work in a four-year college—then transfer to a four-year college.

Why start a four-year degree in a two-year college?

For one thing, there's the price tag. In most states, tuition at a community college is less than half that at a four-year public college, and just over 10 percent of the cost at a four-year private college. On top of that, families who have very low incomes can receive aid at a community college, and other families can use federal income tax credits to defray the cost of community tuition and fees.

Does a bargain tuition get you a bargain-basement education? Definitely not. Both teaching quality and student results at two-year colleges are top-notch.

Teaching quality: Chances are, a community college will offer fairly small classes and faculty who are focused on teaching. "Our faculty is expected to help students learn," says Bill Wenrich, the chancellor emeritus of the Dallas County Community College District. "That's the only thing they are paid to do."

Income and career results: Researchers from the University of Illinois at Chicago and Penn State compared college grads from similar backgrounds who began college in two-year and in four-year institutions. On average, the two groups ended up with similar salaries, in careers that offered similar job prestige, stability, and satisfaction.

Would a community college fit me?

Consider:

- Do you want to live at home? There's probably a community college close by.
- Do you have a strong academic background (decent grades, solid high school courses)? Keep yourself challenged: Look for a two-year college with an honors program designed for students who'll transfer to a four-year institution.
- Did your high school grades slip? At a community college, you can work to build an all-new academic record that will put you into the four-year university you want.
- Is English your second language? Community colleges have special programs that will help you build your English skills.
- Do you have family or work obligations? Community college administrators love to brag about ways their colleges fit the complex lives of their students, offering classes at night, on weekends—even on the Web.
- Are you ready for college? A community college can offer what you might have missed in high school—missing skills, or missing credits such as the math preparation a four-year college requires. It can help overcome the disadvantages of a not-so-challenging high school education.

Karla Gastelum, of Nogales, Arizona, was a pretty typical community college student. She chose Pima Community College because "it was less intimidating, and cheaper" than a big university. Later she transferred to Arizona State and then returned to Pima to pick up one last course before graduating. "Pima was a good transition," Karla says. "It took away all the anxiety of being away from home for the first time. Pima offered a lot more individual attention. There a class may be 30 to 40 students at most—[instead of] lecture classes of 160 or more."

Your experience at a community college is likely to be different from—not necessarily better or worse than, but different from—a four-year college experience. Example: At four-year colleges, freshmen are often 18 years old. In a community college, you'll probably study with people of all ages (the average community college student is 29).

Bill Wenrich, the Dallas-area chancellor emeritus, says, "Our students are complex. There are a lot of single parents. Probably 75 percent are employed. An amazing number of international students come to community colleges. And we have close to 50 percent ethnic diversity." These students bring a whole different outlook to class.

Interested in a community college?

When looking at community colleges, do your research just as if you were choosing a four-year college. After all, no two community colleges are exactly alike. To find one that fits you, consider its academic programs, campus life, diversity, and mission—and, of course, its transfer arrangements. Read the college's catalog, look at its Web site, and talk to its admissions officers. Make sure the college is accredited: All the colleges described in the two-year colleges section of this *Handbook* are. And do visit the campus.

If you choose a two-year college, you'll be in good company. Community college grads include generals and judges, poets and pilots, astronauts and even actors (Tom Hanks, Jim Belushi, Annette Bening). Two-year colleges gave them all a great start. How about you?

Victoria L. Chapman
Producer, *College Times* magazine

Taking college admissions and placement tests

In your junior or senior year of high school, you will probably have to take either the SAT or ACT to satisfy the admissions requirements at the colleges you are considering. This chapter will help you understand the difference between those tests, and give you advice on how to prepare and register for the test once you've chosen between the two.

You may also want to take college-level exams in specific subjects in order to strengthen your application portfolio, place out of introductory college courses, get college credit for your high school work, or all three. At the end of this chapter, you'll find an introduction to the two most widely recognized college credit-by-exam programs.

Which test should I take: SAT or ACT?

The two widely used college admissions tests are the SAT and ACT. Many colleges accept either one, but some require one or the other, so it's essential to check on the policy at the colleges you're considering.

You may find that you have to take both the SAT and ACT if you plan to apply to several colleges with different admissions policies. Some colleges also require one or more SAT Subject Tests in addition to, or instead of, the SAT Reasoning Test™. Finally, if you take the ACT, be sure to find out whether colleges require you to take the optional writing test. It may sound confusing, but don't worry: These requirements are all spelled out in the *Handbook* descriptions for each college.

When you know which test(s) to take, you'll find a schedule of registration and administration dates on page 18. Your school counselor can tell you where the SAT and/or the ACT will be administered close to your home and school. You can also find SAT information and preparation tools at www.collegeboard.com/sat.

What are SAT Subject Tests™?

SAT Subject Tests are one-hour exams offered in 20 subjects that measure your achievement in foreign languages, mathematics, sciences, history, and literature.

If your grades in college-preparatory courses are good, you may want to take one or several of these tests to demonstrate the content mastery you've achieved. The best time to take a Subject Test is after you have completed all the course(s) in that subject. A number of colleges use SAT Subject Test scores for various purposes:

- **Admission:** Some colleges require Subject Tests for admission for all students. Others require them only for certain applicants, such as students who were homeschooled in high school. If they do, their *Handbook* descriptions will indicate this in the bulleted list of key facts and in the "Basis for selection" section.
- **Placement in honors programs:** A college might require Subject Tests for placement in an honors college or other special program.
- **Scholarship awards:** Merit scholarships may be awarded partly on the basis of Subject Test scores. Information about each college's merit scholarships and their requirements is included in the *College Board Guide to Getting Financial Aid 2007*.
- **Advanced placement:** Some colleges will allow you to skip introductory courses if your Subject Test score is sufficient.

For help preparing for your test(s), visit the SAT Subject Tests Learning Center on www.collegeboard.com, or get the *The Official Study Guide for all SAT Subject Tests™*, which is available in bookstores and libraries everywhere.

How do the SAT and ACT differ?

The SAT Reasoning Test measures verbal reasoning, critical thinking, math problem solving, and your ability to construct a reasoned, written argument. It tells you how well you use the skills and knowledge you have attained so far, including what you've learned both in and out of school. It gives you information about yourself that is more far-reaching than tests that only measure knowledge you've acquired in specific subjects.

The ACT is an achievement test—that is, it measures what you have learned in your English, science, social studies, and mathematics classes. This is useful information for you and for colleges, but the test may not give you information about yourself that you don't already know from your high school test scores.

You may prefer one admissions test over the other, but the deciding factor is, of course, which one the college requires. If you've taken one test and a college you're applying to requires the other, register for that test as soon as possible. If you find you've missed the deadline, contact the college to ask if they will either accept your scores for the test you've taken, or accept scores for the test they require after the application deadline.

Taking the test

Once you've decided which test to take, you should register for an upcoming administration and do your best to prepare for it. A calendar of SAT and ACT administrations in 2006-07, with the registration deadlines, appears on page 18.

When should I take the test?

Many students decide that the end of their junior year is a logical point at which to take a college admissions test for the first time. By then, you've been studying English, math, science, social studies, and other courses for more than 11 years! You've been reading, studying, and taking tests regularly during that time. And if you took the PSAT/NMSQT® in October of your junior year, your memory will be fresh from the experience.

How to register

The best way to register is online. It's fast and easy, and it helps you avoid late fees or missed postmark deadlines. You can even register for next year's tests over the summer. SAT registration may be completed at www.collegeboard.com and ACT registration at www.actstudent.org.

To register for the SAT by mail, complete the paper registration form included in the *SAT Registration Bulletin* and send it with your test fee payment. You can get a *Registration Bulletin* in your school's guidance office. Registration deadlines are about four weeks before the test date. There are also late-registration deadlines, and it's possible to register on a standby basis. Both of these involve an additional fee.

Test-prep tips

The best way to prepare for a college admissions test is to take as many challenging courses as you can, study hard in all of them, and read as much general literature as you can outside of class. But it also helps to be familiar with the test you will take. Here are some tips on how to do that.

- **Take the PSAT/NMSQT** in the fall of your junior year. Not only are the questions very similar to those on the SAT, but taking the test also qualifies you for the National Merit Scholarship Competition. The Score Report your counselor will give you after you take the test will point out areas where you should drill and practice to improve before taking the SAT.
- **Get the *SAT Preparation Booklet*™** or *Preparing for the ACT* for free from your school's guidance office, or go online to www.collegeboard.com or www.actstudent.org to download your own copy.
- **Familiarize yourself with all aspects of the test,** including:
  - Directions for taking the test.
  - All question types.
  - Information on how the test is scored—will your score go down if you answer a question wrong, or are you free to guess with no penalty?

2006–2007 SAT Program Test Calendar

Test Dates	**Oct. 14***	**Nov. 4**	**Dec. 2**	**Jan. 27***	**Mar. 10**	**May 5**	**June 2**
Registration Deadlines							
Regular	Sept. 12	Sept. 29	Nov. 1	Dec. 20	Feb. 2	Mar. 29	Apr. 27
Late	Sept. 20	Oct. 11	Nov. 9	Jan. 4	Feb. 14	Apr. 11	May 9
SAT Reasoning Test	■	■	■	■	■	■	■
SAT Subject Tests							
Literature	■	■	■	■		■	■
United States (U.S.) History	■	■	■	■		■	■
World History			■				■
Mathematics Level 1†	■	■	■	■		■	■
Mathematics Level 2†	■	■	■	■		■	■
Biology E/M (Ecological/Molecular)	■	■	■	■		■	■
Chemistry	■	■	■	■		■	■
Physics	■	■	■	■		■	■
Languages: Reading Only							
French	■		■	■		■	■
German							■
Modern Hebrew							■
Italian			■				
Latin			■				■
Spanish	■		■	■		■	■
Languages: Reading and Listening							
Chinese		■					
French		■					
German		■					
Japanese		■					
Korean		■					
Spanish		■					

* Question and Answer Service available.
†Calculator required
NOTE: Sunday test dates follow each Saturday test date for students who cannot test on Saturday because of a religious observance. The October Sunday test date is October 22, to avoid conflict with the Jewish holiday Simchat Torah.

SERVICES FOR STUDENTS WITH DISABILITIES

Students may receive accommodations (extended time, large print, etc.) on College Board exams if they submit an eligibility form and meet the eligibility requirements. **Students must: 1)** have a disability that requires testing accommodations; **2)** have documentation on file that supports the need for accommodations; and **3)** receive and use the requested accommodations for school-based tests. (See program material regarding the Guidelines for Documentation, and for exceptions to the above requirements.)

Contacts (all College Board programs):

Voice	609 771-7137
TTY	609 882-4118
Fax	609 771-7944
E-mail	sat.ssd@ets.org

2006–2007 ACT Assessment Registration Calendar

Test Dates	**9/16***	**10/28**	**12/9**	**2/10****	**4/14**	**6/9**
Registration Deadlines						
Regular	8/18*	9/22	11/3	1/5**	3/9	5/4
Late	8/25*	9/23	11/16	1/19**	3/23	5/18

*Available only in: AZ, CA, FL, GA, IL, IN, MD, NV, NC, PA, SC, TX, and WA
**Not available in NY

- **Take a full-length practice test** that uses official questions (the College Board and ACT preparation booklets each provide one). Take it under real conditions—in one sitting, in a quiet place, and without having looked through the questions first.
- **If you want** to take additional practice tests or drill for a certain type of question, you don't need to break the bank.
  - The College Board publishes *The Official SAT Study Guide*™, which is available in bookstores and libraries everywhere.
  - The College Board also offers The Official SAT Online Course™ through its Web site. (The book you're reading gives you a $10 discount on a four-month subscription to the course. See the inside back cover for details.)
  - ACT also offers several paid test-prep resources, which it lists on its Web site.
- **Remember** that your test scores aren't going to be the most important thing in your life, or even on your college application. Don't study for an admissions test at the expense of your high school course work.

Should I take an admissions test more than once?

Many students who take a college admissions test the second time improve their scores. If you take a test over and over again, your scores may fluctuate—slightly up one time, down the next, and eventually clustering around the point that represents your "true score."

If you take an admissions test in the spring of your junior year and earn a score that satisfies the requirements at colleges that interest you, you may not need to take the test again. But you may find that you want to reach beyond the requirements for various reasons: to qualify for a scholarship or honors program, perhaps, or just to make your application more competitive.

If you do decide to take an admissions test a second time, here are some tips:

- If you take an admissions test in the spring of your junior year and want to try to improve your scores, take it again in the early fall. The experience of having already taken the test may help to improve your performance the second time.
- If you take the SAT in October, January, or May, you can order the Question and Answer Service. This report gives you a copy of your SAT test, the test booklet, your answers and the correct answers, scoring instructions, and information about the questions. Reviewing this information carefully could help you improve your score the next time you take the test.
- Don't worry if your score fluctuates downward the second time you take the test. Many colleges only look at your best score when reviewing your application.

Earning college credit by examination

Most colleges allow you to place out of introductory courses in subject areas where you have already done college-level work, either in high school or through your own life experiences. For example, you might be able to skip the first year of college Spanish and go straight to intermediate-level courses. In order to demonstrate your knowledge, the college usually requires you to either take a nationally offered standardized test, such as an AP Examination or a CLEP exam, or to take an exam offered by the college on campus. (You often have a choice of doing either—that is, if you haven't taken the AP Spanish Language Exam, you can take the college's Spanish placement test as an alternative.)

If you take an AP or CLEP exam, many colleges also allow you to earn credit based on your exam score. To use the same example as above, you wouldn't just place into second-year Spanish; you would also earn credits toward graduation as if you had taken first-year Spanish there on campus. If you have qualifying scores on enough exams, some colleges will even grant you "sophomore standing," meaning you are treated as a sophomore for academic purposes such as when you get to register for courses. (You still have to obey the college's other rules for freshmen, though, so don't expect to be given a single dorm room and a parking permit just because you have sophomore standing through AP.)

More about the Advanced Placement Program® (AP®)

The AP Program offers a wide range of college-level courses that are taught in high schools by high school teachers; a national exam is given for each subject every year in May. AP courses give you a chance to do college-level work while still in high school. Research studies have shown that students with AP experience succeed in college at a rate significantly higher than the average student.

In all, there are 37 courses and exams offered in 22 subject areas. Even if an AP course is not offered at your school, you can still take the exam if you make arrangements with your school's AP Coordinator (usually a school counselor or a teacher). If your school doesn't offer AP at all, or you are homeschooled, you can still make arrangements to take an AP Exam at a nearby school that offers AP.

Many colleges grant credit or advanced placement to incoming freshmen who have qualifying scores on AP Exams. Some even grant sophomore standing if you've earned qualifying grades on a requisite number of exams. You can find out specific AP policies for each exam at every college at www.collegeboard.com/ap/creditpolicy.

AP courses can be a lot of work—after all, you're doing college-level work in high school! But they can also be very rewarding. If you're not sure whether you should take an AP course, talk to your teachers, your school counselor, and your parents. You might also want to obtain a copy of the College Board publication *The Value of AP* or the bilingual booklet *Get with the Program/Avanza con el Programa*. Your school should be able to order copies of these for you and your parents to read.

More About the College-Level Examination Program® (CLEP®)

CLEP, as the program is familiarly known, is the most widely accepted college credit-by-examination program in the country. Approximately 2,900 accredited colleges and universities award credit for qualifying scores on CLEP exams.

Unlike AP Exams, CLEP exams do not correspond to courses that you take in high school. Rather, CLEP offers 33 exams in the areas of business, English composition and literature, foreign languages, history and social studies, and science and mathematics. You can take a CLEP exam at any time during your college career. You can learn about specific CLEP policies for each exam at every college using the College Search on www.collegeboard.com.

AP Course Calendar

Spring before starting an AP course	Well ahead of time, you need to start thinking about what AP courses you might want to take. Discuss your plans with your parents, teachers, and school counselor.
Summer	Some AP teachers require you to complete work (like reading) during the summer months to prepare for their course. For example, for AP English you may be given a reading list. Make sure you complete these assignments so that you're up to speed when the class begins.
January	Talk to your AP teachers and/or AP Coordinator about taking the exams. Contact the disabilities (SSD) coordinator at your school if you will need testing accommodations.
March	Deadlines for homeschooled students and students whose schools do not offer AP to arrange for testing at a nearby school. Deadlines for students with disabilities to show eligibility for testing accommodations.
May 7–11 and May 14–18, 2006	Exam dates.
May 23–25, 2006	Late-testing dates.
June 15, 2006	Deadline for receipt of requests for grade withholding, grade cancellation, or a change in a college grade report recipient.
Early–Mid July	AP Grade Reports released to designated colleges, and to students and their high schools.

All CLEP examinations are administered on the computer. The computer-based CLEP provides you with instant score reports, so you know that day if you will be awarded credit for your performance. To get used to the format of the computer-based test, visit www.collegeboard.com/clep and download the CLEP Sampler. The Sampler gives you a tutorial for taking CLEP on the computer as well as test-taking tips, examination information, and more. Study guides for individual CLEP exams are also available for downloading through collegeboard.com.

Applying to colleges

After you've gone through some exploration and preliminary research, it's time to sit down and apply! In order to successfully apply, you'll need to budget and manage your time, follow each college's instructions to a tee and, most important, take a good hard look at yourself and your interests.

Managing your time

Most applications for regular admissions deadlines are due in early January or February, and most early application deadlines are in November or December. (To learn more about Early Decision plans, see the article "Should I apply early?" by Susan Biemeret on page 25.) For any application, you'll need to fill out forms and request that your transcript and standardized test scores be sent to the college. For most applications to selective colleges, you'll also need to ask teachers and your counselor for recommendations, write an essay or personal statement, and maybe even schedule an interview with the admissions office. You may also want to take the SAT or ACT that semester, or take some SAT Subject Tests in November or December. Meanwhile, you'll be in the middle of your senior year, with academic, extracurricular, and social commitments all over your calendar.

The first thing you should do once you decide which colleges you're applying to is make a checklist, showing the application deadlines and all the tasks you'll have to accomplish for the applications. Then you should fill in the dates by which you need to complete those tasks. Remember to budget time for other people to do things. Teachers won't write recommendations overnight, and testing organizations will need a few weeks to send official score reports to colleges.

For some sample checklists and a college application calendar, read the articles in the "Applying to College" section of www.collegeboard.com. If you like, you can also sign up for a free account and use the MyOrganizer feature of the site, which will help you plan and remind you of upcoming deadlines.

Filling out the application

In addition to the traditional typed or handwritten application, many schools today accept online applications (if they do, it will say so in their *Handbook* description). You may also be able to fill out the Common Application and send it to several schools—though you should be aware that some Common Application subscribers also require a supplementary form of their own.

A typical application will ask you to provide some personal information; a list of schools you have attended; brief descriptions of your extracurricular activities, jobs, and any academic honors you have earned; and standardized test scores. They will also ask for information about your family and their education background, which they may use to determine whether you merit special consideration as a first-generation college student or a "legacy" applicant. Finally, most applications give you the option of affiliating yourself with a race or ethnic group. If you choose to do so, they may take that into consideration when reviewing your application, but however you answer won't hurt your chances of admission.

Finally, all applications will ask whether and when you plan to file for financial aid. Checking this box does not mean you have applied for financial aid! It just lets the admissions office know that they should coordinate with the financial aid office later on. For more information on financial aid and how to apply for it, read the articles in the "Pay for College" section of www.collegeboard.com, or get the *College Board Guide to Getting Financial Aid 2007*.

Besides the application form, there are several things that need to be included with your application. You will have to send some of them with the form; others will be sent to the college by other people.

Application fee

The average college application fee is around $25. (Some colleges charge up to $60, while others don't have an application fee at all.) The fee is usually nonrefundable, even if you're not offered admission. Many colleges offer fee waivers for applicants from low-income families. If you need a fee waiver, call the college's admissions office for more information.

High school transcript

This form is filled out by an official of your high school. If it comes with your admissions materials, you should give it to the guidance office to complete as early as possible. Some colleges send this form directly to your school after receiving your application.

Admissions test scores

If you need to submit standardized test scores, you must make sure the testing agency itself sends an official score report. Writing your scores on your application or sending a photocopy of your own personal score report will not suffice. When you take the SAT or the ACT, you are entitled to four official score reports, which are sent to the colleges you choose. This service is included in the fee you pay to take either test.

Letters of recommendation

Some colleges ask you to submit one or more letters of recommendation from a teacher, counselor, or other adult who knows you well. Usually the person writing the letter will send it directly to the college, though sometimes your school counselor will assemble the letters and send them with your transcript.

Essays short and long

If you're applying to selective colleges, your essay often plays a very important role. Whether you're writing an autobiographical statement or an essay on a specific theme, take the opportunity to express your individuality in a way that sets you apart from other applicants.

Some applications will ask you to attach a separate essay of one or two pages, others will ask you to fill in some one-paragraph short responses directly on the application form, and others will ask for both. Whichever type of question you're answering, give it some thought; draft, revise, and edit your response before putting it with the application; and be sure to type or (if you must) print legibly. (The "fun" fonts that came with your word processor are usually not legible.)

In many cases, you'll be able to reuse the same essay for several college applications (and maybe even use it for a scholarship application or two as well). If you do this, be sure that the essay you want to use really does answer the question on each application, and that you change any references to the college from application to application.

How to ask for recommendations

The key to getting a great recommendation is to be a great student. But showing good manners helps.

- Typically, you know your teachers well enough to know who can provide a favorable review of your accomplishments. That said, Mary Lee Hoganson, a counselor at Homewood-Flossmoor High School in Flossmoor, Illinois, says you should "be sure to ask in a way that allows a teacher to decline comfortably if he or she does not have time to do an adequate job. For example: 'Do you feel you know me well enough, and do you have enough time to write a supportive letter of recommendation?'"
- Respect the time constraints of those you're asking for this favor. Hoganson says that "teachers should always receive a minimum of two weeks' notice, prior to the postmark date."
- Provide teachers and counselors with a deadline for each recommendation that you are requesting, especially noting the earliest deadline.
- Offer them a "brag sheet" or résumé reminding them of your accomplishments over the years. They might know your work in their classes very well, but they might not remember that you were also responsible for organizing the school talent show your junior year.
- Include addressed and stamped envelopes for each school to which you're applying.
- On the application form, waive your right to view recommendation letters. This makes the recommendation more credible in the eyes of the college.
- To ensure recommendations have been mailed or to see if your recommendation writers need additional information from you, follow up with them a week or so before your first deadline.
- Once you have decided which college to attend, write thank-you notes to everyone who provided a recommendation and tell them where you've decided to go to college. Be sure to do this before you leave high school.

Your parents, school counselors, and teachers may have some helpful insights into things you should talk about in your essays. For tips and strategies on how to approach different types of essay questions, general advice on the writing process, and information about how admissions officers evaluate essays, obtain a copy of Sarah Myers McGinty's *The College Application Essay* (College Board, 2004).

Interview

An interview is required or recommended by some colleges. Even if it's not required, it's a good idea to set up an interview because it gives you a chance to make a personal connection with someone who will have a voice in deciding whether or not you'll be offered admission. If you're too far away for an on-campus interview, try to arrange to meet with an alumnus in your community.

Try to schedule interviews early in your senior year—if you wait until December, you may not have time to make the appointment before the application is due. Also, scheduling an interview late in the year may make the college think that your decision to apply there was an afterthought.

For tips on preparing for interviews and getting the most out of them, obtain a copy of Zola Dincin Schneider's *Campus Visits & College Interviews* (College Board, 2002), or read the articles in the "Apply to College" section of the College Board Web site.

Auditions, portfolios, and other supplementary materials

If you're applying for a fine or performing arts program in music, studio art, or graphic design, you may have to document prior work by auditioning on campus or submitting an audiotape, slides, or some other sample of your work to demonstrate your ability. Talk to a teacher or mentor in your subject for advice on both how to assemble a portfolio and which of your pieces to include. Be sure to check the deadlines for auditions—they are often different from the deadlines for applications.

In some cases, a college will ask all students to submit an academic writing sample, either instead of or in addition to a personal statement. You should send a graded essay, presentation, or lab report that you did well on, preferably a copy that has your teacher's comments and the grade you received on it.

Should I apply early?

Early application plans have been around for decades. However, they've only become hot topics among college-bound families over the past 10 years and, today, they are actually the driving force behind some students' college planning. To understand how early plans have taken center stage for some students, you need to first understand how the college application calendar works. Generally speaking, there are three different college application timelines:

Regular admissions. You apply by a midwinter deadline, hear from colleges in early April, and make your decision and notify colleges by May 1 (known as the universal candidate reply date) about whether or not you will attend. This was the norm until fairly recently.

Rolling admissions. You apply and usually receive an admissions decision within two to six weeks from the time you submit your application. Most public universities and many private colleges use this timeline. It's by far the most widely used calendar today—and popular with students because it reduces the period of uncertainty.

Early application. Essentially, two types of early plans—one nonbinding and the other binding—are offered by several hundred colleges that also use the regular application calendar. Here's how they differ:

- **Early Action (EA).** This is a nonbinding plan that requires you to submit your application in early fall (usually by November 1 or 15). The college lets you know whether or not you're accepted by early January, but you have the right to wait until May 1 before responding. This gives you time to compare colleges, including their financial aid offers, before making a decision, since an EA application doesn't commit you to enroll if offered admission.

- **Early Decision (ED).** This is considered binding, so it's essential that you be certain about wanting to enroll at that college. As with Early Action plans, you submit an application in early fall. Sometime between mid-December and the beginning of January, the college notifies you whether you have been admitted, deferred to the pool of regular applicants for a spring decision, or denied admission to the college.

  By applying under an ED plan, you have made a commitment to attend that college and surrendered the right to wait until May 1 to make a decision. High school counselors and college admissions officers take that commitment very seriously. Reneging on your agreement after being offered ED admission could result in other colleges refusing to admit you.

  Most ED plans share the following features:

  - You may apply for Early Decision to only one college.
  - You may also apply for Early Action or regular admission to other colleges during the fall, but once you are admitted under an ED plan, all applications to other colleges must be withdrawn immediately.
  - You are only released from an ED decision if the college is unable to meet your need for financial aid as demonstrated by the completion of a financial aid form. It is vitally important for you and your family to understand that "need," as used in the college admissions process, does not refer to a subjective determination of a family's willingness to pay, but rather to the federal and institutional financial aid methodologies used to determine a family's ability to pay.

In most cases, students may apply EA to more than one college, and even apply ED to one other school. However, some colleges, in an attempt to curb the mania of early applications, are restricting their EA plans. These new plans are called *Early Application/Single Choice* or, sometimes, *Early Application with Restrictions*. Be sure to check each college's policies for EA, as they may vary.

What are the advantages of utilizing an early plan? For students who have found their "ideal" college, applying early allows them to bypass the regular spring notification deadline, avoid the time and expense of submitting multiple applications, and reduce the time spent waiting for a decision. Students who have already completed their college search can accelerate the admissions calendar by applying under an early plan. Being admitted under an early plan may sometimes be somewhat less competitive than competing with all other applicants in the spring, just as letting a college know of your intense desire to attend can be a positive factor in the admissions decision.

Colleges and universities, too, benefit from early plans. Under the ED plan, admitting committed students early in the admissions cycle is a great way to build a strong freshman class. Also, some colleges find that they can stretch their limited financial aid budgets by admitting students who are not only bright and committed to their school, but who also are "full pay" students, i.e., ones who are not relying on financial aid.

So why are early plans such a controversial topic among admissions professionals today? There is a growing concern that the increased publicity about and the popularity of early plans are causing some students to make premature college decisions and some colleges to fill their classes with a disproportionate number of early applicants.

In fact, students even feel compelled to apply early in order to take advantage of the perceived competitive edge ED offers. What was originally designed to be a stress reducer has become a stress enhancer, as students focus more on the *strategy* of ED plans rather than the *opportunity* ED plans offer to the very focused student. In another vein, some students who apply early might find themselves disconnecting from their academic work during their last semester of high school. This particular strain of "senioritis" has created a national concern among high school and college educators alike. Students are expected to remain engaged in their course work throughout their eight semesters of high school; applying early was never designed to lessen a student's academic participation during the spring of senior year.

Simply stated, early plans are wonderful options for students who have found a perfect fit between themselves and a particular college. However, because of media or peer pressure, some students who aren't absolutely certain that one college is the clear winner on their list may find it tempting to apply under an early plan—even if it isn't right for them.

For students who aren't ready to make a binding commitment, applying ED is extremely inappropriate because it forces them to make serious decisions long before they've explored all their options. Another potential disadvantage is that students are not able to wait until the spring of their senior year to compare financial aid packages among colleges that have offered them admission. Therefore, if financial aid is a priority, applying ED is probably not a good idea because it might eliminate, or greatly reduce, aid possibilities.

If you're just starting the college admissions search, we encourage you to keep a few points in mind:

- Remember that the best college for you is the one that fits you best. A good match between your academic, personal, social, and philosophical interests and a college or university's environment is what you are seeking. Get to know yourself well this year, and get to know individual colleges well by reading about them, visiting them, and speaking to their admissions counselors.
- Applying under an early plan is not a mandate, but simply an option. If you find one college that appeals to you more than any other and fits you like a glove, consider using an early plan as you begin the application timetable early in your senior year. However, if you want to take more time to explore a variety of options, that's OK!
- Include your parents in the early plan decision. It is imperative that your parents understand the financial ramifications of applying under a binding ED plan. Make sure your parents have discussed their financial need with the college's financial aid office before you apply under a binding ED plan.
- Include your school counselor in the process. You don't want to make such a weighty decision without the help of a trained professional who can be objective about this decision. Your counselor is your strongest advocate in the college search process!

You'll find a table beginning on page 2013 that provides a list of colleges that offer ED and EA plans, including application deadlines and notification dates.

Susan Biemeret
Coordinator of College Counseling
Adlai E. Stevenson High School
Lincolnshire, Illinois

Life on campus

A college isn't just a place where you'll take classes for two or four years. You'll also be spending a great deal of your time there—and if you're a residential student, you'll even be living there. When you're making your final choice on where to attend, academics may come first, but you'll also want to take into account the housing options, local transit, and whether the campus feels safe.

Housing options

Choices abound for today's college student who is living away from home. You may choose an on-campus "residence hall" (a.k.a. dormitory, or dorm), an off-campus apartment, or a fraternity/sorority house.

On-campus residence halls provide you with more than just a place to sleep; they offer a complete living and learning environment. Living on campus puts you in the heart of a campus community, and campus life is most accessible. The campus, indeed, becomes a new home, and you can build a life there.

Residence hall life has changed over the years. At one time, two-person dormitory rooms with communal bathroom facilities were standard. Colleges and universities now offer a wide variety of living options, including suite living, which resembles an apartment-like environment accommodating four to six students per suite. Residence halls are normally coeducational, segregated by alternate rooms, floors, or wings. Most residence halls maintain common areas that provide entertainment, computers, a kitchen, and reading areas.

When you visit colleges/universities, you should ask about the benefits of living on campus:

- How are the rooms furnished? Are they complete with telephone service for free local calls or basic cable TV service? Is direct, fast Internet access available from individual dorm rooms? Are the rooms equipped with any appliances?
- Are there a variety of social activities, with opportunities to meet new people and to get involved?
- Are there computer rooms in the dorms? Are there convenient and quiet study areas?
- Are resident advisers available, as well as programs that support personal growth, academic advising, student development, campus issues, and individual needs?
- Are meal plans flexible? What are the dining choices?

Where available, you may choose to live in theme-related residence halls. These theme or special-interest residence hall programs give you choices about living in communities with other students who share similar interests in a field of study, culture, hobby, or personal value. Among the living options that may be offered are diversity programs, engineering and science programs, language programs, leadership programs, academic programs, international programs, and outdoor programs, as well as positive choice programs, which focus on wellness and personal responsibility activities.

Social organizations such as fraternities and sororities offer a midsize living experience where students reside together in a large house that has been divided into living units. Although the prevailing Greek stereotype continues to have some validity, campus Greek Living Councils are actively working to eliminate negative traditions and to emphasize the positive aspects of this living experience.

Most colleges and universities require freshmen to live on campus. Before arriving on campus, you will be asked to list your living preferences on questionnaires provided by the college or university's Department of Housing. This information is used to make housing placement decisions.

For upperclassmen (sophomores, juniors, and seniors) who desire more independence and control over their living situations, off-campus housing is a popular choice. Students may reside off campus in single rooms or in apartments; however, off-campus living requires decisions regarding proximity to campus, selection and number of roommates, cost, safety, and guidelines for behavior and necessary chores.

In preparation for living away from home, you should thoughtfully consider your options and make choices that match your academic, personal, and social interests and needs.

Transportation

Getting *to* campus can be a big issue for both residential students and commuter students, but for different reasons. If you're going to live on campus, you will have to bring all your personal belongings with you, or have your parents ship them to you. You'll also have to budget for transportation to and from campus for holidays.

If you're going to commute from your home to a local college, you don't have to worry about making several big trips each year, but you do need to budget for daily transportation costs. If you're going to drive to school, you also need to make arrangements for a parking permit. Finally, commuter students often need to pay more attention to scheduling their study time than residential students—it's harder to run back to the library to check one last thing before turning in a term paper if doing so requires a half hour on the bus.

Getting *around* campus is usually easy, but there are some things that both commuters and residential students will want to know:

- Are classrooms, libraries, and recreational facilities within walking distance of one another? Where are they in relation to the residence halls?
- Is there bus or shuttle service (particularly important on a large campus)? Are such services free?
- Is it safe to ride a bicycle around campus? Are there bike stands near classroom buildings, libraries, and residence halls? Is bike theft a big problem on campus?

Campus safety

It's important for you to feel comfortable with the college, and a big, though often overlooked, aspect of that is campus security. Whether the campus is rural, suburban, or urban, you need to feel safe in order to thrive there.

Before enrolling, try to visit and make sure that you feel safe walking around, both during the day and at night. Look for the following features:

- Are the pathways, bus stops, parking lots, and other public areas well lit at night?
- Are there emergency phones (connecting directly to the police) in public areas?
- Are there security systems in place to prevent nonresidents from walking into a residence hall? Are ground-floor windows in the residence halls secured?
- Do campus security guards or local police patrol the campus?
- Are there student groups dedicated to safety and crime prevention on campus?

You can also obtain a copy of the campus's crime report, a federally mandated report of crime statistics, from the administrative offices. Student-run college newspapers also report crime on and near the campus; often, you can read back issues online.

Packing advice

Going away to college? Here are some tips on how to pack wisely for your first year. For a checklist of items students often find useful, read the articles in the "Plan for College" section of the College Board Web site.

- Shop early—it minimizes stress. You don't want to spend your last few weeks at home arguing with Mom and Dad about what you're planning to take with you.
- Don't forget the things that will make your dorm room feel like home—photographs of family and friends, important mementos, or anything else that will make your new room your own space.
- Don't bring a full four-season wardrobe. Remember that most dorm room closets are fairly small. You'll be able to retrieve extra stuff from home during breaks.
- Don't overestimate how often you'll be doing laundry—21 pairs of socks may seem like a lot, but three weeks fly by when you're busy settling into college life.
- Be realistic about your lifestyle. If you never iron and your idea of getting dressed up is changing from torn jeans to khakis, then you won't want to fill up your limited closet space with an ironing board you won't use or dress clothes you're not going to wear.
- Check with roommates to avoid duplication—space is tight (so are electric outlets, generally) so divvy up the large items.
- Duffle bags are great. They can be stored under a mattress when not in use. (Just don't forget they're there!)

Glossary

Definitions of commonly used terms vary from college to college. Consult specific college catalogs or their Web sites for more detailed information.

Accelerated study. A college program of study completed in less time than is usually required, most often by attending classes in summer or by taking extra courses during the regular academic terms. Completion of a bachelor's degree program in three years is an example of acceleration.

Accreditation. Recognition by an accrediting organization or agency that a college meets certain acceptable standards in its education programs, services, and facilities. Regional accreditation applies to a college as a whole and not to any particular programs or courses of study. Accreditation of specific types of schools, such as Bible colleges or trade and technical schools, may also be determined by a national organization. Institutional accreditation by regional accrediting associations and by national accrediting organizations is included in the *Handbook*'s descriptions of colleges. See page 8 for more information about accreditation and the names and addresses of the national and regional accrediting associations.

ACT Assessment. The group of college admissions tests from ACT, Inc., formerly known as the American College Testing Program, given at test centers in the United States and other countries on specified dates throughout the year. It includes tests in English, mathematics, reading, and science reasoning. The ACT composite score referred to in some colleges' descriptions is the average of students' scores on these four tests.

Advanced placement. Admission or assignment of a freshman to an advanced course in a certain subject on the basis of evidence that the student has already completed the equivalent of the college's freshman course in that subject.

Advanced Placement Program® (AP®). A program of the College Board that provides high schools with course descriptions of college subjects and AP Examinations in those subjects. The AP Program offers 37 exams in 22 subject areas. High schools offer the courses and administer the examinations to interested students, who are then eligible for advanced placement, college credit, or both on the basis of satisfactory grades. Most colleges and universities in the United States accept qualifying AP Exam grades for credit, advanced standing, or both.

Articulation agreement. A formal agreement between two higher education institutions, stating specific policies relating to transfer and recognition of academic achievement in order to facilitate the successful transfer of students without duplication of course work.

Associate degree. A degree granted by a college or university after the satisfactory completion of the equivalent of a two-year full-time program of study. In general, the associate of arts (A.A.) or associate of science (A.S.) degree is granted after completing a program of study similar to the first two years of a four-year college curriculum. The associate in applied science (A.A.S.) is awarded by many colleges on completion of technological or vocational programs of study.

Bachelor's, or baccalaureate, degree. A degree received after the satisfactory completion of a four- or five-year full-time program of study (or its part-time equivalent) at a college or university. The bachelor of arts (B.A.) and bachelor of science (B.S.) are the most common baccalaureates. There is no absolute difference between the degrees, and policies concerning their award vary from college to college.

Bible college. An undergraduate institution whose program, in addition to a general education in the liberal arts, includes a significant element of Bible study. Most Bible colleges seek to prepare their students for vocational or lay Christian ministry.

Calendar. The system by which an institution divides its year into shorter periods for instruction and awarding credit. The most common calendars are those based on the semester, trimester, quarter, and 4-1-4.

Candidates Reply Date Agreement (CRDA). A college subscribing to this College Board–sponsored agreement will not require any applicants offered admission as freshmen to notify the college of their decision to attend (or to accept an offer of financial aid) before

May 1 of the year the applicants apply. The purpose of the agreement is to give applicants time to hear from all the colleges to which they have applied before having to make a commitment to any of them.

CB code. A four-digit College Board code number that students use to designate colleges or scholarship programs to receive their SAT score reports.

College-Level Examination Program® (CLEP®). A series of examinations in undergraduate college courses that provides students of any age the opportunity to demonstrate college-level achievement, thereby reducing costs and time to degree completion. The examinations, which are sponsored by the College Board, are administered at colleges year-round. All CLEP exams are delivered on computer, providing test-takers instant score results.

College-preparatory subjects. A term used to describe subjects required for admission to, or recommended as preparation for, college. It is usually understood to mean subjects from the fields of English, history and social studies, foreign languages, mathematics, science, and the arts.

College Scholarship Service® (CSS®). A unit of the College Board that assists postsecondary institutions, state scholarship programs, and private scholarship organizations in the equitable and efficient distribution of student financial aid funds.

Combined bachelor's/graduate degree. A program in which students complete a bachelor's degree and a master's degree or first-professional degree in less than the usual amount of time. In most programs, students apply to the graduate program during their first three years of undergraduate study, and begin the graduate program in their fourth year of college. Successful completion results in awarding of both bachelor's and graduate degrees. At some colleges, this option is called a joint degree program.

Common Application. The standard application form distributed by the National Association of Secondary School Principals to private colleges who are subscribers to the Common Application Group.

Community/junior college. A college that offers only the first two years of undergraduate study. Community colleges are public institutions, whereas junior colleges are privately operated on a not-for-profit basis. Both usually offer both terminal (or "vocational") programs and transfer programs.

Cooperative education. A program that provides for alternative class attendance and employment in business, industry, or government. Students are typically paid for their work. Under a cooperative plan, five years are normally required to complete a bachelor's degree, but graduates have the advantage of about a year's practical work experience in addition to their studies.

Cooperative housing. College-owned, operated, or affiliated housing in which students share room and board expenses and participate in household chores to reduce living expenses.

Credit hour. A unit of measure representing an hour (50 minutes) of instruction over a 15-week period in a semester or trimester system, or a 10-week period in a quarter system. It is applied toward the total number of hours needed for completing the requirements of a degree, diploma, certificate, or other formal award.

Credit/placement by examination. Academic credit or placement out of introductory courses granted by a college to entering students who have demonstrated proficiency in college-level studies through examinations such as those sponsored by the College Board's AP and CLEP programs.

Cross-registration. The practice, through agreements between colleges, of permitting students enrolled at one college or university to enroll in courses at another institution without formally applying for admission to the second institution.

CSS/Financial Aid PROFILE®. A form and service offered by the College Board and used by some colleges, universities, and private scholarship programs to award their own private financial aid funds. Students pay a fee to register for PROFILE and send reports to institutions and programs that use it. Students register with CSS® by calling a toll-free telephone service or by connecting to College Board on the Web: www.collegeboard.com. CSS provides a customized application for each registrant, based on the individual's information and the requirements of the colleges and programs from which she or he is seeking aid. Students complete and submit the customized application and supplements, if required, to CSS for processing and reporting to institutions. CSS/Financial Aid PROFILE is not a federal form and may not be used to apply for federal student aid.

Deferred admission. The practice of permitting students to postpone enrollment, usually for one year, after acceptance to the college.

Distance learning. An option for earning course credit off campus via cable television, the Internet, satellite classes, videotapes, correspondence courses, or other means. *See also* Virtual university.

Doctoral degree (doctorate). *See* Graduate degree.

Dormitory. *See* Residence hall.

Double major. Any program in which a student completes the requirements of two majors concurrently.

Dual enrollment. The practice of students enrolling in college courses while still in high school.

Early Action (EA). Students who apply under a college's Early Action plan receive a decision earlier than the standard response date but are not required to accept the admissions offer or to make a deposit prior to May 1. See the Early Decision/Early Action table on page 2013 for a list of colleges that offer Early Action plans, including application deadlines and notification dates.

Early admission. The policy of some colleges of admitting certain students who have not completed high school—usually students of exceptional ability who have completed their junior year. These students are enrolled full-time in college.

Early Decision (ED). Students who apply under Early Decision make a commitment to enroll at the college if admitted and offered a satisfactory financial aid package. Application deadlines are usually in November or December with a mid-to-late-December notification date. Some colleges have two rounds of Early Decision. See the Early Decision/Early Action table for details.

Early Decision Plan (EDPA). Colleges that subscribe to this College Board–sponsored plan agree to follow a common schedule for Early Decision applicants. A student applying under EDPA must withdraw applications from all other colleges as soon as he or she is notified of acceptance by the first-choice college. Applications (including financial aid applications) must be received by a specified date no later than November 15, and the college agrees to notify the applicant by a specified date no later than December 15. Colleges that subscribe to EDPA are indicated in the Early Decision/Early Action table.

Exchange student program. Any arrangement that permits a student to study for a semester or more at another college in the United States without extending the amount of time required for a degree.

External degree program. A system of study whereby a student earns credit toward a degree through independent study, college courses, proficiency examinations, and personal experience. External degree colleges generally have no campus or classroom facilities.

FAFSA. *See* Free Application for Federal Student Aid.

Federal Work-Study Program. *See* Work-study.

First-professional degree. A degree granted upon completion of academic requirements to become licensed in a recognized profession. The programs of study require at least two years of previous college work for entrance, and at least six years of total college work for completion. The medical doctorate (M.D.) is one kind of first-professional degree.

For-profit college. A private institution operated by its owners as a profit-making enterprise.

4-1-4 calendar. A variation of the semester calendar system, the 4-1-4 calendar consists of two terms of about 16 weeks each, separated by a one-month intersession used for intensive short courses, independent study, off-campus work, or other types of instruction.

Free Application for Federal Student Aid (FAFSA). A form completed by all applicants for federal student aid. In many states, completion of the FAFSA is also sufficient to establish eligibility for state-sponsored aid programs. There is no charge to students for completing the FAFSA. Forms are widely available in high schools and colleges, and may be filed any time after January 1 of the year for which one is seeking aid (e.g., after January 1, 2007, for academic year 2007-08 assistance).

General Educational Development (GED). A series of five tests that individuals who did not complete high school may take through their state education system to qualify for a high school equivalency certificate. The tests cover correctness and effectiveness of expression, interpretation of reading materials in the natural sciences and the social sciences, interpretation of literary materials, and general mathematics ability. Many colleges accept satisfactory GED test results in lieu of high school graduation. Some colleges require homeschooled students to take the GED.

Grade point average (GPA) or ratio. A system used by many schools for evaluating the overall scholastic performance of students. Grade points are determined by first multiplying the number of hours given for a course by the numerical value of the grade and then dividing the sum of all grade points by the total number of hours carried. The most common system of numerical values for grades is A = 4, B = 3, C = 2, D = 1, and E or F = 0. Also called quality point average or ratio.

Graduate degree. A degree pursued after a student has earned a bachelor's degree. The master's degree, which requires one to three years of study, is usually the degree earned after the bachelor's. The doctoral degree requires further study. First-professional degrees are also graduate degrees.

Hispanic-serving college. A college where Hispanic students comprise at least 25 percent of the full-time undergraduate enrollment.

Historically black college. An institution founded before 1964 whose mission was historically, and remains, the education of African Americans.

Homeschooled. For purposes of the application requirements described in the "basis for selection" entries of the college descriptions, this refers to homeschooling during the four years of secondary school (grades 9–12).

Honors program. Any special program for very able students that offers the opportunity for education enrichment, independent study, acceleration, or some combination of these.

Independent student. For financial aid purposes, a student who is not dependent on financial support from his or her parents. Also called self-supporting student.

Independent study. Academic work chosen or designed by the student with the approval of the department concerned, under an instructor's supervision. This work is usually undertaken outside of the regular classroom structure.

International Baccalaureate (IB). A comprehensive and rigorous two-year curriculum (usually taken in the final two years of high school) that is similar to the final year of secondary school in Europe. Some colleges award credit or advanced placement to students who have completed an IB program.

Internship. A short-term, supervised work experience, usually related to a student's major field, for which the student earns academic credit. The work can be full- or part-time, on or off campus, paid or unpaid. Student teaching and apprenticeships are examples.

Intersession term. A short term offered between semesters. *See also* 4-1-4 calendar.

Junior college. *See* Community/junior college.

Liberal arts. The study of the humanities (literature, the arts, and philosophy), history, foreign languages, social sciences, mathematics, and natural sciences. Study of the liberal arts and humanities prepares students to develop general knowledge and reasoning ability rather than specific skills.

Liberal arts/career combination. A program of study in which a student typically completes three years of study in a liberal arts field followed by two years of professional/technical study (for example, engineering) at the end of which the student is awarded bachelor of arts and bachelor of science degrees. The combination is also referred to as a 3+2 program.

Major. A student's academic field of specialization. In general, most courses in the major are taken during the junior and senior years.

Master's degree. *See* Graduate degree.

Military college. An institution that, in addition to offering a liberal arts or engineering curriculum, prepares its students to become military officers.

Need-based financial aid. Financial aid (scholarships, grants, loans, or work-study opportunities) given to students who have demonstrated financial need, calculated by subtracting the student's expected family contribution from a college's total costs. The expected family contribution is derived from a need analysis of the family's overall financial circumstances, using either a Federal Methodology to determine a student's eligibility for federal student aid, or an Institutional Methodology to determine eligibility for nonfederal financial aid.

Open admissions. The college admissions policy of admitting high school graduates and other adults generally without regard to conventional academic qualifications, such as high school subjects, high school grades, and admissions test scores. Virtually all applicants with high school diplomas or their equivalent are accepted, space permitting.

Placement by examination. *See* Credit/placement by examination.

Private college. Institutions described in this book as "private" are operated on a not-for-profit basis. They may be independent or church-affiliated. *See also* Proprietary college.

PROFILE. *See* CSS/Financial Aid PROFILE.

Proprietary college. *See* For-profit college.

PSAT/NMSQT® (Preliminary SAT/National Merit Scholarship Qualifying Test). A shorter version of the SAT Reasoning Test that includes a writing skills section as well as feedback on academic skills based on test performance. Administered by high schools to sophomores and juniors each year in October, the PSAT/NMSQT helps students prepare for the SAT, aids high schools in the early guidance of students planning for college, and serves as the qualifying test for National Merit Scholarship Corporation programs.

Public college/university. An institution that is supported by taxes and other public revenue and governed by a county, state, or federal government agency.

Quality point average. *See* Grade point average.

Quarter. An academic calendar period of about 12 weeks. Four quarters make up an academic year, but at colleges using the quarter system, students make normal academic progress by attending three quarters each year. In some colleges, students can accelerate their programs by attending all four quarters in one or more years.

Rabbinical college. *See* Seminary/rabbinical college.

Regional accreditation. *See* Accreditation.

Reserve Officers Training Corps (ROTC). Programs conducted by certain colleges in cooperation with the United States Air Force, Army, and Navy. Naval ROTC includes the Marine Corps (the Coast Guard and Merchant Marine do not sponsor ROTC programs). Local recruiting offices of the services themselves can supply detailed information about these programs, as can participating colleges.

Residence hall. An on-campus living facility. Also known as a dormitory (or "dorm").

Residency requirement. The minimum number of terms that a student must spend taking courses on campus (as opposed to independent study, transfer credits from other colleges, or credit by examination) to be eligible for graduation. Can also refer to the minimum amount of time a student must have lived in-state in order to qualify for the in-state tuition rate at a public college or university.

Rolling admissions. An admissions procedure by which the college considers each student's application as soon as all the required credentials, such as school record and test scores, have been received. The college usually notifies an applicant of its decision without delay. At many colleges, rolling admissions allows for early notification and works much like nonbinding Early Action programs.

Room and board. The combined cost of housing and meals for students who reside on campus and/or dine in college-operated meal halls.

SAT® Question and Answer Service. A service of the College Board that provides students with a copy of their SAT Reasoning Test, their answers and the correct answers, scoring instructions, and information about the questions. The service is only available for certain test dates.

SAT Reasoning Test™ (SAT). The College Board's test of developed verbal and mathematical reasoning abilities, given on specified dates throughout the year at test centers in the United States and other countries. The SAT Reasoning Test, formerly known as the SAT I, is required by many colleges and sponsors of financial aid programs.

SAT Subject Tests™. College Board tests in specific subjects, given at test centers in the United States and other countries on specified dates throughout the year. Used by colleges not only to help with decisions about admission but also in course placement and exemption of enrolled freshmen.

Semester. A period of about 16 weeks. Colleges on a semester system offer two semesters of instruction a year; there may be an additional summer session.

Semester at sea. A program for credit, usually for students with majors in oceanography or marine-related fields, in which students live on a ship, frequently a research vessel, for part of a semester. Academic courses are generally taken in conjunction with the sea experience or at separate times during the semester.

Seminary/rabbinical college. An institution that prepares its student for professional religious ministry. Most seminaries are graduate-only institutions that offer first-professional degrees in divinity or rabbinical studies. The seminaries described in this book also offer undergraduate programs in philosophy, theology, Bible studies, or other related liberal arts.

Student Aid Report (SAR). A report produced by the U.S. Department of Education and sent to students in response to their having filed the Free Application for Federal Student Aid (FAFSA). The SAR contains information the student provided on the FAFSA as well as the federally calculated result, which the financial aid office will use in determining the student's eligibility for a Federal Pell Grant and other federal student aid programs.

Student-designed major. An academic program that allows a student to construct a major field of study not formally offered by the college. Often nontraditional and interdisciplinary in nature, the major is developed by the student with the approval of a designated college officer or committee.

Study abroad. Any arrangement by which a student completes part of the college program—typically the junior year but sometimes only a semester or a summer—studying in another country. A college may operate a campus abroad, or it may have a cooperative agreement with some other U.S. college or an institution of the other country.

Teacher certification. A college program designed to prepare students to meet the requirements for certification as teachers in elementary and secondary schools.

Terminal degree. The highest degree level attainable in a particular field. For most teaching faculty this is a doctoral degree. In certain fields, however, a master's degree is the highest level.

Terminal program. An education program designed to prepare students for immediate employment. These programs usually can be completed in less than four years beyond high school and are available in most community colleges and vocational-technical institutes.

3+2 program. *See* Liberal arts/career combination.

Transcript. A copy of a student's official academic record listing all courses taken and grades received.

Transfer program. An education program in a two-year college (or a four-year college that offers associate degrees), primarily for students who plan to continue their studies in a four-year college or university.

Transfer student. A student who has attended another college for any period, which may be defined by various colleges as any time from a single term up to three years. A transfer student may receive credit for all or some of the courses successfully completed before the transfer.

Trimester. An academic calendar period of about 15 weeks. Three trimesters make up one year. Students normally progress by attending two of the trimesters each year and in some colleges can accelerate their programs by attending all three trimesters in one or more years.

Tuition. The price of instruction at a college. Tuition may be charged per term or per credit hour.

Two-year college. *See* Community/junior college; Upper-division college.

United Nations semester. A program in which students generally take courses at a college in the New York City metropolitan area while participating in an internship program at the United Nations.

Upper division. The junior and senior years of study.

Upper-division college. A college offering bachelor's degree programs that begin with the junior year. Entering students must have completed their freshman and sophomore years at other colleges.

Urban semester. A program for credit in which students of diverse majors spend a semester in a major city, such as New York, Philadelphia, Chicago, Denver, or San Francisco, experiencing the complexities of an urban center through course work, seminars, and/or internships related to their major.

Virtual university. A degree-granting, accredited institution wherein all courses are delivered by distance learning, with no physical campus.

Vocational program. *See* Terminal program.

Wait list. A list of students who meet the admissions requirements, but will only be offered a place in the class if space becomes available. See the wait-list table on page 2025 for a list of colleges that placed students on a wait list last year, along with the number of students who were eventually accepted off of that list.

Washington semester. A program in which students participate in an internship program with a government agency or department in the Washington, D.C., metropolitan area. Students earn field service credit for their work and frequently take courses at area colleges.

Weekend college. A program that allows students to take a complete course of study and attend classes only on weekends. These programs are generally restricted to a few areas of study at a college and require more than the traditional number of years to complete.

Work-study. An arrangement by which a student combines employment and college study. The employment may be an integral part of the academic program (as in cooperative education and internships) or simply a means of paying for college (as in the Federal Work-Study Program).

Four-year colleges

Alabama

Alabama Agricultural and Mechanical University
Huntsville, Alabama
www.aamu.edu
CB member
CB code: 1003

- Public 4-year university and agricultural college
- Residential campus in small city
- 5,047 degree-seeking undergraduates: 8% part-time, 53% women, 94% African American, 3% international
- 1,135 degree-seeking graduate students
- SAT or ACT (ACT writing optional) required
- 38% graduate within 6 years

General. Founded in 1875. Regionally accredited. Bachelor of technical studies available to adult learners in nontraditional fields. Campus located near Redstone Arsenal-Defense Research/Space Research Center. **Degrees:** 600 bachelor's awarded; master's, doctoral offered. **ROTC:** Army, Navy. **Location:** 2 miles from downtown Huntsville, 95 miles from Birmingham. **Calendar:** Semester, extensive summer session. **Full-time faculty:** 307 total; 49% have terminal degrees, 34% women. **Part-time faculty:** 98 total; 18% have terminal degrees, 56% women. **Special facilities:** State Black archives research center and museum.

Freshman class profile.

Mid 50% test scores		**Out-of-state:**	42%
ACT:	16-19	**Live on campus:**	87%
Return as sophomores:	66%	**International:**	1%

Basis for selection. GED not accepted. 2.0 GPA required. Test scores important, but may be waived dependent upon evaluation of GPA and other achievements. Interview, essay recommended. **Homeschooled:** Must meet Alabama State Department of Education requirements.

High school preparation. Required units include English 4, mathematics 4 and science 2.

2005-2006 Annual costs. Tuition/fees: $4,940; $8,840 out-of-state. Part-time student required fees are $350. Room/board: $3,592. Books/supplies: $850. Personal expenses: $950.

Financial aid. **Non-need-based:** Scholarships awarded for athletics, minority status.

Application procedures. **Admission:** Priority date 5/1; deadline 7/15 (receipt date). $10 fee. Application may be submitted online. Admission notification on a rolling basis. **Financial aid:** FAFSA, institutional form required. Applicants notified on a rolling basis; must reply within 2 week(s) of notification.

Academics. **Special study options:** Accelerated study, cooperative education, distance learning, dual enrollment of high school students, study abroad, teacher certification program, Washington semester, weekend college. **Credit/placement by examination:** AP, CLEP, institutional tests. 9 credit hours maximum toward bachelor's degree. Scores from DANTES, CLEP, ACE, and similar tests, and work experiences considered for credit toward degree. **Support services:** Learning center, pre-admission summer program, reduced course load, remedial instruction, study skills assistance, tutoring.

Honors college/program. Second semester freshmen with ACT score of 20-21 (SAT 1030) may be considered for admission if they have at least 3.5 GPA in minimum of 12 credit hours completed at the university, and a cumulative high school average of 3.3. The academic program consists of honors core courses.

Majors. **Agriculture:** Economics. **Architecture:** Urban/community planning. **Biology:** General. **Business:** General, accounting, business admin, finance, marketing, office management, public finance. **Communications:** Journalism. **Communications technology:** General, graphic/printing. **Computer sciences:** General. **Education:** General, business, early childhood, elementary, music, physical, school counseling, secondary, special, speech impaired. **Engineering:** Civil, mechanical. **Engineering technology:** Civil. **English:** English lit. **Family/consumer sciences:** General. **Math:** General. **Physical sciences:** Chemistry, physics. **Psychology:** General. **Public administration:** Social work. **Social sciences:** Political science, sociology. **Visual/performing arts:** Art, conducting, music performance.

Computing on campus. 611 workstations in dormitories, library, computer center, student center. Dormitories linked to campus network. Helpline available.

Student life. **Freshman orientation:** Mandatory, $100 fee. Preregistration for classes offered. **Housing:** Guaranteed on-campus for all undergraduates. Single-sex dorms available. $100 deposit, deadline 8/1. **Activities:** Bands, choral groups, dance, drama, film society, music ensembles, radio station, student government, student newspaper, TV station, Christian student organization, honor society, service clubs, NAACP, African-American political club, Baptist student union, Islamic association, Caribbean students association, International Association of Nigerian Students.

Athletics. NCAA. **Intercollegiate:** Baseball M, basketball, bowling W, cross-country, football (tackle) M, golf, soccer, softball W, tennis, track and field, volleyball W. **Intramural:** Basketball, football (tackle) M, soccer W, softball, volleyball. **Team name:** Bulldogs.

Student services. Adult student services, career counseling, student employment services, health services, personal counseling, placement for graduates, veterans' counselor. **Physically disabled:** Services for visually, speech, hearing impaired.

Contact. E-mail: aboyle@aamu.edu
Phone: (256) 372-5245 Toll-free number: (256) 372-5245
Fax: (256) 372-5249
Antonio Boyle, Director of Admissions, Alabama Agricultural and Mechanical University, Box 908, Normal, AL 35762

Alabama State University
Montgomery, Alabama
www.alasu.edu
CB member
CB code: 1006

- Public 4-year university
- Residential campus in small city
- 4,455 degree-seeking undergraduates: 11% part-time, 60% women, 96% African American
- 908 degree-seeking graduate students
- 67% of applicants admitted
- Interview required

General. Founded in 1867. Regionally accredited. **Degrees:** 520 bachelor's awarded; master's, doctoral offered. **ROTC:** Army, Air Force. **Location:** 91 miles from Birmingham, 162 miles from Atlanta. **Calendar:** Semester, limited summer session. **Full-time faculty:** 228 total; 60% have terminal degrees, 60% minority, 52% women. **Part-time faculty:** 180 total; 26% have terminal degrees, 78% minority, 62% women. **Special facilities:** Black history collection, E. D. Nixon papers from civil rights movement of 1960s.

Freshman class profile. 6,202 applied, 4,154 admitted, 1,213 enrolled.

Mid 50% test scores			
SAT verbal:	330-430	GPA 2.0-2.99:	68%
SAT math:	330-430	Return as sophomores:	64%
ACT:	13-17	Out-of-state:	40%
GPA 3.50 or higher:	7%	Live on campus:	81%
GPA 3.0-3.49:	24%	International:	1%

Basis for selection. School record and test scores important. All applicants must have minimum 2.20 GPA from accredited high school. Interview and essay recommended. Audition required of music majors. Portfolio recommended for art majors. **Homeschooled:** Transcript of courses and grades required. Applicants must score 20 or above on the ACT. **Learning Disabled:** Students with learning disabilities must submit appropriate documentation in order to be given special consideration.

High school preparation. 14 units recommended. Recommended units include English 4, mathematics 3, science 3 and foreign language 3.

2006-2007 Annual costs. Tuition/fees: $4,008; $8,016 out-of-state. Room/board: $3,600. Books/supplies: $1,000. Personal expenses: $1,380.

2005-2006 Financial aid. Need-based: 1,101 full-time freshmen applied for aid; 1,016 were judged to have need; 981 of these received aid. Average need met was 63%. Average scholarship/grant was $3,644; average loan $2,589. 47% of total undergraduate aid awarded as scholarships/grants, 53% as loans/jobs. **Non-need-based:** Awarded to 1,149 full-time undergraduates, including 350 freshmen. Scholarships awarded for academics, art, athletics, minority status, music/drama, ROTC.

Application procedures. Admission: Priority date 7/1; deadline 8/1 (postmark date). No application fee. Application may be submitted online. Admission notification on a rolling basis beginning on or about 8/30. **Financial aid:** Priority date 5/1; no closing date. FAFSA required. Applicants notified on a rolling basis starting 6/1.

Academics. Special study options: Combined bachelor's/graduate degree, cooperative education, cross-registration, double major, honors, internships, liberal arts/career combination, teacher certification program. **Credit/placement by examination:** AP, CLEP, ACT, institutional tests. 45 credit hours maximum toward bachelor's degree. Students must have approval of the academic advisor, department head, dean and vice president for academic affairs prior to taking CLEP exam. **Support services:** Learning center, remedial instruction, study skills assistance, tutoring, writing center.

Honors college/program. Minimum requirements are 3.3 GPA and 24 ACT or 1100 SAT. 34 freshmen admitted.

Majors. Biology: General, marine. **Business:** Accounting, business admin, finance, marketing. **Communications:** General. **Computer sciences:** Computer science, information systems. **Education:** Early childhood, elementary, music, physical, secondary, special. **English:** English lit. **Health:** Medical records admin. **History:** General. **Math:** General. **Parks/recreation:** Facilities management. **Physical sciences:** Chemistry, physics. **Protective services:** Criminal justice. **Psychology:** General. **Public administration:** Social work. **Social sciences:** Political science, sociology. **Visual/performing arts:** Art, dramatic.

Most popular majors. Biology 6%, business/marketing 13%, communications/journalism 8%, computer/information sciences 14%, education 27%, public administration/social services 7%, security/protective services 9%.

Computing on campus. 405 workstations in library, computer center. Online course registration, online library, helpline, wireless network available.

Student life. Freshman orientation: Mandatory, $55 fee. Preregistration for classes offered. **Policies:** Freshmen permitted cars on campus. **Housing:** Single-sex dorms, apartments, substance-free housing available. $200 deposit, deadline 5/31. Housing for nontraditional students available. **Activities:** Bands, choral groups, dance, drama, music ensembles, musical theater, opera, radio station, student government, student newspaper, Student Christian Association.

Athletics. NCAA. **Intercollegiate:** Baseball M, basketball, bowling W, cross-country, football (tackle) M, golf, soccer W, softball W, tennis, track and field, volleyball W. **Intramural:** Baseball M, basketball, softball, swimming, tennis, track and field, volleyball W. **Team name:** Hornets.

Student services. Adult student services, alcohol/substance abuse counseling, career counseling, services for economically disadvantaged, student employment services, financial aid counseling, health services, minority student services, personal counseling, placement for graduates, veterans' counselor. **Physically disabled:** Services for visually impaired. **Learning disabled:** Comprehensive services available.

Contact. E-mail: dcrump@alasu.edu
Phone: (334) 229-4291 Toll-free number: (800) 253-5037
Fax: (334) 229-4984
Danielle Kennedy-Lamar, Director of Admissions and Recruitment, Alabama State University, PO Box 271, Montgomery, AL 36101-0271

American Sentinel University

Birmingham, Alabama
www.accis.edu **CB code: 3806**

- For-profit 4-year technical college
- Very large city
- 4,500 undergraduates

General. Accredited by DETC. Distance education with a revolving enrollment policy allows students to begin their studies immediately after enrolling. **Degrees:** 105 bachelor's awarded; master's offered. **Calendar:** Continuous. **Full-time faculty:** 5 total. **Part-time faculty:** 40 total.

Basis for selection. Open admission, but selective for some programs.

2006-2007 Annual costs. Total cost of typical bachelor's program: $30,750; includes application fee, technology fee, and books.

Application procedures. Admission: No deadline. $40 fee. Application may be submitted online. Admission notification on a rolling basis.

Academics. Special study options: Distance learning, honors, independent study, liberal arts/career combination. **Credit/placement by examination:** AP, CLEP. **Support services:** Tutoring.

Majors. Business: Management information systems. **Computer sciences:** General, computer science, information systems, information technology, system admin.

Computing on campus. PC or laptop required.

Student life. Freshman orientation: Available.

Contact. E-mail: admiss@accis.edu
Phone: (205) 323-6191 Toll-free number: (800) 729-2427
Fax: (205) 328-2229
David Lenhart, Director of Admissions, American Sentinel University, 2101 Magnolia Avenue, Suite 200, Birmingham, AL 35205-2827

Andrew Jackson University

Birmingham, Alabama
www.aju.edu **CB code: 3877**

- For-profit 4-year virtual university, business and liberal arts college
- Very large city
- 250 degree-seeking undergraduates
- Application essay required

General. Accredited by DETC. **Degrees:** 5 bachelor's awarded; master's offered. **Calendar:** Continuous. **Part-time faculty:** 46 total.

Basis for selection. Open admission. **Homeschooled:** State high school equivalency certificate, letter of recommendation (nonparent) required.

2005-2006 Annual costs. Tuition/fees: $3,900. Books/supplies: $1,000.

Application procedures. Admission: No deadline. $75 fee. Application may be submitted online. Admission notification on a rolling basis. Must reply by May 1 or within 12 week(s) if notified thereafter.

Academics. Special study options: Accelerated study, distance learning, independent study. **Credit/placement by examination:** AP, CLEP. 30 credit hours maximum toward associate degree, 60 toward bachelor's. **Support services:** Reduced course load.

Majors. Business: General. **Communications:** General. **Protective services:** Criminal justice.

Contact. E-mail: admissions@aju.edu
Phone: (205) 871-9288 Toll-free number: (800) 429-9300
Fax: (205) 871-9294
Betty Howell, Director of Admissions, Andrew Jackson University, 10 Old Montgomery Highway, Suite 225, Birmingham, AL 35209

Athens State University
Athens, Alabama
www.athens.edu **CB code: 0706**

- Public upper-division business and teachers college
- Commuter campus in large town
- 72% of applicants admitted

General. Founded in 1822. Regionally accredited. State's only 2-year senior college serving transfers from junior, community, technical colleges and other 4-year accredited institutions. **Degrees:** 618 bachelor's awarded. **Articulation:** Agreements with state schools through the Alabama Articulation and General Studies Committee. **Location:** 14 miles from Decatur, 24 miles from Huntsville. **Calendar:** Semester, extensive summer session. **Full-time faculty:** 64 total; 73% have terminal degrees, 9% minority, 47% women. **Part-time faculty:** 86 total; 8% have terminal degrees, 12% minority, 54% women. **Class size:** 44% < 20, 44% 20-39, 4% 40-49, 3% 50-99, 5% >100.

Student profile. 2,496 degree-seeking undergraduates. 806 applied as first time-transfer students, 578 admitted, 228 enrolled. 81% transferred from two-year, 19% transferred from four-year institutions.

African American:	11%	**Out-of-state:**	6%
Asian American:	1%	**Live on campus:**	1%
Hispanic American:	1%	**25 or older:**	69%
Native American:	3%		

Basis for selection. College transcript required. Upper-division institution; all students admitted at junior level or above. ELPT recommended for applicants who are not native speakers of English. Transfer accepted as juniors, seniors.

2005-2006 Annual costs. Tuition/fees: $3,870; $7,200 out-of-state. Books/supplies: $800.

Financial aid. **Need-based:** 21% of total undergraduate aid awarded as scholarships/grants, 79% as loans/jobs. **Non-need-based:** Scholarships awarded for academics, alumni affiliation, art, athletics, leadership, minority status.

Application procedures. **Admission:** Rolling admission. $30 fee. **Financial aid:** FAFSA required.

Academics. **Special study options:** Cooperative education, distance learning, double major, dual enrollment of high school students, independent study, study abroad, teacher certification program, weekend college. **Credit/placement by examination:** AP, CLEP.

Majors. **Biology:** General. **Business:** Accounting, business admin, human resources, information resources management. **Computer sciences:** General. **Education:** General, biology, chemistry, early childhood, elementary, English, history, mathematics, middle, physical, physics, science, secondary, social science, social studies, special, trade/industrial. **Engineering technology:** Instrumentation. **History:** General. **Interdisciplinary:** Behavioral sciences. **Liberal arts:** Arts/sciences. **Math:** General. **Philosophy/religion:** Religion. **Physical sciences:** Chemistry, physics. **Protective services:** Criminal justice. **Psychology:** General. **Social sciences:** Political science, sociology. **Visual/performing arts:** Art.

Most popular majors. Business/marketing 31%, computer/information sciences 6%, education 34%, interdisciplinary studies 6%, liberal arts 6%.

Computing on campus. 150 workstations in library, computer center, student center. Dormitories wired for high-speed internet access and linked to campus network. Commuter students can connect to campus network. Online library available.

Student life. **Housing:** Coed dorms available. $75 deposit. **Activities:** Drama, student government, student newspaper, African-American history association, BACCHUS, Centurions, Athenian Hosts/Hostesses, Fellowship of Christian students, campus ministries/Cross Seekers.

Athletics. **Team name:** Bears.

Student services. Career counseling, student employment services, financial aid counseling, minority student services, placement for graduates, veterans' counselor. **Physically disabled:** Services for visually, speech, hearing impaired.

Contact. E-mail: admissions@athens.edu
Phone: (256) 233-8220 Toll-free number: (800) 522-0272
Fax: (256) 233-6565
Necedah Henderson, Coordinator of Admissions, Athens State University, 300 North Beaty Street, Athens, AL 35611

Auburn University
Auburn, Alabama **CB member**
www.auburn.edu **CB code: 1005**

- Public 4-year university
- Commuter campus in large town
- 19,222 degree-seeking undergraduates: 8% part-time, 49% women, 8% African American, 2% Asian American, 2% Hispanic American, 1% Native American, 1% international
- 4,035 degree-seeking graduate students
- 82% of applicants admitted
- SAT or ACT (ACT writing optional) required
- 65% graduate within 6 years

General. Founded in 1856. Regionally accredited. **Degrees:** 3,919 bachelor's awarded; master's, doctoral, first professional offered. **ROTC:** Army, Navy, Air Force. **Location:** 55 miles from Montgomery, 110 miles from Atlanta. **Calendar:** Semester, extensive summer session. **Full-time faculty:** 1,176 total; 90% have terminal degrees, 16% minority, 29% women. **Part-time faculty:** 155 total; 48% have terminal degrees, 8% minority, 47% women. **Class size:** 27% < 20, 54% 20-39, 5% 40-49, 8% 50-99, 5% >100. **Special facilities:** Space power institute, electron microscopes, rhizotron, nuclear science center, arboretum, torsatron, center for arts and humanities, sports museum.

Freshman class profile. 14,249 applied, 11,616 admitted, 4,197 enrolled.

Mid 50% test scores		**Rank in top quarter:**	55%
SAT verbal:	500-600	**Rank in top tenth:**	31%
SAT math:	520-620	**Return as sophomores:**	85%
ACT:	21-27	**Out-of-state:**	41%
GPA 3.50 or higher:	53%	**Live on campus:**	46%
GPA 3.0-3.49:	34%	**Fraternities:**	24%
GPA 2.0-2.99:	13%	**Sororities:**	41%

Basis for selection. High school GPA and test scores considered equally. Preference given to alumni children. SAT or ACT must be received by August 1 or 3 weeks prior to start of semester.

High school preparation. 12 units required; 15 recommended. Required and recommended units include English 4, mathematics 3, social studies 3-4, science 2-3 and foreign language 2. Mathematics must include algebra I, algebra II, and either geometry, trigonometry, calculus or analysis. Science must include biology and a physical science.

2005-2006 Annual costs. Tuition/fees: $5,278; $14,878 out-of-state. Room/board: $6,952. Books/supplies: $900. Personal expenses: $1,988.

2004-2005 Financial aid. **Need-based:** 1,757 full-time freshmen applied for aid; 1,212 were judged to have need; 1,124 of these received aid. Average need met was 46%. Average scholarship/grant was $4,417; average loan $2,935. 34% of total undergraduate aid awarded as scholarships/grants, 66% as loans/jobs. **Non-need-based:** Awarded to 1,420 full-time undergraduates, including 464 freshmen. **Additional information:** State of Alabama has pre-paid college tuition plan for residents.

Application procedures. **Admission:** Closing date 8/1 (postmark date). $25 fee. Application may be submitted online. Admission notification on a rolling basis. Must reply by May 1 or within 4 week(s) if notified thereafter. Early action closing date is 3 weeks prior to start of semester; early action notification is continuous. **Financial aid:** Priority date 3/1; no closing date. FAFSA, institutional form required. Applicants notified on a rolling basis starting 5/1; must reply within 2 week(s) of notification.

Academics. **Special study options:** Accelerated study, cooperative education, distance learning, double major, dual enrollment of high school students, ESL, honors, independent study, internships, liberal arts/career combination, study abroad, teacher certification program. DVM/master's in veterinary specialty, dual option program in education/subject areas. **Credit/placement by examination:** AP, CLEP, institutional tests. **Support services:** Learning center, reduced course load, study skills assistance, tutoring, writing center.

Honors college/program. Minimum 29 ACT or 1280 SAT (exclusive of Writing) and GPA 3.5 required. 3.4 GPA considered. Approximately 200 freshmen accepted last year.

Majors. **Agriculture:** Animal sciences, aquaculture, economics, horticultural science, poultry, soil science. **Architecture:** Architecture, environmental design, interior, landscape. **Biology:** General, bacteriology, biochemistry, botany, entomology, marine, molecular, zoology. **Business:** Accounting, business admin, communications, finance, human resources, international, logistics, managerial economics, marketing, operations. **Communications:**

Journalism, public relations, radio/tv. **Computer sciences:** General. **Conservation:** Environmental science, forest sciences, wildlife. **Education:** Adult/continuing, early childhood, elementary, English, foreign languages, health, mathematics, music, physical, science, social science, special, voc/tech. **Engineering:** Aerospace, agricultural, architectural, chemical, civil, computer, electrical, materials, mechanical, software, textile. **Family/consumer sciences:** Apparel marketing, food/nutrition, housing. **Foreign languages:** French, German, Spanish. **Health:** Audiology/speech pathology, communication disorders, health care admin, nursing (RN), premedicine. **History:** General. **Math:** General, applied. **Parks/recreation:** Exercise sciences. **Philosophy/religion:** Philosophy, religion. **Physical sciences:** Chemistry, geology, physics. **Psychology:** General. **Public administration:** General, social work. **Science technology:** Biological. **Social sciences:** Anthropology, criminology, economics, geography, political science, sociology. **Transportation:** Aviation management. **Visual/performing arts:** Design, dramatic, industrial design, studio arts.

Most popular majors. Business/marketing 26%, education 9%, engineering/engineering technologies 15%, social sciences 8%.

Computing on campus. 600 workstations in dormitories, library, computer center, student center. Dormitories linked to campus network. Commuter students can connect to campus network. Online course registration, online library, helpline, repair service available.

Student life. Freshman orientation: Available, $75 fee. Preregistration for classes offered. **Policies:** Freshmen permitted cars on campus. **Housing:** Coed dorms, single-sex dorms, special housing for disabled, apartments, fraternity/sorority housing available. $100 deposit. Honors housing available. **Activities:** Bands, choral groups, dance, drama, film society, literary magazine, music ensembles, musical theater, opera, radio station, student government, student newspaper, symphony orchestra, TV station, over 300 religious, political, ethnic, and social service organizations.

Athletics. NCAA. **Intercollegiate:** Baseball M, basketball, cross-country, diving, equestrian W, football (tackle) M, golf, gymnastics W, soccer W, softball W, swimming, tennis, track and field, volleyball W. **Intramural:** Badminton, basketball, bowling, cheerleading, football (non-tackle), golf, gymnastics, lacrosse, racquetball, rugby, skiing, soccer, softball, swimming, table tennis, tennis, track and field, volleyball, wrestling M. **Team name:** Tigers.

Student services. Adult student services, alcohol/substance abuse counseling, career counseling, student employment services, financial aid counseling, health services, minority student services, personal counseling, placement for graduates, veterans' counselor, women's services. **Physically disabled:** Services for visually, speech, hearing impaired.

Contact. E-mail: admissions@auburn.edu
Phone: (334) 844-4080 Toll-free number: (800) 282-8769
Fax: (334) 844-6436
Doyle Bickers, Director, Auburn University, 108 Mary Martin Hall, Auburn, AL 36849

Auburn University at Montgomery

Montgomery, Alabama — **CB member**
www.aum.edu — **CB code: 1036**

- Public 4-year university
- Commuter campus in small city
- 4,118 degree-seeking undergraduates: 35% part-time, 65% women, 33% African American, 2% Asian American, 1% Hispanic American, 1% Native American
- 750 degree-seeking graduate students
- 98% of applicants admitted
- SAT or ACT (ACT writing optional) required

General. Founded in 1967. Regionally accredited. **Degrees:** 621 bachelor's awarded; master's, doctoral offered. **ROTC:** Army, Air Force. **Location:** 7 miles from downtown. **Calendar:** Semester, extensive summer session. **Full-time faculty:** 186 total; 80% have terminal degrees, 12% minority, 40% women. **Part-time faculty:** 119 total; 24% have terminal degrees, 9% minority, 57% women. **Class size:** 50% < 20, 47% 20-39, 2% 40-49, less than 1% 50-99.

Freshman class profile. 814 applied, 798 admitted, 758 enrolled.

Mid 50% test scores			
ACT:	18-23	**Live on campus:**	22%
Out-of-state:	4%	**Fraternities:**	16%
		Sororities:	8%

Basis for selection. GPA and ACT/SAT scores considered for admission. Provisional admission may be available for students who do not meet requirements for regular admission. C average after 18 hours of academic courses required for provisional students to become regular students.

High school preparation. College-preparatory program recommended. Recommended units include English 4, mathematics 3, social studies 2, history 2, science 2 (laboratory 2) and foreign language 2.

2005-2006 Annual costs. Tuition/fees: $4,720; $13,690 out-of-state. Room/board: $4,890. Books/supplies: $600. Personal expenses: $1,060.

2004-2005 Financial aid. Need-based: 382 full-time freshmen applied for aid; 374 were judged to have need; 291 of these received aid. Average scholarship/grant was $3,450; average loan $2,327. 26% of total undergraduate aid awarded as scholarships/grants, 74% as loans/jobs. **Non-need-based:** Scholarships awarded for academics, alumni affiliation, art, athletics, job skills, leadership, minority status, music/drama, state residency.

Application procedures. Admission: No deadline. $25 fee. Application may be submitted online. Admission notification on a rolling basis. **Financial aid:** Priority date 3/1; no closing date. FAFSA, institutional form required. Applicants notified on a rolling basis; must reply within 2 week(s) of notification.

Academics. Interdisciplinary Master of Liberal Arts available. **Special study options:** Accelerated study, cooperative education, cross-registration, distance learning, double major, dual enrollment of high school students, ESL, exchange student, honors, independent study, internships, liberal arts/career combination, study abroad, teacher certification program, weekend college. Joint Ph.D. in public administration with Auburn University; cooperative doctoral program in Educational Leadership with Auburn University (Ed.D.). **Credit/placement by examination:** AP, CLEP, IB, ACT, institutional tests. 60 credit hours maximum toward bachelor's degree. **Support services:** Learning center, reduced course load, remedial instruction, tutoring.

Majors. Biology: General. **Business:** General, accounting, business admin, finance, human resources, management information systems, managerial economics, marketing. **Communications:** General. **Education:** Elementary, secondary. **English:** English lit. **Foreign languages:** General. **Health:** Nursing (RN). **History:** General. **Liberal arts:** Arts/sciences. **Math:** General. **Physical sciences:** General. **Protective services:** Criminal justice. **Psychology:** General. **Social sciences:** Political science, sociology. **Visual/performing arts:** Art.

Most popular majors. Business/marketing 36%, education 17%, health sciences 11%, psychology 6%, security/protective services 6%.

Computing on campus. 300 workstations in library, computer center, student center. Dormitories wired for high-speed internet access and linked to campus network. Commuter students can connect to campus network. Online course registration, online library, repair service, student web hosting available.

Student life. Freshman orientation: Mandatory, $40 fee. Preregistration for classes offered. Programs held 2 days before start of each semester. 2 sessions, one hour each, morning and evening. **Policies:** Students are required to conform to all policies and regulations of the university by October registration. Freshmen permitted cars on campus. **Housing:** Special housing for disabled, apartments available. $100 nonrefundable deposit. **Activities:** Choral groups, dance, drama, literary magazine, musical theater, student government, student newspaper, College Democratic international student association, Baptist campus ministry, choir, Landmark Campus ministry, American Humanics, Caunterbury Society, Disciples of Christ, Circle K, NAACP, international student association.

Athletics. NAIA. **Intercollegiate:** Baseball M, basketball, soccer, tennis. **Intramural:** Baseball, basketball M, bowling, football (non-tackle), softball, tennis, volleyball. **Team name:** Senators.

Student services. Adult student services, career counseling, student employment services, health services, personal counseling, placement for graduates, veterans' counselor. **Physically disabled:** Services for visually, speech, hearing impaired.

Contact. E-mail: auminfo@mail.aum.edu
Phone: (334) 244-3614 Toll-free number: (800) 227-2649
Fax: (334) 244-3795
Valerie Crawford, Associate Director of Enrollment Services, Auburn University at Montgomery, 7400 East Drive, Montgomery, AL 36124-4023

Birmingham-Southern College

Birmingham, Alabama — **CB member**
www.bsc.edu — **CB code: 1064**

- Private 4-year liberal arts college affiliated with United Methodist Church
- Residential campus in very large city

- 1,356 degree-seeking undergraduates: 2% part-time, 58% women, 6% African American, 3% Asian American, 1% Hispanic American
- 97 degree-seeking graduate students
- 83% of applicants admitted
- SAT or ACT (ACT writing optional), application essay required
- 70% graduate within 6 years

General. Founded in 1856. Regionally accredited. **Degrees:** 299 bachelor's awarded; master's offered. **ROTC:** Army, Air Force. **Location:** 3 miles from downtown. **Calendar:** 4-1-4, limited summer session. **Full-time faculty:** 96 total; 95% have terminal degrees, 2% minority, 40% women. **Part-time faculty:** 28 total; 18% have terminal degrees, 39% women. **Class size:** 61% < 20, 36% 20-39, 3% 40-49, less than 1% 50-99. **Special facilities:** Planetarium, Academic Resource Center, Science Laboratory center, Southern Environmental Center and Interactive Museum, Ecoscape Garden, Striplin Fitness Center.

Freshman class profile. 1,157 applied, 956 admitted, 367 enrolled.

Mid 50% test scores		**Rank in top tenth:**	31%
SAT verbal:	550-670	**Out-of-state:**	23%
SAT math:	540-640	**Live on campus:**	93%
ACT:	24-30	**Fraternities:**	51%
Rank in top quarter:	64%	**Sororities:**	58%

Basis for selection. High school record most important, followed by test scores, recommendations, and required essay. Interview required for early admission; recommended for borderline applicants. Auditions required for music, theater, dance majors. **Homeschooled:** Interviews recommended.

High school preparation. 16 units required. Required and recommended units include English 4, mathematics 4, social studies 2, history 2, science 4, foreign language 2 and academic electives 10.

2005-2006 Annual costs. Tuition/fees: $21,450. Room/board: $7,230. Books/supplies: $1,000. Personal expenses: $500.

2005-2006 Financial aid. Need-based: 272 full-time freshmen applied for aid; 187 were judged to have need; 187 of these received aid. Average need met was 78%. Average scholarship/grant was $12,222; average loan $3,736. 41% of total undergraduate aid awarded as scholarships/grants, 59% as loans/jobs. **Non-need-based:** Awarded to 1,004 full-time undergraduates, including 267 freshmen. Scholarships awarded for academics, alumni affiliation, art, athletics, job skills, leadership, minority status, music/drama, religious affiliation, ROTC, state residency. **Additional information:** Auditions required for music, theater, dance applicants seeking scholarships. Portfolios required for art applicants seeking scholarships, and essays recommended for all applicants seeking scholarships.

Application procedures. Admission: Priority date 1/15; no deadline. $25 fee, may be waived for applicants with need. Application may be submitted online. Admission notification on a rolling basis beginning on or about 10/1. Must reply by May 1 or within 2 week(s) if notified thereafter. **Financial aid:** Priority date 3/1, closing date 8/1. Applicants notified on a rolling basis starting 3/30.

Academics. Special study options: Combined bachelor's/graduate degree, cooperative education, cross-registration, double major, dual enrollment of high school students, exchange student, honors, independent study, internships, liberal arts/career combination, semester at sea, student-designed major, study abroad, teacher certification program, Washington semester. 4-1-4 in nursing with Vanderbilt; 3-2 in engineering with Washington University, Columbia University, University of Alabama, and Auburn University; 3-2 in environment studies with Duke University. **Credit/placement by examination:** AP, CLEP, IB, institutional tests. 64 credit hours maximum toward bachelor's degree. **Support services:** Pre-admission summer program, reduced course load, study skills assistance, tutoring, writing center.

Majors. Biology: General. **Business:** General, accounting, finance, international, marketing. **Computer sciences:** General, computer science. **Conservation:** Environmental studies. **Education:** General, art, early childhood, elementary, music, special. **Foreign languages:** French, German, Spanish. **History:** General. **Interdisciplinary:** Math/computer science. **Math:** General. **Philosophy/religion:** Philosophy, religion. **Physical sciences:** Chemistry, physics. **Psychology:** General. **Social sciences:** Economics, political science, sociology. **Theology:** Sacred music. **Visual/performing arts:** General, art, art history/conservation, dance, dramatic, drawing, music history, music theory/composition, painting, photography, piano/organ, sculpture, voice/opera.

Computing on campus. 252 workstations in dormitories, library, computer center, student center. Dormitories linked to campus network. Commuter students can connect to campus network.

Student life. Freshman orientation: Mandatory. Preregistration for classes offered. One day mini-session in June and 4 day session prior to beginning of classes. **Policies:** Freshmen permitted cars on campus. **Housing:** Guaranteed on-campus for all undergraduates. Single-sex dorms, special housing for disabled, apartments, fraternity/sorority housing, substance-free housing available. $100 deposit, deadline 5/1. Handicapped students accommodated on individual basis. **Activities:** Bands, choral groups, dance, drama, literary magazine, musical theater, radio station, student government, student newspaper, International Student Association, Fellowship of Christian Athletes, Young Republicans, Black Student Union, Allies, S.O.S. (students offering support).

Athletics. NCAA. **Intercollegiate:** Baseball M, basketball, cross-country, golf, rifle W, soccer, softball W, tennis, volleyball W. **Intramural:** Basketball, racquetball, soccer, softball, table tennis, volleyball. **Team name:** Panthers.

Student services. Adult student services, campus ministries, career counseling, student employment services, health services, personal counseling, placement for graduates, veterans' counselor.

Contact. E-mail: admission@bsc.edu
Phone: (205) 226-4698 Toll-free number: (800) 523-5793
Fax: (205) 226-3074
Sheri Salmon, Vice President for Admission, Birmingham-Southern College, 900 Arkadelphia Road, Birmingham, AL 35254

Columbia Southern University
Orange Beach, Alabama
www.columbiasouthern.edu **CB code: 3878**

- For-profit 4-year virtual business college
- Small town
- 6,100 degree-seeking undergraduates
- 2,550 graduate students

General. Accredited by DETC. **Degrees:** 660 bachelor's awarded; master's offered. **Location:** 60 miles from Mobile. **Calendar:** Continuous. **Full-time faculty:** 4 total. **Part-time faculty:** 60 total.

Basis for selection. Open admission.

2005-2006 Annual costs. Tuition/fees: $3,770.

Application procedures. Admission: No deadline. $25 fee.

Academics. Credit/placement by examination: CLEP.

Majors. Business: Business admin. **Protective services:** Law enforcement admin.

Student life. Activities: Student newspaper.

Contact. E-mail: admissions@columbiasouthern.edu
Phone: (251) 981-3771 Toll-free number: (800) 977-8449
Fax: (251) 981-3815
Tommy Cooley, Director of Admissions, Columbia Southern University, 25326 Canal Road, Orange Beach, AL 36561

Concordia College
Selma, Alabama
www.concordiaselma.edu **CB code: 1989**

- Private 4-year liberal arts college affiliated with Lutheran Church - Missouri Synod
- Residential campus in large town
- 850 degree-seeking undergraduates

General. Founded in 1922. Regionally accredited. **Degrees:** 25 bachelor's, 30 associate awarded. **Location:** 50 miles from Montgomery. **Calendar:** Semester, limited summer session. **Full-time faculty:** 18 total. **Part-time faculty:** 31 total.

Basis for selection. Open admission. 2.0 GPA required for unconditional admission. Students who do not fulfill requirements may be admitted on conditional basis.

High school preparation. 20 units recommended. Recommended units include English 4, mathematics 2, social studies 3, science 2 and foreign language 1.

2005-2006 Annual costs. Tuition/fees: $6,167. Room/board: $3,600. Books/supplies: $400.

2005-2006 Financial aid. All financial aid based on need.

Application procedures. **Admission:** Priority date 8/1; deadline 8/15. $10 fee, may be waived for applicants with need. Admission notification on a rolling basis beginning on or about 8/15. **Financial aid:** Priority date 4/1; no closing date. FAFSA, institutional form, CSS PROFILE required. Applicants notified on a rolling basis starting 6/15; must reply within 2 week(s) of notification.

Academics. **Special study options:** Independent study, liberal arts/career combination. **Credit/placement by examination:** CLEP, institutional tests. **Support services:** Learning center, pre-admission summer program, reduced course load, remedial instruction, tutoring.

Majors. **Business:** Business admin. **Education:** Early childhood, elementary.

Most popular majors. Biology 18%, education 82%.

Computing on campus. 30 workstations in library, computer center.

Student life. **Freshman orientation:** Mandatory. Preregistration for classes offered. **Housing:** Single-sex dorms available. **Activities:** Choral groups, drama, music ensembles, student government, student newspaper, Phi Theta Kappa, Gentlemen Care Group Club, Ambassador's Club, American Red Cross Club.

Athletics. **Intercollegiate:** Baseball M, basketball, softball W. **Intramural:** Baseball M, basketball, football (tackle) M, softball, table tennis, tennis, volleyball. **Team name:** Hornets.

Student services. Adult student services, career counseling, student employment services, health services, personal counseling, placement for graduates, veterans' counselor.

Contact. Phone: (334) 874-5700
Evelyn Pickens, Director of Admissions, Concordia College, 1804 Green Street, Selma, AL 36701

Faulkner University
Montgomery, Alabama
www.faulkner.edu **CB code: 1034**

- Private 4-year university and liberal arts college affiliated with Church of Christ
- Residential campus in small city
- 2,144 degree-seeking undergraduates: 27% part-time, 65% women, 43% African American, 1% Hispanic American
- 382 degree-seeking graduate students
- 50% of applicants admitted
- SAT or ACT (ACT writing optional) required
- 32% graduate within 6 years

General. Founded in 1942. Regionally accredited. Extension centers in Birmingham, Huntsville, and Mobile offer associate degrees. **Degrees:** 572 bachelor's, 61 associate awarded; master's, first professional offered. **ROTC:** Army, Air Force. **Location:** 5 miles from downtown. **Calendar:** Semester, limited summer session. **Full-time faculty:** 60 total. **Part-time faculty:** 300 total. **Class size:** 77% < 20, 18% 20-39, 3% 40-49, 2% 50-99, less than 1% >100.

Freshman class profile. 624 applied, 311 admitted, 205 enrolled.

Mid 50% test scores			
SAT verbal:	480-570	Rank in top quarter:	38%
SAT math:	410-590	Rank in top tenth:	22%
ACT:	19-27	End year in good standing:	86%
GPA 3.50 or higher:	44%	Return as sophomores:	61%
GPA 3.0-3.49:	32%	Out-of-state:	33%
GPA 2.0-2.99:	23%	Live on campus:	58%

Basis for selection. Academic record, test scores, and personal or career goals most important. Interview, essay recommended.

High school preparation. 15 units required. Required units include English 3. 9 units from among social sciences, foreign language, mathematics and science required.

2005-2006 Annual costs. Tuition/fees: $10,500. Room/board: $5,200. Books/supplies: $1,200. Personal expenses: $1,200.

2004-2005 Financial aid. **Need-based:** 170 full-time freshmen applied for aid; 136 were judged to have need; 136 of these received aid. Average need met was 60%. Average scholarship/grant was $2,450; average loan $2,625. 33% of total undergraduate aid awarded as scholarships/grants, 67% as loans/jobs. **Non-need-based:** Awarded to 825 full-time undergraduates, including 115 freshmen. Scholarships awarded for academics, alumni affiliation, art, athletics, leadership, music/drama, religious affiliation, ROTC, state residency.

Application procedures. **Admission:** Priority date 2/15; no deadline. $10 fee, may be waived for applicants with need. Application may be submitted online. Admission notification on a rolling basis beginning on or about 8/15. **Financial aid:** Priority date 5/1; no closing date. FAFSA, institutional form required. Applicants notified on a rolling basis starting 6/1; must reply within 3 week(s) of notification.

Academics. Full-time students required to take 1 Bible course per semester. **Special study options:** Combined bachelor's/graduate degree, cooperative education, cross-registration, distance learning, double major, dual enrollment of high school students, honors, independent study, internships, liberal arts/career combination, teacher certification program, weekend college. **Credit/placement by examination:** AP, CLEP, institutional tests. 16 credit hours maximum toward associate degree, 32 toward bachelor's. **Support services:** Learning center, reduced course load, remedial instruction, study skills assistance, tutoring.

Majors. **Area/ethnic studies:** American. **Biology:** General. **Business:** General, accounting, business admin, human resources, marketing, office management. **Computer sciences:** Information systems. **Education:** General, biology, chemistry, elementary, English, history, mathematics, middle, physical, science, secondary, social studies. **Health:** Predentistry, premedicine, preveterinary. **History:** General. **Interdisciplinary:** Biological/physical sciences. **Legal studies:** Prelaw. **Liberal arts:** Arts/sciences. **Math:** General. **Parks/recreation:** Sports admin. **Philosophy/religion:** Religion. **Protective services:** Criminal justice. **Psychology:** General. **Theology:** Bible, religious ed, theology. **Visual/performing arts:** General, studio arts.

Computing on campus. 250 workstations in dormitories, library, computer center, student center. Dormitories wired for high-speed internet access and linked to campus network. Online library, helpline available.

Student life. **Freshman orientation:** Mandatory. Preregistration for classes offered. **Policies:** Religious observance required. Freshmen permitted cars on campus. **Housing:** Guaranteed on-campus for all undergraduates. Single-sex dorms, special housing for disabled, apartments available. $50 fully refundable deposit. **Activities:** Choral groups, drama, music ensembles, musical theater, student government, student newspaper, minister's club, service organizations, religious organizations.

Athletics. NAIA, NCCAA. **Intercollegiate:** Baseball M, basketball M, cross-country, golf M, softball W. **Intramural:** Badminton, basketball, softball, table tennis, tennis, track and field, volleyball. **Team name:** Eagles.

Student services. Adult student services, career counseling, student employment services, health services, personal counseling, placement for graduates, veterans' counselor.

Contact. Phone: (334) 386-7200 Toll-free number: (800) 879-9816
Fax: (334) 386-7137
Keith Mock, Director of Admissions, Faulkner University, 5345 Atlanta Highway, Montgomery, AL 36109-3398

Heritage Christian University
Florence, Alabama
www.hcu.edu **CB code: 0805**

- Private 4-year Bible college affiliated with Church of Christ
- Commuter campus in large town
- 97 degree-seeking undergraduates: 56% part-time, 18% women, 19% African American, 6% international
- 11 degree-seeking graduate students

General. Founded in 1971. Accredited by ABHE. **Degrees:** 23 bachelor's, 10 associate awarded; master's offered. **Location:** 125 miles from Birmingham, 50 miles from Huntsville. **Calendar:** Semester, limited summer session. **Full-time faculty:** 4 total; 50% have terminal degrees. **Part-time faculty:** 12 total; 42% have terminal degrees, 50% women. **Class size:** 96% < 20, 4% 20-39.

Freshman class profile.

Out-of-state:	40%	Live on campus:	10%

Basis for selection. Open admission. Religious affiliation and recommendations very important, school achievement considered. Interview recommended.

2005-2006 Annual costs. Tuition/fees: $8,940. Room only: $1,650.

2004-2005 Financial aid. **Need-based:** 2 full-time freshmen applied for aid; 2 were judged to have need; 2 of these received aid. Average need met was 63%. Average loan was $2,625. **Non-need-based:** Awarded to 44 full-time undergraduates, including 6 freshmen.

Application procedures. **Admission:** No deadline. $25 fee. Admission notification on a rolling basis. **Financial aid:** Priority date 6/1; no closing date. FAFSA required. Applicants notified on a rolling basis starting 6/1; must reply within 2 week(s) of notification.

Academics. **Special study options:** Accelerated study, distance learning, dual enrollment of high school students, independent study, internships. **Credit/placement by examination:** AP, CLEP, institutional tests. 24 credit hours maximum toward associate degree, 24 toward bachelor's. **Support services:** Reduced course load, remedial instruction, study skills assistance, tutoring.

Majors. **Theology:** Bible.

Computing on campus. 12 workstations in library, computer center. Wireless network available.

Student life. **Freshman orientation:** Mandatory. Preregistration for classes offered. 2 semester hour course. **Policies:** Freshmen permitted cars on campus. **Housing:** Guaranteed on-campus for freshmen. Single-sex dorms, apartments, substance-free housing available. **Activities:** Student government, Christian service program, mission club.

Student services. Career counseling, student employment services, personal counseling, placement for graduates, veterans' counselor.

Contact. E-mail: hcu@hcu.edu
Phone: (256) 766-6610 Toll-free number: (800) 367-3565
Fax: (256) 766-9289
Nathan Hunnicutt, Director of Admissions, Heritage Christian University, 3625 Helton Drive, Florence, AL 35630

Herzing College

Birmingham, Alabama
www.herzing.edu **CB code: 2851**

- For-profit 4-year business and technical college
- Very large city
- 430 degree-seeking undergraduates

General. Accredited by ACCSCT. **Degrees:** 57 bachelor's, 69 associate awarded. **Calendar:** Semester, extensive summer session. **Full-time faculty:** 10 total. **Part-time faculty:** 24 total.

Basis for selection. Students must submit high school transcript or GED, interview with an admissions representative, pass an admissions exam or have an SAT score of 850 or higher (exclusive of Writing), or an ACT score of 17 or higher.

2005-2006 Annual costs. Per-credit-hour charge ranges from $255 to $300 depending on program.

Financial aid. All financial aid based on need.

Application procedures. **Admission:** No deadline. No application fee. **Financial aid:** FAFSA required.

Academics. **Credit/placement by examination:** CLEP.

Majors. **Computer sciences:** General, information systems, LAN/WAN management. **Engineering technology:** Computer systems.

Contact. E-mail: admiss@bhm.herzing.edu
Phone: (205) 916-2800 Fax: (205) 916-2807
Kim Conway, Director of Admissions, Herzing College, 280 West Valley Avenue, Birmingham, AL 35209

Huntingdon College

Montgomery, Alabama **CB member**
www.huntingdon.edu **CB code: 1303**

- Private 4-year liberal arts college affiliated with United Methodist Church
- Residential campus in small city
- 750 degree-seeking undergraduates
- 63% of applicants admitted
- SAT or ACT (ACT writing optional) required

General. Founded in 1854. Regionally accredited. **Degrees:** 111 bachelor's awarded. **ROTC:** Army, Air Force. **Location:** 90 miles from Birmingham, 180 miles from Atlanta. **Calendar:** Semester, limited summer session. **Full-time faculty:** 34 total. **Part-time faculty:** 20 total. **Special facilities:** Recital hall with individual practice studios, 3 theater/performance stages, super conducting 200 MHz Fourier transform nuclear magnetic resonance spectrometer, gas chromatograph-mass spectrometer, Fourier transform infrared spectrophotometer, ecological center, sports medicine/athletic training facilities, United Methodist Church archives, psychology animal behavior lab, smart classrooms with audio/video equipment and wireless laptops.

Freshman class profile. 776 applied, 492 admitted, 186 enrolled.

Mid 50% test scores		**ACT:**	20-25
SAT verbal:	460-570	**Rank in top quarter:**	55%
SAT math:	430-550	**Rank in top tenth:**	26%

Basis for selection. GPA and test scores important. Marginal cases require essay, letters of recommendation, interview and other documentation. Interview, essay recommended. Audition required of music, drama, dance, musical theater majors; portfolio recommended for art, technical theater majors.

High school preparation. 15 units recommended. Recommended units include English 4, mathematics 3, social studies 2, science 2 (laboratory 2) and foreign language 2. 2 units in humanities recommended.

2006-2007 Annual costs. Tuition/fees: $16,690. Room/board: $6,400. Books/supplies: $700. Personal expenses: $865.

Financial aid. **Non-need-based:** Scholarships awarded for academics, alumni affiliation, art, leadership, music/drama, religious affiliation, ROTC, state residency.

Application procedures. **Admission:** Closing date 8/1. $20 fee, may be waived for applicants with need. Application may be submitted online. Admission notification on a rolling basis beginning on or about 9/15. Must reply by May 1 or within 4 week(s) if notified thereafter. **Financial aid:** Priority date 4/15; no closing date. FAFSA, institutional form required. Applicants notified on a rolling basis starting 3/1; must reply by 5/1 or within 4 week(s) of notification.

Academics. 4-part, 12-hour Liberal Arts Symposium core curriculum. **Special study options:** Combined bachelor's/graduate degree, cross-registration, double major, dual enrollment of high school students, honors, independent study, internships, liberal arts/career combination, student-designed major, study abroad, teacher certification program, Washington semester. Dual engineering degree with Auburn University and exchange student program with universities in Korea and Ireland; travel/study opportunities provided to all full-time juniors and seniors within regular educational costs or for nominal additional fees. **Credit/placement by examination:** AP, CLEP, IB. 30 credit hours maximum toward bachelor's degree. **Support services:** Learning center, reduced course load, study skills assistance, tutoring, writing center.

Majors. **Area/ethnic studies:** American, European, women's. **Biology:** General, cell/histology. **Business:** General, accounting, business admin, finance, international, managerial economics, marketing. **Communications:** General. **Computer sciences:** Computer graphics, computer science. **Conservation:** Environmental science. **Education:** Art, early childhood, elementary, middle, multi-level teacher, music, physical. **English:** Creative writing, speech/rhetoric. **Foreign languages:** Spanish. **Health:** Athletic training, predentistry, premedicine, prepharmacy, preveterinary. **History:** General. **Interdisciplinary:** Global studies. **Legal studies:** Prelaw. **Liberal arts:** Arts/sciences. **Math:** General. **Parks/recreation:** General, exercise sciences, health/fitness, sports admin. **Philosophy/religion:** Religion. **Physical sciences:** Chemistry. **Psychology:** General. **Public administration:** General, policy analysis. **Social sciences:** Political science. **Visual/performing arts:** Art, dramatic, music performance, music theory/composition, piano/organ, studio arts, voice/opera.

Computing on campus. PC or laptop required. 75 workstations in dormitories, library, computer center. Dormitories wired for high-speed internet access and linked to campus network. Commuter students can connect to campus network. Helpline, repair service, student web hosting, wireless network available.

Student life. **Freshman orientation:** Mandatory. Preregistration for classes offered. Orientation includes 2-day off-campus retreat prior to start of classes and ongoing seminars during first semester freshman year. **Policies:** Freshmen permitted cars on campus. **Housing:** Guaranteed on-campus for all undergraduates. Coed dorms, special housing for disabled available. $50 deposit. Students under age 21 must live on campus unless living with parent in metropolitan area. **Activities:** Jazz band, choral groups, dance, drama, literary magazine, music ensembles, musical theater, opera, student government, student newspaper, 50 clubs and organizations.

Athletics. NAIA. **Intercollegiate:** Baseball M, basketball, cross-country, football (tackle) M, golf M, soccer, softball W, tennis, volleyball W. **Intramural:** Baseball, basketball, fencing, football (non-tackle), football (tackle) M, golf, rugby, soccer, softball, table tennis, tennis, track and field, volleyball, weight lifting. **Team name:** Hawks.

Student services. Adult student services, alcohol/substance abuse counseling, campus ministries, career counseling, student employment services, financial aid counseling, health services, personal counseling, placement for graduates. **Physically disabled:** Services for visually, hearing impaired.

Contact. E-mail: admiss@huntingdon.edu
Phone: (334) 833-4497 Toll-free number: (800) 763-0313
Fax: (334) 833-4347
Christy Mehaffey, Director of Admissions, Huntingdon College, 1500 East Fairview Avenue, Montgomery, AL 36106-2148

Huntsville Bible College
Huntsville, Alabama
www.huntsvillebiblecollege.com/

- Private 4-year Bible college
- Small city
- 70 degree-seeking undergraduates

General. Accredited by ABHE. **Degrees:** 1 bachelor's, 2 associate awarded. **Location:** 87 miles from Birmingham, 100 miles from Nashville, Tennessee. **Calendar:** Semester. **Part-time faculty:** 13 total.

Freshman class profile. 15 enrolled.

Basis for selection. Open admission.

2005-2006 Annual costs. Tuition/fees: $2,250.

Application procedures. **Admission:** Closing date 9/1. $10 fee.

Academics. **Credit/placement by examination:** CLEP.

Majors. **Theology:** Bible, theology.

Contact. E-mail: students@huntsvillebiblecollege.com
Phone: (256) 539-0834 Fax: (256) 539-0854
Willie Brown, Director of Admissions, Huntsville Bible College, 904 Oakwood Avenue, Huntsville, AL 35811

ITT Technical Institute: Birmingham
Bessemer, Alabama
www.itt-tech.edu **CB code: 2696**

- For-profit 4-year technical college
- Commuter campus in very large city

General. Accredited by ACICS. **Calendar:** Quarter.

Annual costs/financial aid. Tuition varies by program, $260-$368 per credit hour.

Contact. Phone: (205) 991-5410
Director of Recruitment, 6270 Park South Drive, Bessemer, AL 35022

Jacksonville State University
Jacksonville, Alabama
www.jsu.edu **CB code: 1736**

- Public 4-year university
- Commuter campus in small town
- 6,937 degree-seeking undergraduates: 18% part-time, 58% women, 24% African American, 1% Asian American, 1% Hispanic American, 1% Native American, 1% international
- 1,825 degree-seeking graduate students
- 88% of applicants admitted
- SAT or ACT required

General. Founded in 1883. Regionally accredited. **Degrees:** 1,154 bachelor's awarded; master's offered. **ROTC:** Army. **Location:** 75 miles from Birmingham, 100 miles from Atlanta. **Calendar:** Semester, extensive summer session. **Full-time faculty:** 305 total; 66% have terminal degrees, 10% minority, 44% women. **Part-time faculty:** 129 total; 26% have terminal degrees, 3% minority, 37% women. **Class size:** 50% < 20, 37% 20-39, 6% 40-49, 6% 50-99, less than 1% >100. **Special facilities:** Space observatory, Little River Canyon field school, International House, extensive library.

Freshman class profile. 2,839 applied, 2,499 admitted, 1,151 enrolled.

Mid 50% test scores		**Live on campus:**	60%
SAT verbal:	420-530	**International:**	1%
SAT math:	410-520	**Fraternities:**	9%
ACT:	17-22	**Sororities:**	9%
Out-of-state:	12%		

Basis for selection. High school record and test scores important. ACT score of at least 16 or SAT score of at least 750 (exclusive of Writing) required for conditional admission. ACT score of at least 19 or SAT score of at least 900 (exclusive of Writing) required for unconditional admission. SAT/ACT scores must be submitted by beginning of term.

High school preparation. 15 units required. Required units include English 3 and academic electives 4. 8 units required in mathematics, science, foreign language, social studies/history.

2005-2006 Annual costs. Tuition/fees: $4,040; $8,080 out-of-state. Room/board: $4,094. Books/supplies: $1,089. Personal expenses: $2,903.

2005-2006 Financial aid. **Need-based:** 95% of total undergraduate aid awarded as scholarships/grants, 5% as loans/jobs. **Non-need-based:** Scholarships awarded for academics, alumni affiliation, art, athletics, music/drama, ROTC.

Application procedures. **Admission:** No deadline. $20 fee. Application may be submitted online. Admission notification on a rolling basis. **Financial aid:** Priority date 3/15; no closing date. FAFSA, institutional form required. Applicants notified on a rolling basis starting 5/15; must reply within 2 week(s) of notification.

Academics. **Special study options:** Accelerated study, combined bachelor's/graduate degree, cooperative education, distance learning, double major, dual enrollment of high school students, ESL, honors, independent study, internships, teacher certification program. **Credit/placement by examination:** AP, CLEP, institutional tests. 46 credit hours maximum toward bachelor's degree. Maximum credit hours awarded through CLEP examinations: 31 for general tests, 15 through subject tests. **Support services:** Learning center, pre-admission summer program, remedial instruction, tutoring.

Majors. **Biology:** General. **Business:** Accounting, business admin, finance, managerial economics, marketing. **Communications:** Radio/tv. **Computer sciences:** General. **Education:** Elementary, health, physical, secondary, special. **Engineering technology:** Electrical, manufacturing, occupational safety. **Family/consumer sciences:** General. **Foreign languages:** General. **Health:** Nursing (RN). **History:** General. **Liberal arts:** Arts/sciences. **Math:** General. **Parks/recreation:** General. **Physical sciences:** Chemistry, physics. **Protective services:** Criminal justice. **Psychology:** General. **Public administration:** Social work. **Social sciences:** Economics, geography, political science, sociology. **Visual/performing arts:** Art, dramatic.

Most popular majors. Business/marketing 12%, education 41%, health sciences 6%, public administration/social services 7%, security/protective services 7%.

Computing on campus. 330 workstations in library, computer center, student center. Dormitories linked to campus network. Commuter students can connect to campus network. Online course registration, helpline available.

Student life. **Freshman orientation:** Available, $40 fee. Preregistration for classes offered. **Policies:** Freshmen permitted cars on campus. **Housing:** Coed dorms, single-sex dorms, apartments, fraternity/sorority housing available. $100 deposit. **Activities:** Bands, choral groups, drama, music ensembles, musical theater, radio station, student government, student newspaper, symphony orchestra, TV station, Panhellenic council, adult learners forum, peer counselors, African American association, international student organization, book club.

Athletics. NCAA. **Intercollegiate:** Baseball M, basketball, cross-country, football (tackle) M, golf, rifle, soccer W, softball W, tennis, track and field, volleyball W. **Intramural:** Basketball, bowling, football (tackle) M, racquetball, rugby M, softball, tennis, track and field, volleyball. **Team name:** Gamecocks.

Student services. Career counseling, student employment services, financial aid counseling, health services, minority student services, on-campus daycare, personal counseling, placement for graduates, veterans' counselor. **Physically disabled:** Services for visually, speech, hearing impaired.

Contact. E-mail: info@jsucc.jsu.edu
Phone: (256) 782-5268 Toll-free number: (800) 231-5291
Fax: (256) 782-5121
Martha Mitchell, Director of Admissions, Jacksonville State University, 700 Pelham Road North, Jacksonville, AL 36265-1602

Judson College
Marion, Alabama
www.judson.edu **CB code: 1349**

- Private 4-year liberal arts college for women affiliated with Baptist faith
- Residential campus in small town
- 331 degree-seeking undergraduates: 22% part-time, 96% women
- 76% of applicants admitted
- SAT or ACT (ACT writing optional), interview required
- 51% graduate within 6 years; 23% enter graduate study

General. Founded in 1838. Regionally accredited. Men accepted for distance learning program only. **Degrees:** 72 bachelor's awarded. **ROTC:** Army. **Location:** 75 miles from Birmingham and Montgomery. **Calendar:** 2 semesters and one 7 1/2-week session. Limited summer session. **Full-time faculty:** 28 total; 71% have terminal degrees, 4% minority, 46% women. **Part-time faculty:** 6 total; 50% have terminal degrees, 50% women. **Class size:** 94% < 20, 6% 20-39. **Special facilities:** Alabama Women's Hall of Fame, Baptist missionary memorabilia, equestrian facilities.

Freshman class profile. 280 applied, 214 admitted, 79 enrolled.

Mid 50% test scores			
SAT verbal:	460-650	Rank in top quarter:	56%
SAT math:	450-620	Rank in top tenth:	28%
ACT:	18-25	End year in good standing:	77%
GPA 3.50 or higher:	32%	Return as sophomores:	64%
GPA 3.0-3.49:	36%	Out-of-state:	12%
GPA 2.0-2.99:	32%	Live on campus:	94%
		International:	1%

Basis for selection. Academic record, recommendations, test scores considered. Interview required.

High school preparation. 16 units required; 20 recommended. Required and recommended units include English 4, mathematics 2-4, social studies 3-4, history 2, science 2-4, foreign language 2 and academic electives 5.

2006-2007 Annual costs. Tuition/fees (projected): $10,670. Room/board: $6,600. Books/supplies: $800. Personal expenses: $1,600.

2004-2005 Financial aid. Need-based: 79 full-time freshmen applied for aid; 66 were judged to have need; 66 of these received aid. Average need met was 77%. Average scholarship/grant was $7,376; average loan $2,611. 62% of total undergraduate aid awarded as scholarships/grants, 38% as loans/jobs. **Non-need-based:** Awarded to 48 full-time undergraduates, including 19 freshmen. Scholarships awarded for academics, art, athletics, leadership, music/drama, religious affiliation, state residency.

Application procedures. Admission: No deadline. $30 fee, may be waived for applicants with need. Application may be submitted online. Admission notification on a rolling basis beginning on or about 9/1. **Financial aid:** Priority date 3/15; no closing date. FAFSA, institutional form required. Applicants notified on a rolling basis starting 3/15; must reply within 2 week(s) of notification.

Academics. Special study options: Accelerated study, cross-registration, distance learning, double major, dual enrollment of high school students, independent study, internships, student-designed major, study abroad, teacher certification program, Washington semester. **Credit/placement by examination:** AP, CLEP, institutional tests. 30 credit hours maximum toward bachelor's degree. No student may receive more than 30 semester hours of non-attendance credit from all sources, or more than six semester hours in any one department. Maximum permitted from CLEP General Examinations is 15 of 30 hours. **Support services:** Reduced course load, remedial instruction, study skills assistance, tutoring, writing center.

Majors. Biology: General. **Business:** General, business admin. **Education:** Elementary, English, mathematics, music, science, secondary, social science, social studies. **English:** English lit. **Foreign languages:** General. **History:** General. **Math:** General. **Philosophy/religion:** Religion. **Physical sciences:** Chemistry. **Protective services:** Law enforcement admin. **Psychology:** General. **Theology:** Theology. **Visual/performing arts:** Art.

Most popular majors. Biology 18%, business/marketing 9%, English 6%, history 15%, physical sciences 8%, psychology 15%, security/protective services 8%, visual/performing arts 8%.

Computing on campus. 65 workstations in library, computer center, student center. Dormitories wired for high-speed internet access. Online library, helpline available.

Student life. Freshman orientation: Mandatory. Preregistration for classes offered. Orientation includes placement tests, academic registration. **Policies:** Freshmen permitted cars on campus. **Housing:** Guaranteed on-campus for all undergraduates. Substance-free housing available. $100 nonrefundable deposit. **Activities:** Choral groups, dance, drama, literary magazine, music ensembles, musical theater, student government, student newspaper, campus ministries, students in free enterprise, College Democrats, College Republicans, Psych-Key Club, Cahaba River Society, Judson Ambassadors.

Athletics. USCAA. **Intercollegiate:** Basketball W, equestrian W, softball W, tennis W, volleyball W. **Intramural:** Basketball W, equestrian W, field hockey W, softball W, swimming W, table tennis W, tennis W, volleyball W. **Team name:** Lady Eagles.

Student services. Adult student services, alcohol/substance abuse counseling, campus ministries, career counseling, student employment services, financial aid counseling, health services, personal counseling.

Contact. E-mail: admissions@judson.edu
Phone: (334) 683-5110 Toll-free number: (800) 447-9472
Fax: (334) 683-5147
Michael Scotto, Director of Admissions, Judson College, 302 Bibb Street, Marion, AL 36756

Miles College
Birmingham, Alabama
www.miles.edu **CB code: 1468**

- Private 4-year liberal arts college affiliated with Christian Methodist Episcopal Church
- Commuter campus in very large city
- 1,758 degree-seeking undergraduates

General. Founded in 1905. Regionally accredited. **Degrees:** 183 bachelor's awarded. **ROTC:** Army, Navy, Air Force. **Location:** 6 miles from downtown. **Calendar:** Semester, limited summer session. **Full-time faculty:** 96 total. **Part-time faculty:** 44 total. **Special facilities:** Afro-American materials center, media center.

Basis for selection. Open admission, but selective for some programs. Admission to education program based on 2.0 high school GPA, ACT composite score of 16 and recommendations; 3 letters of recommendation required of all.

High school preparation. 20 units recommended. Recommended units include English 4, mathematics 4, social studies 4, history 4 and science 4. 4 units mathematics and science recommended, particularly, for natural science applicants.

2005-2006 Annual costs. Tuition/fees: $5,826. Room/board: $4,068. Books/supplies: $400. Personal expenses: $1,000.

Financial aid. All financial aid based on need.

Application procedures. Admission: Closing date 6/15. No application fee. **Financial aid:** Priority date 4/15; no closing date. FAFSA required. Applicants notified on a rolling basis starting 7/15; must reply within 2 week(s) of notification.

Academics. Special study options: Cooperative education, cross-registration, double major, dual enrollment of high school students, exchange student, honors, independent study, internships. **Credit/placement by examination:** CLEP, institutional tests. **Support services:** Reduced course load, remedial instruction, study skills assistance, tutoring, writing center.

Majors. Biology: General. **Business:** Accounting, business admin, purchasing. **Communications:** General. **Computer sciences:** General. **Conservation:** Environmental science. **Education:** Elementary, English, instructional media, mathematics, science, secondary, social science, social studies. **English:** English lit. **History:** General. **Math:** General. **Physical sciences:** Chemistry. **Public administration:** Social work. **Social sciences:** Political science.

Student life. Freshman orientation: Available, $100 fee. Preregistration for classes offered. **Policies:** Students must maintain a 2.0 grade point average to participate in student activities on campus. Freshmen permitted cars on campus. **Housing:** Single-sex dorms, apartments, substance-free housing available. **Activities:** Marching band, choral groups, drama, music ensembles, radio station, student government, student newspaper, TV station, interdenominational ministerial association.

Athletics. NCAA. **Intercollegiate:** Baseball M, basketball, cross-country, football (tackle) M, softball W, track and field, volleyball W. **Intramural:** Badminton, basketball, softball, tennis, volleyball. **Team name:** Golden Bears.

Student services. Adult student services, campus ministries, career counseling, student employment services, financial aid counseling, health services, personal counseling, placement for graduates.

Contact. E-mail: admissions@miles.edu
Phone: (205) 929-1655 Fax: (205) 923-9292
Christopher Robertson, Director of Admissions and Recruitment, Miles College, 5500 Myron-Massey Boulevard, Fairfield, AL 35064

Oakwood College

Huntsville, Alabama — **CB member**
www.oakwood.edu — **CB code: 1586**

- Private 4-year liberal arts college affiliated with Seventh-day Adventists
- Residential campus in small city
- 1,751 degree-seeking undergraduates: 11% part-time, 57% women, 90% African American, 7% international
- SAT or ACT (ACT writing optional) required

General. Founded in 1896. Regionally accredited. **Degrees:** 369 bachelor's, 5 associate awarded. **Location:** 5 miles from Huntsville. **Calendar:** Semester, limited summer session. **Full-time faculty:** 105 total. **Part-time faculty:** 63 total.

Freshman class profile. 410 enrolled.

Mid 50% test scores		**GPA 2.0-2.99:**	43%
SAT verbal:	410-520	**Rank in top quarter:**	21%
SAT math:	370-480	**Rank in top tenth:**	6%
ACT:	16-21	**Return as sophomores:**	70%
GPA 3.50 or higher:	23%	**International:**	6%
GPA 3.0-3.49:	27%		

Basis for selection. Applicants with GPA of at least 2.0 considered for acceptance. Special consideration for exceptional applicants. **Homeschooled:** Transcript of courses and grades, letter of recommendation (nonparent) required.

High school preparation. College-preparatory program recommended. 18 units recommended. Recommended units include English 4, mathematics 2, social studies 1, history 1, science 2 (laboratory 1) and foreign language 2. One typing or computer applications recommended.

2005-2006 Annual costs. Tuition/fees: $11,722. Room/board: $6,630.

Financial aid. Non-need-based: Scholarships awarded for academics, leadership, religious affiliation, state residency.

Application procedures. Admission: Priority date 6/30; no deadline. $20 fee, may be waived for applicants with need. Admission notification on a rolling basis beginning on or about 12/1. **Financial aid:** Priority date 3/31; no closing date. FAFSA required. Applicants notified on a rolling basis starting 4/1.

Academics. Special study options: Double major, honors, internships, study abroad, teacher certification program. **Credit/placement by examination:** CLEP, SAT, ACT, institutional tests. **Support services:** Learning center, reduced course load, remedial instruction, study skills assistance, tutoring, writing center.

Majors. Biology: General, biochemistry. **Business:** Accounting, business admin, finance, office management. **Communications:** General. **Computer sciences:** General, computer science, information systems. **Education:** Biology, business, chemistry, elementary, English, family/consumer sciences, history, mathematics, music, physical, science, social science. **Family/consumer sciences:** General, family studies, food/nutrition. **Foreign languages:** French, Spanish. **Health:** Cytotechnology. **History:** General. **Interdisciplinary:** Math/computer science, natural sciences. **Liberal arts:** Arts/sciences. **Math:** General, applied. **Philosophy/religion:** Religion. **Physical sciences:** Chemistry. **Psychology:** General. **Public administration:** Social work. **Theology:** Religious ed, theology.

Computing on campus. 300 workstations in dormitories, library. Dormitories linked to campus network. Commuter students can connect to campus network.

Student life. Freshman orientation: Mandatory. **Policies:** Students sit on most faculty and administrative committees. Religious observance required. **Housing:** Single-sex dorms, apartments available. **Activities:** Choral groups, music ensembles, radio station, student government, student newspaper, Outreach, NAACP.

Athletics. Intramural: Baseball M, basketball, golf, gymnastics, soccer, softball, tennis, volleyball. **Team name:** Ambassadors.

Student services. Adult student services, campus ministries, career counseling, student employment services, financial aid counseling, health services, on-campus daycare, personal counseling, placement for graduates, veterans' counselor.

Contact. E-mail: admission@oakwood.edu
Phone: (256) 726-7030 Toll-free number: (800) 824-5312
Fax: (256) 726-7154
Jason McCracken, Director of Enrollment Management, Oakwood College, 7000 Adventist Boulevard, NW, Huntsville, AL 35896

Samford University

Birmingham, Alabama — **CB member**
www.samford.edu — **CB code: 1302**

- Private 4-year university affiliated with Southern Baptist Convention
- Residential campus in very large city
- 2,879 degree-seeking undergraduates: 5% part-time, 65% women, 6% African American, 1% Asian American, 1% Hispanic American, 1% international
- 1,541 degree-seeking graduate students
- 65% of applicants admitted
- SAT or ACT (ACT writing recommended), application essay required
- 68% graduate within 6 years

General. Founded in 1841. Regionally accredited. Students taught to integrate Christian faith with learning and living. **Degrees:** 627 bachelor's, 15 associate awarded; master's, doctoral, first professional offered. **ROTC:** Army, Air Force. **Location:** 6 miles from downtown. **Calendar:** 4-1-4, extensive summer session. **Full-time faculty:** 278 total; 80% have terminal degrees, 8% minority, 42% women. **Part-time faculty:** 147 total; 33% have terminal degrees, 8% minority, 58% women. **Class size:** 56% < 20, 40% 20-39, 2% 40-49, 2% 50-99. **Special facilities:** Computer-assisted journalism laboratory, geographic information system, observatory, global center, planetarium, conservatory.

Freshman class profile. 2,025 applied, 1,315 admitted, 702 enrolled.

Mid 50% test scores		**Rank in top tenth:**	36%
SAT verbal:	530-630	**End year in good standing:**	94%
SAT math:	530-630	**Return as sophomores:**	85%
ACT:	23-28	**Out-of-state:**	64%
GPA 3.50 or higher:	62%	**Live on campus:**	94%
GPA 3.0-3.49:	29%	**Fraternities:**	27%
GPA 2.0-2.99:	9%	**Sororities:**	43%
Rank in top quarter:	66%		

Basis for selection. High school GPA, courses selected and rigor, test scores, recommendations, essay, academic content and trend of high school grades are important. Interview recommended. Audition required for music majors. Portfolio recommended for art and journalism majors. **Homeschooled:** Statement describing homeschool structure and mission, transcript of courses and grades, letter of recommendation (nonparent) required. Leadership resume, SAT or ACT scores also required.

High school preparation. Required and recommended units include English 4, mathematics 3, social studies 2, history 2, science 3 (laboratory 2) and foreign language 2.

2006-2007 Annual costs. Tuition/fees: $16,000. Room/board: $6,060. Books/supplies: $840. Personal expenses: $2,642.

2004-2005 Financial aid. Need-based: 457 full-time freshmen applied for aid; 276 were judged to have need; 271 of these received aid. Average need met was 76%. Average scholarship/grant was $8,149; average loan $3,169. 54% of total undergraduate aid awarded as scholarships/grants, 46% as loans/jobs. **Non-need-based:** Awarded to 725 full-time undergraduates,

including 202 freshmen. Scholarships awarded for academics, athletics, leadership, music/drama, religious affiliation, ROTC, state residency. **Additional information:** Consideration for merit scholarships automatically given to students with admission files completed by December 15.

Application procedures. **Admission:** Priority date 3/1; no deadline. $25 fee, may be waived for applicants with need. Application may be submitted online. Admission notification on a rolling basis beginning on or about 11/1. Must reply by May 1 or within 2 week(s) if notified thereafter. **Financial aid:** Priority date 3/1; no closing date. FAFSA required. Applicants notified on a rolling basis starting 5/1.

Academics. **Special study options:** Accelerated study, combined bachelor's/graduate degree, cooperative education, cross-registration, double major, exchange student, honors, independent study, internships, liberal arts/career combination, study abroad, teacher certification program. Semester offered at Samford London Study Center. **Credit/placement by examination:** AP, CLEP, IB, SAT, ACT, institutional tests. 30 credit hours maximum toward associate degree, 30 toward bachelor's. **Support services:** Learning center, reduced course load, study skills assistance, tutoring, writing center.

Majors. **Area/ethnic studies:** Asian, Latin American. **Biology:** General, biochemistry, marine. **Business:** Accounting, business admin, human resources, international. **Communications:** General, journalism. **Computer sciences:** Computer science. **Conservation:** Environmental science, environmental studies. **Education:** Biology, English, history, multi-level teacher, music, physical, science, social science, speech. **Engineering:** Physics. **English:** English lit, speech/rhetoric. **Family/consumer sciences:** Family studies, human nutrition. **Foreign languages:** General, ancient Greek, French, German, Latin, Spanish. **Health:** Athletic training, nursing (RN), premedicine. **History:** General. **Interdisciplinary:** Classical/archaeology, nutrition sciences, science/society. **Math:** General. **Parks/recreation:** Exercise sciences, health/fitness. **Philosophy/religion:** Philosophy, religion. **Physical sciences:** Chemistry, physics. **Protective services:** Law enforcement admin. **Psychology:** General. **Public administration:** General, community org/advocacy. **Social sciences:** General, cartography, geography, international relations, political science, sociology. **Theology:** Sacred music. **Visual/performing arts:** Art, commercial/advertising art, dramatic, interior design, music performance, music theory/composition, piano/organ, voice/opera.

Most popular majors. Biology 7%, business/marketing 17%, communications/journalism 8%, education 12%, family/consumer sciences 7%, health sciences 7%, social sciences 7%, visual/performing arts 6%.

Computing on campus. 350 workstations in library, computer center, student center. Dormitories wired for high-speed internet access and linked to campus network. Commuter students can connect to campus network. Online library, helpline, repair service available.

Student life. **Freshman orientation:** Mandatory, $150 fee. Preregistration for classes offered. 4 orientation sessions lasting 1 and a half days in summer; includes students and parents. **Policies:** Student code of values observed. Religious observance required. Freshmen permitted cars on campus. **Housing:** Guaranteed on-campus for freshmen. Single-sex dorms, special housing for disabled, fraternity/sorority housing, substance-free housing available. $200 nonrefundable deposit, deadline 5/1. **Activities:** Bands, choral groups, dance, drama, literary magazine, music ensembles, musical theater, radio station, student government, student newspaper, symphony orchestra, Amnesty International, Circle K, Habitat for Humanity, Gamma Sigma Sigma, Alpha Phi Omega, College Republicans, international club, Samford Ambassadors, Beta Beta Beta, Ville Crew.

Athletics. NCAA. **Intercollegiate:** Baseball M, basketball, cross-country, football (tackle) M, golf, soccer W, softball W, tennis, track and field, volleyball W. **Intramural:** Basketball, bowling, cheerleading, football (non-tackle) M, football (tackle), golf, racquetball, soccer, softball, table tennis, tennis, volleyball, water polo. **Team name:** Bulldogs.

Student services. Adult student services, campus ministries, career counseling, student employment services, financial aid counseling, health services, personal counseling, placement for graduates. **Physically disabled:** Services for visually, speech, hearing impaired. **Learning disabled:** Comprehensive services available.

Contact. E-mail: admiss@samford.edu
Phone: (205) 726-3673 Toll-free number: (800) 888-7218
Fax: (205) 726-2171
R Kimrey, Dean of Admission, Samford University, 800 Lakeshore Drive, Birmingham, AL 35229

Selma University
Selma, Alabama
CB code: 1792

- Private 4-year university affiliated with Alabama Baptist Convention
- Large town

General. Founded in 1878. Candidate for regional accreditation. **Location:** 50 miles from Montgomery. **Calendar:** Semester.

Annual costs/financial aid. Tuition/fees (2005-2006): $3,585. Books/supplies: $600. Personal expenses: $600.

Contact. Phone: (334) 872-2533
Registrar, 1501 Lapsley Street, Selma, AL 36701

South University
Montgomery, Alabama
www.southuniversity.edu **CB code: 3947**

- For-profit 4-year business and health science college
- Commuter campus in small city
- 408 degree-seeking undergraduates: 43% part-time, 75% women, 67% African American, 1% Hispanic American
- 9 graduate students
- 95% of applicants admitted
- SAT or ACT (ACT writing recommended), interview required

General. Founded in 1887. Regionally accredited. **Degrees:** 9 bachelor's, 64 associate awarded; master's offered. **Location:** 100 miles from Birmingham, 160 miles from Atlanta. **Calendar:** Quarter, extensive summer session. **Full-time faculty:** 14 total; 36% have terminal degrees, 7% minority, 64% women. **Part-time faculty:** 23 total; 9% have terminal degrees, 26% minority, 35% women. **Class size:** 69% < 20, 31% 20-39.

Freshman class profile. 253 applied, 240 admitted, 127 enrolled.

Basis for selection. High school diploma or GED required. Entrance test most important. CPT (school-administered entrance test) or SAT/ACT required for admission, unless applicant is a transfer student with at least 30 quarter hours and a GPA of at least 2.0.

2005-2006 Annual costs. Tuition/fees: $11,475. Books/supplies: $900. Personal expenses: $1,622.

2004-2005 Financial aid. All financial aid based on need. 22% of total undergraduate aid awarded as scholarships/grants, 78% as loans/jobs.

Application procedures. **Admission:** No deadline. $25 fee. Application may be submitted online. Admission notification on a rolling basis. **Financial aid:** No deadline. FAFSA required. Applicants notified on a rolling basis starting 6/1.

Academics. **Special study options:** Distance learning, double major, internships. **Credit/placement by examination:** CLEP, institutional tests. **Support services:** Remedial instruction, study skills assistance, tutoring.

Majors. **Business:** Business admin. **Computer sciences:** Information technology. **Legal studies:** General.

Computing on campus. 58 workstations in library, computer center. Online library, repair service, wireless network available.

Student life. **Freshman orientation:** Mandatory. Preregistration for classes offered.

Student services. Career counseling, financial aid counseling, personal counseling, placement for graduates, veterans' counselor.

Contact. E-mail: apearson@southuniversity.edu
Phone: (334) 395-8800 Fax: (334) 395-8859
Anna Pearson, Director of Admissions, South University, 5355 Vaughn Road, Montgomery, AL 36116-1120

Southeastern Bible College
Birmingham, Alabama
www.sebc.edu **CB code: 1723**

- Private 4-year Bible college affiliated with interdenominational tradition
- Commuter campus in very large city
- 232 degree-seeking undergraduates
- 72% of applicants admitted
- SAT or ACT (ACT writing recommended) required

General. Founded in 1935. Accredited by ABHE. **Degrees:** 35 bachelor's, 3 associate awarded; first professional offered. **Location:** 10 miles from downtown. **Calendar:** Semester, limited summer session. **Full-time faculty:** 15 total. **Part-time faculty:** 15 total. **Class size:** 82% < 20, 17% 20-39, 2% 50-99. **Special facilities:** Homiletics (preaching) video laboratory.

Freshman class profile. 150 applied, 108 admitted, 65 enrolled.

Out-of-state:	20%	**Live on campus:**	10%

Basis for selection. Minimum 2.0 GPA required; serious commitment to Christian life and service; 2 recommendations important. Interview recommended. **Learning Disabled:** Students should meet with equity coordinator if desired.

High school preparation. 16 units recommended. Recommended units include English 4, mathematics 1, social studies 1, science 2 and foreign language 2.

2005-2006 Annual costs. Tuition/fees: $9,015. Room/board: $4,300. Books/supplies: $500.

Financial aid. **Non-need-based:** Scholarships awarded for academics.

Application procedures. **Admission:** Priority date 5/1; deadline 7/15 (postmark date). $20 fee. Application may be submitted online. Admission notification on a rolling basis. Must reply by May 1 or within 2 week(s) if notified thereafter. **Financial aid:** Priority date 5/1, closing date 8/15. FAFSA, institutional form required. Applicants notified by 7/15; must reply within 2 week(s) of notification.

Academics. **Special study options:** Double major, dual enrollment of high school students, independent study, internships, teacher certification program. **Credit/placement by examination:** AP, CLEP, institutional tests. 15 credit hours maximum toward associate degree, 30 toward bachelor's. **Support services:** Reduced course load, remedial instruction, study skills assistance, tutoring.

Majors. **Education:** Elementary. **Theology:** Bible, missionary, pastoral counseling, religious ed, sacred music, theology.

Most popular majors. Education 43%, philosophy/religious studies 43%, social sciences 14%.

Computing on campus. 25 workstations in library, computer center, student center. Dormitories linked to campus network. Online library available.

Student life. **Freshman orientation:** Mandatory. Preregistration for classes offered. 2 days prior to registration. **Policies:** Religious observance required. Freshmen permitted cars on campus. **Housing:** Single-sex dorms, apartments, substance-free housing available. $150 deposit, deadline 8/1. **Activities:** Choral groups, music ensembles, student government, student missions fellowships.

Athletics. **Intramural:** Baseball M, basketball, football (non-tackle), soccer, softball, table tennis, volleyball, weight lifting. **Team name:** Sabers.

Student services. Adult student services, campus ministries, career counseling, student employment services, financial aid counseling, health services, personal counseling, placement for graduates, women's services. **Physically disabled:** Services for visually, speech, hearing impaired.

Contact. E-mail: info@sebc.edu
Phone: (205) 970-9210 Toll-free number: (800) 749-8878
Fax: (205) 970-9207
Joel Dunn, Director of Admissions, Southeastern Bible College, 2545 Valleydale Road, Birmingham, AL 35244

Southern Christian University

Montgomery, Alabama
www.southernchristian.edu **CB code: 7001**

- Private 4-year university and seminary college affiliated with Church of Christ
- Commuter campus in small city
- 371 degree-seeking undergraduates: 15% part-time, 52% women, 31% African American, 4% Hispanic American
- 349 degree-seeking graduate students

General. Founded in 1967. Regionally accredited. Participant in the U.S. Department of Education's Distance Education Demonstration Program. All degree programs available via distance learning. Participating institution in eArmyU initiative. **Degrees:** 135 bachelor's awarded; master's, doctoral, first professional offered. **Location:** 100 miles from Birmingham, 150 miles from Atlanta. **Calendar:** Semester, extensive summer session. **Full-time faculty:** 76 total. **Part-time faculty:** 12 total.

Basis for selection. Open admission, but selective for some programs. Students admitted under conditional admission must earn a 2.0 during the first 24 semester hours attempted.

High school preparation. 15 units recommended.

2005-2006 Annual costs. Tuition/fees: $10,400. Undergraduates taking a minimum of 12 hours in a given semester receive scholarships in the amount of $2,400 per student. Books/supplies: $800. Personal expenses: $1,739.

2004-2005 Financial aid. **Need-based:** 2% of total undergraduate aid awarded as scholarships/grants, 98% as loans/jobs. **Non-need-based:** Scholarships awarded for academics, leadership. **Additional information:** Scholarships based on need and grades. Half-tuition scholarship is available for full-time undergraduate students.

Application procedures. **Admission:** No deadline. $50 fee. Application may be submitted online. Admission notification on a rolling basis. **Financial aid:** Priority date 5/1, closing date 6/30. FAFSA, institutional form required. Applicants notified by 6/30; must reply by 8/15 or within 2 week(s) of notification.

Academics. **Special study options:** Accelerated study, distance learning, double major, independent study, internships. **Credit/placement by examination:** CLEP. 36 credit hours maximum toward bachelor's degree. **Support services:** Tutoring.

Majors. **Theology:** Bible.

Computing on campus. PC or laptop required. 25 workstations in library, computer center. Online course registration, online library, helpline available.

Student life. **Freshman orientation:** Available. Online orientation available 24 hours a day, seven days a week.

Student services. Financial aid counseling, placement for graduates, veterans' counselor.

Contact. E-mail: admissions@southernchristian.edu
Phone: (334) 387-7513 Toll-free number: (800) 351-4040 ext. 7513
Fax: (334) 387-3878
Rick Johnson, Director of Enrollment Management, Southern Christian University, 1200 Taylor Road, Montgomery, AL 36117-3553

Spring Hill College

Mobile, Alabama **CB member**
www.shc.edu **CB code: 1733**

- Private 4-year liberal arts college affiliated with Roman Catholic Church
- Residential campus in large city
- 1,174 degree-seeking undergraduates: 9% part-time, 64% women, 15% African American, 1% Asian American, 5% Hispanic American, 1% Native American, 1% international
- 175 degree-seeking graduate students
- 80% of applicants admitted
- SAT or ACT (ACT writing recommended), application essay required
- 61% graduate within 6 years; 33% enter graduate study

General. Founded in 1830. Regionally accredited. College in the Jesuit tradition. **Degrees:** 212 bachelor's awarded; master's offered. **ROTC:** Army, Air Force. **Location:** 140 miles from New Orleans, Louisiana. **Calendar:** Semester, limited summer session. **Full-time faculty:** 72 total; 86% have terminal degrees, 3% minority, 44% women. **Part-time faculty:** 66 total; 41% have terminal degrees, 14% minority, 50% women. **Class size:** 47% < 20, 49% 20-39, 4% 40-49, less than 1% 50-99. **Special facilities:** Theater, national historic buildings, public radio broadcasting station, 450-acre wooded campus, 18-hole golf course.

Freshman class profile. 1,190 applied, 953 admitted, 275 enrolled.

Mid 50% test scores		**Rank in top quarter:**	50%
SAT verbal:	480-600	**Rank in top tenth:**	28%
SAT math:	460-610	**End year in good standing:**	87%
ACT:	21-26	**Return as sophomores:**	84%
GPA 3.50 or higher:	48%	**Out-of-state:**	67%
GPA 3.0-3.49:	32%	**Live on campus:**	94%
GPA 2.0-2.99:	20%		

Basis for selection. Grades, test scores, and achievements/ accomplishments outside the classroom important. Interview recommended; portfolio recommended of art majors. **Homeschooled:** Statement describing homeschool structure and mission, transcript of courses and grades, interview required. Portfolio should include thorough explanation of all coursework, how it was graded, a comprehensive reading list, documentation of any program affiliation, and personal assessments provided by both the student and the primary teacher. Information on any independent research project, community outreach, or unique experience that enriched the homeschooling experience may be included.

High school preparation. 15 units recommended. Recommended units include English 4, mathematics 3, social studies 2, history 1, science 3 (laboratory 1) and foreign language 2.

2006-2007 Annual costs. Tuition/fees: $22,000. Room/board: $8,120.

2005-2006 Financial aid. Need-based: 228 full-time freshmen applied for aid; 188 were judged to have need; 188 of these received aid. Average need met was 83%. Average scholarship/grant was $14,874; average loan $3,583. 72% of total undergraduate aid awarded as scholarships/grants, 28% as loans/jobs. **Non-need-based:** Awarded to 895 full-time undergraduates, including 228 freshmen. Scholarships awarded for academics, alumni affiliation, athletics, job skills, leadership, state residency.

Application procedures. Admission: Priority date 1/15; deadline 7/15 (postmark date). $25 fee, may be waived for applicants with need. Application may be submitted online. Admission notification on a rolling basis beginning on or about 11/1. Must reply by May 1 or within 2 week(s) if notified thereafter. **Financial aid:** Priority date 3/1; no closing date. FAFSA, institutional form required. Applicants notified on a rolling basis starting 2/15; must reply by 5/1 or within 2 week(s) of notification.

Academics. Special study options: Accelerated study, combined bachelor's/graduate degree, distance learning, double major, dual enrollment of high school students, honors, independent study, internships, student-designed major, study abroad, teacher certification program, Washington semester. Marine biology majors take credit courses at the Dauphin Island Sea Laboratory of the Marine Environmental Sciences Consortium; 3-2 engineering with Auburn University, University of Alabama at Birmingham, Marquette University, University of Florida, and Texas A & M University; 3-3 B.S./M.S.physical therapy and occupational therapy programs with Rockhurst University and Nova Southeastern University. **Credit/placement by examination:** AP, CLEP, IB, SAT, ACT, institutional tests. 30 credit hours maximum toward bachelor's degree. **Support services:** Remedial instruction, study skills assistance, tutoring.

Majors. Biology: General, biochemistry, marine. **Business:** Accounting, business admin, finance, international, marketing. **Communications:** General, journalism, radio/tv. **Computer sciences:** General. **Education:** Early childhood, elementary, secondary. **English:** English lit. **Foreign languages:** Spanish. **Health:** Art therapy, nursing (RN), predentistry, premedicine, preveterinary. **History:** General. **Liberal arts:** Humanities. **Math:** General. **Philosophy/religion:** Philosophy. **Physical sciences:** Chemistry. **Psychology:** General. **Social sciences:** General, international relations, political science, sociology. **Theology:** Theology. **Visual/performing arts:** Arts management, dramatic, graphic design, studio arts.

Most popular majors. Biology 12%, business/marketing 19%, communications/journalism 11%, education 6%, English 6%, psychology 10%, social sciences 6%.

Computing on campus. 194 workstations in dormitories, library, computer center, student center. Dormitories wired for high-speed internet access and linked to campus network. Commuter students can connect to campus network. Online course registration, online library, helpline, student web hosting, wireless network available.

Student life. Freshman orientation: Mandatory, $225 fee. Preregistration for classes offered. Weekend program held in the summer for students and parents. **Policies:** Freshmen permitted cars on campus. **Housing:** Guaranteed on-campus for all undergraduates. Coed dorms, single-sex dorms, apartments available. $150 fully refundable deposit, deadline 5/1. **Activities:** Choral groups, dance, drama, literary magazine, student government, student newspaper, Amnesty International, Circle K, College Democrats, College Republicans, Habitat for Humanity, multicultural student union, Pro-Life club, student government association, Troubadours, Up 'til Dawn.

Athletics. NAIA. **Intercollegiate:** Baseball M, basketball, cross-country, golf, soccer, softball W, swimming, tennis, volleyball W. **Intramural:** Basketball, football (non-tackle), golf, racquetball, soccer, softball, table tennis, volleyball. **Team name:** Badgers.

Student services. Adult student services, alcohol/substance abuse counseling, campus ministries, career counseling, student employment services, financial aid counseling, health services, personal counseling, placement for graduates.

Contact. E-mail: admit@shc.edu
Phone: (251) 380-3030 Toll-free number: (800) 742-6704
Fax: (251) 460-2186
Florence Hines, Vice President of Enrollment Management and Communications, Spring Hill College, 4000 Dauphin Street, Mobile, AL 36608-1791

Stillman College

Tuscaloosa, Alabama — **CB member**
www.stillman.edu — **CB code: 1739**

- Private 4-year liberal arts college affiliated with Presbyterian Church (USA)
- Residential campus in small city
- 850 degree-seeking undergraduates
- SAT or ACT required

General. Founded in 1876. Regionally accredited. **Degrees:** 170 bachelor's awarded. **ROTC:** Army, Navy, Air Force. **Location:** 60 miles from Birmingham. **Calendar:** Semester, limited summer session. **Full-time faculty:** 72 total. **Part-time faculty:** 25 total. **Special facilities:** Museum.

Freshman class profile.

Mid 50% test scores		**SAT math:**	320-430
SAT verbal:	310-410	**ACT:**	15-19

Basis for selection. School achievement record most important. Class rank, test scores, essay, extracurricular activities also important. **Homeschooled:** Students unable to present a high school transcript may enroll upon presentation of satisfactory passing score on GED.

High school preparation. 24 units required. Required units include English 4, mathematics 2, social studies 2 and science 1.

2005-2006 Annual costs. Tuition/fees: $11,605. Room/board: $5,500.

Financial aid. All financial aid based on need.

Application procedures. Admission: Closing date 5/1 (receipt date). $25 fee, may be waived for applicants with need. Admission notification on a rolling basis. Admitted applicants must reply within 5 days of notification of acceptance. **Financial aid:** Priority date 6/1; no closing date. FAFSA, institutional form required. Applicants notified on a rolling basis; must reply within 4 week(s) of notification.

Academics. Special study options: Accelerated study, cooperative education, double major, dual enrollment of high school students, honors, independent study, internships, student-designed major, study abroad, teacher certification program. Cooperative programs with University of Alabama, University of Alabama at Birmingham. **Credit/placement by examination:** AP, CLEP, institutional tests. 30 credit hours maximum toward bachelor's degree. **Support services:** Learning center, reduced course load, remedial instruction, tutoring, writing center.

Honors college/program. Minimum high school average of A-, demonstrated success in arts, SAT of 1075 (exclusive of Writing), or ACT of 23, demonstrated leadership activity, strong performance in sciences, and original essay.

Majors. Biology: General. **Business:** Business admin. **Computer sciences:** General. **Education:** Elementary, health. **History:** General. **Math:** General. **Visual/performing arts:** Art.

Computing on campus. PC or laptop required. 225 workstations in dormitories, library, computer center, student center. Dormitories linked to campus network. Commuter students can connect to campus network. Online course registration, online library, helpline, student web hosting, wireless network available.

Student life. Freshman orientation: Available, $40 fee. Preregistration for classes offered. **Policies:** Religious observance required. Freshmen permitted cars on campus. **Housing:** Guaranteed on-campus for freshmen. Single-sex dorms available. $100 deposit, deadline 7/1. **Activities:** Bands, choral groups, drama, music ensembles, radio station, student government, student newspaper, Christian Student Association, Chancellorettes, Chancellors.

Athletics. NCAA. **Intercollegiate:** Baseball M, basketball, cross-country, football (tackle) M, softball W, tennis, track and field, volleyball W. **Intramural:** Basketball, softball, volleyball. **Team name:** Tigers.

Student services. Campus ministries, career counseling, student employment services, financial aid counseling, health services, personal counseling, placement for graduates, veterans' counselor.

Contact. E-mail: mbonner@stillman.edu
Phone: (205) 366-8817 Toll-free number: (800) 841-5722
Fax: (205) 366-8156
Mason Bonner, Director of Admissions, Stillman College, 3600 Stillman Boulevard, Tuscaloosa, AL 35403

Talladega College

Talladega, Alabama — **CB member**
www.talladega.edu — **CB code: 1800**

- Private 4-year liberal arts college affiliated with United Church of Christ
- Residential campus in large town
- 368 degree-seeking undergraduates: 8% part-time, 61% women, 92% African American
- 38% of applicants admitted
- SAT or ACT (ACT writing optional), application essay required
- 41% graduate within 6 years; 25% enter graduate study

General. Founded in 1867. Regionally accredited. **Degrees:** 70 bachelor's awarded. **ROTC:** Army. **Location:** 55 miles from Birmingham, 120 miles from Atlanta. **Calendar:** Semester, limited summer session. **Full-time faculty:** 35 total; 60% have terminal degrees, 66% minority, 37% women. **Part-time faculty:** 9 total; 11% have terminal degrees, 78% minority, 67% women. **Class size:** 76% < 20, 18% 20-39, 4% 40-49, 1% 50-99. **Special facilities:** Indoor pool, driving range, Amistad murals.

Freshman class profile. 1,960 applied, 744 admitted, 178 enrolled.

Mid 50% test scores			
SAT verbal:	320-460	GPA 2.0-2.99:	50%
SAT math:	340-410	End year in good standing:	58%
ACT:	16-19	Return as sophomores:	43%
GPA 3.50 or higher:	15%	Out-of-state:	58%
GPA 3.0-3.49:	22%	Live on campus:	82%

Basis for selection. Rank in top half of graduating class and minimum 18 ACT, equivalent SAT or 2.0 GPA required. Test scores considered for scholarships. Audition required of music majors. **Homeschooled:** Transcript of courses and grades, state high school equivalency certificate required.

High school preparation. 22 units required. Required units include English 4, mathematics 2, social studies 3, science 2 and academic electives 2. 2 units required in health/physical education.

2005-2006 Annual costs. Tuition/fees: $7,128. Room/board: $4,420. Books/supplies: $1,178. Personal expenses: $1,100.

2004-2005 Financial aid. All financial aid based on need. 235 full-time freshmen applied for aid; 235 were judged to have need; 235 of these received aid. Average need met was 75%. Average loan was $2,625. 56% of total undergraduate aid awarded as scholarships/grants, 44% as loans/jobs.

Application procedures. Admission: No deadline. $25 fee, may be waived for applicants with need. Application may be submitted online. Admission notification on a rolling basis. **Financial aid:** Priority date 4/15; no closing date. FAFSA, institutional form, CSS PROFILE required. Applicants notified on a rolling basis; must reply within 2 week(s) of notification.

Academics. Special study options: Cooperative education, double major, dual enrollment of high school students, independent study, internships, teacher certification program. Dual degree linkage programs with other colleges in nursing, engineering, pharmacy, veterinary sciences, geology, and allied health. **Credit/placement by examination:** AP, CLEP, institutional tests. 12 credit hours maximum toward bachelor's degree. **Support services:** Learning center, pre-admission summer program, reduced course load, remedial instruction, study skills assistance, tutoring, writing center.

Majors. Area/ethnic studies: African-American. **Biology:** General. **Business:** Accounting, business admin, finance, managerial economics, marketing. **Communications:** Journalism, media studies. **Computer sciences:** General. **Education:** Biology, chemistry, English, French, history, mathematics, music, secondary. **English:** English lit. **Foreign languages:** French, Spanish. **History:** General. **Legal studies:** Prelaw. **Math:** General. **Physical sciences:** Chemistry, physics. **Psychology:** General. **Public administration:** General, social work. **Social sciences:** Economics, sociology. **Visual/performing arts:** Piano/organ, studio arts, voice/opera.

Most popular majors. Biology 24%, business/marketing 25%, education 6%, English 7%, public administration/social services 6%, social sciences 13%.

Computing on campus. 200 workstations in dormitories, library, computer center. Dormitories wired for high-speed internet access and linked to campus network. Commuter students can connect to campus network. Online library available.

Student life. Freshman orientation: Mandatory. Preregistration for classes offered. Held one week prior to school opening. **Policies:** Religious observance required. **Housing:** Guaranteed on-campus for freshmen. Single-sex dorms, substance-free housing available. $200 partly refundable deposit. Dorms for honors students, seniors, athletes. **Activities:** Concert band, choral groups, dance, drama, student government, Arna Bontempts Historical Society, biology club, business and economics club, chemistry club, debate club, Faith Outreach Campus Ministry, foreign language club, mathematics club, National Association of Negro Musicians, psychology club.

Athletics. Intramural: Baseball M, basketball M, football (tackle) M, softball W, table tennis, tennis, volleyball W. **Team name:** Tornadoes.

Student services. Alcohol/substance abuse counseling, campus ministries, career counseling, student employment services, financial aid counseling, health services, personal counseling, placement for graduates, veterans' counselor. **Physically disabled:** Services for visually, hearing impaired.

Contact. E-mail: admissions@talladega.edu
Phone: (205) 761-6235 Toll-free number: (800) 633-2440
Fax: (205) 362-0274
Monroe Thornton, Director of Admissions, Talladega College, 627 West Battle Street, Talladega, AL 35160

Troy University

Troy, Alabama — **CB member**
www.troy.edu — **CB code: 1738**

- Public 4-year university
- Commuter campus in large town
- 18,501 degree-seeking undergraduates: 55% part-time, 54% women, 36% African American, 1% Asian American, 4% Hispanic American, 1% Native American, 2% international
- 8,053 degree-seeking graduate students
- SAT or ACT (ACT writing optional) required

General. Founded in 1887. Regionally accredited. Branch schools responsible for administration of all out-of-state military education programs and locations. Contracts and arrangements with the Department of Defense, which provides instruction and services to selected military at home and abroad. Alabama branch campuses in Dothan, Montgomery, and Phenix City. **Degrees:** 2,260 bachelor's, 454 associate awarded; master's offered. **ROTC:** Army, Air Force. **Location:** 50 miles from Montgomery. **Calendar:** Semester, extensive summer session. **Full-time faculty:** 456 total; 56% have terminal degrees, 41% women. **Part-time faculty:** 949 total; 45% women. **Special facilities:** Rosa Parks Library and Museum.

Freshman class profile.

Out-of-state:	12%	Fraternities:	8%
Live on campus:	57%	Sororities:	12%
International:	7%		

Basis for selection. Minimum 2.0 GPA and test scores important. Audition required of music education majors.

High school preparation. 15 units required. Required units include English 3.

2005-2006 Annual costs. Tuition/fees: $4,678; $8,682 out-of-state. Room/board: $5,157. Books/supplies: $820.

2005-2006 Financial aid. Need-based: 888 full-time freshmen applied for aid; 759 were judged to have need; 759 of these received aid. Average scholarship/grant was $3,244; average loan $2,884. 13% of total undergraduate aid awarded as scholarships/grants, 87% as loans/jobs. **Non-need-based:** Awarded to 3,394 full-time undergraduates, including 784 freshmen. Scholarships awarded for academics, athletics, ROTC.

Application procedures. Admission: No deadline. $20 fee. Application may be submitted online. Admission notification on a rolling basis. **Financial aid:** Closing date 5/1. FAFSA, institutional form required. Applicants notified on a rolling basis starting 5/1; must reply within 2 week(s) of notification.

Academics. Special study options: Distance learning, double major, dual enrollment of high school students, ESL, external degree, honors, independent study, internships, study abroad, teacher certification program, weekend college. **Credit/placement by examination:** AP, CLEP, institutional tests. 45 credit hours maximum toward associate degree, 90 toward bachelor's. **Support services:** Learning center, pre-admission summer program, reduced course load, remedial instruction, study skills assistance, tutoring, writing center.

Majors. Biology: General, marine. **Business:** General, accounting, business admin, finance, management information systems, marketing. **Communications:** Journalism, radio/tv. **Computer sciences:** General. **Conservation:** Environmental science. **Education:** Early childhood, elementary, kindergarten/preschool, multi-level teacher, secondary. **Engineering technology:** Electrical, surveying. **English:** English lit, speech/rhetoric. **Health:** Athletic training, nursing (RN). **History:** General. **Liberal arts:** Arts/sciences. **Math:** General. **Parks/recreation:** Sports admin. **Physical sciences:** Chemistry. **Protective services:** Criminal justice. **Psychology:** General. **Public administration:** Social work. **Social sciences:** General, political science, sociology. **Visual/performing arts:** Art.

Most popular majors. Business/marketing 43%, computer/information sciences 7%, education 9%, psychology 9%, security/protective services 11%, social sciences 9%.

Computing on campus. 487 workstations in library, computer center, student center. Online course registration, online library, helpline available.

Student life. Freshman orientation: Mandatory, $55 fee. Preregistration for classes offered. 2-day sessions held during summer. During spring and summer terms, new students can attend orientation session prior to registration for classes. **Policies:** Freshmen permitted cars on campus. **Housing:** Coed dorms, single-sex dorms, apartments, fraternity/sorority housing available. $50 deposit. Substance-abuse-free housing, honor student housing available. **Activities:** Bands, choral groups, dance, drama, music ensembles, musical theater, student government, student newspaper, TV station, Several religious, service and professional organizations, international student organization, honor societies, Young Democrats, Young Republicans.

Athletics. NCAA. **Intercollegiate:** Baseball M, basketball, cheerleading, cross-country, football (tackle) M, golf, rodeo, soccer W, softball W, tennis, track and field, volleyball W. **Intramural:** Basketball, cross-country, diving, field hockey W, golf, softball, swimming, tennis, track and field, volleyball W. **Team name:** Trojans.

Student services. Campus ministries, career counseling, student employment services, financial aid counseling, health services, on-campus daycare, personal counseling, placement for graduates, veterans' counselor, women's services. **Physically disabled:** Services for visually, hearing impaired.

Contact. E-mail: bstar@troy.edu
Phone: (334) 670-3179 Toll-free number: (800) 551-9716
Fax: (334) 670-3733
Buddy Starling, Dean of Enrollment Management, Troy University, University Avenue, Adams Administration 111, Troy, AL 36082

Tuskegee University

Tuskegee, Alabama — **CB member**
www.tuskegee.edu — **CB code: 1813**

- Private 4-year university and liberal arts college
- Residential campus in small town
- 2,510 degree-seeking undergraduates: 5% part-time, 54% women
- 370 degree-seeking graduate students
- 81% of applicants admitted
- SAT or ACT (ACT writing optional) required
- 51% graduate within 6 years; 61% enter graduate study

General. Founded in 1881. Regionally accredited. **Degrees:** 397 bachelor's awarded; master's, doctoral, first professional offered. **ROTC:** Army, Air Force. **Location:** 30 miles from Montgomery, 162 miles from Atlanta. **Calendar:** Semester, limited summer session. **Full-time faculty:** 222 total; 78% have terminal degrees, 57% minority, 32% women. **Part-time faculty:** 41 total; 42% have terminal degrees, 90% minority, 54% women. **Class size:** 55% < 20, 27% 20-39, 7% 40-49, 10% 50-99, less than 1% >100. **Special facilities:** George Washington Carver museum, aerospace science and health education center.

Freshman class profile. 2,037 applied, 1,640 admitted, 737 enrolled.

Mid 50% test scores		**Rank in top quarter:**	59%
SAT verbal:	390-500	**Rank in top tenth:**	20%
SAT math:	390-500	**End year in good standing:**	85%
ACT:	17-21	**Return as sophomores:**	71%
GPA 3.50 or higher:	19%	**Out-of-state:**	52%
GPA 3.0-3.49:	29%	**Live on campus:**	98%
GPA 2.0-2.99:	50%	**International:**	1%

Basis for selection. School achievement record and test scores important. Minimum SAT combined score of 800 (exclusive of Writing) or equivalent ACT required for engineering and nursing applicants, 700 for other applicants. National League for Nursing Guidance Examination required of nursing applicants. Essay recommended; interview recommended for veterinary medicine majors.

High school preparation. 16 units required. Required units include English 4, mathematics 3, social studies 3, science 2 and academic electives 4.

2006-2007 Annual costs. Tuition/fees: $12,985. Room/board: $7,110. Books/supplies: $873. Personal expenses: $1,596.

2005-2006 Financial aid. Need-based: 664 full-time freshmen applied for aid; 564 were judged to have need; 479 of these received aid. Average need met was 85%. Average scholarship/grant was $8,000; average loan $5,625. 37% of total undergraduate aid awarded as scholarships/grants, 63% as loans/jobs. **Non-need-based:** Awarded to 1,368 full-time undergraduates, including 588 freshmen. Scholarships awarded for academics, athletics, ROTC, state residency.

Application procedures. Admission: Priority date 5/15; deadline 7/15. $25 fee. Application may be submitted online. Admission notification on a rolling basis beginning on or about 3/1. Must reply by May 1 or within 2 week(s) if notified thereafter. **Financial aid:** Closing date 3/31. FAFSA, institutional form, CSS PROFILE required. Applicants notified on a rolling basis starting 5/15; must reply within 2 week(s) of notification.

Academics. Special study options: Combined bachelor's/graduate degree, cooperative education, double major, honors, independent study, internships, liberal arts/career combination, teacher certification program. Engineering program with 2-year colleges. **Credit/placement by examination:** AP, CLEP, SAT, ACT. Credit-by-examination policies determined individually by dean. **Support services:** Learning center, pre-admission summer program, reduced course load, remedial instruction, study skills assistance, tutoring.

Majors. Agriculture: Animal sciences, plant sciences, poultry, soil science. **Architecture:** Architecture. **Biology:** General, ecology. **Business:** Accounting, business admin, finance, hospitality admin, management science. **Computer sciences:** General. **Conservation:** General, forestry. **Education:** General, biology, early childhood, elementary, mathematics, mentally handicapped, physical, science, voc/tech. **Engineering:** Aerospace, chemical, electrical, mechanical. **Engineering technology:** Construction. **Family/consumer sciences:** Food/nutrition. **Health:** Clinical lab science. **History:** General. **Math:** General. **Physical sciences:** Chemistry, physics. **Psychology:** General. **Public administration:** Social work. **Social sciences:** Economics, political science, sociology.

Most popular majors. Agriculture 10%, biology 14%, business/marketing 6%, education 6%, engineering/engineering technologies 13%, psychology 8%, social sciences 14%.

Computing on campus. 1,000 workstations in dormitories, library, computer center. Dormitories wired for high-speed internet access and linked to campus network. Online course registration, helpline, repair service, wireless network available.

Student life. Freshman orientation: Available. **Housing:** Single-sex dorms, apartments available. $300 deposit. Honors dormitories available. Freshmen and sophomores not living with parents or guardians required to reside on campus. **Activities:** Bands, choral groups, dance, drama, film society, student government, student newspaper.

Athletics. NCAA. **Intercollegiate:** Baseball M, basketball, cross-country, football (tackle) M, softball W, tennis, track and field, volleyball W. **Intramural:** Basketball M, rifle. **Team name:** Golden Tigers.

Student services. Campus ministries, career counseling, financial aid counseling, health services, on-campus daycare, personal counseling, placement for graduates, veterans' counselor.

Contact. E-mail: adm@tuskegee.edu
Phone: (334) 727-8500 Toll-free number: (800) 622-6531
Fax: (334) 724-4402
Robert Laney, Vice President/Director of Admissions and Enrollment Managements, Tuskegee University, 102 Old Administration Building, Tuskegee, AL 36088

United States Sports Academy

Daphne, Alabama
www.ussa.edu

- Private upper-division university
- Large town

General. Regionally accredited. **Calendar:** Semester.

Annual costs/financial aid. Tuition/fees (projected): $18,000.

Contact. Phone: (251) 626-3303
One Academy Drive, Daphne, AL 36526

University of Alabama

Tuscaloosa, Alabama **CB member**
www.ua.edu **CB code: 1830**

- Public 4-year university
- Residential campus in small city
- 17,374 degree-seeking undergraduates: 9% part-time, 53% women, 12% African American, 1% Asian American, 2% Hispanic American, 1% Native American, 1% international
- 4,010 degree-seeking graduate students
- 74% of applicants admitted
- SAT or ACT (ACT writing optional) required
- 63% graduate within 6 years

General. Founded in 1831. Regionally accredited. **Degrees:** 2,931 bachelor's awarded; master's, doctoral, first professional offered. **ROTC:** Army, Air Force. **Location:** 60 miles from Birmingham. **Calendar:** Semester, extensive summer session. **Full-time faculty:** 922 total; 90% have terminal degrees, 14% minority, 37% women. **Part-time faculty:** 226 total; 67% have terminal degrees, 6% minority, 53% women. **Class size:** 38% < 20, 39% 20-39, 7% 40-49, 9% 50-99, 6% >100. **Special facilities:** Museum of natural history, arboretum, marine science laboratory, archeological park, observatory, access to CRAY X-UP/24 supercomputer in Huntsville, simulated coal mine setting, concert hall.

Freshman class profile. 10,451 applied, 7,715 admitted, 3,735 enrolled.

Mid 50% test scores		**Rank in top tenth:**	24%
SAT verbal:	500-630	**Return as sophomores:**	86%
SAT math:	500-630	**Out-of-state:**	27%
ACT:	21-27	**Live on campus:**	70%
GPA 3.50 or higher:	46%	**International:**	1%
GPA 3.0-3.49:	28%	**Fraternities:**	33%
GPA 2.0-2.99:	26%	**Sororities:**	39%
Rank in top quarter:	46%		

Basis for selection. Test scores, high school GPA in academic courses most important. Typically, students with 3.0 GPA and 20 ACT composite or 970 combined SAT (exclusive of Writing) will be admitted. Tests are not required of freshman applicants who are 25 years of age or older. Audition required for some performance programs. **Homeschooled:** GED required if program is not certified. **Learning Disabled:** Documentation concerning disability should be submitted to the Office of Disability Services upon admission.

High school preparation. 15 units required. Required units include English 4, mathematics 3, social studies 3, history 1, science 3 (laboratory 2), foreign language 1 and academic electives 5.

2005-2006 Annual costs. Tuition/fees: $4,864; $13,516 out-of-state. Room/board: $5,024. Books/supplies: $900. Personal expenses: $2,020.

2004-2005 Financial aid. Need-based: 2,547 full-time freshmen applied for aid; 1,210 were judged to have need; 1,191 of these received aid. Average need met was 67%. Average scholarship/grant was $3,847; average loan $3,367. 34% of total undergraduate aid awarded as scholarships/grants, 66% as loans/jobs. **Non-need-based:** Awarded to 5,688 full-time undergraduates, including 1,543 freshmen. Scholarships awarded for academics, alumni affiliation, art, athletics, leadership, minority status, music/drama, ROTC, state residency.

Application procedures. Admission: Priority date 6/1; no deadline. $35 fee, may be waived for applicants with need. Application may be submitted online. Admission notification on a rolling basis beginning on or about 7/1. **Financial aid:** Priority date 3/1; no closing date. FAFSA required. Applicants notified on a rolling basis starting 4/1; must reply within 3 week(s) of notification.

Academics. Special study options: Accelerated study, combined bachelor's/graduate degree, cooperative education, cross-registration, distance learning, double major, dual enrollment of high school students, ESL, exchange student, external degree, honors, independent study, internships, liberal arts/career combination, student-designed major, study abroad, teacher certification program, Washington semester, weekend college. **Credit/placement by examination:** AP, CLEP, IB, institutional tests. 45 total semester hours are accepted from: AP; CLEP; placement in English; placement/performance in foreign languages; credit for prior military service; USAFI and DANTES credit. Test scores must be sent directly to the Office of Undergraduate Admissions from the testing agencies. **Support services:** Learning center, pre-admission summer program, remedial instruction, study skills assistance, tutoring, writing center.

Majors. Area/ethnic studies: American, Asian, Latin American. **Biology:** General, marine, microbiology. **Business:** Accounting, business admin, finance, management information systems, management science, managerial economics, marketing, restaurant/food services. **Communications:** General, advertising, journalism, public relations, radio/tv. **Computer sciences:** General. **Conservation:** Environmental science. **Education:** Early childhood, elementary, music, physical, secondary, special. **Engineering:** Aerospace, chemical, civil, electrical, industrial, mechanical, metallurgical. **English:** English lit. **Family/consumer sciences:** General, clothing/textiles, family resources, family studies. **Foreign languages:** Classics, French, German, Russian, Spanish. **Health:** Athletic training, audiology/speech pathology, dietetics, facilities admin, nursing (RN). **History:** General. **Interdisciplinary:** Biological/physical sciences. **Math:** General. **Philosophy/religion:** Philosophy, religion. **Physical sciences:** Chemistry, geology, physics. **Protective services:** Criminal justice. **Psychology:** General. **Public administration:** Social work. **Social sciences:** Anthropology, geography, international relations, political science, sociology. **Visual/performing arts:** Art history/conservation, dance, dramatic, interior design, studio arts.

Most popular majors. Business/marketing 29%, communications/journalism 11%, education 7%, engineering/engineering technologies 6%, family/consumer sciences 8%, health sciences 7%.

Computing on campus. 1,500 workstations in dormitories, library, computer center, student center. Dormitories wired for high-speed internet access and linked to campus network. Commuter students can connect to campus network. Online course registration, online library, helpline, repair service, student web hosting, wireless network available.

Student life. Freshman orientation: Mandatory, $90 fee. Preregistration for classes offered. 12 sessions for 2 days each throughout the summer. **Policies:** Services available for learning impaired students. Freshmen permitted cars on campus. **Housing:** Guaranteed on-campus for freshmen. Coed dorms, single-sex dorms, special housing for disabled, apartments, fraternity/sorority housing, substance-free housing available. $200 partly refundable deposit, deadline 3/1. Apartments for visiting scholars. **Activities:** Bands, choral groups, dance, drama, film society, literary magazine, music ensembles, musical theater, opera, radio station, student government, student newspaper, symphony orchestra, TV station, College Republicans, College Democrats, NAACP, African American Association, international student association, SGA, FCA, Golden Key, National Society of Black Engineers, campus ministries.

Athletics. NCAA. **Intercollegiate:** Baseball M, basketball, cheerleading, cross-country, diving, football (tackle) M, golf, gymnastics W, rowing (crew) W, soccer W, softball W, swimming, tennis, track and field, volleyball W. **Intramural:** Badminton, basketball, bowling, football (non-tackle), football (tackle), golf, racquetball, soccer, softball, squash, table tennis, tennis, track and field, volleyball. **Team name:** Crimson Tide.

Student services. Adult student services, alcohol/substance abuse counseling, campus ministries, career counseling, services for economically disadvantaged, student employment services, financial aid counseling, health services, legal services, minority student services, on-campus daycare, personal counseling, placement for graduates, veterans' counselor, women's services. **Physically disabled:** Services for visually, speech, hearing impaired.

Contact. E-mail: admissions@ua.edu
Phone: (205) 348-5666 Toll-free number: (800) 933-2262
Fax: (205) 348-9046
Mary Spiegel, Director of Undergraduate Admissions, University of Alabama, Box 870132, Tuscaloosa, AL 35487-0132

University of Alabama at Birmingham

Birmingham, Alabama **CB member**
www.uab.edu **CB code: 1856**

- Public 4-year university
- Commuter campus in very large city
- 11,060 degree-seeking undergraduates: 28% part-time, 61% women, 32% African American, 3% Asian American, 1% Hispanic American, 2% international
- 4,589 degree-seeking graduate students
- 88% of applicants admitted
- SAT or ACT (ACT writing optional) required
- 38% graduate within 6 years

General. Founded in 1969. Regionally accredited. **Degrees:** 1,622 bachelor's awarded; master's, doctoral, first professional offered. **ROTC:** Army, Air Force. **Location:** Downtown. **Calendar:** Semester, extensive summer session. **Full-time faculty:** 777 total; 88% have terminal degrees, 17% minority, 39% women. **Part-time faculty:** 103 total; 84% have terminal degrees, 10% minority, 31% women. **Class size:** 34% < 20, 40% 20-39, 9% 40-49, 13% 50-99, 5% >100. **Special facilities:** Alabama Museum of Health Sciences.

Freshman class profile. 4,255 applied, 3,731 admitted, 1,587 enrolled.

Mid 50% test scores			
ACT:	20-26	Return as sophomores:	77%
GPA 3.50 or higher:	44%	Out-of-state:	8%
GPA 3.0-3.49:	22%	Live on campus:	47%
GPA 2.0-2.99:	33%	International:	2%
Rank in top quarter:	49%	Fraternities:	17%
Rank in top tenth:	23%	Sororities:	12%

Basis for selection. High school record and test scores most important. Nontraditional students (typically older students) not required to submit standardized test scores for admission. **Homeschooled:** Statement describing homeschool structure and mission required.

High school preparation. College-preparatory program recommended. 12 units required. Required units include English 4, mathematics 4, social studies 4, science 2 and foreign language 1.

2005-2006 Annual costs. Tuition/fees: $4,792; $10,732 out-of-state. Room/board: $4,490. Books/supplies: $900. Personal expenses: $1,500.

2004-2005 Financial aid. Need-based: 1,226 full-time freshmen applied for aid; 813 were judged to have need; 804 of these received aid. Average need met was 39%. Average scholarship/grant was $3,204; average loan $2,962. 33% of total undergraduate aid awarded as scholarships/grants, 67% as loans/jobs. **Non-need-based:** Awarded to 2,637 full-time undergraduates, including 640 freshmen. Scholarships awarded for academics, alumni affiliation, art, athletics, leadership, minority status, music/drama, ROTC.

Application procedures. Admission: Closing date 3/1 (receipt date). $30 fee, may be waived for applicants with need. Application may be submitted online. Admission notification on a rolling basis beginning on or about 9/1. **Financial aid:** Priority date 4/1; no closing date. FAFSA, institutional form required. Applicants notified on a rolling basis starting 4/1; must reply within 4 week(s) of notification.

Academics. Special study options: Combined bachelor's/graduate degree, cooperative education, cross-registration, distance learning, double major, dual enrollment of high school students, honors, independent study, internships, student-designed major, study abroad, teacher certification program, weekend college. **Credit/placement by examination:** AP, CLEP, IB, SAT, ACT, institutional tests. 45 credit hours maximum toward bachelor's degree. **Support services:** Reduced course load, remedial instruction, study skills assistance, tutoring.

Majors. Area/ethnic studies: African-American. **Biology:** General. **Business:** Accounting, business admin, finance, management information systems, managerial economics, marketing. **Communications:** General. **Computer sciences:** General. **Education:** Early childhood, elementary, health, physical, secondary, special. **Engineering:** Biomedical, civil, electrical, materials, mechanical. **English:** English lit. **Foreign languages:** General. **Health:** Clinical lab science, cytotechnology, health services, medical radiologic technology/radiation therapy, medical records admin, nuclear medical technology, nursing (RN), respiratory therapy technology. **History:** General. **Interdisciplinary:** Biological/physical sciences, natural sciences. **Math:** General. **Philosophy/religion:** Philosophy. **Physical sciences:** Chemistry, physics. **Psychology:** General. **Public administration:** Social work. **Social sciences:** Anthropology, international relations, political science, sociology. **Visual/performing arts:** General, art.

Most popular majors. Business/marketing 24%, education 7%, health sciences 18%, psychology 8%.

Computing on campus. 400 workstations in library, computer center. Dormitories wired for high-speed internet access and linked to campus network. Commuter students can connect to campus network. Online course registration, helpline, student web hosting, wireless network available.

Student life. Freshman orientation: Mandatory, $40 fee. Preregistration for classes offered. 2-day program offered various times between June and August. **Policies:** Freshmen permitted cars on campus. **Housing:** Coed dorms, single-sex dorms, apartments available. $250 fully refundable deposit, deadline 5/1. **Activities:** Bands, choral groups, dance, drama, literary magazine, music ensembles, musical theater, radio station, student government, student newspaper, Young Democrats, College Republicans, campus civitan club, veterans student organization, Catholic student association, United Methodist campus ministry, Baptist campus ministry, Muslim student association, Chinese student association, African student association.

Athletics. NCAA. **Intercollegiate:** Baseball M, basketball, cross-country W, football (tackle) M, golf, rifle, soccer, softball W, synchronized swimming W, tennis, track and field W, volleyball W. **Intramural:** Badminton, basketball, bowling, football (non-tackle), racquetball, skiing, soccer, softball, squash, swimming, table tennis, tennis, track and field, volleyball, water polo, wrestling M. **Team name:** Blazers.

Student services. Adult student services, career counseling, student employment services, financial aid counseling, health services, minority student services, on-campus daycare, personal counseling, placement for graduates, veterans' counselor, women's services. **Physically disabled:** Services for visually, speech, hearing impaired.

Contact. E-mail: UndergradAdmit@uab.edu
Phone: (205) 934-8221 Toll-free number: (800) 421-8743
Fax: (205) 975-7114
Chenise Ryan, Director of Admission, University of Alabama at Birmingham, 260 HUC, 1530 3rd Avenue South, Birmingham, AL 35294-1150

University of Alabama in Huntsville

Huntsville, Alabama — **CB member**
www.uah.edu — **CB code: 1854**

- Public 4-year university
- Residential campus in small city
- 5,232 degree-seeking undergraduates: 26% part-time, 49% women, 14% African American, 3% Asian American, 2% Hispanic American, 1% Native American, 4% international
- 1,268 degree-seeking graduate students
- 87% of applicants admitted
- SAT or ACT (ACT writing optional) required
- 44% graduate within 6 years

General. Founded in 1950. Regionally accredited. Research centers employ undergraduate students and allow them to do work with research projects on the campus and in the community. Co-op program with U.S. Army Redstone Arsenal, NASA Marshall Space Flight Center, U.S. Army Missile Command, over 50 Fortune 500 companies. **Degrees:** 798 bachelor's awarded; master's, doctoral offered. **ROTC:** Army. **Location:** 100 miles from Birmingham, 100 miles from Nashville, Tennessee. **Calendar:** Semester, extensive summer session. **Full-time faculty:** 280 total; 91% have terminal degrees, 18% minority, 38% women. **Part-time faculty:** 188 total; 42% have terminal degrees, 7% minority, 43% women. **Class size:** 37% < 20, 44% 20-39, 9% 40-49, 9% 50-99, 1% >100. **Special facilities:** Centers for: applied optics, micro-gravity research, robotics, solar research, space plasma, aeronomic research, art gallery, observatory with vector magnetograph.

Freshman class profile. 1,698 applied, 1,480 admitted, 660 enrolled.

Mid 50% test scores		Rank in top tenth:	31%
SAT verbal:	520-630	End year in good standing:	84%
SAT math:	510-650	Return as sophomores:	75%
ACT:	22-28	Out-of-state:	17%
GPA 3.50 or higher:	46%	Live on campus:	43%
GPA 3.0-3.49:	30%	International:	3%
GPA 2.0-2.99:	24%	Fraternities:	8%
Rank in top quarter:	57%	Sororities:	5%

Basis for selection. School achievement record and test scores are the most important factors for admission. Conditional admission may be available for applicants with evidence of a serious commitment to academic pursuits, yet not meeting the requirements for regular admission. **Homeschooled:** Official high school record of courses completed should contain the titles of courses in each subject area, beginning with grade nine; record should contain annotation of the general content in the academic courses and the textbooks used; teaching credentials of the home school teacher should also be included with the application for admission.

High school preparation. College-preparatory program required. 20 units required. Required units include English 4, mathematics 3, social studies 4, science 3 and academic electives 6.

2005-2006 Annual costs. Tuition/fees: $4,688; $9,886 out-of-state. Room/board: $5,320. Books/supplies: $720. Personal expenses: $1,200.

2004-2005 Financial aid. Need-based: 590 full-time freshmen applied for aid; 265 were judged to have need; 257 of these received aid. Average need met was 51%. Average scholarship/grant was $2,866; average loan $2,247. 30% of total undergraduate aid awarded as scholarships/grants, 70%

as loans/jobs. **Non-need-based:** Awarded to 1,730 full-time undergraduates, including 495 freshmen. Scholarships awarded for academics, art, athletics, leadership, minority status, music/drama, ROTC. **Additional information:** Application deadline for institutional scholarships is February 1.

Application procedures. **Admission:** Closing date 8/15. $30 fee, may be waived for applicants with need. Application may be submitted online. Admission notification on a rolling basis. **Financial aid:** Priority date 4/1, closing date 7/31. FAFSA, institutional form required. Applicants notified on a rolling basis starting 4/1; must reply within 2 week(s) of notification.

Academics. **Special study options:** Combined bachelor's/graduate degree, cooperative education, cross-registration, distance learning, double major, dual enrollment of high school students, ESL, honors, independent study, internships, liberal arts/career combination, teacher certification program. 3-2 program in engineering. **Credit/placement by examination:** AP, CLEP, IB, SAT, ACT, institutional tests. 32 credit hours maximum toward bachelor's degree. **Support services:** Learning center, reduced course load, remedial instruction, study skills assistance, tutoring, writing center.

Majors. **Biology:** General. **Business:** Accounting, business admin, finance, management information systems, marketing. **Computer sciences:** General. **Education:** Elementary. **Engineering:** Chemical, civil, computer, electrical, mechanical. **English:** Speech/rhetoric. **Foreign languages:** General. **Health:** Nursing (RN). **History:** General. **Math:** General. **Philosophy/religion:** Philosophy. **Physical sciences:** Chemistry, optics, physics. **Psychology:** General. **Social sciences:** Political science, sociology. **Visual/performing arts:** Art.

Most popular majors. Biology 6%, business/marketing 27%, engineering/engineering technologies 24%, health sciences 17%.

Computing on campus. 1,091 workstations in dormitories, library, computer center, student center. Dormitories wired for high-speed internet access and linked to campus network. Commuter students can connect to campus network. Online course registration, online library, helpline, wireless network available.

Student life. **Freshman orientation:** Available, $65 fee. Preregistration for classes offered. 1-1/2 day residential program for students and parents held during the summer. **Policies:** Freshmen permitted cars on campus. **Housing:** Coed dorms, apartments, fraternity/sorority housing, substance-free housing available. $125 partly refundable deposit, deadline 4/1. **Activities:** Bands, choral groups, dance, drama, literary magazine, music ensembles, musical theater, opera, student government, student newspaper, symphony orchestra, Baptist campus ministries, black student association, Campus Crusade for Christ, Catholic student fellowship, Circle K International, College Democrats, Indian students organization, international cultural organization, National Society of Black Engineers, political science club.

Athletics. NCAA. **Intercollegiate:** Baseball M, basketball, cross-country, ice hockey M, soccer, softball W, tennis, track and field, volleyball W. **Intramural:** Badminton, basketball, football (non-tackle), golf, racquetball, soccer, softball, table tennis, volleyball. **Team name:** Chargers.

Student services. Alcohol/substance abuse counseling, career counseling, student employment services, financial aid counseling, health services, minority student services, on-campus daycare, personal counseling, placement for graduates. **Physically disabled:** Services for visually, hearing impaired.

Contact. E-mail: admitme@uah.edu
Phone: (256) 824-6070 Toll-free number: (800) 824-2255
Fax: (256) 824-6073
John Maxon, University of Alabama in Huntsville, 301 Sparkman Drive, Huntsville, AL 35899

University of Mobile
Mobile, Alabama
www.umobile.edu **CB code: 1515**

- Private 4-year university and liberal arts college affiliated with Alabama Baptist Convention
- Commuter campus in small city
- 1,549 degree-seeking undergraduates: 18% part-time, 65% women, 23% African American, 1% Asian American, 1% Hispanic American, 2% Native American, 4% international
- 209 degree-seeking graduate students
- 54% of applicants admitted
- SAT or ACT (ACT writing optional) required
- 46% graduate within 6 years

General. Founded in 1961. Regionally accredited. **Degrees:** 258 bachelor's, 58 associate awarded; master's offered. **ROTC:** Army, Air Force. **Location:** 12 miles from downtown, 170 miles from New Orleans. **Calendar:** Semester, extensive summer session. **Full-time faculty:** 92 total; 60% have terminal degrees, 3% minority, 55% women. **Part-time faculty:** 86 total; 10% have terminal degrees, 49% women. **Class size:** 60% < 20, 36% 20-39, 3% 40-49, less than 1% 50-99. **Special facilities:** Forest Learning Center, comprised of 125 acres with nature trails.

Freshman class profile. 504 applied, 270 admitted, 260 enrolled.

Mid 50% test scores		**Out-of-state:**	25%
ACT:	18-22	**Live on campus:**	28%
Rank in top quarter:	42%	**International:**	7%
Rank in top tenth:	20%		

Basis for selection. Admission decisions based on test scores, high school record. Interview recommended for nursing majors; audition recommended for music majors; portfolio recommended for art majors.

High school preparation. College-preparatory program recommended. 22 units recommended. Recommended units include English 4, mathematics 3, social studies 3 and foreign language 2.

2006-2007 Annual costs. Tuition/fees (projected): $12,330. Room/board: $6,790. Books/supplies: $500. Personal expenses: $1,000.

2005-2006 Financial aid. **Need-based:** 248 full-time freshmen applied for aid; 248 were judged to have need; 248 of these received aid. Average need met was 64%. Average scholarship/grant was $4,283; average loan $2,625. 37% of total undergraduate aid awarded as scholarships/grants, 63% as loans/jobs. **Non-need-based:** Awarded to 729 full-time undergraduates, including 328 freshmen. Scholarships awarded for academics, alumni affiliation, art, athletics, job skills, leadership, minority status, music/drama, religious affiliation, ROTC, state residency.

Application procedures. **Admission:** Priority date 3/31; no deadline. $30 fee. Admission notification on a rolling basis beginning on or about 11/1. Students with 26 or greater ACT may apply for early admission and scholarships. Early applicants invited to attend private luncheon hosted by president; also receive top consideration for scholarship monies. **Financial aid:** Priority date 3/31; no closing date. FAFSA, institutional form required. Applicants notified on a rolling basis; must reply within 2 week(s) of notification.

Academics. **Special study options:** Accelerated study, combined bachelor's/graduate degree, distance learning, double major, honors, independent study, internships, liberal arts/career combination, teacher certification program. **Credit/placement by examination:** AP, CLEP, IB, institutional tests. 30 credit hours maximum toward bachelor's degree. **Support services:** Learning center, pre-admission summer program, reduced course load, remedial instruction, study skills assistance, tutoring, writing center.

Majors. **Biology:** General, marine. **Business:** General, accounting, business admin, marketing. **Communications:** General. **Computer sciences:** General. **Education:** Biology, chemistry, early childhood, elementary, English, history, mathematics, music, physical, social studies. **Health:** Athletic training, nursing (RN). **History:** General. **Liberal arts:** Humanities. **Math:** General. **Parks/recreation:** Health/fitness. **Philosophy/religion:** Religion. **Psychology:** General. **Social sciences:** General, political science, sociology. **Theology:** Theology. **Visual/performing arts:** General, art, dramatic.

Most popular majors. Business/marketing 9%, education 15%, health sciences 9%, interdisciplinary studies 17%.

Computing on campus. 110 workstations in library, computer center.

Student life. **Freshman orientation:** Mandatory. Preregistration for classes offered. **Policies:** Religious observance required. Freshmen permitted cars on campus. **Housing:** Guaranteed on-campus for freshmen. Single-sex dorms, substance-free housing available. $150 nonrefundable deposit. **Activities:** Bands, choral groups, dance, drama, music ensembles, musical theater, opera, student government, symphony orchestra, Ministerial association, Baptist student union, honor societies, academic organizations, Fellowship of Christian Athletes, multicultural club.

Athletics. NAIA. **Intercollegiate:** Baseball M, basketball, cross-country, golf, soccer, softball W, tennis W. **Intramural:** Basketball, softball, table tennis, volleyball. **Team name:** Rams.

Student services. Adult student services, campus ministries, career counseling, student employment services, financial aid counseling, health services, personal counseling, veterans' counselor.

Contact. E-mail: adminfo@umobile.edu
Phone: (251) 442-2287 Toll-free number: (800) 946-7267
Fax: (251) 442-2498
Kris Nelson, Director of Admissions, University of Mobile, 5735 College Parkway, Mobile, AL 36613-2842

University of Montevallo

Montevallo, Alabama **CB member**
www.montevallo.edu **CB code: 1004**

- Public 4-year university and liberal arts college
- Residential campus in small town
- 2,557 degree-seeking undergraduates: 9% part-time, 68% women, 13% African American, 1% Asian American, 1% Hispanic American, 1% Native American, 2% international
- 319 degree-seeking graduate students
- 74% of applicants admitted
- SAT or ACT (ACT writing optional) required
- 45% graduate within 6 years

General. Founded in 1896. Regionally accredited. A National Historic District. **Degrees:** 462 bachelor's awarded; master's offered. **ROTC:** Army, Air Force. **Location:** 30 miles from Birmingham. **Calendar:** Semester, extensive summer session. **Full-time faculty:** 140 total; 84% have terminal degrees, 9% minority, 48% women. **Part-time faculty:** 60 total; 12% have terminal degrees, 2% minority, 58% women. **Class size:** 41% < 20, 51% 20-39, 5% 40-49, 2% 50-99. **Special facilities:** Foreign language laboratory, child development center, mass communication production center, traffic safety center.

Freshman class profile. 1,426 applied, 1,054 admitted, 496 enrolled.

Mid 50% test scores			
ACT:	19-24	**Return as sophomores:**	73%
GPA 3.50 or higher:	39%	**Out-of-state:**	3%
GPA 3.0-3.49:	29%	**Live on campus:**	64%
GPA 2.0-2.99:	32%	**International:**	2%
End year in good standing:	82%	**Fraternities:**	19%
		Sororities:	16%

Basis for selection. High school record and test scores essential factors in individual evaluation. Interview recommended. Audition required of music majors; portfolio required of art majors. **Homeschooled:** Transcript of courses and grades required. **Learning Disabled:** Students with disabilities must meet the same admissions requirements as other students. Conditional admission may be an option if standard requirements are not met. Reasonable accommodations will be provided as necessary. Enrolled students needing disability accommodations and services must provide current documentation and make requests through the Services for Students with Disabiltiies Office.

High school preparation. College-preparatory program recommended. 16 units required. Required and recommended units include English 4, mathematics 2-3, social studies 2, history 2, science 2-3, foreign language 2 and academic electives 4.

2005-2006 Annual costs. Tuition/fees: $5,664; $11,124 out-of-state. Room/board: $3,966. Books/supplies: $600. Personal expenses: $1,622.

2004-2005 Financial aid. Need-based: 420 full-time freshmen applied for aid; 312 were judged to have need; 309 of these received aid. Average need met was 46%. Average scholarship/grant was $4,511; average loan $1,653. 39% of total undergraduate aid awarded as scholarships/grants, 61% as loans/jobs. **Non-need-based:** Awarded to 680 full-time undergraduates, including 179 freshmen. Scholarships awarded for academics, art, athletics, leadership, minority status, music/drama, ROTC.

Application procedures. Admission: Closing date 8/20. $25 fee, may be waived for applicants with need. Application may be submitted online. Admission notification on a rolling basis. **Financial aid:** Priority date 4/15; no closing date. FAFSA required. Applicants notified by 6/1; must reply within 2 week(s) of notification.

Academics. Academic support programs available to all first-generation college students from low-income families and students with disabilities. **Special study options:** Accelerated study, cross-registration, double major, dual enrollment of high school students, exchange student, honors, independent study, internships, study abroad, teacher certification program. **Credit/placement by examination:** AP, CLEP, institutional tests. 45 credit hours maximum toward bachelor's degree. **Support services:** Learning center, pre-admission summer program, reduced course load, remedial instruction, study skills assistance, tutoring, writing center.

Majors. Biology: General. **Business:** Accounting, business admin, finance, management information systems, marketing. **Communications:** Radio/tv. **Education:** Early childhood, elementary. **English:** English lit, speech/rhetoric. **Family/consumer sciences:** General. **Foreign languages:** General. **Health:** Audiology/hearing, speech pathology. **History:** General. **Math:** General. **Parks/recreation:** Health/fitness. **Physical sciences:** Chemistry. **Psychology:** General. **Public administration:** Social work. **Social sciences:** General, political science, sociology. **Visual/performing arts:** Art, dramatic, music pedagogy.

Most popular majors. Business/marketing 19%, communications/journalism 6%, education 10%, English 7%, family/consumer sciences 8%, history 6%, psychology 6%, social sciences 7%, visual/performing arts 11%.

Computing on campus. 340 workstations in dormitories, library, computer center. Dormitories wired for high-speed internet access and linked to campus network. Commuter students can connect to campus network. Online course registration, online library, helpline, wireless network available.

Student life. Freshman orientation: Mandatory. Preregistration for classes offered. Fall Semester freshmen attend one of two preregistration sessions during the summer and return to campus for Freshman Orientation immediately prior to the beginning of Fall Semester classes. **Policies:** Freshmen permitted cars on campus. **Housing:** Guaranteed on-campus for freshmen. Coed dorms, single-sex dorms, apartments available. $100 fully refundable deposit. Several rooms are handicapped accessible. **Activities:** Bands, choral groups, dance, drama, literary magazine, music ensembles, musical theater, student government, student newspaper, TV station, African-American Society, association of international students, Young Republicans, Young Democrats, Baptist campus ministries, campus outreach, Catholic campus ministry, Presbyterian campus ministry, Methodist campus ministry.

Athletics. NAIA, NCAA. **Intercollegiate:** Baseball M, basketball, cross-country W, golf, soccer, tennis W, volleyball W. **Intramural:** Basketball, bowling, soccer, softball, volleyball. **Team name:** Falcons.

Student services. Adult student services, alcohol/substance abuse counseling, campus ministries, career counseling, student employment services, health services, minority student services, personal counseling, placement for graduates, veterans' counselor. **Physically disabled:** Services for visually, speech, hearing impaired.

Contact. E-mail: admissions@montevallo.edu
Phone: (205) 665-6030 Toll-free number: (800) 292-4349
Fax: (205) 665-6032
Ira Gurganus, Director of Admissions, University of Montevallo, Station 6030, Montevallo, AL 35115-6030

University of North Alabama

Florence, Alabama **CB member**
www.una.edu **CB code: 1735**

- Public 4-year university
- Commuter campus in large town
- 5,016 degree-seeking undergraduates: 12% part-time, 57% women
- 974 degree-seeking graduate students
- 80% of applicants admitted
- SAT or ACT required
- 55% graduate within 6 years

General. Founded in 1830. Regionally accredited. **Degrees:** 819 bachelor's awarded; master's offered. **ROTC:** Army. **Location:** 116 miles from Birmingham. **Calendar:** Semester, extensive summer session. **Full-time faculty:** 209 total; 74% have terminal degrees, 13% minority, 41% women. **Part-time faculty:** 113 total; 14% have terminal degrees, 4% minority, 54% women. **Class size:** 48% < 20, 40% 20-39, 9% 40-49, 3% 50-99, less than 1% >100. **Special facilities:** Planetarium-observatory, laboratory school.

Freshman class profile. 2,125 applied, 1,704 admitted, 931 enrolled.

Mid 50% test scores		**Rank in top quarter:**	44%
ACT:	18-23	**Return as sophomores:**	68%
GPA 3.50 or higher:	26%	**Out-of-state:**	14%
GPA 3.0-3.49:	24%	**International:**	8%
GPA 2.0-2.99:	39%		

Basis for selection. Minimum 18 ACT or 700 SAT (exclusive of Writing), or rank in upper 50 percent of high school class, or minimum 35 on each section of GED, or average of 45 on all GED test sections required. Auditions required of music majors. Interviews recommended for education, nursing, social work, preprofessional programs. Portfolios recommended for art majors.

High school preparation. 13 units required. Required units include English 4, mathematics 2, social studies 3, science 2 and foreign language 2.

2005-2006 Annual costs. Tuition/fees: $4,282; $7,930 out-of-state. Room/board: $4,710. Books/supplies: $830.

2004-2005 Financial aid. Need-based: 549 full-time freshmen applied for aid; 412 were judged to have need; 389 of these received aid. Average need met was 35%. Average scholarship/grant was $3,297; average loan $2,983. 39% of total undergraduate aid awarded as scholarships/grants, 61% as loans/jobs. **Non-need-based:** Scholarships awarded for academics, art, athletics, leadership, minority status, music/drama, ROTC, state residency.

Application procedures. Admission: Priority date 8/1; no deadline. $25 fee. Application may be submitted online. Admission notification on a rolling basis beginning on or about 6/15. **Financial aid:** Priority date 4/1; no closing date. FAFSA required. Applicants notified on a rolling basis starting 5/31; must reply within 2 week(s) of notification.

Academics. Special study options: Accelerated study, cooperative education, distance learning, double major, dual enrollment of high school students, ESL, honors, independent study, internships, student-designed major, teacher certification program, weekend college. **Credit/placement by examination:** AP, CLEP, institutional tests. 34 credit hours maximum toward bachelor's degree. **Support services:** Learning center, pre-admission summer program, reduced course load, remedial instruction, study skills assistance, tutoring.

Majors. Biology: General, marine. **Business:** Accounting, business admin, finance, management information systems, managerial economics, marketing. **Computer sciences:** General. **Education:** Elementary, multi-level teacher, secondary. **English:** English lit, speech/rhetoric. **Family/consumer sciences:** General. **Foreign languages:** General. **Health:** Nursing (RN). **History:** General. **Math:** General. **Parks/recreation:** General. **Physical sciences:** Chemistry, geology, physics. **Protective services:** Law enforcement admin. **Psychology:** General. **Public administration:** Social work. **Social sciences:** Geography, political science, sociology. **Visual/performing arts:** Studio arts.

Most popular majors. Business/marketing 29%, education 15%, English 8%, health sciences 14%, social sciences 7%.

Computing on campus. 500 workstations in dormitories, library, computer center, student center. Dormitories wired for high-speed internet access and linked to campus network. Commuter students can connect to campus network. Online course registration, online library, helpline available.

Student life. Freshman orientation: Mandatory, $25 fee. Preregistration for classes offered. 2-day sessions in June and July include orientation, academic advisement. **Policies:** Freshmen permitted cars on campus. **Housing:** Coed dorms, single-sex dorms, apartments, fraternity/sorority housing available. $100 deposit. **Activities:** Bands, choral groups, drama, literary magazine, music ensembles, musical theater, radio station, student government, student newspaper, Young Democrats, Young Republicans, Circle-K, Gold Triangle (honorary service organization), Black Student Alliance, Christian Student Fellowship, Baptist Campus Ministries.

Athletics. NCAA. **Intercollegiate:** Baseball M, basketball, cross-country, football (tackle) M, golf M, soccer W, softball W, tennis, volleyball W. **Intramural:** Badminton, baseball M, basketball, bowling, cross-country, football (tackle) M, golf M, racquetball, softball W, swimming, table tennis, tennis, volleyball. **Team name:** Lions.

Student services. Adult student services, alcohol/substance abuse counseling, campus ministries, career counseling, student employment services, financial aid counseling, health services, minority student services, on-campus daycare, personal counseling, placement for graduates, veterans' counselor, women's services. **Physically disabled:** Services for visually, speech, hearing impaired.

Contact. E-mail: admissions@una.edu
Phone: (256) 765-4608 Toll-free number: (800) 825-5862
Fax: (256) 765-4329
Kim Mauldin, Director of Admissions, University of North Alabama, UNA - Box 5011, Florence, AL 35632-0001

University of South Alabama

Mobile, Alabama
www.southalabama.edu **CB code: 1880**

- Public 4-year university
- Commuter campus in small city
- 9,957 degree-seeking undergraduates: 25% part-time, 60% women
- 2,978 degree-seeking graduate students
- 86% of applicants admitted
- SAT or ACT required
- 33% graduate within 6 years

General. Founded in 1963. Regionally accredited. **Degrees:** 1,365 bachelor's awarded; master's, doctoral, first professional offered. **ROTC:** Army, Air Force. **Location:** 10 miles from downtown, 150 miles from New Orleans. **Calendar:** Semester, extensive summer session. **Full-time faculty:** 485 total. **Part-time faculty:** 250 total. **Special facilities:** Sea laboratory.

Freshman class profile. 2,627 applied, 2,269 admitted, 1,258 enrolled.

Mid 50% test scores		Return as sophomores:	70%
SAT verbal:	460-610	International:	6%
SAT math:	470-570	Fraternities:	10%
ACT:	18-24	Sororities:	10%

Basis for selection. School achievement record and test scores important. Auditions required of music majors. **Learning Disabled:** Submit required documentation to special student services office if requesting services.

High school preparation. 16 units recommended. Recommended units include English 4, mathematics 3, social studies 2, science 2 and academic electives 2.

2005-2006 Annual costs. Tuition/fees: $4,502; $8,312 out-of-state. Room/board: $4,648. Books/supplies: $1,000.

2005-2006 Financial aid. Need-based: Average need met was 23%. Average scholarship/grant was $1,702; average loan $1,301. 36% of total undergraduate aid awarded as scholarships/grants, 64% as loans/jobs. **Non-need-based:** Scholarships awarded for academics, alumni affiliation, art, athletics, minority status, music/drama, ROTC, state residency.

Application procedures. Admission: Closing date 8/10. $25 fee. Application must be submitted on paper. Admission notification on a rolling basis. **Financial aid:** Priority date 5/1; no closing date. FAFSA, institutional form required. Applicants notified on a rolling basis starting 5/15.

Academics. Students in entry-level programming courses must own a laptop. **Special study options:** Cooperative education, distance learning, double major, ESL, honors, independent study, internships, student-designed major, study abroad, teacher certification program, weekend college. **Credit/placement by examination:** AP, CLEP, institutional tests. Maximum of 32 credit hours can be awarded under any combination of AP and CLEP examination credits. **Support services:** Learning center, remedial instruction, study skills assistance, tutoring, writing center.

Honors college/program. Minimum ACT of 27, high school GPA of 3.5, two letters of recommendation and essay required. Program includes honors coursework, extracurricular activities, faculty mentoring.

Majors. Biology: General, biomedical sciences. **Business:** General, accounting, business admin, e-commerce, finance, marketing. **Communications:** General. **Computer sciences:** General. **Education:** Early childhood, elementary, health, physical, secondary, special. **Engineering:** Chemical, civil, computer, electrical, mechanical. **English:** English lit. **Foreign languages:** General. **Health:** Audiology/speech pathology, clinical lab science, medical radiologic technology/radiation therapy, nursing (RN), respiratory therapy technology. **History:** General. **Liberal arts:** Arts/sciences. **Math:** Statistics. **Parks/recreation:** General. **Philosophy/religion:** Philosophy. **Physical sciences:** Atmospheric science, chemistry, geology, physics. **Protective services:** Criminal justice. **Psychology:** General. **Social sciences:** Anthropology, geography, political science, sociology. **Visual/performing arts:** Art, dramatic.

Most popular majors. Biology 6%, business/marketing 16%, education 15%, engineering/engineering technologies 7%, health sciences 22%.

Computing on campus. 500 workstations in library, computer center, student center. Dormitories wired for high-speed internet access and linked to campus network. Commuter students can connect to campus network. Online course registration, online library, helpline available.

Student life. Freshman orientation: Mandatory, $75 fee. **Policies:** Freshmen permitted cars on campus. **Housing:** Coed dorms, special housing for disabled, apartments, fraternity/sorority housing available. $200 deposit. **Activities:** Bands, choral groups, dance, drama, film society, literary magazine, music ensembles, musical theater, opera, student government, student newspaper, symphony orchestra, TV station.

Athletics. NCAA. **Intercollegiate:** Baseball M, basketball, cross-country, golf, soccer W, softball W, tennis, track and field, volleyball W. **Intramural:** Basketball, bowling, football (non-tackle), golf, racquetball, soccer, softball, table tennis, tennis, volleyball, water polo. **Team name:** Jaguars.

Student services. Adult student services, alcohol/substance abuse counseling, campus ministries, career counseling, services for economically disadvantaged, student employment services, financial aid counseling, health

services, minority student services, personal counseling, placement for graduates, veterans' counselor. **Physically disabled:** Services for visually, speech, hearing impaired.

Contact. E-mail: admiss@usouthal.edu
Phone: (251) 460-6141 Toll-free number: (800) 872-5247
Fax: (251) 460-7876
Melissa Haab, Director of Admissions, University of South Alabama, 182 Administration Building, Mobile, AL 36688-0002

University of West Alabama

Livingston, Alabama
www.uwa.edu **CB code: 1737**

- Public 4-year university
- Residential campus in small town
- 1,645 degree-seeking undergraduates: 8% part-time, 54% women
- 1,349 degree-seeking graduate students
- 78% of applicants admitted
- ACT (writing recommended) required

General. Founded in 1835. Regionally accredited. **Degrees:** 228 bachelor's, 41 associate awarded; master's offered. **ROTC:** Air Force. **Location:** 60 miles from Tuscaloosa. **Calendar:** Semester, limited summer session. **Full-time faculty:** 93 total; 68% have terminal degrees, 11% minority, 42% women. **Part-time faculty:** 7 total; 14% have terminal degrees, 43% women. **Special facilities:** Nature trail, herbarium, greenhouses, wildflower gardens, bluebird trail.

Freshman class profile. 832 applied, 646 admitted, 366 enrolled.

Mid 50% test scores		Out-of-state:	12%
ACT:	15-22	International:	1%

Basis for selection. School achievement record and test scores most important.

High school preparation. 15 units required. Required units include English 3, mathematics 3, social studies 3, science 3 and academic electives 3.

2005-2006 Annual costs. Tuition/fees: $4,778; $8,616 out-of-state. Room/board: $3,318. Books/supplies: $900. Personal expenses: $1,200.

2005-2006 Financial aid. **Need-based:** 24% of total undergraduate aid awarded as scholarships/grants, 76% as loans/jobs. **Non-need-based:** Scholarships awarded for academics, alumni affiliation, athletics, leadership, music/drama, state residency.

Application procedures. **Admission:** No deadline. $20 fee. Admission notification on a rolling basis. **Financial aid:** Priority date 4/1; no closing date. FAFSA required. Applicants notified on a rolling basis starting 6/1; must reply within 2 week(s) of notification.

Academics. **Special study options:** Accelerated study, cooperative education, distance learning, double major, dual enrollment of high school students, honors, internships, teacher certification program. **Credit/placement by examination:** AP, CLEP, institutional tests. 15 credit hours maximum toward associate degree, 30 toward bachelor's. **Support services:** Learning center, reduced course load, remedial instruction, study skills assistance, tutoring, writing center.

Majors. **Biology:** General, marine. **Business:** Accounting, business admin, management information systems. **Conservation:** General. **Education:** Early childhood, elementary, physical, secondary, special. **Engineering technology:** Manufacturing. **Health:** Athletic training. **History:** General. **Math:** General. **Physical sciences:** Chemistry. **Psychology:** General. **Social sciences:** Sociology.

Most popular majors. Business/marketing 21%, education 30%, engineering/engineering technologies 8%, English 9%, psychology 8%, social sciences 10%.

Computing on campus. 310 workstations in dormitories, library, computer center, student center. Dormitories wired for high-speed internet access and linked to campus network. Commuter students can connect to campus network. Online library, helpline, wireless network available.

Student life. **Freshman orientation:** Mandatory, $40 fee. Preregistration for classes offered. **Policies:** Freshmen permitted cars on campus. **Housing:** Guaranteed on-campus for all undergraduates. Coed dorms, single-sex dorms, apartments available. $100 deposit. **Activities:** Bands, choral groups, drama, student government, student newspaper, Baptist campus ministries, Wesley Foundation, campus outreach, Fellowship of Christian Athletes, student support services club, African-American cultural association.

Athletics. NCAA. **Intercollegiate:** Baseball M, basketball, cross-country, football (tackle) M, rodeo, softball W, tennis, volleyball W. **Intramural:** Basketball, softball, table tennis, tennis, volleyball, wrestling M. **Team name:** Tigers.

Student services. Career counseling, student employment services, health services, personal counseling, placement for graduates, veterans' counselor. **Physically disabled:** Services for visually, hearing impaired.

Contact. Phone: (205) 652-3578 Fax: (205) 652-3708
Richard Hester, Director of Admissions, University of West Alabama, Station 4, Livingston, AL 35470

Virginia College

Birmingham, Alabama
www.vc.edu **CB code: 2596**

- For-profit 4-year technical college
- Commuter campus in very large city
- 1,879 degree-seeking undergraduates: 45% part-time, 67% women
- 50 degree-seeking graduate students
- Interview required
- 40% graduate within 6 years

General. Founded in 1975. Accredited by ACICS. **Degrees:** 88 bachelor's, 527 associate awarded; master's offered. **Calendar:** Quarter, extensive summer session. **Full-time faculty:** 110 total. **Part-time faculty:** 120 total. **Special facilities:** Full service restaurant and bakery operated by Culinary Institute.

Freshman class profile. 561 applied, 503 admitted, 503 enrolled.

Basis for selection. Open admission, but selective for some programs. High school record, interview and essay evaluated. **Homeschooled:** Diploma and transcript required. **Learning Disabled:** Documentation for untimed testing required.

2005-2006 Annual costs. Per-credit-hour charge ranges from $255-$350 depending on program and includes fees and books. Personal expenses: $100.

Application procedures. **Admission:** No deadline. $100 fee. Admission notification on a rolling basis. **Financial aid:** No deadline.

Academics. **Special study options:** Accelerated study, distance learning, independent study, internships. **Credit/placement by examination:** CLEP, institutional tests. 45 credit hours maximum toward associate degree. **Support services:** Learning center, study skills assistance, tutoring.

Majors. **Business:** Accounting, business admin, management information systems. **Health:** Health care admin. **Visual/performing arts:** Graphic design, interior design.

Computing on campus. 1,000 workstations in library, computer center. Online library, repair service available.

Student life. **Freshman orientation:** Mandatory. Preregistration for classes offered.

Student services. Career counseling, student employment services, financial aid counseling, placement for graduates, veterans' counselor.

Contact. Phone: (205) 802-1200 Fax: (205) 802-7045
Bunty Cantwell, Director of Admissions, Virginia College, Box 19249, Birmingham, AL 35219

Virginia College at Huntsville

Huntsville, Alabama
www.vc.edu **CB code: 3451**

- For-profit 4-year business and technical college
- Small city
- 760 degree-seeking undergraduates

General. Accredited by ACICS. **Degrees:** 20 bachelor's, 131 associate awarded. **Calendar:** Continuous. **Full-time faculty:** 25 total. **Part-time faculty:** 60 total.

Basis for selection. Open admission.

2005-2006 Annual costs. Tuition varies by program. Per-credit-hour charge ranges from $255 to $285. Personal expenses: $2,978.

Application procedures. Admission: No deadline. $100 fee. **Financial aid:** No deadline. FAFSA, institutional form required. Applicants notified on a rolling basis.

Academics. Credit/placement by examination: CLEP.

Contact. Phone: (256) 533-7387
Pat Foster, Vice President of Enrollment, Virginia College at Huntsville, 2800 Bob Wallace Avenue, Huntsville, AL 35805

Alaska

Alaska Bible College

Glennallen, Alaska
www.akbible.edu **CB code: 1237**

- Private 4-year Bible college affiliated with nondenominational tradition
- Residential campus in rural community
- 43 degree-seeking undergraduates
- SAT or ACT, application essay, interview required

General. Founded in 1966. Accredited by ABHE. **Degrees:** 12 bachelor's, 1 associate awarded. **Location:** 187 miles from Anchorage, 250 miles from Fairbanks. **Calendar:** Semester. **Full-time faculty:** 3 total. **Part-time faculty:** 8 total. **Class size:** 92% < 20, 8% 20-39. **Special facilities:** Largest theological library collection in Alaska, Alaskan book collection.

Freshman class profile. 4 applied, 4 admitted, 4 enrolled.

Out-of-state:	40%	**Live on campus:**	100%

Basis for selection. Open admission, but selective for some programs. Applicants considered on a case-by-case basis. References and indications of religious commitment most important, followed by school grade record. Test scores and extracurricular activities also considered. **Homeschooled:** Applicants need to have documentation of high school equivalence.

High school preparation. Recommended units include English 4, mathematics 4, social studies 4, history 4, science 4 and foreign language 2.

2006-2007 Annual costs. Tuition/fees: $5,950. Room/board: $4,750. Books/supplies: $425. Personal expenses: $1,000.

2005-2006 Financial aid. All financial aid based on need. 31% of total undergraduate aid awarded as scholarships/grants, 69% as loans/jobs.

Application procedures. Admission: Closing date 7/1 (postmark date). $35 fee. Admission notification on a rolling basis. Must reply by 7/15. **Financial aid:** Priority date 4/30, closing date 8/1. Institutional form required. Applicants notified on a rolling basis; must reply within 2 week(s) of notification.

Academics. Special study options: Double major, dual enrollment of high school students, independent study, internships. **Credit/placement by examination:** AP, CLEP, institutional tests. **Support services:** Remedial instruction, tutoring.

Majors. Education: ESL. **Theology:** Bible.

Computing on campus. 10 workstations in library, computer center.

Student life. Freshman orientation: Mandatory. Preregistration for classes offered. **Policies:** Religious observance required. Freshmen permitted cars on campus. **Housing:** Guaranteed on-campus for freshmen. Single-sex dorms, apartments available. $150 deposit, deadline 7/1. **Activities:** Radio station, student government.

Athletics. Intramural: Basketball, volleyball.

Student services. Campus ministries, financial aid counseling, health services.

Contact. E-mail: info@akbible.edu
Phone: (907) 822-3201 Toll-free number: (800) 478-7884
Fax: (907) 822-5027
Carol Ridley, Director of Admissions, Alaska Bible College, Box 289, Glennallen, AK 99588-0289

Alaska Pacific University

Anchorage, Alaska
www.alaskapacific.edu **CB code: 4201**

- Private 4-year university and liberal arts college
- Commuter campus in large city
- 471 degree-seeking undergraduates: 37% part-time, 68% women, 6% African American, 4% Asian American, 4% Hispanic American, 16% Native American
- 161 degree-seeking graduate students
- 44% of applicants admitted
- SAT or ACT with writing, application essay required
- 30% graduate within 6 years

General. Founded in 1957. Regionally accredited. **Degrees:** 89 bachelor's, 2 associate awarded; master's offered. **Calendar:** Differs by program. Full semester of 15 weeks or optional 4 week block and 11-week session. Limited summer session. **Full-time faculty:** 44 total; 61% have terminal degrees, 7% minority, 46% women. **Part-time faculty:** 40 total; 18% have terminal degrees, 5% minority, 32% women. **Class size:** 95% < 20, 5% 20-39. **Special facilities:** Climbing wall, trails (connecting with the city trail system) for walking, running, biking and skiing, lake for canoeing and kayaking, Alaskana collection.

Freshman class profile. 122 applied, 54 admitted, 52 enrolled.

Mid 50% test scores		**Rank in top quarter:**	50%
SAT verbal:	450-570	**Rank in top tenth:**	11%
SAT math:	440-560	**End year in good standing:**	76%
ACT:	19-24	**Return as sophomores:**	53%
GPA 3.50 or higher:	37%	**Out-of-state:**	60%
GPA 3.0-3.49:	40%	**Live on campus:**	81%
GPA 2.0-2.99:	23%		

Basis for selection. High school record, level of involvement in school and community activities, test scores, writing samples, recommendations most important. Interviews recommended. **Learning Disabled:** Documentation verifying the disability condition required.

High school preparation. College-preparatory program recommended. 14 units recommended. Recommended units include English 4, mathematics 3, social studies 1, history 1, science 2 (laboratory 1) and foreign language 2.

2006-2007 Annual costs. Tuition/fees (projected): $19,610. Room/board: $6,800. Books/supplies: $840. Personal expenses: $1,111.

2005-2006 Financial aid. Need-based: 36 full-time freshmen applied for aid; 33 were judged to have need; 33 of these received aid. Average need met was 86%. Average scholarship/grant was $2,945; average loan $2,625. 46% of total undergraduate aid awarded as scholarships/grants, 54% as loans/jobs. **Non-need-based:** Awarded to 275 full-time undergraduates, including 32 freshmen. Scholarships awarded for academics, alumni affiliation, leadership, religious affiliation, state residency.

Application procedures. Admission: Priority date 12/1; deadline 8/15. $25 fee, may be waived for applicants with need. Application may be submitted online. Admission notification on a rolling basis beginning on or about 1/15. **Financial aid:** Priority date 4/15; no closing date. FAFSA required. Applicants notified on a rolling basis starting 2/1; must reply within 4 week(s) of notification.

Academics. Special study options: Accelerated study, distance learning, double major, independent study, internships, liberal arts/career combination, student-designed major, study abroad, teacher certification program. Eco-League exchange program for Environmental Sciences with Prescott College, Northland College, College of the Atlantic, Antioch College, Green Mountain College. **Credit/placement by examination:** AP, CLEP, IB, institutional tests. 22 credit hours maximum toward associate degree, 45 toward bachelor's. Sophomore standing available through AP and IB examinations by earning equivalent of 32 semester hours. **Support services:** Learning center, reduced course load, remedial instruction, study skills assistance, tutoring, writing center.

Majors. Biology: Marine. **Business:** Business admin. **Conservation:** General, environmental science. **Education:** Elementary, middle. **Health:** Health care admin. **Legal studies:** Prelaw. **Liberal arts:** Arts/sciences. **Parks/recreation:** Facilities management. **Psychology:** General. **Public administration:** Social work.

Most popular majors. Business/marketing 9%, education 21%, liberal arts 12%, natural resources/environmental science 16%, parks/recreation 23%, psychology 14%.

Computing on campus. 50 workstations in dormitories, library, computer center, student center. Dormitories wired for high-speed internet access. Online library available.

Student life. Freshman orientation: Mandatory. Usually 10 days long, includes outdoor camping events and placement testing. **Policies:** Student representation on faculty committees and councils stressed. Freshmen permitted cars on campus. **Housing:** Guaranteed on-campus for freshmen. Coed dorms, cooperative housing, substance-free housing available. $300 fully refundable deposit, deadline 4/30. **Activities:** Choral groups, drama, literary magazine, music ensembles, student government, student newspaper, art club, business club, campus ministry, environmental club, photgraphy club, psychology club, internaional students organization, service club, soccer club, volleyball club, student government.

Student services. Campus ministries, career counseling, student employment services, financial aid counseling, minority student services, personal counseling.

Contact. E-mail: admissions@alaskapacific.edu
Phone: (907) 564-8248 Toll-free number: (800) 252-7528
Fax: (907) 562-4276
Michael Warner, Director of Admissions, Alaska Pacific University, 4101 University Drive, Anchorage, AK 99508

Charter College
Anchorage, Alaska
www.chartercollege.edu **CB code: 3453**

- Private 4-year junior and technical college
- Commuter campus in large city
- 475 degree-seeking undergraduates

General. Accredited by ACICS. **Degrees:** 20 bachelor's, 51 associate awarded. **Calendar:** Continuous. **Full-time faculty:** 12 total. **Part-time faculty:** 25 total.

Basis for selection. Open admission.

2005-2006 Annual costs. Tuition ranges from $19,000 to $23,000 for associates and from $38,000 to $44,000 for bachelors depending on program; includes books and supplies. Books/supplies: $700.

Application procedures. Admission: No deadline. $20 fee. Admission notification on a rolling basis. **Financial aid:** No deadline. FAFSA required. Applicants notified on a rolling basis; must reply within 5 week(s) of notification.

Academics. Special study options: Double major, internships. **Credit/placement by examination:** CLEP. Up to 33% of total required credits for associate degree may be earned through examination. **Support services:** Tutoring.

Majors. Business: Business admin. **Computer sciences:** Information systems.

Computing on campus. Online library available.

Student life. Freshman orientation: Available.

Student services. Career counseling, student employment services, financial aid counseling.

Contact. Phone: (907) 277-1000
Lily Sirianni, Admissions Director, Charter College, 2221 East Northern Lights Boulevard, Suite 120, Anchorage, AK 99508

Sheldon Jackson College
Sitka, Alaska
www.sj-alaska.edu **CB code: 4742**

- Private 4-year liberal arts and teachers college affiliated with Presbyterian Church (USA)
- Residential campus in small town
- 122 degree-seeking undergraduates

General. Founded in 1878. Regionally accredited. **Degrees:** 14 bachelor's, 10 associate awarded. **Location:** 90 miles from Juneau, 882 air miles from Seattle. **Calendar:** Semester. **Full-time faculty:** 20 total. **Part-time faculty:** 25 total. **Class size:** 91% < 20, 7% 20-39, 1% 40-49. **Special facilities:** Salmon hatchery, sea kayaks, center for outdoor education in Southeast Alaska.

Basis for selection. Open admission. Students with GPA below 2.0 asked to participate in achievement program.

High school preparation. Recommended units include English 4, mathematics 2, social studies 4 and science 2.

2005-2006 Annual costs. Tuition/fees: $11,300. Room/board: $7,300. Books/supplies: $750. Personal expenses: $1,000.

Financial aid. Additional information: Financial aid available from Bureau of Indian Affairs and Alaska State Loan Program.

Application procedures. Admission: Priority date 5/1; no deadline. $25 fee, may be waived for applicants with need. Application may be submitted online. Admission notification on a rolling basis beginning on or about 10/1. **Financial aid:** Priority date 3/15; no closing date. FAFSA required. Applicants notified on a rolling basis starting 4/1; must reply within 3 week(s) of notification.

Academics. Consortium courses available with Alaska Public Safety Academy and University of Alaska Southeast. **Special study options:** Cooperative education, cross-registration, double major, dual enrollment of high school students, independent study, internships, liberal arts/career combination, student-designed major, teacher certification program. **Credit/placement by examination:** AP, CLEP, institutional tests. 40 credit hours maximum toward associate degree, 100 toward bachelor's. Students not submitting SAT/ACT scores must take college-administered placement tests. Test scores not required of applicants out of high school 2 or more years. **Support services:** Learning center, remedial instruction, tutoring.

Majors. Agriculture: Aquaculture. **Biology:** Ecology, marine. **Business:** Business admin. **Conservation:** General, fisheries. **Education:** Elementary, secondary. **Liberal arts:** Arts/sciences. **Parks/recreation:** General. **Public administration:** Human services.

Most popular majors. Education 58%, interdisciplinary studies 8%, natural resources/environmental science 33%.

Computing on campus. 20 workstations in dormitories, library, computer center. Dormitories linked to campus network. Commuter students can connect to campus network.

Student life. Freshman orientation: Available. Preregistration for classes offered. **Policies:** Freshmen permitted cars on campus. **Housing:** Guaranteed on-campus for freshmen. Coed dorms, single-sex dorms, apartments available. $200 deposit, deadline 6/1. Married student apartments very limited. **Activities:** Choral groups, drama, literary magazine, music ensembles, musical theater, student government, symphony orchestra, religious student group, drama club, Alaska native (culture) club, social justice club, outdoor club.

Athletics. Intramural: Badminton, basketball, handball, racquetball, soccer, swimming, table tennis, volleyball, water polo.

Student services. Campus ministries, health services, on-campus daycare, personal counseling, veterans' counselor. **Physically disabled:** Services for visually impaired.

Contact. E-mail: admissions@sj-alaska.edu
Phone: (907) 747-5221 Toll-free number: (800) 478-4556
Fax: (907) 747-6366
Andy Lee, Director of Admissions, Sheldon Jackson College, 801 Lincoln Street, Sitka, AK 99835

University of Alaska Anchorage
Anchorage, Alaska
www.uaa.alaska.edu **CB code: 4896**

- Public 4-year university
- Commuter campus in large city
- 11,398 degree-seeking undergraduates
- 74% of applicants admitted
- SAT or ACT with writing required

General. Founded in 1954. Regionally accredited. **Degrees:** 778 bachelor's, 512 associate awarded; master's offered. **ROTC:** Air Force. **Location:** 3 miles from downtown. **Calendar:** Semester, extensive summer session. **Full-time faculty:** 530 total. **Part-time faculty:** 675 total. **Class size:** 58% < 20, 34% 20-39, 5% 40-49, 3% 50-99, less than 1% >100. **Special facilities:** Environment and natural resources institute, film library, center for international business, center for alcohol and addiction studies, center for high latitude health research, institute for circumpolar health, institute for social and economic research.

Freshman class profile. 2,760 applied, 2,056 admitted, 1,561 enrolled.

Mid 50% test scores			
SAT verbal:	440-580	Rank in top tenth:	12%
SAT math:	450-570	Out-of-state:	6%
ACT:	18-24	Live on campus:	23%
Rank in top quarter:	32%	Fraternities:	1%

Basis for selection. Secondary school record, test scores important; 2.0 high school GPA required. Open admission for non-degree seeking applicants. Interview required of nursing majors; portfolio required of art majors.

High school preparation. Recommended units include English 4, mathematics 2, social studies 3, history 1, science 3 and foreign language 1. 1-2 computer science, 1-2 art also recommended. Specific recommendations vary by program.

2005-2006 Annual costs. Tuition/fees: $3,734; $11,354 out-of-state. Room/board: $6,730. Books/supplies: $912. Personal expenses: $1,194.

2005-2006 Financial aid. Need-based: 842 full-time freshmen applied for aid; 402 were judged to have need; 371 of these received aid. Average need met was 66%. Average scholarship/grant was $3,906; average loan $5,460. 28% of total undergraduate aid awarded as scholarships/grants, 72% as loans/jobs. **Non-need-based:** Awarded to 727 full-time undergraduates, including 195 freshmen. Scholarships awarded for academics, athletics.

Application procedures. Admission: Priority date 3/15; deadline 8/1. $40 fee ($45 out-of-state), may be waived for applicants with need. Admission notification on a rolling basis. Freshman early admit plan allows students to apply early but wait as long as 2 years to enroll. **Financial aid:** Priority date 4/1, closing date 8/1. FAFSA, institutional form required. Applicants notified on a rolling basis starting 3/15; must reply within 4 week(s) of notification.

Academics. Many programs to assist nontraditional and/or at-risk students for college success. **Special study options:** Cooperative education, cross-registration, distance learning, double major, dual enrollment of high school students, ESL, exchange student, honors, independent study, internships, liberal arts/career combination, student-designed major, study abroad, teacher certification program. **Credit/placement by examination:** AP, CLEP, IB, institutional tests. 24 credit hours maximum toward associate degree, 24 toward bachelor's. **Support services:** Learning center, remedial instruction, study skills assistance, tutoring.

Majors. Biology: General. **Business:** Accounting, business admin, entrepreneurial studies, finance, hospitality admin, logistics, management information systems, marketing. **Communications:** Journalism. **Computer sciences:** General, computer science. **Education:** Elementary, music, physical. **Engineering:** Civil, electrical. **Engineering technology:** Electrical, surveying. **Foreign languages:** General, French, German, Japanese, Russian, Spanish. **Health:** Nursing (RN). **History:** General. **Interdisciplinary:** Biological/physical sciences, natural sciences. **Liberal arts:** Arts/sciences. **Math:** General. **Mechanic/repair:** Aircraft. **Personal/culinary services:** Culinary arts. **Physical sciences:** Chemistry. **Psychology:** General. **Public administration:** Human services, social work. **Social sciences:** Anthropology, economics, political science, sociology. **Transportation:** General, air traffic control, aviation, aviation management. **Visual/performing arts:** General, art, dramatic, music performance, studio arts.

Most popular majors. Business/marketing 21%, English 6%, health sciences 17%, psychology 8%, security/protective services 7%, social sciences 12%.

Computing on campus. 851 workstations in dormitories, library, computer center, student center. Dormitories wired for high-speed internet access and linked to campus network. Commuter students can connect to campus network. Helpline, repair service available.

Student life. Freshman orientation: Available. Preregistration for classes offered. **Policies:** Freshmen permitted cars on campus. **Housing:** Coed dorms, special housing for disabled, apartments available. $150 deposit. Separate floors for: Alaska natives studying engineering, nursing students, honor students, language & cultures, first-year students under age 20, healthy lifestyle, quiet lifestyle, WWAME program, Far East exchange program. **Activities:** Jazz band, choral groups, dance, drama, literary magazine, music ensembles, radio station, student government, student newspaper, university community ministry, Alaska Native student organization, African American student associations, Baha'i club, College Republicans, Korean Campus Crusade for Christ, Intervarsity Christian Fellowship, disability awareness club, Student Organization Against Racism (SOAR).

Athletics. NCAA. **Intercollegiate:** Basketball, cross-country, gymnastics W, ice hockey M, skiing, track and field, volleyball W. **Intramural:** Basketball, fencing, ice hockey, racquetball, skiing, soccer, softball, volleyball. **Team name:** Seawolves.

Student services. Adult student services, alcohol/substance abuse counseling, career counseling, student employment services, financial aid counseling, health services, minority student services, personal counseling, veterans' counselor. **Physically disabled:** Services for visually, speech, hearing impaired. **Learning disabled:** Comprehensive services available.

Contact. E-mail: enroll@uaa.alaska.edu
Phone: (907) 786-1480 Fax: (907) 786-4888
Mary Howard, Admissions Manager, University of Alaska Anchorage, 3211 Providence Drive, #158, Anchorage, AK 99508-8046

University of Alaska Fairbanks

Fairbanks, Alaska — **CB member**
www.uaf.edu — **CB code: 4866**

- Public 4-year university
- Commuter campus in small city
- 4,862 degree-seeking undergraduates: 32% part-time, 57% women, 3% African American, 3% Asian American, 3% Hispanic American, 19% Native American, 3% international
- 1,044 degree-seeking graduate students
- 78% of applicants admitted
- SAT or ACT (ACT writing optional) required

General. Founded in 1917. Regionally accredited. 22 campuses and sites located across Alaska. **Degrees:** 432 bachelor's, 206 associate awarded; master's, doctoral offered. **ROTC:** Army. **Location:** 4 miles from downtown. **Calendar:** Semester, limited summer session. **Full-time faculty:** 288 total; 7% have terminal degrees, 16% minority, 38% women. **Part-time faculty:** 7 total; 57% women. **Class size:** 67% < 20, 27% 20-39, 3% 40-49, 2% 50-99, less than 1% >100. **Special facilities:** Art and natural history museum, geophysical institute, bioscience library, Cray super computers, international arctic research center, research range.

Freshman class profile. 1,777 applied, 1,383 admitted, 1,000 enrolled.

Mid 50% test scores			
SAT verbal:	450-600	Rank in top quarter:	34%
SAT math:	450-580	Rank in top tenth:	15%
ACT:	17-23	End year in good standing:	77%
GPA 3.50 or higher:	44%	Return as sophomores:	68%
GPA 3.0-3.49:	40%	Out-of-state:	8%
GPA 2.0-2.99:	16%	Live on campus:	43%
		International:	2%

Basis for selection. GED not accepted. Minimum 2.0 high school GPA; 2.5 GPA in 16 core classes, for bachelor's degree-seeking students. Open admissions for associate degree applicants over age 18. **Learning Disabled:** Contact UAF Disability Services for assistance.

High school preparation. College-preparatory program required. 16 units required. Required and recommended units include English 4, mathematics 3, social studies 3, science 3 (laboratory 1), foreign language 2 and academic electives 3. Mathematics should include 3 from algebra, geometry and trigonometry, precalculus or calculus.

2005-2006 Annual costs. Tuition/fees: $3,946; $11,566 out-of-state. Room/board: $5,580. Books/supplies: $700. Personal expenses: $300.

2005-2006 Financial aid. Need-based: 729 full-time freshmen applied for aid; 302 were judged to have need; 280 of these received aid. Average need met was 62%. Average scholarship/grant was $3,768; average loan $5,690. 27% of total undergraduate aid awarded as scholarships/grants, 73% as loans/jobs. **Non-need-based:** Awarded to 678 full-time undergraduates, including 157 freshmen. Scholarships awarded for academics, art, athletics, job skills, ROTC, state residency.

Application procedures. Admission: Priority date 2/1; deadline 8/1 (postmark date). $40 fee, may be waived for applicants with need. Application may be submitted online. Admission notification on a rolling basis. **Financial aid:** Priority date 7/1; no closing date. FAFSA required. Applicants notified on a rolling basis starting 3/1; must reply within 2 week(s) of notification.

Academics. Special study options: Accelerated study, cooperative education, distance learning, double major, dual enrollment of high school students, ESL, exchange student, honors, independent study, internships, semester at sea, student-designed major, study abroad, teacher certification program. **Credit/placement by examination:** AP, CLEP, IB, SAT, ACT, institutional tests. 15 credit hours maximum toward associate degree, 30 toward bachelor's. 25% of degree requirements awarded for prior work or life experience. Credit awarded for CEEB Advanced Placement Test scores of 3 or greater CLEP, DANTES-DSST, local credit by exam. **Support services:** Learning center, remedial instruction, study skills assistance, tutoring, writing center.

Honors college/program. High school GPA greater than 3.6, composite SAT 1270 (exclusive of Writing), composite ACT 28 required.

Majors. Area/ethnic studies: Native American, Russian/Slavic. **Biology:** General. **Business:** Accounting, business admin, managerial economics. **Communications:** General, journalism. **Computer sciences:** Computer science. **Conservation:** General, fisheries, forestry, management/policy, wildlife. **Education:** General, music, physical. **Engineering:** Civil, electrical, geological, geotechnical, industrial, mechanical, mining, petroleum. **English:** English lit, speech/rhetoric. **Foreign languages:** General, Japanese, linguistics, Native American, Russian. **History:** General. **Interdisciplinary:** Biological/physical sciences. **Liberal arts:** Arts/sciences. **Math:** General, applied, statistics. **Parks/recreation:** Exercise sciences. **Philosophy/religion:** Philosophy. **Physical sciences:** Chemistry, geology, physics, planetary. **Protective services:** Criminal justice. **Psychology:** General. **Public administration:** Community org/advocacy, social work. **Social sciences:** Anthropology, economics, geography, political science, sociology. **Visual/performing arts:** Art, dramatic, music performance, theater design.

Most popular majors. Biology 7%, business/marketing 9%, communications/journalism 7%, engineering/engineering technologies 12%, English 6%, psychology 6%, public administration/social services 6%.

Computing on campus. 60 workstations in dormitories, library, computer center. Dormitories wired for high-speed internet access and linked to campus network. Commuter students can connect to campus network. Online course registration, helpline, repair service, student web hosting, wireless network available.

Student life. Freshman orientation: Available, $30 fee. Preregistration for classes offered. 3 days prior to first day of fall and spring semesters. **Policies:** Freshmen permitted cars on campus. **Housing:** Coed dorms, special housing for disabled, apartments, substance-free housing available. $225 partly refundable deposit, deadline 8/1. Alaska native culture housing. **Activities:** Bands, choral groups, dance, drama, film society, literary magazine, music ensembles, musical theater, opera, radio station, student government, student newspaper, symphony orchestra, TV station, United Campus Ministry, Black Awareness, Young Republicans, Young Democrats, Alaska Native student organization, disabled students association, North Star Chinese association, recreational hockey association, Alaska alpine club, snowboarding association.

Athletics. NCAA. **Intercollegiate:** Basketball, cross-country, ice hockey M, rifle, skiing, swimming W, volleyball W. **Intramural:** Badminton, basketball, bowling, cross-country, football (non-tackle), ice hockey, lacrosse, racquetball, rifle, skiing, soccer, softball, swimming, table tennis, tennis, volleyball, water polo. **Team name:** Nanooks.

Student services. Adult student services, alcohol/substance abuse counseling, campus ministries, career counseling, services for economically disadvantaged, student employment services, financial aid counseling, health services, legal services, minority student services, on-campus daycare, personal counseling, placement for graduates, veterans' counselor, women's services. **Physically disabled:** Services for visually, speech, hearing impaired.

Contact. E-mail: admissions@uaf.edu
Phone: (907) 474-7500 Toll-free number: (800) 478-1823
Fax: (907) 474-5379
Nancy Dix, Director of Admissions, University of Alaska Fairbanks, PO Box 757480, Fairbanks, AK 99775-7480

Freshman class profile. 383 applied, 242 admitted, 190 enrolled.

Mid 50% test scores			
SAT verbal:	440-610	Rank in top quarter:	24%
SAT math:	440-600	Rank in top tenth:	7%
ACT:	19-25	End year in good standing:	76%
GPA 3.50 or higher:	23%	Return as sophomores:	63%
GPA 3.0-3.49:	23%	Out-of-state:	18%
GPA 2.0-2.99:	46%	International:	1%

Basis for selection. High school record most important. Students not meeting B.A. requirements counseled to A.A. or certificate program with possibility of later transfer to B.A. program. Some B.A. programs admit students as pre-majors and upon satisfying prerequisites may be admitted to major. Financial statement and immunization records required of international applicants as well as a statement of educational equivalency written in English. SAT or ACT required for all bachelor degree programs. **Homeschooled:** Student must graduate from an accredited home school program, otherwise GED required.

High school preparation. Recommended units include English 4, mathematics 2, social studies 3, science 1 (laboratory 1).

2005-2006 Annual costs. Tuition/fees: $3,798; $11,418 out-of-state. Room/board: $5,780. Books/supplies: $550. Personal expenses: $1,643.

2005-2006 Financial aid. Need-based: 40% of total undergraduate aid awarded as scholarships/grants, 60% as loans/jobs. **Non-need-based:** Scholarships awarded for academics, leadership. **Additional information:** Transfer, continuing, and freshman scholarship deadline March 1.

Application procedures. Admission: Priority date 8/1; no deadline. $40 fee, may be waived for applicants with need. Application may be submitted online. Admission notification on a rolling basis. Housing deposit refundable if written letter of cancellation is provided prior to July 1st. **Financial aid:** Priority date 6/1; no closing date. FAFSA required. Applicants notified on a rolling basis starting 2/15; must reply within 3 week(s) of notification.

Academics. Special study options: Combined bachelor's/graduate degree, cooperative education, distance learning, dual enrollment of high school students, exchange student, external degree, independent study, internships, liberal arts/career combination, study abroad, teacher certification program. **Credit/placement by examination:** AP, CLEP, institutional tests. 15 credit hours maximum toward associate degree, 30 toward bachelor's. **Support services:** Learning center, pre-admission summer program, remedial instruction, study skills assistance, tutoring, writing center.

University of Alaska Southeast

Juneau, Alaska — **CB member**
www.uas.alaska.edu — **CB code: 4897**

- Public 4-year university
- Commuter campus in large town
- 1,280 degree-seeking undergraduates: 43% part-time, 65% women, 1% African American, 5% Asian American, 3% Hispanic American, 18% Native American, 1% international
- 168 degree-seeking graduate students
- 63% of applicants admitted

General. Founded in 1972. Regionally accredited. All campuses accessible only by ferry or air. **Degrees:** 94 bachelor's, 64 associate awarded; master's offered. **Calendar:** Semester, limited summer session. **Full-time faculty:** 101 total; 35% have terminal degrees, 5% minority, 46% women. **Part-time faculty:** 128 total; 6% have terminal degrees, 12% minority, 60% women. **Class size:** 76% < 20, 22% 20-39, less than 1% 40-49, 1% 50-99. **Special facilities:** Juneau ice field.

Majors. Biology: General, marine. **Business:** General, accounting, management science, marketing. **Communications:** General. **Computer sciences:** Networking. **Conservation:** Environmental science. **Education:** Elementary. **English:** English lit. **Liberal arts:** Arts/sciences. **Math:** General. **Social sciences:** General, political science. **Visual/performing arts:** Art.

Most popular majors. Biology 7%, business/marketing 46%, liberal arts 30%.

Computing on campus. 225 workstations in dormitories, library, computer center, student center. Dormitories wired for high-speed internet access and linked to campus network. Commuter students can connect to campus network. Online course registration, online library, helpline, repair service, student web hosting, wireless network available.

Student life. Freshman orientation: Mandatory, $75 fee. Preregistration for classes offered. 3 day orientation including outdoor experiences. **Policies:** Freshmen permitted cars on campus. **Housing:** Coed dorms, special housing for disabled, apartments, substance-free housing available. $200 fully refundable deposit. **Activities:** Dance, student government, student newspaper, Global Connections Club, Amnesty International, backcountry skiing club, gay organization, swing dancing club, rock climbing club, English club, Wooch Een Native student organization.

Athletics. Intramural: Badminton, basketball, football (non-tackle) M, racquetball, skiing, softball, tennis, volleyball, weight lifting.

Student services. Adult student services, alcohol/substance abuse counseling, career counseling, student employment services, financial aid counseling, health services, minority student services, personal counseling, placement for graduates, veterans' counselor. **Physically disabled:** Services for visually, hearing impaired.

Contact. E-mail: admissions@uas.alaska.edu
Phone: (907) 796-6100 Toll-free number: (877) 465-4827
Fax: (907) 796-6365
Shontay King, Admissions Director, University of Alaska Southeast, 11120 Glacier Highway, Juneau, AK 99801-8681

Arizona

American Indian College of the Assemblies of God

Phoenix, Arizona
www.aicag.edu **CB code: 2597**

- Private 4-year Bible and teachers college affiliated with Assemblies of God
- Residential campus in very large city
- 30 degree-seeking undergraduates
- SAT or ACT (ACT writing optional), application essay required

General. Founded in 1957. Regionally accredited. **Degrees:** 11 bachelor's, 3 associate awarded. **Location:** 15 miles from downtown. **Calendar:** Semester. **Full-time faculty:** 5 total; 60% have terminal degrees, 20% women. **Part-time faculty:** 15 total; 13% have terminal degrees, 27% minority, 40% women.

Freshman class profile.

Out-of-state:	45%	**Live on campus:**	78%

Basis for selection. Applicants must show Christian commitment, willingness to abide by Student Handbook, and favorable reference from home pastor. Must also show ability to complete college-level instruction through SAT/ACT score and transcripts. ACT/SAT requirement may be waived by approval of Academic Dean when other evidence of student ability available. **Homeschooled:** Favorable pastoral reference required.

2005-2006 Annual costs. Tuition/fees: $5,575. Room/board: $3,850. Books/supplies: $500. Personal expenses: $2,570.

Application procedures. Admission: No deadline. No application fee. Application may be submitted online. Admission notification on a rolling basis. Students admitted with proper paperwork through first week of semester. **Financial aid:** Priority date 4/1; no closing date. FAFSA required. Applicants notified on a rolling basis starting 7/15.

Academics. Special study options: Double major, ESL, independent study, internships, liberal arts/career combination, teacher certification program. **Credit/placement by examination:** CLEP, institutional tests. **Support services:** Learning center, pre-admission summer program, reduced course load, remedial instruction, study skills assistance, tutoring.

Majors. Education: Elementary. **Theology:** Theology.

Most popular majors. Education 43%, philosophy/religious studies 57%.

Computing on campus. 39 workstations in library, computer center, student center.

Student life. Freshman orientation: Mandatory. Pre-registration orientation and 3 credit hours of instruction. **Policies:** Religious observance required. Freshmen permitted cars on campus. **Housing:** Guaranteed on-campus for freshmen. Single-sex dorms, special housing for disabled available. Pets allowed in dorm rooms. **Activities:** Choral groups, music ensembles, student government, Associated Student Body, Campus Missions Fellowship.

Athletics. Intercollegiate: Basketball. **Intramural:** Basketball. **Team name:** Warriors.

Student services. Adult student services, campus ministries, career counseling, student employment services, financial aid counseling, personal counseling, placement for graduates.

Contact. E-mail: aicadm@aicag.edu
Phone: (602) 943-335 ext. 232 Toll-free number: (800) 933-3828 ext. 232
Fax: (602) 943-8299
Steve Clindaniel, Admissions Director, American Indian College of the Assemblies of God, 10020 North 15th Avenue, Phoenix, AZ 85021-2199

Arizona State University

Tempe, Arizona **CB member**
www.asu.edu **CB code: 4007**

- Public 4-year university
- Commuter campus in small city
- 39,649 degree-seeking undergraduates: 17% part-time, 51% women, 4% African American, 5% Asian American, 13% Hispanic American, 2% Native American, 3% international
- 8,912 degree-seeking graduate students
- 91% of applicants admitted
- SAT or ACT (ACT writing recommended) required
- 55% graduate within 6 years

General. Founded in 1885. Regionally accredited. **Degrees:** 7,498 bachelor's awarded; master's, doctoral, first professional offered. **ROTC:** Army, Air Force. **Location:** 10 miles from downtown Phoenix. **Calendar:** Semester, extensive summer session. **Full-time faculty:** 1,878 total; 84% have terminal degrees, 20% minority, 39% women. **Part-time faculty:** 404 total; 24% have terminal degrees, 19% minority, 50% women. **Class size:** 41% < 20, 35% 20-39, 9% 40-49, 9% 50-99, 6% >100. **Special facilities:** Center for meteorite studies, solar energy research laboratory, center for solid state science, art collections, herbarium, biodesign institute.

Freshman class profile. 19,914 applied, 18,126 admitted, 7,706 enrolled.

Mid 50% test scores		**Rank in top quarter:**	53%
SAT verbal:	490-610	**Rank in top tenth:**	27%
SAT math:	500-620	**End year in good standing:**	92%
ACT:	20-26	**Return as sophomores:**	79%
GPA 3.50 or higher:	40%	**Out-of-state:**	35%
GPA 3.0-3.49:	33%	**Live on campus:**	51%
GPA 2.0-2.99:	27%	**International:**	2%

Basis for selection. In-state applicants: rank in top 25% of class, 3.0 GPA, minimum 22 ACT or 1040 SAT (exclusive of writing) required. Out-of-state: 24 ACT or 1110 SAT (exclusive of writing) required. Additional requirements for some programs. Auditions required of music, dance, theater majors. Portfolios required of graphic design, architecture, environmental design majors.

High school preparation. 16 units required. Required units include English 4, mathematics 4, social studies 1, history 1, science 3 (laboratory 3) and foreign language 2. One unit American history recommended, 1 fine arts required. 2 foreign languages recommended for College of Liberal Arts and Sciences. One each physics and chemistry required for nursing. 4 mathematics, including calculus recommended for engineering.

2005-2006 Annual costs. Tuition/fees: $4,407; $15,095 out-of-state. Room/board: $7,150. Books/supplies: $948. Personal expenses: $2,526.

2004-2005 Financial aid. Need-based: 3,851 full-time freshmen applied for aid; 2,628 were judged to have need; 2,628 of these received aid. Average need met was 64%. Average scholarship/grant was $5,946; average loan $2,729. 47% of total undergraduate aid awarded as scholarships/grants, 53% as loans/jobs. **Non-need-based:** Awarded to 5,071 full-time undergraduates, including 1,879 freshmen. Scholarships awarded for academics, art, athletics, leadership, music/drama, ROTC.

Application procedures. Admission: Priority date 2/1; no deadline. $25 fee ($50 out-of-state). Application may be submitted online. Admission notification on a rolling basis. Apply for housing as soon as admitted. **Financial aid:** Priority date 3/1; no closing date. FAFSA required. Applicants notified on a rolling basis.

Academics. Special study options: Accelerated study, cooperative education, distance learning, double major, dual enrollment of high school students, exchange student, honors, independent study, internships, study abroad, teacher certification program, Washington semester, weekend college. **Credit/placement by examination:** AP, CLEP, IB, SAT, ACT, institutional tests. 60 credit hours maximum toward bachelor's degree. **Support services:** Learning center, study skills assistance, tutoring, writing center.

Honors college/program. Rank in top 5% of high school class, 1300 SAT (exclusive of writing) or 29 ACT required. Separate application required. Dual enrollment in college of student's disciplinary major.

Majors. Architecture: Architecture, interior, landscape, urban/community planning. **Area/ethnic studies:** African-American, Hispanic-American/Latino/Chicano, Native American, women's. **Biology:** General, bacteriology, biochemistry, botany, conservation, molecular. **Business:** Accounting, business admin, construction management, finance, management information systems, marketing, purchasing. **Communications:** General, media studies. **Computer sciences:** Computer science. **Education:** Art, biology, business, chemistry, early childhood, elementary, English, family/consumer sciences, foreign languages, French, German, history, mathematics, music, physical, physics, secondary, social studies, Spanish, special. **Engineering:** Aerospace, biomedical, chemical, civil, computer, electrical, industrial, materials, mechanical. **English:** English lit. **Family/consumer sciences:** Family resources. **Foreign languages:** East Asian, French, German, Italian, Russian, Spanish. **Health:** Clinical lab science, communication disorders, music therapy, nursing (RN), premedicine. **History:** General. **Interdisciplinary:** Global studies. **Legal studies:** Prelaw. **Liberal arts:** Humanities. **Math:** General, applied. **Parks/recreation:** General, exercise sciences. **Philosophy/religion:** Philosophy, religion. **Physical sciences:** Chemistry, geology, physics. **Protective services:** Criminal justice. **Psychology:** General. **Public administration:** Social work. **Social sciences:** Anthropology, economics, geography, political science, sociology. **Visual/performing arts:** Art, dance, dramatic, film/cinema, graphic design, industrial design, music performance, music theory/composition.

Most popular majors. Business/marketing 19%, communications/journalism 10%, education 9%, engineering/engineering technologies 7%, interdisciplinary studies 10%, social sciences 7%, visual/performing arts 6%.

Computing on campus. Dormitories wired for high-speed internet access and linked to campus network. Commuter students can connect to campus network. Online course registration, online library, helpline, wireless network available.

Student life. **Freshman orientation:** Available. Preregistration for classes offered. Charge varies by orientation program. **Policies:** Freshmen permitted cars on campus. **Housing:** Coed dorms, special housing for disabled, apartments, fraternity/sorority housing available. $75 nonrefundable deposit. **Activities:** Bands, choral groups, dance, drama, literary magazine, music ensembles, musical theater, opera, radio station, student government, student newspaper, symphony orchestra, TV station, over 300 organizations.

Athletics. NCAA. **Intercollegiate:** Baseball M, basketball, cross-country, diving, football (tackle) M, golf, gymnastics W, soccer W, softball W, swimming, tennis, track and field, volleyball W, water polo W, wrestling M. **Intramural:** Basketball, cross-country, football (non-tackle), golf, racquetball, soccer, softball, table tennis, tennis, volleyball. **Team name:** Sun Devils.

Student services. Adult student services, career counseling, student employment services, health services, on-campus daycare, personal counseling, placement for graduates, veterans' counselor. **Physically disabled:** Services for visually, speech, hearing impaired.

Contact. E-mail: ugradinq@asu.edu
Phone: (480) 965-7788
Martha Byrd, Dean, Undergraduate Admissions, Arizona State University, Box 870112, Tempe, AZ 85287-0112

Arizona State University West

Phoenix, Arizona
www.west.asu.edu **CB code: 3882**

- Public 4-year university
- Commuter campus in small city
- 5,551 degree-seeking undergraduates: 27% part-time, 66% women, 5% African American, 4% Asian American, 19% Hispanic American, 2% Native American, 1% international
- 653 degree-seeking graduate students
- 63% of applicants admitted
- SAT or ACT (ACT writing recommended) required

General. Regionally accredited. **Degrees:** 1,486 bachelor's awarded; master's offered. **Calendar:** Semester, limited summer session. **Full-time faculty:** 233 total; 88% have terminal degrees, 22% minority, 51% women. **Part-time faculty:** 155 total; 37% have terminal degrees, 16% minority, 61% women. **Class size:** 21% < 20, 58% 20-39, 14% 40-49, 6% 50-99, less than 1% >100.

Freshman class profile. 1,403 applied, 882 admitted, 487 enrolled.

Mid 50% test scores			
SAT verbal:	460-580	Rank in top quarter:	60%
SAT math:	470-570	Rank in top tenth:	31%
ACT:	19-24	End year in good standing:	73%
GPA 3.50 or higher:	44%	Return as sophomores:	73%
GPA 3.0-3.49:	37%	Out-of-state:	14%
GPA 2.0-2.99:	18%	Live on campus:	21%

Basis for selection. Applicant must rank in top quarter of class, have minimum 22 ACT score or 1040 SAT score (exclusive of Writing), and minimum 3.0 GPA. Out-of-state students must have minimum 24 ACT score or 1110 SAT score.

High school preparation. 16 units required. Required units include English 4, mathematics 4, social studies 1, history 1, science 3 (laboratory 3) and foreign language 2. One fine arts.

2005-2006 Annual costs. Tuition/fees: $4,343; $15,092 out-of-state. Books/supplies: $948. Personal expenses: $2,526.

2004-2005 Financial aid. **Need-based:** 239 full-time freshmen applied for aid; 184 were judged to have need; 184 of these received aid. Average need met was 63%. Average scholarship/grant was $5,776; average loan $2,447. 40% of total undergraduate aid awarded as scholarships/grants, 60% as loans/jobs. **Non-need-based:** Awarded to 307 full-time undergraduates, including 73 freshmen. Scholarships awarded for academics.

Application procedures. **Admission:** Priority date 2/1; no deadline. $50 fee. Application may be submitted online. Admission notification on a rolling basis. **Financial aid:** Closing date 3/1. FAFSA required. Applicants notified on a rolling basis starting 3/15; must reply within 4 week(s) of notification.

Academics. **Special study options:** Distance learning, double major, dual enrollment of high school students, honors, independent study, internships, student-designed major, study abroad, teacher certification program. **Credit/placement by examination:** AP, CLEP, IB, SAT, ACT, institutional tests. 60 credit hours maximum toward bachelor's degree. **Support services:** Learning center, study skills assistance, tutoring, writing center.

Honors college/program. For freshmen students, requirements include GPA of 3.8 and above, top 5 percent of high school graduating class, 29 composite ACT score or a 1300 composite SAT score, exclusive of writing. For transfer students, enter at junior level with a cumulative GPA of 3.5 or better. Freshmen must complete 36 hours of honors coursework and transfer students must complete 18 hours of honors coursework. Three percent of first time freshmen in fall 2005 were admitted to the Honors College.

Majors. **Area/ethnic studies:** American, women's. **Biology:** General. **Business:** Accounting, international. **Communications:** General. **Education:** Elementary, secondary, special. **English:** English lit. **Foreign languages:** Spanish. **History:** General. **Parks/recreation:** General. **Protective services:** Law enforcement admin. **Psychology:** General. **Public administration:** Social work. **Social sciences:** General, political science, sociology. **Visual/performing arts:** General.

Most popular majors. Business/marketing 29%, communications/journalism 6%, education 25%, psychology 7%, security/protective services 7%.

Computing on campus. 674 workstations in dormitories, library, computer center. Dormitories wired for high-speed internet access and linked to campus network. Commuter students can connect to campus network. Online course registration, online library, helpline, student web hosting, wireless network available.

Student life. **Freshman orientation:** Mandatory. Preregistration for classes offered. Provides students with the opportunity to meet academic advisors, select and register for classes, investigate financial aid, discover campus resources/services and tour campus. **Policies:** Freshmen permitted cars on campus. **Housing:** Coed dorms, special housing for disabled, apartments, substance-free housing available. $75 nonrefundable deposit. **Activities:** Drama, literary magazine, student government, student newspaper, Latter-Day Saints student association, Muslim student association, Young Life, Campus Democrats, Campus Republicans, Black Student Union, Hispanic Honor Society/Latino Students Union, Lions clubs international, cancer awareness resources education, council for exceptional children.

Student services. Career counseling, services for economically disadvantaged, student employment services, financial aid counseling, health services, minority student services, on-campus daycare, personal counseling, veterans' counselor, women's services. **Physically disabled:** Services for visually, speech, hearing impaired.

Contact. E-mail: west-admissions@asu.edu
Phone: (602) 543-9378 Fax: (602) 543-8312
Thomas Cabot, Director of Admissions, Arizona State University West, PO Box 37100 MC 0250, Phoenix, AZ 85069-7100

Art Center Design College

Tucson, Arizona
www.theartcenter.edu **CB code: 3037**

- For-profit 3-year visual arts college
- Commuter campus in very large city
- 578 degree-seeking undergraduates
- SAT or ACT (ACT writing optional), application essay, interview required

General. Accredited by ACCSCT. **Degrees:** 71 bachelor's, 20 associate awarded. **Calendar:** Trimester. **Full-time faculty:** 18 total. **Part-time faculty:** 30 total.

Freshman class profile.

Mid 50% test scores		SAT math:	380-470
SAT verbal:	450-530	ACT:	17-23

Basis for selection. Application for admission includes high school transcripts (GED accepted), ACT or SAT scores, essay, interview, career commitment form, and art work for graphic design and animation programs.

2005-2006 Annual costs. Tuition/fees: $11,376. Books/supplies: $1,250. Personal expenses: $3,204.

Financial aid. All financial aid based on need.

Application procedures. Admission: No deadline. $25 fee, may be waived for applicants with need. Admission notification on a rolling basis. **Financial aid:** No deadline. FAFSA required.

Academics. Special study options: Cooperative education. **Credit/placement by examination:** CLEP.

Majors. Communications technology: Animation/special effects. **Visual/performing arts:** Commercial/advertising art, interior design.

Student life. Freshman orientation: Mandatory. Preregistration for classes offered.

Student services. Adult student services, career counseling, student employment services, financial aid counseling, personal counseling, placement for graduates, veterans' counselor.

Contact. E-mail: inquire@theartcenter.edu
Phone: (520) 325-0123 Toll-free number: (800) 825-8753
Colleen Gimbel-Froebe, Director Admissions and Placement, Art Center Design College, 2525 North Country Club Road, Tucson, AZ 85716

Art Institute of Phoenix

Phoenix, Arizona
www.aipx.edu **CB code: 4003**

- Private 4-year art and technical college
- Commuter campus in very large city

General. Accredited by ACICS. **Calendar:** Quarter.

Annual costs/financial aid. Tuition/fees (2005-2006): $16,705. Books/supplies: $1,323. Personal expenses: $2,880. Need-based financial aid available to full-time and part-time students.

Contact. Phone: (602) 678-4300
Director of Admissions, 2233 West Dunlap Avenue, Phoenix, AZ 85021-2859

Chaparral College

Tucson, Arizona
www.chap-col.edu **CB code: 3458**

- For-profit 4-year business college
- Commuter campus in very large city
- 410 degree-seeking undergraduates
- Interview required

General. Accredited by ACICS. **Degrees:** 56 bachelor's, 104 associate awarded. **Calendar:** Continuous. **Full-time faculty:** 20 total. **Part-time faculty:** 26 total.

Basis for selection. Applicants must first meet with admissions representative for personal interview, then complete the first part of the entrance evaluation, an assessment tool. If prospective student meets or exceeds required score, he/she does not need to take second part of entrance evaluation. Prospective students with a degree are exempt from entrance testing requirements.

2005-2006 Annual costs. Cost of continuous-calendar certificate, associate and bachelor programs varies by program and ranges from $185-$195 per credit hour.

Application procedures. Admission: No deadline. $50 fee.

Academics. Special study options: Distance learning, double major, dual enrollment of high school students, internships. **Credit/placement by examination:** CLEP. **Support services:** Remedial instruction, tutoring.

Majors. Business: Accounting, business admin. **Computer sciences:** Computer science.

Computing on campus. 200 workstations in library.

Student services. Career counseling, financial aid counseling, personal counseling, placement for graduates, veterans' counselor.

Contact. Phone: (520) 327-6866
Becki Rossini, Admissions Director, Chaparral College, 4585 East Speedway Boulevard, Suite 204, Tucson, AZ 85712

College of the Humanities and Sciences

Tempe, Arizona
www.chumsci.edu/

- For-profit 4-year liberal arts college

General. Accredited by DETC.

Contact. Phone: (877) 248-6724
1105 East Broadway Road, Tempe, AZ 85282

Collins College

Tempe, Arizona
www.collinscollege.edu **CB code: 2174**

- For-profit 4-year visual arts and technical college
- Commuter campus in small city
- 1,950 degree-seeking undergraduates
- Application essay, interview required

General. Founded in 1978. Accredited by ACCSCT. Satellite campus in west Phoenix. **Degrees:** 199 bachelor's, 469 associate awarded. **Location:** 5 miles from Phoenix. **Calendar:** Continuous, extensive summer session. **Full-time faculty:** 60 total. **Part-time faculty:** 20 total. **Special facilities:** Photography and video studio, with two full edit bays.

Basis for selection. Open admission. Interview and secondary school record important.

2006-2007 Annual costs. Tuition/fees: $14,550. Required fees vary by program. Books/supplies: $1,800.

Application procedures. Admission: No deadline. $50 fee. Admission notification on a rolling basis.

Academics. Special study options: Liberal arts/career combination. **Credit/placement by examination:** CLEP. **Support services:** Tutoring.

Majors. Communications technology: Animation/special effects. **Computer sciences:** LAN/WAN management, system admin, web page design. **Visual/performing arts:** Commercial/advertising art.

Student life. Freshman orientation: Mandatory. **Activities:** TV station.

Student services. Career counseling, student employment services, placement for graduates.

Contact. Phone: (480) 966-3000 Toll-free number: (800) 876-7070
Fax: (480) 902-0663
Wendy Johnston, Vice President of Admissions and Marketing, Collins College, 1140 South Priest Drive, Tempe, AZ 85281

DeVry University: Phoenix

Phoenix, Arizona
www.devry-phx.edu **CB code: 4277**

- For-profit 4-year university
- Commuter campus in large city
- 1,164 degree-seeking undergraduates: 34% part-time, 23% women
- 216 graduate students
- Interview required

General. Founded in 1967. Regionally accredited. **Degrees:** 420 bachelor's, 61 associate awarded; master's offered. **ROTC:** Air Force. **Calendar:** Semester, extensive summer session. **Full-time faculty:** 39 total; 31% women. **Part-time faculty:** 48 total; 4% minority, 19% women.

Freshman class profile. 268 enrolled.

Basis for selection. Applicants must have high school diploma or equivalent or a degree from accredited postsecondary institution, demonstrate proficiency in basic college-level skills through SAT or ACT scores or institution-administered placement exams, and be at least 17 years of age on the first day of classes. New students may enter at beginning of any semester. SAT or ACT recommended. CPT accepted.

High school preparation. Required units include mathematics 1.

2005-2006 Annual costs. Tuition/fees: $12,140. Books/supplies: $1,100. Personal expenses: $1,996.

2004-2005 Financial aid. All financial aid based on need. 317 full-time freshmen applied for aid; 296 were judged to have need; 290 of these received aid. Average need met was 37%. Average scholarship/grant was $5,256; average loan $4,662. 24% of total undergraduate aid awarded as scholarships/grants, 76% as loans/jobs.

Application procedures. Admission: No deadline. $50 fee. Application may be submitted online. Admission notification on a rolling basis. **Financial aid:** No deadline. FAFSA required. Applicants notified on a rolling basis.

Academics. Special study options: Accelerated study, cooperative education, distance learning, weekend college. **Credit/placement by examination:** CLEP, institutional tests. **Support services:** Learning center, remedial instruction, tutoring.

Majors. Business: Business admin, human resources, management information systems, operations. **Computer sciences:** General, information systems, networking. **Engineering technology:** Computer, electrical.

Most popular majors. Business/marketing 33%, computer/information sciences 45%, engineering/engineering technologies 22%.

Computing on campus. 436 workstations in library, computer center. Online course registration, online library, helpline available.

Student life. Freshman orientation: Mandatory. **Policies:** Freshmen permitted cars on campus. **Activities:** Student government, student newspaper, Institute of Electrical and Electronics Engineers, Campus Crusaders for Christ, travel club, Sigma Beta Delta, computer society, DeVry inventors club, sports compact car club, Tau Alpha Pi, hockey league.

Athletics. Intramural: Field hockey M, golf, softball.

Student services. Career counseling, student employment services, financial aid counseling, placement for graduates, veterans' counselor. **Physically disabled:** Services for visually, hearing impaired.

Contact. E-mail: admissions@phx.devry.edu
Phone: (602) 870-9201 Toll-free number: (800) 528-0250
Fax: (602) 331-1494
Jerry Driskill, Director of Admissions, DeVry University: Phoenix, 2149 West Dunlap Avenue, Phoenix, AZ 85021-2995

Embry-Riddle Aeronautical University: Prescott Campus

Prescott, Arizona
www.embryriddle.edu **CB code: 4305**

- Private 4-year university
- Residential campus in large town
- 1,644 degree-seeking undergraduates: 11% part-time, 17% women, 2% African American, 7% Asian American, 6% Hispanic American, 1% Native American, 3% international
- 32 degree-seeking graduate students
- 89% of applicants admitted
- SAT or ACT (ACT writing optional) required
- 57% graduate within 6 years

General. Founded in 1978. Regionally accredited. Eastern residential campus in Daytona Beach, Florida. More than 130 continuing education centers located throughout the United States and Europe. **Degrees:** 315 bachelor's awarded; master's offered. **ROTC:** Army, Air Force. **Location:** 100 miles from Phoenix. **Calendar:** Semester, extensive summer session. **Full-time faculty:** 96 total; 68% have terminal degrees, 8% minority, 22% women. **Part-time faculty:** 18 total; 28% have terminal degrees, 17% minority, 28% women. **Class size:** 36% < 20, 60% 20-39, 3% 40-49, less than 1% 50-99. **Special facilities:** Supersonic wind tunnel, fleet of 40 aircraft, engineering and technical center, aviation safety center.

Freshman class profile. 1,163 applied, 1,040 admitted, 359 enrolled.

Mid 50% test scores			
SAT verbal:	500-630	**Rank in top quarter:**	51%
SAT math:	530-640	**Rank in top tenth:**	24%
ACT:	22-27	**Return as sophomores:**	78%
GPA 3.50 or higher:	46%	**Out-of-state:**	84%
GPA 3.0-3.49:	36%	**Live on campus:**	97%
GPA 2.0-2.99:	18%	**International:**	1%

Basis for selection. High school GPA, class rank, test scores most important. Specific requirements vary by degree program. Flight program applicants must pass medical examination for Class I or II Federal Aviation Administration Medical Certificate at least 60 calendar days prior to enrollment. Interview and essay recommended.

High school preparation. 15 units required; 18 recommended. Required and recommended units include English 4, mathematics 2-3, social studies 3, history 1-2, science 2-3 (laboratory 2-3), foreign language 2 and academic electives 3.

2005-2006 Annual costs. Tuition/fees: $23,490. Room/board: $6,516. Books/supplies: $900. Personal expenses: $1,220.

2005-2006 Financial aid. Need-based: 319 full-time freshmen applied for aid; 252 were judged to have need; 252 of these received aid. Average scholarship/grant was $7,464; average loan $3,470. 47% of total undergraduate aid awarded as scholarships/grants, 53% as loans/jobs. **Non-need-based:** Scholarships awarded for academics, alumni affiliation, athletics, leadership, ROTC.

Application procedures. Admission: Priority date 1/15; no deadline. $50 fee, may be waived for applicants with need. Application may be submitted online. Admission notification on a rolling basis beginning on or about 11/1. Must reply by May 1 or within 2 week(s) if notified thereafter. Application closing date 60 days prior to start of term. Early application encouraged; available facilities limit enrollment in some programs. **Financial aid:** No deadline. FAFSA required. Applicants notified on a rolling basis starting 3/1; must reply within 4 week(s) of notification.

Academics. Special study options: Cooperative education, distance learning, double major, dual enrollment of high school students, ESL, independent study, internships, study abroad. **Credit/placement by examination:** AP, CLEP, IB, institutional tests. 15 credit hours maximum toward associate degree, 30 toward bachelor's. **Support services:** Remedial instruction, study skills assistance, tutoring.

Majors. Engineering: General, aerospace, computer, electrical, software. **Interdisciplinary:** Science/society. **Physical sciences:** Physics. **Social sciences:** International relations. **Transportation:** Airline/commercial pilot, aviation.

Most popular majors. Engineering/engineering technologies 27%, trade and industry 66%.

Computing on campus. 400 workstations in library, computer center, student center. Dormitories linked to campus network. Helpline available.

Student life. Freshman orientation: Available. Preregistration for classes offered. **Policies:** Freshmen permitted cars on campus. **Housing:** Guaranteed on-campus for freshmen. Coed dorms, apartments available. $200 deposit, deadline 6/15. **Activities:** Jazz band, literary magazine, radio station, student government, student newspaper, Rangers (Army ROTC), Student Activities Association, Angel Flight/Silver Wings, Residence Halls Association, Arnold Air Society, Golden Eagles Flight Team, Greeks, Aerobatic Club, Japanese Anime/Manga.

Athletics. NAIA. **Intercollegiate:** Soccer, volleyball W, wrestling M. **Intramural:** Basketball, bowling, cross-country, football (non-tackle), golf, racquetball, soccer, softball, swimming, table tennis, tennis, track and field, volleyball, weight lifting. **Team name:** Eagles.

Student services. Adult student services, career counseling, student employment services, health services, personal counseling, placement for graduates, veterans' counselor. **Physically disabled:** Services for visually, speech, hearing impaired.

Contact. E-mail: pradmit@erau.edu
Phone: (928) 777-6600 Toll-free number: (800) 888-3728
Fax: (928) 777-6606
Bill Thompson, Director of Admissions and Enrollment Management, Embry-Riddle Aeronautical University: Prescott Campus, 3700 North Willow Creek Road, Prescott, AZ 86301-3720

Grand Canyon University

Phoenix, Arizona
www.gcu.net **CB code: 4331**

- For-profit 4-year university
- Commuter campus in very large city
- 1,700 degree-seeking undergraduates
- 170 graduate students

General. Founded in 1949. Regionally accredited. **Degrees:** 385 bachelor's awarded; master's offered. **ROTC:** Army. **Calendar:** Semester, limited summer session. **Full-time faculty:** 90 total. **Part-time faculty:** 350 total. **Special facilities:** Cadaver laboratory.

Basis for selection. Open admission, but selective for some programs. Audition recommended for music, drama, speech majors. Portfolios recommended for art majors. Interview recommended for all applicants.

High school preparation. Recommended units include English 4, mathematics 4, social studies 2, science 3 (laboratory 1) and foreign language 1.

2005-2006 Annual costs. Tuition/fees: $10,250; $12,500 out-of-state. Room/board: $7,130.

Financial aid. Non-need-based: Scholarships awarded for academics, alumni affiliation, art, athletics, leadership, minority status, music/drama, religious affiliation.

Application procedures. Admission: No deadline. $100 fee. Application may be submitted online. Admission notification on a rolling basis. **Financial aid:** No deadline. FAFSA required. Applicants notified on a rolling basis.

Academics. Special study options: Accelerated study, combined bachelor's/graduate degree, cooperative education, cross-registration, distance learning, double major, dual enrollment of high school students, ESL, exchange student, honors, independent study, internships, liberal arts/career combination, study abroad, teacher certification program. **Credit/placement by examination:** CLEP, institutional tests. 30 credit hours maximum toward bachelor's degree. **Support services:** Learning center, reduced course load, remedial instruction, tutoring, writing center.

Majors. Biology: General, biochemistry. **Business:** Accounting, business admin, finance, international, marketing, organizational behavior. **Communications:** General, broadcast journalism, journalism, public relations. **Computer sciences:** General, computer science. **Education:** General, art, biology, chemistry, drama/dance, elementary, emotionally handicapped, English, history, learning disabled, mathematics, music, physical, physics, science, secondary, social science, special, speech. **English:** Composition. **Health:** Athletic training, nursing (RN), predentistry, premedicine, prepharmacy, preveterinary. **History:** General. **Legal studies:** Prelaw. **Liberal arts:** Arts/sciences. **Math:** General. **Parks/recreation:** Health/fitness, sports admin. **Physical sciences:** Chemistry. **Protective services:** Criminal justice. **Psychology:** General. **Social sciences:** General, political science, sociology. **Theology:** Bible, sacred music, theology. **Visual/performing arts:** Art, commercial/advertising art, conducting, dramatic, music performance, piano/organ, studio arts, voice/opera.

Computing on campus. 100 workstations in library, computer center. Dormitories wired for high-speed internet access. Online library, helpline available.

Student life. Freshman orientation: Mandatory, $55 fee. Preregistration for classes offered. Overview of student life, financial aid, academic advising, and payment options. **Policies:** No alcohol, pets (including fish and caged animals), and/or candles are allowed. Smoking allowed outdoors only. Freshmen permitted cars on campus. **Housing:** Single-sex dorms, apartments, substance-free housing available. $200 fully refundable deposit. **Activities:** Bands, choral groups, drama, literary magazine, music ensembles, musical theater, opera, student government, student newspaper, symphony orchestra, TV station, Baptist Student Union, international student organizations, honors organizations, committee on world awareness, professional clubs, Christ-purposed relationships, ethnic diversity in Christ, wildlife society, student health advocates.

Athletics. NCAA. **Intercollegiate:** Baseball M, basketball, golf, soccer, softball W, tennis W, volleyball W. **Intramural:** Basketball, soccer, softball, swimming, table tennis, tennis, volleyball. **Team name:** 'Lopes.

Student services. Campus ministries, career counseling, student employment services, financial aid counseling, health services, personal counseling, placement for graduates, veterans' counselor. **Physically disabled:** Services for visually, hearing impaired.

Contact. E-mail: admissionsground@gcu.edu
Phone: (602) 589-2885
Karilyn VanOosten, Director of Enrollment, Grand Canyon University, 3300 West Camelback Road, Phoenix, AZ 85017

International Import-Export

Phoenix, Arizona
www.iiei.edu

- Private upper-division virtual university
- Commuter campus in very large city

General. Accredited by DETC.

Annual costs/financial aid. Three-week courses range in cost from $440-$563; Six-week courses range in cost from $785-$1,045.

Contact. Phone: (602) 648-5750
2432 W Peoria Ave, Phoenix, AZ 85029

International Institute of the Americas: Mesa

Mesa, Arizona
www.iia.edu **CB code: 3455**

- Private 4-year business and health science college
- Commuter campus in very large city
- 174 degree-seeking undergraduates: 7% African American, 29% Hispanic American, 17% Native American
- Interview required

General. Accredited by ACICS. Four campuses in Arizona- Phoenix, West Valley (Phoenix), Mesa, Tucson; and one in Albuquerque, New Mexico. **Degrees:** 5 bachelor's, 46 associate awarded. **Location:** 5 miles from Phoenix. **Calendar:** Continuous, extensive summer session. **Full-time faculty:** 7 total. **Part-time faculty:** 26 total. **Special facilities:** Child activities centers for children of students.

Basis for selection. Open admission.

2006-2007 Annual costs. Tuition/fees (projected): $10,050.

Application procedures. Admission: No deadline. $200 fee. Application must be submitted on paper. **Financial aid:** FAFSA, institutional form required.

Academics. Special study options: Distance learning, liberal arts/career combination. **Credit/placement by examination:** CLEP.

Majors. Business: Business admin.

Computing on campus. Commuter students can connect to campus network. Online library available.

Student life. Freshman orientation: Mandatory.

Student services. Career counseling, financial aid counseling, on-campus daycare, placement for graduates.

Contact. Phone: (480) 545-8755 ext. 209 Toll-free number: (888) 744-6340 Fax: (480) 926-1371
John Pechota, Director of Admissions, International Institute of the Americas: Mesa, 925 South Gilbert Road, Suite 201, Mesa, AZ 85204

International Institute of the Americas: Tucson

Tucson, Arizona
www.iia.edu **CB code: 3454**

- Private 4-year business and health science college
- Commuter campus in very large city
- 500 degree-seeking undergraduates: 12% African American, 1% Asian American, 46% Hispanic American, 6% Native American

General. Accredited by ACICS. Institution has five campuses in Phoenix, West Phoenix, Mesa and Tucson, AZ and Albuquerque, NM. **Degrees:** 7 bachelor's, 59 associate awarded. **Calendar:** Continuous. **Full-time faculty:** 10 total. **Part-time faculty:** 25 total. **Special facilities:** Child activity centers for children of students.

Basis for selection. Open admission.

2006-2007 Annual costs. Tuition/fees (projected): $10,050. Tuition and fees may vary by program.

Financial aid. All financial aid based on need.

Application procedures. Admission: No deadline. $200 fee. Application must be submitted on paper. Admission notification on a rolling basis. **Financial aid:** No deadline. FAFSA, institutional form required.

Academics. Special study options: Distance learning, liberal arts/career combination. **Credit/placement by examination:** CLEP. **Support services:** Learning center.

Majors. Business: Business admin. **Computer sciences:** General, information systems.

Computing on campus. 240 workstations in library, computer center. Commuter students can connect to campus network. Online library available.

Student life. Freshman orientation: Mandatory.

Student services. Career counseling, services for economically disadvantaged, student employment services, financial aid counseling, on-campus daycare, placement for graduates.

Contact. E-mail: jpechota@iia.edu
Phone: (520) 748-9799 Toll-free number: (888) 744-6340
Fax: (520) 748-9355
John Pechota, Director of Admissions, International Institute of the Americas: Tucson, 5441 East 22nd Street, Suite 125, Tucson, AZ 85711

International Institute of the Americas: West Valley

Phoenix, Arizona
www.iia.edu

- Private 4-year business and health science college
- Commuter campus in very large city
- 205 degree-seeking undergraduates: 15% African American, 37% Hispanic American, 5% Native American

General. Accredited by ACICS. **Degrees:** 6 bachelor's, 36 associate awarded. **Calendar:** Continuous, extensive summer session. **Full-time faculty:** 7 total. **Part-time faculty:** 23 total. **Special facilities:** Child activity centers for children of students.

Basis for selection. Open admission, but selective for some programs. High school, GED, or pass entrance exam (CPAT). Must finish GED prior to graduating. Selective admissions and $25 application fee required for nursing.

2006-2007 Annual costs. Tuition/fees (projected): $10,050.

Application procedures. Admission: $200 fee. Application must be submitted on paper. **Financial aid:** FAFSA, institutional form required.

Academics. Special study options: Distance learning, liberal arts/career combination. **Credit/placement by examination:** CLEP.

Majors. Business: Business admin.

Computing on campus. Commuter students can connect to campus network. Online library available.

Student life. Freshman orientation: Mandatory.

Student services. Career counseling, financial aid counseling, on-campus daycare, placement for graduates.

Contact. Phone: (623) 849-8208 Toll-free number: (888) 744-6340
Fax: (623) 849-0110
John Pechota, Director of Admissions, International Institute of the Americas: West Valley, 4136 North 75th Avenue, Suite 211, Phoenix, AZ 85033

ITT Technical Institute: Tempe

Tempe, Arizona

- For-profit 4-year technical college
- Commuter campus

General. Accredited by ACICS. **Calendar:** Quarter.

Annual costs/financial aid. Tuition varies by program, $260-$368 per credit hour.

Contact. Phone: (602) 437-7500
Director of Recruitment, 5005 South Wendler Drive, Tempe, AZ 85282

ITT Technical Institute: Tucson

Tucson, Arizona
www.itt-tech.edu **CB code: 3598**

- For-profit 4-year technical college
- Commuter campus in large city

General. Founded in 1984. Accredited by ACICS. **Calendar:** Quarter.

Annual costs/financial aid. Tuition varies by program, $260-$368 per credit hour.

Contact. Phone: (520) 408-7488
Director of Recruitment, 1455 West River Road, Tucson, AZ 85704

Metropolitan College of Court Reporting

Phoenix, Arizona
www.metropolitancollege.edu **CB code: 3068**

- For-profit 4-year technical college
- Commuter campus in very large city
- 140 degree-seeking undergraduates
- Interview required

General. Accredited by ACCSCT. **Degrees:** 9 bachelor's, 4 associate awarded. **Calendar:** Continuous. **Full-time faculty:** 15 total. **Part-time faculty:** 7 total.

Basis for selection. Recommendation by admissions representative required, scholastic evaluation important. 30 words per minute on keyboard test required for Paralegal/Legal Assistant and Medical Transcription programs, 40 words per minute required for Court Reporting programs. Required institutional testing for typing and grammar assessment. Wonderlic test required.

2006-2007 Annual costs. Total cost for Court Reporting program is $24,424, $275 per credit. Total cost for Paralegal Bachelor's degree program is $33,390, $265 per credit. Total cost for Paralegal Associate degree program is $18,285, $265 per credit. Books/supplies: $1,260. Personal expenses: $1,500.

Application procedures. Admission: No deadline. $50 fee. Admission notification on a rolling basis. **Financial aid:** No deadline. FAFSA required.

Academics. Credit/placement by examination: CLEP.

Majors. Legal studies: Paralegal.

Contact. Phone: (602) 955-5900
Tiffany Baynard, Director of Admissions, Metropolitan College of Court Reporting, 4129 East Van Buren Street, Suite 100, Phoenix, AZ 85040

Northcentral University

Prescott, Arizona
www.ncu.edu **CB code: 3883**

- For-profit 4-year virtual university
- Commuter campus in large town
- 128 degree-seeking undergraduates
- 2,089 graduate students
- Application essay required
- 81% graduate within 6 years

General. Regionally accredited. All courses and programs are offered via distance education. **Degrees:** 10 bachelor's awarded; master's, doctoral offered. **Calendar:** Continuous, extensive summer session. **Full-time faculty:** 13 total. **Part-time faculty:** 137 total.

Basis for selection. Essay important, work experience considered.

2005-2006 Annual costs. Students pay $375 per semester credit. Books/supplies: $800.

2005-2006 Financial aid. Need-based: Average need met was 48%. Average loan was $3,912. 13% of total undergraduate aid awarded as scholarships/grants, 87% as loans/jobs.

Application procedures. Admission: No deadline. $50 fee. Application must be submitted online. Admission notification on a rolling basis. **Financial aid:** No deadline. Must reply within 4 week(s) of notification.

Academics. Programs are 100 percent on-line, with one-on-one faculty mentoring and no residency requirement. **Special study options:** Distance learning, internships. **Credit/placement by examination:** AP, CLEP, IB. 69 credit hours maximum toward bachelor's degree. **Support services:** Reduced course load, writing center.

Majors. Business: Business admin, marketing. **Computer sciences:** General. **Psychology:** General. **Public administration:** General.

Most popular majors. Business/marketing 68%, computer/information sciences 16%, psychology 16%.

Computing on campus. Commuter students can connect to campus network. Online course registration, online library, helpline available.

Student services. Financial aid counseling.

Contact. E-mail: info@ncu.edu
Phone: (928) 776-0331 Toll-free number: (866) 776-0331
Fax: (928) 541-7817
Cathy Righter, Admission Director, Northcentral University, 505 West Whipple Street, Prescott, AZ 86301-1747

Northern Arizona University

Flagstaff, Arizona **CB member**
www.nau.edu **CB code: 4006**

- Public 4-year university
- Residential campus in small city
- 13,116 degree-seeking undergraduates: 14% part-time, 60% women, 2% African American, 2% Asian American, 12% Hispanic American, 7% Native American, 2% international
- 5,042 degree-seeking graduate students
- 86% of applicants admitted
- SAT or ACT required
- 48% graduate within 6 years

General. Founded in 1899. Regionally accredited. **Degrees:** 2,853 bachelor's awarded; master's, doctoral, first professional offered. **ROTC:** Army, Air Force. **Location:** 140 miles from Phoenix. **Calendar:** Semester, extensive summer session. **Full-time faculty:** 723 total; 78% have terminal degrees, 13% minority, 43% women. **Part-time faculty:** 651 total; 35% have terminal degrees, 10% minority, 59% women. **Class size:** 39% < 20, 47% 20-39, 5% 40-49, 7% 50-99, 2% >100. **Special facilities:** 400-acre forest, observatory, high altitude training center for athletes.

Freshman class profile. 7,304 applied, 6,312 admitted, 2,279 enrolled.

Mid 50% test scores			
SAT verbal:	460-540	Return as sophomores:	69%
SAT math:	460-540	Out-of-state:	27%
ACT:	19-23	Live on campus:	83%
GPA 3.50 or higher:	44%	International:	1%
GPA 3.0-3.49:	37%	Fraternities:	2%
GPA 2.0-2.99:	18%	Sororities:	2%

Basis for selection. Cumulative high school GPA of 3.0, class rank in top quarter, ACT composite score of 22 (24 out-of-state) or SAT combined score of 1040 (exclusive of Writing) (1110 out-of-state) required for unconditional admission. Conditional admission if cumulative high school GPA is 2.5 to 2.99, class rank is in upper half, and test scores are lower than those for unconditional admission. Audition required of music, music education majors.

High school preparation. Required units include English 4, mathematics 4, social studies 1, history 1, science 3 (laboratory 1), foreign language 2 and academic electives 1. Mathematics must include 2 algebra, 1 geometry and 1 year of math after algebra II. One social science must be U.S. history. One fine arts required.

2005-2006 Annual costs. Tuition/fees: $4,393; $13,023 out-of-state. Room/board: $5,960. Books/supplies: $800. Personal expenses: $2,148.

2004-2005 Financial aid. Need-based: 1,720 full-time freshmen applied for aid; 1,102 were judged to have need; 1,078 of these received aid. Average need met was 62%. Average scholarship/grant was $4,199; average loan $2,465. 44% of total undergraduate aid awarded as scholarships/grants, 56% as loans/jobs. **Non-need-based:** Awarded to 4,583 full-time undergraduates, including 1,329 freshmen. Scholarships awarded for academics, alumni affiliation, art, athletics, music/drama, ROTC.

Application procedures. Admission: Priority date 3/1; no deadline. $25 fee. Application may be submitted online. Admission notification on a rolling basis. Applicants encouraged to apply early. **Financial aid:** Priority date 2/14; no closing date. FAFSA required. Applicants notified on a rolling basis starting 3/15.

Academics. Special study options: Accelerated study, cooperative education, distance learning, double major, dual enrollment of high school students, ESL, exchange student, external degree, honors, independent study, internships, study abroad, teacher certification program. **Credit/placement by examination:** AP, CLEP, IB, SAT, ACT, institutional tests. 30 credit hours maximum toward bachelor's degree. **Support services:** Learning center, pre-admission summer program, reduced course load, remedial instruction, study skills assistance, tutoring, writing center.

Honors college/program. New students applying to Honors Program must complete separate application and have either ACT composite score of 29 or higher, SAT combined score of 1290 or higher (exclusive of Writing), or graduation in top five percent of high school class. Students who do not meet criteria can petition for admission to honors program by submitting a completed application and unofficial high school transcript, letter of recommendation, and essay. Transfer students must complete a separate application and have a cumulative grade point average of 3.50 or higher.

Majors. Area/ethnic studies: American, Native American, women's. **Biology:** General, animal behavior, aquatic, bacteriology, botany, cell/histology, cellular/molecular, ecology, microbiology, molecular, physiology, wildlife, zoology. **Business:** Accounting, business admin, construction management, fashion, finance, hospitality admin, hotel/motel admin, management information systems, managerial economics, marketing. **Communications:** General, advertising, broadcast journalism, digital media, journalism, public relations, radio/tv. **Computer sciences:** General, computer science. **Conservation:** Environmental science, environmental studies, forest sciences, forestry, wildlife. **Education:** General, art, biology, chemistry, drama/dance, elementary, English, French, German, health, history, mathematics, music, physical, physics, Spanish, special, speech, technology/industrial arts, trade/industrial, voc/tech. **Engineering:** General, civil, computer, electrical, environmental, mechanical, physics. **Engineering technology:** Computer systems, construction. **English:** English lit, speech/rhetoric. **Foreign languages:** General, French, German, Spanish. **Health:** Athletic training, dental hygiene, health care admin, nursing (RN), premedicine, preveterinary. **History:** General. **Interdisciplinary:** Behavioral sciences, biological/physical sciences. **Legal studies:** Prelaw. **Liberal arts:** Arts/sciences, humanities. **Math:** General, probability. **Parks/recreation:** General, exercise sciences, facilities management, health/fitness. **Philosophy/religion:** Philosophy, religion. **Physical sciences:** General, astronomy, astrophysics, chemistry, geochemistry, geology, hydrology, paleontology, physics, planetary, theoretical physics. **Protective services:** Criminal justice, law enforcement admin. **Psychology:** General. **Public administration:** Policy analysis, social work. **Social sciences:** General, anthropology, cartography, economics, geography, international relations, political science, sociology, U.S. government.

Visual/performing arts: General, art, art history/conservation, arts management, ceramics, design, dramatic, interior design, metal/jewelry, music history, music performance, painting, photography, printmaking, sculpture, studio arts, voice/opera.

Most popular majors. Business/marketing 19%, communications/journalism 6%, education 24%, liberal arts 6%, visual/performing arts 6%.

Computing on campus. 903 workstations in dormitories, library, computer center, student center. Dormitories wired for high-speed internet access and linked to campus network. Commuter students can connect to campus network. Online course registration, online library, helpline, repair service, student web hosting, wireless network available.

Student life. Freshman orientation: Available, $150 fee. Preregistration for classes offered. New Student Orientation gives students an introduction to the University community and an opportunity to locate student support services and meet faculty, staff and peer mentors. **Policies:** Organizations required to register annually, have 12 or more members with cumulative GPA of 2.0 to start club, have constitution and bylaws, be approved by ASNAU Senate and Office of Student Life, and officers must have cumulative GPA of 2.25. Freshmen permitted cars on campus. **Housing:** Guaranteed on-campus for all undergraduates. Coed dorms, single-sex dorms, special housing for disabled, apartments, fraternity/sorority housing available. $100 nonrefundable deposit, deadline 5/1. Honor halls, floors for students 21 years of age and older available. **Activities:** Bands, dance, drama, music ensembles, musical theater, opera, radio station, student government, student newspaper, symphony orchestra, TV station, Campus Crusade for Christ, Baptist Student Ministry, Holy Trinity Catholic Newman Center, Hillel at NAU, Episcopal Canterbury Fellowship, Hispanic Honor Society, African students organization, Asian Americans United, Japanese Association.

Athletics. NCAA. **Intercollegiate:** Basketball, cross-country, diving W, football (tackle) M, golf W, soccer W, swimming W, tennis, track and field, volleyball W. **Intramural:** Archery, badminton, baseball M, basketball, bowling, cross-country, football (non-tackle), ice hockey M, lacrosse, racquetball, rugby, skiing, soccer, softball, swimming, table tennis, tennis, track and field, volleyball, water polo M. **Team name:** Lumberjacks, Jacks.

Student services. Alcohol/substance abuse counseling, campus ministries, career counseling, student employment services, financial aid counseling, health services, minority student services, personal counseling, placement for graduates, veterans' counselor. **Physically disabled:** Services for visually, speech, hearing impaired.

Contact. E-mail: undergraduate.admission@nau.edu
Phone: (928) 523-5511 Toll-free number: (888) 667-3628
Fax: (928) 523-0226
Chris Lynch, Director of Admissions, Northern Arizona University, Box 4084, Flagstaff, AZ 86011-4084

Prescott College
Prescott, Arizona
www.prescott.edu **CB code: 0484**

- Private 4-year liberal arts college
- Commuter campus in large town
- 752 degree-seeking undergraduates: 9% part-time, 63% women, 1% African American, 1% Asian American, 6% Hispanic American, 3% Native American
- 251 degree-seeking graduate students
- 88% of applicants admitted
- SAT or ACT (ACT writing optional), application essay required
- 46% graduate within 6 years

General. Founded in 1966. Regionally accredited. Adult degree program designed for working adults to obtain degree on year-round, part-time basis. Master of arts self-study program available. Programs also available at center in Tucson. **Degrees:** 217 bachelor's awarded; master's offered. **Location:** 100 miles from Phoenix. **Calendar:** Semester, limited summer session. **Full-time faculty:** 50 total; 58% have terminal degrees, 4% minority, 32% women. **Part-time faculty:** 37 total; 14% have terminal degrees, 8% minority, 49% women. **Class size:** 100% < 20. **Special facilities:** Facility for marine studies at Kino Bay, Mexico.

Freshman class profile. 147 applied, 129 admitted, 54 enrolled.

Mid 50% test scores			
SAT verbal:	540-680	GPA 2.0-2.99:	36%
SAT math:	490-610	Rank in top quarter:	19%
ACT:	20-28	Rank in top tenth:	12%
GPA 3.50 or higher:	22%	Return as sophomores:	68%
GPA 3.0-3.49:	34%	Out-of-state:	93%

Basis for selection. Essay and GPA most important. Letters of recommendation, any personal additions important. College visit, interview recommended.

High school preparation. 16 units recommended. Recommended units include English 4, mathematics 3, social studies 1, history 2, science 2 and foreign language 3. One arts unit recommended.

2005-2006 Annual costs. Tuition/fees: $18,015. Books/supplies: $650.

2004-2005 Financial aid. Need-based: 25 full-time freshmen applied for aid; 23 were judged to have need; 23 of these received aid. Average need met was 35%. Average scholarship/grant was $4,627; average loan $2,501. 34% of total undergraduate aid awarded as scholarships/grants, 66% as loans/jobs. **Non-need-based:** Scholarships awarded for academics, alumni affiliation, minority status, state residency.

Application procedures. Admission: Priority date 3/1; deadline 8/15. $25 fee, may be waived for applicants with need. Application may be submitted online. Admission notification on a rolling basis beginning on or about 1/1. Must reply by 5/1. **Financial aid:** Priority date 4/1; no closing date. FAFSA, institutional form required. Applicants notified on a rolling basis starting 3/15; must reply within 3 week(s) of notification.

Academics. Special study options: Cross-registration, double major, exchange student, external degree, independent study, internships, liberal arts/career combination, student-designed major, teacher certification program. **Credit/placement by examination:** AP, CLEP, institutional tests. **Support services:** Learning center, reduced course load, tutoring.

Majors. Agriculture: Agronomy, food science, plant breeding, soil science. **Area/ethnic studies:** Latin American, women's. **Biology:** General, ecology. **Business:** General, accounting, business admin. **Communications:** General. **Computer sciences:** General, information systems. **Conservation:** General, environmental studies, management/policy, wildlife. **Education:** General, art, bilingual, biology, curriculum, early childhood, elementary, English, foreign languages, mathematics, multi-level teacher, music, physical, school counseling, science, secondary, social science, social studies, Spanish, special, technology/industrial arts, voc/tech. **English:** Composition, creative writing. **Family/consumer sciences:** Child development. **Foreign languages:** Comparative lit, Spanish. **Interdisciplinary:** Behavioral sciences, biological/physical sciences, natural sciences, peace/conflict. **Liberal arts:** Arts/sciences. **Parks/recreation:** General, facilities management. **Physical sciences:** Geology, planetary. **Psychology:** General. **Public administration:** Community org/advocacy, human services. **Social sciences:** General, anthropology, sociology. **Visual/performing arts:** General, crafts, dance, dramatic, photography, studio arts.

Most popular majors. Education 37%, natural resources/environmental science 13%, psychology 10%, public administration/social services 6%.

Computing on campus. 50 workstations in library, computer center, student center. Online library, helpline, student web hosting, wireless network available.

Student life. Freshman orientation: Mandatory, $575 fee. 3-week intensive wilderness orientation for freshmen and transfer students. **Policies:** Freshmen permitted cars on campus. **Activities:** Dance, drama, literary magazine, music ensembles, student government, student newspaper, student environmental network, Amnesty International, student union, gay and lesbian group, Art and Activism, community garden group, natural history group, martial arts, Indigenous Rights.

Student services. Adult student services, career counseling, financial aid counseling, personal counseling, placement for graduates, veterans' counselor.

Contact. E-mail: admissions@prescott.edu
Phone: (928) 350-2100 Toll-free number: (800) 628-6364
Fax: (928) 776-5242
Tim Robison, Director of Admissions, Prescott College, 220 Grove Avenue, Prescott, AZ 86301

Southwestern College
Phoenix, Arizona
www.swcaz.edu **CB code: 4736**

- Private 4-year Bible college affiliated with Baptist faith
- Very large city
- 281 degree-seeking undergraduates: 10% part-time, 49% women, 3% African American, 2% Asian American, 7% Hispanic American, 1% Native American
- 52% of applicants admitted
- SAT or ACT (ACT writing optional), application essay required
- 52% graduate within 6 years

General. Founded in 1960. Candidate for regional accreditation; also accredited by ABHE. Affiliated with Conservative Baptist Association. **Degrees:** 59 bachelor's awarded. **ROTC:** Navy, Air Force. **Calendar:** Semester, limited summer session. **Full-time faculty:** 12 total. **Part-time faculty:** 25 total.

Freshman class profile. 207 applied, 107 admitted, 58 enrolled.

Basis for selection. School achievement record and recommendations very important. Written testimony of conversion experience required for admission. **Homeschooled:** Transcript of courses and grades required. Must present ACT or SAT scores for admission.

High school preparation. Recommended units include English 4, mathematics 3, social studies 3, science 2 and foreign language 2.

2005-2006 Annual costs. Tuition/fees: $11,560. Room/board: $4,360. Books/supplies: $800. Personal expenses: $1,300.

Financial aid. Non-need-based: Scholarships awarded for academics, alumni affiliation, leadership, music/drama, religious affiliation.

Application procedures. Admission: Closing date 8/15. $25 fee. Application may be submitted online. Admission notification on a rolling basis. **Financial aid:** Priority date 3/15, closing date 8/31. FAFSA required. Applicants notified on a rolling basis.

Academics. Off-campus, noncredit Christian internship work required during each semester. **Special study options:** Internships, teacher certification program. **Credit/placement by examination:** AP, CLEP, ACT. 30 credit hours maximum toward bachelor's degree. **Support services:** Reduced course load, remedial instruction.

Majors. Education: Elementary, secondary. **Philosophy/religion:** Religion. **Theology:** Bible, missionary, religious ed, sacred music, theology.

Computing on campus. 60 workstations in library, computer center. Dormitories wired for high-speed internet access. Online library available.

Student life. Freshman orientation: Mandatory. Preregistration for classes offered. **Policies:** Religious observance required. Freshmen permitted cars on campus. **Housing:** Guaranteed on-campus for all undergraduates. Single-sex dorms, apartments available. $50 deposit, deadline 8/15. **Activities:** Jazz band, choral groups, drama, music ensembles, musical theater, student government, student newspaper, symphony orchestra.

Athletics. NCCAA. **Intercollegiate:** Basketball, volleyball W. **Intramural:** Football (tackle) M, soccer, table tennis, tennis, volleyball. **Team name:** Eagles.

Student services. Student employment services, financial aid counseling, health services, personal counseling, veterans' counselor.

Contact. E-mail: admissions@swcaz.edu
Phone: (602) 992-6101 ext. 100 Toll-free number: (800) 247-2697 ext. 100
Fax: (602) 404-2159
Brian Haehl, Director of Admission, Southwestern College, 2625 East Cactus Road, Phoenix, AZ 85032-7042

Tucson Design College
Tucson, Arizona
www.tucsondesigncollege.edu

- For-profit 4-year technical college
- Residential campus in very large city
- 100 undergraduates
- Application essay, interview required

General. Accredited by ACICS. Free book loan program. **Degrees:** 10 associate awarded. **Location:** 115 miles from Phoenix. **Calendar:** Quarter, limited summer session. **Full-time faculty:** 7 total; 29% have terminal degrees, 14% minority, 86% women. **Part-time faculty:** 9 total; 22% minority, 78% women. **Special facilities:** Fully equipped fashion design lab with industrial sewing machines, sergers, dress forms, computer pattern making software, fully stocked interior design resource room.

Basis for selection. Open admission, but selective for some programs. Applicants must complete an application, sign releases, and request official transcripts from all previous institutions attended. They must also write an essay, show artwork, and complete an interview with an admissions representative. **Homeschooled:** Transcript of courses and grades, interview required.

Application procedures. Admission: No deadline. $35 fee. Application must be submitted on paper. Admission notification on a rolling basis.

Academics. Special study options: Accelerated study. **Credit/placement by examination:** AP, CLEP. **Support services:** Tutoring.

Majors. Visual/performing arts: Interior design.

Computing on campus. 33 workstations in library, computer center. Online library available.

Student life. Freshman orientation: Mandatory. Held the saturday morning before classes begin. **Activities:** American Society of Interior Designers student chapter.

Student services. Career counseling, student employment services, financial aid counseling, personal counseling, placement for graduates, veterans' counselor.

Contact. E-mail: jfullerton@tucsondesigncollege.edu
Phone: (520) 881-2900 Fax: (520) 881-4234
Kelly De Bonis, Director, Tucson Design College, 1030 North Alvernon Way, Tucson, AZ 85711

University of Advancing Technology
Tempe, Arizona
www.uat.edu **CB code: 3608**

- For-profit 4-year university and technical college
- Commuter campus in very large city
- 1,172 degree-seeking undergraduates: 8% women, 4% African American, 4% Asian American, 5% Hispanic American, 1% Native American, 1% international
- 13 degree-seeking graduate students
- SAT or ACT (ACT writing optional), application essay, interview required
- 30% graduate within 6 years

General. Founded in 1983. Accredited by ACICS. Bachelor's degree can be earned in 2 2/3 years. **Degrees:** 156 bachelor's, 16 associate awarded; master's offered. **Location:** 7 miles from Phoenix. **Calendar:** Trimester, extensive summer session. **Full-time faculty:** 28 total. **Part-time faculty:** 26 total. **Special facilities:** Technology lab, motion capture studio.

Freshman class profile.

Return as sophomores:	65%	**Out-of-state:**	20%

Basis for selection. Academic achievements, leadership experience, career aspirations, hobbies and community and extra-curricular involvement considered. Acceptance based on previous education, test scores (ACT/SAT), the student's match with university culture and a passion for technology. SAT or ACT recommended. Test scores are considered during the admissions process, but are not required unless GPA is not satisfactory.

2006-2007 Annual costs. Tuition/fees: $15,500. Books/supplies: $1,000. Personal expenses: $2,900.

2004-2005 Financial aid. Need-based: 213 full-time freshmen applied for aid; 189 were judged to have need; 189 of these received aid. Average need met was 24%. Average scholarship/grant was $2,550; average loan $2,625. 18% of total undergraduate aid awarded as scholarships/grants, 82% as loans/jobs.

Application procedures. Admission: No deadline. No application fee. Application may be submitted online. Admission notification on a rolling basis. **Financial aid:** Priority date 4/15; no closing date. FAFSA required. Applicants notified on a rolling basis; must reply within 2 week(s) of notification.

Academics. **Special study options:** Accelerated study, distance learning, double major, independent study, internships, student-designed major. **Credit/placement by examination:** AP, CLEP, institutional tests. **Support services:** Learning center, tutoring.

Majors. **Computer sciences:** LAN/WAN management, security, web page design, webmaster. **Engineering:** Software.

Computing on campus. 400 workstations in library, computer center, student center. Commuter students can connect to campus network. Online course registration, online library, helpline, student web hosting, wireless network available.

Student life. **Freshman orientation:** Mandatory. Preregistration for classes offered. **Policies:** Freshmen permitted cars on campus. **Housing:** Apartments available. $550 partly refundable deposit. **Activities:** Dance, film society, student government, student newspaper, Bible Study club.

Student services. Career counseling, student employment services, financial aid counseling, personal counseling, placement for graduates.

Contact. E-mail: admissions@uat.edu
Phone: (602) 383-8228 Toll-free number: (800) 658-5744
Fax: (602) 383-8222
Chrys Pistillo, Manger of Admissions, Student Services, University of Advancing Technology, 2625 West Baseline Road, Tempe, AZ 85283-1056

University of Arizona

Tucson, Arizona — **CB member**
www.arizona.edu — **CB code: 4832**

- Public 4-year university
- Residential campus in very large city
- 28,023 degree-seeking undergraduates: 12% part-time, 53% women, 3% African American, 6% Asian American, 15% Hispanic American, 2% Native American, 3% international
- 7,691 degree-seeking graduate students
- 88% of applicants admitted
- SAT or ACT (ACT writing optional) required
- 58% graduate within 6 years

General. Founded in 1885. Regionally accredited. Sierra Vista campus offers credit-bearing classes in general studies and education. Arizona International College offers liberal arts focus within university setting. **Degrees:** 5,751 bachelor's awarded; master's, doctoral, first professional offered. **ROTC:** Army, Navy, Air Force. **Location:** 111 miles from Phoenix. **Calendar:** Semester, extensive summer session. **Full-time faculty:** 1,378 total; 99% have terminal degrees, 13% minority, 31% women. **Part-time faculty:** 46 total; 94% have terminal degrees, 6% minority, 35% women. **Class size:** 30% < 20, 50% 20-39, 5% 40-49, 9% 50-99, 7% >100. **Special facilities:** Geological museum, state anthropological museum, planetarium, observatory, art museum, center for creative photography.

Freshman class profile. 17,904 applied, 15,701 admitted, 5,974 enrolled.

Mid 50% test scores			
SAT verbal:	500-620	Rank in top quarter:	61%
SAT math:	500-630	Rank in top tenth:	34%
ACT:	21-26	Return as sophomores:	79%
GPA 3.50 or higher:	44%	Out-of-state:	35%
GPA 3.0-3.49:	36%	Live on campus:	65%
GPA 2.0-2.99:	19%	International:	2%

Basis for selection. All applicants: top 25% of class or 3.0 cumulative GPA, SAT score (exclusive of Writing) of 1110 (1040 in-state) or ACT score of 24 (22 in-state) important. Conditional admission may be offered to in-state applicants who meet 1 or more of following: top half of class or 2.5 GPA and no more than 1 deficiency in any 2 required subjects, (deficiency not allowed in both mathematics and science). Essays recommended. Auditions required of applied music and all performance majors. Portfolios required for studio art majors. **Homeschooled:** Course work completion information required. **Learning Disabled:** Separate application for fee-based program (SALT).

High school preparation. 16 units required. Required units include English 4, mathematics 4, social studies 1, science 3 (laboratory 3), foreign language 2 and academic electives 1. One unit fine arts required.

2005-2006 Annual costs. Tuition/fees: $4,487; $13,671 out-of-state. Room/board: $7,460. Books/supplies: $714. Personal expenses: $2,212.

2004-2005 Financial aid. **Need-based:** 3,446 full-time freshmen applied for aid; 2,231 were judged to have need; 2,041 of these received aid. Average need met was 66%. Average scholarship/grant was $5,488; average loan $2,468. 41% of total undergraduate aid awarded as scholarships/grants, 59% as loans/jobs. **Non-need-based:** Awarded to 19,997 full-time undergraduates, including 5,224 freshmen. Scholarships awarded for academics, art, athletics, leadership, minority status, music/drama, ROTC, state residency.

Application procedures. **Admission:** Closing date 4/1 (postmark date). $50 fee, may be waived for applicants with need. Application may be submitted online. Admission notification on a rolling basis. Must reply by May 1 or within 4 week(s) if notified thereafter. **Financial aid:** Priority date 3/1; no closing date. FAFSA required. Applicants notified on a rolling basis starting 4/1; must reply within 3 week(s) of notification.

Academics. **Special study options:** Combined bachelor's/graduate degree, cooperative education, cross-registration, distance learning, double major, dual enrollment of high school students, ESL, exchange student, honors, independent study, internships, semester at sea, study abroad, teacher certification program, weekend college. **Credit/placement by examination:** AP, CLEP, IB, SAT, ACT, institutional tests. 60 credit hours maximum toward bachelor's degree. **Support services:** Learning center, preadmission summer program, reduced course load, study skills assistance, tutoring, writing center.

Majors. **Agriculture:** Animal sciences, economics, plant sciences. **Architecture:** Architecture, urban/community planning. **Area/ethnic studies:** East Asian, Hispanic-American/Latino/Chicano, Latin American, Near/Middle Eastern, women's. **Biology:** General, bacteriology, biochemistry, cell/histology, ecology. **Business:** General, accounting, entrepreneurial studies, finance, human resources, management information systems, managerial economics, marketing, operations. **Communications:** General, broadcast journalism, journalism. **Computer sciences:** General. **Conservation:** General, wildlife. **Education:** Agricultural, art, biology, chemistry, drama/dance, early childhood, elementary, English, family/consumer sciences, foreign languages, French, German, health, history, mathematics, music, physical, physics, science, secondary, social science, social studies, Spanish, special, speech. **Engineering:** General, aerospace, agricultural, chemical, civil, computer, electrical, geological, materials science, mechanical, mining, nuclear, physics, systems. **Engineering technology:** Industrial management. **English:** Creative writing, English lit. **Family/consumer sciences:** Family studies. **Foreign languages:** General, classics, French, German, Italian, linguistics, Russian, Spanish. **Health:** Clinical lab science, communication disorders, health care admin, nursing (RN), preveterinary, speech pathology. **History:** General. **Interdisciplinary:** Nutrition sciences. **Math:** General. **Philosophy/religion:** Judaic, philosophy, religion. **Physical sciences:** Astronomy, atmospheric science, chemistry, geology, hydrology, optics, physics. **Protective services:** Law enforcement admin. **Psychology:** General. **Public administration:** General. **Social sciences:** Anthropology, economics, geography, political science, sociology. **Visual/performing arts:** General, art history/conservation, dance, dramatic, music performance, studio arts, theater design.

Most popular majors. Biology 8%, business/marketing 17%, communications/journalism 9%, education 9%, engineering/engineering technologies 7%, psychology 6%, social sciences 9%.

Computing on campus. 1,950 workstations in dormitories, library, computer center, student center. Dormitories wired for high-speed internet access and linked to campus network. Commuter students can connect to campus network. Online course registration, online library, helpline available.

Student life. **Freshman orientation:** Mandatory, $100 fee. Preregistration for classes offered. 2-day program. **Policies:** Freshmen permitted cars on campus. **Housing:** Coed dorms, single-sex dorms, apartments, fraternity/sorority housing available. $250 deposit, deadline 5/1. Special housing for honors students available. **Activities:** Bands, choral groups, dance, drama, music ensembles, radio station, student government, student newspaper, TV station, over 350 clubs and organizations available.

Athletics. NCAA. **Intercollegiate:** Baseball M, basketball, cross-country, diving, football (tackle) M, golf, gymnastics W, lacrosse M, soccer W, softball W, swimming, tennis, track and field, volleyball W. **Intramural:** Badminton, basketball, bowling, cross-country, diving, football (non-tackle), golf, racquetball, soccer, softball, swimming, table tennis, tennis, track and field, volleyball. **Team name:** Wildcats.

Student services. Adult student services, alcohol/substance abuse counseling, campus ministries, career counseling, services for economically disadvantaged, student employment services, financial aid counseling, health services, legal services, minority student services, personal counseling, placement for graduates, veterans' counselor, women's services. **Physically disabled:** Services for visually, speech, hearing impaired. **Learning disabled:** Comprehensive services available.

Contact. E-mail: appinfo@arizona.edu
Phone: (520) 621-3237 Fax: (520) 621-9799
Lori Goldman, Director of Admissions and New Student Enrollment, University of Arizona, Robert L. Nugent Building, Tucson, AZ 85721-0040

University of Phoenix

Phoenix, Arizona **CB member**
www.phoenix.edu **CB code: 1024**

- For-profit 4-year virtual university
- Commuter campus in very large city
- 161,846 degree-seeking undergraduates: 60% women
- 79,965 degree-seeking graduate students

General. Founded in 1976. Regionally accredited. Classes are offered in classroom environment and on-line in over 34 states, Puerto Rico, Vancouver, British Columbia, Mexico and Europe. **Degrees:** 6,462 bachelor's, 847 associate awarded; master's, doctoral offered. **Calendar:** Continuous, extensive summer session.

Basis for selection. Open admission, but selective for some programs. Undergraduate applicants with fewer than 24 transferable credits must be currently employed, or have the equivalent of one year of full-time work experience and current access to a work environment. Undergraduate applicants entering the University with more than 24 transferable credits must be currently employed, or have current access to a work environment.

2005-2006 Annual costs. Tuition/fees: $9,540. Books/supplies: $525.

Application procedures. Admission: No deadline. $110 fee. Application may be submitted online. Admission notification on a rolling basis. **Financial aid:** No deadline. FAFSA, institutional form required. Applicants notified on a rolling basis.

Academics. Special study options: Accelerated study, distance learning, independent study, internships, teacher certification program. **Credit/placement by examination:** CLEP, IB. 30 credit hours maximum toward associate degree, 30 toward bachelor's. **Support services:** Remedial instruction, writing center.

Majors. Business: Accounting, business admin, finance, management information systems, marketing. **Computer sciences:** General, database management, networking, programming. **Education:** Elementary. **Health:** Health care admin, health services. **Protective services:** Criminal justice.

Computing on campus. Commuter students can connect to campus network. Online library available.

Student life. Freshman orientation: Available.

Student services. Adult student services, financial aid counseling, personal counseling.

Contact. E-mail: beth.barilla@phoenix.edu
Phone: (480) 317-6200 Toll-free number: (800) 288-7240
Fax: (480) 594-1758
Beth Barilla, Associate Vice President, Student Admissions & Services, University of Phoenix, 4615 East Elwood Street, Phoenix, AZ 85040-1958

Western International University

Phoenix, Arizona
www.wintu.edu **CB code: 1316**

- For-profit 4-year university and business college
- Commuter campus in very large city
- 1,900 degree-seeking undergraduates

General. Founded in 1978. Regionally accredited. Adult student body. Portfolio evaluation of relevant experience for course credit. **Degrees:** 300 bachelor's, 50 associate awarded; master's offered. **Location:** 7 miles from downtown. **Calendar:** Semester. **Part-time faculty:** 325 total. **Special facilities:** On-line career service database.

Basis for selection. Accomplishments in working world most important. Academic achievement, cumulative GPA, personal interview, recommendation considered. Interview and essay recommended.

High school preparation. Recommended units include English 4, mathematics 3, social studies 2 and science 2.

2005-2006 Annual costs. On-line undergraduate courses are $420 per-credit-hour. Books/supplies: $900.

Application procedures. Admission: No deadline. $85 fee. Admission notification on a rolling basis. **Financial aid:** No deadline. Applicants notified on a rolling basis.

Academics. Teaching sites at corporate facilities. **Special study options:** Accelerated study, distance learning, double major, dual enrollment of high school students, ESL, independent study, study abroad. **Credit/placement by examination:** AP, CLEP, institutional tests. 45 credit hours maximum toward associate degree, 102 toward bachelor's. Maximum of 90 credits by examination and assessment may be counted toward degree; 36 hour residency requirement. **Support services:** Learning center, writing center.

Majors. Business: General, accounting, business admin, finance, international, management information systems, marketing. **Computer sciences:** General. **Liberal arts:** Arts/sciences. **Transportation:** Aviation management.

Most popular majors. Business/marketing 46%, computer/information sciences 24%, liberal arts 24%.

Computing on campus. 45 workstations in library, computer center. Online library, helpline available.

Student life. Policies: Cultural activities and special seminars/workshops available. **Activities:** Student government, International Students Association.

Student services. Adult student services, financial aid counseling, veterans' counselor.

Contact. Phone: (602) 943-2311 Toll-free number: (866) 948-4636
Fax: (602) 371-8637
Jo Arney, Director of University Student Services, Western International University, 9215 North Black Canyon Highway, Phoenix, AZ 85021

Arkansas

Arkansas Baptist College
Little Rock, Arkansas
www.arbaptcol.edu **CB code: 7301**

- Private 4-year liberal arts college affiliated with American Baptist Churches in the USA
- Large city
- 320 degree-seeking undergraduates

General. Founded in 1884. Regionally accredited. Family atmosphere, Christ centered. **Degrees:** 28 bachelor's awarded. **Calendar:** Semester, limited summer session. **Full-time faculty:** 16 total. **Part-time faculty:** 8 total.

Basis for selection. School achievement record, recommendations most important. Interview, special talents, alumni relations important. Academically borderline applicants may be admitted provisionally but must earn 2.0 GPA by end of first semester to continue in good academic standing. Interview recommended.

High school preparation. 18 units recommended. Recommended units include English 4, mathematics 4, social studies 1 and science 2. Vocational and agriculture courses also recommended.

2005-2006 Annual costs. Tuition/fees: $5,074. Room/board: $6,826. Books/supplies: $700. Personal expenses: $850.

Financial aid. All financial aid based on need.

Application procedures. **Admission:** No deadline. $25 fee. Admission notification on a rolling basis beginning on or about 6/30. **Financial aid:** Closing date 5/1. FAFSA required. Applicants notified on a rolling basis starting 6/15.

Academics. **Special study options:** Double major, independent study. **Credit/placement by examination:** CLEP, institutional tests. **Support services:** Tutoring.

Majors. **Business:** Business admin. **Education:** Elementary. **Social sciences:** General.

Student life. **Freshman orientation:** Available, $10 fee. **Policies:** Religious observance required. **Housing:** Single-sex dorms available. **Activities:** Choral groups, student government, Baptist Student Union, student teacher organization.

Athletics. NJCAA. **Intercollegiate:** Basketball, softball. **Team name:** Buffaloes.

Student services. Career counseling, student employment services, health services, on-campus daycare, personal counseling, placement for graduates, veterans' counselor.

Contact. Phone: (501) 374-7856
Freddie Fox, Director of Admissions, Arkansas Baptist College, 1600 Bishop Street, Little Rock, AR 72202

Arkansas State University
State University, Arkansas **CB member**
www.astate.edu **CB code: 6011**

- Public 4-year university
- Commuter campus in small city
- 8,650 degree-seeking undergraduates: 18% part-time, 59% women, 17% African American, 1% Asian American, 1% Hispanic American, 1% international
- 1,199 degree-seeking graduate students
- 65% of applicants admitted
- SAT or ACT (ACT writing optional) required
- 39% graduate within 6 years; 17% enter graduate study

General. Founded in 1909. Regionally accredited. **Degrees:** 1,555 bachelor's, 172 associate awarded; master's, doctoral offered. **ROTC:** Army. **Location:** 70 miles from Memphis, Tennessee. **Calendar:** Semester, extensive summer session. **Full-time faculty:** 447 total; 66% have terminal degrees, 13% minority, 46% women. **Part-time faculty:** 159 total; 8% have terminal degrees, 5% minority, 57% women. **Class size:** 43% < 20, 44% 20-39, 7% 40-49, 5% 50-99, less than 1% >100. **Special facilities:** Environmental ecotoxicology research facility, electron microscope facility, geographic information center facility, museum, equine center.

Freshman class profile. 3,488 applied, 2,259 admitted, 1,584 enrolled.

Mid 50% test scores		**Return as sophomores:**	65%
ACT:	18-24	**Out-of-state:**	12%
GPA 3.50 or higher:	36%	**Live on campus:**	46%
GPA 3.0-3.49:	29%	**International:**	1%
GPA 2.0-2.99:	35%	**Fraternities:**	32%
End year in good standing:	67%	**Sororities:**	18%

Basis for selection. For unconditional admission, must have a minimum of 19 on ACT scores composite, English, math, reading or comparable scores on the SAT, ASSET, or COMPASS and a minimum 2.5 cumulative high school GPA for eight semesters, or 3.75 cumulative high school GPA for six or seven semesters. Students who do not meet the ACT, GPA criteria and state-mandated core for unrestricted admission may seek admission with restrictions if their high school GPA is at least 2.0. Proof of immunization is required. Proof of registration with selective service is required for all males 18 to 25. Students with no ACT or SAT scores may submit ASSET scores. SAT, SAT Subject Tests, ACT scores must be received by first day of classes for fall term admission. Auditions required of music majors; portfolios required of art majors. **Homeschooled:** Must have overall GPA of 2.0. Minimum GED score for restricted admission 500.

High school preparation. 16 units recommended. Recommended units include English 4, mathematics 4, social studies 1, history 2, science 3 (laboratory 3) and foreign language 2.

2005-2006 Annual costs. Tuition/fees: $5,440; $12,145 out-of-state. Room/board: $4,540. Books/supplies: $1,000. Personal expenses: $2,966.

2005-2006 Financial aid. **Need-based:** Average need met was 67%. Average scholarship/grant was $5,900; average loan $3,100. 58% of total undergraduate aid awarded as scholarships/grants, 42% as loans/jobs. **Non-need-based:** Scholarships awarded for academics, alumni affiliation, art, athletics, leadership, minority status, music/drama, ROTC, state residency.

Application procedures. **Admission:** Closing date 8/21. $15 fee. Application may be submitted online. Admission notification on a rolling basis. **Financial aid:** Priority date 2/15, closing date 7/1. FAFSA, institutional form required. Applicants notified on a rolling basis starting 6/1; must reply within 2 week(s) of notification.

Academics. Of the first 59 hours completed in college, students allowed to repeat courses with final grade of less than C. No more than 18 semester hours of course work may be repeated. **Special study options:** Accelerated study, distance learning, double major, dual enrollment of high school students, exchange student, honors, independent study, internships, study abroad, teacher certification program. **Credit/placement by examination:** AP, CLEP, SAT, ACT, institutional tests. 15 credit hours maximum toward associate degree, 30 toward bachelor's. **Support services:** Reduced course load, remedial instruction, study skills assistance, tutoring.

Honors college/program. Students must have a score of 24 or higher on the ACT or a high school GPA of 3.5 or higher.

Majors. **Agriculture:** General, agribusiness operations, animal sciences, plant sciences. **Biology:** General. **Business:** Accounting, business admin, finance, international, managerial economics, marketing, transportation. **Communications:** Digital media, journalism, radio/tv. **Communications technology:** Graphic/printing. **Computer sciences:** General, data processing. **Conservation:** Wildlife. **Education:** Agricultural, art, biology, business, chemistry, early childhood, English, French, health, mathematics, middle, music, physical, physics, social science, Spanish, special, speech. **Engineering:** General. **Engineering technology:** General. **English:** English lit, speech/rhetoric. **Foreign languages:** French, Spanish. **Health:** Athletic training, audiology/speech pathology, clinical lab science, health services, medical radiologic technology/radiation therapy, nursing (RN). **History:** General. **Math:** General. **Parks/recreation:** Exercise sciences, health/fitness, sports admin. **Philosophy/religion:** Philosophy. **Physical sciences:** Chemistry, physics. **Protective services:** Forensics. **Psychology:** General. **Public administration:** Social work. **Social sciences:** Criminology, economics, geography, political science, sociology. **Visual/performing arts:** Art, commercial/advertising art, dramatic, music performance.

Most popular majors. Business/marketing 19%, education 18%, health sciences 11%, social sciences 6%.

Computing on campus. 510 workstations in dormitories, library, computer center, student center. Dormitories linked to campus network. Commuter students can connect to campus network. Online course registration, helpline, wireless network available.

Student life. **Freshman orientation:** Mandatory. Preregistration for classes offered. All day session held on various dates for students to meet academic advisor, register for classes and learn about the university. **Policies:** Freshmen permitted cars on campus. **Housing:** Single-sex dorms, apartments, fraternity/sorority housing, substance-free housing available. $100 fully refundable deposit. Houses are available for graduate, married and single-parent students. **Activities:** Bands, choral groups, dance, drama, music ensembles, musical theater, opera, radio station, student government, student newspaper, symphony orchestra, TV station, College Democrats, Baptist Student Union, College Republicans Club, Church of Christ Student Center, International Students Association, Islamic Association, Black Student Association, Newman Club, Missionary Baptist Student Fellowship, Wesley Foundation.

Athletics. NCAA. **Intercollegiate:** Baseball M, basketball, bowling W, cross-country, football (tackle) M, golf, soccer W, tennis W, track and field, volleyball W. **Intramural:** Archery, badminton, basketball, bowling, golf, racquetball, soccer, softball, table tennis, tennis, volleyball. **Team name:** Indians.

Student services. Adult student services, career counseling, student employment services, financial aid counseling, health services, minority student services, personal counseling, placement for graduates, veterans' counselor. **Physically disabled:** Services for visually, speech, hearing impaired.

Contact. E-mail: admissions@astate.edu
Phone: (870) 972-3024 Toll-free number: (800) 382-3030
Fax: (870) 910-8094
Tammy Fowler, Interim Director of Admissions, Arkansas State University, PO Box 1630, State University, AR 72467

Arkansas Tech University
Russellville, Arkansas
www.atu.edu **CB code: 6010**

- Public 4-year university and liberal arts college
- Commuter campus in large town
- 6,162 degree-seeking undergraduates: 13% part-time, 53% women, 5% African American, 1% Asian American, 2% Hispanic American, 1% Native American, 2% international
- 444 degree-seeking graduate students
- 48% of applicants admitted
- SAT and SAT Subject Tests or ACT (ACT writing optional) required
- 36% graduate within 6 years

General. Founded in 1909. Regionally accredited. **Degrees:** 783 bachelor's, 45 associate awarded; master's offered. **ROTC:** Army. **Location:** 75 miles from Little Rock, 85 miles from Fort Smith. **Calendar:** Semester, extensive summer session. **Full-time faculty:** 252 total; 62% have terminal degrees, 8% minority, 46% women. **Part-time faculty:** 146 total; 9% have terminal degrees, 3% minority, 70% women. **Class size:** 37% < 20, 48% 20-39, 6% 40-49, 9% 50-99. **Special facilities:** Museum, energy center, observatory, technology center.

Freshman class profile. 3,459 applied, 1,673 admitted, 1,529 enrolled.

Mid 50% test scores		Rank in top tenth:	17%
SAT verbal:	410-510	Return as sophomores:	66%
SAT math:	480-550	Out-of-state:	4%
ACT:	19-25	Live on campus:	56%
GPA 3.50 or higher:	38%	International:	4%
GPA 3.0-3.49:	28%	Fraternities:	3%
GPA 2.0-2.99:	33%	Sororities:	4%
Rank in top quarter:	43%		

Basis for selection. Secondary school record and standardized test scores very important; class rank considered. **Homeschooled:** Documentation of home-school completion with a composite ACT of 19.

High school preparation. 21 units required. Required and recommended units include English 4, mathematics 4, social studies 1, history 2, science 3 (laboratory 3), foreign language 2 and academic electives 4.

2005-2006 Annual costs. Tuition/fees: $4,700; $8,990 out-of-state. Room/board: $4,556. Books/supplies: $1,090. Personal expenses: $2,280.

2004-2005 Financial aid. **Need-based:** 1,075 full-time freshmen applied for aid; 899 were judged to have need; 887 of these received aid. Average need met was 37%. Average scholarship/grant was $2,516; average loan $843. 49% of total undergraduate aid awarded as scholarships/grants, 51% as loans/jobs. **Non-need-based:** Awarded to 2,351 full-time undergraduates, including 899 freshmen. Scholarships awarded for academics, art, athletics, leadership, minority status, music/drama, ROTC.

Application procedures. **Admission:** No deadline. No application fee. Application may be submitted online. Admission notification on a rolling basis. **Financial aid:** Priority date 4/15; no closing date. FAFSA required. Applicants notified on a rolling basis starting 5/1; must reply within 2 week(s) of notification.

Academics. **Special study options:** Accelerated study, cooperative education, distance learning, double major, dual enrollment of high school students, ESL, external degree, honors, independent study, internships, student-designed major, teacher certification program, weekend college. **Credit/placement by examination:** AP, CLEP, SAT, ACT, institutional tests. 30 credit hours maximum toward associate degree, 30 toward bachelor's. **Support services:** Learning center, reduced course load, remedial instruction, study skills assistance, tutoring.

Honors college/program. Minimum GPA of 3.5 and ACT score of 23. Target of 23 students per year. Honors students required to take honors classes throughout their stay at ATU.

Majors. **Agriculture:** Agribusiness operations. **Biology:** General, conservation. **Business:** Accounting, business admin, hospitality admin. **Communications:** Journalism. **Computer sciences:** General, systems analysis. **Education:** Art, biology, business, chemistry, early childhood, English, foreign languages, mathematics, middle, music, physical, science, social studies, speech. **Engineering:** Electrical, mechanical, physics. **English:** Creative writing, English lit, speech/rhetoric. **Foreign languages:** General. **Health:** Clinical lab science, medical records admin, nursing (RN). **History:** General. **Interdisciplinary:** Global studies. **Math:** General. **Parks/recreation:** Facilities management. **Physical sciences:** General, chemistry, geology. **Psychology:** General. **Social sciences:** Economics, sociology. **Visual/performing arts:** Art.

Most popular majors. Biology 6%, business/marketing 15%, education 18%, English 7%, health sciences 9%.

Computing on campus. 700 workstations in dormitories, library, computer center, student center. Dormitories wired for high-speed internet access and linked to campus network. Commuter students can connect to campus network. Online course registration, helpline, wireless network available.

Student life. **Freshman orientation:** Available. Preregistration for classes offered. **Policies:** Freshmen permitted cars on campus. **Housing:** Guaranteed on-campus for freshmen. Coed dorms, single-sex dorms, special housing for disabled, apartments, substance-free housing available. $25 nonrefundable deposit. **Activities:** Bands, choral groups, dance, drama, literary magazine, music ensembles, musical theater, opera, radio station, student government, student newspaper, symphony orchestra, TV station.

Athletics. NCAA. **Intercollegiate:** Baseball M, basketball, cross-country W, football (tackle) M, golf, softball W, tennis W, volleyball W. **Intramural:** Basketball, bowling, cheerleading, cross-country, football (tackle), golf, racquetball, soccer, softball, swimming, table tennis, tennis, volleyball. **Team name:** Wonder Boys, Golden Suns.

Student services. Adult student services, alcohol/substance abuse counseling, career counseling, services for economically disadvantaged, student employment services, financial aid counseling, health services, personal counseling, placement for graduates, veterans' counselor. **Physically disabled:** Services for visually, speech, hearing impaired.

Contact. E-mail: tech.enroll@atu.edu
Phone: (479) 968-0343 Toll-free number: (800) 582-6953
Fax: (479) 964-0522
Shauna Donnell, Director of Enrollment Management, Arkansas Tech University, Doc Bryan Student Services Building, Russellville, AR 72801-2222

Central Baptist College
Conway, Arkansas
www.cbc.edu **CB code: 0788**

- Private 4-year Bible and junior college affiliated with Baptist faith
- Residential campus in large town
- 392 degree-seeking undergraduates
- 82% of applicants admitted
- ACT (writing optional) required

General. Founded in 1952. Regionally accredited; also accredited by ABHE. **Degrees:** 50 bachelor's, 22 associate awarded. **ROTC:** Army. **Location:** 30 miles from Little Rock. **Calendar:** Semester, limited summer session. **Full-time faculty:** 17 total. **Part-time faculty:** 34 total.

Freshman class profile. 158 applied, 130 admitted, 104 enrolled.

Mid 50% test scores		Out-of-state:	13%
ACT:	17-23	Live on campus:	85%

Basis for selection. Religious commitment most important, followed by school achievement record. Interview recommended.

High school preparation. 15 units recommended. Recommended units include English 4, mathematics 2, social studies 2 and science 2.

2005-2006 Annual costs. Tuition/fees: $8,450. Room/board: $4,960. Books/supplies: $600. Personal expenses: $800.

Financial aid. **Non-need-based:** Scholarships awarded for academics, state residency.

Application procedures. **Admission:** Closing date 8/15 (postmark date). $25 fee, may be waived for applicants with need. Application may be submitted online. Admission notification on a rolling basis. Must reply by 8/15. **Financial aid:** Priority date 7/1, closing date 8/1. FAFSA required. Applicants notified on a rolling basis starting 4/1.

Academics. **Special study options:** Internships. **Credit/placement by examination:** AP, CLEP, institutional tests. 15 credit hours maximum toward associate degree, 27 toward bachelor's. **Support services:** Learning center, pre-admission summer program, reduced course load, tutoring.

Majors. **Business:** Organizational behavior. **Computer sciences:** Data processing. **Theology:** Bible, religious ed, sacred music, youth ministry. **Visual/performing arts:** Music management.

Computing on campus. Online library available.

Student life. **Freshman orientation:** Mandatory. **Policies:** Religious observance required. Freshmen permitted cars on campus. **Housing:** Guaranteed on-campus for freshmen. Single-sex dorms available. $20 deposit, deadline 8/15. **Activities:** Concert band, choral groups, music ensembles, student government, Association of Baptist Students, College Republicans.

Athletics. NCCAA. **Intercollegiate:** Baseball M, basketball, volleyball W. **Intramural:** Badminton, basketball, bowling, softball, table tennis, volleyball. **Team name:** Mustangs.

Student services. Career counseling, personal counseling, veterans' counselor.

Contact. Phone: (501) 329-6872 Fax: (501) 329-2941
Cory Calhoun, Director of Admissions, Central Baptist College, 1501 College Avenue, Conway, AR 72034

Ecclesia College

Springdale, Arkansas
www.ecollege.edu

- Private 4-year Christian college emphasizing Biblical higher education affiliated with interdenominational tradition
- Residential campus in large town
- 35 undergraduates
- ACT (writing optional) required

General. Accredited by ABHE. **Degrees:** 5 bachelor's awarded. **Calendar:** Semester, limited summer session.

Basis for selection. Open admission, but selective for some programs. Recommendations and personal character very important. **Homeschooled:** State high school equivalency certificate required.

2005-2006 Annual costs. Books/supplies: $300.

Financial aid. **Non-need-based:** Scholarships awarded for academics, athletics, leadership, music/drama.

Application procedures. **Admission:** Closing date 9/8 (receipt date). $50 fee. Application may be submitted online. Admission notification on a rolling basis. **Financial aid:** No deadline. FAFSA required.

Academics. **Credit/placement by examination:** CLEP, ACT. **Support services:** Remedial instruction.

Majors. **Theology:** Bible.

Computing on campus. 15 workstations in library, computer center. Wireless network available.

Student life. **Freshman orientation:** Mandatory. Preregistration for classes offered. **Policies:** Religious observance required. Freshmen permitted cars on campus. **Housing:** Single-sex dorms, apartments, substance-free housing available. Pets allowed in dorm rooms. **Activities:** Choral groups, drama, student government.

Athletics. **Intercollegiate:** Basketball. **Team name:** Royals.

Student services. Alcohol/substance abuse counseling, campus ministries, career counseling, financial aid counseling, personal counseling, placement for graduates.

Contact. E-mail: admissions@ecollege.edu
Phone: (479) 248-7236 ext. 103 Toll-free number: (800) 735-9926
Fax: (479) 248-1455
Titus Hofer, Director of Admissions, Ecclesia College, 9653 Nations Drive, Springdale, AR 72762

Harding University

Searcy, Arkansas
www.harding.edu **CB code: 6267**

- Private 4-year university affiliated with Church of Christ
- Residential campus in large town
- 4,092 degree-seeking undergraduates: 5% part-time, 54% women, 4% African American, 1% Asian American, 1% Hispanic American, 1% Native American, 4% international
- 1,620 degree-seeking graduate students
- 62% of applicants admitted
- SAT or ACT (ACT writing optional), interview required
- 58% graduate within 6 years; 24% enter graduate study

General. Founded in 1924. Regionally accredited. **Degrees:** 777 bachelor's awarded; master's offered. **ROTC:** Army. **Location:** 50 miles from Little Rock, 100 miles from Memphis, Tennessee. **Calendar:** Semester, extensive summer session. **Full-time faculty:** 226 total; 60% have terminal degrees, 2% minority, 33% women. **Part-time faculty:** 106 total; 20% have terminal degrees, 56% women. **Class size:** 51% < 20, 32% 20-39, 6% 40-49, 10% 50-99, less than 1% >100.

Freshman class profile. 1,658 applied, 1,020 admitted, 960 enrolled.

Mid 50% test scores		Rank in top tenth:	27%
SAT verbal:	500-630	End year in good standing:	95%
SAT math:	490-630	Return as sophomores:	83%
ACT:	20-26	Out-of-state:	77%
GPA 3.50 or higher:	58%	Live on campus:	95%
GPA 3.0-3.49:	27%	International:	3%
GPA 2.0-2.99:	13%	Fraternities:	39%
Rank in top quarter:	52%	Sororities:	40%

Basis for selection. Test scores, academic record, references, interview important. Selective admission with limited openings, students must apply early. Students are encouraged to take rigorous classes in high school. Audition recommended for music majors, portfolio for art majors.

High school preparation. 15 units required; 20 recommended. Required and recommended units include English 4, mathematics 3-4, social studies 3-4, science 2-4, foreign language 2 and academic electives 3.

2005-2006 Annual costs. Tuition/fees: $11,200. Additional $142 required fees for campus residents. Room/board: $5,312. Books/supplies: $1,200. Personal expenses: $300.

2004-2005 Financial aid. **Need-based:** 890 full-time freshmen applied for aid; 238 were judged to have need; 238 of these received aid. Average need met was 69%. Average scholarship/grant was $5,100; average loan $3,892. 47% of total undergraduate aid awarded as scholarships/grants, 53% as loans/jobs. **Non-need-based:** Awarded to 1,331 full-time undergraduates, including 280 freshmen. Scholarships awarded for academics, art, athletics, music/drama, religious affiliation, ROTC, state residency. **Additional information:** Music scholarships available, audition required.

Application procedures. **Admission:** Priority date 7/1; deadline 6/1. $35 fee. Application may be submitted online. Admission notification on a rolling basis beginning on or about 5/1. Must reply by 5/1. Early application encouraged. **Financial aid:** Priority date 4/1; no closing date. FAFSA, institutional form required. Applicants notified on a rolling basis starting 2/15; must reply within 2 week(s) of notification.

Academics. **Special study options:** Accelerated study, combined bachelor's/graduate degree, cooperative education, distance learning, double major, dual enrollment of high school students, ESL, honors, independent study, internships, liberal arts/career combination, study abroad, teacher certification program. **Credit/placement by examination:** AP, CLEP, IB, SAT, ACT, institutional tests. 32 credit hours maximum toward bachelor's degree. **Support services:** Learning center, pre-admission summer program, reduced course load, remedial instruction, study skills assistance, tutoring, writing center.

Honors college/program. Honors Scholars Program is open to National Merit finalists, trustee scholarship recipients, and those with ACT score of 31 or higher, or SAT score of 1200 (exclusive of writing) or higher.

Majors. **Area/ethnic studies:** American. **Biology:** General, biochemistry. **Business:** Accounting, business admin, communications, fashion, human resources, international, marketing, sales/distribution, selling. **Communications:** General, advertising, broadcast journalism, digital media, journalism, public relations. **Computer sciences:** General, computer science, information technology. **Education:** Art, biology, chemistry, early childhood, early childhood special, elementary, English, family/consumer sciences, foreign languages, health, learning disabled, mathematics, middle, multi-level teacher, music, physical, reading, school counseling, science, secondary, social studies, Spanish, special, speech. **Engineering:** Computer, electrical, mechanical. **Family/consumer sciences:** General. **Foreign languages:** French, Spanish. **Health:** Art therapy, athletic training, clinical lab science, communication disorders, dietetics, health care admin, marriage/family therapy, nursing (RN), predentistry, premedicine, prepharmacy, preveterinary, speech pathology. **History:** General. **Interdisciplinary:** Global studies. **Legal studies:** General, prelaw. **Liberal arts:** Humanities. **Math:** General. **Parks/recreation:** Exercise sciences, sports admin. **Philosophy/religion:** Christian, religion. **Physical sciences:** Chemistry, physics. **Protective services:** Criminal justice. **Psychology:** General. **Public administration:** General, social work. **Social sciences:** General, economics, international relations, political science. **Theology:** Bible, missionary, religious ed, theology, youth ministry. **Visual/performing arts:** Art, dramatic, fashion design, graphic design, interior design, music performance, painting, studio arts, voice/opera.

Most popular majors. Business/marketing 20%, communications/journalism 6%, computer/information sciences 6%, education 15%, health sciences 9%, theological studies 6%.

Computing on campus. Dormitories wired for high-speed internet access and linked to campus network. Commuter students can connect to campus network. Online course registration, online library, helpline, repair service, wireless network available.

Student life. **Freshman orientation:** Available, $35 fee. Preregistration for classes offered. Two to three days at beginning of fall semester. **Policies:** Freshmen permitted cars on campus. **Housing:** Guaranteed on-campus for freshmen. Single-sex dorms, special housing for disabled, apartments, substance-free housing available. $125 fully refundable deposit, deadline 5/1. Approved off-campus housing. **Activities:** Bands, choral groups, drama, music ensembles, musical theater, radio station, student government, student newspaper, symphony orchestra, TV station, Young Republicans, dactylology club, Good News Singers, HOPE, JOY, Timothy Club, religious mission campaigns.

Athletics. NCAA. **Intercollegiate:** Baseball M, basketball, cheerleading, cross-country, football (tackle) M, golf, soccer, tennis, track and field, volleyball W. **Intramural:** Basketball, bowling, cross-country, football (non-tackle), golf M, gymnastics W, racquetball, soccer, softball, swimming, table tennis, tennis, track and field, volleyball, weight lifting. **Team name:** Bisons.

Student services. Adult student services, campus ministries, career counseling, student employment services, financial aid counseling, health services, on-campus daycare, personal counseling, placement for graduates, veterans' counselor. **Physically disabled:** Services for visually, speech, hearing impaired.

Contact. E-mail: admissions@harding.edu
Phone: (501) 279-4407 Toll-free number: (800) 477-4407
Fax: (501) 279-4129
Glenn Dillard, Director of Enrollment Management, Harding University, 900 East Center, Searcy, AR 72149-0001

Henderson State University

Arkadelphia, Arkansas — **CB member**
www.getreddie.com — **CB code: 6272**

- Public 4-year university and liberal arts college
- Commuter campus in large town
- 2,728 degree-seeking undergraduates: 12% part-time, 58% women, 18% African American, 2% Hispanic American, 1% Native American, 2% international
- 372 degree-seeking graduate students
- 60% of applicants admitted
- SAT and SAT Subject Tests or ACT (ACT writing optional) required

General. Founded in 1890. Regionally accredited. **Degrees:** 405 bachelor's awarded; master's offered. **ROTC:** Army. **Location:** 67 miles from Little Rock. **Calendar:** Semester, limited summer session. **Full-time faculty:** 161 total; 96% have terminal degrees, 10% minority, 36% women. **Part-time faculty:** 68 total; 71% have terminal degrees, 2% minority, 72% women. **Class size:** 56% < 20, 36% 20-39, 6% 40-49, less than 1% 50-99, less than 1% >100. **Special facilities:** Planetarium.

Freshman class profile. 2,020 applied, 1,206 admitted, 425 enrolled.

Mid 50% test scores		**Rank in top quarter:**	43%
SAT verbal:	420-540	**Rank in top tenth:**	16%
SAT math:	460-600	**Return as sophomores:**	63%
ACT:	19-25	**Out-of-state:**	16%
GPA 3.50 or higher:	34%	**Live on campus:**	71%
GPA 3.0-3.49:	39%	**International:**	2%
GPA 2.0-2.99:	27%		

Basis for selection. Applicants must have ACT composite of 19 and minimum 2.5 GPA for unconditional admission. Those not meeting GPA requirement admitted conditionally. Applicants who do not meet minimum test score standards may be admitted through appeal process. Deadline for applying for appeal is July 15. Scores must be on file with Admissions prior to registering for classes. Audition recommended for music and theater arts majors. **Homeschooled:** Minimum ACT composite score of 18, transcript required. Completion of college prep curriculum encouraged. **Learning Disabled:** Student Support Disability Services assesses and assigns needs for students with learning disabilities.

High school preparation. 14 units required; 22 recommended. Required and recommended units include English 4, mathematics 4, social studies 2, history 1 and science 3. Required: 1/2 oral comm, 1/2 fine art, 6 career focus.

2005-2006 Annual costs. Tuition/fees: $4,645; $8,695 out-of-state.

2004-2005 Financial aid. **Need-based:** 410 full-time freshmen applied for aid; 384 were judged to have need; 296 of these received aid. Average need met was 83%. Average scholarship/grant was $4,400; average loan $2,699. 43% of total undergraduate aid awarded as scholarships/grants, 57% as loans/jobs. **Non-need-based:** Awarded to 2,525 full-time undergraduates, including 304 freshmen. Scholarships awarded for academics, alumni affiliation, art, athletics, leadership, minority status, music/drama, state residency.

Application procedures. **Admission:** No deadline. No application fee. Application may be submitted online. Admission notification on a rolling basis beginning on or about 9/1. Application closing date July 15 for applicants with ACT score under 18. **Financial aid:** Priority date 6/1; no closing date. FAFSA required. Applicants notified on a rolling basis starting 4/1; must reply within 2 week(s) of notification.

Academics. **Special study options:** Cross-registration, distance learning, honors, internships, liberal arts/career combination, teacher certification program. **Credit/placement by examination:** AP, CLEP, institutional tests. 30 credit hours maximum toward bachelor's degree. **Support services:** Learning center, remedial instruction, study skills assistance, tutoring.

Honors college/program. Freshmen must have composite ACT of 26 or higher. Approximately 90 admitted. Sophomores must have cumulative GPA of 3.25 or higher to petition committee for admission.

Majors. **Biology:** General. **Business:** General, accounting, management information systems. **Communications:** Journalism. **Computer sciences:** General. **Education:** Art, biology, business, early childhood, elementary, English, middle, social science. **English:** English lit, speech/rhetoric. **Family/consumer sciences:** General. **Foreign languages:** Spanish. **Health:** Athletic training, clinical lab science, nursing (RN). **History:** General. **Math:** General. **Parks/recreation:** Facilities management. **Physical sciences:** Chemistry, physics. **Psychology:** General. **Public administration:** General, social work. **Social sciences:** Political science, sociology. **Transportation:** Airline/commercial pilot. **Visual/performing arts:** Art, dramatic, music performance.

Most popular majors. Business/marketing 25%, education 26%, health sciences 6%, social sciences 9%, visual/performing arts 6%.

Computing on campus. 125 workstations in dormitories, library, computer center, student center. Dormitories linked to campus network. Commuter students can connect to campus network. Helpline available.

Student life. **Freshman orientation:** Mandatory. Preregistration for classes offered. Day-long program for students and parents includes preregistration, signing up for ID and e-mail address. Program held for week in

June, again in July if necessary. **Policies:** Freshmen permitted cars on campus. **Housing:** Coed dorms, single-sex dorms, cooperative housing available. $50 deposit. Special hall for Honors College participants, special floor for freshman interest groups available. On-campus apartments leased by outside firm available. **Activities:** Bands, choral groups, dance, drama, literary magazine, music ensembles, radio station, student government, student newspaper, TV station, College Republicans, Young Democrats, Student Foundation, Heart & Key service organization, several religious organizations.

Athletics. NCAA. **Intercollegiate:** Baseball M, basketball, cross-country W, football (tackle) M, golf, softball W, swimming, tennis W, volleyball W. **Intramural:** Soccer M. **Team name:** Reddies.

Student services. Career counseling, student employment services, health services, personal counseling, placement for graduates, veterans' counselor. **Physically disabled:** Services for visually, speech, hearing impaired.

Contact. E-mail: admissions@hsu.edu
Phone: (870) 230-5028 Toll-free number: (800) 228-7333
Fax: (870) 230-5066
Vikita Hardwrick, Director of Admissions, Henderson State University, 1100 Henderson Street, Arkadelphia, AR 71999-0001

Hendrix College

Conway, Arkansas — **CB member**
www.hendrix.edu — **CB code: 6273**

- Private 4-year liberal arts college affiliated with United Methodist Church
- Residential campus in small city
- 1,010 degree-seeking undergraduates: 1% part-time, 56% women, 4% African American, 3% Asian American, 3% Hispanic American, 1% Native American
- 9 degree-seeking graduate students
- 83% of applicants admitted
- SAT or ACT (ACT writing optional), application essay required
- 61% graduate within 6 years; 60% enter graduate study

General. Founded in 1876. Regionally accredited. **Degrees:** 202 bachelor's awarded; master's offered. **ROTC:** Army. **Location:** 30 miles from Little Rock. **Calendar:** Semester. **Full-time faculty:** 85 total; 100% have terminal degrees, 11% minority, 38% women. **Part-time faculty:** 22 total; 50% have terminal degrees, 50% women. **Class size:** 67% < 20, 31% 20-39, 2% 40-49. **Special facilities:** Teaching theater, two pipe organs, access to elephant farm for research and volunteer service, arboretum, ring laser, hybrid rocket lab.

Freshman class profile. 1,086 applied, 896 admitted, 281 enrolled.

Mid 50% test scores		**Rank in top quarter:**	73%
SAT verbal:	590-700	**Rank in top tenth:**	37%
SAT math:	560-670	**Return as sophomores:**	81%
ACT:	25-30	**Out-of-state:**	47%
GPA 3.50 or higher:	67%	**Live on campus:**	97%
GPA 3.0-3.49:	23%	**International:**	1%
GPA 2.0-2.99:	10%		

Basis for selection. Academic competence, scholastic potential, motivation, character, and high school leadership important. Interview may be required. **Homeschooled:** Portfolio, admission interview required.

High school preparation. 14 units recommended. Recommended units include English 4, mathematics 3, social studies 3, science 2 and foreign language 2.

2006-2007 Annual costs. Tuition/fees: $22,916. Room/board: $6,738. Books/supplies: $900. Personal expenses: $1,330.

2005-2006 Financial aid. Need-based: 229 full-time freshmen applied for aid; 157 were judged to have need; 157 of these received aid. Average need met was 84%. Average scholarship/grant was $13,129; average loan $3,798. 68% of total undergraduate aid awarded as scholarships/grants, 32% as loans/jobs. **Non-need-based:** Awarded to 528 full-time undergraduates, including 162 freshmen. Scholarships awarded for academics, art, leadership, music/drama, religious affiliation.

Application procedures. Admission: Priority date 2/1; deadline 8/1 (postmark date). $40 fee, may be waived for applicants with need. Application may be submitted online. Admission notification on a rolling basis beginning on or about 11/1. Must reply by May 1 or within 4 week(s) if notified thereafter. **Financial aid:** Priority date 2/15; no closing date. FAFSA required. Applicants notified on a rolling basis starting 3/1; must reply by 5/1 or within 2 week(s) of notification.

Academics. Special study options: Double major, exchange student, honors, independent study, internships, liberal arts/career combination, student-designed major, study abroad, teacher certification program, Washington semester. Hendrix-in-Oxford, Hendrix-in-London, programs with Austria and Japan, American University. **Credit/placement by examination:** AP, CLEP, IB, institutional tests. 6 credit hours maximum toward bachelor's degree. **Support services:** Pre-admission summer program, study skills assistance, tutoring, writing center.

Majors. Biology: General. **Business:** Accounting, managerial economics. **Computer sciences:** Computer science. **Education:** Physical. **English:** English lit. **Foreign languages:** French, German, Spanish. **History:** General. **Liberal arts:** Arts/sciences. **Math:** General. **Parks/recreation:** Exercise sciences. **Philosophy/religion:** Philosophy, religion. **Physical sciences:** Chemistry, physics. **Psychology:** General. **Social sciences:** Anthropology, economics, international relations, political science, sociology. **Visual/performing arts:** Art, dramatic.

Most popular majors. Biology 14%, history 11%, physical sciences 6%, psychology 16%, social sciences 22%, visual/performing arts 7%.

Computing on campus. 75 workstations in dormitories, library, computer center. Dormitories wired for high-speed internet access and linked to campus network. Commuter students can connect to campus network. Online course registration, helpline, repair service, student web hosting, wireless network available.

Student life. Freshman orientation: Mandatory, $425 fee. 7-day program prior to fall term. **Policies:** Freshmen permitted cars on campus. **Housing:** Guaranteed on-campus for freshmen. Coed dorms, single-sex dorms, apartments, substance-free housing available. Language house, small suite-style houses available. **Activities:** Bands, choral groups, dance, drama, film society, literary magazine, music ensembles, musical theater, opera, radio station, student government, student newspaper, symphony orchestra, Students for Black Culture, College Republicans, Young Democrats, environmental group, Amnesty International, BACCHUS, Hendrix Peace Links, religious life council, volunteer action center, Students Promoting the Education of Asian Cultures.

Athletics. NCAA. **Intercollegiate:** Baseball M, basketball, cross-country, diving, golf, soccer, softball W, swimming, tennis, track and field, volleyball W. **Intramural:** Badminton, basketball, football (non-tackle), racquetball, soccer, softball, tennis, volleyball. **Team name:** Warriors.

Student services. Alcohol/substance abuse counseling, campus ministries, career counseling, student employment services, financial aid counseling, health services, minority student services, personal counseling, placement for graduates, veterans' counselor.

Contact. E-mail: adm@hendrix.edu/admission
Phone: (501) 450-1362 Toll-free number: (800) 277-9017
Fax: (501) 450-3843
Kevin Kropf, Executive Director of Admission, Hendrix College, 1600 Washington Avenue, Conway, AR 72032-3080

ITT Technical Institute: Little Rock

Little Rock, Arkansas
www.itt-tech.edu — **CB code: 2721**

- For-profit 4-year technical college
- Commuter campus in small city

General. Accredited by ACICS. **Calendar:** Quarter.

Annual costs/financial aid. Tuition varies by program, $260-$368 per credit hour.

Contact. Phone: (501) 565-5550
Director of Recruitment, 4520 S. University Avenue, Little Rock, AR 72204

John Brown University

Siloam Springs, Arkansas
www.jbu.edu — **CB code: 6321**

- Private 4-year liberal arts college affiliated with interdenominational tradition
- Residential campus in large town

- 1,608 degree-seeking undergraduates: 2% part-time, 51% women, 3% African American, 1% Asian American, 3% Hispanic American, 2% Native American, 6% international
- 245 degree-seeking graduate students
- 62% of applicants admitted
- SAT or ACT (ACT writing optional), application essay required
- 58% graduate within 6 years

General. Founded in 1919. Regionally accredited. **Degrees:** 500 bachelor's, 6 associate awarded; master's offered. **ROTC:** Army, Air Force. **Location:** 30 miles from Fayetteville, 75 miles from Tulsa, Oklahoma. **Calendar:** Semester, limited summer session. **Full-time faculty:** 83 total; 74% have terminal degrees, 4% minority, 24% women. **Part-time faculty:** 65 total; 22% have terminal degrees, 2% minority, 31% women. **Class size:** 53% < 20, 43% 20-39, 3% 40-49, less than 1% 50-99.

Freshman class profile. 874 applied, 545 admitted, 262 enrolled.

Mid 50% test scores			
SAT verbal:	540-660	Rank in top quarter:	59%
SAT math:	510-640	Rank in top tenth:	29%
ACT:	22-28	Return as sophomores:	75%
GPA 3.50 or higher:	64%	Out-of-state:	72%
GPA 3.0-3.49:	27%	Live on campus:	93%
GPA 2.0-2.99:	9%	International:	5%

Basis for selection. Test scores, secondary school record, recommendations, essay, interview most important. Special talents, class rank considered. Combined SAT score of 950 (exclusive of Writing), ACT score of 20 or above. Interview recommended. Audition required of music majors; portfolio recommended for art majors. **Homeschooled:** Transcript of courses and grades required.

High school preparation. Recommended units include English 4, mathematics 3, social studies 2, history 1, science 2 (laboratory 1) and foreign language 2. 4 units of mathematics, 3 science for science and engineering majors; 2 foreign language recommended for home educated students.

2005-2006 Annual costs. Tuition/fees: $15,280. Room/board: $5,630. Books/supplies: $700. Personal expenses: $1,350.

2005-2006 Financial aid. Need-based: 221 full-time freshmen applied for aid; 182 were judged to have need; 182 of these received aid. Average need met was 50%. Average scholarship/grant was $5,030; average loan $3,573. 58% of total undergraduate aid awarded as scholarships/grants, 42% as loans/jobs. **Non-need-based:** Awarded to 808 full-time undergraduates, including 233 freshmen. Scholarships awarded for academics, alumni affiliation, art, athletics, leadership, music/drama, ROTC.

Application procedures. Admission: Priority date 5/1; no deadline. $25 fee, may be waived for applicants with need. Application may be submitted online. Admission notification on a rolling basis beginning on or about 12/1. Must reply by May 1 or within 2 week(s) if notified thereafter. **Financial aid:** Priority date 3/1; no closing date. FAFSA, institutional form required. Applicants notified on a rolling basis starting 3/1; must reply by 5/1 or within 4 week(s) of notification.

Academics. Special study options: Accelerated study, distance learning, double major, dual enrollment of high school students, ESL, exchange student, honors, independent study, internships, New York semester, study abroad, teacher certification program, Washington semester. **Credit/placement by examination:** AP, CLEP, IB, SAT, ACT. 15 credit hours maximum toward associate degree, 30 toward bachelor's. **Support services:** Learning center, reduced course load, remedial instruction, study skills assistance, tutoring, writing center.

Honors college/program. Selected by admissions office/honors committee, requirements are high school GPA, SAT/ACT score and interview.

Majors. Biology: General, biochemistry. **Business:** Accounting, business admin, construction management, international, marketing. **Communications:** Broadcast journalism, digital media, journalism, public relations. **Computer sciences:** Computer science. **Conservation:** General. **Education:** Biology, chemistry, early childhood, English, mathematics, middle, music, social studies. **Engineering:** General. **English:** English lit. **Family/consumer sciences:** Family/community services. **Foreign languages:** Spanish. **Health:** Athletic training. **History:** General. **Interdisciplinary:** Global studies. **Math:** General. **Parks/recreation:** Exercise sciences, sports admin. **Physical sciences:** Chemistry. **Psychology:** General. **Social sciences:** Political science. **Theology:** Missionary, sacred music, theology, youth ministry. **Visual/performing arts:** Graphic design, illustration, music performance.

Most popular majors. Business/marketing 58%, communications/journalism 9%, visual/performing arts 6%.

Computing on campus. 200 workstations in dormitories, library, computer center, student center. Dormitories wired for high-speed internet access and linked to campus network. Commuter students can connect to campus network. Online course registration, online library, helpline, wireless network available.

Student life. Freshman orientation: Mandatory, $75 fee. Preregistration for classes offered. Testing sessions, parent sessions, class registration, community service project, small group activities, music auditions, advising sessions, small workshops of college academic life, etc. **Policies:** No alcohol, drugs, tobacco, or dancing allowed on campus; all applicants required to sign community covenant each year. Religious observance required. Freshmen permitted cars on campus. **Housing:** Guaranteed on-campus for freshmen. Coed dorms, single-sex dorms, special housing for disabled, apartments, substance-free housing available. $200 fully refundable deposit. **Activities:** Pep band, choral groups, drama, music ensembles, musical theater, opera, radio station, student government, student newspaper, TV station, council to assist in the unity of student evangelism, Young republicans, Young Democrats, Young Life, Boys & Girls Club volunteer opportunities.

Athletics. NAIA. **Intercollegiate:** Basketball, soccer, swimming W, tennis, volleyball W. **Intramural:** Baseball M, basketball, football (non-tackle), football (tackle) M, racquetball, soccer, softball, tennis, volleyball. **Team name:** Golden Eagles.

Student services. Campus ministries, career counseling, student employment services, financial aid counseling, health services, personal counseling, placement for graduates. **Physically disabled:** Services for visually, hearing impaired.

Contact. E-mail: jbuinfo@jbu.edu
Phone: (479) 524-7286 Toll-free number: (877) 528-4636
Fax: (479) 524-4196
Don Crandall, Vice President for Enrollment Management, John Brown University, 2000 West University Street, Siloam Springs, AR 72761-2121

Lyon College

Batesville, Arkansas — **CB member**
www.lyon.edu — **CB code: 6009**

- Private 4-year liberal arts college affiliated with Presbyterian Church (USA)
- Residential campus in small town
- 484 degree-seeking undergraduates: 5% part-time, 51% women
- 72% of applicants admitted
- SAT or ACT (ACT writing optional) required
- 68% graduate within 6 years; 22% enter graduate study

General. Founded in 1872. Regionally accredited. **Degrees:** 112 bachelor's awarded. **Location:** 90 miles from Little Rock. **Calendar:** Semester, limited summer session. **Full-time faculty:** 44 total; 91% have terminal degrees, 11% minority, 23% women. **Part-time faculty:** 15 total; 7% minority, 53% women. **Class size:** 74% < 20, 25% 20-39, less than 1% 40-49, less than 1% 50-99. **Special facilities:** Ozark Regional Studies Center.

Freshman class profile. 470 applied, 337 admitted, 112 enrolled.

Mid 50% test scores			
SAT verbal:	500-710	Rank in top quarter:	69%
SAT math:	530-650	Rank in top tenth:	29%
ACT:	23-28	End year in good standing:	88%
GPA 3.50 or higher:	58%	Return as sophomores:	75%
GPA 3.0-3.49:	30%	Out-of-state:	22%
GPA 2.0-2.99:	12%	Live on campus:	96%
		International:	1%

Basis for selection. High school academic performance and standardized test scores are the most important. Personal essays and letters of recommendation are considered on a case by case basis. Math proficiency and placement are judged with ACT math subscores. Auditions or portfolios required for fine arts.

High school preparation. 16 units required; 18 recommended. Required and recommended units include English 4, mathematics 3-4, social studies 1, history 2, science 3-4 (laboratory 2), foreign language 2 and academic electives 1.

2006-2007 Annual costs. Tuition/fees: $14,860. Room/board: $6,270. Books/supplies: $1,000. Personal expenses: $900.

2005-2006 Financial aid. Need-based: 87 full-time freshmen applied for aid; 65 were judged to have need; 65 of these received aid. Average need met was 85%. Average scholarship/grant was $10,531; average loan $3,464. 65% of total undergraduate aid awarded as scholarships/grants, 35% as loans/jobs. **Non-need-based:** Awarded to 258 full-time undergraduates,

including 77 freshmen. Scholarships awarded for academics, art, athletics, leadership, minority status, music/drama, religious affiliation, state residency.

Application procedures. Admission: Priority date 1/15; no deadline. $25 fee, may be waived for applicants with need. Application may be submitted online. Admission notification on a rolling basis. Must reply by May 1 or within 2 week(s) if notified thereafter. **Financial aid:** Priority date 3/15; no closing date. FAFSA required. Applicants notified on a rolling basis starting 3/1; must reply by 8/15.

Academics. Academic honor code administered by peer-elected student honor council. **Special study options:** Accelerated study, combined bachelor's/graduate degree, cross-registration, double major, dual enrollment of high school students, independent study, internships, student-designed major, study abroad, teacher certification program, Washington semester. **Credit/placement by examination:** AP, CLEP, SAT, ACT, institutional tests. 33 credit hours maximum toward bachelor's degree. **Support services:** Learning center, study skills assistance, tutoring, writing center.

Majors. Biology: General. **Business:** Accounting, business admin. **Computer sciences:** Computer science. **Conservation:** Environmental studies. **Education:** Early childhood. **English:** English lit. **Foreign languages:** Spanish. **History:** General. **Math:** General. **Philosophy/religion:** Philosophy, religion. **Physical sciences:** Chemistry. **Psychology:** General. **Social sciences:** Economics, political science. **Visual/performing arts:** Art, dramatic.

Most popular majors. Biology 18%, business/marketing 20%, English 10%, history 8%, psychology 13%, social sciences 14%.

Computing on campus. 103 workstations in dormitories, library, computer center, student center. Dormitories wired for high-speed internet access and linked to campus network. Commuter students can connect to campus network. Online course registration, online library, helpline, wireless network available.

Student life. Freshman orientation: Mandatory. **Policies:** Social code administered by peer-elected student social council. Freshmen permitted cars on campus. **Housing:** Guaranteed on-campus for all undergraduates. Coed dorms, single-sex dorms, apartments available. $100 fully refundable deposit. Limited college-owned off-campus housing is available. **Activities:** Choral groups, drama, literary magazine, music ensembles, student government, student newspaper, Black students' association, Catholic campus ministries, Fellowship of Christian Athletes, Baptist Collegiate Ministry, Wesley Fellowship, Presbyterian Fellowship, Episcopalian Fellowship, International students' association.

Athletics. NAIA. **Intercollegiate:** Baseball M, basketball, cheerleading, cross-country, golf, soccer, tennis, volleyball W. **Intramural:** Badminton, basketball, football (non-tackle), softball, table tennis, tennis, volleyball. **Team name:** Scots (M), Pipers (W).

Student services. Campus ministries, career counseling, financial aid counseling, health services, personal counseling, placement for graduates.

Contact. E-mail: admissions@lyon.edu
Phone: (870) 698-4250 Toll-free number: (800) 423-2542
Fax: (870) 793-1791
Denny Bardos, Vice President for Enrollment Services, Lyon College, PO Box 2317, Batesville, AR 72503-2317

Ouachita Baptist University

Arkadelphia, Arkansas
www.obu.edu **CB code: 6549**

- Private 4-year liberal arts college affiliated with Southern Baptist Convention
- Residential campus in large town
- 1,420 degree-seeking undergraduates: 1% part-time, 55% women, 6% African American, 1% Asian American, 2% Hispanic American, 4% international
- 58% of applicants admitted
- SAT or ACT (ACT writing optional) required
- 59% graduate within 6 years; 30% enter graduate study

General. Founded in 1886. Regionally accredited. Strong emphasis on global awareness, international study opportunities and missions, and volunteer service. **Degrees:** 312 bachelor's, 1 associate awarded. **ROTC:** Army. **Location:** 65 miles from Little Rock. **Calendar:** Semester, limited summer session. **Full-time faculty:** 116 total; 78% have terminal degrees, 2% minority, 32% women. **Part-time faculty:** 33 total; 21% have terminal degrees, 3% minority, 61% women. **Special facilities:** Library houses Special Collections that include the papers of an Arkansas governor and members of Congress.

Freshman class profile. 1,058 applied, 613 admitted, 368 enrolled.

Mid 50% test scores		**Rank in top tenth:**	33%
SAT verbal:	490-600	**Return as sophomores:**	75%
SAT math:	470-610	**Out-of-state:**	48%
ACT:	21-26	**Live on campus:**	98%
GPA 3.50 or higher:	60%	**International:**	3%
GPA 3.0-3.49:	25%	**Fraternities:**	30%
GPA 2.0-2.99:	15%	**Sororities:**	45%
Rank in top quarter:	60%		

Basis for selection. Test scores and school achievement record most important. Minimum high school GPA of 2.75 required, ACT score of 20 or higher. Interview recommended. Portfolio recommended for studio art majors.

High school preparation. 15 units required; 19 recommended. Required and recommended units include English 4, mathematics 2-3, social studies 1, history 2, science 2-3, foreign language 2 and academic electives 4.

2006-2007 Annual costs. Tuition/fees: $16,990. Room/board: $5,000. Books/supplies: $775. Personal expenses: $1,400.

2005-2006 Financial aid. Need-based: Average scholarship/grant was $8,472; average loan $2,724. 76% of total undergraduate aid awarded as scholarships/grants, 24% as loans/jobs. **Non-need-based:** Scholarships awarded for academics, athletics, job skills, leadership, minority status, music/drama, religious affiliation, ROTC, state residency.

Application procedures. Admission: No deadline. $50 fee. Application may be submitted online. Admission notification on a rolling basis beginning on or about 12/1. **Financial aid:** Priority date 2/15, closing date 6/1. Institutional form required. Applicants notified on a rolling basis starting 3/31; must reply by 5/1.

Academics. Classes in Arkansas Folkways taught at Old Washington State Park. International exchange programs in Austria, China, England, Germany, Indonesia, Israel, Japan, Morocco, and Russia. **Special study options:** Cross-registration, distance learning, double major, ESL, exchange student, honors, independent study, internships, study abroad, teacher certification program. **Credit/placement by examination:** AP, CLEP, IB, institutional tests. 24 credit hours maximum toward bachelor's degree. **Support services:** Learning center, reduced course load, remedial instruction, study skills assistance, tutoring, writing center.

Majors. Biology: General. **Business:** Accounting, business admin. **Communications:** Media studies. **Computer sciences:** Computer science. **Education:** General, art, biology, business, chemistry, drama/dance, early childhood, English, foreign languages, French, health, history, mathematics, middle, music, physical, physics, science, secondary, social studies, Spanish, speech. **Engineering:** Physics. **English:** English lit, speech/rhetoric. **Foreign languages:** French, Russian, Spanish. **Health:** Athletic training, audiology/speech pathology, dietetics, predentistry, premedicine, prenursing, prepharmacy, preveterinary. **History:** General. **Legal studies:** Prelaw. **Math:** General. **Parks/recreation:** Exercise sciences. **Philosophy/religion:** Philosophy. **Physical sciences:** Chemistry, physics. **Psychology:** General. **Social sciences:** General, political science, sociology. **Theology:** Bible, missionary, pastoral counseling, sacred music, theology, youth ministry. **Visual/performing arts:** Dramatic, graphic design, music history, music performance, music theory/composition, piano/organ, studio arts, voice/opera.

Most popular majors. Biology 6%, business/marketing 16%, communications/journalism 9%, education 7%, health sciences 8%, parks/recreation 7%, theological studies 9%, visual/performing arts 8%.

Computing on campus. 225 workstations in dormitories, library, computer center, student center. Dormitories wired for high-speed internet access and linked to campus network. Commuter students can connect to campus network. Helpline, student web hosting, wireless network available.

Student life. Freshman orientation: Mandatory. Preregistration for classes offered. Three-part program: day-long pre-registration and orientation session for students and parents; 3-day weekend program prior to registration with one session for parents; optional 3-day summer retreat. **Policies:** Students under 22 must live in campus housing unless commuting. Only local fraternities and sororities are permitted. Religious observance required. Freshmen permitted cars on campus. **Housing:** Guaranteed on-campus for all undergraduates. Single-sex dorms, special housing for disabled, apartments, substance-free housing available. $50 deposit, deadline 6/1. **Activities:** Bands, choral groups, drama, literary magazine, music ensembles, musical theater, opera, student government, student newspaper, Campus ministries, Blue Key, College Republicans, Fellowship of Christian Athletes, international student club, Ouachita student foundation, Pew College Society, ROMS (minority students organization), Young Democrats.

Athletics. NCAA. **Intercollegiate:** Baseball M, basketball, cross-country W, diving, football (tackle) M, golf M, soccer, softball W, swimming, tennis, volleyball W. **Intramural:** Basketball, cheerleading, football (non-tackle), handball, racquetball, soccer, softball, table tennis, volleyball. **Team name:** Tigers.

Student services. Alcohol/substance abuse counseling, campus ministries, career counseling, services for economically disadvantaged, student employment services, financial aid counseling, health services, minority student services, personal counseling, placement for graduates, veterans' counselor. **Physically disabled:** Services for visually, speech, hearing impaired.

Contact. E-mail: goodmand@obu.edu
Phone: (870) 245-5110 Toll-free number: (800) 342-5628
Fax: (870) 245-5500
Judy Jones, Director of Admissions/Registrar, Ouachita Baptist University, OBU Box 3776, Arkadelphia, AR 71998-0001

Philander Smith College

Little Rock, Arkansas
www.philander.edu **CB code: 6578**

- Private 4-year liberal arts college affiliated with United Methodist Church
- Commuter campus in small city
- 670 full-time, degree-seeking undergraduates

General. Founded in 1877. Regionally accredited. **Degrees:** 111 bachelor's awarded. **ROTC:** Army. **Calendar:** Semester, limited summer session. **Full-time faculty:** 46 total. **Part-time faculty:** 45 total.

Freshman class profile. 126 enrolled.

Mid 50% test scores			
ACT:	14-18	Out-of-state:	15%
		Live on campus:	15%

Basis for selection. Open admission.

2005-2006 Annual costs. Tuition/fees: $7,766. Room/board: $5,090. Books/supplies: $650. Personal expenses: $600.

2004-2005 Financial aid. All financial aid based on need. 34% of total undergraduate aid awarded as scholarships/grants, 66% as loans/jobs.

Application procedures. Admission: Priority date 3/15; deadline 7/15. $25 fee. Admission notification on a rolling basis. **Financial aid:** Priority date 5/1; no closing date. FAFSA, institutional form required. Applicants notified on a rolling basis starting 5/1; must reply within 2 week(s) of notification.

Academics. Special study options: Cooperative education, independent study, internships, liberal arts/career combination, study abroad, teacher certification program. **Credit/placement by examination:** CLEP. 30 credit hours maximum toward bachelor's degree. **Support services:** Learning center, reduced course load, remedial instruction, tutoring.

Majors. Biology: General. **Business:** Administrative services, business admin. **Computer sciences:** Computer science. **Education:** General, biology, business, elementary, English, mathematics, physical, science, secondary, special. **Interdisciplinary:** Math/computer science. **Math:** General. **Philosophy/religion:** Philosophy, religion. **Physical sciences:** Chemistry. **Psychology:** General. **Public administration:** Social work. **Social sciences:** Political science, sociology.

Computing on campus. 72 workstations in library, computer center.

Student life. Freshman orientation: Mandatory, $75 fee. **Housing:** Single-sex dorms available. $50 deposit, deadline 7/10. **Activities:** Choral groups, drama, student government, student newspaper.

Athletics. Intercollegiate: Baseball M, basketball, volleyball W. **Intramural:** Badminton, basketball, tennis. **Team name:** Panthers.

Student services. Career counseling, student employment services, health services, personal counseling, veterans' counselor. **Physically disabled:** Services for visually, hearing impaired.

Contact. E-mail: admissions@philander.edu
Phone: (501) 370-5221 Toll-free number: (800) 446-6772
Fax: (501) 370-5225
Arnella Hayes, Director of Admissions, Philander Smith College, One Trudie Kibbe Reed Drive, Little Rock, AR 72202-3718

Southern Arkansas University

Magnolia, Arkansas
www.saumag.edu **CB code: 6661**

- Public 4-year university
- Residential campus in large town
- 2,683 degree-seeking undergraduates: 10% part-time, 56% women, 29% African American, 1% Asian American, 1% Hispanic American, 1% Native American, 5% international
- 175 degree-seeking graduate students
- 82% of applicants admitted
- SAT or ACT (ACT writing optional) required
- 38% graduate within 6 years

General. Founded in 1909. Regionally accredited. **Degrees:** 399 bachelor's, 55 associate awarded; master's offered. **Location:** 53 miles from Texarkana, Texas, 70 miles from Shreveport, Louisiana. **Calendar:** Semester, extensive summer session. **Full-time faculty:** 120 total; 66% have terminal degrees, 17% minority, 42% women. **Part-time faculty:** 62 total; 18% have terminal degrees, 6% minority, 55% women. **Class size:** 50% < 20, 37% 20-39, 7% 40-49, 5% 50-99, less than 1% >100. **Special facilities:** University farm.

Freshman class profile. 1,356 applied, 1,107 admitted, 572 enrolled.

Mid 50% test scores		Return as sophomores:	63%
ACT:	17-24	Out-of-state:	20%
GPA 3.50 or higher:	33%	Live on campus:	67%
GPA 3.0-3.49:	31%	International:	8%
GPA 2.0-2.99:	30%		

Basis for selection. For unconditional admission, applicants must have ACT of 19 or higher. ACT of 16 to 18 allows conditional admission. TOEFL required for non-native English speakers. Interview required of nursing majors.

High school preparation. Recommended units include English 4, mathematics 4, social studies 3, science 3 (laboratory 3) and foreign language 2. 0.5 computer science also recommended.

2005-2006 Annual costs. Tuition/fees: $4,310; $6,320 out-of-state. Room/board: $3,790. Books/supplies: $1,000. Personal expenses: $2,000.

2004-2005 Financial aid. Need-based: 50% of total undergraduate aid awarded as scholarships/grants, 50% as loans/jobs. **Non-need-based:** Scholarships awarded for academics, alumni affiliation, art, athletics, leadership, minority status, music/drama, state residency.

Application procedures. Admission: Closing date 8/30 (receipt date). No application fee. Application may be submitted online. Admission notification on a rolling basis. **Financial aid:** Priority date 7/1; no closing date. FAFSA required. Applicants notified on a rolling basis starting 4/15; must reply within 2 week(s) of notification.

Academics. Special study options: Combined bachelor's/graduate degree, cross-registration, distance learning, double major, dual enrollment of high school students, honors, independent study, internships, teacher certification program. **Credit/placement by examination:** AP, CLEP. 15 credit hours maximum toward associate degree, 30 toward bachelor's. **Support services:** Learning center, reduced course load, remedial instruction, tutoring, writing center.

Honors college/program. Composite ACT score of 26 or higher.

Majors. Agriculture: Business. **Biology:** General. **Business:** Accounting, business admin. **Communications:** General. **Computer sciences:** General. **Education:** Agricultural, art, biology, business, chemistry, early childhood, English, mathematics, middle, music, physical, physics, science, social studies, Spanish. **Foreign languages:** Spanish. **Health:** Athletic training, nursing (RN). **History:** General. **Interdisciplinary:** Biological/physical sciences. **Math:** General. **Parks/recreation:** Exercise sciences. **Physical sciences:** Chemistry. **Protective services:** Criminal justice. **Psychology:** General. **Public administration:** Community org/advocacy, social work. **Social sciences:** Political science, sociology. **Visual/performing arts:** Art, dramatic.

Most popular majors. Agriculture 8%, biology 6%, business/marketing 32%, education 16%, security/protective services 10%.

Computing on campus. 202 workstations in dormitories, library, computer center. Dormitories wired for high-speed internet access and linked to campus network. Commuter students can connect to campus network. Online library, helpline, wireless network available.

Student life. Freshman orientation: Mandatory. Preregistration for classes offered. **Policies:** Freshmen permitted cars on campus. **Housing:** Guaranteed on-campus for all undergraduates. Coed dorms, single-sex dorms, apartments, substance-free housing available. $50 deposit. Freshmen required to live on campus unless commuting or living with parents. **Activities:** Bands, choral groups, drama, music ensembles, musical theater, radio station, student government, student newspaper, More than 80 student organizations.

Athletics. NCAA. **Intercollegiate:** Baseball M, basketball, cross-country, football (tackle) M, golf M, softball W, tennis W, track and field, volleyball W. **Intramural:** Badminton, basketball, football (tackle) M, golf M, softball, table tennis, tennis, volleyball. **Team name:** Muleriders.

Student services. Alcohol/substance abuse counseling, career counseling, services for economically disadvantaged, student employment services, financial aid counseling, health services, minority student services, personal counseling, placement for graduates, veterans' counselor, women's services. **Physically disabled:** Services for visually, hearing impaired.

Contact. E-mail: sejennings@saumag.edu
Phone: (870) 235-4040 Toll-free number: (800) 332-7286
Fax: (870) 235-4931
Sarah Jennings, Dean of Enrollment Services, Southern Arkansas University, Box 9382, Magnolia, AR 71754-9382

University of Arkansas

Fayetteville, Arkansas — **CB member**
www.uark.edu — **CB code: 6866**

- Public 4-year university
- Residential campus in small city
- 13,654 degree-seeking undergraduates: 15% part-time, 49% women, 5% African American, 3% Asian American, 2% Hispanic American, 2% Native American, 2% international
- 3,485 degree-seeking graduate students
- 87% of applicants admitted
- SAT or ACT (ACT writing optional) required
- 56% graduate within 6 years

General. Founded in 1871. Regionally accredited. Arkansas Center for Space and Planetary Sciences, GENESIS Technology Incubator program provides tech-based companies with research and development support. **Degrees:** 2,197 bachelor's awarded; master's, doctoral, first professional offered. **ROTC:** Army, Air Force. **Location:** 192 miles from Little Rock, 120 miles from Tulsa, Oklahoma. **Calendar:** Semester, limited summer session. **Full-time faculty:** 787 total; 90% have terminal degrees, 12% minority, 31% women. **Part-time faculty:** 37 total; 43% have terminal degrees, 8% minority, 51% women. **Class size:** 36% < 20, 41% 20-39, 8% 40-49, 11% 50-99, 5% >100. **Special facilities:** Arts center, center of excellence for poultry science, equine pavilion, animal science center.

Freshman class profile. 6,040 applied, 5,283 admitted, 2,752 enrolled.

Mid 50% test scores		**Rank in top tenth:**	32%
SAT verbal:	510-640	**Return as sophomores:**	81%
SAT math:	520-640	**Out-of-state:**	30%
ACT:	22-28	**Live on campus:**	84%
GPA 3.50 or higher:	60%	**International:**	1%
GPA 3.0-3.49:	30%	**Fraternities:**	29%
GPA 2.0-2.99:	10%	**Sororities:**	36%
Rank in top quarter:	61%		

Basis for selection. Secondary school record, class rank, test scores, evidence of commitment to success most important. As mandated by state law, those with ACT subscore of 19 or less in English, Mathematics or Reading are assigned development coursework or required to take institutional placement test.

High school preparation. 16 units required. Required and recommended units include English 4, mathematics 4, social studies 3, science 3 (laboratory 2), foreign language 2 and academic electives 2. Mathematics must include 1 algebra or 2 applied math, and 2 units chosen from algebra II, geometry, calculus/trigonometry. 2 foreign languages strongly recommended for Arts and Sciences applicants.

2005-2006 Annual costs. Tuition/fees: $5,495; $13,222 out-of-state. Room/board: $6,365. Books/supplies: $923. Personal expenses: $1,866.

2004-2005 Financial aid. Need-based: 1,391 full-time freshmen applied for aid; 1,014 were judged to have need; 922 of these received aid. Average need met was 71%. Average scholarship/grant was $4,003; average loan $2,592. 38% of total undergraduate aid awarded as scholarships/grants, 62% as loans/jobs. **Non-need-based:** Awarded to 4,293 full-time undergraduates, including 1,294 freshmen. Scholarships awarded for academics, alumni affiliation, art, athletics, leadership, minority status, music/drama, ROTC, state residency.

Application procedures. Admission: Priority date 2/1; deadline 8/15 (receipt date). $40 fee, may be waived for applicants with need. Application may be submitted online. Admission notification on a rolling basis beginning on or about 10/1. **Financial aid:** Priority date 3/15; no closing date. FAFSA required. Applicants notified on a rolling basis starting 4/1.

Academics. Special study options: Accelerated study, combined bachelor's/graduate degree, cooperative education, distance learning, double major, dual enrollment of high school students, ESL, honors, independent study, internships, study abroad, teacher certification program, United Nations semester. **Credit/placement by examination:** AP, CLEP, IB, ACT, institutional tests. **Support services:** Learning center, reduced course load, remedial instruction, study skills assistance, tutoring, writing center.

Honors college/program. Student must be admitted to an honors program in the college of major. Must have a minimum 28 ACT or SAT equivalent and a minimum high school GPA of 3.5. Walton College of Business requires a 28 ACT or SAT equivalent and a minimum high school GPA of 3.75.

Majors. Agriculture: Agribusiness operations, agronomy, animal sciences, food science, horticultural science, ornamental horticulture, plant protection, poultry. **Architecture:** Architecture, landscape. **Area/ethnic studies:** American, Near/Middle Eastern. **Biology:** General, bacteriology. **Business:** General, accounting, business admin, finance, international, logistics, managerial economics, marketing, operations. **Communications:** General, journalism. **Computer sciences:** General, data processing. **Conservation:** General, environmental studies. **Education:** Agricultural, elementary, English, family/consumer sciences, foreign languages, middle, science, social science, social studies, special, trade/industrial, visually handicapped. **Engineering:** Agricultural, chemical, civil, computer, electrical, mechanical. **English:** English lit. **Family/consumer sciences:** Clothing/textiles, family studies, food/nutrition, housing. **Foreign languages:** Classics, French, German, Spanish. **Health:** Audiology/speech pathology, nursing (RN), premedicine. **History:** General. **Math:** General. **Parks/recreation:** General. **Philosophy/religion:** Philosophy. **Physical sciences:** Chemistry, geology, physics, planetary. **Protective services:** Criminal justice. **Psychology:** General. **Public administration:** General, social work. **Social sciences:** Anthropology, economics, geography, international relations, political science, sociology. **Visual/performing arts:** Art, dramatic, music performance, studio arts.

Most popular majors. Business/marketing 25%, communications/journalism 7%, education 8%, engineering/engineering technologies 11%, social sciences 6%.

Computing on campus. 1,501 workstations in dormitories, library, computer center, student center. Dormitories wired for high-speed internet access and linked to campus network. Commuter students can connect to campus network. Online course registration, online library, helpline, repair service, student web hosting, wireless network available.

Student life. Freshman orientation: Mandatory, $80 fee. Preregistration for classes offered. 2-day orientation session held in summer for students and parents. **Policies:** Freshmen permitted cars on campus. **Housing:** Coed dorms, single-sex dorms, apartments, fraternity/sorority housing, substance-free housing available. $200 partly refundable deposit, deadline 5/15. Honors residence, global issues, special interest floors for academic majors, student outreach and academic resource centers, first-year, substance-free halls, first year experience program area, adaptable housing for disabled students. **Activities:** Bands, choral groups, dance, drama, film society, literary magazine, music ensembles, musical theater, opera, radio station, student government, student newspaper, symphony orchestra, TV station, More than 200 organizations available.

Athletics. NCAA. **Intercollegiate:** Baseball M, basketball, cross-country, diving W, football (tackle) M, golf, gymnastics W, rowing (crew), soccer W, softball W, swimming W, tennis, track and field, volleyball W. **Intramural:** Badminton, basketball, bowling, golf, handball, judo, racquetball, rugby, soccer, softball, squash, swimming, table tennis, tennis, volleyball, water polo. **Team name:** Razorbacks.

Student services. Adult student services, alcohol/substance abuse counseling, campus ministries, career counseling, student employment services, financial aid counseling, health services, legal services, minority student services, personal counseling, placement for graduates, veterans' counselor. **Physically disabled:** Services for visually, speech, hearing impaired. **Learning disabled:** Comprehensive services available.

Contact. E-mail: uofa@uark.edu
Phone: (479) 575-5346 Toll-free number: (800) 377-8632
Fax: (479) 575-7515
Dawn Medley, Director of Admissions, University of Arkansas, 232 Silas Hunt Hall, Fayetteville, AR 72701

University of Arkansas at Fort Smith

Fort Smith, Arkansas — **CB member**
www.uafortsmith.edu — **CB code: 6220**

- Public 4-year university
- Commuter campus in small city
- 5,914 degree-seeking undergraduates: 35% part-time, 61% women

General. Founded in 1928. Regionally accredited. **Degrees:** 248 bachelor's, 519 associate awarded. **ROTC:** Air Force. **Location:** 150 miles from Little Rock, 120 miles from Tulsa, Oklahoma. **Calendar:** Semester, extensive summer session. **Full-time faculty:** 186 total; 38% have terminal degrees, 8% minority, 50% women. **Part-time faculty:** 185 total; 6% minority, 49% women. **Class size:** 34% < 20, 60% 20-39, 5% 40-49, less than 1% 50-99.

Freshman class profile. 2,691 applied, 1,682 admitted, 1,278 enrolled.

Mid 50% test scores		**Rank in top tenth:**	9%
ACT:	18-24	**End year in good standing:**	69%
GPA 3.50 or higher:	33%	**Return as sophomores:**	68%
GPA 3.0-3.49:	29%	**Out-of-state:**	12%
GPA 2.0-2.99:	33%	**Live on campus:**	14%
Rank in top quarter:	32%		

Basis for selection. Open admission, but selective for some programs. Special criteria for health career and education programs. Some applicants required to obtain individual approval of director of admissions and school relations. Conditional enrollment may apply. COMPASS required for placement if ACT/SAT not submitted, or if scores below acceptable minimum (18 on ACT). Interview required of nursing, radiology, surgical technology, paramedic, and dental hygiene majors, as well as teacher education programs.

High school preparation. 13.5 units recommended. Recommended units include English 4, mathematics 4, social studies 0.5, history 2, science 3 (laboratory 3).

2005-2006 Annual costs. Tuition/fees: $2,830; $7,720 out-of-state. Books/supplies: $1,400. Personal expenses: $1,080.

2004-2005 Financial aid. **Need-based:** 829 full-time freshmen applied for aid; 679 were judged to have need; 643 of these received aid. Average need met was 66%. Average scholarship/grant was $3,447; average loan $2,239. 59% of total undergraduate aid awarded as scholarships/grants, 41% as loans/jobs. **Non-need-based:** Awarded to 904 full-time undergraduates, including 410 freshmen. Scholarships awarded for academics, athletics, job skills, leadership, music/drama.

Application procedures. **Admission:** No deadline. No application fee. Application may be submitted online. Admission notification on a rolling basis. Early applications advised for financial aid. **Financial aid:** Priority date 4/1; no closing date. FAFSA required. Applicants notified on a rolling basis starting 3/1; must reply within 4 week(s) of notification.

Academics. **Special study options:** Cooperative education, distance learning, dual enrollment of high school students, external degree, honors, independent study, internships, liberal arts/career combination, study abroad, teacher certification program. Associate of Art through distance learning. **Credit/placement by examination:** AP, CLEP, institutional tests. 30 credit hours maximum toward associate degree, 45 toward bachelor's. Prior work/life experience credits awarded for military transcripts only; maximum 30 hours. **Support services:** Learning center, pre-admission summer program, reduced course load, remedial instruction, study skills assistance, tutoring, writing center.

Majors. **Biology:** General. **Business:** Accounting, business admin. **Computer sciences:** General. **Education:** Biology, chemistry, early childhood, English, history, mathematics, middle, music. **Engineering technology:** Manufacturing. **English:** English lit, technical writing. **Health:** Nursing (RN). **History:** General. **Interdisciplinary:** Science/society. **Liberal arts:** Arts/sciences. **Math:** General. **Physical sciences:** Chemistry. **Protective services:** Law enforcement admin. **Psychology:** General. **Visual/performing arts:** Graphic design.

Most popular majors. Business/marketing 31%, computer/information sciences 8%, education 32%, interdisciplinary studies 6%, liberal arts 8%.

Computing on campus. 1,067 workstations in library, computer center, student center. Commuter students can connect to campus network. Online course registration, online library, helpline, wireless network available.

Student life. **Freshman orientation:** Available. Preregistration for classes offered. . **Policies:** Freshmen permitted cars on campus. **Housing:** Apartments, substance-free housing available. **Activities:** Bands, choral groups, literary magazine, music ensembles, student government, Baptist Collegiate Ministry, College Democrats, College Republicans, Disabled Students Association, Future Educators Organization, Catholic campus ministry, student nurses association, Phi Beta Lambda, OARS, Chi Alpha.

Athletics. NJCAA. **Intercollegiate:** Baseball M, basketball, golf, tennis, volleyball W. **Intramural:** Basketball, bowling, football (tackle), softball, table tennis, volleyball. **Team name:** Lions.

Student services. Adult student services, career counseling, student employment services, financial aid counseling, placement for graduates, veterans' counselor. **Physically disabled:** Services for visually, speech, hearing impaired.

Contact. E-mail: information@uafortsmith.edu
Phone: (479) 788-7120 Toll-free number: (888) 512-5466
Fax: (479) 788-7016
Marion Dunagan, Vice Chancellor, Enrollment Management, University of Arkansas at Fort Smith, P O Box 3649, Fort Smith, AR 72913-3649

University of Arkansas at Little Rock

Little Rock, Arkansas — **CB member**
www.ualr.edu — **CB code: 6368**

- Public 4-year university
- Commuter campus in small city
- 9,349 degree-seeking undergraduates

General. Founded in 1927. Regionally accredited. **Degrees:** 1,036 bachelor's, 177 associate awarded; master's, doctoral, first professional offered. **ROTC:** Army. **Calendar:** Semester, limited summer session. **Full-time faculty:** 442 total; 71% have terminal degrees, 16% minority, 45% women. **Part-time faculty:** 320 total; 12% minority, 52% women. **Special facilities:** Planetarium, observatory, government documents depository, law center, rehearsal hall, concert hall, theater.

Freshman class profile.

Mid 50% test scores	**ACT:**	16-22

Basis for selection. Unconditional admission based on minimum ACT score of 21, enhanced or combined verbal/mathematics SAT score of 990, high school 2.5 GPA or above, and completion of college preparatory curriculum. Students must meet 2 of 3 basic criteria. All students born after January 1, 1957 required to show Arkansas Certificate of Immunization for Institutions of Higher Education. Interview recommended for academically weak applicants.

High school preparation. 15 units required. Required units include English 4, mathematics 3, social studies 3, science 2 (laboratory 2) and foreign language 2. Social studies should include 1 unit each of American history, world history, and civics or American government.

2005-2006 Annual costs. Tuition/fees: $5,213; $12,083 out-of-state. Fees vary depending on student's field of study. Room only: $2,950. Books/supplies: $1,000. Personal expenses: $800.

Application procedures. **Admission:** No deadline. No application fee. Admission notification on a rolling basis. **Financial aid:** Closing date 8/1. FAFSA required. Applicants notified on a rolling basis starting 5/1.

Academics. **Special study options:** Accelerated study, cooperative education, double major, dual enrollment of high school students, ESL, exchange student, honors, independent study, internships, student-designed major, study abroad, teacher certification program, weekend college. **Credit/placement by examination:** AP, CLEP, institutional tests. 30 credit hours maximum toward associate degree, 30 toward bachelor's. **Support services:** Learning center, reduced course load, remedial instruction, tutoring, writing center.

Majors. **Biology:** General. **Business:** General, accounting, business admin, finance, international, management information systems, managerial economics, marketing. **Communications:** General, advertising, broadcast journalism, journalism. **Computer sciences:** General, information systems. **Education:** Early childhood, elementary, ESL, health, middle. **Engineering:** Operations research, systems. **Engineering technology:** Civil, construction, electrical. **English:** Technical writing. **Foreign languages:** French, German, sign language interpretation, Spanish. **Health:** Audiology/speech pathology, environmental health. **History:** General. **Interdisciplinary:** Biological/physical sciences. **Liberal arts:** Arts/sciences. **Math:** General, applied. **Philosophy/religion:** Philosophy. **Physical sciences:** Chemistry, geology, physics. **Protective services:** Criminal justice. **Psychology:** General. **Public administration:** Social work. **Social sciences:** Economics, international relations, political science, sociology. **Visual/performing arts:** Art, art history/conservation, dramatic.

Computing on campus. 500 workstations in dormitories, library, computer center.

Student life. Freshman orientation: Available. **Housing:** Coed dorms available. **Activities:** Bands, choral groups, dance, drama, literary magazine, music ensembles, musical theater, opera, radio station, student government, student newspaper, TV station, Baptist Student Union, University Republicans, Methodist student club, Muslim students association, Young Democrats, Association for Minority Students Education Needs and Development (AMEND), Advocates for People with Disabilities.

Athletics. NCAA. **Intercollegiate:** Baseball M, basketball, cross-country, golf, soccer, swimming, tennis, track and field, volleyball W. **Intramural:** Badminton, basketball, bowling, football (tackle) M, golf, softball, swimming, tennis, volleyball.

Student services. Adult student services, career counseling, student employment services, health services, personal counseling, placement for graduates, veterans' counselor. **Physically disabled:** Services for visually, speech, hearing impaired.

Contact. Phone: (501) 569-3127 Fax: (501) 569-8956
John Noah, Director of Admissions and Financial Aid, University of Arkansas at Little Rock, 208 Administration South, Little Rock, AR 72204

University of Arkansas at Monticello

Monticello, Arkansas
www.uamont.edu **CB code: 6007**

- Public 4-year university and technical college
- Commuter campus in small town
- 2,915 degree-seeking undergraduates

General. Founded in 1909. Regionally accredited. **Degrees:** 307 bachelor's, 173 associate awarded; master's offered. **ROTC:** Army. **Location:** 100 miles from Little Rock, 50 miles from Pine Bluff. **Calendar:** Semester, extensive summer session. **Full-time faculty:** 120 total. **Part-time faculty:** 15 total. **Special facilities:** Museum of natural history, extensive research forest, planetarium, farm.

Freshman class profile. 668 enrolled.

Out-of-state:	8%	**Fraternities:**	9%
Live on campus:	45%	**Sororities:**	10%

Basis for selection. Open admission. **Homeschooled:** Transcript of courses and grades required. ACT or SAT for placement and not for admission.

High school preparation. Recommended units include English 4, mathematics 4, social studies 3, science 3 and foreign language 2.

2005-2006 Annual costs. Tuition/fees: $3,910; $7,660 out-of-state. Room/board: $3,640. Books/supplies: $800. Personal expenses: $1,800.

Financial aid. Non-need-based: Scholarships awarded for academics, athletics, job skills, leadership, music/drama, state residency.

Application procedures. Admission: Priority date 8/10; no deadline. No application fee. Application may be submitted online. Admission notification on a rolling basis. **Financial aid:** No deadline. FAFSA, institutional form required. Applicants notified on a rolling basis starting 4/1; must reply within 2 week(s) of notification.

Academics. Special study options: Combined bachelor's/graduate degree, cross-registration, distance learning, double major, dual enrollment of high school students, independent study, internships, liberal arts/career combination, study abroad, teacher certification program. **Credit/placement by examination:** AP, CLEP, IB, institutional tests. 9 credit hours maximum toward bachelor's degree. **Support services:** Learning center, pre-admission summer program, reduced course load, remedial instruction, study skills assistance, tutoring, writing center.

Majors. Biology: General. **Business:** General, accounting, administrative services, business admin, management information systems. **Conservation:** Forestry, wildlife. **Education:** Art, business, early childhood, English, middle, music, physical, secondary, social studies, special, speech. **Engineering technology:** Surveying. **English:** Speech/rhetoric. **Health:** Athletic training, nursing (RN). **History:** General. **Math:** General. **Physical sciences:** Chemistry. **Protective services:** Criminal justice. **Psychology:** General. **Public administration:** Social work. **Social sciences:** General, political science. **Visual/performing arts:** Art.

Most popular majors. Business/marketing 11%, education 9%, health sciences 12%, liberal arts 34%.

Computing on campus. 400 workstations in dormitories, library, computer center, student center. Dormitories wired for high-speed internet access and linked to campus network. Commuter students can connect to campus network. Online course registration available.

Student life. Freshman orientation: Mandatory. Preregistration for classes offered. One day, beginning of semester. **Policies:** Freshmen permitted cars on campus. **Housing:** Guaranteed on-campus for all undergraduates. Single-sex dorms, special housing for disabled, apartments, substance-free housing available. $60 deposit, deadline 8/15. **Activities:** Bands, choral groups, drama, literary magazine, music ensembles, musical theater, student government, student newspaper, Baptist Student Union, Missionary Baptist Student Fellowship, Wesley Foundation, Christians in Action, Catholic Weevils, and Chi Alpha.

Athletics. NCAA. **Intercollegiate:** Baseball M, basketball, cross-country, football (tackle) M, golf, rodeo, softball W, tennis W, volleyball W. **Intramural:** Archery, badminton, baseball M, basketball, bowling, boxing M, cross-country, football (tackle) M, golf, handball, racquetball, soccer, softball, swimming, table tennis, tennis, track and field, volleyball. **Team name:** Boll Weevils.

Student services. Alcohol/substance abuse counseling, campus ministries, career counseling, student employment services, financial aid counseling, health services, personal counseling, placement for graduates, veterans' counselor. **Physically disabled:** Services for visually, speech, hearing impaired.

Contact. E-mail: whitingm@uamont.edu
Phone: (870) 460-1026 Fax: (870) 460-1926
Mary Whiting, Director of Admissions, University of Arkansas at Monticello, Box 3600, Monticello, AR 71656

University of Arkansas at Pine Bluff

Pine Bluff, Arkansas **CB member**
www.uapb.edu **CB code: 6004**

- Public 4-year university
- Commuter campus in small city
- 3,100 degree-seeking undergraduates: 9% part-time, 56% women, 96% African American, 1% international
- 74 degree-seeking graduate students
- SAT or ACT (ACT writing optional) required

General. Founded in 1873. Regionally accredited. **Degrees:** 420 bachelor's awarded; master's offered. **ROTC:** Army. **Location:** 42 miles from Little Rock. **Calendar:** Semester, limited summer session. **Full-time faculty:** 170 total. **Part-time faculty:** 55 total. **Class size:** 39% < 20, 50% 20-39, 8% 40-49, 3% 50-99. **Special facilities:** 220-acre farm, aquaculture fisheries.

Freshman class profile.

Mid 50% test scores		**ACT:**	14-18
SAT verbal:	360-470	**Out-of-state:**	8%
SAT math:	340-500	**Live on campus:**	55%

Basis for selection. Admission credentials for entering freshmen must include formal application, high school transcript, ACT test information and scores (SAT is accepted) and immunization record.

High school preparation. 21 units required. Required units include English 4, mathematics 3, social studies 3, science 3 (laboratory 2), foreign language 2 and academic electives 4.

2005-2006 Annual costs. Tuition/fees: $4,254; $8,439 out-of-state. Room/board: $5,940. Books/supplies: $800. Personal expenses: $800.

Financial aid. Non-need-based: Scholarships awarded for academics, alumni affiliation, art, athletics, leadership, minority status, music/drama, religious affiliation, ROTC, state residency.

Application procedures. Admission: Priority date 8/1; no deadline. No application fee. Admission notification on a rolling basis. **Financial aid:** Priority date 4/15; no closing date. FAFSA required. Applicants notified on a rolling basis starting 3/1.

Academics. Special study options: Cooperative education, cross-registration, distance learning, double major, dual enrollment of high school students, honors, independent study, internships, teacher certification program. **Credit/placement by examination:** CLEP, IB. 25 credit hours maximum toward bachelor's degree. **Support services:** Learning center, reduced course load, remedial instruction, study skills assistance, tutoring.

Majors. **Biology:** General. **Business:** Accounting, business admin. **Communications:** General. **Computer sciences:** General. **Conservation:** General, fisheries. **Education:** General, agricultural, art, business, curriculum, early childhood, English, family/consumer sciences, mathematics, middle, physical, science, social science, social studies, special, trade/industrial. **English:** Speech/rhetoric. **Family/consumer sciences:** General, family studies. **Health:** Nursing (RN). **History:** General. **Interdisciplinary:** Gerontology. **Liberal arts:** Arts/sciences. **Math:** General, applied. **Parks/recreation:** General, facilities management. **Physical sciences:** Chemistry, physics. **Protective services:** Criminal justice. **Psychology:** General. **Public administration:** Social work. **Social sciences:** Political science, sociology. **Visual/performing arts:** Art.

Computing on campus. 1,000 workstations in dormitories, library, computer center, student center. Dormitories linked to campus network. Commuter students can connect to campus network. Online library, helpline, repair service available.

Student life. **Freshman orientation:** Mandatory. Preregistration for classes offered. **Policies:** Freshmen permitted cars on campus. **Housing:** Single-sex dorms available. $100 deposit. **Activities:** Bands, choral groups, drama, music ensembles, radio station, student government, student newspaper, symphony orchestra, TV station, Baptist Student Union, political science/prelaw club, Church of God in Christ, Wesley Foundation, criminal justice club.

Athletics. NCAA. **Intercollegiate:** Baseball M, basketball, bowling W, cross-country, football (tackle) M, golf, soccer W, softball W, tennis, track and field, volleyball W. **Intramural:** Baseball M, basketball, bowling, cross-country M, football (tackle), golf, gymnastics, handball, racquetball, softball, swimming, table tennis, tennis, volleyball, weight lifting. **Team name:** Golden Lions.

Student services. Adult student services, alcohol/substance abuse counseling, campus ministries, career counseling, services for economically disadvantaged, student employment services, financial aid counseling, health services, on-campus daycare, personal counseling, placement for graduates, veterans' counselor.

Contact. E-mail: fulton_e@uapb.edu
Phone: (870) 575-8493 Toll-free number: (800) 264-6585
Fax: (870) 575-4608
Erica Fulton, Registrar, University of Arkansas at Pine Bluff, 1200 North University Drive, Mail Slot 4981, Pine Bluff, AR 71601-2799

University of Arkansas for Medical Sciences

Little Rock, Arkansas
www.uams.edu **CB code: 0424**

- Public 4-year university and health science college
- Commuter campus in large city
- 820 degree-seeking undergraduates

General. Founded in 1876. Regionally accredited. University has 5 colleges: medicine, nursing, pharmacy, health-related professions, graduate. **Degrees:** 295 bachelor's, 59 associate awarded; master's, doctoral, first professional offered. **Location:** One mile from downtown. **Calendar:** Semester, limited summer session. **Full-time faculty:** 1,230 total.

Basis for selection. Most incoming students must have prior college credit.

2005-2006 Annual costs. Tuition/fees: $5,215; $11,515 out-of-state. Reported tuition and fees are for Health Related Professions Program and majors in dental hygiene, diagnostic medical sonography, nuclear medicine imaging sciences, and radiologic imaging sciences. Tuition and fees vary by program. Room only: $1,620. Books/supplies: $400. Personal expenses: $1,800.

Application procedures. **Admission:** No application fee. Admission notification on a rolling basis. Must reply by May 1 or within 2 week(s) if notified thereafter. Application closing dates vary by program. **Financial aid:** No deadline. FAFSA required. Applicants notified on a rolling basis starting 5/1; must reply within 2 week(s) of notification.

Academics. **Special study options:** Distance learning, independent study. **Credit/placement by examination:** CLEP.

Majors. **Health:** Clinical lab science, cytotechnology, dental hygiene, medical radiologic technology/radiation therapy, nuclear medical technology, nursing (RN).

Student life. **Housing:** Coed dorms, apartments available. **Activities:** Student government, student newspaper.

Student services. Health services, on-campus daycare.

Contact. Phone: (501) 686-5000 Fax: (501) 686-5905
University of Arkansas for Medical Sciences, 4301 West Markham Street, Little Rock, AR 72205

University of Central Arkansas

Conway, Arkansas **CB member**
www.uca.edu **CB code: 6012**

- Public 4-year university and liberal arts college
- Residential campus in large town
- 9,909 degree-seeking undergraduates: 8% part-time, 59% women, 17% African American, 2% Asian American, 1% Hispanic American, 1% Native American, 2% international
- 1,406 degree-seeking graduate students
- 68% of applicants admitted
- SAT or ACT (ACT writing optional) required
- 49% graduate within 6 years

General. Founded in 1907. Regionally accredited. **Degrees:** 1,198 bachelor's, 20 associate awarded; master's, doctoral offered. **ROTC:** Army. **Location:** 30 miles from Little Rock. **Calendar:** Semester, extensive summer session. **Full-time faculty:** 557 total; 38% have terminal degrees, 10% minority, 51% women. **Part-time faculty:** 115 total; 6% minority, 56% women. **Class size:** 43% < 20, 44% 20-39, 10% 40-49, 3% 50-99, less than 1% >100. **Special facilities:** Observatory, greenhouse, honors center, visual arts center, nature preserve.

Freshman class profile. 5,830 applied, 3,966 admitted, 2,503 enrolled.

Mid 50% test scores		**Rank in top quarter:**	44%
SAT verbal:	430-580	**Rank in top tenth:**	21%
SAT math:	470-600	**Return as sophomores:**	93%
ACT:	20-27	**Out-of-state:**	5%
GPA 3.50 or higher:	43%	**Live on campus:**	91%
GPA 3.0-3.49:	26%	**International:**	2%
GPA 2.0-2.99:	29%		

Basis for selection. Test scores, class rank most important.

High school preparation. Recommended units include English 4, mathematics 3, social studies 1, history 2, science 3 and academic electives 10.

2005-2006 Annual costs. Tuition/fees: $5,682; $10,182 out-of-state. Room/board: $4,320. Books/supplies: $1,200. Personal expenses: $1,899.

2004-2005 Financial aid. **Need-based:** 39% of total undergraduate aid awarded as scholarships/grants, 61% as loans/jobs. **Non-need-based:** Scholarships awarded for academics, athletics, music/drama, ROTC, state residency. **Additional information:** Room and board may be paid monthly.

Application procedures. **Admission:** Priority date 5/1; no deadline. No application fee. Admission notification on a rolling basis. **Financial aid:** Priority date 2/15; no closing date. FAFSA required. Applicants notified on a rolling basis starting 5/4.

Academics. **Special study options:** Accelerated study, combined bachelor's/graduate degree, cooperative education, distance learning, double major, dual enrollment of high school students, ESL, honors, independent study, internships, liberal arts/career combination, study abroad, teacher certification program. 5-year professional programs in physical therapy and occupational therapy. **Credit/placement by examination:** AP, CLEP, institutional tests. 30 credit hours maximum toward bachelor's degree. **Support services:** Learning center, pre-admission summer program, remedial instruction, tutoring, writing center.

Honors college/program. Special honors courses and minor in interdisciplinary studies offered. 28 ACT and 3.5 GPA minimum.

Majors. **Biology:** General. **Business:** General, accounting, administrative services, business admin, fashion, finance, human resources, insurance, international marketing, management information systems, management science, managerial economics, marketing. **Communications:** Journalism. **Computer sciences:** General, computer science, data processing, information systems. **Conservation:** General. **Education:** Business, English, family/consumer sciences, health, mathematics, middle, physical, physically handicapped, science, social studies, special. **English:** English lit, speech/rhetoric. **Family/consumer sciences:** General, clothing/textiles. **Foreign languages:** French, German, Spanish. **Health:** Art therapy, audiology/speech pathology, clinical lab technology, dietetics, health care admin, health services, medical radiologic technology/radiation therapy, nuclear medical technology, nursing (RN), occupational health, physics/radiologic health, predentistry, premedicine, prepharmacy, preveterinary, public health ed, recreational therapy, respiratory therapy technology, speech pathology, substance abuse counseling. **History:** General. **Interdisciplinary:** Biological/physical sciences. **Math:** General. **Parks/recreation:** Exercise sciences. **Philosophy/religion:** Philosophy, religion. **Physical sciences:** Chemistry, physics. **Psychology:** General. **Public administration:** General. **Social sciences:** Economics, geography, political science, sociology. **Visual/performing arts:** Art, music performance, piano/organ, studio arts, voice/opera.

Most popular majors. Business/marketing 23%, education 9%, English 7%, family/consumer sciences 8%, health sciences 18%, history 7%, social sciences 7%.

Computing on campus. 1,100 workstations in dormitories, library, computer center, student center. Dormitories linked to campus network. Commuter students can connect to campus network. Online course registration, helpline, repair service available.

Student life. **Freshman orientation:** Available. Preregistration for classes offered. **Policies:** Freshmen permitted cars on campus. **Housing:** Guaranteed on-campus for freshmen. Coed dorms, single-sex dorms, special housing for disabled, apartments, fraternity/sorority housing available. $100 partly refundable deposit, deadline 7/1. **Activities:** Bands, choral groups, dance, drama, film society, literary magazine, music ensembles, musical theater, opera, radio station, student government, student newspaper, symphony orchestra, TV station, Baptist Student Union, Methodist Student Union, Newman Club, Young Democrats, College Republicans, Students for Propagation of Black Culture, Association of Baptist Students, Catholic Campus Ministries, International Friends.

Athletics. NCAA. **Intercollegiate:** Baseball M, basketball, cheerleading, cross-country, football (tackle) M, golf, soccer, softball W, tennis W, track and field W, volleyball W. **Intramural:** Badminton, basketball, bowling, cross-country, football (non-tackle), racquetball, soccer, softball, swimming, table tennis, tennis, track and field, volleyball. **Team name:** Bears.

Student services. Alcohol/substance abuse counseling, campus ministries, career counseling, student employment services, financial aid counseling, health services, minority student services, on-campus daycare, personal counseling, placement for graduates, veterans' counselor. **Physically disabled:** Services for visually, speech, hearing impaired.

Contact. E-mail: admissions@uca.edu
Phone: (501) 450-3128 Toll-free number: (800) 243-8245
Fax: (501) 450-5228
Penny Hatfield, Director of Admissions, University of Central Arkansas, 201 Donaghey Avenue, Conway, AR 72035-0001

University of the Ozarks

Clarksville, Arkansas
www.ozarks.edu **CB code: 6111**

- Private 4-year university and liberal arts college affiliated with Presbyterian Church (USA)
- Residential campus in small town
- 597 degree-seeking undergraduates: 5% African American, 2% Asian American, 4% Hispanic American, 4% Native American, 17% international
- 84% of applicants admitted
- SAT or ACT (ACT writing optional), application essay required
- 52% graduate within 6 years

General. Founded in 1834. Regionally accredited. **Degrees:** 118 bachelor's awarded. **Location:** 100 miles from Little Rock, 65 miles from Fort Smith. **Calendar:** Semester, limited summer session. **Full-time faculty:** 44 total. **Part-time faculty:** 17 total.

Freshman class profile. 632 applied, 530 admitted, 170 enrolled.

Mid 50% test scores		Return as sophomores:	67%
SAT verbal:	450-640	Out-of-state:	47%
SAT math:	440-620	Live on campus:	87%
ACT:	17-27		

Basis for selection. School achievement record and test scores most important. Interview required of those with marginal grades, recommended for all applicants.

High school preparation. 18 units recommended. Recommended units include English 4, mathematics 4, social studies 1, history 2, science 3 (laboratory 2) and foreign language 2.

2006-2007 Annual costs. Tuition/fees (projected): $14,950. Room/board: $5,260. Books/supplies: $600.

2005-2006 Financial aid. **Non-need-based:** Scholarships awarded for academics, alumni affiliation, art, leadership, minority status, music/drama, religious affiliation. **Additional information:** Walton International Scholarship Program provides full scholarships to selected Central American and Mexican residents.

Application procedures. **Admission:** Priority date 4/1; no deadline. $10 fee, may be waived for applicants with need. Application may be submitted online. Admission notification on a rolling basis. **Financial aid:** Priority date 2/15; no closing date. FAFSA required. Applicants notified on a rolling basis starting 3/15; must reply within 2 week(s) of notification.

Academics. **Special study options:** Cooperative education, double major, dual enrollment of high school students, independent study, internships, liberal arts/career combination, study abroad, teacher certification program. **Credit/placement by examination:** CLEP, institutional tests. 30 credit hours maximum toward bachelor's degree. **Support services:** Learning center, remedial instruction, study skills assistance, tutoring.

Majors. **Biology:** General. **Business:** Accounting, business admin, marketing. **Communications:** General. **Conservation:** General, environmental studies. **Education:** General, biology, business, chemistry, drama/dance, early childhood, middle, physical, science, secondary, special. **Health:** Predentistry, premedicine, preveterinary. **History:** General. **Math:** General. **Physical sciences:** Chemistry, physics. **Psychology:** General. **Public administration:** General. **Social sciences:** General, political science, sociology. **Visual/performing arts:** General, art, dramatic.

Most popular majors. Biology 7%, business/marketing 47%, education 14%, liberal arts 8%, social sciences 12%, visual/performing arts 6%.

Computing on campus. 150 workstations in dormitories, library, computer center, student center. Dormitories linked to campus network. Commuter students can connect to campus network. Online course registration, helpline available.

Student life. **Freshman orientation:** Mandatory. Preregistration for classes offered. **Policies:** Freshmen permitted cars on campus. **Housing:** Guaranteed on-campus for freshmen. Coed dorms, single-sex dorms available. $75 deposit, deadline 8/15. **Activities:** Choral groups, drama, literary magazine, music ensembles, musical theater, radio station, student government, student newspaper, TV station, Ozarks Area Mission, other religious, ethnic, and social service organizations.

Athletics. NCAA. **Intercollegiate:** Baseball M, basketball, cheerleading, cross-country, soccer, softball W, tennis. **Intramural:** Badminton, basketball, bowling, football (non-tackle) M, racquetball, soccer, softball, tennis, track and field, volleyball. **Team name:** Eagles.

Student services. Campus ministries, career counseling, student employment services, financial aid counseling, health services, personal counseling, placement for graduates, veterans' counselor. **Learning disabled:** Comprehensive services available.

Contact. E-mail: admiss@ozarks.edu
Phone: (479) 979-1227 Toll-free number: (800) 264-8636
Fax: (479) 979-1355
Jim Decker, Associate Director of Admissions, University of the Ozarks, 415 College Avenue, Clarksville, AR 72830

Williams Baptist College

Walnut Ridge, Arkansas
www.wbcoll.edu **CB code: 6658**

- Private 4-year liberal arts college affiliated with Southern Baptist Convention
- Residential campus in small town
- 512 degree-seeking undergraduates: 4% part-time, 56% women, 3% African American, 1% Hispanic American, 1% international
- 65% of applicants admitted
- SAT or ACT (ACT writing optional) required
- 34% graduate within 6 years

General. Founded in 1941. Regionally accredited. **Degrees:** 128 bachelor's, 8 associate awarded. **ROTC:** Army. **Location:** 30 miles from Jonesboro, 100 miles from Memphis, Tennessee. **Calendar:** Semester, limited summer session. **Full-time faculty:** 29 total; 59% have terminal degrees, 45% women. **Part-time faculty:** 17 total; 6% have terminal degrees, 6% minority, 65% women. **Class size:** 62% < 20, 35% 20-39, 2% 40-49, less than 1% 50-99.

Freshman class profile. 479 applied, 310 admitted, 130 enrolled.

Mid 50% test scores		Out-of-state:	4%
ACT:	18-24	Live on campus:	85%
Return as sophomores:	57%	International:	2%

Basis for selection. ACT score of 19, high school 2.5 GPA required. Interviews and essays recommended. Audition required of music majors.

High school preparation. Recommended units include English 4, mathematics 4, social studies 3, science 3 (laboratory 3) and foreign language 2.

2005-2006 Annual costs. Tuition/fees: $9,250. Room/board: $4,200. Books/supplies: $900. Personal expenses: $1,100.

2004-2005 Financial aid. **Need-based:** 133 full-time freshmen applied for aid; 96 were judged to have need; 96 of these received aid. Average scholarship/grant was $2,540; average loan $1,903. 45% of total undergraduate aid awarded as scholarships/grants, 55% as loans/jobs. **Non-need-based:** Awarded to 535 full-time undergraduates, including 176 freshmen. Scholarships awarded for academics, art, athletics, leadership, minority status, music/drama, religious affiliation, state residency. **Additional information:** Art scholarship applicants must submit portfolio.

Application procedures. **Admission:** No deadline. $20 fee. Admission notification on a rolling basis. Must reply by May 1 or within 3 week(s) if notified thereafter. **Financial aid:** Priority date 5/1; no closing date. FAFSA required. Applicants notified on a rolling basis starting 4/1; must reply within 2 week(s) of notification.

Academics. **Special study options:** Double major, dual enrollment of high school students, independent study, internships, study abroad. **Credit/placement by examination:** AP, CLEP, IB. 30 credit hours maximum toward bachelor's degree. **Support services:** Learning center, reduced course load, remedial instruction, study skills assistance, tutoring.

Majors. **Biology:** General. **Business:** Business admin, finance. **Computer sciences:** General. **Education:** General, art, early childhood, elementary, English, music, physical, secondary, social studies. **History:** General. **Psychology:** General. **Theology:** Bible, missionary, religious ed, sacred music, theology, youth ministry. **Visual/performing arts:** Studio arts.

Most popular majors. Business/marketing 18%, education 39%, liberal arts 6%, psychology 18%, theological studies 11%.

Computing on campus. 70 workstations in library, computer center, student center. Dormitories wired for high-speed internet access and linked to campus network. Online library, wireless network available.

Student life. **Freshman orientation:** Mandatory, $50 fee. Preregistration for classes offered. 2-day program held at beginning of fall semester. **Policies:** Religious observance required. Freshmen permitted cars on campus. **Housing:** Guaranteed on-campus for all undergraduates. Single-sex dorms, apartments available. $75 deposit, deadline 6/1. All full-time students under 21 required to live in college housing, unless commuting. **Activities:** Choral groups, drama, student government, campus ministries, student activities board, international club, student ambassadors, Southerland Hall activity council, College Republicans.

Athletics. NAIA. **Intercollegiate:** Baseball M, basketball, cheerleading, soccer M, softball W, volleyball W. **Intramural:** Baseball M, basketball, football (non-tackle), softball, volleyball. **Team name:** Eagles.

Student services. Alcohol/substance abuse counseling, campus ministries, career counseling, financial aid counseling, health services, personal counseling, veterans' counselor.

Contact. E-mail: admissions@wbcoll.edu
Phone: (870) 759-4121 Toll-free number: (800) 722-4434
Fax: (870) 886-3924
Angela Flippo, Vice President for Enrollment, Williams Baptist College, PO Box 3665, Walnut Ridge, AR 72476

California

Academy of Art University
San Francisco, California
www.academyart.edu **CB code: 1981**

- For-profit 4-year university and visual arts college
- Commuter campus in very large city
- 6,596 degree-seeking undergraduates: 37% part-time, 50% women, 4% African American, 12% Asian American, 7% Hispanic American, 1% Native American, 15% international
- 1,666 degree-seeking graduate students
- Interview required
- 34% graduate within 6 years; 5% enter graduate study

General. Founded in 1929. Accredited by ACICS. Equal emphasis on both fine and applied arts. Accredited by the National Association of Schools of Art and Design. BFA on-campus program Interior Architecture and Design program accredited by FIDER. **Degrees:** 743 bachelor's, 65 associate awarded; master's offered. **Calendar:** Semester, extensive summer session. **Full-time faculty:** 135 total; 11% have terminal degrees, 44% women. **Part-time faculty:** 540 total; 38% women. **Class size:** 80% < 20, 20% 20-39, less than 1% 40-49, less than 1% >100. **Special facilities:** 3 nonprofit galleries, photography darkrooms, Bosch Telecen, green screen stage, interior design resource room, foundry, 50,000-square-foot sculpture center, Final Cut Pro, Media and Avid Express editing stations.

Freshman class profile. 1,226 applied, 1,226 admitted, 716 enrolled.

End year in good standing:	77%	**Live on campus:**	14%
Return as sophomores:	60%	**International:**	8%
Out-of-state:	60%		

Basis for selection. Open admission. Continuing education program offered. Interview can be in person or over the phone. **Learning Disabled:** Reasonable accomodations made for students with disabilities.

High school preparation. Art and design courses recommended.

2006-2007 Annual costs. Tuition/fees (projected): $18,140. Room/board: $12,600. Books/supplies: $1,242. Personal expenses: $1,980.

2004-2005 Financial aid. Need-based: 328 full-time freshmen applied for aid; 279 were judged to have need; 240 of these received aid. Average need met was 25%. Average scholarship/grant was $4,144; average loan $2,555. 27% of total undergraduate aid awarded as scholarships/grants, 73% as loans/jobs. **Non-need-based:** Awarded to 59 full-time undergraduates, including 11 freshmen. Scholarships awarded for academics, art. **Additional information:** Numerous summer grant programs available.

Application procedures. Admission: No deadline. $100 fee. Application may be submitted online. Admission notification on a rolling basis. Accepted applicants may preregister in mid March. **Financial aid:** Priority date 7/10; no closing date. FAFSA, institutional form required. Applicants notified on a rolling basis.

Academics. Special study options: Combined bachelor's/graduate degree, cross-registration, distance learning, dual enrollment of high school students, ESL, honors, independent study, internships, student-designed major, teacher certification program. **Credit/placement by examination:** AP, CLEP, IB. Interview, essay recommended for placement. Portfolio recommended for bachelor of arts applicants. **Support services:** Learning center, pre-admission summer program, reduced course load, remedial instruction, study skills assistance, tutoring, writing center.

Majors. Communications: Advertising. **Communications technology:** Photo/film/video. **Visual/performing arts:** Cinematography, commercial photography, commercial/advertising art, design, drawing, fashion design, fiber arts, graphic design, illustration, industrial design, interior design, multimedia, painting, photography, printmaking, sculpture, studio arts.

Computing on campus. 700 workstations in dormitories, library, computer center. Dormitories wired for high-speed internet access. Commuter students can connect to campus network. Online course registration, online library, helpline, student web hosting, wireless network available.

Student life. Freshman orientation: Mandatory. Preregistration for classes offered. 5-day session the week before start of classes. **Housing:** Guaranteed on-campus for all undergraduates. Coed dorms, single-sex dorms, special housing for disabled, substance-free housing available. $500 deposit, deadline 7/14. **Activities:** Film society, student government, student newspaper, Chinese society, Circle of Nations, international student organization.

Athletics. Intramural: Basketball, soccer.

Student services. Alcohol/substance abuse counseling, career counseling, student employment services, financial aid counseling, health services, personal counseling, placement for graduates, veterans' counselor. **Physically disabled:** Services for visually, hearing impaired.

Contact. E-mail: info@academyart.edu
Phone: (415) 274-2200 Toll-free number: (800) 544-2787
Fax: (415) 263-4130
John Meurer, Vice President of Admissions, Academy of Art University, 79 New Montgomery Street, San Francisco, CA 94105-3410

Alliant International University
San Diego, California **CB member**
www.alliant.edu **CB code: 4039**

- Private upper-division university
- Commuter campus in very large city

General. Founded in 1952. Regionally accredited. Alliant International University focuses on preparing students for professional careers in the applied social sciences. Our faculty, students and alumni are committed to making an impact on society and to results that make a difference in the lives of individuals, couples, families, schools, organizations, companies, and nations. Our institution applies scholarship to solve social problems and has always had an abiding concern for diversity and internationalism. Students may enter as transfers after two years of undergraduate study at San Diego, and as freshmen or transfers at Mexico City. **Degrees:** 118 bachelor's awarded; master's, doctoral offered. **Articulation:** Agreements with Cuyamaca College, Glendale College, Grossmont College, Imperial Valley College, MiraCosta College, Mt. San Antonio College, Mt. San Jacinto College, Palomar College, Pasadena College, Riverside Community College, Saddleback College, San Diego City College, San Diego Mesa College, San Diego Miramar College, Santa Monica College, Southwestern College, Ventura College. **Location:** 16 miles from downtown. **Calendar:** Semester, limited summer session. **Full-time faculty:** 161 total; 100% have terminal degrees, 17% minority, 43% women. **Part-time faculty:** 405 total; 93% have terminal degrees, 12% minority. **Class size:** 71% < 20, 27% 20-39, 2% 40-49.

Student profile. 307 degree-seeking undergraduates, 3,264 graduate students. 45% transferred from two-year, 55% transferred from four-year institutions.

Out-of-state:	16%	**25 or older:**	17%
Live on campus:	38%		

Basis for selection. High school transcript, college transcript required. Transfer accepted as sophomores, juniors, seniors.

2005-2006 Annual costs. Tuition/fees: $19,350. Room/board: $7,800. Books/supplies: $1,260. Personal expenses: $1,818.

Financial aid. Need-based: 44% of total undergraduate aid awarded as scholarships/grants, 56% as loans/jobs. **Non-need-based:** Scholarships awarded for academics, alumni affiliation, athletics, leadership.

Application procedures. Admission: Priority date 3/2. $40 fee, may be waived for applicants with need. Application may be submitted online. **Financial aid:** FAFSA required.

Academics. Special study options: ESL, honors, independent study, internships, liberal arts/career combination, study abroad. **Credit/placement by examination:** AP, CLEP, IB, institutional tests. 27 credit hours maximum toward bachelor's degree. **Support services:** Learning center, reduced course load, remedial instruction, study skills assistance, tutoring, writing center.

Honors college/program. 3.6 GPA required; honors seminars and enrichment activities offered.

Majors. Area/ethnic studies: Latin American. **Business:** Business admin, hospitality/recreation, international, management information systems, tourism promotion. **Communications:** Journalism. **Conservation:** Environmental studies. **Education:** ESL. **Psychology:** General. **Social sciences:** International relations.

Most popular majors. Business/marketing 66%, liberal arts 9%, psychology 9%.

Computing on campus. 100 workstations in library, computer center. Dormitories wired for high-speed internet access and linked to campus network. Commuter students can connect to campus network. Online library, student web hosting available.

Student life. Housing: Guaranteed on-campus for all undergraduates. Coed dorms available. $250 deposit. All dormitories are made up of 2-bedroom suites with a central living room. **Activities:** Student government, student newspaper, Indian student association, Latino student organization, Alliant Turk Society, Center for International Studies/Model United Nations.

Athletics. NAIA. **Intercollegiate:** Cross-country, soccer, tennis, track and field, volleyball W. **Intramural:** Basketball, bowling, soccer, softball, tennis, volleyball. **Team name:** Mountain Lions.

Student services. Adult student services, alcohol/substance abuse counseling, career counseling, student employment services, financial aid counseling, health services, personal counseling, placement for graduates, veterans' counselor, women's services. **Physically disabled:** Services for visually, speech, hearing impaired.

Contact. E-mail: admissions3@alliant.edu
Phone: (866) 825-5426 Toll-free number: (866) 825-5426
Fax: (858) 635-4555
Susan Topham, Systemwide Director of Admissions, Alliant International University, 10455 Pomerado Road, San Diego, CA 92131-1799

Antioch University Los Angeles

Culver City, California
www.antiochla.edu **CB code: 1862**

- Private upper-division branch campus and liberal arts college
- Commuter campus in very large city
- Application essay, interview required

General. Founded in 1972. Regionally accredited. **Degrees:** 65 bachelor's awarded; master's offered. **Articulation:** Agreements with UCLA Extension, Santa Monica College, West Los Angeles College, Compton City College. **Location:** 15 miles from Los Angeles. **Calendar:** Quarter, extensive summer session. **Full-time faculty:** 17 total. **Part-time faculty:** 5 total.

Student profile. 162 degree-seeking undergraduates, 534 graduate students.

Basis for selection. High school transcript, college transcript, application essay, interview required. Admission decision of full or provisional acceptance made by program chair. Transfer accepted as sophomores, juniors, seniors.

2005-2006 Annual costs. Tuition/fees: $13,560. Cost varies with program. Books/supplies: $1,500.

Application procedures. Admission: Deadline 8/1. $60 fee, may be waived for applicants with need. Must reply by 8/15. **Financial aid:** FAFSA, institutional form required.

Academics. Prior experiential learning credits. **Special study options:** Accelerated study, combined bachelor's/graduate degree, cooperative education, cross-registration, double major, independent study, internships, liberal arts/career combination, student-designed major, study abroad, teacher certification program, weekend college. **Credit/placement by examination:** AP, CLEP. 40 credit hours maximum toward bachelor's degree. DANTES examination scores accepted.

Majors. Liberal arts: Arts/sciences.

Computing on campus. 12 workstations in computer center. Commuter students can connect to campus network.

Student life. Activities: Student government.

Athletics. Team name: Radicals.

Student services. Adult student services, career counseling, student employment services, financial aid counseling, personal counseling, veterans' counselor. **Physically disabled:** Services for visually, speech, hearing impaired.

Contact. E-mail: admissions@antiochla.edu
Phone: (800) 726-8462 Toll-free number: (800) 726-8462
Fax: (310) 822-4824
Kathie Rawding, Director of Admissions, Antioch University Los Angeles, 400 Corporate Pointe, Culver City, CA 90230-7615

Antioch University Santa Barbara

Santa Barbara, California
www.antiochsb.edu **CB code: 3071**

- Private upper-division university and liberal arts college
- Commuter campus in small city
- Application essay, interview required

General. Founded in 1852. Regionally accredited. **Degrees:** 35 bachelor's awarded; master's offered. **Articulation:** Agreements with Santa Barbara City College, University of California: Santa Barbara, Ventura CC, Cuesta CC, Allen Hancock CC. **Location:** Downtown. **Calendar:** Quarter, extensive summer session. **Full-time faculty:** 14 total. **Part-time faculty:** 59 total.

Student profile. 97 degree-seeking undergraduates.

Out-of-state:	2%	**25 or older:**	95%

Basis for selection. Open admission. High school transcript, college transcript, application essay, interview required. Transfer accepted as juniors, seniors.

2005-2006 Annual costs. Tuition/fees: $13,188. Books/supplies: $990.

Financial aid. Need-based: 16% of total undergraduate aid awarded as scholarships/grants, 84% as loans/jobs.

Application procedures. Admission: Rolling admission. $60 fee. **Financial aid:** Priority date 4/1, no deadline. FAFSA, institutional form required.

Academics. Special study options: Cross-registration, double major, independent study, internships, liberal arts/career combination, student-designed major, study abroad, teacher certification program, weekend college. **Credit/placement by examination:** AP, CLEP, IB. **Support services:** Remedial instruction.

Majors. Liberal arts: Arts/sciences.

Computing on campus. 10 workstations in computer center. Online library available.

Student services. Adult student services, career counseling, financial aid counseling, personal counseling, veterans' counselor.

Contact. E-mail: admissions@antiochsb.edu
Phone: (805) 962-8179 Toll-free number: (866) 526-8462
Fax: (805) 962-4786
Ankara McPherson, Director of Admissions, Antioch University Santa Barbara, 801 Garden Street, Santa Barbara, CA 93101-1581

Art Center College of Design

Pasadena, California **CB member**
www.artcenter.edu **CB code: 4009**

- Private 4-year visual arts college
- Commuter campus in small city
- 1,512 degree-seeking undergraduates: 14% part-time, 40% women, 2% African American, 37% Asian American, 12% Hispanic American, 16% international
- 130 degree-seeking graduate students
- 74% of applicants admitted
- SAT or ACT, application essay required
- 67% graduate within 6 years

General. Founded in 1930. Regionally accredited. **Degrees:** 413 bachelor's awarded; master's offered. **Location:** 15 miles from Los Angeles. **Calendar:** Trimester, extensive summer session. **Full-time faculty:** 65 total. **Part-time faculty:** 340 total. **Class size:** 90% < 20, 9% 20-39, less than 1% 40-49, less than 1% 50-99. **Special facilities:** 3 galleries; state of the art 3-D modelling and industrial design facilities.

Freshman class profile. 1,079 applied, 796 admitted, 588 enrolled.

End year in good standing:	89%	**Out-of-state:**	23%
Return as sophomores:	89%	**International:**	18%

Basis for selection. Strength of specific portfolio for one major, academic record, standardized test scores. Interviews recommended for local applicants.

High school preparation. Art classes recommended.

2006-2007 Annual costs. Tuition/fees: $26,370. Books/supplies: $2,000.

2005-2006 Financial aid. All financial aid based on need. 28% of total undergraduate aid awarded as scholarships/grants, 72% as loans/jobs. **Additional information:** Students may apply for scholarships after they enroll while progressing through the program.

Application procedures. Admission: Priority date 3/1; no deadline. $45 fee, may be waived for applicants with need. Admission notification on a rolling basis beginning on or about 1/1. Application 4 to 6 months before fall term recommended. **Financial aid:** Priority date 3/1; no closing date. FAFSA required. Applicants notified on a rolling basis starting 5/15; must reply within 4 week(s) of notification.

Academics. Special study options: Cross-registration, independent study, internships, study abroad. **Credit/placement by examination:** CLEP, IB, institutional tests. **Support services:** Tutoring, writing center.

Majors. Architecture: Environmental design. **Communications:** Advertising. **Communications technology:** Animation/special effects, graphics. **Visual/performing arts:** Cinematography, commercial photography, commercial/advertising art, graphic design, illustration, industrial design, interior design, painting, photography, sculpture, studio arts.

Computing on campus. 250 workstations in library, computer center. Online library, wireless network available.

Student life. Freshman orientation: Mandatory. 3-day program including introduction to a mentor and testing. **Policies:** Freshmen permitted cars on campus. **Activities:** Literary magazine, student government, Chroma Contraste, Christian Fellowship; international student organization, Out Network.

Student services. Alcohol/substance abuse counseling, career counseling, student employment services, financial aid counseling, personal counseling, placement for graduates. **Physically disabled:** Services for hearing impaired.

Contact. E-mail: admissions@artcenter.edu
Phone: (626) 396-2373 Fax: (626) 795-0578
Kit Baron, Vice President, Admissions, Art Center College of Design, 1700 Lida Street, Pasadena, CA 91103

Art Institute of California: Orange County

Santa Ana, California
www.aicaoc.artinstitutes.edu **CB code: 3831**

- For-profit 3-year culinary school and visual arts college
- Commuter campus in very large city
- 1,835 degree-seeking undergraduates: 12% part-time, 37% women, 3% African American, 10% Asian American, 16% Hispanic American, 1% Native American
- 45% of applicants admitted
- Application essay, interview required

General. Accredited by ACICS. **Degrees:** 133 bachelor's, 99 associate awarded. **Location:** 40 miles from Los Angeles, 90 miles from San Diego. **Calendar:** Quarter, extensive summer session. **Full-time faculty:** 53 total. **Part-time faculty:** 121 total. **Class size:** 25% < 20, 75% 20-39. **Special facilities:** 4 professional skills kitchens, 11 computer labs, library, interior design resource center, industrial design workshop, student dining lab.

Freshman class profile. 658 applied, 294 admitted, 277 enrolled.

Basis for selection. High school record and general appropriateness of educational background to specific program applied for most important. Portfolio, interview also important. Standardized test scores considered if submitted.

2005-2006 Annual costs. Books/supplies: $1,100. Personal expenses: $2,280.

Financial aid. Non-need-based: Scholarships awarded for academics, art, minority status.

Application procedures. Admission: No deadline. $50 fee. Application may be submitted online. Admission notification on a rolling basis. **Financial aid:** Priority date 3/2; no closing date. FAFSA required. Applicants notified on a rolling basis starting 2/1; must reply within 2 week(s) of notification.

Academics. Special study options: Cooperative education, distance learning, internships. Online courses. **Credit/placement by examination:** CLEP, IB, institutional tests. 3 credit hours maximum toward associate degree, 3 toward bachelor's. **Support services:** Learning center, pre-admission summer program, reduced course load, study skills assistance, tutoring.

Majors. Communications: Digital media. **Communications technology:** Animation/special effects. **Computer sciences:** Computer graphics, web page design. **Personal/culinary services:** Culinary arts, restaurant/catering. **Visual/performing arts:** Commercial/advertising art, graphic design, industrial design, interior design.

Computing on campus. 312 workstations in library, computer center, student center. Online course registration, online library, helpline, repair service, wireless network available.

Student life. Freshman orientation: Mandatory. **Policies:** Freshmen permitted cars on campus. **Housing:** Special housing for disabled, apartments available. School-sponsored housing available. **Activities:** Film society, student newspaper.

Student services. Career counseling, student employment services, financial aid counseling, personal counseling, placement for graduates, veterans' counselor. **Physically disabled:** Services for visually, speech, hearing impaired.

Contact. E-mail: aicaocadm@aii.edu
Phone: (888) 549-3055 Toll-free number: (888) 549-3055
Fax: (714) 556-1923
Vincent David, Director of Admissions, Art Institute of California: Orange County, 3601 West Sunflower Avenue, Santa Ana, CA 92704-9888

Art Institute of California: San Diego

San Diego, California
www.aicasd.artinstitutes.edu **CB code: 3036**

- For-profit 4-year visual arts college
- Residential campus in very large city
- 1,912 degree-seeking undergraduates
- Application essay, interview required

General. Accredited by ACCSCT. **Degrees:** 217 bachelor's, 93 associate awarded. **Calendar:** Quarter. **Full-time faculty:** 113 total; 100% have terminal degrees, 46% women. **Special facilities:** Dining lab run by culinary students.

Basis for selection. High school record and general appropriateness of educational background to specific program applied for most important. Portfolio, interview, standardized test scores also important. **Learning Disabled:** Students requiring assistance should notify Assistant Director of Admissions.

2005-2006 Annual costs. Tuition/fees: $18,864.

Application procedures. Admission: No deadline. $50 fee. Application may be submitted online. Admission notification on a rolling basis.

Academics. Special study options: Accelerated study, double major, internships. **Credit/placement by examination:** AP, CLEP. **Support services:** Study skills assistance, tutoring.

Majors. Communications: Advertising. **Computer sciences:** Computer graphics, web page design, webmaster. **Visual/performing arts:** Commercial/advertising art, graphic design, interior design, multimedia.

Computing on campus. 300 workstations in computer center.

Student life. Freshman orientation: Available. Preregistration for classes offered. **Policies:** Freshmen permitted cars on campus. **Housing:** Single-sex dorms available. **Activities:** Student government.

Student services. Alcohol/substance abuse counseling, career counseling, services for economically disadvantaged, student employment services, financial aid counseling, personal counseling. **Physically disabled:** Services for visually, speech, hearing impaired. **Learning disabled:** Comprehensive services available.

Contact. E-mail: aicaadmin@aii.edu
Phone: (800) 591-2422 Toll-free number: (800) 591-2422
Jo-Ann White, Director of Admissions, Art Institute of California: San Diego, 7650 Mission Valley Road, San Diego, CA 92108-4423

Art Institute of California: San Francisco

San Francisco, California
www.aicasf.aii.edu **CB code: 4421**

- For-profit 4-year visual arts college
- Commuter campus in very large city
- 1,570 degree-seeking undergraduates
- Application essay required

General. Founded in 1939. Accredited by ACICS. **Degrees:** 67 bachelor's, 14 associate awarded. **Location:** Downtown. **Calendar:** Quarter, extensive summer session. **Full-time faculty:** 21 total. **Part-time faculty:** 85 total. **Special facilities:** Computer-aided fashion design and illustration systems, 2D and 3D animation labs, fashion labs, design library.

Basis for selection. High school record and general appropriateness of educational background to specific program applied for most important. Portfolio, interview, standardized test scores also important. Interview recommended. Portfolios recommended.

High school preparation. Recommended units include English 1, mathematics 1, social studies 1 and history 1. One art class recommended.

2005-2006 Annual costs. Tuition/fees: $17,685. Starter kits additional $600 to $675 for all programs. Books/supplies: $1,125.

2005-2006 Financial aid. **Need-based:** 44% of total undergraduate aid awarded as scholarships/grants, 56% as loans/jobs.

Application procedures. **Admission:** No deadline. $50 fee. Application may be submitted online. Admission notification on a rolling basis. **Financial aid:** No deadline. FAFSA required. Applicants notified on a rolling basis.

Academics. **Special study options:** Distance learning, internships. **Credit/placement by examination:** AP, CLEP, IB. **Support services:** Reduced course load, remedial instruction, study skills assistance, tutoring.

Majors. **Business:** Fashion. **Communications technology:** Animation/special effects. **Computer sciences:** Computer graphics, web page design. **Visual/performing arts:** Commercial/advertising art, fashion design, graphic design, interior design.

Student life. **Freshman orientation:** Mandatory. **Housing:** Coed dorms, apartments available. **Activities:** Student government, student newspaper, animation club, society of web architects and programmers, fashion salon, graphic design club, game art and design club, anime club, photography club, eco club, student SIGGRAPH chapter, interior design club.

Student services. Career counseling, student employment services, financial aid counseling, personal counseling, placement for graduates. **Physically disabled:** Services for hearing impaired.

Contact. E-mail: aisfadm@aii.edu
Phone: (415) 865-0198 Toll-free number: (888) 493-3261
Fax: (415) 863-6344
Daniel Cardenas, Director of Admissions, Art Institute of California: San Francisco, 1170 Market Street, San Francisco, CA 94102

Azusa Pacific University

Azusa, California **CB member**
www.apu.edu **CB code: 4596**

- Private 4-year university affiliated with interdenominational tradition
- Residential campus in small city
- 4,602 degree-seeking undergraduates: 14% part-time, 64% women, 3% African American, 6% Asian American, 12% Hispanic American, 2% international
- 3,682 degree-seeking graduate students
- 69% of applicants admitted
- SAT or ACT, application essay required
- 64% graduate within 6 years

General. Founded in 1899. Regionally accredited. Living-learning community stressing spiritual development. **Degrees:** 1,103 bachelor's awarded; master's, doctoral, first professional offered. **ROTC:** Army. **Location:** 30 miles from Los Angeles. **Calendar:** Semester, limited summer session. **Full-time faculty:** 333 total; 70% have terminal degrees, 19% minority, 44% women. **Part-time faculty:** 585 total. **Class size:** 64% < 20, 34% 20-39, 1% 40-49, 1% 50-99, less than 1% >100.

Freshman class profile. 3,127 applied, 2,151 admitted, 881 enrolled.

Mid 50% test scores		**Rank in top quarter:**	74%
SAT verbal:	510-610	**Rank in top tenth:**	41%
SAT math:	500-610	**Return as sophomores:**	82%
ACT:	21-27	**Out-of-state:**	28%
GPA 3.50 or higher:	65%	**Live on campus:**	93%
GPA 3.0-3.49:	26%	**International:**	1%
GPA 2.0-2.99:	8%		

Basis for selection. GPA, test scores, references, statement of agreement, essay important. Auditions required for music applicants. Interviews recommended for borderline applicants. **Homeschooled:** SAT or ACT and transcript from organization required.

High school preparation. College-preparatory program recommended. Recommended units include English 4, mathematics 3, social studies 1, history 2, science 2 and foreign language 3.

2005-2006 Annual costs. Tuition/fees: $22,210. Room/board: $6,980. Books/supplies: $1,242. Personal expenses: $1,980.

2004-2005 Financial aid. **Need-based:** 897 full-time freshmen applied for aid; 567 were judged to have need; 567 of these received aid. Average need met was 70.4%. Average scholarship/grant was $9,499; average loan $3,706. 58% of total undergraduate aid awarded as scholarships/grants, 42% as loans/jobs. **Non-need-based:** Awarded to 1,939 full-time undergraduates, including 562 freshmen. Scholarships awarded for academics, athletics, leadership, minority status, music/drama, religious affiliation, ROTC.

Application procedures. **Admission:** Closing date 2/15 (postmark date). $45 fee, may be waived for applicants with need. Application may be submitted online. Admission notification on a rolling basis. Students with 3.0 high school GPA or higher and 1000 SAT score or higher can apply at completion of junior year and/or before January 1 for admission consideration. **Financial aid:** Closing date 3/2. FAFSA, institutional form required. Applicants notified on a rolling basis starting 3/1; must reply within 3 week(s) of notification.

Academics. More than 20 online masters and credential programs offered for library media teaching. All other online programs are part of individual face to face programs with exception of one course offered completely online. **Special study options:** Accelerated study, cooperative education, distance learning, double major, ESL, exchange student, honors, independent study, internships, study abroad, teacher certification program, urban semester, Washington semester. **Credit/placement by examination:** AP, CLEP, IB, institutional tests. 15 credit hours maximum toward bachelor's degree. Essays required for Analysis and Interpretation of Literature and Freshman College Composition. **Support services:** Learning center, reduced course load, remedial instruction, study skills assistance, tutoring, writing center.

Majors. **Biology:** General, biochemistry. **Business:** General, accounting, business admin, finance, management information systems, marketing. **Communications:** General, broadcast journalism, journalism. **Computer sciences:** General, information systems, web page design. **Education:** General, art, business, elementary, middle, multi-level teacher, physical, secondary. **English:** English lit. **Foreign languages:** Spanish. **Health:** Nurse practitioner, nursing (RN), predentistry, premedicine. **History:** General. **Liberal arts:** Arts/sciences. **Math:** General. **Philosophy/religion:** Philosophy, religion. **Physical sciences:** General, chemistry, physics. **Psychology:** General. **Public administration:** Social work. **Social sciences:** General, international relations, political science, sociology. **Theology:** Bible, religious ed, sacred music, theology. **Visual/performing arts:** Art, dramatic, music performance, music theory/composition, studio arts.

Most popular majors. Business/marketing 22%, communications/journalism 9%, health sciences 6%, liberal arts 27%, philosophy/religious studies 7%, social sciences 6%.

Computing on campus. 268 workstations in library, computer center, student center. Dormitories wired for high-speed internet access and linked to campus network. Commuter students can connect to campus network. Online course registration, helpline, repair service, wireless network available.

Student life. **Freshman orientation:** Mandatory. Preregistration for classes offered. Class taken during first semester. **Policies:** Students will refrain from activities which may be spiritually or morally destructive. Religious observance required. Freshmen permitted cars on campus. **Housing:** Coed dorms, single-sex dorms, apartments available. $250 deposit, deadline 5/1. **Activities:** Bands, choral groups, drama, music ensembles, musical theater, opera, radio station, student government, student newspaper, symphony orchestra, TV station, International students association, minority student association, campus pastor, ministry and services.

Athletics. NAIA. **Intercollegiate:** Baseball M, basketball, cross-country, football (tackle) M, soccer, softball W, tennis M, track and field, volleyball

W. **Intramural:** Basketball, football (tackle) M, skiing, volleyball. **Team name:** Cougars.

Student services. Campus ministries, career counseling, student employment services, financial aid counseling, health services, minority student services, personal counseling, placement for graduates, veterans' counselor. **Physically disabled:** Services for visually, speech, hearing impaired.

Contact. E-mail: admissions@apu.edu
Phone: (626) 812-3016 Toll-free number: (800) 825-5278
Fax: (626) 812-3096
Deana Porterfield, Dean of Undergraduate Admissions, Azusa Pacific University, 901 East Alosta Avenue, Azusa, CA 91702-7000

Bethany University

Scotts Valley, California
www.bethany.edu **CB code: 4021**

- Private 4-year Bible and liberal arts college affiliated with Assemblies of God
- Residential campus in small town
- 461 degree-seeking undergraduates: 17% part-time, 57% women
- 95 degree-seeking graduate students
- 56% of applicants admitted
- SAT or ACT (ACT writing optional), application essay required

General. Founded in 1919. Regionally accredited. Comprehensive Christian college dedicated to training people for ministry. **Degrees:** 96 bachelor's, 1 associate awarded; master's offered. **Location:** 15 miles from San Jose, 75 miles from San Francisco. **Calendar:** Semester, limited summer session. **Full-time faculty:** 21 total. **Part-time faculty:** 31 total. **Class size:** 77% < 20, 18% 20-39, 2% 40-49, 4% 50-99. **Special facilities:** Early childhood learning center.

Freshman class profile. 245 applied, 136 admitted, 82 enrolled.

Mid 50% test scores		ACT:	15-20
SAT verbal:	400-570	Out-of-state:	23%
SAT math:	400-520	Live on campus:	73%

Basis for selection. Recommendations and religious affiliation/commitment very important. Interviews recommended. Auditions recommended for music applicants.

2006-2007 Annual costs. Tuition/fees: $16,330. Room/board: $6,750. Books/supplies: $1,079. Personal expenses: $2,136.

2005-2006 Financial aid. Need-based: 43% of total undergraduate aid awarded as scholarships/grants, 57% as loans/jobs. **Non-need-based:** Scholarships awarded for academics, alumni affiliation, athletics, leadership, minority status, music/drama, religious affiliation.

Application procedures. Admission: Closing date 7/31 (postmark date). $35 fee. Application may be submitted online. Admission notification on a rolling basis. **Financial aid:** Priority date 3/2; no closing date. FAFSA, institutional form required. Applicants notified on a rolling basis starting 4/15; must reply within 2 week(s) of notification.

Academics. Special study options: Combined bachelor's/graduate degree, double major, ESL, external degree, independent study, internships, teacher certification program. **Credit/placement by examination:** CLEP. 18 credit hours maximum toward associate degree, 18 toward bachelor's. **Support services:** Learning center, reduced course load, remedial instruction, study skills assistance, tutoring.

Majors. Business: General. **Education:** Early childhood. **Health:** Substance abuse counseling. **Liberal arts:** Arts/sciences. **Psychology:** General. **Social sciences:** General. **Theology:** Missionary, theology. **Visual/performing arts:** Dramatic.

Computing on campus. 20 workstations in library, computer center, student center. Dormitories wired for high-speed internet access and linked to campus network. Commuter students can connect to campus network. Online course registration, online library available.

Student life. Freshman orientation: Available, $65 fee. 5-day program before beginning of classes. **Policies:** Student ministry opportunities. Religious observance required. Freshmen permitted cars on campus. **Housing:** Guaranteed on-campus for freshmen. Single-sex dorms, apartments available. $100 deposit. **Activities:** Concert band, choral groups, drama, music ensembles, musical theater, radio station, student government, student newspaper, symphony orchestra, international students association, many service organizations.

Athletics. NAIA. **Intercollegiate:** Basketball M, cheerleading, golf M, softball W, volleyball. **Intramural:** Basketball, golf M, softball, volleyball. **Team name:** Bruins.

Student services. Alcohol/substance abuse counseling, campus ministries, career counseling, student employment services, financial aid counseling, on-campus daycare, personal counseling, placement for graduates, veterans' counselor.

Contact. E-mail: admissions@fc.bethany.edu
Phone: (831) 438-3800 ext. 2011 Toll-free number: (800) 843-9410
Fax: (831) 461-1621
Charles Riley, Director of Admissions, Bethany University, 800 Bethany Drive, Scotts Valley, CA 95066-2898

Bethesda Christian University

Anaheim, California
www.bcu.edu **CB code: 3895**

- Private 4-year university and Bible college affiliated with Christian Church
- Large city
- 171 degree-seeking undergraduates
- Application essay, interview required

General. Accredited by ABHE. **Degrees:** 46 bachelor's awarded; master's, first professional offered. **Location:** 30 miles from Los Angeles. **Calendar:** Semester, limited summer session. **Full-time faculty:** 8 total. **Part-time faculty:** 40 total. **Class size:** 33% < 20, 64% 20-39, 3% 40-49. **Special facilities:** Extension campus in Seoul, South Korea.

Freshman class profile. 37 applied, 34 admitted, 29 enrolled.

Basis for selection. Open admission. Admissions decision based on religious affiliation, recommendations, essay and interview. Secondary school record is also important. Auditions required for music majors. Christian experience essay required.

2006-2007 Annual costs. Tuition/fees: $6,420. Books/supplies: $1,000. Personal expenses: $500.

2004-2005 Financial aid. All financial aid based on need. 52% of total undergraduate aid awarded as scholarships/grants, 48% as loans/jobs.

Application procedures. Admission: No deadline. $35 fee ($60 out-of-state). Admission notification on a rolling basis. **Financial aid:** Closing date 6/30. FAFSA, institutional form required. Applicants notified on a rolling basis starting 6/30.

Academics. Special study options: Combined bachelor's/graduate degree, double major, dual enrollment of high school students, ESL, independent study, liberal arts/career combination. **Credit/placement by examination:** CLEP, IB, institutional tests. **Support services:** Reduced course load.

Majors. Computer sciences: Information technology. **Education:** Early childhood. **Foreign languages:** Translation. **Philosophy/religion:** Religion. **Theology:** Bible, missionary, religious ed, sacred music, theology. **Visual/performing arts:** Conducting, design, fashion design, metal/jewelry, music management, music performance, music theory/composition, piano/organ, stringed instruments, voice/opera.

Computing on campus. 50 workstations in dormitories, library, computer center. Dormitories wired for high-speed internet access.

Student life. Freshman orientation: Mandatory. Preregistration for classes offered. **Policies:** Religious observance required. Freshmen permitted cars on campus. **Activities:** Student government.

Student services. Campus ministries, financial aid counseling, personal counseling.

Contact. E-mail: admission@bcu.edu
Phone: (714) 517-1945 Fax: (714) 517-1948
Samuel Jung, Director of Admissions, Bethesda Christian University, 730 North Euclid Street, Anaheim, CA 92801

Biola University

La Mirada, California **CB member**
www.biola.edu **CB code: 4017**

- Private 4-year university and Bible college affiliated with interdenominational tradition
- Residential campus in large town

- 3,240 degree-seeking undergraduates: 3% part-time, 61% women
- 2,209 graduate students
- 82% of applicants admitted
- SAT or ACT (ACT writing recommended), application essay, interview required
- 70% graduate within 6 years

General. Founded in 1908. Regionally accredited. Biblically centered Christian institution. **Degrees:** 772 bachelor's awarded; master's, doctoral, first professional offered. **ROTC:** Army, Air Force. **Location:** 22 miles from downtown Los Angeles. **Calendar:** 4-1-4, extensive summer session. **Full-time faculty:** 191 total; 78% have terminal degrees, 13% minority, 28% women. **Part-time faculty:** 204 total. **Special facilities:** Concert hall with pipe organ, electron microscope, recording studio, film studio, MIDI lab for music composition, electronic piano lab.

Freshman class profile. 2,077 applied, 1,709 admitted, 781 enrolled.

Mid 50% test scores		**GPA 2.0-2.99:**	10%
SAT verbal:	510-630	**Rank in top quarter:**	69%
SAT math:	500-620	**Rank in top tenth:**	36%
ACT:	22-27	**Return as sophomores:**	83%
GPA 3.50 or higher:	59%	**Out-of-state:**	25%
GPA 3.0-3.49:	31%		

Basis for selection. Christian commitment most important; academic record, personal references, test scores next in importance. School, community, church activities helpful. Out-of-state and ethnic students encouraged to apply. Auditions recommended for music applicants. Portfolios recommended for art applicants. **Homeschooled:** Applicants advised to go through an accreditation agency or take GED.

High school preparation. 15 units recommended. Recommended units include English 4, mathematics 3, social studies 2, science 2 and foreign language 4. One algebra and 1 chemistry required of nursing applicants. 2 mathematics, 1 physics, 1 chemistry required of biology applicants. Some deficiencies may be satisfied during freshman year.

2006-2007 Annual costs. Tuition/fees (projected): $22,602. Room/board: $7,114. Books/supplies: $1,242. Personal expenses: $1,980.

2004-2005 Financial aid. **Need-based:** 565 full-time freshmen applied for aid; 469 were judged to have need; 469 of these received aid. Average need met was 67%. Average scholarship/grant was $9,134; average loan $2,479. 55% of total undergraduate aid awarded as scholarships/grants, 45% as loans/jobs. **Non-need-based:** Awarded to 1,827 full-time undergraduates, including 507 freshmen. Scholarships awarded for academics, alumni affiliation, art, athletics, leadership, minority status, music/drama, ROTC.

Application procedures. **Admission:** Closing date 3/1 (receipt date). $45 fee, may be waived for applicants with need. Application may be submitted online. Admission notification on a rolling basis beginning on or about 4/1. Must reply by 5/1. **Financial aid:** Priority date 1/1, closing date 3/1. FAFSA required. Applicants notified on a rolling basis starting 3/1.

Academics. **Special study options:** Double major, ESL, exchange student, honors, internships, study abroad, Washington semester. 3-2 program with Los Angeles College of Chiropractic. 3-2 engineering program with University of Southern California. **Credit/placement by examination:** AP, CLEP, IB, SAT, ACT. Maximum of 32 credits from CLEP, AP, and IB can be counted toward degree. **Support services:** Reduced course load, remedial instruction, study skills assistance, tutoring, writing center.

Honors college/program. Admission to Torrey Honors Institute by invitation, after application to the university. Students trained in rigorous discussion group format, learning high-level writing and critical thinking skills.

Majors. **Biology:** General, biochemistry. **Business:** Accounting, business admin, international, management information systems, marketing. **Communications:** General, broadcast journalism. **Computer sciences:** Computer science. **Education:** General, elementary, music, physical, secondary. **Engineering:** General. **Foreign languages:** Spanish. **Health:** Communication disorders, nursing (RN). **History:** General. **Interdisciplinary:** Intercultural. **Legal studies:** Prelaw. **Liberal arts:** Arts/sciences. **Math:** General. **Philosophy/religion:** Philosophy, religion. **Psychology:** General. **Social sciences:** General, anthropology, sociology. **Theology:** Bible, religious ed, theology. **Visual/performing arts:** Cinematography, commercial/advertising art, dramatic, drawing, music performance, music theory/composition, painting, sculpture, studio arts.

Most popular majors. Business/marketing 12%, communications/journalism 7%, education 10%, health sciences 6%, liberal arts 11%, philosophy/religious studies 12%, physical sciences 15%, psychology 12%.

Computing on campus. 225 workstations in library, computer center. Dormitories wired for high-speed internet access and linked to campus network. Commuter students can connect to campus network. Online course registration, online library, helpline, repair service, student web hosting, wireless network available.

Student life. **Freshman orientation:** Available, $65 fee. Week-long, held week before term begins. Students assigned to core group led by Biola student. **Policies:** All students encouraged to have Christian service assignment. Students adhere to code of conduct. Freshmen and sophomores under 21 required to live on campus unless living with relatives. Religious observance required. Freshmen permitted cars on campus. **Housing:** Single-sex dorms, apartments available. $100 deposit, deadline 5/1. Flex-style dorms with building split into floors/wings designated all male or all female available. **Activities:** Bands, choral groups, dance, drama, film society, literary magazine, music ensembles, musical theater, opera, radio station, student government, student newspaper, symphony orchestra, TV station, Student Missionary Union, Korean Student Association, Marharlika (Filipino club), International Student Association, Evangelism Team, Alpha Omega Service, For All Believers, Society of Christian Philosophy, Socially Together and Naturally Diverse.

Athletics. NAIA. **Intercollegiate:** Baseball M, basketball, cross-country, soccer, softball W, swimming, tennis W, track and field, volleyball W. **Intramural:** Basketball, football (non-tackle), soccer, softball, volleyball. **Team name:** Eagles.

Student services. Adult student services, campus ministries, career counseling, student employment services, financial aid counseling, health services, personal counseling, placement for graduates, veterans' counselor. **Physically disabled:** Services for speech, hearing impaired.

Contact. E-mail: admissions@biola.edu
Phone: (562) 903-4752 Toll-free number: (800) 652-4652
Fax: (562) 903-4709
Greg Vaughan, Director of Enrollment Management, Biola University, 13800 Biola Avenue, La Mirada, CA 90639-0001

Brooks Institute of Photography

Santa Barbara, California
www.brooks.edu **CB code: 4228**

- For-profit 4-year visual arts college
- Commuter campus in small city
- 2,600 degree-seeking undergraduates
- 95% of applicants admitted
- Application essay, interview required

General. Founded in 1945. Accredited by ACICS. Upper-division students can apply to participate in documentary courses in foreign countries; upper-division professional photography students can apply for inclusion in annual undersea photography class. **Degrees:** 280 bachelor's, 16 associate awarded; master's offered. **Location:** 90 miles from Los Angeles. **Calendar:** Trimester. 6 8-week sessions. Extensive summer session. **Full-time faculty:** 50 total. **Part-time faculty:** 75 total. **Special facilities:** 123,000 square feet of studio space for 40 set-ups, 90 cubicles for black and white enlarging, digital labs in both Santa Barbara and Ventura, design lab for visual communication program.

Freshman class profile. 1,422 applied, 1,344 admitted, 402 enrolled.

Basis for selection. School achievement record most important. Photographic experience not required for entrance. Advanced standing may be offered to those with 4X5 view camera experience. Evaluation consists of written examination portfolio and review. TOEFL required of students whose first language is not English. Different standards exist based on paper vs. computer scores and for undergraduate and graduate applicants. At time of matriculation, institution will assess English and math proficiencies for students who have not demonstrated proficiency in both at the college level or by receiving minimum standard scores in national tests. Interviews can be conducted via telephone. Interview and photography portfolio required for advanced standing in core courses. **Homeschooled:** GED required if home schooling not recognized by state. **Learning Disabled:** Protocol for students seeking accommodation is mailed to accepted applicants with provisional acceptance letter.

High school preparation. Recommended units include English 4, mathematics 2, social studies 1, science 1 and foreign language 2. College preparatory program recommended.

2005-2006 Annual costs. Cost of 6 continuously attended 2-month sessions beginning in fall: $23,760 tuition, $600 fees.

Application procedures. Admission: No deadline. $100 fee. Application may be submitted online. Admission notification on a rolling basis. New undergraduate classes begin in January, March, April, May, July, September, November. New graduate classes begin in January, April, September. Students encouraged to apply at least 6 months in advance. **Financial aid:** Priority date 3/2; no closing date. Institutional form required. Applicants notified on a rolling basis starting 5/1.

Academics. Special study options: Accelerated study, distance learning, double major, independent study, internships. **Credit/placement by examination:** CLEP, institutional tests. 54 credit hours maximum toward bachelor's degree. **Support services:** Tutoring.

Majors. Communications technology: Photo/film/video. **Visual/performing arts:** Cinematography, commercial photography, photography.

Computing on campus. 15 workstations in library, computer center. Online library, helpline, wireless network available.

Student life. Freshman orientation: Mandatory. Immediately prior to matriculation; normally 2-4 days of activities. **Policies:** Car necessary for travel between campuses and to assignment locations. Freshmen permitted cars on campus. **Activities:** Student government.

Student services. Career counseling, student employment services, financial aid counseling, personal counseling, placement for graduates.

Contact. E-mail: admissions@brooks.edu
Phone: (888) 304-3456 Toll-free number: (888) 304-3456
Fax: (805) 565-1386
Reza Garajedaghi, Director of Admissions, Brooks Institute of Photography, 801 Alston Road, Santa Barbara, CA 93108

Brooks Institute of Photography: Ventura
Ventura, California

- For-profit 4-year art college
- Small city

General. Accredited by ACICS. **Calendar:** Trimester.

Contact. Phone: (805) 585-8000
801 Alston Road, Ventura, CA 93108

California Baptist University
Riverside, California — **CB member**
www.calbaptist.edu — **CB code: 4094**

- Private 4-year university and liberal arts college affiliated with Southern Baptist Convention
- Commuter campus in large city
- 2,392 degree-seeking undergraduates: 17% part-time, 65% women, 9% African American, 2% Asian American, 17% Hispanic American, 1% Native American, 1% international
- 690 degree-seeking graduate students
- 71% of applicants admitted
- SAT or ACT (ACT writing optional), application essay required
- 68% graduate within 6 years

General. Founded in 1950. Regionally accredited. **Degrees:** 508 bachelor's awarded; master's offered. **ROTC:** Army, Air Force. **Location:** 60 miles from Los Angeles. **Calendar:** Semester. 4-4-1 semester system. Extensive summer session. **Full-time faculty:** 96 total; 64% have terminal degrees, 16% minority, 41% women. **Part-time faculty:** 130 total; 18% have terminal degrees, 25% minority, 49% women. **Class size:** 50% < 20, 40% 20-39, 5% 40-49, 4% 50-99, 1% >100. **Special facilities:** Hymnology collection, performance and recording studios, Nie Wieder! collection.

Freshman class profile. 1,072 applied, 764 admitted, 439 enrolled.

Mid 50% test scores		**Rank in top quarter:**	42%
SAT verbal:	450-560	**Rank in top tenth:**	12%
SAT math:	450-550	**End year in good standing:**	85%
ACT:	18-23	**Return as sophomores:**	86%
GPA 3.50 or higher:	49%	**Out-of-state:**	9%
GPA 3.0-3.49:	32%	**Live on campus:**	75%
GPA 2.0-2.99:	19%	**International:**	3%

Basis for selection. School achievement record, test scores, essays, recommendations very important. Interviews recommended. Auditions required for music, drama applicants. **Homeschooled:** Transcript of courses and grades required.

High school preparation. College-preparatory program recommended. 15 units required; 19 recommended. Required and recommended units include English 4, mathematics 3-4, social studies 2, history 2, science 2-3 (laboratory 1-2), foreign language 2-3 and academic electives 3.

2005-2006 Annual costs. Tuition/fees: $17,470. Room/board: $6,810. Books/supplies: $1,120. Personal expenses: $1,616.

2004-2005 Financial aid. Need-based: 311 full-time freshmen applied for aid; 298 were judged to have need; 298 of these received aid. Average need met was 70%. Average scholarship/grant was $7,700; average loan $2,430. 53% of total undergraduate aid awarded as scholarships/grants, 47% as loans/jobs. **Non-need-based:** Awarded to 2,083 full-time undergraduates, including 329 freshmen. Scholarships awarded for academics, art, athletics, leadership, music/drama, religious affiliation, ROTC.

Application procedures. Admission: Priority date 2/1; no deadline. $45 fee, may be waived for applicants with need. Application may be submitted online. Admission notification on a rolling basis beginning on or about 11/19. **Financial aid:** Priority date 3/2; no closing date. FAFSA required. Applicants notified on a rolling basis starting 3/2; must reply by 5/1 or within 3 week(s) of notification.

Academics. Special study options: Accelerated study, distance learning, double major, dual enrollment of high school students, ESL, exchange student, honors, internships, liberal arts/career combination, study abroad, teacher certification program, Washington semester, weekend college. **Credit/placement by examination:** AP, CLEP, IB, institutional tests. 30 credit hours maximum toward bachelor's degree. Portfolio course available to assist students in documenting work that may be counted for credit by prior learning experiences. **Support services:** Learning center, reduced course load, remedial instruction, study skills assistance, tutoring, writing center.

Majors. Biology: General. **Business:** Business admin, organizational behavior. **Communications:** Digital media, journalism. **Education:** General, physical. **English:** English lit. **History:** General. **Interdisciplinary:** Behavioral sciences, intercultural. **Liberal arts:** Arts/sciences. **Math:** General. **Parks/recreation:** Exercise sciences. **Philosophy/religion:** Christian, philosophy. **Protective services:** Law enforcement admin. **Psychology:** General. **Social sciences:** Political science, sociology. **Theology:** Bible, missionary. **Visual/performing arts:** General, art, graphic design, theater arts management.

Most popular majors. Business/marketing 15%, liberal arts 31%, parks/recreation 6%, psychology 16%.

Computing on campus. 179 workstations in library, computer center. Dormitories wired for high-speed internet access and linked to campus network. Commuter students can connect to campus network. Online course registration, online library, helpline available.

Student life. Freshman orientation: Mandatory, $210 fee. Preregistration for classes offered. New student orientation prior to beginning of each semester and semester-long University Success Course required of first-semester freshmen. **Policies:** Students receiving institutional scholarships required to live in student housing. Religious observance required. Freshmen permitted cars on campus. **Housing:** Guaranteed on-campus for all undergraduates. Single-sex dorms, apartments, cooperative housing available. $250 fully refundable deposit, deadline 8/1. **Activities:** Bands, choral groups, drama, music ensembles, musical theater, student government, student newspaper, symphony orchestra, Christian outreach ministries and service clubs including Young Republicans, Young Democrats, Fellowship of Christian Athletes, Black Student Union, Big Brother, Big Sister, active compassion, elderly ministry, homeless ministry.

Athletics. NAIA. **Intercollegiate:** Baseball M, basketball, diving, golf W, soccer, softball W, swimming, tennis W, volleyball, water polo. **Intramural:** Basketball, bowling, football (non-tackle), golf, softball, table tennis, tennis, volleyball. **Team name:** Lancers.

Student services. Adult student services, campus ministries, career counseling, student employment services, financial aid counseling, personal counseling, placement for graduates, veterans' counselor.

Contact. E-mail: admissions@calbaptist.edu
Phone: (951) 343-4212 Toll-free number: (877) 228-8866
Fax: (951) 343-4525
Allen Johnson, Director, Undergraduate Admissions, California Baptist University, 8432 Magnolia Avenue, Riverside, CA 92504-3297

California College of the Arts
San Francisco, California — **CB member**
www.cca.edu — **CB code: 4031**

- Private 4-year visual arts college
- Commuter campus in very large city

- 1,312 degree-seeking undergraduates: 6% part-time, 59% women, 2% African American, 12% Asian American, 9% Hispanic American, 1% Native American, 7% international
- 304 degree-seeking graduate students
- 78% of applicants admitted
- Application essay, interview required
- 98% graduate within 6 years

General. Founded in 1907. Regionally accredited. 2 campuses located in San Francisco and Oakland. **Degrees:** 258 bachelor's awarded; master's offered. **Location:** 3 miles from downtown. **Calendar:** Semester, limited summer session. **Full-time faculty:** 42 total; 81% have terminal degrees, 24% minority, 38% women. **Part-time faculty:** 328 total; 62% have terminal degrees, 15% minority, 47% women. **Class size:** 85% < 20, 15% 20-39. **Special facilities:** 2 professional galleries, student galleries.

Freshman class profile. 785 applied, 616 admitted, 181 enrolled.

Mid 50% test scores			
SAT verbal:	480-620	Rank in top quarter:	36%
SAT math:	490-600	Rank in top tenth:	9%
ACT:	18-24	Return as sophomores:	79%
GPA 3.50 or higher:	18%	Out-of-state:	40%
GPA 3.0-3.49:	48%	Live on campus:	68%
GPA 2.0-2.99:	34%	International:	9%

Basis for selection. High school achievement (including art/design activities and interests), GPA, personal essay/statement of purpose, interview, and portfolio very important. SAT or ACT recommended. Portfolio required. **Homeschooled:** Transcript of courses and grades required.

2005-2006 Annual costs. Tuition/fees: $26,100. Room only: $8,430. Books/supplies: $1,300. Personal expenses: $1,880.

2005-2006 Financial aid. Need-based: 134 full-time freshmen applied for aid; 116 were judged to have need; 116 of these received aid. Average need met was 61%. Average scholarship/grant was $12,663; average loan $2,798. 71% of total undergraduate aid awarded as scholarships/grants, 29% as loans/jobs. **Non-need-based:** Awarded to 502 full-time undergraduates, including 98 freshmen. Scholarships awarded for academics, art, minority status. **Additional information:** Application deadline for merit scholarships February 15.

Application procedures. Admission: Priority date 2/1; no deadline. $50 fee, may be waived for applicants with need. Application may be submitted online. Admission notification on a rolling basis. Must reply by May 1 or within 2 week(s) if notified thereafter. **Financial aid:** Priority date 3/1; no closing date. FAFSA required. Applicants notified on a rolling basis starting 4/1; must reply by 5/1 or within 3 week(s) of notification.

Academics. Supplementary instruction in humanities and 5-year bachelor of architecture program offered. **Special study options:** Cross-registration, dual enrollment of high school students, exchange student, independent study, internships, student-designed major, study abroad. Association of Independent Colleges of Art and Design (AICAD) mobility program. **Credit/placement by examination:** AP, CLEP, IB, institutional tests. **Support services:** Pre-admission summer program, reduced course load, remedial instruction, study skills assistance, tutoring.

Majors. Architecture: Architecture, interior. **English:** Creative writing. **Visual/performing arts:** Art, ceramics, cinematography, commercial/advertising art, crafts, drawing, fashion design, fiber arts, graphic design, illustration, industrial design, interior design, metal/jewelry, painting, photography, printmaking, sculpture, studio arts.

Most popular majors. Architecture 12%, visual/performing arts 88%.

Computing on campus. 238 workstations in library, computer center. Dormitories wired for high-speed internet access. Helpline, student web hosting available.

Student life. Freshman orientation: Available. Preregistration for classes offered. Educational and social programs offered week before classes start. **Housing:** Coed dorms, apartments available. $750 deposit, deadline 5/15. Dormitory priority assigned to first-year undergraduates and international students. Off-campus college-owned residence hall available. Shuttle service to both campuses provided. **Activities:** Literary magazine, student government, student newspaper, Women's Caucus for Art, international student club, American Institute of Architecture Students, American Institute of Graphic Arts student chapter, ceramics guild, glass league.

Student services. Career counseling, student employment services, financial aid counseling, personal counseling, placement for graduates.

Contact. E-mail: enroll@cca.edu
Phone: (415) 703-9523 Toll-free number: (800) 447-1278
Fax: (415) 703-9539
Robynne Royster, Director of Undergraduate Admissions, California College of the Arts, 1111 Eighth Street, San Francisco, CA 94107-2247

California College: San Diego
San Diego, California

- Private 3-year business and health science college
- Very large city

General. Accredited by ACCSCT. **Calendar:** Continuous.

Contact. Phone: (619) 295-5785
2820 Camino del Rio, South 300, San Diego, CA 92108

California Institute of Integral Studies
San Francisco, California
www.ciis.edu **CB code: 3609**

- Private upper-division liberal arts college
- Commuter campus in very large city
- Application essay required

General. Regionally accredited. **Degrees:** 31 bachelor's awarded; master's, doctoral offered. **Calendar:** Semester, limited summer session. **Full-time faculty:** 51 total. **Part-time faculty:** 170 total.

Student profile. 55 full-time, degree-seeking undergraduates.

Basis for selection. College transcript, application essay required. Transfer accepted as juniors.

2005-2006 Annual costs. Tuition/fees: $12,250. Cost quoted for 2 semesters; 3-semester attendance mandatory.

Application procedures. Admission: Priority date 7/1. $65 fee, may be waived for applicants with need. Application may be submitted online. Application priority dates differ by program.

Academics. Special study options: Distance learning, independent study, internships, weekend college. **Credit/placement by examination:** AP, CLEP. 30 credit hours maximum toward bachelor's degree. **Support services:** Tutoring.

Majors. Liberal arts: Arts/sciences, humanities.

Computing on campus. 20 workstations in computer center. Commuter students can connect to campus network. Online library, helpline available.

Student life. Activities: Student government.

Student services. Minority student services, personal counseling, placement for graduates.

Contact. E-mail: admissions@ciis.edu
Phone: (415) 575-6150
Director of Admissions, California Institute of Integral Studies, 1453 Mission Street, San Francisco, CA 94103

California Institute of Technology
Pasadena, California **CB member**
www.caltech.edu **CB code: 4034**

- Private 4-year university
- Residential campus in small city
- 913 degree-seeking undergraduates: 30% women, 1% African American, 33% Asian American, 7% Hispanic American, 7% international
- 1,256 degree-seeking graduate students
- 20% of applicants admitted
- SAT or ACT with writing, SAT Subject Tests, application essay required
- 90% graduate within 6 years

General. Founded in 1891. Regionally accredited. **Degrees:** 217 bachelor's awarded; master's, doctoral offered. **ROTC:** Army, Air Force. **Location:** 10 miles from downtown Los Angeles. **Calendar:** Quarter. **Full-time**

faculty: 284 total; 97% have terminal degrees, 11% minority, 14% women. **Part-time faculty:** 16 total; 62% have terminal degrees, 31% minority, 50% women. **Class size:** 67% < 20, 20% 20-39, 5% 40-49, 5% 50-99, 3% >100. **Special facilities:** Jet propulsion laboratories, observatory, wind and water tunnels, radio observatory, seismological laboratory, marine biological laboratory.

Freshman class profile. 2,760 applied, 551 admitted, 234 enrolled.

Mid 50% test scores		**Return as sophomores:**	98%
SAT verbal:	700-780	**Out-of-state:**	62%
SAT math:	770-800	**Live on campus:**	100%
Rank in top quarter:	98%	**International:**	9%
Rank in top tenth:	94%		

Basis for selection. High school preparation and record (particularly in mathematics and science), test scores, extracurricular activities (science and nonscience-related), counselors' and teachers' recommendations, and demonstrated interest in mathematics and science are major considerations. SAT Subject Tests in mathematics level IIC and biology (environmental or molecular), chemistry, or physics required.

High school preparation. Required and recommended units include English 3-4, mathematics 4, social studies 1, history 1, science 2-4 (laboratory 1).

2006-2007 Annual costs. Tuition/fees (projected): $29,595. Room/board: $10,308. Books/supplies: $1,077.

2005-2006 Financial aid. **Need-based:** 179 full-time freshmen applied for aid; 124 were judged to have need; 124 of these received aid. Average need met was 100%. Average scholarship/grant was $26,303; average loan $1,503. 94% of total undergraduate aid awarded as scholarships/grants, 6% as loans/jobs. **Non-need-based:** Awarded to 102 full-time undergraduates, including 26 freshmen. Scholarships awarded for academics.

Application procedures. **Admission:** Closing date 1/1 (postmark date). $60 fee, may be waived for applicants with need. Application may be submitted online. Admission notification 4/1. Must reply by 5/1. **Financial aid:** Closing date 1/15. FAFSA, CSS PROFILE required. Applicants notified by 4/15; must reply by 5/1 or within 2 week(s) of notification.

Academics. Remedial services not formally offered. Remediation available for students deficient in basic scientific knowledge or technical skills. **Special study options:** Cross-registration, double major, ESL, exchange student, independent study, liberal arts/career combination, student-designed major, study abroad. **Credit/placement by examination:** AP, CLEP, institutional tests. **Support services:** Pre-admission summer program, reduced course load, tutoring.

Majors. **Biology:** General. **Business:** Managerial economics. **Computer sciences:** Computer science. **Engineering:** General, aerospace, chemical, civil, computer, electrical, mechanical, physics. **History:** General. **Interdisciplinary:** Science/society. **Liberal arts:** Arts/sciences. **Math:** General, applied. **Physical sciences:** Astronomy, chemistry, geochemistry, geology, geophysics, physics, planetary. **Social sciences:** General, economics.

Most popular majors. Biology 13%, computer/information sciences 6%, engineering/engineering technologies 35%, physical sciences 35%, social sciences 6%.

Computing on campus. 112 workstations in dormitories, library, computer center. Dormitories wired for high-speed internet access and linked to campus network. Commuter students can connect to campus network. Online course registration, online library, helpline, repair service, student web hosting, wireless network available.

Student life. **Freshman orientation:** Mandatory. Three-day camp. **Policies:** Freshmen permitted cars on campus. **Housing:** Guaranteed on-campus for all undergraduates. Coed dorms, special housing for disabled, apartments available. Pets allowed in dorm rooms. Single-unit houses available. **Activities:** Bands, choral groups, dance, drama, film society, literary magazine, music ensembles, musical theater, student government, student newspaper, symphony orchestra, Caltech Y, Christian fellowship, Newman Club, Hillel, Amnesty International.

Athletics. NCAA. **Intercollegiate:** Baseball M, basketball, cross-country, diving, fencing, golf M, soccer M, swimming, tennis, track and field, volleyball W, water polo. **Intramural:** Badminton, baseball M, basketball, cheerleading, cricket M, cross-country, football (tackle) M, soccer, softball, squash, swimming, table tennis, tennis, track and field, volleyball, water polo M. **Team name:** Beavers.

Student services. Alcohol/substance abuse counseling, campus ministries, career counseling, student employment services, financial aid counseling, health services, minority student services, on-campus daycare, personal counseling, placement for graduates, women's services. **Physically disabled:** Services for visually, speech, hearing impaired.

Contact. E-mail: ugadmissions@caltech.edu
Phone: (626) 395-6341 Fax: (626) 683-3026
Richard Bischoff, Director of Admissions, California Institute of Technology, 1200 East California Boulevard, Pasadena, CA 91125

California Institute of the Arts

Valencia, California — **CB member**
www.calarts.edu — **CB code: 4049**

- Private 4-year visual arts and performing arts college
- Residential campus in small city
- 803 degree-seeking undergraduates: 1% part-time, 45% women, 7% African American, 10% Asian American, 12% Hispanic American, 1% Native American, 8% international
- 506 degree-seeking graduate students
- 31% of applicants admitted
- Application essay required
- 67% graduate within 6 years

General. Founded in 1961. Regionally accredited. Single complex of 6 professional schools: art, critical studies, dance, film/video, music and theater. Numerous special programs that cross traditional lines. **Degrees:** 175 bachelor's awarded; master's offered. **Location:** 30 miles from Los Angeles. **Calendar:** Semester. **Full-time faculty:** 194 total; 23% minority. **Part-time faculty:** 140 total; 29% women. **Class size:** 75% < 20, 19% 20-39, 4% 40-49, 2% 50-99, less than 1% >100. **Special facilities:** Art studios, galleries, animation studios, concert halls, 6 theaters.

Freshman class profile. 2,979 applied, 923 admitted, 92 enrolled.

End year in good standing:	100%	**Live on campus:**	60%
Return as sophomores:	78%	**International:**	4%
Out-of-state:	58%		

Basis for selection. Admission is talent based. Portfolio required for art/design, film/video, music composition majors, and theater design and production. Auditions required for acting, dance, music majors. Music applicants may submit audio tape recordings in lieu of live audition. Interview recommended for directing/performance/production studies majors. **Homeschooled:** Letter of recommendation (nonparent) required.

2005-2006 Annual costs. Tuition/fees: $27,735. Room/board: $7,697. Books/supplies: $1,900. Personal expenses: $1,000.

2005-2006 Financial aid. **Need-based:** 108 full-time freshmen applied for aid; 78 were judged to have need; 77 of these received aid. Average need met was 86%. Average scholarship/grant was $9,746; average loan $3,586. 49% of total undergraduate aid awarded as scholarships/grants, 51% as loans/jobs. **Non-need-based:** Awarded to 90 full-time undergraduates, including 19 freshmen. Scholarships awarded for academics, art, minority status, music/drama.

Application procedures. **Admission:** Closing date 1/5 (receipt date). $65 fee. Application must be submitted on paper. Admission notification on a rolling basis beginning on or about 3/1. Must reply by May 1 or within 2 week(s) if notified thereafter. Some programs close after January 5. Early audition recommended for dance applicants. **Financial aid:** Priority date 3/1; no closing date. FAFSA required. Applicants notified on a rolling basis starting 4/15; must reply within 3 week(s) of notification.

Academics. **Special study options:** Independent study, internships, student-designed major, study abroad. **Credit/placement by examination:** AP, CLEP, IB, institutional tests. 6 credit hours maximum toward bachelor's degree. **Support services:** Tutoring.

Majors. **Communications technology:** Animation/special effects. **Computer sciences:** Computer graphics. **Visual/performing arts:** General, acting, art, cinematography, commercial/advertising art, dance, dramatic, film/cinema, graphic design, jazz, music performance, music theory/composition, painting, photography, piano/organ, sculpture, stringed instruments, studio arts, theater arts management, theater design, voice/opera.

Computing on campus. 40 workstations in library, computer center. Dormitories wired for high-speed internet access. Commuter students can connect to campus network. Helpline available.

Student life. **Freshman orientation:** Mandatory. **Policies:** Freshmen permitted cars on campus. **Housing:** Coed dorms, special housing for disabled, apartments available. $250 fully refundable deposit. **Activities:** Jazz band, dance, drama, film society, literary magazine, music ensembles, radio station, student government, student newspaper, TV station, black student union, Latino student union, GLBT student union, Asian club, political issues club.

Student services. Career counseling, student employment services, health services, personal counseling, placement for graduates, veterans' counselor. **Physically disabled:** Services for visually, speech, hearing impaired.

Contact. E-mail: admiss@calarts.edu
Phone: (661) 255-1050 ext. 2185 Toll-free number: (800) 545-2787
Fax: (661) 253-7710
Carol Kim, Director of Enrollment Services, California Institute of the Arts, 24700 McBean Parkway, Valencia, CA 91355

California Lutheran University

Thousand Oaks, California **CB member**
www.clunet.edu **CB code: 4088**

- Private 4-year university and liberal arts college affiliated with Evangelical Lutheran Church in America
- Residential campus in small city
- 2,087 degree-seeking undergraduates: 10% part-time, 56% women, 3% African American, 5% Asian American, 17% Hispanic American, 2% Native American, 2% international
- 979 degree-seeking graduate students
- 69% of applicants admitted
- SAT or ACT (ACT writing optional), application essay required
- 66% graduate within 6 years

General. Founded in 1959. Regionally accredited. **Degrees:** 469 bachelor's awarded; master's, doctoral offered. **ROTC:** Army, Air Force. **Location:** 45 miles from Los Angeles. **Calendar:** Semester, limited summer session. **Full-time faculty:** 130 total; 85% have terminal degrees, 18% minority, 45% women. **Part-time faculty:** 130 total; 33% have terminal degrees, 11% minority, 48% women. **Class size:** 64% < 20, 33% 20-39, 1% 40-49, 1% 50-99, less than 1% >100. **Special facilities:** Science facility housing state-of-the-art electronic blackboard, hypermedia computer laboratory, education technology center.

Freshman class profile. 1,977 applied, 1,362 admitted, 385 enrolled.

Mid 50% test scores			
SAT verbal:	490-580	**Rank in top quarter:**	58%
SAT math:	500-600	**Rank in top tenth:**	23%
ACT:	20-25	**Return as sophomores:**	84%
GPA 3.50 or higher:	54%	**Out-of-state:**	28%
GPA 3.0-3.49:	37%	**Live on campus:**	90%
GPA 2.0-2.99:	9%	**International:**	2%

Basis for selection. High school achievement record, rank in class, test scores, essay, letters of recommendation. Interview recommended. Audition recommended for music, drama majors.

High school preparation. College-preparatory program required. Required units include English 4, mathematics 3, social studies 2, science 3 (laboratory 2) and foreign language 2.

2005-2006 Annual costs. Tuition/fees: $23,370. Room/board: $8,320. Books/supplies: $1,285. Personal expenses: $2,009.

2004-2005 Financial aid. Need-based: 350 full-time freshmen applied for aid; 285 were judged to have need; 284 of these received aid. Average need met was 86%. Average scholarship/grant was $16,616; average loan $2,099. 67% of total undergraduate aid awarded as scholarships/grants, 33% as loans/jobs. **Non-need-based:** Awarded to 906 full-time undergraduates, including 261 freshmen. Scholarships awarded for academics, alumni affiliation, art, music/drama, religious affiliation.

Application procedures. Admission: Priority date 3/15; deadline 7/1. $45 fee, may be waived for applicants with need. Application may be submitted online. Admission notification on a rolling basis beginning on or about 11/15. Must reply by May 1 or within 2 week(s) if notified thereafter. **Financial aid:** Priority date 3/2; no closing date. FAFSA required. Applicants notified on a rolling basis starting 3/20; must reply within 2 week(s) of notification.

Academics. Special study options: Accelerated study, cooperative education, double major, dual enrollment of high school students, exchange student, honors, independent study, internships, New York semester, student-designed major, study abroad, teacher certification program, Washington semester. **Credit/placement by examination:** AP, CLEP, IB, SAT, ACT, institutional tests. 30 credit hours maximum toward bachelor's degree. **Support services:** Learning center, reduced course load, study skills assistance, tutoring.

Majors. Biology: General, biochemistry, molecular. **Business:** General, accounting, business admin, finance, managerial economics, marketing. **Communications:** General, advertising, broadcast journalism, journalism, public relations. **Computer sciences:** General, computer graphics, computer science, information systems, programming. **Conservation:** Environmental science. **Education:** General, art, early childhood, elementary, English, foreign languages, mathematics, middle, music, physical, reading, science, secondary, social science, social studies, special. **Engineering:** Biomedical. **English:** Speech/rhetoric. **Foreign languages:** General, French, German, Spanish. **Health:** Athletic training, predentistry, premedicine, prepharmacy, preveterinary. **History:** General. **Interdisciplinary:** Biological/physical sciences, math/computer science. **Legal studies:** Prelaw. **Liberal arts:** Arts/sciences. **Math:** General. **Philosophy/religion:** Philosophy, religion. **Physical sciences:** Chemistry, geology, physics. **Protective services:** Police science. **Psychology:** General. **Science technology:** Biological. **Social sciences:** Criminology, economics, international relations, political science, sociology. **Theology:** Religious ed, theology. **Visual/performing arts:** General, art, commercial/advertising art, dramatic.

Most popular majors. Business/marketing 28%, communications/journalism 11%, liberal arts 6%, psychology 9%, social sciences 11%.

Computing on campus. 92 workstations in dormitories, library, computer center. Dormitories linked to campus network. Commuter students can connect to campus network. Helpline available.

Student life. Freshman orientation: Mandatory. Preregistration for classes offered. **Policies:** Dry campus. Freshmen permitted cars on campus. **Housing:** Guaranteed on-campus for freshmen. Coed dorms, special housing for disabled available. $195 fully refundable deposit, deadline 5/1. **Activities:** Bands, choral groups, dance, drama, literary magazine, music ensembles, musical theater, radio station, student government, student newspaper, symphony orchestra, TV station, Lutheran Church congregation, Circle-K, African American student association, Rotoract, United Students of the World, Latino student union, Habitat for Humanity, Asian American club.

Athletics. NCAA. **Intercollegiate:** Baseball M, basketball, cross-country, football (tackle) M, golf M, soccer, softball W, swimming, tennis, track and field, volleyball W, water polo. **Intramural:** Archery, badminton, equestrian, rugby M, skiing, softball, tennis, volleyball. **Team name:** Kingsmen/Regals.

Student services. Adult student services, alcohol/substance abuse counseling, campus ministries, career counseling, services for economically disadvantaged, student employment services, financial aid counseling, health services, minority student services, personal counseling, placement for graduates, veterans' counselor, women's services. **Physically disabled:** Services for visually, hearing impaired.

Contact. E-mail: cluadm@clunet.edu
Phone: (805) 493-3135 Toll-free number: (877) 258-3678
Fax: (805) 493-3114
Darryl Calkins, Dean for Undergraduate Enrollment, California Lutheran University, 60 West Olsen Road #1350, Thousand Oaks, CA 91360-2787

California Maritime Academy

Vallejo, California **CB member**
www.csum.edu **CB code: 4035**

- Public 4-year university and maritime college
- Residential campus in small city
- 750 degree-seeking undergraduates: 3% African American, 11% Asian American, 7% Hispanic American, 1% Native American
- 60% of applicants admitted
- SAT or ACT required

General. Founded in 1929. Regionally accredited. Highest job placement in the California State University system. Not a military school. All students participate in at least one 2-month training cruise around Pacific Ocean geared toward their major. **Degrees:** 127 bachelor's awarded. **ROTC:** Navy. **Location:** 30 miles from San Francisco. **Calendar:** Semester, limited summer session. **Full-time faculty:** 50 total. **Part-time faculty:** 25 total. **Special facilities:** 500-foot training ship, computer-aided radar simulators, bridge simulator, steam simulator.

Freshman class profile. 1,400 applied, 840 admitted, 233 enrolled.

Out-of-state:	17%	**Live on campus:**	90%

Basis for selection. Applicants must meet California State University Eligibility Index and have strong grades in mathematics and sciences. All accepted students must pass physical examination. Some students required to take ELM/EPT if test scores are not high enough. Interview recommended, supplemental admission form required.

High school preparation. Required and recommended units include English 4, mathematics 3-4, social studies 1, history 1, science 2 (laboratory 2), foreign language 2-3 and academic electives 1. One additional mathematics course recommended for mechanical engineering applicants. Chemistry or physics required. One visual or performing arts elective required.

2005-2006 Annual costs. Tuition/fees: $3,446; $13,616 out-of-state. Mandatory cruise fee for freshmen $3,100; uniform costs for freshman $1,550. Room/board: $7,030.

Financial aid. All financial aid based on need. **Additional information:** US Maritime Administration provides annual incentive payment of $3,000 per student, with certain conditions. Tuition waiver for children of deceased or disabled California veterans.

Application procedures. Admission: Priority date 11/30; no deadline. $55 fee, may be waived for applicants with need. Application may be submitted online. Admission notification on a rolling basis beginning on or about 2/1. Must reply by May 1 or within 2 week(s) if notified thereafter. **Financial aid:** Priority date 3/2; no closing date. FAFSA required. Applicants notified on a rolling basis starting 4/1.

Academics. Center for Excellence and Learning provides free tutoring and free workshops hosted by professors. **Special study options:** Cooperative education, distance learning, double major, ESL, internships. International training cruise on board training ship "Golden Bear". **Credit/placement by examination:** AP, CLEP. 24 credit hours maximum toward bachelor's degree. **Support services:** Learning center, remedial instruction, tutoring.

Majors. Business: Business admin, logistics. **Engineering:** Marine, mechanical. **Engineering technology:** General. **Interdisciplinary:** Global studies. **Social sciences:** Political science.

Most popular majors. Business/marketing 11%, engineering/engineering technologies 37%, interdisciplinary studies 10%, trade and industry 42%.

Computing on campus. 85 workstations in dormitories, library, computer center, student center. Dormitories wired for high-speed internet access and linked to campus network. Helpline, repair service available.

Student life. Freshman orientation: Mandatory, $200 fee. Preregistration for classes offered. Held last week of August. **Policies:** Freshmen permitted cars on campus. **Housing:** Guaranteed on-campus for all undergraduates. Coed dorms available. $500 deposit, deadline 7/1. Students required to live on campus except those married or with children. **Activities:** Student government, student newspaper, Bible club, Circle K.

Athletics. NAIA. **Intercollegiate:** Basketball, rowing (crew), rugby M, sailing, soccer, volleyball W, water polo. **Intramural:** Badminton, baseball M, basketball, boxing M, golf, racquetball, rowing (crew), rugby M, sailing, softball, tennis, volleyball, water polo. **Team name:** Keelhaulers.

Student services. Career counseling, student employment services, financial aid counseling, health services, minority student services, personal counseling, placement for graduates, veterans' counselor.

Contact. E-mail: admission@csum.edu
Phone: (707) 654-1330 Toll-free number: (800) 561-1945
Fax: (707) 654-1336
Chris Krzak, Director of Admissions, California Maritime Academy, 200 Maritime Academy Drive, Vallejo, CA 94590

California National University for Advanced Studies

Northridge, California
www.cnuas.edu **CB code: 3894**

- For-profit 4-year virtual business and engineering college
- Small city
- 175 degree-seeking undergraduates
- 150 graduate students

General. Accredited by DETC. 100% distance learning institute. **Degrees:** 10 bachelor's awarded; master's offered. **Calendar:** Continuous. **Part-time faculty:** 200 total.

2006-2007 Annual costs. Domestic/Canada Undergraduate Tuition: $270.00 per unit; Domestic/Canada Graduate Tuition: $300.00 per unit; Domestic/Canada Application Fee: $75.00. Int'l Undergraduate $300.00 per unit. Int'l Graduate Tuition $350.00 per unit. Int'l Application Fee $100.00.

Application procedures. Admission: $75 fee.

Academics. Special study options: Distance learning. **Credit/placement by examination:** CLEP.

Majors. Business: Business admin. **Computer sciences:** Computer science. **Engineering:** General.

Contact. E-mail: cnuadms@mail.cnuas.edu
Phone: (818) 830-2411 Toll-free number: (800) 782-2422
Fax: (818) 830-2418
California National University for Advanced Studies, 8550 Balboa Boulevard, Suite 210, Northridge, CA 91325

California Polytechnic State University: San Luis Obispo

San Luis Obispo, California **CB member**
www.calpoly.edu **CB code: 4038**

- Public 4-year university
- Residential campus in large town
- 17,385 degree-seeking undergraduates: 5% part-time, 43% women, 1% African American, 11% Asian American, 10% Hispanic American, 1% Native American
- 963 degree-seeking graduate students
- 45% of applicants admitted
- SAT or ACT (ACT writing optional) required
- 69% graduate within 6 years

General. Founded in 1901. Regionally accredited. **Degrees:** 3,410 bachelor's awarded; master's offered. **ROTC:** Army. **Location:** 200 miles from Los Angeles, 250 miles from San Francisco. **Calendar:** Quarter, extensive summer session. **Full-time faculty:** 726 total; 72% have terminal degrees, 15% minority, 26% women. **Part-time faculty:** 520 total; 26% have terminal degrees, 15% minority, 41% women. **Class size:** 18% < 20, 62% 20-39, 10% 40-49, 7% 50-99, 3% >100. **Special facilities:** Printing press museum, university farm, dairy products technical center, architectural design institute.

Freshman class profile. 23,691 applied, 10,551 admitted, 3,372 enrolled.

Mid 50% test scores			
SAT verbal:	540-630	GPA 3.0-3.49:	22%
SAT math:	570-670	GPA 2.0-2.99:	3%
ACT:	23-28	Rank in top quarter:	76%
GPA 3.50 or higher:	75%	Rank in top tenth:	37%
		Return as sophomores:	91%

Basis for selection. Course work, high school GPA, test scores most important. Extracurricular activities considered. Portfolio required for art, design majors.

High school preparation. College-preparatory program required. 15 units required. Required units include English 4, mathematics 3, social studies 2, history 1, science 3 (laboratory 1), foreign language 2 and academic electives 1. One visual and performing arts. History must be US history/government.

2005-2006 Annual costs. Tuition/fees: $4,246; $14,416 out-of-state. Required fees vary by program. Room/board: $8,145. Books/supplies: $1,260. Personal expenses: $1,980.

2004-2005 Financial aid. Need-based: 1,942 full-time freshmen applied for aid; 998 were judged to have need; 911 of these received aid. Average need met was 64%. Average scholarship/grant was $1,459; average loan $2,466. 58% of total undergraduate aid awarded as scholarships/grants, 42% as loans/jobs. **Non-need-based:** Awarded to 650 full-time undergraduates, including 266 freshmen. Scholarships awarded for academics, alumni affiliation, art, athletics, job skills, leadership, music/drama, ROTC, state residency.

Application procedures. Admission: Closing date 11/30 (postmark date). $55 fee, may be waived for applicants with need. Application may be submitted online. Admission notification on a rolling basis beginning on or about 3/1. Must reply by 5/1. **Financial aid:** Priority date 3/1, closing date 6/30. FAFSA, institutional form required. Applicants notified on a rolling basis starting 4/15; must reply within 8 week(s) of notification.

Academics. **Special study options:** Combined bachelor's/graduate degree, cooperative education, cross-registration, distance learning, double major, dual enrollment of high school students, ESL, exchange student, external degree, honors, independent study, internships, semester at sea, study abroad, teacher certification program. **Credit/placement by examination:** AP, CLEP, SAT, ACT, institutional tests. 45 credit hours maximum toward bachelor's degree. **Support services:** Learning center, pre-admission summer program, reduced course load, remedial instruction, study skills assistance, tutoring, writing center.

Majors. **Agriculture:** Animal sciences, business, dairy, food science, horticulture, mechanization, ornamental horticulture, plant sciences, poultry, soil science. **Architecture:** Architecture, landscape, urban/community planning. **Biology:** General, bacteriology, biochemistry, ecology, microbiology. **Business:** Business admin, managerial economics. **Communications:** Journalism. **Communications technology:** Graphic/printing. **Computer sciences:** General, computer science, systems analysis. **Conservation:** General. **Construction:** Maintenance. **Education:** Agricultural, English, social science. **Engineering:** Aerospace, biomedical, civil, computer, electrical, materials, mechanical, metallurgical, science, software. **Engineering technology:** General, electrical. **English:** English lit, speech/rhetoric. **Family/consumer sciences:** General, family studies, food/nutrition. **Foreign languages:** General. **History:** General. **Liberal arts:** Arts/sciences. **Math:** General, statistics. **Parks/recreation:** Facilities management. **Physical sciences:** General, chemistry, physics. **Psychology:** General. **Social sciences:** General, economics, political science. **Visual/performing arts:** Commercial/advertising art.

Most popular majors. Agriculture 15%, architecture 6%, business/marketing 18%, engineering/engineering technologies 20%.

Computing on campus. PC or laptop required. 1,880 workstations in dormitories, library, computer center. Dormitories linked to campus network. Commuter students can connect to campus network. Helpline, repair service available.

Student life. **Freshman orientation:** Available. Held week prior to start of fall term. **Policies:** Freshmen permitted cars on campus. **Housing:** Coed dorms, single-sex dorms, fraternity/sorority housing available. $832 fully refundable deposit, deadline 3/15. Shared, apartment-style housing. **Activities:** Bands, choral groups, dance, drama, literary magazine, music ensembles, musical theater, radio station, student government, student newspaper, TV station, MECHA, Society of Black Engineers and Scientists, minority engineering program.

Athletics. NCAA. **Intercollegiate:** Baseball M, basketball, cross-country, football (tackle) M, golf, gymnastics W, soccer, softball W, swimming, tennis, track and field, volleyball W, wrestling M. **Intramural:** Badminton, baseball M, bowling, equestrian, fencing, golf, gymnastics, lacrosse, racquetball, rowing (crew), rugby M, sailing, soccer, softball, tennis, volleyball, water polo M. **Team name:** Mustangs.

Student services. Adult student services, alcohol/substance abuse counseling, career counseling, student employment services, health services, on-campus daycare, personal counseling, placement for graduates, veterans' counselor. **Physically disabled:** Services for visually, speech, hearing impaired.

Contact. E-mail: admissions@calpoly.edu
Phone: (805) 756-2311 Fax: (805) 756-5400
James Maraviglia, Admissions Officer, California Polytechnic State University: San Luis Obispo, Admissions Office, Cal Poly, San Luis Obispo, CA 93407

California State Polytechnic University: Pomona

Pomona, California — **CB member**
www.csupomona.edu — **CB code: 4082**

- Public 4-year university
- Commuter campus in small city
- 17,306 degree-seeking undergraduates: 16% part-time, 43% women, 4% African American, 31% Asian American, 27% Hispanic American, 3% international
- 1,257 degree-seeking graduate students
- 24% of applicants admitted
- SAT or ACT (ACT writing recommended) required
- 46% graduate within 6 years

General. Founded in 1938. Regionally accredited. **Degrees:** 3,292 bachelor's awarded; master's offered. **ROTC:** Army, Air Force. **Location:** 30 miles from downtown Los Angeles. **Calendar:** Quarter, extensive summer session. **Full-time faculty:** 659 total; 74% have terminal degrees, 29% minority, 38% women. **Part-time faculty:** 622 total; 27% have terminal degrees, 29% minority, 39% women. **Class size:** 36% < 20, 47% 20-39, 9% 40-49, 7% 50-99, 1% >100. **Special facilities:** Electron microscope center, international center, small ruminant center, Arabian horse center, equine research center, land laboratory, ecological reserve, center for regenerative studies, center for community affairs.

Freshman class profile. 17,252 applied, 4,121 admitted, 2,793 enrolled.

Mid 50% test scores			
SAT verbal:	440-550	GPA 2.0-2.99:	30%
SAT math:	460-600	Return as sophomores:	85%
ACT:	17-23	Out-of-state:	2%
GPA 3.50 or higher:	29%	Live on campus:	40%
GPA 3.0-3.49:	41%	International:	1%

Basis for selection. High school GPA, courses, and test scores important.

High school preparation. 15 units required. Required and recommended units include English 4, mathematics 3-4, social studies 1, history 1, science 2 (laboratory 2), foreign language 2 and academic electives 1. 1 visual and performing arts required.

2005-2006 Annual costs. Tuition/fees: $3,018; $13,188 out-of-state. Room/board: $8,478. Books/supplies: $1,260. Personal expenses: $1,740.

2005-2006 Financial aid. **Need-based:** 1,352 full-time freshmen applied for aid; 919 were judged to have need; 813 of these received aid. Average need met was 84%. Average scholarship/grant was $5,099; average loan $6,804. 55% of total undergraduate aid awarded as scholarships/grants, 45% as loans/jobs. **Non-need-based:** Scholarships awarded for academics, alumni affiliation, art, athletics, leadership, music/drama, state residency.

Application procedures. **Admission:** Closing date 11/30 (postmark date). $55 fee, may be waived for applicants with need. Application may be submitted online. Admission notification on a rolling basis beginning on or about 11/1. Must reply by May 1 or within 3 week(s) if notified thereafter. Applications for first time freshmen accepted October 1 through November 30. **Financial aid:** Priority date 3/2; no closing date. FAFSA required. Applicants notified on a rolling basis starting 4/1.

Academics. **Special study options:** Cooperative education, cross-registration, double major, dual enrollment of high school students, ESL, exchange student, external degree, honors, internships, liberal arts/career combination, study abroad, teacher certification program. Ocean studies institute, desert studies consortium. **Credit/placement by examination:** AP, CLEP, institutional tests. 36 credit hours maximum toward bachelor's degree. **Support services:** Learning center, pre-admission summer program, remedial instruction, study skills assistance, tutoring, writing center.

Majors. **Agriculture:** Agronomy, animal sciences, business, food science, horticultural science, landscaping, ornamental horticulture, plant protection, soil science. **Architecture:** Architecture, landscape, urban/community planning. **Biology:** General, biotechnology, botany, environmental, microbiology, zoology. **Business:** Accounting, business admin, finance, hospitality admin, international, marketing, operations. **Communications:** General. **Computer sciences:** Computer science, information technology. **Engineering:** General, aerospace, chemical, civil, computer, electrical, industrial, manufacturing, materials, mechanical. **Engineering technology:** General, construction, electrical. **English:** English lit. **Family/consumer sciences:** Clothing/textiles. **Foreign languages:** Spanish. **Health:** Dietetics, veterinary technology/assistant. **History:** General. **Interdisciplinary:** Behavioral sciences. **Liberal arts:** Arts/sciences. **Math:** General. **Parks/recreation:** Health/fitness. **Philosophy/religion:** Philosophy. **Physical sciences:** Chemistry, geology, physics. **Psychology:** General. **Social sciences:** General, anthropology, economics, geography, political science, sociology. **Visual/performing arts:** Art, dance, dramatic, graphic design.

Most popular majors. Business/marketing 38%, engineering/engineering technologies 17%, liberal arts 6%.

Computing on campus. 280 workstations in library, computer center. Dormitories wired for high-speed internet access and linked to campus network. Commuter students can connect to campus network. Online course registration, helpline, student web hosting available.

Student life. **Freshman orientation:** Mandatory, $40 fee. Preregistration for classes offered. One-day orientation. **Policies:** Freshmen permitted cars on campus. **Housing:** Coed dorms, special housing for disabled, apartments available. $50 fully refundable deposit. **Activities:** Bands, choral groups, dance, drama, literary magazine, music ensembles, musical theater, opera, student government, student newspaper, symphony orchestra, Campus Crusade for Christ, black student union, Hawaiian club, MECHA, Studies of the World, Newman Club, Hillel, Bahai club, Coptic-Orthodox Christian club.

Athletics. NCAA. **Intercollegiate:** Baseball M, basketball, cross-country, soccer, tennis, track and field, volleyball W. **Intramural:** Badminton, basketball, football (non-tackle) M, golf, racquetball, softball, swimming, table tennis, tennis, track and field, volleyball. **Team name:** Broncos.

Student services. Adult student services, career counseling, student employment services, health services, on-campus daycare, personal counseling, placement for graduates, veterans' counselor. **Physically disabled:** Services for visually, speech, hearing impaired.

Contact. E-mail: admissions@csupomona.edu
Phone: (909) 869-3210 Fax: (909) 869-4529
George Bradshaw, Director of Admissions and Outreach, California State Polytechnic University: Pomona, 3801 West Temple Avenue, Pomona, CA 91768-4019

California State University: Bakersfield

Bakersfield, California **CB member**
www.csub.edu **CB code: 4110**

- Public 4-year university and liberal arts college
- Commuter campus in small city
- 4,825 full-time, degree-seeking undergraduates
- 1,589 graduate students
- 49% of applicants admitted

General. Founded in 1965. Regionally accredited. **Degrees:** 1,243 bachelor's awarded; master's offered. **Location:** 112 miles from Los Angeles. **Calendar:** Quarter, limited summer session. **Full-time faculty:** 330 total. **Part-time faculty:** 185 total. **Class size:** 47% < 20, 44% 20-39, 6% 40-49, 2% 50-99, less than 1% >100. **Special facilities:** 40-acre facility for wild animal care, archaeological information center, center for business and economic research, center for economic education, well-sample repository, center for physiological research.

Freshman class profile. 4,390 applied, 2,150 admitted, 782 enrolled.

Mid 50% test scores		ACT:	16-22
SAT verbal:	400-530	Out-of-state:	3%
SAT math:	420-530	Live on campus:	12%

Basis for selection. GPA, test scores, and certain honors courses must place applicant in upper third of California high school graduates (upper sixth for out-of-state applicants) using eligibility index table. Minimum test scores slightly higher for out-of-state students. SAT or ACT not required if GPA is above 3.0 (3.6 if out-of-state).

High school preparation. Required units include English 4, mathematics 3, history 2, science 2 (laboratory 1), foreign language 2 and academic electives 1. One visual and performing arts required; foreign language must be in same language; math must include algebra, geometry, and intermediate algebra; science must include biology and a physical science.

2005-2006 Annual costs. Tuition/fees: $3,268; $13,438 out-of-state. Room/board: $5,946. Books/supplies: $1,224. Personal expenses: $1,854.

Financial aid. All financial aid based on need.

Application procedures. Admission: Priority date 12/1; no deadline. $55 fee, may be waived for applicants with need. Application may be submitted online. Admission notification on a rolling basis beginning on or about 7/1. **Financial aid:** Priority date 3/2, closing date 4/1. FAFSA required. Applicants notified on a rolling basis; must reply within 2 week(s) of notification.

Academics. Most courses are 5 quarter units. Students enrolled in 3 courses are carrying full unit load. **Special study options:** Accelerated study, cooperative education, distance learning, double major, ESL, exchange student, external degree, honors, independent study, internships, liberal arts/career combination, student-designed major, study abroad, teacher certification program. 2+2 at specified locations for liberal studies (teaching) majors. **Credit/placement by examination:** CLEP. Unlimited number of hours of credit by examination may be counted toward degree. **Support services:** Learning center, pre-admission summer program, reduced course load, remedial instruction, study skills assistance, tutoring.

Majors. Biology: General. **Business:** Business admin. **Communications:** General. **Computer sciences:** Computer science. **Conservation:** Land use planning. **Education:** Early childhood. **English:** American lit. **Foreign languages:** Spanish. **Health:** Nursing (RN). **History:** General. **Liberal arts:** Arts/sciences. **Math:** General. **Philosophy/religion:** Philosophy, religion. **Physical sciences:** Chemistry, geology, physics. **Protective services:** Criminal justice. **Psychology:** General. **Public administration:** General. **Social sciences:** Anthropology, criminology, economics, political science, sociology. **Visual/performing arts:** General, art, dramatic.

Most popular majors. Business/marketing 15%, liberal arts 31%, psychology 7%, social sciences 6%.

Computing on campus. 600 workstations in library, computer center, student center. Dormitories linked to campus network. Commuter students can connect to campus network. Online course registration, online library, helpline, student web hosting available.

Student life. Freshman orientation: Available, $15 fee. Preregistration for classes offered. **Policies:** Freshmen permitted cars on campus. **Housing:** Guaranteed on-campus for all undergraduates. Coed dorms, single-sex dorms available. $50 fully refundable deposit. **Activities:** Jazz band, choral groups, dance, drama, literary magazine, music ensembles, musical theater, student government, student newspaper, black student union, Movimiento Estudiantil Chicano de Aztlan, Christian union, student nursing association, Circle-K, Latinos United for Education.

Athletics. NCAA. **Intercollegiate:** Basketball, cross-country W, golf M, soccer, softball W, swimming, tennis W, track and field, volleyball W, water polo W, wrestling M. **Intramural:** Badminton, basketball, golf, handball, racquetball, soccer, softball, tennis, volleyball. **Team name:** Roadrunners.

Student services. Adult student services, alcohol/substance abuse counseling, career counseling, services for economically disadvantaged, student employment services, financial aid counseling, health services, minority student services, on-campus daycare, personal counseling, placement for graduates, veterans' counselor. **Physically disabled:** Services for visually, speech, hearing impaired. **Learning disabled:** Comprehensive services available.

Contact. Phone: (661) 654-3036 Toll-free number: (800) 788-2782
Fax: (661) 654-3389
Jacqueline Mimms, Director of Admissions, California State University: Bakersfield, 9001 Stockdale Highway, Bakersfield, CA 93311-1099

California State University: Channel Islands

Camarillo, California
www.csuci.edu

- Public 4-year university
- Small city

General. Regionally accredited. **Calendar:** Semester.

Contact. Phone: (805) 437-8400
One University Drive, Camarillo, CA 93012

California State University: Chico

Chico, California **CB member**
www.csuchico.edu **CB code: 4048**

- Public 4-year university and liberal arts college
- Residential campus in small city
- 14,526 degree-seeking undergraduates: 10% part-time, 53% women, 2% African American, 5% Asian American, 11% Hispanic American, 1% Native American, 2% international
- 850 degree-seeking graduate students
- 87% of applicants admitted
- SAT or ACT (ACT writing optional) required
- 51% graduate within 6 years

General. Founded in 1887. Regionally accredited. **Degrees:** 2,724 bachelor's awarded; master's offered. **Location:** 90 miles from Sacramento, 175 miles from San Francisco. **Calendar:** Semester, limited summer session. **Full-time faculty:** 499 total; 88% have terminal degrees, 15% minority, 38% women. **Part-time faculty:** 414 total; 33% have terminal degrees, 8% minority, 50% women. **Class size:** 36% < 20, 45% 20-39, 11% 40-49, 7% 50-99, 2% >100. **Special facilities:** 1000-acre farm, 2 museums, planetarium, instructional media center, biology field station, anthropology museum, intercultural studies center, computer graphics lab, assistive technology center, media prep lab, recording arts studio, hydrotherapy pool, echocardiography system, gas displacement chamber.

Freshman class profile. 12,457 applied, 10,881 admitted, 2,335 enrolled.

Mid 50% test scores		Rank in top quarter:	76%
SAT verbal:	460-570	Rank in top tenth:	35%
SAT math:	470-580	End year in good standing:	81%
ACT:	19-23	Return as sophomores:	82%
GPA 3.50 or higher:	24%	Out-of-state:	1%
GPA 3.0-3.49:	43%	Live on campus:	70%
GPA 2.0-2.99:	33%	International:	1%

Basis for selection. Eligibility index derived from high school GPA and test scores. First-time freshmen applicants rank order based on characteristics of applicant pool. GPA determined from 10th and 11th-grade college prep courses only. Nursing program open only to state residents. Portfolio required of fine arts majors. **Homeschooled:** Transcript of courses and grades required. Must be able to verify completion of required college preparatory subject requirements and meet institutional eligibility index. **Learning Disabled:** Students must meet established admission criteria.

High school preparation. 15 units required. Required units include English 4, mathematics 3, social studies 2, science 2 (laboratory 2), foreign language 2 and academic electives 1. 1 visual and performing arts required.

2005-2006 Annual costs. Tuition/fees: $3,370; $13,540 out-of-state. Room/board: $8,312. Books/supplies: $1,219. Personal expenses: $2,132.

2005-2006 Financial aid. Need-based: 1,432 full-time freshmen applied for aid; 871 were judged to have need; 856 of these received aid. Average need met was 79%. Average scholarship/grant was $5,735; average loan $2,361. 52% of total undergraduate aid awarded as scholarships/grants, 48% as loans/jobs. **Non-need-based:** Awarded to 1,461 full-time undergraduates, including 509 freshmen. Scholarships awarded for academics, art, athletics, leadership, minority status, music/drama, religious affiliation.

Application procedures. Admission: Priority date 10/1; deadline 11/30 (postmark date). $55 fee, may be waived for applicants with need. Application may be submitted online. Admission notification 3/1. Must reply by May 1 or within 2 week(s) if notified thereafter. Applications for the following majors must be made during priority periods of October and August: nursing, media arts, graphic design, recording arts, and interior design. All first time freshmen fall applicants should apply between October 1 and November 30. **Financial aid:** Priority date 3/2; no closing date. FAFSA required. Applicants notified on a rolling basis starting 2/15.

Academics. Special study options: Cooperative education, cross-registration, distance learning, double major, dual enrollment of high school students, ESL, exchange student, external degree, honors, independent study, internships, student-designed major, study abroad, teacher certification program. **Credit/placement by examination:** AP, CLEP, IB, SAT, ACT, institutional tests. 30 credit hours maximum toward bachelor's degree. 6 semester hours awarded for each International Baccalaureate higher level exam passed with score of 4 to 7. **Support services:** Learning center, pre-admission summer program, reduced course load, remedial instruction, study skills assistance, tutoring, writing center.

Majors. Agriculture: Agronomy, animal sciences, business, range science. **Architecture:** Urban/community planning. **Area/ethnic studies:** American, Asian, Latin American, women's. **Biology:** General, biochemistry, ecology, microbiology. **Business:** Accounting, business admin, finance, human resources, management information systems, marketing. **Communications:** Journalism, organizational, public relations, radio/tv. **Computer sciences:** Computer graphics, computer science, information technology. **Conservation:** Environmental studies, management/policy. **Education:** Agricultural, art, biology, chemistry, early childhood, English, French, German, health, instructional media, mathematics, music, physical, science, social science, Spanish. **Engineering:** Civil, computer, electrical, mechanical. **Engineering technology:** Construction. **English:** English lit, speech/rhetoric. **Foreign languages:** French, German, linguistics, Spanish. **Health:** Clinical lab science, communication disorders, dietetics, health services, nursing (RN), predentistry, premedicine, prepharmacy, preveterinary, recreational therapy. **History:** General. **Interdisciplinary:** Accounting/computer science, gerontology, intercultural, math/computer science. **Legal studies:** Paralegal. **Liberal arts:** Arts/sciences, humanities. **Math:** General, applied, statistics. **Parks/recreation:** General, exercise sciences, facilities management, health/fitness. **Philosophy/religion:** Judaic, philosophy, religion. **Physical sciences:** Chemistry, geology, hydrology, physics. **Protective services:** Criminal justice. **Psychology:** General. **Public administration:** General, social work. **Social sciences:** General, anthropology, economics, geography, international economics, international relations, political science, sociology. **Visual/performing arts:** Art, art history/conservation, design, dramatic, graphic design, interior design, music performance, music theory/composition, piano/organ, studio arts.

Most popular majors. Business/marketing 16%, engineering/engineering technologies 6%, English 6%, health sciences 6%, liberal arts 12%, social sciences 9%, visual/performing arts 9%.

Computing on campus. 915 workstations in dormitories, library, computer center, student center. Dormitories wired for high-speed internet access and linked to campus network. Commuter students can connect to campus network. Online course registration, online library, helpline, repair service, student web hosting, wireless network available.

Student life. Freshman orientation: Available. Preregistration for classes offered. Orientation sessions offered during June and July for students and parents. One-day session $50, two days $90. **Policies:** Freshmen permitted cars on campus. **Housing:** Coed dorms, special housing for disabled, apartments, fraternity/sorority housing, substance-free housing available. $1,000 fully refundable deposit. Thematic housing available for honors, engineering, minorities in engineering and science, business, math. **Activities:** Bands, choral groups, dance, drama, film society, literary magazine, music ensembles, musical theater, opera, radio station, student government, student newspaper, symphony orchestra, over 200 organizations.

Athletics. NCAA. **Intercollegiate:** Baseball M, basketball, cross-country, golf, soccer, softball W, track and field, volleyball W. **Intramural:** Badminton, basketball, bowling, football (non-tackle), soccer, softball, volleyball. **Team name:** Wildcats.

Student services. Adult student services, alcohol/substance abuse counseling, career counseling, services for economically disadvantaged, student employment services, financial aid counseling, health services, legal services, minority student services, on-campus daycare, personal counseling, placement for graduates, veterans' counselor, women's services. **Physically disabled:** Services for visually, speech, hearing impaired. **Learning disabled:** Comprehensive services available.

Contact. E-mail: info@csuchico.edu
Phone: (530) 898-4428 Toll-free number: (800) 542-4426
Fax: (530) 898-6456
John Swiney, Director of Admissions Office, California State University: Chico, 400 West First Street, Chico, CA 95929-0722

California State University: Dominguez Hills

Carson, California — **CB member**
www.csudh.edu — **CB code: 4098**

- Public 4-year university
- Small city
- 8,943 degree-seeking undergraduates: 40% part-time, 68% women, 26% African American, 9% Asian American, 35% Hispanic American, 1% Native American, 2% international
- 3,414 degree-seeking graduate students
- 45% of applicants admitted
- 35% graduate within 6 years

General. Founded in 1960. Regionally accredited. **Degrees:** 1,717 bachelor's awarded; master's offered. **ROTC:** Army, Air Force. **Location:** 10 miles from Los Angeles. **Calendar:** Semester, extensive summer session. **Full-time faculty:** 320 total. **Part-time faculty:** 445 total. **Class size:** 38% < 20, 48% 20-39, 8% 40-49, 6% 50-99, less than 1% >100. **Special facilities:** Nature preserve, greenhouse, observatory, social systems research center.

Freshman class profile. 2,323 applied, 1,045 admitted, 786 enrolled.

Return as sophomores:	73%	International:	3%
Out-of-state:	1%		

Basis for selection. Academic record and test scores most important. SAT/ACT required of applicants who do not meet minimum requirement based on admissions eligibility index. Interview required of Educational Opportunity Program applicants.

High school preparation. 15 units required. Required units include English 4, mathematics 3, social studies 1, history 1, science 1 (laboratory 1), foreign language 2 and academic electives 3. One visual and performing arts, 1 US history or government also required.

2005-2006 Annual costs. Tuition/fees: $2,991; $13,161 out-of-state. Room/board: $7,770. Books/supplies: $1,206. Personal expenses: $1,854.

Financial aid. Non-need-based: Scholarships awarded for academics, minority status.

Application procedures. Admission: Priority date 3/1; deadline 4/1 (postmark date). $55 fee, may be waived for applicants with need. Admission notification on a rolling basis beginning on or about 9/1. **Financial aid:** Priority date 4/15; no closing date. FAFSA, CSS PROFILE required. Applicants notified on a rolling basis starting 2/15; must reply within 4 week(s) of notification.

Academics. **Special study options:** Accelerated study, cooperative education, double major, dual enrollment of high school students, ESL, exchange student, honors, independent study, internships, student-designed major, study abroad, teacher certification program. **Credit/placement by examination:** AP, CLEP, institutional tests. 30 credit hours maximum toward bachelor's degree. **Support services:** Learning center, pre-admission summer program, reduced course load, remedial instruction, tutoring.

Majors. **Area/ethnic studies:** African-American. **Biology:** General, bacteriology. **Business:** General, accounting, banking/financial services, business admin, entrepreneurial studies, human resources, international, labor relations, management information systems, management science, real estate. **Communications:** General, journalism, public relations. **Computer sciences:** General. **English:** British lit. **Foreign languages:** French, linguistics, Spanish. **Health:** Clinical lab technology, dental assistant, health care admin, nuclear medical technology, nursing (RN), orthotics/prosthetics, physician assistant. **History:** General. **Interdisciplinary:** Gerontology. **Legal studies:** Prelaw. **Liberal arts:** Arts/sciences. **Math:** General. **Parks/recreation:** Facilities management. **Philosophy/religion:** Philosophy. **Physical sciences:** Chemistry, geology, physics, planetary. **Psychology:** General. **Public administration:** Community org/advocacy, human services. **Social sciences:** Anthropology, economics, geography, political science, sociology. **Visual/performing arts:** Art history/conservation, dramatic, music performance, music theory/composition.

Computing on campus. 210 workstations in library, computer center.

Student life. **Freshman orientation:** Mandatory. Preregistration for classes offered. **Housing:** Coed dorms, single-sex dorms, special housing for disabled, apartments available. **Activities:** Bands, choral groups, drama, music ensembles, musical theater, radio station, student government, student newspaper, TV station, accounting society, African-American Business Student Association, dance club, literary club, Phi Alpha Delta, political science club, science society, Hispanic Association of Natural and Social Science, Campus Crusade for Christ, Hillel.

Athletics. NCAA. **Intercollegiate:** Baseball M, basketball, cross-country W, golf M, soccer, softball W, track and field W, volleyball W. **Team name:** Torros.

Student services. Adult student services, career counseling, student employment services, health services, on-campus daycare, personal counseling, placement for graduates, veterans' counselor, women's services. **Physically disabled:** Services for visually, speech, hearing impaired.

Contact. Phone: (310) 243-3645 Fax: (310) 516-3609
James Wood, Director of Admissions, California State University: Dominguez Hills, 1000 East Victoria Street, Carson, CA 90747

California State University: East Bay

Hayward, California — **CB member**
www.csueastbay.edu — **CB code: 4011**

- Public 4-year university
- Commuter campus in small city
- 8,476 degree-seeking undergraduates: 21% part-time, 61% women
- 3,040 degree-seeking graduate students
- 44% graduate within 6 years

General. Founded in 1957. Regionally accredited. Branch campus in Concord. **Degrees:** 2,419 bachelor's awarded; master's offered. **Location:** 30 miles from San Francisco, 30 miles from San Jose. **Calendar:** Quarter, extensive summer session. **Full-time faculty:** 315 total; 29% minority, 44% women. **Part-time faculty:** 362 total; 22% minority, 51% women. **Class size:** 22% < 20, 49% 20-39, 14% 40-49, 13% 50-99, 2% >100. **Special facilities:** Ecological field station, museum of anthropology, marine laboratory, geology summer field camp.

Freshman class profile. 696 enrolled.

Mid 50% test scores			
SAT verbal:	430-580	**ACT:**	18-24
SAT math:	450-600	**Out-of-state:**	2%
		International:	4%

Basis for selection. Eligibility index based on GPA, test results, and 15 units of subject requirements to yield students in top third of California high school graduates. Out-of-state applicants should be in top sixth of high school class. SAT or ACT recommended. Test scores not required for residents with high school GPA above 3.0, nonresidents with high school GPA above 3.61.

High school preparation. 15 units required. Required units include English 4, mathematics 3, history 2, science 2 (laboratory 2), foreign language 2 and academic electives 1. One visual and performing arts. Math must be algebra, geometry, and intermediate algebra. Science must be biology and a physical science. Foreign language units must be in same language.

2005-2006 Annual costs. Tuition/fees: $2,916; $13,086 out-of-state. Room/board: $6,796. Books/supplies: $1,260. Personal expenses: $2,214.

2005-2006 Financial aid. **Need-based:** 275 full-time freshmen applied for aid; 247 were judged to have need; 240 of these received aid. Average need met was 68%. Average scholarship/grant was $7,128; average loan $2,668. 59% of total undergraduate aid awarded as scholarships/grants, 41% as loans/jobs.

Application procedures. **Admission:** Closing date 4/30 (postmark date). $55 fee, may be waived for applicants with need. Application may be submitted online. Admission notification on a rolling basis beginning on or about 3/15. **Financial aid:** Priority date 3/2; no closing date. FAFSA required. Applicants notified on a rolling basis; must reply within 3 week(s) of notification.

Academics. **Special study options:** Accelerated study, cooperative education, cross-registration, distance learning, double major, dual enrollment of high school students, ESL, exchange student, honors, independent study, internships, liberal arts/career combination, student-designed major, study abroad, teacher certification program. **Credit/placement by examination:** AP, CLEP, IB, SAT, ACT, institutional tests. 45 credit hours maximum toward bachelor's degree. 45-unit limitation excludes advanced placement. **Support services:** Learning center, pre-admission summer program, reduced course load, remedial instruction, study skills assistance, tutoring.

Majors. **Area/ethnic studies:** African-American, Asian-American, Hispanic-American/Latino/Chicano, Latin American, Native American. **Biology:** General, biochemistry, biomedical sciences. **Business:** General, accounting, business admin, entrepreneurial studies, finance, human resources, management information systems, managerial economics, purchasing, real estate. **Communications:** General, advertising, broadcast journalism, journalism, public relations. **Computer sciences:** General, computer science, information systems, networking. **Conservation:** General, environmental studies. **Education:** Mathematics, physical, speech. **Engineering:** Software. **English:** American lit, British lit, speech/rhetoric. **Foreign languages:** French, Spanish. **Health:** Athletic training, audiology/speech pathology, clinical lab technology, environmental health, prenursing, recreational therapy. **History:** General. **Liberal arts:** Arts/sciences. **Math:** General, applied, statistics. **Parks/recreation:** General, exercise sciences, facilities management, health/fitness. **Philosophy/religion:** Philosophy, religion. **Physical sciences:** Chemistry, geology, physics. **Protective services:** Corrections, law enforcement admin. **Psychology:** General. **Public administration:** General, policy analysis, social work. **Social sciences:** Anthropology, archaeology, economics, geography, political science, sociology. **Visual/performing arts:** Art, art history/conservation, arts management, ceramics, commercial/advertising art, dance, dramatic, drawing, painting, photography, printmaking, sculpture, studio arts, theater design.

Computing on campus. 1,062 workstations in dormitories, library, computer center. Dormitories wired for high-speed internet access and linked to campus network. Commuter students can connect to campus network. Online course registration, helpline, student web hosting available.

Student life. **Freshman orientation:** Available, $80 fee. Preregistration for classes offered. Two-day program with overnight lodging on campus optional. **Policies:** Community and campus-based volunteer programs available. **Housing:** Apartments available. $660 deposit, deadline 7/16. Private coeducational dormitory adjacent to campus. **Activities:** Bands, choral groups, dance, drama, literary magazine, music ensembles, musical theater, opera, radio station, student government, student newspaper, symphony orchestra, TV station, 90 campus organizations.

Athletics. NAIA, NCAA. **Intercollegiate:** Baseball M, basketball, cross-country, golf, soccer, softball W, swimming W, track and field, volleyball W, water polo W. **Intramural:** Badminton, basketball, golf, gymnastics M, racquetball, soccer, softball, swimming, tennis, volleyball. **Team name:** Pioneers.

Student services. Adult student services, career counseling, services for economically disadvantaged, student employment services, financial aid counseling, health services, legal services, minority student services, on-campus daycare, personal counseling, placement for graduates, veterans' counselor. **Physically disabled:** Services for visually, speech, hearing impaired.

Contact. E-mail: askES@csueastbay.edu
Phone: (510) 885-2784 Fax: (510) 885-4059
Jeffrey Cook, Executive Director, Enrollment Services, California State University: East Bay, 25800 Carlos Bee Boulevard, Hayward, CA 94542-3095

California State University: Fresno

Fresno, California — **CB member**
www.csufresno.edu — **CB code: 4312**

- Public 4-year university
- Commuter campus in very large city
- 17,428 degree-seeking undergraduates: 15% part-time, 58% women, 5% African American, 14% Asian American, 30% Hispanic American, 1% Native American, 2% international
- 2,943 graduate students
- 65% of applicants admitted
- SAT or ACT required
- 43% graduate within 6 years

General. Founded in 1911. Regionally accredited. Designated as an arboretum in 1978. **Degrees:** 3,030 bachelor's awarded; master's, doctoral offered. **ROTC:** Army, Air Force. **Location:** 217 miles from Los Angeles, 172 miles from Sacramento. **Calendar:** Semester, extensive summer session. **Full-time faculty:** 754 total; 24% minority, 39% women. **Part-time faculty:** 513 total; 19% minority, 49% women. **Class size:** 32% < 20, 46% 20-39, 14% 40-49, 7% 50-99, 2% >100. **Special facilities:** 1,190-acre university farm, strength and conditioning center, planetarium.

Freshman class profile. 13,252 applied, 8,656 admitted, 2,438 enrolled.

Mid 50% test scores			
SAT verbal:	400-530	GPA 2.0-2.99:	26%
SAT math:	420-550	End year in good standing:	83%
ACT:	16-22	Return as sophomores:	85%
GPA 3.50 or higher:	32%	Out-of-state:	1%
GPA 3.0-3.49:	42%	Live on campus:	29%
		International:	1%

Basis for selection. Upper third of California high school graduates based on eligibility index and required college preparatory subjects. Tests recommended, but not required, if student has a high school GPA of 3.0 or higher.

High school preparation. 15 units required. Required and recommended units include English 4, mathematics 3, social studies 1, history 1, science 1 (laboratory 1), foreign language 2 and academic electives 3. One visual and performing arts, and 1 US history/government also required.

2005-2006 Annual costs. Tuition/fees: $2,933; $13,103 out-of-state. Room/board: $7,416. Books/supplies: $1,240. Personal expenses: $1,550.

2004-2005 Financial aid. **Need-based:** 1,952 full-time freshmen applied for aid; 1,648 were judged to have need; 1,014 of these received aid. Average need met was 70%. Average scholarship/grant was $4,334; average loan $2,302. 72% of total undergraduate aid awarded as scholarships/grants, 28% as loans/jobs. **Non-need-based:** Awarded to 2,179 full-time undergraduates, including 332 freshmen. Scholarships awarded for academics, alumni affiliation, athletics, leadership, music/drama, state residency.

Application procedures. **Admission:** Closing date 4/1 (receipt date). $55 fee, may be waived for applicants with need. Application may be submitted online. Admission notification on a rolling basis beginning on or about 8/1. **Financial aid:** Priority date 3/1; no closing date. FAFSA required. Applicants notified on a rolling basis starting 4/1; must reply within 3 week(s) of notification.

Academics. **Special study options:** Accelerated study, combined bachelor's/graduate degree, cooperative education, cross-registration, distance learning, double major, dual enrollment of high school students, ESL, exchange student, honors, independent study, internships, student-designed major, study abroad, teacher certification program. **Credit/placement by examination:** AP, CLEP, institutional tests. 30 credit hours maximum toward bachelor's degree. **Support services:** Learning center, pre-admission summer program, reduced course load, remedial instruction, study skills assistance, tutoring, writing center.

Majors. **Agriculture:** General, agronomy, animal health, animal sciences, business, dairy, food science, horticultural science, plant protection, plant sciences. **Area/ethnic studies:** African-American, women's. **Biology:** General, anatomy, bacteriology, cell/histology, ecology, molecular. **Business:** General, accounting, business admin, finance, human resources, international, management information systems, marketing, real estate. **Communications:** General, journalism, public relations. **Computer sciences:** General, computer science, information systems. **Construction:** Maintenance. **Education:** General, Deaf/hearing impaired, physical. **Engineering:** Civil, computer, electrical, mechanical. **Engineering technology:** Civil, construction, electrical, surveying. **Family/consumer sciences:** Child development, food/nutrition. **Foreign languages:** French, linguistics, Spanish. **Health:** Clinical/medical social work, communication disorders, environmental health, health care admin, nursing (RN), occupational health, vocational rehab counseling. **History:** General. **Interdisciplinary:** Natural sciences. **Math:** General. **Parks/recreation:** Exercise sciences, facilities management. **Philosophy/religion:** Philosophy, religion. **Physical sciences:** Chemistry, geology, physics. **Psychology:** General. **Public administration:** General, social work. **Social sciences:** Anthropology, criminology, economics, geography, political science, sociology. **Visual/performing arts:** Art, commercial/advertising art, dance, dramatic, interior design, music theory/composition, theater design.

Most popular majors. Business/marketing 15%, education 7%, engineering/engineering technologies 6%, health sciences 9%, liberal arts 16%, social sciences 8%.

Computing on campus. PC or laptop required. 1,500 workstations in dormitories, library, computer center, student center. Dormitories linked to campus network. Commuter students can connect to campus network. Online library, helpline, repair service available.

Student life. **Freshman orientation:** Available, $25 fee. One-week programs. **Policies:** Freshmen permitted cars on campus. **Housing:** Coed dorms, single-sex dorms, apartments, fraternity/sorority housing available. $150 deposit, deadline 4/1. **Activities:** Bands, choral groups, dance, drama, literary magazine, music ensembles, musical theater, radio station, student government, student newspaper, symphony orchestra, TV station, over 250 student organizations including religious and ethnic groups.

Athletics. NCAA. **Intercollegiate:** Baseball M, basketball, cross-country, equestrian W, football (tackle) M, golf, soccer W, softball W, tennis, track and field, volleyball W, wrestling M. **Intramural:** Basketball, football (non-tackle), racquetball, soccer, softball, tennis, volleyball. **Team name:** Bulldogs.

Student services. Adult student services, career counseling, student employment services, financial aid counseling, health services, minority student services, on-campus daycare, personal counseling, placement for graduates, veterans' counselor, women's services. **Physically disabled:** Services for visually, speech, hearing impaired.

Contact. E-mail: vivian_franco@csufresno.edu
Phone: (559) 278-2261 Fax: (559) 278-4812
Vivian Franco, Director, California State University: Fresno, 5150 North Maple Avenue, M/S JA 57, Fresno, CA 93740-8026

California State University: Fullerton

Fullerton, California — **CB member**
www.fullerton.edu — **CB code: 4589**

- Public 4-year university
- Commuter campus in small city
- 27,917 degree-seeking undergraduates: 24% part-time, 58% women, 4% African American, 22% Asian American, 28% Hispanic American, 4% international
- 4,356 degree-seeking graduate students
- 64% of applicants admitted
- SAT or ACT required
- 49% graduate within 6 years

General. Founded in 1957. Regionally accredited. **Degrees:** 5,761 bachelor's awarded; master's offered. **ROTC:** Army. **Location:** 30 miles from Los Angeles. **Calendar:** Semester, extensive summer session. **Full-time faculty:** 719 total; 85% have terminal degrees, 24% minority, 42% women. **Part-time faculty:** 1,216 total. **Class size:** 27% < 20, 54% 20-39, 11% 40-49, 6% 50-99, 2% >100. **Special facilities:** Wildlife sanctuary, arboretum, desert studies center, economic education center, social science research center, twin studies center, center for children who stutter, California public archeology center, demographic research center, international business center, institute of gerontology, center for oral and public history, ethnographic cultural analysis center, life span development center, center for study of religion in American life, decision research center.

Freshman class profile. 25,525 applied, 16,304 admitted, 3,943 enrolled.

Mid 50% test scores			
SAT verbal:	430-540	Rank in top quarter:	50%
SAT math:	450-560	Rank in top tenth:	18%
ACT:	17-22	End year in good standing:	79%
GPA 3.50 or higher:	23%	Return as sophomores:	82%
GPA 3.0-3.49:	48%	Out-of-state:	2%
GPA 2.0-2.99:	29%	Live on campus:	7%
		International:	2%

Basis for selection. Eligibility index consisting of combination of high school GPA and SAT or ACT score. Audition required of music majors.

High school preparation. 16 units required. Required units include English 4, mathematics 3, social studies 1, history 1, science 2 (laboratory 2), foreign language 2 and academic electives 1. One visual and performing arts unit, 1 unit US history/government required.

2005-2006 Annual costs. Tuition/fees: $2,990; $13,160 out-of-state. Room/board: $7,174. Books/supplies: $1,260. Personal expenses: $2,300.

2005-2006 Financial aid. **Need-based:** 2,781 full-time freshmen applied for aid; 1,904 were judged to have need; 1,211 of these received aid. Average need met was 64%. Average scholarship/grant was $6,956; average loan $2,492. 65% of total undergraduate aid awarded as scholarships/grants, 35% as loans/jobs. **Non-need-based:** Awarded to 1,634 full-time undergraduates, including 390 freshmen. Scholarships awarded for academics. **Additional information:** Fee waiver for children of veterans killed in action or with service-connected disability whose annual income is $5,000 or less.

Application procedures. **Admission:** Closing date 11/30 (postmark date). $55 fee, may be waived for applicants with need. Application may be submitted online. Admission notification on a rolling basis beginning on or about 1/1. Reply date given on notification letter. **Financial aid:** Priority date 3/2, closing date 5/30. FAFSA required. Applicants notified on a rolling basis starting 4/2; must reply within 3 week(s) of notification.

Academics. **Special study options:** Accelerated study, cooperative education, cross-registration, distance learning, double major, dual enrollment of high school students, ESL, honors, independent study, internships, student-designed major, study abroad, teacher certification program. **Credit/placement by examination:** AP, CLEP, IB, SAT, ACT, institutional tests. 30 credit hours maximum toward bachelor's degree. **Support services:** Learning center, pre-admission summer program, reduced course load, remedial instruction, study skills assistance, tutoring, writing center.

Majors. **Area/ethnic studies:** African-American, American, Asian-American, Central/Eastern European, Hispanic-American/Latino/Chicano, Latin American, women's. **Biology:** General, biochemistry. **Business:** General, accounting, business admin, entrepreneurial studies, finance, international, management information systems, management science, managerial economics, marketing, tourism/travel. **Communications:** General, advertising, journalism, media studies, photojournalism, public relations, radio/tv. **Computer sciences:** General, computer science, information systems, information technology. **Education:** Kindergarten/preschool, music, physical. **Engineering:** General, civil, computer, electrical, mechanical, science. **English:** English lit, speech/rhetoric. **Foreign languages:** Comparative lit, French, German, Japanese, linguistics, Spanish. **Health:** Audiology/speech pathology, communication disorders, health services, nursing (RN). **History:** General. **Liberal arts:** Arts/sciences. **Math:** General, applied, statistics. **Parks/recreation:** Exercise sciences, health/fitness. **Philosophy/religion:** Philosophy, religion. **Physical sciences:** Chemistry, geology, physics. **Protective services:** Law enforcement admin. **Psychology:** General. **Public administration:** General, community org/advocacy. **Social sciences:** General, anthropology, economics, geography, political science, sociology. **Visual/performing arts:** Acting, art, art history/conservation, ceramics, commercial photography, commercial/advertising art, dance, directing/producing, dramatic, drawing, music history, music performance, music theory/composition, painting, photography, piano/organ, printmaking, sculpture, stringed instruments, studio arts, theater design, voice/opera.

Most popular majors. Business/marketing 22%, communications/journalism 12%, education 9%, liberal arts 8%, social sciences 7%, visual/performing arts 6%.

Computing on campus. 2,000 workstations in dormitories, library, computer center, student center. Dormitories wired for high-speed internet access and linked to campus network. Commuter students can connect to campus network. Online course registration, helpline, repair service, wireless network available.

Student life. **Freshman orientation:** Mandatory. Preregistration for classes offered. **Policies:** Freshmen permitted cars on campus. **Housing:** Apartments, fraternity/sorority housing available. **Activities:** Bands, choral groups, dance, drama, film society, literary magazine, music ensembles, musical theater, radio station, student government, student newspaper, symphony orchestra, TV station, Chinese Christian fellowship; Christian student association; disabled student association; Fellowship of Christian Athletes; human services student association; Movimiento Estudiantil Chicano de Atlan (MECHA); New Democratic Movement; poltical science student association; Asian, Hispanic, and African-American faculty/staff associations.

Athletics. NCAA. **Intercollegiate:** Baseball M, basketball, cross-country, fencing, gymnastics W, soccer, softball W, tennis W, track and field, volleyball W, wrestling M. **Intramural:** Badminton, basketball, bowling, football (non-tackle), gymnastics, handball M, racquetball, rugby M, skiing, soccer M, softball, swimming, tennis, volleyball, wrestling M. **Team name:** Titans.

Student services. Adult student services, career counseling, student employment services, financial aid counseling, health services, legal services, on-campus daycare, personal counseling, placement for graduates, veterans' counselor, women's services. **Physically disabled:** Services for visually, speech, hearing impaired.

Contact. Phone: (714) 278-2370 Fax: (714) 278-2356
Nancy Dority, Assistant Vice-President of Enrollment Services, California State University: Fullerton, Box 6900, Fullerton, CA 92834-6900

California State University: Long Beach

Long Beach, California — **CB member**
www.csulb.edu — **CB code: 4389**

- Public 4-year university
- Commuter campus in large city
- 28,514 degree-seeking undergraduates: 21% part-time, 60% women
- 4,026 degree-seeking graduate students
- 55% of applicants admitted
- SAT or ACT (ACT writing optional) required
- 48% graduate within 6 years

General. Founded in 1949. Regionally accredited. **Degrees:** 5,790 bachelor's awarded; master's offered. **ROTC:** Army. **Location:** 25 miles from Los Angeles. **Calendar:** Semester, extensive summer session. **Full-time faculty:** 966 total; 88% have terminal degrees, 26% minority, 42% women. **Part-time faculty:** 1,108 total; 26% have terminal degrees, 23% minority, 52% women. **Class size:** 29% < 20, 51% 20-39, 10% 40-49, 6% 50-99, 4% >100. **Special facilities:** Japanese garden, performing arts center, media center, art museum.

Freshman class profile. 38,579 applied, 21,037 admitted, 4,383 enrolled.

Mid 50% test scores		**GPA 2.0-2.99:**	14%
SAT verbal:	450-560	**Rank in top quarter:**	82%
SAT math:	470-580	**Return as sophomores:**	85%
ACT:	17-23	**Out-of-state:**	1%
GPA 3.50 or higher:	35%	**Live on campus:**	30%
GPA 3.0-3.49:	51%	**International:**	3%

Basis for selection. Admission based on secondary school record and standardized test scores. Audition required of dance, music majors. Portfolio required of art, design majors.

High school preparation. 15 units required. Required units include English 4, mathematics 3, social studies 1, history 1, science 2 (laboratory 2), foreign language 2 and academic electives 1. 1 unit fine arts required.

2006-2007 Annual costs. Tuition/fees (projected): $2,864; $13,034 out-of-state. Room/board: $6,648. Books/supplies: $1,314. Personal expenses: $1,868.

2005-2006 Financial aid. **Need-based:** 2,933 full-time freshmen applied for aid; 2,088 were judged to have need; 1,835 of these received aid. Average need met was 78%. Average scholarship/grant was $3,550; average loan $2,258. 61% of total undergraduate aid awarded as scholarships/grants, 39% as loans/jobs. **Non-need-based:** Awarded to 2,891 full-time undergraduates, including 565 freshmen. Scholarships awarded for academics, alumni affiliation, art, athletics, music/drama.

Application procedures. **Admission:** Closing date 11/30 (postmark date). $55 fee, may be waived for applicants with need. Application may be submitted online. Admission notification on a rolling basis beginning on or about 12/1. **Financial aid:** Priority date 3/2; no closing date. FAFSA required. Applicants notified on a rolling basis starting 4/1; must reply within 3 week(s) of notification.

Academics. **Special study options:** Accelerated study, cross-registration, distance learning, double major, dual enrollment of high school students, ESL, honors, independent study, internships, student-designed major, study abroad, teacher certification program, Washington semester. Concurrent enrollment at other CSU campuses. **Credit/placement by examination:** AP, CLEP, IB, institutional tests. **Support services:** Learning center, pre-admission summer program, reduced course load, remedial instruction, study skills assistance, tutoring, writing center.

Majors. **Architecture:** Interior. **Area/ethnic studies:** African-American, Hispanic-American/Latino/Chicano, women's. **Biology:** General, bacteriology, biochemistry, botany, cell/histology, molecular. **Business:** General, accounting, fashion, finance, human resources, international, management science, managerial economics, operations, real estate. **Communications:** Broadcast journalism, journalism, public relations. **Computer sciences:** General, computer science, information systems. **Education:** Art, family/

consumer sciences, physical. **Engineering:** Aerospace, biomedical, chemical, civil, computer, electrical, materials, mechanical. **Engineering technology:** Civil, construction, electrical, manufacturing. **English:** Composition, creative writing, speech/rhetoric. **Family/consumer sciences:** General, clothing/textiles, food/nutrition. **Foreign languages:** Classics, comparative lit, French, German, Japanese, Spanish. **Health:** Medical illustrating, medical radiologic technology/radiation therapy, nursing (RN), public health ed. **History:** General. **Liberal arts:** Arts/sciences. **Math:** General, applied, statistics. **Parks/recreation:** Facilities management. **Philosophy/religion:** Philosophy, religion. **Physical sciences:** Chemistry, geology, physics. **Protective services:** Criminal justice. **Psychology:** General. **Public administration:** Social work. **Social sciences:** Anthropology, economics, geography, sociology. **Visual/performing arts:** Art, art history/conservation, ceramics, cinematography, commercial/advertising art, conducting, dance, design, dramatic, drawing, fiber arts, industrial design, interior design, jazz, metal/jewelry, music history, music performance, painting, photography, piano/organ, printmaking, sculpture, studio arts, theater design, voice/opera.

Most popular majors. Business/marketing 22%, English 8%, liberal arts 9%, psychology 6%, social sciences 6%, visual/performing arts 9%.

Computing on campus. 1,200 workstations in dormitories, library, computer center. Dormitories linked to campus network. Commuter students can connect to campus network. Online course registration available.

Student life. **Freshman orientation:** Available, $45 fee. One-day pre-semester session. **Policies:** Freshmen permitted cars on campus. **Housing:** Coed dorms available. **Activities:** Bands, choral groups, dance, drama, film society, literary magazine, music ensembles, musical theater, opera, radio station, student government, student newspaper, symphony orchestra, TV station, more than 150 political, ethnic, and social service organizations.

Athletics. NCAA. **Intercollegiate:** Baseball M, basketball, cross-country, golf, soccer W, softball W, tennis W, track and field, volleyball, water polo. **Intramural:** Archery, badminton, basketball, bowling, diving, gymnastics, handball, racquetball, rowing (crew), rugby M, sailing, skiing, soccer, softball, swimming, table tennis, tennis, track and field, volleyball W, water polo W. **Team name:** Forty-Niners.

Student services. Adult student services, alcohol/substance abuse counseling, campus ministries, career counseling, services for economically disadvantaged, student employment services, financial aid counseling, health services, minority student services, on-campus daycare, personal counseling, placement for graduates, veterans' counselor, women's services. **Physically disabled:** Services for visually, speech, hearing impaired.

Contact. E-mail: eslb@csulb.edu
Phone: (562) 985-5471 Fax: (562) 985-4973
Thomas Enders, Assistant Vice President for Enrollment Services, California State University: Long Beach, 1250 Bellflower Boulevard, Long Beach, CA 90840-0106

California State University: Los Angeles

Los Angeles, California — **CB member**
www.calstatela.edu — **CB code: 4399**

- Public 4-year university
- Commuter campus in very large city
- 14,955 degree-seeking undergraduates: 27% part-time, 61% women, 8% African American, 21% Asian American, 46% Hispanic American, 4% international
- 5,079 graduate students
- 62% of applicants admitted

General. Founded in 1947. Regionally accredited. **Degrees:** 2,239 bachelor's awarded; master's, doctoral offered. **ROTC:** Army, Air Force. **Location:** 5 miles from downtown. **Calendar:** Quarter, extensive summer session. **Full-time faculty:** 581 total. **Part-time faculty:** 560 total. **Class size:** 36% < 20, 48% 20-39, 9% 40-49, 7% 50-99, 1% >100. **Special facilities:** Baroque pipe organ, 4 megavolt Van de Graaff accelerator.

Freshman class profile. 17,150 applied, 10,617 admitted, 1,458 enrolled.

Mid 50% test scores		GPA 3.0-3.49:	1%
SAT verbal:	380-500	Return as sophomores:	75%
SAT math:	400-520	Out-of-state:	1%
ACT:	15-20	Live on campus:	20%
GPA 3.50 or higher:	99%	International:	3%

Basis for selection. Secondary school record and standardized test scores important. SAT/ACT not required if GPA is 3.0 or above. EPT/ELM required for placement; may be waived based on SAT score. **Homeschooled:** Syllabi and written evaluation of courses completed may be required.

High school preparation. College-preparatory program required. 15 units required. Required units include English 4, mathematics 3, social studies 1, history 1, science 2 (laboratory 2), foreign language 2 and academic electives 1. 1 visual and performing arts required.

2005-2006 Annual costs. Tuition/fees: $3,035; $13,205 out-of-state. Room/board: $7,353. Books/supplies: $1,242. Personal expenses: $2,340.

Application procedures. **Admission:** Closing date 6/15 (postmark date). $55 fee, may be waived for applicants with need. Application may be submitted online. Admission notification on a rolling basis. **Financial aid:** Priority date 3/1; no closing date. FAFSA required. Applicants notified on a rolling basis starting 4/1; must reply within 3 week(s) of notification.

Academics. **Special study options:** Accelerated study, cooperative education, cross-registration, double major, dual enrollment of high school students, exchange student, honors, independent study, internships, student-designed major, study abroad, teacher certification program. **Credit/placement by examination:** AP, CLEP, institutional tests. **Support services:** Learning center, pre-admission summer program, reduced course load, remedial instruction, tutoring.

Majors. **Area/ethnic studies:** African-American, Hispanic-American/Latino/Chicano, Latin American. **Biology:** General, biochemistry, microbiology. **Business:** Business admin. **Communications:** General, radio/tv. **Computer sciences:** General. **Education:** Kindergarten/preschool, physical, technology/industrial arts, trade/industrial. **Engineering:** General, civil, electrical, mechanical. **Engineering technology:** Industrial. **English:** English lit. **Family/consumer sciences:** Food/nutrition. **Foreign languages:** Chinese, French, Japanese, Spanish. **Health:** Communication disorders, nursing (RN). **History:** General. **Interdisciplinary:** Natural sciences. **Liberal arts:** Arts/sciences. **Math:** General. **Philosophy/religion:** Philosophy. **Physical sciences:** Chemistry, geology, physics. **Protective services:** Fire services admin, law enforcement admin. **Psychology:** General. **Public administration:** Social work. **Social sciences:** Anthropology, economics, geography, political science, sociology. **Visual/performing arts:** Art, commercial/advertising art, dramatic, music performance.

Computing on campus. 1,500 workstations in dormitories, library, computer center, student center. Commuter students can connect to campus network. Online library, helpline, repair service, student web hosting available.

Student life. **Freshman orientation:** Available, $35 fee. Preregistration for classes offered. **Housing:** Coed dorms, apartments, fraternity/sorority housing available. $100 deposit, deadline 7/2. International house available. **Activities:** Jazz band, choral groups, dance, drama, literary magazine, music ensembles, musical theater, opera, student government, student newspaper, symphony orchestra, Chicanos for Creative Medicine, Hispanic business society, society of women engineers, Movimiento Estudiantil Chicanos de Aetlar, Asian student union, black student association, Sisters of the African Star, Vietnamese student association, Latin American society, Chinese American service club.

Athletics. NCAA. **Intercollegiate:** Baseball M, basketball, cross-country W, soccer, tennis W, track and field, volleyball W. **Intramural:** Basketball, bowling, gymnastics, handball, judo, racquetball, skiing, soccer, softball, swimming, synchronized swimming, tennis, track and field, volleyball, water polo, wrestling M. **Team name:** Golden Eagles.

Student services. Career counseling, student employment services, health services, on-campus daycare, personal counseling, placement for graduates, veterans' counselor. **Physically disabled:** Services for visually, speech, hearing impaired. **Learning disabled:** Comprehensive services available.

Contact. E-mail: admission@calstatela.edu
Phone: (323) 343-3901 Fax: (323) 343-6306
Joan Woosley, Director of Admissions and University Registrar, California State University: Los Angeles, 5151 State University Drive SA101, Los Angeles, CA 90032

California State University: Monterey Bay

Seaside, California — **CB member**
www.csumb.edu — **CB code: 1945**

- Public 4-year liberal arts and teachers college
- Residential campus in large town
- 3,407 degree-seeking undergraduates
- 366 graduate students
- 59% of applicants admitted

General. Founded in 1995. Regionally accredited. Dedicated to serving low-income, adult learner, first-generation, and underrepresented populations. **Degrees:** 570 bachelor's awarded; master's offered. **Location:** 107 miles from San Francisco, 70 miles from San Jose. **Calendar:** Semester, limited summer session. **Full-time faculty:** 95 total. **Part-time faculty:** 278 total. **Class size:** 37% < 20, 56% 20-39, 2% 40-49, 4% 50-99, less than 1% >100. **Special facilities:** Watershed facilities to complement earth system and policy major, seafloor mapping lab.

Freshman class profile. 6,369 applied, 3,784 admitted, 547 enrolled.

Mid 50% test scores			
SAT verbal:	440-570	Rank in top quarter:	32%
SAT math:	440-570	Rank in top tenth:	10%
ACT:	17-23	Out-of-state:	2%
		Live on campus:	87%

Basis for selection. Students must be high school graduates or GED equivalent, complete the 15-unit "a-g" course pattern of college preparatory study with grades of C or better, earn a qualifiable eligibility index. SAT/ACT test scores are not required for those students who earn a GPA of 3.00 or above in high school; 3.61 or above for non-residents. **Learning Disabled:** Reviewed case-by-case by Student Disabilities Resources Department.

High school preparation. 15 units required. Required units include English 4, mathematics 3, social studies 1, history 1, science 2 (laboratory 2), foreign language 2 and academic electives 2. One unit of Visual and Performing Arts required. Science lab units must include 1 biological, 1 physical.

2005-2006 Annual costs. Tuition/fees: $3,036; $13,206 out-of-state. Room/board: $8,880. Books/supplies: $1,242. Personal expenses: $1,980.

2004-2005 Financial aid. All financial aid based on need. 338 full-time freshmen applied for aid; 232 were judged to have need; 220 of these received aid. Average need met was 65%. Average scholarship/grant was $4,312; average loan $1,327. 61% of total undergraduate aid awarded as scholarships/grants, 39% as loans/jobs.

Application procedures. Admission: Priority date 11/30; no deadline. $55 fee, may be waived for applicants with need. Application may be submitted online. Admission notification on a rolling basis beginning on or about 12/1. **Financial aid:** Priority date 3/2; no closing date. FAFSA required. Applicants notified on a rolling basis starting 4/1.

Academics. Special study options: Cooperative education, cross-registration, distance learning, double major, dual enrollment of high school students, exchange student, honors, independent study, internships, liberal arts/career combination, semester at sea, student-designed major, study abroad, teacher certification program. **Credit/placement by examination:** AP, CLEP, IB. 30 credit hours maximum toward bachelor's degree. **Support services:** Learning center, reduced course load, remedial instruction, study skills assistance, tutoring, writing center.

Majors. Area/ethnic studies: Latin American, women's. **Biology:** Marine. **Business:** General, business admin, international. **Communications:** General. **Computer sciences:** General, computer graphics, information systems. **Conservation:** General, environmental studies, management/policy. **Education:** General, elementary. **Foreign languages:** General, Spanish. **Interdisciplinary:** Behavioral sciences, global studies. **Liberal arts:** Arts/sciences. **Physical sciences:** Oceanography, planetary. **Public administration:** Human services. **Social sciences:** General, anthropology. **Visual/performing arts:** General, art, dramatic, studio arts.

Most popular majors. Business/marketing 13%, communications/journalism 13%, communication technologies 11%, computer/information sciences 8%, liberal arts 25%, social sciences 10%.

Computing on campus. Dormitories wired for high-speed internet access and linked to campus network. Commuter students can connect to campus network. Online course registration, helpline, repair service, student web hosting, wireless network available.

Student life. Freshman orientation: Mandatory. **Policies:** Drug and alcohol policies/regulations. Freshmen permitted cars on campus. **Housing:** Guaranteed on-campus for all undergraduates. Coed dorms, special housing for disabled, apartments available. $100 deposit. **Activities:** Bands, choral groups, dance, drama, film society, music ensembles, radio station, student government, student newspaper, Amnesty International, business club, MECHA, Black Students United, baseball club, Raza Unida, art club, photography club, Asian club, sailing club.

Athletics. NAIA. **Intercollegiate:** Baseball M, basketball, cross-country, golf, sailing, soccer, softball W, volleyball W, water polo W. **Intramural:** Basketball, cheerleading, rugby W, sailing, soccer, softball, volleyball. **Team name:** Otters.

Student services. Adult student services, alcohol/substance abuse counseling, campus ministries, career counseling, services for economically disadvantaged, student employment services, financial aid counseling, health services, minority student services, on-campus daycare, personal counseling, placement for graduates, women's services. **Physically disabled:** Services for visually, speech, hearing impaired.

Contact. E-mail: moreinfo_admissions@csumb.edu
Phone: (831) 582-3518 Fax: (831) 582-3783
Dennis Geyer, Director of Admissions and Records, California State University: Monterey Bay, 100 Campus Center, Building 47, Seaside, CA 93955-8001

California State University: Northridge

Northridge, California
www.csun.edu **CB code: 4707**

- Public 4-year university
- Commuter campus in very large city
- 26,854 degree-seeking undergraduates: 23% part-time, 59% women, 9% African American, 12% Asian American, 28% Hispanic American, 5% international
- 4,515 degree-seeking graduate students
- 75% of applicants admitted
- SAT or ACT required
- 35% graduate within 6 years

General. Founded in 1958. Regionally accredited. University center in Ventura. **Degrees:** 5,488 bachelor's awarded; master's offered. **ROTC:** Army, Air Force. **Location:** 25 miles from Los Angeles. **Calendar:** Semester, limited summer session. **Full-time faculty:** 803 total; 29% minority, 44% women. **Part-time faculty:** 1,019 total; 24% minority, 52% women. **Class size:** 16% < 20, 57% 20-39, 15% 40-49, 10% 50-99, 3% >100. **Special facilities:** Anthropology museum, art botanical gardens, urban archives center, observatory, map library, center for the study of cancer and development biology, National Center on Deafness, planetarium.

Freshman class profile. 18,178 applied, 13,575 admitted, 3,720 enrolled.

Mid 50% test scores			
SAT verbal:	400-530	Out-of-state:	1%
SAT math:	410-550	Live on campus:	10%
Return as sophomores:	77%	International:	3%

Basis for selection. Index using high school GPA and test scores, and completion of subject requirements. In-state applicants should rank in top third of class; out-of-state in the top sixth. Business administration, economics, engineering, computer science, and physical therapy open to California residents only. Applicants with 3.0 GPA not required to submit test scores. ELM score required for math and English placement. Audition required of music majors.

High school preparation. 15 units required. Required units include English 4, mathematics 3, social studies 1, science 1 (laboratory 1) and foreign language 2. One visual and performing arts, 1 US history/government and 3 approved electives also required.

2005-2006 Annual costs. Tuition/fees: $3,036; $13,206 out-of-state. Room/board: $8,880. Books/supplies: $1,242. Personal expenses: $2,500.

2005-2006 Financial aid. Need-based: 53% of total undergraduate aid awarded as scholarships/grants, 47% as loans/jobs. **Non-need-based:** Scholarships awarded for academics, athletics, state residency.

Application procedures. Admission: Closing date 11/30. $55 fee, may be waived for applicants with need. Application may be submitted online. Admission notification on a rolling basis. Applications must be completed by November 30 for business administration, economics and physical therapy programs. **Financial aid:** Priority date 3/1; no closing date. FAFSA required. Applicants notified on a rolling basis starting 5/1.

Academics. Special study options: Accelerated study, cooperative education, distance learning, double major, dual enrollment of high school students, ESL, exchange student, external degree, honors, independent study, internships, liberal arts/career combination, student-designed major, study abroad, teacher certification program. **Credit/placement by examination:** AP, CLEP, institutional tests. **Support services:** Learning center, pre-admission summer program, remedial instruction, tutoring.

Majors. Area/ethnic studies: African-American, Hispanic-American/Latino/Chicano. **Biology:** General, bacteriology, biochemistry, cell/histology, molecular. **Business:** Banking/financial services, business admin, human resources, management information systems, management science, managerial economics, real estate. **Communications:** Broadcast journalism, journalism. **Computer sciences:** General. **Education:** Art, business, English, family/

consumer sciences, foreign languages, health, mathematics, music, physical, social science, social studies, speech impaired. **Engineering:** General, chemical, civil, computer, electrical, materials, mechanical, mechanics. **English:** British lit, creative writing, speech/rhetoric. **Family/consumer sciences:** General, business, child care, clothing/textiles, family studies, family/community services, food/nutrition, housing. **Foreign languages:** Comparative lit, French, German, linguistics, Spanish. **Health:** Nursing (RN), speech pathology. **History:** General. **Liberal arts:** Arts/sciences. **Math:** General, applied, statistics. **Parks/recreation:** General. **Philosophy/religion:** Philosophy, religion. **Physical sciences:** Chemistry, geology, geophysics, physics, planetary. **Psychology:** General. **Social sciences:** Anthropology, economics, geography, political science, sociology, urban studies. **Visual/performing arts:** Art, art history/conservation, ceramics, commercial/advertising art, crafts, dance, dramatic, drawing, metal/jewelry, music history, music performance, music theory/composition, painting, printmaking, sculpture.

Computing on campus. 1,800 workstations in dormitories, library, computer center, student center. Dormitories wired for high-speed internet access and linked to campus network. Commuter students can connect to campus network. Online course registration, online library, helpline, student web hosting available.

Student life. **Freshman orientation:** Available. **Policies:** Freshmen permitted cars on campus. **Housing:** Coed dorms, apartments, fraternity/sorority housing available. **Activities:** Bands, choral groups, dance, drama, film society, literary magazine, musical theater, radio station, student government, student newspaper, symphony orchestra, TV station, women's center, communities, various clubs and organizations.

Athletics. NCAA. **Intercollegiate:** Baseball M, basketball, cross-country, diving, golf, soccer, softball W, swimming, tennis W, track and field, volleyball, water polo W. **Intramural:** Badminton, baseball M, basketball, bowling, cross-country, diving, handball, ice hockey M, racquetball, rugby, sailing, skiing, soccer, softball, swimming, table tennis, tennis, track and field, volleyball. **Team name:** Matadors.

Student services. Adult student services, alcohol/substance abuse counseling, career counseling, student employment services, health services, on-campus daycare, personal counseling, placement for graduates, veterans' counselor, women's services. **Physically disabled:** Services for visually, speech, hearing impaired.

Contact. E-mail: admissions.records@csun.edu
Phone: (818) 677-3700 Fax: (818) 677-3766
Eric Forbes, Director of Admissions and Records, California State University: Northridge, 18111 Nordhoff Street, Northridge, CA 91328-8207

California State University: Sacramento

Sacramento, California — **CB member**
www.csus.edu — **CB code: 4671**

- Public 4-year university
- Commuter campus in very large city
- 23,028 degree-seeking undergraduates: 22% part-time, 57% women, 7% African American, 19% Asian American, 15% Hispanic American, 1% Native American, 1% international
- 3,594 degree-seeking graduate students
- 47% of applicants admitted
- 40% graduate within 6 years

General. Founded in 1947. Regionally accredited. **Degrees:** 4,659 bachelor's awarded; master's, doctoral offered. **ROTC:** Army, Air Force. **Location:** 100 miles from San Francisco. **Calendar:** Semester, extensive summer session. **Full-time faculty:** 724 total. **Part-time faculty:** 742 total. **Class size:** 22% < 20, 50% 20-39, 12% 40-49, 9% 50-99, 2% >100. **Special facilities:** Aquatic center, anthropology museum, art galleries, hellenic collection.

Freshman class profile. 15,980 applied, 7,584 admitted, 2,519 enrolled.

Mid 50% test scores			
SAT verbal:	410-530	Return as sophomores:	81%
SAT math:	430-560	Out-of-state:	1%
ACT:	17-22	Live on campus:	28%
End year in good standing:	81%	International:	1%

Basis for selection. School achievement record, test scores important (GPA weighted 5 times more than test scores). In-state applicants for regular admission normally in top third of class. Test scores not required if high school GPA 3.0 or higher.

High school preparation. 15 units required. Required units include English 4, mathematics 3, social studies 1, history 1, science 2 (laboratory 2), foreign language 2 and academic electives 1. History must be U.S. history/government. 1 visual and performing arts required.

2005-2006 Annual costs. Tuition/fees: $3,072; $13,242 out-of-state. Room/board: $8,392. Books/supplies: $1,260. Personal expenses: $1,789.

2004-2005 Financial aid. **Need-based:** 1,488 full-time freshmen applied for aid; 1,138 were judged to have need; 1,029 of these received aid. Average need met was 68%. Average scholarship/grant was $2,129; average loan $2,498. 61% of total undergraduate aid awarded as scholarships/grants, 39% as loans/jobs. **Non-need-based:** Awarded to 823 full-time undergraduates, including 113 freshmen.

Application procedures. **Admission:** Closing date 11/30 (receipt date). $55 fee, may be waived for applicants with need. Application may be submitted online. Admission notification on a rolling basis beginning on or about 11/1. Must reply by May 1 or within 2 week(s) if notified thereafter. Early action notification on rolling basis beginning November 1. **Financial aid:** Priority date 3/2; no closing date. FAFSA required. Applicants notified on a rolling basis starting 4/1; must reply within 4 week(s) of notification.

Academics. **Special study options:** Accelerated study, cooperative education, cross-registration, distance learning, double major, dual enrollment of high school students, ESL, independent study, internships, student-designed major, study abroad, teacher certification program. **Credit/placement by examination:** AP, CLEP, IB, SAT, ACT, institutional tests. SAT/ACT may be used to exempt students from English/math placement tests. **Support services:** Learning center, remedial instruction, study skills assistance, tutoring, writing center.

Majors. **Area/ethnic studies:** Asian. **Biology:** General, cellular/molecular, conservation, microbiology, molecular. **Business:** General, accounting, business admin, finance, human resources, insurance, international, management information systems, marketing, operations, real estate, taxation. **Communications:** General, journalism. **Computer sciences:** General, computer science. **Conservation:** General, environmental studies. **Education:** Bilingual, early childhood, ESL. **Engineering:** Civil, computer, electrical, mechanical. **Engineering technology:** General, mechanical. **English:** English lit. **Family/consumer sciences:** General, apparel marketing, child development, communication, family studies, food/nutrition. **Foreign languages:** French, Spanish. **Health:** Athletic training, audiology/speech pathology, community health services, health care admin, nursing (RN), occupational health, public health ed. **History:** General. **Interdisciplinary:** Gerontology. **Liberal arts:** Arts/sciences, humanities. **Math:** General. **Parks/recreation:** General, exercise sciences, facilities management, health/fitness. **Philosophy/religion:** Philosophy. **Physical sciences:** General, chemistry, geology, physics. **Protective services:** Criminal justice. **Psychology:** General. **Public administration:** Social work. **Social sciences:** General, anthropology, economics, geography, political science, sociology. **Visual/performing arts:** Art, dance, design, dramatic, graphic design, interior design, music performance, music theory/composition.

Computing on campus. 700 workstations in dormitories, library, computer center, student center. Dormitories wired for high-speed internet access and linked to campus network. Commuter students can connect to campus network. Online course registration, helpline, repair service, student web hosting, wireless network available.

Student life. **Freshman orientation:** Available, $60 fee. Preregistration for classes offered. **Policies:** Freshmen permitted cars on campus. **Housing:** Coed dorms available. **Activities:** Bands, choral groups, dance, drama, music ensembles, musical theater, opera, student government, student newspaper, symphony orchestra, more than 250 clubs, organizations and special interest groups.

Athletics. NCAA. **Intercollegiate:** Baseball M, basketball, cheerleading, cross-country, football (tackle) M, golf, gymnastics W, rowing (crew) W, soccer, softball W, tennis, track and field, volleyball W. **Intramural:** Badminton, basketball, bowling, football (tackle) M, golf, handball, ice hockey M, lacrosse M, racquetball, rowing (crew), skiing, soccer, softball, swimming, table tennis, tennis, volleyball, water polo, weight lifting. **Team name:** Hornets.

Student services. Adult student services, alcohol/substance abuse counseling, career counseling, services for economically disadvantaged, student employment services, financial aid counseling, health services, legal services, on-campus daycare, personal counseling, placement for graduates, veterans' counselor, women's services. **Physically disabled:** Services for visually, speech, hearing impaired.

Contact. E-mail: admissions@csus.edu
Phone: (916) 278-3901 Fax: (916) 278-6853
Emiliano Diaz, Director of Admissions and Outreach, California State University: Sacramento, 6000 J Street, Sacramento, CA 95819-6048

California State University: San Bernardino

San Bernardino, California **CB member**
www.csusb.edu **CB code: 4099**

- Public 4-year university and liberal arts college
- Commuter campus in small city
- 12,464 degree-seeking undergraduates: 17% part-time, 66% women, 12% African American, 8% Asian American, 34% Hispanic American, 1% Native American, 3% international
- 2,478 degree-seeking graduate students
- 25% of applicants admitted
- SAT or ACT (ACT writing optional) required
- 44% graduate within 6 years

General. Founded in 1962. Regionally accredited. School of Social and Behavioral Sciences offers master's in National Security Studies. Palm Desert satellite campus offers day and evening courses in degree and credential programs. **Degrees:** 2,684 bachelor's awarded; master's offered. **ROTC:** Army, Air Force. **Location:** 60 miles from Los Angeles. **Calendar:** Quarter, limited summer session. **Full-time faculty:** 461 total; 23% minority, 46% women. **Part-time faculty:** 164 total; 23% minority, 46% women. **Class size:** 26% < 20, 51% 20-39, 8% 40-49, 10% 50-99, 5% >100. **Special facilities:** Animal house, greenhouse, desert studies center, visual arts museum.

Freshman class profile. 9,629 applied, 2,385 admitted, 1,692 enrolled.

Mid 50% test scores			
SAT verbal:	400-510	Rank in top tenth:	18%
SAT math:	410-520	Return as sophomores:	81%
ACT:	16-21	Out-of-state:	2%
GPA 3.50 or higher:	1%	Live on campus:	22%
GPA 3.0-3.49:	56%	International:	3%
GPA 2.0-2.99:	32%	Fraternities:	6%
Rank in top quarter:	35%	Sororities:	10%

Basis for selection. High school GPA and test scores most important. SAT/ACT not required if high school GPA is 3.0 or higher. Entering undergraduates, except those who qualify for exemption, must take CSU entry-level mathematics (ELM) examination and CSU English placement test (EPT) after admission and before they enroll in classes.

High school preparation. 15 units required. Required units include English 4, mathematics 3, social studies 1, history 1, science 2 (laboratory 2), foreign language 2 and academic electives 1. One visual and performing arts unit also required. Students with disabilities may substitute alternate courses for specific subject requirements.

2005-2006 Annual costs. Tuition/fees: $3,092; $13,262 out-of-state. Room/board: $9,072. Books/supplies: $1,242. Personal expenses: $1,980.

Application procedures. Admission: No deadline. $55 fee, may be waived for applicants with need. Admission notification on a rolling basis. Students may apply as late as 3 weeks into quarter. **Financial aid:** Priority date 3/2; no closing date. FAFSA required. Applicants notified on a rolling basis starting 4/1.

Academics. Special study options: Accelerated study, cooperative education, cross-registration, distance learning, double major, dual enrollment of high school students, exchange student, honors, independent study, internships, study abroad, teacher certification program. **Credit/placement by examination:** AP, CLEP, IB, SAT, ACT, institutional tests. 40 credit hours maximum toward bachelor's degree. **Support services:** Learning center, pre-admission summer program, remedial instruction, tutoring, writing center.

Majors. Area/ethnic studies: African-American, American, Hispanic-American/Latino/Chicano. **Biology:** General, biochemistry. **Business:** Accounting, business admin, finance, human resources, international, management information systems, managerial economics, marketing, operations, organizational behavior, real estate. **Communications:** General, radio/tv. **Computer sciences:** Computer science, systems analysis. **Conservation:** Environmental studies. **Education:** Physical, trade/industrial. **English:** Creative writing, English lit. **Family/consumer sciences:** Child development, family studies, food/nutrition. **Foreign languages:** French, Spanish. **Health:** Environmental health, health care admin, nursing (RN), premedicine. **History:** General. **Interdisciplinary:** Museum. **Liberal arts:** Arts/sciences, humanities. **Math:** General. **Parks/recreation:** Exercise sciences. **Philosophy/religion:** Philosophy. **Physical sciences:** Chemistry, geology, physics. **Protective services:** Law enforcement admin. **Psychology:** General. **Public administration:** General, social work. **Social sciences:** General, anthropology, economics, geography, political science, sociology. **Visual/performing arts:** Art, art history/conservation, commercial/advertising art, dramatic, music history, music performance, musicology, studio arts, theater design, theater history.

Most popular majors. Business/marketing 22%, liberal arts 23%, psychology 7%, security/protective services 6%, social sciences 10%.

Computing on campus. 600 workstations in dormitories, library, computer center, student center. Dormitories wired for high-speed internet access and linked to campus network. Commuter students can connect to campus network. Online course registration, online library available.

Student life. Freshman orientation: Available. Preregistration for classes offered. **Housing:** Coed dorms, single-sex dorms, apartments, substance-free housing available. $50 partly refundable deposit. **Activities:** Jazz band, choral groups, dance, drama, music ensembles, musical theater, radio station, student government, student newspaper, TV station, more than 80 clubs and organizations.

Athletics. NCAA. **Intercollegiate:** Baseball M, basketball, cross-country W, golf M, soccer, softball W, swimming, tennis W, volleyball W, water polo. **Intramural:** Basketball, field hockey W, soccer, softball M, volleyball. **Team name:** Coyotes.

Student services. Adult student services, career counseling, student employment services, financial aid counseling, health services, legal services, minority student services, on-campus daycare, personal counseling, placement for graduates, veterans' counselor, women's services. **Physically disabled:** Services for visually, speech, hearing impaired.

Contact. E-mail: moreinfo@mail.csusb.edu
Phone: (909) 537-5188 Fax: (909) 537-7034
Olivia Rosas, Director of Admissions and Student Recruitment, California State University: San Bernardino, 5500 University Parkway, San Bernardino, CA 92407-2397

California State University: San Marcos

San Marcos, California **CB member**
www.csusm.edu **CB code: 5677**

- Public 4-year university
- Commuter campus in large town
- 6,276 degree-seeking undergraduates: 26% part-time, 61% women
- 629 degree-seeking graduate students
- 44% of applicants admitted
- 38% graduate within 6 years

General. Founded in 1989. Regionally accredited. **Degrees:** 884 bachelor's awarded; master's offered. **ROTC:** Army, Navy, Air Force. **Location:** 30 miles from San Diego. **Calendar:** Semester, limited summer session. **Full-time faculty:** 203 total; 99% have terminal degrees, 39% minority, 52% women. **Part-time faculty:** 220 total; 36% have terminal degrees, 17% minority, 57% women. **Class size:** 21% < 20, 56% 20-39, 14% 40-49, 7% 50-99, 2% >100.

Freshman class profile. 6,586 applied, 2,877 admitted, 804 enrolled.

Mid 50% test scores		Out-of-state:	2%
SAT verbal:	430-530	Live on campus:	31%
SAT math:	450-550	International:	3%
Return as sophomores:	73%		

Basis for selection. Student eligibility index calculated on GPA and test score combination. SAT scores can be used to meet English or math proficiency requirements.

High school preparation. College-preparatory program required. 15 units required; 16 recommended. Required and recommended units include English 4, mathematics 3-4, social studies 1, science 2 (laboratory 2), foreign language 2 and academic electives 1. One visual/performing arts required.

2005-2006 Annual costs. Tuition/fees: $3,062; $13,232 out-of-state. Room/board: $8,616. Books/supplies: $1,260. Personal expenses: $2,304.

2005-2006 Financial aid. Need-based: 61% of total undergraduate aid awarded as scholarships/grants, 39% as loans/jobs.

Application procedures. Admission: Closing date 11/30. $55 fee, may be waived for applicants with need. Application may be submitted online. Admission notification on a rolling basis beginning on or about 11/30. Must reply by May 1 or within 2 week(s) if notified thereafter. **Financial aid:** Priority date 3/2; no closing date. FAFSA required. Applicants notified on a rolling basis starting 4/15.

Academics. Special study options: Cross-registration, distance learning, double major, dual enrollment of high school students, ESL, independent study, internships, student-designed major, study abroad, teacher certification program, weekend college. Guaranteed admission for San Diego Community College students who have completed specific 2-year program at community college, designed for evening students who progress through program in cohort. **Credit/placement by examination:** AP, CLEP, IB, institutional tests. 30 credit hours maximum toward bachelor's degree. **Support services:** Learning center, pre-admission summer program, study skills assistance, tutoring, writing center.

Majors. Area/ethnic studies: Women's. **Biology:** General. **Business:** Business admin. **Communications:** General. **Computer sciences:** General, computer science. **Family/consumer sciences:** Family studies. **Foreign languages:** Spanish. **History:** General. **Liberal arts:** Arts/sciences. **Math:** General. **Physical sciences:** Chemistry. **Psychology:** General. **Social sciences:** General, economics, political science, sociology. **Visual/performing arts:** General.

Computing on campus. 1,300 workstations in library, computer center. Commuter students can connect to campus network. Online course registration, helpline available.

Student life. Freshman orientation: Mandatory, $60 fee. 2-day program. **Housing:** Special housing for disabled, apartments available. **Activities:** Choral groups, dance, drama, music ensembles, student newspaper, American Indian Science Engineering Society, Circle K, InterVarsity Christian Fellowship, Latter-day Saints student association, accounting society, Black Men on Campus, College Democrats, pre-health society, student housing association.

Athletics. NAIA. **Intercollegiate:** Golf M. **Intramural:** Basketball, golf M, soccer, volleyball.

Student services. Adult student services, alcohol/substance abuse counseling, career counseling, services for economically disadvantaged, student employment services, financial aid counseling, health services, on-campus daycare, personal counseling, placement for graduates, veterans' counselor. **Physically disabled:** Services for visually, speech, hearing impaired.

Contact. E-mail: apply@csusm.edu
Phone: (760) 750-4848 Fax: (760) 750-3248
Darren Bush, Associate Vice President of Enrollment Services, California State University: San Marcos, 333 S. Twin Oaks Valley Road, San Marcos, CA 92096-0001

California State University: Stanislaus

Turlock, California
www.csustan.edu **CB code: 4713**

- Public 4-year business and liberal arts college
- Commuter campus in small city
- 6,434 degree-seeking undergraduates: 31% part-time, 66% women, 4% African American, 12% Asian American, 28% Hispanic American, 1% Native American, 1% international
- 962 degree-seeking graduate students
- 65% of applicants admitted
- 52% graduate within 6 years

General. Founded in 1957. Regionally accredited. **Degrees:** 1,454 bachelor's awarded; master's offered. **Location:** 15 miles from Modesto. **Calendar:** 4-1-4, extensive summer session. **Full-time faculty:** 285 total; 20% minority, 45% women. **Part-time faculty:** 210 total; 16% minority, 49% women. **Class size:** 40% < 20, 50% 20-39, 7% 40-49, 2% 50-99, less than 1% >100. **Special facilities:** Observatory, interactive television classrooms, laser laboratory, marine sciences station, greenhouse, mainstage theater, bio-ag eco building.

Freshman class profile. 4,292 applied, 2,778 admitted, 870 enrolled.

Mid 50% test scores			
SAT verbal:	440-590	GPA 2.0-2.99:	29%
SAT math:	450-590	Return as sophomores:	82%
ACT:	18-24	Out-of-state:	1%
GPA 3.50 or higher:	29%	Live on campus:	29%
GPA 3.0-3.49:	41%	International:	1%

Basis for selection. High school GPA, courses taken and test scores. Special consideration for veterans, low-income and minority applicants. For non-native English speakers, ELPT can be substituted for TOEFL for placement. Exemptions result from scoring well on other specified tests or completion of appropriate courses. Test scores required if high school GPA is less than 3.0. Interview recommended for theatre arts, music majors. Audition recommended for music majors. Portfolio recommended for art majors. **Learning Disabled:** Students with diagnosed learning disability or neurological disorder that significantly impairs academic performance in specified area may be eligible for waiver of General Education Breadth (GEB) requirement. Contact Disabled Student Services or submit documentation of disability. Additional coursework required in lieu of GEB.

High school preparation. 15 units required. Required units include English 4, mathematics 3, social studies 1, history 1, science 2 (laboratory 2), foreign language 2 and academic electives 1. 1 unit visual and performing arts required.

2005-2006 Annual costs. Tuition/fees: $3,080; $13,250 out-of-state. Room/board: $8,253.

2005-2006 Financial aid. Need-based: 662 full-time freshmen applied for aid; 494 were judged to have need; 453 of these received aid. Average need met was 66%. Average scholarship/grant was $4,361; average loan $2,654. 61% of total undergraduate aid awarded as scholarships/grants, 39% as loans/jobs. **Non-need-based:** Awarded to 268 full-time undergraduates, including 86 freshmen. Scholarships awarded for academics, alumni affiliation, art, athletics, leadership, minority status, music/drama, state residency.

Application procedures. Admission: Priority date 11/30; deadline 7/1. $55 fee, may be waived for applicants with need. Application may be submitted online. Admission notification on a rolling basis beginning on or about 1/1. Must reply by May 1 or within 2 week(s) if notified thereafter. **Financial aid:** Priority date 3/2; no closing date. FAFSA required. Applicants notified on a rolling basis starting 3/15; must reply within 3 week(s) of notification.

Academics. Special study options: Accelerated study, cooperative education, cross-registration, distance learning, double major, dual enrollment of high school students, ESL, exchange student, external degree, honors, independent study, internships, liberal arts/career combination, student-designed major, study abroad, teacher certification program, weekend college. **Credit/placement by examination:** AP, CLEP, IB, SAT, ACT, institutional tests. 24 credit hours maximum toward bachelor's degree. Credit by examination does not count toward residency requirement. **Support services:** Learning center, pre-admission summer program, reduced course load, remedial instruction, study skills assistance, tutoring, writing center.

Majors. Agriculture: General. **Biology:** General. **Business:** Business admin. **Communications:** General. **Computer sciences:** Computer science, information technology. **Education:** Early childhood. **English:** English lit. **Foreign languages:** French, Spanish. **Health:** Nursing (RN). **History:** General. **Liberal arts:** Arts/sciences. **Math:** General. **Parks/recreation:** Health/fitness. **Philosophy/religion:** Philosophy. **Physical sciences:** General, chemistry, geology, physics. **Protective services:** Criminal justice. **Psychology:** General. **Social sciences:** General, anthropology, economics, geography, political science, sociology. **Visual/performing arts:** Art, dramatic, music performance, studio arts.

Most popular majors. Business/marketing 16%, liberal arts 23%, psychology 8%, security/protective services 7%, social sciences 12%.

Computing on campus. 150 workstations in dormitories, library, computer center, student center. Dormitories wired for high-speed internet access and linked to campus network. Commuter students can connect to campus network. Online course registration, online library, helpline, wireless network available.

Student life. Freshman orientation: Available. Preregistration for classes offered. Held year-round. **Policies:** Freshmen permitted cars on campus. **Housing:** Coed dorms, special housing for disabled, apartments available. $340 partly refundable deposit. Summer housing available and some housing can accomodate disabled students. **Activities:** Bands, choral groups, dance, drama, music ensembles, musical theater, opera, radio station, student government, student newspaper, symphony orchestra, Baha'i club, chinese student association, Chi Alpha Christian Fellowship, College Republicans, CSUS Democrats, Hunger Network, MEChA, Rainbow Alliance, Umoja, women's advocacy organization.

Athletics. NCAA. **Intercollegiate:** Baseball M, basketball, cross-country, golf M, soccer, softball W, track and field, volleyball W. **Intramural:** Basketball, football (non-tackle) M, soccer M, softball, volleyball. **Team name:** Warriors.

Student services. Adult student services, alcohol/substance abuse counseling, career counseling, services for economically disadvantaged, student employment services, financial aid counseling, health services, minority student services, on-campus daycare, personal counseling, placement for graduates, veterans' counselor, women's services. **Physically disabled:** Services for visually, speech, hearing impaired. **Learning disabled:** Comprehensive services available.

Contact. E-mail: outreach_help_desk@csustan.edu
Phone: (209) 667-3070 Toll-free number: (800) 300-7420
Fax: (209) 667-3788
Lisa Bernardo, Director, Admissions and Records, California State University: Stanislaus, 801 West Monte Vista Avenue, Turlock, CA 95382-0256

Chapman University

Orange, California — **CB member**
www.chapman.edu — **CB code: 4047**

- Private 4-year university and liberal arts college affiliated with Christian Church (Disciples of Christ)
- Residential campus in very large city
- 3,839 degree-seeking undergraduates: 5% part-time, 59% women, 2% African American, 8% Asian American, 11% Hispanic American, 1% Native American, 2% international
- 1,859 degree-seeking graduate students
- 53% of applicants admitted
- SAT or ACT with writing required
- 65% graduate within 6 years

General. Founded in 1861. Regionally accredited. Classes offered online and at 27 satellite campuses throughout California and Washington. **Degrees:** 743 bachelor's awarded; master's, doctoral, first professional offered. **ROTC:** Army, Air Force. **Location:** 35 miles from Los Angeles, 60 miles from San Diego. **Calendar:** 4-1-4, limited summer session. **Full-time faculty:** 262 total. **Part-time faculty:** 317 total; 7% minority, 45% women. **Class size:** 39% < 20, 58% 20-39, 2% 40-49, less than 1% 50-99, less than 1% >100. **Special facilities:** Albert Schweitzer collection of photographs, artifacts, and memorabilia; large Berlin Wall artifact on display; center for economic research; human performance laboratory; food science laboratory; center for entrepreneurship; center for international business; social science research laboratory.

Freshman class profile. 3,862 applied, 2,044 admitted, 853 enrolled.

Mid 50% test scores			
SAT verbal:	540-660	GPA 2.0-2.99:	7%
SAT math:	550-660	End year in good standing:	92%
ACT:	23-29	Return as sophomores:	85%
GPA 3.50 or higher:	65%	Out-of-state:	31%
GPA 3.0-3.49:	28%	International:	1%

Basis for selection. Academic course work plus GPA and test scores most important. Recommendations, essay, extracurricular activities also considered. SAT Subject Tests recommended. Interview recommended. Audition required for music, dance, theater majors. Portfolio required for art, film majors. Supplemental application required for film majors.

High school preparation. 11 units required. Required units include English 2, mathematics 2, social studies 3, science 2 (laboratory 1) and foreign language 2.

2006-2007 Annual costs. Tuition/fees: $30,748. Room/board: $10,500. Books/supplies: $1,100. Personal expenses: $1,600.

2004-2005 Financial aid. Need-based: 661 full-time freshmen applied for aid; 474 were judged to have need; 473 of these received aid. Average need met was 100%. Average scholarship/grant was $19,640; average loan $3,557. 73% of total undergraduate aid awarded as scholarships/grants, 27% as loans/jobs. **Non-need-based:** Awarded to 519 full-time undergraduates, including 99 freshmen. Scholarships awarded for academics, alumni affiliation, art, music/drama, religious affiliation, ROTC.

Application procedures. Admission: Closing date 1/31 (postmark date). $55 fee, may be waived for applicants with need. Application may be submitted online. Admission notification on a rolling basis beginning on or about 1/15. Must reply by May 1 or within 2 week(s) if notified thereafter. **Financial aid:** Priority date 3/2; no closing date. FAFSA required. Applicants notified on a rolling basis starting 3/15; must reply within 3 week(s) of notification.

Academics. Special study options: Distance learning, double major, ESL, exchange student, honors, independent study, internships, liberal arts/career combination, semester at sea, student-designed major, study abroad, teacher certification program, Washington semester. **Credit/placement by examination:** AP, CLEP, IB, SAT, ACT, institutional tests. 32 credit hours maximum toward bachelor's degree. **Support services:** Learning center, reduced course load, remedial instruction, study skills assistance, tutoring, writing center.

Majors. Biology: General, biochemistry, exercise physiology, molecular. **Business:** Accounting, business admin, managerial economics, organizational behavior. **Communications:** General, advertising, broadcast journalism. **Computer sciences:** General, computer science. **Education:** Music. **English:** Creative writing, English lit. **Foreign languages:** French, Spanish. **Health:** Athletic training, music therapy, predentistry, premedicine, preveterinary. **History:** American, European, public archives. **Interdisciplinary:** Biopsychology, nutrition sciences, peace/conflict. **Legal studies:** General. **Liberal arts:** Arts/sciences. **Math:** General. **Philosophy/religion:** Philosophy, religion. **Physical sciences:** Chemistry. **Psychology:** General. **Public administration:** Social work. **Social sciences:** International relations, political science, sociology, U.S. government. **Visual/performing arts:** Art, art history/conservation, cinematography, conducting, dance, dramatic, film/cinema, graphic design, music performance, music theory/composition, play/screenwriting, studio arts, voice/opera.

Most popular majors. Business/marketing 20%, communications/journalism 13%, liberal arts 6%, social sciences 6%, visual/performing arts 25%.

Computing on campus. 453 workstations in dormitories, library, computer center. Dormitories wired for high-speed internet access and linked to campus network. Commuter students can connect to campus network. Online course registration, online library, helpline, repair service, student web hosting, wireless network available.

Student life. Freshman orientation: Mandatory, $120 fee. Preregistration for classes offered. 5-day summer program immediately preceding start of semester. **Policies:** Freshmen permitted cars on campus. **Housing:** Guaranteed on-campus for freshmen. Coed dorms, special housing for disabled, apartments, substance-free housing available. $400 nonrefundable deposit, deadline 6/1. Housing for married, single, and students with dependents. **Activities:** Bands, choral groups, dance, drama, film society, literary magazine, music ensembles, musical theater, opera, radio station, student government, student newspaper, symphony orchestra, Hillel, Black student union, Model UN, gay/lesbian/bisexual association, Disciples on Campus, MEChA, Students for Peaceful Empowerment Action and Knowledge, Asian Pacific Student Association, Student Organization of Latinos.

Athletics. NCAA. **Intercollegiate:** Baseball M, basketball, cross-country, football (tackle) M, golf M, rowing (crew) W, soccer, softball W, swimming W, tennis, track and field W, volleyball W, water polo. **Intramural:** Basketball, soccer, tennis, volleyball. **Team name:** Panthers.

Student services. Adult student services, alcohol/substance abuse counseling, campus ministries, career counseling, student employment services, financial aid counseling, health services, on-campus daycare, personal counseling, placement for graduates, veterans' counselor. **Physically disabled:** Services for visually, speech, hearing impaired.

Contact. E-mail: admit@chapman.edu
Phone: (714) 997-6711 Toll-free number: (888) 282-7759
Fax: (714) 997-6713
Michael Drummy, Assistant Vice President and Chief Admission Officer, Chapman University, One University Drive, Orange, CA 92866

Charles R. Drew University of Medicine and Science

Los Angeles, California
www.cdrewu.edu — **CB code: 4982**

- Private 4-year health science college
- Very large city
- 200 degree-seeking undergraduates
- 10 graduate students
- 51% of applicants admitted

General. Regionally accredited. **Degrees:** 19 bachelor's, 28 associate awarded; master's offered. **Calendar:** Semester. **Full-time faculty:** 420 total. **Part-time faculty:** 25 total.

Freshman class profile. 408 applied, 207 admitted, 148 enrolled.

Basis for selection. High school/college transcripts, performance on institutional examination if required by program, essay if required all considered.

Application procedures. Admission: $35 fee. Application deadlines vary by program.

Academics. Credit/placement by examination: CLEP.

Majors. **Biology:** Biomedical sciences. **Health:** Nuclear medical technology, physician assistant, radiologic technology/medical imaging, sonography.

Contact. Phone: (323) 563-4800
Charles R. Drew University of Medicine and Science, 1731 East 120th Street, Los Angeles, CA 90059

Claremont McKenna College

Claremont, California — **CB member**
www.claremontmckenna.edu — **CB code: 4054**

- Private 4-year liberal arts college
- Residential campus in large town
- 1,140 degree-seeking undergraduates: 46% women, 4% African American, 15% Asian American, 12% Hispanic American, 4% international
- 21% of applicants admitted
- SAT or ACT with writing, application essay required

General. Founded in 1946. Regionally accredited. One of a cluster of 5 undergraduate and 2 graduate schools on adjoining campuses. Campuses share facilities. Cross-enrollment available at any of the 5 colleges, which include Claremont McKenna, Harvey Mudd, Pitzer, Pomona, and Scripps. **Degrees:** 286 bachelor's awarded. **ROTC:** Army, Air Force. **Location:** 35 miles from Los Angeles. **Calendar:** Semester. **Full-time faculty:** 116 total; 96% have terminal degrees, 16% minority, 36% women. **Part-time faculty:** 18 total; 78% have terminal degrees, 28% minority, 39% women. **Special facilities:** 11 research institutes, athenaeum (center of intellectual, cultural, and social activities), science center, leadership laboratory.

Freshman class profile. 3,734 applied, 786 admitted, 271 enrolled.

Mid 50% test scores			
SAT verbal:	630-740	Rank in top quarter:	95%
SAT math:	640-740	Rank in top tenth:	83%
ACT:	29-33	Out-of-state:	55%
		Live on campus:	100%

Basis for selection. School achievement record and test scores most important. Extracurricular activities, curriculum, recommendations, essays, interview, and motivation considered. SAT Subject Tests recommended. **Homeschooled:** Interview required. SAT Subject Tests required in three subjects (math, English, and one of choice).

High school preparation. College-preparatory program required. 15 units required. Required and recommended units include English 4, mathematics 3-4, social studies 2, history 1-3, science 2-3 and foreign language 3-4. Management-engineering candidates and science majors should have had both physics and chemistry.

2005-2006 Annual costs. Tuition/fees: $30,800. Room/board: $10,270. Books/supplies: $850. Personal expenses: $1,000.

2005-2006 Financial aid. All financial aid based on need. 164 full-time freshmen applied for aid; 127 were judged to have need; 127 of these received aid. Average need met was 100%. Average scholarship/grant was $23,460; average loan $2,991. 90% of total undergraduate aid awarded as scholarships/grants, 10% as loans/jobs.

Application procedures. **Admission:** Closing date 1/2 (postmark date). $60 fee, may be waived for applicants with need. Application may be submitted online. Admission notification 4/1. Must reply by 5/1. **Financial aid:** Closing date 2/1. FAFSA, CSS PROFILE required. Applicants notified by 4/1; must reply by 5/1.

Academics. Politics, philosophy, and economics (PPE) major patterned after program at Oxford University available to 12-15 new students each year. Students accepted spring of sophomore year. Environment, economics, and politics major also offered. **Special study options:** Accelerated study, combined bachelor's/graduate degree, cross-registration, double major, exchange student, independent study, internships, liberal arts/career combination, student-designed major, study abroad, Washington semester. **Credit/placement by examination:** AP, CLEP, IB, institutional tests. 16 credit hours maximum toward bachelor's degree. **Support services:** Tutoring, writing center.

Majors. **Area/ethnic studies:** African-American, American, Asian, Asian-American, European, gay/lesbian, Hispanic-American/Latino/Chicano, Latin American, Pacific, regional, South Asian, Southeast Asian, Spanish/Iberian, Western European, women's. **Biology:** General, biochemistry. **Business:** Accounting, accounting/business management, managerial economics. **Communications:** Media studies. **Computer sciences:** Computer science. **Conservation:** Environmental science, environmental studies. **Engineering:** General. **English:** English lit. **Foreign languages:** Chinese, classics, French, German, Italian, Japanese, Russian, Spanish. **Health:** Premedicine. **History:** General. **Interdisciplinary:** Math/computer science, neuroscience. **Legal studies:** General, prelaw. **Math:** General. **Philosophy/religion:** Philosophy, religion. **Physical sciences:** Chemistry, physics. **Psychology:** General. **Social sciences:** Economics, international relations, political science. **Visual/performing arts:** Art, dance, dramatic.

Most popular majors. Biology 9%, English 7%, foreign language 6%, history 11%, interdisciplinary studies 12%, psychology 11%, social sciences 60%.

Computing on campus. 156 workstations in dormitories, library, computer center, student center. Dormitories wired for high-speed internet access and linked to campus network. Commuter students can connect to campus network. Online library, helpline, repair service, student web hosting, wireless network available.

Student life. **Freshman orientation:** Mandatory. 5-day program. Parents invited for first day. **Policies:** Full-time rabbi, priest, and Protestant minister on campus. Also services for Mormon, Islamic, Christian Science, Quaker, and B'hai faiths. Freshmen permitted cars on campus. **Housing:** Guaranteed on-campus for all undergraduates. Coed dorms, apartments, substance-free housing available. $500 nonrefundable deposit, deadline 7/1. No married family (students with children) housing available on campus. **Activities:** Bands, choral groups, dance, drama, film society, literary magazine, music ensembles, musical theater, radio station, student government, student newspaper, symphony orchestra, debate/forensics, volunteer service, Young Republicans, Young Democrats, Pan-African Students Association, MECHA, Asian American Student Alliance, religious activities center, intervarsity faith team (Christian nondenominational), Hillel.

Athletics. NCAA. **Intercollegiate:** Baseball M, basketball, cross-country, diving, football (tackle) M, golf M, lacrosse W, soccer, softball W, swimming, tennis, track and field, volleyball W, water polo. **Intramural:** Badminton, basketball, bowling, fencing, golf W, racquetball, rugby, sailing, skiing, soccer, softball, squash, swimming, tennis, volleyball, water polo M, weight lifting. **Team name:** Stags (M), Athenas (W).

Student services. Campus ministries, career counseling, student employment services, financial aid counseling, health services, minority student services, personal counseling, placement for graduates, women's services. **Physically disabled:** Services for visually, speech, hearing impaired. **Learning disabled:** Comprehensive services available.

Contact. E-mail: admission@claremontmckenna.edu
Phone: (909) 621-8088 Fax: (909) 621-8516
Richard Vos, Vice President and Dean of Admissions and Financial Aid, Claremont McKenna College, 890 Columbia Avenue, Claremont, CA 91711-6425

Cogswell Polytechnical College

Sunnyvale, California
www.cogswell.edu/ — **CB code: 4057**

- Private 4-year visual arts and engineering college
- Commuter campus in small city
- 282 degree-seeking undergraduates: 52% part-time, 12% women
- 81% of applicants admitted
- Application essay required

General. Founded in 1887. Regionally accredited. Program fusion of art and engineering. **Degrees:** 66 bachelor's awarded. **Location:** 45 miles from San Francisco, 4 miles from San Jose. **Calendar:** Semester, extensive summer session. **Full-time faculty:** 14 total; 43% have terminal degrees, 36% women. **Part-time faculty:** 27 total; 11% have terminal degrees, 33% women. **Class size:** 98% < 20, 2% 20-39. **Special facilities:** Electronic music laboratories, sound/recording studio, video studio, editing studio, computer imaging laboratories, SGI laboratory, MIDI laboratory, sculpture studio, drawing/painting studio, 2D and 3D animation laboratories.

Freshman class profile. 48 applied, 39 admitted, 31 enrolled.

Basis for selection. Motivation, 2.7 GPA in academic subjects, and test scores. Recommendations, mathematics and science background also considered. SAT or ACT recommended. SAT recommended and used primarily for placement. Interview recommended. Portfolio required for all programs.

High school preparation. 7 units required. Required units include English 3, mathematics 3 and science 1. One chemistry, 2 physics, 2 algebra, 1 geometry, 1 trigonometry required for engineering program. 2 arts, 2 mathematics required for arts program.

2005-2006 Annual costs. Tuition/fees: $13,720. Books/supplies: $1,168. Personal expenses: $2,512.

2004-2005 Financial aid. **Need-based:** 43% of total undergraduate aid awarded as scholarships/grants, 57% as loans/jobs.

Application procedures. **Admission:** No deadline. $55 fee. Admission notification on a rolling basis. **Financial aid:** Priority date 3/2; no closing date. FAFSA, institutional form required. Applicants notified on a rolling basis starting 4/30; must reply within 4 week(s) of notification.

Academics. **Special study options:** Cross-registration, distance learning, external degree, independent study, internships. **Credit/placement by examination:** AP, CLEP, IB, institutional tests. 16 credit hours maximum toward bachelor's degree. **Support services:** Reduced course load, remedial instruction, tutoring.

Majors. **Communications technology:** Animation/special effects. **Engineering:** Electrical, software. **Protective services:** Fire safety technology, fire services admin. **Visual/performing arts:** Cinematography.

Computing on campus. 100 workstations in library, computer center. Online library, wireless network available.

Student life. **Freshman orientation:** Mandatory. **Policies:** Freshmen permitted cars on campus. **Housing:** Apartments available. $400 deposit. Arrangement with local apartment facility available. **Activities:** Student government, student newspaper.

Athletics. **Intramural:** Skiing, table tennis.

Student services. Alcohol/substance abuse counseling, career counseling, student employment services, financial aid counseling, personal counseling, placement for graduates, veterans' counselor.

Contact. E-mail: info@cogswell.edu
Phone: (408) 541-0100 Fax: (408) 747-0764
Valarie Brown, Director of Enrollment Services, Cogswell Polytechnical College, 1175 Bordeaux Drive, Sunnyvale, CA 94089-1299

Coleman College

La Mesa, California
www.coleman.edu **CB code: 0955**

- Private 4-year technical college
- Commuter campus in small city
- 430 degree-seeking undergraduates
- 17 graduate students
- Interview required

General. Founded in 1963. Accredited by ACICS. College uses inverted curriculum with major taken before general curriculum. Vast majority of students are transfers. **Degrees:** 108 bachelor's, 121 associate awarded; master's offered. **Location:** 5 miles from San Diego. **Calendar:** Continuous. **Full-time faculty:** 95 total. **Part-time faculty:** 40 total.

Basis for selection. Open admission, but selective for some programs. Test score and interview important. In special cases school record, special talents, recommendations will be taken into account. Test scores recommended for placement and credit. Institutionally administered aptitude test required. Skills test given during interview.

2005-2006 Annual costs. Tuition $26,460 for 13-month associate degree program in computer information science. Costs vary depending on program. Books/supplies: $425. Personal expenses: $1,206.

Financial aid. All financial aid based on need.

Application procedures. **Admission:** No deadline. No application fee. Admission notification on a rolling basis. **Financial aid:** Priority date 3/2; no closing date. FAFSA, institutional form required. Applicants notified on a rolling basis.

Academics. **Special study options:** Accelerated study, distance learning, double major. **Credit/placement by examination:** CLEP. 26 credit hours maximum toward associate degree, 36 toward bachelor's. **Support services:** Reduced course load, tutoring.

Majors. **Business:** Business admin. **Computer sciences:** General. **Engineering:** Computer. **Engineering technology:** Computer.

Most popular majors. Computer/information sciences 95%.

Computing on campus. 365 workstations in library, computer center.

Student life. **Activities:** Student government, student activities committee, international student association.

Student services. Career counseling, personal counseling, placement for graduates, veterans' counselor.

Contact. E-mail: admis@coleman.edu
Phone: (619) 465-3990 Toll-free number: (800) 430-2030
Fax: (619) 463-0162
Amy Collins, Director of Admissions, Coleman College, 7380 Parkway Drive, La Mesa, CA 91942-1500

Columbia College: Hollywood

Tarzana, California
www.columbiacollege.edu **CB code: 1247**

- Private 4-year visual arts and technical college
- Commuter campus in very large city
- 211 degree-seeking undergraduates

General. Founded in 1952. Accredited by ACCSCT. Most classes held in evening, taught by professionals in motion picture and television/video industries. **Degrees:** 30 bachelor's, 1 associate awarded. **Location:** 10 miles from downtown Los Angeles. **Calendar:** Quarter, limited summer session. **Part-time faculty:** 30 total; 10% have terminal degrees. **Special facilities:** Film and electronic editing facilities, production facilities, dubbing theater, transfer room (video and audio).

Basis for selection. Open admission, but selective for some programs. References, high school record, and demonstrated interest in communications most important. On-site proficiency tests used to determine reading/ mathematics proficiencies. Interviews recommended.

2005-2006 Annual costs. Tuition/fees: $11,625.

Financial aid. **Additional information:** All financial aid forms due by second week of classes.

Application procedures. **Admission:** Priority date 6/30; no deadline. $50 fee. Admission notification on a rolling basis. **Financial aid:** Priority date 2/1; no closing date. FAFSA, institutional form required. Applicants notified on a rolling basis starting 7/15; must reply within 3 week(s) of notification.

Academics. **Special study options:** Accelerated study, internships. **Credit/ placement by examination:** CLEP.

Majors. **Communications:** Broadcast journalism. **Communications technology:** General. **Visual/performing arts:** Cinematography, film/cinema.

Computing on campus. 12 workstations in library, computer center.

Student life. **Activities:** Film society, student newspaper, TV station.

Student services. Adult student services, career counseling, personal counseling, placement for graduates, veterans' counselor.

Contact. E-mail: cchadmin@columbiacollege.edu
Phone: (818) 345-8414 ext. 105 Toll-free number: (800) 785-0585 ext. 105
Fax: (818) 851-6401
Carmen Munoz, Student Affairs and Admissions Director, Columbia College: Hollywood, 18618 Oxnard Street, Tarzana, CA 91356

Concordia University

Irvine, California **CB member**
www.cui.edu **CB code: 4069**

- Private 4-year university and liberal arts college affiliated with Lutheran Church - Missouri Synod
- Residential campus in small city
- 1,357 degree-seeking undergraduates: 4% part-time, 63% women, 4% African American, 4% Asian American, 13% Hispanic American, 1% Native American, 2% international
- 571 degree-seeking graduate students
- 68% of applicants admitted
- SAT or ACT with writing required
- 56% graduate within 6 years

General. Founded in 1972. Regionally accredited. Part of nationwide 10-campus Concordia University System which provides interactive distance learning classes between campuses and simultaneous enrollment, allowing students to spend semester or year at another Concordia campus. **Degrees:** 334 bachelor's, 2 associate awarded; master's offered. **Location:** 40 miles from Los Angeles, 80 miles from San Diego. **Calendar:** Semester, limited summer session. **Full-time faculty:** 77 total; 62% have terminal degrees, 35% women. **Part-time faculty:** 131 total; 19% have terminal degrees, 44% women. **Class size:** 51% < 20, 45% 20-39, 1% 40-49, 2% 50-99, less than 1% >100.

Freshman class profile. 998 applied, 680 admitted, 265 enrolled.

Mid 50% test scores		**GPA 2.0-2.99:**	4%
SAT verbal:	470-570	**Rank in top quarter:**	53%
SAT math:	470-580	**Rank in top tenth:**	15%
ACT:	20-25	**Return as sophomores:**	78%
GPA 3.50 or higher:	51%	**Out-of-state:**	22%
GPA 3.0-3.49:	45%	**Live on campus:**	95%

Basis for selection. Secondary school record, class rank, standardized test scores most important. Recommendations and character/personal qualities also important. Audition required for music majors.

High school preparation. 16 units required. Required and recommended units include English 4, mathematics 3, social studies 2-4, science 3 (laboratory 2) and foreign language 2. Biology, chemistry, algebra I and II, and geometry specifically recommended.

2006-2007 Annual costs. Tuition/fees: $21,130. Room/board: $7,270. Books/supplies: $1,000. Personal expenses: $1,900.

2004-2005 Financial aid. Need-based: 273 full-time freshmen applied for aid; 200 were judged to have need; 200 of these received aid. Average need met was 70%. Average scholarship/grant was $10,657; average loan $2,583. 74% of total undergraduate aid awarded as scholarships/grants, 26% as loans/jobs. **Non-need-based:** Awarded to 435 full-time undergraduates, including 87 freshmen. Scholarships awarded for academics, alumni affiliation, art, athletics, leadership, music/drama, religious affiliation.

Application procedures. Admission: Priority date 3/2; no deadline. $50 fee, may be waived for applicants with need. Application may be submitted online. Admission notification on a rolling basis. Must reply by May 1 or within 4 week(s) if notified thereafter. **Financial aid:** Priority date 3/2, closing date 4/1. FAFSA, institutional form required. Applicants notified on a rolling basis starting 2/1; must reply within 4 week(s) of notification.

Academics. Special study options: Accelerated study, cross-registration, distance learning, double major, dual enrollment of high school students, ESL, exchange student, honors, independent study, internships, student-designed major, study abroad, teacher certification program. **Credit/placement by examination:** AP, CLEP, IB. 32 credit hours maximum toward bachelor's degree. **Support services:** Learning center, tutoring, writing center.

Majors. Biology: General. **Business:** Business admin, international. **Communications:** General. **Computer sciences:** Information technology. **Education:** General. **English:** English lit. **History:** General. **Interdisciplinary:** Behavioral sciences, global studies. **Legal studies:** Prelaw. **Liberal arts:** Arts/sciences, humanities. **Math:** General. **Parks/recreation:** Exercise sciences. **Physical sciences:** Chemistry. **Psychology:** General. **Social sciences:** Political science. **Theology:** Theology. **Visual/performing arts:** Art, dramatic.

Most popular majors. Business/marketing 18%, communications/journalism 6%, education 17%, liberal arts 17%, philosophy/religious studies 7%, social sciences 11%, visual/performing arts 6%.

Computing on campus. 69 workstations in dormitories, library, computer center, student center. Dormitories wired for high-speed internet access and linked to campus network. Commuter students can connect to campus network. Online library, helpline, wireless network available.

Student life. Freshman orientation: Available. Preregistration for classes offered. **Policies:** Freshmen permitted cars on campus. **Housing:** Guaranteed on-campus for freshmen. Single-sex dorms, special housing for disabled available. $300 fully refundable deposit, deadline 6/30. **Activities:** Pep band, choral groups, dance, drama, film society, literary magazine, music ensembles, musical theater, radio station, student government, student newspaper, Spiritual Life Inreach, Spiritual Life Outreach, Mission Unstoppable, campus church, environmental club, youth ministry team, praise band, gospel choir, Cross Cultural Link, Nuestro Voz.

Athletics. NAIA. **Intercollegiate:** Baseball M, basketball, cross-country, golf, soccer, softball W, tennis, track and field, volleyball W. **Intramural:** Basketball, bowling, football (non-tackle), soccer, softball, table tennis, track and field, volleyball. **Team name:** Eagles.

Student services. Adult student services, alcohol/substance abuse counseling, campus ministries, financial aid counseling, health services, minority student services, personal counseling.

Contact. E-mail: admission@cui.edu
Phone: (949) 854-8002 ext. 1106 Toll-free number: (800) 229-1200
Fax: (949) 854-6894
Lori McDonald, Director of Enrollment Services, Concordia University, 1530 Concordia West, Irvine, CA 92612-3299

Design Institute of San Diego

San Diego, California
www.disd.edu **CB code: 3492**

- For-profit 4-year technical college
- Very large city
- 500 degree-seeking undergraduates
- 40% of applicants admitted
- Application essay, interview required

General. Accredited by ACICS. **Degrees:** 38 bachelor's awarded. **Calendar:** Semester. **Full-time faculty:** 4 total. **Part-time faculty:** 59 total.

Freshman class profile. 25 applied, 10 admitted, 10 enrolled.

Basis for selection. High school/college grades, 2 professional references considered.

2006-2007 Annual costs. Tuition/fees: $14,400. Books/supplies: $800. Personal expenses: $4,626.

Application procedures. Admission: No deadline. No application fee. Admission notification on a rolling basis. **Financial aid:** No deadline. Applicants notified on a rolling basis.

Academics. Credit/placement by examination: CLEP.

Majors. Visual/performing arts: Interior design.

Contact. Phone: (858) 566-1200 Toll-free number: (800) 619-4337
Fax: (858) 566-2711
Paula Parrish, Director of Admissions, Design Institute of San Diego, 8555 Commerce Avenue, San Diego, CA 92121

DeVry University: Fremont

Fremont, California
www.devry.edu **CB code: 0520**

- For-profit 4-year university
- Commuter campus in small city
- 1,446 degree-seeking undergraduates: 35% part-time, 30% women
- 132 graduate students
- 36% graduate within 6 years

General. Regionally accredited. **Degrees:** 346 bachelor's, 26 associate awarded; master's offered. **Location:** 15 miles from San Jose. **Calendar:** Semester, extensive summer session. **Full-time faculty:** 46 total; 65% minority, 17% women. **Part-time faculty:** 32 total; 53% minority, 22% women.

Freshman class profile. 271 enrolled.

Basis for selection. Applicant must have high school diploma or equivalent, degree from accredited postsecondary institution, pass institutional placement examination, or submit acceptable test scores and be 17 years of age. New students may enter at beginning of any semester. Applicants may also take institution-administered admissions test.

2005-2006 Annual costs. Tuition/fees: $13,410. Books/supplies: $1,100. Personal expenses: $1,996.

2004-2005 Financial aid. All financial aid based on need. 264 full-time freshmen applied for aid; 255 were judged to have need; 231 of these received aid. Average need met was 41%. Average scholarship/grant was $6,702; average loan $6,752. 28% of total undergraduate aid awarded as scholarships/grants, 72% as loans/jobs.

Application procedures. Admission: No deadline. $50 fee. Admission notification on a rolling basis. **Financial aid:** No deadline. FAFSA required. Applicants notified on a rolling basis.

Academics. Special study options: Accelerated study, cooperative education, distance learning. **Credit/placement by examination:** CLEP, institutional tests. **Support services:** Learning center, remedial instruction, tutoring.

Majors. **Biology:** Bioinformatics. **Business:** General. **Computer sciences:** Networking, systems analysis. **Engineering technology:** Biomedical, computer, electrical.

Most popular majors. Business/marketing 38%, computer/information sciences 30%, engineering/engineering technologies 32%.

Computing on campus. 350 workstations in library, computer center. Online course registration, online library, helpline available.

Student life. **Freshman orientation:** Mandatory. **Policies:** Freshmen permitted cars on campus. **Housing:** Private apartments, student-plan housing, private rooms available. **Activities:** Institute of Electronic and Electrical Engineers, Hmong Organization on Technology, network communications club, Tau Alpha Pi national honor society for engineering technologies, women's organization, game development, Latino American student organization, Phi Beta Lambda national organization for business majors, chess club, self-defense club.

Athletics. **Intramural:** Soccer.

Student services. Career counseling, student employment services, financial aid counseling, placement for graduates, veterans' counselor. **Physically disabled:** Services for visually, hearing impaired.

Contact. Phone: (510) 574-1200 Toll-free number: (888) 393-3879
Marc Martin, Director of Admission, DeVry University: Fremont, 6600 Dumbarton Circle, Fremont, CA 94555-3615

DeVry University: Long Beach

Long Beach, California
www.devry.edu **CB code: 2053**

- For-profit 4-year university
- Commuter campus in large town
- 1,022 degree-seeking undergraduates: 40% part-time, 34% women
- 178 graduate students
- Interview required
- 36% graduate within 6 years

General. Regionally accredited. **Degrees:** 476 bachelor's, 47 associate awarded; master's offered. **Location:** 26 miles from Los Angeles. **Calendar:** Semester, extensive summer session. **Full-time faculty:** 27 total; 37% minority, 11% women. **Part-time faculty:** 124 total; 23% minority, 23% women.

Freshman class profile. 194 enrolled.

Return as sophomores:	53%	International:	1%

Basis for selection. Applicant must have high school diploma or equivalent, degree from an accredited postsecondary institution, or submit acceptable test scores and be at least 17 years of age on the first day of classes. New students may enter at beginning of any semester. Applicants may also take institution-administered admissions test.

High school preparation. College-preparatory program recommended.

2005-2006 Annual costs. Tuition/fees: $12,800. Books/supplies: $1,200. Personal expenses: $2,090.

2004-2005 Financial aid. All financial aid based on need. 244 full-time freshmen applied for aid; 230 were judged to have need; 224 of these received aid. Average need met was 38%. Average scholarship/grant was $5,906; average loan $4,615. 27% of total undergraduate aid awarded as scholarships/grants, 73% as loans/jobs.

Application procedures. **Admission:** No deadline. $50 fee. Application may be submitted online. Admission notification on a rolling basis. **Financial aid:** No deadline. FAFSA required. Applicants notified on a rolling basis.

Academics. **Special study options:** Accelerated study, cooperative education, distance learning. **Credit/placement by examination:** CLEP. **Support services:** Learning center, remedial instruction, tutoring.

Majors. **Biology:** Bioinformatics. **Business:** Business admin, operations. **Computer sciences:** Information technology, networking, systems analysis. **Engineering technology:** Computer, electrical.

Most popular majors. Business/marketing 36%, computer/information sciences 47%, engineering/engineering technologies 17%.

Computing on campus. 463 workstations in library, computer center. Online course registration, online library, helpline available.

Student life. **Freshman orientation:** Mandatory. **Policies:** Freshmen permitted cars on campus. **Housing:** Private apartments, student-plan housing, private rooms available. **Activities:** Associate Student Body Advocates, Society of Hispanic Professional Engineers, Epsilon Delta Pi, United Islands, Tau Alpha Pi, business and accounting association, National Society of Black Engineers (NSBE), Institute of Electronic and Electrical Engineers (IEEE).

Student services. Career counseling, student employment services, financial aid counseling, placement for graduates, veterans' counselor. **Physically disabled:** Services for visually, hearing impaired.

Contact. Phone: (562) 427-4162 Toll-free number: (800) 597-0444
Elaine Francisco, Director of Admissions, DeVry University: Long Beach, 3880 Kilroy Airport Way, Long Beach, CA 90806

DeVry University: Pomona

Pomona, California
www.devry.edu **CB code: 4214**

- For-profit 4-year university
- Commuter campus in small city
- 1,720 degree-seeking undergraduates: 44% part-time, 30% women
- 178 graduate students
- Interview required
- 36% graduate within 6 years

General. Founded in 1983. Regionally accredited. **Degrees:** 476 bachelor's, 47 associate awarded; master's offered. **Location:** 13 miles from Los Angeles. **Calendar:** Semester, extensive summer session. **Full-time faculty:** 38 total; 42% minority, 13% women. **Part-time faculty:** 42 total; 40% minority, 21% women.

Freshman class profile. 284 enrolled.

Basis for selection. Applicant must have high school diploma or equivalent, degree from an accredited postsecondary institution, or submit acceptable test scores and be at least 17 years of age on the first day of classes. New students may enter at the beginning of any semester. Applicants may also take institution-administered admissions test.

High school preparation. College-preparatory program recommended.

2005-2006 Annual costs. Tuition/fees: $12,800. Books/supplies: $1,100. Personal expenses: $1,996.

2004-2005 Financial aid. All financial aid based on need. 313 full-time freshmen applied for aid; 295 were judged to have need; 292 of these received aid. Average need met was 39%. Average scholarship/grant was $5,259; average loan $5,182. 25% of total undergraduate aid awarded as scholarships/grants, 75% as loans/jobs.

Application procedures. **Admission:** No deadline. $50 fee. Application may be submitted online. Admission notification on a rolling basis. **Financial aid:** No deadline. FAFSA required. Applicants notified on a rolling basis.

Academics. **Special study options:** Accelerated study, cooperative education, distance learning. **Credit/placement by examination:** CLEP, institutional tests. **Support services:** Learning center, remedial instruction, tutoring.

Majors. **Business:** General. **Computer sciences:** General, networking. **Engineering technology:** Biomedical, computer, electrical.

Most popular majors. Business/marketing 41%, computer/information sciences 45%, engineering/engineering technologies 14%.

Computing on campus. 517 workstations in library, computer center. Online course registration, online library, helpline available.

Student life. **Freshman orientation:** Mandatory. **Policies:** Freshmen permitted cars on campus. **Housing:** Private apartments, student-plan housing, private rooms available. **Activities:** Gaming association, Institute for Electrical and Electronic Engineers, Living in Truth, National Society of Black Engineers, Phi Beta Lambda, Society of Hispanic Professional Engineers, networking professional association, Toastmasters.

Student services. Career counseling, student employment services, financial aid counseling, placement for graduates, veterans' counselor. **Physically disabled:** Services for visually, hearing impaired.

Contact. Phone: (909) 868-4240
Jere Thrasher, Director of Admissions, DeVry University: Pomona, 901 Corporate Center Drive, Pomona, CA 91768-2642

DeVry University: West Hills

West Hills, California
www.devry.edu **CB code: 2800**

- For-profit 4-year university
- Commuter campus in large city
- 670 degree-seeking undergraduates: 51% part-time, 26% women
- 98 graduate students
- Interview required
- 36% graduate within 6 years

General. Regionally accredited. **Degrees:** 185 bachelor's, 18 associate awarded; master's offered. **Location:** 30 miles from Los Angeles. **Calendar:** Semester, extensive summer session. **Full-time faculty:** 17 total; 12% minority, 12% women. **Part-time faculty:** 44 total; 18% minority, 27% women.

Freshman class profile. 79 enrolled.

Return as sophomores:	53%	**International:**	3%

Basis for selection. Applicant must have high school diploma or equivalent, degree from an accredited postsecondary institution, or submit acceptable test scores and be at least 17 years of age on the first day of classes. New students may enter at the beginning of any semester. Applicants may also take institution-administered admissions test.

High school preparation. College-preparatory program recommended.

2005-2006 Annual costs. Tuition/fees: $12,800. Books/supplies: $1,100. Personal expenses: $1,996.

2004-2005 Financial aid. All financial aid based on need. 101 full-time freshmen applied for aid; 90 were judged to have need; 89 of these received aid. Average need met was 38%. Average scholarship/grant was $5,981; average loan $4,302. 24% of total undergraduate aid awarded as scholarships/grants, 76% as loans/jobs.

Application procedures. Admission: No deadline. $50 fee. Application may be submitted online. Admission notification on a rolling basis. **Financial aid:** No deadline. FAFSA required. Applicants notified on a rolling basis.

Academics. Special study options: Accelerated study, cooperative education, distance learning. **Credit/placement by examination:** CLEP, institutional tests. **Support services:** Learning center, remedial instruction, tutoring.

Majors. Business: General. **Computer sciences:** Networking. **Engineering technology:** Biomedical, computer, electrical.

Most popular majors. Business/marketing 41%, computer/information sciences 43%, engineering/engineering technologies 16%.

Computing on campus. 412 workstations in library, computer center. Online course registration, online library, helpline available.

Student life. Freshman orientation: Mandatory. **Policies:** Freshmen permitted cars on campus. **Housing:** Private apartments, student-plan housing, private rooms available. **Activities:** Student government, student newspaper, Institution of Electrical & Electronic Engineers, Society of Hispanic Professional Engineers, Students Under Mass Organization, Progressive Advancement in Life, Diverse National Alliance, bowling club, Omega Sigma Phi, Phi Theta Kappa, Epsilon Delta Pi, Japanese anime club.

Athletics. Intramural: Softball.

Student services. Career counseling, student employment services, financial aid counseling, placement for graduates, veterans' counselor. **Physically disabled:** Services for visually, hearing impaired.

Contact. Phone: (818) 587-6227 Toll-free number: (888) 610-0800
Dewey McGuirk, Director of Admissions, DeVry University: West Hills, 22801 Roscoe Boulevard, West Hills, CA 91304-3200

Dominican School of Philosophy and Theology

Berkeley, California
www.dspt.edu **CB code: 0877**

- Private upper-division seminary college affiliated with Roman Catholic Church
- Commuter campus in small city
- Application essay required

General. Founded in 1932. Regionally accredited; also accredited by ATS. Part of Graduate Theological Union. **Degrees:** 1 bachelor's awarded; master's, first professional offered. **Location:** 10 miles from San Francisco. **Calendar:** Semester, limited summer session. **Full-time faculty:** 15 total. **Part-time faculty:** 9 total. **Class size:** 60% < 20, 40% 20-39.

Student profile. 10 degree-seeking undergraduates. 100% entered as juniors. 30% transferred from two-year, 70% transferred from four-year institutions.

Out-of-state:	27%	**25 or older:**	72%
Live on campus:	18%		

Basis for selection. High school transcript, college transcript, application essay required. Admission based on GPA and recommendations. Student must have completed 60 units satisfactorily (2.5 GPA) to enter BA philosophy program. Transfer accepted as juniors, seniors.

2005-2006 Annual costs. Tuition/fees: $13,250. Required medical insurance for otherwise uninsured students costs approximately $610 per semester. Books/supplies: $1,020. Personal expenses: $3,048.

Financial aid. All financial aid based on need. **Additional information:** Limited financial aid. Support available from religious orders.

Application procedures. Admission: Priority date 3/15. $30 fee, may be waived for applicants with need. **Financial aid:** Closing date 4/1. FAFSA, institutional form required.

Academics. Special study options: Cross-registration, double major, independent study, study abroad, Washington semester. **Credit/placement by examination:** CLEP. **Support services:** Reduced course load.

Majors. Philosophy/religion: Philosophy.

Computing on campus. 5 workstations in computer center. Helpline available.

Student life. Housing: Apartments, cooperative housing available. Limited student housing available near campus in apartment complex. **Activities:** Music ensembles, student government.

Student services. Campus ministries, career counseling, student employment services, financial aid counseling, health services, personal counseling, placement for graduates, women's services.

Contact. E-mail: admissions@dspt.edu
Phone: (510) 883-2073 Fax: (510) 849-1372
John Knutsen, Director of Admissions and Recruitment, Dominican School of Philosophy and Theology, 2301 Vine Street, Berkeley, CA 94708

Dominican University of California

San Rafael, California **CB member**
www.dominican.edu **CB code: 4284**

- Private 4-year university and nursing college affiliated with Roman Catholic Church
- Residential campus in small city
- 1,363 degree-seeking undergraduates: 20% part-time, 76% women, 8% African American, 18% Asian American, 15% Hispanic American, 1% Native American, 2% international
- 543 degree-seeking graduate students
- 53% of applicants admitted
- SAT or ACT with writing, application essay required
- 51% graduate within 6 years

General. Founded in 1890. Regionally accredited. **Degrees:** 203 bachelor's awarded; master's offered. **Location:** 11 miles from San Francisco. **Calendar:** Semester, limited summer session. **Full-time faculty:** 71 total; 83% have terminal degrees, 24% minority, 63% women. **Part-time faculty:**

216 total; 40% have terminal degrees, 10% minority, 65% women. **Class size:** 67% < 20, 32% 20-39, less than 1% 40-49.

Freshman class profile. 2,576 applied, 1,359 admitted, 227 enrolled.

Mid 50% test scores		End year in good standing:	91%
SAT verbal:	450-570	Return as sophomores:	74%
SAT math:	440-560	Out-of-state:	6%
ACT:	18-24	Live on campus:	86%
Rank in top quarter:	51%	International:	2%
Rank in top tenth:	24%		

Basis for selection. School achievement record (2.5 high school GPA), recommendations, test scores, essay, extracurricular activities most important. Class rank and work experience considered. SAT Subject Tests recommended. Interview recommended for borderline applicants. Audition recommended for music majors. Portfolio recommended for art majors.

High school preparation. 11 units required. Required units include English 4, mathematics 2, history 1, science 1 (laboratory 1) and foreign language 2.

2005-2006 Annual costs. Tuition/fees: $26,150. Room/board: $10,888. Books/supplies: $1,242. Personal expenses: $1,980.

2005-2006 Financial aid. Need-based: 193 full-time freshmen applied for aid; 157 were judged to have need; 156 of these received aid. Average need met was 67%. Average scholarship/grant was $14,371; average loan $2,785. 76% of total undergraduate aid awarded as scholarships/grants, 24% as loans/jobs. **Non-need-based:** Awarded to 217 full-time undergraduates, including 43 freshmen. Scholarships awarded for academics, athletics, minority status, music/drama. **Additional information:** 4-year guarantee program.

Application procedures. Admission: Priority date 2/1; no deadline. $40 fee, may be waived for applicants with need. Application may be submitted online. Admission notification on a rolling basis beginning on or about 10/15. **Financial aid:** Priority date 3/2; no closing date. FAFSA, institutional form required. Applicants notified on a rolling basis starting 3/15; must reply within 2 week(s) of notification.

Academics. Special study options: Accelerated study, combined bachelor's/graduate degree, cross-registration, double major, dual enrollment of high school students, ESL, exchange student, honors, independent study, internships, liberal arts/career combination, student-designed major, study abroad, teacher certification program, weekend college. Pathways Program (evening/weekend degree program for working adults), semester available at Aquinas College (MI), St. Thomas Aquinas College (NY), Barry University (FL), cross-registration with University of California, Berkeley. **Credit/placement by examination:** AP, CLEP, IB, institutional tests. No more than 30 units can come from one of the following sources: CLEP/Regents College Exams, ACE/PONSI review courses, experiential learning portfolios. No more than 12 units from challenging courses. No more than 38 units from NLN exams. **Support services:** Learning center, study skills assistance, tutoring.

Majors. Biology: General. **Business:** General, business admin, e-commerce, human resources, international. **Communications:** General. **Computer sciences:** Computer graphics. **Conservation:** Environmental science. **English:** Composition, creative writing, English lit. **Health:** Nursing (RN). **History:** General. **Liberal arts:** Arts/sciences, humanities. **Philosophy/religion:** Religion. **Psychology:** General. **Social sciences:** Political science. **Visual/performing arts:** Art, art history/conservation, music performance.

Most popular majors. Biology 7%, business/marketing 16%, health sciences 24%, liberal arts 14%, psychology 16%, public administration/social services 6%.

Computing on campus. 45 workstations in library, computer center, student center. Dormitories wired for high-speed internet access and linked to campus network. Commuter students can connect to campus network. Helpline, repair service, wireless network available.

Student life. Freshman orientation: Available. Preregistration for classes offered. Fall program held week prior to start of classes. **Policies:** Freshmen permitted cars on campus. **Housing:** Coed dorms, substance-free housing available. $250 deposit. **Activities:** Jazz band, choral groups, drama, literary magazine, music ensembles, radio station, student government, student newspaper, SPDI (Campus Ministry), BASIC (Campus Ministry), student government association, Republican club, Democratic club, Perceptions (Cultural Diversity), ROTERACT, various multicultural groups.

Athletics. NAIA. **Intercollegiate:** Basketball, golf, lacrosse M, soccer, softball W, tennis, volleyball W. **Team name:** Penguins.

Student services. Adult student services, alcohol/substance abuse counseling, campus ministries, career counseling, student employment services, financial aid counseling, health services, personal counseling, placement for graduates. **Physically disabled:** Services for visually impaired.

Contact. E-mail: enroll@dominican.edu
Phone: (415) 485-3204 Toll-free number: (888) 323-6763
Fax: (415) 485-3214
Art Criss, Director of Admissions, Dominican University of California, 50 Acacia Avenue, San Rafael, CA 94901-2298

Everest College

Rancho Cucamonga, California
www.everest-college.com

- For-profit 4-year business college
- Small city

General. Accredited by ACICS. **Calendar:** Quarter.

Annual costs/financial aid. Books/supplies: $750.

Contact. Phone: (909) 484-4311
Director of Admissions, 9616 Archibald Avenue, Suite 100, Rancho Cucamonga, CA 91730

Fresno Pacific University

Fresno, California
www.fresno.edu **CB code: 4616**

- Private 4-year university and liberal arts college affiliated with Mennonite Brethren Church
- Residential campus in large city
- 1,399 degree-seeking undergraduates: 11% part-time, 65% women, 4% African American, 4% Asian American, 26% Hispanic American, 1% Native American, 3% international
- 472 degree-seeking graduate students
- 68% of applicants admitted
- SAT and SAT Subject Tests or ACT (ACT writing optional) required
- 55% graduate within 6 years; 39% enter graduate study

General. Founded in 1944. Regionally accredited. All programs emphasize values, in keeping with college identity as a distinctively Christian institution. **Degrees:** 390 bachelor's awarded; master's offered. **Location:** 150 miles from San Francisco. **Calendar:** Semester, limited summer session. **Full-time faculty:** 84 total; 63% have terminal degrees, 12% minority. **Part-time faculty:** 118 total. **Class size:** 67% < 20, 22% 20-39, 4% 40-49, 7% 50-99. **Special facilities:** Center for Mennonite Brethren studies, center for conflict studies and peacemaking.

Freshman class profile. 608 applied, 413 admitted, 212 enrolled.

Mid 50% test scores		Rank in top quarter:	64%
SAT verbal:	460-550	Rank in top tenth:	35%
SAT math:	460-550	End year in good standing:	84%
ACT:	17-23	Return as sophomores:	76%
GPA 3.50 or higher:	56%	Out-of-state:	3%
GPA 3.0-3.49:	28%	Live on campus:	74%
GPA 2.0-2.99:	16%	International:	5%

Basis for selection. School achievement record and test scores very important, minimum 3.1 high school GPA. Recommendations, autobiography also considered. Interview recommended for academically weak applicants. Auditions for music, English (with drama emphasis) majors.

High school preparation. 13 units required. Required units include English 4, mathematics 3, social studies 2, science 1 (laboratory 1) and foreign language 2. One year of visual or performing arts.

2006-2007 Annual costs. Tuition/fees: $20,790. Room/board: $5,990. Books/supplies: $1,242. Personal expenses: $1,980.

2004-2005 Financial aid. Need-based: 148 full-time freshmen applied for aid; 130 were judged to have need; 130 of these received aid. Average need met was 81%. Average scholarship/grant was $12,814; average loan $2,726. 68% of total undergraduate aid awarded as scholarships/grants, 32% as loans/jobs. **Non-need-based:** Awarded to 465 full-time undergraduates, including 126 freshmen. Scholarships awarded for academics, athletics, music/drama.

Application procedures. Admission: Priority date 12/1; deadline 7/31 (postmark date). $40 fee, may be waived for applicants with need. Application may be submitted online. Admission notification on a rolling basis beginning on or about 12/1. **Financial aid:** Priority date 3/2; no closing date. FAFSA, institutional form required. Applicants notified on a rolling basis starting 3/2; must reply by 7/30 or within 3 week(s) of notification.

Academics. **Special study options:** Accelerated study, cross-registration, distance learning, double major, ESL, independent study, internships, liberal arts/career combination, student-designed major, study abroad, teacher certification program, Washington semester. **Credit/placement by examination:** AP, CLEP, IB. 30 credit hours maximum toward associate degree, 30 toward bachelor's. **Support services:** Learning center, reduced course load, remedial instruction, study skills assistance, tutoring, writing center.

Majors. **Biology:** General. **Business:** General, accounting, business admin, human resources, international, management information systems, marketing, nonprofit/public, organizational behavior. **Communications:** General. **Computer sciences:** Computer science. **Conservation:** Environmental science, environmental studies. **Education:** Biology, business, elementary, English, mathematics, music, physical, science, social science. **English:** Creative writing. **Foreign languages:** Spanish. **Health:** Athletic training, premedicine. **History:** General. **Liberal arts:** Arts/sciences. **Math:** General, applied. **Parks/recreation:** Health/fitness, sports admin. **Philosophy/religion:** Philosophy. **Physical sciences:** Chemistry. **Psychology:** General. **Public administration:** Social work. **Social sciences:** General, political science, sociology. **Theology:** Bible. **Visual/performing arts:** Art, dramatic, music performance, music theory/composition.

Most popular majors. Business/marketing 34%, education 35%, theological studies 8%.

Computing on campus. 90 workstations in dormitories, library, computer center, student center. Dormitories wired for high-speed internet access and linked to campus network. Commuter students can connect to campus network. Helpline, student web hosting, wireless network available.

Student life. **Freshman orientation:** Mandatory. Preregistration for classes offered. 4-day fall orientation, 1-day spring. **Housing:** Single-sex dorms, special housing for disabled, apartments, substance-free housing available. $100 deposit, deadline 6/1. Several college-rented apartments available nearby. Resident freshmen under age 23 required to live on campus. **Activities:** Bands, choral groups, dance, drama, music ensembles, student government, student newspaper, Summer Harvest, Shalom Covenant, Kids Klub, Amigos Unidos, Students In Free Enterprise, student chaplains, Daughters of Christ, Faith Project, social work club, international students club.

Athletics. NAIA. **Intercollegiate:** Baseball M, basketball, cross-country, soccer, tennis, track and field, volleyball W. **Intramural:** Basketball, bowling, football (non-tackle), racquetball, soccer, table tennis, volleyball. **Team name:** Sunbirds.

Student services. Adult student services, alcohol/substance abuse counseling, campus ministries, career counseling, student employment services, financial aid counseling, health services, personal counseling. **Physically disabled:** Services for visually, hearing impaired.

Contact. E-mail: ugadmis@fresno.edu
Phone: (559) 453-2039 Toll-free number: (800) 660-6089
Fax: (559) 453-2007
Suzana Dobric-Veiss, Director of Freshmen Admissions, Fresno Pacific University, 1717 South Chestnut Avenue, Fresno, CA 93702

Golden Gate University

San Francisco, California
www.ggu.edu **CB code: 4329**

- Private 4-year university
- Commuter campus in very large city
- 567 degree-seeking undergraduates: 76% part-time, 53% women
- 3,294 degree-seeking graduate students
- 100% of applicants admitted

General. Founded in 1853. Regionally accredited. Evening and weekend degree programs available in San Francisco, San Jose, Walnut Creek, Sacramento, Monterey Bay, Los Angeles, and Seattle (WA). Program length differs by location. **Degrees:** 190 bachelor's, 1 associate awarded; master's, doctoral, first professional offered. **Calendar:** Trimester, extensive summer session. **Full-time faculty:** 76 total. **Part-time faculty:** 680 total.

Freshman class profile. 12 applied, 12 admitted, 5 enrolled.

Basis for selection. School achievement record most important. Work history or military service factor in determining admission of adult students. SAT recommended. Interviews recommended for undecided major applicants.

High school preparation. 14 units recommended. Recommended units include English 4, mathematics 3, social studies 1, history 1, science 2 (laboratory 1) and foreign language 2.

2005-2006 Annual costs. Tuition/fees: $13,500.

Financial aid. **Non-need-based:** Scholarships awarded for academics, alumni affiliation.

Application procedures. **Admission:** Priority date 7/1; no deadline. $55 fee. Application may be submitted online. Admission notification on a rolling basis. Students may be admitted up to 1 year (3 trimesters) before they intend to enroll. **Financial aid:** No deadline. FAFSA required. Applicants notified on a rolling basis starting 4/1; must reply within 3 week(s) of notification.

Academics. Professional degree, certification, and lifelong learning programs in business, law, tax, technology and related professions. **Special study options:** Accelerated study, cooperative education, distance learning, ESL, internships. **Credit/placement by examination:** AP, CLEP, IB, institutional tests. **Support services:** Reduced course load, tutoring, writing center.

Majors. **Business:** Accounting, business admin, finance, human resources, information resources management, international, marketing, operations. **Computer sciences:** Information technology.

Computing on campus. 300 workstations in library, computer center. Commuter students can connect to campus network. Online course registration, online library, wireless network available.

Student life. **Activities:** Student government, student newspaper, Phi Alpha Delta law fraternity, Chi Pi Alpha, Indonesian students organization, Malayan students association, Chinese students club, student government, Indian student association, Korean student association, American Marketing Association, Toastmasters.

Student services. Adult student services, career counseling, student employment services, personal counseling, veterans' counselor. **Physically disabled:** Services for visually, speech, hearing impaired.

Contact. E-mail: info@ggu.edu
Phone: (415) 442-7800 Fax: (415) 442-7807
Cherron Hoppes, Director of Admissions, Golden Gate University, 536 Mission Street, San Francisco, CA 94105-2968

Harvey Mudd College

Claremont, California **CB member**
www.hmc.edu **CB code: 4341**

- Private 4-year engineering and liberal arts college
- Residential campus in small city
- 743 degree-seeking undergraduates
- 36% of applicants admitted
- SAT and SAT Subject Tests, application essay required

General. Founded in 1955. Regionally accredited. One of a cluster of 5 undergraduate and 2 graduate schools on adjoining campuses. Campuses share facilities. Cross-enrollment available at any of the 5 undergraduate colleges, which include Claremont-McKenna, Harvey Mudd, Pitzer, Pomona, and Scripps. **Degrees:** 155 bachelor's awarded. **ROTC:** Army, Air Force. **Location:** 35 miles from Los Angeles. **Calendar:** Semester, limited summer session. **Full-time faculty:** 79 total. **Part-time faculty:** 14 total. **Class size:** 67% < 20, 26% 20-39, 2% 40-49, 3% 50-99, 3% >100. **Special facilities:** Observatory, biological field station, high performance parallel processor.

Freshman class profile. 1,899 applied, 683 admitted, 195 enrolled.

Mid 50% test scores		**Rank in top tenth:**	91%
SAT verbal:	670-760	**Out-of-state:**	55%
SAT math:	760-800	**Live on campus:**	100%
Rank in top quarter:	100%		

Basis for selection. School achievement record important, especially in mathematics and science. Test scores, recommendations, school and community activities important, interviews highly recommended. Students who take SAT must also submit SAT Subject Tests in Math Level 2 and in another subject of their choice. **Homeschooled:** Portfolio suggested describing texts used, curriculum format, how instruction was given. Recommend lab science and foreign language courses be taken at high school or college.

High school preparation. 15 units required. Required and recommended units include English 4, mathematics 4, social studies 1, history 2, science 3 (laboratory 3) and foreign language 2. Calculus, 1 year chemistry, 1 year physics also required.

2006-2007 Annual costs. Tuition/fees (projected): $31,940. Room/board: $10,412. Books/supplies: $800. Personal expenses: $900.

2004-2005 Financial aid. **Need-based:** 87% of total undergraduate aid awarded as scholarships/grants, 13% as loans/jobs. **Non-need-based:** Scholarships awarded for academics.

Application procedures. **Admission:** Closing date 1/15 (postmark date). $50 fee, may be waived for applicants with need. Application may be submitted online. Admission notification 4/1. Must reply by May 1 or within 2 week(s) if notified thereafter. **Financial aid:** Closing date 2/1. FAFSA, CSS PROFILE required. Applicants notified on a rolling basis starting 4/1; must reply by 5/1 or within 2 week(s) of notification.

Academics. Course work divided equally between technical core, major, and humanities and social sciences. **Special study options:** Combined bachelor's/graduate degree, cross-registration, double major, exchange student, independent study, internships, liberal arts/career combination, student-designed major, study abroad. Applied engineering, mathematics and computer science clinics, 4+1 BS/MBA with Claremont Graduate University. **Credit/placement by examination:** AP, CLEP, IB, institutional tests. **Support services:** Learning center, pre-admission summer program, reduced course load, study skills assistance, tutoring, writing center.

Majors. **Biology:** General. **Computer sciences:** General. **Engineering:** General. **Interdisciplinary:** Biological/physical sciences. **Math:** General, applied. **Physical sciences:** Chemistry, physics.

Computing on campus. 360 workstations in dormitories, library, computer center. Dormitories wired for high-speed internet access and linked to campus network. Commuter students can connect to campus network. Online course registration, online library, helpline, student web hosting, wireless network available.

Student life. **Freshman orientation:** Mandatory. 5-day residential introduction. **Policies:** Student-directed honor code governs academic and non-academic life on campus. Freshmen permitted cars on campus. **Housing:** Guaranteed on-campus for freshmen. Coed dorms, special housing for disabled, apartments, substance-free housing available. $150 deposit, deadline 7/1. **Activities:** Bands, choral groups, dance, drama, film society, music ensembles, musical theater, radio station, student government, student newspaper, symphony orchestra, InterVarsity Christian Fellowship, Hillel, Society of Women Engineers, AIDS Awareness, Asian American student alliance, Korean student union, Muslim student association, Society of Hispanic Engineers, National Society of Black Engineers.

Athletics. NCAA. **Intercollegiate:** Baseball M, basketball, cross-country, diving, football (tackle) M, golf M, soccer, softball W, swimming, tennis, track and field, volleyball W, water polo. **Intramural:** Basketball, lacrosse, soccer, softball, tennis, volleyball, water polo. **Team name:** Athenas/Stags.

Student services. Alcohol/substance abuse counseling, campus ministries, career counseling, student employment services, financial aid counseling, health services, minority student services, personal counseling, placement for graduates, women's services.

Contact. E-mail: admission@hmc.edu
Phone: (909) 621-8011 Fax: (909) 607-7046
Peter Osgood, Director of Admission, Harvey Mudd College, Kingston Hall, 301 Platt Boulevard, Claremont, CA 91711-5901

Holy Names University

Oakland, California
www.hnu.edu **CB code: 4059**

- Private 4-year university affiliated with Roman Catholic Church
- Commuter campus in large city
- 657 degree-seeking undergraduates: 33% part-time, 73% women, 26% African American, 9% Asian American, 18% Hispanic American, 1% Native American, 6% international
- 278 degree-seeking graduate students
- 76% of applicants admitted
- SAT or ACT (ACT writing optional), application essay required
- 30% graduate within 6 years

General. Founded in 1868. Regionally accredited. Trimester weekend and evening programs offered. **Degrees:** 175 bachelor's awarded; master's offered. **ROTC:** Army, Air Force. **Location:** 14 miles from San Francisco. **Calendar:** Semester, limited summer session. **Full-time faculty:** 34 total; 85% have terminal degrees, 18% minority, 65% women. **Part-time faculty:** 106 total; 42% have terminal degrees, 21% minority, 60% women. **Class size:** 64% < 20, 35% 20-39, less than 1% 40-49. **Special facilities:** Folk music collection, learning institute for learning disabled, art gallery.

Freshman class profile. 308 applied, 235 admitted, 90 enrolled.

Mid 50% test scores		**Rank in top quarter:**	41%
SAT verbal:	480-520	**Rank in top tenth:**	21%
SAT math:	470-510	**End year in good standing:**	94%
ACT:	18-22	**Return as sophomores:**	64%
GPA 3.50 or higher:	34%	**Out-of-state:**	18%
GPA 3.0-3.49:	36%	**Live on campus:**	72%
GPA 2.0-2.99:	30%	**International:**	12%

Basis for selection. Applicants considered for admission based on overall strength of high school preparation, SAT or ACT scores, personal essay, letter of recommendation, extracurricular activities and individual talents and achievements. For non-native English speakers, ESL Center proficiency report certifying completion of Level 107 or higher may be substituted for TOEFL. Proficiency exams in theory, sight-singing, dictation and piano are required of all students entering the music program. Exams offered during week prior to beginning of each semester. Music major applicant must also audition for a faculty jury. **Homeschooled:** Transcript of courses and grades, letter of recommendation (nonparent) required. Must submit transcript documentation from the primary instructor demonstrating completion of basic credit hours for high school. Transcript should demonstrate academic completion along with short evaluation from primary instructor. May require additional portfolio or performance-based assessments to document competency.

High school preparation. College-preparatory program required. 15 units required. Required and recommended units include English 4, mathematics 3, history 1, science 1 (laboratory 1), foreign language 2-3 and academic electives 3. U.S. history or government required, plus 1 additional year of mathematics, foreign language or lab science.

2006-2007 Annual costs. Tuition/fees (projected): $22,710. Books/supplies: $1,032. Personal expenses: $2,826.

2005-2006 Financial aid. **Need-based:** 89 full-time freshmen applied for aid; 83 were judged to have need; 78 of these received aid. Average need met was 67%. Average scholarship/grant was $8,558; average loan $2,842. 71% of total undergraduate aid awarded as scholarships/grants, 29% as loans/jobs. **Non-need-based:** Awarded to 444 full-time undergraduates, including 49 freshmen. Scholarships awarded for academics, athletics, leadership, music/drama, religious affiliation.

Application procedures. **Admission:** Priority date 3/1; deadline 8/1 (postmark date). $50 fee, may be waived for applicants with need. Application may be submitted online. Admission notification on a rolling basis beginning on or about 10/1. Must reply by May 1 or within 2 week(s) if notified thereafter. **Financial aid:** Priority date 3/2, closing date 6/30. FAFSA required. Applicants notified on a rolling basis starting 9/1; must reply by 5/1 or within 2 week(s) of notification.

Academics. All undergraduate students must satisfy general education requirements. First component is Foundation in Critical Thinking and Communication. Remaining components use thematic and disciplinary approaches to learning. **Special study options:** Accelerated study, cross-registration, distance learning, double major, ESL, exchange student, independent study, internships, liberal arts/career combination, student-designed major, study abroad, weekend college. **Credit/placement by examination:** AP, CLEP, IB, institutional tests. 6 credit hours maximum toward bachelor's degree. Maximum of 6 credit hours per general exam awarded. **Support services:** Learning center, reduced course load, remedial instruction, study skills assistance, tutoring.

Majors. **Biology:** General. **Business:** Business admin, communications, human resources, marketing. **English:** English lit. **Foreign languages:** Spanish. **Health:** Nursing (RN). **History:** General. **Interdisciplinary:** Biopsychology. **Liberal arts:** Arts/sciences, humanities. **Philosophy/religion:** Philosophy, religion. **Psychology:** General. **Social sciences:** International relations, sociology. **Visual/performing arts:** Music pedagogy, music performance.

Most popular majors. Business/marketing 20%, health sciences 30%, liberal arts 8%, psychology 9%, social sciences 9%.

Computing on campus. 86 workstations in dormitories, library, computer center. Dormitories wired for high-speed internet access and linked to campus network. Online library, helpline, student web hosting, wireless network available.

Student life. **Freshman orientation:** Mandatory, $50 fee. Preregistration for classes offered. 2-3 day weekend event prior to start of term. All new students (first-year, transfer, adult, nursing and graduate students) invited to arrive for events on Thursday. Unique student/community event each evening. Fee includes night lodging for residents and meals/activities for all new freshmen and transfers. **Policies:** Freshmen permitted cars on campus. **Housing:** Guaranteed on-campus for all undergraduates. Coed dorms, substance-free housing available. $100 fully refundable deposit, deadline 8/18. **Activities:** Choral groups, drama, music ensembles, student government, symphony orchestra, Asian Pacific International, Black Student Union, Drama Club, Hawks Speech and Debate Team, Holy Names Construction, Global Outlook, International Village, Latinos Unidos, Operation Total Anime, OPAL (Organization of Poetry Appreciation and Learning/Spoken Word).

Athletics. NAIA. **Intercollegiate:** Basketball, cross-country, golf M, soccer, volleyball. **Team name:** Hawks.

Student services. Adult student services, campus ministries, career counseling, student employment services, financial aid counseling, personal counseling. **Physically disabled:** Services for visually impaired.

Contact. E-mail: admission@hnu.edu
Phone: (510) 436-1351 Toll-free number: (800) 430-1321
Fax: (510) 436-1325
Lonnie Morris, Vice President for Enrollment Services, Holy Names University, 3500 Mountain Boulevard, Oakland, CA 94619-1699

Hope International University

Fullerton, California
www.hiu.edu **CB code: 4614**

- Private 4-year university and liberal arts college affiliated with Christian Churches and Churches of Christ
- Residential campus in small city
- 825 degree-seeking undergraduates: 21% part-time, 63% women, 8% African American, 4% Asian American, 18% Hispanic American, 1% Native American, 3% international
- 293 degree-seeking graduate students
- 100% of applicants admitted
- SAT or ACT (ACT writing optional), application essay required
- 36% graduate within 6 years

General. Founded in 1928. Regionally accredited. Emphasis on field-based interactive learning combined with direct professional involvement with students. **Degrees:** 163 bachelor's, 4 associate awarded; master's offered. **Location:** 45 miles from Los Angeles. **Calendar:** 4-1-4, limited summer session. **Full-time faculty:** 28 total; 68% have terminal degrees, 7% minority. **Part-time faculty:** 188 total; 46% have terminal degrees, 14% minority. **Class size:** 77% < 20, 19% 20-39, 2% 40-49, 1% 50-99.

Freshman class profile. 133 applied, 133 admitted, 120 enrolled.

Mid 50% test scores		**GPA 2.0-2.99:**	32%
SAT verbal:	440-550	**End year in good standing:**	77%
SAT math:	440-550	**Return as sophomores:**	64%
ACT:	17-23	**Out-of-state:**	28%
GPA 3.50 or higher:	40%	**International:**	8%
GPA 3.0-3.49:	26%		

Basis for selection. Essay, religious commitment, school achievement, and recommendations important. Test scores and extracurricular activities also considered along with all factors bearing on potential success. Interviews recommended for academically borderline applicants. **Homeschooled:** If schooled under auspices of organization that can offer transcripts, will accept that and SAT/ACT scores. If not, GED score and SAT/ACT scores required in application process.

High school preparation. 14 units recommended. Recommended units include English 4, mathematics 2, social studies 1, history 1, science 1 (laboratory 1), foreign language 1 and academic electives 3. Half-unit speech and .5 computer science or literacy recommended.

2005-2006 Annual costs. Tuition/fees: $18,000. Room/board: $6,860.

2005-2006 Financial aid. Need-based: Average need met was 30%. Average scholarship/grant was $7,365; average loan $2,365. 56% of total undergraduate aid awarded as scholarships/grants, 44% as loans/jobs. **Non-need-based:** Scholarships awarded for academics, alumni affiliation, athletics, leadership, music/drama, religious affiliation.

Application procedures. Admission: Priority date 7/1; no deadline. $40 fee, may be waived for applicants with need. Application must be submitted on paper. Admission notification on a rolling basis. **Financial aid:** Priority date 3/2; no closing date. FAFSA, institutional form required. Applicants notified on a rolling basis starting 3/15; must reply within 2 week(s) of notification.

Academics. Special study options: Accelerated study, cross-registration, distance learning, double major, dual enrollment of high school students, ESL, honors, independent study, internships, liberal arts/career combination, student-designed major, study abroad, teacher certification program. **Credit/placement by examination:** AP, CLEP, IB, institutional tests. 30 credit hours maximum toward bachelor's degree. **Support services:** Learning center, reduced course load, remedial instruction, tutoring.

Majors. Business: Business admin. **Education:** Elementary, music, social science. **Family/consumer sciences:** Family studies. **Health:** Athletic training. **Psychology:** General. **Public administration:** Human services. **Social sciences:** General. **Theology:** Bible, missionary, sacred music, theology, youth ministry.

Most popular majors. Business/marketing 15%, family/consumer sciences 49%, theological studies 25%.

Computing on campus. 57 workstations in dormitories, library. Dormitories wired for high-speed internet access. Online library available.

Student life. Freshman orientation: Mandatory, $75 fee. Preregistration for classes offered. Fall and spring terms orientation held 3 days before beginning of term. **Policies:** Alcohol and smoking policies: no alcohol permitted, smoking discouraged. Religious observance required. Freshmen permitted cars on campus. **Housing:** Guaranteed on-campus for freshmen. Single-sex dorms, substance-free housing available. $200 fully refundable deposit, deadline 7/1. Single students required to live on campus until they are 21 years old or have junior standing, unless living at home or given special approval. **Activities:** Choral groups, drama, music ensembles, musical theater, student government, student newspaper, international student association, school outreach, minority students association, business club.

Athletics. NAIA. **Intercollegiate:** Basketball, cheerleading M, soccer, softball W, tennis, volleyball. **Intramural:** Badminton, basketball, football (non-tackle) W, volleyball. **Team name:** Royals.

Student services. Adult student services, campus ministries, career counseling, student employment services, financial aid counseling, health services, personal counseling, placement for graduates, veterans' counselor.

Contact. E-mail: ug-admissions@hiu.edu
Phone: (714) 879-3901 ext. 2215 Toll-free number: (800) 762-1294
Fax: (714) 681-7423
Butch Ellis, Dean of Enrollment Management, Hope International University, 2500 East Nutwood Avenue, Fullerton, CA 92831-3199

Humboldt State University

Arcata, California
www.humboldt.edu **CB code: 4345**

- Public 4-year university
- Residential campus in large town
- 6,245 degree-seeking undergraduates: 9% part-time, 54% women, 3% African American, 4% Asian American, 10% Hispanic American, 2% Native American, 1% international
- 934 degree-seeking graduate students
- 69% of applicants admitted
- 45% graduate within 6 years

General. Founded in 1913. Regionally accredited. **Degrees:** 1,377 bachelor's awarded; master's offered. **Location:** 275 miles from San Francisco. **Calendar:** Semester, extensive summer session. **Full-time faculty:** 276 total; 80% have terminal degrees, 13% minority, 36% women. **Part-time faculty:** 257 total; 21% have terminal degrees, 20% minority, 41% women. **Class size:** 44% < 20, 43% 20-39, 7% 40-49, 5% 50-99, 1% >100. **Special facilities:** Marine lab, observatory, natural history museum, marsh and wildlife sanctuary, small lakes and ponds, 280-acre sand dune preserve, research vessel, freshwater fish hatchery, small-game animal pen, fungal genetic stock center, 360-acre experimental forest, 170,000 specimen herbarium, center for appropriate technology, energy research center.

Freshman class profile. 7,206 applied, 4,988 admitted, 827 enrolled.

Mid 50% test scores		**GPA 2.0-2.99:**	39%
SAT verbal:	470-600	**Rank in top quarter:**	36%
SAT math:	460-570	**Rank in top tenth:**	10%
ACT:	19-25	**Return as sophomores:**	71%
GPA 3.50 or higher:	22%	**Out-of-state:**	6%
GPA 3.0-3.49:	39%	**Live on campus:**	83%

Basis for selection. High school GPA and test scores most important. In-state residents with high school GPA of 3.0 or higher or out-of-state applicants with high school GPA over 3.6 do not have to submit test scores for admission. Essay recommended for academically weak, special consideration applicants.

High school preparation. 15 units required. Required units include English 4, mathematics 3, social studies 1, history 1, science 2 (laboratory 2), foreign language 2 and academic electives 1.

2005-2006 Annual costs. Tuition/fees: $3,079; $13,249 out-of-state. Room/board: $7,906. Books/supplies: $1,050. Personal expenses: $1,854.

Financial aid. Non-need-based: Scholarships awarded for academics.

Application procedures. Admission: Priority date 10/1; deadline 11/30. $55 fee, may be waived for applicants with need. Application may be submitted online. Admission notification on a rolling basis beginning on or about 11/15. **Financial aid:** No deadline. FAFSA required. Applicants notified on a rolling basis starting 3/1; must reply within 6 week(s) of notification.

Academics. Indian Teacher and Educational Personnel Program, Indian Natural Resources, Sciences and Engineering Program available. **Special study options:** Cooperative education, cross-registration, distance learning, double major, dual enrollment of high school students, ESL, exchange student, honors, independent study, internships, student-designed major, study abroad, teacher certification program. **Credit/placement by examination:** AP, CLEP, IB, SAT, ACT, institutional tests. 24 credit hours maximum toward bachelor's degree. **Support services:** Learning center, pre-admission summer program, remedial instruction, tutoring, writing center.

Majors. Agriculture: Range science. **Area/ethnic studies:** Native American. **Biology:** General, botany, zoology. **Business:** General, business admin. **Communications:** Journalism. **Computer sciences:** General, information systems. **Conservation:** General, environmental studies, fisheries, forestry, management/policy, wildlife. **Education:** Elementary, physical, trade/industrial. **Engineering:** Science. **English:** Composition, speech/rhetoric. **Foreign languages:** French, German, Spanish. **History:** General. **Liberal arts:** Arts/sciences. **Math:** General. **Parks/recreation:** Facilities management, health/fitness. **Philosophy/religion:** Philosophy, religion. **Physical sciences:** General, chemistry, geology, oceanography, physics. **Psychology:** General. **Public administration:** Social work. **Social sciences:** General, anthropology, economics, geography, political science, sociology. **Visual/performing arts:** Art, dramatic.

Most popular majors. Biology 7%, business/marketing 6%, liberal arts 12%, natural resources/environmental science 14%, psychology 7%, social sciences 11%, visual/performing arts 10%.

Computing on campus. 770 workstations in dormitories, library, computer center, student center. Dormitories linked to campus network. Commuter students can connect to campus network. Online course registration, online library, helpline, student web hosting, wireless network available.

Student life. Freshman orientation: Mandatory, $50 fee. Preregistration for classes offered. Student-directed program held June, July and August. **Policies:** Freshmen permitted cars on campus. **Housing:** Guaranteed on-campus for freshmen. Coed dorms, apartments, fraternity/sorority housing, substance-free housing available. $500 partly refundable deposit, deadline 5/2. Themed residence halls available. **Activities:** Bands, choral groups, dance, drama, film society, literary magazine, music ensembles, musical theater, radio station, student government, student newspaper, symphony orchestra, Newman club, Campus Crusade for Christ, youth educational services, black students union, MECHA, gay, lesbian and bisexual students association, Native American club, Jewish student union, multicultural center, veterans organization.

Athletics. NCAA. **Intercollegiate:** Basketball, cross-country, football (tackle) M, rowing (crew) W, soccer, softball W, track and field, volleyball W. **Intramural:** Badminton, basketball, football (tackle) M, soccer, softball, volleyball. **Team name:** Lumberjacks.

Student services. Adult student services, career counseling, student employment services, health services, on-campus daycare, personal counseling, placement for graduates, veterans' counselor. **Physically disabled:** Services for visually, speech, hearing impaired.

Contact. E-mail: hsuinfo@humboldt.edu
Phone: (707) 826-4402 Toll-free number: (866) 850-9556
Fax: (707) 826-6190
Scott Hagg, Director of Admissions and Student Recruitment, Humboldt State University, Arcata, CA 95521-8299

Humphreys College

Stockton, California
www.humphreys.edu **CB code: 4346**

- Private 4-year business and liberal arts college
- Residential campus in large city
- 893 degree-seeking undergraduates: 38% part-time, 86% women, 17% African American, 12% Asian American, 33% Hispanic American, 1% Native American
- 97 graduate students

General. Founded in 1896. Regionally accredited. **Degrees:** 35 bachelor's, 14 associate awarded; first professional offered. **Location:** 35 miles from Sacramento. **Calendar:** Quarter, extensive summer session. **Full-time faculty:** 19 total; 5% have terminal degrees, 53% women. **Part-time faculty:** 66 total; 3% have terminal degrees, 17% minority, 46% women. **Class size:** 80% < 20, 19% 20-39, 2% 40-49.

Freshman class profile.

Out-of-state:	3%	**International:**	2%
Live on campus:	25%		

Basis for selection. Open admission. ACT used for placement only. **Homeschooled:** State high school equivalency certificate required.

2005-2006 Annual costs. Tuition/fees: $9,900. School-controlled apartment housing cost quoted, not including utilities. Room only: $3,150. Books/supplies: $750. Personal expenses: $1,530.

2005-2006 Financial aid. Need-based: 65 full-time freshmen applied for aid; 60 were judged to have need; 60 of these received aid. Average need met was 75%. Average scholarship/grant was $4. 47% of total undergraduate aid awarded as scholarships/grants, 53% as loans/jobs. **Non-need-based:** Scholarships awarded for academics.

Application procedures. Admission: No deadline. $35 fee, may be waived for applicants with need. Admission notification on a rolling basis. **Financial aid:** Closing date 6/30. FAFSA required. Applicants notified on a rolling basis; must reply within 2 week(s) of notification.

Academics. Special study options: Combined bachelor's/graduate degree, cooperative education, cross-registration, double major, honors, independent study, internships. **Credit/placement by examination:** CLEP, IB, institutional tests. 4 credit hours maximum toward associate degree, 45 toward bachelor's. **Support services:** Learning center, pre-admission summer program, remedial instruction, tutoring, writing center.

Majors. Business: General, accounting, administrative services, business admin, office technology, office/clerical. **Computer sciences:** General. **Health:** Medical secretary. **Legal studies:** Court reporting, legal secretary, paralegal. **Public administration:** Community org/advocacy.

Computing on campus. 25 workstations in computer center.

Student life. Freshman orientation: Available. Held in September. **Policies:** Freshmen permitted cars on campus. **Housing:** Apartments, substance-free housing available. $200 partly refundable deposit, deadline 8/20. **Activities:** Student government, student newspaper, business club.

Student services. Career counseling, student employment services, personal counseling, placement for graduates, veterans' counselor.

Contact. E-mail: ugadmission@humphreys.edu
Phone: (209) 478-0800 Fax: (209) 478-8721
Santa Lopez, Admissions Director, Humphreys College, 6650 Inglewood Avenue, Stockton, CA 95207-3896

Independence University

National City, California
www.cchs.edu **CB code: 3354**

- For-profit 4-year health science college
- Commuter campus in small city

General. Founded in 1975. Accredited by ACCSCT. **Location:** 7 miles from downtown San Diego. **Calendar:** Continuous.

Contact. Phone: (619) 477-4800
2423 Hoover Avenue, National City, CA 91950

Institute of Computer Technology

Los Angeles, California
www.ictcollege.edu **CB code: 3046**

- For-profit 4-year business and technical college
- Commuter campus in very large city
- 200 degree-seeking undergraduates

General. Accredited by ACICS. **Degrees:** 25 bachelor's, 70 associate awarded. **Calendar:** Quarter. **Full-time faculty:** 4 total. **Part-time faculty:** 30 total.

Freshman class profile. 60 applied, 30 admitted, 25 enrolled.

Basis for selection. Open admission. ATB required if no high school diploma.

2006-2007 Annual costs. Tuition/fees (projected): $14,200. Books/supplies: $210.

Application procedures. Admission: No deadline. $50 fee. **Financial aid:** FAFSA, institutional form required.

Academics. Credit/placement by examination: CLEP.

Majors. Business: Business admin. **Computer sciences:** General.

Student life. Freshman orientation: Available. 4 days before start date. **Activities:** Student government.

Contact. Phone: (213) 381-3333 Toll-free number: (800) 574-6428
Fax: (213) 383-9369
Gabriel Choriego, Admissions Director, Institute of Computer Technology, 3200 Wilshire Boulevard Ste#400, Los Angeles, CA 90010-1308

Interior Designers Institute
Newport Beach, California
www.idi.edu **CB code: 2318**

- For-profit 4-year college of interior design
- Large city

General. Accredited by ACCSCT. **Calendar:** Continuous.

Annual costs/financial aid. Certificate program tuition $1,995. Associate and bachelor's degree tuition $14,950. Books/supplies: $1,500.

Contact. Phone: (949) 675-4451
Director of Admission, 1061 Camelback Road, Newport Beach, CA 92660-3228

International Technological University
Sunnyvale, California
www.itu.edu/

- Private upper-division engineering college
- Commuter campus

General. Accredited by ACICS. **Degrees:** 3 bachelor's awarded; master's offered. **Calendar:** Trimester. **Full-time faculty:** 3 total. **Part-time faculty:** 2 total.

Student profile. 20 degree-seeking undergraduates.

2006-2007 Annual costs. Tuition/fees: $8,250. MBA $380 per credit hour; MS engineering $425 per credit hour.

Application procedures. Admission: $50 fee.

Academics. Credit/placement by examination: CLEP.

Majors. Computer sciences: General.

Contact. Phone: (408) 331-1014
Gerald Cory, Admissions Director, International Technological University, 756 San Aleso Avenue, Sunnyvale, CA 94085

ITT Technical Institute: Anaheim
Anaheim, California
www.itt-tech.edu **CB code: 3570**

- For-profit 4-year technical college
- Commuter campus in small city

General. Founded in 1983. Accredited by ACICS. **Location:** 15 miles from Los Angeles. **Calendar:** Quarter.

Annual costs/financial aid. Tuition varies by program, $260-$368 per credit hour.

Contact. Phone: (714) 535-3700
Director of Recruitment, 525 North Muller, Anaheim, CA 92801

ITT Technical Institute: Lathrop
Lathrop, California
www.itt-tech.edu **CB code: 2720**

- For-profit 4-year technical college
- Commuter campus in small town

General. Accredited by ACICS. **Calendar:** Quarter.

Annual costs/financial aid. Tuition varies by program, $260-$368 per credit hour.

Contact. Phone: (209) 858-0077
Director of Recruitment, 16916 South Harlan Road, Lathrop, CA 95330

ITT Technical Institute: Oxnard
Oxnard, California
www.itt-tech.edu **CB code: 2744**

- For-profit 4-year technical college
- Commuter campus in small city

General. Accredited by ACICS. **Location:** 34 miles from Santa Barbara, 52 miles from Los Angeles. **Calendar:** Quarter.

Annual costs/financial aid. Tuition varies by program, $260-$368 per credit hour.

Contact. Phone: (805) 988-0143
Director of Recruitment, 2051 Solar Drive, Building B, Oxnard, CA 93036

ITT Technical Institute: Rancho Cordova
Rancho Cordova, California
www.itt-tech.edu **CB code: 3597**

- For-profit 4-year technical college
- Commuter campus in large city

General. Founded in 1954. Accredited by ACICS. **Location:** 11 miles from Sacramento, 87 miles from San Francisco. **Calendar:** Quarter.

Annual costs/financial aid. Tuition varies by program, $260-$368 per credit hour.

Contact. Phone: (916) 366-3900
Director of Recruitment, 10863 Gold Center Drive, Rancho Cordova, CA 95670

ITT Technical Institute: San Bernardino
San Bernardino, California
www.itt-tech.edu **CB code: 7103**

- For-profit 4-year technical college
- Commuter campus in very large city

General. Accredited by ACICS. **Location:** 60 miles from Los Angeles. **Calendar:** Quarter.

Annual costs/financial aid. Tuition varies by program, $260-$368 per credit hour.

Contact. Phone: (800) 888-3801
Director of Recruitment, 670 East Carnegie Drive, San Bernardino, CA 92408-2800

ITT Technical Institute: San Diego
San Diego, California
www.itt-tech.edu **CB code: 0206**

- For-profit 4-year technical college
- Commuter campus in very large city

General. Founded in 1981. Accredited by ACICS. **Calendar:** Quarter.

Annual costs/financial aid. Tuition varies by program, $260-$368 per credit hour.

Contact. Phone: (858) 571-8500
Director of Recruitment, 9680 Granite Ridge Drive, San Diego, CA 92123

ITT Technical Institute: Sylmar
Sylmar, California
www.itt-tech.edu **CB code: 3571**

- For-profit 4-year technical college
- Commuter campus in very large city

General. Founded in 1982. Accredited by ACICS. **Location:** Within Los Angeles County. **Calendar:** Quarter.

Annual costs/financial aid. Tuition varies by program, $260-$368 per credit hour.

Contact. Phone: (818) 364-5151
Director of Recruitment, 12669 Encinitas Avenue, Sylmar, CA 91342-3664

ITT Technical Institute: Torrance
Torrance, California
www.itt-tech.edu **CB code: 7104**

- For-profit 4-year technical college
- Commuter campus in small city

General. Accredited by ACICS. **Calendar:** Quarter.

Annual costs/financial aid. Tuition varies by program, $260-$368 per credit hour.

Contact. Phone: (310) 380-1555
Director of Recruitment, 20050 South Vermont Avenue, Torrance, CA 90502

ITT Technical Institute: West Covina
West Covina, California
www.itt-tech.edu **CB code: 0216**

- For-profit 4-year technical college
- Commuter campus in small city

General. Founded in 1982. Accredited by ACICS. **Location:** 20 miles from Los Angeles. **Calendar:** Quarter.

Annual costs/financial aid. Tuition varies by program, $260-$368 per credit hour.

Contact. Phone: (626) 960-8681
Director of Recruitment, 1530 West Cameron Avenue, West Covina, CA 91790

John F. Kennedy University
Pleasant Hill, California
www.jfku.edu **CB code: 1362**

- Private 4-year business and liberal arts college
- Commuter campus in large town
- 222 degree-seeking undergraduates
- Interview required

General. Founded in 1964. Regionally accredited. **Degrees:** 51 bachelor's awarded; master's, doctoral, first professional offered. **Location:** 35 miles from San Francisco. **Calendar:** Quarter, limited summer session. **Full-time faculty:** 55 total. **Part-time faculty:** 194 total. **Class size:** 81% < 20, 19% 20-39.

Basis for selection. For upper-division bachelor's degree completion, transcript, interview required for assessment of qualifications.

2005-2006 Annual costs. Tuition/fees: $14,325. Books/supplies: $1,080.

2004-2005 Financial aid. All financial aid based on need.

Application procedures. Admission: No deadline. $55 fee. Admission notification on a rolling basis. **Financial aid:** Priority date 3/2; no closing date. FAFSA, institutional form required. Applicants notified on a rolling basis; must reply within 4 week(s) of notification.

Academics. Special study options: Combined bachelor's/graduate degree, cross-registration, double major, independent study, internships, student-designed major, teacher certification program. **Credit/placement by examination:** CLEP, institutional tests. 105 credit hours maximum toward bachelor's degree. Maximum of 105 units through combination of CLEP, DANTES, 2-year schools, and military training.

Majors. Business: Business admin. **Liberal arts:** Arts/sciences. **Psychology:** General.

Most popular majors. Business/marketing 26%, liberal arts 63%, psychology 11%.

Computing on campus. 25 workstations in library, computer center.

Student life. Activities: Student government, student newspaper.

Student services. Career counseling, student employment services, veterans' counselor. **Physically disabled:** Services for visually, speech, hearing impaired.

Contact. Phone: (925) 969-3330 Fax: (925) 969-3331
Ellena Bloedorn, Director of Admissions and Records, John F. Kennedy University, 100 Ellinwood Way, Pleasant Hill, CA 94523-4817

King's College and Seminary
Los Angeles, California
www.kingscollege.edu **CB code: 3896**

- Private 4-year Bible and seminary college affiliated with nondenominational tradition
- Commuter campus in very large city
- 631 degree-seeking undergraduates
- 321 graduate students
- 87% of applicants admitted
- Application essay required

General. Accredited by ABHE. Evangelical institution. **Degrees:** 22 bachelor's, 4 associate awarded; master's, doctoral, first professional offered. **ROTC:** Army, Navy, Air Force. **Calendar:** Quarter, limited summer session. **Full-time faculty:** 15 total. **Part-time faculty:** 32 total.

Freshman class profile. 31 applied, 27 admitted, 17 enrolled.

Basis for selection. Demonstration of commitment to Christian faith required, essays, references important. Tests recommended, not required. **Homeschooled:** Statement describing homeschool structure and mission, transcript of courses and grades required.

2005-2006 Annual costs. Tuition/fees: $7,455. Seminary students pay $175 per credit hour. Room only: $3,300. Books/supplies: $900.

Financial aid. Non-need-based: Scholarships awarded for academics, leadership. **Additional information:** Specific scholarships may require specific essays.

Application procedures. Admission: No deadline. $45 fee. Application may be submitted online. Admission notification on a rolling basis. **Financial aid:** No deadline. FAFSA required. Applicants notified on a rolling basis.

Academics. Special study options: Distance learning, external degree, internships. **Credit/placement by examination:** AP, CLEP, IB, institutional tests. 45 credit hours maximum toward associate degree, 45 toward bachelor's. **Support services:** Reduced course load, remedial instruction, study skills assistance, tutoring.

Majors. Theology: Bible.

Computing on campus. Online course registration, online library available.

Student life. Freshman orientation: Mandatory. Preregistration for classes offered. **Policies:** Drug- and alcohol-free campus. Religious observance required. **Activities:** Student government, C.S. Lewis club, women in ministry group, Delta Epsilon, National Association of Evangelicals.

Student services. Campus ministries, career counseling, financial aid counseling, personal counseling, placement for graduates, veterans' counselor, women's services.

Contact. E-mail: admissions@kingscollege.edu
Phone: (818) 779-8040 Toll-free number: (888) 779-8040
Fax: (818) 779-8241
Marilyn Chappell, Director of Admissions, King's College and Seminary, 14800 Sherman Way, Los Angeles, CA 91405-2233

La Sierra University

Riverside, California — **CB member**
www.lasierra.edu — **CB code: 4380**

- Private 4-year university affiliated with Seventh-day Adventists
- Residential campus in large city
- 1,586 degree-seeking undergraduates: 9% part-time, 59% women, 9% African American, 22% Asian American, 28% Hispanic American, 1% Native American, 10% international
- 303 degree-seeking graduate students
- 38% of applicants admitted
- SAT or ACT (ACT writing optional), application essay required
- 46% graduate within 6 years

General. Founded in 1922. Regionally accredited. **Degrees:** 186 bachelor's awarded; master's, doctoral, first professional offered. **Location:** 55 miles from Los Angeles. **Calendar:** Quarter, limited summer session. **Full-time faculty:** 88 total; 84% have terminal degrees, 34% minority, 38% women. **Part-time faculty:** 76 total; 25% minority, 49% women. **Class size:** 56% < 20, 30% 20-39, 7% 40-49, 5% 50-99, 1% >100. **Special facilities:** Museum of natural history with large freeze-dried collection (reptiles, mammals, birds), mineral spheres collection, arboretum, observatory, women's resource center.

Freshman class profile. 1,389 applied, 533 admitted, 388 enrolled.

Mid 50% test scores		**Rank in top quarter:**	38%
SAT verbal:	420-540	**Rank in top tenth:**	14%
SAT math:	420-560	**Return as sophomores:**	61%
ACT:	17-22	**Out-of-state:**	12%
GPA 3.50 or higher:	35%	**Live on campus:**	65%
GPA 3.0-3.49:	35%	**International:**	7%
GPA 2.0-2.99:	30%		

Basis for selection. School achievement record, test scores, recommendations, and religious affiliation or commitment important.

High school preparation. 18 units recommended. Recommended units include English 4, mathematics 3, history 2, science 3 (laboratory 3) and foreign language 2. 1 unit of computing, .5 unit of health education.

2006-2007 Annual costs. Tuition/fees: $20,633. Room/board: $5,873. Books/supplies: $1,200. Personal expenses: $2,088.

2004-2005 Financial aid. Need-based: 296 full-time freshmen applied for aid; 264 were judged to have need; 262 of these received aid. Average need met was 71%. Average scholarship/grant was $12,940; average loan $2,995. 60% of total undergraduate aid awarded as scholarships/grants, 40% as loans/jobs. **Non-need-based:** Awarded to 357 full-time undergraduates, including 86 freshmen. Scholarships awarded for academics, leadership, music/drama, religious affiliation.

Application procedures. Admission: Priority date 5/1; no deadline. $30 fee, may be waived for applicants with need. Application may be submitted online. Admission notification on a rolling basis beginning on or about 5/1. **Financial aid:** Priority date 3/2; no closing date. FAFSA required. Applicants notified on a rolling basis starting 4/15; must reply by 9/1.

Academics. Special study options: Accelerated study, cross-registration, distance learning, double major, dual enrollment of high school students, ESL, honors, independent study, internships, student-designed major, study abroad, teacher certification program. **Credit/placement by examination:** AP, CLEP, IB, SAT, ACT, institutional tests. 24 credit hours maximum toward bachelor's degree. **Support services:** Learning center, pre-admission summer program, reduced course load, remedial instruction, study skills assistance, tutoring.

Honors college/program. High school GPA above 3.25 and ACT above 60th percentile. 25 freshmen admitted per year.

Majors. Biology: General, biochemistry, biophysics. **Business:** Accounting, business admin, finance. **Communications:** General. **Computer sciences:** Computer science, information systems. **English:** English lit. **Foreign languages:** Spanish. **History:** General. **Interdisciplinary:** Behavioral sciences. **Liberal arts:** Arts/sciences. **Math:** General. **Parks/recreation:** Exercise sciences, health/fitness. **Philosophy/religion:** Religion. **Physical sciences:** Chemistry. **Psychology:** General. **Public administration:** Social work. **Social sciences:** Sociology. **Visual/performing arts:** Art, commercial/advertising art, studio arts.

Most popular majors. Biology 15%, business/marketing 28%, liberal arts 13%, psychology 11%, public administration/social services 7%.

Computing on campus. 135 workstations in dormitories, library, computer center. Dormitories wired for high-speed internet access and linked to campus network. Commuter students can connect to campus network. Online course registration, helpline, repair service, wireless network available.

Student life. Freshman orientation: Mandatory, $100 fee. Preregistration for classes offered. **Policies:** Smoke- and alcohol-free campus. Religious observance required. Freshmen permitted cars on campus. **Housing:** Guaranteed on-campus for all undergraduates. Single-sex dorms, apartments, substance-free housing available. $100 fully refundable deposit. Honors residence hall available. **Activities:** Bands, choral groups, drama, literary magazine, music ensembles, student government, student newspaper, symphony orchestra, Black student association, campus ministries, Earth Awareness, Amnesty International, international student association, Korean club, Ole club, Students in Free Enterprise, South Asia student association.

Athletics. NCAA, USCAA. **Intercollegiate:** Baseball M, basketball. **Intramural:** Badminton, basketball, football (tackle), golf, gymnastics, soccer, softball, table tennis, volleyball, weight lifting.

Student services. Adult student services, campus ministries, career counseling, student employment services, financial aid counseling, health services, personal counseling, placement for graduates, women's services.

Contact. E-mail: ivy@lasierra.edu
Phone: (951) 785-2176 Toll-free number: (800) 874-5587
Fax: (951) 785-2901
Bobby Brown, Director of Admissions, La Sierra University, 4500 Riverwalk Parkway, Riverside, CA 92515-8247

Laguna College of Art and Design

Laguna Beach, California
www.lagunacollege.edu — **CB code: 7248**

- Private 4-year visual arts college
- Commuter campus in large town
- 295 degree-seeking undergraduates
- 60% of applicants admitted
- SAT or ACT (ACT writing optional), application essay, interview required

General. Founded in 1961. Regionally accredited. Accredited by National Association of Schools of Art and Design. **Degrees:** 61 bachelor's awarded. **Location:** 50 miles from Los Angeles, 75 miles from San Diego. **Calendar:** Semester, limited summer session. **Full-time faculty:** 11 total. **Part-time faculty:** 27 total.

Freshman class profile. 229 applied, 137 admitted, 48 enrolled.

Basis for selection. Selection based on academic record and overall merit of 10-piece portfolio which includes minimum of 4 observational drawings. Application fee waived for online applications. Portfolios required.

High school preparation. 14 units recommended. Recommended units include English 2, mathematics 2, social studies 2, history 2, science 2, foreign language 2 and academic electives 2. 3 units of studio art, drawing and painting recommended.

2006-2007 Annual costs. Tuition/fees: $18,600. Books/supplies: $1,300. Personal expenses: $2,312.

Financial aid. Additional information: Need- and merit-based scholarship deadline March 20.

Application procedures. Admission: Priority date 2/2; no deadline. $45 fee, may be waived for applicants with need. Application may be submitted online. Admission notification on a rolling basis. **Financial aid:** No deadline. FAFSA, institutional form required. Applicants notified on a rolling basis; must reply within 2 week(s) of notification.

Academics. Special study options: Cooperative education, double major, exchange student, independent study, internships, New York semester, study abroad. **Credit/placement by examination:** CLEP. **Support services:** Pre-admission summer program, reduced course load, remedial instruction, tutoring.

Majors. **Visual/performing arts:** Commercial/advertising art, drawing, painting.

Computing on campus. 26 workstations in library, computer center.

Student life. **Policies:** Very strong student government promoting activities on and off campus. Many art-related activities with social gatherings as well. **Activities:** Student government, student newspaper, foreign student organization, cultural diversity organization.

Student services. Career counseling, personal counseling, veterans' counselor.

Contact. Phone: (949) 376-6000 Toll-free number: (800) 255-0762
Fax: (949) 376-6009
Anthony Padilla, Vice President of Enrollment Management, Laguna College of Art and Design, 2222 Laguna Canyon Road, Laguna Beach, CA 92651

LIFE Pacific College

San Dimas, California
www.lifepacific.edu **CB code: 4264**

- Private 4-year Bible college affiliated with International Church of the Foursquare Gospel
- Residential campus in large town
- 475 degree-seeking undergraduates
- 98% of applicants admitted
- SAT or ACT (ACT writing optional), application essay required

General. Founded in 1925. Candidate for regional accreditation; also accredited by ABHE. **Degrees:** 113 bachelor's, 19 associate awarded. **Location:** 30 miles from Los Angeles. **Calendar:** Semester, limited summer session. **Full-time faculty:** 13 total. **Part-time faculty:** 29 total. **Class size:** 63% < 20, 27% 20-39, 3% 40-49, 8% 50-99.

Freshman class profile. 174 applied, 171 admitted, 75 enrolled.

Mid 50% test scores		ACT:	16-22
SAT verbal:	440-550	Out-of-state:	51%
SAT math:	420-530	Live on campus:	93%

Basis for selection. Christian character, motivation, and ability to accord with college's program most important. Cumulative GPA in last school attended and SAT or ACT scores also considered. TOEFL is required for those applicants who are not native speakers of English. **Homeschooled:** Must present official transcript with graduation date. SAT or ACT required. **Learning Disabled:** LIFE Challenges Program is available to students with learning disabilities. Request information.

2006-2007 Annual costs. Tuition/fees: $10,100. Room/board: $5,000. Books/supplies: $1,260. Personal expenses: $1,818.

2004-2005 Financial aid. **Need-based:** 57 full-time freshmen applied for aid; 46 were judged to have need; 42 of these received aid. Average need met was 31%. Average scholarship/grant was $2,680; average loan $2,297. 41% of total undergraduate aid awarded as scholarships/grants, 59% as loans/jobs. **Non-need-based:** Awarded to 42 full-time undergraduates, including 16 freshmen. Scholarships awarded for academics, alumni affiliation.

Application procedures. **Admission:** Closing date 7/1 (postmark date). $35 fee. Application may be submitted online. Admission notification on a rolling basis. **Financial aid:** Closing date 7/1. FAFSA required. Applicants notified on a rolling basis starting 6/1.

Academics. **Special study options:** Cooperative education, distance learning, dual enrollment of high school students, external degree, independent study, internships, study abroad. **Credit/placement by examination:** AP, CLEP, institutional tests. 16 credit hours maximum toward associate degree, 16 toward bachelor's. Credit limited by the number of subjects accepted, course by course basis. **Support services:** Reduced course load, remedial instruction, study skills assistance, tutoring.

Majors. **Theology:** Bible, theology.

Computing on campus. 45 workstations in dormitories, library, computer center. Dormitories wired for high-speed internet access and linked to campus network. Online library, helpline, repair service, student web hosting, wireless network available.

Student life. **Freshman orientation:** Mandatory. One full day (meal provided), includes testing. Registration held the following day. **Policies:** Religious observance required. Freshmen permitted cars on campus. **Housing:** Guaranteed on-campus for freshmen. Single-sex dorms, substance-free housing available. $800 deposit, deadline 7/1. **Activities:** Choral groups, drama, music ensembles, student government, learning center (tutoring for junior high and high school).

Athletics. NCCAA. **Intercollegiate:** Basketball M, volleyball W. **Team name:** Warriors.

Student services. Career counseling, financial aid counseling, personal counseling, placement for graduates, veterans' counselor. **Physically disabled:** Services for speech, hearing impaired.

Contact. E-mail: adm@lifepacific.edu
Phone: (909) 599-5433 ext. 314 Toll-free number: (877) 886-5433 ext. 314
Fax: (909) 706-6690
Gina Nicodemas, Admissions Director, LIFE Pacific College, 1100 Covina Boulevard, San Dimas, CA 91773

Lincoln University

Oakland, California
www.lincolnuca.edu **CB code: 4386**

- Private 4-year university, business and health science college
- Commuter campus in very large city
- 18 degree-seeking undergraduates
- 99 graduate students
- 96% of applicants admitted

General. Founded in 1919. Accredited by ACICS. Institution primarily serves international students. **Degrees:** 10 bachelor's awarded; master's offered. **Calendar:** Semester, limited summer session. **Full-time faculty:** 9 total. **Part-time faculty:** 29 total. **Special facilities:** Language laboratory, media center.

Freshman class profile. 89 applied, 85 admitted, 38 enrolled.

Basis for selection. High school achievement record most important. Prior to enrollment students take the Michigan Test of English Placement. Interview recommended.

2005-2006 Annual costs. Tuition/fees: $9,500. Books/supplies: $600. Personal expenses: $3,600.

Application procedures. **Admission:** No deadline. $75 fee.

Academics. **Special study options:** Cross-registration, ESL, internships. **Credit/placement by examination:** CLEP. **Support services:** Tutoring.

Majors. **Business:** General, accounting, business admin, international, management science. **Computer sciences:** General.

Most popular majors. Business/marketing 80%, computer/information sciences 20%.

Computing on campus. 30 workstations in library, computer center.

Student life. **Activities:** Student government, student newspaper.

Student services. Career counseling, personal counseling.

Contact. E-mail: admissions@lincolnuca.edu
Phone: (510) 628-8010 Toll-free number: (888) 810-9998
Fax: (510) 628-8012
Peggy Au, Associate Dean/Registrar, Lincoln University, 401 15th Street, Oakland, CA 94612

Loma Linda University

Loma Linda, California
www.llu.edu **CB code: 4062**

- Private upper-division health science and nursing college affiliated with Seventh-day Adventists
- Commuter campus in large town

General. Founded in 1905. Regionally accredited. Two undergraduate schools: School of Allied Health and School of Nursing, offering sophomore, junior, senior year study. **Degrees:** 238 bachelor's, 145 associate awarded; master's, doctoral, first professional offered. **Location:** 60 miles from Los Angeles, 50 miles from Palm Springs. **Calendar:** Quarter, limited summer session. **Full-time faculty:** 1,196 total; 33% minority, 36% women. **Part-time faculty:** 382 total; 28% minority, 37% women.

Student profile. 1,119 degree-seeking undergraduates, 2,787 graduate students.

Out-of-state:	12%	**25 or older:**	50%
Live on campus:	27%		

Basis for selection. Application requirements vary by specific allied health program. Nursing school applicants must have at least 10 specific college courses with 3.0 GPA. Application deadline January 1 for physical and occupational therapy programs, March 31 for nursing programs. 96 credits required for baccalaureate admission; 48 for associate degree programs. Transfer accepted as sophomores, juniors.

2005-2006 Annual costs. Tuition/fees: $23,514. Tuition quoted for nursing program. Full-time tuition for dental hygiene program: $18,895. For allied health program $465 per credit hour for first 8 credits, $279 per credit hour after 8 credits. Application fee may vary by program. Room only: $2,232. Books/supplies: $1,100. Personal expenses: $1,260.

Application procedures. Admission: Priority date 3/1. $60 fee. **Financial aid:** FAFSA required.

Academics. Special study options: Combined bachelor's/graduate degree, cross-registration, distance learning, ESL, internships, liberal arts/career combination, study abroad. **Credit/placement by examination:** CLEP. **Support services:** Learning center, reduced course load, remedial instruction, study skills assistance, tutoring, writing center.

Majors. Health: Audiology/speech pathology, clinical lab science, cytotechnology, dental hygiene, dietetics, medical radiologic technology/radiation therapy, medical records admin, nursing (RN), preop/surgical nursing, public health ed. **Physical sciences:** Geology.

Computing on campus. Dormitories linked to campus network. Commuter students can connect to campus network. Helpline available.

Student life. Policies: Religious observance required. **Housing:** Guaranteed on-campus for all undergraduates. Single-sex dorms available. Must reside on campus until age 22 unless living with parents. **Activities:** Student government, student newspaper, Black health professional student association, association of Latin American students, social action corps, Students for International Mission Service.

Student services. Alcohol/substance abuse counseling, campus ministries, financial aid counseling, health services, on-campus daycare, personal counseling. **Physically disabled:** Services for hearing impaired.

Contact. E-mail: admissions.app@llu.edu
Phone: (909) 558-8161
Loma Linda University, Loma Linda, CA 92350

Loyola Marymount University

Los Angeles, California — **CB member**
www.lmu.edu — **CB code: 4403**

- Private 4-year university affiliated with Roman Catholic Church
- Residential campus in very large city
- 5,419 degree-seeking undergraduates: 3% part-time, 59% women, 8% African American, 13% Asian American, 20% Hispanic American, 1% Native American, 2% international
- 3,164 degree-seeking graduate students
- 56% of applicants admitted
- SAT or ACT (ACT writing recommended), application essay required
- 76% graduate within 6 years

General. Founded in 1911. Regionally accredited. University is in the Jesuit and Marymount traditions. **Degrees:** 1,384 bachelor's awarded; master's, doctoral, first professional offered. **ROTC:** Army, Navy, Air Force. **Location:** 15 miles from downtown. **Calendar:** Semester, extensive summer session. **Full-time faculty:** 460 total; 24% minority, 38% women. **Part-time faculty:** 396 total; 21% minority, 46% women. **Class size:** 46% < 20, 52% 20-39, 1% 40-49, 1% 50-99, less than 1% >100. **Special facilities:** Fine arts complex with recital hall and recording arts facilities, Baja California marine station.

Freshman class profile. 7,733 applied, 4,367 admitted, 1,346 enrolled.

Mid 50% test scores		**Rank in top quarter:**	64%
SAT verbal:	530-630	**Rank in top tenth:**	30%
SAT math:	540-640	**Return as sophomores:**	90%
ACT:	22-27	**Out-of-state:**	26%
GPA 3.50 or higher:	60%	**Live on campus:**	94%
GPA 3.0-3.49:	35%	**International:**	1%
GPA 2.0-2.99:	5%		

Basis for selection. High school GPA, curriculum, test scores, recommendations, essays, activities important. Consideration given to children of alumni. Interview recommended for early admission, disabled, academically weak applicants. Portfolio required for animation major applicants.

High school preparation. College-preparatory program recommended. 18 units recommended. Recommended units include English 4, mathematics 3, social studies 3, science 2 (laboratory 2), foreign language 3 and academic electives 1. 4 units of mathematics required of engineering, mathematics, and science majors; physics and chemistry required of engineering and science majors; biology and chemistry required (physics recommended) of biology majors.

2006-2007 Annual costs. Tuition/fees: $29,834. Room/board: $12,640. Books/supplies: $832. Personal expenses: $1,900.

2005-2006 Financial aid. Need-based: 1,086 full-time freshmen applied for aid; 801 were judged to have need; 732 of these received aid. Average need met was 88%. Average scholarship/grant was $17,331; average loan $3,332. 73% of total undergraduate aid awarded as scholarships/grants, 27% as loans/jobs. **Non-need-based:** Scholarships awarded for academics, alumni affiliation, athletics, leadership, music/drama.

Application procedures. Admission: Priority date 1/15; no deadline. $50 fee, may be waived for applicants with need. Application may be submitted online. Admission notification on a rolling basis beginning on or about 11/1. Must reply by May 1 or within 2 week(s) if notified thereafter. Applicants who desire housing or financial aid should apply by January 15. **Financial aid:** Closing date 3/2. FAFSA, CSS PROFILE required. Applicants notified on a rolling basis starting 3/15; must reply by 5/1 or within 4 week(s) of notification.

Academics. Special study options: Cross-registration, distance learning, double major, dual enrollment of high school students, honors, independent study, internships, liberal arts/career combination, semester at sea, study abroad, teacher certification program, Washington semester. Encore Program for adult students. **Credit/placement by examination:** AP, CLEP, IB, institutional tests. **Support services:** Learning center, reduced course load, study skills assistance, tutoring.

Majors. Area/ethnic studies: African-American, Asian, European, Hispanic-American/Latino/Chicano, women's. **Biology:** General, biochemistry. **Business:** General, accounting, business admin. **Communications:** General, radio/tv. **Communications technology:** Animation/special effects, recording arts. **Computer sciences:** General. **Engineering:** General, civil, electrical, mechanical, physics. **English:** English lit. **Foreign languages:** Ancient Greek, classics, French, German, Latin, modern Greek, Spanish. **Health:** Art therapy. **History:** General. **Interdisciplinary:** Ancient studies, natural sciences. **Liberal arts:** Arts/sciences, humanities. **Math:** General, applied. **Philosophy/religion:** Philosophy. **Physical sciences:** Chemistry, physics. **Psychology:** General. **Public administration:** General. **Social sciences:** Economics, political science, sociology, urban studies. **Theology:** Theology. **Visual/performing arts:** Art, art history/conservation, cinematography, dance, design, dramatic, film/cinema, play/screenwriting, studio arts.

Computing on campus. 650 workstations in dormitories, library, computer center, student center. Dormitories wired for high-speed internet access and linked to campus network. Commuter students can connect to campus network. Helpline, student web hosting, wireless network available.

Student life. Freshman orientation: Available, $165 fee. **Policies:** Freshmen permitted cars on campus. **Housing:** Guaranteed on-campus for freshmen. Coed dorms, single-sex dorms, special housing for disabled, apartments, cooperative housing, fraternity/sorority housing available. $450 nonrefundable deposit. **Activities:** Pep band, choral groups, dance, drama, film society, literary magazine, music ensembles, musical theater, radio station, student government, student newspaper, TV station, more than 130 student organizations, clubs, and associations.

Athletics. NCAA. **Intercollegiate:** Baseball M, basketball, cross-country, golf M, rowing (crew), soccer, softball W, swimming W, tennis, track and field, volleyball W, water polo. **Intramural:** Basketball, football (tackle), soccer, softball, table tennis, tennis, volleyball, water polo. **Team name:** Lions.

Student services. Adult student services, alcohol/substance abuse counseling, campus ministries, career counseling, student employment services,

financial aid counseling, health services, minority student services, personal counseling, placement for graduates, veterans' counselor. **Physically disabled:** Services for visually, speech, hearing impaired.

Contact. E-mail: admissions@lmu.edu
Phone: (310) 338-2750 Toll-free number: (800) 568-4636
Fax: (310) 338-2797
Matthew Fissinger, Director of Admissions, Loyola Marymount University, Admissions, 1 LMU Drive, Los Angeles, CA 90045-8350

Master's College

Santa Clarita, California
www.masters.edu **CB code: 4411**

- Private 4-year liberal arts and seminary college affiliated with Christian, Protestant, Conservative Evangelical
- Residential campus in small city
- 1,125 degree-seeking undergraduates: 15% part-time, 50% women, 3% African American, 4% Asian American, 7% Hispanic American, 1% Native American, 3% international
- 398 degree-seeking graduate students
- 84% of applicants admitted
- SAT or ACT with writing, application essay, interview required
- 61% graduate within 6 years

General. Founded in 1927. Regionally accredited. Branch campus in Israel; very strong overseas summer missions program. **Degrees:** 264 bachelor's awarded; master's, doctoral, first professional offered. **Location:** 40 miles from Los Angeles. **Calendar:** Semester, limited summer session. **Full-time faculty:** 76 total; 82% have terminal degrees, 9% minority, 13% women. **Part-time faculty:** 83 total; 24% have terminal degrees, 4% minority, 22% women. **Class size:** 72% < 20, 18% 20-39, 2% 40-49, 7% 50-99, 1% >100. **Special facilities:** Home economics - family and consumer sciences center.

Freshman class profile. 369 applied, 311 admitted, 187 enrolled.

Mid 50% test scores			
SAT verbal:	520-620	Rank in top quarter:	53%
SAT math:	490-630	Rank in top tenth:	33%
ACT:	19-27	Return as sophomores:	77%
GPA 3.50 or higher:	70%	Out-of-state:	35%
GPA 3.0-3.49:	17%	Live on campus:	90%
GPA 2.0-2.99:	13%	International:	1%

Basis for selection. School achievement record, references, religious commitment most important. Applications from all individuals who have placed their faith in Jesus Christ as Lord and Savior are welcome. Audition required of music majors. **Homeschooled:** Transcript of courses and grades, letter of recommendation (nonparent) required. **Learning Disabled:** Must speak with human resources department before attending.

High school preparation. Required and recommended units include English 4, mathematics 3, history 2, science 2 and academic electives 3.

2006-2007 Annual costs. Tuition/fees: $27,670. Room/board: $7,150. Books/supplies: $1,224. Personal expenses: $1,872.

2004-2005 Financial aid. **Need-based:** 153 full-time freshmen applied for aid; 123 were judged to have need; 121 of these received aid. Average need met was 68%. Average scholarship/grant was $9,316; average loan $2,776. 63% of total undergraduate aid awarded as scholarships/grants, 37% as loans/jobs. **Non-need-based:** Awarded to 285 full-time undergraduates, including 92 freshmen. Scholarships awarded for academics, alumni affiliation, art, athletics, leadership, music/drama.

Application procedures. **Admission:** Priority date 3/2; no deadline. $55 fee, may be waived for applicants with need. Application may be submitted online. Admission notification on a rolling basis beginning on or about 3/15. Must reply by May 1 or within 2 week(s) if notified thereafter. **Financial aid:** Priority date 3/2; no closing date. FAFSA, institutional form required. Applicants notified on a rolling basis starting 2/18; must reply by 5/1 or within 2 week(s) of notification.

Academics. Students who attend 4 years earn a minor in Biblical Studies upon graduation. **Special study options:** Accelerated study, cooperative education, double major, independent study, internships, liberal arts/career combination, study abroad, teacher certification program, Washington semester. Israel semester. **Credit/placement by examination:** AP, CLEP, IB, institutional tests. 32 credit hours maximum toward bachelor's degree. **Support services:** Reduced course load, remedial instruction, study skills assistance, tutoring.

Majors. **Biology:** General, environmental. **Business:** Accounting, actuarial science, business admin, finance, management information systems. **Communications:** Media studies, public relations, radio/tv. **Computer sciences:** General. **Education:** General, elementary, ESL, middle, music, physical, science, secondary. **English:** English lit, speech/rhetoric. **Family/consumer sciences:** General, food/nutrition. **Foreign languages:** Biblical. **Health:** Premedicine. **History:** General. **Interdisciplinary:** Biological/physical sciences, natural sciences. **Legal studies:** Prelaw. **Liberal arts:** Arts/sciences. **Math:** General, applied. **Parks/recreation:** Health/fitness. **Philosophy/religion:** Religion. **Physical sciences:** General. **Social sciences:** Political science, U.S. government. **Theology:** Bible, pastoral counseling, religious ed, sacred music, theology. **Visual/performing arts:** Music management, piano/organ, voice/opera.

Most popular majors. Business/marketing 18%, communications/journalism 6%, education 16%, history 8%, philosophy/religious studies 33%.

Computing on campus. PC or laptop required. 60 workstations in library, computer center, student center. Dormitories wired for high-speed internet access and linked to campus network. Commuter students can connect to campus network. Online course registration, online library, helpline, repair service, wireless network available.

Student life. **Freshman orientation:** Mandatory. Preregistration for classes offered. 5-day program before start of classes. **Policies:** Emphasis on Godly lifestyle, character and leadership development, service, learning, cross-cultural education. Religious observance required. Freshmen permitted cars on campus. **Housing:** Single-sex dorms, substance-free housing available. $100 nonrefundable deposit, deadline 5/1. **Activities:** Concert band, choral groups, music ensembles, student government, summer missions, church ministries, outreach team.

Athletics. NAIA, NCCAA. **Intercollegiate:** Baseball M, basketball, cross-country, golf M, soccer, softball W, tennis W, volleyball W. **Intramural:** Basketball, football (non-tackle), golf, softball, tennis, volleyball. **Team name:** Mustangs.

Student services. Adult student services, campus ministries, career counseling, student employment services, financial aid counseling, health services, personal counseling, placement for graduates, veterans' counselor. **Physically disabled:** Services for speech impaired.

Contact. E-mail: admissions@masters.edu
Phone: (661) 259-3540 ext. 3369 Toll-free number: (800) 568-6248 ext. 3369 Fax: (661) 288-1037
Hollie Gorsh, Director of Admissions, Master's College, 21726 Placerita Canyon Road, Santa Clarita, CA 91321-1200

Menlo College

Atherton, California **CB member**
www.menlo.edu **CB code: 4483**

- Private 4-year business and liberal arts college
- Residential campus in small city
- 769 degree-seeking undergraduates: 13% part-time, 40% women, 9% African American, 12% Asian American, 15% Hispanic American, 1% Native American, 10% international
- 69% of applicants admitted
- SAT or ACT (ACT writing recommended), application essay required
- 32% graduate within 6 years

General. Founded in 1927. Regionally accredited. **Degrees:** 128 bachelor's awarded. **ROTC:** Army. **Location:** 30 miles from San Francisco, 30 miles from San Jose. **Calendar:** Semester, extensive summer session. **Full-time faculty:** 23 total; 65% have terminal degrees, 4% minority, 39% women. **Part-time faculty:** 50 total; 24% have terminal degrees, 14% minority, 42% women. **Class size:** 51% < 20, 45% 20-39, less than 1% 50-99.

Freshman class profile. 753 applied, 522 admitted, 172 enrolled.

Mid 50% test scores			
SAT verbal:	410-520	Rank in top quarter:	25.6%
SAT math:	420-530	Rank in top tenth:	6%
ACT:	14-21	End year in good standing:	85%
GPA 3.50 or higher:	18%	Return as sophomores:	64%
GPA 3.0-3.49:	33%	Out-of-state:	24%
GPA 2.0-2.99:	48%	Live on campus:	80%
		International:	8%

Basis for selection. High school record, test scores (minimum SAT combined score of 1000 (exclusive of Writing) or ACT composite score of 21, 1 recommendation, essay, depth of achievement in cocurricular activities considered. **Homeschooled:** Statement describing homeschool structure and mission, transcript of courses and grades, state high school equivalency certificate, letter of recommendation (nonparent) required. **Learning Disabled:** Direct queries to Academic Success Center.

High school preparation. 24 units recommended. Recommended units include English 4, mathematics 3, social studies 3, science 3 and foreign language 2.

2006-2007 Annual costs. Tuition/fees (projected): $26,220. Room/board: $9,800. Books/supplies: $280. Personal expenses: $2,046.

2005-2006 Financial aid. Need-based: 127 full-time freshmen applied for aid; 114 were judged to have need; 114 of these received aid. Average need met was 75%. Average scholarship/grant was $17,676; average loan $3,414. 73% of total undergraduate aid awarded as scholarships/grants, 27% as loans/jobs. **Non-need-based:** Awarded to 211 full-time undergraduates, including 61 freshmen. Scholarships awarded for academics.

Application procedures. Admission: Priority date 2/1; no deadline. $40 fee, may be waived for applicants with need. Application may be submitted online. Admission notification on a rolling basis beginning on or about 12/1. Must reply by May 1 or within 4 week(s) if notified thereafter. **Financial aid:** Priority date 3/2, closing date 8/1. FAFSA required. Applicants notified on a rolling basis starting 12/15; must reply by 5/1 or within 2 week(s) of notification.

Academics. Special study options: Accelerated study, cooperative education, double major, independent study, internships, student-designed major, study abroad. **Credit/placement by examination:** AP, CLEP, IB, institutional tests. 30 credit hours maximum toward bachelor's degree. **Support services:** Learning center, pre-admission summer program, reduced course load, remedial instruction, study skills assistance, tutoring, writing center.

Majors. Business: Business admin. **Communications:** General. **Liberal arts:** Arts/sciences.

Most popular majors. Business/marketing 73%, communications/journalism 14%, liberal arts 13%.

Computing on campus. 100 workstations in library, computer center. Dormitories wired for high-speed internet access and linked to campus network. Commuter students can connect to campus network. Online course registration, online library, helpline, repair service available.

Student life. Freshman orientation: Mandatory. Preregistration for classes offered. Weekend before classes begin. Workshops for both parents and students. **Policies:** Freshmen permitted cars on campus. **Housing:** Guaranteed on-campus for freshmen. Coed dorms, single-sex dorms, special housing for disabled, substance-free housing available. $300 partly refundable deposit, deadline 7/1. All freshmen and sophomores must reside on campus unless living at home, 21 years old, or married. **Activities:** Dance, film society, radio station, student government, student newspaper, TV station, international club, African-American student union, Latino student union, Hawaii club, Asia club, Rotaract, club 411, entrepreneurs club, Chinese culture research club, news club, women's club, Jewish student organization, Alpha Chi Honor Society, French club, Hula club, radio club.

Athletics. NAIA, NCAA. **Intercollegiate:** Baseball M, basketball, cross-country, football (tackle) M, golf M, soccer, softball W, volleyball W, wrestling. **Intramural:** Basketball, football (non-tackle), soccer, table tennis, volleyball. **Team name:** Oaks.

Student services. Adult student services, career counseling, student employment services, financial aid counseling, personal counseling, placement for graduates.

Contact. E-mail: admissions@menlo.edu
Phone: (650) 543-3753 Toll-free number: (800) 556-3656
Fax: (650) 543-4496
Greg Smith, Vice President for Enrollment, Menlo College, 1000 El Camino Real, Atherton, CA 94027

Mills College

Oakland, California — **CB member**
www.mills.edu — **CB code: 4485**

- Private 4-year liberal arts college for women
- Residential campus in large city
- 881 degree-seeking undergraduates: 4% part-time, 100% women, 8% African American, 8% Asian American, 9% Hispanic American, 1% Native American, 6% international
- 491 degree-seeking graduate students
- 77% of applicants admitted
- SAT or ACT (ACT writing optional), application essay required
- 67% graduate within 6 years

General. Founded in 1852. Regionally accredited. Men admitted to graduate programs. **Degrees:** 182 bachelor's awarded; master's, doctoral offered. **Location:** 18 miles from San Francisco, 8 miles from Berkeley. **Calendar:** Semester, limited summer session. **Full-time faculty:** 90 total; 91% have terminal degrees, 21% minority, 59% women. **Part-time faculty:** 94 total; 60% have terminal degrees, 26% minority, 74% women. **Class size:** 82% < 20, 16% 20-39, 1% 40-49, less than 1% 50-99. **Special facilities:** Electronic collaborative learning center, center for contemporary music, art museum, children's school (laboratory schools for student teachers), women's leadership institute, institute for civic leadership, center for the book.

Freshman class profile. 783 applied, 604 admitted, 207 enrolled.

Mid 50% test scores			
SAT verbal:	540-670	Rank in top tenth:	27%
SAT math:	490-610	Return as sophomores:	75%
ACT:	19-27	Out-of-state:	27%
Rank in top quarter:	55%	Live on campus:	95%
		International:	2%

Basis for selection. Minimum 3.0 GPA required, school achievement record most important. All credentials considered. SAT Subject Tests recommended. Interview recommended.

High school preparation. Recommended units include English 4, mathematics 4, social studies 4, history 4, science 4, foreign language 4 and academic electives 4.

2006-2007 Annual costs. Tuition/fees: $31,190. Room/board: $10,290. Books/supplies: $890. Personal expenses: $1,506.

2005-2006 Financial aid. Need-based: 121 full-time freshmen applied for aid; 104 were judged to have need; 104 of these received aid. Average need met was 94%. Average scholarship/grant was $20,108; average loan $3,885. 66% of total undergraduate aid awarded as scholarships/grants, 34% as loans/jobs. **Non-need-based:** Awarded to 610 full-time undergraduates, including 123 freshmen. Scholarships awarded for academics.

Application procedures. Admission: Priority date 2/1; deadline 3/1. $40 fee, may be waived for applicants with need. Application may be submitted online. Admission notification on a rolling basis beginning on or about 1/1. Must reply by May 1 or within 2 week(s) if notified thereafter. **Financial aid:** Priority date 2/1, closing date 2/15. FAFSA, institutional form required. Applicants notified by 4/1; must reply by 5/1 or within 2 week(s) of notification.

Academics. Certificate pre-medicine program available to postbaccalaureate students. **Special study options:** Combined bachelor's/graduate degree, cross-registration, double major, exchange student, independent study, internships, student-designed major, study abroad, teacher certification program, Washington semester. **Credit/placement by examination:** AP, CLEP, IB, institutional tests. 8 credit hours maximum toward bachelor's degree. **Support services:** Pre-admission summer program, tutoring, writing center.

Majors. Area/ethnic studies: American, Hispanic-American/Latino/Chicano, women's. **Biology:** General, biochemistry, molecular biochemistry. **Business:** General, managerial economics. **Communications:** General. **Computer sciences:** General. **Conservation:** General. **Education:** General. **Family/consumer sciences:** Child development. **Foreign languages:** Comparative lit, French, German, Spanish. **History:** General. **Interdisciplinary:** Math/computer science. **Legal studies:** General. **Liberal arts:** Arts/sciences. **Math:** General. **Philosophy/religion:** Philosophy. **Physical sciences:** Chemistry. **Psychology:** General. **Public administration:** Policy analysis. **Social sciences:** General, anthropology, international relations, political science, sociology. **Visual/performing arts:** Art, art history/conservation, dance, studio arts, theater history.

Most popular majors. Area/ethnic studies 9%, business/marketing 6%, English 14%, interdisciplinary studies 9%, psychology 7%, social sciences 11%, visual/performing arts 17%.

Computing on campus. 117 workstations in dormitories, library, computer center, student center. Dormitories wired for high-speed internet access and linked to campus network. Commuter students can connect to campus network. Helpline, wireless network available.

Student life. Freshman orientation: Mandatory. 5 days prior to the start of classes. **Policies:** Freshmen permitted cars on campus. **Housing:** Guaranteed on-campus for all undergraduates. Special housing for disabled, apartments, cooperative housing, substance-free housing available. $150 deposit. French, Spanish, and German language houses. Two-thirds of rooms are singles. Married student housing open to partners of lesbian and gay students. **Activities:** Choral groups, dance, drama, literary magazine, music ensembles, student government, student newspaper, ethnic, political, social service, career-oriented, and feminist student organizations, religious groups.

Athletics. NCAA. **Intercollegiate:** Cross-country W, rowing (crew) W, soccer W, swimming W, tennis W, volleyball W. **Intramural:** Badminton W, basketball W, cross-country W, equestrian W, fencing W, golf W, rugby W, sailing W, soccer W, softball W, swimming W, tennis W, track and field W, volleyball W, water polo W. **Team name:** Cyclones.

Student services. Career counseling, student employment services, financial aid counseling, health services, on-campus daycare, personal counseling, placement for graduates. **Physically disabled:** Services for visually, speech, hearing impaired.

Contact. E-mail: admission@mills.edu
Phone: (510) 430-2135 Toll-free number: (800) 876-4557
Fax: (510) 430-3314
Julie Richardson, Vice President for Enrollment Management, Mills College, 5000 MacArthur Boulevard, Oakland, CA 94613

Monterey Institute of International Studies

Monterey, California
www.miis.edu **CB code: 4507**

- Private upper-division liberal arts college
- Commuter campus in small city

General. Founded in 1955. Regionally accredited. **Location:** 130 miles from San Francisco, 60 miles from San Jose. **Calendar:** Semester.

Annual costs/financial aid. Tuition/fees (2005-2006): $25,700. Books/supplies: $900. Need-based financial aid available to full-time and part-time students.

Contact. Phone: (831) 647-4123
Vice President for Enrollment Management, 460 Pierce Street, Monterey, CA 93940

Mount St. Mary's College

Los Angeles, California **CB member**
www.msmc.la.edu **CB code: 4493**

- Private 4-year liberal arts college for women affiliated with Roman Catholic Church
- Residential campus in very large city
- 1,971 degree-seeking undergraduates: 25% part-time, 94% women, 10% African American, 20% Asian American, 44% Hispanic American, 1% Native American, 1% international
- 500 graduate students
- 85% of applicants admitted
- SAT or ACT (ACT writing optional), application essay required
- 58% graduate within 6 years

General. Founded in 1925. Regionally accredited. Founded by the Sisters of St. Joseph of Carondelet in 1925. Men admitted to undergraduate nursing and music programs, graduate division, weekend college and summer divisions. **Degrees:** 299 bachelor's, 132 associate awarded; master's, doctoral offered. **Location:** 2 miles from Los Angeles. **Calendar:** Semester, limited summer session. **Full-time faculty:** 72 total; 69% have terminal degrees, 10% minority. **Part-time faculty:** 225 total; 10% have terminal degrees, 25% minority, 74% women. **Class size:** 63% < 20, 34% 20-39, 2% 40-49, less than 1% 50-99, less than 1% >100. **Special facilities:** Doheny Mansion.

Freshman class profile. 1,035 applied, 881 admitted, 372 enrolled.

Mid 50% test scores		**GPA 2.0-2.99:**	11%
SAT verbal:	470-560	**Return as sophomores:**	72%
SAT math:	460-550	**Out-of-state:**	7%
GPA 3.50 or higher:	53%	**Live on campus:**	71%
GPA 3.0-3.49:	36%		

Basis for selection. Primary emphasis on school academic record, then test scores, essay, and letters of recommendation. School and community activities also considered. Interview important. Admission requirements considered very competitive in baccalaureate program. SAT recommended. Interviews recommended. Auditions recommended of music majors. Portfolios recommended of art majors. **Learning Disabled:** Documentation of learning disability required.

High school preparation. 25 units required; 30 recommended. Required and recommended units include English 4, mathematics 3-4, social studies 2-3, history 2-3, science 2-3 (laboratory 2-3), foreign language 2-3 and academic electives 2-3. For associate degree applicants, required courses include algebra, geometry, American history/government, and 3 units English.

2005-2006 Annual costs. Tuition/fees: $22,824. Room/board: $8,492. Books/supplies: $648. Personal expenses: $1,170.

2004-2005 Financial aid. Need-based: 168 full-time freshmen applied for aid; 152 were judged to have need; 152 of these received aid. Average need met was 79%. Average scholarship/grant was $7,425; average loan $2,485. 72% of total undergraduate aid awarded as scholarships/grants, 28% as loans/jobs. **Non-need-based:** Awarded to 409 full-time undergraduates, including 174 freshmen. Scholarships awarded for academics, alumni affiliation, art, leadership, music/drama.

Application procedures. Admission: Priority date 12/1; deadline 2/15. $40 fee, may be waived for applicants with need. Application may be submitted online. Admission notification on a rolling basis. Must reply by May 1 or within 2 week(s) if notified thereafter. **Financial aid:** Priority date 3/1; no closing date. FAFSA, institutional form required. Applicants notified on a rolling basis starting 2/1; must reply by 5/1.

Academics. Special study options: Accelerated study, cross-registration, double major, exchange student, honors, independent study, internships, student-designed major, study abroad, teacher certification program, United Nations semester, Washington semester, weekend college. **Credit/placement by examination:** AP, CLEP, IB, institutional tests. 24 credit hours maximum toward associate degree, 30 toward bachelor's. **Support services:** Learning center, pre-admission summer program, reduced course load, remedial instruction, study skills assistance, tutoring, writing center.

Majors. Area/ethnic studies: American. **Biology:** General, biochemistry. **Business:** General, accounting, business admin, international. **Education:** Elementary, middle, secondary. **Foreign languages:** French, Spanish. **Health:** Clinical lab technology, health care admin, nursing (RN), predentistry, premedicine, preveterinary. **History:** General. **Legal studies:** Prelaw. **Math:** General, applied. **Philosophy/religion:** Philosophy, religion. **Physical sciences:** Chemistry. **Psychology:** General. **Social sciences:** General, political science, sociology. **Theology:** Sacred music. **Visual/performing arts:** Music performance, music theory/composition, studio arts.

Most popular majors. Biology 7%, business/marketing 13%, English 8%, health sciences 28%, liberal arts 8%, psychology 8%, social sciences 20%.

Computing on campus. 168 workstations in dormitories, library, computer center, student center. Dormitories wired for high-speed internet access and linked to campus network. Commuter students can connect to campus network. Helpline, student web hosting, wireless network available.

Student life. Freshman orientation: Available. **Policies:** Student resident life largely self-regulated under direction of Residence Council. Freshmen permitted cars on campus. **Housing:** Guaranteed on-campus for freshmen. $100 deposit, deadline 5/1. **Activities:** Choral groups, dance, literary magazine, student government, student newspaper, symphony orchestra, campus ministry, volunteer service, ethnic clubs.

Athletics. Intramural: Basketball W, cross-country W, swimming W, tennis W, track and field W, volleyball W.

Student services. Adult student services, campus ministries, career counseling, student employment services, financial aid counseling, health services, personal counseling, placement for graduates.

Contact. E-mail: admissions@msmc.la.edu
Phone: (310) 954-4250 Toll-free number: (800) 999-9893
Fax: (310) 954-4259
Dean Kilgour, Director of Admissions, Mount St. Mary's College, 12001 Chalon Road, Los Angeles, CA 90049

Mt. Sierra College

Monrovia, California
www.mtsierra.edu **CB code: 3090**

- For-profit 4-year technical college
- Commuter campus in very large city
- 800 degree-seeking undergraduates
- 40% of applicants admitted

General. Accredited by ACCSCT. **Degrees:** 129 bachelor's awarded. **Calendar:** Quarter. **Full-time faculty:** 20 total. **Part-time faculty:** 50 total.

Freshman class profile. 318 applied, 127 admitted, 116 enrolled.

Basis for selection. Minimum score on CPT exams; non-high school graduates may be admitted on ability-to-benefit. Institutional CPT exams waived if SAT verbal/math scores 560 or higher, or ACT verbal/math scores 20 or higher.

2005-2006 Annual costs. Tuition/fees: $12,330. Additional lab fees may apply; varies by program of study. Books/supplies: $2,000.

Application procedures. Admission: No deadline. $20 fee. Application may be submitted online. Admission notification on a rolling basis.

Academics. Special study options: Accelerated study, weekend college. **Credit/placement by examination:** CLEP, IB, institutional tests. **Support services:** Learning center, tutoring, writing center.

Majors. Computer sciences: General, security, web page design.

Computing on campus. PC or laptop required.

Student life. Freshman orientation: Available. Held during first week of classes.

Contact. Phone: (626) 873-2144 Toll-free number: (888) 828-8800
Kimberly Rodriguez, Director of Admissions, Mt. Sierra College, 101 East Huntington Drive, Monrovia, CA 91016

National Hispanic University

San Jose, California — **CB member**
www.nhu.edu — **CB code: 4593**

- Private 4-year university
- Commuter campus in very large city
- 427 degree-seeking undergraduates: 38% part-time, 67% women
- 122 degree-seeking graduate students
- Application essay required

General. Regionally accredited. **Degrees:** 9 bachelor's awarded. **ROTC:** Army, Navy. **Calendar:** Semester, limited summer session. **Full-time faculty:** 15 total. **Part-time faculty:** 40 total. **Class size:** 67% < 20, 33% 20-39.

Freshman class profile. 149 enrolled.

Basis for selection. High school GPA is required, transcript, two letters of recommendation, written essay. **Homeschooled:** State high school equivalency certificate required.

High school preparation. College-preparatory program recommended.

2005-2006 Annual costs. Tuition/fees: $4,850.

Financial aid. Non-need-based: Scholarships awarded for academics.

Application procedures. Admission: No deadline. $50 fee. Application must be submitted on paper. Admission notification on a rolling basis. **Financial aid:** No deadline. FAFSA required.

Academics. Special study options: Dual enrollment of high school students, independent study, teacher certification program. **Credit/placement by examination:** AP, CLEP, IB. **Support services:** Learning center, tutoring, writing center.

Majors. Business: Business admin. **Computer sciences:** General. **Liberal arts:** Arts/sciences.

Computing on campus. Online library, wireless network available.

Student life. Freshman orientation: Mandatory. Preregistration for classes offered. **Policies:** Freshmen permitted cars on campus. **Activities:** Student government.

Student services. Financial aid counseling.

Contact. Phone: (408) 273-2772 Fax: (408) 254-1369
Pamela Bustillo, Director of Admissions/Registrar, National Hispanic University, 14271 Story Road, San Jose, CA 95127-3823

National University

La Jolla, California — **CB member**
www.nu.edu — **CB code: 0470**

- Private 4-year university
- Commuter campus in very large city
- 6,186 degree-seeking undergraduates: 74% part-time, 56% women, 12% African American, 9% Asian American, 18% Hispanic American, 1% Native American, 1% international
- 18,876 degree-seeking graduate students
- Interview required
- 50% graduate within 6 years

General. Founded in 1971. Regionally accredited. Located in 13 major cities; also offers more than 30 degrees and 300 courses online. **Degrees:** 1,003 bachelor's, 19 associate awarded; master's offered. **ROTC:** Army, Navy, Air Force. **Calendar:** Continuous, limited summer session. **Full-time faculty:** 199 total; 79% have terminal degrees, 8% minority, 43% women. **Part-time faculty:** 2,502 total; 25% have terminal degrees, 14% minority, 47% women. **Class size:** 84% < 20, 16% 20-39, less than 1% 40-49.

Freshman class profile. 250 enrolled.

Return as sophomores:	100%	**International:**	1%
Out-of-state:	8%		

Basis for selection. Open admission, but selective for some programs. Interview, previous business and work experience, academic record considered.

2005-2006 Annual costs. Tuition/fees: $8,352. Books/supplies: $1,120. Personal expenses: $1,968.

2004-2005 Financial aid. Need-based: 37% of total undergraduate aid awarded as scholarships/grants, 63% as loans/jobs.

Application procedures. Admission: No deadline. $60 fee. Application may be submitted online. Admission notification on a rolling basis. **Financial aid:** No deadline. FAFSA, institutional form required. Applicants notified on a rolling basis.

Academics. Special study options: Accelerated study, cross-registration, distance learning, double major, ESL, independent study, internships, liberal arts/career combination, teacher certification program, weekend college. **Credit/placement by examination:** AP, CLEP, institutional tests. 14 credit hours maximum toward associate degree, 23 toward bachelor's. **Support services:** Learning center, remedial instruction, tutoring, writing center.

Majors. Business: General, accounting, business admin, construction management, hospitality admin, human resources, operations, organizational behavior. **Communications:** Media studies. **Computer sciences:** General, computer science, information systems. **Conservation:** Environmental studies. **Education:** Mathematics. **Engineering:** Construction, systems. **Engineering technology:** Civil drafting. **English:** English lit. **Family/consumer sciences:** Child development. **Health:** Health care admin, licensed practical nurse, preop/surgical nursing. **History:** Gerneral. **Interdisciplinary:** Biological/physical sciences, global studies, intercultural. **Legal studies:** General. **Liberal arts:** Arts/sciences. **Math:** General. **Parks/recreation:** Facilities management, sports admin. **Physical sciences:** General, geology. **Protective services:** Criminal justice, law enforcement admin, security services. **Psychology:** General. **Public administration:** General. **Social sciences:** Economics, sociology. **Visual/performing arts:** Multimedia.

Most popular majors. Business/marketing 32%, computer/information sciences 13%, interdisciplinary studies 16%, liberal arts 8%, psychology 14%, security/protective services 9%.

Computing on campus. 2,500 workstations in library, computer center, student center. Commuter students can connect to campus network. Online course registration, online library, helpline, wireless network available.

Student life. Freshman orientation: Available. Preregistration for classes offered. **Policies:** Freshmen permitted cars on campus. **Activities:** TV station.

Student services. Adult student services, career counseling, services for economically disadvantaged, student employment services, financial aid counseling, minority student services, placement for graduates, veterans' counselor. **Physically disabled:** Services for visually, speech, hearing impaired.

Contact. E-mail: advisor@nu.edu
Phone: (800) 628-8648 Toll-free number: (800) 628-8648
Fax: (858) 642-8709
Megan Magee, Associate Regional Dean - San Diego, National University, 11255 North Torrey Pines Road, La Jolla, CA 92037-1011

New College of California
San Francisco, California
www.newcollege.edu **CB code: 4555**

- Private 4-year liberal arts college
- Commuter campus in very large city

General. Founded in 1971. Regionally accredited. **Calendar:** Semester.

Annual costs/financial aid. Tuition/fees (2005-2006): $13,184. Books/supplies: $650.

Contact. Phone: (415) 437-3460
777 Valencia Street, San Francisco, CA 94110

NewSchool of Architecture & Design
San Diego, California
www.newschoolarch.edu **CB code: 2419**

- For-profit 5-year visual arts and liberal arts college
- Commuter campus in very large city
- 175 full-time, degree-seeking undergraduates
- 180 graduate students
- 100% of applicants admitted
- Interview required

General. Founded in 1980. Accredited by ACICS. **Degrees:** 12 bachelor's awarded; master's offered. **Location:** 90 miles from Los Angeles, 17 miles from Tijuana, Mexico. **Calendar:** Quarter, extensive summer session. **Full-time faculty:** 15 total. **Part-time faculty:** 30 total. **Special facilities:** Design clinic.

Freshman class profile. 16 applied, 16 admitted, 13 enrolled.

Basis for selection. Resume considered if submitted. Portfolio review required.

2005-2006 Annual costs. Books/supplies: $700.

Financial aid. Non-need-based: Scholarships awarded for academics.

Application procedures. Admission: Priority date 11/1; no deadline. $75 fee, may be waived for applicants with need. Application may be submitted online. Admission notification on a rolling basis. Must reply by May 1 or within 4 week(s) if notified thereafter. **Financial aid:** Priority date 3/2; no closing date. FAFSA required. Applicants notified on a rolling basis.

Academics. Special study options: Accelerated study, cooperative education, double major, internships, liberal arts/career combination. Cooperative program available at nearby U.S. International University, where students can take ESL and general education classes. **Credit/placement by examination:** AP, CLEP. **Support services:** Pre-admission summer program, tutoring.

Majors. Architecture: Architecture.

Computing on campus. 17 workstations in library, computer center.

Student life. Freshman orientation: Available. Preregistration for classes offered. Held 1-2 days before start of classes in fall. **Housing:** Private apartments located near college. Affiliation with U.S. International University (board, room, health services, ESL, transportation). **Activities:** Literary magazine, student government, student newspaper, American Institute of Architects student chapter; annual field trips to Europe and Mexico.

Student services. Career counseling, student employment services, health services, personal counseling, placement for graduates, veterans' counselor.

Contact. E-mail: admissions@newschoolarch.edu
Phone: (619) 235-4100 Fax: (619) 235-4651
Barbara Wingate, Director of Admissions, NewSchool of Architecture & Design, 1249 F Street, San Diego, CA 92101

Northwestern Polytechnic University
Fremont, California
www.npu.edu **CB code: 4335**

- Private 4-year business and engineering college
- Commuter campus in small city
- 114 degree-seeking undergraduates
- 232 graduate students
- 89% of applicants admitted

General. Accredited by ACICS. **Degrees:** 33 bachelor's awarded; master's, doctoral offered. **Location:** 42 miles from San Francisco, 11 miles from San Jose. **Calendar:** Trimester, extensive summer session. **Full-time faculty:** 12 total. **Part-time faculty:** 50 total. **Class size:** 94% < 20, 6% 20-39.

Freshman class profile. 18 applied, 16 admitted, 11 enrolled.

Out-of-state:	20%	**Live on campus:**	10%

Basis for selection. Secondary school record, test scores important; recommendations, interview considered. Pre-calculus is prerequisite. On-campus English placement exam may replace TOEFL; on-campus freshman exam may replace SAT. Institutional English placement examination required of new international students who have not passed standardized tests.

High school preparation. Required and recommended units include English 3, mathematics 2, social studies 1 and science 1. One unit in mathematics required for business programs.

2006-2007 Annual costs. Tuition/fees: $8,390. Books/supplies: $700.

Financial aid. Additional information: Work-study, co-op program, internships available. Employment opportunities with local engineering firms help defray costs.

Application procedures. Admission: Priority date 9/11; deadline 10/9 (postmark date). $60 fee. Application must be submitted on paper. Admission notification on a rolling basis. Must reply by 10/9.

Academics. Special study options: Cooperative education, ESL. **Credit/placement by examination:** AP, CLEP, institutional tests. 12 credit hours maximum toward bachelor's degree. **Support services:** Learning center, tutoring.

Majors. Business: Management information systems. **Engineering:** Electrical, software, systems.

Most popular majors. Business/marketing 48%, engineering/engineering technologies 52%.

Computing on campus. 320 workstations in library, computer center, student center. Commuter students can connect to campus network. Online library, helpline available.

Student life. Freshman orientation: Mandatory. Preregistration for classes offered. One-day program before start of classes. **Policies:** Each student is required to join the Student Association. Freshmen permitted cars on campus. **Housing:** Apartments, substance-free housing available. $300 deposit, deadline 10/1. **Activities:** Literary magazine, student government, student association, United Nations at Silicon Valley student chapter.

Student services. Adult student services, career counseling, student employment services, personal counseling, placement for graduates, veterans' counselor.

Contact. E-mail: admission@npu.edu
Phone: (510) 657-5913 Fax: (510) 657-8975
Dennis Yu, Admission Officer, Northwestern Polytechnic University, 47671 Westinghouse Drive, Fremont, CA 94539

Notre Dame de Namur University
Belmont, California **CB member**
www.ndnu.edu **CB code: 4063**

- Private 4-year liberal arts college affiliated with Roman Catholic Church
- Residential campus in large town
- 886 degree-seeking undergraduates
- 96% of applicants admitted
- SAT or ACT with writing, application essay required

General. Founded in 1851. Regionally accredited. **Degrees:** 232 bachelor's awarded; master's offered. **Location:** 25 miles from San Francisco. **Calendar:** Semester, limited summer session. **Full-time faculty:** 54 total. **Part-time faculty:** 93 total. **Class size:** 67% < 20, 32% 20-39, 2% 40-49.

Freshman class profile. 643 applied, 617 admitted, 145 enrolled.

Mid 50% test scores		ACT:	16-24
SAT verbal:	440-530	Out-of-state:	19%
SAT math:	440-550	Live on campus:	85%

Basis for selection. High school record and GPA most important; test scores also important. Essay, recommendation, and school and community activities considered.

High school preparation. 14 units required; 18 recommended. Required and recommended units include English 4-5, mathematics 2-3, social studies 2-3, science 1-2 and foreign language 2-3. 3 additional units from fine arts, advanced laboratory science, advanced mathematics, or advanced foreign language also required.

2006-2007 Annual costs. Tuition/fees: $23,850. Room/board: $10,380. Books/supplies: $882. Personal expenses: $1,642.

Financial aid. Non-need-based: Scholarships awarded for academics, alumni affiliation, athletics, leadership, music/drama.

Application procedures. Admission: Priority date 3/2; no deadline. $40 fee, may be waived for applicants with need. Application may be submitted online. Admission notification on a rolling basis. Must reply by May 1 or within 3 week(s) if notified thereafter. **Financial aid:** Priority date 3/2; no closing date. FAFSA required. CSS/ PROFILE accepted but not required. Applicants notified on a rolling basis starting 1/15.

Academics. Special study options: Accelerated study, cooperative education, double major, dual enrollment of high school students, ESL, exchange student, independent study, internships, liberal arts/career combination, student-designed major, study abroad, teacher certification program. **Credit/placement by examination:** AP, CLEP, IB, institutional tests. 30 credit hours maximum toward bachelor's degree. **Support services:** Learning center, reduced course load, remedial instruction, study skills assistance, tutoring, writing center.

Majors. Biology: General, biochemistry. **Business:** General, business admin. **Communications:** General. **Computer sciences:** General, computer science. **Engineering:** Software. **Health:** Predentistry, premedicine, prepharmacy, preveterinary. **History:** General. **Interdisciplinary:** Behavioral sciences. **Legal studies:** Prelaw. **Liberal arts:** Arts/sciences. **Philosophy/religion:** Philosophy, religion. **Psychology:** General. **Public administration:** Human services. **Social sciences:** Political science, sociology. **Theology:** Religious ed. **Visual/performing arts:** Art, dramatic, music performance, studio arts.

Computing on campus. 86 workstations in library, computer center. Dormitories wired for high-speed internet access and linked to campus network. Commuter students can connect to campus network. Helpline, repair service, student web hosting available.

Student life. Freshman orientation: Available, $60 fee. 5 days preceding opening of classes. **Policies:** Freshmen permitted cars on campus. **Housing:** Guaranteed on-campus for freshmen. Coed dorms, apartments available. $160 deposit, deadline 7/1. **Activities:** Choral groups, drama, literary magazine, music ensembles, musical theater, opera, student government, student newspaper, symphony orchestra, campus ministry, Hawaiian club, international club, business/career club, Filipino club, Alianza Latina, Black Student Union, outdoor activities club, Amnesty International, science and medical careers club.

Athletics. NAIA. **Intercollegiate:** Basketball, cross-country, golf, lacrosse M, soccer, softball W, volleyball W. **Team name:** Argonauts.

Student services. Adult student services, alcohol/substance abuse counseling, campus ministries, career counseling, student employment services, financial aid counseling, health services, personal counseling, placement for graduates. **Learning disabled:** Comprehensive services available.

Contact. E-mail: admiss@ndnu.edu
Phone: (650) 508-3607 Toll-free number: (800) 263-0545
Fax: (650) 508-3426
Katy Murphy, Director of Admission, Notre Dame de Namur University, 1500 Ralston Avenue, Belmont, CA 94002-1997

Occidental College

Los Angeles, California — **CB member**
www.oxy.edu — **CB code: 4581**

- Private 4-year liberal arts college affiliated with nondenominational tradition
- Residential campus in very large city
- 1,814 degree-seeking undergraduates: 1% part-time, 57% women, 6% African American, 13% Asian American, 14% Hispanic American, 1% Native American, 3% international
- 20 degree-seeking graduate students
- 41% of applicants admitted
- SAT or ACT with writing, application essay required
- 84% graduate within 6 years

General. Founded in 1887. Regionally accredited. **Degrees:** 438 bachelor's awarded; master's offered. **ROTC:** Army, Air Force. **Location:** 5 miles from downtown. **Calendar:** Semester, limited summer session. **Full-time faculty:** 148 total; 94% have terminal degrees, 30% minority, 45% women. **Part-time faculty:** 67 total; 27% minority, 46% women. **Class size:** 64% < 20, 32% 20-39, 3% 40-49, 1% 50-99. **Special facilities:** Theater, studio and art gallery, marine biology with scuba access, plasma physics and fluid dynamics labs, ornithology collection, geological collection, astronomical instruments collection, vivarium, greenhouses.

Freshman class profile. 5,114 applied, 2,086 admitted, 436 enrolled.

Mid 50% test scores		Rank in top tenth:	60%
SAT verbal:	600-690	End year in good standing:	96%
SAT math:	610-690	Return as sophomores:	92%
ACT:	27-31	Out-of-state:	56%
Rank in top quarter:	86%	Live on campus:	100%

Basis for selection. Primary consideration given to academic credentials and holistic qualities such as intellectual curiosity, out-of-class interests, and personal character. SAT Subject Tests recommended. Interview recommended. **Homeschooled:** Taking at least 2 SAT Subject Tests recommended.

High school preparation. 20 units recommended. Recommended units include English 4, mathematics 4, social studies 2, history 2, science 3 (laboratory 2), foreign language 3 and academic electives 2.

2006-2007 Annual costs. Tuition/fees: $33,644. Room/board: $9,552. Books/supplies: $914. Personal expenses: $1,300.

2005-2006 Financial aid. Need-based: 272 full-time freshmen applied for aid; 207 were judged to have need; 206 of these received aid. Average need met was 90%. Average scholarship/grant was $21,416; average loan $4,812. 76% of total undergraduate aid awarded as scholarships/grants, 24% as loans/jobs. **Non-need-based:** Awarded to 508 full-time undergraduates, including 164 freshmen. Scholarships awarded for academics, leadership.

Application procedures. Admission: Closing date 1/10 (postmark date). $50 fee, may be waived for applicants with need. Application may be submitted online. Admission notification 4/1. Must reply by May 1 or within 2 week(s) if notified thereafter. **Financial aid:** Priority date 11/15, closing date 2/1. FAFSA, CSS PROFILE required. Applicants notified by 3/24; must reply by 5/1.

Academics. Special study options: Combined bachelor's/graduate degree, cross-registration, double major, exchange student, honors, independent study, internships, student-designed major, study abroad, United Nations semester, Washington semester. **Credit/placement by examination:** AP, CLEP, IB, institutional tests. **Support services:** Learning center, preadmission summer program, study skills assistance, tutoring, writing center.

Majors. Area/ethnic studies: American, Asian, women's. **Biology:** General, biochemistry. **English:** English lit. **Foreign languages:** General, French, Spanish. **History:** General. **Interdisciplinary:** Cognitive science. **Math:** General. **Parks/recreation:** Exercise sciences. **Philosophy/religion:** Philosophy, religion. **Physical sciences:** Chemistry, geology, geophysics, physics. **Psychology:** General. **Social sciences:** Anthropology, economics, international relations, political science, sociology. **Visual/performing arts:** Art, art history/conservation, dramatic.

Most popular majors. Biology 8%, English 7%, history 6%, psychology 10%, social sciences 30%, visual/performing arts 11%.

Computing on campus. 300 workstations in dormitories, library, computer center. Dormitories linked to campus network. Commuter students can connect to campus network. Online course registration, helpline, repair service, wireless network available.

Student life. Freshman orientation: Mandatory. Preregistration for classes offered. Held 1 week in August prior to start of classes. **Policies:** All residence halls student-run. Freshmen permitted cars on campus. **Housing:** Guaranteed on-campus for freshmen. Coed dorms, single-sex dorms, fraternity/sorority housing, substance-free housing available. **Activities:** Bands, choral groups, dance, drama, film society, literary magazine, music ensembles, musical theater, radio station, student government, student newspaper, symphony orchestra, more than 100 clubs and organizations.

Athletics. NCAA. **Intercollegiate:** Baseball M, basketball, cross-country, diving, football (tackle) M, golf, soccer, softball W, swimming, tennis, track and field, volleyball W, water polo. **Intramural:** Basketball, football (non-tackle), volleyball. **Team name:** Tigers.

Student services. Adult student services, alcohol/substance abuse counseling, campus ministries, career counseling, services for economically disadvantaged, student employment services, financial aid counseling, health services, minority student services, on-campus daycare, personal counseling, women's services. **Physically disabled:** Services for hearing impaired.

Contact. E-mail: admission@oxy.edu
Phone: (323) 259-2700 Toll-free number: (800) 825-5262
Fax: (323) 341-4875
Vince Cuseo, Dean of Admission, Occidental College, 1600 Campus Road, Los Angeles, CA 90041

Otis College of Art and Design

Los Angeles, California — **CB member**
www.otis.edu — **CB code: 4394**

- Private 4-year visual arts college
- Commuter campus in very large city
- 1,023 degree-seeking undergraduates
- 62% of applicants admitted
- SAT or ACT (ACT writing optional), application essay required

General. Founded in 1918. Regionally accredited. **Degrees:** 182 bachelor's awarded; master's offered. **Calendar:** Semester, limited summer session. **Full-time faculty:** 43 total. **Part-time faculty:** 192 total. **Class size:** 78% < 20, 20% 20-39, 2% 50-99. **Special facilities:** Rare art books collection, multi-kiln firing capabilities, full foundry and casting facilities, photographic darkroom, fully equipped printmaking studio, fine art book press room, woodworking and metal working shops, toy design department, digital imaging studio.

Freshman class profile. 829 applied, 517 admitted, 173 enrolled.

Mid 50% test scores			
SAT verbal:	420-550	ACT:	17-22
SAT math:	440-580	Out-of-state:	21%
		Live on campus:	58%

Basis for selection. Portfolio most important, followed by school achievement record, essay and test scores. Activities, leadership, motivation also considered. Portfolio required. Interview recommended. **Homeschooled:** Documentation that student has solid academic foundation, is socially and intellectually mature, and has passion for the arts.

High school preparation. Required and recommended units include English 4, mathematics 3-4, social studies 1-2, history 2-3, science 2-4 (laboratory 1-4) and foreign language 2. Drawing and as much art as possible recommended.

2006-2007 Annual costs. Tuition/fees (projected): $27,596. Books/supplies: $2,400. Personal expenses: $1,300.

2004-2005 Financial aid. Need-based: 72% of total undergraduate aid awarded as scholarships/grants, 28% as loans/jobs. **Non-need-based:** Scholarships awarded for academics, art.

Application procedures. Admission: Priority date 2/15; no deadline. $50 fee, may be waived for applicants with need. Application may be submitted online. Admission notification on a rolling basis. Must reply by May 1 or within 2 week(s) if notified thereafter. **Financial aid:** Priority date 2/15; no closing date. FAFSA required. Applicants notified on a rolling basis starting 3/1; must reply within 2 week(s) of notification.

Academics. Approximately one-third of curriculum consists of liberal arts classes. **Special study options:** ESL, exchange student, honors, independent study, internships, study abroad. **Credit/placement by examination:** AP, CLEP, institutional tests. **Support services:** Pre-admission summer program, reduced course load, remedial instruction, study skills assistance, tutoring.

Majors. Communications technology: Animation/special effects. **Visual/performing arts:** Design, fashion design, studio arts.

Computing on campus. 280 workstations in library, computer center. Helpline, wireless network available.

Student life. Freshman orientation: Mandatory. Orientation held in January and August. **Policies:** Freshmen permitted cars on campus. **Housing:** Apartments available. Otis sponsored off-campus apartments available. **Activities:** Literary magazine, student government, student newspaper, literary organization, Campus Crusade.

Student services. Adult student services, alcohol/substance abuse counseling, career counseling, student employment services, financial aid counseling, personal counseling, placement for graduates. **Physically disabled:** Services for hearing impaired.

Contact. E-mail: admissions@otis.edu
Phone: (310) 665-6820 Toll-free number: (800) 527-6847
Fax: (310) 665-6821
Marc Meredith, Dean of Admissions, Otis College of Art and Design, 9045 Lincoln Boulevard, Los Angeles, CA 90045-9785

Pacific Oaks College

Pasadena, California
www.pacificoaks.edu — **CB code: 0482**

- Private upper-division teachers college
- Commuter campus in small city
- Application essay required

General. Founded in 1951. Regionally accredited. College and children's school founded by Quaker families as community education center. **Degrees:** 95 bachelor's awarded; master's offered. **Articulation:** Agreements with De Anza College, Glendale City College, College of the Canyons, Pasadena City College, Rio Hondo College, Santa Monica College, Santa Barbara College, East Los Angeles College, El Camino College, Mt. San Antonio College, Citrus College, Renton Technical College, South Puget Sound CC. **Location:** 10 miles from downtown Los Angeles. **Calendar:** Semester, limited summer session. **Full-time faculty:** 34 total. **Part-time faculty:** 55 total. **Class size:** 72% < 20, 28% 20-39. **Special facilities:** School for infants through kindergarten.

Student profile. 245 degree-seeking undergraduates. 87% transferred from two-year, 13% transferred from four-year institutions.

Out-of-state:	19%	25 or older:	94%

Basis for selection. College transcript, application essay required. Must have completed equivalent of GED. Transfer accepted as juniors, seniors.

2006-2007 Annual costs. Tuition/fees: $22,050. Books/supplies: $600. Personal expenses: $4,000.

Financial aid. All financial aid based on need. 33% of total undergraduate aid awarded as scholarships/grants, 67% as loans/jobs.

Application procedures. Admission: Priority date 4/15; deadline 6/1. $55 fee, may be waived for applicants with need. Application must be submitted on paper. **Financial aid:** FAFSA, institutional form required.

Academics. Special study options: Accelerated study, distance learning, independent study, internships, teacher certification program, weekend college. **Credit/placement by examination:** CLEP. 30 credit hours maximum toward bachelor's degree. Students age 30-35 without a bachelor's degree may earn credit based on life experience. **Support services:** Learning center, reduced course load, study skills assistance, tutoring, writing center.

Majors. Family/consumer sciences: Family studies.

Computing on campus. 17 workstations in library, computer center. Online library available.

Student life. Activities: Teacher education student association; marriage, family therapy student association.

Student services. Adult student services, career counseling, financial aid counseling. **Physically disabled:** Services for visually, speech, hearing impaired.

Contact. E-mail: admissions@pacificoaks.edu
Phone: (626) 397-1349 Toll-free number: (800) 684-0900
Fax: (626) 577-3502
Teresa Cook, Director of Admissions, Pacific Oaks College, 5 Westmoreland Place, Pasadena, CA 91103

Pacific States University

Los Angeles, California
www.psuca.edu — **CB code: 3547**

- Private 4-year university
- Commuter campus in very large city
- 19 degree-seeking undergraduates: 26% women, 16% Asian American, 79% international
- 102 degree-seeking graduate students

General. Accredited by ACICS. **Degrees:** 16 bachelor's awarded; master's offered. **Location:** 15 miles from North Hollywood. **Calendar:** Quarter, limited summer session. **Full-time faculty:** 5 total. **Part-time faculty:** 25 total.

Basis for selection. Open admission. High school diploma and English proficiency required. TOEFL required of students whose native language is not English. **Homeschooled:** Transcript of courses and grades, state high school equivalency certificate, letter of recommendation (nonparent) required.

2006-2007 Annual costs. Tuition/fees (projected): $10,560. Books/supplies: $800.

Financial aid. All financial aid based on need.

Application procedures. **Admission:** No deadline. $100 fee. Application must be submitted on paper. Admission notification on a rolling basis. **Financial aid:** No deadline. FAFSA required.

Academics. **Special study options:** Combined bachelor's/graduate degree, distance learning, double major, ESL, liberal arts/career combination. **Credit/placement by examination:** CLEP, IB. 45 credit hours maximum toward bachelor's degree. **Support services:** Learning center.

Majors. **Business:** Accounting, business admin. **Computer sciences:** General, computer science.

Computing on campus. Commuter students can connect to campus network. Online course registration, wireless network available.

Student life. **Freshman orientation:** Available. Preregistration for classes offered. Program held each quarter 2 weeks after start of classes. **Policies:** Freshmen permitted cars on campus.

Student services. Personal counseling.

Contact. E-mail: admissions@psuca.edu
Phone: (323) 731-2383 ext. 11 Toll-free number: (888) 200-0383
Fax: (323) 731-7276
Marina Miller, Director of Admissions, Pacific States University, 1516 South Western Avenue, Los Angeles, CA 90006

Pacific Union College
Angwin, California
www.puc.edu — **CB code: 4600**

- Private 4-year liberal arts college affiliated with Seventh-day Adventists
- Residential campus in small town
- 1,420 degree-seeking undergraduates: 9% part-time, 53% women, 4% African American, 22% Asian American, 12% Hispanic American, 1% Native American, 7% international
- 2 degree-seeking graduate students
- SAT or ACT (ACT writing recommended) required
- 23% graduate within 6 years

General. Founded in 1882. Regionally accredited. **Degrees:** 247 bachelor's, 97 associate awarded; master's offered. **Location:** 30 miles from Napa, 75 miles from San Francisco. **Calendar:** Quarter, limited summer session. **Full-time faculty:** 80 total; 61% have terminal degrees, 8% minority, 39% women. **Part-time faculty:** 19 total; 37% have terminal degrees, 47% women. **Class size:** 64% < 20, 27% 20-39, 5% 40-49, 4% 50-99, less than 1% >100. **Special facilities:** Observatory, airport/flight training, biology museum, Pitcairn Island Study Center, 1500-acre nature preserve.

Freshman class profile.

Mid 50% test scores			
SAT verbal:	450-590	GPA 2.0-2.99:	31%
SAT math:	440-580	End year in good standing:	86%
ACT:	18-24	Return as sophomores:	73%
GPA 3.50 or higher:	40%	Out-of-state:	17%
GPA 3.0-3.49:	28%	Live on campus:	98%
		International:	5%

Basis for selection. Minimum GPA of 2.3 and acceptable recommendations. **Learning Disabled:** Documentation if available.

High school preparation. 8 units required. Required and recommended units include English 4, mathematics 2-3, history 1-2, science 1-3 and foreign language 2. Computer literacy strongly recommended.

2005-2006 Annual costs. Tuition/fees: $19,125. Room/board: $5,430. Books/supplies: $1,242. Personal expenses: $1,980.

2005-2006 Financial aid. All financial aid based on need. 73% of total undergraduate aid awarded as scholarships/grants, 27% as loans/jobs.

Application procedures. **Admission:** No deadline. $30 fee, may be waived for applicants with need. Application may be submitted online. Admission notification on a rolling basis beginning on or about 1/15. **Financial aid:** No deadline. FAFSA, institutional form required. Applicants notified on a rolling basis; must reply within 3 week(s) of notification.

Academics. **Special study options:** Combined bachelor's/graduate degree, cooperative education, double major, external degree, honors, independent study, internships, study abroad, teacher certification program. **Credit/placement by examination:** AP, CLEP, IB, SAT, ACT, institutional tests. 24 credit hours maximum toward associate degree, 45 toward bachelor's. **Support services:** Learning center, remedial instruction, study skills assistance, tutoring, writing center.

Majors. **Biology:** General, biochemistry, biophysics. **Business:** General, accounting, business admin, finance, international, management information systems, marketing. **Communications:** General, digital media, journalism, public relations. **Computer sciences:** Computer science. **Education:** Early childhood, elementary, English, mathematics, music, physical. **Foreign languages:** French, Spanish. **Health:** Nursing (RN). **History:** General. **Interdisciplinary:** Natural sciences. **Math:** General. **Philosophy/religion:** Religion. **Physical sciences:** Chemistry, physics. **Psychology:** General. **Public administration:** Social work. **Social sciences:** General. **Theology:** Bible, theology. **Transportation:** Aviation. **Visual/performing arts:** Cinematography, commercial/advertising art, music performance, photography, studio arts.

Computing on campus. 178 workstations in dormitories, library. Dormitories wired for high-speed internet access and linked to campus network. Commuter students can connect to campus network. Online course registration, online library, helpline, repair service, wireless network available.

Student life. **Freshman orientation:** Mandatory. Preregistration for classes offered. **Policies:** Religious observance required. Freshmen permitted cars on campus. **Housing:** Guaranteed on-campus for freshmen. Single-sex dorms, apartments, substance-free housing available. $150 partly refundable deposit. **Activities:** Bands, choral groups, drama, film society, literary magazine, music ensembles, musical theater, radio station, student government, student newspaper, symphony orchestra, assembly, 20 clubs.

Athletics. NAIA. **Intercollegiate:** Basketball, cross-country, soccer, volleyball. **Intramural:** Basketball, softball, volleyball. **Team name:** Pioneers.

Student services. Adult student services, alcohol/substance abuse counseling, campus ministries, career counseling, student employment services, financial aid counseling, health services, on-campus daycare, personal counseling, placement for graduates. **Physically disabled:** Services for visually, speech, hearing impaired.

Contact. E-mail: enroll@puc.edu
Phone: (707) 965-6336 Toll-free number: (800) 862-7080
Fax: (707) 965-6432
Sean Kootsey, Director of Enrollment Services, Pacific Union College, Enrollment Services, Angwin, CA 94508

Patten University
Oakland, California — **CB member**
www.patten.edu — **CB code: 4620**

- Private 4-year Bible and liberal arts college affiliated with interdenominational tradition
- Residential campus in very large city
- 545 degree-seeking undergraduates
- SAT or ACT (ACT writing optional), application essay, interview required

General. Founded in 1944. Regionally accredited. Interdenominational Christian college dedicated to providing liberal arts education with strong biblical studies emphasis. **Degrees:** 37 bachelor's, 19 associate awarded; master's offered. **Location:** 18 miles from San Francisco, 30 miles from San Jose. **Calendar:** Semester, limited summer session. **Full-time faculty:** 20 total. **Part-time faculty:** 145 total.

Freshman class profile.

Mid 50% test scores		ACT:	18-25
SAT verbal:	500-610	Out-of-state:	5%
SAT math:	460-590		

Basis for selection. Christian commitment most important. High school record, interview, essay, test scores, recommendation important.

High school preparation. 22 units required. Required units include English 4, mathematics 2, social studies 4, history 2, science 2 (laboratory 1), foreign language 1 and academic electives 6.

2006-2007 Annual costs. Tuition/fees: $11,880. Room/board: $6,250. Books/supplies: $550. Personal expenses: $1,100.

Financial aid. Non-need-based: Scholarships awarded for academics, athletics, state residency.

Application procedures. Admission: Priority date 3/31; deadline 7/31. $35 fee, may be waived for applicants with need. Admission notification on a rolling basis. **Financial aid:** Priority date 3/31; no closing date. FAFSA, institutional form required. Applicants notified on a rolling basis starting 5/31.

Academics. Courses leading to the B.A. degree are from general, biblical, or professional studies. Students assigned faculty advisor. **Special study options:** Accelerated study, double major, dual enrollment of high school students, independent study, teacher certification program, weekend college. **Credit/placement by examination:** AP, CLEP, institutional tests. **Support services:** Learning center, remedial instruction, tutoring, writing center.

Majors. Business: Business admin. **Education:** Adult/continuing, early childhood. **Liberal arts:** Arts/sciences. **Philosophy/religion:** Religion. **Psychology:** General. **Theology:** Religious ed, sacred music.

Computing on campus. 30 workstations in library, computer center.

Student life. Freshman orientation: Mandatory. 3-day overview of institutional policies and procedures, academic tools, and spriritual formation held week before start of classes. **Policies:** Christian service program designed to involve students in practical ministry. Religious observance required. **Housing:** Guaranteed on-campus for all undergraduates. Single-sex dorms, apartments available. $85 deposit, deadline 7/31. **Activities:** Concert band, choral groups, drama, music ensembles, student government, student newspaper, symphony orchestra, Community of Faith groups, prison ministry.

Athletics. NAIA. **Intercollegiate:** Baseball M, basketball.

Student services. Adult student services, career counseling, student employment services, personal counseling, placement for graduates, veterans' counselor.

Contact. E-mail: admissions@patten.edu
Phone: (510) 261-8500 Toll-free number: (877) 472-8836
Fax: (510) 534-4344
Inez Bailey, Director of Admissions, Patten University, 2433 Coolidge Avenue, Oakland, CA 94601-2699

Pepperdine University

Malibu, California — **CB member**
www.pepperdine.edu — **CB code: 4630**

- Private 4-year university and liberal arts college affiliated with Church of Christ
- Residential campus in small city
- 3,169 degree-seeking undergraduates: 14% part-time, 58% women, 8% African American, 11% Asian American, 11% Hispanic American, 2% Native American, 6% international
- 4,485 degree-seeking graduate students
- 28% of applicants admitted
- SAT or ACT with writing, application essay required
- 79% graduate within 6 years

General. Founded in 1937. Regionally accredited. Education, psychology, business graduate colleges in Los Angeles. Educational centers in Long Beach, Irvine, Encino. 5 campuses in Europe (Germany, England, Italy, Spain, France), 1 in Costa Rica. Part-time, evening, and weekend classes for business undergrad programs. **Degrees:** 887 bachelor's awarded; master's, doctoral, first professional offered. **ROTC:** Army, Air Force. **Location:** 14 miles from Santa Monica, 30 miles from Los Angeles. **Calendar:** Semester, limited summer session. **Full-time faculty:** 400 total; 97% have terminal degrees, 11% minority, 36% women. **Part-time faculty:** 326 total; 95% have terminal degrees, 13% minority, 57% women. **Class size:** 64% < 20, 31% 20-39, 2% 40-49, 1% 50-99, 2% >100. **Special facilities:** Japanese tea ceremony rooms, art museum.

Freshman class profile. 7,307 applied, 2,077 admitted, 765 enrolled.

Mid 50% test scores		GPA 2.0-2.99:	3%
SAT verbal:	550-660	Rank in top quarter:	76%
SAT math:	570-670	Rank in top tenth:	43%
ACT:	24-35	Out-of-state:	48%
GPA 3.50 or higher:	76%	Live on campus:	100%
GPA 3.0-3.49:	21%	International:	6%

Basis for selection. School achievement record and test scores most important. Special talents, school and community activities, letters of recommendation, personal qualities also considered. Audition required for music, theater majors. Portfolio recommended for art majors. **Learning Disabled:** Proper documentation from doctor diagnosing learning disability required.

High school preparation. 28 units recommended. Recommended units include English 4, mathematics 4, social studies 3, history 3, science 4 (laboratory 3), foreign language 3 and academic electives 3. 1 speech recommended.

2005-2006 Annual costs. Tuition/fees: $30,860. Room/board: $9,100. Books/supplies: $800. Personal expenses: $700.

2005-2006 Financial aid. Need-based: 499 full-time freshmen applied for aid; 418 were judged to have need; 410 of these received aid. Average need met was 90%. Average scholarship/grant was $19,996; average loan $6,114. 69% of total undergraduate aid awarded as scholarships/grants, 31% as loans/jobs. **Non-need-based:** Scholarships awarded for academics, art, athletics, minority status, music/drama, religious affiliation.

Application procedures. Admission: Priority date 11/15; deadline 1/15 (postmark date). $65 fee, may be waived for applicants with need. Application must be submitted on paper. Admission notification 4/1. Must reply by 5/1. **Financial aid:** Closing date 2/15. FAFSA, institutional form required. Applicants notified by 4/15; must reply within 2 week(s) of notification.

Academics. Great books colloquium, freshman seminars and first year faculty mentor program for all students. **Special study options:** Double major, honors, independent study, internships, student-designed major, study abroad, teacher certification program, Washington semester, weekend college. 3-2 program in engineering with USC, Washington University, Boston University. **Credit/placement by examination:** AP, CLEP, IB, institutional tests. 32 credit hours maximum toward bachelor's degree. International Baccalaureate credit awarded for higher level exams only: 4 credits for each score of 5 and above; maximum 16. **Support services:** Pre-admission summer program, remedial instruction, tutoring, writing center.

Majors. Biology: General, biochemistry. **Business:** Accounting, business admin, international. **Communications:** General, advertising, broadcast journalism, journalism, public relations. **Education:** General, music, physical. **Engineering:** General. **English:** English lit. **Foreign languages:** French, German, Spanish. **Health:** Athletic training. **History:** General. **Interdisciplinary:** Global studies, math/computer science, natural sciences, nutrition sciences. **Liberal arts:** Arts/sciences, humanities. **Math:** General. **Philosophy/religion:** Philosophy, religion. **Physical sciences:** Chemistry. **Psychology:** General. **Social sciences:** Economics, political science, sociology. **Visual/performing arts:** Art, dramatic, studio arts.

Most popular majors. Business/marketing 40%, communications/journalism 16%, interdisciplinary studies 6%, psychology 7%, social sciences 9%.

Computing on campus. 292 workstations in dormitories, library, computer center, student center. Dormitories wired for high-speed internet access and linked to campus network. Commuter students can connect to campus network. Online library, helpline, repair service, wireless network available.

Student life. Freshman orientation: Available. 2 orientations for Fall in July and August. **Policies:** Students required to attend a weekly convocation. Freshmen permitted cars on campus. **Housing:** Guaranteed on-campus for freshmen. Single-sex dorms, special housing for disabled, apartments available. Freshmen and sophomores live on campus or at home with parent or guardian if single and under 21. **Activities:** Bands, choral groups, dance, drama, film society, literary magazine, music ensembles, musical theater, opera, radio station, student government, student newspaper, symphony orchestra, TV station, Campus Crusade for Christ, College Republicans, Young Democrats, volunteer center, black student union, Latin student association, Hawaiian club, international club, Korean student association, Japan club.

Athletics. NCAA. **Intercollegiate:** Baseball M, basketball, cross-country, diving W, golf, soccer W, swimming W, tennis, track and field W, volleyball, water polo M. **Intramural:** Basketball, football (non-tackle), handball, soccer, swimming, tennis, volleyball. **Team name:** Waves.

Student services. Alcohol/substance abuse counseling, campus ministries, career counseling, student employment services, financial aid counseling, health services, personal counseling, placement for graduates, veterans' counselor. **Physically disabled:** Services for visually, hearing impaired.

Contact. E-mail: admission-seaver@pepperdine.edu
Phone: (310) 506-4392 Fax: (310) 506-4861
Mike Trushke, Director of Admission, Pepperdine University, 24255 Pacific Coast Highway, Malibu, CA 90263-4392

Pitzer College

Claremont, California — **CB member**
www.pitzer.edu — **CB code: 4619**

- Private 4-year liberal arts college
- Residential campus in large town
- 963 degree-seeking undergraduates: 5% part-time, 59% women, 5% African American, 10% Asian American, 15% Hispanic American, 1% Native American, 2% international
- 39% of applicants admitted
- Application essay required
- 70% graduate within 6 years

General. Founded in 1963. Regionally accredited. One of a cluster of 5 undergraduate and 2 graduate institutions on adjoining campuses. Campuses share facilities. Cross-enrollment available at any of the 5 colleges, which include Claremont-McKenna, Harvey Mudd, Pitzer, Pomona, and Scripps. Interdisciplinary curriculum with social responsibility requirement, intercultural education objective; no academic departments. **Degrees:** 221 bachelor's awarded. **ROTC:** Army, Air Force. **Location:** 35 miles from Los Angeles. **Calendar:** Semester, limited summer session. **Full-time faculty:** 68 total; 98% have terminal degrees, 31% minority, 41% women. **Part-time faculty:** 24 total; 88% have terminal degrees, 25% minority, 62% women. **Class size:** 65% < 20, 31% 20-39, 4% 40-49, less than 1% 50-99. **Special facilities:** Ecology center, nature reserve, arboretum, women's studies center, restored arts and crafts home with poetry reading room.

Freshman class profile. 3,251 applied, 1,276 admitted, 239 enrolled.

Mid 50% test scores		**Return as sophomores:**	88%
SAT verbal:	570-680	**Out-of-state:**	49%
SAT math:	560-660	**Live on campus:**	99%
Rank in top quarter:	75%	**International:**	1%
Rank in top tenth:	45%		

Basis for selection. School record, essays (judged for writing ability, independence of thought and spirit), 3 recommendations, test scores, leadership, community service, work experience, talent, involvement in sports considered. SAT/ACT not required of students graduating in top 10% of class, or those with an unweighted cumulative GPA of 3.50 or higher in academic subjects. Otherwise, one of the following required: ACT or SAT scores; 2 SAT Subject Tests (one in mathematics); 2 or more AP test scores of at least 4 (one English or English Language and one mathematics or science); two International Baccalaureate exams (one English 1A and one math); or one recent junior or senior year graded analytical writing sample from a humanities or social science course and one recent graded exam from an advanced mathematics course. The samples must include the teacher's comments, grades, and the assignment. Interview recommended.

High school preparation. Recommended units include English 4, mathematics 3, social studies 2, history 1, science 3 (laboratory 3) and foreign language 3.

2005-2006 Annual costs. Tuition/fees: $33,012. Room/board: $8,632. Books/supplies: $950. Personal expenses: $1,000.

2005-2006 Financial aid. All financial aid based on need. 110 full-time freshmen applied for aid; 94 were judged to have need; 94 of these received aid. Average need met was 100%. Average scholarship/grant was $24,317; average loan $2,801. 79% of total undergraduate aid awarded as scholarships/grants, 21% as loans/jobs.

Application procedures. Admission: Closing date 1/1 (postmark date). $50 fee, may be waived for applicants with need. Application may be submitted online. Admission notification 4/1. Must reply by 5/1. **Financial aid:** Closing date 2/1. FAFSA, CSS PROFILE required. Applicants notified by 4/1; must reply by 5/1.

Academics. Students may take up to one-third of their courses at other Claremont campuses and must take 32 courses for graduation. Can create own courses and academic majors. **Special study options:** Combined bachelor's/graduate degree, cross-registration, double major, ESL, exchange student, honors, independent study, internships, student-designed major, study abroad, urban semester. New Resources (for students over age 25 and nontraditional students), joint science program, joint BA/DO program. **Credit/placement by examination:** AP, CLEP, IB, institutional tests. **Support services:** Tutoring, writing center.

Majors. Area/ethnic studies: African-American, American, Asian, Asian-American, Caribbean, European, Hispanic-American/Latino/Chicano, Latin American, women's. **Biology:** General, biochemistry, biophysics, microbiology. **Business:** Organizational behavior. **Conservation:** Environmental science, environmental studies. **English:** Creative writing, English lit. **Foreign languages:** General, Chinese, classics, French, German, Italian, Japanese, linguistics, Russian, Spanish. **History:** General, American, European. **Interdisciplinary:** Biological/physical sciences, global studies, intercultural, natural sciences, neuroscience, science/society. **Math:** General. **Philosophy/religion:** Philosophy, religion. **Physical sciences:** Chemistry, organic chemistry, physics. **Psychology:** General. **Social sciences:** General, anthropology, economics, international relations, political science, sociology. **Visual/performing arts:** Art, art history/conservation, cinematography, dance, dramatic, film/cinema, studio arts.

Most popular majors. Communication technologies 8%, English 9%, interdisciplinary studies 8%, psychology 13%, social sciences 29%, visual/performing arts 9%.

Computing on campus. 100 workstations in dormitories, library, computer center, student center. Dormitories wired for high-speed internet access and linked to campus network. Commuter students can connect to campus network. Online library, helpline, student web hosting, wireless network available.

Student life. Freshman orientation: Mandatory. Held the week prior to start of fall semester. **Policies:** Strong philosophical framework of social responsibility and self-governance. Freshmen permitted cars on campus. **Housing:** Guaranteed on-campus for freshmen. Coed dorms, special housing for disabled, cooperative housing, substance-free housing available. Theme housing available: hush hall, involvement tower, all female. **Activities:** Choral groups, dance, drama, literary magazine, music ensembles, musical theater, radio station, student government, student newspaper, symphony orchestra, over 75 social service, religious, political, and ethnic organizations.

Athletics. NCAA. **Intercollegiate:** Badminton, baseball M, basketball, cross-country, diving, football (tackle) M, golf, lacrosse, soccer, softball W, swimming, tennis, track and field, volleyball W, water polo. **Intramural:** Archery, badminton, basketball, golf, racquetball, sailing, soccer, softball W, squash, tennis. **Team name:** Sagehens.

Student services. Adult student services, alcohol/substance abuse counseling, campus ministries, career counseling, student employment services, financial aid counseling, health services, minority student services, personal counseling, women's services. **Physically disabled:** Services for visually, speech, hearing impaired.

Contact. E-mail: admission@pitzer.edu
Phone: (909) 621-8129 Toll-free number: (800) 748-9371
Fax: (909) 621-8770
Arnaldo Rodriguez, Vice President of Admission and Financial Aid, Pitzer College, 1050 North Mills Avenue, Claremont, CA 91711-6101

Platt College: Ontario

Ontario, California
www.plattcollege.edu — **CB code: 3015**

- For-profit 4-year branch campus and technical college
- Commuter campus in small city
- 400 degree-seeking undergraduates
- 93% of applicants admitted
- Application essay, interview required

General. Accredited by ACCSCT. Branch of Los Angeles campus. **Degrees:** 48 bachelor's, 175 associate awarded. **Location:** 20 miles from Los Angeles. **Calendar:** Continuous. **Full-time faculty:** 7 total; 57% have terminal degrees, 43% minority, 43% women. **Part-time faculty:** 24 total; 42% have terminal degrees, 50% minority, 29% women. **Class size:** 71% < 20, 29% 20-39. **Special facilities:** Motion capture lab.

Freshman class profile. 162 applied, 151 admitted, 108 enrolled.

Basis for selection. Students admitted based on interview, high school diploma or GED, entrance test and essay, and completion of the admissions process. Math and English workshops available to students upon entrance if desired or recommended. **Learning Disabled:** Students with learning disabilities may request consideration for extra time to complete entrance test.

2006-2007 Annual costs. Annual tuition varies by program: $10,300--$14,230.

Application procedures. Admission: No deadline. $75 fee. Application may be submitted online. Admission notification on a rolling basis. **Financial aid:** Priority date 3/2; no closing date. FAFSA, institutional form required. Applicants notified on a rolling basis starting 1/1.

Academics. Special study options: Accelerated study, cooperative education, internships. **Credit/placement by examination:** CLEP. 48 credit hours maximum toward associate degree, 48 toward bachelor's. **Support services:** Tutoring.

Majors. Communications technology: Animation/special effects, graphics. **Computer sciences:** Computer graphics, web page design. **Legal studies:** Legal secretary, paralegal. **Visual/performing arts:** General, commercial/advertising art, design.

Computing on campus. 12 workstations in library.

Student life. Freshman orientation: Mandatory. Preregistration for classes offered. Held on first day of classes. **Policies:** Freshmen permitted cars on campus. **Activities:** Various student clubs and activities available.

Student services. Adult student services, career counseling, student employment services, financial aid counseling, placement for graduates.

Contact. Phone: (909) 941-9410 Toll-free number: (866) 752-8846
Fax: (909) 941-9660
Carmen da Conceicao, Admissions Director, Platt College: Ontario, 3700 Inland Empire Boulevard, Ontario, CA 91764

Platt College: San Diego

San Diego, California
www.platt.edu **CB code: 3020**

- For-profit 4-year visual arts and technical college
- Commuter campus in very large city
- 252 degree-seeking undergraduates: 23% women, 5% African American, 7% Asian American, 20% Hispanic American
- Application essay, interview required

General. Degrees: 49 bachelor's, 117 associate awarded. **Calendar:** Continuous. **Full-time faculty:** 5 total. **Part-time faculty:** 26 total; 58% have terminal degrees, 15% minority, 42% women. **Class size:** 72% < 20, 28% 20-39.

Freshman class profile. 184 applied, 184 admitted, 184 enrolled.

Basis for selection. Open admission, but selective for some programs and for out-of-state students. Aptitude test used to measure academic preparedness to undertake college-level courses; SAT considered in lieu of test.

2005-2006 Annual costs. Total program cost ranges from $13,900 to $25,400 for diploma programs; associate's and bachelor's degree program costs vary. Books/supplies: $1,224. Personal expenses: $200.

Application procedures. Admission: No deadline. No application fee. Application must be submitted on paper. **Financial aid:** Closing date 3/2. FAFSA, institutional form required. Applicants notified on a rolling basis; must reply within 1 week(s) of notification.

Academics. Special study options: Accelerated study, internships, liberal arts/career combination. **Credit/placement by examination:** AP, CLEP, institutional tests. **Support services:** Study skills assistance, tutoring.

Majors. Visual/performing arts: General, commercial/advertising art.

Computing on campus. 200 workstations in library, computer center. Online library available.

Student life. Freshman orientation: Mandatory. Preregistration for classes offered.

Student services. Career counseling, services for economically disadvantaged, student employment services, financial aid counseling, personal counseling, placement for graduates.

Contact. E-mail: info@platt.edu
Phone: (619) 265-0107 ext. 32 Toll-free number: (866) 752-8826
Fax: (619) 308-0570
Carly Westerfield, Admissions Coordinator, Platt College: San Diego, 6250 El Cajon Boulevard, San Diego, CA 92115

Point Loma Nazarene University

San Diego, California **CB member**
www.ptloma.edu **CB code: 4605**

- Private 4-year university and liberal arts college affiliated with Church of the Nazarene
- Residential campus in very large city
- 2,360 degree-seeking undergraduates: 3% part-time, 60% women, 2% African American, 5% Asian American, 10% Hispanic American, 1% Native American, 1% international
- 712 degree-seeking graduate students
- 65% of applicants admitted
- SAT or ACT (ACT writing optional), application essay, interview required
- 68% graduate within 6 years

General. Founded in 1902. Regionally accredited. **Degrees:** 545 bachelor's awarded; master's offered. **ROTC:** Army, Navy, Air Force. **Location:** 5 miles from downtown. **Calendar:** Semester, limited summer session. **Full-time faculty:** 139 total; 79% have terminal degrees, 40% women. **Part-time faculty:** 199 total; 57% women. **Class size:** 44% < 20, 40% 20-39, 12% 40-49, 3% 50-99.

Freshman class profile. 1,857 applied, 1,216 admitted, 563 enrolled.

Mid 50% test scores		**Rank in top quarter:**	75%
SAT verbal:	520-630	**Rank in top tenth:**	39%
SAT math:	520-640	**Return as sophomores:**	85%
ACT:	21-28	**Out-of-state:**	21%
GPA 3.50 or higher:	75%	**Live on campus:**	96%
GPA 3.0-3.49:	19%	**International:**	1%
GPA 2.0-2.99:	6%		

Basis for selection. Moral character, maturity, intellectual ability, and academic achievement important considerations. Preference given to self-directed applicants who appear to share ideals and objectives of college. SAT recommended.

High school preparation. 10 units required. Required units include English 4, mathematics 2, history 1, science 1 (laboratory 1) and foreign language 2.

2006-2007 Annual costs. Tuition/fees (projected): $22,150. Dorm fund $24 annually. Room/board: $7,160. Books/supplies: $1,260. Personal expenses: $2,096.

2004-2005 Financial aid. Need-based: 1,992 full-time freshmen applied for aid; 995 were judged to have need; 632 of these received aid. Average need met was 28%. Average scholarship/grant was $9,044; average loan $3,502. 62% of total undergraduate aid awarded as scholarships/grants, 38% as loans/jobs. **Non-need-based:** Awarded to 389 full-time undergraduates, including 128 freshmen. Scholarships awarded for academics, alumni affiliation, art, athletics, leadership, music/drama, religious affiliation, state residency.

Application procedures. Admission: Priority date 12/1; deadline 3/1 (receipt date). $50 fee, may be waived for applicants with need. Application may be submitted online. Admission notification on a rolling basis beginning on or about 4/1. Must reply by May 1 or within 3 week(s) if notified thereafter. Early action notification period December 15 through January 15. **Financial aid:** Priority date 3/2; no closing date. FAFSA, institutional form required. Applicants notified on a rolling basis starting 3/1; must reply within 4 week(s) of notification.

Academics. Special study options: Double major, honors, independent study, internships, semester at sea, study abroad, teacher certification program, United Nations semester, Washington semester. **Credit/placement by examination:** AP, CLEP, IB, SAT, ACT, institutional tests. 32 credit hours maximum toward bachelor's degree. Some restrictions apply in special majors. **Support services:** Learning center, pre-admission summer program, reduced course load, remedial instruction, study skills assistance, tutoring, writing center.

Majors. Biology: General, biochemistry. **Business:** Accounting, business admin, communications, management information systems. **Communications:** General, broadcast journalism, journalism, media studies. **Communications technology:** Graphics. **Computer sciences:** Computer science. **Education:** Art, music. **Engineering:** Physics. **English:** English lit. **Family/consumer sciences:** General, child development, family/community services, food/nutrition. **Foreign languages:** Romance, Spanish. **Health:** Athletic training, dietetics, nursing (RN). **History:** General. **Interdisciplinary:** Global studies. **Liberal arts:** Arts/sciences. **Math:** General. **Parks/recreation:** Exercise sciences, health/fitness. **Philosophy/religion:** Philosophy. **Physical**

sciences: Chemistry, physics. **Psychology:** General. **Public administration:** Social work. **Social sciences:** General, international economic development, political science, sociology. **Theology:** Bible, preministerial, sacred music, youth ministry. **Visual/performing arts:** Art, dramatic, graphic design, music performance, music theory/composition.

Most popular majors. Business/marketing 14%, communications/journalism 6%, education 18%, health sciences 7%, liberal arts 8%, psychology 8%, visual/performing arts 6%.

Computing on campus. 225 workstations in dormitories, library, computer center. Dormitories linked to campus network. Commuter students can connect to campus network. Online course registration, helpline, repair service, wireless network available.

Student life. Freshman orientation: Available. **Policies:** Religious observance required. **Housing:** Guaranteed on-campus for freshmen. Single-sex dorms, apartments available. $200 deposit. **Activities:** Bands, choral groups, drama, literary magazine, music ensembles, radio station, student government, student newspaper, urban ministries, Habitat for Humanity, Mexico outreach, elderly outreach, Project AIM (Active In Ministries).

Athletics. NAIA. **Intercollegiate:** Baseball M, basketball, cross-country, golf M, soccer M, softball W, tennis, track and field, volleyball W. **Intramural:** Badminton, basketball, bowling, cross-country, diving, football (non-tackle), football (tackle) M, golf, sailing, soccer, softball, swimming, table tennis, tennis, track and field, volleyball, water polo. **Team name:** Sea Lions.

Student services. Career counseling, student employment services, health services, on-campus daycare, personal counseling, placement for graduates, veterans' counselor. **Physically disabled:** Services for visually, hearing impaired.

Contact. E-mail: admissions@ptloma.edu
Phone: (619) 849-2273 Toll-free number: (800) 733-7770
Fax: (619) 849-2601
Scott Shoemaker, Dean of Admissions, Point Loma Nazarene University, 3900 Lomaland Drive, San Diego, CA 92106-2899

Pomona College

Claremont, California — **CB member**
www.pomona.edu — **CB code: 4607**

- Private 4-year liberal arts college
- Residential campus in large town
- 1,529 degree-seeking undergraduates: 50% women, 6% African American, 14% Asian American, 11% Hispanic American, 2% international
- 19% of applicants admitted
- SAT and SAT Subject Tests or ACT (ACT writing recommended), application essay required
- 95% graduate within 6 years; 30% enter graduate study

General. Founded in 1887. Regionally accredited. One of a cluster of 5 undergraduate and 2 graduate schools on adjoining campuses. Campuses share facilities. Cross-enrollment available at any of the 5 colleges, which include Claremont-McKenna, Harvey Mudd, Pitzer, Pomona, and Scripps. Extensive overseas studies. **Degrees:** 368 bachelor's awarded. **Location:** 35 miles from Los Angeles, 20 miles from Pasadena. **Calendar:** Semester. **Full-time faculty:** 172 total; 95% have terminal degrees, 28% minority, 43% women. **Part-time faculty:** 34 total; 53% have terminal degrees, 26% minority, 41% women. **Class size:** 67% < 20, 30% 20-39, 2% 40-49, less than 1% 50-99. **Special facilities:** Science center, center for modern language and international relations, observatory, biological field station, ecological preserve, botanic garden, social sciences center, Greek theater, multimedia labs.

Freshman class profile. 5,054 applied, 954 admitted, 382 enrolled.

Mid 50% test scores		**Rank in top tenth:**	88%
SAT verbal:	690-770	**Out-of-state:**	63%
SAT math:	680-760	**Live on campus:**	100%
ACT:	29-34	**International:**	3%
Rank in top quarter:	98%		

Basis for selection. School achievement record, test scores, essays, 3 recommendations most important. Special skills in music, art, drama, or athletics; leadership, motivation, and diversity of background also important. Some preference to children of alumni; special consideration for underrepresented groups. School and community activities also considered. Students submitting SAT must also submit 2 SAT Subject Tests in different subject areas. Interview required for early admission applicants, strongly recommended for all applicants. Audition recommended for music, dance, theater majors. Portfolio recommended for studio art majors. **Home-schooled:** SAT and at least 3 SAT Subject Tests required, more recommended. Detailed description of curriculum required.

High school preparation. Required and recommended units include English 4, mathematics 3-4, social studies 3-4, science 3-4 (laboratory 2-3) and foreign language 3-4. 3-4 laboratory science recommended for science applicants. Mathematics through calculus recommended for all applicants.

2006-2007 Annual costs. Tuition/fees: $31,865. Room/board: $11,291. Books/supplies: $850. Personal expenses: $1,000.

2004-2005 Financial aid. All financial aid based on need. 263 full-time freshmen applied for aid; 224 were judged to have need; 224 of these received aid. Average need met was 100%. Average scholarship/grant was $24,400; average loan $2,500. 85% of total undergraduate aid awarded as scholarships/grants, 15% as loans/jobs.

Application procedures. Admission: Closing date 1/2 (receipt date). $60 fee, may be waived for applicants with need. Application may be submitted online. Admission notification 4/10. Must reply by May 1 or within 1 week(s) if notified thereafter. **Financial aid:** Closing date 2/1. FAFSA, CSS PROFILE required. Applicants notified by 4/10; must reply by 5/1.

Academics. Special study options: Cross-registration, double major, exchange student, independent study, internships, student-designed major, study abroad, Washington semester. 3-2 program in engineering with California Institute of Technology and Washington University (MO), 4-1 education certification program with Claremont Graduate University. **Credit/placement by examination:** AP, CLEP, IB, institutional tests. **Support services:** Tutoring, writing center.

Majors. Area/ethnic studies: African-American, American, Asian, Asian-American, German, Latin American, women's. **Biology:** General, molecular. **Communications:** Media studies. **Computer sciences:** Computer science. **Conservation:** Environmental studies. **English:** Creative writing. **Foreign languages:** General, Chinese, classics, French, German, Japanese, linguistics, Russian, Spanish. **History:** General. **Interdisciplinary:** Cognitive science, global studies, math/computer science, neuroscience, science/society. **Math:** General. **Philosophy/religion:** Philosophy, religion. **Physical sciences:** Astronomy, chemistry, geochemistry, geology, physics. **Psychology:** General. **Public administration:** Policy analysis. **Social sciences:** General, anthropology, economics, international relations, political science, sociology. **Visual/performing arts:** General, art, art history/conservation, dance, dramatic, studio arts.

Computing on campus. 180 workstations in dormitories, library, computer center, student center. Dormitories wired for high-speed internet access and linked to campus network. Commuter students can connect to campus network. Online library, helpline, wireless network available.

Student life. Freshman orientation: Mandatory. Held immediately prior to fall semester; preorientation adventure available. **Policies:** Freshmen permitted cars on campus. **Housing:** Guaranteed on-campus for all undergraduates. Coed dorms, substance-free housing available. $500 nonrefundable deposit, deadline 5/1. **Activities:** Bands, choral groups, dance, drama, film society, literary magazine, music ensembles, musical theater, radio station, student government, student newspaper, symphony orchestra, TV station, center for religious activities, international peace, Asian students association, Mortar Board (service organization), women's coalition, gay and lesbian student union.

Athletics. NCAA. **Intercollegiate:** Baseball M, basketball, cross-country, diving, football (tackle) M, golf, soccer, softball W, swimming, tennis, track and field, volleyball W, water polo. **Intramural:** Badminton, basketball, equestrian, handball, racquetball, skiing, soccer, softball, squash, table tennis, track and field, volleyball, water polo. **Team name:** Sagehens.

Student services. Campus ministries, career counseling, services for economically disadvantaged, student employment services, financial aid counseling, health services, minority student services, personal counseling, placement for graduates. **Physically disabled:** Services for visually, hearing impaired.

Contact. E-mail: admissions@pomona.edu
Phone: (909) 621-8134 Fax: (909) 621-8952
Bruce Poch, Vice President and Dean of Admissions, Pomona College, 333 North College Way, Claremont, CA 91711-6312

Remington College: San Diego

San Diego, California
www.remingtoncollege.edu — **CB code: 2574**

- For-profit 4-year university
- Very large city
- 600 degree-seeking undergraduates

General. Accredited by ACICS. **Degrees:** 19 bachelor's, 100 associate awarded; master's offered. **Calendar:** Quarter. **Full-time faculty:** 20 total. **Part-time faculty:** 30 total.

Freshman class profile. 899 applied, 451 admitted, 451 enrolled.

Basis for selection. Open admission, but selective for some programs. Wonderlic exam used for admission.

2005-2006 Annual costs. Tuition and fees for complete associate programs (96 credits) $25,824; for bachelor of science in information technology or in information systems (90 credits) $24,210 with 96 credits transferred from associate degree; for complete bachelor's program (180 credits) $48,420.

Financial aid. Additional information: Application fee may be waived and applied toward tuition.

Application procedures. Admission: No deadline. $50 fee. **Financial aid:** FAFSA required.

Academics. Credit/placement by examination: CLEP.

Majors. Business: Business admin. **Protective services:** Criminal justice. **Psychology:** General.

Student life. Freshman orientation: Available. Held 1 week before start of classes.

Contact. Phone: (619) 686-8600 Toll-free number: (800) 214-7001
Fax: (619) 686-8684
Penny Foye, Admissions Director, Remington College: San Diego, 123 Camino de la Reina, Suite 100, North Building, San Diego, CA 92108-3002

St. Mary's College of California

Moraga, California — **CB member**
www.stmarys-ca.edu — **CB code: 4675**

- Private 4-year liberal arts college affiliated with Roman Catholic Church
- Residential campus in large town
- 3,291 degree-seeking undergraduates: 24% part-time, 63% women
- 1,141 degree-seeking graduate students
- 85% of applicants admitted
- SAT or ACT (ACT writing optional), application essay required
- 66% graduate within 6 years; 15% enter graduate study

General. Founded in 1863. Regionally accredited. **Degrees:** 700 bachelor's awarded; master's, doctoral offered. **ROTC:** Army, Air Force. **Location:** 20 miles from San Francisco. **Calendar:** 4-1-4. **Full-time faculty:** 197 total; 90% have terminal degrees, 14% minority, 48% women. **Part-time faculty:** 345 total; 87% have terminal degrees, 11% minority, 57% women. **Class size:** 46% < 20, 53% 20-39, 1% 40-49. **Special facilities:** Art museum.

Freshman class profile. 3,381 applied, 2,861 admitted, 675 enrolled.

Mid 50% test scores		**GPA 2.0-2.99:**	31%
SAT verbal:	490-600	**End year in good standing:**	75%
SAT math:	490-600	**Return as sophomores:**	88%
ACT:	22-27	**Out-of-state:**	16%
GPA 3.50 or higher:	34%	**Live on campus:**	89%
GPA 3.0-3.49:	35%	**International:**	2%

Basis for selection. School achievement record most important. Interview recommended.

High school preparation. College-preparatory program required. 16 units required; 19 recommended. Required and recommended units include English 4, mathematics 3-4, social studies 1, history 1, science 2-3 (laboratory 1), foreign language 2-3 and academic electives 2. One unit each of chemistry, physics, advanced algebra, and trigonometry required for applicants to school of science.

2005-2006 Annual costs. Tuition/fees: $27,280. Room/board: $10,010. Books/supplies: $1,224. Personal expenses: $1,872.

2005-2006 Financial aid. Need-based: 513 full-time freshmen applied for aid; 428 were judged to have need; 428 of these received aid. Average need met was 71%. Average scholarship/grant was $16,812; average loan $2,986. 68% of total undergraduate aid awarded as scholarships/grants, 32% as loans/jobs. **Non-need-based:** Awarded to 532 full-time undergraduates, including 139 freshmen. Scholarships awarded for academics, alumni affiliation, athletics.

Application procedures. Admission: Priority date 11/30; deadline 2/1 (postmark date). $55 fee, may be waived for applicants with need. Application may be submitted online. Admission notification 3/15. Admission notification on a rolling basis beginning on or about 12/15. Must reply by May 1 or within 2 week(s) if notified thereafter. **Financial aid:** Closing date 3/2. FAFSA required. Applicants notified on a rolling basis starting 3/30; must reply by 5/1 or within 2 week(s) of notification.

Academics. Special study options: Cross-registration, double major, exchange student, external degree, honors, independent study, internships, liberal arts/career combination, student-designed major, study abroad, teacher certification program, weekend college. 4-year interdisciplinary program with Great Books orientation. **Credit/placement by examination:** AP, CLEP, IB, institutional tests. 30 credit hours maximum toward bachelor's degree. **Support services:** Learning center, study skills assistance, tutoring, writing center.

Majors. Area/ethnic studies: European, Latin American, women's. **Biology:** General, biochemistry. **Business:** General, accounting, business admin, finance, international. **Communications:** General. **English:** English lit. **Foreign languages:** General, classics, French, German, Italian, Japanese, Spanish. **Health:** Health care admin. **History:** General. **Interdisciplinary:** Biopsychology, math/computer science. **Legal studies:** General. **Liberal arts:** Arts/sciences. **Math:** General. **Parks/recreation:** Exercise sciences, health/fitness, sports admin. **Philosophy/religion:** Philosophy, religion. **Physical sciences:** Chemistry, physics. **Psychology:** General. **Social sciences:** Anthropology, archaeology, economics, political science, sociology. **Visual/performing arts:** General, art, dance, dramatic.

Most popular majors. Business/marketing 27%, communications/journalism 12%, English 6%, liberal arts 10%, psychology 9%, social sciences 11%.

Computing on campus. 244 workstations in dormitories, library, computer center. Dormitories wired for high-speed internet access and linked to campus network. Commuter students can connect to campus network. Online course registration, helpline, student web hosting, wireless network available.

Student life. Freshman orientation: Mandatory, $150 fee. Preregistration for classes offered. Held in June. **Policies:** Freshmen permitted cars on campus. **Housing:** Guaranteed on-campus for freshmen. Coed dorms, single-sex dorms, special housing for disabled, apartments available. $350 deposit, deadline 5/1. **Activities:** Bands, choral groups, dance, drama, film society, literary magazine, music ensembles, musical theater, radio station, student government, student newspaper, TV station, Catholic Institute for Lasallian Social Action, international club, Habitat for Humanity, Amnesty International, Lasallian Collegians, Intervarsity Christians, MECHA, APASA, multicultural club, GALA.

Athletics. NCAA. **Intercollegiate:** Baseball M, basketball, cross-country, football (tackle) M, golf M, lacrosse W, rowing (crew) W, soccer, softball W, tennis, volleyball W. **Intramural:** Basketball, bowling, football (non-tackle), golf, lacrosse, rowing (crew), skiing, soccer, softball, table tennis, tennis, volleyball, water polo. **Team name:** Gaels.

Student services. Alcohol/substance abuse counseling, campus ministries, career counseling, student employment services, financial aid counseling, health services, personal counseling, placement for graduates, veterans' counselor, women's services. **Physically disabled:** Services for visually, speech, hearing impaired.

Contact. E-mail: smcadmit@stmarys_ca.edu
Phone: (925) 631-4224 Toll-free number: (800) 800-4762
Fax: (925) 376-7193
Dorothy Jones, Dean of Admissions, St. Mary's College of California, Box 4800, Moraga, CA 94575-4800

Samuel Merritt College

Oakland, California — **CB member**
www.samuelmerritt.edu — **CB code: 4750**

- Private upper-division health science and nursing college
- Commuter campus in large city
- 8% of applicants admitted
- Application essay required

General. Founded in 1909. Regionally accredited. Part of Alta Bates Summit Medical Center, a nonprofit, community-based health care organization. Clinical opportunities at Summit as well as many other health care agencies throughout greater Bay area. Nursing degree is intercollegiate with St. Mary's College of California. Most undergraduate students transfer in from other colleges. **Degrees:** 68 bachelor's awarded; master's, doctoral, first professional offered. **Articulation:** Agreements with Holy Names University, Mills

College, Saint Mary's College of California. **ROTC:** Army, Navy, Air Force. **Location:** 15 miles from San Francisco. **Calendar:** Semester, limited summer session. **Full-time faculty:** 63 total; 51% have terminal degrees, 13% minority, 71% women. **Part-time faculty:** 93 total; 19% have terminal degrees, 19% minority, 74% women. **Class size:** 77% < 20, 1% 20-39, 15% 40-49, 7% 50-99. **Special facilities:** Nursing resource laboratory, health education center, health science library, anatomy laboratory, therapeutic exercise laboratory, living skills laboratory, human occupations laboratory.

Student profile. 353 degree-seeking undergraduates, 715 degree-seeking graduate students. 312 applied as first time-transfer students, 25 admitted, 14 enrolled. 3% entered as juniors. 80% transferred from two-year, 20% transferred from four-year institutions.

Women:	90%	**International:**	1%
African American:	5%	**Part-time:**	14%
Asian American:	30%	**Live on campus:**	7%
Hispanic American:	11%	**25 or older:**	52%
Native American:	1%		

Basis for selection. College transcript, application essay required. Must have UC transferable college-level coursework in chemistry, anatomy, physiology, multicultural psychology, English (2) and humanities (2). Applicants with fewer than 30 semester hours of transferable credits will be admitted as freshman. Letter of recommendation and experience in health care environment. Reply date for accepted students is 2 weeks from notification. Transfer accepted as sophomores, juniors.

2005-2006 Annual costs. Tuition/fees: $26,664. Room only: $4,464. Books/supplies: $1,350.

Financial aid. Need-based: Average need met was 70%. 56% of total undergraduate aid awarded as scholarships/grants, 44% as loans/jobs. **Non-need-based:** Scholarships awarded for academics. **Additional information:** Ongoing private scholarships available. Students eligible to work in Medical Center (associated with college).

Application procedures. Admission: Priority date 3/1. $35 fee, may be waived for applicants with need. Application must be submitted on paper. Admission notification 4/1. Must reply by 5/1. **Financial aid:** Priority date 3/1, no deadline. Applicants notified on a rolling basis; must reply within 3 weeks of notification.

Academics. Special study options: Accelerated study, combined bachelor's/graduate degree, cooperative education, cross-registration, distance learning, ESL, independent study, internships, liberal arts/career combination. Joint registration with St. Mary's College of California BSN, Holy Names University and Mills College. **Credit/placement by examination:** CLEP. 80 credit hours maximum toward bachelor's degree.

Majors. Health: Nursing (RN).

Computing on campus. 50 workstations in dormitories, library, computer center. Online library, helpline, wireless network available.

Student life. Housing: Guaranteed on-campus for all undergraduates. Coed dorms available. $100 fully refundable deposit. **Activities:** Student government, student newspaper, multicultural committee, American Physical Therapy Association, California Nursing Students Association, Christian Fellowship, American Occupational Therapy Association, Chi Eta Phi, gay, lesbian, bisexual and transgender group.

Student services. Career counseling, financial aid counseling, health services, personal counseling. **Physically disabled:** Services for visually, speech, hearing impaired.

Contact. E-mail: admission@samuelmerritt.edu
Phone: (510) 869-6576 Toll-free number: (800) 607-6377
Fax: (510) 869-6576
Anne Seed, Director of Admissions, Samuel Merritt College, 370 Hawthorne Avenue, Oakland, CA 94609-9954

San Diego Christian College

El Cajon, California
www.sdcc.edu **CB code: 4150**

- Private 4-year liberal arts college affiliated with nondenominational tradition
- Residential campus in small city
- 550 degree-seeking undergraduates
- 72% of applicants admitted
- SAT or ACT (ACT writing optional), application essay required

General. Founded in 1970. Regionally accredited. **Degrees:** 132 bachelor's awarded. **ROTC:** Army, Air Force. **Location:** 15 miles from downtown San Diego. **Calendar:** Semester, limited summer session. **Full-time faculty:** 35 total. **Part-time faculty:** 25 total. **Class size:** 80% < 20, 18% 20-39, 2% 40-49. **Special facilities:** Museum supporting creationist view, aviation school.

Freshman class profile. 493 applied, 353 admitted, 126 enrolled.

Mid 50% test scores		**ACT:**	18-25
SAT verbal:	435-570	**Out-of-state:**	20%
SAT math:	410-555	**Live on campus:**	59%

Basis for selection. Academic abilities as indicated by school achievement record and test scores. Personal and spiritual qualities as indicated by essays, recommendations, and interview.

High school preparation. 15 units recommended. Recommended units include English 4, mathematics 3, social studies 3, science 3 and foreign language 2.

2006-2007 Annual costs. Tuition/fees: $16,992. Room/board: $7,180. Books/supplies: $1,224. Personal expenses: $1,872.

Financial aid. Non-need-based: Scholarships awarded for academics, athletics, leadership, music/drama, religious affiliation.

Application procedures. Admission: Priority date 7/1; deadline 8/1. $25 fee. Admission notification on a rolling basis. Must reply by May 1 or within 4 week(s) if notified thereafter. **Financial aid:** Priority date 3/2, closing date 7/15. FAFSA required. Applicants notified on a rolling basis starting 4/1; must reply by 5/1 or within 4 week(s) of notification.

Academics. Special study options: Accelerated study, double major, ESL, independent study, internships, study abroad, teacher certification program. **Credit/placement by examination:** AP, CLEP, IB, institutional tests. 15 credit hours maximum toward bachelor's degree. **Support services:** Learning center, reduced course load, remedial instruction, study skills assistance, tutoring, writing center.

Majors. Biology: General. **Business:** Business admin. **Communications:** General. **Education:** General, early childhood, elementary, English, history, mathematics, middle, music, physical, secondary, social science. **Family/consumer sciences:** Family studies. **Health:** Athletic training. **History:** General. **Math:** General. **Psychology:** General. **Social sciences:** General. **Theology:** Bible, missionary. **Visual/performing arts:** Music performance.

Computing on campus. 48 workstations in library, computer center. Dormitories wired for high-speed internet access and linked to campus network. Online library available.

Student life. Freshman orientation: Mandatory, $70 fee. Preregistration for classes offered. Takes place within 2 weeks of start of classes in fall. **Policies:** Religious observance required. **Housing:** Guaranteed on-campus for all undergraduates. Single-sex dorms, apartments available. $100 deposit, deadline 7/1. **Activities:** Choral groups, music ensembles, student government, student newspaper, missions club, art club, aviator's club, Students in Free Enterprise.

Athletics. NAIA, NCCAA. **Intercollegiate:** Basketball, cheerleading W, cross-country, golf M, soccer, volleyball W. **Intramural:** Baseball M, basketball, soccer, softball, tennis, volleyball. **Team name:** Hawks.

Student services. Adult student services, campus ministries, career counseling, student employment services, financial aid counseling, health services, personal counseling, placement for graduates.

Contact. E-mail: admissions@sdcc.edu
Phone: (619) 588-7747 Toll-free number: (800) 676-2242
Fax: (619) 590-1739
Jon Melone, Director of Admissions, San Diego Christian College, 2100 Greenfield Drive, El Cajon, CA 92019-1157

San Diego State University

San Diego, California **CB member**
www.sdsu.edu **CB code: 4682**

- Public 4-year university
- Commuter campus in very large city
- 26,690 degree-seeking undergraduates: 18% part-time, 59% women, 4% African American, 16% Asian American, 22% Hispanic American, 1% Native American, 2% international
- 5,819 degree-seeking graduate students
- 44% of applicants admitted

- SAT or ACT (ACT writing optional) required
- 53% graduate within 6 years

General. Founded in 1897. Regionally accredited. Branch campus at Calexico in Imperial Valley. **Degrees:** 6,325 bachelor's awarded; master's, doctoral offered. **ROTC:** Army, Navy, Air Force. **Location:** 8 miles from downtown. **Calendar:** Semester, extensive summer session. **Full-time faculty:** 969 total; 94% have terminal degrees, 21% minority, 43% women. **Part-time faculty:** 783 total; 23% minority, 52% women. **Class size:** 23% < 20, 49% 20-39, 10% 40-49, 13% 50-99, 5% >100. **Special facilities:** Observatory, electron microscope facility, open-air theater, aquatic center, international student center, American Language Institute, recital hall, field studies stations (off-campus), multimedia interactive fine arts lab.

Freshman class profile. 36,718 applied, 16,266 admitted, 4,105 enrolled.

Mid 50% test scores		Return as sophomores:	84%
SAT verbal:	480-580	Out-of-state:	5%
SAT math:	500-600	Live on campus:	63%
ACT:	20-25	International:	1%
GPA 3.50 or higher:	50%	Fraternities:	17%
GPA 3.0-3.49:	44%	Sororities:	13%
GPA 2.0-2.99:	6%		

Basis for selection. High school GPA and test scores most important; 20% of those admitted selected using faculty-defined criteria, such as socioeconomic status, special talent, and San Diego and Imperial County residency.

High school preparation. 15 units required. Required and recommended units include English 4, mathematics 3-4, social studies 1, history 1, science 2 (laboratory 2), foreign language 2 and academic electives 1. One visual and performing arts required. History must be U.S. history or U.S. government. Science must be 1 biology, 1 physical science.

2005-2006 Annual costs. Tuition/fees: $3,122; $13,292 out-of-state. Room/board: $9,849. Books/supplies: $1,283. Personal expenses: $2,392.

2005-2006 Financial aid. Need-based: Average need met was 66%. Average scholarship/grant was $5,600; average loan $2,300. 51% of total undergraduate aid awarded as scholarships/grants, 49% as loans/jobs. **Non-need-based:** Awarded to 630 full-time undergraduates, including 120 freshmen. Scholarships awarded for academics, alumni affiliation, art, athletics, leadership, music/drama, ROTC, state residency.

Application procedures. Admission: Closing date 11/30 (postmark date). $55 fee, may be waived for applicants with need. Application must be submitted online. Admission notification 3/1. Must reply by 5/1. **Financial aid:** Priority date 3/2; no closing date. FAFSA required. Applicants notified on a rolling basis starting 2/14.

Academics. Special study options: Cross-registration, distance learning, double major, dual enrollment of high school students, ESL, exchange student, honors, independent study, internships, student-designed major, study abroad, teacher certification program. **Credit/placement by examination:** AP, CLEP, IB, SAT, ACT, institutional tests. 30 credit hours maximum toward bachelor's degree. Must be registered in at least 1 course, matriculated and in good standing. Approval of department chair and dean of college required. Restricted to regular undergraduate courses. Does not count toward 30-unit minimum residency requirement. **Support services:** Preadmission summer program, reduced course load, remedial instruction, tutoring.

Majors. Area/ethnic studies: African-American, American, Asian, European, Hispanic-American/Latino/Chicano, Latin American, Russian/Slavic, women's. **Biology:** General, bacteriology, ecology, evolutionary, marine, zoology. **Business:** Accounting, business admin, finance, international, operations, tourism/travel. **Communications:** General, advertising, broadcast journalism, journalism, public relations. **Computer sciences:** General, information systems. **Conservation:** General. **Education:** Art, biology, chemistry, computer, drama/dance, English, foreign languages, French, German, mathematics, physical, sales/marketing, science, social science, voc/tech. **Engineering:** Aerospace, civil, computer, electrical, mechanical. **English:** Speech/rhetoric. **Family/consumer sciences:** Family studies, food/nutrition. **Foreign languages:** Classics, French, German, Japanese, linguistics, Russian, Spanish. **Health:** Communication disorders, nursing (RN). **History:** General. **Interdisciplinary:** Gerontology. **Liberal arts:** Arts/sciences. **Math:** General, applied, statistics. **Parks/recreation:** General. **Philosophy/religion:** Philosophy, religion. **Physical sciences:** Astronomy, chemistry, geochemistry, geology, geophysics, molecular physics, paleontology, physics, theoretical physics. **Protective services:** Law enforcement admin. **Psychology:** General. **Public administration:** Social work. **Social sciences:** General, anthropology, economics, geography, international relations, political science, sociology, urban studies. **Visual/performing arts:** Art, art history/conservation, dance, design, dramatic, interior design, music performance, painting, sculpture, theater design.

Most popular majors. Business/marketing 18%, English 7%, liberal arts 10%, psychology 7%, social sciences 11%, visual/performing arts 6%.

Computing on campus. 400 workstations in dormitories, library, computer center, student center. Dormitories wired for high-speed internet access and linked to campus network. Commuter students can connect to campus network. Online course registration, online library, helpline, repair service available.

Student life. Freshman orientation: Mandatory, $55 fee. Preregistration for classes offered. One-day academic orientation in July and August. Student life orientation held in August. **Policies:** Freshmen permitted cars on campus. **Housing:** Coed dorms, apartments, cooperative housing, fraternity/sorority housing available. $800 partly refundable deposit. **Activities:** Bands, choral groups, dance, drama, film society, literary magazine, music ensembles, musical theater, opera, radio station, student government, student newspaper, symphony orchestra, TV station, more than 300 academic, recreational, sports, ethnic, political, honor, and service clubs on campus.

Athletics. NCAA. **Intercollegiate:** Baseball M, basketball, cross-country W, diving W, football (tackle) M, golf, rowing (crew) W, soccer, softball W, swimming W, tennis, track and field W, volleyball W, water polo W. **Intramural:** Basketball, bowling, football (non-tackle), golf, racquetball, soccer, softball, table tennis, tennis, volleyball. **Team name:** Aztecs.

Student services. Alcohol/substance abuse counseling, campus ministries, career counseling, services for economically disadvantaged, student employment services, financial aid counseling, health services, on-campus daycare, personal counseling, placement for graduates, veterans' counselor, women's services. **Physically disabled:** Services for visually, speech, hearing impaired. **Learning disabled:** Comprehensive services available.

Contact. E-mail: admissions@sdsu.edu
Phone: (619) 594-6336
Beverly Arata, Director of Admissions, San Diego State University, 5500 Campanile Drive, San Diego, CA 92182-7455

San Francisco Art Institute

San Francisco, California
www.sfai.edu **CB code: 4036**

- Private 4-year visual arts college
- Commuter campus in very large city
- 354 degree-seeking undergraduates
- 225 graduate students
- SAT or ACT with writing, application essay required

General. Founded in 1871. Regionally accredited. **Degrees:** 99 bachelor's awarded; master's offered. **Calendar:** Semester, limited summer session. **Full-time faculty:** 38 total. **Part-time faculty:** 95 total. **Class size:** 81% < 20, 17% 20-39, 1% 40-49, less than 1% 50-99. **Special facilities:** EARS XXI high definition research lab, Diego Rivera gallery, Walter & McBean galleries, digital media studio, digital imaging studio, studio production facilities in photography, printmaking, design and technology, and filmmaking, open studio spaces for painting, new genres and sculpture.

Basis for selection. Admission decisions based on evaluation of portfolio, academic credentials including transcripts and standardized test scores, letters of recommendation, and personal statement. Portfolio of artwork required. Interviews recommended, but not required. **Homeschooled:** State high school equivalency certificate, letter of recommendation (nonparent) required.

High school preparation. Strong background in English, humanities, and social sciences as well as extensive high school and extracurricular art education recommended.

2005-2006 Annual costs. Tuition/fees: $25,670. Room charge $6,540 for 12-month contract. Books/supplies: $2,125. Personal expenses: $2,400.

Financial aid. Non-need-based: Scholarships awarded for art.

Application procedures. Admission: Priority date 2/15; no deadline. $65 fee, may be waived for applicants with need. Application must be submitted on paper. Admission notification on a rolling basis. Must reply by May 1 or within 3 week(s) if notified thereafter. **Financial aid:** Priority date 3/1, closing date 9/1. FAFSA required. Applicants notified on a rolling basis starting 4/15; must reply within 3 week(s) of notification.

Academics. **Special study options:** Cooperative education, cross-registration, double major, ESL, exchange student, independent study, internships, New York semester, study abroad. **Credit/placement by examination:** AP, CLEP, IB, institutional tests. 20 credit hours maximum toward bachelor's degree. **Support services:** Learning center, remedial instruction, study skills assistance, tutoring, writing center.

Majors. **Visual/performing arts:** Art, art history/conservation, ceramics, cinematography, film/cinema, multimedia, painting, photography, printmaking, sculpture, studio arts.

Computing on campus. 71 workstations in library, computer center, student center. Wireless network available.

Student life. **Freshman orientation:** Mandatory. Preregistration for classes offered. **Policies:** Freshmen permitted cars on campus. **Housing:** Coed dorms available. $450 deposit, deadline 6/1. **Activities:** Film society, student government.

Student services. Career counseling, student employment services, financial aid counseling, personal counseling, placement for graduates, veterans' counselor. **Physically disabled:** Services for visually, speech, hearing impaired.

Contact. E-mail: admissions@sfai.edu
Phone: (415) 749-4500 Toll-free number: (800) 345-7324
Fax: (415) 749-4592
Paula Farmer, Director of Admissions, San Francisco Art Institute, 800 Chestnut Street, San Francisco, CA 94133-2299

San Francisco Conservatory of Music

San Francisco, California
www.sfcm.edu **CB code: 4744**

- Private 4-year music college
- Commuter campus in very large city
- 173 degree-seeking undergraduates
- 49% of applicants admitted
- Application essay required

General. Founded in 1917. Regionally accredited. All conservatory students receive extensive performance opportunities, both on campus and in the San Francisco Bay area. **Degrees:** 36 bachelor's awarded; master's offered. **Location:** 3 miles from downtown. **Calendar:** Semester. **Full-time faculty:** 25 total. **Part-time faculty:** 75 total. **Class size:** 86% < 20, 11% 20-39, 1% 40-49, 1% 50-99. **Special facilities:** Concert performance facility, music library.

Freshman class profile. 295 applied, 145 admitted, 66 enrolled.

Basis for selection. Most important criterion is music audition, followed by school achievement record, letters of recommendation, and test scores. Musical needs of institution also influence admission decisions. SAT or ACT recommended. SAT or ACT recommended, required for home-schooled students. Audition required.

High school preparation. Recommended units include English 3 and foreign language 3.

2006-2007 Annual costs. Tuition/fees (projected): $28,280. Books/supplies: $800. Personal expenses: $1,800.

Financial aid. All financial aid based on need.

Application procedures. **Admission:** Closing date 1/15 (postmark date). $100 fee. Application may be submitted online. Admission notification on a rolling basis beginning on or about 4/1. Must reply by May 1 or within 2 week(s) if notified thereafter. **Financial aid:** Priority date 3/1; no closing date. FAFSA, institutional form required. Applicants notified by 4/1; must reply by 5/1 or within 2 week(s) of notification.

Academics. **Special study options:** Independent study. **Credit/placement by examination:** CLEP, institutional tests. 60 credit hours maximum toward bachelor's degree. **Support services:** Remedial instruction, study skills assistance, tutoring.

Majors. **Visual/performing arts:** Music performance, music theory/composition, piano/organ, stringed instruments, voice/opera.

Computing on campus. 10 workstations in library, computer center.

Student life. **Freshman orientation:** Mandatory. **Policies:** Freshmen permitted cars on campus. **Activities:** Choral groups, music ensembles, musical theater, opera, student government, symphony orchestra.

Student services. Financial aid counseling, health services, personal counseling.

Contact. E-mail: admit@sfcm.edu
Phone: (415) 759-3431 Fax: (415) 759-3499
Alexander Brose, Director of Admission, San Francisco Conservatory of Music, 1201 Ortega Street, San Francisco, CA 94122-4498

San Francisco State University

San Francisco, California **CB member**
www.sfsu.edu **CB code: 4684**

- Public 4-year university
- Commuter campus in very large city
- 23,074 degree-seeking undergraduates: 22% part-time, 59% women, 6% African American, 31% Asian American, 14% Hispanic American, 1% Native American, 5% international
- 4,581 degree-seeking graduate students
- 67% of applicants admitted
- 40% graduate within 6 years

General. Founded in 1899. Regionally accredited. **Degrees:** 5,183 bachelor's awarded; master's, doctoral offered. **ROTC:** Army, Navy, Air Force. **Location:** 10 miles from downtown. **Calendar:** Semester, limited summer session. **Full-time faculty:** 865 total; 77% have terminal degrees, 36% minority, 45% women. **Part-time faculty:** 860 total; 29% have terminal degrees, 30% minority, 57% women. **Class size:** 25% < 20, 43% 20-39, 11% 40-49, 13% 50-99, 8% >100. **Special facilities:** Access to marine laboratories, environmental studies center, Sierra Nevada field campus, anthropology museum, facility for study of astronomy.

Freshman class profile. 22,219 applied, 14,965 admitted, 3,150 enrolled.

Mid 50% test scores		**Return as sophomores:**	81%
SAT verbal:	440-560	**Out-of-state:**	3%
SAT math:	450-570	**Live on campus:**	40%
ACT:	17-23	**International:**	2%
GPA 3.50 or higher:	24%	**Fraternities:**	1%
GPA 3.0-3.49:	43%	**Sororities:**	1%
GPA 2.0-2.99:	33%		

Basis for selection. School achievement record and score on SAT or ACT most important. Students with GPA over 2.0 may be exempted from SAT/ACT. SAT or ACT scores required if applicant's secondary school GPA is lower than 3.0 for California residents or 3.61 for non-residents. Essay recommended. **Homeschooled:** Local school district verification of completion of secondary schooling; SAT or ACT scores.

High school preparation. Required and recommended units include English 4, mathematics 3, social studies 1, history 1, science 2 (laboratory 2), foreign language 2 and academic electives 1. One visual and performing arts required.

2005-2006 Annual costs. Tuition/fees: $3,128; $13,298 out-of-state. Room/board: $10,458. Books/supplies: $1,400. Personal expenses: $2,400.

2005-2006 Financial aid. All financial aid based on need. 2,582 full-time freshmen applied for aid; 2,004 were judged to have need; 1,853 of these received aid. Average need met was 62%. Average scholarship/grant was $6,341; average loan $1,715. 53% of total undergraduate aid awarded as scholarships/grants, 47% as loans/jobs.

Application procedures. **Admission:** $55 fee, may be waived for applicants with need. Admission notification on a rolling basis beginning on or about 10/15. Must reply by May 1 or within 2 week(s) if notified thereafter. **Financial aid:** Priority date 3/1; no closing date. FAFSA required. Applicants notified on a rolling basis starting 1/15; must reply within 2 week(s) of notification.

Academics. **Special study options:** Combined bachelor's/graduate degree, cooperative education, cross-registration, distance learning, double major, dual enrollment of high school students, ESL, exchange student, honors, independent study, internships, liberal arts/career combination, student-designed major, study abroad, teacher certification program. **Credit/placement by examination:** AP, CLEP, IB, SAT, ACT, institutional tests. 30 credit hours maximum toward bachelor's degree. **Support services:** Learning center, pre-admission summer program, remedial instruction, tutoring.

Majors. **Area/ethnic studies:** African, African-American, American, Asian, Asian-American, Hispanic-American/Latino/Chicano, women's. **Biology:** General, bacteriology, biochemistry, biotechnology, botany, cell/histology, ecology, marine, zoology. **Business:** Accounting, banking/financial services, fashion, finance, hospitality admin, hospitality/recreation, human resources, insurance, international, labor relations, management science, real estate, tourism promotion. **Communications:** Broadcast journalism, journalism. **Computer sciences:** General, computer science. **Education:** Art, biology, chemistry, drama/dance, English, family/consumer sciences, foreign languages, French, German, health, mathematics, music, physical, physics, science, social science, Spanish, speech, speech impaired, technology/industrial arts. **Engineering:** Civil, electrical, mechanical. **English:** Speech/rhetoric, technical writing. **Family/consumer sciences:** General, clothing/textiles, housing. **Foreign languages:** Chinese, classics, comparative lit, French, German, Italian, Japanese, Russian, Spanish. **Health:** Athletic training, audiology/speech pathology, clinical lab science. **History:** General. **Liberal arts:** Arts/sciences. **Math:** General, applied, statistics. **Parks/recreation:** Facilities management, sports admin. **Personal/culinary services:** Culinary arts. **Philosophy/religion:** Philosophy. **Physical sciences:** Astronomy, astrophysics, chemistry, geochemistry, geology, geophysics, physics. **Protective services:** Criminal justice. **Psychology:** General. **Public administration:** Social work. **Social sciences:** General, anthropology, criminology, economics, geography, international relations, political science, sociology, urban studies. **Visual/performing arts:** Art, dance, dramatic, film/cinema, industrial design, music performance, piano/organ, voice/opera.

Most popular majors. Business/marketing 26%, communications/journalism 7%, English 7%, liberal arts 6%, psychology 8%, social sciences 8%, visual/performing arts 10%.

Computing on campus. 500 workstations in library, computer center. Dormitories wired for high-speed internet access. Helpline, repair service available.

Student life. **Freshman orientation:** Available, $28 fee. Preregistration for classes offered. Freshman orientation participants given top priority for registration in fall classes. **Housing:** Coed dorms, special housing for disabled, apartments available. $450 deposit. Theme co-ed housing for science-tech freshmen. **Activities:** Bands, choral groups, dance, drama, film society, literary magazine, music ensembles, musical theater, opera, radio station, student government, student newspaper, symphony orchestra, TV station.

Athletics. NCAA. **Intercollegiate:** Baseball M, basketball, cross-country, soccer, softball W, swimming, tennis W, track and field, volleyball W, wrestling M. **Intramural:** Basketball, wrestling M. **Team name:** Gators.

Student services. Adult student services, alcohol/substance abuse counseling, career counseling, services for economically disadvantaged, student employment services, financial aid counseling, health services, on-campus daycare, personal counseling, placement for graduates, veterans' counselor. **Physically disabled:** Services for visually, speech, hearing impaired.

Contact. E-mail: ugadmit@sfsu.edu
Phone: (415) 338-6486 Fax: (415) 338-3880
Valerie Perry, Director, Undergraduate Admissions, San Francisco State University, 1600 Holloway Avenue, San Francisco, CA 94132

San Jose State University

San Jose, California **CB member**
www.sjsu.edu **CB code: 4687**

- Public 4-year university and liberal arts college
- Commuter campus in very large city
- 22,733 degree-seeking undergraduates: 25% part-time, 51% women, 5% African American, 38% Asian American, 16% Hispanic American, 3% international
- 7,242 degree-seeking graduate students
- 65% of applicants admitted
- 38% graduate within 6 years

General. Founded in 1857. Regionally accredited. **Degrees:** 4,259 bachelor's awarded; master's offered. **ROTC:** Army, Air Force. **Location:** 50 miles from San Francisco. **Calendar:** Semester, limited summer session. **Full-time faculty:** 930 total. **Part-time faculty:** 730 total. **Class size:** 26% < 20, 51% 20-39, 10% 40-49, 11% 50-99, 2% >100. **Special facilities:** Marine laboratory, natural history living museum, nuclear science lab, center for Beethoven studies, Chicano resource center, art metal foundry, deep-sea research ship, electro-acoustic and recording studio.

Freshman class profile. 16,893 applied, 11,004 admitted, 2,551 enrolled.

Mid 50% test scores			
SAT verbal:	410-530	GPA 3.50 or higher:	21%
SAT math:	440-570	GPA 3.0-3.49:	45%
ACT:	16-23	GPA 2.0-2.99:	34%
		Out-of-state:	1%

Basis for selection. High school record and test scores most important. SAT or ACT required for applicants with less than 3.0 GPA.

High school preparation. 15 units required. Required units include English 4, mathematics 3, social studies 1, history 1, science 2 (laboratory 2), foreign language 2 and academic electives 1. One visual and performing arts.

2005-2006 Annual costs. Tuition/fees: $3,292; $13,462 out-of-state. Room/board: $8,718.

Financial aid. All financial aid based on need.

Application procedures. **Admission:** Priority date 11/30; deadline 2/1. $55 fee. Application must be submitted online. Must reply by May 1 or within 2 week(s) if notified thereafter. **Financial aid:** Priority date 3/2; no closing date. FAFSA required. Applicants notified on a rolling basis starting 4/30; must reply within 2 week(s) of notification.

Academics. **Special study options:** Accelerated study, cooperative education, cross-registration, distance learning, double major, dual enrollment of high school students, ESL, honors, independent study, internships, liberal arts/career combination, student-designed major, study abroad, teacher certification program. **Credit/placement by examination:** AP, CLEP.

Majors. **Area/ethnic studies:** African-American. **Biology:** General, biochemistry, conservation, marine, microbiology, molecular, physiology. **Business:** Accounting, business admin, finance, hospitality admin, human resources, international, marketing. **Communications:** Advertising, journalism, public relations, radio/tv. **Computer sciences:** Computer science, information technology. **Conservation:** Environmental studies. **Education:** Early childhood. **Engineering:** General, aerospace, chemical, civil, computer, electrical, industrial, materials, mechanical, software. **Engineering technology:** Quality control. **English:** English lit, speech/rhetoric. **Foreign languages:** Chinese, French, German, Japanese, linguistics, Spanish. **Health:** Communication disorders, dietetics, health care admin, health services, nursing (RN). **History:** General. **Interdisciplinary:** Accounting/computer science, behavioral sciences, natural sciences. **Liberal arts:** Arts/sciences, humanities. **Math:** General, applied. **Parks/recreation:** General, health/fitness. **Philosophy/religion:** Philosophy, religion. **Physical sciences:** Chemistry, geology, physics. **Protective services:** Criminal justice, forensics. **Psychology:** General. **Public administration:** Social work. **Social sciences:** General, anthropology, economics, geography, international relations, political science, sociology. **Transportation:** Aviation. **Visual/performing arts:** General, art, art history/conservation, dance, dramatic, graphic design, industrial design, interior design, music performance, studio arts.

Most popular majors. Business/marketing 33%, communications/journalism 6%, computer/information sciences 6%, engineering/engineering technologies 11%, health sciences 6%, visual/performing arts 8%.

Computing on campus. Dormitories wired for high-speed internet access and linked to campus network. Commuter students can connect to campus network. Online course registration, online library, helpline available.

Student life. **Freshman orientation:** Mandatory. Preregistration for classes offered. Mandatory overnight program for all first-time freshmen. **Policies:** Freshmen permitted cars on campus. **Housing:** Coed dorms, fraternity/sorority housing available. **Activities:** Bands, choral groups, dance, drama, literary magazine, music ensembles, musical theater, opera, radio station, student government, student newspaper, symphony orchestra.

Athletics. NCAA. **Intercollegiate:** Baseball M, basketball, cheerleading, cross-country, diving W, football (tackle) M, golf, gymnastics W, soccer, softball W, swimming W, tennis W, volleyball W, water polo W. **Intramural:** Archery, badminton, baseball M, basketball, bowling, field hockey W, football (non-tackle), lacrosse, racquetball, soccer, softball, swimming, table tennis, tennis, volleyball W, water polo. **Team name:** Spartans.

Student services. Adult student services, alcohol/substance abuse counseling, campus ministries, career counseling, services for economically disadvantaged, student employment services, financial aid counseling, health services, legal services, minority student services, on-campus daycare, personal counseling, placement for graduates, veterans' counselor, women's services. **Physically disabled:** Services for visually, speech, hearing impaired.

Contact. E-mail: contact@sjsu.edu
Phone: (408) 924-2550
Susan Hoagland, Undergraduate & Graduate Admissions Director, San Jose State University, One Washington Square, San Jose, CA 95192-0011

Santa Clara University

Santa Clara, California **CB member**
www.scu.edu **CB code: 4851**

- Private 4-year university affiliated with Roman Catholic Church
- Residential campus in small city

- 4,552 degree-seeking undergraduates: 2% part-time, 56% women, 3% African American, 18% Asian American, 13% Hispanic American, 1% Native American, 3% international
- 3,327 degree-seeking graduate students
- 61% of applicants admitted
- SAT or ACT with writing, application essay required
- 84% graduate within 6 years; 54% enter graduate study

General. Founded in 1851. Regionally accredited. **Degrees:** 1,233 bachelor's awarded; master's, doctoral, first professional offered. **ROTC:** Army, Air Force. **Location:** 45 miles from San Francisco, 1 mile from San Jose. **Calendar:** Quarter, limited summer session. **Full-time faculty:** 447 total; 92% have terminal degrees, 17% minority, 38% women. **Part-time faculty:** 299 total; 59% have terminal degrees, 12% minority, 40% women. **Class size:** 31% < 20, 57% 20-39, 10% 40-49, 2% 50-99, less than 1% >100. **Special facilities:** Historic mission church with artifacts dating from California mission era, applied ethics center, performing arts center, observatory, science and technology center, tennis complex, de Saisset museum, fitness center.

Freshman class profile. 8,904 applied, 5,419 admitted, 1,198 enrolled.

Mid 50% test scores			
SAT verbal:	550-650	Rank in top quarter:	71%
SAT math:	570-670	Rank in top tenth:	40%
ACT:	24-28	End year in good standing:	92%
GPA 3.50 or higher:	61%	Return as sophomores:	94%
GPA 3.0-3.49:	32%	Out-of-state:	41%
GPA 2.0-2.99:	7%	Live on campus:	92%
		International:	1%

Basis for selection. GED not accepted. Rigor of high school curriculum and GPA most important, followed by test scores, teacher's recommendation, personal essay, and extracurricular activities. Ethnicity and alumni affiliations given special consideration. Must take SAT/ACT by January of senior year. Interviews recommended. Audition recommended for music, theater arts majors.

High school preparation. 18 units required; 20 recommended. Required and recommended units include English 4, mathematics 4, social studies 1-2, history 1, science 3-4 (laboratory 2), foreign language 3-4 and academic electives 2-4. Additional mathematics and science courses recommended for applicants in business, engineering, mathematics, science. Fine arts recommended.

2005-2006 Annual costs. Tuition/fees: $29,159. Room/board: $10,032. Books/supplies: $1,260. Personal expenses: $1,828.

2005-2006 Financial aid. **Need-based:** 735 full-time freshmen applied for aid; 457 were judged to have need; 447 of these received aid. Average need met was 71%. Average scholarship/grant was $14,253; average loan $3,622. 80% of total undergraduate aid awarded as scholarships/grants, 20% as loans/jobs. **Non-need-based:** Scholarships awarded for academics, alumni affiliation, athletics, music/drama, ROTC.

Application procedures. **Admission:** Closing date 1/15 (receipt date). $55 fee, may be waived for applicants with need. Application may be submitted online. Admission notification 4/1. Admission notification on a rolling basis. Must reply by 5/1. **Financial aid:** Priority date 2/1; no closing date. FAFSA, CSS PROFILE required. Applicants notified on a rolling basis starting 4/1; must reply by 5/1 or within 2 week(s) of notification.

Academics. **Special study options:** Combined bachelor's/graduate degree, cooperative education, double major, exchange student, honors, independent study, internships, student-designed major, study abroad, teacher certification program, Washington semester. **Credit/placement by examination:** AP, CLEP, IB. No credit by examination awarded to new students. Number of credit hours awarded for International Baccalaureate determined on case-by-case basis. **Support services:** Learning center, reduced course load, study skills assistance, tutoring.

Majors. **Biology:** General. **Business:** Accounting, finance, managerial economics, marketing, organizational behavior. **Communications:** General. **Conservation:** Environmental science, environmental studies. **Education:** Special. **Engineering:** General, civil, computer, electrical, mechanical, software. **English:** English lit. **Foreign languages:** Ancient Greek, classics, French, Italian, Latin, Spanish. **History:** General. **Interdisciplinary:** Ancient studies, math/computer science. **Liberal arts:** Arts/sciences. **Math:** General. **Philosophy/religion:** Philosophy, religion. **Physical sciences:** Chemistry, physics. **Psychology:** General. **Social sciences:** Anthropology, economics, political science, sociology. **Visual/performing arts:** Art history/conservation, dramatic, studio arts.

Most popular majors. Business/marketing 31%, communications/journalism 7%, engineering/engineering technologies 11%, interdisciplinary studies 6%, psychology 8%, social sciences 13%.

Computing on campus. 800 workstations in dormitories, library, computer center, student center. Dormitories wired for high-speed internet access and linked to campus network. Commuter students can connect to campus network. Online course registration, online library, helpline, repair service, student web hosting, wireless network available.

Student life. **Freshman orientation:** Mandatory, $285 fee. Preregistration for classes offered. 2-day session in summer and 2-day session on weekend before school starts. Parents attend separate program. **Policies:** Freshmen permitted cars on campus. **Housing:** Guaranteed on-campus for freshmen. Coed dorms, apartments, substance-free housing available. $300 nonrefundable deposit, deadline 5/1. Housing guaranteed to freshmen, sophomores, juniors. **Activities:** Jazz band, choral groups, dance, drama, literary magazine, music ensembles, musical theater, opera, radio station, student government, student newspaper, symphony orchestra, Asian Pacific student union, Ka Mana o O'Hawaii, community action program, Barkada, Community of Portuguese and Brazilians, MECHA, Chinese student association, National Society of Black Engineers, Bronco Christian Fellowship.

Athletics. NCAA. **Intercollegiate:** Baseball M, basketball, cross-country, golf, rowing (crew), soccer, softball W, tennis, track and field, volleyball W, water polo. **Intramural:** Badminton, basketball, football (non-tackle), soccer, softball, tennis, volleyball. **Team name:** Broncos.

Student services. Alcohol/substance abuse counseling, campus ministries, career counseling, student employment services, financial aid counseling, health services, legal services, minority student services, on-campus daycare, personal counseling, placement for graduates. **Physically disabled:** Services for visually, speech, hearing impaired.

Contact. Phone: (408) 554-4700 Fax: (408) 554-5255
Sandra Hayes, Dean of Undergraduate Admissions, Santa Clara University, 500 El Camino Real, Santa Clara, CA 95053

Scripps College

Claremont, California — **CB member**
www.scrippscollege.edu — **CB code: 4693**

- Private 4-year liberal arts college for women
- Residential campus in large town
- 879 degree-seeking undergraduates: 1% part-time, 100% women, 3% African American, 13% Asian American, 5% Hispanic American, 1% international
- 21 degree-seeking graduate students
- 46% of applicants admitted
- SAT or ACT (ACT writing optional), application essay required
- 84% graduate within 6 years

General. Founded in 1926. Regionally accredited. One of cluster of 5 undergraduate and 2 graduate schools on adjoining campuses. Campuses share facilities. Cross-enrollment available at any of Claremont Colleges: Claremont-McKenna, Harvey Mudd, Pitzer, Pomona, and Scripps. **Degrees:** 181 bachelor's awarded. **ROTC:** Army, Air Force. **Location:** 35 miles from Los Angeles. **Calendar:** Semester, limited summer session. **Full-time faculty:** 66 total; 100% have terminal degrees, 20% minority, 56% women. **Part-time faculty:** 34 total; 85% have terminal degrees, 12% minority, 71% women. **Class size:** 67% < 20, 27% 20-39, 4% 40-49, 2% 50-99. **Special facilities:** Art slide library, biological field station, humanities museum.

Freshman class profile. 1,836 applied, 847 admitted, 234 enrolled.

Mid 50% test scores			
SAT verbal:	650-740	Rank in top quarter:	93%
SAT math:	620-700	Rank in top tenth:	69%
ACT:	26-31	Return as sophomores:	88%
GPA 3.50 or higher:	90%	Out-of-state:	60%
GPA 3.0-3.49:	9%	Live on campus:	100%
GPA 2.0-2.99:	1%	International:	1%

Basis for selection. Rigor of high school curriculum, GPA, class rank, aptitude as reflected in standardized testing most important. Essays, recommendations, required graded writing assignment significant. SAT Subject Tests used for placement in language only; institutional language and math exam used for placement. Interviews recommended. Audition recommended for music, dance majors. Portfolio recommended for art majors. **Homeschooled:** Statement describing homeschool structure and mission, transcript of courses and grades, interview, letter of recommendation (nonparent) required. **Learning Disabled:** Documentation of learning disability necessary.

High school preparation. 16 units required. Required units include English 4, mathematics 3, social studies 3, science 3 and foreign language 3.

2005-2006 Annual costs. Tuition/fees: $31,500. Room/board: $9,500. Books/supplies: $800. Personal expenses: $1,000.

2005-2006 Financial aid. **Need-based:** 142 full-time freshmen applied for aid; 100 were judged to have need; 100 of these received aid. Average need met was 100%. Average scholarship/grant was $22,305; average loan $2,573. 85% of total undergraduate aid awarded as scholarships/grants, 15% as loans/jobs. **Non-need-based:** Awarded to 140 full-time undergraduates, including 38 freshmen. Scholarships awarded for academics, leadership.

Application procedures. **Admission:** Closing date 1/1 (postmark date). $50 fee, may be waived for applicants with need. Application may be submitted online. Admission notification 4/1. Must reply by 5/1. **Financial aid:** Priority date 2/1; no closing date. FAFSA, CSS PROFILE required. Applicants notified by 4/1; must reply by 5/1 or within 2 week(s) of notification.

Academics. Almost half of junior class elects to study abroad for semester or year. **Special study options:** Accelerated study, combined bachelor's/graduate degree, cross-registration, double major, dual enrollment of high school students, exchange student, honors, independent study, internships, liberal arts/career combination, New York semester, student-designed major, study abroad, United Nations semester, Washington semester. Postbaccalaureate pre-medical certificate program, humanities internship program, 3-2 engineering. **Credit/placement by examination:** AP, CLEP, IB, institutional tests. 32 credit hours maximum toward bachelor's degree. SAT Subject Tests recommended for placement. **Support services:** Reduced course load, tutoring, writing center.

Majors. **Area/ethnic studies:** African-American, American, Asian, Asian-American, European, French, German, Hispanic-American/Latino/Chicano, Italian, Latin American, Spanish/Iberian, women's. **Biology:** General, biochemistry, molecular. **Business:** Organizational behavior. **Computer sciences:** Computer science. **Conservation:** Environmental science, environmental studies. **Engineering:** General. **English:** English lit. **Foreign languages:** General, Chinese, classics, French, German, Italian, Japanese, linguistics, Russian, Spanish. **History:** General. **Interdisciplinary:** Biological/physical sciences, neuroscience, science/society. **Legal studies:** General. **Liberal arts:** Humanities. **Math:** General. **Philosophy/religion:** Judaic, philosophy, religion. **Physical sciences:** Chemistry, geology, physics. **Psychology:** General. **Public administration:** Policy analysis. **Social sciences:** Anthropology, econometrics, economics, international relations, political science, sociology. **Visual/performing arts:** Art, art history/conservation, cinematography, dance, dramatic, studio arts, theater history.

Most popular majors. Area/ethnic studies 17%, biology 7%, English 9%, interdisciplinary studies 7%, psychology 11%, social sciences 15%, visual/performing arts 18%.

Computing on campus. 72 workstations in dormitories, library, computer center. Dormitories wired for high-speed internet access and linked to campus network. Commuter students can connect to campus network. Online library, helpline, repair service, student web hosting, wireless network available.

Student life. **Freshman orientation:** Mandatory. 5-day orientation begins last Thursday in August. **Policies:** Freshmen permitted cars on campus. **Housing:** Guaranteed on-campus for freshmen. Special housing for disabled, apartments, substance-free housing available. Most sophomores, most juniors and all seniors have single rooms. Off-campus houses available to single students. **Activities:** Choral groups, dance, drama, literary magazine, music ensembles, radio station, student government, student newspaper, symphony orchestra, more than 200 clubs and organizations available through Claremont College consortium.

Athletics. NCAA. **Intercollegiate:** Basketball W, cross-country W, diving W, golf W, lacrosse W, soccer W, softball W, swimming W, tennis W, track and field W, volleyball W, water polo W. **Intramural:** Basketball W, soccer W, softball W, volleyball W, water polo W. **Team name:** Athenas.

Student services. Adult student services, campus ministries, career counseling, student employment services, financial aid counseling, health services, minority student services, personal counseling, placement for graduates, women's services.

Contact. E-mail: admission@scrippscollege.edu
Phone: (909) 621-8149 Toll-free number: (800) 770-1333
Fax: (909) 607-7508
Amy Abrams, Director of Admissions, Scripps College, 1030 North Columbia Avenue, Claremont, CA 91711

Simpson University
Redding, California
www.simpsonuniversity.edu **CB code: 4698**

- Private 4-year liberal arts college affiliated with Christian and Missionary Alliance
- Residential campus in small city
- 922 degree-seeking undergraduates: 2% part-time, 65% women
- 80 degree-seeking graduate students
- 54% of applicants admitted
- SAT or ACT required
- 50% graduate within 6 years

General. Founded in 1921. Regionally accredited. Christ-centered educational community. **Degrees:** 275 bachelor's, 1 associate awarded; master's offered. **Location:** 170 miles from Sacramento. **Calendar:** Semester, limited summer session. **Full-time faculty:** 40 total; 60% have terminal degrees, 5% minority. **Part-time faculty:** 67 total; 22% have terminal degrees. **Class size:** 66% < 20, 29% 20-39, 2% 40-49, 4% 50-99.

Freshman class profile. 929 applied, 500 admitted, 167 enrolled.

Return as sophomores:	58%	**Out-of-state:**	20%

Basis for selection. Commitment to Jesus Christ as reflected in personal statement and required references, academic achievement, other recommendations, and standardized test scores important. **Homeschooled:** Transcript of courses and grades required.

High school preparation. College-preparatory program recommended. Recommended units include English 4, mathematics 3, social studies 3, science 2 and foreign language 2. College-preparatory program highly recommended; GED required for graduates of nonapproved programs.

2006-2007 Annual costs. Tuition/fees: $17,800. Room/board: $6,200. Books/supplies: $1,200. Personal expenses: $1,760.

2004-2005 Financial aid. **Need-based:** 187 full-time freshmen applied for aid; 165 were judged to have need; 165 of these received aid. Average need met was 71%. Average scholarship/grant was $4,600; average loan $2,625. 69% of total undergraduate aid awarded as scholarships/grants, 31% as loans/jobs. **Non-need-based:** Awarded to 634 full-time undergraduates, including 185 freshmen. Scholarships awarded for academics, alumni affiliation, leadership, minority status, music/drama, religious affiliation, state residency. **Additional information:** Work-study programs available.

Application procedures. **Admission:** No deadline. $40 fee, may be waived for applicants with need. Application may be submitted online. Admission notification on a rolling basis. Must reply by May 1 or within 2 week(s) if notified thereafter. **Financial aid:** Priority date 3/2; no closing date. FAFSA, institutional form required. Applicants notified on a rolling basis starting 3/16; must reply within 3 week(s) of notification.

Academics. 34-semester-hour teacher credential program permits students to earn California Clear Credential for grades K-8 (multiple subjects) or for grades 7-12 (single subject). **Special study options:** Accelerated study, combined bachelor's/graduate degree, distance learning, double major, honors, independent study, internships, student-designed major, study abroad, teacher certification program, Washington semester, weekend college. **Credit/placement by examination:** AP, CLEP, institutional tests. 30 credit hours maximum toward bachelor's degree. Credit by examination granted only to enrolled students. Students may take challenge exam for particular course only once. **Support services:** Reduced course load, remedial instruction, study skills assistance, tutoring, writing center.

Majors. **Business:** Business admin, management information systems, organizational behavior. **Communications:** General. **Education:** Elementary, English, mathematics, music, social science. **English:** English lit. **History:** General. **Liberal arts:** Arts/sciences. **Math:** General. **Philosophy/religion:** Christian, religion. **Psychology:** General. **Social sciences:** General. **Theology:** Bible, missionary, pastoral counseling, theology, youth ministry.

Most popular majors. Business/marketing 25%, liberal arts 25%, psychology 19%, theological studies 14%.

Computing on campus. 50 workstations in dormitories, library, computer center. Dormitories wired for high-speed internet access and linked to campus network. Commuter students can connect to campus network. Online course registration, online library, helpline, repair service, wireless network available.

Student life. **Freshman orientation:** Mandatory. Preregistration for classes offered. Offered in both fall and spring semesters for traditional undergraduate students. Events include placement tests. **Policies:** Religious observance required. Freshmen permitted cars on campus. **Housing:** Guaranteed on-campus for all undergraduates. Single-sex dorms, special housing for disabled, apartments, substance-free housing available. $100 deposit. All single undergraduates under 22 required to live on campus. Request for off-campus living must be approved by Vice President for Student Development. **Activities:** Jazz band, choral groups, dance, drama, music ensembles, student government, student newspaper, Asian fellowship, Hispanic fellowship, summer missions teams, chapel worship team, student senate, spiritual action committee, psychology club, missionary kids association, commuter student association.

Athletics. NAIA, NCCAA. **Intercollegiate:** Baseball M, basketball, softball W, volleyball W. **Intramural:** Basketball, football (tackle), soccer, volleyball. **Team name:** Red Hawks.

Student services. Adult student services, campus ministries, career counseling, student employment services, financial aid counseling, health services, minority student services, personal counseling, veterans' counselor. **Physically disabled:** Services for visually, speech, hearing impaired.

Contact. E-mail: admissions@simpsonuniversity.edu
Phone: (530) 226-4606 Toll-free number: (800) 598-2493
Fax: (530) 226-4861
Ron Cushman, Director of Enrollment Development, Simpson University, 2211 College View Drive, Redding, CA 96003-8606

Soka University of America

Aliso Viejo, California
www.soka.edu/ **CB member**

- Private 4-year university and liberal arts college
- Residential campus in large town
- 365 degree-seeking undergraduates
- 43% of applicants admitted
- SAT or ACT with writing, application essay required

General. **Degrees:** 95 bachelor's awarded; master's offered. **Calendar:** Semester. **Full-time faculty:** 37 total. **Part-time faculty:** 29 total.

Freshman class profile. 277 applied, 118 admitted, 86 enrolled.

Mid 50% test scores			
SAT verbal:	430-590	SAT math:	570-680

Basis for selection. Test scores, essay, recommendations, extracurricular activities important.

2006-2007 Annual costs. Tuition/fees: $20,856. Room/board: $8,400.

Application procedures. **Admission:** Closing date 1/6. $45 fee. Admission notification on a rolling basis beginning on or about 12/1. **Financial aid:** Closing date 3/1. Applicants notified on a rolling basis starting 3/15.

Academics. **Credit/placement by examination:** CLEP.

Majors. **Liberal arts:** Arts/sciences.

Student life. **Housing:** Coed dorms available. Students required to live on campus.

Contact. E-mail: admissions@soka.edu
Phone: (949) 480-4150 Toll-free number: (888) 600-7652
Eric Hauber, Dean of Student Recruitment, Soka University of America, 1 University Drive, Aliso Viejo, CA 92656

Sonoma State University

Rohnert Park, California
www.sonoma.edu **CB code: 4723**

- Public 4-year university and liberal arts college
- Commuter campus in large town
- 6,481 degree-seeking undergraduates: 13% part-time, 63% women, 2% African American, 5% Asian American, 11% Hispanic American, 1% Native American, 1% international
- 602 degree-seeking graduate students
- 61% of applicants admitted
- SAT or ACT (ACT writing optional) required
- 49% graduate within 6 years

General. Founded in 1960. Regionally accredited. **Degrees:** 1,584 bachelor's awarded; master's offered. **ROTC:** Army, Navy, Air Force. **Location:** 50 miles from San Francisco, 10 miles from Santa Rosa. **Calendar:** Semester, extensive summer session. **Full-time faculty:** 277 total; 100% have terminal degrees, 16% minority, 45% women. **Part-time faculty:** 265 total; 31% have terminal degrees, 10% minority, 58% women. **Class size:** 37% < 20, 47% 20-39, 8% 40-49, 7% 50-99, 2% >100. **Special facilities:** Observatory, performing arts center, nature preserve, information technology center.

Freshman class profile. 10,597 applied, 6,444 admitted, 1,053 enrolled.

Mid 50% test scores			
SAT verbal:	470-570	GPA 2.0-2.99:	24%
SAT math:	460-570	End year in good standing:	85%
ACT:	19-24	Return as sophomores:	82%
GPA 3.50 or higher:	27%	Out-of-state:	1%
GPA 3.0-3.49:	49%	Live on campus:	82%
		International:	1%

Basis for selection. School GPA and test scores most important. SAT, ACT, SAT Subject Tests must be received before start of term. Audition required of music majors. Portfolio required of art majors. RN required for graduate nursing. **Learning Disabled:** Applicants with disabilities strongly encouraged to complete college preparatory course requirements if at all possible. If applicant judged unable to fulfill specific course requirement because of disability, alternative college preparatory courses may be substituted for specific subject requirements.

High school preparation. College-preparatory program required. 15 units required. Required units include English 4, mathematics 3, history 2, science 2 (laboratory 1), foreign language 2 and academic electives 1. One visual and performing arts, US government required.

2005-2006 Annual costs. Tuition/fees: $3,624; $13,794 out-of-state. Room/board: $8,820. Books/supplies: $1,242. Personal expenses: $2,340.

2004-2005 Financial aid. **Need-based:** 671 full-time freshmen applied for aid; 369 were judged to have need; 249 of these received aid. Average need met was 80%. Average scholarship/grant was $6,329; average loan $2,574. 48% of total undergraduate aid awarded as scholarships/grants, 52% as loans/jobs. **Non-need-based:** Awarded to 732 full-time undergraduates, including 150 freshmen. Scholarships awarded for academics, alumni affiliation, art, athletics, leadership, minority status, music/drama, state residency.

Application procedures. **Admission:** Priority date 11/30; deadline 1/31 (postmark date). $55 fee, may be waived for applicants with need. Application may be submitted online. Admission notification 3/1. Admission notification on a rolling basis beginning on or about 11/1. Must reply by 5/1. **Financial aid:** Priority date 1/31; no closing date. FAFSA required. Applicants notified on a rolling basis starting 3/15; must reply within 4 week(s) of notification.

Academics. **Special study options:** Accelerated study, combined bachelor's/graduate degree, cross-registration, distance learning, double major, dual enrollment of high school students, ESL, exchange student, external degree, honors, independent study, internships, liberal arts/career combination, New York semester, semester at sea, student-designed major, study abroad, teacher certification program, United Nations semester, urban semester, Washington semester. Combined degree programs: bachelor's/MBA; bachelor's/MPA. **Credit/placement by examination:** AP, CLEP, institutional tests. 30 credit hours maximum toward bachelor's degree. **Support services:** Learning center, pre-admission summer program, reduced course load, remedial instruction, study skills assistance, tutoring, writing center.

Majors. **Area/ethnic studies:** African-American, Hispanic-American/Latino/Chicano, women's. **Biology:** General. **Business:** Business admin. **Communications:** General. **Computer sciences:** Computer science, programming. **Conservation:** General, environmental studies. **Engineering:** Computer. **Family/consumer sciences:** Family studies. **Foreign languages:** French, German, Spanish. **Health:** Nursing (RN). **History:** General. **Interdisciplinary:** Global studies. **Liberal arts:** Arts/sciences. **Math:** General. **Philosophy/religion:** Philosophy. **Physical sciences:** Chemistry, geology, physics. **Protective services:** Law enforcement admin. **Psychology:** General. **Social sciences:** Anthropology, economics, geography, political science, sociology. **Visual/performing arts:** General, art history/conservation, dramatic, studio arts.

Most popular majors. Business/marketing 17%, English 6%, liberal arts 12%, psychology 11%, social sciences 10%.

Computing on campus. PC or laptop required. 400 workstations in library, computer center. Dormitories wired for high-speed internet access and linked to campus network. Commuter students can connect to campus network. Online course registration, online library, helpline, student web hosting, wireless network available.

Student life. **Freshman orientation:** Available. Preregistration for classes offered. 2-day residential program in June. Parents invited. **Policies:** Freshmen permitted cars on campus. **Housing:** Guaranteed on-campus for freshmen. Coed dorms, apartments, substance-free housing available. $1,000 partly refundable deposit. Focus learning communities: freshman seminar dorms, healthy living dorms, women in math/science dorms. **Activities:** Jazz band, choral groups, dance, drama, literary magazine, music ensembles, musical theater, opera, radio station, student government, student newspaper, symphony orchestra, Student Advocates for Education, Model United Nations,

College Republicans, Asian Pacific Islander Organization, Raza Native American Council, El Movimiento Estudiantil Chicano/a de Aztlán, InterVarsity Christian Fellowship, Hillel, Best Buddies, Student Ambassadors.

Athletics. NCAA. **Intercollegiate:** Baseball M, basketball, cross-country W, golf M, soccer, softball W, tennis, track and field W, volleyball W, water polo W. **Intramural:** Basketball, football (non-tackle), soccer, softball, volleyball. **Team name:** Sea Wolves.

Student services. Adult student services, alcohol/substance abuse counseling, career counseling, services for economically disadvantaged, student employment services, financial aid counseling, health services, minority student services, on-campus daycare, personal counseling, placement for graduates, veterans' counselor, women's services. **Physically disabled:** Services for visually, speech, hearing impaired.

Contact. Phone: (707) 664-2778 Fax: (707) 664-2060
Gustavo Flores, Director, Admissions, Sonoma State University, 1801 East Cotati Avenue, Rohnert Park, CA 94928

Southern California Institute of Architecture

Los Angeles, California
www.sciarc.edu **CB code: 1575**

- Private 5-year visual arts and technical college
- Commuter campus in very large city
- 200 degree-seeking undergraduates
- 77% of applicants admitted
- SAT or ACT (ACT writing optional), application essay required

General. Founded in 1972. Regionally accredited. School in Switzerland; exchange programs in Japan, Australia, England, Israel, Netherlands. **Degrees:** 53 bachelor's awarded; master's offered. **Location:** Downtown. **Calendar:** Trimester, extensive summer session. **Full-time faculty:** 80 total. **Special facilities:** Media center, architecture gallery, woodshop and model-making center, metal fabrication shop, graphics center, darkroom, CNC Milling.

Freshman class profile. 52 applied, 40 admitted, 8 enrolled.

Basis for selection. School achievement record, interview, portfolio, recommendations, and statement of purpose. One or 2 prior semesters of college recommended. Applicants should have started their general education requirement at another 2- or 4-year institution. General education requirements must be completed prior to fourth year. Portfolio required. Interview recommended.

High school preparation. Recommended units include English 4, mathematics 3, social studies 2, science 1 and foreign language 2. Art design and architecture courses recommended.

2005-2006 Annual costs. Tuition/fees: $19,416. Books/supplies: $1,502. Personal expenses: $2,048.

Application procedures. Admission: Closing date 2/1. $60 fee, may be waived for applicants with need. Admission notification on a rolling basis beginning on or about 6/1. Must reply by May 1 or within 2 week(s) if notified thereafter. **Financial aid:** Priority date 3/2; no closing date. Institutional form required. Applicants notified on a rolling basis starting 5/1; must reply within 2 week(s) of notification.

Academics. Intensive summer session on introduction to architecture offered to graduates and high school students. **Special study options:** Accelerated study, exchange student, independent study, internships, study abroad. **Credit/placement by examination:** CLEP, institutional tests. 27 credit hours maximum toward bachelor's degree. **Support services:** Pre-admission summer program, reduced course load, tutoring.

Majors. Architecture: Architecture.

Computing on campus. 30 workstations in computer center.

Student life. Policies: Informal weekly gathering of entire school sponsored by student government. **Activities:** Film society, literary magazine, student government, student newspaper, Architects, Designers, and Planners for Social Responsibility, American Institute of Architects student affiliation, Women in Architecture.

Student services. Career counseling, personal counseling. **Physically disabled:** Services for speech, hearing impaired.

Contact. E-mail: admissions@sciarc.edu
Phone: (213) 613-2200 ext. 320 Fax: (213) 613-2260
Wenona Kolinco, Admissions Coordinator, Southern California Institute of Architecture, 960 East 3rd Street, Los Angeles, CA 90013

Southern California Institute of Technology

Anaheim, California
www.scit-scu.edu **CB code: 3034**

- For-profit 4-year business and engineering college
- Residential campus in large city
- 350 degree-seeking undergraduates
- Interview required

General. Accredited by ACCSCT. **Degrees:** 87 bachelor's, 79 associate awarded; master's offered. **Calendar:** Quarter, extensive summer session. **Full-time faculty:** 14 total. **Part-time faculty:** 6 total.

Basis for selection. Open admission. Wonderlic required.

Application procedures. Admission: No deadline. $100 fee. Application must be submitted on paper.

Academics. Special study options: Accelerated study, combined bachelor's/graduate degree, cooperative education, ESL, liberal arts/career combination. **Credit/placement by examination:** CLEP. **Support services:** Tutoring.

Majors. Business: Business admin. **Engineering:** Electrical.

Student life. Freshman orientation: Available. Preregistration for classes offered.

Student services. Career counseling, financial aid counseling, placement for graduates.

Contact. E-mail: ssaboury@scit-scu.edu
Phone: (714) 520-5552 Toll-free number: (877) 693-3822
Fax: (714) 520-4520
Soheila Saboury, Admissions Director, Southern California Institute of Technology, 1900 West Crescent, Building A, Anaheim, CA 92801

Stanford University

Stanford, California **CB member**
www.stanford.edu **CB code: 4704**

- Private 4-year university
- Residential campus in small city
- 6,491 degree-seeking undergraduates: 47% women, 10% African American, 24% Asian American, 11% Hispanic American, 2% Native American, 6% international
- 8,177 degree-seeking graduate students
- 12% of applicants admitted
- SAT or ACT with writing, application essay required
- 94% graduate within 6 years; 35% enter graduate study

General. Founded in 1885. Regionally accredited. **Degrees:** 1,790 bachelor's awarded; master's, doctoral, first professional offered. **ROTC:** Army, Navy, Air Force. **Location:** Adjacent to Palo Alto, 29 miles from San Francisco. **Calendar:** Quarter, extensive summer session. **Full-time faculty:** 1,010 total; 92% have terminal degrees, 16% minority, 22% women. **Part-time faculty:** 21 total; 90% have terminal degrees, 5% minority, 19% women. **Class size:** 366% < 20, 14% 20-39, 5% 40-49, 6% 50-99, 5% >100. **Special facilities:** Museum, linear accelerator, 18 libraries, nature preserve, marine research center, Rodin sculpture garden.

Freshman class profile. 20,192 applied, 2,426 admitted, 1,633 enrolled.

Mid 50% test scores			
SAT verbal:	670-770	Rank in top quarter:	97%
SAT math:	690-780	Rank in top tenth:	89%
ACT:	26-31	Return as sophomores:	98%
GPA 3.50 or higher:	99%	Out-of-state:	60%
GPA 3.0-3.49:	1%	Live on campus:	100%
		International:	7%

Basis for selection. School achievement record, test scores, extracurricular activities, teacher and counselor evaluations, and personal qualifications most important. Rigor and variety of academic program very important. Personal qualities also considered. SAT Subject Tests recommended. Arts students may submit supplementary materials for review. Submissions should have previously received significant recognition at a regional, state, national or international level. **Homeschooled:** Statement describing homeschool structure and mission required. Standardized test scores important. Subject tests recommended.

High school preparation. 20 units recommended. Recommended units include English 4, mathematics 4, social studies 2, history 1, science 3 (laboratory 3) and foreign language 3. Recommended that prospective applicants choose and complete the most rigorous course of study available.

2006-2007 Annual costs. Tuition/fees: $32,994. Room/board: $10,367. Books/supplies: $1,260. Personal expenses: $1,815.

2004-2005 Financial aid. All financial aid based on need. 958 full-time freshmen applied for aid; 690 were judged to have need; 683 of these received aid. Average need met was 100%. Average scholarship/grant was $24,631; average loan $2,569. 84% of total undergraduate aid awarded as scholarships/grants, 16% as loans/jobs.

Application procedures. Admission: Closing date 12/15 (postmark date). $75 fee, may be waived for applicants with need. Application may be submitted online. Admission notification 4/1. Admission notification on a rolling basis. Must reply by 5/1. Early action candidates may not apply to other schools under any type of early action, early decision, or early notification program, but can apply under regular admissions time frame. **Financial aid:** Priority date 2/1; no closing date. FAFSA, CSS PROFILE required. Applicants notified on a rolling basis starting 4/3; must reply by 5/1.

Academics. Undergraduate academic offerings stress access to senior faculty from first days on campus through small-group learning experiences and research opportunities. **Special study options:** Distance learning, double major, exchange student, honors, independent study, internships, student-designed major, study abroad, Washington semester. Undergraduate Research Program grants available for students. **Credit/placement by examination:** AP, CLEP, IB, institutional tests. 45 Advanced Placement units allowed. **Support services:** Learning center, pre-admission summer program, study skills assistance, tutoring, writing center.

Majors. Area/ethnic studies: African, African-American, American, Asian-American, East Asian, German, Hispanic-American/Latino/Chicano, Native American, women's. **Biology:** General. **Communications:** General. **Computer sciences:** General, computer science. **Conservation:** Environmental science. **Engineering:** General, chemical, civil, electrical, environmental, materials, materials science, mechanical, petroleum. **Engineering technology:** Industrial management. **English:** British lit, composition. **Foreign languages:** Chinese, classics, comparative lit, French, German, Italian, Japanese, linguistics, Slavic, Spanish. **History:** General. **Interdisciplinary:** Global studies, intercultural, math/computer science, science/society, systems science. **Liberal arts:** Humanities. **Math:** General. **Philosophy/religion:** Philosophy, religion. **Physical sciences:** Chemistry, geology, geophysics, physics. **Psychology:** General. **Public administration:** Policy analysis. **Social sciences:** Anthropology, archaeology, economics, international relations, political science, sociology, urban studies. **Visual/performing arts:** Art, dramatic, studio arts.

Most popular majors. Biology 7%, computer/information sciences 6%, engineering/engineering technologies 15%, interdisciplinary studies 13%, social sciences 25%.

Computing on campus. 1,000 workstations in dormitories, library, computer center, student center. Dormitories wired for high-speed internet access and linked to campus network. Commuter students can connect to campus network. Online course registration, online library, helpline, repair service, student web hosting, wireless network available.

Student life. Freshman orientation: Mandatory, $425 fee. 6-day academically oriented program held in late September. **Housing:** Guaranteed on-campus for all undergraduates. Coed dorms, single-sex dorms, special housing for disabled, apartments, cooperative housing, fraternity/sorority housing available. Academic, cross-cultural, language theme, and ethnic theme housing available. **Activities:** Bands, choral groups, dance, drama, film society, literary magazine, music ensembles, musical theater, radio station, student government, student newspaper, symphony orchestra, TV station, approximately 640 international, political, environmental, religious, ethnic, academic, and recreational student groups.

Athletics. NCAA. **Intercollegiate:** Baseball M, basketball, cross-country, diving, fencing, field hockey W, football (tackle) M, golf, gymnastics, lacrosse W, rowing (crew), sailing, soccer, softball W, squash W, swimming, synchronized swimming W, tennis, track and field, volleyball, water polo, wrestling M. **Intramural:** Archery, badminton, basketball, bowling, football (non-tackle), handball, soccer, softball, table tennis, tennis, triathlon, volleyball. **Team name:** Cardinal.

Student services. Alcohol/substance abuse counseling, campus ministries, career counseling, student employment services, financial aid counseling, health services, legal services, minority student services, on-campus daycare, personal counseling, placement for graduates, women's services. **Physically disabled:** Services for visually, speech, hearing impaired. **Learning disabled:** Comprehensive services available.

Contact. E-mail: admission@stanford.edu
Phone: (650) 723-2091 Fax: (650) 723-6050
Rick Shaw, Dean of Undergraduate Admission and Financial Aid, Stanford University, Bakewell Building, Stanford, CA 94305-3020

Thomas Aquinas College

Santa Paula, California — **CB member**
www.thomasaquinas.edu — **CB code: 4828**

- Private 4-year liberal arts college affiliated with Roman Catholic Church
- Residential campus in large town
- 359 degree-seeking undergraduates: 51% women, 3% Asian American, 7% Hispanic American, 1% Native American, 7% international
- 81% of applicants admitted
- SAT or ACT (ACT writing optional), application essay required
- 85% graduate within 6 years; 20% enter graduate study

General. Founded in 1971. Regionally accredited. Great Books curriculum. **Degrees:** 63 bachelor's awarded. **Location:** 6 miles from Santa Paula, 25 miles from Ventura. **Calendar:** Semester. **Full-time faculty:** 29 total; 62% have terminal degrees, 10% women. **Part-time faculty:** 5 total; 80% have terminal degrees. **Class size:** 98% < 20, 2% 20-39.

Freshman class profile. 196 applied, 159 admitted, 102 enrolled.

Mid 50% test scores		**Rank in top tenth:**	75%
SAT verbal:	630-740	**End year in good standing:**	95%
SAT math:	570-650	**Return as sophomores:**	91%
ACT:	24-29	**Out-of-state:**	66%
GPA 3.50 or higher:	78%	**Live on campus:**	100%
GPA 3.0-3.49:	22%	**International:**	9%
Rank in top quarter:	75%		

Basis for selection. Faculty Admission Committee reviews each applicant for evidence of likely success in all parts of 4-year program. Required essays and 3 letters of reference supplement academic records and test scores. Interview recommended for early admissions applicants and for those whose academic preparation is uncertain. **Homeschooled:** Applicants not homeschooled through formal programs must provide written records of all studies done from grades 9 through 12.

High school preparation. 11 units required; 18 recommended. Required and recommended units include English 4, mathematics 3-4, history 2, science 3, foreign language 2 and academic electives 3.

2006-2007 Annual costs. Tuition/fees: $19,300. Room/board: $6,000. Books/supplies: $450. Personal expenses: $2,088.

2005-2006 Financial aid. All financial aid based on need. 81 full-time freshmen applied for aid; 77 were judged to have need; 77 of these received aid. Average need met was 100%. Average scholarship/grant was $11,949; average loan $2,519. 65% of total undergraduate aid awarded as scholarships/grants, 35% as loans/jobs.

Application procedures. Admission: No deadline. No application fee. Application must be submitted on paper. Admission notification on a rolling basis beginning on or about 10/1. Must reply by May 1 or within 2 week(s) if notified thereafter. **Financial aid:** Closing date 3/2. FAFSA, institutional form required. Applicants notified on a rolling basis starting 1/1; must reply by 5/1 or within 2 week(s) of notification.

Academics. Required study of logic, rhetoric, grammar, mathematics, experimental science, music, philosophy, theology, and humanities. Great Books of the Western World and disciplined round-table discussions used. **Special study options:** "cross-disciplinary" curriculum of liberal education through reading and analyzing the "Great Books," with special emphasis on theology, philosophy, mathematics, laboratory science, and literature. **Credit/placement by examination:** CLEP.

Majors. Liberal arts: Arts/sciences.

Computing on campus. 17 workstations in dormitories, library. Dormitories linked to campus network.

Student life. Freshman orientation: Mandatory. Preregistration for classes offered. 2-day program immediately before classes begin. **Policies:** Freshmen permitted cars on campus. **Housing:** Guaranteed on-campus for all undergraduates. Single-sex dorms, substance-free housing available. Students living with their families may live off campus. **Activities:** Choral groups, dance, drama, literary magazine, music ensembles, musical theater, Legion of Mary, Pro-Life Ministry, Third Order Dominican, Habitat for Humanity.

Athletics. Intramural: Basketball, football (non-tackle) M, football (tackle) M, soccer, softball, table tennis, tennis, volleyball.

Student services. Campus ministries, career counseling, financial aid counseling, health services, personal counseling, placement for graduates.

Contact. E-mail: admissions@thomasaquinas.edu
Phone: (805) 525-4417 Toll-free number: (800) 634-9797
Fax: (805) 525-9342
Jonathan Daly, Director of Admission, Thomas Aquinas College, 10,000 North Ojai Road, Santa Paula, CA 93060-9621

University of California: Berkeley

Berkeley, California — **CB member**
www.berkeley.edu — **CB code: 4833**

- Public 4-year university
- Residential campus in small city
- 23,447 degree-seeking undergraduates: 4% African American, 41% Asian American, 11% Hispanic American, 1% Native American, 3% international
- 10,036 graduate students
- 26% of applicants admitted
- SAT or ACT with writing, SAT Subject Tests, application essay required
- 87% graduate within 6 years

General. Founded in 1868. Regionally accredited. **Degrees:** 6,767 bachelor's awarded; master's, doctoral, first professional offered. **ROTC:** Army, Navy, Air Force. **Location:** 10 miles from San Francisco. **Calendar:** Semester, extensive summer session. **Full-time faculty:** 1,500 total. **Part-time faculty:** 470 total. **Special facilities:** Museums of art, anthropology, archaeology, paleontology and vertebrate zoology; film archive; observatories; science museum and research center for K-12 education; botanical garden; libraries of rare books, Western, and Latin Americana; seismographic station; herbacia; performing arts facilities.

Freshman class profile. 36,967 applied, 9,764 admitted, 4,189 enrolled.

Mid 50% test scores			
SAT verbal:	580-710	**Rank in top tenth:**	99%
SAT math:	620-740	**Out-of-state:**	7%
Rank in top quarter:	100%	**International:**	2%

Basis for selection. Selection based on thorough review of academic performance; likely contribution to the intellectual and cultural vitality of the campus; diversity in personal background and experience; demonstrated qualities in leadership, motivation, concern for others and community; non-academic achievement in the performing arts, athletics or employment; demonstrated interest in the major. All applicants must complete 2 SAT Subject Tests in different subject areas. If Math SAT Subject Test is taken, must be Level 2. Test scores must meet criteria determined by the applicant's residency and high school GPA.

High school preparation. 15 units required; 19 recommended. Required and recommended units include English 4, mathematics 3-4, social studies 2, history 2, science 2-3 (laboratory 2-3), foreign language 2-3 and academic electives 1. 1 visual and performing arts required.

2006-2007 Annual costs. Tuition/fees (projected): $6,558; $25,242 out-of-state. Room/board: $13,074. Books/supplies: $1,326. Personal expenses: $1,388.

2005-2006 Financial aid. Need-based: 3,168 full-time freshmen applied for aid; 1,994 were judged to have need; 1,934 of these received aid. Average need met was 90%. Average scholarship/grant was $12,021; average loan $4,254. 69% of total undergraduate aid awarded as scholarships/grants, 31% as loans/jobs. **Non-need-based:** Awarded to 1,966 full-time undergraduates, including 468 freshmen. Scholarships awarded for academics.

Application procedures. Admission: Closing date 11/30. $60 fee, may be waived for applicants with need. Application may be submitted online. Admission notification 3/31. Must reply by 5/1. Applications accepted 11/01 through 11/30 only. **Financial aid:** Closing date 3/2. FAFSA required. Applicants notified by 4/15.

Academics. All students required to pass one American cultures class. **Special study options:** Accelerated study, cross-registration, distance learning, double major, dual enrollment of high school students, ESL, exchange student, honors, independent study, internships, student-designed major, study abroad, teacher certification program. Freshman seminar, undergraduate research apprenticeship, university research expeditions. **Credit/placement by examination:** AP, CLEP, IB, institutional tests. **Support services:** Learning center, pre-admission summer program, reduced course load, study skills assistance, tutoring.

Majors. Architecture: Architecture, landscape. **Area/ethnic studies:** African-American, American, Asian, Asian-American, Hispanic-American/Latino/Chicano, Latin American, Native American, Near/Middle Eastern, Southeast Asian, women's. **Biology:** General, botany, cellular/molecular, microbiology, toxicology. **Business:** Business admin. **Communications:** Media studies. **Computer sciences:** Computer science. **Conservation:** General, environmental science, environmental studies, forest management, forestry, management/policy. **Engineering:** Biomedical, chemical, civil, electrical, environmental, geological, manufacturing, materials science, mechanical, nuclear, operations research, physics, science. **English:** English lit, speech/rhetoric. **Foreign languages:** Ancient Greek, Celtic, Chinese, classics, comparative lit, Dutch/Flemish, French, German, Italian, Japanese, Latin, linguistics, Scandinavian, Slavic, Spanish. **History:** General. **Interdisciplinary:** Classical/archaeology, cognitive science, nutrition sciences, peace/conflict. **Legal studies:** General. **Math:** General, applied, statistics. **Philosophy/religion:** Philosophy, religion. **Physical sciences:** General, astrophysics, atmospheric science, chemistry, geology, geophysics, oceanography, physics. **Psychology:** General. **Public administration:** Social work. **Social sciences:** Anthropology, economics, geography, political science, sociology, urban studies. **Visual/performing arts:** Art, art history/conservation, dance, dramatic, film/cinema.

Most popular majors. Biology 12%, business/marketing 6%, engineering/engineering technologies 11%, English 6%, interdisciplinary studies 6%, social sciences 21%.

Computing on campus. Dormitories wired for high-speed internet access and linked to campus network. Commuter students can connect to campus network. Online course registration, online library, helpline, repair service available.

Student life. Freshman orientation: Available, $50 fee. Preregistration for classes offered. **Policies:** Freshmen permitted cars on campus. **Housing:** Guaranteed on-campus for freshmen. Coed dorms, single-sex dorms, special housing for disabled, apartments, cooperative housing, fraternity/sorority housing available. $20 deposit, deadline 5/4. **Activities:** Bands, choral groups, dance, drama, film society, literary magazine, music ensembles, musical theater, radio station, student government, student newspaper, symphony orchestra, TV station, Asian American Christian fellowship, black recruitment and retention center, hiking and outdoor society, Americorps, forensics, Chabad, lesbian and gay alliance, Raza recruitment and retention center, College Democrats, College Republicans.

Athletics. NCAA. **Intercollegiate:** Baseball M, basketball, cross-country, diving, field hockey W, football (tackle) M, golf, gymnastics, lacrosse W, rowing (crew), rugby M, soccer, softball W, swimming, tennis, track and field, volleyball W, water polo. **Intramural:** Basketball, bowling, fencing, field hockey M, football (tackle), handball, ice hockey, lacrosse, racquetball, rowing (crew), sailing, skiing, soccer, softball, squash, tennis, volleyball M. **Team name:** Bears.

Student services. Adult student services, alcohol/substance abuse counseling, campus ministries, career counseling, services for economically disadvantaged, student employment services, financial aid counseling, health services, legal services, minority student services, on-campus daycare, personal counseling, placement for graduates, veterans' counselor, women's services. **Physically disabled:** Services for visually, speech, hearing impaired.

Contact. E-mail: ouars@uclink.berkeley.edu
Phone: (510) 642-3175 Fax: (510) 642-7333
Walter Robinson, Director Undergraduate Admission, University of California: Berkeley, 110 Sproul Hall, #5800, Berkeley, CA 94720-5800

University of California: Davis

Davis, California — **CB member**
www.ucdavis.edu — **CB code: 4834**

- Public 4-year university
- Residential campus in small city
- 22,618 degree-seeking undergraduates: 1% part-time, 55% women, 3% African American, 40% Asian American, 11% Hispanic American, 1% Native American, 2% international
- 6,080 degree-seeking graduate students
- 61% of applicants admitted
- SAT or ACT with writing, SAT Subject Tests, application essay required
- 80% graduate within 6 years

General. Founded in 1905. Regionally accredited. **Degrees:** 6,459 bachelor's awarded; master's, doctoral, first professional offered. **ROTC:** Army, Navy, Air Force. **Location:** 72 miles from San Francisco, 15 miles from Sacramento. **Calendar:** Quarter, extensive summer session. **Full-time faculty:** 1,610 total; 98% have terminal degrees, 18% minority, 30% women. **Part-time faculty:** 273 total; 98% have terminal degrees, 19% minority, 41% women. **Class size:** 35% < 20, 31% 20-39, 6% 40-49, 15% 50-99, 12% >100. **Special facilities:** Museums, 150-acre arboretum, equestrian center, craft center, marine laboratory, nuclear laboratory, California Regional Primate Research Center, natural reserves, raptor center.

Freshman class profile. 30,079 applied, 18,264 admitted, 4,381 enrolled.

Mid 50% test scores			
SAT verbal:	500-630	Rank in top quarter:	100%
SAT math:	560-670	Rank in top tenth:	95%
ACT:	21-27	Return as sophomores:	91%
GPA 3.50 or higher:	78%	Out-of-state:	3%
GPA 3.0-3.49:	21%	Live on campus:	81%
GPA 2.0-2.99:	1%	International:	1%

Basis for selection. Scholastic achievement most important, followed by school and community activities, academic interests, special circumstances, special achievements and awards. Two SAT Subject Tests in two different subject areas of student's choice required: history/social science, English literature, mathematics (Level 2), laboratory science or language other than English.

High school preparation. 15 units required; 18 recommended. Required and recommended units include English 4, mathematics 3-4, social studies 2, science 2-3 (laboratory 2-3), foreign language 2-3 and academic electives 1. Social science/history; visual/performing arts required.

2005-2006 Annual costs. Tuition/fees: $7,457; $25,277 out-of-state. Room/board: $10,791. Books/supplies: $1,513. Personal expenses: $2,125.

2005-2006 Financial aid. All financial aid based on need. Average need met was 73%. Average scholarship/grant was $9,655; average loan $4,425. 72% of total undergraduate aid awarded as scholarships/grants, 28% as loans/jobs.

Application procedures. Admission: Closing date 11/30. $60 fee, may be waived for applicants with need. Application may be submitted online. Admission notification 3/15. Must reply by 5/1. **Financial aid:** Priority date 3/2; no closing date. FAFSA required. Applicants notified on a rolling basis starting 3/15.

Academics. Seventy percent of undergraduates participate in full- and part-time internships. **Special study options:** Accelerated study, cross-registration, double major, dual enrollment of high school students, ESL, honors, independent study, internships, student-designed major, study abroad, teacher certification program, Washington semester. **Credit/placement by examination:** AP, CLEP. 10 credit hours maximum toward bachelor's degree. **Support services:** Learning center, pre-admission summer program, reduced course load, remedial instruction, study skills assistance, tutoring, writing center.

Majors. Agriculture: Agronomy, animal sciences, business, economics, food science, international, plant sciences, range science, soil science. **Architecture:** Environmental design, landscape, urban/community planning. **Area/ethnic studies:** African-American, American, Asian-American, East Asian, Hispanic-American/Latino/Chicano, Native American, women's. **Biology:** General, biotechnology, botany, cell/histology, entomology, environmental toxicology, evolutionary, exercise physiology, genetics, microbiology, molecular biochemistry, neurobiology/physiology, zoology. **Computer sciences:** Computer science. **Conservation:** General, environmental studies, fisheries, management/policy, urban forestry, wildlife. **Engineering:** Aerospace, agricultural, biomedical, chemical, civil, computer, electrical, materials, mechanical. **English:** English lit, speech/rhetoric. **Family/consumer sciences:** Clothing/textiles, family studies, food/nutrition. **Foreign languages:** Chinese, classics, comparative lit, French, German, Italian, Japanese, linguistics, Russian, Spanish. **History:** General. **Interdisciplinary:** Classical/archaeology, medieval/Renaissance, nutrition sciences, science/society. **Math:** General, computational, statistics. **Philosophy/religion:** Philosophy, religion. **Physical sciences:** Atmospheric science, chemistry, geology, hydrology, physics. **Psychology:** General. **Social sciences:** Anthropology, economics, international relations, political science, sociology. **Visual/performing arts:** Art history/conservation, design, dramatic, film/cinema, studio arts.

Most popular majors. Agriculture 8%, biology 18%, communications/journalism 6%, engineering/engineering technologies 10%, psychology 8%, social sciences 20%.

Computing on campus. 544 workstations in dormitories, library, computer center. Dormitories wired for high-speed internet access and linked to campus network. Commuter students can connect to campus network. Online course registration, online library, helpline, repair service, wireless network available.

Student life. Freshman orientation: Available, $215 fee. Preregistration for classes offered. Summer advising June-August. **Housing:** Guaranteed on-campus for freshmen. Coed dorms, single-sex dorms, special housing for disabled, apartments, cooperative housing, substance-free housing available. $450 fully refundable deposit, deadline 6/9. Various theme housing available. **Activities:** Bands, choral groups, dance, drama, film society, literary magazine, music ensembles, musical theater, radio station, student government, student newspaper, symphony orchestra, TV station, 316 student organizations.

Athletics. NCAA. **Intercollegiate:** Baseball M, basketball, cross-country, diving, football (tackle) M, golf, gymnastics W, lacrosse, rowing (crew) W, soccer, softball W, swimming, tennis, track and field, volleyball, water polo, wrestling M. **Intramural:** Badminton, basketball, bowling, golf, racquetball, soccer, softball, squash, table tennis, tennis, volleyball, water polo. **Team name:** Aggies.

Student services. Adult student services, alcohol/substance abuse counseling, campus ministries, career counseling, services for economically disadvantaged, student employment services, financial aid counseling, health services, legal services, minority student services, on-campus daycare, personal counseling, placement for graduates, veterans' counselor, women's services. **Physically disabled:** Services for visually, speech, hearing impaired. **Learning disabled:** Comprehensive services available.

Contact. E-mail: undergraduateadmissions@ucdavis.edu
Phone: (530) 752-2971 Fax: (530) 752-1280
Pamela Burnett, Director of Undergraduate Admissions, University of California: Davis, 178 Mrak Hall, Davis, CA 95616

University of California: Irvine

Irvine, California — **CB member**
www.uci.edu — **CB code: 4859**

- Public 4-year university
- Residential campus in small city
- 19,930 degree-seeking undergraduates: 3% part-time, 51% women, 2% African American, 49% Asian American, 12% Hispanic American, 2% international
- 4,301 degree-seeking graduate students
- 60% of applicants admitted
- SAT and SAT Subject Tests or ACT with writing, application essay required
- 80% graduate within 6 years

General. Founded in 1965. Regionally accredited. **Degrees:** 5,242 bachelor's awarded; master's, doctoral, first professional offered. **ROTC:** Army, Air Force. **Location:** 40 miles from Los Angeles. **Calendar:** Quarter, extensive summer session. **Full-time faculty:** 966 total; 98% have terminal degrees, 26% minority, 30% women. **Part-time faculty:** 304 total; 98% have terminal degrees, 17% minority, 49% women. **Class size:** 34% < 20, 31% 20-39, 5% 40-49, 14% 50-99, 16% >100. **Special facilities:** Outdoor laboratory, ecological preserve, freshwater marsh reserve, fine arts museum, arboretum, center for art and technology, observatory.

Freshman class profile. 34,531 applied, 20,825 admitted, 4,338 enrolled.

Mid 50% test scores			
SAT verbal:	540-630	Return as sophomores:	93%
SAT math:	570-680	Out-of-state:	3%
GPA 3.50 or higher:	81%	Live on campus:	82%
GPA 3.0-3.49:	19%	International:	1%
Rank in top quarter:	100%	Fraternities:	5%
Rank in top tenth:	96%	Sororities:	7%

Basis for selection. Demonstrated record of academic excellence and test scores important. Two SAT Subject Tests required: math and student's choice.

High school preparation. 15 units required; 18 recommended. Required and recommended units include English 4, mathematics 3-4, history 2, science 2-3 (laboratory 2-3), foreign language 2-3 and academic electives 1. One unit visual/performing arts required.

2005-2006 Annual costs. Tuition/fees: $6,770; $24,590 out-of-state. Room/board: $9,202. Books/supplies: $1,593. Personal expenses: $1,584.

2004-2005 Financial aid. **Need-based:** 2,745 full-time freshmen applied for aid; 1,833 were judged to have need; 1,691 of these received aid. Average need met was 85%. Average scholarship/grant was $9,236; average loan $5,130. 69% of total undergraduate aid awarded as scholarships/grants, 31% as loans/jobs. **Non-need-based:** Awarded to 1,107 full-time undergraduates, including 210 freshmen. Scholarships awarded for academics, athletics, state residency.

Application procedures. **Admission:** Closing date 11/30. $60 fee, may be waived for applicants with need. Application must be submitted online. Admission notification 3/31. Must reply by 5/1. **Financial aid:** Closing date 3/1. FAFSA required. Applicants notified by 4/1; must reply by 5/1.

Academics. **Special study options:** Combined bachelor's/graduate degree, distance learning, double major, ESL, honors, independent study, internships, study abroad, teacher certification program, Washington semester. **Credit/placement by examination:** AP, CLEP, IB, institutional tests. **Support services:** Learning center, pre-admission summer program, reduced course load, remedial instruction, study skills assistance, tutoring, writing center.

Majors. **Architecture:** Environmental design. **Area/ethnic studies:** African-American, Asian-American, East Asian, European, German, Hispanic-American/Latino/Chicano, women's. **Biology:** General, Biochemistry/biophysics and molecular biology, botany, cell/histology, ecology, genetics. **Communications:** Journalism. **Computer sciences:** General, computer science, information systems. **Engineering:** General, aerospace, biomedical, chemical, civil, computer, electrical, environmental, materials, mechanical. **English:** English lit. **Foreign languages:** Chinese, classics, comparative lit, French, German, Japanese, linguistics, Russian, Spanish. **History:** General. **Interdisciplinary:** Classical/archaeology, global studies, neuroscience. **Liberal arts:** Humanities. **Math:** General. **Philosophy/religion:** Philosophy. **Physical sciences:** Chemistry, geology, physics. **Psychology:** General. **Social sciences:** General, anthropology, criminology, economics, political science, sociology. **Visual/performing arts:** Art, art history/conservation, dance, dramatic, film/cinema, music performance, studio arts.

Most popular majors. Biology 13%, computer/information sciences 9%, engineering/engineering technologies 8%, interdisciplinary studies 9%, psychology 11%, social sciences 28%, visual/performing arts 7%.

Computing on campus. 1,500 workstations in dormitories, library, computer center, student center. Dormitories wired for high-speed internet access and linked to campus network. Commuter students can connect to campus network. Online course registration, online library, helpline, repair service, student web hosting, wireless network available.

Student life. **Freshman orientation:** Available. Held during summer, one day or 3 day programs. **Policies:** Freshmen permitted cars on campus. **Housing:** Guaranteed on-campus for freshmen. Coed dorms, single-sex dorms, special housing for disabled, apartments, cooperative housing, fraternity/sorority housing, substance-free housing available. $250 partly refundable deposit, deadline 5/1. Academic themed houses. **Activities:** Bands, choral groups, dance, drama, film society, literary magazine, music ensembles, musical theater, opera, radio station, student government, student newspaper, symphony orchestra.

Athletics. NCAA. **Intercollegiate:** Baseball M, basketball, cheerleading, cross-country, diving, golf, rowing (crew), sailing, soccer, swimming, tennis, track and field, volleyball, water polo. **Intramural:** Badminton, basketball, bowling, football (non-tackle), golf, racquetball, soccer, softball, swimming, table tennis, tennis, track and field, volleyball, water polo, wrestling. **Team name:** Anteaters.

Student services. Adult student services, alcohol/substance abuse counseling, campus ministries, career counseling, services for economically disadvantaged, student employment services, financial aid counseling, health services, legal services, minority student services, on-campus daycare, personal counseling, placement for graduates, veterans' counselor, women's services. **Physically disabled:** Services for visually, speech, hearing impaired. **Learning disabled:** Comprehensive services available.

Contact. E-mail: admissions@uci.edu
Phone: (949) 824-6703 Fax: (949) 824-2711
Marguerite Bonous-Hammarth, Director of Admissions, University of California: Irvine, 204 Administration Building, Irvine, CA 92697-1075

University of California: Los Angeles

Los Angeles, California — **CB member**
www.ucla.edu — **CB code: 4837**

- Public 4-year university
- Commuter campus in very large city
- 24,811 degree-seeking undergraduates: 4% part-time, 56% women, 3% African American, 38% Asian American, 15% Hispanic American, 4% international
- 10,814 degree-seeking graduate students
- 27% of applicants admitted
- SAT or ACT with writing, SAT Subject Tests, application essay required
- 87% graduate within 6 years

General. Founded in 1919. Regionally accredited. **Degrees:** 7,336 bachelor's awarded; master's, doctoral, first professional offered. **ROTC:** Army, Navy, Air Force. **Calendar:** Quarter, extensive summer session. **Full-time faculty:** 1,859 total; 98% have terminal degrees, 22% minority, 30% women. **Part-time faculty:** 601 total; 98% have terminal degrees, 27% minority, 38% women. **Class size:** 51% <20, 23% 20-39, 4% 40-49, 10% 50-99, 11% >100. **Special facilities:** Museums with specialized collections, centers for cancer research, plasma physics research labs, film and television archive, high power auroral simulation observatory, lab for embedded collaborative systems, research centers for molecular and neuroscience, graphic and animation labs, nanoscience research labs and centers, cell mimetic space exploration center, particle beam physics lab, southern California particle center, ranch for ecological studies, ethnomusicology archive.

Freshman class profile. 42,208 applied, 11,360 admitted, 4,422 enrolled.

Mid 50% test scores			
SAT verbal:	570-690	Rank in top quarter:	100%
SAT math:	600-720	Rank in top tenth:	97%
ACT:	24-30	Return as sophomores:	97%
GPA 3.50 or higher:	97%	Out-of-state:	4%
GPA 3.0-3.49:	2%	Live on campus:	92%
GPA 2.0-2.99:	1%	International:	2%

Basis for selection. GPA, test scores, course work, number of and performance in honors and AP courses most important. Essay considered. Strong senior program important. Extracurricular activities, honors and awards also reviewed. All applicants must take 2 SAT Subject Tests in different subject areas. If Math SAT Subject Test is taken, must be Level 2. Audition required of music, dance, theater majors. Portfolio required of art majors.

High school preparation. 15 units required; 18 recommended. Required and recommended units include English 4, mathematics 3-4, history 2, science 2-3 (laboratory 2-3), foreign language 2-3 and academic electives 1. 1 visual arts and performing arts required.

2005-2006 Annual costs. Tuition/fees: $6,504; $24,324 out-of-state. Room/board: $11,928. Books/supplies: $1,483. Personal expenses: $2,075.

2005-2006 Financial aid. **Need-based:** 2,371 full-time freshmen applied for aid; 1,842 were judged to have need; 1,824 of these received aid. Average need met was 86%. Average scholarship/grant was $11,316; average loan $4,402. 70% of total undergraduate aid awarded as scholarships/grants, 30% as loans/jobs. **Non-need-based:** Awarded to 1,634 full-time undergraduates, including 355 freshmen. Scholarships awarded for academics, athletics, ROTC.

Application procedures. **Admission:** Closing date 11/30 (postmark date). $60 fee, may be waived for applicants with need. Application may be submitted online. Admission notification on a rolling basis beginning on or about 3/15. Must reply by May 1 or within 3 week(s) if notified thereafter. **Financial aid:** Priority date 3/2; no closing date. FAFSA required. Applicants notified on a rolling basis starting 3/15; must reply within 3 week(s) of notification.

Academics. **Special study options:** Cross-registration, distance learning, double major, dual enrollment of high school students, ESL, exchange student, honors, independent study, internships, liberal arts/career combination, student-designed major, study abroad, teacher certification program, Washington semester. **Credit/placement by examination:** AP, CLEP, IB, SAT, institutional tests. **Support services:** Learning center, tutoring, writing center.

Majors. **Area/ethnic studies:** African-American, Asian, Asian-American, East Asian, European, Hispanic-American/Latino/Chicano, Latin American, Native American, Near/Middle Eastern, Russian/Slavic, Southeast Asian, women's. **Biology:** General, bacteriology, biochemistry, biophysics, biotechnology, botany, cellular/molecular, ecology, evolutionary, marine, molecular biochemistry, molecular genetics, physiology. **Business:** Managerial economics. **Computer sciences:** General. **Engineering:** Aerospace, agricultural, chemical, civil, computer, electrical, geological, manufacturing, materials, mechanical. **English:** American lit, English lit. **Foreign languages:** African, ancient Greek, Arabic, Chinese, comparative lit, East Asian, French, German, Hebrew, Italian, Japanese, Korean, Latin, linguistics, Portuguese,

Russian, Scandinavian, Slavic, Spanish. **History:** General. **Interdisciplinary:** Classical/archaeology, cognitive science, global studies, neuroscience. **Liberal arts:** Arts/sciences. **Math:** General, applied, computational, statistics. **Philosophy/religion:** Judaic, philosophy, religion. **Physical sciences:** Astrophysics, atmospheric science, chemistry, geochemistry, geology, geophysics, physics. **Psychology:** General. **Social sciences:** Anthropology, economics, geography, international economic development, international economics, political science, sociology. **Visual/performing arts:** Art, art history/conservation, design, dramatic, film/cinema, music history, musicology.

Most popular majors. Biology 11%, engineering/engineering technologies 8%, English 6%, history 7%, psychology 13%, social sciences 27%, visual/performing arts 6%.

Computing on campus. Dormitories wired for high-speed internet access and linked to campus network. Commuter students can connect to campus network. Online course registration, helpline, student web hosting, wireless network available.

Student life. Freshman orientation: Available, $340 fee. Preregistration for classes offered. 3-day, 2-night program. **Policies:** Freshmen permitted cars on campus. **Housing:** Guaranteed on-campus for freshmen. Coed dorms, special housing for disabled, apartments, cooperative housing, fraternity/sorority housing available. **Activities:** Bands, choral groups, dance, drama, film society, literary magazine, music ensembles, musical theater, opera, radio station, student government, student newspaper, symphony orchestra, TV station.

Athletics. NCAA. **Intercollegiate:** Baseball M, basketball, cross-country, diving W, football (tackle) M, golf, gymnastics W, rowing (crew) W, soccer, softball W, swimming W, tennis, track and field, volleyball, water polo. **Intramural:** Badminton, basketball, cross-country, field hockey W, golf, gymnastics, ice hockey, lacrosse, rowing (crew), rugby, sailing, skiing, soccer, softball, squash, swimming, table tennis, tennis, track and field, volleyball, water polo. **Team name:** Bruins.

Student services. Alcohol/substance abuse counseling, career counseling, student employment services, financial aid counseling, health services, legal services, on-campus daycare, personal counseling, placement for graduates, veterans' counselor, women's services. **Physically disabled:** Services for visually, hearing impaired.

Contact. E-mail: ugadm@saonet.ucla.edu
Phone: (310) 825-3101 Fax: (310) 206-1206
Vu Tran, Director of Undergraduate Admissions and Relations with Schools, University of California: Los Angeles, 1147 Murphy Hall, Los Angeles, CA 90095-1436

University of California: Merced

Merced, California
www.ucmerced.edu **CB code: 4129**

- Public 4-year university
- Residential campus in small city
- 835 degree-seeking undergraduates: 51% women, 6% African American, 38% Asian American, 25% Hispanic American, 1% Native American
- 24 graduate students
- 86% of applicants admitted
- SAT or ACT with writing, SAT Subject Tests, application essay required

General. Location: 120 miles from San Francisco, 60 miles from Fresno. **Calendar:** Semester, limited summer session. **Full-time faculty:** 64 total; 98% have terminal degrees, 23% minority, 44% women. **Part-time faculty:** 15 total; 100% have terminal degrees, 13% minority, 20% women. **Class size:** 44% < 20, 53% 20-39, 2% 40-49, less than 1% 50-99, less than 1% >100. **Special facilities:** Research institute, world culture institute, research station at Yosemite National Park.

Freshman class profile. 14,052 applied, 12,143 admitted, 705 enrolled.

Mid 50% test scores			
SAT verbal:	460-590	GPA 3.50 or higher:	39%
SAT math:	480-610	GPA 3.0-3.49:	50%
ACT:	18-23	GPA 2.0-2.99:	10%
		Live on campus:	79%

Basis for selection. Academic record and test scores determine eligibility. **Homeschooled:** If school is not accredited by a regional association, student must meet eligibility by examination alone.

High school preparation. 15 units required; 18 recommended. Required and recommended units include English 4, mathematics 3-4, social studies 1, history 1, science 2-3 (laboratory 2-3), foreign language 2-3 and academic electives 1. 1 unit approved visual and performing arts.

2005-2006 Annual costs. Tuition/fees: $6,653; $24,473 out-of-state. Room/board: $9,112. Books/supplies: $1,444. Personal expenses: $1,355.

Financial aid. Non-need-based: Scholarships awarded for academics.

Application procedures. Admission: Closing date 11/30 (postmark date). $60 fee, may be waived for applicants with need. Application may be submitted online. Admission notification 3/31. Must reply by May 1 or within 3 week(s) if notified thereafter. **Financial aid:** Priority date 3/2; no closing date. FAFSA required. Applicants notified by 4/1; must reply by 5/1.

Academics. Special study options: Cross-registration, double major, internships, study abroad, Washington semester. Research opportunities and internships at Lawrence Livermore National Laboratories and Yosemite National Park. **Credit/placement by examination:** AP, CLEP, IB, institutional tests. Credit by examination with the approval of the instructor giving the examination and the dean of the school involved. Some courses may not be deemed appropriate for obtaining credit by examination. **Support services:** Learning center, study skills assistance, tutoring, writing center.

Majors. Biology: General. **Engineering:** Biomedical, computer, environmental, mechanical. **Interdisciplinary:** Cognitive science, intercultural. **Physical sciences:** Chemistry, geology, physics.

Computing on campus. Dormitories wired for high-speed internet access and linked to campus network. Commuter students can connect to campus network. Online course registration, online library, helpline, wireless network available.

Student life. Freshman orientation: Available, $49 fee. Preregistration for classes offered. **Policies:** Freshmen permitted cars on campus. **Housing:** Coed dorms, special housing for disabled, substance-free housing available. $300 partly refundable deposit, deadline 5/6. **Activities:** Marching band, choral groups, dance, film society, radio station, student government, student newspaper, African American student union, liberal activism club, student government advisory committee, Latino students alliance, Filipino student alliance, Circle K International, American Red Cross club, Jewish student union.

Athletics. Intramural: Basketball, football (non-tackle), racquetball, soccer, softball, tennis, volleyball. **Team name:** Golden Bobcats.

Student services. Alcohol/substance abuse counseling, career counseling, services for economically disadvantaged, student employment services, financial aid counseling, health services, minority student services, personal counseling, veterans' counselor, women's services. **Physically disabled:** Services for visually, hearing impaired. **Learning disabled:** Comprehensive services available.

Contact. E-mail: admissions@ucmerced.edu
Phone: (209) 381-7880 Toll-free number: (866) 270-7301
Encarnacion Ruiz, Director, Admissions and Relations with Schools & Colleges, University of California: Merced, PO Box 2039, Merced, CA 95344

University of California: Riverside

Riverside, California **CB member**
www.ucr.edu **CB code: 4839**

- Public 4-year university
- Residential campus in large city
- 14,555 degree-seeking undergraduates: 3% part-time, 53% women, 7% African American, 42% Asian American, 24% Hispanic American, 2% international
- 1,973 degree-seeking graduate students
- 76% of applicants admitted
- SAT or ACT with writing, SAT Subject Tests, application essay required
- 65% graduate within 6 years

General. Founded in 1954. Regionally accredited. **Degrees:** 3,080 bachelor's awarded; master's, doctoral offered. **ROTC:** Army, Air Force. **Location:** 60 miles from Los Angeles. **Calendar:** Quarter, limited summer session. **Full-time faculty:** 709 total; 98% have terminal degrees, 27% minority, 34% women. **Part-time faculty:** 140 total; 99% have terminal degrees, 18% minority, 26% women. **Class size:** 33% < 20, 41% 20-39, 3% 40-49, 11% 50-99, 11% >100. **Special facilities:** Botanical gardens, air pollution research center, photography museum, 8 nature preserves, citrus research center and agricultural experiment station, institute of geophysics and planetary physics, water resources center, salinity lab.

Freshman class profile. 19,060 applied, 14,474 admitted, 2,988 enrolled.

Mid 50% test scores			
SAT verbal:	460-570	GPA 2.0-2.99:	5%
SAT math:	490-630	Rank in top quarter:	100%
ACT:	18-23	Rank in top tenth:	94%
GPA 3.50 or higher:	45%	Return as sophomores:	86%
GPA 3.0-3.49:	50%	Live on campus:	76%
		International:	2%

Basis for selection. Secondary school record, standardized test scores, and essay important. SAT Subject Tests required from 2 different subject areas. Math Subject Test must be Level 2. Portfolio required for art (studio) major. **Homeschooled:** Portfolio describing subjects studied and methods of study required.

High school preparation. 15 units required; 18 recommended. Required and recommended units include English 4, mathematics 3-4, history 2, science 2-3 (laboratory 2-3), foreign language 2-3 and academic electives 2. One year of elective units from 1 of the following: visual/performing arts (non-introductory), history, English, advanced mathematics, laboratory science, foreign language, social science, arts. 2 social science units must include 1 U.S. history or .5 history and .5 civics, and 1 world history, cultures, or geography.

2005-2006 Annual costs. Tuition/fees: $6,590; $24,410 out-of-state. Room/board: $10,200. Books/supplies: $1,650. Personal expenses: $1,650.

2005-2006 Financial aid. Need-based: 2,411 full-time freshmen applied for aid; 1,890 were judged to have need; 1,829 of these received aid. Average need met was 89%. Average scholarship/grant was $11,013; average loan $4,596. 69% of total undergraduate aid awarded as scholarships/grants, 31% as loans/jobs. **Non-need-based:** Awarded to 340 full-time undergraduates, including 149 freshmen. Scholarships awarded for academics, art, athletics, leadership, music/drama.

Application procedures. Admission: Closing date 11/30 (postmark date). $60 fee, may be waived for applicants with need. Application may be submitted online. Admission notification on a rolling basis beginning on or about 3/1. Must reply by May 1 or within 3 week(s) if notified thereafter. **Financial aid:** Closing date 3/2. FAFSA required. Applicants notified on a rolling basis starting 3/1; must reply by 5/1 or within 3 week(s) of notification.

Academics. Special study options: Accelerated study, cooperative education, cross-registration, double major, dual enrollment of high school students, ESL, honors, independent study, internships, liberal arts/career combination, student-designed major, study abroad, teacher certification program, Washington semester. **Credit/placement by examination:** AP, CLEP, IB, SAT, ACT, institutional tests. **Support services:** Learning center, preadmission summer program, reduced course load, remedial instruction, study skills assistance, tutoring, writing center.

Majors. Area/ethnic studies: African-American, Asian, Asian-American, German, Hispanic-American/Latino/Chicano, Latin American, Native American, Russian/Slavic, women's. **Biology:** General, biochemistry, botany, entomology. **Business:** Business admin, managerial economics. **Computer sciences:** Computer science, information systems. **Conservation:** Environmental science. **Engineering:** General, biomedical, chemical, computer, electrical, environmental, mechanical. **English:** Creative writing, English lit. **Foreign languages:** General, classics, comparative lit, French, German, linguistics, Russian, Spanish. **Health:** Premedicine. **History:** General. **Interdisciplinary:** Ancient studies, neuroscience. **Legal studies:** General. **Liberal arts:** Arts/sciences, humanities. **Math:** General, applied, statistics. **Philosophy/religion:** Philosophy, religion. **Physical sciences:** General, chemistry, geology, geophysics, physics. **Psychology:** General. **Public administration:** General. **Social sciences:** Anthropology, economics, geography, international relations, political science, sociology. **Visual/performing arts:** Art, art history/conservation, dance, dramatic, film/cinema, studio arts.

Most popular majors. Biology 12%, business/marketing 26%, liberal arts 8%, psychology 9%, social sciences 18%.

Computing on campus. 1,001 workstations in dormitories, library, computer center, student center. Dormitories wired for high-speed internet access and linked to campus network. Commuter students can connect to campus network. Online course registration, online library, helpline, repair service, student web hosting, wireless network available.

Student life. Freshman orientation: Available. 2-day or 1-day summer programs. **Policies:** Freshmen permitted cars on campus. **Housing:** Guaranteed on-campus for freshmen. Coed dorms, special housing for disabled, apartments available. $250 fully refundable deposit, deadline 6/1. Theme hall communities available. **Activities:** Bands, choral groups, dance, drama, film society, literary magazine, music ensembles, musical theater, radio station, student government, student newspaper, 250 clubs and organizations available.

Athletics. NCAA. **Intercollegiate:** Baseball M, basketball, cross-country, golf, soccer, softball W, tennis, track and field, volleyball W. **Intramural:** Badminton, basketball, bowling, football (non-tackle), golf, racquetball, soccer, softball, squash, table tennis, tennis, volleyball. **Team name:** Highlanders.

Student services. Adult student services, alcohol/substance abuse counseling, career counseling, student employment services, financial aid counseling, health services, minority student services, on-campus daycare, personal counseling, placement for graduates, veterans' counselor, women's services. **Physically disabled:** Services for visually, speech, hearing impaired.

Contact. E-mail: discover@ucr.edu
Phone: (951) 827-3411 Fax: (951) 827-6344
LaRae Lundgren, Director of Undergraduate Admissions, University of California: Riverside, 1120 Hinderaker Hall, Riverside, CA 92521

University of California: San Diego

La Jolla, California — **CB member**
www.ucsd.edu — **CB code: 4836**

- Public 4-year university
- Residential campus in large town
- 20,339 degree-seeking undergraduates: 1% part-time, 52% women, 1% African American, 38% Asian American, 10% Hispanic American, 3% international
- 4,324 degree-seeking graduate students
- 42% of applicants admitted
- SAT or ACT with writing, SAT Subject Tests, application essay required
- 78% graduate within 6 years

General. Founded in 1959. Regionally accredited. Includes 6 small undergraduate cluster colleges, each with housing and different general education requirements. **Degrees:** 4,136 bachelor's awarded; master's, doctoral, first professional offered. **ROTC:** Army, Navy, Air Force. **Location:** 12 miles from San Diego. **Calendar:** Quarter, extensive summer session. **Full-time faculty:** 965 total; 98% have terminal degrees, 18% minority, 24% women. **Part-time faculty:** 184 total; 98% have terminal degrees, 16% minority, 43% women. **Class size:** 47% < 20, 21% 20-39, 5% 40-49, 10% 50-99, 18% >100. **Special facilities:** Aquarium-museum, performing arts center, student-run co-ops, supercomputer center, nature preserves, electron beam lithography facility, art gallery, center for music experiment, structural engineering lab.

Freshman class profile. 41,330 applied, 17,269 admitted, 3,874 enrolled.

Mid 50% test scores			
SAT verbal:	540-660	Return as sophomores:	93%
SAT math:	590-700	Out-of-state:	3%
ACT:	23-29	Live on campus:	95%
GPA 3.50 or higher:	100%	International:	2%
Rank in top quarter:	100%	Fraternities:	10%
Rank in top tenth:	99%	Sororities:	10%

Basis for selection. High school course pattern, GPA, essay and test scores most important. Admission for out-of-state applicants more selective than for residents. All applicants must take 2 SAT Subject Tests in different subject areas. If Math SAT Subject Test is taken, must be Level 2. Interview recommended for music, visual arts, theater majors. Audition recommended for music majors. Portfolio recommended for art majors.

High school preparation. 15 units required. Required and recommended units include English 4, mathematics 3-4, history 2, science 2-3 (laboratory 2-3), foreign language 2-3 and academic electives 1. One unit of visual and performing arts.

2005-2006 Annual costs. Tuition/fees: $6,681; $24,501 out-of-state. Room/board: $9,421. Books/supplies: $1,275. Personal expenses: $1,894.

2005-2006 Financial aid. Need-based: 61% of total undergraduate aid awarded as scholarships/grants, 39% as loans/jobs. **Non-need-based:** Scholarships awarded for academics, art, leadership, music/drama.

Application procedures. Admission: Closing date 11/30 (receipt date). $60 fee, may be waived for applicants with need. Application must be submitted online. Admission notification 3/31. Must reply by 5/1. **Financial aid:** Priority date 3/2, closing date 6/1. FAFSA required. Applicants notified on a rolling basis starting 3/15; must reply within 3 week(s) of notification.

Academics. **Special study options:** Cooperative education, cross-registration, double major, ESL, exchange student, honors, independent study, internships, liberal arts/career combination, semester at sea, student-designed major, study abroad, teacher certification program, Washington semester. In-depth academic assignments working in small groups or one-to-one with faculty; research programs. **Credit/placement by examination:** AP, CLEP, IB, institutional tests. **Support services:** Learning center, pre-admission summer program, reduced course load, study skills assistance, tutoring, writing center.

Majors. **Architecture:** Urban/community planning. **Area/ethnic studies:** Chinese, German, Italian, Japanese, Latin American, Russian/Slavic, women's. **Biology:** General, animal physiology, bacteriology, biochemistry, bioinformatics, biophysics, biotechnology, cell/histology, ecology, evolutionary, molecular. **Business:** Management science. **Communications:** General, digital media. **Computer sciences:** General, computer science, information systems, systems analysis. **Conservation:** Environmental science, environmental studies. **Engineering:** Aerospace, biomedical, chemical, computer, electrical, mechanical, mechanics, physics, science, structural, systems. **Engineering technology:** Aerospace. **English:** American lit, British lit, composition, English lit. **Family/consumer sciences:** Family studies. **Foreign languages:** General, classics, French, German, Italian, Japanese, linguistics, Russian, Spanish. **History:** General. **Interdisciplinary:** Behavioral sciences, cognitive science, math/computer science, neuroscience. **Math:** General, applied. **Philosophy/religion:** Judaic, philosophy, religion. **Physical sciences:** Chemical physics, chemistry, molecular physics, physics, planetary. **Psychology:** General. **Public administration:** Policy analysis. **Social sciences:** Anthropology, archaeology, economics, political science, sociology, U.S. government, urban studies. **Visual/performing arts:** Art history/conservation, dance, dramatic, studio arts.

Most popular majors. Biology 16%, communications/journalism 9%, computer/information sciences 6%, psychology 8%, social sciences 37%, visual/performing arts 7%.

Computing on campus. 1,500 workstations in library, computer center, student center. Dormitories wired for high-speed internet access and linked to campus network. Commuter students can connect to campus network. Online course registration, online library, helpline, student web hosting, wireless network available.

Student life. **Freshman orientation:** Mandatory, $125 fee. Preregistration for classes offered. One- to 2-day program for freshmen and transfers. **Policies:** Freshmen permitted cars on campus. **Housing:** Guaranteed on-campus for freshmen. Coed dorms, special housing for disabled, apartments available. Language, cultural interest and international houses available. **Activities:** Bands, choral groups, dance, drama, film society, literary magazine, music ensembles, musical theater, radio station, student government, student newspaper, TV station, 450 student organizations.

Athletics. NCAA. **Intercollegiate:** Baseball M, basketball, cheerleading, cross-country, diving, fencing, golf, rowing (crew), soccer, softball W, swimming, tennis, track and field, volleyball, water polo. **Intramural:** Badminton, basketball, equestrian, ice hockey, judo, lacrosse M, rugby, sailing, skiing, softball. **Team name:** Tritons.

Student services. Adult student services, alcohol/substance abuse counseling, campus ministries, career counseling, services for economically disadvantaged, student employment services, financial aid counseling, health services, legal services, minority student services, on-campus daycare, personal counseling, placement for graduates, veterans' counselor, women's services. **Physically disabled:** Services for visually, speech, hearing impaired. **Learning disabled:** Comprehensive services available.

Contact. E-mail: admissionsinfo@ucsd.edu
Phone: (858) 534-4831 Fax: (858) 534-5723
Mae Brown, Assistant Vice Chancellor, Admissions & Enrollment Services, University of California: San Diego, 9500 Gilman Drive, 0021, La Jolla, CA 92093-0021

University of California: Santa Barbara

Santa Barbara, California — **CB member**
www.ucsb.edu — **CB code: 4835**

- Public 4-year university
- Residential campus in small city
- 18,058 degree-seeking undergraduates: 3% part-time, 55% women
- 2,939 degree-seeking graduate students
- 53% of applicants admitted
- SAT or ACT with writing, SAT Subject Tests, application essay required

General. Founded in 1909. Regionally accredited. **Degrees:** 5,267 bachelor's awarded; master's, doctoral offered. **ROTC:** Army. **Location:** 10 miles from downtown, 100 miles from Los Angeles. **Calendar:** Quarter, extensive summer session. **Full-time faculty:** 919 total; 16% minority, 30% women. **Part-time faculty:** 135 total; 10% minority, 44% women. **Class size:** 50% < 20, 28% 20-39, 4% 40-49, 9% 50-99, 9% >100. **Special facilities:** Art museum; several nature preserves with research facilities; seawater laboratories; robotics laboratory; free electron laser laboratory; institutes for: polymers and organic solids, neuroscience research, quantum, nuclear particle astrophysics and cosmology, marine science, theoretical physics.

Freshman class profile. 37,451 applied, 19,798 admitted, 3,829 enrolled.

Mid 50% test scores			
SAT verbal:	530-650	Out-of-state:	2%
SAT math:	560-670	Live on campus:	64%
ACT:	22-28	International:	1%

Basis for selection. Eligibility established by high school GPA, course requirement, and SAT scores. Special consideration for disadvantaged students. All applicants must take 2 SAT Subject Tests in different subject areas. If Math SAT Subject Test is taken, must be Level 2. Audition required of music, dance, drama majors. Portfolio required of art majors.

High school preparation. Required and recommended units include English 4, mathematics 3-4, social studies 2, science 2-3 (laboratory 2-3), foreign language 2-3 and academic electives 2. One social science unit should be US history.

2005-2006 Annual costs. Tuition/fees: $6,993; $24,813 out-of-state. Room/board: $10,577.

2004-2005 Financial aid. **Need-based:** 2,846 full-time freshmen applied for aid; 2,002 were judged to have need; 1,782 of these received aid. Average need met was 83%. Average scholarship/grant was $10,641; average loan $5,621. 64% of total undergraduate aid awarded as scholarships/grants, 36% as loans/jobs. **Non-need-based:** Awarded to 670 full-time undergraduates, including 146 freshmen.

Application procedures. **Admission:** Closing date 11/30 (postmark date). $40 fee, may be waived for applicants with need. Application may be submitted online. Admission notification on a rolling basis beginning on or about 3/1. Must reply by 5/1. **Financial aid:** Priority date 3/2, closing date 5/31. FAFSA required. Applicants notified on a rolling basis starting 3/15; must reply within 2 week(s) of notification.

Academics. **Special study options:** Accelerated study, cross-registration, distance learning, double major, dual enrollment of high school students, ESL, exchange student, honors, independent study, internships, student-designed major, study abroad, teacher certification program, Washington semester. **Credit/placement by examination:** AP, CLEP, institutional tests. **Support services:** Learning center, pre-admission summer program, reduced course load, tutoring.

Majors. **Area/ethnic studies:** African-American, Asian, Hispanic-American/Latino/Chicano, Latin American, women's. **Biology:** General, aquatic, bacteriology, biochemistry, cell/histology, ecology, marine, molecular, pharmacology, zoology. **Business:** Managerial economics. **Communications:** General. **Computer sciences:** General. **Conservation:** General, environmental studies. **Engineering:** General, chemical, electrical, mechanical. **Foreign languages:** Chinese, classics, comparative lit, French, German, Italian, Japanese, linguistics, Portuguese, Russian, Slavic, Spanish. **Health:** Audiology/speech pathology. **History:** General. **Interdisciplinary:** Biological/physical sciences, biopsychology, global studies, medieval/Renaissance. **Legal studies:** General. **Math:** General, statistics. **Philosophy/religion:** Philosophy, religion. **Physical sciences:** Chemistry, geology, geophysics, physics. **Psychology:** General. **Social sciences:** Anthropology, economics, geography, political science, sociology. **Visual/performing arts:** General, art, art history/conservation, cinematography, dance, dramatic, film/cinema, studio arts.

Most popular majors. Biology 7%, business/marketing 11%, interdisciplinary studies 10%, psychology 7%, social sciences 21%, visual/performing arts 8%.

Student life. **Freshman orientation:** Available. Preregistration for classes offered. Two-day program; includes sessions for parents. **Housing:** Coed dorms, apartments, cooperative housing, fraternity/sorority housing available. **Activities:** Bands, choral groups, dance, drama, film society, literary magazine, music ensembles, musical theater, opera, radio station, student government, student newspaper, symphony orchestra, over 250 organizations.

Athletics. NCAA. **Intercollegiate:** Baseball M, basketball, cross-country, golf M, gymnastics, soccer, softball W, swimming, tennis, track and field, volleyball, water polo. **Intramural:** Badminton, basketball, bowling, cross-country, football (non-tackle), golf, gymnastics, racquetball, rowing (crew), soccer, softball, squash, tennis, volleyball, water polo. **Team name:** Gauchos.

Student services. Adult student services, career counseling, student employment services, health services, on-campus daycare, personal counseling, placement for graduates, veterans' counselor, women's services. **Physically disabled:** Services for visually, speech, hearing impaired.

Contact. E-mail: appinfo@sa.ucsb.edu
Phone: (805) 893-2881 Fax: (805) 893-2676
Christine Van Gieson, Admissions and Outreach Services, University of California: Santa Barbara, 1234 Cheadle Hall, Santa Barbara, CA 93106-2014

University of California: Santa Cruz

Santa Cruz, California — **CB member**
www.ucsc.edu — **CB code: 4860**

- Public 4-year university
- Residential campus in small city
- 13,588 degree-seeking undergraduates: 4% part-time, 54% women, 3% African American, 19% Asian American, 15% Hispanic American, 1% Native American, 1% international
- 1,387 degree-seeking graduate students
- 75% of applicants admitted
- SAT or ACT with writing, SAT Subject Tests, application essay required
- 69% graduate within 6 years

General. Founded in 1965. Regionally accredited. **Degrees:** 2,991 bachelor's awarded; master's, doctoral offered. **ROTC:** Army, Navy, Air Force. **Location:** 75 miles from San Francisco, 30 miles from San Jose. **Calendar:** Quarter, limited summer session. **Full-time faculty:** 537 total; 98% have terminal degrees, 23% minority, 37% women. **Part-time faculty:** 205 total; 98% have terminal degrees, 12% minority, 50% women. **Class size:** 39% < 20, 38% 20-39, 3% 40-49, 9% 50-99, 11% >100. **Special facilities:** Observatories, arboretum, agroecology farm, campus preserve, nonlinear science center, music center, bilingual research center, institutes of marine sciences, tectonics, particle physics, center for adaptive optics.

Freshman class profile. 23,003 applied, 17,342 admitted, 3,000 enrolled.

Mid 50% test scores			
SAT verbal:	520-630	Rank in top quarter:	100%
SAT math:	530-640	Rank in top tenth:	90%
ACT:	21-27	Return as sophomores:	89%
GPA 3.50 or higher:	52%	Out-of-state:	4%
GPA 3.0-3.49:	44%	Live on campus:	98%
GPA 2.0-2.99:	4%	International:	1%

Basis for selection. Test scores, GPA in required subjects most important. Personal statement very important. All applicants must take 2 SAT Subject Tests in different subject areas. If Math SAT Subject Test is taken, must be Level 2. Audition required for music majors. Portfolio recommended for art majors. **Homeschooled:** Eligibility appraised on basis of entrance examination or previous college-level work. **Learning Disabled:** Any extenuating circumstances should be included in the personal statement.

High school preparation. College-preparatory program required. 15 units required; 18 recommended. Required and recommended units include English 4, mathematics 3-4, social studies 1, history 1, science 2-3 (laboratory 2-3), foreign language 2-3 and academic electives 1. 2 semesters of approved arts courses from single visual and performing arts discipline: dance, drama/theater, music, or visual art. Required elective includes 2 semesters from following areas: visual and performing arts, history, social science, English, advanced mathematics, laboratory science, and language other than English.

2005-2006 Annual costs. Tuition/fees: $6,949; $24,769 out-of-state. Room/board: $11,571. Books/supplies: $1,332. Personal expenses: $1,392.

2004-2005 Financial aid. **Need-based:** 1,799 full-time freshmen applied for aid; 1,679 were judged to have need; 1,605 of these received aid. Average need met was 84%. Average scholarship/grant was $8,889; average loan $4,196. 62% of total undergraduate aid awarded as scholarships/grants, 38% as loans/jobs. **Non-need-based:** Awarded to 133 full-time undergraduates, including 36 freshmen. Scholarships awarded for academics, alumni affiliation, art, leadership, music/drama.

Application procedures. **Admission:** Closing date 11/30 (postmark date). $60 fee, may be waived for applicants with need. Application may be submitted online. Admission notification 4/30. Admission notification on a rolling basis beginning on or about 3/15. Must reply by 5/1. **Financial aid:** Closing date 3/2. FAFSA required. Applicants notified on a rolling basis starting 4/1; must reply within 4 week(s) of notification.

Academics. **Special study options:** Combined bachelor's/graduate degree, cooperative education, double major, dual enrollment of high school students, ESL, exchange student, independent study, internships, student-designed major, study abroad, teacher certification program, Washington semester. **Credit/placement by examination:** AP, CLEP, IB, institutional tests. **Support services:** Learning center, reduced course load, remedial instruction, study skills assistance, tutoring, writing center.

Majors. **Agriculture:** Plant sciences. **Area/ethnic studies:** American, East Asian, German, Hispanic-American/Latino/Chicano, Italian, Latin American, Russian/Slavic, South Asian, Southeast Asian, women's. **Biology:** General, biochemistry, bioinformatics, biometrics, cell/histology, ecology, marine, molecular. **Business:** Accounting, business admin, international finance, management information systems, managerial economics. **Computer sciences:** General, computer science, information systems, systems analysis. **Conservation:** General, environmental studies. **Engineering:** Computer, electrical. **Engineering technology:** Electromechanical. **English:** American lit, British lit. **Foreign languages:** Ancient Greek, Chinese, classics, comparative lit, French, German, Italian, Japanese, Latin, linguistics, Russian, Spanish, translation. **Health:** Health services. **History:** General. **Interdisciplinary:** Biopsychology, math/computer science, neuroscience. **Legal studies:** General. **Math:** General, applied. **Philosophy/religion:** Philosophy, religion. **Physical sciences:** Astrophysics, chemistry, geology, geophysics, physics, planetary. **Psychology:** General. **Social sciences:** Anthropology, economics, political science, sociology. **Visual/performing arts:** Art, dance, design, dramatic, film/cinema, photography, studio arts, theater design.

Most popular majors. Biology 12%, business/marketing 9%, English 8%, psychology 10%, social sciences 19%, visual/performing arts 11%.

Computing on campus. 300 workstations in dormitories, library, computer center, student center. Dormitories wired for high-speed internet access and linked to campus network. Commuter students can connect to campus network. Online course registration, online library, helpline, repair service, student web hosting, wireless network available.

Student life. **Freshman orientation:** Available. Preregistration for classes offered. **Policies:** Students may create own organizations. **Housing:** Guaranteed on-campus for freshmen. Coed dorms, single-sex dorms, apartments, cooperative housing, substance-free housing available. $150 deposit, deadline 5/1. Theme housing. **Activities:** Jazz band, choral groups, dance, drama, film society, literary magazine, music ensembles, musical theater, opera, radio station, student government, student newspaper, symphony orchestra, TV station, over 100 student organizations.

Athletics. NCAA. **Intercollegiate:** Basketball, cross-country W, diving, golf W, soccer, swimming, tennis, volleyball, water polo. **Intramural:** Basketball, football (non-tackle), soccer, volleyball. **Team name:** Banana Slugs.

Student services. Adult student services, alcohol/substance abuse counseling, career counseling, services for economically disadvantaged, student employment services, financial aid counseling, health services, minority student services, on-campus daycare, personal counseling, veterans' counselor, women's services. **Physically disabled:** Services for visually, speech, hearing impaired.

Contact. E-mail: admissions@ucsc.edu
Phone: (831) 459-4008 Fax: (831) 459-4452
Kevin Browne, Executive Director of Admissions and University Registrar, University of California: Santa Cruz, Cook House, 1156 High Street, Santa Cruz, CA 95064

University of Judaism

Bel Air, California
www.uj.edu — **CB code: 4876**

- Private 4-year university and liberal arts college affiliated with Jewish faith
- Residential campus in very large city
- 150 degree-seeking undergraduates
- 85% of applicants admitted
- SAT or ACT, application essay required

General. Founded in 1947. Regionally accredited. **Degrees:** 35 bachelor's awarded; master's, first professional offered. **Calendar:** Semester, limited summer session. **Full-time faculty:** 19 total. **Part-time faculty:** 72 total. **Class size:** 93% < 20, 7% 20-39. **Special facilities:** Jewish community documentation center, educational resources center.

Freshman class profile. 60 applied, 51 admitted, 51 enrolled.

Mid 50% test scores			
SAT verbal:	530-610	ACT:	21-30
SAT math:	500-560	Out-of-state:	31%
		Live on campus:	100%

Basis for selection. 3.2 GPA, 1100 SAT (exclusive of writing), essay, recommendations, school and community activities important. Interview recommended.

High school preparation. 18 units recommended. Recommended units include English 4, mathematics 3, social studies 2, history 2, science 3 (laboratory 2) and foreign language 2.

2006-2007 Annual costs. Tuition/fees: $20,290. Room/board: $10,800. Books/supplies: $882. Personal expenses: $1,476.

Financial aid. Non-need-based: Scholarships awarded for academics, leadership.

Application procedures. Admission: Priority date 1/31; no deadline. $35 fee, may be waived for applicants with need. Admission notification on a rolling basis beginning on or about 2/5. Must reply by May 1 or within 2 week(s) if notified thereafter. **Financial aid:** Priority date 3/1; no closing date. FAFSA, institutional form required. Applicants notified on a rolling basis starting 3/15; must reply within 3 week(s) of notification.

Academics. In addition to majors and general education requirements, students take core curriculum of Jewish and Western Civilization classes. **Special study options:** Accelerated study, combined bachelor's/graduate degree, cross-registration, honors, independent study, internships, student-designed major, study abroad. **Credit/placement by examination:** CLEP, IB, institutional tests. **Support services:** Reduced course load, tutoring.

Majors. Business: General. **Foreign languages:** Comparative lit. **Health:** Ethics. **Liberal arts:** Arts/sciences. **Philosophy/religion:** Judaic. **Social sciences:** Political science.

Most popular majors. Area/ethnic studies 32%, English 18%, liberal arts 9%, psychology 18%.

Computing on campus. 30 workstations in dormitories, computer center.

Student life. Freshman orientation: Mandatory. Preregistration for classes offered. Held 1 week prior to start of class; usually lasts 3 days. **Policies:** Freshmen permitted cars on campus. **Housing:** Guaranteed on-campus for all undergraduates. Coed dorms, apartments available. $300 deposit. Kosher meals on campus. Students required to live on campus unless 21 or living with parents. **Activities:** Choral groups, drama, literary magazine, radio station, student government, student newspaper, residence life council, political science club.

Athletics. Intramural: Baseball M, basketball, football (tackle) M, volleyball.

Student services. Career counseling, student employment services, health services, personal counseling, placement for graduates. **Physically disabled:** Services for hearing impaired.

Contact. E-mail: admissions@uj.edu
Phone: (310) 476-9777 ext. 247 Toll-free number: (888) 853-6763
Fax: (310) 471-3657
Bryan Pisetsky, Admissions Director, University of Judaism, 15600 Mulholland Drive, Bel Air, CA 90077

University of La Verne

La Verne, California — **CB member**
www.ulv.edu — **CB code: 4381**

- Private 4-year university and liberal arts college
- Commuter campus in large town
- 1,666 degree-seeking undergraduates: 5% part-time, 65% women, 9% African American, 5% Asian American, 38% Hispanic American, 1% Native American, 1% international
- 2,264 degree-seeking graduate students
- 62% of applicants admitted
- SAT or ACT with writing, application essay required
- 52% graduate within 6 years

General. Founded in 1891. Regionally accredited. Satellite campuses throughout California provide graduate and professional programs to adult students. **Degrees:** 312 bachelor's awarded; master's, doctoral, first professional offered. **ROTC:** Army. **Location:** 35 miles from Los Angeles. **Calendar:** 4-1-4, limited summer session. **Full-time faculty:** 187 total; 96% have terminal degrees, 17% minority, 46% women. **Part-time faculty:** 211 total; 18% minority. **Class size:** 71% < 20, 29% 20-39, less than 1% 40-49, less than 1% 50-99. **Special facilities:** Natural history museum, archeology laboratory.

Freshman class profile. 1,638 applied, 1,008 admitted, 339 enrolled.

Mid 50% test scores			
SAT verbal:	460-560	GPA 2.0-2.99:	16%
SAT math:	470-570	Rank in top quarter:	68%
ACT:	18-23	Rank in top tenth:	33%
GPA 3.50 or higher:	50%	Return as sophomores:	89%
GPA 3.0-3.49:	34%	Live on campus:	50%

Basis for selection. Secondary school record, recommendations, standardized test scores, and essay very important; extracurricular activities, character or personal qualities also important. Class rank, interview, special talents or abilities, alumni relationships, volunteer work, work experience may be considered as additional factors. College Board Test of Standard Written English (TSWE) and math department placement exam required. Departmental placement exams required in foreign language. Individual departments may require interview, audition, or portfolio for theater, art, music, and forensics scholarships.

High school preparation. College-preparatory program required. 14 units required; 19 recommended. Required and recommended units include English 4, mathematics 3-4, social studies 2, history 3, science 2 (laboratory 1-2), foreign language 2 and academic electives 2.

2006-2007 Annual costs. Tuition/fees (projected): $24,260. Room/board: $9,210. Books/supplies: $1,314. Personal expenses: $3,033.

2005-2006 Financial aid. Need-based: 308 full-time freshmen applied for aid; 282 were judged to have need; 282 of these received aid. Average scholarship/grant was $9,243; average loan $4,417. 79% of total undergraduate aid awarded as scholarships/grants, 21% as loans/jobs. **Non-need-based:** Awarded to 2,706 full-time undergraduates, including 552 freshmen. Scholarships awarded for academics, alumni affiliation, art, leadership, minority status, music/drama, religious affiliation.

Application procedures. Admission: Priority date 2/1; no deadline. $50 fee, may be waived for applicants with need. Application must be submitted on paper. Admission notification on a rolling basis beginning on or about 12/1. Must reply by May 1 or within 2 week(s) if notified thereafter. **Financial aid:** Priority date 3/2; no closing date. FAFSA required. Applicants notified on a rolling basis starting 3/3; must reply within 1 week(s) of notification.

Academics. Main Campus offers a traditional-age undergraduate program and an accelerated program for adults in school of continuing education. Off-campus centers available for degree-seeking students in selected majors. Current centers in Riverside, Orange, and Ventura counties, San Luis Obispo, San Fernando Valley and Bakersfield. Education programs available at additional sites in California. **Special study options:** Accelerated study, combined bachelor's/graduate degree, distance learning, double major, ESL, exchange student, honors, independent study, internships, liberal arts/career combination, student-designed major, study abroad, teacher certification program, weekend college. **Credit/placement by examination:** AP, CLEP, institutional tests. 44 credit hours maximum toward bachelor's degree. **Support services:** Learning center, reduced course load, study skills assistance, tutoring.

Majors. Biology: General. **Business:** Accounting, business admin, e-commerce, international, managerial economics, marketing. **Communications:** General, journalism, radio/tv. **Computer sciences:** General. **Conservation:** Environmental science. **Education:** General, early childhood, elementary, physical, secondary. **English:** English lit. **Family/consumer sciences:** Child care. **Foreign languages:** Comparative lit, French, German, Spanish. **Health:** Athletic training, health care admin. **History:** General. **Interdisciplinary:** Behavioral sciences, biological/physical sciences, natural sciences. **Legal studies:** General. **Liberal arts:** Arts/sciences. **Math:** General. **Philosophy/religion:** Philosophy, religion. **Physical sciences:** Chemistry, physics. **Psychology:** General. **Public administration:** General. **Social sciences:** General, anthropology, criminology, economics, international relations, political science, sociology. **Visual/performing arts:** Art, art history/conservation, dramatic.

Most popular majors. Business/marketing 24%, communications/journalism 11%, education 7%, liberal arts 13%, psychology 12%, social sciences 15%.

Computing on campus. 150 workstations in library, computer center, student center. Dormitories wired for high-speed internet access and linked to campus network. Commuter students can connect to campus network. Online course registration, online library, helpline, student web hosting, wireless network available.

Student life. **Freshman orientation:** Available, $50 fee. Preregistration for classes offered. Residential move-in day with residential orientation followed by a full day of academic orientation. Optional overnight retreat to a mountain camp. Additional orientation held the week prior to start of classes. **Policies:** Students must be in good academic standing to participate in clubs or organizations, including fraternities/sororities. Freshmen not permitted to join fraternities/sororities. Freshmen permitted cars on campus. **Housing:** Coed dorms, single-sex dorms, special housing for disabled available. $240 fully refundable deposit, deadline 5/1. **Activities:** Jazz band, choral groups, dance, drama, literary magazine, music ensembles, musical theater, radio station, student government, student newspaper, TV station, African American student alliance, Latino student forum, model United Nations, international student organization, Circle K, associated student federation, debate team, Asian Pacific American student association, Brothers Forum, Sisters Circle.

Athletics. NCAA. **Intercollegiate:** Baseball M, basketball, cross-country, diving, football (tackle) M, golf M, soccer, softball W, swimming, tennis, track and field, volleyball W, water polo. **Intramural:** Basketball, soccer, softball, table tennis, volleyball. **Team name:** Leopards.

Student services. Adult student services, alcohol/substance abuse counseling, campus ministries, career counseling, services for economically disadvantaged, student employment services, financial aid counseling, health services, minority student services, personal counseling, placement for graduates, veterans' counselor. **Physically disabled:** Services for visually, speech, hearing impaired.

Contact. E-mail: admissions@ulv.edu
Phone: (909) 392-2800 Toll-free number: (800) 876-4858
Fax: (909) 392-2714
Ana Liza Zell, Dean of Admissions, University of La Verne, 1950 Third Street, La Verne, CA 91750

University of Redlands

Redlands, California **CB member**
www.redlands.edu **CB code: 4848**

- Private 4-year university and liberal arts college
- Residential campus in small city
- 2,358 degree-seeking undergraduates: 1% part-time, 59% women, 2% African American, 5% Asian American, 11% Hispanic American, 1% international
- 92 degree-seeking graduate students
- 66% of applicants admitted
- SAT or ACT (ACT writing recommended), application essay required
- 58% graduate within 6 years; 45% enter graduate study

General. Founded in 1907. Regionally accredited. Nontraditional study programs available through Johnston Center for Integrated Studies and schools of business and education. **Degrees:** 834 bachelor's awarded; master's offered. **ROTC:** Army, Navy, Air Force. **Location:** 65 miles from Los Angeles, 40 miles from Palm Springs. **Calendar:** 4-1-4. **Full-time faculty:** 163 total; 86% have terminal degrees. **Part-time faculty:** 162 total; 28% have terminal degrees. **Class size:** 72% < 20, 27% 20-39, less than 1% 40-49, less than 1% 50-99. **Special facilities:** Laboratory of anthropology, geographic information systems laboratory, physics/laser/photonics laboratory, map library.

Freshman class profile. 3,395 applied, 2,226 admitted, 615 enrolled.

Mid 50% test scores		**GPA 2.0-2.99:**	26%
SAT verbal:	530-620	**Rank in top quarter:**	37%
SAT math:	540-630	**Rank in top tenth:**	32%
ACT:	21-26	**Return as sophomores:**	83%
GPA 3.50 or higher:	43%	**Out-of-state:**	37%
GPA 3.0-3.49:	30%	**Live on campus:**	92%

Basis for selection. Course selection and grades important. Recommendations, test scores, essays, extracurricular activities also considered. Interview required of Johnston Center for Integrated Studies applicants, strongly recommended for others. Audition required of music majors. Portfolio recommended of art (slides only), creative writing majors. **Homeschooled:** Transcript of courses and grades required.

High school preparation. College-preparatory program required. Required units include English 4, mathematics 3, social studies 3, science 3 (laboratory 3) and foreign language 3.

2006-2007 Annual costs. Tuition/fees: $28,776. Room/board: $9,360. Books/supplies: $1,250. Personal expenses: $2,650.

2005-2006 Financial aid. **Need-based:** 514 full-time freshmen applied for aid; 400 were judged to have need; 400 of these received aid. Average need met was 91%. Average scholarship/grant was $19,703; average loan $4,770. 70% of total undergraduate aid awarded as scholarships/grants, 30% as loans/jobs. **Non-need-based:** Awarded to 1,329 full-time undergraduates, including 395 freshmen. Scholarships awarded for academics, art, music/drama.

Application procedures. **Admission:** Priority date 12/15; deadline 4/1 (postmark date). $45 fee, may be waived for applicants with need. Application may be submitted online. Admission notification on a rolling basis beginning on or about 11/1. Must reply by May 1 or within 3 week(s) if notified thereafter. **Financial aid:** Priority date 2/15; no closing date. FAFSA required. Applicants notified on a rolling basis starting 2/28; must reply by 5/1.

Academics. **Special study options:** Cross-registration, double major, exchange student, honors, independent study, internships, liberal arts/career combination, New York semester, student-designed major, study abroad, teacher certification program, United Nations semester, Washington semester. **Credit/placement by examination:** AP, CLEP, IB, institutional tests. 16 credit hours maximum toward bachelor's degree. **Support services:** Learning center, reduced course load, study skills assistance, tutoring, writing center.

Majors. **Area/ethnic studies:** Asian, Latin American, women's. **Biology:** General, biochemistry. **Business:** General, accounting, business admin, management information systems, managerial economics. **Computer sciences:** General. **Conservation:** Environmental science, environmental studies, management/policy. **Education:** Elementary, middle, music, secondary, speech impaired. **English:** British lit, creative writing, English lit. **Foreign languages:** French, German, Spanish. **Health:** Audiology/speech pathology. **History:** General. **Liberal arts:** Arts/sciences. **Math:** General. **Philosophy/religion:** Philosophy, religion. **Physical sciences:** Chemistry, physics. **Psychology:** General. **Social sciences:** Anthropology, economics, international relations, political science, sociology. **Visual/performing arts:** Art, art history/conservation, dramatic, music history, music performance, music theory/composition.

Most popular majors. Business/marketing 15%, liberal arts 21%, psychology 6%, social sciences 16%, visual/performing arts 7%.

Computing on campus. 655 workstations in dormitories, library, computer center, student center. Dormitories wired for high-speed internet access and linked to campus network. Commuter students can connect to campus network. Online library, helpline, repair service, student web hosting, wireless network available.

Student life. **Freshman orientation:** Mandatory. One full week preceding academic school year. **Policies:** Freshmen permitted cars on campus. **Housing:** Guaranteed on-campus for freshmen. Coed dorms, single-sex dorms, special housing for disabled, apartments, fraternity/sorority housing, substance-free housing available. Pets allowed in dorm rooms. **Activities:** Bands, choral groups, dance, drama, literary magazine, music ensembles, musical theater, opera, radio station, student government, student newspaper, symphony orchestra, Associated Students, intervarsity Christian fellowship, African American association, Gay, Lesbian, Bisexual student union, women's center, College Republicans, College Democrats, Asian Pacific Islander association, Glenn Wallichs Theater association.

Athletics. NCAA. **Intercollegiate:** Baseball M, basketball, cross-country, diving, football (tackle) M, golf, lacrosse W, soccer, softball W, swimming, tennis, track and field, volleyball W, water polo. **Intramural:** Basketball, football (non-tackle), racquetball, soccer, softball, table tennis, tennis, volleyball, water polo. **Team name:** Bulldogs.

Student services. Adult student services, alcohol/substance abuse counseling, campus ministries, career counseling, student employment services, financial aid counseling, health services, minority student services, personal counseling, placement for graduates, veterans' counselor, women's services. **Physically disabled:** Services for visually, speech, hearing impaired.

Contact. E-mail: admissions@redlands.edu
Phone: (909) 335-4074 Toll-free number: (800) 455-5064
Fax: (909) 335-4089
Paul Driscoll, Dean of Admissions, University of Redlands, 1200 East Colton Avenue, Redlands, CA 92373-0999

University of San Diego

San Diego, California **CB member**
www.sandiego.edu **CB code: 4849**

- Private 4-year university affiliated with Roman Catholic Church
- Residential campus in very large city
- 4,959 degree-seeking undergraduates: 3% part-time, 60% women, 2% African American, 7% Asian American, 13% Hispanic American, 1% Native American, 2% international

- 2,546 degree-seeking graduate students
- 60% of applicants admitted
- SAT or ACT with writing, application essay required
- 73% graduate within 6 years

General. Founded in 1949. Regionally accredited. **Degrees:** 1,147 bachelor's awarded; master's, doctoral, first professional offered. **ROTC:** Army, Navy, Air Force. **Location:** 5 miles from downtown. **Calendar:** 4-1-4, extensive summer session. **Full-time faculty:** 359 total; 96% have terminal degrees, 16% minority, 43% women. **Part-time faculty:** 363 total; 49% have terminal degrees, 14% minority, 51% women. **Class size:** 40% < 20, 55% 20-39, 5% 40-49, less than 1% 50-99. **Special facilities:** Sea World/Hubbs Institute research facilities available to marine studies students, center for science and technology, Old Globe Theatre available to MFA students, institute for peace & justice.

Freshman class profile. 7,862 applied, 4,687 admitted, 1,136 enrolled.

Mid 50% test scores			
SAT verbal:	530-630	Rank in top quarter:	79%
SAT math:	550-650	Rank in top tenth:	41%
ACT:	23-28	Return as sophomores:	83%
GPA 3.50 or higher:	72%	Out-of-state:	43%
GPA 3.0-3.49:	23%	Live on campus:	98%
GPA 2.0-2.99:	5%	International:	2%

Basis for selection. School achievement record, test scores, recommendations, and extracurricular activities important. Out-of-state and international applicants welcome. Advanced Placement English examinations (language or literature) with grade of 4 or 5 may also be used for placement. Audition required of choral scholarship applicants. **Learning Disabled:** Must contact Director of Disability Services.

High school preparation. 20 units recommended. Recommended units include English 4, mathematics 4, social studies 4, science 4 and foreign language 4.

2006-2007 Annual costs. Tuition/fees: $30,704. Room/board: $10,960. Books/supplies: $1,300. Personal expenses: $2,088.

2004-2005 Financial aid. Need-based: 781 full-time freshmen applied for aid; 553 were judged to have need; 553 of these received aid. Average need met was 62%. Average scholarship/grant was $13,137; average loan $3,997. 69% of total undergraduate aid awarded as scholarships/grants, 31% as loans/jobs. **Non-need-based:** Awarded to 1,396 full-time undergraduates, including 411 freshmen. Scholarships awarded for academics, athletics, music/drama, religious affiliation, ROTC.

Application procedures. Admission: Priority date 1/5; deadline 3/1 (postmark date). $55 fee, may be waived for applicants with need. Application may be submitted online. Admission notification 4/15. Must reply by May 1 or within 2 week(s) if notified thereafter. **Financial aid:** Closing date 2/20. FAFSA required. Applicants notified on a rolling basis starting 3/1; must reply within 3 week(s) of notification.

Academics. Special study options: Combined bachelor's/graduate degree, double major, exchange student, honors, independent study, internships, liberal arts/career combination, study abroad, teacher certification program. **Credit/placement by examination:** AP, CLEP, IB, institutional tests. **Support services:** Pre-admission summer program, reduced course load, study skills assistance, tutoring, writing center.

Majors. Biology: General, marine. **Business:** Accounting, business admin, managerial economics. **Communications:** General. **Computer sciences:** Computer science. **Conservation:** Environmental studies. **Engineering:** Electrical, industrial, mechanical. **English:** English lit. **Foreign languages:** French, Spanish. **Health:** Nursing (RN). **History:** General. **Liberal arts:** Arts/sciences, humanities. **Math:** General. **Philosophy/religion:** Philosophy, religion. **Physical sciences:** Chemistry, physics. **Psychology:** General. **Social sciences:** Anthropology, economics, international relations, political science, sociology, urban studies. **Visual/performing arts:** Art history/conservation, dramatic, studio arts.

Most popular majors. Business/marketing 36%, communications/journalism 9%, English 6%, liberal arts 7%, psychology 6%, social sciences 17%.

Computing on campus. 250 workstations in dormitories, library, computer center, student center. Dormitories wired for high-speed internet access and linked to campus network. Commuter students can connect to campus network. Helpline, repair service, student web hosting, wireless network available.

Student life. Freshman orientation: Mandatory. Preregistration for classes offered. 5-day program before start of semester. **Policies:** Freshmen permitted cars on campus. **Housing:** Guaranteed on-campus for all undergraduates. Coed dorms, single-sex dorms, special housing for disabled, apartments, substance-free housing available. $100 partly refundable deposit, deadline 5/1. Freshmen required to live on campus unless living with parents. **Activities:** Bands, choral groups, dance, drama, literary magazine, music ensembles, musical theater, student government, student newspaper, symphony orchestra, TV station, university ministry, international students association, Black student union, Asian student association, Young Democrats, Young Republicans, Hawaiian club, Mecha, FUSO (Filipino student association), United Front multicultural center.

Athletics. NCAA. **Intercollegiate:** Baseball M, basketball, cross-country, diving W, football (tackle) M, golf M, rowing (crew), soccer, softball W, swimming W, tennis, volleyball W. **Intramural:** Badminton, basketball, bowling, cross-country, field hockey, golf, ice hockey M, lacrosse M, rugby M, soccer, softball, swimming, table tennis, tennis, volleyball. **Team name:** Toreros.

Student services. Alcohol/substance abuse counseling, campus ministries, career counseling, services for economically disadvantaged, student employment services, financial aid counseling, health services, legal services, on-campus daycare, personal counseling, placement for graduates, veterans' counselor, women's services. **Physically disabled:** Services for visually impaired.

Contact. E-mail: admissions@sandiego.edu
Phone: (619) 260-4506 Toll-free number: (800) 248-4873
Fax: (619) 260-6836
Stephen Pultz, Director of Admission, University of San Diego, 5998 Alcala Park, San Diego, CA 92110

University of San Francisco

San Francisco, California — **CB member**
www.usfca.edu — **CB code: 4850**

- Private 4-year university affiliated with Roman Catholic Church
- Residential campus in very large city
- 4,451 degree-seeking undergraduates: 3% part-time, 66% women
- 3,192 degree-seeking graduate students
- 72% of applicants admitted
- SAT or ACT with writing, application essay required

General. Founded in 1855. Regionally accredited. Jesuit institution. **Degrees:** 1,147 bachelor's awarded; master's, doctoral, first professional offered. **ROTC:** Army, Air Force. **Location:** 3 miles from downtown. **Calendar:** 4-1-4, extensive summer session. **Full-time faculty:** 348 total; 92% have terminal degrees, 20% minority, 43% women. **Part-time faculty:** 513 total; 71% have terminal degrees, 22% minority, 53% women. **Class size:** 51% < 20, 34% 20-39, 12% 40-49, 3% 50-99, less than 1% >100. **Special facilities:** Rare book room, Institute for Chinese Western Cultural History, electron microscope, separate law library available to all students.

Freshman class profile. 6,090 applied, 4,376 admitted, 934 enrolled.

Mid 50% test scores			
SAT verbal:	510-620	Rank in top tenth:	25%
SAT math:	500-620	Out-of-state:	29%
ACT:	21-26	Live on campus:	90%
Rank in top quarter:	57%	Fraternities:	1%
		Sororities:	1%

Basis for selection. School achievement record, test scores, class rank, school attended, recommendations, extracurricular activities, alumni relationship, personal essay important. Require TOEFL for non-native speakers of English. Writing section from either SAT or ACT will also be used for advising and placement purposes. SAT Subject Test scores taken prior to March 2005 will also be accepted for advising and placement purposes. If both old SAT and new SAT Reasoning scores are submitted, then the higher of the scores will be used. Interviews required for nursing students. **Learning Disabled:** After acceptance, students with disabilities must make appointment with Disabilities Specialist in the office of Disablity Related Services (DRS) if they are interested in receiving services and/or accommodations for their disability.

High school preparation. 20 units required. Required units include English 4, mathematics 3, social studies 3, science 2 (laboratory 2), foreign language 2 and academic electives 6. One chemistry and 1 biology or physics required of nursing and science applicants.

2006-2007 Annual costs. Tuition/fees: $28,580. Room/board: $10,580.

2005-2006 Financial aid. Need-based: 667 full-time freshmen applied for aid; 569 were judged to have need; 548 of these received aid. Average need met was 70%. Average scholarship/grant was $16,227; average loan $3,693. 70% of total undergraduate aid awarded as scholarships/grants, 30% as loans/jobs. **Non-need-based:** Awarded to 932 full-time undergraduates, including 256 freshmen. Scholarships awarded for academics, athletics, ROTC. **Additional information:** Individualized installment plans available.

Application procedures. **Admission:** Priority date 2/1; no deadline. $55 fee, may be waived for applicants with need. Application may be submitted online. Admission notification on a rolling basis. Within 4 weeks of completed application. Must reply by May 1 or within 2 week(s) if notified thereafter. **Financial aid:** Priority date 2/1; no closing date. FAFSA required. Applicants notified on a rolling basis starting 4/1; must reply within 4 week(s) of notification.

Academics. **Special study options:** Accelerated study, combined bachelor's/graduate degree, cooperative education, cross-registration, distance learning, double major, ESL, exchange student, external degree, honors, independent study, internships, liberal arts/career combination, student-designed major, study abroad, teacher certification program, Washington semester. Cooperative work study in Computer Science courses. **Credit/placement by examination:** AP, CLEP, IB, institutional tests. 30 credit hours maximum toward bachelor's degree. **Support services:** Learning center, pre-admission summer program, reduced course load, study skills assistance, tutoring, writing center.

Majors. **Architecture:** Urban/community planning. **Biology:** General. **Business:** General, accounting, business admin, finance, hotel/motel admin, international, management information systems, marketing, organizational behavior, restaurant/food services. **Communications:** General, media studies. **Computer sciences:** General, information systems. **Conservation:** Environmental science, environmental studies. **Foreign languages:** French, Spanish. **Health:** Nursing (RN). **History:** General. **Liberal arts:** Arts/sciences. **Math:** General. **Parks/recreation:** Health/fitness. **Philosophy/religion:** Philosophy. **Physical sciences:** Chemistry, physics. **Psychology:** General. **Public administration:** General. **Social sciences:** Economics, political science, sociology. **Visual/performing arts:** General, art, art history/conservation, arts management, drawing, graphic design, illustration, painting, studio arts.

Computing on campus. 200 workstations in dormitories, library, computer center, student center. Dormitories wired for high-speed internet access and linked to campus network. Commuter students can connect to campus network. Online course registration, online library, helpline, repair service, student web hosting, wireless network available.

Student life. **Freshman orientation:** Mandatory. Preregistration for classes offered. Two-day session including placement tests. **Policies:** Freshmen permitted cars on campus. **Housing:** Guaranteed on-campus for freshmen. Coed dorms, single-sex dorms, special housing for disabled, apartments available. $300 deposit. Freshman and sophomores under 21 required to live in residence halls unless they have permanent address within 20 mile radius of campus. **Activities:** Choral groups, dance, drama, literary magazine, music ensembles, musical theater, radio station, student government, student newspaper, St. Ignatius Institute, International Students Association, 13 ethnic clubs, People Advocating Cultural Endeavors, Phelan Multicultural Community.

Athletics. NCAA. **Intercollegiate:** Baseball M, basketball, cross-country, golf, rifle, soccer, tennis, track and field M, volleyball W. **Intramural:** Basketball, football (non-tackle), racquetball, soccer, softball, swimming, table tennis, tennis, volleyball. **Team name:** Dons.

Student services. Adult student services, alcohol/substance abuse counseling, campus ministries, career counseling, student employment services, financial aid counseling, health services, minority student services, personal counseling, placement for graduates. **Physically disabled:** Services for visually, speech, hearing impaired. **Learning disabled:** Comprehensive services available.

Contact. E-mail: admissions@usfca.edu
Phone: (415) 422-6563 Toll-free number: (800) 225-5873
Fax: (415) 422-2217
Michael Hughes, Director of Admissions, University of San Francisco,
2130 Fulton Street, San Francisco, CA 94117-1046

University of Southern California

Los Angeles, California — **CB member**
www.usc.edu — **CB code: 4852**

- Private 4-year university
- Residential campus in very large city
- 16,428 degree-seeking undergraduates: 3% part-time, 51% women, 6% African American, 21% Asian American, 13% Hispanic American, 1% Native American, 8% international
- 15,065 degree-seeking graduate students
- 27% of applicants admitted
- SAT or ACT with writing, application essay required
- 83% graduate within 6 years

General. Founded in 1880. Regionally accredited. **Degrees:** 4,139 bachelor's awarded; master's, doctoral, first professional offered. **ROTC:** Army, Navy, Air Force. **Location:** 3 miles from downtown. **Calendar:** Semester, limited summer session. **Full-time faculty:** 1,495 total; 89% have terminal degrees, 21% minority, 31% women. **Part-time faculty:** 984 total; 58% have terminal degrees, 22% minority, 36% women. **Class size:** 63% < 20, 21% 20-39, 6% 40-49, 6% 50-99, 4% >100. **Special facilities:** 4 art galleries, marine science center on Santa Catalina Island, permanent facilities for study in Sacramento, special collections library, the Gamble House designed by Greene and Greene, Freeman House designed by Frank Lloyd Wright, integrated media systems center, center for digital arts.

Freshman class profile. 31,634 applied, 8,418 admitted, 2,741 enrolled.

Mid 50% test scores			
SAT verbal:	620-710	Return as sophomores:	95%
SAT math:	650-730	Out-of-state:	46%
ACT:	28-32	Live on campus:	97%
Rank in top quarter:	95%	International:	7%
Rank in top tenth:	85%	Fraternities:	18%
End year in good standing:	94%	Sororities:	19%

Basis for selection. GED not accepted. Academic achievement, curriculum and test scores most important. Recommendations, activities, and interviews considered. Tests not required of international applicants attending foreign institutions. Audition required of music, theater majors. Portfolio required of fine arts and architecture majors.

High school preparation. 16 units required; 20 recommended. Required and recommended units include English 4, mathematics 3-4, social studies 2-3, science 2-3 (laboratory 2-3) and foreign language 2-3.

2006-2007 Annual costs. Tuition/fees: $33,888. Room/board: $10,144. Books/supplies: $750. Personal expenses: $1,634.

2004-2005 Financial aid. **Need-based:** 1,805 full-time freshmen applied for aid; 1,210 were judged to have need; 1,210 of these received aid. Average need met was 99%. Average scholarship/grant was $18,919; average loan $3,767. 75% of total undergraduate aid awarded as scholarships/grants, 25% as loans/jobs. **Non-need-based:** Awarded to 6,594 full-time undergraduates, including 1,485 freshmen. Scholarships awarded for academics, alumni affiliation, art, athletics, leadership, music/drama, ROTC.

Application procedures. **Admission:** Priority date 12/10; deadline 1/10 (postmark date). $65 fee, may be waived for applicants with need. Application may be submitted online. Admission notification 4/1. Must reply by 5/1. **Financial aid:** Closing date 1/20. FAFSA, CSS PROFILE required. Applicants notified on a rolling basis starting 3/15; must reply by 5/1.

Academics. **Special study options:** Combined bachelor's/graduate degree, cooperative education, distance learning, double major, ESL, exchange student, honors, independent study, internships, liberal arts/career combination, student-designed major, study abroad, teacher certification program, Washington semester. Learning communities, thematic option, undergraduate research program, freshman seminar program. **Credit/placement by examination:** AP, CLEP, IB, institutional tests. 32 credit hours maximum toward bachelor's degree. **Support services:** Learning center, reduced course load, study skills assistance, tutoring, writing center.

Majors. **Architecture:** Architecture, landscape. **Area/ethnic studies:** African-American, American, Asian-American, East Asian, Hispanic-American/Latino/Chicano, women's. **Biology:** General, biochemistry, biophysics. **Business:** Accounting, business admin, international. **Communications:** General, broadcast journalism, journalism, public relations, radio/tv. **Computer sciences:** Computer science. **Conservation:** Environmental science, environmental studies. **Education:** General, music. **Engineering:** Aerospace, biomedical, chemical, civil, computer, construction, electrical, environmental, industrial, mechanical, petroleum, polymer, structural, systems, water resource. **English:** American lit, creative writing, English lit. **Foreign languages:** Classics, comparative lit, East Asian, French, German, Italian, linguistics, Russian, Spanish. **Health:** Dental hygiene, physician assistant. **History:** General. **Interdisciplinary:** Biopsychology, gerontology, global studies. **Math:** General. **Parks/recreation:** Exercise sciences. **Philosophy/religion:** Ethics, Judaic, philosophy, religion. **Physical sciences:** General, astronomy, chemistry, geology, physics. **Psychology:** General. **Public administration:** General. **Social sciences:** Anthropology, economics, geography, international relations, political science, sociology. **Visual/performing arts:** Acting, art, art history/conservation, dramatic, film/cinema, jazz, music management, music performance, music theory/composition, piano/organ, play/screenwriting, stringed instruments, studio arts, theater arts management, theater design, voice/opera.

Most popular majors. Business/marketing 25%, communications/journalism 9%, engineering/engineering technologies 7%, psychology 6%, social sciences 15%, visual/performing arts 15%.

Computing on campus. 2,700 workstations in dormitories, library, computer center, student center. Dormitories wired for high-speed internet access and linked to campus network. Commuter students can connect to campus network. Online course registration, online library, helpline, repair service, student web hosting, wireless network available.

Student life. **Freshman orientation:** Available, $140 fee. Preregistration for classes offered. Multiple 2-day sessions run all summer. **Policies:** Every incoming student required to take online alcohol education course and pass final exam prior to arriving on campus. Freshmen permitted cars on campus. **Housing:** Guaranteed on-campus for freshmen. Coed dorms, special housing for disabled, apartments, fraternity/sorority housing, substance-free housing available. $400 fully refundable deposit. Housing options: African-American, Jewish, Latino, LGBT, multicultural floors, business, cinema, environmental, law, women-in-science-and-engineering, faculty-in-residence programs, residential college. **Activities:** Bands, choral groups, dance, drama, film society, literary magazine, music ensembles, musical theater, opera, radio station, student government, student newspaper, symphony orchestra, TV station, academic honors assembly, emerging leaders program, minority consortium, religious council, residential community council, student program board, student volunteers center.

Athletics. NCAA. **Intercollegiate:** Baseball M, basketball, cross-country, diving, football (tackle) M, golf, rowing (crew) W, soccer W, swimming, tennis, track and field, volleyball, water polo. **Intramural:** Badminton, basketball, bowling, cross-country, football (non-tackle), golf, racquetball, soccer, softball, swimming, table tennis, tennis, track and field, volleyball, water polo. **Team name:** Trojans.

Student services. Alcohol/substance abuse counseling, campus ministries, career counseling, services for economically disadvantaged, student employment services, financial aid counseling, health services, minority student services, on-campus daycare, personal counseling, placement for graduates, veterans' counselor, women's services. **Physically disabled:** Services for visually, speech, hearing impaired. **Learning disabled:** Comprehensive services available.

Contact. E-mail: admitusc@usc.edu
Phone: (213) 740-1111 Fax: (213) 740-1556
L. Harrington, Vice Provost/Dean of Admission and Financial Aid, University of Southern California, University of Southern California, Los Angeles, CA 90089-1158

University of the Pacific

Stockton, California — **CB member**
www.pacific.edu — **CB code: 4065**

- Private 4-year university
- Residential campus in large city
- 3,436 degree-seeking undergraduates: 3% part-time, 57% women
- 2,698 degree-seeking graduate students
- 56% of applicants admitted
- SAT or ACT with writing, application essay required
- 65% graduate within 6 years

General. Founded in 1851. Regionally accredited. School of Dentistry in San Francisco. McGeorge School of Law in Sacramento. Historic affiliation with United Methodist Church. **Degrees:** 683 bachelor's awarded; master's, doctoral, first professional offered. **ROTC:** Air Force. **Location:** 80 miles from San Francisco, 40 miles from Sacramento. **Calendar:** Semester, limited summer session. **Full-time faculty:** 392 total. **Part-time faculty:** 260 total. **Special facilities:** Recital facilities, Holt-Atherton Center for Western Studies housing the John Muir papers, music conservatory.

Freshman class profile. 5,869 applied, 3,304 admitted, 800 enrolled.

Mid 50% test scores			
SAT verbal:	530-630	Rank in top quarter:	73%
SAT math:	550-670	Rank in top tenth:	43%
ACT:	23-28	Return as sophomores:	85%
GPA 3.50 or higher:	55%	Out-of-state:	20%
GPA 3.0-3.49:	35%	Live on campus:	90%
GPA 2.0-2.99:	10%	International:	2%

Basis for selection. Secondary school record, standardized test scores, recommendations, essay, extracurricular activities important. SAT Subject Tests recommended. Audition required of music/conservatory majors. **Homeschooled:** Standardized test scores weighted heavily.

High school preparation. 16 units required. Required and recommended units include English 4, mathematics 3, history 1, science 2 (laboratory 2), foreign language 2 and academic electives 3. 1 fine/performing arts required.

2005-2006 Annual costs. Tuition/fees: $26,088. Room/board: $8,292. Books/supplies: $1,242. Personal expenses: $1,980.

2005-2006 Financial aid. **Need-based:** 657 full-time freshmen applied for aid; 656 were judged to have need; 537 of these received aid. Average scholarship/grant was $17,574; average loan $3,814. 71% of total undergraduate aid awarded as scholarships/grants, 29% as loans/jobs. **Non-need-based:** Awarded to 558 full-time undergraduates, including 184 freshmen. Scholarships awarded for academics, athletics, leadership, music/drama, religious affiliation.

Application procedures. **Admission:** Priority date 1/15; no deadline. $60 fee, may be waived for applicants with need. Application may be submitted online. Admission notification on a rolling basis beginning on or about 3/15. Must reply by 5/1. **Financial aid:** Priority date 2/15; no closing date. FAFSA required. Applicants notified on a rolling basis starting 3/15.

Academics. **Special study options:** Accelerated study, combined bachelor's/graduate degree, cooperative education, double major, dual enrollment of high school students, ESL, exchange student, honors, independent study, internships, liberal arts/career combination, student-designed major, study abroad, teacher certification program, United Nations semester, Washington semester. **Credit/placement by examination:** AP, CLEP, IB, SAT, ACT, institutional tests. 20 credit hours maximum toward bachelor's degree. **Support services:** Learning center, pre-admission summer program, reduced course load, remedial instruction, tutoring, writing center.

Majors. **Biology:** General, biochemistry. **Business:** Business admin. **Communications:** General. **Computer sciences:** General, computer science, information systems. **Conservation:** Environmental studies. **Education:** General, curriculum, elementary, multi-level teacher, music, secondary. **Engineering:** General, civil, computer, electrical, mechanical, physics. **Engineering technology:** Industrial management. **English:** English lit. **Foreign languages:** French, German, Japanese, Spanish. **Health:** Dental hygiene, music therapy, speech pathology. **History:** General. **Interdisciplinary:** Biological/physical sciences. **Liberal arts:** Arts/sciences. **Math:** General, applied. **Parks/recreation:** Health/fitness, sports admin. **Philosophy/religion:** Philosophy, religion. **Physical sciences:** Chemistry, geology, physics. **Psychology:** General. **Social sciences:** General, economics, international relations, political science, sociology. **Visual/performing arts:** Art, commercial/advertising art, dramatic, music history, music management, music performance, music theory/composition, piano/organ, studio arts, voice/opera.

Most popular majors. Biology 21%, business/marketing 29%, education 14%, parks/recreation 8%, visual/performing arts 7%.

Computing on campus. 325 workstations in dormitories, library, computer center. Dormitories wired for high-speed internet access and linked to campus network. Online course registration, online library, helpline, wireless network available.

Student life. **Freshman orientation:** Mandatory, $120 fee. Preregistration for classes offered. Offered in January, June, July & August, 2-4 days each. **Policies:** Freshmen permitted cars on campus. **Housing:** Guaranteed on-campus for freshmen. Coed dorms, apartments, fraternity/sorority housing, substance-free housing available. $250 fully refundable deposit. Freshmen and sophomores required to live on campus unless living with parents. **Activities:** Bands, choral groups, dance, drama, film society, literary magazine, music ensembles, musical theater, opera, radio station, student government, student newspaper, symphony orchestra, 100 student organizations and clubs.

Athletics. NCAA. **Intercollegiate:** Baseball M, basketball, cross-country W, field hockey W, golf M, soccer W, softball W, swimming, tennis, volleyball, water polo. **Intramural:** Badminton, basketball, bowling, football (tackle), golf, racquetball, soccer, softball, swimming, tennis, volleyball, water polo. **Team name:** Tigers.

Student services. Adult student services, alcohol/substance abuse counseling, campus ministries, career counseling, services for economically disadvantaged, student employment services, financial aid counseling, health services, personal counseling, placement for graduates, veterans' counselor. **Physically disabled:** Services for visually, speech, hearing impaired.

Contact. E-mail: admissions@pacific.edu
Phone: (209) 946-2211 Toll-free number: (800) 959-2867
Fax: (209) 946-2413
Marc McGee, Director of Admissions, University of the Pacific, 3601 Pacific Avenue, Stockton, CA 95211-0197

Vanguard University of Southern California

Costa Mesa, California
www.vanguard.edu — **CB code: 4701**

- Private 4-year university and liberal arts college affiliated with Assemblies of God
- Residential campus in small city

- 1,814 degree-seeking undergraduates: 18% part-time, 64% women, 4% African American, 4% Asian American, 17% Hispanic American, 1% Native American, 1% international
- 346 degree-seeking graduate students
- 86% of applicants admitted
- Application essay required
- 43% graduate within 6 years

General. Founded in 1920. Regionally accredited. **Degrees:** 464 bachelor's awarded; master's offered. **ROTC:** Air Force. **Location:** 45 miles from Los Angeles, 70 miles from San Diego. **Calendar:** Semester, limited summer session. **Full-time faculty:** 66 total; 79% have terminal degrees, 15% minority, 39% women. **Part-time faculty:** 131 total; 34% have terminal degrees, 13% minority, 42% women. **Class size:** 62% < 20, 27% 20-39, 5% 40-49, 6% 50-99.

Freshman class profile. 903 applied, 775 admitted, 405 enrolled.

Mid 50% test scores			
SAT verbal:	450-570	Rank in top quarter:	53%
SAT math:	430-560	Rank in top tenth:	26%
ACT:	19-24	End year in good standing:	90%
GPA 3.50 or higher:	51%	Return as sophomores:	77%
GPA 3.0-3.49:	35%	Out-of-state:	20%
GPA 2.0-2.99:	14%	Live on campus:	95%
		International:	1%

Basis for selection. Priority given to students with GPA of 2.8 or higher, Christian commitment essay, academic reference, reference from pastor. Applications from Christian students who desire an education that integrates Christian faith with learning and living encouraged. SAT or ACT recommended. Interview recommended for borderline applicants. Audition recommended for music, theater majors. **Homeschooled:** Should take GED to qualify for federal financial aid. Must take ACT or SAT and receive ACT composite minimum of 22 or SAT combined minimum of 1000 (exclusive of Writing) in order to qualify for academic scholarship based on home school GPA.

High school preparation. Recommended units include English 4, mathematics 2, social studies 3 and science 2.

2005-2006 Annual costs. Tuition/fees: $20,315. Room/board: $6,756. Books/supplies: $1,260. Personal expenses: $1,818.

2004-2005 Financial aid. Need-based: 336 full-time freshmen applied for aid; 302 were judged to have need; 302 of these received aid. Average need met was 78%. Average scholarship/grant was $13,567; average loan $3,686. 68% of total undergraduate aid awarded as scholarships/grants, 32% as loans/jobs. **Non-need-based:** Awarded to 1,260 full-time undergraduates, including 320 freshmen. Scholarships awarded for academics, athletics, music/drama.

Application procedures. Admission: Priority date 12/1; no deadline. $45 fee, may be waived for applicants with need. Application may be submitted online. Admission notification on a rolling basis beginning on or about 1/15. Must reply by May 1 or within 3 week(s) if notified thereafter. **Financial aid:** Priority date 3/2; no closing date. FAFSA required. Applicants notified on a rolling basis starting 4/1.

Academics. Special study options: Accelerated study, cooperative education, cross-registration, double major, dual enrollment of high school students, external degree, independent study, internships, study abroad, teacher certification program, Washington semester. **Credit/placement by examination:** AP, CLEP, IB, SAT, ACT. 24 credit hours maximum toward bachelor's degree. **Support services:** Learning center, reduced course load, study skills assistance, tutoring, writing center.

Majors. Biology: General. **Business:** General, accounting, business admin, finance, international, marketing. **Communications:** General, broadcast journalism, digital media. **English:** English lit. **Foreign languages:** Spanish. **History:** General. **Interdisciplinary:** Biological/physical sciences. **Legal studies:** Prelaw. **Liberal arts:** Arts/sciences. **Math:** General. **Parks/recreation:** Exercise sciences, health/fitness. **Philosophy/religion:** Christian, religion. **Physical sciences:** Chemistry. **Psychology:** General. **Social sciences:** General, anthropology, political science, sociology. **Theology:** Bible, missionary, religious ed, theology, youth ministry. **Visual/performing arts:** Cinematography, dramatic, music history, music performance.

Most popular majors. Business/marketing 30%, communications/journalism 7%, education 11%, psychology 16%, social sciences 8%, theological studies 11%.

Computing on campus. 182 workstations in dormitories, library, computer center. Dormitories wired for high-speed internet access and linked to campus network. Commuter students can connect to campus network. Online course registration, helpline, wireless network available.

Student life. Freshman orientation: Mandatory, $70 fee. Preregistration for classes offered. 4-day program prior to first day of fall semester. **Policies:** Religious observance required. Freshmen permitted cars on campus. **Housing:** Guaranteed on-campus for freshmen. Single-sex dorms, special housing for disabled, apartments, substance-free housing available. $200 nonrefundable deposit, deadline 7/6. **Activities:** Bands, choral groups, dance, drama, music ensembles, musical theater, student government, student newspaper, student ministries, College Republicans, College Democrats, El Puente, Polynesian ministry, Students for Social Action, Habitat for Humanity, Spanish club, global outreach ministries.

Athletics. NAIA. **Intercollegiate:** Baseball M, basketball, cross-country, soccer, softball W, tennis, track and field, volleyball W. **Intramural:** Football (non-tackle). **Team name:** Lions.

Student services. Adult student services, alcohol/substance abuse counseling, campus ministries, career counseling, student employment services, financial aid counseling, health services, minority student services, personal counseling, veterans' counselor, women's services. **Physically disabled:** Services for visually, hearing impaired.

Contact. E-mail: admissions@vanguard.edu
Phone: (714) 556-3610 Toll-free number: (800) 722-6279
Fax: (714) 966-5471
Jennifer Purga, Director, Undergraduate Admissions, Vanguard University of Southern California, 55 Fair Drive, Costa Mesa, CA 92626-9601

West Coast University
Los Angeles, California
www.westcoastuniversity.com/

- For-profit 4-year health science college
- 55 degree-seeking undergraduates
- 73% of applicants admitted

General. Accredited by ACICS. **Degrees:** 5 bachelor's, 16 associate awarded. **Calendar:** Semester. **Full-time faculty:** 7 total. **Part-time faculty:** 6 total.

Freshman class profile. 94 applied, 69 admitted, 69 enrolled.

Basis for selection. Academics important.

Academics. Credit/placement by examination: CLEP.

Majors. Health: Health care admin.

Contact. Phone: (877) 505-4928
Tracy Cabaco, Admissions Director, West Coast University, 4021 Rosewood Avenue, Los Angeles, CA 90004

Western Career College: Emeryville
Emeryville, California
www.siliconvalley.edu

- For-profit 4-year technical college
- 300 degree-seeking undergraduates

General. Accredited by ACCSCT. **Degrees:** 22 bachelor's, 68 associate awarded. **Calendar:** Continuous, extensive summer session. **Full-time faculty:** 15 total. **Part-time faculty:** 6 total.

Basis for selection. Open admission. CPAT required.

Application procedures. Admission: No deadline. $75 fee, may be waived for applicants with need. Application may be submitted online. Admission notification on a rolling basis. **Financial aid:** FAFSA required. Applicants notified on a rolling basis.

Academics. Credit/placement by examination: CLEP. **Support services:** Learning center, tutoring.

Majors. Communications technology: Animation/special effects, desktop publishing. **Computer sciences:** Computer graphics.

Student life. Freshman orientation: Mandatory. **Policies:** Freshmen permitted cars on campus.

Student services. Student employment services, financial aid counseling.

Contact. Phone: (510) 601-0133 Toll-free number: (800) 750-5627
Western Career College: Emeryville, 1400 65th Street, Suite 200, Emeryville, CA 94608

Westmont College

Santa Barbara, California **CB member**
www.westmont.edu **CB code: 4950**

- Private 4-year liberal arts college affiliated with interdenominational tradition
- Residential campus in small city
- 1,358 degree-seeking undergraduates: 61% women, 2% African American, 8% Asian American, 10% Hispanic American, 2% Native American
- 6 graduate students
- 68% of applicants admitted
- SAT or ACT with writing, application essay required
- 70% graduate within 6 years

General. Founded in 1937. Regionally accredited. **Degrees:** 312 bachelor's awarded. **ROTC:** Army, Air Force. **Location:** 90 miles from Los Angeles. **Calendar:** Semester, limited summer session. **Full-time faculty:** 91 total; 84% have terminal degrees, 11% minority. **Part-time faculty:** 42 total; 29% have terminal degrees, 21% minority, 57% women. **Class size:** 60% < 20, 29% 20-39, 8% 40-49, 2% 50-99. **Special facilities:** Arts center with theater, observatory, electronic music lab, physiology lab.

Freshman class profile. 1,813 applied, 1,231 admitted, 333 enrolled.

Mid 50% test scores			
SAT verbal:	680-740	Rank in top tenth:	44%
SAT math:	670-710	Return as sophomores:	87%
ACT:	24-30	Out-of-state:	37%
Rank in top quarter:	75%	Live on campus:	100%

Basis for selection. Personal Christian statement, college preparatory high school curriculum, high school rank, test scores, 1 academic recommendation, and essays important. Personal interview, teacher, pastor, and other recommendations may enhance chances. SAT Subject Tests recommended. Test scores must be received by November 1 for Early Action applicants. **Homeschooled:** Applicants encouraged. Evaluation based on individual merit as well as high school achievement. Greater emphasis may be given to SAT or ACT scores.

High school preparation. 16 units required. Required units include English 4, mathematics 3, social studies 1, history 2, science 3 (laboratory 2), foreign language 2 and academic electives 4. Students encouraged to take at least 4 strong elective units. Of 3 mathematics credits recommended, 2 algebra, 1 geometry preferred. Applicants should take composition courses at least 1 semester per year.

2005-2006 Annual costs. Tuition/fees: $27,806. Room/board: $8,866. Books/supplies: $1,242. Personal expenses: $1,980.

2005-2006 Financial aid. **Need-based:** 256 full-time freshmen applied for aid; 197 were judged to have need; 197 of these received aid. Average need met was 64%. Average scholarship/grant was $12,941; average loan $3,928. 67% of total undergraduate aid awarded as scholarships/grants, 33% as loans/jobs. **Non-need-based:** Awarded to 534 full-time undergraduates, including 130 freshmen. Scholarships awarded for academics, art, athletics, leadership, minority status, music/drama.

Application procedures. **Admission:** Priority date 2/15; deadline 2/15 (postmark date). $50 fee, may be waived for applicants with need. Application may be submitted online. Admission notification 4/1. Must reply by May 1 or within 2 week(s) if notified thereafter. Candidates not accepted for Early Action may be considered for admission under Regular Decision. This allows time for submission of additional materials that may strengthen the overall application. **Financial aid:** Closing date 3/1. FAFSA required. Applicants notified by 4/1; must reply by 5/1 or within 2 week(s) of notification.

Academics. **Special study options:** Accelerated study, cooperative education, double major, exchange student, honors, independent study, internships, liberal arts/career combination, semester at sea, student-designed major, study abroad, teacher certification program, urban semester, Washington semester. Cross-cultural studies in Western and Eastern Europe, England, Africa, East Asia, Egypt; semester study available in San Francisco, Los Angeles, Mexico and at one of 12 other member colleges of the Christian College Consortium. **Credit/placement by examination:** AP, CLEP, IB, SAT, ACT, institutional tests. 32 credit hours maximum toward bachelor's degree. **Support services:** Learning center, study skills assistance, tutoring, writing center.

Majors. **Area/ethnic studies:** European. **Biology:** General. **Business:** General. **Communications:** General, broadcast journalism, journalism, media studies, organizational, political. **Computer sciences:** Computer science. **Education:** Elementary. **Engineering:** Physics. **Foreign languages:** French, Spanish. **Health:** Predentistry, premedicine, prenursing, prepharmacy, preveterinary. **History:** General. **Interdisciplinary:** Neuroscience. **Legal studies:** Prelaw. **Math:** General. **Parks/recreation:** Exercise sciences. **Philosophy/religion:** Philosophy, religion. **Physical sciences:** Chemistry, physics. **Psychology:** General. **Social sciences:** General, anthropology, economics, political science, sociology. **Visual/performing arts:** Art, dance, dramatic.

Most popular majors. Biology 11%, business/marketing 7%, communications/journalism 12%, English 13%, liberal arts 6%, philosophy/religious studies 9%, social sciences 10%, visual/performing arts 7%.

Computing on campus. 100 workstations in dormitories, library, computer center. Dormitories wired for high-speed internet access and linked to campus network. Commuter students can connect to campus network. Online library, helpline, repair service, student web hosting, wireless network available.

Student life. **Freshman orientation:** Mandatory. Preregistration for classes offered. Overnight program in the summer. **Policies:** Chapel attendance required on Monday, Wednesday, and Friday. "Dry" campus, tobacco free campus. Religious observance required. **Housing:** Guaranteed on-campus for all undergraduates. Coed dorms, special housing for disabled, apartments available. $500 deposit. Coed dorms segregated by floors and/or suites. Men and women do not share hallways and bathrooms. Selected visiting hours for members of opposite sex. **Activities:** Bands, choral groups, dance, drama, film society, literary magazine, music ensembles, musical theater, opera, radio station, student government, student newspaper, symphony orchestra, Christian Concerns, Student Missionary Fellowship, multicultural student organization, Amnesty International, Habitat for Humanity, Leadership Development Program, political organizations, Fellowship of Christian Athletes, community service organizations.

Athletics. NAIA. **Intercollegiate:** Baseball M, basketball, cross-country, soccer, tennis, track and field, volleyball W. **Intramural:** Badminton, basketball, cross-country, field hockey W, football (non-tackle), golf, lacrosse W, racquetball, soccer, softball, swimming, table tennis, tennis, volleyball, water polo. **Team name:** Warriors.

Student services. Alcohol/substance abuse counseling, campus ministries, career counseling, student employment services, financial aid counseling, health services, minority student services, personal counseling, placement for graduates, veterans' counselor, women's services. **Physically disabled:** Services for visually, speech, hearing impaired.

Contact. E-mail: admissions@westmont.edu
Phone: (805) 565-6200 Toll-free number: (800) 777-9011
Fax: (805) 565-6234
Joyce Luy, Dean of Admission, Westmont College, 955 La Paz Road, Santa Barbara, CA 93108-1089

Westwood College

Anaheim, California
www.westwood.edu

- For-profit 4-year technical college
- Very large city
- 620 degree-seeking undergraduates
- Interview required

General. Accredited by ACCSCT. **Degrees:** 80 bachelor's, 63 associate awarded. **Calendar:** Continuous. **Full-time faculty:** 18 total. **Part-time faculty:** 45 total.

Basis for selection. Admissions decisions based on assessment test and interview.

2005-2006 Annual costs. Cost of 20-month, 8-term associate degree program: $33,927; Cost of 34-month bachelor's degree program: $57,810. Cost includes all fees, books, supplies and lab fees (if applicable) for entire program.

Application procedures. **Admission:** $25 fee. Admission notification on a rolling basis. **Financial aid:** FAFSA required. Applicants notified on a rolling basis.

Academics. **Credit/placement by examination:** AP, CLEP.

Majors. **Business:** Accounting/finance, business admin, marketing. **Computer sciences:** Networking, security, web page design, webmaster. **Visual/performing arts:** Design.

Contact. Phone: (714) 704-2720 Toll-free number: (877) 650-6050
Greg Lam, Director of Admissions, Westwood College, 1551 South Douglass Road, Anaheim, CA 92806

Westwood College of Technology: Inland Empire

Upland, California
www.westwood.edu

- For-profit 3-year business and technical college
- Commuter campus in small city
- 1,145 degree-seeking undergraduates
- Interview required

General. Accredited by ACCSCT. **Degrees:** 82 bachelor's, 60 associate awarded. **Location:** 45 miles from Los Angeles; 22 miles from Riverside. **Calendar:** Continuous, extensive summer session. **Full-time faculty:** 10 total. **Part-time faculty:** 50 total. **Class size:** 64% < 20, 36% 20-39.

Basis for selection. Academic record and standardized test scores most important. SAT or ACT recommended. If SAT or ACT scores are not submitted or do not meet minimum requirements, students must take campus-administered Accuplacer placement exam.

2005-2006 Annual costs. Tuition/fees: $11,745. Books/supplies: $1,464. Personal expenses: $1,840.

2004-2005 Financial aid. Need-based: 293 full-time freshmen applied for aid; 293 were judged to have need; 177 of these received aid. Average need met was 95%. Average scholarship/grant was $2,700; average loan $2,700. 41% of total undergraduate aid awarded as scholarships/grants, 59% as loans/jobs. **Non-need-based:** Awarded to 402 full-time undergraduates, including 90 freshmen. Scholarships awarded for academics.

Application procedures. Admission: Priority date 10/15; deadline 10/21 (receipt date). $25 fee. Application may be submitted online. Admission notification on a rolling basis. **Financial aid:** No deadline. FAFSA, institutional form required. Must reply within 1 week(s) of notification.

Academics. Special study options: Cooperative education, distance learning, independent study, liberal arts/career combination. 3-year bachelor's degree program. **Credit/placement by examination:** AP, CLEP, IB, institutional tests. Students may test out of required courses by passing proficiency exams. **Support services:** Learning center, reduced course load, remedial instruction, tutoring.

Majors. Business: Accounting/business management, e-commerce, marketing. **Communications:** Digital media. **Communications technology:** Animation/special effects. **Computer sciences:** LAN/WAN management, web page design. **Protective services:** Police science. **Visual/performing arts:** Design, interior design.

Computing on campus. 10 workstations in library. Online library available.

Student life. Freshman orientation: Mandatory. One-day orientation before start of term. Students receive policy information, schedules, ID cards and participate in ice breakers. **Policies:** Freshmen permitted cars on campus. **Activities:** Student government, student newspaper.

Student services. Career counseling, services for economically disadvantaged, student employment services, financial aid counseling, placement for graduates, veterans' counselor.

Contact. E-mail: lseavers@westwood.edu
Phone: (909) 931-7550 Toll-free number: (866) 221-5632
Fax: (909) 931-5962
Alma Salazar, Director of Admissions, Westwood College of Technology: Inland Empire, 20 West Seventh Street, Upland, CA 91786

Westwood College: Long Beach

Long Beach, California

- For-profit 4-year technical college
- Large city
- 450 degree-seeking undergraduates

General. Accredited by ACCSCT. **Degrees:** 83 associate awarded. **Calendar:** Continuous. **Full-time faculty:** 4 total. **Part-time faculty:** 47 total.

Basis for selection. Institutional assessment exam required if ACT/SAT not submitted.

Application procedures. Admission: No deadline. $100 fee.

Academics. Credit/placement by examination: CLEP.

Majors. Business: Fashion. **Communications technology:** Animation/special effects, graphics. **Computer sciences:** LAN/WAN management, security. **Protective services:** Criminal justice. **Visual/performing arts:** Interior design.

Contact. Phone: (310) 965-0888
Jesse Kamekona, Admissions Director, Westwood College: Long Beach, 19700 South Vermont Avenue #100, Long Beach, CA 90502

Whittier College

Whittier, California — **CB member**
www.whittier.edu — **CB code: 4952**

- Private 4-year liberal arts college
- Residential campus in small city
- 1,325 degree-seeking undergraduates: 2% part-time, 54% women, 4% African American, 8% Asian American, 27% Hispanic American, 2% Native American, 3% international
- 928 degree-seeking graduate students
- 80% of applicants admitted
- SAT or ACT with writing, application essay required
- 56% graduate within 6 years

General. Founded in 1887. Regionally accredited. Historic affiliation with Quakers. **Degrees:** 258 bachelor's awarded; master's, first professional offered. **ROTC:** Army, Navy, Air Force. **Location:** 18 miles from Los Angeles. **Calendar:** 4-1-4, limited summer session. **Full-time faculty:** 86 total; 100% have terminal degrees, 27% minority, 40% women. **Part-time faculty:** 55 total; 24% have terminal degrees, 24% minority, 74% women. **Class size:** 53% < 20, 44% 20-39, less than 1% 40-49, 2% 50-99, less than 1% >100. **Special facilities:** Collection of Quaker books and materials, John Greenleaf Whittier collection including manuscripts, letters and furniture, collection of Richard M. Nixon gifts, keck image processing laboratory.

Freshman class profile. 1,823 applied, 1,458 admitted, 351 enrolled.

Mid 50% test scores			
SAT verbal:	480-590	Rank in top tenth:	25%
SAT math:	470-600	Return as sophomores:	80%
ACT:	19-25	Out-of-state:	37%
GPA 3.50 or higher:	40%	Live on campus:	88%
GPA 3.0-3.49:	28%	International:	3%
GPA 2.0-2.99:	32%	Fraternities:	2%
Rank in top quarter:	42%	Sororities:	3%

Basis for selection. GPA, course selection, and class rank most important followed by essays, references, interviews, test scores, activities, and geographic considerations. Interview recommended.

High school preparation. Required and recommended units include English 3-4, mathematics 2-3, social studies 1-2, science 1-2 and foreign language 2-3.

2005-2006 Annual costs. Tuition/fees: $26,138. Room/board: $8,368. Books/supplies: $656. Personal expenses: $1,380.

2004-2005 Financial aid. Need-based: 351 full-time freshmen applied for aid; 254 were judged to have need; 254 of these received aid. Average need met was 91%. Average scholarship/grant was $12,535; average loan $6,296. 53% of total undergraduate aid awarded as scholarships/grants, 47% as loans/jobs. **Non-need-based:** Awarded to 724 full-time undergraduates, including 142 freshmen. Scholarships awarded for academics, alumni affiliation, art, music/drama. **Additional information:** Auditions required for talent scholarship applicants.

Application procedures. Admission: Priority date 2/1; no deadline. $50 fee, may be waived for applicants with need. Application may be submitted online. Admission notification on a rolling basis beginning on or about 12/30. Must reply by May 1 or within 2 week(s) if notified thereafter. **Financial aid:** Priority date 3/1; no closing date. FAFSA, CSS PROFILE required. Applicants notified on a rolling basis starting 2/1; must reply within 2 week(s) of notification.

Academics. Special study options: Combined bachelor's/graduate degree, double major, independent study, internships, liberal arts/career combination, semester at sea, student-designed major, study abroad, teacher certification program, Washington semester. **Credit/placement by examination:** AP, CLEP, IB, institutional tests. 30 credit hours maximum toward bachelor's degree. **Support services:** Learning center, study skills assistance, tutoring, writing center.

Majors. **Area/ethnic studies:** Latin American. **Biology:** General. **Business:** General. **Conservation:** General. **Education:** General, early childhood. **English:** American lit, British lit. **Foreign languages:** General, comparative lit, French, Spanish. **Health:** Athletic training, predentistry, premedicine, prepharmacy, preveterinary, recreational therapy. **History:** General. **Legal studies:** Prelaw. **Liberal arts:** Arts/sciences. **Math:** General. **Philosophy/religion:** Philosophy, religion. **Physical sciences:** Chemistry, physics. **Psychology:** General. **Public administration:** Social work. **Social sciences:** Anthropology, international relations, political science, sociology, urban studies. **Visual/performing arts:** Art, art history/conservation, dramatic, music history, theater history.

Most popular majors. Biology 9%, business/marketing 16%, English 11%, family/consumer sciences 9%, history 6%, psychology 6%, social sciences 17%, visual/performing arts 6%.

Computing on campus. 165 workstations in dormitories, library, computer center. Dormitories linked to campus network.

Student life. **Freshman orientation:** Mandatory, $100 fee. **Policies:** Freshmen permitted cars on campus. **Housing:** Guaranteed on-campus for freshmen. Coed dorms, single-sex dorms, substance-free housing available. $100 nonrefundable deposit, deadline 5/1. Multicultural hall, honors floor, living and learning community available. **Activities:** Bands, choral groups, dance, drama, literary magazine, music ensembles, musical theater, radio station, student government, student newspaper, several ethnic, religious, and service groups, international student union, national honor societies.

Athletics. NCAA. **Intercollegiate:** Baseball M, basketball, cross-country, diving, football (tackle) M, golf, lacrosse, soccer, softball W, swimming, tennis, track and field, volleyball W, water polo. **Intramural:** Basketball, handball, racquetball, softball, volleyball. **Team name:** Poets.

Student services. Career counseling, student employment services, health services, on-campus daycare, personal counseling, placement for graduates.

Contact. E-mail: admission@whittier.edu
Phone: (562) 907-4238 Fax: (562) 907-4870
Lisa Meyer, Vice President of Enrollment, Whittier College, 13406 East Philadelphia Street, Whittier, CA 90608-0634

William Jessup University

Rocklin, California
www.jessup.edu **CB code: 4756**

- Private 4-year Bible and liberal arts college affiliated with interdenominational tradition
- Residential campus in small city
- 428 degree-seeking undergraduates: 31% part-time, 53% women
- 5 degree-seeking graduate students
- 62% of applicants admitted
- SAT or ACT (ACT writing recommended), application essay required

General. Founded in 1939. Candidate for regional accreditation; also accredited by ABHE. **Degrees:** 67 bachelor's awarded. **Location:** 20 miles from Sacramento. **Calendar:** Semester, limited summer session. **Full-time faculty:** 19 total; 63% have terminal degrees, 5% minority, 32% women. **Part-time faculty:** 67 total; 24% have terminal degrees, 15% minority, 24% women. **Class size:** 77% < 20, 16% 20-39, less than 1% 40-49, 6% 50-99.

Freshman class profile. 104 applied, 65 admitted, 60 enrolled.

Mid 50% test scores			
SAT verbal:	440-590	Out-of-state:	13%
SAT math:	430-580	Live on campus:	60%
ACT:	18-23	International:	1%

Basis for selection. Applicants must demonstrate a clear desire to grow in understanding of Christian faith and to live and learn in Christ-centered, Bible-based community. Interview strongly recommended, may be required. Audition required for music scholarship (majors only). **Homeschooled:** Extra emphasis placed on SAT/ACT; professional/third-party home educators transcript provider preferred over in-home development of transcripts. **Learning Disabled:** Student must provide documentation of learning disability and meet with an academic skills advisor regularly.

High school preparation. 15 units required; 24 recommended. Required and recommended units include English 4, mathematics 3-4, social studies 1, history 2, science 2-3 (laboratory 2), foreign language 3-4 and academic electives 4. Religion taken for credit at accredited parochial/Christian high school may be given academic consideration.

2005-2006 Annual costs. Tuition/fees: $15,814. Room/board: $6,360. Books/supplies: $1,350. Personal expenses: $2,475.

Financial aid. **Non-need-based:** Scholarships awarded for academics, athletics, music/drama.

Application procedures. **Admission:** Priority date 6/1; deadline 8/1 (postmark date). $35 fee, may be waived for applicants with need. Application may be submitted online. Admission notification on a rolling basis beginning on or about 1/1. Must reply by May 1 or within 2 week(s) if notified thereafter. $250 enrollment deposit is also housing deposit and refundable until May 1 (CDRA). **Financial aid:** Priority date 3/1, closing date 8/1. FAFSA required. Applicants notified on a rolling basis starting 3/1; must reply by 5/1 or within 2 week(s) of notification.

Academics. All ministry-based degrees offer a major in Bible and theology. Emphasis placed on pastoral training, missions, youth ministry, Christian education, music and worship. **Special study options:** Double major, independent study, internships, study abroad, teacher certification program. Degree completion program one night/week for students 25 or older with 48 completed units. **Credit/placement by examination:** AP, CLEP, IB, institutional tests. **Support services:** Reduced course load, remedial instruction, study skills assistance, tutoring.

Majors. **Business:** Business admin. **Education:** Elementary, multi-level teacher. **Philosophy/religion:** Religion. **Theology:** Bible, missionary, pastoral counseling, religious ed, sacred music, youth ministry.

Most popular majors. Business/marketing 29%, philosophy/religious studies 46%, psychology 15%, visual/performing arts 10%.

Computing on campus. Dormitories wired for high-speed internet access and linked to campus network. Commuter students can connect to campus network. Online library, helpline, repair service, wireless network available.

Student life. **Freshman orientation:** Mandatory. Preregistration for classes offered. Three 2-day orientation opportunities in May, July and August, including placement testing. **Policies:** Dry campus. Quiet hours but no curfew. No formal dress code, but appropriate dress recommended. Chapel attendance required. Religious observance required. Freshmen permitted cars on campus. **Housing:** Guaranteed on-campus for all undergraduates. Coed dorms, single-sex dorms available. $250 nonrefundable deposit, deadline 6/1. Coed dorm segregated by suite. Men and women do not share bathrooms or bedrooms. **Activities:** Jazz band, choral groups, music ensembles, student government, spiritual formation groups, multicultural fellowship.

Athletics. NAIA. **Intercollegiate:** Basketball, cross-country, soccer, volleyball W. **Team name:** Warriors.

Student services. Campus ministries, career counseling, personal counseling. **Physically disabled:** Services for visually, hearing impaired.

Contact. E-mail: admissions@jessup.edu
Phone: (916) 577-2222 Toll-free number: (800) 355-7522
Fax: (916) 577-2220
Vance Pascua, Director of Admission, William Jessup University, 333 Sunset Boulevard, Rocklin, CA 95765

Woodbury University

Burbank, California **CB member**
www.woodbury.edu **CB code: 4955**

- Private 4-year university
- Commuter campus in very large city
- 1,258 degree-seeking undergraduates: 18% part-time, 60% women, 6% African American, 11% Asian American, 34% Hispanic American, 6% international
- 169 degree-seeking graduate students
- 80% of applicants admitted
- SAT or ACT (ACT writing optional), application essay required
- 57% graduate within 6 years

General. Founded in 1884. Regionally accredited. Combines professional programs in design, architecture, and business with liberal arts components. **Degrees:** 255 bachelor's awarded; master's offered. **Location:** 15 miles from downtown Los Angeles. **Calendar:** Semester, limited summer session. **Full-time faculty:** 44 total; 89% have terminal degrees, 7% minority, 43% women. **Part-time faculty:** 186 total. **Class size:** 81% < 20, 19% 20-39, less than 1% 40-49. **Special facilities:** Design gallery.

Freshman class profile. 390 applied, 311 admitted, 133 enrolled.

Mid 50% test scores		Out-of-state:	14%
SAT verbal:	400-520	Live on campus:	20%
SAT math:	400-550	International:	5%
Rank in top quarter:	40%	Fraternities:	6%
Rank in top tenth:	10%	Sororities:	11%
Return as sophomores:	73%		

Basis for selection. Primary emphasis placed on applicant's prior academic record and standardized test scores. Interview recommended. **Homeschooled:** State high school equivalency certificate required.

High school preparation. College-preparatory program recommended. 15 units recommended. Recommended units include English 4, mathematics 3, social studies 3, history 2, science 3 (laboratory 2) and foreign language 2.

2006-2007 Annual costs. Tuition/fees: $23,474. Room/board: $8,463. Books/supplies: $1,260. Personal expenses: $1,980.

2005-2006 Financial aid. Need-based: Average need met was 62%. Average scholarship/grant was $15,470; average loan $2,649. 60% of total undergraduate aid awarded as scholarships/grants, 40% as loans/jobs. **Non-need-based:** Scholarships awarded for academics.

Application procedures. Admission: No deadline. $35 fee, may be waived for applicants with need. Application may be submitted online. Admission notification on a rolling basis. Must reply by May 1 or within 4 week(s) if notified thereafter. **Financial aid:** Priority date 3/2; no closing date. FAFSA, institutional form required. Applicants notified on a rolling basis starting 3/15; must reply by 5/1 or within 2 week(s) of notification.

Academics. Special study options: Accelerated study, double major, independent study, internships, liberal arts/career combination, student-designed major, weekend college. **Credit/placement by examination:** AP, CLEP, IB, institutional tests. Institutional/departmental examinations used for placement or counseling. **Support services:** Learning center, reduced course load, remedial instruction, tutoring.

Majors. Architecture: Architecture, interior. **Business:** Accounting, business admin, fashion, marketing, organizational behavior. **Communications:** Media studies. **Communications technology:** Animation/special effects. **Computer sciences:** General. **Psychology:** General. **Visual/performing arts:** Commercial/advertising art, fashion design, graphic design.

Most popular majors. Architecture 29%, business/marketing 34%, social sciences 8%, visual/performing arts 16%.

Computing on campus. 170 workstations in library, computer center. Commuter students can connect to campus network. Online library, helpline, wireless network available.

Student life. Freshman orientation: Mandatory, $75 fee. Preregistration for classes offered. **Policies:** Freshmen permitted cars on campus. **Housing:** Coed dorms, apartments available. $150 fully refundable deposit, deadline 5/1. **Activities:** Film society, student government, student newspaper, Armenian Student Association, International Student Organization, Residence Life Council, LIGHT, fraternities and sororities.

Athletics. Intramural: Football (tackle) M.

Student services. Adult student services, alcohol/substance abuse counseling, career counseling, services for economically disadvantaged, student employment services, financial aid counseling, health services, personal counseling, placement for graduates. **Physically disabled:** Services for visually, speech, hearing impaired.

Contact. E-mail: admissions@woodbury.edu
Phone: (818) 767-0888 ext. 221 Toll-free number: (800) 784-9663
Fax: (818) 767-7520
Mauro Diaz, Director of Admissions, Woodbury University, 7500 Glenoaks Boulevard, Burbank, CA 91510-7846

World Mission University

- Private 4-year Bible college

General. Accredited by ABHE.

Contact. Phone: (213) 385-2322
500 Shatto Place, Los Angeles, CA 90020

Yeshiva Ohr Elchonon Chabad/West Coast Talmudical Seminary

Los Angeles, California

CB code: 1331

- Private 4-year rabbinical college for men affiliated with Jewish faith
- Residential campus in very large city

General. Founded in 1953. Accredited by AARTS. **Calendar:** Semester.

Annual costs/financial aid. Tuition/fees (2005-2006): $9,150. Room/board: $6,250. Books/supplies: $125. Personal expenses: $100.

Contact. Phone: (323) 937-3763
Director of Admissions, 7215 Waring Avenue, Los Angeles, CA 90046

Colorado

Adams State College

Alamosa, Colorado
www.adams.edu **CB code: 4001**

- Public 4-year liberal arts college
- Residential campus in small town
- 2,142 degree-seeking undergraduates: 17% part-time, 56% women, 5% African American, 1% Asian American, 29% Hispanic American, 2% Native American
- 664 degree-seeking graduate students
- 60% of applicants admitted
- SAT or ACT (ACT writing optional) required
- 37% graduate within 6 years

General. Founded in 1921. Regionally accredited. Hispanic-serving institution. **Degrees:** 286 bachelor's, 20 associate awarded; master's offered. **Location:** 225 miles from Denver, 200 miles from Albuquerque, New Mexico. **Calendar:** Semester, limited summer session. **Full-time faculty:** 104 total; 76% have terminal degrees, 17% minority, 61% women. **Part-time faculty:** 81 total; 9% minority, 68% women. **Class size:** 63% < 20, 29% 20-39, 6% 40-49, 2% 50-99. **Special facilities:** Observatory, planetarium, natural history museum, geology museum, cross-cultural center.

Freshman class profile. 1,762 applied, 1,065 admitted, 512 enrolled.

Mid 50% test scores			
SAT verbal:	430-560	GPA 2.0-2.99:	44%
SAT math:	450-550	Rank in top quarter:	24%
ACT:	16-22	Rank in top tenth:	7%
GPA 3.50 or higher:	22%	Return as sophomores:	57%
GPA 3.0-3.49:	31%	Out-of-state:	10%

Basis for selection. Open admissions for associate degree programs only. Bachelor's degree candidates must have either 2.0 high school GPA, or rank in top two-thirds of class with average or above average score on ACT or SAT. Accuplacer tests for math and English required if SAT or ACT not available. Audition required of music majors. Portfolio required of art majors. **Homeschooled:** Transcript of courses and grades required.

High school preparation. College-preparatory program recommended. 15 units required. Required and recommended units include English 4, mathematics 2, social studies 3, history 1, science 2 and foreign language 2. Computer applications: .5 units recommended. Math should include Algebra I and one advanced math course.

2005-2006 Annual costs. Tuition/fees: $2,853; $9,123 out-of-state. Room/board: $6,140. Books/supplies: $1,163. Personal expenses: $1,026.

2004-2005 Financial aid. Need-based: Average scholarship/grant was $2,009; average loan $1,366. 54% of total undergraduate aid awarded as scholarships/grants, 46% as loans/jobs. **Non-need-based:** Scholarships awarded for academics, alumni affiliation, art, athletics, leadership, minority status, music/drama, state residency.

Application procedures. Admission: Priority date 8/1; no deadline. $20 fee, may be waived for applicants with need. Application may be submitted online. Admission notification on a rolling basis. **Financial aid:** Priority date 3/1, closing date 4/15. FAFSA required. Applicants notified on a rolling basis starting 4/30; must reply within 4 week(s) of notification.

Academics. Special study options: Accelerated study, combined bachelor's/graduate degree, distance learning, double major, dual enrollment of high school students, independent study, internships, study abroad, teacher certification program, weekend college. **Credit/placement by examination:** AP, CLEP, IB, SAT, ACT, institutional tests. 30 credit hours maximum toward bachelor's degree. **Support services:** Learning center, reduced course load, remedial instruction, study skills assistance, tutoring, writing center.

Majors. Agriculture: Business. **Biology:** General, bacteriology, botany, exercise physiology, zoology. **Business:** General, accounting, business admin, finance, management information systems, marketing, office/clerical, small business admin. **Communications:** General, advertising. **Computer sciences:** General. **Conservation:** Management/policy. **Education:** General, art, biology, business, chemistry, elementary, English, history, mathematics, middle, multi-level teacher, music, physical, science, secondary, social science, social studies, Spanish, speech. **English:** Creative writing, English lit. **Foreign languages:** Spanish. **Health:** Athletic training, health services, nursing (RN), predentistry, premedicine, prenursing, prepharmacy, preveterinary. **History:** General. **Legal studies:** Prelaw. **Liberal arts:** Arts/sciences. **Math:** General. **Parks/recreation:** Exercise sciences, health/fitness. **Physical sciences:** Chemical physics, chemistry, geology, physics. **Psychology:** General. **Social sciences:** General, criminology, economics, sociology. **Visual/performing arts:** Art, ceramics, dramatic, drawing, metal/jewelry, music performance, music theory/composition, painting, photography, printmaking, sculpture, studio arts, voice/opera.

Most popular majors. Business/marketing 24%, English 6%, liberal arts 26%, parks/recreation 7%, psychology 8%, social sciences 11%, visual/performing arts 7%.

Computing on campus. 191 workstations in dormitories, library, computer center, student center. Dormitories wired for high-speed internet access and linked to campus network. Commuter students can connect to campus network. Online course registration, online library, helpline, student web hosting, wireless network available.

Student life. Freshman orientation: Mandatory. Preregistration for classes offered. Program held weekend before start of fall semester. **Policies:** Freshmen permitted cars on campus. **Housing:** Guaranteed on-campus for freshmen. Coed dorms, single-sex dorms, apartments, substance-free housing available. $150 partly refundable deposit. Learning community house, freshman interest-group housing, drug and alcohol-free learning community, outdoor adventure community, making the grade community (must maintain 3.5 GPA). **Activities:** Bands, choral groups, dance, drama, literary magazine, music ensembles, musical theater, radio station, student government, student newspaper, Circle K, College Republicans, Newman Club, Ski Buffs, Student Ambassadors, Teacher Education Association, Associated Students and Faculty, Phi Beta Lambda.

Athletics. NCAA. **Intercollegiate:** Basketball, cross-country, football (tackle) M, golf, soccer W, softball W, track and field, volleyball W, wrestling M. **Intramural:** Basketball, bowling, racquetball, skiing, soccer, softball, swimming, tennis, volleyball, water polo. **Team name:** Grizzlies.

Student services. Adult student services, career counseling, student employment services, financial aid counseling, health services, on-campus daycare, personal counseling, placement for graduates, veterans' counselor. **Physically disabled:** Services for visually, hearing impaired.

Contact. E-mail: ascadmit@adams.edu
Phone: (719) 587-7712 Toll-free number: (800) 824-6494
Fax: (719) 587-7522
Eric Carpio, Director for Admissions, Adams State College, 208 Edgemont Boulevard, Alamosa, CO 81102

Art Institute of Colorado

Denver, Colorado
www.aic.artinstitutes.edu **CB code: 7150**

- For-profit 4-year visual arts and technical college
- Commuter campus in very large city
- 2,350 degree-seeking undergraduates
- Application essay, interview required

General. Founded in 1952. Accredited by ACICS. **Degrees:** 241 bachelor's, 231 associate awarded. **Location:** Downtown. **Calendar:** Quarter, extensive summer session. **Full-time faculty:** 79 total. **Part-time faculty:** 49 total. **Special facilities:** Student-run restaurant at culinary school.

Basis for selection. Commitment to career most important; essay, interview important; high school transcript considered with GPA. Portfolio required of advanced standing applicants. **Homeschooled:** Documentation of grades and official gradution date required.

2006-2007 Annual costs. Tuition/fees (projected): $19,066. Books/supplies: $2,968.

Financial aid. Additional information: Tuition at time of first enrollment guaranteed to students for 4 years providing student maintains continuous attendance and completes program within 150% of program length.

Application procedures. Admission: No deadline. $50 fee. Application may be submitted online. Admission notification on a rolling basis. **Financial aid:** No deadline. FAFSA, institutional form required. Applicants notified on a rolling basis.

Academics. **Special study options:** Distance learning, independent study, internships, study abroad. **Credit/placement by examination:** CLEP, IB, institutional tests. 30 credit hours maximum toward associate degree. **Support services:** Learning center, remedial instruction.

Majors. **Communications technology:** Animation/special effects. **Computer sciences:** Computer graphics. **Family/consumer sciences:** Food/nutrition, institutional food production. **Personal/culinary services:** Culinary arts. **Visual/performing arts:** Cinematography, commercial photography, commercial/advertising art, design, industrial design, interior design, multimedia, photography.

Computing on campus. 380 workstations in library, computer center. Dormitories wired for high-speed internet access.

Student life. **Freshman orientation:** Mandatory. Preregistration for classes offered. **Policies:** Freshmen permitted cars on campus. **Housing:** Coed dorms, substance-free housing available. $300 fully refundable deposit. **Activities:** Student newspaper.

Student services. Alcohol/substance abuse counseling, career counseling, student employment services, financial aid counseling, personal counseling, placement for graduates, veterans' counselor. **Physically disabled:** Services for visually, speech, hearing impaired.

Contact. E-mail: aicadm@aii.edu
Phone: (303) 837-0825 Toll-free number: (800) 275-2420
Fax: (303) 860-8520
Brian Parker, Director of Admissions, Art Institute of Colorado, 1200 Lincoln Street, Denver, CO 80203

College America: Colorado Springs

Colorado Springs, Colorado
www.collegeamerica.edu

- For-profit 4-year technical college
- Commuter campus

General. Accredited by ACCSCT.

Contact. Phone: (719) 637-0600
3645 Citadel Drive South, Colorado Springs, CO 80909

College America: Fort Collins

Fort Collins, Colorado

- For-profit 4-year technical college
- Commuter campus

General. Accredited by ACCSCT. **Calendar:** Semester.

Contact. Phone: (970) 223-6060
4601 South Mason, Fort Collins, CO 80525

Colorado Christian University

Lakewood, Colorado — **CB member**
www.ccu.edu — **CB code: 4659**

- Private 4-year university and liberal arts college affiliated with nondenominational tradition
- Residential campus in large city
- 1,772 degree-seeking undergraduates: 41% part-time, 60% women, 4% African American, 1% Asian American, 9% Hispanic American, 1% Native American, 1% international
- 302 degree-seeking graduate students
- 77% of applicants admitted
- SAT or ACT (ACT writing optional), application essay required
- 45% graduate within 6 years

General. Founded in 1914. Regionally accredited. Degree completion programs available at Colorado Springs, Grand Junction, Loveland, Denver, and Lakewood campuses. **Degrees:** 380 bachelor's, 13 associate awarded; master's offered. **ROTC:** Army, Air Force. **Location:** 10 miles from Denver. **Calendar:** Semester, limited summer session. **Full-time faculty:** 43 total; 7% minority, 44% women. **Part-time faculty:** 3 total; 67% women. **Class size:** 78% < 20, 18% 20-39, 2% 40-49, 1% 50-99.

Freshman class profile. 946 applied, 729 admitted, 237 enrolled.

Mid 50% test scores			
SAT verbal:	510-630	**GPA 2.0-2.99:**	19%
SAT math:	480-590	**Rank in top quarter:**	46%
ACT:	20-26	**Rank in top tenth:**	22%
GPA 3.50 or higher:	54%	**Return as sophomores:**	72%
GPA 3.0-3.49:	26%	**Out-of-state:**	46%
		Live on campus:	92%

Basis for selection. Applicants must show evidence of commitment to Christian faith through written statement. Course selection, GPA, test scores, leadership or service, and motivation important. SAT or ACT is required for all students who have completed less than 30 credit hours. Interviews encouraged. Audition required of music and theater majors.

High school preparation. 19 units recommended. Recommended units include English 4, mathematics 3, social studies 1, history 2, science 3 (laboratory 2) and foreign language 3. Recommend 1 unit of computer science.

2005-2006 Annual costs. Tuition/fees: $16,740. Room/board: $6,990. Books/supplies: $1,188. Personal expenses: $1,044.

Financial aid. **Non-need-based:** Scholarships awarded for academics, athletics, leadership, music/drama.

Application procedures. **Admission:** Priority date 3/1; deadline 8/1 (postmark date). $50 fee, may be waived for applicants with need. Application may be submitted online. Admission notification on a rolling basis beginning on or about 11/1. Must reply by May 1 or within 4 week(s) if notified thereafter. **Financial aid:** Priority date 3/15; no closing date. FAFSA required. Applicants notified on a rolling basis starting 4/1; must reply by 5/1 or within 4 week(s) of notification.

Academics. **Special study options:** Accelerated study, cooperative education, distance learning, double major, honors, independent study, internships, semester at sea, student-designed major, study abroad, teacher certification program, urban semester, Washington semester, weekend college. American studies program (Washington, D.C.), host university for Institute for Family Studies; China studies program at various sites in China, Latin American program (Costa Rica), Los Angeles film studies center, Middle East studies (Cairo, Egypt), Oxford honors program (University of Oxford, England), Russian studies program at various sites in Russia, Summer Institute of Journalism (Washington DC). **Credit/placement by examination:** AP, CLEP, IB, institutional tests. 15 credit hours maximum toward associate degree, 45 toward bachelor's. **Support services:** Learning center, reduced course load, remedial instruction, study skills assistance, tutoring, writing center.

Majors. **Biology:** General. **Business:** Business admin, management information systems, management science. **Communications:** General. **Computer sciences:** General. **Education:** Music. **English:** English lit. **History:** General. **Interdisciplinary:** Biological/physical sciences, global studies. **Liberal arts:** Arts/sciences. **Math:** General. **Parks/recreation:** Health/fitness. **Physical sciences:** Physics. **Psychology:** General. **Social sciences:** General. **Theology:** Bible, youth ministry. **Visual/performing arts:** Music performance, studio arts.

Most popular majors. Business/marketing 37%, computer/information sciences 16%, education 14%, psychology 7%, theological studies 6%.

Computing on campus. 151 workstations in library, computer center, student center. Dormitories wired for high-speed internet access and linked to campus network. Online course registration, online library, helpline, wireless network available.

Student life. **Freshman orientation:** Mandatory. Preregistration for classes offered. Seminars for students and parents 4 days prior to beginning of classes. **Policies:** Use of alcoholic beverages, illegal drugs, and tobacco prohibited on campus and at college-sponsored activities. Premarital sexual relationships prohibited. Religious observance required. Freshmen permitted cars on campus. **Housing:** Guaranteed on-campus for freshmen. Coed dorms, single-sex dorms, special housing for disabled, apartments, substance-free housing available. $150 fully refundable deposit, deadline 5/1. Theme housing available. **Activities:** Bands, choral groups, drama, literary magazine, music ensembles, musical theater, student government, student newspaper, symphony orchestra, Snappers, Fat Boys, FIRE, West Side, Freedom Ministry, Open Door Ministry, Prayer Ministry, Project CURE, SALT.

Athletics. NCAA. **Intercollegiate:** Baseball M, basketball, cross-country, golf, soccer, tennis, volleyball W. **Intramural:** Basketball, football (non-tackle), soccer, softball, table tennis, tennis, volleyball. **Team name:** Cougars.

Student services. Campus ministries, career counseling, student employment services, financial aid counseling, health services, minority student services, personal counseling, veterans' counselor, women's services. **Physically disabled:** Services for visually impaired.

Contact. E-mail: admission@ccu.edu
Phone: (303) 963-3200 Toll-free number: (800) 443-2484
Fax: (303) 963-3201
Steve Woodburn, Director of Undergraduate Admission, Colorado Christian University, 8787 West Alameda Avenue, Lakewood, CO 80226

Colorado College

Colorado Springs, Colorado **CB member**
www.coloradocollege.edu **CB code: 4072**

- Private 4-year liberal arts college
- Residential campus in large city
- 1,928 degree-seeking undergraduates: 54% women, 2% African American, 4% Asian American, 7% Hispanic American, 1% Native American, 2% international
- 36 degree-seeking graduate students
- 38% of applicants admitted
- SAT or ACT (ACT writing optional), application essay required
- 83% graduate within 6 years

General. Founded in 1874. Regionally accredited. Academic year based on block plan schedule of eight three-and-a-half week blocks wherein students take and faculty teach one course at a time. Mountain cabin located about 35 minutes from campus for class and retreat use. Baca campus in Southern Colorado available for intensive study. **Degrees:** 479 bachelor's awarded; master's offered. **ROTC:** Army. **Location:** 70 miles from Denver. **Calendar:** 8 blocks of 3.5 weeks each. Extensive summer session. **Full-time faculty:** 176 total. **Part-time faculty:** 30 total. **Class size:** 67% < 20, 33% 20-39. **Special facilities:** Electronic music studio, environmental science van equipped for field research, petrographic microscopes, X-ray diffractometer, sedimentology lab, metabolic equipment, hydrostatic weighing equipment, cadaver study in sports science, scanning electron microscope, transmission electron microscope.

Freshman class profile. 4,089 applied, 1,535 admitted, 476 enrolled.

Mid 50% test scores			
SAT verbal:	610-710	Rank in top tenth:	66%
SAT math:	610-690	Return as sophomores:	92%
ACT:	27-31	Out-of-state:	70%
Rank in top quarter:	90%	Live on campus:	99%
		International:	1%

Basis for selection. Personal essays, school achievement record most important. Counselor and teacher recommendations, extracurricular activities and test scores also important. Special talents; geographic, socioeconomic, ethnic diversity considered. Challenging curriculum, including honors/AP/IB courses if available, recommended. Interview optional. **Homeschooled:** Transcript of courses and grades required.

High school preparation. 16 units required; 20 recommended. Required and recommended units include English 4.

2005-2006 Annual costs. Tuition/fees: $30,048. Room/board: $7,820. Books/supplies: $844. Personal expenses: $900.

2005-2006 Financial aid. Need-based: Average need met was 98%. Average scholarship/grant was $24,621; average loan $3,521. 85% of total undergraduate aid awarded as scholarships/grants, 15% as loans/jobs. **Non-need-based:** Scholarships awarded for academics, athletics, state residency. **Additional information:** Need-based financial aid available only to students enrolled half-time or more.

Application procedures. Admission: Closing date 1/15 (postmark date). $50 fee, may be waived for applicants with need. Application may be submitted online. Admission notification 4/1. Must reply by May 1 or within 2 week(s) if notified thereafter. Campus visit recommended. Separate letter requesting early action and explaining reasons for applying early required for early action. **Financial aid:** Closing date 2/15. FAFSA, CSS PROFILE required. Applicants notified by 3/20; must reply by 5/1.

Academics. Special study options: Combined bachelor's/graduate degree, double major, ESL, independent study, internships, liberal arts/career combination, semester at sea, student-designed major, study abroad, teacher certification program, urban semester, Washington semester. Urban studies, urban arts and urban education (Chicago); science semester (Oak Ridge, Tennessee); tropical field research (Costa Rica); wilderness field station (Wisconsin); ACM London-Florence program; study abroad programs in France, Germany, Mexico, Russia, Japan, India, Sweden, the Netherlands, and Wales; ACM program in Tanzania and Zimbabwe. **Credit/placement by examination:** AP, CLEP, IB, institutional tests. 32 credit hours maximum toward bachelor's degree. **Support services:** Learning center, remedial instruction, study skills assistance, tutoring, writing center.

Majors. Area/ethnic studies: Asian, French, regional, Russian/Slavic, Spanish/Iberian, women's. **Biology:** General, biochemistry. **Conservation:** General, environmental science. **Foreign languages:** Classics, comparative lit, German, Spanish. **History:** General. **Interdisciplinary:** Math/computer science, neuroscience. **Liberal arts:** Arts/sciences. **Math:** General. **Philosophy/religion:** Philosophy, religion. **Physical sciences:** Chemistry, geology, physics. **Psychology:** General. **Social sciences:** Anthropology, economics, political science, sociology. **Visual/performing arts:** Art history/conservation, dance, dramatic, film/cinema, studio arts.

Most popular majors. Biology 12%, English 8%, interdisciplinary studies 6%, philosophy/religious studies 6%, psychology 7%, social sciences 28%, visual/performing arts 9%.

Computing on campus. 235 workstations in dormitories, library, computer center, student center. Dormitories wired for high-speed internet access and linked to campus network. Commuter students can connect to campus network. Online course registration, online library, helpline, student web hosting available.

Student life. Freshman orientation: Mandatory. Preregistration for classes offered. Week-long, 4-day service trip in the Southwest for incoming students; parents invited. **Housing:** Guaranteed on-campus for all undergraduates. Coed dorms, single-sex dorms, apartments, substance-free housing available. $175 deposit, deadline 6/24. Theme, project, language houses available. Students required to live on campus first 3 years. **Activities:** Bands, choral groups, dance, drama, film society, literary magazine, music ensembles, radio station, student government, student newspaper, Asian American students union, black student union, Chaverim/Hillel, gay, lesbian, and bisexual alliance, community kitchen, environmental action, Shove Chapel Council, Chicano/Latino organization, victim's assistance team, BreakOut community service trips.

Athletics. NCAA. **Intercollegiate:** Basketball, cross-country, diving, football (tackle) M, ice hockey M, lacrosse, soccer, softball W, swimming, tennis, track and field, volleyball W, water polo W. **Intramural:** Basketball, football (non-tackle), ice hockey, racquetball, soccer, softball, tennis, volleyball. **Team name:** Tigers.

Student services. Alcohol/substance abuse counseling, campus ministries, career counseling, student employment services, financial aid counseling, health services, minority student services, on-campus daycare, personal counseling, women's services. **Physically disabled:** Services for visually, speech, hearing impaired.

Contact. E-mail: admission@coloradocollege.edu
Phone: (719) 389-6344 Toll-free number: (800) 542-7214
Fax: (719) 389-6816
Mark Hatch, Dean of Admissions and Financial Aid, Colorado College, 14 East Cache La Poudre, Colorado Springs, CO 80903

Colorado School of Mines

Golden, Colorado **CB member**
www.mines.edu **CB code: 4073**

- Public 4-year university and engineering college
- Residential campus in large town
- 3,098 degree-seeking undergraduates: 6% part-time, 21% women, 1% African American, 5% Asian American, 7% Hispanic American, 1% Native American, 3% international
- 751 graduate students
- 87% of applicants admitted
- SAT or ACT (ACT writing optional) required
- 68% graduate within 6 years; 27% enter graduate study

General. Founded in 1874. Regionally accredited. **Degrees:** 505 bachelor's awarded; master's, doctoral offered. **ROTC:** Army, Air Force. **Location:** 20 miles from Denver. **Calendar:** Semester, limited summer session. **Full-time faculty:** 196 total; 94% have terminal degrees, 12% minority, 18% women. **Part-time faculty:** 106 total; 36% have terminal degrees, 5% minority, 31% women. **Class size:** 43% < 20, 36% 20-39, 12% 40-49, 5% 50-99, 3% >100. **Special facilities:** Geology museum, geophysical observatory, experimental mine.

Freshman class profile. 2,937 applied, 2,556 admitted, 816 enrolled.

Mid 50% test scores			
SAT verbal:	540-650	End year in good standing:	95%
SAT math:	630-690	Return as sophomores:	84%
ACT:	25-29	Out-of-state:	25%
GPA 3.50 or higher:	80%	Live on campus:	80%
GPA 3.0-3.49:	20%	International:	3%
Rank in top quarter:	81%	Fraternities:	20%
Rank in top tenth:	48%	Sororities:	20%

Basis for selection. Applicants should rank in top third of class, must complete 16 or more academic units, and submit test scores. Both scores and academic record considered with heavier weight given to academic record. Interview and essay recommended. **Homeschooled:** Transcript of courses and grades required. More weight given to ACT or SAT scores.

High school preparation. College-preparatory program required. 16 units required. Required and recommended units include English 4, mathematics 4, social studies 2, science 3, foreign language 2 and academic electives 3. Mathematics units should include 2 algebra, 1 geometry, 1 advanced mathematics (including trigonometry). Science units should include 1 chemistry or physics.

2005-2006 Annual costs. Tuition/fees: $8,143; $20,725 out-of-state. Room/board: $6,750. Books/supplies: $1,300. Personal expenses: $1,800.

2005-2006 Financial aid. Need-based: 639 full-time freshmen applied for aid; 554 were judged to have need; 554 of these received aid. Average need met was 92%. Average scholarship/grant was $5,589; average loan $3,700. 58% of total undergraduate aid awarded as scholarships/grants, 42% as loans/jobs. **Non-need-based:** Awarded to 1,177 full-time undergraduates, including 293 freshmen. Scholarships awarded for academics, alumni affiliation, athletics, music/drama, ROTC, state residency.

Application procedures. Admission: Priority date 4/15; deadline 6/1 (postmark date). $45 fee, may be waived for applicants with need. Application must be submitted on paper. Admission notification on a rolling basis beginning on or about 10/1. Must reply by May 1 or within 4 week(s) if notified thereafter. **Financial aid:** Priority date 2/15; no closing date. FAFSA required. Applicants notified on a rolling basis starting 3/15; must reply by 5/1 or within 2 week(s) of notification.

Academics. Special study options: Accelerated study, combined bachelor's/graduate degree, cooperative education, double major, dual enrollment of high school students, ESL, exchange student, honors, independent study, internships, study abroad. **Credit/placement by examination:** AP, CLEP, IB, institutional tests. **Support services:** Pre-admission summer program, reduced course load, remedial instruction, study skills assistance, tutoring, writing center.

Majors. Computer sciences: General, computer science. **Engineering:** General, chemical, geological, metallurgical, mining, petroleum, physics. **Interdisciplinary:** Math/computer science. **Math:** Applied. **Physical sciences:** Chemistry. **Social sciences:** Economics.

Most popular majors. Computer/information sciences 13%, engineering/engineering technologies 72%, physical sciences 8%.

Computing on campus. 400 workstations in dormitories, library, computer center, student center. Dormitories wired for high-speed internet access and linked to campus network. Commuter students can connect to campus network. Online course registration, helpline, repair service, wireless network available.

Student life. Freshman orientation: Available. Preregistration for classes offered. Two 2-day sessions held during summer; 1-day session held at start of fall semester. **Policies:** Freshmen permitted cars on campus. **Housing:** Guaranteed on-campus for freshmen. Coed dorms, single-sex dorms, apartments, fraternity/sorority housing, substance-free housing available. $50 partly refundable deposit, deadline 5/1. **Activities:** Bands, choral groups, drama, literary magazine, music ensembles, student government, student newspaper, symphony orchestra, American Indian Science and Engineering Society, Asian student association, National Society of Black Engineers, Society of Hispanic Professional Engineers, religious clubs, Blue Key, Society of Women Engineers.

Athletics. NCAA. **Intercollegiate:** Baseball M, basketball, cross-country, football (tackle) M, golf, soccer, softball W, swimming, tennis, track and field, volleyball W, wrestling M. **Intramural:** Badminton, basketball, cross-country, football (non-tackle), handball, racquetball, rugby M, skin diving, soccer, softball, swimming, tennis, track and field, volleyball. **Team name:** Orediggers.

Student services. Alcohol/substance abuse counseling, career counseling, student employment services, financial aid counseling, health services, minority student services, personal counseling, placement for graduates, veterans' counselor. **Physically disabled:** Services for visually, hearing impaired.

Contact. E-mail: admit@mines.edu
Phone: (303) 273-3220 Toll-free number: (888) 446-9489
Fax: (303) 273-3509
Bill Young, Director of Enrollment Management, Colorado School of Mines, Undergraduate Admissions, Golden, CO 80401

Colorado State University

Fort Collins, Colorado — **CB member**
www.colostate.edu — **CB code: 4075**

- Public 4-year university
- Residential campus in small city
- 20,584 degree-seeking undergraduates: 8% part-time, 52% women, 2% African American, 3% Asian American, 6% Hispanic American, 1% Native American, 1% international
- 4,213 degree-seeking graduate students
- 88% of applicants admitted
- SAT or ACT (ACT writing optional) required
- 63% graduate within 6 years

General. Founded in 1870. Regionally accredited. **Degrees:** 4,281 bachelor's awarded; master's, doctoral, first professional offered. **ROTC:** Army, Air Force. **Location:** 60 miles from Denver. **Calendar:** Semester, extensive summer session. **Full-time faculty:** 851 total; 99% have terminal degrees, 12% minority, 29% women. **Part-time faculty:** 30 total; 100% have terminal degrees, 10% minority, 7% women. **Class size:** 37% < 20, 37% 20-39, 8% 40-49, 10% 50-99, 8% >100.

Freshman class profile. 10,770 applied, 9,516 admitted, 3,893 enrolled.

Mid 50% test scores			
SAT verbal:	500-610	Rank in top tenth:	19%
SAT math:	510-620	Return as sophomores:	82%
ACT:	22-26	Out-of-state:	19%
GPA 3.50 or higher:	54%	Live on campus:	93%
GPA 3.0-3.49:	36%	International:	1%
GPA 2.0-2.99:	9%	Fraternities:	11%
Rank in top quarter:	48%	Sororities:	11%

Basis for selection. Admission based on numerical index in which cumulative GPA or class rank, whichever is higher, is weighted along with highest set of test scores. Achievement record, recommendations important; extracurricular activities considered. Essay important if there are discrepancies in academic record. Essay may be required for some students. **Homeschooled:** All homeschool applicants and students from nongraded educational settings must be assigned a 3.3 proxy GPA (on a 4.0 scale), regardless of type of assessment system used by family or curriculum. Admission decision process includes detailed review of actual assessment of student performance. Students must provide information about individual experience and achievements.

High school preparation. 15 units required; 18 recommended. Required and recommended units include English 4, mathematics 3-4, social studies 3, science 2-3 (laboratory 1) and foreign language 2. Additional unit of social science or natural science required. 0.5 trigonometry, chemistry, 1 natural science (physics preferred) required for engineering major. Individual colleges may have additional requirements.

2005-2006 Annual costs. Tuition/fees: $4,562; $15,524 out-of-state. Room/board: $6,316. Books/supplies: $900. Personal expenses: $1,665.

2004-2005 Financial aid. Need-based: 2,328 full-time freshmen applied for aid; 1,448 were judged to have need; 1,448 of these received aid. Average need met was 87%. Average scholarship/grant was $5,707; average loan $3,318. 38% of total undergraduate aid awarded as scholarships/grants, 62% as loans/jobs. **Non-need-based:** Awarded to 1,253 full-time undergraduates, including 348 freshmen. Scholarships awarded for academics, art, athletics, leadership, music/drama, ROTC, state residency.

Application procedures. Admission: Priority date 2/15; deadline 7/1 (receipt date). $50 fee, may be waived for applicants with need. Application may be submitted online. Admission notification on a rolling basis. Early application (once 6th semester transcript is available) encouraged. **Financial aid:** Priority date 3/1; no closing date. FAFSA required. Applicants notified on a rolling basis starting 3/1.

Academics. Special study options: Accelerated study, combined bachelor's/graduate degree, cooperative education, distance learning, double major, dual enrollment of high school students, ESL, exchange student, honors, independent study, internships, liberal arts/career combination, semester at sea, study abroad, teacher certification program. **Credit/placement by examination:** AP, CLEP, IB, institutional tests. 30 credit hours maximum toward bachelor's degree. **Support services:** Learning center, study skills assistance, tutoring, writing center.

Majors. **Agriculture:** Agribusiness operations, agronomy, animal sciences, economics, equestrian studies, farm/ranch, horticultural science, horticulture, landscaping, range science. **Architecture:** Landscape. **Biology:** General, biochemistry, biomedical sciences, botany, microbiology, zoology. **Business:** Business admin. **Communications:** Journalism. **Computer sciences:** General, information systems. **Conservation:** General, fisheries, forest sciences, management/policy, water/wetlands/marine. **Education:** Agricultural. **Engineering:** Chemical, civil, computer, electrical, mechanical, science. **Engineering technology:** Construction. **English:** English lit, speech/rhetoric. **Family/consumer sciences:** General, apparel marketing, family studies, human nutrition. **Health:** Environmental health, music therapy. **History:** General. **Interdisciplinary:** Natural sciences. **Liberal arts:** Arts/sciences. **Math:** General. **Parks/recreation:** Exercise sciences, facilities management. **Philosophy/religion:** Philosophy. **Physical sciences:** Chemistry, geology, physics. **Psychology:** General. **Public administration:** Social work. **Social sciences:** Anthropology, economics, political science, sociology. **Visual/performing arts:** Dramatic, interior design, studio arts.

Most popular majors. Agriculture 6%, biology 7%, business/marketing 17%, engineering/engineering technologies 10%, family/consumer sciences 8%, parks/recreation 6%, social sciences 8%.

Computing on campus. 2,700 workstations in dormitories, library, computer center, student center. Dormitories wired for high-speed internet access and linked to campus network. Commuter students can connect to campus network. Online course registration, online library, helpline, repair service, student web hosting, wireless network available.

Student life. **Freshman orientation:** Available, $83 fee. Preregistration for classes offered. 20 sessions offered from mid-June to mid-July for incoming freshmen,family members, and guests. **Policies:** Freshmen permitted cars on campus. **Housing:** Guaranteed on-campus for freshmen. Coed dorms, special housing for disabled, apartments available. $150 partly refundable deposit. Special interest floors, special floors for transfer students available. **Activities:** Bands, choral groups, dance, drama, literary magazine, music ensembles, musical theater, opera, radio station, student government, student newspaper, symphony orchestra, TV station, Asian/American student services, black student services, El Centro student services, Native American student services, Campus Crusade for Christ, CoPIRG, Sierra club, Habitat for Humanity, Pre Medica.

Athletics. NCAA. **Intercollegiate:** Basketball, cross-country, diving W, football (tackle) M, golf, softball W, swimming W, tennis W, track and field, volleyball W, water polo W. **Intramural:** Basketball, football (non-tackle), golf, racquetball, soccer, softball, swimming, tennis, volleyball, water polo. **Team name:** Rams.

Student services. Adult student services, alcohol/substance abuse counseling, campus ministries, career counseling, student employment services, financial aid counseling, health services, legal services, minority student services, on-campus daycare, personal counseling, placement for graduates, veterans' counselor, women's services. **Physically disabled:** Services for visually, speech, hearing impaired.

Contact. E-mail: admissions@colostate.edu
Phone: (970) 491-6909 Fax: (970) 491-7799
Mary Ontiveros, Executive Director of Admissions, Colorado State University, Spruce Hall, Fort Collins, CO 80523-0015

Colorado State University: Pueblo

Pueblo, Colorado
www.colostate-pueblo.edu **CB code: 4611**

- Public 4-year university
- Commuter campus in small city
- 4,241 degree-seeking undergraduates: 23% part-time, 58% women
- 139 degree-seeking graduate students
- SAT or ACT (ACT writing optional) required

General. Founded in 1933. Regionally accredited. **Degrees:** 722 bachelor's awarded; master's offered. **ROTC:** Army. **Location:** 42 miles from Colorado Springs, 100 miles from Denver. **Calendar:** Semester, extensive summer session. **Full-time faculty:** 145 total. **Part-time faculty:** 150 total. **Class size:** 43% < 20, 44% 20-39, 6% 40-49, 7% 50-99, less than 1% >100. **Special facilities:** 3 electron microscopes, golf course, river trail system, automotive service, ropes course, music amphitheater, TV station.

Freshman class profile.

Mid 50% test scores			
SAT verbal:	430-550	Rank in top tenth:	2%
SAT math:	430-540	Out-of-state:	8%
ACT:	18-23	Live on campus:	10%
Rank in top quarter:	9%	Fraternities:	2%
		Sororities:	2%

Basis for selection. High school achievement record and test scores most important. Auditions for music, portfolios for art required for scholarships.

High school preparation. College-preparatory program recommended. 13 units recommended. Recommended units include English 4, mathematics 3, social studies 2, science 2 (laboratory 1) and foreign language 2.

2005-2006 Annual costs. Tuition/fees: $4,118; $14,758 out-of-state. Students from Alaska, Arizona, Hawaii, Idaho, Montana, Nevada, Oregon, South Dakota, North Dakota, Utah, New Mexico, and Wyoming pay $210 per credit hour and $6279 full time. Differential rate for Business, Nursing, Computer Information Systems, and Engineering courses is $15 more per credit hour. Room/board: $6,088. Books/supplies: $540. Personal expenses: $1,013.

Financial aid. All financial aid based on need.

Application procedures. **Admission:** Closing date 8/1 (receipt date). $25 fee, may be waived for applicants with need. Application may be submitted online. Admission notification on a rolling basis beginning on or about 8/1. **Financial aid:** Priority date 3/1; no closing date. FAFSA required. Applicants notified on a rolling basis starting 3/1; must reply within 3 week(s) of notification.

Academics. **Special study options:** Accelerated study, combined bachelor's/graduate degree, cooperative education, cross-registration, distance learning, double major, dual enrollment of high school students, ESL, exchange student, external degree, honors, independent study, internships, study abroad, teacher certification program, weekend college. **Credit/placement by examination:** AP, CLEP, IB, ACT, institutional tests. 30 credit hours maximum toward bachelor's degree. **Support services:** Learning center, study skills assistance, tutoring, writing center.

Majors. **Biology:** General. **Business:** General, accounting, managerial economics. **Communications:** Media studies. **Computer sciences:** Information systems. **Engineering:** Industrial. **Engineering technology:** Automotive, civil, electrical, industrial, mechanical. **English:** English lit. **Foreign languages:** General. **Health:** Nursing (RN). **History:** General. **Liberal arts:** Arts/sciences. **Math:** General. **Parks/recreation:** Exercise sciences, facilities management. **Physical sciences:** Chemistry, physics. **Psychology:** General. **Public administration:** Social work. **Social sciences:** General, political science, sociology. **Visual/performing arts:** Studio arts.

Most popular majors. Business/marketing 18%, communications/journalism 8%, health sciences 6%, public administration/social services 6%, social sciences 24%.

Computing on campus. 741 workstations in dormitories, library, computer center, student center. Dormitories wired for high-speed internet access and linked to campus network. Commuter students can connect to campus network. Online library, helpline, student web hosting, wireless network available.

Student life. **Freshman orientation:** Mandatory, $50 fee. Preregistration for classes offered. 2-day program held in June, July, or August, during which English and math placement testing is conducted. **Policies:** Freshmen permitted cars on campus. **Housing:** Guaranteed on-campus for freshmen. Coed dorms, special housing for disabled, apartments available. $125 partly refundable deposit, deadline 7/1. **Activities:** Bands, choral groups, dance, literary magazine, music ensembles, radio station, student government, student newspaper, symphony orchestra, TV station, Campus Crusade for Christ, Catholic student union, College Republicans, MAES (Society of Mexican American Engineers and Scientists), MEChA (Movimiento Estudiantil Chicano de Aztlan), United Campus Ministries, Colorado international student association, multicultural center, Tackling Life's Choices.

Athletics. NCAA. **Intercollegiate:** Baseball M, basketball, cross-country W, golf, soccer, softball W, tennis, volleyball W. **Intramural:** Basketball, football (non-tackle), golf, handball, racquetball, soccer, softball, table tennis, volleyball. **Team name:** Thunderwolves.

Student services. Alcohol/substance abuse counseling, campus ministries, career counseling, student employment services, financial aid counseling, health services, on-campus daycare, personal counseling, placement for graduates, veterans' counselor. **Physically disabled:** Services for visually, speech, hearing impaired.

Contact. E-mail: info@colostate-pueblo.edu
Phone: (719) 549-2461 Toll-free number: (877) 872-9653
Fax: (719) 549-2419
Joseph Marshall, Director of Admissions and Records, Colorado State University: Pueblo, 2200 Bonforte Boulevard, Pueblo, CO 81001-4901

Colorado Technical University

Colorado Springs, Colorado
www.coloradotech.edu **CB code: 4133**

- For-profit 4-year university and technical college
- Commuter campus in large city
- 2,000 undergraduates
- Interview required

General. Founded in 1965. Regionally accredited. **Degrees:** 185 bachelor's, 41 associate awarded; master's, doctoral offered. **ROTC:** Army. **Location:** 63 miles from Denver. **Calendar:** Quarter, extensive summer session. **Full-time faculty:** 35 total. **Part-time faculty:** 100 total. **Class size:** 69% < 20, 31% 20-39. **Special facilities:** Extensive laboratories and computer facilities.

Basis for selection. Secondary school record, test scores, interview important. SAT or ACT recommended.

2005-2006 Annual costs. Lab fees $30 per lab class. Books/supplies: $1,300. Personal expenses: $1,215.

Financial aid. Non-need-based: Scholarships awarded for academics, ROTC.

Application procedures. Admission: No deadline. $50 fee. Admission notification on a rolling basis. **Financial aid:** No deadline. FAFSA required. Applicants notified on a rolling basis starting 6/30.

Academics. Special study options: Accelerated study, cooperative education, distance learning, double major, internships, weekend college. **Credit/placement by examination:** CLEP, institutional tests. 30 credit hours maximum toward associate degree, 60 toward bachelor's. Course challenge test offered. Credit for life experience based on evaluation by faculty. **Support services:** Learning center, reduced course load, remedial instruction, tutoring.

Majors. Business: Business admin, e-commerce, human resources, information resources management, logistics, management information systems. **Computer sciences:** General, computer science, information systems, information technology, system admin, systems analysis. **Engineering:** Computer, electrical, software. **Engineering technology:** Electrical.

Most popular majors. Business/marketing 34%, computer/information sciences 32%, engineering/engineering technologies 34%.

Computing on campus. 154 workstations in library, computer center. Commuter students can connect to campus network. Online library, helpline, wireless network available.

Student life. Freshman orientation: Mandatory. Preregistration for classes offered. **Policies:** Students must comply with university's standards of conduct. Freshmen permitted cars on campus. **Activities:** Student government.

Student services. Career counseling, student employment services, financial aid counseling, personal counseling, placement for graduates, veterans' counselor.

Contact. E-mail: cosadmissions@coloradotech.edu
Phone: (719) 598-0200 Fax: (719) 598-3740
Beth Bratten, Director of Admissions, Colorado Technical University, 4435 North Chestnut Street, Colorado Springs, CO 80907

DeVry University: Colorado Springs

Colorado Springs, Colorado
www.cs.devry.edu **CB code: 3136**

- For-profit 4-year university
- Commuter campus in large city
- 215 degree-seeking undergraduates: 59% part-time, 34% women, 18% African American, 5% Asian American, 11% Hispanic American, 1% Native American
- 59 graduate students
- Interview required

General. Accredited by ACCSCT. **Degrees:** 59 bachelor's, 22 associate awarded; master's offered. **Calendar:** Semester. **Full-time faculty:** 1 total; 100% minority, 100% women. **Part-time faculty:** 41 total; 22% minority, 29% women.

Freshman class profile.

Return as sophomores:	36%	Out-of-state:	12%

Basis for selection. Applicants must have high school diploma or equivalent, or degree from an accredited postsecondary institution, demonstrate proficiency in basic college-level skills through test scores and/or institution-administered placement examinations, and be at least 17 years of age on the first day of classes. New students may enter at the beginning of any semester. CPT accepted.

High school preparation. Math unit must be algebra or higher.

2005-2006 Annual costs. Tuition/fees: $12,800. Books/supplies: $1,250. Personal expenses: $1,950.

Financial aid. All financial aid based on need.

Application procedures. Admission: No deadline. $50 fee. Application may be submitted online. Admission notification on a rolling basis. **Financial aid:** No deadline. FAFSA required. Applicants notified on a rolling basis starting 7/1.

Academics. Special study options: Accelerated study, cooperative education, distance learning. **Credit/placement by examination:** CLEP. **Support services:** Learning center, remedial instruction, tutoring.

Majors. Business: General. **Computer sciences:** Systems analysis.

Most popular majors. Business/marketing 75%, computer/information sciences 25%.

Computing on campus. 175 workstations in library, computer center. Online course registration, online library, helpline available.

Student life. Freshman orientation: Mandatory. **Policies:** Freshmen permitted cars on campus. **Activities:** Student newspaper, Phi Beta Lambda, Association of Information Technology Professionals, golf club, hiking club, student activity association.

Student services. Career counseling, student employment services, financial aid counseling, placement for graduates, veterans' counselor. **Physically disabled:** Services for visually, hearing impaired.

Contact. E-mail: admitcs@cs.devry.edu
Phone: (719) 632-3000 Toll-free number: (877) 691-3002
Fax: (719) 866-6770
Brett McKamey, Director of Admissions, DeVry University: Colorado Springs, 225 South Union Boulevard, Colorado Springs, CO 80910-3124

DeVry University: Westminster

Westminster, Colorado
www.den.devry.edu **CB code: 1327**

- For-profit 4-year university
- Commuter campus in very large city
- 616 degree-seeking undergraduates: 35% part-time, 40% women
- 122 graduate students
- Interview required

General. Founded in 1945. Accredited by ACCSCT. **Degrees:** 73 bachelor's, 38 associate awarded; master's offered. **Calendar:** Semester, extensive summer session. **Full-time faculty:** 14 total. **Part-time faculty:** 59 total.

Basis for selection. Applicants must have high school diploma or equivalent or a degree from an accredited postsecondary institution, demonstrate proficiency in basic college-level skills through SAT or ACT scores or institutional-administered placement exams, and be at least 17 years of age. SAT or ACT recommended.

High school preparation. Math unit must be algebra or higher.

2005-2006 Annual costs. Tuition/fees: $12,800. Books/supplies: $1,250. Personal expenses: $1,950.

2004-2005 Financial aid. All financial aid based on need. 161 full-time freshmen applied for aid; 151 were judged to have need; 150 of these received aid. Average need met was 39%. Average scholarship/grant was $4,455;

average loan $6,051. 19% of total undergraduate aid awarded as scholarships/grants, 81% as loans/jobs.

Application procedures. Admission: No deadline. $50 fee. Application may be submitted online. Admission notification on a rolling basis. **Financial aid:** No deadline. FAFSA required. Applicants notified on a rolling basis.

Academics. Special study options: Accelerated study, cooperative education, distance learning. **Credit/placement by examination:** CLEP, institutional tests. **Support services:** Learning center, tutoring.

Majors. Business: Business admin. **Computer sciences:** Information systems. **Engineering:** Computer. **Engineering technology:** Computer, electrical.

Most popular majors. Business/marketing 75%, computer/information sciences 16%, engineering/engineering technologies 9%.

Computing on campus. 308 workstations in library, computer center. Online course registration, online library, helpline available.

Student life. Freshman orientation: Mandatory. **Policies:** Freshmen permitted cars on campus. **Activities:** Student government, student newspaper.

Athletics. Intramural: Basketball, volleyball.

Student services. Career counseling, student employment services, financial aid counseling, placement for graduates, veterans' counselor.

Contact. E-mail: denver-admissions@den.devry.edu
Phone: (303) 280-7600 Toll-free number: (888) 212-1857
Fax: (303) 280-7606
Rick Rodman, Director of Admissions, DeVry University: Westminster, 1870 West 122 Avenue, Westminster, CO 80234-2010

Fort Lewis College

Durango, Colorado — **CB member**
www.fortlewis.edu — **CB code: 4310**

- Public 4-year liberal arts college
- Residential campus in large town
- 3,829 degree-seeking undergraduates: 7% part-time, 48% women, 1% African American, 1% Asian American, 6% Hispanic American, 19% Native American, 1% international
- 74% of applicants admitted
- SAT or ACT (ACT writing optional) required

General. Regionally accredited. **Degrees:** 698 bachelor's, 1 associate awarded. **Location:** 215 miles from Albuquerque, New Mexico, 330 miles from Denver. **Calendar:** Semester, extensive summer session. **Full-time faculty:** 177 total; 78% have terminal degrees, 11% minority, 45% women. **Part-time faculty:** 64 total; 11% minority, 56% women. **Class size:** 42% < 20, 51% 20-39, 5% 40-49, 3% 50-99, less than 1% >100. **Special facilities:** Southwest studies center, nuclear magnetic resonance spectrometer, archaeological dig site, community concert hall, separations and spectroscopy lab, mass spectrometer facilities, tissue culture facility, atomic force microscope.

Freshman class profile. 2,765 applied, 2,042 admitted, 910 enrolled.

Mid 50% test scores			
SAT verbal:	460-560	GPA 2.0-2.99:	50%
SAT math:	450-550	Rank in top quarter:	20%
ACT:	18-23	Rank in top tenth:	4%
GPA 3.50 or higher:	20%	Return as sophomores:	58%
GPA 3.0-3.49:	30%	Out-of-state:	27%
		Live on campus:	86%

Basis for selection. Colorado Commission on Higher Education index score comprised of high school GPA and test scores utilized as part of admission criteria. Essay recommended. **Homeschooled:** Official copy of high school completion records; minimum score of 1010 SAT (exclusive of Writing), 22 ACT.

High school preparation. 15 units recommended. Recommended units include English 4, mathematics 4, social studies 3, science 3, foreign language 2 and academic electives 2. Computer science and performing/visual arts required.

2005-2006 Annual costs. Tuition/fees: $3,298; $13,704 out-of-state. Room/board: $6,524.

2004-2005 Financial aid. Need-based: 599 full-time freshmen applied for aid; 415 were judged to have need; 408 of these received aid. Average need met was 64%. Average scholarship/grant was $3,192; average loan $2,140. 47% of total undergraduate aid awarded as scholarships/grants, 53% as loans/jobs. **Non-need-based:** Awarded to 1,011 full-time undergraduates, including 285 freshmen. Scholarships awarded for academics, alumni affiliation, art, athletics, leadership, minority status, music/drama, state residency. **Additional information:** Tuition waived for Native Americans of federally recognized tribes; census number and CIB (Certificate of Indian Blood) must accompany application.

Application procedures. Admission: Closing date 8/1 (postmark date). $30 fee, may be waived for applicants with need. Application may be submitted online. Admission notification on a rolling basis beginning on or about 10/15. **Financial aid:** Priority date 2/15; no closing date. FAFSA required. Applicants notified on a rolling basis starting 4/1; must reply within 2 week(s) of notification.

Academics. Teacher certification available at elementary and secondary levels, early childhood, ESL and bilingual. **Special study options:** Accelerated study, cooperative education, distance learning, double major, dual enrollment of high school students, ESL, exchange student, honors, independent study, internships, liberal arts/career combination, student-designed major, study abroad, teacher certification program. **Credit/placement by examination:** AP, CLEP, IB, SAT, ACT, institutional tests. **Support services:** Learning center, remedial instruction, study skills assistance, tutoring, writing center.

Majors. Agriculture: Business. **Area/ethnic studies:** American, Asian, Chinese, East Asian, Latin American, regional. **Biology:** General, biochemistry, cellular/molecular, environmental. **Business:** Accounting, business admin, finance, international, management information systems, managerial economics, marketing, tourism/travel. **Computer sciences:** General, computer science, information systems. **Education:** General, art, bilingual, biology, chemistry, early childhood, elementary, English, history, mathematics, middle, music, physical, secondary, Spanish. **Engineering:** Physics. **Engineering technology:** Industrial management. **English:** American lit, English lit. **Foreign languages:** Spanish. **Health:** Athletic training. **History:** General, American, European. **Liberal arts:** Humanities. **Math:** General, applied, statistics. **Parks/recreation:** Exercise sciences, sports admin. **Philosophy/religion:** Philosophy. **Physical sciences:** Chemistry, geology, physics. **Psychology:** General. **Social sciences:** Anthropology, economics, political science, sociology. **Visual/performing arts:** Art, arts management, dramatic, music performance.

Most popular majors. Biology 6%, business/marketing 23%, English 10%, liberal arts 13%, parks/recreation 6%, psychology 7%, social sciences 13%, visual/performing arts 8%.

Computing on campus. 633 workstations in dormitories, library, computer center, student center. Dormitories wired for high-speed internet access and linked to campus network. Commuter students can connect to campus network. Online course registration, online library, helpline, repair service, student web hosting, wireless network available.

Student life. Freshman orientation: Mandatory, $50 fee. Preregistration for classes offered. **Policies:** Freshmen permitted cars on campus. **Housing:** Guaranteed on-campus for all undergraduates. Coed dorms, apartments available. $100 deposit, deadline 7/15. **Activities:** Bands, choral groups, drama, literary magazine, music ensembles, radio station, student government, student newspaper, Newman Club, Circle-K International, campus ministries, international friendship club, business club, American Indian business leaders, American Indian science and engineering society, sociology club, Native American club, Habitat for Humanity.

Athletics. NCAA. **Intercollegiate:** Basketball, cross-country, football (tackle) M, golf M, soccer, softball W, volleyball W. **Intramural:** Badminton, basketball, football (tackle), racquetball, soccer, softball, volleyball. **Team name:** Skyhawks.

Student services. Adult student services, alcohol/substance abuse counseling, campus ministries, career counseling, services for economically disadvantaged, student employment services, financial aid counseling, health services, legal services, minority student services, on-campus daycare, personal counseling, placement for graduates, veterans' counselor, women's services. **Physically disabled:** Services for visually, speech, hearing impaired.

Contact. E-mail: admission@fortlewis.edu
Phone: (970) 247-7184 Fax: (970) 247-7179
Gretchen Foster, Director of Admission, Fort Lewis College, 1000 Rim Drive, Durango, CO 81301-3999

ITT Technical Institute: Thornton

Thornton, Colorado
www.itt-tech.edu — **CB code: 3605**

- For-profit 4-year technical college
- Commuter campus in large city

General. Founded in 1984. Accredited by ACICS. **Calendar:** Quarter.

Annual costs/financial aid. Tuition varies by program, $260-$368 per credit hour.

Contact. Phone: (303) 288-4488
Director of Recruitment, 500 East 84th Avenue, Thornton, CO 80229

Johnson & Wales University
Denver, Colorado
www.jwu.edu **CB code: 3567**

- For-profit 4-year university
- Residential campus in large city
- 1,544 degree-seeking undergraduates: 1% part-time, 49% women, 6% African American, 3% Asian American, 11% Hispanic American, 1% Native American, 3% international
- 84% of applicants admitted

General. Regionally accredited. **Degrees:** 133 bachelor's, 291 associate awarded. **Calendar:** Quarter, limited summer session. **Full-time faculty:** 50 total. **Part-time faculty:** 15 total. **Class size:** 34% < 20, 53% 20-39, 12% 40-49. **Special facilities:** Community Leadership Institute.

Freshman class profile. 3,252 applied, 2,744 admitted, 511 enrolled.

Mid 50% test scores			
SAT verbal:	420-550	Rank in top quarter:	24%
SAT math:	420-560	Rank in top tenth:	7%
GPA 3.50 or higher:	22%	Out-of-state:	33%
GPA 3.0-3.49:	27%	Live on campus:	65%
GPA 2.0-2.99:	50%		

Basis for selection. While academic record (secondary school curriculum, GPA, class rank, test scores) is important, student motivation and interest given strong consideration.

High school preparation. 12 units recommended. Recommended units include English 4, mathematics 3, social studies 2 and science 3.

2006-2007 Annual costs. Tuition/fees (projected): $20,826. Room/board: $8,300. Books/supplies: $825. Personal expenses: $639.

2005-2006 Financial aid. Need-based: 343 full-time freshmen applied for aid; 298 were judged to have need; 297 of these received aid. Average need met was 65%. Average scholarship/grant was $5,180; average loan $6,255. 30% of total undergraduate aid awarded as scholarships/grants, 70% as loans/jobs. **Non-need-based:** Awarded to 1,052 full-time undergraduates, including 274 freshmen. Scholarships awarded for academics, leadership.

Application procedures. Admission: No deadline. No application fee. Application may be submitted online. Admission notification on a rolling basis beginning on or about 10/1. **Financial aid:** No deadline. FAFSA required. Applicants notified on a rolling basis starting 3/1; must reply within 2 week(s) of notification.

Academics. Special study options: Cooperative education, double major, honors, independent study, internships, teacher certification program. **Credit/placement by examination:** CLEP. **Support services:** Learning center, remedial instruction, study skills assistance, tutoring, writing center.

Majors. Business: Accounting, banking/financial services, business admin, entrepreneurial studies, hospitality admin, international, investments/securities, public finance. **Education:** Business, family/consumer sciences. **Family/consumer sciences:** Food/nutrition. **Parks/recreation:** Sports admin. **Personal/culinary services:** Culinary arts, restaurant/catering. **Protective services:** Law enforcement admin.

Most popular majors. Business/marketing 54%, family/consumer sciences 31%, parks/recreation 15%.

Computing on campus. Dormitories wired for high-speed internet access and linked to campus network. Commuter students can connect to campus network. Online course registration, online library, helpline, repair service, wireless network available.

Student life. Freshman orientation: Mandatory, $250 fee. Preregistration for classes offered. **Housing:** Coed dorms available. **Activities:** Choral groups, dance, literary magazine, student government.

Athletics. NAIA. **Intercollegiate:** Basketball, soccer, volleyball M. **Intramural:** Basketball, football (non-tackle), soccer, softball, volleyball. **Team name:** Wildcats.

Student services. Adult student services, alcohol/substance abuse counseling, career counseling, student employment services, financial aid counseling, health services, minority student services, personal counseling, placement for graduates. **Physically disabled:** Services for visually, speech, hearing impaired. **Learning disabled:** Comprehensive services available.

Contact. Phone: (303) 256-9300 Toll-free number: (877) 598-3368
Kim Ostrowski, Director of Admissions & Recruiting, Johnson & Wales University, 7150 Montview Boulevard, Denver, CO 80220

Jones International University
Centennial, Colorado
www.jonesinternational.edu **CB code: 2785**

- For-profit upper-division virtual college
- Large city

General. Regionally accredited. Asynchronous learning, 25 student classroom limit, 24/7 technical support. **Degrees:** 16 bachelor's awarded; master's offered. **Calendar:** Continuous. **Full-time faculty:** 5 total. **Part-time faculty:** 90 total. **Special facilities:** Virtual library, online bookstore.

Student profile. 1,604 undergraduates.

Basis for selection. Open admission. Credits must have been earned regionally or at a DETC accredited institution.

2005-2006 Annual costs. Tuition: $960 per course for bachelor's degrees. Tuition for certificate programs range from $400 to $1500 per course, depending on programs. $65 technology fee per course.

Financial aid. Additional information: Loans available through Sallie Mae and PLATO. Most students have costs reimbursed by employers. GI Bill and VA benefits are also accepted.

Application procedures. Admission: $100 fee. Application may be submitted online. **Financial aid:** FAFSA required.

Academics. 24 hour, seven days per week technical support services. **Special study options:** Accelerated study, combined bachelor's/graduate degree, distance learning. **Credit/placement by examination:** CLEP, IB. 60 credit hours maximum toward bachelor's degree.

Majors. Business: General, business admin, communications, e-commerce, international, small business admin. **Communications:** General, digital media, journalism, organizational, public relations. **Communications technology:** General. **Computer sciences:** General, computer science, database management, programming, system admin, systems analysis. **Engineering:** Computer.

Computing on campus. PC or laptop required.

Student services. Career counseling, financial aid counseling.

Contact. E-mail: admissions@international.edu
Phone: (303) 784-8247 Toll-free number: (800) 811-5663 ext. 8247
Fax: (303) 799-0966
Candice Morrissey, Assistant Director of Admissions, Jones International University, 9697 East Mineral Avenue, Centennial, CO 80112

Mesa State College
Grand Junction, Colorado
www.mesastate.edu **CB code: 4484**

- Public 4-year community and liberal arts college
- Residential campus in large town
- 5,499 degree-seeking undergraduates: 19% part-time, 58% women, 2% African American, 2% Asian American, 8% Hispanic American, 2% Native American, 1% international
- 28 degree-seeking graduate students
- 82% of applicants admitted
- SAT or ACT (ACT writing optional) required

General. Founded in 1925. Regionally accredited. **Degrees:** 617 bachelor's, 124 associate awarded; master's offered. **Location:** 250 miles from Denver, 300 miles from Salt Lake City. **Calendar:** Semester, limited summer session. **Full-time faculty:** 206 total; 82% have terminal degrees, 5% minority, 39% women. **Part-time faculty:** 190 total; 5% minority, 50% women. **Class size:** 53% < 20, 37% 20-39, 4% 40-49, 6% 50-99, less than 1% >100. **Special facilities:** Electron microscope laboratory, herbarium, computer-aided drafting laboratory, technical training facility, environmental restoration laboratory.

Freshman class profile. 4,628 applied, 3,807 admitted, 2,013 enrolled.

Mid 50% test scores			
SAT verbal:	430-540	GPA 2.0-2.99:	44%
SAT math:	430-540	Rank in top quarter:	20%
ACT:	18-23	Rank in top tenth:	6%
		Return as sophomores:	57%
GPA 3.50 or higher:	22%	Out-of-state:	8%
GPA 3.0-3.49:	31%	Live on campus:	50%

Basis for selection. Admission based on matrix system using GPA, ACT/SAT, class rank. Open admissions to most technical associates and certificate programs. Audition required of music, music theater, theater majors. Interview recommended for nursing, allied health, teacher certification majors.

High school preparation. College-preparatory program recommended. 15 units recommended. Recommended units include English 4, mathematics 3, social studies 3, history 2, science 3 (laboratory 2) and foreign language 2.

2005-2006 Annual costs. Tuition/fees: $3,080; $10,267 out-of-state. Room/board: $7,050. Books/supplies: $1,162. Personal expenses: $2,266.

2004-2005 Financial aid. Need-based: 828 full-time freshmen applied for aid; 609 were judged to have need; 609 of these received aid. Average need met was 57%. Average scholarship/grant was $3,126; average loan $2,288. 48% of total undergraduate aid awarded as scholarships/grants, 52% as loans/jobs. **Non-need-based:** Awarded to 692 full-time undergraduates, including 689 freshmen. Scholarships awarded for academics, art, athletics, leadership, music/drama.

Application procedures. Admission: No deadline. $30 fee, may be waived for applicants with need. Application may be submitted online. Admission notification on a rolling basis beginning on or about 9/1. Housing deposit refundable in part until August 1. **Financial aid:** Priority date 3/1; no closing date. FAFSA required. Applicants notified on a rolling basis starting 4/1; must reply within 5 week(s) of notification.

Academics. Special study options: Accelerated study, combined bachelor's/graduate degree, cooperative education, cross-registration, distance learning, double major, dual enrollment of high school students, ESL, exchange student, honors, independent study, internships, teacher certification program. Area vocational school provides training in technical skills. **Credit/placement by examination:** AP, CLEP, IB, SAT, ACT, institutional tests. 12 credit hours maximum toward associate degree, 20 toward bachelor's. **Support services:** Learning center, pre-admission summer program, reduced course load, remedial instruction, study skills assistance, tutoring, writing center.

Majors. Biology: General. **Business:** Accounting, business admin, management information systems. **Communications:** Journalism. **Computer sciences:** General. **Conservation:** Environmental science. **English:** English lit. **Foreign languages:** Spanish. **Health:** Nursing (RN). **History:** General. **Liberal arts:** Arts/sciences. **Math:** General. **Parks/recreation:** Health/fitness. **Physical sciences:** General. **Psychology:** General. **Social sciences:** General, political science, sociology. **Visual/performing arts:** Art, dramatic, graphic design, studio arts.

Most popular majors. Biology 8%, business/marketing 25%, health sciences 8%, liberal arts 7%, parks/recreation 7%, psychology 6%, social sciences 10%, visual/performing arts 10%.

Computing on campus. 500 workstations in dormitories, library, computer center, student center. Dormitories wired for high-speed internet access and linked to campus network. Commuter students can connect to campus network. Online course registration, online library, helpline, student web hosting, wireless network available.

Student life. Freshman orientation: Available, $50 fee. Preregistration for classes offered. **Policies:** Freshmen permitted cars on campus. **Housing:** Coed dorms, apartments, substance-free housing available. $150 partly refundable deposit. Pets allowed in dorm rooms. Suite style housing available for sophomores, juniors and seniors. **Activities:** Bands, choral groups, dance, drama, film society, literary magazine, music ensembles, musical theater, radio station, student government, student newspaper, symphony orchestra, TV station, African American college, La Raza, handicapped student organization, Newman Club, Christian fellowship, Latter-Day Saints student association, Baptist student union, Circle-K, Native American council, Polynesian club.

Athletics. NCAA. **Intercollegiate:** Baseball M, basketball, cross-country W, football (tackle) M, golf W, soccer W, softball W, swimming W, tennis, track and field W, volleyball W. **Intramural:** Badminton, basketball, cross-country, golf, handball, racquetball, skiing, soccer, softball, swimming, tennis, track and field, volleyball, water polo. **Team name:** Mavericks.

Student services. Adult student services, alcohol/substance abuse counseling, campus ministries, career counseling, student employment services, financial aid counseling, health services, on-campus daycare, personal counseling, placement for graduates, veterans' counselor. **Physically disabled:** Services for visually, speech, hearing impaired.

Contact. E-mail: admissions@mesastate.edu
Phone: (970) 248-1875 Toll-free number: (800) 982-6372
Fax: (970) 248-1973
Tyre Camille Bush, Director of Admissions, Mesa State College, Grand Junction, CO 81501

Metropolitan State College of Denver

Denver, Colorado
www.mscd.edu **CB code: 4505**

- Public 4-year liberal arts college
- Commuter campus in very large city
- 20,010 undergraduates
- SAT or ACT (ACT writing recommended) required

General. Founded in 1963. Regionally accredited. Library, student center, physical education facilities, child care center shared with Community College of Denver and University of Colorado at Denver. Degree completion programs offered at off-campus sites in North Glen and Englewood. **Degrees:** 2,280 bachelor's awarded. **ROTC:** Army, Air Force. **Location:** Downtown. **Calendar:** Semester, extensive summer session. **Full-time faculty:** 395 total; 76% have terminal degrees, 18% minority, 43% women. **Part-time faculty:** 746 total; 22% have terminal degrees, 16% minority, 46% women. **Class size:** 32% < 20, 54% 20-39, 6% 40-49, 8% 50-99, less than 1% >100. **Special facilities:** Art galleries, CAD/CAM laboratory, world indoor airport.

Freshman class profile.

Mid 50% test scores			
SAT verbal:	450-560	Rank in top quarter:	16%
SAT math:	440-560	Rank in top tenth:	3.8%
ACT:	17-22	Out-of-state:	23%

Basis for selection. Official high school transcript indicating ACT or SAT test results, GPA, high school class rank, date of graduation required. GED certificates acceptable. ACT/SAT not required of those submitting GED. Open admission for applicants 20 years of age and older who are high school graduates, have GED, or have 30 transferable credits from another college. Admission tests required if under 20 for first-time students.

High school preparation. 15 units recommended. Recommended units include English 4, mathematics 3, social studies 2, history 1, science 3 and foreign language 2.

2005-2006 Annual costs. Tuition/fees: $2,941; $10,720 out-of-state.

2005-2006 Financial aid. Need-based: 1,174 full-time freshmen applied for aid; 868 were judged to have need; 753 of these received aid. Average need met was 62%. Average scholarship/grant was $1,902; average loan $1,371. 35% of total undergraduate aid awarded as scholarships/grants, 65% as loans/jobs. **Non-need-based:** Awarded to 553 full-time undergraduates, including 114 freshmen. Scholarships awarded for academics, art, athletics, job skills, music/drama, state residency.

Application procedures. Admission: Closing date 8/26 (receipt date). $25 fee, may be waived for applicants with need. Application may be submitted online. Admission notification on a rolling basis. **Financial aid:** Priority date 3/1; no closing date. FAFSA required. Applicants notified on a rolling basis starting 3/1.

Academics. Special study options: Accelerated study, cooperative education, cross-registration, distance learning, double major, dual enrollment of high school students, external degree, honors, independent study, internships, liberal arts/career combination, student-designed major, study abroad, teacher certification program, Washington semester. **Credit/placement by examination:** AP, CLEP, IB. 64 credit hours maximum toward bachelor's degree. **Support services:** Pre-admission summer program, study skills assistance, tutoring, writing center.

Majors. Area/ethnic studies: African-American, Hispanic-American/Latino/Chicano. **Biology:** General. **Business:** Accounting, business admin, finance, hospitality admin, hospitality/recreation, marketing, tourism promotion, tourism/travel. **Communications:** General, broadcast journalism, journalism. **Computer sciences:** General, computer science. **Conservation:** General, environmental studies, land use planning. **Education:** Art, music. **Engineering technology:** Civil, electrical, surveying. **English:** Speech/rhetoric. **Foreign languages:** General, Spanish. **Health:** Health care admin, nursing (RN). **History:** General. **Interdisciplinary:** Behavioral sciences, math/computer science. **Math:** General. **Parks/recreation:** General, exercise sciences. **Philosophy/religion:** Philosophy. **Physical sciences:** Atmospheric science, chemistry, physics. **Protective services:** Criminal justice, law enforcement admin. **Psychology:** General. **Public administration:** Human services, social work. **Social sciences:** Anthropology, economics, political science, sociology. **Transportation:** Air traffic control, aviation, aviation management. **Visual/performing arts:** Art, industrial design, music performance.

Most popular majors. Business/marketing 23%, English 9%, interdisciplinary studies 12%, security/protective services 10%, social sciences 9%.

Computing on campus. 700 workstations in library, computer center, student center. Commuter students can connect to campus network. Online course registration, online library, helpline, repair service, wireless network available.

Student life. **Freshman orientation:** Mandatory. Preregistration for classes offered. Several sessions held preceding each semester. **Housing:** Off-campus apartments in area. **Activities:** Jazz band, choral groups, dance, drama, literary magazine, music ensembles, musical theater, radio station, student government, student newspaper, approximately 100 student organizations and clubs.

Athletics. NCAA. **Intercollegiate:** Baseball M, basketball, cross-country, diving, soccer, swimming, tennis, volleyball W. **Intramural:** Basketball, handball, lacrosse M, racquetball, rugby M, skiing, softball, tennis, volleyball. **Team name:** Roadrunners.

Student services. Adult student services, alcohol/substance abuse counseling, campus ministries, career counseling, services for economically disadvantaged, student employment services, financial aid counseling, health services, legal services, on-campus daycare, personal counseling, placement for graduates, veterans' counselor, women's services. **Physically disabled:** Services for visually, speech, hearing impaired. **Learning disabled:** Comprehensive services available.

Contact. Phone: (303) 556-3058 Fax: (303) 556-6345
William Hathaway-Clark, Director of Admissions, Metropolitan State College of Denver, Campus Box 16, Denver, CO 80217

Naropa University
Boulder, Colorado — **CB member**
www.naropa.edu — **CB code: 0908**

- Private 4-year liberal arts college
- Commuter campus in small city
- 451 degree-seeking undergraduates: 11% part-time, 58% women, 1% African American, 2% Asian American, 7% Hispanic American, 1% Native American, 3% international
- 712 degree-seeking graduate students
- 84% of applicants admitted
- Application essay, interview required

General. Founded in 1974. Regionally accredited. Nontraditional, experiential, Buddhist-inspired, non-sectarian college. **Degrees:** 108 bachelor's awarded; master's, first professional offered. **Location:** 35 miles from Denver. **Calendar:** Semester, limited summer session. **Full-time faculty:** 55 total; 56% have terminal degrees, 13% minority, 53% women. **Part-time faculty:** 169 total; 18% have terminal degrees, 11% minority, 61% women. **Class size:** 88% < 20, 10% 20-39, less than 1% 40-49, 1% 50-99. **Special facilities:** Meditation halls, maitri rooms, preschool.

Freshman class profile. 122 applied, 103 admitted, 39 enrolled.

Mid 50% test scores			
SAT verbal:	540-630	GPA 2.0-2.99:	38%
SAT math:	520-580	End year in good standing:	86%
ACT:	22-28	Return as sophomores:	82%
GPA 3.50 or higher:	24%	Out-of-state:	82%
GPA 3.0-3.49:	36%	Live on campus:	64%
		International:	3%

Basis for selection. Holistic approach to admissions decisions. Recommendations and interview required. Assessment of academic background, community service, mission and readiness are reviewed. SAT or ACT recommended. Audition required for BFA.

High school preparation. College-preparatory program recommended. Recommended units include English 4, mathematics 3, social studies 3, history 3, science 3 (laboratory 2), foreign language 3 and academic electives 2. Art/dance/theatre and/or creative writing recommended.

2005-2006 Annual costs. Tuition/fees: $18,500. Room/board: $6,590. Books/supplies: $612. Personal expenses: $2,736.

2005-2006 Financial aid. All financial aid based on need. 21 full-time freshmen applied for aid; 20 were judged to have need; 20 of these received aid. Average need met was 58%. Average scholarship/grant was $12,267; average loan $3,215. 52% of total undergraduate aid awarded as scholarships/grants, 48% as loans/jobs.

Application procedures. **Admission:** Priority date 1/15; no deadline. $50 fee, may be waived for applicants with need. Application may be submitted online. Admission notification on a rolling basis. Must reply by May 1 or within 3 week(s) if notified thereafter. High school students with GED may be admitted early. **Financial aid:** Priority date 3/1; no closing date. FAFSA required. Applicants notified on a rolling basis starting 3/1; must reply within 4 week(s) of notification.

Academics. **Special study options:** Double major, dual enrollment of high school students, independent study, internships, student-designed major, study abroad. **Credit/placement by examination:** AP, CLEP, IB. 30 credit hours maximum toward bachelor's degree. **Support services:** Reduced course load, study skills assistance, tutoring, writing center.

Majors. **Conservation:** Environmental studies. **Education:** Kindergarten/preschool. **English:** English lit. **Health:** Yoga therapy. **Philosophy/religion:** Religion. **Psychology:** General. **Visual/performing arts:** Dramatic, studio arts.

Most popular majors. Education 6%, interdisciplinary studies 22%, psychology 44%, theological studies 8%, visual/performing arts 9%.

Computing on campus. 83 workstations in computer center. Online course registration, online library, wireless network available.

Student life. **Freshman orientation:** Mandatory. Wilderness expedition offered at extra cost. **Policies:** Freshmen permitted cars on campus. **Housing:** Guaranteed on-campus for freshmen. Coed dorms, apartments, substance-free housing available. $300 fully refundable deposit, deadline 5/1. **Activities:** Jazz band, choral groups, dance, drama, literary magazine, music ensembles, student government, student newspaper, diversity awareness working group, student union, Garuda theater, Students for a Free Tibet, Gay/Lesbian/Bi/Trans group, poetry coffee houses, GreenWorks, Naropa volunteer corps, yoga clubs.

Student services. Alcohol/substance abuse counseling, career counseling, financial aid counseling, minority student services, personal counseling. **Physically disabled:** Services for visually, hearing impaired.

Contact. E-mail: admissions@naropa.edu
Phone: (303) 546-3572 Toll-free number: (800) 772-6951
Fax: (303) 546-3583
Susan Boyle, Assistant Vice President of Admissions and Marketing, Naropa University, 2130 Arapahoe Avenue, Boulder, CO 80302

National American University: Denver
Denver, Colorado
www.national.edu — **CB code: 5354**

- For-profit 4-year university and branch campus college
- Commuter campus in very large city
- 250 degree-seeking undergraduates

General. Founded in 1941. Regionally accredited. **Degrees:** 45 bachelor's, 10 associate awarded; master's offered. **Calendar:** Quarter, extensive summer session. **Part-time faculty:** 30 total. **Class size:** 92% < 20, 8% 20-39.

Basis for selection. Open admission.

2006-2007 Annual costs. Tuition/fees: $11,700. Books/supplies: $1,200.

Application procedures. **Admission:** No deadline. $25 fee. Admission notification on a rolling basis. **Financial aid:** No deadline. Applicants notified on a rolling basis.

Academics. **Special study options:** Accelerated study, cooperative education, distance learning, double major, ESL, external degree, independent study, internships, liberal arts/career combination, weekend college. **Credit/placement by examination:** AP, CLEP, institutional tests. 48 credit hours maximum toward bachelor's degree. **Support services:** Remedial instruction.

Majors. **Business:** Accounting, business admin, management information systems, management science. **Computer sciences:** Applications programming, information systems, LAN/WAN management, system admin. **Health:** Facilities admin, health care admin, health services, health services admin.

Computing on campus. Online library available.

Student life. Activities: Student government, Phi Beta Lamda (business club), Data Processing Management Association.

Athletics. Team name: Mavericks.

Student services. Career counseling, placement for graduates.

Contact. E-mail: kwalker@national.edu
Phone: (303) 758-6700 Fax: (303) 758-6810
Karen Walker, Senior Admissions Representative, National American University: Denver, 1325 South Colorado Boulevard, Suite 100, Denver, CO 80222-3308

Nazarene Bible College
Colorado Springs, Colorado
www.nbc.edu **CB code: 0476**

- Private 4-year Bible college affiliated with Church of the Nazarene
- Commuter campus in very large city
- 537 degree-seeking undergraduates: 67% part-time, 33% women
- Application essay required

General. Founded in 1964. Accredited by ABHE. Full programs offered in evening classes. Cater to adult students. Extensive online degree programs offered. **Degrees:** 41 bachelor's, 4 associate awarded. **Location:** 60 miles from Denver. **Calendar:** Trimester, limited summer session. **Full-time faculty:** 14 total. **Part-time faculty:** 35 total.

Basis for selection. Open admission, but selective for some programs. Testimony, 2 recommendations required. **Homeschooled:** Transcript of courses and grades, letter of recommendation (nonparent) required.

2005-2006 Annual costs. Tuition/fees: $7,350. Books/supplies: $900.

Financial aid. Non-need-based: Scholarships awarded for religious affiliation. **Additional information:** Tuition waiver available to students serving as student body officers.

Application procedures. Admission: No deadline. $35 fee, may be waived for applicants with need. Admission notification on a rolling basis beginning on or about 5/1. **Financial aid:** Priority date 6/1; no closing date. FAFSA required. Applicants notified on a rolling basis starting 6/15; must reply within 2 week(s) of notification.

Academics. Special study options: Distance learning, double major, internships. **Credit/placement by examination:** CLEP, institutional tests. **Support services:** Learning center, reduced course load, remedial instruction.

Majors. Theology: Bible, pastoral counseling, religious ed, sacred music.

Computing on campus. 20 workstations in library, computer center.

Student life. Freshman orientation: Mandatory. Preregistration for classes offered. **Policies:** Religious observance required. **Activities:** Concert band, choral groups, music ensembles, student government, Missions in Action Club, Wesley Theological Society.

Student services. Campus ministries, career counseling, services for economically disadvantaged, student employment services, financial aid counseling, personal counseling, placement for graduates, women's services. **Physically disabled:** Services for visually, hearing impaired.

Contact. E-mail: admissions@nbc.edu
Phone: (719) 884-5000 ext. 5065 Toll-free number: (800) 873-3873
Fax: (719) 884-5199
Laurel Matson, Vice President for Enrollment Services, Nazarene Bible College, 1111 Academy Park Loop, Colorado Springs, CO 80910-3717

Regis University
Denver, Colorado **CB member**
www.regis.edu **CB code: 4656**

- Private 4-year university and liberal arts college affiliated with Roman Catholic Church
- Residential campus in very large city
- 1,581 degree-seeking undergraduates: 5% part-time, 63% women, 2% African American, 4% Asian American, 12% Hispanic American, 1% Native American, 1% international
- 134 degree-seeking graduate students
- 82% of applicants admitted
- SAT or ACT (ACT writing optional), application essay required
- 59% graduate within 6 years

General. Founded in 1877. Regionally accredited. College in the Jesuit tradition. Regis University is made up of three separate schools: Regis College is a traditional liberal arts college. Students at Regis College are traditional college aged students who take daytime classes on campus. Rueckert-Hartman School for Health Professions offers healthcare degrees including many nursing options, healthcare leadership, and physical therapy degrees to both traditional and non-traditional students. The School of Professional Studies offers part-time undergraduate, graduate, certificate and corporate education programs to adult students on 6 campuses and online. **Degrees:** 210 bachelor's awarded; master's, doctoral offered. **ROTC:** Army, Navy, Air Force. **Location:** 10 miles from downtown. **Calendar:** Semester, limited summer session. **Full-time faculty:** 91 total; 86% have terminal degrees, 11% minority, 48% women. **Class size:** 57% < 20, 42% 20-39, less than 1% 40-49.

Freshman class profile. 1,828 applied, 1,493 admitted, 402 enrolled.

Mid 50% test scores			
SAT verbal:	480-590	**Rank in top quarter:**	55%
SAT math:	460-570	**Rank in top tenth:**	24%
ACT:	20-26	**Return as sophomores:**	79%
GPA 3.50 or higher:	51%	**Out-of-state:**	42%
GPA 3.0-3.49:	26%	**Live on campus:**	75%
GPA 2.0-2.99:	23%	**International:**	1%

Basis for selection. High school record, test scores, recommendations, essay, school and community activities most important. Interview, campus visit recommended. Audition recommended of music, theater majors.

High school preparation. 15 units required. Required and recommended units include English 3, mathematics 3, social studies 1, history 2, science 2 (laboratory 1) and foreign language 2.

2006-2007 Annual costs. Tuition/fees: $25,200. Room/board: $8,190. Books/supplies: $1,306. Personal expenses: $1,143.

2004-2005 Financial aid. Need-based: 368 full-time freshmen applied for aid; 366 were judged to have need; 249 of these received aid. Average scholarship/grant was $13,830; average loan $1,618. 69% of total undergraduate aid awarded as scholarships/grants, 31% as loans/jobs. **Non-need-based:** Awarded to 867 full-time undergraduates, including 313 freshmen. Scholarships awarded for academics, athletics, leadership, minority status, religious affiliation, ROTC, state residency. **Additional information:** Tuition free for any student maintaining the required amount of credit hours who does not graduate in four years.

Application procedures. Admission: Priority date 3/1; deadline 8/1. $40 fee, may be waived for applicants with need. Application may be submitted online. Admission notification on a rolling basis beginning on or about 9/1. Must reply by May 1 or within 2 week(s) if notified thereafter. **Financial aid:** Priority date 3/1; no closing date. FAFSA required. Applicants notified on a rolling basis starting 3/15.

Academics. Special study options: Accelerated study, combined bachelor's/graduate degree, cooperative education, cross-registration, distance learning, double major, exchange student, honors, independent study, internships, student-designed major, study abroad, teacher certification program. **Credit/placement by examination:** AP, CLEP, IB, institutional tests. 30 credit hours maximum toward bachelor's degree. Regis, CLEP, DANTES, Challenge exams offered. **Support services:** Learning center, preadmission summer program, reduced course load, remedial instruction, study skills assistance, tutoring, writing center.

Majors. Area/ethnic studies: Women's. **Biology:** General, biochemistry. **Business:** General, accounting, business admin. **Communications:** General. **Computer sciences:** General, computer science. **Education:** General, biology, chemistry, elementary, English, history, mathematics, middle, physical, science, secondary, special. **Foreign languages:** French, Spanish. **Health:** Medical records admin, predentistry, premedicine, preveterinary. **History:** General. **Interdisciplinary:** Neuroscience. **Legal studies:** Prelaw. **Liberal arts:** Arts/sciences. **Math:** General. **Philosophy/religion:** Philosophy, religion. **Physical sciences:** Chemistry. **Psychology:** General. **Social sciences:** Criminology, economics, political science, sociology. **Visual/performing arts:** General.

Most popular majors. Biology 6%, business/marketing 27%, communications/journalism 9%, English 6%, interdisciplinary studies 15%, social sciences 13%.

Computing on campus. 300 workstations in dormitories, library, computer center, student center. Dormitories wired for high-speed internet access and linked to campus network. Commuter students can connect to campus network. Online course registration, online library, helpline, wireless network available.

Student life. **Freshman orientation:** Mandatory, $75 fee. Preregistration for classes offered. Held weekend before classes begin. **Policies:** Freshmen and sophomores required to live on campus unless residing with parent, guardian or spouse in Denver metropolitan area. Freshmen permitted cars on campus. **Housing:** Guaranteed on-campus for freshmen. Coed dorms, single-sex dorms, special housing for disabled, apartments, cooperative housing, substance-free housing available. $150 nonrefundable deposit, deadline 5/1. **Activities:** Jazz band, choral groups, dance, drama, literary magazine, music ensembles, musical theater, radio station, student government, student newspaper, peer education, environmental action program, Christian Fellowship, Jewish student group, Asian awareness association, black student alliance, Mi Gente, multicultural awareness committee, Romero House, Young Democrats and Republicans.

Athletics. NCAA. **Intercollegiate:** Baseball M, basketball, cross-country, golf, lacrosse W, rifle W, soccer, softball W, volleyball W. **Intramural:** Basketball, bowling, football (non-tackle), golf M, soccer, softball, tennis, volleyball. **Team name:** Rangers.

Student services. Adult student services, alcohol/substance abuse counseling, campus ministries, career counseling, student employment services, financial aid counseling, health services, minority student services, personal counseling, placement for graduates, veterans' counselor. **Physically disabled:** Services for visually, speech, hearing impaired. **Learning disabled:** Comprehensive services available.

Contact. E-mail: regisadm@regis.edu
Phone: (303) 458-4900 Toll-free number: (800) 388-2366 ext. 4900
Fax: (303) 964-5534
Victor Davolt, Director of Admissions, Regis College, Regis University, 3333 Regis Boulevard, Mail Code A12, Denver, CO 80221-1099

Remington College: Denver

Lakewood, Colorado
www.remingtoncollege.edu **CB code: 2256**

- For-profit 4-year business college
- Very large city

General. Accredited by ACICS. **Calendar:** Continuous.

Annual costs/financial aid. $30,480 for all 2-year associate programs. Tuition includes costs of all books, lab fees, laptop computer. Need-based financial aid available for full-time students.

Contact. Phone: (303) 445-0500
Director of Recruitment, 11011 West Sixth Avenue, Lakewood, CO 80215-5501

Rocky Mountain College of Art & Design

Lakewood, Colorado
www.rmcad.edu **CB code: 1943**

- For-profit 4-year visual arts college
- Commuter campus in very large city
- 446 degree-seeking undergraduates: 18% part-time, 56% women, 2% African American, 2% Asian American, 8% Hispanic American, 1% Native American, 1% international
- 100% of applicants admitted
- Application essay, interview required

General. Founded in 1963. Regionally accredited; also accredited by ACCSCT. **Degrees:** 81 bachelor's awarded. **Calendar:** Semester, extensive summer session. **Full-time faculty:** 25 total. **Part-time faculty:** 40 total. **Class size:** 50% < 20, 45% 20-39, 4% 40-49, less than 1% 50-99. **Special facilities:** Fine arts center exhibition space.

Freshman class profile. 216 applied, 216 admitted, 62 enrolled.

Out-of-state:	33%	**Live on campus:**	50%

Basis for selection. Applicants must show desire to pursue art career. Portfolio, essay, and recommendations required. Test scores required for all degree candidates. Portfolio and essay required. Interview required of local applicants, recommended for others.

High school preparation. Art courses strongly recommended.

2006-2007 Annual costs. Tuition/fees: $18,984. Room/board: $5,427. Books/supplies: $1,200. Personal expenses: $300.

2004-2005 Financial aid. **Need-based:** 34% of total undergraduate aid awarded as scholarships/grants, 66% as loans/jobs. **Non-need-based:** Scholarships awarded for academics, art, state residency.

Application procedures. **Admission:** No deadline. $35 fee. Application may be submitted online. Admission notification on a rolling basis. **Financial aid:** Priority date 3/15; no closing date. FAFSA, institutional form required. Applicants notified on a rolling basis starting 4/15; must reply within 2 week(s) of notification.

Academics. **Special study options:** Double major, internships. **Credit/placement by examination:** CLEP, institutional tests. 64 credit hours maximum toward bachelor's degree. **Support services:** Reduced course load, remedial instruction, study skills assistance, tutoring.

Majors. **Communications technology:** Animation/special effects. **Education:** Art. **Visual/performing arts:** Graphic design, illustration, interior design, painting, sculpture.

Computing on campus. 120 workstations in library, computer center. Online library, helpline, repair service, wireless network available.

Student life. **Freshman orientation:** Mandatory. 2-day program held before start of term. **Policies:** Freshmen permitted cars on campus. **Housing:** Guaranteed on-campus for freshmen. Apartments available. $300 deposit, deadline 4/1. **Activities:** Student government.

Student services. Alcohol/substance abuse counseling, career counseling, student employment services, financial aid counseling, personal counseling, placement for graduates, veterans' counselor.

Contact. E-mail: admissions@rmcad.edu
Phone: (303) 753-6046 Toll-free number: (800) 888-2787
Fax: (303) 759-4970
Marianna Bagge, Director of Admissions, Rocky Mountain College of Art & Design, 1600 Pierce Street, Lakewood, CO 80214

Teikyo Loretto Heights University

Denver, Colorado
www.tlhu.edu **CB code: 4878**

- Private 4-year business and liberal arts college
- Residential campus in very large city
- 234 degree-seeking undergraduates

General. Accredited by ACICS. **Degrees:** 30 associate awarded. **Calendar:** Semester, limited summer session. **Full-time faculty:** 4 total. **Part-time faculty:** 17 total.

Freshman class profile. 58 enrolled.

Basis for selection. High school record, class rank, GPA, recommendations, test scores, and essay most important.

High school preparation. College-preparatory program recommended.

2006-2007 Annual costs. Tuition/fees: $13,600. Room/board: $7,300.

Application procedures. **Admission:** No deadline. $65 fee, may be waived for applicants with need. Admission notification on a rolling basis. **Financial aid:** FAFSA required.

Academics. International students with TOEFL score below 525 must enroll in courses offered by university's intensive English program. **Special study options:** Dual enrollment of high school students, ESL, independent study, internships, liberal arts/career combination, study abroad. **Credit/placement by examination:** CLEP, IB.

Majors. **Business:** International.

Computing on campus. Dormitories linked to campus network.

Student life. **Freshman orientation:** Available. **Policies:** Freshmen permitted cars on campus. **Housing:** Guaranteed on-campus for all undergraduates. Coed dorms, single-sex dorms available.

Student services. Career counseling, student employment services, financial aid counseling, placement for graduates.

Contact. E-mail: info@tlhu.edu
Phone: (303) 937-4513 Fax: (303) 937-4224
Regina Kireva, Director of Admissions, Teikyo Loretto Heights University, 3001 South Federal Boulevard, Denver, CO 80236

United States Air Force Academy

USAF Academy, Colorado **CB member**
www.usafa.edu **CB code: 4830**

- Public 4-year university and military college
- Residential campus in large city
- 4,397 degree-seeking undergraduates
- 18% of applicants admitted
- SAT or ACT with writing, application essay, interview required

General. Founded in 1954. Regionally accredited. **Degrees:** 913 bachelor's awarded. **Location:** 8 miles from Colorado Springs, 60 miles from Denver. **Calendar:** Semester, limited summer session. **Full-time faculty:** 559 total. **Class size:** 65% < 20, 35% 20-39. **Special facilities:** 2 airfields, planetarium, tri-sonic wind tunnel, observatory, aeronautics, instrumentation, research and radio-frequency systems laboratories, consolidated educational training facility, meteorology lab, engineering mechanics laboratory, laser optics center.

Freshman class profile. 9,601 applied, 1,746 admitted, 1,384 enrolled.

Mid 50% test scores			
SAT verbal:	530-660	Rank in top quarter:	84%
SAT math:	560-670	Rank in top tenth:	56%
ACT:	23-29	Out-of-state:	94%
		Live on campus:	100%

Basis for selection. GED not accepted. Must be a citizen of the United States, unmarried with no dependents, between the ages of 17 and 23, and of good moral character. Legal nomination from member of Congress, US President or Vice President or other selected sources required. Secondary school record, test scores, leadership ability, extracurricular activities, character most important. Satisfactory completion of medical exam and fitness test, and personal interview required.

High school preparation. Recommended units include English 4, mathematics 4, social studies 3, history 3, science 4 (laboratory 4) and foreign language 2. One computer science course recommended. English should include college preparatory composition and speech courses. Math should include algebra, geometry, trigonometry, calculus, and functional analysis (if available). Science should include biology, chemistry, physics, computers, and additional science courses. Foreign language instruction should be in a modern language.

2006-2007 Annual costs. Tuition, room, board, medical and dental care paid by U.S. Government. Each cadet receives monthly salary to pay for uniforms, supplies and personal expenses. A government loan is advanced to each member of the freshman class.

Application procedures. Admission: Closing date 1/31 (postmark date). No application fee. Application may be submitted online. Admission notification on a rolling basis beginning on or about 11/15. Must reply by 5/1. Several stages of application process; begin junior year.

Academics. Credit/placement by examination: AP, CLEP, institutional tests.

Majors. Biology: General. **Business:** Management science. **Computer sciences:** Computer science. **Engineering:** General, aerospace, civil, computer, electrical, environmental, mechanical, mechanics, operations research, systems. **English:** English lit. **History:** General. **Interdisciplinary:** Behavioral sciences, math/computer science. **Legal studies:** General. **Liberal arts:** Humanities. **Physical sciences:** Atmospheric science, chemistry, physics. **Social sciences:** General, economics, geography, political science.

Most popular majors. Business/marketing 21%, engineering/engineering technologies 31%, interdisciplinary studies 10%, social sciences 17%.

Computing on campus. PC or laptop required. Dormitories wired for high-speed internet access and linked to campus network. Online library, helpline, repair service available.

Student life. Freshman orientation: Available. Three 2-day appointee orientation sessions held in April. **Housing:** Guaranteed on-campus for all undergraduates. Coed dorms available.

Athletics. NCAA. **Intercollegiate:** Baseball M, basketball, boxing M, cheerleading, cross-country, diving, fencing, football (tackle) M, golf M, gymnastics, ice hockey M, lacrosse M, rifle, soccer, swimming, tennis, track and field, volleyball W, water polo M, wrestling M. **Intramural:** Basketball, boxing M, cross-country, football (non-tackle), racquetball, rugby, soccer, softball, tennis, volleyball. **Team name:** Falcons.

Student services. Alcohol/substance abuse counseling, campus ministries, health services, legal services, personal counseling.

Contact. E-mail: rr_webmail@usafa.af.mil
Phone: (719) 333-2520 Toll-free number: (800) 443-9266
Fax: (719) 333-3647
United States Air Force Academy, HQ USAF/RRS, 2304 Cadet Drive, Suite 200, USAF Academy, CO 80840

University of Colorado at Boulder

Boulder, Colorado **CB member**
www.colorado.edu **CB code: 4841**

- Public 4-year university
- Residential campus in small city
- 25,205 degree-seeking undergraduates: 7% part-time, 47% women, 2% African American, 6% Asian American, 6% Hispanic American, 1% Native American, 1% international
- 4,775 degree-seeking graduate students
- 88% of applicants admitted
- SAT or ACT (ACT writing optional) required
- 66% graduate within 6 years; 38% enter graduate study

General. Founded in 1876. Regionally accredited. **Degrees:** 5,124 bachelor's awarded; master's, doctoral, first professional offered. **ROTC:** Army, Navy, Air Force. **Location:** 30 miles from Denver. **Calendar:** Semester, extensive summer session. **Full-time faculty:** 1,227 total; 91% have terminal degrees, 14% minority, 34% women. **Part-time faculty:** 559 total; 38% have terminal degrees, 9% minority, 50% women. **Class size:** 47% < 20, 32% 20-39, 6% 40-49, 8% 50-99, 7% >100. **Special facilities:** Museum, observatory, planetarium and science center, electron microscope, outdoor theater, video interactive foreign language laboratory, mountain research station, centrifuge, engineering lab, multipurpose conference center, concert hall, multi-disciplinary IT center.

Freshman class profile. 17,111 applied, 15,003 admitted, 5,047 enrolled.

Mid 50% test scores			
SAT verbal:	530-630	Rank in top tenth:	22%
SAT math:	550-650	End year in good standing:	90%
ACT:	23-28	Return as sophomores:	83%
GPA 3.50 or higher:	55%	Out-of-state:	37%
GPA 3.0-3.49:	37%	Live on campus:	94%
GPA 2.0-2.99:	8%	International:	1%
Rank in top quarter:	54%	Fraternities:	7%
		Sororities:	10%

Basis for selection. Secondary school record (breadth and rigor of courses, grades, class rank) most important. Tests scores also very important. Personal statement, recommendations, and personal attributes and talents considered. Audition required of music majors. **Homeschooled:** Applicants will receive individual consideration.

High school preparation. 16 units required. Required units include English 4, mathematics 3, social studies 2, history 1, science 3 (laboratory 2) and foreign language 3. Physics or chemistry with lab, geography, 3 years single foreign language required for Colleges of Arts, Sciences and Business. 4 mathematics, 1 physics, 1 chemistry required for College of Engineering. 4 mathematics required for College of Business. 2 years single foreign language required for Colleges of Engineering, Music, Architecture and Planning.

2005-2006 Annual costs. Tuition/fees: $5,372; $22,826 out-of-state. Room/board: $7,980. Books/supplies: $1,306. Personal expenses: $2,853.

2004-2005 Financial aid. Need-based: 3,364 full-time freshmen applied for aid; 1,999 were judged to have need; 1,953 of these received aid. Average need met was 91%. Average scholarship/grant was $5,256; average loan $3,490. 41% of total undergraduate aid awarded as scholarships/grants, 59% as loans/jobs. **Non-need-based:** Awarded to 4,186 full-time undergraduates, including 1,128 freshmen. Scholarships awarded for academics, alumni affiliation, art, athletics, leadership, music/drama, ROTC, state residency.

Application procedures. Admission: Closing date 1/15 (postmark date). $50 fee, may be waived for applicants with need. Application may be submitted online. Admission notification on a rolling basis. Must reply by May 1 or within 2 week(s) if notified thereafter. **Financial aid:** Priority date 4/1; no closing date. FAFSA required. Applicants notified on a rolling basis starting 2/1; must reply within 3 week(s) of notification.

Academics. Special study options: Accelerated study, combined bachelor's/graduate degree, cooperative education, cross-registration, distance learning, double major, dual enrollment of high school students, ESL, exchange student, honors, independent study, internships, liberal arts/career combination, semester at sea, student-designed major, study abroad, teacher certification program. **Credit/placement by examination:** AP, CLEP, IB, institutional tests. Policies vary by department. **Support services:** Learning center, pre-admission summer program, reduced course load, study skills assistance, tutoring, writing center.

Majors. Architecture: Environmental design. **Area/ethnic studies:** Asian, Russian/Slavic, women's. **Biology:** General, biochemistry, cell/histology, cellular/molecular, ecology, environmental, evolutionary, population, systematic. **Business:** Accounting, business admin, finance, human resources, international, marketing, real estate, small business admin, tourism/travel. **Communications:** General, journalism. **Computer sciences:** General, computer science. **Conservation:** Environmental studies. **Education:** Music. **Engineering:** Aerospace, architectural, chemical, civil, computer, electrical, environmental, mechanical, physics. **English:** English lit. **Foreign languages:** Chinese, classics, French, German, Germanic, Italian, Japanese, linguistics, Spanish. **Health:** Communication disorders. **History:** General. **Interdisciplinary:** Global studies. **Liberal arts:** Humanities. **Math:** General, applied. **Parks/recreation:** Exercise sciences. **Philosophy/religion:** Philosophy, religion. **Physical sciences:** Astronomy, chemistry, geology, physics, planetary. **Psychology:** General. **Social sciences:** Anthropology, economics, geography, political science, sociology. **Visual/performing arts:** Dance, dramatic, film/cinema, music performance, studio arts.

Most popular majors. Biology 9%, business/marketing 15%, communications/journalism 10%, engineering/engineering technologies 8%, psychology 9%, social sciences 16%, visual/performing arts 6%.

Computing on campus. 2,300 workstations in dormitories, library, computer center, student center. Dormitories wired for high-speed internet access and linked to campus network. Commuter students can connect to campus network. Online course registration, online library, helpline, repair service, student web hosting, wireless network available.

Student life. Freshman orientation: Mandatory. Preregistration for classes offered. 2-day programs for students and parents held throughout summer, and in January for students entering in the spring. **Policies:** Honor code, Colorado Creed (a lifestyle code of conduct), and 2-Strikes disciplinary policy regarding alcohol violations. Freshmen permitted cars on campus. **Housing:** Guaranteed on-campus for freshmen. Coed dorms, special housing for disabled, apartments, fraternity/sorority housing, substance-free housing available. $250 partly refundable deposit. Engineering dormitories, residential academic programs, honors section. **Activities:** Bands, choral groups, dance, drama, film society, literary magazine, music ensembles, musical theater, opera, radio station, student government, student newspaper, symphony orchestra, TV station, hundreds of student organizations available on campus.

Athletics. NCAA. **Intercollegiate:** Basketball, cross-country, football (tackle) M, golf, skiing, soccer W, tennis, track and field, volleyball W. **Intramural:** Badminton, basketball, football (non-tackle), ice hockey, soccer, softball, volleyball, water polo. **Team name:** Colorado Buffaloes.

Student services. Adult student services, alcohol/substance abuse counseling, campus ministries, career counseling, student employment services, financial aid counseling, health services, legal services, minority student services, on-campus daycare, personal counseling, placement for graduates, veterans' counselor, women's services. **Physically disabled:** Services for visually, speech, hearing impaired.

Contact. Phone: (303) 492-6301 Fax: (303) 492-7115
Kevin McLennan, Interim Director of Admissions, University of Colorado at Boulder, 552 UCB, Boulder, CO 80309-0552

University of Colorado at Colorado Springs

Colorado Springs, Colorado
www.uccs.edu **CB code: 4874**

- Public 4-year university
- Commuter campus in large city
- 6,077 degree-seeking undergraduates: 21% part-time, 61% women, 4% African American, 5% Asian American, 9% Hispanic American, 1% Native American
- 1,496 degree-seeking graduate students
- 76% of applicants admitted
- SAT or ACT (ACT writing optional) required
- 40% graduate within 6 years; 29% enter graduate study

General. Founded in 1965. Regionally accredited. **Degrees:** 1,026 bachelor's awarded; master's, doctoral offered. **ROTC:** Army. **Location:** 60 miles from Denver. **Calendar:** Semester, limited summer session. **Full-time faculty:** 283 total; 12% minority, 45% women. **Part-time faculty:** 32 total; 9% minority, 72% women. **Class size:** 36% < 20, 37% 20-39, 14% 40-49, 11% 50-99, 2% >100.

Freshman class profile. 1,899 applied, 1,449 admitted, 939 enrolled.

Mid 50% test scores			
SAT verbal:	490-600	Rank in top quarter:	42%
SAT math:	480-590	Rank in top tenth:	15%
ACT:	21-25	End year in good standing:	79%
GPA 3.50 or higher:	39%	Return as sophomores:	67%
GPA 3.0-3.49:	37%	Out-of-state:	11%
GPA 2.0-2.99:	24%	Live on campus:	41%

Basis for selection. Priority given to applicants who ranked in top 40% of graduating class, earned 1080 or higher on the SAT (exclusive of Writing) or 24 or higher on the ACT, earned a minimum 2.8 GPA in high school, and completed all high school course units as required by the college to which they applied. Test of Standard Written English required of liberal arts applicants.

High school preparation. College-preparatory program required. 15 units required; 16 recommended. Required and recommended units include English 4, mathematics 3-4, social studies 2, science 3 (laboratory 2), foreign language 2 and academic electives 1. Requirements vary slightly according to college.

2005-2006 Annual costs. Tuition/fees: $4,888; $16,182 out-of-state. Room/board: $6,418. Books/supplies: $1,200.

2005-2006 Financial aid. Need-based: Average need met was 59%. Average scholarship/grant was $4,749; average loan $2,619. 37% of total undergraduate aid awarded as scholarships/grants, 63% as loans/jobs. **Non-need-based:** Scholarships awarded for academics, athletics, leadership, state residency.

Application procedures. Admission: Priority date 4/1; deadline 7/1. $50 fee. Application may be submitted online. Admission notification on a rolling basis. **Financial aid:** Priority date 4/1; no closing date. FAFSA required. Applicants notified on a rolling basis starting 4/15.

Academics. Special study options: Accelerated study, combined bachelor's/graduate degree, cooperative education, cross-registration, distance learning, double major, exchange student, independent study, internships, liberal arts/career combination, student-designed major, study abroad, teacher certification program. **Credit/placement by examination:** AP, CLEP, IB. 30 credit hours maximum toward bachelor's degree. **Support services:** Learning center, study skills assistance, tutoring, writing center.

Majors. Biology: General. **Business:** Accounting, business admin, finance, human resources. **Communications:** General. **Computer sciences:** Computer science. **Education:** Special. **Engineering:** General, computer, electrical, mechanical. **English:** English lit. **Foreign languages:** Spanish. **Health:** Health services, nursing (RN). **History:** General. **Math:** General. **Philosophy/religion:** Philosophy. **Physical sciences:** Chemistry, physics. **Psychology:** General. **Social sciences:** Anthropology, economics, geography, political science, sociology. **Visual/performing arts:** Studio arts.

Most popular majors. Biology 7%, business/marketing 19%, communications/journalism 11%, health sciences 11%, psychology 10%, social sciences 16%.

Computing on campus. 250 workstations in dormitories, library, computer center. Dormitories wired for high-speed internet access and linked to campus network. Commuter students can connect to campus network. Online course registration, online library, helpline, repair service, wireless network available.

Student life. Freshman orientation: Mandatory, $45 fee. One-day sessions throughout summer. **Policies:** Freshmen permitted cars on campus. **Housing:** Coed dorms, single-sex dorms, special housing for disabled, apartments available. $150 partly refundable deposit. **Activities:** Jazz band, choral groups, dance, drama, film society, literary magazine, music ensembles, musical theater, radio station, student government, student newspaper, advocating women's assistance resources education, counseling honor society (Chi SIgma Iota), club hockey, cycling club, math club, chemistry honor society, Black Student Union, international student club, Latino Student Union, Inter-Varsity Christian Fellowship.

Athletics. NCAA. **Intercollegiate:** Basketball, cross-country, golf M, soccer M, softball W, tennis, track and field, volleyball W. **Intramural:** Badminton, basketball, bowling, cross-country, fencing, football (non-tackle), racquetball, soccer, softball, swimming, table tennis, tennis, volleyball. **Team name:** Mountain Lions.

Student services. Adult student services, career counseling, student employment services, financial aid counseling, health services, minority student services, on-campus daycare, personal counseling, veterans' counselor. **Physically disabled:** Services for visually, speech, hearing impaired.

Contact. E-mail: admrec@uccs.edu
Phone: (719) 262-3383 Toll-free number: (800) 990-8227 ext. 3383
Fax: (719) 262-3116
Steve Ellis, Director of Admissions, University of Colorado at Colorado Springs, PO Box 7150, Colorado Springs, CO 80933-7150

University of Colorado at Denver and Health Sciences Center

Denver, Colorado — **CB member**
www.ucdhsc.edu — **CB code: 4875**

- Public 4-year university
- Commuter campus in very large city
- 7,780 degree-seeking undergraduates: 27% part-time, 55% women, 4% African American, 10% Asian American, 11% Hispanic American, 1% Native American, 2% international
- 7,323 degree-seeking graduate students
- 69% of applicants admitted
- SAT or ACT (ACT writing optional) required
- 42% graduate within 6 years; 37% enter graduate study

General. Founded in 1912. Regionally accredited. Library, student center, and classrooms shared with Metropolitan State College and Community College of Denver. **Degrees:** 1,551 bachelor's awarded; master's, doctoral, first professional offered. **ROTC:** Army, Air Force. **Calendar:** Semester, extensive summer session. **Full-time faculty:** 579 total; 82% have terminal degrees, 12% minority, 41% women. **Part-time faculty:** 783 total; 38% have terminal degrees, 9% minority, 53% women. **Class size:** 34% < 20, 45% 20-39, 13% 40-49, 8% 50-99, less than 1% >100. **Special facilities:** Centers for computational mathematics, applied psychology, environmental science, transportation research, Fourth World Center for study of indigenous law and politics.

Freshman class profile. 2,681 applied, 1,852 admitted, 787 enrolled.

Mid 50% test scores			
SAT verbal:	490-590	GPA 2.0-2.99:	29%
SAT math:	490-600	Rank in top quarter:	37%
ACT:	20-25	Rank in top tenth:	13%
GPA 3.50 or higher:	33%	Return as sophomores:	69%
GPA 3.0-3.49:	38%	Out-of-state:	5%

Basis for selection. Previous academic performance including high school course work and GPA; evidence of academic ability and accomplishments as indicated by test scores; and evidence of maturity, motivation, potential for academic success most important. Audition required of music majors.

High school preparation. 16 units required. Required units include English 4, mathematics 3, social studies 2, history 1, science 3, foreign language 2 and academic electives 1. 4 math required for engineering and business students.

2005-2006 Annual costs. Tuition/fees: $5,021; $16,191 out-of-state. Tuition varies by program. Books/supplies: $1,300. Personal expenses: $2,718.

2004-2005 Financial aid. Need-based: 451 full-time freshmen applied for aid; 322 were judged to have need; 285 of these received aid. Average need met was 61%. Average scholarship/grant was $4,296; average loan $2,264. 35% of total undergraduate aid awarded as scholarships/grants, 65% as loans/jobs. **Non-need-based:** Awarded to 169 full-time undergraduates, including 30 freshmen. Scholarships awarded for academics, art, leadership, music/drama.

Application procedures. Admission: Priority date 7/22; deadline 9/1. $50 fee, may be waived for applicants with need. Application may be submitted online. Admission notification on a rolling basis. **Financial aid:** Closing date 4/1. FAFSA, institutional form required. Applicants notified on a rolling basis starting 5/1.

Academics. Learning opportunities through center for internships and cooperative education. **Special study options:** Accelerated study, combined bachelor's/graduate degree, cooperative education, cross-registration, distance learning, double major, ESL, honors, independent study, internships, liberal arts/career combination, student-designed major, study abroad, teacher certification program, weekend college. **Credit/placement by examination:** AP, CLEP, IB, institutional tests. 30 credit hours maximum toward bachelor's degree. **Support services:** Learning center, study skills assistance, tutoring, writing center.

Majors. Biology: General, biomedical sciences. **Business:** General. **Communications:** General. **Computer sciences:** General. **Engineering:** Civil, electrical, mechanical. **English:** Composition, English lit. **Foreign languages:** French, Spanish. **Health:** Dental hygiene, nursing (RN). **History:** General. **Interdisciplinary:** Global studies. **Math:** General. **Philosophy/religion:** Philosophy. **Physical sciences:** Chemistry, physics. **Psychology:** General. **Social sciences:** Anthropology, economics, geography, political science, sociology. **Visual/performing arts:** Dramatic, studio arts.

Most popular majors. Business/marketing 23%, communications/journalism 8%, engineering/engineering technologies 6%, health sciences 12%, psychology 6%, social sciences 14%, visual/performing arts 10%.

Computing on campus. 205 workstations in library, computer center, student center. Commuter students can connect to campus network. Online course registration, online library, helpline, student web hosting, wireless network available.

Student life. Freshman orientation: Mandatory. **Policies:** Freshmen permitted cars on campus. **Housing:** Limited housing available. **Activities:** Jazz band, choral groups, dance, drama, music ensembles, musical theater, student government, student newspaper, more than 60 groups available.

Athletics. Intramural: Basketball M, football (tackle) M, tennis.

Student services. Alcohol/substance abuse counseling, career counseling, student employment services, financial aid counseling, health services, legal services, minority student services, on-campus daycare, personal counseling, placement for graduates, veterans' counselor, women's services. **Physically disabled:** Services for visually, speech, hearing impaired.

Contact. E-mail: admissions@cudenver.edu
Phone: (303) 556-3287 Fax: (303) 556-4838
Barbara Edwards, Director of Admissions, University of Colorado at Denver and Health Sciences Center, Box 173364, Campus Box 167, Denver, CO 80217-3364

University of Denver

Denver, Colorado — **CB member**
www.du.edu — **CB code: 4842**

- Private 4-year university affiliated with United Methodist Church
- Residential campus in very large city
- 4,813 degree-seeking undergraduates: 9% part-time, 55% women
- 4,786 degree-seeking graduate students
- 82% of applicants admitted
- SAT or ACT (ACT writing optional), application essay, interview required
- 69% graduate within 6 years

General. Founded in 1864. Regionally accredited. **Degrees:** 909 bachelor's awarded; master's, doctoral, first professional offered. **ROTC:** Army, Air Force. **Location:** 8 miles from downtown. **Calendar:** Quarter, limited summer session. **Full-time faculty:** 463 total; 93% have terminal degrees, 13% minority, 40% women. **Part-time faculty:** 534 total. **Class size:** 59% < 20, 31% 20-39, 7% 40-49, 2% 50-99, 1% >100. **Special facilities:** Observatory, high altitude research laboratory, centers for gifted children.

Freshman class profile. 4,038 applied, 3,304 admitted, 1,097 enrolled.

Mid 50% test scores		Rank in top quarter:	69%
SAT verbal:	530-630	Rank in top tenth:	36%
SAT math:	530-640	Return as sophomores:	87%
ACT:	23-28	Out-of-state:	55%
GPA 3.50 or higher:	61%	Live on campus:	92%
GPA 3.0-3.49:	30%	Fraternities:	17%
GPA 2.0-2.99:	9%	Sororities:	19%

Basis for selection. High school GPA, test scores and strength of curriculum most important. Interview, academic maturity, contributions to school and community activities, leadership also important; recommendations from teacher and counselor, personal essay considered. Interview required. Audition required of music majors. Portfolio recommended of art majors. **Homeschooled:** Letter of recommendation (nonparent) required.

High school preparation. Recommended units include English 4, mathematics 4, social studies 2, history 2, science 4 (laboratory 2) and foreign language 3.

2005-2006 Annual costs. Tuition/fees: $28,410. Room/board: $8,748. Books/supplies: $1,306. Personal expenses: $1,143.

2004-2005 Financial aid. Need-based: 612 full-time freshmen applied for aid; 458 were judged to have need; 458 of these received aid. Average need met was 75%. Average scholarship/grant was $14,582; average loan $3,581. 70% of total undergraduate aid awarded as scholarships/grants, 30%

as loans/jobs. **Non-need-based:** Awarded to 1,349 full-time undergraduates, including 352 freshmen. Scholarships awarded for academics, alumni affiliation, art, athletics, leadership, minority status, music/drama.

Application procedures. Admission: Closing date 1/15 (postmark date). $50 fee, may be waived for applicants with need. Application may be submitted online. Admission notification 3/15. Must reply by 5/1. **Financial aid:** Priority date 2/15; no closing date. FAFSA required. Applicants notified by 4/1; must reply within 3 week(s) of notification.

Academics. Special inter-term courses for focused concentration on a subject for 3 weeks. **Special study options:** Accelerated study, combined bachelor's/graduate degree, cooperative education, double major, dual enrollment of high school students, ESL, honors, independent study, internships, liberal arts/career combination, semester at sea, student-designed major, study abroad, teacher certification program, Washington semester. **Credit/placement by examination:** AP, CLEP, IB, institutional tests. 45 credit hours maximum toward bachelor's degree. **Support services:** Learning center, tutoring.

Majors. Agriculture: Animal sciences. **Area/ethnic studies:** Asian-American, women's. **Biology:** General, biochemistry, bioinformatics, ecology, molecular. **Business:** General, accounting, construction management, finance, hospitality admin, international, managerial economics, marketing, real estate, statistics, tourism/travel. **Communications:** General, digital media, journalism. **Computer sciences:** General, computer science, systems analysis. **Conservation:** Environmental science. **Education:** Art. **Engineering:** General, computer, electrical, mechanical. **English:** English lit. **Foreign languages:** French, German, Italian, Russian, Spanish. **History:** General. **Interdisciplinary:** Biological/physical sciences, intercultural. **Math:** General. **Philosophy/religion:** Philosophy, religion. **Physical sciences:** Chemistry, physics. **Psychology:** General. **Public administration:** Policy analysis. **Social sciences:** General, anthropology, criminology, economics, geography, international relations, political science, sociology. **Visual/performing arts:** Art, art history/conservation, dramatic, graphic design, music performance, musicology, studio arts.

Most popular majors. Biology 6%, business/marketing 44%, communications/journalism 11%, psychology 6%, social sciences 10%, visual/performing arts 6%.

Computing on campus. PC or laptop required. 390 workstations in dormitories, library, computer center, student center. Dormitories wired for high-speed internet access and linked to campus network. Commuter students can connect to campus network. Online course registration, helpline, wireless network available.

Student life. Freshman orientation: Available. **Housing:** Coed dorms, special housing for disabled, apartments, fraternity/sorority housing available. $200 nonrefundable deposit, deadline 5/1. **Activities:** Bands, choral groups, dance, drama, literary magazine, music ensembles, musical theater, opera, radio station, student government, student newspaper, symphony orchestra, 120 clubs and organizations.

Athletics. NCAA. **Intercollegiate:** Baseball M, basketball, cross-country, diving, golf, gymnastics W, ice hockey M, lacrosse, skiing, soccer, swimming, tennis, volleyball W. **Intramural:** Badminton, basketball, bowling, cross-country, golf, ice hockey M, lacrosse, racquetball, rugby, skiing, soccer, softball, tennis, volleyball, wrestling M. **Team name:** Pioneers.

Student services. Career counseling, student employment services, health services, personal counseling, placement for graduates, veterans' counselor. **Physically disabled:** Services for visually, speech, hearing impaired.

Contact. E-mail: admission@du.edu
Phone: (303) 871-2036 Toll-free number: (800) 525-9495
Fax: (303) 871-3301
Thomas Willoughby, Vice Chancellor, Enrollment, University of Denver, 2197 South University Boulevard, Denver, CO 80208

University of Northern Colorado

Greeley, Colorado
www.unco.edu **CB code: 4074**

- Public 4-year university
- Commuter campus in small city
- 10,407 degree-seeking undergraduates: 7% part-time, 60% women, 2% African American, 3% Asian American, 8% Hispanic American, 1% Native American
- 1,906 degree-seeking graduate students
- 82% of applicants admitted
- SAT or ACT (ACT writing optional) required
- 45% graduate within 6 years; 5% enter graduate study

General. Founded in 1889. Regionally accredited. **Degrees:** 2,047 bachelor's awarded; master's, doctoral offered. **ROTC:** Army, Air Force. **Location:** 50 miles from Denver, 50 miles from Cheyenne, Wyoming. **Calendar:** Semester, limited summer session. **Full-time faculty:** 400 total; 80% have terminal degrees, 12% minority, 46% women. **Part-time faculty:** 201 total; 23% have terminal degrees, 5% minority, 67% women. **Class size:** 28% < 20, 49% 20-39, 7% 40-49, 14% 50-99, 2% >100. **Special facilities:** African-American cultural center, Hispanic cultural center.

Freshman class profile. 7,318 applied, 6,025 admitted, 2,494 enrolled.

Mid 50% test scores		**Rank in top quarter:**	32%
SAT verbal:	480-580	**Rank in top tenth:**	10%
SAT math:	470-580	**End year in good standing:**	79%
ACT:	20-24	**Return as sophomores:**	71%
GPA 3.50 or higher:	33%	**Out-of-state:**	10%
GPA 3.0-3.49:	34%	**Live on campus:**	92%
GPA 2.0-2.99:	33%		

Basis for selection. Expected cumulative GPA of 2.9 or higher; ACT composite score of 21 or combined SAT score of 970 (exclusive of Writing). Higher ACT/SAT score can compensate for lower GPA and higher GPA can compensate for lower test score. Audition required of music majors.

High school preparation. 15 units required. Required and recommended units include English 4, mathematics 3, social studies 3, science 3 (laboratory 1). Mathematics should include 2 algebra, additional higher level mathematics unit.

2005-2006 Annual costs. Tuition/fees: $3,837; $12,381 out-of-state. Room/board: $6,744. Books/supplies: $931. Personal expenses: $1,143.

2004-2005 Financial aid. Need-based: 2,003 full-time freshmen applied for aid; 1,058 were judged to have need; 1,048 of these received aid. Average need met was 95%. Average scholarship/grant was $3,379; average loan $3,134. 34% of total undergraduate aid awarded as scholarships/grants, 66% as loans/jobs. **Non-need-based:** Awarded to 2,598 full-time undergraduates, including 769 freshmen. Scholarships awarded for academics, athletics, music/drama.

Application procedures. Admission: Priority date 8/1; no deadline. $40 fee, may be waived for applicants with need. Application may be submitted online. Admission notification on a rolling basis. **Financial aid:** Priority date 3/1; no closing date. FAFSA required. Applicants notified on a rolling basis starting 4/15; must reply within 4 week(s) of notification.

Academics. Special study options: Cooperative education, cross-registration, distance learning, double major, ESL, exchange student, external degree, honors, independent study, internships, semester at sea, student-designed major, study abroad, teacher certification program. **Credit/placement by examination:** AP, CLEP, IB, institutional tests. 30 credit hours maximum toward bachelor's degree. **Support services:** Learning center, reduced course load, remedial instruction, study skills assistance, tutoring, writing center.

Majors. Area/ethnic studies: African-American, Hispanic-American/Latino/Chicano. **Biology:** General. **Business:** Business admin. **Communications:** General, journalism. **Education:** Music, special. **English:** English lit. **Family/consumer sciences:** Aging. **Foreign languages:** General, Spanish. **Health:** Audiology/hearing, audiology/speech pathology, dietetics, health care admin, health services, nursing (RN), public health ed, speech pathology, vocational rehab counseling. **History:** General. **Math:** General. **Parks/recreation:** Exercise sciences, facilities management. **Philosophy/religion:** Philosophy. **Physical sciences:** Chemistry, geology, physics. **Protective services:** Criminal justice. **Psychology:** General. **Public administration:** Human services. **Social sciences:** General, anthropology, economics, geography, political science, sociology. **Visual/performing arts:** Dramatic, studio arts.

Most popular majors. Business/marketing 13%, communications/journalism 9%, health sciences 10%, interdisciplinary studies 15%, parks/recreation 7%, psychology 7%, social sciences 11%, visual/performing arts 8%.

Computing on campus. 565 workstations in dormitories, library, computer center, student center. Dormitories wired for high-speed internet access and linked to campus network. Commuter students can connect to campus network. Online course registration, online library, helpline, repair service, wireless network available.

Student life. Freshman orientation: Available, $55 fee. Preregistration for classes offered. **Policies:** Freshmen permitted cars on campus. **Housing:** Guaranteed on-campus for all undergraduates. Coed dorms, single-sex dorms, special housing for disabled, apartments, fraternity/sorority housing, substance-free housing available. $250 nonrefundable deposit. **Activities:** Bands, choral groups, dance, drama, film society, literary magazine, music ensembles, musical theater, opera, radio station, student government, student newspaper, symphony orchestra, black student union, Hispanic students organization, international students association, Native American student services, Asian/Pacific American student services.

Athletics. NCAA. **Intercollegiate:** Baseball M, basketball, cross-country W, diving W, football (tackle) M, golf, soccer W, softball W, swimming W, tennis, track and field, volleyball W, wrestling M. **Intramural:** Basketball, football (non-tackle), golf, racquetball, soccer, softball, table tennis, tennis, volleyball, water polo. **Team name:** Bears.

Student services. Adult student services, alcohol/substance abuse counseling, campus ministries, career counseling, student employment services, financial aid counseling, health services, legal services, minority student services, personal counseling, placement for graduates, veterans' counselor, women's services. **Physically disabled:** Services for visually, speech, hearing impaired.

Contact. E-mail: admissions.help@unco.edu
Phone: (970) 351-2881 Toll-free number: (888) 700-4862
Fax: (970) 351-2984
Gary Gullickson, Director of Admissions, University of Northern Colorado, Campus Box 10, Greeley, CO 80639

Western State College of Colorado

Gunnison, Colorado — **CB member**
www.western.edu — **CB code: 4946**

- Public 4-year liberal arts college
- Residential campus in small town
- 2,277 degree-seeking undergraduates
- SAT or ACT (ACT writing optional) required

General. Founded in 1901. Regionally accredited. College-based mountain search and rescue team. **Degrees:** 485 bachelor's awarded. **Location:** 200 miles from Denver. **Calendar:** Semester, limited summer session. **Full-time faculty:** 109 total; 76% have terminal degrees, 4% minority, 35% women. **Part-time faculty:** 26 total; 12% have terminal degrees, 4% minority, 50% women. **Class size:** 46% < 20, 44% 20-39, 10% 40-49, less than 1% 50-99. **Special facilities:** Botanical gardens, archaeological site, dinosaur reconstruction lab.

Freshman class profile.

Mid 50% test scores			
SAT verbal:	440-550	Rank in top quarter:	21%
SAT math:	460-550	Rank in top tenth:	5%
ACT:	18-23	Out-of-state:	30%
		Live on campus:	91%

Basis for selection. School achievement record, test scores very important; recommendations considered. Essay recommended. Interview recommended for academically weak applicants.

High school preparation. Required and recommended units include English 4, mathematics 3-4, social studies 2-3, history 2-3, science 2-3 (laboratory 2), foreign language 2 and academic electives 3.

2005-2006 Annual costs. Tuition/fees: $3,138; $11,754 out-of-state. Room/board: $6,804. Books/supplies: $950. Personal expenses: $1,226.

2005-2006 Financial aid. Need-based: 368 full-time freshmen applied for aid; 294 were judged to have need; 249 of these received aid. Average need met was 45%. Average scholarship/grant was $2,500; average loan $2,625. 44% of total undergraduate aid awarded as scholarships/grants, 56% as loans/jobs. **Non-need-based:** Awarded to 848 full-time undergraduates, including 272 freshmen. Scholarships awarded for academics, alumni affiliation, art, athletics, leadership, music/drama.

Application procedures. Admission: Priority date 5/1; deadline 8/1 (postmark date). $40 fee, may be waived for applicants with need. Application may be submitted online. Admission notification on a rolling basis beginning on or about 11/1. Must reply by May 1 or within 2 week(s) if notified thereafter. **Financial aid:** Priority date 4/15; no closing date. FAFSA required. Applicants notified on a rolling basis starting 4/15; must reply within 3 week(s) of notification.

Academics. Special study options: Combined bachelor's/graduate degree, cooperative education, distance learning, double major, dual enrollment of high school students, exchange student, honors, independent study, internships, liberal arts/career combination, semester at sea, study abroad, teacher certification program. **Credit/placement by examination:** AP, CLEP, IB, institutional tests. 30 credit hours maximum toward bachelor's degree. **Support services:** Study skills assistance, tutoring, writing center.

Majors. Biology: General. **Business:** Accounting, business admin, management information systems. **Communications:** General. **Conservation:** Environmental studies. **Foreign languages:** Spanish. **History:** General. **Legal studies:** Prelaw. **Math:** General. **Parks/recreation:** General, exercise sciences. **Physical sciences:** Chemistry, geology. **Protective services:** Criminal justice, police science. **Psychology:** General. **Social sciences:** Anthropology, economics, political science, sociology. **Visual/performing arts:** Art, music management, studio arts.

Most popular majors. Biology 7%, business/marketing 31%, parks/recreation 14%, psychology 8%, social sciences 13%, visual/performing arts 10%.

Computing on campus. 168 workstations in dormitories, library, student center. Dormitories linked to campus network. Commuter students can connect to campus network. Online course registration available.

Student life. Freshman orientation: Available, $65 fee. Preregistration for classes offered. Wilderness-based orientation available. **Policies:** Freshmen permitted cars on campus. **Housing:** Guaranteed on-campus for freshmen. Coed dorms, single-sex dorms, apartments, fraternity/sorority housing available. $100 deposit. Theme housing (honors, art, wilderness/outdoor activities) available. **Activities:** Bands, choral groups, drama, literary magazine, music ensembles, radio station, student government, student newspaper, symphony orchestra, TV station, Hillel, Black student alliance, Amigos, Campus Crusade, Hui-O-Ka-Aina, Lesbian-Gay-Bisexual alliance, Newman Club, Baptist student union, Christian athletes fellowship, Women's Action Coalition.

Athletics. NCAA. **Intercollegiate:** Basketball, cross-country, football (tackle) M, skiing, track and field, volleyball W, wrestling M. **Intramural:** Baseball M, basketball, golf, ice hockey M, lacrosse, rugby, skiing, soccer, softball, swimming, tennis, track and field, volleyball, wrestling M. **Team name:** Mountaineers.

Student services. Adult student services, career counseling, health services, on-campus daycare, personal counseling, veterans' counselor. **Physically disabled:** Services for visually, hearing impaired. **Learning disabled:** Comprehensive services available.

Contact. E-mail: discover@western.edu
Phone: (970) 943-2119 Toll-free number: (800) 876-5309
Fax: (970) 943-2212
Tim Albers, Director of Admissions, Western State College of Colorado, 600 North Adams Street, Gunnison, CO 81231

Westwood College of Technology

Denver, Colorado
www.westwood.edu — **CB code: 3948**

- For-profit 3-year technical college
- Commuter campus in very large city
- 932 degree-seeking undergraduates
- Interview required

General. Founded in 1953. Accredited by ACCSCT. **Degrees:** 140 bachelor's, 356 associate awarded. **Location:** 5 miles from downtown. **Calendar:** 5 ten-week terms per year. Extensive summer session. **Full-time faculty:** 50 total. **Part-time faculty:** 80 total.

Basis for selection. Institutional test (Accuplacer) and interview most important. Developmental courses may be required for those who do not pass entrance examination. SAT or ACT recommended. Accuplacer waived for students with sufficient scores on SAT or ACT.

High school preparation. At least 1 algebra required for electronics, drafting and surveying programs. General mathematics required for all other programs.

2005-2006 Annual costs. One-time tool charge ranges from $35 to $3,300. Required fees $150. Lab fees vary by program from $600 to $925 per year. Personal expenses: $2,000.

Financial aid. Non-need-based: Scholarships awarded for academics, state residency.

Application procedures. Admission: No deadline. $25 fee. Application may be submitted online. Admission notification on a rolling basis. **Financial aid:** No deadline. FAFSA, institutional form required. Applicants notified on a rolling basis starting 1/1; must reply within 2 week(s) of notification.

Academics. Instruction and emphasis on laboratory work and practical application. **Special study options:** Accelerated study, cooperative education, distance learning, independent study, internships, liberal arts/career combination. **Credit/placement by examination:** CLEP, institutional tests. 69 credit hours maximum toward associate degree, 140 toward bachelor's. **Support services:** Learning center, remedial instruction, study skills assistance, tutoring.

Majors. Architecture: Interior. **Business:** General, accounting, business admin, e-commerce, management information systems, marketing. **Communications:** General. **Communications technology:** Graphic/printing. **Computer sciences:** General, computer graphics, information systems, networking, security, web page design, webmaster. **Engineering:** Electrical. **Engineering technology:** Electrical. **Mechanic/repair:** Electronics/electrical. **Protective services:** Law enforcement admin. **Visual/performing arts:** Commercial/advertising art, design, graphic design.

Most popular majors. Business/marketing 20%, computer/information sciences 44%, engineering/engineering technologies 15%, visual/performing arts 21%.

Computing on campus. 50 workstations in library, computer center. Online library available.

Student life. Freshman orientation: Mandatory. Preregistration for classes offered. **Policies:** No-tolerance drug/alcohol policy. Freshmen permitted cars on campus.

Athletics. Intramural: Baseball.

Student services. Career counseling, student employment services, financial aid counseling, placement for graduates, veterans' counselor. **Physically disabled:** Services for visually impaired.

Contact. E-mail: rpierson@westwood.edu
Phone: (303) 650-5050 Fax: (303) 487-0214
Rob Peirson, Director of Admissions, Westwood College of Technology, 7350 North Broadway, Denver, CO 80221

Westwood College of Technology: South
Denver, Colorado
www.westwood.edu

- For-profit 4-year technical college
- Commuter campus in very large city
- 363 degree-seeking undergraduates: 15% part-time, 39% women, 5% African American, 4% Asian American, 12% Hispanic American, 1% Native American
- 69% of applicants admitted
- Interview required

General. Accredited by ACCSCT. **Degrees:** 43 bachelor's, 53 associate awarded. **Calendar:** Continuous, extensive summer session. **Full-time faculty:** 11 total. **Part-time faculty:** 23 total.

Freshman class profile. 185 applied, 127 admitted, 77 enrolled.

Basis for selection. Admission based on scores from Accuplacer exam. Non-native English speakers must take ESL course, TOEFL score of 475, have a HS diploma or GED in the U.S., or proof of completion of an accredited college program in the U.S. Accuplacer exam can be waived if student scores 17 on ACT or SAT equivalent.

2005-2006 Annual costs. Tuition/fees: $20,425. Books/supplies: $1,250.

Application procedures. Admission: No deadline. $25 fee. Application may be submitted online. Admission notification on a rolling basis. **Financial aid:** No deadline. FAFSA, institutional form required. Applicants notified on a rolling basis; must reply within 2 week(s) of notification.

Academics. Special study options: Accelerated study, distance learning, independent study, weekend college. **Credit/placement by examination:** CLEP, institutional tests. 67 credit hours maximum toward associate degree, 135 toward bachelor's. **Support services:** Reduced course load, remedial instruction, study skills assistance, tutoring, writing center.

Majors. Architecture: Interior. **Business:** E-commerce, fashion. **Communications technology:** Animation/special effects, desktop publishing, graphics. **Computer sciences:** Computer graphics, LAN/WAN management, networking, security, system admin, web page design, webmaster. **Protective services:** Law enforcement admin. **Visual/performing arts:** Commercial/advertising art, design, graphic design, interior design.

Computing on campus. 300 workstations in library, computer center. Commuter students can connect to campus network. Online course registration, online library available.

Student life. Freshman orientation: Mandatory. Preregistration for classes offered. **Policies:** Freshmen permitted cars on campus.

Student services. Adult student services, career counseling, student employment services, financial aid counseling, placement for graduates.

Contact. Phone: (303) 934-1122 Fax: (303) 934-2583
Ron DeJong, Director of Admissions, Westwood College of Technology: South, 3150 South Sheridan Boulevard, Denver, CO 80227-5507

Yeshiva Toras Chaim Talmudical Seminary
Denver, Colorado
CB code: 7008

- Private 4-year rabbinical college for men affiliated with Jewish faith
- Very large city

General. Accredited by AARTS. **Calendar:** Trimester.

Contact. Phone: (303) 629-8200
1555 Stuart Street PO Box 40067, Denver, CO 80204

Connecticut

Albertus Magnus College

New Haven, Connecticut CB member
www.albertus.edu CB code: 3001

- Private 4-year liberal arts college affiliated with Roman Catholic Church
- Residential campus in small city
- 1,695 degree-seeking undergraduates: 71% women, 28% African American, 1% Asian American, 11% Hispanic American
- 366 degree-seeking graduate students
- 83% of applicants admitted
- SAT or ACT (ACT writing optional) required

General. Founded in 1925. Regionally accredited. Majority of students enrolled in adult education and graduate programs. **Degrees:** 372 bachelor's, 149 associate awarded; master's offered. **Location:** 90 miles from New York City. **Calendar:** Semester, limited summer session. **Full-time faculty:** 34 total. **Part-time faculty:** 20 total. **Class size:** 69% < 20, 31% 20-39. **Special facilities:** Center for science, art, and technology.

Freshman class profile. 534 applied, 443 admitted, 126 enrolled.

Mid 50% test scores		Out-of-state:	15%
SAT verbal:	490-540	Live on campus:	56%
SAT math:	470-520		

Basis for selection. School achievement record most important. Recommendations, then test scores, interview, school and community activities also considered.

High school preparation. 16 units required. Required and recommended units include English 4, mathematics 3, social studies 2, science 2 and foreign language 2.

2005-2006 Annual costs. Tuition/fees: $17,836. Room/board: $7,928. Books/supplies: $620. Personal expenses: $940.

2004-2005 Financial aid. Need-based: Average need met was 46%. Average scholarship/grant was $6,720; average loan $3,550. 63% of total undergraduate aid awarded as scholarships/grants, 37% as loans/jobs. **Non-need-based:** Scholarships awarded for academics, art, athletics, leadership, music/drama, religious affiliation, state residency.

Application procedures. Admission: No deadline. $35 fee, may be waived for applicants with need. Application may be submitted online. Admission notification on a rolling basis beginning on or about 12/15. Must reply by May 1 or within 4 week(s) if notified thereafter. **Financial aid:** Priority date 2/28, closing date 8/15. FAFSA, institutional form required. Applicants notified on a rolling basis starting 3/1; must reply within 2 week(s) of notification.

Academics. Special study options: Accelerated study, double major, dual enrollment of high school students, ESL, honors, independent study, internships, liberal arts/career combination, student-designed major, study abroad, teacher certification program. **Credit/placement by examination:** AP, CLEP, institutional tests. 21 credit hours maximum toward associate degree, 45 toward bachelor's. **Support services:** Learning center, reduced course load, study skills assistance, tutoring, writing center.

Majors. Biology: General. **Business:** Accounting, business admin, finance, international, management information systems, managerial economics. **Communications:** General. **Computer sciences:** Information systems. **Education:** General, art, biology, business, chemistry, English, history, mathematics, middle, science, secondary, social studies, Spanish. **English:** British lit, creative writing. **Health:** Art therapy, premedicine. **History:** General. **Legal studies:** Prelaw. **Liberal arts:** Arts/sciences. **Math:** General. **Philosophy/religion:** Philosophy, religion. **Physical sciences:** Chemistry. **Protective services:** Criminal justice. **Psychology:** General. **Public administration:** Human services. **Social sciences:** General, economics, political science, sociology. **Visual/performing arts:** General, art, art history/conservation, commercial/advertising art, dramatic, photography, studio arts.

Computing on campus. 175 workstations in library, computer center, student center. Dormitories wired for high-speed internet access. Commuter students can connect to campus network. Online library, helpline, repair service, wireless network available.

Student life. Freshman orientation: Mandatory. Preregistration for classes offered. **Policies:** Freshmen permitted cars on campus. **Housing:** Guaranteed on-campus for all undergraduates. Coed dorms, single-sex dorms, substance-free housing available. $400 deposit, deadline 7/1. **Activities:** Choral groups, dance, drama, literary magazine, musical theater, student government, campus ministry, outspoken alliance, multi-cultural student union.

Athletics. NCAA. **Intercollegiate:** Baseball M, basketball, cross-country, soccer, softball W, swimming W, tennis, volleyball W. **Team name:** Falcons.

Student services. Adult student services, campus ministries, career counseling, student employment services, financial aid counseling, health services, personal counseling, placement for graduates, veterans' counselor.

Contact. E-mail: admissions@albertus.edu
Phone: (203) 773-8501 Toll-free number: (800) 578-9160
Fax: (203) 773-5248
Richard LoLatte, Dean of Admissions and Enrollment Management, Albertus Magnus College, 700 Prospect Street, New Haven, CT 06511-1189

Briarwood College

Southington, Connecticut
www.briarwood.edu CB code: 3121

- For-profit 4-year junior college
- Commuter campus in large town
- 600 degree-seeking undergraduates
- Application essay required

General. Founded in 1966. Regionally accredited. **Degrees:** 130 associate awarded. **Location:** 19 miles from Hartford. **Calendar:** Semester, limited summer session. **Full-time faculty:** 24 total; 8% have terminal degrees, 88% women. **Part-time faculty:** 58 total; 10% have terminal degrees, 3% minority, 59% women.

Basis for selection. Open admission, but selective for some programs. Special requirements, interviews recommended for occupational therapy assistant program. 3 placement tests (English grammar, reading, math) and essay required of all new students.

High school preparation. For occupational therapy assistant program, 2 math, 2 science, including 1 in biological science, required.

2005-2006 Annual costs. Tuition/fees: $15,925. Room only: $3,320. Books/supplies: $1,000. Personal expenses: $2,400.

Financial aid. Non-need-based: Scholarships awarded for academics, alumni affiliation, leadership.

Application procedures. Admission: No deadline. $25 fee, may be waived for applicants with need. Application may be submitted online. Admission notification on a rolling basis beginning on or about 9/15. **Financial aid:** Priority date 4/30; no closing date. FAFSA required. Applicants notified on a rolling basis starting 3/15; must reply within 2 week(s) of notification.

Academics. Special study options: Double major, ESL, independent study, internships, liberal arts/career combination, weekend college. **Credit/placement by examination:** AP, CLEP, institutional tests. 29 credit hours maximum toward associate degree. **Support services:** Learning center, preadmission summer program, reduced course load, remedial instruction, study skills assistance, tutoring, writing center.

Majors. Personal/culinary services: Mortuary science. **Protective services:** Criminal justice.

Computing on campus. 66 workstations in library, computer center. Dormitories wired for high-speed internet access.

Student life. Freshman orientation: Mandatory. **Policies:** Freshmen permitted cars on campus. **Housing:** Coed dorms, apartments available. $100 deposit. Townhouse apartments with kitchens available. **Activities:** Choral groups, radio station, student government, psychology honor society, allied health club.

Athletics. Intramural: Basketball, cheerleading W, softball.

Student services. Career counseling, student employment services, financial aid counseling, health services, personal counseling, placement for graduates, veterans' counselor. **Physically disabled:** Services for visually, hearing impaired.

Contact. E-mail: admis@briarwood.edu
Phone: (860) 628-4751 ext. 108 Toll-free number: (800) 952-2444 ext. 108
Fax: (860) 628-6444
Donna Yamanis, Director of Enrollment Management, Briarwood College, 2279 Mount Vernon Road, Southington, CT 06489-1057

Central Connecticut State University

New Britain, Connecticut — **CB member**
www.ccsu.edu — **CB code: 3898**

- Public 4-year university
- Commuter campus in small city
- 9,143 degree-seeking undergraduates: 19% part-time, 51% women, 8% African American, 3% Asian American, 6% Hispanic American, 1% Native American, 1% international
- 2,188 degree-seeking graduate students
- 62% of applicants admitted
- SAT or ACT with writing, application essay required
- 40% graduate within 6 years

General. Founded in 1849. Regionally accredited. **Degrees:** 1,530 bachelor's awarded; master's, doctoral offered. **ROTC:** Army, Air Force. **Location:** 9 miles from Hartford. **Calendar:** Semester, extensive summer session. **Full-time faculty:** 416 total; 73% have terminal degrees, 18% minority, 40% women. **Part-time faculty:** 434 total; 5% have terminal degrees, 5% minority, 43% women. **Class size:** 41% < 20, 57% 20-39, 1% 40-49, 1% 50-99, less than 1% >100. **Special facilities:** Observatory, planetarium.

Freshman class profile. 5,549 applied, 3,421 admitted, 1,356 enrolled.

Mid 50% test scores		**Return as sophomores:**	80%
SAT verbal:	470-560	**Out-of-state:**	7%
SAT math:	470-570	**Live on campus:**	51%
Rank in top quarter:	27%	**International:**	1%
Rank in top tenth:	7%		

Basis for selection. High school record, class rank, SAT scores most important. Letters of recommendation, the optional student essay, and resumes of activities to assess applicant's attitude toward future success also considered. School of Business, social work program, communication program, and School of Education programs require acceptance into majors after admission to the university. Interview optional but would be considered. Audition required for music.

High school preparation. 13 units required. Required and recommended units include English 4, mathematics 3, social studies 2, history 1, science 2 (laboratory 1) and foreign language 3. Social science should include US history; mathematics should include algebra I and II and geometry.

2005-2006 Annual costs. Tuition/fees: $6,163; $14,102 out-of-state. Room/board: $7,456. Books/supplies: $1,010. Personal expenses: $1,744.

2004-2005 Financial aid. All financial aid based on need. Average need met was 77%. Average scholarship/grant was $5,077; average loan $2,734. 39% of total undergraduate aid awarded as scholarships/grants, 61% as loans/jobs.

Application procedures. Admission: Priority date 10/1; deadline 6/1. $50 fee, may be waived for applicants with need. Admission notification on a rolling basis beginning on or about 12/1. Must reply by May 1 or within 2 week(s) if notified thereafter. **Financial aid:** Priority date 2/15, closing date 9/15. FAFSA required. Applicants notified on a rolling basis starting 3/15; must reply within 2 week(s) of notification.

Academics. Special study options: Cooperative education, cross-registration, distance learning, double major, dual enrollment of high school students, ESL, exchange student, honors, independent study, internships, student-designed major, study abroad, teacher certification program. Undergraduates may take graduate classes. **Credit/placement by examination:** AP, CLEP, IB, institutional tests. 30 credit hours maximum toward bachelor's degree. **Support services:** Learning center, pre-admission summer program, reduced course load, remedial instruction, study skills assistance, tutoring, writing center.

Honors college/program. Honor Program provides interdisciplinary, team-taught approach to general education. Limited scholarships available.

Majors. Biology: General, molecular. **Business:** Accounting, business admin, construction management, finance, international, management information systems, marketing, organizational behavior, travel services. **Communications:** General. **Computer sciences:** General. **Education:** Art, elementary, music, secondary, technology/industrial arts. **Engineering:** Electrical. **Engineering technology:** Civil, computer, industrial, manufacturing, mechanical. **English:** English lit. **Foreign languages:** French, German, Italian, Spanish. **Health:** Athletic training, nursing (RN). **History:** General. **Interdisciplinary:** Global studies. **Math:** General. **Philosophy/religion:** Philosophy. **Physical sciences:** Chemistry, geology, physics. **Psychology:** General. **Public administration:** Social work. **Social sciences:** General, anthropology, criminology, economics, geography, political science, sociology. **Visual/performing arts:** Art, design, dramatic.

Most popular majors. Business/marketing 28%, education 10%, engineering/engineering technologies 6%, psychology 8%, social sciences 12%, visual/performing arts 6%.

Computing on campus. 875 workstations in dormitories, library, computer center, student center. Dormitories wired for high-speed internet access and linked to campus network. Commuter students can connect to campus network. Online course registration, online library, helpline, repair service, wireless network available.

Student life. Freshman orientation: Available, $65 fee. Preregistration for classes offered. One-day orientation, late June and early July. **Policies:** Freshmen permitted cars on campus. **Housing:** Coed dorms, single-sex dorms available. $250 deposit, deadline 5/1. **Activities:** Bands, choral groups, dance, drama, film society, literary magazine, music ensembles, musical theater, radio station, student government, student newspaper, TV station, Newman Club, Union of Jewish Students, Christian Fellowship, Christian Science Organization, Afro-American and African students, Latin American student association.

Athletics. NCAA. **Intercollegiate:** Baseball M, basketball, cross-country, diving W, football (tackle) M, golf, lacrosse W, soccer, softball W, swimming W, track and field, volleyball W. **Intramural:** Badminton, basketball, field hockey W, football (tackle) M, gymnastics W, lacrosse M, rugby, soccer, softball W, tennis, volleyball, water polo M. **Team name:** Blue Devils.

Student services. Adult student services, alcohol/substance abuse counseling, campus ministries, career counseling, student employment services, financial aid counseling, health services, minority student services, on-campus daycare, personal counseling, placement for graduates, veterans' counselor, women's services. **Physically disabled:** Services for visually, speech, hearing impaired.

Contact. E-mail: admissions@ccsu.edu
Phone: (860) 832-2278 Fax: (860) 832-2295
Richard Bishop, Director of Admissions, Central Connecticut State University, 1615 Stanley Street, New Britain, CT 06050

Charter Oak State College

New Britain, Connecticut — **CB member**
www.charteroak.edu — **CB code: 0870**

- Public 4-year virtual liberal arts college
- Commuter campus in small city
- 1,902 degree-seeking undergraduates: 100% part-time, 60% women, 10% African American, 2% Asian American, 6% Hispanic American, 1% Native American

General. Founded in 1973. Regionally accredited. A non-traditional virtual college. Learners complete degrees by taking classroom-based or distance learning courses at any regionally-accredited college or university. College-level exams, special assessment, portfolio assessment, contract learning, certain noncollegiate-sponsored instruction, and distance learning courses offered online by institution. **Degrees:** 437 bachelor's, 82 associate awarded. **Location:** 5 miles from Hartford. **Calendar:** Continuous, limited summer session. **Part-time faculty:** 67 total; 54% have terminal degrees, 9% minority, 45% women. **Class size:** 74% < 20, 26% 20-39.

Basis for selection. 9 college-level credits must be completed before enrolling. May be earned through college courses, testing, or ACE/PONSI recommendations for noncollege-sponsored instruction.

2006-2007 Annual costs. In-state matriculation fee: $985; out-of-state fees: $1300. Since our students do not have to take our courses, the cost of thier education varies.

2004-2005 Financial aid. All financial aid based on need. 32% of total undergraduate aid awarded as scholarships/grants, 68% as loans/jobs.

Application procedures. Admission: No deadline. $60 fee, may be waived for applicants with need. Application may be submitted online. Admission notification on a rolling basis. **Financial aid:** No deadline. FAFSA, institutional form required. Applicants notified on a rolling basis starting 8/23.

Academics. Tutoring and writing center are available online free to students. **Special study options:** Accelerated study, distance learning, dual enrollment of high school students, external degree, independent study, liberal arts/career combination, student-designed major. Students can take courses at any regionally accredited institution. **Credit/placement by examination:** AP, CLEP, institutional tests. 60 credit hours maximum toward associate degree, 120 toward bachelor's. Unlimited number of hours of credit by examination may be counted toward degree. **Support services:** Tutoring, writing center.

Majors. Liberal arts: Arts/sciences.

Computing on campus. Online library, helpline, wireless network available.

Student life. Activities: Student government.

Student services. Adult student services, financial aid counseling, veterans' counselor.

Contact. E-mail: info@charteroak.edu
Phone: (860) 832-3800 Fax: (860) 832-3999
Lori Pendleton, Director of Admission, Charter Oak State College, 55 Paul Manafort Drive, New Britain, CT 06053-2142

Connecticut College

New London, Connecticut — **CB member**
www.conncoll.edu — **CB code: 3284**

- Private 4-year liberal arts college
- Residential campus in large town
- 1,778 degree-seeking undergraduates: 1% part-time, 59% women, 4% African American, 5% Asian American, 5% Hispanic American, 4% international
- 11 degree-seeking graduate students
- 35% of applicants admitted
- Application essay required

General. Founded in 1911. Regionally accredited. Interdisciplinary centers for students to earn a certificate to complement their major(s) available. **Degrees:** 419 bachelor's awarded; master's offered. **Location:** 105 miles from Boston, 124 miles from New York City. **Calendar:** Semester, limited summer session. **Full-time faculty:** 162 total; 91% have terminal degrees, 15% minority, 41% women. **Part-time faculty:** 80 total; 29% have terminal degrees, 12% minority, 48% women. **Special facilities:** 750-acre arboretum, art museum, greenhouse, ion accelerator, refracting telescope and observatory, scanning and transmission electron microscopes, nuclear magnetic resonance spectrometer, tunable diode laser spectroscopy laboratory, preschool, Center for the Electronic and Digital Sound, neuroscience and animal behavior laboratories, clinical and social psychology research observation suites.

Freshman class profile. 4,183 applied, 1,477 admitted, 492 enrolled.

Mid 50% test scores		Rank in top quarter:	83%
SAT verbal:	630-700	Rank in top tenth:	54%
SAT math:	620-690	Out-of-state:	82%
ACT:	26-29	Live on campus:	100%

Basis for selection. School achievement record is most important. Recommendations, personal qualities, personal essay, special talents, extracurricular activities are also significant. ACT or two SAT Subject Tests required. Other tests are optional and are considered if requested by the student. Interview recommended. Audition recommended of those intending a dance or music major. Portfolio recommended of intended art majors. **Homeschooled:** State high school equivalency certificate, letter of recommendation (nonparent) required. Extracurricular activities encouraged.

High school preparation. 22 units recommended. Recommended units include English 4, mathematics 4, social studies 2, history 3, science 4, foreign language 2 and academic electives 3.

2005-2006 Annual costs. Comprehensive fee: $41,975. Books/supplies: $800.

2005-2006 Financial aid. All financial aid based on need. 246 full-time freshmen applied for aid; 201 were judged to have need; 201 of these received aid. Average need met was 100%. Average scholarship/grant was $24,997; average loan $2,865. 84% of total undergraduate aid awarded as scholarships/grants, 16% as loans/jobs.

Application procedures. Admission: Closing date 1/1 (postmark date). $60 fee, may be waived for applicants with need. Application may be submitted online. Admission notification 3/31. Must reply by 5/1. **Financial aid:** Priority date 11/15, closing date 1/15. FAFSA, CSS PROFILE required. Applicants notified by 4/1; must reply by 5/1.

Academics. Special study options: Accelerated study, cross-registration, double major, dual enrollment of high school students, exchange student, honors, independent study, internships, student-designed major, study abroad, teacher certification program, Washington semester. 12-college exchange, National Theater Institute, Mystic Seaport Program in American Maritime Studies, Institute for Architecture and Urban Studies, American Academy in Rome, Associated Kyoto Program, cross-registration with U.S. Coast Guard Academy, Trinity College and Wesleyan University, study away-teach away opportunities, specially funded student research opportunities. **Credit/placement by examination:** AP, CLEP, IB, institutional tests. 32 credit hours maximum toward bachelor's degree. Students may use AP credit to repair credit deficiencies that arise from voluntary course withdrawals or failing grades, or to accelerate. **Support services:** Study skills assistance, tutoring, writing center.

Majors. Architecture: Architecture. **Area/ethnic studies:** African, American, Chinese, East Asian, German, Hispanic-American/Latino/Chicano, Italian, Japanese, Latin American, Slavic, women's. **Biology:** General, biochemistry, Biochemistry/biophysics and molecular biology, botany, cell/histology, cellular/molecular, molecular, zoology. **Computer sciences:** Computer science. **Conservation:** Environmental studies. **Engineering:** Physics. **Family/consumer sciences:** Family studies. **Foreign languages:** Chinese, classics, French, German, Italian, Japanese, Slavic, Spanish. **History:** General. **Interdisciplinary:** Medieval/Renaissance, neuroscience. **Math:** General. **Philosophy/religion:** Philosophy, religion. **Physical sciences:** Astrophysics, chemistry, physics. **Psychology:** General. **Social sciences:** Anthropology, economics, international relations, political science, sociology, urban studies. **Visual/performing arts:** Art history/conservation, dance, dramatic.

Most popular majors. Biology 10%, English 6%, foreign language 6%, philosophy/religious studies 6%, psychology 7%, social sciences 32%, visual/performing arts 10%.

Computing on campus. 350 workstations in library, computer center. Dormitories wired for high-speed internet access and linked to campus network. Commuter students can connect to campus network. Online library, helpline, repair service, student web hosting, wireless network available.

Student life. Freshman orientation: Mandatory. Preregistration for classes offered. Held week prior to the start of classes. Optional outdoor orientation prior to full orientation. **Policies:** Freshmen permitted cars on campus. **Housing:** Guaranteed on-campus for all undergraduates. Coed dorms, special housing for disabled, cooperative housing, substance-free housing available. $500 nonrefundable deposit, deadline 5/1. Theme dormitories, quiet housing, men's and women's floors within dormitories, living and learning experience are available. **Activities:** Bands, choral groups, dance, drama, film society, literary magazine, music ensembles, radio station, student government, student newspaper, symphony orchestra, College Democrats, College Republicans, Hillel, Intervarsity Christian Fellowship, multi-faith student council, Muslim student association, Connecticut College Asian/Asian American student association, Latino American student association, Sexual Orientations United for Liberation, African/African American Student Association.

Athletics. NCAA. **Intercollegiate:** Basketball, cross-country, diving, field hockey W, ice hockey, lacrosse, rowing (crew), sailing, soccer, squash, swimming, tennis, track and field, volleyball W, water polo. **Intramural:** Baseball M, basketball, football (non-tackle) M, racquetball, soccer, softball, squash, tennis, volleyball. **Team name:** Camels.

Student services. Adult student services, alcohol/substance abuse counseling, campus ministries, career counseling, student employment services, financial aid counseling, health services, minority student services, personal counseling, placement for graduates. **Physically disabled:** Services for visually, speech, hearing impaired. **Learning disabled:** Comprehensive services available.

Contact. E-mail: admission@conncoll.edu
Phone: (860) 439-2200 Fax: (860) 439-4301
Martha Merrill, Dean of Admissions/Financial Aid, Connecticut College, 270 Mohegan Avenue, New London, CT 06320-4196

Eastern Connecticut State University

Willimantic, Connecticut — **CB member**
www.easternct.edu — **CB code: 3966**

- Public 4-year university and liberal arts college
- Residential campus in large town

- 4,606 degree-seeking undergraduates: 19% part-time, 56% women, 7% African American, 2% Asian American, 5% Hispanic American, 1% Native American, 1% international
- 335 degree-seeking graduate students
- 69% of applicants admitted
- SAT or ACT with writing required
- 41% graduate within 6 years; 35% enter graduate study

General. Founded in 1889. Regionally accredited. **Degrees:** 860 bachelor's, 10 associate awarded; master's offered. **ROTC:** Army, Air Force. **Location:** 29 miles from Hartford, 50 miles from New Haven. **Calendar:** Semester, extensive summer session. **Full-time faculty:** 188 total; 93% have terminal degrees, 23% minority, 41% women. **Part-time faculty:** 209 total; 53% have terminal degrees, 10% minority, 47% women. **Class size:** 35% < 20, 56% 20-39, 9% 40-49, less than 1% 50-99. **Special facilities:** Planetarium, 2 electron microscopes, institute for sustainable energy.

Freshman class profile. 3,066 applied, 2,130 admitted, 925 enrolled.

Mid 50% test scores		**End year in good standing:**	80%
SAT verbal:	460-560	**Return as sophomores:**	78%
SAT math:	460-550	**Out-of-state:**	9%
Rank in top quarter:	21%	**Live on campus:**	88%
Rank in top tenth:	5%	**International:**	1%

Basis for selection. Applicants should be in top half of high school class and recommended by high school. Quality of course work very important; minimum 2.5 GPA in college preparatory program. SAT score also important. Extracurricular activities considered. Prueba de Evaluacion y Admission Universataria may be taken in lieu of SAT. Interview and essay recommended. Interview recommended of special admissions applicants. Audition required of music majors. Portfolio recommended of art majors.

High school preparation. Required units include English 4, mathematics 3, social studies 2, history 3, science 2 (laboratory 1) and foreign language 2.

2005-2006 Annual costs. Tuition/fees: $5,964; $13,902 out-of-state. Room/board: $7,590.

2004-2005 Financial aid. **Need-based:** 630 full-time freshmen applied for aid; 504 were judged to have need; 418 of these received aid. Average need met was 59%. Average scholarship/grant was $4,730; average loan $3,035. 40% of total undergraduate aid awarded as scholarships/grants, 60% as loans/jobs. **Non-need-based:** Awarded to 543 full-time undergraduates, including 189 freshmen. Scholarships awarded for academics. **Additional information:** Tuition waiver for veterans and members of National Guard.

Application procedures. **Admission:** Priority date 5/1; no deadline. $50 fee, may be waived for applicants with need. Application must be submitted on paper. Admission notification on a rolling basis beginning on or about 12/1. Must reply by May 1 or within 2 week(s) if notified thereafter. **Financial aid:** Priority date 3/15; no closing date. FAFSA, institutional form required. Applicants notified on a rolling basis starting 2/15; must reply within 2 week(s) of notification.

Academics. **Special study options:** Accelerated study, cooperative education, cross-registration, distance learning, double major, dual enrollment of high school students, exchange student, honors, independent study, internships, student-designed major, study abroad, teacher certification program, weekend college. National Student Exchange (NSE). **Credit/placement by examination:** AP, CLEP, institutional tests. 30 credit hours maximum toward associate degree, 60 toward bachelor's. Institutional placement test required for all entering freshmen. **Support services:** Learning center, preadmission summer program, reduced course load, remedial instruction, tutoring, writing center.

Majors. **Biology:** General, biochemistry. **Business:** Accounting, business admin, management information systems. **Communications:** General. **Computer sciences:** General. **Conservation:** Environmental science. **Education:** Early childhood, elementary, middle, physical, secondary. **Foreign languages:** Spanish. **History:** General. **Math:** General. **Parks/recreation:** Sports admin. **Psychology:** General. **Public administration:** Social work. **Social sciences:** Economics, political science, sociology. **Visual/performing arts:** General, studio arts.

Most popular majors. Business/marketing 13%, communications/journalism 8%, education 7%, English 6%, interdisciplinary studies 6%, liberal arts 8%, psychology 14%, social sciences 14%.

Computing on campus. 637 workstations in dormitories, library, computer center. Dormitories linked to campus network. Commuter students can connect to campus network. Repair service available.

Student life. **Freshman orientation:** Mandatory. Preregistration for classes offered. **Housing:** Coed dorms, single-sex dorms, apartments available. $250 nonrefundable deposit. **Activities:** Concert band, choral groups, dance, drama, literary magazine, music ensembles, musical theater, radio station, student government, student newspaper, TV station, over 60 organizations.

Athletics. NCAA. **Intercollegiate:** Baseball M, basketball, cheerleading M, cross-country, field hockey W, lacrosse, soccer, softball W, swimming W, track and field, volleyball W. **Intramural:** Badminton, basketball, bowling, cross-country, football (tackle) M, gymnastics W, racquetball, rugby, skiing, soccer, softball, swimming, tennis, track and field, volleyball, water polo. **Team name:** Warriors.

Student services. Adult student services, alcohol/substance abuse counseling, campus ministries, career counseling, services for economically disadvantaged, student employment services, financial aid counseling, health services, minority student services, on-campus daycare, personal counseling, placement for graduates, veterans' counselor, women's services. **Physically disabled:** Services for visually, speech, hearing impaired. **Learning disabled:** Comprehensive services available.

Contact. E-mail: admissions@easternct.edu
Phone: (860) 465-5286 Toll-free number: (877) 353-3278
Fax: (860) 465-5544
Kimberly Crone, Director of Admissions and Enrollment Planning, Eastern Connecticut State University, 83 Windham Street, Willimantic, CT 06226-2295

Fairfield University

Fairfield, Connecticut — **CB member**
www.fairfield.edu — **CB code: 3390**

- Private 4-year university affiliated with Roman Catholic Church
- Residential campus in small city
- 3,688 degree-seeking undergraduates: 7% part-time, 57% women
- 1,050 degree-seeking graduate students
- 74% of applicants admitted
- SAT or ACT (ACT writing optional), application essay required
- 84% graduate within 6 years; 20% enter graduate study

General. Founded in 1942. Regionally accredited. **Degrees:** 849 bachelor's, 12 associate awarded; master's offered. **ROTC:** Army. **Location:** 50 miles from New York City. **Calendar:** Semester, limited summer session. **Full-time faculty:** 226 total; 93% have terminal degrees, 8% minority, 48% women. **Part-time faculty:** 187 total; 35% have terminal degrees, 44% women. **Class size:** 34% < 20, 64% 20-39, less than 1% 40-49, 1% 50-99. **Special facilities:** Fine arts center containing 2 theaters, campus ministry center.

Freshman class profile. 6,895 applied, 5,130 admitted, 940 enrolled.

Mid 50% test scores		**Rank in top quarter:**	69%
SAT verbal:	550-630	**Rank in top tenth:**	31%
SAT math:	560-640	**End year in good standing:**	91%
ACT:	23-27	**Return as sophomores:**	91%
GPA 3.50 or higher:	39%	**Out-of-state:**	81%
GPA 3.0-3.49:	42%	**Live on campus:**	98%
GPA 2.0-2.99:	18%	**International:**	1%

Basis for selection. GED not accepted. School achievement record, test scores, recommendations, school activities, class rank important. Special consideration given to minority groups and relatives of alumni. SAT Subject Tests in English, math, and language recommended for placement. SAT Subject Tests in biology and chemistry recommended for nursing and science majors. Interview recommended.

High school preparation. College-preparatory program required. 15 units required; 17 recommended. Required and recommended units include English 4, mathematics 3-4, social studies 3-4, history 1, science 3-4 (laboratory 3) and foreign language 2-4. 1 additional mathematics and 2 science recommended for mathematics, business and science. Portfolio highly recommended for music majors, resume for theatre majors.

2005-2006 Annual costs. Tuition/fees: $30,235. Room/board: $9,600. Books/supplies: $500. Personal expenses: $900.

2005-2006 Financial aid. **Need-based:** 673 full-time freshmen applied for aid; 501 were judged to have need; 497 of these received aid. Average need met was 69%. Average scholarship/grant was $13,151; average loan $3,484. 71% of total undergraduate aid awarded as scholarships/grants, 29% as loans/jobs. **Non-need-based:** Awarded to 815 full-time undergraduates, including 240 freshmen. Scholarships awarded for academics, alumni affiliation, art, athletics, leadership, music/drama.

Application procedures. Admission: Closing date 1/15 (postmark date). $55 fee, may be waived for applicants with need. Application may be submitted online. Admission notification 4/1. Must reply by 5/1. Deadline for those applying for merit scholarships is December 1. **Financial aid:** Closing date 2/15. FAFSA, CSS PROFILE required. Applicants notified on a rolling basis starting 4/1; must reply by 5/1 or within 2 week(s) of notification.

Academics. Associate's program is a part-time evening program for non-traditional students. **Special study options:** Combined bachelor's/graduate degree, double major, exchange student, honors, independent study, internships, semester at sea, student-designed major, study abroad, teacher certification program, Washington semester. 3-2 engineering program with University of Connecticut, Rensselaer Polytechnic Institute, Columbia University, and Stevens Institute of Technology. **Credit/placement by examination:** AP, CLEP, IB, institutional tests. 15 credit hours maximum toward bachelor's degree. **Support services:** Study skills assistance, tutoring, writing center.

Majors. Area/ethnic studies: American. **Biology:** General. **Business:** Accounting, business admin, finance, international, management information systems, marketing. **Communications:** General. **Computer sciences:** General, computer science. **Engineering:** General, chemical, computer, electrical, mechanical. **Foreign languages:** Chinese, French, German, Hebrew, Italian, Japanese, Russian, Spanish. **Health:** Nursing (RN). **History:** General. **Math:** General. **Philosophy/religion:** Philosophy, religion. **Physical sciences:** Chemistry, physics. **Psychology:** General. **Social sciences:** Economics, international relations, political science, sociology. **Visual/performing arts:** General, art history/conservation, dramatic, studio arts.

Most popular majors. Business/marketing 34%, communications/journalism 9%, English 8%, health sciences 7%, psychology 7%, social sciences 14%.

Computing on campus. 230 workstations in dormitories, library, computer center, student center. Dormitories wired for high-speed internet access and linked to campus network. Commuter students can connect to campus network. Online library, helpline, repair service available.

Student life. Freshman orientation: Available, $230 fee. Preregistration for classes offered. 2-day program in late June/early July for students and parents. **Policies:** Juniors and seniors may enter lottery to move off-campus. Campus ministry sponsors activities that enable students to travel to other parts of country, Central America, and neighboring urban centers as community service volunteers. **Housing:** Guaranteed on-campus for freshmen. Coed dorms, special housing for disabled, apartments, substance-free housing available. $200 nonrefundable deposit, deadline 5/1. Wellness floor offered (substance free) in freshmen residence halls. **Activities:** Bands, choral groups, dance, drama, literary magazine, music ensembles, radio station, student government, student newspaper, symphony orchestra, TV station, AHANA (Asian, Hispanic, Afro-American, Native American), Peer Education, Appalachian Volunteers, campus ministry, College Democrats, College Republicans, Circle K, international relations club.

Athletics. NCAA. **Intercollegiate:** Baseball M, basketball, cross-country, diving, field hockey W, golf, lacrosse, rowing (crew) W, skiing, soccer, softball W, swimming, tennis, volleyball W. **Intramural:** Basketball, fencing, football (non-tackle), racquetball, soccer M, softball W, table tennis, tennis, track and field, volleyball. **Team name:** Stags.

Student services. Adult student services, alcohol/substance abuse counseling, campus ministries, career counseling, student employment services, financial aid counseling, health services, minority student services, personal counseling, placement for graduates, veterans' counselor. **Physically disabled:** Services for visually, hearing impaired.

Contact. E-mail: admis@mail.fairfield.edu
Phone: (203) 254-4100 Fax: (203) 254-4199
Karen Pellegrino, Director of Admission, Fairfield University, 1073 North Benson Road, Fairfield, CT 06824-5195

Holy Apostles College and Seminary

Cromwell, Connecticut
www.holyapostles.edu **CB code: 0921**

- Private 4-year liberal arts and seminary college affiliated with Roman Catholic Church
- Commuter campus in small town
- 21 degree-seeking undergraduates: 57% part-time, 33% women, 10% Asian American, 10% Hispanic American, 10% international
- 196 degree-seeking graduate students
- SAT, interview required

General. Founded in 1956. Regionally accredited. 75% of students are lay students, 25% are seminarians. **Degrees:** 5 bachelor's awarded; master's, first professional offered. **Location:** 13 miles from Hartford. **Calendar:** Semester, limited summer session. **Full-time faculty:** 14 total; 79% have terminal degrees, 7% minority, 21% women. **Part-time faculty:** 11 total; 91% have terminal degrees, 27% women.

Freshman class profile. 9 enrolled.

End year in good standing:	90%	**Return as sophomores:**	50%

Basis for selection. Interview and recommendations most important. No mandatory minimum SAT score. **Homeschooled:** State high school equivalency certificate required.

2005-2006 Annual costs. Tuition/fees: $9,350. Room/board: $7,550. Books/supplies: $630.

2004-2005 Financial aid. All financial aid based on need. 40% of total undergraduate aid awarded as scholarships/grants, 60% as loans/jobs.

Application procedures. Admission: Priority date 8/15; no deadline. $25 fee, may be waived for applicants with need. Application must be submitted on paper. Admission notification on a rolling basis. Applications accepted up to one week before the beginning of the semester in which the applicant plans to enroll. **Financial aid:** No deadline. FAFSA, institutional form required. Applicants notified on a rolling basis starting 9/15.

Academics. 54-credit core curriculum required of all undergraduates. **Special study options:** Cooperative education, distance learning, double major, ESL, independent study. **Credit/placement by examination:** AP, CLEP. 30 credit hours maximum toward bachelor's degree. **Support services:** Reduced course load, remedial instruction, tutoring.

Majors. Liberal arts: Humanities. **Philosophy/religion:** Philosophy, religion. **Social sciences:** General.

Computing on campus. 10 workstations in library.

Student life. Freshman orientation: Available. Preregistration for classes offered. **Policies:** Freshmen permitted cars on campus. **Activities:** Choral groups, student government, Life League.

Student services. Campus ministries, financial aid counseling, personal counseling.

Contact. E-mail: admissions@holyapostles.edu
Phone: (860) 632-3033 Fax: (860) 632-3075
Very Rev. Douglas Mosey, President-Rector, Holy Apostles College and Seminary, 33 Prospect Hill Road, Cromwell, CT 06416-2005

Lyme Academy College of Fine Arts

Old Lyme, Connecticut **CB member**
www.lymeacademy.edu **CB code: 1791**

- Private 4-year visual arts college
- Commuter campus in small town
- 96 degree-seeking undergraduates: 17% part-time, 54% women
- 6 degree-seeking graduate students
- 95% of applicants admitted
- SAT or ACT (ACT writing recommended), application essay, interview required

General. Founded in 1976. Regionally accredited. **Degrees:** 19 bachelor's awarded. **Location:** 100 miles from New York City and Boston. **Calendar:** Semester, limited summer session. **Full-time faculty:** 7 total; 43% women. **Part-time faculty:** 10 total; 10% have terminal degrees, 10% women. **Class size:** 91% < 20, 9% 20-39.

Freshman class profile. 63 applied, 60 admitted, 12 enrolled.

Mid 50% test scores		**GPA 2.0-2.99:**	8%
SAT verbal:	510-590	**End year in good standing:**	100%
SAT math:	470-510	**Return as sophomores:**	87%
GPA 3.50 or higher:	34%	**Out-of-state:**	59%
GPA 3.0-3.49:	58%		

Basis for selection. Admissions based on portfolio, interview, GPA, SAT/ACT scores and recommendations. Portfolio, two letters of recommendation required. Campus visit highly recommended. **Homeschooled:** Statement describing homeschool structure and mission, transcript of courses and grades, state high school equivalency certificate, interview, letter of recommendation (nonparent) required.

2006-2007 Annual costs. Tuition/fees: $18,168. Books/supplies: $1,000. Personal expenses: $500.

2005-2006 Financial aid. Need-based: 9 full-time freshmen applied for aid; 9 were judged to have need; 9 of these received aid. Average scholarship/grant was $3,072. 52% of total undergraduate aid awarded as scholarships/grants, 48% as loans/jobs. **Non-need-based:** Scholarships awarded for academics, art.

Application procedures. Admission: Priority date 2/15; no deadline. $35 fee, may be waived for applicants with need. Application may be submitted online. Admission notification on a rolling basis. Must reply by May 1 or within 2 week(s) if notified thereafter. **Financial aid:** Closing date 2/15. FAFSA, institutional form required. CSS PROFILE required of all new students. Applicants notified on a rolling basis; must reply within 2 week(s) of notification.

Academics. Special study options: Double major, independent study. **Credit/placement by examination:** CLEP, SAT, ACT. **Support services:** Pre-admission summer program, study skills assistance, writing center.

Majors. Visual/performing arts: Painting, sculpture.

Computing on campus. 6 workstations in library.

Student life. Freshman orientation: Mandatory. Preregistration for classes offered. Usually one day before the start of classes in the Fall semester. **Policies:** Freshmen permitted cars on campus.

Athletics. Intramural: Table tennis, volleyball.

Student services. Alcohol/substance abuse counseling, career counseling, financial aid counseling, personal counseling, veterans' counselor, women's services.

Contact. E-mail: dsigmon@lymeacademy.edu
Phone: (860) 434-5232 Fax: (860) 434-8725
Debbie Sigmon, Director of Admissions, Lyme Academy College of Fine Arts, 84 Lyme Street, Old Lyme, CT 06371

Mitchell College

New London, Connecticut — **CB member**
www.mitchell.edu — **CB code: 3528**

- Private 4-year liberal arts college
- Residential campus in small city
- 704 degree-seeking undergraduates: 9% part-time, 50% women
- 60% of applicants admitted
- SAT or ACT (ACT writing optional), application essay required

General. Founded in 1938. Regionally accredited. Free professional tutoring in all disciplines. **Degrees:** 38 bachelor's, 95 associate awarded. **Location:** 100 miles from New York City and Boston. **Calendar:** Semester, limited summer session. **Full-time faculty:** 29 total; 55% have terminal degrees. **Part-time faculty:** 45 total; 11% have terminal degrees. **Special facilities:** Two private beaches, private dock with fleet of sailboats, academic support center, learning resource center for students with learning disabilities, hiking trails.

Freshman class profile. 1,115 applied, 664 admitted, 245 enrolled.

Mid 50% test scores			
SAT verbal:	360-460	Rank in top tenth:	3%
SAT math:	350-460	Out-of-state:	45%
Rank in top quarter:	9%	Live on campus:	95%

Basis for selection. High school achievement, recommendations, interview very important.

High school preparation. Recommended units include English 4, mathematics 3, social studies 3, history 2, science 3, foreign language 1 and academic electives 4.

2005-2006 Annual costs. Tuition/fees: $20,705. $6,500 additional fee for students in comprehensive program at learning center for learning disabilities. Room/board: $9,330. Books/supplies: $900. Personal expenses: $1,050.

Financial aid. Non-need-based: Scholarships awarded for academics, alumni affiliation, athletics, leadership.

Application procedures. Admission: Priority date 4/1; no deadline. $30 fee, may be waived for applicants with need. Application may be submitted online. Admission notification on a rolling basis. Must reply by May 1 or within 2 week(s) if notified thereafter. **Financial aid:** Priority date 3/1; no closing date. FAFSA required. Applicants notified on a rolling basis starting 2/15; must reply within 2 week(s) of notification.

Academics. Special study options: Dual enrollment of high school students, ESL, internships. **Credit/placement by examination:** CLEP, institutional tests. 30 credit hours maximum toward associate degree. **Support services:** Learning center, pre-admission summer program, reduced course load, study skills assistance, tutoring, writing center.

Majors. Business: Business admin. **Education:** Early childhood, kindergarten/preschool. **Family/consumer sciences:** Family studies. **Liberal arts:** Arts/sciences. **Parks/recreation:** Sports admin. **Psychology:** General. **Social sciences:** Criminology.

Most popular majors. Liberal arts 61%, social sciences 39%.

Computing on campus. 155 workstations in dormitories, library, computer center, student center. Dormitories wired for high-speed internet access and linked to campus network. Commuter students can connect to campus network. Helpline, repair service available.

Student life. Freshman orientation: Mandatory. Preregistration for classes offered. 2-day orientation held in June, September, and January. **Policies:** Freshmen permitted cars on campus. **Housing:** Guaranteed on-campus for all undergraduates. Coed dorms, single-sex dorms, special housing for disabled available. $300 deposit, deadline 5/1. **Activities:** Choral groups, dance, drama, student government, student newspaper, multicultural club, Hillel, spirituality club, African American alliance, campus ministry.

Athletics. NCAA, NJCAA. **Intercollegiate:** Baseball M, basketball, cross-country, golf, lacrosse M, sailing, soccer, softball W, tennis, volleyball W. **Intramural:** Basketball, sailing, soccer, softball, table tennis, tennis, volleyball. **Team name:** Pequots.

Student services. Adult student services, career counseling, services for economically disadvantaged, student employment services, financial aid counseling, health services, minority student services, on-campus daycare, personal counseling, placement for graduates, veterans' counselor. **Physically disabled:** Services for visually, speech, hearing impaired. **Learning disabled:** Comprehensive services available.

Contact. E-mail: admissions@mitchell.edu
Phone: (860) 701-5037 Toll-free number: (800) 443-2811
Fax: (860) 444-1209
Kevin Mayne, Vice President for Enrollment Management and Marketing, Mitchell College, 437 Pequot Avenue, New London, CT 06320-4498

Paier College of Art

Hamden, Connecticut
www.paiercollegeofart.edu — **CB code: 3699**

- For-profit 4-year visual arts college
- Commuter campus in small city
- 248 degree-seeking undergraduates: 23% part-time, 60% women
- 80% of applicants admitted
- SAT or ACT, interview required
- 56% graduate within 6 years; 20% enter graduate study

General. Founded in 1946. Accredited by ACCSCT. **Degrees:** 36 bachelor's, 7 associate awarded. **Location:** 2 miles from New Haven. **Calendar:** Semester, limited summer session. **Full-time faculty:** 10 total; 30% have terminal degrees, 10% women. **Part-time faculty:** 36 total; 53% have terminal degrees, 3% minority, 31% women. **Class size:** 81% < 20, 19% 20-39. **Special facilities:** Extensive image picture reference file.

Freshman class profile. 101 applied, 81 admitted, 49 enrolled.

Mid 50% test scores			
SAT verbal:	420-510	Rank in top tenth:	10%
SAT math:	380-510	End year in good standing:	85%
Rank in top quarter:	10%	Return as sophomores:	42%

Basis for selection. Artistic ability, interest, and potential, as demonstrated in admission interview and portfolio review most important elements. SAT/ACT requirement waived for international students previously matriculated at another accredited institution in the U.S. Portfolio of 8 to 10 works of art required; essay recommended.

High school preparation. Art classes recommended.

2005-2006 Annual costs. Tuition/fees: $11,565. Books/supplies: $1,000. Personal expenses: $600.

2004-2005 Financial aid. **Need-based:** 24 full-time freshmen applied for aid; 21 were judged to have need; 20 of these received aid. Average need met was 58%. Average scholarship/grant was $4,417; average loan $2,444. 52% of total undergraduate aid awarded as scholarships/grants, 48% as loans/jobs.

Application procedures. **Admission:** No deadline. $25 fee, may be waived for applicants with need. Admission notification on a rolling basis beginning on or about 2/15. **Financial aid:** Priority date 4/15; no closing date. FAFSA required. Applicants notified on a rolling basis starting 6/1; must reply within 3 week(s) of notification.

Academics. Academics required for BFA degrees include: 4 art histories, English I and II, 1 requirement each in the humanities, math, physical and social sciences, and 1 academic elective. **Special study options:** Independent study. **Credit/placement by examination:** AP, CLEP, IB. 5 credit hours maximum toward associate degree, 10 toward bachelor's. **Support services:** Reduced course load, remedial instruction, study skills assistance, tutoring.

Majors. **Visual/performing arts:** Commercial photography, commercial/advertising art, design, graphic design, illustration, interior design, painting, photography, studio arts.

Computing on campus. 60 workstations in library, computer center.

Student life. **Freshman orientation:** Available. Preregistration for classes offered. Open to incoming students and their parents/guardians. Separate 1-hour library orientation. **Policies:** Freshmen permitted cars on campus. **Housing:** Affiliation with neighboring Albertus Magnus College provides an option for dormitory housing and student services (library, gym, health center, student dining). **Activities:** Student government.

Student services. Career counseling, student employment services, financial aid counseling, personal counseling, placement for graduates, veterans' counselor.

Contact. E-mail: paier.admission@snet.net
Phone: (203) 287-3031 Fax: (203) 287-3021
Daniel Paier, Dean of Admissions, Paier College of Art, 20 Gorham Avenue, Hamden, CT 06514-3902

Post University

Waterbury, Connecticut — **CB member**
www.post.edu — **CB code: 3698**

- For-profit 4-year university and business college
- Residential campus in small city
- 1,100 degree-seeking undergraduates
- 62% of applicants admitted
- SAT or ACT (ACT writing optional), interview required

General. Founded in 1890. Regionally accredited. **Degrees:** 193 bachelor's, 39 associate awarded. **ROTC:** Army, Navy. **Location:** 32 miles from Hartford, 80 miles from New York City. **Calendar:** Semester, limited summer session. **Full-time faculty:** 30 total. **Part-time faculty:** 35 total.

Freshman class profile. 1,254 applied, 782 admitted, 188 enrolled.

Mid 50% test scores		Out-of-state:	44%
SAT verbal:	420-510	Live on campus:	66%
SAT math:	430-510		

Basis for selection. Secondary school transcript, interview, and class rank in top half of graduating class most important. Letter of recommendation required. Counselor's recommendation also important. School and community activities and test scores also reviewed and considered. TOEFL also accepted. **Homeschooled:** Interview required.

High school preparation. 13 units required. Required units include English 4, mathematics 3, social studies 3, science 3 (laboratory 1).

2005-2006 Annual costs. Tuition/fees: $20,200. Room/board: $8,300. Books/supplies: $1,000. Personal expenses: $1,200.

Financial aid. **Additional information:** Academic merit scholarships available based on GPA and test scores. Renewable contingent upon maintaining specific GPA.

Application procedures. **Admission:** Priority date 5/1; no deadline. $40 fee, may be waived for applicants with need. Application may be submitted online. Admission notification on a rolling basis. **Financial aid:** Priority date 3/15; no closing date. FAFSA required. Applicants notified on a rolling basis starting 4/15; must reply by 5/1 or within 3 week(s) of notification.

Academics. **Special study options:** Accelerated study, combined bachelor's/graduate degree, cooperative education, cross-registration, distance learning, double major, dual enrollment of high school students, ESL, honors, independent study, internships, liberal arts/career combination, student-designed major, study abroad, weekend college. **Credit/placement by examination:** AP, CLEP, institutional tests. 15 credit hours maximum toward associate degree, 30 toward bachelor's. **Support services:** Learning center, reduced course load, remedial instruction, study skills assistance, tutoring, writing center.

Majors. **Agriculture:** Equestrian studies. **Biology:** General. **Business:** General, accounting, business admin, finance, international. **Computer sciences:** General. **Conservation:** General, environmental studies. **History:** General. **Legal studies:** Paralegal, prelaw. **Psychology:** General. **Public administration:** Human services. **Social sciences:** Sociology.

Computing on campus. 72 workstations in library, computer center, student center. Dormitories wired for high-speed internet access and linked to campus network. Online library available.

Student life. **Freshman orientation:** Mandatory, $100 fee. Preregistration for classes offered. **Policies:** Student leadership opportunities encouraged and supported throughout student's experience. Freshmen permitted cars on campus. **Housing:** Guaranteed on-campus for all undergraduates. Coed dorms available. $100 deposit, deadline 5/1. **Activities:** Choral groups, drama, literary magazine, student government, student newspaper, Phi Theta Kappa, black student union, Student Ambassadors, peer advisors, international student organization, Collegiate Religion Coalition, Hispanic Awareness.

Athletics. NCAA. **Intercollegiate:** Baseball M, basketball, cross-country, equestrian, golf M, soccer, softball W, tennis M, volleyball W. **Intramural:** Baseball M, basketball, football (tackle) M, racquetball, softball, swimming, tennis, volleyball. **Team name:** Eagles.

Student services. Adult student services, alcohol/substance abuse counseling, career counseling, student employment services, financial aid counseling, health services, minority student services, personal counseling, placement for graduates, veterans' counselor. **Physically disabled:** Services for visually impaired.

Contact. E-mail: admissions@post.edu
Phone: (203) 596-4520 Toll-free number: (800) 345-2562
Fax: (203) 756-5810
Dominick Miciotta, Vice President Enrollment Management, Post University, 800 Country Club Road, Waterbury, CT 06723-2540

Quinnipiac University

Hamden, Connecticut — **CB member**
www.quinnipiac.edu — **CB code: 3712**

- Private 4-year university
- Residential campus in small city
- 5,542 degree-seeking undergraduates: 5% part-time, 61% women, 2% African American, 2% Asian American, 4% Hispanic American, 1% international
- 1,536 degree-seeking graduate students
- 53% of applicants admitted
- SAT or ACT (ACT writing recommended), application essay required
- 67% graduate within 6 years; 30% enter graduate study

General. Founded in 1929. Regionally accredited. **Degrees:** 1,147 bachelor's, 3 associate awarded; master's, first professional offered. **ROTC:** Army, Air Force. **Location:** 8 miles from New Haven, 30 miles from Hartford. **Calendar:** Semester, limited summer session. **Full-time faculty:** 280 total; 80% have terminal degrees, 9% minority, 48% women. **Part-time faculty:** 460 total; 49% women. **Class size:** 59% < 20, 41% 20-39, less than 1% 40-49. **Special facilities:** Financial technology center, digital television production studio, polling institute, institute for community health education, critical care simulation laboratory, motion analysis lab, Irish Famine museum, Albert Schweitzer Institute.

Freshman class profile. 11,397 applied, 6,011 admitted, 1,361 enrolled.

Mid 50% test scores		End year in good standing:	93%
SAT verbal:	510-590	Return as sophomores:	87%
SAT math:	540-610	Out-of-state:	75%
ACT:	22-26	Live on campus:	95%
Rank in top quarter:	56%	International:	1%
Rank in top tenth:	22%		

Four-Year Colleges

Basis for selection. School achievement record, course selection, test scores, and class rank most important. Interview recommended, extracurricular activities also considered. Campus visit recommended for interview, group information session, or open house. **Homeschooled:** Statement describing homeschool structure and mission, transcript of courses and grades required. Evaluation of education completed and SAT and/or ACT scores required.

High school preparation. 16 units required. Required units include English 4, mathematics 3, social studies 2, science 3 (laboratory 2), foreign language 2 and academic electives 2. 4 laboratory science including physics, 4 years math required for physical therapy program; 4 science and 4 math required for occupational therapy and physician assistant.

2006-2007 Annual costs. Tuition/fees: $26,280. Room/board: $10,700. Books/supplies: $800. Personal expenses: $900.

2005-2006 Financial aid. Need-based: 1,057 full-time freshmen applied for aid; 799 were judged to have need; 796 of these received aid. Average need met was 65%. Average scholarship/grant was $10,537; average loan $2,856. 54% of total undergraduate aid awarded as scholarships/grants, 46% as loans/jobs. **Non-need-based:** Awarded to 1,897 full-time undergraduates, including 462 freshmen. Scholarships awarded for academics, athletics.

Application procedures. Admission: Closing date 2/1 (receipt date). $45 fee, may be waived for applicants with need. Application may be submitted online. Admission notification on a rolling basis beginning on or about 12/10. Must reply by May 1 or within 2 week(s) if notified thereafter. Applicants to physician assistant, physical therapy, and occupational therapy programs should apply by 12/1, postmark date. **Financial aid:** Priority date 3/1; no closing date. FAFSA required. Applicants notified on a rolling basis starting 2/15; must reply by 5/1 or within 2 week(s) of notification.

Academics. Incoming students must purchase a university recommended laptop computer. **Special study options:** Combined bachelor's/graduate degree, distance learning, double major, honors, independent study, internships, liberal arts/career combination, semester at sea, student-designed major, study abroad, teacher certification program, Washington semester. Online and blended courses offered during the summer sessions. **Credit/placement by examination:** AP, CLEP, IB, institutional tests. 32 credit hours maximum toward bachelor's degree. **Support services:** Learning center, tutoring.

Majors. Biology: General, biochemistry, biomedical sciences, biotechnology. **Business:** General, accounting, business admin, communications, entrepreneurial studies, finance, human resources, international, international marketing, management information systems, management science, managerial economics, marketing, nonprofit/public, office management. **Communications:** General, advertising, broadcast journalism, digital media, journalism, public relations. **Computer sciences:** General, applications programming, computer graphics, computer science. **Education:** Biology, chemistry, elementary, English, foreign languages, history, mathematics, middle, multi-level teacher, science, secondary, social studies, Spanish. **English:** Composition. **Foreign languages:** Spanish. **Health:** Athletic training, health care admin, nursing (RN), physician assistant, predentistry, premedicine, preveterinary, respiratory therapy technology, veterinary technology/assistant. **History:** General. **Interdisciplinary:** Biopsychology, gerontology, math/computer science. **Legal studies:** General, legal secretary, paralegal, prelaw. **Math:** General. **Physical sciences:** Chemistry. **Protective services:** Criminal justice. **Psychology:** General. **Science technology:** Biological. **Social sciences:** General, criminology, economics, political science, sociology.

Most popular majors. Business/marketing 24%, communications/journalism 17%, health sciences 19%, psychology 8%, social sciences 8%.

Computing on campus. PC or laptop required. 300 workstations in library, computer center. Dormitories wired for high-speed internet access and linked to campus network. Commuter students can connect to campus network. Online course registration, online library, helpline, repair service, student web hosting, wireless network available.

Student life. Freshman orientation: Mandatory. Preregistration for classes offered. One of 3 weekends in June (Friday to Sunday) or the 2 days prior to classes in the fall. **Policies:** Free shuttle system to area shopping, restaurants, multiplex cinema, New Haven, Metro North/Amtrak train station. **Housing:** Guaranteed on-campus for freshmen. Coed dorms, apartments, substance-free housing available. $550 partly refundable deposit, deadline 5/1. **Activities:** Pep band, choral groups, dance, drama, literary magazine, radio station, student government, student newspaper, TV station, Hillel, Catholic Community, Black Student Union, Greenpeace, Amnesty International, SADD, women's center, Asian and Pacific Islander club, Hispanic student organization, Christian Fellowship.

Athletics. NCAA. **Intercollegiate:** Baseball M, basketball, cross-country, field hockey W, golf M, ice hockey, lacrosse, soccer, softball W, tennis, track and field, volleyball W. **Intramural:** Archery, badminton, baseball M, basketball, bowling, field hockey W, football (tackle) M, soccer, softball, table tennis, tennis, volleyball. **Team name:** Bobcats.

Student services. Adult student services, campus ministries, career counseling, student employment services, financial aid counseling, health services, minority student services, personal counseling, placement for graduates.

Contact. E-mail: admissions@quinnipiac.edu
Phone: (203) 582-8600 Toll-free number: (800) 462-1944
Fax: (203) 582-8906
Carla Knowlton, Director of Admisssions, Quinnipiac University, 275 Mount Carmel Avenue, Hamden, CT 06518-1908

Sacred Heart University

Fairfield, Connecticut — **CB member**
www.sacredheart.edu — **CB code: 3780**

- Private 4-year university and liberal arts college affiliated with Roman Catholic Church
- Residential campus in large town
- 4,045 degree-seeking undergraduates: 20% part-time, 61% women, 5% African American, 1% Asian American, 6% Hispanic American, 1% international
- 1,456 degree-seeking graduate students
- 64% of applicants admitted
- SAT or ACT with writing, application essay required
- 63% graduate within 6 years; 45% enter graduate study

General. Founded in 1963. Regionally accredited. **Degrees:** 794 bachelor's, 45 associate awarded; master's offered. **ROTC:** Army. **Location:** 55 miles from New York City. **Calendar:** Semester, extensive summer session. **Full-time faculty:** 186 total; 78% have terminal degrees, 13% minority, 47% women. **Part-time faculty:** 286 total; 29% have terminal degrees, 8% minority, 49% women. **Class size:** 53% < 20, 46% 20-39, 1% 40-49. **Special facilities:** Performing arts center, multipurpose communication studios, 36-hole golf course, rehabilitation clinics for occupational and physical therapies, contemporary art gallery.

Freshman class profile. 5,856 applied, 3,731 admitted, 886 enrolled.

Mid 50% test scores		**Rank in top tenth:**	8%
SAT verbal:	490-570	**Return as sophomores:**	84%
SAT math:	500-580	**Out-of-state:**	80%
GPA 3.50 or higher:	41%	**Live on campus:**	95%
GPA 3.0-3.49:	39%	**International:**	1%
GPA 2.0-2.99:	20%	**Fraternities:**	5%
Rank in top quarter:	29%	**Sororities:**	7%

Basis for selection. High school record and college preparatory curriculum most important. Interview required for early decision candidates, recommended for all other candidates.

High school preparation. College-preparatory program required. 22 units required; 30 recommended. Required and recommended units include English 4, mathematics 3-4, social studies 3-4, history 3-4, science 3-4 (laboratory 1-2), foreign language 2-4 and academic electives 3-4.

2005-2006 Annual costs. Tuition/fees: $23,750. Room/board: $9,654. Books/supplies: $700. Personal expenses: $700.

2005-2006 Financial aid. Need-based: 812 full-time freshmen applied for aid; 636 were judged to have need; 623 of these received aid. Average need met was 66%. Average scholarship/grant was $9,266; average loan $5,051. 60% of total undergraduate aid awarded as scholarships/grants, 40% as loans/jobs. **Non-need-based:** Awarded to 930 full-time undergraduates, including 328 freshmen. Scholarships awarded for academics, alumni affiliation, art, athletics, leadership, minority status, music/drama, ROTC.

Application procedures. Admission: Priority date 2/1; no deadline. $50 fee, may be waived for applicants with need. Application may be submitted online. Admission notification on a rolling basis beginning on or about 1/1. Must reply by May 1 or within 2 week(s) if notified thereafter. **Financial aid:** Priority date 2/15; no closing date. FAFSA, CSS PROFILE required. Applicants notified on a rolling basis starting 3/1; must reply within 2 week(s) of notification.

Academics. Special study options: Accelerated study, combined bachelor's/graduate degree, cooperative education, cross-registration, distance learning, double major, dual enrollment of high school students, ESL, honors, independent study, internships, liberal arts/career combination, student-designed major, study abroad, teacher certification program, United Nations semester, Washington semester, weekend college. Luxembourg semester, study abroad program in Ireland. **Credit/placement by examination:** AP, CLEP,

IB, SAT, ACT, institutional tests. 30 credit hours maximum toward bachelor's degree. **Support services:** Learning center, reduced course load, remedial instruction, study skills assistance, tutoring, writing center.

Honors college/program. 3.4 GPA, 1250 combined SAT (exclusive of Writing) with at least a 600 verbal; rank in top 10% of high school class.

Majors. **Biology:** General, biochemistry. **Business:** General, accounting, finance. **Communications:** General, media studies. **Communications technology:** General. **Computer sciences:** General, computer science. **Conservation:** General, environmental science. **English:** English lit. **Foreign languages:** Spanish. **Health:** Athletic training, nursing (RN), preop/surgical nursing. **History:** General. **Liberal arts:** Arts/sciences. **Math:** General. **Parks/recreation:** Sports admin. **Philosophy/religion:** Philosophy, religion. **Physical sciences:** Chemistry. **Psychology:** General. **Public administration:** Social work. **Social sciences:** Criminology, economics, political science, sociology. **Visual/performing arts:** Art, commercial/advertising art, design, painting.

Most popular majors. Business/marketing 35%, communications/journalism 6%, health sciences 9%, psychology 16%.

Computing on campus. PC or laptop required. 300 workstations in dormitories, library, computer center, student center. Dormitories wired for high-speed internet access and linked to campus network. Commuter students can connect to campus network. Online course registration, online library, helpline, repair service, student web hosting, wireless network available.

Student life. **Freshman orientation:** Mandatory. Preregistration for classes offered. Overnight 2-day program in late spring for both parents and students. **Housing:** Guaranteed on-campus for all undergraduates. Coed dorms, special housing for disabled, apartments, substance-free housing available. $1,000 nonrefundable deposit, deadline 5/1. **Activities:** Bands, choral groups, dance, drama, film society, literary magazine, music ensembles, musical theater, radio station, student government, student newspaper, campus ministry, La Hispanidad, Habitat for Humanity, UMOJA, Circle K, Best Buddies, international club, debate society.

Athletics. NCAA. **Intercollegiate:** Baseball M, basketball, bowling, cross-country, equestrian W, fencing, field hockey W, football (tackle) M, golf, ice hockey, lacrosse, rowing (crew) W, soccer, softball W, swimming W, tennis, track and field, volleyball, wrestling M. **Intramural:** Basketball, bowling, cheerleading W, field hockey W, football (non-tackle), golf, gymnastics W, skiing, soccer W, tennis, volleyball. **Team name:** Pioneers.

Student services. Adult student services, alcohol/substance abuse counseling, campus ministries, career counseling, services for economically disadvantaged, student employment services, financial aid counseling, health services, minority student services, personal counseling, placement for graduates, women's services. **Physically disabled:** Services for visually, speech, hearing impaired.

Contact. E-mail: enroll@sacredheart.edu
Phone: (203) 371-7880 Fax: (203) 365-7607
Karen Guastelle, Dean of Undergraduate Admissions, Sacred Heart University, 5151 Park Avenue, Fairfield, CT 06825

St. Joseph College

West Hartford, Connecticut — **CB member**
www.sjc.edu — **CB code: 3754**

- Private 4-year liberal arts college for women affiliated with Roman Catholic Church
- Residential campus in large town
- 1,125 degree-seeking undergraduates: 23% part-time, 99% women, 14% African American, 2% Asian American, 8% Hispanic American
- 562 degree-seeking graduate students
- 72% of applicants admitted
- SAT or ACT required
- 53% graduate within 6 years

General. Founded in 1932. Regionally accredited. Men admitted as part-time students and graduate students. **Degrees:** 229 bachelor's awarded; master's offered. **Location:** 3 miles from Hartford. **Calendar:** Semester, limited summer session. **Full-time faculty:** 77 total; 90% have terminal degrees, 69% women. **Part-time faculty:** 11 total; 27% have terminal degrees, 91% women. **Class size:** 77% < 20, 21% 20-39, less than 1% 40-49, 1% 50-99. **Special facilities:** 2 laboratory schools, nursing laboratory, arts and humanities center.

Freshman class profile. 1,051 applied, 755 admitted, 251 enrolled.

Mid 50% test scores			
SAT verbal:	450-570	Rank in top quarter:	43%
SAT math:	440-540	Rank in top tenth:	15%
GPA 3.50 or higher:	25%	End year in good standing:	60%
GPA 3.0-3.49:	36%	Return as sophomores:	68%
GPA 2.0-2.99:	38%	Out-of-state:	20%
		Live on campus:	71%

Basis for selection. School achievement record most important, then test scores. School and community activities and recommendation also considered but not required.

High school preparation. 16 units required. Required units include English 4, mathematics 3, social studies 3, science 3 and foreign language 3.

2006-2007 Annual costs. Tuition/fees (projected): $23,490. Room/board: $10,167. Books/supplies: $850. Personal expenses: $700.

2005-2006 Financial aid. **Need-based:** Average scholarship/grant was $13,844; average loan $5,023. 55% of total undergraduate aid awarded as scholarships/grants, 45% as loans/jobs. **Non-need-based:** Scholarships awarded for academics, leadership.

Application procedures. **Admission:** No deadline. $35 fee, may be waived for applicants with need. Application may be submitted online. Admission notification on a rolling basis. **Financial aid:** Priority date 2/15, closing date 6/30. FAFSA required. Applicants notified on a rolling basis starting 2/1; must reply within 2 week(s) of notification.

Academics. Seminar offered to introduce students to college experience and philosophy of education. **Special study options:** Combined bachelor's/graduate degree, cross-registration, distance learning, double major, dual enrollment of high school students, honors, independent study, internships, liberal arts/career combination, student-designed major, study abroad, teacher certification program, weekend college. **Credit/placement by examination:** AP, CLEP, institutional tests. 30 credit hours maximum toward bachelor's degree. **Support services:** Learning center, pre-admission summer program, reduced course load, study skills assistance, tutoring, writing center.

Majors. **Area/ethnic studies:** American. **Biology:** General, biochemistry. **Business:** Business admin. **Computer sciences:** Computer science. **Conservation:** Environmental studies. **Education:** Art, family/consumer sciences, kindergarten/preschool, music, special. **English:** English lit. **Family/consumer sciences:** General, child development, consumer economics, food/nutrition. **Foreign languages:** French, Spanish. **Health:** Dietetics, nursing (RN), premedicine. **History:** General. **Interdisciplinary:** Natural sciences. **Legal studies:** Prelaw. **Liberal arts:** Arts/sciences. **Math:** General. **Philosophy/religion:** Philosophy, religion. **Physical sciences:** Chemistry. **Psychology:** General. **Public administration:** Social work. **Social sciences:** General, economics, political science, sociology. **Visual/performing arts:** Art history/conservation, studio arts.

Most popular majors. Education 6%, health sciences 19%, psychology 12%, public administration/social services 13%, social sciences 17%.

Computing on campus. 150 workstations in dormitories, library, computer center, student center. Dormitories linked to campus network. Commuter students can connect to campus network. Online course registration, online library, helpline available.

Student life. **Freshman orientation:** Available. **Policies:** Freshmen permitted cars on campus. **Housing:** Special housing for disabled, substance-free housing available. $250 nonrefundable deposit. Single rooms available for nontraditional students. Medical singles with private bathrooms available on a limited basis. **Activities:** Choral groups, dance, drama, literary magazine, music ensembles, opera, student government, Faith in Action, Nubian Sisters United, multicultural alliance, campus ministry, mentoring circle.

Athletics. NCAA. **Intercollegiate:** Basketball W, cross-country W, diving W, lacrosse W, soccer W, softball W, swimming W, tennis W, volleyball W. **Intramural:** Badminton W, basketball W, soccer W, softball W, tennis W, track and field W, volleyball W. **Team name:** Blue Jays.

Student services. Adult student services, alcohol/substance abuse counseling, campus ministries, career counseling, student employment services, financial aid counseling, health services, on-campus daycare, personal counseling, placement for graduates, women's services. **Physically disabled:** Services for hearing impaired.

Contact. E-mail: admissions@sjc.edu
Phone: (860) 231-5216 Toll-free number: (866) 442-8752
Fax: (860) 231-5744
Alan Chesterton, Associate Vice President for Admission and Enrollment Services, St. Joseph College, 1678 Asylum Avenue, West Hartford, CT 06117-2791

Four-Year Colleges

Southern Connecticut State University

New Haven, Connecticut **CB member**
www.southernct.edu **CB code: 3662**

- Public 4-year university
- Residential campus in small city
- 8,309 degree-seeking undergraduates: 19% part-time, 62% women
- 3,849 degree-seeking graduate students
- 54% of applicants admitted
- SAT or ACT with writing, application essay required
- 36% graduate within 6 years

General. Founded in 1893. Regionally accredited. **Degrees:** 1,180 bachelor's awarded; master's offered. **ROTC:** Army, Air Force. **Location:** 75 miles from New York City. **Calendar:** Semester, extensive summer session. **Full-time faculty:** 403 total; 90% have terminal degrees, 14% minority, 45% women. **Part-time faculty:** 410 total; 15% minority, 55% women. **Class size:** 32% < 20, 57% 20-39, 10% 40-49, less than 1% 50-99, less than 1% >100. **Special facilities:** Planetarium, photonics laboratory, geospatial technology laboratory.

Freshman class profile. 5,037 applied, 2,722 admitted, 1,340 enrolled.

Mid 50% test scores			
SAT verbal:	430-530	Return as sophomores:	75%
SAT math:	420-520	Out-of-state:	7%
Rank in top quarter:	22%	Live on campus:	61%
Rank in top tenth:	6%	Fraternities:	1%
End year in good standing:	62%	Sororities:	1%

Basis for selection. School achievement record, test scores most important. Special consideration to culturally disadvantaged students. **Homeschooled:** Statement describing homeschool structure and mission, transcript of courses and grades, letter of recommendation (nonparent) required.

High school preparation. 16 units required. Required and recommended units include English 4, mathematics 3-4, social studies 2, history 2, science 2 (laboratory 1) and foreign language 2-3. One unit of algebra II required.

2005-2006 Annual costs. Tuition/fees: $5,814; $13,752 out-of-state. Room/board: $7,698. Books/supplies: $750. Personal expenses: $300.

2004-2005 Financial aid. Need-based: 1,142 full-time freshmen applied for aid; 696 were judged to have need; 661 of these received aid. Average need met was 81%. Average scholarship/grant was $4,937; average loan $2,613. 37% of total undergraduate aid awarded as scholarships/grants, 63% as loans/jobs. **Non-need-based:** Awarded to 874 full-time undergraduates, including 260 freshmen. Scholarships awarded for academics, alumni affiliation, athletics, ROTC.

Application procedures. Admission: Closing date 7/1 (postmark date). $50 fee, may be waived for applicants with need. Application may be submitted online. Admission notification on a rolling basis beginning on or about 12/1. Must reply by May 1 or within 2 week(s) if notified thereafter. **Financial aid:** Closing date 3/10. FAFSA required. Applicants notified on a rolling basis; must reply within 2 week(s) of notification.

Academics. Special study options: Accelerated study, cooperative education, cross-registration, distance learning, double major, exchange student, honors, independent study, internships, student-designed major, study abroad, teacher certification program. **Credit/placement by examination:** AP, CLEP, institutional tests. 30 credit hours maximum toward associate degree, 30 toward bachelor's. **Support services:** Learning center, preadmission summer program, reduced course load, remedial instruction, study skills assistance, tutoring, writing center.

Majors. Biology: General, bacteriology, botany, marine, zoology. **Business:** Accounting, business admin, finance, management science, managerial economics, marketing. **Communications:** General, journalism. **Computer sciences:** General. **Education:** General, art, biology, chemistry, elementary, English, history, mathematics, physical, physics, science, secondary, social science, social studies, Spanish. **English:** Composition. **Foreign languages:** General, French, German, Italian, Spanish. **Health:** Nursing (RN), predentistry, premedicine, prepharmacy, preveterinary. **History:** General. **Legal studies:** Prelaw. **Liberal arts:** Arts/sciences, library science. **Math:** General. **Parks/recreation:** General, exercise sciences. **Philosophy/religion:** Philosophy. **Physical sciences:** Chemistry, physics, planetary. **Psychology:** General. **Public administration:** Social work. **Social sciences:** Geography, political science, sociology. **Visual/performing arts:** Art, art history/conservation, dramatic.

Most popular majors. Business/marketing 13%, communications/journalism 10%, education 11%, health sciences 8%, liberal arts 8%, psychology 14%, social sciences 8%.

Computing on campus. 750 workstations in dormitories, library, computer center, student center. Dormitories wired for high-speed internet access and linked to campus network. Commuter students can connect to campus network. Online course registration, online library, helpline, student web hosting, wireless network available.

Student life. Freshman orientation: Mandatory. Preregistration for classes offered. **Policies:** Freshmen permitted cars on campus. **Housing:** Guaranteed on-campus for all undergraduates. Coed dorms, special housing for disabled, apartments, substance-free housing available. $250 nonrefundable deposit. Students must be 19 or older to live in upper-classmen apartments. **Activities:** Bands, choral groups, dance, drama, film society, literary magazine, music ensembles, radio station, student government, student newspaper, symphony orchestra, Christian Fellowship, Newman Club, United Ministries, Organization of Latin American Students, Black Student Union, People to People, Students for Disability Rights, veterans club.

Athletics. NCAA. **Intercollegiate:** Baseball M, basketball, cross-country, field hockey W, football (tackle) M, golf M, gymnastics, ice hockey M, lacrosse W, rugby, soccer, softball, swimming, track and field, volleyball, wrestling M. **Intramural:** Badminton, basketball, cross-country, diving, golf, gymnastics, ice hockey M, lacrosse, rugby, skiing, skin diving, soccer, softball, swimming, volleyball. **Team name:** Owls.

Student services. Adult student services, alcohol/substance abuse counseling, campus ministries, career counseling, student employment services, financial aid counseling, health services, personal counseling, placement for graduates, veterans' counselor, women's services. **Physically disabled:** Services for visually, speech, hearing impaired.

Contact. Phone: (203) 392-5644 Toll-free number: (888) 500-7278
Fax: (203) 392-5727
Sharon Brennan, Director of Admissions and Enrollment Management, Southern Connecticut State University, 131 Farnham Avenue, New Haven, CT 06515-1202

Trinity College

Hartford, Connecticut **CB member**
www.trincoll.edu **CB code: 3899**

- Private 4-year liberal arts college
- Residential campus in large city
- 2,181 degree-seeking undergraduates: 2% part-time, 50% women
- 127 degree-seeking graduate students
- 39% of applicants admitted
- SAT or ACT (ACT writing recommended), application essay required
- 85% graduate within 6 years

General. Founded in 1823. Regionally accredited. **Degrees:** 470 bachelor's awarded; master's offered. **ROTC:** Army. **Location:** 125 miles from New York City, 100 miles from Boston. **Calendar:** Semester, limited summer session. **Full-time faculty:** 183 total; 92% have terminal degrees, 17% minority, 42% women. **Part-time faculty:** 75 total; 61% have terminal degrees, 13% minority, 40% women. **Class size:** 63% < 20, 30% 20-39, 4% 40-49, 3% 50-99, less than 1% >100. **Special facilities:** Library collections on Native Americans, maritime history, early American texts; nuclear magnetic spectrometer, mass spectrometer, electronic microscope, plasma spectrometer, optical diagnostics and communications laboratory, natural science field station.

Freshman class profile. 5,744 applied, 2,265 admitted, 573 enrolled.

Mid 50% test scores			
SAT verbal:	610-700	End year in good standing:	88%
SAT math:	610-700	Return as sophomores:	92%
ACT:	25-29	Out-of-state:	84%
Rank in top quarter:	89%	Live on campus:	99%
Rank in top tenth:	53%	International:	3%

Basis for selection. School record and recommendations most important. Require one of the following: ACT, SAT, or 3 SAT Subject Tests. Interview recommended.

High school preparation. 16 units required. Required units include English 4, mathematics 3, history 2, science 2 (laboratory 2) and foreign language 2.

2005-2006 Annual costs. Tuition/fees: $33,630. Room/board: $8,590. Books/supplies: $850. Personal expenses: $850.

2005-2006 Financial aid. All financial aid based on need. 195 full-time freshmen applied for aid; 160 were judged to have need; 160 of these received aid. Average need met was 100%. Average scholarship/grant was $25,464; average loan $2,688. 84% of total undergraduate aid awarded as scholarships/grants, 16% as loans/jobs.

Application procedures. Admission: Closing date 1/1 (postmark date). $60 fee, may be waived for applicants with need. Application may be submitted online. Admission notification 4/1. Must reply by 5/1. **Financial aid:** Closing date 2/1. FAFSA, CSS PROFILE required. Applicants notified by 4/1; must reply by 5/1 or within 2 week(s) of notification.

Academics. Special study options: Accelerated study, combined bachelor's/graduate degree, cross-registration, double major, exchange student, honors, independent study, internships, liberal arts/career combination, New York semester, semester at sea, student-designed major, study abroad, teacher certification program, United Nations semester, urban semester, Washington semester. 5-year BS/MS in electrical and mechanical engineering with Rensselaer Polytechnic Institute, cross-registration for biomedical engineering courses through Biomedical Engineering Alliance of Connecticut (BEACON). **Credit/placement by examination:** AP, CLEP, IB, institutional tests. **Support services:** Remedial instruction, study skills assistance, tutoring, writing center.

Majors. Area/ethnic studies: African, African-American, American, Asian, Latin American, Near/Middle Eastern, Russian/Slavic, women's. **Biology:** General, biochemistry. **Computer sciences:** General, computer science. **Conservation:** Environmental science. **Education:** General. **Engineering:** General, biomedical, electrical, mechanical. **English:** English lit. **Foreign languages:** General, Chinese, classics, comparative lit, French, German, Italian, Japanese, Russian, Spanish. **Health:** Premedicine. **History:** General. **Interdisciplinary:** Neuroscience. **Legal studies:** Prelaw. **Math:** General. **Philosophy/religion:** Judaic, philosophy, religion. **Physical sciences:** Chemistry, physics. **Psychology:** General. **Public administration:** Policy analysis. **Social sciences:** General, anthropology, economics, international relations, political science, sociology, urban studies. **Visual/performing arts:** General, art, art history/conservation, dance, dramatic, film/cinema, studio arts.

Most popular majors. English 10%, history 6%, psychology 7%, social sciences 31%, visual/performing arts 7%.

Computing on campus. 315 workstations in library, computer center. Dormitories wired for high-speed internet access and linked to campus network. Commuter students can connect to campus network. Online course registration, online library, helpline, student web hosting, wireless network available.

Student life. Freshman orientation: Available. **Housing:** Guaranteed on-campus for all undergraduates. Coed dorms, fraternity/sorority housing, substance-free housing available. Community service dorm, quiet dorm, 21+, cooking, themed housing available. All dorms are non-smoking. **Activities:** Jazz band, choral groups, dance, drama, film society, literary magazine, music ensembles, musical theater, radio station, student government, student newspaper, TV station, Hillel, Newman Club, Christian Fellowship, La Voz Latina, community outreach, Imani (black student union), Asian-American students association, women's center, Trinity College Black women's organization, Encouraging Respect Of Sexualities.

Athletics. NCAA. **Intercollegiate:** Baseball M, basketball, cross-country, diving, field hockey W, football (non-tackle) M, football (tackle) M, golf M, ice hockey, lacrosse, rowing (crew), soccer, softball W, squash, swimming, tennis, track and field, volleyball W, wrestling M. **Intramural:** Basketball, cheerleading, cross-country, fencing, field hockey, football (non-tackle) M, judo, soccer, softball, squash, swimming, tennis, track and field, triathlon, volleyball, weight lifting. **Team name:** Bantams.

Student services. Adult student services, alcohol/substance abuse counseling, campus ministries, career counseling, services for economically disadvantaged, student employment services, financial aid counseling, health services, minority student services, on-campus daycare, personal counseling, placement for graduates, women's services.

Contact. E-mail: admissions.office@trincoll.edu
Phone: (860) 297-2180 Fax: (860) 297-2287
Larry Dow, Dean of Admissions and Financial Aid, Trinity College, 300 Summit Street, Hartford, CT 06106

United States Coast Guard Academy

New London, Connecticut — **CB member**
www.cga.edu — **CB code: 5807**

- Public 4-year engineering and military college
- Residential campus in small city
- 1,012 degree-seeking undergraduates: 28% women, 3% African American, 5% Asian American, 4% Hispanic American, 1% Native American, 1% international
- 26% of applicants admitted
- SAT or ACT with writing, application essay required
- 59% graduate within 6 years

General. Founded in 1876. Regionally accredited. Each student issued a laptop computer. Summers involve introductory and advanced Coast Guard/professional training including opportunities to sail aboard Eagle, fly Coast Guard aircraft, become small arms qualified (rifle and pistol), learn basic shipboard fire fighting and flooding control, and perform actual search and rescue coordination at Coast Guard units. Summer between junior and senior years typically involves piloting and navigation of Coast Guard Cutters and integration into all aspects of operational afloat Coast Guard missions. All graduates commissioned as officers in US Coast Guard. **Degrees:** 215 bachelor's awarded. **Location:** 120 miles from New York City, 130 miles from Boston. **Calendar:** Semester, limited summer session. **Full-time faculty:** 100 total; 49% have terminal degrees, 8% minority, 24% women. **Part-time faculty:** 18 total; 89% have terminal degrees, 11% minority, 22% women. **Class size:** 63% < 20, 37% 20-39. **Special facilities:** Museum, research and development center, 295 foot tall ship, ship navigation simulation facilities with bridge simulator, 10,000 gallon circulating water channel, ship model towing tank, observatory with reflector telescope.

Freshman class profile. 1,597 applied, 422 admitted, 307 enrolled.

Mid 50% test scores		**Rank in top quarter:**	85%
SAT verbal:	590-680	**Rank in top tenth:**	47%
SAT math:	620-690	**End year in good standing:**	92%
ACT:	25-29	**Return as sophomores:**	94%
GPA 3.50 or higher:	80%	**Out-of-state:**	93%
GPA 3.0-3.49:	17%	**Live on campus:**	100%
GPA 2.0-2.99:	3%	**International:**	1%

Basis for selection. Test scores, high school class rank, recommendations, essay, leadership potential as demonstrated by extracurricular activities, athletics, community affairs, and part-time employment considered. Congressional nomination not required. Applicants required to pass medical and physical fitness exams. Interview recommended. **Homeschooled:** AP and SAT Subject Tests recommended. Application should include detailed account of curriculum and course content. Students advised to take courses in math and science at a local college and have professor submit a recommendation. Recommendations from other adults required. Essay should include reasons for undertaking homeschooling, benefits realized, and how experience prepared student to succeed in college.

High school preparation. Required units include English 4, mathematics 4, science 3 (laboratory 3). Math units should include algebra, quadratics, plane or coordinate geometry, or equivalent. Calculus and pre-calculus recommended. Sciences should include chemistry and physics.

2006-2007 Annual costs. All tuition, room and board paid for by U.S. government. Students make one-time entrance deposit of $3,000 to help defray cost of uniforms, books, supplies and personal computer. All students paid monthly stipend of $734.

Application procedures. Admission: Closing date 3/1 (postmark date). No application fee. Application must be submitted online. Admission notification on a rolling basis. Must reply by May 1 or within 2 week(s) if notified thereafter. Application by 11/01 recommended to allow time to complete essays and supplemental forms, obtain teacher recommendations, and schedule required physical. **Financial aid:** No deadline.

Academics. Five-year obligatory military service after graduation, serving as commissioned officer in U.S. Coast Guard. **Special study options:** Double major, exchange student, honors, independent study, internships. **Credit/placement by examination:** CLEP, institutional tests. **Support services:** Learning center, pre-admission summer program, reduced course load, remedial instruction, study skills assistance, tutoring, writing center.

Majors. Business: Business admin. **Engineering:** Civil, electrical, marine, mechanical. **Physical sciences:** Oceanography. **Social sciences:** Political science.

Most popular majors. Biology 18%, business/marketing 16%, engineering/engineering technologies 35%, mathematics 14%, social sciences 18%.

Computing on campus. PC or laptop required. 325 workstations in dormitories, library, computer center. Dormitories wired for high-speed internet access and linked to campus network. Online course registration, online library, helpline, repair service, student web hosting, wireless network available.

Student life. Freshman orientation: Mandatory. 7-week "swab summer," including one week onboard the Coast Guard Cutter Eagle. **Policies:** Students part of corps of cadets. On-campus residence mandatory. **Housing:**

Guaranteed on-campus for all undergraduates. Coed dorms, substance-free housing available. **Activities:** Bands, choral groups, dance, drama, music ensembles, musical theater, student government, student newspaper, Officers Christian Fellowship, multicultural club, Fellowship of Christian Athletes, Big Brothers and Big Sisters, Boy Scouts, Genesis Club.

Athletics. NCAA. **Intercollegiate:** Baseball M, basketball, cheerleading M, cross-country, diving, football (tackle) M, rifle, rowing (crew), sailing, soccer, softball W, swimming, tennis M, track and field, volleyball W, wrestling M. **Intramural:** Basketball, bowling, football (non-tackle), golf, ice hockey M, racquetball, soccer, softball, swimming, tennis, volleyball, water polo M. **Team name:** Bears.

Student services. Alcohol/substance abuse counseling, campus ministries, career counseling, health services, legal services, minority student services, on-campus daycare, personal counseling, placement for graduates.

Contact. E-mail: admissions@exmail.uscga.edu
Phone: (860) 444-8500 Toll-free number: (800) 883-8724
Fax: (860) 701-6700
Capt. Susan Bibeau, Director of Admissions, United States Coast Guard Academy, 31 Mohegan Avenue, New London, CT 06320

University of Bridgeport

Bridgeport, Connecticut — **CB member**
www.bridgeport.edu — **CB code: 3914**

- Private 4-year university
- Residential campus in small city
- 1,676 degree-seeking undergraduates: 26% part-time, 64% women, 33% African American, 4% Asian American, 14% Hispanic American, 13% international
- 1,950 degree-seeking graduate students
- 73% of applicants admitted
- SAT or ACT (ACT writing optional), application essay required
- 54% graduate within 6 years; 50% enter graduate study

General. Founded in 1927. Regionally accredited. Off-campus facilities in Stamford and Waterbury. **Degrees:** 176 bachelor's, 37 associate awarded; master's, doctoral, first professional offered. **ROTC:** Army. **Location:** 60 miles from New York City. **Calendar:** Semester, extensive summer session. **Full-time faculty:** 89 total; 84% have terminal degrees, 21% minority, 26% women. **Part-time faculty:** 257 total; 12% minority, 46% women. **Class size:** 66% < 20, 29% 20-39, 4% 40-49, 1% 50-99. **Special facilities:** Theater, recital halls, studios, exhibit rooms.

Freshman class profile. 2,332 applied, 1,709 admitted, 365 enrolled.

Mid 50% test scores			
SAT verbal:	380-490	**Rank in top quarter:**	25%
SAT math:	390-490	**Rank in top tenth:**	1%
ACT:	15-20	**Out-of-state:**	58%
GPA 3.50 or higher:	14%	**Live on campus:**	75%
GPA 3.0-3.49:	24%	**International:**	13%
GPA 2.0-2.99:	55%	**Fraternities:**	1%
		Sororities:	1%

Basis for selection. School achievement record most important, followed by test scores, activities, trend of grades and curriculum in high school. Audition required of music majors. Portfolio required of fine and applied arts majors. Interview recommended of dental hygiene, basic studies majors.

High school preparation. College-preparatory program recommended. 16 units required. Required units include English 4, mathematics 3, social studies 2, science 2 (laboratory 2) and academic electives 5. 4 math required for math, science, computer science and engineering applicants. Chemistry required for dental hygiene.

2005-2006 Annual costs. Tuition/fees: $20,595. Room/board: $9,000. Books/supplies: $1,200. Personal expenses: $2,147.

Financial aid. Non-need-based: Scholarships awarded for academics, athletics, state residency.

Application procedures. Admission: Priority date 4/1; no deadline. $25 fee, may be waived for applicants with need. Application may be submitted online. Admission notification on a rolling basis. Must reply by May 1 or within 2 week(s) if notified thereafter. **Financial aid:** Priority date 4/1; no closing date. FAFSA, institutional form required. Applicants notified on a rolling basis starting 4/1; must reply within 4 week(s) of notification.

Academics. Special study options: Accelerated study, combined bachelor's/graduate degree, cooperative education, cross-registration, distance learning, double major, dual enrollment of high school students, ESL, exchange student, honors, independent study, internships, liberal arts/career combination, New York semester, student-designed major, study abroad, teacher certification program, United Nations semester, Washington semester, weekend college. **Credit/placement by examination:** AP, CLEP, IB, SAT, ACT, institutional tests. 30 credit hours maximum toward associate degree, 30 toward bachelor's. **Support services:** Learning center, pre-admission summer program, reduced course load, remedial instruction, study skills assistance, tutoring, writing center.

Majors. Area/ethnic studies: East Asian. **Biology:** General. **Business:** General, accounting, fashion, finance, international, labor relations, management information systems, marketing. **Communications:** General, advertising, journalism, media studies, public relations. **Computer sciences:** General. **Engineering:** Computer. **English:** Creative writing. **Health:** Dental hygiene. **Liberal arts:** Arts/sciences, humanities. **Math:** General. **Philosophy/religion:** Religion. **Physical sciences:** General. **Psychology:** General. **Public administration:** Community org/advocacy. **Social sciences:** General, international relations, political science, sociology. **Visual/performing arts:** Graphic design, illustration, industrial design, interior design.

Most popular majors. Business/marketing 24%, health sciences 7%, liberal arts 26%, psychology 8%, public administration/social services 6%, visual/performing arts 12%.

Computing on campus. 600 workstations in dormitories, library, computer center, student center. Dormitories wired for high-speed internet access and linked to campus network. Commuter students can connect to campus network. Online library, helpline, repair service, student web hosting, wireless network available.

Student life. Freshman orientation: Mandatory, $100 fee. Preregistration for classes offered. Placement listing, registration, and orientation held during the summer with final program just prior to class. **Policies:** Student and dormitory governments plan student life activities. Freshmen permitted cars on campus. **Housing:** Guaranteed on-campus for all undergraduates. Coed dorms, substance-free housing available. $200 nonrefundable deposit, deadline 5/1. Dormitories have special facilities (e.g., dark rooms, exercise rooms) arranged by interested groups of students. **Activities:** Choral groups, film society, literary magazine, music ensembles, student government, student newspaper, interfaith center, black student alliance, international relations club, social service sorority, Newman Center, Hillel, Protestant fellowship, Home Base Community Service Project.

Athletics. NCAA. **Intercollegiate:** Baseball M, basketball, cross-country, gymnastics W, soccer, softball W, swimming W, volleyball W. **Intramural:** Basketball, racquetball, soccer, softball, tennis, volleyball. **Team name:** Purple Knights.

Student services. Adult student services, alcohol/substance abuse counseling, campus ministries, career counseling, student employment services, financial aid counseling, health services, minority student services, personal counseling, placement for graduates, veterans' counselor. **Physically disabled:** Services for visually, speech, hearing impaired.

Contact. E-mail: admit@bridgeport.edu
Phone: (203) 576-4552 Toll-free number: (800) 392-3582
Fax: (203) 576-4941
Audrey Ashton-Savage, Vice President Enrollment Management, University of Bridgeport, 126 Park Avenue, Bridgeport, CT 06604

University of Connecticut

Storrs, Connecticut — **CB member**
www.uconn.edu — **CB code: 3915**

- Public 4-year university
- Residential campus in large town
- 15,709 degree-seeking undergraduates: 3% part-time, 53% women, 5% African American, 7% Asian American, 5% Hispanic American, 1% international
- 6,470 degree-seeking graduate students
- 51% of applicants admitted
- SAT or ACT with writing, application essay required
- 72% graduate within 6 years; 27% enter graduate study

General. Founded in 1881. Regionally accredited. Students may take courses at nonresidential campuses in Groton, Hartford, Stamford, Waterbury, and Torrington. **Degrees:** 3,816 bachelor's, 29 associate awarded; master's, doctoral, first professional offered. **ROTC:** Army, Air Force. **Location:** 26 miles from Hartford, 80 miles from Boston. **Calendar:** Semester, extensive summer session. **Full-time faculty:** 975 total; 93% have terminal degrees, 17% minority, 33% women. **Part-time faculty:** 290 total; 29% have terminal degrees, 3% minority, 53% women. **Class size:** 42% < 20, 35% 20-39, 7%

40-49, 9% 50-99, 7% >100. **Special facilities:** Museum of natural history, research center, ice hockey/skating rink, dairy bar.

Freshman class profile. 18,608 applied, 9,498 admitted, 3,260 enrolled.

Mid 50% test scores		Return as sophomores:	92%
SAT verbal:	540-630	Out-of-state:	28%
SAT math:	550-650	Live on campus:	97%
ACT:	23-27	International:	1%
Rank in top quarter:	80%	Fraternities:	5%
Rank in top tenth:	37%	Sororities:	4%

Basis for selection. Curriculum, grades, rank in class most important, followed by test scores. Particular consideration given to first generation college and/or socio-economically disadvantaged applicants and applicants with special talents. Audition required of music, acting, puppetry majors. **Homeschooled:** Statement describing homeschool structure and mission, transcript of courses and grades, state high school equivalency certificate required.

High school preparation. College-preparatory program required. 16 units required. Required and recommended units include English 4, mathematics 3, social studies 2, science 2 (laboratory 2), foreign language 2-3 and academic electives 3. Some programs may require units in addition to those listed.

2006-2007 Annual costs. Tuition/fees (projected): $8,359; $21,559 out-of-state. Out-of-state New England residents pay 150% of in-state tuition rate for programs of study not offered at their home state university. Room/board: $8,266. Books/supplies: $726. Personal expenses: $1,500.

2005-2006 Financial aid. Need-based: 2,628 full-time freshmen applied for aid; 1,627 were judged to have need; 1,560 of these received aid. Average need met was 70%. Average scholarship/grant was $6,393; average loan $4,219. 45% of total undergraduate aid awarded as scholarships/grants, 55% as loans/jobs. **Non-need-based:** Awarded to 4,421 full-time undergraduates, including 1,339 freshmen. Scholarships awarded for academics, art, athletics, leadership, minority status, music/drama. **Additional information:** Institution offers variety of need-based financial aid programs. Financial assistance packages may include grants, loans and work-study awards.

Application procedures. Admission: Closing date 2/1 (receipt date). $70 fee, may be waived for applicants with need. Application may be submitted online. Admission notification on a rolling basis beginning on or about 1/1. Must reply by May 1 or within 2 week(s) if notified thereafter. **Financial aid:** Priority date 3/1; no closing date. FAFSA required. Applicants notified on a rolling basis starting 3/1; must reply within 4 week(s) of notification.

Academics. 5-year program available combining engineering and the German language, including a 6-month internship in Germany. **Special study options:** Accelerated study, combined bachelor's/graduate degree, cooperative education, distance learning, double major, dual enrollment of high school students, ESL, exchange student, honors, independent study, internships, liberal arts/career combination, semester at sea, student-designed major, study abroad, teacher certification program, urban semester. Winter intersession, summer session, urban semester. **Credit/placement by examination:** AP, CLEP, IB, SAT, institutional tests. 30 credit hours maximum toward bachelor's degree. **Support services:** Learning center, pre-admission summer program, study skills assistance, tutoring, writing center.

Majors. Agriculture: Agronomy, animal sciences, economics, horticultural science. **Architecture:** Landscape. **Area/ethnic studies:** American, Latin American, Near/Middle Eastern, women's. **Biology:** General, animal physiology, biophysics, cellular/molecular, ecology, marine, pathology. **Business:** General, accounting, actuarial science, business admin, finance, insurance, management information systems, marketing, real estate. **Communications:** General, journalism. **Computer sciences:** Computer science. **Conservation:** General, environmental science. **Education:** Agricultural, elementary, music, physical, special. **Engineering:** Biomedical, chemical, civil, computer, electrical, environmental, industrial, materials, materials science, mechanical, physics. **English:** English lit. **Family/consumer sciences:** Family studies. **Foreign languages:** Classics, French, German, Italian, linguistics, Spanish. **Health:** Clinical lab science, cytotechnology, dietetics, gene therapy, health care admin, nursing (RN), prepharmacy. **History:** General. **Interdisciplinary:** Cognitive science, nutrition sciences. **Math:** General, applied, statistics. **Parks/recreation:** Facilities management. **Philosophy/religion:** Philosophy. **Physical sciences:** Chemistry, geology, physics. **Psychology:** General. **Social sciences:** Anthropology, economics, geography, political science, sociology, urban studies. **Visual/performing arts:** Acting, art history/conservation, dramatic, studio arts, theater design.

Most popular majors. Business/marketing 15%, engineering/engineering technologies 6%, family/consumer sciences 6%, health sciences 7%, liberal arts 8%, psychology 8%, social sciences 15%.

Computing on campus. 1,318 workstations in dormitories, library, computer center. Dormitories linked to campus network. Online course registration, helpline available.

Student life. Freshman orientation: Available, $60 fee. Preregistration for classes offered. 12 two-day sessions extending from late May to early July. **Housing:** Coed dorms, single-sex dorms, special housing for disabled, apartments, fraternity/sorority housing, substance-free housing available. $150 nonrefundable deposit, deadline 5/1. Foreign language house, Living Learning Center, laboratory science house, engineering floors, designated floors for older students, honors, special interest floors. **Activities:** Bands, choral groups, dance, drama, film society, literary magazine, music ensembles, musical theater, opera, radio station, student government, student newspaper, symphony orchestra, TV station, over 300 organizations available.

Athletics. NCAA. **Intercollegiate:** Baseball M, basketball, cross-country, diving, field hockey W, football (tackle) M, golf M, ice hockey, lacrosse W, rowing (crew) W, soccer, softball W, swimming, tennis, track and field, volleyball W. **Intramural:** Badminton, baseball M, basketball, bowling, cross-country, diving, equestrian, fencing, football (non-tackle), football (tackle) M, ice hockey, lacrosse, racquetball, rowing (crew), rugby, sailing, skiing, soccer, softball, squash, swimming, table tennis, tennis, track and field, volleyball, water polo, weight lifting M. **Team name:** Huskies.

Student services. Adult student services, alcohol/substance abuse counseling, campus ministries, career counseling, student employment services, financial aid counseling, health services, minority student services, on-campus daycare, personal counseling, placement for graduates, veterans' counselor, women's services. **Physically disabled:** Services for visually, speech, hearing impaired.

Contact. E-mail: beahusky@uconnvm.uconn.edu
Phone: (860) 486-3137 Fax: (860) 486-1476
Lee Melvin, Director of Admission, University of Connecticut, 2131 Hillside Road, Unit 3088, Storrs, CT 06269-3088

University of Hartford

West Hartford, Connecticut — **CB member**
www.hartford.edu — **CB code: 3436**

- Private 4-year university
- Residential campus in small city
- 5,289 degree-seeking undergraduates: 12% part-time, 51% women, 10% African American, 3% Asian American, 5% Hispanic American, 3% international
- 1,542 degree-seeking graduate students
- 66% of applicants admitted
- SAT or ACT with writing required
- 54% graduate within 6 years

General. Founded in 1877. Regionally accredited. **Degrees:** 934 bachelor's, 177 associate awarded; master's, doctoral offered. **ROTC:** Army, Air Force. **Location:** 4 miles from downtown. **Calendar:** Semester, extensive summer session. **Full-time faculty:** 325 total; 81% have terminal degrees, 11% minority, 36% women. **Part-time faculty:** 428 total; 4% minority, 48% women. **Class size:** 60% < 20, 39% 20-39, less than 1% 40-49, less than 1% 50-99, less than 1% >100. **Special facilities:** Science center, museum of American political life, engineering applications center, humanities center.

Freshman class profile. 12,065 applied, 7,973 admitted, 1,469 enrolled.

Mid 50% test scores		Return as sophomores:	78%
SAT verbal:	480-580	Out-of-state:	69%
SAT math:	490-590	Live on campus:	90%
ACT:	21-25	International:	2%

Basis for selection. Quality of academic program, school achievement record, class rank important. Test scores secondary. Employment, extracurricular activities, and community service considered. Writing samples and interview also considered. Admission committee can offer admission to alternative program. SAT or ACT can be submitted on a rolling basis. Interview and essay recommended. Audition required of music, dance, acting majors. Portfolio required of art majors.

High school preparation. 16 units required. Required and recommended units include English 4, mathematics 2-3, social studies 2, history 2, science 2-3, foreign language 2 and academic electives 4. Physics, chemistry, and 3.5 math (including trigonometry) recommended for engineering and science applicants.

2006-2007 Annual costs. Tuition/fees: $25,766. Room/board: $9,922. Books/supplies: $860. Personal expenses: $1,350.

2004-2005 Financial aid. **Need-based:** 991 full-time freshmen applied for aid; 865 were judged to have need; 863 of these received aid. Average need met was 60%. Average scholarship/grant was $11,833; average loan $3,061. 57% of total undergraduate aid awarded as scholarships/grants, 43% as loans/jobs. **Non-need-based:** Awarded to 2,531 full-time undergraduates, including 736 freshmen. Scholarships awarded for academics, art, athletics, music/drama.

Application procedures. **Admission:** No deadline. $35 fee, may be waived for applicants with need. Application may be submitted online. Admission notification on a rolling basis beginning on or about 10/1. Must reply by May 1 or within 2 week(s) if notified thereafter. **Financial aid:** Priority date 2/1; no closing date. FAFSA, institutional form required. Applicants notified on a rolling basis starting 3/1; must reply by 5/1.

Academics. **Special study options:** Combined bachelor's/graduate degree, cooperative education, cross-registration, distance learning, double major, dual enrollment of high school students, ESL, exchange student, honors, independent study, internships, liberal arts/career combination, student-designed major, study abroad, teacher certification program, Washington semester. **Credit/placement by examination:** AP, CLEP, SAT, institutional tests. 30 credit hours maximum toward associate degree, 60 toward bachelor's. **Support services:** Learning center, reduced course load, tutoring, writing center.

Majors. **Area/ethnic studies:** Women's. **Biology:** General. **Business:** Accounting, business admin, entrepreneurial studies, finance, insurance, management information systems, marketing. **Communications:** General. **Computer sciences:** General, information systems. **Education:** Early childhood, elementary, music, secondary, special. **Engineering:** General, civil, computer, electrical, mechanical. **Engineering technology:** General, architectural, computer, electrical, environmental, mechanical. **English:** English lit, technical writing. **Foreign languages:** General. **Health:** Clinical lab science, medical radiologic technology/radiation therapy, nursing (RN), respiratory therapy technology. **History:** General. **Legal studies:** General. **Math:** General. **Philosophy/religion:** Judaic, philosophy. **Physical sciences:** Chemistry, physics. **Protective services:** Police science. **Psychology:** General. **Public administration:** Community org/advocacy. **Social sciences:** Economics, international economics, political science, sociology. **Visual/performing arts:** General, acting, art history/conservation, ceramics, cinematography, commercial/advertising art, dance, design, dramatic, drawing, film/cinema, jazz, music history, music management, music performance, music theory/composition, painting, photography, printmaking, sculpture.

Most popular majors. Business/marketing 18%, communications/journalism 10%, education 9%, engineering/engineering technologies 12%, health sciences 10%, visual/performing arts 19%.

Computing on campus. 300 workstations in dormitories, library, computer center. Dormitories wired for high-speed internet access and linked to campus network. Commuter students can connect to campus network. Online course registration, online library, helpline, repair service, student web hosting, wireless network available.

Student life. **Freshman orientation:** Mandatory. **Policies:** Freshmen permitted cars on campus. **Housing:** Guaranteed on-campus for freshmen. Coed dorms, single-sex dorms, special housing for disabled, apartments available. $200 deposit, deadline 2/1. Dormitories with resident faculty members, International residential college, residential college for the arts available. **Activities:** Bands, choral groups, dance, drama, literary magazine, music ensembles, musical theater, opera, radio station, student government, student newspaper, symphony orchestra, TV station, Hillel foundation, Protestant student organization, Newman Club, African American students association, academic department clubs, prelaw and premedical societies, Brothers and Sisters United, Global Friends Association, Malaysian student association, Turkish student association.

Athletics. NCAA. **Intercollegiate:** Baseball M, basketball, cross-country, golf, lacrosse M, soccer, softball W, tennis, track and field, volleyball W. **Intramural:** Basketball, football (non-tackle), handball, racquetball, soccer, softball, tennis, volleyball, water polo. **Team name:** Hawks.

Student services. Campus ministries, career counseling, student employment services, financial aid counseling, health services, minority student services, personal counseling, placement for graduates, veterans' counselor.

Contact. Phone: (860) 768-4296 Fax: (860) 768-4961
Richard Zeiser, Dean of Admission, University of Hartford, Bates House, West Hartford, CT 06117-1599

University of New Haven

West Haven, Connecticut — **CB member**
www.newhaven.edu — **CB code: 3663**

- Private 4-year university
- Residential campus in small city
- 2,744 degree-seeking undergraduates: 16% part-time, 49% women, 8% African American, 2% Asian American, 6% Hispanic American, 2% international
- 1,664 degree-seeking graduate students
- 73% of applicants admitted
- SAT or ACT (ACT writing optional), application essay required
- 44% graduate within 6 years

General. Founded in 1920. Regionally accredited. **Degrees:** 385 bachelor's, 58 associate awarded; master's offered. **Location:** 3 miles from downtown, 75 miles from New York City. **Calendar:** 4-1-4, limited summer session. **Full-time faculty:** 162 total; 85% have terminal degrees, 13% minority, 23% women. **Part-time faculty:** 308 total; 19% have terminal degrees, 6% minority, 40% women. **Class size:** 44% < 20, 53% 20-39, 3% 40-49, less than 1% 50-99. **Special facilities:** Theater, music and sound recording studio, shoreline environmental study preserve, institute of forensic science.

Freshman class profile. 3,051 applied, 2,233 admitted, 664 enrolled.

Mid 50% test scores		Return as sophomores:	77%
SAT verbal:	460-570	Out-of-state:	54%
SAT math:	470-580	Live on campus:	81%
GPA 3.0-3.49:	55%	International:	1%
GPA 2.0-2.99:	45%	Fraternities:	5%
Rank in top quarter:	41%	Sororities:	8%
Rank in top tenth:	16%		

Basis for selection. Academic record, recommendations, test scores, personal essay, advanced placement or honor courses, and extracurricular activities reviewed. **Learning Disabled:** No special admissions requirements or procedures. Students required to meet with the Disability Services Office in order to receive accommodations and/or services.

High school preparation. Required units include English 4, mathematics 3, social studies 2, science 2 (laboratory 2) and foreign language 2.

2005-2006 Annual costs. Tuition/fees: $22,982. Room/board: $9,550. Books/supplies: $750. Personal expenses: $1,000.

2005-2006 Financial aid. **Need-based:** 577 full-time freshmen applied for aid; 505 were judged to have need; 505 of these received aid. Average need met was 68%. Average scholarship/grant was $12,317; average loan $3,320. 73% of total undergraduate aid awarded as scholarships/grants, 27% as loans/jobs. **Non-need-based:** Awarded to 490 full-time undergraduates, including 172 freshmen. Scholarships awarded for academics, athletics.

Application procedures. **Admission:** No deadline. $50 fee, may be waived for applicants with need. Application may be submitted online. Admission notification on a rolling basis beginning on or about 12/1. Must reply by May 1 or within 2 week(s) if notified thereafter. **Financial aid:** Closing date 3/1. FAFSA, institutional form required. Applicants notified on a rolling basis starting 3/15; must reply by 5/1 or within 2 week(s) of notification.

Academics. **Special study options:** Accelerated study, combined bachelor's/graduate degree, cooperative education, distance learning, double major, honors, independent study, internships, study abroad, teacher certification program. **Credit/placement by examination:** AP, CLEP, IB, institutional tests. **Support services:** Learning center, reduced course load, remedial instruction, study skills assistance, tutoring, writing center.

Majors. **Architecture:** Interior. **Biology:** General, ecology, marine. **Business:** Accounting, business admin, finance, hospitality admin, hotel/motel admin, international, managerial economics, marketing. **Communications:** General. **Computer sciences:** General, information systems. **Conservation:** General. **Engineering:** General, chemical, civil, computer, electrical, mechanical. **Engineering technology:** Occupational safety. **English:** English lit. **Health:** Dental hygiene, dietetics. **History:** General. **Interdisciplinary:** Nutrition sciences. **Legal studies:** General. **Liberal arts:** Arts/sciences. **Math:** General, applied. **Parks/recreation:** Sports admin. **Physical sciences:** Chemistry. **Protective services:** Fire safety technology, firefighting, forensics, law enforcement admin. **Psychology:** General. **Public administration:** General. **Science technology:** Biological. **Social sciences:** Political science. **Visual/performing arts:** Graphic design, interior design, music management, studio arts.

Most popular majors. Business/marketing 20%, engineering/engineering technologies 12%, security/protective services 40%, visual/performing arts 8%.

Computing on campus. 300 workstations in dormitories, library, computer center, student center. Dormitories wired for high-speed internet access and linked to campus network. Helpline available.

Student life. **Freshman orientation:** Available. **Housing:** Coed dorms, apartments available. $200 nonrefundable deposit, deadline 5/1. Living/Learning Community available for freshmen engineering majors. **Activities:** Pep band, choral groups, dance, drama, literary magazine, radio station, student government, student newspaper.

Athletics. NCAA. **Intercollegiate:** Baseball M, basketball, cheerleading, cross-country, golf M, lacrosse W, soccer, softball, tennis W, track and field, volleyball. **Intramural:** Basketball, bowling, cross-country, football (non-tackle) M, lacrosse M, racquetball, soccer, softball W, table tennis, tennis, volleyball, weight lifting. **Team name:** Chargers.

Student services. Career counseling, student employment services, financial aid counseling, health services, minority student services, personal counseling, placement for graduates, veterans' counselor, women's services. **Physically disabled:** Services for visually, speech, hearing impaired.

Contact. E-mail: adminfo@newhaven.edu
Phone: (203) 932-7319 Toll-free number: (800) 342-5864
Fax: (203) 931-6093
Jane Sangeloty, Director of Undergraduate Admissions, University of New Haven, 300 Boston Post Road, West Haven, CT 06516

Wesleyan University

Middletown, Connecticut — **CB member**
www.wesleyan.edu — **CB code: 3959**

- Private 4-year university and liberal arts college
- Residential campus in large town
- 2,737 degree-seeking undergraduates: 52% women, 7% African American, 10% Asian American, 7% Hispanic American, 6% international
- 269 degree-seeking graduate students
- 28% of applicants admitted
- SAT and SAT Subject Tests or ACT (ACT writing optional), application essay required
- 90% graduate within 6 years

General. Founded in 1831. Regionally accredited. **Degrees:** 725 bachelor's awarded; master's, doctoral offered. **ROTC:** Air Force. **Location:** 15 miles from Hartford, 25 miles from New Haven. **Calendar:** Semester, limited summer session. **Full-time faculty:** 325 total; 17% minority, 38% women. **Part-time faculty:** 43 total; 14% minority, 46% women. **Class size:** 66% < 20, 26% 20-39, 4% 40-49, 3% 50-99, 1% >100. **Special facilities:** 11-building arts center, observatory, science center with electron microscopes and nuclear magnetic resonance spectrometers, film archives, center for humanities, East Asian Studies Center, Center for African-American Studies.

Freshman class profile. 6,879 applied, 1,902 admitted, 717 enrolled.

Mid 50% test scores		Return as sophomores:	96%
SAT verbal:	650-750	Out-of-state:	90%
SAT math:	650-740	Live on campus:	100%
ACT:	28-32	International:	7%
Rank in top tenth:	71%		

Basis for selection. GED not accepted. High school transcript, class rank, test scores, extracurricular activities, 2 teacher evaluations, personal statement, and other evidence of outstanding accomplishments considered. If SAT scores are submitted, candidates must also submit scores from 2 SAT Subject Tests. Interview recommended. **Homeschooled:** Campus interview strongly recommended.

High school preparation. 16 units required; 20 recommended. Required and recommended units include English 4, mathematics 3-4, social studies 3-4, science 3-4 (laboratory 3) and foreign language 3-4.

2006-2007 Annual costs. Tuition/fees: $35,144. Room/board: $9,540.

2004-2005 Financial aid. All financial aid based on need. 403 full-time freshmen applied for aid; 327 were judged to have need; 327 of these received aid. Average need met was 100%. Average scholarship/grant was $23,568; average loan $2,595. 78% of total undergraduate aid awarded as scholarships/grants, 22% as loans/jobs.

Application procedures. **Admission:** Closing date 1/1 (receipt date). $55 fee, may be waived for applicants with need. Application may be submitted online. Admission notification 4/1. Must reply by 5/1. **Financial aid:** Closing date 2/15. FAFSA, institutional form, CSS PROFILE required. Applicants notified by 4/1; must reply by 5/1 or within 2 week(s) of notification.

Academics. Students expected to complete 3 classes in each of following areas before graduation: natural sciences and mathematics, arts and humanities, social and behavioral sciences. **Special study options:** Combined bachelor's/graduate degree, cross-registration, double major, dual enrollment of high school students, exchange student, honors, independent study, internships, liberal arts/career combination, semester at sea, student-designed major, study abroad, urban semester, Washington semester. 12-college exchange, semester in environmental science at the Marine Biological Laboratory-Woods Hole, Wesleyan-Trinity-Connecticut College Consortium, 3-2 program in science and engineering, teaching apprentice program. **Credit/placement by examination:** AP, CLEP, IB, institutional tests. 2 credit hours maximum toward bachelor's degree. **Support services:** Reduced course load, tutoring, writing center.

Majors. **Area/ethnic studies:** African-American, American, Central/Eastern European, East Asian, Latin American, Russian/Slavic, women's. **Biology:** General, biochemistry, molecular. **Computer sciences:** General. **Conservation:** General. **Foreign languages:** Classics, French, German, Italian, Romance, Russian, Spanish. **History:** General. **Interdisciplinary:** Ancient studies, medieval/Renaissance, neuroscience, science/society. **Liberal arts:** Arts/sciences. **Math:** General. **Philosophy/religion:** Philosophy, religion. **Physical sciences:** Astronomy, chemistry, geology, physics, planetary. **Psychology:** General. **Social sciences:** Anthropology, archaeology, economics, political science, sociology. **Visual/performing arts:** Art history/conservation, dance, dramatic, film/cinema, studio arts.

Most popular majors. Area/ethnic studies 13%, English 11%, psychology 11%, social sciences 27%, visual/performing arts 12%.

Computing on campus. 300 workstations in library, computer center, student center. Dormitories wired for high-speed internet access and linked to campus network. Commuter students can connect to campus network. Online course registration, helpline, repair service, wireless network available.

Student life. **Freshman orientation:** Mandatory. Preregistration for classes offered. Held a week before start of fall classes. **Policies:** Freshmen permitted cars on campus. **Housing:** Guaranteed on-campus for all undergraduates. Coed dorms, special housing for disabled, apartments, fraternity/sorority housing, substance-free housing available. 29 special interest housing options for upperclass students. **Activities:** Bands, choral groups, dance, drama, film society, literary magazine, music ensembles, musical theater, radio station, student government, student newspaper, symphony orchestra, more than 230 religious, political, ethnic, and social service organizations.

Athletics. NCAA. **Intercollegiate:** Baseball M, basketball, cross-country, diving, field hockey W, football (tackle) M, golf M, ice hockey, lacrosse, rowing (crew), soccer, softball W, squash, swimming, tennis, track and field, volleyball W, wrestling M. **Intramural:** Ice hockey M, soccer, volleyball. **Team name:** Cardinals.

Student services. Adult student services, alcohol/substance abuse counseling, campus ministries, career counseling, student employment services, financial aid counseling, health services, minority student services, on-campus daycare, personal counseling, placement for graduates, women's services. **Physically disabled:** Services for visually, speech, hearing impaired.

Contact. E-mail: admissions@wesleyan.edu
Phone: (860) 685-3000 Fax: (860) 685-3001
Nancy Meislahn, Dean of Admission and Financial Aid, Wesleyan University, 70 Wyllys Avenue, Middletown, CT 06459-0260

Western Connecticut State University

Danbury, Connecticut
www.wcsu.edu — **CB code: 3350**

- Public 4-year university
- Commuter campus in small city
- 4,720 degree-seeking undergraduates: 16% part-time, 56% women, 6% African American, 3% Asian American, 6% Hispanic American, 1% international
- 604 degree-seeking graduate students
- 58% of applicants admitted
- SAT or ACT with writing required

General. Founded in 1903. Regionally accredited. **Degrees:** 683 bachelor's, 11 associate awarded; master's, doctoral offered. **ROTC:** Army, Air Force. **Location:** 65 miles from New York City, 50 miles from Hartford. **Calendar:** Semester, extensive summer session. **Full-time faculty:** 223 total. **Part-time faculty:** 320 total. **Class size:** 27% < 20, 66% 20-39, 7% 40-49, less than 1% 50-99. **Special facilities:** Weather station, motorized astronomical observatory, nature preserve, computer-enhanced classrooms.

Freshman class profile. 3,469 applied, 2,029 admitted, 788 enrolled.

Mid 50% test scores		Rank in top tenth:	7%
SAT verbal:	450-550	Out-of-state:	13%
SAT math:	440-540	Live on campus:	59%
Rank in top quarter:	25%		

Basis for selection. Limited freshman class spaces given to students with strongest academic and extracurricular backgrounds, including test results. Freshman class will be filled on a "first-come" basis by major. Essay and interview recommended. Audition required of music majors. Portfolio recommended of graphic design majors.

High school preparation. 13 units required. Required and recommended units include English 4, mathematics 3, social studies 1, history 1, science 2 (laboratory 2) and foreign language 2-3. Additional credits in fine arts and computer science recommended.

2005-2006 Annual costs. Tuition/fees: $5,800; $13,739 out-of-state. Room/board: $7,353. Books/supplies: $1,000. Personal expenses: $1,750.

2004-2005 Financial aid. **Need-based:** 43% of total undergraduate aid awarded as scholarships/grants, 57% as loans/jobs. **Non-need-based:** Scholarships awarded for academics.

Application procedures. **Admission:** Priority date 4/1; no deadline. $40 fee, may be waived for applicants with need. Application may be submitted online. Admission notification on a rolling basis beginning on or about 12/1. Must reply by May 1 or within 2 week(s) if notified thereafter. **Financial aid:** Priority date 3/15, closing date 4/15. FAFSA, institutional form required. Applicants notified on a rolling basis starting 3/15; must reply by 5/1 or within 2 week(s) of notification.

Academics. Math/computer science clinic available. **Special study options:** Accelerated study, cooperative education, cross-registration, distance learning, double major, dual enrollment of high school students, ESL, honors, independent study, internships, student-designed major, study abroad, teacher certification program. **Credit/placement by examination:** AP, CLEP, IB, institutional tests. 30 credit hours maximum toward associate degree, 60 toward bachelor's. **Support services:** Learning center, pre-admission summer program, reduced course load, remedial instruction, study skills assistance, tutoring, writing center.

Majors. **Area/ethnic studies:** American. **Biology:** General. **Business:** Accounting, business admin, finance, management information systems, marketing. **Communications:** General. **Computer sciences:** General. **Education:** Elementary, health, music, secondary. **English:** Composition. **Foreign languages:** Spanish. **Health:** Clinical lab science, community health services, nursing (RN). **History:** General. **Interdisciplinary:** Math/computer science. **Liberal arts:** Arts/sciences. **Math:** General. **Physical sciences:** Atmospheric science, chemistry, planetary. **Protective services:** Law enforcement admin, police science. **Psychology:** General. **Public administration:** Social work. **Social sciences:** General, anthropology, economics, political science, sociology. **Visual/performing arts:** Art, commercial/advertising art, dramatic, music theory/composition.

Most popular majors. Business/marketing 26%, communications/journalism 8%, education 11%, health sciences 9%, psychology 6%, security/protective services 11%, social sciences 12%.

Computing on campus. 430 workstations in library, computer center, student center. Dormitories wired for high-speed internet access and linked to campus network. Commuter students can connect to campus network. Student web hosting available.

Student life. **Freshman orientation:** Available. Preregistration for classes offered. 2-day program for students and parents held the weekend before classes start. **Policies:** Freshmen permitted cars on campus. **Housing:** Guaranteed on-campus for all undergraduates. Coed dorms, single-sex dorms, apartments available. $200 deposit. **Activities:** Bands, choral groups, dance, drama, literary magazine, music ensembles, musical theater, opera, radio station, student government, student newspaper, symphony orchestra, black student alliance, religious groups, nontraditional student, international student associations, Habitat for Humanity, Latin American student organizations.

Athletics. NCAA. **Intercollegiate:** Baseball M, basketball, field hockey W, football (tackle) M, lacrosse, soccer, softball W, swimming W, tennis, volleyball W. **Intramural:** Basketball, football (non-tackle) M, soccer, softball, triathlon, volleyball. **Team name:** Colonials.

Student services. Adult student services, alcohol/substance abuse counseling, campus ministries, career counseling, student employment services, financial aid counseling, health services, minority student services, on-campus daycare, personal counseling, placement for graduates, veterans' counselor. **Physically disabled:** Services for visually, speech, hearing impaired.

Contact. Phone: (203) 837-9000 Toll-free number: (877) 837-9278
Fax: (203) 837-8338
William Hawkins, Enrollment Management Officer, Western Connecticut State University, 181 White Street, Danbury, CT 06810

Yale University

New Haven, Connecticut — **CB member**
www.yale.edu — **CB code: 3987**

- Private 4-year university
- Residential campus in small city
- 5,349 degree-seeking undergraduates: 49% women, 8% African American, 14% Asian American, 7% Hispanic American, 1% Native American, 8% international
- 5,989 degree-seeking graduate students
- 10% of applicants admitted
- SAT and SAT Subject Tests or ACT (ACT writing optional), application essay required
- 96% graduate within 6 years; 13% enter graduate study

General. Founded in 1701. Regionally accredited. **Degrees:** 1,291 bachelor's awarded; master's, doctoral, first professional offered. **ROTC:** Army, Air Force. **Location:** 75 miles from New York City. **Calendar:** Semester, limited summer session. **Full-time faculty:** 1,054 total; 90% have terminal degrees, 16% minority, 33% women. **Part-time faculty:** 376 total; 72% have terminal degrees, 11% minority, 38% women. **Class size:** 76% < 20, 14% 20-39, 2% 40-49, 5% 50-99, 3% >100. **Special facilities:** Natural history museum, clean room, wind tunnel, engine testing facility, graphic workstations, robotics labs, crystal growth, nuclear accelerators, nuclear magnetic resonance spectrometers, optical spectroscopy instruments, high-resolution mass spectrometer, x-ray diffraction instruments, electron microscopes, observatories, marine studies field station, Institute for Biospheric Studies, 10,000 acres of forest.

Freshman class profile. 19,451 applied, 1,880 admitted, 1,321 enrolled.

Mid 50% test scores		Rank in top tenth:	95%
SAT verbal:	700-790	Return as sophomores:	98%
SAT math:	700-790	Out-of-state:	93%
ACT:	31-34	Live on campus:	100%
Rank in top quarter:	99%	International:	7%

Basis for selection. First criterion is evidence of ability to do successful academic work. Diversity of interests, background and special talents also sought. Successful candidates usually have done honors work at secondary level, have high SAT scores, and present high degree of accomplishment in one or more nonacademic areas. Interview recommended. **Homeschooled:** Require 2 recommendations from teachers of courses taken outside home, such as community college courses.

High school preparation. No prescribed high school program required, but students recommended to take richest possible mix of demanding academic offerings.

2006-2007 Annual costs. Tuition/fees: $33,030. Room/board: $10,020. Books/supplies: $2,520.

2004-2005 Financial aid. All financial aid based on need. 802 full-time freshmen applied for aid; 578 were judged to have need; 578 of these received aid. Average need met was 100%. Average scholarship/grant was $25,415; average loan $1,447. 85% of total undergraduate aid awarded as scholarships/grants, 15% as loans/jobs. **Additional information:** All scholarships based on demonstrated need.

Application procedures. **Admission:** Closing date 12/31 (postmark date). $65 fee, may be waived for applicants with need. Application must be submitted on paper. Admission notification 4/1. Must reply by 5/1. **Financial aid:** Closing date 3/1. FAFSA, CSS PROFILE required. Applicants notified by 4/1; must reply by 5/1 or within 1 week(s) of notification.

Academics. **Special study options:** Accelerated study, combined bachelor's/graduate degree, double major, ESL, exchange student, honors, independent study, internships, student-designed major, study abroad, teacher certification program. **Credit/placement by examination:** AP, CLEP, IB, institutional tests. **Support services:** Study skills assistance, tutoring, writing center.

Majors. **Architecture:** Architecture. **Area/ethnic studies:** African, African-American, American, East Asian, European, Latin American, Russian/Slavic, women's. **Biology:** General, biochemistry, Biochemistry/biophysics and molecular biology, molecular. **Computer sciences:** General. **Engineering:** Biomedical, chemical, electrical, environmental, mechanical, physics, science. **English:** English lit. **Foreign languages:** Ancient Greek, Biblical, Chinese, classics, French, German, Italian, Japanese, Latin, linguistics, Portuguese, Russian, Spanish. **History:** General, science/technology. **Interdisciplinary:** Ancient studies, cognitive science, math/computer science, medieval/ Renaissance. **Liberal arts:** Humanities. **Math:** General, applied. **Philosophy/ religion:** Judaic, philosophy, religion. **Physical sciences:** Astronomy, astrophysics, chemistry, geology, physics. **Psychology:** General. **Social sciences:** Anthropology, archaeology, economics, political science, sociology. **Visual/performing arts:** Art, art history/conservation, dramatic, film/ cinema.

Most popular majors. Area/ethnic studies 6%, biology 8%, English 9%, history 13%, interdisciplinary studies 8%, psychology 6%, social sciences 27%, visual/performing arts 8%.

Computing on campus. 400 workstations in dormitories, library, computer center, student center. Dormitories wired for high-speed internet access and linked to campus network. Commuter students can connect to campus network. Online course registration, online library, helpline, student web hosting, wireless network available.

Student life. Freshman orientation: Mandatory. **Policies:** Freshmen permitted cars on campus. **Housing:** Guaranteed on-campus for freshmen. Coed dorms, special housing for disabled available. **Activities:** Bands, choral groups, dance, drama, film society, literary magazine, music ensembles, musical theater, opera, radio station, student government, student newspaper, symphony orchestra, TV station, over 135 organizations available.

Athletics. NCAA. **Intercollegiate:** Baseball M, basketball, cross-country, diving, fencing, field hockey W, football (tackle) M, golf, gymnastics W, ice hockey, lacrosse, rowing (crew), soccer, softball W, squash, swimming, tennis, track and field, volleyball W. **Intramural:** Baseball M, basketball, bowling, cross-country, field hockey W, football (tackle) M, golf, ice hockey, racquetball, rowing (crew), soccer, softball, squash, swimming, table tennis, tennis, volleyball, water polo, wrestling M. **Team name:** Bulldogs.

Student services. Alcohol/substance abuse counseling, campus ministries, career counseling, student employment services, financial aid counseling, health services, minority student services, personal counseling, placement for graduates, women's services. **Physically disabled:** Services for visually, speech, hearing impaired.

Contact. E-mail: undergraduate.admissions@yale.edu
Phone: (203) 432-9300 Fax: (203) 432-9392
Jeffrey Brenzel, Dean of Undergraduate Admissions, Yale University, Box 208234, New Haven, CT 06520-8234

Delaware

Delaware State University
Dover, Delaware **CB member**
www.desu.edu **CB code: 5153**

- Public 4-year university and liberal arts college
- Commuter campus in large town
- 3,440 degree-seeking undergraduates: 14% part-time, 58% women
- 282 degree-seeking graduate students
- 64% of applicants admitted
- SAT or ACT (ACT writing optional) required

General. Founded in 1891. Regionally accredited. University has its own fleet of planes. **Degrees:** 368 bachelor's awarded; master's, doctoral offered. **ROTC:** Army, Air Force. **Location:** 46 miles from Wilmington, 100 miles from Washington, D.C. **Calendar:** Semester, extensive summer session. **Full-time faculty:** 177 total. **Part-time faculty:** 107 total. **Special facilities:** Science center, observatory, herbarium.

Freshman class profile. 3,691 applied, 2,378 admitted, 940 enrolled.

Mid 50% test scores			
SAT verbal:	360-450	ACT:	14-17
SAT math:	360-450	Out-of-state:	59%
		Live on campus:	77%

Basis for selection. High school curriculum and GPA most important. Test scores only used in conjunction with GPA. Class rank considered. Interview recommended for nursing majors, some academically weak applicants.

High school preparation. 16 units required. Required units include English 4, mathematics 3, social studies 2, science 3 (laboratory 3) and academic electives 4. Math units must include 2 courses in algebra and course in geometry.

2005-2006 Annual costs. Tuition/fees: $5,480; $11,704 out-of-state. Room/board: $7,642. Books/supplies: $1,050. Personal expenses: $777.

2005-2006 Financial aid. All financial aid based on need. 33% of total undergraduate aid awarded as scholarships/grants, 67% as loans/jobs.

Application procedures. Admission: No deadline. $25 fee. Admission notification on a rolling basis beginning on or about 9/1. **Financial aid:** Priority date 3/1, closing date 4/17. FAFSA required. Applicants notified on a rolling basis starting 4/1.

Academics. Special study options: Accelerated study, cooperative education, distance learning, double major, ESL, exchange student, honors, independent study, internships, study abroad, teacher certification program, weekend college. **Credit/placement by examination:** CLEP, IB. 30 credit hours maximum toward bachelor's degree. **Support services:** Learning center, pre-admission summer program, reduced course load, remedial instruction, study skills assistance, tutoring.

Majors. Agriculture: Business, plant sciences, soil science. **Biology:** General, biotechnology. **Business:** Accounting, finance, hospitality admin, marketing. **Communications:** Broadcast journalism, journalism, public relations. **Computer sciences:** General, computer science, information systems. **Conservation:** Fisheries, management/policy, wildlife. **Education:** General, art, biology, business, early childhood, elementary, English, foreign languages, French, gifted/talented, health, mathematics, middle, music, physical, physics, science, social studies, Spanish, special, trade/industrial. **Engineering technology:** Civil, electrical. **English:** Speech/rhetoric. **Family/consumer sciences:** Clothing/textiles, food/nutrition. **Foreign languages:** French, Spanish. **Health:** Environmental health, nursing (RN), preveterinary. **History:** General. **Interdisciplinary:** Historic preservation, math/computer science. **Math:** General. **Parks/recreation:** Facilities management, health/fitness, sports admin. **Physical sciences:** Chemistry, physics. **Protective services:** Criminal justice. **Psychology:** General. **Public administration:** Social work. **Social sciences:** Political science, sociology. **Transportation:** Aviation, aviation management. **Visual/performing arts:** Art, arts management, dramatic.

Computing on campus. 361 workstations in library, computer center. Dormitories linked to campus network. Helpline, repair service available.

Student life. Freshman orientation: Mandatory. **Housing:** Coed dorms, single-sex dorms, apartments available. $200 deposit, deadline 4/15. Suite style accommodations available for upper class students and honor students, residence hall available for honors students. **Activities:** Bands, choral groups, dance, music ensembles, radio station, student government, student newspaper, TV station, Wesley Foundation, United Campus Ministry, commuters club, NAACP, international students association, black studies club, student government association, honor societies, Greek letter organizations, student ambassadors.

Athletics. NCAA. **Intercollegiate:** Baseball M, basketball, bowling W, cross-country, football (tackle) M, soccer W, softball W, tennis, track and field, volleyball W, wrestling M. **Intramural:** Basketball, bowling, soccer, softball, swimming, table tennis, tennis, track and field, volleyball. **Team name:** Hornets.

Student services. Adult student services, career counseling, health services, on-campus daycare, personal counseling, placement for graduates, veterans' counselor. **Physically disabled:** Services for visually, speech, hearing impaired.

Contact. E-mail: admissions@desu.edu
Phone: (302) 857-6351 Toll-free number: (800) 845-2544
Fax: (302) 857-6352
L. Germaine Scott-Cheatham, Director of Admissions, Delaware State University, 1200 North DuPont Highway, Dover, DE 19901

Goldey-Beacom College
Wilmington, Delaware **CB member**
www.gbc.edu **CB code: 5255**

- Private 4-year business college
- Commuter campus in small city
- 450 full-time, degree-seeking undergraduates
- 225 graduate students

General. Founded in 1886. Regionally accredited. **Degrees:** 193 bachelor's, 45 associate awarded; master's offered. **Location:** 15 miles from downtown, 36 miles from Philadelphia. **Calendar:** Semester, limited summer session. **Full-time faculty:** 30 total. **Part-time faculty:** 40 total.

Freshman class profile.

Out-of-state:	60%	Live on campus:	46%

Basis for selection. School record most important. Test scores important for bachelor's degree applicants. Associate degree applicants may be required to take placement tests. Interview recommended.

High school preparation. 16 units recommended. Recommended units include English 4, mathematics 3 and science 3. 3 math units required for bachelor's degree applicants.

2005-2006 Annual costs. Tuition/fees: $13,736. Room only: $4,240. Books/supplies: $600. Personal expenses: $1,068.

Financial aid. All financial aid based on need. **Additional information:** Essays required for scholarship applicants.

Application procedures. Admission: Priority date 5/1; deadline 8/15. $30 fee, may be waived for applicants with need. Admission notification on a rolling basis beginning on or about 10/1. Must reply by May 1 or within 2 week(s) if notified thereafter. SAT not required but recommended for associate degree applicants for placement and counseling. **Financial aid:** Priority date 4/1; no closing date. FAFSA required. Applicants notified on a rolling basis starting 2/15; must reply within 2 week(s) of notification.

Academics. Special study options: Accelerated study, combined bachelor's/graduate degree, cooperative education, cross-registration, distance learning, double major, honors, independent study, internships, liberal arts/career combination. **Credit/placement by examination:** AP, CLEP, IB, institutional tests. **Support services:** Learning center, reduced course load, remedial instruction, tutoring.

Majors. Business: Accounting, business admin, international, management information systems, management science, marketing. **Computer sciences:** General.

Most popular majors. Business/marketing 89%, computer/information sciences 11%.

Computing on campus. 200 workstations in dormitories, library, computer center. Dormitories wired for high-speed internet access and linked to campus network. Commuter students can connect to campus network. Online library, wireless network available.

Student life. Freshman orientation: Available. Preregistration for classes offered. **Policies:** Freshmen permitted cars on campus. **Housing:** Guaranteed on-campus for all undergraduates. Coed dorms, special housing for disabled, apartments, fraternity/sorority housing, substance-free housing available. $395 deposit. Apartment-style residence halls. **Activities:** Choral groups, drama, student government, student newspaper, Christian Fellowship, minority student union, Circle-K, international student association.

Athletics. NAIA, NCAA. **Intercollegiate:** Basketball, cross-country, golf M, soccer, softball W, tennis W, volleyball W. **Intramural:** Basketball M, cheerleading W, soccer M, softball, volleyball. **Team name:** Lightning.

Student services. Career counseling, student employment services, financial aid counseling, health services, personal counseling, placement for graduates. **Physically disabled:** Services for visually, speech, hearing impaired.

Contact. E-mail: admissions@gbc.edu
Phone: (302) 225-6248 Toll-free number: (800) 833-4877
Fax: (302) 996-5408
Stacey Schwartz, Assistant Director of Admission, Goldey-Beacom College, 4701 Limestone Road, Wilmington, DE 19808

University of Delaware

Newark, Delaware — **CB member**
www.udel.edu — **CB code: 5811**

- Public 4-year university
- Residential campus in large town
- 15,742 degree-seeking undergraduates: 5% part-time, 58% women, 6% African American, 3% Asian American, 4% Hispanic American, 1% international
- 3,238 degree-seeking graduate students
- 47% of applicants admitted
- SAT or ACT with writing, application essay required
- 76% graduate within 6 years

General. Founded in 1743. Regionally accredited. **Degrees:** 3,602 bachelor's, 14 associate awarded; master's, doctoral offered. **ROTC:** Army, Air Force. **Location:** 12 miles from Wilmington, 30 miles from Philadelphia. **Calendar:** 4-1-4, limited summer session. **Full-time faculty:** 1,126 total; 84% have terminal degrees, 15% minority, 37% women. **Part-time faculty:** 244 total; 35% have terminal degrees, 9% minority, 48% women. **Class size:** 34% < 20, 41% 20-39, 8% 40-49, 12% 50-99, 5% >100. **Special facilities:** Science development center, human performance laboratory, greenhouse, preschool lab, nutrition clinic, engineering research centers, 400-acre agriculture research complex, center for composites manufacturing and research, apparel design laboratory, simulated hospital rooms for nursing, physical therapy clinic, applied coastal research, Delaware biotechnology institute.

Freshman class profile. 21,617 applied, 10,256 admitted, 3,522 enrolled.

Mid 50% test scores			
SAT verbal:	550-640	GPA 2.0-2.99:	10%
SAT math:	560-660	Rank in top quarter:	76%
ACT:	24-29	Rank in top tenth:	37%
GPA 3.50 or higher:	61%	Return as sophomores:	89%
GPA 3.0-3.49:	29%	Out-of-state:	67%
		Live on campus:	93%

Basis for selection. High school record, program of study, test scores most important. References, essay, extracurricular accomplishments considered. SAT Subject Tests recommended. Particularly recommended that honors program applicants take SAT Subject Tests. Audition or portfolio required for music or art. **Homeschooled:** Transcript of courses and grades required. Students should provide reading lists for home-schooled courses they have completed. Sample portfolio of work or sample research paper recommended. Home-schooled applicants should submit at least 2 SAT Subject Tests of their choice. In lieu of SAT Reasoning Test and SAT Subject Tests, students may submit ACT with Writing score.

High school preparation. 18 units required; 22 recommended. Required and recommended units include English 4, mathematics 3-4, social studies 2, history 2, science 3-4 (laboratory 2-3), foreign language 2-4 and academic electives 2. 4 math strongly recommended for engineering, business, science or math applicants. 4 laboratory science strongly recommended for science, nursing, and engineering applicants.

2005-2006 Annual costs. Tuition/fees: $7,318; $17,474 out-of-state. Room/board: $6,824. Books/supplies: $800. Personal expenses: $1,500.

2005-2006 Financial aid. All financial aid based on need. 2,597 full-time freshmen applied for aid; 1,391 were judged to have need; 1,391 of these received aid. Average need met was 77%. Average scholarship/grant was $6,600; average loan $4,000. 48% of total undergraduate aid awarded as scholarships/grants, 52% as loans/jobs. **Additional information:** December 15 application deadline to receive scholarship consideration. Sibling/parent tuition credit plan. Senior citizen tuition credit for state residents over 60.

Application procedures. Admission: Priority date 12/15; deadline 1/15 (postmark date). $60 fee, may be waived for applicants with need. Application may be submitted online. Admission notification 3/15. Must reply by May 1 or within 3 week(s) if notified thereafter. **Financial aid:** Priority date 2/1, closing date 3/15. FAFSA required. Applicants notified on a rolling basis starting 3/15; must reply by 5/1 or within 3 week(s) of notification.

Academics. Special study options: Accelerated study, cooperative education, distance learning, double major, dual enrollment of high school students, ESL, honors, independent study, internships, liberal arts/career combination, student-designed major, study abroad, teacher certification program, Washington semester. Research program, minors in 68 disciplines, five-year engineering/liberal arts option. **Credit/placement by examination:** AP, CLEP, IB, SAT, institutional tests. For credit/placement to be awarded for International Baccalaureate, applicant must have taken higher level courses and have minimum score of 4 on exams. **Support services:** Pre-admission summer program, reduced course load, remedial instruction, study skills assistance, tutoring, writing center.

Honors college/program. Program emphasizes small classes, undergraduate research, honors housing, special scholarship opportunities. Special application required.

Majors. Agriculture: Agribusiness operations, agronomy, animal sciences, business, economics, food science, ornamental horticulture, plant sciences, soil science. **Area/ethnic studies:** Latin American, women's. **Biology:** General, biochemistry, biotechnology, entomology, plant pathology. **Business:** Accounting, business admin, fashion, finance, management information systems, operations. **Communications:** General, journalism. **Computer sciences:** General. **Conservation:** General, management/policy, wildlife. **Education:** General, agricultural, biology, chemistry, early childhood, elementary, English, ESL, family/consumer sciences, foreign languages, French, geography, German, health, history, mathematics, middle, music, physical, physics, psychology, science, secondary, social science, Spanish, special. **Engineering:** Aerospace, agricultural, biomedical, chemical, civil, computer, electrical, environmental, mechanical, operations research. **Family/consumer sciences:** General, child care, family studies, family/community services, food/nutrition. **Foreign languages:** General, Biblical, classics, comparative lit, French, German, Italian, Latin, Russian, Spanish. **Health:** Athletic training, clinical lab science, clinical lab technology, nursing (RN), predentistry, premedicine, prepharmacy, preveterinary. **History:** General. **Interdisciplinary:** Historic preservation, nutrition sciences. **Legal studies:** Prelaw. **Liberal arts:** Arts/sciences. **Math:** General, statistics. **Parks/recreation:** Exercise sciences, facilities management, health/fitness, sports admin. **Philosophy/religion:** Philosophy. **Physical sciences:** Astronomy, chemistry, geology, geophysics, physics, planetary. **Protective services:** Criminal justice. **Psychology:** General. **Social sciences:** Anthropology, economics, geography, international relations, political science, sociology. **Visual/performing arts:** Art, art history/conservation, commercial/advertising art, fashion design, music performance, music theory/composition, piano/organ, studio arts, theater design, theater history, voice/opera.

Most popular majors. Business/marketing 17%, education 12%, engineering/engineering technologies 7%, English 6%, family/consumer sciences 6%, health sciences 6%, psychology 6%, social sciences 14%.

Computing on campus. 900 workstations in dormitories, library, computer center. Dormitories wired for high-speed internet access and linked to campus network. Commuter students can connect to campus network. Online course registration, online library, helpline, repair service, student web hosting, wireless network available.

Student life. Freshman orientation: Mandatory, $65 fee. Preregistration for classes offered. One-day summer program, plus 3-day program before start of classes. **Policies:** Freshmen permitted cars on campus. **Housing:** Guaranteed on-campus for all undergraduates. Coed dorms, single-sex dorms, special housing for disabled, apartments, fraternity/sorority housing, substance-free housing available. $100 partly refundable deposit, deadline 5/1. Special interest housing including language houses, humanities house, honors hall, music house, international house, farmhouse, education house. Alcohol- and smoke-free residence hall available. Freshmen under the age of 21 must live on-campus or at home with parent or guardian. **Activities:** Bands, choral groups, dance, drama, literary magazine, music ensembles, musical theater, opera, radio station, student government, student newspaper, symphony orchestra, TV station, black student union, Asian student association, Cosmopolitan Club, Hillel, Hispanic student association, Indian student association, lesbian, gay, bisexual student union, returning adult student association, honorary academic clubs.

Athletics. NCAA. **Intercollegiate:** Baseball M, basketball, cheerleading, cross-country, diving, field hockey W, football (tackle) M, golf M, lacrosse, rowing (crew) W, soccer, softball W, swimming, tennis, track and field, volleyball W. **Intramural:** Badminton, basketball, cross-country, fencing, field hockey W, golf, lacrosse, racquetball, soccer, softball, table tennis, tennis, volleyball, water polo M. **Team name:** Fightin' Blue Hens.

Student services. Adult student services, alcohol/substance abuse counseling, campus ministries, career counseling, services for economically disadvantaged, student employment services, financial aid counseling, health services, minority student services, personal counseling, placement for graduates, veterans' counselor, women's services. **Physically disabled:** Services for visually, speech, hearing impaired.

Contact. E-mail: admissions@udel.edu
Phone: (302) 831-8123 Fax: (302) 831-6905
Lou Hirsh, Director of Admission, University of Delaware, 116 Hullihen Hall, Newark, DE 19716

Wesley College

Dover, Delaware **CB member**
www.wesley.edu **CB code: 5894**

- Private 4-year liberal arts college affiliated with United Methodist Church
- Residential campus in large town
- 1,864 degree-seeking undergraduates
- 173 graduate students
- 57% of applicants admitted

General. Founded in 1873. Regionally accredited. **Degrees:** 247 bachelor's, 80 associate awarded; master's offered. **ROTC:** Army. **Location:** 75 miles from Philadelphia, 90 miles from Washington, D.C. **Calendar:** Semester, limited summer session. **Full-time faculty:** 61 total; 87% have terminal degrees, 8% minority, 46% women. **Part-time faculty:** 74 total; 27% have terminal degrees, 4% minority, 43% women. **Class size:** 48% < 20, 52% 20-39.

Freshman class profile. 2,408 applied, 1,363 admitted, 529 enrolled.

Mid 50% test scores			
SAT verbal:	460-530	Out-of-state:	75%
SAT math:	470-530	Live on campus:	80%
Rank in top quarter:	42%	Fraternities:	1%
Rank in top tenth:	17%	Sororities:	1%

Basis for selection. High school performance most important. Campus interview very important. Extracurricular activities important. SAT or ACT recommended.

High school preparation. 16 units required. Required and recommended units include English 4, mathematics 2, social studies 2, history 2, science 2 (laboratory 2), foreign language 2 and academic electives 2.

2005-2006 Annual costs. Tuition/fees: $15,379. Room/board: $6,960. Books/supplies: $1,000. Personal expenses: $750.

2005-2006 Financial aid. All financial aid based on need. 466 full-time freshmen applied for aid; 389 were judged to have need; 389 of these received aid. Average need met was 85%. Average scholarship/grant was $5,500; average loan $2,200. 53% of total undergraduate aid awarded as scholarships/grants, 47% as loans/jobs.

Application procedures. Admission: Priority date 4/1; deadline 8/20. $25 fee. Application may be submitted online. Admission notification on a rolling basis beginning on or about 10/1. Must reply by May 1 or within 4 week(s) if notified thereafter. **Financial aid:** Priority date 4/15; no closing date. FAFSA, institutional form required. Applicants notified on a rolling basis starting 3/15; must reply within 2 week(s) of notification.

Academics. Credit requirement for bachelor's degree varies according to program. **Special study options:** Double major, ESL, exchange student, independent study, internships, liberal arts/career combination, study abroad, teacher certification program. **Credit/placement by examination:** AP, CLEP, institutional tests. 15 credit hours maximum toward associate degree, 33 toward bachelor's. **Support services:** Learning center, reduced course load, remedial instruction, study skills assistance, tutoring, writing center.

Majors. Area/ethnic studies: American. **Biology:** General. **Business:** Accounting, business admin, sales/distribution. **Communications:** General. **Conservation:** Environmental studies. **Education:** General, elementary, physical. **Health:** Clinical lab science, nursing (RN). **History:** General. **Legal studies:** Paralegal. **Liberal arts:** Arts/sciences. **Parks/recreation:** Health/fitness. **Psychology:** General. **Social sciences:** Economics, political science.

Most popular majors. Business/marketing 43%, communications/journalism 6%, education 16%, parks/recreation 8%, psychology 11%, social sciences 6%.

Computing on campus. 225 workstations in library. Dormitories wired for high-speed internet access and linked to campus network. Commuter students can connect to campus network. Online course registration, online library, helpline, repair service available.

Student life. Freshman orientation: Mandatory. Preregistration for classes offered. **Policies:** Freshmen permitted cars on campus. **Housing:** Coed dorms, single-sex dorms, apartments, substance-free housing available. $175 deposit, deadline 8/20. Floors in coed dorms are single-sex. **Activities:** Jazz band, choral groups, drama, literary magazine, music ensembles, student government, student newspaper, TV station, community action, Christian student associations, student activity board, National Coed Community Service Organization, black student union.

Athletics. NCAA. **Intercollegiate:** Baseball M, basketball, cheerleading, cross-country, field hockey W, football (tackle) M, golf, lacrosse, soccer, softball W, tennis, volleyball W. **Intramural:** Basketball, cross-country, soccer M, volleyball. **Team name:** Wolverines.

Student services. Campus ministries, career counseling, student employment services, financial aid counseling, health services, personal counseling, placement for graduates. **Physically disabled:** Services for speech impaired.

Contact. E-mail: admissions@wesley.edu
Phone: (302) 736-2400 Toll-free number: (800) 937-5398
Fax: (302) 736-2400
Arthur Jacobs, Director of Admissions, Wesley College, 120 North State Street, Dover, DE 19901-3875

Wilmington College

New Castle, Delaware **CB member**
www.wilmcoll.edu **CB code: 5925**

- Private 4-year liberal arts college
- Commuter campus in large town
- 4,220 degree-seeking undergraduates
- 2,765 graduate students

General. Founded in 1967. Regionally accredited. Two 7-week sessions within each trimester in addition to regular trimester sessions and weekend modules. **Degrees:** 810 bachelor's, 34 associate awarded; master's, doctoral offered. **ROTC:** Army, Air Force. **Location:** 7 miles from Wilmington. **Calendar:** Trimester, limited summer session. **Full-time faculty:** 67 total; 4% minority, 46% women. **Part-time faculty:** 488 total; 48% women. **Class size:** 76% < 20, 24% 20-39.

Basis for selection. Open admission. Math and English skills testing required of all freshmen. Interview recommended. **Homeschooled:** GED recommended for nonaccredited programs.

2005-2006 Annual costs. Tuition/fees: $7,670. Books/supplies: $1,000. Personal expenses: $165.

2005-2006 Financial aid. Need-based: 10% of total undergraduate aid awarded as scholarships/grants, 90% as loans/jobs. **Non-need-based:** Scholarships awarded for academics, athletics.

Application procedures. Admission: No deadline. $25 fee, may be waived for applicants with need. Admission notification on a rolling basis. **Financial aid:** Priority date 4/30; no closing date. FAFSA required. Applicants notified on a rolling basis starting 8/5; must reply within 2 week(s) of notification.

Academics. Mentoring program for all interested incoming freshmen. **Special study options:** Accelerated study, distance learning, double major, independent study, internships, liberal arts/career combination, teacher certification program, weekend college. **Credit/placement by examination:** AP, CLEP, institutional tests. 15 credit hours maximum toward associate degree, 15 toward bachelor's. **Support services:** Learning center, remedial instruction, tutoring, writing center.

Majors. Business: Accounting, finance, human resources, information resources management, marketing. **Computer sciences:** General, programming, web page design. **Education:** Early childhood, elementary. **Engineering technology:** Software. **Health:** Preop/surgical nursing. **Interdisciplinary:** Behavioral sciences. **Legal studies:** Prelaw. **Liberal arts:** Arts/sciences. **Protective services:** Criminal justice. **Psychology:** General. **Transportation:** Aviation, aviation management.

Computing on campus. 516 workstations in library, computer center.

Student life. Freshman orientation: Available. Videotaped orientation distributed to all new students. Two new student orientations offered in the fall. **Policies:** Adherence to student handbook expected. **Activities:** Student government, professional fraternities/organizations, Sigma Theta Tau Nursing Society, Business Professionals of America, Alpha Delta Chi, criminal justice club.

Athletics. NCAA. **Intercollegiate:** Baseball M, basketball, cross-country, golf M, lacrosse W, soccer, softball W, volleyball W. **Team name:** Wildcats.

Student services. Career counseling, student employment services, financial aid counseling, placement for graduates.

Contact. E-mail: inquire@wilmcoll.edu
Phone: (302) 328-9447 Toll-free number: (877) 967-5464
Fax: (302) 328-5902
Christopher Ferguson, Director of Admissions, Wilmington College, 320 Dupont Highway, New Castle, DE 19720

District of Columbia

American University
Washington, District of Columbia **CB member**
www.american.edu **CB code: 5007**

- Private 4-year university affiliated with United Methodist Church
- Residential campus in very large city
- 5,788 degree-seeking undergraduates: 4% part-time, 62% women, 6% African American, 5% Asian American, 5% Hispanic American, 6% international
- 5,145 degree-seeking graduate students
- 51% of applicants admitted
- SAT or ACT with writing, application essay required
- 71% graduate within 6 years

General. Founded in 1893. Regionally accredited. **Degrees:** 1,419 bachelor's awarded; master's, doctoral, first professional offered. **ROTC:** Army, Air Force. **Location:** 2 miles from downtown. **Calendar:** Semester, extensive summer session. **Full-time faculty:** 509 total; 95% have terminal degrees, 18% minority, 45% women. **Part-time faculty:** 513 total; 96% have terminal degrees, 45% women. **Class size:** 44% < 20, 46% 20-39, 6% 40-49, 3% 50-99, less than 1% >100. **Special facilities:** Art galleries, theatres, spiritual life center, NPR affiliated radio.

Freshman class profile. 13,583 applied, 6,973 admitted, 1,223 enrolled.

Mid 50% test scores		**Rank in top quarter:**	82%
SAT verbal:	600-690	**Rank in top tenth:**	47%
SAT math:	580-670	**Return as sophomores:**	89%
ACT:	26-30	**Out-of-state:**	88%
GPA 3.50 or higher:	53%	**Live on campus:**	99%
GPA 3.0-3.49:	40%	**International:**	2%
GPA 2.0-2.99:	7%		

Basis for selection. High school record, GPA, test scores, writing sample, recommendations most important. Breadth and rigor of curriculum, 4-year trend (grade improvement) also important. Extracurricular activities, class rank, and leadership roles considered. SAT Subject Tests recommended. Interview recommended. Audition/interview required of music and music theater majors. Portfolio required of fine arts majors. **Homeschooled:** Should submit at least three SAT Subject Test scores, including math. **Learning Disabled:** Supplementary application, diagnostic reports, and high school transcript required for freshman learning services program. All other LD/ADD students have access to full range of services.

High school preparation. 16 units required; 18 recommended. Required and recommended units include English 4, mathematics 3-4, social studies 2-4, science 2-4 (laboratory 2), foreign language 2-3 and academic electives 3-4.

2006-2007 Annual costs. Tuition/fees (projected): $29,673. Room/board: $11,240. Books/supplies: $600. Personal expenses: $1,300.

2005-2006 Financial aid. All financial aid based on need. 911 full-time freshmen applied for aid; 630 were judged to have need; 629 of these received aid. Average need met was 68%. Average scholarship/grant was $13,745; average loan $5,784. 55% of total undergraduate aid awarded as scholarships/grants, 45% as loans/jobs. **Additional information:** Early decision applicants must submit estimated AU Institutional financial aid application by 11/15 and a FASFA as soon as possible after Jan 1.

Application procedures. Admission: Closing date 1/15 (receipt date). $45 fee, may be waived for applicants with need. Application must be submitted on paper. Admission notification 4/1. Must reply by May 1 or within 4 week(s) if notified thereafter. **Financial aid:** Closing date 2/15. FAFSA, institutional form required. Applicants notified by 4/1; must reply by 5/1 or within 4 week(s) of notification.

Academics. Academic integrity code. **Special study options:** Accelerated study, combined bachelor's/graduate degree, cooperative education, cross-registration, double major, exchange student, honors, independent study, internships, student-designed major, study abroad, teacher certification program, Washington semester, weekend college. AU's study abroad program sends students to 48 different countries on 84 different programs including (but not limited to) programs in Peru, Chile, Brazil, London, Rome, Brussels, Copenhagen, Beijing/Hong Kong, Buenos Aires, Paris, Madrid, Madrid and the Mediterranean, Moscow, Prague, Poland, South Africa, Scotland, Turkey, Italy, Canada, Mexico City and Monterey, and Australia/New Zealand. AU also offers other study abroad programs such as Alternative Break Programs and specialized programs in AU's School of International Service, KOGOD School of Business, and Washington College of Law. **Credit/placement by examination:** AP, CLEP, IB, institutional tests. 30 credit hours maximum toward bachelor's degree. Credit awarded for some international high school learning programs such as BritishAlevelsor GermanArbitur; Advanced Placement, International Baccalaureate higher level tests only. **Support services:** Learning center, pre-admission summer program, reduced course load, study skills assistance, tutoring, writing center.

Majors. Area/ethnic studies: American, French, German, Latin American, Russian/Slavic, women's. **Biology:** General, biochemistry, environmental, marine, toxicology. **Business:** Accounting, business admin, finance, management information systems. **Communications:** Journalism, media studies, public relations, radio/tv. **Communications technology:** Animation/special effects, recording arts. **Computer sciences:** General, computer graphics, computer science, webmaster. **Conservation:** Environmental studies. **Education:** Elementary, secondary. **English:** English lit. **Foreign languages:** French, German, Russian, Spanish. **Health:** Predentistry, premedicine, prenursing, prepharmacy, preveterinary. **History:** General. **Interdisciplinary:** Biological/physical sciences, global studies. **Legal studies:** General, prelaw. **Liberal arts:** Arts/sciences. **Math:** General, applied, statistics. **Parks/recreation:** Health/fitness, sports admin. **Philosophy/religion:** Judaic, philosophy. **Physical sciences:** Acoustics, chemistry, physics. **Protective services:** Criminal justice, police science. **Psychology:** General. **Social sciences:** Anthropology, economics, international relations, political science, sociology. **Visual/performing arts:** General, art, art history/conservation, cinematography, design, dramatic, film/cinema, graphic design, multimedia, music history, music performance, music theory/composition, studio arts.

Most popular majors. Business/marketing 18%, communications/journalism 12%, social sciences 35%, visual/performing arts 7%.

Computing on campus. 650 workstations in dormitories, library, computer center, student center. Dormitories wired for high-speed internet access and linked to campus network. Commuter students can connect to campus network. Online course registration, online library, helpline, repair service, student web hosting, wireless network available.

Student life. Freshman orientation: Available, $110 fee. Preregistration for classes offered. 2-day programs in late June and early July. Students take placement exams, meet advisers. Parents may attend. **Housing:** Guaranteed on-campus for freshmen. Coed dorms, special housing for disabled, apartments, substance-free housing available. $200 deposit, deadline 5/1. Honors floors, wellness floor, and intercultural/international hall available. Housing for handicapped students handled individually; community service floor available. Some single-sex floors in coed dorms. **Activities:** Bands, choral groups, dance, drama, film society, literary magazine, music ensembles, musical theater, opera, radio station, student government, student newspaper, symphony orchestra, TV station, NAACP, Kennedy Political Union (nonpartisan), Amnesty International, Habitat for Humanity, Asia Students Association, Student Confederation, Concert Choir, Hillel, Latin American Student Organization.

Athletics. NCAA. **Intercollegiate:** Basketball, cross-country, diving, field hockey W, golf M, lacrosse W, soccer, swimming, tennis, track and field, volleyball W, wrestling M. **Intramural:** Basketball, bowling, cheerleading W, equestrian, football (non-tackle) M, sailing, soccer, softball, volleyball. **Team name:** Eagles.

Student services. Adult student services, alcohol/substance abuse counseling, campus ministries, career counseling, student employment services, financial aid counseling, health services, minority student services, on-campus daycare, personal counseling, placement for graduates, veterans' counselor, women's services. **Physically disabled:** Services for visually, speech, hearing impaired.

Contact. E-mail: admissions@american.edu
Phone: (202) 885-6000 Fax: (202) 885-6014
Sharon Alston, Director of Admissions, American University, 4400 Massachusetts Avenue NW, Washington, DC 20016-8001

Catholic University of America
Washington, District of Columbia **CB member**
www.cua.edu **CB code: 5104**

- Private 4-year university affiliated with Roman Catholic Church
- Residential campus in very large city
- 3,007 degree-seeking undergraduates: 8% part-time, 57% women, 7% African American, 3% Asian American, 5% Hispanic American, 2% international

- 2,955 degree-seeking graduate students
- 81% of applicants admitted
- SAT or ACT with writing, application essay required
- 73% graduate within 6 years; 41% enter graduate study

General. Founded in 1887. Regionally accredited. Internship and study opportunities with Congress, federal agencies, and international embassies. **Degrees:** 563 bachelor's awarded; master's, doctoral, first professional offered. **ROTC:** Army, Navy, Air Force. **Calendar:** Semester, limited summer session. **Full-time faculty:** 344 total; 98% have terminal degrees, 10% minority, 36% women. **Part-time faculty:** 370 total; 3% minority, 38% women. **Class size:** 57% < 20, 35% 20-39, 4% 40-49, 4% 50-99. **Special facilities:** Anthropology and art department museums, rare book collection, university archives, on-campus nuclear reactor and vitreous state laboratory.

Freshman class profile. 3,152 applied, 2,561 admitted, 792 enrolled.

Mid 50% test scores		**Rank in top tenth:**	23%
SAT verbal:	530-630	**Return as sophomores:**	82%
SAT math:	510-620	**Out-of-state:**	98%
ACT:	21-27	**Live on campus:**	94%
GPA 3.50 or higher:	43%	**International:**	3%
GPA 3.0-3.49:	31%	**Fraternities:**	1%
GPA 2.0-2.99:	26%	**Sororities:**	1%
Rank in top quarter:	54%		

Basis for selection. GED not accepted. School achievement record, class rank, test scores most important. Recommendations, extracurricular activities also important. SAT Subject Tests recommended. Applicants to School of Arts and Sciences and School of Philosophy should submit SAT Subject Test foreign language score. Audition required of music majors. **Homeschooled:** Statement describing homeschool structure and mission, transcript of courses and grades, state high school equivalency certificate, interview, letter of recommendation (nonparent) required. **Learning Disabled:** Students who submit documented evidence of learning disabilities may receive special consideration.

High school preparation. 17 units recommended. Recommended units include English 4, mathematics 3, social studies 4, history 1, science 3 (laboratory 1) and foreign language 2.

2006-2007 Annual costs. Tuition/fees: $27,440. Full-time tuition for the School of Engineering is $26,400. Full-time tuition for the School of Architecture is $26,800. Part-time tuition for the School of Architecture is $1,000 per-credit-hour. Room/board: $10,330. Books/supplies: $1,000. Personal expenses: $1,500.

2005-2006 Financial aid. Need-based: 587 full-time freshmen applied for aid; 448 were judged to have need; 447 of these received aid. Average need met was 84%. Average scholarship/grant was $13,234; average loan $3,730. 59% of total undergraduate aid awarded as scholarships/grants, 41% as loans/jobs. **Non-need-based:** Awarded to 1,105 full-time undergraduates, including 319 freshmen. Scholarships awarded for academics, alumni affiliation, leadership, music/drama, religious affiliation, state residency.

Application procedures. Admission: Closing date 2/1 (postmark date). $55 fee, may be waived for applicants with need. Application may be submitted online. Admission notification 3/1. Must reply by May 1 or within 2 week(s) if notified thereafter. **Financial aid:** Priority date 2/1, closing date 4/15. FAFSA required. Applicants notified on a rolling basis starting 4/1; must reply by 5/1 or within 2 week(s) of notification.

Academics. Students must have minimum cumulative GPA of 2.0 at end of semester to be in good academic standing. **Special study options:** Accelerated study, combined bachelor's/graduate degree, cross-registration, double major, dual enrollment of high school students, ESL, honors, independent study, internships, study abroad, teacher certification program, Washington semester. **Credit/placement by examination:** AP, CLEP, IB, institutional tests. All credit-by-examination awarded on case-by-case basis. No credit by outside examination given to matriculated students. **Support services:** Learning center, pre-admission summer program, reduced course load, study skills assistance, tutoring, writing center.

Majors. Architecture: Architecture. **Biology:** General, biochemistry. **Business:** General, accounting, finance, human resources, international finance, management science. **Communications:** General. **Computer sciences:** General. **Education:** General, biology, chemistry, drama/dance, early childhood, elementary, English, ESL, history, mathematics, music, secondary, Spanish. **Engineering:** Biomedical, civil, computer, electrical, mechanical. **Foreign languages:** Classics, French, German, Latin, modern Greek, Spanish. **Health:** Clinical lab science, nursing (RN). **History:** General. **Interdisciplinary:** Medieval/Renaissance. **Liberal arts:** Arts/sciences. **Math:** General. **Philosophy/religion:** Philosophy, religion. **Physical sciences:** Chemistry, molecular physics, physics. **Psychology:** General. **Public administration:** Social work. **Social sciences:** Anthropology, economics, political science, sociology. **Visual/performing arts:** Art, art history/conservation, dramatic, music history, music performance, music theory/composition, piano/organ, voice/opera.

Most popular majors. Architecture 12%, business/marketing 7%, communications/journalism 8%, history 7%, psychology 9%, social sciences 11%, visual/performing arts 11%.

Computing on campus. 500 workstations in dormitories, library, computer center, student center. Dormitories wired for high-speed internet access and linked to campus network. Commuter students can connect to campus network. Online course registration, online library, helpline, repair service, student web hosting, wireless network available.

Student life. Freshman orientation: Mandatory. Held Thursday-Sunday before start of fall semester. **Housing:** Coed dorms, single-sex dorms, apartments available. $400 nonrefundable deposit, deadline 5/15. Residential college, thematic housing, honors housing available. **Activities:** Bands, choral groups, dance, drama, film society, literary magazine, music ensembles, musical theater, opera, radio station, student government, student newspaper, symphony orchestra, Community Action Network, Black Organization of Students, Best Buddies, Muslim Student Association, Hispanic Association, Young Republicans, Young Democrats, program board, campus ministry.

Athletics. NCAA. **Intercollegiate:** Baseball M, basketball, cross-country, field hockey W, football (tackle) M, lacrosse, soccer, softball W, swimming, tennis, track and field, volleyball W. **Intramural:** Basketball, football (tackle), racquetball, soccer, softball, tennis, volleyball. **Team name:** Cardinals.

Student services. Adult student services, alcohol/substance abuse counseling, campus ministries, career counseling, student employment services, health services, legal services, minority student services, personal counseling, placement for graduates, veterans' counselor. **Physically disabled:** Services for visually, speech, hearing impaired.

Contact. E-mail: cua-admissions@cua.edu
Phone: (202) 319-5305 Toll-free number: (800) 673-2772
Fax: (202) 319-6533
Christine Mica, Director of University Admissions, Catholic University of America, Office of Undergraduate Admissions, Washington, DC 20064

Corcoran College of Art and Design

Washington, District of Columbia — **CB member**
www.corcoran.edu — **CB code: 5705**

- Private 4-year visual arts college
- Commuter campus in very large city
- 393 degree-seeking undergraduates: 13% part-time, 65% women, 8% African American, 10% Asian American, 8% Hispanic American
- 70 degree-seeking graduate students
- 61% of applicants admitted
- SAT or ACT (ACT writing optional) required
- 64% graduate within 6 years

General. Founded in 1890. Regionally accredited. **Degrees:** 75 bachelor's, 5 associate awarded; master's offered. **Calendar:** Semester, limited summer session. **Full-time faculty:** 34 total; 41% have terminal degrees, 44% women. **Part-time faculty:** 187 total; 33% have terminal degrees, 55% women. **Class size:** 94% < 20, 6% 20-39. **Special facilities:** Student and alumni exhibition spaces.

Freshman class profile. 233 applied, 143 admitted, 52 enrolled.

Mid 50% test scores		**Rank in top quarter:**	35%
SAT verbal:	490-620	**Rank in top tenth:**	20%
SAT math:	470-540	**End year in good standing:**	98%
ACT:	14-23	**Return as sophomores:**	69%
GPA 3.50 or higher:	22%	**Out-of-state:**	90%
GPA 3.0-3.49:	45%	**Live on campus:**	79%
GPA 2.0-2.99:	33%		

Basis for selection. Class rank, school achievement record, art portfolio, interview, motivation important. Letters of recommendation and personal statement encouraged. School and community activities, test scores considered. Portfolio required (slides or CD may replace original portfolio). Essay recommended. Interview required of Washington, DC-area (within 200 miles) resident applicants.

High school preparation. Recommended units include English 4 and history 4. Advanced art courses also recommended.

2005-2006 Annual costs. Tuition/fees: $22,800. Room only: $8,150. Books/supplies: $2,300. Personal expenses: $1,050.

2004-2005 Financial aid. **Need-based:** 67 full-time freshmen applied for aid; 67 were judged to have need; 67 of these received aid. Average need met was 42%. Average scholarship/grant was $4,640; average loan $3,506. 53% of total undergraduate aid awarded as scholarships/grants, 47% as loans/jobs. **Non-need-based:** Awarded to 264 full-time undergraduates, including 49 freshmen. Scholarships awarded for academics, art.

Application procedures. **Admission:** Priority date 3/15; no deadline. $40 fee, may be waived for applicants with need. Application may be submitted online. Admission notification on a rolling basis. Must reply by May 1 or within 2 week(s) if notified thereafter. **Financial aid:** Priority date 4/15; no closing date. FAFSA, institutional form required. Applicants notified on a rolling basis starting 4/15; must reply by 5/1 or within 2 week(s) of notification.

Academics. **Special study options:** Combined bachelor's/graduate degree, exchange student, internships, study abroad. Mobility programs with 11 member schools of Art College Exchange and 8 members of the Association of Independent Colleges of Art and Design. **Credit/placement by examination:** AP, CLEP, IB, SAT, ACT. 15 credit hours maximum toward bachelor's degree. **Support services:** Reduced course load, study skills assistance, tutoring, writing center.

Majors. **Education:** Art. **Visual/performing arts:** General, art, graphic design, photography, studio arts.

Computing on campus. PC or laptop required. 89 workstations in library, computer center, student center. Dormitories wired for high-speed internet access. Commuter students can connect to campus network. Online library, wireless network available.

Student life. **Freshman orientation:** Mandatory. Preregistration for classes offered. Mandatory session introducing college, museum, faculty, majors, city. **Policies:** Freshmen permitted cars on campus. **Housing:** Guaranteed on-campus for freshmen. Coed dorms, apartments available. $400 nonrefundable deposit, deadline 5/15. **Activities:** Film society, student government.

Student services. Alcohol/substance abuse counseling, career counseling, student employment services, financial aid counseling, personal counseling, placement for graduates, veterans' counselor.

Contact. E-mail: admissions@corcoran.org
Phone: (202) 639-1814 Toll-free number: (888) 267-2672
Fax: (202) 639-1830
Elizabeth Paladino, Director of Admissions, Corcoran College of Art and Design, 500 17th Street, N.W., Washington, DC 20006-4804

Gallaudet University

Washington, District of Columbia
www.gallaudet.edu **CB code: 5240**

- Private 4-year university and liberal arts college
- Residential campus in very large city
- 1,213 degree-seeking undergraduates
- 76% of applicants admitted
- SAT or ACT (ACT writing optional), application essay required

General. Founded in 1857. Regionally accredited. Only liberal arts university in the world designed exclusively for deaf and hard of hearing students. Bilingual (English/American Sign Language), multicultural environment, assistive devices (TTY's or campus phones, closed captioned television and campus films), specially-designed classrooms and dormitories available. **Degrees:** 172 bachelor's awarded; master's, doctoral offered. **Calendar:** Semester, limited summer session. **Full-time faculty:** 235 total. **Class size:** 92% < 20, 8% 20-39. **Special facilities:** Gallaudet Interpreting Services (GIS) provides interpreters for university-related events.

Freshman class profile. 478 applied, 361 admitted, 280 enrolled.

Mid 50% test scores			
SAT verbal:	320-550	ACT:	14-18
SAT math:	360-520	Out-of-state:	99%

Basis for selection. Applicants with hearing loss who show evidence of academic ability and motivation considered. Test scores, grades, class rank, essay, recommendation important. Interview recommended. **Learning Disabled:** Untimed tests, psychological evaluations confirming disabilities required.

High school preparation. 16 units recommended. Recommended units include English 4, mathematics 4, social studies 4, history 4, science 4 (laboratory 2).

2005-2006 Annual costs. Tuition/fees: $10,150. Non-resident alien tuition reduction to $14,445 for students in developing countries, if approved. Room/board: $8,650. Books/supplies: $834. Personal expenses: $2,852.

2005-2006 Financial aid. **Need-based:** 84% of total undergraduate aid awarded as scholarships/grants, 16% as loans/jobs. **Non-need-based:** Scholarships awarded for academics. **Additional information:** Institution receives substantial aid from state vocational rehabilitation agencies, supplemented by institutional grants when needed.

Application procedures. **Admission:** No deadline. $50 fee, may be waived for applicants with need. Application may be submitted online. Admission notification on a rolling basis. **Financial aid:** Priority date 7/1; no closing date. FAFSA, institutional form required. Applicants notified on a rolling basis starting 4/1; must reply within 4 week(s) of notification.

Academics. Undergraduate degree program open to deaf and hard of hearing students and a limited number of hearing students; visiting and exchange student programs available to any qualified student. **Special study options:** Accelerated study, combined bachelor's/graduate degree, cooperative education, cross-registration, double major, dual enrollment of high school students, ESL, exchange student, honors, independent study, internships, liberal arts/career combination, student-designed major, study abroad, teacher certification program. Experiential programs off-campus including orientation program for employers of deaf students and paraprofessional jobs on campus, programs for interpreter-assisted mainstreaming of students into area colleges such as Georgetown University, George Mason University, Catholic University, Howard University. **Credit/placement by examination:** AP, CLEP, institutional tests. **Support services:** Learning center, preadmission summer program, reduced course load, remedial instruction, study skills assistance, tutoring, writing center.

Majors. **Biology:** General. **Business:** General, accounting, business admin, entrepreneurial studies, management information systems. **Communications:** General, broadcast journalism. **Computer sciences:** General, computer science, information systems. **Education:** General, art, Deaf/hearing impaired, early childhood, elementary, family/consumer sciences, multiple handicapped, physical, secondary. **English:** British lit. **Family/consumer sciences:** General, child care, food/nutrition. **Foreign languages:** American Sign Language, French, Spanish. **Health:** Recreational therapy. **History:** General. **Math:** General. **Parks/recreation:** Facilities management. **Philosophy/religion:** Philosophy. **Physical sciences:** Chemistry, physics. **Psychology:** General. **Public administration:** Social work. **Social sciences:** Criminology, economics, political science, sociology. **Visual/performing arts:** General, art history/conservation, commercial/advertising art, dramatic, studio arts.

Most popular majors. Education 26%, health sciences 9%, psychology 15%, security/protective services 11%.

Computing on campus. 352 workstations in dormitories, library, computer center, student center. Dormitories wired for high-speed internet access and linked to campus network. Commuter students can connect to campus network. Online course registration, online library, helpline, repair service, student web hosting, wireless network available.

Student life. **Freshman orientation:** Mandatory. Preregistration for classes offered. Held 1 week before beginning of semester. **Policies:** Freshman dorms are "dry." No smoking in residence halls. Students must be full time to reside in dorm. Freshmen permitted cars on campus. **Housing:** Guaranteed on-campus for freshmen. Coed dorms, special housing for disabled, apartments available. $150 deposit, deadline 6/1. All dormitories equipped for deaf and hard of hearing students. **Activities:** Dance, drama, film society, literary magazine, student government, student newspaper, TV station, Asian Pacific Association, Black Deaf Student Union, Hispanic Student Association, International Student Club, Literary Society.

Athletics. NCAA. **Intercollegiate:** Baseball M, basketball, cross-country, football (tackle) M, soccer, softball W, swimming, tennis, track and field, volleyball, wrestling M. **Intramural:** Basketball, football (non-tackle) M, softball, volleyball. **Team name:** Bisons.

Student services. Adult student services, alcohol/substance abuse counseling, campus ministries, career counseling, student employment services, health services, minority student services, on-campus daycare, personal counseling, placement for graduates. **Physically disabled:** Services for visually, speech, hearing impaired.

Contact. E-mail: admissions@gallaudet.edu
Phone: (202) 651-5750 Toll-free number: (800) 995-0550
Fax: (202) 651-5774
Charity Reedy-Hines, Director of Admissions, Gallaudet University, 800 Florida Avenue, NE, Washington, DC 20002

George Washington University

Washington, District of Columbia **CB member**
www.gwu.edu **CB code: 5246**

- Private 4-year university
- Residential campus in very large city
- 10,394 degree-seeking undergraduates: 7% part-time, 56% women, 6% African American, 9% Asian American, 5% Hispanic American, 4% international
- 12,630 degree-seeking graduate students
- 37% of applicants admitted
- SAT or ACT (ACT writing recommended), application essay required
- 78% graduate within 6 years

General. Founded in 1821. Regionally accredited. **Degrees:** 2,421 bachelor's, 134 associate awarded; master's, doctoral, first professional offered. **ROTC:** Army, Navy, Air Force. **Calendar:** Semester, extensive summer session. **Full-time faculty:** 826 total; 92% have terminal degrees, 17% minority, 35% women. **Part-time faculty:** 1,210 total; 24% have terminal degrees, 15% minority, 43% women. **Class size:** 54% < 20, 29% 20-39, 6% 40-49, 9% 50-99, 3% >100. **Special facilities:** Observatory.

Freshman class profile. 19,406 applied, 7,275 admitted, 2,411 enrolled.

Mid 50% test scores		**Return as sophomores:**	92%
SAT verbal:	600-700	**Out-of-state:**	99%
SAT math:	600-690	**Live on campus:**	93%
Rank in top quarter:	88%	**International:**	4%
Rank in top tenth:	63%		

Basis for selection. GED not accepted. Strong college-preparatory program, GPA of 3.0 and class rank in top third important. Teacher and counselor recommendation and personal statement required. SAT Subject Tests required for applicants to 7-year BA/MD and integrated engineering/MD programs(any math and any science); early admission applicants (any math, student's choice); and recommended for all for admission and placement. Interview recommended for all, and required of early admission applicants. Audition required of bachelor of music applicants.

High school preparation. Required and recommended units include English 4, mathematics 2-4, social studies 2-4, science 2-4 (laboratory 1) and foreign language 2-4. One physics, 1 chemistry, and additional 1 unit in mathematics required for School of Engineering and Applied Science.

2006-2007 Annual costs. Tuition/fees (projected): $37,820. Tuition stays fixed until student graduates, for a maximum of five years. Room/board: $11,000. Books/supplies: $1,000. Personal expenses: $1,350.

2004-2005 Financial aid. Need-based: 1,605 full-time freshmen applied for aid; 1,072 were judged to have need; 1,060 of these received aid. Average need met was 93%. Average scholarship/grant was $19,024; average loan $5,340. 67% of total undergraduate aid awarded as scholarships/ grants, 33% as loans/jobs. **Non-need-based:** Awarded to 3,359 full-time undergraduates, including 898 freshmen. Scholarships awarded for academics, art, athletics, music/drama, ROTC. **Additional information:** Auditions required for performing arts scholarships.

Application procedures. Admission: Priority date 12/1; deadline 1/10. $70 fee, may be waived for applicants with need. Admission notification 3/31. Admission notification on a rolling basis. Must reply by May 1 or within 2 week(s) if notified thereafter. Applications received after 2/1 reviewed on a space available basis. Supplemental applications required for honors program, 7-year integrated engineering/law program, integrated engineering/MD program. **Financial aid:** Closing date 2/1. FAFSA, CSS PROFILE required. Applicants notified on a rolling basis starting 3/24; must reply by 5/1.

Academics. Special study options: Accelerated study, cooperative education, cross-registration, distance learning, double major, dual enrollment of high school students, honors, independent study, internships, liberal arts/ career combination, student-designed major, study abroad. 7-year integrated BA/MD liberal arts program, 8-year integrated engineering/JD and engineering/MD programs. **Credit/placement by examination:** AP, CLEP, IB, institutional tests. 30 credit hours maximum toward bachelor's degree. **Support services:** Pre-admission summer program, reduced course load, tutoring.

Majors. Area/ethnic studies: American, European, Latin American, Near/ Middle Eastern. **Biology:** General, biomedical sciences, biophysics, pharmacology. **Business:** Accounting, business admin, finance, international, management information systems, tourism promotion. **Communications:** General, journalism, political. **Computer sciences:** General, information systems. **Conservation:** General, environmental studies. **Education:** Physical. **Engineering:** General, biomedical, civil, computer, electrical, mechanical. **Foreign languages:** General, Arabic, Chinese, classics, French, German, Hebrew, Italian, Japanese, Latin, Portuguese, Romance, Russian, Spanish. **Health:** Audiology/speech pathology, cytotechnology, nuclear medical technology, physician assistant, sonography. **History:** General. **Liberal arts:** Arts/ sciences. **Math:** General, applied, statistics. **Parks/recreation:** Exercise sciences. **Philosophy/religion:** Judaic, philosophy, religion. **Physical sciences:** Chemistry, geology, physics. **Protective services:** Criminal justice, police science. **Psychology:** General. **Public administration:** Human services, policy analysis. **Social sciences:** Anthropology, archaeology, economics, geography, international relations, political science, sociology. **Visual/ performing arts:** General, art history/conservation, dance, dramatic, interior design, studio arts, theater history.

Most popular majors. Business/marketing 17%, English 6%, psychology 8%, social sciences 33%.

Computing on campus. 600 workstations in dormitories, library, computer center, student center. Dormitories linked to campus network. Commuter students can connect to campus network. Repair service available.

Student life. Housing: Guaranteed on-campus for freshmen. Coed dorms, apartments, fraternity/sorority housing available. $800 nonrefundable deposit, deadline 5/1. Residential programs available in politics and values, Roots of Western Civilization; multilingual floors, creative and performing arts floors, healthy living floors, disabled student housing available. **Activities:** Bands, choral groups, dance, drama, film society, literary magazine, music ensembles, musical theater, radio station, student government, student newspaper, TV station, religious groups, national political party organizations, ethnic, social action, public affairs groups.

Athletics. NCAA. **Intercollegiate:** Baseball M, basketball, cross-country, diving, golf M, gymnastics W, lacrosse W, rowing (crew), soccer, softball W, squash W, swimming, tennis, volleyball W, water polo. **Intramural:** Basketball, football (tackle) M, golf, racquetball, soccer, softball, table tennis, tennis, volleyball. **Team name:** Colonials.

Student services. Alcohol/substance abuse counseling, career counseling, student employment services, financial aid counseling, health services, on-campus daycare, personal counseling, placement for graduates, veterans' counselor. **Physically disabled:** Services for visually, speech, hearing impaired.

Contact. E-mail: gwadm@gwu.edu
Phone: (202) 994-6040 Toll-free number: (800) 447-3765
Fax: (202) 994-0325
Kathryn Napper, Director of Admissions, George Washington University, 2121 I Street NW, Suite 201, Washington, DC 20052

Georgetown University

Washington, District of Columbia **CB member**
www.georgetown.edu **CB code: 5244**

- Private 4-year university affiliated with Roman Catholic Church
- Residential campus in very large city
- 6,395 degree-seeking undergraduates: 2% part-time, 54% women, 7% African American, 9% Asian American, 6% Hispanic American, 4% international
- 6,785 degree-seeking graduate students
- 21% of applicants admitted
- SAT or ACT (ACT writing optional), application essay, interview required
- 93% graduate within 6 years; 26% enter graduate study

General. Founded in 1789. Regionally accredited. **Degrees:** 1,679 bachelor's awarded; master's, doctoral, first professional offered. **ROTC:** Army, Navy, Air Force. **Location:** 1.5 miles from downtown. **Calendar:** Semester, extensive summer session. **Full-time faculty:** 752 total; 92% have terminal degrees, 16% minority, 37% women. **Part-time faculty:** 506 total; 58% have terminal degrees, 10% minority, 33% women. **Class size:** 57% < 20, 26% 20-39, 9% 40-49, 6% 50-99, 2% >100. **Special facilities:** Observatory; language learning technology lab with satellite link; library with special collections including archives, rare books, prints, manuscripts dealing with medieval and early modern periods, and American history.

Freshman class profile. 15,285 applied, 3,286 admitted, 1,551 enrolled.

Mid 50% test scores		Rank in top quarter:	97%
SAT verbal:	640-750	Rank in top tenth:	86%
SAT math:	650-740	End year in good standing:	100%
ACT:	27-32	Return as sophomores:	98%
GPA 3.50 or higher:	86%	Out-of-state:	99%
GPA 3.0-3.49:	11%	Live on campus:	99%
GPA 2.0-2.99:	3%	International:	3%

Basis for selection. School academic record most important, in addition to test scores, essays, extracurricular activities, interview, and recommendations. Special consideration given to qualified minorities, athletes, internationals, and alumni relatives. SAT Subject Tests recommended. Interview required unless not possible to assign based on geographic area; portfolio recommended for fine arts majors.

High school preparation. College-preparatory program recommended. Required units include English 4, mathematics 2, social studies 2, history 2, science 1 and foreign language 2. Additional units in science, mathematics, and foreign language recommended for some programs.

2005-2006 Annual costs. Tuition/fees: $32,024. Room/board: $10,739. Books/supplies: $980. Personal expenses: $1,522.

2005-2006 Financial aid. Need-based: 862 full-time freshmen applied for aid; 646 were judged to have need; 642 of these received aid. Average need met was 100%. Average scholarship/grant was $23,000; average loan $1,800. 77% of total undergraduate aid awarded as scholarships/grants, 23% as loans/jobs. **Non-need-based:** Awarded to 180 full-time undergraduates, including 51 freshmen. Scholarships awarded for athletics.

Application procedures. Admission: Closing date 1/10 (receipt date). $60 fee, may be waived for applicants with need. Application must be submitted on paper. Admission notification 4/1. Must reply by May 1 or within 2 week(s) if notified thereafter. **Financial aid:** Closing date 2/1. FAFSA, CSS PROFILE required. Applicants notified by 4/1; must reply by 5/1 or within 2 week(s) of notification.

Academics. Early assurance program to university's medical and law schools. **Special study options:** Combined bachelor's/graduate degree, cross-registration, double major, ESL, honors, independent study, internships, student-designed major, study abroad, Washington semester. **Credit/placement by examination:** AP, CLEP, IB, institutional tests. **Support services:** Learning center, pre-admission summer program, study skills assistance, tutoring, writing center.

Majors. Area/ethnic studies: American, women's. **Biology:** General, biochemistry. **Business:** Accounting, business admin, finance, international, marketing. **Computer sciences:** Computer science. **English:** English lit. **Foreign languages:** Arabic, Chinese, classics, comparative lit, French, German, Italian, Japanese, linguistics, Portuguese, Russian, Spanish. **Health:** Nursing (RN). **History:** General. **Interdisciplinary:** Medieval/Renaissance, peace/conflict, science/society. **Liberal arts:** Arts/sciences. **Math:** General. **Philosophy/religion:** Philosophy, religion. **Physical sciences:** Chemistry, physics. **Psychology:** General. **Social sciences:** Anthropology, economics, international relations, political science, sociology. **Visual/performing arts:** Art, art history/conservation, studio arts.

Most popular majors. Business/marketing 18%, English 9%, foreign language 7%, health sciences 9%, social sciences 34%.

Computing on campus. 355 workstations in dormitories, library, computer center. Dormitories wired for high-speed internet access and linked to campus network. Commuter students can connect to campus network. Online course registration, helpline, repair service, wireless network available.

Student life. Freshman orientation: Mandatory, $160 fee. Preregistration for classes offered. Student volunteer-led program. **Policies:** Freshmen and sophomores required to live on campus. Upperclass students obtain housing via a lottery process. **Housing:** Guaranteed on-campus for freshmen. Coed dorms, special housing for disabled, apartments, substance-free housing available. **Activities:** Bands, choral groups, dance, drama, film society, literary magazine, music ensembles, musical theater, radio station, student government, student newspaper, symphony orchestra, TV station, over 120 student organizations.

Athletics. NCAA. **Intercollegiate:** Baseball M, basketball, cross-country, diving, field hockey W, football (tackle) M, golf, lacrosse, rowing (crew), sailing, soccer, softball W, swimming, tennis, track and field, volleyball W. **Intramural:** Basketball, cross-country, football (non-tackle), golf, handball, racquetball, skiing, soccer, softball, squash, table tennis, tennis, volleyball. **Team name:** Hoyas.

Student services. Alcohol/substance abuse counseling, campus ministries, career counseling, student employment services, financial aid counseling, health services, minority student services, on-campus daycare, personal counseling, placement for graduates, women's services. **Physically disabled:** Services for visually, hearing impaired.

Contact. Phone: (202) 687-3600 Fax: (202) 687-5084
Charles Deacon, Dean of Admissions, Georgetown University, 103 White-Gravenor, Washington, DC 20057-1002

Howard University

Washington, District of Columbia — **CB member**
www.howard.edu — **CB code: 5297**

- Private 4-year university
- Residential campus in very large city
- 7,164 degree-seeking undergraduates: 6% part-time, 67% women
- 3,699 degree-seeking graduate students
- 44% of applicants admitted
- SAT or ACT with writing required

General. Founded in 1867. Regionally accredited. 5 campuses. 25 major research centers and several special programs. **Degrees:** 1,395 bachelor's awarded; master's, doctoral, first professional offered. **ROTC:** Army, Air Force. **Location:** 38 miles from Baltimore; 105 miles from Richmond, Virginia. **Calendar:** Semester, extensive summer session. **Full-time faculty:** 1,069 total. **Part-time faculty:** 604 total. **Class size:** 64% < 20, 26% 20-39, 6% 40-49, 3% 50-99, less than 1% >100. **Special facilities:** Research center, including museum and archives, with collections on Africa and persons of African descent; international affairs center.

Freshman class profile. 9,542 applied, 4,227 admitted, 1,410 enrolled.

Mid 50% test scores		Rank in top tenth:	23%
SAT verbal:	460-680	Return as sophomores:	90%
SAT math:	450-690	Out-of-state:	93%
ACT:	19-28	Live on campus:	92%
Rank in top quarter:	49%	International:	7%

Basis for selection. High school achievement record, test scores most important. Requirements vary from college to college. SAT Subject Tests recommended. Dental Hygiene Aptitude Test required of dental hygiene applicants. Essay recommended; required of Early Action applicants. Audition required of music, drama majors. Portfolio required of art, architecture majors. Interview recommended for pharmacy and pharmaceutical programs, physician assistant majors. **Homeschooled:** Must have GED.

High school preparation. 14 units required; 21 recommended. Required and recommended units include English 4, mathematics 2-3, social studies 2, science 2, foreign language 2 and academic electives 4.

2005-2006 Annual costs. Tuition/fees: $12,295. Room/board: $6,186. Books/supplies: $1,100. Personal expenses: $1,800.

2004-2005 Financial aid. All financial aid based on need. 5% of total undergraduate aid awarded as scholarships/grants, 95% as loans/jobs.

Application procedures. Admission: Priority date 11/1; deadline 2/15 (receipt date). $45 fee. Admission notification on a rolling basis beginning on or about 4/15. Must reply by May 1 or within 4 week(s) if notified thereafter. **Financial aid:** Priority date 2/15, closing date 8/15. FAFSA, institutional form required. Applicants notified by 4/1; must reply by 8/1 or within 4 week(s) of notification.

Academics. Special study options: Accelerated study, combined bachelor's/graduate degree, cooperative education, cross-registration, distance learning, double major, dual enrollment of high school students, exchange student, honors, independent study, internships, student-designed major, study abroad, teacher certification program. **Credit/placement by examination:** AP, CLEP, SAT, ACT, institutional tests. 60 credit hours maximum toward bachelor's degree. **Support services:** Learning center, reduced course load, remedial instruction, study skills assistance, tutoring.

Majors. Architecture: Architecture. **Area/ethnic studies:** African, African-American. **Biology:** General. **Business:** Accounting, business admin, fashion, finance, hospitality admin, hospitality/recreation, insurance, international, management information systems, market research. **Communications:** General, broadcast journalism, journalism, radio/tv. **Computer sciences:** Information systems, systems analysis. **Education:** Art, English, health, music, physical. **Engineering:** Chemical, civil, computer, electrical, mechanical, systems. **Foreign languages:** Ancient Greek, classics, French, German, modern Greek, Russian, Spanish. **Health:** Clinical lab science, medical radiologic technology/radiation therapy, music therapy, physician assistant, recreational therapy. **History:** General. **Interdisciplinary:** Nutrition sciences. **Math:** General. **Parks/recreation:** General. **Philosophy/religion:** Philosophy. **Physical sciences:** Chemistry, physics. **Psychology:** General. **Social sciences:** Anthropology, economics, political science, sociology. **Visual/**

performing arts: General, art, art history/conservation, arts management, conducting, dance, design, interior design, jazz, music history, music management, music theory/composition, piano/organ, theater arts management, theater design, theater history, voice/opera.

Most popular majors. Biology 9%, business/marketing 18%, communications/journalism 14%, computer/information sciences 7%, health sciences 14%, psychology 7%, social sciences 9%, visual/performing arts 6%.

Computing on campus. 6,343 workstations in dormitories, library, computer center, student center. Dormitories wired for high-speed internet access and linked to campus network. Commuter students can connect to campus network. Online course registration, online library, helpline, student web hosting, wireless network available.

Student life. Freshman orientation: Mandatory. Preregistration for classes offered. **Policies:** Freshmen permitted cars on campus. **Housing:** Guaranteed on-campus for freshmen. Coed dorms, single-sex dorms, apartments available. $50 deposit, deadline 4/1. **Activities:** Bands, choral groups, dance, drama, film society, literary magazine, music ensembles, musical theater, opera, radio station, student government, student newspaper, symphony orchestra, TV station, Absalom Jones Student Association, Adventist Committee, Baptist Student Union, Christian Science Organization, Christian Fellowship-Igbimo Otito, Lutheran Student Organization, Muslim Students, Wesley Foundation Methodist Fellowship, William J. Seymour Pentacostal Fellowship, academic honorary societies.

Athletics. NCAA. **Intercollegiate:** Baseball M, basketball, bowling, cross-country, diving, football (tackle) M, golf W, gymnastics, lacrosse W, soccer, softball W, swimming, tennis, track and field, volleyball W, wrestling M. **Intramural:** Badminton W, basketball, bowling, soccer W, softball, table tennis. **Team name:** Bison.

Student services. Campus ministries, career counseling, student employment services, financial aid counseling, health services, on-campus daycare, personal counseling, placement for graduates, veterans' counselor. **Physically disabled:** Services for visually, speech impaired.

Contact. E-mail: admissions@howard.edu
Phone: (202) 806-2755 Toll-free number: (800) 822-6363
Fax: (202) 806-4467
Linda Saunders-Hawkins, Associate Director of Admissions, Howard University, 2400 Sixth Street Northwest, Washington, DC 20059

Potomac College
Washington, District of Columbia
www.potomac.edu **CB code: 3569**

- For-profit 3-year business and technical college
- Commuter campus in very large city
- 210 full-time, degree-seeking undergraduates

General. Candidate for regional accreditation; also accredited by ACICS. Credit earned for work-related research projects. **Degrees:** 30 bachelor's awarded. **Calendar:** Continuous, extensive summer session. **Full-time faculty:** 10 total. **Part-time faculty:** 15 total.

Basis for selection. Must have High School diploma or GED equivalent.

2005-2006 Annual costs. Tuition/fees: $17,220. Books/supplies: $630.

Application procedures. Admission: No deadline. $15 fee, may be waived for applicants with need. Application may be submitted online. Admission notification on a rolling basis. **Financial aid:** No deadline. FAFSA, institutional form required. Applicants notified on a rolling basis; must reply within 4 week(s) of notification.

Academics. Special study options: Accelerated study, independent study, weekend college. **Credit/placement by examination:** CLEP, institutional tests. 30 credit hours maximum toward bachelor's degree. **Support services:** Learning center.

Majors. Business: Management science. **Computer sciences:** General.

Computing on campus. 23 workstations in library, computer center. Online library available..

Student life. Freshman orientation: Mandatory. Preregistration for classes offered.

Student services. Adult student services.

Contact. E-mail: info@potomac.edu
Phone: (202) 686-0876 Fax: (202) 686-0818
Michael Mella, Director of Admissions, Potomac College, 4000 Chesapeake Street NW, Washington, DC 20016

Southeastern University
Washington, District of Columbia
www.seu.edu **CB code: 5622**

- Private 4-year university and business college
- Commuter campus in very large city
- 651 degree-seeking undergraduates
- 257 graduate students
- 40% graduate within 6 years

General. Founded in 1879. Regionally accredited. Weekend college degree available for all programs. **Degrees:** 157 bachelor's, 75 associate awarded; master's offered. **Calendar:** Quarter, extensive summer session. **Full-time faculty:** 9 total; 67% have terminal degrees, 44% minority, 22% women. **Part-time faculty:** 95 total; 26% have terminal degrees, 63% minority, 26% women. **Class size:** 67% < 20, 32% 20-39, 1% 40-49.

Freshman class profile. 200 applied, 141 admitted, 141 enrolled.

End year in good standing:	70%	**Out-of-state:**	23%
Return as sophomores:	65%		

Basis for selection. Open admission. TOEFL used for non-English speakers.

High school preparation. Recommended units include English 4, mathematics 3, social studies 2 and foreign language 2.

2005-2006 Annual costs. Tuition/fees: $12,525. Reduction in fees available for early registration. Online programs: $305 per credit hour. Books/supplies: $1,200. Personal expenses: $1,359.

Financial aid. Non-need-based: Scholarships awarded for academics, state residency.

Application procedures. Admission: No deadline. $45 fee, may be waived for applicants with need. Application may be submitted online. Admission notification on a rolling basis. **Financial aid:** Closing date 8/15. FAFSA, institutional form required. Applicants notified on a rolling basis; must reply within 2 week(s) of notification.

Academics. Special study options: Accelerated study, cooperative education, cross-registration, double major, dual enrollment of high school students, honors, independent study, weekend college. **Credit/placement by examination:** CLEP, IB, institutional tests. 9 credit hours maximum toward associate degree, 9 toward bachelor's. **Support services:** Learning center, pre-admission summer program, reduced course load, remedial instruction, study skills assistance, tutoring, writing center.

Majors. Business: General, accounting, banking/financial services, business admin, management information systems, management science, market research, statistics, tourism/travel. **Computer sciences:** Programming, systems analysis. **Family/consumer sciences:** Child development. **Health:** Health care admin. **Liberal arts:** Arts/sciences. **Protective services:** Police science. **Public administration:** General. **Social sciences:** Economics.

Most popular majors. Business/marketing 38%, computer/information sciences 30%, health sciences 6%, liberal arts 28%.

Computing on campus. 137 workstations in library, computer center.

Student life. Freshman orientation: Mandatory, $255 fee. Preregistration for classes offered. **Activities:** Student government, student newspaper.

Student services. Career counseling, student employment services, financial aid counseling, personal counseling, placement for graduates, veterans' counselor. **Physically disabled:** Services for visually, hearing impaired.

Contact. E-mail: admissions@admin.seu.edu
Phone: (202) 478-8210 ext. 210 Fax: (202) 488-3172
Ronald Burleson, Director of Admissions, Southeastern University, 501 I Street Southwest, Washington, DC 20024

Strayer University
Washington, District of Columbia
www.strayer.edu **CB code: 5632**

- For-profit 4-year university and business college
- Commuter campus in very large city
- 27,309 undergraduates

General. Founded in 1892. Regionally accredited. Additional campuses in Maryland, North Carolina and Virginia. **Degrees:** 1,299 bachelor's, 123 associate awarded; master's offered. **Location:** Downtown. **Calendar:** Quarter, extensive summer session. **Full-time faculty:** 140 total. **Part-time faculty:** 900 total. **Class size:** 41% < 20, 57% 20-39, 2% 40-49.

Basis for selection. Institutional placement tests required. Students with SAT scores of 400 or above in verbal and/or mathematics or who have prior college level mathematics/English credits, can waive placement tests. Interview recommended.

High school preparation. 14 units recommended. Recommended units include English 3, mathematics 3, social studies 1, history 1, foreign language 2 and academic electives 4. 1 unit of sociology or psychology recommended; 3 units of art, music, or literature recommended.

2005-2006 Annual costs. Tuition/fees: $11,520. Books/supplies: $1,200.

Financial aid. Additional information: 10/03 closing date for academic scholarship applications.

Application procedures. Admission: No deadline. $50 fee. Admission notification on a rolling basis. **Financial aid:** No deadline. FAFSA required. Applicants notified on a rolling basis; must reply within 2 week(s) of notification.

Academics. Special study options: Accelerated study, cooperative education, distance learning, double major, internships, weekend college. **Credit/placement by examination:** AP, CLEP, institutional tests. 63 credit hours maximum toward associate degree, 126 toward bachelor's. **Support services:** Learning center, remedial instruction, tutoring.

Majors. Business: Accounting, business admin. **Computer sciences:** Information systems. **Social sciences:** Economics.

Computing on campus. 760 workstations in library, computer center. Online course registration, online library, helpline available.

Student life. Activities: Student newspaper, accounting club, international club, data processing management association, business administration club, marketing club, human resource management club, Alpha Chi National Honor Society, Alpha Sigma Lambda National Honor Society, Sigma Gamma Rho Sorority, Thai Student Association.

Student services. Career counseling, student employment services, placement for graduates, veterans' counselor. **Physically disabled:** Services for visually, hearing impaired.

Contact. E-mail: washington@strayer.edu
Phone: (202) 408-2400 Toll-free number: (888) 478-7293
Ed Dobson, Campus Director, Strayer University, 1133 15th Sreet NW, Washington, DC 20005

Trinity University
Washington, District of Columbia **CB member**
www.trinitydc.edu **CB code: 5796**

- Private 4-year liberal arts college for women affiliated with Roman Catholic Church
- Residential campus in very large city
- 948 degree-seeking undergraduates
- 92% of applicants admitted
- Application essay, interview required

General. Founded in 1897. Regionally accredited. **Degrees:** 149 bachelor's awarded; master's offered. **ROTC:** Army. **Calendar:** Semester, extensive summer session. **Full-time faculty:** 55 total. **Part-time faculty:** 115 total. **Class size:** 70% < 20, 30% 20-39.

Freshman class profile. 423 applied, 388 admitted, 140 enrolled.

Mid 50% test scores		ACT:	13-18
SAT verbal:	360-480	Out-of-state:	49%
SAT math:	330-480	Live on campus:	42%

Basis for selection. School achievement record, test scores, recommendations, interview, school and community activities important. 3.0 GPA preferred. SAT and SAT Subject Tests or ACT recommended.

High school preparation. 16 units required. Required units include English 4, mathematics 3, social studies 3, history 2, science 2 (laboratory 1) and foreign language 2.

2006-2007 Annual costs. Tuition/fees (projected): $17,715. Room/board: $7,800. Books/supplies: $1,000. Personal expenses: $1,500.

2005-2006 Financial aid. Need-based: 3% of total undergraduate aid awarded as scholarships/grants, 97% as loans/jobs. **Non-need-based:** Scholarships awarded for academics, alumni affiliation, leadership.

Application procedures. Admission: Priority date 3/1; no deadline. $35 fee, may be waived for applicants with need. Admission notification on a rolling basis beginning on or about 10/1. Must reply by May 1 or within 3 week(s) if notified thereafter. **Financial aid:** Priority date 3/1; no closing date. FAFSA required. Applicants notified on a rolling basis starting 2/1; must reply within 2 week(s) of notification.

Academics. Special study options: Accelerated study, cross-registration, distance learning, double major, dual enrollment of high school students, honors, independent study, internships, student-designed major, study abroad, teacher certification program, Washington semester, weekend college. **Credit/placement by examination:** AP, CLEP, institutional tests. **Support services:** Learning center, pre-admission summer program, reduced course load, remedial instruction, tutoring.

Majors. Area/ethnic studies: American, Latin American. **Biology:** General, biochemistry. **Business:** Business admin, operations. **Communications:** General. **Conservation:** General. **English:** British lit. **Foreign languages:** French, Spanish. **History:** General. **Interdisciplinary:** Biological/physical sciences. **Liberal arts:** Arts/sciences. **Math:** General. **Physical sciences:** Chemistry. **Protective services:** Law enforcement admin. **Psychology:** General. **Social sciences:** Economics, international relations, political science, sociology. **Visual/performing arts:** Art history/conservation.

Most popular majors. Business/marketing 24%, communications/journalism 10%, psychology 40%, social sciences 12%.

Computing on campus. 70 workstations in dormitories, library, computer center.

Student life. Freshman orientation: Available. **Policies:** Student life mostly self-governed. Honor code exists. **Housing:** Guaranteed on-campus for all undergraduates. **Activities:** Choral groups, dance, drama, film society, literary magazine, student government, student newspaper, Young Democrats, Young Republicans, Black Student Alliance, international student association, Inter-American Club, peer ministry.

Athletics. NCAA. **Intercollegiate:** Basketball W, field hockey W, lacrosse W, rowing (crew) W, soccer W, softball W, tennis W, track and field W, volleyball W. **Intramural:** Golf W, lacrosse W, soccer W, softball W, swimming W, tennis W, volleyball W.

Student services. Adult student services, career counseling, student employment services, health services, on-campus daycare, personal counseling, placement for graduates, veterans' counselor. **Physically disabled:** Services for visually, speech, hearing impaired.

Contact. E-mail: admissions@trinitydc.edu
Phone: (202) 884-9400 Toll-free number: (800) 492-6882
Fax: (202) 884-9229
Renee Orlick, Director of Admissions, Trinity University, 125 Michigan Avenue, NE, Washington, DC 20017

University of the District of Columbia
Washington, District of Columbia **CB member**
www.udc.edu **CB code: 5929**

- Public 4-year university and liberal arts college
- Commuter campus in very large city
- 5,170 degree-seeking undergraduates: 62% part-time, 65% women, 80% African American, 2% Asian American, 6% Hispanic American
- 194 degree-seeking graduate students
- 25% graduate within 6 years

General. Founded in 1976. Regionally accredited. **Degrees:** 294 bachelor's, 172 associate awarded; master's offered. **ROTC:** Army, Navy, Air Force. **Calendar:** Semester, limited summer session. **Full-time faculty:** 235 total. **Part-time faculty:** 250 total.

Freshman class profile. 2,026 applied, 1,746 admitted, 1,136 enrolled.

Out-of-state:	21%	**Sororities:**	2%
Fraternities:	1%		

Basis for selection. Open admission, but selective for some programs. Special requirements for nursing, art, and music programs. First-time students must take placement test prior to enrollment. Interview recommended for nursing majors. Audition recommended for music majors. Portfolio recommended for art majors.

High school preparation. Recommended units include English 4, mathematics 2, social studies 2, history 1, science 2, foreign language 2 and academic electives 3.

2005-2006 Annual costs. Tuition/fees: $2,520; $4,710 out-of-state. Books/supplies: $800. Personal expenses: $1,600.

Financial aid. All financial aid based on need.

Application procedures. Admission: Closing date 6/14 (postmark date). $20 fee, may be waived for applicants with need. Admission notification on a rolling basis. **Financial aid:** Priority date 3/15; no closing date. FAFSA required. Applicants notified on a rolling basis starting 5/1; must reply within 2 week(s) of notification.

Academics. Special study options: Cooperative education, cross-registration, double major, dual enrollment of high school students, ESL, honors, independent study, internships, teacher certification program, weekend college. **Credit/placement by examination:** AP, CLEP, IB, institutional tests. **Support services:** Learning center, pre-admission summer program, remedial instruction, tutoring.

Majors. Architecture: Architecture, urban/community planning. **Biology:** General. **Business:** Accounting, business admin, finance, office management. **Communications technology:** Graphic/printing. **Computer sciences:** General, computer science. **Conservation:** General. **Education:** Art, business, early childhood, elementary, health, physical. **Engineering:** Civil, electrical, mechanical. **Family/consumer sciences:** General, family studies, food/nutrition. **Foreign languages:** French, Spanish. **Health:** Nursing (RN), speech pathology. **History:** General. **Math:** General. **Parks/recreation:** General. **Philosophy/religion:** Philosophy. **Physical sciences:** Chemistry, physics. **Protective services:** Fire services admin. **Psychology:** General. **Public administration:** Social work. **Social sciences:** Anthropology, economics, geography, political science, sociology, urban studies. **Transportation:** Aviation. **Visual/performing arts:** Dramatic, studio arts.

Most popular majors. Business/marketing 19%, computer/information sciences 17%, health sciences 9%, legal studies 14%, mathematics 16%, visual/performing arts 8%.

Computing on campus. 2 workstations in library, computer center. Helpline, repair service available.

Student life. Freshman orientation: Mandatory. Preregistration for classes offered. **Policies:** Freshmen permitted cars on campus. **Activities:** Bands, choral groups, dance, drama, student government, student newspaper, symphony orchestra, TV station.

Athletics. NCAA. **Intercollegiate:** Basketball, cross-country, soccer, tennis, track and field, volleyball W. **Intramural:** Basketball, softball, swimming, tennis, volleyball W. **Team name:** Firebirds.

Student services. Career counseling, student employment services, health services, personal counseling, placement for graduates, veterans' counselor. **Physically disabled:** Services for visually, speech, hearing impaired.

Contact. Phone: (202) 274-6110 Fax: (202) 274-5552
LaVerne Hill-Flannigan, Director of Enrollment Services, University of the District of Columbia, 4200 Connecticut Avenue NW, Washington, DC 20008

Florida

Art Institute of Fort Lauderdale

Ft. Lauderdale, Florida
www.artinstitute.edu **CB code: 5040**

- For-profit 4-year visual arts and technical college
- Commuter campus in large city
- 2,893 degree-seeking undergraduates: 48% part-time, 50% women, 17% African American, 2% Asian American, 33% Hispanic American
- Application essay, interview required
- 437% graduate within 6 years

General. Founded in 1968. Accredited by ACICS. **Degrees:** 293 bachelor's, 320 associate awarded. **Location:** 25 miles from Miami, 30 miles from West Palm Beach. **Calendar:** Quarter, extensive summer session. **Full-time faculty:** 103 total; 56% have terminal degrees, 12% minority, 40% women. **Part-time faculty:** 17 total; 53% have terminal degrees, 18% minority, 18% women. **Special facilities:** Broadcasting studio, silicon graphics lab, full culinary kitchens.

Freshman class profile.

Out-of-state:	50%	Live on campus:	10%

Basis for selection. Interview, essay important. MELP exam required for placement of non-native English speakers. Portfolio recommended. **Learning Disabled:** Documentation must be submitted if student has special needs to be accommodated.

High school preparation. Prefer students with background in chosen major.

2005-2006 Annual costs. Tuition/fees: $17,325. Books/supplies: $1,227. Personal expenses: $1,980.

2004-2005 Financial aid. All financial aid based on need. **Additional information:** Internal scholarships available. Financial planning program allows personalized service to budget and meet college costs through individualized payment plans.

Application procedures. Admission: No deadline. $50 fee. Application may be submitted online. Admission notification on a rolling basis. **Financial aid:** No deadline. FAFSA required.

Academics. Academic program designed to simulate working environment. After completion of associate degree students may continue to earn a bachelor of science. **Special study options:** ESL, honors, independent study, internships. **Credit/placement by examination:** AP, CLEP, IB. SAT or ACT preferred for placement but ACCUPLACER accepted in lieu of either. **Support services:** Remedial instruction, tutoring, writing center.

Majors. Business: Fashion. **Computer sciences:** General, programming. **Personal/culinary services:** Culinary arts. **Visual/performing arts:** Commercial/advertising art, graphic design, illustration, industrial design, interior design, multimedia.

Most popular majors. Architecture 14%, computer/information sciences 35%, interdisciplinary studies 12%, visual/performing arts 36%.

Computing on campus. Dormitories wired for high-speed internet access and linked to campus network. Online course registration, online library, helpline, repair service, student web hosting, wireless network available.

Student life. Freshman orientation: Available. Preregistration for classes offered. **Policies:** Freshmen permitted cars on campus. **Housing:** Guaranteed on-campus for all undergraduates. Coed dorms, apartments, substance-free housing available. $275 deposit. **Activities:** Radio station, student government, TV station, student chapter of American Society of Interior Designers, photography club, fashion club, Distributive Education Club, junior collegiate chapter, music and video club, Professional Photographers of America, student chapter, international student organization.

Student services. Career counseling, student employment services, financial aid counseling, personal counseling, placement for graduates. **Physically disabled:** Services for hearing impaired.

Contact. E-mail: northroe@aii.edu
Phone: (954) 463-3000 ext. 2149 Toll-free number: (800) 275-7603
Fax: (954) 728-8637
Eileen Northrop, Vice President, Director of Admissions, Art Institute of Fort Lauderdale, 1799 Southeast 17th Street, Fort Lauderdale, FL 33316

Baptist College of Florida

Graceville, Florida
www.baptistcollege.edu **CB code: 7322**

- Private 4-year Bible and teachers college affiliated with Southern Baptist Convention
- Residential campus in small town
- 593 degree-seeking undergraduates: 28% part-time, 37% women, 5% African American, 1% Asian American, 3% Hispanic American, 1% Native American
- 78% of applicants admitted
- SAT or ACT with writing required

General. Founded in 1943. Regionally accredited. **Degrees:** 76 bachelor's, 1 associate awarded. **Location:** 90 miles from Tallahassee, 60 miles from Panama City. **Calendar:** Semester, limited summer session. **Full-time faculty:** 26 total; 69% have terminal degrees, 27% women. **Part-time faculty:** 43 total; 46% have terminal degrees, 16% women. **Class size:** 71% < 20, 23% 20-39, 2% 40-49, 4% 50-99.

Freshman class profile. 72 applied, 56 admitted, 46 enrolled.

Mid 50% test scores		Rank in top quarter:	27%
SAT verbal:	430-500	Rank in top tenth:	10%
SAT math:	360-530	Out-of-state:	28%
ACT:	17-21	Live on campus:	76%

Basis for selection. Applicant must be member in good standing of church affiliated with Southern Baptist Convention or other evangelical body. Special program for non-high school graduates. Recommendations very important. Letter of testimony required. Audition required of music applicants. Interview recommended. **Homeschooled:** Transcript of courses and grades required. Present ACT or SAT test scores no more than 5 years old. Minimum 2.5 GPA, evidence of having earned minimum of 20 units with at least 14 units from the fields of English, math, social and natural sciences required.

High school preparation. Recommended units include English 4, mathematics 4, social studies 1, history 2 and science 3.

2005-2006 Annual costs. Tuition/fees: $7,250. Room/board: $3,570. Books/supplies: $900. Personal expenses: $400.

2004-2005 Financial aid. Need-based: 51 full-time freshmen applied for aid; 42 were judged to have need; 42 of these received aid. Average need met was 50%. Average loan was $1,551. 51% of total undergraduate aid awarded as scholarships/grants, 49% as loans/jobs. **Non-need-based:** Awarded to 81 full-time undergraduates, including 23 freshmen. Scholarships awarded for academics, minority status, music/drama, religious affiliation.

Application procedures. Admission: Priority date 6/30; deadline 8/1 (receipt date). $20 fee. Application may be submitted online. Admission notification on a rolling basis beginning on or about 9/1. **Financial aid:** Priority date 4/1, closing date 4/15. FAFSA, institutional form required. Applicants notified on a rolling basis starting 6/15; must reply within 4 week(s) of notification.

Academics. Special study options: Distance learning, double major, independent study, internships, liberal arts/career combination, teacher certification program, weekend college. **Credit/placement by examination:** AP, CLEP, IB, SAT, ACT, institutional tests. 30 credit hours maximum toward bachelor's degree. **Support services:** Learning center, reduced course load, remedial instruction, study skills assistance, tutoring.

Majors. Education: Elementary, music. **Philosophy/religion:** Religion. **Theology:** Bible, pastoral counseling, religious ed, sacred music, theology.

Computing on campus. 25 workstations in library, computer center. Commuter students can connect to campus network. Online course registration, online library, wireless network available.

Student life. Freshman orientation: Mandatory. Preregistration for classes offered. Held the week before classes begin in fall and spring, for 1-2 days, depending on major. **Policies:** Religious observance required. Freshmen permitted cars on campus. **Housing:** Single-sex dorms, apartments available. $100 fully refundable deposit. **Activities:** Bands, choral groups, drama, music ensembles, radio station, student government, Baptist Collegiate Ministry, Women of Worth, student government association.

Athletics. Intramural: Basketball, football (non-tackle), golf, soccer, softball, table tennis, volleyball.

Student services. Campus ministries, career counseling, student employment services, financial aid counseling, personal counseling, veterans' counselor. **Physically disabled:** Services for visually, speech, hearing impaired.

Contact. E-mail: admissions@baptistcollege.edu
Phone: (850) 263-3261 ext. 460 Toll-free number: (800) 328-2660 ext. 460
Fax: (850) 263-7506
Chris Bishop, Director of Admissions, Baptist College of Florida, 5400 College Drive, Graceville, FL 32440-3306

Barry University

Miami Shores, Florida — **CB member**
www.barry.edu — **CB code: 5053**

- Private 4-year university affiliated with Roman Catholic Church
- Commuter campus in large town
- 5,677 degree-seeking undergraduates: 20% part-time, 68% women, 23% African American, 1% Asian American, 33% Hispanic American, 5% international
- 3,282 degree-seeking graduate students
- 72% of applicants admitted
- SAT or ACT (ACT writing optional) required
- 38% graduate within 6 years

General. Founded in 1940. Regionally accredited. 22 off-campus sites for adult and continuing education and some graduate degrees. Center for Dominician Studies. **Degrees:** 1,503 bachelor's awarded; master's, doctoral, first professional offered. **ROTC:** Army, Air Force. **Location:** 14 miles from Fort Lauderdale, 7 miles from Miami. **Calendar:** Semester, limited summer session. **Full-time faculty:** 353 total; 85% have terminal degrees, 27% minority, 52% women. **Part-time faculty:** 518 total. **Class size:** 68% < 20, 31% 20-39, less than 1% 40-49, less than 1% 50-99, less than 1% >100. **Special facilities:** Human performance laboratory, athletic training room, cell biology/biotechnology lab, classroom of tomorrow, photography facilities, lighting studio, dark room, imaging lab, performing arts center, biomechanics lab.

Freshman class profile. 3,802 applied, 2,728 admitted, 563 enrolled.

Mid 50% test scores		**GPA 3.0-3.49:**	32%
SAT verbal:	480-540	**GPA 2.0-2.99:**	41%
SAT math:	480-530	**Return as sophomores:**	64%
ACT:	18-22	**Out-of-state:**	54%
GPA 3.50 or higher:	27%	**Live on campus:**	70%

Basis for selection. Test scores and GPA. Higher test score and GPA requirements for biology, nursing, mathematics, international business and pre-engineering majors. **Homeschooled:** All files reviewed by Director of Admissions--academic portfolio or GED, transcripts of any traditional high school work, SAT/ACT, copy of home school rules of the state which home school is chartered. **Learning Disabled:** Students must apply directly to the comprehensive service program.

High school preparation. 12 units recommended. Recommended units include English 4, mathematics 3, social studies 3 and science 3. For nursing program, 1 chemistry, 1 biology, algebra II required. For biology and allied health programs, 2 laboratory science including biology and chemistry, 3.5 mathematics required. For mathematics program, 3.5 mathematics (algebra, geometry, trigonometry, required). For chemistry program, 3 mathematics, 1 chemistry with lab required.

2005-2006 Annual costs. Tuition/fees: $22,430. Room/board: $7,620.

2005-2006 Financial aid. Need-based: Average need met was 70%. Average scholarship/grant was $9,215; average loan $2,664. 52% of total undergraduate aid awarded as scholarships/grants, 48% as loans/jobs. **Non-need-based:** Scholarships awarded for academics, art, athletics, music/drama.

Application procedures. Admission: No deadline. $30 fee, may be waived for applicants with need. Application may be submitted online. Admission notification on a rolling basis beginning on or about 9/5. Must reply by May 1 or within 2 week(s) if notified thereafter. **Financial aid:** No deadline. FAFSA required. Applicants notified on a rolling basis starting 1/25.

Academics. Special study options: Accelerated study, combined bachelor's/graduate degree, distance learning, double major, dual enrollment of high school students, ESL, honors, independent study, internships, semester at sea, study abroad, teacher certification program, United Nations semester, Washington semester. Semesters in Paris, London, Mexico, Monaco, Madrid available through bilateral exchange program. **Credit/placement by examination:** AP, CLEP, IB, institutional tests. 30 credit hours maximum toward bachelor's degree. All credit by examination should be completed prior to junior status. **Support services:** Learning center, reduced course load, remedial instruction, study skills assistance, tutoring, writing center.

Majors. Biology: General, marine, radiobiology. **Business:** Accounting, business admin, international, management information systems, managerial economics. **Communications:** General, advertising, public relations, radio/tv. **Computer sciences:** Computer science, information systems. **Conservation:** Environmental science. **Education:** Early childhood, elementary, physical, special. **Engineering:** General. **English:** English lit. **Foreign languages:** French, Spanish. **Health:** Athletic training, cardiovascular technology, clinical lab science, cytotechnology, health care admin, nuclear medical technology, nursing (RN), nursing admin, predentistry, premedicine, prepharmacy, preveterinary, sonography. **History:** General. **Legal studies:** General, prelaw. **Liberal arts:** Arts/sciences. **Math:** General. **Parks/recreation:** Exercise sciences, health/fitness, sports admin. **Philosophy/religion:** Philosophy. **Physical sciences:** Chemistry. **Protective services:** Criminal justice. **Psychology:** General. **Public administration:** General, social work. **Social sciences:** Economics, political science, sociology. **Theology:** Theology. **Visual/performing arts:** Art, dramatic, photography.

Most popular majors. Business/marketing 19%, computer/information sciences 8%, education 22%, health sciences 12%, liberal arts 14%, security/protective services 6%.

Computing on campus. 368 workstations in library, computer center. Dormitories wired for high-speed internet access and linked to campus network. Commuter students can connect to campus network. Online library, helpline, repair service, wireless network available.

Student life. Freshman orientation: Mandatory. Preregistration for classes offered. **Policies:** Freshmen permitted cars on campus. **Housing:** Coed dorms, single-sex dorms, special housing for disabled available. $200 deposit. **Activities:** Choral groups, dance, drama, literary magazine, music ensembles, musical theater, radio station, student government, student newspaper, TV station, Circle-K International, Jamaican association, Habitat for Humanity, Caribbean student organization, Haitian intercultural association, Jewish/Christian/Muslim interfaith group, Latter-Day Saints student association, Best Buddies, Spanish club, Baptist Dialogue Group.

Athletics. NCAA. **Intercollegiate:** Baseball M, basketball, golf, rowing (crew) W, soccer, softball W, tennis, volleyball W. **Intramural:** Basketball, golf, skin diving, soccer, softball, volleyball. **Team name:** Buccaneers.

Student services. Adult student services, alcohol/substance abuse counseling, campus ministries, career counseling, student employment services, financial aid counseling, health services, personal counseling, placement for graduates. **Physically disabled:** Services for visually, speech, hearing impaired. **Learning disabled:** Comprehensive services available.

Contact. E-mail: admissions@mail.barry.edu
Phone: (305) 899-3100 Toll-free number: (800) 695-2279
Fax: (305) 899-2971
Helen Corpuz, Director of Admissions, Barry University, 11300 Northeast Second Avenue, Miami Shores, FL 33161-6695

Beacon College

Leesburg, Florida
www.beaconcollege.edu — **CB code: 3611**

- Private 4-year liberal arts college
- Residential campus in large town
- 99 degree-seeking undergraduates: 41% women, 12% African American, 3% Asian American, 6% Hispanic American
- 58% of applicants admitted
- Application essay, interview required
- 63% graduate within 6 years; 36% enter graduate study

General. Regionally accredited. College solely for students with learning disabilities. **Degrees:** 16 bachelor's, 14 associate awarded. **Location:** 50 miles from Orlando. **Calendar:** Semester, limited summer session. **Full-time faculty:** 12 total; 33% have terminal degrees, 8% minority, 33% women. **Part-time faculty:** 4 total; 75% have terminal degrees, 50% minority, 50% women. **Class size:** 100% < 20.

Freshman class profile. 59 applied, 34 admitted, 20 enrolled.

End year in good standing:	93%	**Out-of-state:**	74%
Return as sophomores:	100%	**Live on campus:**	100%

Basis for selection. TOEFL of 500 or better would be used to provide proof of English proficiency for those whose first language is not English.

SAT or ACT recommended. **Learning Disabled:** Students accepted by committee decision based on psycho-educational evaluation documenting learning disability, academic potential, evaluation of high school records, references, and campus interviews with assessments as part of admissions process. Students must provide current psycho-educational report (within 3 years) documenting learning disability as primary handicapping condition, including WAIS score.

High school preparation. 12 units required. Required and recommended units include English 4, mathematics 1, social studies 1, history 2-3, science 1-2 and academic electives 3.

2005-2006 Annual costs. Tuition/fees: $23,000. Room/board: $6,860. Books/supplies: $600. Personal expenses: $2,565.

2004-2005 Financial aid. Need-based: 3 full-time freshmen applied for aid; 3 were judged to have need; 3 of these received aid. Average need met was 80%. Average scholarship/grant was $7,000; average loan $2,625. 67% of total undergraduate aid awarded as scholarships/grants, 33% as loans/jobs. **Non-need-based:** Scholarships awarded for academics. **Additional information:** Work-study programs offered based on financial need.

Application procedures. Admission: Priority date 5/1; deadline 8/1 (receipt date). $50 fee. Application must be submitted on paper. Admission notification on a rolling basis. Must reply by May 1 or within 2 week(s) if notified thereafter. **Financial aid:** Priority date 4/1; no closing date. FAFSA, institutional form required. Applicants notified on a rolling basis starting 4/1; must reply within 2 week(s) of notification.

Academics. Provides remedial coursework in writing, reading, and math. **Special study options:** Double major, independent study, internships, liberal arts/career combination, study abroad. **Credit/placement by examination:** AP, CLEP, institutional tests. **Support services:** Learning center, reduced course load, remedial instruction, study skills assistance, tutoring, writing center.

Majors. Liberal arts: Arts/sciences. **Public administration:** Human services.

Computing on campus. 32 workstations in library, computer center, student center. Dormitories wired for high-speed internet access and linked to campus network. Commuter students can connect to campus network. Online library, helpline, repair service, student web hosting, wireless network available.

Student life. Freshman orientation: Mandatory. Preregistration for classes offered. **Policies:** Freshmen permitted cars on campus. **Housing:** Guaranteed on-campus for all undergraduates. Apartments, substance-free housing available. $750 nonrefundable deposit, deadline 5/1. **Activities:** Literary magazine, student government, student newspaper.

Athletics. Team name: Wildcats.

Student services. Career counseling, student employment services, financial aid counseling, personal counseling, placement for graduates. **Physically disabled:** Services for visually, speech, hearing impaired. **Learning disabled:** Comprehensive services available.

Contact. E-mail: admissions@beaconcollege.edu
Phone: (352) 787-7249 Fax: (352) 787-0721
Carolyn Scott, Director of Admissions, Beacon College, 105 East Main Street, Leesburg, FL 34748

Bethune-Cookman College

Daytona Beach, Florida — **CB member**
www.bethune.cookman.edu — **CB code: 5061**

- Private 4-year liberal arts college affiliated with United Methodist Church
- Residential campus in small city
- 3,090 degree-seeking undergraduates: 10% part-time, 59% women, 91% African American, 1% Hispanic American, 4% international
- 74% of applicants admitted
- SAT or ACT (ACT writing optional), application essay required
- 39% graduate within 6 years; 30% enter graduate study

General. Founded in 1904. Regionally accredited. **Degrees:** 322 bachelor's awarded. **ROTC:** Army, Air Force. **Location:** 60 miles from Orlando. **Calendar:** Semester, limited summer session. **Full-time faculty:** 147 total; 5% have terminal degrees, 60% minority, 46% women. **Part-time faculty:** 56 total; 36% minority, 64% women. **Class size:** 47% < 20, 49% 20-39, 2% 40-49, 1% 50-99, less than 1% >100. **Special facilities:** Founder Mary McLeod Bethune's home and gravesite (national historic landmarks).

Freshman class profile. 3,974 applied, 2,925 admitted, 949 enrolled.

Mid 50% test scores			
SAT verbal:	360-460	Rank in top quarter:	22%
SAT math:	360-460	Rank in top tenth:	6%
ACT:	14-17	Return as sophomores:	71%
GPA 3.50 or higher:	7%	Out-of-state:	35%
GPA 3.0-3.49:	22%	Live on campus:	72%
GPA 2.0-2.99:	70%	International:	1%

Basis for selection. School achievement record most important. Test scores and letters of recommendation important. Interview required of music majors.

High school preparation. 19 units required. Required and recommended units include English 4, mathematics 3, social studies 1, history 2, science 3 (laboratory 1), foreign language 2 and academic electives 6. 1 unit computer literacy.

2005-2006 Annual costs. Tuition/fees: $11,230. Room/board: $6,692. Books/supplies: $820. Personal expenses: $2,700.

2005-2006 Financial aid. All financial aid based on need. 905 full-time freshmen applied for aid; 893 were judged to have need; 887 of these received aid. Average need met was 69%. Average scholarship/grant was $6,150; average loan $2,604. 61% of total undergraduate aid awarded as scholarships/grants, 39% as loans/jobs.

Application procedures. Admission: Priority date 6/30; no deadline. $25 fee, may be waived for applicants with need. Application must be submitted on paper. Admission notification on a rolling basis. **Financial aid:** Priority date 4/1; no closing date. FAFSA required. Applicants notified on a rolling basis starting 4/1; must reply within 3 week(s) of notification.

Academics. Special study options: Accelerated study, cooperative education, distance learning, double major, honors, independent study, internships, study abroad, teacher certification program, weekend college. **Credit/placement by examination:** AP, CLEP, IB, SAT, ACT, institutional tests. 30 credit hours maximum toward bachelor's degree. **Support services:** Learning center, reduced course load, remedial instruction, study skills assistance, tutoring, writing center.

Majors. Biology: General. **Business:** Accounting, business admin, hotel/motel admin, international. **Communications:** Journalism. **Computer sciences:** Computer science, information systems. **Education:** General, biology, business, chemistry, elementary, English, learning disabled, music, physical, physics, social studies. **Engineering:** Computer. **English:** English lit, speech/rhetoric. **Health:** Clinical lab science, nursing (RN). **History:** General. **Interdisciplinary:** Gerontology. **Liberal arts:** Arts/sciences. **Math:** General. **Philosophy/religion:** Christian. **Physical sciences:** Chemistry, physics. **Protective services:** Law enforcement admin. **Psychology:** General. **Social sciences:** International relations, political science, sociology. **Visual/performing arts:** Music performance.

Most popular majors. Business/marketing 20%, education 17%, health sciences 8%, psychology 11%, security/protective services 13%, social sciences 6%.

Computing on campus. 502 workstations in dormitories, library, computer center. Dormitories wired for high-speed internet access and linked to campus network. Commuter students can connect to campus network. Online course registration, online library, helpline, wireless network available.

Student life. Freshman orientation: Mandatory. Preregistration for classes offered. One-week program in beginning of fall. **Housing:** Guaranteed on-campus for all undergraduates. Single-sex dorms available. $200 nonrefundable deposit, deadline 8/15. Special wings in dormitories reserved for honor students and social organization members. **Activities:** Bands, choral groups, drama, music ensembles, radio station, student government, student newspaper, YM/YWCA, Religious Life Fellowship, Pre-seminarian club, Greek letter organization, Gamma Sigma Sigma National Service sorority, Kappa Kappa Psi Nat'l Band fraternity, The Voice newspaper, Alpha Chi honor sorority, Alpha Kappa Mu honor sorority.

Athletics. NCAA. **Intercollegiate:** Baseball M, basketball, bowling W, cross-country, football (tackle) M, golf, softball W, tennis, track and field, volleyball W. **Intramural:** Basketball, football (tackle) M. **Team name:** Wildcats.

Student services. Adult student services, campus ministries, career counseling, student employment services, financial aid counseling, health services, personal counseling, placement for graduates, veterans' counselor.

Contact. E-mail: admissions@cookman.edu
Phone: (386) 481-2600 Toll-free number: (800) 448-0228
Fax: (386) 481-2601
Les Ferrier, Director of Admissions, Bethune-Cookman College, Dr. Mary McLeod Bethune Boulevard, Daytona Beach, FL 32114-3099

Carlos Albizu University
Miami, Florida
www.albizu.edu **CB code: 2102**

- Private 4-year university and branch campus college
- Commuter campus in very large city
- 457 degree-seeking undergraduates
- Application essay, interview required

General. Founded in 1980. Regionally accredited. **Degrees:** 111 bachelor's awarded; master's, doctoral offered. **Calendar:** 3 sessions of 15 weeks each. Extensive summer session. **Full-time faculty:** 17 total. **Part-time faculty:** 75 total. **Class size:** 39% < 20, 61% 20-39.

Basis for selection. Open admission. Minimum 2.0 GPA required. **Homeschooled:** State high school equivalency certificate required.

2005-2006 Annual costs. Tuition/fees: $7,406. Reported tuition, fees and per-credit-hour charge are for Bachelor's degree program in business. Other programs individually priced. Books/supplies: $690. Personal expenses: $1,800.

Financial aid. All financial aid based on need.

Application procedures. **Admission:** No deadline. $25 fee, may be waived for applicants with need. Admission notification on a rolling basis. **Financial aid:** Priority date 6/1; no closing date. FAFSA, institutional form required. Applicants notified on a rolling basis starting 2/1.

Academics. **Special study options:** Accelerated study, cooperative education, cross-registration, distance learning, dual enrollment of high school students, ESL, independent study, internships, study abroad, weekend college. **Credit/placement by examination:** CLEP, IB. 12 credit hours maximum toward bachelor's degree. 6 for foreign language, 6 for other foundation courses. **Support services:** Learning center, remedial instruction, study skills assistance, tutoring, writing center.

Majors. **Business:** General. **Education:** Elementary. **Psychology:** General.

Computing on campus. 50 workstations in library, computer center, student center. Commuter students can connect to campus network. Online library, wireless network available.

Student life. **Freshman orientation:** Mandatory. Preregistration for classes offered. Held each session (spring, summer, fall) for 2 hours. **Policies:** Freshmen permitted cars on campus. **Activities:** Student government, student newspaper.

Student services. Adult student services, career counseling, services for economically disadvantaged, student employment services, financial aid counseling, minority student services.

Contact. E-mail: webmaster@albizu.edu
Phone: (305) 593-1223 ext. 137 Toll-free number: (800) 672-3246
Fax: (305) 593-1854
Gerardo Alvarado, Director of Recruitment and Outreach, Carlos Albizu University, 2173 NW 99th Avenue, Miami, FL 33172

Chipola College
Marianna, Florida
www.chipola.edu **CB code: 5106**

- Public 4-year community and junior college
- Commuter campus in small town
- 1,527 degree-seeking undergraduates: 40% part-time, 62% women

General. Founded in 1947. Regionally accredited. **Degrees:** 6 bachelor's, 267 associate awarded. **Location:** 70 miles from Tallahassee. **Calendar:** Semester, limited summer session. **Full-time faculty:** 61 total; 25% have terminal degrees, 5% minority, 61% women. **Part-time faculty:** 78 total; 12% minority, 22% women.

Basis for selection. Open admission, but selective for some programs.

High school preparation. Recommended units include English 4, mathematics 3, social studies 3 and science 3.

2005-2006 Annual costs. Tuition/fees: $1,920; $5,790 out-of-state. Books/supplies: $800. Personal expenses: $1,500.

2005-2006 Financial aid. **Need-based:** 92% of total undergraduate aid awarded as scholarships/grants, 8% as loans/jobs. **Non-need-based:** Scholarships awarded for academics, alumni affiliation, art, athletics, job skills, leadership, minority status, music/drama.

Application procedures. **Admission:** Priority date 8/1; no deadline. No application fee. Admission notification on a rolling basis. **Financial aid:** Priority date 5/1; no closing date. FAFSA, institutional form required. Applicants notified on a rolling basis starting 1/2; must reply within 2 week(s) of notification.

Academics. **Special study options:** Accelerated study, cooperative education, distance learning, dual enrollment of high school students, honors, independent study, internships, liberal arts/career combination, teacher certification program. **Credit/placement by examination:** AP, CLEP, IB. 45 credit hours maximum toward associate degree, 45 toward bachelor's. **Support services:** Remedial instruction, study skills assistance, tutoring, writing center.

Majors. **Biology:** General. **Education:** Mathematics, middle, science, secondary. **Math:** General.

Computing on campus. 150 workstations in library. Dormitories linked to campus network. Online library available.

Student life. **Freshman orientation:** Mandatory. Preregistration for classes offered. **Policies:** Freshmen permitted cars on campus. **Housing:** Men's and women's athletic dorms only. **Activities:** Jazz band, choral groups, dance, drama, musical theater, student government, student newspaper, Baptist Campus Ministry, The Vine (interdenominational organization), Black Student Union.

Athletics. NJCAA. **Intercollegiate:** Baseball M, basketball, softball W. **Team name:** Indians.

Student services. Career counseling. **Physically disabled:** Services for visually, hearing impaired.

Contact. Phone: (850) 526-2761 Fax: (850) 718-2287
Jayne Roberts, Dean of Enrollment Services, Chipola College, 3094 Indian Circle, Marianna, FL 32446

City College
Fort Lauderdale, Florida
www.citycollege.edu **CB code: 3578**

- Private 4-year business and technical college
- Commuter campus in very large city
- 977 degree-seeking undergraduates
- Application essay, interview required

General. Accredited by ACICS. **Degrees:** 36 bachelor's, 207 associate awarded. **Calendar:** Quarter. **Full-time faculty:** 6 total. **Part-time faculty:** 75 total.

Basis for selection. Open admission, but selective for some programs. Interviews and essay important.

2005-2006 Annual costs. Books/supplies: $1,044. Personal expenses: $2,931.

Application procedures. **Admission:** No deadline. $25 fee, may be waived for applicants with need. Admission notification on a rolling basis.

Academics. **Special study options:** Double major, independent study, internships. **Credit/placement by examination:** CLEP, IB, institutional tests. 15 credit hours maximum toward associate degree, 30 toward bachelor's.

Majors. **Business:** Business admin.

Student life. **Freshman orientation:** Mandatory. Preregistration for classes offered.

Student services. Adult student services, alcohol/substance abuse counseling, career counseling, student employment services, financial aid counseling, personal counseling, placement for graduates.

Contact. Phone: (954) 492-5353 Fax: (954) 491-1965
Ron Lohrmann, Director of Admissions, City College, 1401 West Cypress Creek Road, Fort Lauderdale, FL 33309

Clearwater Christian College

Clearwater, Florida
www.clearwater.edu **CB code: 5142**

- Private 4-year liberal arts college affiliated with nondenominational tradition
- Residential campus in small city
- 564 degree-seeking undergraduates
- 83% of applicants admitted
- SAT or ACT, application essay required

General. Founded in 1966. Regionally accredited. **Degrees:** 108 bachelor's, 2 associate awarded. **ROTC:** Army. **Location:** 20 miles from Tampa, 15 miles from St. Petersburg. **Calendar:** Semester, limited summer session. **Full-time faculty:** 31 total. **Part-time faculty:** 12 total. **Class size:** 55% < 20, 31% 20-39, 4% 40-49, 10% 50-99.

Freshman class profile. 498 applied, 412 admitted, 213 enrolled.

Mid 50% test scores		SAT math:	510-550
SAT verbal:	540-590	ACT:	23-26

Basis for selection. Recommendations, Christian testimony, minimum 2.0 high school GPA, minimum 870 SAT or 18 ACT. Interview recommended. Audition recommended for music majors. **Homeschooled:** GED required Liberal-arts/college preparatory program recommended. Academic placement testing may be administered.

High school preparation. Recommended units include English 4, mathematics 3, social studies 3, science 3 and foreign language 2.

2006-2007 Annual costs. Tuition/fees: $12,500. Room/board: $5,330. Books/supplies: $850. Personal expenses: $1,750.

2005-2006 Financial aid. Need-based: 47% of total undergraduate aid awarded as scholarships/grants, 53% as loans/jobs. **Non-need-based:** Scholarships awarded for academics, music/drama, religious affiliation. **Additional information:** Special consideration for financial aid given to children of Christian service workers.

Application procedures. Admission: Closing date 8/1 (receipt date). $35 fee. Admission notification on a rolling basis. **Financial aid:** Priority date 3/15; no closing date. FAFSA, institutional form required. Applicants notified on a rolling basis starting 4/15; must reply within 2 week(s) of notification.

Academics. All students completing 4-year degree earn 20-hour minor in Bible. Scripture integrated into various subject areas. **Special study options:** Double major, dual enrollment of high school students, internships, liberal arts/career combination, study abroad, teacher certification program. **Credit/placement by examination:** AP, CLEP, institutional tests. 24 credit hours maximum toward associate degree, 24 toward bachelor's. **Support services:** Reduced course load, remedial instruction, study skills assistance, tutoring.

Majors. Biology: General. **Business:** Accounting, business admin, office management. **Communications:** General. **Education:** Biology, elementary, English, mathematics, music, physical, social studies, special. **Health:** Premedicine. **History:** General. **Legal studies:** Prelaw. **Liberal arts:** Arts/sciences. **Math:** General. **Psychology:** General. **Theology:** Bible, religious ed, sacred music, theology.

Most popular majors. Biology 7%, business/marketing 22%, education 13%, English 6%, liberal arts 8%, psychology 8%.

Computing on campus. 38 workstations in dormitories, library, computer center. Dormitories linked to campus network. Commuter students can connect to campus network. Repair service available.

Student life. Freshman orientation: Mandatory. Preregistration for classes offered. Non-credit 2-day freshman orientation prior to opening of fall classes. **Policies:** Daily chapel service. Attendance at evening group devotions and prayer meetings required of dormitory residents. Religious observance required. Freshmen permitted cars on campus. **Housing:** Guaranteed on-campus for all undergraduates. Single-sex dorms available. $100 deposit. **Activities:** Choral groups, drama, music ensembles, student government, symphony orchestra, Christian service organizations, student missionary fellowship, College Republicans, science club, drama club.

Athletics. NCCAA. **Intercollegiate:** Baseball M, basketball, football (non-tackle) M, soccer M, softball W, volleyball W. **Intramural:** Basketball, soccer, volleyball. **Team name:** Cougars.

Student services. Career counseling, student employment services, personal counseling, placement for graduates. **Physically disabled:** Services for speech impaired.

Contact. E-mail: admissions@clearwater.edu
Phone: (727) 726-1153 Toll-free number: (800) 348-4463
Fax: (727) 726-8597
Benjamin Puckett, Dean of Enrollment Services, Clearwater Christian College, 3400 Gulf-to-Bay Boulevard, Clearwater, FL 33759-4595

College for Professional Studies

Boca Raton, Florida
CB code: 3907

- For-profit 4-year business college

General. Accredited by DETC.

Contact. Phone: (561) 994-2522
6409 Congress Avenue, Boca Raton, FL 33487

DeVry University: Miramar

Miramar, Florida
www.mir.devry.edu **CB code: 4134**

- For-profit 4-year university
- Commuter campus in large town
- 969 degree-seeking undergraduates: 33% part-time, 58% women
- 99 graduate students
- Interview required

General. Degrees: 54 bachelor's, 11 associate awarded; master's offered. **Calendar:** Semester, extensive summer session. **Full-time faculty:** 34 total; 65% minority, 26% women. **Part-time faculty:** 22 total; 46% minority, 23% women.

Freshman class profile. 188 enrolled.

Return as sophomores:	43%	International:	4%

Basis for selection. Applicants must have high school diploma or equivalent, or a degree from accredited postsecondary institution, demonstrate proficiency in basic college-level skills through SAT or ACT scores or institution-administered placement exams, and be at least 17 years of age. New students may enter at beginning of any semester. SAT or ACT recommended. CPT also accepted.

High school preparation. Required units include mathematics 1.

2005-2006 Annual costs. Tuition/fees: $12,800. Books/supplies: $1,100. Personal expenses: $1,816.

2004-2005 Financial aid. All financial aid based on need. 106 full-time freshmen applied for aid; 101 were judged to have need; 97 of these received aid. Average need met was 44%. Average scholarship/grant was $5,299; average loan $5,065. 19% of total undergraduate aid awarded as scholarships/grants, 81% as loans/jobs.

Application procedures. Admission: No deadline. $50 fee. Application may be submitted online. Admission notification on a rolling basis. **Financial aid:** No deadline. FAFSA required. Applicants notified on a rolling basis.

Academics. Special study options: Accelerated study, cooperative education, distance learning. **Credit/placement by examination:** CLEP. **Support services:** Learning center, remedial instruction, tutoring.

Majors. Business: Business admin, operations. **Computer sciences:** Information systems, LAN/WAN management. **Engineering technology:** Computer, electrical.

Most popular majors. Business/marketing 78%, computer/information sciences 20%.

Computing on campus. Online course registration, online library, helpline available.

Student life. Policies: Freshmen permitted cars on campus. **Activities:** Student government, student newspaper.

Student services. Career counseling, student employment services, financial aid counseling, placement for graduates, veterans' counselor. **Physically disabled:** Services for visually, hearing impaired.

Contact. E-mail: openhouse@mir.devry.edu
Phone: (954) 499-9700 Toll-free number: (866) 793-3879
Fax: (954) 499-9723
Aaron McCardell, Director of Admission, DeVry University: Miramar, 2300 Southwest 145th Avenue, Miramar, FL 33027

DeVry University: Orlando

Orlando, Florida
www.orl.devry.edu **CB code: 2881**

- For-profit 4-year university
- Commuter campus in very large city
- 1,048 degree-seeking undergraduates: 33% part-time, 51% women
- 133 graduate students
- Interview required

General. Regionally accredited. **Degrees:** 230 bachelor's, 39 associate awarded; master's offered. **Calendar:** Semester, extensive summer session. **Full-time faculty:** 37 total; 24% minority, 14% women. **Part-time faculty:** 54 total; 22% minority, 54% women.

Freshman class profile. 159 enrolled.

Return as sophomores:	43%	**International:**	3%

Basis for selection. Applicants must have high school diploma or equivalent, or degree from an accredited postsecondary institution. New students may enter at the beginning of any semester. SAT or ACT recommended. SAT or ACT or institution-administered placement examination used to determine proficiency in basic college-level skills.

High school preparation. Required units include mathematics 1. Math unit must be algebra or higher.

2005-2006 Annual costs. Tuition/fees: $12,800. Books/supplies: $1,100. Personal expenses: $1,750.

2004-2005 Financial aid. All financial aid based on need. 131 full-time freshmen applied for aid; 125 were judged to have need; 125 of these received aid. Average need met was 41%. Average scholarship/grant was $4,432; average loan $5,684. 17% of total undergraduate aid awarded as scholarships/grants, 83% as loans/jobs.

Application procedures. Admission: No deadline. $50 fee. Application may be submitted online. Admission notification on a rolling basis. **Financial aid:** No deadline. FAFSA required. Applicants notified on a rolling basis starting 7/2.

Academics. Special study options: Accelerated study, cooperative education, distance learning. **Credit/placement by examination:** CLEP, institutional tests. **Support services:** Learning center, remedial instruction, tutoring.

Majors. Business: Business admin. **Computer sciences:** Information systems, LAN/WAN management. **Engineering technology:** Computer systems, electrical.

Most popular majors. Business/marketing 40%, computer/information sciences 42%, engineering/engineering technologies 18%.

Computing on campus. 303 workstations in library, computer center. Online course registration, online library, helpline available.

Student life. Freshman orientation: Mandatory. **Policies:** Freshmen permitted cars on campus. **Activities:** Student newspaper, student activities council, National Society of Black Engineers, Association for IT Professionals, chess club, Technology Forum, Millenia Engineering Students Association.

Student services. Career counseling, student employment services, financial aid counseling, placement for graduates, veterans' counselor. **Physically disabled:** Services for visually, hearing impaired.

Contact. E-mail: krochford@orl.devry.edu
Phone: (407) 370-3131 Toll-free number: (866) 353-3879
Fax: (407) 370-3198
Jody Wasmer, Director of Admissions, DeVry University: Orlando, 4000 Millennia Boulevard, Orlando, FL 32839-2426

Eckerd College

St. Petersburg, Florida **CB member**
www.eckerd.edu **CB code: 5223**

- Private 4-year liberal arts college affiliated with Presbyterian Church (USA)
- Residential campus in large city
- 1,756 degree-seeking undergraduates: 1% part-time, 57% women, 3% African American, 2% Asian American, 4% Hispanic American, 5% international
- 72% of applicants admitted
- SAT or ACT (ACT writing optional), application essay required

General. Founded in 1958. Regionally accredited. **Degrees:** 330 bachelor's awarded. **ROTC:** Army, Air Force. **Location:** 25 miles from Tampa. **Calendar:** 4-1-4, limited summer session. **Full-time faculty:** 107 total; 92% have terminal degrees, 13% minority, 36% women. **Part-time faculty:** 54 total; 30% women. **Class size:** 46% < 20, 51% 20-39, 1% 40-49, less than 1% 50-99. **Special facilities:** Marine science laboratory, waterfront program.

Freshman class profile. 2,740 applied, 1,962 admitted, 502 enrolled.

Mid 50% test scores		**GPA 2.0-2.99:**	30%
SAT verbal:	510-630	**Rank in top quarter:**	46%
SAT math:	510-610	**Rank in top tenth:**	19%
ACT:	22-27	**Out-of-state:**	78%
GPA 3.50 or higher:	35%	**Live on campus:**	96%
GPA 3.0-3.49:	35%	**International:**	2%

Basis for selection. School achievement record, school/community involvement, student's character, test scores most important. Students from Puerto Rico may take the PAA in lieu of the SAT or ACT. Interview recommended. Audition tapes for music and theatre majors accepted, portfolios accepted for art majors. **Homeschooled:** Statement describing homeschool structure and mission, transcript of courses and grades, state high school equivalency certificate, letter of recommendation (nonparent) required. **Learning Disabled:** Students should provide proper documentation for any disability they wish to inform the college about.

High school preparation. College-preparatory program required. 18 units required; 22 recommended. Required and recommended units include English 4, mathematics 3-4, social studies 2, history 1-2, science 3-4 (laboratory 2-3), foreign language 2-3 and academic electives 3.

2006-2007 Annual costs. Tuition/fees: $27,624. Room/board: $7,868. Books/supplies: $1,000. Personal expenses: $1,400.

2005-2006 Financial aid. Need-based: 347 full-time freshmen applied for aid; 273 were judged to have need; 273 of these received aid. Average need met was 87%. Average scholarship/grant was $17,956; average loan $2,204. 69% of total undergraduate aid awarded as scholarships/grants, 31% as loans/jobs. **Non-need-based:** Awarded to 579 full-time undergraduates, including 97 freshmen. Scholarships awarded for academics, alumni affiliation, art, athletics, leadership, minority status, music/drama, religious affiliation, ROTC, state residency.

Application procedures. Admission: No deadline. $35 fee, may be waived for applicants with need. Application may be submitted online. Admission notification on a rolling basis beginning on or about 10/1. Must reply by May 1 or within 2 week(s) if notified thereafter. **Financial aid:** Priority date 2/15; no closing date. FAFSA required. Applicants notified on a rolling basis starting 2/1.

Academics. Special study options: Accelerated study, combined bachelor's/graduate degree, cross-registration, double major, dual enrollment of high school students, ESL, exchange student, honors, independent study, internships, liberal arts/career combination, semester at sea, student-designed major, study abroad, United Nations semester, Washington semester. Winter term exchange with other 4-1-4 colleges, 3-2 in engineering with Columbia University, Washington University (MO), University of Miami, and Auburn. **Credit/placement by examination:** AP, CLEP, IB, institutional tests. 63 credit hours maximum toward bachelor's degree. **Support services:** Reduced course load, tutoring, writing center.

Majors. Area/ethnic studies: American, East Asian, women's. **Biology:** General, biochemistry, environmental, marine. **Business:** Business admin, international, management science. **Communications:** General. **Computer sciences:** General. **Conservation:** Environmental studies. **English:** Creative writing, English lit. **Family/consumer sciences:** Family studies. **Foreign languages:** General, comparative lit, French, German, Spanish. **History:** General. **Interdisciplinary:** Global studies. **Liberal arts:** Humanities.

Math: General. **Philosophy/religion:** Philosophy, religion. **Physical sciences:** Chemistry, physics. **Psychology:** General. **Social sciences:** Anthropology, economics, international relations, political science, sociology. **Visual/performing arts:** Dramatic, studio arts.

Most popular majors. Biology 17%, business/marketing 21%, natural resources/environmental science 8%, psychology 6%, social sciences 14%, visual/performing arts 6%.

Computing on campus. 300 workstations in dormitories, library. Dormitories wired for high-speed internet access and linked to campus network. Commuter students can connect to campus network. Online course registration, online library, helpline, repair service, student web hosting, wireless network available.

Student life. **Freshman orientation:** Mandatory. Preregistration for classes offered. 3-week autumn term includes both orientation and 1 academic course. **Policies:** Freshmen permitted cars on campus. **Housing:** Guaranteed on-campus for all undergraduates. Coed dorms, single-sex dorms, apartments, substance-free housing available. Pets allowed in dorm rooms. **Activities:** Choral groups, drama, film society, literary magazine, music ensembles, musical theater, radio station, student government, student newspaper, TV station, Phi Beta Kappa, Afro-American Society, international students association, Eckerd college search and rescue team, student religious organizations, Circle-K, honor societies, Earth society, Model United Nations.

Athletics. NCAA. **Intercollegiate:** Baseball M, basketball, golf, sailing, soccer, softball W, tennis, volleyball W. **Intramural:** Baseball M, basketball, bowling, sailing, soccer, softball, swimming, table tennis, tennis, volleyball. **Team name:** Tritons.

Student services. Adult student services, alcohol/substance abuse counseling, campus ministries, career counseling, student employment services, financial aid counseling, health services, minority student services, personal counseling, placement for graduates, veterans' counselor, women's services.

Contact. E-mail: admissions@eckerd.edu
Phone: (727) 864-8331 Toll-free number: (800) 456-9009
Fax: (727) 866-2304
John Sullivan, Director of Admissions, Eckerd College, 4200 54th Avenue South, St. Petersburg, FL 33711-4700

Edward Waters College

Jacksonville, Florida
www.ewc.edu **CB code: 5182**

- Private 4-year liberal arts college affiliated with African Methodist Episcopal Church
- Commuter campus in very large city
- 837 degree-seeking undergraduates: 2% part-time, 48% women, 92% African American, 1% Hispanic American, 1% international
- 15% graduate within 6 years

General. Founded in 1866. Regionally accredited. **Degrees:** 141 bachelor's awarded. **ROTC:** Army. **Location:** 150 miles from Orlando, 90 miles from Savannah, Georgia. **Calendar:** Semester, extensive summer session. **Full-time faculty:** 35 total; 54% have terminal degrees. **Part-time faculty:** 12 total. **Class size:** 100% < 20. **Special facilities:** African art collection, three computer centers.

Freshman class profile.

Out-of-state:	31%	**International:**	1%

Basis for selection. Open admission. All students who successfuly complete High School with a Standard High School Diploma or a GED is admitted.

High school preparation. 15 units recommended. Recommended units include English 4, mathematics 3, social studies 3, science 2 and academic electives 5.

2005-2006 Annual costs. Tuition/fees: $9,176. Room/board: $6,474. Books/supplies: $500. Personal expenses: $750.

Financial aid. **Non-need-based:** Scholarships awarded for academics, athletics, minority status, state residency.

Application procedures. **Admission:** No deadline. $25 fee, may be waived for applicants with need. Admission notification on a rolling basis. Must reply by May 1 or within 4 week(s) if notified thereafter. **Financial aid:** Closing date 4/15. FAFSA, institutional form required. Applicants notified on a rolling basis starting 5/1; must reply within 2 week(s) of notification.

Academics. **Special study options:** Accelerated study, combined bachelor's/graduate degree, cooperative education, cross-registration, double major, dual enrollment of high school students, independent study, internships, liberal arts/career combination, teacher certification program, weekend college. **Credit/placement by examination:** AP, CLEP. 30 credit hours maximum toward bachelor's degree. **Support services:** Learning center, pre-admission summer program, remedial instruction, study skills assistance, tutoring.

Majors. **Biology:** General. **Business:** Accounting, business admin. **Communications:** General, journalism. **Computer sciences:** Computer science. **Education:** General, mathematics, mentally handicapped, physical, special. **History:** General. **Legal studies:** Prelaw. **Liberal arts:** Arts/sciences. **Math:** General. **Philosophy/religion:** Religion. **Protective services:** Law enforcement admin. **Psychology:** General. **Public administration:** Social work. **Social sciences:** Sociology.

Most popular majors. Business/marketing 57%, education 11%, legal studies 8%.

Computing on campus. 120 workstations in library, computer center. Dormitories wired for high-speed internet access and linked to campus network. Repair service, wireless network available.

Student life. **Freshman orientation:** Mandatory. Preregistration for classes offered. **Policies:** Religious observance required. Freshmen permitted cars on campus. **Housing:** Guaranteed on-campus for freshmen. Coed dorms, single-sex dorms, substance-free housing available. $100 deposit, deadline 7/31. **Activities:** Bands, choral groups, dance, drama, music ensembles, student government, student newspaper, NAACP, international student organization, ministerial alliance, debate club, pre-alumni club.

Athletics. NAIA. **Intercollegiate:** Baseball M, basketball, cheerleading, cross-country M, diving W, football (tackle) M, golf, softball W, track and field M, volleyball W. **Intramural:** Table tennis, volleyball. **Team name:** Fighting Tigers.

Student services. Adult student services, campus ministries, career counseling, student employment services, financial aid counseling, health services, personal counseling, placement for graduates, veterans' counselor.

Contact. E-mail: Admissions@ewc.edu
Phone: (904) 470-8000 Toll-free number: (888) 898-3191
Fax: (904) 470-8041
Terri Little-Berry, Associate Director, Edward Waters College, 1658 Kings Road, Jacksonville, FL 32209

Embry-Riddle Aeronautical University

Daytona Beach, Florida **CB member**
www.embryriddle.edu **CB code: 5190**

- Private 4-year university
- Residential campus in small city
- 4,352 degree-seeking undergraduates: 6% part-time, 17% women, 5% African American, 5% Asian American, 7% Hispanic American, 8% international
- 391 degree-seeking graduate students
- 84% of applicants admitted
- SAT or ACT (ACT writing optional) required
- 59% graduate within 6 years

General. Founded in 1926. Regionally accredited. Over 130 teaching centers across the United States and Europe. **Degrees:** 844 bachelor's, 9 associate awarded; master's offered. **ROTC:** Army, Navy, Air Force. **Location:** 50 miles from Orlando. **Calendar:** Semester, extensive summer session. **Full-time faculty:** 227 total; 65% have terminal degrees, 12% minority, 18% women. **Part-time faculty:** 87 total; 12% have terminal degrees, 3% minority, 41% women. **Class size:** 23% < 20, 68% 20-39, 6% 40-49, 3% 50-99. **Special facilities:** Airway science simulation lab.

Freshman class profile. 3,527 applied, 2,978 admitted, 977 enrolled.

Mid 50% test scores		**Rank in top tenth:**	20%
SAT verbal:	480-600	**Return as sophomores:**	75%
SAT math:	510-630	**Out-of-state:**	73%
ACT:	21-27	**Live on campus:**	95%
GPA 3.50 or higher:	38%	**International:**	6%
GPA 3.0-3.49:	36%	**Fraternities:**	10%
GPA 2.0-2.99:	25%	**Sororities:**	13%
Rank in top quarter:	48%		

Basis for selection. High school GPA, rank in class, and test scores important. Specific requirements vary by degree program. Interview and essay recommended.

High school preparation. 15 units required; 19 recommended. Required and recommended units include English 4, mathematics 3-4, social studies 2, history 1-2, science 2-3 (laboratory 2), foreign language 1 and academic electives 3.

2005-2006 Annual costs. Tuition/fees: $23,500. Room/board: $6,936. Books/supplies: $920. Personal expenses: $1,250.

2005-2006 Financial aid. **Need-based:** 806 full-time freshmen applied for aid; 667 were judged to have need; 667 of these received aid. Average scholarship/grant was $7,380; average loan $3,169. 41% of total undergraduate aid awarded as scholarships/grants, 59% as loans/jobs. **Non-need-based:** Scholarships awarded for academics, alumni affiliation, athletics, leadership, ROTC.

Application procedures. **Admission:** No deadline. $50 fee, may be waived for applicants with need. Application may be submitted online. Admission notification on a rolling basis beginning on or about 11/1. Early application encouraged since available facilities limit enrollment in some programs. **Financial aid:** No deadline. FAFSA required. Applicants notified on a rolling basis starting 3/1; must reply within 4 week(s) of notification.

Academics. **Special study options:** Accelerated study, cooperative education, distance learning, double major, dual enrollment of high school students, ESL, honors, independent study, internships, student-designed major, study abroad. **Credit/placement by examination:** AP, CLEP, IB, institutional tests. 30 credit hours maximum toward bachelor's degree. **Support services:** Pre-admission summer program, remedial instruction, study skills assistance, tutoring.

Majors. **Business:** Business admin. **Communications:** General. **Computer sciences:** General, computer science. **Engineering:** General, aerospace, civil, computer, electrical, mechanical, physics, software. **Engineering technology:** Aerospace, electrical, occupational safety. **Mechanic/repair:** Aircraft powerplant. **Physical sciences:** Atmospheric science, physics. **Transportation:** Air traffic control, airline/commercial pilot, aviation, aviation management.

Most popular majors. Business/marketing 8%, engineering/engineering technologies 32%, trade and industry 52%.

Computing on campus. 890 workstations in library, computer center. Dormitories linked to campus network. Commuter students can connect to campus network. Helpline, student web hosting available.

Student life. **Freshman orientation:** Available. Preregistration for classes offered. **Policies:** Freshmen permitted cars on campus. **Housing:** Guaranteed on-campus for freshmen. Coed dorms available. $250 deposit, deadline 11/1. Special units available in regular coed dorms. **Activities:** Pep band, choral groups, dance, drama, radio station, student government, student newspaper, more than 100 clubs and organizations available.

Athletics. NAIA. **Intercollegiate:** Baseball M, basketball M, cheerleading, cross-country, golf, soccer, tennis, track and field, volleyball W. **Intramural:** Badminton, basketball, bowling, football (non-tackle), golf, racquetball, soccer, table tennis, volleyball. **Team name:** Eagles.

Student services. Alcohol/substance abuse counseling, campus ministries, career counseling, student employment services, financial aid counseling, health services, personal counseling, placement for graduates, veterans' counselor. **Physically disabled:** Services for visually, speech, hearing impaired.

Contact. E-mail: dbadmit@erau.edu
Phone: (386) 226-6100 Toll-free number: (800) 862-2416
Fax: (386) 226-7070
Rich Clarke, Director of Admissions, Embry-Riddle Aeronautical University, 600 South Clyde Morris Boulevard, Daytona Beach, FL 32114-3900

Embry-Riddle Aeronautical University: Extended Campus

Daytona Beach, Florida
www.embryriddle.edu **CB code: 5036**

- Private 4-year university
- Commuter campus in small city
- 10,776 degree-seeking undergraduates: 81% part-time, 11% women, 8% African American, 3% Asian American, 8% Hispanic American, 1% Native American, 1% international
- 3,604 degree-seeking graduate students

General. Regionally accredited. Campus is a network of more than 130 centers and teaching sites in the United States and Europe, with virtual presence via distance learning covering every continent. **Degrees:** 1,858 bachelor's, 421 associate awarded; master's offered. **Calendar:** Varies by location. Extensive summer session. **Full-time faculty:** 137 total; 47% have terminal degrees, 9% minority, 18% women. **Part-time faculty:** 1,967 total; 17% have terminal degrees, 14% minority, 18% women.

Basis for selection. High school GPA, rank in class, and test scores important. Specific requirements vary by degree program.

2005-2006 Annual costs. Per credit hour charges range from $176 to $274.

2005-2006 Financial aid. **Need-based:** 18 full-time freshmen applied for aid; 16 were judged to have need; 16 of these received aid. Average scholarship/grant was $3,623; average loan $2,606. 20% of total undergraduate aid awarded as scholarships/grants, 80% as loans/jobs. **Non-need-based:** Scholarships awarded for academics.

Application procedures. **Admission:** No deadline. $50 fee, may be waived for applicants with need. Admission notification on a rolling basis. **Financial aid:** Priority date 4/15; no closing date. FAFSA required. Applicants notified on a rolling basis starting 3/1; must reply within 4 week(s) of notification.

Academics. **Special study options:** Distance learning. **Credit/placement by examination:** AP, CLEP.

Majors. **Business:** Business admin. **Mechanic/repair:** Aircraft powerplant. **Transportation:** Aviation, aviation management.

Most popular majors. Business/marketing 13%, trade and industry 87%.

Student life. **Activities:** Student newspaper.

Contact. E-mail: ecinfo@erau.edu
Phone: (386) 225-6910 Toll-free number: (800) 522-6787
Fax: (386) 226-6984
Pamela Thomas, Director of Admissions, Embry-Riddle Aeronautical University: Extended Campus, 600 South Clyde Morris Boulevard, Daytona Beach, FL 32114-3900

Everglades University

Boca Raton, Florida
www.evergladesuniversity.edu **CB code: 3191**

- Private 4-year university
- Commuter campus in large city
- 360 degree-seeking undergraduates
- 40 graduate students

General. Accredited by ACCSCT. **Degrees:** 91 bachelor's, 5 associate awarded; master's offered. **Calendar:** Semester, extensive summer session. **Full-time faculty:** 24 total; 71% have terminal degrees, 33% women. **Part-time faculty:** 93 total; 45% have terminal degrees, 40% women.

Basis for selection. Students without an associate degree must either obtain a passing score on college administered entrance exam, provide an SAT score of at least 800 (exclusive of Writing) or provide an ACT score of at least 17.

2005-2006 Annual costs. Tuition/fees: $12,500. Books/supplies: $500. Personal expenses: $500.

Financial aid. **Additional information:** Federal Pell Grant, Federal Direct Stafford Student Loan, Federal Family Education Loan (Stafford Student Loan), Unsubsidized Federal Direct and FFEL Stafford Loans and Federal Plus Loans offered.

Application procedures. **Admission:** No deadline. $55 fee. Application may be submitted online. Admission notification on a rolling basis. **Financial aid:** No deadline. FAFSA required. Applicants notified on a rolling basis.

Academics. **Special study options:** Distance learning. **Credit/placement by examination:** CLEP.

Majors. **Business:** Business admin, construction management. **Computer sciences:** Information technology. **Transportation:** Aviation, aviation management.

Computing on campus. 25 workstations in library, computer center. Online library, helpline, wireless network available.

Student life. Freshman orientation: Mandatory. **Policies:** Freshmen permitted cars on campus. **Activities:** Student government.

Student services. Career counseling, student employment services, placement for graduates.

Contact. E-mail: admissions-boca@evergladesuniversity.edu
Phone: (561) 912-1211 Toll-free number: (888) 772-6077
Fax: (561) 912-1211
Jean Graham, Director of Admissions, Everglades University, 5002 T-REX Avenue, Suite 100, Boca Raton, FL 33431

Flagler College

St. Augustine, Florida **CB member**
www.flagler.edu **CB code: 5235**

- Private 4-year liberal arts college
- Residential campus in large town
- 2,157 degree-seeking undergraduates: 3% part-time, 62% women, 2% African American, 1% Asian American, 4% Hispanic American, 3% international
- SAT or ACT (ACT writing recommended), application essay required
- 56% graduate within 6 years; 20% enter graduate study

General. Founded in 1968. Regionally accredited. Center for Historic Research co-sponsored by Flagler College and St. Augustine Foundation on campus. **Degrees:** 449 bachelor's awarded. **Location:** 35 miles from Jacksonville, 50 miles from Daytona Beach. **Calendar:** Semester, limited summer session. **Full-time faculty:** 74 total; 64% have terminal degrees, 4% minority, 42% women. **Part-time faculty:** 109 total; 19% have terminal degrees, 38% women. **Class size:** 42% < 20, 56% 20-39, 1% 40-49, less than 1% 50-99.

Freshman class profile.

Mid 50% test scores			
SAT verbal:	530-620	GPA 2.0-2.99:	34%
SAT math:	530-600	Rank in top quarter:	51%
ACT:	22-26	Rank in top tenth:	16%
GPA 3.50 or higher:	26%	Return as sophomores:	69%
GPA 3.0-3.49:	40%	Out-of-state:	32%
		Live on campus:	81%

Basis for selection. Academic record, including pattern of courses and class rank, most important, followed by test scores. Extracurricular activities, recommendations, and intended major also considered. Education applicants must score at or above 45th percentile on SAT or ACT. Interview required for early admission applicants; recommended for all others.

High school preparation. 16 units required; 20 recommended. Required and recommended units include English 4, mathematics 3-4, social studies 3-4, history 2-3, science 2-3 (laboratory 1-2), foreign language 2 and academic electives 1-2.

2006-2007 Annual costs. Tuition/fees: $9,450. Room/board: $5,760. Books/supplies: $800. Personal expenses: $1,200.

2005-2006 Financial aid. Need-based: 333 full-time freshmen applied for aid; 209 were judged to have need; 206 of these received aid. Average need met was 75%. Average scholarship/grant was $3,152; average loan $2,721. 51% of total undergraduate aid awarded as scholarships/grants, 49% as loans/jobs. **Non-need-based:** Awarded to 896 full-time undergraduates, including 203 freshmen. Scholarships awarded for academics, art, athletics, job skills, leadership, minority status, music/drama, state residency.

Application procedures. Admission: Priority date 1/15; deadline 3/1 (postmark date). $40 fee, may be waived for applicants with need. Application may be submitted online. Admission notification 3/15. Must reply by May 1 or within 3 week(s) if notified thereafter. **Financial aid:** Priority date 4/1; no closing date. FAFSA, institutional form required. Applicants notified on a rolling basis starting 3/1; must reply within 2 week(s) of notification.

Academics. Freshmen must earn at least 24 semester hours credit for good academic standing. **Special study options:** Double major, independent study, internships, study abroad, teacher certification program. Deaf education majors work directly with faculty and students at nearby Florida School for the Deaf and Blind. **Credit/placement by examination:** AP, CLEP, IB, SAT, ACT, institutional tests. 30 credit hours maximum toward bachelor's degree. **Support services:** Reduced course load, remedial instruction, study skills assistance, writing center.

Majors. Area/ethnic studies: Latin American. **Business:** Accounting, business admin. **Communications:** General. **Education:** Art, Deaf/hearing impaired, drama/dance, elementary, English, history, multi-level teacher, secondary, social science, social studies, special. **Foreign languages:** Spanish. **History:** General. **Liberal arts:** Arts/sciences. **Parks/recreation:** Sports admin. **Philosophy/religion:** Philosophy. **Psychology:** General. **Public administration:** General. **Social sciences:** Political science, sociology. **Visual/performing arts:** General, dramatic, studio arts.

Most popular majors. Business/marketing 23%, communications/journalism 15%, education 10%, English 7%, psychology 6%, social sciences 8%, visual/performing arts 15%.

Computing on campus. 205 workstations in library, computer center. Dormitories wired for high-speed internet access and linked to campus network. Commuter students can connect to campus network. Online course registration, online library, helpline, student web hosting, wireless network available.

Student life. Freshman orientation: Mandatory. Preregistration for classes offered. 3-day program held each semester. **Policies:** Interdorm visitation not allowed in residence halls. Alcohol prohibited on campus. No smoking in buildings, including residence halls. Freshmen permitted cars on campus. **Housing:** Guaranteed on-campus for freshmen. Single-sex dorms available. $200 nonrefundable deposit, deadline 5/1. **Activities:** Choral groups, drama, literary magazine, radio station, student government, student newspaper, Rotaract, Intervarsity Christian Fellowship, Catholic College Fellowship, Society for Advancement of Management, Students in Free Enterprises, deaf awareness club, sport management club, AIGA, SPIRIT, The Home Team.

Athletics. NAIA. **Intercollegiate:** Baseball M, basketball, cheerleading, cross-country, golf, soccer, tennis, volleyball W. **Intramural:** Badminton, basketball, bowling, football (non-tackle), golf, soccer, softball, table tennis, tennis, volleyball, weight lifting. **Team name:** Saints.

Student services. Career counseling, student employment services, financial aid counseling, health services, personal counseling, veterans' counselor. **Physically disabled:** Services for visually, speech, hearing impaired.

Contact. E-mail: admiss@flagler.edu
Phone: (904) 829-6220 Toll-free number: (800) 304-4208
Fax: (904) 829-6838
Marc Williar, Director of Admissions, Flagler College, 74 King Street, St. Augustine, FL 32084

Florida Agricultural and Mechanical University

Tallahassee, Florida **CB member**
www.famu.edu **CB code: 5215**

- Public 4-year university
- Residential campus in small city
- 10,372 degree-seeking undergraduates
- 71% of applicants admitted
- SAT or ACT with writing, application essay required

General. Founded in 1887. Regionally accredited. **Degrees:** 1,353 bachelor's, 83 associate awarded; master's, doctoral, first professional offered. **ROTC:** Army, Navy, Air Force. **Location:** 169 miles from Jacksonville. **Calendar:** Semester, extensive summer session. **Full-time faculty:** 623 total. **Part-time faculty:** 169 total. **Class size:** 37% < 20, 42% 20-39, 9% 40-49, 8% 50-99, 4% >100. **Special facilities:** African American archives research center and museum, observatory.

Freshman class profile. 4,493 applied, 3,172 admitted, 1,459 enrolled.

Mid 50% test scores			
SAT verbal:	410-550	ACT:	15-21
SAT math:	410-520	Out-of-state:	5%
		Live on campus:	80%

Basis for selection. School achievement record and test scores most important. Minimum 2.5 GPA required. Essay required of borderline applicants. Interview recommended for nursing, physical therapy, architecture, pharmacy, engineering majors. Audition required of music majors. Portfolio required of architecture majors. **Homeschooled:** Applicant may be asked to complete GED.

High school preparation. Required units include English 4, mathematics 3, social studies 3, science 3 (laboratory 1), foreign language 2 and academic electives 4.

2005-2006 Annual costs. Tuition/fees: $3,188; $15,177 out-of-state. Room/board: $5,667. Books/supplies: $800. Personal expenses: $2,400.

2005-2006 Financial aid. Need-based: 56% of total undergraduate aid awarded as scholarships/grants, 44% as loans/jobs. **Non-need-based:** Scholarships awarded for academics, art, leadership.

Application procedures. **Admission:** Priority date 3/9; deadline 5/18. $20 fee. Admission notification on a rolling basis. **Financial aid:** Priority date 3/1, closing date 6/30. FAFSA required. Applicants notified on a rolling basis starting 3/1; must reply within 2 week(s) of notification.

Academics. **Special study options:** Accelerated study, combined bachelor's/graduate degree, cooperative education, distance learning, double major, dual enrollment of high school students, external degree, honors, independent study, internships, liberal arts/career combination, study abroad, teacher certification program, weekend college. **Credit/placement by examination:** AP, CLEP, IB. 30 credit hours maximum toward associate degree, 30 toward bachelor's. Student must have passing scores (determined by state) for AP and CLEP exams. **Support services:** Learning center, pre-admission summer program, reduced course load, remedial instruction, study skills assistance, tutoring, writing center.

Majors. **Agriculture:** Agribusiness operations, agronomy, animal sciences, food science, horticultural science, horticulture, landscaping, ornamental horticulture, plant protection. **Architecture:** Architecture. **Area/ethnic studies:** African-American. **Biology:** General. **Business:** Accounting, business admin, managerial economics. **Communications:** Broadcast journalism, journalism, public relations. **Computer sciences:** General. **Conservation:** Environmental science. **Education:** Art, business, early childhood, elementary, English, mathematics, music, physical, science, social studies, trade/industrial. **Engineering:** Agricultural, chemical, civil, electrical, mechanical. **Engineering technology:** Civil, construction, electrical. **Foreign languages:** French, Spanish. **Health:** Health care admin, medical records admin, nursing (RN), respiratory therapy technology. **History:** General. **Math:** General. **Philosophy/religion:** Philosophy, religion. **Physical sciences:** Chemistry, physics. **Protective services:** Criminal justice. **Psychology:** General. **Public administration:** Social work. **Social sciences:** Economics, political science, sociology. **Visual/performing arts:** General, commercial/advertising art, dramatic, music performance.

Most popular majors. Business/marketing 23%, communications/journalism 6%, education 10%, engineering/engineering technologies 7%, health sciences 11%, psychology 6%, security/protective services 8%, social sciences 7%.

Computing on campus. Dormitories wired for high-speed internet access and linked to campus network. Commuter students can connect to campus network. Online course registration, online library, helpline, repair service, wireless network available.

Student life. **Freshman orientation:** Mandatory, $15 fee. Preregistration for classes offered. Five-day orientation for fall, one-day orientation for spring. Cost contingent on whether student stays on campus or off. **Housing:** Single-sex dorms, apartments available. $350 deposit, deadline 6/1. **Activities:** Bands, choral groups, dance, drama, music ensembles, radio station, student government, student newspaper, symphony orchestra, TV station, religious, honorary and scholastic organizations, marketing club, student social workers.

Athletics. NCAA. **Intercollegiate:** Baseball M, basketball, bowling W, cross-country, football (tackle) M, golf, softball W, swimming, tennis, track and field, volleyball W. **Intramural:** Badminton, basketball, bowling, football (tackle) M, gymnastics, racquetball, soccer, softball, table tennis, tennis, track and field, volleyball, weight lifting. **Team name:** Rattlers.

Student services. Alcohol/substance abuse counseling, career counseling, student employment services, financial aid counseling, health services, on-campus daycare, personal counseling, placement for graduates, veterans' counselor. **Physically disabled:** Services for visually, hearing impaired.

Contact. E-mail: barbara.cox@famu.edu
Phone: (850) 599-3796 Fax: (850) 599-3069
Barbara Cox, Director of Admissions, Florida Agricultural and Mechanical University, FHAC, G-9, Tallahassee, FL 32307-3200

Florida Atlantic University

Boca Raton, Florida — **CB member**
www.fau.edu — **CB code: 5229**

- Public 4-year university
- Commuter campus in small city
- 19,951 degree-seeking undergraduates: 41% part-time, 60% women, 18% African American, 4% Asian American, 17% Hispanic American, 4% international
- 3,386 degree-seeking graduate students
- 56% of applicants admitted
- SAT or ACT (ACT writing optional), application essay required
- 37% graduate within 6 years

General. Founded in 1961. Regionally accredited. Courses and degree programs offered at additional sites in Palm Beach, Broward, St. Lucie and Indian River Counties. **Degrees:** 4,022 bachelor's, 172 associate awarded; master's, doctoral offered. **ROTC:** Army, Air Force. **Location:** 17 miles from Fort Lauderdale, 45 miles from Miami. **Calendar:** Semester, extensive summer session. **Full-time faculty:** 740 total; 86% have terminal degrees, 19% minority, 39% women. **Part-time faculty:** 551 total; 15% minority, 50% women. **Class size:** 38% < 20, 46% 20-39, 5% 40-49, 8% 50-99, 3% >100. **Special facilities:** Environmental center, native fish research center, ocean engineering laboratory, marine research facility, robotics laboratory, art museums.

Freshman class profile. 13,033 applied, 7,287 admitted, 2,478 enrolled.

Mid 50% test scores		**Return as sophomores:**	72%
SAT verbal:	480-570	**Out-of-state:**	9%
SAT math:	480-570	**Live on campus:**	50%
ACT:	19-24	**International:**	2%
GPA 3.50 or higher:	28%	**Fraternities:**	3%
GPA 3.0-3.49:	30%	**Sororities:**	4%
GPA 2.0-2.99:	40%		

Basis for selection. Secondary school record, standardized test scores most important. Recommendation, talent, ability also important. Top 20% of state high school graduates guaranteed admission. Audition recommended for theater majors. Portfolio recommended for art majors. **Homeschooled:** State high school equivalency certificate required.

High school preparation. 18 units required. Required and recommended units include English 4, mathematics 3-4, social studies 1, history 2, science 3-4 (laboratory 1-2), foreign language 2 and academic electives 3.

2005-2006 Annual costs. Tuition/fees: $3,259; $15,765 out-of-state. Additional $625 in fees for out-of-state students. Room/board: $6,783. Books/supplies: $700. Personal expenses: $1,410.

2005-2006 Financial aid. **Need-based:** 1,793 full-time freshmen applied for aid; 1,007 were judged to have need; 966 of these received aid. Average need met was 82%. Average scholarship/grant was $5,768; average loan $2,345. 57% of total undergraduate aid awarded as scholarships/grants, 43% as loans/jobs. **Non-need-based:** Awarded to 575 full-time undergraduates, including 114 freshmen. Scholarships awarded for academics, athletics, state residency.

Application procedures. **Admission:** Closing date 6/1 (receipt date). $30 fee, may be waived for applicants with need. Application may be submitted online. Admission notification on a rolling basis. **Financial aid:** Priority date 3/1; no closing date. FAFSA required. Applicants notified on a rolling basis starting 5/1; must reply within 3 week(s) of notification.

Academics. Certificate programs available in child welfare, classical studies, gerontology, non-profit management, public administration, ethnic studies, film and video, Judaic studies, Latin American studies, peace studies, women's studies, environmental education, actuarial science, environmental studies, GIS, and statistics. **Special study options:** Accelerated study, combined bachelor's/graduate degree, cooperative education, cross-registration, distance learning, double major, dual enrollment of high school students, ESL, exchange student, honors, independent study, internships, liberal arts/career combination, student-designed major, study abroad, teacher certification program, weekend college. **Credit/placement by examination:** AP, CLEP, IB. 45 credit hours maximum toward bachelor's degree. **Support services:** Learning center, pre-admission summer program, reduced course load, study skills assistance, tutoring, writing center.

Honors college/program. Most applicants will have a 3.5 GPA, 1280 SAT (exclusive of Writing) or 29 on Enhanced ACT. Exceptional applicants who do not meet these criteria may be admitted on an individual basis by Admissions Committee.

Majors. **Architecture:** Architecture, urban/community planning. **Biology:** General. **Business:** Accounting, business admin, finance, hospitality admin, human resources, international, management information systems, marketing, real estate. **Communications:** General, digital media. **Computer sciences:** General. **Education:** Elementary, English, mathematics, music, science, social science, special. **Engineering:** Civil, computer, electrical, mechanical, ocean. **English:** English lit. **Foreign languages:** French, German, linguistics, Spanish. **Health:** Health care admin, health services, nursing (RN). **History:** General. **Liberal arts:** Arts/sciences. **Math:** General. **Parks/recreation:** Exercise sciences. **Philosophy/religion:** Judaic, philosophy. **Physical sciences:** Chemistry, geology, physics. **Protective services:** Criminal justice. **Psychology:** General. **Public administration:** General, social work. **Social sciences:** General, anthropology, economics, geography, political science, sociology. **Visual/performing arts:** Art, dramatic.

Most popular majors. Business/marketing 31%, education 10%, English 6%, health sciences 8%, psychology 6%, social sciences 8%.

Computing on campus. 822 workstations in dormitories, library, computer center, student center. Dormitories wired for high-speed internet access and linked to campus network. Commuter students can connect to campus network. Online course registration, helpline, repair service, wireless network available.

Student life. Freshman orientation: Mandatory, $35 fee. Preregistration for classes offered. Held 2 different dates before semester starts. **Policies:** Freshmen permitted cars on campus. **Housing:** Guaranteed on-campus for freshmen. Coed dorms, single-sex dorms, special housing for disabled, apartments available. $200 deposit, deadline 8/1. **Activities:** Bands, choral groups, dance, drama, music ensembles, musical theater, opera, radio station, student government, student newspaper, symphony orchestra, TV station, Circle K, College Democrats, College Republicans, B'nai B'rith Hillel, Neumann Club, Christian College Fellowship, Human Rights Organization, European Student Association, NAACP, Peace Finders.

Athletics. NCAA. **Intercollegiate:** Baseball M, basketball, cheerleading, cross-country, football (tackle) M, golf, soccer, softball W, swimming, tennis, track and field W, volleyball W. **Intramural:** Basketball, diving, football (non-tackle), rugby, soccer M, softball, table tennis, volleyball M. **Team name:** Owls.

Student services. Adult student services, alcohol/substance abuse counseling, campus ministries, career counseling, student employment services, financial aid counseling, health services, minority student services, on-campus daycare, personal counseling, placement for graduates, veterans' counselor, women's services. **Physically disabled:** Services for visually, speech, hearing impaired. **Learning disabled:** Comprehensive services available.

Contact. E-mail: admisweb@fau.edu
Phone: (561) 297-3040 Toll-free number: (800) 299-4328
Fax: (561) 297-2758
Barbara Pletcher, Director of Admissions, Florida Atlantic University, 777 Glades Road, Boca Raton, FL 33431

Florida Christian College

Kissimmee, Florida
www.fcc.edu **CB code: 2167**

- Private 4-year Bible and teachers college affiliated with Independent Christian Church and Church of Christ
- Residential campus in small city
- 278 degree-seeking undergraduates
- 71% of applicants admitted
- SAT or ACT, application essay required

General. Founded in 1975. Candidate for regional accreditation; also accredited by ABHE. **Degrees:** 41 bachelor's, 9 associate awarded. **Location:** 20 miles from Orlando. **Calendar:** Semester, limited summer session. **Full-time faculty:** 10 total; 30% women. **Part-time faculty:** 30 total; 47% women. **Class size:** 70% < 20, 21% 20-39, 8% 40-49, 2% 50-99.

Freshman class profile. 119 applied, 84 admitted, 47 enrolled.

Out-of-state:	16%	**Live on campus:**	80%

Basis for selection. Autobiographical essays, personal recommendation, and church references required. Taylor-Johnson Temperament Analysis required. **Homeschooled:** State high school equivalency certificate, letter of recommendation (nonparent) required.

High school preparation. 24 units recommended. Recommended units include English 4, mathematics 3, social studies 3, science 3 and foreign language 2.

2005-2006 Annual costs. Tuition/fees: $8,950. Room/board: $4,000. Books/supplies: $850. Personal expenses: $895.

2004-2005 Financial aid. Need-based: 71 full-time freshmen applied for aid; 60 were judged to have need; 58 of these received aid. Average scholarship/grant was $3,424; average loan $2,576. 43% of total undergraduate aid awarded as scholarships/grants, 57% as loans/jobs. **Non-need-based:** Awarded to 189 full-time undergraduates, including 62 freshmen. Scholarships awarded for academics, alumni affiliation, leadership, music/drama, religious affiliation, state residency.

Application procedures. Admission: Priority date 7/15; deadline 8/1 (postmark date). $35 fee, may be waived for applicants with need. Application may be submitted online. Admission notification on a rolling basis. **Financial aid:** Priority date 5/1, closing date 7/15. FAFSA, institutional form required. Applicants notified on a rolling basis starting 3/1.

Academics. Special study options: Accelerated study, combined bachelor's/graduate degree, distance learning, dual enrollment of high school students, independent study, internships, student-designed major, teacher certification program. **Credit/placement by examination:** AP, CLEP, SAT, ACT, institutional tests. **Support services:** Reduced course load, study skills assistance, tutoring.

Majors. Education: Elementary. **Philosophy/religion:** Philosophy, religion. **Theology:** Bible, missionary, pastoral counseling, sacred music, theology.

Computing on campus. 8 workstations in library, student center. Dormitories wired for high-speed internet access and linked to campus network. Online course registration, online library, helpline, repair service, student web hosting, wireless network available.

Student life. Freshman orientation: Mandatory. **Policies:** Religious observance required. Freshmen permitted cars on campus. **Housing:** Special housing for disabled, apartments, substance-free housing available. $100 nonrefundable deposit, deadline 7/15. **Activities:** Choral groups, drama, music ensembles, student government, Christian service activities, mission group.

Athletics. NCCAA. **Intercollegiate:** Basketball M, volleyball W. **Intramural:** Football (non-tackle), soccer, softball, table tennis. **Team name:** Suns.

Student services. Career counseling, financial aid counseling, personal counseling, veterans' counselor. **Physically disabled:** Services for visually impaired.

Contact. E-mail: katie.french@fcc.edu
Phone: (407) 569-1172 Toll-free number: (877) 468-6322
Fax: (321) 206-2007
Philip Vincent, Dean of Enrollment Management, Florida Christian College, 1011 Bill Beck Boulevard, Kissimmee, FL 34744-4402

Florida College

Temple Terrace, Florida
www.floridacollege.edu **CB code: 5216**

- Private 4-year liberal arts college
- Residential campus in large town
- 456 degree-seeking undergraduates: 4% part-time, 50% women, 3% African American, 3% Hispanic American, 2% international
- 72% of applicants admitted
- SAT or ACT (ACT writing optional) required

General. Founded in 1944. Regionally accredited. **Degrees:** 27 bachelor's, 121 associate awarded. **ROTC:** Army, Air Force. **Location:** 2 miles from Tampa. **Calendar:** Semester, limited summer session. **Full-time faculty:** 31 total; 29% have terminal degrees, 23% women. **Part-time faculty:** 6 total; 33% women. **Class size:** 75% < 20, 16% 20-39, 5% 40-49, 3% 50-99.

Freshman class profile. 299 applied, 214 admitted, 214 enrolled.

Mid 50% test scores		**ACT:**	19-25
SAT verbal:	480-610	**International:**	2%
SAT math:	470-600		

Basis for selection. 2 recommendations, 2.0 high school GPA required. Test scores, moral character important. Interview and essay recommended. Portfolio required for art majors. **Homeschooled:** High school course requirements, essay and ACT minimum requirements. **Learning Disabled:** Provide voluntary declaration of disability form and documentation.

High school preparation. College-preparatory program required. 16 units required. Required and recommended units include English 4, mathematics 3, social studies 2-3, science 2 (laboratory 2) and foreign language 2.

2005-2006 Annual costs. Tuition/fees: $11,130. Room/board: $5,260. Books/supplies: $1,760. Personal expenses: $2,200.

2004-2005 Financial aid. Need-based: 141 full-time freshmen applied for aid; 60 were judged to have need; 60 of these received aid. Average need met was 40%. Average scholarship/grant was $3,316; average loan $1,789. 72% of total undergraduate aid awarded as scholarships/grants, 28% as loans/jobs. **Non-need-based:** Awarded to 217 full-time undergraduates, including 109 freshmen. Scholarships awarded for academics, athletics, state residency. **Additional information:** Music and forensic scholarships available. Audition required for music scholarships.

Application procedures. **Admission:** Priority date 4/1; deadline 8/1. $25 fee. Admission notification on a rolling basis. **Financial aid:** Priority date 4/1, closing date 6/1. FAFSA, institutional form required. Applicants notified on a rolling basis starting 3/1; must reply within 2 week(s) of notification.

Academics. **Special study options:** Cross-registration, independent study, teacher certification program. **Credit/placement by examination:** AP, CLEP, IB, SAT, ACT, institutional tests. 30 credit hours maximum toward associate degree, 30 toward bachelor's. **Support services:** Reduced course load, remedial instruction, study skills assistance, tutoring, writing center.

Majors. **Education:** Elementary. **Liberal arts:** Arts/sciences. **Theology:** Bible.

Most popular majors. Education 19%, liberal arts 22%, philosophy/religious studies 40%.

Computing on campus. 76 workstations in library, computer center. Dormitories wired for high-speed internet access and linked to campus network. Wireless network available.

Student life. **Freshman orientation:** Mandatory. **Policies:** All campus residents expected to attend Sunday worship services. Freshmen permitted cars on campus. **Housing:** Guaranteed on-campus for freshmen. Single-sex dorms available. $150 deposit, deadline 8/1. **Activities:** Bands, choral groups, drama, literary magazine, music ensembles, musical theater, student government, religious organizations, honor society, social clubs.

Athletics. USCAA. **Intercollegiate:** Baseball M, basketball M, cheerleading M, volleyball W. **Intramural:** Basketball, football (non-tackle), soccer, softball, volleyball. **Team name:** Falcons.

Student services. Financial aid counseling, health services, personal counseling, veterans' counselor.

Contact. E-mail: admission@floridacollege.edu
Phone: (813) 899-6716 Toll-free number: (800) 326-7655
Fax: (813) 899-6772
Matthew Qualls, Director of Admissions, Florida College, 119 North Glen Arven Avenue, Temple Terrace, FL 33617

Florida Gulf Coast University

Ft. Myers, Florida — **CB member**
www.fgcu.edu — **CB code: 5221**

- Public 4-year university
- Commuter campus in small city
- 5,974 degree-seeking undergraduates: 23% part-time, 62% women, 6% African American, 2% Asian American, 10% Hispanic American, 1% international
- 762 degree-seeking graduate students
- 76% of applicants admitted
- SAT or ACT with writing required
- 37% graduate within 6 years

General. Regionally accredited. **Degrees:** 832 bachelor's, 96 associate awarded; master's offered. **Location:** 100 miles from Tampa, 125 miles from Miami. **Calendar:** Semester, extensive summer session. **Full-time faculty:** 253 total; 78% have terminal degrees, 17% minority, 49% women. **Part-time faculty:** 188 total; 8% minority, 45% women. **Class size:** 33% < 20, 58% 20-39, 4% 40-49, 4% 50-99, less than 1% >100. **Special facilities:** Natural wetlands, observatory.

Freshman class profile. 3,449 applied, 2,617 admitted, 1,343 enrolled.

Mid 50% test scores			
SAT verbal:	470-560	Rank in top tenth:	20%
SAT math:	470-570	End year in good standing:	90%
ACT:	19-23	Return as sophomores:	72%
GPA 3.50 or higher:	42%	Out-of-state:	10%
GPA 3.0-3.49:	36%	Live on campus:	65%
GPA 2.0-2.99:	22%	International:	1%
Rank in top quarter:	49%	Fraternities:	1%
		Sororities:	2%

Basis for selection. Grades in academic units, test scores very important. Writing test required for students who graduate high school in 2006 or later. Flexible enforcement in 2006; strict enforcement anticipated by 2008. Interview and essay recommended for academically weak. **Homeschooled:** Transcript of courses and grades required. Must score 1010 on the SAT (exclusive of Writing) or 21 on the ACT.

High school preparation. 18 units required. Required units include English 4, mathematics 3, social studies 3, science 3 (laboratory 2), foreign language 2 and academic electives 3.

2005-2006 Annual costs. Tuition/fees: $3,191; $15,287 out-of-state. Room/board: $7,460. Books/supplies: $700. Personal expenses: $1,400.

2004-2005 Financial aid. **Need-based:** 760 full-time freshmen applied for aid; 339 were judged to have need; 339 of these received aid. Average need met was 66%. Average scholarship/grant was $3,044; average loan $2,351. 28% of total undergraduate aid awarded as scholarships/grants, 72% as loans/jobs. **Non-need-based:** Awarded to 1,937 full-time undergraduates, including 673 freshmen. Scholarships awarded for academics, athletics, leadership, minority status, music/drama, state residency.

Application procedures. **Admission:** Priority date 11/15; deadline 8/1 (postmark date). $30 fee, may be waived for applicants with need. Application may be submitted online. Admission notification on a rolling basis. 12 months prior. **Financial aid:** Priority date 2/1, closing date 3/15. FAFSA, institutional form required. Applicants notified on a rolling basis starting 2/15.

Academics. **Special study options:** Accelerated study, combined bachelor's/graduate degree, cooperative education, cross-registration, distance learning, double major, dual enrollment of high school students, honors, independent study, internships, study abroad, teacher certification program, Washington semester. **Credit/placement by examination:** AP, CLEP, IB, SAT, ACT, institutional tests. 45 credit hours maximum toward bachelor's degree. Credit received from one exam program may not be duplicated by another, nor duplicated through dual enrollment credit. **Support services:** Learning center, reduced course load, remedial instruction, study skills assistance, tutoring, writing center.

Majors. **Biology:** General, biotechnology. **Business:** Accounting, business admin, finance, management information systems, marketing, resort management. **Communications:** General. **Computer sciences:** General. **Conservation:** Environmental science. **Education:** Early childhood, elementary, special. **Engineering:** Agricultural, civil, environmental. **English:** English lit. **Foreign languages:** Spanish. **Health:** Athletic training, community health, health services, nursing (RN). **Interdisciplinary:** Biological/physical sciences. **Legal studies:** Paralegal. **Liberal arts:** Arts/sciences. **Math:** General. **Parks/recreation:** Exercise sciences. **Physical sciences:** Chemistry. **Protective services:** Criminal justice, criminalistics. **Psychology:** General. **Public administration:** Human services, social work. **Social sciences:** General, political science. **Visual/performing arts:** Dramatic, studio arts.

Most popular majors. Business/marketing 27%, education 12%, health sciences 15%, liberal arts 34%, security/protective services 6%.

Computing on campus. 302 workstations in dormitories, library, computer center. Dormitories wired for high-speed internet access and linked to campus network. Commuter students can connect to campus network. Online course registration, online library, helpline, student web hosting, wireless network available.

Student life. **Freshman orientation:** Mandatory, $35 fee. Preregistration for classes offered. 2-day summer program prior to fall semester. Families invited. **Policies:** Student code of conduct in effect. Freshmen permitted cars on campus. **Housing:** Coed dorms, special housing for disabled, apartments, substance-free housing available. $150 fully refundable deposit, deadline 4/15. Honors and other special interest dorms available. **Activities:** Choral groups, dance, drama, literary magazine, radio station, student government, student newspaper, College Republicans, College Democrats, Christian Campus Fellowship, Intervarsity Christian Fellowship, Navigators, Model United Nations, colleges against cancer, American Association of University Women Student affiliates, human services student organization.

Athletics. NCAA. **Intercollegiate:** Baseball M, basketball, cross-country, golf, softball W, tennis, volleyball W. **Intramural:** Basketball, cross-country, football (non-tackle), soccer, softball, table tennis, tennis, volleyball, water polo. **Team name:** Eagles.

Student services. Adult student services, alcohol/substance abuse counseling, career counseling, student employment services, financial aid counseling, health services, minority student services, on-campus daycare, personal counseling, placement for graduates, veterans' counselor, women's services. **Physically disabled:** Services for visually, speech, hearing impaired.

Contact. E-mail: admissions@fgcu.edu
Phone: (239) 590-7878 Toll-free number: (888) 889-1095
Fax: (239) 590-7894
Marc Laviolette, Director of Admissions and Records, Florida Gulf Coast University, 10501 FGCU Boulevard South, Ft. Myers, FL 33965-6565

Florida Hospital College of Health Sciences
Orlando, Florida
www.fhchs.edu **CB code: 3614**

- Private 4-year health science and nursing college affiliated with Seventh-day Adventists
- Commuter campus in large city
- 1,943 degree-seeking undergraduates
- SAT and SAT Subject Tests or ACT (ACT writing optional), application essay required

General. Regionally accredited. Florida Hopsital College of Health Sciences is an affiliate of Florida Hospital, a Seventh-day Adventist institution. **Degrees:** 145 bachelor's, 160 associate awarded. **Location:** Downtown Orlando. **Calendar:** Semester, extensive summer session. **Full-time faculty:** 49 total; 20% minority, 74% women. **Part-time faculty:** 43 total. **Class size:** 57% < 20, 32% 20-39, 9% 40-49, 2% 50-99. **Special facilities:** Students utilize human patient simulators to practice skills in our professional program learning labs.

Basis for selection. Students are admitted first to take general education/prerequisite courses; then to specific professional programs. A minimum GPA of 2.5 and satisfactory recommendations are required for general college admission. ACT/SAT scores are required for advising and placement purposes. Professional program admission requirements vary and may be obtained by contacting the Admission Office. Students transferring with 24 or more semester hours with a minimum GPA of 2.50 from a regionally accredited college are not required to submit ACT/SAT scores. ACT test scores are required for professional program admission for those students with less than 24 hours of college credit. **Homeschooled:** Curriculum must be regionally accredited. **Learning Disabled:** Contact the Office of Disability Services prior to enrollment at the college.

High school preparation. 21 units recommended. Recommended units include English 4, mathematics 3, social studies 3, history 3, science 3 (laboratory 3) and foreign language 2.

2006-2007 Annual costs. Tuition/fees (projected): $7,450. Room only: $4,200. Books/supplies: $1,950. Personal expenses: $1,206.

Application procedures. Admission: Closing date 7/10 (postmark date). $20 fee, may be waived for applicants with need. Application must be submitted on paper. Admission notification on a rolling basis. Students accepted into Professional Programs have deadline dates to reply. **Financial aid:** Priority date 4/12; no closing date. FAFSA, institutional form required. Applicants notified on a rolling basis starting 3/1.

Academics. Special study options: Combined bachelor's/graduate degree, distance learning, dual enrollment of high school students, independent study. **Credit/placement by examination:** AP, CLEP, ACT, institutional tests. **Support services:** Learning center, pre-admission summer program, remedial instruction, study skills assistance, tutoring.

Majors. Health: Health services, nursing (RN), radiologic technology/medical imaging.

Computing on campus. 45 workstations in dormitories, library, computer center, student center. Commuter students can connect to campus network. Online library, wireless network available.

Student life. Freshman orientation: Mandatory. All new students and students entering a professional program are required to attend a day-long orientation program. **Policies:** No-use policy for alcohol, drugs, smoking, and illegal substances. Freshmen permitted cars on campus. **Housing:** Apartments, substance-free housing available. $200 partly refundable deposit, deadline 8/1. **Activities:** Drama, literary magazine, student government, student newspaper.

Athletics. Intramural: Basketball, football (non-tackle) M, volleyball.

Student services. Alcohol/substance abuse counseling, campus ministries, career counseling, student employment services, financial aid counseling, health services, personal counseling. **Physically disabled:** Services for visually, speech, hearing impaired.

Contact. Phone: (407) 303-9798 Toll-free number: (800) 500-7747
Fax: (407) 303-9408
Janet Calderon, Director of Admissions, Florida Hospital College of Health Sciences, 800 Lake Estelle Drive, Orlando, FL 32803

Florida Institute of Technology
Melbourne, Florida **CB member**
www.fit.edu **CB code: 5080**

- Private 4-year university
- Residential campus in small city
- 2,337 degree-seeking undergraduates: 3% part-time, 31% women, 4% African American, 3% Asian American, 7% Hispanic American, 14% international
- 2,265 degree-seeking graduate students
- 83% of applicants admitted
- SAT or ACT (ACT writing optional) required
- 52% graduate within 6 years; 38% enter graduate study

General. Founded in 1958. Regionally accredited. Located near Kennedy Space Center with opportunities for research with NASA. **Degrees:** 461 bachelor's awarded; master's, doctoral offered. **ROTC:** Army. **Location:** 76 miles from Orlando, 35 miles from Cape Kennedy. **Calendar:** Semester, limited summer session. **Full-time faculty:** 215 total; 90% have terminal degrees, 11% minority, 18% women. **Part-time faculty:** 193 total; 67% have terminal degrees, 3% minority, 17% women. **Class size:** 54% < 20, 42% 20-39, 1% 40-49, 3% 50-99, less than 1% >100. **Special facilities:** Observatory, botanical gardens, research vessel, anchorage, medical genetics lab, wind and hurricane impact research lab, electron microscope.

Freshman class profile. 2,463 applied, 2,051 admitted, 604 enrolled.

Mid 50% test scores		**Rank in top tenth:**	32%
SAT verbal:	510-630	**Return as sophomores:**	78%
SAT math:	550-660	**Out-of-state:**	69%
ACT:	22-29	**Live on campus:**	92%
GPA 3.50 or higher:	55%	**International:**	10%
GPA 3.0-3.49:	27%	**Fraternities:**	26%
GPA 2.0-2.99:	18%	**Sororities:**	8%
Rank in top quarter:	66%		

Basis for selection. GPA, test scores, class rank, specific course grades considered. Marginal applicants reviewed by academic departments. Minimum requirements vary depending on intended program. Students in college-preparatory programs may be informed of admission after completion of junior year. Interview and essays recommended. **Homeschooled:** Transcript of courses and grades required. Self-descriptive 1 page essay, proof of research project participation required. SAT Subject Test strongly recommended (English composition, math level II, any sciences related to desired area of study).

High school preparation. 12 units required. Required and recommended units include English 4, mathematics 4, science 3-4 (laboratory 2-3). College-preparatory mathematics through trigonometry required. Precalculus or calculus required of engineering applicants.

2005-2006 Annual costs. Tuition/fees: $25,150. Tuition $22,920 for aeronautics, business, psychology, and humanities programs. Room/board: $6,800. Books/supplies: $2,000.

2005-2006 Financial aid. Need-based: 525 full-time freshmen applied for aid; 437 were judged to have need; 437 of these received aid. Average need met was 86%. Average scholarship/grant was $15,091; average loan $3,927. 56% of total undergraduate aid awarded as scholarships/grants, 44% as loans/jobs. **Non-need-based:** Awarded to 1,788 full-time undergraduates, including 592 freshmen. Scholarships awarded for academics, alumni affiliation, athletics, leadership, ROTC.

Application procedures. Admission: No deadline. $50 fee. Application may be submitted online. Admission notification on a rolling basis beginning on or about 9/1. **Financial aid:** Priority date 3/15; no closing date. FAFSA required. Applicants notified on a rolling basis starting 2/15; must reply by 5/1 or within 4 week(s) of notification.

Academics. Special study options: Accelerated study, cooperative education, double major, dual enrollment of high school students, ESL, internships, study abroad, teacher certification program. Dual degrees in computer engineering/electrical engineering, chemical engineering/chemistry, molecular/marine biology. **Credit/placement by examination:** AP, CLEP, IB, institutional tests. **Support services:** Learning center, pre-admission summer program, remedial instruction, study skills assistance, tutoring.

Majors. Biology: General, aquatic, biochemistry, biomedical sciences, biotechnology, cellular/molecular, ecology, marine, molecular. **Business:** Accounting, business admin, management information systems. **Communications:** General. **Computer sciences:** Computer science, information systems.

Conservation: Environmental science. **Education:** Biology, chemistry, computer, mathematics, physics, science. **Engineering:** General, aerospace, chemical, civil, computer, electrical, mechanical, ocean, software, systems. **Interdisciplinary:** Biological/physical sciences. **Liberal arts:** Humanities. **Math:** General, applied. **Physical sciences:** Analytical chemistry, astronomy, astrophysics, chemistry, hydrology, meteorology, oceanography, physics. **Psychology:** General. **Transportation:** Aviation, aviation management.

Most popular majors. Biology 10%, business/marketing 6%, computer/information sciences 9%, engineering/engineering technologies 39%, physical sciences 9%, trade and industry 15%.

Computing on campus. 400 workstations in library, computer center, student center. Dormitories wired for high-speed internet access and linked to campus network. Commuter students can connect to campus network. Online course registration, online library, helpline, repair service, student web hosting, wireless network available.

Student life. **Freshman orientation:** Mandatory. Preregistration for classes offered. 8-day program in late August. **Policies:** Function in accordance with written constitution and bylaws approved by Director of Student Activities. Freshmen permitted cars on campus. **Housing:** Guaranteed on-campus for freshmen. Coed dorms, single-sex dorms, special housing for disabled available. $200 fully refundable deposit, deadline 8/1. **Activities:** Bands, choral groups, dance, drama, film society, literary magazine, radio station, student government, student newspaper, TV station, Newman Club, Unite, International student service organization, Chinese student association, Saudi Student House, National Society of Black Engineers, Society of Women Engineers, Society of Hispanic Professional Engineers, French Connexion, Caribbean students association, Women in Aviation.

Athletics. NCAA. **Intercollegiate:** Baseball M, basketball, cross-country, golf, rowing (crew) W, soccer, softball W, tennis, volleyball W. **Intramural:** Badminton, basketball, cricket, football (non-tackle), golf, racquetball, soccer, softball, tennis, volleyball, water polo, weight lifting. **Team name:** Panthers.

Student services. Alcohol/substance abuse counseling, campus ministries, career counseling, student employment services, financial aid counseling, health services, personal counseling, veterans' counselor. **Physically disabled:** Services for visually, speech, hearing impaired.

Contact. E-mail: admission@fit.edu
Phone: (321) 674-8030 Toll-free number: (800) 888-4348
Fax: (321) 723-9468
Judith Marino, Director, Undergraduate Admissions, Florida Institute of Technology, 150 West University Boulevard, Melbourne, FL 32901-6975

Florida International University

Miami, Florida — **CB member**
www.fiu.edu — **CB code: 5206**

- Public 4-year university
- Commuter campus in very large city
- 28,405 degree-seeking undergraduates: 36% part-time, 57% women
- 5,084 degree-seeking graduate students
- 47% of applicants admitted
- SAT or ACT (ACT writing optional) required

General. Founded in 1965. Regionally accredited. **Degrees:** 4,862 bachelor's awarded; master's, doctoral, first professional offered. **ROTC:** Army, Air Force. **Location:** 10 miles from downtown. **Calendar:** Semester, extensive summer session. **Full-time faculty:** 757 total; 79% have terminal degrees, 35% minority, 33% women. **Part-time faculty:** 672 total; 5% have terminal degrees, 49% minority, 47% women. **Class size:** 30% < 20, 41% 20-39, 9% 40-49, 17% 50-99, 3% >100. **Special facilities:** Nature preserve, museum.

Freshman class profile. 10,223 applied, 4,833 admitted, 2,506 enrolled.

Mid 50% test scores			
SAT verbal:	520-590	GPA 2.0-2.99:	36%
SAT math:	510-590	Out-of-state:	15%
ACT:	21-25	Live on campus:	8%
GPA 3.50 or higher:	24%	Fraternities:	14%
GPA 3.0-3.49:	40%	Sororities:	14%

Basis for selection. Minimum high school GPA 3.0. Lower GPA considered with higher test score. Lower test score considered with higher GPA. Audition required of music performance, theater, dance majors. Portfolio required of art majors. Interview and essay recommended for academically marginal applicants.

High school preparation. 19 units required. Required units include English 4, mathematics 3, social studies 3, science 3 (laboratory 2), foreign language 2 and academic electives 4.

2005-2006 Annual costs. Tuition/fees: $3,210; $15,609 out-of-state. Room/board: $9,480. Books/supplies: $1,080. Personal expenses: $2,100.

Financial aid. **Non-need-based:** Scholarships awarded for academics, art, athletics, minority status, music/drama, state residency.

Application procedures. **Admission:** Priority date 3/15; no deadline. $30 fee, may be waived for applicants with need. Admission notification on a rolling basis beginning on or about 9/1. **Financial aid:** Priority date 3/1; no closing date. FAFSA required. Applicants notified on a rolling basis starting 4/15; must reply within 4 week(s) of notification.

Academics. **Special study options:** Distance learning, double major, dual enrollment of high school students, exchange student, honors, independent study, internships, study abroad, teacher certification program, weekend college. **Credit/placement by examination:** AP, CLEP, IB, institutional tests. 45 credit hours maximum toward bachelor's degree. **Support services:** Learning center, pre-admission summer program, study skills assistance, tutoring.

Honors college/program. Freshmen must have a 3.5 GPA. Transfer and continuing students must have a 3.3 GPA in all college level work. Students may pursue any major while completing the honors curriculum.

Majors. **Architecture:** Architecture. **Area/ethnic studies:** Asian, women's. **Biology:** General, marine. **Business:** Accounting, business admin, finance, hospitality admin, human resources, insurance, international, management information systems, marketing, real estate, tourism/travel. **Communications:** General. **Computer sciences:** General, information technology. **Conservation:** General. **Education:** Art, elementary, emotionally handicapped, English, family/consumer sciences, foreign languages, health, learning disabled, mathematics, mentally handicapped, music, physical, science, social science, social studies, trade/industrial. **Engineering:** Biomedical, chemical, civil, computer, electrical, mechanical, systems. **Engineering technology:** Construction. **Foreign languages:** French, German, Italian, Portuguese, Spanish. **Health:** Health care admin, medical records admin, nursing (RN), orthotics/prosthetics. **History:** General. **Liberal arts:** Arts/sciences. **Math:** General, applied, statistics. **Parks/recreation:** Exercise sciences, facilities management. **Philosophy/religion:** Philosophy, religion. **Physical sciences:** Chemistry, geology, physics. **Protective services:** Criminal justice. **Psychology:** General. **Public administration:** General, social work. **Social sciences:** Economics, geography, international relations, political science, sociology. **Visual/performing arts:** Art history/conservation, dance, dramatic, interior design, studio arts.

Most popular majors. Business/marketing 35%, communications/journalism 6%, education 9%, engineering/engineering technologies 6%, health sciences 8%, psychology 8%, security/protective services 7%, social sciences 6%.

Computing on campus. 1,800 workstations in library, computer center. Dormitories linked to campus network. Commuter students can connect to campus network. Online course registration available.

Student life. **Freshman orientation:** Mandatory, $50 fee. **Policies:** Freshmen permitted cars on campus. **Housing:** Coed dorms, apartments available. **Activities:** Bands, choral groups, dance, drama, music ensembles, musical theater, radio station, student government, student newspaper, symphony orchestra, over 190 clubs available.

Athletics. NCAA. **Intercollegiate:** Baseball M, basketball, cross-country, football (tackle) M, golf, soccer, softball W, swimming W, tennis W, track and field, volleyball W. **Intramural:** Basketball, bowling, cross-country, football (tackle) M, golf, lacrosse M, racquetball M, rugby M, sailing, skin diving, soccer, softball, swimming, tennis, volleyball, water polo M. **Team name:** Golden Panthers.

Student services. Adult student services, alcohol/substance abuse counseling, campus ministries, career counseling, student employment services, financial aid counseling, health services, minority student services, on-campus daycare, personal counseling, placement for graduates, veterans' counselor. **Physically disabled:** Services for visually, speech, hearing impaired.

Contact. E-mail: admiss@fiu.edu
Phone: (305) 348-2363 Fax: (305) 348-3648
Carmen Brown, Director of Admissions, Florida International University, University Park Campus, PC 140, Miami, FL 33199

Florida Memorial University

Miami, Florida — **CB member**
www.fmuniv.edu — **CB code: 5217**

- Private 4-year liberal arts college affiliated with American Baptist Churches in the USA
- Residential campus in very large city

- 1,945 degree-seeking undergraduates: 9% part-time, 66% women
- 59 degree-seeking graduate students
- SAT or ACT with writing, application essay required
- 65% graduate within 6 years

General. Founded in 1879. Regionally accredited. Christian principles emphasized. 4 branch campuses. **Degrees:** 398 bachelor's awarded; master's offered. **ROTC:** Army. **Location:** 15 miles from downtown Miami. **Calendar:** Semester, limited summer session. **Full-time faculty:** 112 total; 71% have terminal degrees. **Special facilities:** Black archives, airway science building with simulator and control tower.

Freshman class profile.

Out-of-state:	20%	Live on campus:	80%

Basis for selection. High school GPA of 2.0 required. School achievement record, test scores, interview, recommendations, alumni affiliation considered. Interview recommended.

High school preparation. 15 units recommended. Recommended units include English 4, mathematics 4, social studies 2, science 3 and foreign language 2. College-preparatory program strongly recommended.

2006-2007 Annual costs. Tuition/fees (projected): $11,782. Room/board: $5,134. Books/supplies: $1,000.

Financial aid. Additional information: Need-based financial aid available to part-time students taking 6 credits or more per semester.

Application procedures. Admission: No deadline. $15 fee, may be waived for applicants with need. Admission notification on a rolling basis. **Financial aid:** Priority date 4/15; no closing date. Applicants notified on a rolling basis; must reply within 2 week(s) of notification.

Academics. Special study options: Combined bachelor's/graduate degree, cooperative education, double major, dual enrollment of high school students, honors, independent study, internships, study abroad, teacher certification program, weekend college. **Credit/placement by examination:** CLEP, institutional tests. 30 credit hours maximum toward bachelor's degree. **Support services:** Learning center, pre-admission summer program, remedial instruction, tutoring, writing center.

Majors. Biology: General. **Business:** Accounting, business admin, management information systems. **Computer sciences:** General, computer science. **Education:** Elementary, physical. **Health:** Clinical lab science. **Math:** General. **Psychology:** General. **Public administration:** General. **Social sciences:** Sociology. **Transportation:** Aviation.

Most popular majors. Business/marketing 50%, computer/information sciences 8%, education 7%, social sciences 25%.

Computing on campus. 150 workstations in dormitories, library, computer center, student center. Dormitories wired for high-speed internet access and linked to campus network. Commuter students can connect to campus network. Online library, helpline, repair service, wireless network available.

Student life. Freshman orientation: Mandatory. Preregistration for classes offered. **Policies:** Freshmen permitted cars on campus. **Housing:** Guaranteed on-campus for freshmen. Single-sex dorms available. **Activities:** Jazz band, choral groups, music ensembles, musical theater, student government, student newspaper, TV station, Christian Student Union, international students, broadcasting club, Junior NAACP, Toastmasters, Professional Women of Tomorrow.

Athletics. NAIA. **Intercollegiate:** Baseball M, basketball, track and field, volleyball W. **Intramural:** Baseball M, basketball, soccer M, softball W, swimming, tennis, volleyball. **Team name:** Figthing lions.

Student services. Campus ministries, career counseling, student employment services, health services, minority student services, personal counseling, placement for graduates.

Contact. E-mail: admit@fmuniv.edu
Phone: (305) 626-3750 Fax: (305) 623-1462
Peggy Martin, Director of Admissions, Florida Memorial University, 15800 Northwest 42 Avenue, Miami, FL 33054

Florida Metropolitan University: Brandon Campus

Tampa, Florida
www.fmu.edu **CB code: 3585**

- For-profit 4-year university and business college
- Commuter campus in very large city
- 907 degree-seeking undergraduates: 59% part-time, 76% women
- 52 degree-seeking graduate students

General. Accredited by ACICS. **Degrees:** 81 bachelor's, 175 associate awarded; master's offered. **Calendar:** Quarter. **Full-time faculty:** 12 total. **Part-time faculty:** 56 total.

Basis for selection. CPAT required.

2005-2006 Annual costs. Tuition/fees: $12,615. Books/supplies: $600. Personal expenses: $184.

Financial aid. All financial aid based on need.

Application procedures. Admission: No deadline. $25 fee, may be waived for applicants with need. Admission notification on a rolling basis. **Financial aid:** No deadline. FAFSA, institutional form required. Applicants notified on a rolling basis; must reply within 2 week(s) of notification.

Academics. Special study options: Cooperative education, distance learning, ESL. **Credit/placement by examination:** AP, CLEP.

Majors. Business: General, accounting. **Computer sciences:** General. **Legal studies:** Paralegal. **Protective services:** Police science.

Most popular majors. Business/marketing 58%, computer/information sciences 13%, security/protective services 25%.

Contact. E-mail: SPointer@cci.edu
Phone: (813) 621-0041 Toll-free number: (877) 338-0068
Fax: (813) 628-0919
Shandretta Pointer, Director of Admissions, Florida Metropolitan University: Brandon Campus, 3924 Coconut Palm Drive, Tampa, FL 33619

Florida Metropolitan University: Jacksonville

Jacksonville, Florida
www.fmu.edu **CB code: 3801**

- For-profit 4-year business college
- Commuter campus in large city
- 300 degree-seeking undergraduates

General. Accredited by ACICS. **Degrees:** 31 bachelor's, 112 associate awarded; master's offered. **Calendar:** Semester.

Academics. Credit/placement by examination: CLEP.

Majors. Business: Accounting, business admin, hospitality admin, marketing. **Protective services:** Law enforcement admin.

Contact. Phone: (904) 731-4949
Robin Manning, Director of Admissions, Florida Metropolitan University: Jacksonville, 8226 Phillips Highway, Jacksonville, FL 32256

Florida Metropolitan University: Melbourne Campus

Melbourne, Florida
www.cci.edu **CB code: 3586**

- For-profit 4-year business college
- Commuter campus in small city
- 950 degree-seeking undergraduates
- 75% of applicants admitted

General. Accredited by ACICS. **Degrees:** 79 bachelor's, 123 associate awarded; master's offered. **Calendar:** Quarter, extensive summer session. **Full-time faculty:** 11 total. **Part-time faculty:** 45 total. **Class size:** 64% < 20, 32% 20-39, 3% 40-49.

Freshman class profile. 300 applied, 225 admitted, 200 enrolled.

Basis for selection. Minimum 120 CPAT required.

2005-2006 Annual costs. Books/supplies: $600. Personal expenses: $1,764.

Financial aid. Non-need-based: Scholarships awarded for academics.

Application procedures. Admission: No deadline. $25 fee. Admission notification on a rolling basis. **Financial aid:** No deadline. FAFSA required.

Applicants notified on a rolling basis; must reply within 3 week(s) of notification.

Academics. **Special study options:** Combined bachelor's/graduate degree, distance learning, independent study, liberal arts/career combination. **Credit/placement by examination:** CLEP. 24 credit hours maximum toward associate degree, 48 toward bachelor's. **Support services:** Reduced course load, tutoring.

Majors. **Business:** Accounting, business admin. **Computer sciences:** General.

Most popular majors. Business/marketing 30%, computer/information sciences 33%, security/protective services 37%.

Computing on campus. 50 workstations in library, computer center. Online library available.

Student life. **Freshman orientation:** Mandatory.

Student services. Career counseling, student employment services, financial aid counseling, placement for graduates, veterans' counselor.

Contact. E-mail: talexand@cci.edu
Phone: (321) 253-2929 Toll-free number: (866) 355-2959
Fax: (321) 255-2017
Tim Alexander, Director of Admission, Florida Metropolitan University: Melbourne Campus, 2401 North Harbor City Boulevard, Melbourne, FL 32935

Florida Metropolitan University: Orange Park

Orange Park, Florida
www.fmu.edu

- For-profit 4-year business college
- Commuter campus in small city
- 608 degree-seeking undergraduates

General. Accredited by ACICS. **Degrees:** 3 associate awarded. **Calendar:** Semester. **Full-time faculty:** 4 total. **Part-time faculty:** 34 total.

Application procedures. **Admission:** $25 fee.

Academics. **Credit/placement by examination:** CLEP.

Majors. **Business:** Business admin. **Protective services:** Criminal justice, law enforcement admin, security management.

Contact. Phone: (904) 264-9122
Florida Metropolitan University: Orange Park, 805 Wells Road, Orange Park, FL 32073

Florida Metropolitan University: Orlando College North

Orlando, Florida
www.cci.edu **CB code: 0742**

- For-profit 4-year business college
- Commuter campus in very large city
- 1,257 degree-seeking undergraduates
- Interview required

General. Founded in 1918. Accredited by ACICS. Additional campus south of downtown Orlando. **Degrees:** 72 bachelor's, 249 associate awarded; master's offered. **Location:** 2 miles from downtown. **Calendar:** Quarter, extensive summer session. **Full-time faculty:** 9 total. **Part-time faculty:** 69 total.

Basis for selection. CPAT exam, interview important. SAT or ACT may be substituted for CPAT.

2005-2006 Annual costs. Books/supplies: $700. Personal expenses: $1,764.

Application procedures. **Admission:** No deadline. No application fee. Admission notification on a rolling basis. **Financial aid:** No deadline. FAFSA required. Applicants notified on a rolling basis starting 6/1.

Academics. **Special study options:** Accelerated study, cooperative education, distance learning, independent study, internships. **Credit/placement by examination:** CLEP, institutional tests. 24 credit hours maximum toward associate degree, 48 toward bachelor's.

Majors. **Business:** General, accounting, business admin, marketing. **Computer sciences:** General.

Most popular majors. Business/marketing 72%, computer/information sciences 28%.

Computing on campus. 25 workstations in library, computer center.

Student life. **Freshman orientation:** Mandatory.

Student services. Placement for graduates.

Contact. E-mail: jdweber@cci.edu
Phone: (407) 628-5870 Fax: (407) 628-1344
Joann Derosa-Weber, Director of Admissions, Florida Metropolitan University: Orlando College North, 5421 Diplomat Circle, Orlando, FL 32810

Florida Metropolitan University: Orlando College South

Orlando, Florida
www.fmu.edu **CB code: 3587**

- For-profit 4-year university and business college
- Very large city
- 1,851 degree-seeking undergraduates
- SAT or ACT, interview required

General. Accredited by ACICS. **Degrees:** 152 bachelor's, 508 associate awarded; master's offered. **Calendar:** Quarter, extensive summer session. **Full-time faculty:** 22 total. **Part-time faculty:** 78 total.

Basis for selection. At least one of the following three criteria required for admission: ACT of 15; SAT of 700 (exclusive of Writing); passing grade on the university administered assessment examination.

2005-2006 Annual costs. Tuition/fees: $9,900. Books/supplies: $800. Personal expenses: $1,764.

Application procedures. **Admission:** No deadline. No application fee. **Financial aid:** No deadline.

Academics. **Credit/placement by examination:** CLEP.

Majors. **Business:** Business admin.

Contact. Phone: (407) 851-2525
Annette Cloin, Director of Admissions, Florida Metropolitan University: Orlando College South, 9200 Southpark Center Loop, Orlando, FL 32819

Florida Metropolitan University: Pinellas

Clearwater, Florida
www.fmu.edu **CB code: 3583**

- For-profit 5-year university and business college
- Commuter campus in large city
- 924 degree-seeking undergraduates
- Interview required

General. Accredited by ACICS. **Degrees:** 51 bachelor's, 125 associate awarded; master's offered. **Location:** 15 miles west of Tampa. **Calendar:** Quarter, extensive summer session. **Full-time faculty:** 5 total. **Part-time faculty:** 76 total. **Class size:** 64% < 20, 34% 20-39, 2% 40-49.

Basis for selection. Students with no SAT, SAT Subject Test or ACT scores must pass CPAT entrance examination. International students must meet TOEFL requirements.

High school preparation. Required units include English 4, mathematics 4, social studies 4 and history 4.

2005-2006 Annual costs. Books/supplies: $500.

Application procedures. **Admission:** No deadline. No application fee. Admission notification on a rolling basis. **Financial aid:** No deadline. FAFSA, institutional form required. Applicants notified on a rolling basis.

Academics. **Special study options:** Cooperative education, distance learning, double major, ESL, independent study, internships. **Credit/placement**

by examination: CLEP. 24 credit hours maximum toward associate degree, 48 toward bachelor's. **Support services:** Remedial instruction, study skills assistance, tutoring.

Majors. Business: Accounting, business admin, international, marketing. **Computer sciences:** General.

Most popular majors. Business/marketing 35%, computer/information sciences 10%, visual/performing arts 47%.

Computing on campus. 75 workstations in library, computer center. Online library available.

Student life. Freshman orientation: Mandatory. **Activities:** American Market Association, Student Human Resource Association, "EXXTEND" (service), Criminal Justice Fraternity, Medical Assisting Drs.

Student services. Adult student services, alcohol/substance abuse counseling, career counseling, student employment services, financial aid counseling, personal counseling, placement for graduates, veterans' counselor.

Contact. Phone: (727) 725-2688 Toll-free number: (800) 353-3687
Fax: (727) 725-3827
Director of Admissions, Florida Metropolitan University: Pinellas, 2471 McMullen Booth Road, Suite 200, Clearwater, FL 33759

Florida Metropolitan University: Pompano Beach

Pompano Beach, Florida
www.fmu.edu **CB code: 5171**

- For-profit 4-year business college
- Small city
- 1,500 degree-seeking undergraduates
- Interview required

General. Founded in 1940. Accredited by ACICS. **Degrees:** 114 bachelor's, 114 associate awarded; master's offered. **Location:** 35 miles from Miami. **Calendar:** Quarter, extensive summer session. **Full-time faculty:** 8 total. **Part-time faculty:** 84 total.

Freshman class profile.

Out-of-state:	78%	Live on campus:	40%

Basis for selection. School achievement record, interview considered. School entrance examination required.

2005-2006 Annual costs. Tuition may vary by program. Books/supplies: $600. Personal expenses: $1,584.

Application procedures. Admission: No deadline. $25 fee. Admission notification on a rolling basis. **Financial aid:** No deadline. FAFSA, institutional form required. Applicants notified on a rolling basis starting 6/1.

Academics. Special study options: Accelerated study, cooperative education, double major, independent study, internships, student-designed major. **Credit/placement by examination:** CLEP, institutional tests. 24 credit hours maximum toward associate degree, 48 toward bachelor's. **Support services:** Learning center, reduced course load, tutoring.

Majors. Business: General, accounting, business admin, hospitality admin, international, management information systems, management science, marketing.

Student life. Housing: Apartments available. **Activities:** Student government, student newspaper.

Athletics. Intramural: Basketball, soccer M, softball, volleyball.

Student services. Career counseling, student employment services, personal counseling, placement for graduates, veterans' counselor.

Contact. Phone: (954) 783-7339
Tony Wallace, Director of Admissions, Florida Metropolitan University: Pompano Beach, 225 North Federal Highway, Pompano Beach, FL 33062

Florida Metropolitan University: Tampa College

Tampa, Florida
www.fmu.edu **CB code: 0428**

- For-profit 4-year university and business college
- Commuter campus in large city
- 1,398 degree-seeking undergraduates

General. Founded in 1890. Accredited by ACICS. **Degrees:** 63 bachelor's, 233 associate awarded; master's offered. **Location:** 85 miles from Orlando. **Calendar:** Quarter, extensive summer session. **Full-time faculty:** 20 total. **Part-time faculty:** 61 total.

Basis for selection. Open admission.

2005-2006 Annual costs. Cost of tuition may vary with program. Books/supplies: $540. Personal expenses: $1,710.

Financial aid. All financial aid based on need.

Application procedures. Admission: No deadline. No application fee. Admission notification on a rolling basis. **Financial aid:** No deadline. FAFSA required. Applicants notified on a rolling basis.

Academics. Special study options: Accelerated study, distance learning, double major, ESL, independent study, internships. **Credit/placement by examination:** CLEP, institutional tests. **Support services:** Tutoring.

Majors. Business: General, accounting, business admin, marketing. **Computer sciences:** General, information systems, programming. **Protective services:** Criminal justice.

Computing on campus. 50 workstations in library, computer center.

Student life. Freshman orientation: Mandatory. **Activities:** Student newspaper.

Student services. Career counseling, student employment services, personal counseling, placement for graduates, veterans' counselor.

Contact. Phone: (813) 879-6000 Fax: (813) 871-2483
Donald Broughton, Director of Admissions, Florida Metropolitan University: Tampa College, 3319 West Hillsborough Avenue, Tampa, FL 33614

Florida Metropolitan University: Tampa College Lakeland

Lakeland, Florida
www.cci.edu **CB code: 3584**

- Private 4-year university and branch campus college
- Small city
- 716 degree-seeking undergraduates

General. Accredited by ACICS. **Degrees:** 19 bachelor's, 85 associate awarded; master's offered. **Calendar:** Quarter, extensive summer session. **Full-time faculty:** 7 total. **Part-time faculty:** 37 total.

Basis for selection. At least one of the following required for admission: ACT of 15; SAT of 700 (exclusive of Writing); passing grade on the university-administered assessment examination.

2005-2006 Annual costs. Tuition/fees: $12,375.

Financial aid. All financial aid based on need.

Application procedures. Admission: No deadline. $25 fee, may be waived for applicants with need. Admission notification on a rolling basis. **Financial aid:** No deadline.

Academics. Credit/placement by examination: CLEP.

Majors. Business: Accounting, business admin. **Computer sciences:** General. **Protective services:** Criminal justice.

Student life. Freshman orientation: Mandatory.

Contact. Phone: (863) 686-1444
Stephanie Andrews, Registrar, Florida Metropolitan University: Tampa College Lakeland, 995 East Memorial Boulevard, Suite 110, Lakeland, FL 33801-1919

Florida Southern College

Lakeland, Florida **CB member**
www.flsouthern.edu **CB code: 5218**

- Private 4-year liberal arts college affiliated with United Methodist Church
- Residential campus in small city

- 1,816 degree-seeking undergraduates: 3% part-time, 61% women, 6% African American, 1% Asian American, 6% Hispanic American, 4% international
- 105 degree-seeking graduate students
- 73% of applicants admitted
- SAT or ACT (ACT writing optional), application essay required
- 57% graduate within 6 years; 11% enter graduate study

General. Founded in 1885. Regionally accredited. Campus designed by Frank Lloyd Wright; contains world's largest collection of his buildings. **Degrees:** 512 bachelor's awarded; master's offered. **ROTC:** Army, Air Force. **Location:** 30 miles from Tampa, 50 miles from Orlando. **Calendar:** Semester, limited summer session. **Full-time faculty:** 107 total; 83% have terminal degrees, 8% minority, 35% women. **Part-time faculty:** 59 total; 20% have terminal degrees, 12% minority, 41% women. **Class size:** 64% < 20, 34% 20-39, 2% 40-49. **Special facilities:** Wellness center, planetarium, art gallery.

Freshman class profile. 1,829 applied, 1,343 admitted, 464 enrolled.

Mid 50% test scores		**Rank in top tenth:**	23%
SAT verbal:	470-580	**End year in good standing:**	78%
SAT math:	480-590	**Return as sophomores:**	67%
ACT:	20-26	**Out-of-state:**	34%
GPA 3.50 or higher:	53%	**Live on campus:**	82%
GPA 3.0-3.49:	25%	**International:**	4%
GPA 2.0-2.99:	22%	**Fraternities:**	3%
Rank in top quarter:	47%	**Sororities:**	8%

Basis for selection. School achievement record most important, followed by test scores and recommendations. Character and motivation, extracurricular activities are also important. Interview recommended. Audition recommended for music, theater majors. Portfolio recommended for art majors. Faculty interview required for athletic training program.

High school preparation. 18 units required. Required and recommended units include English 4, mathematics 3, social studies 3, history 3, science 3, foreign language 2 and academic electives 2.

2005-2006 Annual costs. Tuition/fees: $19,165. Room/board: $6,800. Books/supplies: $1,000. Personal expenses: $800.

2005-2006 Financial aid. Need-based: 395 full-time freshmen applied for aid; 310 were judged to have need; 309 of these received aid. Average need met was 72%. Average scholarship/grant was $14,611; average loan $4,331. 76% of total undergraduate aid awarded as scholarships/grants, 24% as loans/jobs. **Non-need-based:** Awarded to 923 full-time undergraduates, including 306 freshmen. Scholarships awarded for academics, alumni affiliation, art, athletics, job skills, leadership, minority status, music/drama, religious affiliation, ROTC, state residency.

Application procedures. Admission: Closing date 4/1 (receipt date). $30 fee, may be waived for applicants with need. Application may be submitted online. Admission notification on a rolling basis. Must reply by 5/1. Housing deposit refundable only through May 1. **Financial aid:** Priority date 4/1, closing date 8/1. FAFSA, institutional form required. Applicants notified on a rolling basis starting 3/15.

Academics. Special study options: Combined bachelor's/graduate degree, double major, dual enrollment of high school students, honors, independent study, internships, liberal arts/career combination, New York semester, study abroad, teacher certification program, United Nations semester, Washington semester. **Credit/placement by examination:** AP, CLEP, IB, SAT, ACT. 60 credit hours maximum toward bachelor's degree. **Support services:** Reduced course load, study skills assistance, tutoring, writing center.

Majors. Agriculture: General, business, horticultural science, ornamental horticulture, turf management. **Biology:** General. **Business:** General, accounting, business admin, finance, human resources, international, management information systems, marketing, operations. **Communications:** General, advertising, journalism, public relations. **Computer sciences:** Computer science. **Conservation:** General. **Education:** General, art, early childhood, elementary, learning disabled, music, physical, secondary. **English:** Composition, English lit. **Foreign languages:** Spanish. **Health:** Athletic training, nursing (RN), premedicine. **History:** General. **Interdisciplinary:** Biological/physical sciences. **Liberal arts:** Arts/sciences. **Math:** General. **Philosophy/religion:** Philosophy, religion. **Physical sciences:** Chemistry. **Protective services:** Criminal justice. **Psychology:** General. **Social sciences:** General, economics, political science, sociology. **Theology:** Religious ed, sacred music. **Visual/performing arts:** Art, commercial/advertising art, dramatic, music management, music theory/composition, studio arts, theater design.

Most popular majors. Biology 6%, business/marketing 35%, communications/journalism 9%, education 11%, psychology 6%, visual/performing arts 6%.

Computing on campus. 300 workstations in dormitories, library, computer center. Dormitories wired for high-speed internet access and linked to campus network. Commuter students can connect to campus network. Online course registration, online library, helpline, wireless network available.

Student life. Freshman orientation: Mandatory. Preregistration for classes offered. 4 days prior to classes for fall semester and 1 day prior to classes for spring semester. Includes social and academic programming and common reading. **Policies:** Freshmen permitted cars on campus. **Housing:** Guaranteed on-campus for all undergraduates. Coed dorms, single-sex dorms, special housing for disabled, apartments, fraternity/sorority housing, substance-free housing available. $500 deposit, deadline 5/1. Seniors have option to live off-campus independently. Freshmen required to live on campus unless living with relatives. **Activities:** Bands, choral groups, dance, drama, literary magazine, music ensembles, musical theater, opera, student government, student newspaper, symphony orchestra, Wesley Fellowship, international club, community tutorial service organizations, Fellowship of Christian Athletes, All-Campus Fellowship, Upper Room Ministries, Antioch 2, Beyond Campus Ministries, Newman Club, reformed university fellowship.

Athletics. NCAA. **Intercollegiate:** Baseball M, basketball, cross-country, golf, soccer, softball W, swimming, tennis, track and field, volleyball W. **Intramural:** Basketball, bowling, football (non-tackle), golf, soccer, softball, tennis, volleyball. **Team name:** Moccasins.

Student services. Adult student services, alcohol/substance abuse counseling, campus ministries, career counseling, student employment services, financial aid counseling, health services, minority student services, personal counseling, placement for graduates.

Contact. E-mail: fscadm@flsouthern.edu
Phone: (863) 680-4131 Toll-free number: (800) 274-4131
Fax: (863) 680-4120
Bill Langston, Director of Admission, Florida Southern College, 111 Lake Hollingsworth Drive, Lakeland, FL 33801-5698

Florida State University

Tallahassee, Florida — **CB member**
www.fsu.edu — **CB code: 5219**

- Public 4-year university
- Residential campus in small city
- 30,206 degree-seeking undergraduates: 10% part-time, 57% women, 12% African American, 3% Asian American, 10% Hispanic American, 1% international
- 7,749 degree-seeking graduate students
- 62% of applicants admitted
- SAT or ACT with writing, application essay required

General. Founded in 1851. Regionally accredited. **Degrees:** 6,856 bachelor's awarded; master's, doctoral, first professional offered. **ROTC:** Army, Navy, Air Force. **Location:** 191 miles from Pensacola, 163 miles from Jacksonville. **Calendar:** Semester, extensive summer session. **Full-time faculty:** 1,265 total; 92% have terminal degrees, 14% minority, 35% women. **Part-time faculty:** 327 total; 92% have terminal degrees, 9% minority, 54% women. **Class size:** 36% < 20, 41% 20-39, 8% 40-49, 9% 50-99, 5% >100. **Special facilities:** Marine laboratory/aquarium, geophysical fluid dynamics institute, high magnetic field laboratory, music research center, supercomputer, accelerator, oceanographic institute, art museum, planetarium, Imax theater, reservation, golf course.

Freshman class profile. 22,450 applied, 14,016 admitted, 6,067 enrolled.

Mid 50% test scores		**GPA 2.0-2.99:**	3%
SAT verbal:	530-620	**Rank in top quarter:**	61%
SAT math:	540-630	**Rank in top tenth:**	26%
ACT:	23-27	**Return as sophomores:**	89%
GPA 3.50 or higher:	68%	**Out-of-state:**	13%
GPA 3.0-3.49:	29%	**Live on campus:**	54%

Basis for selection. Most Florida students accepted have at least a B+ average in all academic subjects (grades 9-12) and test scores of at least 25 composite on the ACT or 1100 combined SAT (exclusive of Writing). Out-of-state applicants held to higher standards. Audition required of music, dance, BFA theater majors. Portfolio required of BFA art, interior design majors. Departmental application required for motion picture, television, and recording art programs may be submitted either with regular university application or after admission. **Homeschooled:** Must provide detailed information regarding academic program, including names of textbooks used, and complete course descriptions.

High school preparation. College-preparatory program required. 18 units required; 22 recommended. Required and recommended units include English 4, mathematics 3-4, social studies 1, history 2, science 3-4 (laboratory 2), foreign language 2-4 and academic electives 3. Mathematics courses must be algebra I and above; two units of same foreign language required; at least 3 units English with substantial writing requirements, social studies must include history. Additional consideration given for completion of higher level courses (AP, IB, honors, calculus and/or foreign language IV or V), and for completion of 4 or more senior academic courses.

2005-2006 Annual costs. Tuition/fees: $3,208; $16,340 out-of-state. Room/board: $6,778.

2005-2006 Financial aid. Need-based: 3,835 full-time freshmen applied for aid; 2,019 were judged to have need; 2,107 of these received aid. Average need met was 65%. Average scholarship/grant was $2,817; average loan $2,160. 60% of total undergraduate aid awarded as scholarships/grants, 40% as loans/jobs. **Non-need-based:** Awarded to 7,856 full-time undergraduates, including 2,613 freshmen. Scholarships awarded for academics, athletics, state residency. **Additional information:** Out-of-state tuition costs waived for National Merit and National Achievement students and National Hispanic Scholars, and some southwest Georgia residents.

Application procedures. Admission: Priority date 10/1; deadline 3/1 (receipt date). $30 fee. Application may be submitted online. Must reply by May 1 or within 2 week(s) if notified thereafter. Students strongly encouraged to apply early. Those applying before November 30 who are denied admission are given additional opportunities to improve application standing. **Financial aid:** Priority date 2/15; no closing date. FAFSA required. Applicants notified on a rolling basis starting 3/15; must reply within 2 week(s) of notification.

Academics. 2+2 distance learning available in cooperation with selected Florida community colleges includes programs in computer science, interdisciplinary social sciences, and nursing (RN to BSN). **Special study options:** Accelerated study, combined bachelor's/graduate degree, cooperative education, cross-registration, distance learning, double major, dual enrollment of high school students, ESL, honors, independent study, internships, study abroad, teacher certification program. Cooperative programs with Florida Agricultural and Mechanical University and Tallahassee Community College; degree in three years; International year abroad, year-round study abroad in England, Italy, Panama, Spain; summer study abroad in Belize, Bolivia, China, Costa Rica, Croatia, Czech Republic, England, France, Ireland, Japan, Lebenon, Russia, Switzerland. **Credit/placement by examination:** AP, CLEP, IB, SAT, ACT, institutional tests. 30 credit hours maximum toward associate degree, 60 toward bachelor's. English AP credit not awarded for more than 1 exam. **Support services:** Learning center, reduced course load, study skills assistance, tutoring, writing center.

Majors. Area/ethnic studies: American, Asian, Caribbean, Central/Eastern European, Latin American, Russian/Slavic, women's. **Biology:** General, biochemistry, biophysics, ecology, marine, zoology. **Business:** Accounting, actuarial science, finance, hospitality admin, human resources, insurance, international, management information systems, management science, marketing, operations, real estate. **Communications:** Advertising, media studies, public relations. **Computer sciences:** General, computer science, information systems, information technology. **Conservation:** Environmental science, environmental studies. **Education:** Art, bilingual, early childhood, elementary, emotionally handicapped, English, family/consumer sciences, foreign languages, health, learning disabled, mathematics, mentally handicapped, multicultural, music, physical, physics, science, social science, visually handicapped. **Engineering:** Biomedical, chemical, civil, computer, electrical, environmental, industrial, materials, mechanical, software. **English:** Creative writing, English lit. **Family/consumer sciences:** Child development, clothing/textiles, family studies, food/nutrition, housing, merchandising. **Foreign languages:** Ancient Greek, classics, French, German, Italian, Latin, Russian, Spanish. **Health:** Athletic training, audiology/speech pathology, dietetics, music therapy, nursing (RN), predentistry, premedicine, prepharmacy, preveterinary, vocational rehab counseling. **History:** General. **Interdisciplinary:** Nutrition sciences. **Legal studies:** Prelaw. **Liberal arts:** Humanities. **Math:** General, applied, computational, statistics. **Parks/recreation:** Exercise sciences, facilities management, health/fitness, sports admin. **Philosophy/religion:** Philosophy, religion. **Physical sciences:** Atmospheric science, chemistry, geology, physics. **Protective services:** Criminal justice. **Psychology:** General. **Public administration:** Social work. **Social sciences:** General, anthropology, applied economics, criminology, economics, geography, international relations, political science, sociology. **Visual/performing arts:** Acting, art history/conservation, cinematography, dance, dramatic, fashion design, interior design, jazz, music history, music performance, music theory/composition, piano/organ, stringed instruments, studio arts, theater design, voice/opera.

Most popular majors. Business/marketing 21%, education 7%, family/consumer sciences 8%, security/protective services 6%, social sciences 15%, visual/performing arts 6%.

Computing on campus. PC or laptop required. 2,958 workstations in dormitories, library, computer center, student center. Dormitories wired for high-speed internet access and linked to campus network. Commuter students can connect to campus network. Online course registration, online library, helpline, student web hosting, wireless network available.

Student life. Freshman orientation: Mandatory, $25 fee. Preregistration for classes offered. Orientation for fall term conducted during summer. **Policies:** Freshmen permitted cars on campus. **Housing:** Coed dorms, single-sex dorms, special housing for disabled, apartments, fraternity/sorority housing, substance-free housing available. $225 partly refundable deposit. Honor residences and living and learning communities on campus. Off campus, cooperative living through the Southern Scholarship Foundation and several private residence halls available. **Activities:** Bands, choral groups, dance, drama, film society, literary magazine, music ensembles, musical theater, opera, radio station, student government, student newspaper, symphony orchestra, TV station, campus ministries, Hillel, Christian student association, Catholic Student Union, Campus Crusade for Christ, College Democrats, College Republicans, Black Student Union, El Centro (Hispanic Student Union), American Civil Liberties Union.

Athletics. NCAA. **Intercollegiate:** Baseball M, basketball, cheerleading, cross-country, diving, football (tackle) M, golf, soccer W, softball W, swimming, tennis, track and field, volleyball W. **Intramural:** Basketball, bowling, cross-country, football (non-tackle), golf, racquetball, soccer, softball, swimming, table tennis, tennis, track and field, volleyball, weight lifting, wrestling. **Team name:** Seminoles.

Student services. Adult student services, alcohol/substance abuse counseling, campus ministries, career counseling, student employment services, financial aid counseling, health services, legal services, minority student services, on-campus daycare, personal counseling, placement for graduates, veterans' counselor, women's services. **Physically disabled:** Services for visually, speech, hearing impaired.

Contact. E-mail: admissions@admin.fsu.edu
Phone: (850) 644-6200 Fax: (850) 644-0197
Janice Finney, Director of Admissions, Florida State University, A2500 University Center, Tallahassee, FL 32306-2400

Herzing College
Winter Park, Florida
www.herzing.edu

- For-profit 4-year business and technical college

General. Accredited by ACICS.

Annual costs/financial aid. Tuition varies by program, per-credit-hour charge $325; required fees $100.

Contact. Phone: (407) 478-0500
1595 South Semoran Boulevard, Suite 1501, Winter Park, FL 32792

Hobe Sound Bible College
Hobe Sound, Florida
www.hsbc.edu **CB code: 5306**

- Private 4-year Bible college affiliated with interdenominational tradition
- Residential campus in small town
- 133 degree-seeking undergraduates
- 31% of applicants admitted
- SAT or ACT (ACT writing optional) required

General. Founded in 1960. Accredited by ABHE. **Degrees:** 19 bachelor's, 6 associate awarded. **Location:** 25 miles from West Palm Beach. **Calendar:** 4-1-4, limited summer session. **Full-time faculty:** 25 total. **Part-time faculty:** 10 total.

Freshman class profile. 98 applied, 30 admitted, 30 enrolled.

Mid 50% test scores		SAT math:	560-670
SAT verbal:	460-520	ACT:	19-23

Basis for selection. Recommendations, essay, religious commitment important. **Homeschooled:** Must submit official transcripts from reputable organizations documenting completion of all academic coursework required for high school diploma.

2005-2006 Annual costs. Tuition/fees: $4,320. Room/board: $3,240. Books/supplies: $450. Personal expenses: $2,000.

2005-2006 Financial aid. Non-need-based: Scholarships awarded for academics, leadership.

Application procedures. **Admission:** Closing date 8/25. $25 fee, may be waived for applicants with need. Admission notification on a rolling basis beginning on or about 3/1. **Financial aid:** Closing date 8/1.

Academics. Double major required of all students in 4-year programs. All students complete major in Bible as well as major in Christian vocational field. **Special study options:** Distance learning, double major, dual enrollment of high school students, ESL, external degree, internships, teacher certification program. **Credit/placement by examination:** CLEP, institutional tests. **Support services:** Reduced course load, remedial instruction.

Majors. **Education:** Elementary, English, mathematics, music. **Philosophy/religion:** Religion. **Theology:** Bible, missionary, sacred music, theology. **Visual/performing arts:** Music performance, piano/organ.

Computing on campus. 10 workstations in computer center.

Student life. **Freshman orientation:** Mandatory. **Policies:** Religious observance required. Freshmen permitted cars on campus. **Housing:** Guaranteed on-campus for all undergraduates. Single-sex dorms, apartments available. Unmarried students under 25 required to live in campus dormitories or with parents. **Activities:** Concert band, choral groups, music ensembles, student government, Christian service organizations.

Athletics. **Intramural:** Basketball, football (tackle) M, racquetball, soccer, softball, tennis, volleyball.

Student services. Health services, personal counseling.

Contact. E-mail: admissions@hsbc.edu
Phone: (772) 546-5534 ext. 1015 Toll-free number: (800) 881-5534
Fax: (772) 545-1422
Judy Fay, Director of Admissions, Hobe Sound Bible College, Box 1065, Hobe Sound, FL 33475

International Academy of Design and Technology: Orlando

Orlando, Florida
www.iadt.edu **CB code: 4366**

- For-profit 4-year technical college
- Very large city
- 1,022 degree-seeking undergraduates

General. Accredited by ACICS. **Degrees:** 189 bachelor's awarded. **Calendar:** Quarter, extensive summer session. **Full-time faculty:** 12 total. **Part-time faculty:** 78 total.

Basis for selection. Open admission.

2006-2007 Annual costs. Tuition/fees (projected): $15,936.

2005-2006 Financial aid. **Need-based:** 30% of total undergraduate aid awarded as scholarships/grants, 70% as loans/jobs.

Application procedures. **Admission:** No deadline. $50 fee. **Financial aid:** No deadline. FAFSA required.

Academics. **Credit/placement by examination:** CLEP.

Majors. **Business:** Fashion, marketing. **Computer sciences:** Computer graphics, LAN/WAN management, webmaster. **Visual/performing arts:** Interior design.

Contact. Phone: (407) 857-2300
John Dietrich, Director of Admissions, International Academy of Design and Technology: Orlando, 5959 Lake Ellenor Drive, Orlando, FL 32809

International Academy of Design and Technology: Tampa

Tampa, Florida
www.academy.edu **CB code: 7114**

- For-profit 4-year visual arts and technical college
- Commuter campus in very large city
- 2,400 degree-seeking undergraduates
- Interview required

General. Accredited by ACICS. **Degrees:** 220 bachelor's, 390 associate awarded. **Location:** Downtown. **Calendar:** Quarter, extensive summer session. **Full-time faculty:** 20 total. **Part-time faculty:** 147 total.

Basis for selection. Personal interview required. School achievement considered. Essay recommended. **Learning Disabled:** Submit Auxiliary Aid Application.

2006-2007 Annual costs. Tuition/fees (projected): $17,820.

Financial aid. **Non-need-based:** Scholarships awarded for academics.

Application procedures. **Admission:** No deadline. $50 fee, may be waived for applicants with need. Admission notification on a rolling basis. **Financial aid:** No deadline. FAFSA required.

Academics. **Special study options:** Accelerated study, cooperative education, internships, study abroad. **Credit/placement by examination:** AP, CLEP, institutional tests. 67 credit hours maximum toward associate degree, 135 toward bachelor's. **Support services:** Learning center, study skills assistance, tutoring.

Majors. **Business:** Merchandising. **Visual/performing arts:** Fashion design, interior design.

Computing on campus. Wireless network available.

Student life. **Freshman orientation:** Mandatory. Preregistration for classes offered. **Policies:** Freshmen permitted cars on campus.

Student services. Adult student services, student employment services, financial aid counseling, placement for graduates, veterans' counselor.

Contact. E-mail: admissions@academy.edu
Phone: (813) 881-0007 Toll-free number: (800) 222-3369
Fax: (813) 881-0008
Richard Costa, Vice President of Admissions and Marketing, International Academy of Design and Technology: Tampa, 5104 Eisenhower Boulevard, Tampa, FL 33634

International College

Naples, Florida
www.internationalcollege.edu **CB code: 7113**

- Private 4-year business college
- Commuter campus in small city
- 1,452 degree-seeking undergraduates: 25% part-time, 70% women
- 185 degree-seeking graduate students

General. Founded in 1990. Regionally accredited. **Degrees:** 288 bachelor's, 113 associate awarded; master's offered. **Location:** 110 miles from Miami, 180 miles from Tampa. **Calendar:** Trimester, extensive summer session. **Full-time faculty:** 53 total; 62% have terminal degrees, 23% minority, 38% women. **Part-time faculty:** 54 total; 35% have terminal degrees, 13% minority, 39% women. **Class size:** 84% < 20, 16% 20-39.

Basis for selection. Open admission.

2005-2006 Annual costs. Books/supplies: $1,000. Personal expenses: $944.

Financial aid. **Non-need-based:** Scholarships awarded for academics, leadership, state residency.

Application procedures. **Admission:** No deadline. $20 fee. Admission notification on a rolling basis. **Financial aid:** No deadline. FAFSA required. Applicants notified on a rolling basis.

Academics. On-line classes and programs available. **Special study options:** Accelerated study, combined bachelor's/graduate degree, distance learning, double major, ESL. **Credit/placement by examination:** AP, CLEP, IB, institutional tests. **Support services:** Remedial instruction, tutoring.

Majors. **Business:** Accounting, business admin. **Computer sciences:** Information technology. **Health:** Health care admin. **Legal studies:** Paralegal. **Protective services:** Criminal justice.

Most popular majors. Business/marketing 67%, computer/information sciences 9%, interdisciplinary studies 12%, legal studies 11%.

Computing on campus. 500 workstations in library, computer center. Wireless network available.

Student life. **Freshman orientation:** Mandatory. **Activities:** Literary magazine.

Student services. Financial aid counseling, personal counseling, placement for graduates.

Contact. E-mail: admit@internationalcollege.edu
Phone: (239) 513-1122 Toll-free number: (800) 466-8017
Fax: (239) 513-9071
Rita Lampus, Vice President of Student Enrollment Management, International College, 2655 Northbrooke Drive, Naples, FL 34119

ITT Technical Institute: Ft. Lauderdale

Ft. Lauderdale, Florida
www.itt-tech.edu **CB code: 2700**

- For-profit 4-year technical college
- Commuter campus in small city

General. Accredited by ACICS. **Calendar:** Quarter.

Annual costs/financial aid. Tuition varies by program, $260-$368 per credit hour.

Contact. Phone: (954) 476-9300
Director of Recruitment, 3401 South University Drive, Ft. Lauderdale, FL 33328

ITT Technical Institute: Jacksonville

Jacksonville, Florida
www.itt-tech.edu **CB code: 2716**

- For-profit 4-year technical college
- Commuter campus in very large city

General. Accredited by ACICS. **Calendar:** Quarter.

Annual costs/financial aid. Tuition varies by program, $260-$368 per credit hour.

Contact. Phone: (904) 573-9100
Director of Recruitment, 6600-10 Youngerman Circle, Jacksonville, FL 32244

ITT Technical Institute: Lake Mary

Lake Mary, Florida
www.itt-tech.edu

- For-profit 4-year technical college
- Commuter campus

General. Accredited by ACICS. **Calendar:** Quarter.

Annual costs/financial aid. Tuition varies by program, $260-$368 per credit hour.

Contact. Phone: (407) 660-2900
Director of Recruitment, 1400 International Parkway South, Lake Mary, FL 32746

ITT Technical Institute: Miami

Miami, Florida
www.itt-tech.edu **CB code: 2733**

- For-profit 4-year technical college
- Commuter campus in large city

General. Accredited by ACICS. **Calendar:** Quarter.

Annual costs/financial aid. Tuition varies by program, $260-$368 per credit hour.

Contact. Phone: (305) 477-3080
Director of Recruitment, 7955 12th Street, Suite 119, Miami, FL 33126

ITT Technical Institute: Tampa

Tampa, Florida
www.itt-tech.edu **CB code: 2145**

- For-profit 4-year technical college
- Commuter campus in large city

General. Founded in 1981. Accredited by ACICS. **Calendar:** Quarter.

Annual costs/financial aid. Tuition varies by program, $260-$368 per credit hour.

Contact. Phone: (813) 885-2244
Director of Recruitment, 4809 Memorial Highway, Tampa, FL 33634

Jacksonville University

Jacksonville, Florida **CB member**
www.jacksonville.edu **CB code: 5331**

- Private 4-year university and liberal arts college
- Residential campus in very large city
- 2,113 degree-seeking undergraduates: 10% part-time, 51% women
- 310 degree-seeking graduate students
- 67% of applicants admitted
- SAT or ACT (ACT writing optional) required
- 44% graduate within 6 years

General. Founded in 1934. Regionally accredited. **Degrees:** 660 bachelor's awarded; master's offered. **ROTC:** Navy. **Calendar:** Semester, limited summer session. **Full-time faculty:** 134 total; 77% have terminal degrees, 4% minority, 42% women. **Part-time faculty:** 85 total; 29% have terminal degrees, 5% minority, 48% women. **Class size:** 58% < 20, 39% 20-39, 2% 40-49, 1% 50-99. **Special facilities:** Art museum, marine science research vessels, observatory, cybercafe.

Freshman class profile. 2,621 applied, 1,753 admitted, 539 enrolled.

Mid 50% test scores		Rank in top quarter:	33%
SAT verbal:	450-560	Rank in top tenth:	11%
SAT math:	450-560	Out-of-state:	46%
ACT:	18-24	Live on campus:	87%
GPA 3.50 or higher:	21%	International:	5%
GPA 3.0-3.49:	35%	Fraternities:	21%
GPA 2.0-2.99:	43%	Sororities:	16%

Basis for selection. School achievement record most important, followed by test scores. Audition required of music, dance, theater majors. Portfolio required for art, computer art and design. **Homeschooled:** Transcript of courses and grades, interview, letter of recommendation (nonparent) required. SAT or ACT scores with established freshman application and admission guidelines, two letters of recommendation evaluating the student's academic potential from a qualified educator or evaluator outside of the home school environment, a portfolio that includes two writing samples of not less than 100 words, a bibliography of reading completed and text used, and a description of the curriculum for grades 9 through 12, and a personal interview with the Office of Admissions.

High school preparation. 13 units required; 16 recommended. Required and recommended units include English 4, mathematics 3-4, social studies 3, science 3 (laboratory 2) and foreign language 2. History units may be included for satisfaction of social studies requirement.

2005-2006 Annual costs. Tuition/fees: $19,970. $540 mandatory health insurance fee charged unless proof of other coverage is provided. Room/board: $6,600. Books/supplies: $600. Personal expenses: $600.

2005-2006 Financial aid. Need-based: 439 full-time freshmen applied for aid; 382 were judged to have need; 382 of these received aid. Average need met was 81%. Average scholarship/grant was $7,103; average loan $4,291. 62% of total undergraduate aid awarded as scholarships/grants, 38% as loans/jobs. **Non-need-based:** Scholarships awarded for academics, art, athletics, job skills, music/drama, ROTC, state residency.

Application procedures. Admission: Priority date 3/1; no deadline. $30 fee, may be waived for applicants with need. Application may be submitted online. Admission notification on a rolling basis beginning on or about 12/15. Must reply by May 1 or within 2 week(s) if notified thereafter. **Financial aid:** Priority date 2/1, closing date 3/15. FAFSA required. Applicants notified on a rolling basis starting 2/1; must reply by 5/1 or within 3 week(s) of notification.

Academics. Special study options: Accelerated study, combined bachelor's/graduate degree, cooperative education, distance learning, double major, honors, independent study, internships, liberal arts/career combination, semester at sea, student-designed major, study abroad, teacher certification program, Washington semester. Dual degree programs in engineering with Columbia University, Georgia Institute of Technology, University of Florida, University of Miami, Mercer University, Washington University in St. Louis, Stevens Institute of Technology. **Credit/placement by examination:** AP, CLEP, IB, institutional tests. 30 credit hours maximum toward associate degree, 30 toward bachelor's. **Support services:** Learning center, remedial instruction, study skills assistance, tutoring, writing center.

Majors. Biology: General, marine. **Business:** General, accounting, business admin, finance, international, marketing. **Communications:** General. **Computer sciences:** General. **Education:** General, drama/dance, elementary, music, physical, secondary. **Engineering:** Electrical, mechanical, physics. **English:** English lit. **Foreign languages:** French, Spanish. **Health:** Nursing (RN), predentistry, premedicine, prenursing, preveterinary. **History:** General. **Legal studies:** Prelaw. **Liberal arts:** Arts/sciences, humanities. **Math:** General. **Parks/recreation:** Exercise sciences. **Philosophy/religion:** Philosophy. **Physical sciences:** Chemistry, physics. **Psychology:** General. **Social sciences:** Economics, geography, political science, sociology. **Theology:** Sacred music. **Transportation:** Airline/commercial pilot, aviation management. **Visual/performing arts:** Art, art history/conservation, dance, design, dramatic, music management, music performance, music theory/ composition, studio arts, voice/opera.

Most popular majors. Business/marketing 24%, health sciences 30%, trade and industry 6%, visual/performing arts 7%.

Computing on campus. 450 workstations in dormitories, library, computer center. Dormitories wired for high-speed internet access and linked to campus network. Commuter students can connect to campus network. Online course registration, online library, helpline, wireless network available.

Student life. Freshman orientation: Mandatory. Preregistration for classes offered. Spring program available for pre-registration; formal freshmen orientation program occurs in the few days preceding the first day of class. **Policies:** Freshmen permitted cars on campus. **Housing:** Guaranteed on-campus for freshmen. Coed dorms, single-sex dorms, special housing for disabled, apartments, fraternity/sorority housing available. $200 deposit, deadline 5/1. **Activities:** Bands, choral groups, dance, drama, literary magazine, music ensembles, musical theater, radio station, student government, student newspaper, TV station, Political Science Society, Black Student Union, Baptist Campus Ministry, Hillel, Circle-K, Rotaract, Caribbean Student Group, Dolphin Diversity.

Athletics. NCAA. **Intercollegiate:** Baseball M, basketball, cross-country, football (tackle) M, golf, rowing (crew) W, soccer, softball W, tennis, track and field W, volleyball W. **Intramural:** Basketball, bowling, football (non-tackle), soccer, softball, table tennis, tennis, volleyball. **Team name:** Dolphins.

Student services. Adult student services, alcohol/substance abuse counseling, campus ministries, career counseling, student employment services, financial aid counseling, health services, minority student services, personal counseling, placement for graduates. **Physically disabled:** Services for visually, speech, hearing impaired.

Contact. E-mail: admissions@ju.edu
Phone: (904) 256-7000 Toll-free number: (800) 225-2027
Fax: (904) 256-7012
Lisa Becker, Director of First Year Admissions and Enrollment, Jacksonville University, 2800 University Boulevard North, Jacksonville, FL 32211-3394

Johnson & Wales University

North Miami, Florida
www.jwu.edu/florida **CB code: 3441**

- Private 4-year university
- Residential campus in large city
- 2,452 degree-seeking undergraduates: 6% part-time, 53% women, 31% African American, 2% Asian American, 20% Hispanic American, 7% international
- 73% of applicants admitted

General. Regionally accredited. **Degrees:** 190 bachelor's, 388 associate awarded. **Calendar:** Quarter, extensive summer session. **Full-time faculty:** 59 total; 25% minority. **Part-time faculty:** 17 total; 53% minority. **Class size:** 26% < 20, 55% 20-39, 19% 40-49. **Special facilities:** University-operated hotel.

Freshman class profile. 7,628 applied, 5,601 admitted, 829 enrolled.

Mid 50% test scores		GPA 2.0-2.99:	54%
SAT verbal:	390-510	Rank in top quarter:	14%
SAT math:	390-500	Rank in top tenth:	3%
GPA 3.50 or higher:	23%	Out-of-state:	45%
GPA 3.0-3.49:	21%		

Basis for selection. While academic record (secondary school curriculum, GPA, class rank, test scores) is important, student motivation and interest are given strong consideration. SAT or ACT, SAT Subject Tests recommended. SAT and ACT scores are not required for general admission but are strongly recommended for candidates in the honors international business or education program for acceptance consideration.

High school preparation. 12 units recommended. Recommended units include English 4, mathematics 3, social studies 2 and science 3.

2006-2007 Annual costs. Tuition/fees (projected): $20,826. Weekend meal plan is optional for $954. Room/board: $9,300. Books/supplies: $750. Personal expenses: $1,250.

2005-2006 Financial aid. Need-based: 622 full-time freshmen applied for aid; 590 were judged to have need; 581 of these received aid. Average need met was 65%. Average scholarship/grant was $6,734; average loan $6,857. 37% of total undergraduate aid awarded as scholarships/grants, 63% as loans/jobs. **Non-need-based:** Awarded to 1,294 full-time undergraduates, including 424 freshmen. Scholarships awarded for academics, alumni affiliation, job skills, leadership, state residency.

Application procedures. Admission: No deadline. No application fee. Application may be submitted online. Admission notification on a rolling basis. Must reply by May 1 or within 2 week(s) if notified thereafter. **Financial aid:** No deadline. FAFSA required. Applicants notified on a rolling basis starting 3/1; must reply within 2 week(s) of notification.

Academics. Special study options: Accelerated study, cooperative education, dual enrollment of high school students, honors, independent study, internships, study abroad, weekend college. **Credit/placement by examination:** CLEP. **Support services:** Learning center, pre-admission summer program, reduced course load, remedial instruction, study skills assistance, tutoring, writing center.

Majors. Business: Accounting, business admin, hospitality admin, hospitality/ recreation, investments/securities, marketing. **Parks/recreation:** Sports admin. **Personal/culinary services:** General, restaurant/catering. **Protective services:** Law enforcement admin.

Most popular majors. Business/marketing 55%, family/consumer sciences 25%, parks/recreation 8%, personal/culinary services 8%.

Computing on campus. 60 workstations in library, computer center, student center. Dormitories wired for high-speed internet access and linked to campus network. Commuter students can connect to campus network. Online course registration, online library, helpline, repair service, wireless network available.

Student life. Freshman orientation: Mandatory, $250 fee. Preregistration for classes offered. **Policies:** Freshmen permitted cars on campus. **Housing:** Guaranteed on-campus for freshmen. Coed dorms, substance-free housing available. $300 deposit. All housing is accessible for disabled students. **Activities:** Dance, drama, student government, student newspaper.

Athletics. NAIA. **Intramural:** Basketball M, bowling, football (non-tackle), soccer, softball, volleyball. **Team name:** Wildcats.

Student services. Adult student services, alcohol/substance abuse counseling, career counseling, student employment services, financial aid counseling, health services, personal counseling, placement for graduates, veterans' counselor. **Physically disabled:** Services for visually, speech, hearing impaired.

Contact. E-mail: admissions.mia@jwu.edu
Phone: (305) 892-7600 Toll-free number: (866) 598-3567
Fax: (305) 892-7020
Jeff Greenip, Director, Johnson & Wales University, 1701 Northeast 127th Street, North Miami, FL 33181

Jones College

Jacksonville, Florida
www.jones.edu **CB code: 5343**

- Private 4-year business college
- Commuter campus in very large city
- 652 degree-seeking undergraduates: 76% part-time, 78% women
- Interview required

General. Founded in 1918. Accredited by ACICS. Branch campus in Miami. 2 campuses in Jacksonville. Distance Learning classes available. **Degrees:** 87 bachelor's, 36 associate awarded. **Calendar:** Trimester, extensive summer session. **Full-time faculty:** 10 total. **Part-time faculty:** 50 total. **Class size:** 91% < 20, 9% 20-39.

Basis for selection. Open admission. Score on institutional test most important.

2005-2006 Annual costs. Tuition/fees: $8,340.

Financial aid. All financial aid based on need.

Application procedures. Admission: No deadline. No application fee. Application may be submitted online. Admission notification on a rolling basis. **Financial aid:** No deadline. FAFSA required. Applicants notified on a rolling basis.

Academics. Special study options: Accelerated study, distance learning, double major, independent study, internships, student-designed major, weekend college. **Credit/placement by examination:** CLEP, institutional tests. 15 credit hours maximum toward associate degree, 15 toward bachelor's. Life experience: 21.0 hours if in bachelor's degree programs, 9.0 hours if in associate degree programs. **Support services:** Reduced course load, remedial instruction, study skills assistance, tutoring.

Majors. Business: Accounting, business admin. **Computer sciences:** General. **Education:** Elementary. **Health:** Medical assistant. **Legal studies:** Paralegal.

Most popular majors. Business/marketing 72%, computer/information sciences 11%, health sciences 8%, legal studies 8%.

Computing on campus. 166 workstations in library, computer center. Commuter students can connect to campus network. Wireless network available.

Student life. Freshman orientation: Mandatory. Preregistration for classes offered. **Policies:** Freshmen permitted cars on campus. **Activities:** Radio station.

Student services. Career counseling, student employment services, financial aid counseling, personal counseling, placement for graduates, veterans' counselor.

Contact. E-mail: Lwade@jones.edu
Phone: (904) 743-1122 ext. 213 Toll-free number: (800) 331-0176
Fax: (904) 743-4446
Len Wade, Director of Admissions, Jones College, 5353 Arlington Expressway, Jacksonville, FL 32211

Jones College: Miami

Miami, Florida
www.jones.edu **CB code: 3444**

- Private 4-year business and health science college
- Commuter campus in very large city

General. Accredited by ACICS. **Location:** 30 miles from downtown. **Calendar:** Semester.

Annual costs/financial aid. Tuition/fees (2005-2006): $8,340. Books/supplies: $750. Personal expenses: $1,700. Need-based financial aid available to full-time and part-time students.

Contact. Phone: (305) 275-9996
Admissions Representative, 11430 North Kendall Drive, Suite 200, Miami, FL 33176

Lynn University

Boca Raton, Florida **CB member**
www.lynn.edu **CB code: 5437**

- Private 4-year university
- Residential campus in small city
- 2,281 degree-seeking undergraduates: 14% part-time, 50% women
- 464 graduate students
- 80% of applicants admitted
- SAT or ACT (ACT writing optional), application essay required
- 45% graduate within 6 years

General. Founded in 1962. Regionally accredited. **Degrees:** 381 bachelor's awarded; master's, doctoral offered. **ROTC:** Air Force. **Location:** 20 miles from Fort Lauderdale, 20 miles from Palm Beach. **Calendar:** Semester, extensive summer session. **Full-time faculty:** 74 total; 58% have terminal degrees, 12% minority, 50% women. **Part-time faculty:** 178 total; 8% have terminal degrees, 90% minority, 51% women. **Class size:** 53% < 20, 47% 20-39. **Special facilities:** University club (private dining room that serves as laboratory for hotel and restaurant management students), flight simulator, conservatory of music.

Freshman class profile. 2,939 applied, 2,339 admitted, 655 enrolled.

Mid 50% test scores			
SAT verbal:	410-510	**Rank in top quarter:**	33%
SAT math:	400-510	**Rank in top tenth:**	8%
ACT:	16-21	**Out-of-state:**	72%
		Live on campus:	95%

Basis for selection. School achievement record, high school counselor's recommendation, test scores important; class rank, school and community activities considered. Special consideration given to foreign and minority applicants. Interview and essay recommended. Portfolio recommended for art and graphic design majors. **Learning Disabled:** Submit psychological testing in addition to other admission documents.

High school preparation. College-preparatory program recommended. 16 units required; 20 recommended. Required and recommended units include English 4, mathematics 4, social studies 2, history 2 and science 4.

2006-2007 Annual costs. Tuition/fees (projected): $27,700. Room/board: $9,650. Books/supplies: $800. Personal expenses: $1,100.

2005-2006 Financial aid. Need-based: 273 full-time freshmen applied for aid; 212 were judged to have need; 209 of these received aid. Average need met was 51%. Average scholarship/grant was $11,591; average loan $3,084. 59% of total undergraduate aid awarded as scholarships/grants, 41% as loans/jobs. **Non-need-based:** Awarded to 592 full-time undergraduates, including 287 freshmen. Scholarships awarded for academics, art, athletics, leadership, music/drama, religious affiliation.

Application procedures. Admission: Priority date 5/1; no deadline. $35 fee, may be waived for applicants with need. Application may be submitted online. Admission notification on a rolling basis beginning on or about 9/1. Must reply by May 1 or within 2 week(s) if notified thereafter. **Financial aid:** Priority date 3/1; no closing date. FAFSA, institutional form required. Applicants notified on a rolling basis starting 2/1; must reply within 2 week(s) of notification.

Academics. Special study options: Accelerated study, cooperative education, cross-registration, distance learning, double major, dual enrollment of high school students, ESL, honors, independent study, internships, study abroad, Washington semester. Students in Bachelor of Arts in Education prepare for certification exam. **Credit/placement by examination:** AP, CLEP, IB, institutional tests. 30 credit hours maximum toward associate degree, 30 toward bachelor's. **Support services:** Learning center, reduced course load, tutoring, writing center.

Majors. Biology: General. **Business:** Accounting, business admin, fashion, hospitality admin, international, management information systems, management science, marketing, tourism promotion, tourism/travel. **Communications:** Broadcast journalism, media studies. **Education:** Early childhood, elementary, multi-level teacher, secondary, special. **English:** English lit. **Health:** Health care admin, premedicine, preop/surgical nursing. **History:** General. **Interdisciplinary:** Behavioral sciences, gerontology, natural sciences. **Liberal arts:** Arts/sciences. **Parks/recreation:** Facilities management, sports admin. **Protective services:** Criminal justice, law enforcement admin. **Psychology:** General. **Public administration:** Community org/advocacy. **Social sciences:** International relations, political science. **Transportation:** Aviation management. **Visual/performing arts:** General, commercial/advertising art, fashion design, music performance.

Computing on campus. 220 workstations in dormitories, library, computer center. Dormitories wired for high-speed internet access and linked to campus network. Online library, helpline, repair service, wireless network available.

Student life. Freshman orientation: Mandatory. **Policies:** Freshmen permitted cars on campus. **Housing:** Guaranteed on-campus for all undergraduates. Coed dorms, special housing for disabled, substance-free housing available. $300 fully refundable deposit. **Activities:** Bands, choral groups, dance, drama, film society, literary magazine, music ensembles, radio station, student government, student newspaper, symphony orchestra, TV station, black student union, debate team, gay-straight alliance, Hillel, honors colloquium, hospitality club, international relations club, Knights of the Roundtable.

Athletics. NCAA. **Intercollegiate:** Baseball M, basketball, cross-country, golf, rowing (crew) M, soccer, softball W, tennis, volleyball W. **Intramural:** Basketball, bowling, cross-country, equestrian, golf, handball, ice hockey, lacrosse, rugby M, soccer, softball, swimming, table tennis, tennis, volleyball, water polo. **Team name:** Fighting Knights.

Student services. Adult student services, campus ministries, career counseling, student employment services, health services, personal counseling, placement for graduates, veterans' counselor.

Contact. E-mail: admissions@lynn.edu
Phone: (561) 237-7900 Toll-free number: (800) 888-5966 ext. 1
Fax: (561) 237-7100
Brett Ormandy, Director of Admissions, Lynn University, 3601 North Military Trail, Boca Raton, FL 33431-5598

Miami International University of Art and Design

Miami, Florida
www.aimiami.aii.edu **CB code: 5327**

- For-profit 3-year visual arts college
- Commuter campus in very large city
- 316 degree-seeking undergraduates: 72% women
- 54 degree-seeking graduate students
- 98% of applicants admitted
- Application essay, interview required

General. Founded in 1965. Regionally accredited. **Degrees:** 170 bachelor's, 150 associate awarded; master's offered. **Location:** 2 miles from downtown. **Calendar:** Quarter, extensive summer session. **Full-time faculty:** 50 total. **Part-time faculty:** 60 total.

Freshman class profile. 952 applied, 933 admitted, 313 enrolled.

Out-of-state:	74%	**Live on campus:**	33%

Basis for selection. Keen interest in fashion, merchandising, art, interior design, or related areas. Secondary school record, recommendations, essay important. Portfolio recommended.

2005-2006 Annual costs. $15,000 per year for film, graphic design, interior design and visual arts; $11,940 per year for fashion program; $16,500 per year for computer animation. Fees vary according to program. Books/supplies: $1,500. Personal expenses: $1,200.

Application procedures. Admission: No deadline. $50 fee. Admission notification on a rolling basis. **Financial aid:** Priority date 7/1; no closing date. FAFSA, CSS PROFILE required. Applicants notified on a rolling basis starting 8/1.

Academics. Special study options: ESL, internships, study abroad. **Credit/placement by examination:** CLEP. **Support services:** Learning center, preadmission summer program, reduced course load, remedial instruction, tutoring.

Majors. Communications technology: Animation/special effects. **Visual/performing arts:** General, cinematography.

Computing on campus. 87 workstations in computer center. Wireless network available.

Student life. Freshman orientation: Mandatory. Held first week of semester for approximately 4 hours. **Housing:** Coed dorms, single-sex dorms available. **Activities:** Dance, student government, student newspaper.

Student services. Career counseling, student employment services, personal counseling, placement for graduates.

Contact. E-mail: admissions@aii.edu
Phone: (305) 428-5700 Toll-free number: (800) 225-9023
Fax: (305) 374-5933
Carmen Topper, 2nd Director of Admissions, Miami International University of Art and Design, 1501 Biscayne Boulevard Suite 100, Miami, FL 33132-1418

New College of Florida

Sarasota, Florida **CB member**
www.ncf.edu **CB code: 5506**

- Public 4-year liberal arts college
- Residential campus in small city
- 761 degree-seeking undergraduates: 61% women, 2% African American, 3% Asian American, 9% Hispanic American, 2% international
- 60% of applicants admitted
- SAT or ACT (ACT writing optional), application essay required

General. Founded in 1960. Regionally accredited. Institution is the Honors College of Florida State University System. Emphasis on individualized learning. **Degrees:** 125 bachelor's awarded. **Location:** 50 miles from Tampa. **Calendar:** 4-1-4. **Full-time faculty:** 68 total; 98% have terminal degrees, 15% minority, 47% women. **Part-time faculty:** 9 total; 67% have terminal degrees, 11% minority, 56% women. **Class size:** 64% < 20, 32% 20-39, 2% 40-49, 2% 50-99. **Special facilities:** High-field nuclear magnetic resonance spectrometer, hardware/software system for brain function analysis, scanning electron microscope, UV-visible and infrared spectrophotometer, inert atmosphere glove box, fine arts center (practice rooms, recital hall, electronic music studio, dark room, 2- and 3-D studio facilities), laboratories for environmental studies, anthropology, psychology, marine biology facility.

Freshman class profile. 684 applied, 408 admitted, 218 enrolled.

Mid 50% test scores		**Rank in top quarter:**	80%
SAT verbal:	630-720	**Rank in top tenth:**	44%
SAT math:	580-670	**End year in good standing:**	96%
ACT:	25-29	**Return as sophomores:**	84%
GPA 3.50 or higher:	88%	**Out-of-state:**	21%
GPA 3.0-3.49:	11%	**Live on campus:**	91%
GPA 2.0-2.99:	1%	**International:**	1%

Basis for selection. Challenging courses, strong grades, test scores, recommendations, and writing ability important. Class rank, extracurricular activities considered. Interview recommended; graded analytical paper optional. **Homeschooled:** GED and documentation of required high school credits, either by accredited agency or by program supervisor required. Interview, additional recommendations, additional writing samples, samples of creative work, and/or SAT Subject Tests optional. **Learning Disabled:** Voluntary documentaton of disability must be provided.

High school preparation. 18 units required; 20 recommended. Required and recommended units include English 4, mathematics 3, social studies 3, science 3, foreign language 2 and academic electives 3-5. Advanced courses recommended.

2005-2006 Annual costs. Tuition/fees: $3,013; $15,520 out-of-state. Additional $625 required fees for out-of-state students. Room/board: $6,330. Books/supplies: $800. Personal expenses: $2,700.

2005-2006 Financial aid. Need-based: 144 full-time freshmen applied for aid; 76 were judged to have need; 76 of these received aid. Average need met was 96%. Average scholarship/grant was $8,439; average loan $2,215. 63% of total undergraduate aid awarded as scholarships/grants, 37% as loans/jobs. **Non-need-based:** Awarded to 425 full-time undergraduates, including 168 freshmen. Scholarships awarded for academics, leadership, state residency.

Application procedures. Admission: Priority date 2/1; deadline 5/1 (postmark date). $30 fee, may be waived for applicants with need. Application may be submitted online. Admission notification on a rolling basis beginning on or about 1/1. Must reply by May 1 or within 4 week(s) if notified thereafter. **Financial aid:** Priority date 3/1; no closing date. FAFSA required. Applicants notified on a rolling basis starting 1/1; must reply by 5/1 or within 4 week(s) of notification.

Academics. All students required to completed three 4-week independent study projects, a senior thesis, and an oral baccalaureate exam before a committee of faculty. Other individualized work is common (and generally expected) in the form of self-designed academic projects done for credit as either tutorials or independent reading projects during the semester. **Special study options:** Accelerated study, cross-registration, double major, exchange student, honors, independent study, internships, student-designed major, study abroad. **Credit/placement by examination:** AP, CLEP, institutional tests. AP exam scores, IB higher-level exam scores, and CLEP scores at certain levels may be used toward exemptions from Liberal Arts Curriculum requirements. **Support services:** Tutoring, writing center.

Majors. Area/ethnic studies: French. **Biology:** General. **Conservation:** Environmental studies. **English:** English lit. **Foreign languages:** General, classics, French, German, Russian, Spanish. **History:** General. **Interdisciplinary:** Global studies, medieval/Renaissance, natural sciences. **Liberal arts:** Arts/sciences, humanities. **Math:** General. **Philosophy/religion:** Philosophy, religion. **Physical sciences:** Chemistry, physics. **Psychology:** General. **Public administration:** Policy analysis. **Social sciences:** General, anthropology, economics, political science, sociology, urban studies. **Visual/performing arts:** Art, art history/conservation, studio arts.

Computing on campus. 41 workstations in library, computer center, student center. Dormitories wired for high-speed internet access and linked to campus network. Commuter students can connect to campus network. Online library, helpline, student web hosting, wireless network available.

Student life. Freshman orientation: Mandatory, $125 fee. 7-day program. **Policies:** Freshmen permitted cars on campus. **Housing:** Guaranteed on-campus for freshmen. Coed dorms, special housing for disabled, apartments, substance-free housing available. $100 nonrefundable deposit, deadline 5/1. Wellness housing; specialized housing options may be arranged in response to student interest. **Activities:** Choral groups, dance, drama, film society, literary magazine, music ensembles, radio station, student government, student newspaper, Best Buddies, Black Student Union, farmworkers alliance, Feminist Majority leadership alliance, Hillel, Hispanic Achievers, Intervarsity Christian Fellowship, Multifaith Council, College Greens/Dems/Republicans.

Athletics. **Intramural:** Basketball, fencing, football (non-tackle), lacrosse, racquetball, rowing (crew), sailing, swimming, synchronized swimming, table tennis, tennis, volleyball, weight lifting, wrestling.

Student services. Alcohol/substance abuse counseling, campus ministries, career counseling, student employment services, financial aid counseling, health services, minority student services, personal counseling, placement for graduates, veterans' counselor, women's services. **Physically disabled:** Services for visually, speech, hearing impaired.

Contact. E-mail: admissions@ncf.edu
Phone: (941) 359-4269 Fax: (941) 359-4435
Kathleen Killion, Dean of Admissions and Financial Aid, New College of Florida, 5700 North Tamiami Trail, Sarasota, FL 34243-2197

Northwood University: Florida Campus

West Palm Beach, Florida
www.northwood.edu **CB code: 5162**

- Private 4-year university and business college
- Residential campus in small city
- 721 degree-seeking undergraduates: 4% part-time, 38% women, 10% African American, 2% Asian American, 8% Hispanic American, 25% international
- 60% of applicants admitted
- SAT or ACT (ACT writing optional), application essay required

General. Regionally accredited. Three residential campuses in Texas, Florida, and Michigan and 44 program centers. **Degrees:** 139 bachelor's, 124 associate awarded. **Location:** 75 miles from Miami. **Calendar:** Quarter, limited summer session. **Full-time faculty:** 19 total; 26% have terminal degrees, 5% minority, 32% women. **Part-time faculty:** 31 total; 10% have terminal degrees, 10% minority, 48% women. **Class size:** 51% < 20, 47% 20-39, 3% 40-49.

Freshman class profile. 913 applied, 550 admitted, 160 enrolled.

Mid 50% test scores			
SAT verbal:	420-520	Rank in top quarter:	13%
SAT math:	430-520	Rank in top tenth:	4%
ACT:	18-21	End year in good standing:	49%
GPA 3.50 or higher:	10%	Return as sophomores:	59%
GPA 3.0-3.49:	37%	Out-of-state:	57%
GPA 2.0-2.99:	50%	Live on campus:	74%
		International:	9%

Basis for selection. School achievement record, test scores, business academic interest most important; interview, school and community activities considered. Interview recommended. **Homeschooled:** Transcript of courses and grades required.

High school preparation. College-preparatory program recommended. 16 units recommended. Recommended units include English 4, mathematics 3, social studies 3, science 2 (laboratory 1) and foreign language 3.

2005-2006 Annual costs. Tuition/fees: $15,183. Room/board: $7,488.

2005-2006 Financial aid. **Need-based:** 97 full-time freshmen applied for aid; 89 were judged to have need; 89 of these received aid. Average need met was 67%. Average scholarship/grant was $6,092; average loan $2,555. 60% of total undergraduate aid awarded as scholarships/grants, 40% as loans/jobs. **Non-need-based:** Awarded to 331 full-time undergraduates, including 64 freshmen. Scholarships awarded for academics, alumni affiliation, athletics, leadership, minority status, state residency.

Application procedures. **Admission:** No deadline. $25 fee, may be waived for applicants with need. Application may be submitted online. Admission notification on a rolling basis. **Financial aid:** No deadline. FAFSA required. Applicants notified on a rolling basis starting 3/1.

Academics. Writing, math and accounting labs available. **Special study options:** Accelerated study, combined bachelor's/graduate degree, distance learning, double major, dual enrollment of high school students, ESL, external degree, honors, independent study, internships, study abroad, weekend college. **Credit/placement by examination:** AP, CLEP, IB, SAT, ACT, institutional tests. 12 credit hours maximum toward associate degree, 12 toward bachelor's. **Support services:** Reduced course load, remedial instruction, study skills assistance, tutoring, writing center.

Majors. **Business:** Accounting, banking/financial services, business admin, hotel/motel admin, international, management information systems, marketing, vehicle parts marketing. **Communications:** Advertising. **Computer sciences:** General. **Parks/recreation:** Sports admin.

Most popular majors. Business/marketing 89%, parks/recreation 7%.

Computing on campus. 89 workstations in dormitories, library, computer center, student center. Dormitories wired for high-speed internet access and linked to campus network. Commuter students can connect to campus network. Online course registration, online library, helpline, student web hosting, wireless network available.

Student life. **Freshman orientation:** Mandatory, $125 fee. Preregistration for classes offered. 3-day program in early September. **Policies:** Adheres to all federal and state laws concerning alcohol and drugs. Freshman and sophomores not living at home must live on campus. Freshmen permitted cars on campus. **Housing:** Guaranteed on-campus for freshmen. Single-sex dorms, special housing for disabled, substance-free housing available. $100 partly refundable deposit. **Activities:** Student government, international club, student government association, residence hall association, ambassador club.

Athletics. NAIA. **Intercollegiate:** Baseball M, golf, soccer, softball W, tennis, volleyball W. **Intramural:** Basketball, bowling, football (non-tackle), racquetball, tennis. **Team name:** Seahawks.

Student services. Adult student services, alcohol/substance abuse counseling, career counseling, student employment services, financial aid counseling, health services, personal counseling, placement for graduates. **Physically disabled:** Services for hearing impaired.

Contact. E-mail: fladmit@northwood.edu
Phone: (561) 478-5500 Toll-free number: (800) 458-8325
Fax: (561) 640-3328
Jack Letvintchuk, Director of Admissions, Northwood University: Florida Campus, 2600 North Military Trail, West Palm Beach, FL 33409-2911

Nova Southeastern University

Fort Lauderdale, Florida **CB member**
www.nova.edu **CB code: 5514**

- Private 4-year university
- Commuter campus in small city
- 5,275 degree-seeking undergraduates: 36% part-time, 73% women
- 20,528 degree-seeking graduate students
- 54% of applicants admitted
- SAT or ACT required
- 45% graduate within 6 years

General. Founded in 1964. Regionally accredited. Field-based programs throughout Florida, the nation, and in selected international sites. **Degrees:** 1,173 bachelor's, 5 associate awarded; master's, doctoral, first professional offered. **Location:** 10 miles from Fort Lauderdale. **Calendar:** Trimester, limited summer session. **Full-time faculty:** 582 total; 18% minority, 45% women. **Part-time faculty:** 1,033 total. **Class size:** 69% < 20, 30% 20-39, less than 1% 50-99. **Special facilities:** Oceanographic center, law center, university school (K-12).

Freshman class profile. 2,429 applied, 1,315 admitted, 457 enrolled.

Mid 50% test scores			
SAT verbal:	470-560	Rank in top tenth:	20%
SAT math:	470-580	Return as sophomores:	63%
Rank in top quarter:	44%	Out-of-state:	18%
		Live on campus:	45%

Basis for selection. Test scores, high school GPA important, interview recommended. Career Development Program (adult and evening/weekend) exempt from test score requirement and requires only high school diploma or GED. Interviews and essays are suggested, but not required. **Homeschooled:** Provide SAT or ACT scores, information about home school program of study pursued and GED score to demonstrate high school equivalence.

High school preparation. College-preparatory program recommended. Required and recommended units include English 4, mathematics 3, social studies 1, history 2, science 3, foreign language 2 and academic electives 1. One computer course recommended.

2005-2006 Annual costs. Tuition/fees: $17,580. Room/board: $8,126. Books/supplies: $1,200. Personal expenses: $4,340.

2004-2005 Financial aid. **Need-based:** 317 full-time freshmen applied for aid; 288 were judged to have need; 288 of these received aid. Average scholarship/grant was $9,407; average loan $2,545. 52% of total undergraduate aid awarded as scholarships/grants, 48% as loans/jobs. **Non-need-based:** Awarded to 2,619 full-time undergraduates, including 301 freshmen. Scholarships awarded for academics, athletics, leadership.

Application procedures. Admission: No deadline. $50 fee, may be waived for applicants with need. Application may be submitted online. Admission notification on a rolling basis. **Financial aid:** Priority date 4/15; no closing date. FAFSA, institutional form required. Applicants notified on a rolling basis starting 3/15.

Academics. Two undergraduate programs: college of professional and liberal studies for traditional daytime students, college of career development for adult evening and weekend students. Core curriculum of liberal-arts based courses plus general education required. **Special study options:** Accelerated study, combined bachelor's/graduate degree, cooperative education, distance learning, double major, dual enrollment of high school students, honors, internships, study abroad, teacher certification program. Dual admission with NSU graduate/professional programs. **Credit/placement by examination:** AP, CLEP, IB, SAT, ACT, institutional tests. 90 credit hours maximum toward bachelor's degree. **Support services:** Learning center, reduced course load, remedial instruction, study skills assistance, tutoring, writing center.

Majors. Biology: General, marine. **Business:** Accounting, business admin, finance. **Communications:** General. **Computer sciences:** General, computer science. **Conservation:** Environmental science, environmental studies. **Education:** Early childhood, elementary, special. **English:** English lit. **Health:** Athletic training, health services, nursing (RN), premedicine. **History:** General. **Legal studies:** General, paralegal, prelaw. **Liberal arts:** Arts/sciences, humanities. **Parks/recreation:** Sports admin. **Protective services:** Police science. **Psychology:** General. **Visual/performing arts:** Theater arts management.

Most popular majors. Biology 7%, business/marketing 41%, education 12%, health sciences 13%, liberal arts 8%, psychology 12%.

Computing on campus. 2,443 workstations in dormitories, library, computer center, student center. Dormitories wired for high-speed internet access and linked to campus network. Commuter students can connect to campus network. Online course registration, online library, helpline, student web hosting, wireless network available.

Student life. Freshman orientation: Mandatory. Preregistration for classes offered. Sessions offered 3 times in summer, twice in winter. Summer sessions last 2 days, 1 night. Winter sessions 1 full day with special evening session for evening students. **Policies:** Freshmen permitted cars on campus. **Housing:** Guaranteed on-campus for freshmen. Coed dorms, special housing for disabled, apartments, substance-free housing available. $500 partly refundable deposit. **Activities:** Choral groups, drama, literary magazine, radio station, student government, student newspaper, Black student association, international student association, psychology club, Hillel, pre-med society, Alpha Phi Omega, Salsa, Indian student association, international Muslim association.

Athletics. NCAA. **Intercollegiate:** Baseball M, basketball, cheerleading M, cross-country, golf, rowing (crew) W, soccer, softball W, tennis W, volleyball W. **Intramural:** Basketball M, cross-country, football (tackle) M, golf M, soccer, softball W, tennis, volleyball W. **Team name:** Sharks.

Student services. Adult student services, career counseling, student employment services, financial aid counseling, health services, personal counseling, veterans' counselor, women's services. **Physically disabled:** Services for visually, speech, hearing impaired.

Contact. E-mail: ncsinfo@nova.edu
Phone: (954) 262-8000 Toll-free number: (800) 338-4723 ext. 8000
Fax: (954) 262-3811
Maria Dillard, Director of Undergraduate Admissions, Nova Southeastern University, 3301 College Avenue, Fort Lauderdale, FL 33314

Okaloosa-Walton College

Niceville, Florida
www.owc.edu **CB code: 5526**

- Public 4-year business and community college
- Commuter campus in large town
- 4,134 degree-seeking undergraduates

General. Founded in 1963. Regionally accredited. Additional teaching centers at Ft. Walton Beach, Eglin Air Force Base, Hurlburt Field, DeFuniak Springs and Crestview. **Degrees:** 999 associate awarded. **ROTC:** Army. **Location:** 55 miles from Pensacola. **Calendar:** Semester, extensive summer session. **Full-time faculty:** 75 total. **Part-time faculty:** 170 total. **Class size:** 3% < 20, 97% 20-39. **Special facilities:** Fine and performing arts center with 2 theaters and 2 art galleries.

Basis for selection. Open admission. Applicants without high school diploma may be admitted to credit-bearing certificate programs.

High school preparation. Recommended units include English 4, mathematics 3, social studies 3 and science 3.

2005-2006 Annual costs. Tuition/fees: $1,745; $6,326 out-of-state. Books/supplies: $812.

Financial aid. Non-need-based: Scholarships awarded for academics, art, athletics, leadership, minority status, music/drama.

Application procedures. Admission: Priority date 7/25; no deadline. No application fee. Admission notification on a rolling basis. **Financial aid:** Priority date 4/1; no closing date. FAFSA, institutional form required. Applicants notified on a rolling basis starting 2/1; must reply within 2 week(s) of notification.

Academics. Special study options: Combined bachelor's/graduate degree, cooperative education, cross-registration, distance learning, dual enrollment of high school students, ESL, independent study, internships, student-designed major. **Credit/placement by examination:** AP, CLEP, institutional tests. 32 credit hours maximum toward associate degree. **Support services:** Learning center, remedial instruction, study skills assistance, tutoring.

Majors. Health: Nursing assistant.

Computing on campus. 800 workstations in library, computer center. Commuter students can connect to campus network. Online course registration, online library, wireless network available.

Student life. Freshman orientation: Mandatory. Preregistration for classes offered. Orientation can be completed online. **Policies:** Freshmen permitted cars on campus. **Activities:** Bands, choral groups, dance, drama, literary magazine, music ensembles, musical theater, student government, symphony orchestra, Student Christian Fellowship, Baptist Campus Ministry, African-American Student Association, Circle-K, College Republicans, environmental club.

Athletics. NJCAA. **Intercollegiate:** Baseball M, basketball, softball W. **Intramural:** Softball, volleyball. **Team name:** Raiders.

Student services. Adult student services, career counseling, student employment services, on-campus daycare, personal counseling, placement for graduates, veterans' counselor. **Physically disabled:** Services for visually, speech, hearing impaired.

Contact. E-mail: registrar@owcc.net
Phone: (850) 729-5373 Fax: (850) 729-5215
Christine Bishop, Registrar, Okaloosa-Walton College, 100 College Boulevard, Niceville, FL 32578-1295

Palm Beach Atlantic University

West Palm Beach, Florida
www.pba.edu **CB code: 5553**

- Private 4-year university and liberal arts college affiliated with nondenominational tradition
- Residential campus in large city
- 2,461 degree-seeking undergraduates: 7% part-time, 63% women, 15% African American, 2% Asian American, 8% Hispanic American, 2% international
- 685 degree-seeking graduate students
- 44% of applicants admitted
- SAT or ACT (ACT writing optional), application essay, interview required
- 44% graduate within 6 years

General. Founded in 1968. Regionally accredited. Distinctly Christian university with an emphasis on student community service. University offers mission trips around the world, weekly worship services, and student-led prayer groups. **Degrees:** 524 bachelor's, 30 associate awarded; master's, first professional offered. **Location:** 60 miles from Miami, 180 miles from Orlando. **Calendar:** Semester, limited summer session. **Full-time faculty:** 138 total; 72% have terminal degrees, 9% minority, 43% women. **Part-time faculty:** 130 total; 30% have terminal degrees, 7% minority, 42% women. **Class size:** 57% < 20, 39% 20-39, less than 1% 40-49, 3% 50-99, less than 1% >100.

Freshman class profile. 2,224 applied, 974 admitted, 528 enrolled.

Mid 50% test scores		Rank in top quarter:	47%
SAT verbal:	490-670	Rank in top tenth:	21%
SAT math:	490-660	Return as sophomores:	71%
ACT:	20-25	Out-of-state:	44%
GPA 3.50 or higher:	55%	Live on campus:	89%
GPA 3.0-3.49:	32%	International:	1%
GPA 2.0-2.99:	13%		

Basis for selection. Secondary school record, recommendations, test scores, interview, autobiographical essay important. Some areas also require audition. Audition required of music, theater and dance majors.

High school preparation. 18 units recommended. Recommended units include English 4, mathematics 3, social studies 3, science 3 (laboratory 3).

2006-2007 Annual costs. Tuition/fees: $18,740. Per-credit-hour charge ranges from $395 to $760 depending on the number of credits. Room/board: $7,100. Books/supplies: $1,000. Personal expenses: $1,500.

2004-2005 Financial aid. Need-based: 371 full-time freshmen applied for aid; 283 were judged to have need; 283 of these received aid. Average need met was 64%. Average scholarship/grant was $3,568; average loan $2,462. 40% of total undergraduate aid awarded as scholarships/grants, 60% as loans/jobs. **Non-need-based:** Awarded to 1,835 full-time undergraduates, including 274 freshmen. Scholarships awarded for academics, alumni affiliation, athletics, minority status, music/drama, state residency.

Application procedures. Admission: Priority date 2/1; no deadline. $25 fee, may be waived for applicants with need. Application may be submitted online. Admission notification on a rolling basis beginning on or about 12/15. **Financial aid:** Priority date 2/1; no closing date. FAFSA required. Applicants notified on a rolling basis starting 2/15; must reply within 1 week(s) of notification.

Academics. Special study options: Accelerated study, combined bachelor's/graduate degree, cooperative education, cross-registration, double major, dual enrollment of high school students, exchange student, honors, independent study, internships, study abroad, teacher certification program, Washington semester. **Credit/placement by examination:** AP, CLEP, IB, SAT, ACT. 30 credit hours maximum toward bachelor's degree. If enrolled in one of the undergraduate evening adult programs, the aggregate of credit by examination or Professional Education Credit may not exceed 45 semester hours. **Support services:** Writing center.

Majors. Biology: General. **Business:** Accounting/finance, business admin, entrepreneurial studies, international, marketing, nonprofit/public. **Communications:** General, broadcast journalism, journalism, organizational, radio/tv. **Computer sciences:** General. **Education:** General, art, biology, drama/dance, English, history, mathematics, music, physical, social science. **English:** English lit. **Health:** Athletic training, nursing (RN). **History:** General. **Legal studies:** Prelaw. **Math:** General. **Philosophy/religion:** Philosophy, religion. **Psychology:** General. **Social sciences:** Political science. **Theology:** Bible, sacred music, theology. **Visual/performing arts:** General, acting, dance, dramatic, graphic design, music performance, music theory/composition, piano/organ, play/screenwriting, studio arts, voice/opera.

Most popular majors. Biology 6%, business/marketing 42%, communications/journalism 12%, education 9%, psychology 6%, theological studies 6%, visual/performing arts 6%.

Computing on campus. 300 workstations in dormitories, library, computer center, student center. Dormitories wired for high-speed internet access and linked to campus network. Commuter students can connect to campus network. Online course registration, online library, helpline, wireless network available.

Student life. Freshman orientation: Mandatory, $80 fee. Preregistration for classes offered. Student-led and organized. **Policies:** Undergraduate students required to donate 45 hours of community service for each year of attendance. Chapel attendance required of all students. Religious observance required. Freshmen permitted cars on campus. **Housing:** Guaranteed on-campus for freshmen. Single-sex dorms, substance-free housing available. $200 fully refundable deposit, deadline 5/1. Off campus apartments. **Activities:** Bands, choral groups, dance, drama, film society, literary magazine, music ensembles, musical theater, student government, student newspaper, symphony orchestra, students in free enterprise, Newman Club, Kappa Delta Epsilon, Kappa Psi, Lambda Pi Eta, Theta Alpha Kappa, American Society of Health System Pharmacists, American association of Christian counselors, Alpha Psi Omega, campus programming association.

Athletics. NCAA. **Intercollegiate:** Baseball M, basketball, cheerleading, cross-country, golf, soccer, softball W, tennis, volleyball W. **Intramural:** Basketball, bowling, football (non-tackle), golf, racquetball, soccer, softball, table tennis, volleyball. **Team name:** Sailfish.

Student services. Campus ministries, career counseling, student employment services, financial aid counseling, health services, personal counseling, veterans' counselor.

Contact. E-mail: admit@pba.edu
Phone: (561) 803-2000 Toll-free number: (888) 468-6722
Fax: (561) 803-2115
Buckley James, Vice President for Enrollment Services, Palm Beach Atlantic University, PO Box 24708, West Palm Beach, FL 33416-4708

Remington College: Jacksonville

Jacksonville, Florida
www.remingtoncollege.edu

- For-profit 4-year technical college
- Commuter campus in small city
- 310 degree-seeking undergraduates
- Interview required

General. Accredited by ACCSCT. **Degrees:** 26 bachelor's, 88 associate awarded. **Calendar:** Differs by program. **Full-time faculty:** 20 total. **Part-time faculty:** 4 total.

Basis for selection. Open admission, but selective for some programs. Admission to bachelor's degree program in operations management requires associate degree in technical or business field with minimum of 90 credit hours. **Homeschooled:** Various entrance examinations that must be successfully passed in order to be accepted into a program.

Financial aid. Additional information: Participates in the Title IV Federal Financial Aid program. Financial aid is available to those who qualify. Approved for program participation by the Veterans Administration and certain other government-sponsored student assistance programs.

Application procedures. Admission: No deadline. $50 fee. **Financial aid:** No deadline. FAFSA required.

Academics. Special study options: Distance learning, internships. **Credit/placement by examination:** CLEP. **Support services:** Remedial instruction, tutoring.

Majors. Computer sciences: Information systems.

Computing on campus. 60 workstations in library. Online library, helpline, repair service, wireless network available.

Student life. Freshman orientation: Mandatory. Preregistration for classes offered. **Activities:** Student government, student newspaper.

Student services. Career counseling, student employment services, financial aid counseling, placement for graduates. **Physically disabled:** Services for visually, speech, hearing impaired.

Contact. Phone: (904) 296-3435 Fax: (904) 296-9097
Remington College: Jacksonville, 7011 AC Skinner Parkway, Suite 140, Jacksonville, FL 32256-6954

Remington College: Largo

Largo, Florida
www.remingtoncollege.edu/largo

- For-profit 4-year technical college
- Commuter campus in small city
- 138 degree-seeking undergraduates: 41% women
- Interview required

General. Accredited by ACCSCT. **Degrees:** 4 bachelor's, 136 associate awarded. **Location:** 18 miles from Tampa. **Calendar:** Differs by program, extensive summer session. **Full-time faculty:** 10 total; 30% have terminal degrees, 20% minority, 50% women. **Part-time faculty:** 7 total; 14% have terminal degrees, 29% minority, 57% women. **Class size:** 68% < 20, 32% 20-39.

Freshman class profile.

End year in good standing:	62%	International:	1%

Basis for selection. Open admission, but selective for some programs. Admission requires acceptable score on an entrance examination.

2005-2006 Annual costs. Tuition/fees: $15,745. Includes all fees, books and supplies.

Application procedures. **Admission:** No deadline. $50 fee. Application must be submitted on paper.

Academics. **Credit/placement by examination:** AP, CLEP. **Support services:** Tutoring.

Majors. **Business:** Operations. **Computer sciences:** General, information technology, LAN/WAN management, system admin.

Computing on campus. 75 workstations in library, computer center. Online library, repair service, wireless network available.

Student life. **Freshman orientation:** Available.

Student services. Career counseling, student employment services, financial aid counseling, placement for graduates. **Physically disabled:** Services for visually, speech, hearing impaired.

Contact. Phone: (727) 532-1999 Toll-free number: (888) 900-2343
Kathy McCabe, Director of Recruitment, Remington College: Largo, 8550 Ulmerton Road, Largo, FL 33771

Remington College: Tampa

Tampa, Florida
www.remingtoncollege.edu **CB code: 0123**

- For-profit 4-year technical college
- Commuter campus in very large city
- 586 degree-seeking undergraduates: 33% women
- 71% of applicants admitted
- Interview required

General. Founded in 1948. Accredited by ACCSCT. **Degrees:** 123 bachelor's, 463 associate awarded. **Calendar:** Quarter, extensive summer session. **Full-time faculty:** 42 total. **Part-time faculty:** 3 total.

Freshman class profile. 115 applied, 82 admitted, 82 enrolled.

Basis for selection. Interview required; recommendations considered; Wonderlic test used. Non-native speakers of English must show English proficiency.

2005-2006 Annual costs. Tuition/fees: $12,711. Tuition includes cost of books. Some programs have additional fees that cover cost of a laptop computer. Personal expenses: $1,200.

Financial aid. All financial aid based on need.

Application procedures. **Admission:** No deadline. $50 fee. Application may be submitted online. Admission notification on a rolling basis. **Financial aid:** No deadline. FAFSA, institutional form required.

Academics. **Special study options:** Accelerated study, combined bachelor's/graduate degree, distance learning. **Credit/placement by examination:** CLEP. **Support services:** Remedial instruction, tutoring.

Majors. **Engineering technology:** Electrical.

Computing on campus. 350 workstations in library, computer center. Online library, helpline, repair service, wireless network available.

Student life. **Freshman orientation:** Mandatory. Preregistration for classes offered.

Student services. Career counseling, student employment services, financial aid counseling, personal counseling, placement for graduates.

Contact. E-mail: kathleen.miller@remingtoncollege.edu
Phone: (813) 935-5700 Toll-free number: (800) 992-4850
Fax: (813) 935-7415
Kathy Miller, Director of Admissions, Remington College: Tampa, 2410 East Busch Boulevard, Tampa, FL 33612

Ringling School of Art and Design

Sarasota, Florida **CB member**
www.ringling.edu **CB code: 5573**

- Private 4-year visual arts college
- Residential campus in small city
- 1,088 degree-seeking undergraduates: 3% part-time, 49% women, 3% African American, 4% Asian American, 11% Hispanic American, 1% Native American, 5% international
- Application essay required
- 70% graduate within 6 years

General. Founded in 1931. Regionally accredited. **Degrees:** 196 bachelor's awarded. **Location:** 50 miles from Tampa. **Calendar:** Semester. **Full-time faculty:** 60 total; 70% have terminal degrees, 2% minority, 35% women. **Part-time faculty:** 59 total; 51% have terminal degrees, 39% women. **Class size:** 56% < 20, 41% 20-39, 2% 40-49, 1% 50-99. **Special facilities:** Art library.

Freshman class profile.

Mid 50% test scores		**Return as sophomores:**	86%
SAT verbal:	480-600	**Out-of-state:**	46%
SAT math:	450-580	**Live on campus:**	76%
ACT:	19-26	**International:**	5%
GPA 3.50 or higher:	24%	**Fraternities:**	3%
GPA 3.0-3.49:	32%	**Sororities:**	2%
GPA 2.0-2.99:	43%		

Basis for selection. Portfolio, school achievement record, statement of purpose, and recommendations important. Interview recommended. Portfolio required. **Learning Disabled:** Students seeking special accommodations for learning disabilities must provide documentation of disability.

2005-2006 Annual costs. Tuition/fees: $21,400. Room/board: $9,165. Books/supplies: $1,850. Personal expenses: $2,300.

2005-2006 Financial aid. All financial aid based on need. 165 full-time freshmen applied for aid; 139 were judged to have need; 138 of these received aid. Average need met was 30%. Average scholarship/grant was $6,897; average loan $2,426. 33% of total undergraduate aid awarded as scholarships/grants, 67% as loans/jobs.

Application procedures. **Admission:** Priority date 3/1; no deadline. $35 fee, may be waived for applicants with need. Application may be submitted online. Admission notification on a rolling basis beginning on or about 9/1. **Financial aid:** Priority date 3/1; no closing date. FAFSA required. Applicants notified on a rolling basis starting 5/1; must reply by 8/1.

Academics. **Special study options:** Dual enrollment of high school students, exchange student, independent study, internships, New York semester, study abroad. **Credit/placement by examination:** AP, CLEP, IB. 24 credit hours maximum toward bachelor's degree. **Support services:** Learning center, pre-admission summer program, remedial instruction, study skills assistance, tutoring, writing center.

Majors. **Communications technology:** Animation/special effects. **Visual/performing arts:** Commercial/advertising art, interior design, photography, studio arts.

Computing on campus. 350 workstations in dormitories, library, computer center. Dormitories linked to campus network. Commuter students can connect to campus network.

Student life. **Freshman orientation:** Mandatory. Orientation held week prior to classes. **Policies:** Freshmen permitted cars on campus. **Housing:** Coed dorms, single-sex dorms, special housing for disabled, apartments available. $100 deposit. **Activities:** Dance, drama, student government.

Athletics. **Intramural:** Baseball, basketball, soccer, softball, table tennis, volleyball.

Student services. Campus ministries, career counseling, student employment services, financial aid counseling, personal counseling, placement for graduates, veterans' counselor. **Physically disabled:** Services for visually, hearing impaired.

Contact. E-mail: admissions@ringling.edu
Phone: (941) 351-5100 Toll-free number: (800) 255-7695
Fax: (941) 359-7517
James Dean, Dean of Admissions, Ringling School of Art and Design, 2700 North Tamiami Trail, Sarasota, FL 34234

Rollins College

Winter Park, Florida **CB member**
www.rollins.edu **CB code: 5572**

- Private 4-year liberal arts college
- Residential campus in large town
- 1,719 degree-seeking undergraduates: 60% women, 5% African American, 4% Asian American, 8% Hispanic American, 1% Native American, 2% international

- 774 degree-seeking graduate students
- 53% of applicants admitted
- SAT or ACT (ACT writing recommended), application essay required
- 63% graduate within 6 years; 25% enter graduate study

General. Founded in 1885. Regionally accredited. International business major featuring language training, internships and study abroad available; pre-professional support services. **Degrees:** 394 bachelor's awarded; master's offered. **Location:** 5 miles from Orlando. **Calendar:** Semester, limited summer session. **Full-time faculty:** 180 total. **Part-time faculty:** 50 total. **Class size:** 65% < 20, 35% 20-39. **Special facilities:** Art museum, 2 theaters, child development center, center for psychology, greenhouse.

Freshman class profile. 2,958 applied, 1,578 admitted, 464 enrolled.

Mid 50% test scores		**GPA 2.0-2.99:**	26%
SAT verbal:	540-650	**Rank in top quarter:**	67%
SAT math:	540-640	**Rank in top tenth:**	34%
ACT:	22-27	**Return as sophomores:**	84%
GPA 3.50 or higher:	34%	**Out-of-state:**	52%
GPA 3.0-3.49:	40%	**Live on campus:**	90%

Basis for selection. School achievement record most important, followed by test scores, activities, essay, recommendations, interview. Audition recommended for music, theater arts majors. **Homeschooled:** Transcript of courses and grades, letter of recommendation (nonparent) required. Complete three SAT Subject Tests.

High school preparation. College-preparatory program recommended. 17 units required; 24 recommended. Required and recommended units include English 4, mathematics 3-4, social studies 2-3, history 2-3, science 2-4, foreign language 2-3 and academic electives 2-3.

2006-2007 Annual costs. Tuition/fees: $30,860. Room/board: $9,626. Books/supplies: $538. Personal expenses: $2,210.

2005-2006 Financial aid. Need-based: 249 full-time freshmen applied for aid; 209 were judged to have need; 209 of these received aid. Average need met was 90%. Average scholarship/grant was $24,085; average loan $3,739. 82% of total undergraduate aid awarded as scholarships/grants, 18% as loans/jobs. **Non-need-based:** Awarded to 383 full-time undergraduates, including 107 freshmen. Scholarships awarded for academics, art, athletics, leadership, music/drama, state residency. **Additional information:** Audition required for theater arts and music scholarship applicants. Portfolio required for art scholarships.

Application procedures. Admission: Closing date 2/15 (postmark date). $40 fee. Application may be submitted online. Admission notification 4/1. Must reply by 5/1. **Financial aid:** Priority date 2/15, closing date 3/1. FAFSA, institutional form required. Applicants notified on a rolling basis starting 3/1.

Academics. Special study options: Accelerated study, combined bachelor's/graduate degree, cross-registration, double major, dual enrollment of high school students, honors, independent study, internships, semester at sea, student-designed major, study abroad, teacher certification program, Washington semester. **Credit/placement by examination:** AP, CLEP, IB. 76 credit hours maximum toward bachelor's degree. **Support services:** Learning center, reduced course load, study skills assistance, tutoring, writing center.

Honors college/program. Top 10% of entering freshman class admitted.

Majors. Area/ethnic studies: Latin American. **Biology:** General, Biochemistry/biophysics and molecular biology. **Business:** International. **Computer sciences:** General. **Conservation:** Environmental studies. **Education:** General. **English:** English lit. **Foreign languages:** Classics, French, Spanish. **History:** General. **Math:** General. **Philosophy/religion:** Philosophy, religion. **Physical sciences:** Chemistry, physics. **Psychology:** General. **Social sciences:** Anthropology, economics, international relations, political science, sociology. **Visual/performing arts:** Art, art history/conservation, dramatic.

Most popular majors. Biology 7%, business/marketing 10%, English 6%, psychology 14%, social sciences 28%, visual/performing arts 14%.

Computing on campus. 205 workstations in dormitories, library, computer center, student center. Dormitories wired for high-speed internet access and linked to campus network. Online course registration, online library, helpline, repair service, student web hosting, wireless network available.

Student life. Freshman orientation: Mandatory. Preregistration for classes offered. Held just prior to fall semester. **Housing:** Guaranteed on-campus for freshmen. Coed dorms, single-sex dorms, special housing for disabled, apartments, fraternity/sorority housing available. $200 nonrefundable deposit, deadline 5/15. Special interest group housing available. **Activities:** Pep band, choral groups, dance, drama, film society, literary magazine, music ensembles, musical theater, radio station, student government, student newspaper, TV station, Gay, Lesbian, Bisexual, Transgender, ally alliance, Muslim student association, Hillel, Rollins, Habitat for Humanity, 5 Stones, cultural action committee, College Republicans, College Democrats, Black Student Union.

Athletics. NCAA. **Intercollegiate:** Baseball M, basketball, cheerleading M, cross-country, golf, rowing (crew), sailing, skiing, soccer, softball W, swimming, tennis, volleyball W. **Intramural:** Basketball M, football (non-tackle), soccer, softball, table tennis, tennis, volleyball. **Team name:** Tars.

Student services. Alcohol/substance abuse counseling, campus ministries, career counseling, student employment services, financial aid counseling, health services, personal counseling, placement for graduates, veterans' counselor. **Physically disabled:** Services for visually, speech, hearing impaired.

Contact. E-mail: admission@rollins.edu
Phone: (407) 646-2161 Fax: (407) 646-1502
Mike Lynch, Director of Admission, Rollins College, 1000 Holt Avenue, Winter Park, FL 32789

St. John Vianney College Seminary
Miami, Florida
www.sjvcs.edu **CB code: 5650**

- Private 4-year liberal arts and seminary college for men affiliated with Roman Catholic Church
- Residential campus in very large city
- 55 undergraduates
- Interview required

General. Founded in 1959. Regionally accredited. Women students admitted on part-time or full-time basis, by exception. **Degrees:** 12 bachelor's awarded. **Location:** 12 miles from downtown. **Calendar:** Semester, limited summer session. **Full-time faculty:** 7 total. **Part-time faculty:** 12 total. **Class size:** 100% < 20.

Freshman class profile.

Out-of-state:	2%	**Live on campus:**	100%

Basis for selection. Interview, academic record, recommendations required. Those to be formed for priesthood should present evidence of vocation for priesthood and submit psychological and physical evaluations. Applicants referred by home (church) Diocesan Offices of Vocations.

High school preparation. 20 units required. Required units include English 4, mathematics 2, social studies 2, history 2, science 2, foreign language 2 and academic electives 6.

2005-2006 Annual costs. Tuition/fees: $11,000. Room/board: $6,500. Books/supplies: $600. Personal expenses: $990.

Application procedures. Admission: Priority date 6/30; deadline 7/15 (receipt date). No application fee. Admission notification on a rolling basis. **Financial aid:** No deadline. FAFSA required. Applicants notified on a rolling basis.

Academics. Fluency in both English and Spanish must be achieved. Students required to take at least 1 course in alternate language each semester. **Special study options:** Cross-registration, ESL, independent study. **Credit/placement by examination:** AP, CLEP, institutional tests. **Support services:** Pre-admission summer program, reduced course load, remedial instruction, study skills assistance, tutoring.

Majors. Philosophy/religion: Philosophy.

Computing on campus. 12 workstations in library, computer center.

Student life. Freshman orientation: Mandatory, $2,000 fee. Preregistration for classes offered. 3 weeks during August. **Policies:** All sophomores and upperclassmen assigned weekly apostolic work at various locations. Religious observance required. Freshmen permitted cars on campus. **Housing:** Guaranteed on-campus for all undergraduates. **Activities:** Choral groups, drama, music ensembles, student government, student newspaper, apostolic works program.

Athletics. Intramural: Baseball M, basketball M, handball M, racquetball M, soccer M, softball M, swimming M, table tennis M, tennis M, volleyball M, weight lifting M.

Student services. Adult student services, career counseling, financial aid counseling, health services, personal counseling.

Contact. Phone: (305) 223-4561 Fax: (305) 223-0650
Edward van Merrienboer, Academic Dean, St. John Vianney College Seminary, 2900 Southwest 87 Avenue, Miami, FL 33165-3244

St. Leo University

Saint Leo, Florida **CB member**
www.saintleo.edu **CB code: 5638**

- Private 4-year university affiliated with Roman Catholic Church
- Residential campus in rural community
- 1,382 degree-seeking undergraduates: 3% part-time, 55% women, 8% African American, 1% Asian American, 9% Hispanic American, 1% Native American, 8% international
- 854 degree-seeking graduate students
- 43% of applicants admitted
- SAT or ACT (ACT writing optional), application essay required
- 41% graduate within 6 years

General. Founded in 1889. Regionally accredited. **Degrees:** 180 bachelor's, 10 associate awarded; master's offered. **ROTC:** Army, Air Force. **Location:** 25 miles from Tampa. **Calendar:** Semester, limited summer session. **Full-time faculty:** 66 total; 82% have terminal degrees, 6% minority, 32% women. **Part-time faculty:** 56 total; 27% have terminal degrees, 7% minority, 43% women. **Class size:** 53% < 20, 47% 20-39. **Special facilities:** Wetlands nearby for field studies in environmental science, Center for Catholic and Jewish Studies.

Freshman class profile. 3,248 applied, 1,409 admitted, 454 enrolled.

Mid 50% test scores			
SAT verbal:	460-540	Rank in top quarter:	30%
SAT math:	460-550	Rank in top tenth:	8%
ACT:	19-24	End year in good standing:	77%
GPA 3.50 or higher:	28%	Return as sophomores:	71%
GPA 3.0-3.49:	34%	Out-of-state:	40%
GPA 2.0-2.99:	37%	Live on campus:	88%
		International:	9%

Basis for selection. Test scores, GPA, guidance counselor's recommendation, high school curriculum, essay important. Interview recommended. **Homeschooled:** Transcript of courses and grades required. Bibliography of all high school reading material, 2 letters of recommendation, SAT or ACT scores, portfolio of sample work, interview (in person or via phone) required.

High school preparation. 16 units recommended. Recommended units include English 4, mathematics 3, social studies 3, science 2, foreign language 2 and academic electives 2. Social studies units should include history. No more than 4 nonacademic units. Algebra I and II, geometry strongly recommended.

2005-2006 Annual costs. Tuition/fees: $14,680. Room/board: $7,460. Books/supplies: $1,200. Personal expenses: $900.

2005-2006 Financial aid. Need-based: 398 full-time freshmen applied for aid; 297 were judged to have need; 296 of these received aid. Average need met was 85%. Average scholarship/grant was $10,787; average loan $2,740. 66% of total undergraduate aid awarded as scholarships/grants, 34% as loans/jobs. **Non-need-based:** Awarded to 175 full-time undergraduates, including 52 freshmen. Scholarships awarded for academics, alumni affiliation, athletics, leadership, minority status, music/drama, religious affiliation, state residency.

Application procedures. Admission: Priority date 3/1; deadline 8/15 (postmark date). $35 fee, may be waived for applicants with need. Application may be submitted online. Admission notification on a rolling basis beginning on or about 10/15. Must reply by May 1 or within 2 week(s) if notified thereafter. **Financial aid:** Priority date 4/1; no closing date. FAFSA required. Applicants notified on a rolling basis starting 1/31.

Academics. Special study options: Combined bachelor's/graduate degree, distance learning, double major, dual enrollment of high school students, honors, independent study, internships, liberal arts/career combination, study abroad, teacher certification program, weekend college. Opportunity to study abroad in Italy, Switzerland, France, Ecuador, Spain, United Kingdom, Ireland and Australia, Germany. **Credit/placement by examination:** AP, CLEP, IB, SAT, ACT, institutional tests. 40 credit hours maximum toward associate degree, 40 toward bachelor's. **Support services:** Learning center, pre-admission summer program, reduced course load, remedial instruction, study skills assistance, tutoring, writing center.

Honors college/program. 3.0 high school GPA, 50 TSWE or 1150 SAT (exclusive of Writing) or 25 ACT required.

Majors. Biology: General. **Business:** Accounting, business admin, hospitality admin, human resources, international, management information systems, management science, marketing, operations. **Communications:** Media studies. **Conservation:** Environmental studies. **Education:** Elementary, middle. **English:** Creative writing, English lit. **Health:** Clinical lab science, facilities admin, health care admin. **History:** General. **Math:** General. **Parks/recreation:** Sports admin. **Protective services:** Criminal justice. **Psychology:** General. **Public administration:** Community org/advocacy, social work. **Social sciences:** International relations, political science, sociology. **Theology:** Theology.

Most popular majors. Biology 6%, business/marketing 33%, education 14%, history 7%, psychology 9%, public administration/social services 7%, social sciences 13%.

Computing on campus. 1,230 workstations in dormitories, library, student center. Dormitories wired for high-speed internet access and linked to campus network. Commuter students can connect to campus network. Online course registration, online library, helpline, repair service, student web hosting, wireless network available.

Student life. Freshman orientation: Mandatory, $200 fee. Preregistration for classes offered. Advising, testing, introduction to student life in mid-July. 4-day program in August includes team-building, personal responsibility activities. **Policies:** Fish aquariums allowed in residence hall rooms. Freshmen permitted cars on campus. **Housing:** Guaranteed on-campus for all undergraduates. Coed dorms, single-sex dorms, special housing for disabled, apartments, fraternity/sorority housing, substance-free housing available. $200 nonrefundable deposit, deadline 8/1. Freshmen only housing available. **Activities:** Concert band, choral groups, dance, drama, literary magazine, music ensembles, radio station, student government, student newspaper, TV station, Circle-K, Samaritans, intercultural student association, Ambassadors, Best Buddies, student chaplain program, Pi Sigma Alpha, Brothers and Sisters United, social work club.

Athletics. NCAA. **Intercollegiate:** Baseball M, basketball, cross-country, golf, lacrosse M, soccer, softball W, swimming, tennis, volleyball W. **Intramural:** Basketball, football (non-tackle), softball. **Team name:** Lions.

Student services. Adult student services, alcohol/substance abuse counseling, campus ministries, career counseling, student employment services, financial aid counseling, health services, personal counseling. **Physically disabled:** Services for visually impaired.

Contact. E-mail: admission@saintleo.edu
Phone: (352) 588-8283 Toll-free number: (800) 334-5532
Fax: (352) 588-8257
Gary Bracken, Vice President for Enrollment, St. Leo University, Office of Admission, Saint Leo, FL 33574-6665

St. Thomas University

Miami Gardens, Florida
www.stu.edu **CB code: 5076**

- Private 4-year university affiliated with Roman Catholic Church
- Commuter campus in very large city
- 1,158 degree-seeking undergraduates: 5% part-time, 58% women
- 1,534 degree-seeking graduate students
- 91% of applicants admitted
- SAT or ACT (ACT writing recommended) required
- 36% graduate within 6 years

General. Founded in 1961. Regionally accredited. Multi-location institution. Affiliated with Archdiocese of Miami. **Degrees:** 325 bachelor's awarded; master's, first professional offered. **Location:** 10 miles from Miami. **Calendar:** Semester, extensive summer session. **Full-time faculty:** 95 total; 87% have terminal degrees, 28% minority, 39% women. **Part-time faculty:** 156 total; 44% have terminal degrees, 44% minority, 38% women. **Class size:** 63% < 20, 36% 20-39, less than 1% 40-49, less than 1% 50-99.

Freshman class profile. 551 applied, 499 admitted, 206 enrolled.

Mid 50% test scores			
SAT verbal:	400-500	GPA 2.0-2.99:	52%
SAT math:	380-510	Return as sophomores:	69%
ACT:	16-23	Out-of-state:	17%
GPA 3.50 or higher:	15%	Live on campus:	22%
GPA 3.0-3.49:	32%	International:	5%

Basis for selection. High school grades, test scores primary factors. Class rank, interview, school, community activities, recommendations also considered. Interview recommended.

High school preparation. Required units include English 4, mathematics 3, social studies 3, science 2 and academic electives 6.

2005-2006 Annual costs. Tuition/fees: $17,860. Room/board: $5,630. Books/supplies: $1,000. Personal expenses: $1,870.

2005-2006 Financial aid. **Need-based:** 189 full-time freshmen applied for aid; 177 were judged to have need; 177 of these received aid. Average scholarship/grant was $1,820; average loan $2,837. 73% of total undergraduate aid awarded as scholarships/grants, 27% as loans/jobs. **Non-need-based:** Awarded to 949 full-time undergraduates, including 184 freshmen. Scholarships awarded for academics, athletics, leadership, music/drama, state residency.

Application procedures. **Admission:** No deadline. $40 fee, may be waived for applicants with need. Application may be submitted online. Admission notification on a rolling basis. Must reply by May 1 or within 2 week(s) if notified thereafter. Applicants needing on-campus housing strongly encouraged to apply before May 15. **Financial aid:** Priority date 4/1; no closing date. FAFSA required. Applicants notified on a rolling basis starting 3/1.

Academics. **Special study options:** Combined bachelor's/graduate degree, distance learning, double major, dual enrollment of high school students, honors, independent study, internships, liberal arts/career combination, teacher certification program. **Credit/placement by examination:** AP, CLEP, SAT, ACT, institutional tests. 45 credit hours maximum toward bachelor's degree. **Support services:** Learning center, pre-admission summer program, reduced course load, remedial instruction, study skills assistance, tutoring.

Majors. **Biology:** General. **Business:** Accounting, business admin, finance, hospitality admin, international, organizational behavior, tourism/travel. **Communications:** General, media studies. **Computer sciences:** General, computer science. **Education:** Elementary, secondary, social studies. **English:** English lit. **Health:** Health care admin, premedicine, preveterinary. **History:** General. **Legal studies:** Prelaw. **Liberal arts:** Arts/sciences. **Parks/recreation:** Sports admin. **Philosophy/religion:** Religion. **Protective services:** Criminal justice. **Psychology:** General. **Social sciences:** Political science. **Theology:** Religious ed.

Computing on campus. 123 workstations in library, computer center. Dormitories linked to campus network. Online course registration, helpline, wireless network available.

Student life. **Freshman orientation:** Mandatory. **Policies:** Freshmen permitted cars on campus. **Housing:** Single-sex dorms available. $225 fully refundable deposit. **Activities:** Choral groups, literary magazine, music ensembles, student government, TV station, international student organization, political action club, Students for Global Preservation, prelaw society, premedicine club, accounting club.

Athletics. NAIA. **Intercollegiate:** Baseball M, cross-country, golf, soccer, softball W, tennis, volleyball W. **Intramural:** Golf, soccer M, softball, tennis, volleyball. **Team name:** Bobcats.

Student services. Adult student services, alcohol/substance abuse counseling, campus ministries, career counseling, student employment services, financial aid counseling, health services, personal counseling, placement for graduates. **Physically disabled:** Services for visually, hearing impaired.

Contact. E-mail: signup@stu.edu
Phone: (305) 628-6546 Toll-free number: (800) 367-9010
Fax: (305) 628-6591
Lydia Amy, Dean, Enrollment Services, St. Thomas University, 16401 Northwest 37th Avenue, Miami Gardens, FL 33054-6459

Schiller International University

Dunedin, Florida
www.schiller.edu **CB code: 0601**

- For-profit 4-year university
- Residential campus in large town
- 81 degree-seeking undergraduates: 9% part-time, 43% women
- 69 degree-seeking graduate students
- Application essay required

General. Founded in 1964. Accredited by ACICS. 8 campuses in 6 countries located in or near major urban areas: Dunedin, London, Paris, Madrid, Heidelberg, Strasbourg, Engelberg and Leysin. Students may transfer without loss of credit. **Degrees:** 34 bachelor's, 5 associate awarded; master's offered. **Location:** 20 miles from Tampa. **Calendar:** Semester, extensive summer session. **Full-time faculty:** 5 total. **Part-time faculty:** 45 total. **Special facilities:** University owned and operated hotels.

Basis for selection. Open admission. Graduate students must have a four year Bachelor's degree, and undergraduate students must have the equivalency of the U.S. high school diploma or GED. TOEFL required for all foreign students; on-campus English Placement Exam available for those without TOEFL. English language school available on campus.

2006-2007 Annual costs. Tuition/fees (projected): $17,650. Room/board: $7,600. Books/supplies: $1,250. Personal expenses: $2,600.

Financial aid. **Non-need-based:** Scholarships awarded for academics, alumni affiliation, leadership, minority status, state residency. **Additional information:** Special scholarship program for U.S. college students studying abroad at European campuses of Schiller. Work-study available to students taking 2 or more courses.

Application procedures. **Admission:** No deadline. $50 fee. Application must be submitted on paper. Admission notification on a rolling basis. **Financial aid:** Closing date 4/1. FAFSA, institutional form required. Applicants notified on a rolling basis starting 5/1; must reply within 3 week(s) of notification.

Academics. Completion of intermediate level of at least one foreign language required for most undergraduate degree programs. **Special study options:** Accelerated study, cooperative education, distance learning, double major, dual enrollment of high school students, ESL, exchange student, independent study, internships, liberal arts/career combination, study abroad, weekend college. **Credit/placement by examination:** AP, CLEP, IB, institutional tests. 16 credit hours maximum toward associate degree, 16 toward bachelor's. **Support services:** Learning center, reduced course load, study skills assistance, tutoring.

Majors. **Area/ethnic studies:** European. **Business:** General, banking/financial services, business admin, finance, hotel/motel admin, international, international marketing, management information systems, marketing, tourism/travel. **Computer sciences:** Information technology, systems analysis. **Foreign languages:** French, German. **Interdisciplinary:** Global studies. **Psychology:** General. **Social sciences:** International economics, international relations.

Most popular majors. Business/marketing 85%, social sciences 12%.

Computing on campus. 35 workstations in library, computer center, student center. Commuter students can connect to campus network. Online library, repair service, wireless network available.

Student life. **Freshman orientation:** Mandatory. Preregistration for classes offered. 2-day program, 2 days before registration. **Policies:** Alcohol use banned; smoking limited to specific locations. No heating devices allowed. Freshmen permitted cars on campus. **Housing:** Guaranteed on-campus for freshmen. Coed dorms, substance-free housing available. $400 deposit, deadline 8/5. Students may also live with host families at some campuses. **Activities:** Student government, student newspaper, Model United Nations, Rotaract, Young Skal, honors society, Society for Human Resource Management, student council.

Athletics. **Intramural:** Baseball, basketball, soccer.

Student services. Adult student services, career counseling, services for economically disadvantaged, student employment services, financial aid counseling, legal services, personal counseling, placement for graduates.

Contact. E-mail: admissions@schiller.edu
Phone: (727) 736-5082 ext. 240 Toll-free number: (800) 336-4133
Fax: (727) 734-0359
Kamala Dontamsetti, Associate Director of Admissions, Schiller International University, 453 Edgewater Drive, Dunedin, FL 34698

South Florida Bible College and Theological Seminary

Deerfield Beach, Florida
www.sfbc.edu

- Private 4-year Bible and seminary college affiliated with interdenominational tradition
- Small city

General. Accredited by ABHE. **Location:** 10 miles from Ft. Lauderdale. **Calendar:** Quarter.

Annual costs/financial aid. Tuition/fees (2005-2006): $4,880.

Contact. Phone: (954) 426-8652 ext. 209
747 South Federal Highway, Deerfield Beach, FL 33441

South University: West Palm Beach Campus

West Palm Beach, Florida
www.southuniversity.edu **CB code: 5321**

- For-profit 4-year business and health science college
- Commuter campus in large city
- 502 degree-seeking undergraduates: 31% part-time, 86% women
- 67% of applicants admitted
- Interview required

General. Regionally accredited. **Degrees:** 44 bachelor's, 72 associate awarded; master's offered. **Location:** 3 miles from downtown, 29 miles from Fort Lauderdale. **Calendar:** Quarter, extensive summer session. **Full-time faculty:** 18 total. **Part-time faculty:** 40 total.

Freshman class profile. 253 applied, 169 admitted, 130 enrolled.

Basis for selection. Test scores most important. Satisfactory score on college-administered entrance exams (CPT), or combined SAT score of 660 (exclusive of Writing) or ACT of 14 required. Some programs have higher requirements. SAT and SAT Subject Tests or ACT recommended.

2005-2006 Annual costs. Tuition/fees: $11,085. Books/supplies: $900. Personal expenses: $1,476.

Financial aid. Non-need-based: Scholarships awarded for academics.

Application procedures. Admission: Priority date 10/1; no deadline. $25 fee, may be waived for applicants with need. Admission notification on a rolling basis. **Financial aid:** No deadline. FAFSA, institutional form required. Applicants notified on a rolling basis; must reply within 2 week(s) of notification.

Academics. Special study options: Accelerated study, double major, dual enrollment of high school students, internships. **Credit/placement by examination:** CLEP, SAT, ACT, institutional tests. No more than 60% of any program requirements may be earned through credits by examinations. **Support services:** Remedial instruction, study skills assistance, tutoring.

Majors. Business: Business admin, finance. **Computer sciences:** Information systems. **Health:** Nursing (RN). **Legal studies:** Paralegal.

Most popular majors. Business/marketing 25%, health sciences 35%, legal studies 40%.

Computing on campus. 75 workstations in library, computer center. Online library available.

Student life. Freshman orientation: Mandatory. **Policies:** Freshmen permitted cars on campus. **Activities:** Student government, student newspaper, paralegal club,honor society,student goverment.

Student services. Adult student services, career counseling, student employment services, personal counseling, placement for graduates, veterans' counselor.

Contact. E-mail: wpbadmis@southuniversity.edu
Phone: (561) 697-9200 Fax: (561) 697-9944
Joseph Rogalski, Director of Admissions, South University: West Palm Beach Campus, 1760 North Congress Avenue, West Palm Beach, FL 33409-5178

Southeastern College of the Assemblies of God

Lakeland, Florida
www.seuniversity.edu **CB code: 5621**

- Private 4-year liberal arts and teachers college affiliated with Assemblies of God
- Residential campus in small city
- 2,297 degree-seeking undergraduates: 5% part-time, 57% women, 7% African American, 1% Asian American, 12% Hispanic American
- 39 graduate students
- 36% graduate within 6 years

General. Founded in 1935. Regionally accredited; also accredited by ABHE. **Degrees:** 254 bachelor's awarded. **ROTC:** Army. **Location:** 40 miles from Tampa, 50 miles from Orlando. **Calendar:** Semester, limited summer session. **Full-time faculty:** 54 total; 63% have terminal degrees, 17% minority, 32% women. **Part-time faculty:** 83 total; 4% minority, 45% women. **Class size:** 35% < 20, 42% 20-39, 7% 40-49, 15% 50-99, 1% >100.

Freshman class profile. 984 applied, 785 admitted, 521 enrolled.

Mid 50% test scores		Return as sophomores:	65%
ACT:	18-24	Out-of-state:	56%

Basis for selection. Open admission, but selective for some programs. Christian character important. SAT or ACT test scores are used for placement purposes in Math, English; also used to determine scholarship eligibility. Accuplacer may be used in lieu of SAT/ACT. Essay recommended. Interview recommended for academically weak applicants.

2006-2007 Annual costs. Tuition/fees: $12,280. Room/board: $6,028. Books/supplies: $800. Personal expenses: $800.

2005-2006 Financial aid. Need-based: 47% of total undergraduate aid awarded as scholarships/grants, 53% as loans/jobs. **Non-need-based:** Scholarships awarded for academics, leadership, music/drama.

Application procedures. Admission: Priority date 8/1; no deadline. $40 fee, may be waived for applicants with need. Application must be submitted on paper. Admission notification on a rolling basis. **Financial aid:** Priority date 5/15; no closing date. FAFSA, institutional form required. Applicants notified on a rolling basis starting 5/10; must reply within 3 week(s) of notification.

Academics. Special study options: Accelerated study, distance learning, double major, dual enrollment of high school students, independent study, internships, liberal arts/career combination, study abroad, teacher certification program. **Credit/placement by examination:** AP, CLEP, IB, institutional tests. 45 credit hours maximum toward bachelor's degree. **Support services:** Reduced course load, remedial instruction, study skills assistance, tutoring, writing center.

Majors. Biology: General. **Business:** Accounting, business admin, finance, marketing. **Communications:** General. **Education:** Biology, early childhood, elementary, English, mathematics, middle, music, science, secondary, social studies. **English:** English lit. **History:** General. **Legal studies:** Prelaw. **Math:** General. **Philosophy/religion:** Religion. **Psychology:** General. **Public administration:** Social work. **Theology:** Bible, missionary, pastoral counseling, religious ed, sacred music, theology. **Visual/performing arts:** Piano/organ, voice/opera.

Most popular majors. Business/marketing 18%, communications/journalism 6%, education 17%, philosophy/religious studies 34%, psychology 11%.

Computing on campus. Dormitories wired for high-speed internet access and linked to campus network. Commuter students can connect to campus network. Online course registration, online library, helpline, wireless network available.

Student life. Freshman orientation: Mandatory. Preregistration for classes offered. **Policies:** Religious observance required. Freshmen permitted cars on campus. **Housing:** Guaranteed on-campus for freshmen. Single-sex dorms available. **Activities:** Bands, choral groups, drama, literary magazine, music ensembles, musical theater, opera, radio station, student government, student newspaper, TV station.

Athletics. NCCAA. **Intercollegiate:** Basketball, golf M, soccer M, tennis W, volleyball W. **Intramural:** Baseball M, basketball M, bowling, football (non-tackle) M, soccer, softball, tennis, volleyball, weight lifting. **Team name:** Fire.

Student services. Adult student services, campus ministries, career counseling, student employment services, financial aid counseling, health services, personal counseling, placement for graduates.

Contact. E-mail: admission@seuniversity.edu
Phone: (863) 667-5018 Toll-free number: (800) 500-8760
Fax: (863) 667-5200
Omar Rashed, Director of Admission, Southeastern College of the Assemblies of God, 1000 Longfellow Boulevard, Lakeland, FL 33801

Stetson University

DeLand, Florida **CB member**
www.stetson.edu **CB code: 5630**

- Private 4-year university
- Residential campus in large town
- 2,199 degree-seeking undergraduates: 3% part-time, 58% women, 4% African American, 2% Asian American, 7% Hispanic American, 3% international

- 1,430 graduate students
- 69% of applicants admitted
- SAT or ACT (ACT writing optional), application essay required
- 65% graduate within 6 years; 48% enter graduate study

General. Founded in 1883. Regionally accredited. **Degrees:** 454 bachelor's awarded; master's, first professional offered. **ROTC:** Army. **Location:** 20 miles from Daytona Beach, 40 miles from Orlando. **Calendar:** Semester, limited summer session. **Full-time faculty:** 186 total; 90% have terminal degrees, 11% minority, 41% women. **Part-time faculty:** 76 total; 9% minority, 45% women. **Class size:** 59% < 20, 39% 20-39, 1% 40-49, less than 1% 50-99. **Special facilities:** Geological museum, greenhouse with growth chambers, digital arts laboratory.

Freshman class profile. 2,777 applied, 1,918 admitted, 550 enrolled.

Mid 50% test scores		Return as sophomores:	77%
SAT verbal:	520-620	Out-of-state:	21%
SAT math:	520-610	Live on campus:	91%
ACT:	22-27	International:	3%
GPA 3.50 or higher:	71%	Fraternities:	20%
GPA 3.0-3.49:	22%	Sororities:	20%
GPA 2.0-2.99:	7%		

Basis for selection. High school record most important, followed by class rank, standardized test scores, and secondary school's recommendation. Extracurricular activities and particular talents or abilities also important. Interview recommended. Audition required of music majors. Portfolio recommended for art majors.

High school preparation. 14 units required. Required units include English 4, mathematics 3, social studies 2, science 3, foreign language 2 and academic electives 2.

2005-2006 Annual costs. Tuition/fees: $25,450. Room/board: $7,275. Books/supplies: $800. Personal expenses: $1,620.

2004-2005 Financial aid. Need-based: 428 full-time freshmen applied for aid; 345 were judged to have need; 345 of these received aid. Average need met was 87%. Average scholarship/grant was $17,501; average loan $4,087. 67% of total undergraduate aid awarded as scholarships/grants, 33% as loans/jobs. **Non-need-based:** Awarded to 2,026 full-time undergraduates, including 611 freshmen. Scholarships awarded for academics, alumni affiliation, art, athletics, leadership, minority status, music/drama, religious affiliation, ROTC, state residency.

Application procedures. Admission: Priority date 3/1; no deadline. $40 fee, may be waived for applicants with need. Application may be submitted online. Admission notification on a rolling basis beginning on or about 11/15. Must reply by May 1 or within 3 week(s) if notified thereafter. **Financial aid:** Priority date 3/15; no closing date. FAFSA, institutional form required. Applicants notified on a rolling basis.

Academics. Special study options: Accelerated study, combined bachelor's/graduate degree, double major, honors, independent study, internships, liberal arts/career combination, student-designed major, study abroad, teacher certification program, Washington semester. **Credit/placement by examination:** AP, CLEP, IB, institutional tests. **Support services:** Reduced course load, study skills assistance, tutoring, writing center.

Majors. Area/ethnic studies: American, Latin American, Russian/Slavic. **Biology:** General, aquatic, biochemistry, molecular. **Business:** Accounting, business admin, e-commerce, entrepreneurial studies, finance, international, management science, managerial economics, marketing. **Communications:** General. **Computer sciences:** Computer science, web page design. **Conservation:** Environmental science. **Education:** General, biology, chemistry, elementary, English, foreign languages, French, German, mathematics, music, secondary, social science, Spanish. **English:** English lit. **Foreign languages:** French, German, Spanish. **Health:** Clinical lab science, health services. **History:** General. **Liberal arts:** Humanities. **Math:** General. **Parks/recreation:** Exercise sciences, sports admin. **Philosophy/religion:** Philosophy, religion. **Physical sciences:** Chemistry, physics. **Psychology:** General. **Social sciences:** General, economics, geography, international relations, political science, sociology. **Visual/performing arts:** Art, dramatic, music performance, music theory/composition, piano/organ, stringed instruments, studio arts, voice/opera.

Most popular majors. Biology 7%, business/marketing 36%, education 6%, social sciences 7%, visual/performing arts 9%.

Computing on campus. 320 workstations in library, computer center. Dormitories wired for high-speed internet access and linked to campus network. Commuter students can connect to campus network. Online library, helpline, student web hosting available.

Student life. Freshman orientation: Mandatory. Preregistration for classes offered. Fall orientation held four days prior to the first day of classes. Spring orientation is an abbreviated version held in one day before classes begin. **Policies:** Freshmen permitted cars on campus. **Housing:** Guaranteed on-campus for all undergraduates. Coed dorms, single-sex dorms, fraternity/sorority housing, substance-free housing available. Foreign language houses available. **Activities:** Bands, choral groups, dance, drama, literary magazine, music ensembles, musical theater, opera, radio station, student government, student newspaper, symphony orchestra, multiple religious groups, Best Buddies, Black Student Association, Caribbean Club, Habitat for Humanity, Indian Student Association, Roots and Shoots, Multicultural Student Council, College Democrats, College Republicans.

Athletics. NCAA. **Intercollegiate:** Baseball M, basketball, cross-country, golf, rowing (crew), soccer, softball W, tennis, volleyball W. **Intramural:** Basketball, bowling, football (non-tackle), soccer, softball, swimming, table tennis, volleyball, water polo. **Team name:** Hatters.

Student services. Campus ministries, career counseling, student employment services, financial aid counseling, health services, minority student services, personal counseling, placement for graduates, women's services. **Physically disabled:** Services for visually, speech impaired.

Contact. E-mail: admissions@stetson.edu
Phone: (386) 822-7100 Toll-free number: (800) 688-0101
Fax: (386) 822-7112
Deborah Thompson, Vice President for Enrollment Management, Stetson University, Campus Box 8378, DeLand, FL 32723

Talmudic College of Florida

Miami Beach, Florida
www.talmudicu.edu **CB code: 0514**

- Private 4-year rabbinical college for men affiliated with Jewish faith
- Very large city

General. Founded in 1974. Accredited by AARTS. **Calendar:** Semester.

Annual costs/financial aid. Costs for 11 months: tuition $6,500, fees $200, room and board $4,300. Books/supplies: $900. Need-based financial aid available to full-time and part-time students.

Contact. Phone: (305) 534-0803
Financial Aid Officer, 1910 Alton Road, Miami Beach, FL 33139

Trinity College of Florida

Trinity, Florida
www.trinitycollege.edu **CB code: 3975**

- Private 4-year Bible college affiliated with interdenominational tradition
- Commuter campus in small city
- 160 degree-seeking undergraduates
- 30% of applicants admitted
- Application essay, interview required

General. Accredited by ABHE. **Degrees:** 10 bachelor's, 4 associate awarded. **Location:** 25 miles from of Tampa. **Calendar:** Semester, limited summer session. **Full-time faculty:** 21 total. **Part-time faculty:** 38 total. **Class size:** 22% < 20, 47% 20-39, 16% 40-49, 16% 50-99.

Freshman class profile. 151 applied, 45 admitted, 45 enrolled.

Mid 50% test scores		SAT math:	400-510
SAT verbal:	440-560	ACT:	18-25

Basis for selection. Applicants must provide evidence of Christian character and witness, as well as academic ability largely based upon GPA and SAT/ACT scores. SAT or ACT recommended. **Homeschooled:** If the student is not registered with the local superintendent or under an umbrella school, GED is required.

2005-2006 Annual costs. Tuition/fees: $8,474. Room/board: $4,970. Books/supplies: $500.

2005-2006 Financial aid. All financial aid based on need.

Application procedures. Admission: Closing date 8/2 (receipt date). $25 fee, may be waived for applicants with need. Application may be submitted online. Admission notification on a rolling basis. Must reply by 7/26. **Financial aid:** Closing date 8/2. FAFSA, institutional form required. Applicants notified on a rolling basis.

Academics. Special study options: Cooperative education, double major, dual enrollment of high school students, honors, internships, teacher certification program. **Credit/placement by examination:** AP, CLEP, SAT, ACT, institutional tests. **Support services:** Reduced course load, remedial instruction, tutoring.

Majors. Education: General. **Philosophy/religion:** Christian. **Theology:** Bible, missionary, pastoral counseling, youth ministry.

Most popular majors. Education 25%, philosophy/religious studies 50%.

Computing on campus. 15 workstations in library, computer center. Dormitories wired for high-speed internet access and linked to campus network. Online library, repair service, wireless network available.

Student life. Freshman orientation: Mandatory. Preregistration for classes offered. **Policies:** Religious observance required. Freshmen permitted cars on campus. **Housing:** Guaranteed on-campus for all undergraduates. Single-sex dorms, apartments, substance-free housing available. $150 fully refundable deposit, deadline 7/26. **Activities:** Choral groups, drama, student government.

Athletics. NCCAA. **Intercollegiate:** Basketball M. **Intramural:** Basketball M. **Team name:** Tigers.

Student services. Campus ministries, financial aid counseling, personal counseling.

Contact. E-mail: admissions@trinitycollege.edu
Phone: (727) 569-1411 Toll-free number: (800) 388-0869
Fax: (727) 569-1410
Kevin Bonsignore, Assistant Director of Admissions, Trinity College of Florida, 2430 Welbilt Boulevard, Trinity, FL 34655

Universidad FLET

Miami, Florida
www.flet.edu

- Private 4-year university and Bible college
- Large city
- 165 degree-seeking undergraduates
- 16 graduate students

General. Accredited by DETC. **Degrees:** 64 bachelor's, 1 associate awarded; master's offered. **Calendar:** Continuous. **Full-time faculty:** 5 total. **Part-time faculty:** 15 total.

Basis for selection. Open admission. **Homeschooled:** Letter of recommendation (nonparent) required.

2005-2006 Annual costs. Tuition varies by program. Per-credit-hour charge $30.

Application procedures. Admission: No deadline. $20 fee, may be waived for applicants with need. Application may be submitted online. **Financial aid:** No deadline.

Academics. Special study options: Distance learning. **Credit/placement by examination:** CLEP.

Majors. Theology: Bible, theology.

Student life. Freshman orientation: Available. Preregistration for classes offered.

Contact. E-mail: admisiones@flet.edu
Phone: (305) 378-8700 Toll-free number: (888) 376-3538
Fax: (305) 232-5832
Janet Ramirez, Director of Admission, Universidad FLET, 14540 SW 136th Street, Suite 202, Miami, FL 33186

University of Central Florida

Orlando, Florida **CB member**
www.ucf.edu **CB code: 5233**

- Public 4-year university
- Residential campus in very large city
- 37,568 degree-seeking undergraduates: 24% part-time, 55% women, 9% African American, 5% Asian American, 13% Hispanic American, 1% international
- 6,328 degree-seeking graduate students
- 62% of applicants admitted
- SAT or ACT with writing required
- 57% graduate within 6 years; 34% enter graduate study

General. Founded in 1963. Regionally accredited. **Degrees:** 7,330 bachelor's, 223 associate awarded; master's, doctoral offered. **ROTC:** Army, Air Force. **Location:** 13 miles from downtown. **Calendar:** Semester, extensive summer session. **Full-time faculty:** 1,192 total; 79% have terminal degrees, 22% minority, 38% women. **Part-time faculty:** 445 total; 33% have terminal degrees, 14% minority, 49% women. **Class size:** 27% < 20, 39% 20-39, 13% 40-49, 15% 50-99, 6% >100. **Special facilities:** Florida Solar Energy Center, Institute for Simulation and Training, Center for Research/Education in Optics and Lasers, Space Education and Research Center, Biomolecular Sciences Center, National Center for Forensic Science, arboretum, observatory.

Freshman class profile. 20,265 applied, 12,542 admitted, 6,359 enrolled.

Mid 50% test scores		**Rank in top tenth:**	35%
SAT verbal:	520-610	**End year in good standing:**	97%
SAT math:	530-620	**Return as sophomores:**	83%
ACT:	22-26	**Out-of-state:**	7%
GPA 3.50 or higher:	56%	**Live on campus:**	61%
GPA 3.0-3.49:	34%	**International:**	1%
GPA 2.0-2.99:	10%	**Fraternities:**	8%
Rank in top quarter:	75%	**Sororities:**	6%

Basis for selection. 2/3 of admission offers made via review of GPA and standardized test scores. 1/3 are made via review of factors such as grades, strength of coursework, essays, letters of recommendation, special talents. TOEFL may be required of applicants who are not native speakers of English. Essay recommended. Audition required of music majors. Portfolio recommended for art majors. **Homeschooled:** Provide detail about coursework and teaching process. Applications will be reviewed on a case-by-case basis.

High school preparation. College-preparatory program required. 19 units required. Required units include English 4, mathematics 3, social studies 3, science 3 (laboratory 2), foreign language 2 and academic electives 4.

2005-2006 Annual costs. Tuition/fees: $3,359; $16,491 out-of-state. Room/board: $7,529. Books/supplies: $860. Personal expenses: $2,136.

2004-2005 Financial aid. Need-based: 3,860 full-time freshmen applied for aid; 3,597 were judged to have need; 3,506 of these received aid. Average need met was 70%. Average scholarship/grant was $3,215; average loan $2,621. 44% of total undergraduate aid awarded as scholarships/grants, 56% as loans/jobs. **Non-need-based:** Awarded to 13,382 full-time undergraduates, including 4,552 freshmen. Scholarships awarded for academics, alumni affiliation, athletics, leadership, ROTC, state residency.

Application procedures. Admission: Priority date 1/1; deadline 5/1 (postmark date). $30 fee, may be waived for applicants with need. Application may be submitted online. Admission notification on a rolling basis beginning on or about 10/1. Must reply by May 1 or within 3 week(s) if notified thereafter. **Financial aid:** Priority date 3/1, closing date 6/30. FAFSA required. Applicants notified on a rolling basis starting 3/15; must reply within 3 week(s) of notification.

Academics. Special study options: Accelerated study, combined bachelor's/graduate degree, cooperative education, distance learning, double major, dual enrollment of high school students, ESL, honors, independent study, internships, study abroad, teacher certification program. Lead Scholars program. **Credit/placement by examination:** AP, CLEP, IB, SAT, ACT, institutional tests. 45 credit hours maximum toward bachelor's degree. **Support services:** Learning center, pre-admission summer program, reduced course load, study skills assistance, tutoring, writing center.

Honors college/program. Requires separate application, admission based on GPA, test scores and class rank. Small general and specialized honors courses, honors building, and residence hall available. Accept approximately 700 freshmen in the Fall.

Majors. Biology: General, bacteriology. **Business:** General, accounting, actuarial science, business admin, finance, hospitality admin, management information systems, managerial economics, marketing, restaurant/food services. **Communications:** Advertising, journalism, media studies, radio/tv. **Computer sciences:** General, information technology. **Education:** Art, early childhood, elementary, English, foreign languages, mathematics, music, physical, science, social science, special, trade/industrial. **Engineering:** Aerospace, civil, computer, electrical, environmental, industrial, mechanical. **Engineering technology:** General, computer systems, electrical. **English:** English lit, speech/rhetoric. **Foreign languages:** General, French, Spanish. **Health:** Audiology/speech pathology, clinical lab science, health care admin, health services, medical radiologic technology/radiation therapy, medical records admin, nursing (RN), predentistry, premedicine, prepharmacy, preveterinary, respiratory therapy technology. **History:** General. **Legal studies:** Paralegal. **Liberal arts:** Arts/sciences, humanities. **Math:** General, statistics. **Philosophy/religion:** Philosophy. **Physical sciences:** Chemistry, physics. **Protective services:** Criminal justice, forensics. **Psychology:** General. **Public administration:** General, social work. **Social sciences:** General, anthropology, economics, political science, sociology. **Visual/performing arts:** Art, cinematography, dramatic, multimedia, music performance, photography, studio arts.

Most popular majors. Business/marketing 27%, education 9%, engineering/engineering technologies 7%, health sciences 8%, liberal arts 7%, psychology 10%.

Computing on campus. 2,926 workstations in library, computer center, student center. Dormitories wired for high-speed internet access and linked to campus network. Commuter students can connect to campus network. Online course registration, online library, helpline, repair service, student web hosting, wireless network available.

Student life. **Freshman orientation:** Mandatory, $20 fee. Preregistration for classes offered. 10 sessions offered throughout spring and summer. 2-day event including financial aid presentation, advising. **Policies:** Freshmen permitted cars on campus. **Housing:** Coed dorms, single-sex dorms, apartments, fraternity/sorority housing available. $100 nonrefundable deposit, deadline 3/1. Affiliated student residence housing. Students under guidance of university housing resident assistants considered part of on-campus housing. **Activities:** Bands, choral groups, drama, film society, literary magazine, music ensembles, musical theater, radio station, student government, student newspaper, symphony orchestra, campus activities board, African American Student Union, international student association, orientation team, Hispanic American student association, Korean student association, Indian student association, Christian student association, Jewish Student Union.

Athletics. NCAA. **Intercollegiate:** Baseball M, basketball, cheerleading, cross-country, football (tackle) M, golf, rowing (crew) W, soccer, softball W, tennis, track and field W, volleyball W. **Intramural:** Badminton, baseball M, basketball, bowling, football (non-tackle), golf, racquetball, soccer, softball, tennis, volleyball, weight lifting, wrestling M. **Team name:** Golden Knights.

Student services. Adult student services, alcohol/substance abuse counseling, campus ministries, career counseling, student employment services, financial aid counseling, health services, legal services, minority student services, on-campus daycare, personal counseling, placement for graduates, veterans' counselor, women's services. **Physically disabled:** Services for visually, speech, hearing impaired.

Contact. E-mail: admission@mail.ucf.edu
Phone: (407) 823-3000 Fax: (407) 823-5625
Gordon Chavis, Executive Director of Admissions, University of Central Florida, Box 160111, Orlando, FL 32816-0111

University of Florida

Gainesville, Florida **CB member**
www.ufl.edu **CB code: 5812**

- Public 4-year university
- Residential campus in small city
- 34,088 degree-seeking undergraduates: 7% part-time, 54% women, 9% African American, 7% Asian American, 13% Hispanic American, 1% international
- 14,278 degree-seeking graduate students
- 53% of applicants admitted
- SAT or ACT with writing required
- 78% graduate within 6 years

General. Founded in 1853. Regionally accredited. **Degrees:** 8,417 bachelor's, 447 associate awarded; master's, doctoral, first professional offered. **ROTC:** Army, Navy, Air Force. **Location:** 70 miles from Jacksonville. **Calendar:** Semester, limited summer session. **Full-time faculty:** 1,622 total; 90% have terminal degrees, 16% minority, 26% women. **Part-time faculty:** 32 total; 97% have terminal degrees, 12% minority, 41% women. **Class size:** 37% < 20, 34% 20-39, 7% 40-49, 11% 50-99, 10% >100. **Special facilities:** Natural history museum, art museum, astronomical research facility, marine laboratory, wildlife sanctuary, citrus research center, bell carillon, pipe organ, center for performing arts, hyperbaric chamber, microkelvin laboratory, brain institute, engineering and industrial experiment station.

Freshman class profile. 22,458 applied, 11,928 admitted, 6,745 enrolled.

Mid 50% test scores		**Return as sophomores:**	94%
SAT verbal:	570-670	**Out-of-state:**	9%
SAT math:	590-690	**Live on campus:**	90%
ACT:	25-29	**Fraternities:**	28%
Rank in top quarter:	90%	**Sororities:**	28%
Rank in top tenth:	81%		

Basis for selection. High school grades, academic course selection, SAT/ACT scores, extracurricular activities, awards, honors, recognitions, special talents and recommendations considered.

High school preparation. 15 units required. Required units include English 4, mathematics 3, social studies 3, science 3 (laboratory 2) and foreign language 2. English must include substantial writing. Mathematics must include algebra I and II, and geometry. Foreign language must be 2 units of same language.

2005-2006 Annual costs. Tuition/fees: $3,094; $16,579 out-of-state. Additional $643 in required fees for out-of-state students. Room/board: $6,260. Books/supplies: $790. Personal expenses: $2,620.

2004-2005 Financial aid. **Need-based:** 4,144 full-time freshmen applied for aid; 2,498 were judged to have need; 2,485 of these received aid. Average need met was 84%. Average scholarship/grant was $4,335; average loan $2,668. 53% of total undergraduate aid awarded as scholarships/grants, 47% as loans/jobs. **Non-need-based:** Awarded to 25,885 full-time undergraduates, including 6,018 freshmen. Scholarships awarded for academics, art, athletics, leadership, minority status, music/drama, ROTC, state residency.

Application procedures. **Admission:** Closing date 1/14. $30 fee. Application may be submitted online. Admission notification on a rolling basis. Must reply by May 1 or within 3 week(s) if notified thereafter. **Financial aid:** Priority date 3/15; no closing date. FAFSA required. Applicants notified on a rolling basis starting 4/1.

Academics. **Special study options:** Accelerated study, cooperative education, cross-registration, distance learning, double major, dual enrollment of high school students, ESL, exchange student, external degree, honors, independent study, internships, liberal arts/career combination, student-designed major, study abroad, teacher certification program, weekend college. **Credit/placement by examination:** CLEP, institutional tests. 30 credit hours maximum toward bachelor's degree. **Support services:** Learning center, reduced course load, study skills assistance, tutoring, writing center.

Majors. **Agriculture:** Animal sciences, economics, farm/ranch, food science, horticultural science, plant sciences, soil science. **Architecture:** Architecture, landscape. **Area/ethnic studies:** Latin American. **Biology:** Bacteriology, biochemistry, botany, cellular/molecular, ecology, entomology, plant pathology, zoology. **Business:** General, accounting, finance, insurance, management science, marketing, real estate. **Communications:** Advertising, journalism, public relations. **Computer sciences:** General. **Conservation:** General, forestry, wildlife. **Education:** Agricultural, art, college student counseling, curriculum, elementary, English, foreign languages, foundations, mathematics, music, reading, science, social science, special, statistics. **Engineering:** Aerospace, agricultural, biomedical, chemical, civil, computer, electrical, environmental, materials, mechanical, mechanics, nuclear, ocean, science, systems. **Engineering technology:** Construction, surveying. **Family/consumer sciences:** Family/community services. **Foreign languages:** Classics, French, German, Latin, linguistics, Spanish. **Health:** Audiology/hearing, audiology/speech pathology, health services, nursing (RN), physician assistant, vocational rehab counseling. **History:** General. **Interdisciplinary:** Museum. **Math:** General, statistics. **Parks/recreation:** Exercise sciences, facilities management. **Philosophy/religion:** Judaic, philosophy, religion. **Physical sciences:** Astronomy, chemistry, geology, physics. **Protective services:** Criminal justice. **Psychology:** General. **Social sciences:** Anthropology, economics, geography, political science, sociology. **Visual/performing arts:** Art history/conservation, commercial/advertising art, dance, dramatic, interior design.

Most popular majors. Agriculture 6%, business/marketing 20%, communications/journalism 9%, engineering/engineering technologies 12%, health sciences 7%, social sciences 13%.

Computing on campus. PC or laptop required. Dormitories linked to campus network. Commuter students can connect to campus network. Online course registration, helpline available.

Student life. **Freshman orientation:** Mandatory. Students must attend orientation before they can register for classes. **Policies:** Freshmen permitted cars on campus. **Housing:** Coed dorms, special housing for disabled, apartments, cooperative housing, fraternity/sorority housing available. $200 partly refundable deposit. Pets allowed in dorm rooms. Undergraduate honor halls, "quiet/study" floors, faculty-in-residence program, first-year experience program, wellness floor, no-visitation by opposite sex floor available. **Activities:** Bands, choral groups, dance, drama, film society, literary magazine, music ensembles, musical theater, radio station, student government, student newspaper, symphony orchestra, TV station, over 500 student groups on campus.

Athletics. NCAA. **Intercollegiate:** Baseball M, basketball, cross-country, diving, football (tackle) M, golf, gymnastics W, soccer W, softball W, swimming, tennis, track and field, volleyball W. **Intramural:** Archery, badminton, basketball, bowling, cross-country, fencing, field hockey W, football (tackle) M, golf, handball, racquetball, sailing, soccer, softball, swimming, tennis, track and field, volleyball. **Team name:** Gators.

Student services. Adult student services, alcohol/substance abuse counseling, campus ministries, career counseling, student employment services, health services, legal services, on-campus daycare, personal counseling, placement for graduates, veterans' counselor. **Physically disabled:** Services for visually, speech, hearing impaired.

Contact. Phone: (352) 392-1365
Patrick Herring, Director of Admissions, University of Florida, 201 Criser Hall, Gainesville, FL 32611-4000

University of Miami

Coral Gables, Florida — **CB member**
www.miami.edu — **CB code: 5815**

- Private 4-year university
- Commuter campus in small city
- 10,132 degree-seeking undergraduates: 5% part-time, 57% women, 9% African American, 5% Asian American, 23% Hispanic American, 6% international
- 4,999 degree-seeking graduate students
- 46% of applicants admitted
- SAT or ACT (ACT writing optional), application essay required
- 71% graduate within 6 years; 37% enter graduate study

General. Founded in 1925. Regionally accredited. **Degrees:** 2,392 bachelor's awarded; master's, doctoral, first professional offered. **ROTC:** Army, Air Force. **Location:** 7 miles from downtown. **Calendar:** Semester, extensive summer session. **Full-time faculty:** 892 total; 87% have terminal degrees, 22% minority, 32% women. **Part-time faculty:** 383 total; 56% have terminal degrees, 27% minority, 46% women. **Class size:** 45% < 20, 44% 20-39, 4% 40-49, 4% 50-99, 2% >100. **Special facilities:** Art museum, cinema, observatory, palmetum, marine science research vessels, broadcasting studios, concert hall, arboretum, performing arts theater, film studios, sound stage.

Freshman class profile. 18,807 applied, 8,679 admitted, 2,277 enrolled.

Mid 50% test scores			
SAT verbal:	570-670	Rank in top tenth:	62%
SAT math:	590-690	End year in good standing:	95%
ACT:	26-30	Return as sophomores:	89%
GPA 3.50 or higher:	86%	Out-of-state:	56%
GPA 3.0-3.49:	12%	Live on campus:	83%
GPA 2.0-2.99:	2%	International:	4%
Rank in top quarter:	89%	Fraternities:	13%
		Sororities:	21%

Basis for selection. Secondary school record most important. Test scores, recommendations, essay also important. Extracurricular activities considered. SAT Subject Tests (English, Math, & Science) for our Dual Degree Honors Programs in Medicine. Auditions required for all School of Music and Theatre Arts applicants. **Homeschooled:** Interview required.

High school preparation. 16 units recommended. Recommended units include English 4, mathematics 4, social studies 3, history 2, science 3 (laboratory 2) and foreign language 2.

2006-2007 Annual costs. Tuition/fees: $31,288. Room/board: $9,334. Books/supplies: $830. Personal expenses: $1,200.

2004-2005 Financial aid. Need-based: 1,496 full-time freshmen applied for aid; 1,171 were judged to have need; 1,171 of these received aid. Average need met was 80%. Average scholarship/grant was $17,512; average loan $3,534. 65% of total undergraduate aid awarded as scholarships/grants, 35% as loans/jobs. **Non-need-based:** Awarded to 3,653 full-time undergraduates, including 921 freshmen. Scholarships awarded for academics, athletics, music/drama.

Application procedures. Admission: Closing date 2/1 (postmark date). $65 fee, may be waived for applicants with need. Application may be submitted online. Admission notification 4/15. Must reply by May 1 or within 2 week(s) if notified thereafter. **Financial aid:** Priority date 2/15; no closing date. FAFSA required. Applicants notified on a rolling basis starting 3/1.

Academics. Special study options: Accelerated study, combined bachelor's/graduate degree, distance learning, double major, dual enrollment of high school students, ESL, honors, independent study, internships, student-designed major, study abroad, teacher certification program, Washington semester, weekend college. Learning Communities. **Credit/placement by examination:** AP, CLEP, IB, SAT, institutional tests. 60 credit hours maximum toward bachelor's degree. **Support services:** Learning center, pre-admission summer program, reduced course load, remedial instruction, study skills assistance, tutoring, writing center.

Majors. Architecture: Architecture. **Area/ethnic studies:** African-American, American, Latin American, women's. **Biology:** General, bacteriology, biochemistry, biophysics, ecology, marine, neurobiology/physiology. **Business:** Accounting, business admin, entrepreneurial studies, finance, human resources, international, management science, managerial economics, marketing. **Communications:** General, advertising, broadcast journalism, journalism, media studies, organizational, public relations, radio/tv. **Computer sciences:** Computer graphics, computer science, information systems, security. **Conservation:** Management/policy. **Education:** Elementary, music, special. **Engineering:** Aerospace, architectural, biomedical, civil, computer, electrical, environmental, industrial, manufacturing, mechanical, science. **English:** British lit, creative writing, English lit. **Foreign languages:** French, German, Italian, Spanish. **Health:** Athletic training, music therapy, nursing (RN), premedicine, prepharmacy, preveterinary. **History:** General. **Interdisciplinary:** Neuroscience. **Legal studies:** General. **Math:** General, applied, probability. **Parks/recreation:** Exercise sciences, sports admin. **Philosophy/religion:** Judaic, philosophy, religion. **Physical sciences:** Atmospheric science, chemistry, geology, meteorology, oceanography, physics, theoretical physics. **Psychology:** General. **Social sciences:** Anthropology, criminology, economics, geography, international relations, political science, sociology. **Visual/performing arts:** General, acting, art, art history/conservation, ceramics, cinematography, design, directing/producing, dramatic, film/cinema, graphic design, jazz, multimedia, music performance, music theory/composition, musicology, painting, photography, piano/organ, printmaking, sculpture, studio arts, theater arts management, theater design, voice/opera.

Most popular majors. Biology 10%, business/marketing 19%, communications/journalism 10%, engineering/engineering technologies 7%, health sciences 8%, psychology 8%, social sciences 8%, visual/performing arts 12%.

Computing on campus. 1,800 workstations in dormitories, library, computer center, student center. Dormitories wired for high-speed internet access and linked to campus network. Commuter students can connect to campus network. Online library, helpline, repair service, student web hosting, wireless network available.

Student life. Freshman orientation: Mandatory. Preregistration for classes offered. 3-day program in August. **Policies:** Honor Code is a student initiated and administered code designed to protect academic integrity by encouraging consistent ethical behavior among undergraduates. Freshmen permitted cars on campus. **Housing:** Guaranteed on-campus for all undergraduates. Coed dorms, special housing for disabled, apartments, fraternity/sorority housing, substance-free housing available. $250 nonrefundable deposit, deadline 5/1. Residential college system available to all undergraduates. Students live with faculty members and their families in 5 residential colleges. **Activities:** Bands, choral groups, dance, drama, film society, literary magazine, music ensembles, musical theater, opera, radio station, student government, student newspaper, symphony orchestra, TV station, 220 clubs and organizations.

Athletics. NCAA. **Intercollegiate:** Baseball M, basketball, cheerleading, cross-country, diving, football (tackle) M, golf W, rowing (crew) W, soccer W, swimming, tennis, track and field, volleyball. **Intramural:** Badminton, basketball, football (non-tackle), golf, racquetball, soccer, softball, squash, tennis, track and field, volleyball, water polo, weight lifting. **Team name:** Hurricanes.

Student services. Adult student services, alcohol/substance abuse counseling, campus ministries, career counseling, student employment services, financial aid counseling, health services, minority student services, on-campus daycare, personal counseling, placement for graduates, veterans' counselor, women's services. **Physically disabled:** Services for visually, hearing impaired.

Contact. E-mail: admission@miami.edu
Phone: (305) 284-4323 Fax: (305) 284-2507
Edward Gillis, Vice President for Enrollment Management/ Executive Director of Admissions, University of Miami, 132 Ashe Building, Coral Gables, FL 33124-4616

University of North Florida

Jacksonville, Florida **CB member**
www.unf.edu **CB code: 5490**

- Public 4-year university
- Commuter campus in very large city
- 13,065 degree-seeking undergraduates: 28% part-time, 58% women, 10% African American, 5% Asian American, 6% Hispanic American, 1% international
- 1,615 degree-seeking graduate students
- 62% of applicants admitted
- SAT or ACT with writing required

General. Founded in 1965. Regionally accredited. **Degrees:** 2,262 bachelor's, 750 associate awarded; master's, doctoral offered. **ROTC:** Navy. **Location:** 12 miles from downtown. **Calendar:** Semester, extensive summer session. **Full-time faculty:** 448 total; 93% have terminal degrees, 14% minority, 40% women. **Part-time faculty:** 252 total; 13% minority, 56% women. **Class size:** 23% < 20, 55% 20-39, 10% 40-49, 7% 50-99, 4% >100. **Special facilities:** Nature trails, designated bird sanctuary, fine arts center.

Freshman class profile. 9,147 applied, 5,668 admitted, 2,388 enrolled.

Mid 50% test scores		**Rank in top tenth:**	23%
SAT verbal:	510-610	**End year in good standing:**	75%
SAT math:	500-600	**Return as sophomores:**	75%
ACT:	20-24	**Out-of-state:**	3%
GPA 3.50 or higher:	49%	**Live on campus:**	68%
GPA 3.0-3.49:	31%	**Fraternities:**	36%
GPA 2.0-2.99:	20%	**Sororities:**	28%
Rank in top quarter:	55%		

Basis for selection. SAT or ACT score and high school GPA based on 19 academic units very important. High school academic courses (not including electives) used for calculating GPA. Summer program available for some students who do not meet fall admissions criteria; students admitted on probation. Audition required for music majors. **Homeschooled:** Required to pass all sections of the GED.

High school preparation. College-preparatory program required. 19 units required. Required units include English 4, mathematics 3, social studies 3, science 3 (laboratory 1), foreign language 2 and academic electives 4.

2005-2006 Annual costs. Tuition/fees: $3,268; $14,356 out-of-state. Additional $554 required fees for out-of-state students. Room/board: $7,030. Books/supplies: $600. Personal expenses: $819.

2005-2006 Financial aid. Need-based: 1,328 full-time freshmen applied for aid; 329 were judged to have need; 326 of these received aid. Average need met was 89%. Average scholarship/grant was $1,018; average loan $778. 48% of total undergraduate aid awarded as scholarships/grants, 52% as loans/jobs. **Non-need-based:** Awarded to 1,714 full-time undergraduates, including 528 freshmen. Scholarships awarded for academics, athletics, leadership, minority status, music/drama, state residency.

Application procedures. Admission: Priority date 11/14; deadline 7/2 (receipt date). $30 fee, may be waived for applicants with need. Application may be submitted online. Admission notification on a rolling basis. Must reply by 7/31. **Financial aid:** Priority date 4/1; no closing date. FAFSA required. Applicants notified on a rolling basis starting 3/15; must reply within 2 week(s) of notification.

Academics. Special study options: Accelerated study, combined bachelor's/graduate degree, cooperative education, distance learning, double major, dual enrollment of high school students, ESL, honors, independent study, internships, student-designed major, study abroad, teacher certification program, Washington semester, weekend college. Learning communities. **Credit/placement by examination:** AP, CLEP, IB, SAT, ACT, institutional tests. 45 credit hours maximum toward bachelor's degree. **Support services:** Learning center, pre-admission summer program, reduced course load, study skills assistance, tutoring, writing center.

Honors college/program. Must be in top 10% of graduating class, have 3.75 GPA or higher, 1250 SAT (exclusive of Writing) or 30 ACT. 200 students admitted per year.

Majors. Biology: General. **Business:** Accounting, banking/financial services, business admin, finance, international, managerial economics, marketing, transportation. **Communications:** Media studies. **Computer sciences:** General. **Education:** Art, elementary, mathematics, middle, music, physical, science, secondary, special, trade/industrial. **Engineering:** Civil, electrical, mechanical. **Engineering technology:** Construction. **English:** English lit. **Foreign languages:** Spanish. **Health:** Athletic training, health services, nursing (RN). **History:** General. **Interdisciplinary:** Biological/physical sciences. **Liberal arts:** Arts/sciences. **Math:** General, statistics. **Philosophy/religion:** Philosophy. **Physical sciences:** Chemistry, physics. **Protective services:** Criminal justice. **Psychology:** General. **Social sciences:** Anthropology, economics, international relations, political science, sociology. **Visual/performing arts:** Art, jazz, music performance, studio arts.

Most popular majors. Business/marketing 27%, communications/journalism 9%, education 10%, health sciences 11%, psychology 7%, social sciences 7%.

Computing on campus. 850 workstations in library, computer center, student center. Dormitories wired for high-speed internet access and linked to campus network. Commuter students can connect to campus network. Online course registration, online library, helpline, student web hosting, wireless network available.

Student life. Freshman orientation: Available, $25 fee. Preregistration for classes offered. One-and-one-half day program several times during summer. **Policies:** Students must abide by drug/alcohol policy, student code of conduct, model bill of rights and responsibilities. Freshmen permitted cars on campus. **Housing:** Coed dorms, special housing for disabled, apartments, fraternity/sorority housing available. $150 deposit, deadline 4/15. Suite style housing available. **Activities:** Bands, choral groups, dance, drama, literary magazine, music ensembles, radio station, student government, student newspaper, TV station, African-American student union, international student association, Jewish student union, InterVarsity Christian Fellowship, College Republicans, Jeffersonian Society, The New Left, Muslim student association, Filipino student association, Golden Key International Honor Society.

Athletics. NCAA. **Intercollegiate:** Baseball M, basketball, cross-country, diving W, golf M, soccer, softball W, swimming W, tennis, track and field, volleyball W. **Intramural:** Basketball, football (non-tackle), racquetball, soccer, softball, tennis, track and field, volleyball. **Team name:** Ospreys.

Student services. Adult student services, alcohol/substance abuse counseling, campus ministries, career counseling, student employment services, financial aid counseling, health services, minority student services, on-campus daycare, personal counseling, placement for graduates, veterans' counselor, women's services. **Physically disabled:** Services for visually, speech, hearing impaired.

Contact. E-mail: admissions@unf.edu
Phone: (904) 620-2624 Fax: (904) 620-2414
John Yancey, Director, University of North Florida, 4567 St. Johns Bluff Road, South, Jacksonville, FL 32224-2645

University of South Florida

Tampa, Florida **CB member**
www.usf.edu **CB code: 5828**

- Public 4-year university
- Commuter campus in very large city
- 32,898 degree-seeking undergraduates: 28% part-time, 59% women, 13% African American, 6% Asian American, 11% Hispanic American, 3% international
- 7,871 degree-seeking graduate students
- 58% of applicants admitted
- SAT or ACT with writing required
- 47% graduate within 6 years; 22% enter graduate study

General. Founded in 1956. Regionally accredited. Regional campuses in St. Petersburg, Sarasota/Manatee, and Lakeland, plus off-campus sites in Pasco/Hernando County and at a Downtown Center. **Degrees:** 5,719 bachelor's awarded; master's, doctoral, first professional offered. **ROTC:** Army, Navy, Air Force. **Location:** 10 miles from downtown. **Calendar:** Semester, extensive summer session. **Full-time faculty:** 1,640 total. **Part-time faculty:** 160 total. **Class size:** 30% < 20, 50% 20-39, 7% 40-49, 9% 50-99, 3% >100. **Special facilities:** Art museum, weather station, botanical garden, art galleries, anthropology museum.

Freshman class profile. 18,307 applied, 10,664 admitted, 4,311 enrolled.

Mid 50% test scores		Rank in top tenth:	23%
SAT verbal:	510-600	Return as sophomores:	82%
SAT math:	520-610	Out-of-state:	6%
ACT:	21-26	Live on campus:	50%
GPA 3.50 or higher:	54%	International:	1%
GPA 3.0-3.49:	31%	Fraternities:	7%
GPA 2.0-2.99:	15%	Sororities:	6%
Rank in top quarter:	59%		

Basis for selection. High school GPA and test scores most important. On sliding scale, higher grades compensate for lower test scores. Requirements higher for several degree programs. SAT or ACT writing scores required for all applicants graduating from high school in 2006 or later. Audition required of music majors. Portfolio required of art majors.

High school preparation. 19 units required. Required units include English 4, mathematics 3, social studies 3, science 3 (laboratory 2), foreign language 2 and academic electives 3. Foreign language units must be in 1 language.

2005-2006 Annual costs. Tuition/fees: $3,236; $15,045 out-of-state. Some additional required fees for out-of-state students. Room/board: $6,900. Books/supplies: $800. Personal expenses: $2,710.

2004-2005 Financial aid. Need-based: 2,554 full-time freshmen applied for aid; 1,873 were judged to have need; 1,856 of these received aid. Average need met was 31%. Average scholarship/grant was $4,020; average loan $2,440. 42% of total undergraduate aid awarded as scholarships/grants, 58% as loans/jobs. **Non-need-based:** Awarded to 4,948 full-time undergraduates, including 1,563 freshmen. Scholarships awarded for academics, art, athletics, leadership, minority status, music/drama. **Additional information:** Deferred tuition payment plan available for late financial aid recipients.

Application procedures. Admission: Priority date 4/15; no deadline. $30 fee, may be waived for applicants with need. Application may be submitted online. Admission notification on a rolling basis. Must reply by May 1 or within 2 week(s) if notified thereafter. **Financial aid:** Priority date 3/1; no closing date. FAFSA required. Applicants notified on a rolling basis starting 3/15; must reply within 4 week(s) of notification.

Academics. Special study options: Accelerated study, combined bachelor's/graduate degree, cooperative education, cross-registration, distance learning, double major, dual enrollment of high school students, exchange student, honors, internships, study abroad, teacher certification program, Washington semester, weekend college. **Credit/placement by examination:** AP, CLEP, IB, SAT, ACT, institutional tests. 45 credit hours maximum toward bachelor's degree. **Support services:** Learning center, preadmission summer program, tutoring.

Majors. Area/ethnic studies: African-American, American, women's. **Biology:** General, bacteriology, biomedical sciences. **Business:** General, accounting, business admin, finance, hospitality admin, international, management information systems, managerial economics, marketing. **Communications:** General. **Computer sciences:** General, information systems, information technology. **Conservation:** General. **Education:** General, art, business, drama/dance, early childhood, elementary, emotionally handicapped, English, foreign languages, learning disabled, mathematics, mentally handicapped, music, physical, science, social science, special, trade/industrial. **Engineering:** General, chemical, civil, computer, electrical, manufacturing, mechanical. **English:** English lit, speech/rhetoric. **Foreign languages:** Classics, French, German, Italian, Russian, Spanish. **Health:** Athletic training, audiology/speech pathology, clinical lab science, nursing (RN). **History:** General. **Interdisciplinary:** Biological/physical sciences, gerontology. **Liberal arts:** Arts/sciences, humanities. **Math:** General. **Philosophy/religion:** Philosophy, religion. **Physical sciences:** Chemistry, geology, physics. **Protective services:** Criminal justice. **Psychology:** General. **Public administration:** Social work. **Social sciences:** General, anthropology, criminology, economics, geography, international relations, political science, sociology. **Visual/performing arts:** Art, art history/conservation, dance, dramatic, music performance, studio arts.

Most popular majors. Biology 6%, business/marketing 25%, education 10%, engineering/engineering technologies 6%, English 7%, psychology 8%, security/protective services 7%, social sciences 12%.

Computing on campus. 500 workstations in dormitories, library, computer center, student center. Dormitories wired for high-speed internet access and linked to campus network. Commuter students can connect to campus network. Online course registration, helpline, wireless network available.

Student life. Freshman orientation: Mandatory, $35 fee. Preregistration for classes offered. **Policies:** Freshmen permitted cars on campus. **Housing:** Coed dorms, single-sex dorms, special housing for disabled, apartments, cooperative housing, fraternity/sorority housing, substance-free housing available. $225 partly refundable deposit, deadline 8/1. Grad students only; medical students only. **Activities:** Bands, choral groups, dance, drama, film society, literary magazine, music ensembles, musical theater, opera, radio station, student government, student newspaper, symphony orchestra, TV station, approximately 300 student organizations available.

Athletics. NCAA. **Intercollegiate:** Baseball M, basketball, cross-country, football (tackle) M, golf, sailing, soccer, softball W, tennis, track and field, volleyball W. **Intramural:** Badminton, basketball, bowling, cross-country, fencing, football (tackle) M, golf, handball, ice hockey, lacrosse, racquetball, rugby, sailing, soccer, softball W, swimming, table tennis, tennis, track and field, volleyball, wrestling M. **Team name:** Bulls.

Student services. Adult student services, campus ministries, career counseling, student employment services, financial aid counseling, health services, legal services, on-campus daycare, personal counseling, placement for graduates, veterans' counselor. **Physically disabled:** Services for visually, speech, hearing impaired.

Contact. Phone: (813) 974-3350 Toll-free number: (877) 873-2855
Fax: (813) 974-9689
J. Spatig, Director of Admissions, University of South Florida, 4202 East Fowler Avenue, SVC 1036, Tampa, FL 33620-9951

University of Tampa

Tampa, Florida — **CB member**
www.ut.edu — **CB code: 5819**

- Private 4-year university and liberal arts college
- Residential campus in large city
- 4,602 degree-seeking undergraduates: 9% part-time, 62% women, 6% African American, 2% Asian American, 9% Hispanic American, 5% international
- 553 degree-seeking graduate students
- 50% of applicants admitted
- SAT or ACT (ACT writing recommended), application essay required
- 56% graduate within 6 years; 8% enter graduate study

General. Founded in 1931. Regionally accredited. **Degrees:** 784 bachelor's, 1 associate awarded; master's offered. **ROTC:** Army, Navy, Air Force. **Location:** 20 miles from St. Petersburg, 70 miles from Orlando. **Calendar:** Semester, extensive summer session. **Full-time faculty:** 208 total; 90% have terminal degrees, 4% minority, 40% women. **Part-time faculty:** 217 total; 37% have terminal degrees, 12% minority, 57% women. **Class size:** 41% < 20, 57% 20-39, 2% 40-49, less than 1% 50-99. **Special facilities:** Art and furniture museum, dance studio, art studio, marine science research vessel, marine science research laboratory.

Freshman class profile. 6,365 applied, 3,202 admitted, 1,010 enrolled.

Mid 50% test scores		Rank in top tenth:	20%
SAT verbal:	490-580	End year in good standing:	82%
SAT math:	500-600	Return as sophomores:	77%
ACT:	20-25	Out-of-state:	68%
GPA 3.50 or higher:	28%	Live on campus:	88%
GPA 3.0-3.49:	44%	International:	4%
GPA 2.0-2.99:	27%	Fraternities:	13%
Rank in top quarter:	50%	Sororities:	17%

Basis for selection. Secondary school record, test scores most important. Recommendations, interview, talent/ability, character/personal qualities considered. TOEFL required for non-native English speakers. Interview recommended. Auditions required of music and performing arts majors. Portfolio recommended for art majors. **Learning Disabled:** Dean of Students coordinates assistance for students with disabilities. It is the responsibility of the student to request accommodations for each term. Documentation is required.

High school preparation. College-preparatory program required. Required units include English 4, mathematics 3, social studies 2, science 3 (laboratory 2), foreign language 2 and academic electives 3.

2005-2006 Annual costs. Tuition/fees: $18,848. Room/board: $6,936. Books/supplies: $870. Personal expenses: $1,238.

2005-2006 Financial aid. Need-based: 699 full-time freshmen applied for aid; 547 were judged to have need; 547 of these received aid. Average need met was 82%. Average scholarship/grant was $7,185; average loan $3,612. 64% of total undergraduate aid awarded as scholarships/grants, 36% as loans/jobs. **Non-need-based:** Awarded to 1,982 full-time undergraduates, including 613 freshmen. Scholarships awarded for academics, alumni affiliation, art, athletics, leadership, music/drama, ROTC, state residency. **Additional information:** Early aid estimator service.

Application procedures. Admission: No deadline. $35 fee, may be waived for applicants with need. Application must be submitted on paper. Admission notification on a rolling basis beginning on or about 9/1. Must reply by May 1 or within 3 week(s) if notified thereafter. **Financial aid:** No deadline. FAFSA required. Applicants notified on a rolling basis starting 2/1; must reply within 3 week(s) of notification.

Academics. Special study options: Combined bachelor's/graduate degree, double major, dual enrollment of high school students, ESL, exchange student, honors, independent study, internships, study abroad, teacher certification program, Washington semester, weekend college. **Credit/placement by examination:** AP, CLEP, IB, SAT, ACT, institutional tests. 30 credit hours maximum toward associate degree, 30 toward bachelor's. **Support services:** Learning center, reduced course load, study skills assistance, tutoring, writing center.

Majors. Biology: General, biochemistry, marine. **Business:** Accounting, business admin, finance, international, marketing. **Communications:** General. **Computer sciences:** General, computer graphics. **Conservation:** Environmental science. **Education:** General, elementary, music. **English:** Creative writing, English lit. **Foreign languages:** Spanish. **Health:** Athletic training, nursing (RN), predentistry, premedicine, preveterinary. **History:** General. **Interdisciplinary:** Math/computer science. **Legal studies:** Prelaw. **Liberal arts:** Arts/sciences. **Math:** General. **Parks/recreation:** Exercise sciences, sports admin. **Physical sciences:** Chemistry. **Psychology:** General. **Social sciences:** General, criminology, economics, political science, sociology. **Visual/performing arts:** General, art, commercial/advertising art, graphic design, music performance, music theory/composition.

Most popular majors. Biology 7%, business/marketing 28%, communications/journalism 11%, computer/information sciences 6%, psychology 7%, social sciences 15%, visual/performing arts 6%.

Computing on campus. 472 workstations in dormitories, library, computer center, student center. Dormitories wired for high-speed internet access and linked to campus network. Commuter students can connect to campus network. Online course registration, online library, helpline, student web hosting, wireless network available.

Student life. Freshman orientation: Mandatory, $60 fee. Preregistration for classes offered. **Policies:** Freshmen permitted cars on campus. **Housing:** Coed dorms, special housing for disabled, apartments, substance-free housing available. $125 nonrefundable deposit, deadline 5/1. **Activities:** Bands, choral groups, dance, drama, literary magazine, music ensembles, musical theater, radio station, student government, student newspaper, symphony orchestra, TV station, 120 student organizations.

Athletics. NCAA. **Intercollegiate:** Baseball M, basketball, cross-country, golf M, rowing (crew) W, soccer, softball W, swimming, tennis W, track and field, volleyball W. **Intramural:** Basketball, football (non-tackle) W, football (tackle) M, golf, soccer, softball, tennis, volleyball. **Team name:** Spartans.

Student services. Adult student services, career counseling, student employment services, financial aid counseling, health services, personal counseling, placement for graduates, veterans' counselor.

Contact. E-mail: admissions@ut.edu
Phone: (813) 253-6211 Toll-free number: (888) 646-2738
Fax: (813) 258-7398
Barbara Strickler, Vice President for Enrollment, University of Tampa, 401 West Kennedy Boulevard, Tampa, FL 33606-1490

University of West Florida

Pensacola, Florida — **CB member**
www.uwf.edu — **CB code: 5833**

- Public 4-year university
- Commuter campus in small city
- 7,783 degree-seeking undergraduates: 28% part-time, 60% women, 9% African American, 4% Asian American, 5% Hispanic American, 1% Native American, 1% international
- 1,235 degree-seeking graduate students
- 68% of applicants admitted
- SAT or ACT (ACT writing optional) required

General. Founded in 1963. Regionally accredited. **Degrees:** 1,642 bachelor's, 160 associate awarded; master's, doctoral offered. **ROTC:** Army, Air Force. **Location:** 10 miles from downtown. **Calendar:** Semester, extensive summer session. **Full-time faculty:** 308 total; 85% have terminal degrees, 15% minority, 40% women. **Part-time faculty:** 219 total; 9% minority, 49% women. **Class size:** 37% < 20, 49% 20-39, 7% 40-49, 7% 50-99, 1% >100. **Special facilities:** Archaeology museum, nature preserve.

Freshman class profile. 3,401 applied, 2,316 admitted, 924 enrolled.

Mid 50% test scores			
SAT verbal:	500-600	Return as sophomores:	73%
SAT math:	490-600	Out-of-state:	14%
ACT:	19-25	Live on campus:	51%
Rank in top quarter:	85%	International:	1%
Rank in top tenth:	40%	Fraternities:	5%
		Sororities:	5%

Basis for selection. School achievement record, test scores, school curriculum most important. **Learning Disabled:** If requesting special consideration due to disability, student must provide documentation.

High school preparation. 19 units required. Required units include English 4, mathematics 3, social studies 3, science 3 (laboratory 2), foreign language 2 and academic electives 4. 4 academic electives includes courses chosen from list above. Social studies includes history, economics, government, psychology, sociology and geography.

2005-2006 Annual costs. Tuition/fees: $3,198; $15,704 out-of-state. Room/board: $6,528. Books/supplies: $800. Personal expenses: $1,950.

2004-2005 Financial aid. Need-based: 46% of total undergraduate aid awarded as scholarships/grants, 54% as loans/jobs. **Non-need-based:** Scholarships awarded for academics, alumni affiliation, art, athletics, minority status, music/drama, ROTC.

Application procedures. Admission: Closing date 6/30 (postmark date). $30 fee, may be waived for applicants with need. Application may be submitted online. Admission notification on a rolling basis beginning on or about 10/1. Students may apply up to one year in advance but, for scholarship consideration, they must apply by January. **Financial aid:** Priority date 3/1; no closing date. FAFSA, institutional form required. Applicants notified on a rolling basis starting 2/1.

Academics. Weekend program in nursing (BSN) available. **Special study options:** Cooperative education, distance learning, double major, dual enrollment of high school students, exchange student, honors, independent study, internships, study abroad, teacher certification program, Washington semester. Joint electrical engineering and computer engineering with the University of Florida. **Credit/placement by examination:** AP, CLEP, IB, institutional tests. 30 credit hours maximum toward associate degree, 30 toward bachelor's. **Support services:** Learning center, study skills assistance, tutoring, writing center.

Majors. Biology: General, marine. **Business:** Accounting, business admin, finance, hospitality admin, management information systems, managerial economics, marketing. **Communications:** Media studies. **Computer sciences:** General, information technology. **Conservation:** Environmental science. **Education:** Art, early childhood, elementary, English, mathematics, mentally handicapped, middle, special, trade/industrial. **Engineering:** Computer, electrical. **Engineering technology:** General. **English:** English lit. **Health:** Community health services, nursing (RN). **History:** General. **Interdisciplinary:** Biological/physical sciences. **Legal studies:** Paralegal. **Liberal arts:** Humanities. **Math:** General. **Parks/recreation:** Health/fitness. **Philosophy/religion:** Philosophy. **Physical sciences:** Chemistry, oceanography, physics. **Protective services:** Criminal justice. **Psychology:** General. **Public administration:** Social work. **Social sciences:** General, anthropology, international relations, political science, sociology. **Visual/performing arts:** Art, dramatic, music performance, studio arts.

Most popular majors. Business/marketing 18%, communication technologies 10%, computer/information sciences 6%, education 11%, psychology 9%, security/protective services 11%, social sciences 7%.

Computing on campus. 115 workstations in dormitories, library, computer center, student center. Dormitories wired for high-speed internet access and linked to campus network. Commuter students can connect to campus network. Online course registration, online library, helpline, wireless network available.

Student life. Freshman orientation: Mandatory, $75 fee. Preregistration for classes offered. 2-day program includes parents. Sessions held throughout summer. **Policies:** Freshmen permitted cars on campus. **Housing:** Coed dorms, apartments, fraternity/sorority housing available. $150 deposit. **Activities:** Bands, choral groups, dance, drama, music ensembles, musical theater, radio station, student government, student newspaper, symphony orchestra, TV station, Black student union, CLOVE, recreation clubs, international student organization, College Republicans, Catholic Ministries, Baptist Collegiate Ministries.

Athletics. NCAA. **Intercollegiate:** Baseball M, basketball, cross-country, golf, soccer, softball W, tennis, track and field, volleyball W. **Intramural:** Badminton, bowling, cheerleading, diving M, fencing, football (non-tackle), handball, racquetball, rugby, sailing, soccer, swimming, table tennis, volleyball, water polo, weight lifting. **Team name:** Argonauts.

Student services. Alcohol/substance abuse counseling, campus ministries, career counseling, student employment services, financial aid counseling, health services, minority student services, on-campus daycare, personal counseling, placement for graduates, veterans' counselor. **Physically disabled:** Services for visually, speech, hearing impaired.

Contact. E-mail: admissions@uwf.edu
Phone: (850) 474-2230 Toll-free number: (800) 263-1074
Fax: (850) 474-3360
Matt Hulett, Director, University of West Florida, 11000 University Parkway, Pensacola, FL 32514

Warner Southern College

Lake Wales, Florida
www.warner.edu **CB code: 5883**

- Private 4-year liberal arts college affiliated with Church of God
- Commuter campus in small town
- 903 degree-seeking undergraduates: 14% part-time, 57% women, 21% African American, 1% Asian American, 10% Hispanic American, 2% international
- 48 degree-seeking graduate students
- 58% of applicants admitted
- SAT or ACT (ACT writing optional) required
- 43% graduate within 6 years

General. Founded in 1968. Regionally accredited. Evening courses offered at classroom sites in Deland, Orlando, Lake Wales, Lakeland, Titusville, Port St. Lucie, Leesburg, Altamonte Springs, and Melbourne for bachelor's degree in organizational management. Online distance learning opportunities are available for those interested in Organizational Management or Church Ministry. **Degrees:** 303 bachelor's, 11 associate awarded; master's offered. **Location:** 60 miles from Tampa, 55 miles from Orlando. **Calendar:** Semester, limited summer session. **Full-time faculty:** 35 total; 60% have terminal degrees, 6% minority, 31% women. **Part-time faculty:** 54 total; 37% have terminal degrees, 11% minority, 48% women. **Class size:** 72% < 20, 27% 20-39, less than 1% 40-49, less than 1% 50-99.

Freshman class profile. 391 applied, 226 admitted, 109 enrolled.

Mid 50% test scores		**GPA 2.0-2.99:**	39%
SAT verbal:	350-580	**Rank in top quarter:**	28%
SAT math:	370-590	**Rank in top tenth:**	11%
ACT:	15-23	**Return as sophomores:**	57%
GPA 3.50 or higher:	34%	**Out-of-state:**	9%
GPA 3.0-3.49:	24%	**Live on campus:**	69%

Basis for selection. Applicants must meet 2 of 3 admission criteria: 2.25 GPA, top 50% of high school class, or minimum 18 ACT or 870 SAT (exclusive of Writing). TOEFL required for non-native English speakers. Will administer the ACT Residual test to those without scores or with scores too low. Interview recommended. Audition required of music majors. **Homeschooled:** GED, standardized tests, or portfolio required of applicants without transcripts. ACT or SAT also required.

High school preparation. 13 units required; 15 recommended. Required and recommended units include English 4, mathematics 3, social studies 2, history 2, science 2 and foreign language 2.

2006-2007 Annual costs. Tuition/fees (projected): $12,590. One-time $50 security deposit for incoming freshmen living on campus. Room/board: $5,876. Books/supplies: $1,000. Personal expenses: $1,792.

2004-2005 Financial aid. Need-based: 43 full-time freshmen applied for aid; 36 were judged to have need; 36 of these received aid. Average scholarship/grant was $3,641; average loan $3,670. 30% of total undergraduate aid awarded as scholarships/grants, 70% as loans/jobs. **Non-need-based:** Awarded to 965 full-time undergraduates, including 64 freshmen. Scholarships awarded for academics, alumni affiliation, art, athletics, leadership, music/drama, religious affiliation, state residency.

Application procedures. Admission: No deadline. $20 fee, may be waived for applicants with need. Admission notification on a rolling basis beginning on or about 9/15. **Financial aid:** Priority date 5/1; no closing date. FAFSA required. Applicants notified by 1/15; Applicants notified on a rolling basis starting 3/15; must reply within 2 week(s) of notification.

Academics. Special study options: Accelerated study, distance learning, double major, dual enrollment of high school students, ESL, independent study, internships, New York semester, semester at sea, study abroad, teacher certification program, Washington semester. **Credit/placement by examination:** AP, CLEP, IB, SAT, ACT, institutional tests. CLEP, Dantes, AP accepted. **Support services:** Learning center, remedial instruction, study skills assistance, tutoring.

Majors. Biology: General. **Business:** Accounting, business admin, finance, marketing, organizational behavior. **Communications:** General. **Education:** Business, elementary, English, music, physical, science, social science, special. **English:** English lit. **History:** General. **Parks/recreation:** Exercise sciences, sports admin. **Psychology:** General. **Public administration:** Social work. **Theology:** Bible, pastoral counseling, sacred music.

Most popular majors. Business/marketing 74%, education 8%.

Computing on campus. 80 workstations in library, computer center, student center. Online library, helpline available.

Student life. Freshman orientation: Mandatory. Preregistration for classes offered. 3-day program at start of fall semester. **Policies:** Student Lifestyle agreement keeping with the moral and spiritual nature of the Institution. Religious observance required. Freshmen permitted cars on campus. **Housing:** Guaranteed on-campus for all undergraduates. Single-sex dorms, apartments, substance-free housing available. $50 fully refundable deposit, deadline 8/15. **Activities:** Choral groups, music ensembles, student government, student newspaper, star throwers, missions, outreach ministries, Young Americans.

Athletics. NAIA. **Intercollegiate:** Baseball M, basketball, cheerleading, cross-country, golf, soccer, softball W, tennis, track and field, volleyball W. **Intramural:** Basketball, football (non-tackle), soccer, volleyball. **Team name:** Royals.

Student services. Alcohol/substance abuse counseling, campus ministries, career counseling, student employment services, financial aid counseling, health services, personal counseling, placement for graduates.

Contact. E-mail: admission@warner.edu
Phone: (863) 638-7212 Toll-free number: (800) 309-9563
Fax: (863) 638-7290
Jason Roe, Director of Admissions, Warner Southern College, 13895 Hwy. 27, Lake Wales, FL 33859

Webber International University

Babson Park, Florida
www.webber.edu **CB code: 5893**

- Private 4-year university and business college
- Residential campus in rural community
- 556 degree-seeking undergraduates: 9% part-time, 39% women
- 60 degree-seeking graduate students
- SAT or ACT (ACT writing optional) required

General. Founded in 1927. Regionally accredited. **Degrees:** 133 bachelor's, 9 associate awarded; master's offered. **Location:** 50 miles from Orlando, 60 miles from Tampa. **Calendar:** Semester, limited summer session. **Full-time faculty:** 19 total; 84% have terminal degrees, 5% minority, 32% women. **Part-time faculty:** 20 total; 40% have terminal degrees, 5% minority, 35% women. **Class size:** 40% < 20, 59% 20-39, 2% 40-49. **Special facilities:** Audubon society nature preserve.

Freshman class profile.

Mid 50% test scores		**Rank in top tenth:**	4%
SAT verbal:	380-480	**Out-of-state:**	6%
SAT math:	370-490	**Live on campus:**	85%
ACT:	14-19	**International:**	19%
Rank in top quarter:	29%		

Basis for selection. Secondary school record, recommendations, standardized test scores, and GPA very important. Interview recommended. **Homeschooled:** Transcript of courses and grades required. Proof of graduation with 2.0 or better. **Learning Disabled:** Documentation of disability required in order to adequately assist student in studies.

High school preparation. 15 units recommended. Required and recommended units include English 4, mathematics 2-3, social studies 2, history 2, science 1-3, foreign language 1 and academic electives 4. 2 business courses recommended.

2005-2006 Annual costs. Tuition/fees: $13,950. Room/board: $4,700. Books/supplies: $700. Personal expenses: $2,530.

Four-Year Colleges

2005-2006 Financial aid. Need-based: 85 full-time freshmen applied for aid; 74 were judged to have need; 74 of these received aid. Average need met was 62%. Average scholarship/grant was $8,504; average loan $2,556. 58% of total undergraduate aid awarded as scholarships/grants, 42% as loans/jobs. **Non-need-based:** Awarded to 331 full-time undergraduates, including 94 freshmen. Scholarships awarded for academics, alumni affiliation, athletics, leadership, state residency.

Application procedures. Admission: Priority date 5/1; deadline 8/1 (postmark date). $35 fee, may be waived for applicants with need. Application may be submitted online. Admission notification on a rolling basis beginning on or about 12/1. Must reply by May 1 or within 4 week(s) if notified thereafter. **Financial aid:** Priority date 5/1; no closing date. FAFSA required. Applicants notified on a rolling basis starting 3/15; must reply within 4 week(s) of notification.

Academics. Special study options: Combined bachelor's/graduate degree, cross-registration, double major, dual enrollment of high school students, ESL, exchange student, internships, liberal arts/career combination, study abroad, weekend college. **Credit/placement by examination:** AP, CLEP, IB, institutional tests. 30 credit hours maximum toward associate degree, 30 toward bachelor's. No more than 6 semester hours credit awarded in each of 5 areas (English, humanities, science, social science, mathematics). **Support services:** Reduced course load, remedial instruction, tutoring.

Majors. Business: General, accounting, business admin, finance, hospitality admin, marketing. **Computer sciences:** General. **Legal studies:** Prelaw. **Parks/recreation:** Facilities management.

Most popular majors. Business/marketing 87%, parks/recreation 13%.

Computing on campus. 100 workstations in library, computer center. Online library, helpline available.

Student life. Freshman orientation: Mandatory. 3-day program immediately preceding semester opening. **Policies:** Freshmen permitted cars on campus. **Housing:** Guaranteed on-campus for freshmen. Single-sex dorms available. $205 deposit, deadline 8/1. **Activities:** Student government, student newspaper, service clubs, professional development organizations.

Athletics. NAIA. **Intercollegiate:** Baseball M, basketball, cross-country, football (tackle) M, golf, soccer, softball W, tennis, track and field, volleyball W. **Intramural:** Basketball, bowling, soccer, softball, table tennis. **Team name:** Warriors.

Student services. Adult student services, alcohol/substance abuse counseling, career counseling, student employment services, financial aid counseling, health services, personal counseling, placement for graduates, veterans' counselor, women's services.

Contact. E-mail: admissions@webber.edu
Phone: (863) 638-2910 Toll-free number: (800) 741-1844
Fax: (863) 638-1591
Julie Ragans, Director of Admission, Webber International University, 1201 North Scenic Highway, Babson Park, FL 33827-0096

Webster College

Ocala, Florida
www.webstercollege.edu **CB code: 3502**

- For-profit 4-year business college
- Small city
- 345 degree-seeking undergraduates

General. Accredited by ACICS. **Degrees:** 10 bachelor's, 124 associate awarded. **Calendar:** Quarter. **Full-time faculty:** 5 total. **Part-time faculty:** 18 total.

Basis for selection. Open admission. COMPASS used for placement.

2005-2006 Annual costs. Personal expenses: $2,856.

Application procedures. Admission: No deadline. Admission notification on a rolling basis. **Financial aid:** Institutional form required. Applicants notified on a rolling basis; must reply within 1 week(s) of notification.

Academics. Credit/placement by examination: CLEP.

Majors. Business: Business admin.

Contact. E-mail: rfinelli@webstercollege.edu
Phone: (352) 629-1941 Fax: (352) 629-0926
Peggy Meyers, Director of Admissions, Webster College, 2221 Southwest 19th Avenue Road, Ocala, FL 34474-7051

Webster College: Holiday

Holiday, Florida
www.webstercollege.edu **CB code: 3503**

- For-profit 4-year business college
- Small city
- 225 degree-seeking undergraduates
- Interview required

General. Accredited by ACICS. **Degrees:** 5 bachelor's, 70 associate awarded. **Location:** 30 miles from Tampa. **Calendar:** Quarter. **Full-time faculty:** 5 total. **Part-time faculty:** 14 total.

Basis for selection. Open admission. COMPASS used for placement.

2005-2006 Annual costs. Books/supplies: $203. Personal expenses: $2,448.

Financial aid. All financial aid based on need.

Application procedures. Admission: No deadline. $20 fee. Application may be submitted online. Admission notification on a rolling basis. **Financial aid:** No deadline. FAFSA, institutional form required.

Academics. Credit/placement by examination: CLEP.

Majors. Business: Business admin.

Contact. E-mail: sstiles@webstercollege.com
Phone: (727) 942-0069 Toll-free number: (888) 729-7247
Fax: (727) 938-5709
Sheila Stiles, Director of Admissions, Webster College: Holiday, 2127 Grand Boulevard, Holiday, FL 34691

Yeshiva Gedolah Rabbinical College

Miami Beach, Florida

- Private 4-year rabbinical college for men affiliated with Jewish faith
- Very large city
- 52 degree-seeking undergraduates
- 100% of applicants admitted

General. Accredited by AARTS. **Full-time faculty:** 3 total. **Part-time faculty:** 2 total.

Freshman class profile. 11 applied, 11 admitted, 11 enrolled.

Academics. Credit/placement by examination: CLEP.

Majors. Philosophy/religion: Judaic. **Theology:** Religious ed, Talmudic.

Contact. Phone: (305) 673-5664
Yeshiva Gedolah Rabbinical College, 1140 Alton Road, Miami Beach, FL 33139

Georgia

Agnes Scott College

Decatur, Georgia **CB member**
www.agnesscott.edu **CB code: 5002**

- Private 4-year liberal arts college for women affiliated with Presbyterian Church (USA)
- Residential campus in very large city
- 875 degree-seeking undergraduates: 3% part-time, 100% women, 19% African American, 5% Asian American, 3% Hispanic American, 6% international
- 13 degree-seeking graduate students
- 53% of applicants admitted
- SAT or ACT (ACT writing recommended), application essay required
- 66% graduate within 6 years; 25% enter graduate study

General. Founded in 1889. Regionally accredited. **Degrees:** 187 bachelor's awarded; master's offered. **ROTC:** Army, Air Force. **Location:** 6 miles from downtown Atlanta. **Calendar:** Semester, limited summer session. **Full-time faculty:** 81 total; 96% have terminal degrees, 21% minority, 56% women. **Part-time faculty:** 29 total; 66% have terminal degrees, 21% minority, 79% women. **Class size:** 73% < 20, 26% 20-39, less than 1% 40-49, less than 1% 50-99. **Special facilities:** Observatory, planetarium, art collection, electron microscope, 30-inch Beck telescope, center for writing and speaking, interactive learning center, multi-media classrooms, GALILEO project of the University System of Georgia.

Freshman class profile. 1,526 applied, 812 admitted, 229 enrolled.

Mid 50% test scores			
SAT verbal:	570-690	Rank in top quarter:	75%
SAT math:	540-650	Rank in top tenth:	48%
ACT:	24-29	End year in good standing:	95%
GPA 3.50 or higher:	70%	Return as sophomores:	84%
GPA 3.0-3.49:	28%	Out-of-state:	52%
GPA 2.0-2.99:	2%	Live on campus:	98%
		International:	2%

Basis for selection. High school record, class rank, test scores, counselor recommendation, personal qualities, and extracurricular activities considered. Interview recommended. Audition required for music scholarship. **Homeschooled:** Statement describing homeschool structure and mission, interview required. SAT Subject Test scores must be submitted.

High school preparation. 16 units recommended. Recommended units include English 4, mathematics 3, social studies 2, science 2 (laboratory 2) and foreign language 2.

2006-2007 Annual costs. Tuition/fees: $25,410. Room/board: $8,990. Books/supplies: $700. Personal expenses: $900.

2005-2006 Financial aid. Need-based: 193 full-time freshmen applied for aid; 151 were judged to have need; 151 of these received aid. Average need met was 96%. Average scholarship/grant was $17,390; average loan $2,606. 77% of total undergraduate aid awarded as scholarships/grants, 23% as loans/jobs. **Non-need-based:** Awarded to 453 full-time undergraduates, including 147 freshmen. Scholarships awarded for academics, leadership, music/drama, religious affiliation, state residency. **Additional information:** Middle Income Assistance Grants available. Auditions required for music scholarship applicants.

Application procedures. Admission: Closing date 3/1 (postmark date). $35 fee, may be waived for applicants with need. Application must be submitted on paper. Admission notification on a rolling basis. Must reply by 5/1. Must reply by May 1 or within 2 week(s) if notified thereafter. Scholarship applicants must apply for regular admission by January 15. **Financial aid:** Priority date 2/15, closing date 5/1. FAFSA, institutional form, CSS PROFILE required. Applicants notified on a rolling basis starting 3/1; must reply by 5/1 or within 2 week(s) of notification.

Academics. Global Awareness and Global Connections programs offer opportunities to visit other regions of the world. Internships opportunity guaranteed; over 250 internships and externships available in Atlanta and other cities. Atlanta Semester allows Agnes Scott students to focus on women, leadership and social change. Language Across the Curriculum links foreign languages to other disciplines. Membership in International Student Exchange Program (ISEP) gives students opportunities to study at over 123 universities in 33 countries. **Special study options:** Accelerated study, combined bachelor's/graduate degree, cross-registration, double major, dual enrollment of high school students, exchange student, independent study, internships, semester at sea, student-designed major, study abroad, teacher certification program, United Nations semester, Washington semester. Woodruff Scholars program for women beyond traditional college age, exchange program with Mills College, Atlanta Semester, exchange program with 123 institutions in 33 countries. **Credit/placement by examination:** AP, CLEP, IB, SAT, ACT, institutional tests. 32 credit hours maximum toward bachelor's degree. **Support services:** Learning center, reduced course load, study skills assistance, tutoring, writing center.

Majors. Area/ethnic studies: Women's. **Biology:** General, biochemistry. **Business:** General. **Foreign languages:** Classics, French, German, Spanish. **History:** General. **Math:** General. **Philosophy/religion:** Philosophy, religion. **Physical sciences:** Astrophysics, chemistry, physics. **Psychology:** General. **Social sciences:** Anthropology, economics, international relations, political science, sociology. **Visual/performing arts:** Art, dramatic, studio arts.

Most popular majors. English 6%, foreign language 9%, history 8%, physical sciences 15%, social sciences 35%, visual/performing arts 10%.

Computing on campus. 458 workstations in dormitories, library, computer center, student center. Dormitories wired for high-speed internet access and linked to campus network. Commuter students can connect to campus network. Online library, helpline, repair service, wireless network available.

Student life. Freshman orientation: Mandatory. Five days prior to the start of the semester, includes signing of Honor Code, breakfast with college president and introduction to Big/Little Sister program. **Policies:** Traditions include Black Cat, capping, sophomore ring ceremony, and senior investiture. Freshmen permitted cars on campus. **Housing:** Guaranteed on-campus for all undergraduates. Apartments, substance-free housing available. $100 partly refundable deposit, deadline 5/1. College-owned houses for nontraditional students, theme houses, CHOICE housing (Choosing Healthy Options in a Community Environment) available. **Activities:** Bands, choral groups, dance, drama, literary magazine, music ensembles, musical theater, student government, student newspaper, symphony orchestra, TV station, Religious Life Council, Conservative Forum, College Democrats, International Student Organization, Green Earth Organization, Circle-K, Witkaze (African American student group), Asian Cultural Awareness Association, Amnesty International.

Athletics. NCAA. **Intercollegiate:** Basketball W, cross-country W, soccer W, softball W, swimming W, tennis W, volleyball W. **Intramural:** Basketball W, cheerleading W, fencing W, field hockey W, football (non-tackle) W, soccer W, swimming W, tennis W, track and field W, volleyball W, weight lifting W. **Team name:** Scotties.

Student services. Adult student services, alcohol/substance abuse counseling, campus ministries, career counseling, student employment services, financial aid counseling, health services, minority student services, personal counseling, placement for graduates, women's services. **Physically disabled:** Services for visually, speech, hearing impaired.

Contact. E-mail: admission@agnesscott.edu
Phone: (404) 471-6285 Toll-free number: (800) 868-8602
Fax: (404) 471-6414
Stephanie Balmer, Dean of Admission, Agnes Scott College, 141 East College Avenue, Decatur, GA 30030-3797

Albany State University

Albany, Georgia **CB member**
www.asuweb.asurams.edu **CB code: 5004**

- Public 4-year liberal arts college
- Residential campus in small city
- 3,228 degree-seeking undergraduates
- 90% of applicants admitted
- SAT or ACT with writing required

General. Founded in 1903. Regionally accredited. **Degrees:** 546 bachelor's awarded; master's offered. **ROTC:** Army. **Location:** 180 miles from Atlanta. **Calendar:** Semester, limited summer session. **Full-time faculty:** 142 total. **Part-time faculty:** 69 total.

Freshman class profile. 2,025 applied, 1,828 admitted, 843 enrolled.

Mid 50% test scores			
SAT verbal:	430-500	SAT math:	420-500
		ACT:	17-20

Basis for selection. Minimum 430 SAT verbal score or 18 ACT English, or 400 SAT math score or 16 ACT math and 2.0 high school GPA.

High school preparation. 16 units required. Required units include English 4, mathematics 4, social studies 1, history 2 and foreign language 2. 2 units in same language required for foreign language.

2005-2006 Annual costs. Tuition/fees: $3,022; $10,338 out-of-state. Room/board: $4,064. Books/supplies: $750. Personal expenses: $925.

2004-2005 Financial aid. Need-based: 46% of total undergraduate aid awarded as scholarships/grants, 54% as loans/jobs. **Non-need-based:** Scholarships awarded for academics, athletics, ROTC, state residency.

Application procedures. Admission: Closing date 7/1. $20 fee, may be waived for applicants with need. Admission notification on a rolling basis. **Financial aid:** Closing date 4/15. FAFSA, institutional form required. Applicants notified on a rolling basis starting 7/1; must reply within 2 week(s) of notification.

Academics. Special study options: Cooperative education, cross-registration, distance learning, double major, dual enrollment of high school students, honors, independent study, internships, liberal arts/career combination, study abroad, teacher certification program, weekend college. 3+2 and 2+2 engineering program with Georgia Institute of Technology. **Credit/placement by examination:** CLEP, institutional tests. 45 credit hours maximum toward bachelor's degree. **Support services:** Learning center, remedial instruction, study skills assistance, tutoring, writing center.

Majors. Biology: General. **Business:** Accounting, administrative services, business admin, management information systems, marketing. **Communications:** Journalism. **Computer sciences:** General. **Education:** General, early childhood, middle, physical, science, special. **English:** Speech/rhetoric. **Foreign languages:** French, Spanish. **Health:** Nursing (RN). **History:** General. **Math:** General. **Physical sciences:** Chemistry. **Protective services:** Criminal justice. **Psychology:** General. **Public administration:** Social work. **Social sciences:** Political science, sociology. **Visual/performing arts:** Drawing.

Most popular majors. Business/marketing 17%, education 20%, health sciences 14%, psychology 8%, security/protective services 17%, social sciences 12%.

Computing on campus. Dormitories wired for high-speed internet access. Online course registration, helpline, student web hosting, wireless network available.

Student life. Freshman orientation: Mandatory. Preregistration for classes offered. 3 1/2 days in mid-July, August and January. **Policies:** Freshmen permitted cars on campus. **Housing:** Single-sex dorms available. $150 deposit, deadline 7/1. **Activities:** Bands, choral groups, dance, drama, music ensembles, musical theater, student government, student newspaper, Anointed Students in Unity, Baptist Student Union, ASU, Renewed Gospel Choir, religious life organization.

Athletics. NCAA. **Intercollegiate:** Baseball M, basketball, cross-country, football (tackle) M, softball W, tennis W, track and field, volleyball W. **Intramural:** Basketball, football (non-tackle) M, track and field W. **Team name:** Rams.

Student services. Campus ministries, career counseling, student employment services, financial aid counseling, health services, personal counseling, placement for graduates, veterans' counselor.

Contact. E-mail: robin.mcdermott@asurams.edu
Phone: (229) 430-4646 Toll-free number: (800) 822-7267
Fax: (229) 430-3936
Fred Shuttles, Director of Recruitment and Admissions, Albany State University, 504 College Drive, Albany, GA 31705-2796

American InterContinental University

Atlanta, Georgia
www.aiuniv.edu **CB code: 2486**

- For-profit 4-year university
- Commuter campus in very large city

General. Founded in 1977. Regionally accredited. **Calendar:** Quarter.

Annual costs/financial aid. Tuition/fees (2005-2006): $16,386. Costs vary by program. Room: $4,800. Books/supplies: $1,500. Personal expenses: $960.

Contact. Phone: (404) 965-5700
Director of Admissions, Buckhead Campus, 3330 Peachtree Road Northeast, Atlanta, GA 30326-1016

Armstrong Atlantic State University

Savannah, Georgia **CB member**
www.armstrong.edu **CB code: 5012**

- Public 4-year university
- Commuter campus in small city
- 5,878 degree-seeking undergraduates: 38% part-time, 68% women, 21% African American, 3% Asian American, 3% Hispanic American, 2% international
- 788 degree-seeking graduate students
- 100% of applicants admitted
- SAT or ACT with writing required
- 18% graduate within 6 years

General. Founded in 1935. Regionally accredited. **Degrees:** 657 bachelor's, 64 associate awarded; master's offered. **ROTC:** Army, Navy. **Location:** 250 miles from Atlanta. **Calendar:** Semester, extensive summer session. **Full-time faculty:** 224 total; 59% have terminal degrees, 18% minority, 53% women. **Part-time faculty:** 200 total; 22% have terminal degrees, 10% minority, 66% women. **Class size:** 52% < 20, 38% 20-39, 8% 40-49, 2% 50-99, less than 1% >100.

Freshman class profile. 800 applied, 799 admitted, 799 enrolled.

Mid 50% test scores		**GPA 3.0-3.49:**	29%
SAT verbal:	460-550	**GPA 2.0-2.99:**	46%
SAT math:	460-550	**Return as sophomores:**	67%
ACT:	18-22	**Out-of-state:**	5%
GPA 3.50 or higher:	24%	**International:**	1%

Basis for selection. Minimum SAT math score of 430 and verbal of 460 and 2.0 GPA required for regular admissions. Conditional admission possible with 1.8 GPA and lower test scores. **Homeschooled:** Applicants who meet all other freshmen admission requirements have the option of validating CPC requirements by passing SAT subject tests as indicated above or enrolling in specified freshmen level courses earning a grade of C or higher.

High school preparation. Required units include English 4, mathematics 4, social studies 3, science 3 (laboratory 2) and foreign language 2.

2005-2006 Annual costs. Tuition/fees: $2,924; $10,240 out-of-state. Room only: $4,500. Books/supplies: $1,000.

2004-2005 Financial aid. Need-based: Average need met was 90%. Average scholarship/grant was $2,668; average loan $2,184. 38% of total undergraduate aid awarded as scholarships/grants, 62% as loans/jobs. **Non-need-based:** Scholarships awarded for academics, athletics, ROTC, state residency.

Application procedures. Admission: Closing date 6/30. $20 fee. Application may be submitted online. Admission notification on a rolling basis beginning on or about 1/1. **Financial aid:** Priority date 3/15; no closing date. FAFSA required. Applicants notified on a rolling basis starting 2/1; must reply within 2 week(s) of notification.

Academics. Special study options: Combined bachelor's/graduate degree, cooperative education, distance learning, double major, dual enrollment of high school students, honors, independent study, internships, study abroad, teacher certification program, weekend college. **Credit/placement by examination:** AP, CLEP, IB, institutional tests. 30 credit hours maximum toward associate degree, 30 toward bachelor's. **Support services:** Learning center, reduced course load, remedial instruction, study skills assistance, tutoring, writing center.

Majors. Biology: General. **Computer sciences:** General, information technology. **Education:** Art, business, early childhood, elementary, English, health, learning disabled, mathematics, middle, music, physical, science, secondary, social science, special, speech impaired. **English:** English lit. **Foreign languages:** Spanish. **Health:** Clinical lab science, communication disorders, dental hygiene, health services, medical radiologic technology/radiation therapy, nuclear medical technology, nursing (RN), respiratory therapy technology, sonography. **History:** General. **Math:** Applied. **Parks/recreation:** Health/fitness. **Physical sciences:** Chemistry, physics. **Protective services:** Police science. **Psychology:** General. **Social sciences:** Economics, political science. **Visual/performing arts:** General, art, dramatic.

Most popular majors. Education 18%, health sciences 31%, liberal arts 14%, social sciences 7%.

Computing on campus. Dormitories wired for high-speed internet access. Online course registration, helpline available.

Student life. Freshman orientation: Available. Preregistration for classes offered. One day event scheduled for new students prior to registration for spring and summer semesters. **Policies:** Freshmen permitted cars on campus. **Housing:** Apartments, substance-free housing available. $235 partly refundable deposit. **Activities:** Bands, choral groups, drama, music ensembles, musical theater, student government, student newspaper, symphony orchestra, NAACP, Baptist Student Union, Hispanic outreach and leadership, Cercle Francais, international student organization, Newman Club, Wesley Foundation, College Democrats, College Republicans.

Athletics. NCAA. **Intercollegiate:** Baseball M, basketball, golf, softball W, tennis, volleyball W. **Intramural:** Badminton, basketball, bowling, cheerleading, football (non-tackle), golf, racquetball, soccer, softball, swimming, table tennis, tennis, volleyball. **Team name:** Pirates.

Student services. Adult student services, alcohol/substance abuse counseling, career counseling, student employment services, financial aid counseling, health services, minority student services, personal counseling, placement for graduates, veterans' counselor. **Physically disabled:** Services for visually, hearing impaired.

Contact. E-mail: adm-info@mail.armstrong.edu
Phone: (912) 927-5277 Toll-free number: (800) 633-2349
Fax: (912) 921-5462
Kim West, Registrar/Director of Admissions, Armstrong Atlantic State University, 11935 Abercorn Street, Savannah, GA 31419-1997

Art Institute of Atlanta

Atlanta, Georgia — **CB member**
www.aia.artinstitutes.edu — **CB code: 5429**

- For-profit 4-year art college
- Commuter campus in very large city

General. Founded in 1949. Regionally accredited. **Location:** 12 miles from city center. **Calendar:** Quarter.

Annual costs/financial aid. Tuition/fees (2005-2006): $18,000. Students purchase starting kits for programs; costs vary depending on programs. Some programs require lab fees. Room: $7,311. Books/supplies: $1,551. Need-based financial aid available to full-time and part-time students.

Contact. Phone: (770) 394-8300
V.P., Admissions, 6600 Peachtree Dunwoody Road, Atlanta, GA 30328

Atlanta Christian College

East Point, Georgia
www.acc.edu — **CB code: 5029**

- Private 4-year Bible and liberal arts college affiliated with Christian Church
- Residential campus in small city
- 415 degree-seeking undergraduates: 51% women
- 35% of applicants admitted
- SAT or ACT (ACT writing optional) required

General. Founded in 1937. Regionally accredited. **Degrees:** 61 bachelor's, 2 associate awarded. **Location:** 10 miles from Atlanta. **Calendar:** Semester, limited summer session. **Full-time faculty:** 24 total. **Part-time faculty:** 31 total.

Freshman class profile. 806 applied, 282 admitted, 99 enrolled.

Basis for selection. Recommendations, scholastic ability, and test scores most important.

2005-2006 Annual costs. Tuition/fees: $12,380. Room/board: $4,800. Books/supplies: $400. Personal expenses: $500.

Application procedures. Admission: Priority date 11/15; deadline 8/1 (receipt date). $25 fee. Application may be submitted online. Admission notification on a rolling basis. **Financial aid:** Priority date 6/1, closing date 8/1. FAFSA required. Applicants notified on a rolling basis starting 3/1; must reply within 3 week(s) of notification.

Academics. Special study options: Double major, dual enrollment of high school students, independent study, internships, liberal arts/career combination, study abroad. **Credit/placement by examination:** AP, CLEP, IB, SAT, ACT. 16 credit hours maximum toward associate degree, 32 toward bachelor's. **Support services:** Reduced course load, remedial instruction, study skills assistance, tutoring, writing center.

Majors. Business: General, business admin. **Education:** Business, early childhood, elementary. **English:** English lit. **Interdisciplinary:** Intercultural. **Liberal arts:** Arts/sciences. **Psychology:** General. **Theology:** Bible, theology.

Computing on campus. 30 workstations in library, computer center, student center. Dormitories wired for high-speed internet access and linked to campus network. Commuter students can connect to campus network. Online library, helpline, repair service, wireless network available.

Student life. Freshman orientation: Mandatory. Preregistration for classes offered. **Policies:** Religious observance required. Freshmen permitted cars on campus. **Housing:** Single-sex dorms, special housing for disabled, apartments, substance-free housing available. $50 nonrefundable deposit. **Activities:** Choral groups, dance, drama, music ensembles, student government, student newspaper, religious organizations, Christian service clubs, service-oriented fraternities and sororities.

Athletics. NCCAA. **Intercollegiate:** Baseball M, basketball, golf M, soccer, track and field, volleyball W. **Intramural:** Basketball, football (non-tackle), volleyball. **Team name:** Chargers.

Student services. Alcohol/substance abuse counseling, campus ministries, career counseling, financial aid counseling, health services, personal counseling, placement for graduates.

Contact. E-mail: kwagner@acc.edu
Phone: (404) 669-3202 Toll-free number: (800) 776-1222
Fax: (404) 460-2451
Keith Wagner, Director of Admissions, Atlanta Christian College, 2605 Ben Hill Road, East Point, GA 30344

Augusta State University

Augusta, Georgia — **CB member**
www.aug.edu — **CB code: 5336**

- Public 4-year liberal arts college
- Commuter campus in small city
- 5,386 degree-seeking undergraduates: 32% part-time, 64% women, 26% African American, 3% Asian American, 3% Hispanic American, 1% international
- 788 degree-seeking graduate students
- 63% of applicants admitted
- SAT or ACT (ACT writing optional) required

General. Founded in 1925. Regionally accredited. **Degrees:** 529 bachelor's, 75 associate awarded; master's offered. **ROTC:** Army. **Location:** 145 miles from Atlanta. **Calendar:** Semester, extensive summer session. **Full-time faculty:** 215 total; 67% have terminal degrees, 14% minority, 51% women. **Part-time faculty:** 115 total; 30% have terminal degrees, 16% minority, 48% women. **Class size:** 34% < 20, 58% 20-39, 7% 40-49, less than 1% 50-99, less than 1% >100. **Special facilities:** History walk and museum, 18-hole golf course.

Freshman class profile. 2,076 applied, 1,305 admitted, 988 enrolled.

Mid 50% test scores		**GPA 2.0-2.99:**	53%
SAT verbal:	430-540	**Return as sophomores:**	65%
SAT math:	430-540	**Out-of-state:**	9%
ACT:	16-21	**International:**	1%
GPA 3.50 or higher:	15%	**Fraternities:**	1%
GPA 3.0-3.49:	29%	**Sororities:**	1%

Basis for selection. Minimum 430 SAT verbal or 17 ACT English, and 400 SAT mathematics or 17 ACT mathematics. SAT Subject Tests required of GED recipients or graduates of non-accredited high schools.

High school preparation. 18 units required. Required units include English 4, mathematics 4, social studies 3, science 3, foreign language 2 and academic electives 2.

2005-2006 Annual costs. Tuition/fees: $2,920; $10,236 out-of-state.

2004-2005 Financial aid. Need-based: 727 full-time freshmen applied for aid; 542 were judged to have need; 525 of these received aid. Average need met was 70%. Average scholarship/grant was $6,991; average loan $5,353. 52% of total undergraduate aid awarded as scholarships/grants, 48% as loans/jobs. **Non-need-based:** Awarded to 1,433 full-time undergraduates, including 499 freshmen. Scholarships awarded for academics, art, athletics, leadership, minority status, music/drama, ROTC, state residency.

Application procedures. Admission: Priority date 7/1; no deadline. $20 fee, may be waived for applicants with need. Application must be submitted on paper. Admission notification on a rolling basis. **Financial aid:** Closing date 6/1. FAFSA, institutional form required. Applicants notified on a rolling basis starting 3/1; must reply within 4 week(s) of notification.

Academics. Special study options: Cooperative education, cross-registration, distance learning, double major, dual enrollment of high school students, ESL, honors, independent study, internships, study abroad, teacher certification program. Paralegal certificate. **Credit/placement by examination:** AP, CLEP, institutional tests. 30 credit hours maximum toward associate degree, 30 toward bachelor's. **Support services:** Learning center, pre-admission summer program, reduced course load, remedial instruction, study skills assistance, tutoring, writing center.

Majors. Biology: General. **Business:** Accounting, business admin, finance, management information systems, marketing. **Communications:** General. **Computer sciences:** General. **Education:** Early childhood, mentally handicapped, middle, music, physical, special. **Foreign languages:** French, Spanish. **Health:** Clinical lab science. **History:** General. **Math:** General. **Physical sciences:** Chemistry, physics. **Protective services:** Criminal justice. **Psychology:** General. **Public administration:** Social work. **Social sciences:** Political science, sociology. **Visual/performing arts:** Multimedia, music performance.

Most popular majors. Biology 6%, business/marketing 25%, communications/journalism 7%, education 18%, psychology 9%, social sciences 11%.

Computing on campus. 300 workstations in library, computer center, student center. Commuter students can connect to campus network. Online course registration, online library, helpline, student web hosting, wireless network available.

Student life. Freshman orientation: Available. Preregistration for classes offered. **Housing:** Apartments available. Private off-campus housing reserved for students. **Activities:** Bands, choral groups, drama, literary magazine, radio station, student government, student newspaper, Black Student Union, Los Amigos Hispanos, Le Cercle Francais, international club, Muslim Student Association, Circle K, chess club, anime club, College Conservatives, Baptist Student Union.

Athletics. NCAA. **Intercollegiate:** Baseball M, basketball, cross-country, golf, softball W, tennis, volleyball W. **Intramural:** Basketball M. **Team name:** Jaguars.

Student services. Adult student services, alcohol/substance abuse counseling, career counseling, student employment services, financial aid counseling, minority student services, personal counseling, placement for graduates, veterans' counselor. **Physically disabled:** Services for visually, hearing impaired.

Contact. E-mail: admissio@aug.edu
Phone: (706) 737-1632 Toll-free number: (800) 341-4373
Fax: (706) 667-4355
Katherine Sweeney, Registrar and Director of Admissions, Augusta State University, 2500 Walton Way, Augusta, GA 30904-2200

Bauder College

Atlanta, Georgia
www.bauder.edu — **CB code: 5070**

- For-profit 4-year college of fashion, design, criminal justice, business, and technology
- Commuter campus in very large city
- 794 degree-seeking undergraduates
- Application essay, interview required

General. Founded in 1964. Regionally accredited. **Degrees:** 374 associate awarded. **Location:** 5 miles from downtown Atlanta. **Calendar:** Quarter, limited summer session. **Full-time faculty:** 43 total. **Part-time faculty:** 24 total.

Freshman class profile.

Out-of-state:	14%	**Live on campus:**	50%

Basis for selection. Open admission. Portfolio recommended for interior and fashion design majors. **Homeschooled:** GED recommended.

2005-2006 Annual costs. Cost of tuition for design majors in 18-21 month associate degree program is $25,632; books $2,300; $50 administrative fee, $350 student activity fee; $250 technology fee; $250 graduation fee. Tuition only for the associate degree programs varies from $21,498 -$25,632. Tuition for newly instituted bachelor of science in business program is $42,996. Books/supplies: $900. Personal expenses: $1,100.

Financial aid. All financial aid based on need.

Application procedures. Admission: No deadline. $100 fee. Application must be submitted on paper. Admission notification on a rolling basis. **Financial aid:** No deadline. FAFSA, institutional form required. Applicants notified on a rolling basis starting 7/15.

Academics. Special study options: Double major, internships, liberal arts/career combination, study abroad. **Credit/placement by examination:** AP, CLEP. **Support services:** Reduced course load, remedial instruction, tutoring.

Majors. Business: Business admin.

Computing on campus. 38 workstations in library, computer center, student center. Online library, wireless network available.

Student life. Freshman orientation: Mandatory. Preregistration for classes offered. **Policies:** Freshmen permitted cars on campus. **Housing:** Cooperative housing available. **Activities:** Student government, student newspaper.

Student services. Alcohol/substance abuse counseling, career counseling, services for economically disadvantaged, student employment services, financial aid counseling, personal counseling, placement for graduates.

Contact. E-mail: admissions@bauder.edu
Phone: (404) 237-7573 Toll-free number: (800) 241-3797
Fax: (404) 237-1619
Victor Tedoff, Director of Admissions, Bauder College, 384 Northyards Boulevard NW, Ste 190, Atlanta, GA 30313

Berry College

Mount Berry, Georgia — **CB member**
www.berry.edu — **CB code: 5059**

- Private 4-year liberal arts college
- Residential campus in large town
- 1,855 degree-seeking undergraduates: 2% part-time, 64% women, 3% African American, 2% Asian American, 2% Hispanic American, 2% international
- 107 degree-seeking graduate students
- 83% of applicants admitted
- SAT or ACT with writing required
- 67% graduate within 6 years

General. Founded in 1902. Regionally accredited. **Degrees:** 379 bachelor's awarded; master's offered. **Location:** 65 miles from Atlanta. **Calendar:** Semester, limited summer session. **Full-time faculty:** 126 total; 94% have terminal degrees, 6% minority, 40% women. **Part-time faculty:** 68 total; 35% have terminal degrees, 3% minority, 41% women. **Class size:** 60% < 20, 38% 20-39, 2% 40-49, less than 1% 50-99. **Special facilities:** Oak Hill founder's home, Martha Berry Museum, research center for animal science, nature preserve of 400 acres containing riding trails and stables, government depository containing over 89,000 documents.

Freshman class profile. 1,827 applied, 1,517 admitted, 514 enrolled.

Mid 50% test scores		**Rank in top quarter:**	59%
SAT verbal:	520-630	**Rank in top tenth:**	28%
SAT math:	520-620	**End year in good standing:**	74%
ACT:	23-28	**Return as sophomores:**	78%
GPA 3.50 or higher:	55%	**Out-of-state:**	15%
GPA 3.0-3.49:	29%	**International:**	1%
GPA 2.0-2.99:	16%		

Basis for selection. School achievement record and test scores most important. Class rank, recommendations and essays considered. Interview recommended; auditions required of music and theatre majors; portfolio recommended for art majors. **Homeschooled:** Transcript of courses and grades, letter of recommendation (nonparent) required.

High school preparation. 20 units required. Required units include English 4, mathematics 4, social studies 3, science 3 and foreign language 2. Algebra I, geometry or trigonometry, algebra II and fourth year higher than algebra II required.

2005-2006 Annual costs. Tuition/fees: $17,620. Room/board: $6,772. Books/supplies: $900. Personal expenses: $1,870.

2005-2006 Financial aid. Need-based: 406 full-time freshmen applied for aid; 300 were judged to have need; 300 of these received aid. Average need met was 82%. Average scholarship/grant was $11,582; average loan $2,694. 73% of total undergraduate aid awarded as scholarships/grants, 27%

as loans/jobs. **Non-need-based:** Awarded to 1,057 full-time undergraduates, including 315 freshmen. Scholarships awarded for academics, art, athletics, minority status, music/drama. **Additional information:** All students are encouraged to work on-campus up to 20 hours per week. Jobs available in over 100 different areas.

Application procedures. Admission: Priority date 2/1; deadline 7/21 (receipt date). $50 fee, may be waived for applicants with need. Application must be submitted on paper. Admission notification on a rolling basis beginning on or about 10/15. Must reply by 5/1. Must reply by May 1 or within 4 week(s) if notified thereafter. Students are encouraged to reply within one month of acceptance. **Financial aid:** Priority date 4/1; no closing date. Institutional form required. Applicants notified on a rolling basis starting 3/15; must reply by 5/1 or within 4 week(s) of notification.

Academics. Special study options: Combined bachelor's/graduate degree, cooperative education, cross-registration, double major, dual enrollment of high school students, honors, independent study, internships, liberal arts/career combination, student-designed major, study abroad, teacher certification program, Washington semester. 3-2 nursing with Emory University, 3-2 engineering with Georgia Institute of Technology, Mercer University. **Credit/placement by examination:** AP, CLEP, IB, institutional tests. **Support services:** Remedial instruction, study skills assistance, tutoring, writing center.

Majors. Agriculture: Animal sciences. **Biology:** General, biochemistry. **Business:** Accounting, business admin, finance, marketing. **Communications:** General. **Computer sciences:** Computer science. **Conservation:** Environmental science. **Education:** Early childhood, mathematics, middle, music, physical. **Engineering technology:** General. **English:** English lit. **Foreign languages:** French, German, Spanish. **Health:** Nursing (RN). **History:** General. **Math:** General. **Philosophy/religion:** Religion. **Physical sciences:** Chemistry, physics. **Psychology:** General. **Social sciences:** General, anthropology, economics, international relations, political science, sociology. **Visual/performing arts:** Art, music management, music performance, theater arts management.

Most popular majors. Business/marketing 14%, communication technologies 9%, education 12%, psychology 12%, social sciences 10%, visual/performing arts 6%.

Computing on campus. 158 workstations in library, computer center, student center. Dormitories wired for high-speed internet access and linked to campus network. Commuter students can connect to campus network. Online library, helpline, repair service, student web hosting, wireless network available.

Student life. Freshman orientation: Mandatory, $90 fee. Preregistration for classes offered. Orientation for new students and parents in June, July, or August based on date of prepayment. Additional student orientation for four days prior to the start of classes. **Policies:** Limited visitation hours. Dry campus. Freshmen permitted cars on campus. **Housing:** Guaranteed on-campus for freshmen. Coed dorms, single-sex dorms, special housing for disabled, apartments, substance-free housing available. $100 deposit, deadline 5/1. Special-interest houses for Women in Math and Science. **Activities:** Bands, choral groups, dance, drama, literary magazine, music ensembles, musical theater, student government, student newspaper, TV station, Amnesty International, Baptist student union, international club, Wesley Foundation, Catholic student association, Habitat for Humanity, Canterbury Club, campus outreach, Presbyterian student fellowship, Young Democrats, Berry Republicans.

Athletics. NAIA. **Intercollegiate:** Baseball M, basketball, cheerleading, cross-country, golf, soccer, tennis, track and field, volleyball W. **Intramural:** Badminton, baseball M, basketball, bowling, cross-country, football (non-tackle), golf, racquetball, rowing (crew), soccer, softball, swimming, table tennis, tennis, volleyball. **Team name:** Vikings.

Student services. Alcohol/substance abuse counseling, campus ministries, career counseling, student employment services, financial aid counseling, health services, minority student services, on-campus daycare, personal counseling, placement for graduates, veterans' counselor, women's services. **Physically disabled:** Services for visually, hearing impaired.

Contact. E-mail: admissions@berry.edu
Phone: (706) 236-2215 Toll-free number: (800) 237-7942
Fax: (706) 290-2178
Garreth Johnson, Director of Admissions, Berry College, PO Box 490159, Mount Berry, GA 30149-0159

Beulah Heights Bible College

Atlanta, Georgia
www.beulah.org — **CB code: 5082**

- Private 4-year Bible college affiliated with International Pentecostal Church of Christ
- Commuter campus in very large city
- 372 degree-seeking undergraduates
- Application essay required

General. Accredited by ABHE. **Degrees:** 80 bachelor's, 40 associate awarded. **Calendar:** Semester, extensive summer session. **Full-time faculty:** 9 total. **Part-time faculty:** 35 total.

Basis for selection. Open admission. Applicants must have accepted Christ, although personal denomination is not considered. Pastoral and personal references required. Applicants can be accepted prior to completing GED, but must complete GED before graduation to be eligible for a degree. SAT or ACT recommended.

2006-2007 Annual costs. Tuition/fees (projected): $6,470. Room only: $2,400.

Application procedures. Admission: No deadline. $20 fee. Admission notification on a rolling basis.

Academics. Special study options: Double major, ESL, internships. **Credit/placement by examination:** CLEP. **Support services:** Study skills assistance, tutoring, writing center.

Majors. Theology: Bible.

Student life. Freshman orientation: Mandatory. **Policies:** Religious observance required. Freshmen permitted cars on campus. **Housing:** Single-sex dorms, apartments, substance-free housing available. **Activities:** Student government.

Student services. Campus ministries, personal counseling.

Contact. E-mail: admissions@beulah.org
Phone: (404) 627-2681 ext. 104 Toll-free number: (888) 777-2422
Fax: (404) 627-0702
Jackie Armstrong, Registrar and Director of Admissions, Beulah Heights Bible College, 892 Berne Street SE, Atlanta, GA 30316

Brenau University

Gainesville, Georgia — **CB member**
www.brenau.edu — **CB code: 5066**

- Private 4-year liberal arts college for women
- Residential campus in small city
- 696 degree-seeking undergraduates: 4% part-time, 100% women, 16% African American, 2% Asian American, 3% Hispanic American, 1% Native American, 4% international
- 32 degree-seeking graduate students
- 38% of applicants admitted
- SAT or ACT (ACT writing recommended) required
- 53% graduate within 6 years

General. Founded in 1878. Regionally accredited. Composed of 4 educational units: the Women's College (main campus), the Academy (women's secondary school), the Evening and Weekend College (coeducational), and the Online College. Performing arts and nursing daytime programs are coeducational. Male students may enroll in several Women's College programs through the Evening and Weekend College. **Degrees:** 146 bachelor's awarded; master's offered. **Location:** 45 miles from Atlanta. **Calendar:** Semester, limited summer session. **Full-time faculty:** 72 total; 86% have terminal degrees, 7% minority, 65% women. **Part-time faculty:** 33 total; 27% have terminal degrees, 6% minority, 76% women. **Class size:** 77% < 20, 21% 20-39, 2% 40-49. **Special facilities:** Visual arts center, performing arts center, regional history museum, vintage clothing museum.

Freshman class profile. 2,063 applied, 778 admitted, 176 enrolled.

Mid 50% test scores		Return as sophomores:	73%
SAT verbal:	460-560	Out-of-state:	14%
SAT math:	450-540	Live on campus:	79%
ACT:	18-23	International:	4%
End year in good standing:	75%	Sororities:	24%

Basis for selection. Course selection is most important factor, followed by GPA, standardized test scores, recommendations, and student's personal statement. Admission policies for Evening/Weekend College differ from Women's College. SAT or ACT used for placement into mathematics courses. If student has been out of high school for over 7 years, institutional placement test may be substituted. Auditions required of performing arts majors. **Homeschooled:** Standardized test scores, transcripts and an interview are required. **Learning Disabled:** Learning disability must be professionally diagnosed.

2006-2007 Annual costs. Tuition/fees: $16,590. Room/board: $8,550. Books/supplies: $800. Personal expenses: $1,200.

2005-2006 Financial aid. Need-based: 83% of total undergraduate aid awarded as scholarships/grants, 17% as loans/jobs. **Non-need-based:** Scholarships awarded for academics, art, athletics, leadership, music/drama.

Application procedures. Admission: No deadline. $35 fee, may be waived for applicants with need. Application may be submitted online. Admission notification on a rolling basis. **Financial aid:** Priority date 3/15; no closing date. FAFSA required. Applicants notified on a rolling basis starting 3/1.

Academics. Leadership curriculum available. **Special study options:** Accelerated study, combined bachelor's/graduate degree, cross-registration, distance learning, double major, dual enrollment of high school students, exchange student, external degree, honors, independent study, internships, liberal arts/career combination, student-designed major, study abroad, teacher certification program, weekend college. **Credit/placement by examination:** AP, CLEP, IB, SAT, ACT, institutional tests. 27 credit hours maximum toward bachelor's degree. Total of 27 hours for non-traditional students allowed. **Support services:** Learning center, pre-admission summer program, reduced course load, remedial instruction, study skills assistance, tutoring, writing center.

Majors. Biology: General, environmental. **Business:** Accounting, business admin, fashion, marketing. **Communications:** Media studies. **Education:** Art, drama/dance, elementary, mentally handicapped, middle, music. **English:** English lit. **Health:** Nursing (RN). **History:** General. **Legal studies:** Prelaw. **Liberal arts:** Arts/sciences. **Parks/recreation:** Exercise sciences. **Psychology:** General. **Social sciences:** International relations. **Visual/performing arts:** Arts management, dance, dramatic, fashion design, graphic design, interior design, music performance, studio arts.

Most popular majors. Business/marketing 10%, communications/journalism 7%, education 13%, health sciences 30%, psychology 8%, visual/performing arts 21%.

Computing on campus. 200 workstations in dormitories, library, computer center, student center. Dormitories wired for high-speed internet access and linked to campus network. Commuter students can connect to campus network. Online course registration, online library, helpline, student web hosting, wireless network available.

Student life. Freshman orientation: Mandatory. Preregistration for classes offered. **Policies:** Single students under 22 years of age required to live on campus unless living with family or legal guardian; alcohol-free campus; required convocation attendance. Freshmen permitted cars on campus. **Housing:** Guaranteed on-campus for all undergraduates. Special housing for disabled, apartments, fraternity/sorority housing, substance-free housing available. $100 nonrefundable deposit, deadline 6/15. **Activities:** Choral groups, dance, drama, musical theater, radio station, student government, student newspaper, symphony orchestra, TV station, Brenau Fellowship Association, Fellowship of Christian Athletes, College Republicans, College Democrats, Circle K International, Silhouettes, Eco-Friends, international club, volunteer center, student alumni council, Devoted Individuals Visualizing Awareness and Sensibility, Greek-letter service organizations.

Athletics. NAIA. **Intercollegiate:** Basketball W, cross-country W, soccer W, softball W, tennis W, volleyball W. **Team name:** Golden Tigers.

Student services. Alcohol/substance abuse counseling, campus ministries, career counseling, student employment services, financial aid counseling, health services, minority student services, personal counseling, placement for graduates, women's services. **Physically disabled:** Services for visually, speech, hearing impaired. **Learning disabled:** Comprehensive services available.

Contact. E-mail: wcadmissions@lib.brenau.edu
Phone: (770) 534-6100 Toll-free number: (800) 252-5119
Fax: (770) 538-4306
Christina White, Coordinator of Women's College Admissions, Brenau University, 500 Washington Street SE, Gainesville, GA 30501

Brewton-Parker College

Mount Vernon, Georgia — **CB member**
www.bpc.edu — **CB code: 5068**

- Private 4-year liberal arts college affiliated with Southern Baptist Convention
- Residential campus in small town
- 1,094 degree-seeking undergraduates: 23% part-time, 64% women
- 97% of applicants admitted
- SAT or ACT (ACT writing optional) required

General. Founded in 1904. Regionally accredited. **Degrees:** 171 bachelor's, 32 associate awarded. **Location:** 90 miles from Macon and Savannah. **Calendar:** Semester, limited summer session. **Full-time faculty:** 50 total; 76% have terminal degrees, 32% women. **Part-time faculty:** 87 total; 49% women. **Class size:** 86% < 20, 14% 20-39, less than 1% 40-49. **Special facilities:** Living history museum; recital hall, greenhouse.

Freshman class profile. 435 applied, 424 admitted, 257 enrolled.

Mid 50% test scores		**Return as sophomores:**	52%
SAT verbal:	420-530	**Out-of-state:**	5%
SAT math:	420-550	**Live on campus:**	52%
ACT:	16-22	**International:**	1%
Rank in top quarter:	19%	**Fraternities:**	5%
Rank in top tenth:	18%	**Sororities:**	7%

Basis for selection. Students evaluated on SAT/ACT scores and high school performance. Not required for non-traditional students. Audition and interview required of music and drama majors.

High school preparation. College-preparatory program recommended. 13 units required. Required units include English 4, mathematics 3, social studies 3 and science 3.

2005-2006 Annual costs. Tuition/fees: $11,984. Additional $130 per credit fee for applied music majors; matriculation fee of $700. Room/board: $4,820. Books/supplies: $1,000. Personal expenses: $1,900.

2005-2006 Financial aid. Need-based: Average need met was 62%. Average scholarship/grant was $6,851; average loan $2,250. 56% of total undergraduate aid awarded as scholarships/grants, 44% as loans/jobs. **Non-need-based:** Scholarships awarded for academics, art, athletics, leadership, music/drama, religious affiliation, state residency.

Application procedures. Admission: No deadline. $25 fee. Application may be submitted online. Admission notification on a rolling basis beginning on or about 9/1. **Financial aid:** Priority date 4/1; no closing date. FAFSA required. Applicants notified on a rolling basis starting 2/27.

Academics. Special study options: Accelerated study, double major, dual enrollment of high school students, exchange student, external degree, honors, independent study, internships, teacher certification program, weekend college. **Credit/placement by examination:** AP, CLEP, SAT, ACT. 30 credit hours maximum toward associate degree, 30 toward bachelor's. **Support services:** Learning center, reduced course load, remedial instruction, study skills assistance, tutoring, writing center.

Majors. Biology: General. **Business:** Accounting, business admin. **Communications:** General. **Computer sciences:** Information systems. **Education:** General, biology, early childhood, English, history, mathematics, middle, music, physical, science, secondary. **English:** English lit. **History:** General. **Legal studies:** Prelaw. **Math:** General. **Parks/recreation:** Health/fitness. **Philosophy/religion:** Religion. **Psychology:** General. **Social sciences:** General, political science, sociology. **Theology:** Theology. **Visual/performing arts:** Music performance.

Most popular majors. Business/marketing 14%, education 36%, liberal arts 15%, psychology 6%, social sciences 12%, theological studies 6%.

Computing on campus. 87 workstations in library, computer center. Dormitories wired for high-speed internet access. Online course registration, online library, helpline, repair service available.

Student life. Freshman orientation: Available, $100 fee. Four days prior to start of classes. **Policies:** All day students required to live on campus except seniors, students residing with parents, students 22 or older. Religious observance required. Freshmen permitted cars on campus. **Housing:** Guaranteed on-campus for freshmen. Single-sex dorms available. $100 nonrefundable deposit. **Activities:** Bands, choral groups, drama, literary magazine, music ensembles, musical theater, student government, student newspaper, Baptist Student Union, ministerial association, Fellowship of Christian Athletes, Christian Fraternities and Sororities, Rotaract, Circle K, student government association.

Athletics. NAIA. **Intercollegiate:** Baseball M, basketball, cheerleading, soccer, softball W, volleyball W. **Intramural:** Basketball, football (non-tackle), softball, table tennis, tennis, volleyball. **Team name:** Barons.

Student services. Alcohol/substance abuse counseling, campus ministries, career counseling, student employment services, financial aid counseling, health services, personal counseling, placement for graduates, veterans' counselor. **Physically disabled:** Services for visually, speech, hearing impaired.

Contact. E-mail: admissions@bpc.edu
Phone: (912) 583-3265 Toll-free number: (800) 342-1087 ext. 265
Fax: (912) 583-3598
Brad Kissell, Dean of Enrollment Management, Brewton-Parker College, PO Box 197, #2011, Mount Vernon, GA 30445-0197

Carver Bible College

Atlanta, Georgia
www.carver.edu/default.asp

- Private 4-year Bible college

General. Accredited by ABHE.

Contact. Phone: (404) 527-4520
437 Nelson Street, Atlanta, GA 30313

Clark Atlanta University

Atlanta, Georgia **CB member**
www.cau.edu **CB code: 5110**

- Private 4-year university affiliated with United Methodist Church
- Commuter campus in very large city
- 3,253 degree-seeking undergraduates: 5% part-time, 78% women, 93% African American
- 226 degree-seeking graduate students
- 48% of applicants admitted
- SAT or ACT with writing, application essay required
- 69% graduate within 6 years

General. Founded in 1869. Regionally accredited. Clark Atlanta University is a member of a nationallly recognized consortium known as the Atlanta University Center. It is the largest consortium of black private education institutions in the nation. **Degrees:** 594 bachelor's awarded; master's, doctoral offered. **ROTC:** Army, Navy, Air Force. **Location:** 2 miles from downtown. **Calendar:** Semester, limited summer session. **Full-time faculty:** 236 total; 86% have terminal degrees, 40% women. **Part-time faculty:** 3 total; 33% have terminal degrees, 33% women. **Class size:** 42% < 20, 47% 20-39, 8% 40-49, 1% 50-99, 2% >100. **Special facilities:** Exhibition gallery, research center for science and technology.

Freshman class profile. 9,330 applied, 4,469 admitted, 4,349 enrolled.

Mid 50% test scores			
SAT verbal:	330-590	SAT math:	360-580
		ACT:	14-25

Basis for selection. Secondary school record most important. Test scores, recommendations, essay also important. SAT Subject Tests recommended. Interview recommended. Audition recommended for music and drama majors. **Homeschooled:** SAT, SAT Subject Tests or ACT, portfolio required.

High school preparation. 17 units required. Required units include English 4, mathematics 3, social studies 3, science 2, foreign language 2 and academic electives 3.

2005-2006 Annual costs. Tuition/fees: $14,522. Room/board: $7,415. Books/supplies: $1,000. Personal expenses: $2,374.

2005-2006 Financial aid. Need-based: Average need met was 7%. Average scholarship/grant was $3,618; average loan $2,905. 72% of total undergraduate aid awarded as scholarships/grants, 28% as loans/jobs. **Non-need-based:** Scholarships awarded for academics, alumni affiliation, art, athletics, job skills, leadership, minority status, music/drama, religious affiliation, ROTC, state residency.

Application procedures. Admission: Priority date 3/1; deadline 7/1 (postmark date). $35 fee ($35 out-of-state), may be waived for applicants with need. Application may be submitted online. Admission notification on a rolling basis beginning on or about 1/1. Must reply by 8/1. **Financial aid:** Priority date 3/1, closing date 4/1. FAFSA required. Applicants notified on a rolling basis starting 2/1; must reply within 2 week(s) of notification.

Academics. Special study options: Accelerated study, combined bachelor's/graduate degree, cooperative education, cross-registration, distance learning, double major, dual enrollment of high school students, exchange student, honors, independent study, internships, liberal arts/career combination, study abroad, teacher certification program, Washington semester, weekend college. **Credit/placement by examination:** AP, CLEP, IB, ACT, institutional tests. 45 credit hours maximum toward bachelor's degree. **Support services:** Learning center, pre-admission summer program, reduced course load, remedial instruction, study skills assistance, tutoring, writing center.

Majors. Biology: General. **Business:** Accounting, business admin, fashion, hospitality admin, managerial economics. **Communications:** General, advertising, broadcast journalism, journalism, media studies, public relations. **Communications technology:** General. **Computer sciences:** General, computer science. **Education:** General, art, business, early childhood, elementary, English, health, mathematics, middle, music, physical, reading, secondary, social science, special. **Engineering:** General. **English:** Speech/rhetoric. **Foreign languages:** General, French, German, Spanish. **Health:** Medical illustrating, medical records admin, medical records technology. **History:** General. **Interdisciplinary:** Math/computer science, nutrition sciences. **Math:** General. **Philosophy/religion:** Philosophy, religion. **Physical sciences:** Chemistry, physics. **Psychology:** General. **Public administration:** Social work. **Social sciences:** General, criminology, economics, political science, sociology. **Visual/performing arts:** Art, dramatic, studio arts.

Computing on campus. 640 workstations in dormitories, library, computer center. Dormitories wired for high-speed internet access and linked to campus network. Commuter students can connect to campus network. Online course registration, online library, helpline, repair service available.

Student life. Freshman orientation: Mandatory, $150 fee. Preregistration for classes offered. **Policies:** Drug/alcohol policy, sanctions for violations, policies governing Greek and other student organizations. **Housing:** Guaranteed on-campus for freshmen. Coed dorms, single-sex dorms, special housing for disabled, apartments, substance-free housing available. $300 nonrefundable deposit, deadline 6/1. **Activities:** Bands, choral groups, dance, drama, film society, literary magazine, music ensembles, musical theater, radio station, student government, student newspaper, symphony orchestra, TV station, NAACP, pan-Hellenic council, Anointed Students in Fellowship, Campus Crusade for Christ, Christian Fellowship, National Council of Negro Women, Forensic Society, Gamma Sigma Sigma, Caribbean-oriented student organization.

Athletics. NCAA. **Intercollegiate:** Baseball M, basketball, cheerleading M, cross-country, football (tackle) M, softball W, tennis, track and field, volleyball W. **Intramural:** Basketball, football (non-tackle), swimming, tennis, track and field. **Team name:** Panthers.

Student services. Alcohol/substance abuse counseling, campus ministries, career counseling, student employment services, financial aid counseling, health services, legal services, personal counseling, placement for graduates, veterans' counselor, women's services. **Physically disabled:** Services for visually, speech, hearing impaired.

Contact. E-mail: admissions@cau.edu
Phone: (404) 880-6605 Toll-free number: (800) 688-3228
Fax: (404) 880-6174
Julius Dodds, Director of Admissions, Clark Atlanta University, 223 James P. Brawley Drive, SW, Atlanta, GA 30314

Clayton State University

Morrow, Georgia **CB member**
www.clayton.edu **CB code: 5145**

- Public 4-year liberal arts and technical college
- Commuter campus in small city
- 6,212 degree-seeking undergraduates
- 49% of applicants admitted

General. Founded in 1969. Regionally accredited. **Degrees:** 558 bachelor's, 235 associate awarded. **ROTC:** Army, Navy, Air Force. **Location:** 12 miles from Atlanta. **Calendar:** Semester, extensive summer session. **Full-time faculty:** 197 total. **Part-time faculty:** 154 total. **Class size:** 42% < 20, 48% 20-39, 6% 40-49, 4% 50-99, less than 1% >100. **Special facilities:** Concert hall, wellness center.

Freshman class profile. 1,688 applied, 833 admitted, 592 enrolled.

Mid 50% test scores			
SAT verbal:	450-540	Out-of-state:	9%
SAT math:	430-520	Live on campus:	30%
ACT:	17-22	Fraternities:	8%
		Sororities:	2%

Basis for selection. Minimum ACT score of 17 or minimum SAT of 400 math and 430 verbal required. In health sciences, music, teacher education, and business programs, secondary school record also very important. Auditions recommended for music majors. **Homeschooled:** Must validate the completion of a college prep curriculum. SAT tests may be used to do so.

High school preparation. 16 units required; 22 recommended. Required and recommended units include English 4, mathematics 4, social studies 3, history 2, science 3-4 (laboratory 3), foreign language 2-3 and academic electives 2. Students not meeting college-preparatory requirements must take remedial classes before entering any program.

2005-2006 Annual costs. Tuition/fees: $2,962; $10,278 out-of-state. Books/supplies: $1,000. Personal expenses: $3,440.

2005-2006 Financial aid. Need-based: 38% of total undergraduate aid awarded as scholarships/grants, 62% as loans/jobs. **Non-need-based:** Scholarships awarded for academics.

Application procedures. Admission: Priority date 2/15; no deadline. $15 fee, may be waived for applicants with need. Application may be submitted online. Admission notification on a rolling basis beginning on or about 1/1. **Financial aid:** Priority date 7/18; no closing date. FAFSA required. Applicants notified on a rolling basis starting 3/12.

Academics. Special study options: Cooperative education, cross-registration, distance learning, double major, dual enrollment of high school students, exchange student, honors, independent study, internships, liberal arts/career combination, student-designed major, study abroad, teacher certification program. **Credit/placement by examination:** AP, CLEP, IB, institutional tests. **Support services:** Learning center, reduced course load, remedial instruction, study skills assistance, tutoring.

Majors. Biology: General. **Business:** General, accounting, business admin, marketing, office management, operations. **Communications:** General. **Computer sciences:** General, data processing, information systems, programming, systems analysis. **Education:** Middle, music. **Health:** Dental assistant, dental hygiene, facilities admin, health care admin, nursing admin. **History:** General. **Liberal arts:** Arts/sciences. **Protective services:** Criminal justice. **Psychology:** General. **Visual/performing arts:** Music performance, music theory/composition.

Most popular majors. Business/marketing 36%, computer/information sciences 15%, health sciences 23%, psychology 11%.

Computing on campus. PC or laptop required. Online course registration, online library, helpline, repair service, student web hosting, wireless network available.

Student life. Freshman orientation: Mandatory, $30 fee. Preregistration for classes offered. **Policies:** Freshmen permitted cars on campus. **Housing:** Apartments available. Housing available adjacent to campus includes computer hook-ups, roommate plans. Selection of student housing is responsibility of student and his/her guardians. **Activities:** Jazz band, choral groups, drama, literary magazine, music ensembles, musical theater, opera, student government, student newspaper, Approximately 20 student groups.

Athletics. NAIA, NCAA. **Intercollegiate:** Basketball, cross-country, golf M, soccer, tennis W, track and field. **Team name:** Lakers.

Student services. Adult student services, alcohol/substance abuse counseling, career counseling, student employment services, financial aid counseling, health services, minority student services, personal counseling, placement for graduates, veterans' counselor. **Physically disabled:** Services for visually, speech, hearing impaired.

Contact. E-mail: ccsu-info@mail.clayton.edu
Phone: (770) 961-3500 Fax: (770) 961-3700
Anne Meservey, Director of Admissions, Clayton State University, 5900 North Lee Street, Morrow, GA 30260-0285

Columbus State University

Columbus, Georgia — **CB member**
www.colstate.edu — **CB code: 5123**

- Public 4-year university and liberal arts college
- Commuter campus in large city
- 6,543 degree-seeking undergraduates: 33% part-time, 62% women, 32% African American, 2% Asian American, 3% Hispanic American, 1% international
- 823 degree-seeking graduate students
- 64% of applicants admitted
- SAT or ACT (ACT writing optional) required

General. Founded in 1958. Regionally accredited. **Degrees:** 654 bachelor's, 18 associate awarded; master's offered. **ROTC:** Army. **Location:** 100 miles from Atlanta. **Calendar:** Semester, extensive summer session. **Full-time faculty:** 216 total; 76% have terminal degrees, 20% minority, 47% women. **Part-time faculty:** 195 total; 25% have terminal degrees, 14% minority, 51% women. **Class size:** 30% < 20, 57% 20-39, 7% 40-49, 6% 50-99, less than 1% >100. **Special facilities:** Environmental learning center, space science center, performing arts center, international house.

Freshman class profile. 3,005 applied, 1,921 admitted, 1,184 enrolled.

Mid 50% test scores		End year in good standing:	88%
SAT verbal:	450-560	Return as sophomores:	72%
SAT math:	430-550	Out-of-state:	11%
ACT:	17-22	Live on campus:	34%
GPA 3.50 or higher:	22%	Fraternities:	1%
GPA 3.0-3.49:	30%	Sororities:	1%
GPA 2.0-2.99:	47%		

Basis for selection. GED not accepted. Minimum SAT math 420 or ACT math 17, or SAT verbal 450 or ACT English 18 required. Students must be on track to graduate with college preparatory seal. Students with college prep deficiencies will be considered on individual basis. Interviews required of nursing and music majors. Audition required of music majors. Portfolio recommended for art majors. **Homeschooled:** Must submit combined SAT (exclusive of Writing) score of 1000, official transcripts from any high school and colleges attended, Home School Credit Evaluation Table, letter from primary teacher certifying completion of high school and date of graduation and two letters of recommendation from non-family members.

High school preparation. 16 units required. Required units include English 4, mathematics 4, social studies 3, science 3 (laboratory 2) and foreign language 2. Social studies units required include U.S. history and world studies.

2005-2006 Annual costs. Tuition/fees: $2,944; $10,260 out-of-state. Room/board: $5,720. Books/supplies: $800. Personal expenses: $1,676.

2005-2006 Financial aid. Need-based: 680 full-time freshmen applied for aid; 496 were judged to have need; 430 of these received aid. Average need met was 58%. Average scholarship/grant was $2,491; average loan $2,620. 21% of total undergraduate aid awarded as scholarships/grants, 79% as loans/jobs. **Non-need-based:** Awarded to 2,775 full-time undergraduates, including 670 freshmen. Scholarships awarded for academics, alumni affiliation, art, athletics, job skills, leadership, music/drama, ROTC.

Application procedures. Admission: Priority date 7/1; deadline 7/1 (receipt date). $25 fee, may be waived for applicants with need. Application may be submitted online. Admission notification on a rolling basis beginning on or about 9/1. **Financial aid:** Priority date 5/1; no closing date. FAFSA required. Applicants notified on a rolling basis starting 2/1; must reply within 4 week(s) of notification.

Academics. Special study options: Accelerated study, cooperative education, distance learning, double major, dual enrollment of high school students, honors, independent study, internships, liberal arts/career combination, study abroad, teacher certification program. **Credit/placement by examination:** AP, CLEP, institutional tests. 30 credit hours maximum toward associate degree, 60 toward bachelor's. **Support services:** Learning center, reduced course load, remedial instruction, study skills assistance, tutoring, writing center.

Majors. Biology: General, biomedical sciences. **Business:** General, accounting, business admin, finance, marketing. **Computer sciences:** General. **Education:** Art, drama/dance, early childhood, emotionally handicapped, English, learning disabled, mathematics, mentally handicapped, middle, music, physical, science, secondary, social science, social studies. **English:** English lit, speech/rhetoric. **Foreign languages:** French, Spanish. **Health:** Nursing (RN). **History:** General. **Math:** General. **Parks/recreation:** Exercise sciences. **Physical sciences:** Chemistry, geology. **Protective services:** Criminal justice. **Psychology:** General. **Social sciences:** Political science, sociology. **Visual/performing arts:** Art, dramatic, music performance.

Most popular majors. Biology 8%, business/marketing 22%, computer/information sciences 11%, education 15%, English 7%, health sciences 7%, security/protective services 9%.

Computing on campus. 625 workstations in library, computer center, student center. Dormitories wired for high-speed internet access and linked to campus network. Commuter students can connect to campus network. Online course registration, online library, helpline, repair service, wireless network available.

Student life. Freshman orientation: Mandatory, $35 fee. Preregistration for classes offered. **Policies:** Freshmen permitted cars on campus. **Housing:** Coed dorms, single-sex dorms, special housing for disabled, apartments, fraternity/sorority housing, substance-free housing available. $225 partly refundable deposit, deadline 7/1. Apartments take place of traditional dorms; weekday meals are included in fee. **Activities:** Bands, choral groups, dance, drama, literary magazine, music ensembles, musical theater, opera, student government, student newspaper, symphony orchestra, College Republicans, CSU Islamic Association, Freethought Society.

Athletics. NCAA. **Intercollegiate:** Baseball M, basketball, cross-country, golf M, soccer W, softball W, tennis. **Intramural:** Badminton, basketball, football (tackle) M, skiing, soccer, softball, table tennis, tennis, volleyball. **Team name:** Cougars.

Student services. Adult student services, alcohol/substance abuse counseling, career counseling, student employment services, financial aid counseling, health services, minority student services, personal counseling, placement for graduates, veterans' counselor, women's services. **Physically disabled:** Services for visually, speech, hearing impaired.

Contact. E-mail: admissions@colstate.edu
Phone: (706) 568-2035 Toll-free number: (866) 264-2035
Fax: (706) 568-5091
Susan Lovell, Director of Admissions, Columbus State University, 4225 University Avenue, Columbus, GA 31907-5645

Covenant College

Lookout Mountain, Georgia
www.covenant.edu **CB code: 6124**

- Private 4-year liberal arts college affiliated with Presbyterian Church in America
- Residential campus in small city
- 902 degree-seeking undergraduates: 3% part-time, 57% women, 2% African American, 1% Asian American, 2% Hispanic American, 2% international
- 74 graduate students
- 66% of applicants admitted
- SAT or ACT with writing, application essay required
- 59% graduate within 6 years

General. Founded in 1955. Regionally accredited. **Degrees:** 338 bachelor's awarded; master's offered. **Location:** 120 miles from Atlanta, 5 miles from Chattanooga, Tennessee. **Calendar:** Semester, limited summer session. **Full-time faculty:** 56 total; 86% have terminal degrees, 5% minority, 16% women. **Part-time faculty:** 27 total; 30% have terminal degrees, 26% women.

Freshman class profile. 817 applied, 543 admitted, 271 enrolled.

Mid 50% test scores			
SAT verbal:	540-660	Rank in top quarter:	50%
SAT math:	520-610	Rank in top tenth:	18%
ACT:	21-28	Return as sophomores:	73%
GPA 3.50 or higher:	70%	Out-of-state:	9%
GPA 3.0-3.49:	18%	Live on campus:	99%
GPA 2.0-2.99:	12%	International:	3%

Basis for selection. Minimum SAT 1500 (including written portion) or ACT 21, minimum 2.5 high school GPA or 2.0 college transfer, plus academic evaluation, church evaluation, and a personal testimony of faith. Those students that do not meet the minimum scores above may be asked to provide additional information. Auditions required for music and voice majors. **Homeschooled:** Transcript of courses and grades required.

High school preparation. College-preparatory program recommended. 16 units recommended. Recommended units include English 4, mathematics 3, social studies 2, science 2, foreign language 2 and academic electives 3.

2006-2007 Annual costs. Tuition/fees (projected): $21,850. Room/board: $6,180. Books/supplies: $600. Personal expenses: $500.

Financial aid. Non-need-based: Scholarships awarded for academics, alumni affiliation, art, athletics, leadership, minority status, music/drama, religious affiliation, state residency.

Application procedures. Admission: Priority date 5/1; no deadline. $35 fee, may be waived for applicants with need. Application must be submitted on paper. Admission notification on a rolling basis beginning on or about 1/1. Must reply by May 1 or within 8 week(s) if notified thereafter. **Financial aid:** Priority date 3/1, closing date 3/31. FAFSA, institutional form required. Applicants notified on a rolling basis starting 4/15; must reply within 3 week(s) of notification.

Academics. Organizational management program designed for adult students with minimum of 5 years of work experience who have completed at least 2 years of college. Maximum of 32 credit hours given for assessment of life experience learning. All classes held in evenings, with degree completion taking just over 1 year. **Special study options:** Double major, dual enrollment of high school students, exchange student, independent study, internships, liberal arts/career combination, student-designed major, study abroad, teacher certification program, Washington semester. Dual engineering degree with Georgia Tech, cooperative program with school of nursing at Emory University and Chattanooga State; bridge program leading to master of nursing science at Vanderbilt University. **Credit/placement by examination:** AP, CLEP, IB, institutional tests. 30 credit hours maximum toward associate degree, 30 toward bachelor's. **Support services:** Reduced course load, remedial instruction, tutoring, writing center.

Majors. Biology: General. **Business:** General, organizational behavior. **Computer sciences:** General, computer science. **Education:** Biology, early childhood, elementary, English, history, mathematics, middle, science, secondary. **English:** English lit. **Health:** Nursing (RN), prenursing. **History:** General. **Interdisciplinary:** Natural sciences. **Math:** General. **Philosophy/religion:** Philosophy. **Physical sciences:** Chemistry, physics. **Psychology:** General. **Social sciences:** Economics, international economic development, sociology. **Theology:** Bible, missionary. **Visual/performing arts:** Art, music performance, studio arts.

Computing on campus. 135 workstations in dormitories, library, computer center. Dormitories linked to campus network. Commuter students can connect to campus network. Online library, helpline, wireless network available.

Student life. Freshman orientation: Mandatory, $65 fee. Preregistration for classes offered. One week prior to beginning of classes. **Policies:** Smoking, alcoholic beverages, and drugs prohibited. Students are to use wisdom and Christ-like discretion in the application of Biblical principles to decisions regarding all areas of life such as the involvement with various forms of media, all non-college organizations, social interaction (including dance) and the physical expression of intimacy in relationships. Religious observance required. Freshmen permitted cars on campus. **Housing:** Guaranteed on-campus for freshmen. Single-sex dorms, apartments available. $300 nonrefundable deposit. **Activities:** Choral groups, dance, drama, film society, literary magazine, music ensembles, student government, student newspaper, symphony orchestra, Rotaract, campus ministries, inner-city ministries, Young Life, nursing home ministries, widows ministry, pre-law club, Psi Chi, Reformed University Fellowship, evangelism club.

Athletics. NAIA. **Intercollegiate:** Basketball, cross-country, golf M, soccer, volleyball W. **Intramural:** Basketball, football (non-tackle), football (tackle) M, soccer, tennis, volleyball. **Team name:** Scots.

Student services. Adult student services, campus ministries, career counseling, student employment services, financial aid counseling, health services, personal counseling, placement for graduates.

Contact. E-mail: admissions@covenant.edu
Phone: (706) 419-1148 Toll-free number: (888) 451-2683
Fax: (706) 820-0893
Jan Weaver, Assistant Director of Admissions, Covenant College, 14049 Scenic Highway, Lookout Mountain, GA 30750

Dalton State College

Dalton, Georgia
www.daltonstate.edu **CB code: 5167**

- Public 4-year liberal arts and technical college
- Commuter campus in large town
- 4,267 degree-seeking undergraduates: 55% part-time, 62% women
- 69% of applicants admitted
- SAT or ACT required

General. Founded in 1963. Regionally accredited. **Degrees:** 53 bachelor's, 289 associate awarded. **Location:** 90 miles from Atlanta. **Calendar:** Semester, limited summer session. **Full-time faculty:** 115 total; 49% have terminal degrees, 7% minority, 48% women. **Part-time faculty:** 43 total.

Freshman class profile. 1,941 applied, 1,347 admitted, 1,165 enrolled.

Basis for selection. Must meet test score minimums or have 1.8 high school GPA for transfer associate degree programs. **Homeschooled:** State high school equivalency certificate required.

High school preparation. 16 units required. Required units include English 4, mathematics 4, social studies 3, science 3 and foreign language 2.

2005-2006 Annual costs. Tuition/fees: $1,666; $6,290 out-of-state.

2004-2005 Financial aid. Need-based: 96% of total undergraduate aid awarded as scholarships/grants, 4% as loans/jobs. **Non-need-based:** Scholarships awarded for academics, minority status, state residency.

Application procedures. Admission: No deadline. $25 fee, may be waived for applicants with need. Application may be submitted online. Admission notification on a rolling basis. **Financial aid:** Priority date 7/1; no

closing date. FAFSA, institutional form required. Applicants notified on a rolling basis starting 7/1.

Academics. **Special study options:** Cooperative education, double major, dual enrollment of high school students, ESL, external degree, honors, independent study, internships, study abroad, weekend college. **Credit/placement by examination:** CLEP, institutional tests. Credit is awarded only to admitted students and recorded only for those who enroll for credit courses. Credit is awarded only for offered courses. **Support services:** Remedial instruction, study skills assistance, tutoring, writing center.

Honors college/program. For early admission, first-time freshmen and early enrollment students need a minimum high school GPA of 3.5, combined SAT score of 1100 or above (exclusive of Writing) with verbal score of 580, ACT composite score of 24 or above. Must submit an honors essay and 2 letters of recommendation; interview with the honors program director and committee representatives also required.

Majors. **Business:** Management information systems, management science, marketing, operations. **Computer sciences:** General. **Education:** Elementary. **Family/consumer sciences:** Work/family studies. **Public administration:** Social work.

Computing on campus. 800 workstations in library, computer center, student center. Commuter students can connect to campus network. Online library, helpline available.

Student life. **Freshman orientation:** Mandatory. Preregistration for classes offered. **Policies:** Freshmen permitted cars on campus. **Activities:** Literary magazine, student government, student newspaper, Baptist Student Union, Students in Free Enterprise, international students association, Spanish club, Phi Theta Kappa, Funny Healers, social work club, College Republicans.

Athletics. **Intramural:** Badminton, basketball, football (non-tackle) M, racquetball, softball, swimming, table tennis, tennis, volleyball.

Student services. Adult student services, career counseling, student employment services, financial aid counseling, personal counseling, placement for graduates, veterans' counselor. **Physically disabled:** Services for hearing impaired.

Contact. E-mail: aharris@daltonstate.edu
Phone: (706) 272-4436 Toll-free number: (800) 829-4436
Fax: (706) 272-2530
Jodi Johnson, Vice President for Enrollment Services, Dalton State College, 650 College Drive, Dalton, GA 30720

DeVry University: Alpharetta

Alpharetta, Georgia
www.atl.devry.edu **CB code: 0077**

- For-profit 4-year university
- Commuter campus in large town
- 848 degree-seeking undergraduates: 47% part-time, 42% women
- 193 graduate students
- Interview required
- 28% graduate within 6 years

General. Regionally accredited. **Degrees:** 254 bachelor's, 9 associate awarded; master's offered. **Location:** 18 miles from Atlanta. **Calendar:** Semester, extensive summer session. **Full-time faculty:** 36 total; 33% minority, 39% women. **Part-time faculty:** 40 total; 28% minority, 55% women.

Freshman class profile. 73 enrolled.

Return as sophomores:	43%	**International:**	3%

Basis for selection. Applicants must have high school diploma or equivalent, or degree from an accredited postsecondary institution, demonstrate proficiency in basic college-level skills through ACT, SAT, or institution-administered placement examinations, and be at least 17 years of age. New students may enter at the beginning of any semester. Applicants may also take a DeVry administered admissions test.

High school preparation. College-preparatory program recommended. Required units include mathematics 1. Math unit must be algebra or higher.

2005-2006 Annual costs. Tuition/fees: $12,140. Books/supplies: $1,100. Personal expenses: $1,750.

2004-2005 Financial aid. All financial aid based on need. 130 full-time freshmen applied for aid; 120 were judged to have need; 120 of these received aid. Average need met was 45%. Average scholarship/grant was $4,931; average loan $5,348. 25% of total undergraduate aid awarded as scholarships/grants, 75% as loans/jobs.

Application procedures. **Admission:** No deadline. $50 fee. Application may be submitted online. Admission notification on a rolling basis. **Financial aid:** No deadline. FAFSA required. Applicants notified on a rolling basis.

Academics. **Special study options:** Accelerated study, cooperative education, distance learning. **Credit/placement by examination:** CLEP, institutional tests. **Support services:** Learning center, remedial instruction, tutoring.

Majors. **Business:** Business admin, human resources, management information systems, operations. **Computer sciences:** Information systems, networking. **Engineering technology:** Computer, electrical.

Most popular majors. Business/marketing 41%, computer/information sciences 46%, engineering/engineering technologies 13%.

Computing on campus. 218 workstations in library, computer center. Online course registration, online library, helpline available.

Student life. **Freshman orientation:** Mandatory. **Policies:** Freshmen permitted cars on campus. **Activities:** Alpha Sigma Lambda, Toastmasters International, international student organization, National Society of Black Engineers, Alpha Beta Kappa, Delta Pi Chi, Epsilon Delta Pi, Tau Alpha Pi, Future Business Leaders of America.

Athletics. **Intramural:** Basketball, football (non-tackle), softball, volleyball.

Student services. Career counseling, student employment services, financial aid counseling, placement for graduates, veterans' counselor. **Physically disabled:** Services for visually, hearing impaired.

Contact. E-mail: admissions@devry.edu
Phone: (770) 664-9520 Toll-free number: (800) 221-4771
Fax: (770) 664-8824
Gerry Purcell, Director of Admissions, DeVry University: Alpharetta, 2555 Northwinds Parkway, Alpharetta, GA 30004

DeVry University: Decatur

Decatur, Georgia
www.atl.devry.edu **CB code: 5715**

- For-profit 4-year university
- Commuter campus in large town
- 1,865 degree-seeking undergraduates: 48% part-time, 34% women
- 329 graduate students
- Interview required
- 28% graduate within 6 years

General. Founded in 1969. Regionally accredited. **Degrees:** 467 bachelor's, 55 associate awarded; master's offered. **Location:** 15 miles from Atlanta. **Calendar:** Semester, extensive summer session. **Full-time faculty:** 53 total; 42% minority, 36% women. **Part-time faculty:** 80 total; 61% minority, 46% women.

Freshman class profile. 339 enrolled.

Basis for selection. Applicants must have high school diploma or equivalent, or degree from accredited post-secondary institution, demonstrate proficiency in basic college-level skills through SAT or ACT scores or institution-administered placement examinations, and be at least 17 years of age. New students may enter at beginning of any semester. Applicants may also take a DeVry administered admissions test.

High school preparation. College-preparatory program recommended. Required units include mathematics 1. Math unit must be algebra or higher.

2005-2006 Annual costs. Tuition/fees: $12,140. Books/supplies: $1,100. Personal expenses: $1,750.

Financial aid. All financial aid based on need.

Application procedures. **Admission:** No deadline. $50 fee. Application may be submitted online. Admission notification on a rolling basis. **Financial aid:** No deadline. FAFSA required. Applicants notified on a rolling basis.

Academics. **Special study options:** Accelerated study, cooperative education, distance learning. **Credit/placement by examination:** CLEP, institutional tests. **Support services:** Learning center, remedial instruction, tutoring.

Majors. **Business:** Business admin, operations. **Computer sciences:** Information systems, networking. **Engineering technology:** Computer, electrical.

Most popular majors. Business/marketing 51%, computer/information sciences 37%, engineering/engineering technologies 12%.

Computing on campus. 300 workstations in library, computer center. Online course registration, online library, helpline available.

Student life. **Freshman orientation:** Mandatory. **Policies:** Freshmen permitted cars on campus. **Activities:** Toastmasters International, National Society of Black Engineers, International Student Organization, Delta Pi Chi, Tau Alpha Pi, Sigma Beta Delta, Alpha Beta Kappa.

Athletics. **Intramural:** Basketball, football (non-tackle), softball, volleyball.

Student services. Career counseling, student employment services, financial aid counseling, placement for graduates, veterans' counselor. **Physically disabled:** Services for visually, hearing impaired.

Contact. E-mail: dsilva@admin.atl.devry.edu
Phone: (404) 292-2645 Toll-free number: (800) 221-4771
Fax: (404) 292-7011
Barbara Silva, Director of Admissions, DeVry University: Decatur, 250 North Arcadia Avenue, Decatur, GA 30030-2198

Emmanuel College

Franklin Springs, Georgia — **CB member**
www.emmanuelcollege.edu — **CB code: 5184**

- Private 4-year liberal arts college affiliated with Pentecostal Holiness Church
- Residential campus in rural community
- 707 degree-seeking undergraduates: 16% part-time, 57% women, 15% African American, 1% Asian American, 1% Hispanic American, 1% international
- 38% of applicants admitted
- SAT or ACT (ACT writing optional) required
- 36% graduate within 6 years

General. Founded in 1919. Regionally accredited. **Degrees:** 113 bachelor's, 12 associate awarded. **Location:** 30 miles from Athens, 90 miles from Atlanta. **Calendar:** Semester, limited summer session. **Full-time faculty:** 44 total; 70% have terminal degrees, 4% minority, 34% women. **Part-time faculty:** 24 total; 21% have terminal degrees, 33% women. **Class size:** 69% < 20, 28% 20-39, 2% 40-49, 1% 50-99.

Freshman class profile. 1,039 applied, 391 admitted, 231 enrolled.

Mid 50% test scores			
SAT verbal:	440-570	Return as sophomores:	71%
SAT math:	430-530	Out-of-state:	23%
		Live on campus:	47%

Basis for selection. High school record and SAT/ACT scores important. Audition required and interview recommended for music majors. **Learning Disabled:** Must submit documentation of disability from professional.

High school preparation. College-preparatory program recommended.

2005-2006 Annual costs. Tuition/fees: $10,150. Room/board: $4,700. Books/supplies: $600. Personal expenses: $900.

2004-2005 Financial aid. **Need-based:** 120 full-time freshmen applied for aid; 103 were judged to have need; 103 of these received aid. Average need met was 35%. Average scholarship/grant was $3,273; average loan $2,421. 35% of total undergraduate aid awarded as scholarships/grants, 65% as loans/jobs. **Non-need-based:** Awarded to 606 full-time undergraduates, including 134 freshmen. Scholarships awarded for academics, art, athletics, leadership, music/drama, religious affiliation, state residency.

Application procedures. **Admission:** Closing date 8/1 (receipt date). $25 fee, may be waived for applicants with need. Application may be submitted online. Admission notification on a rolling basis beginning on or about 1/1. **Financial aid:** Priority date 5/1; no closing date. FAFSA, institutional form required. Applicants notified on a rolling basis starting 3/1; must reply within 2 week(s) of notification.

Academics. **Special study options:** Dual enrollment of high school students, honors, independent study, internships, teacher certification program. **Credit/placement by examination:** AP, CLEP, institutional tests. 24 credit hours maximum toward associate degree, 24 toward bachelor's. **Support services:** Remedial instruction, study skills assistance, tutoring, writing center.

Majors. **Biology:** General. **Business:** Business admin. **Communications:** General. **Computer sciences:** General. **Education:** Business, elementary, English, mathematics, middle, music, social science. **English:** English lit. **Health:** Premedicine. **History:** General. **Legal studies:** Prelaw. **Math:** General. **Parks/recreation:** Exercise sciences, sports admin. **Psychology:** General. **Theology:** Bible, pastoral counseling, sacred music, youth ministry.

Most popular majors. Business/marketing 19%, education 28%, psychology 10%, theological studies 16%.

Computing on campus. 50 workstations in dormitories, library, computer center. Dormitories wired for high-speed internet access and linked to campus network. Commuter students can connect to campus network. Online course registration, online library, repair service available.

Student life. **Freshman orientation:** Mandatory. Preregistration for classes offered. First 2 days of semester. **Policies:** Chapel attendance required for all full-time students. Students not living at home must reside in college housing through junior year. Religious observance required. Freshmen permitted cars on campus. **Housing:** Guaranteed on-campus for all undergraduates. Single-sex dorms, apartments, substance-free housing available. $150 fully refundable deposit, deadline 8/1. **Activities:** Concert band, choral groups, drama, literary magazine, music ensembles, musical theater, student government, student newspaper, ministerial fellowship, missions fellowship, Students in Free Enterprise.

Athletics. NAIA, NCCAA. **Intercollegiate:** Baseball M, basketball, soccer, softball W, tennis. **Intramural:** Basketball, soccer, softball, table tennis, tennis, track and field, volleyball. **Team name:** Lions.

Student services. Adult student services, campus ministries, career counseling, financial aid counseling, health services, personal counseling, veterans' counselor.

Contact. E-mail: admission@emmanuelcollege.edu
Phone: (706) 245-7226 Toll-free number: (800) 860-8800
Fax: (706) 245-4424
Kirk McConnell, Director of Admissions, Emmanuel College, 181 Spring Street, Franklin Springs, GA 30639-0129

Emory University

Atlanta, Georgia — **CB member**
www.emory.edu — **CB code: 5187**

- Private 4-year university affiliated with United Methodist Church
- Residential campus in very large city
- 6,378 degree-seeking undergraduates: 1% part-time, 58% women, 9% African American, 16% Asian American, 3% Hispanic American, 4% international
- 5,354 degree-seeking graduate students
- 37% of applicants admitted
- SAT or ACT with writing, application essay required
- 89% graduate within 6 years; 47% enter graduate study

General. Founded in 1836. Regionally accredited. **Degrees:** 1,476 bachelor's, 250 associate awarded; master's, doctoral, first professional offered. **ROTC:** Army, Navy, Air Force. **Location:** 5 miles from downtown Atlanta. **Calendar:** Semester, limited summer session. **Full-time faculty:** 1,236 total; 100% have terminal degrees, 19% minority, 39% women. **Part-time faculty:** 199 total; 98% have terminal degrees, 15% minority, 52% women. **Class size:** 64% < 20, 25% 20-39, 4% 40-49, 6% 50-99, 2% >100. **Special facilities:** Museum of art and archeology, biological field station, primate research center, 185-acre park, planetarium, Emory Healthcare facilities, affiliation with nearby Carter Presidential Center.

Freshman class profile. 12,011 applied, 4,395 admitted, 1,259 enrolled.

Mid 50% test scores			
SAT verbal:	640-730	Rank in top tenth:	90%
SAT math:	660-740	Return as sophomores:	94%
ACT:	29-33	Out-of-state:	83%
GPA 3.50 or higher:	82%	Live on campus:	97%
GPA 3.0-3.49:	18%	International:	6%
Rank in top quarter:	98%	Fraternities:	39%
		Sororities:	40%

Basis for selection. GED not accepted. Primarily school achievement record, program content and rigor of coursework. Test scores, prior academic success, as well as character and maturity are important. Diversity of interests, background, and special talents are sought. Campus visits or other indications of interest are encouraged. SAT Subject Tests recommended. **Homeschooled:** Interview required. SAT Subject Tests required.

High school preparation. 16 units required. Required and recommended units include English 4, mathematics 3-4, social studies 2, science 2-3 (laboratory 2), foreign language 2-3 and academic electives 2. At least 2 units required in either social studies or history, including history of a country/region other than the U.S. 4 units mathematics and science, with at least 3 units laboratory science, are recommended for students concentrating in science or mathematics.

2006-2007 Annual costs. Tuition/fees: $32,506. Room/board: $9,938. Books/supplies: $1,000. Personal expenses: $800.

2005-2006 Financial aid. Need-based: 832 full-time freshmen applied for aid; 629 were judged to have need; 629 of these received aid. Average need met was 100%. Average scholarship/grant was $21,616; average loan $3,529. 78% of total undergraduate aid awarded as scholarships/grants, 22% as loans/jobs. **Non-need-based:** Awarded to 1,403 full-time undergraduates, including 336 freshmen. Scholarships awarded for academics, art, leadership, music/drama, religious affiliation, state residency. **Additional information:** Private Emory loan programs assist families in financing tuition. Fixed tuition program also available.

Application procedures. Admission: Closing date 1/15 (postmark date). $50 fee, may be waived for applicants with need. Application may be submitted online. Admission notification 4/1. Must reply by May 1 or within 1 week(s) if notified thereafter. **Financial aid:** Priority date 2/15, closing date 4/1. FAFSA required. All applicants wishing to be considered for institutionally funded need-based grant aid must file the CSS PROFILE. Applicants notified by 4/15; must reply by 5/1 or within 4 week(s) of notification.

Academics. Special study options: Accelerated study, combined bachelor's/graduate degree, cooperative education, double major, dual enrollment of high school students, exchange student, honors, independent study, internships, study abroad, teacher certification program, Washington semester. 3-2 dual-degree program in engineering with Georgia Institute of Technology. **Credit/placement by examination:** AP, CLEP, IB, institutional tests. **Support services:** Learning center, study skills assistance, tutoring, writing center.

Majors. Area/ethnic studies: African, African-American, Asian, Caribbean, Central/Eastern European, French, German, Italian, Latin American, Russian/Slavic, women's. **Biology:** General. **Business:** General, accounting, business admin, finance, management science, marketing. **Communications:** Journalism. **Computer sciences:** Computer science. **Conservation:** Environmental studies. **Education:** General. **English:** Creative writing, English lit. **Foreign languages:** Chinese, classics, comparative lit, French, German, Italian, Japanese, Latin, linguistics, Russian, Spanish. **History:** General. **Interdisciplinary:** Math/computer science, medieval/Renaissance. **Math:** General. **Philosophy/religion:** Judaic, philosophy, religion. **Physical sciences:** Astronomy, chemistry, physics. **Psychology:** General. **Social sciences:** Anthropology, economics, international relations, political science, sociology. **Visual/performing arts:** Art history/conservation, dance, dramatic, film/cinema.

Most popular majors. Biology 8%, business/marketing 15%, English 6%, health sciences 6%, interdisciplinary studies 7%, psychology 9%, social sciences 28%.

Computing on campus. 700 workstations in dormitories, library, computer center, student center. Dormitories wired for high-speed internet access and linked to campus network. Commuter students can connect to campus network. Online course registration, online library, helpline, repair service, student web hosting, wireless network available.

Student life. Freshman orientation: Mandatory. Typically held over 5 days immediately prior to the first day of classes. New students receive orientation information by mail in June. **Policies:** Two -year residency requirement. **Housing:** Guaranteed on-campus for all undergraduates. Coed dorms, single-sex dorms, special housing for disabled, apartments, fraternity/sorority housing, substance-free housing available. $200 fully refundable deposit, deadline 5/1. Theme halls are available. **Activities:** Bands, choral groups, dance, drama, film society, literary magazine, music ensembles, musical theater, radio station, student government, student newspaper, symphony orchestra, TV station, over 220 student clubs and organizations are available.

Athletics. NCAA. **Intercollegiate:** Baseball M, basketball, cross-country, diving, golf M, soccer, softball W, swimming, tennis, track and field, volleyball W. **Intramural:** Badminton, basketball, diving, football (non-tackle), golf, handball, racquetball, soccer, softball, squash, swimming, table tennis, tennis, track and field, volleyball, wrestling. **Team name:** Eagles.

Student services. Alcohol/substance abuse counseling, campus ministries, career counseling, student employment services, financial aid counseling, health services, legal services, minority student services, on-campus daycare, personal counseling, placement for graduates, women's services. **Physically disabled:** Services for visually, speech, hearing impaired.

Contact. E-mail: admiss@learnlink.emory.edu
Phone: (404) 727-6036 Toll-free number: (800) 727-6036
Fax: (404) 727-4303
Daniel Walls, Dean of Admissions, Emory University, 200 Boisfeuillet Jones Center, Atlanta, GA 30322

Fort Valley State University

Fort Valley, Georgia — **CB member**
www.fvsu.edu — **CB code: 5220**

- Public 4-year liberal arts and teachers college
- Residential campus in small town
- 1,943 degree-seeking undergraduates: 13% part-time, 55% women
- 177 graduate students
- 36% of applicants admitted
- SAT or ACT (ACT writing optional) required

General. Founded in 1895. Regionally accredited. 1890 land-grant institution. **Degrees:** 246 bachelor's, 13 associate awarded; master's, first professional offered. **ROTC:** Army. **Location:** 30 miles from Macon. **Calendar:** Semester, limited summer session. **Full-time faculty:** 120 total. **Part-time faculty:** 15 total. **Class size:** 33% < 20, 56% 20-39, 9% 40-49, 2% 50-99.

Freshman class profile. 2,190 applied, 793 admitted, 354 enrolled.

Mid 50% test scores		ACT:	16-22
SAT verbal:	350-550	Out-of-state:	6%
SAT math:	330-570	Live on campus:	58%

Basis for selection. High school transcript, test scores, physical examination important. Audition recommended for music education majors.

High school preparation. 19 units required; 21 recommended. Required and recommended units include English 4, mathematics 3-4, social studies 3-4, science 3-4 and foreign language 2.

2005-2006 Annual costs. Tuition/fees: $3,044; $10,360 out-of-state. Room/board: $4,496. Books/supplies: $790. Personal expenses: $1,425.

Financial aid. Need-based: Average need met was 90%. Average scholarship/grant was $3,040; average loan $1,200. **Non-need-based:** Scholarships awarded for academics, athletics, ROTC, state residency.

Application procedures. Admission: No deadline. $20 fee. Application may be submitted online. Admission notification on a rolling basis. Must reply by May 1 or within 4 week(s) if notified thereafter. **Financial aid:** Priority date 4/1; no closing date. FAFSA, institutional form required. Applicants notified by 6/15; must reply within 1 week(s) of notification.

Academics. Special study options: Cooperative education, double major, dual enrollment of high school students, external degree, honors, independent study, internships, liberal arts/career combination, student-designed major, study abroad, teacher certification program, weekend college. **Credit/placement by examination:** CLEP, institutional tests. 20 credit hours maximum toward associate degree, 45 toward bachelor's. **Support services:** Learning center, reduced course load, remedial instruction, tutoring, writing center.

Majors. Agriculture: Animal sciences, economics, farm/ranch, horticultural science, plant sciences. **Biology:** General. **Business:** General, accounting, business admin, marketing, office management. **Communications:** Journalism, public relations. **Computer sciences:** General, information systems. **Education:** Agricultural, elementary, English, family/consumer sciences, foreign languages, French, mathematics, middle, music, physical, secondary. **Engineering:** Agricultural. **Engineering technology:** Electrical. **Family/consumer sciences:** General, child care, child development, family studies, food/nutrition. **Health:** Medical assistant, veterinary technology/assistant. **Liberal arts:** Arts/sciences. **Math:** General. **Physical sciences:** Chemistry. **Psychology:** General. **Public administration:** Human services, social work. **Social sciences:** Economics, political science, sociology.

Most popular majors. Biology 7%, business/marketing 12%, education 7%, psychology 9%, security/protective services 12%, visual/performing arts 28%.

Computing on campus. Dormitories linked to campus network. Commuter students can connect to campus network. Helpline available.

Student life. Freshman orientation: Mandatory. Preregistration for classes offered. **Policies:** Freshmen permitted cars on campus. **Housing:** Single-sex dorms available. $50 deposit. **Activities:** Bands, choral groups, dance, drama, music ensembles, musical theater, student government, student newspaper.

Athletics. NCAA. **Intercollegiate:** Basketball, cross-country, football (tackle) M, softball W, tennis, track and field, volleyball W. **Intramural:** Basketball, softball, swimming, tennis, track and field, volleyball. **Team name:** Wildcats.

Student services. Adult student services, career counseling, student employment services, health services, on-campus daycare, personal counseling, placement for graduates, veterans' counselor.

Contact. E-mail: admissap@fvsu.edu
Phone: (478) 825-6307 Toll-free number: (877) 462-3878
Fax: (478) 825-6394
Debra McGhee, Director of Admissions, Fort Valley State University, 1005 State University Drive, Fort Valley, GA 31030-4313

Georgia College and State University

Milledgeville, Georgia — **CB member**
www.gcsu.edu — **CB code: 5252**

- Public 4-year university and liberal arts college
- Residential campus in large town
- 4,782 degree-seeking undergraduates: 11% part-time, 59% women, 8% African American, 1% Asian American, 1% Hispanic American, 2% international
- 861 degree-seeking graduate students
- 60% of applicants admitted
- SAT or ACT with writing, application essay required
- 45% graduate within 6 years; 67% enter graduate study

General. Founded in 1889. Regionally accredited. Branch campuses in Macon and Warner Robins offering junior, senior, and graduate level options. **Degrees:** 794 bachelor's awarded; master's offered. **ROTC:** Army. **Location:** 95 miles from Atlanta, 30 miles from Macon. **Calendar:** Semester, limited summer session. **Full-time faculty:** 268 total; 75% have terminal degrees, 10% minority, 48% women. **Part-time faculty:** 134 total; 13% minority, 57% women. **Class size:** 37% < 20, 54% 20-39, 8% 40-49, 1% 50-99. **Special facilities:** Art galleries, greenhouse, challenge/ropes course, former Governor's mansion, Flannery O'Connor collection, Georgia education museum and archives.

Freshman class profile. 3,236 applied, 1,954 admitted, 1,030 enrolled.

Mid 50% test scores			
SAT verbal:	520-600	Rank in top tenth:	16%
SAT math:	510-600	End year in good standing:	97%
ACT:	20-24	Return as sophomores:	84%
GPA 3.50 or higher:	33%	Out-of-state:	1%
GPA 3.0-3.49:	42%	Live on campus:	99%
GPA 2.0-2.99:	25%	International:	1%
Rank in top quarter:	46%	Fraternities:	16%
		Sororities:	16%

Basis for selection. Admission decisions are based on the total student portfolio and demonstrated potential for contribution to the university and probability for success. International students must show English proficiency with a TOEFL score, or completion of the E.L.S. Language Center Level 112 or the University of Georgia American Language Program Level Five. SAT or ACT also required of international applicants who wish to participate in intercollegiate athletics. Test scores used in academic advising for honors program consideration. Audition required of music and drama majors. **Homeschooled:** Transcript of courses and grades required. SAT/ACT score equal to or above the average score of the previous year's entering freshmen class. Other documentation may be required. **Learning Disabled:** Students must identify themselves as disabled during the admissions process.

High school preparation. 16 units required. Required units include English 4, mathematics 4, social studies 3, science 3 (laboratory 2) and foreign language 2. Additional courses selected from the following areas are strongly recommended: Trigonometry, third course in foreign language, additional laboratory course in science, fine arts and computer technology.

2005-2006 Annual costs. Tuition/fees: $4,142; $14,354 out-of-state. Room/board: $6,878. Books/supplies: $800. Personal expenses: $2,088.

2004-2005 Financial aid. **Need-based:** 885 full-time freshmen applied for aid; 309 were judged to have need; 307 of these received aid. Average need met was 71%. Average scholarship/grant was $2,620; average loan $2,630. 29% of total undergraduate aid awarded as scholarships/grants, 71% as loans/jobs. **Non-need-based:** Awarded to 1,734 full-time undergraduates, including 367 freshmen. Scholarships awarded for academics, alumni affiliation, art, athletics, job skills, leadership, minority status, music/drama, religious affiliation, ROTC, state residency.

Application procedures. **Admission:** Closing date 4/1 (postmark date). $25 fee. Application may be submitted online. Admission notification on a rolling basis beginning on or about 1/1. Students encouraged to apply early to be considered for admission, university housing, scholarship funding, and financial aid. **Financial aid:** Priority date 3/1; no closing date. FAFSA required. Applicants notified on a rolling basis starting 3/1; must reply within 2 week(s) of notification.

Academics. Department of Academic Assistance supports students in academic success. **Special study options:** Accelerated study, distance learning, double major, ESL, external degree, honors, independent study, internships, liberal arts/career combination, semester at sea, student-designed major, study abroad, teacher certification program, Washington semester. 3-2 engineering program with Georgia Institute of Technology. **Credit/placement by examination:** AP, CLEP, SAT, ACT, institutional tests. 30 credit hours maximum toward bachelor's degree. **Support services:** Learning center, reduced course load, remedial instruction, study skills assistance, tutoring, writing center.

Majors. **Biology:** General. **Business:** General, accounting, business admin, international, managerial economics, marketing, office management. **Communications:** Journalism. **Computer sciences:** General. **Education:** Early childhood, health, middle, music, social science, special. **Foreign languages:** French, Spanish. **Health:** Music therapy, nursing (RN). **History:** General. **Liberal arts:** Arts/sciences. **Math:** General. **Parks/recreation:** General. **Physical sciences:** Chemistry. **Protective services:** Law enforcement admin. **Psychology:** General. **Social sciences:** Political science, sociology. **Visual/performing arts:** Art, dramatic, music performance, voice/opera.

Most popular majors. Business/marketing 26%, communications/journalism 6%, education 20%, health sciences 10%, psychology 9%, social sciences 6%.

Computing on campus. 500 workstations in dormitories, library, computer center, student center. Dormitories wired for high-speed internet access and linked to campus network. Commuter students can connect to campus network. Online course registration, online library, helpline, wireless network available.

Student life. **Freshman orientation:** Available, $60 fee. Preregistration for classes offered. One-day program that offers new students opportunity to establish a link with faculty in their intended major and become familiar with the campus and programs available. $25 fee for parents/guests. **Policies:** Students who choose student housing must remain in dormitories for full academic year. Meal plan purchase required of all on-campus residents. Freshmen permitted cars on campus. **Housing:** Guaranteed on-campus for freshmen. Coed dorms, apartments, substance-free housing available. $200 partly refundable deposit, deadline 5/1. **Activities:** Bands, choral groups, dance, drama, literary magazine, music ensembles, musical theater, radio station, student government, student newspaper, TV station, Baptist student union, Give Center, Habitat for Humanity, Big Brother/Big Sister, Delta Sigma Theta, Black Student Alliance.

Athletics. NCAA. **Intercollegiate:** Baseball M, basketball, cheerleading, cross-country, golf M, soccer W, softball W, tennis. **Intramural:** Basketball, bowling, football (non-tackle), golf, racquetball, soccer, softball, swimming, tennis, volleyball. **Team name:** Bobcats.

Student services. Adult student services, campus ministries, career counseling, student employment services, financial aid counseling, health services, minority student services, personal counseling, placement for graduates, veterans' counselor, women's services. **Physically disabled:** Services for visually, hearing impaired.

Contact. E-mail: info@gcsu.edu
Phone: (478) 445-2774 Toll-free number: (800) 342-0471
Fax: (478) 445-1914
Mike Augustine, Director, Georgia College and State University, Campus Box 23, Milledgeville, GA 31061-0490

Georgia Institute of Technology

Atlanta, Georgia — **CB member**
www.gatech.edu — **CB code: 5248**

- Public 4-year university
- Residential campus in very large city
- 11,624 degree-seeking undergraduates: 6% part-time, 28% women, 7% African American, 15% Asian American, 4% Hispanic American, 5% international
- 5,202 degree-seeking graduate students
- 67% of applicants admitted

- SAT or ACT with writing, application essay required
- 76% graduate within 6 years; 24% enter graduate study

General. Founded in 1885. Regionally accredited. **Degrees:** 2,512 bachelor's awarded; master's, doctoral offered. **ROTC:** Army, Navy, Air Force. **Calendar:** Semester, extensive summer session. **Full-time faculty:** 810 total; 97% have terminal degrees, 24% minority, 17% women. **Part-time faculty:** 27 total; 78% have terminal degrees, 15% minority, 37% women. **Class size:** 39% < 20, 33% 20-39, 8% 40-49, 13% 50-99, 8% >100. **Special facilities:** Advanced technology development center, research institute, ovarian cancer institute, electron microscope, paper museum.

Freshman class profile. 9,172 applied, 6,191 admitted, 2,425 enrolled.

Mid 50% test scores			
SAT verbal:	600-700	End year in good standing:	87%
SAT math:	650-740	Return as sophomores:	92%
ACT:	26-30	Out-of-state:	31%
GPA 3.50 or higher:	77%	Live on campus:	98%
GPA 3.0-3.49:	22%	International:	3%
GPA 2.0-2.99:	1%	Fraternities:	23%
		Sororities:	26%

Basis for selection. School achievement record and SAT math score most important, followed by SAT verbal score. Activities, leadership, and personal statement required. SAT preferred. **Homeschooled:** Official documentation of all subjects studied, credit earned per subject, time span of each unit, bibliography of all textbooks used, and grades required, along with verification of completion of college preparatory curriculum.

High school preparation. College-preparatory program required. 16 units required. Required units include English 4, mathematics 4, social studies 3, science 3 (laboratory 2) and foreign language 2.

2005-2006 Annual costs. Tuition/fees: $4,648; $18,990 out-of-state. Room/board: $6,802.

2005-2006 Financial aid. Need-based: 1,855 full-time freshmen applied for aid; 742 were judged to have need; 730 of these received aid. Average need met was 76%. Average scholarship/grant was $5,224; average loan $3,504. 53% of total undergraduate aid awarded as scholarships/grants, 47% as loans/jobs. **Non-need-based:** Awarded to 2,710 full-time undergraduates, including 786 freshmen. Scholarships awarded for academics, alumni affiliation, athletics, job skills, leadership, music/drama, ROTC, state residency.

Application procedures. Admission: Closing date 1/15 (postmark date). $50 fee, may be waived for applicants with need. Application may be submitted online. Admission notification 3/15. Admission notification on a rolling basis. Must reply by May 1 or within 2 week(s) if notified thereafter. Nonresident applicants advised to apply early. **Financial aid:** Closing date 3/1. FAFSA, institutional form required. Applicants notified on a rolling basis starting 4/1; must reply by 5/1.

Academics. Special study options: Accelerated study, combined bachelor's/graduate degree, cooperative education, cross-registration, distance learning, double major, dual enrollment of high school students, ESL, honors, independent study, internships, student-designed major, study abroad. Dual degree program (3-2) with approximately 90 liberal arts colleges and universities, Regents Engineering Transfer Program with 11 Georgia colleges; Georgia Tech Regional Engineering Program. **Credit/placement by examination:** AP, CLEP, IB, SAT, ACT, institutional tests. **Support services:** Learning center, pre-admission summer program, reduced course load, remedial instruction, study skills assistance, tutoring, writing center.

Majors. Architecture: Architecture. **Biology:** General. **Business:** Business admin, managerial economics, operations. **Communications:** Digital media. **Computer sciences:** General. **Engineering:** Aerospace, biomedical, chemical, civil, computer, electrical, industrial, materials, mechanical, nuclear, textile. **History:** Science/technology. **Interdisciplinary:** Global studies, science/society. **Math:** Applied. **Physical sciences:** Chemistry, geology, physics, polymer chemistry. **Public administration:** Policy analysis. **Social sciences:** International relations. **Visual/performing arts:** Industrial design.

Most popular majors. Business/marketing 14%, computer/information sciences 12%, engineering/engineering technologies 54%.

Computing on campus. PC or laptop required. 1,355 workstations in dormitories, library, computer center, student center. Dormitories wired for high-speed internet access and linked to campus network. Commuter students can connect to campus network. Online course registration, online library, helpline, student web hosting, wireless network available.

Student life. Freshman orientation: Available, $105 fee. Preregistration for classes offered. 2-day program. Spring and Summer orientations are one-day programs. **Policies:** First-time, first-year students are not allowed to have a car on campus during their first semester only. **Housing:** Guaranteed on-campus for freshmen. Coed dorms, single-sex dorms, special housing for disabled, apartments, fraternity/sorority housing, substance-free housing available. $600 partly refundable deposit, deadline 5/1. First year housing guaranteed to all new students who submit their housing deposit by May 1. **Activities:** Bands, choral groups, dance, drama, film society, literary magazine, music ensembles, musical theater, opera, radio station, student government, student newspaper, symphony orchestra, TV station, Campus Crusade for Christ, Christian Campus Fellowship, Catholic, Jewish, Muslim, African Student Associations, Asian Christian Fellowship, College Democrats, College Republicans.

Athletics. NCAA. **Intercollegiate:** Baseball M, basketball, cross-country, diving, football (tackle) M, golf M, softball W, swimming, tennis, track and field, volleyball W. **Intramural:** Archery, badminton, basketball, bowling, diving, equestrian, fencing, football (non-tackle), football (tackle) M, golf, gymnastics, lacrosse, racquetball, rowing (crew), sailing, skiing, soccer, softball W, squash, swimming, table tennis, tennis, track and field, volleyball, water polo, weight lifting. **Team name:** Yellow Jackets.

Student services. Alcohol/substance abuse counseling, campus ministries, career counseling, student employment services, financial aid counseling, health services, legal services, minority student services, on-campus daycare, personal counseling, placement for graduates, women's services. **Physically disabled:** Services for visually, speech, hearing impaired. **Learning disabled:** Comprehensive services available.

Contact. E-mail: admission@gatech.edu
Phone: (404) 894-4154 Fax: (404) 894-9511
Ingrid Hayes, Director of Undergraduate Admissions, Georgia Institute of Technology, 225 North Avenue NW, Atlanta, GA 30332-0320

Georgia Southern University

Statesboro, Georgia — **CB member**
www.georgiasouthern.edu — **CB code: 5253**

- Public 4-year university
- Residential campus in large town
- 13,975 degree-seeking undergraduates: 7% part-time, 49% women, 22% African American, 1% Asian American, 1% Hispanic American, 1% international
- 1,758 degree-seeking graduate students
- 55% of applicants admitted
- SAT or ACT (ACT writing recommended) required
- 41% graduate within 6 years

General. Founded in 1906. Regionally accredited. **Degrees:** 2,172 bachelor's awarded; master's, doctoral offered. **ROTC:** Army. **Location:** 50 miles from Savannah, 200 miles from Atlanta. **Calendar:** Semester, extensive summer session. **Full-time faculty:** 660 total; 76% have terminal degrees, 14% minority, 45% women. **Part-time faculty:** 53 total; 30% have terminal degrees, 2% minority, 66% women. **Class size:** 28% < 20, 53% 20-39, 8% 40-49, 9% 50-99, 3% >100. **Special facilities:** Planetarium, electron microscope, woodland nature preserve, museum, eagle sanctuary, national tick collection, wildlife education center, raptor center, botanical garden, family life center, center for international studies.

Freshman class profile. 8,302 applied, 4,585 admitted, 3,145 enrolled.

Mid 50% test scores			
SAT verbal:	510-580	End year in good standing:	76%
SAT math:	510-590	Return as sophomores:	78%
ACT:	20-23	Out-of-state:	6%
GPA 3.50 or higher:	21%	Live on campus:	68%
GPA 3.0-3.49:	37%	International:	1%
GPA 2.0-2.99:	42%	Fraternities:	12%
		Sororities:	14%

Basis for selection. GED not accepted. Test scores, high school GPA, and college preparatory curriculum are considered. Students may be required to take placement exams. **Homeschooled:** A minimum SAT score of 1100 (exclusive of Writing) or a minimum ACT score of 24 is required. **Learning Disabled:** Admissions of learning disabled students is coordinated through the Student Disability Resource Center.

High school preparation. 16 units required. Required units include English 4, mathematics 4, social studies 3, science 3 (laboratory 2) and foreign language 2. Additional college prep courses required.

2005-2006 Annual costs. Tuition/fees: $3,462; $10,778 out-of-state. Room/board: $6,300. Books/supplies: $1,000. Personal expenses: $2,466.

2004-2005 Financial aid. Need-based: 2,812 full-time freshmen applied for aid; 1,465 were judged to have need; 1,441 of these received aid. Average need met was 66%. Average scholarship/grant was $4,871; average loan $3,414. 47% of total undergraduate aid awarded as scholarships/grants, 53% as loans/jobs. **Non-need-based:** Awarded to 896 full-time undergraduates, including 288 freshmen. Scholarships awarded for academics, alumni affiliation, art, athletics, leadership, minority status, music/drama, ROTC, state residency. **Additional information:** The majority of scholarships available are need-blind.

Application procedures. Admission: Closing date 5/1 (postmark date). $50 fee, may be waived for applicants with need. Application may be submitted online. Admission notification on a rolling basis. **Financial aid:** Priority date 3/31; no closing date. FAFSA required. Applicants notified on a rolling basis starting 4/15.

Academics. Special study options: Accelerated study, combined bachelor's/graduate degree, cooperative education, cross-registration, distance learning, double major, dual enrollment of high school students, ESL, external degree, honors, independent study, internships, student-designed major, study abroad, teacher certification program, weekend college. **Credit/placement by examination:** AP, CLEP, IB, institutional tests. 30 credit hours maximum toward bachelor's degree. For AP exams, more credit hours will be awarded for higher-than-minimum scores. **Support services:** Learning center, pre-admission summer program, reduced course load, remedial instruction, study skills assistance, tutoring, writing center.

Majors. Biology: General. **Business:** General, accounting, finance, hotel/motel admin, international, logistics, management information systems, managerial economics, marketing. **Communications:** General, journalism, public relations, radio/tv. **Communications technology:** Graphic/printing. **Computer sciences:** General. **Education:** General, art, biology, business, chemistry, English, family/consumer sciences, French, German, history, kindergarten/preschool, mathematics, middle, music, physical, physics, Spanish, special, technology/industrial arts. **Engineering technology:** Civil, construction, electrical, industrial, mechanical. **English:** English lit, speech/rhetoric. **Family/consumer sciences:** Clothing/textiles, family studies, food/nutrition. **Foreign languages:** French, German, Spanish. **Health:** Athletic training, clinical lab science, nursing (RN), public health ed. **History:** General. **Math:** General. **Parks/recreation:** General, exercise sciences, health/fitness, sports admin. **Philosophy/religion:** Philosophy. **Physical sciences:** Chemistry, geology, physics. **Protective services:** Criminal justice. **Psychology:** General. **Social sciences:** Anthropology, economics, geography, international economic development, international relations, political science, sociology. **Visual/performing arts:** Art, dramatic, interior design, music performance, music theory/composition.

Most popular majors. Business/marketing 29%, communications/journalism 6%, education 11%, health sciences 7%, parks/recreation 7%.

Computing on campus. 1,600 workstations in dormitories, library, student center. Dormitories wired for high-speed internet access and linked to campus network. Online course registration, online library, helpline, student web hosting, wireless network available.

Student life. Freshman orientation: Mandatory, $60 fee. Preregistration for classes offered. Freshman/parent program held for 2 days. $30 fee for first parent; $10 fee for each additional guest. **Policies:** Freshmen permitted cars on campus. **Housing:** Coed dorms, special housing for disabled, apartments, fraternity/sorority housing, substance-free housing available. $300 deposit. **Activities:** Bands, choral groups, dance, drama, film society, literary magazine, music ensembles, musical theater, opera, radio station, student government, student newspaper, symphony orchestra, over 200 clubs and organizations available.

Athletics. NCAA. **Intercollegiate:** Baseball M, basketball, cheerleading, cross-country W, diving W, football (tackle) M, golf M, soccer, softball W, swimming W, tennis, track and field W, volleyball W. **Intramural:** Basketball, bowling, football (non-tackle), golf, soccer, softball, tennis, volleyball. **Team name:** Eagles.

Student services. Adult student services, career counseling, services for economically disadvantaged, student employment services, financial aid counseling, health services, minority student services, personal counseling, veterans' counselor, women's services. **Physically disabled:** Services for visually, speech, hearing impaired. **Learning disabled:** Comprehensive services available.

Contact. E-mail: admissions@georgiasouthern.edu
Phone: (912) 681-5391 Fax: (912) 486-7240
Susan Davies, Director, Georgia Southern University, PO Box 8024, Statesboro, GA 30460

Georgia Southwestern State University

Americus, Georgia — **CB member**
www.gsw.edu — **CB code: 5250**

- Public 4-year university and liberal arts college
- Residential campus in large town
- 2,183 degree-seeking undergraduates: 22% part-time, 65% women, 34% African American, 1% Asian American, 1% Hispanic American, 1% Native American, 2% international
- 163 degree-seeking graduate students
- 74% of applicants admitted
- SAT or ACT (ACT writing optional) required
- 32% graduate within 6 years

General. Founded in 1906. Regionally accredited. **Degrees:** 335 bachelor's, 8 associate awarded; master's offered. **Location:** 135 miles from Atlanta. **Calendar:** Semester, limited summer session. **Full-time faculty:** 96 total; 78% have terminal degrees, 19% minority, 46% women. **Part-time faculty:** 55 total; 27% have terminal degrees, 6% minority, 54% women. **Class size:** 49% < 20, 44% 20-39, 5% 40-49, 2% 50-99. **Special facilities:** Observatory, glass blowing studio, GSW-I-TECH (internet & intranet consulting, development, and installation; application development; system integration), golf course.

Freshman class profile. 1,083 applied, 797 admitted, 385 enrolled.

Mid 50% test scores			
SAT verbal:	450-540	Rank in top tenth:	14%
SAT math:	460-530	Return as sophomores:	71%
ACT:	18-21	Out-of-state:	2%
GPA 3.50 or higher:	24%	Live on campus:	57%
GPA 3.0-3.49:	30%	International:	2%
GPA 2.0-2.99:	46%	Fraternities:	20%
Rank in top quarter:	40%	Sororities:	16%

Basis for selection. School achievement record, test scores most important. Interview and essay recommended. **Homeschooled:** Must submit 7 SAT Subject Tests along with SAT or complete home-schooled application alternative.

High school preparation. College-preparatory program required. 16 units required. Required and recommended units include English 4, mathematics 4, social studies 1, history 2, science 3 (laboratory 2), foreign language 2 and academic electives 2.

2005-2006 Annual costs. Tuition/fees: $3,034; $10,350 out-of-state. Room/board: $4,810. Books/supplies: $1,000.

Financial aid. Non-need-based: Scholarships awarded for academics, athletics, leadership.

Application procedures. Admission: Closing date 7/21 (postmark date). $25 fee, may be waived for applicants with need. Application may be submitted online. Admission notification on a rolling basis beginning on or about 8/1. Must reply by May 1 or within 2 week(s) if notified thereafter. **Financial aid:** Priority date 4/1, closing date 6/1. FAFSA, institutional form required. Applicants notified on a rolling basis starting 3/1.

Academics. Credit hours required for major vary per program. **Special study options:** Accelerated study, cooperative education, distance learning, double major, dual enrollment of high school students, ESL, honors, independent study, internships, liberal arts/career combination, study abroad, teacher certification program. Associate degree program in trade and industry with South Georgia Technical College in Americas, Albany Area Technical College in Albany, GA and Middle Georgia in Warner Robins, GA; 3-2 program in engineering with Georgia Institute of Technology. **Credit/placement by examination:** AP, CLEP, institutional tests. 45 credit hours maximum toward bachelor's degree. **Support services:** Learning center, reduced course load, remedial instruction, study skills assistance, tutoring.

Majors. Biology: General. **Business:** General, accounting, business admin, finance, human resources, marketing. **Computer sciences:** General, computer science. **Education:** Elementary, middle, physical, special. **Engineering technology:** Computer. **English:** English lit. **Health:** Nursing (RN). **History:** General. **Math:** General. **Parks/recreation:** Facilities management. **Physical sciences:** Chemistry, geology. **Psychology:** General. **Social sciences:** Political science, sociology. **Visual/performing arts:** Art, dramatic.

Most popular majors. Business/marketing 26%, education 34%, health sciences 6%, psychology 8%.

Computing on campus. 550 workstations in dormitories, library, computer center, student center. Dormitories wired for high-speed internet access and linked to campus network. Commuter students can connect to campus network. Online library, wireless network available.

Student life. Freshman orientation: Available, $55 fee. Preregistration for classes offered. 2 sessions in summer; includes parents program. **Policies:** Freshmen permitted cars on campus. **Housing:** Guaranteed on-campus for freshmen. Coed dorms, single-sex dorms, special housing for disabled, fraternity/sorority housing available. $75 deposit. **Activities:** Bands, choral groups, dance, drama, literary magazine, music ensembles, musical theater, student government, student newspaper, TV station, Baptist Student Union, Wesley Foundation, Young Republicans, Young Democrats, SABU, Habitat for Humanity, campus activity board, ZEPHYR recruitment team, College Republicans, Presbyterian campus ministry.

Athletics. NAIA. **Intercollegiate:** Baseball M, basketball, golf, soccer, softball W, tennis, track and field W. **Intramural:** Badminton, basketball, football (non-tackle), golf, soccer, softball, table tennis, tennis, volleyball, weight lifting, wrestling M. **Team name:** Hurricanes.

Student services. Adult student services, alcohol/substance abuse counseling, campus ministries, career counseling, services for economically disadvantaged, student employment services, financial aid counseling, health services, minority student services, personal counseling, placement for graduates, veterans' counselor. **Physically disabled:** Services for visually, speech, hearing impaired.

Contact. E-mail: gswapps@canes.gsw.edu
Phone: (229) 928-1273 Toll-free number: (800) 338-0082
Fax: (229) 931-2059
Gaye Hayes, Dean of Students & Admissions Services, Georgia Southwestern State University, 800 Georgia Southwestern State University Drive, Americus, GA 31709-9957

Georgia State University

Atlanta, Georgia **CB member**
www.gsu.edu **CB code: 5251**

- Public 4-year university
- Commuter campus in very large city
- 18,480 degree-seeking undergraduates: 26% part-time, 61% women, 31% African American, 10% Asian American, 3% Hispanic American, 3% international
- 6,570 degree-seeking graduate students
- 50% of applicants admitted
- SAT or ACT with writing required
- 39% graduate within 6 years

General. Founded in 1913. Regionally accredited. Courses offered at the Alpharetta Center. Distance learning and web courses available in the College of Health and Human Sciences. **Degrees:** 3,337 bachelor's awarded; master's, doctoral, first professional offered. **ROTC:** Army, Navy, Air Force. **Location:** Downtown. **Calendar:** Semester, extensive summer session. **Full-time faculty:** 1,054 total; 85% have terminal degrees, 19% minority, 44% women. **Part-time faculty:** 376 total. **Class size:** 16% < 20, 48% 20-39, 22% 40-49, 9% 50-99, 4% >100. **Special facilities:** Digital aquarium, biotechnology and drug design center, digital arts and entertainment laboratory, cartography production laboratory, art galleries, performing arts center, recital hall, military science leadership laboratory, language research center, digital arts and media research center, viral immunology center, middle east center for peace, culture, and development, Hellenic studies center, learning disorders center, language research center.

Freshman class profile. 8,313 applied, 4,117 admitted, 2,291 enrolled.

Mid 50% test scores			
SAT verbal:	490-590	GPA 3.0-3.49:	53%
SAT math:	500-590	GPA 2.0-2.99:	18%
ACT:	19-24	Return as sophomores:	80%
GPA 3.50 or higher:	29%	Out-of-state:	3%
		International:	2%

Basis for selection. GED not accepted. Minimum 2.8 high school grade point average calculated on the 16 required courses; minimum combined SAT verbal/math score of 900 with at least 430 verbal and 400 math or ACT scores (including Writing Test) with a minimum composite score of 19 with at least 17 English and 17 math. Essay recommended. Audition and an interview is required for music majors. A portfolio is required for art majors. **Homeschooled:** Validation of completion of 16 unit college preparatory curriculum required.

High school preparation. 16 units required. Required units include English 4, mathematics 4, social studies 2, history 1, science 3 (laboratory 2) and foreign language 2. 1 life sciences lab, 1 physical sciences lab plus additional science unit; foreign language units must be same language; mathematics units must be Algebra I, Geometry, Algebra II, and higher.

2005-2006 Annual costs. Tuition/fees: $4,464; $15,378 out-of-state. Room/board: $6,980. Books/supplies: $1,000. Personal expenses: $2,166.

2005-2006 Financial aid. All financial aid based on need. 2,157 full-time freshmen applied for aid; 1,330 were judged to have need; 1,330 of these received aid. Average need met was 24%. Average scholarship/grant was $3,227; average loan $2,650. 40% of total undergraduate aid awarded as scholarships/grants, 60% as loans/jobs.

Application procedures. Admission: Priority date 2/1; deadline 3/1 (postmark date). $50 fee, may be waived for applicants with need. Application may be submitted online. Admission notification on a rolling basis beginning on or about 10/1. **Financial aid:** Priority date 4/1, closing date 11/1. FAFSA required. Applicants notified on a rolling basis starting 3/30; must reply within 2 week(s) of notification.

Academics. Special study options: Accelerated study, cooperative education, cross-registration, distance learning, double major, dual enrollment of high school students, ESL, exchange student, honors, independent study, internships, study abroad, teacher certification program. Freshman learning communities. **Credit/placement by examination:** AP, CLEP, IB, institutional tests. 30 credit hours maximum toward bachelor's degree. Credit awarded for some DANTES program subject examinations, Advanced Placement Examination and CLEP. **Support services:** Learning center, pre-admission summer program, reduced course load, remedial instruction, study skills assistance, tutoring, writing center.

Honors college/program. High school GPA of 3.3 and a combined SAT score of 1800 or 26 or above on the ACT. Transfers and students already enrolled at the university should have a cumulative GPA of at least 3.3 based on a minimum of 12 semester hours.

Majors. Area/ethnic studies: African-American, women's. **Biology:** General. **Business:** Accounting, actuarial science, business admin, finance, hotel/motel admin, insurance, managerial economics, marketing, real estate. **Communications:** General, journalism. **Computer sciences:** General, computer science. **Education:** Art, early childhood, middle, physical. **English:** English lit, speech/rhetoric. **Family/consumer sciences:** Food/nutrition. **Foreign languages:** Classics, French, German, Spanish. **Health:** Nursing (RN), respiratory therapy technology. **History:** General. **Math:** General, applied. **Parks/recreation:** Exercise sciences, facilities management, health/fitness. **Philosophy/religion:** Philosophy, religion. **Physical sciences:** Chemistry, geology, physics. **Protective services:** Criminal justice. **Psychology:** General. **Public administration:** Social work. **Social sciences:** Anthropology, economics, geography, political science, sociology, urban studies. **Visual/performing arts:** Art, film/cinema, music management, music performance.

Most popular majors. Business/marketing 31%, communications/journalism 6%, education 6%, psychology 9%, social sciences 13%, visual/performing arts 7%.

Computing on campus. 395 workstations in library, computer center. Dormitories wired for high-speed internet access and linked to campus network. Commuter students can connect to campus network. Online course registration, online library, helpline, student web hosting, wireless network available.

Student life. Freshman orientation: Mandatory, $56 fee. Preregistration for classes offered. Offered at the beginning of each semester. **Policies:** Freshmen permitted cars on campus. **Housing:** Coed dorms, apartments, substance-free housing available. $475 nonrefundable deposit, deadline 5/1. **Activities:** Bands, choral groups, dance, drama, film society, literary magazine, music ensembles, radio station, student government, student newspaper, TV station, Amnesty International club, Black Student Alliance, Campus Civitan, Campus Crusade for Christ, council on Interfaith concerns, global outreach campus Ministries, College Republicans, international student association council, Toastmasters, Young Democrats.

Athletics. NCAA. **Intercollegiate:** Baseball M, basketball, cross-country, golf, soccer, softball W, tennis, track and field, volleyball W. **Intramural:** Basketball, bowling, football (non-tackle), golf, racquetball, soccer, softball, table tennis, tennis, volleyball. **Team name:** Panthers.

Student services. Career counseling, student employment services, financial aid counseling, health services, minority student services, on-campus daycare, personal counseling, placement for graduates, veterans' counselor, women's services. **Physically disabled:** Services for visually, speech, hearing impaired.

Contact. E-mail: admissions@gsu.edu
Phone: (404) 651-2365 Fax: (404) 651-4811
Diane Weber, Director of Admissions, Georgia State University, Box 4009, Atlanta, GA 30302-4009

Herzing College

Atlanta, Georgia
www.herzing.edu **CB code: 2342**

- For-profit 3-year business and technical college
- Commuter campus in very large city

General. Founded in 1949. Accredited by ACICS. **Location:** 120 miles from Birmingham, Alabama, 70 miles from Chattanooga, Tennessee. **Calendar:** Semester.

Annual costs/financial aid. Tuition/fees (2005-2006): $9,000. Tuition includes use of books. One-time $100 fee for technology programs; one-time $300 fee for engineering programs. On-line courses are an additional $30 per hour. Need-based financial aid available to full-time and part-time students.

Contact. Phone: (404) 816-4533
Director of Admissions, 3393 Peachtree Road, N.E., Atlanta, GA 30326

ITT Technical Institute: Duluth
Duluth, Georgia

- For-profit 4-year technical college
- Commuter campus

General. Accredited by ACICS. **Calendar:** Quarter.

Annual costs/financial aid. Tuition varies by program, $260-$368 per credit hour.

Contact. Phone: (866) 489-8818
Director of Recruitment, 10700 Abbotts Bridge Road, Duluth, GA 30097

Kennesaw State University
Kennesaw, Georgia — **CB member**
www.kennesaw.edu — **CB code: 5359**

- Public 4-year university
- Commuter campus in large town
- 16,599 degree-seeking undergraduates: 32% part-time, 61% women, 8% African American, 2% Asian American, 2% Hispanic American, 8% international
- 1,719 degree-seeking graduate students
- 62% of applicants admitted
- SAT or ACT (ACT writing optional) required
- 32% graduate within 6 years

General. Founded in 1963. Regionally accredited. **Degrees:** 1,908 bachelor's awarded; master's offered. **ROTC:** Army, Air Force. **Location:** 20 miles from Atlanta. **Calendar:** Semester, limited summer session. **Full-time faculty:** 586 total; 71% have terminal degrees, 21% minority, 51% women. **Part-time faculty:** 329 total; 22% have terminal degrees, 10% minority, 60% women. **Class size:** 21% < 20, 58% 20-39, 10% 40-49, 9% 50-99, 1% >100. **Special facilities:** Theater, educational technology center, presentation technology department, teacher resource and activity center, 2 art galleries, multimedia laboratories.

Freshman class profile. 6,658 applied, 4,119 admitted, 2,348 enrolled.

Mid 50% test scores		**Rank in top tenth:**	21%
SAT verbal:	490-570	**Return as sophomores:**	74%
SAT math:	490-560	**Out-of-state:**	4%
ACT:	20-23	**Live on campus:**	41%
GPA 3.50 or higher:	25%	**International:**	6%
GPA 3.0-3.49:	40%	**Fraternities:**	1%
GPA 2.0-2.99:	35%	**Sororities:**	1%
Rank in top quarter:	53%		

Basis for selection. GED not accepted. Applicants must have 2.5 high school GPA in college prep courses and minimum SAT scores of 490 verbal, 460 math, or ACT scores of 20 English, 19 math. Freshman applicants with SAT verbal scores less than 490 and/or math scores less than 460 must take institutional placement exams in appropriate subject areas. Audition required of music majors. Portfolio required of art majors. **Homeschooled:** Students considered based on portfolio, standardized tests scores, extracurricular activities, and recommendations.

High school preparation. 16 units required. Required units include English 4, mathematics 4, social studies 3, science 3 (laboratory 2) and foreign language 2.

2005-2006 Annual costs. Tuition/fees: $3,044; $10,360 out-of-state. Room only: $4,900. Books/supplies: $1,000.

2005-2006 Financial aid. Need-based: 1,836 full-time freshmen applied for aid; 710 were judged to have need; 710 of these received aid. Average need met was 19%. Average scholarship/grant was $2,698; average loan $2,366. 32% of total undergraduate aid awarded as scholarships/grants, 68% as loans/jobs. **Non-need-based:** Scholarships awarded for academics, alumni affiliation, art, athletics, job skills, leadership, minority status, music/drama, state residency.

Application procedures. Admission: Closing date 5/19 (receipt date). $40 fee, may be waived for applicants with need. Application may be submitted online. Admission notification on a rolling basis beginning on or about 1/1. **Financial aid:** Priority date 4/1, closing date 7/1. FAFSA required. Applicants notified on a rolling basis starting 5/15.

Academics. Special study options: Cooperative education, cross-registration, distance learning, double major, ESL, honors, independent study, internships, study abroad, teacher certification program, weekend college. **Credit/placement by examination:** AP, CLEP, IB, institutional tests. 30 credit hours maximum toward bachelor's degree. **Support services:** Learning center, reduced course load, remedial instruction, study skills assistance, tutoring, writing center.

Honors college/program. GPA of 3.5 or higher and 1200+ SAT (exclusive of Writing) for freshmen, and 3.7+ GPA for transfers with 30-60 semester hours of credit. Joint enrollment honors program for high school junior and seniors. Minimum requirements are 3.0 GPA (academic), 530 verbal/530 math SAT scores (1100 or above exclusive of writing) or ACT composite of 25, with minimum English 24 and Math 20 subscores.

Majors. Biology: General, biochemistry, biotechnology. **Business:** Accounting, business admin, finance, managerial economics, marketing, operations. **Communications:** General. **Computer sciences:** General, information systems. **Education:** Art, biology, chemistry, elementary, English, mathematics, middle, music, physical, social studies. **English:** English lit. **Foreign languages:** Romance. **Health:** Nursing (RN). **History:** General. **Math:** General. **Parks/recreation:** Exercise sciences, sports admin. **Physical sciences:** Chemistry. **Protective services:** Criminal justice. **Psychology:** General. **Public administration:** Human services. **Social sciences:** Cartography, international relations, political science, sociology. **Visual/performing arts:** Art, dramatic, music performance.

Most popular majors. Business/marketing 26%, communications/journalism 6%, computer/information sciences 8%, education 20%, health sciences 7%, psychology 6%, social sciences 6%.

Computing on campus. 1,175 workstations in dormitories, library, computer center, student center. Dormitories wired for high-speed internet access. Commuter students can connect to campus network. Online course registration, online library, helpline, wireless network available.

Student life. Freshman orientation: Available, $25 fee. Preregistration for classes offered. Orientation held prior to each semester. **Policies:** Freshmen permitted cars on campus. **Housing:** Apartments available. $340 nonrefundable deposit. On- and off-campus apartment contracts available through third party. **Activities:** Bands, choral groups, dance, drama, literary magazine, music ensembles, musical theater, student government, student newspaper, symphony orchestra, Baptist Student Union, International Student Association, Student Nurses Association, College Ambassadors, Volunteer Kennesaw State, American Marketing Association, African American Student Alliance, Circle K, Catholic Student Association.

Athletics. NCAA. **Intercollegiate:** Baseball M, basketball, cheerleading M, cross-country, golf, ice hockey M, soccer W, softball W, tennis W, track and field. **Intramural:** Basketball, bowling, soccer, softball, swimming, table tennis, tennis, volleyball, wrestling. **Team name:** Fighting Owls.

Student services. Adult student services, alcohol/substance abuse counseling, campus ministries, career counseling, student employment services, financial aid counseling, health services, minority student services, personal counseling, placement for graduates, veterans' counselor. **Physically disabled:** Services for visually, speech, hearing impaired.

Contact. E-mail: ksuadmit@kennesaw.edu
Phone: (770) 423-6300 Fax: (770) 420-4435
Joe Head, Dean of Enrollment Services and Director of Admissions, Kennesaw State University, 1000 Chastain Road, Kennesaw, GA 30144-5591

LaGrange College
LaGrange, Georgia — **CB member**
www.lagrange.edu — **CB code: 5362**

- Private 4-year liberal arts college affiliated with United Methodist Church
- Residential campus in large town
- 986 degree-seeking undergraduates: 9% part-time, 61% women, 20% African American, 1% Asian American, 1% Hispanic American, 1% Native American, 1% international

- 60 degree-seeking graduate students
- 48% of applicants admitted
- SAT or ACT with writing, application essay required
- 39% graduate within 6 years; 18% enter graduate study

General. Founded in 1831. Regionally accredited. **Degrees:** 212 bachelor's, 8 associate awarded; master's offered. **Location:** 70 miles from Atlanta, 45 miles from Columbus. **Calendar:** 4-1-4, limited summer session. **Full-time faculty:** 65 total; 82% have terminal degrees, 8% minority, 43% women. **Part-time faculty:** 64 total; 27% have terminal degrees, 8% minority, 53% women. **Class size:** 86% < 20, 13% 20-39, less than 1% 50-99. **Special facilities:** 750 seat auditorium, natatorium, museum, historical archives.

Freshman class profile. 1,247 applied, 604 admitted, 204 enrolled.

Mid 50% test scores		**Rank in top tenth:**	21%
SAT verbal:	450-570	**End year in good standing:**	94%
SAT math:	460-560	**Return as sophomores:**	78%
ACT:	18-24	**Out-of-state:**	8%
GPA 3.50 or higher:	32%	**Live on campus:**	82%
GPA 3.0-3.49:	34%	**International:**	5%
GPA 2.0-2.99:	34%	**Fraternities:**	36%
Rank in top quarter:	40%	**Sororities:**	40%

Basis for selection. School achievement record and test scores most important. Interview and recommendations considered. Separate application typically during sophomore year for nursing applicants. Students undergo a writing sample and math placement test prior to registration. **Homeschooled:** Bibliography of high school readings, including textbooks, 2 letters of recommendation, one from outside the home, required. Interview suggested.

High school preparation. 16 units required. Required units include English 4, mathematics 4, social studies 3, science 3 and foreign language 2.

2005-2006 Annual costs. Tuition/fees: $16,200. Room/board: $6,675. Books/supplies: $750. Personal expenses: $1,800.

2004-2005 Financial aid. Need-based: 194 full-time freshmen applied for aid; 164 were judged to have need; 164 of these received aid. Average need met was 86%. Average scholarship/grant was $12,796; average loan $2,717. 67% of total undergraduate aid awarded as scholarships/grants, 33% as loans/jobs. **Non-need-based:** Awarded to 289 full-time undergraduates, including 95 freshmen. Scholarships awarded for academics, art, leadership, minority status, music/drama, religious affiliation, state residency.

Application procedures. Admission: No deadline. $20 fee, may be waived for applicants with need. Admission notification on a rolling basis beginning on or about 9/15. Early admission candidates must be highly recommended by counselors and parents. **Financial aid:** Closing date 3/15. FAFSA, institutional form required. Applicants notified on a rolling basis starting 3/1; must reply by 8/15 or within 2 week(s) of notification.

Academics. Special study options: Accelerated study, double major, dual enrollment of high school students, independent study, internships, liberal arts/career combination, study abroad, teacher certification program. **Credit/placement by examination:** AP, CLEP, IB, SAT, institutional tests. 27 credit hours maximum toward bachelor's degree. **Support services:** Tutoring, writing center.

Majors. Biology: General, biochemistry. **Business:** General, accounting, business admin. **Computer sciences:** General, computer science. **Education:** General, early childhood, elementary, middle. **English:** English lit. **Foreign languages:** Spanish. **Health:** Nursing (RN). **History:** General. **Math:** General. **Philosophy/religion:** Religion. **Physical sciences:** Chemistry. **Psychology:** General. **Public administration:** Social work. **Social sciences:** Political science. **Theology:** Religious ed. **Visual/performing arts:** General, dramatic.

Most popular majors. Biology 7%, business/marketing 41%, education 7%, health sciences 7%, psychology 7%, public administration/social services 7%, visual/performing arts 11%.

Computing on campus. 175 workstations in dormitories, library, computer center. Dormitories wired for high-speed internet access and linked to campus network. Commuter students can connect to campus network. Online course registration, helpline, student web hosting available.

Student life. Freshman orientation: Mandatory. Preregistration for classes offered. Number of 1-day summer orientation sessions available. **Policies:** Freshmen permitted cars on campus. **Housing:** Guaranteed on-campus for freshmen. Coed dorms, single-sex dorms, apartments, substance-free housing available. $100 deposit, deadline 5/1. **Activities:** Choral groups, drama, literary magazine, music ensembles, musical theater, student government, student newspaper, Wesley Fellowship, Baptist Student Union, Circle-K, Rotaract, Interfaith Council, volunteer corps, Habitat for Humanity, Catholic group.

Athletics. NCAA. **Intercollegiate:** Baseball M, basketball, cheerleading M, cross-country, football (tackle) M, golf M, soccer, softball W, swimming, tennis, volleyball W. **Intramural:** Basketball, football (tackle) M, softball, volleyball. **Team name:** Panthers.

Student services. Adult student services, campus ministries, career counseling, student employment services, financial aid counseling, personal counseling, placement for graduates.

Contact. E-mail: admission@lagrange.edu
Phone: (706) 880-8005 Toll-free number: (800) 593-2885
Fax: (706) 880-8010
Wells Shepard, Director of Admissions, LaGrange College, 601 Broad Street, LaGrange, GA 30240-2999

Life University
Marietta, Georgia
www.life.edu **CB code: 7006**

- Private 4-year university
- Large city
- 476 degree-seeking undergraduates: 6% African American, 2% Asian American, 1% Hispanic American
- 997 graduate students
- SAT or ACT (ACT writing optional) required

General. Accredited by ACCSCT. **Degrees:** 59 bachelor's, 1 associate awarded; master's, first professional offered. **Location:** 10 miles from downtown Atlanta. **Calendar:** Quarter, limited summer session. **Full-time faculty:** 93 total; 86% have terminal degrees, 31% minority, 34% women. **Part-time faculty:** 15 total. **Class size:** 63% < 20, 23% 20-39, 1% 40-49, 13% 50-99.

Freshman class profile. 430 applied, 257 admitted, 157 enrolled.

Mid 50% test scores		**SAT math:**	440-500
SAT verbal:	420-530	**ACT:**	17-21

Basis for selection. Open admission, but selective for some programs. Standardized test scores and high school record most important. High School GPA of 2.0 or better and SAT score of 1430 (including writing) or ACT score of 18. **Homeschooled:** Transcript of courses and grades required. **Learning Disabled:** Letter from doctor required.

2006-2007 Annual costs. Tuition/fees (projected): $6,975. Books/supplies: $760.

2004-2005 Financial aid. Need-based: 78 full-time freshmen applied for aid; 71 were judged to have need; 68 of these received aid. Average need met was 38%. Average scholarship/grant was $4,200; average loan $3,100. 26% of total undergraduate aid awarded as scholarships/grants, 74% as loans/jobs. **Non-need-based:** Awarded to 121 full-time undergraduates, including 35 freshmen. Scholarships awarded for academics.

Application procedures. Admission: Closing date 9/1 (postmark date). $50 fee, may be waived for applicants with need. Application may be submitted online. Admission notification on a rolling basis. **Financial aid:** Priority date 3/1; no closing date. FAFSA, institutional form required. Applicants notified on a rolling basis.

Academics. Special study options: Accelerated study, double major, ESL, independent study, internships. **Credit/placement by examination:** AP, CLEP, SAT, ACT. **Support services:** Learning center, reduced course load, remedial instruction, study skills assistance, tutoring, writing center.

Majors. Biology: General. **Business:** General, business admin. **Computer sciences:** Information systems. **Education:** General. **Health:** Health care admin. **Interdisciplinary:** Nutrition sciences. **Parks/recreation:** Exercise sciences.

Computing on campus. Commuter students can connect to campus network. Online course registration, online library, wireless network available.

Student life. Freshman orientation: Mandatory. Orientation is held quarterly. It is a two-day orientation usually held on Thursday & Friday before each quarter begins. **Policies:** Freshmen permitted cars on campus. **Housing:** Apartments available. **Activities:** Student government.

Athletics. Intramural: Basketball, football (tackle), volleyball. **Team name:** Eagles.

Student services. Alcohol/substance abuse counseling, financial aid counseling, personal counseling.

Contact. E-mail: admissions@life.edu
Phone: (770) 426-2884 Toll-free number: (800) 543-3202
Fax: (770) 428-9886
Deborah Heairlston, Director of New Student Development, Life University, 1269 Barclay Circle, Marietta, GA 30060

Macon State College

Macon, Georgia — **CB member**
www.maconstate.edu — **CB code: 5439**

- Public 4-year business and health science college
- Commuter campus in small city
- 5,894 degree-seeking undergraduates: 53% part-time, 69% women, 40% African American, 2% Asian American, 2% Hispanic American
- 82% of applicants admitted

General. Founded in 1968. Regionally accredited. **Degrees:** 227 bachelor's, 363 associate awarded. **Location:** 85 miles from Atlanta. **Calendar:** Semester, extensive summer session. **Full-time faculty:** 172 total; 56% have terminal degrees, 58% women. **Part-time faculty:** 98 total. **Class size:** 40% < 20, 56% 20-39, 4% 40-49. **Special facilities:** Botanical gardens.

Freshman class profile. 1,201 applied, 989 admitted, 953 enrolled.

Mid 50% test scores		ACT:	16-19
SAT verbal:	400-520	Out-of-state:	2%
SAT math:	390-510		

Basis for selection. For unconditional admission SAT verbal 480 or ACT English 21, or SAT math 440 or ACT math 19 required. For early admission applicants or joint high school enrollment applicants, minimum SAT composite (exclusive of writing) of 1010, SAT verbal 530 and 3.0 academic high school GPA required. College-preparatory requirements waived for students in career programs and adult applicants. SAT or ACT recommended. Interview required for respiratory therapy, health information technology, health information management, health services administration, and technology programs. **Homeschooled:** Recent GED or home-schooled applicants must submit SAT and provide portfolio indicating courses taken from grades 9-12.

High school preparation. College-preparatory program required. 16 units required. Required units include English 4, mathematics 4, social studies 1, history 2, science 3 (laboratory 2) and foreign language 2.

2005-2006 Annual costs. Tuition/fees: $1,730; $6,354 out-of-state. Books/supplies: $800. Personal expenses: $3,000.

2004-2005 Financial aid. All financial aid based on need. Average scholarship/grant was $3,152; average loan $2,158. 55% of total undergraduate aid awarded as scholarships/grants, 45% as loans/jobs.

Application procedures. Admission: Closing date 7/23 (receipt date). $20 fee, may be waived for applicants with need. Application may be submitted online. Admission notification on a rolling basis. **Financial aid:** Priority date 4/1; no closing date. FAFSA required. Applicants notified on a rolling basis starting 4/15; must reply within 2 week(s) of notification.

Academics. Special study options: Distance learning, dual enrollment of high school students, honors, internships, liberal arts/career combination, study abroad, teacher certification program. **Credit/placement by examination:** AP, CLEP, IB, institutional tests. 40 credit hours maximum toward associate degree, 40 toward bachelor's. **Support services:** Learning center, pre-admission summer program, reduced course load, remedial instruction, study skills assistance, tutoring, writing center.

Majors. Business: Business admin. **Communications:** General. **Computer sciences:** Applications programming, information systems, programming. **Education:** Early childhood. **Health:** Health care admin, health services, medical records admin, nursing (RN). **Public administration:** Human services.

Most popular majors. Business/marketing 37%, computer/information sciences 40%, health sciences 11%, public administration/social services 9%.

Computing on campus. 150 workstations in library, computer center, student center. Commuter students can connect to campus network. Online course registration, online library, helpline, wireless network available.

Student life. Freshman orientation: Available, $25 fee. Preregistration for classes offered. **Policies:** Freshmen permitted cars on campus. **Activities:** Choral groups, drama, literary magazine, music ensembles, musical theater, student government, student newspaper, TV station, Black Student Unification, Association of Nursing Students, Spanish club, Baptist student union, astronomy club, pre-med club, honors student association, Amnesty International, information technology club.

Athletics. Intramural: Basketball, bowling, golf, softball, swimming, table tennis, tennis, volleyball.

Student services. Career counseling, student employment services, financial aid counseling, health services, minority student services, personal counseling, veterans' counselor.

Contact. E-mail: mscinfo@mail.maconstate.edu
Phone: (478) 471-2800 Toll-free number: (800) 272-7619
Fax: (478) 471-5343
Dee Minter, Associate Vice President for Enrollment Management, Macon State College, 100 College Station Drive, Macon, GA 31206-5145

Medical College of Georgia

Augusta, Georgia — **CB member**
www.mcg.edu — **CB code: 5406**

- Public upper-division health science college
- Commuter campus in large city
- 28% of applicants admitted
- Test scores, application essay required

General. Founded in 1828. Regionally accredited. **Degrees:** 366 bachelor's awarded; master's, doctoral, first professional offered. **Location:** 157 miles from Atlanta. **Calendar:** Semester. **Full-time faculty:** 667 total; 87% have terminal degrees, 20% minority, 32% women. **Part-time faculty:** 129 total; 88% have terminal degrees, 12% minority, 39% women. **Special facilities:** 600-bed teaching hospital, over 80 clinics.

Student profile. 717 degree-seeking undergraduates, 1,396 degree-seeking graduate students. 3,794 applied as first time-transfer students, 1,071 admitted, 775 enrolled.

Women:	84%	International:	2%
African American:	14%	Part-time:	8%
Asian American:	3%	Out-of-state:	7%
Hispanic American:	2%	Live on campus:	10%
Native American:	1%	25 or older:	53%

Basis for selection. College transcript, application essay, standardized test scores required. Admission based on GPA, math and science test scores, 3 references, and statement of purpose. SAT or ACT and personal interview required. Minimum of 60 semester hours of transferable prescribed liberal arts courses required. Closing dates and score reports vary by program. Transfer accepted as juniors.

2005-2006 Annual costs. Tuition/fees: $4,224; $15,138 out-of-state. Room only: $2,586.

Financial aid. Need-based: Average need met was 51%. 30% of total undergraduate aid awarded as scholarships/grants, 70% as loans/jobs. **Non-need-based:** Scholarships awarded for academics, state residency. **Additional information:** State Hope scholarships only available to Georgia residents.

Application procedures. Admission: Rolling admission. $30 fee. **Financial aid:** Priority date 3/31, closing date 5/30.

Academics. Special study options: Distance learning, internships, liberal arts/career combination, study abroad. Cooperative program with Augusta State University. **Credit/placement by examination:** AP, CLEP.

Majors. Health: Clinical lab technology, dental hygiene, medical radiologic technology/radiation therapy, medical records admin, physician assistant, preop/surgical nursing, respiratory therapy technology, sonography.

Computing on campus. 323 workstations in library, student center. Commuter students can connect to campus network. Online library, wireless network available.

Student life. Housing: Coed dorms, apartments, substance-free housing available. **Activities:** Student government, student newspaper, Christian Medical Society, Black Student Medical Alliance.

Athletics. Intramural: Badminton, basketball, football (non-tackle), golf, racquetball, soccer, softball, table tennis, volleyball, weight lifting.

Student services. Career counseling, student employment services, health services, minority student services, on-campus daycare, personal counseling.

Contact. E-mail: underadm@mcg.edu
Phone: (706) 721-2725 Toll-free number: (800) 519-3388
Fax: (706) 721-7279
Carol Nobles, Director of Student Recruitment and Admissions, Medical College of Georgia, Office of Academic Admissions, Room 170 Kelly Building, Augusta, GA 30912-7310

Mercer University

Macon, Georgia — **CB member**
www.mercer.edu — **CB code: 5409**

- Private 4-year university affiliated with Baptist faith
- Residential campus in small city
- 2,355 degree-seeking undergraduates: 2% part-time, 55% women, 16% African American, 5% Asian American, 2% Hispanic American, 2% international
- 2,265 degree-seeking graduate students
- 80% of applicants admitted
- SAT or ACT (ACT writing recommended) required
- 54% graduate within 6 years; 20% enter graduate study

General. Founded in 1833. Regionally accredited. Undergraduate profile based on traditional program at Macon campus. Evening and weekend continuing education programs available at 4 regional academic centers; transfer degree programs offered at Atlanta campus. **Degrees:** 1,089 bachelor's awarded; master's, doctoral, first professional offered. **ROTC:** Army. **Location:** 85 miles from Atlanta. **Calendar:** Semester, extensive summer session. **Full-time faculty:** 345 total; 86% have terminal degrees, 14% minority, 39% women. **Part-time faculty:** 269 total; 42% have terminal degrees, 18% minority, 50% women. **Class size:** 56% < 20, 40% 20-39, 2% 40-49, 2% 50-99, less than 1% >100.

Freshman class profile. 3,108 applied, 2,486 admitted, 616 enrolled.

Mid 50% test scores		**Rank in top tenth:**	48%
SAT verbal:	530-640	**End year in good standing:**	85%
SAT math:	550-640	**Return as sophomores:**	80%
ACT:	22-27	**Out-of-state:**	25%
GPA 3.50 or higher:	68%	**Live on campus:**	90%
GPA 3.0-3.49:	26%	**International:**	1%
GPA 2.0-2.99:	6%	**Fraternities:**	19%
Rank in top quarter:	74%	**Sororities:**	24%

Basis for selection. GED not accepted. Based on academic merit. GPA and SAT scores important. Extracurricular activities also important. Interview recommended. Audition recommended for music majors. **Homeschooled:** Minimum SAT of 1100 (exclusive of Writing), certified transcript indicating college-preparatory curriculum including name and title of textbooks used, interview. SAT exams may be substituted for certified transcript. **Learning Disabled:** Documentation from licensed professional required.

High school preparation. 16 units required. Required units include English 4, mathematics 4, social studies 1, history 2, science 3 and foreign language 2.

2005-2006 Annual costs. Tuition/fees: $23,460. Room/board: $7,413. Books/supplies: $900. Personal expenses: $800.

2005-2006 Financial aid. Need-based: 537 full-time freshmen applied for aid; 418 were judged to have need; 417 of these received aid. Average need met was 93%. Average scholarship/grant was $15,670; average loan $5,006. 74% of total undergraduate aid awarded as scholarships/grants, 26% as loans/jobs. **Non-need-based:** Awarded to 1,340 full-time undergraduates, including 379 freshmen. Scholarships awarded for academics, art, athletics, job skills, leadership, music/drama, religious affiliation, ROTC, state residency.

Application procedures. Admission: Priority date 4/1; deadline 7/1 (postmark date). $50 fee, may be waived for applicants with need. Application may be submitted online. Admission notification on a rolling basis beginning on or about 11/1. Must reply by May 1 or within 4 week(s) if notified thereafter. **Financial aid:** Priority date 4/1; no closing date. FAFSA, institutional form required. Applicants notified on a rolling basis starting 3/15; must reply within 2 week(s) of notification.

Academics. Special study options: Accelerated study, combined bachelor's/graduate degree, cooperative education, cross-registration, double major, dual enrollment of high school students, honors, independent study, internships, liberal arts/career combination, student-designed major, study abroad, teacher certification program. Great Books Program alternative to standard requirements. **Credit/placement by examination:** AP, CLEP, IB, SAT, ACT. 32 credit hours maximum toward bachelor's degree. **Support services:** Learning center, pre-admission summer program, reduced course load, study skills assistance, tutoring, writing center.

Majors. Area/ethnic studies: African-American, regional. **Biology:** General, biochemistry. **Business:** General. **Communications:** Journalism, media studies. **Computer sciences:** Computer science, information systems. **Conservation:** Environmental science. **Education:** Elementary, middle, music. **Engineering:** General. **English:** English lit. **Foreign languages:** Classics, French, German, Latin, Spanish. **Health:** Nursing (RN), predentistry, premedicine. **History:** General. **Liberal arts:** Arts/sciences. **Math:** General. **Philosophy/religion:** Christian, philosophy. **Physical sciences:** Chemistry, physics. **Protective services:** Criminal justice. **Psychology:** General. **Public administration:** Community org/advocacy. **Social sciences:** Economics, international relations, political science, sociology. **Visual/performing arts:** Art, dramatic, music performance.

Most popular majors. Business/marketing 22%, communication technologies 8%, education 7%, engineering/engineering technologies 18%, psychology 7%, social sciences 10%.

Computing on campus. 930 workstations in dormitories, library, computer center, student center. Dormitories wired for high-speed internet access and linked to campus network. Commuter students can connect to campus network. Online course registration, online library, helpline, repair service, wireless network available.

Student life. Freshman orientation: Mandatory, $100 fee. Preregistration for classes offered. One-day summer orientation and 4 days in the fall before semester begins. **Policies:** Alcohol not permitted on campus. Freshmen permitted cars on campus. **Housing:** Guaranteed on-campus for freshmen. Coed dorms, single-sex dorms, special housing for disabled, apartments, fraternity/sorority housing available. . **Activities:** Bands, choral groups, dance, drama, film society, literary magazine, music ensembles, opera, student government, student newspaper, Baptist Student Union, Reformed University Fellowship, Habitat for Humanity, Organization of Black Students, International Student Association, Catholic Newman Center, College Republicans, College Democrats, Hispanic Latino Student Union, Islamic student organization.

Athletics. NCAA. **Intercollegiate:** Baseball M, basketball, cross-country, golf, rifle, soccer, softball W, tennis, volleyball W. **Intramural:** Basketball, bowling, football (non-tackle), golf, racquetball, soccer, softball, tennis, volleyball, water polo. **Team name:** Bears.

Student services. Adult student services, alcohol/substance abuse counseling, campus ministries, career counseling, services for economically disadvantaged, student employment services, financial aid counseling, health services, minority student services, personal counseling, placement for graduates. **Physically disabled:** Services for visually, speech, hearing impaired.

Contact. E-mail: admissions@mercer.edu
Phone: (478) 301-2650 Toll-free number: (800) 637-2378
Fax: (478) 301-2828
John Cole, Vice President, University Admissions, Mercer University, 1400 Coleman Avenue, Macon, GA 31207-0001

Morehouse College

Atlanta, Georgia — **CB member**
www.morehouse.edu — **CB code: 5415**

- Private 4-year liberal arts college for men
- Residential campus in very large city
- 3,029 degree-seeking undergraduates: 6% part-time, 96% African American, 1% international
- 53% of applicants admitted
- SAT or ACT with writing required
- 50% graduate within 6 years

General. Founded in 1867. Regionally accredited. One of 5 members of Atlanta University Center sharing facilities including library. **Degrees:** 434 bachelor's awarded. **ROTC:** Army, Navy, Air Force. **Calendar:** Semester, limited summer session. **Full-time faculty:** 167 total; 62% have terminal degrees, 82% minority, 34% women. **Part-time faculty:** 56 total; 71% have terminal degrees, 89% minority, 29% women. **Class size:** 41% < 20, 53% 20-39, 3% 40-49, 2% 50-99, 1% >100. **Special facilities:** Chapels, meditation room.

Freshman class profile. 2,520 applied, 1,327 admitted, 682 enrolled.

Mid 50% test scores		Rank in top quarter:	41%
SAT verbal:	470-580	Rank in top tenth:	18%
SAT math:	470-590	End year in good standing:	83%
ACT:	19-24	Return as sophomores:	84%
GPA 3.50 or higher:	30%	Out-of-state:	73%
GPA 3.0-3.49:	38%	Live on campus:	93%
GPA 2.0-2.99:	28%	International:	3%

Basis for selection. School academic record most important, followed by test scores, counselor recommendation, school and community activities, and student leadership. Interview recommended.

High school preparation. 13 units required; 16 recommended. Required and recommended units include English 4, mathematics 3, social studies 2, science 2 and foreign language 2. 3 additional units may be from any academic discipline.

2005-2006 Annual costs. Tuition/fees: $16,684. Room/board: $9,066. Books/supplies: $850. Personal expenses: $3,800.

2005-2006 Financial aid. **Need-based:** Average need met was 58%. Average scholarship/grant was $3,819; average loan $2,625. 23% of total undergraduate aid awarded as scholarships/grants, 77% as loans/jobs. **Non-need-based:** Scholarships awarded for academics, alumni affiliation, art, athletics, leadership, music/drama, ROTC, state residency.

Application procedures. **Admission:** Priority date 11/1; deadline 2/15. $45 fee, may be waived for applicants with need. Application must be submitted on paper. Admission notification 4/1. Admission notification on a rolling basis. Must reply by 5/15. **Financial aid:** Closing date 4/1. FAFSA, institutional form, CSS PROFILE required. Applicants notified by 5/1.

Academics. **Special study options:** Combined bachelor's/graduate degree, cooperative education, cross-registration, double major, dual enrollment of high school students, exchange student, honors, internships, liberal arts/career combination, semester at sea, study abroad. Dual degree program in engineering and architecture with other institutions. **Credit/placement by examination:** AP, CLEP, SAT, ACT, institutional tests. 30 credit hours maximum toward bachelor's degree. **Support services:** Learning center, pre-admission summer program, reduced course load, remedial instruction, study skills assistance, tutoring, writing center.

Majors. **Area/ethnic studies:** African-American. **Biology:** General. **Business:** Business admin, managerial economics. **Computer sciences:** General. **Education:** General, elementary, middle, physical, secondary. **Engineering:** General. **English:** English lit. **Foreign languages:** French, German, linguistics, Spanish. **History:** General. **Math:** General. **Parks/recreation:** Health/fitness. **Philosophy/religion:** Philosophy, religion. **Physical sciences:** Chemistry, physics. **Psychology:** General. **Social sciences:** Economics, international relations, political science, sociology, urban studies. **Visual/performing arts:** Dramatic, studio arts.

Most popular majors. Biology 6%, business/marketing 35%, English 7%, mathematics 6%, psychology 7%, social sciences 19%.

Computing on campus. 300 workstations in dormitories, library, computer center. Dormitories linked to campus network. Commuter students can connect to campus network. Online course registration, online library, helpline, repair service, wireless network available.

Student life. **Freshman orientation:** Mandatory. Preregistration for classes offered. Held several days before class begins each fall. **Policies:** Freshmen permitted cars on campus. **Housing:** Guaranteed on-campus for freshmen. Apartments, substance-free housing available. $7,725 partly refundable deposit, deadline 6/24. **Activities:** Bands, choral groups, drama, literary magazine, music ensembles, student government, student newspaper, Martin Luther King International Chapel Assistants, international student association, mentoring program, Frederick Douglass Tutorial Program, political science club, New Life Inspirational Gospel Choir, NAACP, Eagle Scout Association.

Athletics. NCAA. **Intercollegiate:** Baseball M, basketball M, cross-country M, football (tackle) M, golf M, soccer M, tennis M, track and field M. **Intramural:** Baseball M, basketball M, bowling M, soccer M, softball M, swimming M, table tennis M, tennis M. **Team name:** Maroon Tigers.

Student services. Alcohol/substance abuse counseling, campus ministries, career counseling, student employment services, financial aid counseling, health services, personal counseling, placement for graduates, veterans' counselor. **Physically disabled:** Services for visually, speech, hearing impaired.

Contact. E-mail: admissions@morehouse.edu
Phone: (404) 681-2800 ext. 2632 Toll-free number: (800) 851-1254
Fax: (404) 524-5635
Terrance Dixon, Associate Dean of Admissions and Records, Morehouse College, 830 Westview Drive SW, Atlanta, GA 30314

North Georgia College & State University

Dahlonega, Georgia — CB member
www.ngcsu.edu — CB code: 5497

- Public 4-year comprehensive state university with military college
- Commuter campus in small town
- 4,144 degree-seeking undergraduates: 19% part-time, 62% women, 3% African American, 1% Asian American, 3% Hispanic American, 1% international
- 575 graduate students
- 68% of applicants admitted
- SAT or ACT (ACT writing optional) required
- 45% graduate within 6 years

General. Founded in 1873. Regionally accredited. 4 years Army ROTC required of all resident male undergraduate students. Military service following graduation not mandatory. **Degrees:** 669 bachelor's, 117 associate awarded; master's offered. **ROTC:** Army. **Location:** 70 miles from Atlanta. **Calendar:** Semester, extensive summer session. **Full-time faculty:** 191 total; 68% have terminal degrees, 7% minority, 49% women. **Part-time faculty:** 123 total; 48% have terminal degrees, 3% minority, 58% women. **Class size:** 38% < 20, 54% 20-39, 6% 40-49, 3% 50-99. **Special facilities:** Observatory, rappeling tower, planetarium, nature preserve.

Freshman class profile. 2,081 applied, 1,413 admitted, 731 enrolled.

Mid 50% test scores		GPA 2.0-2.99:	23%
SAT verbal:	500-590	Rank in top quarter:	57%
SAT math:	490-570	Rank in top tenth:	24%
ACT:	20-24	Out-of-state:	6%
GPA 3.50 or higher:	38%	Live on campus:	56%
GPA 3.0-3.49:	39%	International:	1%

Basis for selection. High school academic record, test scores important, disciplinary record considered. Students must provide certification of immunization against communicable diseases. Commuting students must apply for permission to commute. Audition recommended for music majors. Portfolio recommended for art majors. **Homeschooled:** SAT Subject Tests required.

High school preparation. 17 units required. Required units include English 4, mathematics 4, social studies 3, science 3 (laboratory 1) and foreign language 2.

2005-2006 Annual costs. Tuition/fees: $3,044; $10,360 out-of-state. Room/board: $4,596. Books/supplies: $500. Personal expenses: $1,000.

2004-2005 Financial aid. **Need-based:** 214 full-time freshmen applied for aid; 214 were judged to have need; 214 of these received aid. Average need met was 35%. Average scholarship/grant was $2,562; average loan $2,009. 42% of total undergraduate aid awarded as scholarships/grants, 58% as loans/jobs. **Non-need-based:** Awarded to 2,163 full-time undergraduates, including 642 freshmen. Scholarships awarded for academics, alumni affiliation, art, athletics, leadership, music/drama, ROTC, state residency. **Additional information:** Aid to international students limited to fee waiver for cadets.

Application procedures. **Admission:** Closing date 7/1. $25 fee, may be waived for applicants with need. Application may be submitted online. Admission notification on a rolling basis. Must reply by 5/1. **Financial aid:** Priority date 5/1; no closing date. FAFSA, institutional form required. Applicants notified on a rolling basis starting 5/15; must reply within 3 week(s) of notification.

Academics. **Special study options:** Combined bachelor's/graduate degree, cooperative education, distance learning, double major, dual enrollment of high school students, external degree, honors, independent study, internships, liberal arts/career combination, study abroad, teacher certification program. Dual degree program in engineering with Georgia Institute of Technology and Clemson University. **Credit/placement by examination:** AP, CLEP, SAT, ACT, institutional tests. 30 credit hours maximum toward associate degree, 30 toward bachelor's. **Support services:** Learning center, pre-admission summer program, reduced course load, remedial instruction, study skills assistance, tutoring, writing center.

Majors. **Biology:** General. **Business:** Accounting, business admin, finance, marketing. **Computer sciences:** General. **Education:** Art, early childhood, middle, music, physical, special. **Foreign languages:** French, German, Spanish. **Health:** Athletic training, nursing (RN). **History:** General. **Math:** General. **Parks/recreation:** Health/fitness. **Physical sciences:** Chemistry, physics. **Psychology:** General. **Social sciences:** Political science, sociology.

Most popular majors. Biology 7%, business/marketing 30%, education 19%, psychology 6%, social sciences 9%.

Computing on campus. 470 workstations in dormitories, library, computer center, student center. Dormitories linked to campus network. Commuter students can connect to campus network. Online course registration, online library, helpline, student web hosting available.

Student life. Freshman orientation: Available. Preregistration for classes offered. 2.5-day program held 4 times during June, July, August; students stay in residence halls. **Policies:** All male residents must join Corps of Cadets, female residents may join if they desire. Freshmen permitted cars on campus. **Housing:** Coed dorms, single-sex dorms, apartments available. $250 fully refundable deposit, deadline 5/1. **Activities:** Bands, choral groups, drama, literary magazine, music ensembles, student government, student newspaper, symphony orchestra, Students for Social Awareness, Baptist student union, commuter council, Muslim student association, Newman Club, international student association, Model UN, Habitat for Humanity.

Athletics. NCAA. **Intercollegiate:** Baseball M, basketball, cheerleading M, cross-country, rifle, soccer, softball W, tennis, track and field. **Intramural:** Basketball, football (non-tackle) W, football (tackle) M, golf, softball W, table tennis, volleyball, water polo. **Team name:** Saints.

Student services. Alcohol/substance abuse counseling, campus ministries, career counseling, student employment services, financial aid counseling, health services, minority student services, personal counseling, placement for graduates, veterans' counselor. **Physically disabled:** Services for visually, hearing impaired.

Contact. E-mail: admissions@ngcsu.edu
Phone: (706) 864-1800 Toll-free number: (800) 498-9581
Fax: (706) 864-1478
Jennifer Collins, Director of Admissions, North Georgia College & State University, 82 College Circle, Dahlonega, GA 30597

Oglethorpe University

Atlanta, Georgia — **CB member**
www.oglethorpe.edu — **CB code: 5521**

- Private 4-year university and liberal arts college
- Residential campus in very large city
- 975 degree-seeking undergraduates: 12% part-time, 64% women, 21% African American, 4% Asian American, 1% Hispanic American, 2% international
- 65 degree-seeking graduate students
- 64% of applicants admitted
- SAT or ACT (ACT writing recommended) required
- 60% graduate within 6 years

General. Founded in 1835. Regionally accredited. Academic buildings feature English gothic architecture; campus home to Georgia Shakespeare Festival. **Degrees:** 150 bachelor's awarded; master's offered. **Location:** 10 miles from downtown Atlanta. **Calendar:** Semester, limited summer session. **Full-time faculty:** 56 total; 95% have terminal degrees, 9% minority, 34% women. **Part-time faculty:** 59 total; 76% have terminal degrees, 8% minority, 51% women. **Class size:** 79% < 20, 21% 20-39. **Special facilities:** Art museum.

Freshman class profile. 1,236 applied, 794 admitted, 233 enrolled.

Mid 50% test scores			
SAT verbal:	500-630	Rank in top quarter:	57%
SAT math:	470-610	Rank in top tenth:	27%
ACT:	21-27	Return as sophomores:	79%
GPA 3.50 or higher:	46%	Out-of-state:	32%
GPA 3.0-3.49:	35%	Live on campus:	86%
GPA 2.0-2.99:	19%	Fraternities:	33%
		Sororities:	25%

Basis for selection. High school GPA and general academic record most important, followed by test scores. Recommendations required. Activities considered. International students may submit TOEFL in place of SAT or ACT. Interview recommended.

High school preparation. 18 units required. Required and recommended units include English 4, mathematics 3, social studies 3, science 2 and foreign language 2. Honors, AP, IB recommended where available.

2005-2006 Annual costs. Tuition/fees: $22,300. Room/board: $8,000. Books/supplies: $600. Personal expenses: $1,200.

Financial aid. Non-need-based: Scholarships awarded for academics, art, leadership, music/drama.

Application procedures. Admission: No deadline. $35 fee, may be waived for applicants with need. Admission notification on a rolling basis beginning on or about 2/1. Must reply by May 1 or within 3 week(s) if notified thereafter. **Financial aid:** No deadline. FAFSA, institutional form required. Applicants notified on a rolling basis starting 3/1; must reply within 3 week(s) of notification.

Academics. Special study options: Accelerated study, cooperative education, cross-registration, double major, dual enrollment of high school students, honors, independent study, internships, liberal arts/career combination, student-designed major, study abroad, Washington semester. Dual engineering degree program with Auburn University, Georgia Institute of Technology, University of Florida, and University of Southern California; dual art degree program with Atlanta College of Art; Urban Leadership Program. **Credit/placement by examination:** AP, CLEP, institutional tests. 30 credit hours maximum toward bachelor's degree. **Support services:** Learning center.

Majors. Area/ethnic studies: American. **Biology:** General. **Business:** Accounting, managerial economics, organizational behavior. **Communications:** General. **Education:** Early childhood, elementary, middle, secondary. **Health:** Clinical lab science, predentistry, premedicine, prepharmacy, preveterinary. **History:** General. **Interdisciplinary:** Math/computer science. **Legal studies:** Prelaw. **Liberal arts:** Arts/sciences. **Math:** General. **Philosophy/religion:** Philosophy. **Physical sciences:** Chemistry, physics. **Psychology:** General. **Public administration:** Social work. **Social sciences:** Economics, international relations, political science, sociology. **Visual/performing arts:** Art.

Most popular majors. Biology 8%, business/marketing 32%, English 21%, history 6%, psychology 11%, social sciences 9%, visual/performing arts 6%.

Computing on campus. 57 workstations in library, computer center. Dormitories linked to campus network. Commuter students can connect to campus network. Helpline available.

Student life. Housing: Guaranteed on-campus for freshmen. Coed dorms, single-sex dorms, fraternity/sorority housing available. $200 nonrefundable deposit. **Activities:** Choral groups, dance, drama, film society, literary magazine, musical theater, radio station, student government, student newspaper, Catholic Student Association, Black Student Caucus, Oglethorpe Christian Fellowship, International Club, Environmentally Concerned Oglethorpe Students, Oglethorpe Academic Team.

Athletics. NCAA. **Intercollegiate:** Baseball M, basketball, cross-country, golf, soccer, tennis, track and field, volleyball W. **Intramural:** Badminton, basketball, softball, tennis, volleyball.

Student services. Adult student services, career counseling, student employment services, health services, personal counseling, placement for graduates, veterans' counselor. **Physically disabled:** Services for visually impaired.

Contact. E-mail: admission@oglethorpe.edu
Phone: (404) 364-8307 Toll-free number: (800) 428-4484
Fax: (404) 364-8500
Dennis Matthews, Associate Dean for Enrollment Management, Oglethorpe University, 4484 Peachtree Road NE, Atlanta, GA 30319-2797

Paine College

Augusta, Georgia — **CB member**
www.paine.edu — **CB code: 5530**

- Private 4-year liberal arts college affiliated with Christian Methodist Episcopal Church and United Methodist Church
- Residential campus in large city
- 812 degree-seeking undergraduates: 7% part-time, 70% women, 98% African American
- 31% of applicants admitted
- SAT or ACT (ACT writing optional), application essay required
- 28% graduate within 6 years

General. Founded in 1882. Regionally accredited. **Degrees:** 98 bachelor's awarded. **ROTC:** Army. **Location:** 72 miles from Columbia, South Carolina, 150 miles from Atlanta. **Calendar:** Semester, limited summer session. **Full-time faculty:** 74 total; 51% have terminal degrees, 76% minority, 30% women. **Part-time faculty:** 17 total; 29% have terminal degrees, 82% minority, 41% women. **Class size:** 78% < 20, 22% 20-39.

Freshman class profile. 3,683 applied, 1,131 admitted, 1,081 enrolled.

Mid 50% test scores			
SAT verbal:	370-460	GPA 3.0-3.49:	26%
SAT math:	360-450	GPA 2.0-2.99:	53%
ACT:	14-17	Return as sophomores:	60%
GPA 3.50 or higher:	18%	Out-of-state:	18%
		Live on campus:	89%

Basis for selection. School achievement record, test scores, and recommendations considered. Minimum 2.0 high school GPA. College-preparatory program preferred. Interview recommended. Audition required of music education majors if they apply for a scholarship.

High school preparation. College-preparatory program recommended. 16 units recommended. Recommended units include English 4, mathematics 2, social studies 2, science 2 (laboratory 2). Social science recommendation includes 1 history. 6 electives required.

2005-2006 Annual costs. Tuition/fees: $9,690. Room/board: $4,728. Books/supplies: $700. Personal expenses: $2,864.

2005-2006 Financial aid. Need-based: Average need met was 57%. Average scholarship/grant was $6,775; average loan $2,228. 55% of total undergraduate aid awarded as scholarships/grants, 45% as loans/jobs. **Non-need-based:** Scholarships awarded for academics, alumni affiliation, athletics, music/drama, religious affiliation, ROTC.

Application procedures. Admission: Closing date 8/1 (receipt date). $20 fee, may be waived for applicants with need. Application may be submitted online. Admission notification on a rolling basis. **Financial aid:** Priority date 3/1; no closing date. FAFSA, institutional form required. Applicants notified on a rolling basis starting 5/1; must reply within 2 week(s) of notification.

Academics. Special study options: Combined bachelor's/graduate degree, cooperative education, cross-registration, dual enrollment of high school students, honors, independent study, internships, liberal arts/career combination, study abroad, teacher certification program. Dual degree in engineering and mathematics with Florida Agriculture and Mechanical University, Tuskegee University, Tennessee State University. **Credit/placement by examination:** AP, CLEP, SAT, ACT, institutional tests. **Support services:** Learning center, pre-admission summer program, reduced course load, remedial instruction, study skills assistance, tutoring.

Majors. Biology: General. **Business:** Accounting, business admin, international, management information systems, marketing. **Communications:** Broadcast journalism, journalism, public relations. **Conservation:** Environmental science. **Education:** Biology, elementary, English, history, mathematics, middle. **English:** English lit. **History:** General. **Interdisciplinary:** Math/computer science. **Math:** General. **Philosophy/religion:** Philosophy, religion. **Physical sciences:** Chemistry. **Psychology:** General, counseling. **Social sciences:** Criminology, sociology. **Visual/performing arts:** Dramatic.

Most popular majors. Biology 11%, business/marketing 25%, communications/journalism 6%, psychology 8%, social sciences 33%.

Computing on campus. 125 workstations in dormitories, library, computer center, student center. Dormitories wired for high-speed internet access and linked to campus network. Commuter students can connect to campus network. Online course registration, online library, repair service, wireless network available.

Student life. Freshman orientation: Mandatory, $96 fee. Preregistration for classes offered. One week at the beginning of the semester. **Policies:** Freshmen permitted cars on campus. **Housing:** Single-sex dorms, substance-free housing available. $75 nonrefundable deposit, deadline 8/1. **Activities:** Bands, choral groups, dance, drama, literary magazine, music ensembles, student government, student newspaper, Baptist student union, Methodist student union, NAACP, pre-alumni club, international student organization, National Pan Hellenic Council, Alpha Kappa Mu honor society.

Athletics. NCAA. **Intercollegiate:** Baseball M, basketball, cross-country, golf M, softball W, track and field, volleyball W. **Intramural:** Badminton, baseball M, basketball, cross-country, football (tackle) M, softball, table tennis, tennis, track and field, volleyball, weight lifting. **Team name:** Lions.

Student services. Alcohol/substance abuse counseling, campus ministries, career counseling, student employment services, financial aid counseling, health services, personal counseling, placement for graduates, veterans' counselor.

Contact. E-mail: tinsleyj@mail.paine.edu
Phone: (706) 821-8320 Toll-free number: (800) 476-7703
Fax: (706) 821-8648
Joseph Tinsley, Director of Admissions, Paine College, 1235 15th Street, Augusta, GA 30901-3182

Piedmont College

Demorest, Georgia — **CB member**
www.piedmont.edu — **CB code: 5537**

- Private 4-year liberal arts and teachers college affiliated with Congregational Christian Churches of America
- Residential campus in rural community
- 939 degree-seeking undergraduates: 10% part-time, 64% women, 6% African American, 1% Asian American, 2% Hispanic American
- 999 graduate students
- 66% of applicants admitted
- SAT or ACT required
- 42% graduate within 6 years

General. Founded in 1897. Regionally accredited. **Degrees:** 257 bachelor's awarded; master's offered. **Location:** 30 miles from Gainesville, 75 miles from Atlanta. **Calendar:** Semester. **Full-time faculty:** 98 total; 76% have terminal degrees, 5% minority, 51% women. **Part-time faculty:** 100 total; 51% have terminal degrees, 7% minority, 49% women. **Class size:** 83% < 20, 16% 20-39, less than 1% 50-99. **Special facilities:** Science and technology center, botanical center, pipe organ, center for worship and music.

Freshman class profile. 485 applied, 322 admitted, 166 enrolled.

Mid 50% test scores		**GPA 2.0-2.99:**	15%
SAT verbal:	480-570	**Rank in top quarter:**	41%
SAT math:	460-570	**Rank in top tenth:**	18%
ACT:	17-23	**Return as sophomores:**	69%
GPA 3.50 or higher:	47%	**Out-of-state:**	1%
GPA 3.0-3.49:	38%	**Live on campus:**	77%

Basis for selection. Test scores and GPA most important. Essay recommended. Interview recommended for academically weak. **Homeschooled:** Transcript or portfolio detailing high school coursework completed, two letters of recommendation from sources outside home who have knowledge of student's academic/extracurricular achievements, possible interview with student and family.

High school preparation. College-preparatory program recommended. 21 units recommended. Recommended units include English 4, mathematics 3, social studies 1, history 2, science 3 and foreign language 2.

2006-2007 Annual costs. Tuition/fees (projected): $15,500. Room/board: $5,000. Books/supplies: $1,250. Personal expenses: $2,350.

2005-2006 Financial aid. Need-based: 144 full-time freshmen applied for aid; 106 were judged to have need; 106 of these received aid. Average need met was 61%. Average scholarship/grant was $2,097; average loan $2,034. 45% of total undergraduate aid awarded as scholarships/grants, 55% as loans/jobs. **Non-need-based:** Awarded to 660 full-time undergraduates, including 130 freshmen. Scholarships awarded for academics, art, leadership, music/drama, religious affiliation, state residency. **Additional information:** College meets 100% of unmet direct financial need for early applicants through grants, scholarships, and loan programs.

Application procedures. Admission: Closing date 7/1. No application fee. Admission notification 7/1. **Financial aid:** Priority date 5/1; no closing date. FAFSA, institutional form required. Applicants notified on a rolling basis; must reply within 2 week(s) of notification.

Academics. Experiential learning credit allows students to document work experience for college credit as appropriate. **Special study options:** Accelerated study, combined bachelor's/graduate degree, distance learning, double major, dual enrollment of high school students, honors, independent study, internships, student-designed major, study abroad, teacher certification program. **Credit/placement by examination:** AP, CLEP. 30 credit hours maximum toward bachelor's degree. **Support services:** Learning center, study skills assistance, tutoring, writing center.

Majors. Biology: General. **Business:** Business admin. **Communications:** Media studies. **Conservation:** Environmental science. **Education:** Early childhood, middle, special. **English:** English lit. **Foreign languages:** Spanish. **Health:** Nursing (RN). **History:** General. **Interdisciplinary:** Math/computer science. **Math:** General. **Philosophy/religion:** Philosophy, religion. **Physical sciences:** Chemistry. **Protective services:** Criminal justice. **Psychology:** General. **Social sciences:** General, political science, sociology. **Visual/performing arts:** Art, dramatic, studio arts.

Most popular majors. Business/marketing 23%, education 32%, psychology 6%, social sciences 11%.

Computing on campus. 200 workstations in dormitories, library, computer center, student center. Dormitories wired for high-speed internet access and linked to campus network. Commuter students can connect to campus network. Online library available.

Student life. Freshman orientation: Mandatory, $40 fee. Preregistration for classes offered. 3-day weekend with activities for students, resident assistants, faculty and staff. **Policies:** Freshmen permitted cars on campus. **Housing:** Guaranteed on-campus for all undergraduates. Coed dorms, single-sex dorms, special housing for disabled, apartments, substance-free housing available. $100 deposit. Unmarried students under 21 must live in dormitories or with blood relatives. **Activities:** Choral groups, drama, film society, music ensembles, radio station, student government, student newspaper, symphony orchestra, TV station, psychology club, Students in Free Enterprise, Baptist student union, Student Association of Educators, literary society, art club, science club, environmental club, Rotaract, history society.

Athletics. NCAA, NCCAA. **Intercollegiate:** Baseball M, basketball, cross-country, golf, soccer, softball W, tennis, volleyball W. **Intramural:** Basketball, football (non-tackle), soccer, softball, table tennis, volleyball. **Team name:** Lions.

Student services. Campus ministries, career counseling, financial aid counseling, health services, personal counseling, placement for graduates, veterans' counselor.

Contact. E-mail: ugrad@piedmont.edu
Phone: (706) 776-0103 Toll-free number: (800) 277-7020
Fax: (706) 776-6635
Cynthia Peterson, Director of Admissions, Piedmont College, 165 Central Avenue, Demorest, GA 30535-0010

Reinhardt College

Waleska, Georgia — **CB member**
www.reinhardt.edu — **CB code: 5568**

- Private 4-year business and teachers college affiliated with United Methodist Church
- Commuter campus in rural community
- 1,008 degree-seeking undergraduates: 12% part-time, 58% women
- SAT or ACT, application essay required
- 29% graduate within 6 years

General. Founded in 1883. Regionally accredited. Off-campus centers in Alpharetta and Woodstock. **Degrees:** 181 bachelor's, 26 associate awarded. **Location:** 50 miles from Atlanta. **Calendar:** Semester, extensive summer session. **Full-time faculty:** 56 total. **Part-time faculty:** 58 total. **Class size:** 69% < 20, 31% 20-39. **Special facilities:** Indian history museum, visual arts center, performing arts center.

Freshman class profile. 813 applied, 425 admitted, 218 enrolled.

Mid 50% test scores		**Return as sophomores:**	59%
SAT verbal:	450-550	**Out-of-state:**	7%
SAT math:	430-540	**Live on campus:**	60%
End year in good standing:	77%		

Basis for selection. Open admission, but selective for some programs. School achievement record most important, followed by test scores, then recommendations. Interview recommended. Audition required of music majors. Portfolio required of art majors. **Homeschooled:** Transcript of courses and grades, interview required. **Learning Disabled:** Recommend that students be counseled by Academic Support Office.

High school preparation. College-preparatory program recommended. 14 units recommended. Recommended units include English 4, mathematics 4, social studies 3, science 3 and foreign language 2.

2005-2006 Annual costs. Tuition/fees: $13,090. Room/board: $5,900. Books/supplies: $500.

2005-2006 Financial aid. Need-based: 227 full-time freshmen applied for aid; 162 were judged to have need; 162 of these received aid. Average need met was 39%. Average scholarship/grant was $949; average loan $2,090. 37% of total undergraduate aid awarded as scholarships/grants, 63% as loans/jobs. **Non-need-based:** Awarded to 227 full-time undergraduates, including 141 freshmen. Scholarships awarded for academics, alumni affiliation, art, athletics.

Application procedures. Admission: No deadline. $25 fee, may be waived for applicants with need. Application may be submitted online. Admission notification on a rolling basis. **Financial aid:** Priority date 5/1; no closing date. FAFSA, institutional form required. Applicants notified on a rolling basis starting 4/1; must reply within 2 week(s) of notification.

Academics. Emphasis on computer literacy throughout coursework. **Special study options:** Accelerated study, combined bachelor's/graduate degree, double major, dual enrollment of high school students, external degree, honors, independent study, internships, study abroad, teacher certification program. **Credit/placement by examination:** AP, CLEP. 15 credit hours maximum toward associate degree, 30 toward bachelor's. **Support services:** Learning center, pre-admission summer program, reduced course load, remedial instruction, tutoring, writing center.

Majors. Biology: General. **Business:** General, accounting, business admin. **Communications:** General. **Computer sciences:** Information systems. **Education:** Biology, early childhood, elementary, English, middle, music, physical. **History:** General. **Liberal arts:** Arts/sciences. **Parks/recreation:** Sports admin. **Philosophy/religion:** Religion. **Psychology:** General. **Social sciences:** Sociology. **Visual/performing arts:** Studio arts.

Most popular majors. Business/marketing 37%, communications/journalism 7%, education 21%, psychology 7%.

Computing on campus. 165 workstations in dormitories, library, computer center. Dormitories wired for high-speed internet access and linked to campus network. Commuter students can connect to campus network. Online course registration, online library, helpline, repair service, student web hosting, wireless network available.

Student life. Freshman orientation: Mandatory, $35 fee. Preregistration for classes offered. 1-2 day program. **Policies:** Freshmen permitted cars on campus. **Housing:** Guaranteed on-campus for freshmen. Coed dorms, single-sex dorms, apartments, substance-free housing available. $150 partly refundable deposit, deadline 8/1. Honors housing. **Activities:** Choral groups, film society, music ensembles, student government, student newspaper, TV station, Baptist student union, Wesley Foundation, fellowship of Christian athletes, Catholic campus ministry, Reach Out Reinhardt, Phi Theta Kappa, Circle-K.

Athletics. NAIA. **Intercollegiate:** Baseball M, basketball, cheerleading, cross-country, golf M, soccer, softball W, tennis. **Intramural:** Basketball, football (non-tackle), soccer, softball, volleyball. **Team name:** Eagles.

Student services. Adult student services, alcohol/substance abuse counseling, campus ministries, career counseling, student employment services, financial aid counseling, health services, personal counseling, placement for graduates, veterans' counselor. **Physically disabled:** Services for visually, speech, hearing impaired.

Contact. E-mail: admissions@mail.reinhardt.edu
Phone: (770) 720-5526 Toll-free number: (877) 343-4273
Fax: (770) 720-5602
Julie Cook, Director of Admissions, Reinhardt College, 7300 Reinhardt College Circle, Waleska, GA 30183

Savannah College of Art and Design

Savannah, Georgia — **CB member**
www.scad.edu — **CB code: 5631**

- Private 4-year visual arts college
- Commuter campus in small city
- 6,062 degree-seeking undergraduates: 9% part-time, 52% women, 5% African American, 2% Asian American, 4% Hispanic American, 4% international
- 1,214 degree-seeking graduate students
- 68% of applicants admitted
- SAT or ACT (ACT writing optional) required
- 61% graduate within 6 years; 10% enter graduate study

General. Founded in 1978. Regionally accredited. Extensive study abroad program in France at Lacoste School of the Arts. **Degrees:** 1,071 bachelor's awarded; master's offered. **Location:** 150 miles from Jacksonville, Florida, 250 miles from Atlanta. **Calendar:** Quarter, limited summer session. **Full-time faculty:** 366 total; 78% have terminal degrees, 8% minority, 41% women. **Part-time faculty:** 53 total; 91% have terminal degrees, 9% minority, 47% women. **Class size:** 75% < 20, 25% 20-39. **Special facilities:** British American studies center, 2 vintage diners, 10 exhibition galleries, amphitheater, restored 1943 theater.

Freshman class profile. 4,782 applied, 3,251 admitted, 1,407 enrolled.

Mid 50% test scores		**Return as sophomores:**	81%
SAT verbal:	490-600	**Out-of-state:**	85%
SAT math:	480-580	**Live on campus:**	87%
ACT:	20-26	**International:**	2%
End year in good standing:	90%		

Basis for selection. Entrance test scores, 3 letters of recommendation, and high school transcript required. TOEFL is required of all entering students whose first language is not English. Interview, portfolio recommended. Essay recommended for historic preservation, art history, and architectural history programs only. **Homeschooled:** Statement describing homeschool structure and mission, transcript of courses and grades, state high school equivalency certificate required. **Learning Disabled:** Students with learning disabilities are evaluated on an individual basis. Documentation of the specific nature of the disability is required.

2006-2007 Annual costs. Tuition/fees: $22,950. A one-time matriculation fee of $500 is required of all students. Room/board: $9,600. Books/supplies: $1,500. Personal expenses: $1,500.

2005-2006 Financial aid. Need-based: 990 full-time freshmen applied for aid; 762 were judged to have need; 747 of these received aid. Average need met was 10%. Average scholarship/grant was $3,220; average loan $2,590. 24% of total undergraduate aid awarded as scholarships/grants, 76% as loans/jobs. **Non-need-based:** Awarded to 4,057 full-time undergraduates, including 1,152 freshmen. Scholarships awarded for academics, art, music/drama. **Additional information:** Degree-seeking students may be awarded maximum of one scholarship from college, but may receive additional scholarships from other sources, as well as additional forms of financial aid. Scholarships based on academic achievement are awarded through admission office.

Application procedures. Admission: Priority date 4/1; no deadline. $50 fee. Application may be submitted online. Admission notification on a rolling basis. Students encouraged to apply early to gain priority for housing. **Financial aid:** Priority date 2/15; no closing date. FAFSA, institutional form required. Applicants notified on a rolling basis starting 6/1; must reply within 4 week(s) of notification.

Academics. Strong fine arts foundation along with strong liberal arts curriculum. **Special study options:** Distance learning, double major, dual enrollment of high school students, ESL, independent study, internships, New York semester, study abroad. Off-campus programs in Europe and other art centers. **Credit/placement by examination:** AP, CLEP, IB. 15 credit hours maximum toward bachelor's degree. **Support services:** Learning center, pre-admission summer program, reduced course load, study skills assistance, tutoring, writing center.

Majors. Architecture: Architecture, history/criticism. **Communications technology:** Animation/special effects, recording arts. **Computer sciences:** Computer graphics. **Interdisciplinary:** Historic preservation. **Production:** Furniture. **Visual/performing arts:** General, art history/conservation, cinematography, commercial/advertising art, dramatic, fashion design, fiber arts, graphic design, illustration, industrial design, interior design, metal/jewelry, painting, photography.

Most popular majors. Communication technologies 10%, computer/information sciences 10%, visual/performing arts 72%.

Computing on campus. 2,800 workstations in dormitories, library, computer center. Dormitories wired for high-speed internet access and linked to campus network. Commuter students can connect to campus network. Online course registration, online library, helpline, repair service, wireless network available.

Student life. Freshman orientation: Available. Preregistration for classes offered. 2-day program, parents included, summer orientation options available. **Policies:** Freshmen permitted cars on campus. **Housing:** Coed dorms, single-sex dorms, apartments, substance-free housing available. $250 nonrefundable deposit, deadline 6/1. Some apartment-style residence halls with full kitchen facilities available. Students with disabilities are accommodated on an individual basis. **Activities:** Choral groups, dance, drama, music ensembles, musical theater, radio station, student government, student newspaper, TV station, American Institute of Architecture Students, student chapter of American Society of Interior Designers, united student forum, interclub council, inter-hall council, student activities council, intercultural student association, American Society of Heating, Refrigeration and Air Conditioning, engineers student chapter, society of illustrators, art history society, society for collegiate journalists.

Athletics. NAIA. **Intercollegiate:** Baseball M, basketball, cheerleading, cross-country, equestrian, golf, rowing (crew), soccer, softball W, swimming, tennis, volleyball. **Intramural:** Basketball, football (non-tackle), rowing (crew), soccer, softball, volleyball. **Team name:** Bees.

Student services. Adult student services, alcohol/substance abuse counseling, career counseling, student employment services, financial aid counseling, health services, personal counseling, placement for graduates. **Physically disabled:** Services for visually, speech, hearing impaired.

Contact. E-mail: admission@scad.edu
Phone: (912) 525-5100 Toll-free number: (800) 869-7223
Fax: (912) 525-5986
Pamela Rhame, Vice President for Admission, Savannah College of Art and Design, Admission Department, Savannah, GA 31402-2072

Savannah State University

Savannah, Georgia — **CB member**
www.savstate.edu — **CB code: 5609**

- Public 4-year business and liberal arts college
- Commuter campus in small city
- 2,975 degree-seeking undergraduates
- 78% of applicants admitted
- SAT or ACT (ACT writing optional) required

General. Founded in 1890. Regionally accredited. **Degrees:** 293 bachelor's awarded; master's offered. **ROTC:** Army, Navy. **Location:** 250 miles from Atlanta, 120 miles from Jacksonville, Florida. **Calendar:** Semester, extensive summer session. **Full-time faculty:** 123 total. **Part-time faculty:** 43 total. **Special facilities:** Marine biology dock, college archives, natural estuary.

Freshman class profile. 2,689 applied, 2,084 admitted, 1,067 enrolled.

Mid 50% test scores		**Out-of-state:**	18%
SAT verbal:	400-480	**Live on campus:**	50%
SAT math:	400-480		

Basis for selection. Test scores and high school GPA considered.

High school preparation. 15 units required. Required units include English 4, mathematics 3, social studies 3, science 3 and foreign language 2. Students lacking complete college-preparatory requirements admitted on provisional basis.

2005-2006 Annual costs. Tuition/fees: $3,056; $10,372 out-of-state. Room/board: $4,716. Books/supplies: $750. Personal expenses: $800.

2005-2006 Financial aid. Non-need-based: Scholarships awarded for academics, alumni affiliation, music/drama.

Application procedures. Admission: Closing date 7/1. $20 fee, may be waived for applicants with need. Admission notification on a rolling basis beginning on or about 3/1. **Financial aid:** Closing date 4/1. FAFSA required. Applicants notified on a rolling basis starting 4/15; must reply within 2 week(s) of notification.

Academics. Special study options: Cooperative education, cross-registration, double major, dual enrollment of high school students, exchange student, honors, independent study, internships. **Credit/placement by examination:** AP, CLEP, institutional tests. 45 credit hours maximum toward associate degree, 45 toward bachelor's. **Support services:** Learning center, remedial instruction, tutoring.

Majors. Biology: General, marine. **Business:** Accounting, hospitality/recreation, international, management science. **Communications:** General. **Computer sciences:** General, computer science, information systems. **Education:** Early childhood. **Engineering technology:** Civil, electrical. **Health:** Clinical lab science. **History:** General. **Math:** General. **Parks/recreation:** General. **Physical sciences:** Chemistry. **Public administration:** Social work. **Social sciences:** Political science, sociology. **Visual/performing arts:** Music performance.

Computing on campus. 300 workstations in library, computer center. Commuter students can connect to campus network.

Student life. Housing: Single-sex dorms, apartments available. $100 deposit. **Activities:** Bands, choral groups, dance, drama, literary magazine, music ensembles, radio station, student government, student newspaper.

Athletics. NCAA. **Intercollegiate:** Baseball M, basketball, bowling W, cross-country, football (tackle) M, golf, softball W, tennis, track and field, volleyball W. **Intramural:** Baseball M, bowling, softball W, table tennis.

Student services. Campus ministries, student employment services, health services, on-campus daycare, personal counseling, placement for graduates, veterans' counselor.

Contact. E-mail: ssvadms@savstate.edu
Phone: (912) 356-2181 Fax: (912) 356-2256
Gwendolyn Moore, Director of Admissions, Savannah State University, State College Branch, Savannah, GA 31404

Shorter College

Rome, Georgia — **CB member**
www.shorter.edu — **CB code: 5616**

- Private 4-year liberal arts college affiliated with Southern Baptist Convention
- Residential campus in large town
- 948 degree-seeking undergraduates: 3% part-time, 50% women, 9% African American, 1% Asian American, 2% Hispanic American, 4% international
- 75% of applicants admitted

- SAT or ACT (ACT writing optional), application essay required
- 51% graduate within 6 years

General. Founded in 1873. Regionally accredited. **Degrees:** 179 bachelor's awarded. **Location:** 70 miles from Atlanta, 65 miles from Chattanooga, Tennessee. **Calendar:** Semester, limited summer session. **Full-time faculty:** 65 total; 77% have terminal degrees, 6% minority, 37% women. **Part-time faculty:** 55 total; 7% have terminal degrees, 51% women. **Class size:** 62% < 20, 36% 20-39, 1% 40-49, less than 1% 50-99, less than 1% >100. **Special facilities:** Extensive music collection, microfilm archive of local history.

Freshman class profile. 1,031 applied, 769 admitted, 291 enrolled.

Mid 50% test scores			
SAT verbal:	460-570	Rank in top tenth:	19%
SAT math:	460-560	End year in good standing:	87%
ACT:	17-23	Return as sophomores:	71%
GPA 3.50 or higher:	40%	Out-of-state:	9%
GPA 3.0-3.49:	29%	Live on campus:	76%
GPA 2.0-2.99:	31%	International:	1%
Rank in top quarter:	46%	Fraternities:	6%
		Sororities:	35%

Basis for selection. High school achievement, curriculum most important. Test scores, essay, counselor recommendation also considered. Auditions required of music and drama majors. Portfolios required of art majors. **Homeschooled:** Applicants will be reviewed individually according to materials submitted. A personal interview may be required.

High school preparation. College-preparatory program required. 16 units required. Required units include English 4, mathematics 4, history 3, science 3 and foreign language 2. Mathematics units should include 2 algebra, 1 geometry.

2005-2006 Annual costs. Tuition/fees: $13,500. Room/board: $6,200. Books/supplies: $700. Personal expenses: $2,300.

2004-2005 Financial aid. Need-based: 260 full-time freshmen applied for aid; 215 were judged to have need; 215 of these received aid. Average need met was 66%. Average scholarship/grant was $9,685; average loan $2,470. 64% of total undergraduate aid awarded as scholarships/grants, 36% as loans/jobs. **Non-need-based:** Awarded to 502 full-time undergraduates, including 163 freshmen. Scholarships awarded for academics, alumni affiliation, art, athletics, leadership, minority status, music/drama, religious affiliation, state residency. **Additional information:** Cost is reduced for all in-state students by state tuition equalization grant program. College matches for out-of-state full-time students.

Application procedures. Admission: Priority date 3/15; deadline 8/25 (receipt date). $25 fee, may be waived for applicants with need. Application must be submitted on paper. Admission notification on a rolling basis beginning on or about 11/1. **Financial aid:** Priority date 4/1; no closing date. FAFSA, institutional form required. Applicants notified on a rolling basis starting 3/1; must reply within 2 week(s) of notification.

Academics. Special study options: Cross-registration, double major, dual enrollment of high school students, honors, independent study, internships, student-designed major, study abroad, teacher certification program. Annual extended seacoast field trips in natural science. **Credit/placement by examination:** AP, CLEP, IB, institutional tests. 30 credit hours maximum toward bachelor's degree. **Support services:** Remedial instruction, study skills assistance, tutoring.

Majors. Biology: General. **Business:** Accounting, business admin, managerial economics. **Communications:** General, public relations. **Computer sciences:** General. **Conservation:** General, environmental studies. **Education:** Art, elementary, mathematics, middle, music. **English:** English lit. **Foreign languages:** French, Spanish. **History:** General. **Interdisciplinary:** Global studies. **Liberal arts:** Arts/sciences. **Math:** General. **Parks/recreation:** General. **Philosophy/religion:** Religion. **Physical sciences:** Chemistry. **Psychology:** General. **Social sciences:** General, sociology. **Theology:** Sacred music, theology. **Visual/performing arts:** Dramatic, piano/organ, studio arts, voice/opera.

Most popular majors. Biology 13%, business/marketing 21%, communications/journalism 10%, education 19%, visual/performing arts 10%.

Computing on campus. 50 workstations in library, computer center. Dormitories linked to campus network. Helpline, wireless network available.

Student life. Freshman orientation: Mandatory, $60 fee. Preregistration for classes offered. Several summer overnight sessions from June to August. Freshmen take placement exams. **Policies:** Religious observance required. Freshmen permitted cars on campus. **Housing:** Guaranteed on-campus for freshmen. Single-sex dorms, apartments available. $200 fully refundable deposit, deadline 8/20. **Activities:** Concert band, choral groups, dance, drama, film society, literary magazine, music ensembles, musical theater, opera, radio station, student government, student newspaper, TV station, Baptist student union, Shorter Relations Society, fellowship of Christian athletes, international student organization.

Athletics. NAIA. **Intercollegiate:** Baseball M, basketball, cheerleading, cross-country, football (tackle) M, golf W, soccer, softball W, tennis, track and field, volleyball W. **Intramural:** Basketball, bowling, football (non-tackle), soccer, softball, table tennis, tennis, track and field, volleyball. **Team name:** Hawks.

Student services. Adult student services, alcohol/substance abuse counseling, campus ministries, career counseling, student employment services, financial aid counseling, health services, personal counseling, placement for graduates. **Physically disabled:** Services for visually, hearing impaired.

Contact. E-mail: admissions@shorter.edu
Phone: (706) 233-7319 Toll-free number: (800) 868-6980
Fax: (706) 233-7224
John Head, Vice President for Enrollment Management, Shorter College, 315 Shorter Avenue, Rome, GA 30165

South University
Savannah, Georgia
www.southuniversity.edu **CB code: 5157**

- For-profit 4-year business and health science college
- Commuter campus in small city
- 1,148 degree-seeking undergraduates
- SAT or ACT, interview required

General. Founded in 1899. Regionally accredited. **Degrees:** 118 bachelor's, 237 associate awarded; master's, doctoral, first professional offered. **Location:** 225 miles from Atlanta, 165 miles from Jacksonville, Florida. **Calendar:** Quarter, extensive summer session. **Full-time faculty:** 18 total; 28% have terminal degrees, 17% minority, 56% women. **Part-time faculty:** 43 total; 30% have terminal degrees, 9% minority, 56% women.

Basis for selection. Test scores and school achievement record considered. Physician assistant students must have completed two years of a science based curriculum. Computerized Placement Test may be submitted in place of test scores for admission. Essays are required for the physician assistant and physical therapist assistant programs.

2005-2006 Annual costs. Tuition for bachelor degrees in Business Administration, Legal Studies, Information Technology, Healthcare Management, Medical Assisting, Allied Health and Physical Therapist Assisting is $11,475 per year. Physician Assistant bachelor's program is $16,485 per year. BSN in Nursing is $16,485 per year. Cost of paralegal certificate is $7595 per program. Books/supplies: $750.

Financial aid. Non-need-based: Scholarships awarded for state residency.

Application procedures. Admission: No deadline. $25 fee. Admission notification on a rolling basis. **Financial aid:** No deadline. FAFSA required. Applicants notified on a rolling basis starting 9/1.

Academics. Special study options: Accelerated study, combined bachelor's/graduate degree, distance learning, double major, dual enrollment of high school students, independent study, internships, liberal arts/career combination. **Credit/placement by examination:** AP, CLEP, IB, institutional tests. 45 credit hours maximum toward associate degree, 90 toward bachelor's. 60% of total credits, 50% of major credits may be earned by examination. **Support services:** Learning center, reduced course load, remedial instruction, study skills assistance, tutoring.

Majors. Business: Accounting, business admin. **Computer sciences:** Information technology. **Health:** Physician assistant. **Legal studies:** General.

Computing on campus. 50 workstations in library, computer center. Commuter students can connect to campus network. Online library, helpline, repair service, wireless network available.

Student life. Freshman orientation: Mandatory. Preregistration for classes offered. **Policies:** Freshmen permitted cars on campus. **Housing:** Apartments available.

Student services. Career counseling, student employment services, financial aid counseling, personal counseling, placement for graduates, veterans' counselor.

Contact. Phone: (912) 201-8100 Toll-free number: (866) 629-2901
Fax: (912) 201-8070
Matthew Mills, Director of Admissions, South University, 709 Mall Boulevard, Savannah, GA 31406

Southern Polytechnic State University

Marietta, Georgia **CB member**
www.spsu.edu **CB code: 5626**

- Public 4-year university and engineering college
- Commuter campus in large city
- 3,299 degree-seeking undergraduates: 34% part-time, 17% women, 21% African American, 6% Asian American, 3% Hispanic American, 6% international
- 476 graduate students
- 62% of applicants admitted
- SAT or ACT with writing required

General. Founded in 1948. Regionally accredited. **Degrees:** 421 bachelor's, 5 associate awarded; master's offered. **ROTC:** Army, Navy, Air Force. **Location:** 15 miles from Atlanta. **Calendar:** Semester, extensive summer session. **Full-time faculty:** 137 total; 62% have terminal degrees, 23% minority, 17% women. **Part-time faculty:** 89 total; 17% minority, 33% women. **Class size:** 36% < 20, 57% 20-39, 5% 40-49, 1% 50-99.

Freshman class profile. 1,069 applied, 668 admitted, 436 enrolled.

Mid 50% test scores			
SAT verbal:	500-610	Out-of-state:	2%
SAT math:	530-630	Live on campus:	57%
ACT:	19-25	International:	4%
Return as sophomores:	68%	Fraternities:	7%
		Sororities:	1%

Basis for selection. GED not accepted. Test scores, high school units, and GPA important. SAT Subject Tests required of students not graduating from approved accredited high school.

High school preparation. 18 units required. Required units include English 4, mathematics 4, social studies 3, history 2, science 3 (laboratory 2), foreign language 2 and academic electives 2. Social studies units must include 2 history (1 U.S., 1 world). Foreign language must include 2 years same language. Mathematics must include 2 algebra, 1 geometry.

2005-2006 Annual costs. Tuition/fees: $3,174; $11,038 out-of-state. Room/board: $5,490. Books/supplies: $1,500. Personal expenses: $1,500.

2005-2006 Financial aid. Need-based: Average need met was 68%. Average scholarship/grant was $2,364; average loan $2,531. 40% of total undergraduate aid awarded as scholarships/grants, 60% as loans/jobs. **Non-need-based:** Scholarships awarded for academics, athletics.

Application procedures. Admission: Closing date 8/1 (postmark date). $20 fee, may be waived for applicants with need. Application may be submitted online. Admission notification on a rolling basis. **Financial aid:** Priority date 4/15; no closing date. FAFSA required. Applicants notified on a rolling basis starting 6/1.

Academics. Special study options: Cooperative education, cross-registration, distance learning, double major, dual enrollment of high school students, honors, independent study, internships, liberal arts/career combination, study abroad. **Credit/placement by examination:** AP, CLEP, IB, institutional tests. **Support services:** Learning center, reduced course load, study skills assistance, tutoring.

Majors. Architecture: Architecture. **Biology:** General. **Business:** Construction management, entrepreneurial studies, organizational behavior. **Communications:** General. **Computer sciences:** Computer science, information technology. **Engineering:** Software. **Engineering technology:** General, civil, computer, electrical, industrial, mechanical, surveying, telecommunications. **Math:** General. **Physical sciences:** Physics. **Social sciences:** International relations.

Most popular majors. Architecture 7%, business/marketing 18%, computer/information sciences 23%, engineering/engineering technologies 48%.

Computing on campus. 800 workstations in dormitories, library, computer center, student center. Dormitories wired for high-speed internet access and linked to campus network. Commuter students can connect to campus network. Online course registration, online library, helpline, student web hosting, wireless network available.

Student life. Freshman orientation: Available, $50 fee. Preregistration for classes offered. One-and-a-half day program held 2 times prior to beginning of semester. Price includes 1 night in a dorm. **Policies:** Freshmen permitted cars on campus. **Housing:** Coed dorms, apartments available. $150 deposit. Privately-owned apartments are available on campus. **Activities:** Bands, radio station, student government, student newspaper, campus activities board, international student association, National Society of Black Engineers, Baptist Student Union, African students association, Bahai Club, Black student association, Japanese Friendship Society, Muslim student association.

Athletics. NAIA. **Intercollegiate:** Baseball M, basketball. **Intramural:** Badminton, basketball, football (non-tackle), golf, racquetball, softball, table tennis, tennis, volleyball. **Team name:** Runnin' Hornets.

Student services. Alcohol/substance abuse counseling, career counseling, student employment services, financial aid counseling, health services, minority student services, personal counseling, placement for graduates, veterans' counselor. **Physically disabled:** Services for visually, speech, hearing impaired.

Contact. E-mail: admissions@spsu.edu
Phone: (678) 915-4188 Toll-free number: (800) 635-3204
Fax: (678) 915-7292
Virginia Head, Director of Admissions, Southern Polytechnic State University, 1100 South Marietta Parkway, Marietta, GA 30060-2896

Spelman College

Atlanta, Georgia **CB member**
www.spelman.edu **CB code: 5628**

- Private 4-year liberal arts college for women
- Residential campus in very large city
- 2,229 degree-seeking undergraduates: 4% part-time, 100% women, 95% African American, 2% international
- 39% of applicants admitted
- SAT or ACT (ACT writing optional), application essay required
- 76% graduate within 6 years

General. Founded in 1881. Regionally accredited. One of 6 members of Atlanta University Center sharing facilities, resources, and activities. Students may take courses at the other undergraduate schools in the Atlanta University Consortium. **Degrees:** 474 bachelor's awarded. **ROTC:** Army, Navy, Air Force. **Location:** 2 miles from downtown. **Calendar:** Semester. **Full-time faculty:** 169 total; 85% have terminal degrees, 79% minority, 66% women. **Part-time faculty:** 76 total; 20% have terminal degrees, 72% minority, 59% women. **Class size:** 57% < 20, 41% 20-39, 1% 40-49, 1% 50-99. **Special facilities:** Women's research and resource center, museum of fine art.

Freshman class profile. 4,534 applied, 1,771 admitted, 531 enrolled.

Mid 50% test scores			
SAT verbal:	510-600	Rank in top quarter:	71%
SAT math:	500-580	Rank in top tenth:	33%
ACT:	21-25	Return as sophomores:	90%
GPA 3.50 or higher:	58%	Out-of-state:	83%
GPA 3.0-3.49:	35%	Live on campus:	93%
GPA 2.0-2.99:	7%	International:	3%

Basis for selection. School achievement record, letters of recommendation, test scores, leadership, activities, essay are all important.

High school preparation. 15 units required; 16 recommended. Required and recommended units include English 4, mathematics 2-3, social studies 2, science 2-3 (laboratory 1) and foreign language 2-4. Mathematics units must include algebra and geometry. Must have 2 years of the same foreign language.

2005-2006 Annual costs. Tuition/fees: $16,195. Room/board: $8,455. Books/supplies: $1,150. Personal expenses: $2,100.

2005-2006 Financial aid. Need-based: 488 full-time freshmen applied for aid; 435 were judged to have need; 435 of these received aid. Average need met was 67%. Average scholarship/grant was $2,500; average loan $2,625. 49% of total undergraduate aid awarded as scholarships/grants, 51% as loans/jobs. **Non-need-based:** Awarded to 330 full-time undergraduates, including 67 freshmen. Scholarships awarded for academics, alumni affiliation, music/drama, state residency.

Application procedures. Admission: Closing date 2/1 (postmark date). $35 fee, may be waived for applicants with need. Application may be submitted online. Admission notification 4/1. Admission notification on a rolling basis beginning on or about 12/1. Must reply by 5/1. All students not accepted under early action plan are moved into regular application pool. **Financial aid:** Priority date 3/1; no closing date. FAFSA, institutional form, CSS PROFILE required. Applicants notified on a rolling basis starting 2/15; must reply within 2 week(s) of notification.

Academics. Special study options: Cross-registration, double major, dual enrollment of high school students, exchange student, honors, independent study, internships, New York semester, student-designed major, study abroad, teacher certification program, Washington semester. **Credit/placement by examination:** AP, CLEP, IB, institutional tests. 16 credit hours maximum toward bachelor's degree. **Support services:** Learning center, pre-admission summer program, tutoring, writing center.

Majors. Area/ethnic studies: Women's. **Biology:** General, biochemistry. **Computer sciences:** General. **Conservation:** Environmental science. **Education:** Early childhood. **Engineering:** General. **English:** English lit. **Family/consumer sciences:** Child care. **Foreign languages:** French, Spanish. **History:** General. **Interdisciplinary:** Biological/physical sciences, global studies. **Math:** General. **Philosophy/religion:** Philosophy, religion. **Physical sciences:** Chemistry, physics. **Psychology:** General. **Public administration:** Human services. **Social sciences:** Economics, political science, sociology. **Visual/performing arts:** Dramatic, studio arts.

Most popular majors. Biology 13%, English 11%, psychology 19%, social sciences 28%.

Computing on campus. 102 workstations in dormitories, library, computer center, student center. Dormitories wired for high-speed internet access and linked to campus network. Commuter students can connect to campus network. Helpline, wireless network available.

Student life. Freshman orientation: Mandatory. One-week program prior to registration. **Housing:** Guaranteed on-campus for freshmen. $100 nonrefundable deposit, deadline 5/1. **Activities:** Bands, choral groups, dance, drama, literary magazine, music ensembles, musical theater, student government, student newspaper, subject-related clubs, community services office.

Athletics. NCAA. **Intercollegiate:** Basketball W, cross-country W, soccer W, softball W, tennis W, track and field W, volleyball W. **Intramural:** Basketball W, bowling W, golf W, soccer W, softball W, swimming W, tennis W, track and field W, volleyball W. **Team name:** Jaguars.

Student services. Adult student services, campus ministries, career counseling, student employment services, health services, on-campus daycare, personal counseling, placement for graduates, women's services. **Physically disabled:** Services for visually, speech, hearing impaired.

Contact. E-mail: admiss@spelman.edu
Phone: (404) 270-5193 Toll-free number: (800) 982-2411
Fax: (404) 270-5201
Janet Ashley, Director of Admissions, Spelman College, 350 Spelman Lane Southwest Campus Box 277, Atlanta, GA 30314

Thomas University
Thomasville, Georgia
www.thomasu.edu **CB code: 5072**

- Private 4-year university and liberal arts college
- Commuter campus in large town
- 607 degree-seeking undergraduates: 37% African American, 1% Asian American, 1% Hispanic American, 1% Native American, 4% international
- 104 graduate students
- 32% graduate within 6 years

General. Founded in 1950. Regionally accredited. **Degrees:** 140 bachelor's, 7 associate awarded; master's offered. **Location:** 60 miles from Albany, 35 miles from Tallahassee, Florida. **Calendar:** Semester, extensive summer session. **Full-time faculty:** 41 total; 56% have terminal degrees, 10% minority, 58% women. **Part-time faculty:** 32 total; 28% have terminal degrees, 16% minority, 47% women. **Class size:** 89% < 20, 11% 20-39, less than 1% 40-49.

Freshman class profile. 124 applied, 85 admitted, 67 enrolled.

End year in good standing:	97%	**Out-of-state:**	8%
Return as sophomores:	49%	**Live on campus:**	25%

Basis for selection. Open admission, but selective for some programs. All students must take the Multiple Assessment Programs & Services examination and successfully complete remedial courses before enrolling in academic courses. **Homeschooled:** Transcript of courses and grades, state high school equivalency certificate required.

2006-2007 Annual costs. Tuition/fees: $10,570. Room only: $2,500. Books/supplies: $900. Personal expenses: $1,000.

2004-2005 Financial aid. Need-based: 25% of total undergraduate aid awarded as scholarships/grants, 75% as loans/jobs. **Non-need-based:** Scholarships awarded for academics, athletics, ROTC, state residency.

Application procedures. Admission: No deadline. $25 fee. Application may be submitted online. Admission notification on a rolling basis. **Financial aid:** Priority date 7/1; no closing date. FAFSA, institutional form required. Applicants notified on a rolling basis.

Academics. Special study options: Distance learning, dual enrollment of high school students, internships, liberal arts/career combination, teacher certification program. **Credit/placement by examination:** AP, CLEP, institutional tests. 40 credit hours maximum toward associate degree, 40 toward bachelor's. Total of 40 hours applies to credit by examination and prior work/life experience credit combined. **Support services:** Learning center, reduced course load, remedial instruction, study skills assistance, tutoring, writing center.

Majors. Biology: General. **Business:** General, accounting, management information systems, marketing. **Education:** Early childhood, elementary, middle, music, secondary. **Health:** Nursing (RN), staff services technology. **History:** General. **Liberal arts:** Arts/sciences. **Protective services:** Criminal justice. **Psychology:** General. **Public administration:** Social work. **Social sciences:** General, anthropology.

Most popular majors. Business/marketing 13%, education 26%, health sciences 9%, psychology 6%, public administration/social services 36%.

Computing on campus. 50 workstations in library, computer center. Dormitories wired for high-speed internet access and linked to campus network. Commuter students can connect to campus network. Online library, wireless network available.

Student life. Freshman orientation: Available. Preregistration for classes offered. Half-day every semester. **Policies:** Freshmen permitted cars on campus. **Housing:** Guaranteed on-campus for freshmen. Coed dorms, apartments available. $250 fully refundable deposit, deadline 8/1. **Activities:** Jazz band, choral groups, drama, literary magazine, music ensembles, student government, student newspaper.

Athletics. NAIA. **Intercollegiate:** Baseball M, golf, soccer, softball W. **Team name:** Night Hawks.

Student services. Adult student services, alcohol/substance abuse counseling, career counseling, student employment services, financial aid counseling, personal counseling, placement for graduates, veterans' counselor. **Physically disabled:** Services for visually, hearing impaired.

Contact. E-mail: admissions@thomasu.edu
Phone: (229) 226-1621 ext. 124 Toll-free number: (800) 538-9784 ext. 124
Fax: (229) 226-1653
Heather Mueller, Executive Director for Enrollment Management and Student Affairs, Thomas University, 1501 Millpond Road, Thomasville, GA 31792-7499

Toccoa Falls College
Toccoa Falls, Georgia
www.tfc.edu **CB code: 5799**

- Private 4-year Bible and liberal arts college affiliated with Christian and Missionary Alliance
- Residential campus in large town
- 910 degree-seeking undergraduates: 5% part-time, 58% women, 3% African American, 7% Asian American, 2% Hispanic American, 2% international
- 61% of applicants admitted
- SAT or ACT (ACT writing optional), application essay required
- 46% graduate within 6 years

General. Founded in 1907. Regionally accredited; also accredited by ABHE. **Degrees:** 148 bachelor's, 10 associate awarded. **Location:** 60 miles from Greenville, South Carolina, 90 miles from Atlanta. **Calendar:** 4-1-4, limited summer session. **Full-time faculty:** 45 total; 62% have terminal degrees, 7% minority, 20% women. **Part-time faculty:** 38 total; 16% have terminal degrees, 3% minority, 34% women. **Class size:** 60% < 20, 27% 20-39, 7% 40-49, 6% 50-99, less than 1% >100. **Special facilities:** 186-foot waterfall, power house, electric generator built in 1898.

Freshman class profile. 815 applied, 496 admitted, 271 enrolled.

Mid 50% test scores		Rank in top quarter:	40%
SAT verbal:	450-590	Rank in top tenth:	18%
SAT math:	430-570	End year in good standing:	87%
ACT:	19-26	Return as sophomores:	71%
GPA 3.50 or higher:	49%	Out-of-state:	43%
GPA 3.0-3.49:	29%	Live on campus:	83%
GPA 2.0-2.99:	22%		

Basis for selection. Evidence of Christian commitment, character, as well as the capacity and desire to learn, considered in selecting students for admission. All applicants must graduate from a regular high school program. Office of Admissions determines index score by multiplying final high school unweighted grade point average by the best total standardized test score. Minimum index score is 2000. Students with a score of at least 48 on the GED also considered. Personal statement of Christian faith required of all applicants. **Homeschooled:** Must submit SAT or ACT test results.

High school preparation. 19 units recommended. Recommended units include English 4, mathematics 3, social studies 3, science 3 and academic electives 6.

2005-2006 Annual costs. Tuition/fees: $12,050. Room/board: $4,600. Books/supplies: $855. Personal expenses: $2,327.

2005-2006 Financial aid. Need-based: Average need met was 61%. Average scholarship/grant was $6,920; average loan $2,085. 57% of total undergraduate aid awarded as scholarships/grants, 43% as loans/jobs. **Non-need-based:** Scholarships awarded for academics, alumni affiliation, leadership, music/drama, religious affiliation, state residency.

Application procedures. Admission: Priority date 5/1; deadline 8/1 (postmark date). $20 fee, may be waived for applicants with need. Application may be submitted online. Admission notification on a rolling basis beginning on or about 3/1. Must reply by May 1 or within 2 week(s) if notified thereafter. **Financial aid:** Priority date 5/1; no closing date. FAFSA required. Applicants notified on a rolling basis starting 3/1; must reply within 2 week(s) of notification.

Academics. All students complete at least 30 credit hours of Bible courses (18 credit hours for associate degrees), attend weekly church services and participate in student ministry field assignments. **Special study options:** Distance learning, double major, independent study, internships, teacher certification program. **Credit/placement by examination:** AP, CLEP, institutional tests. 30 credit hours maximum toward associate degree, 45 toward bachelor's. **Support services:** Learning center, reduced course load, study skills assistance, tutoring.

Majors. Biology: General. **Business:** Business admin. **Communications:** General, media studies. **Education:** Early childhood, English, history, middle, music. **English:** English lit. **Legal studies:** Prelaw. **Philosophy/religion:** Religion. **Psychology:** General. **Theology:** Bible, missionary, pastoral counseling, religious ed, sacred music, youth ministry. **Visual/performing arts:** Music performance.

Most popular majors. Business/marketing 7%, education 15%, psychology 19%, theological studies 45%.

Computing on campus. 60 workstations in library, computer center. Dormitories wired for high-speed internet access and linked to campus network. Commuter students can connect to campus network. Online course registration, online library, helpline, student web hosting, wireless network available.

Student life. Freshman orientation: Mandatory. Preregistration for classes offered. Held one week in the fall and throughout the spring semester. **Policies:** Over 50 different ministry opportunities for students. Religious observance required. Freshmen permitted cars on campus. **Housing:** Guaranteed on-campus for freshmen. Single-sex dorms, apartments, substance-free housing available. $200 nonrefundable deposit. Trailers available on campus lots for married students. **Activities:** Bands, choral groups, drama, music ensembles, radio station, student government, student newspaper.

Athletics. NCCAA. **Intercollegiate:** Baseball M, basketball, cross-country, golf, soccer, volleyball W. **Intramural:** Basketball, football (non-tackle), soccer, softball, volleyball. **Team name:** Eagles.

Student services. Campus ministries, student employment services, financial aid counseling, health services, personal counseling. **Physically disabled:** Services for visually impaired.

Contact. E-mail: admissions@tfc.edu
Phone: (706) 886-6831 ext. 5380 Fax: (706) 282-6012
Christy Meadows, Director of Admissions, Toccoa Falls College, Office of Admissions, Toccoa Falls, GA 30598-0368

Truett-McConnell College

Cleveland, Georgia — **CB member**
www.truett.edu — **CB code: 5798**

- Private 4-year liberal arts college affiliated with Southern Baptist Convention
- Residential campus in rural community
- 353 degree-seeking undergraduates: 4% part-time, 44% women
- 42% of applicants admitted
- SAT or ACT required

General. Founded in 1946. Regionally accredited. Associated with Baptist Convention of the State of Georgia. **Degrees:** 2 bachelor's, 42 associate awarded. **Location:** 75 miles from Atlanta, 25 miles from Gainesville, Florida. **Calendar:** Semester, limited summer session. **Full-time faculty:** 25 total; 44% have terminal degrees, 44% women. **Part-time faculty:** 19 total; 47% women. **Class size:** 75% < 20, 25% 20-39.

Freshman class profile. 604 applied, 254 admitted, 171 enrolled.

Mid 50% test scores		GPA 3.0-3.49:	32%
SAT verbal:	420-510	GPA 2.0-2.99:	54%
SAT math:	390-500	Return as sophomores:	54%
ACT:	16-20	Out-of-state:	5%
GPA 3.50 or higher:	13%	Live on campus:	87%

Basis for selection. Secondary school record, test scores. Minimum 2.0 GPA in core classes required. Minimum combined SAT of 720 or ACT composite of 15 required. Students with scores that do not meet criteria may apply to academic enrichment program. Audition required of music majors. **Homeschooled:** Transcript of courses and grades required. SAT score of at least 720 or ACT score of 15, letter from local school board stating that student has completed home-school program requirements, and placement exams required. **Learning Disabled:** Students may request accommodations upon presentation of appropriate documentation of disability. Determination of reasonable accommodations made on an individual student basis.

High school preparation. Recommended units include English 4, mathematics 3, social studies 3, science 3 and foreign language 2.

2005-2006 Annual costs. Tuition/fees: $11,550. Room/board: $4,600. Books/supplies: $1,000. Personal expenses: $1,150.

Financial aid. Non-need-based: Scholarships awarded for academics, athletics, music/drama, religious affiliation, state residency. **Additional information:** Installment plan available through AMS.

Application procedures. Admission: Closing date 8/1 (receipt date). $25 fee, may be waived for applicants with need. Admission notification on a rolling basis. Must reply by May 1 or within 1 week(s) if notified thereafter. **Financial aid:** Priority date 6/1; no closing date. FAFSA, institutional form required. Applicants notified on a rolling basis starting 4/1; must reply within 2 week(s) of notification.

Academics. Special study options: Double major, dual enrollment of high school students, honors, independent study, study abroad. **Credit/placement by examination:** AP, CLEP, SAT, ACT. 30 credit hours maximum toward associate degree, 30 toward bachelor's. **Support services:** Remedial instruction, tutoring.

Computing on campus. 38 workstations in library, computer center, student center. Dormitories linked to campus network. Commuter students can connect to campus network.

Student life. Freshman orientation: Mandatory, $100 fee. Preregistration for classes offered. Held for one day during July and August. **Policies:** Religious observance required. Freshmen permitted cars on campus. **Housing:** Single-sex dorms, substance-free housing available. $75 deposit. **Activities:** Bands, choral groups, music ensembles, student government, Baptist Student Union, Phi Theta Kappa, Impact Teams and Majesty, Phi Beta Lambda, Ministerial Association, Student Professional Association of Georgia Educators, Fellowship of Christian Athletes.

Athletics. NJCAA. **Intercollegiate:** Baseball M, basketball, cross-country, golf M, soccer, softball W. **Intramural:** Basketball, soccer. **Team name:** Bears.

Student services. Campus ministries, financial aid counseling, veterans' counselor. **Physically disabled:** Services for visually, speech, hearing impaired.

Contact. E-mail: admissions@truett.edu
Phone: (706) 865-2134 Toll-free number: (800) 226-8621
Fax: (706) 865-7615
Penny Loggins, Dean for Admissions, Truett-McConnell College, 100 Alumni Drive, Cleveland, GA 30528

University of Georgia

Athens, Georgia **CB member**
www.uga.edu **CB code: 5813**

- Public 4-year university
- Commuter campus in small city
- 24,791 degree-seeking undergraduates: 9% part-time, 57% women, 5% African American, 5% Asian American, 2% Hispanic American, 1% international
- 7,826 degree-seeking graduate students
- 65% of applicants admitted
- SAT or ACT with writing, application essay required
- 75% graduate within 6 years

General. Founded in 1785. Regionally accredited. **Degrees:** 6,160 bachelor's awarded; master's, doctoral, first professional offered. **ROTC:** Army, Air Force. **Location:** 60 miles from of Atlanta. **Calendar:** Semester, extensive summer session. **Full-time faculty:** 1,691 total; 93% have terminal degrees, 15% minority, 31% women. **Part-time faculty:** 420 total; 58% have terminal degrees, 10% minority, 42% women. **Class size:** 35% < 20, 48% 20-39, 6% 40-49, 6% 50-99, 5% >100. **Special facilities:** Art museum, botanical garden, theater, golf course.

Freshman class profile. 12,326 applied, 7,982 admitted, 4,712 enrolled.

Mid 50% test scores		Rank in top tenth:	52%
SAT verbal:	560-660	Return as sophomores:	93%
SAT math:	570-670	Out-of-state:	12%
ACT:	24-28	Live on campus:	97%
GPA 3.50 or higher:	75%	International:	1%
GPA 3.0-3.49:	22%	Fraternities:	21%
GPA 2.0-2.99:	3%	Sororities:	27%
Rank in top quarter:	84%		

Basis for selection. The academic review of first-year applications centers on three criteria: student's GPA in core academic courses, rigor of student's course selection, and best combination of scores on the SAT or ACT. Applications are reviewed for conduct issues, recommendations; satisfactory completion of all courses and completion of the required college preparatory courses. SAT Subject Tests recommended. Audition required of music majors.

High school preparation. 16 units required; 18 recommended. Required and recommended units include English 4, mathematics 4, social studies 3, history 2, science 3 (laboratory 2), foreign language 2-3 and academic electives 1.

2005-2006 Annual costs. Tuition/fees: $4,628; $16,848 out-of-state. Room/board: $6,376. Books/supplies: $800.

2005-2006 Financial aid. Need-based: 2,836 full-time freshmen applied for aid; 1,275 were judged to have need; 1,261 of these received aid. Average need met was 81%. Average scholarship/grant was $6,148; average loan $2,558. 58% of total undergraduate aid awarded as scholarships/grants, 42% as loans/jobs. **Non-need-based:** Awarded to 2,748 full-time undergraduates, including 842 freshmen. Scholarships awarded for academics, athletics, ROTC, state residency.

Application procedures. Admission: Priority date 10/15; deadline 1/15 (postmark date). $50 fee, may be waived for applicants with need. Application may be submitted online. Admission notification 2/15. Must reply by May 1 or within 2 week(s) if notified thereafter. **Financial aid:** Priority date 3/1; no closing date. FAFSA required. Applicants notified on a rolling basis starting 5/15; must reply within 2 week(s) of notification.

Academics. Special study options: Accelerated study, combined bachelor's/graduate degree, cooperative education, cross-registration, distance learning, double major, dual enrollment of high school students, exchange student, external degree, honors, independent study, internships, liberal arts/career combination, student-designed major, study abroad, teacher certification program, Washington semester. **Credit/placement by examination:** AP, CLEP, IB, SAT, ACT, institutional tests. Unlimited number of hours of credit by examination may be counted toward bachelor's degree. **Support services:** Learning center, pre-admission summer program, reduced course load, remedial instruction, study skills assistance, tutoring, writing center.

Majors. Agriculture: General, agribusiness operations, animal sciences, communications, dairy, economics, food science, horticulture, landscaping, poultry, turf management. **Architecture:** Landscape. **Area/ethnic studies:** African-American, women's. **Biology:** General, biochemistry, biotechnology, botany, cell/histology, ecology, entomology, genetics, microbiology. **Business:** General, accounting, business admin, fashion, finance, insurance, international, management information systems, managerial economics, marketing, real estate. **Communications:** Advertising, broadcast journalism, journalism, public relations. **Communications technology:** Radio/tv. **Computer sciences:** Computer science. **Conservation:** Environmental studies, fisheries, forestry, wildlife. **Education:** Agricultural, business, English, family/consumer sciences, foreign languages, health, kindergarten/preschool, mathematics, middle, music, physical, sales/marketing, science, social science, special, technology/industrial arts. **Engineering:** General, agricultural, chemical, computer, environmental. **English:** English lit, speech/rhetoric. **Family/consumer sciences:** Child development, communication, consumer economics, family studies, food/nutrition, housing. **Foreign languages:** Ancient Greek, classics, comparative lit, French, German, Italian, Japanese, Latin, linguistics, Romance, Russian, Spanish. **Health:** Communication disorders, dietetics, environmental health, music therapy, public health ed. **History:** General. **Interdisciplinary:** Biological/physical sciences. **Liberal arts:** Arts/sciences. **Math:** General, statistics. **Parks/recreation:** Sports admin. **Philosophy/religion:** Philosophy, religion. **Physical sciences:** Astronomy, chemistry, geology, physics. **Protective services:** Criminal justice. **Psychology:** General. **Public administration:** Social work. **Social sciences:** Anthropology, economics, geography, international relations, political science, sociology. **Visual/performing arts:** Art, art history/conservation, dance, dramatic, film/cinema, music performance, music theory/composition, studio arts.

Most popular majors. Biology 7%, business/marketing 21%, communications/journalism 7%, education 10%, family/consumer sciences 7%, psychology 6%, social sciences 11%.

Computing on campus. 2,600 workstations in dormitories, library, computer center, student center. Dormitories wired for high-speed internet access and linked to campus network. Commuter students can connect to campus network. Online course registration, online library, helpline, repair service, student web hosting, wireless network available.

Student life. Freshman orientation: Mandatory. Preregistration for classes offered. 2-day sessions offered in the summer. **Policies:** Freshmen permitted cars on campus. **Housing:** Guaranteed on-campus for freshmen. Coed dorms, single-sex dorms, special housing for disabled, apartments, fraternity/sorority housing available. $275 fully refundable deposit. Honors and language focused housing available. **Activities:** Bands, choral groups, dance, drama, film society, literary magazine, music ensembles, musical theater, opera, radio station, student government, student newspaper, symphony orchestra, TV station.

Athletics. NCAA. **Intercollegiate:** Baseball M, basketball, cross-country, diving, equestrian W, football (tackle) M, golf, gymnastics W, soccer W, softball W, swimming, tennis, track and field, volleyball W. **Intramural:** Basketball, cross-country, football (non-tackle), football (tackle) M, golf, racquetball, soccer, softball, squash, tennis, track and field, volleyball, wrestling M. **Team name:** Bulldogs.

Student services. Adult student services, alcohol/substance abuse counseling, campus ministries, career counseling, student employment services, financial aid counseling, health services, legal services, minority student services, on-campus daycare, personal counseling, placement for graduates, veterans' counselor, women's services. **Physically disabled:** Services for visually, speech, hearing impaired. **Learning disabled:** Comprehensive services available.

Contact. E-mail: undergrad@admissions.uga.edu
Phone: (706) 542-8776 Fax: (706) 542-1466
Nancy McDuff, Associate Vice President for Admissions and Enrollment Management, University of Georgia, Office of Undergraduate Admissions, Athens, GA 30602-1633

University of West Georgia

Carrollton, Georgia **CB member**
www.westga.edu **CB code: 5900**

- Public 4-year university and liberal arts college
- Commuter campus in large town
- 8,346 degree-seeking undergraduates: 17% part-time, 60% women, 23% African American, 1% Asian American, 2% Hispanic American, 1% international
- 1,808 graduate students
- 55% of applicants admitted
- SAT or ACT with writing required
- 31% graduate within 6 years

General. Founded in 1906. Regionally accredited. Off-campus sites in Dalton (graduate) and Newnan (undergraduate). Advanced Academy of Georgia for academically accelerated high school juniors and seniors. **Degrees:**

1,137 bachelor's awarded; master's, doctoral offered. **ROTC:** Army. **Location:** 50 miles from Atlanta. **Calendar:** Semester, extensive summer session. **Full-time faculty:** 383 total; 78% have terminal degrees, 15% minority, 49% women. **Part-time faculty:** 135 total; 37% have terminal degrees, 12% minority, 61% women. **Class size:** 39% < 20, 41% 20-39, 9% 40-49, 8% 50-99, 3% >100. **Special facilities:** Observatory, performing arts center, archaeological laboratory, technology enhanced learning center.

Freshman class profile. 5,175 applied, 2,859 admitted, 1,983 enrolled.

Mid 50% test scores			
SAT verbal:	470-560	Return as sophomores:	71%
SAT math:	460-550	Out-of-state:	2%
ACT:	18-22	Live on campus:	66%
GPA 3.50 or higher:	20%	International:	1%
GPA 3.0-3.49:	33%	Fraternities:	10%
GPA 2.0-2.99:	46%	Sororities:	10%

Basis for selection. GED not accepted. Freshman admission is based on standardized test scores, such as the SAT or ACT, high school GPA in college preparatory subjects, system mandated college preparatory curriculum. **Homeschooled:** Home schooled or graduates from non-accredited high schools may apply for admission if SAT composite score (verbal & math) is equal to or greater than average SAT score of the previous fall freshman class. Minimum SAT score of 430 verbal and 410 math; minimum ACT score of 17 English and 17 math required. In lieu of high school transcript, must present portfolio of all 16 required college prep courses.

High school preparation. 16 units required. Required units include English 4, mathematics 4, social studies 1, history 2, science 3 (laboratory 2) and foreign language 2.

2005-2006 Annual costs. Tuition/fees: $3,270; $10,586 out-of-state. Room/board: $5,568. Books/supplies: $900.

2005-2006 Financial aid. **Need-based:** Average need met was 66%. Average scholarship/grant was $4,348; average loan $2,121. 54% of total undergraduate aid awarded as scholarships/grants, 46% as loans/jobs. **Non-need-based:** Scholarships awarded for academics, alumni affiliation, art, athletics, leadership, music/drama.

Application procedures. **Admission:** Priority date 4/1; deadline 7/1. $20 fee, may be waived for applicants with need. Application must be submitted on paper. Admission notification on a rolling basis beginning on or about 9/1. **Financial aid:** Priority date 4/1; no closing date. FAFSA required. Applicants notified by 3/1; Applicants notified on a rolling basis starting 3/1; must reply by 5/1.

Academics. **Special study options:** Accelerated study, cooperative education, distance learning, double major, dual enrollment of high school students, external degree, honors, independent study, internships, New York semester, study abroad, teacher certification program. **Credit/placement by examination:** AP, CLEP, IB, SAT, ACT, institutional tests. 30 credit hours maximum toward bachelor's degree. **Support services:** Learning center, pre-admission summer program, reduced course load, remedial instruction, study skills assistance, tutoring, writing center.

Majors. **Biology:** General, zoology. **Business:** Accounting, business admin, finance, management information systems, managerial economics, marketing, real estate. **Communications:** Journalism. **Computer sciences:** General. **Conservation:** Environmental science, environmental studies. **Education:** Biology, business, chemistry, elementary, mentally handicapped, middle, music, physical, physics, secondary. **English:** English lit. **Foreign languages:** French, German, Spanish. **Health:** Nursing (RN), premedicine, prepharmacy, speech pathology. **History:** General. **Legal studies:** Prelaw. **Math:** General. **Parks/recreation:** Facilities management. **Philosophy/religion:** Philosophy. **Physical sciences:** Chemistry, geology, physics. **Protective services:** Criminal justice. **Psychology:** General. **Social sciences:** Anthropology, criminology, economics, geography, international economics, international relations, political science, sociology. **Visual/performing arts:** Art, dramatic, music performance, music theory/composition.

Most popular majors. Business/marketing 26%, education 22%, health sciences 7%, psychology 6%, social sciences 14%.

Computing on campus. 745 workstations in dormitories, library, computer center, student center. Dormitories wired for high-speed internet access and linked to campus network. Online course registration, online library, helpline, repair service, student web hosting, wireless network available.

Student life. **Freshman orientation:** Mandatory, $60 fee. Preregistration for classes offered. **Policies:** Freshmen permitted cars on campus. **Housing:** Guaranteed on-campus for freshmen. Coed dorms, single-sex dorms, special housing for disabled, fraternity/sorority housing available. $250 deposit. All freshmen required to reside on-campus unless married or living with parents, relatives, or legal guardians. **Activities:** Bands, choral groups, dance, drama, literary magazine, music ensembles, musical theater, opera, radio station, student government, student newspaper, TV station, Baptist Student Union, Catholic student life, Muslim student alliance, Latter-Day Saint student association, Jewish student group, Black Students Alliance, Democratic organization, Republican organization.

Athletics. NCAA. **Intercollegiate:** Baseball M, basketball, cheerleading, cross-country, football (tackle) M, golf, soccer W, softball W, volleyball W. **Intramural:** Basketball, bowling, football (non-tackle), golf, soccer, softball, swimming, table tennis, tennis, track and field, volleyball, water polo, weight lifting. **Team name:** Wolves.

Student services. Adult student services, career counseling, student employment services, financial aid counseling, health services, minority student services, on-campus daycare, personal counseling, placement for graduates, veterans' counselor. **Physically disabled:** Services for visually, speech, hearing impaired.

Contact. E-mail: admiss@westga.edu
Phone: (678) 839-4000 Fax: (678) 839-4747
Bobby Johnson, Director of Admissions, University of West Georgia, 1601 Maple Street, Carrollton, GA 30118-0001

Valdosta State University

Valdosta, Georgia — **CB member**
www.valdosta.edu — **CB code: 5855**

- Public 4-year university
- Commuter campus in small city
- 9,015 degree-seeking undergraduates: 17% part-time, 59% women, 22% African American, 1% Asian American, 2% Hispanic American, 1% international
- 1,294 degree-seeking graduate students
- 63% of applicants admitted
- SAT or ACT (ACT writing optional) required
- 41% graduate within 6 years

General. Founded in 1906. Regionally accredited. **Degrees:** 1,391 bachelor's, 79 associate awarded; master's, doctoral offered. **ROTC:** Air Force. **Location:** 235 miles from Atlanta, 138 miles from Jacksonville, Florida. **Calendar:** Semester, extensive summer session. **Full-time faculty:** 435 total; 10% minority, 45% women. **Part-time faculty:** 110 total; 52% minority, 63% women. **Class size:** 29% < 20, 56% 20-39, 9% 40-49, 4% 50-99, less than 1% >100. **Special facilities:** Planetarium, herbarium, observatory, art gallery.

Freshman class profile. 5,782 applied, 3,643 admitted, 1,757 enrolled.

Mid 50% test scores			
SAT verbal:	480-560	Return as sophomores:	76%
SAT math:	470-570	Out-of-state:	1%
ACT:	20-23	Live on campus:	64%
GPA 3.50 or higher:	20%	International:	1%
GPA 3.0-3.49:	33%	Fraternities:	13%
GPA 2.0-2.99:	47%	Sororities:	13%

Basis for selection. GED not accepted. Admission requirements: SAT Verbal 440, SAT Math 410, ACT English 18, ACT Math 17. Require Freshmen Index of 2040, based on high school academic GPA multiplied by 500 added to the SAT verbal and math scores. **Homeschooled:** SAT total 1050 or higher (440 Verbal/410 Math) or ACT Composite score of 23 or higher (18 English/17 Math), declaration of intent to homeschool filed with Board of Education, portfolio, letter from primary teacher. **Learning Disabled:** Must meet minimum admission standards. Will accept untimed SAT/ACT tests.

High school preparation. 16 units required. Required units include English 4, mathematics 4, social studies 3, science 3 (laboratory 2) and foreign language 2.

2005-2006 Annual costs. Tuition/fees: $3,278; $10,594 out-of-state. Room/board: $5,524. Books/supplies: $1,000. Personal expenses: $2,400.

2004-2005 Financial aid. **Need-based:** 1,681 full-time freshmen applied for aid; 941 were judged to have need; 941 of these received aid. Average need met was 82%. Average scholarship/grant was $4,413; average loan $2,176. 47% of total undergraduate aid awarded as scholarships/grants, 53% as loans/jobs. **Non-need-based:** Awarded to 3,623 full-time undergraduates, including 926 freshmen. Scholarships awarded for academics, art, athletics, leadership, music/drama, ROTC, state residency.

Application procedures. **Admission:** Closing date 7/15 (receipt date). $20 fee, may be waived for applicants with need. Application may be submitted online. Admission notification on a rolling basis beginning on or about 8/1. **Financial aid:** Priority date 5/1; no closing date. FAFSA required. Applicants notified on a rolling basis starting 5/15.

Academics. Special study options: Cooperative education, distance learning, double major, dual enrollment of high school students, ESL, external degree, honors, independent study, internships, liberal arts/career combination, study abroad, teacher certification program, weekend college. **Credit/placement by examination:** AP, CLEP, IB. 30 credit hours maximum toward associate degree, 30 toward bachelor's. **Support services:** Study skills assistance, tutoring, writing center.

Majors. Biology: General. **Business:** Accounting, administrative services, business admin, finance, managerial economics, marketing. **Communications:** Media studies. **Computer sciences:** General, information systems. **Conservation:** Environmental science. **Education:** Art, business, early childhood, middle, music, physical, secondary, special, trade/industrial. **Engineering technology:** General. **English:** English lit, speech/rhetoric. **Foreign languages:** French, sign language interpretation, Spanish. **Health:** Athletic training, nursing (RN). **History:** General. **Legal studies:** Paralegal. **Liberal arts:** Arts/sciences. **Math:** General, applied. **Parks/recreation:** Exercise sciences. **Philosophy/religion:** Philosophy. **Physical sciences:** Astronomy, chemistry, physics. **Protective services:** Criminal justice. **Psychology:** General. **Social sciences:** Political science, sociology. **Visual/performing arts:** General, art, interior design, music performance.

Most popular majors. Business/marketing 22%, education 23%, health sciences 8%, social sciences 7%.

Computing on campus. 1,600 workstations in library, computer center. Dormitories wired for high-speed internet access and linked to campus network. Commuter students can connect to campus network. Online course registration, online library, helpline, repair service, student web hosting, wireless network available.

Student life. Freshman orientation: Available, $50 fee. Preregistration for classes offered. One-day programs held in June, July, and August. **Policies:** Freshmen permitted cars on campus. **Housing:** Coed dorms, single-sex dorms, special housing for disabled, apartments, substance-free housing available. $300 fully refundable deposit, deadline 3/1. Honors wing available. **Activities:** Bands, choral groups, dance, drama, literary magazine, music ensembles, musical theater, radio station, student government, student newspaper, symphony orchestra, TV station, Black Student League, several religious and social service organizations, outdoor adventure club, Habitat for Humanity.

Athletics. NCAA. **Intercollegiate:** Baseball M, basketball, cross-country, football (tackle) M, golf M, softball W, tennis, volleyball W. **Intramural:** Basketball, football (non-tackle), golf, racquetball, soccer, softball, swimming, tennis, volleyball, water polo. **Team name:** Blazers.

Student services. Adult student services, alcohol/substance abuse counseling, career counseling, student employment services, financial aid counseling, health services, minority student services, personal counseling, placement for graduates, veterans' counselor. **Physically disabled:** Services for visually, speech, hearing impaired. **Learning disabled:** Comprehensive services available.

Contact. E-mail: admissions@valdosta.edu
Phone: (229) 333-5791 Toll-free number: (800) 618-1878
Fax: (229) 333-5482
Walter Peacock, Director of Admissions, Valdosta State University, 1500 North Patterson Street, Valdosta, GA 31698

Wesleyan College

Macon, Georgia — **CB member**
www.wesleyancollege.edu — **CB code: 5895**

- Private 4-year liberal arts college for women affiliated with United Methodist Church
- Residential campus in small city
- 530 degree-seeking undergraduates: 26% part-time, 100% women
- 89 graduate students
- 55% of applicants admitted
- SAT or ACT (ACT writing optional), application essay required
- 45% graduate within 6 years

General. Founded in 1836. Regionally accredited. Chartered in 1836, the world's first college to grant degrees to women. **Degrees:** 132 bachelor's awarded; master's offered. **Location:** 75 miles from Atlanta. **Calendar:** Semester, limited summer session. **Full-time faculty:** 47 total; 96% have terminal degrees, 11% minority, 49% women. **Part-time faculty:** 33 total; 39% have terminal degrees, 6% minority, 76% women. **Class size:** 89% < 20, 11% 20-39. **Special facilities:** Equestrian facilities, arboretum, lake.

Freshman class profile. 483 applied, 267 admitted, 113 enrolled.

Mid 50% test scores		Rank in top tenth:	34%
SAT verbal:	500-630	Return as sophomores:	64%
SAT math:	490-600	Out-of-state:	25%
ACT:	21-26	Live on campus:	95%
Rank in top quarter:	57%	International:	9%

Basis for selection. Admission committee reviews applicants for admission based on academic performance in college preparatory courses, standardized test scores, extra-curricular activities and recommendations. Interview recommended, but required for scholarship competitions. Audition required of music or theater students interested in a performance arts scholarship. Portfolio required of art majors. **Homeschooled:** Statement describing homeschool structure and mission, transcript of courses and grades, letter of recommendation (nonparent) required. Must take SAT or ACT. Diplomas issued by the parents are recognized. Student may provide biography of high school literature and essay to evaluate his/her exposure and thinking skills. Extra-curricular activities and counselor interviews considered. GED or additional testing not required.

High school preparation. 15 units required; 22 recommended. Required and recommended units include English 4, mathematics 3-4, social studies 3-4, science 3-4 (laboratory 2-3), foreign language 2-4 and academic electives 2.

2005-2006 Annual costs. Tuition/fees: $12,110. Room/board: $7,450. Books/supplies: $800. Personal expenses: $1,000.

2004-2005 Financial aid. Need-based: 59 full-time freshmen applied for aid; 46 were judged to have need; 46 of these received aid. Average need met was 81%. Average scholarship/grant was $7,469; average loan $2,302. 59% of total undergraduate aid awarded as scholarships/grants, 41% as loans/jobs. **Non-need-based:** Awarded to 199 full-time undergraduates, including 43 freshmen. Scholarships awarded for academics, alumni affiliation, art, job skills, leadership, minority status, music/drama, religious affiliation, state residency. **Additional information:** Fellowships available based on number of hours and cumulative GPA transferred in, with minimum 30 semester or 45 quarter hours and 3.0 GPA required.

Application procedures. Admission: Priority date 2/1; deadline 5/1 (postmark date). $30 fee, may be waived for applicants with need. Application may be submitted online. Admission notification on a rolling basis beginning on or about 10/1. Must reply by May 1 or within 2 week(s) if notified thereafter. **Financial aid:** Priority date 4/1; no closing date. FAFSA, institutional form required. Applicants notified on a rolling basis starting 3/1; must reply by 5/1 or within 3 week(s) of notification.

Academics. Special study options: Accelerated study, cross-registration, double major, dual enrollment of high school students, exchange student, honors, independent study, internships, liberal arts/career combination, student-designed major, study abroad, teacher certification program, weekend college. **Credit/placement by examination:** AP, CLEP, IB, institutional tests. 30 credit hours maximum toward bachelor's degree. **Support services:** Learning center, study skills assistance, tutoring, writing center.

Majors. Area/ethnic studies: American. **Biology:** General. **Business:** Business admin, international. **Communications:** General, advertising. **Computer sciences:** General. **Education:** Early childhood, middle. **English:** English lit. **Foreign languages:** French, Spanish. **History:** General. **Liberal arts:** Arts/sciences. **Math:** General. **Philosophy/religion:** Philosophy, religion. **Physical sciences:** Chemistry, physics. **Psychology:** General. **Social sciences:** General, economics, international relations, sociology. **Theology:** Preministerial. **Visual/performing arts:** Art history/conservation, dramatic, studio arts.

Most popular majors. Biology 8%, business/marketing 24%, communications/journalism 9%, education 11%, psychology 16%, social sciences 7%.

Computing on campus. PC or laptop required. 100 workstations in library, computer center, student center. Dormitories wired for high-speed internet access and linked to campus network. Commuter students can connect to campus network. Online course registration, online library, helpline, repair service, wireless network available.

Student life. Freshman orientation: Mandatory. Preregistration for classes offered. Summer Orientation is held in June for all new students. Fall Orientation is held in August, prior to the start of classes. This orientation focuses on transitioning to college. **Policies:** Students required to live on campus unless married or living with immediate family in the local area. Freshmen permitted cars on campus. **Housing:** Guaranteed on-campus for all undergraduates. Special housing for disabled, apartments available. $150 fully refundable deposit, deadline 6/1. **Activities:** Choral groups, dance, drama, literary magazine, music ensembles, student government, student newspaper, Honor Council, Mortar Board, International Club, Young Democrats, Circle K, College Republicans, Council on Religions Concerns, Young Democrates, American Chemical Society, Model UN.

Athletics. NCAA. **Intercollegiate:** Basketball W, equestrian W, soccer W, softball W, tennis W, volleyball W. **Intramural:** Basketball W, soccer W, softball W, volleyball W. **Team name:** Pioneers.

Student services. Adult student services, alcohol/substance abuse counseling, campus ministries, career counseling, services for economically disadvantaged, student employment services, financial aid counseling, health services, minority student services, personal counseling, women's services.

Contact. E-mail: admission@wesleyancollege.edu
Phone: (478) 757-5206 Toll-free number: (800) 447-6610
Fax: (478) 757-4030
Patricia Gibbs, Vice President for Enrollment and Student Services, Wesleyan College, 4760 Forsyth Road, Macon, GA 31210-4462

Westwood College - Atlanta Midtown
Atlanta, Georgia

- For-profit 3-year technical college
- Very large city

General. Accredited by ACICS. **Calendar:** Differs by program.

Annual costs/financial aid. Tuition/fees (2005-2006): $12,255.

Contact. Phone: (404) 745-9096
1100 Spring Street, Suite 200, Atlanta, GA 30309

Hawaii

Brigham Young University-Hawaii

Laie, Hawaii **CB member**
www.byuh.edu **CB code: 4106**

- Private 4-year university and liberal arts college affiliated with Church of Jesus Christ of Latter-day Saints
- Residential campus in small town
- 2,398 degree-seeking undergraduates: 7% part-time, 58% women, 1% African American, 22% Asian American, 2% Hispanic American, 1% Native American, 47% international
- 31% of applicants admitted
- Application essay, interview required
- 38% graduate within 6 years

General. Founded in 1955. Regionally accredited. Mission is to educate students from the Asia and Pacific Rim. **Degrees:** 551 bachelor's, 4 associate awarded. **ROTC:** Army, Air Force. **Location:** 38 miles from Honolulu. **Calendar:** Semester, limited summer session. **Full-time faculty:** 115 total. **Part-time faculty:** 110 total. **Class size:** 57% < 20, 36% 20-39, 3% 40-49, 4% 50-99, less than 1% >100. **Special facilities:** Natural history museum, Polynesian Cultural Center, artifact collection housed in library, Institute for Pacific Studies.

Freshman class profile. 841 applied, 257 admitted, 220 enrolled.

Mid 50% test scores			
SAT verbal:	420-510	Rank in top tenth:	17%
SAT math:	450-550	Return as sophomores:	74%
ACT:	20-26	Out-of-state:	24%
Rank in top quarter:	55%	Live on campus:	100%
		International:	41%

Basis for selection. GED not accepted. Interview, essay, recommendations very important. Test scores also important. 3.0 GPA required for local students. ACT recommended. Audition required for music majors. Portfolio required for art majors. Ecclesiastical interviews required for all students. Essays may make difference in admission.

High school preparation. Recommended units include English 4, mathematics 2, social studies 3, history 2 and science 2.

2005-2006 Annual costs. Tuition/fees: $2,760. 50% higher tuition and per-credit-hour charges for students who are not members of The Church of Jesus Christ of Latter-day Saints. Room/board: $4,980. Books/supplies: $800. Personal expenses: $1,600.

Financial aid. Non-need-based: Scholarships awarded for academics, art, athletics, leadership, music/drama, state residency. **Additional information:** Closing date for scholarship applications May 1.

Application procedures. Admission: Closing date 2/15 (receipt date). $30 fee. Application may be submitted online. Admission notification on a rolling basis beginning on or about 4/1. Must reply by 8/25. **Financial aid:** Closing date 5/30. FAFSA required. Applicants notified by 5/1; must reply by 8/31.

Academics. Special study options: Cooperative education, double major, ESL, honors, independent study, internships, student-designed major, teacher certification program. **Credit/placement by examination:** AP, CLEP, IB, institutional tests. **Support services:** Learning center, remedial instruction, study skills assistance, tutoring, writing center.

Majors. Area/ethnic studies: Pacific. **Biology:** General, biochemistry. **Business:** Accounting, hospitality admin, hotel/motel admin, international, tourism/travel. **Computer sciences:** Computer science, information systems. **Education:** Art, biology, business, chemistry, elementary, English, ESL, mathematics, music, physical, physics, science, secondary, social science, special. **English:** English lit. **History:** General. **Interdisciplinary:** Intercultural. **Math:** General. **Parks/recreation:** Exercise sciences, health/fitness. **Psychology:** General. **Public administration:** Social work. **Science technology:** Biological. **Social sciences:** Political science. **Visual/performing arts:** Art, piano/organ, studio arts, voice/opera.

Most popular majors. Business/marketing 24%, computer/information sciences 12%, education 11%, interdisciplinary studies 12%, parks/recreation 6%, psychology 8%, public administration/social services 6%, visual/performing arts 6%.

Computing on campus. 465 workstations in dormitories, library, computer center, student center. Dormitories wired for high-speed internet access and linked to campus network. Online course registration, online library, helpline, repair service, wireless network available.

Student life. Freshman orientation: Mandatory. Preregistration for classes offered. 2 weeks at beginning of semester, includes luau, campus and island tour. **Policies:** Religious observance required. Freshmen permitted cars on campus. **Housing:** Guaranteed on-campus for freshmen. Single-sex dorms, apartments, substance-free housing available. $50 deposit, deadline 4/30. All first-time, non-local freshmen required to live on campus until sophomore standing achieved. **Activities:** Bands, choral groups, dance, drama, film society, literary magazine, music ensembles, student government, student newspaper, African club, Brasil club, Cambodian club, Fijian club, Filipino club, Hawaiian club, Hong Kong club, Indian club, Japanese club, Korean club.

Athletics. NCAA. **Intercollegiate:** Basketball M, cross-country, golf, softball W, tennis, volleyball W, water polo M. **Intramural:** Basketball, bowling, cross-country, golf, racquetball, rugby, soccer, softball, swimming, table tennis, tennis, volleyball, water polo M, weight lifting. **Team name:** Seasiders.

Student services. Campus ministries, career counseling, student employment services, financial aid counseling, health services, personal counseling, placement for graduates, veterans' counselor, women's services. **Physically disabled:** Services for visually, speech, hearing impaired.

Contact. E-mail: admissions@byuh.edu
Phone: (808) 293-3738 Fax: (808) 293-3741
Jeffery Bunker, Dean of Admissions and Records, Brigham Young University-Hawaii, 55-220 Kulanui Street, #1973, Laie, HI 96762-1294

Chaminade University of Honolulu

Honolulu, Hawaii **CB member**
www.chaminade.edu **CB code: 4105**

- Private 4-year university affiliated with Roman Catholic Church
- Commuter campus in large city
- 1,079 degree-seeking undergraduates: 4% part-time, 69% women, 4% African American, 64% Asian American, 7% Hispanic American, 1% Native American, 2% international
- 704 degree-seeking graduate students
- 96% of applicants admitted
- SAT or ACT (ACT writing optional), application essay required
- 38% graduate within 6 years

General. Founded in 1955. Regionally accredited. Campus shared with St. Louis School. **Degrees:** 276 bachelor's, 171 associate awarded; master's offered. **ROTC:** Army, Air Force. **Location:** 2 miles from Waikiki. **Calendar:** Semester, limited summer session. **Full-time faculty:** 82 total; 58% have terminal degrees, 34% minority, 39% women. **Part-time faculty:** 49 total; 20% have terminal degrees, 37% minority, 45% women. **Class size:** 63% < 20, 36% 20-39, 1% 40-49. **Special facilities:** Montessori laboratory preschool, observatory, theatre.

Freshman class profile. 904 applied, 870 admitted, 268 enrolled.

Mid 50% test scores		Rank in top quarter:	35%
SAT verbal:	430-530	Rank in top tenth:	11%
SAT math:	410-530	End year in good standing:	81%
ACT:	18-23	Return as sophomores:	69%
GPA 3.50 or higher:	25%	Out-of-state:	57%
GPA 3.0-3.49:	33%	Live on campus:	65%
GPA 2.0-2.99:	42%		

Basis for selection. School achievement record, test scores, statement of purpose important. Interview recommended for marginal students.

High school preparation. College-preparatory program recommended. Recommended units include English 4, mathematics 3, social studies 3, science 2 and academic electives 4.

2005-2006 Annual costs. Tuition/fees: $14,450. Room/board: $8,870. Books/supplies: $720. Personal expenses: $1,104.

2004-2005 Financial aid. Need-based: 202 full-time freshmen applied for aid; 167 were judged to have need; 167 of these received aid. Average need met was 65%. Average scholarship/grant was $8,258; average loan $2,879. 60% of total undergraduate aid awarded as scholarships/grants, 40%

as loans/jobs. **Non-need-based:** Awarded to 275 full-time undergraduates, including 56 freshmen. Scholarships awarded for academics, art, athletics, leadership, religious affiliation, ROTC, state residency. **Additional information:** For students whose eligibility for federal and institutional aid does not meet entire costs, alternative student loans may be secured for eligible applicants.

Application procedures. Admission: No deadline. $50 fee. Application may be submitted online. Admission notification on a rolling basis. **Financial aid:** Priority date 2/15; no closing date. FAFSA required. Applicants notified on a rolling basis starting 2/15; must reply within 4 week(s) of notification.

Academics. Special study options: Accelerated study, distance learning, double major, exchange student, independent study, internships, semester at sea, student-designed major, teacher certification program. Accelerated sessions in evening division. **Credit/placement by examination:** AP, CLEP, IB, SAT, ACT, institutional tests. 30 credit hours maximum toward associate degree, 30 toward bachelor's. **Support services:** Learning center, preadmission summer program, remedial instruction, study skills assistance, tutoring.

Majors. Biology: General. **Business:** Accounting, business admin, marketing. **Communications:** General, broadcast journalism, media studies, public relations. **Computer sciences:** General, computer science. **Conservation:** Environmental studies. **Education:** Early childhood, elementary, secondary. **English:** English lit. **History:** General. **Interdisciplinary:** Behavioral sciences. **Liberal arts:** Arts/sciences. **Philosophy/religion:** Religion. **Protective services:** Criminalistics, forensics. **Psychology:** General. **Social sciences:** General, international relations, political science. **Visual/performing arts:** Interior design.

Most popular majors. Business/marketing 11%, education 16%, English 8%, history 11%, psychology 11%, security/protective services 27%.

Computing on campus. 96 workstations in dormitories, library, computer center, student center. Dormitories wired for high-speed internet access. Online library, helpline, repair service, wireless network available.

Student life. Freshman orientation: Mandatory, $115 fee. Preregistration for classes offered. **Policies:** Freshmen permitted cars on campus. **Housing:** Guaranteed on-campus for freshmen. Coed dorms, single-sex dorms, special housing for disabled, apartments, substance-free housing available. $300 nonrefundable deposit, deadline 5/1. **Activities:** Choral groups, dance, drama, literary magazine, musical theater, student government, student newspaper, Samoan club, Hawaiian club, Rotaract club, accounting club, Black Student Union, Filipino club, CJ Sleuths, communications club, surf club, sailing club.

Athletics. NCAA. **Intercollegiate:** Basketball M, cross-country, golf, softball W, tennis, volleyball W, water polo M. **Intramural:** Cheerleading. **Team name:** Silverswords.

Student services. Adult student services, alcohol/substance abuse counseling, campus ministries, career counseling, student employment services, financial aid counseling, health services, personal counseling, placement for graduates. **Physically disabled:** Services for visually, speech, hearing impaired.

Contact. E-mail: admissions@chaminade.edu
Phone: (808) 735-4735 Toll-free number: (800) 735-3733
Fax: (808) 739-4647
Joy Bouey, Dean of Enrollment Management, Chaminade University of Honolulu, 3140 Waialae Avenue, Honolulu, HI 96816

Hawaii Pacific University

Honolulu, Hawaii
www.hpu.edu **CB code: 4352**

- Private 4-year university and liberal arts college
- Commuter campus in large city
- 6,296 degree-seeking undergraduates: 36% part-time, 60% women
- 1,109 degree-seeking graduate students
- 82% of applicants admitted
- SAT or ACT (ACT writing optional) required
- 41% graduate within 6 years

General. Founded in 1965. Regionally accredited. 2 main campuses connected by free shuttle service. Programs offered for military personnel and their dependents and for older students. Satellite campus on 6 military installations on Oahu. Affiliated with the Oceanic Institute. **Degrees:** 1,012 bachelor's, 203 associate awarded; master's offered. **ROTC:** Army, Air Force. **Calendar:** Semester, extensive summer session. **Full-time faculty:** 238 total; 65% have terminal degrees, 22% minority, 45% women. **Part-time faculty:** 374 total; 29% have terminal degrees, 36% minority, 46% women. **Class size:** 47% < 20, 53% 20-39, less than 1% 40-49. **Special facilities:** Research boat, theater.

Freshman class profile. 3,094 applied, 2,541 admitted, 657 enrolled.

Mid 50% test scores		**Rank in top quarter:**	50%
SAT verbal:	420-560	**Rank in top tenth:**	22%
SAT math:	440-570	**End year in good standing:**	93%
ACT:	17-24	**Return as sophomores:**	66%
GPA 3.50 or higher:	40%	**Out-of-state:**	60%
GPA 3.0-3.49:	30%	**Live on campus:**	27%
GPA 2.0-2.99:	30%	**International:**	10%

Basis for selection. Academic record, test scores most important. Interview also important, recommendations considered. Essay recommended. **Homeschooled:** Transcript of courses and grades, interview, letter of recommendation (nonparent) required. ACT or SAT scores required.

High school preparation. College-preparatory program recommended. 14 units recommended. Recommended units include English 4, mathematics 3, social studies 2, history 2, science 2 and foreign language 1. Additional science and mathematics required for nursing and marine science.

2005-2006 Annual costs. Tuition/fees: $11,630. Room/board: $9,450. Books/supplies: $1,300. Personal expenses: $800.

2005-2006 Financial aid. Need-based: 518 full-time freshmen applied for aid; 299 were judged to have need; 280 of these received aid. Average need met was 80%. Average scholarship/grant was $4,033; average loan $3,109. 21% of total undergraduate aid awarded as scholarships/grants, 79% as loans/jobs. **Non-need-based:** Awarded to 1,447 full-time undergraduates, including 318 freshmen. Scholarships awarded for academics, athletics, job skills, leadership, music/drama, religious affiliation, ROTC.

Application procedures. Admission: Priority date 3/1; no deadline. $50 fee, may be waived for applicants with need. Application may be submitted online. Admission notification on a rolling basis. Must reply by May 1 or within 4 week(s) if notified thereafter. **Financial aid:** Priority date 3/1; no closing date. FAFSA required. Applicants notified on a rolling basis starting 4/1; must reply within 3 week(s) of notification.

Academics. All students complete core requirements based on following themes: global systems, world cultures, communication skills, research/epistemology, values and choices. **Special study options:** Accelerated study, combined bachelor's/graduate degree, cooperative education, distance learning, double major, dual enrollment of high school students, ESL, honors, independent study, internships, liberal arts/career combination, student-designed major, study abroad, teacher certification program, weekend college. 3-2 engineering program with University of Southern California (CA), Washington University, St. Louis (MO). **Credit/placement by examination:** AP, CLEP, IB, SAT, ACT, institutional tests. 36 credit hours maximum toward associate degree, 36 toward bachelor's. **Support services:** Learning center, pre-admission summer program, reduced course load, remedial instruction, study skills assistance, tutoring.

Honors college/program. 3.5 minimum high school GPA, minimum 24 ACT or 1100 SAT (exclusive of Writing) required. 40-50 admitted and enrolled each fall.

Majors. Biology: General, marine. **Business:** General, accounting, banking/financial services, business admin, communications, finance, human resources, international, international finance, management information systems, managerial economics, marketing, tourism/travel. **Communications:** General, advertising, journalism, public relations. **Computer sciences:** General, computer science. **Conservation:** General, environmental science, environmental studies. **Education:** ESL. **Family/consumer sciences:** Family studies. **Foreign languages:** Comparative lit. **Health:** Nursing (RN), premedicine. **History:** General. **Interdisciplinary:** Behavioral sciences. **Liberal arts:** Arts/sciences. **Math:** Applied. **Physical sciences:** Oceanography. **Protective services:** Law enforcement admin. **Psychology:** General. **Public administration:** General, human services, social work. **Social sciences:** General, anthropology, economics, international relations, political science, sociology.

Most popular majors. Business/marketing 44%, computer/information sciences 9%, health sciences 14%, legal studies 6%.

Computing on campus. PC or laptop required. 590 workstations in library, computer center, student center. Dormitories wired for high-speed internet access and linked to campus network. Commuter students can connect to campus network. Online course registration, online library, helpline, student web hosting, wireless network available.

Student life. Freshman orientation: Available, $70 fee. Preregistration for classes offered. Week of activities that include on-campus sessions and off-campus activities. **Policies:** Freshmen permitted cars on campus. **Housing:** Coed dorms, single-sex dorms, apartments, substance-free housing available. $500 deposit. Homestay program also available. **Activities:** Pep band, choral groups, dance, drama, film society, literary magazine, music ensembles, musical theater, student government, student newspaper, Rotaract, President's Hosts, international student organization, Christian Fellowship, American marketing association, hiking club, honors societies, computing club, students In free enterprise.

Athletics. NCAA. **Intercollegiate:** Baseball M, basketball M, cross-country, golf, softball W, tennis, volleyball W. **Intramural:** Soccer, volleyball. **Team name:** Sea Warriors.

Student services. Adult student services, alcohol/substance abuse counseling, campus ministries, career counseling, student employment services, financial aid counseling, health services, personal counseling, placement for graduates, veterans' counselor.

Contact. E-mail: admissions@hpu.edu
Phone: (808) 544-0238 Toll-free number: (800) 669-4724
Fax: (808) 544-1136
Sara Sato, Director of Admissions, Hawaii Pacific University, 1164 Bishop Street, Honolulu, HI 96813

University of Hawaii at Hilo

Hilo, Hawaii — **CB member**
www.uhh.hawaii.edu — **CB code: 4869**

- Public 4-year university
- Commuter campus in large town
- 3,363 undergraduates
- SAT or ACT (ACT writing optional) required

General. Founded in 1970. Regionally accredited. **Degrees:** 453 bachelor's awarded; master's offered. **Location:** 200 miles from Honolulu. **Calendar:** Semester, limited summer session. **Full-time faculty:** 197 total. **Part-time faculty:** 93 total. **Class size:** 41% < 20, 47% 20-39, 8% 40-49, 5% 50-99. **Special facilities:** Active volcanoes study center, space science center, small business development center, marine education center, 110-acre farm laboratory.

Freshman class profile.

Mid 50% test scores			
SAT verbal:	420-540	Out-of-state:	39%
SAT math:	440-560	Live on campus:	64%
ACT:	18-23		

Basis for selection. High school GPA in academic subjects, SAT/ACT test scores, class rank, and school recommendation considered.

High school preparation. 17 units required. Required and recommended units include English 4, mathematics 3, social studies 2, history 2, science 3, foreign language 2 and academic electives 7. 3 mathematics beyond pre-algebra, 7 academic electives not including physical education or ROTC. 4 math and 4 science recommended for science and business majors.

2005-2006 Annual costs. Tuition/fees: $2,603; $8,171 out-of-state. Room/board: $5,472. Books/supplies: $1,017. Personal expenses: $1,166.

Financial aid. Additional information: Hawaii student incentive grants and tuition waivers (merit and need-based) available to Hawaii residents at participating institutions.

Application procedures. Admission: Priority date 3/1; deadline 7/1 (postmark date). $40 fee, may be waived for applicants with need. Application may be submitted online. Admission notification on a rolling basis beginning on or about 10/1. Must reply by May 1 or within 2 week(s) if notified thereafter. **Financial aid:** Priority date 3/1; no closing date. FAFSA required. Applicants notified on a rolling basis starting 4/15; must reply within 2 week(s) of notification.

Academics. Special study options: Cross-registration, distance learning, double major, dual enrollment of high school students, exchange student, honors, independent study, internships, student-designed major, study abroad, teacher certification program. Marine sciences and astronomy summer programs. **Credit/placement by examination:** CLEP, IB, institutional tests. 30 credit hours maximum toward bachelor's degree. **Support services:** Learning center, tutoring, writing center.

Majors. Agriculture: Agribusiness operations, agronomy, animal sciences, horticultural science, plant protection, soil science. **Area/ethnic studies:** Native American. **Biology:** General, marine. **Business:** General, accounting, business admin, finance, marketing. **Communications:** General. **Computer sciences:** General. **English:** Speech/rhetoric. **Foreign languages:** Japanese, linguistics. **Health:** Premedicine. **History:** General. **Interdisciplinary:** Natural sciences. **Liberal arts:** Arts/sciences. **Math:** General. **Parks/recreation:** Facilities management, health/fitness. **Philosophy/religion:** Philosophy, religion. **Physical sciences:** Astronomy, chemistry, geology, physics. **Psychology:** General. **Public administration:** General. **Social sciences:** Anthropology, economics, geography, political science, sociology. **Visual/performing arts:** Art.

Most popular majors. Agriculture 7%, biology 8%, business/marketing 13%, interdisciplinary studies 8%, psychology 18%, social sciences 21%.

Computing on campus. 600 workstations in dormitories, library, computer center, student center. Commuter students can connect to campus network. Online course registration, online library, helpline, repair service available.

Student life. Freshman orientation: Available. Preregistration for classes offered. 1-week program before start of classes. **Housing:** Coed dorms, special housing for disabled, apartments available. $20 deposit, deadline 7/15. Student housing units available for mobility-impaired students. **Activities:** Bands, choral groups, dance, drama, literary magazine, music ensembles, musical theater, student government, student newspaper, international student association, Samoan club, Delta Sigma Pi business fraternity, World Hope, Rotoract, Bayanihan club, Bahai Club, Chuukese Student Association, Earth Action, Nihon no kai.

Athletics. NCAA. **Intercollegiate:** Baseball M, basketball M, cross-country, golf, softball W, tennis, volleyball W. **Intramural:** Archery, badminton, basketball, bowling, cross-country, golf, softball, table tennis, tennis, volleyball. **Team name:** Vulcans.

Student services. Career counseling, services for economically disadvantaged, student employment services, financial aid counseling, health services, minority student services, personal counseling, placement for graduates, women's services. **Physically disabled:** Services for visually, speech, hearing impaired.

Contact. E-mail: uhhadm@hawaii.edu
Phone: (808) 974-7414 Toll-free number: (800) 897-4456
Fax: (808) 933-0861
James Cromwell, Director of Admissions, University of Hawaii at Hilo, 200 West Kawili Street, Hilo, HI 96720-4091

University of Hawaii at Manoa

Honolulu, Hawaii — **CB member**
www.manoa.hawaii.edu — **CB code: 4867**

- Public 4-year university
- Commuter campus in very large city
- 13,831 degree-seeking undergraduates: 17% part-time, 55% women, 1% African American, 65% Asian American, 2% Hispanic American, 3% international
- 5,409 degree-seeking graduate students
- 68% of applicants admitted
- SAT or ACT with writing required
- 56% graduate within 6 years; 65% enter graduate study

General. Founded in 1907. Regionally accredited. **Degrees:** 2,647 bachelor's awarded; master's, doctoral, first professional offered. **ROTC:** Army, Air Force. **Location:** 3 miles from downtown. **Calendar:** Semester, extensive summer session. **Full-time faculty:** 1,086 total; 80% have terminal degrees, 32% minority, 38% women. **Part-time faculty:** 83 total; 78% have terminal degrees, 40% minority, 41% women. **Class size:** 46% < 20, 39% 20-39, 6% 40-49, 5% 50-99, 4% >100. **Special facilities:** Institute for Astronomy, observatories, arboretum, art museum, East-West Center, Japanese tea house and garden, Hawaiian Studies Center, Korean Studies Center.

Freshman class profile. 6,896 applied, 4,679 admitted, 2,022 enrolled.

Mid 50% test scores			
SAT verbal:	480-580	Rank in top tenth:	25%
SAT math:	520-620	End year in good standing:	83%
ACT:	21-25	Return as sophomores:	75%
GPA 3.50 or higher:	44%	Out-of-state:	25%
GPA 3.0-3.49:	42%	Live on campus:	15%
GPA 2.0-2.99:	14%	International:	1%
Rank in top quarter:	61%	Fraternities:	1%
		Sororities:	1%

Basis for selection. School achievement record, test scores, class rank most important. **Homeschooled:** In absence of official transcript from accredited school, students must submit GED results in addition to other requirements.

High school preparation. College-preparatory program required. 22 units required. Required and recommended units include English 4, mathematics 3, social studies 3, science 3 (laboratory 1), foreign language 2 and academic electives 4.

2005-2006 Annual costs. Tuition/fees: $3,697; $10,177 out-of-state. Room/board: $6,717. Books/supplies: $1,112. Personal expenses: $1,189.

2004-2005 Financial aid. **Need-based:** 1,264 full-time freshmen applied for aid; 686 were judged to have need; 626 of these received aid. Average need met was 62%. Average scholarship/grant was $3,516; average loan $2,575. 45% of total undergraduate aid awarded as scholarships/grants, 55% as loans/jobs. **Non-need-based:** Awarded to 2,017 full-time undergraduates, including 357 freshmen. Scholarships awarded for academics, alumni affiliation, art, athletics, job skills, leadership, minority status, music/drama, religious affiliation, ROTC, state residency. **Additional information:** Hawaii student incentive grants and tuition waivers (merit and need-based) available to Hawaii residents at participating institutions.

Application procedures. **Admission:** Priority date 2/1; deadline 5/1 (receipt date). $50 fee, may be waived for applicants with need. Application may be submitted online. Admission notification on a rolling basis beginning on or about 12/1. Must reply by May 1 or within 2 week(s) if notified thereafter. **Financial aid:** Priority date 3/1; no closing date. FAFSA required. Applicants notified on a rolling basis starting 3/15; must reply within 4 week(s) of notification.

Academics. **Special study options:** Cooperative education, distance learning, double major, ESL, exchange student, honors, independent study, internships, student-designed major, study abroad, teacher certification program. **Credit/placement by examination:** AP, CLEP, IB, SAT, ACT, institutional tests. 30 credit hours maximum toward bachelor's degree. **Support services:** Learning center, pre-admission summer program, remedial instruction, study skills assistance, tutoring, writing center.

Majors. **Agriculture:** Animal sciences, plant protection. **Area/ethnic studies:** American, Asian, Native American. **Biology:** General, botany, marine, microbiology, zoology. **Business:** General, accounting, business admin, finance, human resources, international, management information systems, marketing, tourism/travel. **Communications:** General, journalism. **Computer sciences:** General, computer science. **Conservation:** Environmental science, management/policy. **Education:** Elementary, secondary, special. **Engineering:** Agricultural, civil, electrical, mechanical. **English:** English lit. **Family/consumer sciences:** General, clothing/textiles. **Foreign languages:** Chinese, classics, Filipino/Tagalog, French, German, Japanese, Korean, Native American, Russian, Spanish. **Health:** Athletic training, audiology/speech pathology, clinical lab science, dental hygiene, nursing (RN). **History:** General. **Interdisciplinary:** Nutrition sciences. **Liberal arts:** Arts/sciences. **Math:** General. **Parks/recreation:** Exercise sciences. **Philosophy/religion:** Philosophy, religion. **Physical sciences:** Chemistry, geology, meteorology, physics. **Psychology:** General. **Public administration:** Social work. **Social sciences:** Anthropology, economics, geography, political science, sociology. **Visual/performing arts:** Art, dance, dramatic.

Most popular majors. Business/marketing 23%, education 7%, psychology 7%, social sciences 11%.

Computing on campus. 1,400 workstations in dormitories, library, computer center. Dormitories wired for high-speed internet access and linked to campus network. Commuter students can connect to campus network. Online course registration, online library, helpline, repair service, student web hosting, wireless network available.

Student life. **Freshman orientation:** Available, $80 fee. Preregistration for classes offered. 2-day program. **Policies:** Freshmen permitted cars on campus. **Housing:** Guaranteed on-campus for freshmen. Coed dorms, apartments, substance-free housing available. $225 fully refundable deposit, deadline 5/1. Some modified units within student housing facilities available for disabled students. **Activities:** Bands, choral groups, dance, drama, literary magazine, music ensembles, radio station, student government, student newspaper, symphony orchestra, TV station, 150+ registered organizations.

Athletics. NCAA. **Intercollegiate:** Baseball M, basketball, cheerleading, cross-country W, diving, football (tackle) M, golf, sailing, soccer W, softball W, swimming, tennis, track and field W, volleyball, water polo W. **Intramural:** Badminton, basketball, cross-country, golf, soccer, softball, table tennis, tennis, track and field W, volleyball, weight lifting. **Team name:** Warriors, Rainbow Warriors, Rainbows, Rainbow Wahine.

Student services. Adult student services, alcohol/substance abuse counseling, career counseling, services for economically disadvantaged, student employment services, financial aid counseling, health services, minority student services, on-campus daycare, personal counseling, placement for graduates, veterans' counselor, women's services. **Physically disabled:** Services for visually, speech, hearing impaired.

Contact. E-mail: ar-info@hawaii.edu
Phone: (808) 956-8975 Toll-free number: (800) 823-9771
Fax: (808) 956-4148
Jan Heu, Interim Director of Admissions and Records, University of Hawaii at Manoa, 2600 Campus Road, QLC Rm 001, Honolulu, HI 96822

University of Hawaii: West Oahu

Pearl City, Hawaii — **CB member**
www.uhwo.hawaii.edu — **CB code: 1042**

- Public upper-division liberal arts college
- Commuter campus in large town
- 86% of applicants admitted

General. Founded in 1976. Regionally accredited. Campus shared with community college. **Degrees:** 193 bachelor's awarded. **ROTC:** Army, Air Force. **Location:** 10 miles from Honolulu. **Calendar:** Semester, limited summer session. **Full-time faculty:** 28 total; 96% have terminal degrees, 32% women. **Part-time faculty:** 20 total; 85% have terminal degrees, 35% women. **Class size:** 36% < 20, 62% 20-39, 2% 40-49.

Student profile. 838 degree-seeking undergraduates. 436 applied as first time-transfer students, 377 admitted, 305 enrolled.

Women:	69%	**Native American:**	1%
African American:	2%	**Part-time:**	66%
Asian American:	59%	**Out-of-state:**	6%
Hispanic American:	3%	**25 or older:**	72%

Basis for selection. College transcript required. Transfer accepted as juniors, seniors.

2005-2006 Annual costs. Tuition/fees: $2,266; $7,402 out-of-state. Foreign students pay out-of-state tuition rates, except for applicants from countries with reciprocity agreements. Books/supplies: $1,048. Personal expenses: $1,029.

Financial aid. **Need-based:** 54% of total undergraduate aid awarded as scholarships/grants, 46% as loans/jobs. **Non-need-based:** Scholarships awarded for academics, leadership, state residency. **Additional information:** Tuition waivers (merit and need-based) available to Hawaii residents.

Application procedures. **Admission:** Priority date 8/1. $50 fee. Application must be submitted on paper. **Financial aid:** Priority date 4/1, no deadline. Applicants notified by 7/1.

Academics. **Special study options:** Cross-registration, distance learning, double major, independent study, internships, study abroad. **Credit/placement by examination:** AP, CLEP, institutional tests. 42 credit hours maximum toward bachelor's degree. 21 lower division and 21 upper division credits may be earned through examination.

Majors. **Area/ethnic studies:** Pacific. **Business:** Accounting, business admin. **History:** General. **Philosophy/religion:** Philosophy. **Protective services:** Law enforcement admin. **Psychology:** General. **Public administration:** General. **Social sciences:** General, anthropology, economics, political science, sociology.

Most popular majors. Business/marketing 24%, psychology 26%, public administration/social services 7%, security/protective services 15%, social sciences 21%.

Computing on campus. 18 workstations in computer center. Commuter students can connect to campus network. Helpline, wireless network available.

Student life. **Activities:** Student government, various interest clubs available.

Student services. Career counseling, student employment services, financial aid counseling, veterans' counselor. **Physically disabled:** Services for visually, hearing impaired.

Contact. E-mail: info@uhwo.hawaii.edu
Phone: (808) 454-4700 Fax: (808) 453-6075
Terri Ota, Registrar, University of Hawaii: West Oahu, 96-129 Ala Ike, Pearl City, HI 96782

Idaho

Albertson College of Idaho

Caldwell, Idaho
www.albertson.edu

CB member
CB code: 4060

- Private 4-year liberal arts college
- Residential campus in large town
- 788 degree-seeking undergraduates: 3% part-time, 58% women, 1% African American, 3% Asian American, 5% Hispanic American, 1% Native American, 2% international
- 18 graduate students
- 84% of applicants admitted
- SAT or ACT with writing, application essay required
- 56% graduate within 6 years

General. Founded in 1891. Regionally accredited. Founded by Presbyterian Church. **Degrees:** 174 bachelor's awarded; master's offered. **ROTC:** Army. **Location:** 30 miles from Boise, 400 miles from Salt Lake City. **Calendar:** 13-6-13. **Full-time faculty:** 66 total; 83% have terminal degrees, 6% minority, 39% women. **Part-time faculty:** 5 total; 100% have terminal degrees, 20% minority, 40% women. **Class size:** 72% < 20, 25% 20-39, less than 1% 40-49, 2% 50-99, less than 1% >100. **Special facilities:** Natural history museum, mineral and gem collection, planetarium, observatory, nuclear magnetic resonance spectrometer, performing and fine arts center.

Freshman class profile. 924 applied, 777 admitted, 196 enrolled.

Mid 50% test scores			
SAT verbal:	520-640	Rank in top quarter:	70%
SAT math:	530-640	Rank in top tenth:	34%
ACT:	23-28	Return as sophomores:	76%
GPA 3.50 or higher:	71%	Out-of-state:	28%
GPA 3.0-3.49:	22%	Live on campus:	88%
GPA 2.0-2.99:	7%	International:	1%

Basis for selection. Academic record, test scores, extracurricular activities, essay, teacher recommendation important. Interview and essay recommended. Audition required of music, theater majors. Portfolio required of art majors. **Homeschooled:** Writing, ACT critical reading.

High school preparation. Required and recommended units include English 4, mathematics 3, social studies 3, history 3, science 2-3 (laboratory 2) and foreign language 2.

2006-2007 Annual costs. Tuition/fees: $16,625. Room/board: $6,191. Books/supplies: $900. Personal expenses: $700.

2005-2006 Financial aid. Need-based: 157 full-time freshmen applied for aid; 139 were judged to have need; 139 of these received aid. Average need met was 89%. Average scholarship/grant was $3,737; average loan $3,515. 51% of total undergraduate aid awarded as scholarships/grants, 49% as loans/jobs. **Non-need-based:** Awarded to 874 full-time undergraduates, including 244 freshmen. Scholarships awarded for academics, alumni affiliation, art, athletics, job skills, leadership, minority status, music/drama, religious affiliation.

Application procedures. Admission: Priority date 11/15; deadline 6/1 (postmark date). $50 fee, may be waived for applicants with need. Application may be submitted online. Admission notification on a rolling basis beginning on or about 11/15. Must reply by 5/1. **Financial aid:** Priority date 2/15; no closing date. FAFSA, institutional form required. Applicants notified on a rolling basis starting 3/1; must reply within 3 week(s) of notification.

Academics. All freshmen participate in first-year experience course and receive a book to read over summer as preparation. Program for learning-disabled students available through partnership with Lee Pesky Learning Center. **Special study options:** Combined bachelor's/graduate degree, cross-registration, double major, dual enrollment of high school students, exchange student, honors, independent study, internships, liberal arts/career combination, semester at sea, student-designed major, study abroad, teacher certification program. Bachelor's/graduate program in law with University of Idaho; MBA with Gonzaga University (WA), Boise State University; bachelor's/master's degrees in accountancy with University of Idaho, management with Willamette University (OR), natural resources with University of Idaho, economics with University of Idaho; bachelor's in engineering with University of Idaho, Boise State University, Columbia University (NY), Washington University (MO); 5th-year teaching internship, cooperative nursing program with Idaho State University. **Credit/placement by examination:** AP, CLEP, IB, institutional tests. **Support services:** Learning center, reduced course load, remedial instruction, study skills assistance, tutoring, writing center.

Majors. Biology: General. **Business:** Accounting, business admin, international. **Conservation:** Environmental studies. **Education:** Physical. **Engineering:** General. **English:** Creative writing, English lit. **Foreign languages:** Spanish. **Health:** Prenursing. **History:** General. **Interdisciplinary:** Math/computer science. **Liberal arts:** Arts/sciences. **Math:** General, applied. **Parks/recreation:** Exercise sciences, health/fitness, sports admin. **Philosophy/religion:** Philosophy, religion. **Physical sciences:** Chemistry. **Psychology:** General. **Social sciences:** Anthropology, economics, international relations, political science, sociology. **Visual/performing arts:** Art, dramatic.

Most popular majors. Biology 8%, business/marketing 21%, history 12%, interdisciplinary studies 6%, psychology 9%, social sciences 12%, visual/performing arts 9%.

Computing on campus. PC or laptop required. 276 workstations in dormitories, library, computer center, student center. Dormitories wired for high-speed internet access and linked to campus network. Commuter students can connect to campus network. Online library, helpline, repair service, student web hosting, wireless network available.

Student life. Freshman orientation: Mandatory. Preregistration for classes offered. Several 1-day sessions are scheduled over the summer for registration, orientation, and tuition payment; 3-day fall orientation in nearby mountains before the start of fall semester. **Policies:** Freshman and sophomores under age 21 must live on campus unless living with parents or relatives. Freshmen permitted cars on campus. **Housing:** Guaranteed on-campus for freshmen. Coed dorms, special housing for disabled, fraternity/sorority housing available. $300 deposit, deadline 9/1. Pets allowed in dorm rooms. Honors residence available for students with superior academic records. **Activities:** Bands, choral groups, dance, drama, film society, literary magazine, music ensembles, musical theater, opera, radio station, student government, student newspaper, symphony orchestra, Young Democrats, College Republicans, Terra, Intercollegiate Knights, Kiwanis International, progressive student alliance, Philotech, Gay-Straight aampus alliance, Fellowship of Christian Athletes.

Athletics. NAIA. **Intercollegiate:** Baseball M, basketball, cross-country, golf, skiing, soccer, softball W, swimming, tennis W, track and field, volleyball W. **Intramural:** Badminton, basketball, football (non-tackle), soccer, softball, swimming, table tennis, tennis, volleyball. **Team name:** Coyotes.

Student services. Alcohol/substance abuse counseling, campus ministries, career counseling, student employment services, financial aid counseling, health services, minority student services, personal counseling, placement for graduates, women's services. **Physically disabled:** Services for visually impaired.

Contact. E-mail: admission@albertson.edu
Phone: (208) 459-5305 Toll-free number: (800) 224-3246
Fax: (208) 459-5116
Charlene Brown, Director of Admissions, Albertson College of Idaho, 2112 Cleveland Boulevard, Caldwell, ID 83605

Boise Bible College

Boise, Idaho
www.boisebible.edu

CB code: 0891

- Private 4-year Bible college affiliated with nondenominational tradition
- Residential campus in small city
- 171 degree-seeking undergraduates
- 100% of applicants admitted
- SAT or ACT (ACT writing optional), application essay required

General. Founded in 1945. Accredited by ABHE. **Degrees:** 11 bachelor's, 9 associate awarded. **Location:** 4 miles from downtown. **Calendar:** Semester. **Full-time faculty:** 8 total. **Part-time faculty:** 7 total. **Class size:** 74% < 20, 21% 20-39, 5% 40-49.

Freshman class profile. 78 applied, 78 admitted, 62 enrolled.

Mid 50% test scores		Rank in top quarter:	25%
SAT verbal:	420-560	Rank in top tenth:	15%
SAT math:	440-530	Live on campus:	74%
ACT:	19-25		

Basis for selection. Christian conduct or ethical code standards based on signed student statement, recommendation of home church minister, 1 employment reference required. School achievement important. **Homeschooled:** GED or transcripts from homeschooling agency recommended. Applicants submitting home-prepared transcripts advised to consult admissions office.

High school preparation. Recommended units include English 4, mathematics 2, history 2 and foreign language 1.

2005-2006 Annual costs. Tuition/fees: $6,500. Room/board: $4,200. Books/supplies: $605. Personal expenses: $1,210.

Financial aid. Non-need-based: Scholarships awarded for academics, leadership, music/drama, religious affiliation.

Application procedures. Admission: Priority date 5/1; deadline 8/15 (receipt date). $25 fee. Application must be submitted on paper. Admission notification on a rolling basis. Must reply by May 1 or within 3 week(s) if notified thereafter. **Financial aid:** Priority date 5/1; no closing date. FAFSA, institutional form required. Applicants notified on a rolling basis starting 5/2; must reply by 8/1 or within 2 week(s) of notification.

Academics. Special study options: Distance learning, double major, independent study, internships, study abroad. Church leadership weekend seminars. **Credit/placement by examination:** AP, CLEP, IB, institutional tests. AABC Bible Knowledge Test, institutional English placement test required. **Support services:** Reduced course load, remedial instruction.

Majors. Theology: Bible, missionary, pastoral counseling, religious ed, sacred music, theology, youth ministry.

Computing on campus. 7 workstations in library, computer center.

Student life. Freshman orientation: Mandatory. Preregistration for classes offered. 2 days of training and testing, followed by white-water boat trip. **Policies:** Religious observance required. Freshmen permitted cars on campus. **Housing:** Guaranteed on-campus for freshmen. Single-sex dorms available. $150 deposit, deadline 8/15. Trailer hookups for married students. **Activities:** Choral groups, music ensembles, student government, student newspaper, Christian service missions club.

Athletics. Intramural: Basketball, football (non-tackle) M, soccer M, softball, table tennis, volleyball. **Team name:** Lions.

Student services. Adult student services, career counseling, student employment services, financial aid counseling, health services, personal counseling, placement for graduates, veterans' counselor.

Contact. E-mail: boisebible@boisebible.edu
Phone: (208) 376-7731 Toll-free number: (800) 893-7755
Martin Flaherty, Admissions Director, Boise Bible College, 8695 Marigold Street, Boise, ID 83714-1220

Boise State University

Boise, Idaho — **CB member**
www.boisestate.edu — **CB code: 4018**

- Public 4-year university and technical college
- Commuter campus in small city
- 15,676 degree-seeking undergraduates: 31% part-time, 54% women, 1% African American, 3% Asian American, 6% Hispanic American, 1% Native American, 1% international
- 1,485 degree-seeking graduate students
- 90% of applicants admitted
- SAT or ACT (ACT writing optional) required

General. Founded in 1932. Regionally accredited. **Degrees:** 1,663 bachelor's, 447 associate awarded; master's, doctoral offered. **ROTC:** Army. **Location:** Downtown. **Calendar:** Semester, limited summer session. **Full-time faculty:** 578 total; 82% have terminal degrees, 7% minority, 42% women. **Part-time faculty:** 549 total; 43% have terminal degrees, 6% minority, 44% women. **Class size:** 46% < 20, 41% 20-39, 7% 40-49, 5% 50-99, 2% >100. **Special facilities:** Performing arts center, technology center, natural area and world center for birds of prey research.

Freshman class profile. 3,340 applied, 2,991 admitted, 2,501 enrolled.

Mid 50% test scores		Rank in top tenth:	9%
SAT verbal:	460-590	End year in good standing:	95%
SAT math:	500-550	Return as sophomores:	63%
ACT:	17-26	Out-of-state:	9%
GPA 3.50 or higher:	32%	Live on campus:	8%
GPA 3.0-3.49:	36%	International:	1%
GPA 2.0-2.99:	30%	Fraternities:	1%
Rank in top quarter:	28%	Sororities:	1%

Basis for selection. Admission based on high school GPA and ACT or SAT score. Applicants without high school diploma or GED may petition for admission. Interview required for vocational-technical, nursing majors. **Homeschooled:** State high school equivalency certificate required.

High school preparation. 15 units required. Required and recommended units include English 4, mathematics 3, social studies 3, science 3 and foreign language 1. One unit foreign language, humanities, or fine arts and 1.5 units other college preparatory also recommended.

2005-2006 Annual costs. Tuition/fees: $3,872; $11,280 out-of-state. Out-of-state students (undergraduate and graduate) taking less than 8 credit hours pay in-state rate. Room/board: $4,908. Books/supplies: $1,000. Personal expenses: $2,258.

2005-2006 Financial aid. Need-based: Average need met was 60%. Average scholarship/grant was $2,934; average loan $2,685. 33% of total undergraduate aid awarded as scholarships/grants, 67% as loans/jobs. **Non-need-based:** Scholarships awarded for academics, athletics, music/drama, ROTC, state residency.

Application procedures. Admission: Closing date 7/14. $30 fee. Application may be submitted online. Admission notification on a rolling basis beginning on or about 2/15. Strongly recommended that students apply January-March. **Financial aid:** Priority date 4/1; no closing date. FAFSA required. Applicants notified on a rolling basis starting 6/1; must reply within 2 week(s) of notification.

Academics. Basque studies program abroad. **Special study options:** Distance learning, double major, dual enrollment of high school students, exchange student, honors, independent study, internships, student-designed major, study abroad, teacher certification program, weekend college. **Credit/placement by examination:** AP, CLEP, SAT, ACT, institutional tests. 21 credit hours maximum toward associate degree, 42 toward bachelor's. **Support services:** Learning center, pre-admission summer program, reduced course load, remedial instruction, study skills assistance, tutoring.

Majors. Biology: General. **Business:** Accounting, construction management, finance, human resources, international, management information systems, managerial economics, market research, marketing, operations. **Communications:** General, journalism. **Computer sciences:** Computer science, information systems. **Education:** General, art, bilingual, business, elementary, music, physical, special. **Engineering:** Civil, electrical, mechanical. **Engineering technology:** Construction. **English:** American lit, British lit. **Foreign languages:** French, German, Spanish. **Health:** Athletic training, environmental health, medical radiologic technology/radiation therapy, medical records admin, nursing (RN), predentistry, premedicine, preveterinary, respiratory therapy technology. **History:** General. **Liberal arts:** Arts/sciences. **Math:** General, applied. **Parks/recreation:** Exercise sciences, health/fitness. **Philosophy/religion:** Philosophy. **Physical sciences:** Chemistry, geology, geophysics, physics, planetary. **Protective services:** Law enforcement admin. **Psychology:** General. **Public administration:** Social work. **Social sciences:** General, anthropology, economics, political science, sociology. **Visual/performing arts:** Art, commercial/advertising art, dramatic, music management, music performance, music theory/composition.

Most popular majors. Business/marketing 22%, communications/journalism 6%, education 9%, health sciences 12%, social sciences 8%.

Computing on campus. 900 workstations in dormitories, library, computer center. Dormitories linked to campus network. Commuter students can connect to campus network. Online course registration, wireless network available.

Student life. Freshman orientation: Available. Preregistration for classes offered. **Policies:** Freshmen permitted cars on campus. **Housing:** Coed dorms, single-sex dorms, special housing for disabled, apartments, fraternity/sorority housing, substance-free housing available. $75 deposit, deadline 7/15. **Activities:** Bands, choral groups, dance, drama, literary magazine, music ensembles, musical theater, radio station, student government, student newspaper, symphony orchestra, TV station, Black Student Union, Native American Association, Organization de Estudiantes Latino-Americanos, International Student Association, Latter-day Saints Student Association, Alternative Mobility Adventure Seekers.

Athletics. NCAA. **Intercollegiate:** Basketball, cheerleading, cross-country, football (tackle) M, golf, gymnastics W, rodeo, skiing W, soccer W, tennis, track and field, volleyball W, wrestling M. **Intramural:** Baseball M, basketball, bowling, handball, racquetball, soccer M, softball, swimming, tennis, volleyball. **Team name:** Broncos.

Student services. Adult student services, career counseling, student employment services, health services, on-campus daycare, personal counseling, placement for graduates, veterans' counselor. **Physically disabled:** Services for visually, speech, hearing impaired.

Contact. E-mail: bsuinfo@boisestate.edu
Phone: (208) 426-1156 Toll-free number: (800) 824-7017
Fax: (208) 426-3765
Barbara Fortin, Director of Admissions, Boise State University, 1910 University Drive, Boise, ID 83725

Brigham Young University-Idaho

Rexburg, Idaho
www.byui.edu **CB code: 4657**

- Private 4-year university affiliated with Church of Jesus Christ of Latter-day Saints
- Residential campus in large town
- 12,295 degree-seeking undergraduates: 9% part-time, 55% women, 2% Asian American, 3% Hispanic American, 1% Native American, 3% international
- 74% of applicants admitted
- ACT (writing optional), application essay required

General. Founded in 1888. Regionally accredited. **Degrees:** 1,867 bachelor's, 1,105 associate awarded. **ROTC:** Army. **Location:** 30 miles from Idaho Falls, 240 miles from Salt Lake City. **Calendar:** Semester, extensive summer session. **Full-time faculty:** 470 total; 58% have terminal degrees, 17% women. **Part-time faculty:** 132 total; 61% women. **Class size:** 28% < 20, 49% 20-39, 9% 40-49, 14% 50-99, 1% >100. **Special facilities:** Observatory, planetarium, livestock center, off-campus outdoor educational facility, leadership and service institute.

Freshman class profile. 10,439 applied, 7,744 admitted, 4,364 enrolled.

Mid 50% test scores			
SAT verbal:	480-600	Out-of-state:	72%
SAT math:	490-600	Live on campus:	21%
ACT:	20-26	International:	2%

Basis for selection. Religious affiliation, recommendations most important. High school record, test scores, personal essay, extracurricular activities also important. Interview with student's ecclesiastical leader required. Auditions required for music, dance, theater majors. **Homeschooled:** GED required; may be waived for home-schooled students with 24 ACT composite score.

2005-2006 Annual costs. Tuition/fees: $3,170. Tuition for students who are not members of The Church of Jesus Christ of Latter-day Saints is $4,130 per academic year, $172 per credit hour. Room/board: $5,500. Books/supplies: $920. Personal expenses: $1,400.

Financial aid. Non-need-based: Scholarships awarded for academics, athletics, leadership. **Additional information:** Application deadline for merit scholarships 03/01.

Application procedures. Admission: Closing date 2/15 (receipt date). $25 fee. Application may be submitted online. Admission notification on a rolling basis beginning on or about 12/1. **Financial aid:** Priority date 5/1; no closing date. FAFSA required. Applicants notified on a rolling basis starting 2/1.

Academics. Special study options: Accelerated study, distance learning, double major, honors, independent study, internships, student-designed major, study abroad, teacher certification program, urban semester. **Credit/placement by examination:** AP, CLEP, IB, institutional tests. **Support services:** Learning center, reduced course load, remedial instruction, study skills assistance, tutoring, writing center.

Majors. Agriculture: Agronomy, animal sciences, horticulture. **Biology:** General, zoology. **Business:** Accounting, business admin. **Communications:** General, advertising, broadcast journalism, journalism, public relations. **Computer sciences:** General, computer science. **Education:** Elementary. **Engineering:** Computer, mechanical. **English:** Composition. **Health:** Nursing (RN), predentistry, premedicine, prepharmacy, preveterinary. **History:** General. **Math:** General. **Parks/recreation:** General. **Physical sciences:** Geology, physics. **Psychology:** General. **Social sciences:** Economics, political science, sociology. **Visual/performing arts:** Art, interior design.

Most popular majors. Business/marketing 18%, communications/journalism 9%, education 22%, health sciences 6%, liberal arts 10%.

Computing on campus. 2,500 workstations in dormitories, library, computer center, student center. Dormitories wired for high-speed internet access and linked to campus network. Commuter students can connect to campus network. Online course registration, online library, helpline, student web hosting, wireless network available.

Student life. Freshman orientation: Available. **Policies:** Students encouraged to attend weekly devotional at which noted church leaders speak. Religious observance required. Freshmen permitted cars on campus. **Housing:** Single-sex dorms, apartments, substance-free housing available. $175 deposit. **Activities:** Bands, choral groups, dance, drama, literary magazine, music ensembles, musical theater, radio station, student government, student newspaper, symphony orchestra, TV station, international student club, Lambda Delta Sigma, Sigma Gamma Chi, business club, Married Student Association, outdoor club.

Athletics. Intramural: Archery, badminton, baseball, basketball, bowling, cheerleading, cross-country, diving, fencing, field hockey, football (non-tackle), football (tackle), golf, ice hockey, racquetball, skiing, skin diving, soccer, softball, swimming, table tennis, tennis, track and field, volleyball, water polo, wrestling M. **Team name:** Vikings.

Student services. Career counseling, student employment services, health services, personal counseling, placement for graduates, veterans' counselor. **Physically disabled:** Services for visually, hearing impaired.

Contact. E-mail: admissionser@byui.edu
Phone: (208) 496-1020 Fax: (208) 496-1185
Gordon Westenskow, Director of Admissions, Brigham Young University-Idaho, 120 Kimball Building, Rexburg, ID 83460-1615

Idaho State University

Pocatello, Idaho **CB member**
www.isu.edu **CB code: 4355**

- Public 4-year university
- Commuter campus in small city
- 10,376 degree-seeking undergraduates: 25% part-time, 56% women, 1% African American, 1% Asian American, 5% Hispanic American, 2% Native American, 2% international
- 1,745 degree-seeking graduate students
- 77% of applicants admitted
- SAT or ACT (ACT writing optional) required

General. Founded in 1901. Regionally accredited. Designated by State Board of Education as institution specializing in health-related programs. Only College of Pharmacy in Idaho. **Degrees:** 1,119 bachelor's, 323 associate awarded; master's, doctoral, first professional offered. **ROTC:** Army. **Location:** 150 miles from Salt Lake City, 230 miles from Boise. **Calendar:** Semester, limited summer session. **Full-time faculty:** 550 total. **Part-time faculty:** 200 total. **Class size:** 62% < 20, 29% 20-39, 5% 40-49, 3% 50-99, less than 1% >100. **Special facilities:** Natural history museum, planetarium, accelerator center, geographical information systems center, performing arts center.

Freshman class profile. 3,566 applied, 2,731 admitted, 2,490 enrolled.

Mid 50% test scores			
SAT verbal:	440-570	Rank in top tenth:	13%
SAT math:	470-610	Return as sophomores:	57%
ACT:	18-24	Out-of-state:	4%
GPA 3.50 or higher:	35%	Live on campus:	23%
GPA 3.0-3.49:	28%	International:	1%
GPA 2.0-2.99:	33%	Fraternities:	1%
Rank in top quarter:	32%	Sororities:	1%

Basis for selection. For general admissions, predicted GPA of 2.0 (predicted based on core GPA and test scores). Students not meeting those standards can be admitted through various levels and by petition. For international students, TOEFL, IELTS, Compass English, and SAT Critical Reading is required. U.S. High School graduates with an "A" or "B" in English are exempted. Students who complete ELS Language Centers level 112 are exempted. Students from countries where English is the official language can be exempted based on academic performance. ACT preferred. Interview recommended. Audition recommended for music majors. Portfolio recommended for experiential credit-seeking applicants. **Homeschooled:** Students need to complete their GED along with taking the ACT or SAT test.

High school preparation. 16 units required. Required and recommended units include English 4, mathematics 3-4, social studies 2, science 3 (laboratory 1) and foreign language 1. Humanities also recommended.

2005-2006 Annual costs. Tuition/fees: $4,000; $11,700 out-of-state. Refundable $330 per semester or $660 per year charge for health insurance. Room/board: $4,870. Books/supplies: $900. Personal expenses: $1,840.

2005-2006 Financial aid. **Need-based:** Average need met was 57%. Average scholarship/grant was $2,503; average loan $2,065. 42% of total undergraduate aid awarded as scholarships/grants, 58% as loans/jobs. **Non-need-based:** Scholarships awarded for academics, alumni affiliation, art, athletics, leadership, minority status, music/drama, ROTC, state residency.

Application procedures. **Admission:** No deadline. $40 fee, may be waived for applicants with need. Application may be submitted online. Admission notification on a rolling basis. High school students who graduate early may petition admissions committee to enroll full time. **Financial aid:** Priority date 2/20; no closing date. FAFSA required. Applicants notified on a rolling basis starting 4/1.

Academics. **Special study options:** Accelerated study, combined bachelor's/graduate degree, cooperative education, cross-registration, distance learning, double major, dual enrollment of high school students, ESL, exchange student, honors, independent study, internships, liberal arts/career combination, student-designed major, study abroad, teacher certification program. **Credit/placement by examination:** AP, CLEP, IB, ACT, institutional tests. 48 credit hours maximum toward bachelor's degree. **Support services:** Learning center, remedial instruction, study skills assistance, tutoring, writing center.

Majors. **Area/ethnic studies:** American. **Biology:** General, biochemistry, botany, ecology, microbiology, zoology. **Business:** General, accounting, business admin, finance, human resources, marketing. **Communications:** General, media studies. **Computer sciences:** General, information systems. **Education:** Early childhood, elementary, health, music, physical, secondary, special. **Engineering:** Civil, electrical, mechanical, nuclear. **Engineering technology:** Surveying. **English:** English lit. **Family/consumer sciences:** General. **Foreign languages:** French, German, sign language interpretation, Spanish. **Health:** Audiology/speech pathology, clinical lab science, dental hygiene, dietetics, health care admin, health services, medical radiologic technology/radiation therapy, nursing (RN). **History:** General. **Math:** General. **Philosophy/religion:** Philosophy. **Physical sciences:** Chemistry, geology, physics. **Psychology:** General. **Public administration:** Social work. **Social sciences:** Anthropology, economics, international relations, political science, sociology. **Visual/performing arts:** Art, dramatic, music performance.

Most popular majors. Biology 8%, business/marketing 18%, education 18%, history 18%, trade and industry 7%.

Computing on campus. 507 workstations in dormitories, library, computer center, student center. Dormitories wired for high-speed internet access and linked to campus network. Commuter students can connect to campus network. Online course registration, online library, helpline, repair service, student web hosting, wireless network available.

Student life. **Freshman orientation:** Available, $35 fee. Preregistration for classes offered. **Policies:** Freshmen permitted cars on campus. **Housing:** Coed dorms, single-sex dorms, special housing for disabled, apartments, fraternity/sorority housing, substance-free housing available. $150 partly refundable deposit. Housing modified for handicapped available on request, subject to waiting list. **Activities:** Bands, choral groups, dance, drama, musical theater, radio station, student government, student newspaper, symphony orchestra, TV station, campus ministry, Newman Center, Latter-Day Saints Institute, Student Ambassadors, Young Democrats, Young Republicans, Campus Crusade for Christ, Associated Black Students, Native Americans United, Cooperative Wilderness Handicapped Outdoor Group.

Athletics. NCAA. **Intercollegiate:** Basketball, cheerleading, cross-country, football (tackle) M, golf, soccer W, tennis, track and field, volleyball W. **Intramural:** Badminton, basketball, bowling, fencing, racquetball, soccer, softball, table tennis, tennis, volleyball. **Team name:** Bengals.

Student services. Adult student services, alcohol/substance abuse counseling, career counseling, student employment services, financial aid counseling, health services, legal services, minority student services, on-campus daycare, personal counseling, placement for graduates, veterans' counselor, women's services. **Physically disabled:** Services for visually, speech, hearing impaired.

Contact. E-mail: info@isu.edu
Phone: (208) 282-2475 Fax: (208) 282-4511
Nathan Peterson, Director, Idaho State University, PO Box 8270, Museum Natural History 319, Pocatello, ID 83209-8270

ITT Technical Institute: Boise

Boise, Idaho
www.itt-tech.edu **CB code: 3596**

- For-profit 4-year technical college
- Commuter campus in small city

General. Founded in 1906. Accredited by ACICS. **Calendar:** Quarter.

Annual costs/financial aid. Tuition varies by program, $260-$368 per credit hour.

Contact. Phone: (208) 322-8844
Director of Recruitment, 12302 West Explorer Drive, Boise, ID 83713-1529

Lewis-Clark State College

Lewiston, Idaho
www.lcsc.edu **CB code: 4385**

- Public 4-year liberal arts and technical college
- Commuter campus in small city
- 2,944 degree-seeking undergraduates: 23% part-time, 61% women, 1% African American, 1% Asian American, 5% Hispanic American, 5% Native American, 3% international
- 46% of applicants admitted
- 29% graduate within 6 years

General. Founded in 1893. Regionally accredited. Courses offered at outreach centers (Orofino, Grangeville, Coeur d'Alene, Kamiah, and Lapwai). **Degrees:** 388 bachelor's, 138 associate awarded. **ROTC:** Army, Navy, Air Force. **Location:** 300 miles from Boise, 100 miles from Spokane, Washington. **Calendar:** Semester, limited summer session. **Full-time faculty:** 158 total; 65% have terminal degrees, 6% minority, 49% women. **Part-time faculty:** 71 total; 1% have terminal degrees, 37% women. **Class size:** 70% < 20, 28% 20-39, 2% 40-49, less than 1% 50-99, less than 1% >100. **Special facilities:** Biodiversity museum and collection, geographical information systems center, observatory.

Freshman class profile. 1,108 applied, 512 admitted, 504 enrolled.

Mid 50% test scores		**GPA 2.0-2.99:**	43%
SAT verbal:	420-540	**Rank in top quarter:**	26%
SAT math:	440-570	**Rank in top tenth:**	9%
ACT:	17-22	**Return as sophomores:**	57%
GPA 3.50 or higher:	24%	**Out-of-state:**	21%
GPA 3.0-3.49:	29%	**Live on campus:**	22%

Basis for selection. High school courses, GPA, test scores considered. Non-native speakers may be required to take ESL classes until they can pass TOEFL. ACT and SAT may be accepted for all students. Students may be asked to take COMPASS test under certain circumstances. **Home-schooled:** Must have predicted college GPA of 2.0 based on ACT or SAT. Must have acceptable performance on 2 testing indicators: GED score of 500 (50 if tested before 2002) or higher, or other standardized diagnostic test such as ACT, SAT, COMPASS, ASSET, or CPT.

High school preparation. College-preparatory program recommended. 15 units required. Required and recommended units include English 4, mathematics 3, social studies 2, science 3 (laboratory 2), foreign language 1 and academic electives 1. 1 fine arts.

2005-2006 Annual costs. Tuition/fees: $3,714; $10,266 out-of-state. Room/board: $5,400. Books/supplies: $1,500. Personal expenses: $1,462.

2004-2005 Financial aid. **Need-based:** 393 full-time freshmen applied for aid; 338 were judged to have need; 332 of these received aid. Average need met was 7%. Average scholarship/grant was $3,018; average loan $2,203. 45% of total undergraduate aid awarded as scholarships/grants, 55% as loans/jobs. **Non-need-based:** Awarded to 632 full-time undergraduates, including 227 freshmen. Scholarships awarded for academics, alumni affiliation, art, athletics, leadership, minority status, music/drama.

Application procedures. **Admission:** Priority date 3/1; no deadline. $35 fee. Application may be submitted online. Admission notification on a rolling basis. **Financial aid:** Priority date 3/1; no closing date. FAFSA required. Applicants notified on a rolling basis starting 4/15; must reply within 2 week(s) of notification.

Academics. Communications/speech lab to help students prepare for speeches and presentations. **Special study options:** Accelerated study, cooperative education, distance learning, double major, dual enrollment of high school students, ESL, honors, independent study, internships, student-designed major, study abroad, teacher certification program, weekend college. **Credit/placement by examination:** AP, CLEP, IB, SAT, ACT, institutional tests. 16 credit hours maximum toward associate degree, 32 toward bachelor's. **Support services:** Learning center, reduced course load, remedial instruction, study skills assistance, tutoring, writing center.

Majors. Biology: General. **Business:** Accounting technology, administrative services, business admin, hospitality admin, small business admin. **Communications:** General. **Communications technology:** Graphic/printing. **Computer sciences:** General, computer science, webmaster. **Education:** Elementary, English, mathematics, physical, science, social science. **Engineering technology:** Drafting, manufacturing. **English:** Creative writing, English lit. **Family/consumer sciences:** Child development. **Health:** Management/clinical assistant, nursing (RN), office assistant. **Interdisciplinary:** Natural sciences. **Legal studies:** Legal secretary, paralegal. **Math:** General. **Mechanic/repair:** General, auto body, automotive, diesel, electronics/electrical, heating/ac/refrig, industrial electronics. **Parks/recreation:** Exercise sciences. **Physical sciences:** Chemistry. **Production:** Welding. **Protective services:** Corrections, criminal justice, firefighting. **Psychology:** General. **Public administration:** Social work. **Social sciences:** General.

Computing on campus. 455 workstations in dormitories, library, computer center, student center. Dormitories wired for high-speed internet access and linked to campus network. Commuter students can connect to campus network. Online course registration, helpline, repair service, student web hosting, wireless network available.

Student life. Freshman orientation: Mandatory. Preregistration for classes offered. One-day session held in August. **Policies:** Freshmen permitted cars on campus. **Housing:** Coed dorms, apartments available. $100 partly refundable deposit. **Activities:** Jazz band, choral groups, dance, drama, film society, literary magazine, music ensembles, radio station, student government, student newspaper, TV station, Native American Indian student organization, international student club, Ambassadors' club, criminal justice society, Idaho student lobby, Baptist student ministries, business students organization, Latter-day Saints student association, College Democrats, College Republicans.

Athletics. NAIA. **Intercollegiate:** Baseball M, basketball, cross-country, golf, tennis, volleyball W. **Intramural:** Badminton, baseball, basketball, bowling, field hockey, football (non-tackle), golf, lacrosse, racquetball, rugby M, skiing, soccer, softball, table tennis, tennis, volleyball, weight lifting. **Team name:** Warriors.

Student services. Adult student services, alcohol/substance abuse counseling, career counseling, services for economically disadvantaged, student employment services, financial aid counseling, health services, minority student services, on-campus daycare, personal counseling, placement for graduates, veterans' counselor, women's services. **Physically disabled:** Services for visually, speech, hearing impaired.

Contact. E-mail: admissions@lcsc.edu
Phone: (208) 792-2210 Toll-free number: (800) 933-5272
Fax: (208) 792-2876
Steven Bussolini, Director of Admission and Market Development,
Lewis-Clark State College, 500 Eighth Avenue, Lewiston, ID 83501-2698

Northwest Nazarene University

Nampa, Idaho
www.nnu.edu **CB code: 4544**

- Private 4-year university affiliated with Church of the Nazarene
- Residential campus in small city
- 1,128 degree-seeking undergraduates: 6% part-time, 61% women, 1% African American, 1% Asian American, 2% Hispanic American, 1% Native American, 1% international
- 459 degree-seeking graduate students
- 60% of applicants admitted
- ACT (writing optional), application essay required
- 49% graduate within 6 years

General. Founded in 1913. Regionally accredited. **Degrees:** 240 bachelor's awarded; master's offered. **ROTC:** Army, Air Force. **Location:** 18 miles from Boise. **Calendar:** Semester, extensive summer session. **Full-time faculty:** 95 total; 74% have terminal degrees, 3% minority, 37% women. **Part-time faculty:** 5 total; 40% have terminal degrees, 60% women. **Class size:** 63% < 20, 29% 20-39, 3% 40-49, 5% 50-99. **Special facilities:** Depository for federal government publications.

Freshman class profile. 923 applied, 556 admitted, 277 enrolled.

Mid 50% test scores			
SAT verbal:	470-570	GPA 2.0-2.99:	19%
SAT math:	440-480	Rank in top quarter:	49%
ACT:	19-26	Rank in top tenth:	24%
GPA 3.50 or higher:	52%	Return as sophomores:	71%
GPA 3.0-3.49:	28%	Out-of-state:	62%
		Live on campus:	93%

Basis for selection. 2 letters of recommendation including 1 character recommendation from pastor or teacher required. For unconditional admission 2 of following criteria must be met: minimum 2.5 high school GPA, class rank in top 50 percent, minimum ACT score of 18. Provisional admission available. Interview recommended for students with provisional admission. **Homeschooled:** ACT required.

High school preparation. 15 units recommended. Recommended units include English 4, mathematics 3, social studies 2, history 1, science 3 and foreign language 2.

2006-2007 Annual costs. Tuition/fees (projected): $18,770. Room/board: $5,010. Books/supplies: $900. Personal expenses: $870.

2005-2006 Financial aid. Need-based: Average need met was 75%. Average scholarship/grant was $2,524; average loan $3,742. 48% of total undergraduate aid awarded as scholarships/grants, 52% as loans/jobs. **Non-need-based:** Scholarships awarded for academics, alumni affiliation, art, athletics, leadership, music/drama, religious affiliation, ROTC, state residency.

Application procedures. Admission: Priority date 3/1; deadline 8/8. $25 fee, may be waived for applicants with need. Application may be submitted online. Admission notification on a rolling basis beginning on or about 9/1. **Financial aid:** Priority date 3/1; no closing date. FAFSA, institutional form required. Applicants notified on a rolling basis starting 4/1; must reply within 3 week(s) of notification.

Academics. Special study options: Accelerated study, combined bachelor's/graduate degree, cooperative education, cross-registration, distance learning, double major, exchange student, honors, independent study, internships, liberal arts/career combination, student-designed major, study abroad, teacher certification program. **Credit/placement by examination:** AP, CLEP, IB, SAT, ACT, institutional tests. 31 credit hours maximum toward bachelor's degree. **Support services:** Learning center, reduced course load, remedial instruction, study skills assistance, tutoring, writing center.

Majors. Biology: General. **Business:** Accounting, business admin, international marketing, management information systems. **Communications:** Journalism. **Computer sciences:** General. **Education:** Art, biology, chemistry, elementary, English, health, history, mathematics, middle, music, physical, science, secondary, social science, Spanish. **Engineering:** Physics. **English:** Speech/rhetoric. **Foreign languages:** Spanish. **Health:** Nursing (RN), predentistry, premedicine, preveterinary. **History:** General. **Interdisciplinary:** Biological/physical sciences. **Legal studies:** Prelaw. **Liberal arts:** Arts/sciences. **Math:** General. **Parks/recreation:** Facilities management, health/fitness. **Philosophy/religion:** Philosophy, religion. **Physical sciences:** Chemistry, physics. **Psychology:** General. **Public administration:** Social work. **Social sciences:** General, international relations, political science. **Theology:** Missionary, religious ed, sacred music, theology. **Visual/performing arts:** Commercial/advertising art, music performance, music theory/composition, painting, sculpture.

Most popular majors. Biology 6%, business/marketing 20%, education 20%, English 6%, health sciences 6%, psychology 6%, social sciences 7%, theological studies 9%, visual/performing arts 6%.

Computing on campus. 275 workstations in dormitories, library, computer center, student center. Dormitories wired for high-speed internet access and linked to campus network. Commuter students can connect to campus network. Online course registration, online library, helpline, repair service, student web hosting, wireless network available.

Student life. Freshman orientation: Mandatory. Preregistration for classes offered. **Policies:** All students required to live on campus until senior year or age 21. Religious observance required. Freshmen permitted cars on campus. **Housing:** Guaranteed on-campus for all undergraduates. Single-sex dorms, apartments available. $50 deposit, deadline 5/1. Some rental units available. **Activities:** Bands, choral groups, drama, literary magazine, music ensembles, musical theater, student government, student newspaper, symphony orchestra, summer ministries, Circle-K, urban ministries club, social work clubs, Angels Ministry, PALS ministry, AIDS ministry, Fellowship of Christian Athletes, multicultural affairs club, international students club.

Athletics. NCAA. **Intercollegiate:** Baseball M, basketball, cross-country, golf M, soccer W, softball W, track and field, volleyball W. **Intramural:** Archery, badminton, basketball, bowling, cross-country, football (non-tackle) M, racquetball, softball, swimming, table tennis, volleyball. **Team name:** Crusaders.

Student services. Adult student services, alcohol/substance abuse counseling, campus ministries, career counseling, student employment services, financial aid counseling, health services, minority student services, personal counseling, placement for graduates. **Physically disabled:** Services for visually, hearing impaired.

Contact. E-mail: admissions@nnu.edu
Phone: (208) 467-8496 Toll-free number: (877) 668-4968
Fax: (208) 467-8645
Dianna Gibney, Director of Admissions, Northwest Nazarene University, 623 Holly Street, Nampa, ID 83686-5897

University of Idaho

Moscow, Idaho — **CB member**
www.uidaho.edu — **CB code: 4843**

- Public 4-year university
- Residential campus in large town
- 8,978 degree-seeking undergraduates: 8% part-time, 46% women, 1% African American, 2% Asian American, 4% Hispanic American, 1% Native American, 2% international
- 2,632 degree-seeking graduate students
- 82% of applicants admitted
- SAT or ACT (ACT writing optional) required
- 56% graduate within 6 years

General. Founded in 1889. Regionally accredited. Residential land-grant university. **Degrees:** 1,774 bachelor's awarded; master's, doctoral, first professional offered. **ROTC:** Army, Navy, Air Force. **Location:** 85 miles from Spokane, Washington. **Calendar:** Semester, extensive summer session. **Full-time faculty:** 564 total; 78% have terminal degrees, 9% minority, 26% women. **Part-time faculty:** 22 total; 54% have terminal degrees, 9% minority, 32% women. **Class size:** 50% < 20, 36% 20-39, 6% 40-49, 6% 50-99, 2% >100. **Special facilities:** Arboretum, 18-hole golf course.

Freshman class profile. 4,444 applied, 3,660 admitted, 1,745 enrolled.

Mid 50% test scores			
SAT verbal:	490-610	GPA 2.0-2.99:	23%
SAT math:	490-610	Rank in top quarter:	46%
ACT:	20-26	Rank in top tenth:	20%
GPA 3.50 or higher:	45%	Out-of-state:	34%
GPA 3.0-3.49:	31%	International:	1%

Basis for selection. Applicants must have 3.0 high school GPA or 2.2 to 3.0 high school GPA with high SAT/ACT scores. Recommendations, essay required of applicants with nonstandard high school diploma and adults long out of high school.

High school preparation. 15 units required. Required units include English 4, mathematics 3, social studies 3, science 3 (laboratory 1), foreign language 1 and academic electives 2. Up to 1 unit of history, literature, philosophy, or fine arts may be substituted for foreign language requirement, but foreign language strongly recommended.

2005-2006 Annual costs. Tuition/fees: $3,968; $12,738 out-of-state. Room/board: $5,888. Books/supplies: $1,286. Personal expenses: $2,326.

2004-2005 Financial aid. Need-based: 1,303 full-time freshmen applied for aid; 947 were judged to have need; 940 of these received aid. Average need met was 80%. Average scholarship/grant was $3,263; average loan $3,337. 35% of total undergraduate aid awarded as scholarships/grants, 65% as loans/jobs. **Non-need-based:** Awarded to 6,201 full-time undergraduates, including 1,542 freshmen. Scholarships awarded for academics, alumni affiliation, leadership, minority status, music/drama, ROTC, state residency.

Application procedures. Admission: Priority date 2/15; deadline 8/1. $40 fee. Application may be submitted online. Admission notification on a rolling basis. **Financial aid:** Priority date 2/15; no closing date. FAFSA required. Applicants notified on a rolling basis starting 3/30; must reply within 3 week(s) of notification.

Academics. Special study options: Accelerated study, combined bachelor's/graduate degree, cooperative education, cross-registration, distance learning, double major, dual enrollment of high school students, ESL, exchange student, honors, independent study, internships, student-designed major, study abroad, teacher certification program. **Credit/placement by examination:** AP, CLEP, IB, SAT, ACT, institutional tests. 48 credit hours maximum toward bachelor's degree. **Support services:** Learning center, pre-admission summer program, reduced course load, study skills assistance, tutoring, writing center.

Majors. Agriculture: Agronomy, animal sciences, business, dairy, economics, food science, horticultural science, plant protection, plant sciences, range science, soil science. **Architecture:** Architecture, landscape. **Area/ethnic studies:** American, Latin American. **Biology:** General, bacteriology, biomedical sciences, botany, entomology, molecular, zoology. **Business:** Accounting, administrative services, finance, human resources, management information systems, managerial economics, marketing, operations. **Communications:** General, journalism. **Computer sciences:** General. **Conservation:** General, fisheries, forest resources, forestry, management/policy, wildlife. **Education:** Agricultural, art, business, elementary, health, instructional media, music, physical, sales/marketing, secondary, special, technology/industrial arts, trade/industrial, voc/tech. **Engineering:** Agricultural, biomedical, chemical, civil, computer, electrical, geological, mechanical, metallurgical, mining. **Family/consumer sciences:** Clothing/textiles, family studies, food/nutrition. **Foreign languages:** General, classics, French, German, Latin, Spanish. **Health:** Athletic training, predentistry, premedicine. **History:** General. **Liberal arts:** Arts/sciences. **Math:** General, applied. **Parks/recreation:** General. **Philosophy/religion:** Philosophy. **Physical sciences:** Chemistry, geology, physics. **Protective services:** Criminal justice. **Psychology:** General. **Social sciences:** Anthropology, cartography, economics, geography, political science, sociology. **Visual/performing arts:** Art, dance, design, dramatic, interior design, music history, music management, music performance, music theory/composition, voice/opera.

Most popular majors. Business/marketing 13%, communications/journalism 7%, education 12%, engineering/engineering technologies 9%, natural resources/environmental science 7%, social sciences 9%.

Computing on campus. 750 workstations in dormitories, library, computer center, student center. Dormitories wired for high-speed internet access and linked to campus network. Commuter students can connect to campus network. Online course registration, helpline, repair service, student web hosting, wireless network available.

Student life. Freshman orientation: Available. Preregistration for classes offered. **Policies:** Freshmen permitted cars on campus. **Housing:** Coed dorms, single-sex dorms, special housing for disabled, apartments, cooperative housing, fraternity/sorority housing available. $120 partly refundable deposit. **Activities:** Bands, choral groups, dance, drama, film society, literary magazine, music ensembles, musical theater, opera, radio station, student government, student newspaper, symphony orchestra, TV station, campus Christian center, St. Augustine's Catholic center, Latter-day Saint Institute, MECHA (Hispanic students), The Republicans, American Indian science and engineering society, Golden Key national honorary society, Pi Chi, environmental club, society of women engineers.

Athletics. NCAA. **Intercollegiate:** Basketball, cross-country, football (tackle) M, golf, soccer W, swimming W, tennis, track and field, volleyball W. **Intramural:** Badminton, basketball, golf, racquetball, rifle, skiing, soccer, softball, table tennis, tennis, wrestling M. **Team name:** Vandals.

Student services. Adult student services, alcohol/substance abuse counseling, career counseling, student employment services, health services, legal services, minority student services, on-campus daycare, personal counseling, placement for graduates, veterans' counselor, women's services. **Physically disabled:** Services for visually, speech, hearing impaired.

Contact. E-mail: admappl@uidaho.edu
Phone: (208) 885-6326 Toll-free number: (888) 884-3246
Fax: (208) 885-9119
Dan Davenport, Director of Admissions and Financial Aid, University of Idaho, PO Box 444264, Moscow, ID 83844-4264

Four-Year Colleges

Illinois

American Academy of Art
Chicago, Illinois
www.aaart.edu **CB code: 1013**

- For-profit 4-year visual arts college
- Commuter campus in very large city
- 410 degree-seeking undergraduates
- Interview required

General. Founded in 1923. Accredited by ACCSCT. **Degrees:** 57 bachelor's awarded; master's offered. **Location:** Downtown. **Calendar:** Semester, extensive summer session. **Full-time faculty:** 28 total. **Part-time faculty:** 32 total. **Class size:** 76% < 20, 24% 20-39. **Special facilities:** Art gallery.

Basis for selection. Open admission, but selective for some programs.

2005-2006 Annual costs. Tuition/fees: $19,805. Fees vary by program. Books/supplies: $800.

Financial aid. Non-need-based: Scholarships awarded for art.

Application procedures. Admission: No deadline. $25 fee, may be waived for applicants with need. Application may be submitted online. Admission notification on a rolling basis. Essay explaining desire to enter art school used for counseling purposes. **Financial aid:** No deadline. FAFSA, institutional form required. Applicants notified on a rolling basis.

Academics. Special study options: Accelerated study, independent study, internships, study abroad. **Credit/placement by examination:** CLEP, institutional tests. **Support services:** Pre-admission summer program, tutoring.

Majors. Communications: Advertising. **Computer sciences:** Computer graphics. **Visual/performing arts:** General, commercial/advertising art, design, drawing, multimedia, painting, studio arts.

Computing on campus. 70 workstations in library, computer center.

Student life. Freshman orientation: Mandatory. Preregistration for classes offered. 1-day orientation held in week before classes start. **Activities:** Film society.

Student services. Career counseling, student employment services, personal counseling, placement for graduates, veterans' counselor.

Contact. E-mail: info@aaart.edu
Phone: (312) 461-0600 Toll-free number: (888) 461-0600
Fax: (312) 294-9570
Stuart Rosenbloom, Director of Admissions, American Academy of Art, 332 South Michigan Avenue, Suite 300, Chicago, IL 60604-4302

Argosy University
Chicago, Illinois
www.auchicago.net **CB code: 3922**

- For-profit 4-year university
- Very large city
- 72 undergraduates

General. Regionally accredited. Additional campuses in Northwest Chicago, Washington, DC, Atlanta, Seattle, Tampa, Minneapolis/St. Paul, San Francisco bay area, Dallas, Honolulu, Nashville, Phoenix, Sarasota, Orange County, CA. **Degrees:** 6 bachelor's awarded; master's, doctoral offered. **Calendar:** 4-1-4. **Full-time faculty:** 40 total.

2005-2006 Annual costs. Tuition/fees: $12,050. Costs vary by program.

Application procedures. Admission: No deadline. $50 fee.

Academics. Special study options: Distance learning. **Credit/placement by examination:** CLEP.

Majors. Psychology: General.

Computing on campus. Online library available.

Contact. Phone: (312) 201-0200 Toll-free number: (800) 626-4123
Argosy University, Two First National Plaza, 20 South Clark Street, 3rd Floor, Chicago, IL 60603

Augustana College
Rock Island, Illinois **CB member**
www.augustana.edu **CB code: 1025**

- Private 4-year liberal arts college affiliated with Evangelical Lutheran Church in America
- Residential campus in large city
- 2,364 degree-seeking undergraduates: 1% part-time, 58% women, 2% African American, 2% Asian American, 3% Hispanic American, 1% international
- 84% of applicants admitted
- SAT or ACT (ACT writing optional) required
- 76% graduate within 6 years; 33% enter graduate study

General. Founded in 1860. Regionally accredited. Ecumenical in nature, Augustana was founded by Swedish Lutheran immigrants. **Degrees:** 493 bachelor's awarded. **Location:** 165 miles from Chicago. **Calendar:** Quarter, limited summer session. **Full-time faculty:** 149 total; 96% have terminal degrees, 11% minority, 40% women. **Part-time faculty:** 86 total; 23% have terminal degrees, 6% minority, 49% women. **Class size:** 49% < 20, 45% 20-39, 4% 40-49, 3% 50-99. **Special facilities:** Educational technology center, planetarium/observatory, map library, geology museum, Swedish immigration research center, research foundation, language laboratory, 500 acres of environmental laboratories, recreational center, scanning electron mircroscope, High-Field NMR, X-ray diffractometer, scanning tunneling microscope, HeliFlux Station Magnetometer.

Freshman class profile. 2,921 applied, 2,462 admitted, 679 enrolled.

Mid 50% test scores			
ACT:	24-29	Rank in top tenth:	29%
GPA 3.50 or higher:	62%	Return as sophomores:	85%
GPA 3.0-3.49:	29%	Out-of-state:	11%
GPA 2.0-2.99:	9%	Live on campus:	94%
Rank in top quarter:	63%	International:	1%

Basis for selection. GPA, class rank, test scores, high school curriculum most important. Extracurricular activities and essay important. Academic honors and special qualifications also considered. Interview and essay required of freshman honors program applicants, recommended for all applicants. Essay also required of academically marginal applicants and for certain departmental programs. Portfolio required of applicants to some art programs. Audition recommended for music and theater majors.

High school preparation. College-preparatory program recommended. 16 units recommended. Recommended units include English 4, mathematics 3, social studies 1, history 1, science 2, foreign language 1 and academic electives 4. Engineering, science, and mathematics majors should have 3 units mathematics: 1.5 algebra, 1 plane geometry, .5 trigonometry.

2006-2007 Annual costs. Tuition/fees (projected): $23,457. Room/board: $6,405. Books/supplies: $675. Personal expenses: $800.

2005-2006 Financial aid. Need-based: 579 full-time freshmen applied for aid; 455 were judged to have need; 453 of these received aid. Average need met was 88%. Average scholarship/grant was $12,816; average loan $3,801. 61% of total undergraduate aid awarded as scholarships/grants, 39% as loans/jobs. **Non-need-based:** Awarded to 1,592 full-time undergraduates, including 513 freshmen. Scholarships awarded for academics, alumni affiliation, art, leadership, music/drama, religious affiliation.

Application procedures. Admission: Priority date 2/1; no deadline. $25 fee, may be waived for applicants with need. Application may be submitted online. Admission notification on a rolling basis. **Financial aid:** Priority date 4/1; no closing date. FAFSA, institutional form required. Applicants notified on a rolling basis; must reply by 5/11.

Academics. Term-abroad programs in Asia, Europe, and South America. Internship programs in cities throughout United States and in South America, Europe, Asia, Africa, and Australia. Exchange programs with universities in People's Republic of China, Peru, and Sweden. Summer language study programs in Sweden, France, Ecuador and Israel. Team-taught, interdisciplinary honors sequence available. June registration for classes. **Special study options:** Accelerated study, combined bachelor's/graduate degree, cooperative education, double major, honors, independent study, internships, liberal arts/career combination, study abroad, teacher certification program. 3-2 forestry and environmental management program with Duke University (NC), 3-2 landscape architecture program with University of Illinois at Urbana-Champaign, 3-2 engineering program with Washington University (MO), Iowa State University, University of Illinois at Urbana-Champaign, and Purdue University, 3-2 occupational therapy program with Washington University, early selection programs in dentistry with University of Iowa, study abroad programs in Asia, Europe, and South America. **Credit/placement by examination:** AP, CLEP, IB, ACT, institutional tests. More than 18 hours of credit by examination must be approved by the Dean of the College. **Support services:** Learning center, pre-admission summer program, reduced course load, study skills assistance, tutoring, writing center.

Majors. Area/ethnic studies: Asian. **Biology:** General. **Business:** General, accounting, business admin, finance, international, management information systems, marketing. **Communications:** General. **Computer sciences:** Computer science. **Conservation:** General. **Education:** General, art, biology, chemistry, elementary, English, foreign languages, French, German, history, mathematics, middle, music, physical, physics, science, secondary, social science, Spanish, speech. **Engineering:** Physics. **English:** Speech/rhetoric. **Foreign languages:** Ancient Greek, classics, French, German, Latin, Scandinavian, Spanish. **Health:** Audiology/speech pathology, predentistry, premedicine. **History:** General. **Interdisciplinary:** Math/computer science. **Legal studies:** Prelaw. **Liberal arts:** Arts/sciences. **Math:** General. **Philosophy/religion:** Philosophy, religion. **Physical sciences:** Chemistry, geology, physics, planetary. **Psychology:** General. **Public administration:** General. **Social sciences:** Economics, geography, political science, sociology. **Visual/performing arts:** Art, art history/conservation, dramatic, jazz, music performance, piano/organ, studio arts, voice/opera.

Most popular majors. Biology 15%, business/marketing 20%, education 6%, English 8%, health sciences 6%, psychology 8%, social sciences 11%.

Computing on campus. 500 workstations in dormitories, library, computer center, student center. Dormitories wired for high-speed internet access and linked to campus network. Commuter students can connect to campus network. Online library, helpline, repair service, student web hosting, wireless network available.

Student life. Freshman orientation: Mandatory, $100 fee. Preregistration for classes offered. 3-day program before start of fall classes. **Policies:** Students represented on all major faculty/administrative committees and act as observers at Board of Trustees meetings. Student life governed by Bill of Student Rights and code of social conduct. Campus judiciary process includes student participation. Lower-division students not living with parents required to live on campus unless released to live off-campus by student services office. Freshmen permitted cars on campus. **Housing:** Guaranteed on-campus for all undergraduates. Coed dorms, single-sex dorms, apartments, substance-free housing available. $100 fully refundable deposit. Theme housing available. **Activities:** Bands, choral groups, dance, drama, literary magazine, music ensembles, musical theater, opera, radio station, student government, student newspaper, symphony orchestra, Black student union, Asian student organization, Latinos Unidos, Latin American Council, international club, multicultural programming board, feminist forum, Global Affect, Campus Ministries, Intervarsity Christian Fellowship, Catholic organization, Muslim student association, Viking Volunteers, College Republicans/Democrats, Habitat for Humanity, Amnesty International.

Athletics. NCAA. **Intercollegiate:** Baseball M, basketball, cross-country, diving, football (tackle) M, golf, soccer, softball W, swimming, tennis, track and field, volleyball W, wrestling M. **Intramural:** Badminton, basketball, bowling, cross-country, football (non-tackle), golf, handball, racquetball, rowing (crew), skiing, soccer, softball, swimming M, table tennis, tennis, track and field, volleyball, water polo, wrestling M. **Team name:** Vikings.

Student services. Alcohol/substance abuse counseling, campus ministries, career counseling, student employment services, financial aid counseling, health services, minority student services, personal counseling, placement for graduates, women's services. **Physically disabled:** Services for visually, speech, hearing impaired.

Contact. E-mail: admissions@augustana.edu
Phone: (309) 794-7341 Toll-free number: (800) 798-8100
Fax: (309) 794-7422
Kent Barnds, Vice President of Enrollment, Augustana College, 639 38th Street, Rock Island, IL 61201-2296

Aurora University

Aurora, Illinois
www.aurora.edu **CB code: 1027**

- Private 4-year university
- Commuter campus in small city
- 1,897 degree-seeking undergraduates: 11% part-time, 66% women, 13% African American, 2% Asian American, 12% Hispanic American
- 1,559 degree-seeking graduate students
- 74% of applicants admitted
- 53% graduate within 6 years

General. Founded in 1893. Regionally accredited. Additional 241-acre campus in Williams Bay, Wisconsin. **Degrees:** 388 bachelor's awarded; master's, doctoral offered. **ROTC:** Army. **Location:** 40 miles from Chicago. **Calendar:** Semester, limited summer session. **Full-time faculty:** 95 total; 84% have terminal degrees, 5% minority, 53% women. **Part-time faculty:** 176 total; 25% have terminal degrees, 57% women. **Class size:** 34% < 20, 66% 20-39, less than 1% 40-49. **Special facilities:** Museum of Native American history, television studio.

Freshman class profile. 1,405 applied, 1,036 admitted, 383 enrolled.

Mid 50% test scores			
SAT verbal:	470-540	Rank in top quarter:	37%
SAT math:	460-580	Rank in top tenth:	11%
ACT:	19-23	Return as sophomores:	71%
GPA 3.50 or higher:	32%	Out-of-state:	8%
GPA 3.0-3.49:	27%	Live on campus:	70%
GPA 2.0-2.99:	39%	Sororities:	1%

Basis for selection. School achievement record most important, followed by test scores. Interview and recommendation also considered. SAT and SAT Subject Tests or ACT recommended. Interview and essay recommended.

High school preparation. 16 units recommended. Recommended units include English 4, mathematics 3, social studies 3, science 3 and academic electives 3.

2006-2007 Annual costs. Tuition/fees (projected): $16,190. Room/board: $6,590. Books/supplies: $1,000. Personal expenses: $1,100.

2005-2006 Financial aid. Need-based: 383 full-time freshmen applied for aid; 318 were judged to have need; 318 of these received aid. Average need met was 90%. Average scholarship/grant was $6,095; average loan $2,455. 53% of total undergraduate aid awarded as scholarships/grants, 47% as loans/jobs. **Non-need-based:** Awarded to 1,579 full-time undergraduates, including 375 freshmen. Scholarships awarded for academics, alumni affiliation, art, religious affiliation, state residency.

Application procedures. Admission: No deadline. $25 fee, may be waived for applicants with need. Application may be submitted online. Admission notification on a rolling basis beginning on or about 9/1. Candidates may apply early and have until May 1 to have tuition and housing deposits refunded. **Financial aid:** Priority date 4/15; no closing date. FAFSA required. Applicants notified on a rolling basis starting 3/1; must reply by 5/1 or within 3 week(s) of notification.

Academics. Special study options: Accelerated study, cross-registration, double major, dual enrollment of high school students, honors, independent study, internships, liberal arts/career combination, student-designed major, study abroad, teacher certification program, weekend college. **Credit/placement by examination:** AP, CLEP, institutional tests. 30 credit hours maximum toward bachelor's degree. **Support services:** Learning center, pre-admission summer program, reduced course load, remedial instruction, study skills assistance, tutoring, writing center.

Majors. Biology: General. **Business:** General, accounting, finance, management information systems, marketing, operations. **Communications:** General. **Computer sciences:** General, networking. **Conservation:** General. **Education:** Elementary, physical, secondary. **Engineering technology:** Industrial management. **English:** Composition. **Foreign languages:** Spanish. **Health:** Clinical lab science, nursing (RN). **History:** General. **Legal studies:** Prelaw. **Liberal arts:** Arts/sciences. **Math:** General. **Parks/recreation:** General. **Protective services:** Criminal justice, law enforcement admin. **Psychology:** General. **Public administration:** Social work. **Social sciences:** Economics, political science, sociology.

Most popular majors. Business/marketing 26%, communications/journalism 6%, education 20%, health sciences 10%, psychology 8%, public administration/social services 8%, security/protective services 6%.

Computing on campus. 90 workstations in library, computer center, student center. Dormitories wired for high-speed internet access and linked to campus network. Commuter students can connect to campus network. Online library, helpline, student web hosting, wireless network available.

Student life. Freshman orientation: Mandatory. Preregistration for classes offered. Held each summer. Day-long sessions include advising appointments. **Policies:** Freshmen permitted cars on campus. **Housing:** Coed dorms, special housing for disabled, substance-free housing available. **Activities:** Choral groups, dance, literary magazine, student government, student newspaper, Black student association, Latin American student organization, Native American club, GLOBAL, Students for Wellness, Fellowship of Christian Athletes, Circle K International, InterVarsity Christian Fellowship, political science club.

Athletics. NCAA. **Intercollegiate:** Baseball M, basketball, cross-country, football (tackle) M, golf, soccer, softball W, tennis, track and field, volleyball W. **Intramural:** Basketball, football (non-tackle), volleyball. **Team name:** Spartans.

Student services. Adult student services, alcohol/substance abuse counseling, campus ministries, career counseling, student employment services, financial aid counseling, health services, personal counseling, placement for graduates. **Physically disabled:** Services for visually, speech, hearing impaired.

Contact. E-mail: admission@aurora.edu
Phone: (630) 844-5533 Toll-free number: (800) 742-5281
Fax: (630) 844-5535
James Lancaster, Director of Freshman Admission, Aurora University, 347 South Gladstone Avenue, Aurora, IL 60506-4892

Benedictine University
Lisle, Illinois
www.ben.edu **CB code: 1707**

- Private 4-year university and liberal arts college affiliated with Roman Catholic Church
- Commuter campus in large town
- 2,213 degree-seeking undergraduates: 32% part-time, 60% women, 10% African American, 14% Asian American, 7% Hispanic American, 1% international
- 977 degree-seeking graduate students
- 82% of applicants admitted
- SAT or ACT (ACT writing optional), application essay required
- 52% graduate within 6 years

General. Founded in 1887. Regionally accredited. **Degrees:** 443 bachelor's, 16 associate awarded; master's, doctoral offered. **ROTC:** Army. **Location:** 25 miles from Chicago. **Calendar:** Semester, extensive summer session. **Full-time faculty:** 87 total; 91% have terminal degrees, 10% minority, 34% women. **Part-time faculty:** 266 total; 12% minority, 49% women. **Class size:** 61% < 20, 38% 20-39, 1% 40-49. **Special facilities:** Nature museum, Benedictine abbey, arboretum, Fermi Nuclear Accelerator Laboratories, Argonne National Laboratories.

Freshman class profile. 972 applied, 800 admitted, 311 enrolled.

Mid 50% test scores		**Rank in top tenth:**	20%
ACT:	20-25	**End year in good standing:**	83%
GPA 3.50 or higher:	42%	**Return as sophomores:**	76%
GPA 3.0-3.49:	28%	**Out-of-state:**	4%
GPA 2.0-2.99:	30%	**Live on campus:**	48%
Rank in top quarter:	45%		

Basis for selection. Require rank in top half of class and minimum 21 ACT. Candidates falling below these criteria reviewed by admissions committee. Audition required of musical instrument and voice majors.

High school preparation. College-preparatory program recommended. 16 units required. Required and recommended units include English 4, mathematics 3-4, history 1, science 2-3 (laboratory 1-2) and foreign language 2.

2005-2006 Annual costs. Tuition/fees: $19,720. Room/board: $6,770. Books/supplies: $700. Personal expenses: $1,500.

2005-2006 Financial aid. Need-based: 235 full-time freshmen applied for aid; 234 were judged to have need; 232 of these received aid. Average need met was 86%. Average scholarship/grant was $6,118; average loan $3,617. 69% of total undergraduate aid awarded as scholarships/grants, 31% as loans/jobs. **Non-need-based:** Awarded to 1,216 full-time undergraduates, including 288 freshmen. Scholarships awarded for academics, alumni affiliation, minority status, music/drama, ROTC. **Additional information:** Need-based financial aid available to part-time students who are enrolled at least half-time.

Application procedures. Admission: No deadline. $40 fee, may be waived for applicants with need. Application may be submitted online. Admission notification on a rolling basis. Must reply by May 1 or within 2 week(s) if notified thereafter. **Financial aid:** Priority date 4/15; no closing date. FAFSA, institutional form required. Applicants notified on a rolling basis starting 2/15; must reply within 2 week(s) of notification.

Academics. Special study options: Accelerated study, combined bachelor's/graduate degree, cross-registration, distance learning, double major, dual enrollment of high school students, honors, independent study, internships, liberal arts/career combination, study abroad, teacher certification program, weekend college. Engineering degree program with Illinois Institute of Technology. **Credit/placement by examination:** AP, CLEP, institutional tests. 30 credit hours maximum toward bachelor's degree. **Support services:** Learning center, study skills assistance, tutoring, writing center.

Majors. Biology: General, biochemistry, molecular. **Business:** Accounting, finance, international, managerial economics, marketing, organizational behavior. **Communications:** General, publishing. **Computer sciences:** Computer science, information systems. **Conservation:** Environmental studies. **Education:** Elementary, special. **Engineering:** Science. **English:** English lit. **Foreign languages:** Spanish. **Health:** Clinical lab science, health care admin, nuclear medical technology, nursing (RN). **History:** General. **Math:** General. **Philosophy/religion:** Philosophy. **Physical sciences:** Chemistry, physics. **Psychology:** General. **Social sciences:** General, economics, political science, sociology. **Visual/performing arts:** Arts management, studio arts.

Most popular majors. Biology 8%, business/marketing 35%, communications/journalism 7%, education 8%, health sciences 9%, psychology 9%, social sciences 8%.

Computing on campus. 200 workstations in dormitories, library, computer center, student center. Dormitories wired for high-speed internet access and linked to campus network. Commuter students can connect to campus network. Online course registration, online library, helpline, wireless network available.

Student life. Freshman orientation: Mandatory, $125 fee. Preregistration for classes offered. **Policies:** Freshmen permitted cars on campus. **Housing:** Coed dorms, single-sex dorms, apartments, substance-free housing available. $100 deposit. **Activities:** Bands, choral groups, film society, literary magazine, music ensembles, student government, student newspaper, symphony orchestra, TV station, Muslim Student Association, African-American Student Union, Knights of Columbus, Mediterranean Club, Daughters of Isabella, Students for Life, Relay for Life, Best Buddies, South Asian Student Association.

Athletics. NCAA. **Intercollegiate:** Baseball M, basketball, cross-country, diving, football (tackle) M, golf M, soccer, softball W, swimming, tennis W, track and field, volleyball W. **Intramural:** Badminton, basketball, bowling, tennis, water polo. **Team name:** Eagles.

Student services. Adult student services, campus ministries, career counseling, student employment services, financial aid counseling, health services, personal counseling, placement for graduates. **Physically disabled:** Services for visually, speech, hearing impaired. **Learning disabled:** Comprehensive services available.

Contact. E-mail: admissions@ben.edu
Phone: (630) 829-6300 Toll-free number: (888) 829-6363
Fax: (630) 829-6301
Kari Gibbons, Dean of Enrollment, Benedictine University, 5700 College Road, Lisle, IL 60532

Blackburn College
Carlinville, Illinois **CB member**
www.blackburn.edu **CB code: 1065**

- Private 4-year liberal arts college affiliated with Presbyterian Church (USA)
- Residential campus in small town
- 598 degree-seeking undergraduates: 2% part-time, 53% women, 7% African American, 1% Asian American, 1% Hispanic American, 1% international
- 62% of applicants admitted
- SAT or ACT (ACT writing optional) required
- 40% graduate within 6 years

General. Founded in 1837. Regionally accredited. Participation in student-managed work program required for all resident students. Resident students work 160 hours per semester to reduce costs and gain valuable career skills. **Degrees:** 140 bachelor's awarded. **Location:** 40 miles from Springfield, 60 miles from St. Louis. **Calendar:** Semester, limited summer session. **Full-time faculty:** 35 total; 91% have terminal degrees, 3% minority, 40% women. **Part-time faculty:** 36 total; 28% have terminal degrees, 6% minority, 56% women. **Class size:** 69% < 20, 28% 20-39, 2% 40-49, 2% 50-99.

Freshman class profile. 937 applied, 583 admitted, 211 enrolled.

Mid 50% test scores		Rank in top quarter:	44%
SAT verbal:	480-540	Rank in top tenth:	17%
SAT math:	480-540	End year in good standing:	71%
ACT:	19-24	Return as sophomores:	64%
GPA 3.50 or higher:	35%	Out-of-state:	12%
GPA 3.0-3.49:	30%	Live on campus:	82%
GPA 2.0-2.99:	35%		

Basis for selection. High school academic record, substantiated by test scores, most important. Interview recommended. Audition recommended for music majors. Portfolio recommended for art majors. **Homeschooled:** Statement describing homeschool structure and mission, transcript of courses and grades, state high school equivalency certificate required.

High school preparation. College-preparatory program recommended. 16 units recommended. Recommended units include English 4, mathematics 3, social studies 2, history 2, science 3 and foreign language 2.

2005-2006 Annual costs. Tuition/fees: $15,040. All on-campus students participate in a work program which reduces net tuition costs. Room/board: $3,695. Books/supplies: $700. Personal expenses: $800.

2004-2005 Financial aid. Need-based: 169 full-time freshmen applied for aid; 152 were judged to have need; 152 of these received aid. Average need met was 91%. Average scholarship/grant was $8,802; average loan $1,779. 68% of total undergraduate aid awarded as scholarships/grants, 32% as loans/jobs. **Non-need-based:** Awarded to 126 full-time undergraduates, including 44 freshmen. Scholarships awarded for academics, state residency. **Additional information:** Each resident student works 160 hours per semester.

Application procedures. Admission: No deadline. No application fee. Application may be submitted online. Admission notification on a rolling basis beginning on or about 10/15. **Financial aid:** Priority date 4/1; no closing date. FAFSA required. Applicants notified on a rolling basis starting 3/1; must reply within 4 week(s) of notification.

Academics. Special study options: Accelerated study, cooperative education, double major, dual enrollment of high school students, independent study, internships, student-designed major, study abroad, teacher certification program, Washington semester. British studies semester, Mexico studies semester. **Credit/placement by examination:** AP, CLEP, SAT, ACT, institutional tests. 30 credit hours maximum toward bachelor's degree. **Support services:** Learning center, reduced course load, remedial instruction, study skills assistance, tutoring, writing center.

Majors. Area/ethnic studies: Latin American. **Biology:** General. **Business:** Accounting, business admin, management information systems, marketing. **Communications:** General. **Computer sciences:** General, programming. **Education:** General, art, biology, elementary, English, history, mathematics, multi-level teacher, physical, science, secondary, social science, social studies. **English:** British lit. **Foreign languages:** Spanish. **Health:** Clinical lab technology, predentistry, premedicine, preveterinary. **History:** General. **Legal studies:** Prelaw. **Math:** General. **Physical sciences:** Chemistry. **Protective services:** Criminal justice. **Psychology:** General. **Public administration:** General. **Social sciences:** Criminology, political science. **Visual/performing arts:** Art, music performance, studio arts.

Most popular majors. Biology 9%, business/marketing 15%, communications/journalism 6%, computer/information sciences 6%, education 25%, psychology 6%.

Computing on campus. 82 workstations in library, computer center. Dormitories linked to campus network. Helpline available.

Student life. Freshman orientation: Mandatory. Preregistration for classes offered. One day summer orientation and two day orientation prior to the beginning of fall semester. **Policies:** Alcohol allowed for students 21 and older. Freshmen permitted cars on campus. **Housing:** Guaranteed on-campus for all undergraduates. Coed dorms, single-sex dorms, substance-free housing available. $50 nonrefundable deposit, deadline 7/31. Alcohol-free, quiet study housing available. **Activities:** Concert band, choral groups, dance, drama, music ensembles, student government, student newspaper, Cultural Expressions, Habitat for Humanity chapter, Catacombs, Baptist Fellowship Group, Newman Club, Catholic Fellowship and Service Group, common ground, SADD, Republican club, health and wellness club.

Athletics. NCAA. **Intercollegiate:** Baseball M, basketball, cross-country, football (tackle) M, golf M, soccer, softball W, tennis W, volleyball W. **Intramural:** Badminton, basketball, bowling, racquetball, softball, tennis, volleyball, water polo. **Team name:** Beavers.

Student services. Adult student services, alcohol/substance abuse counseling, career counseling, student employment services, financial aid counseling, minority student services, personal counseling, placement for graduates.

Contact. E-mail: jmali@blackburn.edu
Phone: (217) 854-3231 Toll-free number: (800) 233-3550
Fax: (217) 854-3713
John Malin, Dean of Enrollment Management, Blackburn College, 700 College Avenue, Carlinville, IL 62626

Blessing-Reiman College of Nursing

Quincy, Illinois
www.brcn.edu **CB code: 0139**

- Private 4-year nursing college
- Commuter campus in large town
- 211 degree-seeking undergraduates: 9% part-time, 93% women, 2% African American, 4% Asian American
- SAT or ACT (ACT writing optional) required

General. Founded in 1891. Regionally accredited. Joint degree programs with Culver-Stockton College (MO) and Quincy University (IL) leading to Bachelor of Science in Nursing degree. General education classes held at partner campus, with nursing classes at B-RCN campus and regional medical center. **Degrees:** 40 bachelor's awarded. **Location:** 120 miles from St. Louis, 100 miles from Springfield. **Calendar:** Semester, limited summer session. **Full-time faculty:** 18 total; 22% have terminal degrees, 100% women. **Part-time faculty:** 11 total; 100% women. **Class size:** 68% < 20, 29% 20-39, 3% 40-49.

Freshman class profile.

Mid 50% test scores		Out-of-state:	44%
ACT:	21-25	Live on campus:	82%
Return as sophomores:	70%		

Basis for selection. 3.0 GPA and at least 22 ACT composite score required for nursing majors.

High school preparation. Required units include English 4, mathematics 2, social studies 3, science 3 (laboratory 2). Biology, chemistry, algebra required.

2005-2006 Annual costs. Partnered with Quincy University and Culver-Stockton College. Freshmen and sophomores pay partnering school's tuition rate: $17,800 at Quincy, $14,250 at Culver-Stockton. Books/supplies: $600. Personal expenses: $1,725.

2004-2005 Financial aid. Need-based: 35% of total undergraduate aid awarded as scholarships/grants, 65% as loans/jobs. **Additional information:** Financial aid for freshmen and sophomores administered by Culver-Stockton College and Quincy University.

Application procedures. Admission: No deadline. No application fee. Application may be submitted online. Admission notification on a rolling basis. **Financial aid:** Priority date 3/1; no closing date. FAFSA required. Applicants notified on a rolling basis starting 7/1.

Academics. Special study options: Accelerated study, combined bachelor's/graduate degree, internships. **Credit/placement by examination:** AP, CLEP, institutional tests. **Support services:** Study skills assistance, tutoring.

Majors. Health: Nursing (RN).

Computing on campus. 25 workstations in dormitories, library, computer center. Dormitories linked to campus network. Online library available.

Student life. Freshman orientation: Mandatory. Preregistration for classes offered. Inclusive of all classes. **Policies:** Immunization and background check required for sophomore level and up. Freshmen permitted cars on campus. **Housing:** Apartments, substance-free housing available. Men's and women's dormitories available at Culver-Stockton College and Quincy University. **Activities:** Literary magazine, student government, Student Nurses Organization, club and intramural sports, fraternities and sororities available at Culver-Stockton College and Quincy University.

Student services. Alcohol/substance abuse counseling, career counseling, student employment services, financial aid counseling, health services, on-campus daycare, personal counseling, placement for graduates.

Contact. E-mail: admissions@brcn.edu
Phone: (217) 228-5520 ext. 6949 Toll-free number: (800) 877-9140 ext. 6949 Fax: (217) 223-4661
Pam Brown, President, Blessing-Reiman College of Nursing, PO Box 7005, Quincy, IL 62305-7005

Four-Year Colleges

Bradley University

Peoria, Illinois **CB member**
www.bradley.edu **CB code: 1070**

- Private 4-year university and engineering college
- Residential campus in large city
- 5,343 degree-seeking undergraduates: 5% part-time, 55% women, 6% African American, 3% Asian American, 2% Hispanic American, 1% international
- 653 degree-seeking graduate students
- 91% of applicants admitted
- SAT or ACT (ACT writing recommended), application essay required
- 72% graduate within 6 years; 16% enter graduate study

General. Founded in 1897. Regionally accredited. **Degrees:** 1,329 bachelor's awarded; master's, doctoral offered. **ROTC:** Army. **Location:** 157 miles from Chicago, 164 miles from St. Louis. **Calendar:** Semester, limited summer session. **Full-time faculty:** 326 total; 85% have terminal degrees, 14% minority, 35% women. **Part-time faculty:** 224 total; 5% minority, 52% women. **Class size:** 46% < 20, 45% 20-39, 5% 40-49, 3% 50-99, less than 1% >100. **Special facilities:** Global communications center, 2 art galleries.

Freshman class profile. 4,218 applied, 3,820 admitted, 1,136 enrolled.

Mid 50% test scores			
SAT verbal:	500-630	Return as sophomores:	87%
SAT math:	520-640	Out-of-state:	14%
ACT:	23-27	Live on campus:	94%
Rank in top quarter:	59%	International:	1%
Rank in top tenth:	28%	Fraternities:	40%
		Sororities:	35%

Basis for selection. High school curriculum and achievement, test scores, special talents, co-curricular activities and involvement, letters of recommendation and personal statement, and educational goals important. Student's academic interest, motivational level, and quality of secondary school education also considered. Interview recommended. Audition required of music majors, recommended for theater majors. Portfolio recommended for art majors. **Homeschooled:** Applicants must submit ACT or SAT score, record of courses taken, grades earned, personal statement, letter of recommendation and record of activities or club memberships. Interview may be required and highly recommended.

High school preparation. College-preparatory program required. 16 units required. Required and recommended units include English 4-5, mathematics 3-4, social studies 2-3, science 2-3 (laboratory 2-3) and foreign language 2. Additional requirements for business, science, engineering, liberal arts, music, nursing, and physical therapy majors.

2005-2006 Annual costs. Tuition/fees: $18,630. Room/board: $6,450. Personal expenses: $1,500.

2004-2005 Financial aid. **Need-based:** 931 full-time freshmen applied for aid; 679 were judged to have need; 679 of these received aid. Average need met was 81.96%. Average scholarship/grant was $10,648; average loan $3,699. 63% of total undergraduate aid awarded as scholarships/grants, 37% as loans/jobs. **Non-need-based:** Awarded to 1,457 full-time undergraduates, including 347 freshmen. Scholarships awarded for academics, alumni affiliation, art, athletics, leadership, music/drama, state residency.

Application procedures. **Admission:** Priority date 3/1; deadline 8/1 (postmark date). $35 fee, may be waived for applicants with need. Application may be submitted online. Admission notification on a rolling basis beginning on or about 10/1. Must reply by May 1 or within 2 week(s) if notified thereafter. **Financial aid:** Priority date 3/1; no closing date. FAFSA required. Applicants notified on a rolling basis starting 2/15.

Academics. Academic Exploration Program assists undergraduates in choosing major. **Special study options:** Accelerated study, combined bachelor's/graduate degree, cooperative education, double major, honors, independent study, internships, liberal arts/career combination, student-designed major, study abroad, teacher certification program, Washington semester. **Credit/placement by examination:** AP, CLEP, IB, institutional tests. 60 credit hours maximum toward bachelor's degree. **Support services:** Learning center, study skills assistance, tutoring, writing center.

Majors. **Biology:** General, biochemistry, cellular/molecular. **Business:** Accounting, actuarial science, business admin, entrepreneurial studies, finance, human resources, insurance, international, management information systems, managerial economics, marketing, selling, small business admin. **Communications:** General, advertising, digital media, journalism, photojournalism, public relations, radio/tv. **Communications technology:** Animation/special effects. **Computer sciences:** Computer science, information systems. **Conservation:** Environmental science. **Education:** Art, biology, chemistry, drama/dance, early childhood, elementary, English, family/consumer sciences, French, German, history, learning disabled, mentally handicapped, music, physics, psychology, science, Spanish, speech. **Engineering:** Civil, computer, construction, electrical, environmental, industrial, manufacturing, mechanical, physics. **Engineering technology:** Electrical, manufacturing. **English:** English lit. **Family/consumer sciences:** General, merchandising. **Foreign languages:** French, German, Spanish. **Health:** Clinical lab science, dietetics, nursing (RN). **History:** General. **Liberal arts:** Arts/sciences, humanities. **Math:** General. **Philosophy/religion:** Philosophy, religion. **Physical sciences:** Chemistry, geology, physics. **Protective services:** Corrections. **Psychology:** General. **Public administration:** Social work. **Social sciences:** Economics, international relations, political science, sociology. **Visual/performing arts:** Acting, art, art history/conservation, ceramics, directing/producing, dramatic, drawing, graphic design, music management, music performance, music theory/composition, painting, photography, printmaking, sculpture, studio arts.

Most popular majors. Business/marketing 24%, communications/journalism 13%, education 9%, engineering/engineering technologies 12%, family/consumer sciences 9%, health sciences 7%.

Computing on campus. 900 workstations in dormitories, library, computer center. Dormitories wired for high-speed internet access and linked to campus network. Commuter students can connect to campus network. Online course registration, helpline, repair service, student web hosting, wireless network available.

Student life. **Freshman orientation:** Mandatory, $115 fee. Preregistration for classes offered. 13 sessions throughout summer. **Policies:** Freshmen permitted cars on campus. **Housing:** Guaranteed on-campus for freshmen. Coed dorms, single-sex dorms, apartments, fraternity/sorority housing, substance-free housing available. $100 deposit, deadline 5/1. **Activities:** Bands, choral groups, dance, drama, film society, literary magazine, music ensembles, musical theater, opera, radio station, student government, student newspaper, symphony orchestra, TV station, Alpha Phi Omega, center for student leadership and public services, Hillel, InterVarsity Christian Fellowship, mock trial, Model UN, Amnesty International, Habitat for Humanity, Beyond Prejudice.

Athletics. NCAA. **Intercollegiate:** Baseball M, basketball, cross-country, golf, soccer M, softball W, tennis, track and field W, volleyball W. **Intramural:** Badminton, basketball, bowling, fencing, football (tackle) M, golf, handball, racquetball, soccer, softball, swimming, table tennis, tennis, volleyball, water polo, wrestling M. **Team name:** Braves.

Student services. Alcohol/substance abuse counseling, career counseling, student employment services, financial aid counseling, health services, minority student services, personal counseling, placement for graduates, veterans' counselor.

Contact. E-mail: admissions@bradley.edu
Phone: (309) 677-1000 Toll-free number: (800) 447-6460
Fax: (309) 677-2797
Rodney San Jose, Director of Admissions, Bradley University, 1501 West Bradley Avenue, Peoria, IL 61625

Chicago State University

Chicago, Illinois **CB member**
www.csu.edu **CB code: 1118**

- Public 4-year university
- Commuter campus in very large city
- 5,096 degree-seeking undergraduates: 32% part-time, 72% women, 87% African American, 1% Asian American, 6% Hispanic American, 1% international
- 938 degree-seeking graduate students
- 47% of applicants admitted
- SAT or ACT required

General. Founded in 1867. Regionally accredited. **Degrees:** 699 bachelor's awarded; master's offered. **ROTC:** Army. **Location:** 12 miles from downtown. **Calendar:** Semester, limited summer session. **Full-time faculty:** 307 total. **Part-time faculty:** 127 total. **Class size:** 48% < 20, 51% 20-39, less than 1% 40-49, less than 1% 50-99. **Special facilities:** Electron microscopy laboratory, video conference room, center of African heritage and culture.

Freshman class profile. 2,969 applied, 1,401 admitted, 451 enrolled.

Mid 50% test scores			
ACT:	16-19	Rank in top tenth:	13%
Rank in top quarter:	35%	Out-of-state:	6%
		Live on campus:	23%

Basis for selection. High school GPA, standardized test scores, and subject/units completed.

High school preparation. 15 units required. Required units include English 4, mathematics 3, social studies 3, science 3 and academic electives 2. 2 units foreign language, music, vocational education or art.

2005-2006 Annual costs. Tuition/fees: $6,625; $11,815 out-of-state. Rates are guaranteed for all four years. Tuition quoted is for first-time freshmen. Room/board: $6,212. Books/supplies: $1,400. Personal expenses: $2,800.

Financial aid. Non-need-based: Scholarships awarded for academics, athletics, ROTC, state residency. **Additional information:** Freshmen of outstanding academic ability and talent eligible for Scholars Program full-tuition scholarship.

Application procedures. Admission: Closing date 7/15 (receipt date). $25 fee, may be waived for applicants with need. Admission notification on a rolling basis. **Financial aid:** No deadline. FAFSA, institutional form required.

Academics. Special study options: Cooperative education, distance learning, double major, ESL, honors, independent study, internships, liberal arts/career combination, student-designed major, study abroad, teacher certification program. Programs for mature adults (University Without Walls, individualized curriculum, Board of Governors degree program). **Credit/placement by examination:** AP, CLEP, institutional tests. 60 credit hours maximum toward bachelor's degree. **Support services:** Learning center, remedial instruction, study skills assistance, tutoring, writing center.

Majors. Area/ethnic studies: African-American. **Biology:** General, bacteriology, biochemistry, environmental, molecular. **Business:** Accounting, business admin, fashion, finance, management information systems. **Communications:** Broadcast journalism. **Computer sciences:** General, data processing, information systems. **Education:** General, art, biology, business, chemistry, early childhood, elementary, English, health, history, mathematics, mentally handicapped, multi-level teacher, music, physical, secondary, special, technology/industrial arts. **English:** Speech/rhetoric, technical writing. **Foreign languages:** Spanish. **Health:** Medical records admin, nursing (RN). **History:** General. **Math:** General. **Parks/recreation:** Health/fitness. **Physical sciences:** Chemistry, physics. **Psychology:** General. **Social sciences:** Anthropology, economics, geography, political science, sociology. **Visual/performing arts:** Art, commercial/advertising art.

Most popular majors. Business/marketing 14%, education 11%, health sciences 9%, liberal arts 30%, psychology 8%, security/protective services 7%, social sciences 6%.

Computing on campus. 156 workstations in dormitories, library, computer center, student center. Dormitories wired for high-speed internet access. Commuter students can connect to campus network. Online course registration, online library available.

Student life. Freshman orientation: Mandatory. Preregistration for classes offered. One-day programs in July and August. **Policies:** Freshmen permitted cars on campus. **Housing:** Coed dorms available. $125 deposit, deadline 8/1. **Activities:** Bands, choral groups, dance, drama, literary magazine, music ensembles, radio station, student government, student newspaper, TV station, 47 clubs and organizations.

Athletics. NCAA. **Intercollegiate:** Baseball M, basketball, cross-country, golf, tennis, track and field, volleyball W. **Intramural:** Basketball, gymnastics, swimming, volleyball. **Team name:** Cougars.

Student services. Adult student services, alcohol/substance abuse counseling, campus ministries, career counseling, student employment services, financial aid counseling, health services, minority student services, on-campus daycare, personal counseling, placement for graduates, veterans' counselor, women's services.

Contact. E-mail: ug-admissions@csu.edu
Phone: (773) 995-2513 Fax: (773) 995-3820
Addie Epps, Director of Admissions, Chicago State University, 9501 South King Drive, Chicago, IL 60628

Columbia College Chicago

Chicago, Illinois — **CB member**
www.colum.edu — **CB code: 1135**

- Private 4-year visual arts and liberal arts college
- Commuter campus in very large city
- 10,039 degree-seeking undergraduates: 13% part-time, 51% women
- 690 degree-seeking graduate students
- Application essay required
- 30% graduate within 6 years

General. Founded in 1890. Regionally accredited. **Degrees:** 1,560 bachelor's awarded; master's offered. **Location:** Downtown. **Calendar:** Semester, limited summer session. **Full-time faculty:** 299 total; 19% minority, 44% women. **Part-time faculty:** 1,327 total; 13% minority, 46% women. **Class size:** 77% < 20, 22% 20-39, 1% 40-49, less than 1% 50-99, less than 1% >100. **Special facilities:** Museum of contemporary photography, photography studios, film/video sound stage, dance performance space, theater, audio technology center, Center for Book and Paper Arts, Center for Black Music Research, Glass Curtain Gallery, C33 Gallery, Multimedia Center/Conaway Center, Urban Fusion.

Freshman class profile. 3,428 applied, 3,111 admitted, 1,829 enrolled.

Mid 50% test scores		**Rank in top tenth:**	7%
ACT:	17-24	**End year in good standing:**	92%
GPA 3.50 or higher:	18%	**Return as sophomores:**	68%
GPA 3.0-3.49:	27%	**Out-of-state:**	39%
GPA 2.0-2.99:	46%	**Live on campus:**	55%
Rank in top quarter:	23%		

Basis for selection. Open admission, but selective for some programs. Proof of high school graduation (or earned GED), letter of recommendation, and essay required for placement/counseling. Students with less than 2.0 GPA may be required to attend special summer program. All freshmen take COMPASS placement test on campus. Interview recommended, portfolio not required. **Homeschooled:** Transcript of courses and grades required. **Learning Disabled:** Student must have regular earned GED or HS diploma and may have to complete BRIDGE program.

2005-2006 Annual costs. Tuition/fees: $15,998. Room/board: $9,356. Books/supplies: $1,300. Personal expenses: $3,654.

2004-2005 Financial aid. Need-based: 34% of total undergraduate aid awarded as scholarships/grants, 66% as loans/jobs. **Non-need-based:** Scholarships awarded for academics, art, leadership, music/drama, state residency.

Application procedures. Admission: Priority date 6/15; no deadline. $35 fee. Application may be submitted online. Admission notification on a rolling basis. **Financial aid:** Priority date 7/1; no closing date. FAFSA, institutional form required. Applicants notified on a rolling basis.

Academics. Special study options: Cooperative education, distance learning, dual enrollment of high school students, ESL, independent study, internships, liberal arts/career combination, student-designed major, study abroad, teacher certification program. **Credit/placement by examination:** AP, CLEP, IB, institutional tests. 62 credit hours maximum toward bachelor's degree. **Support services:** Learning center, pre-admission summer program, reduced course load, remedial instruction, study skills assistance, tutoring, writing center.

Majors. Architecture: Interior. **Business:** Business admin, fashion, marketing. **Communications:** Advertising, broadcast journalism, journalism, public relations. **Communications technology:** Recording arts. **Computer sciences:** Web page design. **Education:** Early childhood, kindergarten/preschool. **English:** Creative writing. **Liberal arts:** Arts/sciences. **Visual/performing arts:** General, art, arts management, cinematography, commercial/advertising art, dance, design, dramatic, fashion design, film/cinema, interior design, jazz, multimedia, music management, music performance, photography, play/screenwriting, studio arts, theater design, voice/opera.

Computing on campus. 851 workstations in dormitories, library, computer center. Dormitories wired for high-speed internet access and linked to campus network. Commuter students can connect to campus network. Online course registration, helpline, wireless network available.

Student life. Freshman orientation: Mandatory, $50 fee. Preregistration for classes offered. **Policies:** Freshmen permitted cars on campus. **Housing:** Coed dorms, substance-free housing available. $500 fully refundable deposit, deadline 5/2. Student housing available at nearby colleges and universities. **Activities:** Bands, choral groups, dance, drama, film society, literary magazine, music ensembles, musical theater, radio station, student government, student newspaper, TV station, Association of Black Journalists, Umoja, Black Actor's Guild, Black Ink, Latino Alliance, Campus Christian Ministry, environmental campus organization, Hillel, international student organization, Not In Our Name.

Athletics. Intramural: Basketball, soccer.

Student services. Alcohol/substance abuse counseling, career counseling, services for economically disadvantaged, student employment services, financial aid counseling, health services, minority student services, personal counseling, placement for graduates, veterans' counselor. **Physically disabled:** Services for visually, speech, hearing impaired.

Contact. E-mail: admissions@colum.edu
Phone: (312) 663-1600 ext. 7131 Fax: (312) 344-8024
Murphy Monroe, Executive Director of Admissions, Columbia College Chicago, 600 South Michigan Avenue, Chicago, IL 60605-1996

Concordia University

River Forest, Illinois — **CB member**
www.curf.edu — **CB code: 1140**

- Private 4-year university and teachers college affiliated with Lutheran Church - Missouri Synod
- Residential campus in large town
- 961 degree-seeking undergraduates
- 62% of applicants admitted
- ACT (writing optional) required

General. Founded in 1864. Regionally accredited. **Degrees:** 216 bachelor's awarded; master's, doctoral offered. **Location:** 10 miles from Chicago. **Calendar:** Semester, limited summer session. **Full-time faculty:** 80 total. **Part-time faculty:** 140 total. **Class size:** 71% < 20, 28% 20-39, less than 1% 40-49, less than 1% 50-99. **Special facilities:** Early childhood education laboratory school, curriculum center (teacher's resource), human performance laboratory.

Freshman class profile. 1,005 applied, 628 admitted, 210 enrolled.

Mid 50% test scores			
SAT verbal:	450-590	ACT:	19-25
SAT math:	460-590	Out-of-state:	42%

Basis for selection. School achievement record, character reference most important. 2.0 GPA in college preparatory classes and rank in top half of class with a minimum 20 ACT composite score required. Interview recommended. Essay and interview required for students who do not meet academic admission requirements.

High school preparation. 15 units required. Required and recommended units include English 4, mathematics 3, social studies 2, history 1, science 2-4 (laboratory 1) and foreign language 2.

2006-2007 Annual costs. Tuition/fees (projected): $20,400. Room/board: $6,600. Books/supplies: $600. Personal expenses: $400.

Financial aid. Non-need-based: Scholarships awarded for academics, alumni affiliation, minority status, music/drama.

Application procedures. Admission: No deadline. No application fee. Application may be submitted online. Admission notification on a rolling basis beginning on or about 9/4. **Financial aid:** Closing date 4/1. FAFSA, institutional form required. Applicants notified on a rolling basis; must reply within 4 week(s) of notification.

Academics. Special study options: Cross-registration, distance learning, double major, exchange student, honors, independent study, internships, study abroad, teacher certification program. Adult degree completion program. **Credit/placement by examination:** CLEP, IB, institutional tests. **Support services:** Learning center, reduced course load, study skills assistance, tutoring, writing center.

Majors. Biology: General. **Business:** General, accounting, business admin, marketing. **Communications:** General, advertising. **Computer sciences:** General, computer science. **Education:** General, biology, chemistry, computer, early childhood, elementary, English, history, multi-level teacher, music, physical, science, secondary, social science, social studies. **Foreign languages:** Ancient Greek, Hebrew, Latin. **Health:** Prenursing. **History:** General. **Interdisciplinary:** Natural sciences. **Math:** General. **Parks/recreation:** Exercise sciences. **Philosophy/religion:** Philosophy. **Physical sciences:** Chemistry. **Protective services:** Criminal justice, law enforcement admin, police science. **Psychology:** General. **Public administration:** Social work. **Social sciences:** Geography, political science, sociology. **Theology:** Religious ed, sacred music, theology. **Visual/performing arts:** Art, music performance, music theory/composition.

Computing on campus. 70 workstations in library, computer center, student center. Dormitories linked to campus network. Commuter students can connect to campus network. Helpline available.

Student life. Freshman orientation: Mandatory. Preregistration for classes offered. **Policies:** Freshmen permitted cars on campus. **Housing:** Guaranteed on-campus for freshmen. Coed dorms, single-sex dorms, apartments available. $100 deposit. **Activities:** Bands, choral groups, drama, literary magazine, music ensembles, musical theater, student government, student newspaper, TV station, minority student alliance, Concordia Youth Ministry, Ambassadors for Christ, sociology/social service club, Fellowship of Christian Athletes, environmental awareness club, Pace Jail Ministries, Latin student union.

Athletics. NCAA. **Intercollegiate:** Baseball M, basketball, cross-country, football (tackle) M, soccer, softball W, tennis, track and field, volleyball W. **Intramural:** Badminton, basketball, bowling, cross-country, softball, swimming, tennis, track and field, volleyball. **Team name:** Cougars.

Student services. Campus ministries, career counseling, student employment services, financial aid counseling, health services, on-campus daycare, personal counseling, placement for graduates.

Contact. E-mail: crfadmis@curf.edu
Phone: (708) 209-3100 Toll-free number: (866) 462-2873
Fax: (708) 209-3473
James Malley, Dean of Admission, Concordia University, 7400 Augusta Street, River Forest, IL 60305-1499

DePaul University

Chicago, Illinois — **CB member**
www.depaul.edu — **CB code: 1165**

- Private 4-year university affiliated with Roman Catholic Church
- Residential campus in very large city
- 14,277 degree-seeking undergraduates: 21% part-time, 57% women, 10% African American, 9% Asian American, 13% Hispanic American, 1% international
- 8,249 degree-seeking graduate students
- 71% of applicants admitted
- SAT or ACT (ACT writing optional) required
- 64% graduate within 6 years

General. Founded in 1898. Regionally accredited. Largest Catholic university in the United States. **Degrees:** 2,683 bachelor's awarded; master's, doctoral, first professional offered. **ROTC:** Army. **Location:** Downtown. **Calendar:** Quarter, extensive summer session. **Full-time faculty:** 834 total; 80% have terminal degrees, 20% minority, 41% women. **Part-time faculty:** 643 total; 14% minority, 47% women. **Class size:** 39% < 20, 50% 20-39, 10% 40-49, less than 1% 50-99. **Special facilities:** Theater, fitness center.

Freshman class profile. 9,744 applied, 6,948 admitted, 2,400 enrolled.

Mid 50% test scores		Rank in top quarter:	43%
SAT verbal:	530-630	Rank in top tenth:	12%
SAT math:	510-620	End year in good standing:	93%
ACT:	22-27	Return as sophomores:	85%
GPA 3.50 or higher:	44%	Out-of-state:	29%
GPA 3.0-3.49:	32%	Live on campus:	70%
GPA 2.0-2.99:	24%	International:	1%

Basis for selection. Secondary school record and character are most important; class rank, recommendations, test scores, essay, extracurricular activities, talent/ability, volunteer and work experience also important. Interview, alumni/ae relation, geographical location, state residency, religious affiliation, racial or ethnic status also considered. Interview required of acting, theater technologies, and recording sound technology majors. Auditions required of music and theater majors. Portfolios required of theater technology and design majors. **Homeschooled:** Transcript of courses and grades required. ACT or SAT, official community college transcripts for any courses taken. Listing of textbooks used, especially in math and science, is recommended.

High school preparation. College-preparatory program recommended. 16 units required. Required units include English 4, mathematics 2, social studies 2, science 2 (laboratory 2) and academic electives 4.

2005-2006 Annual costs. Tuition/fees: $21,100. Room/board: $9,656. Books/supplies: $1,000.

2005-2006 Financial aid. Need-based: 1,826 full-time freshmen applied for aid; 1,509 were judged to have need; 1,442 of these received aid. Average need met was 69%. Average scholarship/grant was $11,853; average loan $3,248. 51% of total undergraduate aid awarded as scholarships/grants, 49% as loans/jobs. **Non-need-based:** Awarded to 2,998 full-time undergraduates, including 960 freshmen. Scholarships awarded for academics, art, athletics, leadership, minority status, music/drama.

Application procedures. Admission: Priority date 2/1; no deadline. $40 fee, may be waived for applicants with need. Application may be submitted online. Admission notification on a rolling basis beginning on or about 5/1. Must reply by May 1 or within 2 week(s) if notified thereafter. Early action applicants receive early financial aid estimates, priority registration, and priority housing. **Financial aid:** Closing date 5/1. FAFSA required. Applicants notified on a rolling basis starting 2/15; must reply by 5/1 or within 4 week(s) of notification.

Academics. Honors programs offered in arts and sciences, business. Conservatory program in theater and music provides professional training. **Special study options:** Accelerated study, combined bachelor's/graduate degree, cooperative education, distance learning, double major, ESL, honors, independent study, internships, liberal arts/career combination, study abroad, teacher certification program, weekend college. **Credit/placement by examination:** AP, CLEP, IB, SAT, ACT, institutional tests. 99 credit hours maximum toward bachelor's degree. Senior year residency requirement excludes CLEP, AP or IB credits. For transfer students, CLEP, IB or AP credits combined with transfer credits from 2-year institutions may total no more than 99 hours, and combined with transfer credits from 4-year institutions may total no more than 132 hours. **Support services:** Learning center, preadmission summer program, reduced course load, remedial instruction, study skills assistance, tutoring, writing center.

Majors. Area/ethnic studies: African-American, American, East Asian, Latin American, women's. **Biology:** General. **Business:** General, accounting, banking/financial services, business admin, finance, human resources, managerial economics, operations. **Communications:** General. **Communications technology:** Recording arts. **Computer sciences:** General, computer graphics, computer science, information systems, networking, web page design. **Conservation:** General, environmental science. **Education:** Early childhood, elementary, kindergarten/preschool, music, physical, secondary. **Foreign languages:** French, German, Italian, Spanish. **Health:** Clinical lab science, nursing (RN). **History:** General. **Liberal arts:** Arts/sciences. **Math:** General. **Philosophy/religion:** Judaic, philosophy, religion. **Physical sciences:** Chemistry, physics. **Psychology:** General. **Public administration:** Policy analysis. **Social sciences:** General, economics, geography, international relations, political science, sociology, urban studies. **Visual/performing arts:** Art history/conservation, dramatic, music management, music performance, music theory/composition, musicology, play/screenwriting, theater design, theater history.

Most popular majors. Business/marketing 31%, communications/journalism 7%, computer/information sciences 11%, liberal arts 14%, psychology 6%, social sciences 9%, visual/performing arts 7%.

Computing on campus. 1,758 workstations in dormitories, library, computer center, student center. Dormitories wired for high-speed internet access and linked to campus network. Commuter students can connect to campus network. Online course registration, online library, helpline, student web hosting, wireless network available.

Student life. Freshman orientation: Mandatory, $65 fee. Preregistration for classes offered. 2 day summer orientation program designed for first-year students and their families where students meet with an academic advisor and register for classes. **Policies:** Freshmen permitted cars on campus. **Housing:** Coed dorms, apartments, fraternity/sorority housing, substance-free housing available. $500 fully refundable deposit, deadline 3/1. Theme housing available. **Activities:** Bands, choral groups, dance, drama, film society, music ensembles, musical theater, opera, student government, student newspaper, symphony orchestra, over 70 clubs and organizations.

Athletics. NCAA. **Intercollegiate:** Basketball, cross-country, golf M, soccer, softball W, tennis, track and field, volleyball W. **Intramural:** Basketball, football (non-tackle), handball, racquetball, skiing, soccer, softball, swimming, volleyball. **Team name:** Blue Demons.

Student services. Adult student services, alcohol/substance abuse counseling, campus ministries, career counseling, services for economically disadvantaged, student employment services, financial aid counseling, health services, legal services, minority student services, personal counseling, placement for graduates, veterans' counselor, women's services. **Physically disabled:** Services for visually, speech, hearing impaired.

Contact. E-mail: admitdpu@depaul.edu
Phone: (312) 362-8300 Toll-free number: (800) 433-7285
Fax: (312) 362-5749
Carlene Klaas, Director of Undergraduate Admissions, DePaul University, One East Jackson Boulevard, Chicago, IL 60604-2287

DeVry University: Addison

Addison, Illinois
www.dpg.devry.edu CB code: 3204

- For-profit 4-year university
- Commuter campus in large town
- 1,574 degree-seeking undergraduates: 28% part-time, 40% women
- Interview required
- 38% graduate within 6 years

General. Founded in 1982. Regionally accredited. **Degrees:** 549 bachelor's, 52 associate awarded. **Location:** 20 miles from Chicago. **Calendar:** Semester, extensive summer session. **Full-time faculty:** 51 total; 24% minority, 33% women. **Part-time faculty:** 61 total; 28% minority, 33% women.

Freshman class profile. 236 enrolled.

Basis for selection. Applicants must have high school diploma or equivalent, or degree from an accredited postsecondary institution and demonstrate proficiency in basic college-level skills through test scores and/or institution-administered placement examinations, and be at least 17 years of age. New students may enter at the beginning of any semester. Applicants may also take a DeVry administered admissions test.

High school preparation. College-preparatory program recommended. Required units include mathematics 1. Math unit must be algebra or higher.

2005-2006 Annual costs. Tuition/fees: $12,240. Books/supplies: $1,100. Personal expenses: $1,750.

2004-2005 Financial aid. All financial aid based on need. 333 full-time freshmen applied for aid; 297 were judged to have need; 293 of these received aid. Average need met was 48%. Average scholarship/grant was $6,193; average loan $4,825. 25% of total undergraduate aid awarded as scholarships/grants, 75% as loans/jobs.

Application procedures. Admission: No deadline. $50 fee. Application may be submitted online. Admission notification on a rolling basis. **Financial aid:** No deadline. FAFSA required. Applicants notified on a rolling basis.

Academics. Special study options: Accelerated study, cooperative education, distance learning. **Credit/placement by examination:** CLEP, institutional tests. **Support services:** Learning center, remedial instruction, tutoring.

Majors. Business: Business admin, operations. **Computer sciences:** Information systems, information technology, networking. **Engineering technology:** Computer, electrical.

Most popular majors. Business/marketing 30%, computer/information sciences 57%, engineering/engineering technologies 13%.

Computing on campus. 548 workstations in library, computer center. Online course registration, online library, helpline available.

Student life. Freshman orientation: Mandatory. **Policies:** Freshmen permitted cars on campus. **Activities:** Literary magazine, student government, student newspaper, Muslim student association, Alpha Sigma Lambda, DeVry Christian Fellowship, Chi Pi Alpha, Epsilon Delta Pi, international student organization, Phi Theta Kappa, Institute of Electrical and Electronics Engineers, computer users group.

Athletics. Intramural: Basketball, soccer M, softball, tennis.

Student services. Career counseling, student employment services, financial aid counseling, placement for graduates, veterans' counselor. **Physically disabled:** Services for visually, hearing impaired.

Contact. E-mail: mbutler@dpg.devry.edu
Phone: (630) 953-2000 Toll-free number: (800) 346-5420
Fax: (630) 953-1236
Sandra Stack, Director of Admissions, DeVry University: Addison, 1221 North Swift Road, Addison, IL 60101-6106

DeVry University: Chicago

Chicago, Illinois
www.chi.devry.edu CB code: 1171

- For-profit 4-year university
- Commuter campus in very large city
- 2,042 degree-seeking undergraduates: 37% part-time, 41% women
- Interview required
- 38% graduate within 6 years

General. Founded in 1931. Regionally accredited. **Degrees:** 498 bachelor's, 71 associate awarded. **Location:** 6 miles from downtown. **Calendar:** Semester, extensive summer session. **Full-time faculty:** 53 total; 26% minority, 26% women. **Part-time faculty:** 60 total; 33% minority, 45% women.

Freshman class profile. 334 enrolled.

Return as sophomores:	48%	**International:**	1%

Basis for selection. Applicants must have high school diploma or equivalent, or degree from an accredited postsecondary institution, demonstrate proficiency in basic college-level skills through ACT scores or institution-administered placement examinations, and be at least 17 years of age. New students may enter at beginning of any semester. Applicants may also take a DeVry administered admissions test.

High school preparation. College-preparatory program recommended. Required units include mathematics 1. Math unit must be algebra or higher.

2005-2006 Annual costs. Tuition/fees: $12,240. Books/supplies: $1,100. Personal expenses: $1,816.

2004-2005 Financial aid. All financial aid based on need. 279 full-time freshmen applied for aid; 268 were judged to have need; 262 of these received aid. Average need met was 48%. Average scholarship/grant was $7,316; average loan $4,169. 34% of total undergraduate aid awarded as scholarships/grants, 66% as loans/jobs.

Application procedures. **Admission:** No deadline. $50 fee. Application may be submitted online. Admission notification on a rolling basis. **Financial aid:** No deadline. FAFSA required. Applicants notified on a rolling basis.

Academics. **Special study options:** Accelerated study, cooperative education, distance learning. **Credit/placement by examination:** CLEP, institutional tests. **Support services:** Learning center, remedial instruction, tutoring.

Majors. **Business:** General, business admin. **Computer sciences:** Information systems, information technology, networking. **Engineering technology:** Computer, electrical.

Most popular majors. Business/marketing 34%, computer/information sciences 48%, engineering/engineering technologies 18%.

Computing on campus. 600 workstations in library, computer center. Online course registration, online library, helpline available.

Student life. **Freshman orientation:** Mandatory. **Policies:** Freshmen permitted cars on campus. **Activities:** Student government, student newspaper, Muslim Student Association, Alpha Beta Gamma, Alpha Chi, DeVry Bible Club, National Society of Black Engineers, Tau Alpha Pi.

Student services. Career counseling, student employment services, financial aid counseling, placement for graduates, veterans' counselor. **Physically disabled:** Services for visually, hearing impaired.

Contact. E-mail: admissions2@devry.edu
Phone: (773) 929-6550 Toll-free number: (800) 383-3879
Fax: (773) 697-2710
Christine Hierl, Director of Admissions, DeVry University: Chicago, 3300 North Campbell Avenue, Chicago, IL 60618-5994

DeVry University: Tinley Park

Tinley Park, Illinois
www.tp.devry.edu **CB code: 2818**

- For-profit 4-year university
- Commuter campus in large town
- 1,047 degree-seeking undergraduates: 33% part-time, 40% women
- 236 graduate students
- Interview required
- 38% graduate within 6 years

General. Regionally accredited. **Degrees:** 223 bachelor's, 57 associate awarded; master's offered. **Location:** 20 miles from Chicago. **Calendar:** Semester, extensive summer session. **Full-time faculty:** 33 total; 12% minority, 24% women. **Part-time faculty:** 41 total; 34% minority, 34% women.

Freshman class profile. 195 enrolled.

Basis for selection. Applicants must have high school diploma or equivalent, or degree from an accredited postsecondary institution and demonstrate proficiency in basic college-level skills through test scores and/or institution-administered placement examinations, and be at least 17 years of age. New students may enter at the beginning of any semester. Applicants may also take a DeVry administered admissions test.

High school preparation. College-preparatory program recommended. Required units include mathematics 1. Math unit must be algebra or higher.

2005-2006 Annual costs. Tuition/fees: $12,240. Books/supplies: $1,100. Personal expenses: $1,816.

2004-2005 Financial aid. All financial aid based on need. 179 full-time freshmen applied for aid; 162 were judged to have need; 158 of these received aid. Average need met was 48%. Average scholarship/grant was $6,298; average loan $4,681. 28% of total undergraduate aid awarded as scholarships/grants, 72% as loans/jobs.

Application procedures. **Admission:** No deadline. $50 fee. Application may be submitted online. Admission notification on a rolling basis. **Financial aid:** No deadline. FAFSA required. Applicants notified on a rolling basis.

Academics. **Special study options:** Accelerated study, cooperative education, distance learning. **Credit/placement by examination:** CLEP. **Support services:** Learning center, remedial instruction, tutoring.

Majors. **Business:** Business admin, human resources, management information systems. **Computer sciences:** Information systems, networking. **Engineering technology:** Computer, electrical.

Most popular majors. Business/marketing 23%, computer/information sciences 60%, engineering/engineering technologies 17%.

Computing on campus. 344 workstations in library, computer center. Online course registration, online library, helpline available.

Student life. **Freshman orientation:** Mandatory. **Policies:** Freshmen permitted cars on campus. **Activities:** Student Activities Association, Student Leadership Group, Women in Technology.

Student services. Career counseling, student employment services, financial aid counseling, placement for graduates, veterans' counselor. **Physically disabled:** Services for visually, hearing impaired.

Contact. E-mail: imccauley@tp.devry.edu
Phone: (708) 342-3100 Toll-free number: (877) 305-8184
Fax: (708) 342-3505
Bruce Jones, Director of Admissions, DeVry University: Tinley Park, 18624 West Creek Drive, Tinley Park, IL 60477-6243

Dominican University

River Forest, Illinois **CB member**
www.dom.edu **CB code: 1667**

- Private 4-year university and liberal arts college affiliated with Roman Catholic Church
- Commuter campus in large town
- 1,273 degree-seeking undergraduates: 11% part-time, 70% women, 7% African American, 3% Asian American, 19% Hispanic American, 1% international
- 1,708 degree-seeking graduate students
- 81% of applicants admitted
- SAT or ACT (ACT writing optional), application essay required
- 67% graduate within 6 years; 30% enter graduate study

General. Founded in 1901. Regionally accredited. **Degrees:** 269 bachelor's awarded; master's offered. **Location:** 10 miles from downtown. **Calendar:** Semester, extensive summer session. **Full-time faculty:** 109 total; 84% have terminal degrees, 13% minority, 61% women. **Part-time faculty:** 200 total; 29% have terminal degrees, 4% minority, 59% women. **Class size:** 70% < 20, 29% 20-39, less than 1% 40-49, less than 1% 50-99. **Special facilities:** Language laboratory, food science laboratory.

Freshman class profile. 993 applied, 808 admitted, 271 enrolled.

Mid 50% test scores		**End year in good standing:**	94%
SAT verbal:	500-610	**Return as sophomores:**	83%
SAT math:	500-600	**Out-of-state:**	11%
ACT:	20-25	**Live on campus:**	55%
Rank in top quarter:	47%	**International:**	1%
Rank in top tenth:	19%		

Basis for selection. Students must rank in upper half of class, have minimum GPA of 2.75, have ACT composite or SAT combined scores at or above the national average, and have completed 16 units of college prep work. Interview recommended.

High school preparation. College-preparatory program required. 16 units required. Required and recommended units include English 4, mathematics 3, social studies 1, history 2, science 3 (laboratory 2) and foreign language

2. 14 credits must be in English, mathematics, social science, laboratory science, and foreign languages.

2006-2007 Annual costs. Tuition/fees: $21,250. Room/board: $6,620. Books/supplies: $800. Personal expenses: $900.

2005-2006 Financial aid. Need-based: 68% of total undergraduate aid awarded as scholarships/grants, 32% as loans/jobs. **Non-need-based:** Scholarships awarded for academics, alumni affiliation, leadership.

Application procedures. Admission: Priority date 6/1; no deadline. $25 fee, may be waived for applicants with need. Application may be submitted online. Admission notification on a rolling basis beginning on or about 10/1. Must reply by May 1 or within 2 week(s) if notified thereafter. **Financial aid:** Priority date 6/1; no closing date. FAFSA required. Applicants notified on a rolling basis starting 2/15; must reply within 2 week(s) of notification.

Academics. Special study options: Accelerated study, combined bachelor's/graduate degree, cross-registration, distance learning, double major, dual enrollment of high school students, ESL, honors, independent study, internships, liberal arts/career combination, study abroad, teacher certification program, Washington semester. 2+2 nursing with Rush University, 5-year BA/BS engineering program with Illinois Institute of Technology, license preparation in gerontology on-campus, 5 year program in occupational therapy with Rush University leading to master's degree. **Credit/placement by examination:** AP, CLEP, IB, institutional tests. 28 credit hours maximum toward bachelor's degree. **Support services:** Pre-admission summer program, reduced course load, remedial instruction, study skills assistance, tutoring, writing center.

Majors. Area/ethnic studies: African-American, American. **Biology:** General, biochemistry. **Business:** Accounting, business admin, communications, fashion, international. **Communications:** General, journalism. **Computer sciences:** General, computer science, information systems. **Conservation:** Environmental science, environmental studies. **Education:** Early childhood. **Engineering:** Architectural, chemical, civil, computer, electrical, mechanical. **English:** English lit, technical writing. **Family/consumer sciences:** Food/nutrition. **Foreign languages:** French, Italian, Spanish. **Health:** Predentistry, premedicine, prenursing, prepharmacy, preveterinary, substance abuse counseling. **History:** General. **Interdisciplinary:** Gerontology, math/computer science, nutrition sciences. **Math:** General. **Philosophy/religion:** Philosophy. **Physical sciences:** Chemistry. **Psychology:** General. **Social sciences:** General, criminology, economics, international relations, political science, sociology. **Theology:** Theology. **Visual/performing arts:** Art, art history/conservation, commercial/advertising art, dramatic, fashion design, photography, studio arts.

Most popular majors. Business/marketing 33%, psychology 10%, social sciences 16%, visual/performing arts 9%.

Computing on campus. 309 workstations in dormitories, library, computer center. Dormitories wired for high-speed internet access and linked to campus network. Commuter students can connect to campus network. Online library, helpline, wireless network available.

Student life. Freshman orientation: Mandatory. Preregistration for classes offered. 2-day program with overnight on campus. **Policies:** Freshmen permitted cars on campus. **Housing:** Guaranteed on-campus for freshmen. Coed dorms, substance-free housing available. $100 deposit. **Activities:** Choral groups, dance, drama, literary magazine, musical theater, student government, student newspaper, campus ministry, Organization of Latino Americans, social service organization, business club, Italian club, International club, Black Student Union, psychology club, education club.

Athletics. NCAA. **Intercollegiate:** Baseball M, basketball, cross-country, soccer, softball W, tennis, volleyball W. **Intramural:** Basketball, bowling, cheerleading, racquetball, soccer, softball W, table tennis, volleyball, water polo. **Team name:** Stars.

Student services. Adult student services, alcohol/substance abuse counseling, campus ministries, career counseling, student employment services, financial aid counseling, health services, minority student services, on-campus daycare, personal counseling, placement for graduates, veterans' counselor. **Physically disabled:** Services for visually, hearing impaired.

Contact. E-mail: domadmis@dom.edu
Phone: (708) 524-6800 Toll-free number: (800) 828-8475
Fax: (708) 524-6864
Glenn Hamilton, Director of Freshman Admission, Dominican University, 7900 West Division Street, River Forest, IL 60305-1099

East-West University
Chicago, Illinois
www.eastwest.edu **CB code: 0798**

- Private 4-year university
- Commuter campus in very large city
- 1,035 degree-seeking undergraduates
- Interview required

General. Founded in 1978. Regionally accredited. **Degrees:** 54 bachelor's, 51 associate awarded. **Calendar:** Quarter, limited summer session. **Full-time faculty:** 12 total; 100% have terminal degrees, 42% minority, 50% women. **Part-time faculty:** 67 total; 100% have terminal degrees, 70% minority, 49% women.

Basis for selection. Open admission.

2006-2007 Annual costs. Tuition/fees (projected): $12,045. Books/supplies: $1,000. Personal expenses: $1,800.

Financial aid. Non-need-based: Scholarships awarded for academics. **Additional information:** Foreign students eligible for institutional scholarship.

Application procedures. Admission: No deadline. $30 fee, may be waived for applicants with need. Admission notification on a rolling basis. **Financial aid:** No deadline. FAFSA required. Applicants notified on a rolling basis starting 1/4; must reply within 4 week(s) of notification.

Academics. Special study options: Cooperative education, double major, independent study, internships. **Credit/placement by examination:** CLEP, institutional tests. Interview recommended for placement. **Support services:** Tutoring.

Majors. Business: Business admin. **Computer sciences:** General. **Engineering technology:** Electrical. **English:** Composition. **Liberal arts:** Arts/sciences. **Math:** General.

Computing on campus. 10 workstations in computer center. Online library available.

Student life. Freshman orientation: Available. **Activities:** Drama, student government, student newspaper.

Athletics. Team name: Phantom.

Student services. Career counseling.

Contact. E-mail: seeyou@eastwest.edu
Phone: (312) 939-0111 Toll-free number: (877) 398-9376
Fax: (312) 939-0083
William Link, Director of Admissions, East-West University, 816 South Michigan Avenue, Chicago, IL 60605

Eastern Illinois University
Charleston, Illinois
www.eiu.edu **CB code: 1199**

- Public 4-year university and teachers college
- Residential campus in large town
- 10,243 degree-seeking undergraduates: 11% part-time, 58% women, 7% African American, 1% Asian American, 2% Hispanic American
- 1,646 degree-seeking graduate students
- 78% of applicants admitted
- SAT or ACT (ACT writing optional) required
- 62% graduate within 6 years

General. Founded in 1895. Regionally accredited. Off-campus sites in Champaign, Danville, Decatur, Effingham, Olney, Rantoul, Robinson, St. Joseph, Centralia, Mattoon, Taylorville. **Degrees:** 1,970 bachelor's awarded; master's offered. **ROTC:** Army. **Location:** 200 miles from Chicago, 145 miles from St. Louis. **Calendar:** Semester, limited summer session. **Full-time faculty:** 610 total; 70% have terminal degrees, 11% minority, 45% women. **Part-time faculty:** 145 total; 12% have terminal degrees, 5% minority, 56% women. **Class size:** 30% < 20, 59% 20-39, 6% 40-49, 3% 50-99, 1% >100. **Special facilities:** Arts center, greenhouse, electron microscope.

Freshman class profile. 7,682 applied, 5,975 admitted, 1,668 enrolled.

Mid 50% test scores		**Rank in top tenth:**	7%
ACT:	19-24	**Return as sophomores:**	81%
GPA 3.50 or higher:	19%	**Out-of-state:**	1%
GPA 3.0-3.49:	27%	**Live on campus:**	99%
GPA 2.0-2.99:	53%	**Fraternities:**	14%
Rank in top quarter:	24%	**Sororities:**	18%

Basis for selection. Applicants must be in top quarter of high school class and have ACT score of at least 18, in top half of high school class and ACT score of at least 19, or be in upper three-quarters of high school class with ACT score of at least 22. Gateway admissions program for students with ACT composite score of 14 or above and GPA of 2.0 or above. Audition required of music majors. **Homeschooled:** GED requirement may be waived with acceptable ACT score for home-schooled students who present recognized diploma.

High school preparation. College-preparatory program required. 15 units required. Required and recommended units include English 4, mathematics 3, social studies 3, science 3 (laboratory 3), foreign language 2 and academic electives 2. Significant science lab experience required.

2005-2006 Annual costs. Tuition/fees: $6,373; $15,631 out-of-state. New students will have a guaranteed tuition rate for 4 years. Room/board: $6,196. Books/supplies: $120. Personal expenses: $1,460.

2005-2006 Financial aid. Need-based: 1,306 full-time freshmen applied for aid; 944 were judged to have need; 837 of these received aid. Average need met was 17%. Average scholarship/grant was $2,750; average loan $2,436. 43% of total undergraduate aid awarded as scholarships/grants, 57% as loans/jobs. **Non-need-based:** Awarded to 2,293 full-time undergraduates, including 516 freshmen. Scholarships awarded for academics, art, athletics, music/drama.

Application procedures. Admission: No deadline. $30 fee, may be waived for applicants with need. Application may be submitted online. Admission notification on a rolling basis. Consult university for possible early cut-off date. **Financial aid:** Priority date 3/1; no closing date. FAFSA required. Applicants notified on a rolling basis starting 3/1; must reply within 2 week(s) of notification.

Academics. Special study options: Distance learning, double major, dual enrollment of high school students, honors, independent study, internships, study abroad, teacher certification program. Cooperative program in engineering with University of Illinois. **Credit/placement by examination:** AP, CLEP. **Support services:** Learning center, reduced course load, study skills assistance, tutoring, writing center.

Majors. Area/ethnic studies: African-American. **Biology:** General. **Business:** Accounting, business admin, finance, management information systems, management science, marketing. **Communications:** Journalism. **Education:** Biology, early childhood, elementary, health, physical, science, social science, special, voc/tech. **Engineering technology:** Industrial. **English:** English lit, speech/rhetoric. **Family/consumer sciences:** General. **Foreign languages:** General. **Health:** Clinical lab science, communication disorders. **History:** General. **Interdisciplinary:** Math/computer science. **Liberal arts:** Arts/sciences. **Math:** General. **Parks/recreation:** Facilities management. **Philosophy/religion:** Philosophy. **Physical sciences:** Chemistry, geology, physics. **Psychology:** General. **Social sciences:** Economics, geography, political science, sociology. **Visual/performing arts:** Art, dramatic.

Most popular majors. Business/marketing 14%, education 26%, English 10%, liberal arts 8%, social sciences 8%.

Computing on campus. 1,219 workstations in dormitories, library, computer center. Dormitories wired for high-speed internet access and linked to campus network. Commuter students can connect to campus network. Online course registration, helpline, student web hosting, wireless network available.

Student life. Freshman orientation: Mandatory. Preregistration for classes offered. New students are required to attend an EIU Debut program designed to provide an orientation to campus, allow students to meet w/an academic advisor and register for classes. All day sessions held on various dates from May-August. **Policies:** Freshmen permitted cars on campus. **Housing:** Guaranteed on-campus for freshmen. Coed dorms, single-sex dorms, special housing for disabled, apartments, fraternity/sorority housing, substance-free housing available. $50 partly refundable deposit. Quiet study floors available. **Activities:** Bands, choral groups, dance, drama, literary magazine, music ensembles, musical theater, radio station, student government, student newspaper, symphony orchestra, TV station, United Campus Ministry, Newman Community, College Democrats, veterans association, Young Republicans, Black Student Union, Latin American student organization, international student association.

Athletics. NCAA. **Intercollegiate:** Baseball M, basketball, cross-country, diving, football (tackle) M, golf, rugby W, soccer, softball W, swimming, tennis, track and field, volleyball W, wrestling M. **Intramural:** Badminton, basketball, bowling, cross-country, football (non-tackle), racquetball, soccer, softball, table tennis, volleyball, weight lifting. **Team name:** Panthers.

Student services. Adult student services, alcohol/substance abuse counseling, career counseling, services for economically disadvantaged, student employment services, health services, legal services, minority student services, personal counseling, placement for graduates, veterans' counselor, women's services. **Physically disabled:** Services for visually, speech, hearing impaired.

Contact. E-mail: admissns@eiu.edu
Phone: (217) 581-2223 Toll-free number: (800) 252-5711
Fax: (217) 581-7060
Brenda Major, Director of Admissions, Eastern Illinois University, 600 Lincoln Avenue, Charleston, IL 61920-3099

Elmhurst College

Elmhurst, Illinois — **CB member**
www.elmhurst.edu — **CB code: 1204**

- Private 4-year liberal arts college affiliated with United Church of Christ
- Commuter campus in large town
- 2,601 degree-seeking undergraduates: 10% part-time, 65% women
- 227 degree-seeking graduate students
- 75% of applicants admitted
- SAT or ACT (ACT writing optional) required

General. Founded in 1871. Regionally accredited. **Degrees:** 611 bachelor's awarded; master's offered. **ROTC:** Army, Air Force. **Location:** 15 miles from downtown Chicago. **Calendar:** 4-1-4, limited summer session. **Full-time faculty:** 117 total. **Part-time faculty:** 180 total. **Class size:** 66% < 20, 34% 20-39, less than 1% 40-49. **Special facilities:** 2 nuclear accelerators, 4 electron microscopes, collection of Impressionist art, computer science and technology center, media center, sound studio, greenhouse.

Freshman class profile. 1,700 applied, 1,278 admitted, 472 enrolled.

Mid 50% test scores		Live on campus:	67%
ACT:	20-26	Fraternities:	17%
Out-of-state:	12%	Sororities:	20%

Basis for selection. School achievement record, including grades and course levels, most important, followed by test scores. Applicants should rank in top half of class. Activities and counselor recommendations also important. Interview and essay recommended for all applicants, required of academically marginal applicants. Audition required of music majors. Portfolio recommended for art majors.

High school preparation. College-preparatory program required. 16 units required; 21 recommended. Required and recommended units include English 4, mathematics 2-3, social studies 2-3, history 1-2, science 2-3 (laboratory 2-3), foreign language 1-2 and academic electives 4. Chemistry required for nursing applicants. 3 mathematics required for most business administration and computer-related specialties applicants.

2006-2007 Annual costs. Tuition/fees (projected): $23,160. Room/board: $6,825. Books/supplies: $1,000. Personal expenses: $1,200.

2005-2006 Financial aid. Need-based: 395 full-time freshmen applied for aid; 325 were judged to have need; 325 of these received aid. Average need met was 93%. Average scholarship/grant was $14,284; average loan $3,500. 68% of total undergraduate aid awarded as scholarships/grants, 32% as loans/jobs. **Non-need-based:** Awarded to 677 full-time undergraduates, including 165 freshmen. Scholarships awarded for academics, art, minority status, music/drama, religious affiliation.

Application procedures. Admission: Priority date 4/15; no deadline. No application fee. Application may be submitted online. Admission notification on a rolling basis beginning on or about 11/1. Must reply by May 1 or within 2 week(s) if notified thereafter. **Financial aid:** Priority date 4/15; no closing date. FAFSA required. Applicants notified on a rolling basis starting 3/1; must reply within 3 week(s) of notification.

Academics. Special study options: Accelerated study, cooperative education, double major, dual enrollment of high school students, honors, independent study, internships, liberal arts/career combination, study abroad, teacher certification program, Washington semester. 3+2 engineering with Illinois Institute of Technology, University of Illinois at Urbana-Champaign, and Washington University (MO). **Credit/placement by examination:** AP, CLEP, IB, institutional tests. 48 credit hours maximum toward bachelor's degree. **Support services:** Learning center, pre-admission summer program, reduced course load, study skills assistance, tutoring.

Majors. Area/ethnic studies: American. **Biology:** General. **Business:** Accounting, business admin, finance, international, logistics, marketing. **Communications:** General. **Computer sciences:** Computer science, information systems. **Conservation:** Management/policy. **Education:** General, agricultural, art, biology, chemistry, early childhood, elementary, English, French, German, history, kindergarten/preschool, mathematics, music, physical, physics, secondary, Spanish, special. **English:** English lit. **Foreign languages:** French, German, Spanish. **Health:** Nursing (RN), predentistry, premedicine, prepharmacy, preveterinary, speech pathology. **History:** General. **Legal studies:** Prelaw. **Liberal arts:** Arts/sciences. **Math:** General. **Parks/**

recreation: Exercise sciences, health/fitness, sports admin. **Philosophy/religion:** Philosophy. **Physical sciences:** Chemistry, physics. **Psychology:** General. **Social sciences:** Economics, geography, political science, sociology, urban studies. **Theology:** Preministerial, theology. **Visual/performing arts:** Art, dramatic, music management.

Computing on campus. 440 workstations in library, computer center, student center. Dormitories wired for high-speed internet access and linked to campus network. Commuter students can connect to campus network. Online library, helpline, repair service, wireless network available.

Student life. **Freshman orientation:** Mandatory. 3-day orientation program held immediately prior to fall term. **Policies:** Freshmen permitted cars on campus. **Housing:** Coed dorms, apartments available. $150 deposit, deadline 5/1. Each residence hall is self-governing. **Activities:** Bands, choral groups, drama, literary magazine, music ensembles, musical theater, radio station, student government, student newspaper, Over 90 organizations.

Athletics. NCAA. **Intercollegiate:** Baseball M, basketball, bowling W, cross-country, football (tackle) M, golf, soccer, softball W, tennis, track and field, volleyball W, wrestling M. **Intramural:** Basketball, football (tackle) M, golf, racquetball, softball, volleyball. **Team name:** Blue Jays.

Student services. Adult student services, campus ministries, career counseling, student employment services, financial aid counseling, health services, minority student services, on-campus daycare, personal counseling, placement for graduates.

Contact. E-mail: admit@elmhurst.edu
Phone: (630) 617-3400 Toll-free number: (800) 697-1871
Fax: (630) 617-5501
Stephanie Levenson, Director of Admission, Elmhurst College, 190 South Prospect Avenue, Elmhurst, IL 60126-3296

Eureka College

Eureka, Illinois — **CB member**
www.eureka.edu — **CB code: 1206**

- Private 4-year liberal arts college affiliated with Christian Church (Disciples of Christ)
- Residential campus in small town
- 538 degree-seeking undergraduates
- SAT or ACT (ACT writing recommended) required

General. Founded in 1855. Regionally accredited. **Degrees:** 138 bachelor's awarded. **Location:** 140 miles from Chicago. **Calendar:** Semester, limited summer session. **Full-time faculty:** 42 total. **Part-time faculty:** 27 total. **Class size:** 69% < 20, 31% 20-39. **Special facilities:** Ronald Reagan Museum, Ronald Reagan Trail, Ronald Reagan Peace Garden, 2 buildings on National Register of Historic Places, lilac arboretum, labyrinth.

Freshman class profile.

Out-of-state:	12%	Live on campus:	95%

Basis for selection. Class rank, high school GPA, ACT scores, and high school curriculum most important. Recommendations and interviews also important. Audition required for music and drama scholarships. Portfolio required for art scholarship. **Homeschooled:** Interview required.

High school preparation. 14 units recommended. Recommended units include English 4, mathematics 3, social studies 3, science 2 and foreign language 2.

2006-2007 Annual costs. Tuition/fees: $14,230. Room/board: $6,220. Books/supplies: $800. Personal expenses: $510.

2005-2006 Financial aid. **Need-based:** Average need met was 80%. Average scholarship/grant was $11,896; average loan $1,906. 74% of total undergraduate aid awarded as scholarships/grants, 26% as loans/jobs. **Non-need-based:** Scholarships awarded for academics, alumni affiliation, art, leadership, music/drama, religious affiliation.

Application procedures. **Admission:** Priority date 5/1; deadline 8/10 (postmark date). No application fee. Application may be submitted online. Admission notification on a rolling basis. Must reply by May 1 or within 3 week(s) if notified thereafter. **Financial aid:** Priority date 4/15; no closing date. FAFSA required. Applicants notified on a rolling basis starting 2/15; must reply by 5/1 or within 3 week(s) of notification.

Academics. **Special study options:** Cooperative education, double major, dual enrollment of high school students, honors, independent study, internships, liberal arts/career combination, student-designed major, study abroad, teacher certification program, Washington semester. Students who began as freshmen, have a record of leadership and service, and hold a 3.5 GPA at the end of their sophomore year qualify for a mentorship paid for by the college. **Credit/placement by examination:** AP, CLEP, institutional tests. **Support services:** Learning center, reduced course load, remedial instruction, study skills assistance, tutoring, writing center.

Honors college/program. Admitted by invitation, includes advanced and special classes, advanced general education requirements along with thesis preparation and presentation, honors seminars on special topics.

Majors. **Biology:** General, environmental. **Business:** General, accounting, business admin, finance, management information systems, marketing. **Communications:** General, media studies, public relations. **Computer sciences:** General, computer science. **Education:** General, elementary, middle, multi-level teacher, secondary, special. **Engineering:** General. **English:** Composition, creative writing, English lit. **Health:** Predentistry, premedicine, prenursing, preveterinary. **History:** General. **Interdisciplinary:** Math/computer science. **Legal studies:** Prelaw. **Liberal arts:** Arts/sciences. **Math:** General. **Philosophy/religion:** Philosophy, religion. **Physical sciences:** Chemistry. **Protective services:** Law enforcement admin. **Psychology:** General. **Social sciences:** Political science. **Visual/performing arts:** Art, arts management, dramatic, music performance.

Computing on campus. 50 workstations in dormitories, library, computer center, student center. Dormitories wired for high-speed internet access and linked to campus network. Commuter students can connect to campus network. Online library, helpline, repair service available.

Student life. **Freshman orientation:** Mandatory. Preregistration for classes offered. Orientation for new students held at start of school year. **Policies:** All single students under 24 not living with parents required to live on campus. Freshmen permitted cars on campus. **Housing:** Guaranteed on-campus for all undergraduates. Coed dorms, single-sex dorms, special housing for disabled, fraternity/sorority housing, substance-free housing available. $200 deposit, deadline 8/14. **Activities:** Bands, choral groups, dance, drama, film society, literary magazine, music ensembles, musical theater, student government, student newspaper, Disciples on Campus, PRIDE, Young Republicans, Campus Democrats, Catholic Salve Regina Newman Center, Campus Crusade for Christ, Black student union, Habitat for Humanity, Student Foundation, International Healthcare Development Program.

Athletics. NCAA. **Intercollegiate:** Baseball M, basketball, cross-country, diving, football (tackle) M, golf, soccer, softball W, swimming, tennis, track and field, volleyball W. **Intramural:** Badminton, basketball, bowling, football (non-tackle), golf, softball, swimming, table tennis, tennis, volleyball. **Team name:** Red Devils.

Student services. Adult student services, alcohol/substance abuse counseling, campus ministries, career counseling, student employment services, financial aid counseling, health services, personal counseling, placement for graduates.

Contact. E-mail: admissions@eureka.edu
Phone: (309) 467-6350 Toll-free number: (888) 438-7352
Fax: (309) 467-6576
Brian Sajko, Dean of Admissions and Financial Aid, Eureka College, 300 East College Avenue, Eureka, IL 61530-1500

Governors State University

University Park, Illinois
www.govst.edu — **CB code: 0807**

- Public upper-division university
- Commuter campus in large town
- 78% of applicants admitted

General. Founded in 1969. Regionally accredited. Over one-half of students are in graduate programs. **Degrees:** 634 bachelor's awarded; master's offered. **Articulation:** Agreements with Prairie State College, Joliet Junior College, Kankakee CC, Moraine Valley CC, South Suburban College of Cook County, College of DuPage, Morton College, City Colleges of Chicago, Waubonsee CC, Triton College, Parkland College, College of Lake County, Illinois Valley College, Ivy Tech State College (IN). **ROTC:** Army, Air Force. **Location:** 30 miles from Chicago. **Calendar:** Semester, extensive summer session. **Full-time faculty:** 187 total; 82% have terminal degrees, 26% minority, 43% women. **Part-time faculty:** 32 total; 38% have terminal degrees, 34% minority, 47% women. **Special facilities:** 750-acre campus, nature trails, 6 lakes, sculpture park.

Student profile. 2,632 degree-seeking undergraduates, 2,773 graduate students. 2,331 applied as first time-transfer students, 1,818 admitted, 1,305 enrolled. 63% transferred from two-year, 37% transferred from four-year institutions.

Women:	68%	**Out-of-state:**	3%
Part-time:	67%	**25 or older:**	61%

Basis for selection. College transcript required. Minimum 60 semester hours or associate degree required. Additional special criteria for selected undergraduate majors. Applicants notified of decisions on rolling basis. Special admissions for applicants not meeting stated requirements available by petition. Institutional examinations required of nursing applicants. ACT/PEP required of nursing applicants from diploma program. Transfer accepted as juniors, seniors.

2006-2007 Annual costs. Tuition/fees (projected): $5,230; $14,530 out-of-state. Books/supplies: $700. Personal expenses: $800.

Financial aid. **Non-need-based:** Scholarships awarded for academics, ROTC, state residency.

Application procedures. **Admission:** Priority date 6/1. No application fee. Application may be submitted online. **Financial aid:** No aid for second bachelor's or second master's degree. FAFSA required.

Academics. **Special study options:** Distance learning, dual enrollment of high school students, external degree, honors, independent study, internships, student-designed major, study abroad, teacher certification program, weekend college. Board of Governors degree program, dual enrollment with several community colleges. **Credit/placement by examination:** AP, CLEP. 60 credit hours maximum toward bachelor's degree.

Majors. **Biology:** General. **Business:** Accounting, business admin, finance, human resources, international, international marketing, management information systems. **Communications:** General, broadcast journalism, journalism. **Computer sciences:** General, computer science. **Education:** Biology, chemistry, early childhood, elementary, English, mathematics. **Health:** Health care admin, preop/surgical nursing, speech pathology. **Liberal arts:** Arts/sciences. **Math:** General. **Physical sciences:** Chemistry. **Protective services:** Criminal justice. **Psychology:** General. **Public administration:** General, social work. **Social sciences:** General. **Visual/performing arts:** Art, art history/conservation.

Computing on campus. 280 workstations in library, computer center, student center. Commuter students can connect to campus network. Online library, helpline available.

Student life. **Activities:** Choral groups, film society, literary magazine, student government, student newspaper, TV station, veterans organization, several international student organizations, Union of African Peoples, naturalist club, 30-plus cocurricular professional service organizations.

Athletics. **Intramural:** Badminton, basketball, handball, racquetball, skiing, soccer, softball, table tennis, volleyball.

Student services. Career counseling, student employment services, financial aid counseling, minority student services, on-campus daycare, personal counseling, placement for graduates, veterans' counselor. **Physically disabled:** Services for visually, speech, hearing impaired.

Contact. E-mail: gsunow@govst.edu
Phone: (708) 534-4490 Fax: (708) 534-1640
Governors State University, One University Parkway, University Park, IL 60466

Greenville College

Greenville, Illinois
www.greenville.edu **CB code: 1256**

- Private 4-year liberal arts college affiliated with Free Methodist Church of North America
- Residential campus in small town
- 1,197 degree-seeking undergraduates: 2% part-time, 54% women
- 133 degree-seeking graduate students
- 90% of applicants admitted
- SAT or ACT (ACT writing optional), application essay required
- 52% graduate within 6 years

General. Founded in 1892. Regionally accredited. Academic and Christian values emphasized. **Degrees:** 294 bachelor's awarded; master's offered. **Location:** 50 miles from St. Louis, 190 miles from Indianapolis. **Calendar:** 4-1-4, limited summer session. **Full-time faculty:** 55 total; 69% have terminal degrees, 7% minority, 33% women. **Part-time faculty:** 77 total; 25% have terminal degrees, 4% minority, 32% women. **Class size:** 58% < 20, 32% 20-39, 5% 40-49, 5% 50-99, less than 1% >100. **Special facilities:** Sculpture museum, science field station.

Freshman class profile. 633 applied, 570 admitted, 252 enrolled.

Mid 50% test scores		**Rank in top quarter:**	37%
SAT verbal:	450-590	**Rank in top tenth:**	16%
SAT math:	430-560	**Return as sophomores:**	73%
ACT:	19-25	**Out-of-state:**	46%
GPA 3.50 or higher:	42%	**Live on campus:**	95%
GPA 3.0-3.49:	28%	**International:**	2%
GPA 2.0-2.99:	28%		

Basis for selection. Secondary school record, class rank, standardized test scores, essay, character/personal qualities, and religious affiliation or commitment all very important. Recommendations, extracurricular activities, talent/ability and alumni/ae relation considered. Interview required of academically weak applicants. Audition recommended for music majors.

High school preparation. 11 units recommended. Recommended units include English 4, mathematics 2, history 1, science 1 (laboratory 1) and foreign language 2. Mathematics recommendation includes algebra and geometry.

2005-2006 Annual costs. Tuition/fees: $17,242. Per-credit-hour charges vary between $361 and $723 according to number of credits taken. Room/board: $5,904. Books/supplies: $800. Personal expenses: $1,200.

2004-2005 Financial aid. **Need-based:** Average need met was 81%. Average scholarship/grant was $10,483; average loan $3,385. 66% of total undergraduate aid awarded as scholarships/grants, 34% as loans/jobs. **Non-need-based:** Scholarships awarded for academics, alumni affiliation, art, leadership, minority status, music/drama, religious affiliation, state residency.

Application procedures. **Admission:** Closing date 8/15. $25 fee, may be waived for applicants with need. Application may be submitted online. Admission notification on a rolling basis beginning on or about 10/15. **Financial aid:** Priority date 5/1; no closing date. FAFSA required. Applicants notified on a rolling basis starting 3/15; must reply within 3 week(s) of notification.

Academics. **Special study options:** Accelerated study, cooperative education, cross-registration, double major, external degree, honors, independent study, internships, liberal arts/career combination, semester at sea, student-designed major, study abroad, teacher certification program, urban semester, Washington semester. **Credit/placement by examination:** AP, CLEP, IB, SAT, ACT, institutional tests. 32 credit hours maximum toward bachelor's degree. **Support services:** Learning center, reduced course load, remedial instruction, study skills assistance, tutoring.

Majors. **Biology:** General, environmental. **Business:** Accounting, business admin, management information systems, marketing, organizational behavior. **Communications:** Media studies, public relations. **Computer sciences:** Computer science. **Education:** Biology, chemistry, early childhood, elementary, English, history, mathematics, music, physical, physics, Spanish, special. **English:** English lit, speech/rhetoric. **Foreign languages:** Spanish. **Health:** Predentistry, premedicine, preveterinary. **Liberal arts:** Arts/sciences. **Math:** General. **Parks/recreation:** General, exercise sciences, sports admin. **Philosophy/religion:** Philosophy, religion. **Physical sciences:** Chemistry, physics. **Protective services:** Law enforcement admin. **Psychology:** General. **Public administration:** Social work. **Social sciences:** Sociology. **Theology:** Pastoral counseling, youth ministry. **Visual/performing arts:** Art, dramatic.

Most popular majors. Business/marketing 40%, education 12%, visual/performing arts 8%.

Computing on campus. 100 workstations in library, computer center. Dormitories wired for high-speed internet access and linked to campus network. Commuter students can connect to campus network. Helpline, repair service, wireless network available.

Student life. **Freshman orientation:** Mandatory. Preregistration for classes offered. Begins Friday morning, before classes begin on Wednesday and ends Tuesday evening. A special service project is also conducted over the weekend. **Policies:** Signed statements of Christian values and academic honesty requested. Required chapel. All single students not living at home must live in college housing. Religious observance required. Freshmen permitted cars on campus. **Housing:** Guaranteed on-campus for all undergraduates. Single-sex dorms, apartments, substance-free housing available. $200 deposit. **Activities:** Bands, choral groups, drama, music ensembles, musical theater, radio station, student government, student newspaper, Habitat for Humanity, Fellowship of Christian Athletes, campus activities board, student outreach, Agape Music Festival, Circle K, E-cafe', Mosaic, Young Republicans, Big Brother Big Sister Program.

Athletics. NCAA, NCCAA. **Intercollegiate:** Baseball M, basketball, cross-country, football (tackle) M, soccer, softball W, tennis, track and field, volleyball W. **Intramural:** Badminton, basketball, football (non-tackle), soccer, softball, table tennis, tennis, volleyball. **Team name:** Panthers.

Student services. Adult student services, campus ministries, career counseling, student employment services, financial aid counseling, personal counseling, placement for graduates.

Contact. E-mail: admissions@greenville.edu
Phone: (618) 664-7100 Toll-free number: (800) 345-4440
Fax: (618) 664-9841
Michael Ritter, Director of Admissions, Greenville College, 315 East College Avenue, Greenville, IL 62246-0159

Harrington College of Design

Chicago, Illinois
www.harringtoncollege.com **CB code: 0940**

- For-profit 4-year visual arts college
- Commuter campus in very large city
- 1,563 degree-seeking undergraduates: 6% African American, 4% Asian American, 9% Hispanic American
- Interview required

General. Founded in 1931. Accredited by Foundation for Interior Design Education Research and National Association of Schools of Art and Design. **Degrees:** 124 bachelor's, 102 associate awarded. **Location:** Downtown Chicago. **Calendar:** Semester, extensive summer session. **Full-time faculty:** 10 total. **Part-time faculty:** 115 total. **Class size:** 84% < 20, 16% 20-39. **Special facilities:** Access to Chicago Merchandise Mart's wholesale showroom.

Basis for selection. Open admission. Personal interview, commitment to career, 2.0 GPA most important.

2005-2006 Annual costs. Tuition/fees: $16,750. Required fees vary from $250 to $500, depending on program. Books/supplies: $850. Personal expenses: $2,500.

Financial aid. All financial aid based on need.

Application procedures. **Admission:** Priority date 6/1; no deadline. $60 fee, may be waived for applicants with need. Application may be submitted online. Admission notification on a rolling basis. **Financial aid:** Closing date 7/15. FAFSA required. Applicants notified on a rolling basis; must reply within 2 week(s) of notification.

Academics. Exchange program with Interior Architecture Department, Rotterdam College of Art and Design, The Netherlands. **Special study options:** Cooperative education, internships, study abroad. **Credit/placement by examination:** CLEP. **Support services:** Tutoring, writing center.

Majors. **Architecture:** Interior. **Visual/performing arts:** Interior design.

Computing on campus. 35 workstations in library, computer center.

Student life. **Freshman orientation:** Mandatory. One-day program held 1 or 2 weeks before classes begin. **Housing:** Students may reside at Crown Center Residence at nearby Roosevelt University. **Activities:** Student government, American Society of Interior Design student chapter.

Student services. Career counseling, financial aid counseling, personal counseling, placement for graduates, veterans' counselor.

Contact. E-mail: admissions@interiordesign.edu
Phone: (312) 939-4975 Toll-free number: (877) 939-4975
Fax: (312) 939-8005
Wendi Franczyk, Vice President of Admissions, Harrington College of Design, 200 West Madison Avenue, Chicago, IL 60606

Hebrew Theological College

Skokie, Illinois
www.htcnet.edu **CB code: 0817**

- Private 4-year rabbinical college
- 50 degree-seeking undergraduates

General. Regionally accredited. **Degrees:** 33 bachelor's awarded. **Calendar:** Semester.

2005-2006 Annual costs. Tuition/fees: $15,410.

Academics. **Credit/placement by examination:** CLEP.

Contact. E-mail: htc@htcnet.edu
Phone: (847) 982-2500 Fax: (847) 674-6381
Hebrew Theological College, 7135 North Carpenter Road, Skokie, IL 60077

Illinois College

Jacksonville, Illinois **CB member**
www.ic.edu **CB code: 1315**

- Private 4-year liberal arts college affiliated with United Church of Christ and Presbyterian Church (USA)
- Residential campus in large town
- 1,019 degree-seeking undergraduates: 1% part-time, 53% women, 3% African American, 1% Asian American, 1% Hispanic American, 2% international
- 65% of applicants admitted
- SAT or ACT (ACT writing optional) required
- 57% graduate within 6 years

General. Founded in 1829. Regionally accredited. **Degrees:** 170 bachelor's awarded. **Location:** 35 miles from Springfield, 100 miles from St. Louis. **Calendar:** Semester, limited summer session. **Full-time faculty:** 61 total. **Part-time faculty:** 32 total. **Class size:** 71% < 20, 28% 20-39, less than 1% 40-49, less than 1% 50-99, less than 1% >100. **Special facilities:** Biology station, observatory.

Freshman class profile. 1,145 applied, 740 admitted, 256 enrolled.

Mid 50% test scores		Rank in top tenth:	23%
ACT:	21-27	End year in good standing:	80%
GPA 3.50 or higher:	43%	Return as sophomores:	74%
GPA 3.0-3.49:	35%	Out-of-state:	5%
GPA 2.0-2.99:	22%	Live on campus:	89%
Rank in top quarter:	53%	International:	2%

Basis for selection. Test scores, rank in top half of class, 1 letter of recommendation from teacher, 1 letter of recommendation from guidance counselor. Interview recommended. Essay considered. **Homeschooled:** Transcript of courses and grades required.

High school preparation. College-preparatory program recommended. 15 units required. Required and recommended units include English 3-4, mathematics 1-3, social studies 1, history 1-2, science 1-2, foreign language 2 and academic electives 3.

2005-2006 Annual costs. Tuition/fees: $15,500. Room/board: $6,400. Books/supplies: $800. Personal expenses: $900.

2005-2006 Financial aid. **Need-based:** 241 full-time freshmen applied for aid; 197 were judged to have need; 197 of these received aid. Average need met was 82%. Average scholarship/grant was $6,176; average loan $3,556. 65% of total undergraduate aid awarded as scholarships/grants, 35% as loans/jobs. **Non-need-based:** Awarded to 802 full-time undergraduates, including 225 freshmen. Scholarships awarded for academics, art, leadership, minority status, music/drama.

Application procedures. **Admission:** Priority date 3/15; deadline 8/15 (postmark date). $25 fee, may be waived for applicants with need. Application may be submitted online. Admission notification on a rolling basis beginning on or about 10/15. Must reply by 5/1. **Financial aid:** Priority date 3/1; no closing date. FAFSA required. Applicants notified on a rolling basis starting 3/1; must reply within 2 week(s) of notification.

Academics. **Special study options:** Combined bachelor's/graduate degree, double major, dual enrollment of high school students, independent study, internships, liberal arts/career combination, student-designed major, study abroad, teacher certification program, Washington semester. Intercultural exchange program with Ritsumeikan University, Japan. **Credit/placement by examination:** AP, CLEP, IB, ACT, institutional tests. 84 credit hours maximum toward bachelor's degree. **Support services:** Reduced course load, tutoring, writing center.

Majors. **Biology:** General. **Business:** General, accounting, finance, management information systems. **Computer sciences:** General. **Conservation:** Environmental science, forestry. **Education:** Early childhood, elementary, physical. **Engineering:** General. **English:** Speech/rhetoric. **Foreign languages:** French, German, Spanish. **Health:** Clinical lab science, cytotechnology. **History:** General. **Math:** General. **Parks/recreation:** Sports admin. **Philosophy/religion:** Philosophy, religion. **Physical sciences:** Chemistry, physics. **Psychology:** General. **Social sciences:** Economics, international relations, political science, sociology. **Visual/performing arts:** General, art.

Computing on campus. 111 workstations in library, computer center. Dormitories wired for high-speed internet access and linked to campus network. Commuter students can connect to campus network. Helpline available.

Student life. Freshman orientation: Mandatory. Preregistration for classes offered. 4 2-day summer sessions available. **Policies:** Student representation on faculty committees. Freshmen permitted cars on campus. **Housing:** Guaranteed on-campus for all undergraduates. Coed dorms, single-sex dorms available. $100 fully refundable deposit, deadline 5/1. **Activities:** Bands, choral groups, drama, literary magazine, music ensembles, musical theater, student government, student newspaper, symphony orchestra, TV station, Young Republicans, Young Democrats, Alpha Phi Omega, minority students' union, men's and women's literary societies, international club, Model United Nations, debate club, Action Jacksonville.

Athletics. NCAA. **Intercollegiate:** Baseball M, basketball, cheerleading, cross-country, football (tackle) M, golf, soccer, softball W, tennis, track and field, volleyball W, wrestling M. **Intramural:** Basketball, football (non-tackle) M, handball, racquetball, softball, volleyball. **Team name:** Blueboys, Lady Blues.

Student services. Campus ministries, career counseling, student employment services, financial aid counseling, health services, personal counseling, placement for graduates. **Physically disabled:** Services for visually, hearing impaired.

Contact. E-mail: admissions@hilltop.ic.edu
Phone: (217) 245-3030 Toll-free number: (866) 464-5265
Fax: (217) 245-3034
Scott Belobrajdic, Vice President for Enrollment, Illinois College, 1101 West College Avenue, Jacksonville, IL 62650

Illinois Institute of Art-Chicago

Chicago, Illinois
www.ilic.artinstitutes.edu **CB code: 2908**

- For-profit 4-year art college
- Very large city

General. Founded in 1916. Accredited by ACCSCT. **Calendar:** Semester.

Annual costs/financial aid. Tuition/fees (2005-2006): $18,390. Books/supplies: $1,000. Personal expenses: $1,260. Need-based financial aid available to full-time and part-time students.

Contact. Phone: (312) 280-3500
V.P., Director of Admissions, 350 North Orleans Street, Chicago, IL 60654

Illinois Institute of Art-Schaumburg

Schaumburg, Illinois
www.ilis.aii.edu **CB code: 3043**

- For-profit 4-year visual arts college
- Commuter campus in small city
- 290 full-time, degree-seeking undergraduates
- Application essay, interview required

General. Accredited by ACCSCT. **Degrees:** 244 bachelor's awarded. **Location:** 26 miles west of Chicago. **Calendar:** Continuous. **Full-time faculty:** 45 total. **Part-time faculty:** 30 total.

Basis for selection. Essay and interview most important.

2005-2006 Annual costs. Tuition/fees: $17,100. Room/board: $6,000. Books/supplies: $987. Personal expenses: $1,788.

Financial aid. Non-need-based: Scholarships awarded for art. **Additional information:** Merit scholarships based on GPA; talent-based scholarships.

Application procedures. Admission: No deadline. $50 fee. Application may be submitted online. Admission notification on a rolling basis. **Financial aid:** No deadline. FAFSA required.

Academics. Special study options: Accelerated study, internships, liberal arts/career combination. **Credit/placement by examination:** CLEP. **Support services:** Learning center, pre-admission summer program, reduced course load, remedial instruction, study skills assistance, tutoring.

Majors. Architecture: Interior. **Communications:** Advertising. **Computer sciences:** Computer graphics. **Visual/performing arts:** General, art, commercial/advertising art, design, interior design, multimedia.

Student life. Freshman orientation: Mandatory. **Policies:** Freshmen permitted cars on campus. **Housing:** Single-sex dorms available. $200 deposit. Dormitory-style living in college-leased apartments. **Activities:** Jazz band, student government.

Student services. Career counseling, student employment services, financial aid counseling, personal counseling, placement for graduates.

Contact. E-mail: rmckinney@aii.edu
Phone: (847) 619-3450 Toll-free number: (800) 314-3450
Ron McKinney, Director of Admissions, Illinois Institute of Art-Schaumburg, 1000 North Plaza Drive, Schaumburg, IL 60173

Illinois Institute of Technology

Chicago, Illinois **CB member**
www.iit.edu **CB code: 1318**

- Private 4-year university and engineering college
- Residential campus in very large city
- 2,156 degree-seeking undergraduates: 8% part-time, 25% women, 5% African American, 14% Asian American, 7% Hispanic American, 16% international
- 3,933 degree-seeking graduate students
- 63% of applicants admitted
- SAT or ACT (ACT writing optional), application essay required
- 69% graduate within 6 years

General. Founded in 1890. Regionally accredited. **Degrees:** 370 bachelor's awarded; master's, doctoral, first professional offered. **ROTC:** Army, Navy, Air Force. **Location:** 3 miles from downtown. **Calendar:** Semester, extensive summer session. **Full-time faculty:** 303 total; 86% have terminal degrees, 14% minority, 21% women. **Part-time faculty:** 277 total; 57% have terminal degrees, 11% minority, 23% women. **Class size:** 68% < 20, 26% 20-39, 3% 40-49, 3% 50-99, less than 1% >100. **Special facilities:** Wind tunnel, polymer science and engineering center, center for study of ethics in the professions, center for synchrotron radiation research and instrumentation.

Freshman class profile. 2,514 applied, 1,588 admitted, 415 enrolled.

Mid 50% test scores			
SAT verbal:	560-660	Rank in top tenth:	37%
SAT math:	620-720	Return as sophomores:	81%
ACT:	25-30	Out-of-state:	36%
Rank in top quarter:	70%	International:	6%

Basis for selection. GED not accepted. Academic performance, test scores, counselor recommendations and essay most important. Class rank and interview, extracurricular activities, alumni relationship, volunteer and work experience also considered. Interview and portfolio recommended.

High school preparation. Required units include English 4, mathematics 4, social studies 2, history 2, science 3 (laboratory 2). Computer course required for computer-related majors.

2005-2006 Annual costs. Tuition/fees: $22,982. Tuition and fees cover unlimited number of courses during academic year and include library and computer usage fees. Room/board: $7,520. Books/supplies: $1,000. Personal expenses: $3,300.

2004-2005 Financial aid. Need-based: 339 full-time freshmen applied for aid; 290 were judged to have need; 288 of these received aid. Average need met was 89%. Average scholarship/grant was $13,991; average loan $4,456. 74% of total undergraduate aid awarded as scholarships/grants, 26% as loans/jobs. **Non-need-based:** Awarded to 906 full-time undergraduates, including 177 freshmen. Scholarships awarded for academics, alumni affiliation, athletics, leadership, minority status, ROTC.

Application procedures. Admission: Priority date 12/1; no deadline. $30 fee, may be waived for applicants with need. Application may be submitted online. Admission notification on a rolling basis beginning on or about 9/15. Must reply by May 1 or within 2 week(s) if notified thereafter. **Financial aid:** Priority date 4/15; no closing date. FAFSA required. Applicants notified on a rolling basis starting 3/1; must reply by 5/1 or within 2 week(s) of notification.

Academics. Special study options: Combined bachelor's/graduate degree, cooperative education, cross-registration, distance learning, double major, ESL, independent study, liberal arts/career combination, study abroad, teacher certification program. Joint enrollment at 2 institutions for 2 degrees. **Credit/placement by examination:** AP, CLEP, IB, institutional tests. 18 credit hours maximum toward bachelor's degree. No limit for advanced placement credit. **Support services:** Learning center, study skills assistance, tutoring, writing center.

Majors. Architecture: Architecture. **Biology:** General, Biochemistry/biophysics and molecular biology, biophysics. **Business:** General. **Computer sciences:** Computer science, information technology. **Engineering:** Aerospace, architectural, chemical, civil, computer, electrical, environmental, materials, mechanical, metallurgical. **Engineering technology:** Industrial management, manufacturing. **English:** Technical writing. **Health:** Premedicine, prepharmacy. **Legal studies:** Prelaw. **Physical sciences:** Chemistry, physics. **Psychology:** General.

Most popular majors. Business/marketing 14%, computer/information sciences 16%, engineering/engineering technologies 31%, legal studies 21%.

Computing on campus. 560 workstations in dormitories, library, computer center, student center. Dormitories wired for high-speed internet access and linked to campus network. Commuter students can connect to campus network. Online course registration, online library, helpline, repair service, student web hosting, wireless network available.

Student life. Freshman orientation: Mandatory, $100 fee. Preregistration for classes offered. 3-day program prior to start of fall classes. **Policies:** Freshmen permitted cars on campus. **Housing:** Guaranteed on-campus for freshmen. Coed dorms, single-sex dorms, special housing for disabled, apartments, fraternity/sorority housing available. $300 deposit, deadline 7/1. **Activities:** Drama, film society, literary magazine, musical theater, radio station, student government, student newspaper, National Society of Black Engineers, Latinos Involved in Further Education, international student association, Union Board, Techmate, Greek Council, society of women engineers.

Athletics. NAIA. **Intercollegiate:** Baseball M, basketball, cross-country, diving, soccer, swimming, volleyball W. **Intramural:** Badminton, basketball, racquetball, table tennis, volleyball. **Team name:** Scarlet Hawks.

Student services. Alcohol/substance abuse counseling, campus ministries, career counseling, student employment services, financial aid counseling, health services, minority student services, personal counseling, placement for graduates, women's services. **Physically disabled:** Services for visually, hearing impaired.

Contact. E-mail: admission@iit.edu
Phone: (312) 567-3025 Toll-free number: (800) 448-2329
Fax: (312) 567-6939
Mary Ann Rowan, Vice President of Enrollment Management, Illinois Institute of Technology, 10 West 33rd Street, Chicago, IL 60616

Illinois State University

Normal, Illinois — **CB member**
www.ilstu.edu — **CB code: 1319**

- Public 4-year university
- Residential campus in small city
- 17,795 degree-seeking undergraduates: 7% part-time, 58% women, 6% African American, 2% Asian American, 3% Hispanic American, 1% international
- 2,374 degree-seeking graduate students
- 77% of applicants admitted
- SAT or ACT (ACT writing optional), application essay required

General. Founded in 1857. Regionally accredited. **Degrees:** 4,274 bachelor's awarded; master's, doctoral offered. **ROTC:** Army. **Location:** 132 miles from Chicago, 168 miles from St. Louis. **Calendar:** Semester, limited summer session. **Full-time faculty:** 829 total; 84% have terminal degrees, 11% minority, 44% women. **Part-time faculty:** 274 total; 30% have terminal degrees, 5% minority, 53% women. **Class size:** 32% < 20, 53% 20-39, 4% 40-49, 7% 50-99, 5% >100. **Special facilities:** 310-acre farm, school museum, planetarium, museum of nations, laboratory school.

Freshman class profile. 10,414 applied, 8,030 admitted, 3,179 enrolled.

Mid 50% test scores		Rank in top tenth:	11%
ACT:	22-26	Return as sophomores:	85%
GPA 3.50 or higher:	39%	Out-of-state:	.6%
GPA 3.0-3.49:	43%	Live on campus:	97%
GPA 2.0-2.99:	18%	Fraternities:	9%
Rank in top quarter:	36%	Sororities:	6%

Basis for selection. School achievement record and test scores most important. Interview required of special admission applicants. Audition recommended for music majors. Portfolio recommended for art majors.

High school preparation. College-preparatory program required. 15 units required. Required units include English 4, mathematics 3, social studies 2, science 2 (laboratory 2), foreign language 2 and academic electives 2. 2 units required in foreign language and/or fine arts, 2 units in social studies and/or history. Electives may include fundamentals of computing or vocational education courses.

2005-2006 Annual costs. Tuition/fees: $7,091; $12,971 out-of-state. Tuition for incoming freshmen is guaranteed for 4 years. Room/board: $5,762. Books/supplies: $828. Personal expenses: $2,073.

2005-2006 Financial aid. Need-based: 2,421 full-time freshmen applied for aid; 1,378 were judged to have need; 1,339 of these received aid. Average need met was 79%. Average scholarship/grant was $6,496; average loan $3,988. 51% of total undergraduate aid awarded as scholarships/grants, 49% as loans/jobs. **Non-need-based:** Awarded to 2,216 full-time undergraduates, including 489 freshmen. Scholarships awarded for academics, art, athletics, leadership, music/drama.

Application procedures. Admission: Priority date 11/15; deadline 3/1 (receipt date). $30 fee, may be waived for applicants with need. Application may be submitted online. Admission notification on a rolling basis beginning on or about 9/1. **Financial aid:** Priority date 3/1; no closing date. FAFSA required. Applicants notified on a rolling basis starting 4/1; must reply within 2 week(s) of notification.

Academics. Special study options: Accelerated study, combined bachelor's/graduate degree, cooperative education, distance learning, double major, dual enrollment of high school students, ESL, exchange student, honors, independent study, internships, student-designed major, study abroad, teacher certification program, Washington semester. **Credit/placement by examination:** AP, CLEP, SAT, ACT, institutional tests. 26 credit hours maximum toward bachelor's degree. **Support services:** Learning center, preadmission summer program, tutoring.

Majors. Agriculture: Agribusiness operations. **Biology:** General, biochemistry. **Business:** Accounting, business admin, finance, insurance, international, management science, marketing. **Communications:** Journalism, public relations. **Computer sciences:** Computer science, information technology, networking. **Education:** Business, early childhood, elementary, health, middle, music, physical, social studies, special, technology/industrial arts. **Engineering technology:** Industrial. **English:** Speech/rhetoric. **Family/consumer sciences:** General. **Foreign languages:** French, German, Spanish. **Health:** Athletic training, audiology/speech pathology, clinical lab science, environmental health, medical records admin, nursing (RN), occupational health. **History:** General. **Liberal arts:** Arts/sciences. **Math:** General. **Parks/recreation:** Exercise sciences, facilities management. **Philosophy/religion:** Philosophy. **Physical sciences:** Chemistry, geology, physics. **Protective services:** Criminal justice. **Psychology:** General. **Public administration:** Social work. **Social sciences:** Anthropology, economics, geography, political science, sociology. **Visual/performing arts:** Art, dramatic, music history, music performance, studio arts.

Most popular majors. Business/marketing 20%, communications/journalism 6%, education 21%, health sciences 7%, social sciences 7%.

Computing on campus. PC or laptop required. 2,530 workstations in dormitories, library, computer center, student center. Dormitories wired for high-speed internet access and linked to campus network. Commuter students can connect to campus network. Online course registration, helpline, student web hosting, wireless network available.

Student life. Freshman orientation: Mandatory, $50 fee. Preregistration for classes offered. Consists of 12 sessions (2 days each), held each week from mid-June to end of July. Students meet with advisers, register, and take placement exams. **Policies:** Freshmen permitted cars on campus. **Housing:** Guaranteed on-campus for freshmen. Coed dorms, single-sex dorms, special housing for disabled, apartments, fraternity/sorority housing, substance-free housing available. $150 deposit. **Activities:** Bands, choral groups, dance, drama, film society, literary magazine, music ensembles, musical theater, radio station, student government, student newspaper, symphony orchestra, TV station, 250 student organizations.

Athletics. NCAA. **Intercollegiate:** Baseball M, basketball, cross-country, diving W, football (tackle) M, golf, gymnastics W, soccer W, softball W, swimming W, tennis, track and field, volleyball W. **Intramural:** Badminton, basketball, football (tackle), golf, racquetball, soccer, softball, volleyball. **Team name:** Redbirds.

Student services. Adult student services, alcohol/substance abuse counseling, career counseling, student employment services, financial aid counseling, health services, legal services, minority student services, on-campus daycare, personal counseling, placement for graduates, veterans' counselor. **Physically disabled:** Services for visually, speech, hearing impaired.

Contact. E-mail: admissions@ilstu.edu
Phone: (309) 438-2181 Toll-free number: (800) 366-2478
Fax: (309) 438-3932
Molly Arnold, Director of Admissions, Illinois State University, Campus Box 2200, Normal, IL 61790-2200

Illinois Wesleyan University

Bloomington, Illinois **CB member**
www.iwu.edu **CB code: 1320**

- Private 4-year university and liberal arts college affiliated with United Methodist Church
- Residential campus in small city
- 2,139 degree-seeking undergraduates: 57% women, 4% African American, 3% Asian American, 3% Hispanic American, 2% international
- 57% of applicants admitted
- SAT or ACT (ACT writing optional), application essay required
- 82% graduate within 6 years; 30% enter graduate study

General. Founded in 1850. Regionally accredited. 1-month optional May term provides travel and internship experiences as well as on-campus courses. Interdisciplinary study, individual student research, internships, and study abroad are supported and encouraged throughout the academic year. **Degrees:** 474 bachelor's awarded. **ROTC:** Army. **Location:** 125 miles from Chicago, 165 miles from St. Louis. **Calendar:** 4-4-1 (2 semesters plus May Term). **Full-time faculty:** 161 total; 92% have terminal degrees, 16% minority, 42% women. **Part-time faculty:** 61 total; 52% have terminal degrees, 8% minority, 54% women. **Class size:** 60% < 20, 36% 20-39, 2% 40-49, 1% 50-99, less than 1% >100. **Special facilities:** Observatory, natural sciences research labs, art galleries, computerized music lab, visual anthropology lab, library archives and special collections, student-managed real-dollar investment portfolio program, nursing lab, Action Research Center (supporting community-based student research).

Freshman class profile. 2,770 applied, 1,580 admitted, 565 enrolled.

Mid 50% test scores		**Rank in top tenth:**	47%
SAT verbal:	600-690	**End year in good standing:**	99%
SAT math:	590-690	**Return as sophomores:**	92%
ACT:	26-31	**Out-of-state:**	15%
GPA 3.50 or higher:	79%	**Live on campus:**	100%
GPA 3.0-3.49:	19%	**International:**	3%
GPA 2.0-2.99:	2%	**Fraternities:**	23%
Rank in top quarter:	81%	**Sororities:**	20%

Basis for selection. Test scores, class rank, high school record, and essay or personal statement are most important. Interview strongly recommended. Audition with program faculty required for bachelor of music and BFA in theater or music theater programs. Portfolio review by art faculty required for BFA in art program. **Homeschooled:** Transcript of courses and grades required. Applicants must provide official standardized test scores (either ACT or SAT). **Learning Disabled:** Students welcome to submit information on learning disabilities as part of the application review process. Once admitted, individual needs are addressed by associate provost.

High school preparation. 15 units required. Required units include English 4, mathematics 3, social studies 2, science 3 (laboratory 2) and foreign language 3. Biology and chemistry are required for admission to nursing and biology.

2006-2007 Annual costs. Tuition/fees (projected): $29,136. Additional expense-based fees are charged for the University's semester abroad programs in London and Madrid. Room/board: $6,714. Books/supplies: $650. Personal expenses: $780.

2005-2006 Financial aid. **Need-based:** 429 full-time freshmen applied for aid; 337 were judged to have need; 336 of these received aid. Average need met was 91%. Average scholarship/grant was $14,847; average loan $4,197. 70% of total undergraduate aid awarded as scholarships/grants, 30% as loans/jobs. **Non-need-based:** Awarded to 749 full-time undergraduates, including 204 freshmen. Scholarships awarded for academics, art, music/drama.

Application procedures. **Admission:** Priority date 11/1; no deadline. No application fee. Application may be submitted online. Admission notification on a rolling basis beginning on or about 12/15. Must reply by May 1 or within 3 week(s) if notified thereafter. **Financial aid:** Closing date 3/1. FAFSA, institutional form required. Applicants notified on a rolling basis starting 2/1; must reply by 5/1 or within 3 week(s) of notification.

Academics. Optional 3-week May Term provides opportunities for students to pursue experimental courses, travel courses, interships, or independent research projects. About 2/3 of the student body chooses to take a May Term course each year; about 20% are typically enrolled in off-campus domestic or international travel courses. Illinois Wesleyan also offers Fall Term in London and Spring Term in Madrid; led by Illinois Wesleyan faculty members--students may earn General Education credit during these terms. **Special study options:** Combined bachelor's/graduate degree, double major, exchange student, honors, independent study, internships, liberal arts/career combination, New York semester, student-designed major, study abroad, teacher certification program, United Nations semester, urban semester, Washington semester. 3-2 cooperative program in engineering with Washington University, Case Western Reserve University, and Northwestern University; 3-2 program in forestry and environmental management with Duke University; 3-2 program in occupational therapy with Washington University, 2-2 program in engineering with the University of Illinois, and a nonguaranteed cooperative program in engineering with Dartmouth College. **Credit/placement by examination:** AP, CLEP, IB, institutional tests. 32 credit hours maximum toward bachelor's degree. Limit of 16 hours may count toward general education credit. Up to 16 additional hours (equivalent to a total of four courses) can be awarded as elective credit. **Support services:** Reduced course load, study skills assistance, tutoring, writing center.

Majors. **Area/ethnic studies:** African, American, Asian, Central/Eastern European, Latin American, Russian/Slavic, Western European, women's. **Biology:** General. **Business:** Accounting, business admin, insurance, international. **Computer sciences:** General. **Conservation:** Environmental studies. **Education:** General, biology, chemistry, elementary, English, French, history, mathematics, music, physics, Spanish. **English:** English lit. **Foreign languages:** Classics, French, German, Spanish. **Health:** Nursing (RN). **History:** General. **Math:** General. **Philosophy/religion:** Philosophy, religion. **Physical sciences:** Chemistry, physics. **Psychology:** General. **Social sciences:** Anthropology, economics, political science, sociology. **Visual/performing arts:** Acting, art, dramatic, music performance, music theory/composition, piano/organ, stringed instruments, theater design, voice/opera.

Most popular majors. Biology 8%, business/marketing 22%, education 8%, English 6%, history 6%, psychology 8%, social sciences 13%, visual/performing arts 9%.

Computing on campus. 420 workstations in dormitories, library, computer center, student center. Dormitories wired for high-speed internet access and linked to campus network. Commuter students can connect to campus network. Online course registration, online library, helpline, repair service, student web hosting, wireless network available.

Student life. **Freshman orientation:** Mandatory. Preregistration for classes offered. Orientation for parents held in June. New student orientation held 5-6 days prior to the start of fall classes. **Policies:** No smoking is permitted in residence halls. Beer and wine are permitted in designated areas on campus, including individual student rooms, for students who are of legal age. Freshmen permitted cars on campus. **Housing:** Guaranteed on-campus for freshmen. Coed dorms, special housing for disabled, fraternity/sorority housing, substance-free housing available. Theme housing available. **Activities:** Bands, choral groups, dance, drama, film society, literary magazine, music ensembles, musical theater, opera, radio station, student government, student newspaper, symphony orchestra, TV station, Black Student Union, InterVarsity Christian Fellowship, Alpha Phi Omega, Council of Latin American student enrichment, Habitat for Humanity, environmental concerns organization, Amnesty International, Muslim student association, Southeast Asian student association.

Athletics. NCAA. **Intercollegiate:** Baseball M, basketball, cross-country, diving, football (tackle) M, golf, soccer, softball W, swimming, tennis, track and field, volleyball W. **Intramural:** Badminton, basketball, football (non-tackle), golf M, soccer, softball, volleyball. **Team name:** Titans.

Student services. Alcohol/substance abuse counseling, campus ministries, career counseling, student employment services, financial aid counseling, health services, minority student services, personal counseling, placement for graduates. **Physically disabled:** Services for visually, speech, hearing impaired.

Contact. E-mail: iwuadmit@iwu.edu
Phone: (309) 556-3031 Toll-free number: (800) 332-2498
Fax: (309) 556-3820
Tony Bankston, Acting Dean of Admission, Illinois Wesleyan University, PO Box 2900, Bloomington, IL 61702-2900

International Academy of Design and Technology: Chicago

Chicago, Illinois
www.iadtchicago.edu **CB code: 3363**

- For-profit 4-year visual arts and technical college
- Commuter campus in very large city

- 2,768 degree-seeking undergraduates: 13% part-time, 69% women, 33% African American, 3% Asian American, 20% Hispanic American, 2% international
- Interview required

General. Founded in 1977. Accredited by ACICS. **Degrees:** 268 bachelor's, 100 associate awarded. **Location:** Downtown Chicago. **Calendar:** Quarter, extensive summer session. **Full-time faculty:** 2 total. **Part-time faculty:** 160 total. **Class size:** 54% < 20, 39% 20-39, 7% 40-49, less than 1% 50-99.

Freshman class profile. 1,713 applied, 1,699 admitted, 675 enrolled.

End year in good standing:	90%	**Out-of-state:**	7%
Return as sophomores:	34%	**International:**	1%

Basis for selection. Open admission, but selective for some programs. Students must meet with an admissions representative and go through interview process. **Homeschooled:** Transcript of courses and grades required. Should be registered with state or accrediting agency.

2006-2007 Annual costs. Tuition/fees (projected): $16,350. Books/supplies: $1,600. Personal expenses: $1,428.

2004-2005 Financial aid. All financial aid based on need. 20% of total undergraduate aid awarded as scholarships/grants, 80% as loans/jobs. **Additional information:** College work study programs available to day and evening students.

Application procedures. Admission: No deadline. $50 fee, may be waived for applicants with need. Application may be submitted online. Admission notification on a rolling basis. **Financial aid:** No deadline. FAFSA, institutional form required. Applicants notified on a rolling basis starting 1/6; must reply within 2 week(s) of notification.

Academics. Special study options: Cooperative education, independent study, internships, study abroad, weekend college. **Credit/placement by examination:** AP, CLEP, IB, institutional tests. 40 credit hours maximum toward associate degree, 100 toward bachelor's. **Support services:** Learning center, reduced course load, remedial instruction, study skills assistance, tutoring.

Majors. Business: Fashion. **Communications technology:** Animation/special effects. **Computer sciences:** Information technology. **Visual/performing arts:** Commercial/advertising art, fashion design, graphic design, interior design.

Most popular majors. Business/marketing 25%, visual/performing arts 74%.

Computing on campus. 386 workstations in library, computer center. Online library available.

Student life. Freshman orientation: Mandatory. **Activities:** Student government, student newspaper, the fashion council, merchandising management club, information technology club, video and animation club, Omega Pi Delta, International Interior Design Association, graphic design club, international club, chess club, movie club.

Student services. Adult student services, career counseling, student employment services, financial aid counseling, personal counseling, placement for graduates, veterans' counselor.

Contact. E-mail: academy@iadtchicago.com
Phone: (312) 980-9200 Toll-free number: (877) 222-3369
Fax: (312) 541-3929
Doug Lochbaum, Assistant Vice President of Marketing and Admissions, International Academy of Design and Technology: Chicago, One North State Street, Suite 500, Chicago, IL 60602

International Academy of Design and Technology: Schaumburg

Schaumburg, Illinois
www.iadtschaumburg.com

- For-profit 4-year visual arts and technical college
- Commuter campus
- 217 degree-seeking undergraduates

General. Accredited by ACICS. **Degrees:** 1 bachelor's awarded.

2005-2006 Annual costs. Bachelor's degree program is $64,000 plus books and fees.

Academics. Credit/placement by examination: CLEP.

Majors. Communications technology: Animation/special effects. **Computer sciences:** Web page design. **Visual/performing arts:** Fashion design, interior design.

Contact. Phone: (847) 969-2800 Fax: (847) 969-0599
Tom Claxton, Director of Admissions, International Academy of Design and Technology: Schaumburg, 915 National Parkway, Schaumburg, IL 60173

ITT Technical Institute: Burr Ridge

Burr Ridge, Illinois
www.itt-tech.edu **CB code: 2698**

- For-profit 4-year technical college
- Commuter campus in small town

General. Accredited by ACICS. **Calendar:** Quarter.

Annual costs/financial aid. Tuition varies by program, $260-$368 per credit hour.

Contact. Phone: (630) 455-6470
Director of Recruitment, 7040 High Grove Boulevard, Burr Ridge, IL 60527

ITT Technical Institute: Matteson

Matteson, Illinois
www.itt-tech.edu **CB code: 2729**

- For-profit 4-year technical college
- Commuter campus in large town

General. Accredited by ACICS. **Calendar:** Quarter.

Annual costs/financial aid. Tuition varies by program, $260-$368 per credit hour.

Contact. Phone: (708) 747-2571
Director of Recruitment, 600 Holiday Plaza Drive, Matteson, IL 60443

ITT Technical Institute: Mount Prospect

Mount Prospect, Illinois
www.itt-tech.edu **CB code: 4271**

- For-profit 4-year technical college
- Commuter campus in small city

General. Founded in 1986. Accredited by ACICS. **Location:** 20 miles from Chicago. **Calendar:** Quarter.

Annual costs/financial aid. Tuition varies by program, $260-$368 per credit hour.

Contact. Phone: (847) 375-8800
Director of Recruitment, 1401 Feehanville Drive, Mount Prospect, IL 60056

Judson College

Elgin, Illinois
www.judsoncollege.edu **CB code: 1351**

- Private 4-year liberal arts college affiliated with American Baptist Churches in the USA
- Residential campus in small city
- 1,125 degree-seeking undergraduates: 20% part-time, 58% women, 4% African American, 1% Asian American, 5% Hispanic American, 3% international
- 50 degree-seeking graduate students
- 79% of applicants admitted
- SAT or ACT (ACT writing optional), application essay required

General. Founded in 1963. Regionally accredited. **Degrees:** 339 bachelor's awarded; master's offered. **Location:** 40 miles from Chicago. **Calendar:** Semester, limited summer session. **Full-time faculty:** 54 total; 67% have terminal degrees, 13% minority, 35% women. **Part-time faculty:** 57 total; 25% have terminal degrees, 4% minority, 46% women. **Class size:**

66% < 20, 32% 20-39, less than 1% 40-49, 2% 50-99. **Special facilities:** Computer-aided graphics laboratory, cadaver room, gene splicing laboratory, music technology laboratory.

Freshman class profile. 457 applied, 361 admitted, 135 enrolled.

Mid 50% test scores		End year in good standing:	78%
SAT verbal:	430-600	Return as sophomores:	83%
SAT math:	440-660	International:	4%
ACT:	20-26		

Basis for selection. School achievement record and test scores important. Counselor's reference also considered. Audition recommended for performing arts majors. Portfolio recommended for art majors. Essay required for architecture majors. **Homeschooled:** Transcript of courses and grades required.

High school preparation. Recommended units include English 4, mathematics 3, social studies 2, science 2 (laboratory 2).

2006-2007 Annual costs. Tuition/fees: $19,450. Room/board: $6,900.

2004-2005 Financial aid. Need-based: 115 full-time freshmen applied for aid; 100 were judged to have need; 100 of these received aid. Average need met was 40%. Average scholarship/grant was $7,212; average loan $2,569. 54% of total undergraduate aid awarded as scholarships/grants, 46% as loans/jobs. **Non-need-based:** Awarded to 186 full-time undergraduates, including 49 freshmen. Scholarships awarded for academics, athletics, music/drama.

Application procedures. Admission: No deadline. $35 fee, may be waived for applicants with need. Application may be submitted online. Admission notification on a rolling basis beginning on or about 7/1. **Financial aid:** Priority date 3/1; no closing date. FAFSA required. Applicants notified on a rolling basis starting 3/1; must reply within 4 week(s) of notification.

Academics. Special study options: Accelerated study, combined bachelor's/graduate degree, distance learning, double major, honors, independent study, internships, study abroad, teacher certification program, Washington semester. **Credit/placement by examination:** AP, CLEP, SAT, ACT, institutional tests. 30 credit hours maximum toward bachelor's degree. **Support services:** Learning center, reduced course load, remedial instruction, study skills assistance, tutoring.

Majors. Architecture: Architecture. **Biology:** General. **Business:** General, accounting, accounting/finance, business admin, international, management information systems, marketing. **Communications:** General, journalism, media studies. **Computer sciences:** General, computer science. **Education:** Chemistry, early childhood, elementary, English, mathematics, middle, multi-level teacher, music, physical, physics, science, secondary. **English:** Speech/rhetoric. **Foreign languages:** Linguistics. **Health:** Predentistry, premedicine. **History:** General. **Legal studies:** Prelaw. **Math:** General. **Parks/recreation:** Health/fitness, sports admin. **Philosophy/religion:** Philosophy, religion. **Physical sciences:** Chemistry, physics. **Psychology:** General. **Public administration:** Human services. **Social sciences:** Anthropology, political science, sociology. **Theology:** Bible, preministerial, sacred music, youth ministry. **Visual/performing arts:** Art, ceramics, commercial photography, commercial/advertising art, design, dramatic, drawing, graphic design, illustration, interior design, music performance, photography, piano/organ, sculpture, studio arts, voice/opera.

Computing on campus. 200 workstations in dormitories, library, computer center, student center. Dormitories wired for high-speed internet access and linked to campus network. Online library, helpline, wireless network available.

Student life. Freshman orientation: Mandatory. Preregistration for classes offered. **Policies:** Chapel services held 3 mornings a week. Religious observance required. Freshmen permitted cars on campus. **Housing:** Guaranteed on-campus for all undergraduates. Coed dorms, single-sex dorms, special housing for disabled, apartments, substance-free housing available. $100 nonrefundable deposit, deadline 6/1. **Activities:** Concert band, choral groups, drama, music ensembles, student government, student newspaper, symphony orchestra.

Athletics. NAIA, NCCAA. **Intercollegiate:** Baseball M, basketball, cross-country, soccer, softball W, tennis, volleyball W. **Intramural:** Badminton, basketball, racquetball, soccer, softball, table tennis, tennis, volleyball. **Team name:** Eagles.

Student services. Adult student services, campus ministries, career counseling, student employment services, financial aid counseling, health services, personal counseling, placement for graduates.

Contact. E-mail: admissions@judsoncollege.edu
Phone: (847) 628-2510 Toll-free number: (800) 879-5376
Fax: (847) 628-2526
William Dean, Director of Admissions, Judson College, 1151 North State Street, Elgin, IL 60123-1404

Kendall College
Chicago, Illinois
www.kendall.edu **CB code: 1366**

- Private 4-year culinary school and business college affiliated with United Methodist Church
- Commuter campus in very large city
- 780 degree-seeking undergraduates: 36% part-time, 59% women
- 30% of applicants admitted
- SAT or ACT (ACT writing optional) required

General. Founded in 1934. Regionally accredited. Internships required in every major. **Degrees:** 50 bachelor's, 75 associate awarded. **Calendar:** Quarter, extensive summer session. **Full-time faculty:** 37 total; 14% minority, 38% women. **Part-time faculty:** 43 total; 30% minority, 54% women. **Special facilities:** New Riverworks Campus features wireless classrooms and renovated campus in downtown Chicago.

Freshman class profile. 605 applied, 180 admitted, 177 enrolled.

Basis for selection. High school record most important, followed by test scores, class rank, recommendations and interview. Placement test may be required. Interview recommended.

High school preparation. College-preparatory program recommended. Recommended units include English 4, mathematics 2, social studies 2, science 2 and foreign language 2. Specific academic units required for certain majors.

2005-2006 Annual costs. Tuition costs range from $15,750 to $25,400 per academic year. Required fees: $470. Room/board: $9,000.

Financial aid. Non-need-based: Scholarships awarded for academics, athletics, religious affiliation.

Application procedures. Admission: No deadline. $75 fee, may be waived for applicants with need. Application may be submitted online. Admission notification on a rolling basis. Must reply by May 1 or within 4 week(s) if notified thereafter. **Financial aid:** Priority date 6/1; no closing date. FAFSA required. Applicants notified on a rolling basis starting 4/1; must reply within 2 week(s) of notification.

Academics. Special study options: Accelerated study, cooperative education, double major, ESL, independent study, internships, student-designed major, study abroad, teacher certification program. **Credit/placement by examination:** AP, CLEP, IB, institutional tests. 24 credit hours maximum toward associate degree, 48 toward bachelor's. **Support services:** Learning center, reduced course load, remedial instruction, study skills assistance, tutoring, writing center.

Majors. Business: Business admin, entrepreneurial studies, hospitality admin, hotel/motel admin, nonprofit/public. **Education:** Early childhood. **Personal/culinary services:** Culinary arts.

Computing on campus. Dormitories wired for high-speed internet access and linked to campus network. Commuter students can connect to campus network. Online course registration, online library, helpline, wireless network available.

Student life. Freshman orientation: Mandatory. Preregistration for classes offered. One-day event held 1 week before the start of the quarter. **Policies:** Freshmen permitted cars on campus. **Housing:** Coed dorms available. $350 deposit. **Activities:** Student government, student newspaper.

Student services. Alcohol/substance abuse counseling, career counseling, student employment services, financial aid counseling, personal counseling, placement for graduates.

Contact. E-mail: admissions@kendall.edu
Phone: (312) 752-2020 Toll-free number: (888) 653-6325
Fax: (312) 752-2021
Tom Fitzgibbon, Director of Admissions, Kendall College, 900 North Branch Street North, Chicago, IL 60622-4278

Knox College

Galesburg, Illinois — **CB member**
www.knox.edu — **CB code: 1372**

- Private 4-year liberal arts college
- Residential campus in large town
- 1,205 degree-seeking undergraduates: 54% women, 4% African American, 5% Asian American, 4% Hispanic American, 7% international
- 76% of applicants admitted
- Application essay required
- 75% graduate within 6 years; 22% enter graduate study

General. Founded in 1837. Regionally accredited. Extensive overseas study centers with more than 30 international and off-campus study programs. Significant independent research opportunities with funding for projects. Repertory theater, psychology, and Green Oaks (environmental) terms. **Degrees:** 224 bachelor's awarded. **Location:** 180 miles from Chicago, 200 miles from St. Louis. **Calendar:** Trimester. **Full-time faculty:** 95 total; 94% have terminal degrees, 10% minority, 43% women. **Part-time faculty:** 22 total; 50% have terminal degrees, 18% minority, 50% women. **Class size:** 66% < 20, 31% 20-39, 3% 40-49, less than 1% 50-99. **Special facilities:** Electron microscope, greenhouse, studio and large-scale production theaters, 760-acre biological field station, ceramics, sculpture, painting, and printmaking studios, fieldhouse.

Freshman class profile. 1,771 applied, 1,338 admitted, 325 enrolled.

Mid 50% test scores		**Return as sophomores:**	85%
SAT verbal:	580-700	**Out-of-state:**	49%
SAT math:	540-660	**Live on campus:**	98%
ACT:	25-30	**International:**	6%
Rank in top quarter:	61%	**Fraternities:**	21%
Rank in top tenth:	33%	**Sororities:**	6%
End year in good standing:	91%		

Basis for selection. Course of study, grades, essay, and recommendations most important. Class rank, extracurricular activities, special skills, talents and personal qualities, and interview also considered. Submission of ACT/SAT scores is optional; scores will be considered if submitted. Preference given to students who have taken advantage of academic opportunities offered by high school, including honors, Advanced Placement, and International Baccalaureate, if available. SAT or ACT score submission is optional for most applicants. If students elect to submit scores, they will be considered. Home-schooled students or applicants from secondary schools that do not provide grades are asked to submit test scores. Interview strongly recommended. **Homeschooled:** Statement describing homeschool structure and mission, transcript of courses and grades, state high school equivalency certificate required. Applicants should provide detailed documentation of coursework completed, including course syllabi as appropriate. ACT and/or SAT scores are required for all home-schooled students.

High school preparation. 15 units required; 18 recommended. Required and recommended units include English 4, mathematics 4, social studies 2, history 2, science 3 (laboratory 2) and foreign language 3.

2006-2007 Annual costs. Tuition/fees: $27,900. Room/board: $5,925. Books/supplies: $900. Personal expenses: $600.

2005-2006 Financial aid. **Need-based:** 271 full-time freshmen applied for aid; 216 were judged to have need; 216 of these received aid. Average need met was 95%. Average scholarship/grant was $16,474; average loan $4,424. 76% of total undergraduate aid awarded as scholarships/grants, 24% as loans/jobs. **Non-need-based:** Awarded to 456 full-time undergraduates, including 129 freshmen. Scholarships awarded for academics, art, music/drama.

Application procedures. **Admission:** Closing date 2/1 (postmark date). $40 fee, may be waived for applicants with need. Application may be submitted online. Admission notification 3/31. Must reply by May 1 or within 2 week(s) if notified thereafter. **Financial aid:** Priority date 2/15; no closing date. FAFSA, institutional form required. Applicants notified on a rolling basis starting 3/15; must reply by 5/1 or within 2 week(s) of notification.

Academics. Academic work conducted under honor system, placing primary responsibility for academic honesty on student. Examinations not proctored. **Special study options:** Combined bachelor's/graduate degree, double major, dual enrollment of high school students, honors, independent study, internships, liberal arts/career combination, student-designed major, study abroad, teacher certification program, urban semester, Washington semester. **Credit/placement by examination:** AP, CLEP, IB, SAT, ACT, institutional tests. 9 credit hours maximum toward bachelor's degree. Up to 25% of required credits may be obtained through examination. **Support services:** Learning center, reduced course load, study skills assistance, tutoring, writing center.

Majors. **Area/ethnic studies:** African-American, American, women's. **Biology:** General, biochemistry. **Computer sciences:** Computer science. **Conservation:** Environmental studies. **Education:** General, social science. **English:** Creative writing, English lit. **Foreign languages:** General, classics, French, German, Spanish. **History:** General. **Interdisciplinary:** Global studies. **Math:** General, applied. **Philosophy/religion:** Philosophy. **Physical sciences:** Chemistry, physics. **Psychology:** General. **Social sciences:** Anthropology, economics, international relations, political science, sociology. **Visual/performing arts:** Art history/conservation, dramatic, studio arts.

Most popular majors. Biology 7%, education 6%, English 10%, foreign language 6%, physical sciences 6%, psychology 10%, social sciences 26%, visual/performing arts 10%.

Computing on campus. 335 workstations in library, computer center, student center. Dormitories wired for high-speed internet access and linked to campus network. Commuter students can connect to campus network. Online course registration, online library, helpline, student web hosting, wireless network available.

Student life. **Freshman orientation:** Mandatory. Preregistration for classes offered. 1 week before beginning of fall term. Additional orientation held for international students. **Policies:** Students actively engaged in college governance. All students requred to live on campus. Freshmen permitted cars on campus. **Housing:** Guaranteed on-campus for all undergraduates. Coed dorms, single-sex dorms, apartments, fraternity/sorority housing, substance-free housing available. $200 nonrefundable deposit, deadline 5/1. **Activities:** Bands, choral groups, dance, drama, literary magazine, music ensembles, radio station, student government, student newspaper, symphony orchestra, Christian Fellowship, Amnesty International, Latin American Concerns, Allied Blacks for Liberty and Equality, Lo Nuestro (Hispanic student group), Habitat for Humanity, Common Ground, environmental group.

Athletics. NCAA. **Intercollegiate:** Baseball M, basketball, cross-country, diving, football (tackle) M, golf, soccer, softball W, swimming, tennis, track and field, volleyball W, wrestling M. **Intramural:** Basketball, football (tackle), soccer, softball, swimming, tennis, track and field, volleyball. **Team name:** Prairie Fire.

Student services. Alcohol/substance abuse counseling, career counseling, services for economically disadvantaged, student employment services, financial aid counseling, health services, minority student services, personal counseling. **Physically disabled:** Services for visually, hearing impaired.

Contact. E-mail: admission@knox.edu
Phone: (309) 341-7100 Toll-free number: (800) 678-5669
Fax: (309) 341-7070
Paul Steenis, Dean of Admission, Knox College, Campus Box 148, Galesburg, IL 61401-4999

Lake Forest College

Lake Forest, Illinois — **CB member**
www.lakeforest.edu — **CB code: 1392**

- Private 4-year liberal arts college affiliated with Presbyterian Church (USA)
- Residential campus in large town
- 1,383 degree-seeking undergraduates: 1% part-time, 58% women, 5% African American, 3% Asian American, 6% Hispanic American, 8% international
- 17 degree-seeking graduate students
- 65% of applicants admitted
- SAT or ACT (ACT writing optional), application essay required
- 70% graduate within 6 years; 22% enter graduate study

General. Founded in 1857. Regionally accredited. **Degrees:** 306 bachelor's awarded; master's offered. **Location:** 30 miles from Chicago. **Calendar:** Semester, limited summer session. **Full-time faculty:** 89 total; 93% have terminal degrees, 10% minority, 33% women. **Part-time faculty:** 69 total; 54% have terminal degrees, 7% minority, 55% women. **Class size:** 59% < 20, 40% 20-39, 1% 40-49. **Special facilities:** Electron microscope, NMR spectrometer, neutron howitzer, multimedia language laboratory, electronic music studio.

Freshman class profile. 2,195 applied, 1,431 admitted, 358 enrolled.

Mid 50% test scores			
SAT verbal:	540-640	Rank in top quarter:	54%
SAT math:	530-650	Rank in top tenth:	32%
ACT:	23-28	End year in good standing:	90%
GPA 3.50 or higher:	48%	Return as sophomores:	82%
GPA 3.0-3.49:	35%	Out-of-state:	60%
GPA 2.0-2.99:	17%	Live on campus:	88%
		International:	7%

Basis for selection. Secondary school curriculum and record most important, followed by school and community activities, essay. Recommendations considered carefully. Copy of graded paper required. Interview required for merit scholarships in leadership and science, recommended for all. Audition required for theater and music scholarships. Portfolio required for art, foreign language and writing scholarships.

High school preparation. 16 units required; 19 recommended. Required and recommended units include English 4, mathematics 3-4, social studies 1-2, history 1-2, science 2-3 (laboratory 2-3), foreign language 2-4 and academic electives 3.

2005-2006 Annual costs. Tuition/fees: $27,334. Room/board: $6,526. Books/supplies: $700. Personal expenses: $750.

2005-2006 Financial aid. **Need-based:** 329 full-time freshmen applied for aid; 292 were judged to have need; 292 of these received aid. Average need met was 100%. Average scholarship/grant was $18,006; average loan $4,159. 79% of total undergraduate aid awarded as scholarships/grants, 21% as loans/jobs. **Non-need-based:** Awarded to 204 full-time undergraduates, including 34 freshmen. Scholarships awarded for academics, alumni affiliation, art, leadership, music/drama.

Application procedures. **Admission:** Priority date 2/15; no deadline. $40 fee, may be waived for applicants with need. Application may be submitted online. Admission notification on a rolling basis beginning on or about 3/15. Must reply by May 1 or within 3 week(s) if notified thereafter. **Financial aid:** Priority date 2/15; no closing date. FAFSA required. Applicants notified on a rolling basis starting 2/15; must reply by 5/1 or within 3 week(s) of notification.

Academics. In freshman studies program students select 1 of 4 fall courses from designated set, usually 25 to 30, with class size limit of 12 students. Faculty member teaching course serves as student's academic adviser. **Special study options:** Combined bachelor's/graduate degree, double major, honors, independent study, internships, liberal arts/career combination, semester at sea, student-designed major, study abroad, teacher certification program, urban semester, Washington semester. International internship program in Paris and Santiago, Chile; 3-2 engineering program with Washington University. **Credit/placement by examination:** AP, CLEP, IB, SAT, ACT, institutional tests. **Support services:** Learning center, study skills assistance, tutoring, writing center.

Majors. **Area/ethnic studies:** American, Asian, Latin American. **Biology:** General. **Business:** General. **Communications:** General. **Computer sciences:** Computer science. **Conservation:** Environmental studies. **Education:** General. **English:** English lit. **Foreign languages:** French, Spanish. **History:** General. **Math:** General. **Philosophy/religion:** Philosophy. **Physical sciences:** Chemistry, physics. **Psychology:** General. **Social sciences:** Anthropology, economics, international relations, political science, sociology. **Visual/performing arts:** Art.

Most popular majors. Biology 6%, business/marketing 11%, communications/journalism 16%, English 7%, foreign language 6%, interdisciplinary studies 8%, psychology 7%, social sciences 18%.

Computing on campus. 200 workstations in library, computer center, student center. Dormitories wired for high-speed internet access and linked to campus network. Commuter students can connect to campus network. Online library, helpline, repair service, student web hosting, wireless network available.

Student life. **Freshman orientation:** Mandatory. Preregistration for classes offered. **Housing:** Guaranteed on-campus for freshmen. Coed dorms, single-sex dorms, substance-free housing available. $200 deposit, deadline 5/1. **Activities:** Jazz band, choral groups, dance, drama, film society, literary magazine, music ensembles, musical theater, radio station, student government, student newspaper, Christian Fellowship, Interfaith Council, Amnesty International, League for Environmental Awareness and Protection, United Black Association, Women's Issues Table, Latinos Unidos, Asian interest group, diversity advocates (ALLY), anti-racism group (STAR), Hillel.

Athletics. NCAA. **Intercollegiate:** Basketball, cross-country, diving, football (tackle) M, handball, ice hockey, soccer, softball W, swimming, tennis, volleyball W. **Intramural:** Basketball, football (non-tackle), racquetball, soccer, softball, tennis, volleyball. **Team name:** Foresters.

Student services. Adult student services, alcohol/substance abuse counseling, career counseling, student employment services, financial aid counseling, health services, minority student services, personal counseling, placement for graduates, veterans' counselor, women's services. **Physically disabled:** Services for visually, hearing impaired.

Contact. E-mail: admissions@lakeforest.edu
Phone: (847) 735-5000 Toll-free number: (800) 828-4751
Fax: (847) 735-6271
William Motzer, Vice President for Admissions and Career Services, Lake Forest College, 555 North Sheridan Road, Lake Forest, IL 60045-2399

Lakeview College of Nursing

Danville, Illinois
www.lakeviewcol.edu **CB code: 0149**

- Private upper-division nursing college
- Commuter campus in large town
- Application essay required

General. Founded in 1894. Regionally accredited. **Degrees:** 50 bachelor's awarded. **Articulation:** Agreements with Danville Area CC and Eastern Illinois University. **Location:** 35 miles from Urbana-Champaign, 130 miles from Chicago. **Calendar:** Semester, limited summer session. **Full-time faculty:** 9 total. **Part-time faculty:** 12 total. **Special facilities:** Free clinic, nature preserve.

Student profile. 235 degree-seeking undergraduates.

Out-of-state:	2%	25 or older:	83%

Basis for selection. Open admission. High school transcript, college transcript, application essay required. Based on interview, references, and transcripts. Applicant must have completed 33 credit hours of general course work with 2.5 GPA prior to admission. Transfer accepted as sophomores, juniors.

2005-2006 Annual costs. Tuition/fees: $10,650. Books/supplies: $582.

Financial aid. All financial aid based on need.

Application procedures. **Admission:** Rolling admission. $50 fee, may be waived for applicants with need. National League for Nursing examinations used to determine advanced placement for entering students who already have RN degree. **Financial aid:** Priority date 4/15, no deadline. FAFSA, institutional form required.

Academics. BS in nursing requires total of 125 credit hours. 95% of entering students complete degree in 5 years or less. **Special study options:** Distance learning, honors, independent study. **Credit/placement by examination:** CLEP. **Support services:** Reduced course load, study skills assistance, tutoring.

Majors. **Health:** Nursing (RN).

Computing on campus. 12 workstations in library, computer center.

Student life. **Activities:** Student government, student newspaper, Illinois Student Nurses Association, National Student Nurses Association.

Student services. Adult student services, career counseling, financial aid counseling, health services, personal counseling, veterans' counselor.

Contact. E-mail: cyoung@lakeviewcol.edu
Phone: (217) 554-6899 Fax: (217) 442-2279
Connie Young, Registrar, Lakeview College of Nursing, 903 North Logan Avenue, Danville, IL 61832

Lewis University

Romeoville, Illinois **CB member**
www.lewisu.edu **CB code: 1404**

- Private 4-year university affiliated with Roman Catholic Church
- Residential campus in large town
- 3,543 degree-seeking undergraduates: 25% part-time, 61% women, 12% African American, 4% Asian American, 9% Hispanic American, 3% international
- 1,472 degree-seeking graduate students
- 69% of applicants admitted
- SAT or ACT required
- 50% graduate within 6 years

General. Founded in 1932. Regionally accredited. Sponsored by De La Salle Christian Brothers. **Degrees:** 698 bachelor's, 1 associate awarded; master's, doctoral offered. **ROTC:** Army, Air Force. **Location:** 30 miles from Chicago. **Calendar:** Semester, extensive summer session. **Full-time faculty:** 151 total; 60% have terminal degrees, 9% minority, 47% women. **Part-time faculty:** 308 total; 14% have terminal degrees, 6% minority, 51% women. **Class size:** 68% < 20, 30% 20-39, 2% 40-49, less than 1% 50-99. **Special facilities:** Campus airport, aeronautical training center, all digital radio station.

Freshman class profile. 2,014 applied, 1,398 admitted, 561 enrolled.

Mid 50% test scores			
SAT verbal:	500-570	Rank in top tenth:	15%
SAT math:	510-570	Return as sophomores:	75%
ACT:	19-25	Out-of-state:	10%
GPA 3.50 or higher:	33%	Live on campus:	58%
GPA 3.0-3.49:	31%	International:	3%
GPA 2.0-2.99:	36%	Fraternities:	6%
Rank in top quarter:	40%	Sororities:	9%

Basis for selection. Applicants must graduate from approved high school. Must have 2.0 minimum GPA, class rank and ACT or SAT score indicating strong likelihood of success in university studies. Minimum ACT composite score of 20 required for admission to nursing program. TOEFL required for non-native speakers of English. Interview recommended.

High school preparation. 18 units required. Required and recommended units include English 3-4, mathematics 3, social studies 2, history 1, science 2 (laboratory 1), foreign language 2 and academic electives 4. 1 year chemistry and 2 years math at 2.0 level or above strongly recommended for nursing applicants.

2005-2006 Annual costs. Tuition/fees: $18,075. Room/board: $7,400. Books/supplies: $500. Personal expenses: $1,320.

2005-2006 Financial aid. Need-based: 488 full-time freshmen applied for aid; 387 were judged to have need; 387 of these received aid. Average need met was 77%. Average scholarship/grant was $6,818; average loan $2,195. 44% of total undergraduate aid awarded as scholarships/grants, 56% as loans/jobs. **Non-need-based:** Scholarships awarded for academics, alumni affiliation, art, athletics, leadership, music/drama, ROTC.

Application procedures. Admission: Priority date 3/1; no deadline. $40 fee, may be waived for applicants with need. Application may be submitted online. Admission notification on a rolling basis beginning on or about 10/1. Must reply by May 1 or within 2 week(s) if notified thereafter. **Financial aid:** Priority date 5/1; no closing date. FAFSA required. Applicants notified on a rolling basis starting 2/15; must reply by 5/1 or within 2 week(s) of notification.

Academics. Accelerated degree completion program available to students 24 years and older. **Special study options:** Accelerated study, combined bachelor's/graduate degree, cooperative education, distance learning, double major, dual enrollment of high school students, ESL, exchange student, honors, independent study, internships, liberal arts/career combination, student-designed major, study abroad, teacher certification program. **Credit/placement by examination:** AP, CLEP, ACT, institutional tests. 60 credit hours maximum toward bachelor's degree. **Support services:** Learning center, pre-admission summer program, reduced course load, remedial instruction, study skills assistance, tutoring, writing center.

Majors. Area/ethnic studies: American. **Biology:** General, biochemistry, environmental. **Business:** General, accounting, business admin, finance, human resources, international, management information systems, management science, managerial economics, marketing. **Communications:** General, broadcast journalism, journalism, public relations, radio/tv. **Communications technology:** General, radio/tv. **Computer sciences:** General, computer graphics, computer science, information systems. **Conservation:** General. **Education:** General, elementary, special. **English:** Composition, creative writing, speech/rhetoric. **Health:** Athletic training, nursing (RN), predentistry, preveterinary. **History:** General. **Interdisciplinary:** Global studies. **Legal studies:** Prelaw. **Liberal arts:** Arts/sciences. **Math:** General. **Mechanic/repair:** Aircraft, avionics. **Parks/recreation:** Sports admin. **Philosophy/religion:** Philosophy, religion. **Physical sciences:** Chemistry, physics. **Protective services:** Correctional facilities, criminal justice, forensics, law enforcement admin, police science, security services. **Psychology:** General. **Public administration:** General, human services, social work. **Social sciences:** Economics, political science, sociology. **Transportation:** Airline/commercial pilot, aviation, aviation management. **Visual/performing arts:** Art, commercial/advertising art, dramatic, drawing, graphic design, illustration, music management, painting, studio arts, theater arts management.

Most popular majors. Business/marketing 25%, education 6%, health sciences 16%, psychology 6%, public administration/social services 6%, security/protective services 12%, trade and industry 8%.

Computing on campus. 350 workstations in library, computer center. Dormitories wired for high-speed internet access and linked to campus network. Commuter students can connect to campus network. Online course registration, online library, helpline, wireless network available.

Student life. Freshman orientation: Mandatory, $80 fee. Preregistration for classes offered. 2-day program includes transition seminars, assessment, and academic advising. Summer/winter orientations (overnight optional), includes parent orientations and welcome weekend before first day of classes. **Policies:** Freshmen permitted cars on campus. **Housing:** Guaranteed on-campus for all undergraduates. Coed dorms available. $100 nonrefundable deposit, deadline 8/1. Handicapped accessibility available in most residence halls. **Activities:** Bands, choral groups, dance, drama, literary magazine, music ensembles, musical theater, radio station, student government, student newspaper, symphony orchestra, TV station, Fellowship of Justice, Black student union, international student association, Latin American student organization, InterFratority Council, National Panhellenic Council, American Association of Airport Executives, Coffey Aviation student organization, student nurses association, Teachers of Tomorrow.

Athletics. NCAA. **Intercollegiate:** Baseball M, basketball, cheerleading, cross-country, golf, soccer, softball W, swimming, tennis, track and field, volleyball. **Intramural:** Basketball, bowling, field hockey, football (non-tackle), golf, handball, racquetball, soccer, softball, table tennis, tennis, volleyball. **Team name:** Flyers.

Student services. Adult student services, alcohol/substance abuse counseling, campus ministries, career counseling, student employment services, financial aid counseling, health services, minority student services, personal counseling, placement for graduates, veterans' counselor.

Contact. E-mail: admissions@lewisu.edu
Phone: (815) 836-5250 Toll-free number: (800) 897-9000
Fax: (815) 836-5002
Andrew Sison, Dean of Admission, Lewis University, One University Parkway, Romeoville, IL 60446-2200

Lexington College
Chicago, Illinois
www.lexingtoncollege.edu **CB code: 3843**

- Private 4-year hospitality management college for women affiliated with Roman Catholic Church
- Commuter campus in very large city
- 56 degree-seeking undergraduates
- 67% of applicants admitted
- SAT or ACT, application essay required

General. Founded in 1977. Regionally accredited. **Degrees:** 4 bachelor's, 3 associate awarded. **Location:** Downtown. **Calendar:** Semester. **Full-time faculty:** 4 total; 100% have terminal degrees, 100% minority, 100% women. **Part-time faculty:** 13 total; 100% have terminal degrees, 77% minority, 77% women. **Class size:** 100% < 20. **Special facilities:** Culinary demonstration laboratory, computer laboratory.

Freshman class profile. 60 applied, 40 admitted, 35 enrolled.

Mid 50% test scores			
ACT:	18-22	Out-of-state:	12%

Basis for selection. School achievement record, essay, and interview most important. Character and work experience considered. **Home-schooled:** Must submit GED with scores.

High school preparation. 10 units recommended. Recommended units include English 4, mathematics 2, social studies 2 and science 2.

2006-2007 Annual costs. Tuition/fees (projected): $17,000. Books/supplies: $1,500. Personal expenses: $400.

Financial aid. All financial aid based on need. **Additional information:** Work-study is available.

Application procedures. Admission: No deadline. $30 fee, may be waived for applicants with need. Admission notification on a rolling basis. **Financial aid:** Priority date 5/15; no closing date. FAFSA required. Applicants notified on a rolling basis starting 7/1; must reply within 2 week(s) of notification.

Academics. Special study options: Cooperative education, internships. **Credit/placement by examination:** AP, CLEP. **Support services:** Remedial instruction, study skills assistance, tutoring.

Majors. Business: Business admin, hotel/motel admin, restaurant/food services. **Family/consumer sciences:** Institutional food production.

Computing on campus. 30 workstations in library, computer center.

Student life. Freshman orientation: Mandatory. Preregistration for classes offered. 2-day program before classes begin. **Activities:** Student government, campus ministry.

Student services. Campus ministries, career counseling, student employment services, financial aid counseling, personal counseling, placement for graduates.

Contact. E-mail: admissions@lexingtoncollege.edu
Phone: (312) 226-6294 Fax: (312) 226-6405
Tammy Schofield, Director of Enrollment and Communication, Lexington College, 310 South Peoria Street, Suite 512, Chicago, IL 60607-3534

Lincoln Christian College and Seminary

Lincoln, Illinois
www.lccs.edu **CB code: 1405**

- Private 4-year Bible and seminary college affiliated with Christian Church
- Residential campus in large town
- 696 degree-seeking undergraduates: 12% part-time, 48% women, 3% African American, 1% Hispanic American, 1% international
- 316 degree-seeking graduate students
- 78% of applicants admitted
- SAT or ACT (ACT writing optional) required
- 47% graduate within 6 years

General. Founded in 1944. Regionally accredited; also accredited by ABHE, ATS. **Degrees:** 139 bachelor's, 26 associate awarded; master's, first professional offered. **Location:** 30 miles from Springfield. **Calendar:** Semester, limited summer session. **Full-time faculty:** 56 total; 45% have terminal degrees, 27% women. **Part-time faculty:** 22 total; 36% have terminal degrees, 14% minority, 36% women.

Freshman class profile. 269 applied, 210 admitted, 152 enrolled.

Mid 50% test scores		Rank in top tenth:	18%
ACT:	19-26	Out-of-state:	40%
Rank in top quarter:	32%	Live on campus:	90%

Basis for selection. Recommendation of applicant's church leaders as to suitability for church-related vocations very important. High school record and ACT test scores also considered. Interview recommended. Audition required of music majors. **Learning Disabled:** Students who volunteer information re: learning disabilities are usually recommended to Learning Resource Center.

High school preparation. 14 units recommended. Recommended units include English 4, mathematics 3, social studies 3, science 2 and foreign language 2.

2005-2006 Annual costs. Tuition/fees: $9,750. Room/board: $4,750. Books/supplies: $600. Personal expenses: $1,700.

Application procedures. Admission: No deadline. $20 fee, may be waived for applicants with need. Application may be submitted online. Admission notification on a rolling basis. **Financial aid:** Priority date 8/10; no closing date. FAFSA required. Applicants notified on a rolling basis starting 3/1; must reply within 2 week(s) of notification.

Academics. Special study options: Combined bachelor's/graduate degree, distance learning, double major, honors, independent study, internships, teacher certification program, weekend college. Teacher preparatory program through University of Illinois at Springfield, Illinois State University, and Greenville College. **Credit/placement by examination:** AP, CLEP, ACT. **Support services:** Learning center, reduced course load, remedial instruction, study skills assistance, tutoring, writing center.

Majors. Business: Business admin. **Education:** Secondary. **Philosophy/religion:** Religion. **Theology:** Bible, missionary, religious ed, sacred music, theology, youth ministry.

Most popular majors. Business/marketing 15%, education 10%, philosophy/religious studies 10%, theological studies 75%.

Computing on campus. 51 workstations in dormitories, library, computer center, student center. Dormitories linked to campus network. Commuter students can connect to campus network. Online library, helpline, wireless network available.

Student life. Freshman orientation: Mandatory, $60 fee. Preregistration for classes offered. **Policies:** Religious observance required. Freshmen permitted cars on campus. **Housing:** Guaranteed on-campus for freshmen. Single-sex dorms, apartments, substance-free housing available. $150 fully refundable deposit, deadline 8/1. **Activities:** Choral groups, drama, music ensembles, musical theater, student government, volunteer groups in local health care institutions, missions interest groups, Christian service and outreach groups.

Athletics. NCAA, NCCAA. **Intercollegiate:** Baseball M, basketball, cross-country, soccer, softball W, volleyball W. **Intramural:** Basketball, cheerleading, tennis, volleyball.

Student services. Adult student services, campus ministries, career counseling, student employment services, financial aid counseling, health services, personal counseling, placement for graduates. **Physically disabled:** Services for visually, hearing impaired.

Contact. E-mail: coladmis@lccs.edu
Phone: (217) 732-3168 ext. 2251 Toll-free number: (888) 522-5228
Fax: (217) 732-4199
Greg Taylor, Director of Admissions, Lincoln Christian College and Seminary, 100 Campus View Drive, Lincoln, IL 62656

Loyola University of Chicago

Chicago, Illinois **CB member**
www.luc.edu **CB code: 1412**

- Private 4-year university affiliated with Roman Catholic Church
- Residential campus in very large city
- 8,616 degree-seeking undergraduates: 7% part-time, 65% women, 6% African American, 11% Asian American, 10% Hispanic American, 2% international
- 5,324 degree-seeking graduate students
- 81% of applicants admitted
- SAT or ACT (ACT writing optional) required
- 66% graduate within 6 years

General. Founded in 1870. Regionally accredited. College in the Jesuit tradition. Extensive degree program for returning adults. Lake Shore and Water Tower campuses in Chicago, and medical center campus in suburbs. **Degrees:** 1,436 bachelor's awarded; master's, doctoral, first professional offered. **ROTC:** Army, Navy. **Calendar:** Semester, extensive summer session. **Full-time faculty:** 523 total; 9% minority, 43% women. **Part-time faculty:** 583 total; 12% minority, 54% women. **Class size:** 37% < 20, 37% 20-39, 19% 40-49, 5% 50-99, 2% >100. **Special facilities:** Gallery of medieval and renaissance art, nursing resource center, seismograph station, theater, electron microscope.

Freshman class profile. 13,163 applied, 10,722 admitted, 2,080 enrolled.

Mid 50% test scores		Rank in top tenth:	30%
SAT verbal:	540-640	Return as sophomores:	83%
SAT math:	530-640	Out-of-state:	39%
ACT:	22-27	Live on campus:	79%
GPA 3.50 or higher:	56%	International:	1%
GPA 3.0-3.49:	36%	Fraternities:	9%
GPA 2.0-2.99:	8%	Sororities:	7%
Rank in top quarter:	63%		

Basis for selection. GPA, test scores, and rigor of high school curriculum important. Interview recommended. Essay required for honors program applicants.

High school preparation. 15 units required; 20 recommended. Required and recommended units include English 4, mathematics 2-4, social studies 2-3, history 1-2, science 2-3, foreign language 2 and academic electives 1-3. Additional requirements for certain majors.

2006-2007 Annual costs. Tuition/fees (projected): $26,886. Room/board: $9,614. Books/supplies: $1,200. Personal expenses: $1,600.

2005-2006 Financial aid. Need-based: 1,807 full-time freshmen applied for aid; 1,531 were judged to have need; 1,526 of these received aid. Average need met was 80%. Average scholarship/grant was $12,434; average loan $2,739. 66% of total undergraduate aid awarded as scholarships/grants, 34% as loans/jobs. **Non-need-based:** Awarded to 959 full-time undergraduates, including 335 freshmen. Scholarships awarded for academics, athletics, leadership, music/drama.

Application procedures. Admission: Priority date 4/1; no deadline. $25 fee, may be waived for applicants with need. Application may be submitted online. Admission notification on a rolling basis beginning on or about 10/1.

Must reply by May 1 or within 2 week(s) if notified thereafter. Honors program applicants must apply by March 1. **Financial aid:** Priority date 3/1; no closing date. FAFSA required. Applicants notified on a rolling basis starting 2/15; must reply within 3 week(s) of notification.

Academics. **Special study options:** Accelerated study, combined bachelor's/graduate degree, double major, ESL, honors, independent study, internships, study abroad, teacher certification program, Washington semester. School of professional studies offers part-time evening programs leading to bachelor's degrees; cooperative programs with Erikson Institute for Early Education and St. Joseph's Seminary; study abroad in Italy and Mexico available. **Credit/placement by examination:** AP, CLEP, IB, institutional tests. **Support services:** Learning center, pre-admission summer program, reduced course load, remedial instruction, study skills assistance, tutoring, writing center.

Majors. **Biology:** General, bioinformatics. **Business:** Accounting, finance, human resources, international, management information systems, managerial economics, marketing, operations. **Communications:** General, journalism, media studies, public relations. **Computer sciences:** General, security. **Conservation:** Environmental science. **Education:** Bilingual, elementary, mathematics, secondary, special. **English:** English lit. **Foreign languages:** Ancient Greek, classics, French, German, Italian, Latin, Spanish. **Health:** Clinical nutrition, nursing (RN). **History:** General. **Interdisciplinary:** Math/computer science. **Math:** General, statistics. **Philosophy/religion:** Philosophy. **Physical sciences:** Chemistry, physics. **Protective services:** Criminal justice, forensics. **Psychology:** General. **Public administration:** Human services, social work. **Social sciences:** Anthropology, international relations, political science, sociology. **Theology:** Theology. **Visual/performing arts:** Dramatic, studio arts.

Most popular majors. Biology 11%, business/marketing 23%, health sciences 7%, psychology 12%, social sciences 10%.

Computing on campus. 451 workstations in dormitories, library, computer center, student center. Dormitories wired for high-speed internet access and linked to campus network. Commuter students can connect to campus network. Online course registration, helpline, repair service, student web hosting, wireless network available.

Student life. **Freshman orientation:** Mandatory, $245 fee. Preregistration for classes offered. 1-day orientation program at Lake Shore campus. **Policies:** Freshmen permitted cars on campus. **Housing:** Guaranteed on-campus for freshmen. Coed dorms, single-sex dorms, special housing for disabled, apartments, fraternity/sorority housing, substance-free housing available. $150 fully refundable deposit, deadline 6/1. 24-hour quiet facility available. **Activities:** Bands, choral groups, drama, literary magazine, music ensembles, radio station, student government, student newspaper, symphony orchestra, over 125 clubs and organizations.

Athletics. NCAA. **Intercollegiate:** Basketball, cross-country, golf, soccer, softball W, track and field, volleyball. **Intramural:** Badminton, baseball M, basketball, cross-country, football (non-tackle), golf, racquetball, rugby M, skiing W, soccer, softball, swimming, table tennis, tennis, volleyball. **Team name:** Ramblers.

Student services. Adult student services, alcohol/substance abuse counseling, campus ministries, career counseling, student employment services, financial aid counseling, health services, minority student services, on-campus daycare, personal counseling, placement for graduates, veterans' counselor. **Physically disabled:** Services for visually, hearing impaired.

Contact. E-mail: admission@luc.edu
Phone: (312) 915-6500 Toll-free number: (800) 262-2373
Fax: (312) 915-7216
April Hansen, Director of Admissions, Loyola University of Chicago, 820 North Michigan Avenue, Chicago, IL 60611-9810

MacMurray College

Jacksonville, Illinois — **CB member**
www.mac.edu — **CB code: 1435**

- Private 4-year liberal arts college affiliated with United Methodist Church
- Residential campus in large town
- 683 degree-seeking undergraduates: 6% part-time, 60% women, 11% African American, 3% Hispanic American, 1% Native American, 1% international
- 57% of applicants admitted
- SAT or ACT required
- 56% graduate within 6 years

General. Founded in 1846. Regionally accredited. **Degrees:** 128 bachelor's, 5 associate awarded. **Location:** 30 miles from Springfield. **Calendar:** Semester, limited summer session. **Full-time faculty:** 45 total; 62% have terminal degrees, 2% minority, 58% women. **Part-time faculty:** 31 total; 16% have terminal degrees, 64% women. **Class size:** 66% < 20, 28% 20-39, 4% 40-49, 2% 50-99.

Freshman class profile. 1,421 applied, 806 admitted, 160 enrolled.

Mid 50% test scores		Return as sophomores:	56%
SAT verbal:	430-710	Out-of-state:	21%
SAT math:	450-590	Live on campus:	46%
ACT:	20-24	Fraternities:	6%
Rank in top quarter:	10%	Sororities:	18%
Rank in top tenth:	10%		

Basis for selection. ACT composite score of 23 or higher, or class ranking in top 25%, or ACT composite of 20 and class ranking in top 50%. Applicants with ACT 20-22 and in lower 50% of high school class, or ACT composite scores of 17-19 (with no subtest score below 16) and high school grade point average of at least 2.0 reviewed by faculty admission committee. SAT results (equivalent to ACT cutoffs) also considered. Participation in school, community, and church activities, and recommendations also important. Minimum ACT score of 20 required for nursing applicants. Interview recommended for academically deficient applicants. Audition recommended for music scholarship. Portfolio recommended for art scholarship. **Homeschooled:** ACT or SAT required.

High school preparation. 13 units recommended. Recommended units include English 4, mathematics 3, social studies 2, science 2 and foreign language 2.

2006-2007 Annual costs. Tuition/fees: $15,750. Room/board: $5,928. Books/supplies: $875. Personal expenses: $650.

2005-2006 Financial aid. **Need-based:** 167 full-time freshmen applied for aid; 150 were judged to have need; 150 of these received aid. Average need met was 72%. Average scholarship/grant was $10,204; average loan $3,111. 64% of total undergraduate aid awarded as scholarships/grants, 36% as loans/jobs. **Non-need-based:** Awarded to 105 full-time undergraduates, including 32 freshmen. Scholarships awarded for academics, alumni affiliation, art, leadership, minority status, music/drama, religious affiliation. **Additional information:** Merit scholarships for accepted, enrolled freshman based on academic record. Need-based program meets 100% of direct tuition charges after family contribution and financial aid.

Application procedures. **Admission:** No deadline. No application fee. Application may be submitted online. Admission notification on a rolling basis. Decisions on a rolling basis. Admission decision issued when applicant meets requirements. Prospect must maintain eligibility status. **Financial aid:** Priority date 5/1, closing date 8/1. FAFSA required. Applicants notified on a rolling basis starting 3/1; must reply by 5/1 or within 4 week(s) of notification.

Academics. **Special study options:** Combined bachelor's/graduate degree, cross-registration, double major, dual enrollment of high school students, honors, independent study, internships, liberal arts/career combination, study abroad, teacher certification program, Washington semester. 3-2 programs in engineering with Washington University (MO) and Columbia University (NY). **Credit/placement by examination:** AP, CLEP, IB, institutional tests. 32 credit hours maximum toward bachelor's degree. **Support services:** Learning center, reduced course load, remedial instruction, study skills assistance, tutoring, writing center.

Majors. **Biology:** General. **Business:** Accounting, business admin, finance, management information systems. **Communications:** Journalism. **Computer sciences:** General, computer science. **Education:** Biology, Deaf/hearing impaired, elementary, emotionally handicapped, English, history, learning disabled, mathematics, music, physical, secondary, Spanish, special. **Engineering:** General. **Foreign languages:** French, sign language interpretation, Spanish. **Health:** Predentistry, premedicine, preveterinary. **History:** General. **Math:** General. **Parks/recreation:** Sports admin. **Philosophy/religion:** Philosophy, religion. **Physical sciences:** Chemistry, physics. **Psychology:** General. **Public administration:** Social work. **Social sciences:** International relations, political science. **Visual/performing arts:** Art, dramatic.

Computing on campus. 75 workstations in dormitories, library, computer center. Dormitories wired for high-speed internet access and linked to campus network. Online library available.

Student life. **Freshman orientation:** Mandatory. Preregistration for classes offered. 2-day acclimation to campus life prior to start of classes. **Policies:** Freshmen permitted cars on campus. **Housing:** Guaranteed on-campus for all undergraduates. Coed dorms, single-sex dorms, special housing for disabled, substance-free housing available. $150 deposit. **Activities:** Choral groups, dance, drama, literary magazine, music ensembles, student government, student newspaper, symphony orchestra, NAACP, Alpha Phi Omega, Circle-K, Holy Fools, Newman Club.

Athletics. NCAA. **Intercollegiate:** Baseball M, basketball, cross-country, football (tackle) M, golf, soccer, softball W, tennis, volleyball W, wrestling M. **Intramural:** Basketball, cheerleading, cross-country, soccer, table tennis, volleyball. **Team name:** Highlanders.

Student services. Alcohol/substance abuse counseling, campus ministries, career counseling, student employment services, financial aid counseling, health services, personal counseling, placement for graduates. **Physically disabled:** Services for visually, hearing impaired.

Contact. E-mail: admissions@mac.edu
Phone: (217) 479-7056 Toll-free number: (800) 252-7485
Fax: (217) 291-0702
Rhonda Cors, Vice President for Enrollment Management, MacMurray College, 447 East College Avenue, Jacksonville, IL 62650-2590

McKendree College

Lebanon, Illinois
www.mckendree.edu **CB code: 1456**

- Private 4-year liberal arts college affiliated with United Methodist Church
- Residential campus in small town
- 2,218 degree-seeking undergraduates: 27% part-time, 56% women, 13% African American, 1% Asian American, 2% Hispanic American, 2% international
- 288 degree-seeking graduate students
- 66% of applicants admitted
- SAT or ACT, application essay required
- 61% graduate within 6 years; 28% enter graduate study

General. Founded in 1828. Regionally accredited. **Degrees:** 513 bachelor's awarded; master's offered. **ROTC:** Army, Air Force. **Location:** 12 miles from Belleville, 23 miles from St. Louis. **Calendar:** Semester, limited summer session. **Full-time faculty:** 77 total; 83% have terminal degrees, 4% minority, 52% women. **Part-time faculty:** 130 total; 23% have terminal degrees, 9% minority, 58% women. **Class size:** 68% < 20, 32% 20-39. **Special facilities:** Completely networked faculty and classroom buildings.

Freshman class profile. 1,465 applied, 968 admitted, 274 enrolled.

Mid 50% test scores		**Rank in top tenth:**	22%
SAT verbal:	430-560	**End year in good standing:**	80%
SAT math:	480-560	**Return as sophomores:**	80%
ACT:	19-26	**Out-of-state:**	16%
GPA 3.50 or higher:	60%	**Live on campus:**	77%
GPA 3.0-3.49:	31%	**International:**	4%
GPA 2.0-2.99:	9%	**Fraternities:**	8%
Rank in top quarter:	59%	**Sororities:**	20%

Basis for selection. Holistic approach to admissions; variety of criteria considered including GPA, rigor of secondary school record, standardized test scores, and interview, when possible. Middle 50% of admitted students are between a 23-27 ACT score and 3.2-3.7 academic GPA. RN required of Nursing Completion Program applicants. Interviews recommended. Audition required of music majors and minors. Portfolio recommended for art majors. **Homeschooled:** Applicants must submit description of courses studied, 3 letters of recommendation (not including that of parents), as well as official ACT or SAT score.

High school preparation. College-preparatory program recommended. 14 units recommended. Recommended units include English 4, mathematics 3, social studies 2, history 1, science 3 and foreign language 1.

2005-2006 Annual costs. Tuition/fees: $17,800. Room/board: $7,000. Books/supplies: $1,000. Personal expenses: $600.

2005-2006 Financial aid. Need-based: 238 full-time freshmen applied for aid; 207 were judged to have need; 207 of these received aid. Average need met was 86%. Average scholarship/grant was $14,846; average loan $2,323. 70% of total undergraduate aid awarded as scholarships/grants, 30% as loans/jobs. **Non-need-based:** Scholarships awarded for academics, art, athletics, leadership, minority status, music/drama, religious affiliation.

Application procedures. Admission: No deadline. $40 fee, may be waived for applicants with need. Application may be submitted online. Admission notification on a rolling basis. **Financial aid:** Priority date 5/31; no closing date. FAFSA required. Applicants notified on a rolling basis starting 3/1; must reply within 4 week(s) of notification.

Academics. Special study options: Accelerated study, combined bachelor's/graduate degree, cooperative education, double major, external degree, honors, independent study, internships, liberal arts/career combination, semester at sea, student-designed major, study abroad, teacher certification program, Washington semester. 3-2 and 3-3 occupational therapy program with Washington University. **Credit/placement by examination:** AP, CLEP, institutional tests. 70 credit hours maximum toward associate degree, 70 toward bachelor's. **Support services:** Learning center, reduced course load, remedial instruction, study skills assistance, tutoring, writing center.

Honors college/program. 3.6 GPA or higher, 27 ACT or higher, top 10% of class; approximately 20 freshmen.

Majors. Biology: General. **Business:** Accounting, business admin, management science, marketing. **Communications:** General. **Computer sciences:** General, computer science, information systems, information technology. **Education:** General, art, business, elementary, health, history, music, physical, science. **English:** English lit, speech/rhetoric. **Health:** Athletic training, clinical lab science, nursing (RN). **History:** General. **Liberal arts:** Arts/sciences. **Math:** General. **Philosophy/religion:** Philosophy, religion. **Physical sciences:** Chemistry. **Psychology:** General. **Social sciences:** General, economics, international relations, political science, sociology. **Visual/performing arts:** Studio arts.

Most popular majors. Business/marketing 32%, computer/information sciences 8%, education 13%, health sciences 18%, psychology 8%.

Computing on campus. 450 workstations in library, computer center, student center. Dormitories wired for high-speed internet access and linked to campus network. Commuter students can connect to campus network. Online course registration, online library, helpline, repair service, student web hosting, wireless network available.

Student life. Freshman orientation: Mandatory, $50 fee. Preregistration for classes offered. 3 days, held the weekend before start of classes. **Policies:** On-campus residency requirement for first year. Freshmen permitted cars on campus. **Housing:** Guaranteed on-campus for all undergraduates. Coed dorms, single-sex dorms, special housing for disabled, apartments, substance-free housing available. $200 nonrefundable deposit. **Activities:** Bands, choral groups, dance, drama, film society, literary magazine, music ensembles, musical theater, opera, student government, student newspaper, Model United Nations, Campus Christian Fellowship, Students Against Social Injustice, Black student organization, student government association, service organizations, resident hall association, Intergreek Council, Community Service Fellows.

Athletics. NAIA. **Intercollegiate:** Baseball M, basketball, bowling, cheerleading, cross-country, football (tackle) M, golf, ice hockey, soccer, softball W, tennis, track and field, volleyball W, wrestling M. **Intramural:** Basketball, football (non-tackle), softball, volleyball. **Team name:** Bearcats.

Student services. Alcohol/substance abuse counseling, campus ministries, career counseling, student employment services, financial aid counseling, health services, minority student services, personal counseling, placement for graduates, veterans' counselor. **Physically disabled:** Services for visually, hearing impaired.

Contact. E-mail: inquiry@mckendree.edu
Phone: (618) 537-6831 Toll-free number: (800) 232-7228 ext. 6831
Fax: (618) 537-6496
Mark Campbell, Vice President for Enrollment Management, McKendree College, 701 College Road, Lebanon, IL 62254

Midstate College

Peoria, Illinois
www.midstate.edu **CB code: 3329**

- For-profit 4-year business college
- Commuter campus in small city
- 598 degree-seeking undergraduates: 59% part-time, 85% women, 21% African American, 1% Hispanic American
- Application essay, interview required

General. Founded in 1888. Regionally accredited. **Degrees:** 25 bachelor's, 71 associate awarded. **Location:** 165 miles from Chicago. **Calendar:** Quarter, extensive summer session. **Full-time faculty:** 18 total. **Part-time faculty:** 37 total.

Basis for selection. Midstate College Entrance Exam, including writing sample, and math placement tests administered to all applicants. Necessity for remedial support determined from results.

2005-2006 Annual costs. Tuition/fees: $10,203. Fees vary according to program.

Financial aid. **Additional information:** Work-study program available.

Application procedures. **Admission:** No deadline. $25 fee, may be waived for applicants with need. Admission notification on a rolling basis. **Financial aid:** No deadline. FAFSA, institutional form required. Applicants notified on a rolling basis; must reply within 4 week(s) of notification.

Academics. **Special study options:** Distance learning, double major, dual enrollment of high school students, internships. **Credit/placement by examination:** AP, CLEP, institutional tests. 24 credit hours maximum toward associate degree, 46 toward bachelor's. **Support services:** Learning center, reduced course load, remedial instruction, study skills assistance, tutoring.

Majors. **Business:** Accounting, business admin. **Computer sciences:** Information systems.

Computing on campus. 70 workstations in library, computer center. Commuter students can connect to campus network. Online course registration, online library, helpline, repair service, wireless network available.

Student life. **Freshman orientation:** Mandatory. Preregistration for classes offered. Held first day of each quarter as well as at mid-term for the miniterm. **Activities:** Student government.

Student services. Career counseling, student employment services, financial aid counseling, personal counseling, placement for graduates, veterans' counselor.

Contact. E-mail: midstate@midstate.edu
Phone: (309) 692-4092 Toll-free number: (800) 251-1299
Fax: (309) 692-3893
Jessica Hancock, Director of Admissions, Midstate College, 411 West Northmoor Road, Peoria, IL 61614-3558

Millikin University
Decatur, Illinois
www.millikin.edu **CB code: 1470**

- Private 4-year university affiliated with Presbyterian Church (USA)
- Residential campus in small city
- 2,597 degree-seeking undergraduates
- 75% of applicants admitted
- SAT or ACT (ACT writing optional) required

General. Founded in 1901. Regionally accredited. **Degrees:** 676 bachelor's awarded; master's offered. **Location:** 180 miles from Chicago, 120 miles from St. Louis. **Calendar:** Semester, limited summer session. **Full-time faculty:** 145 total. **Part-time faculty:** 137 total. **Class size:** 52% < 20, 44% 20-39, 2% 40-49, 2% 50-99. **Special facilities:** Porcelain, glass and decorative arts museum, 32-track recording studio, computer imaging center, greenhouse, observatory, 2,000 seat performance center.

Freshman class profile. 2,719 applied, 2,033 admitted, 573 enrolled.

Mid 50% test scores			
SAT verbal:	450-510	Rank in top tenth:	17%
SAT math:	450-580	Out-of-state:	15%
ACT:	20-26	Live on campus:	84%
Rank in top quarter:	45%	Fraternities:	18%
		Sororities:	17%

Basis for selection. School achievement record most important. Class rank, recommendation, test scores important. Applicant should rank in top half of class. Character references considered. Test scores not required for transfers who have completed 28 or more acceptable transfer credits. Interview recommended. Audition required of music, music/theater majors. Portfolio required of art majors.

High school preparation. 16 units recommended. Recommended units include English 4, mathematics 3, social studies 2, history 2, science 3 and foreign language 2.

2006-2007 Annual costs. Tuition/fees (projected): $22,069. Room/board: $6,773. Books/supplies: $800.

2005-2006 Financial aid. **Need-based:** 66% of total undergraduate aid awarded as scholarships/grants, 34% as loans/jobs. **Non-need-based:** Scholarships awarded for academics, art, leadership, music/drama, state residency.

Application procedures. **Admission:** No deadline. No application fee. Application may be submitted online. Admission notification on a rolling basis beginning on or about 9/15. **Financial aid:** Priority date 4/1, closing date 6/1. FAFSA required. Applicants notified on a rolling basis starting 3/1; must reply within 4 week(s) of notification.

Academics. **Special study options:** Combined bachelor's/graduate degree, double major, exchange student, honors, independent study, internships, student-designed major, study abroad, teacher certification program, United Nations semester, urban semester, Washington semester. **Credit/placement by examination:** AP, CLEP, IB, institutional tests. 24 credit hours maximum toward bachelor's degree. To receive CLEP credit student must not have attended secondary school in the past 3 years. **Support services:** Learning center, reduced course load, study skills assistance, tutoring, writing center.

Majors. **Area/ethnic studies:** American. **Biology:** General. **Business:** Accounting, business admin, finance, human resources, international, management information systems, managerial economics, marketing. **Communications:** General. **Computer sciences:** Computer science. **Education:** General, early childhood, elementary, music, physical, social science. **English:** Creative writing, English lit. **Foreign languages:** General, French, Spanish. **Health:** Art therapy, athletic training, nursing (RN), predentistry, premedicine, prepharmacy, preveterinary. **History:** General. **Legal studies:** Prelaw. **Math:** General, applied. **Parks/recreation:** Sports admin. **Philosophy/religion:** Philosophy. **Physical sciences:** Chemistry, physics. **Psychology:** General. **Public administration:** Human services. **Social sciences:** International relations, political science, sociology. **Visual/performing arts:** Arts management, commercial/advertising art, dramatic, music management, music performance, piano/organ, studio arts, theater design, voice/opera.

Computing on campus. 193 workstations in dormitories, library, computer center, student center. Dormitories wired for high-speed internet access and linked to campus network. Commuter students can connect to campus network. Helpline, student web hosting available.

Student life. **Freshman orientation:** Mandatory, $75 fee. Held 5 days before beginning of classes. **Policies:** Freshmen may petition to have a car on campus. **Housing:** Guaranteed on-campus for freshmen. Coed dorms, single-sex dorms, special housing for disabled, apartments, fraternity/sorority housing available. $150 deposit. **Activities:** Bands, choral groups, dance, drama, film society, literary magazine, music ensembles, musical theater, opera, radio station, student government, student newspaper, symphony orchestra, Hand-in-Hand, Fellowship of Christian Athletes, Alpha Phi Omega, Newman Catholic, Sister Circle, Model Illinois Government, Circle K, Christian Fellowship, Black Student Union, Latin American Student Association.

Athletics. NCAA. **Intercollegiate:** Baseball M, basketball, cross-country, football (tackle) M, golf, soccer, softball W, swimming, tennis W, track and field, volleyball W, wrestling M. **Intramural:** Basketball, bowling, softball, table tennis, volleyball. **Team name:** Big Blue.

Student services. Alcohol/substance abuse counseling, campus ministries, career counseling, student employment services, financial aid counseling, health services, minority student services, personal counseling, women's services. **Physically disabled:** Services for visually, speech impaired.

Contact. E-mail: admis@mail.millikin.edu
Phone: (217) 424-6210 Toll-free number: (800) 373-7733
Fax: (217) 425-4669
Lin Stoner, Dean of Admission, Millikin University, 1184 West Main Street, Decatur, IL 62522-2084

Monmouth College
Monmouth, Illinois **CB member**
www.monm.edu **CB code: 1484**

- Private 4-year liberal arts college affiliated with Presbyterian Church (USA)
- Residential campus in large town
- 1,336 degree-seeking undergraduates
- 79% of applicants admitted
- SAT or ACT (ACT writing optional) required

General. Founded in 1853. Regionally accredited. **Degrees:** 220 bachelor's awarded. **ROTC:** Army. **Location:** 180 miles from Chicago, 60 miles from Peoria. **Calendar:** Semester. **Full-time faculty:** 87 total. **Part-time faculty:** 46 total. **Class size:** 51% < 20, 47% 20-39, 2% 40-49, less than 1% 50-99. **Special facilities:** Ecological field station on the Mississippi River, biology field station, nature preserve, art collection.

Freshman class profile. 1,634 applied, 1,293 admitted, 368 enrolled.

Mid 50% test scores			
SAT verbal:	550-580	Rank in top tenth:	12%
SAT math:	560-580	Out-of-state:	10%
ACT:	20-26	Live on campus:	91%
Rank in top quarter:	37%	Fraternities:	18%
		Sororities:	17%

Four-Year Colleges

Basis for selection. Test scores and school achievement record most important, followed by recommendations of counselor and teacher, test scores, and interview. Interview and essay recommended.

High school preparation. 14 units required; 20 recommended. Required and recommended units include English 4, mathematics 3-4, social studies 2-3, history 1-2, science 2-4 (laboratory 1-2) and foreign language 2-3.

2006-2007 Annual costs. Tuition/fees (projected): $21,150. Room/board: $6,150. Books/supplies: $650. Personal expenses: $400.

2004-2005 Financial aid. Need-based: 77% of total undergraduate aid awarded as scholarships/grants, 23% as loans/jobs. **Non-need-based:** Scholarships awarded for academics, art, music/drama, state residency.

Application procedures. Admission: Priority date 4/1; no deadline. No application fee. Application may be submitted online. Admission notification on a rolling basis beginning on or about 9/1. **Financial aid:** Priority date 3/1; no closing date. FAFSA required. Applicants notified on a rolling basis starting 2/15; must reply by 8/1.

Academics. Special study options: Combined bachelor's/graduate degree, double major, honors, independent study, internships, liberal arts/career combination, student-designed major, study abroad, teacher certification program, urban semester, Washington semester. Off-campus programs in cooperation with Associated Colleges of the Midwest, institutional off-campus programs. **Credit/placement by examination:** AP, CLEP, IB, institutional tests. 5 credit hours maximum toward bachelor's degree. **Support services:** Learning center, tutoring, writing center.

Majors. Biology: General, biochemistry. **Business:** Accounting, business admin, international, management information systems, managerial economics. **Communications:** General, public relations. **Computer sciences:** General, computer science. **Conservation:** General, environmental science. **Education:** General, art, elementary, history, multi-level teacher, music, physical, science, secondary, social studies. **Engineering:** General. **English:** Speech/rhetoric. **Foreign languages:** Ancient Greek, classics, French, Latin, Spanish. **History:** General. **Interdisciplinary:** Biopsychology. **Legal studies:** Prelaw. **Liberal arts:** Arts/sciences. **Math:** General. **Physical sciences:** Chemistry, physics. **Psychology:** General. **Social sciences:** Economics, international relations, political science, sociology. **Visual/performing arts:** Art, studio arts.

Computing on campus. 300 workstations in dormitories, library, computer center, student center. Dormitories wired for high-speed internet access and linked to campus network. Online course registration, online library, helpline, student web hosting, wireless network available.

Student life. Freshman orientation: Mandatory, $110 fee. Preregistration for classes offered. **Policies:** Freshmen permitted cars on campus. **Housing:** Guaranteed on-campus for all undergraduates. Coed dorms, single-sex dorms, special housing for disabled, apartments, cooperative housing, fraternity/sorority housing, substance-free housing available. $150 deposit, deadline 5/1. Theme housing available. **Activities:** Bands, choral groups, dance, drama, film society, literary magazine, music ensembles, radio station, student government, student newspaper, TV station, Coalition for Ethnic Awareness, Christian fellowship groups, interdenominational religious group, College Republicans, College Democrats, Students Organized for Service.

Athletics. NCAA. **Intercollegiate:** Baseball M, basketball, cheerleading, cross-country, football (tackle) M, golf, soccer, softball W, swimming, tennis, track and field, volleyball W. **Intramural:** Archery, badminton, basketball, cross-country, golf, soccer, softball, swimming, tennis, track and field, volleyball, weight lifting. **Team name:** Fighting Scots.

Student services. Alcohol/substance abuse counseling, campus ministries, career counseling, student employment services, financial aid counseling, health services, minority student services, personal counseling, placement for graduates.

Contact. E-mail: admit@monm.edu
Phone: (309) 457-2131 Toll-free number: (800) 747-2687
Fax: (309) 457-2141
Christine Johnston, Director of New Student Enrollment, Monmouth College, 700 East Broadway, Monmouth, IL 61462-9989

Moody Bible Institute
Chicago, Illinois
www.moody.edu **CB code: 1486**

- Private 4-year Bible college affiliated with interdenominational tradition
- Residential campus in very large city
- 1,634 degree-seeking undergraduates: 7% part-time, 43% women, 4% African American, 3% Asian American, 5% Hispanic American, 5% international
- 305 degree-seeking graduate students
- SAT or ACT, application essay required
- 75% graduate within 6 years

General. Founded in 1886. Regionally accredited; also accredited by ABHE. **Degrees:** 375 bachelor's, 38 associate awarded; master's, first professional offered. **Location:** Downtown. **Calendar:** Semester, limited summer session. **Full-time faculty:** 75 total.

Freshman class profile.

Return as sophomores:	86%	**Live on campus:**	98%
Out-of-state:	81%	**International:**	6%

Basis for selection. Rank in top half of graduating class and/or high school GPA above 2.3. Applicants must have been Christians for at least 1 year. Membership in Evangelical Protestant Church and recommendation from church leadership required. Interview recommended. Audition required of music majors. **Homeschooled:** ACT plus GED or SAT.

High school preparation. 12 units recommended.

2005-2006 Annual costs. Undergraduates are not charged tuition because it is paid from external funding. Students must pay fees of $2,468 and room and board costs of $7030. Books/supplies: $600. Personal expenses: $500.

Financial aid. All financial aid based on need. **Additional information:** Aid available to upperclassmen is based on private and not federal/state sources.

Application procedures. Admission: Priority date 12/1; deadline 3/1 (postmark date). $35 fee, may be waived for applicants with need. Admission notification 4/1. Must reply by May 1 or within 6 week(s) if notified thereafter. **Financial aid:** No deadline.

Academics. Special study options: Distance learning, double major, dual enrollment of high school students, external degree, independent study, internships, study abroad, teacher certification program. Exchange program with International Christian College, Scotland; European Bible Institute, France; Belfast Bible College, Ireland; Spanish Bible Institute, Barcelona, Spain. **Credit/placement by examination:** AP, CLEP, IB, institutional tests. 9 credit hours maximum toward associate degree, 12 toward bachelor's. **Support services:** Learning center, pre-admission summer program, reduced course load, study skills assistance, tutoring.

Majors. Communications: General. **Education:** General, ESL. **Foreign languages:** Ancient Greek, Hebrew, linguistics. **Mechanic/repair:** Aircraft. **Philosophy/religion:** Judaic, religion. **Theology:** Bible, missionary, religious ed, sacred music, theology. **Visual/performing arts:** Music performance, music theory/composition, piano/organ, voice/opera.

Computing on campus. 40 workstations in library, computer center. Dormitories linked to campus network. Commuter students can connect to campus network. Repair service available.

Student life. Freshman orientation: Mandatory. **Policies:** Religious observance required. **Housing:** Guaranteed on-campus for all undergraduates. Single-sex dorms, apartments available. $100 deposit, deadline 5/1. **Activities:** Concert band, choral groups, drama, music ensembles, radio station, student government, student newspaper, symphony orchestra, Student Missionary Fellowship, Gospel Teams, Afro Awareness Fellowship, International Student Fellowship, Big Brother/Big Sister Program, pre-aviation club, married students fellowship, residence activities council, Hispanic Student Fellowship.

Athletics. NCCAA. **Intercollegiate:** Basketball, soccer M, volleyball. **Intramural:** Badminton, basketball, cross-country, football (non-tackle) M, racquetball, soccer, swimming, table tennis, volleyball, water polo. **Team name:** Archers.

Student services. Career counseling, student employment services, health services, minority student services, on-campus daycare, personal counseling, placement for graduates, veterans' counselor. **Physically disabled:** Services for visually impaired. **Learning disabled:** Comprehensive services available.

Contact. E-mail: admissions@moody.edu
Phone: (312) 329-4400 Toll-free number: (800) 967-4624
Fax: (312) 329-8987
Annette Moy, Dean of Enrollment Management, Moody Bible Institute, 820 North La Salle Boulevard, Chicago, IL 60610

National University of Health Sciences

Lombard, Illinois
www.nuhs.edu **CB code: 1567**

- Private 4-year university and health science college
- Commuter campus in large town
- 124 degree-seeking undergraduates
- 382 graduate students

General. Regionally accredited. College of Professional Studies offers doctor of chiropractic, with a doctor of naturopathy, and master's degrees in acupuncture and Oriental Medicine. Primary undergraduate enrollment is in certificate programs in massage therapy and chiropractic assistance. Accelerated prerequisite program available for students needing to complete science entrance requirements. Bachelor of science completion program. Students in first professional degree programs may earn second B.S. in biomedical science. **Degrees:** 51 bachelor's awarded; first professional offered. **Location:** 20 miles from Chicago. **Calendar:** Trimester. **Full-time faculty:** 41 total; 93% have terminal degrees, 22% women. **Part-time faculty:** 12 total; 100% have terminal degrees, 25% women. **Special facilities:** Learning resource center, medical library.

Basis for selection. College of Professional Studies and the first professional program require bachelor's degree with a GPA of 2.5; specific course requirements apply. Certificate programs require high school diploma with a cumulative GPA of 2.0 or GED. Must be 18 years of age and of good moral character.

2005-2006 Annual costs. Tuition/fees: $7,049. Room only: $3,694.

Financial aid. Additional information: Massage Therapy certificate program is eligible for Title IV financial aid. Program is half-time and qualifies for half-time and less-than-half-time Pell grants, federal work-study, FSEOG, federal Perkins grants, and prorated federal Stafford loans.

Academics. Special study options: Internships. **Credit/placement by examination:** CLEP. **Support services:** Learning center, tutoring.

Computing on campus. 75 workstations in library, computer center. Commuter students can connect to campus network. Helpline, wireless network available.

Student life. Policies: Must be 21 to live on campus. Freshmen permitted cars on campus. **Housing:** Coed dorms available. Pets allowed in dorm rooms. **Activities:** Student government, student newspaper, student chiropractic organizations, professional sororities and fraternities, christian chiropractic association.

Athletics. Intramural: Basketball, golf, soccer, softball, tennis, volleyball.

Student services. Financial aid counseling, health services.

Contact. E-mail: admissions@nuhs.edu
Phone: (630) 889-6566 Toll-free number: (800) 826-6285
Fax: (630) 889-6554
Victoria Sweeney, Director of Communications and Enrollment Services, National University of Health Sciences, 200 East Roosevelt Road, Lombard, IL 60148-4583

National-Louis University

Chicago, Illinois **CB member**
www.nl.edu **CB code: 1551**

- Private 4-year university and teachers college
- Commuter campus in small city
- 2,064 degree-seeking undergraduates: 24% part-time, 75% women, 25% African American, 2% Asian American, 7% Hispanic American
- 4,536 degree-seeking graduate students
- 95% of applicants admitted
- SAT or ACT required
- 30% graduate within 6 years

General. Founded in 1886. Regionally accredited. Illinois locations in Evanston, Wheeling, downtown Chicago, Lisle and Elgin. Field programs available on and off campus. Out-of-state campuses offering selected undergraduate and graduate programs located in Milwaukee/Beloit (WI), McLean (VA), Washington DC, and Tampa (FL). **Degrees:** 892 bachelor's awarded; master's, doctoral offered. **Location:** 10 miles from Chicago. **Calendar:** Quarter, limited summer session. **Full-time faculty:** 250 total; 10% minority, 63% women. **Part-time faculty:** 626 total; 12% minority, 67% women. **Class size:** 92% < 20, 8% 20-39, less than 1% 50-99. **Special facilities:** Elementary demonstration school for practice teaching and observation.

Freshman class profile. 60 applied, 57 admitted, 35 enrolled.

Return as sophomores:	40%	Live on campus:	3%

Basis for selection. Applicants should rank in top half of high school class, score 19 or above on ACT, 750 or above on SAT (exclusive of Writing) and submit 2 letters of recommendation from counselors or teachers. Entering students whose native language is not English assessed by Language Institute counselors. Such testing may be used in place of TOEFL for nonresident international students. Interview and essay recommended.

High school preparation. Recommended units include English 4, mathematics 3, social studies 3, science 2 (laboratory 1) and foreign language 2. One unit U.S. government or U.S. history recommended.

2006-2007 Annual costs. Tuition/fees (projected): $17,550. Books/supplies: $992. Personal expenses: $1,305.

Financial aid. Non-need-based: Scholarships awarded for academics.

Application procedures. Admission: No deadline. $40 fee, may be waived for applicants with need. Application may be submitted online. Admission notification on a rolling basis. **Financial aid:** Priority date 4/15; no closing date. FAFSA, institutional form required. Applicants notified on a rolling basis starting 5/1; must reply within 2 week(s) of notification.

Academics. Degree-completion programs available in allied health leadership, management, and applied behavioral science. Field classes offered evenings/weekends. **Special study options:** Accelerated study, combined bachelor's/graduate degree, distance learning, double major, dual enrollment of high school students, ESL, honors, independent study, internships, liberal arts/career combination, teacher certification program. **Credit/placement by examination:** AP, CLEP. 132 credit hours maximum toward bachelor's degree. **Support services:** Learning center, pre-admission summer program, reduced course load, remedial instruction, tutoring.

Majors. Biology: General. **Business:** Accounting, business admin. **Computer sciences:** Information systems. **Education:** Early childhood, elementary. **Health:** Clinical lab science, health care admin, medical radiologic technology/radiation therapy, respiratory therapy technology, substance abuse counseling. **Interdisciplinary:** Behavioral sciences, biological/physical sciences. **Liberal arts:** Arts/sciences. **Math:** General, applied. **Psychology:** General. **Public administration:** Human services. **Social sciences:** General, anthropology, economics. **Visual/performing arts:** Dramatic, studio arts.

Most popular majors. Business/marketing 49%, education 10%, health sciences 8%, interdisciplinary studies 27%.

Computing on campus. 500 workstations in library, computer center. Commuter students can connect to campus network. Online course registration, online library, helpline, repair service available.

Student life. Freshman orientation: Available. **Housing:** Coed dorms available. $50 deposit, deadline 7/30. **Activities:** Drama, musical theater, student government, student newspaper, Chinese club, Polish club, educational club, social science club, school psychology club, drama club, educational honorary society.

Student services. Adult student services, career counseling, student employment services, health services, personal counseling, placement for graduates. **Physically disabled:** Services for visually, speech, hearing impaired.

Contact. E-mail: nluinfo@wheeling1.nl.edu
Phone: (847) 475-1100 ext. 5151 Toll-free number: (800) 443-5522
Fax: (847) 256-1057
Patricia Petillo, Director of Recruitment and Admissions Response, National-Louis University, 122 South Michigan Avenue, Chicago, IL 60603

North Central College

Naperville, Illinois **CB member**
www.northcentralcollege.edu **CB code: 1555**

- Private 4-year liberal arts college affiliated with United Methodist Church
- Residential campus in small city
- 2,045 degree-seeking undergraduates: 7% part-time, 59% women, 4% African American, 3% Asian American, 5% Hispanic American, 2% international
- 297 degree-seeking graduate students
- 70% of applicants admitted

- SAT or ACT (ACT writing optional) required
- 63% graduate within 6 years

General. Founded in 1861. Regionally accredited. **Degrees:** 503 bachelor's awarded; master's offered. **ROTC:** Army, Air Force. **Location:** 25 miles from Chicago. **Calendar:** Quarter, limited summer session. **Full-time faculty:** 111 total; 86% have terminal degrees, 7% minority, 45% women. **Part-time faculty:** 92 total; 38% have terminal degrees, 8% minority, 56% women. **Class size:** 45% < 20, 54% 20-39, less than 1% 40-49, less than 1% 50-99. **Special facilities:** Accelerator laboratory, Argonne laboratory, arboretum.

Freshman class profile. 1,936 applied, 1,348 admitted, 425 enrolled.

Mid 50% test scores			
SAT verbal:	510-630	Rank in top quarter:	49%
SAT math:	510-650	Rank in top tenth:	21%
ACT:	22-27	End year in good standing:	80%
GPA 3.50 or higher:	50%	Return as sophomores:	79%
GPA 3.0-3.49:	33%	Out-of-state:	12%
GPA 2.0-2.99:	17%	Live on campus:	76%
		International:	1%

Basis for selection. Academic record, rank in top half of class, SAT or ACT scores, personal character all considered important. Interview and essay recommended for marginal students. **Learning Disabled:** Students who self-identify are referred to the academic support center.

High school preparation. College-preparatory program recommended. 17 units required; 22 recommended. Required and recommended units include English 4, mathematics 3, social studies 2, history 1, science 3 (laboratory 1-3), foreign language 3 and academic electives 3.

2005-2006 Annual costs. Tuition/fees: $21,933. Room/board: $6,993. Books/supplies: $750. Personal expenses: $1,182.

2005-2006 Financial aid. Need-based: 369 full-time freshmen applied for aid; 288 were judged to have need; 288 of these received aid. Average need met was 89%. Average scholarship/grant was $13,890; average loan $5,167. 72% of total undergraduate aid awarded as scholarships/grants, 28% as loans/jobs. **Non-need-based:** Awarded to 561 full-time undergraduates, including 145 freshmen. Scholarships awarded for academics, art, music/drama, religious affiliation. **Additional information:** Part-time students, non-degree-seeking students, and degree-seeking students primarily attending night or weekend classes may apply for special student status at discounted rate.

Application procedures. Admission: Priority date 6/1; no deadline. $25 fee, may be waived for applicants with need. Application may be submitted online. Admission notification on a rolling basis beginning on or about 10/1. Must reply by May 1 or within 4 week(s) if notified thereafter. **Financial aid:** Priority date 4/1; no closing date. FAFSA, institutional form required. Applicants notified on a rolling basis starting 3/1; must reply within 4 week(s) of notification.

Academics. Special study options: Accelerated study, combined bachelor's/graduate degree, cooperative education, cross-registration, double major, dual enrollment of high school students, ESL, exchange student, honors, independent study, internships, New York semester, student-designed major, study abroad, teacher certification program, United Nations semester, Washington semester, weekend college. Richter Fellowship Program: grants for independent study projects. 3-2 engineering program with University of Illiinois and Washington University. **Credit/placement by examination:** AP, CLEP, IB, SAT, ACT, institutional tests. 28 credit hours maximum toward bachelor's degree. **Support services:** Pre-admission summer program, reduced course load, remedial instruction, study skills assistance, tutoring, writing center.

Majors. Area/ethnic studies: East Asian. **Biology:** General, biochemistry. **Business:** General, accounting, actuarial science, finance, human resources, international, management information systems, marketing, small business admin. **Communications:** General, journalism, organizational, radio/tv. **Computer sciences:** General. **Education:** General, art, elementary, music, physical. **English:** Creative writing, English lit, speech/rhetoric. **Foreign languages:** Classics, French, German, Japanese, Spanish. **Health:** Athletic training, medical radiologic technology/radiation therapy, nuclear medical technology. **History:** General. **Interdisciplinary:** Biological/physical sciences. **Liberal arts:** Arts/sciences, humanities. **Math:** General, applied. **Parks/recreation:** Exercise sciences, health/fitness, sports admin. **Philosophy/religion:** Philosophy, religion. **Physical sciences:** Chemistry, physics. **Psychology:** General. **Social sciences:** Anthropology, economics, international relations, political science, sociology. **Visual/performing arts:** General, art, dramatic, jazz, studio arts.

Most popular majors. Business/marketing 27%, communications/journalism 10%, education 15%, psychology 8%, social sciences 10%.

Computing on campus. 325 workstations in dormitories, library, computer center, student center. Dormitories wired for high-speed internet access and linked to campus network. Commuter students can connect to campus network. Online library, helpline, student web hosting, wireless network available.

Student life. Freshman orientation: Available, $125 fee. Students meet with faculty advisor in small groups and one-on-one settings to explore possible course choices. **Policies:** Freshmen permitted cars on campus. **Housing:** Coed dorms, single-sex dorms, special housing for disabled, substance-free housing available. $100 fully refundable deposit. Substance-free housing, learning communities. **Activities:** Bands, choral groups, drama, literary magazine, music ensembles, musical theater, radio station, student government, student newspaper, United Methodist student organization, Black student organization, La Familia, Fellowship of Christian Athletes, Raza Unida, Cardinals in Action, NCC Green, commuter student organization, Model United Nations, students in free enterprise.

Athletics. NCAA. **Intercollegiate:** Baseball M, basketball, cross-country, football (tackle) M, golf, soccer, softball W, swimming, tennis, track and field, volleyball W, wrestling M. **Intramural:** Basketball, bowling, cheerleading, football (tackle) M, golf, softball, table tennis, volleyball. **Team name:** Cardinals.

Student services. Adult student services, campus ministries, career counseling, student employment services, financial aid counseling, health services, minority student services, personal counseling, placement for graduates. **Physically disabled:** Services for visually, hearing impaired.

Contact. E-mail: admissions@noctrl.edu
Phone: (630) 637-5800 Toll-free number: (800) 411-1861
Fax: (630) 637-5819
Marty Sauer, Dean of Admissions and Financial Aid, North Central College, Office of Admissions, Naperville, IL 60566-7063

North Park University

Chicago, Illinois — **CB member**
www.northpark.edu — **CB code: 1556**

- Private 4-year university and liberal arts college affiliated with Evangelical Covenant Church of America
- Residential campus in very large city
- 1,850 degree-seeking undergraduates: 16% part-time, 64% women, 11% African American, 7% Asian American, 10% Hispanic American, 1% Native American, 3% international
- 653 degree-seeking graduate students
- 69% of applicants admitted
- SAT or ACT (ACT writing recommended), application essay required
- 54% graduate within 6 years

General. Founded in 1891. Regionally accredited. **Degrees:** 355 bachelor's awarded; master's, doctoral, first professional offered. **Location:** 6 miles from downtown Chicago. **Calendar:** Semester, limited summer session. **Full-time faculty:** 122 total; 81% have terminal degrees, 17% minority, 55% women. **Part-time faculty:** 217 total; 16% minority, 46% women. **Class size:** 58% < 20, 37% 20-39, 4% 40-49, less than 1% 50-99, less than 1% >100.

Freshman class profile. 1,386 applied, 954 admitted, 359 enrolled.

Mid 50% test scores			
SAT verbal:	510-630	Rank in top quarter:	42%
SAT math:	490-640	Rank in top tenth:	16%
ACT:	19-26	Return as sophomores:	76%
GPA 3.50 or higher:	36%	Out-of-state:	46%
GPA 3.0-3.49:	29%	Live on campus:	73%
GPA 2.0-2.99:	33%	International:	5%

Basis for selection. Admission based on achievement record, class rank, test scores, school, recommendations, and community involvement. No statement of faith or religious belief required. Interview required for some applicants. All students who visit campus are interviewed. **Homeschooled:** Transcript of courses and grades, letter of recommendation (nonparent) required. **Learning Disabled:** Students should contact office of academic advising.

High school preparation. Recommended units include English 4, mathematics 3, social studies 1, history 1, science 3 and foreign language 2.

2006-2007 Annual costs. Tuition/fees: $14,900. Room/board: $7,110. Books/supplies: $950. Personal expenses: $1,350.

2004-2005 Financial aid. Need-based: 299 full-time freshmen applied for aid; 254 were judged to have need; 254 of these received aid. Average

need met was 73%. Average scholarship/grant was $4,600; average loan $2,720. 63% of total undergraduate aid awarded as scholarships/grants, 37% as loans/jobs. **Non-need-based:** Scholarships awarded for academics, art, music/drama, religious affiliation.

Application procedures. Admission: Priority date 4/1; deadline 7/1 (receipt date). $40 fee, may be waived for applicants with need. Application may be submitted online. Admission notification on a rolling basis beginning on or about 9/15. Must reply by May 1 or within 4 week(s) if notified thereafter. **Financial aid:** Priority date 5/1, closing date 8/1. FAFSA required. Applicants notified on a rolling basis starting 3/10; must reply by 5/1 or within 3 week(s) of notification.

Academics. Intensive summer ESL program. **Special study options:** Accelerated study, combined bachelor's/graduate degree, distance learning, double major, ESL, exchange student, honors, independent study, internships, liberal arts/career combination, student-designed major, study abroad, teacher certification program, Washington semester. **Credit/placement by examination:** AP, CLEP, IB, SAT, ACT, institutional tests. 60 credit hours maximum toward bachelor's degree. **Support services:** Learning center, pre-admission summer program, reduced course load, remedial instruction, study skills assistance, tutoring, writing center.

Majors. Biology: General. **Business:** General, accounting, business admin, finance, international, marketing, organizational behavior. **Communications:** General, advertising. **Computer sciences:** General. **Education:** Early childhood, elementary, middle, multi-level teacher. **Foreign languages:** French, Scandinavian, Spanish. **Health:** Clinical lab science, nursing (RN), predentistry, premedicine, prepharmacy, preveterinary. **History:** General. **Liberal arts:** Arts/sciences. **Math:** General, applied. **Philosophy/religion:** Christian, philosophy, religion. **Physical sciences:** Chemistry, physics. **Psychology:** General. **Social sciences:** General, anthropology, economics, international relations, political science, sociology, urban studies. **Theology:** Bible, youth ministry. **Visual/performing arts:** Art, art history/conservation, commercial/advertising art, dramatic, music history, music performance, piano/organ, studio arts.

Computing on campus. 100 workstations in dormitories, library, computer center, student center. Dormitories wired for high-speed internet access and linked to campus network. Commuter students can connect to campus network. Online course registration, helpline, wireless network available.

Student life. Freshman orientation: Mandatory. Preregistration for classes offered. Begins 5 days before the start of classes. **Housing:** Guaranteed on-campus for freshmen. Single-sex dorms, apartments, substance-free housing available. $250 deposit. **Activities:** Bands, choral groups, drama, literary magazine, music ensembles, musical theater, opera, student government, student newspaper, symphony orchestra, Gospel teams, Black student association, Latino student association, Korean student association, campus ministries, Outreach Ministries, Catholic association, Middle Eastern student association.

Athletics. NCAA. **Intercollegiate:** Baseball M, basketball, cross-country, football (tackle) M, golf, rowing (crew) W, soccer, softball W, track and field, volleyball W. **Intramural:** Basketball, cheerleading W, football (non-tackle), soccer, tennis, volleyball. **Team name:** Vikings.

Student services. Adult student services, alcohol/substance abuse counseling, campus ministries, career counseling, services for economically disadvantaged, student employment services, financial aid counseling, health services, minority student services, personal counseling, placement for graduates.

Contact. E-mail: admission@northpark.edu
Phone: (773) 244-5500 Toll-free number: (800) 888-6728
Fax: (773) 244-5243
Shari Clemens, Director, Undergraduate Admission, North Park University, 3225 West Foster Avenue, Chicago, IL 60625-4895

Northeastern Illinois University

Chicago, Illinois — **CB member**
www.neiu.edu — **CB code: 1090**

- Public 4-year university
- Commuter campus in very large city
- 9,166 degree-seeking undergraduates: 44% part-time, 62% women, 12% African American, 11% Asian American, 29% Hispanic American, 2% international
- 2,241 degree-seeking graduate students
- 75% of applicants admitted
- SAT or ACT (ACT writing optional) required

General. Founded in 1961. Regionally accredited. 2 extension centers serving Hispanic and African-American communities. **Degrees:** 1,247 bachelor's awarded; master's offered. **ROTC:** Army, Air Force. **Calendar:** Semester, limited summer session. **Full-time faculty:** 415 total; 72% have terminal degrees, 25% minority, 47% women. **Part-time faculty:** 265 total; 24% have terminal degrees, 28% minority, 49% women. **Class size:** 45% < 20, 48% 20-39, 4% 40-49, 3% 50-99, less than 1% >100.

Freshman class profile. 3,071 applied, 2,298 admitted, 1,058 enrolled.

Mid 50% test scores		**Rank in top quarter:**	16%
ACT:	16-21	**Rank in top tenth:**	7%
GPA 3.50 or higher:	14%	**Return as sophomores:**	69%
GPA 3.0-3.49:	21%	**Out-of-state:**	1%
GPA 2.0-2.99:	45%		

Basis for selection. Rank in top half of graduating class or minimum enhanced 19 ACT or equivalent SAT required. Audition recommended for dance and music majors. Portfolio recommended for art majors.

High school preparation. 15 units required. Required units include English 4, mathematics 3, social studies 3 and science 3. 2 additional units in fine arts, music, art, foreign languages, or vocational education. (Only 1 vocational education course accepted.).

2005-2006 Annual costs. Tuition/fees: $5,646; $10,446 out-of-state. Books/supplies: $1,152. Personal expenses: $2,628.

2005-2006 Financial aid. Need-based: 704 full-time freshmen applied for aid; 495 were judged to have need; 488 of these received aid. Average need met was 62%. Average scholarship/grant was $5,674; average loan $2,447. 70% of total undergraduate aid awarded as scholarships/grants, 30% as loans/jobs. **Non-need-based:** Awarded to 348 full-time undergraduates, including 56 freshmen. Scholarships awarded for academics, art, leadership, music/drama.

Application procedures. Admission: Closing date 7/1 (receipt date). $25 fee, may be waived for applicants with need. Application may be submitted online. Admission notification on a rolling basis beginning on or about 9/1. **Financial aid:** Priority date 3/1; no closing date. FAFSA, institutional form required. Applicants notified on a rolling basis starting 4/1; must reply within 3 week(s) of notification.

Academics. Special study options: Cooperative education, distance learning, double major, dual enrollment of high school students, exchange student, honors, independent study, student-designed major, study abroad, teacher certification program. Board of Governors degree program, University Without Walls. **Credit/placement by examination:** AP, CLEP, IB, ACT, institutional tests. 30 credit hours maximum toward bachelor's degree. **Support services:** Learning center, pre-admission summer program, remedial instruction, study skills assistance, tutoring, writing center.

Majors. Area/ethnic studies: Women's. **Biology:** General. **Business:** General, accounting, business admin, finance, marketing. **Computer sciences:** Computer science. **Conservation:** Environmental studies. **Education:** Bilingual, early childhood, elementary, physical, special. **English:** English lit, speech/rhetoric. **Foreign languages:** French, linguistics, Spanish. **Health:** Community health services. **History:** General. **Liberal arts:** Arts/sciences. **Math:** General. **Philosophy/religion:** Philosophy. **Physical sciences:** Chemistry, geology, physics. **Protective services:** Criminal justice. **Psychology:** General. **Public administration:** Social work. **Social sciences:** General, anthropology, economics, geography, political science, sociology. **Visual/performing arts:** Art.

Most popular majors. Business/marketing 14%, computer/information sciences 7%, education 17%, English 7%, liberal arts 16%, social sciences 9%.

Computing on campus. 315 workstations in library, computer center, student center. Commuter students can connect to campus network. Online course registration, helpline available.

Student life. Freshman orientation: Available. **Policies:** Freshmen permitted cars on campus. **Activities:** Bands, choral groups, dance, drama, literary magazine, music ensembles, musical theater, opera, radio station, student government, student newspaper, symphony orchestra, Muslim Student Association, Black heritage club, politics club, Chimexla Student Union, Indian student association, University bible association, Northeastern program board, Union of Puerto Rican Students, Hillel, outdoor adventure club.

Athletics. Intramural: Badminton, basketball, cross-country, racquetball, soccer, softball, table tennis, tennis, volleyball, weight lifting. **Team name:** Eagles.

Student services. Adult student services, career counseling, student employment services, financial aid counseling, health services, minority student services, on-campus daycare, personal counseling, placement for graduates, veterans' counselor, women's services. **Physically disabled:** Services for visually, speech impaired.

Contact. E-mail: admerc@neiu.edu
Phone: (773) 442-4000 Fax: (773) 442-4020
Janice Harring Hendon, Director of Admissions and Records, Northeastern Illinois University, 5500 North St. Louis Avenue, Chicago, IL 60625

Northern Illinois University

DeKalb, Illinois — **CB member**
www.niu.edu — **CB code: 1559**

- Public 4-year university
- Residential campus in large town
- 18,459 degree-seeking undergraduates: 10% part-time, 52% women, 12% African American, 5% Asian American, 7% Hispanic American, 1% international
- 5,454 degree-seeking graduate students
- 66% of applicants admitted
- SAT or ACT required
- 51% graduate within 6 years

General. Founded in 1895. Regionally accredited. Classes also held at Loredo Taft Field campus in Oregon. **Degrees:** 3,626 bachelor's awarded; master's, doctoral, first professional offered. **ROTC:** Army. **Location:** 65 miles from Chicago. **Calendar:** Semester, extensive summer session. **Full-time faculty:** 894 total; 83% have terminal degrees, 14% minority, 43% women. **Part-time faculty:** 299 total; 38% have terminal degrees, 5% minority, 54% women. **Class size:** 39% < 20, 44% 20-39, 5% 40-49, 9% 50-99, 3% >100.

Freshman class profile. 15,007 applied, 9,917 admitted, 3,179 enrolled.

Mid 50% test scores		**End year in good standing:**	95%
ACT:	19-24	**Return as sophomores:**	79%
Rank in top quarter:	31%	**Out-of-state:**	3%
Rank in top tenth:	9%	**Live on campus:**	92%

Basis for selection. Minimum ACT composite score of 19 required of applicants who rank in top half of class, 23 required of applicants in top two-thirds of class or with high school equivalency certificate. Interview required of CHANCE program applicants. Audition required of music majors. Portfolio recommended for art majors.

High school preparation. 15 units required. Required and recommended units include English 4, mathematics 2-4, social studies 2-3, history 1, science 2-4 (laboratory 1-2) and foreign language 1-2. One unit of art, film, music, theater, or foreign language required. Mathematics must include algebra and/or geometry. Social sciences must include US history or a combination of US history and government.

2005-2006 Annual costs. Tuition/fees: $6,638; $11,699 out-of-state. Room/board: $6,924. Books/supplies: $700. Personal expenses: $1,584.

Financial aid. Non-need-based: Scholarships awarded for academics, athletics, ROTC.

Application procedures. Admission: Priority date 3/1; deadline 8/1. No application fee. Application may be submitted online. Admission notification on a rolling basis. **Financial aid:** Priority date 3/1; no closing date. FAFSA, institutional form required. Applicants notified on a rolling basis starting 4/15.

Academics. Special study options: Cooperative education, distance learning, double major, dual enrollment of high school students, honors, independent study, internships, student-designed major, study abroad, teacher certification program. **Credit/placement by examination:** AP, CLEP, institutional tests. Credit by examination not awarded for courses that are prerequisites for courses for which the student already has credit or is currently enrolled. **Support services:** Tutoring.

Majors. Biology: General. **Business:** General, accounting, finance, marketing, operations. **Communications:** General, journalism. **Computer sciences:** General, computer science. **Education:** General, art, elementary, family/consumer sciences, health, physical, special. **Engineering:** Electrical, industrial, mechanical. **Engineering technology:** Industrial. **English:** English lit. **Family/consumer sciences:** Clothing/textiles, family studies, food/nutrition. **Foreign languages:** French, German, Russian, Spanish. **Health:** Clinical lab science, communication disorders, nursing (RN), public health nursing. **History:** General. **Liberal arts:** Arts/sciences. **Math:** General, applied, computational, probability. **Philosophy/religion:** Philosophy. **Physical sciences:** Atmospheric science, chemistry, geology, physics. **Psychology:** General. **Social sciences:** Anthropology, economics, geography, political science, sociology. **Visual/performing arts:** Art, art history/conservation, dramatic, studio arts.

Most popular majors. Business/marketing 22%, communications/journalism 8%, education 14%, engineering/engineering technologies 6%, health sciences 8%, social sciences 10%, visual/performing arts 6%.

Computing on campus. 550 workstations in dormitories, library, computer center, student center. Commuter students can connect to campus network. Helpline available.

Student life. Freshman orientation: Mandatory, $60 fee. **Housing:** Guaranteed on-campus for freshmen. Coed dorms, special housing for disabled, apartments, fraternity/sorority housing available. $150 deposit. Quiet and alcohol-free lifestyle floors, 21 and over/graduates student floors, honors floors available. **Activities:** Bands, choral groups, dance, drama, film society, opera, radio station, student government, student newspaper, symphony orchestra, TV station, numerous religious, political, ethnic, social service organizations.

Athletics. NCAA. **Intercollegiate:** Baseball M, basketball, cross-country W, football (tackle) M, golf, gymnastics W, soccer, softball W, swimming, tennis, track and field W, volleyball W, wrestling M. **Intramural:** Badminton, baseball M, basketball, football (tackle) M, golf, ice hockey M, racquetball, sailing, soccer, softball, table tennis, tennis, volleyball, wrestling M. **Team name:** Huskies.

Student services. Campus ministries, career counseling, student employment services, health services, legal services, minority student services, on-campus daycare, personal counseling, placement for graduates, veterans' counselor, women's services. **Physically disabled:** Services for visually, speech, hearing impaired.

Contact. E-mail: admission-info@niu.edu
Phone: (815) 753-0446 Toll-free number: (800) 892-3050
Fax: (815) 753-8312
Robert Burk, Director of Admissions, Northern Illinois University, DeKalb, IL 60115-2854

Northwestern University

Evanston, Illinois — **CB member**
www.northwestern.edu — **CB code: 1565**

- Private 4-year university
- Residential campus in small city
- 7,902 degree-seeking undergraduates: 1% part-time, 53% women, 5% African American, 17% Asian American, 6% Hispanic American, 5% international
- 8,848 degree-seeking graduate students
- 30% of applicants admitted
- SAT or ACT with writing, application essay required
- 92% graduate within 6 years; 13% enter graduate study

General. Founded in 1851. Regionally accredited. **Degrees:** 2,083 bachelor's awarded; master's, doctoral, first professional offered. **ROTC:** Army, Navy, Air Force. **Location:** 12 miles from downtown Chicago. **Calendar:** Quarter, limited summer session. **Full-time faculty:** 938 total; 100% have terminal degrees, 15% minority, 27% women. **Part-time faculty:** 207 total; 100% have terminal degrees, 7% minority, 46% women. **Class size:** 72% < 20, 16% 20-39, 3% 40-49, 5% 50-99, 4% >100. **Special facilities:** Fine-arts complex, dance center, art museum, observatory, engineering design center, tennis center.

Freshman class profile. 16,221 applied, 4,819 admitted, 1,952 enrolled.

Mid 50% test scores		**Return as sophomores:**	97%
SAT verbal:	650-740	**Out-of-state:**	75%
SAT math:	670-760	**Live on campus:**	99%
ACT:	29-33	**International:**	5%
Rank in top quarter:	96%	**Fraternities:**	25%
Rank in top tenth:	82%	**Sororities:**	34%

Basis for selection. Academic record, essays, test scores, activity record, school recommendations important. SAT Subject Tests recommended. SAT Subject Tests in Math Level 2 and Chemistry required of all applicants for honors program in medical education. Applicants to integrated science program must take SAT Subject Tests in Chemistry or Physics, Math Level 2, plus second science. Audition required for music majors. **Homeschooled:** 3 SAT Subject Tests required. Math Level 1 or 2 for students who plan to study sciences or engineering, Math Level 2 preferable, plus two other SAT Subject Tests of applicant's choice from different subject areas are required.

High school preparation. College-preparatory program recommended. 16 units recommended. Recommended units include English 4, mathematics 3, social studies 2, science 2 (laboratory 2), foreign language 2 and academic electives 1. 4 units of mathematics recommended for engineering applicants. Applicants typically have 20 academic high school units.

2006-2007 Annual costs. Tuition/fees: $33,559. Room/board: $10,266. Books/supplies: $1,488. Personal expenses: $1,698.

2005-2006 Financial aid. All financial aid based on need. 1,065 full-time freshmen applied for aid; 903 were judged to have need; 903 of these received aid. Average need met was 100%. Average scholarship/grant was $21,691; average loan $3,284. 78% of total undergraduate aid awarded as scholarships/grants, 22% as loans/jobs.

Application procedures. Admission: Closing date 1/1 (postmark date). $65 fee, may be waived for applicants with need. Application may be submitted online. Admission notification 4/15. Must reply by May 1 or within 2 week(s) if notified thereafter. **Financial aid:** Closing date 2/1. FAFSA, CSS PROFILE required. Applicants notified by 4/15; must reply by 5/1 or within 2 week(s) of notification.

Academics. University awards 1 unit of credit for each course; 45-48 units required for graduation. **Special study options:** Accelerated study, combined bachelor's/graduate degree, cooperative education, double major, honors, independent study, internships, liberal arts/career combination, student-designed major, study abroad, teacher certification program. 3-year integrated science program; 4-year mathematical methods in social sciences bachelor's program; honors programs in undergraduate research engineering, engineering and management, medical education; 7-year BA/MD program resulting in both an undergraduate degree and MD. **Credit/placement by examination:** AP, CLEP, IB, institutional tests. **Support services:** Study skills assistance, tutoring, writing center.

Majors. Area/ethnic studies: African-American, American, Asian, European, women's. **Biology:** General, ecology. **Business:** Organizational behavior. **Communications:** General, broadcast journalism, journalism, radio/tv. **Computer sciences:** General, computer science, information systems. **Conservation:** Environmental science, environmental studies. **Education:** General, foundations, learning disabled, mathematics, music, secondary. **Engineering:** General, biomedical, chemical, civil, computer, electrical, environmental, industrial, manufacturing, materials, materials science, mechanical, science. **English:** Creative writing, English lit. **Foreign languages:** Classics, comparative lit, French, German, Italian, linguistics, Slavic, Spanish. **Health:** Communication disorders, premedicine. **History:** General. **Interdisciplinary:** Biological/physical sciences, neuroscience, science/society. **Legal studies:** General. **Liberal arts:** Arts/sciences. **Math:** General, applied, statistics. **Philosophy/religion:** Philosophy, religion. **Physical sciences:** Chemistry, geology, physics. **Psychology:** General. **Public administration:** Community org/advocacy, policy analysis. **Social sciences:** Anthropology, economics, geography, international relations, political science, sociology, urban studies. **Visual/performing arts:** General, art, art history/conservation, dance, dramatic, jazz, music performance, music theory/composition, musicology, piano/organ, stringed instruments, theater history, voice/opera.

Most popular majors. Communications/journalism 19%, engineering/engineering technologies 14%, psychology 10%, social sciences 17%, visual/performing arts 10%.

Computing on campus. 678 workstations in dormitories, library, computer center, student center. Dormitories wired for high-speed internet access and linked to campus network. Commuter students can connect to campus network. Online course registration, helpline, repair service, student web hosting, wireless network available.

Student life. Freshman orientation: Mandatory. Held for 5 days prior to start of classes. **Housing:** Guaranteed on-campus for freshmen. Coed dorms, single-sex dorms, fraternity/sorority housing available. $200 nonrefundable deposit, deadline 5/25. Residential colleges devoted to particular themes and two nonthematic residential colleges available. **Activities:** Bands, choral groups, dance, drama, film society, literary magazine, music ensembles, musical theater, opera, radio station, student government, student newspaper, symphony orchestra, TV station, over 300 organizations.

Athletics. NCAA. **Intercollegiate:** Baseball M, basketball, cheerleading, cross-country W, diving, fencing W, field hockey W, football (tackle) M, golf, lacrosse W, soccer, softball W, swimming, tennis, volleyball W, wrestling M. **Intramural:** Basketball, football (non-tackle), ice hockey, racquetball, soccer, softball, table tennis, tennis, volleyball. **Team name:** Wildcats.

Student services. Adult student services, alcohol/substance abuse counseling, campus ministries, career counseling, student employment services, financial aid counseling, health services, minority student services, personal counseling, placement for graduates, women's services. **Physically disabled:** Services for visually, speech, hearing impaired.

Contact. E-mail: ug-admission@northwestern.edu
Phone: (847) 491-7271
Carol Lunkenheimer, Dean of Undergraduate Admissions, Northwestern University, 1801 Hinman Avenue, Evanston, IL 60204-3060

Olivet Nazarene University

Bourbonnais, Illinois — **CB member**
www.olivet.edu — **CB code: 1596**

- Private 4-year university and liberal arts college affiliated with Church of the Nazarene
- Residential campus in small city
- 2,897 degree-seeking undergraduates
- 78% of applicants admitted
- ACT (writing optional) required

General. Founded in 1907. Regionally accredited. Evangelical liberal arts institution emphasizing Christian values. **Degrees:** 455 bachelor's, 39 associate awarded; master's offered. **ROTC:** Army. **Location:** 60 miles from Chicago. **Calendar:** Semester, extensive summer session. **Full-time faculty:** 106 total. **Part-time faculty:** 193 total. **Special facilities:** Planetarium, observatory, science museum, distance learning classroom.

Freshman class profile. 2,063 applied, 1,601 admitted, 671 enrolled.

Mid 50% test scores		Out-of-state:	52%
ACT:	19-26	Live on campus:	90%

Basis for selection. Minimum 2.0 GPA in college-preparatory subjects, ranking in top three-quarters of class, ACT of 18, 2 recommendations required. Interview recommended. Audition required of music majors. Art portfolios required for art scholarship applicants. **Homeschooled:** ACT required.

High school preparation. 15 units required. Required and recommended units include English 4, mathematics 3, social studies 4, history 2, science 3 and foreign language 2.

2006-2007 Annual costs. Tuition/fees: $17,590. Room/board: $6,800. Books/supplies: $800. Personal expenses: $400.

2004-2005 Financial aid. Need-based: 42% of total undergraduate aid awarded as scholarships/grants, 58% as loans/jobs. **Non-need-based:** Scholarships awarded for academics, art, athletics, leadership, music/drama, religious affiliation, ROTC, state residency.

Application procedures. Admission: Closing date 5/15 (postmark date). No application fee. Application may be submitted online. Admission notification on a rolling basis. **Financial aid:** Priority date 3/1; no closing date. FAFSA, institutional form required. Applicants notified on a rolling basis starting 1/15; must reply within 2 week(s) of notification.

Academics. Special study options: Accelerated study, distance learning, double major, independent study, internships, liberal arts/career combination, student-designed major, study abroad, teacher certification program, Washington semester. Council of Christian Colleges and Universities study programs, adult studies degree program. **Credit/placement by examination:** AP, CLEP, IB, institutional tests. **Support services:** Learning center, pre-admission summer program, reduced course load, remedial instruction, tutoring.

Majors. Biology: General, zoology. **Business:** General, accounting, business admin, fashion, finance, international, marketing. **Communications:** General, broadcast journalism, journalism. **Computer sciences:** General, computer science, information systems, programming. **Conservation:** Environmental studies. **Education:** Art, biology, chemistry, early childhood, elementary, English, family/consumer sciences, foreign languages, health, history, mathematics, music, physical, science, secondary, social science, social studies, Spanish. **Engineering:** General. **Family/consumer sciences:** General, family/community services, housing. **Foreign languages:** General, Spanish. **Health:** Athletic training. **History:** General. **Interdisciplinary:** Biological/physical sciences. **Liberal arts:** Arts/sciences. **Math:** General. **Parks/recreation:** Exercise sciences, sports admin. **Philosophy/religion:** Religion. **Physical sciences:** Chemistry, geology. **Protective services:** Criminal justice. **Psychology:** General. **Public administration:** Policy analysis, social work. **Social sciences:** General, economics, political science, sociology. **Theology:** Bible, religious ed, sacred music, theology. **Visual/performing arts:** Art, music performance, piano/organ, voice/opera.

Computing on campus. 125 workstations in library, computer center, student center. Dormitories wired for high-speed internet access and linked to campus network. Commuter students can connect to campus network. Online library, helpline, repair service, student web hosting, wireless network available.

Student life. Freshman orientation: Mandatory. Preregistration for classes offered. 3-day program held on second and third weekends in June. Comprehensive for students and parents. **Policies:** Chapel convocations held twice weekly. Religious observance required. Freshmen permitted cars on campus. **Housing:** Guaranteed on-campus for all undergraduates. Single-sex dorms, special housing for disabled, apartments available. $30 deposit, deadline 8/1. Pets allowed in dorm rooms. **Activities:** Bands, choral groups, drama, literary magazine, music ensembles, musical theater, radio station, student government, student newspaper, symphony orchestra, social service clubs, spiritual life groups.

Athletics. NAIA, NCCAA. **Intercollegiate:** Baseball M, basketball, cheerleading, cross-country, football (tackle) M, golf M, soccer, softball W, tennis, track and field, volleyball W. **Intramural:** Badminton, basketball, bowling, cross-country, football (non-tackle) W, golf, handball, racquetball, soccer, softball, table tennis, tennis, track and field, volleyball. **Team name:** Tigers.

Student services. Adult student services, alcohol/substance abuse counseling, campus ministries, career counseling, services for economically disadvantaged, student employment services, financial aid counseling, health services, personal counseling, placement for graduates, veterans' counselor.

Contact. E-mail: admissions@olivet.edu
Phone: (815) 939-5203 Toll-free number: (800) 648-1463
Fax: (815) 939-5069
Brian Parker, Director of Admissions, Olivet Nazarene University, One University Avenue, Bourbonnais, IL 60914

Principia College

Elsah, Illinois — **CB member**
www.prin.edu — **CB code: 1630**

- Private 4-year liberal arts college affiliated with Christian Science (unaffiliated with Christian Science Church)
- Residential campus in rural community
- 542 degree-seeking undergraduates: 1% part-time, 52% women, 1% African American, 1% Asian American, 1% Hispanic American, 13% international
- 89% of applicants admitted
- SAT or ACT with writing, application essay required
- 87% graduate within 6 years; 29% enter graduate study

General. Founded in 1910. Regionally accredited. Principia College is the only school of higher education in the world which serves students who are Christian Scientists. All faculty, staff, and students are Christian Scientists. **Degrees:** 118 bachelor's awarded. **Location:** 35 miles from St. Louis. **Calendar:** Quarter. **Full-time faculty:** 55 total; 46% have terminal degrees, 2% minority, 42% women. **Part-time faculty:** 11 total; 36% have terminal degrees, 27% women. **Class size:** 94% < 20, 6% 20-39. **Special facilities:** School of Nations museum, observatory, fully equipped media center, tropical aviary, 39 bronze bell carillon, language lab, campus designated as National Historic Landmark.

Freshman class profile. 242 applied, 216 admitted, 139 enrolled.

Mid 50% test scores			
SAT verbal:	530-660	Rank in top quarter:	63%
SAT math:	520-650	Rank in top tenth:	38%
ACT:	21-29	End year in good standing:	93%
GPA 3.50 or higher:	51%	Return as sophomores:	78%
GPA 3.0-3.49:	17%	Out-of-state:	90%
GPA 2.0-2.99:	31%	Live on campus:	100%
		International:	11%

Basis for selection. School achievement record and essay or personal statement most important. Applicant must be practicing Christian Scientist. Test scores important. Foreign language SAT Subject Test required for placement purposes. Interview recommended. Portfolio recommended for art majors. **Homeschooled:** Must submit curricula program from accredited high school or accepted agency, plus GED and SAT or ACT test scores.

High school preparation. 16 units required; 20 recommended. Required and recommended units include English 4, mathematics 3, social studies 2, history 1-2, science 2-3 (laboratory 2), foreign language 2-3 and academic electives 2.

2006-2007 Annual costs. Tuition/fees: $21,450. Room/board: $7,896. Books/supplies: $900. Personal expenses: $750.

2005-2006 Financial aid. **Need-based:** 93 full-time freshmen applied for aid; 89 were judged to have need; 89 of these received aid. Average need met was 95%. Average scholarship/grant was $13,410; average loan $4,111. 81% of total undergraduate aid awarded as scholarships/grants, 19% as loans/jobs. **Non-need-based:** Awarded to 254 full-time undergraduates, including 77 freshmen. Scholarships awarded for academics, alumni affiliation. **Additional information:** Need-based tuition reduction work plan combines job with grant.

Application procedures. **Admission:** Priority date 11/15; deadline 3/1 (postmark date). No application fee. Application may be submitted online. Admission notification on a rolling basis beginning on or about 10/15. Must reply by May 1 or within 2 week(s) if notified thereafter. Admissions, scholarship, and financial aid decisions will be given by December 1 to those who complete all three applications by November 15th. **Financial aid:** Closing date 3/1. Institutional form, CSS PROFILE required. Applicants notified by 4/1.

Academics. First year experience and pre-fall writing program for all students. Emphasis on character education, interdisciplinary curriculum, and individual skill development. Principia abroad and internship programs available. **Special study options:** Double major, independent study, internships, liberal arts/career combination, student-designed major, study abroad, teacher certification program. 3-2 engineering with Washington University, University of Southern California, Southern Illinois University at Edwardswille. **Credit/placement by examination:** AP, CLEP, IB, institutional tests. **Support services:** Learning center, study skills assistance, tutoring, writing center.

Majors. **Biology:** General. **Business:** Business admin. **Communications:** Media studies. **Computer sciences:** General, computer science. **Conservation:** General. **Education:** Elementary. **Engineering:** Science. **English:** English lit. **Foreign languages:** General, French, German, Spanish. **History:** General. **Interdisciplinary:** Global studies. **Liberal arts:** Arts/sciences, humanities. **Math:** General. **Parks/recreation:** Sports admin. **Philosophy/religion:** Philosophy, religion. **Physical sciences:** Chemistry, physics. **Social sciences:** General, anthropology, economics, political science, sociology. **Visual/performing arts:** Art history/conservation, dramatic, studio arts.

Most popular majors. Biology 6%, business/marketing 10%, computer/information sciences 7%, liberal arts 8%, physical sciences 6%, social sciences 26%, visual/performing arts 14%.

Computing on campus. 250 workstations in dormitories, library, computer center, student center. Dormitories wired for high-speed internet access and linked to campus network. Online course registration, online library, helpline, student web hosting available.

Student life. **Freshman orientation:** Mandatory. Preregistration for classes offered. Pre-fall writing and orientation program immediately precedes start of classes. **Policies:** Students required to comply with standards of Christian Science. No alcoholic beverages, smoking, drugs. High moral standards and behavior expected. Standards maintained regarding abstinence from premarital sex or homosexual activity. Religious observance required. Freshmen permitted cars on campus. **Housing:** Guaranteed on-campus for all undergraduates. Single-sex dorms, apartments, substance-free housing available. $100 deposit, deadline 5/1. Housing with single-sex wings, 8 person cottages for nontraditional students, and theme houses available. **Activities:** Jazz band, choral groups, dance, drama, music ensembles, musical theater, radio station, student government, student newspaper, TV station, Christian Science Organization, Black student union, Latin American student organization, Soc 50, student volunteer program.

Athletics. NCAA. **Intercollegiate:** Baseball M, basketball, cross-country, diving, football (tackle) M, golf M, soccer, swimming, tennis, track and field, volleyball W. **Intramural:** Basketball, soccer, softball, volleyball W. **Team name:** Panthers.

Student services. Adult student services, career counseling, student employment services, financial aid counseling, health services, on-campus daycare, personal counseling.

Contact. E-mail: collegeadmissions@prin.edu
Phone: (618) 374-5181 Toll-free number: (800) 277-4648 ext. 2802
Fax: (618) 374-4000
Martha Quirk, Dean of Admissions, Principia College, One Maybeck Place, Elsah, IL 62028-9799

Quincy University

Quincy, Illinois
www.quincy.edu — **CB code: 1645**

- Private 4-year university and liberal arts college affiliated with Roman Catholic Church
- Residential campus in large town
- 1,000 degree-seeking undergraduates: 7% part-time, 57% women, 6% African American, 1% Asian American, 2% Hispanic American, 1% international
- 182 degree-seeking graduate students
- 94% of applicants admitted
- SAT or ACT (ACT writing recommended), application essay required

General. Founded in 1860. Regionally accredited. Associate's degrees are offered in all majors by arrangement with institution. **Degrees:** 228 bachelor's awarded; master's offered. **Location:** 280 miles from Chicago, 120 miles from St. Louis. **Calendar:** Semester, limited summer session. **Full-time faculty:** 54 total; 83% have terminal degrees, 6% minority, 30% women. **Part-time faculty:** 73 total; 32% have terminal degrees, 52% women. **Class size:** 71% < 20, 29% 20-39, less than 1% 40-49, less than 1% 50-99. **Special facilities:** College-operated national public radio station.

Freshman class profile. 986 applied, 926 admitted, 202 enrolled.

Mid 50% test scores		**Rank in top quarter:**	30%
SAT verbal:	440-540	**Rank in top tenth:**	9%
SAT math:	460-560	**End year in good standing:**	89%
ACT:	20-24	**Return as sophomores:**	68%
GPA 3.50 or higher:	29%	**Out-of-state:**	32%
GPA 3.0-3.49:	30%	**Live on campus:**	77%
GPA 2.0-2.99:	40%	**International:**	1%

Basis for selection. School achievement record and test scores most important. Applicants for BS in nursing must have minimum ACT score of 22 and minimum 3.0 GPA on a 4.0 scale. All applicants must submit a letter of recommendation and a personal statement on why they would like to attend Quincy University. Audition required of music majors. Portfolio recommended for art majors. **Homeschooled:** Transcript of courses and grades, letter of recommendation (nonparent) required. **Learning Disabled:** Submit documentation of disability.

High school preparation. 16 units recommended. Required and recommended units include English 4, mathematics 3, social studies 4, science 3 and foreign language 2.

2006-2007 Annual costs. Tuition/fees: $19,010. Room/board: $6,980. Books/supplies: $1,000. Personal expenses: $1,000.

2004-2005 Financial aid. Need-based: 71% of total undergraduate aid awarded as scholarships/grants, 29% as loans/jobs. **Non-need-based:** Scholarships awarded for academics, art, athletics, music/drama.

Application procedures. Admission: No deadline. $25 fee, may be waived for applicants with need. Application may be submitted online. Admission notification on a rolling basis. **Financial aid:** Priority date 4/15; no closing date. FAFSA required. Applicants notified on a rolling basis starting 2/15; must reply by 5/1 or within 2 week(s) of notification.

Academics. Special study options: Accelerated study, distance learning, double major, dual enrollment of high school students, ESL, honors, independent study, internships, liberal arts/career combination, student-designed major, study abroad, teacher certification program. 3-2 in engineering with Washington University; 3-1 in medical technology with various hospitals. **Credit/placement by examination:** AP, CLEP, IB, institutional tests. 40 credit hours maximum toward bachelor's degree. Combined total of 40 semester hours of credit from nontraditional sources accepted toward degree. **Support services:** Learning center, pre-admission summer program, reduced course load, remedial instruction, study skills assistance, tutoring, writing center.

Majors. Biology: General. **Business:** Accounting, business admin, finance, marketing. **Communications:** General, broadcast journalism, journalism. **Computer sciences:** Computer science, information systems. **Education:** Elementary, music, physical, special. **English:** English lit. **Health:** Clinical lab science, nursing (RN). **History:** General. **Liberal arts:** Humanities. **Math:** General. **Parks/recreation:** Sports admin. **Physical sciences:** Chemistry. **Protective services:** Criminal justice. **Psychology:** General. **Public administration:** Human services, social work. **Social sciences:** Political science. **Theology:** Theology. **Transportation:** Airline/commercial pilot, aviation management. **Visual/performing arts:** General, art, graphic design.

Most popular majors. Biology 6%, business/marketing 22%, education 19%, health sciences 10%, psychology 6%, security/protective services 6%.

Computing on campus. 200 workstations in dormitories, library, computer center, student center. Dormitories wired for high-speed internet access and linked to campus network. Commuter students can connect to campus network. Online course registration, online library, helpline, student web hosting available.

Student life. Freshman orientation: Mandatory, $100 fee. Preregistration for classes offered. Academic year begins with 1-2 week registration and advisement program and 1-week social program. **Policies:** Freshmen permitted cars on campus. **Housing:** Guaranteed on-campus for all undergraduates. Coed dorms, single-sex dorms, apartments, fraternity/sorority housing available. $150 deposit. **Activities:** Bands, choral groups, dance, drama, film society, literary magazine, music ensembles, musical theater, opera, radio station, student government, student newspaper, symphony orchestra, TV station, campus ministry, Circle-K, Black Student Perspective, entrepreneur club, student volunteer services, BACCHUS, inter-cultural exchange, Needs of Our World, Amnesty International.

Athletics. NAIA, NCAA. **Intercollegiate:** Baseball M, basketball, football (tackle) M, golf, soccer, softball W, tennis, volleyball. **Intramural:** Basketball, bowling, football (non-tackle), racquetball, softball, volleyball. **Team name:** Hawks.

Student services. Alcohol/substance abuse counseling, campus ministries, career counseling, student employment services, financial aid counseling, health services, minority student services, personal counseling, placement for graduates. **Physically disabled:** Services for visually, hearing impaired.

Contact. E-mail: admissions@quincy.edu
Phone: (217) 228-5210 Toll-free number: (800) 688-4295
Fax: (217) 228-5479
Mark Clynes, Vice President for Enrollment Management, Quincy University, 1800 College Avenue, Quincy, IL 62301-2699

Robert Morris College: Chicago

Chicago, Illinois — **CB member**
www.robertmorris.edu — **CB code: 1670**

- Private 4-year business and technical college
- Commuter campus in very large city
- 4,847 degree-seeking undergraduates: 3% part-time, 65% women, 37% African American, 2% Asian American, 24% Hispanic American
- 95% graduate within 6 years

General. Founded in 1913. Regionally accredited. Branch campuses in DuPage, Lake County, O'Hare, Orland Park, Peoria, and Springfield. **Degrees:** 954 bachelor's, 1,394 associate awarded; master's offered. **ROTC:** Army. **Location:** Downtown. **Calendar:** 5 10-week sessions. Extensive summer session. **Full-time faculty:** 133 total; 20% have terminal degrees, 26% minority, 50% women. **Part-time faculty:** 235 total; 22% have terminal degrees, 24% minority, 40% women. **Class size:** 41% < 20, 54% 20-39, 4% 40-49, 1% 50-99, less than 1% >100.

Freshman class profile. 2,714 applied, 2,167 admitted, 977 enrolled.

GPA 3.50 or higher:	15%	**End year in good standing:**	56%
GPA 3.0-3.49:	17%	**Return as sophomores:**	56%
GPA 2.0-2.99:	50%	**Out-of-state:**	1%
Rank in top quarter:	23%	**Live on campus:**	10%
Rank in top tenth:	7%		

Basis for selection. Open admission, but selective for some programs. Applicants must submit high school transcript for review and are encouraged to meet with admissions counselor. Strongly recommend meeting with admissions counselor and campus visit. **Homeschooled:** Must submit a transcript of classes, curriculum documentation, and state certification. In addition, student must take a nationally normed standardized examination demonstrating an acceptable achievement level.

2006-2007 Annual costs. Tuition/fees: $15,900. Lab fees vary by program. Books/supplies: $1,350. Personal expenses: $1,047.

2005-2006 Financial aid. Need-based: 867 full-time freshmen applied for aid; 839 were judged to have need; 827 of these received aid. Average need met was 50%. Average scholarship/grant was $8,318; average loan $2,511. 58% of total undergraduate aid awarded as scholarships/grants, 42% as loans/jobs. **Non-need-based:** Awarded to 339 full-time undergraduates, including 65 freshmen. Scholarships awarded for academics, art, athletics, state residency.

Application procedures. Admission: No deadline. $30 fee, may be waived for applicants with need. Application may be submitted online. Admission notification on a rolling basis. **Financial aid:** No deadline. FAFSA required. Applicants notified on a rolling basis.

Academics. Special study options: Accelerated study, cooperative education, distance learning, dual enrollment of high school students, honors, internships, study abroad. **Credit/placement by examination:** AP, CLEP, institutional tests. 36 credit hours maximum toward associate degree, 44 toward bachelor's. **Support services:** Learning center, study skills assistance, tutoring, writing center.

Majors. Business: Business admin. **Computer sciences:** Information technology. **Visual/performing arts:** Graphic design.

Most popular majors. Business/marketing 79%, computer/information sciences 13%, visual/performing arts 8%.

Computing on campus. 1,809 workstations in library, computer center, student center. Dormitories linked to campus network. Commuter students can connect to campus network. Online library, helpline, repair service, wireless network available.

Student life. **Freshman orientation:** Mandatory. Held 1-4 weeks prior to commencement of classes. Students required to attend one 2 1/2-hour session. **Policies:** Students required to comply with college dress and attendance policies. Freshmen permitted cars on campus. **Housing:** Guaranteed on-campus for all undergraduates. Coed dorms, substance-free housing available. $300 nonrefundable deposit, deadline 5/1. **Activities:** Dance, drama, literary magazine, student newspaper.

Athletics. NAIA, USCAA. **Intercollegiate:** Baseball M, basketball, bowling W, cross-country, golf, soccer, softball W, tennis W, track and field W, volleyball W. **Team name:** Eagles.

Student services. Adult student services, career counseling, services for economically disadvantaged, student employment services, financial aid counseling, personal counseling, placement for graduates, veterans' counselor. **Physically disabled:** Services for visually, hearing impaired.

Contact. E-mail: enroll@robertmorris.edu
Phone: (800) 762-5960 Toll-free number: (800) 762-5960
Fax: (312) 935-6819
Candace Goodwin, Senior Vice President for Enrollment, Robert Morris College: Chicago, 401South State Street, Chicago, IL 60605

Rockford College

Rockford, Illinois **CB member**
www.rockford.edu **CB code: 1665**

- Private 4-year liberal arts college
- Residential campus in small city
- 852 degree-seeking undergraduates: 14% part-time, 64% women, 7% African American, 2% Asian American, 5% Hispanic American, 2% international
- 222 degree-seeking graduate students
- SAT or ACT required
- 46% graduate within 6 years

General. Founded in 1847. Regionally accredited. Accrediting institution for Regent's College, London, England. **Degrees:** 217 bachelor's awarded; master's offered. **ROTC:** Army. **Location:** 90 miles from Chicago and Milwaukee. **Calendar:** Semester, limited summer session. **Full-time faculty:** 68 total; 6% minority, 44% women. **Part-time faculty:** 92 total; 73% women. **Class size:** 79% < 20, 19% 20-39, 1% 40-49. **Special facilities:** Theater, nursing computer lab, black box theater.

Freshman class profile.

Out-of-state:	12%	**International:**	1%
Live on campus:	83%		

Basis for selection. School achievement record, test scores most important. Recommendations and activities also considered. Interview and essay recommended. Audition required of theater arts and musical theater performance majors. **Homeschooled:** Must score 18 or better on ACT with no subscore below 17.

High school preparation. 16 units required. Required and recommended units include English 4, mathematics 2-3, social studies 3, history 1, science 2 (laboratory 1) and foreign language 2. Biology, 2 years algebra, and chemistry required for nursing bachelor's program.

2005-2006 Annual costs. Tuition/fees: $22,460. Room/board: $7,190. Books/supplies: $880. Personal expenses: $1,745.

Financial aid. **Non-need-based:** Scholarships awarded for academics, alumni affiliation. **Additional information:** Will attempt to meet 100% of student's demonstrated financial need. Full tuition scholarships available, separate application and interview process required.

Application procedures. **Admission:** Closing date 8/15 (postmark date). $35 fee, may be waived for applicants with need. Application may be submitted online. Admission notification on a rolling basis beginning on or about 9/1. Must reply by May 1 or within 2 week(s) if notified thereafter. **Financial aid:** Priority date 4/15; no closing date. FAFSA, institutional form required. Applicants notified on a rolling basis starting 4/15; must reply within 3 week(s) of notification.

Academics. English Language Study Center open to international students. **Special study options:** Accelerated study, combined bachelor's/graduate degree, cooperative education, double major, ESL, exchange student, honors, independent study, internships, liberal arts/career combination, study abroad, teacher certification program, Washington semester. **Credit/placement by examination:** AP, CLEP, IB, institutional tests. 30 credit hours maximum toward bachelor's degree. No more than 64 hours of combined general and subject hours allowed. **Support services:** Learning center, reduced course load, remedial instruction, study skills assistance, tutoring, writing center.

Majors. **Biology:** General, biochemistry. **Business:** General, accounting, business admin, human resources, management information systems, managerial economics, marketing. **Computer sciences:** General, computer science, information systems. **Education:** General, elementary, physical. **Foreign languages:** General, ancient Greek, classics, French, Latin, Spanish. **Health:** Nursing (RN), predentistry, premedicine, preop/surgical nursing, prepharmacy, preveterinary. **History:** General. **Interdisciplinary:** Math/computer science. **Legal studies:** Prelaw. **Math:** General. **Philosophy/religion:** Philosophy. **Physical sciences:** Chemistry. **Psychology:** General. **Social sciences:** General, anthropology, economics, political science, sociology, urban studies. **Visual/performing arts:** General, art, art history/conservation, ceramics, dramatic, drawing, music history, painting, printmaking, sculpture, studio arts, theater design.

Computing on campus. 75 workstations in dormitories, library, computer center, student center. Dormitories linked to campus network. Commuter students can connect to campus network. Helpline, wireless network available.

Student life. **Freshman orientation:** Mandatory. Preregistration for classes offered. Held 4 days before classes begin. **Policies:** Freshmen permitted cars on campus. **Housing:** Guaranteed on-campus for freshmen. Coed dorms, single-sex dorms, substance-free housing available. $100 deposit, deadline 5/1. Students not living with family must live on campus, unless age 21 or older. **Activities:** Jazz band, choral groups, dance, drama, literary magazine, music ensembles, musical theater, radio station, student government, student newspaper, Brothers and Sisters in Christ, Volunteer Service Corps, Commuter Student Organization, intercultural club, Psychology Society, Nursing Student Organization, art club, Alpha Helix Science Society, residence hall association, entertainment council, Cross Roads.

Athletics. NCAA. **Intercollegiate:** Baseball M, basketball, cross-country, football (tackle) M, golf M, soccer, softball W, tennis, track and field, volleyball W. **Intramural:** Badminton, basketball, bowling, football (non-tackle) M, soccer, softball, table tennis, tennis, volleyball. **Team name:** Regents.

Student services. Campus ministries, career counseling, student employment services, financial aid counseling, health services, personal counseling, placement for graduates. **Physically disabled:** Services for visually, hearing impaired.

Contact. E-mail: admission@rockford.edu
Phone: (815) 226-4050 Toll-free number: (800) 892-2984
Fax: (815) 226-2822
Michael Plocinski, Director of Admission, Rockford College, 5050 East State Street, Rockford, IL 61108-2393

Roosevelt University

Chicago, Illinois **CB member**
www.roosevelt.edu **CB code: 1666**

- Private 4-year university
- Commuter campus in very large city
- 3,907 degree-seeking undergraduates: 48% part-time, 67% women, 24% African American, 5% Asian American, 11% Hispanic American, 2% international
- 3,161 graduate students
- 60% of applicants admitted
- SAT or ACT, application essay required
- 37% graduate within 6 years

General. Founded in 1945. Regionally accredited. **Degrees:** 863 bachelor's awarded; master's, doctoral offered. **Location:** Downtown. **Calendar:** Semester, extensive summer session. **Full-time faculty:** 212 total; 75% have terminal degrees, 9% minority, 39% women. **Part-time faculty:** 437 total; 43% women. **Class size:** 63% < 20, 35% 20-39, 1% 40-49, less than 1% 50-99, less than 1% >100.

Freshman class profile. 1,390 applied, 832 admitted, 326 enrolled.

Mid 50% test scores		Rank in top tenth:	3%
SAT verbal:	500-630	Return as sophomores:	70%
SAT math:	470-590	Out-of-state:	29%
ACT:	19-25	Live on campus:	56%
GPA 3.50 or higher:	31%	International:	5%
GPA 3.0-3.49:	28%	Fraternities:	4%
GPA 2.0-2.99:	35%	Sororities:	2%
Rank in top quarter:	11%		

Basis for selection. Recent secondary school performance most crucial. Required essays and recommended interviews can be used to communicate special circumstances. Placement evaluation required for all admitted, degree-seeking undergraduate students. Institutional examination accepted in lieu of SAT or ACT for those applicants out of secondary school at least 5 years. Interview recommended for early admission and borderline applicants. Audition required of music and theater majors. Portfolio recommended for art and theater majors.

High school preparation. College-preparatory program recommended. 15 units required; 19 recommended. Required and recommended units include English 4, mathematics 3-4, social studies 2, history 1-2, science 3 (laboratory 2), foreign language 2 and academic electives 2. Extensive work in English, history, mathematics, foreign language, and science recommended.

2005-2006 Annual costs. Tuition/fees: $14,430. Chicago College of the Performing Arts is $19,630 per year or $575 per semester hour for undergraduates. Room/board: $7,990. Books/supplies: $1,200. Personal expenses: $1,500.

2004-2005 Financial aid. Need-based: 218 full-time freshmen applied for aid; 190 were judged to have need; 178 of these received aid. Average need met was 75%. Average scholarship/grant was $5,740. 36% of total undergraduate aid awarded as scholarships/grants, 64% as loans/jobs. **Non-need-based:** Awarded to 675 full-time undergraduates, including 157 freshmen. Scholarships awarded for academics, alumni affiliation, leadership, minority status, music/drama, state residency.

Application procedures. Admission: Priority date 8/15; deadline 9/1. $25 fee, may be waived for applicants with need. Admission notification on a rolling basis beginning on or about 10/15. **Financial aid:** Priority date 4/1; no closing date. FAFSA, institutional form required. Applicants notified on a rolling basis starting 3/15; must reply within 2 week(s) of notification.

Academics. Special study options: Accelerated study, combined bachelor's/graduate degree, distance learning, double major, dual enrollment of high school students, ESL, honors, independent study, internships, student-designed major, study abroad, teacher certification program. Early admission agreement with John Marshall Law School. **Credit/placement by examination:** AP, CLEP, ACT, institutional tests. 30 credit hours maximum toward bachelor's degree. **Support services:** Learning center, preadmission summer program, reduced course load, remedial instruction, tutoring.

Majors. Area/ethnic studies: African-American, American, women's. **Biology:** General. **Business:** General, accounting, actuarial science, business admin, communications, finance, hospitality admin, human resources, insurance, international, labor relations, management science, managerial economics, marketing, tourism/travel. **Communications:** General, journalism, public relations. **Computer sciences:** General, computer science, information systems. **Conservation:** Environmental studies. **Education:** Biology, chemistry, early childhood, elementary, English, French, history, mathematics, multi-level teacher, music, secondary, social science, Spanish. **Engineering technology:** Electrical. **English:** Speech/rhetoric. **Foreign languages:** General, comparative lit, Spanish. **Health:** Clinical lab technology, health care admin, health services, nuclear medical technology, predentistry, premedicine, prepharmacy, preveterinary. **History:** General. **Interdisciplinary:** Gerontology, math/computer science. **Legal studies:** General, prelaw. **Liberal arts:** Arts/sciences. **Math:** General, statistics. **Philosophy/religion:** Philosophy. **Physical sciences:** Chemistry, physics. **Protective services:** Criminal justice. **Psychology:** General. **Public administration:** Social work. **Social sciences:** General, criminology, economics, geography, international relations, political science, sociology, urban studies. **Visual/performing arts:** General, art history/conservation, arts management, conducting, dramatic, jazz, music history, music management, music performance, music theory/composition, piano/organ, voice/opera.

Most popular majors. Business/marketing 32%, communications/journalism 8%, communication technologies 9%, education 8%, liberal arts 6%, psychology 12%, social sciences 8%, visual/performing arts 6%.

Computing on campus. 180 workstations in library, computer center. Commuter students can connect to campus network. Helpline available.

Student life. Freshman orientation: Available. **Housing:** Guaranteed on-campus for all undergraduates. Coed dorms available. $250 deposit, deadline 8/1. High-rise residence hall in cooperation with University Center of Chicago available. **Activities:** Dance, literary magazine, radio station, student government, student newspaper, Christian Bible Groups, theater club, Black Student Union, Hispanic Organization, international student union, residence hall council, Asociacion de Latinos Unidos.

Athletics. Intramural: Badminton, basketball, table tennis.

Student services. Adult student services, career counseling, student employment services, personal counseling, placement for graduates, veterans' counselor. **Physically disabled:** Services for visually, hearing impaired.

Contact. E-mail: applyru@roosevelt.edu
Phone: (312) 341-3515 Toll-free number: (877) 277-5978
Fax: (312) 341-4316
Brian Lynch, Director of Admission, Roosevelt University, 430 South Michigan Avenue, Chicago, IL 60605-1394

Rosalind Franklin University of Medicine and Science

North Chicago, Illinois
www.rosalindfranklin.edu **CB code: 0768**

- Private upper-division university and health science college
- Commuter campus in large town
- Application essay required

General. Founded in 1912. Regionally accredited. **Location:** 40 miles from Chicago. **Calendar:** Quarter, limited summer session. **Full-time faculty:** 142 total; 38% women. **Part-time faculty:** 54 total; 30% women. **Special facilities:** 14 fully equipped patient examination rooms, museum, fitness center, anatomy lab.

Student profile. 9 degree-seeking undergraduates, 1,659 degree-seeking graduate students. 9 applied as first time-transfer students. 100% entered as juniors. 78% transferred from two-year, 22% transferred from four-year institutions.

Women:	56%	Asian American:	33%
African American:	22%	Part-time:	11%

Basis for selection. College transcript, application essay required. Undergraduate education must be completed in an accredited college or university, with at least a "C" in required courses. Proficiency in written and spoken English required. Transfer accepted as juniors.

2005-2006 Annual costs. Tuition/fees: $14,118. Books/supplies: $300.

Financial aid. All financial aid based on need.

Application procedures. Admission: Deadline 7/1. $20 fee, may be waived for applicants with need. Application must be submitted on paper. **Financial aid:** FAFSA, institutional form required.

Academics. Special study options: Accelerated study, cooperative education, cross-registration, distance learning, double major, dual enrollment of high school students, internships. **Credit/placement by examination:** AP, CLEP, institutional tests. **Support services:** Learning center, reduced course load, study skills assistance, tutoring.

Majors. Health: Clinical lab technology.

Computing on campus. 106 workstations in library, computer center, student center. Dormitories wired for high-speed internet access and linked to campus network. Commuter students can connect to campus network. Helpline, repair service, wireless network available.

Student life. Housing: Apartments available. $500 partly refundable deposit. Limited on-campus housing available. **Activities:** Choral groups, literary magazine, student government, student newspaper, Asian Pacific American medical atudent association, Adolescent Substance Abuse Prevention, Christian Medical Association, Hillel, internal health/medicine interest groups, Lesbian, Gay, Bisexual and Transgendered People in Medicine, Middle Eastern medical student association, South Asian Medical Association, Salud Ofrecida A Latinos.

Student services. Alcohol/substance abuse counseling, career counseling, financial aid counseling, health services, minority student services, personal counseling, placement for graduates, veterans' counselor.

Contact. E-mail: grad.admissions@rosalindfranklin.edu
Phone: (847) 578-3209
Maryann DeCaire, Executive Director of Admissions, Records & Financial Aid, Rosalind Franklin University of Medicine and Science, Graduate Admissions Office, North Chicago, IL 60064-3095

Rush University
Chicago, Illinois
www.rushu.rush.edu **CB code: 3262**

- Private upper-division health professions university
- Commuter campus in very large city
- 53% of applicants admitted
- Application essay required

General. Founded in 1971. Regionally accredited. Educational component of Rush University Medical Center. Students use clinical and laboratory facilities of the medical center, affiliated hospitals, and community health centers. **Degrees:** 111 bachelor's awarded; master's, doctoral, first professional offered. **Articulation:** Agreements with College of DuPage, Triton College, Parkland College, Moraine Valley Community College, Oakton Community College, William Rainey Harper College, Kankakee Community College. **Location:** 2 miles from the Chicago loop. **Calendar:** Quarter, limited summer session. **Full-time faculty:** 450 total. **Part-time faculty:** 350 total. **Class size:** 67% < 20, 14% 20-39, 19% 50-99.

Student profile. 240 degree-seeking undergraduates, 1,123 degree-seeking graduate students. 208 applied as first time-transfer students, 111 admitted, 87 enrolled. 100% entered as juniors.

Women:	87%	**Part-time:**	4%
African American:	5%	**Out-of-state:**	17%
Asian American:	13%	**Live on campus:**	15%
Hispanic American:	4%	**25 or older:**	47%
International:	2%		

Basis for selection. College transcript, application essay required. Admission based on GPA and letters of recommendation. Application closing dates: nursing April 1, clinical lab sciences/medical technology June 1, perfusion technology, March 1. Transfer accepted as juniors.

2005-2006 Annual costs. Tuition/fees: $18,195. Tuition costs vary by program. Room only: $7,704. Books/supplies: $700. Personal expenses: $1,220.

Financial aid. Need-based: 33% of total undergraduate aid awarded as scholarships/grants, 67% as loans/jobs.

Application procedures. Admission: Rolling admission. $40 fee, may be waived for applicants with need. Application may be submitted online. **Financial aid:** FAFSA, institutional form required.

Academics. Special study options: Accelerated study, combined bachelor's/graduate degree, distance learning, liberal arts/career combination. Registered nurse completion program. **Credit/placement by examination:** AP, CLEP, institutional tests. 45 credit hours maximum toward bachelor's degree.

Majors. Health: Clinical lab science, nursing (RN), perfusion technology.

Computing on campus. 120 workstations in library, computer center, student center. Commuter students can connect to campus network. Online library, helpline, wireless network available.

Student life. Policies: Funds available for official student groups. Student Affairs staff presides over decisions. **Housing:** Apartments available. $200 fully refundable deposit. **Activities:** Student government, student newspaper, Christian Fellowship, rape victim advocate program, medical technicians club, National Student Nurses' association chapter, Lesbian/Gay/Bisexual/Allies, health science students for choice.

Student services. Alcohol/substance abuse counseling, career counseling, student employment services, financial aid counseling, health services, on-campus daycare, personal counseling.

Contact. E-mail: Rush_Admissions@rush.edu
Phone: (312) 942-7100 Fax: (312) 942-2219
Hicela Woods, Director of College Admission Services, Rush University, College Admissions, Chicago, IL 60612

Saint Anthony College of Nursing
Rockford, Illinois
www.sacn.edu **CB code: 3923**

- Private upper-division nursing college affiliated with Roman Catholic Church
- Commuter campus in large city
- 28% of applicants admitted
- Application essay, interview required

General. Regionally accredited. **Degrees:** 47 bachelor's awarded. **Articulation:** Formal agreements with Rock Valley College, McHenry County College, Sauk Valley Community College, Kishwaukee College, Elgin Community College, Blackhawk Technical College, Highland Community College. **Location:** 90 miles from Chicago. **Calendar:** Semester, limited summer session. **Full-time faculty:** 10 total; 10% minority, 100% women. **Part-time faculty:** 5 total; 20% have terminal degrees, 80% women. **Class size:** 25% < 20, 75% 20-39.

Student profile. 124 degree-seeking undergraduates. 142 applied as first time-transfer students, 40 admitted, 33 enrolled. 100% entered as juniors. 88% transferred from two-year, 12% transferred from four-year institutions.

Women:	91%	**Out-of-state:**	6%
Part-time:	13%	**25 or older:**	56%

Basis for selection. College transcript, application essay, interview required. 64 credits required in specific pre-nursing and general education courses. Transfer accepted as juniors.

2006-2007 Annual costs. Tuition/fees: $16,282. Required fees vary from $112-$262. Books/supplies: $1,500.

Financial aid. Need-based: 124 applied for aid; 124 were judged to have need; 124 of these received aid. Average need met was 15%. 28% of total undergraduate aid awarded as scholarships/grants, 72% as loans/jobs. **Non-need-based:** Awarded to 125 undergraduates. Scholarships awarded for academics, leadership, state residency.

Application procedures. Admission: Deadline 8/15. $50 fee. Application may be submitted online. Admission notification 9/15. Must reply by 10/15. **Financial aid:** No deadline. Applicants notified on a rolling basis starting 8/18. FAFSA required.

Academics. Special study options: Independent study, liberal arts/career combination. **Credit/placement by examination:** AP, CLEP.

Majors. Health: Adult health nursing.

Computing on campus. 18 workstations in library, computer center. Commuter students can connect to campus network.

Student life. Activities: Student government.

Contact. E-mail: deborahdenny@sacn.edu
Phone: (815) 227-2141 Fax: (815) 227-2730
Nancy Sanders, Assistant Dean for Admissions and Student Affairs, Saint Anthony College of Nursing, 5658 East State Street, Rockford, IL 61108-2468

St. Augustine College
Chicago, Illinois
www.staugustinecollege.edu **CB code: 0697**

- Private 4-year liberal arts college affiliated with Episcopal Church
- Commuter campus in very large city
- 1,542 degree-seeking undergraduates

General. Founded in 1980. Regionally accredited. **Degrees:** 16 bachelor's, 236 associate awarded. **Calendar:** Semester, limited summer session. **Full-time faculty:** 29 total. **Part-time faculty:** 130 total.

Basis for selection. Open admission. Ability to benefit test scores considered for students over 17 years old who have not completed high school. High school diploma or GED required for students entering respiratory therapy technician program. Applicants without high school diploma or GED at time of enrollment must earn GED by end of first year of study. **Home-schooled:** Placement test in English, Math, and Spanish.

2005-2006 Annual costs. Tuition/fees: $8,910. Cost includes tuition, fees, books.

Application procedures. Admission: No deadline. No application fee. Admission notification on a rolling basis. **Financial aid:** No deadline. FAFSA, institutional form required. Applicants notified on a rolling basis.

Academics. Curriculum offers several elective courses in English language addressed primarily to Hispanic students. **Special study options:** Combined bachelor's/graduate degree, cooperative education, double major, ESL, independent study, internships, liberal arts/career combination. **Credit/**

placement by examination: CLEP, IB, institutional tests. **Support services:** Learning center, pre-admission summer program, remedial instruction, tutoring.

Majors. Public administration: Social work.

Computing on campus. 100 workstations in library, computer center.

Student life. Freshman orientation: Mandatory. Preregistration for classes offered. **Policies:** Freshmen permitted cars on campus. **Activities:** Student government, student newspaper.

Athletics. Intercollegiate: Soccer M.

Student services. Adult student services, alcohol/substance abuse counseling, career counseling, financial aid counseling, minority student services, on-campus daycare, personal counseling, placement for graduates.

Contact. Phone: (773) 878-8756 Fax: (773) 878-9032
Soledad Ruiz, Assistant Dean of Admissions and Records, St. Augustine College, 1345 West Argyle, Chicago, IL 60640-3501

St. Francis Medical Center College of Nursing

Peoria, Illinois
www.sfmccon.edu **CB code: 1756**

- Private upper-division nursing college affiliated with Roman Catholic Church
- Commuter campus in small city
- 40% of applicants admitted
- Application essay required

General. Founded in 1905. Regionally accredited. Located at large medical center. National League of Nursing accredited. NCA accredited. Offers experience at Tazewell County, Fulton County, Peoria City/County Health Departments, Human Service Center and various other community agencies. **Degrees:** 97 bachelor's awarded; master's offered. **Location:** 180 miles from Chicago, 160 miles from St. Louis. **Calendar:** Semester, limited summer session. **Full-time faculty:** 20 total; 35% have terminal degrees, 100% women. **Part-time faculty:** 8 total; 100% women. **Class size:** 35% < 20, 20% 20-39, 15% 40-49, 30% 50-99.

Student profile. 223 degree-seeking undergraduates, 58 degree-seeking graduate students. 148 applied as first time-transfer students, 59 admitted, 59 enrolled. 100% entered as juniors. 90% transferred from two-year, 10% transferred from four-year institutions.

Women:	85%	**Part-time:**	16%
African American:	2%	**25 or older:**	51%
Hispanic American:	2%		

Basis for selection. High school transcript, college transcript, application essay required. Enrollment depends on satisfactory completion of 62 semester hours of a specified prenursing curriculum. Applications may be submitted after satisfactory completion of 30 semester hours of required prenursing courses. Must include 8 semester hours of physical/life sciences. Require minimum cumulative GPA of 2.50. Transfer accepted as juniors.

2006-2007 Annual costs. Students enter at the junior-level. Cost for 2006/2007 academic year: $13,200 (tuition), $220 (required fees). Room only: $1,880. Books/supplies: $1,173. Personal expenses: $3,033.

Financial aid. Need-based: 160 applied for aid; 132 were judged to have need; 132 of these received aid. Average need met was 80%. 63% of total undergraduate aid awarded as scholarships/grants, 37% as loans/jobs. **Non-need-based:** Awarded to 58 undergraduates. Scholarships awarded for academics, alumni affiliation. **Additional information:** Modified Education Employment Program available to full-time students on a limited basis. Tuition waiver program for hospital employees available.

Application procedures. Admission: Deadline 9/1. $50 fee. **Financial aid:** No deadline. Applicants notified on a rolling basis starting 5/15; must reply within 2 weeks of notification. FAFSA, institutional form required.

Academics. Special study options: Distance learning. **Credit/placement by examination:** CLEP.

Majors. Health: Nursing (RN).

Computing on campus. 22 workstations in library, computer center. Dormitories linked to campus network. Commuter students can connect to campus network. Online library, helpline, repair service available.

Student life. Housing: Guaranteed on-campus for all undergraduates. Coed dorms, substance-free housing available. **Activities:** Student government, Christian Fellowship, Student Nurses' Association, student senate.

Student services. Adult student services, financial aid counseling, health services, personal counseling.

Contact. E-mail: janice.farquharson@osfhealthcare.org
Phone: (309) 655-2245 Fax: (309) 624-8973
Janice Farquharson, Director of Admissions and Recruitment, St. Francis Medical Center College of Nursing, 511 NE Greenleaf Street, Peoria, IL 61603-3783

St. John's College

Springfield, Illinois

- Private upper-division nursing college
- Commuter campus

Annual costs/financial aid. Tuition/fees (2005-2006): $10,332.

Contact. Phone: (217) 525-5628
421 North Ninth Street, Springfield, IL 62702

St. Xavier University

Chicago, Illinois **CB member**
www.sxu.edu **CB code: 1708**

- Private 4-year university affiliated with Roman Catholic Church
- Commuter campus in very large city
- 3,131 degree-seeking undergraduates: 24% part-time, 72% women, 18% African American, 2% Asian American, 13% Hispanic American
- 2,370 degree-seeking graduate students
- 69% of applicants admitted
- SAT or ACT (ACT writing optional) required
- 53% graduate within 6 years

General. Founded in 1847. Regionally accredited. Affiliated with Sisters of Mercy. **Degrees:** 663 bachelor's awarded; master's offered. **ROTC:** Air Force. **Location:** 20 miles from downtown. **Calendar:** Semester, limited summer session. **Full-time faculty:** 168 total; 85% have terminal degrees, 11% minority, 56% women. **Part-time faculty:** 258 total; 30% have terminal degrees, 5% minority, 64% women. **Class size:** 45% < 20, 52% 20-39, 2% 40-49, less than 1% 50-99. **Special facilities:** Music performance studio, reading clinic, speech clinic, learning disabilities clinic, mathematics laboratory, chapel.

Freshman class profile. 1,998 applied, 1,385 admitted, 422 enrolled.

Mid 50% test scores		**GPA 2.0-2.99:**	36%
SAT verbal:	470-590	**Rank in top quarter:**	43%
SAT math:	480-590	**Rank in top tenth:**	14%
ACT:	20-25	**Out-of-state:**	9%
GPA 3.50 or higher:	34%	**Live on campus:**	46%
GPA 3.0-3.49:	29%		

Basis for selection. GPA, test scores most important. Counselor recommendation, class rank considered. Interview recommended for borderline applicants. Audition required of music majors.

High school preparation. 16 units recommended. Recommended units include English 4, mathematics 3, foreign language 2 and academic electives 3. 4 units of science and social studies combined.

2005-2006 Annual costs. Tuition/fees: $18,520. Room/board: $7,058. Books/supplies: $900. Personal expenses: $862.

2004-2005 Financial aid. Need-based: 385 full-time freshmen applied for aid; 340 were judged to have need; 340 of these received aid. Average need met was 88%. Average scholarship/grant was $10,853; average loan $2,714. 48% of total undergraduate aid awarded as scholarships/grants, 52% as loans/jobs. **Non-need-based:** Awarded to 2,120 full-time undergraduates, including 391 freshmen. Scholarships awarded for academics, athletics, music/drama.

Application procedures. Admission: No deadline. $25 fee, may be waived for applicants with need. Application may be submitted online. Admission notification on a rolling basis. Must reply by May 1 or within 4 week(s) if notified thereafter. **Financial aid:** Priority date 3/1; no closing date. FAFSA required. Applicants notified on a rolling basis starting 2/1; must reply by 5/1 or within 2 week(s) of notification.

Academics. Special study options: Accelerated study, combined bachelor's/graduate degree, cooperative education, distance learning, dual enrollment of high school students, ESL, external degree, honors, independent study, internships, liberal arts/career combination, student-designed major, study abroad, teacher certification program. **Credit/placement by examination:** AP, CLEP, institutional tests. 27 credit hours maximum toward bachelor's degree. **Support services:** Learning center, pre-admission summer program, reduced course load, remedial instruction, study skills assistance, tutoring, writing center.

Majors. Biology: General, botany. **Business:** General, accounting, actuarial science, international. **Communications:** General. **Computer sciences:** General, computer science. **Education:** General, art, biology, history, mathematics, music, secondary, social science, Spanish. **Foreign languages:** Spanish. **Health:** Nursing (RN), premedicine, prepharmacy, preveterinary, speech pathology. **History:** General. **Interdisciplinary:** Biological/physical sciences. **Legal studies:** Prelaw. **Liberal arts:** Arts/sciences. **Math:** General. **Philosophy/religion:** Philosophy, religion. **Physical sciences:** Chemistry. **Protective services:** Criminal justice. **Psychology:** General. **Social sciences:** General, international relations, political science, sociology. **Theology:** Theology. **Visual/performing arts:** Studio arts, voice/opera.

Most popular majors. Business/marketing 21%, education 20%, health sciences 16%, liberal arts 9%, psychology 7%.

Computing on campus. 306 workstations in dormitories, library, computer center, student center. Dormitories wired for high-speed internet access and linked to campus network. Commuter students can connect to campus network. Online course registration, helpline, student web hosting, wireless network available.

Student life. Freshman orientation: Mandatory. Preregistration for classes offered. Two day overnight orientation held in the summer. **Policies:** Freshmen permitted cars on campus. **Housing:** Coed dorms available. $100 nonrefundable deposit, deadline 5/1. **Activities:** Bands, choral groups, film society, literary magazine, music ensembles, radio station, student government, student newspaper, symphony orchestra, Black student organization, Hispanic student organization, international student organization, student activities board, student nurses association, Muslim student association, Celtic Connection, campus ministry, Fellowship of Christian Athletes, Xi Delta.

Athletics. NAIA. **Intercollegiate:** Baseball M, basketball, cross-country, football (tackle) M, soccer, softball W, volleyball W. **Intramural:** Basketball M, bowling, volleyball. **Team name:** Cougars.

Student services. Adult student services, alcohol/substance abuse counseling, campus ministries, career counseling, services for economically disadvantaged, student employment services, financial aid counseling, health services, on-campus daycare, personal counseling, placement for graduates. **Physically disabled:** Services for speech impaired.

Contact. E-mail: admissions@sxu.edu
Phone: (773) 298-3050 Toll-free number: (800) 462-9288
Fax: (773) 298-3076
Beth Gierach, Associate Vice President of Enrollment Services, St. Xavier University, 3700 West 103rd Street, Chicago, IL 60655

School of the Art Institute of Chicago

Chicago, Illinois — **CB member**
www.artic.edu/saic — **CB code: 1713**

- Private 4-year visual arts college
- Commuter campus in very large city
- 2,008 degree-seeking undergraduates: 6% part-time, 65% women, 3% African American, 10% Asian American, 7% Hispanic American, 1% Native American, 16% international
- 552 degree-seeking graduate students
- 84% of applicants admitted
- SAT or ACT (ACT writing optional), application essay required
- 53% graduate within 6 years

General. Founded in 1866. Regionally accredited. Interdisciplinary curriculum. Credit/no credit grading option, 6 credit off campus study requirement. **Degrees:** 379 bachelor's awarded; master's offered. **Location:** Downtown Chicago. **Calendar:** Semester, extensive summer session. **Full-time faculty:** 124 total; 90% have terminal degrees, 13% minority, 41% women. **Part-time faculty:** 344 total; 46% women. **Class size:** 76% < 20, 21% 20-39, 1% 40-49, 1% 50-99, less than 1% >100. **Special facilities:** Film center, art collection, architecture library, video data bank, student galleries, poetry center, fashion resource center, artists' books collection, visiting artists' program archives.

Freshman class profile. 1,354 applied, 1,136 admitted, 356 enrolled.

Return as sophomores:	77%	**Live on campus:**	85%
Out-of-state:	81%	**International:**	16%

Basis for selection. Portfolio most important; statement of purpose, minimum 500 SAT verbal or 20 ACT English, academic credentials, and recommendations also considered. Interview recommended. Portfolio required. **Learning Disabled:** For students with proper documentation, liberal arts placement test offered in lieu of ACT or SAT minimum.

High school preparation. Advanced-level study of art recommended.

2006-2007 Annual costs. Tuition/fees (projected): $27,400. Students will be required to purchase a laptop through SAIC. Costs range from $2,000 to $2,200. Room only: $8,200. Books/supplies: $2,340. Personal expenses: $2,460.

2005-2006 Financial aid. Need-based: 268 full-time freshmen applied for aid; 179 were judged to have need; 178 of these received aid. Average scholarship/grant was $10,895; average loan $3,415. 64% of total undergraduate aid awarded as scholarships/grants, 36% as loans/jobs. **Non-need-based:** Scholarships awarded for academics, art.

Application procedures. Admission: Priority date 3/1; no deadline. $65 fee, may be waived for applicants with need. Application may be submitted online. Admission notification on a rolling basis beginning on or about 10/1. **Financial aid:** Priority date 3/15; no closing date. FAFSA required. Applicants notified on a rolling basis starting 3/1.

Academics. Interdisciplinary curriculum allows students to personalize education or concentrate on single discipline. **Special study options:** Cooperative education, cross-registration, double major, dual enrollment of high school students, ESL, exchange student, independent study, internships, New York semester, student-designed major, study abroad, teacher certification program. **Credit/placement by examination:** AP, CLEP, IB. 18 credit hours maximum toward bachelor's degree. DANTES scores accepted. **Support services:** Learning center, pre-admission summer program, reduced course load, remedial instruction, study skills assistance, tutoring.

Majors. Architecture: Interior. **Communications:** Digital media. **Communications technology:** Recording arts. **Education:** Art. **English:** Creative writing. **Visual/performing arts:** General, art history/conservation, ceramics, cinematography, design, drawing, fashion design, fiber arts, graphic design, multimedia, painting, photography, printmaking, sculpture, studio arts.

Computing on campus. PC or laptop required. 430 workstations in dormitories, library, computer center. Dormitories wired for high-speed internet access and linked to campus network. Commuter students can connect to campus network. Online library, helpline, student web hosting, wireless network available.

Student life. Freshman orientation: Mandatory, $50 fee. Preregistration for classes offered. Orientation is held 4 days prior to the beginning of class. The first day of orientation is open to parent, family and friends. **Policies:** Student government officers are elected each spring to promote student interests and concerns. Student government provides funds for the 40+ officially-recognized student groups on campus. Freshmen permitted cars on campus. **Housing:** Coed dorms, special housing for disabled, substance-free housing available. $500 nonrefundable deposit. **Activities:** Dance, drama, film society, literary magazine, music ensembles, radio station, student government, student newspaper, TV station, Campus Crusade for Christ, Chinese culture association, Grounded: A Green Concept Group, Korean student association, Latino American student organization, Native American student organization, African American women's organization, Hillel, Student Organization for the Advancement of Philosophy.

Student services. Alcohol/substance abuse counseling, career counseling, student employment services, financial aid counseling, health services, minority student services, personal counseling, veterans' counselor. **Physically disabled:** Services for visually, speech, hearing impaired.

Contact. E-mail: admiss@artic.edu
Phone: (312) 899-5219 Toll-free number: (800) 232-7242
Fax: (312) 899-1840
Scott Ramon, Director, Undergraduate Admissions, School of the Art Institute of Chicago, 37 South Wabash Avenue, Chicago, IL 60603

Shimer College

Waukegan, Illinois
www.shimer.edu — **CB code: 1717**

- Private 4-year liberal arts college
- Residential campus in small city
- 107 degree-seeking undergraduates

- 96% of applicants admitted
- Application essay, interview required

General. Founded in 1853. Regionally accredited. **Degrees:** 16 bachelor's awarded. **Calendar:** Semester. **Full-time faculty:** 13 total; 92% have terminal degrees, 31% women. **Part-time faculty:** 3 total; 33% have terminal degrees, 33% women.

Freshman class profile. 23 applied, 22 admitted, 19 enrolled.

Out-of-state:	80%	**Live on campus:**	98%

Basis for selection. Essays and interviews most important. Test scores, GPA, recommendations, motivation, maturity considered. Demonstrated writing skills and interest in and enthusiasm about Shimer's Great Books curriculum and discussion method are important. Early entrants and other applicants who do not have high school diplomas may be required to take the GED; applicants without high school diplomas who are too young to take the GED may be required to complete additional approved testing in order to comply with financial aid regulations.

2005-2006 Annual costs. Tuition/fees: $19,450. Room only: $3,000.

Financial aid. Non-need-based: Scholarships awarded for academics.

Application procedures. Admission: Priority date 6/1; deadline 8/1 (receipt date). $25 fee, may be waived for applicants with need. Application may be submitted online. Admission notification on a rolling basis. **Financial aid:** Priority date 4/15, closing date 7/31. FAFSA required. Applicants notified on a rolling basis; must reply by 8/1.

Academics. Special study options: Cross-registration, double major, dual enrollment of high school students, independent study, internships, study abroad, weekend college. Shimer-in-Oxford Program, Partnership for Service/Learning Program. **Credit/placement by examination:** CLEP, institutional tests. **Support services:** Reduced course load, study skills assistance, tutoring, writing center.

Majors. Interdisciplinary: Natural sciences. **Liberal arts:** Arts/sciences, humanities. **Social sciences:** General.

Computing on campus. 25 workstations in dormitories, computer center. Dormitories wired for high-speed internet access and linked to campus network. Commuter students can connect to campus network. Helpline, wireless network available.

Student life. Freshman orientation: Mandatory. Held in the 3-4 days prior to classes beginning each semester. Meetings on campus life and community, demonstration class, placement exams, social gatherings. **Policies:** Freshmen permitted cars on campus. **Housing:** Guaranteed on-campus for freshmen. Coed dorms, substance-free housing available. Pets allowed in dorm rooms. **Activities:** Drama, film society, literary magazine, student government, student newspaper.

Athletics. Intramural: Basketball, football (non-tackle), softball, volleyball.

Student services. Adult student services, alcohol/substance abuse counseling, career counseling, student employment services, financial aid counseling, health services, personal counseling, placement for graduates.

Contact. E-mail: admissions@shimer.edu
Phone: (847) 623-8400 Toll-free number: (800) 215-7173
Fax: (847) 249-8798
Anne Penway, Director of Admissions, Shimer College, 414 North Sheridan Road, Waukegan, IL 60085

Southern Illinois University Carbondale

Carbondale, Illinois — **CB member**
www.siuc.edu — **CB code: 1726**

- Public 4-year university
- Residential campus in large town
- 16,617 degree-seeking undergraduates: 10% part-time, 43% women, 16% African American, 2% Asian American, 4% Hispanic American, 1% Native American, 2% international
- 4,210 degree-seeking graduate students
- 77% of applicants admitted
- SAT or ACT (ACT writing recommended) required
- 41% graduate within 6 years

General. Founded in 1869. Regionally accredited. **Degrees:** 4,373 bachelor's, 87 associate awarded; master's, doctoral, first professional offered. **ROTC:** Army, Air Force. **Location:** 100 miles from St. Louis. **Calendar:** Semester, extensive summer session. **Full-time faculty:** 901 total; 84% have terminal degrees, 14% minority, 35% women. **Part-time faculty:** 180 total; 49% have terminal degrees, 11% minority, 39% women. **Class size:** 47% < 20, 44% 20-39, 3% 40-49, 4% 50-99, 1% >100. **Special facilities:** Museum, university press, coal research center, materials technology center, outdoor education laboratory, university farms, center for study of crime, electron microscopy center, cooperative wildlife research laboratory, cooperative fisheries research laboratory, vivarium, airport training facility, theatre and laboratory theatre, child development laboratory, center for archaeological investigations, small business incubator, Public Policy Institute, dental and medical clinics, public radio, television stations, environmental center.

Freshman class profile. 9,285 applied, 7,173 admitted, 2,470 enrolled.

Mid 50% test scores		**Rank in top tenth:**	9%
SAT verbal:	450-590	**Out-of-state:**	8%
SAT math:	460-580	**International:**	1%
ACT:	19-24	**Fraternities:**	7%
Rank in top quarter:	27%	**Sororities:**	5%

Basis for selection. High school class rank and ACT scores most important. **Homeschooled:** Transcript of courses and grades required. Submit standardized test score. **Learning Disabled:** Requirements for Disability Support Services can be found at DSSsiu@siu.edu. Requirements for the Achieve Program can be found at achieve@siu.edu.

High school preparation. 15 units required. Required and recommended units include English 4, mathematics 3, social studies 3, science 3 (laboratory 3), foreign language 2 and academic electives 2.

2005-2006 Annual costs. Tuition/fees: $6,831; $14,796 out-of-state. Room/board: $5,560. Books/supplies: $840. Personal expenses: $1,297.

2005-2006 Financial aid. Need-based: 1,948 full-time freshmen applied for aid; 1,413 were judged to have need; 1,390 of these received aid. Average need met was 97%. Average scholarship/grant was $6,609; average loan $3,439. 50% of total undergraduate aid awarded as scholarships/grants, 50% as loans/jobs. **Non-need-based:** Awarded to 4,422 full-time undergraduates, including 750 freshmen. Scholarships awarded for academics, alumni affiliation, art, athletics, job skills, leadership, minority status, music/drama, ROTC, state residency. **Additional information:** Need-based financial aid available to part-time students enrolled in minimum of 6 semester hours.

Application procedures. Admission: Priority date 6/1; deadline 8/22 (receipt date). $30 fee, may be waived for applicants with need. Application may be submitted online. Admission notification on a rolling basis beginning on or about 10/1. Must reply by May 1 or within 4 week(s) if notified thereafter. **Financial aid:** Priority date 4/1; no closing date. FAFSA required. Applicants notified on a rolling basis starting 3/15; must reply within 3 week(s) of notification.

Academics. Special study options: Cooperative education, distance learning, double major, ESL, honors, independent study, internships, student-designed major, study abroad, teacher certification program, Washington semester. **Credit/placement by examination:** AP, CLEP, IB, SAT, ACT, institutional tests. 15 credit hours maximum toward associate degree, 30 toward bachelor's. Proficiency examinations. **Support services:** Learning center, pre-admission summer program, remedial instruction, study skills assistance, tutoring, writing center.

Majors. Agriculture: General, animal sciences, economics, plant sciences. **Architecture:** Architecture. **Biology:** General, botany, microbiology, physiology, zoology. **Business:** Accounting, business admin, finance, management science, managerial economics, marketing. **Communications:** Journalism, radio/tv. **Computer sciences:** Computer science, information systems. **Conservation:** Forestry. **Education:** Early childhood, elementary, health, physical, special, trade/industrial. **Engineering:** Civil, computer, electrical, mechanical, mining. **Engineering technology:** General, automotive, industrial. **English:** English lit, speech/rhetoric. **Family/consumer sciences:** Clothing/textiles, food/nutrition. **Foreign languages:** Classics, French, German, linguistics, Russian, Spanish. **Health:** Communication disorders, dental hygiene, health care admin, medical radiologic technology/radiation therapy, physician assistant. **History:** General. **Legal studies:** Paralegal. **Liberal arts:** Arts/sciences. **Math:** General. **Mechanic/repair:** Avionics. **Parks/recreation:** General. **Personal/culinary services:** Mortuary science. **Philosophy/religion:** Philosophy. **Physical sciences:** Chemistry, geology, physics. **Protective services:** Fire services admin, law enforcement admin. **Psychology:** General. **Public administration:** Social work. **Social sciences:** General, anthropology, economics, geography, political science, sociology. **Transportation:** Aviation management. **Visual/performing arts:** Art, cinematography, design, dramatic, interior design, studio arts.

Most popular majors. Business/marketing 8%, education 22%, engineering/engineering technologies 11%, health sciences 8%, visual/performing arts 6%.

Computing on campus. 1,851 workstations in dormitories, library, computer center, student center. Dormitories wired for high-speed internet access and linked to campus network. Commuter students can connect to campus network. Online course registration, online library, helpline, student web hosting, wireless network available.

Student life. Freshman orientation: Mandatory, $75 fee. Preregistration for classes offered. Several 1-day seminars offered April through July; includes academic expectations, involvement opportunities, transitional issues for first-time students, campus overview, and more. **Policies:** Freshmen permitted cars on campus. **Housing:** Guaranteed on-campus for freshmen. Coed dorms, single-sex dorms, special housing for disabled, apartments, fraternity/sorority housing, substance-free housing available. $325 partly refundable deposit, deadline 6/1. Many privately owned facilities within walking distance of campus available. **Activities:** Bands, choral groups, dance, drama, film society, literary magazine, music ensembles, musical theater, opera, radio station, student government, student newspaper, symphony orchestra, TV station, Over 400 student organizations, including Black Affairs Council, International Student Council, Fellowship of Christian Athletes, College Democrats, College Republicans, Student Bible Fellowship, Saluki Volunteer Corps, Inter-Greek Council, Society of Women Engineers, wildlife society.

Athletics. NCAA. **Intercollegiate:** Baseball M, basketball, cheerleading, cross-country, diving, football (tackle) M, golf, softball W, swimming, tennis, track and field, volleyball W. **Intramural:** Badminton, basketball, cricket, cross-country, football (non-tackle), golf, handball, racquetball, soccer, softball, squash, table tennis, tennis, triathlon, volleyball, water polo, wrestling M. **Team name:** Salukis.

Student services. Adult student services, alcohol/substance abuse counseling, campus ministries, career counseling, services for economically disadvantaged, student employment services, financial aid counseling, health services, legal services, minority student services, on-campus daycare, personal counseling, placement for graduates, veterans' counselor, women's services. **Physically disabled:** Services for visually, speech, hearing impaired. **Learning disabled:** Comprehensive services available.

Contact. E-mail: admrec@siu.edu
Phone: (618) 453-4381 Fax: (618) 453-3250
Anne De Luca, Assistant Vice Chancellor, Student Affairs and Enrollment Management and Director of Admissions, Southern Illinois University Carbondale, Mailcode 4701, Carbondale, IL 62901-4701

Southern Illinois University Edwardsville

Edwardsville, Illinois — **CB member**
www.siue.edu — **CB code: 1759**

- Public 4-year university
- Commuter campus in very large city
- 10,855 degree-seeking undergraduates: 15% part-time, 55% women, 10% African American, 2% Asian American, 2% Hispanic American, 1% international
- 2,385 degree-seeking graduate students
- 77% of applicants admitted
- 45% graduate within 6 years

General. Founded in 1957. Regionally accredited. **Degrees:** 722 bachelor's, 7 associate awarded; master's, first professional offered. **ROTC:** Army, Air Force. **Location:** 18 miles from St. Louis. **Calendar:** Semester, extensive summer session. **Full-time faculty:** 556 total; 83% have terminal degrees, 14% minority, 44% women. **Part-time faculty:** 263 total; 9% minority, 47% women. **Class size:** 38% < 20, 41% 20-39, 10% 40-49, 11% 50-99, 1% >100. **Special facilities:** Museum collections, arboretum, greenhouse, engineering labs, on-campus clinical facility for nursing instruction, observatory.

Freshman class profile. 5,379 applied, 4,149 admitted, 1,749 enrolled.

Mid 50% test scores		Return as sophomores:	76%
ACT:	20-25	Out-of-state:	9%
Rank in top quarter:	43%	Live on campus:	62%
Rank in top tenth:	16%	International:	1%

Basis for selection. Recent high school graduates admitted if GPA is equal to 2.5 and ACT score is greater than or equal to 21 (SAT equivalent = 970-1000, exclusive of Writing), or student is in top 25 percent of high school class. Applicants who do not meet this requirement may be considered for admission but are subject to additional review. SAT or ACT recommended. Audition recommended for music majors and portfolio recommended for art majors for admission to major.

High school preparation. 15 units required. Required and recommended units include English 4, mathematics 3, social studies 3, science 3 (laboratory 3), foreign language 2 and academic electives 2. 2 years of foreign language, music, dance, theater, art, or vocational education (1 year maximum) electives required. 2 years of 1 foreign language and 1 year of music and/or art recommended. 1 year of chemistry and 1 year of biology required. At least 2 years of history or government required.

2005-2006 Annual costs. Tuition/fees: $5,209; $11,734 out-of-state. Required fees include book rental. Room/board: $5,790. Books/supplies: $652. Personal expenses: $1,404.

2004-2005 Financial aid. All financial aid based on need. 1,249 full-time freshmen applied for aid; 850 were judged to have need; 806 of these received aid. Average need met was 76%. Average scholarship/grant was $5,573; average loan $2,369. 51% of total undergraduate aid awarded as scholarships/grants, 49% as loans/jobs.

Application procedures. Admission: Priority date 12/1; deadline 5/1 (postmark date). $30 fee, may be waived for applicants with need. Application may be submitted online. Admission notification on a rolling basis beginning on or about 9/1. Application and all official documents required to be on file 3 weeks before beginning of term. **Financial aid:** Priority date 3/1, closing date 6/1. FAFSA required. Applicants notified on a rolling basis starting 3/15; must reply within 4 week(s) of notification.

Academics. An undergraduate research academy and required senior project add to classroom experience. **Special study options:** Accelerated study, combined bachelor's/graduate degree, cooperative education, cross-registration, distance learning, double major, ESL, honors, independent study, internships, student-designed major, study abroad, teacher certification program, weekend college. **Credit/placement by examination:** AP, CLEP, institutional tests. 32 credit hours maximum toward bachelor's degree. Placement tests required for some students in reading, writing and/or math; determination based on test scores and GPA. **Support services:** Learning center, pre-admission summer program, reduced course load, remedial instruction, study skills assistance, tutoring, writing center.

Majors. Biology: General. **Business:** Accounting, business admin, management information systems, managerial economics. **Communications:** Media studies. **Computer sciences:** General, computer science. **Education:** Early childhood, elementary, health, science, special. **Engineering:** Civil, computer, electrical, industrial, manufacturing, mechanical. **Engineering technology:** Construction. **English:** Speech/rhetoric. **Foreign languages:** General. **Health:** Audiology/speech pathology, nursing (RN). **History:** General. **Liberal arts:** Arts/sciences. **Math:** General. **Parks/recreation:** Health/fitness. **Philosophy/religion:** Philosophy. **Physical sciences:** Chemistry, physics. **Protective services:** Criminal justice. **Psychology:** General. **Public administration:** Social work. **Social sciences:** Anthropology, economics, geography, political science, sociology. **Visual/performing arts:** Art, dance, dramatic, studio arts.

Most popular majors. Business/marketing 26%, education 11%, engineering/engineering technologies 6%, health sciences 6%, psychology 7%, social sciences 6%, visual/performing arts 6%.

Computing on campus. 600 workstations in dormitories, library, computer center, student center. Dormitories linked to campus network. Commuter students can connect to campus network. Online course registration, online library, helpline, wireless network available.

Student life. Freshman orientation: Available. Preregistration for classes offered. Offer summer pre-entry advisement and registration program in addition to freshman orientation. **Policies:** Freshmen permitted cars on campus. **Housing:** Coed dorms, special housing for disabled, apartments, fraternity/sorority housing, substance-free housing available. $300 deposit, deadline 5/1. Focused-interest communities. **Activities:** Bands, choral groups, dance, drama, film society, literary magazine, music ensembles, musical theater, opera, radio station, student government, student newspaper, symphony orchestra, TV station, 170 departmental, professional, religious, political, ethnic, and social organizations and honor societies.

Athletics. NCAA. **Intercollegiate:** Baseball M, basketball, cross-country, golf, soccer, softball W, tennis, track and field, volleyball W, wrestling M. **Intramural:** Badminton, basketball, bowling, fencing, football (non-tackle), golf, racquetball, soccer, softball, table tennis, tennis, volleyball, water polo. **Team name:** Cougars.

Student services. Alcohol/substance abuse counseling, campus ministries, career counseling, services for economically disadvantaged, student employment services, financial aid counseling, health services, legal services, on-campus daycare, personal counseling, placement for graduates, veterans' counselor. **Physically disabled:** Services for visually, speech, hearing impaired. **Learning disabled:** Comprehensive services available.

Contact. E-mail: admissions@siue.edu
Phone: (618) 650-3705 Toll-free number: (800) 447-7483
Fax: (618) 650-5013
Todd Burrell, Director of Admissions, Southern Illinois University Edwardsville, Campus Box 1600, Rendleman Hall, Rm 2120, Edwardsville, IL 62026-1600

Telshe Yeshiva-Chicago

Chicago, Illinois

CB code: 7009

- Private 4-year rabbinical college for men affiliated with Jewish faith
- Very large city
- 58 degree-seeking undergraduates
- 100% of applicants admitted

General. Accredited by AARTS. **Degrees:** 1 bachelor's awarded; first professional offered. **Calendar:** Continuous. **Full-time faculty:** 5 total. **Part-time faculty:** 1 total.

Freshman class profile. 17 applied, 17 admitted, 17 enrolled.

2006-2007 Annual costs. Comprehensive fee: $11,000.

Application procedures. Admission: No deadline. No application fee.

Academics. Credit/placement by examination: CLEP.

Majors. Theology: Talmudic.

Contact. Phone: (773) 463-7738 Fax: (773) 463-2894
Director of Admissions, Telshe Yeshiva-Chicago, 3535 West Foster Avenue, Chicago, IL 60625

Trinity Christian College

Palos Heights, Illinois
www.trnty.edu

CB code: 1820

- Private 4-year liberal arts college affiliated with Reformed (unaffiliated)
- Residential campus in very large city
- 1,148 degree-seeking undergraduates: 14% part-time, 66% women, 8% African American, 2% Asian American, 5% Hispanic American, 1% international
- 96% of applicants admitted
- SAT or ACT (ACT writing optional), application essay, interview required
- 53% graduate within 6 years; 12% enter graduate study

General. Founded in 1959. Regionally accredited. **Degrees:** 244 bachelor's awarded. **Location:** 20 miles from Chicago. **Calendar:** Semester, limited summer session. **Full-time faculty:** 76 total; 62% have terminal degrees, 60% minority, 41% women. **Part-time faculty:** 51 total; 20% have terminal degrees, 14% minority, 41% women. **Class size:** 64% < 20, 35% 20-39, less than 1% 40-49, less than 1% 50-99. **Special facilities:** Dutch heritage center archives.

Freshman class profile. 559 applied, 535 admitted, 229 enrolled.

Mid 50% test scores		**Rank in top quarter:**	33%
SAT verbal:	470-600	**Rank in top tenth:**	14%
SAT math:	440-570	**End year in good standing:**	86%
ACT:	19-25	**Return as sophomores:**	80%
GPA 3.50 or higher:	42%	**Out-of-state:**	52%
GPA 3.0-3.49:	25%	**Live on campus:**	90%
GPA 2.0-2.99:	32%		

Basis for selection. Recommended high school GPA 3.0, minimum 2.0 in English and mathematics, and ACT composite score of 22 (minimum 16) or SAT combined score of 950 (exclusive of Writing) required. Statement of religious faith recommended.

High school preparation. College-preparatory program recommended. 16 units required; 18 recommended. Required and recommended units include English 3-4, mathematics 3-4, social studies 2-3, history 2, science 2-3 and foreign language 2. One 3-year major in mathematics, science, or social studies, and 2 2-year minors in mathematics, science, social studies, or foreign language recommended.

2005-2006 Annual costs. Tuition/fees: $17,135. Room/board: $6,600. Books/supplies: $925. Personal expenses: $1,547.

2004-2005 Financial aid. Need-based: 196 full-time freshmen applied for aid; 163 were judged to have need; 163 of these received aid. Average need met was 8%. Average scholarship/grant was $3,995; average loan $2,994. 58% of total undergraduate aid awarded as scholarships/grants, 42% as loans/jobs. **Non-need-based:** Awarded to 774 full-time undergraduates, including 206 freshmen. Scholarships awarded for academics, art, athletics, leadership, minority status, music/drama, religious affiliation. **Additional information:** High school transcripts and ACT or SAT scores required for merit scholarships.

Application procedures. Admission: No deadline. $20 fee, may be waived for applicants with need. Application may be submitted online. Admission notification on a rolling basis beginning on or about 9/1. Must reply by May 1 or within 2 week(s) if notified thereafter. **Financial aid:** Priority date 2/15, closing date 4/15. FAFSA, institutional form required. Applicants notified by 2/28; must reply by 5/1 or within 2 week(s) of notification.

Academics. Special study options: Cooperative education, double major, honors, independent study, internships, liberal arts/career combination, study abroad, teacher certification program, urban semester, Washington semester. **Credit/placement by examination:** AP, CLEP, IB, SAT, ACT, institutional tests. 30 credit hours maximum toward bachelor's degree. **Support services:** Learning center, pre-admission summer program, reduced course load, remedial instruction, study skills assistance, tutoring, writing center.

Honors college/program. Must have 28 ACT, be in top 10% of high school class, and have 3.5 high school GPA. 13-19 semester hours of unique courses. Approximately 15 freshmen admitted each year.

Majors. Biology: General. **Business:** General, accounting, communications, management information systems, organizational behavior. **Communications:** General. **Computer sciences:** Computer science, information systems. **Education:** General, art, biology, business, chemistry, elementary, English, history, mathematics, music, physical, science, Spanish, special. **English:** English lit. **Foreign languages:** Spanish. **Health:** Nursing (RN). **History:** General. **Math:** General. **Parks/recreation:** Exercise sciences, health/fitness. **Philosophy/religion:** Philosophy. **Physical sciences:** Chemistry. **Psychology:** General. **Public administration:** Social work. **Social sciences:** Political science, sociology. **Theology:** Religious ed, theology. **Visual/performing arts:** Art, music performance, studio arts.

Most popular majors. Business/marketing 17%, education 34%, health sciences 6%, psychology 6%, theological studies 8%.

Computing on campus. 140 workstations in dormitories, library, computer center. Dormitories wired for high-speed internet access and linked to campus network. Commuter students can connect to campus network. Online library, helpline, wireless network available.

Student life. Freshman orientation: Mandatory, $150 fee. Preregistration for classes offered. 2-day program in early July and 2 week program in late August. **Policies:** Freshmen permitted cars on campus. **Housing:** Guaranteed on-campus for freshmen. Coed dorms, substance-free housing available. $75 fully refundable deposit, deadline 9/1. **Activities:** Bands, choral groups, dance, drama, literary magazine, music ensembles, student government, student newspaper, Christian ministry club, religious drama club, theology club, pro-life, Bread for the World, Inter-Varsity Fellowship, Big Brother Big Sister, Association for Public Justice, PACE literacy program in Cook County Jail.

Athletics. NAIA, NCCAA. **Intercollegiate:** Baseball M, basketball, cross-country, soccer, softball W, track and field, volleyball W. **Intramural:** Basketball, racquetball, soccer, volleyball. **Team name:** Trolls.

Student services. Adult student services, alcohol/substance abuse counseling, campus ministries, career counseling, student employment services, financial aid counseling, minority student services, personal counseling, placement for graduates, veterans' counselor. **Physically disabled:** Services for visually, speech, hearing impaired.

Contact. E-mail: adm@trnty.edu
Phone: (708) 239-4708 Toll-free number: (800) 748-0085
Fax: (708) 239-4826
Josh Lenarz, Director of Admissions, Trinity Christian College, 6601 West College Drive, Palos Heights, IL 60463

Trinity College of Nursing and Health Sciences

Rock Island, Illinois

CB code: 2555

- Private 4-year nursing college

Annual costs/financial aid. Tuition/fees (2005-2006): $8,050.

Contact. Phone: (309) 779-7710
2122 25th Avenue, Rock Island, IL 61201

Trinity International University

Deerfield, Illinois **CB member**
www.tiu.edu **CB code: 1810**

- Private 4-year university and liberal arts college affiliated with Evangelical Free Church of America
- Residential campus in large town
- 1,249 degree-seeking undergraduates: 13% part-time, 60% women, 13% African American, 4% Asian American, 4% Hispanic American, 1% international
- 1,370 degree-seeking graduate students
- 82% of applicants admitted
- SAT or ACT (ACT writing optional), application essay required
- 55% graduate within 6 years; 21% enter graduate study

General. Founded in 1897. Regionally accredited. Off-campus programs available through Christian College Consortium. **Degrees:** 210 bachelor's awarded; master's, doctoral, first professional offered. **Location:** 25 miles from Chicago. **Calendar:** Semester, limited summer session. **Full-time faculty:** 86 total; 80% have terminal degrees, 12% minority, 22% women. **Part-time faculty:** 274 total; 47% have terminal degrees, 23% minority, 34% women. **Class size:** 65% < 20, 28% 20-39, 5% 40-49, 2% 50-99. **Special facilities:** Seminary facilities.

Freshman class profile. 459 applied, 377 admitted, 160 enrolled.

Mid 50% test scores			
SAT verbal:	450-590	GPA 2.0-2.99:	27%
SAT math:	500-590	Rank in top quarter:	38%
ACT:	21-24	Rank in top tenth:	15%
GPA 3.50 or higher:	43%	Return as sophomores:	71%
GPA 3.0-3.49:	28%	Out-of-state:	41%
		Live on campus:	85%

Basis for selection. School achievement record, test scores, recommendations, evidence of Christian commitment, essays most important. Rank in top half of class recommended. Interview recommended for borderline applicants. **Homeschooled:** Transcript of courses and grades required.

High school preparation. College-preparatory program required. 15 units required. Required units include English 3, mathematics 2, social studies 2, science 2 (laboratory 1), foreign language 2 and academic electives 3.

2005-2006 Annual costs. Tuition/fees: $19,366. Room/board: $6,320. Books/supplies: $910. Personal expenses: $1,130.

2005-2006 Financial aid. Need-based: 183 full-time freshmen applied for aid; 153 were judged to have need; 153 of these received aid. Average need met was 16%. Average scholarship/grant was $5,897; average loan $3,121. 56% of total undergraduate aid awarded as scholarships/grants, 44% as loans/jobs. **Non-need-based:** Awarded to 857 full-time undergraduates, including 196 freshmen. Scholarships awarded for academics, alumni affiliation, athletics, minority status, music/drama, religious affiliation.

Application procedures. Admission: No deadline. $25 fee, may be waived for applicants with need. Application may be submitted online. Admission notification on a rolling basis beginning on or about 9/1. **Financial aid:** Priority date 4/1; no closing date. FAFSA required. Applicants notified on a rolling basis starting 2/15; must reply within 4 week(s) of notification.

Academics. Special study options: Accelerated study, cooperative education, cross-registration, distance learning, double major, dual enrollment of high school students, exchange student, honors, independent study, internships, liberal arts/career combination, student-designed major, study abroad, teacher certification program, urban semester, Washington semester. REACH (for nontraditional students with previous college credit), graduate courses available to undergraduates with junior or senior standing. **Credit/placement by examination:** AP, CLEP, IB, SAT, ACT, institutional tests. Permission and approval by department chair required. May not be used to satisfy senior residency requirement. **Support services:** Learning center, remedial instruction, study skills assistance, tutoring, writing center.

Majors. Biology: General. **Business:** General, accounting, human resources, management science, marketing, nonprofit/public, organizational behavior, training/development. **Communications:** General. **Education:** Biology, elementary, English, history, mathematics, music, physical, secondary. **Health:** Athletic training, premedicine. **History:** General. **Legal studies:** Prelaw. **Liberal arts:** Humanities. **Math:** General. **Parks/recreation:** Health/fitness. **Philosophy/religion:** Philosophy. **Physical sciences:** Chemistry. **Psychology:** General. **Social sciences:** General. **Theology:** Bible, pastoral counseling, preministerial, religious ed, sacred music, theology, youth ministry. **Visual/performing arts:** Music pedagogy, music performance, music theory/composition, piano/organ, voice/opera.

Most popular majors. Business/marketing 17%, education 25%, liberal arts 13%, psychology 6%, theological studies 20%.

Computing on campus. 100 workstations in library, computer center, student center. Dormitories wired for high-speed internet access and linked to campus network. Commuter students can connect to campus network. Online course registration, online library, helpline, repair service, student web hosting, wireless network available.

Student life. Freshman orientation: Mandatory, $30 fee. Preregistration for classes offered. Orientation held the week before classes each fall and spring. Generally lasts entire week. **Policies:** Community expectations, general patterns of Christian lifestyle, policy on drug and alcohol abuse. Religious observance required. Freshmen permitted cars on campus. **Housing:** Guaranteed on-campus for freshmen. Single-sex dorms, special housing for disabled, apartments, substance-free housing available. $50 deposit. **Activities:** Bands, choral groups, dance, drama, literary magazine, music ensembles, musical theater, opera, student government, student newspaper, symphony orchestra, Association of Believers for Black America, Global Christian Movement, Kappa Tau, Discipleship Cabinet, FAT Thursdays, Chapel Cabinet, Kids on Kampus, Fellowship of International Women, Wives Fellowship, Men's Ministry.

Athletics. NAIA, NCCAA. **Intercollegiate:** Baseball M, basketball, football (tackle) M, soccer, softball W, volleyball W. **Intramural:** Baseball M, basketball, bowling, football (non-tackle) M, racquetball, rugby M, soccer, softball, volleyball. **Team name:** Trojans.

Student services. Alcohol/substance abuse counseling, campus ministries, career counseling, student employment services, financial aid counseling, health services, minority student services, on-campus daycare, personal counseling, placement for graduates. **Physically disabled:** Services for visually impaired.

Contact. E-mail: tcadmissions@tiu.edu
Phone: (847) 317-7000 Toll-free number: (800) 822-3225
Fax: (847) 317-8097
Matt Yoder, Director of Admissions, Trinity International University, 2065 Half Day Road, Deerfield, IL 60015

University of Chicago

Chicago, Illinois **CB member**
www.uchicago.edu **CB code: 1832**

- Private 4-year university and liberal arts college
- Residential campus in very large city
- 4,638 degree-seeking undergraduates: 1% part-time, 51% women, 4% African American, 14% Asian American, 8% Hispanic American, 7% international
- 9,046 degree-seeking graduate students
- 40% of applicants admitted
- SAT or ACT (ACT writing optional), application essay required
- 89% graduate within 6 years

General. Founded in 1891. Regionally accredited. **Degrees:** 1,072 bachelor's awarded; master's, doctoral, first professional offered. **ROTC:** Army, Air Force. **Location:** 7 miles from Chicago. **Calendar:** Quarter, extensive summer session. **Full-time faculty:** 1,057 total; 98% have terminal degrees, 15% minority, 28% women. **Part-time faculty:** 530 total; 64% have terminal degrees, 14% minority, 32% women. **Class size:** 57% < 20, 33% 20-39, 3% 40-49, 5% 50-99, 1% >100. **Special facilities:** Oriental Institute, Argonne National Laboratory, library of sciences, Fermi National Accelerator Laboratory, theater, film studies center, National Opinion Research Center, art museum, observatory.

Freshman class profile. 9,011 applied, 3,628 admitted, 1,205 enrolled.

Mid 50% test scores			
SAT verbal:	680-770	Rank in top tenth:	79%
SAT math:	670-760	End year in good standing:	98%
ACT:	29-33	Return as sophomores:	96%
Rank in top quarter:	95%	Out-of-state:	83%
		International:	7%

Basis for selection. Secondary school record, recommendations, essay very important, as are talent/ability and character/ personal qualities. Interview recommended.

High school preparation. Recommended units include English 4, mathematics 4, social studies 2, history 2, science 4 and foreign language 3.

2005-2006 Annual costs. Tuition/fees: $32,265. Room/board: $10,104. Books/supplies: $950. Personal expenses: $1,736.

2004-2005 Financial aid. **Need-based:** 78% of total undergraduate aid awarded as scholarships/grants, 22% as loans/jobs. **Non-need-based:** Scholarships awarded for academics, leadership.

Application procedures. **Admission:** Closing date 1/1 (postmark date). $60 fee, may be waived for applicants with need. Application may be submitted online. Admission notification 4/1. Must reply by 5/1. **Financial aid:** Closing date 2/1. FAFSA, institutional form, CSS PROFILE required. Applicants notified by 4/5; must reply by 5/1.

Academics. **Special study options:** Accelerated study, combined bachelor's/graduate degree, double major, independent study, internships, student-designed major, study abroad, teacher certification program, Washington semester. **Credit/placement by examination:** AP, CLEP, IB, institutional tests. **Support services:** Study skills assistance, tutoring.

Majors. **Area/ethnic studies:** African, African-American, German, Latin American, Near/Middle Eastern, Russian/Slavic, Slavic, South Asian. **Biology:** General, biochemistry. **Computer sciences:** General. **Conservation:** Environmental studies. **Foreign languages:** Ancient Greek, Arabic, Biblical, classics, comparative lit, East Asian, French, German, Hebrew, Italian, Latin, linguistics, Portuguese, Russian, Scandinavian, Slavic, South Asian, Spanish. **History:** General. **Liberal arts:** Arts/sciences. **Math:** General, applied, statistics. **Philosophy/religion:** Judaic, philosophy, religion. **Physical sciences:** Chemistry, geophysics, physics. **Psychology:** General. **Public administration:** Policy analysis. **Social sciences:** Anthropology, economics, geography, international relations, political science, sociology. **Visual/performing arts:** General, art history/conservation, film/cinema.

Most popular majors. Biology 11%, English 6%, history 6%, mathematics 7%, physical sciences 6%, psychology 6%, social sciences 39%.

Computing on campus. 1,000 workstations in dormitories, library, computer center, student center. Dormitories wired for high-speed internet access and linked to campus network. Commuter students can connect to campus network. Online course registration, online library, helpline, repair service, student web hosting, wireless network available.

Student life. **Freshman orientation:** Mandatory, $440 fee. Held 10 days before classes begin in the fall. **Housing:** Guaranteed on-campus for all undergraduates. Coed dorms, apartments, fraternity/sorority housing available. $150 deposit, deadline 5/1. **Activities:** Bands, choral groups, dance, drama, film society, literary magazine, music ensembles, musical theater, radio station, student government, student newspaper, symphony orchestra, over 350 organizations.

Athletics. NCAA. **Intercollegiate:** Baseball M, basketball, cross-country, football (tackle) M, soccer, softball W, swimming, tennis, track and field, volleyball W, wrestling M. **Intramural:** Archery, badminton, basketball, cross-country, fencing, handball, racquetball, soccer, softball, swimming, table tennis, tennis, track and field, volleyball. **Team name:** Maroons.

Student services. Adult student services, alcohol/substance abuse counseling, campus ministries, career counseling, services for economically disadvantaged, student employment services, financial aid counseling, health services, minority student services, personal counseling, placement for graduates, veterans' counselor, women's services. **Physically disabled:** Services for visually, hearing impaired.

Contact. E-mail: questions@phoenix.uchicago.edu
Phone: (773) 702-8650 Fax: (773) 702-4199
Theodore O'Neill, Dean of Admissions, University of Chicago, 1101 East 58th Street, Chicago, IL 60637

University of Illinois at Chicago

Chicago, Illinois — **CB member**
www.uic.edu — **CB code: 1851**

- Public 4-year university
- Commuter campus in very large city
- 15,029 degree-seeking undergraduates: 9% part-time, 53% women, 9% African American, 25% Asian American, 17% Hispanic American, 1% international
- 8,756 degree-seeking graduate students
- 58% of applicants admitted
- SAT or ACT (ACT writing recommended) required
- 50% graduate within 6 years

General. Founded in 1946. Regionally accredited. Medical, dental, nursing and pharmacy colleges, and medical center within university complex. **Degrees:** 3,149 bachelor's awarded; master's, doctoral, first professional offered. **ROTC:** Army, Navy, Air Force. **Location:** One mile from downtown. **Calendar:** Semester, limited summer session. **Full-time faculty:** 1,206 total; 74% have terminal degrees, 22% minority, 40% women. **Part-time faculty:** 288 total; 48% have terminal degrees, 17% minority, 48% women. **Class size:** 36% < 20, 39% 20-39, 7% 40-49, 9% 50-99, 8% >100. **Special facilities:** Jane Addams' Hull House, prairie preserve, health sciences library, software technologies research facility, numerous computer labs, cultural centers, art galleries.

Freshman class profile. 12,692 applied, 7,418 admitted, 2,776 enrolled.

Mid 50% test scores		**Out-of-state:**	4%
ACT:	20-26	**Live on campus:**	25%
Rank in top quarter:	57%	**International:**	2%
Rank in top tenth:	25%	**Fraternities:**	1%
Return as sophomores:	78%	**Sororities:**	1%

Basis for selection. Class rank and test scores most important. High school course selection, GPA and personal statement considered. Essay required of human nutrition and dietetics, health information management, education majors. Auditions required of music and theater majors. Portfolio required of art majors. **Homeschooled:** Transcript of courses and grades required. Students must satisfy all of the requirements for a beginning freshman applicant. **Learning Disabled:** Students may add learning disability information to personal essay.

High school preparation. 16 units required. Required and recommended units include English 4, mathematics 3-4, social studies 3, science 3 (laboratory 3) and foreign language 4. Additional course requirements vary with college and program.

2005-2006 Annual costs. Tuition/fees: $8,302; $20,692 out-of-state. Room/board: $7,954. Books/supplies: $900. Personal expenses: $2,000.

2004-2005 Financial aid. **Need-based:** 2,181 full-time freshmen applied for aid; 1,594 were judged to have need; 1,584 of these received aid. Average need met was 94%. Average scholarship/grant was $8,860; average loan $2,822. 58% of total undergraduate aid awarded as scholarships/grants, 42% as loans/jobs. **Non-need-based:** Awarded to 2,592 full-time undergraduates, including 724 freshmen. Scholarships awarded for academics, art, athletics, music/drama, ROTC, state residency.

Application procedures. **Admission:** Closing date 1/15 (postmark date). $40 fee, may be waived for applicants with need. Application may be submitted online. Admission notification on a rolling basis. **Financial aid:** Priority date 3/1; no closing date. FAFSA required. Applicants notified on a rolling basis starting 4/15; must reply within 2 week(s) of notification.

Academics. **Special study options:** Accelerated study, combined bachelor's/graduate degree, cooperative education, distance learning, double major, dual enrollment of high school students, exchange student, honors, independent study, internships, student-designed major, study abroad, teacher certification program. Concurrent registration at another campus of University of Illinois. **Credit/placement by examination:** AP, CLEP, IB, institutional tests. 30 credit hours maximum toward bachelor's degree. **Support services:** Learning center, pre-admission summer program, remedial instruction, study skills assistance, tutoring, writing center.

Honors college/program. Minimum ACT of 28; top 15% of high school class. About 450 freshmen admitted each year. Students must complete an honors activity each term and maintain a minimum cumulative GPA of 3.25 on 4.0 scale. Transfer students with a GPA of 3.50 on 4.0 scale and continuing UIC students with a minimum cumulative GPA of 3.25 who have at least three semesters remaining before graduation are also encouraged to apply to the Honors College.

Majors. **Area/ethnic studies:** African-American, Latin American. **Biology:** General, biochemistry. **Business:** Accounting, entrepreneurial studies, finance, management information systems, marketing. **Computer sciences:** General. **Education:** Art, chemistry, elementary, English, foreign languages, French, German, history, mathematics, physics, Spanish. **Engineering:** Biomedical, chemical, civil, computer, electrical, mechanical, physics. **Engineering technology:** Industrial management. **English:** Speech/rhetoric. **Foreign languages:** Classics, French, German, Italian, Polish, Russian, Spanish. **Health:** Clinical lab science, dietetics, medical records admin, nursing (RN), predentistry. **History:** General. **Interdisciplinary:** Math/computer science. **Liberal arts:** Arts/sciences. **Math:** General, statistics. **Parks/recreation:** Exercise sciences. **Philosophy/religion:** Philosophy. **Physical sciences:** Chemistry, geology, physics. **Protective services:** Criminal justice. **Psychology:** General. **Public administration:** Social work. **Social sciences:** Anthropology, economics, political science, sociology. **Visual/performing arts:** Art history/conservation, commercial/advertising art, dramatic, industrial design, photography, studio arts.

Most popular majors. Biology 11%, business/marketing 20%, education 6%, engineering/engineering technologies 10%, health sciences 8%, psychology 9%, social sciences 8%.

Computing on campus. 1,100 workstations in dormitories, library, computer center, student center. Dormitories wired for high-speed internet access and linked to campus network. Commuter students can connect to campus network. Online course registration, online library, helpline, wireless network available.

Student life. Freshman orientation: Mandatory, $99 fee. Preregistration for classes offered. 2-day, overnight offered 12 times from early June to mid-August. **Policies:** Freshmen permitted cars on campus. **Housing:** Coed dorms, special housing for disabled, apartments available. $125 partly refundable deposit, deadline 4/1. Honors floors, Presidential Award House, special interest floors available. **Activities:** Bands, choral groups, dance, drama, literary magazine, music ensembles, musical theater, radio station, student government, student newspaper, over 200 student groups including academic, professional, governing, ethnic, religious, literary, political, social service, special interest organizations.

Athletics. NCAA. **Intercollegiate:** Baseball M, basketball, cross-country, diving, gymnastics, soccer M, softball W, swimming, tennis, track and field, volleyball W. **Intramural:** Badminton, basketball, bowling, cross-country, fencing, football (non-tackle), golf, racquetball, soccer, softball, squash, table tennis, tennis, volleyball, wrestling M. **Team name:** Flames.

Student services. Adult student services, alcohol/substance abuse counseling, campus ministries, career counseling, services for economically disadvantaged, student employment services, financial aid counseling, health services, legal services, minority student services, on-campus daycare, personal counseling, placement for graduates, veterans' counselor, women's services. **Physically disabled:** Services for visually, speech, hearing impaired.

Contact. E-mail: uicadmit@uic.edu
Phone: (312) 996-4350 Fax: (312) 413-7628
Thomas Glenn, Executive Director Admissions and Records, University of Illinois at Chicago, PO Box 5220, Chicago, IL 60680

University of Illinois at Urbana-Champaign

Champaign, Illinois — **CB member**
www.uiuc.edu — **CB code: 1836**

- Public 4-year university
- Residential campus in small city
- 30,251 degree-seeking undergraduates: 2% part-time, 47% women, 7% African American, 13% Asian American, 6% Hispanic American, 4% international
- 10,494 degree-seeking graduate students
- 75% of applicants admitted
- SAT or ACT (ACT writing recommended), application essay required
- 80% graduate within 6 years; 30% enter graduate study

General. Founded in 1867. Regionally accredited. 16 colleges and schools and more than 80 research centers and labs. **Degrees:** 6,752 bachelor's awarded; master's, doctoral, first professional offered. **ROTC:** Army, Navy, Air Force. **Location:** 130 miles from Chicago, 180 miles from St. Louis. **Calendar:** Semester, extensive summer session. **Full-time faculty:** 2,271 total; 87% have terminal degrees, 19% minority, 31% women. **Part-time faculty:** 430 total; 63% have terminal degrees, 19% minority, 41% women. **Class size:** 34% < 20, 42% 20-39, 6% 40-49, 9% 50-99, 9% >100. **Special facilities:** Natural history museum, museum of world history and culture, performing and visual arts centers, institute for advanced science and technology, computer science center, national center for supercomputing applications, arboretum, observatory, hiking trails, Japanese house and gardens.

Freshman class profile. 18,987 applied, 14,326 admitted, 8,577 enrolled.

Mid 50% test scores			
SAT verbal:	550-670	Return as sophomores:	93%
SAT math:	620-730	Out-of-state:	11%
ACT:	26-31	Live on campus:	99%
Rank in top quarter:	86%	International:	4%
Rank in top tenth:	48%	Fraternities:	25%
End year in good standing:	98%	Sororities:	27%

Basis for selection. High school course work, personal essay, class rank, SAT/ACT test scores most important. Audition required of dance, music, theater (performance) majors. Professional interest statement required of all applicants. **Homeschooled:** The more information about the home school environment/coursework descriptions the better; aplicants should contact admissions office early in high school career with any questions or concerns. **Learning Disabled:** Recommended that students with learning disabilities address disability and any accommodations they receive in required personal statement section.

High school preparation. 15 units required. Required units include English 4, mathematics 3, social studies 2, science 2 (laboratory 2), foreign language 2 and academic electives 2. Specific subject requirements vary with college and program.

2005-2006 Annual costs. Tuition/fees: $8,688; $22,774 out-of-state. Room/board: $7,176. Books/supplies: $950. Personal expenses: $2,020.

2004-2005 Financial aid. Need-based: 4,994 full-time freshmen applied for aid; 3,084 were judged to have need; 2,927 of these received aid. Average need met was 90%. Average scholarship/grant was $6,680; average loan $3,290. 46% of total undergraduate aid awarded as scholarships/grants, 54% as loans/jobs. **Non-need-based:** Awarded to 12,510 full-time undergraduates, including 4,265 freshmen. Scholarships awarded for academics, alumni affiliation, art, athletics, leadership, music/drama, ROTC, state residency.

Application procedures. Admission: Closing date 1/2 (postmark date). $40 fee, may be waived for applicants with need. Application may be submitted online. Admission notification on a rolling basis beginning on or about 10/1. Must reply by 5/1. Application filing period October 1 to January 2. Applicants encouraged to have complete application on file by November 15. **Financial aid:** Priority date 3/15; no closing date. FAFSA required. Applicants notified on a rolling basis starting 3/15.

Academics. Students generally declare a major upon enrollment. Students without a declared major may apply for general curriculum option in College of Liberal Arts and Science. **Special study options:** Accelerated study, combined bachelor's/graduate degree, cooperative education, cross-registration, distance learning, double major, dual enrollment of high school students, ESL, exchange student, honors, independent study, internships, liberal arts/career combination, student-designed major, study abroad, teacher certification program, Washington semester. Illinois Leadership program. **Credit/placement by examination:** AP, CLEP, IB, SAT, ACT, institutional tests. Unlimited credit hours may be counted toward a degree. **Support services:** Learning center, pre-admission summer program, reduced course load, study skills assistance, tutoring, writing center.

Majors. Agriculture: Agronomy, animal husbandry, animal sciences, business, communications, economics, education services, farm/ranch, food processing, food science, horticultural science, horticulture, mechanization, ornamental horticulture. **Architecture:** Architecture, landscape, urban/community planning. **Area/ethnic studies:** East Asian, Latin American, Russian/Slavic, women's. **Biology:** General, biochemistry, biomedical sciences, biophysics, biotechnology, botany, cell/histology, cellular/molecular, entomology, microbiology, physiology, plant molecular. **Business:** General, accounting, accounting/business management, actuarial science, auditing, banking/financial services, business admin, entrepreneurial studies, finance, financial planning, hospitality admin, human resources, insurance, logistics, management information systems, management science, market research, marketing, operations, organizational behavior, purchasing, real estate, sales/distribution. **Communications:** General, advertising, broadcast journalism, journalism, media studies, organizational. **Computer sciences:** General, computer science, programming, security. **Conservation:** General, environmental science, forest sciences, management/policy, urban forestry, wildlife. **Education:** Agricultural, art, biology, chemistry, early childhood, early childhood special, elementary, English, foreign languages, French, German, history, kindergarten/preschool, Latin, mathematics, multi-level teacher, multiple handicapped, music, physical, physics, secondary, Spanish, special. **Engineering:** General, aerospace, agricultural, architectural, biomedical, ceramic, chemical, civil, computer, electrical, geotechnical, industrial, materials, materials science, mechanical, mechanics, metallurgical, nuclear, physics, polymer, structural. **English:** Composition, English lit, speech/rhetoric. **Family/consumer sciences:** Child development, clothing/textiles, consumer economics, family studies, human nutrition. **Foreign languages:** Classics, comparative lit, East Asian, French, German, Hebrew, Italian, linguistics, Portuguese, Russian, Spanish. **Health:** Athletic training, audiology/hearing, audiology/speech pathology, community health, dietetics, environmental health, health services admin, preveterinary, vocational rehab counseling. **History:** General. **Interdisciplinary:** Global studies, math/computer science. **Legal studies:** Prelaw. **Liberal arts:** Arts/sciences, humanities. **Math:** General, computational, statistics. **Parks/recreation:** General, exercise sciences. **Philosophy/religion:** Philosophy, religion. **Physical sciences:** Astronomy, chemistry, geology, physics. **Psychology:** General. **Social sciences:** Anthropology, economics, geography, political science, sociology. **Transportation:** Airline/commercial pilot, aviation management. **Visual/performing arts:** Art history/conservation, crafts, dance, dramatic, film/cinema, graphic design, music history, music performance, music theory/composition, painting, photography, sculpture, studio arts, theater history, voice/opera.

Most popular majors. Biology 7%, business/marketing 16%, engineering/engineering technologies 14%, English 7%, psychology 7%, social sciences 10%.

Computing on campus. 4,420 workstations in dormitories, library, computer center, student center. Dormitories wired for high-speed internet access and linked to campus network. Commuter students can connect to campus network. Online course registration, online library, helpline, repair service, student web hosting, wireless network available.

Student life. Freshman orientation: Mandatory, $96 fee. Preregistration for classes offered. One-day program, held June 1 to July 13. **Policies:** Freshmen required to live on campus unless over 21 years, married, or living with parents. Freshmen permitted cars on campus. **Housing:** Guaranteed on-campus for freshmen. Coed dorms, single-sex dorms, special housing for disabled, apartments, cooperative housing, fraternity/sorority housing, substance-free housing available. $100 fully refundable deposit, deadline 5/1. Living and learning communities and private housing are available. **Activities:** Bands, choral groups, dance, drama, literary magazine, music ensembles, musical theater, opera, radio station, student government, student newspaper, symphony orchestra, TV station, more than 1,000 registered student organizations.

Athletics. NCAA. **Intercollegiate:** Baseball M, basketball, cheerleading, cross-country, diving W, football (tackle) M, golf, gymnastics, soccer W, softball W, swimming W, tennis, track and field, volleyball W, wrestling M. **Intramural:** Badminton, basketball, cross-country, football (non-tackle), golf, racquetball, soccer, softball, tennis, volleyball. **Team name:** Illini.

Student services. Alcohol/substance abuse counseling, campus ministries, career counseling, services for economically disadvantaged, student employment services, financial aid counseling, health services, legal services, minority student services, on-campus daycare, personal counseling, placement for graduates, veterans' counselor, women's services. **Physically disabled:** Services for visually, speech, hearing impaired. **Learning disabled:** Comprehensive services available.

Contact. E-mail: ugradadmissioins@uiuc.edu
Phone: (217) 333-0302 Fax: (217) 244-0903
Keith Marshall, Associate Provost, University of Illinois at Urbana-Champaign, 901 West Illinois, Urbana, IL 61801-3028

University of Illinois: Springfield

Springfield, Illinois — **CB member**
www.uis.edu — **CB code: 0834**

- Public 4-year university and liberal arts college
- Commuter campus in small city
- 2,446 degree-seeking undergraduates: 38% part-time, 59% women, 9% African American, 3% Asian American, 2% Hispanic American, 1% international
- 1,619 degree-seeking graduate students
- 63% of applicants admitted
- SAT or ACT (ACT writing recommended) required

General. Founded in 1969. Regionally accredited. Third campus of University of Illinois system with emphasis on public affairs and a liberal arts mission. **Degrees:** 672 bachelor's awarded; master's, doctoral offered. **Location:** 95 miles from St. Louis, 200 miles from Chicago. **Calendar:** Semester, extensive summer session. **Full-time faculty:** 179 total; 91% have terminal degrees, 16% minority, 42% women. **Part-time faculty:** 152 total; 32% have terminal degrees, 10% minority, 52% women. **Class size:** 65% < 20, 34% 20-39, 1% 40-49. **Special facilities:** Observatory, studio theatre, visual arts gallery.

Freshman class profile. 493 applied, 311 admitted, 138 enrolled.

Mid 50% test scores		**End year in good standing:**	83%
ACT:	22-27	**Return as sophomores:**	84%
Rank in top quarter:	52%	**Out-of-state:**	4%
Rank in top tenth:	20%	**International:**	1%

Basis for selection. Secondary school GPA, rank, and record; completion of college-preparatory program, recommendations, admission test scores, and formal demonstration of competencies all fully considered. Personal or telephone interview may be part of the selection process.

High school preparation. Required units include English 4, mathematics 3, social studies 3, science 2 (laboratory 2) and foreign language 2.

2005-2006 Annual costs. Tuition/fees: $5,375; $14,525 out-of-state. Room/board: $6,960. Books/supplies: $1,200. Personal expenses: $1,950.

2004-2005 Financial aid. Need-based: 87 full-time freshmen applied for aid; 55 were judged to have need; 55 of these received aid. Average need met was 88%. Average scholarship/grant was $4,719; average loan $2,361. 49% of total undergraduate aid awarded as scholarships/grants, 51% as loans/jobs. **Non-need-based:** Awarded to 594 full-time undergraduates, including 98 freshmen. Scholarships awarded for academics, alumni affiliation, art, athletics, job skills, leadership, minority status, music/drama, state residency.

Application procedures. Admission: Priority date 1/15; no deadline. $40 fee, may be waived for applicants with need. Application may be submitted online. Admission notification on a rolling basis beginning on or about 9/15. Must reply by May 1 or we will accept notification until the class is filled. **Financial aid:** Priority date 4/1, closing date 11/15. FAFSA required. Applicants notified on a rolling basis starting 1/1; must reply within 3 week(s) of notification.

Academics. Special study options: Distance learning, double major, external degree, independent study, internships, student-designed major, study abroad, teacher certification program. **Credit/placement by examination:** AP, CLEP, IB, institutional tests. **Support services:** Learning center, reduced course load, study skills assistance, tutoring, writing center.

Majors. Biology: General. **Business:** Accounting, business admin. **Communications:** General. **Computer sciences:** Computer science. **English:** English lit. **Health:** Clinical lab science. **History:** General. **Legal studies:** General. **Liberal arts:** Arts/sciences. **Math:** General. **Philosophy/religion:** Philosophy. **Physical sciences:** Chemistry. **Protective services:** Criminal justice. **Psychology:** General. **Public administration:** Social work. **Social sciences:** General, economics, political science. **Visual/performing arts:** Studio arts.

Most popular majors. Business/marketing 29%, communications/journalism 8%, computer/information sciences 6%, liberal arts 9%, psychology 12%, security/protective services 6%, social sciences 6%.

Computing on campus. 132 workstations in library, computer center. Dormitories wired for high-speed internet access and linked to campus network. Commuter students can connect to campus network. Online course registration, online library, helpline, wireless network available.

Student life. Freshman orientation: Mandatory. **Policies:** Freshmen permitted cars on campus. **Housing:** Guaranteed on-campus for freshmen. Coed dorms, apartments, substance-free housing available. $150 partly refundable deposit, deadline 5/1. **Activities:** Concert band, choral groups, drama, film society, music ensembles, student government, student newspaper, Chinese student association, Christian student fellowship, ACLU, Indian student organization, Habitat for Humanity, Living Word Bible Study, college Democrats, college Republicans, Polish club.

Athletics. NAIA. **Intercollegiate:** Basketball, soccer M, softball W, tennis, volleyball W. **Intramural:** Badminton, basketball, football (tackle), soccer, softball, tennis, volleyball. **Team name:** Prairie Stars.

Student services. Alcohol/substance abuse counseling, career counseling, student employment services, financial aid counseling, health services, minority student services, on-campus daycare, personal counseling, women's services. **Physically disabled:** Services for visually, speech, hearing impaired.

Contact. E-mail: admissions@uis.edu
Phone: (217) 206-4847 Toll-free number: (888) 977-4847
Fax: (217) 206-6620
Director, University of Illinois: Springfield, One University Plaza, MS UHB 1080, Springfield, IL 62703

University of St. Francis

Joliet, Illinois
www.stfrancis.edu — **CB code: 1130**

- Private 4-year university and liberal arts college affiliated with Roman Catholic Church
- Commuter campus in small city
- 1,249 degree-seeking undergraduates: 9% part-time, 69% women, 9% African American, 4% Asian American, 7% Hispanic American, 1% international
- 745 degree-seeking graduate students
- 57% of applicants admitted
- SAT or ACT (ACT writing optional) required
- 56% graduate within 6 years; 15% enter graduate study

General. Founded in 1920. Regionally accredited. Affiliated with Argonne National Laboratories, Morton Arboretum, Will County Forest Preserve, Midewin Tallgrass Prairie, Shedd Aquarium. **Degrees:** 288 bachelor's awarded; master's offered. **Location:** 45 miles from Chicago. **Calendar:** Semester, limited summer session. **Full-time faculty:** 74 total; 60% have terminal degrees, 8% minority, 58% women. **Part-time faculty:** 145 total; 23% have terminal degrees, 7% minority, 52% women. **Class size:** 68% < 20, 31% 20-39, 1% 40-49. **Special facilities:** Performing arts center, greenhouse.

Freshman class profile. 759 applied, 429 admitted, 190 enrolled.

Mid 50% test scores		Rank in top tenth:	18%
ACT:	20-24	End year in good standing:	90%
GPA 3.50 or higher:	27%	Return as sophomores:	80%
GPA 3.0-3.49:	39%	Out-of-state:	2%
GPA 2.0-2.99:	34%	Live on campus:	56%
Rank in top quarter:	43%		

Basis for selection. High school record and rank; test scores important. Essay and letters of recommendation required and interview recommended for academically weak applicants. **Homeschooled:** Transcript of courses and grades, state high school equivalency certificate required.

High school preparation. College-preparatory program required. 16 units required. Required and recommended units include English 4, mathematics 2, social studies 2, science 2 (laboratory 1), foreign language 1 and academic electives 3. 3 units required from 2 areas: language, music or arts, or computer science.

2005-2006 Annual costs. Tuition/fees: $18,530. Room/board: $6,380.

2005-2006 Financial aid. Need-based: 175 full-time freshmen applied for aid; 144 were judged to have need; 144 of these received aid. Average need met was 91%. Average scholarship/grant was $7,030; average loan $2,692. 66% of total undergraduate aid awarded as scholarships/grants, 34% as loans/jobs. **Non-need-based:** Awarded to 914 full-time undergraduates, including 187 freshmen. Scholarships awarded for academics, alumni affiliation, art, athletics, leadership, music/drama, religious affiliation, state residency.

Application procedures. Admission: Priority date 5/1; deadline 8/1 (receipt date). $30 fee, may be waived for applicants with need. Application may be submitted online. Admission notification on a rolling basis beginning on or about 9/1. Must reply by 5/1. **Financial aid:** Priority date 4/1; no closing date. FAFSA, institutional form required. Applicants notified on a rolling basis starting 2/15.

Academics. Special study options: Accelerated study, combined bachelor's/graduate degree, distance learning, double major, honors, independent study, internships, student-designed major, study abroad, teacher certification program, Washington semester. **Credit/placement by examination:** AP, CLEP, IB, SAT, ACT, institutional tests. 33 credit hours maximum toward bachelor's degree. **Support services:** Learning center, pre-admission summer program, reduced course load, remedial instruction, study skills assistance, tutoring, writing center.

Majors. Biology: General. **Business:** Accounting, actuarial science, business admin, finance, human resources, marketing, organizational behavior. **Communications:** Advertising, broadcast journalism, media studies, public relations, radio/tv. **Computer sciences:** Computer science, information technology, webmaster. **Conservation:** Environmental science. **Education:** Elementary, English, mathematics, music, science, social studies, special. **English:** English lit. **Health:** Clinical lab science, health care admin, medical radiologic technology/radiation therapy, nuclear medical technology, nursing (RN), predentistry, premedicine, preveterinary, radiologic technology/medical imaging, recreational therapy. **History:** General. **Interdisciplinary:** Math/computer science. **Liberal arts:** Arts/sciences. **Math:** General. **Parks/recreation:** Facilities management. **Psychology:** General. **Public administration:** Social work. **Social sciences:** Political science. **Theology:** Theology. **Visual/performing arts:** General, music performance.

Most popular majors. Business/marketing 19%, education 25%, health sciences 17%.

Computing on campus. 365 workstations in dormitories, library, computer center. Dormitories wired for high-speed internet access and linked to campus network. Commuter students can connect to campus network. Online course registration, online library, helpline, wireless network available.

Student life. Freshman orientation: Mandatory, $40 fee. Orientation is part of semester-long Core I program. **Policies:** Freshmen permitted cars on campus. **Housing:** Guaranteed on-campus for freshmen. Coed dorms, substance-free housing available. $50 fully refundable deposit, deadline 6/30. **Activities:** Choral groups, dance, drama, literary magazine, music ensembles, musical theater, radio station, student government, student newspaper, symphony orchestra, TV station, Ministry Council, social work club, Black Student Association, student business association, Association of Republican Students, Council for Environmental and Social Awareness, Council for Social Activism, Unidos Vamos Alcanzar, student government association, student nurses association.

Athletics. NAIA. **Intercollegiate:** Baseball M, basketball, cheerleading M, cross-country W, football (tackle) M, golf, soccer, softball W, tennis, track and field W, volleyball W. **Intramural:** Basketball, bowling, golf, racquetball, skiing, table tennis, volleyball. **Team name:** Saints.

Student services. Adult student services, campus ministries, career counseling, student employment services, financial aid counseling, health services, minority student services, personal counseling, placement for graduates. **Physically disabled:** Services for visually, speech, hearing impaired.

Contact. E-mail: information@stfrancis.edu
Phone: (815) 740-5037 Toll-free number: (800) 735-7500
Fax: (815) 740-5032
Meghan Connolly, Director Undergraduate Admissions, University of St. Francis, 500 Wilcox Street, Joliet, IL 60435

VanderCook College of Music

Chicago, Illinois
www.vandercook.edu **CB code: 1872**

- Private 4-year music and teachers college
- Residential campus in very large city
- 110 degree-seeking undergraduates: 5% part-time, 50% women, 14% African American, 2% Asian American, 13% Hispanic American, 2% international
- 37 degree-seeking graduate students
- 50% of applicants admitted
- SAT or ACT (ACT writing recommended), application essay, interview required
- 39% graduate within 6 years

General. Founded in 1909. Regionally accredited. Provides one of largest summer programs for music teachers in nation. **Degrees:** 8 bachelor's awarded; master's offered. **Location:** Central Chicago. **Calendar:** Semester. **Full-time faculty:** 11 total. **Part-time faculty:** 31 total. **Class size:** 67% < 20, 30% 20-39, 3% 50-99. **Special facilities:** MIDI/electronic music laboratory, listening booths equipped with cassette, compact disc and LP formats, access to student services at Illinois Institute of Technology.

Freshman class profile. 82 applied, 41 admitted, 31 enrolled.

Mid 50% test scores		Return as sophomores:	89%
SAT verbal:	440-540	Out-of-state:	37%
SAT math:	490-540	International:	5%
ACT:	16-22		

Basis for selection. Academic credentials, SAT or ACT scores and recommendations are weighed along with student's musical audition and interview. Institutional test required. Audition required. **Homeschooled:** Should obtain experience performing with a concert band or chorus.

High school preparation. 15 units required. Required units include English 3, mathematics 2, social studies 3, science 2, foreign language 2 and academic electives 3. Evidence of participation in curricular or extracurricular music ensembles and lessons.

2005-2006 Annual costs. Tuition/fees: $16,610. Room/board: $7,200. Books/supplies: $1,500. Personal expenses: $1,850.

2004-2005 Financial aid. Need-based: 46% of total undergraduate aid awarded as scholarships/grants, 54% as loans/jobs. **Non-need-based:** Scholarships awarded for academics, alumni affiliation, leadership, minority status, music/drama, state residency. **Additional information:** Musical talent considered for partial tuition waiver.

Application procedures. Admission: Priority date 3/15; deadline 5/1 (receipt date). $35 fee. Admission notification on a rolling basis. Must reply by 6/1. **Financial aid:** Priority date 3/1, closing date 4/30. FAFSA required. Applicants notified on a rolling basis starting 5/15; must reply within 2 week(s) of notification.

Academics. Special study options: Teacher certification program. **Credit/placement by examination:** CLEP, institutional tests.

Majors. Education: Music.

Computing on campus. 10 workstations in dormitories, library, computer center, student center.

Student life. Freshman orientation: Mandatory. **Policies:** Student life focuses around musical activities at VanderCook and on the Illinois Institue of Technology campus. **Housing:** Guaranteed on-campus for all undergraduates. Coed dorms, apartments, fraternity/sorority housing available. $100 deposit. **Activities:** Bands, choral groups, music ensembles, musical theater.

Student services. Career counseling, student employment services, health services, personal counseling, placement for graduates.

Contact. E-mail: admissions@vandercook.edu
Phone: (312) 225-6288 ext. 230 Toll-free number: (800) 448-2655 ext. 230
Fax: (312) 225-5211
Patty O'Kelley, Student Recruiter, VanderCook College of Music, 3140 South Federal Street, Chicago, IL 60616-3731

West Suburban College of Nursing

Oak Park, Illinois
www.wscn.edu **CB code: 1927**

- Private upper-division nursing college affiliated with Roman Catholic Church
- Commuter campus in very large city
- Test scores, application essay required

General. Founded in 1982. Regionally accredited. Facilities located in West Suburban Medical Center. **Degrees:** 36 bachelor's awarded. **Location:** 10 miles from downtown Chicago. **Calendar:** Semester, limited summer session. **Full-time faculty:** 11 total. **Part-time faculty:** 6 total. **Class size:** 38% < 20, 38% 20-39, 24% 40-49. **Special facilities:** In-hospital location, health sciences library, nursing clinical skills laboratory.

Student profile. 136 degree-seeking undergraduates, 2 degree-seeking graduate students. 29 applied as first time-transfer students.

Women:	90%	**Hispanic American:**	14%
African American:	20%	**Part-time:**	21%
Asian American:	25%		

Basis for selection. College transcript, application essay, standardized test scores required. Natural and behavioral science grades are more heavily weighted. Recommendation and essay required. Must have science GPA of 2.75 cum/4.0. Transfer accepted as juniors, seniors.

2005-2006 Annual costs. Tuition/fees: $19,034. 16 month fast track nursing program available for $30,628. Books/supplies: $400. Personal expenses: $600.

Financial aid. Additional information: Financial aid administered through Concordia University.

Application procedures. Admission: No application fee. Application may be submitted online. **Financial aid:** FAFSA required.

Academics. Small class sizes offer excellent faculty-to-student ratios allowing for personalized attention. **Special study options:** Accelerated study, independent study. BS completion program for registered nurses. **Credit/placement by examination:** CLEP.

Majors. Health: Nursing (RN).

Computing on campus. 10 workstations in library, computer center. Online library available.

Athletics. Intercollegiate: Baseball M, basketball, cross-country M, field hockey W, football (tackle) M, tennis, track and field, volleyball W, wrestling M. **Intramural:** Basketball M, field hockey W, soccer, softball, swimming, tennis, volleyball.

Student services. Career counseling, student employment services, health services, on-campus daycare, personal counseling, placement for graduates, veterans' counselor.

Contact. E-mail: wsadmis@wscn.edu
Phone: (708) 763-6530 Fax: (708) 763-1531
Cindy Valdez, Director of Admissions and Records/Registrar, West Suburban College of Nursing, 3 Erie Court, Oak Park, IL 60302

Western Illinois University

Macomb, Illinois
www.wiu.edu **CB code: 1900**

- Public 4-year university
- Residential campus in large town
- 11,276 degree-seeking undergraduates: 9% part-time, 49% women, 7% African American, 1% Asian American, 4% Hispanic American, 1% international
- 1,984 degree-seeking graduate students
- 72% of applicants admitted
- SAT or ACT (ACT writing optional) required
- 55% graduate within 6 years

General. Founded in 1899. Regionally accredited. **Degrees:** 2,376 bachelor's awarded; master's, doctoral offered. **ROTC:** Army. **Location:** 83 miles from Rock Island, 78 miles from Peoria. **Calendar:** Semester, limited summer session. **Full-time faculty:** 624 total; 70% have terminal degrees, 10% minority, 38% women. **Part-time faculty:** 61 total; 25% have terminal degrees, 3% minority, 44% women. **Class size:** 29% < 20, 53% 20-39, 9% 40-49, 7% 50-99, 2% >100. **Special facilities:** Geology museum, art gallery.

Freshman class profile. 7,286 applied, 5,224 admitted, 1,816 enrolled.

Mid 50% test scores		**Return as sophomores:**	79%
ACT:	19-24	**Out-of-state:**	4%
Rank in top quarter:	22%	**Live on campus:**	93%
Rank in top tenth:	5%	**International:**	1%
End year in good standing:	89%		

Basis for selection. Standardized test scores, class rank very important. Audition required for music majors.

High school preparation. 15 units recommended. Recommended units include English 4, mathematics 3, social studies 3, science 3 and academic electives 2. 2 units of art, film, foreign language, music, speech, theater, journalism, religion, philosophy or vocational education also recommended.

2005-2006 Annual costs. Tuition/fees: $6,411; $8,895 out-of-state. Residents of nearby counties in Iowa and Missouri pay in-state tuition during first year. Incoming freshmen guaranteed the first year tuition rate for their entire 4 years, provided they are continually enrolled. Room/board: $6,143. Books/supplies: $1,000. Personal expenses: $1,568.

2005-2006 Financial aid. Need-based: 1,341 full-time freshmen applied for aid; 990 were judged to have need; 951 of these received aid. Average need met was 63%. Average scholarship/grant was $6,423; average loan $2,517. 51% of total undergraduate aid awarded as scholarships/grants, 49% as loans/jobs. **Non-need-based:** Awarded to 813 full-time undergraduates, including 172 freshmen. Scholarships awarded for academics, alumni affiliation, art, athletics, leadership, minority status, music/drama, ROTC.

Application procedures. Admission: $30 fee. Application may be submitted online. Admission notification on a rolling basis. **Financial aid:** Priority date 2/15; no closing date. FAFSA required. Applicants notified on a rolling basis starting 1/15.

Academics. Special study options: Distance learning, double major, dual enrollment of high school students, ESL, external degree, honors, independent study, internships, student-designed major, study abroad, teacher certification program, weekend college. **Credit/placement by examination:** AP, CLEP, IB. 30 credit hours maximum toward bachelor's degree. **Support services:** Remedial instruction, study skills assistance, tutoring, writing center.

Majors. Area/ethnic studies: African-American, women's. **Biology:** General. **Business:** Accounting, business admin, construction management, finance, human resources, management information systems, managerial economics, marketing. **Communications:** General, journalism, radio/tv. **Communications technology:** Graphic/printing. **Computer sciences:** General. **Education:** Bilingual, elementary, health, instructional media, special. **Engineering technology:** Industrial. **English:** English lit. **Family/consumer sciences:** General. **Foreign languages:** French, Spanish. **Health:** Clinical lab science, communication disorders, health care admin. **History:** General. **Liberal arts:** Arts/sciences. **Math:** General. **Parks/recreation:** Exercise sciences, facilities management. **Philosophy/religion:** Philosophy. **Physical sciences:** Chemistry, geology, meteorology, physics. **Protective services:** Law enforcement admin. **Psychology:** General. **Public administration:** Social work. **Social sciences:** Economics, geography, political science, sociology. **Visual/performing arts:** Art, dramatic, music performance, studio arts.

Most popular majors. Business/marketing 13%, communications/journalism 7%, education 14%, liberal arts 15%, security/protective services 13%.

Computing on campus. 1,000 workstations in dormitories, library, computer center. Dormitories wired for high-speed internet access and linked to campus network. Commuter students can connect to campus network. Online course registration, online library, helpline, wireless network available.

Student life. Freshman orientation: Mandatory, $15 fee. Preregistration for classes offered. The First Year Experience program is held the week prior to the beginning of fall semester. **Policies:** Freshmen permitted cars on campus. **Housing:** Guaranteed on-campus for all undergraduates. Coed dorms, single-sex dorms, apartments, fraternity/sorority housing, substance-free housing available. $50 nonrefundable deposit. **Activities:** Bands, choral groups, dance, drama, music ensembles, musical theater, radio station, student government, student newspaper, symphony orchestra, TV station, 67 special-interest organizations, 5 service organizations, 14 religious organizations, 32 national honorary and professional fraternities.

Athletics. NCAA. **Intercollegiate:** Baseball M, basketball, cheerleading, cross-country, diving, football (tackle) M, golf, soccer, softball W, swimming, tennis, track and field, volleyball W. **Intramural:** Badminton, basketball, bowling, cross-country, football (non-tackle), football (tackle) M, golf, handball, lacrosse M, racquetball, rugby, skin diving, soccer, softball, swimming, table tennis, tennis, volleyball, water polo. **Team name:** Leathernecks (men), Westerwinds (women).

Student services. Adult student services, career counseling, student employment services, financial aid counseling, health services, legal services, minority student services, on-campus daycare, personal counseling, placement for graduates, veterans' counselor, women's services. **Physically disabled:** Services for visually, speech, hearing impaired.

Contact. E-mail: wiuadm@wiu.edu
Phone: (309) 298-3157 Toll-free number: (877) 742-5948
Fax: (309) 298-3111
Karen Helmers, Director of Admissions, Western Illinois University, One University Circle, Macomb, IL 61455-1390

Westwood College - Chicago Loop

Chicago, Illinois
www.westwood.edu

- For-profit 4-year technical college
- Very large city
- 70 undergraduates

General. Accredited by ACICS. **Degrees:** 8 associate awarded. **Calendar:** Continuous. 5-10 week terms.

2005-2006 Annual costs. $3,729 Per term; 5 terms per year.

Academics. Credit/placement by examination: CLEP.

Majors. Business: Marketing. **Communications technology:** Animation/special effects. **Computer sciences:** Security. **Protective services:** Police science. **Visual/performing arts:** Design.

Contact. Phone: (312) 739-0850 Toll-free number: (800) 281-2978
Fax: (312) 739-1004
Jeff Hill, Director of Admissions, Westwood College - Chicago Loop, 17 North State Street, Suite 300, Chicago, IL 60602

Westwood College - DuPage

Woodridge, Illinois
www.westwood.edu

- For-profit 4-year technical college
- Large city
- 581 degree-seeking undergraduates
- 36% of applicants admitted
- SAT or ACT (ACT writing optional), interview required

General. Accredited by ACICS. **Degrees:** 139 bachelor's, 11 associate awarded. **Location:** 20 miles from downtown Chicago. **Calendar:** Quarter. **Full-time faculty:** 4 total. **Part-time faculty:** 46 total.

Freshman class profile. 556 applied, 201 admitted, 178 enrolled.

Basis for selection. Interview and applicant's level of interest are most important criteria for admission.

2006-2007 Annual costs. Comprehensive fee: (projected) $27,047.

2004-2005 Financial aid. Need-based: 56% of total undergraduate aid awarded as scholarships/grants, 44% as loans/jobs.

Application procedures. Admission: No deadline. $100 fee. Application may be submitted online.

Academics. Special study options: Accelerated study. **Credit/placement by examination:** CLEP.

Contact. Phone: (630) 434-8244 Toll-free number: (866) 721-7646
Fax: (630) 434-8255
Scott Kawall, Director of Admissions, Westwood College - DuPage, 7155 Janes Avenue, Woodridge, IL 60517

Westwood College of Technology: O'Hare

Chicago, Illinois
www.westwood.edu

- For-profit 4-year health science and technical college
- Commuter campus in large city
- 516 degree-seeking undergraduates
- Interview required

General. Accredited by ACICS. **Degrees:** 25 bachelor's, 96 associate awarded. **Calendar:** Continuous, extensive summer session. **Full-time faculty:** 10 total. **Part-time faculty:** 34 total.

Basis for selection. Placement test required.

2005-2006 Annual costs. Tuition/fees: $18,645. Total cost of associate degree program including books, supplies and fees: $29,773, graphic design; $33,610, networking program.

Application procedures. Admission: No deadline. $25 fee. **Financial aid:** FAFSA required.

Academics. Credit/placement by examination: AP, CLEP, SAT, ACT. **Support services:** Tutoring.

Majors. Architecture: Environmental design, interior, urban/community planning. **Business:** Marketing. **Communications technology:** Animation/special effects. **Computer sciences:** General, information technology. **Legal studies:** General, legal secretary, prelaw. **Protective services:** Correctional facilities, corrections, criminal justice, criminalistics, forensics, juvenile corrections, law enforcement admin, police science, security management, security services. **Public administration:** General, community org/advocacy, human services, policy analysis. **Social sciences:** Criminology. **Visual/performing arts:** Design, graphic design, interior design.

Most popular majors. Computer/information sciences 60%, visual/performing arts 40%.

Computing on campus. Online library available.

Student life. Freshman orientation: Mandatory. Preregistration for classes offered. **Activities:** Student government, student newspaper.

Student services. Adult student services, alcohol/substance abuse counseling, career counseling, student employment services, financial aid counseling, personal counseling, placement for graduates.

Contact. Phone: (773) 380-6800 Toll-free number: (877) 877-8857
Fax: (773) 714-0828
David Traub, Director of Admissions, Westwood College of Technology: O'Hare, 8501 West Higgins Road, Chicago, IL 60631

Westwood College of Technology: River Oaks

Calumet City, Illinois
www.westwood.edu

- For-profit 4-year technical college
- 750 degree-seeking undergraduates

General. Accredited by ACICS. **Calendar:** Continuous.

2005-2006 Annual costs. Associate degree program is $32,450; Bachelor's is $62,910. Costs include tuition, fees and books for entire 2 or 4 year program.

Academics. Credit/placement by examination: CLEP.

Contact. Phone: (708) 832-1988
Westwood College of Technology: River Oaks, 80 River Oaks Center, Suite D-49, Calumet City, IL 60409

Wheaton College

Wheaton, Illinois — **CB member**
www.wheaton.edu — **CB code: 1905**

- Private 4-year liberal arts college affiliated with nondenominational tradition
- Residential campus in small city

- 2,392 degree-seeking undergraduates: 2% part-time, 51% women, 2% African American, 7% Asian American, 3% Hispanic American, 1% international
- 404 degree-seeking graduate students
- 51% of applicants admitted
- SAT or ACT with writing, application essay required
- 56% graduate within 6 years; 31% enter graduate study

General. Founded in 1860. Regionally accredited. **Degrees:** 592 bachelor's awarded; master's, doctoral offered. **ROTC:** Army, Air Force. **Location:** 25 miles from Chicago. **Calendar:** Semester, limited summer session. **Full-time faculty:** 191 total; 93% have terminal degrees, 9% minority, 27% women. **Part-time faculty:** 96 total; 24% have terminal degrees, 7% minority, 43% women. **Class size:** 51% < 20, 40% 20-39, 7% 40-49, 2% 50-99, less than 1% >100. **Special facilities:** Billy Graham Museum, Black Hills Science Station, HoneyRock Christian residential camp, collection of books and papers of 7 British authors, Center for Applied Christian Ethics.

Freshman class profile. 2,163 applied, 1,097 admitted, 578 enrolled.

Mid 50% test scores		**Rank in top quarter:**	81%
SAT verbal:	630-730	**Rank in top tenth:**	54%
SAT math:	620-710	**Return as sophomores:**	95%
ACT:	27-31	**Out-of-state:**	82%
GPA 3.50 or higher:	81%	**Live on campus:**	100%
GPA 3.0-3.49:	18%	**International:**	1%
GPA 2.0-2.99:	1%		

Basis for selection. Evidence of a vital Christian experience, moral character, personal integrity, social concern, academic ability, and desire for a liberal arts education as defined by the college are most important. Interview recommended. Audition required of music majors. **Homeschooled:** Applicants advised to take the ACT to satisfy the "Ability to Benefit" requirements. **Learning Disabled:** Personal interview required. Student must contact Registrar to request services or equipment and provide documentation/ diagnosis of disability.

High school preparation. 15 units required; 18 recommended. Required and recommended units include English 4, mathematics 4, social studies 4, science 4 and foreign language 3.

2006-2007 Annual costs. Tuition/fees: $22,450. Room/board: $7,040. Books/supplies: $714. Personal expenses: $1,860.

2005-2006 Financial aid. Need-based: 461 full-time freshmen applied for aid; 287 were judged to have need; 282 of these received aid. Average need met was 87%. Average scholarship/grant was $13,546; average loan $4,808. 68% of total undergraduate aid awarded as scholarships/grants, 32% as loans/jobs. **Non-need-based:** Awarded to 844 full-time undergraduates, including 257 freshmen. Scholarships awarded for academics, alumni affiliation, art, minority status, music/drama, ROTC.

Application procedures. Admission: Priority date 11/1; deadline 1/15 (receipt date). $50 fee, may be waived for applicants with need. Application may be submitted online. Admission notification 4/1. Must reply by May 1 or within 3 week(s) if notified thereafter. **Financial aid:** Priority date 2/15; no closing date. FAFSA, institutional form required. Applicants notified on a rolling basis starting 3/1.

Academics. Special study options: Combined bachelor's/graduate degree, cross-registration, double major, exchange student, independent study, internships, liberal arts/career combination, student-designed major, study abroad, teacher certification program, urban semester, Washington semester. **Credit/placement by examination:** AP, CLEP, IB, SAT, ACT, institutional tests. 76 credit hours maximum toward bachelor's degree. **Support services:** Study skills assistance, writing center.

Majors. Biology: General. **Business:** Managerial economics. **Communications:** General. **Computer sciences:** Computer science. **Conservation:** Environmental studies. **Education:** Elementary, music. **Engineering:** General. **English:** English lit. **Foreign languages:** Classics, French, German, Spanish. **History:** General. **Math:** General. **Parks/recreation:** Exercise sciences. **Philosophy/religion:** Philosophy, religion. **Physical sciences:** Chemistry, geology, physics. **Psychology:** General. **Social sciences:** Anthropology, archaeology, economics, international relations, political science, sociology. **Theology:** Bible, religious ed. **Visual/performing arts:** Art, music history, music performance, music theory/composition.

Most popular majors. Business/marketing 8%, communications/ journalism 7%, education 9%, English 8%, psychology 7%, social sciences 15%, theological studies 9%.

Computing on campus. 201 workstations in dormitories, library, computer center, student center. Dormitories wired for high-speed internet access and linked to campus network. Commuter students can connect to campus network. Online library, helpline, wireless network available.

Student life. Freshman orientation: Mandatory. Preregistration for classes offered. 4-day program during the week before classes begin. **Policies:** All college and college-related functions are alcohol and tobacco free. Religious observance required. **Housing:** Guaranteed on-campus for freshmen. Single-sex dorms, special housing for disabled, apartments, cooperative housing, substance-free housing available. **Activities:** Bands, choral groups, drama, literary magazine, music ensembles, musical theater, opera, radio station, student government, student newspaper, symphony orchestra, TV station, Christian Service Council, Student Missionary Project, Youth Hostel Ministries, World Christian Fellowship, Students for Biblical Equality, Amnesty International, Earthkeepers, Jonathan Blanchard Society, Unidad Christiana, Koinonia.

Athletics. NCAA. **Intercollegiate:** Baseball M, basketball, cross-country, football (tackle) M, golf, soccer, softball W, swimming, tennis, track and field, volleyball W, water polo W, wrestling M. **Intramural:** Basketball, bowling, football (non-tackle) W, football (tackle) M, golf, soccer, softball, table tennis, tennis, volleyball, water polo, weight lifting. **Team name:** Thunder.

Student services. Campus ministries, career counseling, student employment services, financial aid counseling, health services, minority student services, personal counseling, placement for graduates, veterans' counselor. **Physically disabled:** Services for visually, speech, hearing impaired.

Contact. E-mail: admissions@wheaton.edu
Phone: (630) 752-5005 Toll-free number: (800) 222-2419
Fax: (630) 752-5285
Shawn Leftwich, Director of Undergraduate Admissions, Wheaton College, 501 College Avenue, Wheaton, IL 60187-5593

Indiana

American Conservatory of Music

Hammond, Indiana
www.americanconservatory.edu **CB code: 1014**

- Private 4-year music college affiliated with Orthodox Church
- Commuter campus in very large city
- 55 undergraduates
- 30 graduate students
- Application essay, interview required

General. Founded in 1886. **Location:** 25 miles from downtown. **Calendar:** Semester, extensive summer session. **Full-time faculty:** 10 total. **Part-time faculty:** 30 total. **Special facilities:** Recordings and video holdings, recording studio.

Basis for selection. Institutional entrance examination most important. School record and test scores considered. SAT or ACT recommended. Audition required; portfolio recommended.

High school preparation. Participation in school music program recommended.

2005-2006 Annual costs. Annual full-time cost ranges from $10,000-$18,000 depending on teacher. Books/supplies: $500. Personal expenses: $1,200.

Financial aid. Non-need-based: Scholarships awarded for music/drama.

Application procedures. Admission: Closing date 7/1. $50 fee, may be waived for applicants with need. Admission notification on a rolling basis beginning on or about 4/1. **Financial aid:** No deadline. FAFSA required. Applicants notified on a rolling basis.

Academics. Special study options: Accelerated study, double major, ESL. **Credit/placement by examination:** CLEP, IB, institutional tests. 12 credit hours maximum toward associate degree, 12 toward bachelor's. Life experience credit available. Advanced placement determined by institutional placement tests. **Support services:** Reduced course load, remedial instruction.

Majors. Visual/performing arts: Jazz, music history, music performance, music theory/composition, piano/organ, voice/opera.

Computing on campus. 3 workstations in library.

Student life. Freshman orientation: Available. **Activities:** Bands, choral groups, music ensembles, opera, student government, symphony orchestra.

Student services. Student employment services.

Contact. Phone: (219) 931-6000 Fax: (219) 931-6089
Joseph Miller, Admissions Director, American Conservatory of Music, 252 Wildwood Road, Hammond, IN 46324

Anderson University

Anderson, Indiana **CB member**
www.anderson.edu **CB code: 1016**

- Private 4-year liberal arts college affiliated with Church of God
- Residential campus in small city
- 2,329 degree-seeking undergraduates: 8% part-time, 58% women, 5% African American, 1% Hispanic American, 1% Native American, 2% international
- 464 degree-seeking graduate students
- 90% of applicants admitted
- SAT or ACT with writing required
- 59% graduate within 6 years

General. Founded in 1917. Regionally accredited. **Degrees:** 344 bachelor's, 4 associate awarded; master's, doctoral, first professional offered. **Location:** 45 miles from Indianapolis. **Calendar:** Semester, limited summer session. **Full-time faculty:** 137 total; 62% have terminal degrees, 3% minority, 43% women. **Part-time faculty:** 117 total; 2% have terminal degrees, 7% minority, 47% women. **Class size:** 47% < 20, 44% 20-39, 6% 40-49, 4% 50-99, less than 1% >100. **Special facilities:** Religious art collection, art galleries, Bible museum, glass studio.

Freshman class profile. 1,110 applied, 1,003 admitted, 580 enrolled.

Mid 50% test scores		**Rank in top quarter:**	52%
SAT verbal:	480-590	**Rank in top tenth:**	24%
SAT math:	490-580	**Return as sophomores:**	74%
ACT:	21-26	**Out-of-state:**	40%
GPA 3.50 or higher:	51%	**Live on campus:**	91%
GPA 3.0-3.49:	27%	**International:**	2%
GPA 2.0-2.99:	21%		

Basis for selection. GED not accepted. Rank in top half of class, test scores, reference important. School, church, and community activities also considered. Additional requirements for entry into nursing, athletic training, and educational programs. Essay recommended. Interview required of academically weak applicants. Audition required of music majors. Portfolio recommended for art majors. **Homeschooled:** Interview may be required.

High school preparation. College-preparatory program recommended. 17 units required; 28 recommended. Required and recommended units include English 4, mathematics 3-4, social studies 1-2, history 1-2, science 3-4 (laboratory 3-4), foreign language 2-3 and academic electives 5.

2005-2006 Annual costs. Tuition/fees: $18,900. Room/board: $6,150. Books/supplies: $850. Personal expenses: $1,350.

Financial aid. Non-need-based: Scholarships awarded for academics, leadership, minority status, music/drama, state residency.

Application procedures. Admission: Priority date 1/15; deadline 7/1. $20 fee, may be waived for applicants with need. Application may be submitted online. Admission notification on a rolling basis beginning on or about 9/1. Must reply by May 1 or within 2 week(s) if notified thereafter. **Financial aid:** Priority date 3/1; no closing date. FAFSA required. Applicants notified on a rolling basis starting 3/1.

Academics. Special study options: Accelerated study, combined bachelor's/graduate degree, cross-registration, double major, honors, independent study, internships, student-designed major, study abroad, teacher certification program, urban semester. **Credit/placement by examination:** AP, CLEP, IB, institutional tests. 30 credit hours maximum toward bachelor's degree. **Support services:** Learning center, pre-admission summer program, reduced course load, tutoring.

Majors. Biology: General, biochemistry. **Business:** Accounting, business admin, finance, managerial economics, marketing. **Communications:** Journalism. **Computer sciences:** Computer science, information systems. **Education:** General, art, drama/dance, elementary, English, French, health, mathematics, music, physical, science, social studies, Spanish. **English:** English lit. **Family/consumer sciences:** Family systems. **Foreign languages:** French, Spanish. **Health:** Athletic training, nursing (RN). **History:** General. **Interdisciplinary:** Math/computer science. **Legal studies:** Prelaw. **Math:** General. **Parks/recreation:** Exercise sciences, health/fitness. **Philosophy/religion:** Philosophy, religion. **Physical sciences:** Chemistry, physics. **Protective services:** Criminal justice. **Psychology:** General. **Public administration:** Social work. **Social sciences:** Econometrics, political science, sociology. **Theology:** Bible, sacred music, theology. **Visual/performing arts:** Commercial/advertising art, dramatic, music management, music performance, studio arts.

Most popular majors. Business/marketing 20%, education 13%, health sciences 7%, public administration/social services 6%, visual/performing arts 7%.

Computing on campus. 225 workstations in dormitories, library, computer center, student center. Dormitories linked to campus network. Commuter students can connect to campus network.

Student life. Freshman orientation: Available. Preregistration for classes offered. **Policies:** Religious observance required. Freshmen permitted cars on campus. **Housing:** Single-sex dorms available. $100 deposit, deadline 5/1. **Activities:** Bands, choral groups, dance, drama, literary magazine, music ensembles, musical theater, radio station, student government, student newspaper, symphony orchestra, multicultural student union, Religious Life Council, business club, women's clubs, men's clubs, international student association.

Athletics. NCAA. **Intercollegiate:** Baseball M, basketball, cross-country, football (tackle) M, golf, soccer, softball W, tennis, track and field, volleyball W. **Intramural:** Basketball, rugby M, softball, swimming, tennis, volleyball. **Team name:** Ravens.

Student services. Adult student services, campus ministries, career counseling, student employment services, health services, minority student services, personal counseling, placement for graduates, veterans' counselor. **Physically disabled:** Services for visually, speech impaired.

Contact. E-mail: info@anderson.edu
Phone: (765) 641-4080 Toll-free number: (800) 428-6414
Fax: (765) 641-4091
Jim King, Director of Admissions, Anderson University, 1100 East Fifth, Anderson, IN 46012

Ball State University

Muncie, Indiana — **CB member**
www.bsu.edu — **CB code: 1051**

- Public 4-year university
- Residential campus in small city
- 17,269 degree-seeking undergraduates: 7% part-time, 52% women, 7% African American, 1% Asian American, 2% Hispanic American
- 2,558 degree-seeking graduate students
- 80% of applicants admitted
- SAT or ACT with writing required
- 52% graduate within 6 years

General. Founded in 1918. Regionally accredited. **Degrees:** 3,238 bachelor's, 359 associate awarded; master's, doctoral offered. **ROTC:** Army. **Location:** 56 miles from Indianapolis. **Calendar:** Semester, extensive summer session. **Full-time faculty:** 910 total; 76% have terminal degrees, 10% minority, 40% women. **Part-time faculty:** 243 total; 22% have terminal degrees, 3% minority, 51% women. **Class size:** 32% < 20, 50% 20-39, 8% 40-49, 6% 50-99, 4% >100. **Special facilities:** Planetarium, nature preserves, wellness institute, Center for Energy Research, Education, and Service (CERES), art museum.

Freshman class profile. 9,889 applied, 7,944 admitted, 3,692 enrolled.

Mid 50% test scores			
SAT verbal:	470-570	Return as sophomores:	77%
SAT math:	470-570	Out-of-state:	8%
ACT:	19-25	Live on campus:	89%
Rank in top quarter:	41%	Fraternities:	8%
Rank in top tenth:	14%	Sororities:	9%

Basis for selection. Curriculum, GPA, test scores most important; academic index calculated by BSU admissions. Credentials of non-traditional students (age 23 or older) evaluated for admission on individual basis. Personal statement required of all non-traditional students. Test for placement required for transfers and non-traditional freshmen. Interview and essay recommended. Audition required of music and theater majors. Portfolio recommended for art and architecture majors.

High school preparation. College-preparatory program required. Required and recommended units include English 4, mathematics 3, social studies 3, science 3 (laboratory 2) and foreign language 3.

2005-2006 Annual costs. Tuition/fees: $6,458; $16,218 out-of-state. Room/board: $6,680. Books/supplies: $880. Personal expenses: $1,380.

2005-2006 Financial aid. Need-based: 3,113 full-time freshmen applied for aid; 2,143 were judged to have need; 2,117 of these received aid. Average need met was 61%. Average scholarship/grant was $4,522; average loan $2,794. 49% of total undergraduate aid awarded as scholarships/grants, 51% as loans/jobs. **Non-need-based:** Awarded to 4,777 full-time undergraduates, including 1,853 freshmen. Scholarships awarded for academics, athletics, leadership, minority status, music/drama, ROTC, state residency.

Application procedures. Admission: Priority date 5/1; no deadline. $25 fee, may be waived for applicants with need. Application may be submitted online. Admission notification on a rolling basis. Must reply by May 1 or within 2 week(s) if notified thereafter. **Financial aid:** Priority date 3/10; no closing date. FAFSA required. Applicants notified on a rolling basis starting 4/1.

Academics. Minimum credit hours in major for associate degree range from 30 to 45; for bachelor's, 45 to 65. All undergraduates must meet writing competency requirement. **Special study options:** Cooperative education, distance learning, double major, dual enrollment of high school students, ESL, exchange student, honors, independent study, internships, liberal arts/career combination, student-designed major, study abroad, teacher certification program, Washington semester. **Credit/placement by examination:** AP, CLEP, IB, SAT, ACT, institutional tests. 15 credit hours maximum toward associate degree, 63 toward bachelor's. **Support services:** Learning center, pre-admission summer program, reduced course load, study skills assistance, tutoring, writing center.

Honors college/program. Separate curriculum, undergraduate research fellowships, and study abroad programs; 281 freshmen students were admitted in Fall 2005.

Majors. Architecture: Architecture, environmental design, landscape, urban/community planning. **Area/ethnic studies:** Women's. **Biology:** General. **Business:** General, accounting, actuarial science, administrative services, business admin, finance, managerial economics, marketing, office management. **Communications:** Journalism. **Computer sciences:** General. **Conservation:** General. **Education:** Art, business, elementary, health, kindergarten/preschool, multiple handicapped, physical, science, technology/industrial arts. **Engineering:** General. **Engineering technology:** Industrial. **English:** English lit, speech/rhetoric. **Family/consumer sciences:** General, food/nutrition. **Foreign languages:** Classics, French, German, Japanese, Latin, Spanish. **Health:** Audiology/speech pathology, clinical lab science, dietetics, nursing (RN), predentistry, premedicine, respiratory therapy technology. **History:** General. **Legal studies:** Prelaw. **Liberal arts:** Arts/sciences, library science. **Math:** General. **Parks/recreation:** Health/fitness. **Philosophy/religion:** Philosophy, religion. **Physical sciences:** Chemistry, geology, physics. **Protective services:** Criminal justice. **Psychology:** General. **Public administration:** Social work. **Social sciences:** Anthropology, criminology, economics, geography, political science, sociology, urban studies. **Visual/performing arts:** Art, dance, dramatic.

Most popular majors. Business/marketing 13%, communications/journalism 11%, education 16%, health sciences 6%, liberal arts 11%.

Computing on campus. 1,450 workstations in dormitories, library, computer center, student center. Dormitories wired for high-speed internet access and linked to campus network. Commuter students can connect to campus network. Online library, helpline, repair service, student web hosting, wireless network available.

Student life. Freshman orientation: Mandatory. Preregistration for classes offered. 2-day program. **Policies:** Freshmen permitted cars on campus. **Housing:** Guaranteed on-campus for freshmen. Coed dorms, single-sex dorms, special housing for disabled, apartments, cooperative housing, fraternity/sorority housing, substance-free housing available. $125 nonrefundable deposit. Freshmen and sophomore transfer students required to live on campus unless living with parents or guardian, or 21 years of age or older. **Activities:** Bands, choral groups, dance, drama, film society, literary magazine, music ensembles, musical theater, radio station, student government, student newspaper, symphony orchestra, TV station, over 300 student organizations.

Athletics. NCAA. **Intercollegiate:** Baseball M, basketball, cheerleading, cross-country, diving, equestrian, field hockey W, football (tackle) M, golf, gymnastics W, soccer W, softball W, swimming, tennis, track and field, volleyball. **Intramural:** Archery, badminton, baseball M, basketball, bowling, cross-country, diving, fencing, football (tackle) M, golf M, gymnastics W, handball, lacrosse, racquetball, rowing (crew), rugby, sailing, skiing, soccer, softball, swimming, table tennis, tennis, track and field, volleyball, wrestling M. **Team name:** Cardinals.

Student services. Adult student services, alcohol/substance abuse counseling, career counseling, student employment services, financial aid counseling, health services, legal services, minority student services, on-campus daycare, personal counseling, placement for graduates, veterans' counselor, women's services. **Physically disabled:** Services for visually, speech, hearing impaired.

Contact. E-mail: askus@bsu.edu
Phone: (765) 285-8300 Toll-free number: (800) 428-4278
Fax: (765) 285-1632
Lawrence Waters, Dean of Admissions and Enrollment Services, Ball State University, 2000 University Avenue, Muncie, IN 47306-1022

Bethel College

Mishawaka, Indiana
www.bethelcollege.edu — **CB code: 1079**

- Private 4-year liberal arts college affiliated with Missionary Church
- Commuter campus in large town
- 1,930 degree-seeking undergraduates
- 70 graduate students
- SAT or ACT (ACT writing optional) required

General. Founded in 1947. Regionally accredited. **Degrees:** 313 bachelor's, 75 associate awarded; master's offered. **Location:** 140 miles from Indianapolis, 90 miles from Chicago. **Calendar:** Semester, limited summer session. **Full-time faculty:** 74 total. **Part-time faculty:** 102 total.

Freshman class profile.

Mid 50% test scores			
SAT verbal:	470-580	ACT:	19-26
SAT math:	460-590	Out-of-state:	31%

Basis for selection. School achievement record, test scores, character recommendations, personal statement important. Interview recommended. Audition required of music majors and scholarship candidates. Portfolio recommended for returning adults, fine arts majors.

High school preparation. 17 units recommended. Recommended units include English 4, mathematics 3, social studies 1, history 1, science 3 (laboratory 2), foreign language 2 and academic electives 2.

2005-2006 Annual costs. Tuition/fees: $16,396. All first-time, full-time students must pay a one-time fee of $600. Room/board: $5,330. Books/supplies: $600. Personal expenses: $700.

Financial aid. Non-need-based: Scholarships awarded for academics, art, athletics, minority status, music/drama, ROTC, state residency.

Application procedures. Admission: Priority date 5/1; deadline 8/1 (receipt date). $25 fee, may be waived for applicants with need. Application may be submitted online. Admission notification on a rolling basis. **Financial aid:** Priority date 3/1; no closing date. Institutional form, CSS PROFILE required. Applicants notified on a rolling basis starting 2/15; must reply within 2 week(s) of notification.

Academics. Special study options: Accelerated study, cross-registration, double major, independent study, internships, study abroad, teacher certification program, urban semester, Washington semester, weekend college. **Credit/placement by examination:** CLEP, IB. 20 credit hours maximum toward bachelor's degree. **Support services:** Learning center, reduced course load, remedial instruction, study skills assistance, tutoring.

Majors. Biology: General. **Business:** Accounting, business admin, human resources. **Communications:** General. **Computer sciences:** Information systems. **Conservation:** General. **Education:** Business, elementary, English, mathematics, music, physical, science, social studies. **Engineering:** General. **Foreign languages:** Sign language interpretation. **Health:** Nursing (RN), predentistry, premedicine. **History:** General. **Liberal arts:** Arts/sciences. **Math:** General. **Parks/recreation:** Facilities management. **Philosophy/religion:** Philosophy, religion. **Physical sciences:** Chemistry. **Psychology:** General. **Public administration:** Human services. **Social sciences:** General, international relations, sociology. **Theology:** Bible, sacred music, theology. **Visual/performing arts:** Art, design, dramatic.

Computing on campus. 215 workstations in dormitories, library, computer center.

Student life. Freshman orientation: Mandatory. **Policies:** Religious observance required. **Housing:** Single-sex dorms, apartments available. $200 deposit. **Activities:** Bands, choral groups, drama, music ensembles, musical theater, opera, radio station, student government, student newspaper, symphony orchestra, Fellowship of Christian Athletes, ministerial association, interest clubs.

Athletics. NAIA, NCCAA. **Intercollegiate:** Baseball M, basketball, cross-country, golf M, soccer M, softball W, tennis, track and field, volleyball W. **Intramural:** Basketball M, football (tackle) M, soccer, table tennis, volleyball. **Team name:** Pilots.

Student services. Adult student services, campus ministries, career counseling, student employment services, financial aid counseling, health services, minority student services, personal counseling, placement for graduates. **Physically disabled:** Services for hearing impaired.

Contact. Phone: (574) 257-3339 Fax: (574) 257-3326
Randy Beachy, Director of Admissions, Bethel College, 1001 West McKinley Avenue, Mishawaka, IN 46545

Butler University

Indianapolis, Indiana
www.butler.edu

CB member
CB code: 1073

- Private 4-year university
- Residential campus in very large city
- 3,635 degree-seeking undergraduates: 2% part-time, 62% women, 3% African American, 2% Asian American, 2% Hispanic American, 3% international
- 626 degree-seeking graduate students
- 72% of applicants admitted
- SAT or ACT with writing, application essay required
- 70% graduate within 6 years; 23% enter graduate study

General. Founded in 1855. Regionally accredited. **Degrees:** 638 bachelor's, 1 associate awarded; master's, first professional offered. **ROTC:** Army, Air Force. **Location:** 5 miles from downtown. **Calendar:** Semester, limited summer session. **Full-time faculty:** 279 total; 85% have terminal degrees, 11% minority, 39% women. **Part-time faculty:** 155 total; 23% have terminal degrees, 7% minority, 48% women. **Class size:** 56% < 20, 39% 20-39, 2% 40-49, 2% 50-99, less than 1% >100. **Special facilities:** Observatory, planetarium, herbarium.

Freshman class profile. 4,782 applied, 3,458 admitted, 867 enrolled.

Mid 50% test scores			
SAT verbal:	540-630	Rank in top quarter:	74%
SAT math:	540-650	Rank in top tenth:	43%
ACT:	24-29	End year in good standing:	95%
GPA 3.50 or higher:	64%	Return as sophomores:	87%
GPA 3.0-3.49:	26%	Out-of-state:	43%
GPA 2.0-2.99:	10%	Live on campus:	97%
		International:	2%

Basis for selection. Test scores, high school record most important. Recommendations, activities considered. Audition required of dance, drama, music majors. **Homeschooled:** Statement describing homeschool structure and mission, transcript of courses and grades, state high school equivalency certificate, letter of recommendation (nonparent) required.

High school preparation. College-preparatory program required. 16 units required. Required units include English 4, mathematics 3, history 2, science 3, foreign language 2 and academic electives 2. 4 mathematics units for business administration majors.

2005-2006 Annual costs. Tuition/fees: $23,774. Room/board: $7,920. Books/supplies: $800. Personal expenses: $1,450.

2005-2006 Financial aid. Need-based: 801 full-time freshmen applied for aid; 541 were judged to have need; 541 of these received aid. Average need met was 81%. Average scholarship/grant was $13,800; average loan $3,590. 65% of total undergraduate aid awarded as scholarships/grants, 35% as loans/jobs. **Non-need-based:** Scholarships awarded for academics, athletics, music/drama.

Application procedures. Admission: No deadline. $35 fee, may be waived for applicants with need. Application must be submitted on paper. Admission notification on a rolling basis beginning on or about 10/1. Must reply by May 1 or within 2 week(s) if notified thereafter. **Financial aid:** Priority date 3/1, closing date 8/1. FAFSA required. Applicants notified on a rolling basis starting 3/15; must reply within 3 week(s) of notification.

Academics. Special study options: Combined bachelor's/graduate degree, cooperative education, cross-registration, double major, dual enrollment of high school students, ESL, exchange student, honors, independent study, internships, student-designed major, study abroad, teacher certification program, Washington semester. Dual-degree engineering program with Purdue University. **Credit/placement by examination:** AP, CLEP, SAT, ACT. **Support services:** Learning center, reduced course load, study skills assistance, tutoring, writing center.

Majors. Biology: General. **Business:** Accounting, actuarial science, finance, international, marketing. **Communications:** General, journalism, radio/tv. **Computer sciences:** General, information systems. **Education:** Early childhood, elementary, kindergarten/preschool, middle, music, secondary. **Engineering:** Physics. **English:** Creative writing, English lit, speech/rhetoric. **Foreign languages:** French, German, Latin, modern Greek, Spanish. **Health:** Communication disorders, physician assistant. **History:** General. **Interdisciplinary:** Science/society. **Liberal arts:** Arts/sciences. **Math:** General. **Philosophy/religion:** Philosophy, religion. **Physical sciences:** Chemistry, physics. **Protective services:** Criminal justice. **Psychology:** General. **Social sciences:** Anthropology, criminology, economics, international relations, political science, sociology, urban studies. **Visual/performing arts:** Arts management, dance, dramatic, music management, music pedagogy, music performance, music theory/composition, piano/organ, stringed instruments, voice/opera.

Most popular majors. Business/marketing 16%, communications/journalism 13%, education 10%, health sciences 16%, social sciences 7%, visual/performing arts 8%.

Computing on campus. 430 workstations in dormitories, library, computer center, student center. Dormitories wired for high-speed internet access and linked to campus network. Commuter students can connect to campus network. Online course registration, helpline available.

Student life. Freshman orientation: Mandatory, $75 fee. Preregistration for classes offered. 3-day program held in August. **Policies:** Freshmen permitted cars on campus. **Housing:** Guaranteed on-campus for freshmen. Coed dorms, single-sex dorms, apartments, fraternity/sorority housing, substance-free housing available. $100 fully refundable deposit. Service learning residence available. **Activities:** Bands, choral groups, dance, drama, literary magazine, music ensembles, opera, student government, student newspaper, symphony orchestra, volunteer center, Black Student Union, Campus Crusade for Christ, YMCA, College Republicans, Mortar Board, academic honoraries, Alpha Phi Omega.

Athletics. NCAA. **Intercollegiate:** Baseball M, basketball, cross-country, football (tackle) M, golf, lacrosse M, soccer, softball W, swimming, tennis, track and field, volleyball W. **Intramural:** Badminton, baseball M, basketball, bowling, football (tackle) M, golf, soccer, softball, swimming, table tennis, tennis, track and field, volleyball, weight lifting. **Team name:** Bulldogs.

Student services. Alcohol/substance abuse counseling, career counseling, student employment services, financial aid counseling, health services, minority student services, on-campus daycare, personal counseling, placement for graduates. **Physically disabled:** Services for visually, speech impaired.

Contact. E-mail: admission@butler.edu
Phone: (317) 940-8100 Toll-free number: (888) 940-8100
Fax: (317) 940-8150
Scott McIntyre, Director of Admissions, Butler University, 4600 Sunset Avenue, Indianapolis, IN 46208

Calumet College of St. Joseph

Whiting, Indiana
www.ccsj.edu **CB code: 1776**

- Private 4-year liberal arts college affiliated with Roman Catholic Church
- Commuter campus in small city
- 1,125 degree-seeking undergraduates: 58% part-time, 57% women
- 83 degree-seeking graduate students
- Application essay required

General. Founded in 1951. Regionally accredited. **Degrees:** 291 bachelor's, 20 associate awarded; master's offered. **Location:** 20 miles from Chicago. **Calendar:** Semester, limited summer session. **Full-time faculty:** 31 total; 13% minority, 23% women. **Part-time faculty:** 98 total; 19% minority, 46% women. **Class size:** 78% < 20, 18% 20-39, 3% 40-49.

Freshman class profile. 60 enrolled.

Basis for selection. High school record most important. ACT/COMPASS Assessment Test required for all applicants, top half of class, minimum 2.0 GPA. SAT or ACT recommended. Interview recommended. **Homeschooled:** State high school equivalency certificate required.

High school preparation. 15 units recommended. Recommended units include English 4, mathematics 3, social studies 3, science 2 (laboratory 1) and foreign language 1.

2005-2006 Annual costs. Tuition/fees: $9,975. Books/supplies: $1,050. Personal expenses: $690.

2004-2005 Financial aid. Need-based: 104 full-time freshmen applied for aid; 91 were judged to have need; 91 of these received aid. 54% of total undergraduate aid awarded as scholarships/grants, 46% as loans/jobs. **Non-need-based:** Awarded to 140 full-time undergraduates, including 48 freshmen. Scholarships awarded for academics, alumni affiliation, religious affiliation. **Additional information:** Immediate computerized estimate of financial aid eligibility available to students applying in person.

Application procedures. Admission: No deadline. No application fee. Application may be submitted online. Admission notification on a rolling basis. **Financial aid:** Priority date 3/1; no closing date. FAFSA required. Applicants notified on a rolling basis; must reply within 2 week(s) of notification.

Academics. Special study options: Accelerated study, cooperative education, double major, dual enrollment of high school students, ESL, honors, independent study, internships, liberal arts/career combination, student-designed major, teacher certification program, weekend college. **Credit/placement by examination:** AP, CLEP, institutional tests. 30 credit hours maximum toward associate degree, 60 toward bachelor's. **Support services:** Learning center, reduced course load, remedial instruction, study skills assistance, tutoring, writing center.

Majors. Business: General, accounting, business admin, organizational behavior. **Communications:** General, media studies. **Computer sciences:** General. **Education:** General, elementary, science, secondary. **English:** English lit. **Health:** Health care admin. **Legal studies:** Paralegal. **Liberal arts:** Arts/sciences. **Philosophy/religion:** Religion. **Protective services:** Police science. **Psychology:** General. **Public administration:** Human services. **Social sciences:** General. **Visual/performing arts:** Studio arts.

Computing on campus. 72 workstations in library, computer center. Online library, wireless network available.

Student life. Freshman orientation: Mandatory. Preregistration for classes offered. Held one week before classes begin. Followed up by mentoring program. **Policies:** Freshmen permitted cars on campus. **Activities:** Choral groups, drama, literary magazine, student government, student newspaper, Los Amigos, Black student organization, criminal justice club, drama club, media and fine arts club, creative writing club, paralegal studies club, booster club, human services club, educators club.

Athletics. NAIA. **Intercollegiate:** Baseball M, basketball, cross-country, golf, soccer, softball W, volleyball. **Team name:** Crimson Wave.

Student services. Campus ministries, career counseling, student employment services, financial aid counseling, on-campus daycare, personal counseling, placement for graduates, veterans' counselor.

Contact. E-mail: admissions@ccsj.edu
Phone: (219) 473-4215 Toll-free number: (877) 700-9100
Fax: (219) 473-4259
Chuck Walz, Director of Admissions, Calumet College of St. Joseph, 2400 New York Avenue, Whiting, IN 46394-2195

College of Court Reporting

Hobart, Indiana
www.ccredu.com **CB code: 3532**

- Private 3-year business and technical college
- Small city
- 175 degree-seeking undergraduates

General. Accredited by ACICS. **Degrees:** 15 associate awarded. **Calendar:** Semester. **Full-time faculty:** 15 total. **Part-time faculty:** 5 total.

Basis for selection. Open admission.

2006-2007 Annual costs. Tuition/fees: $5,760.

Application procedures. Admission: Closing date 9/30. $50 fee.

Academics. Credit/placement by examination: CLEP.

Contact. E-mail: information@ccredu.com
Phone: (219) 942-1459 Fax: (219) 942-1631
College of Court Reporting, 111 West 10th Street, Suite 111, Hobart, IN 46342

DePauw University

Greencastle, Indiana **CB member**
www.depauw.edu **CB code: 1166**

- Private 4-year music and liberal arts college affiliated with United Methodist Church
- Residential campus in small town
- 2,345 degree-seeking undergraduates: 55% women, 6% African American, 2% Asian American, 3% Hispanic American, 2% international
- 66% of applicants admitted
- SAT or ACT with writing, application essay required
- 79% graduate within 6 years; 29% enter graduate study

General. Founded in 1837. Regionally accredited. Honor students can participate in selective programs in management, entrepreneurship, media studies, and science research. **Degrees:** 516 bachelor's awarded; master's offered. **ROTC:** Army, Air Force. **Location:** 45 miles from Indianapolis. **Calendar:** 4-1-4. **Full-time faculty:** 213 total; 94% have terminal degrees, 13% minority, 42% women. **Part-time faculty:** 41 total; 42% have terminal degrees, 24% minority, 54% women. **Class size:** 64% < 20, 35% 20-39, less than 1% 40-49. **Special facilities:** Nature park and arboretum; 4 art galleries; Asian and anthropology ethnographic museums; 24 hour radio station; commercial-quality, closed circuit tv studio facilities; music instructional technology studio; digital media laboratory; visual resources library with digital image collection; digital video studio; observatory; two theaters and full scene shop; two music concert halls; concert pipe organ.

Freshman class profile. 3,440 applied, 2,269 admitted, 586 enrolled.

Mid 50% test scores			
SAT verbal:	550-660	Rank in top tenth:	53%
SAT math:	570-660	Return as sophomores:	92%
ACT:	23-29	Out-of-state:	52%
Rank in top quarter:	85%	Live on campus:	100%
		International:	1%

Basis for selection. Academic achievement and preparation, demonstrated verbal and quantitative skills, evidence of continuing commitment to learning most important. TOEFL recommended for international students. Interview strongly recommended. Audition required for school of music candidates. **Homeschooled:** Interview required.

High school preparation. 32 units recommended. Recommended units include English 4, mathematics 4, social studies 3, history 3, science 4 (laboratory 2), foreign language 3 and academic electives 10.

2006-2007 Annual costs. Tuition/fees: $27,780. Room/board: $7,800. Books/supplies: $700. Personal expenses: $1,000.

2005-2006 Financial aid. Need-based: 463 full-time freshmen applied for aid; 355 were judged to have need; 355 of these received aid. Average need met was 98%. Average scholarship/grant was $13,514; average loan $3,550. 77% of total undergraduate aid awarded as scholarships/grants, 23% as loans/jobs. **Non-need-based:** Awarded to 2,122 full-time undergraduates, including 526 freshmen. Scholarships awarded for academics, alumni affiliation, leadership, minority status, music/drama, ROTC.

Application procedures. Admission: Closing date 2/1 (postmark date). $40 fee, may be waived for applicants with need. Application may be submitted online. Admission notification 4/1. Must reply by 5/1. **Financial aid:** Closing date 2/15. FAFSA, institutional form required. Applicants notified by 3/27; must reply by 5/1.

Academics. Demonstrated competence in writing, quantitative reasoning, and oral communication required of all students. Seminar, thesis, project, or comprehensive examination in major also required. More than 700 students participate in off-campus winter term programs; 40% study off-campus. **Special study options:** Combined bachelor's/graduate degree, double major, dual enrollment of high school students, exchange student, honors, independent study, internships, New York semester, student-designed major, study abroad, teacher certification program, urban semester, Washington semester. **Credit/placement by examination:** AP, CLEP, IB, institutional tests. 32 credit hours maximum toward bachelor's degree. **Support services:** Learning center, study skills assistance, tutoring, writing center.

Majors. Area/ethnic studies: African-American, East Asian, Russian/Slavic, women's. **Biology:** General, biochemistry. **Communications:** Media studies. **Computer sciences:** Computer science. **Conservation:** Environmental science. **Education:** Elementary, music, physical. **English:** Composition, English lit. **Foreign languages:** Ancient Greek, classics, French, German, Latin, Romance, Spanish. **Health:** Athletic training. **History:** General. **Interdisciplinary:** Peace/conflict. **Math:** General. **Parks/recreation:** Exercise sciences. **Philosophy/religion:** Philosophy, religion. **Physical sciences:** Chemistry, geology, physics. **Psychology:** General. **Social sciences:** Anthropology, economics, political science, sociology. **Visual/performing arts:** Art history/conservation, dramatic, music management, music performance, music theory/composition, studio arts.

Computing on campus. PC or laptop required. 424 workstations in dormitories, library, computer center, student center. Dormitories wired for high-speed internet access and linked to campus network. Commuter students can connect to campus network. Online course registration, online library, helpline, repair service, student web hosting, wireless network available.

Student life. Freshman orientation: Mandatory. Preregistration for classes offered. 4-day program in August. **Policies:** Freshmen permitted cars on campus. **Housing:** Guaranteed on-campus for all undergraduates. Coed dorms, apartments, fraternity/sorority housing, substance-free housing available. $400 deposit, deadline 5/1. **Activities:** Bands, choral groups, dance, drama, film society, literary magazine, music ensembles, musical theater, opera, radio station, student government, student newspaper, symphony orchestra, TV station, Association of African American Students, international students association, Union Board, Coalition for Women's Concerns, College Republicans, College Democrats, Habitat for Humanity, JC Christian Fellowship, United DePauw (GLBTQ students and allies), Committee for Latino Concerns.

Athletics. NCAA. **Intercollegiate:** Baseball M, basketball, cross-country, diving, field hockey W, football (tackle) M, golf, soccer, softball W, swimming, tennis, track and field, volleyball W. **Intramural:** Badminton, basketball, bowling, football (non-tackle), golf M, racquetball, soccer, softball, table tennis, tennis, volleyball. **Team name:** Tigers.

Student services. Alcohol/substance abuse counseling, campus ministries, career counseling, student employment services, financial aid counseling, health services, minority student services, personal counseling, placement for graduates. **Physically disabled:** Services for visually, hearing impaired.

Contact. E-mail: admission@depauw.edu
Phone: (765) 658-4006 Toll-free number: (800) 447-2495
Fax: (765) 658-4007
Stefanie Niles, Dean of Admission, DePauw University, 101 East Seminary Street, Greencastle, IN 46135-1611

DeVry University: Indianapolis
Indianapolis, Indiana
www.devry.com

- For-profit 4-year university
- Commuter campus
- 72 degree-seeking undergraduates: 71% part-time, 51% women, 33% African American, 4% Hispanic American, 3% international
- 71 graduate students

General. Degrees: 67 bachelor's, 207 associate awarded; master's offered. **Calendar:** Semester. **Part-time faculty:** 27 total; 15% minority, 15% women.

Freshman class profile. 8 enrolled.

Basis for selection. Interview most important, GPA and standardized test scores considered.

2005-2006 Annual costs. Tuition/fees: $11,900. Books/supplies: $1,250. Personal expenses: $1,740.

Application procedures. Admission: No deadline. $50 fee. Admission notification on a rolling basis.

Academics. Credit/placement by examination: CLEP.

Contact. Phone: (866) 513-3879
DeVry University: Indianapolis, 9100 Keystone Crossing, Indianapolis, IN 46240

Earlham College
Richmond, Indiana — **CB member**
www.earlham.edu — **CB code: 1195**

- Private 4-year liberal arts and seminary college affiliated with Society of Friends (Quaker)
- Residential campus in large town
- 1,185 degree-seeking undergraduates: 1% part-time, 58% women, 7% African American, 2% Asian American, 3% Hispanic American, 7% international
- 122 degree-seeking graduate students
- 70% of applicants admitted
- SAT or ACT with writing, application essay required
- 68% graduate within 6 years; 17% enter graduate study

General. Founded in 1847. Regionally accredited; also accredited by ATS. **Degrees:** 226 bachelor's awarded; master's, first professional offered. **Location:** 70 miles from Indianapolis, 45 miles from Dayton, Ohio. **Calendar:** Semester. **Full-time faculty:** 93 total; 97% have terminal degrees, 23% minority, 45% women. **Part-time faculty:** 15 total; 40% have terminal degrees, 13% minority, 33% women. **Class size:** 71% < 20, 23% 20-39, 2% 40-49, 4% 50-99. **Special facilities:** Natural history museum, observatory, planetarium, herbarium, working farm, biological field stations.

Freshman class profile. 1,554 applied, 1,092 admitted, 324 enrolled.

Mid 50% test scores			
SAT verbal:	570-700	Rank in top quarter:	61%
SAT math:	530-650	Rank in top tenth:	30%
ACT:	23-29	End year in good standing:	85%
GPA 3.50 or higher:	52%	Return as sophomores:	83%
GPA 3.0-3.49:	32%	Out-of-state:	75%
GPA 2.0-2.99:	16%	Live on campus:	99%
		International:	10%

Basis for selection. Secondary school record, recommendations, essay, and character very important. Interview recommended. **Homeschooled:** Portfolio or other evidence of learning, test scores, letters of recommendations, and essay.

High school preparation. 15 units required; 20 recommended. Required and recommended units include English 4, mathematics 3-4, social studies 2-3, history 1, science 3-4 (laboratory 2) and foreign language 2-4.

2006-2007 Annual costs. Tuition/fees: $29,320. Room/board: $6,200. Books/supplies: $850. Personal expenses: $1,000.

2004-2005 Financial aid. Need-based: 236 full-time freshmen applied for aid; 197 were judged to have need; 197 of these received aid. Average need met was 85%. Average scholarship/grant was $12,422; average loan $3,257. 77% of total undergraduate aid awarded as scholarships/grants, 23% as loans/jobs. **Non-need-based:** Awarded to 697 full-time undergraduates, including 210 freshmen. Scholarships awarded for academics, minority status, religious affiliation.

Application procedures. Admission: Closing date 2/15 (postmark date). $30 fee, may be waived for applicants with need. Application may be submitted online. Admission notification 3/15. Must reply by May 1 or within 2 week(s) if notified thereafter. **Financial aid:** Closing date 3/1. FAFSA, institutional form required. Applicants notified on a rolling basis starting 3/1.

Academics. Special study options: Accelerated study, cross-registration, double major, ESL, independent study, internships, New York semester, student-designed major, study abroad, urban semester. **Credit/placement by examination:** AP, CLEP, IB, institutional tests. 18 credit hours maximum toward bachelor's degree. **Support services:** Learning center, pre-admission summer program, study skills assistance, tutoring, writing center.

Majors. Area/ethnic studies: African-American, Asian, Latin American, women's. **Biology:** General, biochemistry. **Business:** Business admin. **Computer sciences:** General. **Conservation:** Environmental studies. **English:** English lit. **Foreign languages:** Classics, comparative lit, French, German, Spanish. **Health:** Premedicine. **History:** General. **Interdisciplinary:** Biopsychology, peace/conflict. **Math:** General. **Philosophy/religion:** Philosophy, religion. **Physical sciences:** Chemistry, geology, physics. **Psychology:** General. **Social sciences:** Anthropology, sociology. **Visual/performing arts:** General, art, dramatic, music history, music performance.

Most popular majors. Area/ethnic studies 9%, biology 15%, English 6%, foreign language 8%, interdisciplinary studies 11%, psychology 8%, social sciences 15%, visual/performing arts 12%.

Computing on campus. 164 workstations in library, computer center. Dormitories wired for high-speed internet access and linked to campus network. Online library, helpline, repair service, student web hosting, wireless network available.

Student life. Freshman orientation: Mandatory. Preregistration for classes offered. 5-day program held just prior to beginning of fall semester. **Policies:** Community and academic honor codes exist based on values such as peace and social justice, respect for the individual, simplicity and cooperative learning. Freshmen permitted cars on campus. **Housing:** Guaranteed on-campus for all undergraduates. Coed dorms, special housing for disabled, cooperative housing, substance-free housing available. 28 college-owned off-campus language and special interest houses (e.g. Japan House, German House, Peace House) available to upperclassmen. Living/Learning halls in some residence halls. Single sex halls in some co-ed dorms. **Activities:** Bands, choral groups, dance, drama, film society, literary magazine, music ensembles, musical theater, radio station, student government, student newspaper, symphony orchestra, Fellowship of Christian Athletes, Earlham Young Friends, Jewish Students' Union, Black Leadership Action Coalition, Black Men United, Bahai Club, Sociedad de Estudiantes Latinos (SEL), Committee for Justice in Middle East, Volunteer Exchange, Action Against Rape.

Athletics. NCAA. **Intercollegiate:** Baseball M, basketball, cross-country, field hockey W, football (tackle) M, soccer, tennis, track and field, volleyball W. **Intramural:** Basketball, football (non-tackle), racquetball, soccer, softball, tennis, triathlon, volleyball. **Team name:** Quakers.

Student services. Campus ministries, career counseling, student employment services, financial aid counseling, health services, minority student services, on-campus daycare, personal counseling, placement for graduates, women's services. **Physically disabled:** Services for visually, speech, hearing impaired.

Contact. E-mail: admission@earlham.edu
Phone: (765) 983-1600 Toll-free number: (800) 327-5426
Fax: (765) 983-1560
Jeffrey Rickey, Dean of Admissions and Financial Aid, Earlham College, 801 National Road West, Richmond, IN 47374-4095

Franklin College

Franklin, Indiana — **CB member**
www.franklincollege.edu — **CB code: 1228**

- Private 4-year liberal arts college affiliated with American Baptist Churches in the USA
- Residential campus in large town
- 1,003 degree-seeking undergraduates: 6% part-time, 48% women, 4% African American, 1% Hispanic American, 1% international
- 78% of applicants admitted
- SAT or ACT with writing, application essay required
- 56% graduate within 6 years; 14% enter graduate study

General. Founded in 1834. Regionally accredited. **Degrees:** 196 bachelor's awarded. **ROTC:** Army. **Location:** 20 miles from Indianapolis. **Calendar:** 4-1-4, limited summer session. **Full-time faculty:** 65 total; 83% have terminal degrees, 5% minority, 35% women. **Part-time faculty:** 45 total; 18% have terminal degrees, 2% minority, 47% women. **Class size:** 65% < 20, 34% 20-39, 1% 40-49.

Freshman class profile. 1,009 applied, 790 admitted, 273 enrolled.

Mid 50% test scores		**Rank in top tenth:**	20%
SAT verbal:	460-560	**End year in good standing:**	85%
SAT math:	460-580	**Return as sophomores:**	76%
ACT:	19-25	**Out-of-state:**	3%
GPA 3.50 or higher:	35%	**Live on campus:**	85%
GPA 3.0-3.49:	30%	**Fraternities:**	35%
GPA 2.0-2.99:	28%	**Sororities:**	42%
Rank in top quarter:	54%		

Basis for selection. Class rank, test scores, essay and counselor recommendations important. Extracurricular activities considered. Interview recommended for all. **Homeschooled:** Transcript of courses and grades, interview, letter of recommendation (nonparent) required. Submit research paper(s), art work, community service projects, educational trip or programs, writing samples, other pertinent documents. Formal interview on campus required. **Learning Disabled:** Students with learning disabilities asked to schedule meeting with Director of Academic Support Services.

High school preparation. Required and recommended units include English 4, mathematics 4, social studies 3, science 2 and foreign language 2.

2005-2006 Annual costs. Tuition/fees: $19,275. Room/board: $5,730.

2004-2005 Financial aid. Need-based: 281 full-time freshmen applied for aid; 246 were judged to have need; 245 of these received aid. Average need met was 87%. Average scholarship/grant was $11,507; average loan $3,730. 72% of total undergraduate aid awarded as scholarships/grants, 28% as loans/jobs. **Non-need-based:** Awarded to 280 full-time undergraduates, including 92 freshmen. Scholarships awarded for academics, alumni affiliation, leadership, minority status, religious affiliation, state residency.

Application procedures. Admission: Priority date 1/15; no deadline. $30 fee, may be waived for applicants with need. Application may be submitted online. Admission notification on a rolling basis beginning on or about 10/5. **Financial aid:** Closing date 3/1. FAFSA, institutional form required. Applicants notified by 4/1; must reply by 5/1 or within 4 week(s) of notification.

Academics. Special study options: Cross-registration, double major, dual enrollment of high school students, exchange student, independent study, internships, semester at sea, study abroad, teacher certification program, United Nations semester, Washington semester. **Credit/placement by examination:** AP, CLEP, institutional tests. 30 credit hours maximum toward bachelor's degree. **Support services:** Learning center, remedial instruction, study skills assistance, tutoring, writing center.

Majors. Area/ethnic studies: American, Canadian. **Biology:** General. **Business:** General, accounting. **Communications:** Journalism. **Computer sciences:** General, computer science. **Education:** Biology, chemistry, elementary, English, French, mathematics, physical, Spanish. **English:** English lit. **Foreign languages:** French, Spanish. **Health:** Athletic training. **History:** General. **Math:** General. **Parks/recreation:** General. **Philosophy/religion:** Philosophy, religion. **Physical sciences:** Chemistry. **Psychology:** General. **Social sciences:** Economics, political science, sociology. **Visual/performing arts:** Dramatic.

Most popular majors. Biology 6%, business/marketing 11%, communications/journalism 22%, education 19%, social sciences 16%.

Computing on campus. 250 workstations in dormitories, library, student center. Dormitories wired for high-speed internet access and linked to campus network. Commuter students can connect to campus network. Online course registration, online library, helpline, student web hosting, wireless network available.

Student life. Freshman orientation: Mandatory, $50 fee. Preregistration for classes offered. Orientation for all students held 4 days prior to start of classes. **Policies:** Freshmen permitted cars on campus. **Housing:** Guaranteed on-campus for all undergraduates. Coed dorms, special housing for disabled, fraternity/sorority housing, substance-free housing available. All students must live on campus until senior year unless living with family. **Activities:** Pep band, choral groups, dance, drama, literary magazine, musical theater, radio station, student government, student newspaper, TV station, student association for the support of multiculturalism, Habitat for Humanity, college mentors for kids, Fellowship of Christian Athletes, ODK Leadership, international club.

Athletics. NCAA. **Intercollegiate:** Baseball M, basketball, cheerleading M, cross-country, football (tackle) M, golf, soccer, softball W, tennis, track and field, volleyball W. **Intramural:** Basketball, football (non-tackle), racquetball, softball, volleyball. **Team name:** Grizzlies.

Student services. Alcohol/substance abuse counseling, campus ministries, career counseling, student employment services, financial aid counseling, health services, minority student services, personal counseling, placement for graduates, veterans' counselor, women's services.

Contact. E-mail: admissions@franklincollege.edu
Phone: (317) 738-8062 Toll-free number: (800) 852-0232
Fax: (317) 738-8274
Jacqueline Acosta, Director of Admissions, Franklin College, 101 Branigin Boulevard, Franklin, IN 46131-2623

Goshen College

Goshen, Indiana
www.goshen.edu **CB code: 1251**

- Private 4-year liberal arts college affiliated with Mennonite Church
- Residential campus in large town
- 899 degree-seeking undergraduates: 8% part-time, 62% women
- 76% of applicants admitted
- SAT or ACT (ACT writing optional), application essay required
- 60% graduate within 6 years

General. Founded in 1894. Regionally accredited. 1150 acre environmental study facility located 30 miles from campus. **Degrees:** 209 bachelor's awarded. **Location:** 25 miles from South Bend, 150 miles from Chicago. **Calendar:** Semester, limited summer session. **Full-time faculty:** 72 total; 62% have terminal degrees, 4% minority, 46% women. **Part-time faculty:** 32 total; 12% have terminal degrees, 16% minority, 53% women. **Class size:** 65% < 20, 27% 20-39, 4% 40-49, 4% 50-99. **Special facilities:** X-ray precision laboratory, nature preserve, marine biology laboratory in Florida Keys, Mennonite Historical Library.

Freshman class profile. 493 applied, 375 admitted, 200 enrolled.

Mid 50% test scores			
SAT verbal:	500-630	Rank in top quarter:	63%
SAT math:	490-640	Rank in top tenth:	30%
ACT:	23-29	End year in good standing:	96%
GPA 3.50 or higher:	65%	Return as sophomores:	80%
GPA 3.0-3.49:	26%	Out-of-state:	60%
GPA 2.0-2.99:	9%	Live on campus:	86%

Basis for selection. School achievement record most important. Applicants should rank in top half of class and must have minimum GPA of 2.3, SAT of 920 or ACT score of 19. Personal reference important. Essay encouraged. Minimum score of TOEFL 550 if student does not have at least two years of high school in U.S. and English is not first language. Tests not required if out of high school five(+) years. Interview recommended. **Homeschooled:** Transcript of courses and grades required. **Learning Disabled:** Documentation of disability and special requirements dated within last 3 years required. Exit interview with high school special needs counselor, if working with one, required.

High school preparation. 12 units required; 16 recommended. Required and recommended units include English 4, mathematics 2-3, social studies 2, history 2, science 2-3 and foreign language 2.

2006-2007 Annual costs. Tuition/fees: $20,300. Room/board: $6,700. Books/supplies: $700.

2004-2005 Financial aid. Need-based: 195 full-time freshmen applied for aid; 147 were judged to have need; 147 of these received aid. Average need met was 88%. Average scholarship/grant was $12,537; average loan $3,558. 61% of total undergraduate aid awarded as scholarships/grants, 39% as loans/jobs. **Non-need-based:** Awarded to 595 full-time undergraduates, including 165 freshmen. Scholarships awarded for academics, athletics, state residency.

Application procedures. Admission: Priority date 2/15; deadline 8/15 (postmark date). $25 fee, may be waived for applicants with need. Application may be submitted online. Admission notification on a rolling basis beginning on or about 9/15. Must reply by May 1 or within 2 week(s) if notified thereafter. **Financial aid:** Priority date 2/11; no closing date. FAFSA, institutional form required. Applicants notified by 3/1; must reply by 5/1 or within 2 week(s) of notification.

Academics. Practicum and ethics course required in major. International education through on-campus courses or study abroad required. Study abroad incorporates language study, academic and cultural learning and service. Students live in homes of country where studying for one semester. **Special study options:** Combined bachelor's/graduate degree, cross-registration, double major, dual enrollment of high school students, honors, independent study, internships, liberal arts/career combination, student-designed major, study abroad, teacher certification program, urban semester, Washington semester. Adult degree completion program (one evening per week, concentrated study). **Credit/placement by examination:** AP, CLEP, IB, SAT, ACT, institutional tests. **Support services:** Learning center, reduced course load, remedial instruction, study skills assistance, tutoring, writing center.

Majors. Biology: General, molecular. **Business:** General, accounting, business admin, management science. **Communications:** General. **Computer sciences:** General, computer science, information systems. **Conservation:** General, environmental studies. **Education:** General, art, biology, business, chemistry, computer, elementary, English, ESL, foreign languages, history, mathematics, middle, music, physical, physics, psychology, science, secondary, social science, Spanish, special. **English:** English lit. **Foreign languages:** General, American Sign Language, sign language interpretation, Spanish. **Health:** Nursing (RN). **History:** General. **Interdisciplinary:** Peace/conflict. **Math:** General, applied. **Parks/recreation:** Health/fitness. **Physical sciences:** Chemistry, physics. **Psychology:** General. **Public administration:** Social work. **Social sciences:** Anthropology, sociology. **Theology:** Theology. **Visual/performing arts:** General, art, dramatic, music performance.

Most popular majors. Business/marketing 20%, communications/journalism 7%, computer/information sciences 8%, education 7%, health sciences 10%, psychology 7%, visual/performing arts 8%.

Computing on campus. 160 workstations in dormitories, library, computer center, student center. Dormitories wired for high-speed internet access and linked to campus network. Commuter students can connect to campus network. Online library, helpline, student web hosting, wireless network available.

Student life. Freshman orientation: Mandatory. Preregistration for classes offered. 4 days before semester begins. **Policies:** No smoking or drinking alcoholic beverages on campus. Freshmen permitted cars on campus. **Housing:** Guaranteed on-campus for all undergraduates. Coed dorms, single-sex dorms, special housing for disabled, apartments, substance-free housing available. $200 fully refundable deposit, deadline 5/1. **Activities:** Jazz band, choral groups, drama, music ensembles, musical theater, opera, radio station, student government, student newspaper, symphony orchestra, Black student union, Latin student union, international student club, women's association, Third Culture Support Group, World Christian Fellowship, nontraditional student network, Environmental Concerns club, Peace (Pax) club, Fellowship of Christian Athletes.

Athletics. NAIA. **Intercollegiate:** Baseball M, basketball, cross-country, golf M, soccer, softball W, tennis, track and field, volleyball W. **Intramural:** Badminton, basketball, cross-country, racquetball, skiing, soccer, softball, swimming, table tennis, tennis, volleyball. **Team name:** Maple Leafs.

Student services. Adult student services, alcohol/substance abuse counseling, campus ministries, career counseling, student employment services, financial aid counseling, health services, minority student services, on-campus daycare, personal counseling, placement for graduates, veterans' counselor, women's services. **Physically disabled:** Services for visually, speech, hearing impaired.

Contact. E-mail: admissions@goshen.edu
Phone: (574) 535-7535 Toll-free number: (800) 348-7422
Fax: (574) 535-7609
Galen Graber, Executive Director of Enrollment Services, Goshen College, 1700 South Main Street, Goshen, IN 46526

Grace College and Seminary

Winona Lake, Indiana
www.grace.edu **CB code: 1252**

- Private 4-year Bible and liberal arts college affiliated with Brethren Church
- Residential campus in small town
- 1,062 degree-seeking undergraduates: 8% part-time, 45% women, 10% African American, 1% Asian American, 2% Hispanic American, 1% Native American, 1% international

- 62 degree-seeking graduate students
- 73% of applicants admitted
- SAT or ACT (ACT writing optional) required
- 65% graduate within 6 years

General. Founded in 1948. Regionally accredited. **Degrees:** 208 bachelor's, 30 associate awarded; master's, doctoral, first professional offered. **Location:** 40 miles from Fort Wayne. **Calendar:** Semester, limited summer session. **Full-time faculty:** 43 total; 70% have terminal degrees, 9% minority, 19% women. **Part-time faculty:** 78 total; 9% have terminal degrees, 3% minority, 28% women. **Class size:** 57% < 20, 36% 20-39, 5% 40-49, 1% 50-99, less than 1% >100. **Special facilities:** Westminster Hall building on National Register of Historic Places, Reneker Museum, Creation Center.

Freshman class profile. 837 applied, 609 admitted, 218 enrolled.

Mid 50% test scores			
SAT verbal:	480-590	GPA 3.0-3.49:	31%
SAT math:	450-590	GPA 2.0-2.99:	20%
ACT:	20-25	Rank in top quarter:	53%
GPA 3.50 or higher:	48%	Rank in top tenth:	24%
		Out-of-state:	50%

Basis for selection. References, religious affiliation/commitment, high school class rank, test scores most important. Interview recommended for music and art majors. Audition recommended for music majors. Portfolio recommended for art majors. **Homeschooled:** Must take ACT or SAT.

High school preparation. College-preparatory program recommended. 14 units recommended. Recommended units include English 4, mathematics 2, social studies 2, history 1, science 2 (laboratory 1) and foreign language 2.

2005-2006 Annual costs. Tuition/fees: $16,020. Room/board: $6,150. Books/supplies: $800. Personal expenses: $800.

2005-2006 Financial aid. Need-based: 198 full-time freshmen applied for aid; 170 were judged to have need; 170 of these received aid. Average need met was 80%. Average scholarship/grant was $7,932; average loan $4,381. 55% of total undergraduate aid awarded as scholarships/grants, 45% as loans/jobs. **Non-need-based:** Scholarships awarded for academics, art, athletics, leadership, music/drama.

Application procedures. Admission: Priority date 6/1; deadline 8/15 (postmark date). $20 fee, may be waived for applicants with need. Application may be submitted online. Admission notification on a rolling basis beginning on or about 9/1. Must reply by May 1 or within 2 week(s) if notified thereafter. **Financial aid:** Priority date 3/10; no closing date. FAFSA required. Applicants notified on a rolling basis starting 3/1.

Academics. Special study options: Combined bachelor's/graduate degree, cooperative education, cross-registration, distance learning, double major, dual enrollment of high school students, exchange student, honors, independent study, internships, liberal arts/career combination, study abroad, teacher certification program. **Credit/placement by examination:** AP, CLEP, IB, SAT, ACT, institutional tests. 30 credit hours maximum toward associate degree, 30 toward bachelor's. **Support services:** Reduced course load, remedial instruction, study skills assistance, tutoring, writing center.

Majors. Biology: General. **Business:** General, accounting, administrative services, business admin, finance, international, management information systems, marketing. **Communications:** General, journalism. **Computer sciences:** Information technology. **Education:** Art, business, elementary, English, French, German, mathematics, music, physical, science, social studies, Spanish, special. **English:** English lit. **Foreign languages:** General, French, German, Spanish. **Math:** General. **Parks/recreation:** Health/fitness, sports admin. **Physical sciences:** General. **Protective services:** Criminal justice. **Psychology:** General. **Public administration:** Social work. **Social sciences:** Sociology. **Theology:** Bible, youth ministry. **Visual/performing arts:** Drawing, graphic design, illustration, music performance.

Most popular majors. Business/marketing 21%, communications/journalism 7%, education 27%, psychology 11%, theological studies 6%, visual/performing arts 12%.

Computing on campus. 62 workstations in dormitories, library, computer center, student center. Dormitories wired for high-speed internet access and linked to campus network. Commuter students can connect to campus network. Online course registration, helpline available.

Student life. Freshman orientation: Mandatory. **Policies:** Religious observance required. Freshmen permitted cars on campus. **Housing:** Guaranteed on-campus for all undergraduates. Single-sex dorms, apartments, substance-free housing available. $200 fully refundable deposit, deadline 5/1. **Activities:** Concert band, choral groups, drama, music ensembles, musical theater, opera, student government, student newspaper, symphony orchestra, Christian outreach groups.

Athletics. NAIA, NCCAA. **Intercollegiate:** Baseball M, basketball, cross-country, golf M, soccer, softball W, tennis, track and field, volleyball W. **Intramural:** Basketball, soccer, softball, volleyball. **Team name:** Lancers.

Student services. Campus ministries, career counseling, student employment services, health services, personal counseling, placement for graduates, veterans' counselor.

Contact. E-mail: enroll@grace.edu
Phone: (574) 372-5100 ext. 6008 Toll-free number: (800) 544-7223 ext. 6008 Fax: (574) 372-5120
Anecia Miller, Director of Admissions/Registrar, Grace College and Seminary, 200 Seminary Drive, Winona Lake, IN 46590

Hanover College

Hanover, Indiana — **CB member**
www.hanover.edu — **CB code: 1290**

- Private 4-year liberal arts college affiliated with Presbyterian Church (USA)
- Residential campus in rural community
- 999 degree-seeking undergraduates: 56% women, 1% African American, 3% Asian American, 1% Hispanic American, 5% international
- 70% of applicants admitted
- SAT or ACT with writing, application essay required
- 70% graduate within 6 years; 29% enter graduate study

General. Founded in 1827. Regionally accredited. **Degrees:** 196 bachelor's awarded. **Location:** 85 miles from Indianapolis, 40 miles from Louisville, Kentucky. **Calendar:** Trimester. **Full-time faculty:** 95 total; 98% have terminal degrees, 10% minority, 36% women. **Part-time faculty:** 8 total; 62% have terminal degrees, 38% women. **Class size:** 84% < 20, 16% 20-39, less than 1% 40-49. **Special facilities:** Geology museum, observatory.

Freshman class profile. 1,680 applied, 1,168 admitted, 265 enrolled.

Mid 50% test scores			
SAT verbal:	540-650	Rank in top tenth:	44%
SAT math:	550-650	Return as sophomores:	78%
ACT:	23-29	Out-of-state:	38%
Rank in top quarter:	80%	Live on campus:	98%
		International:	5%

Basis for selection. GED not accepted. Selection of and performance in academic courses most important. Interview recommended.

High school preparation. 19 units required; 28 recommended. Required and recommended units include English 3-4, mathematics 3-4, social studies 2-3, history 2-3, science 3-4 (laboratory 2-3), foreign language 2-4 and academic electives 2-3.

2006-2007 Annual costs. Tuition/fees: $22,700. Room/board: $6,800. Books/supplies: $900.

2004-2005 Financial aid. Need-based: 354 full-time freshmen applied for aid; 303 were judged to have need; 303 of these received aid. Average need met was 77%. Average scholarship/grant was $14,421; average loan $2,765. 85% of total undergraduate aid awarded as scholarships/grants, 15% as loans/jobs. **Non-need-based:** Awarded to 419 full-time undergraduates, including 135 freshmen. Scholarships awarded for academics, alumni affiliation, leadership, minority status, music/drama, religious affiliation, state residency.

Application procedures. Admission: Closing date 3/1 (postmark date). $35 fee, may be waived for applicants with need. Application may be submitted online. Admission notification on a rolling basis beginning on or about 1/15. Must reply by May 1 or within 2 week(s) if notified thereafter. **Financial aid:** Priority date 3/1; no closing date. FAFSA required. Applicants notified on a rolling basis starting 3/1; must reply by 5/1.

Academics. Students take only one course in the 4-week spring term. **Special study options:** Double major, dual enrollment of high school students, independent study, internships, student-designed major, study abroad, teacher certification program, Washington semester. Philadelphia and Washington Semester Programs, Center for Business Preparation. **Credit/placement by examination:** AP, CLEP, IB, institutional tests. **Support services:** Reduced course load, tutoring, writing center.

Majors. Area/ethnic studies: Latin American. **Biology:** General. **Business:** Business admin. **Communications:** General. **Computer sciences:** General. **Education:** Physical. **English:** English lit. **Foreign languages:** Classics, French, German, Spanish. **History:** General. **Interdisciplinary:** Medieval/Renaissance. **Math:** General. **Parks/recreation:** Exercise sciences. **Philosophy/**

religion: Philosophy. **Physical sciences:** Chemistry, geology, physics. **Psychology:** General. **Social sciences:** Anthropology, economics, political science, sociology. **Theology:** Theology. **Visual/performing arts:** Art history/conservation, dramatic, studio arts.

Most popular majors. Biology 9%, business/marketing 10%, communications/journalism 6%, education 8%, English 6%, history 7%, psychology 10%, social sciences 20%, visual/performing arts 6%.

Computing on campus. 195 workstations in library, computer center, student center. Dormitories wired for high-speed internet access and linked to campus network. Commuter students can connect to campus network. Online course registration, online library, helpline, student web hosting, wireless network available.

Student life. Freshman orientation: Available. Preregistration for classes offered. Two 1-day orientation sessions in June. An all-freshmen orientation starts 1 week before classes begin. **Housing:** Guaranteed on-campus for freshmen. Coed dorms, single-sex dorms, apartments, fraternity/sorority housing, substance-free housing available. $250 fully refundable deposit, deadline 5/1. Theme housing available. **Activities:** Bands, choral groups, dance, drama, film society, literary magazine, music ensembles, musical theater, radio station, student government, student newspaper, symphony orchestra, TV station, Campus Fellowship, political and social service organizations, international club, academic clubs, Christian Life, Love Out Loud.

Athletics. NCAA. **Intercollegiate:** Baseball M, basketball, cross-country, football (tackle) M, golf, soccer, softball W, tennis, track and field, volleyball W. **Intramural:** Basketball, football (non-tackle) W, football (tackle) M, soccer, softball, volleyball. **Team name:** Panthers.

Student services. Alcohol/substance abuse counseling, campus ministries, career counseling, student employment services, financial aid counseling, health services, personal counseling, placement for graduates.

Contact. E-mail: admission@hanover.edu
Phone: (812) 866-7021 Toll-free number: (800) 213-2178
Fax: (812) 866-7098
William Preble, Dean of Admission and Financial Assistance, Hanover College, PO Box 108, Hanover, IN 47243-0108

Holy Cross College

Notre Dame, Indiana
www.hcc-nd.edu
CB member
CB code: 1309

- Private 4-year liberal arts college affiliated with Roman Catholic Church
- Residential campus in small city
- 440 degree-seeking undergraduates
- SAT or ACT (ACT writing optional), application essay required

General. Founded in 1966. Regionally accredited. **Degrees:** 14 bachelor's, 91 associate awarded. **ROTC:** Army, Air Force. **Location:** One mile from South Bend, 80 miles from Chicago. **Calendar:** Semester, limited summer session. **Full-time faculty:** 24 total. **Part-time faculty:** 21 total.

Freshman class profile.

Mid 50% test scores		Out-of-state:	49%
SAT verbal:	420-520	Live on campus:	49%
SAT math:	450-560		

Basis for selection. School achievement and student's perception of value of program for future plans most important. Interview recommended.

High school preparation. Required and recommended units include English 4, mathematics 3-4, social studies 2-4, science 2-4 and foreign language 2.

2005-2006 Annual costs. Tuition/fees: $11,000. Room/board: $8,050. Books/supplies: $500.

Financial aid. Non-need-based: Scholarships awarded for academics, leadership.

Application procedures. Admission: Priority date 7/1; deadline 8/15. $50 fee, may be waived for applicants with need. Application may be submitted online. Admission notification on a rolling basis. **Financial aid:** Priority date 3/1; no closing date. FAFSA required. Applicants notified on a rolling basis starting 5/1; must reply within 2 week(s) of notification.

Academics. Special study options: Accelerated study, cross-registration, ESL, honors, study abroad. **Credit/placement by examination:** AP, CLEP, SAT, ACT, institutional tests. 30 credit hours maximum toward associate degree. **Support services:** Learning center, pre-admission summer program, reduced course load, remedial instruction, study skills assistance, tutoring, writing center.

Majors. Liberal arts: Arts/sciences.

Computing on campus. 32 workstations in computer center, student center. Dormitories wired for high-speed internet access and linked to campus network. Commuter students can connect to campus network. Online library, repair service, wireless network available.

Student life. Freshman orientation: Mandatory. Preregistration for classes offered. **Policies:** Freshmen permitted cars on campus. **Housing:** Coed dorms, single-sex dorms, special housing for disabled, apartments available. $500 partly refundable deposit, deadline 8/15. **Activities:** Marching band, choral groups, drama, literary magazine, music ensembles, student government, student newspaper, campus ministry, student advisory committee, Flip Side.

Athletics. NAIA. **Intercollegiate:** Cross-country M. **Intramural:** Basketball, cheerleading, football (non-tackle), football (tackle) M, golf, lacrosse M, soccer, volleyball. **Team name:** Saints.

Student services. Alcohol/substance abuse counseling, campus ministries, career counseling, financial aid counseling, health services, personal counseling.

Contact. E-mail: admissions@hcc-nd.edu
Phone: (574) 239-8400 Fax: (574) 239-8323
Vincent Duke, Director of Admissions, Holy Cross College, 54515 State Road 933N, Notre Dame, IN 46556-0308

Huntington University

Huntington, Indiana
www.huntington.edu
CB code: 1304

- Private 4-year university and liberal arts college affiliated with United Brethren in Christ
- Residential campus in large town
- 908 degree-seeking undergraduates: 9% part-time, 55% women
- 70 graduate students
- 93% of applicants admitted
- SAT or ACT with writing, application essay required
- 69% graduate within 6 years; 10% enter graduate study

General. Founded in 1897. Regionally accredited. **Degrees:** 182 bachelor's, 14 associate awarded; master's offered. **Location:** 20 miles from Fort Wayne. **Calendar:** 4-1-4, limited summer session. **Full-time faculty:** 59 total; 90% have terminal degrees, 34% women. **Part-time faculty:** 63 total; 11% have terminal degrees, 2% minority, 46% women. **Class size:** 74% < 20, 26% 20-39, 3% 40-49, less than 1% 50-99. **Special facilities:** Nature preserve, greenhouse.

Freshman class profile. 692 applied, 641 admitted, 229 enrolled.

Mid 50% test scores		Rank in top quarter:	26%
SAT verbal:	460-630	Rank in top tenth:	26%
SAT math:	440-620	End year in good standing:	88%
ACT:	19-27	Return as sophomores:	78%
GPA 3.50 or higher:	39%	Out-of-state:	20%
GPA 3.0-3.49:	44%	Live on campus:	91%
GPA 2.0-2.99:	17%		

Basis for selection. Class rank in top half, satisfactory test scores, GPA of 2.3 most important. Selected students with SAT score of 860 (exclusive of Writing) or more, GPA of 2.0, or rank in top 50% of class may be admitted on minimum load. Interview recommended. Audition required of music majors. Portfolio required for art scholarships. Essay required for presidential scholarships. Education majors also must apply separately to the Education Department before entering those major classes. Performance grants also require a separate application process for those majoring in Music, Theatre, Art, and Communications.

High school preparation. Required and recommended units include English 4, mathematics 2-3, social studies 3, history 2, science 2-3 (laboratory 1-2) and foreign language 2.

2006-2007 Annual costs. Tuition/fees: $18,860. Room/board: $6,530. Books/supplies: $750. Personal expenses: $1,150.

2005-2006 Financial aid. Need-based: 203 full-time freshmen applied for aid; 173 were judged to have need; 173 of these received aid. Average need met was 77%. Average scholarship/grant was $11,883; average loan $3,067. 63% of total undergraduate aid awarded as scholarships/grants, 37%

as loans/jobs. **Non-need-based:** Awarded to 293 full-time undergraduates, including 115 freshmen. Scholarships awarded for academics, alumni affiliation, art, athletics, leadership, music/drama, religious affiliation.

Application procedures. Admission: Priority date 3/1; deadline 8/1 (receipt date). $20 fee. Application may be submitted online. Admission notification on a rolling basis beginning on or about 7/1. **Financial aid:** Priority date 3/1; no closing date. FAFSA required. Applicants notified on a rolling basis starting 3/1; must reply by 5/1 or within 2 week(s) of notification.

Academics. Special study options: Double major, independent study, internships, liberal arts/career combination, study abroad, teacher certification program, Washington semester. **Credit/placement by examination:** AP, CLEP, SAT, ACT. 38 credit hours maximum toward bachelor's degree. **Support services:** Learning center, pre-admission summer program, reduced course load, remedial instruction, study skills assistance, tutoring, writing center.

Majors. Biology: General. **Business:** General, accounting, accounting/finance, business admin, entrepreneurial studies, managerial economics, nonprofit/public, small business admin. **Communications:** General, broadcast journalism, digital media, journalism, media studies, public relations, radio/tv. **Computer sciences:** General, computer science. **Conservation:** Environmental science. **Education:** General, art, biology, business, chemistry, elementary, English, mathematics, music, physical, science, secondary, social studies, special. **English:** English lit, speech/rhetoric. **Health:** Premedicine. **History:** General. **Interdisciplinary:** Math/computer science, natural sciences. **Legal studies:** Prelaw. **Math:** General. **Parks/recreation:** Exercise sciences, facilities management, sports admin. **Philosophy/religion:** Philosophy, religion. **Physical sciences:** Chemistry. **Psychology:** General. **Public administration:** Social work. **Social sciences:** Sociology. **Theology:** Bible, missionary, religious ed, sacred music, youth ministry. **Visual/performing arts:** Art, commercial/advertising art, dramatic, film/cinema, graphic design, music management, music pedagogy, music performance, music theory/composition, piano/organ, studio arts, theater arts management, theater design, voice/opera.

Most popular majors. Business/marketing 21%, communications/journalism 6%, education 20%, parks/recreation 9%, psychology 9%, theological studies 11%, visual/performing arts 7%.

Computing on campus. 187 workstations in dormitories, library, computer center, student center. Dormitories wired for high-speed internet access and linked to campus network. Commuter students can connect to campus network. Online library, helpline, student web hosting, wireless network available.

Student life. Freshman orientation: Mandatory. 3-day orientation held immediately before first semester. **Policies:** No social dancing. Chapel/convocation attendance required 2 out of 4 weekly programs. Use of alcohol, drugs, tobacco prohibited. Religious observance required. Freshmen permitted cars on campus. **Housing:** Guaranteed on-campus for all undergraduates. Single-sex dorms, apartments, substance-free housing available. $100 fully refundable deposit, deadline 8/1. College-owned houses. **Activities:** Bands, choral groups, dance, drama, film society, literary magazine, music ensembles, musical theater, opera, radio station, student government, student newspaper, TV station, minority student fellowship, Collegians for Life, international club, center for volunteerism, Habitat for Humanity.

Athletics. NAIA, NCCAA. **Intercollegiate:** Baseball M, basketball, cross-country, golf M, soccer, softball W, tennis, track and field, volleyball W. **Intramural:** Basketball, football (non-tackle) M, racquetball, softball, volleyball. **Team name:** Foresters.

Student services. Adult student services, alcohol/substance abuse counseling, campus ministries, career counseling, student employment services, financial aid counseling, health services, minority student services, on-campus daycare, personal counseling, placement for graduates, women's services. **Physically disabled:** Services for visually, speech, hearing impaired.

Contact. E-mail: admissions@huntington.edu
Phone: (260) 359-4000 Toll-free number: (800) 642-6493
Fax: (260) 358-3699
Jeff Berggren, Vice President of Enrollment Management & Marketing, Huntington University, 2303 College Avenue, Huntington, IN 46750-1237

Indiana Institute of Technology

Fort Wayne, Indiana — **CB member**
www.indianatech.edu — **CB code: 1323**

- Private 4-year business and engineering college
- Residential campus in large city
- 2,828 degree-seeking undergraduates: 44% part-time, 56% women
- 372 degree-seeking graduate students
- 54% of applicants admitted
- SAT or ACT required

General. Founded in 1930. Regionally accredited. ABET accreditation for electrical engineering and mechanical engineering. **Degrees:** 379 bachelor's, 208 associate awarded; master's offered. **Location:** 120 miles from Indianapolis. **Calendar:** Semester, limited summer session. **Full-time faculty:** 41 total; 37% have terminal degrees, 17% minority, 37% women. **Part-time faculty:** 239 total; 4% have terminal degrees, 10% minority, 34% women. **Class size:** 85% < 20, 15% 20-39, less than 1% 40-49. **Special facilities:** Computer-aided design center, amphitheater.

Freshman class profile. 2,251 applied, 1,213 admitted, 317 enrolled.

Mid 50% test scores		**Rank in top quarter:**	27%
SAT verbal:	440-470	**Rank in top tenth:**	8%
SAT math:	470-500	**Out-of-state:**	49%
ACT:	17-18	**Live on campus:**	73%
GPA 3.50 or higher:	16%	**Fraternities:**	10%
GPA 3.0-3.49:	26%	**Sororities:**	5%
GPA 2.0-2.99:	46%		

Basis for selection. GPA and test scores most important. Interview recommended.

High school preparation. Required and recommended units include English 4, mathematics 2-4, science 2-3 and academic electives 7. Engineering and computer science majors require 13.5 units including 4 English; 3.5 mathematics; 2 physical science; 4 history, social studies, or language.

2006-2007 Annual costs. Tuition/fees: $18,560. Room/board: $7,088. Personal expenses: $3,000.

2005-2006 Financial aid. Need-based: Average need met was 71%. Average scholarship/grant was $8,828; average loan $3,251. 41% of total undergraduate aid awarded as scholarships/grants, 59% as loans/jobs. **Non-need-based:** Scholarships awarded for academics, alumni affiliation, athletics, leadership, minority status, music/drama, state residency.

Application procedures. Admission: No deadline. $50 fee, may be waived for applicants with need. Application may be submitted online. Admission notification on a rolling basis beginning on or about 10/15. **Financial aid:** Closing date 3/10. FAFSA, institutional form required. Applicants notified on a rolling basis starting 2/2; must reply within 2 week(s) of notification.

Academics. Special study options: Accelerated study, combined bachelor's/graduate degree, cross-registration, double major, dual enrollment of high school students, external degree, independent study, internships, student-designed major. **Credit/placement by examination:** AP, CLEP, IB, institutional tests. 45 credit hours maximum toward associate degree, 90 toward bachelor's. **Support services:** Learning center, reduced course load, remedial instruction, study skills assistance, tutoring.

Majors. Business: General, accounting, business admin, human resources, management information systems, marketing, operations. **Computer sciences:** General, computer science, information systems. **Engineering:** Biomedical, computer, electrical, industrial, mechanical. **Health:** Recreational therapy. **Parks/recreation:** Facilities management, sports admin. **Psychology:** General. **Public administration:** Human services.

Most popular majors. Business/marketing 86%.

Computing on campus. PC or laptop required. 270 workstations in library, computer center. Dormitories wired for high-speed internet access and linked to campus network. Commuter students can connect to campus network. Online library, helpline, repair service, student web hosting available.

Student life. Freshman orientation: Mandatory. Preregistration for classes offered. 1-day program. **Policies:** Freshmen permitted cars on campus. **Housing:** Guaranteed on-campus for freshmen. Coed dorms, apartments, fraternity/sorority housing available. $350 deposit. **Activities:** Pep band, choral groups, dance, student government, student newspaper, Student Board, Black Student Association, Campus Ministries, Nova Society, Society for Women Engineers, American Society of Mechanical Engineers, Society for Human Resource Management, Society of Automotive Engineering, Institute of Electrical and Electronics Engineers, Society for Manufacturing Engineers.

Athletics. NAIA. **Intercollegiate:** Baseball M, basketball, soccer, softball W. **Intramural:** Badminton, basketball, bowling, soccer, softball, volleyball. **Team name:** Warriors.

Student services. Adult student services, campus ministries, career counseling, student employment services, financial aid counseling, personal counseling, placement for graduates, veterans' counselor.

Contact. E-mail: admissions@indianatech.edu
Phone: (260) 422-5561 ext. 2251 Toll-free number: (800) 937-2448
Fax: (260) 422-7696
Allison Carnahan, Interim Vice President of Enrollment Management, Indiana Institute of Technology, 1600 East Washington Boulevard, Fort Wayne, IN 46803-1297

Indiana State University

Terre Haute, Indiana **CB member**
www.indstate.edu **CB code: 1322**

- Public 4-year university
- Residential campus in small city
- 8,531 degree-seeking undergraduates: 11% part-time, 52% women, 11% African American, 1% Asian American, 1% Hispanic American, 1% international
- 1,976 degree-seeking graduate students
- 80% of applicants admitted
- SAT or ACT with writing required
- 40% graduate within 6 years

General. Founded in 1865. Regionally accredited. **Degrees:** 1,459 bachelor's, 190 associate awarded; master's, doctoral offered. **ROTC:** Army, Air Force. **Location:** 70 miles from Indianapolis. **Calendar:** Semester, extensive summer session. **Full-time faculty:** 489 total; 77% have terminal degrees, 10% minority, 40% women. **Part-time faculty:** 173 total; 20% have terminal degrees, 6% minority, 47% women. **Class size:** 44% < 20, 33% 20-39, 6% 40-49, 4% 50-99, less than 1% >100. **Special facilities:** Observatory, museum, flight simulator.

Freshman class profile. 5,351 applied, 4,279 admitted, 1,642 enrolled.

Mid 50% test scores			
SAT verbal:	420-530	**Rank in top quarter:**	28%
SAT math:	420-520	**Rank in top tenth:**	10%
ACT:	17-23	**End year in good standing:**	69%
GPA 3.50 or higher:	21%	**Return as sophomores:**	67%
GPA 3.0-3.49:	27%	**Out-of-state:**	9%
GPA 2.0-2.99:	51%	**Live on campus:**	68%
		International:	1%

Basis for selection. Students who rank in top 50% of high school class usually admitted. High school curriculum, GPA, test scores, class rank, type of high school, and interview all considered. Interview required of some scholarship applicants, recommended for applicants below 50th percentile of high school graduating class. Essay recommended. Audition required of music majors. Portfolio recommended for art majors.

High school preparation. 20 units recommended. Recommended units include English 4, mathematics 3, social studies 2, history 1, science 3 (laboratory 3), foreign language 1 and academic electives 1. Three or more courses recommended in career area.

2005-2006 Annual costs. Tuition/fees: $5,864; $12,860 out-of-state. Room/board: $5,615.

2004-2005 Financial aid. All financial aid based on need. 1,575 full-time freshmen applied for aid; 1,245 were judged to have need; 1,159 of these received aid. Average need met was 72%. Average scholarship/grant was $4,790; average loan $2,615. 48% of total undergraduate aid awarded as scholarships/grants, 52% as loans/jobs. **Additional information:** Financial aid application deadline March 1 for Indiana residents applying for state grant.

Application procedures. Admission: Priority date 7/1; deadline 8/15. $25 fee, may be waived for applicants with need. Application may be submitted online. Admission notification on a rolling basis. Must reply by 5/1. **Financial aid:** Priority date 3/1; no closing date. FAFSA required. Applicants notified on a rolling basis starting 4/15.

Academics. Special study options: Accelerated study, cooperative education, distance learning, double major, dual enrollment of high school students, ESL, honors, independent study, internships, study abroad, teacher certification program. **Credit/placement by examination:** AP, CLEP, institutional tests. 31 credit hours maximum toward bachelor's degree. **Support services:** Learning center, pre-admission summer program, study skills assistance, tutoring, writing center.

Majors. Architecture: Interior. **Area/ethnic studies:** African-American. **Biology:** General. **Business:** Accounting, business admin, finance, human resources, insurance, management information systems, marketing, office management, operations. **Communications:** General, journalism, organizational, radio/tv. **Computer sciences:** General, information technology. **Education:** Elementary, physical, social studies, special, trade/industrial. **Engineering technology:** Architectural, automotive, computer, electrical, industrial, manufacturing, mechanical, occupational safety, robotics. **English:** English lit. **Family/consumer sciences:** General, clothing/textiles, family studies, food/nutrition. **Foreign languages:** French, German, linguistics, Spanish. **Health:** Athletic training, clinical lab science, community health services, environmental health, nursing (RN). **History:** General. **Liberal arts:** Arts/sciences. **Math:** General. **Parks/recreation:** Facilities management. **Philosophy/religion:** Philosophy. **Physical sciences:** Chemistry, geology, physics. **Psychology:** General. **Public administration:** Social work. **Social sciences:** Anthropology, criminology, economics, geography, political science, sociology. **Transportation:** Airline/commercial pilot, aviation management. **Visual/performing arts:** Art, dramatic, music performance, studio arts.

Most popular majors. Business/marketing 17%, education 18%, engineering/engineering technologies 8%, health sciences 6%, social sciences 12%.

Computing on campus. 415 workstations in dormitories, library, computer center, student center. Dormitories wired for high-speed internet access and linked to campus network. Commuter students can connect to campus network. Online course registration, helpline, repair service, student web hosting, wireless network available.

Student life. Freshman orientation: Mandatory. Preregistration for classes offered. One-day program includes registration, question and answer sessions, placement testing, campus tour, and meeting with advisers. Parents encouraged to attend. **Policies:** Freshmen permitted cars on campus. **Housing:** Guaranteed on-campus for freshmen. Coed dorms, single-sex dorms, special housing for disabled, apartments, fraternity/sorority housing, substance-free housing available. Special housing for freshmen. **Activities:** Bands, choral groups, dance, drama, film society, literary magazine, music ensembles, musical theater, radio station, student government, student newspaper, symphony orchestra, over 130 student organizations available.

Athletics. NCAA. **Intercollegiate:** Baseball M, basketball, cross-country, football (tackle) M, golf W, soccer W, softball W, tennis, track and field, volleyball W. **Intramural:** Badminton, basketball, bowling, football (non-tackle), golf, racquetball, soccer, softball, swimming, table tennis, tennis, track and field, volleyball. **Team name:** Sycamores.

Student services. Adult student services, campus ministries, career counseling, student employment services, financial aid counseling, health services, minority student services, on-campus daycare, personal counseling, placement for graduates, women's services. **Physically disabled:** Services for visually, speech, hearing impaired.

Contact. E-mail: ADMISU@indstate.edu
Phone: (812) 237-2121 Toll-free number: (800) 742-0891
Fax: (812) 237-8023
Richard Toomey, Director, Indiana State University, Office of Admissions, Tirey Hall 134, Terre Haute, IN 47809-9989

Indiana University Bloomington

Bloomington, Indiana **CB member**
www.iub.edu **CB code: 1324**

- Public 4-year university
- Residential campus in small city
- 29,120 degree-seeking undergraduates: 4% part-time, 52% women, 5% African American, 3% Asian American, 2% Hispanic American, 4% international
- 7,904 degree-seeking graduate students
- 85% of applicants admitted
- SAT or ACT with writing required
- 72% graduate within 6 years

General. Founded in 1820. Regionally accredited. Big Ten research university. **Degrees:** 6,069 bachelor's, 55 associate awarded; master's, doctoral, first professional offered. **ROTC:** Army, Air Force. **Location:** 50 miles from Indianapolis. **Calendar:** Semester, extensive summer session. **Full-time faculty:** 1,562 total; 79% have terminal degrees, 14% minority, 33% women. **Class size:** 40% < 20, 37% 20-39, 4% 40-49, 12% 50-99, 7% >100. **Special facilities:** Cyclotron, 2 observatories, museum of anthropology, history, and folklore, rare book library, outdoor educational center, center for excellence in education, garden and nature center, arboretum, CAVE Automated Virtual Environment.

Freshman class profile. 21,974 applied, 18,602 admitted, 6,949 enrolled.

Mid 50% test scores		Rank in top tenth:	25%
SAT verbal:	490-610	Return as sophomores:	87%
SAT math:	500-620	Out-of-state:	32%
ACT:	21-27	Live on campus:	96%
Rank in top quarter:	57%	International:	3%

Basis for selection. Strength of student's college preparatory program, senior year program, grade trends in academic program, class rank, if provided, and SAT or ACT test scores important. SAT Subject Tests recommended. Campus visit encouraged. Audition required for majority of music majors. **Learning Disabled:** Current and comprehensive documentation of disability required to receive services.

High school preparation. 14 units required; 19 recommended. Required and recommended units include English 4, mathematics 3-4, social studies 2-3, science 1-3 (laboratory 1), foreign language 3 and academic electives 4. Residents should have at least 3 year-long academic courses in different subject areas in senior year. Nonresidents should schedule 4.

2005-2006 Annual costs. Tuition/fees: $7,112; $19,508 out-of-state. Room/board: $6,240. Books/supplies: $740. Personal expenses: $2,200.

2004-2005 Financial aid. Need-based: 5,460 full-time freshmen applied for aid; 2,919 were judged to have need; 2,833 of these received aid. Average need met was 66%. Average scholarship/grant was $4,964; average loan $3,076. 43% of total undergraduate aid awarded as scholarships/grants, 57% as loans/jobs. **Non-need-based:** Awarded to 7,988 full-time undergraduates, including 2,680 freshmen. Scholarships awarded for academics, art, athletics, leadership, minority status, music/drama, religious affiliation, state residency. **Additional information:** Majority of institutional gift aid merit-based. Some need-based grants go to merit winners with financial need.

Application procedures. Admission: Priority date 4/1; no deadline. $50 fee, may be waived for applicants with need. Application may be submitted online. Admission notification on a rolling basis. Must reply by May 1 or within 3 week(s) if notified thereafter. **Financial aid:** Priority date 3/1; no closing date. FAFSA required. Applicants notified on a rolling basis starting 4/1.

Academics. Special study options: Accelerated study, combined bachelor's/graduate degree, cooperative education, distance learning, double major, dual enrollment of high school students, ESL, external degree, honors, independent study, internships, liberal arts/career combination, semester at sea, student-designed major, study abroad, teacher certification program, United Nations semester, Washington semester. **Credit/placement by examination:** AP, CLEP, IB, institutional tests. **Support services:** Learning center, pre-admission summer program, reduced course load, remedial instruction, study skills assistance, tutoring, writing center.

Honors college/program. Top 5 percent of high school graduating class or minimum 1350 SAT or 31 ACT. Qualified students will receive application to Honors College Scholarship automatically. Completed applications reviewed by faculty panel. Honors College participants complete at least 3 approved honors courses during first 4 semesters on campus.

Majors. Area/ethnic studies: African-American, East Asian, women's. **Biology:** General, bacteriology, biochemistry. **Business:** General, accounting, business admin, finance, labor relations. **Communications:** General, digital media, journalism. **Communications technology:** Recording arts. **Computer sciences:** General. **Conservation:** General, environmental science. **Education:** General, art, biology, chemistry, early childhood, elementary, English, French, German, health, Latin, mathematics, multi-level teacher, music, physical, physics, science, secondary, social studies, Spanish, special, speech. **English:** Composition. **Family/consumer sciences:** Clothing/textiles. **Foreign languages:** General, African, ancient Greek, comparative lit, East Asian, French, German, Italian, Latin, linguistics, Portuguese, Slavic, Spanish. **Health:** Audiology/hearing, audiology/speech pathology, cytotechnology, dental hygiene, health care admin, medical radiologic technology/radiation therapy, medical records technology, nuclear medical technology, nursing (RN), respiratory therapy technology, sonography. **History:** General. **Interdisciplinary:** Science/society, systems science. **Liberal arts:** Arts/sciences. **Math:** General. **Parks/recreation:** General, facilities management. **Philosophy/religion:** Judaic, philosophy, religion. **Physical sciences:** Astronomy, astrophysics, chemistry, geology, physics. **Protective services:** Criminal justice. **Psychology:** General. **Public administration:** General. **Social sciences:** General, anthropology, economics, geography, political science, sociology. **Visual/performing arts:** General, art history/conservation, commercial/advertising art, conducting, dance, dramatic, interior design, jazz, music performance, music theory/composition, piano/organ, studio arts, voice/opera.

Most popular majors. Biology 6%, business/marketing 20%, communications/journalism 10%, education 16%, public administration/social services 7%, social sciences 7%.

Computing on campus. 2,262 workstations in dormitories, library, computer center, student center. Dormitories wired for high-speed internet access and linked to campus network. Commuter students can connect to campus network. Online course registration, helpline, repair service, student web hosting, wireless network available.

Student life. Freshman orientation: Mandatory, $104 fee. Preregistration for classes offered. 2-day program held between June 14 and July 20. **Policies:** Freshmen permitted cars on campus. **Housing:** Guaranteed on-campus for freshmen. Coed dorms, single-sex dorms, special housing for disabled, apartments, cooperative housing, fraternity/sorority housing, substance-free housing available. $400 deposit. Residential language houses, living/learning centers, wellness center, African-American living/learning center, honors college floors, first-year academic interest group housing available. **Activities:** Bands, choral groups, dance, drama, literary magazine, music ensembles, musical theater, opera, radio station, student government, student newspaper, symphony orchestra, TV station, College Democrats, College Republicans, Young Americans for Freedom, Black Student Union, Latinos Unidos, Asian-American Association, Alpha Phi Omega, Volunteers Student Bureau, College Mentors for Kids, Golden Key.

Athletics. NCAA. **Intercollegiate:** Baseball M, basketball, cross-country, diving, field hockey W, football (tackle) M, golf, rowing (crew) W, soccer, softball W, swimming, tennis, track and field, volleyball W, water polo W, wrestling M. **Intramural:** Archery, badminton, basketball, bowling, cross-country, diving, equestrian, fencing, field hockey W, gymnastics, handball, ice hockey M, lacrosse, racquetball, rifle, rowing (crew), rugby, sailing, skiing, skin diving, soccer, softball, squash, swimming, table tennis, tennis, track and field, volleyball, water polo, wrestling M. **Team name:** Hoosiers.

Student services. Adult student services, alcohol/substance abuse counseling, campus ministries, career counseling, services for economically disadvantaged, student employment services, financial aid counseling, health services, legal services, minority student services, on-campus daycare, personal counseling, placement for graduates, veterans' counselor, women's services. **Physically disabled:** Services for visually, speech, hearing impaired.

Contact. E-mail: iuadmit@indiana.edu
Phone: (812) 855-0661 Fax: (812) 855-5102
Mary Ellen Anderson, Director of Undergraduate Admissions, Indiana University Bloomington, 300 North Jordan Avenue, Bloomington, IN 47405

Indiana University East
Richmond, Indiana
www.iue.edu **CB code: 1194**

- Public 4-year university and branch campus college
- Commuter campus in large town
- 2,128 degree-seeking undergraduates: 40% part-time, 69% women, 4% African American, 1% Asian American, 1% Hispanic American
- 67 graduate students
- 88% of applicants admitted
- SAT or ACT with writing required

General. Founded in 1971. Regionally accredited. **Degrees:** 156 bachelor's, 86 associate awarded. **Location:** 70 miles from Indianapolis, 40 miles from Dayton, Ohio. **Calendar:** Semester, extensive summer session. **Full-time faculty:** 75 total. **Class size:** 68% < 20, 29% 20-39, 2% 40-49, less than 1% 50-99.

Freshman class profile. 491 applied, 434 admitted, 372 enrolled.

Mid 50% test scores		Rank in top quarter:	26%
SAT verbal:	400-530	Rank in top tenth:	8%
SAT math:	390-510	Return as sophomores:	54%
ACT:	16-20	Out-of-state:	18%

Basis for selection. Selective admission criteria for nursing program. Traditional students (3 years or less after high school graduation) required to take SAT or ACT for placement. May attend 1 semester while waiting to take test. Interview recommended. **Homeschooled:** Must graduate from national accredited home school program or take GED.

High school preparation. College-preparatory program recommended. 14 units required; 16 recommended. Required and recommended units include English 4, mathematics 3, social studies 2, science 1 (laboratory 1) and academic electives 4. 4 units in some combination of additional mathematics, laboratory science, social science, computer science, and other courses of college preparatory nature. Foreign language strongly recommended.

2005-2006 Annual costs. Tuition/fees: $4,806; $11,484 out-of-state. Books/supplies: $800. Personal expenses: $1,300.

2004-2005 Financial aid. **Need-based:** 280 full-time freshmen applied for aid; 216 were judged to have need; 194 of these received aid. Average need met was 55%. Average scholarship/grant was $4,408; average loan $2,351. 60% of total undergraduate aid awarded as scholarships/grants, 40% as loans/jobs. **Non-need-based:** Awarded to 322 full-time undergraduates, including 114 freshmen. Scholarships awarded for academics, alumni affiliation, minority status.

Application procedures. **Admission:** No deadline. $25 fee, may be waived for applicants with need. Application may be submitted online. Admission notification on a rolling basis. **Financial aid:** Priority date 3/1; no closing date. FAFSA, institutional form required. Applicants notified on a rolling basis starting 5/1; must reply within 2 week(s) of notification.

Academics. **Special study options:** Cooperative education, cross-registration, distance learning, double major, dual enrollment of high school students, external degree, independent study, internships, teacher certification program, weekend college. State-wide technology program with Purdue University. **Credit/placement by examination:** AP, CLEP, SAT, ACT, institutional tests. **Support services:** Remedial instruction, study skills assistance, tutoring, writing center.

Majors. **Biology:** General. **Business:** Accounting, business admin, management information systems, marketing. **Communications:** General. **Education:** Elementary, secondary. **English:** English lit. **Health:** Nursing (RN). **Interdisciplinary:** Biological/physical sciences, natural sciences. **Liberal arts:** Humanities. **Protective services:** Criminal justice. **Psychology:** General. **Public administration:** Social work. **Social sciences:** Sociology.

Most popular majors. Education 21%, health sciences 18%, liberal arts 16%, philosophy/religious studies 15%, public administration/social services 6%.

Computing on campus. 120 workstations in library, computer center.

Student life. **Freshman orientation:** Mandatory. Preregistration for classes offered. **Policies:** Freshmen permitted cars on campus. **Activities:** Drama, student government, student newspaper, TV station.

Athletics. **Intramural:** Basketball, softball, volleyball. **Team name:** Pioneers.

Student services. Adult student services, career counseling, student employment services, financial aid counseling, health services, on-campus daycare, personal counseling, placement for graduates. **Physically disabled:** Services for visually, speech, hearing impaired.

Contact. E-mail: eaadmit@indiana.edu
Phone: (765) 973-8208 Toll-free number: (800) 959-3278
Fax: (765) 973-8288
James Bland, Director, Admissions and Financial Aid, Indiana University East, 2325 Chester Boulevard, Richmond, IN 47374-1289

Indiana University Kokomo

Kokomo, Indiana
www.iuk.edu **CB code: 1337**

- Public 4-year university
- Commuter campus in large town
- 2,525 degree-seeking undergraduates: 44% part-time, 72% women, 3% African American, 1% Asian American, 1% Hispanic American, 1% Native American
- 77 degree-seeking graduate students
- 82% of applicants admitted
- SAT or ACT with writing required
- 32% graduate within 6 years

General. Founded in 1945. Regionally accredited. **Degrees:** 222 bachelor's, 194 associate awarded; master's offered. **Location:** 50 miles from Indianapolis. **Calendar:** Semester, limited summer session. **Full-time faculty:** 83 total; 71% have terminal degrees, 11% minority, 57% women. **Class size:** 44% < 20, 43% 20-39, 10% 40-49, 2% 50-99, less than 1% >100. **Special facilities:** Observatory.

Freshman class profile. 717 applied, 587 admitted, 476 enrolled.

Mid 50% test scores		**Rank in top quarter:**	20%
SAT verbal:	440-540	**Rank in top tenth:**	5%
SAT math:	430-540	**Return as sophomores:**	56%
ACT:	17-22		

Basis for selection. Test scores, class rank, course work important; 2 out of 3 should be met for admission. In-state applicants should be in top half of graduating class (top third for out-of-state applicants).

High school preparation. 14 units required. Required and recommended units include English 4, mathematics 3, social studies 2, history 2, science 1 and foreign language 2. Additional 4 units required from math, science, social sciences, and foreign language.

2005-2006 Annual costs. Tuition/fees: $4,835; $11,513 out-of-state. Books/supplies: $840. Personal expenses: $1,130.

2004-2005 Financial aid. **Need-based:** 244 full-time freshmen applied for aid; 164 were judged to have need; 155 of these received aid. Average need met was 68%. Average scholarship/grant was $4,476; average loan $2,283. 58% of total undergraduate aid awarded as scholarships/grants, 42% as loans/jobs. **Non-need-based:** Awarded to 195 full-time undergraduates, including 108 freshmen. Scholarships awarded for academics.

Application procedures. **Admission:** Priority date 8/3; no deadline. $30 fee, may be waived for applicants with need. Application must be submitted on paper. Admission notification on a rolling basis. **Financial aid:** Closing date 3/1. FAFSA, institutional form required. Applicants notified on a rolling basis starting 5/1; must reply within 4 week(s) of notification.

Academics. **Special study options:** Accelerated study, cross-registration, distance learning, double major, dual enrollment of high school students, external degree, honors, independent study, internships, study abroad, teacher certification program. **Credit/placement by examination:** AP, CLEP, institutional tests. **Support services:** Learning center, reduced course load, remedial instruction, tutoring.

Majors. **Biology:** General. **Business:** General, accounting, business admin, labor relations, marketing. **Communications:** General. **Computer sciences:** General. **Education:** Elementary. **English:** English lit. **Health:** Nursing (RN). **Interdisciplinary:** Behavioral sciences, biological/physical sciences, gerontology. **Liberal arts:** Humanities. **Math:** General. **Physical sciences:** Chemistry. **Protective services:** Criminal justice. **Psychology:** General. **Public administration:** General. **Social sciences:** General, sociology.

Most popular majors. Business/marketing 16%, computer/information sciences 7%, education 19%, health sciences 18%, liberal arts 18%, security/protective services 7%.

Computing on campus. 100 workstations in library, computer center, student center. Online course registration, helpline available.

Student life. **Freshman orientation:** Available, $25 fee. Preregistration for classes offered. **Policies:** Freshmen permitted cars on campus. **Activities:** Choral groups, drama, music ensembles, student government, student newspaper.

Athletics. **Intramural:** Basketball M, soccer, softball, volleyball.

Student services. Adult student services, career counseling, student employment services, financial aid counseling, minority student services, on-campus daycare, personal counseling, placement for graduates, veterans' counselor. **Physically disabled:** Services for visually, hearing impaired.

Contact. E-mail: iuadmis@iuk.edu
Phone: (765) 455-9217 Toll-free number: (888) 875-4485
Fax: (765) 455-9537
Jackie Kennedy-Fletcher, Director of Admissions, Indiana University Kokomo, Box 9003, KC 230A, Kokomo, IN 46904-9003

Indiana University Northwest

Gary, Indiana
www.iun.edu **CB code: 1338**

- Public 4-year university
- Commuter campus in small city
- 4,042 degree-seeking undergraduates: 40% part-time, 71% women, 22% African American, 1% Asian American, 12% Hispanic American
- 386 degree-seeking graduate students
- 75% of applicants admitted
- SAT or ACT required
- 31% graduate within 6 years

General. Founded in 1948. Regionally accredited. **Degrees:** 367 bachelor's, 247 associate awarded; master's offered. **ROTC:** Army. **Location:** 35 miles from Chicago. **Calendar:** Semester, limited summer session. **Full-time faculty:** 164 total; 65% have terminal degrees, 18% minority, 48% women. **Class size:** 57% < 20, 36% 20-39, 4% 40-49, 4% 50-99, less than 1% >100.

Freshman class profile. 1,062 applied, 795 admitted, 604 enrolled.

Mid 50% test scores		Rank in top quarter:	21%
SAT verbal:	400-510	Rank in top tenth:	6%
SAT math:	390-510	Return as sophomores:	58%
ACT:	16-21	Out-of-state:	1%

Basis for selection. School achievement record and test scores most important. Applicants should be in top half of class and have 2.0 high school GPA or better.

High school preparation. College-preparatory program recommended. 16 units required. Required and recommended units include English 4, mathematics 3, social studies 2, science 1, foreign language 2 and academic electives 4.

2005-2006 Annual costs. Tuition/fees: $4,902. Books/supplies: $720. Personal expenses: $2,630.

2004-2005 Financial aid. **Need-based:** 486 full-time freshmen applied for aid; 392 were judged to have need; 352 of these received aid. Average need met was 65.8%. Average scholarship/grant was $4,170; average loan $2,352. 47% of total undergraduate aid awarded as scholarships/grants, 53% as loans/jobs. **Non-need-based:** Awarded to 370 full-time undergraduates, including 63 freshmen. Scholarships awarded for academics, athletics.

Application procedures. **Admission:** Priority date 8/1; no deadline. $35 fee, may be waived for applicants with need. Admission notification on a rolling basis. **Financial aid:** Priority date 3/1; no closing date. FAFSA, institutional form required. Applicants notified on a rolling basis starting 5/1; must reply within 2 week(s) of notification.

Academics. **Special study options:** Accelerated study, cooperative education, distance learning, double major, dual enrollment of high school students, external degree, independent study, internships, liberal arts/career combination, student-designed major, study abroad, teacher certification program, Washington semester, weekend college. **Credit/placement by examination:** AP, CLEP, institutional tests. **Support services:** Learning center, preadmission summer program, reduced course load, remedial instruction, tutoring.

Majors. **Area/ethnic studies:** African-American. **Biology:** General. **Business:** General, actuarial science, labor relations. **Communications:** General. **Computer sciences:** Data processing. **Education:** Elementary, English, mathematics, secondary, social studies, Spanish. **English:** English lit. **Foreign languages:** French, Spanish. **Health:** Health care admin, medical records admin, nursing (RN). **History:** General. **Math:** General. **Philosophy/religion:** Philosophy. **Physical sciences:** Chemistry, geology. **Protective services:** Criminal justice. **Psychology:** General. **Public administration:** General. **Social sciences:** Economics, political science, sociology. **Visual/performing arts:** Art, dramatic.

Most popular majors. Business/marketing 16%, education 15%, health sciences 15%, liberal arts 12%, security/protective services 12%.

Computing on campus. 170 workstations in library, computer center, student center. Commuter students can connect to campus network. Online course registration, helpline available.

Student life. **Freshman orientation:** Available. Preregistration for classes offered. **Policies:** Freshmen permitted cars on campus. **Activities:** Choral groups, drama, literary magazine, student government, student newspaper, Christian Student Fellowship, Young Republicans, Young Democrats, Women with a Challenge, Student Guide Services, Black Student Union.

Athletics. NAIA. **Intercollegiate:** Basketball, golf, volleyball W. **Intramural:** Baseball M, basketball M, bowling, cheerleading W, golf. **Team name:** Red Hawks.

Student services. Adult student services, career counseling, student employment services, financial aid counseling, on-campus daycare, personal counseling, placement for graduates, veterans' counselor, women's services. **Physically disabled:** Services for visually impaired.

Contact. Phone: (219) 980-6991 Toll-free number: (800) 968-7486
Fax: (219) 981-4219
Linda Templeton, Director of Admissions, Indiana University Northwest, 3400 Broadway, Gary, IN 46408

Indiana University South Bend

South Bend, Indiana
www.iusb.edu **CB code: 1339**

- Public 4-year university
- Commuter campus in small city
- 5,818 degree-seeking undergraduates: 38% part-time, 63% women, 7% African American, 1% Asian American, 3% Hispanic American, 2% international
- 812 degree-seeking graduate students
- 88% of applicants admitted
- SAT or ACT required

General. Founded in 1922. Regionally accredited. Off-campus course offerings in Elkhart, Warsaw, Plymouth. **Degrees:** 575 bachelor's, 194 associate awarded; master's offered. **ROTC:** Army, Navy, Air Force. **Location:** 90 miles from Chicago, 120 miles from Indianapolis. **Calendar:** Semester, limited summer session. **Full-time faculty:** 237 total; 69% have terminal degrees, 16% minority, 50% women. **Class size:** 50% < 20, 41% 20-39, 5% 40-49, 4% 50-99, less than 1% >100.

Freshman class profile. 1,560 applied, 1,374 admitted, 1,006 enrolled.

Mid 50% test scores		Rank in top tenth:	7%
SAT verbal:	430-540	Return as sophomores:	64%
SAT math:	420-530	Out-of-state:	2%
ACT:	18-23	International:	1%
Rank in top quarter:	24%		

Basis for selection. Rank in top half of class important. Core 40 completion with "C" or higher. Interview recommended for academically weak applicants or those with unusual circumstances. Audition required of music majors. Portfolios required for some majors. **Homeschooled:** Applicants to degree-seeking programs must meet institution's requirement for college-prep courses.

High school preparation. 13 units required. Required and recommended units include English 4, mathematics 3, social studies 2, science 1 (laboratory 1) and foreign language 2. Strong preparation in mathematics and sciences recommended.

2005-2006 Annual costs. Tuition/fees: $4,989; $12,408 out-of-state. Books/supplies: $976. Personal expenses: $1,604.

2004-2005 Financial aid. **Need-based:** 563 full-time freshmen applied for aid; 461 were judged to have need; 400 of these received aid. Average need met was 48%. Average scholarship/grant was $3,978; average loan $2,275. 49% of total undergraduate aid awarded as scholarships/grants, 51% as loans/jobs. **Non-need-based:** Awarded to 343 full-time undergraduates, including 145 freshmen. Scholarships awarded for academics, athletics.

Application procedures. **Admission:** Priority date 7/1; no deadline. $43 fee, may be waived for applicants with need. Application may be submitted online. Admission notification on a rolling basis. **Financial aid:** Closing date 3/1. FAFSA, institutional form required. Applicants notified on a rolling basis starting 5/1.

Academics. Most allied health programs must be completed at Indianapolis campus. **Special study options:** Accelerated study, cross-registration, distance learning, double major, ESL, external degree, honors, internships, liberal arts/career combination, study abroad, teacher certification program, weekend college. Electrical, mechanical engineering, computer technology with Purdue University on Indiana University South Bend campus; Northern Indiana Consortium for Education (NICE) - IUSB is one of 6 member institutions sharing library resources, faculty expertise, and academic strengths. **Credit/placement by examination:** AP, CLEP, IB, institutional tests. 90 credit hours maximum toward bachelor's degree. **Support services:** Learning center, pre-admission summer program, reduced course load, remedial instruction, tutoring, writing center.

Majors. **Area/ethnic studies:** Women's. **Biology:** General. **Business:** General, actuarial science, business admin, finance, labor relations, labor studies, marketing. **Communications:** Media studies. **Computer sciences:** General. **Education:** Biology, chemistry, elementary, mathematics, music, physics, science, secondary, social studies, Spanish, special. **English:** Composition, English lit, speech/rhetoric. **Foreign languages:** French, German, Spanish. **Health:** Health care admin, nursing (RN). **History:** General. **Math:** General, applied. **Philosophy/religion:** Philosophy. **Physical sciences:** Chemistry, physics. **Protective services:** Criminal justice. **Psychology:** General. **Public administration:** General. **Social sciences:** Economics, political science, sociology. **Visual/performing arts:** Art, dramatic, music performance, studio arts.

Most popular majors. Business/marketing 16%, education 22%, health sciences 12%, liberal arts 13%, security/protective services 7%.

Computing on campus. 325 workstations in library, computer center. Commuter students can connect to campus network. Online library, helpline available.

Student life. **Freshman orientation:** Available, $21 fee. Preregistration for classes offered. Two and a half hour sessions held in May, June, July and August. **Policies:** Freshmen permitted cars on campus. **Housing:** Some housing for athletes and visiting scholars. **Activities:** Jazz band, choral groups, drama, film society, literary magazine, music ensembles, musical theater, opera, student government, student newspaper, symphony orchestra, student educational association, black student union, student council for exceptional children, campus ministry, Latino student union, Asian student union, women's student union, Habitat for Humanity, international student organization, departmental clubs.

Athletics. NAIA. **Intercollegiate:** Basketball. **Intramural:** Badminton, basketball, bowling, football (tackle), racquetball, softball, table tennis, tennis, volleyball. **Team name:** Titans.

Student services. Adult student services, campus ministries, career counseling, student employment services, on-campus daycare, personal counseling, placement for graduates, veterans' counselor. **Physically disabled:** Services for visually, speech, hearing impaired.

Contact. E-mail: admissio@iusb.edu
Phone: (574) 520-4480 Fax: (574) 520-4834
Jeff Johnston, Director Recruitment/Admissions, Indiana University South Bend, 1700 Mishawaka Avenue, South Bend, IN 46634-7111

Indiana University Southeast

New Albany, Indiana — **CB member**
www.ius.edu — **CB code: 1314**

- Public 4-year university
- Commuter campus in large town
- 5,079 degree-seeking undergraduates: 37% part-time, 64% women, 4% African American, 1% Asian American, 1% Hispanic American
- 646 degree-seeking graduate students
- 89% of applicants admitted
- SAT or ACT with writing required
- 34% graduate within 6 years

General. Founded in 1941. Regionally accredited. **Degrees:** 614 bachelor's, 116 associate awarded; master's offered. **ROTC:** Army, Air Force. **Location:** 10 miles from Louisville, Kentucky. **Calendar:** Semester, limited summer session. **Full-time faculty:** 173 total; 71% have terminal degrees, 13% minority, 46% women. **Class size:** 44% < 20, 50% 20-39, 5% 40-49, 1% 50-99. **Special facilities:** Cultural and community center.

Freshman class profile. 1,194 applied, 1,066 admitted, 753 enrolled.

Mid 50% test scores			
SAT verbal:	430-540	Rank in top tenth:	8%
SAT math:	430-530	Return as sophomores:	65%
ACT:	17-22	Out-of-state:	14%
Rank in top quarter:	28%	Fraternities:	3%
		Sororities:	4%

Basis for selection. Rank in top half of class for in-state applicants. Interview recommended.

High school preparation. 14 units required; 19 recommended. Required and recommended units include English 4, mathematics 3-4, social studies 2, history 1, science 1-2 (laboratory 1-2), foreign language 2 and academic electives 4.

2005-2006 Annual costs. Tuition/fees: $4,880; $11,558 out-of-state. Books/supplies: $576. Personal expenses: $990.

2004-2005 Financial aid. Need-based: 586 full-time freshmen applied for aid; 450 were judged to have need; 423 of these received aid. Average need met was 55%. Average scholarship/grant was $3,972; average loan $2,166. 46% of total undergraduate aid awarded as scholarships/grants, 54% as loans/jobs. **Non-need-based:** Awarded to 581 full-time undergraduates, including 224 freshmen. Scholarships awarded for academics, art, athletics, leadership, minority status, music/drama.

Application procedures. Admission: Priority date 7/15; no deadline. $30 fee, may be waived for applicants with need. Application may be submitted online. Admission notification on a rolling basis. **Financial aid:** Priority date 3/1; no closing date. FAFSA required. Applicants notified on a rolling basis starting 5/1; must reply within 3 week(s) of notification.

Academics. Special study options: Accelerated study, cross-registration, double major, dual enrollment of high school students, external degree, independent study, internships, student-designed major, study abroad, teacher certification program, weekend college. Member of Metroversity consortium of institutions of higher education in Louisville area. **Credit/placement by examination:** AP, CLEP, IB, institutional tests. **Support services:** Reduced course load, remedial instruction, study skills assistance, tutoring, writing center.

Majors. Biology: General. **Business:** General, accounting, accounting technology, labor relations. **Communications:** General, journalism. **Computer sciences:** General. **Education:** General, biology, elementary, English, mathematics, science, secondary, social studies, special. **English:** English lit. **Foreign languages:** French, German, Spanish. **Health:** Clinical lab science, nursing (RN). **History:** General. **Math:** General. **Philosophy/religion:** Philosophy. **Physical sciences:** Chemistry, physics. **Psychology:** General. **Social sciences:** Economics, geography, international relations, political science, sociology. **Visual/performing arts:** Art, studio arts.

Most popular majors. Business/marketing 24%, education 23%, health sciences 6%, liberal arts 16%, psychology 7%.

Computing on campus. 165 workstations in library, computer center, student center. Commuter students can connect to campus network. Online course registration, online library, helpline, student web hosting, wireless network available.

Student life. Freshman orientation: Mandatory. Preregistration for classes offered. One-day summer program. **Policies:** Freshmen permitted cars on campus. **Activities:** Concert band, choral groups, drama, literary magazine, music ensembles, student government, student newspaper, symphony orchestra, Christian fellowship, Students for World Peace, multicultural student union.

Athletics. NAIA. **Intercollegiate:** Baseball M, basketball, cross-country, tennis, volleyball W. **Intramural:** Basketball, bowling, softball, tennis, volleyball. **Team name:** Grenadier.

Student services. Adult student services, alcohol/substance abuse counseling, campus ministries, career counseling, student employment services, financial aid counseling, minority student services, on-campus daycare, personal counseling, placement for graduates, veterans' counselor. **Physically disabled:** Services for visually, speech, hearing impaired.

Contact. E-mail: admissions@ius.edu
Phone: (812) 941-2212 Toll-free number: (800) 852-8835
Fax: (812) 941-2595
Anne Skuce, Assistant Vice Chancellor for Enrollment Mgmt./Dir. of Admission, Indiana University Southeast, 4201 Grant Line Road, New Albany, IN 47150-6405

Indiana University-Purdue University Fort Wayne

Fort Wayne, Indiana — **CB member**
www.ipfw.edu — **CB code: 1336**

- Public 4-year university and branch campus college
- Commuter campus in small city
- 10,694 degree-seeking undergraduates: 37% part-time, 57% women, 5% African American, 2% Asian American, 3% Hispanic American, 1% international
- 653 degree-seeking graduate students
- 96% of applicants admitted
- SAT or ACT (ACT writing optional) required

General. Founded in 1964. Regionally accredited. Degrees awarded through Indiana University or Purdue University, depending on course of study. **Degrees:** 907 bachelor's, 572 associate awarded; master's offered. **Location:** 110 miles from Indianapolis. **Calendar:** Semester, limited summer session. **Full-time faculty:** 372 total; 82% have terminal degrees, 10% minority, 41% women. **Part-time faculty:** 394 total; 10% have terminal degrees, 5% minority, 54% women. **Class size:** 46% < 20, 47% 20-39, 4% 40-49, 3% 50-99, less than 1% >100. **Special facilities:** Lake biological research station.

Freshman class profile. 2,786 applied, 2,681 admitted, 1,895 enrolled.

Mid 50% test scores			
SAT verbal:	430-540	Rank in top quarter:	28%
SAT math:	440-550	Rank in top tenth:	9%
ACT:	18-24	End year in good standing:	95%
GPA 3.50 or higher:	25%	Return as sophomores:	64%
GPA 3.0-3.49:	29%	Out-of-state:	6%
GPA 2.0-2.99:	44%	Live on campus:	16%
		International:	1%

Basis for selection. In-state applicants should rank in top half of high school class, out-of-state in top third. Test scores important. TOEFL or Michigan Test may be used to assess English proficiency. Audition required of music majors. Portfolio required of visual arts majors. **Homeschooled:** Transcript of courses and grades required.

High school preparation. College-preparatory program recommended. 20 units required. Required units include English 4, mathematics 3, social studies 5, science 2 (laboratory 1) and academic electives 5. Additional requirements vary by program.

2005-2006 Annual costs. Tuition/fees: $5,630; $12,984 out-of-state. Room only: $4,750. Books/supplies: $1,096. Personal expenses: $3,224.

2004-2005 Financial aid. **Need-based:** 1,296 full-time freshmen applied for aid; 984 were judged to have need; 914 of these received aid. Average need met was 69%. Average scholarship/grant was $3,786; average loan $2,333. 45% of total undergraduate aid awarded as scholarships/grants, 55% as loans/jobs. **Non-need-based:** Awarded to 1,342 full-time undergraduates, including 375 freshmen. Scholarships awarded for academics, athletics, state residency.

Application procedures. **Admission:** Priority date 8/1; no deadline. $30 fee, may be waived for applicants with need. Application may be submitted online. Admission notification on a rolling basis. **Financial aid:** Priority date 3/10; no closing date. FAFSA required. Applicants notified on a rolling basis starting 5/15; must reply within 3 week(s) of notification.

Academics. **Special study options:** Accelerated study, cooperative education, distance learning, double major, ESL, exchange student, honors, independent study, internships, liberal arts/career combination, student-designed major, study abroad, teacher certification program, Washington semester, weekend college. **Credit/placement by examination:** AP, CLEP, IB, institutional tests. Hours of credit awarded by examination varies by program. **Support services:** Learning center, pre-admission summer program, remedial instruction, study skills assistance, tutoring, writing center.

Majors. **Area/ethnic studies:** Women's. **Biology:** General. **Business:** Accounting, business admin, finance, hospitality admin, labor studies, managerial economics, marketing, operations. **Communications:** General, media studies, organizational. **Computer sciences:** Computer science, information systems. **Education:** Art, biology, chemistry, drama/dance, elementary, English, French, German, history, mathematics, music, physics, science, secondary, social studies, Spanish, speech. **Engineering:** Computer, electrical, mechanical. **Engineering technology:** Computer, construction, electrical, industrial, mechanical. **English:** British lit, composition, English lit, technical writing. **Foreign languages:** French, German, Spanish. **Health:** Audiology/hearing, clinical lab science, clinical lab technology, community health services, health care admin, health services admin, mental health services, music therapy, nursing (RN), predentistry, premedicine, preveterinary, recreational therapy, substance abuse counseling. **History:** General. **Interdisciplinary:** Math/computer science. **Legal studies:** General. **Math:** General, computational, statistics. **Philosophy/religion:** Philosophy. **Physical sciences:** Chemistry, geology, physics. **Protective services:** Law enforcement admin. **Psychology:** General. **Public administration:** General, policy analysis. **Social sciences:** Anthropology, economics, political science, sociology. **Visual/performing arts:** Commercial/advertising art, crafts, dramatic, drawing, graphic design, painting, photography, piano/organ, printmaking, sculpture, studio arts, voice/opera.

Most popular majors. Business/marketing 19%, education 21%, engineering/engineering technologies 9%, liberal arts 14%, psychology 6%.

Computing on campus. 285 workstations in dormitories, library, computer center, student center. Dormitories wired for high-speed internet access and linked to campus network. Commuter students can connect to campus network. Online course registration, online library, helpline, student web hosting, wireless network available.

Student life. **Freshman orientation:** Mandatory, $20 fee. Preregistration for classes offered. 4-hour program; 10-12 dates between June and August. **Policies:** Freshmen permitted cars on campus. **Housing:** Coed dorms, apartments, substance-free housing available. $150 fully refundable deposit. **Activities:** Bands, choral groups, dance, drama, literary magazine, music ensembles, musical theater, opera, student government, student newspaper, symphony orchestra, TV station, Black Collegian Caucus, Disabled Students Excelling in Leadership, Hispanos Unidos, InterVarsity Christian Fellowship, Muslim student association, Graduate Business Council, international students' organization.

Athletics. NCAA. **Intercollegiate:** Baseball M, basketball, cross-country, golf, soccer, softball W, tennis, track and field W, volleyball. **Intramural:** Basketball, football (non-tackle), football (tackle) M, golf, handball, racquetball, soccer, softball, table tennis, tennis, volleyball. **Team name:** Mastodons.

Student services. Adult student services, alcohol/substance abuse counseling, campus ministries, career counseling, student employment services, financial aid counseling, health services, minority student services, on-campus daycare, personal counseling, placement for graduates, veterans' counselor, women's services. **Physically disabled:** Services for visually, speech, hearing impaired.

Contact. E-mail: ipfwadms@ipfw.edu
Phone: (260) 481-6812 Toll-free number: (800) 324-4739
Fax: (260) 481-6880
Carol Isaacs, Director of Admissions, Indiana University-Purdue University Fort Wayne, 2101 East Coliseum Boulevard, Fort Wayne, IN 46805-1499

Indiana University-Purdue University Indianapolis

Indianapolis, Indiana — **CB member**
www.iupui.edu — **CB code: 1325**

- Public 4-year university
- Commuter campus in very large city
- 20,537 degree-seeking undergraduates: 34% part-time, 59% women, 11% African American, 2% Asian American, 2% Hispanic American, 2% international
- 7,288 degree-seeking graduate students
- 74% of applicants admitted
- SAT or ACT with writing required

General. Founded in 1969. Regionally accredited. **Degrees:** 2,713 bachelor's, 603 associate awarded; master's, doctoral, first professional offered. **ROTC:** Army, Navy, Air Force. **Calendar:** Semester, extensive summer session. **Full-time faculty:** 850 total. **Class size:** 41% < 20, 43% 20-39, 7% 40-49, 8% 50-99, 1% >100.

Freshman class profile. 6,136 applied, 4,525 admitted, 2,746 enrolled.

Mid 50% test scores		**Return as sophomores:**	65%
SAT verbal:	440-550	**Out-of-state:**	2%
SAT math:	440-560	**Live on campus:**	12%
ACT:	18-23	**International:**	2%
Rank in top quarter:	33%	**Fraternities:**	1%
Rank in top tenth:	9%	**Sororities:**	1%

Basis for selection. Course curriculum, grades, trend in grades, and test scores are the factors used. Portfolio recommended for some art applicants.

High school preparation. 17 units required; 22 recommended. Required and recommended units include English 4, mathematics 3-4, social studies 1, history 2, science 3-4 (laboratory 3), foreign language 3 and academic electives 4. Additional mathematics and science units required for science, engineering and nursing programs. 4 additional units required in some combination of foreign language, laboratory science, mathematics, social science, or computer science. Courses that develop writing composition skills strongly recommended.

2005-2006 Annual costs. Tuition/fees: $6,219; $16,547 out-of-state. Room/board: $4,740. Books/supplies: $576. Personal expenses: $2,084.

2004-2005 Financial aid. **Need-based:** 1,683 full-time freshmen applied for aid; 1,358 were judged to have need; 1,192 of these received aid. Average need met was 41%. Average scholarship/grant was $4,984; average loan $2,449. 49% of total undergraduate aid awarded as scholarships/grants, 51% as loans/jobs. **Non-need-based:** Awarded to 2,185 full-time undergraduates, including 708 freshmen. Scholarships awarded for academics.

Application procedures. **Admission:** Closing date 6/1. $50 fee, may be waived for applicants with need. Application may be submitted online. Admission notification on a rolling basis. Application deadlines for nursing and allied health programs range from October 15 to February 1. **Financial aid:** Priority date 3/1; no closing date. FAFSA required. Applicants notified on a rolling basis starting 4/1.

Academics. **Special study options:** Accelerated study, cooperative education, cross-registration, distance learning, double major, dual enrollment of high school students, ESL, external degree, honors, independent study, internships, student-designed major, study abroad, teacher certification program, weekend college. **Credit/placement by examination:** AP, CLEP, IB, institutional tests. Policy varies by school. **Support services:** Learning center, reduced course load, remedial instruction, tutoring, writing center.

Majors. **Biology:** General. **Business:** General, accounting, finance, human resources, international, labor relations, labor studies, management information systems, market research, nonprofit/public, tourism/travel. **Communications:** General, advertising, journalism, public relations. **Computer sciences:** General, computer graphics, information systems, system admin, web page design, webmaster. **Conservation:** Environmental science. **Education:** Art, biology, chemistry, elementary, English, ESL, French, German, health occupations, mathematics, physical, physics, secondary, social studies, Spanish, speech. **Engineering:** General, biomedical, computer, electrical, mechanical. **Engineering technology:** Computer, computer hardware, computer systems, construction, electrical, mechanical, robotics, software.

English: English lit. **Foreign languages:** American Sign Language, French, German, Spanish. **Health:** Clinical lab science, cytotechnology, dental hygiene, medical informatics, medical radiologic technology/radiation therapy, medical records admin, nuclear medical technology, nursing (RN), predentistry, premedicine, prenursing, prepharmacy, preveterinary, radiologic technology/medical imaging, respiratory therapy assistant. **History:** General. **Legal studies:** Prelaw. **Liberal arts:** Arts/sciences. **Math:** General. **Parks/recreation:** Exercise sciences. **Philosophy/religion:** Philosophy, religion. **Physical sciences:** Chemistry, geology, physics. **Protective services:** Criminal justice, forensics. **Psychology:** General. **Public administration:** General, social work. **Social sciences:** Anthropology, economics, geography, political science, sociology. **Visual/performing arts:** Art, art history/conservation, ceramics, design, interior design, painting, photography, printmaking, sculpture, studio arts.

Most popular majors. Business/marketing 17%, communications/journalism 6%, computer/information sciences 6%, education 10%, engineering/engineering technologies 7%, health sciences 14%, liberal arts 15%.

Computing on campus. 750 workstations in library, computer center, student center. Dormitories wired for high-speed internet access and linked to campus network. Commuter students can connect to campus network. Online course registration, helpline, repair service, wireless network available.

Student life. **Freshman orientation:** Mandatory, $100 fee. Preregistration for classes offered. **Policies:** Smoking policy, code of conduct. Freshmen permitted cars on campus. **Housing:** Coed dorms, apartments available. $35 deposit. **Activities:** Bands, choral groups, dance, drama, literary magazine, music ensembles, student government, student newspaper, Black Student Union, international affairs club.

Athletics. NCAA. **Intercollegiate:** Basketball, cheerleading, cross-country, diving, golf, soccer, softball W, swimming, tennis, volleyball W. **Intramural:** Basketball, football (non-tackle), golf, ice hockey, racquetball, soccer, softball, tennis, volleyball. **Team name:** Jaguars.

Student services. Adult student services, campus ministries, career counseling, student employment services, financial aid counseling, health services, minority student services, on-campus daycare, personal counseling, placement for graduates, veterans' counselor, women's services. **Physically disabled:** Services for visually, speech, hearing impaired. **Learning disabled:** Comprehensive services available.

Contact. E-mail: apply@iupui.edu
Phone: (317) 274-4591 Fax: (317) 278-1862
Michael Donahue, Director of Admissions, Indiana University-Purdue University Indianapolis, 425 North University Boulevard, Cavanaugh Hall R129, Indianapolis, IN 46202-5143

Indiana Wesleyan University

Marion, Indiana
www.indwes.edu **CB code: 1446**

- Private 4-year university and liberal arts college affiliated with Wesleyan Church
- Residential campus in large town
- 8,447 degree-seeking undergraduates: 7% part-time, 64% women
- 4,185 degree-seeking graduate students
- 82% of applicants admitted
- SAT or ACT with writing, application essay required
- 65% graduate within 6 years

General. Founded in 1920. Regionally accredited. Education centers in Indianapolis, Fort Wayne, Columbus (IN), Shelbyville (IN), Cleveland, Cincinnati, Louisville and Dayton. **Degrees:** 1,460 bachelor's, 453 associate awarded; master's, doctoral offered. **ROTC:** Army. **Location:** 65 miles from Indianapolis. **Calendar:** Differs by program, limited summer session. **Full-time faculty:** 127 total; 56% have terminal degrees, 35% women. **Part-time faculty:** 102 total; 54% women. **Class size:** 67% < 20, 25% 20-39, 4% 40-49, 3% 50-99, less than 1% >100. **Special facilities:** History museum, nature preserve, museum of European oil paintings, Camponigro photograph collection.

Freshman class profile. 2,105 applied, 1,721 admitted, 1,432 enrolled.

Mid 50% test scores		**Rank in top quarter:**	47%
SAT verbal:	470-630	**Rank in top tenth:**	22%
SAT math:	450-650	**End year in good standing:**	98%
ACT:	20-29	**Return as sophomores:**	80%
GPA 3.50 or higher:	35%	**Out-of-state:**	36%
GPA 3.0-3.49:	29%	**Live on campus:**	92%
GPA 2.0-2.99:	30%		

Basis for selection. High school record, class rank, and test scores. Recommendations required. Standardized tests and insitutional tests used to assist students in selecting classes appropriate to their preparation, designated scores determine placement in Math and English. Audition recommended for music majors. Portfolio recommended for art majors. **Homeschooled:** Transcript of courses and grades, letter of recommendation (nonparent) required. The transcript must have the GPA on a 4.0 scale. Recommendation from a pastor required.

High school preparation. 20 units recommended. Recommended units include English 4, mathematics 4, social studies 2, history 2, science 3, foreign language 2 and academic electives 3.

2006-2007 Annual costs. Tuition/fees: $17,164. Required fees vary by program but are minimal. Room/board: $6,124. Books/supplies: $800. Personal expenses: $800.

2005-2006 Financial aid. **Non-need-based:** Scholarships awarded for academics, alumni affiliation, art, athletics, music/drama, ROTC.

Application procedures. **Admission:** Priority date 12/1; deadline 8/1 (receipt date). $25 fee, may be waived for applicants with need. Application may be submitted online. Admission notification on a rolling basis. **Financial aid:** Closing date 3/1. FAFSA required. Applicants notified by 4/1.

Academics. **Special study options:** Accelerated study, cross-registration, distance learning, dual enrollment of high school students, honors, independent study, internships, liberal arts/career combination, student-designed major, study abroad, teacher certification program. **Credit/placement by examination:** AP, CLEP, IB, SAT, ACT. Students must complete at least 30 hours in residence. **Support services:** Learning center, reduced course load, remedial instruction, study skills assistance, tutoring, writing center.

Honors college/program. The Honors College admits students based on a competitive applicaiton process. In order to apply, one must be accepted into IWU, possess at least a combined score of 1250 on the SAT (Math/Critical Reading) or 28 on the ACT, hold at least a 3.6 high school G.P.A. or class rank in the top 10 percent, and desire to participate in an interdisciplinary community of committed learners.

Majors. **Biology:** General. **Business:** Accounting, business admin, finance, management information systems, managerial economics, marketing. **Communications:** General. **Computer sciences:** General, applications programming. **Education:** Art, business, elementary, English, mathematics, middle, music, physical, science, secondary, social studies. **English:** Creative writing. **Foreign languages:** Spanish. **Health:** Athletic training, nursing (RN), predentistry, premedicine, prepharmacy, preveterinary, substance abuse counseling. **History:** General. **Legal studies:** Prelaw. **Math:** General. **Parks/recreation:** Exercise sciences, facilities management, health/fitness, sports admin. **Philosophy/religion:** Philosophy, religion. **Physical sciences:** Chemistry. **Protective services:** Criminal justice. **Psychology:** General. **Public administration:** Social work. **Social sciences:** General, criminology, economics, international relations, political science, urban studies. **Theology:** Bible, religious ed, sacred music, theology. **Visual/performing arts:** Art history/conservation, music performance, music theory/composition, studio arts.

Most popular majors. Business/marketing 10%, education 12%, philosophy/religious studies 17%, psychology 6%, social sciences 6%.

Computing on campus. 591 workstations in dormitories, library, computer center, student center. Dormitories wired for high-speed internet access and linked to campus network. Commuter students can connect to campus network. Online library, helpline, repair service, student web hosting, wireless network available.

Student life. **Freshman orientation:** Mandatory. Students register for classes during summer. Freshman orientation is set the weekend before school begins. **Policies:** No alcohol allowed on campus, students attend chapel services three times weekly. Religious observance required. Freshmen permitted cars on campus. **Housing:** Guaranteed on-campus for all undergraduates. Single-sex dorms, special housing for disabled, apartments, substance-free housing available. $100 fully refundable deposit. **Activities:** Bands, choral groups, drama, film society, literary magazine, music ensembles, musical theater, opera, radio station, student government, student newspaper, symphony orchestra, TV station, World Christian Fellowship, Fellowship of Christian Athletes, International Student Organization, Habitat for Humanity, Young Republicans, College Libertarians, IWU Democrats.

Athletics. NAIA, NCCAA. **Intercollegiate:** Baseball M, basketball, cross-country, golf M, soccer, softball W, tennis, track and field, volleyball W. **Intramural:** Badminton, basketball, bowling, football (non-tackle), golf, racquetball, soccer, softball, swimming, table tennis, tennis, volleyball, water polo, weight lifting. **Team name:** Wildcats.

Student services. Adult student services, alcohol/substance abuse counseling, campus ministries, career counseling, services for economically disadvantaged, student employment services, financial aid counseling, health services, minority student services, personal counseling, placement for graduates. **Physically disabled:** Services for visually, speech, hearing impaired. **Learning disabled:** Comprehensive services available.

Contact. E-mail: admissions@indwes.edu
Phone: (765) 677-2138 Toll-free number: (800) 332-6901
Fax: (765) 677-2333
Daniel Solms, Director of Admissions, Indiana Wesleyan University, 4201 South Washington Street, Marion, IN 46953-4999

International Business College

Fort Wayne, Indiana

CB code: 1330

- For-profit 4-year business and community college
- Small city
- 575 degree-seeking undergraduates

General. Founded in 1889. Accredited by ACICS. Branch campus located in Indianapolis. **Degrees:** 52 bachelor's, 112 associate awarded. **Location:** 4 miles from downtown. **Calendar:** Semester, extensive summer session. **Full-time faculty:** 10 total. **Part-time faculty:** 40 total.

Freshman class profile.

Out-of-state:	30%	**Live on campus:**	40%

Basis for selection. School achievement record and personal interview most important. Recommendations important.

2005-2006 Annual costs. Lab fee for medical assisting program $1060. Room only: $5,000. Books/supplies: $900.

Application procedures. Admission: No deadline. $50 fee. Admission notification on a rolling basis. **Financial aid:** Closing date 5/1. Applicants notified by 9/15.

Academics. Special study options: Independent study, internships. **Credit/placement by examination:** CLEP. **Support services:** Tutoring.

Majors. Business: General.

Computing on campus. 146 workstations in library, computer center.

Student life. Freshman orientation: Available. **Housing:** Coed dorms, single-sex dorms available. **Activities:** Student government, accounting club, secretarial club.

Student services. Career counseling, student employment services, personal counseling, placement for graduates.

Contact. Phone: (260) 459-4500 Toll-free number: (800) 589-6363
Fax: (260) 436-1896
Steve Kinzer, Director of Admissions, International Business College, 5699 Coventry Lane, Fort Wayne, IN 46804

ITT Technical Institute: Fort Wayne

Fort Wayne, Indiana
www.itt-tech.edu **CB code: 0650**

- For-profit 4-year technical college
- Commuter campus in large city

General. Founded in 1967. Accredited by ACICS. **Location:** 122 miles from Indianapolis. **Calendar:** Quarter.

Annual costs/financial aid. Tuition varies by program, $260-$368 per credit hour.

Contact. Phone: (260) 484-4107
Director of Recruitment, 2810 Dupont Commerce Court, Fort Wayne, IN 46825

ITT Technical Institute: Indianapolis

Indianapolis, Indiana
www.itt-tech.edu **CB code: 0640**

- For-profit 4-year technical college
- Commuter campus in very large city

General. Founded in 1956. Accredited by ACICS. **Location:** 10 miles from downtown. **Calendar:** Quarter.

Annual costs/financial aid. Tuition varies by program, $260-$368 per credit hour.

Contact. Phone: (317) 875-8640
Director of Recruitment, 9511 Angola Court, Indianapolis, IN 46268-1119

Manchester College

North Manchester, Indiana **CB member**
www.manchester.edu **CB code: 1440**

- Private 4-year liberal arts college affiliated with Church of the Brethren
- Residential campus in small town
- 1,058 degree-seeking undergraduates: 1% part-time, 53% women, 3% African American, 1% Asian American, 2% Hispanic American, 6% international
- 10 degree-seeking graduate students
- 73% of applicants admitted
- SAT or ACT (ACT writing optional) required

General. Founded in 1889. Regionally accredited. **Degrees:** 221 bachelor's, 3 associate awarded; master's offered. **Location:** 35 miles from Fort Wayne, 100 miles from Indianapolis. **Calendar:** 4-1-4, limited summer session. **Full-time faculty:** 68 total; 93% have terminal degrees, 6% minority, 40% women. **Part-time faculty:** 21 total; 24% have terminal degrees, 10% minority, 33% women. **Class size:** 58% < 20, 38% 20-39, 3% 40-49, less than 1% 50-99. **Special facilities:** Observatory, 100-acre environmental studies and retreat center.

Freshman class profile. 1,487 applied, 1,089 admitted, 330 enrolled.

Mid 50% test scores		**Rank in top tenth:**	22%
SAT verbal:	460-580	**Out-of-state:**	8%
SAT math:	470-580	**Live on campus:**	95%
ACT:	18-24	**International:**	3%
Rank in top quarter:	45%		

Basis for selection. School achievement record most important, with emphasis on college-preparatory courses, followed by SAT or ACT scores, class rank, recommendations. Interview recommended. Essay recommended for academically borderline applicants. Audition recommended for music majors. **Homeschooled:** Provide full information in detailed cover letter with application. **Learning Disabled:** School reviews ability to meet student needs.

High school preparation. 14 units required; 17 recommended. Required and recommended units include English 4, mathematics 2-3, social studies 2, history 1-2, science 2-3 (laboratory 2-3), foreign language 2 and academic electives 1-2.

2006-2007 Annual costs. Tuition/fees (projected): $20,500. Room/board: $7,260. Books/supplies: $550. Personal expenses: $900.

2005-2006 Financial aid. Need-based: 318 full-time freshmen applied for aid; 283 were judged to have need; 283 of these received aid. Average need met was 93%. Average scholarship/grant was $15,334; average loan $2,213. 76% of total undergraduate aid awarded as scholarships/grants, 24% as loans/jobs. **Non-need-based:** Awarded to 712 full-time undergraduates, including 247 freshmen. Scholarships awarded for academics, alumni affiliation, art, leadership, minority status, music/drama, religious affiliation. **Additional information:** Students are automatically considered for all scholarship programs.

Application procedures. Admission: Priority date 5/1; no deadline. $20 fee, may be waived for applicants with need. Application may be submitted online. Admission notification on a rolling basis beginning on or about 9/1. Must reply by May 1 or within 2 week(s) if notified thereafter. **Financial**

aid: Priority date 3/1; no closing date. FAFSA required. Applicants notified on a rolling basis starting 2/15.

Academics. Students are required to earn 2 credits in Values, Ideas and the Arts. **Special study options:** Double major, dual enrollment of high school students, exchange student, honors, independent study, internships, liberal arts/career combination, student-designed major, study abroad, teacher certification program, urban semester. Medical technology programs with area hospitals, 3-2 engineering dual-degree program with Washington University (MO) and others, 2-2 nursing program with Goshen College. **Credit/placement by examination:** AP, CLEP, IB, institutional tests. First year students take college proficiency tests to place out of the first year of modern language. Unlimited credit hours by examination may be counted toward associate or bachelor's degree. **Support services:** Learning center, reduced course load, study skills assistance, tutoring, writing center.

Majors. Area/ethnic studies: Women's. **Biology:** General, biochemistry. **Business:** General, accounting, banking/financial services, business admin, marketing, nonprofit/public. **Communications:** General, broadcast journalism, journalism. **Computer sciences:** General, computer science. **Conservation:** General, environmental studies. **Education:** General, biology, chemistry, elementary, English, foreign languages, French, German, health, history, mathematics, mentally handicapped, middle, multi-level teacher, music, physical, physics, science, secondary, social science, social studies, Spanish, special. **Engineering:** Science. **Foreign languages:** General, French, German, Spanish. **Health:** Clinical lab science, predentistry, premedicine, prepharmacy, preveterinary. **History:** General. **Interdisciplinary:** Global studies, math/computer science, peace/conflict. **Legal studies:** Prelaw. **Liberal arts:** Arts/sciences. **Math:** General. **Philosophy/religion:** Philosophy, religion. **Physical sciences:** Chemistry, physics. **Psychology:** General. **Public administration:** Social work. **Social sciences:** General, economics, political science, sociology. **Theology:** Sacred music. **Visual/performing arts:** Art, music performance.

Most popular majors. Business/marketing 24%, education 36%, psychology 6%, social sciences 6%.

Computing on campus. 165 workstations in dormitories, library, computer center. Dormitories wired for high-speed internet access and linked to campus network. Helpline, student web hosting available.

Student life. Freshman orientation: Mandatory, $100 fee. Preregistration for classes offered. 3 days prior to start of fall classes. **Policies:** Significant student involvement in governance, programming, activities, and administrative services such as security, health, and residence hall management. Freshmen permitted cars on campus. **Housing:** Guaranteed on-campus for freshmen. Coed dorms, single-sex dorms, special housing for disabled, apartments, substance-free housing available. $50 deposit. All students over 21 may live off-campus. Other students required to live on-campus unless living with family. **Activities:** Bands, choral groups, dance, drama, literary magazine, music ensembles, musical theater, radio station, student government, student newspaper, symphony orchestra, campus ministry board, political clubs, Black Student Union, Hispanos Unidos, Manchester College International Association, Habitat for Humanity, volunteer corps, Intercollegiate Ministries, Amnesty International, Manchester Environmental Club.

Athletics. NCAA. **Intercollegiate:** Baseball M, basketball, cross-country, football (tackle) M, golf, soccer, softball W, tennis, track and field, volleyball W, wrestling M. **Intramural:** Badminton, basketball, bowling, cross-country, golf, racquetball, soccer, softball, swimming, table tennis, tennis, track and field, volleyball, wrestling M. **Team name:** Spartans.

Student services. Campus ministries, career counseling, student employment services, financial aid counseling, health services, minority student services, personal counseling, placement for graduates, veterans' counselor. **Physically disabled:** Services for visually, hearing impaired.

Contact. E-mail: admitinfo@manchester.edu
Phone: (260) 982-5055 Toll-free number: (800) 852-3648
Fax: (260) 982-5239
Jolane Rohr, Director of Admissions, Manchester College, 604 East College Avenue, North Manchester, IN 46962-0365

Marian College

Indianapolis, Indiana — **CB member**
www.marian.edu — **CB code: 1442**

- Private 4-year liberal arts college affiliated with Roman Catholic Church
- Residential campus in very large city
- 1,573 degree-seeking undergraduates: 31% part-time, 73% women, 18% African American, 1% Asian American, 2% Hispanic American, 1% Native American
- 12 degree-seeking graduate students
- 85% of applicants admitted
- SAT or ACT with writing required
- 51% graduate within 6 years

General. Founded in 1851. Regionally accredited. **Degrees:** 218 bachelor's, 80 associate awarded; master's offered. **ROTC:** Army. **Location:** 4 miles from downtown. **Calendar:** Semester, limited summer session. **Full-time faculty:** 79 total; 51% have terminal degrees, 2% minority, 48% women. **Part-time faculty:** 70 total; 17% have terminal degrees, 6% minority, 46% women. **Class size:** 67% < 20, 28% 20-39, 3% 40-49, 2% 50-99. **Special facilities:** Archives (materials on development of education in Archdiocese), 35 acre wetlands biology/ecology laboratory, Allison and Wheeler-Stokely Mansions, Japanese tea house and garden.

Freshman class profile. 657 applied, 557 admitted, 191 enrolled.

Mid 50% test scores		**GPA 2.0-2.99:**	30%
SAT verbal:	460-560	**Rank in top quarter:**	42%
SAT math:	450-570	**Rank in top tenth:**	15%
ACT:	18-23	**Return as sophomores:**	71%
GPA 3.50 or higher:	40%	**Out-of-state:**	7%
GPA 3.0-3.49:	30%	**Live on campus:**	61%

Basis for selection. School achievement record, test scores, recommendations important. TOEFL required for nonnative speakers of English. Interview recommended. Essay recommended for academically weak applicants. **Homeschooled:** Please contact our Home Schooled Counselor for details.

High school preparation. 20 units required. Required and recommended units include English 4, mathematics 2-3, social studies 1-2, history 1-2, science 2-3, foreign language 1-2 and academic electives 9.

2005-2006 Annual costs. Tuition/fees: $19,060. Room/board: $6,300. Books/supplies: $700. Personal expenses: $900.

2004-2005 Financial aid. Need-based: 215 full-time freshmen applied for aid; 191 were judged to have need; 191 of these received aid. Average scholarship/grant was $9,156; average loan $3,014. **Non-need-based:** Scholarships awarded for academics, alumni affiliation, art, athletics, leadership, minority status, music/drama, religious affiliation.

Application procedures. Admission: Priority date 5/1; deadline 8/1 (postmark date). $20 fee, may be waived for applicants with need. Application may be submitted online. Admission notification on a rolling basis beginning on or about 9/15. Must reply by May 1 or within 3 week(s) if notified thereafter. **Financial aid:** Priority date 3/10; no closing date. FAFSA, institutional form required. Applicants notified on a rolling basis starting 3/15; must reply within 3 week(s) of notification.

Academics. Special study options: Accelerated study, cooperative education, cross-registration, double major, dual enrollment of high school students, honors, independent study, internships, liberal arts/career combination, study abroad, teacher certification program. **Credit/placement by examination:** AP, CLEP, IB, SAT, ACT, institutional tests. 30 credit hours maximum toward associate degree, 60 toward bachelor's. **Support services:** Learning center, reduced course load, remedial instruction, study skills assistance, tutoring, writing center.

Majors. Biology: General. **Business:** General, accounting, finance, management information systems, marketing. **Communications:** General. **Computer sciences:** Computer science. **Conservation:** Environmental studies. **Education:** Elementary, physical. **English:** English lit. **Foreign languages:** French, Spanish. **Health:** Nursing (RN). **History:** General. **Math:** General. **Parks/recreation:** Sports admin. **Philosophy/religion:** Philosophy. **Physical sciences:** Chemistry. **Psychology:** General. **Social sciences:** Economics, political science, sociology. **Theology:** Religious ed, theology. **Visual/performing arts:** Art, art history/conservation, commercial/advertising art.

Most popular majors. Business/marketing 34%, education 9%, health sciences 17%, parks/recreation 8%, psychology 6%, visual/performing arts 6%.

Computing on campus. 160 workstations in dormitories, library, computer center, student center. Dormitories wired for high-speed internet access and linked to campus network. Online library, helpline available.

Student life. Freshman orientation: Mandatory. Preregistration for classes offered. Held weekend prior to start of school. Community service project required. **Policies:** Drinking under the age of 21 on campus prohibited. Freshmen permitted cars on campus. **Housing:** Guaranteed on-campus for freshmen. Coed dorms, single-sex dorms, apartments, substance-free housing available. $125 fully refundable deposit, deadline 6/1. College-owned apartments for students 21 or older, voluntary spiritual living community, nonsmoking areas, suite-style rooms, singles available. **Activities:** Bands, choral groups, dance, drama, literary magazine, music ensembles, musical theater, student government, student newspaper, campus ministry, service organization, Campus America Life League, BACCHUS, Project Earth, community ministries, Union for Black Identity, Fellowship of Christian Athletes, student association, Campus Crusade for Christ.

Athletics. NAIA. **Intercollegiate:** Baseball M, basketball, cheerleading, cross-country, golf, soccer, softball W, tennis, track and field, volleyball W. **Intramural:** Basketball, football (non-tackle) M, handball, racquetball, softball, table tennis, tennis, volleyball. **Team name:** Knights.

Student services. Adult student services, alcohol/substance abuse counseling, campus ministries, career counseling, student employment services, financial aid counseling, health services, personal counseling, placement for graduates. **Physically disabled:** Services for visually, hearing impaired.

Contact. E-mail: admissions@marian.edu
Phone: (317) 955-6300 Toll-free number: (800) 772-7264
Fax: (317) 955-6401
Luann Brames, Director of Enrollment, Marian College, 3200 Cold Spring Road, Indianapolis, IN 46222-1960

Martin University
Indianapolis, Indiana
www.martin.edu **CB code: 1379**

- Private 4-year university and liberal arts college
- Commuter campus in very large city
- 506 degree-seeking undergraduates
- Interview required

General. Founded in 1977. Regionally accredited. **Degrees:** 37 bachelor's awarded; master's offered. **Calendar:** Semester, extensive summer session. **Full-time faculty:** 30 total. **Part-time faculty:** 9 total.

Freshman class profile. 67 enrolled.

Basis for selection. Essay most important. Standardized test scores also important.

2005-2006 Annual costs. Tuition/fees: $11,720. Books/supplies: $820. Personal expenses: $1,114.

Application procedures. Admission: Priority date 3/1; no deadline. $25 fee, may be waived for applicants with need. Admission notification on a rolling basis. **Financial aid:** Priority date 5/1; no closing date. FAFSA required. Applicants notified on a rolling basis starting 6/1; must reply within 2 week(s) of notification.

Academics. Special study options: Accelerated study, cross-registration, double major, internships, liberal arts/career combination, student-designed major. **Credit/placement by examination:** CLEP. **Support services:** Learning center, remedial instruction, tutoring.

Majors. Area/ethnic studies: African, African-American. **Biology:** General. **Business:** General, accounting, insurance. **Communications:** General. **Communications technology:** General. **Conservation:** Environmental science. **Education:** Adult/continuing, early childhood. **English:** Composition. **Foreign languages:** Spanish. **Health:** Genetic counseling. **History:** General. **Liberal arts:** Arts/sciences. **Math:** General. **Philosophy/religion:** Religion. **Psychology:** General. **Social sciences:** General, political science, sociology. **Theology:** Religious ed. **Visual/performing arts:** Music performance, piano/organ, studio arts.

Computing on campus. 14 workstations in computer center.

Student life. Activities: Choral groups, dance, drama, music ensembles, opera, GIFT of Brightwood (neighborhood youth services), Healthy Babies (pre- and post-natal education).

Student services. Adult student services, career counseling, student employment services, health services, personal counseling, placement for graduates, veterans' counselor.

Contact. Phone: (317) 543-3238 Fax: (317) 543-3257
Charlesetta Stanley, Director of Admissions, Martin University, 2171 Avondale Place, Indianapolis, IN 46218

Oakland City University
Oakland City, Indiana
www.oak.edu **CB code: 1585**

- Private 4-year university affiliated with General Association of General Baptists
- Commuter campus in small town
- 1,566 degree-seeking undergraduates: 19% part-time, 54% women, 10% African American, 1% Asian American, 2% Hispanic American, 2% international
- 334 degree-seeking graduate students
- SAT or ACT (ACT writing optional) required

General. Founded in 1885. Regionally accredited. Branches in Bedford and at Branchville Training Center. Accelerated degrees offered at several off-campus sites (National Guard bases and civilian locations), Rockville Training Center, Miami Correctional Center. **Degrees:** 233 bachelor's, 184 associate awarded; master's, doctoral, first professional offered. **Location:** 30 miles from Evansville. **Calendar:** Semester, limited summer session. **Full-time faculty:** 15 total. **Part-time faculty:** 165 total. **Class size:** 87% < 20, 12% 20-39, less than 1% 40-49, less than 1% 50-99.

Freshman class profile. 207 applied, 155 admitted, 127 enrolled.

Mid 50% test scores		**GPA 2.0-2.99:**	16%
SAT verbal:	430-580	**Rank in top quarter:**	26%
SAT math:	440-600	**Rank in top tenth:**	7%
ACT:	17-23	**Out-of-state:**	4%
GPA 3.50 or higher:	35%	**Live on campus:**	50%
GPA 3.0-3.49:	49%	**International:**	6%

Basis for selection. Open admission, but selective for some programs. High school GPA of 2.5 and SAT or ACT test scores most important. Recommendations considered. Interview and essay recommended. **Homeschooled:** Transcript of courses and grades required.

High school preparation. 12 units recommended. Recommended units include English 4, mathematics 3, social studies 2 and science 3.

2006-2007 Annual costs. Tuition/fees (projected): $14,220. Room/board: $5,400. Books/supplies: $1,500. Personal expenses: $1,500.

2005-2006 Financial aid. Need-based: 68% of total undergraduate aid awarded as scholarships/grants, 32% as loans/jobs. **Non-need-based:** Scholarships awarded for academics, alumni affiliation, art, athletics, minority status, music/drama, religious affiliation.

Application procedures. Admission: No deadline. $35 fee, may be waived for applicants with need. Admission notification on a rolling basis. **Financial aid:** Closing date 3/1. FAFSA required. Applicants notified on a rolling basis starting 6/1.

Academics. Special study options: Accelerated study, combined bachelor's/graduate degree, cooperative education, distance learning, double major, dual enrollment of high school students, external degree, honors, independent study, internships, liberal arts/career combination, teacher certification program. Combined bachelor's/graduate degree: M.S. in Management. **Credit/placement by examination:** AP, CLEP, IB, institutional tests. 16 credit hours maximum toward associate degree, 32 toward bachelor's. **Support services:** Learning center, reduced course load, remedial instruction, tutoring.

Majors. Biology: General. **Business:** General, accounting, business admin, human resources, management information systems, organizational behavior. **Computer sciences:** General, computer science. **Education:** Art, biology, business, elementary, English, history, mathematics, music, physical, psychology, science, social studies, special. **History:** General. **Liberal arts:** Arts/sciences. **Math:** Applied. **Parks/recreation:** Health/fitness. **Philosophy/religion:** Religion. **Protective services:** Criminal justice. **Psychology:** General. **Social sciences:** General. **Theology:** Sacred music. **Visual/performing arts:** Art, commercial/advertising art, industrial design, music performance, studio arts.

Most popular majors. Business/marketing 60%, education 17%, philosophy/religious studies 6%.

Computing on campus. 92 workstations in library, computer center, student center. Dormitories linked to campus network. Online library available.

Student life. Freshman orientation: Mandatory, $75 fee. Preregistration for classes offered. One day immediately before each semester. **Policies:** Freshmen permitted cars on campus. **Housing:** Guaranteed on-campus for all undergraduates. Single-sex dorms, apartments, substance-free housing available. $100 fully refundable deposit, deadline 7/21. **Activities:** Pep band, choral groups, drama, music ensembles, student government, student newspaper, mental health assistance group, Circle-K, Student Christian Association, Fellowship of Christian Athletes, Theologs, student education association.

Athletics. NCAA, NCCAA. **Intercollegiate:** Baseball M, basketball, cheerleading M, cross-country, golf, soccer, softball W, tennis, volleyball W. **Intramural:** Basketball, cross-country, football (non-tackle), golf, softball, table tennis, tennis, volleyball. **Team name:** Oaks.

Student services. Adult student services, campus ministries, career counseling, services for economically disadvantaged, student employment services, financial aid counseling, personal counseling, placement for graduates, veterans' counselor.

Contact. E-mail: ocuadmit@oak.edu
Phone: (812) 749-4781 ext. 222 Toll-free number: (800) 737-5125
Fax: (812) 749-1233
Brian Baker, Director of Admissions, Oakland City University, 138 North Lucretia Street, Oakland City, IN 47660

Purdue University

West Lafayette, Indiana — **CB member**
www.purdue.edu — **CB code: 1631**

- Public 4-year university
- Residential campus in small city
- 30,545 degree-seeking undergraduates: 5% part-time, 41% women, 4% African American, 5% Asian American, 3% Hispanic American, 6% international
- 7,623 degree-seeking graduate students
- 85% of applicants admitted
- SAT or ACT with writing required
- 68% graduate within 6 years

General. Founded in 1869. Regionally accredited. **Degrees:** 6,197 bachelor's, 543 associate awarded; master's, doctoral, first professional offered. **ROTC:** Army, Navy, Air Force. **Location:** 65 miles from Indianapolis. **Calendar:** Semester, limited summer session. **Full-time faculty:** 1,960 total; 98% have terminal degrees, 15% minority, 26% women. **Part-time faculty:** 333 total; 86% have terminal degrees, 11% minority, 51% women. **Class size:** 33% < 20, 42% 20-39, 7% 40-49, 10% 50-99, 8% >100. **Special facilities:** Linear accelerator, horticultural park, concert hall, 3 theaters, outdoor concert facility, 2 professional golf courses, on-campus airport.

Freshman class profile. 24,052 applied, 20,432 admitted, 7,191 enrolled.

Mid 50% test scores		**GPA 2.0-2.99:**	13%
SAT verbal:	500-610	**Rank in top quarter:**	58%
SAT math:	530-650	**Rank in top tenth:**	27%
ACT:	23-28	**Return as sophomores:**	85%
GPA 3.50 or higher:	54%	**Out-of-state:**	29%
GPA 3.0-3.49:	33%	**International:**	6%

Basis for selection. Class rank, curriculum, high school GPA, test scores most important. Applicants generally must be in top half of senior class, engineering applicants in top quarter. Out-of-state students with alumni affiliation reviewed on in-state basis. Some programs close without notice. Early application recommended. Interview required of veterinary medicine, veterinary technology and pharmacy applicants; recommended for flight technology and nursing applicants.

High school preparation. Required and recommended units include English 4, mathematics 3, science 2-3 (laboratory 2-3) and foreign language 2. 2 units in history or social science recommended.

2005-2006 Annual costs. Tuition/fees: $6,458; $19,824 out-of-state. Engineering students pay additional $564 fee per year.Technology students pay $137.60 fee per year. Management students pay $882.00 fee per year. Room/board: $7,160. Books/supplies: $980. Personal expenses: $1,040.

2005-2006 Financial aid. Need-based: 5,161 full-time freshmen applied for aid; 3,089 were judged to have need; 3,083 of these received aid. Average need met was 92%. Average scholarship/grant was $9,745; average loan $3,072. 53% of total undergraduate aid awarded as scholarships/grants, 47% as loans/jobs. **Non-need-based:** Awarded to 6,147 full-time undergraduates, including 2,176 freshmen. Scholarships awarded for academics, athletics, leadership, minority status, music/drama, ROTC, state residency. **Additional information:** Cooperative work for credit available in many programs.

Application procedures. Admission: Priority date 3/1; no deadline. $30 fee, may be waived for applicants with need. Application may be submitted online. Admission notification on a rolling basis beginning on or about 9/1. Must reply by May 1 or within 3 week(s) if notified thereafter. November 15 deadline for flight technology program and deadine for veterinary technology program. **Financial aid:** Priority date 3/1; no closing date. FAFSA required. Applicants notified by 4/15.

Academics. Minimal number of courses outside major allowed on pass/fail basis, not to exceed 20 percent of total credit hours required. **Special study options:** Accelerated study, cooperative education, cross-registration, distance learning, double major, dual enrollment of high school students, ESL, exchange student, honors, independent study, internships, liberal arts/career combination, study abroad, teacher certification program, weekend college. **Credit/placement by examination:** AP, CLEP, IB, SAT, ACT, institutional tests. **Support services:** Learning center, pre-admission summer program, reduced course load, remedial instruction, study skills assistance, tutoring, writing center.

Majors. Agriculture: General, agronomy, animal sciences, economics, food science, horticultural science, mechanization. **Architecture:** Landscape. **Area/ethnic studies:** African-American. **Biology:** General, biochemistry, botany, entomology. **Business:** Accounting, business admin, hotel/motel admin, operations. **Communications:** General. **Computer sciences:** General. **Conservation:** General, forestry, wildlife. **Education:** General, agricultural, early childhood, elementary, kindergarten/preschool, physical, technology/industrial arts. **Engineering:** Aerospace, agricultural, biomedical, chemical, civil, computer, construction, electrical, industrial, materials, mechanical, nuclear. **Engineering technology:** Architectural, electrical, mechanical drafting, robotics, surveying. **English:** English lit. **Family/consumer sciences:** General, clothing/textiles, family studies, food/nutrition. **Foreign languages:** General. **Health:** Audiology/speech pathology, clinical lab science, nursing (RN), premedicine, veterinary technology/assistant. **History:** General. **Interdisciplinary:** Biological/physical sciences. **Liberal arts:** Humanities. **Math:** General, statistics. **Philosophy/religion:** Philosophy. **Physical sciences:** Chemistry, geology, physics. **Psychology:** General. **Social sciences:** General, political science, sociology. **Transportation:** Aviation. **Visual/performing arts:** Art, design, dramatic, film/cinema, photography.

Most popular majors. Business/marketing 16%, education 7%, engineering/engineering technologies 28%, family/consumer sciences 6%.

Computing on campus. 2,100 workstations in dormitories, library, computer center. Dormitories wired for high-speed internet access and linked to campus network. Commuter students can connect to campus network.

Student life. Freshman orientation: Available, $195 fee. Preregistration for classes offered. **Policies:** Nondiscrimination, antiharassment, antihazing policies; bill of students' rights. **Housing:** Coed dorms, single-sex dorms, special housing for disabled, apartments, cooperative housing, fraternity/sorority housing available. $75 deposit, deadline 3/1. **Activities:** Bands, choral groups, dance, drama, literary magazine, music ensembles, musical theater, radio station, student government, student newspaper, symphony orchestra, TV station, more than 630 organizations.

Athletics. NCAA. **Intercollegiate:** Baseball M, basketball, cross-country, diving, football (tackle) M, golf, soccer W, softball W, swimming, tennis, track and field, volleyball W, wrestling M. **Intramural:** Archery, badminton, basketball, bowling, cross-country, golf, handball, racquetball, rifle, soccer, softball, squash M, swimming, table tennis, tennis, track and field, volleyball, water polo. **Team name:** Boilermakers.

Student services. Adult student services, alcohol/substance abuse counseling, campus ministries, career counseling, student employment services, financial aid counseling, health services, on-campus daycare, personal counseling, placement for graduates, veterans' counselor, women's services. **Physically disabled:** Services for visually, speech, hearing impaired.

Contact. E-mail: admissions@purdue.edu
Phone: (765) 494-1776 Fax: (765) 494-0544
Douglas Christiansen, Dean of Admissions, Purdue University, 475 Stadium Mall Dr., West Lafayette, IN 47907-2050

Purdue University: Calumet

Hammond, Indiana — **CB member**
www.calumet.purdue.edu — **CB code: 1638**

- Public 4-year university and branch campus college
- Commuter campus in small city
- 7,879 degree-seeking undergraduates: 36% part-time, 57% women, 16% African American, 1% Asian American, 14% Hispanic American, 1% international
- 698 degree-seeking graduate students
- 80% of applicants admitted
- 24% graduate within 6 years

General. Founded in 1943. Regionally accredited. **Degrees:** 773 bachelor's, 308 associate awarded; master's offered. **ROTC:** Army. **Location:** 20 miles from Chicago. **Calendar:** Semester, extensive summer session. **Full-time faculty:** 270 total; 65% have terminal degrees, 23% minority, 47% women. **Part-time faculty:** 201 total; 2% have terminal degrees, 12% minority, 56% women. **Class size:** 25% < 20, 65% 20-39, 4% 40-49, 5% 50-99, less than 1% >100.

Freshman class profile. 2,405 applied, 1,916 admitted, 1,252 enrolled.

Mid 50% test scores		**End year in good standing:**	78%
SAT verbal:	400-510	**Return as sophomores:**	64%
SAT math:	390-510	**Out-of-state:**	11%
Rank in top quarter:	22%	**International:**	1%
Rank in top tenth:	7%		

Basis for selection. Quality is determined by considering a combination of class rank, grade average in subjects related to degree objectives, trends in achievement throughout high school, satisfactory high school subject matter requirements, strength of college preparatory program, and standardized test results. Graduation from high school with a minimum of 15 units of credit is required. Beginning applicants who have graduated high school within the last year must take SAT/ACT. Those who have been out of high school more than 1 year must take appropriate placement tests offered through school Skills Assessment and Development Center. Individuals transferring from non-Purdue school may be required to take math and/or English placement tests. **Homeschooled:** Transcript of courses and grades required.

High school preparation. 14 units recommended. Recommended units include English 8, mathematics 2, social studies 2, history 2, science 2 and foreign language 2. Course requirements vary according to program.

2005-2006 Annual costs. Tuition/fees: $5,071; $11,371 out-of-state.

2004-2005 Financial aid. Need-based: 777 full-time freshmen applied for aid; 528 were judged to have need; 476 of these received aid. Average need met was 18%. Average scholarship/grant was $5,748; average loan $2,763. 43% of total undergraduate aid awarded as scholarships/grants, 57% as loans/jobs. **Non-need-based:** Awarded to 550 full-time undergraduates, including 95 freshmen. Scholarships awarded for academics, athletics.

Application procedures. Admission: No deadline. No application fee. Application may be submitted online. Admission notification on a rolling basis. **Financial aid:** Priority date 3/10, closing date 6/30. FAFSA required. Applicants notified on a rolling basis starting 5/1; must reply within 2 week(s) of notification.

Academics. Special study options: Accelerated study, combined bachelor's/graduate degree, cooperative education, cross-registration, distance learning, double major, dual enrollment of high school students, ESL, exchange student, honors, independent study, internships, study abroad, teacher certification program, weekend college. **Credit/placement by examination:** AP, CLEP, SAT, ACT, institutional tests. **Support services:** Learning center, reduced course load, remedial instruction, study skills assistance, tutoring, writing center.

Honors college/program. To apply for the Honors Program, a students should have a minimum high school GPA of 3.5/4.0, ACT score of 27 or higher, or a 1200 SAT (verbal + math) or higher. Current students Purdue University Calumet students should have a cumulative GPA of at least 3.5. Must maintain a cumulative GPA of 3.5/4.0. Factors taken into consideration include outstanding academic achievement, strength of academic program, ACT or SAT scores, demonstrated leadership, creativity, community involvement, essay, and letter(s) of recommendation.

Majors. Biology: General. **Business:** General, accounting, business admin, entrepreneurial studies, finance, human resources, retailing, small business admin. **Communications:** General, broadcast journalism, journalism, public relations. **Computer sciences:** General, computer graphics, computer science, database management, information systems, networking, programming. **Education:** General, biology, chemistry, early childhood, elementary, English, French, multi-level teacher, physics, science, secondary, social science, social studies, special. **Engineering:** General, computer, electrical, mechanical, mechanics, software. **Engineering technology:** Construction, electrical, industrial management. **English:** American lit, composition. **Foreign languages:** General, French, Spanish. **Health:** Clinical lab science, nursing (RN), premedicine, preop/surgical nursing, prepharmacy, preveterinary. **History:** General. **Interdisciplinary:** Gerontology, math/computer science. **Legal studies:** Prelaw. **Math:** General, applied. **Philosophy/religion:** Philosophy. **Physical sciences:** Chemistry, physics. **Protective services:** Law enforcement admin. **Psychology:** General. **Social sciences:** Political science, sociology.

Most popular majors. Communications/journalism 10%, computer/information sciences 12%, education 11%, engineering/engineering technologies 25%, psychology 9%, social sciences 17%.

Computing on campus. 1,500 workstations in library, computer center, student center. Dormitories wired for high-speed internet access and linked to campus network. Commuter students can connect to campus network. Online course registration, online library, helpline, wireless network available.

Student life. Freshman orientation: Mandatory. Preregistration for classes offered. **Policies:** Freshmen permitted cars on campus. **Housing:** Substance-free housing available. **Activities:** Choral groups, drama, literary magazine, musical theater, student government, student newspaper, Black Student Union, Los Latinos, Society of Professional Hispanic Engineers, InterVarsity Christian Fellowship, Muslim Student Association, New Life Ministries, National Society of Black Engineers, Purdue Indian Students Association, Korean Student Organization, Social Justice Club.

Athletics. NAIA. **Intercollegiate:** Basketball, cheerleading. **Intramural:** Basketball, bowling, golf, racquetball, sailing, soccer, softball, table tennis, volleyball, weight lifting. **Team name:** Peregrines.

Student services. Adult student services, career counseling, student employment services, financial aid counseling, health services, on-campus daycare, personal counseling, placement for graduates, veterans' counselor. **Physically disabled:** Services for visually, speech, hearing impaired.

Contact. E-mail: adms@calumet.purdue.edu
Phone: (219) 989-2213 Toll-free number: (800) 447-76383 ext. 2213
Fax: (219) 989-2775
Paul McGuinness, Director of Admissions, Purdue University: Calumet, 2200 169th Street, Hammond, IN 46323-2094

Purdue University: North Central Campus

Westville, Indiana — **CB member**
www.pnc.edu — **CB code: 1640**

- Public 4-year branch campus college
- Commuter campus in rural community
- 3,450 degree-seeking undergraduates

General. Founded in 1943. Regionally accredited. **Degrees:** 243 bachelor's, 235 associate awarded; master's offered. **Location:** 10 miles from Michigan City, 13 miles from Laporte. **Calendar:** Semester, limited summer session. **Full-time faculty:** 103 total. **Part-time faculty:** 150 total. **Class size:** 41% < 20, 54% 20-39, 2% 40-49, 3% 50-99, less than 1% >100.

Basis for selection. High school record, class rank, test scores important. Admission requirements are reduced for community college division. SAT or ACT recommended. Interview recommended for academically weak applicants.

High school preparation. 17 units required; 26 recommended. Required and recommended units include English 4, mathematics 3-4, social studies 1-2, history 1, science 2-3 (laboratory 2-3), foreign language 4 and academic electives 5.

2005-2006 Annual costs. Tuition/fees: $5,195; $12,215 out-of-state. Additional $50 per course fee for classes at Valparaiso Academic Center. Books/supplies: $600. Personal expenses: $1,200.

Financial aid. All financial aid based on need.

Application procedures. Admission: Priority date 8/1; no deadline. $30 fee. Application may be submitted online. Admission notification on a rolling basis beginning on or about 8/1. **Financial aid:** Priority date 3/1; no closing date. FAFSA required. Applicants notified on a rolling basis starting 5/31; must reply within 2 week(s) of notification.

Academics. Special study options: Combined bachelor's/graduate degree, distance learning, dual enrollment of high school students, independent study, internships, liberal arts/career combination, teacher certification program. **Credit/placement by examination:** CLEP, institutional tests. **Support services:** Learning center, reduced course load, remedial instruction, tutoring.

Majors. Biology: General. **Business:** General, accounting, human resources, labor relations, operations. **Education:** Elementary. **Liberal arts:** Arts/sciences.

Computing on campus. 240 workstations in library, computer center.

Student life. Freshman orientation: Available. **Activities:** Student government, student newspaper, Campus Crusade for Christ, computer club, photography club, accounting club, student cultural society, Students in Fall Enterprise.

Athletics. Intercollegiate: Baseball M, basketball M, cross-country M. **Intramural:** Basketball, bowling, cross-country, football (tackle) M, golf, skiing, softball, table tennis, tennis, volleyball. **Team name:** Panthers.

Student services. Career counseling, student employment services, on-campus daycare, personal counseling, placement for graduates. **Physically disabled:** Services for visually, hearing impaired.

Contact. E-mail: admissions@purduenc.edu
Phone: (219) 785-5455 Toll-free number: (800) 872-1231
Fax: (219) 785-5538
Cathy Buckman, Director of Enrollment Services, Purdue University: North Central Campus, 1401 South US Highway 421, Westville, IN 46391-9528

Rose-Hulman Institute of Technology

Terre Haute, Indiana — **CB member**
www.rose-hulman.edu — **CB code: 1668**

- Private 4-year engineering college
- Residential campus in small city
- 1,768 degree-seeking undergraduates: 18% women, 2% African American, 4% Asian American, 1% Hispanic American, 1% international
- 112 degree-seeking graduate students
- 69% of applicants admitted
- SAT or ACT (ACT writing optional) required
- 82% graduate within 6 years; 19% enter graduate study

General. Founded in 1874. Regionally accredited. **Degrees:** 368 bachelor's awarded; master's offered. **ROTC:** Army, Air Force. **Location:** 73 miles from Indianapolis. **Calendar:** Quarter, limited summer session. **Full-time faculty:** 148 total; 100% have terminal degrees, 7% minority, 18% women. **Part-time faculty:** 9 total; 67% have terminal degrees, 22% women. **Class size:** 38% < 20, 62% 20-39. **Special facilities:** Advanced learning center, observatory, center for technological research with industry.

Freshman class profile. 3,294 applied, 2,288 admitted, 448 enrolled.

Mid 50% test scores		**Return as sophomores:**	92%
SAT verbal:	570-680	**Out-of-state:**	58%
SAT math:	640-720	**Live on campus:**	98%
ACT:	27-32	**International:**	2%
Rank in top quarter:	93%	**Fraternities:**	32%
Rank in top tenth:	64%	**Sororities:**	41%
End year in good standing:	89%		

Basis for selection. GED not accepted. Primary consideration given to school achievement record and subjects taken. Applicants must rank in top quarter of graduating class. Test scores also very important. Recommendations important. Extracurricular and leadership activities, alumni ties considered. Interviews, although not required, can be determining factor. **Homeschooled:** Statement describing homeschool structure and mission, transcript of courses and grades, state high school equivalency certificate, letter of recommendation (nonparent) required. Lab courses must have been taken at high school or community college.

High school preparation. College-preparatory program required. 16 units required. Required and recommended units include English 4, mathematics 4-5, social studies 2, science 2-3 (laboratory 2) and academic electives 4.

2005-2006 Annual costs. Tuition/fees: $27,138. Laptop computer $3,200. Room/board: $7,449. Books/supplies: $1,200. Personal expenses: $1,200.

2005-2006 Financial aid. Need-based: 401 full-time freshmen applied for aid; 320 were judged to have need; 320 of these received aid. Average need met was 83%. Average scholarship/grant was $15,300; average loan $8,104. 56% of total undergraduate aid awarded as scholarships/grants, 44% as loans/jobs. **Non-need-based:** Awarded to 480 full-time undergraduates, including 107 freshmen. Scholarships awarded for academics, minority status, ROTC.

Application procedures. Admission: Priority date 12/1; deadline 3/1 (postmark date). $40 fee, may be waived for applicants with need. Application may be submitted online. Admission notification on a rolling basis beginning on or about 9/15. Must reply by 5/1. **Financial aid:** Priority date 3/1; no closing date. FAFSA required. Applicants notified on a rolling basis starting 3/10.

Academics. Area minor programs in science, engineering, humanities and social sciences. Additional certificate and interdisciplinary programs available in imaging systems, German technical translation, consulting engineering, and management studies. **Special study options:** Accelerated study, cooperative education, cross-registration, double major, independent study, study abroad. **Credit/placement by examination:** AP, CLEP, IB, institutional tests. **Support services:** Learning center, reduced course load, study skills assistance, tutoring, writing center.

Majors. Biology: General. **Computer sciences:** Computer science. **Engineering:** Biomedical, chemical, civil, computer, electrical, mechanical, physics, software. **Math:** General. **Physical sciences:** Chemistry, physics. **Social sciences:** Economics.

Most popular majors. Computer/information sciences 10%, engineering/engineering technologies 78%.

Computing on campus. PC or laptop required. 20 workstations in library. Dormitories wired for high-speed internet access and linked to campus network. Commuter students can connect to campus network. Online course registration, online library, helpline, repair service, student web hosting, wireless network available.

Student life. Freshman orientation: Mandatory. **Policies:** Freshmen permitted cars on campus. **Housing:** Guaranteed on-campus for freshmen. Coed dorms, single-sex dorms, apartments, fraternity/sorority housing available. $75 nonrefundable deposit, deadline 6/6. **Activities:** Bands, choral groups, dance, drama, literary magazine, music ensembles, musical theater, radio station, student government, student newspaper, Inter-Varsity Christian Fellowship, international student association, Circle K, National Society of Black Engineers, Spanish club, student activities board, Society of Woman Engineers, Alpha Phi Omega Service Fraternity, Catholic campus ministry.

Athletics. NCAA. **Intercollegiate:** Baseball M, basketball, cheerleading M, cross-country, diving, football (tackle) M, golf, rifle, soccer, softball W, swimming, tennis, track and field, volleyball W, wrestling M. **Intramural:** Basketball, cross-country, football (non-tackle), golf, racquetball, soccer, softball, tennis, volleyball. **Team name:** Fightin' Engineers.

Student services. Alcohol/substance abuse counseling, career counseling, student employment services, financial aid counseling, health services, personal counseling, placement for graduates.

Contact. E-mail: admis.ofc@rose-hulman.edu
Phone: (812) 877-8213 Toll-free number: (800) 248-7448
Fax: (812) 877-8941
James Goecker, Dean of Admissions and Financial Aid, Rose-Hulman Institute of Technology, Office of Admissions, Terre Haute, IN 47803-3999

St. Joseph's College

Rensselaer, Indiana — **CB member**
www.saintjoe.edu — **CB code: 1697**

- Private 4-year liberal arts college affiliated with Roman Catholic Church
- Residential campus in small town
- 991 degree-seeking undergraduates: 11% part-time, 62% women, 6% African American, 3% Hispanic American, 1% international
- 78% of applicants admitted
- SAT or ACT (ACT writing optional) required
- 52% graduate within 6 years; 14% enter graduate study

General. Founded in 1889. Regionally accredited. Core curriculum is interdisciplinary sequence of general education courses spread over 8 semesters. **Degrees:** 160 bachelor's awarded; master's offered. **Location:** 80 miles from Chicago, 90 miles from Indianapolis. **Calendar:** Semester, limited summer session. **Full-time faculty:** 56 total; 79% have terminal degrees, 7% minority, 41% women. **Part-time faculty:** 21 total; 19% have terminal degrees, 5% minority, 43% women. **Class size:** 82% < 20, 16% 20-39, 2% 40-49, less than 1% 50-99.

Freshman class profile. 1,363 applied, 1,061 admitted, 233 enrolled.

Mid 50% test scores		**Rank in top quarter:**	40%
SAT verbal:	430-550	**Rank in top tenth:**	13%
SAT math:	450-550	**End year in good standing:**	94%
ACT:	19-24	**Return as sophomores:**	71%
GPA 3.50 or higher:	28%	**Out-of-state:**	34%
GPA 3.0-3.49:	33%	**Live on campus:**	90%
GPA 2.0-2.99:	37%		

Basis for selection. For those applicants with requirement deficiencies, the admissions decision may be deferred until additional requirements (which may include an interview, recommendations, further course work, or an essay) are evaluated. A limited number of these applicants will be admitted under the Freshman Academic Support Program. **Homeschooled:** ACT or SAT test scores and transcript of high school equivalent course work over 6 semesters minimum with description of courses are required. **Learning Disabled:** Documentation of learning disability not considered in application process. After admission, documentation of learning disability must be submitted to Director of Counseling Services in order to receive academic accommodations.

High school preparation. College-preparatory program recommended. 15 units recommended. Recommended units include English 4, mathematics 3, social studies 3, science 3 (laboratory 2) and foreign language 2. 10 recommended units must be from English, foreign language, social studies, mathematics, and natural science. 3 units distributed among social studies, history, and academic electives.

2005-2006 Annual costs. Tuition/fees: $20,120. Room/board: $6,480. Books/supplies: $700. Personal expenses: $650.

2004-2005 Financial aid. **Need-based:** 203 full-time freshmen applied for aid; 165 were judged to have need; 165 of these received aid. Average need met was 80%. Average scholarship/grant was $12,307; average loan $3,269. 70% of total undergraduate aid awarded as scholarships/grants, 30% as loans/jobs. **Non-need-based:** Awarded to 341 full-time undergraduates, including 91 freshmen. Scholarships awarded for academics, alumni affiliation, athletics, minority status, music/drama.

Application procedures. **Admission:** Priority date 12/1; no deadline. $25 fee, may be waived for applicants with need. Application may be submitted online. Admission notification on a rolling basis beginning on or about 12/1. Must reply by May 1 or within 2 week(s) if notified thereafter. **Financial aid:** Priority date 3/1; no closing date. FAFSA required. Applicants notified on a rolling basis starting 3/1; must reply by 5/1 or within 2 week(s) of notification.

Academics. Core program is a sequence of 10 interdisciplinary courses and seeks to integrate Christian humanism with critical appraisal of human condition. **Special study options:** Accelerated study, cross-registration, double major, dual enrollment of high school students, honors, independent study, internships, liberal arts/career combination, student-designed major, study abroad, teacher certification program, Washington semester. **Credit/placement by examination:** AP, CLEP, institutional tests. Current policy is being reevaluated. **Support services:** Learning center, reduced course load, study skills assistance, tutoring.

Majors. **Biology:** General, biochemistry. **Business:** General, accounting, management information systems. **Communications:** Media studies. **Computer sciences:** General. **Conservation:** Environmental science. **Education:** Art, elementary, physical, secondary. **English:** Creative writing, English lit. **Health:** Clinical lab science, nursing (RN), predentistry, premedicine, preveterinary. **History:** General. **Interdisciplinary:** Math/computer science. **Legal studies:** Prelaw. **Math:** General. **Philosophy/religion:** Philosophy. **Physical sciences:** Chemistry. **Protective services:** Criminal justice. **Psychology:** General. **Public administration:** Social work. **Social sciences:** Economics, international relations, political science, sociology. **Theology:** Pastoral counseling, sacred music. **Visual/performing arts:** Directing/producing, music history, music management, studio arts.

Most popular majors. Business/marketing 21%, education 16%, psychology 7%, security/protective services 11%, social sciences 7%.

Computing on campus. 69 workstations in library, computer center, student center. Dormitories wired for high-speed internet access and linked to campus network. Helpline, student web hosting, wireless network available.

Student life. **Freshman orientation:** Mandatory. Preregistration for classes offered. One-day early registrations in June and July; 4-day orientation in August. **Policies:** Freshmen permitted cars on campus. **Housing:** Guaranteed on-campus for all undergraduates. Coed dorms, single-sex dorms, special housing for disabled, apartments available. $200 nonrefundable deposit, deadline 5/1. Special dormitories available for non-traditional full-time students. **Activities:** Bands, choral groups, dance, drama, film society, literary magazine, music ensembles, musical theater, radio station, student government, student newspaper, TV station, Gallagher Charitable Society, Habitat for Humanity, Kairos Team, College Republicans, College Democrats, Peer Ministry, Right to Life, Volunteer Corps, Diversity Coalition, St. Thomas Aquinas Catholic Society.

Athletics. NCAA. **Intercollegiate:** Baseball M, basketball, cross-country, football (tackle) M, golf, soccer, softball W, tennis, track and field, volleyball W. **Intramural:** Basketball, football (non-tackle), soccer, softball, volleyball. **Team name:** Pumas.

Student services. Campus ministries, career counseling, financial aid counseling, health services, personal counseling, placement for graduates.

Contact. E-mail: admissions@saintjoe.edu
Phone: (219) 866-6170 Toll-free number: (800) 447-8781
Fax: (219) 866-6122
Karen Raftus, Director of Admissions, St. Joseph's College, Box 890, Rensselaer, IN 47978

St. Mary-of-the-Woods College

St. Mary-of-the-Woods, Indiana — **CB member**
www.smwc.edu — **CB code: 1704**

- Private 4-year liberal arts college for women affiliated with Roman Catholic Church
- Residential campus in small city
- 1,595 degree-seeking undergraduates: 68% part-time, 100% women, 3% African American, 1% Hispanic American, 1% Native American
- 131 degree-seeking graduate students
- 61% of applicants admitted
- Application essay required
- 54% graduate within 6 years

General. Founded in 1840. Regionally accredited. Distance education program available in over 20 majors. **Degrees:** 132 bachelor's, 9 associate awarded; master's offered. **ROTC:** Army, Air Force. **Location:** 4 miles from Terre Haute, 70 miles from Indianapolis. **Calendar:** Semester, limited summer session. **Full-time faculty:** 61 total. **Part-time faculty:** 5 total. **Class size:** 92% < 20, 8% 20-39. **Special facilities:** Equine indoor and outdoor arenas, wildlife habitat restoration areas.

Freshman class profile. 268 applied, 163 admitted, 80 enrolled.

Mid 50% test scores		**GPA 2.0-2.99:**	24%
SAT verbal:	450-580	**Rank in top quarter:**	49%
SAT math:	420-560	**Rank in top tenth:**	23%
ACT:	19-25	**Return as sophomores:**	64%
GPA 3.50 or higher:	42%	**Out-of-state:**	20%
GPA 3.0-3.49:	34%	**Live on campus:**	70%

Basis for selection. School achievement record, test scores most important. Recommendations, evaluation of potential for college success considered. Interview recommended. Audition required of music majors. Portfolio required of art and journalism majors. **Homeschooled:** Statement describing homeschool structure and mission, state high school equivalency certificate required. **Learning Disabled:** Meeting with Learning Resource Coordinate strongly recommended.

High school preparation. College-preparatory program required. 13 units required; 16 recommended. Required and recommended units include English 4, mathematics 3, social studies 3, science 3 (laboratory 3) and foreign language 2.

2005-2006 Annual costs. Tuition/fees: $18,660. External degree program tuition $342 per credit hour. Room/board: $6,820. Books/supplies: $900.

2004-2005 Financial aid. **Need-based:** 50% of total undergraduate aid awarded as scholarships/grants, 50% as loans/jobs. **Non-need-based:** Scholarships awarded for academics, alumni affiliation, art, athletics, leadership, minority status, music/drama, state residency. **Additional information:** Portfolio or audition required of applicants who wish to be considered for Creative Arts Scholarship.

Application procedures. **Admission:** Closing date 8/15. $30 fee, may be waived for applicants with need. Application may be submitted online. Admission notification on a rolling basis beginning on or about 9/1. Must reply by 5/1. **Financial aid:** Priority date 3/1; no closing date. FAFSA required. Applicants notified on a rolling basis starting 12/1; must reply within 6 week(s) of notification.

Academics. **Special study options:** Accelerated study, cross-registration, distance learning, double major, external degree, independent study, internships, student-designed major, study abroad, teacher certification program, weekend college. Women's External Degree Program: students throughout country visit campus 1 or 2 days twice a year and do course work at home. Exchange program with Providence University in Taiwan. Study abroad program. **Credit/placement by examination:** AP, CLEP, IB, institutional tests. 30 credit hours maximum toward associate degree, 60 toward bachelor's. **Support services:** Learning center, pre-admission summer program, reduced course load, study skills assistance, tutoring, writing center.

Majors. **Agriculture:** Animal husbandry, equestrian studies, equine science. **Biology:** General. **Business:** General, accounting, business admin, communications, e-commerce, human resources, marketing, nonprofit/public. **Communications:** Journalism, media studies, public relations. **Communications technology:** General, graphics. **Computer sciences:** General, information technology. **Education:** General, art, biology, early childhood, elementary, English, foreign languages, kindergarten/preschool, mathematics, music, science, secondary, social science, social studies, Spanish, special. **English:** Creative writing, English lit. **Family/consumer sciences:** Aging, family studies. **Foreign languages:** French, Spanish. **Health:** Music therapy, predentistry, premedicine, prepharmacy, preveterinary. **History:** General. **Interdisciplinary:** Biological/physical sciences. **Legal studies:** Paralegal, prelaw. **Liberal arts:** Arts/sciences, humanities. **Math:** General. **Philosophy/religion:** Religion. **Psychology:** General. **Public administration:** Human services. **Social sciences:** General. **Theology:** Pastoral counseling, theology. **Visual/performing arts:** Art, design, dramatic, graphic design, music performance, photography.

Most popular majors. Business/marketing 21%, education 29%, psychology 11%.

Computing on campus. 90 workstations in dormitories, library, computer center, student center. Dormitories wired for high-speed internet access and linked to campus network. Commuter students can connect to campus network. Online course registration, online library, helpline, wireless network available.

Student life. **Freshman orientation:** Mandatory. Preregistration for classes offered. First 3 days of fall semester. Requires service component. **Policies:** Freshmen permitted cars on campus. **Housing:** Guaranteed on-campus for all undergraduates. Substance-free housing available. $100 fully refundable deposit. Single mothers with children ages 3-10 may live in college housing. **Activities:** Bands, choral groups, dance, drama, literary magazine, music ensembles, musical theater, student government, student newspaper, symphony orchestra, Campus ministry, Habitat for Humanity, literacy volunteers, environmentalist activities, peace and justice committee, arts and issues committee, Race-for-the-Cure, United Way.

Athletics. USCAA. **Intercollegiate:** Basketball W, equestrian W, soccer W, softball W. **Team name:** Pomeroys.

Student services. Adult student services, alcohol/substance abuse counseling, campus ministries, career counseling, student employment services, financial aid counseling, health services, on-campus daycare, personal counseling, placement for graduates. **Physically disabled:** Services for visually, hearing impaired.

Contact. E-mail: smwcadms@smwc.edu
Phone: (812) 535-5106 Toll-free number: (800) 926-7692
Fax: (812) 535-5010
Theresa Denton, Chief Enrollment Services & Marketing Officer, St. Mary-of-the-Woods College, Guerin Hall, SMWC, St. Mary-of-the-Woods, IN 47876

Saint Mary's College

Notre Dame, Indiana — CB member
www.saintmarys.edu — CB code: 1702

- Private 4-year liberal arts college for women affiliated with Roman Catholic Church
- Residential campus in small city
- 1,366 degree-seeking undergraduates: 100% women, 1% African American, 2% Asian American, 4% Hispanic American, 1% Native American, 1% international
- 81% of applicants admitted
- SAT or ACT (ACT writing optional), application essay required
- 74% graduate within 6 years; 70% enter graduate study

General. Founded in 1844. Regionally accredited. College has campus in Rome, Italy and sponsors programs in Ireland, India, Spain, France and Australia. Summer European study tour. Co-exchange enrollment with the University of Notre Dame. Volunteer service opportunities in the United States and abroad. **Degrees:** 376 bachelor's awarded. **ROTC:** Army, Navy, Air Force. **Location:** 1 mile from South Bend. **Calendar:** Semester, limited summer session. **Full-time faculty:** 125 total; 75% have terminal degrees, 9% minority, 61% women. **Part-time faculty:** 73 total; 19% have terminal degrees, 10% minority, 68% women. **Class size:** 63% < 20, 34% 20-39, 1% 40-49, 2% 50-99. **Special facilities:** Nature trail, performing arts center, art gallery, greenhouse.

Freshman class profile. 997 applied, 807 admitted, 377 enrolled.

Mid 50% test scores			
SAT verbal:	530-630	Rank in top quarter:	66%
SAT math:	520-610	Rank in top tenth:	32%
ACT:	23-27	End year in good standing:	94%
GPA 3.50 or higher:	66%	Return as sophomores:	87%
GPA 3.0-3.49:	31%	Out-of-state:	76%
GPA 2.0-2.99:	3%	Live on campus:	97%

Basis for selection. School achievement record, high school transcript, GPA, class rank, test scores, and activities most important. Essay and school recommendations considered. Students must submit at least one writing component. Interview recommended. Audition recommended for music majors. Portfolio recommended for art majors. **Homeschooled:** Students are encouraged to apply. Candidate should contact the Admission Office for details.

High school preparation. 16 units required. Required and recommended units include English 4, mathematics 3-4, social studies 2, science 2-4 (laboratory 2), foreign language 2-4 and academic electives 4. Science and nursing programs require more science and mathematics. All students must take an additional 4 units distributed among English, math, science, foreign language, and social studies.

2005-2006 Annual costs. Tuition/fees: $24,358. Room/board: $8,180. Books/supplies: $1,000. Personal expenses: $1,200.

2005-2006 Financial aid. **Need-based:** Average need met was 80%. Average scholarship/grant was $9,557; average loan $2,436. 69% of total undergraduate aid awarded as scholarships/grants, 31% as loans/jobs. **Non-need-based:** Scholarships awarded for academics, ROTC.

Application procedures. **Admission:** Priority date 3/1; no deadline. $30 fee, may be waived for applicants with need. Application may be submitted online. Admission notification on a rolling basis beginning on or about 1/15. $200 Housing deposit refunded if letter sent in by May 1. Housing deposit nonrefundable for early decision. **Financial aid:** Priority date 3/1; no closing date. FAFSA, CSS PROFILE required. Applicants notified on a rolling basis starting 12/15; must reply by 5/1.

Academics. Department of Religious Studies coordinated with Department of Theology at University of Notre Dame. After first year, student can take courses in either department. **Special study options:** Accelerated study, cross-registration, double major, exchange student, independent study, internships, liberal arts/career combination, student-designed major, study abroad, teacher certification program, Washington semester. **Credit/placement by examination:** AP, CLEP, IB, institutional tests. 30 credit hours maximum toward bachelor's degree. **Support services:** Reduced course load, tutoring, writing center.

Majors. **Biology:** General. **Business:** Accounting, business admin, management information systems. **Communications:** General. **Education:** Elementary. **English:** British lit, creative writing. **Foreign languages:** French, Spanish. **Health:** Cytotechnology, nursing (RN). **History:** General. **Interdisciplinary:** Math/computer science. **Liberal arts:** Humanities. **Math:** General, applied, statistics. **Philosophy/religion:** Philosophy, religion. **Physical sciences:** Chemistry. **Psychology:** General. **Public administration:** Social work. **Social sciences:** Economics, political science, sociology. **Visual/performing arts:** Art, dramatic, studio arts.

Most popular majors. Biology 7%, business/marketing 14%, communications/journalism 11%, education 15%, English 9%, health sciences 6%, psychology 7%, social sciences 8%, visual/performing arts 6%.

Computing on campus. 200 workstations in dormitories, library, computer center, student center. Dormitories wired for high-speed internet access and linked to campus network. Commuter students can connect to campus network. Online course registration, online library, helpline, repair service, student web hosting, wireless network available.

Student life. **Freshman orientation:** Mandatory. Preregistration for classes offered. Held during weekend prior to beginning of fall semester. Preorientation sessions held for fall admits during summer months. **Policies:** Educational judicial system guaranteeing certain due process rights to all students involved in discipline situation; student judicial board provides opportunity for peer review system. Freshmen permitted cars on campus. **Housing:** Guaranteed on-campus for all undergraduates. Apartments available. $200 deposit. **Activities:** Marching band, choral groups, dance, drama, literary magazine, music ensembles, musical theater, opera, radio station, student government, student newspaper, TV station, neighborhood study help program, Community of International Lay Apostolate, Urban Plunge community program, Circle-K, World Hunger Coalition, Student Alliance for Women's Colleges, Right to Life, Women for the Environment, Sisters of Nefertiti, Fuerza y Union Entre las Razas.

Athletics. NCAA. **Intercollegiate:** Basketball W, cross-country W, diving W, golf W, soccer W, softball W, swimming W, tennis W, volleyball W. **Intramural:** Basketball W, bowling W, football (non-tackle) W, lacrosse W, racquetball W, soccer W, tennis W, triathlon W, volleyball W. **Team name:** Belles.

Student services. Adult student services, campus ministries, career counseling, student employment services, financial aid counseling, health services, minority student services, on-campus daycare, personal counseling, placement for graduates. **Physically disabled:** Services for visually, hearing impaired.

Contact. E-mail: admission@saintmarys.edu
Phone: (574) 284-4587 Toll-free number: (800) 551-7621
Fax: (574) 284-4841
Mona Bowe, Director of Admissions, Saint Mary's College, Admission Office, Notre Dame, IN 46556-5001

Taylor University

Upland, Indiana — CB member
www.taylor.edu — CB code: 1802

- Private 4-year liberal arts college affiliated with interdenominational tradition
- Residential campus in small town

- 1,829 degree-seeking undergraduates: 2% part-time, 55% women
- 14 degree-seeking graduate students
- 82% of applicants admitted
- SAT or ACT (ACT writing recommended), application essay, interview required
- 80% graduate within 6 years

General. Founded in 1846. Regionally accredited. Christ-centered, covenant community committed to service. **Degrees:** 417 bachelor's, 5 associate awarded; master's offered. **Location:** 20 miles from Muncie, 65 miles from Indianapolis. **Calendar:** 4-1-4, limited summer session. **Full-time faculty:** 127 total; 74% have terminal degrees, 5% minority, 25% women. **Part-time faculty:** 60 total; 22% have terminal degrees, 2% minority, 57% women. **Class size:** 55% < 20, 37% 20-39, 6% 40-49, 1% 50-99, 1% >100. **Special facilities:** Arboretum, environmental studies laboratory, NASA-approved clean room, particle accelerator, NASA project space research equipment, C.S. Lewis Collection of original manuscripts.

Freshman class profile. 1,517 applied, 1,237 admitted, 464 enrolled.

Mid 50% test scores			
SAT verbal:	530-660	Rank in top tenth:	37%
SAT math:	550-660	Return as sophomores:	88%
ACT:	24-29	Out-of-state:	70%
Rank in top quarter:	68%	Live on campus:	99%

Basis for selection. High school transcript, test scores important. Recommend rank in top 25% of graduating class with GPA of 3.3 and SAT combined score of 1000 (exculsive of writing). Essay and personal statement required. Recommendations from applicant's pastor and counselor required. Cocurricular activities considered. Audition required of music majors. Portfolio recommended for art majors.

High school preparation. 15 units required. Required and recommended units include English 4, mathematics 3-4, social studies 2-3, science 3-4 (laboratory 3-4), foreign language 2 and academic electives 3.

2005-2006 Annual costs. Tuition/fees: $20,746. Room/board: $5,630. Books/supplies: $800. Personal expenses: $1,600.

2005-2006 Financial aid. Need-based: 361 full-time freshmen applied for aid; 268 were judged to have need; 268 of these received aid. Average need met was 74%. Average scholarship/grant was $10,644; average loan $4,260. 65% of total undergraduate aid awarded as scholarships/grants, 35% as loans/jobs. **Non-need-based:** Awarded to 574 full-time undergraduates, including 154 freshmen. Scholarships awarded for academics, alumni affiliation, art, athletics, leadership, minority status, music/drama, religious affiliation, state residency. **Additional information:** Reduced rates for high school students during academic year. Tuition waivers for children of alumni during summer session.

Application procedures. Admission: No deadline. $25 fee, may be waived for applicants with need. Application may be submitted online. Admission notification on a rolling basis beginning on or about 10/1. Must reply by May 1 or within 2 week(s) if notified thereafter. **Financial aid:** Closing date 3/10. FAFSA, institutional form required. Applicants notified on a rolling basis starting 3/1; must reply by 5/1.

Academics. Special study options: Combined bachelor's/graduate degree, double major, dual enrollment of high school students, exchange student, honors, independent study, internships, liberal arts/career combination, semester at sea, student-designed major, study abroad, teacher certification program, urban semester, Washington semester. **Credit/placement by examination:** AP, CLEP, institutional tests. 30 credit hours maximum toward associate degree, 30 toward bachelor's. **Support services:** Learning center, remedial instruction, study skills assistance, tutoring, writing center.

Majors. Biology: General. **Business:** Accounting, business admin, finance, financial planning, human resources, international, management science, managerial economics, marketing. **Communications:** General, broadcast journalism, journalism, media studies. **Computer sciences:** General, computer graphics, computer science. **Conservation:** Environmental science. **Education:** Art, biology, chemistry, elementary, English, French, history, mathematics, music, physical, physics, science, social science, social studies, Spanish. **Engineering:** Computer, environmental, physics. **Foreign languages:** French, Spanish. **History:** General. **Interdisciplinary:** Biological/physical sciences, math/computer science. **Math:** General. **Parks/recreation:** Exercise sciences, health/fitness, sports admin. **Philosophy/religion:** Philosophy. **Physical sciences:** General, chemistry, physics. **Psychology:** General. **Public administration:** Social work. **Social sciences:** General, economics, geography, political science, sociology. **Theology:** Bible, youth ministry. **Visual/performing arts:** Art, dramatic, music management, music performance.

Most popular majors. Business/marketing 17%, communications/journalism 9%, computer/information sciences 6%, education 17%, psychology 12%, theological studies 8%.

Computing on campus. 228 workstations in library, computer center. Dormitories wired for high-speed internet access and linked to campus network. Commuter students can connect to campus network. Online course registration, online library, helpline, repair service, wireless network available.

Student life. Freshman orientation: Available. Preregistration for classes offered. **Policies:** Students and faculty sign Life Together Covenant explaining expectations and responsibilities of living in Christian community where faith is integrated with academic progress. Religious observance required. Freshmen permitted cars on campus. **Housing:** Guaranteed on-campus for freshmen. Single-sex dorms, apartments, substance-free housing available. $200 fully refundable deposit, deadline 5/1. Some off-campus apartments available to upperclassmen with special permission. **Activities:** Bands, choral groups, drama, film society, literary magazine, music ensembles, musical theater, opera, radio station, student government, student newspaper, symphony orchestra, TV station, missions service program, multicultural society, Missionary Kids Organizations, community outreach, Campus Life/Young Life, international student society, Habitat for Humanity, ReaLife Inner City Children's Ministry, high school youth conference, Acting on AIDS.

Athletics. NAIA, NCCAA. **Intercollegiate:** Baseball M, basketball, cross-country, football (tackle) M, golf M, soccer, softball W, tennis, track and field, volleyball W. **Intramural:** Badminton, basketball, football (non-tackle), golf, racquetball, soccer, softball, table tennis, tennis, volleyball. **Team name:** Trojans.

Student services. Campus ministries, career counseling, student employment services, financial aid counseling, health services, minority student services, personal counseling, placement for graduates. **Physically disabled:** Services for visually, speech, hearing impaired.

Contact. E-mail: admissions_u@tayloru.edu
Phone: (765) 998-5134 Toll-free number: (800) 882-3456
Fax: (765) 998-4925
Stephen Mortland, Director of Admissions, Taylor University, 236 West Reade Avenue, Upland, IN 46989-1001

Taylor University: Fort Wayne

Fort Wayne, Indiana
http://fw.taylor.edu **CB code: 1227**

- Private 4-year liberal arts college affiliated with Christian interdenominational tradition
- Residential campus in large city
- 408 degree-seeking undergraduates: 17% part-time, 59% women
- 38 degree-seeking graduate students
- 83% of applicants admitted
- SAT or ACT, application essay required
- 49% graduate within 6 years

General. Regionally accredited. **Degrees:** 89 bachelor's, 8 associate awarded; master's offered. **Location:** 109 miles from Indianapolis. **Calendar:** 4-1-4, limited summer session. **Full-time faculty:** 31 total; 68% have terminal degrees, 3% minority, 32% women. **Part-time faculty:** 29 total; 34% have terminal degrees, 52% women. **Class size:** 70% < 20, 27% 20-39, 2% 40-49, less than 1% 50-99.

Freshman class profile. 266 applied, 221 admitted, 83 enrolled.

Mid 50% test scores			
SAT verbal:	450-590	Rank in top quarter:	27%
SAT math:	430-580	Rank in top tenth:	13%
ACT:	18-26	End year in good standing:	71%
GPA 3.50 or higher:	39%	Return as sophomores:	70%
GPA 3.0-3.49:	26%	Out-of-state:	28%
GPA 2.0-2.99:	24%	Live on campus:	93%

Basis for selection. High school record and religious affiliation most important.

High school preparation. 14 units required; 16 recommended. Required and recommended units include English 4, mathematics 3, social studies 2, history 2, science 3 and foreign language 2. Recommend 2 units of fine arts.

2005-2006 Annual costs. Tuition/fees: $17,714. Room/board: $4,960. Books/supplies: $800. Personal expenses: $1,600.

2005-2006 Financial aid. Need-based: 59 full-time freshmen applied for aid; 53 were judged to have need; 53 of these received aid. Average need met was 86%. Average scholarship/grant was $11,573; average loan

$4,083. 64% of total undergraduate aid awarded as scholarships/grants, 36% as loans/jobs. **Non-need-based:** Awarded to 70 full-time undergraduates, including 19 freshmen. Scholarships awarded for academics, alumni affiliation, athletics, leadership, religious affiliation, state residency.

Application procedures. Admission: No deadline. $20 fee, may be waived for applicants with need. Application may be submitted online. Admission notification on a rolling basis. Must reply by May 1 or within 2 week(s) if notified thereafter. **Financial aid:** Closing date 3/1. FAFSA, institutional form required. Applicants notified on a rolling basis starting 3/1; must reply by 5/1 or within 2 week(s) of notification.

Academics. Special study options: Accelerated study, combined bachelor's/graduate degree, cooperative education, distance learning, double major, dual enrollment of high school students, ESL, exchange student, external degree, independent study, internships, liberal arts/career combination, student-designed major, study abroad, teacher certification program. **Credit/placement by examination:** AP, CLEP, SAT, ACT, institutional tests. 30 credit hours maximum toward bachelor's degree. **Support services:** Learning center, reduced course load, remedial instruction, study skills assistance, tutoring, writing center.

Majors. Business: Business admin, international, management science, market research. **Communications:** Public relations. **Computer sciences:** Computer science. **Education:** Elementary. **Legal studies:** Prelaw. **Protective services:** Law enforcement admin. **Psychology:** General. **Public administration:** Social work. **Theology:** Bible, missionary, religious ed, theology.

Most popular majors. Education 24%, English 7%, philosophy/religious studies 30%, public administration/social services 7%, security/protective services 16%.

Computing on campus. 69 workstations in dormitories, library, computer center, student center. Dormitories wired for high-speed internet access and linked to campus network. Commuter students can connect to campus network. Online library, helpline, wireless network available.

Student life. Freshman orientation: Mandatory. Preregistration for classes offered. Held the weekend before classes start. **Policies:** Religious observance required. Freshmen permitted cars on campus. **Housing:** Guaranteed on-campus for freshmen. Single-sex dorms, apartments, substance-free housing available. $50 deposit. **Activities:** Jazz band, choral groups, drama, music ensembles, student government, student newspaper, world outreach, student organization, multicultural activities council, student activities council, adult fellowship, prayer council, dorm council, theatre organization, Sanctity of Life organization.

Athletics. USCAA. **Intercollegiate:** Basketball, soccer M, volleyball W. **Intramural:** Basketball, football (non-tackle), table tennis, volleyball. **Team name:** Falcons.

Student services. Adult student services, alcohol/substance abuse counseling, campus ministries, career counseling, services for economically disadvantaged, student employment services, financial aid counseling, health services, personal counseling, placement for graduates. **Physically disabled:** Services for visually, speech, hearing impaired.

Contact. E-mail: admissions@fw.taylor.edu
Phone: (260) 744-8689 Toll-free number: (800) 233-3922
Fax: (260) 744-8850
Leo Gonot, Associate Vice President for Enrollment Management, Taylor University: Fort Wayne, 1025 West Rudisill Boulevard, Fort Wayne, IN 46807

Tri-State University

Angola, Indiana — **CB member**
www.tristate.edu — **CB code: 1811**

- Private 4-year university
- Residential campus in small town
- 1,126 degree-seeking undergraduates: 12% part-time, 34% women
- 4 degree-seeking graduate students
- 75% of applicants admitted
- SAT or ACT (ACT writing optional) required
- 51% graduate within 6 years; 40% enter graduate study

General. Founded in 1884. Regionally accredited. **Degrees:** 216 bachelor's, 23 associate awarded; master's offered. **Location:** 40 miles from Fort Wayne, 80 miles from Toledo, Ohio. **Calendar:** Semester, limited summer session. **Full-time faculty:** 69 total; 65% have terminal degrees, 4% minority, 25% women. **Part-time faculty:** 30 total; 17% have terminal degrees, 3% minority, 30% women. **Class size:** 60% < 20, 40% 20-39. **Special facilities:** Museum, educational media resource center, golf course.

Freshman class profile. 1,649 applied, 1,229 admitted, 305 enrolled.

Mid 50% test scores			
SAT verbal:	450-570	Rank in top quarter:	44%
SAT math:	490-600	Rank in top tenth:	17%
ACT:	20-25	Out-of-state:	38%
GPA 3.50 or higher:	39%	Live on campus:	87%
GPA 3.0-3.49:	32%	Fraternities:	5%
GPA 2.0-2.99:	28%	Sororities:	1%

Basis for selection. School achievement, class rank, test scores, school and community activities, and recommendations important. Interview recommended.

High school preparation. College-preparatory program required. 17 units required. Required units include English 4, mathematics 3, social studies 2, history 2, science 2 (laboratory 2) and academic electives 5. 3 1/2 years of mathematics, physics, and chemistry required for engineering, mathematics and computer science majors.

2005-2006 Annual costs. Tuition/fees: $20,200. Room/board: $6,000. Books/supplies: $1,000. Personal expenses: $1,850.

2005-2006 Financial aid. Need-based: 271 full-time freshmen applied for aid; 271 were judged to have need; 271 of these received aid. Average need met was 58%. Average scholarship/grant was $3,600; average loan $2,682. 52% of total undergraduate aid awarded as scholarships/grants, 48% as loans/jobs. **Non-need-based:** Awarded to 1,071 full-time undergraduates, including 271 freshmen. Scholarships awarded for academics.

Application procedures. Admission: No application fee. Application must be submitted online. Admission notification on a rolling basis. **Financial aid:** Closing date 3/10. FAFSA required. Applicants notified on a rolling basis starting 2/1; must reply by 5/1 or within 2 week(s) of notification.

Academics. Special study options: Cooperative education, distance learning, double major, dual enrollment of high school students, honors, internships, study abroad, teacher certification program. **Credit/placement by examination:** AP, CLEP, IB, institutional tests. **Support services:** Preadmission summer program, reduced course load, remedial instruction, study skills assistance, tutoring, writing center.

Majors. Biology: General. **Business:** Accounting, business admin, finance, management information systems, operations. **Communications:** General. **Computer sciences:** General, computer science. **Conservation:** General. **Education:** Elementary, English, health, mathematics, middle, physical, science, social studies. **Engineering:** Chemical, civil, electrical, mechanical. **Engineering technology:** Drafting, industrial management. **English:** English lit. **Health:** Premedicine. **Math:** General. **Parks/recreation:** Health/fitness, sports admin. **Physical sciences:** Chemistry. **Protective services:** Criminal justice, forensics. **Psychology:** General. **Social sciences:** General.

Most popular majors. Business/marketing 16%, education 17%, engineering/engineering technologies 38%, security/protective services 10%.

Computing on campus. 150 workstations in dormitories, library, computer center. Dormitories wired for high-speed internet access and linked to campus network. Commuter students can connect to campus network. Online library, helpline, wireless network available.

Student life. Freshman orientation: Mandatory. Preregistration for classes offered. 3 days at the start of the fall semester. **Policies:** Freshmen permitted cars on campus. **Housing:** Guaranteed on-campus for freshmen. Coed dorms, apartments available. $150 deposit, deadline 7/26. Independent fraternity/sorority housing available. **Activities:** Pep band, choral groups, drama, radio station, student government, student newspaper, Circle K, Newman Fellowship, InterVarsity Christian Fellowship, international student association, multicultural student association, Students Against Destructive Decisions, Habitat for Humanity.

Athletics. NCAA. **Intercollegiate:** Baseball M, basketball, cross-country, football (tackle) M, golf, soccer, softball W, swimming M, tennis, track and field, volleyball W, wrestling M. **Intramural:** Badminton, basketball, football (non-tackle) M, golf, handball, racquetball, softball, table tennis, volleyball. **Team name:** Thunder.

Student services. Career counseling, student employment services, financial aid counseling, personal counseling, placement for graduates, veterans' counselor.

Contact. E-mail: admit@tristate.edu
Phone: (260) 665-4132 Toll-free number: (800) 347-4878
Fax: (260) 665-4578
Scott Goplin, Dean of Admission, Tri-State University, One University Avenue, Angola, IN 46703

Trinity College of the Bible and Theological Seminary

Newburgh, Indiana
www.trinitysem.edu/

- Private 4-year Bible and seminary college

Contact. Phone: (812) 853-0611
4233 Medwel Drive, Newburgh, IN 47630

University of Evansville

Evansville, Indiana — **CB member**
www.evansville.edu — **CB code: 1208**

- Private 4-year university and liberal arts college affiliated with United Methodist Church
- Residential campus in small city
- 2,552 degree-seeking undergraduates: 5% part-time, 61% women, 2% African American, 1% Asian American, 1% Hispanic American, 5% international
- 69 degree-seeking graduate students
- 91% of applicants admitted
- SAT or ACT with writing required
- 61% graduate within 6 years; 18% enter graduate study

General. Founded in 1854. Regionally accredited. Campus in Grantham, England. **Degrees:** 396 bachelor's, 4 associate awarded; master's offered. **Location:** 180 miles from Indianapolis, 170 miles from St. Louis. **Calendar:** Semester, limited summer session. **Full-time faculty:** 175 total; 88% have terminal degrees, 6% minority, 33% women. **Part-time faculty:** 59 total; 41% have terminal degrees, 61% women. **Class size:** 50% < 20, 42% 20-39, 5% 40-49, 2% 50-99. **Special facilities:** Institute for global enterprise.

Freshman class profile. 2,583 applied, 2,339 admitted, 670 enrolled.

Mid 50% test scores		Rank in top tenth:	35%
SAT verbal:	520-630	End year in good standing:	91%
SAT math:	520-640	Return as sophomores:	81%
ACT:	22-28	Out-of-state:	38%
GPA 3.50 or higher:	62%	Live on campus:	88%
GPA 3.0-3.49:	22%	International:	4%
GPA 2.0-2.99:	16%	Fraternities:	25%
Rank in top quarter:	65%	Sororities:	24%

Basis for selection. Weighted GPA calculated using academic courses only. Extracurricular activities important. Interview recommended. Audition required of music and theatre majors. Portfolio required of art majors. **Homeschooled:** Transcript of courses and grades, letter of recommendation (nonparent) required. **Learning Disabled:** Students requesting accomodations must provide documentation of the disability and the significant impact of the disability on academic functioning.

High school preparation. 10 units required; 14 recommended. Required and recommended units include English 4, mathematics 3-4, history 1, science 2-3 (laboratory 2) and foreign language 2. One or more years of physics, additional chemistry and math, and 2 or more years of a foreign language recommended for engineering programs.

2005-2006 Annual costs. Tuition/fees: $21,660. Room/board: $6,660. Books/supplies: $800. Personal expenses: $850.

2005-2006 Financial aid. Need-based: 580 full-time freshmen applied for aid; 491 were judged to have need; 491 of these received aid. Average need met was 96%. Average scholarship/grant was $16,730; average loan $3,835. 75% of total undergraduate aid awarded as scholarships/grants, 25% as loans/jobs. **Non-need-based:** Awarded to 1,866 full-time undergraduates, including 570 freshmen. Scholarships awarded for academics, alumni affiliation, art, athletics, leadership, minority status, music/drama, religious affiliation. **Additional information:** Early financial planning service allows prospective students to get free estimate of available aid.

Application procedures. Admission: Priority date 12/1; deadline 2/1 (postmark date). $35 fee, may be waived for applicants with need. Application may be submitted online. Admission notification 3/1. Admission notification on a rolling basis. Must reply by May 1 or within 2 week(s) if notified thereafter. **Financial aid:** Priority date 3/10; no closing date. FAFSA required. CSS PROFILE accepted but not required. Applicants notified on a rolling basis starting 3/21.

Academics. Special study options: Accelerated study, combined bachelor's/graduate degree, cooperative education, double major, dual enrollment of high school students, ESL, external degree, honors, independent study, internships, semester at sea, student-designed major, study abroad, teacher certification program, Washington semester. Italian archeological excavation program, British campus at Harlaxton College, British Parliament internship, American University semester study, US Pentagon internship, research program for undergraduates. **Credit/placement by examination:** AP, CLEP, IB, ACT, institutional tests. 6 credit hours maximum toward associate degree, 6 toward bachelor's. **Support services:** Learning center, preadmission summer program, study skills assistance, tutoring, writing center.

Majors. Biology: General, biochemistry. **Business:** General, accounting, business admin, finance, international, managerial economics, marketing. **Communications:** General, media studies. **Computer sciences:** General, programming. **Conservation:** Environmental science, environmental studies. **Education:** General, art, biology, chemistry, drama/dance, elementary, English, French, German, mathematics, music, physical, physics, science, social science, social studies, Spanish, special. **Engineering:** Civil, computer, electrical, mechanical. **Engineering technology:** Industrial management. **English:** Composition, creative writing, English lit. **Foreign languages:** Classics, French, German, Spanish. **Health:** Athletic training, health services admin, music therapy, nursing (RN), predentistry, premedicine, prepharmacy, preveterinary. **History:** General. **Interdisciplinary:** Cognitive science. **Legal studies:** General. **Liberal arts:** Arts/sciences. **Math:** General. **Parks/recreation:** Exercise sciences, health/fitness. **Philosophy/religion:** Philosophy. **Physical sciences:** Chemistry, physics. **Psychology:** General. **Social sciences:** Archaeology, economics, international relations, political science, sociology. **Theology:** Bible, theology. **Visual/performing arts:** Art, art history/conservation, design, dramatic, graphic design, music management, music performance, theater arts management.

Most popular majors. Business/marketing 11%, education 11%, engineering/engineering technologies 11%, health sciences 14%, liberal arts 10%, social sciences 8%, visual/performing arts 12%.

Computing on campus. 300 workstations in dormitories, library, student center. Dormitories wired for high-speed internet access and linked to campus network. Commuter students can connect to campus network. Online library, helpline, student web hosting, wireless network available.

Student life. Freshman orientation: Mandatory. Preregistration for classes offered. 2 programs available: one in summer includes testing, advising, and registration; another 3 1/2 day program held prior to beginning of semester. **Policies:** Freshmen permitted cars on campus. **Housing:** Guaranteed on-campus for freshmen. Coed dorms, single-sex dorms, apartments, fraternity/sorority housing, substance-free housing available. $100 partly refundable deposit, deadline 5/1. Honors housing. **Activities:** Bands, choral groups, dance, drama, film society, literary magazine, music ensembles, musical theater, opera, radio station, student government, student newspaper, symphony orchestra, Baptist Collegiate Ministry, Black Student Union, Hillel, international students club, Kappa Chi (service), Amnesty International, Habitat for Humanity, Circle K, College Democrats, College Republicans.

Athletics. NCAA. **Intercollegiate:** Baseball M, basketball, cross-country, diving, golf, soccer, softball W, swimming, tennis W, volleyball W. **Intramural:** Basketball, bowling, cross-country, football (non-tackle), golf, racquetball, soccer, softball, swimming, table tennis, tennis, volleyball. **Team name:** Purple Aces.

Student services. Adult student services, alcohol/substance abuse counseling, campus ministries, career counseling, student employment services, financial aid counseling, health services, minority student services, personal counseling, placement for graduates, veterans' counselor. **Physically disabled:** Services for visually impaired.

Contact. E-mail: admission@evansville.edu
Phone: (812) 488-2468 Toll-free number: (800) 423-8633 ext. 2468
Fax: (812) 474-4076
Don Vos, Dean of Admission, University of Evansville, 1800 Lincoln Avenue, Evansville, IN 47722

University of Indianapolis

Indianapolis, Indiana — **CB member**
www.uindy.edu — **CB code: 1321**

- Private 4-year university and liberal arts college affiliated with United Methodist Church
- Residential campus in very large city
- 3,317 degree-seeking undergraduates: 28% part-time, 68% women, 11% African American, 1% Asian American, 2% Hispanic American, 2% international
- 1,090 degree-seeking graduate students
- 83% of applicants admitted
- SAT or ACT (ACT writing optional) required
- 53% graduate within 6 years; 25% enter graduate study

General. Founded in 1902. Regionally accredited. **Degrees:** 454 bachelor's, 68 associate awarded; master's, doctoral offered. **ROTC:** Army. **Location:** 4 miles from downtown. **Calendar:** Semester, limited summer session. **Full-time faculty:** 166 total; 74% have terminal degrees, 9% minority, 51% women. **Part-time faculty:** 250 total; 39% have terminal degrees, 8% minority, 46% women. **Class size:** 61% < 20, 37% 20-39, less than 1% 40-49, less than 1% 50-99, less than 1% >100. **Special facilities:** Observatory, fine arts center.

Freshman class profile. 2,884 applied, 2,404 admitted, 737 enrolled.

Mid 50% test scores			
SAT verbal:	450-570	Rank in top quarter:	54%
SAT math:	460-570	Rank in top tenth:	20%
ACT:	19-24	Return as sophomores:	74%
GPA 3.50 or higher:	28%	Out-of-state:	9%
GPA 3.0-3.49:	30%	Live on campus:	75%
GPA 2.0-2.99:	41%	International:	2%

Basis for selection. Recommendations, GPA, SAT/ACT scores, class rank important. Involvements and extracurricular activities considered. Essay recommended. Interview recommended for borderline applicants. Audition required of music majors. Portfolio recommended for art majors. **Homeschooled:** Transcript of courses and grades required. **Learning Disabled:** Students with learning disabilities may apply to the BUILD program through separate application process.

High school preparation. 30 units required; 36 recommended. Required and recommended units include English 8, mathematics 6-8, social studies 2, history 2, science 4-6 (laboratory 2-4), foreign language 4 and academic electives 6.

2005-2006 Annual costs. Tuition/fees: $17,980. Room/board: $7,010. Books/supplies: $600. Personal expenses: $1,200.

2004-2005 Financial aid. Need-based: Average need met was 82%. Average scholarship/grant was $7,850; average loan $3,003. 43% of total undergraduate aid awarded as scholarships/grants, 57% as loans/jobs. **Non-need-based:** Scholarships awarded for academics, alumni affiliation, art, athletics, job skills, leadership, music/drama, religious affiliation, state residency.

Application procedures. Admission: No deadline. $20 fee, may be waived for applicants with need. Application may be submitted online. Admission notification on a rolling basis. Must reply by May 1 or within 2 week(s) if notified thereafter. **Financial aid:** Closing date 3/1. FAFSA, institutional form required. Applicants notified on a rolling basis starting 3/1; must reply within 3 week(s) of notification.

Academics. Special study options: Accelerated study, cross-registration, double major, dual enrollment of high school students, ESL, honors, independent study, internships, liberal arts/career combination, student-designed major, study abroad, teacher certification program, weekend college. Third-year medical technology program at Methodist Hospital, Baccalaureate for University of Indianapolis Learning Disabled (BUILD). **Credit/placement by examination:** AP, CLEP, IB, SAT, ACT, institutional tests. 3 to 8 hours awarded for International Baccalaureate based on scores. **Support services:** Learning center, pre-admission summer program, reduced course load, remedial instruction, study skills assistance, tutoring, writing center.

Majors. Biology: General, cell/histology. **Business:** Accounting, business admin, international, management information systems, managerial economics, marketing, tourism/travel. **Communications:** General. **Computer sciences:** General, computer science, information systems. **Education:** General, art, biology, business, chemistry, elementary, English, foreign languages, French, history, mathematics, music, physical, physics, science, secondary, social studies, Spanish, speech. **English:** English lit. **Foreign languages:** French, German, Spanish. **Health:** Art therapy, athletic training, clinical lab technology, nursing (RN), respiratory therapy technology. **History:** General. **Math:** General. **Parks/recreation:** Exercise sciences, sports admin. **Philosophy/religion:** Philosophy, religion. **Physical sciences:** Chemistry, geology, physics. **Protective services:** Law enforcement admin. **Psychology:** General. **Public administration:** Social work. **Social sciences:** Anthropology, archaeology, economics, international relations, political science, sociology. **Visual/performing arts:** Art, commercial/advertising art, design, dramatic, music performance.

Most popular majors. Business/marketing 25%, education 16%, health sciences 7%, liberal arts 6%, psychology 13%, social sciences 6%, visual/performing arts 6%.

Computing on campus. 222 workstations in library, computer center. Dormitories wired for high-speed internet access and linked to campus network. Commuter students can connect to campus network. Online library, helpline, wireless network available.

Student life. Freshman orientation: Mandatory, $40 fee. Preregistration for classes offered. Student attends one of 6 summer registration programs. **Policies:** Freshmen permitted cars on campus. **Housing:** Coed dorms, single-sex dorms, apartments, substance-free housing available. $50 fully refundable deposit, deadline 5/1. **Activities:** Bands, choral groups, dance, drama, literary magazine, music ensembles, musical theater, opera, radio station, student government, student newspaper, TV station, Young Democrats, Young Republicans, Fellowship of Christian Athletes, Circle-K, social service and honorary societies.

Athletics. NCAA. **Intercollegiate:** Baseball M, basketball, cross-country, diving, football (tackle) M, golf, soccer, softball W, swimming, tennis, track and field, volleyball W, wrestling M. **Intramural:** Basketball, football (non-tackle) M, soccer, softball, volleyball. **Team name:** Greyhounds.

Student services. Adult student services, campus ministries, career counseling, student employment services, health services, personal counseling, placement for graduates, veterans' counselor. **Physically disabled:** Services for visually, speech, hearing impaired. **Learning disabled:** Comprehensive services available.

Contact. E-mail: admissions@uindy.edu
Phone: (317) 788-3216 Toll-free number: (800) 232-8634
Fax: (317) 788-3300
Ron Wilks, Director of Admissions, University of Indianapolis, 1400 East Hanna Avenue, Indianapolis, IN 46227-3697

University of Notre Dame

Notre Dame, Indiana — **CB member**
www.nd.edu — **CB code: 1841**

- Private 4-year university affiliated with Roman Catholic Church
- Residential campus in small city
- 8,266 degree-seeking undergraduates: 47% women, 4% African American, 6% Asian American, 9% Hispanic American, 1% Native American, 3% international
- 3,016 degree-seeking graduate students
- 32% of applicants admitted
- SAT or ACT (ACT writing optional), application essay required

General. Founded in 1842. Regionally accredited. Notre Dame Study Centers in Washington, DC; Dublin, Ireland; London, England; Rome, Italy; and Jerusalem; as well as several other countries. **Degrees:** 2,167 bachelor's awarded; master's, doctoral, first professional offered. **ROTC:** Army, Navy, Air Force. **Location:** 90 miles from Chicago. **Calendar:** Semester, extensive summer session. **Full-time faculty:** 780 total; 99% have terminal degrees, 13% minority, 23% women. **Part-time faculty:** 410 total; 61% have terminal degrees, 7% minority, 31% women. **Class size:** 50% < 20, 30% 20-39, 8% 40-49, 8% 50-99, 3% >100. **Special facilities:** Art museum, theater, germ-free research facility, radiation laboratory, nature preserve for biological research, wind-tunnel research facility.

Freshman class profile. 11,317 applied, 3,582 admitted, 2,002 enrolled.

Mid 50% test scores			
SAT verbal:	630-730	Rank in top tenth:	86%
SAT math:	660-740	Out-of-state:	89%
ACT:	30-33	Live on campus:	100%
Rank in top quarter:	97%	International:	3%

Basis for selection. GED not accepted. Demonstrated academic achievement and test scores most important. Essay, teacher recommendations, extracurricular activities, and personal statement also important. Audition recommended for music majors. Portfolio recommended for art majors.

High school preparation. 16 units required; 20 recommended. Required and recommended units include English 4, mathematics 3-4, history 2-4, science 2-4, foreign language 2-4 and academic electives 3. Precalculus or calculus, chemistry and physics recommended for architecture, engineering and science programs. Social studies requirement should include history.

2006-2007 Annual costs. Tuition/fees: $33,407. Room/board: $8,730. Books/supplies: $850. Personal expenses: $900.

2005-2006 Financial aid. Need-based: 1,381 full-time freshmen applied for aid; 1,050 were judged to have need; 1,050 of these received aid. Average need met was 100%. Average scholarship/grant was $19,058; average loan $3,603. 76% of total undergraduate aid awarded as scholarships/grants, 24% as loans/jobs. **Non-need-based:** Awarded to 1,913 full-time undergraduates, including 560 freshmen. Scholarships awarded for athletics, ROTC. **Additional information:** ROTC scholarships and athletic grants are available to qualified applicants on competitive basis.

Application procedures. Admission: Closing date 12/31 (postmark date). $50 fee, may be waived for applicants with need. Application may be submitted online. Admission notification 4/10. Must reply by 5/1. **Financial aid:** Closing date 2/15. FAFSA, CSS PROFILE required. Applicants notified on a rolling basis starting 3/15; must reply by 5/1.

Academics. Special study options: Accelerated study, cross-registration, distance learning, double major, honors, independent study, internships, liberal arts/career combination, student-designed major, study abroad, teacher certification program, Washington semester. Teacher certification available only through cross-registration with St. Mary's College; triple majors, quadruple majors, triple degrees, double majors within dual degrees. **Credit/placement by examination:** AP, CLEP, IB. Students with HL score of 6 or 7 eligible to receive credit in anthropology, biology, chemistry, English, French, German, Greek, American history, Latin, mathematics, music, physics, psychology, and Spanish. **Support services:** Learning center, study skills assistance, tutoring, writing center.

Majors. Architecture: Architecture. **Area/ethnic studies:** American. **Biology:** General, biochemistry. **Business:** General, accounting, finance, management information systems, marketing. **Computer sciences:** General. **Conservation:** Environmental science. **Education:** Physics, science. **Engineering:** Aerospace, chemical, civil, computer, electrical, environmental, mechanical. **English:** English lit. **Foreign languages:** Ancient Greek, Arabic, Chinese, classics, French, German, Italian, Japanese, Latin, Romance, Russian, Spanish. **Health:** Physics/radiologic health, premedicine. **History:** General. **Interdisciplinary:** Medieval/Renaissance. **Liberal arts:** Arts/sciences. **Math:** General. **Philosophy/religion:** Philosophy. **Physical sciences:** Chemistry, geology, physics. **Psychology:** General. **Social sciences:** Anthropology, economics, political science, sociology. **Theology:** Theology. **Visual/performing arts:** Art history/conservation, design, dramatic, studio arts.

Most popular majors. Business/marketing 22%, engineering/engineering technologies 8%, foreign language 6%, health sciences 7%, psychology 6%, social sciences 18%.

Computing on campus. 265 workstations in dormitories, library, computer center, student center. Dormitories linked to campus network. Commuter students can connect to campus network. Online course registration, helpline, repair service, wireless network available.

Student life. Freshman orientation: Mandatory. Preregistration for classes offered. **Housing:** Guaranteed on-campus for freshmen. Single-sex dorms available. $50 deposit, deadline 5/1. Requests for ground level housing or housing that will suit a disabled student will be honored. **Activities:** Bands, choral groups, dance, drama, film society, literary magazine, music ensembles, musical theater, opera, radio station, student government, student newspaper, symphony orchestra, more than 260 clubs and organizations available.

Athletics. NCAA. **Intercollegiate:** Baseball M, basketball, cross-country, diving, fencing, football (tackle) M, golf, ice hockey M, lacrosse, rowing (crew) W, soccer, softball W, swimming, tennis, track and field, volleyball W. **Intramural:** Badminton, baseball M, basketball, cross-country, football (tackle), golf, ice hockey M, racquetball, soccer, softball, squash, table tennis, tennis, volleyball, water polo. **Team name:** Fighting Irish.

Student services. Alcohol/substance abuse counseling, campus ministries, career counseling, student employment services, health services, minority student services, on-campus daycare, personal counseling, placement for graduates, women's services. **Physically disabled:** Services for visually, hearing impaired.

Contact. E-mail: admissions@nd.edu
Phone: (574) 631-7505 Fax: (574) 631-8865
Daniel Saracino, Director of Admissions, University of Notre Dame, 220 Main Building, Notre Dame, IN 46556

University of St. Francis

Fort Wayne, Indiana
www.sf.edu **CB code: 1693**

- Private 4-year university and liberal arts college affiliated with Roman Catholic Church
- Commuter campus in small city
- 1,736 degree-seeking undergraduates: 23% part-time, 70% women, 4% African American, 1% Asian American, 2% Hispanic American, 1% Native American
- 223 degree-seeking graduate students
- 59% of applicants admitted
- SAT or ACT (ACT writing optional) required
- 43% graduate within 6 years

General. Founded in 1890. Regionally accredited. **Degrees:** 140 bachelor's, 124 associate awarded; master's offered. **Location:** 150 miles from Chicago, Detroit, and Cincinnati. **Calendar:** Semester, limited summer session. **Full-time faculty:** 100 total. **Part-time faculty:** 10 total. **Class size:** 62% < 20, 33% 20-39, 4% 40-49, 1% 50-99. **Special facilities:** Planetarium, nature preserve.

Freshman class profile. 1,129 applied, 664 admitted, 319 enrolled.

Mid 50% test scores		**GPA 3.0-3.49:**	32%
SAT verbal:	430-570	**GPA 2.0-2.99:**	33%
SAT math:	450-590	**Rank in top quarter:**	34%
ACT:	18-23	**Rank in top tenth:**	10%
GPA 3.50 or higher:	34%	**Return as sophomores:**	78%

Basis for selection. School achievement record, rank in top half of class, and test scores most important. Additional requirements for health care majors, education majors. Admission procedures may vary among schools within the university. Essay and portfolio recommended. Interview recommended for underprepared applicants. **Homeschooled:** State high school equivalency certificate, letter of recommendation (nonparent) required. Bibliography of books read, extracurricular activities.

High school preparation. 20 units required; 26 recommended. Required and recommended units include English 4, mathematics 2-3, social studies 2-3, history 1, science 2-3 and academic electives 1-4.

2005-2006 Annual costs. Tuition/fees: $17,468. Room/board: $5,610. Books/supplies: $1,000. Personal expenses: $1,100.

2004-2005 Financial aid. Need-based: 280 full-time freshmen applied for aid; 242 were judged to have need; 242 of these received aid. Average need met was 75%. Average scholarship/grant was $9,470; average loan $2,354. 54% of total undergraduate aid awarded as scholarships/grants, 46% as loans/jobs. **Non-need-based:** Awarded to 352 full-time undergraduates, including 115 freshmen. Scholarships awarded for academics, alumni affiliation, art, athletics, music/drama.

Application procedures. Admission: Priority date 8/1; no deadline. $20 fee, may be waived for applicants with need. Application may be submitted online. Admission notification on a rolling basis beginning on or about 8/1. **Financial aid:** Priority date 3/10; no closing date. FAFSA required. Applicants notified on a rolling basis starting 3/1.

Academics. Special study options: Combined bachelor's/graduate degree, cross-registration, double major, dual enrollment of high school students, exchange student, honors, independent study, internships, liberal arts/career combination, teacher certification program. **Credit/placement by examination:** AP, CLEP, SAT, ACT, institutional tests. 16 credit hours maximum toward associate degree, 32 toward bachelor's. **Support services:** Learning center, reduced course load, remedial instruction, study skills assistance, tutoring, writing center.

Majors. Business: Accounting, business admin, human resources. **Communications:** General. **Conservation:** General, environmental studies. **Education:** Art, business, chemistry, elementary, English, health, science, social studies, special. **English:** English lit. **Health:** Clinical lab science, nursing (RN), physician assistant, prepharmacy. **History:** General. **Legal studies:** Prelaw. **Liberal arts:** Arts/sciences. **Philosophy/religion:** Religion. **Psychology:** General. **Public administration:** Social work. **Visual/performing arts:** Art, commercial/advertising art.

Most popular majors. Business/marketing 21%, education 18%, health sciences 21%, liberal arts 7%, visual/performing arts 13%.

Computing on campus. 211 workstations in dormitories, library, computer center, student center. Dormitories wired for high-speed internet access and linked to campus network. Commuter students can connect to campus network. Online course registration, online library, helpline, repair service, wireless network available.

Student life. Freshman orientation: Mandatory, $30 fee. 3-day program during weekend prior to beginning of classes. **Policies:** No alcohol allowed in residence halls, no smoking in campus buildings. Freshmen permitted cars on campus. **Housing:** Guaranteed on-campus for freshmen. Coed dorms, apartments available. $100 fully refundable deposit. Full-time students under 21 not living at home or with adult relatives must live in residence halls. **Activities:** Pep band, choral groups, dance, drama, film society, student government, student newspaper, campus ministry, Educators in Action, student nursing association, peer ministers, Fellowship of Christian Athletes.

Athletics. NAIA. **Intercollegiate:** Baseball M, basketball, cheerleading, cross-country, football (tackle) M, golf, soccer, softball W, tennis W, track and field, volleyball W. **Intramural:** Basketball, bowling, volleyball. **Team name:** Cougars.

Student services. Adult student services, campus ministries, career counseling, student employment services, financial aid counseling, health services, personal counseling, placement for graduates. **Physically disabled:** Services for visually, hearing impaired.

Contact. E-mail: admiss@sf.edu
Phone: (260) 434-3279 Toll-free number: (800) 729-4732
Fax: (260) 434-7590
Ron Schumacher, Vice President, Enrollment Management, University of St. Francis, 2701 Spring Street, Fort Wayne, IN 46808

University of Southern Indiana
Evansville, Indiana
www.usi.edu **CB code: 1335**

- Public 4-year university and liberal arts college
- Commuter campus in small city
- 8,977 degree-seeking undergraduates: 17% part-time, 60% women, 5% African American, 1% Asian American, 1% Hispanic American, 1% international
- 341 degree-seeking graduate students
- 91% of applicants admitted
- SAT or ACT with writing required
- 33% graduate within 6 years

General. Founded in 1965. Regionally accredited. Credit courses offered at various off-campus sites in Evansville and surrounding areas. **Degrees:** 1,151 bachelor's, 159 associate awarded; master's offered. **ROTC:** Army. **Location:** 150 miles from Indianapolis, 100 miles from Louisville, Kentucky. **Calendar:** Semester, limited summer session. **Full-time faculty:** 303 total; 63% have terminal degrees, 9% minority, 49% women. **Part-time faculty:** 316 total; 19% have terminal degrees, 5% minority, 58% women. **Class size:** 38% < 20, 55% 20-39, 3% 40-49, 2% 50-99, 2% >100. **Special facilities:** Restored historic town managed by university.

Freshman class profile. 4,807 applied, 4,356 admitted, 2,148 enrolled.

Mid 50% test scores		**Rank in top quarter:**	25%
SAT verbal:	420-530	**Rank in top tenth:**	7%
SAT math:	420-540	**End year in good standing:**	71%
ACT:	18-23	**Return as sophomores:**	59%
GPA 3.50 or higher:	20%	**Out-of-state:**	4%
GPA 3.0-3.49:	26%	**Live on campus:**	64%
GPA 2.0-2.99:	48%		

Basis for selection. 2.0 GPA for out-of-state applicants. Combined SAT score of 900 (exclusive of Writing) for applicants to health programs. Students accepted at 1 of 3 levels based on academic record and test scores. Placement test administered prior to registration. SAT/ACT used to place students at 1 of 3 levels within institution. **Homeschooled:** Transcript of courses and grades required.

High school preparation. 18 units recommended. Recommended units include English 4, mathematics 4, social studies 2, history 2, science 3, foreign language 2 and academic electives 2. 2 units computer and/or art recommended.

2005-2006 Annual costs. Tuition/fees: $4,379; $10,253 out-of-state. Room/board: $6,368. Books/supplies: $900. Personal expenses: $1,822.

2005-2006 Financial aid. Need-based: 1,772 full-time freshmen applied for aid; 1,217 were judged to have need; 1,096 of these received aid. Average need met was 54%. Average scholarship/grant was $4,506; average loan $2,412. 50% of total undergraduate aid awarded as scholarships/grants, 50% as loans/jobs. **Non-need-based:** Awarded to 1,247 full-time undergraduates, including 382 freshmen. Scholarships awarded for academics, alumni affiliation, art, athletics, job skills, leadership, music/drama, state residency.

Application procedures. Admission: Closing date 8/15 (receipt date). $25 fee, may be waived for applicants with need. Application may be submitted online. Admission notification on a rolling basis beginning on or about 7/1. Applicants accepted through first week of classes, but encouraged to apply by August 15 for fall and January 1 for spring. **Financial aid:** Closing date 3/1. FAFSA, institutional form required. Applicants notified on a rolling basis starting 4/15.

Academics. Special study options: Combined bachelor's/graduate degree, cooperative education, distance learning, double major, dual enrollment of high school students, ESL, honors, independent study, internships, study abroad, teacher certification program. **Credit/placement by examination:** AP, CLEP, SAT, ACT, institutional tests. 96 credit hours maximum toward bachelor's degree. **Support services:** Learning center, reduced course load, remedial instruction, study skills assistance, tutoring, writing center.

Majors. Biology: General, biophysics. **Business:** General, accounting, business admin, entrepreneurial studies, finance, marketing, office management. **Communications:** Advertising, journalism, media studies, radio/tv. **Computer sciences:** General, data processing. **Education:** Business, early childhood, elementary, physical. **Engineering:** General. **English:** English lit. **Foreign languages:** French, German, Spanish. **Health:** Dental hygiene, nursing (RN). **History:** General. **Interdisciplinary:** Biological/physical sciences. **Liberal arts:** Arts/sciences. **Math:** General. **Parks/recreation:** Exercise sciences. **Philosophy/religion:** Philosophy. **Physical sciences:** Chemistry, geology. **Psychology:** General. **Public administration:** Social work. **Social sciences:** General, economics, international relations, political science, sociology. **Visual/performing arts:** Art, dramatic.

Most popular majors. Business/marketing 23%, communications/journalism 11%, education 15%, health sciences 14%, psychology 6%, social sciences 7%.

Computing on campus. 161 workstations in dormitories, library, computer center, student center. Dormitories linked to campus network. Commuter students can connect to campus network. Online course registration, helpline, wireless network available.

Student life. Freshman orientation: Mandatory, $62 fee. Preregistration for classes offered. 2-day program (parent participation). Lunch and dinner included first day. **Policies:** Freshmen permitted cars on campus. **Housing:** Coed dorms, special housing for disabled, apartments, fraternity/sorority housing, substance-free housing available. $200 fully refundable deposit, deadline 3/1. **Activities:** Jazz band, choral groups, dance, drama, literary magazine, radio station, student government, student newspaper, Black Student Union, International Student Club, Habitat for Humanity, Kappa Chi (Christian Service Fraternity), Baptist Student Ministry, Newman Catholic Student Organization, Collegiate Democrats, Collegiate Republicans, campus ministry.

Athletics. NCAA. **Intercollegiate:** Baseball M, basketball, cheerleading, cross-country, golf, soccer, softball W, tennis, track and field, volleyball W. **Intramural:** Badminton, basketball, bowling, cross-country, football (tackle), golf, soccer M, softball, table tennis, tennis, volleyball. **Team name:** Screaming Eagles.

Student services. Adult student services, campus ministries, career counseling, student employment services, financial aid counseling, health services, minority student services, on-campus daycare, personal counseling, placement for graduates, veterans' counselor. **Physically disabled:** Services for visually, speech, hearing impaired.

Contact. E-mail: enroll@usi.edu
Phone: (812) 464-1765 Toll-free number: (800) 467-1965
Fax: (812) 465-7154
Eric Otto, Director of Admission, University of Southern Indiana, 8600 University Boulevard, Evansville, IN 47712

Valparaiso University
Valparaiso, Indiana **CB member**
www.valpo.edu **CB code: 1874**

- Private 4-year university affiliated with Lutheran Church
- Residential campus in large town
- 2,918 degree-seeking undergraduates: 4% part-time, 52% women, 4% African American, 2% Asian American, 3% Hispanic American, 2% international
- 868 degree-seeking graduate students
- 83% of applicants admitted
- SAT or ACT with writing, application essay required
- 71% graduate within 6 years; 25% enter graduate study

General. Founded in 1859. Regionally accredited. **Degrees:** 654 bachelor's, 2 associate awarded; master's, first professional offered. **ROTC:** Air Force. **Location:** 55 miles from Chicago. **Calendar:** Semester, limited summer session. **Full-time faculty:** 243 total; 89% have terminal degrees, 5% minority, 35% women. **Part-time faculty:** 119 total; 58% have terminal degrees, 5% minority, 50% women. **Class size:** 52% < 20, 42% 20-39, 2% 40-49, 3% 50-99, less than 1% >100. **Special facilities:** Electron microscope, observatory, storm chasing equipment, weather station, Doppler Radar facility, planetarium, center for learning and information resources, virtual nursing learning center, scientific visualization laboratory.

Freshman class profile. 3,532 applied, 2,931 admitted, 673 enrolled.

Mid 50% test scores		Rank in top tenth:	34%
SAT verbal:	520-630	End year in good standing:	90%
SAT math:	520-640	Return as sophomores:	84%
ACT:	23-28	Out-of-state:	67%
GPA 3.50 or higher:	47%	Live on campus:	90%
GPA 3.0-3.49:	28%	International:	1%
GPA 2.0-2.99:	25%	Fraternities:	26%
Rank in top quarter:	60%	Sororities:	25%

Basis for selection. High school record most important. Test scores next in importance, followed by recommendations and activities. Nature of high school program considered. Interview recommended. Audition required of music majors. Portfolio recommended for art majors. **Homeschooled:** Transcript of courses and grades required. SAT/ACT scores directly from testing center. Specify primary educator. Course description list or reading list required. **Learning Disabled:** Student should submit suitable documentation to the Disability Support Services Office following admission into the University in order to determine eligibility of services.

High school preparation. Required and recommended units include English 4, mathematics 3-4, social studies 3, science 2-3 (laboratory 2-3), foreign language 2 and academic electives 3.

2006-2007 Annual costs. Tuition/fees: $24,000. College of Engineering sophomores, juniors, and seniors: engineering fee - $690; Nursing lab and test fee: beginning of sophomore year - $430; Nursing lab and test fee: beginning of sophomore year: $430; General fee for part-time students: $130. Room/board: $6,640. Books/supplies: $1,000. Personal expenses: $870.

2005-2006 Financial aid. Need-based: 599 full-time freshmen applied for aid; 482 were judged to have need; 482 of these received aid. Average need met was 92%. Average scholarship/grant was $13,799; average loan $4,660. 73% of total undergraduate aid awarded as scholarships/grants, 27% as loans/jobs. **Non-need-based:** Awarded to 1,065 full-time undergraduates, including 258 freshmen. Scholarships awarded for academics, alumni affiliation, art, athletics, leadership, music/drama, religious affiliation, ROTC. **Additional information:** Financial assistance based on need, academic record, talent, etc., available through University.

Application procedures. Admission: Priority date 1/15; deadline 8/15 (receipt date). $30 fee, may be waived for applicants with need. Application may be submitted online. Admission notification on a rolling basis beginning on or about 12/1. Must reply by May 1 or within 4 week(s) if notified thereafter. **Financial aid:** Priority date 3/1; no closing date. FAFSA required. Applicants notified on a rolling basis starting 3/1.

Academics. Special study options: Accelerated study, combined bachelor's/graduate degree, cooperative education, cross-registration, distance learning, double major, dual enrollment of high school students, ESL, exchange student, honors, independent study, internships, liberal arts/career combination, student-designed major, study abroad, teacher certification program, United Nations semester, urban semester, Washington semester. **Credit/placement by examination:** AP, CLEP, IB, institutional tests. **Support services:** Learning center, reduced course load, study skills assistance, tutoring, writing center.

Honors college/program. Approximately 80 students enroll per year. Must demonstrate academic excellence in high school, intellectual curiosity, and leadership skills. Program integrates history, literature, philosophy, religion, and art.

Majors. Area/ethnic studies: American, East Asian. **Biology:** General, biochemistry. **Business:** Accounting, actuarial science, finance, international, management science, marketing. **Communications:** Journalism, media studies, organizational, public relations, radio/tv. **Computer sciences:** Computer science. **Conservation:** Environmental science. **Education:** Art, biology, chemistry, drama/dance, elementary, English, foreign languages, French, geography, German, history, mathematics, middle, music, physical, physics, psychology, science, secondary, social science, Spanish. **Engineering:** Civil, computer, electrical, mechanical. **English:** Creative writing, English lit, technical writing. **Foreign languages:** Classics, French, German, Spanish. **Health:** Nursing (RN). **History:** General. **Math:** General. **Parks/recreation:** Exercise sciences, health/fitness, sports admin. **Philosophy/religion:** Philosophy. **Physical sciences:** Atmospheric science, chemistry, geology, physics. **Psychology:** General. **Public administration:** Social work. **Social sciences:** Criminology, economics, geography, international economics, international relations, political science, sociology. **Theology:** Theology, youth ministry. **Visual/performing arts:** Art, dramatic, music management, music performance, music theory/composition, piano/organ, voice/opera.

Most popular majors. Business/marketing 12%, education 9%, engineering/engineering technologies 9%, health sciences 7%, physical sciences 7%, social sciences 10%, visual/performing arts 7%.

Computing on campus. 820 workstations in dormitories, library, computer center, student center. Dormitories wired for high-speed internet access and linked to campus network. Commuter students can connect to campus network. Online course registration, helpline, student web hosting, wireless network available.

Student life. Freshman orientation: Available, $80 fee. Preregistration for classes offered. Overnight program held in June. **Housing:** Guaranteed on-campus for all undergraduates. Coed dorms, single-sex dorms, apartments, fraternity/sorority housing, substance-free housing available. $100 fully refundable deposit, deadline 5/1. Residence hall for German language students. **Activities:** Bands, choral groups, dance, drama, film society, literary magazine, music ensembles, musical theater, radio station, student government, student newspaper, symphony orchestra, Chapel Ministry, Alpha Phi Omega, InterVarsity Christian Fellowship, St. Teresa of Avila, Black Student Organization, International Student Association, Habitat for Humanity, Asian American Association, Latinos in Valparaiso for Excellence, College Democrats.

Athletics. NCAA. **Intercollegiate:** Baseball M, basketball, cross-country, diving, football (tackle) M, soccer, softball W, swimming, tennis, track and field, volleyball W. **Intramural:** Badminton, basketball, bowling, football (tackle) M, golf, racquetball, soccer, softball, swimming, table tennis, tennis, volleyball. **Team name:** Crusaders.

Student services. Adult student services, alcohol/substance abuse counseling, campus ministries, career counseling, student employment services, financial aid counseling, health services, legal services, minority student services, personal counseling, placement for graduates. **Physically disabled:** Services for visually impaired.

Contact. E-mail: undergrad.admissions@valpo.edu
Phone: (219) 464-5011 Toll-free number: (888) 468-2576
Fax: (219) 464-6898
Joyce Lantz, Director of Admission, Valparaiso University, Kretzmann Hall, 1700 Chapel Drive, Valparaiso, IN 46383-6493

Wabash College

Crawfordsville, Indiana — **CB member**
www.wabash.edu — **CB code: 1895**

- Private 4-year liberal arts college for men
- Residential campus in large town
- 869 degree-seeking undergraduates: 6% African American, 3% Asian American, 4% Hispanic American, 4% international
- 51% of applicants admitted
- SAT or ACT (ACT writing optional), application essay required
- 70% graduate within 6 years; 36% enter graduate study

General. Founded in 1832. Regionally accredited. **Degrees:** 163 bachelor's awarded. **ROTC:** Army. **Location:** 45 miles from Indianapolis. **Calendar:** Semester. **Full-time faculty:** 87 total; 97% have terminal degrees, 6% minority, 20% women. **Part-time faculty:** 2 total; 50% have terminal degrees, 50% women. **Class size:** 74% < 20, 19% 20-39, 2% 40-49, less than 1% 50-99. **Special facilities:** 180-acre biology field station, Wabash Center for Teaching and Learning in Theology and Religion, qualitative and quantitative skills center, electron microscope, parallel computer, Center of Academic Enrichment, Center of Inquiry in the Liberal Arts, Ramsay Archival Center.

Freshman class profile. 1,358 applied, 691 admitted, 249 enrolled.

Mid 50% test scores		Rank in top tenth:	29%
SAT verbal:	530-650	End year in good standing:	92%
SAT math:	550-660	Return as sophomores:	89%
ACT:	23-28	Out-of-state:	29%
GPA 3.50 or higher:	60%	Live on campus:	100%
GPA 3.0-3.49:	30%	International:	3%
GPA 2.0-2.99:	10%	Fraternities:	65%
Rank in top quarter:	69%		

Basis for selection. Class rank, school achievement, recommendation, essay and test scores important. Interview recommended. Character and personal qualities considered. TOEFL required of non-native speakers of English. **Homeschooled:** Case-by-case basis. **Learning Disabled:** All students considered on a case-by-case basis.

High school preparation. 17 units recommended. Recommended units include English 4, mathematics 4, social studies 2, science 2 (laboratory 2), foreign language 2 and academic electives 3.

2006-2007 Annual costs. Tuition/fees: $24,792. Room/board: $7,776. Books/supplies: $1,000. Personal expenses: $1,000.

2004-2005 Financial aid. Need-based: 217 full-time freshmen applied for aid; 179 were judged to have need; 179 of these received aid. Average need met was 100%. Average scholarship/grant was $17,396; average loan $1,506. 83% of total undergraduate aid awarded as scholarships/grants, 17% as loans/jobs. **Non-need-based:** Awarded to 325 full-time undergraduates, including 96 freshmen. Scholarships awarded for academics, art, leadership, minority status, music/drama, state residency. **Additional information:** Unlimited President's Scholarships based on class rank, SAT scores. Extensive merit awards including Leadership Scholarships, Fine Arts Fellowships, Lilly Awards.

Application procedures. Admission: Priority date 12/15; no deadline. $30 fee, may be waived for applicants with need. Application may be submitted online. Admission notification on a rolling basis beginning on or about 12/15. Must reply by May 1 or within 2 week(s) if notified thereafter. **Financial aid:** Priority date 2/15, closing date 3/1. FAFSA, CSS PROFILE required. Applicants notified by 4/1; must reply by 5/1 or within 2 week(s) of notification.

Academics. Special study options: Combined bachelor's/graduate degree, double major, independent study, internships, liberal arts/career combination, New York semester, semester at sea, student-designed major, study abroad, teacher certification program, United Nations semester, urban semester, Washington semester. Cooperative law program with Columbia University (NY), International and Domestic Study Program of Great Lakes Colleges Association, 3-2 engineering program with Columbia University and Washington University. **Credit/placement by examination:** AP, CLEP, institutional tests. AP credit not given solely based on AP exam scores. Scores used in conjunction with in-house exams and subsequent coursework. **Support services:** Learning center, pre-admission summer program, study skills assistance, tutoring, writing center.

Majors. Biology: General. **English:** Speech/rhetoric. **Foreign languages:** Ancient Greek, classics, French, German, Latin, Spanish. **History:** General. **Liberal arts:** Arts/sciences. **Math:** General. **Philosophy/religion:** Philosophy, religion. **Physical sciences:** Chemistry, physics. **Psychology:** General. **Social sciences:** Economics, political science. **Visual/performing arts:** Art, dramatic.

Most popular majors. Biology 8%, English 17%, foreign language 8%, history 14%, mathematics 7%, philosophy/religious studies 10%, physical sciences 7%, psychology 11%, social sciences 16%.

Computing on campus. 330 workstations in dormitories, library, computer center, student center. Dormitories wired for high-speed internet access and linked to campus network. Commuter students can connect to campus network. Online library, helpline, repair service, student web hosting, wireless network available.

Student life. Freshman orientation: Mandatory. Preregistration for classes offered. 5-day program orients students to library and computer resources, the Gentleman's Rule, and includes all class members in community service projects. **Policies:** The Gentleman's Rule is the College's only rule. Freshmen permitted cars on campus. **Housing:** Guaranteed on-campus for all undergraduates. Apartments, fraternity/sorority housing, substance-free housing available. $150 nonrefundable deposit, deadline 7/1. Pets allowed in dorm rooms. Limited wheelchair accessibility available. **Activities:** Bands, choral groups, drama, film society, literary magazine, music ensembles, musical theater, radio station, student government, student newspaper, symphony orchestra, Malcolm X Institute for Black Studies, political groups, Newman Center, Alpha Phi Omega, Fellowship of Christian Athletes, Muslim student association, Wabash Christian Fellowship, model U.N., Pre-Law Society, moot court competition, Sphinx Club.

Athletics. NCAA. **Intercollegiate:** Baseball M, basketball M, cross-country M, diving M, football (tackle) M, golf M, soccer M, swimming M, tennis M, track and field M, wrestling M. **Intramural:** Badminton M, basketball M, bowling M, cross-country M, diving M, football (non-tackle) M, golf M, handball M, racquetball M, soccer M, softball M, swimming M, table tennis M, tennis M, track and field M, volleyball M, wrestling M. **Team name:** Little Giants.

Student services. Alcohol/substance abuse counseling, campus ministries, career counseling, student employment services, financial aid counseling, health services, minority student services, personal counseling, placement for graduates. **Physically disabled:** Services for visually impaired.

Contact. E-mail: admissions@wabash.edu
Phone: (765) 361-6225 Toll-free number: (800) 345-5385
Fax: (765) 361-6437
Steven Klein, Dean of Admissions, Wabash College, PO Box 352, Crawfordsville, IN 47933

Iowa

Allen College

Waterloo, Iowa
www.allencollege.edu **CB code: 3610**

- Private 4-year health science and nursing college
- Commuter campus in small city
- 374 degree-seeking undergraduates: 15% part-time, 94% women, 1% African American, 1% Asian American, 1% Hispanic American
- 30 degree-seeking graduate students
- 73% of applicants admitted
- SAT or ACT required
- 75% graduate within 6 years; 5% enter graduate study

General. Regionally accredited. Students take general education courses at University of Northern Iowa. **Degrees:** 45 bachelor's, 11 associate awarded; master's offered. **ROTC:** Army. **Calendar:** Semester, limited summer session. **Full-time faculty:** 16 total; 19% have terminal degrees, 6% minority, 100% women. **Part-time faculty:** 10 total; 100% women. **Class size:** 39% < 20, 37% 20-39, 7% 40-49, 17% 50-99.

Freshman class profile. 51 applied, 37 admitted, 18 enrolled.

Mid 50% test scores		**Rank in top tenth:**	17%
ACT:	19-23	**End year in good standing:**	95%
GPA 3.50 or higher:	67%	**Return as sophomores:**	84%
GPA 3.0-3.49:	33%	**Live on campus:**	33%
Rank in top quarter:	50%		

Basis for selection. Secondary school record, class rank, test scores important; recommendations, essay considered, when required. Competitive admission to all programs. Admission requirements are minimum standards. Meeting the requirements does not guarantee admission to any program. TOEFL required of applicants who are not native speakers of English. **Homeschooled:** Complete ACT.

High school preparation. 4 units required. Required units include English 4, mathematics 3, social studies 3, science 3 (laboratory 2).

2006-2007 Annual costs. Tuition/fees (projected): $13,928. Room/board: $5,712. Books/supplies: $891. Personal expenses: $2,724.

2004-2005 Financial aid. Need-based: 33 full-time freshmen applied for aid; 24 were judged to have need; 24 of these received aid. Average need met was 58%. Average scholarship/grant was $3,113; average loan $1,849. 43% of total undergraduate aid awarded as scholarships/grants, 57% as loans/jobs. **Non-need-based:** Awarded to 29 full-time undergraduates, including 6 freshmen. Scholarships awarded for academics, leadership, minority status, ROTC.

Application procedures. Admission: Closing date 3/1 (receipt date). $50 fee, may be waived for applicants with need. Application may be submitted online. Admission notification on a rolling basis. Must reply by May 1 or within 4 week(s) if notified thereafter. Accepted applicants must reply within 30 days of notification. **Financial aid:** Priority date 6/1; no closing date. FAFSA, institutional form required. Applicants notified on a rolling basis starting 4/1; must reply within 2 week(s) of notification.

Academics. Special study options: Accelerated study, cooperative education, distance learning, external degree, honors, independent study, internships, liberal arts/career combination. **Credit/placement by examination:** AP, CLEP, IB. **Support services:** Learning center, study skills assistance, tutoring, writing center.

Majors. Health: Nursing (RN).

Computing on campus. 26 workstations in dormitories, library, computer center. Online library, helpline available.

Student life. Freshman orientation: Mandatory. Includes registration, assessment testing, and completion of mandatory health career training. **Policies:** Freshmen permitted cars on campus. **Housing:** Coed dorms, single-sex dorms, special housing for disabled, apartments, cooperative housing, substance-free housing available. $200 nonrefundable deposit. On-campus suite housing available and dorm-style housing is offered at cooperating institutions. **Activities:** Student government, student newspaper.

Student services. Alcohol/substance abuse counseling, campus ministries, career counseling, financial aid counseling, health services, on-campus daycare, personal counseling, placement for graduates, women's services. **Physically disabled:** Services for visually, speech, hearing impaired.

Contact. E-mail: AllenCollegeAdmissions@ihs.org
Phone: (319) 226-2000 Fax: (319) 226-2051
Holly Risetter, Admissions Counselor, Allen College, 1825 Logan Avenue, Waterloo, IA 50703

Ashford University

Clinton, Iowa
www.ashford.edu **CB code: 6418**

- For-profit 4-year university affiliated with Roman Catholic Church
- Commuter campus in large town
- 376 degree-seeking undergraduates
- 72% of applicants admitted
- SAT or ACT (ACT writing optional) required

General. Founded in 1918. Regionally accredited. **Degrees:** 91 bachelor's, 4 associate awarded; master's offered. **Location:** 35 miles from Davenport, 138 miles from Chicago. **Calendar:** Differs by program, limited summer session. **Full-time faculty:** 22 total. **Part-time faculty:** 20 total. **Class size:** 71% < 20, 29% 20-39. **Special facilities:** Restored prairie land adjacent to campus.

Freshman class profile. 278 applied, 200 admitted, 63 enrolled.

Mid 50% test scores		**Out-of-state:**	40%
ACT:	15-21	**Live on campus:**	60%

Basis for selection. High school record, GPA, class rank, test scores all considered. Applicants not meeting selection criteria may be admitted conditionally. Interview required for teacher education majors. Audition recommended for fine arts. Portfolio recommended for art majors. Essay recommended for academically weak applicants.

High school preparation. 20 units recommended. Recommended units include English 4, mathematics 3, social studies 3, history 3, science 3 (laboratory 2) and foreign language 2.

2006-2007 Annual costs. Tuition/fees: $13,920. Books/supplies: $600. Personal expenses: $600.

2005-2006 Financial aid. Non-need-based: Scholarships awarded for academics, alumni affiliation, art, athletics, leadership, minority status, music/drama, religious affiliation.

Application procedures. Admission: Priority date 5/1; no deadline. $20 fee, may be waived for applicants with need. Application may be submitted online. Admission notification on a rolling basis beginning on or about 9/1. **Financial aid:** Priority date 3/1, closing date 8/1. FAFSA required. Applicants notified on a rolling basis starting 3/15; must reply within 3 week(s) of notification.

Academics. Liberal arts program has interdisciplinary approach. Freshmen take a freshman experience course that teaches them effective study habits, time management, adjustment to college, and an introduction to Franciscanism. **Special study options:** Distance learning, double major, ESL, honors, independent study, internships, student-designed major, study abroad, teacher certification program. Off campus study, senior capstone or culminating academic experience, advanced placement credit, student designed major summer school. **Credit/placement by examination:** CLEP, institutional tests. 32 credit hours maximum toward associate degree, 32 toward bachelor's. **Support services:** Learning center, reduced course load, remedial instruction, tutoring.

Majors. Biology: General. **Business:** General, accounting, business admin, communications, finance, human resources, marketing. **Communications:** General. **Computer sciences:** General. **Conservation:** Environmental studies. **Education:** Biology, chemistry, early childhood, elementary, English, history, mathematics, middle, music, reading, science, secondary, social science, social studies. **Health:** Cytotechnology, health care admin, premedicine. **Interdisciplinary:** Math/computer science. **Legal studies:** Prelaw. **Liberal arts:** Arts/sciences. **Philosophy/religion:** Religion. **Psychology:** General. **Social sciences:** General. **Visual/performing arts:** Graphic design, studio arts.

Computing on campus. 109 workstations in dormitories, library, computer center. Dormitories wired for high-speed internet access and linked to campus network. Helpline, repair service available.

Student life. Freshman orientation: Mandatory. Preregistration for classes offered. 2-day orientation program held in the summer prior to beginning of fall classes. **Policies:** Freshmen permitted cars on campus. **Housing:** Guaranteed on-campus for all undergraduates. Coed dorms available. $125 deposit. **Activities:** Choral groups, music ensembles, student government, student newspaper, Christian Fellowship club, international club, Campus Ministry, Hispanic American Leadership Organization, Circle K, Black Student Union, State Iowa Education Association.

Athletics. NAIA. **Intercollegiate:** Baseball M, basketball, cross-country, golf M, soccer, softball W, track and field, volleyball W. **Intramural:** Basketball, bowling, football (non-tackle), swimming, volleyball. **Team name:** Saints.

Student services. Adult student services, campus ministries, career counseling, student employment services, financial aid counseling, minority student services, on-campus daycare, placement for graduates.

Contact. E-mail: admissns@ashford.edu
Phone: (563) 242-4153 Toll-free number: (800) 242-4153
Fax: (563) 243-6102
Waunita Sullivan, Director of Enrollment, Ashford University, 400 North Bluff Boulevard, Clinton, IA 52733-2967

Briar Cliff University
Sioux City, Iowa
www.briarcliff.edu **CB code: 6046**

- Private 4-year liberal arts college affiliated with Roman Catholic Church
- Residential campus in small city
- 1,081 degree-seeking undergraduates: 10% part-time, 61% women, 2% African American, 2% Asian American, 4% Hispanic American, 1% Native American
- 29 degree-seeking graduate students
- 76% of applicants admitted
- ACT (writing optional) required
- 52% graduate within 6 years

General. Founded in 1930. Regionally accredited. Academic calendar consists of three 10-week terms (Sept-May), with two 5-week summer sessions also available, giving semester hours of credit. **Degrees:** 177 bachelor's awarded; master's offered. **Location:** 90 miles from Omaha, Nebraska. **Calendar:** Trimester, limited summer session. **Full-time faculty:** 56 total; 57% have terminal degrees, 2% minority, 52% women. **Part-time faculty:** 40 total; 18% have terminal degrees, 58% women. **Class size:** 62% < 20, 34% 20-39, 3% 40-49, 1% 50-99. **Special facilities:** Prairie nature preserve, human anatomy/cadaver laboratory, integrated media lab, nursing simulation lab.

Freshman class profile. 1,275 applied, 971 admitted, 251 enrolled.

Mid 50% test scores		**Rank in top quarter:**	36%
SAT verbal:	420-560	**Rank in top tenth:**	15%
SAT math:	390-650	**End year in good standing:**	82%
ACT:	19-24	**Return as sophomores:**	72%
GPA 3.50 or higher:	38%	**Out-of-state:**	56%
GPA 3.0-3.49:	29%	**Live on campus:**	92%
GPA 2.0-2.99:	29%		

Basis for selection. GPA of 2.0 and minimum ACT 18 required for full acceptance. Students not meeting requirement may be accepted conditionally or may appeal admission decision if not accepted. Interview and essay recommended. **Homeschooled:** A transcript of high school work can be obtained from the school district where the student resides full time. **Learning Disabled:** Students should submit official documentation directly to Student Support Services office, which determines how the university can assist the student.

High school preparation. 16 units recommended. Recommended units include English 4, mathematics 3, social studies 3, science 3, foreign language 2 and academic electives 1.

2005-2006 Annual costs. Tuition/fees: $17,985. Room/board: $5,565. Books/supplies: $825. Personal expenses: $1,935.

2005-2006 Financial aid. Need-based: 251 full-time freshmen applied for aid; 203 were judged to have need; 203 of these received aid. Average need met was 98%. Average scholarship/grant was $9,177; average loan $3,150. 38% of total undergraduate aid awarded as scholarships/grants, 62% as loans/jobs. **Non-need-based:** Awarded to 2,658 full-time undergraduates, including 704 freshmen. Scholarships awarded for academics, alumni affiliation, art, athletics, leadership, music/drama, religious affiliation, state residency. **Additional information:** 97% of Briar Cliff's student body receive some sort of aid.

Application procedures. Admission: Priority date 4/1; no deadline. $20 fee, may be waived for applicants with need. Application may be submitted online. Admission notification on a rolling basis beginning on or about 6/1. **Financial aid:** Priority date 3/15; no closing date. FAFSA required. Applicants notified on a rolling basis starting 3/15; must reply by 5/1 or within 2 week(s) of notification.

Academics. Special study options: Accelerated study, cross-registration, double major, honors, independent study, internships, liberal arts/career combination, student-designed major, study abroad, teacher certification program, urban semester, Washington semester, weekend college. Radiologic technology 1-2-1 program, medical technology 3-1 program. **Credit/placement by examination:** AP, CLEP, ACT, institutional tests. 45 credit hours maximum toward bachelor's degree. Examinations must be taken before student enters last 30 hours of study. **Support services:** Learning center, pre-admission summer program, reduced course load, remedial instruction, study skills assistance, tutoring, writing center.

Majors. Biology: General. **Business:** Accounting, business admin, human resources, management information systems. **Communications:** Digital media, media studies. **Communications technology:** Graphics. **Computer sciences:** General, computer science. **Conservation:** Environmental science. **Education:** General, art, biology, chemistry, elementary, English, history, mathematics, music, physical, reading, science, secondary, social science. **English:** Composition, creative writing, English lit. **Foreign languages:** Spanish. **Health:** Clinical lab science, medical radiologic technology/radiation therapy, nursing (RN). **History:** General. **Interdisciplinary:** Biological/physical sciences. **Legal studies:** Prelaw. **Math:** General. **Parks/recreation:** Exercise sciences, health/fitness, sports admin. **Philosophy/religion:** Religion. **Physical sciences:** Chemistry. **Protective services:** Law enforcement admin. **Psychology:** General. **Public administration:** Social work. **Social sciences:** Political science, sociology. **Theology:** Theology. **Visual/performing arts:** Art, dramatic, graphic design.

Most popular majors. Biology 6%, business/marketing 27%, education 14%, health sciences 12%, parks/recreation 6%, visual/performing arts 10%.

Computing on campus. 121 workstations in dormitories, library, computer center, student center. Dormitories wired for high-speed internet access and linked to campus network. Commuter students can connect to campus network. Online library, helpline, repair service, student web hosting, wireless network available.

Student life. Freshman orientation: Mandatory, $75 fee. Preregistration for classes offered. Held weekends during the summer for students and parents. Includes placement testing, advising, and programs with staff and student leaders that introduce campus, campus life and student services. Parents are oriented to the campus, meet with financial aid advisors, and are introduced to senior administrators and staff who introduce services, programs and policies. **Policies:** Freshmen permitted cars on campus. **Housing:** Guaranteed on-campus for freshmen. Coed dorms available. $150 deposit. **Activities:** Choral groups, dance, drama, literary magazine, music ensembles, musical theater, opera, radio station, student government, student newspaper, Best Buddies, BCCares, Champions of Characters Council of Athletes, College Democrats, College Republicans, criminal justice club, departmental clubs, ethnic relations club, mentors in violence prevention, student government association.

Athletics. NAIA. **Intercollegiate:** Baseball M, basketball, cheerleading M, cross-country, football (tackle) M, golf, soccer, softball W, tennis W, track and field, volleyball W, wrestling M. **Intramural:** Badminton, basketball, bowling, cross-country, football (non-tackle) M, golf, handball, racquetball, soccer, softball, table tennis, tennis, track and field, volleyball. **Team name:** Chargers.

Student services. Campus ministries, career counseling, services for economically disadvantaged, student employment services, financial aid counseling, health services, personal counseling, placement for graduates. **Physically disabled:** Services for visually impaired.

Contact. E-mail: admissions@briarcliff.edu
Phone: (712) 279-5200 Toll-free number: (800) 662-3303 ext. 5200
Fax: (712) 279-1632
Sharisue Wilcoxon, Vice President for Enrollment Management, Briar Cliff University, 3303 Rebecca Street, Sioux City, IA 51104-2100

Buena Vista University

Storm Lake, Iowa
www.bvu.edu **CB code: 6047**

- Private 4-year liberal arts college affiliated with Presbyterian Church (USA)
- Residential campus in large town
- 1,198 degree-seeking undergraduates: 52% women, 3% African American, 2% Asian American, 2% Hispanic American
- 64 degree-seeking graduate students
- 83% of applicants admitted
- SAT or ACT (ACT writing optional) required
- 57% graduate within 6 years; 14% enter graduate study

General. Founded in 1891. Regionally accredited. 15 branch campuses throughout Iowa provide educational opportunities for nontraditional students. **Degrees:** 871 bachelor's awarded; master's offered. **Location:** 150 miles from Des Moines, 80 miles from Sioux City. **Calendar:** 4-1-4, limited summer session. **Full-time faculty:** 81 total; 69% have terminal degrees, 4% minority, 44% women. **Part-time faculty:** 40 total; 5% have terminal degrees, 2% minority, 50% women. **Class size:** 70% < 20, 28% 20-39, less than 1% 40-49, less than 1% 50-99. **Special facilities:** Multimedia production facilities, underground buildings, information technology center, digitally-controlled acoustic music practice rooms, wireless technology.

Freshman class profile. 1,183 applied, 984 admitted, 287 enrolled.

Mid 50% test scores		**Rank in top quarter:**	38%
ACT:	19-25	**Rank in top tenth:**	16%
GPA 3.50 or higher:	42%	**Return as sophomores:**	76%
GPA 3.0-3.49:	31%	**Out-of-state:**	23%
GPA 2.0-2.99:	27%	**Live on campus:**	96%

Basis for selection. High school GPA and curriculum, rank in class, standardized test scores, interview, school and community activities important. Essay recommended.

High school preparation. College-preparatory program recommended. 15 units required. Required and recommended units include English 4, mathematics 4, social studies 2, history 2, science 2-4 and foreign language 2. One unit computer science also recommended.

2005-2006 Annual costs. Tuition/fees: $21,688. Room/board: $6,054. Books/supplies: $500. Personal expenses: $1,000.

2005-2006 Financial aid. Need-based: 282 full-time freshmen applied for aid; 265 were judged to have need; 265 of these received aid. Average need met was 90%. Average scholarship/grant was $7,463; average loan $4,149. 68% of total undergraduate aid awarded as scholarships/grants, 32% as loans/jobs. **Non-need-based:** Awarded to 874 full-time undergraduates, including 263 freshmen. Scholarships awarded for academics, art, leadership, minority status, music/drama, religious affiliation, state residency. **Additional information:** Portfolio required of art scholarship applicants, audition required of music and drama scholarship applicants.

Application procedures. Admission: No deadline. $25 fee, may be waived for applicants with need. Application may be submitted online. Admission notification on a rolling basis. **Financial aid:** Priority date 6/1; no closing date. FAFSA required. Applicants notified on a rolling basis starting 2/20; must reply by 5/1 or within 2 week(s) of notification.

Academics. Students must earn credit by attending the Academic and Cultural Events Series, featuring lectures by national and international leaders and performances by world-famous classical performing groups and artists. **Special study options:** Combined bachelor's/graduate degree, distance learning, double major, dual enrollment of high school students, ESL, exchange student, honors, independent study, internships, liberal arts/career combination, student-designed major, study abroad, teacher certification program, Washington semester. Rollins Fellows (competitive international internships). **Credit/placement by examination:** AP, CLEP, IB. 20 credit hours maximum toward bachelor's degree. **Support services:** Learning center, reduced course load, remedial instruction, study skills assistance, tutoring, writing center.

Majors. Biology: General. **Business:** Accounting, banking/financial services, entrepreneurial studies, international, management information systems, managerial economics, marketing. **Communications:** General, media studies, organizational. **Computer sciences:** Computer science. **Education:** Art, biology, business, chemistry, computer, elementary, English, history, mathematics, multi-level teacher, music, physical, physics, reading, science, secondary, social science, Spanish, special, speech. **English:** English lit. **Foreign languages:** Spanish. **Health:** Athletic training, premedicine. **History:** General. **Interdisciplinary:** Biological/physical sciences. **Math:** General. **Parks/recreation:** Exercise sciences, sports admin. **Personal/culinary services:** Embalming. **Physical sciences:** Chemistry, physics. **Protective services:** Criminal justice. **Psychology:** General. **Public administration:** General, social work. **Social sciences:** General, political science, sociology. **Visual/performing arts:** Art, arts management, commercial/advertising art, music performance, theater history.

Most popular majors. Business/marketing 29%, education 21%, interdisciplinary studies 13%, psychology 13%.

Computing on campus. 400 workstations in dormitories, library, computer center, student center. Dormitories wired for high-speed internet access and linked to campus network. Commuter students can connect to campus network. Online course registration, online library, helpline, repair service, wireless network available.

Student life. Freshman orientation: Mandatory. Preregistration for classes offered. 2-day orientation offered during summer. **Policies:** Freshmen permitted cars on campus. **Housing:** Guaranteed on-campus for all undergraduates. Coed dorms, single-sex dorms, apartments, substance-free housing available. $150 deposit. **Activities:** Bands, choral groups, drama, music ensembles, musical theater, radio station, student government, student newspaper, symphony orchestra, TV station, Circle-K, Students Concerned about Tomorrow's Environment, intervarsity multicultural club, international club, Fellowship of Christian Athletes, College Democrats, College Republicans, Reshaping our campus community (ROCC).

Athletics. NCAA. **Intercollegiate:** Baseball M, basketball, cross-country, football (tackle) M, golf, soccer, softball W, tennis, track and field, volleyball W, wrestling M. **Intramural:** Basketball, football (non-tackle) M, handball, racquetball, soccer, softball, swimming, table tennis, volleyball. **Team name:** Beavers.

Student services. Adult student services, alcohol/substance abuse counseling, campus ministries, career counseling, student employment services, financial aid counseling, health services, minority student services, personal counseling, placement for graduates, veterans' counselor. **Physically disabled:** Services for visually, speech, hearing impaired.

Contact. E-mail: admissions@bvu.edu
Phone: (712) 749-2235 Toll-free number: (800) 383-9600
Fax: (712) 749-2037
Chris Coons, Director of Admissions, Buena Vista University, 610 West Fourth Street, Storm Lake, IA 50588

Central College

Pella, Iowa **CB member**
www.central.edu **CB code: 6087**

- Private 4-year liberal arts college affiliated with Reformed Church in America
- Residential campus in large town
- 1,502 degree-seeking undergraduates: 1% part-time, 54% women, 1% African American, 1% Asian American, 1% Hispanic American, 1% international
- 84% of applicants admitted
- SAT or ACT (ACT writing optional) required
- 64% graduate within 6 years

General. Founded in 1853. Regionally accredited. Study centers in France, Austria, Spain, England, Wales, Mexico, China, and the Netherlands. More than 40% of students spend a semester or year outside the United States. **Degrees:** 368 bachelor's awarded. **Location:** 45 miles from Des Moines. **Calendar:** Semester, limited summer session. **Full-time faculty:** 94 total; 89% have terminal degrees, 11% minority, 36% women. **Part-time faculty:** 46 total; 28% have terminal degrees, 33% women. **Class size:** 62% < 20, 38% 20-39, less than 1% 40-49, less than 1% 50-99. **Special facilities:** Glass-blowing studio, cross-cultural study center, center for communication and theater.

Freshman class profile. 1,641 applied, 1,375 admitted, 367 enrolled.

Return as sophomores:	81%	**International:**	1%
Out-of-state:	17%	**Fraternities:**	15%
Live on campus:	98%	**Sororities:**	9%

Basis for selection. High school curriculum, GPA, class rank, test scores important. Recommendations, school and community activities, alumni affiliation also considered. Interview and essay recommended. Audition recommended for music and theater majors. Portfolio recommended for art majors. **Homeschooled:** Contact admission office for specific requirements. **Learning Disabled:** Special Assistance for students with physical and learning disabilities.

High school preparation. College-preparatory program recommended. 15 units recommended. Required and recommended units include English 4, mathematics 2-3, social studies 3, history 2, science 2-3 (laboratory 2) and foreign language 2.

2006-2007 Annual costs. Tuition/fees: $21,222. Costs provided are for main campus only. International location costs may vary by program location. Room/board: $7,224. Books/supplies: $750. Personal expenses: $1,500.

Financial aid. Non-need-based: Scholarships awarded for academics, alumni affiliation, art, leadership, minority status, music/drama, religious affiliation, state residency. **Additional information:** Institutional parent loan program and interest-earning, tuition prepayment savings account available. Auditions required for music and theater scholarships, portfolios required for art scholarships. Monthly payment plan available.

Application procedures. Admission: No deadline. $25 fee, may be waived for applicants with need. Application may be submitted online. Admission notification on a rolling basis. **Financial aid:** Priority date 3/1; no closing date. FAFSA required. Applicants notified on a rolling basis starting 3/10; must reply by 5/1 or within 2 week(s) of notification.

Academics. Special study options: Combined bachelor's/graduate degree, cooperative education, cross-registration, double major, dual enrollment of high school students, honors, independent study, internships, liberal arts/career combination, student-designed major, study abroad, teacher certification program, urban semester, Washington semester. Chicago semester. **Credit/placement by examination:** AP, CLEP, IB, institutional tests. **Support services:** Learning center, reduced course load, study skills assistance, tutoring, writing center.

Majors. Biology: General. **Business:** Accounting, business admin, international. **Communications:** General. **Computer sciences:** General, information systems. **Conservation:** Environmental studies. **Education:** Elementary, music. **English:** English lit. **Foreign languages:** French, German, linguistics, Spanish. **History:** General. **Interdisciplinary:** Global studies, math/computer science, natural sciences. **Math:** General. **Parks/recreation:** Exercise sciences. **Philosophy/religion:** Philosophy, religion. **Physical sciences:** Chemistry, physics. **Psychology:** General. **Social sciences:** General, anthropology, economics, political science, sociology. **Visual/performing arts:** Art, dramatic.

Most popular majors. Business/marketing 15%, communications/journalism 6%, computer/information sciences 6%, education 11%, parks/recreation 10%, physical sciences 6%, social sciences 11%.

Computing on campus. 256 workstations in dormitories, library, computer center, student center. Dormitories wired for high-speed internet access and linked to campus network. Commuter students can connect to campus network. Online library, helpline, repair service, student web hosting, wireless network available.

Student life. Freshman orientation: Mandatory. Preregistration for classes offered. Held weekends in June. **Policies:** Freshmen permitted cars on campus. **Housing:** Guaranteed on-campus for all undergraduates. Coed dorms, single-sex dorms, apartments, fraternity/sorority housing available. $200 deposit, deadline 5/1. Pets allowed in dorm rooms. 24 town houses, each housing 16 to 32 students, available to juniors and seniors. French, German, and Spanish houses available to language majors. **Activities:** Bands, choral groups, drama, literary magazine, music ensembles, musical theater, radio station, student government, student newspaper, symphony orchestra, Young Democrats, Young Republicans, Fellowship of Christian Athletes, Inter-Varsity Christian Fellowship, Alcohol Awareness Committee, Coalition for a Multicultural Campus, Circle-K, Amnesty International, Students Against Apartheid, Students Concerned About the Environment.

Athletics. NCAA. **Intercollegiate:** Baseball M, basketball, cross-country, football (tackle) M, golf, soccer, softball W, tennis, track and field, volleyball W, wrestling M. **Intramural:** Basketball, racquetball, rugby, softball, volleyball. **Team name:** Dutch.

Student services. Alcohol/substance abuse counseling, campus ministries, career counseling, services for economically disadvantaged, student employment services, financial aid counseling, health services, minority student services, personal counseling, placement for graduates, veterans' counselor. **Physically disabled:** Services for visually, speech, hearing impaired. **Learning disabled:** Comprehensive services available.

Contact. E-mail: admissions@central.edu
Phone: (641) 628-5286 Toll-free number: (877) 462-3687
Fax: (641) 628-5316
Carol Williamson, Dean of Admission, Central College, 812 University Street, Pella, IA 50219-1999

Clarke College
Dubuque, Iowa
www.clarke.edu **CB code: 6099**

- Private 4-year liberal arts college affiliated with Roman Catholic Church
- Residential campus in small city
- 982 degree-seeking undergraduates: 13% part-time, 71% women, 2% African American, 3% Hispanic American, 1% international
- 225 degree-seeking graduate students
- 61% of applicants admitted
- SAT or ACT (ACT writing optional) required
- 56% graduate within 6 years; 23% enter graduate study

General. Founded in 1843. Regionally accredited. **Degrees:** 191 bachelor's, 2 associate awarded; master's, doctoral offered. **ROTC:** Army. **Location:** 150 miles from Chicago. **Calendar:** Semester, extensive summer session. **Full-time faculty:** 83 total; 54% have terminal degrees, 1% minority, 63% women. **Part-time faculty:** 54 total; 20% have terminal degrees, 57% women. **Class size:** 81% < 20, 18% 20-39, less than 1% 50-99. **Special facilities:** Planetarium, art and communications laboratory, on-line writing center, art slide library, computerized mathematics laboratory, nursing laboratory, multimedia classroom, human gross anatomy laboratory with A.D.A.M. software, computerized foreign language lab.

Freshman class profile. 784 applied, 478 admitted, 158 enrolled.

Mid 50% test scores		GPA 2.0-2.99:	26%
SAT verbal:	470-630	Rank in top quarter:	34%
SAT math:	470-640	Rank in top tenth:	13%
ACT:	20-25	Return as sophomores:	79%
GPA 3.50 or higher:	41%	Out-of-state:	50%
GPA 3.0-3.49:	32%	Live on campus:	60%

Basis for selection. High school record of primary importance. Particular attention paid to grades on college preparatory course work and test scores. Interview required of the academically weak. Auditions required of music and drama majors. Portfolio required of art majors. **Homeschooled:** Must take ACT or SAT.

High school preparation. 21 units required. Required and recommended units include English 4, mathematics 3-4, social studies 3, science 3-4 (laboratory 2), foreign language 2 and academic electives 4. 4 college preparatory mathematics and science, including 3 lab, required for physical therapy program.

2005-2006 Annual costs. Tuition/fees: $18,945. Room/board: $6,445. Books/supplies: $700. Personal expenses: $700.

2005-2006 Financial aid. Need-based: 155 full-time freshmen applied for aid; 148 were judged to have need; 148 of these received aid. Average need met was 100%. Average scholarship/grant was $16,125; average loan $2,776. 72% of total undergraduate aid awarded as scholarships/grants, 28% as loans/jobs. **Non-need-based:** Awarded to 720 full-time undergraduates, including 150 freshmen. Scholarships awarded for academics, alumni affiliation, art, leadership, music/drama. **Additional information:** Reduced tuition for family members of BVMs.

Application procedures. Admission: No deadline. $25 fee, may be waived for applicants with need. Application may be submitted online. Admission notification on a rolling basis beginning on or about 1/15. Must reply by May 1 or within 3 week(s) if notified thereafter. **Financial aid:** Priority date 4/15; no closing date. FAFSA required. Applicants notified on a rolling basis starting 3/15; must reply by 5/1 or within 2 week(s) of notification.

Academics. Special study options: Accelerated study, combined bachelor's/graduate degree, cooperative education, cross-registration, distance learning, double major, ESL, honors, independent study, internships, liberal arts/career combination, student-designed major, study abroad, teacher certification program. **Credit/placement by examination:** AP, CLEP, IB, SAT, ACT. 15 credit hours maximum toward associate degree, 30 toward bachelor's. **Support services:** Learning center, reduced course load, study skills assistance, tutoring, writing center.

Majors. Biology: General. **Business:** Accounting, business admin, finance, international, management information systems, marketing. **Communications:** General. **Computer sciences:** General, computer science. **Education:** General, art, biology, chemistry, early childhood, elementary, English, history, mathematics, middle, multiple handicapped, music, physical, science, secondary, social studies, Spanish, special. **Foreign languages:** Spanish. **Health:** Predentistry, premedicine, prepharmacy, preveterinary. **History:** General. **Interdisciplinary:** Biological/physical sciences, peace/conflict. **Math:** General. **Parks/recreation:** Exercise sciences. **Philosophy/**

religion: Philosophy, religion. **Physical sciences:** Chemistry. **Psychology:** General. **Public administration:** Social work. **Social sciences:** Political science, sociology. **Visual/performing arts:** Art, art history/conservation, commercial/advertising art, dramatic, studio arts.

Most popular majors. Business/marketing 17%, communications/journalism 10%, computer/information sciences 7%, education 22%, health sciences 14%, psychology 7%, visual/performing arts 7%.

Computing on campus. 237 workstations in dormitories, library, computer center, student center. Dormitories linked to campus network. Commuter students can connect to campus network. Online course registration, online library, helpline, wireless network available.

Student life. Freshman orientation: Mandatory. **Housing:** Guaranteed on-campus for freshmen. Coed dorms, single-sex dorms, apartments available. $100 fully refundable deposit, deadline 7/15. **Activities:** Jazz band, choral groups, drama, literary magazine, music ensembles, musical theater, radio station, student government, student newspaper, campus ministry, Amnesty International, peace and justice, peer ministry program, minority student organization, Walden Society (political discussion group), international student organization.

Athletics. NCAA. **Intercollegiate:** Baseball M, basketball, cross-country, golf, soccer, softball W, tennis, track and field, volleyball. **Intramural:** Badminton, basketball, bowling, golf, racquetball, skiing, soccer, softball, swimming, table tennis, tennis, volleyball, water polo, weight lifting. **Team name:** Crusaders.

Student services. Adult student services, alcohol/substance abuse counseling, campus ministries, career counseling, student employment services, financial aid counseling, health services, minority student services, personal counseling, placement for graduates. **Physically disabled:** Services for visually, hearing impaired.

Contact. E-mail: admissions@clarke.edu
Phone: (563) 588-6316 Toll-free number: (800) 383-2345
Fax: (563) 588-6789
Sharon Lyons, Director of Admission, Clarke College, 1550 Clarke Drive, Dubuque, IA 52001-3198

Coe College

Cedar Rapids, Iowa — **CB member**
www.coe.edu — **CB code: 6101**

- Private 4-year liberal arts college affiliated with Presbyterian Church (USA)
- Residential campus in small city
- 1,331 degree-seeking undergraduates: 6% part-time, 57% women, 2% African American, 1% Asian American, 2% Hispanic American, 4% international
- 24 degree-seeking graduate students
- 72% of applicants admitted
- SAT or ACT (ACT writing optional), application essay required
- 73% graduate within 6 years

General. Founded in 1851. Regionally accredited. **Degrees:** 254 bachelor's awarded; master's offered. **ROTC:** Army, Air Force. **Location:** 230 miles from Chicago, 300 miles from Minneapolis-St. Paul. **Calendar:** Semester, limited summer session. **Full-time faculty:** 76 total; 96% have terminal degrees, 4% minority, 29% women. **Part-time faculty:** 49 total; 41% have terminal degrees, 4% minority, 65% women. **Class size:** 71% < 20, 27% 20-39, less than 1% 40-49, less than 1% 50-99. **Special facilities:** Bird museum, infrared spectrometer, analytical physiology units, music library, wilderness field station.

Freshman class profile. 1,278 applied, 922 admitted, 316 enrolled.

Mid 50% test scores		**Rank in top quarter:**	67%
SAT verbal:	540-660	**Rank in top tenth:**	30%
SAT math:	540-650	**Return as sophomores:**	81%
ACT:	23-28	**Out-of-state:**	41%
GPA 3.50 or higher:	72%	**Live on campus:**	97%
GPA 3.0-3.49:	26%	**International:**	3%
GPA 2.0-2.99:	2%	**Fraternities:**	17%

Basis for selection. School achievement record and test scores most important. Recommendations and school activities also important. Interview and community activities considered. **Homeschooled:** GED, test scores, and portfolio required. **Learning Disabled:** Submission of disability assessment required.

High school preparation. College-preparatory program recommended. 18 units recommended. Recommended units include English 4, mathematics 3, social studies 3, science 3 (laboratory 1), foreign language 2 and academic electives 2.

2006-2007 Annual costs. Tuition/fees (projected): $25,120. Part-time classes are $1,120 per course. Room/board: $6,550. Books/supplies: $600. Personal expenses: $1,100.

2005-2006 Financial aid. Need-based: 283 full-time freshmen applied for aid; 253 were judged to have need; 253 of these received aid. Average need met was 96%. Average scholarship/grant was $16,012; average loan $4,727. 70% of total undergraduate aid awarded as scholarships/grants, 30% as loans/jobs. **Non-need-based:** Awarded to 382 full-time undergraduates, including 124 freshmen. Scholarships awarded for academics, alumni affiliation, art, leadership, music/drama, ROTC.

Application procedures. Admission: Priority date 12/10; deadline 3/1 (postmark date). $30 fee, may be waived for applicants with need. Application may be submitted online. Admission notification 3/15. Must reply by May 1 or within 2 week(s) if notified thereafter. **Financial aid:** Priority date 3/1; no closing date. FAFSA required. Applicants notified on a rolling basis starting 3/15; must reply by 5/1 or within 2 week(s) of notification.

Academics. Writing emphasis courses required. Semester practicum required for all students. **Special study options:** Accelerated study, combined bachelor's/graduate degree, cross-registration, double major, dual enrollment of high school students, ESL, exchange student, honors, independent study, internships, New York semester, student-designed major, study abroad, teacher certification program, urban semester, Washington semester. Oak Ridge science semester; research program at the Coe College wilderness field station- Minnesota Superior National Forest; tropical field research in Costa Rica; travel abroad to England, Hong Kong, India, Italy, Japan, Russia, Latin America, Czech Republic, Tanzania, Germany, Sweden, Spain, France, Korea, Thailand, Ireland. **Credit/placement by examination:** AP, CLEP, IB, institutional tests. 16 credit hours maximum toward bachelor's degree. **Support services:** Pre-admission summer program, reduced course load, study skills assistance, tutoring, writing center.

Majors. Area/ethnic studies: African-American, American, Asian, French, German, Spanish/Iberian. **Biology:** General, biochemistry, molecular. **Business:** Accounting, business admin. **Communications:** General, public relations. **Computer sciences:** Computer science. **Conservation:** Environmental science. **Education:** General, art, elementary, middle, music, physical, science, secondary. **English:** Creative writing, English lit, speech/rhetoric. **Foreign languages:** Classics, French, German, Spanish. **Health:** Athletic training, nursing (RN), predentistry, premedicine, preveterinary. **History:** General. **Interdisciplinary:** Accounting/computer science, biological/physical sciences, math/computer science. **Legal studies:** Prelaw. **Math:** General. **Parks/recreation:** Health/fitness. **Philosophy/religion:** Philosophy, religion. **Physical sciences:** General, chemistry, physics. **Psychology:** General. **Social sciences:** Economics, political science, sociology. **Visual/performing arts:** Acting, art, ceramics, directing/producing, dramatic, music performance, music theory/composition, painting, photography, studio arts, theater design.

Most popular majors. Biology 7%, business/marketing 15%, education 6%, English 8%, health sciences 8%, psychology 10%, social sciences 17%, visual/performing arts 10%.

Computing on campus. 275 workstations in dormitories, library, computer center, student center. Dormitories wired for high-speed internet access and linked to campus network. Commuter students can connect to campus network. Online course registration, online library, helpline, student web hosting available.

Student life. Freshman orientation: Mandatory, $75 fee. 4-5 day program. **Policies:** Students must live on campus unless residing with relatives or granted off-campus permission by Department of Residence Life. Freshmen permitted cars on campus. **Housing:** Guaranteed on-campus for all undergraduates. Coed dorms, single-sex dorms, apartments, fraternity/sorority housing, substance-free housing available. $200 nonrefundable deposit, deadline 5/1. **Activities:** Bands, choral groups, drama, literary magazine, music ensembles, radio station, student government, student newspaper, symphony orchestra, Black Self-Education Organization, international club, Coe Friends, Coe Egalitarians Supporting the Advancement of Women, Coe Christian Fellowship, College Republicans, Habitat for Humanity, Coe Greens, College Democrats, Fellowship of Christian Athletes.

Athletics. NCAA. **Intercollegiate:** Baseball M, basketball, cheerleading M, cross-country, diving, football (tackle) M, golf, soccer, softball W, swimming, tennis, track and field, volleyball W, wrestling M. **Intramural:** Badminton, basketball, football (non-tackle) M, racquetball, soccer, softball, squash, table tennis, tennis, volleyball, wrestling M. **Team name:** Kohawks.

Student services. Adult student services, alcohol/substance abuse counseling, campus ministries, career counseling, student employment services,

financial aid counseling, health services, minority student services, personal counseling, placement for graduates.

Contact. E-mail: admission@coe.edu
Phone: (319) 399-8500 Toll-free number: (877) 225-5263
Fax: (319) 399-8816
John Grundig, Dean of Admission, Coe College, 1220 First Avenue, NE, Cedar Rapids, IA 52402

Cornell College

Mount Vernon, Iowa — **CB member**
www.cornellcollege.edu — **CB code: 6119**

- Private 4-year liberal arts college affiliated with United Methodist Church
- Residential campus in small town
- 1,171 degree-seeking undergraduates: 1% part-time, 55% women, 4% African American, 1% Asian American, 3% Hispanic American, 2% international
- 66% of applicants admitted
- SAT or ACT (ACT writing optional), application essay required
- 67% graduate within 6 years

General. Founded in 1853. Regionally accredited. **Degrees:** 220 bachelor's awarded. **Location:** 15 miles from Cedar Rapids, Iowa, 20 miles from Iowa City, Iowa. **Calendar:** Nine terms of 3 and 1/2 weeks, one course per term. **Full-time faculty:** 94 total; 89% have terminal degrees, 6% minority, 47% women. **Part-time faculty:** 18 total; 39% have terminal degrees, 11% minority, 39% women. **Class size:** 59% < 20, 41% 20-39. **Special facilities:** Geology museum, nearby state park for biology and environmental science research.

Freshman class profile. 1,653 applied, 1,096 admitted, 319 enrolled.

Mid 50% test scores		**Rank in top quarter:**	56%
SAT verbal:	560-680	**Rank in top tenth:**	24%
SAT math:	550-680	**Return as sophomores:**	79%
ACT:	23-29	**Out-of-state:**	73%
GPA 3.50 or higher:	62%	**Live on campus:**	99%
GPA 3.0-3.49:	26%	**International:**	2%
GPA 2.0-2.99:	12%		

Basis for selection. Academic record, statement of purpose, interview weighed on individual basis. Test scores often secondary. Institution uses the University of Michigan's English Placement Test. **Homeschooled:** Transcript of courses and grades, letter of recommendation (nonparent) required. Applicants are asked to provide as many documents pertaining to their education as possible, requirements are same as for all first-time first year degree seeking applicants. **Learning Disabled:** Must have documentation of their disability if they plan on requiring any special arrangements in the academic setting during their career at our college.

High school preparation. College-preparatory program recommended. 15 units recommended. Recommended units include English 4, mathematics 3, social studies 1, science 3 (laboratory 2) and foreign language 2. We recommend as many advanced, honors, or AP courses as possible.

2006-2007 Annual costs. Tuition/fees: $24,800. Room/board: $6,660. Books/supplies: $920. Personal expenses: $540.

2005-2006 Financial aid. Need-based: 268 full-time freshmen applied for aid; 222 were judged to have need; 222 of these received aid. Average need met was 100%. Average scholarship/grant was $17,905; average loan $3,155. 81% of total undergraduate aid awarded as scholarships/grants, 19% as loans/jobs. **Non-need-based:** Awarded to 1,068 full-time undergraduates, including 292 freshmen. Scholarships awarded for academics, art, leadership, music/drama, religious affiliation, state residency. **Additional information:** Portfolio required for art scholarship applicants. Audition required for music scholarship applicants.

Application procedures. Admission: Priority date 12/1; deadline 3/1 (postmark date). $30 fee, may be waived for applicants with need. Application may be submitted online. Admission notification on a rolling basis. Must reply by May 1 or within 2 week(s) if notified thereafter. **Financial aid:** Closing date 3/1. FAFSA, institutional form required. Applicants notified on a rolling basis starting 3/1; must reply by 5/1 or within 2 week(s) of notification.

Academics. Special study options: Accelerated study, combined bachelor's/graduate degree, double major, ESL, exchange student, independent study, internships, liberal arts/career combination, semester at sea, student-designed major, study abroad, teacher certification program, urban semester, Washington semester. **Credit/placement by examination:** AP, CLEP, IB, institutional tests. **Support services:** Learning center, study skills assistance, tutoring, writing center.

Majors. Area/ethnic studies: French, Latin American, women's. **Biology:** General, Biochemistry/biophysics and molecular biology. **Computer sciences:** Computer science. **Conservation:** Environmental studies, forestry, management/policy. **Education:** General, art, biology, chemistry, elementary, English, French, German, history, mathematics, middle, music, physical, physics, science, secondary, social science, social studies, Spanish. **English:** English lit. **Foreign languages:** General, classics, French, German, Latin, Russian, Spanish. **History:** General. **Math:** General. **Parks/recreation:** Health/fitness. **Philosophy/religion:** Philosophy, religion. **Physical sciences:** Chemistry, geology, physics. **Psychology:** General. **Social sciences:** Economics, international relations, political science, sociology. **Visual/performing arts:** Art, dramatic, music performance.

Most popular majors. Biology 7%, education 11%, history 7%, interdisciplinary studies 7%, psychology 9%, social sciences 21%, visual/performing arts 7%.

Computing on campus. 132 workstations in dormitories, library, computer center, student center. Dormitories wired for high-speed internet access and linked to campus network. Commuter students can connect to campus network. Online library, helpline, repair service, student web hosting, wireless network available.

Student life. Freshman orientation: Mandatory. Five-day orientation just before fall classes begin. **Policies:** Freshmen permitted cars on campus. **Housing:** Guaranteed on-campus for freshmen. Coed dorms, single-sex dorms, apartments, substance-free housing available. $300 nonrefundable deposit. First-year halls or first year only floors available. **Activities:** Bands, choral groups, dance, drama, literary magazine, music ensembles, musical theater, opera, radio station, student government, student newspaper, symphony orchestra, Alpha Phi Omega, alumni student association, fellowship of Christian athletes, Black Awareness Cultural Organization, women's action group, Young Democrats, College Republicans, Habitat for Humanity, women's social groups, men's social groups, lunch buddies/youth mentoring.

Athletics. NCAA. **Intercollegiate:** Baseball M, basketball, cross-country, football (tackle) M, golf, soccer, softball W, tennis, track and field, volleyball W, wrestling M. **Intramural:** Badminton, basketball, bowling, cross-country, fencing, golf, racquetball, soccer, softball, table tennis, tennis, track and field, volleyball, water polo, wrestling. **Team name:** Rams.

Student services. Adult student services, alcohol/substance abuse counseling, campus ministries, career counseling, student employment services, financial aid counseling, health services, minority student services, personal counseling, women's services. **Physically disabled:** Services for visually impaired.

Contact. E-mail: admissions@cornellcollege.edu
Phone: (319) 895-4477 Toll-free number: (800) 747-1112
Fax: (319) 895-4451
Jonathan Stroud, Vice President for Enrollment - Dean of Admissions and Financial Aid, Cornell College, 600 First Street, SW, Mount Vernon, IA 52314-1098

Divine Word College

Epworth, Iowa
www.dwci.edu — **CB code: 6174**

- Private 4-year liberal arts and seminary college for men affiliated with Roman Catholic Church
- Rural community
- 54 degree-seeking undergraduates
- 100% of applicants admitted
- Application essay, interview required

General. Founded in 1912. Regionally accredited. **Degrees:** 7 bachelor's, 1 associate awarded. **Location:** 15 miles from Dubuque. **Calendar:** Semester. **Full-time faculty:** 22 total. **Part-time faculty:** 3 total.

Freshman class profile. 9 applied, 9 admitted, 9 enrolled.

Mid 50% test scores		**SAT math:**	520-570
SAT verbal:	520-620		

Basis for selection. Interview and religious commitment most important. School achievement record, test scores, recommendations, and school and community activities also considered. Minnesota Multiphasic Personality Inventory (MMPI) used for admission and counseling.

High school preparation. 16 units required. Required units include English 4, social studies 1 and science 1.

2006-2007 Annual costs. Tuition/fees (projected): $9,825. Room/board: $2,400. Books/supplies: $500.

2004-2005 Financial aid. Need-based: 69% of total undergraduate aid awarded as scholarships/grants, 31% as loans/jobs.

Application procedures. Admission: Closing date 7/15. $25 fee, may be waived for applicants with need. Admission notification on a rolling basis beginning on or about 1/1. Must reply by 8/1. **Financial aid:** Priority date 8/31; no closing date. Applicants notified on a rolling basis starting 8/1.

Academics. Special study options: Double major, dual enrollment of high school students, independent study, study abroad. **Credit/placement by examination:** AP, CLEP, institutional tests. **Support services:** Reduced course load, remedial instruction, tutoring.

Majors. Interdisciplinary: Intercultural. **Philosophy/religion:** Philosophy.

Computing on campus. 26 workstations in computer center.

Student life. Policies: Religious observance required. **Housing:** All students live in dormitories on campus. **Activities:** Choral groups, drama, student government, Social Justice Committee.

Athletics. Intramural: Baseball M, basketball M, handball M, ice hockey M, soccer M, softball M, swimming M, table tennis M, tennis M, volleyball M.

Student services. Career counseling, health services, personal counseling.

Contact. Phone: (563) 876-3332
Len Uhal, Vice President for Recruitment and Admissions, Divine Word College, 102 Jacoby Drive Southwest, Epworth, IA 52045

Dordt College

Sioux Center, Iowa
www.dordt.edu **CB code: 6171**

- Private 4-year liberal arts college affiliated with Christian Reformed Church
- Residential campus in small town
- 1,233 degree-seeking undergraduates: 3% part-time, 54% women
- 7 degree-seeking graduate students
- 92% of applicants admitted
- SAT or ACT (ACT writing recommended) required
- 63% graduate within 6 years; 15% enter graduate study

General. Founded in 1955. Regionally accredited. Classes for master's degree program in summer only. **Degrees:** 210 bachelor's, 27 associate awarded; master's offered. **Location:** 45 miles from Sioux City. **Calendar:** Semester. **Full-time faculty:** 73 total; 93% have terminal degrees, 8% minority, 22% women. **Part-time faculty:** 32 total; 12% have terminal degrees, 50% women. **Class size:** 63% < 20, 26% 20-39, 6% 40-49, 4% 50-99, less than 1% >100. **Special facilities:** Farm.

Freshman class profile. 774 applied, 712 admitted, 367 enrolled.

Mid 50% test scores			
SAT verbal:	490-640	Rank in top quarter:	38%
SAT math:	510-650	Rank in top tenth:	16%
ACT:	21-27	End year in good standing:	95%
GPA 3.50 or higher:	46%	Return as sophomores:	80%
GPA 3.0-3.49:	35%	Out-of-state:	65%
GPA 2.0-2.99:	18%	Live on campus:	95%

Basis for selection. School achievement record, high school GPA, test scores, religious affiliation or commitment. Test required of all students except international students. Interview recommended for academically borderline applicants. **Homeschooled:** Must submit ACT or SAT scores and certified GPA. **Learning Disabled:** Copies of prior testing and interview with learning disabilities advisor required.

High school preparation. 17 units required; 25 recommended. Required and recommended units include English 3-4, mathematics 2-3, social studies 1, history 2, science 2-4, foreign language 2-3 and academic electives 6. 10 units must be in social science, English, foreign language, natural science, or mathematics; 2 mathematics units required: algebra, geometry.

2005-2006 Annual costs. Tuition/fees: $17,640. Room/board: $4,900. Books/supplies: $650. Personal expenses: $1,900.

2004-2005 Financial aid. Need-based: 320 full-time freshmen applied for aid; 278 were judged to have need; 278 of these received aid. Average scholarship/grant was $9,623; average loan $4,173. 50% of total undergraduate aid awarded as scholarships/grants, 50% as loans/jobs. **Non-need-based:** Awarded to 293 full-time undergraduates, including 92 freshmen. Scholarships awarded for academics, alumni affiliation, art, athletics, leadership, minority status, music/drama, religious affiliation, state residency.

Application procedures. Admission: Closing date 7/31. $25 fee, may be waived for applicants with need. Application may be submitted online. Admission notification on a rolling basis beginning on or about 10/1. Must reply by May 1 or within 1 week(s) if notified thereafter. Applicants with high school GPA under 2.25 considered on individual basis, may be admitted on probation. **Financial aid:** Priority date 4/1; no closing date. FAFSA, institutional form required. Applicants notified on a rolling basis starting 3/15; must reply within 3 week(s) of notification.

Academics. Special study options: Combined bachelor's/graduate degree, distance learning, double major, ESL, honors, independent study, internships, liberal arts/career combination, student-designed major, study abroad, teacher certification program, urban semester, Washington semester. Iowa Legislative Intern program; China, England, Costa Rica, Russia, Latin America, Netherlands, and Germany semesters; Los Angeles-Film Institute semester, Chicago Metro semester, American Studies semester. **Credit/placement by examination:** AP, CLEP, IB, SAT, ACT, institutional tests. Registrar makes determination on case-by-case basis. **Support services:** Learning center, reduced course load, remedial instruction, study skills assistance, tutoring.

Majors. Agriculture: Agribusiness operations, animal sciences, business, plant sciences. **Biology:** General. **Business:** General, accounting, accounting/business management, information resources management, marketing. **Communications:** General, broadcast journalism, journalism, public relations. **Communications technology:** Graphics. **Computer sciences:** General, computer science, information systems, LAN/WAN management, system admin. **Conservation:** General, environmental studies. **Education:** General, art, biology, business, chemistry, drama/dance, elementary, English, foreign languages, health, history, mathematics, middle, music, physical, physics, reading, science, secondary, social science, social studies, Spanish, special, speech. **Engineering:** General, agricultural, biomedical, civil, computer, electrical, mechanical. **English:** Composition, English lit, speech/rhetoric. **Foreign languages:** Dutch/Flemish, Spanish. **Health:** Athletic training, clinical lab science, clinical lab technology, health services. **History:** General. **Legal studies:** Prelaw. **Liberal arts:** Arts/sciences. **Math:** General. **Parks/recreation:** General, exercise sciences, health/fitness. **Philosophy/religion:** Philosophy, religion. **Physical sciences:** General, chemistry, physics. **Protective services:** Police science. **Psychology:** General. **Public administration:** General, social work. **Social sciences:** General, political science. **Theology:** Missionary, sacred music, theology, youth ministry. **Visual/performing arts:** Art, commercial/advertising art, design, dramatic, piano/organ, stringed instruments, voice/opera.

Most popular majors. Business/marketing 28%, education 20%, English 9%, visual/performing arts 8%.

Computing on campus. 225 workstations in dormitories, library, computer center, student center. Dormitories wired for high-speed internet access and linked to campus network. Online course registration, online library, helpline, wireless network available.

Student life. Freshman orientation: Mandatory. Preregistration for classes offered. 3 days prior to the beginning of classes. **Policies:** Religious observance required. Freshmen permitted cars on campus. **Housing:** Guaranteed on-campus for all undergraduates. Single-sex dorms, special housing for disabled, apartments, substance-free housing available. $100 fully refundable deposit, deadline 6/1. **Activities:** Bands, choral groups, dance, drama, film society, literary magazine, music ensembles, musical theater, opera, radio station, student government, student newspaper, symphony orchestra, 40 clubs and student organizations.

Athletics. NAIA. **Intercollegiate:** Baseball M, basketball, cross-country, football (tackle) M; golf M, ice hockey M, soccer, softball W, tennis, track and field, volleyball W. **Intramural:** Badminton, basketball, bowling, cross-country, field hockey W, golf, racquetball, soccer, softball, swimming, tennis, volleyball. **Team name:** Defenders.

Student services. Adult student services, alcohol/substance abuse counseling, campus ministries, career counseling, student employment services, financial aid counseling, health services, personal counseling, placement for graduates, veterans' counselor. **Physically disabled:** Services for visually, speech, hearing impaired. **Learning disabled:** Comprehensive services available.

Contact. E-mail: admission@dordt.edu
Phone: (712) 722-6080 Toll-free number: (800) 343-6738
Fax: (712) 722-1967
Quentin Van Essen, Director of Admissions, Dordt College, 498 Fourth Avenue, NE, Sioux Center, IA 51250

Four-Year Colleges

Drake University

Des Moines, Iowa **CB member**
www.drake.edu **CB code: 6168**

- Private 4-year university
- Residential campus in large city
- 3,015 degree-seeking undergraduates: 5% part-time, 57% women, 3% African American, 4% Asian American, 2% Hispanic American, 5% international
- 1,933 degree-seeking graduate students
- 82% of applicants admitted
- SAT or ACT (ACT writing optional) required
- 66% graduate within 6 years; 38% enter graduate study

General. Founded in 1881. Regionally accredited. **Degrees:** 647 bachelor's awarded; master's, doctoral, first professional offered. **ROTC:** Army, Air Force. **Location:** 243 miles from Minneapolis-St. Paul, 150 miles from Omaha, Nebraska. **Calendar:** Semester, extensive summer session. **Full-time faculty:** 246 total; 96% have terminal degrees, 11% minority, 39% women. **Part-time faculty:** 142 total; 49% women. **Class size:** 44% < 20, 33% 20-39, 14% 40-49, 5% 50-99, 4% >100. **Special facilities:** Observatory, green house.

Freshman class profile. 3,668 applied, 3,006 admitted, 809 enrolled.

Mid 50% test scores			
SAT verbal:	520-660	Rank in top tenth:	37%
SAT math:	510-650	End year in good standing:	95%
ACT:	24-29	Return as sophomores:	85%
GPA 3.50 or higher:	75%	Out-of-state:	66%
GPA 3.0-3.49:	20%	Live on campus:	94%
GPA 2.0-2.99:	5%	International:	3%
Rank in top quarter:	73%	Fraternities:	12%
		Sororities:	18%

Basis for selection. High school academic record, test scores, extracurricular activities, counselor recommendation, optional essay. Interview and essay recommended. Audition required of music majors. Portfolio recommended for art majors.

High school preparation. College-preparatory program recommended. 16 units recommended. Recommended units include English 4, mathematics 3, social studies 4, science 2 and foreign language 2.

2006-2007 Annual costs. Tuition/fees: $22,682. Room/board: $6,500. Books/supplies: $700. Personal expenses: $1,500.

2004-2005 Financial aid. Need-based: 691 full-time freshmen applied for aid; 532 were judged to have need; 532 of these received aid. Average need met was 88%. Average scholarship/grant was $11,768; average loan $4,783. 58% of total undergraduate aid awarded as scholarships/grants, 42% as loans/jobs. **Non-need-based:** Awarded to 1,422 full-time undergraduates, including 380 freshmen. Scholarships awarded for academics, alumni affiliation, art, athletics, music/drama, ROTC, state residency.

Application procedures. Admission: Priority date 3/1; no deadline. $25 fee, may be waived for applicants with need. Application may be submitted online. Admission notification on a rolling basis beginning on or about 10/1. Must reply by May 1 or within 2 week(s) if notified thereafter. **Financial aid:** Priority date 3/1; no closing date. FAFSA required. Applicants notified on a rolling basis starting 3/1; must reply by 5/1 or within 3 week(s) of notification.

Academics. Peer support through academic departments and residence halls offered. **Special study options:** Accelerated study, combined bachelor's/graduate degree, cooperative education, cross-registration, distance learning, double major, dual enrollment of high school students, ESL, exchange student, honors, independent study, internships, liberal arts/career combination, student-designed major, study abroad, teacher certification program, Washington semester. Extended campus programs, internal exchange program. **Credit/placement by examination:** AP, CLEP, IB, institutional tests. 39 credit hours maximum toward bachelor's degree. **Support services:** Study skills assistance, tutoring, writing center.

Majors. Biology: General, biochemistry, cellular/molecular, pharmacology. **Business:** General, accounting, actuarial science, finance, international, management information systems, management science, managerial economics, marketing. **Communications:** General, advertising, broadcast journalism, journalism, media studies, public relations, radio/tv. **Computer sciences:** General, computer science, information technology. **Conservation:** Environmental science, management/policy. **Education:** General, curriculum, drama/dance, early childhood, elementary, mathematics, music, secondary, special. **English:** British lit, composition, speech/rhetoric. **History:** General. **Legal studies:** General. **Math:** General. **Philosophy/religion:** Ethics, philosophy, religion. **Physical sciences:** Astronomy, chemistry, physics. **Psychology:** General. **Social sciences:** General, anthropology, economics, international relations, political science, sociology. **Visual/performing arts:** Acting, art, art history/conservation, commercial/advertising art, directing/producing, dramatic, drawing, music management, music pedagogy, music performance, painting, piano/organ, printmaking, sculpture, studio arts, theater design, voice/opera.

Most popular majors. Biology 7%, business/marketing 29%, communications/journalism 17%, education 8%, English 6%, social sciences 11%, visual/performing arts 8%.

Computing on campus. 360 workstations in library, student center. Dormitories wired for high-speed internet access and linked to campus network. Commuter students can connect to campus network. Online course registration, online library, helpline, repair service, student web hosting, wireless network available.

Student life. Freshman orientation: Available, $75 fee. Preregistration for classes offered. 4 2-1/2 day sessions; all held in June (parents included). **Policies:** Student leaders must maintain a 2.0 cumulative GPA. Students must live on campus the first two years following high school. Freshmen permitted cars on campus. **Housing:** Guaranteed on-campus for freshmen. Coed dorms, apartments, fraternity/sorority housing, substance-free housing available. $100 fully refundable deposit, deadline 5/1. Houses available. **Activities:** Bands, choral groups, dance, drama, film society, literary magazine, music ensembles, musical theater, radio station, student government, student newspaper, symphony orchestra, TV station, Habitat for Humanity, volunteer programs, Coalition of Black Students, Black Law Students Association, international students association, Best Buddies, College Republicans, College Democrats, La Fuerza Latina, Alpha Phi Omega.

Athletics. NCAA. **Intercollegiate:** Basketball, cheerleading, cross-country, football (tackle) M, golf, rowing (crew) W, soccer, softball W, tennis, track and field, volleyball W. **Intramural:** Badminton, basketball, football (non-tackle), golf, racquetball, soccer, softball, swimming, table tennis, tennis, track and field, volleyball. **Team name:** Bulldogs.

Student services. Campus ministries, career counseling, student employment services, financial aid counseling, health services, legal services, personal counseling, placement for graduates. **Physically disabled:** Services for visually, speech, hearing impaired.

Contact. E-mail: admission@drake.edu
Phone: (515) 271-3181 Toll-free number: (800) 443-7253
Fax: (515) 271-2831
Laura Linn, Director of Admission, Drake University, 2507 University Avenue, Des Moines, IA 50311-4505

Emmaus Bible College

Dubuque, Iowa
www.emmaus.edu **CB code: 1215**

- Private 4-year Bible college affiliated with Brethren Church
- Residential campus in small city
- 251 degree-seeking undergraduates: 8% part-time, 53% women, 1% African American, 2% Asian American, 2% Hispanic American

General. Founded in 1942. Accredited by ABHE. **Degrees:** 39 bachelor's, 1 associate awarded. **Location:** 90 miles from Waterloo, 150 miles from Chicago. **Calendar:** Semester. **Full-time faculty:** 26 total; 12% have terminal degrees, 12% minority, 19% women. **Part-time faculty:** 6 total; 67% have terminal degrees, 67% women.

Freshman class profile.

Mid 50% test scores			
SAT verbal:	490-660	ACT:	16-26
SAT math:	490-640	Out-of-state:	71%
		Live on campus:	99%

Basis for selection. Recommendations and essay most important. GPA also important. All high school students admitted, some may be placed on academic probation. Interview recommended. **Homeschooled:** Must submit transcript.

2005-2006 Annual costs. Tuition/fees: $8,210. Room/board: $4,162. Books/supplies: $450. Personal expenses: $850.

Financial aid. Non-need-based: Scholarships awarded for academics, music/drama.

Application procedures. Admission: Priority date 7/1; no deadline. $25 fee. Admission notification on a rolling basis. Must reply by May 1 or within 2 week(s) if notified thereafter. **Financial aid:** Priority date 5/15, closing date 7/1. FAFSA, institutional form required. Applicants notified on a rolling basis starting 3/1; must reply within 2 week(s) of notification.

Academics. **Special study options:** Combined bachelor's/graduate degree, distance learning, double major, ESL, internships, teacher certification program. **Credit/placement by examination:** AP, CLEP, IB, institutional tests. 18 credit hours maximum toward bachelor's degree. **Support services:** Study skills assistance, tutoring.

Majors. **Computer sciences:** General. **Education:** Elementary. **Theology:** Bible, missionary, theology, youth ministry.

Most popular majors. Computer/information sciences 6%, education 56%, philosophy/religious studies 18%, theological studies 19%.

Computing on campus. 60 workstations in library, computer center.

Student life. **Freshman orientation:** Mandatory. 4 days immediately preceding first day of class. **Policies:** No smoking, alcohol consumption, dancing. Freshmen permitted cars on campus. **Housing:** Guaranteed on-campus for freshmen. Single-sex dorms available. $400 deposit, deadline 7/1. **Activities:** Choral groups, drama, radio station, student government.

Athletics. NCCAA. **Intercollegiate:** Basketball. **Intramural:** Basketball, cross-country, handball, racquetball, soccer, softball, table tennis, tennis, volleyball. **Team name:** Eagles.

Student services. Career counseling, student employment services, health services, personal counseling, veterans' counselor.

Contact. E-mail: sschimpf@emmaus.edu
Phone: (563) 588-8000 ext. 1310 Fax: (563) 588-1216
Steve Schimpf, Director of Admissions, Emmaus Bible College, 2570 Asbury Road, Dubuque, IA 52001

Faith Baptist Bible College and Theological Seminary

Ankeny, Iowa
www.faith.edu **CB code: 6214**

- Private 4-year Bible and seminary college affiliated with General Association of Regular Baptist Churches
- Residential campus in large town
- 324 degree-seeking undergraduates: 11% part-time, 53% women, 2% Asian American, 1% Hispanic American, 1% international
- 160 graduate students
- SAT or ACT (ACT writing optional), application essay required
- 53% graduate within 6 years; 37% enter graduate study

General. Founded in 1921. Regionally accredited; also accredited by ABHE. **Degrees:** 64 bachelor's, 17 associate awarded; master's, first professional offered. **Location:** 6 miles from Des Moines. **Calendar:** Semester, limited summer session. **Full-time faculty:** 21 total; 52% have terminal degrees, 10% minority, 14% women. **Part-time faculty:** 16 total; 31% have terminal degrees, 6% minority, 38% women. **Class size:** 65% < 20, 19% 20-39, 5% 40-49, 9% 50-99, 2% >100.

Freshman class profile. 156 applied, 101 admitted, 86 enrolled.

Mid 50% test scores			
SAT verbal:	480-620	Rank in top quarter:	31%
SAT math:	440-600	Rank in top tenth:	10%
ACT:	19-24	Return as sophomores:	76%
GPA 3.50 or higher:	40%	Out-of-state:	52%
GPA 3.0-3.49:	25%	Live on campus:	98%
GPA 2.0-2.99:	33%	International:	2%

Basis for selection. Open admission, but selective for some programs. Recommendations, church affiliation, character qualities important. Interview recommended for borderline applicants. **Homeschooled:** Transcript of courses and grades required. Validation by third-party testing recommended, such as SAT, ACT, GED. **Learning Disabled:** Request for accommodation must be submitted.

High school preparation. 4 units required. Required and recommended units include English 4, mathematics 3, social studies 2, history 2 and science 3.

2005-2006 Annual costs. Tuition/fees: $11,204. Room/board: $4,316. Books/supplies: $830. Personal expenses: $1,510.

2004-2005 Financial aid. **Need-based:** 62% of total undergraduate aid awarded as scholarships/grants, 38% as loans/jobs. **Non-need-based:** Scholarships awarded for academics, leadership, music/drama.

Application procedures. **Admission:** Closing date 8/1 (postmark date). $25 fee, may be waived for applicants with need. Application must be submitted on paper. Admission notification on a rolling basis. **Financial aid:** Priority date 4/1; no closing date. FAFSA required. Applicants notified on a rolling basis starting 3/15.

Academics. **Special study options:** Combined bachelor's/graduate degree, double major, internships, liberal arts/career combination, study abroad, teacher certification program. **Credit/placement by examination:** AP, CLEP, institutional tests. 6 credit hours maximum toward associate degree, 12 toward bachelor's. **Support services:** Learning center, reduced course load, remedial instruction, study skills assistance, tutoring.

Majors. **Education:** Elementary, English, middle, music, secondary. **Theology:** Bible, missionary, religious ed, sacred music, theology.

Most popular majors. Education 32%, theological studies 66%.

Computing on campus. 46 workstations in library, computer center. Dormitories wired for high-speed internet access and linked to campus network. Repair service available.

Student life. **Freshman orientation:** Mandatory. Preregistration for classes offered. Weekend before classes start in fall. **Policies:** Religious observance required. Freshmen permitted cars on campus. **Housing:** Guaranteed on-campus for freshmen. Single-sex dorms, apartments available. $200 deposit, deadline 6/1. All single students under the age of 26 and not living at home must live in the residence halls. **Activities:** Bands, choral groups, drama, music ensembles, student government, student missionary fellowship, missionary kids fellowship, missions ambassadors, student association, Future Christian Teachers Association, ladies fellowship.

Athletics. NCCAA. **Intercollegiate:** Basketball, soccer, volleyball W. **Intramural:** Basketball, football (tackle). **Team name:** Eagles.

Student services. Career counseling, financial aid counseling, health services, personal counseling, placement for graduates, veterans' counselor.

Contact. E-mail: admissions@faith.edu
Phone: (515) 964-0601 ext. 233 Toll-free number: (888) 324-8448
Fax: (515) 964-1638
Tim Nilius, Vice President Enrollment/Constituency Services, Faith Baptist Bible College and Theological Seminary, 1900 NW Fourth Street, Ankeny, IA 50023

Graceland University

Lamoni, Iowa
www.graceland.edu **CB code: 6249**

- Private 4-year university and liberal arts college affiliated with Community of Christ
- Residential campus in rural community
- 1,916 degree-seeking undergraduates: 25% part-time, 62% women, 5% African American, 2% Asian American, 2% Hispanic American, 9% international
- 595 degree-seeking graduate students
- 63% of applicants admitted
- SAT or ACT required
- 48% graduate within 6 years

General. Founded in 1895. Regionally accredited. Campus in Independence, Missouri. Evening and weekend programs offered at Indian Hills Community College in Centerville, North Central Missouri College in Trenton, Missouri. **Degrees:** 423 bachelor's awarded; master's offered. **Location:** 75 miles from Des Moines, 110 miles from Kansas City. **Calendar:** 4-1-4, limited summer session. **Full-time faculty:** 94 total; 55% have terminal degrees, 2% minority, 51% women. **Part-time faculty:** 24 total; 17% have terminal degrees, 4% minority, 58% women. **Class size:** 63% < 20, 31% 20-39, 4% 40-49, 2% 50-99. **Special facilities:** Electron microscope, communications network, international health center, center for study of Korean War.

Freshman class profile. 1,004 applied, 629 admitted, 262 enrolled.

Mid 50% test scores			
SAT verbal:	450-560	Rank in top quarter:	21%
SAT math:	450-510	Rank in top tenth:	15%
ACT:	18-24	Return as sophomores:	70%
GPA 3.50 or higher:	35%	Out-of-state:	75%
GPA 3.0-3.49:	28%	Live on campus:	98%
GPA 2.0-2.99:	34%	International:	13%

Basis for selection. Rank in upper 50% of class, 2.5 GPA or above, ACT minimum score of 21 or SAT score of 960 (exclusive of writing) important. Interview required of applicants who do not meet admissions requirements, recommended for others. Portfolio recommended of art majors. Auditions required for music, theater and athletic performance areas. **Homeschooled:** Certificate of completion of home study program recognized by home state, ACT or SAT test scores required. **Learning Disabled:** Applicants who do not meet admissions criteria may be considered individually. If accepted, they will be required to take developmental courses. Some applicants may be requested to test for Chance Program prior to being considered for acceptance.

High school preparation. 16 units recommended. Recommended units include English 3, mathematics 2, social studies 2, science 2, foreign language 2 and academic electives 5.

2006-2007 Annual costs. Tuition/fees (projected): $17,050. Room/board: $5,650. Books/supplies: $900. Personal expenses: $1,300.

2004-2005 Financial aid. Need-based: 214 full-time freshmen applied for aid; 181 were judged to have need; 179 of these received aid. Average need met was 88%. Average scholarship/grant was $12,468; average loan $4,489. 54% of total undergraduate aid awarded as scholarships/grants, 46% as loans/jobs. **Non-need-based:** Awarded to 903 full-time undergraduates, including 199 freshmen. Scholarships awarded for academics, alumni affiliation, art, athletics, job skills, leadership, music/drama, religious affiliation.

Application procedures. Admission: No deadline. $50 fee, may be waived for applicants with need. Application may be submitted online. Admission notification on a rolling basis. **Financial aid:** Priority date 3/1; no closing date. FAFSA required. Applicants notified on a rolling basis starting 2/1; must reply within 2 week(s) of notification.

Academics. Distance Learning programs delivered through directed independent study (correspondence), online cohorts, and multiple off-campus locations. Nursing program delivered through directed independent study and on-campus residency sessions, and available only to individuals licensed as registered nurses in the U.S. **Special study options:** Accelerated study, combined bachelor's/graduate degree, distance learning, double major, dual enrollment of high school students, ESL, external degree, honors, independent study, internships, liberal arts/career combination, student-designed major, study abroad, teacher certification program. Accelerated program for nursing only. **Credit/placement by examination:** AP, CLEP, IB, institutional tests. 30 credit hours maximum toward bachelor's degree. Credit by standardized examinations is awarded based on American Council on Education recommendations. **Support services:** Learning center, reduced course load, remedial instruction, tutoring.

Majors. Biology: General. **Business:** Accounting, business admin, international. **Communications technology:** Desktop publishing. **Computer sciences:** General, computer science, information systems. **Education:** Elementary. **Engineering:** Computer. **English:** Composition, speech/rhetoric. **Family/consumer sciences:** Food/nutrition. **Foreign languages:** General, comparative lit, German, Spanish. **Health:** Athletic training, clinical lab science, nursing (RN), preop/surgical nursing, substance abuse counseling. **History:** General. **Liberal arts:** Arts/sciences. **Math:** General. **Parks/recreation:** General, health/fitness, sports admin. **Philosophy/religion:** Religion. **Physical sciences:** Chemistry. **Protective services:** Criminal justice. **Psychology:** General. **Public administration:** Human services. **Social sciences:** General, economics, sociology. **Visual/performing arts:** General, commercial/advertising art, dramatic, studio arts.

Most popular majors. Business/marketing 27%, education 26%, health sciences 21%, liberal arts 8%.

Computing on campus. 106 workstations in dormitories, library, computer center, student center. Dormitories wired for high-speed internet access and linked to campus network. Commuter students can connect to campus network. Online library, helpline, student web hosting, wireless network available.

Student life. Freshman orientation: Mandatory. Preregistration for classes offered. Early orientation sessions in spring and summer (1 day each). Additional 2-3 day orientation at beginning of semester, and quarter-long orientation class, "Orientation to College Life.". **Policies:** No tobacco, alcohol, or drug use on campus. Students required to live on campus through sophomore year unless married or living with relatives. Freshmen permitted cars on campus. **Housing:** Guaranteed on-campus for all undergraduates. Single-sex dorms, special housing for disabled, apartments, substance-free housing available. $200 deposit, deadline 6/1. **Activities:** Bands, choral groups, drama, music ensembles, musical theater, radio station, student government, student newspaper, symphony orchestra, Religious Life Program, social service projects, peace organization, Amnesty International, OASIS, Students for Free Enterprise, Habitat for Humanity, Young Republicans, Young Democrats.

Athletics. NAIA. **Intercollegiate:** Baseball M, basketball, cross-country, football (tackle) M, golf, soccer, softball W, tennis, track and field, volleyball. **Intramural:** Badminton, baseball M, basketball, cross-country, football (non-tackle), golf, handball, racquetball, soccer, softball, swimming, table tennis, tennis, track and field, volleyball. **Team name:** Yellowjackets.

Student services. Adult student services, alcohol/substance abuse counseling, campus ministries, career counseling, student employment services, financial aid counseling, health services, minority student services, personal counseling, placement for graduates, veterans' counselor. **Physically disabled:** Services for visually impaired.

Contact. E-mail: admissions@graceland.edu
Phone: (641) 784-5196 Toll-free number: (866) 472-2352
Fax: (641) 784-5480
Brian Shantz, Vice President for Enrollment, Graceland University, One University Place, Lamoni, IA 50140

Grand View College

Des Moines, Iowa **CB member**
www.gvc.edu **CB code: 6251**

- Private 4-year liberal arts college affiliated with Evangelical Lutheran Church in America
- Commuter campus in large city
- 1,709 degree-seeking undergraduates: 20% part-time, 69% women, 4% African American, 3% Asian American, 2% Hispanic American, 1% international
- 95% of applicants admitted
- SAT or ACT (ACT writing recommended) required
- 36% graduate within 6 years

General. Founded in 1896. Regionally accredited. **Degrees:** 361 bachelor's, 1 associate awarded. **ROTC:** Army, Air Force. **Location:** 200 miles from Kansas City, Missouri, 250 miles from Minneapolis-St. Paul. **Calendar:** Semester, extensive summer session. **Full-time faculty:** 86 total; 58% have terminal degrees, 6% minority, 58% women. **Part-time faculty:** 116 total; 24% have terminal degrees, 5% minority, 54% women. **Class size:** 80% < 20, 20% 20-39, less than 1% 50-99.

Freshman class profile. 442 applied, 421 admitted, 221 enrolled.

Mid 50% test scores			
SAT verbal:	400-520	Rank in top quarter:	32%
SAT math:	410-500	Rank in top tenth:	11%
ACT:	18-22	Return as sophomores:	68%
GPA 3.50 or higher:	26%	Out-of-state:	15%
GPA 3.0-3.49:	27%	Live on campus:	67%
GPA 2.0-2.99:	43%	International:	2%

Basis for selection. Admissions based on individualized evaluation of applicant's secondary school record and SAT or ACT score. Interview required of nursing, education, human services majors. Essay required of education, nursing majors. Audition recommended for drama majors. Portfolio recommended for graphic design and fine arts majors.

High school preparation. College-preparatory program recommended. 15 units recommended. Recommended units include English 4, mathematics 3, social studies 3, science 3 and foreign language 2.

2005-2006 Annual costs. Tuition/fees: $16,060. Room/board: $5,422. Books/supplies: $800. Personal expenses: $2,000.

2005-2006 Financial aid. Need-based: 202 full-time freshmen applied for aid; 165 were judged to have need; 163 of these received aid. Average need met was 80%. Average scholarship/grant was $10,895; average loan $3,000. 55% of total undergraduate aid awarded as scholarships/grants, 45% as loans/jobs. **Non-need-based:** Awarded to 400 full-time undergraduates, including 89 freshmen. Scholarships awarded for academics, alumni affiliation, art, athletics, leadership, music/drama, religious affiliation.

Application procedures. Admission: Closing date 8/15 (receipt date). $35 fee, may be waived for applicants with need. Application may be submitted online. Admission notification on a rolling basis beginning on or about 9/15. **Financial aid:** Priority date 3/1; no closing date. FAFSA required. Applicants notified on a rolling basis starting 3/1; must reply by 5/1 or within 4 week(s) of notification.

Academics. College emphasizes integration of liberal arts core with career-related majors. Internships are a primary focus in many majors. **Special study options:** Accelerated study, combined bachelor's/graduate degree, cooperative education, cross-registration, distance learning, double major, dual enrollment of high school students, honors, independent study, internships, liberal arts/career combination, student-designed major, study abroad, teacher certification program, Washington semester, weekend college. **Credit/placement by examination:** AP, CLEP, IB, institutional tests. 32 credit hours maximum toward bachelor's degree. ACT PEP credit accepted, DANTES accepted. **Support services:** Learning center, reduced course load, remedial instruction, study skills assistance, tutoring, writing center.

Majors. Biology: General. **Business:** General, accounting. **Communications:** Broadcast journalism, journalism, media studies, radio/tv. **Communications technology:** Graphics. **Computer sciences:** General, programming. **Education:** Elementary, secondary. **English:** English lit. **Health:** Health services, nursing (RN), premedicine, prepharmacy. **Legal studies:** Prelaw. **Liberal arts:** Arts/sciences. **Math:** Applied. **Philosophy/religion:** Religion. **Physical sciences:** General. **Protective services:** Criminal justice. **Psychology:** General. **Public administration:** Human services. **Social sciences:** General, political science. **Visual/performing arts:** Dramatic, graphic design, studio arts.

Most popular majors. Business/marketing 18%, education 9%, health sciences 26%, liberal arts 12%, security/protective services 7%, visual/performing arts 8%.

Computing on campus. Dormitories wired for high-speed internet access and linked to campus network. Commuter students can connect to campus network. Online library, student web hosting, wireless network available.

Student life. Freshman orientation: Mandatory. Preregistration for classes offered. Program includes low ropes course at nearby camp. 3 day program just before start of fall semester. **Policies:** Freshmen permitted cars on campus. **Housing:** Coed dorms, apartments available. College owned on-campus houses available. **Activities:** Choral groups, dance, drama, literary magazine, music ensembles, radio station, student government, student newspaper, TV station, Concerned Black Students, student political awareness alliance, art club, Key Club, environmental club, human services club, education club, nursing club, Habitat for Humanity, College Republicans.

Athletics. NAIA. **Intercollegiate:** Baseball M, basketball, cross-country, golf, soccer, softball W, track and field, volleyball W. **Intramural:** Badminton, basketball, cheerleading W, football (non-tackle), soccer, softball, swimming, table tennis, tennis, track and field, volleyball. **Team name:** Vikings.

Student services. Adult student services, alcohol/substance abuse counseling, campus ministries, career counseling, student employment services, financial aid counseling, health services, minority student services, personal counseling, placement for graduates, veterans' counselor. **Physically disabled:** Services for visually, speech, hearing impaired.

Contact. E-mail: admissions@gvc.edu
Phone: (515) 263-2810 Toll-free number: (800) 444-6083
Fax: (515) 263-2974
Diane Johnson, Director of Admissions, Grand View College, 1200 Grandview Avenue, Des Moines, IA 50316-1599

Grinnell College

Grinnell, Iowa — **CB member**
www.grinnell.edu — **CB code: 6252**

- Private 4-year liberal arts college
- Residential campus in small town
- 1,546 degree-seeking undergraduates: 54% women, 4% African American, 6% Asian American, 4% Hispanic American, 11% international
- 45% of applicants admitted
- SAT or ACT (ACT writing optional), application essay required
- 87% graduate within 6 years; 45% enter graduate study

General. Founded in 1846. Regionally accredited. **Degrees:** 319 bachelor's awarded. **Location:** 55 miles from Des Moines. **Calendar:** Semester, limited summer session. **Full-time faculty:** 156 total; 96% have terminal degrees, 13% minority, 46% women. **Part-time faculty:** 43 total; 49% have terminal degrees, 14% minority, 49% women. **Class size:** 63% < 20, 36% 20-39, less than 1% 40-49, less than 1% 50-99. **Special facilities:** 365-acre environmental research area, research telescope, 2 theaters.

Freshman class profile. 3,121 applied, 1,398 admitted, 387 enrolled.

Mid 50% test scores			
SAT verbal:	640-750	End year in good standing:	99%
SAT math:	640-730	Return as sophomores:	92%
ACT:	29-33	Out-of-state:	81%
Rank in top quarter:	93%	Live on campus:	100%
Rank in top tenth:	73%	International:	10%

Basis for selection. Scholastic ability plus extracurricular pursuits, accomplishments most important. Curiosity, motivation, persistence stressed. Interview recommended. **Homeschooled:** Copy of curriculum, writing sample, interview, letter of reference required. SAT Subject Tests strongly recommended.

High school preparation. College-preparatory program recommended. 20 units recommended. Recommended units include English 4, mathematics 4, social studies 4, science 4 (laboratory 3) and foreign language 4.

2006-2007 Annual costs. Tuition/fees: $29,030. Room/board: $7,700. Books/supplies: $600. Personal expenses: $400.

2005-2006 Financial aid. Need-based: 310 full-time freshmen applied for aid; 236 were judged to have need; 236 of these received aid. Average need met was 100%. Average scholarship/grant was $18,952; average loan $4,384. 79% of total undergraduate aid awarded as scholarships/grants, 21% as loans/jobs. **Non-need-based:** Awarded to 624 full-time undergraduates, including 180 freshmen. Scholarships awarded for academics. **Additional information:** Students may apply financial aid to off-campus study programs.

Application procedures. Admission: Closing date 1/20 (receipt date). $30 fee, may be waived for applicants with need. Application may be submitted online. Admission notification 4/1. Must reply by 5/1. **Financial aid:** Closing date 2/1. FAFSA, institutional form required. Applicants notified by 4/1; must reply by 5/1.

Academics. Internships available in public agencies, private organizations, and corporations. **Special study options:** Accelerated study, combined bachelor's/graduate degree, double major, exchange student, independent study, internships, liberal arts/career combination, student-designed major, study abroad, teacher certification program, urban semester, Washington semester. **Credit/placement by examination:** AP, CLEP, IB, institutional tests. 24 credit hours maximum toward bachelor's degree. **Support services:** Reduced course load, study skills assistance, tutoring, writing center.

Majors. Area/ethnic studies: African-American, American, East Asian, Latin American, Russian/Slavic, Western European, women's. **Biology:** General, biochemistry. **Computer sciences:** Computer science. **Foreign languages:** Chinese, classics, French, German, Japanese, Russian, Spanish. **History:** General. **Interdisciplinary:** Biological/physical sciences. **Math:** General. **Philosophy/religion:** Philosophy, religion. **Physical sciences:** Chemistry, physics. **Psychology:** General. **Social sciences:** Anthropology, economics, political science, sociology. **Visual/performing arts:** Art, dramatic.

Most popular majors. Biology 11%, English 7%, foreign language 14%, mathematics 6%, physical sciences 6%, psychology 6%, social sciences 24%, visual/performing arts 7%.

Computing on campus. 134 workstations in dormitories, library, computer center. Dormitories wired for high-speed internet access and linked to campus network. Online library, helpline, student web hosting, wireless network available.

Student life. Freshman orientation: Mandatory. 4-day program. **Policies:** Freshmen permitted cars on campus. **Housing:** Guaranteed on-campus for all undergraduates. Coed dorms, cooperative housing, substance-free housing available. $200 deposit, deadline 5/1. All residence halls and college-owned off-campus houses self-governing: residents decide how their individual hall will operate and share responsibility for budget, quiet hours, social policy, regulations. **Activities:** Bands, choral groups, dance, drama, film society, literary magazine, music ensembles, musical theater, radio station, student government, student newspaper, symphony orchestra, Muslim prayer group, Chalutzim, friends silent meeting, Concerned Black Students, Asian Students in alliance, Student Organization of Latino/as, Campus Democrats, College Republicans, Palastinian solidarity group, Alternative Break (intensive volunteer experience).

Athletics. NCAA. **Intercollegiate:** Baseball M, basketball, cross-country, diving, football (tackle) M, golf, soccer, softball W, swimming, tennis, track and field, volleyball W. **Intramural:** Basketball, fencing, field hockey, rugby, soccer, softball, tennis, volleyball, water polo. **Team name:** Pioneers.

Student services. Alcohol/substance abuse counseling, campus ministries, career counseling, financial aid counseling, health services, minority student services, personal counseling, placement for graduates, veterans' counselor. **Physically disabled:** Services for visually, hearing impaired.

Contact. E-mail: askgrin@grinnell.edu
Phone: (641) 269-3600 Toll-free number: (800) 247-0113
Fax: (641) 269-4800
James Sumner, Dean of Admission and Financial Aid, Grinnell College, 1103 Park Street, Grinnell, IA 50112-1690

Hamilton College

Urbandale, Iowa
www.hamiltonia.edu **CB code: 3388**

- For-profit 4-year business and technical college
- Commuter campus in large city
- 865 degree-seeking undergraduates
- Interview required

General. Accredited by ACICS. **Degrees:** 27 bachelor's, 167 associate awarded. **Location:** 4 miles from Des Moines. **Calendar:** Quarter, extensive summer session. **Full-time faculty:** 20 total; 100% have terminal degrees, 60% women. **Part-time faculty:** 41 total; 100% have terminal degrees.

Basis for selection. Student must have minimum 17 ACT, pass entrance exam, or have associate degree. ACT recommended.

2005-2006 Annual costs. Tuition/fees: $16,000. Tuition includes books and fees. Personal expenses: $1,500.

Financial aid. All financial aid based on need.

Application procedures. Admission: No deadline. $25 fee, may be waived for applicants with need. Application must be submitted on paper. Admission notification on a rolling basis. **Financial aid:** No deadline. FAFSA, institutional form required.

Academics. Special study options: Accelerated study, distance learning, independent study, internships, liberal arts/career combination. **Credit/placement by examination:** AP, CLEP, institutional tests. 32 credit hours maximum toward associate degree, 32 toward bachelor's. **Support services:** Learning center, remedial instruction, study skills assistance, tutoring.

Majors. Business: Accounting, business admin. **Computer sciences:** Information technology.

Computing on campus. 195 workstations in library, computer center. Commuter students can connect to campus network. Online library, repair service available.

Student life. Freshman orientation: Mandatory. Preregistration for classes offered. **Policies:** Freshmen permitted cars on campus. **Activities:** Student government, student newspaper.

Student services. Adult student services, career counseling, student employment services, financial aid counseling, placement for graduates.

Contact. E-mail: erogan@hamiltonia.edu
Phone: (515) 727-2100 Toll-free number: (800) 383-0253
Fax: (515) 727-2115
Amy Vokoun, Director of Admissions, Hamilton College, 4655 121st Street, Urbandale, IA 50323

Hamilton College: Cedar Falls

Cedar Falls, Iowa
www.hamiltoncf.com

- For-profit 4-year business and technical college
- Commuter campus in large town
- 679 degree-seeking undergraduates: 20% part-time, 76% women
- Application essay, interview required

General. Accredited by ACICS. **Degrees:** 34 bachelor's, 94 associate awarded. **Calendar:** Quarter. **Full-time faculty:** 17 total; 12% minority, 65% women. **Part-time faculty:** 20 total; 10% minority, 35% women. **Class size:** 55% < 20, 36% 20-39, 7% 40-49, 2% 50-99.

Freshman class profile. 94 enrolled.

Basis for selection. Open admission, but selective for some programs. High School or GED and entrance test is required in most programs. 2-year degree, ACT with a score of 17+, SAT score of 830+ (exclusive of writing) will be accepted in place of school-administered entrance exam.

2005-2006 Annual costs. Costs vary by program.

2004-2005 Financial aid. All financial aid based on need. 39% of total undergraduate aid awarded as scholarships/grants, 61% as loans/jobs. **Additional information:** Freshman deadline for filing required financial aid forms is 30 days after start of classes.

Application procedures. Admission: No deadline. $25 fee. Application must be submitted on paper. Admission notification on a rolling basis. **Financial aid:** No deadline. FAFSA, institutional form required.

Academics. Special study options: Cooperative education, distance learning. **Credit/placement by examination:** AP, CLEP. **Support services:** Learning center, tutoring.

Majors. Computer sciences: Information technology.

Student life. Freshman orientation: Available. **Activities:** Student newspaper.

Student services. Student employment services, financial aid counseling.

Contact. Phone: (319) 277-0220 Toll-free number: (800) 728-1220
Jill Lines, Director, Admissions, Hamilton College: Cedar Falls, 7009 Nordic Drive, Cedar Falls, IA 50613

Hamilton College: Cedar Rapids

Cedar Rapids, Iowa
www.hamiltonia.edu **CB code: 3384**

- For-profit 4-year business college
- Commuter campus in small city
- 706 degree-seeking undergraduates: 19% part-time, 73% women, 9% African American, 2% Asian American, 1% Hispanic American, 1% Native American
- Application essay, interview required
- 34% graduate within 6 years

General. Accredited by ACICS. **Degrees:** 48 bachelor's, 118 associate awarded. **Calendar:** Quarter, extensive summer session. **Full-time faculty:** 18 total; 6% have terminal degrees, 6% minority, 67% women. **Part-time faculty:** 29 total; 3% have terminal degrees, 10% minority, 55% women. **Class size:** 66% < 20, 34% 20-39.

Freshman class profile. 206 applied, 200 admitted, 61 enrolled.

Basis for selection. Open admission, but selective for some programs. **Homeschooled:** Transcript of courses and grades, state high school equivalency certificate required.

2005-2006 Annual costs. Personal expenses: $1,692.

2004-2005 Financial aid. Need-based: 253 full-time freshmen applied for aid; 250 were judged to have need; 207 of these received aid. Average scholarship/grant was $2,142; average loan $1,846. 76% of total undergraduate aid awarded as scholarships/grants, 24% as loans/jobs. **Non-need-based:** Awarded to 91 full-time undergraduates, including 24 freshmen. Scholarships awarded for academics.

Application procedures. Admission: No deadline. $25 fee, may be waived for applicants with need. Application must be submitted on paper. Admission notification on a rolling basis. **Financial aid:** Priority date 6/30; no closing date. FAFSA, institutional form required. Applicants notified on a rolling basis.

Academics. Special study options: Cooperative education, distance learning, double major, internships, liberal arts/career combination. **Credit/placement by examination:** AP, CLEP, institutional tests. **Support services:** Learning center, tutoring.

Majors. Business: Business admin.

Computing on campus. 161 workstations in library, computer center.

Student life. Freshman orientation: Mandatory. Preregistration for classes offered. 2-hour sessions held a week before quarter starts and again at midterm. **Policies:** Freshmen permitted cars on campus.

Student services. Adult student services, career counseling, student employment services, financial aid counseling, placement for graduates. **Physically disabled:** Services for speech, hearing impaired.

Contact. E-mail: servin@hamiltonia.edu
Phone: (319) 363-0481 Toll-free number: (800) 728-0481
Fax: (319) 363-3812
Scott Ervin, Director of Admissions, Hamilton College: Cedar Rapids, 3165 Edgewood Parkway SW, Cedar Rapids, IA 52404

Hamilton College: Mason City

Mason City, Iowa
www.hamiltoncollegemc.com **CB code: 6289**

- For-profit 4-year business and technical college
- Large town

General. Accredited by ACICS. **Location:** 127 miles from Des Moines. **Calendar:** Quarter.

Annual costs/financial aid. Yearly tuition and fees range from $12,000 to $13,500 (including books) depending on program.

Contact. Phone: (641) 423-2530
Director of Admissions, 100 First Street Northwest, Mason City, IA 50401

Hamilton Technical College

Davenport, Iowa
www.hamiltontechcollege.com **CB code: 1588**

- For-profit 3-year technical college
- Commuter campus in small city
- 226 degree-seeking undergraduates
- Interview required

General. Founded in 1969. Accredited by ACCSCT. **Degrees:** 61 bachelor's, 146 associate awarded. **Location:** 190 miles from Des Moines, 175 miles from Chicago. **Calendar:** Semester. **Full-time faculty:** 15 total. **Part-time faculty:** 1 total.

Basis for selection. Interview most important, recommendations considered. Pseudoisochromatic Color Plates and Wonderlic required.

2005-2006 Annual costs. Medical assistant diploma program tuition: $6750.

Application procedures. Admission: No deadline. $25 fee. Admission notification on a rolling basis. **Financial aid:** No deadline. FAFSA, institutional form required. Applicants notified on a rolling basis.

Academics. Credit/placement by examination: CLEP. 35 credit hours maximum toward associate degree, 60 toward bachelor's. **Support services:** Tutoring.

Majors. Engineering technology: Electrical.

Student services. Career counseling, placement for graduates.

Contact. E-mail: cnelson@hamiltontechcollege.com
Phone: (563) 386-3570 Fax: (563) 386-6756
Chad Nelson, Admissions Director, Hamilton Technical College, 1011 East 53rd Street, Davenport, IA 52807

Iowa State University

Ames, Iowa **CB member**
www.iastate.edu **CB code: 6306**

- Public 4-year university
- Residential campus in small city
- 20,364 degree-seeking undergraduates: 5% part-time, 43% women, 3% African American, 3% Asian American, 2% Hispanic American, 3% international
- 5,009 degree-seeking graduate students
- 90% of applicants admitted
- SAT or ACT (ACT writing optional) required
- 68% graduate within 6 years

General. Founded in 1858. Regionally accredited. Classes offered over the Internet, by videotape, at distant locations through the state's fiber-optic communication network, and at off-campus locations taught in person by the university's professors. **Degrees:** 4,679 bachelor's awarded; master's, doctoral, first professional offered. **ROTC:** Army, Navy, Air Force. **Location:** 30 miles from Des Moines. **Calendar:** Semester, extensive summer session. **Full-time faculty:** 1,419 total; 91% have terminal degrees, 16% minority, 31% women. **Part-time faculty:** 217 total; 65% have terminal degrees, 13% minority, 48% women. **Class size:** 33% < 20, 37% 20-39, 10% 40-49, 11% 50-99, 9% >100. **Special facilities:** Observatory, nature preserve, research park, molecular biology building, computation center, center for designing foods, Ames Laboratory of the Department of Energy, virtual reality applications center, center for crop utilization, center for transportation research and education, lakeside laboratory, Reiman Gardens.

Freshman class profile. 9,101 applied, 8,216 admitted, 4,845 enrolled.

Mid 50% test scores		**Rank in top quarter:**	52%
SAT verbal:	530-660	**Rank in top tenth:**	24%
SAT math:	550-690	**End year in good standing:**	86%
ACT:	22-27	**Return as sophomores:**	86%
GPA 3.50 or higher:	54%	**Out-of-state:**	26%
GPA 3.0-3.49:	31%	**Live on campus:**	86%
GPA 2.0-2.99:	15%	**International:**	1%

Basis for selection. Rank in top half of graduating class and completion of prescribed set of college-preparatory high school courses. Test scores considered alternative criterion to class rank in some instances. Level of difficulty of courses also considered. **Homeschooled:** Emphasis placed on standardized examinations.

High school preparation. College-preparatory program required. Required and recommended units include English 4, mathematics 3-4, social studies 2-4, science 3-4 (laboratory 2-3) and foreign language 4. 2 years foreign language and 3 years social studies required for the College of Liberal Arts & Sciences.

2005-2006 Annual costs. Tuition/fees: $5,634; $15,724 out-of-state. Additional $224 in fees for engineering program; additional $138 in fees for computer science and management information systems. Room/board: $6,197. Books/supplies: $892. Personal expenses: $2,586.

2005-2006 Financial aid. Need-based: 3,046 full-time freshmen applied for aid; 1,907 were judged to have need; 1,877 of these received aid. Average need met was 76%. Average scholarship/grant was $3,399; average loan $3,403. 38% of total undergraduate aid awarded as scholarships/grants, 62% as loans/jobs. **Non-need-based:** Awarded to 7,637 full-time undergraduates, including 2,089 freshmen. Scholarships awarded for academics, art, athletics, leadership, minority status, music/drama, ROTC, state residency. **Additional information:** Short-term loan program available to meet unplanned needs. Financial counseling clinic provides budget and credit education assistance.

Application procedures. Admission: Closing date 8/1. $30 fee. Application may be submitted online. Admission notification on a rolling basis beginning on or about 9/1. Must reply by May 1 or within 2 week(s) if notified thereafter. **Financial aid:** Priority date 3/1; no closing date. FAFSA required. Applicants notified on a rolling basis starting 4/1; must reply by 5/1.

Academics. Special study options: Accelerated study, combined bachelor's/graduate degree, cooperative education, cross-registration, distance learning, double major, dual enrollment of high school students, ESL, exchange student, external degree, honors, independent study, internships, liberal arts/career combination, student-designed major, study abroad, teacher certification program, Washington semester, weekend college. National Collegiate Honors Council Honors Semester. Combined bachelor's/graduate programs include: landscape architecture, agriculture and biosystems engineering, biochemistry and biophysics, electrical and computer engineering, civil and construction engineering, chemical engineering, food science and human nutrition, material science engineering, zoology and genetics. **Credit/placement by examination:** AP, CLEP, IB, SAT, ACT, institutional tests. No limit on number of hours of credit by examination that may be counted toward degree. **Support services:** Learning center, pre-admission summer program, reduced course load, remedial instruction, study skills assistance, tutoring, writing center.

Majors. Agriculture: Agribusiness operations, agronomy, animal sciences, dairy, education services, farm/ranch, horticulture, international, mechanization, plant protection, plant sciences. **Architecture:** Architecture, landscape, urban/community planning. **Area/ethnic studies:** Russian/Slavic, women's. **Biology:** General, biochemistry, biophysics, entomology, genetics, microbiology. **Business:** General, accounting, finance, hospitality admin, international, logistics, management information systems, marketing, operations, statistics. **Communications:** General, advertising, journalism. **Computer sciences:** General. **Conservation:** Environmental science, environmental studies, forestry. **Education:** General, agricultural, early childhood, elementary, family/consumer sciences, health, kindergarten/preschool, music, technology/industrial arts, trade/industrial. **Engineering:** General, aerospace, agricultural, chemical, civil, computer, construction, electrical, industrial, materials, materials science, mechanical. **English:** English lit, speech/rhetoric, technical writing. **Family/consumer sciences:** General, apparel marketing, clothing/textiles, family resources, family/community services, housing, human nutrition, textile manufacture. **Foreign languages:** French, German, linguistics, Russian, Spanish. **Health:** Dietetics, medical illustrating, premedicine, preveterinary. **History:** General. **Liberal arts:** Arts/sciences. **Math:** General, statistics. **Parks/recreation:** Health/fitness. **Philosophy/religion:** Philosophy, religion. **Physical sciences:** Chemistry, geology, physics, planetary. **Psychology:** General. **Social sciences:** Anthropology, economics, international relations, political science, sociology. **Visual/performing arts:** General, art, commercial/advertising art, design, fashion design, graphic design, interior design.

Most popular majors. Agriculture 9%, business/marketing 21%, education 7%, engineering/engineering technologies 17%, visual/performing arts 7%.

Computing on campus. 2,700 workstations in dormitories, library, computer center, student center. Dormitories wired for high-speed internet access and linked to campus network. Commuter students can connect to campus network. Online course registration, online library, helpline, repair service, wireless network available.

Student life. **Freshman orientation:** Available. Preregistration for classes offered. 2-day, overnight program. **Policies:** Freshmen permitted cars on campus. **Housing:** Guaranteed on-campus for all undergraduates. Coed dorms, single-sex dorms, special housing for disabled, apartments, fraternity/sorority housing, substance-free housing available. $135 fully refundable deposit, deadline 5/1. Learning communities, family, quiet, non-smoking, alcohol-free, housing available. **Activities:** Bands, choral groups, dance, drama, film society, literary magazine, music ensembles, musical theater, opera, radio station, student government, student newspaper, symphony orchestra, TV station, More than 500 clubs and organizations.

Athletics. NCAA. **Intercollegiate:** Basketball, cross-country, football (tackle) M, golf, gymnastics W, soccer W, softball W, swimming W, tennis W, track and field, volleyball W, wrestling M. **Intramural:** Badminton, basketball, bowling, boxing M, cross-country, diving, golf, handball, ice hockey, racquetball, skiing, soccer, softball, squash, swimming, table tennis, tennis, volleyball, water polo, weight lifting, wrestling. **Team name:** Cyclones.

Student services. Adult student services, alcohol/substance abuse counseling, campus ministries, career counseling, student employment services, financial aid counseling, health services, legal services, minority student services, on-campus daycare, personal counseling, placement for graduates, veterans' counselor, women's services. **Physically disabled:** Services for visually, speech, hearing impaired. **Learning disabled:** Comprehensive services available.

Contact. E-mail: admissions@iastate.edu
Phone: (515) 294-5836 Toll-free number: (800) 262-3810
Fax: (515) 294-2592
Marc Harding, Director of Admissions, Iowa State University, 100 Alumni Hall, Ames, IA 50011-2011

Iowa Wesleyan College

Mount Pleasant, Iowa — **CB member**
www.iwc.edu — **CB code: 6308**

- Private 4-year liberal arts college affiliated with United Methodist Church
- Residential campus in small town
- 844 degree-seeking undergraduates: 28% part-time, 61% women
- 59% of applicants admitted
- SAT or ACT (ACT writing optional) required

General. Founded in 1842. Regionally accredited. **Degrees:** 132 bachelor's awarded. **Location:** 47 miles from Iowa City, 25 miles from Burlington. **Calendar:** Semester, limited summer session. **Full-time faculty:** 47 total; 49% have terminal degrees, 4% minority, 43% women. **Part-time faculty:** 42 total; 7% have terminal degrees, 67% women. **Class size:** 86% < 20, 14% 20-39. **Special facilities:** Public Interest Institute (Iowa's only state-level, independent, research organization).

Freshman class profile. 727 applied, 426 admitted, 135 enrolled.

Out-of-state:	55%	**Fraternities:**	3%
Live on campus:	91%	**Sororities:**	8%

Basis for selection. Upper 50% class rank preferred. Automatic acceptance: 2.5 GPA and 19 ACT. Conditional acceptance: 2.0 GPA and 16-18 ACT. All others not meeting this criteria will go to committee. Interviews recommended. Audition recommended for music majors. Portfolio recommended for art, creative programs majors. Essay recommended for applicants who do not meet regular admission requirements. **Homeschooled:** Transcript of courses and grades required. GED or portfolio may be substituted for high school transcript requirement.

High school preparation. 16 units recommended. Recommended units include English 4, mathematics 3, social studies 3, science 2 (laboratory 2) and academic electives 4.

2005-2006 Annual costs. Tuition/fees: $16,950. Room/board: $5,360. Books/supplies: $800.

Financial aid. **Non-need-based:** Scholarships awarded for academics, alumni affiliation, art, athletics, job skills, leadership, minority status, music/drama, religious affiliation, state residency.

Application procedures. **Admission:** Priority date 4/1; no deadline. No application fee. Application may be submitted online. Admission notification on a rolling basis beginning on or about 8/15. Must reply by May 1 or within 2 week(s) if notified thereafter. **Financial aid:** Priority date 4/1; no closing date. FAFSA required. Applicants notified on a rolling basis starting 3/1; must reply within 2 week(s) of notification.

Academics. **Special study options:** Combined bachelor's/graduate degree, cross-registration, distance learning, double major, dual enrollment of high school students, exchange student, independent study, internships, liberal arts/career combination, student-designed major, study abroad, teacher certification program, Washington semester. **Credit/placement by examination:** AP, CLEP, IB, institutional tests. 30 credit hours maximum toward bachelor's degree. **Support services:** Learning center, reduced course load, study skills assistance, tutoring, writing center.

Majors. **Biology:** General. **Business:** General, accounting, business admin. **Communications:** General, broadcast journalism, journalism. **Computer sciences:** General, computer science. **Conservation:** Forestry. **Education:** General, art, biology, chemistry, early childhood, elementary, English, health, mathematics, middle, music, physical, secondary. **Engineering:** General. **Health:** Environmental health, nursing (RN), predentistry, premedicine, prepharmacy, preveterinary. **History:** General. **Legal studies:** Prelaw. **Liberal arts:** Library science. **Math:** General. **Parks/recreation:** Exercise sciences, health/fitness, sports admin. **Philosophy/religion:** Christian, philosophy, religion. **Physical sciences:** Chemistry. **Protective services:** Criminal justice. **Psychology:** General. **Social sciences:** Sociology. **Visual/performing arts:** Design, studio arts.

Most popular majors. Business/marketing 23%, education 32%, health sciences 10%, parks/recreation 6%, psychology 10%.

Computing on campus. 90 workstations in dormitories, library, computer center. Dormitories wired for high-speed internet access and linked to campus network. Commuter students can connect to campus network. Repair service available.

Student life. **Freshman orientation:** Mandatory. Preregistration for classes offered. Orientation program held weekend before classes begin lasting 3 days with special events held throughout the weekend. **Policies:** Freshmen permitted cars on campus. **Housing:** Guaranteed on-campus for all undergraduates. Coed dorms, single-sex dorms, substance-free housing available. $100 fully refundable deposit, deadline 8/20. Pets allowed in dorm rooms. **Activities:** Bands, choral groups, dance, drama, literary magazine, music ensembles, radio station, student government, student newspaper, symphony orchestra, campus ministries, Black Awareness Organization, Fellowship of Christian Athletics, Bacchus, Unidad, International Club.

Athletics. NAIA. **Intercollegiate:** Baseball M, basketball, football (tackle) M, golf, soccer, softball W, track and field, volleyball W. **Intramural:** Badminton, basketball, bowling, football (non-tackle), softball, table tennis, tennis, volleyball. **Team name:** Tigers.

Student services. Adult student services, alcohol/substance abuse counseling, campus ministries, career counseling, student employment services, financial aid counseling, health services, personal counseling, placement for graduates.

Contact. E-mail: admit@iwc.edu
Phone: (319) 385-6231 Toll-free number: (800) 582-2383 ext. 6231
Fax: (319) 385-6240
Cary Owens, Dean of Enrollment Management, Iowa Wesleyan College, 601 North Main Street, Mount Pleasant, IA 52641-1398

Kaplan University

Davenport, Iowa
www.kaplan.edu/ku — **CB code: 5848**

- For-profit 4-year university
- Residential campus in large city

- 19,953 degree-seeking undergraduates: 74% part-time, 74% women, 1% African American
- 81 degree-seeking graduate students
- Interview required
- 52% graduate within 6 years

General. Founded in 1937. Regionally accredited. **Degrees:** 165 bachelor's, 731 associate awarded; master's offered. **Location:** 165 miles from Des Moines, 180 miles from Chicago. **Calendar:** Quarter, extensive summer session. **Full-time faculty:** 64 total; 3% minority, 61% women. **Part-time faculty:** 1,002 total; 6% minority, 50% women.

Freshman class profile.

Return as sophomores:	40%	Out-of-state:	25%

Basis for selection. Open admission.

2005-2006 Annual costs. Tuition/fees: $12,000. Tuition figure includes fees and books. Personal expenses: $1,485.

Financial aid. Non-need-based: Scholarships awarded for academics.

Application procedures. Admission: No deadline. $25 fee, may be waived for applicants with need. Application may be submitted online. Admission notification on a rolling basis. **Financial aid:** Priority date 5/15; no closing date. FAFSA, institutional form required. Applicants notified on a rolling basis starting 3/4; must reply by 6/15 or within 2 week(s) of notification.

Academics. Special study options: Distance learning, double major, internships. **Credit/placement by examination:** AP, CLEP, institutional tests. Up to 25% of all credit in a particular program can be earned through examination. **Support services:** Learning center, reduced course load, remedial instruction, study skills assistance, tutoring.

Majors. Business: General, business admin, management information systems. **Computer sciences:** Information technology. **Legal studies:** Paralegal. **Protective services:** Criminal justice.

Most popular majors. Business/marketing 88%, computer/information sciences 8%.

Computing on campus. 114 workstations in library, student center. Online course registration, online library, helpline, student web hosting, wireless network available.

Student life. Freshman orientation: Available. **Activities:** Student government, student newspaper.

Student services. Career counseling, student employment services, financial aid counseling, personal counseling, placement for graduates.

Contact. E-mail: rhoffmann@kucampus.edu
Phone: (563) 355-3500 Toll-free number: (800) 747-1035
Fax: (563) 355-1320
Robert Hoffmann, Director of Admissions, Kaplan University, 1801 East Kimberly Road, Suite 1, Davenport, IA 52807-2095

Loras College
Dubuque, Iowa
www.loras.edu **CB code: 6370**

- Private 4-year liberal arts college affiliated with Roman Catholic Church
- Residential campus in small city
- 1,565 degree-seeking undergraduates: 3% part-time, 50% women, 1% African American, 1% Asian American, 1% Hispanic American, 3% international
- 74 degree-seeking graduate students
- 82% of applicants admitted
- SAT or ACT (ACT writing optional) required
- 65% graduate within 6 years; 17% enter graduate study

General. Founded in 1839. Regionally accredited. **Degrees:** 319 bachelor's awarded; master's offered. **ROTC:** Army. **Location:** 180 miles from Chicago. **Calendar:** Semester, extensive summer session. **Full-time faculty:** 111 total; 100% have terminal degrees, 3% minority, 31% women. **Part-time faculty:** 35 total; 57% women. **Class size:** 57% < 20, 43% 20-39. **Special facilities:** Planetarium, observatory, residential arts complex.

Freshman class profile. 1,402 applied, 1,152 admitted, 366 enrolled.

Mid 50% test scores			
SAT verbal:	450-580	Rank in top quarter:	34%
SAT math:	500-630	Rank in top tenth:	13%
ACT:	20-25	End year in good standing:	90%
GPA 3.50 or higher:	40%	Return as sophomores:	68%
GPA 3.0-3.49:	30%	Out-of-state:	48%
GPA 2.0-2.99:	30%	Live on campus:	94%
		International:	10%

Basis for selection. High school academic record and test scores most important. Interview and essay recommended. **Homeschooled:** Considered by admissions committee on individual basis. **Learning Disabled:** All students applying for the enhanced learning disabilities program must have materials submitted by the required date. All files are reviewed by the learning disabilities program.

High school preparation. 16 units recommended. Recommended units include English 4, mathematics 3, social studies 3, history 3 and science 3.

2005-2006 Annual costs. Tuition/fees: $20,198. Room/board: $6,100. Books/supplies: $800. Personal expenses: $600.

2005-2006 Financial aid. Need-based: 342 full-time freshmen applied for aid; 328 were judged to have need; 328 of these received aid. Average need met was 85%. Average scholarship/grant was $8,192; average loan $4,242. 68% of total undergraduate aid awarded as scholarships/grants, 32% as loans/jobs. **Non-need-based:** Awarded to 1,484 full-time undergraduates, including 357 freshmen. Scholarships awarded for academics, alumni affiliation, music/drama. **Additional information:** Audition or portfolio recommended for music and art financial aid applicants.

Application procedures. Admission: No deadline. $25 fee, may be waived for applicants with need. Application may be submitted online. Admission notification on a rolling basis. Must reply by May 1 or within 2 week(s) if notified thereafter. **Financial aid:** Priority date 4/15; no closing date. FAFSA required. Applicants notified on a rolling basis starting 3/1; must reply within 3 week(s) of notification.

Academics. Special study options: Cooperative education, cross-registration, double major, dual enrollment of high school students, exchange student, honors, independent study, internships, student-designed major, study abroad, teacher certification program, urban semester, Washington semester. **Credit/placement by examination:** AP, CLEP, IB. **Support services:** Learning center, reduced course load, remedial instruction, study skills assistance, tutoring, writing center.

Majors. Biology: General, biochemistry. **Business:** General, accounting, business admin, finance, human resources, international, management information systems, marketing. **Communications:** Journalism, media studies, public relations. **Computer sciences:** Computer science. **Education:** General, art, early childhood, elementary, emotionally handicapped, mentally handicapped, multi-level teacher, physical, secondary, special. **Engineering:** Electrical, physics. **English:** Creative writing, English lit. **Foreign languages:** Spanish. **Health:** Athletic training, clinical lab science, nuclear medical technology. **History:** General. **Legal studies:** Prelaw. **Liberal arts:** Arts/sciences. **Math:** General. **Parks/recreation:** Exercise sciences. **Philosophy/religion:** Philosophy, religion. **Physical sciences:** General, chemistry, physics. **Protective services:** Criminal justice. **Psychology:** General. **Public administration:** Social work. **Social sciences:** Economics, international relations, political science, sociology. **Visual/performing arts:** General, studio arts.

Most popular majors. Business/marketing 28%, education 25%, security/protective services 9%, social sciences 8%.

Computing on campus. PC or laptop required. 20 workstations in library, computer center, student center. Dormitories wired for high-speed internet access and linked to campus network. Commuter students can connect to campus network. Online course registration, online library, helpline, repair service, student web hosting, wireless network available.

Student life. Freshman orientation: Mandatory. Preregistration for classes offered. Held from early June through end of July. **Policies:** Freshmen permitted cars on campus. **Housing:** Guaranteed on-campus for freshmen. Coed dorms, single-sex dorms, apartments available. $100 deposit. **Activities:** Bands, choral groups, dance, drama, film society, literary magazine, music ensembles, musical theater, radio station, student government, student newspaper, TV station, Peace and Justice, African Hispanic Asian Native American, Amnesty International, environmental action forum, international student organization, fellowship of Christian athletes.

Athletics. NCAA. **Intercollegiate:** Baseball M, basketball, cross-country, diving, football (tackle) M, golf, soccer, softball W, swimming, tennis, track and field, volleyball W, wrestling M. **Intramural:** Badminton, baseball M, basketball, bowling, cross-country, diving, football (non-tackle), golf, handball, racquetball, soccer, softball, swimming, table tennis, tennis, track and field, volleyball, water polo, weight lifting, wrestling M. **Team name:** Duhawks.

Student services. Adult student services, alcohol/substance abuse counseling, campus ministries, career counseling, student employment services, financial aid counseling, health services, minority student services, personal counseling, placement for graduates, veterans' counselor. **Learning disabled:** Comprehensive services available.

Contact. E-mail: adms@loras.edu
Phone: (563) 588-7236 Toll-free number: (800) 245-6727
Fax: (563) 588-7119
Mary Weck, Director of Admissions, Loras College, 1450 Alta Vista Street, Dubuque, IA 52004-0178

Luther College

Decorah, Iowa — **CB member**
www.luther.edu — **CB code: 6375**

- Private 4-year liberal arts college affiliated with Evangelical Lutheran Church in America
- Residential campus in small town
- 2,466 degree-seeking undergraduates: 1% part-time, 58% women, 1% African American, 2% Asian American, 1% Hispanic American, 3% international
- 75% of applicants admitted
- SAT or ACT (ACT writing optional), application essay required
- 75% graduate within 6 years; 21% enter graduate study

General. Founded in 1861. Regionally accredited. All students receive a solid foundation in the liberal arts through the all-college PAIDEIA program, including a common yearlong interdisciplinary course for first-year students and an upper-class values seminar. **Degrees:** 570 bachelor's awarded. **Location:** 70 miles from Rochester, Minnesota, 50 miles from LaCrosse, Wisconsin. **Calendar:** 4-1-4, limited summer session. **Full-time faculty:** 179 total; 88% have terminal degrees, 7% minority, 38% women. **Part-time faculty:** 60 total; 28% have terminal degrees, 5% minority, 58% women. **Class size:** 50% < 20, 46% 20-39, 2% 40-49, 2% 50-99, less than 1% >100. **Special facilities:** Live animal center, planetarium, art galleries, Norwegian-American museum, extensive biology field study areas, cadaver laboratory, wellness center with climbing wall.

Freshman class profile. 2,121 applied, 1,593 admitted, 630 enrolled.

Mid 50% test scores			
SAT verbal:	550-670	**Rank in top quarter:**	61%
SAT math:	550-670	**Rank in top tenth:**	32%
ACT:	22-28	**End year in good standing:**	91%
GPA 3.50 or higher:	65%	**Return as sophomores:**	84%
GPA 3.0-3.49:	22%	**Out-of-state:**	63%
GPA 2.0-2.99:	13%	**Live on campus:**	99%
		International:	2%

Basis for selection. Rigor of high school curriculum most important, followed by test scores and teacher recommendation(s). Applicants should rank in top half of high school class. Extracurricular activities considered. Audition recommended for music scholarships. Portfolio recommended for art majors. Interview recommended for borderline students.

High school preparation. College-preparatory program recommended. 14 units recommended. Recommended units include English 4, mathematics 3, social studies 3, science 2 (laboratory 1) and foreign language 2.

2006-2007 Annual costs. Tuition/fees: $26,380. Room/board: $4,290. Books/supplies: $830. Personal expenses: $1,510.

2005-2006 Financial aid. Need-based: 564 full-time freshmen applied for aid; 458 were judged to have need; 458 of these received aid. Average need met was 90%. Average scholarship/grant was $18,463; average loan $4,640. 69% of total undergraduate aid awarded as scholarships/grants, 31% as loans/jobs. **Non-need-based:** Awarded to 785 full-time undergraduates, including 181 freshmen. Scholarships awarded for academics, alumni affiliation, art, minority status, music/drama.

Application procedures. Admission: No deadline. $25 fee, may be waived for applicants with need. Application may be submitted online. Admission notification on a rolling basis beginning on or about 11/1. Must reply by May 1 or within 4 week(s) if notified thereafter. **Financial aid:** Priority date 3/1; no closing date. FAFSA, institutional form required. Applicants notified on a rolling basis starting 3/15.

Academics. Special study options: Combined bachelor's/graduate degree, double major, dual enrollment of high school students, honors, independent study, internships, student-designed major, study abroad, teacher certification program, Washington semester. **Credit/placement by examination:** AP, CLEP, IB, institutional tests. No limit but must satisfy Luther's residency requirement. **Support services:** Learning center, reduced course load, remedial instruction, study skills assistance, tutoring, writing center.

Majors. Area/ethnic studies: African-American, Scandinavian. **Biology:** General. **Business:** Accounting, business admin, management information systems. **Communications:** Media studies. **Computer sciences:** Computer science. **Education:** Elementary, health, physical. **English:** English lit. **Foreign languages:** Ancient Greek, Biblical, classics, French, German, Latin, Spanish. **Health:** Nursing (RN). **History:** General. **Math:** General, statistics. **Parks/recreation:** Health/fitness, sports admin. **Philosophy/religion:** Philosophy, religion. **Physical sciences:** Chemistry, physics. **Psychology:** General. **Public administration:** Social work. **Social sciences:** Anthropology, economics, political science, sociology. **Visual/performing arts:** Art, dramatic.

Most popular majors. Biology 10%, business/marketing 16%, education 6%, parks/recreation 6%, psychology 8%, social sciences 8%, visual/performing arts 12%.

Computing on campus. 500 workstations in dormitories, library, computer center, student center. Dormitories wired for high-speed internet access and linked to campus network. Online course registration, helpline, wireless network available.

Student life. Freshman orientation: Mandatory. **Policies:** Freshmen permitted cars on campus. **Housing:** Guaranteed on-campus for all undergraduates. Coed dorms, special housing for disabled, apartments, substance-free housing available. $200 nonrefundable deposit. International language houses (French, German, Spanish), clusters, quiet floors, chemical-free/wellness floor options available. Honors floor. **Activities:** Bands, choral groups, dance, drama, film society, literary magazine, music ensembles, musical theater, radio station, student government, student newspaper, symphony orchestra, major religious denominations and political parties represented, Black Student Union, Asian Student Association, international student association, Hispanic/Latino Student Association, Phi Beta Kappa.

Athletics. NCAA. **Intercollegiate:** Baseball M, basketball, cross-country, football (tackle) M, golf, soccer, softball W, swimming, tennis, track and field, volleyball W, wrestling M. **Intramural:** Archery, badminton, basketball, bowling, football (non-tackle), golf, handball, racquetball, rugby, skiing, soccer, softball, table tennis, tennis, track and field, volleyball, water polo. **Team name:** The Norse.

Student services. Alcohol/substance abuse counseling, campus ministries, career counseling, student employment services, financial aid counseling, health services, minority student services, personal counseling, placement for graduates. **Physically disabled:** Services for visually, hearing impaired.

Contact. E-mail: admissions@luther.edu
Phone: (563) 387-1287 Toll-free number: (800) 458-8437
Fax: (563) 387-2159
Jon Lund, Vice President for Enrollment, Luther College, 700 College Drive, Decorah, IA 52101-1042

Maharishi University of Management

Fairfield, Iowa
www.mum.edu — **CB code: 4497**

- Private 4-year university and liberal arts college
- Residential campus in small town
- 218 degree-seeking undergraduates: 6% part-time, 41% women
- 523 graduate students
- 66% of applicants admitted
- Application essay required
- 52% graduate within 6 years

General. Founded in 1971. Regionally accredited. Provides Consciousness-Based education and incorporates group practice of the Maharishi Transcendental Meditation technique into a traditional academic program. Curriculum is taught one course at a time in a four-week block system. **Degrees:** 44 bachelor's awarded; master's, doctoral offered. **Location:** 60 miles from Iowa City, 110 miles from Des Moines. **Calendar:** Semester, limited summer session. **Full-time faculty:** 45 total. **Part-time faculty:** 15 total. **Class size:** 85% < 20, 13% 20-39, 1% 40-49, 1% 50-99. **Special facilities:** Scanning electron microscope, two large domes for transcendental meditation, greenhouses for botany study, college prep-school on campus, indoor rock-climbing wall.

Freshman class profile. 58 applied, 38 admitted, 25 enrolled.

Mid 50% test scores		Return as sophomores:	85%
SAT verbal:	510-640	Out-of-state:	39%
SAT math:	470-620	Live on campus:	95%
ACT:	19-25		

Basis for selection. Academics, grades, SAT or ACT scores, recommendations, extracurricular activities, work experience, and essay important. Interview with admissions officer recommended. SAT or ACT recommended. Students encouraged to visit campus for 3-day weekend. **Homeschooled:** Must supply a detailed record of courses and objectives.

High school preparation. 15 units recommended. Recommended units include English 4, mathematics 3, social studies 3, science 3 and foreign language 2.

2005-2006 Annual costs. Tuition/fees: $24,430. Room/board: $6,000. Books/supplies: $800. Personal expenses: $1,500.

Financial aid. Non-need-based: Scholarships awarded for academics, alumni affiliation, music/drama, state residency. **Additional information:** Students may earn scholarships through volunteer staff program.

Application procedures. Admission: Priority date 4/15; deadline 8/1 (receipt date). $15 fee, may be waived for applicants with need. Application may be submitted online. Admission notification on a rolling basis. Online application fee is $15. **Financial aid:** Priority date 4/15; no closing date. FAFSA required. Applicants notified on a rolling basis starting 3/1; must reply within 4 week(s) of notification.

Academics. Innovative modular block system in which students study one subject at a time. **Special study options:** Double major, exchange student, honors, independent study, internships, liberal arts/career combination, study abroad, teacher certification program. Rotating university: several one-month blocks out of each academic year, a course is offered abroad, e.g. students spend one month with professor studying art in Italy, literature in Switzerland, or business in Japan. **Credit/placement by examination:** CLEP, IB, institutional tests. 12 credit hours maximum toward bachelor's degree. **Support services:** Study skills assistance.

Majors. Agriculture: General. **Biology:** General, ecology, environmental. **Business:** Business admin. **Conservation:** Environmental studies. **Education:** Elementary, secondary. **Physical sciences:** Physics. **Visual/performing arts:** General, art, dramatic, studio arts.

Most popular majors. Business/marketing 32%, computer/information sciences 8%, education 6%, health sciences 8%, liberal arts 8%, visual/performing arts 26%.

Computing on campus. 400 workstations in library, computer center, student center. Dormitories wired for high-speed internet access and linked to campus network. Commuter students can connect to campus network. Online library, helpline available.

Student life. Freshman orientation: Mandatory. **Policies:** Daily practice of transcendental meditation by all students, faculty, and staff fosters a fulfilling and harmonious campus life. Drugs and alcohol not permitted on campus. Freshmen permitted cars on campus. **Housing:** Guaranteed on-campus for all undergraduates. Single-sex dorms, special housing for disabled, apartments available. On-campus privately operated 200 units of family housing, rental arranged by students. Quiet dorms available. **Activities:** Choral groups, dance, drama, music ensembles, musical theater, radio station, student government, student newspaper, Adventures in Art Club, athletics club, ceramics club, choreography club, Circus Club: Expressions of Creative Movement, Ethiopian Social Activities Association, fencing club, Go Club, Green Technology Club, hockey club, Indo-American Association, Intenders Club, knitting club, music club, The Not Funny Club, Peace Club, soccer club, theater club, Ultimate Frisbee Club.

Athletics. Intercollegiate: Golf. **Intramural:** Golf. **Team name:** Flyers.

Student services. Career counseling, financial aid counseling, health services, on-campus daycare, personal counseling, placement for graduates.

Contact. E-mail: admissions@mum.edu
Phone: (641) 472-1110 Toll-free number: (800) 369-6480
Fax: (641) 472-1179
Barbara Rainbow, Director of Admissions, Maharishi University of Management, Fairfield, IA 52557

Mercy College of Health Sciences

Des Moines, Iowa
www.mchs.edu **CB code: 2803**

- For-profit 4-year health science college affiliated with Roman Catholic Church
- Commuter campus in small city
- 656 degree-seeking undergraduates
- 59% of applicants admitted
- SAT or ACT (ACT writing optional) required

General. Regionally accredited. **Degrees:** 26 bachelor's, 200 associate awarded. **Calendar:** Semester. **Full-time faculty:** 29 total; 28% have terminal degrees, 3% minority, 86% women. **Part-time faculty:** 28 total; 4% have terminal degrees, 96% women.

Freshman class profile. 925 applied, 549 admitted, 45 enrolled.

Mid 50% test scores	ACT:	20-23

Basis for selection. Admission decisions based primarily on secondary school record and standardized test scores. Recommendations and interview also important.

2005-2006 Annual costs. Tuition/fees: $11,700. Books/supplies: $400.

Financial aid. Non-need-based: Scholarships awarded for academics.

Application procedures. Admission: Priority date 7/20; deadline 11/15 (postmark date). $25 fee, may be waived for applicants with need. Application may be submitted online. Admission notification on a rolling basis. **Financial aid:** Closing date 7/1. FAFSA required.

Academics. Special study options: Combined bachelor's/graduate degree. **Credit/placement by examination:** AP, CLEP. **Support services:** Tutoring, writing center.

Majors. Health: Health care admin, preop/surgical nursing.

Computing on campus. 40 workstations in library, computer center. Commuter students can connect to campus network. Online library available.

Student life. Freshman orientation: Mandatory. Preregistration for classes offered. Orientation and registration sessions last one day and are held at various times before the beginning of each term.

Student services. Financial aid counseling, minority student services.

Contact. E-mail: admissions@mchs.edu
Phone: (515) 643-6715 Toll-free number: (800) 637-2994 ext. 33180
Sandi Nagel, Admissions Rep, Mercy College of Health Sciences, 928 Sixth Avenue, Des Moines, IA 50309

Morningside College

Sioux City, Iowa
www.morningside.edu **CB code: 6415**

- Private 4-year liberal arts college affiliated with United Methodist Church
- Residential campus in small city
- 1,101 degree-seeking undergraduates: 4% part-time, 54% women, 2% African American, 1% Asian American, 3% Hispanic American, 2% international
- 88 degree-seeking graduate students
- 76% of applicants admitted
- SAT or ACT (ACT writing optional) required
- 57% graduate within 6 years; 8% enter graduate study

General. Founded in 1894. Regionally accredited. All full-time students receive notebook computers. **Degrees:** 123 bachelor's awarded; master's offered. **Location:** 90 miles from Omaha, Nebraska, 90 miles from Sioux Falls, South Dakota. **Calendar:** Semester, limited summer session. **Full-time faculty:** 66 total; 80% have terminal degrees, 3% minority, 42% women. **Part-time faculty:** 66 total; 2% minority, 64% women. **Class size:** 47% < 20, 50% 20-39, 2% 40-49, less than 1% 50-99. **Special facilities:** Biology research station.

Freshman class profile. 1,267 applied, 957 admitted, 309 enrolled.

Mid 50% test scores		End year in good standing:	84%
ACT:	19-25	Return as sophomores:	65%
GPA 3.50 or higher:	44%	Out-of-state:	34%
GPA 3.0-3.49:	29%	Live on campus:	91%
GPA 2.0-2.99:	27%	International:	2%
Rank in top quarter:	39%	Fraternities:	4%
Rank in top tenth:	17%	Sororities:	3%

Basis for selection. Minimum composite ACT of 20, or SAT of 930 (exclusive of Writing), and either ranked in top half of their class or have a high school GPA of 2.5 or better. Interview recommended. Audition or audition tape required for music majors, recommended for theater applicants. Portfolio recommended for art majors. **Homeschooled:** Must complete the application for admission and submit offical ACT or SAT results along with satisfactory transcript evaluation. In lieu of a transcript, a completed "Home School Credit Evaluation" form from Office of Admissions is accepted. **Learning Disabled:** Achievement Center staff will interview students and review recent aptitude and/or achievement test results. If requested, the staff will test students.

High school preparation. College-preparatory program recommended. 10 units recommended. Recommended units include English 3, mathematics 2, social studies 3 and science 2. Students wishing to pursue careers in math or science-related fields should complete 4 years of math and science in high school.

2005-2006 Annual costs. Tuition/fees: $18,080. Room/board: $5,624. Books/supplies: $800. Personal expenses: $1,500.

2005-2006 Financial aid. **Need-based:** 307 full-time freshmen applied for aid; 280 were judged to have need; 278 of these received aid. Average need met was 83%. Average scholarship/grant was $5,850; average loan $3,676. 53% of total undergraduate aid awarded as scholarships/grants, 47% as loans/jobs. **Non-need-based:** Awarded to 1,334 full-time undergraduates, including 502 freshmen. Scholarships awarded for academics, alumni affiliation, art, athletics, job skills, leadership, music/drama, religious affiliation, ROTC, state residency.

Application procedures. **Admission:** Priority date 8/15; no deadline. $25 fee, may be waived for applicants with need. Application may be submitted online. Admission notification on a rolling basis. **Financial aid:** Priority date 3/1; no closing date. FAFSA required. Applicants notified on a rolling basis starting 3/31.

Academics. **Special study options:** Distance learning, double major, dual enrollment of high school students, ESL, honors, independent study, internships, liberal arts/career combination, student-designed major, study abroad, teacher certification program, United Nations semester, Washington semester. **Credit/placement by examination:** AP, CLEP, IB, institutional tests. 32 credit hours maximum toward bachelor's degree. Maximum 12 hours may be used for general studies core requirements. **Support services:** Learning center, reduced course load, remedial instruction, study skills assistance, tutoring.

Majors. **Biology:** General. **Business:** Accounting, business admin, communications, finance, human resources, international, marketing. **Communications:** Advertising, broadcast journalism, journalism, media studies, radio/tv. **Computer sciences:** Programming. **Education:** General, art, biology, chemistry, elementary, emotionally handicapped, English, foreign languages, history, mathematics, mentally handicapped, multiple handicapped, music, physics, science, secondary, social science, Spanish, special. **Engineering:** Physics. **English:** English lit. **Foreign languages:** Spanish. **Health:** Clinical lab technology, nursing (RN), predentistry, premedicine, prepharmacy, preveterinary. **History:** General, American. **Interdisciplinary:** Biopsychology. **Math:** General. **Philosophy/religion:** Philosophy, religion. **Physical sciences:** Chemistry, physics. **Psychology:** General. **Social sciences:** International relations, political science. **Visual/performing arts:** Commercial/advertising art, dramatic, music performance, photography, studio arts.

Most popular majors. Business/marketing 27%, education 28%, health sciences 12%, visual/performing arts 8%.

Computing on campus. PC or laptop required. Dormitories wired for high-speed internet access and linked to campus network. Commuter students can connect to campus network. Online library, helpline, repair service, student web hosting, wireless network available.

Student life. **Freshman orientation:** Mandatory. Preregistration for classes offered. Held 4 days before school begins, followed by a mandatory freshman transition seminar. **Policies:** Freshmen permitted cars on campus. **Housing:** Guaranteed on-campus for freshmen. Coed dorms, apartments, fraternity/sorority housing available. $100 fully refundable deposit. Apartments for adult non-traditional students available. **Activities:** Bands, choral groups, dance, drama, literary magazine, music ensembles, musical theater, radio station, student government, student newspaper, symphony orchestra, TV station, Morningside Civic Union, Project Hope, Fellowship of Christian Athletes, Peace and Justice at Morningside, Mission Trips, Cross by Color, Spanish Club.

Athletics. NAIA. **Intercollegiate:** Baseball M, basketball, cross-country, football (tackle) M, golf, soccer, softball W, swimming, tennis, track and field, volleyball W. **Intramural:** Basketball, bowling, football (non-tackle), golf, soccer, softball, swimming, tennis, track and field, volleyball. **Team name:** Mustangs.

Student services. Alcohol/substance abuse counseling, campus ministries, career counseling, student employment services, financial aid counseling, health services, minority student services, personal counseling, placement for graduates, veterans' counselor. **Physically disabled:** Services for visually, speech, hearing impaired. **Learning disabled:** Comprehensive services available.

Contact. E-mail: mscadm@morningside.edu
Phone: (712) 274-5000 ext. 5111 Toll-free
number: (800) 831-0806 ext. 5111 Fax: (712) 274-5101
Joel Weyand, Director of Admissions, Morningside College, 1501 Morningside Avenue, Sioux City, IA 51106

Mount Mercy College

Cedar Rapids, Iowa
www.mtmercy.edu **CB code: 6417**

- Private 4-year liberal arts college affiliated with Roman Catholic Church
- Residential campus in small city
- 1,490 degree-seeking undergraduates
- 85% of applicants admitted
- SAT or ACT (ACT writing optional) required
- 61% graduate within 6 years

General. Founded in 1928. Regionally accredited. **Degrees:** 389 bachelor's awarded. **Location:** 220 miles from Chicago. **Calendar:** 4-1-4, limited summer session. **Full-time faculty:** 73 total; 81% have terminal degrees, 59% women. **Part-time faculty:** 78 total; 59% women. **Class size:** 77% < 20, 22% 20-39, less than 1% 40-49. **Special facilities:** Campus buildings connected by tunnel system.

Freshman class profile. 415 applied, 354 admitted, 181 enrolled.

Mid 50% test scores		**Rank in top quarter:**	41%
ACT:	20-24	**Rank in top tenth:**	19%
GPA 3.50 or higher:	44%	**Return as sophomores:**	76%
GPA 3.0-3.49:	40%	**Out-of-state:**	10%
GPA 2.0-2.99:	16%	**Live on campus:**	94%

Basis for selection. Minimum criteria for acceptance: GPA 2.5 or above, class rank in top half of high school class, ACT of 19 or above. **Homeschooled:** Transcript of courses and grades required. Submit records of high school and college-level studies or a detailed account of subjects studied and materials used and ACT scores.

High school preparation. Recommended units include English 4, mathematics 3, social studies 3, history 3, science 3 (laboratory 1) and foreign language 2.

2005-2006 Annual costs. Tuition/fees: $18,030. Room/board: $5,680. Books/supplies: $810. Personal expenses: $1,674.

2005-2006 Financial aid. **Need-based:** 176 full-time freshmen applied for aid; 151 were judged to have need; 151 of these received aid. Average need met was 87%. Average scholarship/grant was $11,614; average loan $4,738. **Non-need-based:** Scholarships awarded for academics, art, leadership, music/drama.

Application procedures. **Admission:** Priority date 8/15; deadline 8/25 (receipt date). $20 fee, may be waived for applicants with need. Application may be submitted online. Admission notification on a rolling basis. Must reply by May 1 or within 2 week(s) if notified thereafter. **Financial aid:** Priority date 3/1; no closing date. FAFSA required. Applicants notified on a rolling basis starting 3/15; must reply by 5/1 or within 3 week(s) of notification.

Academics. **Special study options:** Accelerated study, cross-registration, double major, dual enrollment of high school students, honors, independent study, internships, liberal arts/career combination, study abroad, teacher certification program. **Credit/placement by examination:** AP, CLEP, ACT, institutional tests. 60 credit hours maximum toward bachelor's degree. **Support services:** Learning center, remedial instruction, study skills assistance, tutoring, writing center.

Majors. **Biology:** General. **Business:** General, accounting, business admin. **Communications:** General. **Computer sciences:** General, computer science. **Education:** Elementary, secondary. **English:** Speech/rhetoric. **Health:** Clinical lab technology. **History:** General. **Legal studies:** Prelaw. **Liberal arts:** Arts/sciences. **Math:** General. **Philosophy/religion:** Philosophy, religion. **Psychology:** General. **Social sciences:** Sociology, urban studies. **Visual/performing arts:** Art, commercial/advertising art.

Most popular majors. Business/marketing 41%, education 13%, health sciences 11%.

Computing on campus. 135 workstations in dormitories, library, computer center. Dormitories wired for high-speed internet access and linked to

campus network. Commuter students can connect to campus network. Online library, helpline, wireless network available.

Student life. Freshman orientation: Mandatory. Preregistration for classes offered. 3-day orientation held prior to start of fall term freshman year. **Policies:** Freshmen permitted cars on campus. **Housing:** Guaranteed on-campus for all undergraduates. Coed dorms, apartments available. $50 fully refundable deposit, deadline 8/1. **Activities:** Choral groups, drama, literary magazine, musical theater, student government, student newspaper, volunteer association, campus ministry, social work organization, Bacchus.

Athletics. NAIA. **Intercollegiate:** Baseball M, basketball, cheerleading M, cross-country, golf, soccer, softball W, track and field, volleyball W. **Intramural:** Basketball, football (non-tackle) M, racquetball, soccer, softball, table tennis, tennis, volleyball. **Team name:** Mustangs.

Student services. Adult student services, alcohol/substance abuse counseling, campus ministries, career counseling, student employment services, financial aid counseling, health services, personal counseling, placement for graduates, veterans' counselor. **Physically disabled:** Services for visually, speech, hearing impaired.

Contact. E-mail: admission@mtmercy.edu
Phone: (319) 368-6460 Toll-free number: (800) 248-4504
Fax: (319) 363-5270
Jim Krystofiak, Dean of Admission, Mount Mercy College, 1330 Elmhurst Drive NE, Cedar Rapids, IA 52402-4797

Northwestern College
Orange City, Iowa
www.nwciowa.edu **CB code: 6490**

- Private 4-year liberal arts college affiliated with Reformed Church in America
- Residential campus in small town
- 1,247 degree-seeking undergraduates: 2% part-time, 62% women, 1% African American, 1% Asian American, 1% Hispanic American, 2% international
- 93% of applicants admitted
- SAT or ACT required
- 60% graduate within 6 years

General. Founded in 1882. Regionally accredited. **Degrees:** 285 bachelor's, 4 associate awarded. **Location:** 40 miles from Sioux City, 75 miles from Sioux Falls, South Dakota. **Calendar:** Semester, limited summer session. **Full-time faculty:** 78 total; 80% have terminal degrees, 3% minority, 32% women. **Part-time faculty:** 50 total; 4% have terminal degrees, 64% women. **Class size:** 67% < 20, 55% 20-39, 2% 40-49, less than 1% 50-99. **Special facilities:** Natural prairie restoration project.

Freshman class profile. 1,185 applied, 1,101 admitted, 374 enrolled.

Mid 50% test scores		**Return as sophomores:**	76%
ACT:	21-27	**Out-of-state:**	49%
Rank in top quarter:	58%	**Live on campus:**	95%
Rank in top tenth:	26%	**International:**	1%

Basis for selection. Top half of class and test scores above fiftieth percentile most important. Recommendations also important. Must have GPA of 2.0 on 4.0 scale to be considered. Interview and essay recommended. Audition recommended for theater, music majors. Portfolio recommended for art majors. **Homeschooled:** Transcript of courses and grades required. **Learning Disabled:** Prospective students with a documented learning disability are asked to provide such documentation to the Director of Academic Support upon admittance, as it is used to assist with meeting student learning needs.

High school preparation. 16 units recommended. Recommended units include English 4, mathematics 3, social studies 3, science 3 and foreign language 3.

2005-2006 Annual costs. Tuition/fees: $17,260. 1-4 credits $365 per credit hour; 5-8 credits $545 per credit hour; 9-11 credits $725 per credit hour. Room/board: $4,914. Books/supplies: $900. Personal expenses: $2,026.

2004-2005 Financial aid. Need-based: 341 full-time freshmen applied for aid; 289 were judged to have need; 289 of these received aid. Average need met was 95%. Average scholarship/grant was $4,931; average loan $3,414. 54% of total undergraduate aid awarded as scholarships/grants, 46% as loans/jobs. **Non-need-based:** Awarded to 1,447 full-time undergraduates, including 467 freshmen. Scholarships awarded for academics, art, athletics, music/drama, religious affiliation, state residency.

Application procedures. Admission: Priority date 6/2; no deadline. $25 fee, may be waived for applicants with need. Application may be submitted online. Admission notification on a rolling basis beginning on or about 10/1. Must reply by May 1 or within 3 week(s) if notified thereafter. **Financial aid:** Priority date 4/1, closing date 6/30. FAFSA required. Applicants notified on a rolling basis starting 3/15; must reply within 3 week(s) of notification.

Academics. Special study options: Combined bachelor's/graduate degree, double major, ESL, honors, independent study, internships, liberal arts/career combination, student-designed major, study abroad, teacher certification program, Washington semester. Off-campus study programs: American Studies Program (Washington, D.C.), AuSable Inst of Environmental Studies Program (Michigan), Los Angeles Film Studies Semester, Chicago Metropolitan Studies Program (Chicago), China Studies Program (Xiaman, China), Middle East Studies Program (Cairo, Egypt), Oxford Summer Program (Oxford, England), Russian Studies Program, Contemporary Music Center (Martha's Vineyard, MA), Latin American Studies Program (Costa Rica), Oxford Honours Programme (England), Trinity Christian College: Semester in Spain, Creation Care Study Program, and Summer Institute of Journalism (Washington, DC). **Credit/placement by examination:** AP, CLEP, IB, institutional tests. 24 credit hours maximum toward associate degree, 24 toward bachelor's. **Support services:** Learning center, reduced course load, remedial instruction, tutoring, writing center.

Majors. Agriculture: Business. **Biology:** General. **Business:** Accounting, actuarial science, business admin, finance, managerial economics, marketing. **Communications:** General. **Computer sciences:** General, computer science. **Conservation:** General. **Education:** General, elementary. **English:** Speech/rhetoric. **Foreign languages:** Spanish. **Health:** Athletic training, clinical lab technology, predentistry, premedicine, preveterinary. **History:** General. **Liberal arts:** Arts/sciences. **Math:** General. **Parks/recreation:** Exercise sciences, health/fitness. **Philosophy/religion:** Philosophy, religion. **Physical sciences:** Chemistry. **Psychology:** General. **Public administration:** Social work. **Social sciences:** Economics, political science, sociology. **Theology:** Religious ed. **Visual/performing arts:** Art.

Most popular majors. Biology 7%, business/marketing 22%, education 20%, visual/performing arts 6%.

Computing on campus. 250 workstations in dormitories, library, computer center. Dormitories linked to campus network. Commuter students can connect to campus network. Online course registration, helpline, repair service, wireless network available.

Student life. Freshman orientation: Available. Preregistration for classes offered. One-day orientation program in late May. **Policies:** Use of alcohol prohibited on campus. Resident living required for all students unless granted commuting status or living with parents. Religious observance required. Freshmen permitted cars on campus. **Housing:** Guaranteed on-campus for all undergraduates. Single-sex dorms, special housing for disabled, apartments available. $100 deposit, deadline 8/1. **Activities:** Bands, choral groups, dance, drama, literary magazine, music ensembles, student government, student newspaper, symphony orchestra, TV station, student activities council, Fellowship of Christian Athletes, College Republicans, Campus Democrats, Phi Beta Lambda, Sigma Tau, Spanish club, education club, student ministries, international student organization.

Athletics. NAIA. **Intercollegiate:** Baseball M, basketball, cross-country, football (tackle) M, golf, soccer, softball W, tennis, track and field, volleyball W, wrestling M. **Intramural:** Badminton, basketball, bowling, football (non-tackle), golf, racquetball, soccer, softball, table tennis, tennis, volleyball. **Team name:** Red Raiders.

Student services. Alcohol/substance abuse counseling, campus ministries, career counseling, student employment services, financial aid counseling, health services, personal counseling, placement for graduates. **Physically disabled:** Services for visually, speech, hearing impaired.

Contact. E-mail: admissions@nwciowa.edu
Phone: (712) 707-7130 Toll-free number: (800) 747-4757
Fax: (712) 707-7164
Mark Bloemendaal, Director of Admissions, Northwestern College, 101 7th Street, SW, Orange City, IA 51041

St. Ambrose University
Davenport, Iowa
www.sau.edu **CB code: 6617**

- Private 4-year university and liberal arts college affiliated with Roman Catholic Church
- Residential campus in small city
- 2,634 degree-seeking undergraduates: 17% part-time, 60% women, 3% African American, 1% Asian American, 3% Hispanic American, 1% international

- 831 degree-seeking graduate students
- 84% of applicants admitted
- SAT or ACT with writing required
- 58% graduate within 6 years; 22% enter graduate study

General. Founded in 1882. Regionally accredited. **Degrees:** 553 bachelor's awarded; master's, doctoral offered. **Location:** 180 miles from Des Moines, 175 miles from Chicago. **Calendar:** 4-1-4, limited summer session. **Full-time faculty:** 157 total; 81% have terminal degrees, 7% minority, 42% women. **Part-time faculty:** 130 total; 6% have terminal degrees, 6% minority, 47% women. **Class size:** 60% < 20, 40% 20-39, less than 1% 40-49. **Special facilities:** Transmission electron microscope, cable television channel, observatory, national prairie garden.

Freshman class profile. 1,634 applied, 1,373 admitted, 474 enrolled.

Mid 50% test scores		**Rank in top tenth:**	16%
ACT:	19-25	**End year in good standing:**	90%
GPA 3.50 or higher:	33%	**Return as sophomores:**	485%
GPA 3.0-3.49:	28%	**Out-of-state:**	53%
GPA 2.0-2.99:	39%	**Live on campus:**	93%
Rank in top quarter:	36%	**International:**	1%

Basis for selection. Minimum high school GPA 2.5; SAT combined score 780 (exclusive of writing), ACT 20 required, or rank in top half of class. Interview recommended. Portfolio required for art majors. **Homeschooled:** Prospective students who do not have a high school diploma required to score 50 or higher on GED with ACT composite score of 18 or SAT score of 860.

High school preparation. College-preparatory program recommended. 18 units recommended. Recommended units include English 4, mathematics 3, social studies 1, history 1, science 2 (laboratory 2), foreign language 1 and academic electives 4.

2005-2006 Annual costs. Tuition/fees: $18,530. Room/board: $6,965. Books/supplies: $800. Personal expenses: $1,035.

2005-2006 Financial aid. Need-based: 468 full-time freshmen applied for aid; 403 were judged to have need; 403 of these received aid. Average need met was 21%. Average scholarship/grant was $9,150; average loan $2,742. 41% of total undergraduate aid awarded as scholarships/grants, 59% as loans/jobs. **Non-need-based:** Awarded to 1,233 full-time undergraduates, including 161 freshmen. Scholarships awarded for academics, alumni affiliation, art, athletics, job skills, music/drama. **Additional information:** Iowa applicants must apply for financial aid by July 1. Audition required for music, drama scholarship applicants.

Application procedures. Admission: No deadline. $25 fee, may be waived for applicants with need. Application may be submitted online. Admission notification on a rolling basis beginning on or about 10/1. Must reply by May 1 or within 2 week(s) if notified thereafter. **Financial aid:** Priority date 3/15; no closing date. FAFSA required. Applicants notified on a rolling basis starting 2/1; must reply within 2 week(s) of notification.

Academics. Service learning program provides opportunities for community service, coordinated by faculty and community agencies. **Special study options:** Accelerated study, combined bachelor's/graduate degree, cooperative education, distance learning, double major, independent study, internships, liberal arts/career combination, student-designed major, study abroad, teacher certification program. Service learning program in which students work as volunteers for community and earn 1-3 semester hours credit, license preparation for occupational therapy on campus, accounting majors volunteer to work on income tax forms for low income families on campus. **Credit/placement by examination:** AP, CLEP, IB, SAT, ACT, institutional tests. 60 credit hours maximum toward bachelor's degree. **Support services:** Learning center, pre-admission summer program, reduced course load, remedial instruction, study skills assistance, tutoring, writing center.

Majors. Biology: General. **Business:** General, accounting, business admin, finance, international, management science, marketing, organizational behavior. **Communications:** General, advertising, broadcast journalism, journalism, media studies, public relations, radio/tv. **Computer sciences:** General, computer science, information systems, LAN/WAN management, security, systems analysis. **Education:** General, art, biology, business, chemistry, early childhood, elementary, English, foreign languages, French, German, health, history, mathematics, music, physical, physics, psychology, science, secondary, social science, Spanish. **Engineering:** Industrial, physics. **English:** Speech/rhetoric. **Foreign languages:** French, German, Spanish. **Health:** Nursing (RN). **History:** General. **Interdisciplinary:** Biological/physical sciences, natural sciences, neuroscience. **Math:** General. **Parks/recreation:** Health/fitness, sports admin. **Philosophy/religion:** Philosophy. **Physical sciences:** Chemistry, physics. **Protective services:** Criminal justice, criminalistics. **Psychology:** General. **Public administration:** General. **Social sciences:** Economics, political science, sociology. **Visual/performing arts:** Commercial/advertising art, dramatic, graphic design, multimedia, studio arts, theater arts management.

Most popular majors. Business/marketing 28%, communications/journalism 7%, education 15%, psychology 11%.

Computing on campus. 190 workstations in library, computer center, student center. Dormitories wired for high-speed internet access and linked to campus network. Commuter students can connect to campus network. Online course registration, online library, helpline, repair service, wireless network available.

Student life. Freshman orientation: Mandatory. Preregistration for classes offered. Held April through August, 2 days per month. **Policies:** Campus smoke-free in all buildings. Freshmen permitted cars on campus. **Housing:** Guaranteed on-campus for freshmen. Coed dorms, single-sex dorms, special housing for disabled, apartments, substance-free housing available. $250 partly refundable deposit, deadline 5/1. Townhouses for seniors available. Juniors, seniors and graduates may rent space in college-owned houses near campus. **Activities:** Bands, choral groups, dance, drama, literary magazine, music ensembles, musical theater, opera, radio station, student government, student newspaper, symphony orchestra, TV station, Fellowship of Christian Athletes, black student union, philosophy club, Young Republicans, Young Democrats, veterans club, art club, music club, psychology club, multicultural club.

Athletics. NAIA. **Intercollegiate:** Baseball M, basketball, cheerleading, cross-country, football (tackle) M, golf, soccer, softball W, tennis, track and field, volleyball. **Intramural:** Badminton, basketball, bowling, football (non-tackle), golf, handball, racquetball, softball, tennis, triathlon, volleyball. **Team name:** Fighting Bees.

Student services. Adult student services, alcohol/substance abuse counseling, campus ministries, career counseling, student employment services, financial aid counseling, health services, minority student services, on-campus daycare, personal counseling, placement for graduates, veterans' counselor, women's services. **Physically disabled:** Services for visually, speech, hearing impaired.

Contact. E-mail: admit@sau.edu
Phone: (563) 333-6300 Toll-free number: (800) 383-2627
Fax: (563) 333-6243
Meg Halligan, Director of Admissions, St. Ambrose University, 518 West Locust Street, Davenport, IA 52803-2898

Simpson College

Indianola, Iowa **CB member**
www.simpson.edu **CB code: 6650**

- Private 4-year liberal arts college affiliated with United Methodist Church
- Residential campus in large town
- 1,899 degree-seeking undergraduates: 22% part-time, 59% women
- 25 degree-seeking graduate students
- 87% of applicants admitted
- SAT or ACT (ACT writing optional) required
- 70% graduate within 6 years; 16% enter graduate study

General. Founded in 1860. Regionally accredited. **Degrees:** 342 bachelor's awarded. **Location:** 12 miles from Des Moines. **Calendar:** 4-4-1. Limited summer session. **Full-time faculty:** 87 total; 90% have terminal degrees, 5% minority, 38% women. **Part-time faculty:** 83 total; 40% have terminal degrees, 35% women. **Class size:** 68% < 20, 31% 20-39, less than 1% 40-49, less than 1% 50-99. **Special facilities:** Extensive Antebellum Era collection, cadaver laboratory, mock classroom.

Freshman class profile. 1,216 applied, 1,055 admitted, 336 enrolled.

Mid 50% test scores		**Return as sophomores:**	82%
ACT:	22-27	**Out-of-state:**	12%
Rank in top quarter:	61%	**Live on campus:**	93%
Rank in top tenth:	30%	**Fraternities:**	20%
End year in good standing:	88%	**Sororities:**	25%

Basis for selection. High school academic record, including college preparatory courses taken and grades received in those courses, class rank, and ACT/SAT scores most important. Recommendations also considered. Interview recommended. Audition recommended for music, drama majors. Portfolio recommended for art majors. Auditions and portfolios required for scholarships in music, theater, or art. **Homeschooled:** Must submit GED or high school diploma and ACT or SAT scores.

High school preparation. 16 units recommended. Recommended units include English 4, mathematics 3, social studies 3, science 3 (laboratory 3) and foreign language 3.

2005-2006 Annual costs. Tuition/fees: $20,911. Room/board: $5,922. Books/supplies: $900. Personal expenses: $1,300.

2004-2005 Financial aid. **Need-based:** 336 full-time freshmen applied for aid; 290 were judged to have need; 290 of these received aid. Average need met was 87%. Average scholarship/grant was $13,935; average loan $3,208. 69% of total undergraduate aid awarded as scholarships/grants, 31% as loans/jobs. **Non-need-based:** Awarded to 363 full-time undergraduates, including 81 freshmen. Scholarships awarded for academics, alumni affiliation, art, leadership, minority status, music/drama, religious affiliation, state residency. **Additional information:** Music and theater scholarships based on audition. Art scholarships based on portfolio.

Application procedures. **Admission:** Priority date 5/1; no deadline. No application fee. Application may be submitted online. Admission notification on a rolling basis. **Financial aid:** Priority date 4/1; no closing date. FAFSA required. Applicants notified on a rolling basis starting 3/15; must reply by 5/1 or within 3 week(s) of notification.

Academics. **Special study options:** Accelerated study, combined bachelor's/graduate degree, cooperative education, distance learning, double major, dual enrollment of high school students, external degree, honors, independent study, internships, liberal arts/career combination, study abroad, teacher certification program, United Nations semester, Washington semester, weekend college. 3-2 and 4-2 engineering program with Washington University in St. Louis, Iowa State University, and University of Minnesota. **Credit/placement by examination:** AP, CLEP, IB, institutional tests. 24 credit hours maximum toward bachelor's degree. **Support services:** Learning center, study skills assistance, tutoring, writing center.

Majors. **Biology:** General, biochemistry. **Business:** Accounting, business admin, international, managerial economics, marketing. **Communications:** General, journalism, media studies, public relations. **Computer sciences:** Computer science, information systems. **Conservation:** Environmental science. **Education:** General, art, early childhood, elementary, middle, music, physical, secondary. **English:** English lit. **Foreign languages:** French, German, Spanish. **Health:** Athletic training, predentistry, premedicine, prepharmacy, preveterinary. **History:** General. **Legal studies:** Prelaw. **Liberal arts:** Arts/sciences. **Math:** General. **Parks/recreation:** Health/fitness, sports admin. **Philosophy/religion:** Philosophy, religion. **Physical sciences:** Chemistry, physics. **Protective services:** Criminal justice, forensics. **Psychology:** General. **Social sciences:** Economics, international relations, political science, sociology. **Visual/performing arts:** Art, dramatic, music performance.

Most popular majors. Business/marketing 28%, education 7%, liberal arts 6%, social sciences 10%.

Computing on campus. 286 workstations in dormitories, library, computer center, student center. Dormitories wired for high-speed internet access and linked to campus network. Commuter students can connect to campus network. Online library, repair service, wireless network available.

Student life. **Freshman orientation:** Mandatory. Preregistration for classes offered. Students attend 1 of 4 summer registration/orientation one day programs in June. **Policies:** Freshmen permitted cars on campus. **Housing:** Guaranteed on-campus for all undergraduates. Coed dorms, single-sex dorms, apartments, fraternity/sorority housing, substance-free housing available. $200 deposit. Theme housing available. **Activities:** Bands, choral groups, dance, drama, literary magazine, music ensembles, musical theater, opera, radio station, student government, student newspaper, Religious Life Community, concerned multicultural students, Alpha Phi Omega, Young Democrats, Young Republicans, Fellowship of Christian Athletes, students embracing responsible volunteer experiences, Habitat for Humanity, Amnesty International.

Athletics. NCAA. **Intercollegiate:** Baseball M, basketball, cheerleading, cross-country, football (tackle) M, golf, soccer, softball W, swimming W, tennis, track and field, volleyball W, wrestling M. **Intramural:** Badminton, basketball, football (non-tackle), golf, racquetball, soccer, softball, swimming, table tennis, tennis, volleyball, weight lifting. **Team name:** Storm.

Student services. Adult student services, campus ministries, career counseling, student employment services, financial aid counseling, health services, minority student services, personal counseling, placement for graduates. **Physically disabled:** Services for visually, speech, hearing impaired.

Contact. E-mail: admiss@simpson.edu
Phone: (515) 961-1624 Toll-free number: (800) 362-2454
Fax: (515) 961-1870
Deborah Tierney, Vice President for Enrollment, Simpson College, 701 North C Street, Indianola, IA 50125

University of Dubuque

Dubuque, Iowa — **CB member**
www.dbq.edu — **CB code: 6869**

- Private 4-year university and seminary college affiliated with Presbyterian Church (USA)
- Residential campus in small city
- 1,175 degree-seeking undergraduates: 4% part-time, 38% women, 12% African American, 1% Asian American, 4% Hispanic American, 2% Native American, 1% international
- 262 degree-seeking graduate students
- 77% of applicants admitted
- SAT or ACT (ACT writing optional), application essay required
- 59% graduate within 6 years; 24% enter graduate study

General. Founded in 1852. Regionally accredited. **Degrees:** 180 bachelor's, 1 associate awarded; master's, doctoral, first professional offered. **ROTC:** Army. **Location:** 180 miles from Chicago. **Calendar:** Semester, limited summer session. **Full-time faculty:** 70 total; 74% have terminal degrees, 10% minority, 39% women. **Part-time faculty:** 88 total; 30% have terminal degrees, 2% minority, 49% women. **Class size:** 59% < 20, 40% 20-39, less than 1% 40-49, less than 1% 50-99. **Special facilities:** Floating laboratory on Mississippi River, curriculum laboratory for teachers, aviation operations center, studio laboratory for animation program, wetland area management.

Freshman class profile. 885 applied, 681 admitted, 309 enrolled.

Mid 50% test scores		**Rank in top tenth:**	7%
SAT verbal:	400-540	**End year in good standing:**	99%
SAT math:	410-560	**Return as sophomores:**	65%
ACT:	18-23	**Out-of-state:**	60%
GPA 3.50 or higher:	20%	**Live on campus:**	71%
GPA 3.0-3.49:	20%	**Fraternities:**	18%
GPA 2.0-2.99:	60%	**Sororities:**	14%
Rank in top quarter:	21%		

Basis for selection. Minimum ACT score 18, SAT score 860 (exclusive of writing), rank in top half of class most important for admission. 2.0 GPA in college preparatory classes also considered. Recommendations required. **Learning Disabled:** Students must request assistance.

High school preparation. College-preparatory program recommended. 10 units required; 15 recommended. Required and recommended units include English 4, mathematics 2-3, social studies 2-3, science 2-3 and foreign language 2.

2005-2006 Annual costs. Tuition/fees: $17,470. Room/board: $5,950. Books/supplies: $750.

2005-2006 Financial aid. **Need-based:** 290 full-time freshmen applied for aid; 266 were judged to have need; 264 of these received aid. Average need met was 87%. Average scholarship/grant was $9,189; average loan $9,302. 50% of total undergraduate aid awarded as scholarships/grants, 50% as loans/jobs. **Non-need-based:** Scholarships awarded for academics, alumni affiliation, music/drama, ROTC.

Application procedures. **Admission:** No deadline. $25 fee, may be waived for applicants with need. Application may be submitted online. Admission notification on a rolling basis. Must reply by May 1 or within 3 week(s) if notified thereafter. **Financial aid:** Priority date 4/1; no closing date. FAFSA required. Applicants notified on a rolling basis starting 3/1; must reply within 3 week(s) of notification.

Academics. **Special study options:** Combined bachelor's/graduate degree, cooperative education, cross-registration, double major, dual enrollment of high school students, independent study, internships, liberal arts/career combination, study abroad, teacher certification program, urban semester. Undergraduate students may take graduate courses. **Credit/placement by examination:** AP, CLEP, IB, SAT, ACT, institutional tests. 24 credit hours maximum toward associate degree, 24 toward bachelor's. **Support services:** Learning center, reduced course load, remedial instruction, study skills assistance, tutoring, writing center.

Majors. **Biology:** General, ecology. **Business:** Accounting, business admin. **Communications:** General. **Computer sciences:** General, computer graphics. **Conservation:** General, environmental studies. **Education:** Elementary, physical. **English:** Speech/rhetoric. **Health:** Nursing (RN). **Parks/recreation:** General. **Philosophy/religion:** Philosophy, religion. **Physical sciences:** Planetary. **Protective services:** Criminal justice. **Psychology:** General. **Social sciences:** Sociology. **Transportation:** Aviation, aviation management, flight instructor. **Visual/performing arts:** Commercial/advertising art, graphic design.

Most popular majors. Business/marketing 15%, computer/information sciences 20%, education 10%, health sciences 10%, physical sciences 7%, psychology 6%, social sciences 6%.

Computing on campus. 200 workstations in dormitories, library, computer center, student center. Dormitories wired for high-speed internet access and linked to campus network. Commuter students can connect to campus network. Online course registration, online library, helpline, student web hosting available.

Student life. Freshman orientation: Mandatory, $60 fee. Preregistration for classes offered. 4 days prior to beginning of class. **Policies:** Students are required to live on-campus through their junior year or until they reach 21 years of age. Student's whose home is within 50 miles of campus are exempt. Freshmen permitted cars on campus. **Housing:** Guaranteed on-campus for freshmen. Coed dorms, special housing for disabled, apartments, substance-free housing available. $200 fully refundable deposit, deadline 6/1. Houses and townhouses available. **Activities:** Pep band, choral groups, dance, drama, film society, music ensembles, student government, student newspaper, campus ministry, social service and international organizations, service fraternity, Web of Life (environmental group), student activities board, College Republicans, College Democrats.

Athletics. NCAA. **Intercollegiate:** Baseball M, basketball, cross-country, football (tackle) M, golf, soccer, softball W, tennis, track and field, volleyball W, wrestling M. **Intramural:** Archery, badminton, baseball M, basketball, bowling, cheerleading, football (non-tackle) M, golf, racquetball, soccer, softball, table tennis, tennis, volleyball. **Team name:** Spartans.

Student services. Alcohol/substance abuse counseling, campus ministries, career counseling, student employment services, financial aid counseling, health services, minority student services, personal counseling, placement for graduates, veterans' counselor.

Contact. E-mail: admssns@dbq.edu
Phone: (563) 589-3200 Toll-free number: (800) 722-5583
Fax: (563) 589-3690
Jesse James, Director of Admission, University of Dubuque, 2000 University Avenue, Dubuque, IA 52001-5099

University of Iowa

Iowa City, Iowa **CB member**
www.uiowa.edu **CB code: 6681**

- Public 4-year university
- Residential campus in small city
- 19,566 degree-seeking undergraduates: 7% part-time, 53% women, 2% African American, 4% Asian American, 2% Hispanic American, 1% international
- 8,126 graduate students
- 84% of applicants admitted
- SAT or ACT (ACT writing optional) required
- 66% graduate within 6 years

General. Founded in 1847. Regionally accredited. **Degrees:** 4,041 bachelor's awarded; master's, doctoral, first professional offered. **ROTC:** Army, Air Force. **Location:** 20 miles from Cedar Rapids, 110 miles from Des Moines. **Calendar:** Semester, extensive summer session. **Full-time faculty:** 1,595 total; 96% have terminal degrees, 14% minority, 28% women. **Part-time faculty:** 98 total; 96% have terminal degrees, 5% minority, 24% women. **Class size:** 49% < 20, 37% 20-39, 4% 40-49, 6% 50-99, 4% >100. **Special facilities:** Art museum, field campus, accelerator, observatory, natural history museum, driving simulator.

Freshman class profile. 13,241 applied, 11,122 admitted, 3,849 enrolled.

Mid 50% test scores		**Rank in top quarter:**	53%
SAT verbal:	520-650	**Rank in top tenth:**	22%
SAT math:	540-660	**Return as sophomores:**	84%
ACT:	22-27	**Out-of-state:**	39%
GPA 3.50 or higher:	57%	**Live on campus:**	90%
GPA 3.0-3.49:	36%	**International:**	1%
GPA 2.0-2.99:	7%		

Basis for selection. For in-state applicants, rank in top half of class or acceptable admission index score (combination of class rank and test scores). For nonresidents, rank in top 30% or acceptable admission index score. Students must have completed specific high school course units. Audition required of music, dance majors.

High school preparation. College-preparatory program required. 15 units required. Required and recommended units include English 4, mathematics 3, social studies 3, science 3 and foreign language 2-4. Mathematics units must include 2 algebra, 1 geometry; engineering majors require fourth unit of higher mathematics. Science units must include 1 from any 2 of the following: biology, chemistry, and physics. Engineering requires 1 unit chemistry and 1 unit physics. Engineering majors require only 2 units social studies.

2005-2006 Annual costs. Tuition/fees: $5,612; $16,998 out-of-state. Room/board: $6,073. Books/supplies: $840. Personal expenses: $2,400.

Financial aid. Non-need-based: Scholarships awarded for academics, athletics, leadership, minority status, music/drama.

Application procedures. Admission: Priority date 2/1; deadline 4/1 (postmark date). $40 fee, may be waived for applicants with need. Application may be submitted online. Admission notification on a rolling basis beginning on or about 9/15. Must reply by May 1 or within 2 week(s) if notified thereafter. **Financial aid:** Priority date 1/1; no closing date. FAFSA, institutional form required. Applicants notified on a rolling basis starting 3/1.

Academics. Distance learning programs available via several options; bachelor of liberal studies degree may be earned with distance education course work. **Special study options:** Accelerated study, combined bachelor's/graduate degree, cooperative education, distance learning, double major, dual enrollment of high school students, ESL, exchange student, external degree, honors, independent study, internships, student-designed major, study abroad, teacher certification program, Washington semester. **Credit/placement by examination:** AP, CLEP, IB, SAT, ACT, institutional tests. 30 credit hours maximum toward bachelor's degree. **Support services:** Learning center, pre-admission summer program, reduced course load, remedial instruction, study skills assistance, tutoring, writing center.

Majors. Area/ethnic studies: African, African-American, American, Asian, Russian/Slavic, women's. **Biology:** General, biochemistry, microbiology. **Business:** Accounting, actuarial science, business admin, finance, human resources, labor relations, management information systems, management science, managerial economics, marketing. **Communications:** General, journalism, media studies. **Computer sciences:** General, computer science. **Conservation:** Environmental science, environmental studies. **Education:** Elementary. **Engineering:** General, biomedical, chemical, civil, electrical, industrial, mechanical. **English:** Speech/rhetoric. **Foreign languages:** Ancient Greek, Chinese, classics, comparative lit, French, German, Italian, Japanese, Latin, linguistics, Portuguese, Russian, Sanskrit, Spanish. **Health:** Athletic training, audiology/hearing, clinical lab science, music therapy, nuclear medical technology, nursing (RN), predentistry, premedicine, prenursing, prepharmacy, preveterinary, radiologic technology/medical imaging, recreational therapy. **History:** General. **Interdisciplinary:** Ancient studies, global studies. **Legal studies:** Prelaw. **Liberal arts:** Arts/sciences. **Math:** General, applied, statistics. **Parks/recreation:** General, exercise sciences, facilities management, sports admin. **Philosophy/religion:** Philosophy, religion. **Physical sciences:** Astronomy, chemistry, geology, physics. **Psychology:** General. **Public administration:** Social work. **Social sciences:** Anthropology, economics, geography, political science, sociology. **Visual/performing arts:** Art, art history/conservation, arts management, ceramics, cinematography, dance, dramatic, drawing, film/cinema, jazz, metal/jewelry, music management, music performance, music theory/composition, painting, photography, piano/organ, printmaking, sculpture, stringed instruments, studio arts, voice/opera.

Most popular majors. Business/marketing 19%, communications/journalism 10%, English 6%, psychology 8%, social sciences 15%, visual/performing arts 7%.

Computing on campus. 1,100 workstations in dormitories, library, computer center, student center. Dormitories wired for high-speed internet access and linked to campus network. Commuter students can connect to campus network. Online course registration, helpline, repair service, student web hosting, wireless network available.

Student life. Freshman orientation: Mandatory, $175 fee. Preregistration for classes offered. 2-day summer program. **Policies:** Freshmen permitted cars on campus. **Housing:** Coed dorms, special housing for disabled, apartments, fraternity/sorority housing, substance-free housing available. $50 deposit. International, freshman and transfer honors, and quiet houses available. Special house for women in science and engineering. Special floors for men in engineering; students in prebusiness, performing arts, health/science, writing. Healthy lifestyle floors. **Activities:** Bands, choral groups, dance, drama, film society, literary magazine, music ensembles, musical theater, opera, radio station, student government, student newspaper, symphony orchestra, College Republicans, University Democrats, American Indian Student association, Hispanic Society, Black Student Union, Amnesty International.

Athletics. NCAA. **Intercollegiate:** Baseball M, basketball, cheerleading, cross-country, diving, field hockey W, football (tackle) M, golf, gymnastics, rowing (crew) W, soccer W, softball W, swimming, tennis, track and field, volleyball W, wrestling M. **Intramural:** Badminton, basketball, bowling, football (non-tackle), golf, racquetball, soccer, softball, table tennis, tennis, volleyball, wrestling. **Team name:** Hawkeyes.

Student services. Adult student services, alcohol/substance abuse counseling, campus ministries, career counseling, student employment services, financial aid counseling, health services, legal services, minority student services, on-campus daycare, personal counseling, placement for graduates, veterans' counselor, women's services. **Physically disabled:** Services for visually, speech, hearing impaired.

Contact. E-mail: admissions@uiowa.edu
Phone: (319) 335-3847 Toll-free number: (800) 553-4692
Fax: (319) 335-1535
Michael Barron, Assistant Provost for Enrollment Services, University of Iowa, 107 Calvin Hall, Iowa City, IA 52242

University of Northern Iowa

Cedar Falls, Iowa
www.uni.edu **CB code: 6307**

- Public 4-year university
- Residential campus in small city
- 10,734 degree-seeking undergraduates: 10% part-time, 57% women, 3% African American, 1% Asian American, 1% Hispanic American, 2% international
- 1,348 degree-seeking graduate students
- 78% of applicants admitted
- SAT or ACT (ACT writing optional) required
- 65% graduate within 6 years

General. Founded in 1876. Regionally accredited. **Degrees:** 2,669 bachelor's awarded; master's, doctoral offered. **ROTC:** Army. **Location:** 63 miles from Cedar Rapids. **Calendar:** Semester, limited summer session. **Full-time faculty:** 641 total; 81% have terminal degrees, 12% minority, 43% women. **Part-time faculty:** 188 total; 29% have terminal degrees, 4% minority, 50% women. **Class size:** 33% < 20, 51% 20-39, 7% 40-49, 7% 50-99, 2% >100. **Special facilities:** Performing arts center, domed stadium, center for energy and environmental education, NASA teacher resource center, museum, observatory, wellness and recreation center, natural preserve.

Freshman class profile. 4,360 applied, 3,422 admitted, 1,737 enrolled.

Mid 50% test scores		Return as sophomores:	81%
SAT verbal:	470-590	Out-of-state:	8%
SAT math:	490-640	Live on campus:	89%
ACT:	20-25	International:	1%
Rank in top quarter:	48%	Fraternities:	6%
Rank in top tenth:	19%	Sororities:	3%
End year in good standing:	95%		

Basis for selection. Rank in top half of class, completion of high school curriculum requirements most important factors for admission. In the absence of class rank, standardized test scores may carry greater weight in the admissions process. Audition required of music majors. Interview may be recommended for borderline applicants who do not meet admission requirements. **Homeschooled:** Statement describing homeschool structure and mission, transcript of courses and grades required.

High school preparation. 15 units required. Required and recommended units include English 4, mathematics 3, social studies 3, science 3 (laboratory 1), foreign language 2 and academic electives 2. English units must include 1 composition. Mathematics units must include algebra, geometry and advanced algebra. Two electives required in subjects listed above and/or fine arts.

2005-2006 Annual costs. Tuition/fees: $5,602; $13,214 out-of-state. Room/board: $5,531. Books/supplies: $838. Personal expenses: $2,545.

2005-2006 Financial aid. Need-based: 1,460 full-time freshmen applied for aid; 949 were judged to have need; 913 of these received aid. Average need met was 65%. Average scholarship/grant was $2,556; average loan $2,701. 30% of total undergraduate aid awarded as scholarships/grants, 70% as loans/jobs. **Non-need-based:** Awarded to 2,569 full-time undergraduates, including 795 freshmen. Scholarships awarded for academics, alumni affiliation, art, athletics, leadership, minority status, music/drama, ROTC, state residency.

Application procedures. Admission: Closing date 8/15 (postmark date). $30 fee. Application may be submitted online. Admission notification on a rolling basis beginning on or about 9/1. **Financial aid:** No deadline. FAFSA required. Applicants notified on a rolling basis starting 3/1.

Academics. 15 master's degrees, 2 undergraduate degrees available through distance learning within Iowa. Coursework delivered through Iowa Communications Network (ICN) and World Wide Web. Many programs also have on-campus components. Bachelor of Liberal Studies (BLS) degree is external undergraduate degree completion program available to Iowan and nonresident students. **Special study options:** Accelerated study, combined bachelor's/graduate degree, cooperative education, distance learning, double major, dual enrollment of high school students, ESL, exchange student, external degree, honors, independent study, internships, liberal arts/career combination, student-designed major, study abroad, teacher certification program, Washington semester. **Credit/placement by examination:** AP, CLEP, IB, institutional tests. 32 credit hours maximum toward bachelor's degree. **Support services:** Learning center, pre-admission summer program, reduced course load, remedial instruction, study skills assistance, tutoring, writing center.

Majors. Area/ethnic studies: American, Asian, European, Latin American, Russian/Slavic. **Biology:** General, biochemistry, bioinformatics, biomedical sciences, biotechnology, ecology, microbiology. **Business:** Accounting, actuarial science, business admin, construction management, finance, management information systems, marketing, real estate. **Communications:** General, digital media, organizational, public relations. **Communications technology:** Graphics. **Computer sciences:** General, computer science, networking. **Conservation:** Environmental science. **Education:** Business, elementary, ESL, foreign languages, health, kindergarten/preschool, middle, music, physical, reading, science, social science, speech, technology/industrial arts. **Engineering:** Physics. **Engineering technology:** Electromechanical, industrial, manufacturing. **English:** English lit, speech/rhetoric. **Family/consumer sciences:** Clothing/textiles, family/community services. **Foreign languages:** General, French, German, Russian, Spanish. **Health:** Athletic training, speech pathology. **History:** General. **Interdisciplinary:** Biological/physical sciences, gerontology. **Liberal arts:** Arts/sciences, humanities. **Math:** General, applied. **Parks/recreation:** General, health/fitness. **Philosophy/religion:** Philosophy, religion. **Physical sciences:** Chemistry, geology, physics. **Psychology:** General. **Public administration:** General, social work. **Social sciences:** Anthropology, applied economics, criminology, econometrics, economics, geography, political science, sociology. **Visual/performing arts:** Acting, art, art history/conservation, dramatic, interior design, music performance, music theory/composition, studio arts, theater design.

Most popular majors. Business/marketing 23%, education 18%, social sciences 8%, visual/performing arts 6%.

Computing on campus. 1,900 workstations in dormitories, library, computer center, student center. Dormitories wired for high-speed internet access and linked to campus network. Commuter students can connect to campus network. Online course registration, online library, helpline, student web hosting, wireless network available.

Student life. Freshman orientation: Available, $90 fee. Preregistration for classes offered. 10 - 2 day orientation sessions in summer and immediately preceding beginning of fall/spring semesters. **Policies:** Freshmen permitted cars on campus. **Housing:** Guaranteed on-campus for freshmen. Coed dorms, single-sex dorms, special housing for disabled, apartments, fraternity/sorority housing, substance-free housing available. **Activities:** Bands, choral groups, dance, drama, literary magazine, music ensembles, musical theater, opera, radio station, student government, student newspaper, symphony orchestra, Amnesty International, Asian American student union, Black student union, Campus Crusade for Christ, Catholic student association, College Republicans, conservation club, Fellowship of Christian Athletes, Habitat for Humanity, Northern Iowa Democrats.

Athletics. NCAA. **Intercollegiate:** Baseball M, basketball, cross-country, diving W, football (tackle) M, golf, soccer W, softball W, swimming W, tennis W, track and field, volleyball W, wrestling M. **Intramural:** Badminton, basketball, bowling, cheerleading, cross-country, football (tackle) M, golf, ice hockey M, lacrosse W, racquetball, rowing (crew), rugby, skiing, soccer, softball, swimming, table tennis, tennis, track and field, volleyball, water polo, wrestling M. **Team name:** Panthers.

Student services. Adult student services, alcohol/substance abuse counseling, campus ministries, career counseling, student employment services, financial aid counseling, health services, minority student services, on-campus daycare, personal counseling, placement for graduates, veterans' counselor. **Physically disabled:** Services for visually, speech, hearing impaired.

Contact. E-mail: admissions@uni.edu
Phone: (319) 273-2281 Toll-free number: (800) 772-2037
Fax: (319) 273-2885
Roland Carrillo, Executive Director, Enrollment Services, University of Northern Iowa, 120 Gilchrist Hall, Cedar Falls, IA 50614-0018

Upper Iowa University

Fayette, Iowa
www.uiu.edu **CB code: 6885**

- Private 4-year university
- Residential campus in rural community
- 691 degree-seeking undergraduates
- SAT or ACT (ACT writing recommended) required
- 36% graduate within 6 years

Four-Year Colleges

General. Founded in 1857. Regionally accredited. 2 consecutive 8-week terms equal one semester. **Degrees:** 992 bachelor's, 44 associate awarded; master's offered. **Location:** 50 miles from Waterloo, 70 miles from Cedar Rapids. **Calendar:** Semester, limited summer session. **Full-time faculty:** 36 total. **Part-time faculty:** 2 total. **Special facilities:** Electron microscope lab, greenhouse, television and media lab with computer animation suite.

Freshman class profile. 691 applied, 464 admitted, 132 enrolled.

Mid 50% test scores		**Return as sophomores:**	67%
SAT verbal:	370-520	**Out-of-state:**	45%
SAT math:	380-490		

Basis for selection. Open admission, but selective for some programs. Minimum 2.0 high school GPA, ACT composite score of 16, SAT score of 760 (exclusive of writing) important. Early application is recommended because of a limited enrollment policy. Interview recommended for academically weak applicants. Portfolio recommended for art majors. **Homeschooled:** Letters of recommendation are strongly encouraged. GED or proof of completed coursework is required. ACT or SAT test score required.

High school preparation. 14 units recommended. Recommended units include English 4, mathematics 3, social studies 2, history 1, science 3 (laboratory 1).

2006-2007 Annual costs. Tuition/fees (projected): $18,797. Room/board: $5,815. Books/supplies: $1,050. Personal expenses: $1,600.

2004-2005 Financial aid. Need-based: 38% of total undergraduate aid awarded as scholarships/grants, 62% as loans/jobs. **Non-need-based:** Scholarships awarded for academics.

Application procedures. Admission: No deadline. No application fee. Application may be submitted online. Admission notification on a rolling basis. **Financial aid:** Priority date 6/1; no closing date. FAFSA required. Applicants notified on a rolling basis starting 4/1.

Academics. Special study options: Accelerated study, combined bachelor's/graduate degree, cooperative education, double major, dual enrollment of high school students, exchange student, external degree, independent study, internships, liberal arts/career combination, student-designed major, study abroad, teacher certification program. **Credit/placement by examination:** AP, CLEP, IB, institutional tests. 30 credit hours maximum toward bachelor's degree. **Support services:** Learning center, tutoring.

Majors. Area/ethnic studies: American. **Biology:** General. **Business:** General, accounting, business admin, management information systems. **Communications:** General. **Conservation:** General, environmental science, forestry, management/policy. **Education:** General, biology, chemistry, early childhood, elementary, health, history, kindergarten/preschool, middle, physical, reading, science, secondary, social science, social studies, special. **Health:** Athletic training, facilities admin, health care admin, physical therapy assistant, predentistry, premedicine, prepharmacy, preveterinary. **Legal studies:** Prelaw. **Math:** General. **Parks/recreation:** Facilities management, health/fitness. **Personal/culinary services:** Mortuary science. **Physical sciences:** Chemistry. **Protective services:** Criminal justice. **Psychology:** General. **Public administration:** Human services. **Social sciences:** General, criminology, sociology. **Visual/performing arts:** Art, arts management, commercial/advertising art, studio arts.

Computing on campus. 3 workstations in dormitories, library, computer center, student center. Dormitories wired for high-speed internet access.

Student life. Freshman orientation: Mandatory. Preregistration for classes offered. Held during summer, includes financial aid counseling. **Policies:** Freshmen permitted cars on campus. **Housing:** Guaranteed on-campus for all undergraduates. Coed dorms, single-sex dorms available. $100 deposit. **Activities:** Drama, student government, student newspaper, various political, academic, religious, and ethnic organizations.

Athletics. NCAA. **Intercollegiate:** Baseball M, basketball, cheerleading, cross-country, football (tackle) M, golf, soccer, softball W, tennis, track and field, volleyball W, wrestling M. **Intramural:** Badminton, basketball, softball, table tennis, volleyball. **Team name:** Peacocks.

Student services. Campus ministries, career counseling, student employment services, financial aid counseling, health services, personal counseling, placement for graduates.

Contact. E-mail: admission@uiu.edu
Phone: (563) 425-5281 Toll-free number: (800) 553-4150 ext. 2
Fax: (563) 425-5323
Linda Hoopes, Director of Admission, Upper Iowa University, Parker Fox Hall, Fayette, IA 52142

Vennard College

University Park, Iowa
www.vennard.edu **CB code: 6094**

- Private 4-year Bible college affiliated with interdenominational tradition
- Residential campus in large town
- 77 degree-seeking undergraduates: 9% part-time, 47% women, 1% Asian American, 1% Hispanic American, 1% international
- 62% of applicants admitted
- SAT or ACT (ACT writing optional) required
- 44% graduate within 6 years; 3% enter graduate study

General. Founded in 1910. Regionally accredited; also accredited by ABHE. Dedicated to education in basic Christian doctrine and to preparing students for service in church-related ministries, or as lay persons in a Christian context. **Degrees:** 12 bachelor's, 3 associate awarded. **Location:** 65 miles from Des Moines. **Calendar:** Semester, limited summer session. **Full-time faculty:** 4 total; 25% have terminal degrees, 25% women. **Part-time faculty:** 13 total; 8% have terminal degrees, 23% women.

Freshman class profile. 40 applied, 25 admitted, 19 enrolled.

Mid 50% test scores		**Rank in top quarter:**	38%
SAT verbal:	430-620	**End year in good standing:**	95%
SAT math:	400-570	**Return as sophomores:**	53%
ACT:	18-23	**Out-of-state:**	52%
GPA 3.50 or higher:	37%	**Live on campus:**	76%
GPA 3.0-3.49:	10%	**International:**	5%
GPA 2.0-2.99:	48%		

Basis for selection. Applicant's statement of Christian experience and recommendation of pastor are major factors. The student's GPA in core academic courses and national test scores are used to evaluate student's ability to succeed academically. Character references are carefully considered. Minimum ACT score and GPA flexible, depending on other factors as considered by admissions office and academic departments. Essay recommended. **Homeschooled:** Students without an official high school transcript must take the ASSET test as an A.T.B. test to make them eligible for financial aid. The home-school code is also required, if the state of the home-schooler requires one. **Learning Disabled:** In order to receive the required academic tutoring or considerations, the student is responsible to provide the college with certification of the learning disability and the recommended learning aid strategies.

2005-2006 Annual costs. Tuition/fees: $9,150. Room/board: $4,600. Books/supplies: $500. Personal expenses: $1,390.

2004-2005 Financial aid. Need-based: 42% of total undergraduate aid awarded as scholarships/grants, 58% as loans/jobs.

Application procedures. Admission: No deadline. $20 fee, may be waived for applicants with need. Application may be submitted online. Admission notification on a rolling basis. **Financial aid:** Priority date 7/1; no closing date. FAFSA required. Applicants notified on a rolling basis starting 8/29; must reply within 1 week(s) of notification.

Academics. All students choose double major, one of which must be Bible. Individualized tutoring available. **Special study options:** Accelerated study, distance learning, double major, dual enrollment of high school students, independent study, internships, teacher certification program. **Credit/placement by examination:** AP, CLEP, SAT, ACT, institutional tests. 18 credit hours maximum toward associate degree, 18 toward bachelor's. Courses that are requirements in one's major will need the permission of the Program Coordinator. **Support services:** Learning center, reduced course load, remedial instruction, study skills assistance, tutoring.

Majors. Business: Human resources. **Psychology:** General. **Theology:** Missionary, pastoral counseling, religious ed, theology, youth ministry.

Computing on campus. 20 workstations in library, computer center. Online library, wireless network available.

Student life. Freshman orientation: Mandatory. Preregistration for classes offered. Held two or three days before classes begin each semester; placement tests are given. **Policies:** College emphasizes social life disciplines as they relate to Christian life. Religious observance required. Freshmen permitted cars on campus. **Housing:** Single-sex dorms, apartments available. $50 nonrefundable deposit. Single students over 25 may petition for permission to live off campus. **Activities:** Choral groups, music ensembles, student government, World Christian Fellowship, Ministerial Association.

Athletics. NCCAA. **Intercollegiate:** Basketball, cross-country M, soccer M, volleyball W. **Intramural:** Basketball, table tennis, tennis, volleyball. **Team name:** Cougars.

Student services. Campus ministries, financial aid counseling, personal counseling.

Contact. E-mail: admiss@vennard.edu
Phone: (641) 673-8391 ext. 106 Toll-free number: (800) 686-8365
Fax: (641) 673-8365
Robyn Chrisman, Director of Admissions, Vennard College, Box 29, University Park, IA 52595-0029

Waldorf College

Forest City, Iowa **CB member**
www.waldorf.edu **CB code: 6925**

- Private 4-year liberal arts college affiliated with Evangelical Lutheran Church in America
- Residential campus in small town
- 581 degree-seeking undergraduates: 2% part-time, 49% women, 6% African American, 1% Asian American, 2% Hispanic American, 7% international
- 63% of applicants admitted
- SAT or ACT (ACT writing optional) required
- 29% graduate within 6 years

General. Founded in 1903. Regionally accredited. **Degrees:** 62 bachelor's, 17 associate awarded. **Location:** 125 miles from Des Moines and Minneapolis-St. Paul. **Calendar:** Semester, limited summer session. **Full-time faculty:** 39 total; 51% have terminal degrees, 44% women. **Class size:** 59% < 20, 41% 20-39, less than 1% 50-99. **Special facilities:** Multimedia lab for video, digital editing and communications.

Freshman class profile. 761 applied, 476 admitted, 197 enrolled.

Mid 50% test scores			
SAT verbal:	420-500	Rank in top quarter:	30%
SAT math:	380-410	Rank in top tenth:	6%
ACT:	18-24	End year in good standing:	88%
GPA 3.50 or higher:	11%	Return as sophomores:	82%
GPA 3.0-3.49:	29%	Out-of-state:	42%
GPA 2.0-2.99:	54%	Live on campus:	94%
		International:	6%

Basis for selection. School record and test scores most important, recommendations important, class rank and interview considered. Interview recommended. Audition and portfolio recommended for music, theater majors. **Homeschooled:** Must submit ACT or SAT scores.

High school preparation. College-preparatory program recommended. 16 units recommended. Recommended units include English 4, mathematics 3, social studies 4, science 3 and foreign language 2.

2005-2006 Annual costs. Tuition/fees: $15,720. Room/board: $4,620. Books/supplies: $775. Personal expenses: $1,500.

2004-2005 Financial aid. Need-based: 168 full-time freshmen applied for aid; 153 were judged to have need; 152 of these received aid. Average need met was 85%. Average scholarship/grant was $9,126; average loan $3,421. 63% of total undergraduate aid awarded as scholarships/grants, 37% as loans/jobs. **Non-need-based:** Awarded to 194 full-time undergraduates, including 81 freshmen. Scholarships awarded for academics, alumni affiliation, athletics, job skills, leadership, music/drama, religious affiliation, state residency.

Application procedures. Admission: No deadline. No application fee. Application may be submitted online. Admission notification on a rolling basis beginning on or about 10/6. **Financial aid:** Priority date 3/1; no closing date. FAFSA required. Applicants notified on a rolling basis starting 3/1; must reply within 2 week(s) of notification.

Academics. Internships required in all baccalaureate programs. **Special study options:** Accelerated study, combined bachelor's/graduate degree, double major, dual enrollment of high school students, ESL, honors, independent study, internships, liberal arts/career combination, study abroad, teacher certification program. **Credit/placement by examination:** AP, CLEP, SAT, ACT, institutional tests. 8 credit hours maximum toward associate degree, 8 toward bachelor's. **Support services:** Learning center, reduced course load, remedial instruction, study skills assistance, tutoring, writing center.

Majors. Biology: General. **Business:** General, business admin, finance, marketing. **Communications:** Broadcast journalism, journalism, media studies, radio/tv. **Communications technology:** General. **Computer sciences:** General, information systems. **Education:** Drama/dance, elementary, English, history, middle, multi-level teacher, music, secondary, social studies. **English:** British lit, composition, creative writing, English lit. **Family/consumer sciences:** Food/nutrition. **History:** General. **Legal studies:** Prelaw. **Liberal arts:** Arts/sciences, humanities. **Psychology:** General. **Social sciences:** General, political science. **Visual/performing arts:** General, arts management, dramatic, music management, music performance, piano/organ, theater arts management, voice/opera.

Most popular majors. Business/marketing 31%, communications/journalism 21%, education 21%, health sciences 10%, interdisciplinary studies 6%.

Computing on campus. PC or laptop required. Dormitories wired for high-speed internet access and linked to campus network. Online library, helpline, repair service, wireless network available.

Student life. Freshman orientation: Mandatory. Preregistration for classes offered. Held 2 days prior to the start of school. **Policies:** No alcohol on campus. Freshmen permitted cars on campus. **Housing:** Guaranteed on-campus for all undergraduates. Coed dorms, single-sex dorms, special housing for disabled available. $100 deposit, deadline 9/6. One house near campus available for upperclassmen. **Activities:** Bands, choral groups, drama, literary magazine, music ensembles, musical theater, radio station, student government, student newspaper, TV station, Lutheran youth encounter, fellowship of Christian athletes, science club, student senate, youth ministry, culture club, Amnesty International, social warriors activities team, awareness ambassadors.

Athletics. NAIA. **Intercollegiate:** Baseball M, basketball, football (tackle) M, golf, soccer, softball W, volleyball W, wrestling M. **Intramural:** Badminton, basketball, racquetball, rugby W, skiing, soccer, softball, table tennis, volleyball, weight lifting. **Team name:** Warriors.

Student services. Alcohol/substance abuse counseling, campus ministries, career counseling, student employment services, financial aid counseling, health services, minority student services, personal counseling, placement for graduates, veterans' counselor. **Physically disabled:** Services for visually, speech, hearing impaired.

Contact. E-mail: admissions@waldorf.edu
Phone: (641) 585-8112 Toll-free number: (800) 292-1903
Fax: (641) 585-8125
Steve Lovik, Vice President of Enrollment Management, Waldorf College, 106 South Sixth Street, Forest City, IA 50436-1713

Wartburg College

Waverly, Iowa
www.wartburg.edu **CB code: 6926**

- Private 4-year liberal arts college affiliated with Evangelical Lutheran Church in America
- Residential campus in small town
- 1,768 degree-seeking undergraduates: 2% part-time, 53% women, 3% African American, 1% Asian American, 1% Hispanic American, 5% international
- 88% of applicants admitted
- SAT or ACT (ACT writing optional) required
- 68% graduate within 6 years; 19% enter graduate study

General. Founded in 1852. Regionally accredited. **Degrees:** 368 bachelor's awarded. **Location:** 15 miles from Waterloo-Cedar Falls. **Calendar:** 4-4-1 semester system. Limited summer session. **Full-time faculty:** 106 total; 80% have terminal degrees, 7% minority, 43% women. **Part-time faculty:** 73 total; 11% have terminal degrees, 6% minority, 58% women. **Class size:** 43% < 20, 50% 20-39, 4% 40-49, 2% 50-99, less than 1% >100. **Special facilities:** Planetarium/observatory, prairie preserve, fine arts center, journalism laboratory, mathematics simulation laboratory, institute for leadership education, international museum, music laboratory, state-of-the-art learning library, science center, Center for Community Engagement.

Freshman class profile. 1,681 applied, 1,472 admitted, 519 enrolled.

Mid 50% test scores			
SAT verbal:	500-600	Rank in top quarter:	61%
SAT math:	500-650	Rank in top tenth:	31%
ACT:	21-26	Return as sophomores:	77%
GPA 3.50 or higher:	61%	Out-of-state:	25%
GPA 3.0-3.49:	29%	Live on campus:	99%
GPA 2.0-2.99:	10%	International:	3%

Basis for selection. Class rank, GPA, courses taken, test scores, recommendations important. Students with 18 ACT composite and below or who rank in lower half of their high school class are reviewed by admission and scholarship committee for final decision. Interview recommended. Audition recommended for music majors. Portfolio recommended for art majors. **Learning Disabled:** Documentation of disability required.

High school preparation. 15 units recommended. Recommended units include English 4, mathematics 3, social studies 2, science 3 and foreign language 2. Computer course required.

2005-2006 Annual costs. Tuition/fees: $21,130. Room/board: $5,600.

2005-2006 Financial aid. Need-based: 464 full-time freshmen applied for aid; 398 were judged to have need; 398 of these received aid. Average need met was 90%. Average scholarship/grant was $13,851; average loan $3,966. 72% of total undergraduate aid awarded as scholarships/grants, 28% as loans/jobs. **Non-need-based:** Awarded to 560 full-time undergraduates, including 174 freshmen. Scholarships awarded for academics, alumni affiliation, job skills, music/drama, religious affiliation, state residency.

Application procedures. Admission: Priority date 5/1; no deadline. $20 fee, may be waived for applicants with need. Admission notification on a rolling basis beginning on or about 7/1. **Financial aid:** Priority date 3/1; no closing date. FAFSA required. Applicants notified on a rolling basis starting 3/21; must reply within 2 week(s) of notification.

Academics. Special study options: Accelerated study, double major, dual enrollment of high school students, honors, independent study, internships, student-designed major, study abroad, teacher certification program, urban semester, Washington semester. Spring term consortium (students may enroll at any of 11 member colleges), Wartburg West urban academic internship experience in Denver, CO; Washington Center Academic Internship Program; cultural immersions in U.S. and around the world; Leadership Certificate Program; 3-2 engineering agreements; deferred admission program with the University of Iowa College of Dentistry. **Credit/placement by examination:** AP, CLEP, SAT, ACT, institutional tests. 42 credit hours maximum toward bachelor's degree. **Support services:** Learning center, reduced course load, remedial instruction, study skills assistance, tutoring, writing center.

Majors. Biology: General, biochemistry. **Business:** Accounting, business admin, finance, international, marketing. **Communications:** General, broadcast journalism, journalism, public relations. **Computer sciences:** General, information systems. **Education:** Art, elementary, history, music, physical. **Engineering:** Science. **English:** Composition, speech/rhetoric. **Foreign languages:** French, German, Spanish. **Health:** Clinical lab science, music therapy. **History:** General. **Math:** General. **Parks/recreation:** Sports admin. **Philosophy/religion:** Philosophy, religion. **Physical sciences:** Chemistry, physics. **Psychology:** General. **Public administration:** Social work. **Social sciences:** Economics, international relations, political science, sociology. **Theology:** Pastoral counseling, religious ed, sacred music. **Visual/performing arts:** Art, commercial/advertising art, dramatic, music performance, music theory/composition.

Most popular majors. Biology 10%, business/marketing 19%, communications/journalism 11%, education 15%, social sciences 6%.

Computing on campus. 275 workstations in dormitories, library, computer center, student center. Dormitories wired for high-speed internet access and linked to campus network. Commuter students can connect to campus network. Online course registration, online library, helpline, wireless network available.

Student life. Freshman orientation: Mandatory. Preregistration for classes offered. Two-day program in summer, continues in fall for 3 days, plus extended activities throughout the term. **Policies:** Students actively assist in residential-life design and food-service planning. Freshmen permitted cars on campus. **Housing:** Guaranteed on-campus for freshmen. Coed dorms, single-sex dorms, apartments available. $100 deposit, deadline 5/1. Townhomes for single senior students available. **Activities:** Bands, choral groups, dance, drama, film society, literary magazine, music ensembles, musical theater, opera, radio station, student government, student newspaper, symphony orchestra, TV station, Campus Ministry Board, Campus Crusade for Christ, Young Democrats, Young Republicans, Cultural Awareness Center/Organization, Habitat for Humanity, international club, Students for Peace and Justice, Fellowship of Christian Athletes, Volunteer Action Center.

Athletics. NCAA. **Intercollegiate:** Baseball M, basketball, cross-country, football (tackle) M, golf, soccer, softball W, tennis, track and field, volleyball W, wrestling M. **Intramural:** Badminton, basketball, football (non-tackle), golf, racquetball, softball, tennis, volleyball. **Team name:** Knights.

Student services. Alcohol/substance abuse counseling, campus ministries, career counseling, student employment services, financial aid counseling, health services, minority student services, personal counseling.

Contact. E-mail: admissions@wartburg.edu
Phone: (319) 352-8264 Toll-free number: (800) 772-2085
Fax: (319) 352-8579
Brent Matthias, Dean of Admissions/Financial Aid, Wartburg College, 100 Wartburg Boulevard, PO Box 1003, Waverly, IA 50677-0903

William Penn University
Oskaloosa, Iowa
www.wmpenn.edu **CB code: 6943**

- Private 4-year liberal arts college affiliated with Society of Friends (Quaker)
- Residential campus in large town
- 1,795 degree-seeking undergraduates
- 43% of applicants admitted
- SAT or ACT (ACT writing optional) required

General. Founded in 1873. Regionally accredited. College for working adults degree program. **Degrees:** 254 bachelor's, 20 associate awarded. **Location:** 60 miles from Des Moines. **Calendar:** Semester, limited summer session. **Full-time faculty:** 48 total. **Part-time faculty:** 171 total. **Class size:** 61% < 20, 31% 20-39, 4% 40-49, 3% 50-99. **Special facilities:** Middle Eastern art collection.

Freshman class profile. 586 applied, 253 admitted, 166 enrolled.

Mid 50% test scores		**Out-of-state:**	50%
SAT verbal:	340-510	**Live on campus:**	85%
SAT math:	340-520	**Fraternities:**	5%
ACT:	17-22	**Sororities:**	5%
Rank in top quarter:	21%		

Basis for selection. Class rank, test scores, high school GPA important. Extracurricular activities, alumni relationship, recommendation, personal essay considered. Interview and essay recommended for academically marginal applicants. Audition recommended for music grants.

High school preparation. 15 units required. Required and recommended units include English 4, mathematics 2, social studies 2, history 2, science 2 and academic electives 3.

2005-2006 Annual costs. Tuition/fees: $15,334. Room/board: $4,896. Books/supplies: $800. Personal expenses: $900.

2004-2005 Financial aid. Need-based: 61% of total undergraduate aid awarded as scholarships/grants, 39% as loans/jobs. **Non-need-based:** Scholarships awarded for academics, alumni affiliation, athletics, leadership, music/drama, religious affiliation.

Application procedures. Admission: No deadline. $20 fee, may be waived for applicants with need. Application may be submitted online. Admission notification on a rolling basis beginning on or about 11/1. **Financial aid:** Priority date 7/1; no closing date. FAFSA required. Applicants notified on a rolling basis starting 1/1; must reply within 2 week(s) of notification.

Academics. Special study options: Accelerated study, distance learning, double major, dual enrollment of high school students, independent study, internships, liberal arts/career combination, teacher certification program. 3-2 engineering program offered with Iowa State University. **Credit/placement by examination:** AP, CLEP, IB, institutional tests. 32 credit hours maximum toward bachelor's degree. **Support services:** Learning center, reduced course load, remedial instruction, study skills assistance, tutoring, writing center.

Majors. Biology: General. **Business:** Accounting, business admin. **Communications:** General, journalism, public relations. **Computer sciences:** General. **Education:** General, biology, business, chemistry, driver/safety, elementary, English, ESL, health, history, mathematics, physical, physics, science, secondary, social science, social studies, special, technology/industrial arts, trade/industrial. **Engineering:** Mechanical. **History:** General, American. **Interdisciplinary:** Biological/physical sciences. **Legal studies:** Prelaw. **Liberal arts:** Arts/sciences. **Math:** General. **Parks/recreation:** Health/fitness, sports admin. **Protective services:** Criminal justice. **Psychology:** General. **Public administration:** Human services. **Social sciences:** General, political science, sociology. **Visual/performing arts:** General.

Computing on campus. 70 workstations in dormitories, library, computer center, student center. Dormitories wired for high-speed internet access and linked to campus network. Repair service, wireless network available.

Student life. Freshman orientation: Mandatory. Preregistration for classes offered. 3-day orientation activities before classes begin in fall. **Policies:**

Freshmen permitted cars on campus. **Housing:** Guaranteed on-campus for freshmen. Coed dorms, single-sex dorms, special housing for disabled, apartments available. $100 deposit, deadline 8/1. **Activities:** Jazz band, choral groups, dance, drama, literary magazine, music ensembles, musical theater, radio station, student government, student newspaper, Fellowship of Christian Athletes, Students for Minority Interests, international relations club, honor societies, computer club, various religious activity groups.

Athletics. NAIA. **Intercollegiate:** Baseball M, basketball, cheerleading M, cross-country, football (tackle) M, golf M, soccer, softball W, track and field, volleyball W, wrestling M. **Intramural:** Basketball, bowling, football (non-tackle) M, softball, table tennis, tennis, volleyball. **Team name:** Statesmen.

Student services. Adult student services, alcohol/substance abuse counseling, campus ministries, career counseling, financial aid counseling, personal counseling, veterans' counselor.

Contact. E-mail: admissions@wmpenn.edu
Phone: (641) 673-1012 Toll-free number: (800) 779-7366
Fax: (641) 673-2113
John Ottosson, Vice President for Enrollment Management, William Penn University, 201 Trueblood Avenue, Oskaloosa, IA 52577

Kansas

Baker University
Baldwin City, Kansas
www.bakeru.edu
CB member
CB code: 6031

- Private 4-year liberal arts college affiliated with United Methodist Church
- Residential campus in small town
- 870 degree-seeking undergraduates: 2% part-time, 52% women, 8% African American, 1% Asian American, 3% Hispanic American, 1% Native American
- 63% of applicants admitted
- SAT or ACT (ACT writing optional) required
- 63% graduate within 6 years

General. Founded in 1858. Regionally accredited. School of Nursing confers Bachelor's of Science in Nursing (BSN) degree; operates in a clinical setting in Topeka, KS. Associate, Bachelor's and Master's degrees also conferred through the School of Professional and Graduate Studies. **Degrees:** 152 bachelor's awarded. **ROTC:** Army, Air Force. **Location:** 15 miles from Lawrence; 35 miles from Kansas City, Missouri. **Calendar:** 4-1-4, limited summer session. **Full-time faculty:** 73 total; 71% have terminal degrees, 38% women. **Part-time faculty:** 38 total; 18% have terminal degrees, 45% women. **Class size:** 78% < 20, 18% 20-39, 3% 40-49, 1% 50-99. **Special facilities:** Wetlands, old castle museum, bible collections, retail art gallery.

Freshman class profile. 1,051 applied, 666 admitted, 239 enrolled.

Mid 50% test scores		**Rank in top tenth:**	25%
ACT:	21-26	**Return as sophomores:**	81%
GPA 3.50 or higher:	51%	**Out-of-state:**	26%
GPA 3.0-3.49:	33%	**Live on campus:**	93%
GPA 2.0-2.99:	16%	**Fraternities:**	49%
Rank in top quarter:	52%	**Sororities:**	45%

Basis for selection. Strong core curriculum during high school very important. GPA, class rank, course selection, ACT or SAT, and recommendation from high school core teacher or guidance counselor important. Involvement in school, community and church activities considered. Interview and essay recommended. Audition recommended for music and theater majors. Portfolio recommended for art majors.

High school preparation. 17 units recommended. Recommended units include English 4, mathematics 3, social studies 3, science 3 (laboratory 1) and foreign language 2. One fine arts and one computing course recommended.

2005-2006 Annual costs. Tuition/fees: $16,560. Room/board: $5,630. Books/supplies: $1,000. Personal expenses: $1,400.

2005-2006 Financial aid. Need-based: 222 full-time freshmen applied for aid; 183 were judged to have need; 183 of these received aid. Average need met was 85%. Average scholarship/grant was $7,981; average loan $3,052. 56% of total undergraduate aid awarded as scholarships/grants, 44% as loans/jobs. **Non-need-based:** Awarded to 517 full-time undergraduates, including 141 freshmen. Scholarships awarded for academics, alumni affiliation, art, athletics, leadership, music/drama, religious affiliation, ROTC.

Application procedures. Admission: No deadline. No application fee. Application may be submitted online. Admission notification on a rolling basis. **Financial aid:** Priority date 3/1; no closing date. FAFSA, institutional form required. Applicants notified on a rolling basis starting 3/1; must reply by 5/1 or within 6 week(s) of notification.

Academics. Liberal arts core consisting of 9 hours stressing critical thinking skills, strong writing ability, and application of these skills to various academic disciplines required. **Special study options:** Accelerated study, double major, honors, independent study, internships, liberal arts/career combination, student-designed major, study abroad, teacher certification program. **Credit/placement by examination:** AP, CLEP, IB, SAT, ACT. **Support services:** Learning center, reduced course load, study skills assistance, tutoring, writing center.

Majors. Biology: General, molecular, wildlife. **Business:** General, accounting, international. **Communications:** General, media studies. **Computer sciences:** Computer science, information systems. **Education:** Art, elementary, music, secondary. **English:** English lit. **Foreign languages:** French, German, Spanish. **History:** General. **Interdisciplinary:** Global studies. **Math:** General. **Parks/recreation:** Exercise sciences, health/fitness. **Philosophy/religion:** Philosophy, religion. **Physical sciences:** Chemistry, physics. **Psychology:** General. **Social sciences:** Economics, political science, sociology. **Visual/performing arts:** Art history/conservation, dramatic, studio arts.

Most popular majors. Biology 11%, business/marketing 24%, communications/journalism 10%, education 12%, parks/recreation 7%, social sciences 8%.

Computing on campus. 222 workstations in dormitories, library, computer center. Dormitories wired for high-speed internet access and linked to campus network. Online library, helpline, repair service, student web hosting, wireless network available.

Student life. Freshman orientation: Available. Preregistration for classes offered. 2-day program in summer and 4-day program prior to start of fall term. **Policies:** Students required to live in campus or Greek housing unless granted permission to live off-campus. Freshmen not allowed to live in Greek housing. Freshmen permitted cars on campus. **Housing:** Guaranteed on-campus for freshmen. Coed dorms, single-sex dorms, special housing for disabled, apartments, fraternity/sorority housing available. $100 fully refundable deposit. **Activities:** Bands, choral groups, drama, literary magazine, music ensembles, radio station, student government, student newspaper, TV station, Mungano (minority student organization), Fellowship of Christian Athletes, Parmentors, Ambassadors, Earth We Are, College Republicans, Young Democrats, Bacchus.

Athletics. NAIA. **Intercollegiate:** Baseball M, basketball, cheerleading, cross-country, football (tackle) M, golf, soccer, softball W, tennis, track and field, volleyball W. **Intramural:** Basketball, football (non-tackle), softball, table tennis, volleyball. **Team name:** Wildcats.

Student services. Alcohol/substance abuse counseling, campus ministries, career counseling, student employment services, financial aid counseling, health services, minority student services, personal counseling, placement for graduates, veterans' counselor. **Physically disabled:** Services for visually, hearing impaired.

Contact. E-mail: admissions@bakeru.edu
Phone: (785) 594-8307 Toll-free number: (800) 873-4282
Fax: (785) 594-8372
Daniel McKinney, Director of Admissions, Baker University, 618 Eighth Street, Baldwin City, KS 66006-0065

Barclay College
Haviland, Kansas
www.barclaycollege.edu
CB code: 6228

- Private 4-year Bible college affiliated with Evangelical Friends Alliance and Friends United Meeting
- Residential campus in rural community
- 122 degree-seeking undergraduates: 26% part-time, 49% women, 3% African American, 2% Asian American, 3% Hispanic American, 1% Native American, 1% international
- 79% of applicants admitted
- ACT (writing optional), application essay required

General. Founded in 1917. Accredited by ABHE. **Degrees:** 47 bachelor's, 2 associate awarded. **Location:** 100 miles from Wichita, 65 miles from Dodge City. **Calendar:** Semester, limited summer session. **Full-time faculty:** 6 total; 17% have terminal degrees, 17% minority, 33% women. **Part-time faculty:** 23 total; 13% have terminal degrees, 26% women. **Class size:** 89% < 20, 11% 20-39.

Freshman class profile. 48 applied, 38 admitted, 22 enrolled.

Mid 50% test scores		**Return as sophomores:**	71%
ACT:	16-24	**Out-of-state:**	59%
End year in good standing:	76%	**Live on campus:**	100%

Basis for selection. Personal references and commitment to Christian vocation important. Committee reviews file and conducts phone interview. Audition recommended for music majors.

2006-2007 Annual costs. Tuition/fees (projected): $12,730. Room/board: $5,100. Books/supplies: $800. Personal expenses: $1,000.

2005-2006 Financial aid. **Need-based:** 41% of total undergraduate aid awarded as scholarships/grants, 59% as loans/jobs. **Non-need-based:** Scholarships awarded for academics, alumni affiliation, leadership, music/drama, state residency.

Application procedures. **Admission:** Closing date 9/1. $25 fee, may be waived for applicants with need. Application may be submitted online. Admission notification on a rolling basis. **Financial aid:** Priority date 5/31, closing date 7/15. FAFSA, institutional form required. Applicants notified on a rolling basis starting 1/1; must reply within 4 week(s) of notification.

Academics. Each student has Bible major in addition to individually chosen major. Emphasis on practicums and internships. **Special study options:** Cross-registration, distance learning, double major, independent study, internships, liberal arts/career combination, teacher certification program. Cooperative classes with Pratt Community College. **Credit/placement by examination:** AP, CLEP, IB, SAT, ACT, institutional tests. 15 credit hours maximum toward associate degree, 30 toward bachelor's. **Support services:** Remedial instruction, study skills assistance, tutoring.

Majors. **Business:** General, business admin. **Education:** Elementary. **Philosophy/religion:** Religion. **Psychology:** General. **Theology:** Bible, missionary, pastoral counseling, sacred music, theology, youth ministry.

Most popular majors. Business/marketing 9%, psychology 32%, theological studies 55%.

Computing on campus. 18 workstations in library, computer center. Dormitories wired for high-speed internet access and linked to campus network. Online library, repair service available.

Student life. **Freshman orientation:** Mandatory. Preregistration for classes offered. **Policies:** Christian and social work required. Religious observance required. Freshmen permitted cars on campus. **Housing:** Guaranteed on-campus for freshmen. Single-sex dorms available. $50 fully refundable deposit. **Activities:** Choral groups, drama, music ensembles, student government.

Athletics. NCCAA. **Intercollegiate:** Baseball M, basketball, golf, soccer M, tennis, volleyball W. **Intramural:** Basketball, bowling, softball, volleyball. **Team name:** Bears.

Student services. Student employment services, health services, personal counseling, placement for graduates.

Contact. E-mail: admissions@barclaycollege.edu
Phone: (620) 862-5252 ext. 21 Toll-free number: (800) 862-0226
Fax: (620) 862-5242
Ryan Kendall, Director of Admissions, Barclay College, 607 North Kingman, Haviland, KS 67059

Benedictine College

Atchison, Kansas — **CB member**
www.benedictine.edu — **CB code: 6056**

- Private 4-year liberal arts college affiliated with Roman Catholic Church
- Residential campus in large town
- 1,176 degree-seeking undergraduates
- SAT or ACT (ACT writing optional) required

General. Founded in 1858. Regionally accredited. Affiliated with Benedictine monastic order. Institution offers additional associate degree and bachelors degree programs in Hong Kong. **Degrees:** 187 bachelor's awarded; master's offered. **ROTC:** Army. **Location:** 45 miles from Kansas City, Missouri. **Calendar:** Semester, limited summer session. **Full-time faculty:** 59 total; 78% have terminal degrees, 12% minority, 30% women. **Part-time faculty:** 40 total; 20% have terminal degrees, 38% women. **Class size:** 49% < 20, 49% 20-39, 1% 40-49, less than 1% 50-99. **Special facilities:** Biological research area, high-tech classrooms, 2 performing arts theaters.

Freshman class profile.

Mid 50% test scores			
SAT verbal:	470-600	Rank in top quarter:	15%
SAT math:	460-570	Rank in top tenth:	5%
ACT:	21-27	Out-of-state:	60%
		Live on campus:	98%

Basis for selection. Applicant must satisfy 2 of following requirements: GPA above 2.0, rank in top half of class, requisite ACT or SAT scores. Recommendations and interview considered. Interview recommended for academically weak applicants.

High school preparation. Required and recommended units include English 4, mathematics 3-4, social studies 2, history 2, science 2-4 and foreign language 2-4.

2005-2006 Annual costs. Tuition/fees: $15,760. Room/board: $6,478. Books/supplies: $2,400. Personal expenses: $2,800.

2005-2006 Financial aid. **Need-based:** 313 full-time freshmen applied for aid; 243 were judged to have need; 243 of these received aid. Average need met was 74%. Average scholarship/grant was $8,883; average loan $3,855. 60% of total undergraduate aid awarded as scholarships/grants, 40% as loans/jobs. **Non-need-based:** Awarded to 73 full-time undergraduates, including 27 freshmen. Scholarships awarded for academics, alumni affiliation, art, athletics, job skills, leadership, minority status, music/drama, religious affiliation, ROTC.

Application procedures. **Admission:** No deadline. $25 fee, may be waived for applicants with need. Application may be submitted online. Admission notification on a rolling basis. Must reply by May 1 or within 4 week(s) if notified thereafter. **Financial aid:** Priority date 3/15; no closing date. FAFSA required. Applicants notified on a rolling basis starting 2/1; must reply within 2 week(s) of notification.

Academics. **Special study options:** Combined bachelor's/graduate degree, cooperative education, double major, dual enrollment of high school students, ESL, exchange student, independent study, internships, liberal arts/career combination, student-designed major, study abroad, teacher certification program. **Credit/placement by examination:** AP, CLEP, IB, institutional tests. 30 credit hours maximum toward associate degree, 30 toward bachelor's. **Support services:** Learning center, reduced course load, remedial instruction, study skills assistance, tutoring.

Majors. **Biology:** General, biochemistry. **Business:** Accounting, business admin. **Communications:** Media studies. **Computer sciences:** Computer science. **Education:** Elementary, music, physical, special. **Foreign languages:** French, Spanish. **Health:** Athletic training. **History:** General. **Interdisciplinary:** Natural sciences. **Liberal arts:** Arts/sciences. **Math:** General. **Philosophy/religion:** Philosophy, religion. **Physical sciences:** Astronomy, chemistry, physics. **Psychology:** General. **Social sciences:** General, economics, political science, sociology. **Theology:** Youth ministry. **Visual/performing arts:** Dramatic, music management, theater arts management.

Most popular majors. Biology 9%, business/marketing 18%, communications/journalism 8%, education 16%, philosophy/religious studies 15%, social sciences 14%.

Computing on campus. 83 workstations in dormitories, library, computer center. Dormitories wired for high-speed internet access and linked to campus network. Helpline, repair service available.

Student life. **Freshman orientation:** Mandatory. Preregistration for classes offered. Weekend program before classes commence. **Policies:** Freshmen permitted cars on campus. **Housing:** Guaranteed on-campus for freshmen. Coed dorms, single-sex dorms available. $100 deposit. Off-campus college-owned housing available. **Activities:** Bands, choral groups, dance, drama, literary magazine, music ensembles, musical theater, student government, student newspaper, symphony orchestra, Ravens Respect Life, Young Democrats, Young Republicans, Knights of Columbus, hunger coalition, Fellowship of Catholic University Students, campus ministry, Students in Free Enterprise, Black student union, Amnesty International.

Athletics. NAIA. **Intercollegiate:** Baseball M, basketball, cheerleading, cross-country, football (tackle) M, golf, soccer, softball W, tennis, track and field, volleyball W. **Intramural:** Baseball M, basketball, handball, racquetball, soccer, softball, table tennis, tennis, volleyball. **Team name:** Ravens.

Student services. Alcohol/substance abuse counseling, campus ministries, career counseling, student employment services, financial aid counseling, health services, personal counseling, placement for graduates, veterans' counselor. **Physically disabled:** Services for visually, speech, hearing impaired.

Contact. E-mail: bcadmiss@benedictine.edu
Phone: (913) 360-7476 Toll-free number: (800) 467-5340
Fax: (913) 367-5462
Kelly Vowels, Dean of Enrollment Management, Benedictine College, 1020 North Second Street, Atchison, KS 66002-1499

Bethany College

Lindsborg, Kansas
www.bethanylb.edu — **CB code: 6034**

- Private 4-year liberal arts college affiliated with Evangelical Lutheran Church in America
- Residential campus in small town

- 563 degree-seeking undergraduates: 2% part-time, 45% women, 8% African American, 1% Asian American, 5% Hispanic American, 1% Native American, 4% international
- 63% of applicants admitted
- SAT or ACT required
- 47% graduate within 6 years

General. Founded in 1881. Regionally accredited. **Degrees:** 129 bachelor's awarded. **Location:** 20 miles from Salina, 60 miles from Wichita. **Calendar:** 4-1-4, limited summer session. **Full-time faculty:** 40 total; 60% have terminal degrees, 40% women. **Part-time faculty:** 30 total; 20% have terminal degrees, 53% women. **Class size:** 81% < 20, 17% 20-39, 2% 40-49. **Special facilities:** Art galleries.

Freshman class profile. 868 applied, 548 admitted, 148 enrolled.

Mid 50% test scores			
ACT:	19-25	Return as sophomores:	61%
GPA 3.50 or higher:	44%	Out-of-state:	44%
GPA 3.0-3.49:	34%	Live on campus:	91%
GPA 2.0-2.99:	22%	International:	9%
Rank in top quarter:	41%	Fraternities:	2%
Rank in top tenth:	17%	Sororities:	1%

Basis for selection. High school GPA, course selection, trends in grades, class rank, standardized test scores very important. Interview, letters of recommendation, leadership, curriculum, involvement considered. Interview and essay recommended for some. Audition required of music and theater majors. Portfolio required of art majors.

High school preparation. College-preparatory program recommended. Recommended units include English 4, mathematics 3, social studies 3, science 3 (laboratory 2) and foreign language 2.

2006-2007 Annual costs. Tuition/fees (projected): $16,210. Room/board: $5,250. Books/supplies: $900. Personal expenses: $1,900.

2005-2006 Financial aid. Need-based: 143 full-time freshmen applied for aid; 116 were judged to have need; 116 of these received aid. Average need met was 97%. Average scholarship/grant was $4,942; average loan $4,430. 50% of total undergraduate aid awarded as scholarships/grants, 50% as loans/jobs. **Non-need-based:** Awarded to 205 full-time undergraduates, including 59 freshmen. Scholarships awarded for academics, alumni affiliation, art, athletics, leadership, music/drama, religious affiliation. **Additional information:** State financial aid deadline March 15.

Application procedures. Admission: Priority date 2/1; deadline 6/15 (postmark date). $20 fee, may be waived for applicants with need. Application may be submitted online. Admission notification on a rolling basis beginning on or about 10/1. **Financial aid:** Priority date 3/15; no closing date. FAFSA required. Applicants notified on a rolling basis starting 2/1; must reply within 3 week(s) of notification.

Academics. Special study options: Accelerated study, combined bachelor's/graduate degree, cross-registration, double major, dual enrollment of high school students, exchange student, honors, independent study, internships, liberal arts/career combination, student-designed major, study abroad, teacher certification program, urban semester, Washington semester. Special education program with Associated Colleges of Central Kansas. **Credit/placement by examination:** AP, CLEP, IB, institutional tests. 32 credit hours maximum toward bachelor's degree. **Support services:** Learning center, reduced course load, study skills assistance, tutoring, writing center.

Majors. Biology: General. **Business:** Accounting, business admin, managerial economics. **Communications:** General. **Education:** General, art, biology, business, chemistry, elementary, English, health, history, mathematics, music, physical, secondary, social science. **English:** Speech/rhetoric. **History:** General. **Liberal arts:** Arts/sciences. **Math:** General. **Parks/recreation:** Facilities management, sports admin. **Philosophy/religion:** Christian. **Physical sciences:** Chemistry. **Protective services:** Criminal justice, police science. **Psychology:** General. **Public administration:** Social work. **Social sciences:** General, economics, sociology. **Visual/performing arts:** Art, music performance.

Most popular majors. Biology 13%, business/marketing 17%, education 25%, public administration/social services 6%, visual/performing arts 12%.

Computing on campus. 40 workstations in library, computer center. Dormitories wired for high-speed internet access and linked to campus network. Commuter students can connect to campus network. Online library available.

Student life. Freshman orientation: Mandatory. Preregistration for classes offered. 3 days of activities; planned and organized by returning students. **Policies:** No alcohol allowed on campus. Freshmen permitted cars on campus. **Housing:** Coed dorms, single-sex dorms, substance-free housing available. $100 deposit, deadline 8/1. Full-time students required to live on campus. Special interest housing available. Perimeter houses occupied by groups of students who bid on them. Bids include house improvements and community service pledge. **Activities:** Bands, choral groups, dance, drama, music ensembles, musical theater, student government, student newspaper, symphony orchestra, SOAR (Student Outreach or Active Response), Blue Key, Gold Key, multicultural student association, Alpha Omega (men's Christian fellowship), Bethany youth ministry program, Bread for the World, campus ministry, departmental organizations, honorary societies.

Athletics. NAIA. **Intercollegiate:** Baseball M, basketball, cross-country, football (tackle) M, golf M, soccer, softball W, tennis, track and field, volleyball W. **Intramural:** Basketball, football (non-tackle), racquetball, soccer, softball, table tennis, volleyball, weight lifting. **Team name:** Swedes.

Student services. Alcohol/substance abuse counseling, campus ministries, career counseling, student employment services, financial aid counseling, health services, minority student services, personal counseling, placement for graduates, veterans' counselor.

Contact. E-mail: admissions@bethanylb.edu
Phone: (785) 227-3380 ext. 8113 Toll-free number: (800) 826-2281
Fax: (785) 227-8993
Thandabantu Maceo, Dean for Enrollment Management, Bethany College, 421 North First Street, Lindsborg, KS 67456-1897

Bethel College

North Newton, Kansas
www.bethelks.edu **CB code: 6037**

- Private 4-year liberal arts college affiliated with Mennonite Church
- Residential campus in large town
- 514 degree-seeking undergraduates: 7% part-time, 51% women
- 72% of applicants admitted
- SAT or ACT (ACT writing optional) required
- 53% graduate within 6 years

General. Founded in 1887. Regionally accredited. **Degrees:** 113 bachelor's awarded. **Location:** 25 miles from Wichita. **Calendar:** 4-1-4, limited summer session. **Full-time faculty:** 47 total; 57% have terminal degrees, 43% women. **Part-time faculty:** 19 total; 21% have terminal degrees, 63% women. **Class size:** 75% < 20, 19% 20-39, 4% 40-49, less than 1% 50-99, less than 1% >100. **Special facilities:** Natural history museum, 80-acre natural history field laboratory, institute for peace and conflict resolution, Mennonite library and archives, observatory, conservatory.

Freshman class profile. 581 applied, 418 admitted, 96 enrolled.

Mid 50% test scores		Rank in top quarter:	46%
SAT verbal:	410-630	Rank in top tenth:	17%
SAT math:	450-650	End year in good standing:	84%
ACT:	20-25	Return as sophomores:	66%
GPA 3.50 or higher:	57%	Out-of-state:	29%
GPA 3.0-3.49:	31%	Live on campus:	99%
GPA 2.0-2.99:	12%	International:	1%

Basis for selection. Automatic admission generally given to students with high school GPA of 2.5 and ACT score of at least 19 or SAT of at least 890 (exclusive of writing). Essay recommended for academically weak applicants. Audition recommended for drama and music majors. **Homeschooled:** Evaluative transcript or GED score. Personal interview, essay, references may be required.

High school preparation. College-preparatory program recommended. 18 units recommended. Recommended units include English 4, mathematics 4, social studies 3, history 1, science 3 and foreign language 2. 1 unit computer technology recommended.

2005-2006 Annual costs. Tuition/fees: $15,550. Room/board: $6,100.

2004-2005 Financial aid. Need-based: 106 full-time freshmen applied for aid; 100 were judged to have need; 100 of these received aid. Average need met was 90%. Average scholarship/grant was $4,464; average loan $3,817. 36% of total undergraduate aid awarded as scholarships/grants, 64% as loans/jobs. **Non-need-based:** Awarded to 565 full-time undergraduates, including 174 freshmen. Scholarships awarded for academics, alumni affiliation, art, athletics, minority status, music/drama, religious affiliation, state residency.

Application procedures. Admission: No deadline. $20 fee, may be waived for applicants with need. Application may be submitted online. Admission notification on a rolling basis beginning on or about 9/1. **Financial**

aid: Priority date 4/1; no closing date. FAFSA required. Applicants notified on a rolling basis starting 2/15; must reply within 2 week(s) of notification.

Academics. Curriculum founded on general education program in liberal arts and sciences; geared toward students of moderate to high ability. Distinctive elements include cross-cultural learning requirement and senior capstone course focusing on basic issues of faith and life. **Special study options:** Cross-registration, double major, dual enrollment of high school students, independent study, internships, liberal arts/career combination, study abroad, teacher certification program, urban semester, Washington semester. **Credit/ placement by examination:** AP, CLEP, IB, institutional tests. **Support services:** Learning center, study skills assistance, tutoring.

Majors. Biology: General. **Business:** General. **Communications:** Media studies. **Computer sciences:** Computer science. **Education:** Elementary. **English:** English lit. **Foreign languages:** German, Spanish. **Health:** Athletic training, nursing (RN). **History:** General. **Interdisciplinary:** Natural sciences. **Math:** General. **Parks/recreation:** Health/fitness. **Philosophy/ religion:** Religion. **Physical sciences:** Chemistry, physics. **Psychology:** General. **Public administration:** Social work. **Visual/performing arts:** Studio arts.

Most popular majors. Business/marketing 8%, education 6%, health sciences 24%, interdisciplinary studies 6%, physical sciences 6%, public administration/social services 7%, visual/performing arts 7%.

Computing on campus. 56 workstations in library, computer center. Dormitories wired for high-speed internet access and linked to campus network. Commuter students can connect to campus network. Helpline, repair service, student web hosting, wireless network available.

Student life. Freshman orientation: Mandatory. Preregistration for classes offered. Held the Thursday through Monday before classes begin. **Policies:** Chapel services voluntary. 2 weekly convocations required and credited as part of general education. Freshmen permitted cars on campus. **Housing:** Guaranteed on-campus for all undergraduates. Coed dorms, special housing for disabled, apartments, substance-free housing available. **Activities:** Bands, choral groups, dance, drama, literary magazine, music ensembles, musical theater, opera, radio station, student government, student newspaper, symphony orchestra, Student Community Action Network for voluntary services, peace club, Bethel Christian Fellowship, service corps-disaster response, Fellowship of Christian Athletes, Amnesty International, environmental action club, multicultural organization, Catholic student organization, international students club.

Athletics. NAIA. **Intercollegiate:** Basketball, football (tackle) M, golf, soccer, tennis, track and field, volleyball W. **Intramural:** Badminton, baseball M, basketball, bowling, football (non-tackle), golf, soccer, softball, table tennis, tennis, volleyball. **Team name:** Threshers.

Student services. Alcohol/substance abuse counseling, campus ministries, career counseling, student employment services, financial aid counseling, health services, minority student services, personal counseling. **Physically disabled:** Services for visually, hearing impaired.

Contact. E-mail: admissions@bethelks.edu
Phone: (316) 284-5230 Toll-free number: (800) 522-1887 ext. 230
Fax: (316) 284-5870
Allan Bartel, Director of Admissions and Enrollment, Bethel College, 300 E 27th Street, North Newton, KS 67117-0531

Central Christian College of Kansas

McPherson, Kansas
www.centralchristian.edu **CB code: 6088**

- Private 4-year liberal arts college affiliated with Free Methodist Church of North America
- Residential campus in large town
- 314 degree-seeking undergraduates: 54% women, 9% African American, 7% Hispanic American, 2% Native American, 3% international
- 45% of applicants admitted
- 54% graduate within 6 years; 2% enter graduate study

General. Founded in 1884. Regionally accredited. **Degrees:** 55 bachelor's, 19 associate awarded. **Location:** 55 miles from Wichita. **Calendar:** 4-1-4. **Full-time faculty:** 18 total; 11% have terminal degrees, 28% women. **Part-time faculty:** 20 total; 15% have terminal degrees, 35% women. **Class size:** 75% < 20, 18% 20-39, 4% 40-49, 2% 50-99, 2% >100.

Freshman class profile. 626 applied, 283 admitted, 97 enrolled.

Mid 50% test scores		**Rank in top quarter:**	42%
SAT verbal:	450-610	**Rank in top tenth:**	15%
SAT math:	400-560	**End year in good standing:**	83%
ACT:	20-26	**Return as sophomores:**	58%
GPA 3.50 or higher:	54%	**Out-of-state:**	60%
GPA 3.0-3.49:	27%	**Live on campus:**	98%
GPA 2.0-2.99:	18%	**International:**	3%

Basis for selection. Secondary school record, recommendations very important; test scores important. SAT or ACT recommended. Applicants whose high school GPA is lower than 2.5 must submit ACT or SAT score for acceptance consideration. Interview and essay recommended. **Homeschooled:** Transcript required. **Learning Disabled:** Provide Individualized Education Program (IEP).

High school preparation. College-preparatory program recommended. 22 units recommended. Recommended units include English 4, mathematics 2, social studies 2, history 1, science 1 (laboratory 1). 1 computer technology recommended.

2006-2007 Annual costs. Tuition/fees (projected): $15,000. Room/ board: $5,000. Books/supplies: $800. Personal expenses: $1,000.

2005-2006 Financial aid. Need-based: 90 full-time freshmen applied for aid; 82 were judged to have need; 82 of these received aid. Average need met was 62%. Average scholarship/grant was $3,888; average loan $3,929. 39% of total undergraduate aid awarded as scholarships/grants, 61% as loans/jobs. **Non-need-based:** Awarded to 406 full-time undergraduates, including 140 freshmen. Scholarships awarded for academics, alumni affiliation, athletics, leadership, music/drama, religious affiliation.

Application procedures. Admission: Closing date 7/1. $20 fee, may be waived for applicants with need. Application may be submitted online. Admission notification on a rolling basis. **Financial aid:** Priority date 3/1; no closing date. FAFSA required. Applicants notified on a rolling basis starting 3/1; must reply within 4 week(s) of notification.

Academics. Special study options: Cooperative education, cross-registration, double major, dual enrollment of high school students, independent study, internships, liberal arts/career combination, student-designed major, urban semester, Washington semester. **Credit/placement by examination:** AP, CLEP, IB. 30 credit hours maximum toward associate degree, 30 toward bachelor's. **Support services:** Learning center, reduced course load, remedial instruction, study skills assistance, tutoring.

Majors. Area/ethnic studies: Western European. **Biology:** General, exercise physiology. **Business:** General, accounting, accounting/business management, business admin, entrepreneurial studies, managerial economics, office management, small business admin. **Communications:** General, broadcast journalism, journalism, media studies. **Health:** Health services. **Interdisciplinary:** Accounting/computer science, natural sciences. **Liberal arts:** Arts/sciences. **Math:** General. **Parks/recreation:** Exercise sciences, facilities management, sports admin. **Philosophy/religion:** Religion. **Physical sciences:** Chemistry. **Protective services:** Law enforcement admin, security management. **Psychology:** General. **Social sciences:** General. **Theology:** Bible, missionary, pastoral counseling, religious ed, sacred music, theology, youth ministry. **Visual/performing arts:** General, acting, dramatic, music performance, play/screenwriting, theater arts management, theater design.

Most popular majors. Business/marketing 42%, liberal arts 30%, theological studies 20%.

Computing on campus. 18 workstations in library, computer center, student center. Online course registration, online library, helpline, repair service available.

Student life. Freshman orientation: Mandatory. Preregistration for classes offered. Held at beginning of interterm and spring sessions, 1-2 days. **Policies:** Students must sign a life-style covenant. Alcohol, smoking, drugs not allowed on campus. Freshmen permitted cars on campus. **Housing:** Guaranteed on-campus for all undergraduates. Coed dorms, single-sex dorms, apartments, substance-free housing available. $150 fully refundable deposit, deadline 8/1. Students 23 years of age or older can live off campus. **Activities:** Bands, choral groups, drama, music ensembles, musical theater, radio station, student government, student newspaper, symphony orchestra, Christian service organization, Flying Tigers, prison ministries, performing arts club, Share teams, C.O.L.O.R.S., PBL, student activities council.

Athletics. NAIA. **Intercollegiate:** Baseball M, basketball, cheerleading, cross-country, golf, soccer, softball W, tennis, volleyball W. **Intramural:** Badminton, basketball, bowling, football (non-tackle) M, golf, soccer, softball, table tennis, tennis, volleyball. **Team name:** Tigers.

Student services. Campus ministries, career counseling, student employment services, financial aid counseling, health services, personal counseling, placement for graduates.

Contact. E-mail: admissions@centralchristian.edu
Phone: (316) 241-0723 ext. 337 Toll-free number: (800) 835-0078 ext. 337
Fax: (316) 241-6032
J. Ferrell, Dean of Enrollment, Central Christian College of Kansas, 1200 South Main, McPherson, KS 67460-5740

Emporia State University
Emporia, Kansas
www.emporia.edu **CB code: 6335**

- Public 4-year university and teachers college
- Residential campus in large town
- 4,159 degree-seeking undergraduates: 9% part-time, 62% women, 4% African American, 1% Asian American, 5% Hispanic American, 1% Native American, 2% international
- 1,512 degree-seeking graduate students
- 78% of applicants admitted
- SAT or ACT (ACT writing optional) required
- 43% graduate within 6 years; 18% enter graduate study

General. Founded in 1863. Regionally accredited. **Degrees:** 741 bachelor's awarded; master's, doctoral offered. **Location:** 50 miles from Topeka, 77 miles from Wichita. **Calendar:** Semester, extensive summer session. **Full-time faculty:** 253 total; 81% have terminal degrees, 8% minority, 40% women. **Part-time faculty:** 30 total; 33% have terminal degrees, 7% minority, 63% women. **Class size:** 46% < 20, 38% 20-39, 10% 40-49, 6% 50-99, less than 1% >100. **Special facilities:** Planetarium, natural history reserve, natural history museum, National Teachers Hall of Fame, Great Plains study center.

Freshman class profile. 1,188 applied, 931 admitted, 739 enrolled.

Mid 50% test scores		**Live on campus:**	86%
ACT:	19-25	**International:**	1%
End year in good standing:	78%	**Fraternities:**	14%
Return as sophomores:	68%	**Sororities:**	10%
Out-of-state:	7%		

Basis for selection. Applicants must have one of following: minimum ACT score of 21, rank in top third of high school class, minimum 2.0 GPA in Kansas Core Curriculum for in-state students, or 2.5 GPA for out-of-state students. Limited number of students who do not meet qualifications may be admitted through 10% exceptions window. ACT scores must be received by end of first semester of study. **Homeschooled:** GED must be submitted.

High school preparation. College-preparatory program recommended. Required units include English 4, mathematics 3, social studies 3, science 3 and academic electives 1. 1 computer technology recommended. These units required for students who do not have minimum ACT score of 21, or in top 1/3 of high school class.

2005-2006 Annual costs. Tuition/fees: $3,306; $10,658 out-of-state. Room/board: $4,787. Books/supplies: $900. Personal expenses: $1,854.

2004-2005 Financial aid. Need-based: 665 full-time freshmen applied for aid; 427 were judged to have need; 427 of these received aid. Average need met was 63%. Average scholarship/grant was $1,474; average loan $2,135. 38% of total undergraduate aid awarded as scholarships/grants, 62% as loans/jobs. **Non-need-based:** Awarded to 1,407 full-time undergraduates, including 434 freshmen. Scholarships awarded for academics, alumni affiliation, art, athletics, job skills, leadership, minority status, music/drama, religious affiliation, state residency. **Additional information:** Institution's own payment plan is available.

Application procedures. Admission: No deadline. $30 fee, may be waived for applicants with need. Application may be submitted online. Admission notification on a rolling basis. **Financial aid:** Priority date 3/15; no closing date. FAFSA required. Applicants notified on a rolling basis starting 2/2; must reply within 2 week(s) of notification.

Academics. Special study options: Distance learning, double major, dual enrollment of high school students, ESL, honors, independent study, internships, student-designed major, study abroad, teacher certification program. Career development center and programs, continuing education courses, evening program, interdisciplinary or interdepartmental courses of study, learning assistance programs, pass-fail grading option, service members' opportunity college, summer sessions, tutorial program, trio programs. **Credit/placement by examination:** AP, CLEP, IB, ACT, institutional tests. 30 credit hours maximum toward bachelor's degree. **Support services:** Remedial instruction, writing center.

Majors. Biology: General, biochemistry. **Business:** Accounting, business admin, marketing. **Communications:** General. **Computer sciences:** General, information systems. **Education:** Elementary, music, secondary. **Foreign languages:** General. **Health:** Athletic training, nursing (RN), vocational rehab counseling. **History:** General. **Liberal arts:** Arts/sciences. **Math:** General. **Parks/recreation:** General. **Physical sciences:** General, chemistry, geology, physics. **Psychology:** General. **Social sciences:** General, economics, political science, sociology. **Visual/performing arts:** Art, dramatic.

Most popular majors. Business/marketing 19%, education 29%, health sciences 8%, social sciences 12%.

Computing on campus. 410 workstations in dormitories, library, computer center, student center. Dormitories wired for high-speed internet access and linked to campus network. Commuter students can connect to campus network. Online library, helpline, student web hosting, wireless network available.

Student life. Freshman orientation: Available, $35 fee. Preregistration for classes offered. One-day program for students and parents; held during summer and prior to start of classes. **Policies:** Freshmen permitted cars on campus. **Housing:** Guaranteed on-campus for freshmen. Coed dorms, special housing for disabled, apartments, fraternity/sorority housing, substance-free housing available. $145 partly refundable deposit. **Activities:** Bands, choral groups, dance, drama, film society, literary magazine, music ensembles, musical theater, opera, student government, student newspaper, symphony orchestra, Black Student Union, International Club, Hispanic American leadership organization, Catholic Campus Community, Christian student center, Black women's network, Muslim student association, Fellowship of Christian Athletes, Arabic language club, East Asian club, Campus Crusade for Christ.

Athletics. NCAA. **Intercollegiate:** Baseball M, basketball, cheerleading, cross-country, football (tackle) M, soccer W, softball W, tennis, track and field, volleyball W. **Intramural:** Badminton, basketball, football (non-tackle), softball, table tennis, tennis, volleyball. **Team name:** Hornets.

Student services. Adult student services, alcohol/substance abuse counseling, campus ministries, career counseling, services for economically disadvantaged, student employment services, financial aid counseling, health services, legal services, minority student services, on-campus daycare, personal counseling, placement for graduates, veterans' counselor, women's services. **Physically disabled:** Services for visually, speech, hearing impaired.

Contact. E-mail: go2esu@emporia.edu
Phone: (620) 341-5465 Toll-free number: (877) 468-6378
Fax: (620) 341-5599
Laura Eddy, Director of Admisisons, Emporia State University, 1200 Commercial, Campus Box 4034, Emporia, KS 66801-5087

Fort Hays State University
Hays, Kansas
www.fhsu.edu **CB code: 6218**

- Public 4-year university
- Commuter campus in large town
- 7,614 degree-seeking undergraduates: 44% part-time, 55% women, 2% African American, 2% Hispanic American, 31% international
- 837 degree-seeking graduate students
- SAT or ACT with writing required
- 49% graduate within 6 years

General. Founded in 1902. Regionally accredited. **Degrees:** 1,064 bachelor's, 56 associate awarded; master's offered. **Location:** 170 miles from Wichita, 270 miles from Kansas City. **Calendar:** Semester, extensive summer session. **Full-time faculty:** 258 total. **Part-time faculty:** 45 total. **Class size:** 48% < 20, 44% 20-39, 5% 40-49, 4% 50-99, less than 1% >100. **Special facilities:** Observatory; paleontology, natural history, archeology, history, geology, botanical-zoological museums.

Freshman class profile.

Mid 50% test scores		**Out-of-state:**	10%
SAT verbal:	430-540	**Live on campus:**	67%
SAT math:	470-590	**International:**	1%
ACT:	19-24	**Fraternities:**	2%
Rank in top quarter:	31%	**Sororities:**	4%
Rank in top tenth:	9%		

Basis for selection. One of following required: minimum ACT composite score of 21, rank in top third of high school class, or minimum 2.0 GPA on Kansas pre-college curriculum (2.5 GPA for out-of-state students). Audition recommended for music majors.

High school preparation. 14 units recommended. Recommended units include English 4, mathematics 3, social studies 2, history 1 and science 3. 1 computer technology recommended.

2005-2006 Annual costs. Tuition/fees: $3,053; $9,576 out-of-state. Room/board: $5,314. Books/supplies: $800. Personal expenses: $2,082.

2004-2005 Financial aid. Need-based: 597 full-time freshmen applied for aid; 471 were judged to have need; 461 of these received aid. Average need met was 64%. Average scholarship/grant was $3,401; average loan $2,394. 35% of total undergraduate aid awarded as scholarships/grants, 65% as loans/jobs. **Non-need-based:** Awarded to 1,412 full-time undergraduates, including 381 freshmen.

Application procedures. Admission: No deadline. $30 fee. Application may be submitted online. Admission notification on a rolling basis. **Financial aid:** Priority date 3/15, closing date 5/30. FAFSA required. Applicants notified on a rolling basis starting 3/15; must reply within 3 week(s) of notification.

Academics. Special study options: Distance learning, double major, dual enrollment of high school students, ESL, exchange student, external degree, honors, independent study, internships, liberal arts/career combination, student-designed major, study abroad, teacher certification program, United Nations semester. **Credit/placement by examination:** AP, CLEP, institutional tests. **Support services:** Learning center, pre-admission summer program, reduced course load, remedial instruction, study skills assistance, tutoring, writing center.

Majors. Agriculture: Business. **Biology:** General. **Business:** General, accounting, business admin, market research, marketing, office management. **Communications:** General. **Computer sciences:** General. **Education:** Business, elementary, music, physical, technology/industrial arts, trade/industrial. **Foreign languages:** General. **Health:** Physical therapy assistant, sonography. **History:** General. **Interdisciplinary:** Biological/physical sciences. **Math:** General. **Philosophy/religion:** Philosophy. **Physical sciences:** Chemistry, geology, physics. **Protective services:** Criminal justice. **Psychology:** General. **Public administration:** Social work. **Social sciences:** Economics, political science, sociology. **Visual/performing arts:** Art.

Computing on campus. 1,400 workstations in dormitories, library, computer center, student center. Dormitories linked to campus network. Commuter students can connect to campus network. Online course registration, helpline available.

Student life. Freshman orientation: Mandatory, $25 fee. Preregistration for classes offered. 3-day program before start of classes; includes skills training. **Housing:** Guaranteed on-campus for freshmen. Coed dorms, single-sex dorms, apartments, fraternity/sorority housing available. $100 deposit, deadline 7/1. **Activities:** Bands, choral groups, dance, drama, music ensembles, musical theater, radio station, student government, student newspaper, symphony orchestra, TV station, Campus Crusade for Christ, Disciples of the Catholic Campus Center, Black Student Union, Hispanic American leadership organization, Young Republicans, Young Democrats.

Athletics. NCAA. **Intercollegiate:** Baseball M, basketball, cross-country, football (tackle) M, golf, gymnastics W, rodeo, softball W, tennis, track and field, volleyball W, wrestling M. **Intramural:** Archery, badminton, baseball M, basketball, bowling, cross-country, diving, fencing, field hockey W, gymnastics W, racquetball, soccer, softball, swimming, table tennis, tennis, track and field, volleyball, water polo, wrestling M.

Student services. Adult student services, career counseling, student employment services, financial aid counseling, health services, on-campus daycare, personal counseling, placement for graduates, veterans' counselor. **Physically disabled:** Services for visually, speech, hearing impaired.

Contact. E-mail: tigers@fshu.edu
Phone: (785) 628-5666 Toll-free number: (800) 628-3478
Fax: (785) 432-0248
Roger Schieferecke, Director of Admissions Counseling, Fort Hays State University, 600 Park Street, Hays, KS 67601

Friends University

Wichita, Kansas
www.friends.edu CB code: 6224

- Private 4-year business and liberal arts college affiliated with nondenominational tradition
- Commuter campus in large city
- 2,166 degree-seeking undergraduates
- SAT or ACT (ACT writing optional) required

General. Founded in 1898. Regionally accredited. **Degrees:** 586 bachelor's, 46 associate awarded; master's offered. **Location:** 1 mile from downtown. **Calendar:** Semester, limited summer session. **Full-time faculty:** 80 total. **Part-time faculty:** 155 total. **Special facilities:** Quaker collection, art center, observatory.

Freshman class profile.

Mid 50% test scores		**ACT:**	18-24
SAT verbal:	400-570	**Out-of-state:**	20%
SAT math:	420-620	**Live on campus:**	24%

Basis for selection. ACT score multiplied by GPA must equal 45 or above for admission. Those with score between 20 and 29 admitted provisionally. Audition required of music majors. Portfolio recommended for art majors.

High school preparation. 11 units required. Required units include English 4, social studies 2 and science 2.

2005-2006 Annual costs. Tuition/fees: $15,270. Room/board: $4,920. Books/supplies: $750. Personal expenses: $2,765.

2005-2006 Financial aid. Need-based: 40% of total undergraduate aid awarded as scholarships/grants, 60% as loans/jobs. **Additional information:** Scholarships for clergy/family of clergy available.

Application procedures. Admission: No deadline. $15 fee, may be waived for applicants with need. Admission notification on a rolling basis. **Financial aid:** Priority date 3/15; no closing date. FAFSA, institutional form required. Applicants notified on a rolling basis; must reply within 3 week(s) of notification.

Academics. Special study options: Cross-registration, double major, dual enrollment of high school students, external degree, honors, independent study, liberal arts/career combination, student-designed major, study abroad, teacher certification program. Degree completion program for working adults. **Credit/placement by examination:** CLEP. 60 credit hours maximum toward bachelor's degree. **Support services:** Reduced course load, study skills assistance, tutoring, writing center.

Majors. Biology: General. **Business:** Accounting, business admin, human resources, international, management information systems. **Communications:** General. **Computer sciences:** General. **Education:** Art, early childhood, elementary, English, mathematics, middle, music, physical, science, secondary, social science, Spanish. **Foreign languages:** Spanish. **Health:** Health care admin, medical radiologic technology/radiation therapy. **History:** General. **Liberal arts:** Arts/sciences. **Math:** General. **Parks/recreation:** Facilities management, health/fitness. **Physical sciences:** Chemistry. **Psychology:** General. **Social sciences:** Political science, sociology. **Theology:** Youth ministry. **Visual/performing arts:** Art, dance, dramatic, music performance.

Computing on campus. 142 workstations in dormitories, library, computer center. Dormitories linked to campus network. Commuter students can connect to campus network.

Student life. Freshman orientation: Mandatory. **Housing:** Single-sex dorms, apartments available. $100 deposit. **Activities:** Bands, choral groups, dance, drama, literary magazine, music ensembles, musical theater, opera, student government, symphony orchestra, international relations club, Phi Beta Lambda.

Athletics. NAIA. **Intercollegiate:** Baseball M, basketball, football (tackle) M, golf M, soccer, softball W, tennis, volleyball W. **Intramural:** Basketball, bowling, racquetball, soccer, softball, table tennis, volleyball. **Team name:** Falcons.

Student services. Adult student services, career counseling, student employment services, health services, personal counseling, placement for graduates, veterans' counselor. **Physically disabled:** Services for visually, speech, hearing impaired.

Contact. E-mail: learn@friends.edu
Phone: (316) 295-5100 Toll-free number: (800) 577-2233
Fax: (316) 295-5101
Tony Myers, Director of Admissions, Friends University, 2100 University, Wichita, KS 67213

Haskell Indian Nations University

Lawrence, Kansas
www.haskell.edu CB code: 0919

- Public 4-year university
- Small city

- 900 degree-seeking undergraduates
- SAT or ACT (ACT writing optional) required

General. Founded in 1884. Regionally accredited. Federally owned and operated college provides educational benefits to North American Indians who are under jurisdiction of Bureau of Indian Affairs. Students receive tuition, books, and some college housing. **Degrees:** 67 bachelor's, 94 associate awarded. **ROTC:** Air Force. **Location:** 38 miles from Kansas City, Missouri. **Calendar:** Semester, limited summer session. **Full-time faculty:** 42 total. **Part-time faculty:** 15 total. **Special facilities:** Wetlands south of campus.

Freshman class profile.

Out-of-state:	90%	**Live on campus:**	90%

Basis for selection. For bachelor's programs, secondary school record, class rank important; recommendations, test scores considered. Associate degree programs are open admission. Students must be certified by Bureau of Indian Affairs as member of federally-recognized tribe or quarter degree descendant of tribal member. SAT/ACT scores not used in admission decisions for associate programs. **Learning Disabled:** Must provide IEP from high school and test scores not more than 2 years old.

2005-2006 Annual costs. Federally subsidized college for Native Americans: no tuition; required fees $420, room and board $140. Books/supplies: $220.

Financial aid. Additional information: Some personal expenses may be offset by Bureau of Indian Affairs grants. Most students qualify for only minimum Pell grant.

Application procedures. Admission: Closing date 6/30 (postmark date). $10 fee, may be waived for applicants with need. Admission notification on a rolling basis beginning on or about 3/10. **Financial aid:** Priority date 5/15; no closing date. FAFSA required. Applicants notified on a rolling basis starting 3/15; must reply within 9 week(s) of notification.

Academics. Special study options: Cooperative education, independent study, internships. **Credit/placement by examination:** CLEP. 10 credit hours maximum toward associate degree. **Support services:** Learning center, reduced course load, remedial instruction, tutoring, writing center.

Majors. Area/ethnic studies: Native American. **Business:** Business admin. **Conservation:** General. **Education:** General, elementary.

Computing on campus. 45 workstations in dormitories, library, computer center, student center.

Student life. Freshman orientation: Mandatory. Preregistration for classes offered. 3 days preceding start of classes. **Policies:** Freshmen permitted cars on campus. **Housing:** Coed dorms, single-sex dorms available. $35 deposit. **Activities:** Choral groups, drama, student government, student newspaper, Native American clubs, Phi Beta Lambda (service organization), Baptist Student Union, LIGHT House (Lutheran organization), Catholic Center.

Athletics. NAIA. **Intercollegiate:** Basketball, cross-country, football (tackle) M, golf M, track and field, volleyball. **Intramural:** Basketball, bowling, racquetball, softball, volleyball, wrestling M. **Team name:** Indians.

Student services. Adult student services, alcohol/substance abuse counseling, career counseling, student employment services, financial aid counseling, health services, personal counseling, placement for graduates, veterans' counselor, women's services.

Contact. Phone: (785) 749-8454 Fax: (913) 749-8429
Ellen Allen, Director of Admissions and Records, Haskell Indian Nations University, 155 Indian Avenue #5031, Lawrence, KS 66046-4800

Kansas State University

Manhattan, Kansas — **CB member**
www.ksu.edu — **CB code: 6334**

- Public 4-year university and technical college
- Commuter campus in large town
- 18,605 degree-seeking undergraduates: 11% part-time, 49% women, 3% African American, 1% Asian American, 3% Hispanic American, 1% Native American, 1% international
- 3,176 degree-seeking graduate students
- 59% of applicants admitted
- SAT or ACT (ACT writing optional) required

General. Founded in 1863. Regionally accredited. Additional campus at Salina. Off-campus site at Fort Riley army base. **Degrees:** 3,612 bachelor's, 93 associate awarded; master's, doctoral, first professional offered. **ROTC:** Army, Air Force. **Location:** 120 miles from Kansas City, Missouri. **Calendar:** Semester, extensive summer session. **Full-time faculty:** 890 total; 85% have terminal degrees, 14% minority, 33% women. **Part-time faculty:** 161 total; 50% have terminal degrees, 5% minority, 56% women. **Class size:** 50% < 20, 43% 20-39, 6% 40-49, 5% 50-99, 5% >100. **Special facilities:** Nuclear reactor, prairie for biological research, laser laboratory, cancer research center, art museum.

Freshman class profile. 8,207 applied, 4,806 admitted, 3,309 enrolled.

Mid 50% test scores		**Rank in top tenth:**	32%
ACT:	21-26	**International:**	1%
Rank in top quarter:	54%		

Basis for selection. One of following required: minimum ACT score of 21, rank in top third of high school class, or minimum 2.0 GPA on Kansas pre-college curriculum (2.5 GPA for out-of-state students). Audition recommended for music and theater majors. Portfolio recommended for art and architecture majors.

High school preparation. 14 units recommended. Recommended units include English 4, mathematics 3, social studies 2, history 1 and science 3. One unit of technology recommended.

2005-2006 Annual costs. Tuition/fees: $5,124; $14,454 out-of-state. Room/board: $5,772. Books/supplies: $1,061. Personal expenses: $3,183.

2004-2005 Financial aid. Need-based: 2,404 full-time freshmen applied for aid; 1,678 were judged to have need; 1,665 of these received aid. Average need met was 63%. Average scholarship/grant was $3,034; average loan $2,862. 36% of total undergraduate aid awarded as scholarships/grants, 64% as loans/jobs. **Non-need-based:** Awarded to 4,766 full-time undergraduates, including 1,508 freshmen. Scholarships awarded for academics, alumni affiliation, art, athletics, leadership, music/drama, ROTC.

Application procedures. Admission: No deadline. $30 fee, may be waived for applicants with need. Application may be submitted online. Admission notification on a rolling basis beginning on or about 6/1. **Financial aid:** Priority date 3/1; no closing date. FAFSA required. Applicants notified on a rolling basis starting 3/15; must reply within 2 week(s) of notification.

Academics. Special study options: Accelerated study, cooperative education, distance learning, double major, ESL, exchange student, honors, independent study, internships, study abroad, teacher certification program. **Credit/placement by examination:** AP, CLEP, IB, ACT. 10 credit hours maximum toward associate degree, 20 toward bachelor's. PEP, DANTES exams accepted for credit. **Support services:** Learning center, preadmission summer program, reduced course load, remedial instruction, study skills assistance, tutoring, writing center.

Majors. Agriculture: Agronomy, animal sciences, business, communications, economics, food science, horticultural science. **Architecture:** Architecture, interior, landscape. **Biology:** General, biochemistry, microbiology, wildlife. **Business:** General, accounting, business admin, finance. **Communications:** General, journalism, media studies. **Computer sciences:** General, information systems, networking. **Education:** Agricultural, art, elementary, family/consumer sciences, music, secondary. **Engineering:** Agricultural, architectural, chemical, civil, computer, electrical, industrial, manufacturing, mechanical. **Engineering technology:** General, industrial management. **English:** English lit. **Family/consumer sciences:** General, child development, clothing/textiles, communication, family studies, human nutrition. **Foreign languages:** General. **Health:** Athletic training, communication disorders, dietetics, preveterinary. **History:** General. **Liberal arts:** Humanities. **Math:** General, statistics. **Mechanic/repair:** Aircraft. **Parks/recreation:** Exercise sciences, facilities management. **Philosophy/religion:** Philosophy. **Physical sciences:** General, chemistry, geology, physics. **Psychology:** General. **Public administration:** Social work. **Social sciences:** General, anthropology, economics, geography, political science, sociology. **Transportation:** Airline/commercial pilot, aviation management. **Visual/performing arts:** Dramatic, interior design, music performance, studio arts.

Most popular majors. Agriculture 9%, business/marketing 17%, education 11%, engineering/engineering technologies 12%, family/consumer sciences 7%, social sciences 10%.

Computing on campus. 547 workstations in dormitories, library, computer center. Dormitories linked to campus network. Commuter students can connect to campus network. Online course registration, helpline, repair service available.

Student life. Freshman orientation: Available, $25 fee. **Policies:** Freshmen permitted cars on campus. **Housing:** Coed dorms, single-sex dorms, apartments, cooperative housing, fraternity/sorority housing available. $25 deposit. **Activities:** Bands, choral groups, dance, drama, music ensembles, musical theater, radio station, student government, student newspaper, symphony orchestra, TV station, 340 religious, political, ethnic, and social service clubs and organizations available.

Athletics. NCAA. **Intercollegiate:** Baseball M, basketball, cross-country, equestrian W, football (tackle) M, golf, rowing (crew) W, tennis W, track and field, volleyball W. **Intramural:** Badminton, basketball, bowling, cross-country, golf, handball, soccer, softball, squash, swimming, table tennis, tennis, track and field, volleyball, water polo, wrestling M. **Team name:** Wildcats.

Student services. Adult student services, career counseling, student employment services, health services, on-campus daycare, personal counseling, placement for graduates, veterans' counselor. **Physically disabled:** Services for visually, speech, hearing impaired.

Contact. E-mail: kstate@ksu.edu
Phone: (785) 532-6250 Fax: (785) 532-6393
Larry Moeder, Director of Admissions, Kansas State University, 119 Anderson Hall, Manhattan, KS 66506

Kansas Wesleyan University

Salina, Kansas
www.kwu.edu **CB code: 6337**

- Private 4-year liberal arts college affiliated with United Methodist Church
- Residential campus in large town
- 897 degree-seeking undergraduates
- SAT or ACT (ACT writing optional) required

General. Founded in 1886. Regionally accredited. **Degrees:** 142 bachelor's, 30 associate awarded; master's offered. **Location:** 90 miles from Wichita, 180 miles from Kansas City. **Calendar:** Semester, limited summer session. **Full-time faculty:** 40 total. **Part-time faculty:** 30 total. **Class size:** 66% < 20, 26% 20-39, 6% 40-49, 1% 50-99, less than 1% >100. **Special facilities:** Observatory with 16-inch Cassegrain telescope.

Freshman class profile.

Mid 50% test scores			
SAT verbal:	470-550	ACT:	21-25
SAT math:	480-620	Out-of-state:	32%
		Live on campus:	67%

Basis for selection. Applicant must have ACT composite score of 18 or SAT combined score of 850 (exclusive of Writing) and high school GPA of 2.5 or rank in top half of class. Interview recommended for academically weak applicants. Audition recommended for music majors. Portfolio recommended for art majors.

2005-2006 Annual costs. Tuition/fees: $15,800. $200 per-credit-hour charge for 1-5 credit hours; $1,800 per semester for 6-8 credit hours; $3,600 per semester for 9-11 credit hours. Room/board: $5,600. Books/supplies: $800. Personal expenses: $500.

Financial aid. Non-need-based: Scholarships awarded for academics, alumni affiliation, art, athletics, music/drama, state residency. **Additional information:** Awards available for residence hall students: minimum $7,000 for 3.0 GPA plus ACT score of 22 or SAT of 950 (exclusive of Writing); minimum $8,000 for 3.5 GPA plus ACT score of 22 or SAT score of 1030 (exclusive of Writing); minimum $9,000 for 3.75 GPA plus ACT score of 25 or SAT score of 1140 (exclusive of Writing). Application deadline March 15.

Application procedures. Admission: No deadline. $20 fee. Admission notification on a rolling basis. **Financial aid:** Closing date 3/15. FAFSA required. Applicants notified on a rolling basis starting 1/1; must reply by 8/1 or within 3 week(s) of notification.

Academics. Special study options: Accelerated study, cross-registration, double major, ESL, independent study, internships, liberal arts/career combination, student-designed major, teacher certification program. **Credit/placement by examination:** AP, CLEP, institutional tests. 30 credit hours maximum toward bachelor's degree. **Support services:** Learning center, reduced course load, remedial instruction, tutoring, writing center.

Majors. Biology: General. **Business:** General, accounting. **Communications:** General, public relations. **Computer sciences:** General, computer science. **Education:** Art, elementary, English, secondary. **English:** Speech/rhetoric. **Foreign languages:** General, German, Spanish. **Health:** Preop/surgical nursing. **History:** General. **Math:** General. **Parks/recreation:** Health/fitness. **Philosophy/religion:** Religion. **Physical sciences:** Chemistry, physics. **Protective services:** Criminal justice. **Psychology:** General. **Social sciences:** Sociology. **Theology:** Religious ed. **Visual/performing arts:** Arts management, dramatic, music performance, studio arts.

Most popular majors. Business/marketing 32%, education 9%, health sciences 9%, parks/recreation 7%, physical sciences 7%, social sciences 7%.

Computing on campus. 50 workstations in library, computer center. Dormitories wired for high-speed internet access and linked to campus network. Online library available.

Student life. Freshman orientation: Available. Preregistration for classes offered. **Policies:** Freshmen permitted cars on campus. **Housing:** Guaranteed on-campus for freshmen. Single-sex dorms, apartments available. $100 deposit. **Activities:** Jazz band, choral groups, dance, drama, literary magazine, music ensembles, musical theater, radio station, student government, student newspaper, Fellowship of Christian Athletes, Religious Life Committee.

Athletics. NAIA. **Intercollegiate:** Baseball M, basketball, cross-country, football (tackle) M, golf, soccer, softball W, tennis, track and field, volleyball W. **Intramural:** Basketball, softball, volleyball, weight lifting. **Team name:** Coyotes.

Student services. Adult student services, career counseling, student employment services, financial aid counseling, personal counseling, placement for graduates, veterans' counselor. **Physically disabled:** Services for visually impaired.

Contact. E-mail: admissions@kwu.edu
Phone: (785) 827-5541 ext. 1285 Toll-free number: (800) 874-1154
Fax: (785) 827-0927
Jim Allen, Director of Admissions, Kansas Wesleyan University, 100 East Claflin Avenue, Salina, KS 67401-6196

Manhattan Christian College

Manhattan, Kansas
www.mccks.edu **CB code: 6392**

- Private 4-year Bible college affiliated with Christian Church
- Residential campus in large town
- 305 degree-seeking undergraduates
- SAT or ACT (ACT writing optional), application essay required

General. Founded in 1927. Regionally accredited; also accredited by ABHE. Students have access to Kansas State University library and facilities at student rates. **Degrees:** 65 bachelor's, 8 associate awarded. **ROTC:** Army, Air Force. **Location:** 130 miles from Kansas City. **Calendar:** Semester, limited summer session. **Full-time faculty:** 10 total. **Part-time faculty:** 20 total.

Freshman class profile.

Out-of-state:	38%	Live on campus:	98%

Basis for selection. High school record, test scores, recommendations important. Character recommendations required. Interview recommended. Audition required for music majors.

High school preparation. Recommended units include English 4, mathematics 2 and science 2.

2005-2006 Annual costs. Tuition/fees: $9,494. Additional $6 required fee per-credit-hour, up to $72; $140 per-credit-hour charge for part-time, non-degree-seeking students. Room/board: $5,590. Books/supplies: $1,150. Personal expenses: $1,067.

Financial aid. Non-need-based: Scholarships awarded for academics, leadership, music/drama.

Application procedures. Admission: Priority date 4/15; deadline 7/1 (postmark date). $25 fee, may be waived for applicants with need. Admission notification on a rolling basis beginning on or about 10/15. **Financial aid:** Priority date 4/1; no closing date. FAFSA required. Applicants notified on a rolling basis starting 5/1; must reply within 2 week(s) of notification.

Academics. Special study options: Combined bachelor's/graduate degree, double major, dual enrollment of high school students, internships, liberal arts/career combination. Dual degree program with Kansas State University. **Credit/placement by examination:** CLEP, institutional tests. 36 credit hours maximum toward bachelor's degree. **Support services:** Reduced course load, tutoring.

Majors. Business: Business admin. **Philosophy/religion:** Religion. **Theology:** Bible, missionary, pastoral counseling, religious ed, theology.

Most popular majors. Business/marketing 65%, philosophy/religious studies 35%.

Computing on campus. 12 workstations in library, computer center.

Student life. **Freshman orientation:** Mandatory. Preregistration for classes offered. 3-day program held before start of classes. **Policies:** Religious observance required. Freshmen permitted cars on campus. **Housing:** Guaranteed on-campus for freshmen. Single-sex dorms, apartments available. $125 deposit, deadline 6/1. **Activities:** Bands, choral groups, drama, music ensembles, student government.

Athletics. NCCAA. **Intercollegiate:** Basketball, soccer, volleyball W. **Intramural:** Softball. **Team name:** Crusaders.

Student services. Career counseling, student employment services, health services, personal counseling, placement for graduates. **Physically disabled:** Services for speech impaired.

Contact. E-mail: admit@mccks.edu
Phone: (785) 539-3571 Toll-free number: (877) 246-4622
Fax: (785) 776-9251
Eric Ingmire, Director of Admissions, Manhattan Christian College, 1415 Anderson Avenue, Manhattan, KS 66502

McPherson College

McPherson, Kansas
www.mcpherson.edu **CB code: 6404**

- Private 4-year liberal arts college affiliated with Church of the Brethren
- Residential campus in large town
- 466 degree-seeking undergraduates: 9% part-time, 38% women, 6% African American, 6% Hispanic American, 1% Native American
- 85% of applicants admitted
- SAT or ACT (ACT writing optional) required

General. Founded in 1887. Regionally accredited. Only degree program in antique auto restoration in United States. **Degrees:** 82 bachelor's, 22 associate awarded. **Location:** 60 miles from Wichita. **Calendar:** 4-1-4, limited summer session. **Full-time faculty:** 35 total; 63% have terminal degrees, 3% minority, 31% women. **Part-time faculty:** 12 total; 33% have terminal degrees, 25% women. **Class size:** 80% < 20, 19% 20-39, less than 1% 50-99. **Special facilities:** Museum.

Freshman class profile. 495 applied, 421 admitted, 109 enrolled.

Mid 50% test scores			
SAT verbal:	410-560	GPA 2.0-2.99:	22%
SAT math:	410-580	Rank in top quarter:	31%
ACT:	19-24	Rank in top tenth:	26%
GPA 3.50 or higher:	41%	Return as sophomores:	63%
GPA 3.0-3.49:	37%	Out-of-state:	48%
		Live on campus:	93%

Basis for selection. Satisfactory high school performance or completion of GED, corresponding standardized test scores, and appropriate personal qualities. Portfolio required for auto restoration program.

High school preparation. College-preparatory program recommended.

2005-2006 Annual costs. Tuition/fees: $15,160. Room/board: $5,850.

2005-2006 Financial aid. **Need-based:** 105 full-time freshmen applied for aid; 93 were judged to have need; 93 of these received aid. Average need met was 88%. Average scholarship/grant was $5,246; average loan $4,384. 42% of total undergraduate aid awarded as scholarships/grants, 58% as loans/jobs. **Non-need-based:** Awarded to 402 full-time undergraduates, including 102 freshmen. Scholarships awarded for academics, art, athletics, religious affiliation, ROTC, state residency.

Application procedures. **Admission:** Priority date 3/1; no deadline. $25 fee, may be waived for applicants with need. Application may be submitted online. Admission notification on a rolling basis. Must reply by May 1 or within 4 week(s) if notified thereafter. **Financial aid:** Priority date 3/1; no closing date. FAFSA required. Applicants notified on a rolling basis starting 3/1; must reply within 3 week(s) of notification.

Academics. **Special study options:** Combined bachelor's/graduate degree, cross-registration, double major, independent study, internships, liberal arts/career combination, student-designed major, study abroad, teacher certification program, urban semester. **Credit/placement by examination:** AP, CLEP, IB, institutional tests. **Support services:** Learning center, reduced course load, remedial instruction, study skills assistance, tutoring, writing center.

Majors. **Agriculture:** Agribusiness operations, agronomy, animal sciences, farm/ranch. **Biology:** General. **Business:** Accounting, business admin, finance, international. **Communications:** General. **Computer sciences:** Programming. **Conservation:** Environmental studies. **Education:** General, art, biology, business, chemistry, computer, early childhood, elementary, English, foreign languages, history, mathematics, middle, music, physical, science, social studies, Spanish, special, speech, technology/industrial arts. **Foreign languages:** General, Spanish. **Health:** Predentistry, premedicine, prepharmacy, preveterinary. **History:** General. **Legal studies:** Prelaw. **Liberal arts:** Arts/sciences. **Math:** General. **Mechanic/repair:** Automotive. **Parks/recreation:** Health/fitness. **Physical sciences:** Chemistry. **Psychology:** General. **Social sciences:** Sociology. **Visual/performing arts:** Art, dramatic, music performance.

Most popular majors. Biology 8%, business/marketing 25%, education 9%, engineering/engineering technologies 7%, English 6%, history 6%, parks/recreation 7%, social sciences 6%, visual/performing arts 11%.

Computing on campus. 72 workstations in dormitories, library, computer center, student center. Dormitories wired for high-speed internet access and linked to campus network. Commuter students can connect to campus network. Online library, helpline, wireless network available.

Student life. **Freshman orientation:** Mandatory. Preregistration for classes offered. **Policies:** No alcohol permitted on campus. Unmarried students under 23 years old are required to live in residence halls. Freshmen permitted cars on campus. **Housing:** Guaranteed on-campus for all undergraduates. Coed dorms, single-sex dorms, special housing for disabled available. $150 nonrefundable deposit, deadline 5/1. **Activities:** Bands, choral groups, drama, music ensembles, musical theater, student government, student newspaper, 28 clubs and organizations available.

Athletics. NAIA. **Intercollegiate:** Basketball, cheerleading, cross-country, football (tackle) M, softball W, track and field, volleyball W. **Intramural:** Badminton, basketball, football (non-tackle), football (tackle) M, handball, racquetball, soccer, softball, table tennis, volleyball. **Team name:** Bulldogs.

Student services. Adult student services, campus ministries, career counseling, student employment services, financial aid counseling, health services, personal counseling, placement for graduates. **Physically disabled:** Services for hearing impaired.

Contact. E-mail: admiss@mcpherson.edu
Phone: (620) 241-0731 ext. 1270 Toll-free number: (800) 695-7402
Fax: (620) 241-8443
Carol Williams, Director of Admissions and Financial Aid, McPherson College, 1600 East Euclid Street, McPherson, KS 67460-1402

MidAmerica Nazarene University

Olathe, Kansas
www.mnu.edu **CB code: 6437**

- Private 4-year university and liberal arts college affiliated with Church of the Nazarene
- Residential campus in small city
- 1,338 degree-seeking undergraduates: 11% part-time, 52% women, 7% African American, 1% Asian American, 4% Hispanic American, 1% Native American, 1% international
- 315 degree-seeking graduate students
- 69% of applicants admitted
- SAT or ACT (ACT writing optional) required
- 45% graduate within 6 years

General. Founded in 1966. Regionally accredited. **Degrees:** 345 bachelor's, 4 associate awarded; master's offered. **ROTC:** Army, Air Force. **Location:** 19 miles from Kansas City. **Calendar:** Semester, limited summer session. **Full-time faculty:** 71 total; 38% have terminal degrees, 4% minority, 41% women. **Part-time faculty:** 102 total; 10% have terminal degrees, 3% minority, 48% women. **Class size:** 62% < 20, 34% 20-39, 3% 40-49, 2% 50-99.

Freshman class profile. 750 applied, 519 admitted, 216 enrolled.

Mid 50% test scores			
SAT verbal:	460-610	Return as sophomores:	67%
SAT math:	440-610	Out-of-state:	34%
ACT:	19-26	Live on campus:	59%

Basis for selection. Secondary school record, class rank, test scores, moral principles important. Nursing, elementary education, secondary education programs have higher standards for admission. Interview recommended for music, nursing, elementary and secondary education programs. Audition recommended for music majors. **Homeschooled:** Transcript of courses and grades, letter of recommendation (nonparent) required.

High school preparation. 14 units recommended. Recommended units include English 4, mathematics 3, social studies 3, science 3 and foreign language 1.

2006-2007 Annual costs. Tuition/fees (projected): $15,968. Room/board: $5,830. Books/supplies: $1,300. Personal expenses: $2,500.

2005-2006 Financial aid. Need-based: 196 full-time freshmen applied for aid; 166 were judged to have need; 166 of these received aid. Average need met was 62%. Average scholarship/grant was $7,247; average loan $4,149. 49% of total undergraduate aid awarded as scholarships/grants, 51% as loans/jobs. **Non-need-based:** Awarded to 284 full-time undergraduates, including 77 freshmen. Scholarships awarded for academics, art, athletics, leadership, music/drama, religious affiliation, ROTC.

Application procedures. Admission: Priority date 3/1; deadline 8/1 (postmark date). $25 fee. Application may be submitted online. Admission notification on a rolling basis. **Financial aid:** Priority date 3/1; no closing date. FAFSA, institutional form required. Applicants notified on a rolling basis starting 3/30; must reply within 2 week(s) of notification.

Academics. Adults 25 and older may earn bachelor's degree through evening division. **Special study options:** Accelerated study, cross-registration, distance learning, double major, dual enrollment of high school students, independent study, internships, study abroad, teacher certification program, Washington semester. Dual degree program in vocational agriculture with Kansas State University. **Credit/placement by examination:** AP, CLEP, IB, SAT, ACT, institutional tests. 34 credit hours maximum toward associate degree, 34 toward bachelor's. **Support services:** Learning center, reduced course load, remedial instruction, study skills assistance, tutoring.

Majors. Biology: General. **Business:** General, accounting, business admin, communications, human resources. **Communications:** General, media studies, public relations. **Computer sciences:** General, computer science, information systems. **Education:** Biology, business, elementary, English, foreign languages, health, mathematics, middle, music, physical, secondary, social studies, Spanish. **English:** English lit. **Foreign languages:** Spanish. **Health:** Athletic training, nursing (RN). **History:** General. **Math:** General. **Parks/recreation:** Exercise sciences, sports admin. **Philosophy/religion:** Religion. **Physical sciences:** Chemistry, physics. **Protective services:** Law enforcement admin. **Psychology:** General. **Social sciences:** General, criminology, sociology, urban studies. **Theology:** Missionary, religious ed, sacred music, youth ministry. **Visual/performing arts:** General, music performance, voice/opera.

Most popular majors. Business/marketing 48%, education 11%, health sciences 8%, social sciences 6%.

Computing on campus. 90 workstations in dormitories, library, computer center. Dormitories wired for high-speed internet access and linked to campus network. Commuter students can connect to campus network. Online course registration, online library, helpline, student web hosting, wireless network available.

Student life. Freshman orientation: Mandatory, $44 fee. Preregistration for classes offered. Program concentrates on essential study skills, time management, value of liberal arts learning, career development aids, proficiency assessment. **Policies:** Religious observance required. Freshmen permitted cars on campus. **Housing:** Guaranteed on-campus for freshmen. Single-sex dorms, special housing for disabled, apartments, substance-free housing available. $100 deposit, deadline 8/21. **Activities:** Bands, choral groups, drama, music ensembles, radio station, student government, student newspaper, TV station, Circle K, College Republicans, gospel station, Fellowship of Christian Athletes, multicultural student asociation, BYTE (computer science) club, Psych Incorporated (psychology honors club), medical careers club, covenant groups.

Athletics. NAIA. **Intercollegiate:** Baseball M, basketball, cheerleading, cross-country, football (tackle) M, soccer, softball W, track and field, volleyball W. **Intramural:** Basketball, bowling, football (non-tackle), football (tackle), golf, soccer, softball, table tennis, tennis, track and field, volleyball. **Team name:** Pioneers.

Student services. Campus ministries, career counseling, student employment services, financial aid counseling, health services, personal counseling, placement for graduates, veterans' counselor. **Physically disabled:** Services for visually, speech, hearing impaired.

Contact. E-mail: admissions@mnu.edu
Phone: (913) 791-3380 Toll-free number: (800) 800-8887
Fax: (913) 791-3481
Dennis Troyer, Director of Admissions, MidAmerica Nazarene University, 2030 East College Way, Olathe, KS 66062-1899

Newman University
Wichita, Kansas
www.newmanu.edu **CB code: 6615**

- Private 4-year university and liberal arts college affiliated with Roman Catholic Church
- Commuter campus in large city
- 1,301 degree-seeking undergraduates: 14% part-time, 61% women
- 371 degree-seeking graduate students
- SAT and SAT Subject Tests or ACT (ACT writing optional) required

General. Founded in 1933. Regionally accredited. The university is a sponsored ministry of the Adorers of the Blood of Christ. **Degrees:** 311 bachelor's, 56 associate awarded; master's offered. **Location:** 160 miles from Oklahoma City, 180 miles from Kansas City. **Calendar:** Semester, limited summer session. **Full-time faculty:** 85 total. **Part-time faculty:** 68 total. **Class size:** 71% < 20, 27% 20-39, 2% 40-49, less than 1% 50-99, less than 1% >100. **Special facilities:** Photography laboratory, cadaver laboratory.

Freshman class profile. 753 applied, 637 enrolled.

Basis for selection. Minimum GPA 2.0, minimum ACT composite score of 18, or SAT score of 860 (exclusive of writing). Caliber of high school curriculum important. Portfolio recommended for art majors.

High school preparation. Recommended units include English 4, mathematics 3, social studies 3 and science 3.

2006-2007 Annual costs. Tuition/fees (projected): $17,308. Room/board: $5,372. Books/supplies: $904. Personal expenses: $4,495.

2005-2006 Financial aid. Need-based: 41% of total undergraduate aid awarded as scholarships/grants, 59% as loans/jobs. **Non-need-based:** Scholarships awarded for academics, alumni affiliation, athletics, leadership, minority status, music/drama, religious affiliation.

Application procedures. Admission: No deadline. $20 fee, may be waived for applicants with need. Application may be submitted online. Admission notification on a rolling basis. **Financial aid:** Priority date 3/1; no closing date. FAFSA, institutional form required. Applicants notified on a rolling basis starting 2/1.

Academics. Special study options: Cooperative education, cross-registration, distance learning, double major, dual enrollment of high school students, independent study, internships, liberal arts/career combination, student-designed major, study abroad, teacher certification program. **Credit/placement by examination:** AP, CLEP, IB, institutional tests. 30 credit hours maximum toward bachelor's degree. **Support services:** Learning center, study skills assistance, tutoring, writing center.

Majors. Biology: General. **Business:** Accounting, business admin, management information systems, marketing. **Communications:** Media studies. **Computer sciences:** Information systems. **Education:** General, elementary, middle, secondary. **English:** English lit. **Health:** Nursing (RN), sonography. **History:** General. **Liberal arts:** Arts/sciences. **Math:** General. **Physical sciences:** Chemistry. **Protective services:** Law enforcement admin. **Psychology:** General. **Social sciences:** Sociology. **Theology:** Pastoral counseling. **Visual/performing arts:** Art.

Computing on campus. 90 workstations in dormitories, library, computer center, student center. Dormitories wired for high-speed internet access and linked to campus network. Commuter students can connect to campus network. Online library, helpline, repair service, wireless network available.

Student life. Freshman orientation: Mandatory, $10 fee. Preregistration for classes offered. 2-day program prior to fall term. **Policies:** Freshmen permitted cars on campus. **Housing:** Guaranteed on-campus for freshmen. Coed dorms, apartments available. $100 deposit. Freshmen required to live in college housing for first 2 years if not living with parents. **Activities:** Choral groups, drama, literary magazine, student government, student newspaper, Koinonia, service scholars, Newman Club, international club, Peer Educators, Kansas Catholic College Student Convention, campus ministries, peer ministers.

Athletics. NAIA. **Intercollegiate:** Baseball M, basketball, bowling, cheerleading, cross-country, golf, soccer, softball W, tennis, volleyball. **Intramural:** Baseball M, basketball, football (tackle), table tennis, volleyball, weight lifting. **Team name:** Jets.

Student services. Adult student services, campus ministries, career counseling, student employment services, financial aid counseling, on-campus daycare, personal counseling, placement for graduates. **Physically disabled:** Services for visually, speech, hearing impaired.

Contact. E-mail: admissions@newmanu.edu
Phone: (316) 942-4291 ext. 2144 Toll-free number: (877) 639-6268
Fax: (316) 942-4483
Todd Lucas, Dean of Admissions, Newman University, 3100 McCormick Avenue, Wichita, KS 67213-2097

Ottawa University

Ottawa, Kansas **CB member**
www.ottawa.edu **CB code: 6547**

- Private 4-year liberal arts college affiliated with American Baptist Churches in the USA
- Residential campus in large town
- 416 degree-seeking undergraduates: 6% part-time, 42% women, 10% African American, 1% Asian American, 6% Hispanic American, 3% Native American, 3% international
- SAT or ACT (ACT writing optional) required
- 33% graduate within 6 years

General. Founded in 1865. Regionally accredited. Degree completion programs in Overland Park; Phoenix, AZ; Milwaukee, WI; Jeffersonville, IN and Pacific Rim countries. Master's programs in Overland Park and Phoenix, AZ. **Degrees:** 105 bachelor's awarded. **Location:** 45 miles from Kansas City. **Calendar:** Semester, limited summer session. **Full-time faculty:** 27 total. **Part-time faculty:** 25 total. **Class size:** 63% < 20, 35% 20-39, 2% 40-49, less than 1% 50-99.

Freshman class profile. 113 enrolled.

Mid 50% test scores			
ACT:	19-24	Rank in top quarter:	39%
GPA 3.50 or higher:	38%	Rank in top tenth:	17%
GPA 3.0-3.49:	37%	Out-of-state:	53%
GPA 2.0-2.99:	25%	Live on campus:	99%

Basis for selection. Rank in top half of class, 2.5 GPA, ACT composite score of 18 or above required. Personal recommendation, school and community achievements, interview, special talents considered. Audition recommended for music and drama majors. Portfolio recommended for art majors.

High school preparation. Recommended units include English 4, mathematics 3, social studies 1, history 2, science 3 (laboratory 2) and foreign language 1.

2005-2006 Annual costs. Tuition/fees: $14,800. Room/board: $5,542. Books/supplies: $900. Personal expenses: $1,600.

2005-2006 Financial aid. Need-based: Average need met was 90%. Average scholarship/grant was $10,266; average loan $3,652. 56% of total undergraduate aid awarded as scholarships/grants, 44% as loans/jobs. **Non-need-based:** Scholarships awarded for academics, alumni affiliation, athletics, music/drama, religious affiliation.

Application procedures. Admission: Priority date 6/1; no deadline. $15 fee. Application may be submitted online. Admission notification on a rolling basis. Must reply by May 1 or within 4 week(s) if notified thereafter. **Financial aid:** Priority date 3/15; no closing date. FAFSA required. Applicants notified on a rolling basis starting 2/1; must reply within 4 week(s) of notification.

Academics. Special study options: Double major, dual enrollment of high school students, internships, liberal arts/career combination, student-designed major, teacher certification program. **Credit/placement by examination:** AP, CLEP, IB. 20 credit hours maximum toward bachelor's degree. **Support services:** Learning center, reduced course load, study skills assistance, tutoring.

Majors. Biology: General. **Business:** Accounting/business management, business admin, management information systems. **Communications:** General. **Computer sciences:** Information technology. **Education:** Art, elementary, English, mathematics, music, physical. **History:** General. **Math:** General. **Parks/recreation:** Health/fitness. **Philosophy/religion:** Religion. **Psychology:** General. **Public administration:** Human services. **Social sciences:** Political science, sociology. **Visual/performing arts:** Art, dramatic.

Most popular majors. Biology 10%, business/marketing 24%, communications/journalism 10%, education 11%, health sciences 10%, mathematics 6%, social sciences 14%.

Computing on campus. 71 workstations in dormitories, library, computer center. Dormitories wired for high-speed internet access and linked to campus network. Commuter students can connect to campus network. Online library, helpline available.

Student life. Freshman orientation: Mandatory. Preregistration for classes offered. **Policies:** Freshmen permitted cars on campus. **Housing:** Guaranteed on-campus for freshmen. Coed dorms, single-sex dorms available. $150 deposit, deadline 6/1. Pets allowed in dorm rooms. **Activities:** Jazz band, choral groups, drama, music ensembles, radio station, student government, student newspaper, symphony orchestra, Christian Faith in Action, voluntary service organization, Whole Earth club, Fellowship of Christian Athletes, student activities force, Cognoscenti (literary group), Amnesty International.

Athletics. NAIA. **Intercollegiate:** Baseball M, basketball, cross-country, football (tackle) M, golf M, soccer, softball W, track and field, volleyball W. **Intramural:** Badminton, basketball, bowling, golf, handball, racquetball, soccer, softball, table tennis, tennis, track and field, volleyball. **Team name:** Braves.

Student services. Alcohol/substance abuse counseling, campus ministries, career counseling, student employment services, financial aid counseling, health services, personal counseling, placement for graduates.

Contact. E-mail: admiss@ottawa.edu
Phone: (785) 242-5200 ext. 5421 Toll-free number: (800) 775-5200 ext. 5421 Fax: (785) 242-1008
Fola Akande, Director of Admissions, Ottawa University, 1001 South Cedar Street, #17, Ottawa, KS 66067-3399

Pittsburg State University

Pittsburg, Kansas
www.pittstate.edu **CB code: 6336**

- Public 4-year university
- Residential campus in large town
- 5,357 degree-seeking undergraduates: 5% part-time, 49% women, 2% African American, 1% Asian American, 2% Hispanic American, 2% Native American, 4% international
- 700 degree-seeking graduate students
- 90% of applicants admitted
- ACT (writing optional) required
- 51% graduate within 6 years

General. Founded in 1903. Regionally accredited. Centers in Kansas City and Wichita. **Degrees:** 1,081 bachelor's, 28 associate awarded; master's offered. **ROTC:** Army. **Location:** 120 miles from Kansas City. **Calendar:** Semester, limited summer session. **Full-time faculty:** 291 total; 78% have terminal degrees, 7% minority, 38% women. **Part-time faculty:** 82 total; 18% have terminal degrees, 5% minority, 58% women. **Class size:** 54% < 20, 35% 20-39, 4% 40-49, 7% 50-99, less than 1% >100. **Special facilities:** Planetarium, observatory, field biology reserve, technology center, amphitheater.

Freshman class profile. 1,935 applied, 1,738 admitted, 991 enrolled.

Mid 50% test scores			
ACT:	19-24	GPA 2.0-2.99:	25%
GPA 3.50 or higher:	41%	Out-of-state:	25%
GPA 3.0-3.49:	31%	Live on campus:	70%
		International:	1%

Basis for selection. Kansas residents must have one of following: minimum ACT score of 21, or rank in top 1/3 of high school graduating class, or minimum 2.0 GPA in Kansas precollege curriculum. (Out-of-state students must have a minimum 2.5 GPA or one of the other qualifications listed above.). No ACT scores required for applicants 21 years old or over. **Homeschooled:** GED, record of course content and completion required.

High school preparation. College-preparatory program recommended. 14 units recommended. Recommended units include English 4, mathematics 3, social studies 2, history 1 and science 3. 1 computer technology required.

2005-2006 Annual costs. Tuition/fees: $3,562; $10,444 out-of-state. The College of Technology assesses $14 per credit hour for technology courses with a cap of $140 per semester. Room/board: $4,550. Books/supplies: $800. Personal expenses: $1,980.

2005-2006 Financial aid. Need-based: 739 full-time freshmen applied for aid; 525 were judged to have need; 513 of these received aid. Average need met was 89%. Average scholarship/grant was $3,770; average loan $2,658. 45% of total undergraduate aid awarded as scholarships/grants, 55% as loans/jobs. **Non-need-based:** Awarded to 1,056 full-time undergraduates, including 375 freshmen. Scholarships awarded for academics, alumni affiliation, art, athletics, leadership, music/drama, ROTC.

Application procedures. Admission: No deadline. $30 fee. Application may be submitted online. Admission notification on a rolling basis. **Financial aid:** Priority date 3/1; no closing date. FAFSA, institutional form required. Applicants notified on a rolling basis; must reply within 2 week(s) of notification.

Academics. Special study options: Accelerated study, combined bachelor's/graduate degree, cooperative education, distance learning, double major, dual enrollment of high school students, ESL, exchange student, external degree, honors, independent study, internships, liberal arts/career combination, student-designed major, study abroad, teacher certification program. **Credit/placement by examination:** AP, CLEP, ACT, institutional tests. 24 credit hours maximum toward bachelor's degree. **Support services:** Learning center, tutoring, writing center.

Honors college/program. Separate application required. Criteria for selection include minimum 28 ACT score, minimum 3.5 GPA, recommendations, record of participation in academic and other extracurricular activities.

Majors. Biology: General, biochemistry, cellular/molecular, plant physiology. **Business:** Accounting, actuarial science, business admin, construction management, fashion, finance, international, managerial economics, marketing. **Communications:** General, advertising, digital media, journalism, photojournalism, public relations, radio/tv. **Computer sciences:** Computer science, information technology, security. **Conservation:** Fisheries, management/policy, wildlife. **Education:** Art, biology, chemistry, elementary, English, family/consumer sciences, French, history, mathematics, music, physical, physics, psychology, Spanish, speech, technology/industrial arts, voc/tech. **Engineering technology:** General, construction, electrical, manufacturing, mechanical, plastics. **English:** Creative writing, English lit, technical writing. **Family/consumer sciences:** General, child development, family resources. **Foreign languages:** French, Spanish. **Health:** Clinical lab science, nursing (RN), predentistry, premedicine, prepharmacy, preveterinary. **History:** General. **Legal studies:** Prelaw. **Math:** General. **Mechanic/repair:** Automotive, diesel, motorcycle. **Parks/recreation:** Facilities management, sports admin. **Physical sciences:** Chemistry, physics, polymer chemistry. **Production:** Woodworking. **Protective services:** Criminal justice. **Psychology:** General. **Public administration:** Social work. **Social sciences:** Geography, international relations, political science, sociology. **Visual/performing arts:** Art, ceramics, commercial/advertising art, interior design, metal/jewelry, music performance, painting, voice/opera.

Most popular majors. Business/marketing 13%, education 18%, engineering/engineering technologies 6%, health sciences 6%, psychology 7%, science technologies 12%, trade and industry 6%.

Computing on campus. 320 workstations in library, computer center, student center. Dormitories wired for high-speed internet access and linked to campus network. Commuter students can connect to campus network. Online course registration, online library, wireless network available.

Student life. Freshman orientation: Mandatory, $20 fee. Eight individual sessions are offered and last approximately eight hours each. **Policies:** Freshmen permitted cars on campus. **Housing:** Guaranteed on-campus for all undergraduates. Coed dorms, special housing for disabled, apartments, substance-free housing available. $145 deposit. **Activities:** Bands, choral groups, dance, drama, film society, literary magazine, music ensembles, musical theater, opera, radio station, student government, student newspaper, symphony orchestra, TV station, Over 140 clubs and organizations available.

Athletics. NCAA. **Intercollegiate:** Baseball M, basketball, cross-country, football (tackle) M, golf M, softball W, track and field, volleyball W. **Intramural:** Basketball, football (non-tackle), racquetball, softball, tennis, volleyball. **Team name:** Gorillas.

Student services. Alcohol/substance abuse counseling, campus ministries, career counseling, student employment services, financial aid counseling, health services, legal services, minority student services, personal counseling, placement for graduates, veterans' counselor. **Physically disabled:** Services for visually, speech, hearing impaired.

Contact. E-mail: psuadmit@pittstate.edu
Phone: (620) 235-4251 Toll-free number: (800) 854-7488
Fax: (620) 235-6003
Director of Admission & Enrollment Services, Pittsburg State University, 1701 South Broadway, Pittsburg, KS 66762

Southwestern College

Winfield, Kansas
www.sckans.edu **CB code: 6670**

- Private 4-year liberal arts college affiliated with United Methodist Church
- Residential campus in large town
- 1,213 degree-seeking undergraduates: 53% part-time, 50% women, 8% African American, 1% Asian American, 4% Hispanic American, 2% Native American, 2% international
- 153 degree-seeking graduate students
- SAT or ACT, application essay required
- 52% graduate within 6 years

General. Founded in 1885. Regionally accredited. Laptop computers issued to all students enrolled at main campus. **Degrees:** 347 bachelor's awarded; master's offered. **Location:** 40 miles from Wichita. **Calendar:** Semester, limited summer session. **Full-time faculty:** 46 total; 50% have terminal degrees, 6% minority, 37% women. **Part-time faculty:** 98 total; 8% minority, 45% women. **Special facilities:** Biological field station.

Freshman class profile.

Mid 50% test scores		**Rank in top quarter:**	45%
SAT verbal:	440-550	**Rank in top tenth:**	21%
SAT math:	430-590	**Return as sophomores:**	71%
ACT:	19-26	**Out-of-state:**	40%
GPA 3.50 or higher:	48%	**Live on campus:**	97%
GPA 3.0-3.49:	36%	**International:**	2%
GPA 2.0-2.99:	16%		

Basis for selection. School achievement record, test scores and personal essay statement most important. Portfolio required. Interview recommended for nursing majors. Audition required for music and drama majors.

High school preparation. 12 units required. Required and recommended units include English 4, mathematics 3, social studies 1, history 1, science 2 (laboratory 1) and foreign language 1. Computer or communication unit may be substituted for foreign language.

2005-2006 Annual costs. Tuition/fees: $16,118. Room/board: $5,258. Books/supplies: $600. Personal expenses: $2,178.

2005-2006 Financial aid. Need-based: 123 full-time freshmen applied for aid; 102 were judged to have need; 102 of these received aid. Average need met was 82%. Average scholarship/grant was $10,183; average loan $4,258. 40% of total undergraduate aid awarded as scholarships/grants, 60% as loans/jobs. **Non-need-based:** Awarded to 225 full-time undergraduates, including 83 freshmen. Scholarships awarded for academics, alumni affiliation, athletics, leadership, minority status, music/drama, religious affiliation, state residency. **Additional information:** Academic and activity grants available.

Application procedures. Admission: Priority date 5/1; no deadline. $20 fee, may be waived for applicants with need. Application may be submitted online. Admission notification on a rolling basis beginning on or about 9/15. **Financial aid:** Priority date 4/1; no closing date. FAFSA, institutional form required. Applicants notified on a rolling basis starting 2/1; must reply within 4 week(s) of notification.

Academics. Special study options: Accelerated study, cooperative education, distance learning, double major, dual enrollment of high school students, exchange student, honors, independent study, internships, liberal arts/career combination, student-designed major, study abroad, teacher certification program, urban semester, Washington semester, weekend college. **Credit/placement by examination:** AP, CLEP, institutional tests. 30 credit hours maximum toward bachelor's degree. **Support services:** Learning center, reduced course load, remedial instruction, study skills assistance, tutoring.

Majors. Biology: General, biochemistry, marine. **Business:** Accounting, business admin, communications, human resources, management information systems, management science, marketing, training/development. **Communications:** General, digital media. **Computer sciences:** Computer science, programming. **Education:** General, drama/dance, early childhood, elementary, English, foreign languages, mathematics, music, physical, science, secondary. **Engineering:** Physics, software. **Engineering technology:** Computer systems, manufacturing. **English:** English lit. **Health:** Athletic training, nursing (RN). **History:** General. **Liberal arts:** Arts/sciences. **Math:** General. **Parks/recreation:** Health/fitness, sports admin. **Philosophy/religion:** Christian. **Physical sciences:** Chemistry, physics. **Protective services:** Law enforcement admin, security management. **Psychology:** General. **Theology:** Pastoral counseling. **Visual/performing arts:** Dramatic, film/cinema.

Most popular majors. Biology 10%, business/marketing 16%, education 13%, health sciences 13%, parks/recreation 8%, visual/performing arts 10%.

Computing on campus. PC or laptop required. 50 workstations in dormitories, library, computer center, student center. Dormitories wired for high-speed internet access and linked to campus network. Commuter students can connect to campus network. Online library, helpline, repair service, student web hosting, wireless network available.

Student life. Freshman orientation: Mandatory. Preregistration for classes offered. Overnight orientation held before upper classmen arrive on campus. Includes laptop distribution and training, community service project. **Policies:** Drug and alcohol-free campus. Freshmen permitted cars on campus. **Housing:** Guaranteed on-campus for freshmen. Coed dorms, single-sex dorms, special housing for disabled, apartments available. $100 deposit. Freshmen and sophomores under 20 years old, not veteran or living with parent or guardian, must live on campus. **Activities:** Bands, choral groups, dance, drama, literary magazine, music ensembles, musical theater, radio station, student government, student newspaper, symphony orchestra, TV station, Black Student Union, Campus Council on Ministries, Sharp Ambassadors, Student Activities Association, Business Students Association, Fellowship of Christian Athletes, Discipleship Southwestern, Leadership Southwestern, outreach teams, SC Association of Nursing Students.

Athletics. NAIA. **Intercollegiate:** Basketball, cheerleading, cross-country, football (tackle) M, golf, soccer, softball W, tennis, track and field, volleyball W. **Intramural:** Basketball, bowling, softball, swimming, tennis, volleyball. **Team name:** Moundbuilders.

Student services. Adult student services, alcohol/substance abuse counseling, campus ministries, career counseling, student employment services, financial aid counseling, health services, minority student services, on-campus daycare, personal counseling, placement for graduates. **Physically disabled:** Services for visually, hearing impaired.

Contact. E-mail: scadmit@sckans.edu
Phone: (620) 229-6236 Toll-free number: (800) 846-1543 ext. 6236
Fax: (620) 229-6344
Todd Moore, Director of Admission, Southwestern College, 100 College Street, Winfield, KS 67156

Sterling College
Sterling, Kansas
www.sterling.edu **CB code: 6684**

- Private 4-year liberal arts college affiliated with Presbyterian Church (USA)
- Residential campus in rural community
- 442 degree-seeking undergraduates: 3% part-time, 47% women, 9% African American, 1% Asian American, 6% Hispanic American, 2% Native American, 1% international
- 22 graduate students
- 56% of applicants admitted
- SAT or ACT (ACT writing optional) required
- 63% graduate within 6 years

General. Founded in 1887. Regionally accredited. Christian values of faith and service stressed. Partnerships with Habitat for Humanity and Americorp. **Degrees:** 80 bachelor's awarded. **Location:** 20 miles from Hutchinson, 70 miles from Wichita. **Calendar:** 4-1-4. **Full-time faculty:** 40 total; 50% have terminal degrees, 38% women. **Part-time faculty:** 21 total; 19% have terminal degrees, 5% minority, 33% women. **Class size:** 76% < 20, 22% 20-39, 2% 40-49, less than 1% 50-99. **Special facilities:** Museum collections at campus library.

Freshman class profile. 541 applied, 305 admitted, 127 enrolled.

Mid 50% test scores			
SAT verbal:	420-510	Rank in top quarter:	35%
SAT math:	430-520	Rank in top tenth:	7%
ACT:	19-25	End year in good standing:	80%
GPA 3.50 or higher:	41%	Return as sophomores:	64%
GPA 3.0-3.49:	32%	Out-of-state:	52%
GPA 2.0-2.99:	26%	Live on campus:	95%

Basis for selection. High school record, test scores, recommendations from school counselor and pastor important; commitment to Christian values and service also important. ACT or SAT scores are also recommended for transfer students in teacher licensure programs. Interview recommended. Audition required of performing arts majors. Portfolio recommended for art majors. **Homeschooled:** Transcript of courses and grades required. **Learning Disabled:** Must provide official documentation with recommended accommodations.

High school preparation. 18 units recommended. Recommended units include English 4, mathematics 3, social studies 1, history 2, science 3 (laboratory 2), foreign language 2 and academic electives 1. One computer technology recommended; Physical education recommended.

2005-2006 Annual costs. Tuition/fees: $13,906. $275 per-credit-hour charge for 1-6 credits. Room/board: $6,086. Books/supplies: $600. Personal expenses: $650.

2004-2005 Financial aid. Need-based: 112 full-time freshmen applied for aid; 98 were judged to have need; 98 of these received aid. Average need met was 92%. Average scholarship/grant was $7,789; average loan $3,736. 66% of total undergraduate aid awarded as scholarships/grants, 34% as loans/jobs. **Non-need-based:** Awarded to 109 full-time undergraduates, including 25 freshmen. Scholarships awarded for academics, alumni affiliation, art, athletics, leadership, minority status, music/drama, religious affiliation, state residency. **Additional information:** Twins enrolled at institution pay single tuition.

Application procedures. Admission: Priority date 3/1; deadline 8/1 (postmark date). $25 fee, may be waived for applicants with need. Application may be submitted online. Admission notification 8/1. Admission notification on a rolling basis beginning on or about 9/15. **Financial aid:** Priority date 4/1; no closing date. FAFSA required. Applicants notified on a rolling basis starting 1/1; must reply within 3 week(s) of notification.

Academics. Social entrepreneurship minor available. Habitat for Humanity Fellowships. **Special study options:** Double major, dual enrollment of high school students, honors, independent study, internships, liberal arts/career combination, student-designed major, study abroad, teacher certification program, Washington semester. **Credit/placement by examination:** AP, CLEP, SAT, ACT, institutional tests. **Support services:** Reduced course load, remedial instruction, study skills assistance, tutoring, writing center.

Majors. Biology: General. **Business:** Business admin. **Communications:** General. **Computer sciences:** General. **Education:** Elementary, mathematics, music. **English:** English lit. **Health:** Athletic training. **History:** General. **Interdisciplinary:** Behavioral sciences. **Math:** General. **Parks/recreation:** Health/fitness. **Physical sciences:** Chemistry. **Theology:** Religious ed. **Visual/performing arts:** Art, dramatic.

Most popular majors. Biology 8%, business/marketing 10%, communications/journalism 6%, education 26%, parks/recreation 7%, psychology 6%, theological studies 7%, visual/performing arts 8%.

Computing on campus. 115 workstations in dormitories, library, computer center. Dormitories wired for high-speed internet access and linked to campus network. Online library, wireless network available.

Student life. Freshman orientation: Mandatory. Preregistration for classes offered. 3-day program prior to start of fall classes; includes service project. **Policies:** Prohibition of alcohol and tobacco products. Religious observance required. Freshmen permitted cars on campus. **Housing:** Guaranteed on-campus for all undergraduates. Single-sex dorms, substance-free housing available. $100 fully refundable deposit, deadline 8/15. All students under age 23 required to live in campus dormitories unless married or with dependents, living at home with parents, or 5th-year senior. **Activities:** Bands, choral groups, drama, literary magazine, music ensembles, musical theater, radio station, student government, student newspaper, science club, minority cultural organization, Alpha Phi Omega, Fellowship of Christian Athletes, behavioral science club, Habitat for Humanity, Chi Beta Sigma (business), peace club, student ministries, community service.

Athletics. NAIA. **Intercollegiate:** Baseball M, basketball, cross-country, football (tackle) M, soccer, softball W, track and field, volleyball W. **Intramural:** Basketball, bowling, football (non-tackle), golf, softball, table tennis, volleyball. **Team name:** Warriors.

Student services. Campus ministries, career counseling, student employment services, financial aid counseling, personal counseling.

Contact. E-mail: admissions@sterling.edu
Phone: (620) 278-4275 Toll-free number: (800) 346-1017
Fax: (620) 278-4416
Dennis Dutton, Vice President for Enrollment Services, Sterling College, 125 West Cooper, Sterling, KS 67579

Tabor College
Hillsboro, Kansas
www.tabor.edu **CB code: 6815**

- Private 4-year liberal arts college affiliated with Mennonite Brethren Church
- Residential campus in small town
- 593 degree-seeking undergraduates: 19% part-time, 48% women, 5% African American, 1% Asian American, 4% Hispanic American, 1% Native American, 1% international
- 8 degree-seeking graduate students
- 100% of applicants admitted
- SAT or ACT (ACT writing optional), application essay required
- 48% graduate within 6 years

General. Founded in 1908. Regionally accredited. Off-campus site in Wichita offers accelerated degree completion program. **Degrees:** 137 bachelor's, 1 associate awarded; master's offered. **Location:** 50 miles from Wichita. **Calendar:** 4-1-4, limited summer session. **Full-time faculty:** 34 total; 65% have terminal degrees, 38% women. **Part-time faculty:** 22 total; 9% have terminal degrees, 4% minority, 23% women. **Class size:** 72% < 20, 27% 20-39, 1% 40-49.

Freshman class profile. 234 applied, 234 admitted, 124 enrolled.

Mid 50% test scores		Rank in top quarter:	53%
ACT:	20-27	Rank in top tenth:	24%
GPA 3.50 or higher:	53%	Out-of-state:	38%
GPA 3.0-3.49:	28%	Live on campus:	99%
GPA 2.0-2.99:	18%		

Basis for selection. Life values and objectives, desire for Christian growth, interview, references, formula combining GPA and ACT composite score important. Audition recommended for music and drama majors. **Learning Disabled:** Students asked to provide IEPs if they request special accommodations.

High school preparation. 17 units recommended. Recommended units include English 4, mathematics 3, social studies 2, history 2, science 3 and foreign language 1. 2 units of fine arts also recommended.

2005-2006 Annual costs. Tuition/fees: $15,944. Room/board: $5,670. Books/supplies: $600. Personal expenses: $1,920.

2005-2006 Financial aid. **Need-based:** 121 full-time freshmen applied for aid; 98 were judged to have need; 98 of these received aid. Average need met was 88%. Average scholarship/grant was $3,855; average loan $5,722. 24% of total undergraduate aid awarded as scholarships/grants, 76% as loans/jobs. **Non-need-based:** Scholarships awarded for academics, alumni affiliation, art, athletics, music/drama, religious affiliation, state residency.

Application procedures. **Admission:** No deadline. $20 fee, may be waived for applicants with need. Application may be submitted online. Admission notification on a rolling basis beginning on or about 9/1. **Financial aid:** Priority date 3/1, closing date 8/15. FAFSA required. Applicants notified on a rolling basis starting 3/15; must reply within 4 week(s) of notification.

Academics. **Special study options:** Accelerated study, cross-registration, double major, dual enrollment of high school students, exchange student, independent study, internships, liberal arts/career combination, student-designed major, study abroad, teacher certification program, Washington semester. **Credit/placement by examination:** AP, CLEP, IB, SAT, ACT. 30 credit hours maximum toward bachelor's degree. **Support services:** Learning center, reduced course load, remedial instruction, study skills assistance, tutoring, writing center.

Majors. **Biology:** General, biochemistry. **Business:** Accounting/business management, administrative services, business admin, marketing, office management. **Communications:** General, journalism, organizational, public relations. **Computer sciences:** Computer science, system admin. **Conservation:** Environmental studies. **Education:** General, biology, business, chemistry, developmentally delayed, early childhood special, elementary, emotionally handicapped, English, health, history, kindergarten/preschool, learning disabled, mathematics, mentally handicapped, middle, multi-level teacher, multiple handicapped, music, physical, science, secondary, social science, social studies, special. **Health:** Athletic training, clinical lab technology, predentistry, premedicine, preop/surgical nursing, prepharmacy, preveterinary. **History:** General. **Interdisciplinary:** Biological/physical sciences, math/computer science, natural sciences. **Legal studies:** Prelaw. **Liberal arts:** Humanities. **Math:** General. **Parks/recreation:** General, health/fitness, sports admin. **Philosophy/religion:** Philosophy, religion. **Physical sciences:** Chemistry. **Psychology:** General. **Social sciences:** General, sociology. **Theology:** Bible, theology, youth ministry. **Visual/performing arts:** Commercial/advertising art.

Most popular majors. Business/marketing 19%, communications/journalism 7%, education 16%, health sciences 12%, philosophy/religious studies 9%, theological studies 10%, visual/performing arts 6%.

Computing on campus. 58 workstations in library, computer center, student center. Dormitories wired for high-speed internet access and linked to campus network. Commuter students can connect to campus network. Online library available.

Student life. **Freshman orientation:** Mandatory. Preregistration for classes offered. 3-day program prior to fall semester; includes service day. **Policies:** Convocation attendance required. Freshmen permitted cars on campus. **Housing:** Guaranteed on-campus for freshmen. Single-sex dorms, special housing for disabled, substance-free housing available. $100 deposit, deadline 8/1. **Activities:** Bands, choral groups, drama, music ensembles, musical theater, student government, student newspaper, science club, student music association, Christian student organizations, multicultural student union, international student union, English society, student education association, Fellowship of Christian Athletes.

Athletics. NAIA. **Intercollegiate:** Baseball M, basketball, cheerleading, cross-country, football (tackle) M, soccer, softball W, tennis, track and field, volleyball W. **Intramural:** Basketball, football (non-tackle), football (tackle) M, racquetball, soccer, softball, table tennis, tennis, track and field, volleyball. **Team name:** Blue Jays.

Student services. Alcohol/substance abuse counseling, campus ministries, career counseling, student employment services, financial aid counseling, minority student services, personal counseling, placement for graduates.

Contact. E-mail: admissions@tabor.edu
Phone: (620) 947-3121 ext. 1723 Toll-free number: (800) 822-6799
Fax: (620) 947-6276
Rusty Allen, Dean of Enrollment Management, Tabor College, 400 South Jefferson, Hillsboro, KS 67063-1799

University of Kansas

Lawrence, Kansas — **CB member**
www.ku.edu — **CB code: 6871**

- Public 4-year university
- Commuter campus in small city
- 20,652 degree-seeking undergraduates: 11% part-time, 50% women, 4% African American, 4% Asian American, 4% Hispanic American, 1% Native American, 3% international
- 6,026 graduate students
- SAT or ACT (ACT writing optional) required
- 57% graduate within 6 years; 28% enter graduate study

General. Founded in 1866. Regionally accredited. **Degrees:** 3,647 bachelor's awarded; master's, doctoral, first professional offered. **ROTC:** Army, Navy, Air Force. **Location:** 40 miles from Kansas City. **Calendar:** Semester, extensive summer session. **Full-time faculty:** 955 total; 98% have terminal degrees, 15% minority, 31% women. **Part-time faculty:** 82 total; 74% have terminal degrees, 4% minority, 33% women. **Class size:** 31% < 20, 50% 20-39, 6% 40-49, 6% 50-99, 6% >100. **Special facilities:** 12 libraries including art, engineering, science, music, government documents and maps, rare books, manuscripts, and regional collections; art and natural history museums, space technology center, observatory, institute for life span studies, performing arts center and organ recital hall, Kansas Ecological Reserves, design lab, flight research lab, radar systems and remote sensing lab, film studio, center for the humanities, multicultural resource center.

Freshman class profile. 4,201 enrolled.

Mid 50% test scores		Rank in top tenth:	28%
ACT:	21-27	Return as sophomores:	82%
GPA 3.50 or higher:	51%	Out-of-state:	27%
GPA 3.0-3.49:	31%	Live on campus:	55%
GPA 2.0-2.99:	18%	International:	1%
Rank in top quarter:	56%		

Basis for selection. Admission to College of Liberal Arts and Sciences requires one of following for in-state students: minimum ACT score of 21 or SAT score of 980 (exclusive of writing), rank in top third of high school class, or completion of required college preparatory curriculum with 2.0 GPA. For out-of-state students: minimum test scores are 24 on ACT or 1090 on SAT (exclusive of writing); minimum GPA 2.5 on college preparatory curriculum; rank in top third of high school class. Admission policies for other colleges within university may vary. Audition required for music performance, theater, music education, music therapy majors. **Homeschooled:** Admission based on test scores.

High school preparation. 14 units required; 17 recommended. Required and recommended units include English 4, mathematics 3-4, social studies 3, science 3, foreign language 2 and academic electives 1. One computer technology unit required, 1 science unit must be chemistry or physics. 4 units mathematics recommended for mathematics, engineering and architecture majors. Social studies units include history.

2005-2006 Annual costs. Tuition/fees: $5,413; $13,866 out-of-state. Room/board: $5,852. Books/supplies: $750. Personal expenses: $2,094.

2004-2005 Financial aid. **Need-based:** 2,598 full-time freshmen applied for aid; 1,594 were judged to have need; 1,509 of these received aid. Average need met was 62%. Average scholarship/grant was $3,752; average loan $2,607. 42% of total undergraduate aid awarded as scholarships/grants,

58% as loans/jobs. **Non-need-based:** Awarded to 1,963 full-time undergraduates, including 486 freshmen. Scholarships awarded for academics, alumni affiliation, art, athletics, leadership, minority status, music/drama, ROTC, state residency. **Additional information:** Work study available weekdays.

Application procedures. Admission: Priority date 1/15; deadline 4/1 (receipt date). $30 fee. Application may be submitted online. Admission notification on a rolling basis. Must reply by May 1 or within 2 week(s) if notified thereafter. **Financial aid:** Priority date 3/1; no closing date. FAFSA required. Applicants notified on a rolling basis starting 4/1; must reply within 2 week(s) of notification.

Academics. Special study options: Accelerated study, combined bachelor's/graduate degree, cooperative education, distance learning, double major, dual enrollment of high school students, ESL, honors, independent study, internships, study abroad, teacher certification program, Washington semester. **Credit/placement by examination:** AP, CLEP, IB, institutional tests. **Support services:** Learning center, remedial instruction, study skills assistance, tutoring, writing center.

Honors college/program. Students accepted into any school or college may also be accepted into the honors program.

Majors. Architecture: Architecture, history/criticism. **Area/ethnic studies:** African, African-American, American, European, Latin American, Russian/Slavic, women's. **Biology:** General, Biochemistry/biophysics and molecular biology, microbiology, molecular. **Business:** General, accounting, finance. **Communications:** Journalism. **Computer sciences:** General. **Conservation:** Environmental studies. **Education:** Art, biology, chemistry, elementary, English, French, German, history, Latin, mathematics, middle, music, physical, physics, science, secondary, social studies, Spanish, speech. **Engineering:** Aerospace, architectural, chemical, civil, computer, electrical, mechanical, petroleum, physics. **English:** English lit, speech/rhetoric. **Foreign languages:** Classics, East Asian, French, Germanic, linguistics, Slavic, Spanish. **Health:** Athletic training, communication disorders, community health services, music therapy. **History:** General. **Interdisciplinary:** Ancient studies, behavioral sciences. **Liberal arts:** Arts/sciences, humanities. **Math:** General. **Parks/recreation:** Health/fitness. **Philosophy/religion:** Philosophy, religion. **Physical sciences:** Astronomy, atmospheric science, chemistry, geology, physics. **Psychology:** General. **Public administration:** General, social work. **Social sciences:** Anthropology, economics, geography, international relations, political science, sociology. **Visual/performing arts:** Art history/conservation, ceramics, commercial/advertising art, dance, design, dramatic, fiber arts, graphic design, illustration, industrial design, interior design, metal/jewelry, music history, music performance, music theory/composition, musicology, painting, piano/organ, printmaking, sculpture, stringed instruments, studio arts, theater design, voice/opera.

Most popular majors. Biology 8%, business/marketing 12%, communications/journalism 8%, engineering/engineering technologies 6%, English 11%, psychology 7%, social sciences 10%, visual/performing arts 8%.

Computing on campus. 1,500 workstations in dormitories, library, computer center. Dormitories wired for high-speed internet access and linked to campus network. Commuter students can connect to campus network. Online course registration, online library, helpline, student web hosting, wireless network available.

Student life. Freshman orientation: Available, $55 fee. Preregistration for classes offered. One-day program throughout summer; several 2 day programs available. Additional charges for parent participation and 2 day program. **Policies:** No alcohol permitted on campus, no smoking in any buildings. Parking by permit only. Freshmen permitted cars on campus. **Housing:** Coed dorms, single-sex dorms, apartments, cooperative housing, fraternity/sorority housing, substance-free housing available. $35 nonrefundable deposit, deadline 2/15. Scholarship halls available to students with high scholastic achievement and financial need. **Activities:** Bands, choral groups, dance, drama, literary magazine, music ensembles, musical theater, opera, radio station, student government, student newspaper, symphony orchestra, TV station, over 400 student organizations and activities available.

Athletics. NCAA. **Intercollegiate:** Baseball M, basketball, cross-country, football (tackle) M, golf, rowing (crew) W, soccer W, softball W, swimming W, tennis W, track and field, volleyball W. **Intramural:** Basketball, bowling, golf, racquetball, soccer, softball, table tennis, tennis, volleyball, wrestling M. **Team name:** Jayhawks.

Student services. Adult student services, alcohol/substance abuse counseling, career counseling, services for economically disadvantaged, student employment services, financial aid counseling, health services, legal services, minority student services, on-campus daycare, personal counseling, placement for graduates, veterans' counselor, women's services. **Physically disabled:** Services for visually, speech, hearing impaired.

Contact. E-mail: adm@ku.edu
Phone: (785) 864-3911 Fax: (785) 864-5017
Lisa Pinamonti Kress, Director of Admissions and Scholarships, University of Kansas, 1502 Iowa Street, Lawrence, KS 66045-7576

University of Kansas Medical Center

Kansas City, Kansas
www.kumc.edu **CB code: 0414**

- Public upper-division university and health science college
- Commuter campus in very large city

General. Founded in 1905. Regionally accredited. **Degrees:** 217 bachelor's awarded; master's, doctoral, first professional offered. **Location:** Downtown. **Calendar:** Semester, limited summer session. **Full-time faculty:** 257 total. **Part-time faculty:** 62 total. **Class size:** 78% < 20, 12% 20-39, 3% 40-49, 4% 50-99, 3% >100.

Student profile. 479 degree-seeking undergraduates, 1,527 degree-seeking graduate students.

Women:	88%	**Out-of-state:**	31%
Part-time:	23%	**25 or older:**	34%

Basis for selection. College transcript required. Admissions regulations, policies and application closing dates vary by degree program. Transfer accepted as juniors, seniors.

2005-2006 Annual costs. Tuition/fees: $5,413; $13,866 out-of-state. Annual tuition for medical students: $18,919 (residents) and $34,674 (nonresidents); required fees are $418. Books/supplies: $720.

Financial aid. Need-based: 251 applied for aid; 221 were judged to have need; 219 of these received aid. Average need met was 56%. 37% of total undergraduate aid awarded as scholarships/grants, 63% as loans/jobs. **Non-need-based:** Awarded to 1 undergraduate. Scholarships awarded for academics, leadership, minority status, state residency.

Application procedures. Admission: Rolling admission. $35 fee. Admissions deadlines vary by school and program. **Financial aid:** FAFSA, institutional form required.

Academics. Assessment and reading skills screened. Assistance offered in reviewing APA-style papers. **Special study options:** Combined bachelor's/graduate degree, distance learning, honors, independent study, internships. BOS/MOT in occupational therapy. **Credit/placement by examination:** CLEP.

Majors. Health: Clinical lab science, cytotechnology, medical records admin, preop/surgical nursing, respiratory therapy technology.

Computing on campus. 150 workstations in library, computer center, student center. Commuter students can connect to campus network. Helpline, student web hosting, wireless network available.

Student life. Activities: Literary magazine, student government, allied health student senate, graduate student council, medical student assembly, association of undergraduate nurses, Latino Midwest medical student association, American medical women's association, Students for Women's Wellness, Lifewatch Bible Study (Christian medical/dental society), Students Educating and Advocating for Diversity.

Athletics. Intramural: Basketball, racquetball, soccer, softball, volleyball.

Student services. Campus ministries, financial aid counseling, health services, legal services, personal counseling. **Physically disabled:** Services for visually, speech, hearing impaired.

Contact. E-mail: kumcregistrar@kumc.edu
Phone: (913) 588-7055 Fax: (913) 588-4697
University of Kansas Medical Center, 3901 Rainbow Boulevard, Kansas City, KS 66160-7116

University of St. Mary

Leavenworth, Kansas
www.stmary.edu **CB code: 6630**

- Private 4-year university affiliated with Roman Catholic Church
- Residential campus in large town
- 435 degree-seeking undergraduates: 14% part-time, 56% women, 13% African American, 3% Asian American, 11% Hispanic American, 1% international
- 285 degree-seeking graduate students
- 45% of applicants admitted
- SAT or ACT (ACT writing optional) required
- 39% graduate within 6 years

General. Founded in 1923. Regionally accredited. **Degrees:** 79 bachelor's, 2 associate awarded; master's offered. **ROTC:** Army, Air Force. **Location:** 26 miles from Kansas City. **Calendar:** Semester, limited summer session. **Full-time faculty:** 39 total; 72% have terminal degrees, 5% minority, 56% women. **Part-time faculty:** 50 total; 20% have terminal degrees, 6% minority, 58% women. **Class size:** 76% < 20, 23% 20-39, less than 1% 40-49, less than 1% 50-99. **Special facilities:** On campus library with collections in Sacred Scripture, and History of the Catholic Church in Kansas.

Freshman class profile. 570 applied, 255 admitted, 83 enrolled.

Mid 50% test scores		**Rank in top tenth:**	6%
SAT verbal:	370-490	**Return as sophomores:**	60%
SAT math:	310-550	**Out-of-state:**	50%
ACT:	17-22	**Live on campus:**	73%
Rank in top quarter:	23%		

Basis for selection. Minimum 2.5 high school GPA, 18 ACT, 870 SAT (exclusive of Writing) required. Applicants below required GPA or ACT/SAT may be considered for admission. Portfolio recommended for fine and applied arts majors. **Homeschooled:** ACT or SAT recommended.

High school preparation. 12 units required; 24 recommended. Required and recommended units include English 4, mathematics 2-4, social studies 2, history 2-4, science 2-4 (laboratory 2), foreign language 2 and academic electives 2. 1-2 computer programming recommended.

2005-2006 Annual costs. Tuition/fees: $15,590. Room/board: $5,850. Books/supplies: $1,000. Personal expenses: $1,576.

2005-2006 Financial aid. Need-based: 75 full-time freshmen applied for aid; 64 were judged to have need; 63 of these received aid. Average need met was 65%. Average scholarship/grant was $7,914; average loan $3,838. 54% of total undergraduate aid awarded as scholarships/grants, 46% as loans/jobs. **Non-need-based:** Awarded to 247 full-time undergraduates, including 62 freshmen. Scholarships awarded for academics, art, athletics, leadership, music/drama, ROTC. **Additional information:** Essays may be required for scholarship applicants. Auditions recommended for music and drama scholarship applicants. Portfolio reviews for art award applicants.

Application procedures. Admission: No deadline. $25 fee. Application may be submitted online. Admission notification on a rolling basis. Must reply by May 1 or within 4 week(s) if notified thereafter. **Financial aid:** Priority date 4/1; no closing date. FAFSA required. Applicants notified on a rolling basis starting 2/6; must reply within 2 week(s) of notification.

Academics. Special study options: Accelerated study, cooperative education, distance learning, double major, dual enrollment of high school students, exchange student, honors, independent study, internships, student-designed major, study abroad, teacher certification program. Degree completion programs. **Credit/placement by examination:** AP, CLEP, IB, SAT, ACT, institutional tests. 30 credit hours maximum toward bachelor's degree. **Support services:** Learning center, remedial instruction, study skills assistance, tutoring.

Majors. Biology: General. **Business:** General, accounting, business admin, international. **Communications:** General. **Computer sciences:** Information technology. **Education:** Elementary. **English:** English lit. **Family/consumer sciences:** Child development. **History:** General. **Liberal arts:** Arts/sciences. **Math:** General. **Parks/recreation:** Sports admin. **Physical sciences:** Chemistry. **Psychology:** General. **Social sciences:** Political science, sociology. **Theology:** Pastoral counseling, theology. **Visual/performing arts:** Art, dramatic.

Most popular majors. Business/marketing 20%, computer/information sciences 7%, education 16%, psychology 22%, social sciences 6%, visual/performing arts 9%.

Computing on campus. 95 workstations in dormitories, library, computer center. Dormitories wired for high-speed internet access and linked to campus network. Helpline, student web hosting, wireless network available.

Student life. Freshman orientation: Mandatory. Preregistration for classes offered. 3-day program at beginning of fall semester. **Policies:** Freshmen permitted cars on campus. **Housing:** Guaranteed on-campus for freshmen. Coed dorms available. $100 nonrefundable deposit. **Activities:** Bands, choral groups, drama, literary magazine, music ensembles, musical theater, opera, student government, student newspaper, campus ministry, international club, Bacchus, Aristotle Club, Amnesty International, Students in Free Enterprise, Young Democrats, Campus Republicans.

Athletics. NAIA. **Intercollegiate:** Baseball M, basketball, football (tackle) M, soccer, softball W, volleyball W. **Intramural:** Basketball, bowling, racquetball, softball, table tennis, volleyball. **Team name:** Spires.

Student services. Adult student services, alcohol/substance abuse counseling, campus ministries, career counseling, student employment services, financial aid counseling, health services, on-campus daycare, personal counseling, placement for graduates, veterans' counselor.

Contact. E-mail: admissions@stmary.edu
Phone: (913) 758-6118 Toll-free number: (800) 752-7043
Fax: (913) 758-6140
Jessica Goffinet, Director of Admissions and Financial Aid, University of St. Mary, 4100 South Fourth Street Trafficway, Leavenworth, KS 66048

Washburn University of Topeka

Topeka, Kansas
www.washburn.edu **CB code: 6928**

- Public 4-year university
- Commuter campus in small city
- 5,943 degree-seeking undergraduates: 31% part-time, 62% women
- 837 degree-seeking graduate students
- 66% graduate within 6 years

General. Founded in 1865. Regionally accredited. **Degrees:** 684 bachelor's, 135 associate awarded; master's, first professional offered. **ROTC:** Army, Navy, Air Force. **Location:** 60 miles from Kansas City. **Calendar:** Semester, extensive summer session. **Full-time faculty:** 258 total; 82% have terminal degrees, 13% minority, 45% women. **Part-time faculty:** 252 total; 41% have terminal degrees, 6% minority, 45% women. **Class size:** 40% < 20, 51% 20-39, 6% 40-49, 2% 50-99. **Special facilities:** Art museum, theater, concert hall, observatory, planetarium, 30-acre natural study and research area.

Freshman class profile. 1,576 applied, 1,565 admitted, 863 enrolled.

Mid 50% test scores		**End year in good standing:**	65%
ACT:	19-24	**Return as sophomores:**	69%
GPA 3.50 or higher:	39%	**Out-of-state:**	6%
GPA 3.0-3.49:	28%	**Live on campus:**	42%
GPA 2.0-2.99:	30%	**Fraternities:**	9%
Rank in top quarter:	32%	**Sororities:**	7%
Rank in top tenth:	12%		

Basis for selection. Open admission, but selective for some programs. Special requirements for health science programs, nursing, school of business. ACT or ASSET required of all students for placement purposes. Open admissions policy with regular or conditional admissions granted based on ACT and GPA.

High school preparation. Recommended units include English 4, mathematics 3, social studies 3, history 1, science 3 and foreign language 2. 1 unit computer technology recommended.

2005-2006 Annual costs. Tuition/fees: $4,982; $11,192 out-of-state. Room/board: $4,752. Books/supplies: $976. Personal expenses: $1,332.

2005-2006 Financial aid. Need-based: 620 full-time freshmen applied for aid; 512 were judged to have need; 511 of these received aid. Average need met was 30%. Average scholarship/grant was $3,056; average loan $2,526. 35% of total undergraduate aid awarded as scholarships/grants, 65% as loans/jobs. **Non-need-based:** Awarded to 2,185 full-time undergraduates, including 402 freshmen. Scholarships awarded for academics, alumni affiliation, art, athletics, job skills, leadership, minority status, music/drama, religious affiliation, ROTC, state residency.

Application procedures. Admission: Priority date 7/1; deadline 8/1. $20 fee. Application may be submitted online. Admission notification on a rolling basis beginning on or about 9/1. **Financial aid:** Priority date 2/15; no closing date. FAFSA required. Applicants notified by 3/15; Applicants notified on a rolling basis starting 3/15; must reply within 4 week(s) of notification.

Academics. Special study options: Cooperative education, cross-registration, distance learning, double major, dual enrollment of high school students, ESL, honors, independent study, internships, liberal arts/career combination, student-designed major, study abroad, teacher certification program. **Credit/placement by examination:** AP, CLEP, institutional tests. 40 credit hours maximum toward bachelor's degree. **Support services:** Learning center, remedial instruction, study skills assistance, tutoring, writing center.

Majors. Biology: General. **Business:** General, accounting, business admin, finance, managerial economics, marketing. **Communications:** General, media studies. **Computer sciences:** General, systems analysis. **Education:** General, business, early childhood, elementary, English, foreign languages, health, mathematics, music, physical, science, secondary, social science, social studies. **English:** Speech/rhetoric. **Foreign languages:** French, German, Spanish. **Health:** Athletic training, clinical lab technology, health services, nursing (RN), predentistry, premedicine, prepharmacy, preveterinary, sonography, substance abuse counseling. **History:** General. **Interdisciplinary:** Gerontology. **Legal studies:** Paralegal, prelaw. **Liberal arts:** Arts/sciences. **Math:** General. **Parks/recreation:** Exercise sciences, health/fitness, sports admin. **Philosophy/religion:** Philosophy, religion. **Physical sciences:** General, chemistry, physics. **Protective services:** Corrections, criminal justice, law enforcement admin, police science, security services. **Psychology:** General. **Public administration:** General, social work. **Social sciences:** Anthropology, economics, political science, sociology. **Visual/performing arts:** General, art, art history/conservation, dramatic, music performance, studio arts.

Most popular majors. Business/marketing 23%, communications/journalism 6%, education 8%, health sciences 20%, security/protective services 12%, visual/performing arts 6%.

Computing on campus. 1,000 workstations in dormitories, library, computer center, student center. Dormitories wired for high-speed internet access and linked to campus network. Commuter students can connect to campus network. Online course registration, online library, helpline, student web hosting, wireless network available.

Student life. Freshman orientation: Available. Preregistration for classes offered. Half-day session in summer for pre-registration; 3-day session prior to start of classes. **Policies:** Freshmen permitted cars on campus. **Housing:** Coed dorms, apartments, fraternity/sorority housing, substance-free housing available. $200 deposit. Special interest housing available. **Activities:** Bands, choral groups, dance, drama, film society, literary magazine, music ensembles, musical theater, student government, student newspaper, symphony orchestra, TV station, College Republicans, Young Democrats, Learning in the Community, international student organization, Campus Crusade for Christ, Circle K, Project Equal, Fellowship of Christian Athletes, Hispanic American Leadership Organization, Black Men and Women of Today.

Athletics. NCAA. **Intercollegiate:** Baseball M, basketball, cheerleading, football (tackle) M, golf M, soccer W, softball W, tennis, volleyball W. **Intramural:** Badminton, basketball, cross-country, football (non-tackle), golf, soccer, softball, tennis, volleyball. **Team name:** Ichabods.

Student services. Adult student services, alcohol/substance abuse counseling, career counseling, services for economically disadvantaged, student employment services, financial aid counseling, health services, minority student services, personal counseling, placement for graduates, veterans' counselor. **Physically disabled:** Services for visually, hearing impaired.

Contact. E-mail: admissions@washburn.edu
Phone: (785) 670-1030 Toll-free number: (800) 332-0291
Fax: (785) 670-1113
Kirk Haskins, Director of Admissions, Washburn University of Topeka, 1700 Southwest College, Morgan 114, Topeka, KS 66621

Wichita State University

Wichita, Kansas
www.wichita.edu **CB code: 6884**

- Public 4-year university
- Commuter campus in large city
- 9,974 degree-seeking undergraduates: 29% part-time, 57% women, 7% African American, 7% Asian American, 5% Hispanic American, 1% Native American, 5% international
- 2,571 degree-seeking graduate students
- 84% of applicants admitted
- 37% graduate within 6 years

General. Founded in 1895. Regionally accredited. **Degrees:** 1,870 bachelor's, 111 associate awarded; master's, doctoral offered. **Calendar:** Semester, extensive summer session. **Full-time faculty:** 467 total; 81% have terminal degrees, 12% minority, 38% women. **Part-time faculty:** 48 total; 50% have terminal degrees, 12% minority, 58% women. **Class size:** 52% < 20, 36% 20-39, 5% 40-49, 6% 50-99, 1% >100. **Special facilities:** Sculpture garden, wind tunnels, Marcusson pipe organ, flow-visualization water tunnel, national aviation research institute, observatory.

Freshman class profile. 2,066 applied, 1,734 admitted, 1,241 enrolled.

Mid 50% test scores		**Rank in top tenth:**	19%
SAT verbal:	470-590	**End year in good standing:**	79%
SAT math:	480-610	**Return as sophomores:**	67%
ACT:	20-25	**Out-of-state:**	6%
GPA 3.50 or higher:	46%	**Live on campus:**	26%
GPA 3.0-3.49:	32%	**International:**	4%
GPA 2.0-2.99:	21%	**Fraternities:**	11%
Rank in top quarter:	47%	**Sororities:**	7%

Basis for selection. In-state criteria: 21 ACT or greater, rank in top 1/3 of high school class, or minimum 2.00 GPA in pre-college curriculum. Some academic colleges within WSU require a higher GPA for admission. **Homeschooled:** ACT required.

High school preparation. 14 units required. Required units include English 4, mathematics 3, social studies 3 and science 3. One computer technology required.

2005-2006 Annual costs. Tuition/fees: $4,232; $11,685 out-of-state. Room/board: $5,070. Books/supplies: $800. Personal expenses: $1,570.

2004-2005 Financial aid. Need-based: 902 full-time freshmen applied for aid; 887 were judged to have need; 751 of these received aid. Average need met was 43%. Average scholarship/grant was $2,897; average loan $2,183. 29% of total undergraduate aid awarded as scholarships/grants, 71% as loans/jobs. **Non-need-based:** Awarded to 2,767 full-time undergraduates, including 655 freshmen. Scholarships awarded for academics, alumni affiliation, art, athletics, leadership, music/drama. **Additional information:** Top freshman applicants admitted by October 1 invited to university scholarship competition.

Application procedures. Admission: No deadline. $30 fee. Application may be submitted online. Admission notification on a rolling basis. **Financial aid:** Closing date 3/15. FAFSA required. Applicants notified on a rolling basis starting 3/15; must reply within 2 week(s) of notification.

Academics. 24-hour study room with Internet access. All library databases and other software maintained for student use. **Special study options:** Accelerated study, cooperative education, distance learning, double major, dual enrollment of high school students, ESL, exchange student, honors, independent study, internships, liberal arts/career combination, study abroad, teacher certification program, Washington semester. Peace Corps returnee program. **Credit/placement by examination:** AP, CLEP, IB, SAT, ACT, institutional tests. 30 credit hours maximum toward associate degree, 60 toward bachelor's. **Support services:** Learning center, preadmission summer program, reduced course load, remedial instruction, study skills assistance, tutoring, writing center.

Majors. Area/ethnic studies: Women's. **Biology:** General. **Business:** Accounting, business admin, finance, human resources, international, management information systems, marketing. **Communications:** General. **Computer sciences:** General. **Education:** Art, elementary, music, physical, secondary. **Engineering:** Aerospace, computer, electrical, industrial, manufacturing, mechanical. **Foreign languages:** French, Latin, Spanish. **Health:** Athletic training, audiology/speech pathology, dental hygiene, health care admin, physician assistant, staff services technology. **History:** General. **Interdisciplinary:** Gerontology. **Liberal arts:** Arts/sciences. **Math:** General. **Parks/recreation:** Exercise sciences, sports admin. **Philosophy/religion:** Philosophy. **Physical sciences:** Chemistry, geology, physics. **Protective services:** Criminal justice. **Psychology:** General. **Public administration:** Social work. **Social sciences:** Anthropology, economics, political science, sociology. **Visual/performing arts:** General, art, art history/conservation, commercial/advertising art, dramatic, studio arts.

Most popular majors. Business/marketing 23%, education 12%, engineering/engineering technologies 10%, health sciences 12%, psychology 6%, security/protective services 6%.

Computing on campus. 1,500 workstations in dormitories, library, computer center, student center. Dormitories wired for high-speed internet access and linked to campus network. Commuter students can connect to campus network. Online course registration, online library, helpline, wireless network available.

Student life. Freshman orientation: Mandatory, $10 fee. Preregistration for classes offered. Held prior to fall semester. **Policies:** Freshmen permitted cars on campus. **Housing:** Guaranteed on-campus for freshmen. Coed dorms, special housing for disabled, apartments, fraternity/sorority housing, substance-free housing available. **Activities:** Bands, choral groups, dance, drama, film society, literary magazine, music ensembles, musical theater, opera, radio station, student government, student newspaper, symphony orchestra, TV station, Campus Crusade for Christ, College Republicans, Chinese student friendship association, Black Student Union, Hispanic American leadership association, Students in Free Enterprise, Association of Hindu Students.

Athletics. NCAA. **Intercollegiate:** Baseball M, basketball, cheerleading, cross-country, golf, softball W, tennis, track and field, volleyball W. **Intramural:** Badminton, basketball, football (non-tackle), golf, racquetball, rowing (crew), soccer, softball, swimming, table tennis, tennis, volleyball. **Team name:** Shockers.

Student services. Adult student services, alcohol/substance abuse counseling, campus ministries, career counseling, services for economically disadvantaged, student employment services, financial aid counseling, health services, minority student services, on-campus daycare, personal counseling, placement for graduates, veterans' counselor. **Physically disabled:** Services for visually, speech, hearing impaired.

Contact. E-mail: admissions@wichita.edu
Phone: (316) 978-3085 Toll-free number: (800) 362-2594
Fax: (316) 978-3174
Gina Crabtree, Director of Admissions, Wichita State University, 1845 Fairmount Box 124, Wichita, KS 67260-0124

Kentucky

Alice Lloyd College

Pippa Passes, Kentucky
www.alc.edu **CB code: 1098**

- Private 4-year liberal arts college
- Residential campus in rural community
- 612 degree-seeking undergraduates: 4% part-time, 52% women, 2% African American, 1% Hispanic American
- 59% of applicants admitted
- SAT or ACT (ACT writing optional) required

General. Founded in 1923. Regionally accredited. **Degrees:** 107 bachelor's awarded. **Location:** 150 miles from Lexington; 100 miles from Huntington, West Virginia. **Calendar:** Semester. **Full-time faculty:** 29 total; 55% have terminal degrees, 3% minority, 31% women. **Part-time faculty:** 12 total; 8% have terminal degrees, 50% women. **Class size:** 45% < 20, 48% 20-39, 8% 40-49. **Special facilities:** Appalachian history collection, photographic archives.

Freshman class profile. 1,014 applied, 603 admitted, 188 enrolled.

Mid 50% test scores		**Rank in top tenth:**	24%
ACT:	18-23	**End year in good standing:**	96%
GPA 3.50 or higher:	50%	**Return as sophomores:**	67%
GPA 3.0-3.49:	24%	**Out-of-state:**	21%
GPA 2.0-2.99:	26%	**Live on campus:**	89%
Rank in top quarter:	48%		

Basis for selection. High school record and test scores important. Essay and interview recommended. **Homeschooled:** Transcript of courses and grades, letter of recommendation (nonparent) required. Interview highly recommended.

High school preparation. College-preparatory program required. 12 units required. Required units include English 4, mathematics 3, social studies 2 and science 3.

2005-2006 Annual costs. Tuition/fees: $7,510. Guaranteed tuition for students from 108-county central Appalachian service area in Kentucky, West Virginia, Virginia, Tennessee, and Ohio. Room/board: $3,750. Books/supplies: $850. Personal expenses: $1,300.

2004-2005 Financial aid. Need-based: 175 full-time freshmen applied for aid; 136 were judged to have need; 136 of these received aid. Average need met was 78%. Average scholarship/grant was $7,053; average loan $228. 77% of total undergraduate aid awarded as scholarships/grants, 23% as loans/jobs. **Non-need-based:** Awarded to 166 full-time undergraduates, including 79 freshmen. Scholarships awarded for athletics, minority status, state residency. **Additional information:** All students receive financial aid through student work program. No student denied admission because of inability to pay. All full-time students required to work minimum of 10 hours per week.

Application procedures. Admission: Priority date 5/1; no deadline. No application fee. Application may be submitted online. Admission notification on a rolling basis beginning on or about 9/1. **Financial aid:** Priority date 3/15; no closing date. FAFSA required. Applicants notified on a rolling basis starting 4/1; must reply within 6 week(s) of notification.

Academics. Scholarships for graduate work following graduation. **Special study options:** Double major, independent study, internships, liberal arts/career combination, student-designed major, study abroad, teacher certification program, Washington semester. **Credit/placement by examination:** AP, CLEP, IB, SAT, ACT, institutional tests. 30 credit hours maximum toward bachelor's degree. Limited number of hours of credit by examination may be counted toward degree, decided on individual basis. **Support services:** Learning center, reduced course load, remedial instruction, study skills assistance, tutoring.

Majors. Biology: General. **Business:** Business admin. **Education:** Biology, elementary, English, mathematics, middle, physical, science, secondary, social studies. **English:** English lit. **History:** General. **Interdisciplinary:** Biological/physical sciences. **Parks/recreation:** General. **Physical sciences:** General. **Social sciences:** General.

Most popular majors. Biology 17%, business/marketing 18%, education 30%, history 18%, social sciences 8%.

Computing on campus. 80 workstations in library, computer center. Dormitories wired for high-speed internet access and linked to campus network. Online library, helpline, repair service, wireless network available.

Student life. Freshman orientation: Mandatory. Preregistration for classes offered. Held 3 days before start of first semester. **Policies:** Zero tolerance of on-campus alcohol and/or drug usage or possession. Freshmen permitted cars on campus. **Housing:** Guaranteed on-campus for all undergraduates. Single-sex dorms available. $50 fully refundable deposit, deadline 5/15. **Activities:** Choral groups, drama, radio station, student government, student newspaper, Students for Christ, Baptist Student Union, Cultural Diversity Club, Children's Outreach Club, Community Service Volunteers, Circle K.

Athletics. NAIA. **Intercollegiate:** Baseball M, basketball, cheerleading M, cross-country, softball W. **Intramural:** Basketball, bowling, football (non-tackle), golf, racquetball, soccer, softball, swimming, table tennis, tennis, volleyball, weight lifting. **Team name:** Eagles.

Student services. Alcohol/substance abuse counseling, career counseling, student employment services, financial aid counseling, health services, on-campus daycare, personal counseling, placement for graduates, veterans' counselor.

Contact. E-mail: admissions@alc.edu
Phone: (606) 368-6036 Toll-free number: (888) 280-4252
Fax: (606) 368-6215
Sean Damron, Director of Admissions, Alice Lloyd College, 100 Purpose Road, Pippa Passes, KY 41844

Asbury College

Wilmore, Kentucky **CB member**
www.asbury.edu **CB code: 1019**

- Private 4-year liberal arts college affiliated with interdenominational tradition
- Residential campus in small town
- 1,139 degree-seeking undergraduates: 2% part-time, 59% women, 1% African American, 1% Asian American, 1% Hispanic American, 1% international
- 64 degree-seeking graduate students
- 74% of applicants admitted
- SAT or ACT (ACT writing optional), application essay required
- 69% graduate within 6 years

General. Founded in 1890. Regionally accredited. **Degrees:** 271 bachelor's awarded; master's offered. **ROTC:** Army, Air Force. **Location:** 20 miles from Lexington. **Calendar:** Semester, limited summer session. **Full-time faculty:** 86 total; 80% have terminal degrees, 1% minority, 29% women. **Part-time faculty:** 65 total; 17% have terminal degrees, 5% minority, 45% women. **Class size:** 61% < 20, 36% 20-39, 3% 40-49.

Freshman class profile. 797 applied, 589 admitted, 217 enrolled.

Mid 50% test scores		**Rank in top quarter:**	64%
SAT verbal:	530-660	**Rank in top tenth:**	35%
SAT math:	500-630	**End year in good standing:**	90%
ACT:	21-28	**Return as sophomores:**	79%
GPA 3.50 or higher:	67%	**Out-of-state:**	65%
GPA 3.0-3.49:	24%	**Live on campus:**	94%
GPA 2.0-2.99:	9%	**International:**	1%

Basis for selection. Probationary acceptance possible if GPA below 2.5 or test results below ACT 22 or SAT 1020 (exclusive of Writing). ACT required prior to admission to education department for education majors; both ACT and SAT required for presidential level scholarships. Interview recommended for music majors, academically weak applicants, scholarships. Audition required for music majors. Portfolio recommended for art majors. **Homeschooled:** Transcript of courses and grades, state high school equivalency certificate required.

High school preparation. College-preparatory program recommended. 15 units recommended. Recommended units include English 4, mathematics 3, social studies 1, history 1, science 2 (laboratory 2) and foreign language 2.

2005-2006 Annual costs. Tuition/fees: $18,956. Room/board: $4,806. Books/supplies: $600. Personal expenses: $1,038.

2005-2006 Financial aid. Need-based: 253 full-time freshmen applied for aid; 214 were judged to have need; 213 of these received aid. Average

need met was 81%. Average scholarship/grant was $8,273; average loan $2,696. 49% of total undergraduate aid awarded as scholarships/grants, 51% as loans/jobs. **Non-need-based:** Awarded to 349 full-time undergraduates, including 130 freshmen. Scholarships awarded for academics, athletics, leadership, music/drama, ROTC.

Application procedures. **Admission:** No deadline. $30 fee, may be waived for applicants with need. Application may be submitted online. Admission notification on a rolling basis. Confirmation of intention to enroll requires $200 pre-tuition deposit within 30 days of admission notification. **Financial aid:** Priority date 3/1; no closing date. FAFSA, institutional form required. Applicants notified on a rolling basis starting 2/15; must reply within 4 week(s) of notification.

Academics. **Special study options:** Double major, ESL, internships, study abroad, teacher certification program, Washington semester. Exchange program with colleges in Christian College Consortium, 3-2 programs in engineering with the University of Kentucky. **Credit/placement by examination:** AP, CLEP, IB, SAT, ACT, institutional tests. **Support services:** Remedial instruction, study skills assistance, tutoring, writing center.

Majors. **Biology:** General, biochemistry. **Business:** General, accounting. **Communications:** Journalism. **Communications technology:** Radio/tv. **Education:** Art, elementary, middle, music, physical. **English:** English lit, speech/rhetoric. **Foreign languages:** Ancient Greek, Biblical, classics, French, Latin, Spanish. **Health:** Health services. **History:** General. **Math:** General, computational. **Parks/recreation:** Facilities management, health/fitness, sports admin. **Philosophy/religion:** Philosophy. **Physical sciences:** General, chemistry. **Psychology:** General. **Public administration:** Social work. **Social sciences:** General, sociology. **Theology:** Bible, missionary, religious ed, youth ministry. **Visual/performing arts:** Studio arts.

Most popular majors. Business/marketing 7%, communication technologies 12%, education 8%, English 12%, foreign language 9%, psychology 7%, public administration/social services 6%, theological studies 12%.

Computing on campus. 189 workstations in dormitories, library, computer center, student center. Dormitories wired for high-speed internet access and linked to campus network. Commuter students can connect to campus network. Online library, helpline, repair service available.

Student life. **Freshman orientation:** Mandatory. Preregistration for classes offered. Held weekend before fall semester begins. **Policies:** Christian values stressed. Religious observance required. **Housing:** Guaranteed on-campus for freshmen. Single-sex dorms, special housing for disabled, apartments available. Spanish Language House available. **Activities:** Bands, choral groups, drama, literary magazine, music ensembles, musical theater, opera, radio station, student government, student newspaper, symphony orchestra, TV station, Christian Service Association, Fellowship of Christian Athletes, Salvation Army Student Fellowship, World Gospel Mission Student Fellowship, Impact, Student Fellowship, Asburians for Life, ministerial association, outdoors club, international student fellowship.

Athletics. NAIA, NCCAA. **Intercollegiate:** Basketball, cross-country, diving, soccer, swimming, tennis, volleyball W. **Intramural:** Basketball, football (non-tackle), golf, racquetball, soccer, softball, volleyball. **Team name:** Eagles.

Student services. Campus ministries, career counseling, student employment services, health services, minority student services, personal counseling, placement for graduates, veterans' counselor.

Contact. E-mail: admissions@asbury.edu
Phone: (859) 858-3511 ext. 2142 Toll-free number: (800) 888-1818
Fax: (859) 858-3921
Ronald Anderson, Director of Admissions, Asbury College, One Macklem Drive, Wilmore, KY 40390-1198

Beckfield College

Florence, Kentucky
www.beckfield.edu **CB code: 3404**

- For-profit 4-year business and nursing college
- Commuter campus in large town
- 485 degree-seeking undergraduates: 35% part-time, 80% women, 2% Asian American, 1% Hispanic American
- Interview required

General. Accredited by ACICS. **Degrees:** 84 associate awarded. **Location:** 10 miles from Cincinnati. **Calendar:** Quarter, extensive summer session. **Full-time faculty:** 10 total. **Part-time faculty:** 25 total. **Class size:** 100% < 20.

Freshman class profile.

Out-of-state:	18%	**International:**	2%

Basis for selection. Open admission, but selective for some programs. Admission to programs other than nursing requires minimum composite score of 16 (ACT), 780 (old SAT), or 1150 (new SAT). If ACT or SAT scores do not qualify or are not available, applicants must achieve combined (writing, reading, and mathematics) score of 106 on ACT ASSET test administered by college. Admission to nursing program requires a composite score of 18 (ACT), 870 (old SAT), or 1250 (new SAT). **Homeschooled:** Transcript of courses and grades required.

2005-2006 Annual costs. Tuition/fees: $10,000. Technology fee, where applicable, varies with program. Books/supplies: $950.

Financial aid. All financial aid based on need. **Additional information:** Deadline for filing of financial aid forms is end of first week of classes.

Application procedures. **Admission:** No deadline. No application fee. Application must be submitted on paper. Admission notification on a rolling basis. **Financial aid:** FAFSA required. Applicants notified on a rolling basis.

Academics. **Special study options:** Independent study, internships, liberal arts/career combination. **Credit/placement by examination:** CLEP, IB. **Support services:** Reduced course load, remedial instruction, study skills assistance, tutoring.

Majors. **Business:** Business admin. **Health:** Nursing (RN). **Legal studies:** Paralegal.

Computing on campus. 90 workstations in computer center. Online library, helpline, repair service available.

Student life. **Freshman orientation:** Mandatory. Preregistration for classes offered. Held for half day 3 days before beginning of quarter. **Policies:** Freshmen permitted cars on campus. **Activities:** Student newspaper.

Student services. Career counseling, student employment services, financial aid counseling, personal counseling, placement for graduates, veterans' counselor.

Contact. E-mail: kleeds@beckfield.edu
Phone: (859) 371-9393 Fax: (859) 371-5096
Ken Leeds, Admissions, Beckfield College, 16 Spiral Drive, Florence, KY 41042

Bellarmine University

Louisville, Kentucky **CB member**
www.bellarmine.edu **CB code: 1056**

- Private 4-year university and liberal arts college affiliated with Roman Catholic Church
- Commuter campus in very large city
- 2,004 degree-seeking undergraduates: 3% African American, 2% Asian American, 2% Hispanic American, 2% international
- 71% of applicants admitted
- SAT or ACT (ACT writing recommended), application essay required
- 62% graduate within 6 years; 53% enter graduate study

General. Founded in 1950. Regionally accredited. **Degrees:** 413 bachelor's awarded; master's, doctoral offered. **ROTC:** Army, Air Force. **Location:** 7 miles from downtown, 100 miles from Cincinnati. **Calendar:** Semester, extensive summer session. **Full-time faculty:** 114 total; 73% have terminal degrees, 6% minority, 47% women. **Part-time faculty:** 188 total; 21% have terminal degrees, 10% minority, 67% women. **Class size:** 59% < 20, 40% 20-39, 1% 40-49, less than 1% 50-99. **Special facilities:** 9-hole golf course, service learning clinic for physical therapy students, Thomas Merton museum.

Freshman class profile. 2,024 applied, 1,427 admitted, 431 enrolled.

Mid 50% test scores		**Out-of-state:**	28%
SAT verbal:	500-610	**Live on campus:**	63%
SAT math:	490-610	**International:**	1%
ACT:	21-26	**Fraternities:**	1%
End year in good standing:	90%	**Sororities:**	1%
Return as sophomores:	84%		

Basis for selection. Minimum GPA 2.0, college preparatory curriculum, 21 ACT or 900 SAT (exclusive of Writing), strong high school recommendation, submission of acceptable essay. Applicants not meeting requirements may be admitted on strength of each criterion. School activities also considered. Interview recommended. Audition required of music majors. Portfolio recommended for art majors.

High school preparation. College-preparatory program required. 20 units required; 24 recommended. Required and recommended units include English 4, mathematics 3-4, social studies 2-3, history 1-2, science 2-4 (laboratory 1), foreign language 2 and academic electives 3-4. One unit computer science recommended.

2006-2007 Annual costs. Tuition/fees: $24,150. Room/board: $6,920. Books/supplies: $600. Personal expenses: $1,100.

2004-2005 Financial aid. Need-based: 326 full-time freshmen applied for aid; 269 were judged to have need; 269 of these received aid. Average need met was 89%. Average scholarship/grant was $13,242; average loan $2,719. 74% of total undergraduate aid awarded as scholarships/grants, 26% as loans/jobs. **Non-need-based:** Awarded to 609 full-time undergraduates, including 286 freshmen. Scholarships awarded for academics, alumni affiliation, art, athletics, leadership, minority status, music/drama, religious affiliation, ROTC, state residency.

Application procedures. Admission: Priority date 2/1; deadline 8/15 (postmark date). $25 fee, may be waived for applicants with need. Application may be submitted online. Admission notification on a rolling basis. **Financial aid:** Priority date 3/1; no closing date. FAFSA required. Applicants notified on a rolling basis starting 4/15; must reply by 5/1 or within 3 week(s) of notification.

Academics. Special study options: Accelerated study, combined bachelor's/graduate degree, cross-registration, double major, dual enrollment of high school students, honors, independent study, internships, liberal arts/career combination, semester at sea, study abroad, teacher certification program, Washington semester. **Credit/placement by examination:** AP, CLEP, IB, SAT, ACT, institutional tests. 30 credit hours maximum toward bachelor's degree. **Support services:** Learning center, reduced course load, study skills assistance, tutoring.

Majors. Biology: General. **Business:** Accounting, actuarial science, business admin. **Communications:** General. **Computer sciences:** General, computer science. **Education:** General, art, biology, chemistry, elementary, English, history, mathematics, middle, music, physics, secondary, social studies, special. **Engineering:** Computer. **Foreign languages:** General. **Health:** Clinical lab science, cytotechnology, nursing (RN), predentistry, premedicine, prenursing, prepharmacy, respiratory therapy technology. **History:** General. **Liberal arts:** Arts/sciences. **Math:** General. **Philosophy/religion:** Philosophy. **Physical sciences:** Chemistry. **Psychology:** General. **Social sciences:** Economics, political science, sociology. **Visual/performing arts:** Art, arts management.

Most popular majors. Business/marketing 15%, communications/journalism 6%, English 6%, health sciences 31%, liberal arts 8%.

Computing on campus. 200 workstations in dormitories, library, computer center, student center. Dormitories wired for high-speed internet access and linked to campus network. Commuter students can connect to campus network. Online course registration, helpline, repair service, wireless network available.

Student life. Freshman orientation: Mandatory. Preregistration for classes offered. One day program in summer and 2 days before classes begin in August. **Policies:** Freshmen permitted cars on campus. **Housing:** Guaranteed on-campus for freshmen. Coed dorms, single-sex dorms, special housing for disabled available. $200 deposit, deadline 5/1. Suites available to upperclassmen. **Activities:** Bands, choral groups, dance, drama, literary magazine, music ensembles, musical theater, opera, student government, student newspaper, 50 clubs and organizations available.

Athletics. NCAA. **Intercollegiate:** Baseball M, basketball, cross-country, field hockey W, golf, lacrosse M, soccer, softball W, tennis, track and field, volleyball W. **Intramural:** Basketball, cheerleading, football (non-tackle) M, golf, soccer, softball, swimming, tennis, volleyball, weight lifting. **Team name:** Knights.

Student services. Adult student services, campus ministries, career counseling, student employment services, financial aid counseling, health services, personal counseling, placement for graduates, veterans' counselor. **Physically disabled:** Services for visually, hearing impaired.

Contact. E-mail: admissions@bellarmine.edu
Phone: (502) 452-8131 Toll-free number: (800) 274-4723 ext. 8131
Fax: (502) 452-8002
Timothy Sturgeon, Dean of Admissions, Bellarmine University, 2001 Newburg Road, Louisville, KY 40205

Berea College

Berea, Kentucky — **CB member**
www.berea.edu — **CB code: 1060**

- Private 4-year liberal arts college
- Residential campus in small town
- 1,523 degree-seeking undergraduates: 60% women, 19% African American, 1% Asian American, 2% Hispanic American, 1% Native American, 5% international
- 27% of applicants admitted
- SAT or ACT (ACT writing optional), application essay, interview required
- 62% graduate within 6 years

General. Founded in 1855. Regionally accredited. **Degrees:** 314 bachelor's awarded. **Location:** 40 miles from Lexington, 100 miles from Louisville. **Calendar:** 4-1-4, limited summer session. **Full-time faculty:** 130 total; 91% have terminal degrees, 10% minority, 42% women. **Part-time faculty:** 29 total; 3% minority, 38% women. **Class size:** 66% < 20, 34% 20-39, less than 1% 50-99. **Special facilities:** Geology museum, planetarium with observatory, Ecovillage.

Freshman class profile. 1,908 applied, 511 admitted, 378 enrolled.

Mid 50% test scores		**Rank in top quarter:**	66%
SAT verbal:	510-640	**Rank in top tenth:**	30%
SAT math:	500-620	**Return as sophomores:**	82%
ACT:	21-25	**Out-of-state:**	56%
GPA 3.50 or higher:	54%	**Live on campus:**	98%
GPA 3.0-3.49:	31%	**International:**	5%
GPA 2.0-2.99:	15%		

Basis for selection. Rank in top half of class, recommendations, essays, interviews, test scores, involvement in community and school activities important. Financial need absolute prerequisite for admission. **Homeschooled:** If a transcript is not available, a list of the applicant's homeschooled courses and titles of the textbooks used in courses are required.

High school preparation. 13 units recommended. Recommended units include English 4, mathematics 3, social studies 1, history 1, science 2 and foreign language 2.

2006-2007 Annual costs. Tuition/fees: $22,116. Only those with financial need admitted. All students receive 4-year full tuition scholarship. Students required to earn a portion of their expenses by working a minimum of 10 hours per week on campus. Room/board: $4,980. Books/supplies: $700.

2005-2006 Financial aid. All financial aid based on need. 378 full-time freshmen applied for aid; 378 were judged to have need; 378 of these received aid. Average need met was 93%. Average scholarship/grant was $26,190; average loan $91. 93% of total undergraduate aid awarded as scholarships/grants, 7% as loans/jobs.

Application procedures. Admission: Closing date 4/30. No application fee. Application may be submitted online. Admission notification on a rolling basis beginning on or about 12/20. Must reply by 5/1. **Financial aid:** No deadline. FAFSA required. Applicants notified on a rolling basis starting 4/1.

Academics. All students are provided with a laptop computer that becomes their property upon graduation. **Special study options:** Combined bachelor's/graduate degree, double major, exchange student, honors, independent study, internships, student-designed major, study abroad, teacher certification program. 3-2 engineering program with Washington University (MO) and University of Kentucky. **Credit/placement by examination:** AP, CLEP, SAT, ACT, institutional tests. Unlimited number of credit hours may be counted toward degree. **Support services:** Learning center, remedial instruction, study skills assistance, tutoring, writing center.

Majors. Agriculture: General, agribusiness operations. **Area/ethnic studies:** Women's. **Biology:** General. **Business:** General. **Communications:** General. **Education:** General, art, elementary, family/consumer sciences, middle, music, physical, technology/industrial arts. **Family/consumer sciences:** General. **Foreign languages:** French, German, Latin, Spanish. **Health:** Nursing (RN). **History:** General. **Math:** General. **Philosophy/religion:** Philosophy, religion. **Physical sciences:** Chemistry, physics. **Psychology:** General. **Social sciences:** Economics, political science, sociology. **Visual/performing arts:** Art, dramatic, interior design, music performance, studio arts.

Most popular majors. Biology 6%, business/marketing 10%, education 12%, engineering/engineering technologies 15%, family/consumer sciences 7%, psychology 7%, visual/performing arts 8%.

Computing on campus. Dormitories wired for high-speed internet access and linked to campus network. Online course registration, online library, helpline, repair service available.

Student life. **Freshman orientation:** Mandatory. Preregistration for classes offered. During 3 summer weekends (2 in June, 1 in July). **Housing:** Guaranteed on-campus for all undergraduates. Single-sex dorms, apartments, substance-free housing available. Apartments for single-parent students, group housing for upperclassmen, EcoVillage available. **Activities:** Bands, choral groups, dance, drama, literary magazine, music ensembles, student government, student newspaper, religious organizations: People Who Care, Students for Appalachia, Habitat for Humanity, Black Music Ensemble, Cosmopolitan Club.

Athletics. NAIA. **Intercollegiate:** Baseball M, basketball, cross-country, golf M, soccer, softball W, swimming, tennis, track and field, volleyball W. **Intramural:** Basketball, football (non-tackle), racquetball, soccer, softball, volleyball. **Team name:** Mountaineers.

Student services. Adult student services, alcohol/substance abuse counseling, campus ministries, career counseling, services for economically disadvantaged, student employment services, financial aid counseling, health services, minority student services, on-campus daycare, personal counseling, placement for graduates, veterans' counselor, women's services. **Physically disabled:** Services for visually, speech, hearing impaired.

Contact. E-mail: admissions@berea.edu
Phone: (859) 985-3500 Toll-free number: (800) 326-5948
Fax: (859) 985-3512
Jamie Ealy, Director of Admissions, Berea College, CPO 2220, Berea, KY 40404

Brescia University
Owensboro, Kentucky
www.brescia.edu **CB code: 1071**

- Private 4-year university and liberal arts college affiliated with Roman Catholic Church
- Residential campus in small city
- 467 degree-seeking undergraduates: 12% part-time, 58% women, 4% African American, 1% Hispanic American, 10% international
- 26 degree-seeking graduate students
- 75% of applicants admitted
- SAT or ACT (ACT writing optional), application essay required
- 50% graduate within 6 years

General. Founded in 1950. Regionally accredited. Weekend college for nontraditional students. Lay ministry formation program nationally accredited. **Degrees:** 118 bachelor's, 10 associate awarded; master's offered. **Location:** 120 miles from Louisville; 120 miles from Nashville, Tennessee. **Calendar:** Semester, limited summer session. **Full-time faculty:** 44 total; 57% have terminal degrees, 11% minority, 48% women. **Part-time faculty:** 33 total; 42% women. **Class size:** 84% < 20, 16% 20-39. **Special facilities:** Observatory, greenhouse.

Freshman class profile. 126 applied, 94 admitted, 48 enrolled.

Mid 50% test scores		**GPA 3.0-3.49:**	13%
SAT verbal:	410-600	**GPA 2.0-2.99:**	32%
SAT math:	320-570	**Return as sophomores:**	71%
ACT:	18-23	**Out-of-state:**	13%
GPA 3.50 or higher:	50%	**Live on campus:**	83%

Basis for selection. Test scores, school record most important. Class rank, essay, recommendations also important. TOEFL required of nonnative speakers of English. Interview recommended.

High school preparation. College-preparatory program recommended. 17 units recommended. Recommended units include English 4, mathematics 3, social studies 2, history 2, science 2, foreign language 2 and academic electives 2. 2 units in fine arts, 2 units in computer science also recommended.

2005-2006 Annual costs. Tuition/fees: $12,400. Technology fee: $10/credit hour to maximum of $60 per semester. Room/board: $5,480. Books/supplies: $1,000. Personal expenses: $1,800.

2005-2006 Financial aid. **Need-based:** 96% of total undergraduate aid awarded as scholarships/grants, 4% as loans/jobs. **Non-need-based:** Scholarships awarded for academics, alumni affiliation, art, athletics, minority status, music/drama, religious affiliation, state residency.

Application procedures. **Admission:** No deadline. $25 fee, may be waived for applicants with need. Application may be submitted online. Admission notification on a rolling basis beginning on or about 9/1. **Financial aid:** Priority date 8/1; no closing date. FAFSA required. Applicants notified on a rolling basis starting 3/1; must reply within 3 week(s) of notification.

Academics. **Special study options:** Combined bachelor's/graduate degree, cross-registration, distance learning, double major, ESL, exchange student, honors, independent study, internships, liberal arts/career combination, student-designed major, teacher certification program, weekend college. **Credit/placement by examination:** AP, CLEP, IB, SAT, ACT, institutional tests. 18 credit hours maximum toward associate degree, 36 toward bachelor's. **Support services:** Reduced course load, remedial instruction, study skills assistance, tutoring.

Majors. **Biology:** General. **Business:** General, accounting, business admin. **Computer sciences:** General. **Education:** Art, elementary, middle, secondary, social studies, Spanish, special. **English:** English lit. **Foreign languages:** Spanish. **Health:** Audiology/speech pathology, clinical lab science, health care admin. **History:** General. **Interdisciplinary:** Biological/physical sciences, math/computer science. **Liberal arts:** Arts/sciences. **Math:** Applied. **Philosophy/religion:** Religion. **Physical sciences:** Chemistry. **Psychology:** General. **Public administration:** Social work. **Social sciences:** General, political science, sociology. **Theology:** Pastoral counseling, theology. **Visual/performing arts:** Art, commercial/advertising art.

Most popular majors. Biology 11%, business/marketing 25%, education 17%, liberal arts 9%, public administration/social services 12%.

Computing on campus. 67 workstations in library, computer center, student center. Dormitories wired for high-speed internet access and linked to campus network. Commuter students can connect to campus network. Online library available.

Student life. **Freshman orientation:** Available. Preregistration for classes offered. Activities begin on Sunday prior to classes through Tuesday. **Policies:** Freshmen permitted cars on campus. **Housing:** Guaranteed on-campus for freshmen. Coed dorms, single-sex dorms, special housing for disabled available. $100 fully refundable deposit, deadline 8/23. Shared apartment houses available. **Activities:** Choral groups, dance, drama, literary magazine, student government, student newspaper, Christian Student Union, social work association, council for exceptional children, campus ministry, international student organization.

Athletics. NAIA. **Intercollegiate:** Baseball M, basketball, golf, soccer, softball W, tennis W, volleyball W. **Intramural:** Basketball, racquetball, table tennis, volleyball. **Team name:** Bearcats.

Student services. Adult student services, alcohol/substance abuse counseling, campus ministries, career counseling, services for economically disadvantaged, student employment services, financial aid counseling, personal counseling, placement for graduates, veterans' counselor, women's services. **Physically disabled:** Services for speech impaired.

Contact. E-mail: admissions@brescia.edu
Phone: (270) 686-4241 Toll-free number: (877) 273-7242
Fax: (270) 686-4314
Dean of Enrollment, Brescia University, 717 Frederica Street, Owensboro, KY 42301-3023

Campbellsville University
Campbellsville, Kentucky **CB member**
www.campbellsville.edu **CB code: 1097**

- Private 4-year university affiliated with Baptist faith
- Residential campus in large town
- 1,379 degree-seeking undergraduates: 8% part-time, 53% women, 6% African American, 1% Asian American, 1% Hispanic American, 3% international
- 447 degree-seeking graduate students
- 68% of applicants admitted
- SAT or ACT (ACT writing optional) required
- 34% graduate within 6 years

General. Founded in 1906. Regionally accredited. Affiliated with Kentucky Baptist Convention. **Degrees:** 219 bachelor's, 25 associate awarded; master's offered. **Location:** 80 miles from Louisville, 140 miles from Nashville, Tennessee. **Calendar:** Semester, extensive summer session. **Full-time faculty:** 86 total; 66% have terminal degrees, 5% minority, 46% women. **Part-time faculty:** 131 total; 10% minority, 55% women. **Class size:** 76% < 20, 24% 20-39, less than 1% 40-49. **Special facilities:** Educational and research woodland, American Civil War institute, fine arts center with computer-enhanced practice room with acoustical adjustment system.

Freshman class profile. 1,351 applied, 922 admitted, 356 enrolled.

Mid 50% test scores			
SAT verbal:	430-560	End year in good standing:	84%
SAT math:	440-560	Return as sophomores:	62%
ACT:	18-24	Out-of-state:	16%
Rank in top quarter:	38%	Live on campus:	70%
Rank in top tenth:	16%	International:	2%

Basis for selection. Achievement in strong high school program and satisfactory ACT or SAT scores most important. Special consideration for entry to basic skills program may be given to other highly motivated and potentially successful applicants. Interview and essay recommended.

High school preparation. 21 units recommended. Recommended units include English 4, mathematics 3, social studies 2, history 2, science 3 (laboratory 1), foreign language 1 and academic electives 6. At least 2 units in the arts recommended for academic elective.

2006-2007 Annual costs. Tuition/fees: $16,340. Room/board: $5,932. Books/supplies: $800. Personal expenses: $1,330.

2004-2005 Financial aid. Need-based: 387 full-time freshmen applied for aid; 346 were judged to have need; 344 of these received aid. Average need met was 75%. Average scholarship/grant was $9,632; average loan $2,779. 70% of total undergraduate aid awarded as scholarships/grants, 30% as loans/jobs. **Non-need-based:** Awarded to 404 full-time undergraduates, including 169 freshmen. **Additional information:** Matching scholarships available for students whose church contributes $200 annually. Performance grants available to members of marching band.

Application procedures. Admission: Priority date 4/15; no deadline. $20 fee, may be waived for applicants with need. Application may be submitted online. Admission notification on a rolling basis beginning on or about 1/2. **Financial aid:** Priority date 4/1; no closing date. FAFSA required. Applicants notified on a rolling basis starting 5/15.

Academics. Special study options: Cooperative education, distance learning, double major, dual enrollment of high school students, ESL, exchange student, honors, independent study, internships, study abroad, teacher certification program, Washington semester. London semester. **Credit/placement by examination:** AP, CLEP, institutional tests. 32 credit hours maximum toward bachelor's degree. Institutional/departmental examinations given in some areas. **Support services:** Learning center, preadmission summer program, reduced course load, remedial instruction, study skills assistance, tutoring, writing center.

Majors. Biology: General. **Business:** General, accounting, business admin, marketing, office management. **Communications:** General, broadcast journalism, journalism, public relations. **Computer sciences:** General. **Education:** General, art, biology, chemistry, early childhood, elementary, English, health, history, mathematics, middle, music, physical, physics, reading, science, secondary, social science, social studies. **Health:** Athletic training, predentistry, premedicine, prenursing, prepharmacy, preveterinary. **History:** General. **Legal studies:** Prelaw. **Math:** General. **Parks/recreation:** General, exercise sciences, health/fitness. **Philosophy/religion:** Religion. **Physical sciences:** Chemistry, physics. **Protective services:** Law enforcement admin. **Psychology:** General. **Public administration:** Social work. **Social sciences:** General, economics, political science, sociology. **Theology:** Bible, religious ed, sacred music. **Visual/performing arts:** Art, conducting, dramatic, music performance, music theory/composition, piano/organ, studio arts, voice/opera.

Most popular majors. Biology 6%, business/marketing 19%, education 16%, psychology 6%, public administration/social services 10%, social sciences 8%, theological studies 12%.

Computing on campus. 175 workstations in dormitories, library, computer center, student center. Dormitories wired for high-speed internet access and linked to campus network. Online course registration, online library available.

Student life. Freshman orientation: Mandatory. Preregistration for classes offered. Held in June and July. **Policies:** Religious observance required. Freshmen permitted cars on campus. **Housing:** Guaranteed on-campus for all undergraduates. Single-sex dorms, apartments, substance-free housing available. $100 nonrefundable deposit, deadline 7/1. **Activities:** Bands, choral groups, dance, drama, literary magazine, music ensembles, musical theater, opera, radio station, student government, student newspaper, symphony orchestra, TV station, Baptist Student Union, Young Republicans, Young Democrats, Student Foundation, Fellowship of Christian Athletes, Student Ambassadors, African American Leadership League, World Community Club.

Athletics. NAIA. **Intercollegiate:** Baseball M, basketball, cross-country, football (tackle) M, golf, soccer, softball W, tennis, track and field, volleyball W, wrestling M. **Intramural:** Basketball, racquetball, soccer, softball, table tennis, tennis, volleyball. **Team name:** Tigers.

Student services. Adult student services, alcohol/substance abuse counseling, campus ministries, career counseling, student employment services, financial aid counseling, health services, personal counseling, placement for graduates, veterans' counselor.

Contact. E-mail: admissions@campbellsville.edu
Phone: (270) 789-5220 Toll-free number: (800) 264-6014
Fax: (270) 789-5071
David Walters, Vice President for Admissions, Campbellsville University, 1University Drive, Campbellsville, KY 42718-2799

Centre College

Danville, Kentucky
www.centre.edu
CB member
CB code: 1109

- Private 4-year liberal arts college affiliated with Presbyterian Church (USA)
- Residential campus in large town
- 1,122 degree-seeking undergraduates: 51% women, 2% African American, 2% Asian American, 1% Hispanic American, 2% international
- 63% of applicants admitted
- SAT or ACT (ACT writing optional), application essay required
- 79% graduate within 6 years; 46% enter graduate study

General. Founded in 1819. Regionally accredited. **Degrees:** 230 bachelor's awarded. **ROTC:** Army, Air Force. **Location:** 35 miles from Lexington, 85 miles from Louisville. **Calendar:** 4-1-4. **Full-time faculty:** 96 total; 98% have terminal degrees, 4% minority, 32% women. **Part-time faculty:** 27 total; 37% have terminal degrees, 7% minority, 52% women. **Class size:** 54% < 20, 46% 20-39. **Special facilities:** Performing arts center, visual arts center, physical science center.

Freshman class profile. 1,989 applied, 1,257 admitted, 317 enrolled.

Mid 50% test scores			
SAT verbal:	580-680	Rank in top quarter:	85%
SAT math:	600-670	Rank in top tenth:	55%
ACT:	25-29	Return as sophomores:	92%
GPA 3.50 or higher:	77%	Out-of-state:	34%
GPA 3.0-3.49:	19%	Live on campus:	99%
GPA 2.0-2.99:	4%	International:	3%

Basis for selection. Achievement and quality of high school program most important. Recommendations, test scores, academic and nonacademic interests, experiences considered. Interview recommended.

High school preparation. 14 units required; 17 recommended. Required and recommended units include English 4, mathematics 4, history 2, science 2-3 (laboratory 2-3) and foreign language 2. 1 fine arts recommended.

2006-2007 Annual costs. Comprehensive fee: $33,000. Students wishing to live off-campus must annually seek approval from the Dean of Students; in such cases, a reduced comprehensive fee may be available. Books/supplies: $890. Personal expenses: $700.

2005-2006 Financial aid. Need-based: 252 full-time freshmen applied for aid; 182 were judged to have need; 182 of these received aid. Average need met was 90%. Average scholarship/grant was $17,281; average loan $2,716. 83% of total undergraduate aid awarded as scholarships/grants, 17% as loans/jobs. **Non-need-based:** Awarded to 386 full-time undergraduates, including 124 freshmen. Scholarships awarded for academics, alumni affiliation, minority status, music/drama, ROTC.

Application procedures. Admission: Closing date 2/1 (postmark date). $40 fee, may be waived for applicants with need. Application may be submitted online. Admission notification 3/15. Must reply by May 1 or within 2 week(s) if notified thereafter. **Financial aid:** Priority date 2/15, closing date 3/1. FAFSA, institutional form required. Applicants notified by 3/25; must reply by 5/1 or within 2 week(s) of notification.

Academics. Unusual courses and off-campus study options offered during 3-week winter term. Sites in England, France, Mexico, Japan, and Ireland; other winter-term international locations vary. **Special study options:** Cross-registration, double major, honors, independent study, internships, liberal arts/career combination, student-designed major, study abroad, teacher certification program, Washington semester. Science semester at Oak Ridge National Laboratories, Tennessee, and 5 other national science laboratories; 3-2 engineering program with Columbia University (NY), Washington University (MO), Vanderbilt University (TN), and University of Kentucky. **Credit/placement by examination:** AP, CLEP, IB, SAT, ACT, institutional tests. **Support services:** Reduced course load, tutoring, writing center.

Majors. Biology: General, biochemistry, molecular. **Computer sciences:** Computer science. **Education:** Elementary. **English:** English lit. **Foreign languages:** Classics, French, German, Spanish. **History:** General. **Math:** General. **Philosophy/religion:** Philosophy, religion. **Physical sciences:** Chemical physics, chemistry, physics. **Psychology:** General. **Social sciences:** Anthropology, economics, international relations, political science, sociology. **Visual/performing arts:** Art, dramatic.

Most popular majors. Biology 10%, English 9%, foreign language 6%, history 11%, interdisciplinary studies 6%, philosophy/religious studies 6%, physical sciences 6%, psychology 8%, social sciences 23%, visual/performing arts 8%.

Computing on campus. 170 workstations in dormitories, library, computer center, student center. Dormitories linked to campus network. Online course registration, helpline, repair service, wireless network available.

Student life. Freshman orientation: Mandatory. 3 days available in June; also held at beginning of fall term. **Policies:** Freshmen permitted cars on campus. **Housing:** Guaranteed on-campus for all undergraduates. Coed dorms, single-sex dorms, special housing for disabled, apartments, fraternity/sorority housing, substance-free housing available. Fraternity/sorority housing for officers. **Activities:** Bands, choral groups, dance, drama, film society, literary magazine, music ensembles, musical theater, student government, student newspaper, symphony orchestra, TV station, volunteer services, diversity student union, Fellowship of Christian Athletes, Centre Christian Fellowship, Catholic Campus Ministry, Baptist Campus Ministry, College Life, Centrecycle, LIFT (tutoring and mentoring for at-risk elementary students), international club.

Athletics. NCAA. **Intercollegiate:** Baseball M, basketball, cross-country, diving, field hockey W, football (tackle) M, golf, soccer, softball W, swimming, tennis, track and field, volleyball W. **Intramural:** Badminton, basketball, bowling, cross-country, fencing, field hockey W, football (tackle), golf, racquetball, rugby M, soccer, softball, swimming, table tennis, tennis, track and field, volleyball, wrestling M. **Team name:** Colonels.

Student services. Alcohol/substance abuse counseling, campus ministries, career counseling, student employment services, financial aid counseling, health services, minority student services, personal counseling, placement for graduates. **Physically disabled:** Services for visually, hearing impaired.

Contact. E-mail: admission@centre.edu
Phone: (859) 238-5350 Toll-free number: (800) 423-6236
Fax: (859) 238-5373
J. Carey Thompson, Dean of Admission and Student Financial Planning, Centre College, 600 West Walnut Street, Danville, KY 40422-1394

Clear Creek Baptist Bible College

Pineville, Kentucky
www.ccbbc.edu **CB code: 5975**

- Private 4-year Bible and seminary college affiliated with Southern Baptist Convention
- Residential campus in small town
- 190 degree-seeking undergraduates: 18% part-time, 23% women, 1% African American, 2% international
- Application essay, interview required

General. Founded in 1926. Regionally accredited; also accredited by ABHE. Adult family Bible college affiliated with Kentucky Baptist Convention that trains individuals for ministry in local church. Prefer students to be at least 21 years of age. **Degrees:** 30 bachelor's, 4 associate awarded. **Location:** 110 miles from Lexington; 76 miles from Knoxville, Tennessee. **Calendar:** Semester, limited summer session. **Full-time faculty:** 6 total; 83% have terminal degrees. **Part-time faculty:** 17 total; 35% have terminal degrees, 24% women. **Class size:** 79% < 20, 21% 20-39. **Special facilities:** Family life center.

Freshman class profile.

Out-of-state:	25%	Live on campus:	80%

Basis for selection. Open admission. Demonstrated clear call to Christian ministry necessary. Audition required for music minor. **Homeschooled:** State high school certificate or GED required.

2006-2007 Annual costs. Tuition/fees (projected): $4,870. Room and board fee given for single student. Married student housing fees vary from $160 to $325 per month. Room/board: $3,310. Personal expenses: $1,600.

2004-2005 Financial aid. Need-based: 21 full-time freshmen applied for aid; 13 were judged to have need; 13 of these received aid. Average need met was 38%. 95% of total undergraduate aid awarded as scholarships/grants, 5% as loans/jobs. **Non-need-based:** Awarded to 160 full-time undergraduates, including 9 freshmen. Scholarships awarded for academics.

Application procedures. Admission: Priority date 7/15; deadline 8/2 (receipt date). $40 fee. Application must be submitted on paper. Admission notification on a rolling basis. **Financial aid:** Priority date 6/30; no closing date. FAFSA, institutional form required. Applicants notified on a rolling basis; must reply by 8/1.

Academics. Night classes offered in summer. **Special study options:** Cross-registration, distance learning, double major, dual enrollment of high school students, independent study. **Credit/placement by examination:** AP, CLEP, institutional tests. **Support services:** Reduced course load, remedial instruction, study skills assistance, tutoring.

Majors. Theology: Bible.

Computing on campus. 12 workstations in library, computer center. Dormitories wired for high-speed internet access. Online course registration, online library available.

Student life. Freshman orientation: Available. Preregistration for classes offered. 4-day program held week of registration. **Policies:** Dress code; no tobacco, alcohol, or drugs on campus. Religious observance required. Freshmen permitted cars on campus. **Housing:** Single-sex dorms, apartments, substance-free housing available. $50 partly refundable deposit, deadline 7/25. Cottages, family housing available. **Activities:** Choral groups, drama, music ensembles, radio station, student government, Women's Missionary Union, Brotherhood, Baptist Campus Ministry, Young Disciples, Acteens, Royal Ambassadors, Girls in Action, Mission Friends.

Athletics. Intramural: Basketball, softball, swimming, table tennis, tennis, volleyball.

Student services. Campus ministries, career counseling, student employment services, financial aid counseling, health services, on-campus daycare, personal counseling, placement for graduates, veterans' counselor.

Contact. E-mail: ccbbc@ccbbc.edu
Phone: (606) 337-3196 Toll-free number: (866) 340-3196
Fax: (606) 337-2372
Billy Howell, Director of Admissions, Clear Creek Baptist Bible College, 300 Clear Creek Road, Pineville, KY 40977-9754

Eastern Kentucky University

Richmond, Kentucky **CB member**
www.eku.edu **CB code: 1200**

- Public 4-year university
- Residential campus in large town
- 13,000 degree-seeking undergraduates
- 2,277 graduate students
- 73% of applicants admitted
- ACT required
- 38% graduate within 6 years

General. Founded in 1906. Regionally accredited. Courses offered at additional sites in Corbin, Manchester, London, Somerset and Barbourville. **Degrees:** 1,795 bachelor's, 243 associate awarded; master's offered. **ROTC:** Army, Air Force. **Location:** 28 miles from Lexington, 110 miles from Cincinnati. **Calendar:** Semester, extensive summer session. **Full-time faculty:** 623 total. **Part-time faculty:** 479 total. **Class size:** 49% < 20, 45% 20-39, 4% 40-49, 2% 50-99, less than 1% >100. **Special facilities:** Planetarium, nature preserves, law enforcement facilities, music library.

Freshman class profile. 6,208 applied, 4,552 admitted, 2,500 enrolled.

Mid 50% test scores		Rank in top tenth:	13%
SAT verbal:	450-560	Out-of-state:	3%
SAT math:	440-580	Live on campus:	65%
ACT:	18-23	Fraternities:	9%
Rank in top quarter:	35%	Sororities:	9%

Basis for selection. Out-of-state applicants must rank in top half of graduating class or have 21 ACT or 890 SAT (exclusive of Writing). Resident applicants must have completed specified high school curriculum. Applicants without college preparatory courses subject to remediation. ACT only required for placement for in-state applicants. Interview recommended. Audition recommended for music majors. Portfolio recommended for art and graphic art majors.

High school preparation. 22 units required. Required units include English 4, mathematics 3, social studies 3, history 1, science 3 (laboratory 1) and academic electives 7. Art, drama, music, and computer science also recommended.

2005-2006 Annual costs. Tuition/fees: $4,660; $13,070 out-of-state. Room/board: $4,708. Books/supplies: $800. Personal expenses: $1,550.

2005-2006 Financial aid. Need-based: 1,990 full-time freshmen applied for aid; 1,448 were judged to have need; 1,429 of these received aid. Average need met was 90%. Average scholarship/grant was $4,235; average loan $2,069. 39% of total undergraduate aid awarded as scholarships/grants, 61% as loans/jobs. **Non-need-based:** Awarded to 5,800 full-time undergraduates, including 1,987 freshmen. Scholarships awarded for academics, alumni affiliation, art, athletics, job skills, leadership, minority status, music/drama, ROTC.

Application procedures. Admission: Closing date 8/1. $30 fee, may be waived for applicants with need. Application may be submitted online. Admission notification on a rolling basis. **Financial aid:** Priority date 4/1; no closing date. FAFSA required. Applicants notified on a rolling basis starting 4/1.

Academics. Special study options: Cooperative education, distance learning, double major, ESL, honors, independent study, internships, liberal arts/career combination, study abroad, teacher certification program. **Credit/placement by examination:** AP, CLEP, institutional tests. 30 credit hours maximum toward associate degree, 65 toward bachelor's. **Support services:** Learning center, pre-admission summer program, reduced course load, remedial instruction, study skills assistance, tutoring, writing center.

Majors. Agriculture: Ornamental horticulture, turf management. **Area/ethnic studies:** Canadian. **Biology:** General, bacteriology, ecology. **Business:** General, accounting, business admin, fashion, finance, insurance, management information systems, managerial economics, marketing, office management. **Communications:** General, broadcast journalism, journalism, public relations. **Computer sciences:** General, computer science. **Conservation:** Management/policy, wildlife. **Education:** Art, biology, business, Deaf/hearing impaired, elementary, family/consumer sciences, geography, mathematics, middle, music, physical, science, Spanish, special, speech impaired, technology/industrial arts, trade/industrial. **Engineering:** Science. **Engineering technology:** Architectural, manufacturing, water quality. **English:** Speech/rhetoric. **Family/consumer sciences:** Family studies, food/nutrition, housing. **Foreign languages:** General, French, German, sign language interpretation, Spanish. **Health:** Clinical lab assistant, clinical lab science, clinical lab technology, EMT paramedic, health care admin, medical assistant, medical records admin, medical records technology, nursing (RN), predentistry, premedicine, preop/surgical nursing, prepharmacy. **History:** General. **Legal studies:** Paralegal. **Liberal arts:** Arts/sciences. **Math:** General, statistics. **Parks/recreation:** General, facilities management. **Philosophy/religion:** Philosophy. **Physical sciences:** Chemistry, geology, physics. **Protective services:** Corrections, fire safety technology, forensics, police science, security services. **Psychology:** General. **Public administration:** Social work. **Social sciences:** Anthropology, economics, geography, political science, sociology. **Transportation:** Aviation. **Visual/performing arts:** Art, ceramics, dramatic, drawing, interior design, painting, printmaking, sculpture, studio arts.

Most popular majors. Business/marketing 8%, education 16%, health sciences 16%, security/protective services 18%, social sciences 9%.

Computing on campus. 250 workstations in dormitories, library, computer center, student center. Dormitories wired for high-speed internet access and linked to campus network. Commuter students can connect to campus network. Online course registration, online library, helpline, wireless network available.

Student life. Freshman orientation: Available. Registration and campus tour. **Policies:** Freshmen permitted cars on campus. **Housing:** Guaranteed on-campus for freshmen. Coed dorms, single-sex dorms, apartments, fraternity/sorority housing available. Students required to live on campus until age 21 unless living with parent or guardian. **Activities:** Bands, choral groups, dance, drama, literary magazine, music ensembles, musical theater, radio station, student government, student newspaper, symphony orchestra, 160 religious, political, ethnic, social service, and special interest organizations.

Athletics. NCAA. **Intercollegiate:** Baseball M, basketball, cheerleading, cross-country, football (tackle) M, golf, soccer W, softball W, swimming, tennis, track and field, volleyball W. **Intramural:** Basketball, football (tackle) M, golf, racquetball, softball, tennis, volleyball. **Team name:** Colonels.

Student services. Career counseling, student employment services, health services, personal counseling, placement for graduates, veterans' counselor. **Physically disabled:** Services for visually, speech, hearing impaired.

Contact. E-mail: admissions@eku.edu
Phone: (859) 622-2106 Toll-free number: (800) 465-9191
Fax: (859) 622-8024
Steve Byrn, Director of Admissions, Eastern Kentucky University, SSB CPO 54, 521 Lancaster Avenue, Richmond, KY 40475-3102

Georgetown College

Georgetown, Kentucky
www.georgetowncollege.edu **CB code: 1249**

- Private 4-year liberal arts college affiliated with Southern Baptist Convention
- Residential campus in large town
- 1,364 degree-seeking undergraduates: 4% part-time, 55% women, 4% African American, 1% Asian American, 1% Hispanic American, 1% international
- 487 degree-seeking graduate students
- 95% of applicants admitted
- SAT or ACT (ACT writing optional), application essay required
- 58% graduate within 6 years

General. Founded in 1829. Regionally accredited. **Degrees:** 250 bachelor's awarded; master's offered. **ROTC:** Army, Air Force. **Location:** 12 miles from Lexington, 60 miles from Louisville. **Calendar:** Semester, limited summer session. **Full-time faculty:** 101 total; 88% have terminal degrees, 4% minority, 41% women. **Part-time faculty:** 66 total; 14% have terminal degrees, 4% minority, 59% women. **Class size:** 58% < 20, 41% 20-39, less than 1% 40-49, less than 1% 50-99. **Special facilities:** Planetarium, Foucault pendulum, fine arts building.

Freshman class profile. 1,063 applied, 1,009 admitted, 416 enrolled.

Mid 50% test scores			
SAT verbal:	480-590	Rank in top quarter:	58%
SAT math:	470-590	Rank in top tenth:	31%
ACT:	21-26	Return as sophomores:	85%
GPA 3.50 or higher:	57%	Out-of-state:	14%
GPA 3.0-3.49:	30%	Live on campus:	95%
GPA 2.0-2.99:	13%	International:	1%

Basis for selection. School achievement record, test scores, and rank in top half of class most important. Interview recommended for academically weak or special needs applicants. Audition recommended for music and communication arts majors. Portfolio recommended for art majors.

High school preparation. 20 units recommended. Recommended units include English 4, mathematics 3, social studies 2, science 3 and foreign language 2.

2006-2007 Annual costs. Tuition/fees: $20,700. Per-credit-hour charge for only one course is $630. Room/board: $6,070. Books/supplies: $1,050. Personal expenses: $1,000.

2005-2006 Financial aid. Need-based: 353 full-time freshmen applied for aid; 268 were judged to have need; 268 of these received aid. Average need met was 91%. Average scholarship/grant was $14,359; average loan $3,284. 79% of total undergraduate aid awarded as scholarships/grants, 21% as loans/jobs. **Non-need-based:** Awarded to 705 full-time undergraduates, including 262 freshmen. Scholarships awarded for academics, art, athletics, leadership, minority status, music/drama, religious affiliation, ROTC.

Application procedures. Admission: Priority date 5/1; deadline 8/1 (postmark date). $30 fee, may be waived for applicants with need. Application may be submitted online. Admission notification on a rolling basis beginning on or about 10/1. Must reply by May 1 or within 4 week(s) if notified thereafter. **Financial aid:** Priority date 2/15; no closing date. FAFSA, institutional form required. Applicants notified on a rolling basis starting 3/1; must reply by 5/1.

Academics. Special study options: Accelerated study, cooperative education, double major, dual enrollment of high school students, honors, independent study, internships, liberal arts/career combination, student-designed major, study abroad, teacher certification program. 3-2 nursing program with University of Kentucky. **Credit/placement by examination:** AP, CLEP, IB, SAT, ACT, institutional tests. **Support services:** Study skills assistance, tutoring, writing center.

Majors. Area/ethnic studies: American, European. **Biology:** General, ecology. **Business:** General, accounting, business admin. **Computer sciences:** General. **Education:** Elementary, middle, music. **English:** English lit. **Foreign languages:** French, German, Spanish. **Health:** Athletic training, predentistry, prepharmacy, preveterinary. **History:** General. **Liberal arts:** Arts/sciences. **Math:** General. **Parks/recreation:** Exercise sciences, health/fitness. **Philosophy/religion:** Philosophy, religion. **Physical sciences:** Chemistry, physics. **Psychology:** General. **Social sciences:** Economics, political science, sociology. **Visual/performing arts:** Dramatic, studio arts.

Most popular majors. Biology 12%, business/marketing 15%, communications/journalism 11%, education 8%, psychology 10%, social sciences 8%, visual/performing arts 7%.

Computing on campus. 175 workstations in library, computer center, student center. Dormitories wired for high-speed internet access and linked to campus network. Commuter students can connect to campus network. Online course registration, online library, helpline, repair service, wireless network available.

Student life. **Freshman orientation:** Mandatory, $100 fee. Preregistration for classes offered. 5-day orientation held just prior to beginning of fall semester. **Policies:** Academic honor code enforced. Freshmen permitted cars on campus. **Housing:** Single-sex dorms, apartments, fraternity/sorority housing available. $200 deposit, deadline 5/1. Most students housed in mini-dorms of fewer than 80 students each. New apartments available for seniors. **Activities:** Bands, choral groups, dance, drama, literary magazine, music ensembles, musical theater, radio station, student government, student newspaper, Baptist Student Union, Fellowship of Christian Athletes, Union of Black Leaders, United Nations of Georgetown.

Athletics. NAIA. **Intercollegiate:** Baseball M, basketball, cheerleading M, cross-country, football (tackle) M, golf, soccer, softball W, tennis, track and field, volleyball W. **Intramural:** Basketball, equestrian, football (non-tackle), golf, racquetball, soccer, softball, table tennis, tennis, volleyball. **Team name:** Tigers.

Student services. Alcohol/substance abuse counseling, campus ministries, career counseling, student employment services, financial aid counseling, health services, minority student services, personal counseling, placement for graduates.

Contact. E-mail: admissions@georgetowncollege.edu
Phone: (502) 863-8009 Toll-free number: (800) 788-9985
Fax: (502) 868-7733
Johnnie Johnson, Director of Admissions, Georgetown College, 400 East College Street, Georgetown, KY 40324

ITT Technical Institute: Louisville

Louisville, Kentucky
www.itt-tech.edu **CB code: 2728**

- For-profit 4-year technical college
- Large city

General. Accredited by ACICS. **Calendar:** Quarter.

Annual costs/financial aid. Tuition varies by program, $260-$368 per credit hour.

Contact. Phone: (502) 327-7424
Director of Recruitment, 10509 Timberwood Circle, Louisville, KY 40223

Kentucky Christian University

Grayson, Kentucky
www.kcu.edu **CB code: 1377**

- Private 4-year Bible and liberal arts college affiliated with Christian Church/Church of Christ
- Residential campus in small town
- 550 degree-seeking undergraduates
- 70% of applicants admitted
- SAT or ACT (ACT writing optional), application essay required

General. Founded in 1919. Regionally accredited; also accredited by ABHE. All students required to major in Bible as a second degree. **Degrees:** 103 bachelor's awarded; master's offered. **Location:** 25 miles from Ashland, 100 miles from Lexington. **Calendar:** Semester, limited summer session. **Full-time faculty:** 40 total. **Part-time faculty:** 20 total. **Class size:** 62% < 20, 28% 20-39, 5% 40-49, 5% 50-99.

Freshman class profile. 335 applied, 235 admitted, 142 enrolled.

Mid 50% test scores			
SAT verbal:	440-560	Rank in top quarter:	43%
SAT math:	430-560	Rank in top tenth:	18%
ACT:	18-24	Out-of-state:	74%
		Live on campus:	95%

Basis for selection. High school grades, rank in class, ACT or SAT test scores, personal references, and religious commitment given equal weight. Interview recommended for academically weak.

2005-2006 Annual costs. Tuition/fees: $10,950. Room/board: $4,514. Books/supplies: $900. Personal expenses: $2,012.

Financial aid. **Non-need-based:** Scholarships awarded for academics, alumni affiliation, leadership, music/drama, religious affiliation.

Application procedures. **Admission:** No deadline. $25 fee. Application may be submitted online. Admission notification on a rolling basis. **Financial aid:** Priority date 4/1; no closing date. FAFSA required. Applicants notified on a rolling basis starting 3/15; must reply within 2 week(s) of notification.

Academics. **Special study options:** Cooperative education, distance learning, double major, independent study, internships, liberal arts/career combination, study abroad, teacher certification program. **Credit/placement by examination:** AP, CLEP, IB. **Support services:** Reduced course load, remedial instruction, tutoring, writing center.

Majors. **Business:** Business admin, finance. **Education:** Elementary, middle, music. **History:** General. **Interdisciplinary:** Behavioral sciences. **Liberal arts:** Arts/sciences. **Math:** General. **Philosophy/religion:** Religion. **Psychology:** General. **Public administration:** Social work. **Theology:** Bible, pastoral counseling, religious ed, sacred music, theology. **Visual/performing arts:** Music performance.

Most popular majors. Business/marketing 11%, education 27%, philosophy/religious studies 42%, social sciences 11%.

Computing on campus. 50 workstations in library, computer center, student center. Dormitories linked to campus network. Commuter students can connect to campus network. Online library, helpline, repair service available.

Student life. **Freshman orientation:** Mandatory. **Policies:** Religious observance required. Freshmen permitted cars on campus. **Housing:** Guaranteed on-campus for all undergraduates. Single-sex dorms, apartments available. All students under 26 not living with parents must live in on-campus housing. Honors housing available for upper-class students of good merit. **Activities:** Jazz band, choral groups, drama, music ensembles, student government, Student Council, Rotaract, Pi Chi Delta, Laos Alpha, Matheteuo, Priscillas, Revelation.

Athletics. NCCAA. **Intercollegiate:** Basketball, cross-country, soccer, tennis, volleyball W. **Intramural:** Basketball, football (non-tackle) M, soccer, softball, table tennis, volleyball. **Team name:** Knights.

Student services. Campus ministries, financial aid counseling, health services, minority student services, personal counseling. **Physically disabled:** Services for visually, hearing impaired.

Contact. E-mail: sdeakins@kcu.edu
Phone: (606) 474-3266 Toll-free number: (800) 522-3181
Fax: (606) 474-3155
Sandra Deakins, Vice President of Enrollment Management, Kentucky Christian University, 100 Academic Parkway, Grayson, KY 41143-2205

Kentucky Mountain Bible College

Vancleve, Kentucky
www.kmbc.edu **CB code: 1384**

- Private 4-year Bible college affiliated with Kentucky Mountain Holiness Association
- Residential campus in small town
- 59 degree-seeking undergraduates
- ACT (writing optional), application essay required

General. Founded in 1931. Accredited by ABHE. **Degrees:** 8 bachelor's, 2 associate awarded. **Location:** 75 miles from Lexington. **Calendar:** Semester. **Full-time faculty:** 10 total. **Part-time faculty:** 10 total.

Freshman class profile.

Out-of-state:	86%	Live on campus:	100%

Basis for selection. All students must have C average or above and provide 2 recommendations. 15 ACT required. Provisional admission granted. Interview recommended.

High school preparation. 18 units required. Required and recommended units include English 4, mathematics 2, history 2 and science 2. A total of 10 units in English, math, science or language required out of 18 units.

2006-2007 Annual costs. Tuition/fees (projected): $5,260. Room/board: $3,200. Books/supplies: $400. Personal expenses: $250.

2005-2006 Financial aid. All financial aid based on need.

Application procedures. **Admission:** Priority date 6/1; no deadline. $25 fee. Admission notification on a rolling basis. **Financial aid:** Priority date

4/1, closing date 6/30. FAFSA required. Applicants notified on a rolling basis; must reply by 7/1.

Academics. **Special study options:** Internships. **Credit/placement by examination:** CLEP. **Support services:** Reduced course load.

Majors. **Communications:** General. **Theology:** Missionary, religious ed, sacred music, theology.

Computing on campus. 12 workstations in library, computer center.

Student life. **Freshman orientation:** Mandatory. 2-day program, includes Bible-knowledge testing. **Policies:** Religious observance required. Freshmen permitted cars on campus. **Housing:** Guaranteed on-campus for all undergraduates. Single-sex dorms, apartments available. **Activities:** Choral groups, drama, radio station, student government, Missionary Student Involvement group, Student Council, class organizations.

Student services. Financial aid counseling, personal counseling.

Contact. E-mail: kmbc@kmbc.edu
Phone: (606) 693-5000 Toll-free number: (800) 879-5622
Fax: (606) 693-4884
Jay Wisker, Chief Admissions Counselor, Kentucky Mountain Bible College, Box 10, Vancleve, KY 41385

Kentucky State University

Frankfort, Kentucky — **CB member**
www.kysu.edu — **CB code: 1368**

- Public 4-year university
- Residential campus in large town
- 1,908 degree-seeking undergraduates: 16% part-time, 59% women, 67% African American, 1% Asian American
- 158 degree-seeking graduate students
- SAT or ACT required
- 30% graduate within 6 years; 8% enter graduate study

General. Founded in 1886. Regionally accredited. **Degrees:** 228 bachelor's, 50 associate awarded; master's offered. **ROTC:** Army, Air Force. **Location:** 50 miles from Louisville, 25 miles from Lexington. **Calendar:** Semester, limited summer session. **Full-time faculty:** 146 total; 39% women. **Part-time faculty:** 5 total; 80% women. **Class size:** 64% < 20, 36% 20-39, less than 1% 40-49, less than 1% 50-99. **Special facilities:** Center for study of Kentucky African-Americans, aquaculture program, Land Grant Mission.

Freshman class profile.

Mid 50% test scores		**ACT:**	15-19
SAT verbal:	390-490	**Return as sophomores:**	69%
SAT math:	380-490	**Out-of-state:**	12%

Basis for selection. Unconditional admission for graduates of accredited high schools meeting Pre-College Curriculum (PCC) requirements established by Kentucky Council on Higher Education and having admission index of 430. Interview recommended for nursing majors and applicants to College of Leadership Studies. Audition recommended for music majors. Portfolio recommended for art majors. Essay required of applicants to College of Leadership Studies.

High school preparation. 20 units required. Required and recommended units include English 4, mathematics 3, history 2, science 2 and foreign language 2.

2005-2006 Annual costs. Tuition/fees: $4,170; $10,612 out-of-state. Room/board: $5,688. Books/supplies: $510. Personal expenses: $800.

Financial aid. All financial aid based on need.

Application procedures. **Admission:** No deadline. $22 fee, may be waived for applicants with need. Admission notification on a rolling basis. **Financial aid:** Priority date 4/15, closing date 5/31. FAFSA, institutional form required. Applicants notified by 7/1; must reply by 7/15.

Academics. **Special study options:** Accelerated study, combined bachelor's/graduate degree, cooperative education, distance learning, double major, dual enrollment of high school students, ESL, exchange student, honors, independent study, internships, liberal arts/career combination, student-designed major, study abroad, teacher certification program, weekend college. Liberal studies Great Books program. **Credit/placement by examination:** AP, CLEP, SAT, ACT, institutional tests. 16 credit hours maximum toward associate degree, 32 toward bachelor's. **Support services:** Learning center, preadmission summer program, reduced course load, remedial instruction, study skills assistance, tutoring, writing center.

Majors. **Biology:** General. **Business:** General, accounting, business admin, managerial economics, marketing. **Computer sciences:** General, computer graphics, computer science. **Education:** General, art, biology, early childhood, elementary, English, history, mathematics, music, physical, secondary, social studies. **Family/consumer sciences:** Clothing/textiles, family studies. **Health:** Clinical lab science, nursing (RN). **History:** General. **Liberal arts:** Arts/sciences. **Math:** General. **Physical sciences:** Chemistry. **Protective services:** Criminal justice, police science. **Psychology:** General. **Public administration:** General, social work. **Social sciences:** General, political science, sociology. **Visual/performing arts:** Studio arts.

Most popular majors. Biology 7%, business/marketing 22%, computer/information sciences 11%, education 9%, family/consumer sciences 6%, liberal arts 6%, psychology 7%, security/protective services 10%.

Computing on campus. 125 workstations in dormitories, library, computer center, student center. Dormitories wired for high-speed internet access and linked to campus network. Repair service available.

Student life. **Freshman orientation:** Available. **Policies:** Freshmen permitted cars on campus. **Housing:** Guaranteed on-campus for freshmen. Single-sex dorms available. $208 partly refundable deposit, deadline 8/1. **Activities:** Bands, choral groups, dance, drama, music ensembles, musical theater, opera, student government, student newspaper, Alpha Phi Omega, Wesley Club, Baptist Student Union, Circle-K, international student association, NAACP, Optimist Club, Student Government Association.

Athletics. NCAA. **Intercollegiate:** Baseball M, basketball, cross-country, football (tackle) M, golf M, softball W, tennis, track and field, volleyball W. **Intramural:** Basketball, bowling, football (tackle) M, soccer, softball W, swimming, table tennis, tennis, track and field, volleyball. **Team name:** Thoroughbreds.

Student services. Adult student services, career counseling, student employment services, financial aid counseling, health services, on-campus daycare, personal counseling, placement for graduates, veterans' counselor. **Physically disabled:** Services for visually, hearing impaired.

Contact. Phone: (502) 597-6813 Toll-free number: (800) 633-9413
Fax: (502) 597-6239
James Burrell, Director of Admissions, Kentucky State University, 400 East Main Street, ASB13, Frankfort, KY 40601

Kentucky Wesleyan College

Owensboro, Kentucky — **CB member**
www.kwc.edu — **CB code: 1369**

- Private 4-year liberal arts college affiliated with United Methodist Church
- Residential campus in small city
- 734 degree-seeking undergraduates: 2% part-time, 49% women, 10% African American, 2% Hispanic American, 1% international
- 77% of applicants admitted
- SAT or ACT (ACT writing recommended) required
- 45% graduate within 6 years; 26% enter graduate study

General. Founded in 1858. Regionally accredited. Co-curricular leadership program available. **Degrees:** 97 bachelor's awarded. **Location:** 116 miles from Louisville, 133 miles from Nashville, Tennessee. **Calendar:** Semester, limited summer session. **Full-time faculty:** 36 total; 75% have terminal degrees, 6% minority, 31% women. **Part-time faculty:** 34 total; 24% have terminal degrees, 68% women. **Class size:** 70% < 20, 29% 20-39, less than 1% 40-49. **Special facilities:** Center for the Sciences, Center for the Arts, Health and Recreation Center, criminal justice research center, fully computerized writing workshop, center for business studies.

Freshman class profile. 1,074 applied, 828 admitted, 209 enrolled.

Mid 50% test scores		**Rank in top tenth:**	19%
SAT verbal:	400-570	**End year in good standing:**	85%
SAT math:	460-580	**Return as sophomores:**	71%
ACT:	18-25	**Out-of-state:**	26%
GPA 3.50 or higher:	43%	**Live on campus:**	73%
GPA 3.0-3.49:	27%	**Fraternities:**	18%
GPA 2.0-2.99:	28%	**Sororities:**	27%
Rank in top quarter:	30%		

Basis for selection. Secondary school record very important. Test scores, GPA, class rank, and school activities important. Interview recommended.

High school preparation. College-preparatory program required. 13 units required. Required and recommended units include English 4, mathematics 3, social studies 3, science 3 and foreign language 2.

2005-2006 Annual costs. Tuition/fees: $13,115. Room/board: $5,600. Books/supplies: $1,250. Personal expenses: $2,000.

2004-2005 Financial aid. **Need-based:** 211 full-time freshmen applied for aid; 184 were judged to have need; 183 of these received aid. Average need met was 75%. Average scholarship/grant was $10,420; average loan $2,339. 77% of total undergraduate aid awarded as scholarships/grants, 23% as loans/jobs. **Non-need-based:** Awarded to 182 full-time undergraduates, including 69 freshmen. Scholarships awarded for academics, alumni affiliation, art, athletics, leadership, music/drama, religious affiliation, state residency.

Application procedures. **Admission:** No deadline. No application fee. Application may be submitted online. Admission notification on a rolling basis. **Financial aid:** Priority date 3/15; no closing date. FAFSA required. Applicants notified on a rolling basis starting 2/15; must reply within 2 week(s) of notification.

Academics. **Special study options:** Double major, independent study, internships, liberal arts/career combination, study abroad, teacher certification program, Washington semester. Summer research stipends include toxicology in New Mexico, molecular biology at LSU, science ethics at Yale University; course offerings in New York City during spring break. **Credit/placement by examination:** AP, CLEP, IB, institutional tests. 42 credit hours maximum toward bachelor's degree. International Baccalaureate Diploma credit will be awarded for advanced course scores of 6 or 7, with up to 10 hours of credit awarded. **Support services:** Learning center, reduced course load, remedial instruction, study skills assistance, tutoring, writing center.

Majors. **Biology:** General, zoology. **Business:** General, accounting, business admin. **Communications:** General. **Computer sciences:** General. **Education:** Art, biology, chemistry, elementary, English, mathematics, middle, physical, social studies, Spanish. **English:** English lit. **Foreign languages:** Spanish. **History:** General. **Math:** General. **Parks/recreation:** Sports admin. **Philosophy/religion:** Religion. **Physical sciences:** Chemistry, physics. **Protective services:** Criminal justice. **Psychology:** General. **Public administration:** Human services. **Social sciences:** Political science, sociology. **Visual/performing arts:** Art, studio arts.

Most popular majors. Biology 6%, business/marketing 21%, communications/journalism 15%, education 14%, English 7%, security/protective services 9%.

Computing on campus. Dormitories wired for high-speed internet access and linked to campus network. Commuter students can connect to campus network. Online library, helpline, repair service, wireless network available.

Student life. **Freshman orientation:** Mandatory, $100 fee. Preregistration for classes offered. Held 3 days during opening weekend of fall term. **Policies:** Freshmen permitted cars on campus. **Housing:** Guaranteed on-campus for freshmen. Coed dorms, single-sex dorms, fraternity/sorority housing, substance-free housing available. $100 deposit, deadline 5/1. **Activities:** Bands, choral groups, dance, drama, literary magazine, music ensembles, radio station, student government, student newspaper, student activities programming board, Baptist Student Union, United Methodist Student Fellowship, Brothers and Sisters in Christ, criminal justice association, Campus Ministries Team, Kentucky Wesleyan Singers, College Republicans, Young Democrats.

Athletics. NCAA. **Intercollegiate:** Baseball M, basketball, cheerleading, football (tackle) M, golf, soccer, softball W, tennis W, volleyball W. **Intramural:** Basketball, bowling, football (non-tackle), golf, racquetball, soccer, softball, table tennis, tennis, volleyball. **Team name:** Panthers.

Student services. Alcohol/substance abuse counseling, campus ministries, career counseling, student employment services, financial aid counseling, health services, on-campus daycare, personal counseling, placement for graduates, veterans' counselor.

Contact. E-mail: admitme@kwc.edu
Phone: (270) 852-3120 Toll-free number: (800) 999-0592
Fax: (270) 852-3133
Claude Bacon, Dean of Admissions and Finanancial Aid, Kentucky Wesleyan College, 3000 Frederica Street, Owensboro, KY 42302-1039

Lindsey Wilson College

Columbia, Kentucky
www.lindsey.edu **CB code: 1409**

- Private 4-year liberal arts college affiliated with United Methodist Church
- Residential campus in small town
- 1,611 degree-seeking undergraduates: 10% part-time, 65% women, 8% African American, 1% Asian American, 2% Hispanic American, 3% international
- 280 graduate students
- 80% of applicants admitted
- ACT (writing optional) required

General. Founded in 1903. Regionally accredited. **Degrees:** 233 bachelor's, 49 associate awarded; master's offered. **Location:** 100 miles from Louisville. **Calendar:** Semester, limited summer session. **Full-time faculty:** 73 total; 68% have terminal degrees, 6% minority, 42% women. **Part-time faculty:** 47 total.

Freshman class profile. 1,621 applied, 1,303 admitted, 416 enrolled.

Return as sophomores:	53%	**Live on campus:**	68%
Out-of-state:	3%		

Basis for selection. Selective admission to education and human services programs. ACCUPLACER may be taken for placement instead of ACT. Interview recommended.

2006-2007 Annual costs. Tuition/fees: $14,438. Room/board: $6,163. Books/supplies: $700. Personal expenses: $800.

2004-2005 Financial aid. All financial aid based on need. 405 full-time freshmen applied for aid; 382 were judged to have need; 382 of these received aid. Average scholarship/grant was $6,356; average loan $2,300. 99% of total undergraduate aid awarded as scholarships/grants, 1% as loans/jobs.

Application procedures. **Admission:** Priority date 6/1; no deadline. No application fee. Application may be submitted online. Admission notification on a rolling basis beginning on or about 1/1. **Financial aid:** Priority date 4/15; no closing date. FAFSA, institutional form required. Applicants notified on a rolling basis starting 5/1; must reply within 2 week(s) of notification.

Academics. **Special study options:** Dual enrollment of high school students, independent study, internships, student-designed major, study abroad, teacher certification program, weekend college. On-campus and extension evening program for associate degree in business management and computer science, weekend extension program in human services. **Credit/placement by examination:** AP, CLEP, ACT. 16 credit hours maximum toward associate degree, 32 toward bachelor's. **Support services:** Learning center, reduced course load, remedial instruction, study skills assistance, tutoring, writing center.

Majors. **Area/ethnic studies:** American. **Biology:** General. **Business:** Business admin. **Communications:** General, journalism. **Education:** Art, biology, elementary, English, mathematics, middle, physical, secondary, social science. **History:** General. **Liberal arts:** Humanities. **Math:** General. **Parks/recreation:** Health/fitness. **Philosophy/religion:** Christian. **Protective services:** Criminal justice. **Psychology:** General. **Social sciences:** General. **Visual/performing arts:** Studio arts.

Most popular majors. Biology 7%, business/marketing 7%, education 6%, public administration/social services 63%.

Computing on campus. 100 workstations in library, computer center. Dormitories wired for high-speed internet access and linked to campus network. Commuter students can connect to campus network. Online course registration, online library, wireless network available.

Student life. **Freshman orientation:** Available. Preregistration for classes offered. **Policies:** Freshmen permitted cars on campus. **Housing:** Single-sex dorms, apartments available. $40 deposit. All students not living with family must live in campus housing. **Activities:** Choral groups, drama, literary magazine, music ensembles, student government, student newspaper, Christian student organizations, Student Ambassadors, Black Student Union, Students in Free Enterprise, Raider Republicans, international student association.

Athletics. NAIA. **Intercollegiate:** Baseball M, basketball, bowling, cross-country, golf, soccer, softball W, tennis, track and field, volleyball W. **Intramural:** Basketball, football (tackle), softball, table tennis, tennis, volleyball. **Team name:** Blue Raiders.

Student services. Alcohol/substance abuse counseling, campus ministries, career counseling, student employment services, financial aid counseling, health services, personal counseling, placement for graduates. **Physically disabled:** Services for visually impaired.

Contact. E-mail: admissions@lindsey.edu
Phone: (270) 384-8100 Toll-free number: (800) 264-0138
Fax: (270) 384-8591
Traci Pooler, Director of Admissions, Lindsey Wilson College, 210 Lindsey Wilson Street, Columbia, KY 42728

Mid-Continent University

Mayfield, Kentucky
www.midcontinent.edu **CB code: 0254**

- Private 4-year Bible and liberal arts college affiliated with Southern Baptist Convention
- Commuter campus in large town
- 972 degree-seeking undergraduates: 16% part-time, 53% women
- SAT or ACT, application essay required
- 23% graduate within 6 years

General. Founded in 1949. Regionally accredited. Accelerated programs in organizational leadership for adult learners available. **Degrees:** 128 bachelor's, 59 associate awarded. **Location:** 20 miles from Paducah; 125 from Nashville, Tennessee. **Calendar:** Semester, limited summer session. **Full-time faculty:** 20 total; 70% have terminal degrees, 20% minority, 30% women. **Part-time faculty:** 36 total; 11% have terminal degrees, 11% minority, 17% women. **Class size:** 100% 20-39.

Freshman class profile.

Mid 50% test scores		**Rank in top tenth:**	10%
SAT verbal:	450-490	**End year in good standing:**	75%
SAT math:	510-610	**Return as sophomores:**	56%
ACT:	15-21	**Out-of-state:**	16%
Rank in top quarter:	34%		

Basis for selection. Secondary school record and standardized test scores most important. Entering students tested in mathematics and English. **Homeschooled:** Transcript of courses and grades, letter of recommendation (nonparent) required.

High school preparation. Required units include English 4, mathematics 2, social studies 2, science 2 and foreign language 1.

2005-2006 Annual costs. Tuition/fees: $10,100. Room/board: $5,700. Books/supplies: $800. Personal expenses: $1,300.

2005-2006 Financial aid. Need-based: 76 full-time freshmen applied for aid; 64 were judged to have need; 64 of these received aid. Average need met was 60%. Average scholarship/grant was $4,270; average loan $1,953. 62% of total undergraduate aid awarded as scholarships/grants, 38% as loans/jobs. **Non-need-based:** Scholarships awarded for academics.

Application procedures. Admission: Priority date 8/1; no deadline. $20 fee, may be waived for applicants with need. Application may be submitted online. Admission notification on a rolling basis. **Financial aid:** Priority date 3/15, closing date 5/30. FAFSA, institutional form required. Applicants notified on a rolling basis starting 4/1.

Academics. Bachelor of ministry degree offered after 36 hours above earned baccalaureate degree from regionally accredited institution. **Special study options:** Accelerated study, cooperative education, double major, dual enrollment of high school students, independent study, study abroad, teacher certification program. **Credit/placement by examination:** CLEP, institutional tests. 30 credit hours maximum toward bachelor's degree. **Support services:** Remedial instruction, tutoring.

Majors. Business: Business admin, organizational behavior. **Education:** Elementary. **Psychology:** General. **Social sciences:** General. **Theology:** Bible, missionary, religious ed.

Most popular majors. Business/marketing 32%.

Computing on campus. 24 workstations in dormitories, library, computer center. Dormitories wired for high-speed internet access. Online library available.

Student life. Freshman orientation: Mandatory. Preregistration for classes offered. 2-3 day orientation process at beginning of academic year. **Policies:** Religious observance required. Freshmen permitted cars on campus. **Housing:** Single-sex dorms available. $200 nonrefundable deposit, deadline 8/1. **Activities:** Student government, student newspaper, Baptist Student Union, Fellowship of Christian Athletes, psychology club, international student association.

Athletics. NAIA, NCCAA. **Intercollegiate:** Baseball M, soccer M, softball W. **Team name:** Lady Cougars, Cougars.

Student services. Campus ministries, career counseling, financial aid counseling, personal counseling, veterans' counselor. **Physically disabled:** Services for visually impaired.

Contact. E-mail: admissions@midcontinent.edu
Phone: (270) 247-8521 ext. 238 Toll-free number: (866) 894-8878
Fax: (270) 247-3115
Butch Booth, Director of Admissions, Mid-Continent University, 99 Powell Road East, Mayfield, KY 42066-0357

Midway College

Midway, Kentucky **CB member**
www.midway.edu **CB code: 1467**

- Private 4-year liberal arts college for women affiliated with Christian Church (Disciples of Christ)
- Residential campus in small town
- 1,230 degree-seeking undergraduates: 29% part-time, 88% women, 6% African American, 1% international
- SAT or ACT required
- 34% graduate within 6 years

General. Founded in 1847. Regionally accredited. Men admitted to evening and weekend programs in nursing, business administration, computer information systems, healthcare managment, human resource management. **Degrees:** 218 bachelor's, 61 associate awarded. **ROTC:** Army. **Location:** 12 miles from Lexington, 60 miles from Louisville. **Calendar:** Semester, limited summer session. **Full-time faculty:** 50 total; 44% have terminal degrees, 64% women. **Part-time faculty:** 99 total; 17% have terminal degrees, 63% women. **Class size:** 79% < 20, 19% 20-39, 2% 40-49. **Special facilities:** Equine science center, riding arena, campus farm.

Freshman class profile. 423 applied, 319 admitted, 161 enrolled.

Mid 50% test scores		**Rank in top quarter:**	34%
SAT verbal:	470-660	**Rank in top tenth:**	15%
SAT math:	440-630	**End year in good standing:**	75%
ACT:	17-22	**Return as sophomores:**	53%
GPA 3.50 or higher:	37%	**Out-of-state:**	16%
GPA 3.0-3.49:	24%	**Live on campus:**	33%
GPA 2.0-2.99:	36%		

Basis for selection. Open admission, but selective for some programs. High school record and test scores important. Essay and letters of recommendation encouraged. More competitive requirements established for certain programs such as biology, paralegal, nursing. Interview required for majors in nursing; also required of academically weak. Essay recommended for students who are conditionally admitted.

High school preparation. 15 units required. Required and recommended units include English 4, mathematics 3, social studies 1, history 1 and science 2. Specific college-preparatory program required for some majors.

2005-2006 Annual costs. Tuition/fees: $13,800. Room/board: $6,200. Books/supplies: $1,000. Personal expenses: $1,000.

2005-2006 Financial aid. Need-based: 116 full-time freshmen applied for aid; 105 were judged to have need; 105 of these received aid. Average need met was 57%. Average scholarship/grant was $6,530; average loan $2,475. 49% of total undergraduate aid awarded as scholarships/grants, 51% as loans/jobs. **Non-need-based:** Awarded to 70 full-time undergraduates, including 11 freshmen. Scholarships awarded for academics, alumni affiliation, art, athletics, leadership, minority status, music/drama, religious affiliation. **Additional information:** Audition required of applicants for music scholarships. Portfolio required for art scholarships.

Application procedures. Admission: Priority date 4/1; no deadline. $25 fee, may be waived for applicants with need. Application may be submitted online. Admission notification on a rolling basis. Must reply by May 1 or within 4 week(s) if notified thereafter. **Financial aid:** Priority date 4/1, closing date 8/1. FAFSA, institutional form required. Applicants notified on a rolling basis; must reply within 4 week(s) of notification.

Academics. Special study options: Accelerated study, cooperative education, distance learning, double major, dual enrollment of high school students, independent study, internships, liberal arts/career combination, study abroad, teacher certification program. Evening business program. **Credit/placement by examination:** AP, CLEP, IB, institutional tests. 12 credit hours maximum toward associate degree, 12 toward bachelor's. **Support services:** Learning center, reduced course load, remedial instruction, tutoring, writing center.

Majors. Agriculture: Equestrian studies, equine science. **Biology:** General. **Business:** Banking/financial services, business admin, managerial economics. **Computer sciences:** General. **Conservation:** Environmental science. **Education:** Elementary, multi-level teacher, secondary, special. **English:**

English lit. **Health:** Health care admin, nursing (RN). **Interdisciplinary:** Intercultural. **Math:** General. **Psychology:** General.

Most popular majors. Agriculture 11%, business/marketing 38%, education 34%, health sciences 12%.

Computing on campus. 60 workstations in dormitories, library, computer center, student center. Dormitories linked to campus network. Commuter students can connect to campus network. Helpline, repair service available.

Student life. Freshman orientation: Mandatory. Preregistration for classes offered. 2-3 day orientation prior to start of term. **Policies:** Freshmen permitted cars on campus. **Housing:** Guaranteed on-campus for all undergraduates. Substance-free housing available. $25 deposit, deadline 5/1. All students under 21, unmarried, and not living at home required to live in campus housing. Handicapped accessible dorm. **Activities:** Choral groups, student government, student newspaper, vespers committee, international student organization, Baptist Student Union, Disciples on Campus, Ruth Slack Roach Scholars.

Athletics. NAIA. **Intercollegiate:** Basketball W, equestrian W, softball W, tennis W. **Team name:** Eagles.

Student services. Adult student services, career counseling, student employment services, financial aid counseling, health services, personal counseling, placement for graduates.

Contact. E-mail: admissions@midway.edu
Phone: (859) 846-5346 Toll-free number: (800) 755-0031
Fax: (859) 846-5328
Jim Wombles, Chief Enrollment Officer, Midway College, 512 East Stephen Street, Midway, KY 40347-1120

Morehead State University

Morehead, Kentucky
www.moreheadstate.edu **CB code: 1487**

- Public 4-year university
- Residential campus in small town
- 6,971 degree-seeking undergraduates: 15% part-time, 61% women, 4% African American, 1% Hispanic American
- 1,029 degree-seeking graduate students
- 69% of applicants admitted
- SAT or ACT (ACT writing optional) required
- 38% graduate within 6 years

General. Founded in 1922. Regionally accredited. **Degrees:** 1,038 bachelor's, 125 associate awarded; master's offered. **ROTC:** Army. **Location:** 65 miles from Lexington; 70 miles from Huntington, West Virginia. **Calendar:** Semester, extensive summer session. **Full-time faculty:** 378 total; 65% have terminal degrees, 11% minority, 45% women. **Part-time faculty:** 156 total; 2% minority, 56% women. **Special facilities:** Planetarium, agriculture complex, outdoor learning center at Cave Run, Kentucky folk art center, Space Science Center, space tracking radio telescope.

Freshman class profile. 5,092 applied, 3,529 admitted, 1,300 enrolled.

Mid 50% test scores		**Rank in top tenth:**	17%
ACT:	17-22	**Return as sophomores:**	61%
GPA 3.50 or higher:	36%	**Out-of-state:**	18%
GPA 3.0-3.49:	28%	**Live on campus:**	70%
GPA 2.0-2.99:	32%	**Fraternities:**	20%
Rank in top quarter:	39%	**Sororities:**	20%

Basis for selection. Test scores and GPA used to calculate index to determine admission. Status and review of pre-college curriculum important. ACT recommended. Interview recommended for applicants to specialized allied health programs. Audition recommended for music majors. **Homeschooled:** Statement describing homeschool structure and mission, transcript of courses and grades, interview, letter of recommendation (nonparent) required.

High school preparation. College-preparatory program required. 22 units required. Required and recommended units include English 4, mathematics 3, social studies 3, science 3 (laboratory 1), foreign language 2 and academic electives 7. Recommend 1 unit history and appreciation of fine arts.

2005-2006 Annual costs. Tuition/fees: $4,320; $11,480 out-of-state. Room/board: $4,798. Books/supplies: $500. Personal expenses: $800.

2005-2006 Financial aid. Need-based: 1,137 full-time freshmen applied for aid; 877 were judged to have need; 869 of these received aid. Average need met was 88%. Average scholarship/grant was $4,339; average loan $2,570. 56% of total undergraduate aid awarded as scholarships/grants, 44% as loans/jobs. **Non-need-based:** Awarded to 3,275 full-time undergraduates, including 1,070 freshmen. Scholarships awarded for academics, alumni affiliation, art, athletics, leadership, minority status, music/drama, ROTC, state residency.

Application procedures. Admission: No deadline. No application fee. Application may be submitted online. Admission notification on a rolling basis. **Financial aid:** Priority date 3/15; no closing date. FAFSA, institutional form required. Applicants notified on a rolling basis.

Academics. 2-year transfer programs in prechiropractic, predentistry, preengineering, preforestry, prelaw, premedicine, preoptometry, prepharmacy, prephysical therapy, preveterinary medicine offered. **Special study options:** Accelerated study, cooperative education, distance learning, double major, dual enrollment of high school students, exchange student, honors, independent study, internships, student-designed major, study abroad, teacher certification program, Washington semester, weekend college. **Credit/placement by examination:** AP, CLEP, institutional tests. 16 credit hours maximum toward associate degree, 32 toward bachelor's. **Support services:** Learning center, pre-admission summer program, remedial instruction, study skills assistance, tutoring, writing center.

Majors. Agriculture: General. **Biology:** General, ecology. **Business:** Accounting, business admin, finance, management information systems, managerial economics, marketing, real estate. **Communications:** General. **Computer sciences:** General. **Education:** Business, early childhood, elementary, family/consumer sciences, health, middle, physical, special. **Engineering technology:** Manufacturing. **English:** English lit, speech/rhetoric. **Family/consumer sciences:** Work/family studies. **Foreign languages:** French, Spanish. **Health:** Medical radiologic technology/radiation therapy, nursing (RN). **History:** General. **Legal studies:** Paralegal. **Math:** General. **Parks/recreation:** Exercise sciences. **Philosophy/religion:** Philosophy. **Physical sciences:** Chemistry, geology, physics. **Psychology:** General. **Public administration:** Social work. **Social sciences:** General, geography, political science, sociology. **Visual/performing arts:** Dramatic, studio arts.

Most popular majors. Business/marketing 18%, communications/journalism 7%, education 17%, engineering/engineering technologies 6%, liberal arts 10%, social sciences 7%, visual/performing arts 6%.

Computing on campus. 1,000 workstations in dormitories, library, computer center, student center. Dormitories wired for high-speed internet access and linked to campus network. Commuter students can connect to campus network. Online library, helpline, student web hosting, wireless network available.

Student life. Freshman orientation: Available. Preregistration for classes offered. Offered several times in June and July. **Policies:** Freshmen permitted cars on campus. **Housing:** Coed dorms, single-sex dorms, special housing for disabled, apartments, fraternity/sorority housing available. $100 fully refundable deposit. Limited housing available at agriculture complex for agriculture science students. Housing for handicapped students and private rooms available. **Activities:** Bands, choral groups, dance, drama, literary magazine, music ensembles, musical theater, opera, radio station, student government, student newspaper, symphony orchestra, TV station, seven religious organizations, Young Democrats, Young Republicans, several service organizations.

Athletics. NCAA. **Intercollegiate:** Baseball M, basketball, cross-country, football (tackle) M, golf M, rifle, soccer W, softball W, tennis, track and field, volleyball W. **Intramural:** Archery, badminton, basketball, bowling, football (tackle), golf, racquetball, soccer M, softball, swimming, table tennis, tennis, track and field, volleyball. **Team name:** Eagles.

Student services. Adult student services, alcohol/substance abuse counseling, career counseling, services for economically disadvantaged, student employment services, financial aid counseling, health services, minority student services, on-campus daycare, personal counseling, placement for graduates, veterans' counselor. **Physically disabled:** Services for visually, hearing impaired.

Contact. E-mail: admissions@moreheadstate.edu
Phone: (606) 783-2000 Toll-free number: (800) 585-6781
Fax: (606) 783-5038
Joel Pace, Director of Admissions, Morehead State University, Admissions Center, Morehead, KY 40351

Murray State University

Murray, Kentucky **CB member**
www.murraystate.edu **CB code: 1494**

- Public 4-year university
- Residential campus in large town

- 7,937 degree-seeking undergraduates: 11% part-time, 57% women, 6% African American, 1% Asian American, 1% Hispanic American, 2% international
- 1,416 degree-seeking graduate students
- 64% of applicants admitted
- ACT (writing recommended) required
- 56% graduate within 6 years

General. Founded in 1922. Regionally accredited. Five academic colleges and school of agriculture offering 136 programs of study. **Degrees:** 1,372 bachelor's, 38 associate awarded; master's offered. **ROTC:** Army. **Location:** 115 miles from Nashville, Tennessee. **Calendar:** Semester, limited summer session. **Full-time faculty:** 386 total; 78% have terminal degrees, 9% minority, 37% women. **Part-time faculty:** 151 total; 31% have terminal degrees, 4% minority, 52% women. **Class size:** 50% < 20, 37% 20-39, 8% 40-49, 4% 50-99, less than 1% >100. **Special facilities:** Biological research station, aquatic wildlife area, veterinary diagnostic research center, Center of Excellence for Reservoir Research, NASA-related technology-transfer station, 2 farms, archaeological research and excavation site, West Kentucky regional museum, State Center of Excellence for Telecommunication Systems Management.

Freshman class profile. 3,057 applied, 1,944 admitted, 1,030 enrolled.

Mid 50% test scores		End year in good standing:	94%
ACT:	21-26	Return as sophomores:	80%
GPA 3.50 or higher:	59%	Out-of-state:	32%
GPA 3.0-3.49:	35%	Live on campus:	81%
GPA 2.0-2.99:	6%	International:	1%
Rank in top quarter:	65%	Fraternities:	12%
Rank in top tenth:	28%	Sororities:	10%

Basis for selection. Selective admission to nursing, business and social work programs. Students must rank in the top half of graduating class or have a cumulative GPA of 3.0 or above, a composite ACT score of 18 or above and complete the precollege curriculum. Interview recommended for art, music, nursing majors. Auditions recommended for music majors. Portfolio recommended for art majors. **Homeschooled:** Students may be asked to verify lab experience and provide GED if ACT score is less than average. **Learning Disabled:** Contact office for students with learning disabilities.

High school preparation. 22 units required. Required and recommended units include English 4, mathematics 3-4, social studies 3, science 3-4 (laboratory 1), foreign language 2 and academic electives 5. One unit required in art appreciation. Social sciences must include U.S. history and world civilization. 1 arts and 1 computer science recommended. Mathematics must include 3 units algebra I and above. Sciences must include biology and chemistry or physics.

2005-2006 Annual costs. Tuition/fees: $4,428; $12,036 out-of-state. Room/board: $4,890. Books/supplies: $700. Personal expenses: $790.

2004-2005 Financial aid. Need-based: 1,134 full-time freshmen applied for aid; 680 were judged to have need; 639 of these received aid. Average need met was 94%. Average scholarship/grant was $2,257; average loan $1,850. 46% of total undergraduate aid awarded as scholarships/grants, 54% as loans/jobs. **Non-need-based:** Awarded to 4,023 full-time undergraduates, including 910 freshmen. Scholarships awarded for academics, alumni affiliation, art, athletics, job skills, leadership, minority status, music/drama, ROTC, state residency.

Application procedures. Admission: Closing date 8/1 (postmark date). $30 fee, may be waived for applicants with need. Application may be submitted online. Admission notification on a rolling basis. **Financial aid:** Priority date 4/1; no closing date. FAFSA, institutional form required. Applicants notified on a rolling basis starting 4/15.

Academics. Special study options: Combined bachelor's/graduate degree, cooperative education, cross-registration, distance learning, double major, dual enrollment of high school students, ESL, exchange student, external degree, honors, independent study, internships, liberal arts/career combination, semester at sea, study abroad, teacher certification program, weekend college. Cooperative center for study in Britain, Kentucky Institute for International Studies, national and international student exchange. **Credit/placement by examination:** AP, CLEP, ACT, institutional tests. 96 credit hours maximum toward bachelor's degree. **Support services:** Learning center, pre-admission summer program, reduced course load, remedial instruction, study skills assistance, tutoring, writing center.

Honors college/program. Based on standardized test scores, grade point average, evidence of creative and leadership abilities as displayed in extracurricular interests and activities, and faculty recommendation.

Majors. Agriculture: General. **Biology:** General. **Business:** General, accounting, business admin, finance, international, management information systems, marketing. **Communications:** Advertising, journalism, organizational, public relations, radio/tv. **Communications technology:** Desktop publishing, printing management. **Computer sciences:** General, information systems. **Conservation:** Wildlife. **Education:** Art, early childhood, elementary, health, middle, music, special. **Engineering:** Electrical, physics. **Engineering technology:** Civil, drafting, electromechanical, manufacturing, occupational safety, water quality. **English:** English lit. **Family/consumer sciences:** Food/nutrition. **Foreign languages:** French, German, Spanish. **Health:** Audiology/speech pathology, nursing (RN), veterinary technology/assistant. **History:** General. **Liberal arts:** Arts/sciences. **Math:** General. **Parks/recreation:** Exercise sciences, facilities management, health/fitness. **Philosophy/religion:** Philosophy. **Physical sciences:** Chemistry, geology, physics. **Protective services:** Criminal justice. **Psychology:** General. **Public administration:** Social work. **Social sciences:** Economics, international relations, political science, sociology. **Visual/performing arts:** Dramatic, studio arts.

Most popular majors. Business/marketing 15%, communications/journalism 12%, education 18%, engineering/engineering technologies 6%, health sciences 10%.

Computing on campus. 1,800 workstations in dormitories, library, computer center, student center. Dormitories wired for high-speed internet access and linked to campus network. Commuter students can connect to campus network. Online course registration, online library, helpline, repair service, student web hosting, wireless network available.

Student life. Freshman orientation: Available, $50 fee. Preregistration for classes offered. **Policies:** Freshmen permitted cars on campus. **Housing:** Guaranteed on-campus for freshmen. Coed dorms, single-sex dorms, special housing for disabled, apartments, fraternity/sorority housing, substance-free housing available. $75 deposit, deadline 3/1. **Activities:** Bands, choral groups, dance, drama, film society, literary magazine, music ensembles, musical theater, opera, radio station, student government, student newspaper, symphony orchestra, TV station, Rotaract, Young Democrats, Young Republicans, international student association, Black Student Council, Newman Center, Baptist Student Center, Chi Alpha, Murray Christian Fellowship, United Methodist.

Athletics. NCAA. **Intercollegiate:** Baseball M, basketball, bowling M, cheerleading, cross-country, equestrian, football (tackle) M, golf, rifle, rodeo, rowing (crew) W, soccer W, tennis, track and field, volleyball W. **Intramural:** Basketball, football (non-tackle), golf, racquetball, soccer, softball, tennis, volleyball. **Team name:** Racers.

Student services. Adult student services, alcohol/substance abuse counseling, campus ministries, career counseling, services for economically disadvantaged, student employment services, financial aid counseling, health services, legal services, minority student services, on-campus daycare, personal counseling, placement for graduates, veterans' counselor, women's services. **Physically disabled:** Services for visually, hearing impaired. **Learning disabled:** Comprehensive services available.

Contact. E-mail: admissions@murraystate.edu
Phone: (270) 809-3741 Toll-free number: (800) 272-4678
Fax: (270) 809-3780
Mary Smith, Director of Admission Services, Murray State University, 113 Sparks Hall, Murray, KY 42071

Northern Kentucky University

Highland Heights, Kentucky — **CB member**
www.nku.edu — **CB code: 1574**

- Public 4-year university
- Commuter campus in large city
- 11,611 degree-seeking undergraduates: 22% part-time, 58% women, 5% African American, 1% Asian American, 1% Hispanic American, 2% international
- 1,655 degree-seeking graduate students
- 41% graduate within 6 years; 39% enter graduate study

General. Founded in 1968. Regionally accredited. Introductory-level courses and some graduate-level courses and business seminars available at University College Campus in Covington; Summer NKU Academy gives remediation for denied students. **Degrees:** 1,529 bachelor's, 237 associate awarded; master's, first professional offered. **ROTC:** Army, Air Force. **Location:** 7 miles from Cincinnati. **Calendar:** Semester, extensive summer session. **Full-time faculty:** 567 total; 69% have terminal degrees, 10% minority, 48% women. **Part-time faculty:** 423 total; 8% minority. **Class size:** 35% < 20, 55% 20-39, 7% 40-49, 3% 50-99, less than 1% >100. **Special facilities:** Anthropology museum, biology museum, geology exhibit, wildlife exhibit, cadaver lab.

Freshman class profile. 4,317 applied, 3,242 admitted, 1,777 enrolled.

Mid 50% test scores		Out-of-state:	29%
SAT verbal:	440-540	Live on campus:	32%
SAT math:	440-560	International:	1%
ACT:	18-23	Fraternities:	3%
End year in good standing:	68%	Sororities:	5%
Return as sophomores:	67%		

Basis for selection. Open admission, but selective for some programs. Special requirements for nursing, respiratory care, radiological technology, education, business, biological sciences. High school courses taken and results of standardized test scores (ACT, SAT, COMPASS) reviewed. General college preparatory programs are required for placement, recommended for admission. SAT/ACT scores required for admission to selective programs. **Homeschooled:** Transcript of courses and grades required.

High school preparation. 22 units required. Required units include English 4, mathematics 3, social studies 3, science 3 (laboratory 1), foreign language 2 and academic electives 6. Chemistry and biology required for nursing program. Computer science recommended for all. 1 history and appreciation of visual, performing arts required.

2005-2006 Annual costs. Tuition/fees: $4,968; $9,696 out-of-state. Room/board: $5,358. Books/supplies: $800.

2004-2005 Financial aid. **Need-based:** 1,616 full-time freshmen applied for aid; 1,293 were judged to have need; 1,293 of these received aid. Average need met was 90%. Average scholarship/grant was $4,214; average loan $2,601. 43% of total undergraduate aid awarded as scholarships/grants, 57% as loans/jobs. **Non-need-based:** Awarded to 2,635 full-time undergraduates, including 646 freshmen. Scholarships awarded for academics, alumni affiliation, art, athletics, job skills, leadership, minority status, music/drama, state residency.

Application procedures. **Admission:** Priority date 5/1; deadline 8/1 (postmark date). $30 fee, may be waived for applicants with need. Application may be submitted online. Admission notification on a rolling basis beginning on or about 10/1. **Financial aid:** Priority date 3/1; no closing date. FAFSA required. Applicants notified on a rolling basis starting 4/1; must reply within 3 week(s) of notification.

Academics. **Special study options:** Cooperative education, cross-registration, distance learning, double major, dual enrollment of high school students, exchange student, honors, independent study, internships, liberal arts/career combination, study abroad, teacher certification program, weekend college. **Credit/placement by examination:** AP, CLEP, SAT, ACT, institutional tests. 16 credit hours maximum toward associate degree, 32 toward bachelor's. Credit may be awarded for military, vocational, and National Occupational Competency Testing Institute exams. **Support services:** Learning center, pre-admission summer program, reduced course load, remedial instruction, tutoring, writing center.

Majors. **Biology:** General. **Business:** General, accounting, business admin, finance, labor relations, management information systems, managerial economics, marketing, organizational behavior. **Communications:** Journalism, public relations, radio/tv. **Computer sciences:** General, information technology. **Conservation:** Environmental science. **Education:** Business, elementary, kindergarten/preschool, middle, physical, trade/industrial. **Engineering technology:** Architectural, electrical, industrial. **English:** English lit, speech/rhetoric. **Foreign languages:** French, Spanish. **Health:** Athletic training, mental health services, nursing (RN). **History:** General. **Liberal arts:** Arts/sciences. **Math:** General. **Parks/recreation:** Sports admin. **Philosophy/religion:** Philosophy. **Physical sciences:** Chemistry, geology, physics. **Protective services:** Criminal justice. **Psychology:** General. **Public administration:** Social work. **Social sciences:** General, anthropology, geography, international relations, political science, sociology. **Visual/performing arts:** Commercial/advertising art, dramatic, studio arts.

Most popular majors. Business/marketing 24%, education 13%, English 8%, health sciences 7%, psychology 6%, social sciences 8%, visual/performing arts 6%.

Computing on campus. 1,500 workstations in dormitories, library, computer center, student center. Dormitories wired for high-speed internet access and linked to campus network. Commuter students can connect to campus network. Online course registration, helpline, repair service, student web hosting, wireless network available.

Student life. **Freshman orientation:** Mandatory, $25 fee. All-day program held 12 times a year. **Policies:** Freshmen permitted cars on campus. **Housing:** Coed dorms, single-sex dorms, special housing for disabled, apartments, cooperative housing available. $200 fully refundable deposit, deadline 5/1. One-third of all college housing accessible to handicapped. **Activities:** Bands, choral groups, dance, drama, literary magazine, music ensembles, musical theater, opera, radio station, student government, student newspaper, symphony orchestra, TV station, Young Democrats, Young Republicans, Black United Studies, Baptist Student Union, international student union, Latino Student Union, Alpha Phi Omega.

Athletics. NCAA. **Intercollegiate:** Baseball M, basketball, cross-country, golf, soccer, softball W, tennis, track and field, volleyball W. **Intramural:** Badminton, basketball, football (non-tackle), golf, racquetball, soccer, softball, table tennis, tennis, volleyball, water polo, wrestling M. **Team name:** Norse.

Student services. Adult student services, alcohol/substance abuse counseling, campus ministries, career counseling, services for economically disadvantaged, student employment services, financial aid counseling, health services, legal services, minority student services, on-campus daycare, personal counseling, placement for graduates, veterans' counselor, women's services. **Physically disabled:** Services for visually, speech, hearing impaired.

Contact. E-mail: admitnku@nku.edu
Phone: (859) 572-5220 Toll-free number: (800) 637-9948
Fax: (859) 572-6665
Joel Robinson, Director of Admissions, Northern Kentucky University, Administrative Center 401, Northern Kentucky University, Highland Heights, KY 41099

Pikeville College

Pikeville, Kentucky — **CB member**
www.pc.edu — **CB code: 1625**

- Private 4-year liberal arts college affiliated with Presbyterian Church (USA)
- Residential campus in small town
- 830 degree-seeking undergraduates: 6% part-time, 53% women, 8% African American, 1% Hispanic American, 1% international
- 285 graduate students
- 37% graduate within 6 years; 28% enter graduate study

General. Founded in 1889. Regionally accredited. **Degrees:** 140 bachelor's, 24 associate awarded; first professional offered. **Location:** 150 miles from Lexington; 140 miles from Charleston, West Virginia. **Calendar:** Semester, limited summer session. **Full-time faculty:** 54 total; 52% have terminal degrees, 57% women. **Part-time faculty:** 7 total; 29% have terminal degrees, 43% women. **Class size:** 47% < 20, 50% 20-39, 3% 40-49.

Freshman class profile. 520 applied, 520 admitted, 208 enrolled.

Mid 50% test scores		End year in good standing:	72%
ACT:	17-22	Return as sophomores:	58%
GPA 3.50 or higher:	36%	Out-of-state:	21%
GPA 3.0-3.49:	18%	Live on campus:	52%
GPA 2.0-2.99:	40%		

Basis for selection. Open admission, but selective for some programs. ACT score of 19 required for nursing, ACT score of 21 required for education majors.

High school preparation. College-preparatory program recommended. 13 units recommended. Recommended units include English 4, mathematics 3, social studies 2, history 2 and science 3.

2005-2006 Annual costs. Tuition/fees: $11,500. Room/board: $5,000. Books/supplies: $1,600. Personal expenses: $2,000.

2005-2006 Financial aid. All financial aid based on need. 200 full-time freshmen applied for aid; 200 were judged to have need; 200 of these received aid. Average need met was 90%. Average scholarship/grant was $10,040; average loan $2,530. 72% of total undergraduate aid awarded as scholarships/grants, 28% as loans/jobs.

Application procedures. **Admission:** Priority date 3/15; deadline 8/16 (receipt date). No application fee. Admission notification on a rolling basis beginning on or about 9/15. **Financial aid:** Priority date 3/15; no closing date. FAFSA, institutional form required. Applicants notified on a rolling basis starting 1/15; must reply by 5/1 or within 2 week(s) of notification.

Academics. **Special study options:** Double major, independent study, internships, liberal arts/career combination, study abroad, teacher certification program, Washington semester. **Credit/placement by examination:** AP, CLEP, ACT. 15 credit hours maximum toward associate degree, 15 toward bachelor's. **Support services:** Learning center, reduced course load, remedial instruction, study skills assistance, tutoring, writing center.

Majors. **Biology:** General. **Business:** Business admin. **Communications:** General. **Computer sciences:** General. **Education:** Elementary, middle. **English:** English lit. **History:** General. **Math:** General. **Philosophy/religion:** Religion. **Physical sciences:** Chemistry. **Protective services:** Criminal justice. **Psychology:** General. **Social sciences:** General, sociology. **Visual/performing arts:** Art.

Most popular majors. Biology 7%, business/marketing 19%, communications/journalism 6%, education 16%, English 6%, history 7%, psychology 20%, security/protective services 9%.

Computing on campus. 162 workstations in library, computer center. Dormitories wired for high-speed internet access and linked to campus network. Commuter students can connect to campus network. Online library, student web hosting, wireless network available.

Student life. **Freshman orientation:** Mandatory. Preregistration for classes offered. Held first 3 days before start of classes. **Policies:** No alcohol allowed on campus. Freshmen permitted cars on campus. **Housing:** Guaranteed on-campus for freshmen. Coed dorms, single-sex dorms, apartments available. $50 nonrefundable deposit, deadline 5/30. **Activities:** Bands, choral groups, dance, drama, student government, student newspaper, Academic Team, Appalachian Association for Justice, Baptist Student Union, Blessed Unity of God, Fellowship of Christian Athletes, Lambda Sigma Society, Phi Beta Lambda, Psi Chi, Sigma Tau Delta, Young Republicans Club.

Athletics. NAIA. **Intercollegiate:** Baseball M, basketball, bowling, cheerleading, cross-country, football (tackle) M, golf, soccer, softball W, tennis, volleyball W. **Intramural:** Basketball, bowling, football (non-tackle), softball, tennis, volleyball. **Team name:** Bears.

Student services. Campus ministries, career counseling, student employment services, financial aid counseling, health services, personal counseling, veterans' counselor.

Contact. E-mail: wewantyou@pc.edu
Phone: (606) 218-5251 Toll-free number: (866) 232-7700
Fax: (606) 218-5255
Melinda Lynch, Dean, Enrollment Management, Pikeville College, 147 Sycamore Street, Pikeville, KY 41501-1194

St. Catharine College

St. Catharine, Kentucky
www.sccky.edu **CB code: 1690**

- Private 4-year health science and liberal arts college affiliated with Roman Catholic Church
- Commuter campus in large town
- 682 degree-seeking undergraduates

General. Founded in 1931. Regionally accredited. **Degrees:** 83 associate awarded. **Location:** 60 miles from Louisville and Lexington. **Calendar:** Semester, limited summer session. **Full-time faculty:** 45 total. **Part-time faculty:** 25 total.

Basis for selection. Open admission. Assessment tests in mathematics, English and reading administered upon admission for course placement or remediation.

2005-2006 Annual costs. Tuition/fees: $10,920. Health sciences associate degree programs: $13,740 annual tuition and fees. Room/board: $5,720. Books/supplies: $700. Personal expenses: $1,080.

Financial aid. All financial aid based on need.

Application procedures. **Admission:** No deadline. $15 fee, may be waived for applicants with need. Application must be submitted on paper. Admission notification on a rolling basis. **Financial aid:** Priority date 3/15; no closing date. FAFSA, institutional form required. Applicants notified on a rolling basis; must reply by 8/15.

Academics. **Special study options:** Dual enrollment of high school students, independent study, internships, weekend college. **Credit/placement by examination:** AP, CLEP, institutional tests. 35 credit hours maximum toward associate degree. **Support services:** Learning center, reduced course load, remedial instruction, tutoring.

Majors. **Business:** Business admin. **Health:** Health services, sonography.

Computing on campus. 33 workstations in library, computer center. Dormitories wired for high-speed internet access. Online library available.

Student life. **Freshman orientation:** Mandatory. Preregistration for classes offered. 1-day program before start of classes. Semester-long orientation course. **Policies:** Freshmen permitted cars on campus. **Housing:** Single-sex dorms available. $25 deposit, deadline 8/15. **Activities:** Pep band, choral groups, literary magazine, student government, Phi Theta Kappa, international club, Christian Athletics Club, African-American Club, art club, Students Above Traditional Age, Student Ambassadors, campus ministry, Students in Free Enterprise.

Athletics. NJCAA. **Intercollegiate:** Baseball M, basketball, golf, soccer, softball W. **Team name:** Patriots.

Student services. Campus ministries, career counseling, financial aid counseling, on-campus daycare, personal counseling, veterans' counselor.

Contact. E-mail: twiley@sccky.edu
Phone: (859) 336-5082 ext. 1259 Toll-free number: (800) 599-2000 ext. 1259 Fax: (859) 336-5031
Toni Wiley, Director of Admissions, St. Catharine College, 2735 Bardstown Road, St. Catharine, KY 40061

Spalding University

Louisville, Kentucky **CB member**
www.spalding.edu **CB code: 1552**

- Private 4-year university affiliated with Roman Catholic Church
- Commuter campus in very large city
- 1,660 degree-seeking undergraduates
- SAT or ACT (ACT writing recommended) required

General. Founded in 1814. Regionally accredited. **Degrees:** 227 bachelor's, 11 associate awarded; master's, doctoral offered. **ROTC:** Army, Air Force. **Calendar:** Continuous, extensive summer session. **Full-time faculty:** 65 total. **Part-time faculty:** 130 total. **Special facilities:** Historical collection of Edith Stein works.

Freshman class profile.

Mid 50% test scores		ACT:	16-21
SAT verbal:	410-530	Out-of-state:	13%
SAT math:	440-580	Live on campus:	15%

Basis for selection. Open admission, but selective for some programs. Class rank (top half), academic preparation, and SAT or ACT test scores important. Interview recommended.

High school preparation. 16 units recommended. Recommended units include English 4, mathematics 3, social studies 2, science 2 and foreign language 2. 2 units of social science recommended.

2005-2006 Annual costs. Tuition/fees: $14,400. Room/board: $3,882. Books/supplies: $700.

Financial aid. **Non-need-based:** Scholarships awarded for academics, athletics, religious affiliation, ROTC.

Application procedures. **Admission:** No deadline. $20 fee, may be waived for applicants with need. Application may be submitted online. Admission notification on a rolling basis. **Financial aid:** Priority date 3/1; no closing date. FAFSA required. Applicants notified on a rolling basis starting 3/31; must reply within 2 week(s) of notification.

Academics. **Special study options:** Accelerated study, cross-registration, double major, dual enrollment of high school students, independent study, internships, liberal arts/career combination, study abroad, teacher certification program, weekend college. **Credit/placement by examination:** AP, CLEP, institutional tests. 32 credit hours maximum toward associate degree, 32 toward bachelor's. **Support services:** Learning center, reduced course load, remedial instruction, study skills assistance, tutoring, writing center.

Majors. **Biology:** General. **Business:** General, accounting. **Communications:** General. **Education:** General, art, business, early childhood, elementary, middle, science, social studies, special. **Health:** Nursing (RN). **Liberal arts:** Arts/sciences, humanities. **Psychology:** General. **Public administration:** Social work. **Social sciences:** General. **Visual/performing arts:** Studio arts.

Most popular majors. Business/marketing 43%, communications/journalism 7%, education 13%, health sciences 20%, social sciences 7%.

Computing on campus. 45 workstations in dormitories, library, student center. Dormitories linked to campus network. Online library, helpline available.

Student life. **Freshman orientation:** Available. Preregistration for classes offered. Two-day program with on-campus stay in August. **Policies:** Freshmen permitted cars on campus. **Housing:** Guaranteed on-campus for freshmen. Coed dorms available. $100 deposit. Two floors in residence hall designated for graduate students. **Activities:** Drama, student government, student newspaper, International club, Campus Crusade for Christ, Fellowship of Christian Athletes, Black student association, Spalding Advocates for Campus Accessibility.

Athletics. NAIA. **Intercollegiate:** Baseball M, basketball, soccer, softball W, volleyball W. **Intramural:** Basketball, bowling, soccer, softball W, table tennis, tennis, volleyball, weight lifting. **Team name:** Pelicans.

Student services. Adult student services, alcohol/substance abuse counseling, campus ministries, career counseling, services for economically disadvantaged, student employment services, financial aid counseling, health services, minority student services, personal counseling, placement for graduates. **Physically disabled:** Services for visually impaired.

Contact. E-mail: admissions@spalding.edu
Phone: (502) 585-7111 Toll-free number: (800) 896-8941
Fax: (502) 585-7128
Vickie Prince, Director of Admissions, Spalding University, 851 South Fourth Street, Louisville, KY 40203

Sullivan University

Louisville, Kentucky
www.sullivan.edu **CB code: 0811**

- For-profit 4-year university, culinary school and business college
- Commuter campus in large city
- 4,500 undergraduates
- SAT or ACT (ACT writing optional), interview required

General. Founded in 1962. Regionally accredited. Day classes meet Monday to Thursday; special program on Friday for additional help. Night/Weekend classes meet Monday through Sunday; many graduate and undergraduate classes are offered online. **Degrees:** 354 bachelor's, 395 associate awarded; master's offered. **ROTC:** Air Force. **Calendar:** Quarter, extensive summer session. **Full-time faculty:** 71 total. **Part-time faculty:** 120 total. **Special facilities:** Unversity-operated fine dining restaurant.

Freshman class profile.

Out-of-state:	17%	**Live on campus:**	9%

Basis for selection. Test scores, interview, high school record important. CPAT can be taken on campus for placement and admission if ACT or SAT scores are not available. ACT Career Programs Assessment test required for placement.

2005-2006 Annual costs. Tuition, fees and per-credit-hour charges vary by program. Tuition costs range from $11,760 to $12,750 per academic year. Required fees are $415. Books/supplies: $900. Personal expenses: $1,305.

Financial aid. All financial aid based on need.

Application procedures. **Admission:** No deadline. $90 fee. Admission notification on a rolling basis. **Financial aid:** No deadline. FAFSA required. Applicants notified on a rolling basis starting 1/2.

Academics. **Special study options:** Accelerated study, distance learning, double major, independent study, internships, weekend college. **Credit/placement by examination:** CLEP, institutional tests. **Support services:** Reduced course load, remedial instruction, study skills assistance, tutoring.

Majors. **Business:** Accounting, business admin, tourism promotion. **Computer sciences:** General, applications programming. **Legal studies:** Paralegal. **Personal/culinary services:** Culinary arts.

Most popular majors. Business/marketing 96%.

Computing on campus. 225 workstations in library, computer center. Commuter students can connect to campus network. Online course registration, online library, helpline available.

Student life. **Freshman orientation:** Mandatory. **Policies:** Freshmen permitted cars on campus. **Housing:** Apartments available. Guaranteed housing for freshmen under 21 or who live in more than 75-mile radius from Louisville. **Activities:** Student government, student newspaper, Baptist Student Union, national student business organization, women's service organization, travel club, paralegal association, American Marketing Association, Culinary Competition Team, Data Processing Management Association.

Athletics. **Intramural:** Basketball, bowling, softball, volleyball.

Student services. Career counseling, student employment services, financial aid counseling, personal counseling, placement for graduates, veterans' counselor.

Contact. E-mail: admissions@sullivan.edu
Phone: (502) 456-6505 Toll-free number: (800) 844-1354
Fax: (502) 456-0040
Greg Cawthon, Director of Admissions, Sullivan University, 3101 Bardstown Road, Louisville, KY 40205

Thomas More College

Crestview Hills, Kentucky **CB member**
www.thomasmore.edu **CB code: 1876**

- Private 4-year liberal arts college affiliated with Roman Catholic Church
- Commuter campus in small town
- 1,343 degree-seeking undergraduates
- 91 graduate students
- 63% of applicants admitted
- SAT or ACT (ACT writing optional) required
- 55% graduate within 6 years; 75% enter graduate study

General. Founded in 1921. Regionally accredited. **Degrees:** 228 bachelor's, 57 associate awarded; master's offered. **ROTC:** Army, Air Force. **Location:** 8 miles from Cincinnati. **Calendar:** Semester, limited summer session. **Full-time faculty:** 71 total; 69% have terminal degrees, 7% minority, 48% women. **Part-time faculty:** 63 total. **Class size:** 81% < 20, 19% 20-39, less than 1% 40-49. **Special facilities:** Biology field station, observatory.

Freshman class profile. 1,007 applied, 637 admitted, 227 enrolled.

Mid 50% test scores		**GPA 2.0-2.99:**	29%
SAT verbal:	450-610	**Rank in top quarter:**	37%
SAT math:	460-590	**Rank in top tenth:**	14%
ACT:	19-24	**Return as sophomores:**	87%
GPA 3.50 or higher:	41%	**Out-of-state:**	32%
GPA 3.0-3.49:	29%	**Live on campus:**	49%

Basis for selection. Rank in top half of graduating class, 2.0 GPA (college-preparatory curriculum), and 20 ACT with at least 20 English score, or 1010 SAT (exclusive of writing) with at least 530 verbal score important. Test scores required prior to registration. Interview recommended. Essay recommended for special admissions. **Learning Disabled:** Need to submit legal documentation of disabilities.

High school preparation. 15 units required. Required and recommended units include English 4, mathematics 3, social studies 3, science 3 (laboratory 1), foreign language 2 and academic electives 2. Art appreciation and computer literacy recommended.

2005-2006 Annual costs. Tuition/fees: $18,320. 2006-2007 Costs will not be available until mid March, 2006. Room/board: $6,150. Books/supplies: $800. Personal expenses: $2,800.

2004-2005 Financial aid. **Need-based:** 167 full-time freshmen applied for aid; 167 were judged to have need; 167 of these received aid. Average need met was 87%. Average scholarship/grant was $4,086; average loan $1,962. 37% of total undergraduate aid awarded as scholarships/grants, 63% as loans/jobs. **Non-need-based:** Awarded to 932 full-time undergraduates, including 182 freshmen. Scholarships awarded for academics, alumni affiliation, art, job skills, leadership, minority status, music/drama, religious affiliation, ROTC, state residency.

Application procedures. **Admission:** Priority date 3/15; deadline 8/15 (postmark date). $25 fee, may be waived for applicants with need. Application may be submitted online. Admission notification on a rolling basis. **Financial aid:** Priority date 3/15; no closing date. FAFSA, institutional form required. Applicants notified on a rolling basis; must reply within 4 week(s) of notification.

Academics. **Special study options:** Accelerated study, combined bachelor's/graduate degree, cooperative education, cross-registration, double major, dual enrollment of high school students, honors, independent study, internships, liberal arts/career combination, student-designed major, study abroad, teacher certification program, weekend college. **Credit/placement by examination:** AP, CLEP, IB, SAT, ACT, institutional tests. 30 credit hours maximum toward associate degree, 60 toward bachelor's. **Support services:** Learning center, pre-admission summer program, reduced course load, remedial instruction, study skills assistance, tutoring, writing center.

Majors. **Biology:** General. **Business:** General, accounting. **Communications:** General. **Computer sciences:** General. **Education:** General, art, biology, business, chemistry, computer, elementary, English, mathematics, middle, physics, science, secondary, social studies. **English:** English lit, speech/rhetoric. **Health:** Clinical lab science, nursing (RN), predentistry, premedicine, prepharmacy, preveterinary. **History:** General. **Liberal arts:** Arts/sciences, humanities. **Math:** General. **Philosophy/religion:** Philosophy, religion. **Physical sciences:** Chemistry, physics. **Protective services:** Forensics, law enforcement admin. **Psychology:** General. **Social sciences:** Economics, international relations, political science, sociology. **Visual/performing arts:** General, dramatic, studio arts.

Most popular majors. Business/marketing 50%, education 6%.

Computing on campus. 200 workstations in dormitories, library, computer center, student center. Dormitories wired for high-speed internet access and linked to campus network. Commuter students can connect to campus network. Online course registration, online library, helpline, student web hosting, wireless network available.

Student life. **Freshman orientation:** Mandatory, $125 fee. Preregistration for classes offered. 2-day program held at beginning of fall semester in August. **Policies:** Freshmen permitted cars on campus. **Housing:** Guaranteed on-campus for all undergraduates. Coed dorms, single-sex dorms available. $200 fully refundable deposit, deadline 8/15. **Activities:** Choral groups, drama, literary magazine, student government, Campus Ministry, student activities board, residence hall government association, African American Society, deans council, international student society, service learning, Habitat for Humanity, business society, social issues commune.

Athletics. NCAA. **Intercollegiate:** Baseball M, basketball, cross-country, football (tackle) M, golf, soccer, softball W, tennis, volleyball W. **Intramural:** Basketball, football (non-tackle), golf, racquetball, softball, volleyball. **Team name:** Saints.

Student services. Adult student services, alcohol/substance abuse counseling, campus ministries, career counseling, student employment services, financial aid counseling, health services, minority student services, personal counseling, placement for graduates, veterans' counselor. **Physically disabled:** Services for visually, speech, hearing impaired.

Contact. E-mail: admissions@thomasmore.edu
Phone: (859) 344-3332 Toll-free number: (800) 825-4557
Fax: (859) 344-3444
Angela Griffin Jones, Director of Admissions, Thomas More College, 333 Thomas More Parkway, Crestview Hills, KY 41017-3495

Transylvania University

Lexington, Kentucky **CB member**
www.transy.edu **CB code: 1808**

- Private 4-year liberal arts college affiliated with Christian Church (Disciples of Christ)
- Residential campus in small city
- 1,143 degree-seeking undergraduates: 1% part-time, 60% women, 2% African American, 2% Asian American, 1% Hispanic American
- 84% of applicants admitted
- SAT or ACT (ACT writing optional), application essay required
- 67% graduate within 6 years; 40% enter graduate study

General. Founded in 1780. Regionally accredited. **Degrees:** 232 bachelor's awarded. **ROTC:** Army, Air Force. **Location:** 80 miles from Louisville, 80 miles from Cincinnati. **Calendar:** 4-1-4, limited summer session. **Full-time faculty:** 81 total; 91% have terminal degrees, 4% minority, 37% women. **Part-time faculty:** 15 total; 27% have terminal degrees, 7% minority, 40% women. **Class size:** 59% < 20, 41% 20-39. **Special facilities:** Museum of early scientific apparatus, special library collections of early medical and scientific works and Kentucky books.

Freshman class profile. 1,222 applied, 1,032 admitted, 326 enrolled.

Mid 50% test scores		**End year in good standing:**	94%
SAT verbal:	540-650	**Return as sophomores:**	89%
SAT math:	540-640	**Out-of-state:**	18%
ACT:	23-28	**Live on campus:**	96%
Rank in top quarter:	77%	**Fraternities:**	50%
Rank in top tenth:	44%	**Sororities:**	50%

Basis for selection. Rigor of high school curriculum most important. Minimum 2.75 GPA, 1030 SAT (exclusive of Writing), 22 ACT. Academic recommendations required. Extracurricular activities considered. Essay important. Excellence of character and high personal goals important. Interview recommended. Audition required for music scholarship applicants. Portfolio required for art scholarship applicants. **Homeschooled:** Transcript of courses and grades required. **Learning Disabled:** Meet with coordinator of disability services.

High school preparation. 12 units required; 16 recommended. Required and recommended units include English 4, mathematics 3, social studies 2, history 1, science 3, foreign language 2 and academic electives 1. Broad high school curriculum important to allow full participation in required liberal arts course work. Solid background in English highly recommended.

2005-2006 Annual costs. Tuition/fees: $19,650. Room/board: $6,590. Books/supplies: $750. Personal expenses: $1,250.

2005-2006 Financial aid. **Need-based:** 275 full-time freshmen applied for aid; 222 were judged to have need; 221 of these received aid. Average need met was 88%. Average scholarship/grant was $12,719; average loan $3,080. 75% of total undergraduate aid awarded as scholarships/grants, 25% as loans/jobs. **Non-need-based:** Awarded to 532 full-time undergraduates, including 153 freshmen. Scholarships awarded for academics, art, leadership, minority status, music/drama, religious affiliation, ROTC, state residency. **Additional information:** Auditions and portfolios required for music and art scholarships respectively. Essays required for other scholarship programs. Applications for William T. Young scholarships must be received by December 1.

Application procedures. **Admission:** Priority date 12/1; deadline 2/1 (receipt date). $30 fee, may be waived for applicants with need. Application may be submitted online. Admission notification on a rolling basis beginning on or about 12/15. Must reply by 5/1. **Financial aid:** Priority date 3/1; no closing date. FAFSA required. Applicants notified on a rolling basis starting 3/15; must reply by 5/1 or within 2 week(s) of notification.

Academics. **Special study options:** Combined bachelor's/graduate degree, double major, independent study, internships, liberal arts/career combination, student-designed major, study abroad, teacher certification program, Washington semester. **Credit/placement by examination:** AP, CLEP, IB, institutional tests. **Support services:** Learning center, study skills assistance, tutoring, writing center.

Majors. **Biology:** General. **Business:** General, accounting. **Computer sciences:** General. **Education:** Elementary, middle, music, physical. **Foreign languages:** Classics, French, Spanish. **History:** General. **Liberal arts:** Arts/sciences. **Math:** General. **Parks/recreation:** Exercise sciences. **Philosophy/religion:** Philosophy, religion. **Physical sciences:** Chemistry, physics. **Psychology:** General. **Social sciences:** Anthropology, economics, political science, sociology. **Visual/performing arts:** Dramatic, music performance, studio arts.

Most popular majors. Biology 12%, business/marketing 24%, history 6%, psychology 8%, social sciences 15%.

Computing on campus. 250 workstations in dormitories, library, computer center, student center. Dormitories wired for high-speed internet access and linked to campus network. Commuter students can connect to campus network. Online library, helpline, student web hosting, wireless network available.

Student life. **Freshman orientation:** Mandatory. Preregistration for classes offered. One-day summer event; 4-day program before classes begin. **Policies:** Freshmen permitted cars on campus. **Housing:** Guaranteed on-campus for freshmen. Coed dorms, single-sex dorms, special housing for disabled, apartments, substance-free housing available. $125 deposit, deadline 5/1. Efficiency apartment option for upperclassmen; two units with facilities for disabled students. **Activities:** Bands, choral groups, dance, drama, literary magazine, music ensembles, musical theater, opera, radio station, student government, student newspaper, Circle K, Diversity Action Council, College Democrats, College Republicans, Alternative Spring Break, Campus Crusade, Student Activities Board, Student Alumni Association, Disciples on Campus.

Athletics. NCAA. **Intercollegiate:** Baseball M, basketball, cross-country, diving, field hockey W, golf, soccer, softball W, swimming, tennis, volleyball W. **Intramural:** Badminton, basketball, bowling, cross-country, football (non-tackle), football (tackle), golf, handball, racquetball, soccer, softball, swimming, table tennis, tennis, volleyball. **Team name:** Pioneers.

Student services. Alcohol/substance abuse counseling, campus ministries, career counseling, student employment services, financial aid counseling, health services, minority student services, personal counseling, veterans' counselor. **Physically disabled:** Services for visually, hearing impaired.

Contact. E-mail: admissions@transy.edu
Phone: (859) 233-8242 Toll-free number: (800) 872-6798
Fax: (859) 233-8797
Deana Ison, Interim Director of Admissions, Transylvania University, 300 North Broadway, Lexington, KY 40508-1797

Union College
Barbourville, Kentucky
www.unionky.edu **CB code: 1825**

- Private 4-year liberal arts college affiliated with United Methodist Church
- Residential campus in small town
- 602 degree-seeking undergraduates: 8% part-time, 44% women, 9% African American, 2% Hispanic American, 1% Native American, 4% international
- 381 degree-seeking graduate students
- SAT or ACT (ACT writing recommended) required
- 33% graduate within 6 years

General. Founded in 1879. Regionally accredited. **Degrees:** 146 bachelor's, 1 associate awarded; master's offered. **ROTC:** Army. **Location:** 107 miles from Lexington; 107 miles from Knoxville, Tennessee. **Calendar:** Semester, limited summer session. **Full-time faculty:** 45 total. **Part-time faculty:** 30 total. **Class size:** 79% < 20, 21% 20-39.

Freshman class profile. 596 applied, 384 admitted, 181 enrolled.

Mid 50% test scores			
SAT verbal:	400-490	Rank in top quarter:	28%
SAT math:	370-460	Rank in top tenth:	6%
ACT:	17-21	End year in good standing:	80%
GPA 3.50 or higher:	18%	Return as sophomores:	56%
GPA 3.0-3.49:	31%	Out-of-state:	22%
GPA 2.0-2.99:	48%	Live on campus:	70%
		International:	3%

Basis for selection. Open admission, but selective for some programs. School achievement record, course work, class rank, SAT or ACT scores important. ACT preferred for all, required for teacher education program. Interview recommended. **Learning Disabled:** Students must provide documentation to coordinator of special program to receive necessary accommodations.

High school preparation. 21 units required. Required and recommended units include English 4, mathematics 3, history 2, science 2 (laboratory 2), foreign language 2 and academic electives 8.

2006-2007 Annual costs. Tuition/fees (projected): $15,290. Room/board: $4,600. Books/supplies: $900. Personal expenses: $800.

2005-2006 Financial aid. Need-based: Average need met was 78%. Average scholarship/grant was $10,454; average loan $3,570. 44% of total undergraduate aid awarded as scholarships/grants, 56% as loans/jobs. **Non-need-based:** Scholarships awarded for academics, athletics, leadership, minority status, music/drama, religious affiliation, state residency.

Application procedures. Admission: No deadline. $10 fee, may be waived for applicants with need. Application may be submitted online. Admission notification on a rolling basis. Must reply by May 1 or within 2 week(s) if notified thereafter. **Financial aid:** Priority date 3/15; no closing date. FAFSA required. Applicants notified on a rolling basis starting 4/1; must reply within 2 week(s) of notification.

Academics. Special study options: Cooperative education, double major, dual enrollment of high school students, exchange student, independent study, internships, student-designed major, study abroad, teacher certification program. **Credit/placement by examination:** AP, CLEP, institutional tests. 30 credit hours maximum toward bachelor's degree. **Support services:** Learning center, study skills assistance, tutoring.

Majors. Biology: General. **Business:** Accounting, business admin. **Communications:** General. **Education:** Elementary, health, middle, physical, science, social studies, special. **English:** English lit. **History:** General. **Math:** General. **Parks/recreation:** Facilities management, sports admin. **Philosophy/religion:** Religion. **Physical sciences:** Chemistry. **Protective services:** Law enforcement admin. **Psychology:** General. **Social sciences:** Sociology. **Theology:** Religious ed.

Most popular majors. Business/marketing 28%, education 30%, psychology 12%, security/protective services 8%, social sciences 9%.

Computing on campus. 117 workstations in library, computer center, student center. Dormitories wired for high-speed internet access and linked to campus network. Online course registration, online library, helpline, wireless network available.

Student life. Freshman orientation: Mandatory. Preregistration for classes offered. **Policies:** Freshmen permitted cars on campus. **Housing:** Guaranteed on-campus for freshmen. Single-sex dorms, apartments, substance-free housing available. $50 partly refundable deposit. Private rooms sometimes available to upperclassmen. **Activities:** Pep band, choral groups, drama, literary magazine, music ensembles, student government, student newspaper, TV station, Fellowship of Christian Athletes, Appalachian Wilderness Club, Baptist Student Union, Methodist Student Organizations, Newman Club, Student Ambassadors, science society, philosophy society.

Athletics. NAIA. **Intercollegiate:** Baseball M, basketball, cross-country, football (tackle) M, golf, soccer, softball W, tennis, volleyball W. **Intramural:** Basketball, football (non-tackle), soccer, softball, table tennis, tennis, volleyball. **Team name:** Bulldogs.

Student services. Alcohol/substance abuse counseling, campus ministries, career counseling, services for economically disadvantaged, financial aid counseling, health services, personal counseling, placement for graduates.

Contact. E-mail: enrollme@unionky.edu
Phone: (606) 546-1229 Toll-free number: (800) 489-8646
Fax: (606) 546-1667
Jerry Jackson, Dean of Enrollment Management, Union College, 310 College Street, Barbourville, KY 40906

University of Kentucky
Lexington, Kentucky **CB member**
www.uky.edu **CB code: 1837**

- Public 4-year university
- Commuter campus in large city
- 18,416 degree-seeking undergraduates: 8% part-time, 52% women, 5% African American, 2% Asian American, 1% Hispanic American, 1% international
- 6,532 degree-seeking graduate students
- 82% of applicants admitted
- SAT or ACT (ACT writing optional) required
- 59% graduate within 6 years

General. Founded in 1865. Regionally accredited. **Degrees:** 3,285 bachelor's awarded; master's, doctoral, first professional offered. **ROTC:** Army, Air Force. **Location:** 80 miles from Louisville, 90 miles from Cincinnati. **Calendar:** Semester, limited summer session. **Full-time faculty:** 1,200 total. **Part-time faculty:** 500 total. **Class size:** 23% < 20, 53% 20-39, 6% 40-49, 11% 50-99, 7% >100. **Special facilities:** Center for the arts, Van de Graaff accelerator, equine research center, center for the humanities.

Freshman class profile. 10,508 applied, 8,650 admitted, 3,835 enrolled.

Mid 50% test scores		GPA 2.0-2.99:	11%
SAT verbal:	510-630	Rank in top quarter:	57%
SAT math:	520-640	Rank in top tenth:	28%
ACT:	22-27	Return as sophomores:	79%
GPA 3.50 or higher:	61%	Out-of-state:	20%
GPA 3.0-3.49:	27%		

Basis for selection. Test scores and GPA should indicate potential for academic success. Required course work and extracurricular activities also considered. Students out of high school 2 years or more with no college credit admitted on probationary basis. Audition required of music majors. **Homeschooled:** List of textbooks, attendance record and 2 letters of recommendation from persons outside family required.

High school preparation. 22 units required. Required and recommended units include English 4, mathematics 3-4, social studies 3, science 3-4, foreign language 2 and academic electives 5. 1 fine or performing arts, .5 health, .5 physical education required.

2005-2006 Annual costs. Tuition/fees: $5,812; $12,798 out-of-state. Tuition charges include fees. Upper division tuition is $5980, in-state; $12,970, out-of-state. Room/board: $5,229. Books/supplies: $600. Personal expenses: $1,148.

2005-2006 Financial aid. Need-based: 2,387 full-time freshmen applied for aid; 1,530 were judged to have need; 1,519 of these received aid. Average need met was 79%. Average scholarship/grant was $5,743; average loan $2,599. 58% of total undergraduate aid awarded as scholarships/grants, 42% as loans/jobs. **Non-need-based:** Awarded to 5,153 full-time undergraduates, including 1,773 freshmen. Scholarships awarded for academics, alumni affiliation, art, athletics, job skills, leadership, minority status, music/drama, ROTC, state residency.

Application procedures. Admission: Closing date 2/15 (postmark date). $40 fee, may be waived for applicants with need. Application may be submitted online. Admission notification on a rolling basis beginning on or

about 10/1. Reply by 05/01 preferred. **Financial aid:** Priority date 2/15; no closing date. FAFSA required. Applicants notified on a rolling basis starting 4/1; must reply within 3 week(s) of notification.

Academics. Special study options: Accelerated study, combined bachelor's/graduate degree, cooperative education, distance learning, double major, ESL, exchange student, honors, independent study, internships, study abroad, teacher certification program, weekend college. **Credit/placement by examination:** AP, CLEP, IB, SAT, ACT, institutional tests. Students who receive Advanced Placement credit for a course may apply this credit the same way credit earned by passing a course is applied. **Support services:** Learning center, reduced course load, remedial instruction, tutoring, writing center.

Majors. Agriculture: Agronomy, animal sciences, communications, economics, education services, food science. **Architecture:** Architecture, landscape. **Area/ethnic studies:** Latin American. **Biology:** General. **Business:** General, accounting, finance, hospitality admin, management science, managerial economics, marketing. **Communications:** General, advertising, journalism, radio/tv. **Computer sciences:** General. **Conservation:** General, forest sciences. **Education:** Art, early childhood, elementary, health, mathematics, middle, music, physical, science, special. **Engineering:** Agricultural, chemical, civil, electrical, materials, mechanical, mining. **Family/consumer sciences:** General, food/nutrition. **Foreign languages:** Classics, French, German, linguistics, Russian, Spanish. **Health:** Audiology/speech pathology, clinical lab science, health care admin. **History:** General. **Math:** General. **Philosophy/religion:** Philosophy. **Physical sciences:** Chemistry, geology, physics. **Psychology:** General. **Public administration:** Social work. **Social sciences:** General, anthropology, economics, geography, political science, sociology. **Visual/performing arts:** Art history/conservation, arts management, dramatic, interior design, music history, music performance.

Most popular majors. Business/marketing 22%, communications/journalism 10%, education 8%, engineering/engineering technologies 7%, social sciences 10%.

Computing on campus. 810 workstations in dormitories, library, computer center, student center. Dormitories wired for high-speed internet access and linked to campus network. Commuter students can connect to campus network. Online course registration, online library, helpline, wireless network available.

Student life. Freshman orientation: Mandatory, $40 fee. Preregistration for classes offered. $20 charge per guest. **Policies:** Freshmen permitted cars on campus. **Housing:** Coed dorms, single-sex dorms, special housing for disabled, apartments, fraternity/sorority housing available. $300 partly refundable deposit, deadline 6/1. **Activities:** Bands, choral groups, dance, drama, literary magazine, music ensembles, musical theater, opera, radio station, student government, student newspaper, symphony orchestra, More than 300 organizations.

Athletics. NCAA. **Intercollegiate:** Baseball M, basketball, cross-country, diving, football (tackle) M, golf, gymnastics W, rifle, soccer, softball W, swimming, tennis, track and field, volleyball W. **Intramural:** Archery, badminton, basketball, bowling, cross-country, fencing, field hockey W, football (non-tackle), golf, handball, ice hockey M, lacrosse, racquetball, rugby M, skiing, soccer, softball, squash, swimming, table tennis, tennis, track and field, volleyball, wrestling M. **Team name:** Wildcats.

Student services. Adult student services, career counseling, student employment services, health services, on-campus daycare, personal counseling, placement for graduates, veterans' counselor. **Physically disabled:** Services for visually, speech, hearing impaired.

Contact. E-mail: admisso@uky.edu
Phone: (859) 257-2000 Toll-free number: (800) 432-0967
Fax: (859) 257-3823
Don Witt, Director of Admissions, University of Kentucky, 100 W.D. Funkhouser Building, Lexington, KY 40506-0054

University of Louisville

Louisville, Kentucky — **CB member**
www.louisville.edu — **CB code: 1838**

- Public 4-year university
- Commuter campus in very large city
- 13,893 degree-seeking undergraduates: 19% part-time, 53% women, 14% African American, 3% Asian American, 1% Hispanic American, 1% international
- 5,325 degree-seeking graduate students
- 79% of applicants admitted
- SAT or ACT (ACT writing optional) required
- 37% graduate within 6 years

General. Founded in 1798. Regionally accredited. **Degrees:** 2,148 bachelor's, 48 associate awarded; master's, doctoral, first professional offered. **ROTC:** Army, Air Force. **Location:** 92 miles from Cincinnati, 110 miles from Indianapolis. **Calendar:** Semester, extensive summer session. **Full-time faculty:** 802 total; 89% have terminal degrees, 18% minority, 37% women. **Part-time faculty:** 511 total; 35% have terminal degrees, 13% minority, 46% women. **Class size:** 27% < 20, 53% 20-39, 7% 40-49, 8% 50-99, 4% >100. **Special facilities:** Planetarium, computer-aided engineering building with robotics laboratory, rapid prototype facility with Sinterstation 2000 system.

Freshman class profile. 5,712 applied, 4,515 admitted, 2,318 enrolled.

Mid 50% test scores		**Rank in top tenth:**	22%
SAT verbal:	500-620	**Return as sophomores:**	76%
SAT math:	510-640	**Out-of-state:**	18%
ACT:	21-27	**Live on campus:**	52%
GPA 3.50 or higher:	51%	**International:**	1%
GPA 3.0-3.49:	32%	**Fraternities:**	7%
GPA 2.0-2.99:	17%	**Sororities:**	4%
Rank in top quarter:	51%		

Basis for selection. High school grades, curriculum, class rank and test scores very important. Rank in top half of graduating class. Partnership with local community college for those not meeting unit admission requirements. Diagnostic testing/interview option for those failing to meet minimum. Freshmen must have completed state precollege curriculum. SAT/ACT score reports must be received by registration before the first day of class.

High school preparation. College-preparatory program required. Required and recommended units include English 4, mathematics 3-4, social studies 3, science 3-4 (laboratory 1), foreign language 2 and academic electives 5. 5 electives must be rigorous.

2005-2006 Annual costs. Tuition/fees: $5,532; $15,092 out-of-state. Room/board: $4,868. Books/supplies: $800. Personal expenses: $4,914.

2005-2006 Financial aid. Need-based: 1,564 full-time freshmen applied for aid; 1,277 were judged to have need; 1,261 of these received aid. Average need met was 56%. Average scholarship/grant was $5,876; average loan $2,618. 55% of total undergraduate aid awarded as scholarships/grants, 45% as loans/jobs. **Non-need-based:** Awarded to 2,526 full-time undergraduates, including 733 freshmen. Scholarships awarded for academics, art, athletics, leadership, minority status, music/drama, ROTC.

Application procedures. Admission: Priority date 3/1; deadline 8/22 (receipt date). $30 fee, may be waived for applicants with need. Application may be submitted online. Must reply by May 1 or within 4 week(s) if notified thereafter. **Financial aid:** Priority date 3/15; no closing date. FAFSA required. Applicants notified on a rolling basis starting 4/1; must reply by 5/1.

Academics. Special study options: Accelerated study, combined bachelor's/graduate degree, cooperative education, distance learning, double major, dual enrollment of high school students, ESL, honors, independent study, internships, student-designed major, study abroad, teacher certification program. **Credit/placement by examination:** AP, CLEP, IB, institutional tests. 24 credit hours maximum toward bachelor's degree. Candidates for the nursing program may apply no more than 37 semester hours of CLEP credit toward the bachelor's degree. **Support services:** Learning center, pre-admission summer program, reduced course load, remedial instruction, tutoring.

Majors. Area/ethnic studies: African-American, women's. **Biology:** General. **Business:** Accounting, business admin, finance, management information systems, managerial economics, marketing. **Communications:** General. **Education:** Elementary, music, trade/industrial. **Engineering:** General, chemical, civil, computer, electrical, industrial, mechanical. **English:** English lit. **Foreign languages:** French, Spanish. **Health:** Dental hygiene, music therapy, nursing (RN). **History:** General. **Liberal arts:** Arts/sciences. **Math:** General. **Parks/recreation:** Health/fitness, sports admin. **Philosophy/religion:** Philosophy. **Physical sciences:** Chemistry, physics. **Protective services:** Law enforcement admin. **Psychology:** General. **Social sciences:** Anthropology, economics, geography, political science, sociology. **Visual/performing arts:** Art history/conservation, dramatic, studio arts.

Most popular majors. Business/marketing 22%, communications/journalism 7%, engineering/engineering technologies 9%, health sciences 6%, parks/recreation 6%, psychology 8%, security/protective services 6%, social sciences 10%.

Computing on campus. 327 workstations in dormitories, library, computer center, student center. Dormitories wired for high-speed internet access and linked to campus network. Commuter students can connect to campus network. Online course registration, online library, helpline, repair service, student web hosting, wireless network available.

Student life. **Freshman orientation:** Mandatory, $100 fee. Preregistration for classes offered. **Policies:** Freshmen permitted cars on campus. **Housing:** Coed dorms, special housing for disabled, apartments, fraternity/sorority housing available. Special residence hall floors with in-house computer facilities for honors students, coed suites available. **Activities:** Marching band, choral groups, dance, drama, radio station, student government, student newspaper, Alpha Phi Omega, College Democrats, UNICEF, Common Ground, Fellowship for Christian Athletes, Baptist Student Union, Asian Student Union, College Republicans.

Athletics. NCAA. **Intercollegiate:** Baseball M, basketball, cross-country, diving, field hockey W, football (tackle) M, golf, rowing (crew) W, soccer, softball W, swimming, tennis, track and field, volleyball W. **Intramural:** Badminton, basketball, bowling, cheerleading, cross-country, fencing, golf, racquetball, rugby M, skiing, soccer, softball, swimming, table tennis, tennis, track and field, volleyball. **Team name:** Cardinals.

Student services. Alcohol/substance abuse counseling, campus ministries, career counseling, student employment services, financial aid counseling, health services, legal services, minority student services, personal counseling, placement for graduates, women's services. **Physically disabled:** Services for visually, speech, hearing impaired.

Contact. E-mail: admitme@gwise.louisville.edu
Phone: (502) 852-6531 Toll-free number: (800) 334-8635 ext. 6531
Fax: (502) 852-4776
Jenny Sawyer, Director of Admissions, University of Louisville, 2211 South Brook Street, Louisville, KY 40292

University of the Cumberlands

Williamsburg, Kentucky — **CB member**
www.ucumberlands.edu — **CB code: 1145**

- Private 4-year liberal arts college affiliated with Baptist faith
- Residential campus in small town
- 1,456 degree-seeking undergraduates: 3% part-time, 51% women, 7% African American, 1% Asian American, 2% Hispanic American, 2% international
- 139 degree-seeking graduate students
- 83% of applicants admitted
- SAT or ACT (ACT writing optional), application essay required
- 42% graduate within 6 years; 36% enter graduate study

General. Founded in 1889. Regionally accredited. **Degrees:** 246 bachelor's awarded; master's offered. **ROTC:** Army. **Location:** 100 miles from Lexington; 65 miles from Knoxville, Tennessee. **Calendar:** Semester, limited summer session. **Full-time faculty:** 85 total; 75% have terminal degrees, 5% minority, 36% women. **Part-time faculty:** 42 total; 24% have terminal degrees, 36% women. **Class size:** 64% < 20, 31% 20-39, 2% 40-49, 2% 50-99, less than 1% >100. **Special facilities:** Life science museum, greenhouse, conference center and inn.

Freshman class profile. 984 applied, 818 admitted, 433 enrolled.

Mid 50% test scores			
SAT verbal:	430-550	Rank in top quarter:	42%
SAT math:	450-550	Rank in top tenth:	16%
ACT:	18-23	End year in good standing:	80%
GPA 3.50 or higher:	41%	Return as sophomores:	63%
GPA 3.0-3.49:	28%	Out-of-state:	43%
GPA 2.0-2.99:	30%	Live on campus:	84%
		International:	1%

Basis for selection. School achievement and activities, test scores, recommendations, essay important. **Homeschooled:** Must have GED or high school transcript.

High school preparation. Required and recommended units include English 4, mathematics 3, social studies 1-2 and science 2-3.

2006-2007 Annual costs. Tuition/fees (projected): $13,658. Room/board: $6,326. Books/supplies: $900.

2005-2006 Financial aid. **Need-based:** 402 full-time freshmen applied for aid; 353 were judged to have need; 353 of these received aid. Average need met was 93%. Average scholarship/grant was $6,538; average loan $3,319. 56% of total undergraduate aid awarded as scholarships/grants, 44% as loans/jobs. **Non-need-based:** Awarded to 1,134 full-time undergraduates, including 401 freshmen. Scholarships awarded for academics, alumni affiliation, art, athletics, leadership, music/drama, religious affiliation, ROTC, state residency.

Application procedures. **Admission:** Priority date 3/1; deadline 8/15 (receipt date). $30 fee, may be waived for applicants with need. Application may be submitted online. Admission notification on a rolling basis. Must reply by May 1 or within 2 week(s) if notified thereafter. **Financial aid:** Priority date 3/1; no closing date. FAFSA required. Applicants notified on a rolling basis starting 4/1; must reply within 2 week(s) of notification.

Academics. All students encouraged to take advantage of individualized or computerized tutoring assistance. **Special study options:** Accelerated study, cooperative education, distance learning, double major, honors, independent study, internships, liberal arts/career combination, student-designed major, study abroad, teacher certification program. **Credit/placement by examination:** AP, CLEP, IB, institutional tests. 30 credit hours maximum toward bachelor's degree. **Support services:** Learning center, reduced course load, study skills assistance, tutoring, writing center.

Majors. **Biology:** General. **Business:** General, accounting. **Communications:** General. **Computer sciences:** General. **Education:** Art, business, computer, elementary, health, middle, music, physical, social studies, special. **English:** English lit, speech/rhetoric. **Health:** Community health services. **History:** General. **Math:** General. **Parks/recreation:** Health/fitness. **Physical sciences:** Chemistry, physics. **Psychology:** General. **Public administration:** Social work. **Social sciences:** Political science. **Theology:** Religious ed. **Visual/performing arts:** Dramatic, studio arts.

Most popular majors. Biology 12%, business/marketing 18%, communications/journalism 7%, education 18%, health sciences 7%, psychology 8%, public administration/social services 9%.

Computing on campus. 300 workstations in dormitories, library, computer center, student center. Dormitories wired for high-speed internet access and linked to campus network. Commuter students can connect to campus network. Online library, wireless network available.

Student life. **Freshman orientation:** Mandatory. Preregistration for classes offered. One-day session in summer. **Policies:** All students required to complete 40-hour community service project. Religious observance required. Freshmen permitted cars on campus. **Housing:** Guaranteed on-campus for all undergraduates. Single-sex dorms, substance-free housing available. $125 partly refundable deposit. **Activities:** Bands, choral groups, dance, drama, music ensembles, musical theater, radio station, student government, student newspaper, TV station, Baptist Student Union, Fellowship of Christian Athletes, Appalachian Ministries, Mountain Outreach.

Athletics. NAIA. **Intercollegiate:** Baseball M, basketball, cheerleading, cross-country, football (non-tackle) M, football (tackle) M, golf, judo, soccer, softball W, swimming, tennis, track and field, volleyball W, wrestling. **Intramural:** Basketball, football (non-tackle), golf, soccer, softball, table tennis, volleyball, water polo. **Team name:** Patriots.

Student services. Alcohol/substance abuse counseling, campus ministries, career counseling, student employment services, financial aid counseling, health services, personal counseling, placement for graduates, veterans' counselor, women's services.

Contact. E-mail: admiss@ucumberlands.edu
Phone: (606) 539-4241 Toll-free number: (800) 343-1609
Fax: (606) 539-4303
Erica Harris, Director of Admissions, University of the Cumberlands, 6178 College Station Drive, Williamsburg, KY 40769

Western Kentucky University

Bowling Green, Kentucky — **CB member**
www.wku.edu — **CB code: 1901**

- Public 4-year university
- Commuter campus in small city
- 15,341 degree-seeking undergraduates: 15% part-time, 58% women, 9% African American, 1% Asian American, 1% Hispanic American, 1% international
- 2,068 degree-seeking graduate students
- SAT or ACT (ACT writing optional) required
- 45% graduate within 6 years

General. Founded in 1906. Regionally accredited. Branch campus located in Glasgow, KY, offering general education, nursing, and elementary education programs. Upper division and graduate courses also offered at branch campuses in Owensboro, KY and Fort Knox/Elizabethtown, KY area. **Degrees:** 2,166 bachelor's, 299 associate awarded; master's, doctoral offered. **ROTC:** Army, Air Force. **Location:** 110 miles from Louisville; 65 miles from Nashville, Tennessee. **Calendar:** Semester, limited summer session. **Full-time faculty:** 694 total; 74% have terminal degrees, 12% minority, 44% women. **Part-time faculty:** 413 total; 14% have terminal degrees, 4% minority, 52% women. **Class size:** 39% < 20, 47% 20-39, 8% 40-49, 5% 50-99, less than 1% >100. **Special facilities:** Farm, planetarium.

Freshman class profile. 6,781 applied, 6,220 admitted, 3,150 enrolled.

Mid 50% test scores		Rank in top tenth:	15%
SAT verbal:	450-550	End year in good standing:	74%
SAT math:	440-560	Return as sophomores:	73%
ACT:	18-23	Out-of-state:	16%
GPA 3.50 or higher:	33%	Live on campus:	70%
GPA 3.0-3.49:	28%	International:	2%
GPA 2.0-2.99:	34%	Fraternities:	10%
Rank in top quarter:	36%	Sororities:	8%

Basis for selection. Open admission, but selective for some programs.

High school preparation. 22 units required. Required units include English 4, mathematics 3, social studies 3, science 3 (laboratory 1) and foreign language 2. 0.5 credits required in health & PE, history, performing arts.

2005-2006 Annual costs. Tuition/fees: $5,316; $12,732 out-of-state. Room/board: $5,220. Books/supplies: $800. Personal expenses: $1,600.

2004-2005 Financial aid. **Need-based:** 2,265 full-time freshmen applied for aid; 1,680 were judged to have need; 1,644 of these received aid. Average need met was 29%. Average scholarship/grant was $3,650; average loan $2,330. 49% of total undergraduate aid awarded as scholarships/grants, 51% as loans/jobs. **Non-need-based:** Awarded to 3,612 full-time undergraduates, including 2,266 freshmen. Scholarships awarded for academics, alumni affiliation, art, athletics, job skills, leadership, minority status, music/drama, religious affiliation, ROTC, state residency.

Application procedures. **Admission:** Closing date 8/1 (postmark date). $35 fee, may be waived for applicants with need. Application may be submitted online. Admission notification on a rolling basis. **Financial aid:** Priority date 4/1; no closing date. FAFSA required. Applicants notified on a rolling basis starting 3/1.

Academics. **Special study options:** Cooperative education, distance learning, double major, dual enrollment of high school students, ESL, exchange student, external degree, honors, independent study, internships, New York semester, student-designed major, study abroad, teacher certification program, Washington semester. Learning communities. **Credit/placement by examination:** AP, CLEP, IB, institutional tests. Unlimited number of hours of credit by examination may be counted toward degree. Students 21 and over admitted to community college division may take ACCUPLACER rather than ACT or SAT for placement. **Support services:** Learning center, preadmission summer program, reduced course load, remedial instruction, study skills assistance, tutoring, writing center.

Majors. **Agriculture:** General. **Biology:** General, biochemistry, molecular genetics. **Business:** Accounting, business admin, finance, hospitality admin, management information systems, managerial economics, marketing. **Communications:** General, advertising, journalism, organizational, political, public relations, radio/tv. **Computer sciences:** General. **Education:** Art, business, elementary, family/consumer sciences, middle, physical, special, speech impaired, trade/industrial. **Engineering:** Civil, electrical, mechanical. **Engineering technology:** Civil, environmental, industrial. **English:** English lit. **Family/consumer sciences:** Clothing/textiles. **Foreign languages:** French, German, Spanish. **Health:** Clinical lab science, community health services, dental hygiene, health care admin, nursing (RN). **History:** General. **Math:** General. **Parks/recreation:** Facilities management. **Philosophy/religion:** Philosophy, religion. **Physical sciences:** Chemistry, geology, physics. **Psychology:** General. **Public administration:** Social work. **Social sciences:** General, anthropology, economics, geography, political science, sociology. **Visual/performing arts:** General, dramatic, studio arts.

Most popular majors. Business/marketing 16%, communications/journalism 11%, education 19%, health sciences 6%, liberal arts 9%, social sciences 9%.

Computing on campus. 1,350 workstations in dormitories, library, computer center, student center. Dormitories wired for high-speed internet access and linked to campus network. Commuter students can connect to campus network. Online course registration, online library, helpline, student web hosting, wireless network available.

Student life. **Freshman orientation:** Mandatory. Preregistration for classes offered. One-day program held March through August. **Policies:** Freshmen permitted cars on campus. **Housing:** Guaranteed on-campus for freshmen. Coed dorms, single-sex dorms, special housing for disabled, fraternity/sorority housing, substance-free housing available. $150 partly refundable deposit, deadline 5/29. Learning communities, themed living options-honors, health and fitness, leadership, development, academic enhancement, diversity housing available. **Activities:** Bands, choral groups, dance, drama, film society, literary magazine, music ensembles, musical theater, opera, radio station, student government, student newspaper, symphony orchestra, TV station, College Republicans, Young Democrats, Campus Crusade, Women in Transition, international club, NAACP, Western Association of Asian Students, Green Party, Celebrate Activism Now.

Athletics. NCAA. **Intercollegiate:** Baseball M, basketball, cross-country, diving, football (tackle) M, golf, rifle, soccer, softball W, swimming, tennis, track and field, volleyball W. **Intramural:** Archery, badminton, basketball, bowling, equestrian, football (non-tackle), golf, handball, racquetball, soccer, softball, swimming, table tennis, triathlon, volleyball, water polo, wrestling M. **Team name:** Hilltoppers.

Student services. Adult student services, alcohol/substance abuse counseling, campus ministries, career counseling, services for economically disadvantaged, student employment services, financial aid counseling, health services, minority student services, on-campus daycare, personal counseling, placement for graduates, veterans' counselor, women's services. **Physically disabled:** Services for visually, speech, hearing impaired.

Contact. E-mail: admission@wku.edu
Phone: (270) 745-2551 Toll-free number: (800) 495-8463
Fax: (270) 745-6133
Dean Kahler, Director of Admission and Academic Services, Western Kentucky University, 1906 College Heights Boulevard, Bowling Green, KY 42101

Louisiana

Centenary College of Louisiana

Shreveport, Louisiana **CB member**
www.centenary.edu **CB code: 6082**

- Private 4-year liberal arts college affiliated with United Methodist Church
- Residential campus in small city
- 880 degree-seeking undergraduates: 1% part-time, 62% women, 7% African American, 2% Asian American, 4% Hispanic American, 1% Native American, 2% international
- 114 degree-seeking graduate students
- 64% of applicants admitted
- SAT or ACT (ACT writing optional) required
- 53% graduate within 6 years

General. Founded in 1825. Regionally accredited. **Degrees:** 184 bachelor's awarded; master's offered. **Location:** 325 miles from New Orleans, 189 miles from Dallas. **Calendar:** Semester, extensive summer session. **Full-time faculty:** 68 total; 94% have terminal degrees, 3% minority, 34% women. **Part-time faculty:** 55 total; 34% have terminal degrees, 7% minority, 47% women. **Class size:** 69% < 20, 30% 20-39, less than 1% 40-49. **Special facilities:** Amphitheater, playhouse, music library, archives, museum, Jack London Collection.

Freshman class profile. 1,348 applied, 856 admitted, 233 enrolled.

Mid 50% test scores			
SAT verbal:	510-650	Rank in top tenth:	40%
SAT math:	500-630	End year in good standing:	91%
ACT:	22-27	Return as sophomores:	81%
GPA 3.50 or higher:	57%	Out-of-state:	57%
GPA 3.0-3.49:	26%	Live on campus:	88%
GPA 2.0-2.99:	17%	International:	1%
Rank in top quarter:	70%	Sororities:	21%

Basis for selection. Academic achievement record, high school GPA, test scores, essay, letters of recommendation, interview recommended. Extracurricular activities and leadership ability considered. Audition required of music, theater, dance majors. Portfolio recommended for art majors. **Homeschooled:** Transcript of courses and grades required.

High school preparation. College-preparatory program recommended. 15 units recommended. Recommended units include English 4, mathematics 3, social studies 3, science 3 (laboratory 2) and foreign language 2.

2005-2006 Annual costs. Tuition/fees: $18,390. Room/board: $6,370.

2004-2005 Financial aid. Need-based: 205 full-time freshmen applied for aid; 149 were judged to have need; 149 of these received aid. Average need met was 71%. Average scholarship/grant was $11,168; average loan $2,702. 83% of total undergraduate aid awarded as scholarships/grants, 17% as loans/jobs. **Non-need-based:** Awarded to 585 full-time undergraduates, including 166 freshmen. Scholarships awarded for academics, art, athletics, leadership, music/drama, religious affiliation, state residency.

Application procedures. Admission: Priority date 2/15; deadline 8/1 (postmark date). $30 fee, may be waived for applicants with need. Application may be submitted online. Admission notification on a rolling basis beginning on or about 11/15. Must reply by 5/1. Must reply by May 1 or within 3 week(s) if notified thereafter. **Financial aid:** Priority date 2/15; no closing date. FAFSA, institutional form required. Applicants notified by 3/15; must reply by 5/1.

Academics. Special study options: Combined bachelor's/graduate degree, cross-registration, double major, dual enrollment of high school students, exchange student, honors, independent study, internships, liberal arts/career combination, student-designed major, study abroad, teacher certification program, Washington semester. Oak Ridge National Laboratory semester, 3-2 engineering program, 3-2 communication disorders program. **Credit/placement by examination:** AP, CLEP, IB, institutional tests. 40 credit hours maximum toward bachelor's degree. Credit awarded only when the student has not already attempted to earn credit in a college classroom at or below the level of the subject covered by the exam. **Support services:** Learning center, reduced course load, study skills assistance, tutoring, writing center.

Majors. Biology: General, biochemistry, biophysics. **Business:** Accounting, accounting/business management, accounting/finance, business admin, finance, managerial economics. **Communications:** General, digital media, media studies. **Conservation:** Environmental science. **Education:** Art, biology, chemistry, drama/dance, elementary, English, foreign languages, French, German, health, history, mathematics, middle, multi-level teacher, music, physical, psychology, science, secondary, social studies, Spanish. **English:** English lit. **Foreign languages:** General, classics, French, German, Latin, Spanish. **Health:** Predentistry, premedicine, prepharmacy, preveterinary, speech pathology. **History:** General. **Interdisciplinary:** Neuroscience. **Legal studies:** Prelaw. **Liberal arts:** Arts/sciences. **Math:** General. **Parks/recreation:** Exercise sciences, health/fitness. **Philosophy/religion:** Philosophy, religion. **Physical sciences:** Chemistry, geology, physics. **Psychology:** General. **Social sciences:** Applied economics, economics, political science, sociology. **Theology:** Sacred music. **Visual/performing arts:** General, art, cinematography, dance, dramatic, music performance, music theory/composition, painting, piano/organ, sculpture, studio arts, theater design, voice/opera.

Most popular majors. Biology 13%, business/marketing 17%, communications/journalism 9%, parks/recreation 8%, psychology 10%, social sciences 7%, visual/performing arts 12%.

Computing on campus. 250 workstations in dormitories, library, computer center. Dormitories linked to campus network. Commuter students can connect to campus network. Online course registration, student web hosting available.

Student life. Freshman orientation: Mandatory, $100 fee. 4 days prior to beginning of fall classes. **Policies:** Students participate on enrollment management committee, academic affairs committee, student/faculty discipline and other college-wide committees. Freshmen permitted cars on campus. **Housing:** Guaranteed on-campus for all undergraduates. Coed dorms, single-sex dorms, fraternity/sorority housing available. $200 partly refundable deposit, deadline 7/1. All students 21 years of age or below who are not local residents are required to live in college housing. **Activities:** Bands, choral groups, dance, drama, film society, music ensembles, musical theater, opera, radio station, student government, student newspaper, symphony orchestra, church careers institute, United Methodist student movement, Baptist Collegiate Ministry, Canterbury House, Fellowship of Christian Athletes, student government association, Young Democrats, Young Republicans, students for diversity, tutoring service.

Athletics. NCAA. **Intercollegiate:** Baseball M, basketball, cross-country, golf, gymnastics W, soccer, softball W, swimming, tennis, volleyball W. **Intramural:** Archery, badminton, basketball, bowling, football (non-tackle), golf, lacrosse M, racquetball, rowing (crew), soccer, softball, table tennis, tennis, volleyball. **Team name:** Gents/Ladies.

Student services. Alcohol/substance abuse counseling, campus ministries, career counseling, financial aid counseling, health services, personal counseling, veterans' counselor. **Physically disabled:** Services for visually impaired.

Contact. E-mail: tcrowley@centenary.edu
Phone: (318) 869-5131 Toll-free number: (800) 234-4448
Fax: (318) 869-5005
Tim Crowley, Director of Admissions, Centenary College of Louisiana, Box 41188, Shreveport, LA 71134-1188

Dillard University

New Orleans, Louisiana **CB member**
www.dillard.edu **CB code: 6164**

- Private 4-year university and liberal arts college affiliated with United Church of Christ and United Methodist Church
- Residential campus in very large city
- 2,155 degree-seeking undergraduates
- SAT or ACT with writing, application essay required

General. Founded in 1869. Regionally accredited. Because of higher priorities in the aftermath of Hurricane Katrina, the information in this profile has not been updated for the 2006-2007 academic year. **Degrees:** 345 bachelor's awarded. **ROTC:** Army, Navy, Air Force. **Calendar:** Semester, limited summer session. **Full-time faculty:** 145 total; 68% have terminal degrees, 91% minority, 57% women. **Part-time faculty:** 56 total; 14% have terminal degrees, 77% minority, 55% women. **Class size:** 60% < 20, 34% 20-39, 5% 40-49, 1% 50-99, less than 1% >100. **Special facilities:** Video encyclopedia of 20th century.

Freshman class profile.

Mid 50% test scores			
SAT verbal:	450-530	Rank in top quarter:	44%
SAT math:	440-520	Rank in top tenth:	2%
ACT:	19-22	Out-of-state:	46%

Basis for selection. Preference to applicants in top 25% of class, 2.5 minimum GPA. Test scores, class rank, participation in extracurricular activities and community projects considered. Interview recommended. **Homeschooled:** Recommended that student apply for state diploma.

High school preparation. 19 units required. Required and recommended units include English 4, mathematics 3, social studies 3, science 3, foreign language 2 and academic electives 6.

2005-2006 Annual costs. Tuition/fees: $12,240. Room/board: $7,070. Books/supplies: $1,000. Personal expenses: $1,533.

2005-2006 Financial aid. All financial aid based on need. Average need met was 85%. Average scholarship/grant was $3,834; average loan $2,511. 64% of total undergraduate aid awarded as scholarships/grants, 36% as loans/jobs.

Application procedures. Admission: Priority date 5/1; deadline 7/1 (postmark date). $20 fee, may be waived for applicants with need. Application may be submitted online. Admission notification on a rolling basis. Must reply by May 1 or within 2 week(s) if notified thereafter. **Financial aid:** Priority date 3/1, closing date 5/1. FAFSA, institutional form required. Applicants notified on a rolling basis starting 3/1; must reply by 5/1 or within 2 week(s) of notification.

Academics. Special study options: Combined bachelor's/graduate degree, double major, dual enrollment of high school students, honors, independent study, internships, liberal arts/career combination, study abroad, teacher certification program. **Credit/placement by examination:** AP, CLEP, IB, institutional tests. 20 credit hours maximum toward bachelor's degree. **Support services:** Learning center, pre-admission summer program, reduced course load, remedial instruction, tutoring.

Majors. Area/ethnic studies: African, Japanese. **Biology:** General. **Business:** Accounting, business admin, finance. **Communications:** General. **Computer sciences:** Computer science. **Education:** Brain injured, early childhood, early childhood special, elementary, physical, secondary, special. **English:** English lit. **Foreign languages:** General, French, German, Japanese, Spanish. **Health:** Nursing (RN), premedicine, public health ed. **History:** General. **Math:** General. **Physical sciences:** Chemistry, physics. **Psychology:** General. **Public administration:** Social work. **Social sciences:** Criminology, economics, political science, sociology, urban studies. **Visual/performing arts:** Art, arts management, dramatic, music management.

Computing on campus. 400 workstations in dormitories, library, computer center. Dormitories wired for high-speed internet access and linked to campus network. Commuter students can connect to campus network. Online library, helpline, repair service available.

Student life. Freshman orientation: Mandatory, $200 fee. Preregistration for classes offered. **Policies:** Freshmen permitted cars on campus. **Housing:** Guaranteed on-campus for freshmen. Coed dorms, single-sex dorms, special housing for disabled, apartments, substance-free housing available. $300 deposit, deadline 5/1. **Activities:** Jazz band, choral groups, dance, drama, music ensembles, musical theater, radio station, student government, student newspaper, service sororities and fraternities, honor societies, religious groups, NAACP, Santa Filomena, Young Republicans, Baptist Student Union.

Athletics. NAIA. **Intercollegiate:** Basketball, cross-country, tennis, volleyball W. **Intramural:** Basketball, football (non-tackle), football (tackle) M, soccer, softball, swimming, table tennis, tennis, track and field, volleyball. **Team name:** Blue Devils.

Student services. Campus ministries, career counseling, student employment services, financial aid counseling, health services, personal counseling, placement for graduates.

Contact. Phone: (504) 816-4670 Toll-free number: (800) 216-6637
Fax: (504) 816-4895
Linda Nash, Director of Admissions, Dillard University, 2601 Gentilly Boulevard, New Orleans, LA 70122-3097

Grambling State University

Grambling, Louisiana
www.gram.edu **CB code: 6250**

- Public 4-year university
- Residential campus in small town
- 4,574 degree-seeking undergraduates: 9% part-time, 59% women, 93% African American, 2% international
- 508 degree-seeking graduate students
- 37% graduate within 6 years

General. Founded in 1901. Regionally accredited. **Degrees:** 512 bachelor's, 51 associate awarded; master's, doctoral offered. **ROTC:** Army. **Location:** 35 miles from Monroe, 70 miles from Shreveport. **Calendar:** Semester, limited summer session. **Full-time faculty:** 251 total; 58% have terminal degrees, 76% minority, 46% women. **Part-time faculty:** 12 total; 50% have terminal degrees, 50% minority, 83% women.

Freshman class profile.

Mid 50% test scores			
SAT verbal:	380-460	GPA 2.0-2.99:	61%
SAT math:	370-470	Rank in top quarter:	23%
ACT:	15-18	End year in good standing:	80%
GPA 3.50 or higher:	9%	Return as sophomores:	63%
GPA 3.0-3.49:	20%	Out-of-state:	44%
		International:	1%

Basis for selection. Open admission, but selective for out-of-state students.

High school preparation. 16.5 units recommended. Recommended units include English 4, mathematics 3, history 3, science 3 and foreign language 2. One fine arts and .5 computer science units recommended.

2005-2006 Annual costs. Tuition/fees: $3,506; $8,856 out-of-state. Room/board: $4,034. Books/supplies: $702. Personal expenses: $1,365.

2005-2006 Financial aid. Need-based: 1,085 full-time freshmen applied for aid; 975 were judged to have need; 956 of these received aid. Average need met was 90%. Average scholarship/grant was $2,765; average loan $2,563. 47% of total undergraduate aid awarded as scholarships/grants, 53% as loans/jobs. **Non-need-based:** Awarded to 975 full-time undergraduates, including 251 freshmen. Scholarships awarded for academics, athletics, leadership, minority status, music/drama, ROTC, state residency.

Application procedures. Admission: Priority date 4/1; deadline 7/1. $20 fee. Application may be submitted online. Admission notification on a rolling basis. **Financial aid:** Priority date 4/1, closing date 6/1. FAFSA, institutional form required. Applicants notified on a rolling basis starting 3/1; must reply within 2 week(s) of notification.

Academics. Special study options: Cooperative education, cross-registration, distance learning, double major, exchange student, honors, independent study, internships, study abroad, teacher certification program. **Credit/placement by examination:** CLEP. **Support services:** Learning center, reduced course load, remedial instruction, tutoring.

Honors college/program. Requires minimum ACT score of 25 or SAT equivalent.

Majors. Biology: General. **Business:** Accounting, managerial economics, marketing. **Communications:** Journalism. **Computer sciences:** Computer science, information systems. **Education:** Art, business, early childhood, elementary, English, family/consumer sciences, French, music, physical, social science, special, technology/industrial arts. **Engineering technology:** Construction, drafting, electrical. **Family/consumer sciences:** Institutional food production. **Foreign languages:** French, Spanish. **Health:** Nursing (RN), speech pathology. **History:** General. **Legal studies:** Paralegal, prelaw. **Math:** General. **Parks/recreation:** General. **Physical sciences:** Chemistry, physics. **Protective services:** Criminal justice. **Psychology:** General. **Public administration:** General, social work. **Social sciences:** General, political science, sociology. **Visual/performing arts:** Art, art history/conservation, dramatic, music performance.

Most popular majors. Biology 6%, business/marketing 21%, computer/information sciences 16%, education 7%, health sciences 9%, security/protective services 10%.

Computing on campus. 175 workstations in library, computer center. Dormitories linked to campus network. Online course registration, helpline available.

Student life. Freshman orientation: Available. Preregistration for classes offered. **Housing:** Single-sex dorms, apartments available. $50 deposit. **Activities:** Bands, choral groups, dance, drama, film society, music ensembles, opera, radio station, student government, student newspaper, symphony orchestra, TV station, Bayou Boyz social organization, Favrot student union, College Democrats.

Athletics. NCAA. **Intercollegiate:** Baseball M, basketball, bowling W, cross-country, football (tackle) M, golf, soccer W, softball W, tennis, track and field, volleyball W. **Intramural:** Badminton, baseball M, basketball, bowling, cross-country, golf, gymnastics M, softball W, swimming, tennis, track and field, volleyball. **Team name:** Tigers.

Student services. Career counseling, student employment services, financial aid counseling, health services, personal counseling, placement for graduates, veterans' counselor. **Physically disabled:** Services for visually, speech, hearing impaired.

Contact. E-mail: collierc@gram.edu
Phone: (318) 274-6183 Toll-free number: (888) 863-3655
Fax: (318) 274-3292
Carolyn Collier, Acting Director of Admission, Grambling State University, PO Box 864, Grambling, LA 71245-0864

Herzing College
Kenner, Louisiana
www.herzing.edu **CB code: 3430**

- For-profit 4-year branch campus and technical college
- Commuter campus in very large city

General. Accredited by ACICS. **Location:** 10 miles from downtown New Orleans. **Calendar:** Semester.

Annual costs/financial aid. Tuition costs vary by program, $255-300 per credit hour.

Contact. Phone: (504) 733-0074
Director of Admissions, 2400 Veterans Boulevard, Suite 410, Kenner, LA 70062

ITT Technical Institute: St. Rose
St. Rose, Louisiana
www.itt-tech.edu **CB code: 2766**

- For-profit 4-year technical college
- Commuter campus in small town

General. Accredited by ACICS. **Calendar:** Quarter.

Annual costs/financial aid. Tuition varies by program, $260-$368 per credit hour.

Contact. Phone: (504) 463-0338
Director of Recruitment, 140 James Drive East, St. Rose, LA 70087

Louisiana College
Pineville, Louisiana
www.lacollege.edu **CB code: 6371**

- Private 4-year liberal arts college affiliated with Southern Baptist Convention
- Commuter campus in small city

General. Founded in 1906. Regionally accredited. **Location:** One mile from Alexandria. **Calendar:** Semester.

Annual costs/financial aid. Tuition/fees (2005-2006): $10,300. Room/board: $3,886. Books/supplies: $535. Personal expenses: $1,040. Need-based financial aid available to full-time and part-time students.

Contact. Phone: (318) 487-7011
Director of Enrollment Management and Admissions, 1140 College Drive, Pineville, LA 71359

Louisiana State University and Agricultural and Mechanical College
Baton Rouge, Louisiana **CB member**
www.lsu.edu **CB code: 6373**

- Public 4-year university and agricultural college
- Commuter campus in large city
- 25,301 degree-seeking undergraduates: 7% part-time, 52% women, 9% African American, 3% Asian American, 3% Hispanic American, 2% international
- 5,219 degree-seeking graduate students
- 73% of applicants admitted
- SAT or ACT with writing required
- 58% graduate within 6 years

General. Founded in 1860. Regionally accredited. **Degrees:** 4,449 bachelor's awarded; master's, doctoral, first professional offered. **ROTC:** Army, Navy, Air Force. **Location:** 80 miles from New Orleans. **Calendar:** Semester, extensive summer session. **Full-time faculty:** 1,277 total; 85% have terminal degrees, 12% minority, 33% women. **Part-time faculty:** 190 total; 52% have terminal degrees, 9% minority, 43% women. **Class size:** 31% < 20, 42% 20-39, 7% 40-49, 12% 50-99, 8% >100. **Special facilities:** Mycological herbarium, lichenological herbarium, natural science museum, geoscience museum, rural life museum, Anglo-American art museum, Civil War center, biomedical research center, coastal ecology center, center for advanced microstructures & devices.

Freshman class profile. 10,825 applied, 7,927 admitted, 4,970 enrolled.

Mid 50% test scores			
SAT verbal:	520-630	Rank in top quarter:	53%
SAT math:	540-660	Rank in top tenth:	25%
ACT:	22-27	End year in good standing:	87%
GPA 3.50 or higher:	51%	Return as sophomores:	83%
GPA 3.0-3.49:	39%	Out-of-state:	17%
GPA 2.0-2.99:	10%	Live on campus:	44%
		International:	1%

Basis for selection. Sliding scale admissions criteria include number of academic units earned, GPA on those units, ACT or SAT scores. Students must also meet minimum Board of Regents Master Plan requirements. Applicants not meeting course units and/or grades or test score requirements may be considered by admissions committee. Out-of-state students must score at least 17 on the ACT or 830 on the SAT (exclusive of Writing). ACT/SAT writing component required for scholarship and honors college consideration. Audition required for MDA majors. Portfolio required for Art and Landscape Architecture majors. **Homeschooled:** Statement describing homeschool structure and mission, transcript of courses and grades required. Students with ACT score below 26 will be reviewed by admission committee. **Learning Disabled:** Students with learning disabilities who do not meet regular admission requirements may appeal to the admission committee and submit documentation explaining their positions.

High school preparation. College-preparatory program required. 18 units required. Required and recommended units include English 4, mathematics 3-4, social studies 2, history 1, science 3, foreign language 2 and academic electives 3. Computer literacy (.5 units) also required. Specific courses required in some subject areas.

2005-2006 Annual costs. Tuition/fees: $4,515; $12,815 out-of-state. Room/board: $6,330. Books/supplies: $1,000. Personal expenses: $1,427.

2004-2005 Financial aid. Need-based: 4,835 full-time freshmen applied for aid; 2,465 were judged to have need; 2,419 of these received aid. Average need met was 65%. Average scholarship/grant was $4,460; average loan $2,366. 51% of total undergraduate aid awarded as scholarships/grants, 49% as loans/jobs. **Non-need-based:** Awarded to 9,175 full-time undergraduates, including 2,641 freshmen. Scholarships awarded for academics, alumni affiliation, art, athletics, leadership, music/drama, ROTC, state residency.

Application procedures. Admission: Priority date 11/15; deadline 4/15 (receipt date). $40 fee. Application must be submitted online. Admission notification on a rolling basis. **Financial aid:** No deadline. FAFSA, institutional form required. Applicants notified on a rolling basis starting 3/1; must reply within 3 week(s) of notification.

Academics. Special study options: Accelerated study, cooperative education, cross-registration, distance learning, double major, dual enrollment of high school students, ESL, exchange student, honors, independent study, internships, student-designed major, study abroad, teacher certification program. **Credit/placement by examination:** AP, CLEP, IB, SAT, ACT, institutional tests. 30 credit hours maximum toward bachelor's degree. **Support services:** Learning center, study skills assistance, tutoring, writing center.

Honors college/program. Minimum ACT of 30 composite and 30 English, or 29 composite and 31 English; or SAT of 1320 total (exclusive of Writing) and 660 verbal. High school academic GPA of 3.5 required. Essay required.

Majors. Agriculture: Animal sciences, business, food science, plant sciences. **Architecture:** Architecture, interior, landscape. **Area/ethnic studies:** Women's. **Biology:** General, biochemistry, microbiology. **Business:** Accounting, business admin, construction management, fashion, finance, international, management science, managerial economics, marketing. **Communications:** Media studies. **Computer sciences:** Computer science. **Conservation:** Environmental science, forest management, management/policy. **Education:** Adult/continuing, early childhood, elementary, music, physical, secondary. **Engineering:** Biomedical, chemical, civil, computer, electrical, environmental, industrial, mechanical, petroleum. **English:** English lit, speech/

rhetoric. **Family/consumer sciences:** General. **Foreign languages:** French, German, Latin, Spanish. **Health:** Audiology/speech pathology, dietetics. **History:** General. **Interdisciplinary:** Global studies. **Liberal arts:** Arts/sciences. **Math:** General. **Philosophy/religion:** Philosophy. **Physical sciences:** Chemistry, geology, physics. **Psychology:** General. **Social sciences:** Anthropology, economics, geography, political science, sociology. **Visual/performing arts:** Dramatic, music performance, studio arts.

Most popular majors. Biology 8%, business/marketing 21%, education 10%, engineering/engineering technologies 9%, liberal arts 9%, social sciences 9%.

Computing on campus. 1,000 workstations in dormitories, library, student center. Dormitories wired for high-speed internet access and linked to campus network. Commuter students can connect to campus network. Online course registration, online library, helpline, student web hosting, wireless network available.

Student life. Freshman orientation: Mandatory, $76 fee. Preregistration for classes offered. Held in June, July, and August; testing held in spring. **Policies:** Freshmen permitted cars on campus. **Housing:** Coed dorms, single-sex dorms, special housing for disabled, apartments, fraternity/sorority housing available. **Activities:** Bands, choral groups, dance, drama, film society, literary magazine, music ensembles, musical theater, opera, radio station, student government, student newspaper, symphony orchestra, TV station, Various religious, professional, honorary, political, service, and special interest organizations.

Athletics. NCAA. **Intercollegiate:** Baseball M, basketball, cross-country, football (tackle) M, golf, gymnastics W, soccer W, softball W, swimming, tennis, track and field, volleyball W. **Intramural:** Badminton, basketball, football (non-tackle), golf, racquetball, soccer, softball, table tennis, tennis, volleyball. **Team name:** Tigers.

Student services. Adult student services, alcohol/substance abuse counseling, career counseling, student employment services, financial aid counseling, health services, minority student services, on-campus daycare, personal counseling, placement for graduates, veterans' counselor, women's services. **Physically disabled:** Services for visually, speech, hearing impaired.

Contact. E-mail: admissions@lsu.edu
Phone: (225) 578-1175 Fax: (225) 578-4433
Cleve Brooks, Director, Admissions, Louisiana State University and Agricultural and Mechanical College, 110 Thomas Boyd Hall, Baton Rouge, LA 70803-2750

Louisiana State University at Alexandria

Alexandria, Louisiana
www.lsua.edu **CB code: 1632**

- Public 4-year university
- Commuter campus in small city
- 2,940 degree-seeking undergraduates: 47% part-time, 74% women, 19% African American, 1% Asian American, 1% Hispanic American, 2% Native American

General. Founded in 1959. Regionally accredited. **Degrees:** 87 bachelor's, 197 associate awarded. **ROTC:** Army. **Location:** 10 miles from downtown. **Calendar:** Semester, extensive summer session. **Full-time faculty:** 105 total; 49% have terminal degrees, 10% minority, 52% women. **Part-time faculty:** 75 total; 15% have terminal degrees, 5% minority, 56% women. **Class size:** 42% < 20, 50% 20-39, 4% 40-49, 3% 50-99.

Freshman class profile.

Return as sophomores:	50%	**Out-of-state:**	1%

Basis for selection. Open admission. ACT scores are used to determine placement in Math and English courses. **Homeschooled:** Applicants must submit transcript of high school level work with graduation date and ACT scores.

High school preparation. College-preparatory program recommended. 16.5 units recommended. Recommended units include English 4, mathematics 3, social studies 3, science 3, foreign language 2, academic electives 1.5. .5 units in computer studies and 1 unit in fine arts survey recommended.

2005-2006 Annual costs. Tuition/fees: $3,387; $6,054 out-of-state. Books/supplies: $690. Personal expenses: $1,342.

Financial aid. Non-need-based: Scholarships awarded for academics, state residency.

Application procedures. Admission: Priority date 8/1; no deadline. $20 fee. Admission notification on a rolling basis. **Financial aid:** Priority date 4/1; no closing date. FAFSA, institutional form required. Applicants notified on a rolling basis starting 4/20; must reply within 3 week(s) of notification.

Academics. Special study options: Distance learning, dual enrollment of high school students. **Credit/placement by examination:** AP, CLEP, institutional tests. Credit by examination limited to one-fourth the number of hours required for the degree. **Support services:** Learning center, pre-admission summer program, remedial instruction, study skills assistance, tutoring, writing center.

Majors. Biology: General. **Education:** General. **Liberal arts:** Arts/sciences.

Most popular majors. Education 42%, liberal arts 53%.

Computing on campus. 163 workstations in library, computer center, student center. Commuter students can connect to campus network.

Student life. Freshman orientation: Mandatory. Preregistration for classes offered. **Policies:** Freshmen permitted cars on campus. **Housing:** Apartments available. On-campus apartment housing available Fall 2004. **Activities:** Choral groups, drama, literary magazine, student government, student newspaper, Baptist Ministry, Catholic student organization, Apostolic Student Fellowship, Canterbury Club, College Republicans, College Democrats, international student organization, non-traditional student organization, identity, Circle K.

Athletics. Intramural: Basketball, cross-country, football (non-tackle) M, soccer, softball, tennis, volleyball.

Student services. Adult student services, campus ministries, career counseling, student employment services, financial aid counseling, minority student services, on-campus daycare, personal counseling, placement for graduates, veterans' counselor.

Contact. E-mail: generalinfo@lsua.edu
Phone: (318) 473-6417 Toll-free number: (888) 473-6417
Fax: (318) 473-6418
Leslie Quinn, Registrar, Louisiana State University at Alexandria, 8100 Highway 71 South, Alexandria, LA 71302-9121

Louisiana State University Health Sciences Center

New Orleans, Louisiana
www.lsuhsc.edu **CB code: 1192**

- Public upper-division health science and nursing college
- Commuter campus in very large city

General. Founded in 1931. Regionally accredited. **Degrees:** 231 bachelor's, 6 associate awarded; master's, doctoral, first professional offered. **Articulation:** Agreement with University of New Orleans. **Location:** Downtown. **Calendar:** Differs by program, limited summer session. **Full-time faculty:** 1,242 total. **Part-time faculty:** 138 total.

Student profile. 615 degree-seeking undergraduates.

Out-of-state:	1%	**25 or older:**	28%
Live on campus:	20%		

Basis for selection. College transcript required. Interview required. TOEFL required of applicants for whom English is second language. Selection based on academic record and interview. Application closing, notification, and response dates vary by program. Transfer accepted as sophomores, juniors, seniors.

2005-2006 Annual costs. Tuition/fees: $3,978; $7,110 out-of-state. Room only: $2,210.

Financial aid. Need-based: 4% of total undergraduate aid awarded as scholarships/grants, 96% as loans/jobs. **Non-need-based:** Scholarships awarded for academics.

Application procedures. Financial aid: Priority date 4/15. FAFSA, institutional form required.

Academics. Special study options: Cross-registration, double major, honors, independent study, internships. **Credit/placement by examination:** CLEP.

Majors. Health: Cardiovascular technology, clinical lab science, dental hygiene, dental lab technology, nursing (RN), ophthalmic technology, vocational rehab counseling.

Computing on campus. 227 workstations in dormitories, library, computer center, student center. Dormitories wired for high-speed internet access and linked to campus network. Commuter students can connect to campus network. Online library, helpline, repair service, wireless network available.

Student life. Housing: Coed dorms, apartments, substance-free housing available. **Activities:** Choral groups, student government.

Student services. Alcohol/substance abuse counseling, career counseling, financial aid counseling, health services, personal counseling. **Physically disabled:** Services for visually, speech, hearing impaired.

Contact. Phone: (504) 568-4808
Louisiana State University Health Sciences Center, 433 Bolivar Street, New Orleans, LA 70112-2223

Louisiana State University in Shreveport

Shreveport, Louisiana
www.lsus.edu **CB code: 6355**

- Public 4-year university
- Commuter campus in large city
- 3,764 degree-seeking undergraduates: 32% part-time, 64% women, 23% African American, 2% Asian American, 2% Hispanic American, 1% Native American
- 430 degree-seeking graduate students
- ACT (writing optional) required

General. Founded in 1965. Regionally accredited. **Degrees:** 481 bachelor's awarded; master's offered. **ROTC:** Army. **Location:** 180 miles from Dallas. **Calendar:** Semester, extensive summer session. **Full-time faculty:** 160 total. **Part-time faculty:** 100 total. **Class size:** 37% < 20, 48% 20-39, 9% 40-49, 6% 50-99. **Special facilities:** Life science museum, pioneer heritage center, Northwest Louisiana archives, Noal Memorial collection.

Freshman class profile. 459 enrolled.

Mid 50% test scores			
SAT verbal:	420-590	ACT:	18-23
SAT math:	420-540	Return as sophomores:	62%
		Out-of-state:	4%

Basis for selection. Completion of the Regents' high school core curriculum (currently TOPS core curriculum) of 16.5 course units. In addition, one of the following: high school GPA of 2.0 or greater, or high school graduation rank top 50% of class, or ACT composite score of 20 or greater. No more than one developmental course necessary if ACT English score of 18 or greater, or an ACT mathematics score of 18 or greater. Regardless of age, students who have accumulated at least 12 term hours of non-developmental college credit may transfer to LSUS if they meet all transfer requirements. **Homeschooled:** GED required.

High school preparation. Recommended units include English 4, mathematics 3, social studies 3 and science 3. 1 unit each in humanities, computer science, and speech also recommended.

2005-2006 Annual costs. Tuition/fees: $3,270; $7,600 out-of-state. Room only: $3,510. Books/supplies: $702. Personal expenses: $1,365.

Application procedures. Admission: Closing date 7/15. $10 fee. Application must be submitted on paper. Admission notification on a rolling basis. For early admission, principal's recommendation, ACT score of 27, 15 specific high school units, 3.0 GPA required. **Financial aid:** No deadline. Applicants notified on a rolling basis.

Academics. Special study options: Combined bachelor's/graduate degree, cooperative education, distance learning, double major, dual enrollment of high school students, internships, study abroad, teacher certification program, Washington semester. Cooperative education program with Southern University at Shreveport. **Credit/placement by examination:** AP, CLEP, ACT, institutional tests. 62 credit hours maximum toward bachelor's degree. **Support services:** Learning center, remedial instruction, study skills assistance, tutoring, writing center.

Majors. Biology: Biochemistry. **Business:** Accounting, business admin, finance, managerial economics. **Communications:** Journalism. **Computer sciences:** Computer science. **Conservation:** General. **Education:** Art, biology, chemistry, early childhood, elementary, English, French, mathematics, physical, physics, science, social studies, special. **English:** Speech/rhetoric. **Foreign languages:** French, Spanish. **Health:** Audiology/speech pathology. **History:** General. **Liberal arts:** Arts/sciences. **Math:** General. **Parks/recreation:** Health/fitness. **Physical sciences:** Chemistry, physics. **Protective services:** Criminal justice. **Psychology:** General. **Social sciences:** Geography, political science, sociology. **Visual/performing arts:** Art.

Computing on campus. 250 workstations in library, computer center, student center. Commuter students can connect to campus network. Online course registration, online library, helpline, student web hosting available.

Student life. Freshman orientation: Mandatory. Preregistration for classes offered. **Policies:** Freshmen permitted cars on campus. **Housing:** Guaranteed on-campus for all undergraduates. Apartments available. Pets allowed in dorm rooms. **Activities:** Dance, literary magazine, radio station, student government, student newspaper, Baptist student union, College Republicans, government and law society, Catholic student union, Rotaract, foreign language club, psychology club, Black student association.

Athletics. NAIA. **Intercollegiate:** Baseball M. **Intramural:** Badminton, basketball, football (non-tackle), golf, racquetball, soccer, softball, swimming, table tennis, tennis, track and field, volleyball. **Team name:** Pilots.

Student services. Career counseling, student employment services, financial aid counseling, minority student services, personal counseling, placement for graduates, veterans' counselor. **Physically disabled:** Services for visually, speech, hearing impaired.

Contact. E-mail: admissions@pilot.lsus.edu
Phone: (318) 797-5000 Toll-free number: (800) 229-5957
Fax: (318) 797-5286
Mickey Diez, Registrar, Louisiana State University in Shreveport, One University Place, Shreveport, LA 71115-2399

Louisiana Tech University

Ruston, Louisiana **CB member**
www.latech.edu **CB code: 6372**

- Public 4-year university
- Commuter campus in large town
- 8,892 degree-seeking undergraduates
- 83% of applicants admitted
- SAT or ACT (ACT writing optional) required

General. Founded in 1894. Regionally accredited. **Degrees:** 1,384 bachelor's, 100 associate awarded; master's, doctoral offered. **ROTC:** Army, Navy. **Location:** 70 miles from Shreveport, 30 miles from Monroe. **Calendar:** Quarter, extensive summer session. **Full-time faculty:** 394 total. **Part-time faculty:** 105 total. **Class size:** 37% < 20, 42% 20-39, 11% 40-49, 8% 50-99, 2% >100. **Special facilities:** Natural history museum, on-campus lab school, arboretum, planetarium, rehabilitation science and biomedical engineering center, micromanufacturing institute, water resource center.

Freshman class profile. 3,551 applied, 2,964 admitted, 1,829 enrolled.

Mid 50% test scores			
ACT:	20-25	Fraternities:	9%
Out-of-state:	14%	Sororities:	17%

Basis for selection. High school record, test scores most important. Special talents, school and community activities, recommendations considered. **Homeschooled:** Applicants must have an overall high school GPA of 2.5, ACT of at least 23, or SAT of at least 1060 (exclusive of Writing).

High school preparation. Required units include English 4, mathematics 3, social studies 3, science 3, academic electives 4.5. 2 units algebra required. Social studies must include 1 unit American history. 4.5 units of electives from foreign language, sciences, mathematics, social studies, speech, advanced fine arts, or computer literacy required. Prefer English courses that emphasize grammar, composition, and literature.

2005-2006 Annual costs. Tuition/fees: $4,131; $10,131 out-of-state. Room/board: $4,056. Books/supplies: $660. Personal expenses: $1,440.

2005-2006 Financial aid. Need-based: Average need met was 53%. Average scholarship/grant was $4,271; average loan $2,048. **Non-need-based:** Scholarships awarded for academics, art, athletics, leadership, music/drama, ROTC.

Application procedures. Admission: Priority date 8/1; no deadline. $20 fee, may be waived for applicants with need. Admission notification on a rolling basis beginning on or about 6/1. **Financial aid:** Priority date 4/15; no closing date. FAFSA, institutional form required. Applicants notified on a rolling basis starting 3/18; must reply within 4 week(s) of notification.

Academics. **Special study options:** Combined bachelor's/graduate degree, cooperative education, cross-registration, distance learning, double major, dual enrollment of high school students, ESL, honors, independent study, internships, liberal arts/career combination, study abroad, teacher certification program. Cooperative programs with Grambling State University. **Credit/placement by examination:** AP, CLEP, institutional tests. 30 credit hours maximum toward associate degree, 30 toward bachelor's. **Support services:** Remedial instruction, study skills assistance, tutoring.

Majors. **Agriculture:** Animal sciences, business, plant sciences. **Architecture:** Architecture, interior. **Biology:** General. **Business:** Accounting, business admin, finance, human resources, management information systems, management science, managerial economics, marketing, operations. **Communications:** Journalism. **Computer sciences:** Computer science. **Conservation:** General, forest resources, forestry. **Education:** Art, early childhood, elementary, French, music, physical, secondary, special, speech impaired. **Engineering:** Biomedical, chemical, civil, electrical, mechanical. **Engineering technology:** Civil, electrical. **English:** Speech/rhetoric. **Family/consumer sciences:** Family studies. **Foreign languages:** French, Spanish. **Health:** Audiology/speech pathology, clinical lab science, medical records admin. **History:** General. **Liberal arts:** Arts/sciences. **Math:** General. **Parks/recreation:** Health/fitness. **Physical sciences:** Chemistry, geology, physics. **Psychology:** General. **Social sciences:** Geography, political science, sociology. **Transportation:** Aviation, aviation management. **Visual/performing arts:** Art, commercial/advertising art, music performance, photography.

Computing on campus. 1,800 workstations in dormitories, library, computer center. Dormitories linked to campus network.

Student life. **Freshman orientation:** Available, $55 fee. Preregistration for classes offered. 4 sessions offered during the summer. **Policies:** Freshmen permitted cars on campus. **Housing:** Guaranteed on-campus for freshmen. Single-sex dorms, special housing for disabled, apartments available. $50 deposit, deadline 7/15. **Activities:** Bands, choral groups, dance, drama, music ensembles, musical theater, radio station, student government, Wesley Foundation, Baptist Student Union, Union Board, College Republicans, Campus Crusade for Christ, International Student Association, NAACP, Circle K, Angel Flight.

Athletics. NCAA. **Intercollegiate:** Baseball M, basketball, bowling W, cross-country, football (tackle) M, golf M, soccer W, softball W, tennis W, track and field, volleyball W. **Intramural:** Badminton, basketball, bowling, golf M, racquetball, soccer, softball, tennis, volleyball. **Team name:** Bulldogs (M), Lady Techsters (W).

Student services. Campus ministries, career counseling, student employment services, financial aid counseling, health services, legal services, minority student services, personal counseling, placement for graduates, veterans' counselor, women's services. **Physically disabled:** Services for speech impaired.

Contact. E-mail: bulldog@latech.edu
Phone: (318) 257-3036 Toll-free number: (800) 528-3241
Fax: (318) 257-2499
Jan Albritton, Director of Admissions, College of Basic and Career Studies, Louisiana Tech University, Box 3178, Ruston, LA 71272

Loyola University New Orleans

New Orleans, Louisiana — **CB member**
www.loyno.edu — **CB code: 6374**

- Private 4-year university and liberal arts college affiliated with Roman Catholic Church
- Residential campus in large city
- 3,618 degree-seeking undergraduates
- 68% of applicants admitted
- SAT or ACT with writing, application essay required

General. Founded in 1912. Regionally accredited. College in the Jesuit tradition. Because of higher priorities in the aftermath of Hurricane Katrina, the information in this profile has not been updated for the 2006-2007 academic year. **Degrees:** 784 bachelor's awarded; master's, first professional offered. **ROTC:** Army, Navy, Air Force. **Calendar:** Semester, limited summer session. **Full-time faculty:** 306 total; 85% have terminal degrees, 12% minority, 40% women. **Part-time faculty:** 177 total; 29% have terminal degrees, 10% minority, 37% women. **Class size:** 52% < 20, 42% 20-39, 3% 40-49, 2% 50-99, less than 1% >100. **Special facilities:** Humanities lab with Perseus Project and TLG TV and radio production studios, multimedia classrooms, 24-hour microcomputer lab, graphics lab, visual arts lab, communications lab, audio recording studio.

Freshman class profile. 3,713 applied, 2,522 admitted, 820 enrolled.

Mid 50% test scores			
SAT verbal:	570-680	Rank in top tenth:	28%
SAT math:	560-660	Out-of-state:	67%
ACT:	24-29	Live on campus:	81%
Rank in top quarter:	60%	Fraternities:	18%
		Sororities:	18%

Basis for selection. Freshman admission is based on the credentials submitted by a student for the admissions portfolio. High school performance, test scores, counselor/teacher evaluation, personal essay, extracurricular activity, community involvement and work experience are all considered. Interview recommended. Audition required for music, drama and speech majors. Portfolio required for art program applicants. **Homeschooled:** Require proof of high school graduation or its equivalent.

High school preparation. 10 units required; 15 recommended. Required and recommended units include English 4, mathematics 2-3, social studies 2-3 and science 2-3.

2005-2006 Annual costs. Tuition/fees: $25,246. Room/board: $8,312. Books/supplies: $1,000. Personal expenses: $1,424.

2005-2006 Financial aid. **Need-based:** 612 full-time freshmen applied for aid; 481 were judged to have need; 481 of these received aid. Average need met was 86%. Average scholarship/grant was $14,770; average loan $4,730. 71% of total undergraduate aid awarded as scholarships/grants, 29% as loans/jobs. **Non-need-based:** Awarded to 1,383 full-time undergraduates, including 290 freshmen. Scholarships awarded for academics, alumni affiliation, art, minority status, ROTC.

Application procedures. **Admission:** Priority date 1/15; no deadline. $20 fee, may be waived for applicants with need. Application may be submitted online. Admission notification on a rolling basis beginning on or about 11/1. Must reply by May 1 or within 2 week(s) if notified thereafter. **Financial aid:** Priority date 2/15; no closing date. FAFSA required. Applicants notified on a rolling basis starting 3/1; must reply by 5/1 or within 2 week(s) of notification.

Academics. Institution emphasizes the Jesuit tradition of contributing to the liberal education of the whole person. **Special study options:** Accelerated study, combined bachelor's/graduate degree, cross-registration, distance learning, double major, dual enrollment of high school students, ESL, exchange student, honors, independent study, internships, liberal arts/career combination, student-designed major, study abroad, teacher certification program, Washington semester. 3-2 engineering program with Tulane University. Limited weekend courses available. **Credit/placement by examination:** AP, CLEP, IB, institutional tests. 30 credit hours maximum toward bachelor's degree. **Support services:** Learning center, pre-admission summer program, reduced course load, remedial instruction, study skills assistance, tutoring, writing center.

Majors. **Biology:** General. **Business:** Accounting, business admin, finance, international, managerial economics, marketing. **Communications:** General. **Computer sciences:** General, information systems. **Education:** Elementary, music. **English:** Creative writing, English lit. **Foreign languages:** Ancient Greek, French, German, Russian, Spanish. **Health:** Music therapy, nursing (RN). **History:** General. **Liberal arts:** Arts/sciences. **Math:** General. **Philosophy/religion:** Philosophy, religion. **Physical sciences:** Chemistry, physics. **Protective services:** Criminal justice, forensics. **Psychology:** General. **Social sciences:** General, anthropology, economics, political science, sociology. **Visual/performing arts:** General, art, commercial/advertising art, dramatic, jazz, music history, music management, music performance, music theory/composition, piano/organ, studio arts.

Computing on campus. 458 workstations in dormitories, library, computer center, student center. Dormitories wired for high-speed internet access and linked to campus network. Commuter students can connect to campus network. Online course registration, online library, helpline, repair service, student web hosting, wireless network available.

Student life. **Freshman orientation:** Mandatory, $150 fee. Preregistration for classes offered. Includes placement tests. **Housing:** Guaranteed on-campus for freshmen. Coed dorms, special housing for disabled, apartments available. $100 deposit, deadline 5/1. Honors floors available. Counselors live in each hall to provide spiritual/counseling assistance. **Activities:** Bands, choral groups, dance, drama, film society, literary magazine, music ensembles, opera, student government, student newspaper, symphony orchestra, TV station, Student Government Association, Black Student Union, Community Action Program, International Students Association, La Gente, Asian Student Organization, Student Democrats, Gay/Lesbian Outreach, University Programming Board, Big Brothers/Big Sisters.

Athletics. NAIA. **Intercollegiate:** Baseball M, basketball, cross-country, soccer W, track and field, volleyball W. **Intramural:** Basketball, racquetball, soccer, softball, swimming, tennis, volleyball, water polo, weight lifting. **Team name:** Wolfpack.

Student services. Adult student services, alcohol/substance abuse counseling, campus ministries, career counseling, student employment services, financial aid counseling, health services, on-campus daycare, personal counseling, placement for graduates, women's services. **Physically disabled:** Services for visually, speech, hearing impaired.

Contact. E-mail: admit@loyno.edu
Phone: (504) 865-3240 Toll-free number: (800) 456-9652
Fax: (504) 865-3383
Deborah Stieffel, Dean of Admissions and Enrollment Management, Loyola University New Orleans, 6363 St. Charles Avenue, New Orleans, LA 70118-6195

McNeese State University
Lake Charles, Louisiana
www.mcneese.edu **CB code: 6403**

- Public 4-year university
- Commuter campus in small city

General. Founded in 1939. Regionally accredited. **Location:** 150 miles from Houston. **Calendar:** Semester.

Annual costs/financial aid. Tuition/fees (2005-2006): $3,204; $9,270 out-of-state. Room/board: $3,921. Books/supplies: $1,000. Personal expenses: $2,250. Need-based financial aid available to full-time and part-time students.

Contact. Phone: (337) 475-5356
Dean of Enrollment, 4205 Ryan Street, Lake Charles, LA 70609

New Orleans Baptist Theological Seminary: Leavell College
New Orleans, Louisiana
www.nobts.edu **CB code: 5034**

- Private 4-year Bible and seminary college affiliated with Southern Baptist Convention
- Very large city
- 1,650 degree-seeking undergraduates
- 89% of applicants admitted
- Application essay, interview required

General. Regionally accredited. Because of higher priorities in the aftermath of Hurricane Katrina, the information in this profile has not been updated for the 2006-2007 academic year. **Degrees:** 72 bachelor's, 25 associate awarded; master's, doctoral, first professional offered. **Calendar:** Semester, limited summer session. **Full-time faculty:** 13 total. **Part-time faculty:** 30 total. **Special facilities:** Learning extension centers in Baton Rouge, Lake Charles, and Shreveport. Other centers in Mississippi, Alabama, Florida, and Georgia.

Freshman class profile. 151 applied, 134 admitted, 102 enrolled.

Basis for selection. Must be 21 years old or over and a Christian for at least one year.

2005-2006 Annual costs. Tuition/fees: $3,820. Tuition reported for Southern Baptist students. Other Baptist students pay $4500; non-Baptist students pay $7200. Off-campus students pay additional $300 (Baptists) or $600 (non-Baptists). Certificate programs: $90 per course. Room only: $1,500. Books/supplies: $500.

Application procedures. Admission: No deadline. $25 fee, may be waived for applicants with need. Admission notification on a rolling basis. **Financial aid:** Closing date 6/1. Applicants notified by 8/1.

Academics. Credit/placement by examination: CLEP. 30 credit hours maximum toward bachelor's degree.

Majors. Theology: Bible, religious ed.

Student life. Freshman orientation: Mandatory. **Housing:** Single-sex dorms, apartments available.

Contact. E-mail: leavelladmission@nobts.edu
Phone: (504) 282-4455
Paul Gregoire, Registrar and Director of Admissions, New Orleans Baptist Theological Seminary: Leavell College, 3939 Gentilly Boulevard, New Orleans, LA 70126-4858

Nicholls State University
Thibodaux, Louisiana
www.nicholls.edu **CB code: 6221**

- Public 4-year university
- Commuter campus in large town
- 6,861 degree-seeking undergraduates: 20% part-time, 63% women, 20% African American, 1% Asian American, 1% Hispanic American, 2% Native American, 1% international
- 234 degree-seeking graduate students
- 67% of applicants admitted
- 27% graduate within 6 years

General. Founded in 1948. Regionally accredited. **Degrees:** 749 bachelor's, 159 associate awarded; master's offered. **Location:** 60 miles from New Orleans, 75 miles from Baton Rouge. **Calendar:** Semester, extensive summer session. **Full-time faculty:** 289 total; 55% have terminal degrees, 11% minority, 51% women. **Part-time faculty:** 1 total; 100% have terminal degrees. **Class size:** 39% < 20, 40% 20-39, 9% 40-49, 12% 50-99, 1% >100. **Special facilities:** Marine research facility, culinary institute, center for women and government, marine biology laboratory, center for study of dyslexia, center for economic education, small business development center, center for traditional boat building, economic council.

Freshman class profile. 2,339 applied, 1,566 admitted, 1,301 enrolled.

Mid 50% test scores		**End year in good standing:**	74%
ACT:	18-22	**Return as sophomores:**	62%
GPA 3.50 or higher:	28%	**Out-of-state:**	4%
GPA 3.0-3.49:	33%	**Live on campus:**	31%
GPA 2.0-2.99:	36%	**International:**	1%
Rank in top quarter:	37%	**Fraternities:**	2%
Rank in top tenth:	15%	**Sororities:**	3%

Basis for selection. Admission to four-year program requires a college preparatory program consisting of: 4 units in English, 3 units in mathematics, 3 units in science, 1 unit in social studies, 2 units in history, 7.5 units in academic electives, 2.5 units in health and physical education. Recommended units for a four-year program: 2 units in a foreign language. SAT or ACT recommended.

High school preparation. Required and recommended units include English 4, mathematics 3, social studies 1, history 2, science 3, foreign language 2, academic electives 7.5. 2.5 health and physical education.

2005-2006 Annual costs. Tuition/fees: $3,390; $8,838 out-of-state. Room/board: $3,720. Books/supplies: $1,000. Personal expenses: $1,574.

2004-2005 Financial aid. Need-based: 1,442 full-time freshmen applied for aid; 924 were judged to have need; 911 of these received aid. Average need met was 87%. Average scholarship/grant was $3,094; average loan $2,263. 60% of total undergraduate aid awarded as scholarships/grants, 40% as loans/jobs. **Non-need-based:** Awarded to 792 full-time undergraduates, including 351 freshmen. Scholarships awarded for academics, athletics, state residency.

Application procedures. Admission: Priority date 8/15; no deadline. $20 fee ($30 out-of-state). Application may be submitted online. Admission notification on a rolling basis beginning on or about 9/1. **Financial aid:** Priority date 4/17; no closing date. FAFSA, institutional form required. Applicants notified on a rolling basis; must reply within 2 week(s) of notification.

Academics. Special study options: Cooperative education, cross-registration, distance learning, dual enrollment of high school students, exchange student, honors, independent study, internships, study abroad, teacher certification program. **Credit/placement by examination:** AP, CLEP, SAT, ACT, institutional tests. 15 credit hours maximum toward associate degree, 30 toward bachelor's. **Support services:** Learning center, preadmission summer program, reduced course load, remedial instruction, study skills assistance, tutoring, writing center.

Majors. Agriculture: Business. **Biology:** General, environmental, marine. **Business:** Accounting, business admin, finance, human resources, management information systems, marketing, operations. **Communications:** Journalism. **Computer sciences:** Computer science. **Education:** Art, business, elementary, English, French, mathematics, middle, music, physical, science, secondary, social studies. **Engineering technology:** Manufacturing, petroleum. **English:** Creative writing, English lit, technical writing. **Family/consumer sciences:** General. **Foreign languages:** French. **Health:** Athletic training, audiology/speech pathology, communication disorders, health care admin, health services, nursing (RN), predentistry, premedicine, preveterinary. **History:** General. **Liberal arts:** Arts/sciences. **Math:** General. **Personal/**

culinary services: Culinary arts. **Physical sciences:** Chemistry. **Psychology:** General. **Social sciences:** Political science, sociology. **Visual/performing arts:** Art.

Most popular majors. Business/marketing 21%, education 13%, health sciences 23%, liberal arts 8%.

Computing on campus. 285 workstations in dormitories, library, computer center. Dormitories wired for high-speed internet access and linked to campus network. Commuter students can connect to campus network. Online course registration, online library, wireless network available.

Student life. **Freshman orientation:** Mandatory, $50 fee. Preregistration for classes offered. **Policies:** Freshmen permitted cars on campus. **Housing:** Guaranteed on-campus for all undergraduates. Coed dorms, single-sex dorms, special housing for disabled, apartments, substance-free housing available. $150 fully refundable deposit, deadline 8/15. **Activities:** Bands, choral groups, dance, drama, film society, literary magazine, music ensembles, musical theater, radio station, student government, student newspaper, TV station, Baptist Student Union, Circle K, Young Democrats, Support for Older and Returning Students, Order of Athena, Young Republicans, UNITE, Newman Club, Muslim Student Association.

Athletics. NCAA. **Intercollegiate:** Baseball M, basketball, cross-country, football (tackle) M, golf, soccer W, softball W, tennis, track and field W, volleyball W. **Intramural:** Basketball, football (non-tackle), racquetball, soccer, softball, swimming, tennis, volleyball. **Team name:** Colonels.

Student services. Adult student services, alcohol/substance abuse counseling, campus ministries, career counseling, services for economically disadvantaged, student employment services, financial aid counseling, health services, legal services, minority student services, personal counseling, placement for graduates, veterans' counselor, women's services. **Physically disabled:** Services for visually, speech, hearing impaired.

Contact. E-mail: nicholls@nicholls.edu
Phone: (985) 448-4507 Toll-free number: (877) 642-4655
Fax: (985) 448-4929
Becky Durocher, Director of Admissions, Nicholls State University, PO Box 2004-NSU, Thibodaux, LA 70310

Northwestern State University

Natchitoches, Louisiana — **CB member**
www.nsula.edu — **CB code: 6492**

- Public 4-year university
- Commuter campus in large town
- 8,559 degree-seeking undergraduates: 25% part-time, 67% women, 31% African American, 1% Asian American, 2% Hispanic American, 2% Native American
- 848 degree-seeking graduate students
- 77% of applicants admitted
- SAT or ACT (ACT writing optional) required
- 32% graduate within 6 years

General. Founded in 1884. Regionally accredited. Additional campuses in Shreveport, Leesville, and Alexandria. **Degrees:** 1,061 bachelor's, 275 associate awarded; master's offered. **ROTC:** Army. **Location:** 75 miles from Shreveport, 57 miles from Alexandria. **Calendar:** Semester, extensive summer session. **Full-time faculty:** 309 total; 57% have terminal degrees, 9% minority, 54% women. **Part-time faculty:** 237 total. **Class size:** 38% < 20, 41% 20-39, 9% 40-49, 10% 50-99, less than 1% >100. **Special facilities:** Center for history of education in Louisiana, Louisiana archives, museum, Louisiana scholar's college, Louisiana folklife center, Creole heritage center, center for historic preservation.

Freshman class profile. 2,852 applied, 2,206 admitted, 1,539 enrolled.

Mid 50% test scores			
SAT verbal:	450-570	Rank in top quarter:	35%
SAT math:	450-570	Rank in top tenth:	14%
ACT:	17-22	End year in good standing:	84%
GPA 3.50 or higher:	26%	Return as sophomores:	66%
GPA 3.0-3.49:	30%	Out-of-state:	11%
GPA 2.0-2.99:	42%	Live on campus:	57%

Basis for selection. In general, first-time freshmen must have completed the 16.5 unit college preparatory program, need no more than one developmental class, and must have one of the following: 20 on the ACT (or SAT equivalent), 2.0 high school GPA, or be in the top 50% of their graduating class. Out-of-state students and home-schooled students can be admitted based on ACT/SAT scores alone. Students 21 and older also have their own admission criteria. Finally, NSU does offer exceptions to the admission criteria to some students. The Louisiana Scholars' College has its own admissions criteria. Entering freshmen must submit ACT/SAT scores to be considered for admission; only students 25 or older are exempt from this requirement.

High school preparation. 16.5 units required. Required units include English 4, mathematics 3, social studies 1, history 2, science 3 (laboratory 3), foreign language 2 and academic electives 1. .5 computer literacy.

2005-2006 Annual costs. Tuition/fees: $3,423; $9,501 out-of-state. Room/board: $3,750. Books/supplies: $1,000. Personal expenses: $1,574.

2004-2005 Financial aid. **Need-based:** 1,490 full-time freshmen applied for aid; 1,049 were judged to have need; 1,049 of these received aid. Average need met was 34%. Average scholarship/grant was $7,199; average loan $3,628. 47% of total undergraduate aid awarded as scholarships/grants, 53% as loans/jobs. **Non-need-based:** Awarded to 3,088 full-time undergraduates, including 877 freshmen. Scholarships awarded for academics, alumni affiliation, art, athletics, job skills, leadership, minority status, music/drama, religious affiliation, ROTC, state residency.

Application procedures. **Admission:** Closing date 7/6 (receipt date). $20 fee. Application may be submitted online. Admission notification on a rolling basis. Students are allowed to submit their applications after the fall deadline; however, there is no guarantee that such applications will be acted upon. **Financial aid:** Priority date 5/1; no closing date. FAFSA, institutional form required. Applicants notified on a rolling basis starting 5/1; must reply within 4 week(s) of notification.

Academics. **Special study options:** Cooperative education, distance learning, double major, dual enrollment of high school students, honors, independent study, internships, liberal arts/career combination, study abroad, teacher certification program. **Credit/placement by examination:** AP, CLEP, SAT, ACT, institutional tests. 30 credit hours maximum toward associate degree, 62 toward bachelor's. Maximum semester hours of credit by examination may not exceed half the number of credits required for degree. **Support services:** Learning center, pre-admission summer program, reduced course load, remedial instruction, study skills assistance, tutoring, writing center.

Honors college/program. Student must have ACT 25 or above, or SAT 1130 (exclusive of Writing) or above; must score 20 or higher on each of their subscores on ACT or 480 or higher on SAT verbal and SAT math; and must have 3.0 high school GPA in the Louisiana core curriculum or 3.0 college GPA.

Majors. **Biology:** General. **Business:** Accounting, business admin, hospitality admin. **Communications:** Journalism. **Computer sciences:** Information systems. **Education:** Biology, business, chemistry, early childhood, elementary, English, family/consumer sciences, mathematics, middle, music, physical, physics, social studies, speech. **Engineering technology:** Electrical, industrial. **English:** English lit. **Family/consumer sciences:** General. **Health:** Nursing (RN), radiologic technology/medical imaging, substance abuse counseling. **History:** General. **Interdisciplinary:** Cultural resource management. **Liberal arts:** Arts/sciences. **Math:** General. **Physical sciences:** Chemistry, physics. **Protective services:** Criminal justice. **Psychology:** General. **Public administration:** Social work. **Social sciences:** Anthropology, political science, sociology. **Visual/performing arts:** Dramatic, music performance, studio arts.

Most popular majors. Business/marketing 14%, education 10%, health sciences 16%, liberal arts 15%, psychology 9%.

Computing on campus. Dormitories linked to campus network. Commuter students can connect to campus network. Online course registration, online library, helpline, student web hosting, wireless network available.

Student life. **Freshman orientation:** Available, $75 fee. Preregistration for classes offered. One- to 2-day program held 5 times during the summer; includes program for parents. **Policies:** Freshmen permitted cars on campus. **Housing:** Coed dorms, special housing for disabled, apartments, fraternity/sorority housing, substance-free housing available. $75 nonrefundable deposit, deadline 3/5. Theme housing and privately-owned housing available on campus. **Activities:** Bands, choral groups, dance, drama, literary magazine, music ensembles, musical theater, opera, radio station, student government, student newspaper, symphony orchestra, TV station, Baptist Collegiate Ministries, Catholic student organization, Fellowship of Christian Athletes, The Foundation (a Wesley Westminster Ministry), Latter-day Saints Institute, Blue Key honor society, Purple Jackets, College Republicans, College Democrats, African American caucus.

Athletics. NCAA. **Intercollegiate:** Baseball M, basketball, cross-country, football (tackle) M, soccer W, softball W, tennis W, track and field, volleyball W. **Intramural:** Badminton, baseball, basketball, bowling, football (non-tackle), golf, racquetball, soccer, softball, table tennis, tennis, volleyball, water polo. **Team name:** Demons.

Student services. Adult student services, alcohol/substance abuse counseling, campus ministries, career counseling, services for economically disadvantaged, student employment services, financial aid counseling, health services, minority student services, personal counseling, placement for graduates, veterans' counselor. **Physically disabled:** Services for visually, speech, hearing impaired. **Learning disabled:** Comprehensive services available.

Contact. E-mail: admissions@nsula.edu
Phone: (318) 357-4078 Toll-free number: (800) 767-8115
Fax: (318) 357-4660
Yvette Williams, Associate Registrar for Admissions, Northwestern State University, Roy Hall, Room 209, Natchitoches, LA 71497

Our Lady of Holy Cross College

New Orleans, Louisiana
www.olhcc.edu **CB code: 6002**

- Private 4-year liberal arts college affiliated with Roman Catholic Church
- Commuter campus in very large city
- 1,316 degree-seeking undergraduates
- ACT required

General. Founded in 1916. Regionally accredited. Because of higher priorities in the aftermath of Hurricane Katrina, the information in this profile has not been updated for the 2006-2007 academic year. **Degrees:** 157 bachelor's awarded; master's offered. **ROTC:** Army, Navy, Air Force. **Location:** 3 miles from downtown. **Calendar:** Semester, limited summer session. **Full-time faculty:** 45 total. **Part-time faculty:** 85 total. **Class size:** 51% < 20, 43% 20-39, 3% 40-49, 2% 50-99. **Special facilities:** Training and counseling center; campus offerings available for senior citizens.

Freshman class profile.

Mid 50% test scores		**Out-of-state:**	1%
ACT:	17-21		

Basis for selection. Those with 2.0 GPA and 20 ACT composite unconditionally accepted. Students with less than 2.0 and 16-19 ACT must take learning contract or institutionally-designed schedule. Students entering directly from high school required to take ACT, while others must take institutional test. English and mathematics proficiency tests required.

High school preparation. 17.5 units recommended. Recommended units include English 4, mathematics 2, social studies 3, science 4 and foreign language 2. .5 unit of computer literacy recommended.

2005-2006 Annual costs. Tuition/fees: $8,110. Books/supplies: $700. Personal expenses: $1,264.

Financial aid. Non-need-based: Scholarships awarded for academics, state residency.

Application procedures. Admission: Priority date 12/1; no deadline. $15 fee. Application may be submitted online. Admission notification on a rolling basis. **Financial aid:** Priority date 4/15; no closing date. FAFSA, institutional form required. Applicants notified on a rolling basis starting 5/15; must reply within 2 week(s) of notification.

Academics. Special study options: Cross-registration, distance learning, dual enrollment of high school students, exchange student, independent study, internships, study abroad, teacher certification program. **Credit/placement by examination:** AP, CLEP, institutional tests. 60 credit hours maximum toward bachelor's degree. **Support services:** Learning center, preadmission summer program, reduced course load, remedial instruction, tutoring.

Majors. Biology: General. **Business:** Accounting, business admin. **Education:** Business, elementary, English, mathematics, secondary, social studies, special. **Health:** Medical radiologic technology/radiation therapy, respiratory therapy technology. **History:** General. **Interdisciplinary:** Biological/physical sciences. **Liberal arts:** Arts/sciences. **Social sciences:** General.

Computing on campus. 68 workstations in library, computer center. Commuter students can connect to campus network. Online library, wireless network available.

Student life. Freshman orientation: Mandatory. Preregistration for classes offered. **Activities:** Choral groups, drama, literary magazine, student government, student newspaper, Rotaract Club, various honor societies.

Athletics. Intramural: Bowling, soccer M, softball, volleyball. **Team name:** Hurricanes.

Student services. Adult student services, campus ministries, career counseling, student employment services, financial aid counseling, health services, personal counseling, placement for graduates, veterans' counselor.

Contact. E-mail: admissions@olhcc.edu
Phone: (504) 394-7744 ext. 175 Toll-free number: (800) 259-7744
Fax: (504) 391-2421
Kristine Kopecky, Vice President for Enrollment Services, Our Lady of Holy Cross College, 4123 Woodland Drive, New Orleans, LA 70131-7399

Our Lady of the Lake College

Baton Rouge, Louisiana
www.ololcollege.edu **CB code: 3928**

- Private 4-year nursing and liberal arts college affiliated with Roman Catholic Church
- Commuter campus in large city
- 2,043 degree-seeking undergraduates: 23% African American, 2% Asian American, 2% Hispanic American, 1% Native American
- 40 degree-seeking graduate students
- ACT (writing optional) required

General. Regionally accredited. **Degrees:** 60 bachelor's, 325 associate awarded; master's offered. **ROTC:** Air Force. **Calendar:** Semester, extensive summer session. **Full-time faculty:** 63 total. **Part-time faculty:** 60 total.

Freshman class profile.

Mid 50% test scores		**GPA 2.0-2.99:**	30%
ACT:	17-22	**Rank in top quarter:**	75%
GPA 3.50 or higher:	20%	**Rank in top tenth:**	25%
GPA 3.0-3.49:	50%		

Basis for selection. Open admission, but selective for some programs.

High school preparation. 16 units recommended. Recommended units include English 4, mathematics 4, social studies 2, science 4 (laboratory 2) and academic electives 2.

2005-2006 Annual costs. Tuition/fees: $7,430. Books/supplies: $1,000.

Application procedures. Admission: Closing date 8/1 (receipt date). $35 fee. Application may be submitted online. Admission notification on a rolling basis. **Financial aid:** FAFSA required.

Academics. Special study options: Accelerated study, combined bachelor's/graduate degree, cross-registration, distance learning, liberal arts/career combination. **Credit/placement by examination:** CLEP, ACT, institutional tests. 15 credit hours maximum toward associate degree, 30 toward bachelor's. **Support services:** Learning center, reduced course load, study skills assistance, tutoring.

Majors. Biology: General, biomedical sciences. **Health:** Clinical lab science, facilities admin, health care admin, health services, health services admin, nursing (RN), premedicine. **Liberal arts:** Humanities. **Psychology:** General.

Computing on campus. 150 workstations in library. Commuter students can connect to campus network. Online library, wireless network available.

Student life. Freshman orientation: Mandatory. Preregistration for classes offered. One-day program the week before classes begin. **Policies:** Our Lady of the Lake College is a smoke-free campus. Freshmen permitted cars on campus. **Activities:** Student government, student newspaper, Student Government Association, American College of Healthcare Executives, Beta Epsilon Fraternity of Radiologic Technology Students, Beta Sigma Mu (Human Medicine), Christian Student Fellowship, Clinical Laboratory Scientist Association, Cultural Arts Association, Epsilon Mu Theta, Mathematics and Science Association, Professional Fraternity of Phi Theta Alpha, Student Association of Respiratory Therapist, Student Association of Surgical Technologists, Student Nurses Association.

Student services. Adult student services, campus ministries, career counseling, financial aid counseling.

Contact. Phone: (225) 768-1700
Marvell Nesmith, Director of Admissions, Our Lady of the Lake College, 7434 Perkins Road, Baton Rouge, LA 70808

St. Joseph Seminary College
St. Benedict, Louisiana
www.sjasc.edu **CB code: 6689**

- Private 4-year liberal arts and seminary college for men affiliated with Roman Catholic Church
- Residential campus in rural community
- 67 degree-seeking undergraduates
- ACT (writing optional) required

General. Founded in 1891. Regionally accredited. Because of higher priorities in the aftermath of Hurricane Katrina, the information in this profile has not been updated for the 2006-2007 academic year. **Degrees:** 20 bachelor's awarded. **Location:** 40 miles from New Orleans. **Calendar:** Semester. **Full-time faculty:** 15 total. **Part-time faculty:** 20 total. **Class size:** 88% < 20, 12% 20-39. **Special facilities:** 1200 acres of forest, Romanesque abbey church; non-seminarian, non-degree-seeking students may attend part-time.

Freshman class profile. 29 enrolled.

Out-of-state:	42%	**Live on campus:**	100%

Basis for selection. Recommendation by diocesan bishop, academic standing, and test scores required. MIchigan test used for placement and proficiency. Interview recommended.

High school preparation. 17 units recommended. Recommended units include English 4, mathematics 3, social studies 1, history 1, science 2, foreign language 2 and academic electives 7. Second foreign language recommended.

2005-2006 Annual costs. Tuition/fees: $13,685. St. Joseph Abby subsidizes $2400 per student per year (subject to change). Room/board: $7,415. Books/supplies: $1,000. Personal expenses: $1,387.

Financial aid. Non-need-based: Scholarships awarded for academics, leadership.

Application procedures. Admission: No deadline. No application fee. Admission notification on a rolling basis. **Financial aid:** Priority date 3/15; no closing date. FAFSA required. Applicants notified on a rolling basis starting 7/1; must reply within 4 week(s) of notification.

Academics. Special study options: ESL. **Credit/placement by examination:** AP, CLEP, IB. 24 credit hours maximum toward bachelor's degree. **Support services:** Reduced course load, remedial instruction, tutoring.

Majors. Liberal arts: Arts/sciences.

Computing on campus. 14 workstations in library, computer center. Repair service available.

Student life. Freshman orientation: Mandatory. Preregistration for classes offered. **Policies:** Freshmen permitted cars on campus. **Housing:** Guaranteed on-campus for all undergraduates. All students live on campus. **Activities:** Choral groups, drama, music ensembles, musical theater, student government, community, religious, social service activities.

Athletics. Intramural: Baseball M, basketball M, handball M, racquetball M, soccer M, softball M, squash M, swimming M, table tennis M, tennis M, volleyball M. **Team name:** Ravens.

Student services. Career counseling, health services, personal counseling, veterans' counselor.

Contact. E-mail: acdean@sjasc.edu
Phone: (985) 867-2248 ext. 148 Fax: (985) 867-2270
Russ Pottle, Director of Admissions/Registrar, St. Joseph Seminary College, 75376 River Road, St. Benedict, LA 70457-9990

Southeastern Louisiana University
Hammond, Louisiana
www.selu.edu **CB code: 6656**

- Public 4-year university
- Commuter campus in large town
- 14,334 degree-seeking undergraduates: 19% part-time, 62% women, 18% African American, 1% Asian American, 2% Hispanic American, 1% international
- 1,212 degree-seeking graduate students
- 95% of applicants admitted
- SAT and SAT Subject Tests or ACT (ACT writing optional) required
- 25% graduate within 6 years

General. Founded in 1925. Regionally accredited. **Degrees:** 1,601 bachelor's, 92 associate awarded; master's offered. **ROTC:** Army. **Location:** 55 miles from New Orleans, 40 miles from Baton Rouge. **Calendar:** Semester, extensive summer session. **Full-time faculty:** 496 total; 61% have terminal degrees, 10% minority, 56% women. **Part-time faculty:** 197 total; 24% have terminal degrees, 9% minority, 55% women. **Class size:** 31% < 20, 50% 20-39, 10% 40-49, 7% 50-99, 2% >100. **Special facilities:** Environmental research station, social science research center, maritime museum, theater, contemporary art gallery.

Freshman class profile. 3,286 applied, 3,111 admitted, 2,578 enrolled.

Mid 50% test scores		**Rank in top tenth:**	8%
ACT:	18-22	**End year in good standing:**	60%
GPA 3.50 or higher:	19%	**Return as sophomores:**	68%
GPA 3.0-3.49:	32%	**Out-of-state:**	1%
GPA 2.0-2.99:	47%	**Live on campus:**	39%
Rank in top quarter:	28%	**International:**	1%

Basis for selection. In-state students must meet the following criteria: completion of the Regents High School Core Curriculum; ACT score of at least 20, or high school rank in upper 50% of graduating class, or high school GPA of 2.0; have no more than one developmental course requirement. Out-of-state students must have no more than one developmental course requirement and meet the same criteria as in-state students or meet all of the following criteria: ACT composite of at least a 20, high school rank in the upper 50% of class, and high school GPA of 2.0; or ACT of at least 23. Audition recommended for music majors. **Homeschooled:** Must have GED and minimum of 23 on ACT, as well as no more than one developmental course requirement. **Learning Disabled:** No special requirements or procedures.

High school preparation. 16.5 units required. Required units include English 4, mathematics 3, social studies 3, science 3 and foreign language 2. Fine arts survey 1, computer .5 required.

2005-2006 Annual costs. Tuition/fees: $3,121; $8,449 out-of-state. Room/board: $5,180.

2004-2005 Financial aid. Need-based: 1,900 full-time freshmen applied for aid; 1,382 were judged to have need; 1,216 of these received aid. Average scholarship/grant was $2,943; average loan $2,190. 44% of total undergraduate aid awarded as scholarships/grants, 56% as loans/jobs. **Non-need-based:** Awarded to 1,887 full-time undergraduates, including 608 freshmen. Scholarships awarded for academics, athletics, job skills, leadership, music/drama, state residency.

Application procedures. Admission: Closing date 8/15 (postmark date). $20 fee. Application may be submitted online. Admission notification on a rolling basis beginning on or about 9/1. **Financial aid:** Priority date 5/1; no closing date. FAFSA, institutional form required. Applicants notified on a rolling basis starting 3/1; must reply within 2 week(s) of notification.

Academics. Special study options: Cross-registration, distance learning, double major, dual enrollment of high school students, honors, independent study, internships, liberal arts/career combination, study abroad, teacher certification program. **Credit/placement by examination:** AP, CLEP, SAT, ACT, institutional tests. 30 credit hours maximum toward bachelor's degree. Maximum of 60 hours through all types of nontraditional educational experiences, i.e., advanced standing credit, extension courses, correspondence-study, and military service credits. **Support services:** Learning center, remedial instruction, study skills assistance, tutoring, writing center.

Majors. Agriculture: Horticultural science. **Biology:** General. **Business:** Accounting, business admin, finance, marketing. **Communications:** General. **Computer sciences:** Computer science. **Education:** Art, early childhood, elementary, English, French, mathematics, middle, music, physical, science, social studies, Spanish, special, speech, speech impaired. **Engineering technology:** Industrial, occupational safety. **English:** English lit. **Family/consumer sciences:** General. **Foreign languages:** French, Spanish. **Health:** Athletic training, health services, nursing (RN), public health ed. **History:** General. **Liberal arts:** Arts/sciences. **Math:** General. **Physical sciences:** Chemistry, physics. **Protective services:** Criminal justice. **Psychology:** General. **Public administration:** Social work. **Social sciences:** Political science, sociology. **Visual/performing arts:** Art, arts management, music performance.

Most popular majors. Business/marketing 35%, education 12%, health sciences 9%, liberal arts 10%.

Computing on campus. 717 workstations in library, computer center, student center. Dormitories wired for high-speed internet access and linked to campus network. Commuter students can connect to campus network.

Online course registration, online library, helpline, repair service, student web hosting, wireless network available.

Student life. **Freshman orientation:** Mandatory, $75 fee. Preregistration for classes offered. Students may take orientation either during the summer or at the beginning of their first semester. Must pay room and board for summer session. **Policies:** Freshmen and sophomores must live on campus. Freshmen permitted cars on campus. **Housing:** Coed dorms, apartments, fraternity/sorority housing, substance-free housing available. $150 nonrefundable deposit. **Activities:** Bands, choral groups, dance, drama, music ensembles, musical theater, opera, radio station, student government, student newspaper, symphony orchestra, TV station, gospel choir, Baptist Collegiate Ministries, student government association, international student organization, press club, Wesley Foundation, campus activities board, Black student union, campus outreach, Yellow Ribbon Project.

Athletics. NCAA. **Intercollegiate:** Baseball M, basketball, cheerleading, cross-country, football (tackle) M, golf M, soccer W, softball W, tennis, track and field, volleyball W. **Intramural:** Badminton, basketball, football (non-tackle), rugby M, soccer, softball, table tennis, tennis, volleyball, weight lifting. **Team name:** Lions, Lady Lions.

Student services. Adult student services, alcohol/substance abuse counseling, career counseling, services for economically disadvantaged, student employment services, financial aid counseling, health services, minority student services, personal counseling, placement for graduates, veterans' counselor. **Physically disabled:** Services for visually, speech, hearing impaired.

Contact. E-mail: admissions@selu.edu
Phone: (985) 549-2066 Toll-free number: (800) 222-7358
Fax: (985) 549-5632
Richard Beaugh, Director of Admissions, Southeastern Louisiana University, SLU 10752, Hammond, LA 70402

Southern University and Agricultural and Mechanical College

Baton Rouge, Louisiana
www.subr.edu **CB code: 6663**

- Public 4-year university
- Residential campus in large city
- 8,493 degree-seeking undergraduates: 9% part-time, 61% women, 97% African American, 1% international
- 1,169 degree-seeking graduate students
- 53% of applicants admitted
- SAT or ACT (ACT writing optional) required
- 29% graduate within 6 years; 20% enter graduate study

General. Founded in 1880. Regionally accredited. **Degrees:** 923 bachelor's, 5 associate awarded; master's, doctoral offered. **ROTC:** Army, Navy, Air Force. **Location:** 80 miles from New Orleans. **Calendar:** Semester, extensive summer session. **Full-time faculty:** 420 total; 68% have terminal degrees, 73% minority, 48% women. **Part-time faculty:** 141 total; 38% have terminal degrees, 76% minority, 59% women. **Class size:** 30% < 20, 47% 20-39, 12% 40-49, 2% 50-99, 1% >100. **Special facilities:** Experimental (laboratory) farm, outdoor learning resource center (nature trail), meat processing plant, Black heritage museum.

Freshman class profile. 4,703 applied, 2,479 admitted, 1,486 enrolled.

Mid 50% test scores			
SAT verbal:	380-480	Rank in top quarter:	12%
SAT math:	370-480	Rank in top tenth:	2.8%
ACT:	16-19	End year in good standing:	62%
GPA 3.50 or higher:	10%	Return as sophomores:	68%
GPA 3.0-3.49:	23%	Out-of-state:	28%
GPA 2.0-2.99:	62%	Live on campus:	84%
		International:	3%

Basis for selection. Applicants must have high school GPA of 2.0 (based on 4.0), ACT score of 20 or comparable SAT score, or be in the top 50% of their graduating class, and require no more than 1 remedial course. Auditions required for music program.

High school preparation. 16.5 units required. Required units include English 4, mathematics 3, social studies 2, history 1, science 3 and foreign language 2. .5 computer literacy, 1 fine arts required.

2005-2006 Annual costs. Tuition/fees: $3,592; $9,384 out-of-state. Room/board: $4,646. Books/supplies: $1,600. Personal expenses: $1,545.

2005-2006 Financial aid. **Need-based:** Average need met was 79%. Average scholarship/grant was $1,778; average loan $2,405. 29% of total undergraduate aid awarded as scholarships/grants, 71% as loans/jobs. **Non-need-based:** Scholarships awarded for academics, athletics, ROTC.

Application procedures. **Admission:** Closing date 7/1 (postmark date). $20 fee. Application may be submitted online. Admission notification on a rolling basis. **Financial aid:** Closing date 3/31. FAFSA, institutional form required. Applicants notified on a rolling basis starting 6/30; must reply within 3 week(s) of notification.

Academics. **Special study options:** Combined bachelor's/graduate degree, cooperative education, cross-registration, distance learning, double major, dual enrollment of high school students, exchange student, honors, independent study, internships, liberal arts/career combination, study abroad, teacher certification program. **Credit/placement by examination:** AP, CLEP, SAT, ACT, institutional tests. 30 credit hours maximum toward bachelor's degree. **Support services:** Learning center, pre-admission summer program, reduced course load, remedial instruction, tutoring.

Honors college/program. Must have ACT composite score of 23 (SAT score of 1070 or above, exclusive of Writing) and GPA of 3.0.

Majors. **Agriculture:** Animal sciences, economics. **Architecture:** Architecture. **Biology:** General. **Business:** Accounting, business admin, e-commerce, finance, managerial economics, marketing. **Communications:** Media studies. **Computer sciences:** Computer science. **Conservation:** Urban forestry. **Education:** Agricultural, biology, chemistry, computer, early childhood, elementary, English, French, mathematics, middle, music, physical, physics, science, secondary, social studies, Spanish, special. **Engineering:** Civil, electrical, mechanical. **Engineering technology:** Electrical. **English:** Speech/rhetoric. **Family/consumer sciences:** General. **Foreign languages:** French, Spanish. **Health:** Audiology/speech pathology, nursing (RN), recreational therapy, vocational rehab counseling. **History:** General. **Math:** General. **Physical sciences:** Chemistry, physics. **Protective services:** Criminal justice. **Psychology:** General. **Public administration:** Social work. **Social sciences:** Political science, sociology. **Visual/performing arts:** Dramatic, music performance, studio arts.

Most popular majors. Business/marketing 17%, computer/information sciences 7%, engineering/engineering technologies 10%, family/consumer sciences 6%, health sciences 17%, security/protective services 6%.

Computing on campus. 1,500 workstations in library, computer center. Dormitories linked to campus network. Commuter students can connect to campus network. Online course registration, helpline available.

Student life. **Freshman orientation:** Mandatory. Preregistration for classes offered. 2-day program during registration. **Housing:** Single-sex dorms, special housing for disabled, substance-free housing available. $50 partly refundable deposit, deadline 5/1. **Activities:** Bands, choral groups, dance, drama, literary magazine, music ensembles, musical theater, student government, student newspaper, Catholic student club, Chosen Generation Campus Ministry, Committed to Christ student organization, Love Alive Christian Fellowship, Muslim student organization, Nation of Islam student organization, Sigma Omega Delta social service organization, College Democrats, College Republicans, Collegiant 100 Black Men.

Athletics. NCAA. **Intercollegiate:** Baseball M, basketball, bowling W, cross-country, football (non-tackle) M, football (tackle) M, golf, soccer W, softball W, tennis, track and field, volleyball W. **Intramural:** Football (non-tackle), golf, swimming, volleyball, weight lifting. **Team name:** Jaguars.

Student services. Career counseling, student employment services, financial aid counseling, health services, personal counseling, placement for graduates, veterans' counselor. **Physically disabled:** Services for visually, speech, hearing impaired.

Contact. E-mail: admit@subr.edu
Phone: (225) 771-2430 Toll-free number: (800) 256-1531
Fax: (225) 771-2500
Tracy Abraham, Interim Director, Southern University and Agricultural and Mechanical College, T.H. Harris Hall, Baton Rouge, LA 70813

Southern University at New Orleans

New Orleans, Louisiana
www.suno.edu **CB code: 1647**

- Public 4-year university
- Commuter campus in very large city
- 3,282 degree-seeking undergraduates

General. Founded in 1959. Regionally accredited. Because of higher priorities in the aftermath of Hurricane Katrina, the information in this profile has not been updated for the 2006-2007 academic year. **Degrees:** 484 bachelor's, 12 associate awarded; master's offered. **ROTC:** Army, Navy, Air Force. **Calendar:** Semester, limited summer session. **Full-time faculty:** 150 total. **Part-time faculty:** 85 total. **Class size:** 49% < 20, 47% 20-39, 3% 40-49, less than 1% 50-99, less than 1% >100.

Basis for selection. Open admission. ACT required by state law for placement.

High school preparation. 16 units recommended. Recommended units include English 4, mathematics 3, social studies 3, science 3 (laboratory 2) and foreign language 1.

2005-2006 Annual costs. Tuition/fees: $2,958; $6,696 out-of-state. Books/ supplies: $1,000. Personal expenses: $2,802.

Financial aid. All financial aid based on need.

Application procedures. Admission: Closing date 7/1. $5 fee. Admission notification on a rolling basis. **Financial aid:** Closing date 4/1. FAFSA required. Applicants notified by 5/15; must reply within 1 week(s) of notification.

Academics. Special study options: Cooperative education, cross-registration, double major, dual enrollment of high school students, independent study, internships, teacher certification program, weekend college. **Credit/ placement by examination:** CLEP, ACT. 30 credit hours maximum toward bachelor's degree. **Support services:** Reduced course load, remedial instruction, study skills assistance, tutoring, writing center.

Majors. Biology: General. **Business:** Accounting, business admin, managerial economics. **Computer sciences:** General, systems analysis. **Education:** Art, biology, chemistry, elementary, English, French, mathematics, music, science, secondary, social science, Spanish. **Foreign languages:** French, Spanish. **Health:** Clinical lab technology. **History:** General. **Math:** General. **Physical sciences:** Chemistry, physics. **Protective services:** Law enforcement admin. **Psychology:** General. **Public administration:** Social work. **Social sciences:** General, economics, political science, sociology. **Visual/ performing arts:** General.

Computing on campus. 400 workstations in library, computer center. Helpline available.

Student life. Freshman orientation: Available. **Activities:** Jazz band, choral groups, drama, musical theater, student government, student newspaper.

Athletics. NAIA. **Intercollegiate:** Basketball. **Team name:** Black Knights.

Student services. Campus ministries, career counseling, financial aid counseling, health services, personal counseling, placement for graduates. **Physically disabled:** Services for visually, speech, hearing impaired.

Contact. Phone: (504) 286-5000
Timothea Bailey, Director of Admissions, Southern University at New Orleans, 6400 Press Drive, New Orleans, LA 70126

Southwest University

Kenner, Louisiana
www.southwest.edu

- For-profit 4-year virtual university
- Very large city
- 350 undergraduates

General. Accredited by DETC. Because of higher priorities in the aftermath of Hurricane Katrina, the information in this profile has not been updated for the 2006-2007 academic year. **Degrees:** 21 bachelor's awarded; master's offered. **Calendar:** Continuous.

Basis for selection. Open admission.

2005-2006 Annual costs. Undergraduate tuition is $130 to $250 per credit hour.

Application procedures. Admission: No deadline. $50 fee. Application may be submitted online. Admission notification on a rolling basis.

Academics. Special study options: Accelerated study, distance learning, liberal arts/career combination. **Credit/placement by examination:** CLEP.

Majors. Protective services: Law enforcement admin.

Computing on campus. Online library available.

Student services. Adult student services, veterans' counselor.

Contact. E-mail: admissions@southwest.edu
Phone: (800) 433-5923 Fax: (504) 468-3213
Lydia Ocmand, Director of Admissions, Southwest University, 2200 Veterans Boulevard, Kenner, LA 70062

Tulane University

New Orleans, Louisiana **CB member**
www.tulane.edu **CB code: 6832**

- Private 4-year university
- Residential campus in very large city
- 7,954 degree-seeking undergraduates
- 4,715 graduate students
- 44% of applicants admitted
- SAT or ACT with writing, application essay required

General. Founded in 1834. Regionally accredited. Due to Hurricane Katrina, enrollment information for Fall 2005 is not available; figures in this profile are from Fall 2004. **Degrees:** 1,533 bachelor's, 74 associate awarded; master's, doctoral, first professional offered. **ROTC:** Army, Navy, Air Force. **Location:** 4 miles from downtown. **Calendar:** Semester, limited summer session. **Full-time faculty:** 1,099 total; 92% have terminal degrees, 22% minority, 31% women. **Part-time faculty:** 868 total; 57% have terminal degrees, 13% minority, 42% women. **Class size:** 57% < 20, 30% 20-39, 5% 40-49, 7% 50-99, 1% >100. **Special facilities:** Jazz archive, Louisiana collection of historical materials, Southeastern architecture archive, center for research on women, research center on ethnic minorities, political economy institute, center for Latin American studies, middle American research institute, Gallier house museum, center for bioenvironmental research, performing arts center, Amistad Research Center.

Basis for selection. High school achievement record most important, followed by test scores, recommendation, personal qualities; special consideration for children of alumni and minority applicants. Candidates should be in top third of graduating class with at least 3.5 average. Audition recommended for music majors. Portfolio recommended for architecture, art majors. **Homeschooled:** State high school equivalency certificate, letter of recommendation (nonparent) required. SAT Subject Tests required.

High school preparation. Required and recommended units include English 4, mathematics 3-4, social studies 3, history 3, science 3-4 (laboratory 3-4), foreign language 2-3 and academic electives 2-3. Chemistry and physics recommended for science or engineering majors.

2005-2006 Annual costs. Tuition/fees: $32,946. Room/board: $8,152. Books/supplies: $800.

2004-2005 Financial aid. Need-based: 1,082 full-time freshmen applied for aid; 769 were judged to have need; 768 of these received aid. Average need met was 92%. Average scholarship/grant was $17,764; average loan $4,783. 73% of total undergraduate aid awarded as scholarships/ grants, 27% as loans/jobs. **Non-need-based:** Awarded to 2,532 full-time undergraduates, including 772 freshmen. Scholarships awarded for academics, athletics, ROTC. **Additional information:** Application deadline for merit scholarships December 1.

Application procedures. Admission: Priority date 11/1; deadline 1/15 (postmark date). $55 fee, may be waived for applicants with need. Application may be submitted online. Admission notification 4/15. Must reply by May 1 or within 2 week(s) if notified thereafter. **Financial aid:** Priority date 1/15, closing date 2/1. FAFSA, CSS PROFILE required. Applicants notified on a rolling basis starting 2/1; must reply by 5/1 or within 2 week(s) of notification.

Academics. Special study options: Accelerated study, combined bachelor's/ graduate degree, cross-registration, distance learning, double major, exchange student, honors, independent study, internships, liberal arts/career combination, student-designed major, study abroad, teacher certification program, Washington semester. **Credit/placement by examination:** AP, CLEP, IB, institutional tests. **Support services:** Learning center, study skills assistance, tutoring, writing center.

Majors. Architecture: Architecture. **Area/ethnic studies:** African, American, Asian, German, Latin American, Russian/Slavic, women's. **Biology:** General, biochemistry, cell/histology, ecology, evolutionary, molecular. **Business:** General, accounting, business admin, finance, management information systems, marketing. **Communications:** Media studies. **Conservation:** Environmental science, environmental studies. **Engineering:** Biomedical, chemical. **English:** English lit. **Foreign languages:** Classics, French, German, Italian, linguistics, modern Greek, Portuguese, Russian, Spanish. **History:** General. **Interdisciplinary:** Medieval/Renaissance, neuroscience. **Legal studies:** General. **Math:** General. **Philosophy/religion:** Judaic, philosophy. **Physical sciences:** Chemistry, geology, physics. **Psychology:** General. **Social sciences:** Anthropology, economics, international economics, political science, sociology, urban studies. **Visual/performing arts:** Art, art history/ conservation, dance, dramatic, multimedia, music performance, music theory/ composition, studio arts, theater history.

Most popular majors. Biology 8%, business/marketing 20%, psychology 7%, social sciences 16%, visual/performing arts 6%.

Computing on campus. 562 workstations in library, computer center, student center. Dormitories wired for high-speed internet access and linked to campus network. Commuter students can connect to campus network. Online course registration, online library, helpline, repair service, student web hosting, wireless network available.

Student life. Freshman orientation: Mandatory, $400 fee. Preregistration for classes offered. **Policies:** Alcohol policy. **Housing:** Guaranteed on-campus for freshmen. Coed dorms, single-sex dorms, special housing for disabled, apartments, substance-free housing available. $150 nonrefundable deposit, deadline 5/1. Honors program residence hall, language floors, women in science, healthy lifestyle, engineering and technology, performing and creative arts, pre-med and pre-law special living floors, quiet-study floors, and international living floors available. **Activities:** Bands, choral groups, dance, drama, film society, literary magazine, music ensembles, musical theater, radio station, student government, student newspaper, symphony orchestra, TV station, Hillel, Episcopal Center, Inter-Varsity Christian Fellowship, Catholic Center, Baptist Student Union, African-American Congress, Latin American students association, Amnesty International.

Athletics. NCAA. **Intercollegiate:** Baseball M, basketball, cross-country, diving W, field hockey, football (tackle) M, golf, soccer W, swimming W, tennis, track and field, volleyball W. **Intramural:** Badminton, basketball, bowling, cross-country M, football (tackle) M, golf, handball M, racquetball, soccer, softball, swimming, table tennis M, tennis, track and field M, volleyball, wrestling M. **Team name:** Green Wave.

Student services. Alcohol/substance abuse counseling, campus ministries, career counseling, student employment services, financial aid counseling, health services, legal services, minority student services, personal counseling, women's services. **Physically disabled:** Services for visually, speech, hearing impaired.

Contact. E-mail: undergrad.admission@tulane.edu
Phone: (504) 865-5731 Toll-free number: (800) 873-9283
Fax: (504) 862-8715
Richard Whiteside, Vice President for Enrollment Management and Institutional Research, Tulane University, 6823 St. Charles Avenue, New Orleans, LA 70118-5680

University of Louisiana at Lafayette

Lafayette, Louisiana — **CB member**
www.louisiana.edu — **CB code: 6672**

- Public 4-year university
- Commuter campus in small city
- 15,093 degree-seeking undergraduates: 14% part-time, 58% women
- 1,288 degree-seeking graduate students
- 76% of applicants admitted
- SAT or ACT (ACT writing optional) required
- 38% graduate within 6 years

General. Founded in 1898. Regionally accredited. **Degrees:** 1,964 bachelor's, 3 associate awarded; master's, doctoral offered. **ROTC:** Army. **Location:** 130 miles from New Orleans, 200 miles from Houston. **Calendar:** Semester, extensive summer session. **Full-time faculty:** 564 total; 69% have terminal degrees, 14% minority, 41% women. **Part-time faculty:** 153 total; 26% have terminal degrees, 14% minority, 47% women. **Class size:** 29% < 20, 48% 20-39, 13% 40-49, 6% 50-99, 3% >100. **Special facilities:** 2 nuclear accelerators, 2 electron microscopes, CAD/CAM laboratory, art museum, Acadiana folklore archives, confocal microscope, atomic force microscope.

Freshman class profile. 6,309 applied, 4,782 admitted, 2,819 enrolled.

Mid 50% test scores		**End year in good standing:**	76%
ACT:	19-24	**Return as sophomores:**	71%
GPA 3.50 or higher:	26%	**Out-of-state:**	4%
GPA 3.0-3.49:	36%	**Live on campus:**	30%
GPA 2.0-2.99:	37%	**International:**	1%
Rank in top quarter:	38%	**Sororities:**	5%
Rank in top tenth:	15%		

Basis for selection. 2.0 high school GPA, the state's Board of Regents core courses, and 18 ACT in English or math required; and either 23 ACT, 2.5 high school GPA, or rank in the top 25% of graduating class. Audition required of music majors. Portfolio required of art, architecture majors. Essays required for some applicants.

High school preparation. College-preparatory program required. Required units include English 4, mathematics 3, social studies 2, history 1, science 3, academic electives 4.5. Suggested electives: .5 unit computer science, 1 unit fine arts, 1 unit speech.

2005-2006 Annual costs. Tuition/fees: $3,324; $9,504 out-of-state. Room/board: $3,478. Books/supplies: $1,000. Personal expenses: $1,574.

Financial aid. All financial aid based on need.

Application procedures. Admission: Priority date 7/15; no deadline. $25 fee. Application may be submitted online. Admission notification on a rolling basis. **Financial aid:** Priority date 5/1; no closing date. FAFSA, institutional form required. Applicants notified on a rolling basis starting 4/1; must reply within 2 week(s) of notification.

Academics. Special study options: Accelerated study, cooperative education, cross-registration, distance learning, double major, dual enrollment of high school students, ESL, exchange student, honors, independent study, internships, student-designed major, study abroad, teacher certification program, Washington semester. **Credit/placement by examination:** AP, CLEP, SAT, ACT, institutional tests. 15 credit hours maximum toward associate degree, 30 toward bachelor's. **Support services:** Learning center, reduced course load, remedial instruction, study skills assistance, tutoring, writing center.

Majors. Agriculture: General. **Architecture:** Architecture, interior. **Biology:** General, conservation, microbiology. **Business:** Accounting, business admin, fashion, finance, hospitality admin, insurance, management information systems, managerial economics, marketing. **Communications:** General, media studies, public relations. **Computer sciences:** Computer science. **Conservation:** Land use planning, management/policy. **Education:** Agricultural, art, biology, business, chemistry, early childhood, early childhood special, elementary, English, family/consumer sciences, French, German, mathematics, middle, music, physical, physics, science, social studies, Spanish, special, speech, technology/industrial arts. **Engineering:** Chemical, civil, computer, electrical, mechanical, petroleum. **Engineering technology:** Industrial. **Family/consumer sciences:** Family studies. **Foreign languages:** General. **Health:** Athletic training, audiology/speech pathology, dental hygiene, dietetics, medical records admin, nursing (RN). **History:** General. **Legal studies:** Prelaw. **Math:** General. **Philosophy/religion:** Philosophy. **Physical sciences:** Chemistry, geology, physics. **Protective services:** Criminal justice. **Psychology:** General. **Social sciences:** Anthropology, political science, sociology. **Visual/performing arts:** General, art, industrial design, music performance.

Most popular majors. Business/marketing 23%, education 14%, engineering/engineering technologies 9%, health sciences 7%, liberal arts 13%.

Computing on campus. 2,000 workstations in dormitories, library, computer center, student center. Commuter students can connect to campus network. Online course registration, online library, helpline, wireless network available.

Student life. Freshman orientation: Mandatory, $15 fee. Preregistration for classes offered. **Policies:** Freshmen permitted cars on campus. **Housing:** Guaranteed on-campus for freshmen. Single-sex dorms, special housing for disabled, apartments, fraternity/sorority housing, substance-free housing available. $50 nonrefundable deposit. **Activities:** Bands, choral groups, dance, drama, film society, literary magazine, music ensembles, musical theater, opera, radio station, student government, student newspaper, Wesley Foundation, Catholic Student Center, Baptist Student Union, Young Republicans, Young Democrats, international student organization, Circle-K, Afro-American student groups.

Athletics. NCAA. **Intercollegiate:** Baseball M, basketball, cheerleading, cross-country, football (tackle) M, golf M, soccer W, softball W, tennis, track and field, volleyball W. **Intramural:** Badminton, basketball, bowling, equestrian, golf, racquetball, rugby M, sailing, soccer, softball, swimming, table tennis, tennis, volleyball. **Team name:** Ragin' Cajuns.

Student services. Adult student services, career counseling, student employment services, financial aid counseling, health services, minority student services, on-campus daycare, personal counseling, placement for graduates, veterans' counselor. **Physically disabled:** Services for visually, speech, hearing impaired.

Contact. E-mail: admissions@louisiana.edu
Phone: (337) 482-6467 Toll-free number: (800) 752-6553
Fax: (337) 482-6195
Leroy Broussard, Director of Admissions, University of Louisiana at Lafayette, Box 41210, Lafayette, LA 70504-1210

University of Louisiana at Monroe

Monroe, Louisiana **CB member**
www.ulm.edu **CB code: 6482**

- Public 4-year university
- Commuter campus in small city
- 7,894 degree-seeking undergraduates: 19% part-time, 64% women, 30% African American, 2% Asian American, 1% Hispanic American, 1% international
- 1,160 degree-seeking graduate students
- 87% of applicants admitted
- SAT or ACT (ACT writing optional) required

General. Founded in 1931. Regionally accredited. School of Pharmacy has the only state-supported professional PharmD program in Louisiana; aviation program has state's only FAA qualified Level III full-motion flight simulator. **Degrees:** 953 bachelor's, 50 associate awarded; master's, doctoral, first professional offered. **ROTC:** Army, Air Force. **Location:** 90 miles from Shreveport, 120 miles from Jackson, Mississippi. **Calendar:** Semester, extensive summer session. **Full-time faculty:** 373 total. **Part-time faculty:** 170 total. **Special facilities:** Louisiana State Small Business Development Center, Louisiana State Poison Information Center, National Public Radio station, Louisiana State Cancer Tumor Registry Archives, regional small business development center, weather research center, museum of natural history, art gallery.

Freshman class profile. 2,378 applied, 2,070 admitted, 1,471 enrolled.

Mid 50% test scores			
SAT verbal:	440-530	GPA 2.0-2.99:	35.7%
SAT math:	430-530	Rank in top quarter:	42%
ACT:	18-23	Rank in top tenth:	18%
GPA 3.50 or higher:	30.2%	Out-of-state:	6%
GPA 3.0-3.49:	32.7%	Live on campus:	43%
		International:	1%

Basis for selection. Students who do not meet the defined criteria are evaluated on other evidence of academic promise for admittance by exception. Only a limited number of students will be granted admittance by exception. **Homeschooled:** Must submit official transcript of grades and official proof of graduation or original diploma to admissions office.

High school preparation. 16.5 units required. Required units include English 4, mathematics 3, social studies 1, history 2, science 3 and foreign language 2. .5 unit computer science and 1 unit in arts required.

2005-2006 Annual costs. Tuition/fees: $3,353; $9,305 out-of-state. Room/board: $6,140. Books/supplies: $500.

2004-2005 Financial aid. Non-need-based: Scholarships awarded for academics, alumni affiliation, art, athletics, job skills, leadership, minority status, music/drama, religious affiliation, ROTC, state residency.

Application procedures. Admission: Priority date 4/1; no deadline. $20 fee, may be waived for applicants with need. Application may be submitted online. Admission notification on a rolling basis. **Financial aid:** Priority date 4/1; no closing date. FAFSA required. Applicants notified on a rolling basis starting 6/1; must reply within 2 week(s) of notification.

Academics. Credit hours toward graduation may be earned through examination, military service, correspondence and extension courses taken through accredited extension divisions of other colleges and universities. **Special study options:** Accelerated study, combined bachelor's/graduate degree, cooperative education, distance learning, double major, dual enrollment of high school students, ESL, honors, independent study, internships, study abroad, teacher certification program. Evening college. **Credit/placement by examination:** AP, CLEP, SAT, ACT, institutional tests. 22 credit hours maximum toward associate degree, 43 toward bachelor's. Maximum of one-third of credits required for degree may be earned through examination, military experience, and correspondence courses. **Support services:** Learning center, reduced course load, remedial instruction, study skills assistance, tutoring, writing center.

Majors. Agriculture: Business. **Biology:** General, toxicology. **Business:** Accounting, business admin, entrepreneurial studies, finance, insurance, management information systems, managerial economics, marketing. **Communications:** Media studies. **Computer sciences:** Computer science. **Education:** Art, biology, chemistry, elementary, English, family/consumer sciences, French, mathematics, music, physical, physics, social studies, Spanish, speech. **Engineering technology:** Construction. **English:** English lit, speech/rhetoric. **Family/consumer sciences:** General. **Foreign languages:** French, Spanish. **Health:** Audiology/speech pathology, clinical lab science, dental hygiene, nursing (RN), radiologic technology/medical imaging. **History:** General. **Math:** General. **Physical sciences:** Atmospheric science, chemistry. **Protective services:** Criminal justice. **Psychology:** General. **Public administration:** Social work. **Social sciences:** Political science, sociology. **Transportation:** Airline/commercial pilot. **Visual/performing arts:** Music performance, studio arts.

Computing on campus. Dormitories wired for high-speed internet access and linked to campus network. Commuter students can connect to campus network. Online course registration, online library, helpline, repair service, student web hosting, wireless network available.

Student life. Freshman orientation: Available. Preregistration for classes offered. 5 regular sessions plus one computer PREP session. **Policies:** Freshmen permitted cars on campus. **Housing:** Coed dorms, single-sex dorms, apartments, fraternity/sorority housing, substance-free housing available. $150 deposit, deadline 7/8. **Activities:** Bands, choral groups, dance, drama, literary magazine, music ensembles, musical theater, opera, radio station, student government, student newspaper, symphony orchestra.

Athletics. NCAA. **Intercollegiate:** Baseball M, basketball, cheerleading, cross-country, football (tackle) M, golf, soccer W, softball W, swimming, tennis W, track and field, volleyball W. **Intramural:** Archery, badminton, basketball, bowling, cross-country, football (non-tackle), golf, racquetball, rodeo, soccer, softball, swimming, tennis, track and field, volleyball, weight lifting. **Team name:** Indians.

Student services. Adult student services, alcohol/substance abuse counseling, campus ministries, career counseling, student employment services, financial aid counseling, health services, on-campus daycare, personal counseling, placement for graduates, veterans' counselor. **Physically disabled:** Services for visually, speech, hearing impaired.

Contact. E-mail: admit@ulm.edu
Phone: (318) 342-5430 Toll-free number: (800) 372-5127
Fax: (318) 342-1915
Lisa Miller, Director of Recruitment and Admissions, University of Louisiana at Monroe, 700 University Avenue, Monroe, LA 71209-1160

University of New Orleans

New Orleans, Louisiana **CB member**
www.uno.edu **CB code: 6379**

- Public 4-year university
- Commuter campus in very large city
- 13,225 degree-seeking undergraduates
- 63% of applicants admitted
- SAT or ACT (ACT writing optional) required

General. Founded in 1956. Regionally accredited. Because of higher priorities in the aftermath of Hurricane Katrina, the information in this profile has not been updated for the 2006-2007 academic year. **Degrees:** 1,727 bachelor's awarded; master's, doctoral offered. **ROTC:** Army, Navy, Air Force. **Calendar:** Semester, extensive summer session. **Full-time faculty:** 556 total; 70% have terminal degrees, 14% minority, 38% women. **Part-time faculty:** 229 total; 38% have terminal degrees, 11% minority, 44% women. **Class size:** 40% < 20, 43% 20-39, 8% 40-49, 6% 50-99, 3% >100.

Freshman class profile. 6,197 applied, 3,928 admitted, 2,043 enrolled.

Mid 50% test scores		Rank in top tenth:	11%
SAT verbal:	450-590	Out-of-state:	5%
SAT math:	450-580	Live on campus:	9%
ACT:	18-23	Fraternities:	2%
Rank in top quarter:	32%	Sororities:	2%

Basis for selection. Admission based on minimum ACT score of 20 or SAT score of 950 (exclusive of Writing); or 2.0 GPA in 17.5 units of high school core course work. Applicants with ACT of 15 or SAT of 720 (exclusive of Writing) may be considered for developmental College Life program. Interview, essay recommended. Audition required of music majors. Portfolio required of fine arts/studio majors. **Homeschooled:** Must have graduated from state-approved home study program and received 950 SAT (exclusive of Writing) or 20 ACT (section minimums: English 19, math 18).

High school preparation. Required units include English 4, mathematics 3, social studies 3, science 3, foreign language 2 and academic electives 2. .5 credit computer literacy or computer science required.

2005-2006 Annual costs. Tuition/fees: $3,814; $10,854 out-of-state. Room only: $3,690. Books/supplies: $1,150. Personal expenses: $1,533.

2004-2005 Financial aid. Need-based: 1,767 full-time freshmen applied for aid; 1,766 were judged to have need; 1,271 of these received aid. Average need met was 64%. Average scholarship/grant was $3,231; average loan $2,477. 36% of total undergraduate aid awarded as scholarships/grants,

64% as loans/jobs. **Non-need-based:** Awarded to 1,940 full-time undergraduates, including 738 freshmen. Scholarships awarded for academics, athletics. **Additional information:** Students in good academic and financial standing eligible to participate in Extended Payment Plan option.

Application procedures. Admission: Priority date 7/1; deadline 8/31 (receipt date). $20 fee, may be waived for applicants with need. Application may be submitted online. Admission notification on a rolling basis beginning on or about 9/1. **Financial aid:** Priority date 5/15; no closing date. FAFSA, institutional form required. Applicants notified on a rolling basis starting 4/20; must reply within 4 week(s) of notification.

Academics. Special study options: Cooperative education, cross-registration, distance learning, double major, dual enrollment of high school students, ESL, exchange student, honors, independent study, internships, student-designed major, study abroad, teacher certification program, Washington semester, weekend college. **Credit/placement by examination:** AP, CLEP, IB, institutional tests. 30 credit hours maximum toward bachelor's degree. **Support services:** Learning center, pre-admission summer program, reduced course load, remedial instruction, tutoring.

Majors. Biology: General. **Business:** Accounting, business admin, finance, hospitality admin, management information systems, managerial economics, marketing. **Communications:** General. **Computer sciences:** Computer science. **Conservation:** Environmental studies. **Education:** Chemistry, early childhood, elementary, English, foreign languages, mathematics, middle, music, physical, physics, science, social studies. **Engineering:** Civil, electrical, marine, mechanical, science. **English:** English lit. **Foreign languages:** French, Spanish. **Health:** Clinical lab science. **History:** General. **Interdisciplinary:** Global studies. **Math:** General. **Philosophy/religion:** Philosophy. **Physical sciences:** Chemistry, geology, geophysics, physics. **Psychology:** General. **Social sciences:** Anthropology, economics, geography, political science, sociology, urban studies. **Visual/performing arts:** Art history/conservation, studio arts.

Computing on campus. 1,084 workstations in library, computer center, student center. Dormitories wired for high-speed internet access. Online course registration, helpline, repair service, student web hosting, wireless network available.

Student life. Freshman orientation: Available, $75 fee. Preregistration for classes offered. **Policies:** Freshmen permitted cars on campus. **Housing:** Coed dorms, special housing for disabled, apartments available. $225 deposit. Apartment referral and roommate locator services. **Activities:** Bands, choral groups, dance, drama, film society, literary magazine, music ensembles, musical theater, opera, radio station, student government, student newspaper, African American student union, Circle K, College Republicans, Young Democrats, international student organization, Latin American student association, Muslim student association, religious council.

Athletics. NCAA. **Intercollegiate:** Baseball M, basketball, cross-country, golf, swimming, tennis, track and field, volleyball W. **Intramural:** Badminton, basketball, golf, gymnastics, racquetball, soccer, table tennis, tennis, volleyball. **Team name:** Privateers.

Student services. Adult student services, alcohol/substance abuse counseling, campus ministries, career counseling, student employment services, financial aid counseling, health services, legal services, on-campus daycare, personal counseling, placement for graduates, veterans' counselor, women's services. **Physically disabled:** Services for visually, speech, hearing impaired.

Contact. E-mail: admissions@uno.edu
Phone: (504) 280-6595 Toll-free number: (800) 256-5866
Fax: (504) 280-5522
Roslyn Sheley, Director of Admissions Office, University of New Orleans, Administrative Building Room 103, New Orleans, LA 70148

Xavier University of Louisiana

New Orleans, Louisiana — **CB member**
www.xula.edu — **CB code: 6975**

- Private 4-year university affiliated with Roman Catholic Church
- Commuter campus in very large city
- 3,224 degree-seeking undergraduates
- 83% of applicants admitted
- SAT or ACT with writing required

General. Founded in 1915. Regionally accredited. Due to Hurricane Katrina, the information in this profile has not been updated for the 2006-2007 academic year. **Degrees:** 441 bachelor's awarded; master's, first professional offered. **ROTC:** Army, Navy, Air Force. **Location:** 1 mile from downtown. **Calendar:** Semester, limited summer session. **Full-time faculty:** 241 total; 90% have terminal degrees, 46% minority, 44% women. **Part-time faculty:** 48 total; 27% have terminal degrees, 50% minority, 38% women. **Class size:** 42% < 20, 44% 20-39, 6% 40-49, 3% 50-99, 5% >100.

Freshman class profile. 4,248 applied, 3,516 admitted, 1,001 enrolled.

Mid 50% test scores			
SAT verbal:	440-570	Rank in top quarter:	55%
SAT math:	430-540	Rank in top tenth:	30%
ACT:	18-24	Out-of-state:	63%
		Live on campus:	60%

Basis for selection. High school record or GED scores, standardized test results, and recommendation from counselor important. Interview recommended for academically weak. Audition required for music majors. Portfolio required for art majors.

High school preparation. 16 units required. Required and recommended units include English 4, mathematics 2-4, social studies 1-2, science 1-3, foreign language 1 and academic electives 8. Mathematics must include 1 algebra.

2005-2006 Annual costs. Tuition/fees: $12,900. Room/board: $6,200. Books/supplies: $1,000. Personal expenses: $1,533.

2005-2006 Financial aid. Need-based: 947 full-time freshmen applied for aid; 792 were judged to have need; 791 of these received aid. Average need met was 74%. Average loan was $2,340. 37% of total undergraduate aid awarded as scholarships/grants, 63% as loans/jobs. **Non-need-based:** Scholarships awarded for academics, art, athletics, music/drama, religious affiliation.

Application procedures. Admission: Priority date 3/1; deadline 7/1 (postmark date). $25 fee, may be waived for applicants with need. Application may be submitted online. Admission notification 4/15. Must reply by May 1 or within 2 week(s) if notified thereafter. **Financial aid:** Closing date 1/1. FAFSA required. Applicants notified on a rolling basis starting 4/1; must reply within 2 week(s) of notification.

Academics. Special study options: Accelerated study, combined bachelor's/graduate degree, cross-registration, double major, exchange student, honors, independent study, internships, liberal arts/career combination, study abroad, teacher certification program. **Credit/placement by examination:** AP, CLEP. 30 credit hours maximum toward bachelor's degree. **Support services:** Learning center, pre-admission summer program, reduced course load, remedial instruction, study skills assistance, tutoring, writing center.

Majors. Biology: General, biochemistry, microbiology. **Business:** Accounting, business admin, finance, management science, marketing. **Communications:** Media studies. **Computer sciences:** General, computer science. **Education:** General, art, biology, chemistry, early childhood, elementary, English, foreign languages, French, history, mathematics, multi-level teacher, music, physical, science, social studies, Spanish, special. **Engineering:** Computer. **English:** English lit. **Foreign languages:** French, Spanish. **Health:** Predentistry, premedicine, prepharmacy, preveterinary, speech pathology. **History:** General. **Legal studies:** Prelaw. **Math:** General, statistics. **Parks/recreation:** Health/fitness. **Philosophy/religion:** Philosophy. **Physical sciences:** Chemistry, physics. **Psychology:** General. **Social sciences:** Political science, sociology. **Theology:** Theology. **Visual/performing arts:** Art, music performance, piano/organ, stringed instruments, voice/opera.

Computing on campus. 350 workstations in dormitories, library, computer center. Dormitories wired for high-speed internet access and linked to campus network. Commuter students can connect to campus network. Online course registration, online library, helpline available.

Student life. Freshman orientation: Mandatory. Preregistration for classes offered. One-week program. **Policies:** All recognized student organizations must perform 2 community service activities per semester. **Housing:** Coed dorms, single-sex dorms, substance-free housing available. $100 deposit. **Activities:** Bands, choral groups, dance, literary magazine, music ensembles, opera, student government, student newspaper, symphony orchestra, TV station, over 30 organizations.

Athletics. NAIA. **Intercollegiate:** Basketball, cross-country, tennis, volleyball W. **Intramural:** Basketball, cheerleading, football (non-tackle), softball, swimming, table tennis, tennis, track and field, volleyball. **Team name:** Gold Rush.

Student services. Adult student services, alcohol/substance abuse counseling, campus ministries, career counseling, student employment services, financial aid counseling, health services, personal counseling, placement for graduates, veterans' counselor, women's services. **Physically disabled:** Services for visually, speech, hearing impaired.

Contact. E-mail: apply@xula.edu
Phone: (504) 520-7388 Toll-free number: (877) 928-4378
Fax: (504) 520-7941
Winston Brown, Dean of Admissions, Xavier University of Louisiana, One Drexel Drive, New Orleans, LA 70125-1098

Maine

Bates College

Lewiston, Maine **CB member**
www.bates.edu **CB code: 3076**

- Private 4-year liberal arts college
- Residential campus in large town
- 1,684 degree-seeking undergraduates: 51% women, 3% African American, 4% Asian American, 2% Hispanic American, 5% international
- 29% of applicants admitted
- Application essay required
- 89% graduate within 6 years

General. Founded in 1855. Regionally accredited. **Degrees:** 517 bachelor's awarded. **Location:** 35 miles from Portland. **Calendar:** 4-4-1 semester system. **Full-time faculty:** 164 total; 94% have terminal degrees, 13% minority, 45% women. **Part-time faculty:** 23 total; 83% have terminal degrees, 9% minority, 56% women. **Class size:** 63% < 20, 28% 20-39, 4% 40-49, 5% 50-99. **Special facilities:** Mountain seacoast conservation area, Edmund S. Muskie Archives, art museum, observatory.

Freshman class profile. 4,356 applied, 1,272 admitted, 490 enrolled.

Mid 50% test scores			
SAT verbal:	640-710	End year in good standing:	97%
SAT math:	640-710	Return as sophomores:	94%
Rank in top quarter:	91%	Out-of-state:	90%
Rank in top tenth:	57%	Live on campus:	100%
		International:	4%

Basis for selection. GED not accepted. School achievement record, recommendations, special talents, leadership, essay, interview all important. Submission of standardized test scores is optional for admission. Interviews are strongly recommended.

High school preparation. 15 units required; 19 recommended. Required and recommended units include English 4, mathematics 3-4, social studies 3, science 2-3 (laboratory 1-3) and foreign language 2-4. History included in social studies requirement.

2005-2006 Annual costs. Comprehensive fee: $42,100. Books/supplies: $1,150.

2005-2006 Financial aid. All financial aid based on need. 239 full-time freshmen applied for aid; 208 were judged to have need; 182 of these received aid. Average need met was 100%. Average scholarship/grant was $24,369; average loan $3,282. 84% of total undergraduate aid awarded as scholarships/grants, 16% as loans/jobs. **Additional information:** Priority date for filing required financial aid forms for early decision students is 11/15.

Application procedures. Admission: Closing date 1/1 (postmark date). $60 fee, may be waived for applicants with need. Application may be submitted online. Admission notification 3/31. Must reply by 5/1. **Financial aid:** Closing date 2/1. FAFSA, CSS PROFILE required. Applicants notified by 4/1; must reply by 5/1.

Academics. Special study options: Accelerated study, combined bachelor's/graduate degree, double major, exchange student, honors, independent study, internships, liberal arts/career combination, semester at sea, student-designed major, study abroad, teacher certification program, urban semester, Washington semester. Marine studies program at Mystic Seaport, liberal arts-engineering dual degree program with 5 universities. **Credit/placement by examination:** AP, CLEP, IB, institutional tests. **Support services:** Reduced course load, study skills assistance, tutoring, writing center.

Majors. Area/ethnic studies: African-American, American, East Asian, women's. **Biology:** General, biochemistry. **Conservation:** Environmental studies. **Engineering:** General. **English:** English lit, speech/rhetoric. **Foreign languages:** Chinese, French, German, Japanese, Russian, Spanish. **History:** General. **Interdisciplinary:** Ancient studies, neuroscience. **Math:** General. **Philosophy/religion:** Philosophy, religion. **Physical sciences:** Chemistry, geology, physics. **Psychology:** General. **Social sciences:** Anthropology, economics, political science, sociology. **Visual/performing arts:** Art, dramatic.

Most popular majors. Biology 9%, English 8%, history 6%, interdisciplinary studies 8%, physical sciences 6%, psychology 12%, social sciences 29%.

Computing on campus. 415 workstations in dormitories, library, computer center. Dormitories wired for high-speed internet access and linked to campus network. Commuter students can connect to campus network. Online course registration, helpline, repair service, student web hosting, wireless network available.

Student life. Freshman orientation: Mandatory. Preregistration for classes offered. Held 5 days prior to start of classes. **Policies:** Freshmen permitted cars on campus. **Housing:** Guaranteed on-campus for all undergraduates. Coed dorms, single-sex dorms, substance-free housing available. $300 nonrefundable deposit, deadline 5/1. Quiet study house, chemical-free houses, theme houses. **Activities:** Jazz band, choral groups, dance, drama, film society, literary magazine, music ensembles, musical theater, radio station, student government, student newspaper, symphony orchestra, Africana Club, Amandla!, Bates Christian Fellowship, Bates Democrats, Bates Hindu Awareness group, College Republicans, Hillel, International Club, Latinos Unidos, Mushahada Club, Sangai Asia, Women of Color.

Athletics. NCAA. **Intercollegiate:** Baseball M, basketball, cross-country, diving, field hockey W, football (tackle) M, golf, lacrosse, rowing (crew), skiing, soccer, softball W, squash, swimming, tennis, track and field, volleyball W. **Intramural:** Badminton, baseball M, basketball, football (tackle), golf, handball, ice hockey, lacrosse, racquetball, rugby, sailing, soccer, softball, squash, table tennis, tennis, volleyball. **Team name:** Bobcats.

Student services. Alcohol/substance abuse counseling, campus ministries, career counseling, student employment services, financial aid counseling, health services, minority student services, personal counseling, placement for graduates, women's services. **Physically disabled:** Services for visually, hearing impaired.

Contact. E-mail: admissions@bates.edu
Phone: (207) 786-6000 Fax: (207) 786-6025
Wylie Mitchell, Dean of Admissions, Bates College, Lindholm House, 23 Campus Avenue, Lewiston, ME 04240-9917

Bowdoin College

Brunswick, Maine **CB member**
www.bowdoin.edu **CB code: 3089**

- Private 4-year liberal arts college
- Residential campus in large town
- 1,660 degree-seeking undergraduates: 50% women, 6% African American, 12% Asian American, 7% Hispanic American, 1% Native American, 3% international
- 25% of applicants admitted
- Application essay required
- 94% graduate within 6 years; 15% enter graduate study

General. Founded in 1794. Regionally accredited. **Degrees:** 408 bachelor's awarded. **Location:** 25 miles from Portland, 120 miles from Boston. **Calendar:** Semester. **Full-time faculty:** 157 total; 98% have terminal degrees, 15% minority, 46% women. **Part-time faculty:** 37 total; 78% have terminal degrees, 8% minority, 51% women. **Class size:** 65% < 20, 30% 20-39, 2% 40-49, 3% 50-99. **Special facilities:** Arctic museum, arctic studies center, coastal marine biology and ornithology research facility, scientific station, farm, center for learning and teaching, 2 theaters, visual arts center, hall of music, environmental studies center, outdoor leadership center, community service resource center, African-American center, women's resource center, educational research and development program, career planning center.

Freshman class profile. 5,026 applied, 1,232 admitted, 478 enrolled.

Mid 50% test scores			
SAT verbal:	660-740	Return as sophomores:	97%
SAT math:	660-730	Out-of-state:	88%
End year in good standing:	97%	Live on campus:	100%
		International:	2%

Basis for selection. GED not accepted. Academic record, level of challenge represented in the candidate's course work, counselor/teacher recommendations, interview, quality of application and essay, character and personal qualities, extracurricular activities, talents and abilities, and overall academic potential most important. Test scores considered, but not required. Motivation of candidate also considered. Interview recommended. Candidates with unusual talent in music, theater or visual arts encouraged to complete Arts Supplement when applying for admission. Audition recommended for music majors. Portfolio recommended for art majors. **Homeschooled:** Applicants applying from systems that provide written evaluations rather than grades are required to submit SAT and SAT Subject Tests or ACT test results. SAT Subject Tests should include Math Level 1 or 2 and Science. **Learning Disabled:** No special requirements or procedures for students with learning disabilities who need not identify themselves when applying for admission.

High school preparation. 20 units recommended. Recommended units include English 4, mathematics 4, social studies 4, science 4 (laboratory 3) and foreign language 4. Arts, music and computer science or computer literacy recommended.

2005-2006 Annual costs. Tuition/fees: $32,990. Room/board: $8,670. Books/supplies: $890. Personal expenses: $1,200.

2004-2005 Financial aid. Need-based: 258 full-time freshmen applied for aid; 203 were judged to have need; 203 of these received aid. Average need met was 100%. Average scholarship/grant was $23,702; average loan $3,268. 85% of total undergraduate aid awarded as scholarships/grants, 15% as loans/jobs. **Non-need-based:** Awarded to 62 full-time undergraduates, including 19 freshmen. Scholarships awarded for academics, leadership. **Additional information:** Regardless of financial circumstances, students admitted will receive money they need to attend. International students for regular admission must submit their financial aid applications by January 1st.

Application procedures. Admission: Closing date 1/1 (receipt date). $60 fee, may be waived for applicants with need. Application may be submitted online. Admission notification on a rolling basis beginning on or about 4/5. Must reply by May 1 or within 1 week(s) if notified thereafter. No housing deposit required for first-year, first-time students; however, for returning students, there is a re-enrollment deposit of $400 due by April 1st. This deposit is not an additional fee but goes toward the following year's expenses. **Financial aid:** Closing date 2/15. FAFSA, institutional form, CSS PROFILE required. Applicants notified by 4/5; must reply by 5/1 or within 1 week(s) of notification.

Academics. Most students pursue independent scholarly research, working closely with a faculty advisor, through an independent study or honors project. Students may work towards departmental honors through the honors project. About half of the student body studies abroad for one or 2 semesters, usually during the junior year. First-year seminars are limited to 16 first-year students and emphasize college-level reading and writing. Interdisciplinary majors are available. **Special study options:** Accelerated study, combined bachelor's/graduate degree, double major, exchange student, independent study, liberal arts/career combination, semester at sea, student-designed major, study abroad, teacher certification program, Washington semester. 3-2 engineering degree programs with California Institute of Technology and Columbia University, 3-3 legal studies program with Columbia University Law School, first-year seminars, summer research fellowships, service-learning courses, the Writing Project, Quantitative Skills Program, Legal Studies Advisory Group. **Credit/placement by examination:** AP, CLEP, IB, institutional tests. **Support services:** Learning center, reduced course load, study skills assistance, tutoring, writing center.

Majors. Area/ethnic studies: African, African-American, Asian, Central/Eastern European, Latin American, women's. **Biology:** General, biochemistry. **Computer sciences:** Computer science. **Conservation:** Environmental studies. **English:** English lit. **Foreign languages:** Classics, French, German, Romance, Russian, Spanish. **History:** General. **Interdisciplinary:** Classical/archaeology, math/computer science, neuroscience. **Math:** General. **Philosophy/religion:** Philosophy, religion. **Physical sciences:** Chemical physics, chemistry, geochemistry, geology, geophysics, physics. **Psychology:** General. **Social sciences:** Anthropology, archaeology, econometrics, economics, political science, sociology. **Visual/performing arts:** Art history/conservation, studio arts, theater history.

Most popular majors. Biology 9%, foreign language 13%, history 7%, social sciences 32%, visual/performing arts 7%.

Computing on campus. 400 workstations in dormitories, library, computer center, student center. Dormitories wired for high-speed internet access and linked to campus network. Commuter students can connect to campus network. Online library, helpline, repair service, student web hosting, wireless network available.

Student life. Freshman orientation: Mandatory. 4-5 day program at the end of August, just before the start of classes. Pre-orientation outing trips offered over 4 nights prior to formal orientation; separate charge depending on the trip. **Policies:** Freshmen permitted cars on campus. **Housing:** Guaranteed on-campus for freshmen. Coed dorms, special housing for disabled, apartments, substance-free housing available. Six small college houses and 6 college system houses available. **Activities:** Bands, choral groups, dance, drama, film society, literary magazine, music ensembles, musical theater, radio station, student government, student newspaper, symphony orchestra, TV station, African-American society, Asian student organization, Latin American student organization, Hillel, Catholic student union, Christian fellowship, community service council, Evergreens, Democrats, Republicans.

Athletics. NCAA. **Intercollegiate:** Baseball M, basketball, cross-country, diving, field hockey W, football (tackle) M, golf, ice hockey, lacrosse, rugby W, sailing, skiing, soccer, softball W, squash, swimming, tennis, track and field, volleyball W. **Intramural:** Badminton, basketball, cricket, cross-country, field hockey, football (non-tackle), ice hockey, rugby, soccer, softball, squash, tennis, volleyball, water polo. **Team name:** Polar Bears.

Student services. Alcohol/substance abuse counseling, career counseling, student employment services, health services, minority student services, on-campus daycare, personal counseling, placement for graduates, women's services. **Physically disabled:** Services for visually, speech, hearing impaired.

Contact. E-mail: admissions@bowdoin.edu
Phone: (207) 725-3100 Fax: (207) 725-3101
Richard Steele, Dean of Admissions and Student Aid, Bowdoin College, 5000 College Station, Brunswick, ME 04011-8441

Colby College

Waterville, Maine — **CB member**
www.colby.edu — **CB code: 3280**

- Private 4-year liberal arts college
- Residential campus in large town
- 1,868 degree-seeking undergraduates: 53% women
- 38% of applicants admitted
- SAT or ACT (ACT writing optional), application essay required
- 89% graduate within 6 years; 22% enter graduate study

General. Founded in 1813. Regionally accredited. Off-campus facilities available for teaching and research in biology, ecology, geology. **Degrees:** 484 bachelor's awarded. **ROTC:** Army. **Location:** 180 miles from Boston, 75 miles from Portland. **Calendar:** 4-1-4. **Full-time faculty:** 161 total; 96% have terminal degrees, 15% minority, 44% women. **Part-time faculty:** 64 total; 45% have terminal degrees, 5% minority, 61% women. **Class size:** 58% < 20, 34% 20-39, 3% 40-49, 5% 50-99, less than 1% >100. **Special facilities:** Center for public affairs and civic engagement, public art museum , astronomical observatory, arboretum, rare books and archives, research greenhouses, institute for study of international human rights, scanning and transmission electron microscopes, laser flash photolysis, 400 MHz NMR, x-ray diffractometer, spectrophotometers, chromatographs, electrophoresis, microcalorimeters, piezometers (groundwater monitoring wells), kettlehole research bog, professional blacksmith's forge, woodworking shop, crew rowing center, technical climbing wall, Nordic ski trails, community radio station.

Freshman class profile. 3,874 applied, 1,454 admitted, 511 enrolled.

Mid 50% test scores		**End year in good standing:**	99%
SAT verbal:	640-720	**Return as sophomores:**	94%
SAT math:	640-710	**Out-of-state:**	89%
ACT:	27-31	**Live on campus:**	100%
Rank in top quarter:	92%	**International:**	6%
Rank in top tenth:	67%		

Basis for selection. School record and personal qualities very important. Test scores, recommendations, potential contribution to college life, essay, interview, important. Social, economic, racial, geographic diversity considered.

High school preparation. College-preparatory program recommended. 16 units recommended. Recommended units include English 4, mathematics 3, social studies 2, science 2 (laboratory 2), foreign language 3 and academic electives 2. Social studies units recommended could include history courses.

2005-2006 Annual costs. Comprehensive fee: $41,770. 2005-2006 comprehensive fee is $41,770 which includes room, board, and tuition. Books/supplies: $700. Personal expenses: $800.

2005-2006 Financial aid. All financial aid based on need. 267 full-time freshmen applied for aid; 213 were judged to have need; 213 of these received aid. Average need met was 100%. Average scholarship/grant was $27,190; average loan $3,043. 88% of total undergraduate aid awarded as scholarships/grants, 12% as loans/jobs.

Application procedures. Admission: Closing date 1/1 (postmark date). $55 fee, may be waived for applicants with need. Application may be submitted online. Admission notification 4/1. Must reply by 5/1. **Financial aid:** Closing date 2/1. FAFSA required. Applicants notified by 4/1; must reply by 5/1.

Academics. **Special study options:** Combined bachelor's/graduate degree, cross-registration, double major, exchange student, honors, independent study, internships, semester at sea, student-designed major, study abroad, teacher certification program, Washington semester. Numerous research, service learning, and intership opportunities through the Goldfarb Center for Public Affairs; summer research assistantships; course exchange programs with Bowdoin College, Bates College, Thomas College; stipends to enable student internships; coordinated 3-2 engineering program with Dartmouth; Idea Network of Biomedical Research Excellence (partnerships with Jackson Labs, Mt. Desert Island Biological Labs, and other colleges). **Credit/placement by examination:** AP, CLEP, IB, institutional tests. 30 credit hours maximum toward bachelor's degree. **Support services:** Tutoring, writing center.

Majors. **Area/ethnic studies:** African-American, American, East Asian, Latin American, Russian/Slavic, women's. **Biology:** General, biochemistry, cell/histology, environmental, molecular, molecular biochemistry, neurobiology/physiology. **Computer sciences:** Computer science. **Conservation:** Environmental science, environmental studies. **English:** Creative writing. **Foreign languages:** Classics, French, German, Russian, Spanish. **History:** General. **Interdisciplinary:** Biological/physical sciences, classical/archaeology, math/computer science, neuroscience, science/society. **Math:** General. **Philosophy/religion:** Philosophy, religion. **Physical sciences:** Chemistry, geology, physics. **Psychology:** General. **Social sciences:** Anthropology, econometrics, economics, international relations, political science, sociology. **Visual/performing arts:** Art, art history/conservation, dramatic, studio arts.

Most popular majors. Area/ethnic studies 12%, biology 12%, English 12%, foreign language 7%, history 6%, physical sciences 7%, social sciences 22%.

Computing on campus. 300 workstations in library, computer center. Dormitories wired for high-speed internet access and linked to campus network. Commuter students can connect to campus network. Online course registration, online library, helpline, repair service, student web hosting, wireless network available.

Student life. **Freshman orientation:** Mandatory. Preregistration for classes offered. 4-day optional outdoor component ($175); 3-day on-campus component follows, both held the week before classes begin. **Policies:** Students participate in forming policies and governing social and community activities through student government and serving on official college committees up to and including the Board of Trustees. Freshmen permitted cars on campus. **Housing:** Guaranteed on-campus for all undergraduates. Coed dorms, substance-free housing available. Senior apartments, quiet dormitories, interest housing, chemical-free halls available. **Activities:** Bands, choral groups, dance, drama, film society, literary magazine, music ensembles, musical theater, radio station, student government, student newspaper, symphony orchestra, Black and Hispanic student group, environmental coalition, social service and political organizations, volunteer center, international club, five a capella groups, Amnesty International, women's group, outing club, Habitat for Humanity.

Athletics. NCAA. **Intercollegiate:** Baseball M, basketball, cross-country, diving, field hockey W, football (tackle) M, golf, ice hockey, lacrosse, rowing (crew), skiing, soccer, softball W, squash, swimming, tennis, track and field, volleyball W. **Intramural:** Badminton, basketball, football (non-tackle), ice hockey, sailing, soccer, softball, squash, table tennis, volleyball, weight lifting. **Team name:** White Mules.

Student services. Alcohol/substance abuse counseling, campus ministries, career counseling, student employment services, financial aid counseling, health services, minority student services, personal counseling, placement for graduates, women's services. **Physically disabled:** Services for visually, hearing impaired.

Contact. E-mail: admissions@colby.edu
Phone: (800) 723-3032 Toll-free number: (800) 723-3032
Fax: (207) 859-4828
Parker Beverage, Dean of Admissions and Financial Aid, Colby College, 4800 Mayflower Hill, Waterville, ME 04901-8848

College of the Atlantic

Bar Harbor, Maine
www.coa.edu **CB code: 3305**

- Private 4-year liberal arts college
- Residential campus in small town
- 295 degree-seeking undergraduates: 2% part-time, 65% women, 1% Hispanic American, 17% international
- 2 degree-seeking graduate students
- 66% of applicants admitted
- Application essay required
- 62% graduate within 6 years

General. Founded in 1969. Regionally accredited. **Degrees:** 61 bachelor's awarded; master's offered. **Location:** 300 miles from Boston, 50 miles from Bangor. **Calendar:** Three 10-week terms. **Full-time faculty:** 19 total. **Part-time faculty:** 11 total. **Class size:** 95% < 20, 5% 20-39. **Special facilities:** Natural history museum, herbarium, greenhouse, pier, research boat, organic farm, island research station.

Freshman class profile. 284 applied, 188 admitted, 82 enrolled.

Mid 50% test scores			
SAT verbal:	560-670	Rank in top quarter:	76%
SAT math:	530-630	Rank in top tenth:	36%
ACT:	23-28	Return as sophomores:	86%
GPA 3.50 or higher:	65%	Out-of-state:	72%
GPA 3.0-3.49:	30%	Live on campus:	100%
GPA 2.0-2.99:	5%	International:	13%

Basis for selection. Academic ability, motivation, intellectual enthusiasm, independence, creativity, and commitment to ecological concerns and to goals and philosophies of college as demonstrated by high school record, recommendations, and interview are all important. **Homeschooled:** Thorough outline of topics covered, books read, homework completed, the evaluation process used in assessing work and the progress made over the years required. Standardized test scores recommended. **Learning Disabled:** We recommend students with learning disabilities meet with our dean of academic services to assess COA's fit with their learning styles.

High school preparation. 15 units required; 19 recommended. Required and recommended units include English 4, mathematics 3-4, social studies 2, history 2, science 2-3 (laboratory 2), foreign language 2 and academic electives 1.

2006-2007 Annual costs. Tuition/fees: $28,140. Room/board: $7,710. Books/supplies: $500. Personal expenses: $400.

2005-2006 Financial aid. **Need-based:** 79 full-time freshmen applied for aid; 76 were judged to have need; 76 of these received aid. Average need met was 98%. Average scholarship/grant was $20,017; average loan $2,977. 79% of total undergraduate aid awarded as scholarships/grants, 21% as loans/jobs. **Non-need-based:** Awarded to 61 full-time undergraduates, including 19 freshmen. Scholarships awarded for academics, leadership.

Application procedures. **Admission:** Closing date 2/15 (postmark date). $45 fee, may be waived for applicants with need. Application may be submitted online. Admission notification 4/1. Must reply by May 1 or within 2 week(s) if notified thereafter. **Financial aid:** Closing date 2/15. FAFSA, institutional form required. Applicants notified by 4/1; must reply by 5/1.

Academics. Interdisciplinary curriculum consists of problem-solving course work, seminars, independent study, tutorials, specialized skill courses, and supervised internships away from college. Opportunities for coursework at EcoLeague Institutions. **Special study options:** Independent study, internships, semester at sea, student-designed major, study abroad, teacher certification program. Winter Term program in Yucatan, Mexico. Eco-League - Consortium agreement with five other colleges for student exchanges (Alaska Pacific University, Antioch College, Green Mountain College, Northland College, Prescott College). **Credit/placement by examination:** AP, CLEP, IB. 30 credit hours maximum toward bachelor's degree. **Support services:** Reduced course load, remedial instruction, study skills assistance, tutoring, writing center.

Majors. **Biology:** Botany, ecology, marine, zoology. **Conservation:** General, environmental studies. **Education:** Biology, elementary, social studies. **Social sciences:** General. **Visual/performing arts:** General, music performance, studio arts.

Computing on campus. 50 workstations in library, computer center. Dormitories wired for high-speed internet access and linked to campus network. Online library, student web hosting, wireless network available.

Student life. **Freshman orientation:** Mandatory, $100 fee. Preregistration for classes offered. Academic orientation is 3 days on campus. 6-day optional trips by canoe, bike, kayak, sailboat or backpacking. **Policies:** Students participate in developing college policy and operate student activities fund. Freshmen permitted cars on campus. **Housing:** Guaranteed on-campus for freshmen. Coed dorms, special housing for disabled, substance-free housing available. $150 nonrefundable deposit, deadline 5/1. Pets allowed in dorm rooms. **Activities:** Choral groups, dance, drama, literary magazine, music ensembles, student government, student newspaper, Students for a Free Tibet, SustainUs, outing club, life-drawing club, student drama club.

Athletics. **Intramural:** Badminton, cricket, ice hockey, sailing, soccer, softball, table tennis, volleyball, water polo.

Student services. Alcohol/substance abuse counseling, career counseling, student employment services, financial aid counseling, health services, minority student services, personal counseling, placement for graduates. **Physically disabled:** Services for visually, hearing impaired.

Contact. E-mail: inquiry@ecology.coa.edu
Phone: (207) 288-5015 ext. 230 Toll-free number: (800) 528-0025
Fax: (207) 288-4126
Sarah Baker, Director of Admission, College of the Atlantic, 105 Eden Street, Bar Harbor, ME 04609

Husson College

Bangor, Maine — **CB member**
www.husson.edu — **CB code: 3440**

- Private 4-year business and health science college
- Residential campus in large town
- 1,877 degree-seeking undergraduates: 16% part-time, 61% women
- 268 degree-seeking graduate students
- 95% of applicants admitted
- SAT or ACT with writing, application essay required

General. Founded in 1898. Regionally accredited. **Degrees:** 317 bachelor's, 40 associate awarded; master's, doctoral offered. **ROTC:** Army, Navy. **Location:** 125 miles from Portland. **Calendar:** Semester, extensive summer session. **Full-time faculty:** 50 total; 100% have terminal degrees, 8% minority, 48% women. **Part-time faculty:** 4 total; 25% have terminal degrees, 100% women. **Class size:** 59% < 20, 35% 20-39, 5% 40-49, 1% 50-99. **Special facilities:** Center for family business.

Freshman class profile. 677 applied, 641 admitted, 327 enrolled.

Mid 50% test scores			
SAT verbal:	410-490	GPA 2.0-2.99:	37%
SAT math:	400-510	Rank in top quarter:	28%
ACT:	16-20	Rank in top tenth:	11%
GPA 3.50 or higher:	30%	Out-of-state:	17%
GPA 3.0-3.49:	29%	Live on campus:	62%

Basis for selection. Class rank and school achievement record most important. Counselor recommendations considered. Test scores important for nursing applicants and occupational and physical therapy applicants. Test scores are used only for placement purposes for business and humanities school applicants. SAT recommended but not required for 2-year program. Interview recommended. **Homeschooled:** GED required for financial aid to be awarded. **Learning Disabled:** School must be apprised of special accommodation needs at time of payment of tuition deposit.

High school preparation. College-preparatory program recommended. Recommended units include English 4, mathematics 3, social studies 1, history 1, science 3 (laboratory 2).

2006-2007 Annual costs. Tuition/fees: $11,770. Room/board: $6,240. Books/supplies: $930. Personal expenses: $1,030.

2005-2006 Financial aid. Need-based: Average need met was 75%. Average scholarship/grant was $6,038; average loan $2,304. 52% of total undergraduate aid awarded as scholarships/grants, 48% as loans/jobs. **Non-need-based:** Scholarships awarded for academics, leadership.

Application procedures. Admission: Priority date 3/1; deadline 9/1 (postmark date). $25 fee, may be waived for applicants with need. Application must be submitted on paper. Admission notification on a rolling basis beginning on or about 12/1. Must reply by May 1 or within 2 week(s) if notified thereafter. **Financial aid:** Priority date 4/15; no closing date. FAFSA required. Applicants notified on a rolling basis starting 4/1; must reply by 5/1 or within 2 week(s) of notification.

Academics. Strong liberal arts core within business programs. **Special study options:** Combined bachelor's/graduate degree, cooperative education, double major, ESL, independent study, internships, liberal arts/career combination, student-designed major, teacher certification program, weekend college. **Credit/placement by examination:** AP, CLEP, IB, SAT, ACT, institutional tests. 30 credit hours maximum toward bachelor's degree. **Support services:** Learning center, pre-admission summer program, reduced course load, remedial instruction, study skills assistance, tutoring, writing center.

Majors. Biology: General. **Business:** General, accounting, accounting/business management, banking/financial services, business admin, entrepreneurial studies, finance, hospitality admin, hospitality/recreation, hotel/motel admin, international, international marketing, management information systems, managerial economics, market research, marketing, public finance, sales/distribution, small business admin. **Computer sciences:** Applications programming, programming, systems analysis. **Education:** Biology, elementary, physical. **Health:** Nursing (RN). **Legal studies:** Paralegal. **Liberal arts:** Arts/sciences. **Parks/recreation:** Facilities management, health/fitness, sports admin. **Protective services:** Criminal justice, law enforcement admin. **Psychology:** General. **Social sciences:** Criminology.

Most popular majors. Business/marketing 62%, computer/information sciences 6%, education 6%, health sciences 14%, legal studies 9%.

Computing on campus. 115 workstations in library, computer center, student center. Dormitories wired for high-speed internet access and linked to campus network. Online course registration, online library, helpline, student web hosting, wireless network available.

Student life. Freshman orientation: Mandatory, $50 fee. Preregistration for classes offered. 2 days of meetings with faculty, staff, administration; departmental orientation and activities for students and parents. **Policies:** Freshmen permitted cars on campus. **Housing:** Guaranteed on-campus for all undergraduates. Coed dorms, fraternity/sorority housing, substance-free housing available. **Activities:** Bands, drama, literary magazine, radio station, student government, student newspaper, international club, campus crusade for Christ, Chi Alpha.

Athletics. NCAA. **Intercollegiate:** Baseball M, basketball, field hockey W, football (tackle) M, golf M, soccer, softball W, swimming W, volleyball W. **Intramural:** Basketball, football (non-tackle) M, ice hockey, soccer, swimming W, tennis, volleyball. **Team name:** Eagles.

Student services. Adult student services, alcohol/substance abuse counseling, campus ministries, career counseling, student employment services, financial aid counseling, health services, personal counseling, placement for graduates, veterans' counselor.

Contact. E-mail: admit@husson.edu
Phone: (207) 941-7100 Toll-free number: (800) 448-7766
Fax: (207) 941-7935
Jane Goodwin, Director of Admissions, Husson College, One College Circle, Bangor, ME 04401

Maine College of Art

Portland, Maine — **CB member**
www.meca.edu — **CB code: 3701**

- Private 4-year visual arts college
- Commuter campus in small city
- 449 degree-seeking undergraduates
- SAT or ACT, application essay required

General. Founded in 1882. Regionally accredited. 1- to 2-year foundation program in drawing, color, and 2- and 3-dimensional design, followed by transitional year, and final 2 years in major. Personal studio space with 24-hour access for all juniors and seniors. **Degrees:** 88 bachelor's awarded; master's offered. **Location:** 100 miles from Boston. **Calendar:** Semester, limited summer session. **Full-time faculty:** 30 total; 93% have terminal degrees, 3% minority, 63% women. **Part-time faculty:** 37 total; 54% have terminal degrees, 3% minority, 35% women. **Class size:** 74% < 20, 25% 20-39, less than 1% >100. **Special facilities:** 2 art galleries, largest visual arts library in Northern New England.

Freshman class profile.

Mid 50% test scores			
SAT verbal:	480-610	Rank in top quarter:	19%
SAT math:	440-560	Rank in top tenth:	8%
ACT:	17-23	Out-of-state:	76%
		Live on campus:	90%

Basis for selection. Decision based on interview and portfolio in conjunction with high school achievement record; essay, recommendations important, test scores considered. Interview recommended. Portfolio required. **Homeschooled:** Show evidence through the State Certification of Completion of high school program or GED. **Learning Disabled:** Submit proper documentation to Dean of Students (once accepted) and request specific accomodations.

High school preparation. 27 units recommended. Recommended units include English 4, mathematics 3, social studies 4, history 4, science 3, foreign language 2 and academic electives 3. 4 units of art strongly recommended.

2005-2006 Annual costs. Tuition/fees: $24,030. Studio fees vary per class. Room/board: $8,692. Books/supplies: $1,714. Personal expenses: $1,174.

2005-2006 Financial aid. Need-based: Average need met was 57%. Average scholarship/grant was $11,023; average loan $3,468. 56% of total undergraduate aid awarded as scholarships/grants, 44% as loans/jobs. **Non-need-based:** Scholarships awarded for academics, art.

Application procedures. Admission: Priority date 3/1; no deadline. $40 fee, may be waived for applicants with need. Application may be submitted online. Admission notification on a rolling basis. Must reply by May 1 or within 2 week(s) if notified thereafter. **Financial aid:** Priority date 3/15, closing date 4/15. FAFSA required. Applicants notified on a rolling basis starting 2/15; must reply within 2 week(s) of notification.

Academics. Our foundation program, consisting of 2-dimensional design, 3-dimensional design, drawing, and art history, is nationally recognized for its quality and rigor. **Special study options:** Combined bachelor's/graduate degree, cross-registration, double major, exchange student, independent study, internships, liberal arts/career combination, student-designed major, study abroad, teacher certification program. Mobility program with 36 AICAD (Associated Independent Colleges of Art and Design) across the country and in Canada, cross-registration program with 4 other colleges and universities in the greater Portland area; special exchange program with Hanoi Fine Arts College, Vietnam; BFA credit available through Provincetown, MA Fine Arts Work Center. **Credit/placement by examination:** AP, CLEP, IB. **Support services:** Learning center, pre-admission summer program, study skills assistance, tutoring, writing center.

Majors. Visual/performing arts: Art, ceramics, graphic design, illustration, metal/jewelry, painting, photography, printmaking, sculpture, studio arts.

Computing on campus. 57 workstations in library, computer center, student center. Online library, helpline, student web hosting available.

Student life. Freshman orientation: Mandatory. Preregistration for classes offered. Week-long, includes 2-day trip to artist colony on Deer Isle. Also extended required semester-long first-year seminar. **Policies:** Freshmen permitted cars on campus. **Housing:** Coed dorms, apartments available. $210 deposit, deadline 9/1. **Activities:** Film society, student government, student newspaper, student representative association, ski and snowboard club, outdoor group, bowling club, movie club, peer mentor scholarships, international student union.

Student services. Adult student services, alcohol/substance abuse counseling, career counseling, student employment services, financial aid counseling, health services, minority student services, personal counseling.

Contact. E-mail: admissions@meca.edu
Phone: (207) 775-3052 Toll-free number: (800) 639-4808
Fax: (207) 772-5069
Karen Townsend, Director of Admissions, Maine College of Art, 97 Spring Street, Portland, ME 04101

Maine Maritime Academy
Castine, Maine
www.mainemaritime.edu **CB code: 3505**

- Public 4-year engineering, technical and maritime college
- Residential campus in rural community
- 846 degree-seeking undergraduates: 12% part-time, 16% women
- 15 degree-seeking graduate students
- SAT or ACT with writing required

General. Founded in 1941. Regionally accredited. **Degrees:** 129 bachelor's, 9 associate awarded; master's offered. **ROTC:** Navy. **Location:** 38 miles from Bangor. **Calendar:** Semester, limited summer session. **Full-time faculty:** 50 total. **Part-time faculty:** 16 total. **Special facilities:** 500-foot training ship, 40-foot marine research vessel, ocean going tugboat, two-masted arctic schooner, steam and diesel engine laboratories, power plant simulations, bridge simulator, planetarium, ocean classrooms.

Freshman class profile.

Mid 50% test scores		ACT:	16-24
SAT verbal:	460-570	Out-of-state:	45%
SAT math:	490-590	Live on campus:	95%

Basis for selection. Academic record, test scores most important. Interview, school and community activities, and recommendations also considered. Interview and essay recommended.

High school preparation. Required and recommended units include English 4, mathematics 3-4, science 2-3 (laboratory 2) and foreign language 2. 1 unit computer literacy recommended.

2005-2006 Annual costs. Tuition/fees: $7,620; $10,810 out-of-district; $13,550 out-of-state. Cruise fee of $2,600 for U.S. Coast Guard Licensing Program. Room/board: $6,720. Books/supplies: $900. Personal expenses: $800.

2005-2006 Financial aid. Non-need-based: Scholarships awarded for academics, leadership, state residency.

Application procedures. Admission: Closing date 7/1. $15 fee, may be waived for applicants with need. Application may be submitted online. Admission notification on a rolling basis beginning on or about 1/1. Must reply by 5/1. **Financial aid:** Priority date 4/15; no closing date. FAFSA, institutional form required. Applicants notified on a rolling basis starting 3/1; must reply within 4 week(s) of notification.

Academics. Special study options: Cooperative education, internships, liberal arts/career combination, semester at sea, study abroad. 2-month training cruise. **Credit/placement by examination:** CLEP, institutional tests. **Support services:** Study skills assistance, tutoring, writing center.

Majors. Biology: Marine. **Business:** General, business admin, entrepreneurial studies, international, logistics. **Engineering:** Marine, systems. **Physical sciences:** Oceanography. **Transportation:** Marine science/Merchant Marine.

Most popular majors. Biology 10%, business/marketing 12%, engineering/engineering technologies 52%, trade and industry 26%.

Computing on campus. PC or laptop required. 40 workstations in library, computer center. Dormitories wired for high-speed internet access and linked to campus network.

Student life. Freshman orientation: Mandatory. 8 days immediately preceding start of fall semester. **Policies:** Regimental lifestyle optional for all 2-year programs and those majoring in power engineering, ocean studies, international business, and small vessel operations; mandatory for United States Coast Guard license programs. No military obligation. **Housing:** Guaranteed on-campus for all undergraduates. Coed dorms, apartments available. Students required to live on-campus unless married, over age 24, or have completed 2 or more years of active military service or 6 semesters of study. **Activities:** Bands, drama, student government, student newspaper, Alpha Phi Omega, other service organizations.

Athletics. NCAA. **Intercollegiate:** Basketball, cross-country, football (tackle) M, golf M, lacrosse M, sailing, soccer, softball W, volleyball W. **Intramural:** Basketball, golf, handball, ice hockey M, racquetball, rifle, rugby M, sailing, skiing, skin diving, soccer, softball, squash, tennis, volleyball, water polo. **Team name:** Mariners.

Student services. Alcohol/substance abuse counseling, career counseling, student employment services, health services, personal counseling, placement for graduates, veterans' counselor.

Contact. E-mail: admissions@mma.edu
Phone: (207) 326-2206 Toll-free number: (800) 227-8465
Fax: (207) 326-2515
Jeffrey Wright, Director of Admissions, Maine Maritime Academy, 66 Pleasant Street, Castine, ME 04420

New England School of Communications
Bangor, Maine
www.nescom.edu **CB code: 3101**

- Private 4-year college of communications
- Residential campus in small city
- 305 degree-seeking undergraduates: 3% part-time, 23% women, 2% African American, 1% Asian American
- 69% of applicants admitted
- Application essay, interview required

General. Accredited by ACCSCT. **Degrees:** 8 bachelor's, 28 associate awarded. **ROTC:** Army. **Location:** 250 miles from Boston. **Calendar:** Semester, limited summer session. **Full-time faculty:** 6 total; 33% have terminal degrees. **Part-time faculty:** 30 total; 33% have terminal degrees, 23% women. **Special facilities:** Television studio, sound recording studio, digital photography lab.

Freshman class profile. 310 applied, 213 admitted, 126 enrolled.

Out-of-state:	16%	Live on campus:	75%

Basis for selection. Interview most important. High school record and essay also important. SAT or ACT recommended. Tests are recommended for all applicants, although test results are not required for admission decisions. Timed scholastic placement exam. **Homeschooled:** State high school equivalency certificate, interview, letter of recommendation (nonparent) required. Require GED score if home schooling is not through an accredited curriculum-based program. **Learning Disabled:** Students requiring additional placement test time must provide professional evaluation documentation requesting extra time prior to interview date.

High school preparation. Recommended units include English 4, mathematics 2, social studies 1, history 2, science 2 and foreign language 2. Recommend additional computer, public speaking, creative arts coursework.

2005-2006 Annual costs. Tuition/fees: $9,440. Room/board: $6,030. Books/supplies: $550. Personal expenses: $150.

2005-2006 Financial aid. Need-based: Average need met was 94%. Average scholarship/grant was $1,400; average loan $2,625. 27% of total undergraduate aid awarded as scholarships/grants, 73% as loans/jobs. **Non-need-based:** Scholarships awarded for academics, leadership.

Application procedures. Admission: No deadline. $15 fee, may be waived for applicants with need. Application may be submitted online. Admission notification on a rolling basis. **Financial aid:** Priority date 4/15; no closing date. FAFSA, institutional form required. Applicants notified on a rolling basis starting 2/1; must reply by 8/15.

Academics. Special study options: Cross-registration, double major, internships, liberal arts/career combination, student-designed major. **Credit/placement by examination:** AP, CLEP, institutional tests. 6 credit hours maximum toward associate degree, 15 toward bachelor's. **Support services:** Reduced course load, study skills assistance, tutoring, writing center.

Majors. Communications: General, advertising, broadcast journalism, digital media, photojournalism, public relations, radio/tv. **Communications technology:** General, photo/film/video, radio/tv, recording arts. **Computer sciences:** Web page design. **Visual/performing arts:** Cinematography.

Computing on campus. 170 workstations in dormitories, library, computer center, student center. Dormitories wired for high-speed internet access and linked to campus network. Online library, helpline, wireless network available.

Student life. Freshman orientation: Mandatory. Preregistration for classes offered. 3 days before start of fall session. Spring orientation is held the Monday before classes. **Policies:** Freshmen permitted cars on campus. **Housing:** Guaranteed on-campus for freshmen. Coed dorms, fraternity/sorority housing, substance-free housing available. $50 fully refundable deposit, deadline 7/1. **Activities:** Pep band, choral groups, drama, literary magazine, music ensembles, musical theater, radio station, student government, student newspaper, TV station.

Athletics. Intramural: Baseball, basketball, cheerleading, diving, field hockey, football (non-tackle), skiing, soccer, softball, swimming, table tennis, tennis, volleyball.

Student services. Adult student services, alcohol/substance abuse counseling, campus ministries, career counseling, student employment services, financial aid counseling, health services, personal counseling, placement for graduates, veterans' counselor.

Contact. E-mail: info@nescom.edu
Phone: (207) 941-7176 Toll-free number: (888) 877-1876 ext. 1093
Fax: (207) 947-3987
Louise Grant, Director of Admissions, New England School of Communications, One College Circle, Bangor, ME 04401

St. Joseph's College

Standish, Maine **CB member**
www.sjcme.edu **CB code: 3755**

- Private 4-year liberal arts college affiliated with Roman Catholic Church
- Residential campus in small town
- 944 degree-seeking undergraduates: 2% part-time, 64% women, 2% African American, 1% Hispanic American
- 79% of applicants admitted
- SAT or ACT (ACT writing recommended), application essay required

General. Founded in 1912. Regionally accredited. **Degrees:** 212 bachelor's awarded. **ROTC:** Army. **Location:** 18 miles from Portland, 120 miles from Boston. **Calendar:** Semester, limited summer session. **Full-time faculty:** 64 total. **Part-time faculty:** 44 total. **Class size:** 56% < 20, 43% 20-39, 1% 40-49, less than 1% 50-99. **Special facilities:** Telescope, observatory.

Freshman class profile. 1,107 applied, 874 admitted, 267 enrolled.

Mid 50% test scores			
SAT verbal:	460-560	Rank in top tenth:	13%
SAT math:	460-560	Return as sophomores:	81%
ACT:	19-23	Out-of-state:	45%
Rank in top quarter:	37%	Live on campus:	90%

Basis for selection. School record, class rank, test scores, recommendations, essays, extracurricular activities all considered. Interview optional, but recommended.

High school preparation. 16 units recommended. Recommended units include English 4, mathematics 3, social studies 2, history 2, science 2 (laboratory 2) and foreign language 2. Laboratory biology and laboratory chemistry required of nursing and science applicants. For any intended major, transcripts from candidates for admission should include 16 or more college-preparatory courses.

2006-2007 Annual costs. Tuition/fees (projected): $21,550. Room/board: $8,980. Books/supplies: $800. Personal expenses: $1,330.

2005-2006 Financial aid. Need-based: 62% of total undergraduate aid awarded as scholarships/grants, 38% as loans/jobs. **Non-need-based:** Scholarships awarded for academics, leadership.

Application procedures. Admission: Priority date 3/1; no deadline. $40 fee, may be waived for applicants with need. Application may be submitted online. Admission notification on a rolling basis beginning on or about 12/15. Must reply by May 1 or within 3 week(s) if notified thereafter. Series of on-campus early action days for students completing application process prior to start of rolling admission notification in mid-December. **Financial aid:** Priority date 3/1; no closing date. FAFSA, institutional form required. Applicants notified on a rolling basis starting 3/1; must reply within 3 week(s) of notification.

Academics. College belongs to Greater Portland Alliance, a 5-college consortium with cross registration. **Special study options:** Combined bachelor's/graduate degree, cooperative education, cross-registration, distance learning, double major, honors, independent study, internships, liberal arts/career combination, semester at sea, student-designed major, study abroad, teacher certification program, Washington semester. **Credit/placement by examination:** AP, CLEP, SAT, ACT, institutional tests. 30 credit hours maximum toward bachelor's degree. **Support services:** Study skills assistance, tutoring, writing center.

Majors. Biology: General, marine. **Business:** Accounting, business admin, finance, international, marketing. **Communications:** Advertising, digital media, journalism, public relations. **Computer sciences:** General. **Conservation:** Environmental science, environmental studies. **Education:** Biology, elementary, English, history, mathematics, physical. **English:** English lit. **Health:** Nursing (RN). **History:** General. **Liberal arts:** Arts/sciences. **Math:** General. **Parks/recreation:** Exercise sciences, sports admin. **Philosophy/religion:** Philosophy. **Physical sciences:** Chemistry. **Protective services:** Criminal justice. **Psychology:** General. **Social sciences:** Sociology. **Theology:** Theology.

Most popular majors. Biology 9%, business/marketing 15%, communications/journalism 12%, education 25%, English 7%, health sciences 12%, psychology 6%, social sciences 8%.

Computing on campus. 102 workstations in library, computer center, student center. Dormitories wired for high-speed internet access and linked to campus network. Commuter students can connect to campus network. Helpline, repair service, wireless network available.

Student life. Freshman orientation: Available, $50 fee. Preregistration for classes offered. 2-day session in June or July. **Policies:** Mass available daily on campus. Freshmen permitted cars on campus. **Housing:** Guaranteed on-campus for all undergraduates. Coed dorms, single-sex dorms, substance-free housing available. $100 deposit, deadline 5/1. **Activities:** Choral groups, drama, literary magazine, radio station, student government, student newspaper, 25 clubs and organizations on campus, including Habitat for Humanity, High Adventure, Superkids, business club, campus ministry, culture and heritage club, interhall council, student nurses association.

Athletics. NCAA. **Intercollegiate:** Baseball M, basketball, cross-country, field hockey W, golf M, soccer, softball W, volleyball W. **Intramural:** Basketball, football (non-tackle), soccer, softball, swimming, volleyball. **Team name:** Monks.

Student services. Alcohol/substance abuse counseling, campus ministries, career counseling, student employment services, financial aid counseling, health services, personal counseling, placement for graduates, veterans' counselor. **Physically disabled:** Services for visually, speech, hearing impaired. **Learning disabled:** Comprehensive services available.

Contact. E-mail: admission@sjcme.edu
Phone: (207) 893-7746 Toll-free number: (800) 338-7057
Fax: (207) 893-7862
Vincent Kloskowski, Director of Admission, St. Joseph's College, 278 Whites Bridge Road, Standish, ME 04084

Thomas College
Waterville, Maine
www.thomas.edu
CB member
CB code: 3903

- Private 4-year business and liberal arts college
- Residential campus in large town
- 700 degree-seeking undergraduates: 15% part-time, 51% women, 1% African American, 1% Asian American, 1% Hispanic American, 1% Native American
- 104 degree-seeking graduate students
- 73% of applicants admitted
- Application essay required
- 44% graduate within 6 years

General. Founded in 1894. Regionally accredited. Undergraduate evening courses offered in Pittsfield, graduate courses in Augusta and Portland, limited distance learning. Evening division (undergraduate and graduate) on trimester system. **Degrees:** 125 bachelor's, 22 associate awarded; master's offered. **Location:** 75 miles from Portland. **Calendar:** Semester, limited summer session. **Full-time faculty:** 23 total; 48% have terminal degrees, 35% women. **Part-time faculty:** 55 total; 16% have terminal degrees, 34% women. **Class size:** 45% < 20, 55% 20-39.

Freshman class profile. 628 applied, 458 admitted, 221 enrolled.

Mid 50% test scores		**Rank in top quarter:**	30%
SAT verbal:	430-520	**Rank in top tenth:**	12%
SAT math:	430-540	**End year in good standing:**	77%
ACT:	17-	**Return as sophomores:**	58%
GPA 3.50 or higher:	14%	**Out-of-state:**	24%
GPA 3.0-3.49:	35%	**Live on campus:**	79%
GPA 2.0-2.99:	43%		

Basis for selection. Academic transcripts most important. Letters of recommendation and SAT and/or TOEFL Exam scores are also important. Recommend minimum 2.0 overall GPA, rank in top half of class. Test scores required of bachelor's degree candidates, not required for associate degree candidates. Interview recommended.

High school preparation. 16 units required. Required and recommended units include English 4, mathematics 3, social studies 2, science 3, foreign language 2 and academic electives 2.

2006-2007 Annual costs. Tuition/fees: $17,730. Room/board: $7,430. Books/supplies: $700. Personal expenses: $1,000.

2005-2006 Financial aid. Need-based: 183 full-time freshmen applied for aid; 165 were judged to have need; 165 of these received aid. Average need met was 85%. Average scholarship/grant was $11,129; average loan $3,405. 68% of total undergraduate aid awarded as scholarships/grants, 32% as loans/jobs. **Non-need-based:** Awarded to 141 full-time undergraduates, including 64 freshmen. Scholarships awarded for academics, leadership, state residency.

Application procedures. Admission: No deadline. $50 fee, may be waived for applicants with need. Application may be submitted online. Admission notification on a rolling basis beginning on or about 11/1. Must reply by May 1 or within 2 week(s) if notified thereafter. **Financial aid:** Priority date 2/15; no closing date. FAFSA required. Applicants notified on a rolling basis starting 3/15; must reply within 2 week(s) of notification.

Academics. Special study options: Combined bachelor's/graduate degree, cross-registration, dual enrollment of high school students, exchange student, independent study, internships, study abroad, teacher certification program. New England/Quebec Student Exchange Program; Ecole de Gestion et de Commerce in Nante, France. **Credit/placement by examination:** AP, CLEP. 15 credit hours maximum toward associate degree, 15 toward bachelor's. **Support services:** Learning center, reduced course load, study skills assistance, tutoring.

Majors. Business: Accounting, business admin, finance, hospitality admin, human resources, international, management information systems, marketing. **Communications:** General. **Computer sciences:** General, computer science, information systems. **Education:** Elementary. **Engineering:** Software. **Legal studies:** Prelaw. **Parks/recreation:** Sports admin. **Protective services:** Criminal justice, law enforcement admin. **Psychology:** General. **Social sciences:** Political science.

Most popular majors. Business/marketing 66%, computer/information sciences 12%, education 8%, security/protective services 7%.

Computing on campus. 120 workstations in dormitories, library, computer center, student center. Dormitories wired for high-speed internet access and linked to campus network. Commuter students can connect to campus network. Online course registration, online library, helpline, student web hosting, wireless network available.

Student life. Freshman orientation: Mandatory. Preregistration for classes offered. One credit pass/fail for first year students. **Policies:** Freshmen permitted cars on campus. **Housing:** Guaranteed on-campus for freshmen. Coed dorms, apartments, substance-free housing available. $200 deposit. **Activities:** Choral groups, dance, drama, student government, student newspaper, Newman Club, veterans club, marketing group, nontraditional students group.

Athletics. NCAA. **Intercollegiate:** Baseball M, basketball, field hockey W, golf M, lacrosse, soccer, softball W, tennis M, volleyball W. **Intramural:** Baseball M, basketball, bowling, football (non-tackle) M, soccer, softball, tennis, volleyball, weight lifting. **Team name:** Terriers.

Student services. Alcohol/substance abuse counseling, campus ministries, career counseling, student employment services, financial aid counseling, health services, personal counseling, placement for graduates, veterans' counselor.

Contact. E-mail: admiss@thomas.edu
Phone: (207) 859-1101 Toll-free number: (800) 339-7001
Fax: (207) 859-1114
Wendy Martin, Director of Admissions, Thomas College, 180 West River Road, Waterville, ME 04901

Unity College
Unity, Maine
www.unity.edu
CB member
CB code: 3925

- Private 4-year liberal arts college
- Residential campus in rural community
- 518 degree-seeking undergraduates
- Application essay required

General. Founded in 1965. Regionally accredited. **Degrees:** 89 bachelor's, 4 associate awarded. **ROTC:** Army. **Location:** 20 miles from Waterville. **Calendar:** 4-1-4, limited summer session. **Full-time faculty:** 35 total. **Part-time faculty:** 15 total. **Special facilities:** Indian museum, wetlands research area.

Freshman class profile.

Out-of-state:	65%	**Live on campus:**	90%

Basis for selection. High school transcripts, interviews, recommendations and essay most important. Test scores not required but highly recommended. SAT or ACT recommended.

High school preparation. 18 units recommended. Required and recommended units include English 4, mathematics 4, social studies 4, science 2 and foreign language 2.

2006-2007 Annual costs. Tuition/fees (projected): $18,530. Room/board: $6,970. Books/supplies: $450. Personal expenses: $600.

Financial aid. Non-need-based: Scholarships awarded for academics, leadership, minority status.

Application procedures. Admission: No deadline. $25 fee, may be waived for applicants with need. Application may be submitted online. Admission notification on a rolling basis. **Financial aid:** Priority date 3/1; no closing date. FAFSA required. Applicants notified on a rolling basis starting 2/15.

Academics. Special study options: Accelerated study, cooperative education, double major, dual enrollment of high school students, independent study, internships, liberal arts/career combination, semester at sea, student-designed major, Washington semester. **Credit/placement by examination:** AP, CLEP, institutional tests. 60 credit hours maximum toward bachelor's degree. **Support services:** Learning center, pre-admission summer program, reduced course load, remedial instruction, study skills assistance, tutoring, writing center.

Majors. Agriculture: Aquaculture. **Biology:** Ecology, environmental, marine. **Conservation:** General, environmental science, environmental studies, fisheries, forestry, management/policy, wildlife. **Liberal arts:** Arts/sciences. **Parks/recreation:** Facilities management. **Social sciences:** General.

Computing on campus. 41 workstations in dormitories, library, computer center. Dormitories wired for high-speed internet access and linked to campus network. Commuter students can connect to campus network.

Student life. **Freshman orientation:** Mandatory, $180 fee. A 5-day outdoor orientation program, wilderness-based, designed to introduce new students to Maine, to classmates, and help their transition to college environment. **Housing:** Guaranteed on-campus for all undergraduates. Coed dorms, single-sex dorms available. **Activities:** Drama, radio station, student government, student newspaper, fire-fighting crew, photography club, Environmental Awareness, recycling, community service.

Athletics. **Intercollegiate:** Basketball M, cross-country, soccer, volleyball W. **Intramural:** Baseball M, basketball, cross-country, equestrian, football (tackle) M, ice hockey, lacrosse M, skiing, soccer, softball, volleyball.

Student services. Alcohol/substance abuse counseling, campus ministries, career counseling, student employment services, financial aid counseling, health services, personal counseling, placement for graduates, veterans' counselor.

Contact. E-mail: admissions@unity.edu
Phone: (207) 948-3131 ext. 231 Toll-free number: (800) 624-1024
Fax: (207) 948-6277
John M.B. Craig, Vice President and Dean for Admissions, Unity College, 90 Quaker Hill Road, Unity, ME 04988-0532

University of Maine

Orono, Maine — **CB member**
www.umaine.edu — **CB code: 3916**

- Public 4-year university
- Residential campus in large town
- 8,496 degree-seeking undergraduates: 11% part-time, 50% women, 1% African American, 1% Asian American, 1% Hispanic American, 2% Native American, 2% international
- 1,804 degree-seeking graduate students
- 80% of applicants admitted
- SAT or ACT (ACT writing optional), application essay required
- 53% graduate within 6 years; 25% enter graduate study

General. Founded in 1865. Regionally accredited. **Degrees:** 1,601 bachelor's awarded; master's, doctoral offered. **ROTC:** Army, Navy. **Location:** 12 miles from Bangor. **Calendar:** Semester, extensive summer session. **Full-time faculty:** 496 total; 85% have terminal degrees, 5% minority, 32% women. **Part-time faculty:** 327 total; 24% have terminal degrees, 2% minority, 52% women. **Class size:** 45% < 20, 38% 20-39, 5% 40-49, 8% 50-99, 4% >100. **Special facilities:** Advanced manufacturing center, machine tool lab, laboratory for surface science and technology, planetarium, anthropology museum, woodland preserve, botanical garden, arts center, observatory, environmental research facility, performing arts hall, Canadian-American center, Franco-American center, digital media lab, farm museum, marine lab, aquatic production facility, climbing wall, Laboratory for Surface Science & Technology.

Freshman class profile. 5,702 applied, 4,580 admitted, 1,800 enrolled.

Mid 50% test scores			
SAT verbal:	480-590	Rank in top quarter:	52%
SAT math:	490-600	Rank in top tenth:	22%
ACT:	20-25	End year in good standing:	88%
GPA 3.50 or higher:	33%	Return as sophomores:	79%
GPA 3.0-3.49:	50%	Out-of-state:	18%
GPA 2.0-2.99:	17%	Live on campus:	86%
		International:	2%

Basis for selection. Strong emphasis on grades earned, GPA, and class rank (if available). Academic requirements for admission vary by program. Interview recommended. Audition required of music majors. Portfolio recommended for art majors. **Homeschooled:** Statement describing home-school structure and mission, transcript of courses and grades, state high school equivalency certificate, letter of recommendation (nonparent) required. GED requirement may be waived if thorough home-school records submitted by home-school provider.

High school preparation. 17 units required; 22 recommended. Required and recommended units include English 4, mathematics 3-4, social studies 2, history 1, science 2-4 (laboratory 2-3), foreign language 2 and academic electives 4. 1 unit physical education required of all College of Education candidates.

2005-2006 Annual costs. Tuition/fees: $6,910; $17,050 out-of-state. New England Regional Student Program tuition is 150% of public in-district tuition. Room/board: $6,722. Books/supplies: $700. Personal expenses: $1,100.

2005-2006 Financial aid. **Need-based:** Average need met was 82%. Average scholarship/grant was $5,909; average loan $3,202. 46% of total undergraduate aid awarded as scholarships/grants, 54% as loans/jobs. **Non-need-based:** Scholarships awarded for academics, alumni affiliation, art, athletics, job skills, leadership, minority status, music/drama, religious affiliation, ROTC, state residency. **Additional information:** Financial aid is available for students entering in the spring.

Application procedures. **Admission:** No deadline. $40 fee, may be waived for applicants with need. Application may be submitted online. Admission notification on a rolling basis beginning on or about 1/15. Must reply by May 1 or within 2 week(s) if notified thereafter. **Financial aid:** Priority date 3/1; no closing date. FAFSA required. Applicants notified on a rolling basis starting 3/15; must reply by 5/1 or within 2 week(s) of notification.

Academics. **Special study options:** Accelerated study, combined bachelor's/graduate degree, cooperative education, distance learning, double major, ESL, exchange student, honors, independent study, internships, liberal arts/career combination, semester at sea, student-designed major, study abroad, teacher certification program. **Credit/placement by examination:** AP, CLEP, IB, institutional tests. Duplicate credit may not be granted. Each department may develop or adopt examinations other than CLEP examinations for the purpose of granting credit for specific courses. **Support services:** Reduced course load, remedial instruction, study skills assistance, tutoring.

Honors college/program. Admission for first-time and transfer students based on test scores and high school record.

Majors. **Agriculture:** Animal sciences, business, economics, food science, greenhouse operations, horticultural science, landscaping, nursery operations, ornamental horticulture, plant sciences, soil science, turf management. **Architecture:** Landscape. **Area/ethnic studies:** Women's. **Biology:** General, bacteriology, biochemistry, biomedical sciences, botany, cell/histology, ecology, entomology, marine, molecular, pathology, zoology. **Business:** General, accounting, business admin, finance, labor relations, management information systems, managerial economics. **Communications:** General, journalism. **Computer sciences:** General. **Conservation:** Environmental studies, forest resources, forestry, management/policy, wildlife, wood science. **Education:** General, art, biology, chemistry, elementary, English, foreign languages, French, history, mathematics, music, physical, science, secondary, social studies, Spanish. **Engineering:** General, agricultural, chemical, civil, computer, electrical, forest, mechanical, physics, systems. **Engineering technology:** Civil, electrical, surveying. **English:** Speech/rhetoric. **Family/consumer sciences:** Family/community services, food/nutrition. **Foreign languages:** General, French, German, Latin, Spanish. **Health:** Audiology/speech pathology, clinical lab science, communication disorders, nursing (RN). **History:** General. **Interdisciplinary:** Biological/physical sciences, natural sciences. **Liberal arts:** Arts/sciences. **Math:** General. **Parks/recreation:** Facilities management. **Philosophy/religion:** Philosophy. **Physical sciences:** Chemistry, geology, oceanography, physics. **Psychology:** General. **Public administration:** General, social work. **Social sciences:** Anthropology, economics, international relations, political science, sociology. **Visual/performing arts:** Art history/conservation, dramatic, music performance, studio arts.

Most popular majors. Biology 6%, business/marketing 11%, education 13%, engineering/engineering technologies 12%, health sciences 7%, social sciences 7%.

Computing on campus. 500 workstations in library, computer center, student center. Dormitories wired for high-speed internet access and linked to campus network. Commuter students can connect to campus network. Online course registration, online library, helpline, repair service, student web hosting, wireless network available.

Student life. **Freshman orientation:** Available. Preregistration for classes offered. 2-day events in June, parents invited; 4-day welcome program in fall; additional adventure orientations available. **Policies:** Freshmen permitted cars on campus. **Housing:** Guaranteed on-campus for freshmen. Coed dorms, special housing for disabled, apartments, fraternity/sorority housing, substance-free housing available. Academic grouping wings, substance-free and quiet areas, honors housing, men-only sections, women-only sections available. **Activities:** Bands, choral groups, dance, drama, film society, music ensembles, musical theater, opera, radio station, student government, student newspaper, symphony orchestra, TV station, InterVarsity Christian Fellowship, Campus Crusade for Christ, Catholic Student Association, Hillel, Maine Christian Association, Muslim student organization, Newman Center.

Athletics. NCAA. **Intercollegiate:** Baseball M, basketball, cross-country, diving, field hockey W, football (tackle) M, ice hockey, soccer, softball, swimming, track and field, volleyball W. **Intramural:** Badminton, basketball, cross-country, diving, field hockey W, football (non-tackle) M, golf, racquetball, skiing, soccer, softball, squash, swimming, table tennis, tennis, track and field, triathlon, volleyball, water polo. **Team name:** Black Bears.

Student services. Adult student services, alcohol/substance abuse counseling, campus ministries, career counseling, services for economically disadvantaged, student employment services, financial aid counseling, health services, legal services, minority student services, on-campus daycare, personal counseling, placement for graduates, veterans' counselor, women's services. **Physically disabled:** Services for visually, speech, hearing impaired.

Contact. E-mail: um-admit@maine.edu
Phone: (207) 581-1561 Toll-free number: (877) 486-2364
Fax: (207) 581-1213
Sharon Oliver, Director of Admissions, University of Maine, 5713 Chadbourne Hall, Orono, ME 04469-5713

University of Maine at Augusta

Augusta, Maine **CB member**
www.uma.maine.edu **CB code: 3929**

- Public 4-year university and community college
- Commuter campus in large town
- 4,362 degree-seeking undergraduates: 66% part-time, 76% women, 1% African American, 3% Native American

General. Founded in 1965. Regionally accredited. Additional program and course offerings through centers in Thomaston, Brunswick, Rumford, Saco, Sanford, Ellsworth, East Millinocket. Campuses in Augusta, Lewiston, Bangor and serving students statewide via distance education. **Degrees:** 222 bachelor's, 331 associate awarded. **ROTC:** Army, Navy, Air Force. **Location:** 65 miles from Portland, 75 miles from Bangor. **Calendar:** Semester, extensive summer session. **Full-time faculty:** 95 total; 38% have terminal degrees, 53% women. **Part-time faculty:** 229 total; 48% women. **Class size:** 66% < 20, 31% 20-39, 1% 40-49, 2% 50-99. **Special facilities:** Outdoor leisure center, walking and running trails, art gallery, Holocaust Center.

Freshman class profile. 526 enrolled.

Basis for selection. Open admission, but selective for some programs. High school achievement record and test scores considered for admission to allied health and bachelor's degree programs. Talent/ability assessed for admission to music programs. TOEFL is requested of non-native English speakers. Interviews required of dental hygiene and medical laboratory technology majors. Audition required of music majors. **Homeschooled:** Transcript of courses and grades required. Documentation of high school completion required of all.

High school preparation. Recommended units include English 4, mathematics 2, social studies 2, history 2, science 2 (laboratory 2). Applicants to health science programs must have biology, chemistry, and Algebra II. Business administration and public administration applicants must have Algebra II and geometry.

2005-2006 Annual costs. Tuition/fees: $5,025; $11,115 out-of-state. New England Regional Student Program tuition is 150% of public in-district tuition.

2005-2006 Financial aid. Need-based: 301 full-time freshmen applied for aid; 277 were judged to have need; 264 of these received aid. Average need met was 64%. Average scholarship/grant was $4,128; average loan $2,689. 55% of total undergraduate aid awarded as scholarships/grants, 45% as loans/jobs. **Non-need-based:** Awarded to 156 full-time undergraduates, including 36 freshmen. Scholarships awarded for academics, athletics, leadership, music/drama, state residency.

Application procedures. Admission: Priority date 6/15; deadline 8/30 (receipt date). $40 fee, may be waived for applicants with need. Application may be submitted online. Admission notification on a rolling basis. Must reply by May 1 or within 2 week(s) if notified thereafter. **Financial aid:** Priority date 3/1; no closing date. FAFSA required. Applicants notified on a rolling basis starting 3/15; must reply within 2 week(s) of notification.

Academics. Special study options: Combined bachelor's/graduate degree, cross-registration, distance learning, double major, dual enrollment of high school students, honors, independent study, internships, liberal arts/career combination, student-designed major, study abroad. **Credit/placement by examination:** AP, CLEP, institutional tests. 45 credit hours maximum toward associate degree, 90 toward bachelor's. **Support services:** Reduced course load, remedial instruction, study skills assistance, tutoring.

Majors. Architecture: Technology. **Biology:** General. **Business:** Accounting, business admin, financial planning. **Computer sciences:** General. **English:** English lit. **Health:** Dental hygiene. **Liberal arts:** Library science. **Protective services:** Law enforcement admin. **Public administration:** General. **Social sciences:** General. **Visual/performing arts:** Studio arts.

Most popular majors. Business/marketing 18%, health sciences 45%, library sciences 13%, security/protective services 6%, social sciences 6%.

Computing on campus. 178 workstations in library, computer center. Commuter students can connect to campus network. Online course registration, wireless network available.

Student life. Freshman orientation: Available. Preregistration for classes offered. One-day orientations held 1 week prior to start of each semester and mid-summer. **Policies:** Freshmen permitted cars on campus. **Activities:** Bands, music ensembles, student government, student newspaper, art and architectural student association, Gay Lesbian Bisexual Transgender friends and associates, student government association, honors English program, english society, student nursing association, Pi Alpha Alpha, international student club, college republicans, mental health and human services club, campus crusade.

Athletics. USCAA. **Intercollegiate:** Basketball, soccer W. **Intramural:** Basketball, racquetball, soccer, volleyball. **Team name:** Moose.

Student services. Alcohol/substance abuse counseling, career counseling, financial aid counseling, personal counseling, veterans' counselor. **Physically disabled:** Services for visually, speech, hearing impaired.

Contact. E-mail: umaar@maine.maine.edu
Phone: (207) 621-3185 Toll-free number: (877) 862-1234
Fax: (207) 621-3333
Sheri Fraser, Director of Admissions and Advising, University of Maine at Augusta, 46 University Drive, Augusta, ME 04330

University of Maine at Farmington

Farmington, Maine **CB member**
www.umf.maine.edu **CB code: 3506**

- Public 4-year liberal arts and teachers college
- Residential campus in small town
- 2,278 degree-seeking undergraduates: 8% part-time, 66% women, 1% Asian American, 1% Hispanic American, 1% Native American
- 74% of applicants admitted
- Application essay required
- 57% graduate within 6 years; 20% enter graduate study

General. Founded in 1863. Regionally accredited. **Degrees:** 381 bachelor's awarded. **Location:** 38 miles from Augusta, 80 miles from Portland. **Calendar:** Semester, extensive summer session. **Full-time faculty:** 118 total; 85% have terminal degrees, 3% minority, 48% women. **Part-time faculty:** 57 total; 37% have terminal degrees, 2% minority, 58% women. **Class size:** 65% < 20, 32% 20-39, 1% 40-49, 1% 50-99, less than 1% >100. **Special facilities:** Archaeology research center, campus-wide wireless laptop network, 24/7 computer center, on-site nursery school and day care center teaching labs, multi-media graphics lab, observatory.

Freshman class profile. 1,602 applied, 1,190 admitted, 575 enrolled.

Mid 50% test scores		**Rank in top tenth:**	12%
SAT verbal:	450-580	**Return as sophomores:**	75%
SAT math:	450-550	**Out-of-state:**	23%
Rank in top quarter:	38%	**Live on campus:**	95%

Basis for selection. School achievement record and recommendation most important. School and community activities, interviews and personal essay also important. On campus tests required for those below SAT 490 Verbal, 450 Math. Interview recommended. 13-15 page writing sample required for Creative Writing BFA. **Homeschooled:** GED or SAT required. **Learning Disabled:** Students asked to submit documentation to learning assistance center after acceptance.

High school preparation. 19 units recommended. Required and recommended units include English 4, mathematics 3-4, social studies 2-3, science 2-3 (laboratory 2-3), foreign language 2-3 and academic electives 3. Algebra I and II and geometry required. Two years of same foreign language required. General college preparatory program required for all except those admitted to Program of Basic Studies.

2005-2006 Annual costs. Tuition/fees: $5,541; $12,771 out-of-state. New England Regional Student Program tuition is 150% of public in-district tuition. Room/board: $5,984. Books/supplies: $560. Personal expenses: $2,122.

2004-2005 Financial aid. Need-based: 473 full-time freshmen applied for aid; 358 were judged to have need; 357 of these received aid. Average need met was 69%. Average scholarship/grant was $4,496; average loan $2,849. 45% of total undergraduate aid awarded as scholarships/grants, 55% as loans/jobs. **Non-need-based:** Awarded to 367 full-time undergraduates,

including 96 freshmen. Scholarships awarded for academics, leadership, minority status, state residency. **Additional information:** FAFSA must arrive at Federal processor by 3/1.

Application procedures. Admission: No deadline. $40 fee, may be waived for applicants with need. Application may be submitted online. Admission notification on a rolling basis beginning on or about 12/15. Must reply by May 1 or within 3 week(s) if notified thereafter. **Financial aid:** Priority date 3/1; no closing date. FAFSA required. Applicants notified on a rolling basis starting 3/15; must reply within 2 week(s) of notification.

Academics. Interdisciplinary first year seminar. **Special study options:** Accelerated study, cross-registration, distance learning, double major, dual enrollment of high school students, exchange student, honors, independent study, internships, liberal arts/career combination, semester at sea, student-designed major, study abroad, teacher certification program. **Credit/placement by examination:** AP, CLEP, IB, SAT, institutional tests. 30 credit hours maximum toward bachelor's degree. **Support services:** Learning center, pre-admission summer program, reduced course load, remedial instruction, study skills assistance, tutoring, writing center.

Majors. Area/ethnic studies: Women's. **Biology:** General. **Business:** Managerial economics. **Computer sciences:** Computer science. **Conservation:** Environmental science, land use planning, management/policy. **Education:** Biology, early childhood, early childhood special, elementary, English, health, kindergarten/preschool, mathematics, middle, multi-level teacher, science, secondary, social science, special. **English:** Creative writing. **Health:** Community health, public health ed. **History:** General. **Interdisciplinary:** Math/computer science. **Liberal arts:** Arts/sciences. **Math:** General. **Physical sciences:** Geochemistry. **Psychology:** General. **Social sciences:** General, anthropology, economics, geography, international relations, political science. **Visual/performing arts:** Art, dramatic.

Most popular majors. Education 40%, English 10%, health sciences 7%, interdisciplinary studies 9%, psychology 9%, social sciences 8%.

Computing on campus. 175 workstations in library, computer center, student center. Dormitories wired for high-speed internet access and linked to campus network. Commuter students can connect to campus network. Online course registration, online library, helpline, wireless network available.

Student life. Freshman orientation: Available, $90 fee. Preregistration for classes offered. Held two days before classes; includes academic advising, outdoor activities, and community service. **Policies:** Freshmen permitted cars on campus. **Housing:** Guaranteed on-campus for freshmen. Coed dorms, single-sex dorms, apartments, substance-free housing available. Housing for students maintaining certain GPA, medical single rooms, quiet floors, wellness community, independent living environment housing available. **Activities:** Concert band, choral groups, dance, drama, literary magazine, music ensembles, radio station, student government, student newspaper, symphony orchestra, justice uniting students together, student environmental and political awareness club, Amnesty International, Inter-Varsity Christian Fellowship, student alcohol educators, student admissions club, Alpha Phi Omega, literary guild, Newman club, student-run entertainment board.

Athletics. NAIA, NCAA. **Intercollegiate:** Baseball M, basketball, cross-country, field hockey W, golf M, soccer, softball W, volleyball W. **Intramural:** Basketball, soccer, softball, swimming, tennis, volleyball. **Team name:** Beavers.

Student services. Alcohol/substance abuse counseling, campus ministries, career counseling, student employment services, financial aid counseling, health services, on-campus daycare, personal counseling, placement for graduates, veterans' counselor, women's services. **Physically disabled:** Services for visually, hearing impaired.

Contact. E-mail: umfadmit@maine.edu
Phone: (207) 778-7050 Fax: (207) 778-8182
William Geller, Vice President Student Community Services, University of Maine at Farmington, 246 Main Street, Farmington, ME 04938-1994

University of Maine at Fort Kent

Fort Kent, Maine — **CB member**
www.umfk.maine.edu — **CB code: 3393**

- Public 4-year university
- Commuter campus in small town
- 869 degree-seeking undergraduates: 15% part-time, 62% women
- Application essay required
- 36% graduate within 6 years; 4% enter graduate study

General. Founded in 1878. Regionally accredited. Bilingual Franco-American region. **Degrees:** 254 bachelor's, 42 associate awarded. **Location:** 200 miles from Bangor, 21 miles from Edmundston, Canada. **Calendar:** Semester, limited summer session. **Full-time faculty:** 35 total; 6% minority. **Part-time faculty:** 43 total. **Special facilities:** 16-acre biological park, Acadian Archives, interactive television site, Northern Maine Center for Rural Health Science.

Freshman class profile. 319 applied, 275 admitted, 143 enrolled.

GPA 3.50 or higher:	6%	**Rank in top tenth:**	5%
GPA 3.0-3.49:	29%	**End year in good standing:**	77%
GPA 2.0-2.99:	57%	**International:**	2%
Rank in top quarter:	20%		

Basis for selection. Open admission, but selective for some programs. High school courses and achievement record most important. Recommendations considered. SAT, ACT scores, or on-campus placement exams required. Interview recommended.

High school preparation. 16 units required. Required and recommended units include English 4, mathematics 2, social studies 2, science 2 and foreign language 2. Biology and chemistry required for nursing and environmental studies.

2005-2006 Annual costs. Tuition/fees: $4,844; $10,934 out-of-state. New England Regional tuition is 150% of public in-district tuition. Room/board: $5,984. Books/supplies: $900. Personal expenses: $1,000.

2005-2006 Financial aid. Need-based: Average need met was 70%. Average scholarship/grant was $3,218; average loan $2,647. 53% of total undergraduate aid awarded as scholarships/grants, 47% as loans/jobs. **Non-need-based:** Scholarships awarded for academics.

Application procedures. Admission: No deadline. $40 fee, may be waived for applicants with need. Application may be submitted online. Admission notification on a rolling basis. Must reply by May 1 or within 4 week(s) if notified thereafter. **Financial aid:** Priority date 3/1; no closing date. FAFSA required. Applicants notified on a rolling basis starting 3/15; must reply within 2 week(s) of notification.

Academics. Special study options: Accelerated study, cooperative education, cross-registration, distance learning, double major, dual enrollment of high school students, honors, independent study, internships, liberal arts/career combination, student-designed major, study abroad, teacher certification program. **Credit/placement by examination:** AP, CLEP, IB, institutional tests. 30 credit hours maximum toward associate degree, 90 toward bachelor's. **Support services:** Learning center, pre-admission summer program, reduced course load, remedial instruction, tutoring.

Majors. Area/ethnic studies: Canadian. **Biology:** General. **Business:** General, business admin, e-commerce, management information systems. **Computer sciences:** General, information technology, programming, systems analysis. **Conservation:** Environmental science, management/policy. **Education:** General, business, elementary, English, multi-level teacher, music, science, secondary, social studies. **English:** American lit, British lit. **Foreign languages:** General, comparative lit, French. **Health:** Nursing (RN), predentistry, premedicine, prepharmacy, preveterinary. **Interdisciplinary:** Math/computer science. **Legal studies:** Prelaw. **Liberal arts:** Arts/sciences. **Psychology:** General. **Public administration:** Social work. **Social sciences:** General, sociology.

Most popular majors. Education 75%, health sciences 9%, social sciences 6%.

Computing on campus. 100 workstations in dormitories, library, computer center. Dormitories linked to campus network. Commuter students can connect to campus network. Online course registration, repair service, student web hosting, wireless network available.

Student life. Freshman orientation: Mandatory. Preregistration for classes offered. 3-day social and educational orientation, including workshops. **Policies:** Freshmen permitted cars on campus. **Housing:** Coed dorms available. $100 deposit. **Activities:** Jazz band, choral groups, dance, drama, music ensembles, musical theater, student government, Christian Fellowship, Newman Club.

Athletics. NAIA. **Intercollegiate:** Basketball, skiing, soccer. **Intramural:** Baseball M, basketball, cross-country, golf, ice hockey M, racquetball, skiing, soccer, softball, table tennis, tennis, volleyball, weight lifting. **Team name:** Bengals.

Student services. Adult student services, career counseling, financial aid counseling, health services, personal counseling, placement for graduates, veterans' counselor.

Contact. E-mail: umfkadm@maine.edu
Phone: (207) 834-7600 Toll-free number: (888) 879-8635
Fax: (207) 834-7609
Douglas Barley, Director of Admissions, University of Maine at Fort Kent, 23 University Drive, Fort Kent, ME 04743

University of Maine at Machias

Machias, Maine — **CB member**
www.umm.maine.edu — **CB code: 3956**

- Public 4-year university and liberal arts college
- Commuter campus in rural community
- 578 degree-seeking undergraduates: 21% part-time, 68% women, 1% African American, 1% Asian American, 2% Hispanic American, 4% Native American, 5% international
- 83% of applicants admitted
- SAT or ACT (ACT writing optional), application essay required
- 45% graduate within 6 years

General. Founded in 1909. Regionally accredited. **Degrees:** 94 bachelor's, 12 associate awarded. **Location:** 85 miles from Bangor, 65 miles from Bar Harbor. **Calendar:** Semester, limited summer session. **Full-time faculty:** 40 total; 55% have terminal degrees, 2% minority, 35% women. **Part-time faculty:** 59 total; 30% have terminal degrees, 2% minority, 54% women. **Class size:** 70% < 20, 30% 20-39. **Special facilities:** Institute for applied marine research and education, mariculture student research facility, greenhouse, GIS lab, early childhood center, field station, international park, sail loft.

Freshman class profile. 374 applied, 312 admitted, 120 enrolled.

Mid 50% test scores			
SAT verbal:	430-570	Rank in top tenth:	15%
SAT math:	400-540	Return as sophomores:	67%
ACT:	18-25	Out-of-state:	28%
Rank in top quarter:	31%	Live on campus:	68%
		International:	1%

Basis for selection. Applicants should rank in top half of class and have a B average. Recommendations and test scores are important. Essay and outstanding nonacademic achievement (extracurricular, community, military, life, or work) considered. SAT/ACT not required of applicants for associate of science degree. Test score for fall-term admission must be received before first day of classes. Interview recommended. **Homeschooled:** Statement describing homeschool structure and mission, transcript of courses and grades required. Records of all completed coursework plus documentation verifying proficiency in coursework (such as examples of writing, math skills). Portfolio beneficial for some coursework. Standardized test scores required; campus visit with interview important. **Learning Disabled:** Students evaluated on results of required college preparatory work. Documentation of disability important if seeking assistance from Student Resource Center.

High school preparation. 11 units required. Required and recommended units include English 4, mathematics 3, social studies 2, science 2 (laboratory 2), foreign language 2 and academic electives 3. Social studies may include history. Computer applications, fine arts also recommended.

2005-2006 Annual costs. Tuition/fees: $4,845; $12,195 out-of-state. New England Regional Student Program tuition is 150% of public in-district tuition. Room/board: $5,678. Books/supplies: $650. Personal expenses: $1,600.

2005-2006 Financial aid. Need-based: 76 full-time freshmen applied for aid; 67 were judged to have need; 67 of these received aid. Average need met was 79%. Average scholarship/grant was $5,030; average loan $2,990. 56% of total undergraduate aid awarded as scholarships/grants, 44% as loans/jobs. **Non-need-based:** Awarded to 46 full-time undergraduates, including 10 freshmen. Scholarships awarded for academics, alumni affiliation, art, job skills, leadership, minority status, music/drama, state residency.

Application procedures. Admission: Closing date 8/15 (receipt date). $40 fee, may be waived for applicants with need. Application may be submitted online. Admission notification on a rolling basis. Must reply by May 1 or within 2 week(s) if notified thereafter. **Financial aid:** Priority date 3/1; no closing date. FAFSA required. Applicants notified on a rolling basis starting 2/15; must reply within 2 week(s) of notification.

Academics. Internships and/or cooperative education program available in business studies, recreation management, biology, environmental studies, and behavioral science. **Special study options:** Cooperative education, distance learning, double major, dual enrollment of high school students, honors, independent study, internships, student-designed major, study abroad, teacher certification program. **Credit/placement by examination:** AP, CLEP, SAT, ACT, institutional tests. **Support services:** Learning center, reduced course load, remedial instruction, study skills assistance, tutoring, writing center.

Majors. Biology: General, ecology, marine. **Business:** General, accounting, business admin, hospitality admin, hospitality/recreation, marketing, office management, office/clerical, tourism promotion, tourism/travel. **Conservation:** General, environmental studies. **Education:** Business, elementary, middle. **Health:** Mental health services. **History:** General. **Interdisciplinary:** Behavioral sciences. **Liberal arts:** Arts/sciences. **Parks/recreation:** General, facilities management. **Psychology:** General. **Public administration:** Human services. **Visual/performing arts:** General.

Most popular majors. Biology 13%, business/marketing 20%, education 10%, interdisciplinary studies 14%, liberal arts 13%, natural resources/environmental science 8%, parks/recreation 6%.

Computing on campus. 117 workstations in dormitories, library, computer center. Dormitories wired for high-speed internet access and linked to campus network. Commuter students can connect to campus network. Online course registration, online library, helpline, repair service, wireless network available.

Student life. Freshman orientation: Available. Preregistration for classes offered. Orientation in June, August, and January. **Policies:** Students over 21 may drink in their rooms. Firearms must be stored in safe in Resident Director's office. Freshmen permitted cars on campus. **Housing:** Guaranteed on-campus for all undergraduates. Coed dorms, substance-free housing available. $100 nonrefundable deposit. Pets allowed in dorm rooms. **Activities:** Concert band, choral groups, dance, drama, literary magazine, music ensembles, musical theater, radio station, student government, Newman Club, Students of Service.

Athletics. NAIA. **Intercollegiate:** Basketball, cross-country, soccer, volleyball W. **Intramural:** Basketball, cheerleading W, fencing, football (non-tackle), soccer, softball W, water polo. **Team name:** Clippers.

Student services. Career counseling, student employment services, financial aid counseling, health services, on-campus daycare, personal counseling, placement for graduates, veterans' counselor.

Contact. E-mail: ummadmissions@maine.edu
Phone: (207) 255-1318 Toll-free number: (888) 468-6866
Fax: (207) 255-1363
Stewart Bennett, Director of Admissions, University of Maine at Machias, 9 O'Brien Avenue, Machias, ME 04654

University of Maine at Presque Isle

Presque Isle, Maine — **CB member**
www.umpi.maine.edu — **CB code: 3008**

- Public 4-year university
- Commuter campus in small town
- 1,325 degree-seeking undergraduates: 17% part-time, 65% women, 1% African American, 1% Asian American, 1% Hispanic American, 4% Native American, 9% international
- 86% of applicants admitted
- Application essay required
- 28% graduate within 6 years

General. Founded in 1903. Regionally accredited. **Degrees:** 300 bachelor's, 23 associate awarded. **Location:** 165 miles from Bangor. **Calendar:** Semester, limited summer session. **Full-time faculty:** 54 total; 82% have terminal degrees, 4% minority, 44% women. **Part-time faculty:** 62 total; 16% have terminal degrees, 3% minority, 45% women. **Class size:** 63% < 20, 37% 20-39. **Special facilities:** Small business institute, kinesiology laboratory, local history center, human services laboratory, museum of natural science.

Freshman class profile. 483 applied, 417 admitted, 211 enrolled.

Mid 50% test scores			
SAT verbal:	390-530	Rank in top quarter:	23%
SAT math:	390-500	Rank in top tenth:	8%
GPA 3.50 or higher:	21%	Return as sophomores:	55%
GPA 3.0-3.49:	38%	Out-of-state:	4%
GPA 2.0-2.99:	40%	Live on campus:	38%
		International:	4%

Basis for selection. Admissions based on secondary school record, class rank, recommendations, and essay. Interview also important. Interview recommended for academically borderline. Portfolio required of bachelor of fine arts applicants.

High school preparation. 16 units required. Required units include English 4, mathematics 3, social studies 3, science 2 (laboratory 2), foreign language 2 and academic electives 2. Medical laboratory technology and nursing programs: 4 English, 1 biology w/lab, 1 chemistry w/lab, 2 math, 1 social studies, 6 electives, totaling 15.

2005-2006 Annual costs. Tuition/fees: $4,820; $11,210 out-of-state. Room/board: $5,246. Books/supplies: $800. Personal expenses: $1,100.

2005-2006 Financial aid. **Need-based:** 187 full-time freshmen applied for aid; 160 were judged to have need; 138 of these received aid. Average need met was 89%. Average scholarship/grant was $5,288; average loan $2,499. 58% of total undergraduate aid awarded as scholarships/grants, 42% as loans/jobs. **Non-need-based:** Awarded to 115 full-time undergraduates, including 28 freshmen. Scholarships awarded for academics, alumni affiliation, art, job skills, leadership, minority status, music/drama, state residency.

Application procedures. **Admission:** No deadline. $40 fee, may be waived for applicants with need. Application may be submitted online. Admission notification on a rolling basis. **Financial aid:** Priority date 4/1; no closing date. FAFSA required. Applicants notified on a rolling basis starting 3/1; must reply within 2 week(s) of notification.

Academics. **Special study options:** Accelerated study, combined bachelor's/graduate degree, cooperative education, cross-registration, distance learning, double major, exchange student, honors, independent study, internships, student-designed major, study abroad, teacher certification program. **Credit/placement by examination:** AP, CLEP, IB, SAT, ACT, institutional tests. 30 credit hours maximum toward associate degree, 60 toward bachelor's. Scores of 3, 4, and 5 acceptable on AP tests; hours awarded decided on case-by-case basis. **Support services:** Learning center, reduced course load, remedial instruction, study skills assistance, tutoring, writing center.

Majors. **Biology:** General. **Business:** Accounting, business admin, communications. **Conservation:** Environmental studies. **Education:** General, art, elementary, health, physical, secondary. **Health:** Athletic training. **Interdisciplinary:** Behavioral sciences. **Liberal arts:** Arts/sciences. **Parks/recreation:** General. **Physical sciences:** Geology. **Protective services:** Law enforcement admin. **Psychology:** General. **Public administration:** Social work. **Social sciences:** International relations, political science, sociology. **Visual/performing arts:** Art, studio arts.

Most popular majors. Business/marketing 9%, education 17%, liberal arts 46%.

Computing on campus. 120 workstations in library, computer center. Dormitories wired for high-speed internet access and linked to campus network. Commuter students can connect to campus network. Helpline available.

Student life. **Freshman orientation:** Mandatory, $35 fee. Preregistration for classes offered. Orientation programs for new or transfer students and parents are held during the spring, summer and in January of each year. **Policies:** Freshmen permitted cars on campus. **Housing:** Guaranteed on-campus for freshmen. Coed dorms, apartments available. $100 fully refundable deposit, deadline 8/1. **Activities:** Drama, radio station, student government, student newspaper, Geo-ecology club, honors club, Campus Crusade for Christ, outdoor adventure program, physical education majors club, games club, Big Brothers & Big Sisters, accounting/business/MIS club.

Athletics. **Intercollegiate:** Baseball M, basketball, cross-country, golf M, skiing, soccer, softball W, volleyball W. **Team name:** Owls.

Student services. Adult student services, campus ministries, career counseling, student employment services, financial aid counseling, health services, on-campus daycare, personal counseling, placement for graduates, veterans' counselor. **Physically disabled:** Services for visually, hearing impaired.

Contact. E-mail: adventure@umpi.maine.edu
Phone: (207) 768-9532 Fax: (207) 768-9777
Brian Manter, Director of Admissions, University of Maine at Presque Isle, 181 Main Street, Presque Isle, ME 04769

University of New England

Biddeford, Maine — **CB member**
www.une.edu — **CB code: 3751**

- Private 4-year university
- Residential campus in small city
- 1,599 degree-seeking undergraduates: 7% part-time, 78% women, 1% African American, 1% Asian American, 1% Hispanic American
- 1,506 degree-seeking graduate students
- 92% of applicants admitted
- SAT or ACT required
- 57% graduate within 6 years

General. Founded in 1831. Regionally accredited. **Degrees:** 223 bachelor's, 114 associate awarded; master's, first professional offered. **ROTC:** Army. **Location:** 15 miles from Portland. **Calendar:** Semester, limited summer session. **Full-time faculty:** 137 total; 85% have terminal degrees, 4% minority, 49% women. **Part-time faculty:** 104 total; 4% minority, 52% women. **Class size:** 49% < 20, 43% 20-39, 5% 40-49, 3% 50-99. **Special facilities:** Maine Women Writers collection, osteopathic center, performance enhancement and evaluation center, marine science education and research center.

Freshman class profile. 2,055 applied, 1,888 admitted, 468 enrolled.

Mid 50% test scores		Rank in top quarter:	49%
SAT verbal:	540-570	Rank in top tenth:	17%
SAT math:	470-580	End year in good standing:	82%
GPA 3.50 or higher:	37%	Return as sophomores:	75%
GPA 3.0-3.49:	30%	Out-of-state:	67%
GPA 2.0-2.99:	33%	Live on campus:	92%

Basis for selection. School achievement record most important. Test scores and school and community activities considered. Exposure to health careers recommended if seeking admission to health science majors. Essay recommended. Interview required for nursing program, recommended for all, strongly recommended for academically weaker students.

High school preparation. College-preparatory program recommended. Required and recommended units include English 4, mathematics 3-4, social studies 2, history 2, science 2-4 (laboratory 2), foreign language 2 and academic electives 4.

2005-2006 Annual costs. Tuition/fees: $22,275. Room/board: $8,730. Books/supplies: $1,400. Personal expenses: $1,570.

2005-2006 Financial aid. **Need-based:** 440 full-time freshmen applied for aid; 387 were judged to have need; 387 of these received aid. Average need met was 76%. Average scholarship/grant was $11,382; average loan $4,294. 50% of total undergraduate aid awarded as scholarships/grants, 50% as loans/jobs. **Non-need-based:** Awarded to 312 full-time undergraduates, including 119 freshmen. Scholarships awarded for academics, alumni affiliation, leadership.

Application procedures. **Admission:** Priority date 3/1; deadline 9/1 (postmark date). $40 fee, may be waived for applicants with need. Application may be submitted online. Admission notification on a rolling basis. Must reply by May 1 or within 4 week(s) if notified thereafter. **Financial aid:** Priority date 5/1; no closing date. FAFSA required. Applicants notified on a rolling basis starting 1/25.

Academics. **Special study options:** Combined bachelor's/graduate degree, cooperative education, cross-registration, distance learning, double major, dual enrollment of high school students, independent study, internships, liberal arts/career combination, student-designed major, study abroad, teacher certification program. **Credit/placement by examination:** AP, CLEP, institutional tests. **Support services:** Learning center, reduced course load, remedial instruction, study skills assistance, tutoring.

Majors. **Agriculture:** Aquaculture. **Area/ethnic studies:** American. **Biology:** General, biochemistry, marine. **Business:** Business admin. **Conservation:** Environmental science, environmental studies. **Education:** General, art, elementary. **English:** English lit. **Health:** Athletic training, clinical lab technology, dental hygiene, health services admin, nursing (RN). **History:** General. **Interdisciplinary:** Biopsychology. **Liberal arts:** Arts/sciences. **Math:** General. **Parks/recreation:** Exercise sciences, sports admin. **Physical sciences:** Chemistry. **Psychology:** General. **Social sciences:** Political science, sociology.

Most popular majors. Biology 26%, health sciences 39%, natural resources/environmental science 7%, psychology 10%.

Computing on campus. 150 workstations in dormitories, library, computer center, student center. Dormitories wired for high-speed internet access and linked to campus network. Commuter students can connect to campus network. Online course registration, online library, helpline, student web hosting, wireless network available.

Student life. **Freshman orientation:** Available. Preregistration for classes offered. **Policies:** Freshmen permitted cars on campus. **Housing:** Guaranteed on-campus for freshmen. Coed dorms, single-sex dorms, substance-free housing available. $200 fully refundable deposit, deadline 5/1. **Activities:** Literary magazine, student government, Earth's E.C.O., Rotoract, Marine Animal Stranding Helpline, Make A Wish, EMS, Campus Diversity Club, Intervarsity Christian Fellowship, Cross Seekers, Habitat for Humanity, College Democrats.

Athletics. NCAA. **Intercollegiate:** Basketball, cross-country, field hockey W, golf M, lacrosse, soccer, softball W, swimming W, volleyball W. **Intramural:** Basketball, gymnastics, racquetball, soccer, softball, table tennis, volleyball W, water polo. **Team name:** Nor-easters.

Student services. Adult student services, alcohol/substance abuse counseling, career counseling, financial aid counseling, health services, minority student services, personal counseling, veterans' counselor.

Contact. E-mail: admissions@une.edu
Phone: (207) 283-0170 ext. 2297 Toll-free number: (800) 477-4863
Fax: (207) 602-5900
Robert Pecchia, Associate Dean of Admissions, University of New England, Hills Beach Road, Biddeford, ME 04005

University of Southern Maine

Gorham, Maine — **CB member**
www.usm.maine.edu — **CB code: 3691**

- Public 4-year university and liberal arts college
- Residential campus in small city
- 6,895 degree-seeking undergraduates: 32% part-time, 60% women, 1% African American, 1% Asian American, 1% Hispanic American, 2% Native American
- 1,673 degree-seeking graduate students
- 79% of applicants admitted
- SAT or ACT with writing, application essay required
- 32% graduate within 6 years

General. Founded in 1878. Regionally accredited. **Degrees:** 1,000 bachelor's, 61 associate awarded; master's, doctoral, first professional offered. **ROTC:** Army, Air Force. **Location:** 110 miles from Boston. **Calendar:** Semester, extensive summer session. **Full-time faculty:** 402 total; 80% have terminal degrees, 5% minority, 44% women. **Part-time faculty:** 302 total; 14% have terminal degrees, 1% minority, 53% women. **Special facilities:** Planetarium, cartographic collection, olympic-sized ice arena, concert hall, indoor tennis courts.

Freshman class profile. 3,599 applied, 2,848 admitted, 1,010 enrolled.

Mid 50% test scores			
SAT verbal:	450-570	Rank in top quarter:	31%
SAT math:	450-550	Rank in top tenth:	10%
ACT:	17-22	End year in good standing:	86%
GPA 3.50 or higher:	16%	Return as sophomores:	67%
GPA 3.0-3.49:	34%	Out-of-state:	17%
GPA 2.0-2.99:	49%	Live on campus:	76%

Basis for selection. Level and content of academic program with performance or achievement record, class rank, and standardized test scores most important. Counselor recommendation, essay, and experience outside classroom also important. Interview recommended for all. Audition required of music majors. **Homeschooled:** Transcript of courses and grades, letter of recommendation (nonparent) required. SAT or ACT, annual assessment of courses, and GED required for financial aid purposes. **Learning Disabled:** Must be otherwise qualified to be admitted, may be asked to provide documentation.

High school preparation. 16 units required. Required and recommended units include English 4, mathematics 3-4, social studies 2-3, history 2-3, science 2-3 (laboratory 2-3) and foreign language 2-3. 3 lab sciences for science majors. Math, business and electrical engineering majors require 4 years of math.

2005-2006 Annual costs. Tuition/fees: $5,695; $14,515 out-of-state. New England Regional Student Program tuition is 150% of public in-district tuition. Room/board: $6,689. Books/supplies: $800. Personal expenses: $2,000.

2005-2006 Financial aid. Need-based: 707 full-time freshmen applied for aid; 555 were judged to have need; 531 of these received aid. Average need met was 71%. Average scholarship/grant was $4194.31; average loan $2,988. 37% of total undergraduate aid awarded as scholarships/grants, 63% as loans/jobs. **Non-need-based:** Scholarships awarded for academics, music/drama.

Application procedures. Admission: Priority date 2/15; no deadline. $40 fee, may be waived for applicants with need. Application may be submitted online. Admission notification on a rolling basis beginning on or about 1/1. Must reply by May 1 or within 2 week(s) if notified thereafter. **Financial aid:** Priority date 2/15; no closing date. FAFSA required. Applicants notified on a rolling basis starting 3/15; must reply by 5/1 or within 2 week(s) of notification.

Academics. Special study options: Accelerated study, combined bachelor's/graduate degree, cooperative education, cross-registration, distance learning, double major, ESL, exchange student, honors, independent study, internships, liberal arts/career combination, semester at sea, student-designed major, study abroad, teacher certification program, Washington semester, weekend college. Preengineering program with University of Maine at Orono, living/learning scholars program, Greater Portland Alliance - cross registration with University of New England, St. Joseph's (Maine), Southern Maine Technical College, and Maine College of Art. **Credit/placement by examination:** AP, CLEP, IB, institutional tests. No numerical limit. Students must meet all course requirements and 30 credit residency for BA/BS and 15 credit residency for AA/AS degrees. **Support services:** Learning center, reduced course load, remedial instruction, study skills assistance, tutoring, writing center.

Honors college/program. Honors application required. Several course options available. Interdisciplinary curriculum with small seminar classes.

Majors. Area/ethnic studies: French, German, Hispanic-American/Latino/Chicano, Russian/Slavic, women's. **Biology:** General, biotechnology, radiobiology. **Business:** General, accounting, accounting/finance, business admin, finance, management information systems, marketing, organizational behavior. **Communications:** General, broadcast journalism, journalism, media studies, public relations. **Computer sciences:** General, applications programming, computer science, programming. **Conservation:** General, environmental science, environmental studies. **Education:** General, art, elementary, music, technology/industrial arts, voc/tech. **Engineering:** Electrical, environmental. **Engineering technology:** Electrical, manufacturing, telecommunications. **English:** Composition. **Foreign languages:** General, Arabic, classics, comparative lit, French, linguistics. **Health:** Athletic training, environmental health, medical radiologic technology/radiation therapy, nursing (RN), pediatric nursing, predentistry, premedicine, preop/surgical nursing, preveterinary, psychiatric nursing, recreational therapy. **History:** General. **Interdisciplinary:** Behavioral sciences, global studies, math/computer science, natural sciences. **Legal studies:** Prelaw. **Liberal arts:** Arts/sciences, humanities. **Math:** General. **Parks/recreation:** General, exercise sciences, sports admin. **Philosophy/religion:** Philosophy. **Physical sciences:** Chemistry, geology, physics. **Protective services:** Criminal justice. **Psychology:** General. **Public administration:** Social work. **Social sciences:** General, anthropology, criminology, economics, geography, international relations, political science, sociology. **Visual/performing arts:** General, acting, art, art history/conservation, arts management, cinematography, directing/producing, dramatic, drawing, jazz, music performance, painting, piano/organ, sculpture, stringed instruments, studio arts, theater arts management, voice/opera.

Most popular majors. Business/marketing 11%, health sciences 18%, psychology 6%, social sciences 13%.

Computing on campus. 410 workstations in dormitories, library, computer center, student center. Dormitories wired for high-speed internet access and linked to campus network. Commuter students can connect to campus network. Online course registration, helpline, repair service, wireless network available.

Student life. Freshman orientation: Mandatory, $150 fee. Preregistration for classes offered. Sessions in summer and autumn. **Policies:** Smoking is not allowed within 50 feet of any dormitory. Freshmen permitted cars on campus. **Housing:** Coed dorms, special housing for disabled, apartments, fraternity/sorority housing, substance-free housing available. $75 nonrefundable deposit, deadline 5/1. Substance-free floor, 24 hour quiet floor, living/learning communities, community service, health-fitness, outdoor recreation housing available. **Activities:** Bands, choral groups, dance, drama, literary magazine, music ensembles, musical theater, opera, radio station, student government, student newspaper, symphony orchestra, TV station, Amnesty International, American Indian student association, Environmental Coalition, College Republicans, Alliance of Sexual Diversity, Women's Forum, Bahai Association, international students association, ethnic student association.

Athletics. NCAA. **Intercollegiate:** Baseball M, basketball, cheerleading, cross-country, field hockey W, golf, ice hockey, lacrosse, soccer, softball W, tennis, track and field, volleyball W, wrestling M. **Intramural:** Basketball, cheerleading W, football (non-tackle), football (tackle) M, ice hockey, lacrosse, racquetball, rugby, sailing, skiing, soccer, softball, squash, table tennis, tennis, volleyball, weight lifting. **Team name:** Huskies.

Student services. Adult student services, alcohol/substance abuse counseling, campus ministries, career counseling, services for economically disadvantaged, student employment services, financial aid counseling, health services, legal services, minority student services, on-campus daycare, personal counseling, placement for graduates, veterans' counselor, women's services. **Physically disabled:** Services for visually, speech, hearing impaired.

Contact. E-mail: usmadm@usm.maine.edu
Phone: (207) 780-5670 Toll-free number: (800) 800-4876 ext. 5670
Fax: (207) 780-5640
Denise Gardner, Director of Admission, University of Southern Maine, 37 College Avenue, Gorham, ME 04038

Four-Year Colleges

Maryland

Baltimore Hebrew University

Baltimore, Maryland
www.bhu.edu **CB code: 2165**

- Private 4-year university and teachers college
- Commuter campus in very large city
- 6 degree-seeking undergraduates
- Application essay, interview required

General. Founded in 1919. Regionally accredited. Easy access to regional Jewish community. University population consists primarily of graduate students. **Degrees:** 3 bachelor's awarded; master's, doctoral offered. **Calendar:** Semester, extensive summer session. **Full-time faculty:** 10 total. **Part-time faculty:** 7 total.

Basis for selection. Dean reviews high school record, Jewish communal activity and conducts personal interview.

2006-2007 Annual costs. Tuition/fees: $13,550. Books/supplies: $400. Personal expenses: $1,300.

2004-2005 Financial aid. Need-based: 25% of total undergraduate aid awarded as scholarships/grants, 75% as loans/jobs. **Non-need-based:** Scholarships awarded for academics.

Application procedures. Admission: Closing date 6/1. $35 fee, may be waived for applicants with need. Admission notification on a rolling basis beginning on or about 5/1. **Financial aid:** Priority date 4/15, closing date 6/1. FAFSA, institutional form required. Applicants notified on a rolling basis starting 7/15; must reply by 9/9.

Academics. University-operated Judaic/Hebraic library. **Special study options:** Accelerated study, cross-registration, double major, dual enrollment of high school students, ESL, independent study, internships, teacher certification program. **Credit/placement by examination:** CLEP, IB, institutional tests. 12 credit hours maximum toward bachelor's degree. **Support services:** Pre-admission summer program, study skills assistance.

Majors. Foreign languages: Hebrew. **Philosophy/religion:** Judaic. **Theology:** Talmudic.

Computing on campus. 12 workstations in library, computer center.

Student life. Activities: Dance.

Student services. Adult student services, career counseling, financial aid counseling, veterans' counselor. **Physically disabled:** Services for hearing impaired.

Contact. E-mail: bhu@bhu.edu
Phone: (410) 578-6918 Fax: (410) 578-6940
Laurie Kott, Director of Admissions and Recruitment, Baltimore Hebrew University, 5800 Park Heights Avenue, Baltimore, MD 21215

Baltimore International College

Baltimore, Maryland
www.bic.edu **CB code: 5086**

- Private 4-year culinary school and business college
- Commuter campus in very large city
- 516 degree-seeking undergraduates: 6% part-time, 53% women
- 90% of applicants admitted
- Application essay required
- 42% graduate within 6 years

General. Founded in 1972. Regionally accredited. **Degrees:** 21 bachelor's, 132 associate awarded. **Location:** Downtown. **Calendar:** Semester, limited summer session. **Full-time faculty:** 13 total. **Part-time faculty:** 17 total. **Class size:** 46% < 20, 52% 20-39, 2% 40-49.

Freshman class profile. 306 applied, 274 admitted, 182 enrolled.

End year in good standing:	88%	**Live on campus:**	23%
Return as sophomores:	81%	**International:**	1%
Out-of-state:	18%		

Basis for selection. Institutional placement evaluation most important. School achievement record, interview, test scores, and recommendations also important. SAT or ACT recommended. Interview recommended. **Homeschooled:** Must be an accredited home school program or approved by the local school district.

2005-2006 Annual costs. Tuition/fees: $20,990. Fees shown are for culinary school and include use of computer, culinary supplies, upgrading and maintenance of kitchen equipment and facilities. Day students provided one full meal daily. Business program students pay lower fees. Room/board: $6,608. Books/supplies: $1,500.

2004-2005 Financial aid. Need-based: 51% of total undergraduate aid awarded as scholarships/grants, 49% as loans/jobs. **Non-need-based:** Scholarships awarded for academics, alumni affiliation, athletics, job skills, leadership, state residency.

Application procedures. Admission: No deadline. $35 fee. Application may be submitted online. Admission notification on a rolling basis. **Financial aid:** Priority date 3/1; no closing date. FAFSA, institutional form required. Applicants notified on a rolling basis; must reply within 2 week(s) of notification.

Academics. Special study options: Accelerated study, cooperative education, double major, honors, internships, liberal arts/career combination, study abroad. Honors program available at the Virginia Park campus in Ireland. **Credit/placement by examination:** AP, CLEP, institutional tests. 15 credit hours maximum toward associate degree, 15 toward bachelor's. **Support services:** Remedial instruction, study skills assistance, tutoring.

Majors. Personal/culinary services: Restaurant/catering.

Computing on campus. 45 workstations in dormitories, library, computer center.

Student life. Freshman orientation: Mandatory. Preregistration for classes offered. One-day program held approximately a week before first day of classes. **Policies:** Freshmen under 21, single, with permanent residence more than 50 miles from campus required to live on campus. **Housing:** Guaranteed on-campus for freshmen. Coed dorms, substance-free housing available. $100 deposit. **Activities:** Student government, American Culinary Federation.

Athletics. Team name: Wolfhounds.

Student services. Alcohol/substance abuse counseling, career counseling, services for economically disadvantaged, student employment services, financial aid counseling, health services, minority student services, personal counseling, placement for graduates, veterans' counselor, women's services.

Contact. E-mail: admissions@bic.edu
Phone: (410) 752-4710 ext. 120 Toll-free number: (800) 624-9926 ext. 120
Fax: (410) 752-3730
Kristin Ciarlo, Director of Admissions, Baltimore International College, 17 Commerce Street, Baltimore, MD 21202-3230

Bowie State University

Bowie, Maryland **CB member**
www.bowiestate.edu **CB code: 5401**

- Public 4-year university
- Commuter campus in small city
- 4,023 degree-seeking undergraduates: 18% part-time, 63% women
- 1,299 degree-seeking graduate students
- 46% of applicants admitted
- SAT or ACT (ACT writing optional) required
- 36% graduate within 6 years

General. Founded in 1865. Regionally accredited. University offers limited courses at off-site locations. **Degrees:** 579 bachelor's awarded; master's, doctoral offered. **ROTC:** Army, Air Force. **Location:** 25 miles from Baltimore, 20 miles from Washington, DC. **Calendar:** Semester, limited summer session. **Full-time faculty:** 149 total; 66% have terminal degrees, 70% minority, 43% women. **Part-time faculty:** 194 total; 39% have terminal degrees, 71% minority, 42% women. **Class size:** 50% < 20, 50% 20-39. **Special facilities:** NASA operations and control center.

Freshman class profile. 5,653 applied, 2,606 admitted, 1,227 enrolled.

Mid 50% test scores		Out-of-state:	13%
SAT verbal:	480-560	Live on campus:	53%
SAT math:	500-600		

Basis for selection. School achievement record in college-preparatory curriculum, test scores, minimum GPA of 2.0, counselor/school recommendation important. Audition required for music program. Portfolio required for art program. Praxis I required for education program. **Homeschooled:** Statement describing homeschool structure and mission required.

High school preparation. Required units include English 4, mathematics 3, social studies 1, history 2, science 3 and foreign language 2.

2005-2006 Annual costs. Tuition/fees: $5,481; $14,786 out-of-state. Room/board: $5,837. Books/supplies: $1,388. Personal expenses: $2,186.

2004-2005 Financial aid. Need-based: 521 full-time freshmen applied for aid; 499 were judged to have need; 499 of these received aid. Average need met was 72%. Average scholarship/grant was $4,839; average loan $2,875. 52% of total undergraduate aid awarded as scholarships/grants, 48% as loans/jobs. **Non-need-based:** Awarded to 656 full-time undergraduates, including 153 freshmen. Scholarships awarded for academics, alumni affiliation, art, athletics, leadership, music/drama, ROTC, state residency.

Application procedures. Admission: No deadline. $40 fee, may be waived for applicants with need. Application may be submitted online. Admission notification on a rolling basis. **Financial aid:** Closing date 3/1. FAFSA required. Applicants notified on a rolling basis starting 4/1; must reply within 10 week(s) of notification.

Academics. Special study options: Combined bachelor's/graduate degree, cooperative education, cross-registration, distance learning, double major, dual enrollment of high school students, exchange student, honors, independent study, internships, liberal arts/career combination, study abroad, teacher certification program. Dual degree programs in engineering and dentistry with cooperating universities. **Credit/placement by examination:** AP, CLEP, institutional tests. 60 credit hours maximum toward bachelor's degree. **Support services:** Learning center, pre-admission summer program, reduced course load, remedial instruction, tutoring, writing center.

Majors. Biology: General. **Business:** General, accounting, business admin, finance, management information systems. **Communications:** Journalism. **Communications technology:** General. **Computer sciences:** General, computer science. **Education:** Early childhood, elementary, English, history, mathematics, science. **Health:** Nursing (RN). **History:** General. **Math:** General. **Psychology:** General. **Public administration:** General, social work. **Social sciences:** Economics, political science, sociology. **Visual/performing arts:** Studio arts.

Most popular majors. Business/marketing 25%, communications/journalism 9%, interdisciplinary studies 13%, psychology 10%, social sciences 17%.

Computing on campus. Dormitories wired for high-speed internet access and linked to campus network. Commuter students can connect to campus network. Online course registration, helpline, repair service, wireless network available.

Student life. Freshman orientation: Mandatory, $75 fee. Preregistration for classes offered. **Policies:** Zero tolerance policy for illegal substance use and violence. **Housing:** Coed dorms, single-sex dorms, apartments available. $150 deposit. **Activities:** Bands, choral groups, dance, drama, music ensembles, musical theater, radio station, student government, student newspaper, TV station, NAACP student chapter, greater Washington urban league chapter, international student association, commuter senate, campus ministry organization.

Athletics. NCAA. **Intercollegiate:** Basketball, bowling W, cross-country, football (tackle) M, softball W, tennis W, track and field, volleyball W. **Intramural:** Basketball, football (non-tackle), racquetball, soccer, table tennis, tennis, volleyball, weight lifting. **Team name:** Bulldogs.

Student services. Adult student services, alcohol/substance abuse counseling, campus ministries, career counseling, student employment services, financial aid counseling, health services, personal counseling, placement for graduates, veterans' counselor. **Physically disabled:** Services for visually, hearing impaired.

Contact. E-mail: dkiah@bowiestate.edu
Phone: (301) 860-3415 Fax: (301) 860-3438
Don Kiah, Assistant Vice President, Enrollment Management, Bowie State University, 14000 Jericho Park Road, Bowie, MD 20715

Capitol College

Laurel, Maryland
www.capitol-college.edu **CB code: 5101**

- Private 4-year business and engineering college
- Commuter campus in large town
- 342 degree-seeking undergraduates
- 435 graduate students
- 50% of applicants admitted
- SAT or ACT (ACT writing optional), application essay required

General. Founded in 1964. Regionally accredited. **Degrees:** 72 bachelor's, 5 associate awarded; master's offered. **ROTC:** Army. **Location:** 19 miles from Washington, DC, 22 miles from Baltimore. **Calendar:** Semester, limited summer session. **Full-time faculty:** 20 total. **Part-time faculty:** 60 total. **Special facilities:** Video lab, interactive computer classrooms, two engineering labs, telecommunications lab.

Freshman class profile. 500 applied, 250 admitted, 95 enrolled.

Mid 50% test scores		SAT math:	390-470
SAT verbal:	400-480	Live on campus:	20%

Basis for selection. Academic preparation, school record and test scores most important. Mathematics foundation necessary for successful completion of programs. Interview and essay recommended.

High school preparation. 20 units required. Required and recommended units include English 4, mathematics 3-4, social studies 2, history 2, science 1-3 (laboratory 1-2) and academic electives 2-3. Mathematic units include algebra I, geometry, algebra II/trigonometry. Calculus recommended for advanced standing.

2005-2006 Annual costs. Tuition/fees: $18,308. Room only: $4,084. Books/supplies: $800. Personal expenses: $1,900.

Financial aid. Non-need-based: Scholarships awarded for academics, alumni affiliation, leadership, minority status.

Application procedures. Admission: Priority date 5/1; no deadline. $25 fee, may be waived for applicants with need. Application may be submitted online. Admission notification on a rolling basis beginning on or about 3/1. Must reply by May 1 or within 3 week(s) if notified thereafter. **Financial aid:** Priority date 2/1; no closing date. FAFSA, institutional form required. Applicants notified on a rolling basis starting 6/3; must reply by 5/1 or within 3 week(s) of notification.

Academics. Special study options: Combined bachelor's/graduate degree, cooperative education, distance learning, double major, independent study, liberal arts/career combination, weekend college. **Credit/placement by examination:** AP, CLEP, institutional tests. **Support services:** Learning center, pre-admission summer program, reduced course load, remedial instruction, tutoring.

Majors. Business: Business admin. **Computer sciences:** Computer science. **Engineering:** Computer, electrical, software. **Engineering technology:** Aerospace, electrical, telecommunications.

Most popular majors. Business/marketing 12%, computer/information sciences 29%, engineering/engineering technologies 59%.

Computing on campus. 60 workstations in library, computer center. Dormitories wired for high-speed internet access and linked to campus network. Helpline, wireless network available.

Student life. Freshman orientation: Mandatory. **Policies:** Freshmen permitted cars on campus. **Housing:** Coed dorms available. $200 fully refundable deposit, deadline 5/1. **Activities:** Literary magazine, radio station, student government, student newspaper, computer club, chess club, robotics club, music club, drama club, Society of Black Engineers, Society of Women Engineers.

Athletics. Intramural: Basketball M, boxing M, fencing M, golf M, soccer M, softball M, table tennis, tennis, track and field, volleyball, water polo.

Student services. Adult student services, career counseling, student employment services, personal counseling, placement for graduates, veterans' counselor.

Contact. E-mail: admissions@capitol-college.edu
Phone: (301) 369-2800 Toll-free number: (800) 950-1992
Fax: (301) 953-1442
Darnell Edwards, Director of Admissions, Capitol College, 11301 Springfield Road, Laurel, MD 20708

College of Notre Dame of Maryland

Baltimore, Maryland **CB member**
www.ndm.edu **CB code: 5114**

- Private 4-year liberal arts college for women affiliated with Roman Catholic Church
- Residential campus in very large city
- 1,444 degree-seeking undergraduates
- 1,632 graduate students
- 81% of applicants admitted
- SAT or ACT (ACT writing recommended), application essay required
- 61% graduate within 6 years

General. Founded in 1873. Regionally accredited. Men admitted only to undergraduate and graduate weekend college programs. **Degrees:** 254 bachelor's awarded; master's offered. **ROTC:** Army. **Location:** 37 miles from Washington, D.C.; 5 miles from Baltimore. **Calendar:** Semester, limited summer session. **Full-time faculty:** 82 total; 76% have terminal degrees, 70% women. **Class size:** 78% < 20, 22% 20-39. **Special facilities:** Planetarium, photography laboratories, premier science laboratories, new tv and radio studios.

Freshman class profile. 477 applied, 388 admitted, 147 enrolled.

Mid 50% test scores			
SAT verbal:	460-580	Rank in top quarter:	40%
SAT math:	450-560	Rank in top tenth:	23%
GPA 3.50 or higher:	37%	Return as sophomores:	81%
GPA 3.0-3.49:	36%	Out-of-state:	14%
GPA 2.0-2.99:	27%	Live on campus:	66%

Basis for selection. Careful evaluation of academic record, high school curriculum, test scores, recommendations, personal abilities/talents and goals, intellectual potential and eagerness to learn and be challenged. Students should take SAT by January of senior year. Interview and campus visit highly recommended; visits required for scholarship consideration. Audition recommended for music majors. Portfolio recommended for art, writing majors. **Homeschooled:** Home-school transcript or GED required. **Learning Disabled:** Students with learning disabilities should self-report during admissions process.

High school preparation. 18 units required. Required units include English 4, mathematics 3, social studies 2, science 2 (laboratory 2), foreign language 3 and academic electives 4.

2006-2007 Annual costs. Tuition/fees (projected): $23,000. Room/board: $8,300. Books/supplies: $800. Personal expenses: $800.

2004-2005 Financial aid. **Need-based:** 56% of total undergraduate aid awarded as scholarships/grants, 44% as loans/jobs. **Non-need-based:** Scholarships awarded for academics, alumni affiliation, art, leadership, music/drama, ROTC. **Additional information:** Maximum consideration for financial aid if application received by February 15. Auditions and portfolios in areas of art, music and writing considered for scholarships.

Application procedures. **Admission:** Priority date 2/15; no deadline. $40 fee, may be waived for applicants with need. Application may be submitted online. Admission notification on a rolling basis beginning on or about 10/1. Must reply by May 1 or within 2 week(s) if notified thereafter. **Financial aid:** Priority date 2/15; no closing date. FAFSA required. Applicants notified on a rolling basis starting 3/15; must reply by 5/1 or within 2 week(s) of notification.

Academics. **Special study options:** Accelerated study, combined bachelor's/graduate degree, cross-registration, double major, dual enrollment of high school students, ESL, honors, independent study, internships, liberal arts/career combination, student-designed major, study abroad, teacher certification program, weekend college. 3-2 programs in engineering and nursing with Johns Hopkins University; academic consortium with seven local colleges and universities. **Credit/placement by examination:** AP, CLEP, IB, institutional tests. 30 credit hours maximum toward bachelor's degree. AP, CLEP and IB credits are posted upon admissions to college. Students should send testing information with their admissions application or prior to start of their first semester. **Support services:** Reduced course load, study skills assistance, writing center.

Majors. **Biology:** General. **Business:** General, finance, international, nonprofit/public. **Communications:** General. **Computer sciences:** General, computer science. **Education:** Early childhood, elementary, secondary, special. **Engineering:** General. **English:** English lit. **Foreign languages:** General, classics, French, Spanish. **Health:** Medical radiologic technology/radiation therapy. **History:** General. **Interdisciplinary:** Biopsychology. **Legal studies:** Prelaw. **Liberal arts:** Arts/sciences. **Math:** General. **Philosophy/religion:** Philosophy, religion. **Physical sciences:** Chemistry, physics. **Psychology:** General. **Public administration:** Community org/advocacy. **Social sciences:** Criminology, economics, international relations, political science. **Visual/performing arts:** Art, art history/conservation, photography, studio arts.

Most popular majors. Biology 7%, business/marketing 21%, communications/journalism 8%, education 14%, health sciences 7%, interdisciplinary studies 6%, liberal arts 11%.

Computing on campus. 80 workstations in dormitories, library, computer center, student center. Dormitories wired for high-speed internet access and linked to campus network. Commuter students can connect to campus network. Online library, helpline, repair service, wireless network available.

Student life. **Freshman orientation:** Mandatory. Preregistration for classes offered. 2-day program in June; 4-day program prior to start of school in late August/early September. **Policies:** Must abide by honor code. Freshmen permitted cars on campus. **Housing:** Guaranteed on-campus for all undergraduates. Substance-free housing available. $200 deposit, deadline 5/1. **Activities:** Choral groups, dance, drama, film society, literary magazine, music ensembles, musical theater, radio station, student government, student newspaper, TV station, campus ministries, community service organization, Hispanic society, Black student organization, international student organization, inter-organizational council.

Athletics. NCAA. **Intercollegiate:** Basketball W, field hockey W, lacrosse W, soccer W, swimming W, tennis W, volleyball W. **Intramural:** Basketball W, cross-country W, field hockey W, lacrosse W, soccer W, softball W. **Team name:** Gators.

Student services. Adult student services, alcohol/substance abuse counseling, campus ministries, career counseling, student employment services, financial aid counseling, health services, personal counseling, placement for graduates, veterans' counselor.

Contact. E-mail: admiss@ndm.edu
Phone: (410) 532-5330 Toll-free number: (800) 435-0200
Fax: (410) 532-6287
Christine Beverly, Director of Admissions, College of Notre Dame of Maryland, 4701 North Charles Street, Baltimore, MD 21210

Columbia Union College

Takoma Park, Maryland
www.cuc.edu **CB code: 5890**

- Private 4-year liberal arts college affiliated with Seventh-day Adventists
- Residential campus in large town
- 992 degree-seeking undergraduates: 27% part-time, 64% women, 56% African American, 6% Asian American, 8% Hispanic American, 4% international
- 29 graduate students
- 35% of applicants admitted
- SAT or ACT with writing required

General. Founded in 1904. Regionally accredited. **Degrees:** 230 bachelor's, 10 associate awarded; master's offered. **Location:** 1 mile from Washington, DC. **Calendar:** Semester, limited summer session. **Full-time faculty:** 53 total; 47% have terminal degrees, 34% minority, 43% women. **Part-time faculty:** 3 total; 100% have terminal degrees, 67% minority, 33% women. **Class size:** 81% < 20, 17% 20-39, 2% 40-49, less than 1% 50-99. **Special facilities:** College-operated radio station.

Freshman class profile. 1,351 applied, 469 admitted, 172 enrolled.

Mid 50% test scores			
SAT verbal:	370-490	GPA 2.0-2.99:	53%
SAT math:	370-480	End year in good standing:	81%
ACT:	17-21	Return as sophomores:	59%
GPA 3.50 or higher:	15%	Out-of-state:	62%
GPA 3.0-3.49:	32%	Live on campus:	84%

Basis for selection. High school GPA of 2.5, school achievement record, test scores important; recommendations considered. Audition required of music majors. **Homeschooled:** Transcript of courses and grades required. Recognized high school diploma or GED required. **Learning Disabled:** Students must provide written documentation of disabilities and submit written request for all needed services for review by the Disabilities Coordinator three months before registration. All forms may be obtained from Center for Learning Resources.

High school preparation. 16 units required. Required units include English 4, mathematics 2, history 2, science 2 (laboratory 2) and academic electives 4. One unit of computer science also recommended.

2005-2006 Annual costs. Tuition/fees: $17,586. Room/board: $5,950. Books/supplies: $945.

2004-2005 Financial aid. Need-based: 203 full-time freshmen applied for aid; 203 were judged to have need; 203 of these received aid. Average scholarship/grant was $6,000; average loan $3,665. 48% of total undergraduate aid awarded as scholarships/grants, 52% as loans/jobs. **Non-need-based:** Scholarships awarded for academics, athletics, leadership, music/drama, state residency.

Application procedures. Admission: No deadline. $25 fee, may be waived for applicants with need. Application may be submitted online. Admission notification on a rolling basis. **Financial aid:** Closing date 3/31. FAFSA required. Applicants notified on a rolling basis starting 5/31; must reply within 4 week(s) of notification.

Academics. Special study options: Accelerated study, combined bachelor's/graduate degree, cooperative education, cross-registration, distance learning, double major, ESL, external degree, honors, independent study, internships, liberal arts/career combination, student-designed major, study abroad, teacher certification program, Washington semester. Adult evening program. **Credit/placement by examination:** AP, CLEP, SAT, ACT, institutional tests. 12 credit hours maximum toward associate degree, 24 toward bachelor's. CLEP business exams not accepted for traditional business majors. **Support services:** Learning center, reduced course load, remedial instruction, study skills assistance, tutoring, writing center.

Majors. Biology: General, biochemistry. **Business:** Accounting, business admin, marketing, organizational behavior. **Communications:** General, broadcast journalism, journalism. **Computer sciences:** General, computer science, information systems. **Education:** General, elementary, English, mathematics, music, physical, science, secondary. **Health:** Health care admin, nursing (RN), predentistry, premedicine, prepharmacy, preveterinary. **History:** General. **Liberal arts:** Arts/sciences. **Math:** General. **Parks/recreation:** Health/fitness. **Philosophy/religion:** Religion. **Physical sciences:** Chemistry. **Psychology:** General. **Social sciences:** Political science. **Theology:** Religious ed, theology. **Visual/performing arts:** Music performance.

Most popular majors. Business/marketing 22%, computer/information sciences 9%, health sciences 20%, liberal arts 7%, psychology 25%.

Computing on campus. 60 workstations in dormitories, library, computer center. Dormitories wired for high-speed internet access and linked to campus network. Commuter students can connect to campus network. Online library, wireless network available.

Student life. Freshman orientation: Mandatory. Preregistration for classes offered. **Policies:** Attendance required at weekly chapel service. Resident students required to attend dormitory worships. Religious observance required. Freshmen permitted cars on campus. **Housing:** Guaranteed on-campus for all undergraduates. Single-sex dorms, apartments, substance-free housing available. $200 partly refundable deposit. **Activities:** Concert band, choral groups, literary magazine, music ensembles, musical theater, opera, radio station, student government, student newspaper, symphony orchestra, Metro Ministries, Humanitas, Loaves and Fishes, community ministry, Shepherd's Hands (puppet ministry), Teach-a-Kid, Youth-to-Youth (drug prevention), student mission club.

Athletics. NCAA. **Intercollegiate:** Baseball M, basketball, cross-country, soccer, softball W, track and field. **Team name:** Pioneers.

Student services. Adult student services, campus ministries, career counseling, student employment services, financial aid counseling, health services, personal counseling, placement for graduates, veterans' counselor.

Contact. E-mail: enroll@cuc.edu
Phone: (301) 891-4080 Toll-free number: (800) 835-4212
Fax: (301) 891-4230
Emile John, Director of Admissions, Columbia Union College, 7600 Flower Avenue, Takoma Park, MD 20912

Coppin State University

Baltimore, Maryland — **CB member**
www.coppin.edu — **CB code: 5122**

- Public 4-year liberal arts college
- Commuter campus in very large city
- 3,380 degree-seeking undergraduates
- 855 graduate students
- SAT or ACT (ACT writing optional) required

General. Founded in 1900. Regionally accredited. Manages Rosemont Elementary School; educational corridor between Coppin and selected elementary, middle, and high schools; mentorship program with elementary students. **Degrees:** 315 bachelor's awarded; master's offered. **ROTC:** Army. **Location:** 50 miles from Washington, DC. **Calendar:** Semester, extensive summer session. **Full-time faculty:** 140 total. **Part-time faculty:** 110 total.

Freshman class profile.

Mid 50% test scores			
SAT verbal:	380-460	Out-of-state:	17%
SAT math:	370-450	Live on campus:	43%

Basis for selection. Minimum GPA of 2.5 and predictive index based on test scores and school achievement record. Essay recommended. Interview recommended for nursing majors. Portfolio recommended for art majors. **Homeschooled:** Location must be certified by Maryland Department of Education.

High school preparation. 16 units required. Required units include English 4, mathematics 3, social studies 3, science 2 (laboratory 2) and foreign language 2. 2 years of advanced tech program courses can be substituted for foreign language requirement.

2005-2006 Annual costs. Tuition/fees: $4,714; $11,235 out-of-state. Room/board: $6,239. Books/supplies: $700. Personal expenses: $3,085.

Financial aid. Non-need-based: Scholarships awarded for academics, alumni affiliation, athletics, ROTC, state residency. **Additional information:** Funds allocated by State of Maryland for minority students enrolled for at least 6 credits who are Maryland residents and U.S. citizens (Other Race Grant).

Application procedures. Admission: Priority date 3/15; deadline 7/15. $35 fee, may be waived for applicants with need. Application may be submitted online. Admission notification on a rolling basis beginning on or about 3/15. **Financial aid:** Priority date 3/1; no closing date. FAFSA required. Applicants notified on a rolling basis starting 4/15; must reply within 2 week(s) of notification.

Academics. Special study options: Accelerated study, combined bachelor's/graduate degree, cooperative education, distance learning, double major, dual enrollment of high school students, external degree, honors, independent study, internships, liberal arts/career combination, study abroad, teacher certification program, weekend college. 3-2 programs in engineering, pharmacy, dentistry, physical therapy. **Credit/placement by examination:** AP, CLEP, IB, institutional tests. 30 credit hours maximum toward bachelor's degree. **Support services:** Learning center, pre-admission summer program, remedial instruction, study skills assistance, tutoring, writing center.

Majors. Biology: General. **Business:** Human resources, management science. **Communications:** Media studies. **Computer sciences:** Computer science. **Education:** Biology, chemistry, early childhood, elementary, mathematics, secondary, special. **English:** English lit. **Health:** Nursing (RN), predentistry, prepharmacy. **History:** General. **Liberal arts:** Arts/sciences. **Math:** General. **Parks/recreation:** Sports admin. **Physical sciences:** Chemistry. **Protective services:** Law enforcement admin. **Psychology:** General. **Public administration:** Social work. **Social sciences:** General, political science, sociology. **Visual/performing arts:** Art.

Most popular majors. Business/marketing 16%, computer/information sciences 7%, health sciences 14%, legal studies 13%, liberal arts 11%, psychology 13%, social sciences 14%.

Computing on campus. 371 workstations in dormitories, library, computer center, student center. Dormitories wired for high-speed internet access and linked to campus network. Commuter students can connect to campus network. Online course registration, online library, helpline, repair service, student web hosting, wireless network available.

Student life. Freshman orientation: Mandatory. Preregistration for classes offered. **Housing:** Coed dorms, special housing for disabled, substance-free housing available. $150 deposit. **Activities:** Choral groups, dance, drama, film society, music ensembles, radio station, student government, student newspaper, TV station, Apostolic Collegiate Ministry, student chapel association, international students association, criminal justice club, gospel choir, history club, psychology club, The Union, Thurgood Marshall club, social work association.

Athletics. NCAA. **Intercollegiate:** Baseball M, basketball, bowling W, cheerleading M, cross-country, golf W, softball W, tennis, track and field, volleyball W. **Intramural:** Basketball, football (non-tackle), softball, tennis, volleyball. **Team name:** Eagles.

Student services. Adult student services, alcohol/substance abuse counseling, career counseling, services for economically disadvantaged, student employment services, financial aid counseling, health services, minority student services, personal counseling, placement for graduates, veterans' counselor, women's services. **Physically disabled:** Services for visually, hearing impaired.

Contact. E-mail: admissions@coppin.edu
Phone: (410) 951-3000 Toll-free number: (800) 635-3674
Fax: (410) 523-7351
Michelle Gross, Director of Admissions, Coppin State University, 2500 West North Avenue, Baltimore, MD 21216

DeVry University: Bethesda
Bethesda, Maryland

- For-profit 4-year university
- Commuter campus
- 32 degree-seeking undergraduates: 72% part-time, 53% women, 56% African American, 6% Asian American, 16% Hispanic American, 3% international
- 64 graduate students

General. Degrees: 1 bachelor's awarded; master's offered. **Calendar:** Semester. **Full-time faculty:** 2 total. **Part-time faculty:** 13 total; 8% minority, 46% women.

Basis for selection. Interview important.

2005-2006 Annual costs. Tuition/fees: $13,170. Books/supplies: $1,250. Personal expenses: $1,680.

Application procedures. Admission: No deadline. $50 fee. Admission notification on a rolling basis.

Academics. Special study options: Accelerated study, cooperative education, distance learning. **Credit/placement by examination:** CLEP.

Majors. Business: Business admin. **Computer sciences:** General.

Contact. Phone: (301) 652-8477 Fax: (301) 652-8577
DeVry University: Bethesda, 4550 Montgomery Avenue, Suite 100 N, Bethesda, MD 20814

Frostburg State University
Frostburg, Maryland — **CB member**
www.frostburg.edu — **CB code: 5402**

- Public 4-year university, business, liberal arts and teachers college
- Residential campus in small town
- 4,246 degree-seeking undergraduates: 5% part-time, 49% women, 15% African American, 2% Asian American, 2% Hispanic American, 1% international
- 668 degree-seeking graduate students
- 76% of applicants admitted
- SAT or ACT (ACT writing optional) required
- 47% graduate within 6 years

General. Founded in 1898. Regionally accredited. Center in Hagerstown offers upper-division undergraduate and graduate courses. **Degrees:** 834 bachelor's awarded; master's offered. **Location:** 150 miles from Baltimore, 150 miles from Washington, DC. **Calendar:** Semester, limited summer session. **Full-time faculty:** 233 total; 87% have terminal degrees, 13% minority, 38% women. **Part-time faculty:** 118 total; 20% have terminal degrees, 4% minority, 52% women. **Class size:** 52% < 20, 42% 20-39, 3% 40-49, 3% 50-99. **Special facilities:** Planetarium, arboretum, electron microscope.

Freshman class profile. 3,434 applied, 2,596 admitted, 942 enrolled.

Mid 50% test scores		**Rank in top quarter:**	32%
SAT verbal:	450-550	**Rank in top tenth:**	10%
SAT math:	450-550	**Return as sophomores:**	71%
ACT:	18-21	**Out-of-state:**	11%
GPA 3.50 or higher:	21%	**Live on campus:**	74%
GPA 3.0-3.49:	31%	**International:**	1%
GPA 2.0-2.99:	48%		

Basis for selection. High school record and SAT scores most important. Interview recommended. Audition required of music majors. Portfolio required of art majors.

High school preparation. 15 units required. Required units include English 4, mathematics 3, social studies 3, science 3 (laboratory 2) and foreign language 2.

2005-2006 Annual costs. Tuition/fees: $6,230; $14,480 out-of-state. Room/board: $6,442. Books/supplies: $750. Personal expenses: $900.

2005-2006 Financial aid. Need-based: 742 full-time freshmen applied for aid; 506 were judged to have need; 506 of these received aid. Average need met was 66%. Average scholarship/grant was $4,439; average loan $2,237. 56% of total undergraduate aid awarded as scholarships/grants, 44% as loans/jobs. **Non-need-based:** Awarded to 986 full-time undergraduates, including 331 freshmen. Scholarships awarded for academics, leadership, minority status.

Application procedures. Admission: Priority date 6/1; no deadline. $30 fee, may be waived for applicants with need. Application may be submitted online. Admission notification on a rolling basis beginning on or about 11/1. Must reply by May 1 or within 4 week(s) if notified thereafter. **Financial aid:** Priority date 3/1; no closing date. FAFSA required. Applicants notified on a rolling basis starting 3/15; must reply within 3 week(s) of notification.

Academics. Special study options: Accelerated study, combined bachelor's/graduate degree, cross-registration, distance learning, double major, dual enrollment of high school students, honors, independent study, internships, liberal arts/career combination, study abroad, teacher certification program, weekend college. International student exchange program, dual degree program, combined bachelor's program. **Credit/placement by examination:** AP, CLEP, IB, institutional tests. 30 credit hours maximum toward bachelor's degree. **Support services:** Learning center, reduced course load, remedial instruction, tutoring, writing center.

Majors. Architecture: Urban/community planning. **Biology:** General. **Business:** Accounting, business admin. **Communications:** General. **Computer sciences:** General. **Conservation:** General, environmental studies, fisheries, wildlife. **Education:** Early childhood, elementary, English, mathematics, music, physical, social science. **English:** Speech/rhetoric. **Foreign languages:** General. **Health:** Predentistry, premedicine, prenursing, prepharmacy, preveterinary. **History:** General. **Liberal arts:** Arts/sciences. **Math:** General. **Parks/recreation:** General, exercise sciences, health/fitness, sports admin. **Philosophy/religion:** Philosophy. **Physical sciences:** Chemistry, physics. **Protective services:** Law enforcement admin, police science. **Psychology:** General. **Public administration:** Social work. **Social sciences:** General, economics, geography, international relations, political science, sociology. **Visual/performing arts:** General, commercial/advertising art, dance, dramatic, studio arts.

Most popular majors. Business/marketing 15%, education 14%, liberal arts 6%, parks/recreation 6%, psychology 7%, security/protective services 6%, social sciences 13%, visual/performing arts 8%.

Computing on campus. 668 workstations in dormitories, library, computer center, student center. Dormitories wired for high-speed internet access and linked to campus network. Commuter students can connect to campus network. Online course registration, helpline available.

Student life. Freshman orientation: Mandatory. **Policies:** Freshmen permitted cars on campus. **Housing:** Coed dorms, single-sex dorms, special housing for disabled, substance-free housing available. $100 deposit. Special interest housing. **Activities:** Bands, choral groups, dance, drama, literary magazine, music ensembles, musical theater, radio station, student government, student newspaper, symphony orchestra, TV station, social, religious, political, and ethnic organizations.

Athletics. NCAA. **Intercollegiate:** Baseball M, basketball, cross-country, diving, field hockey W, football (tackle) M, golf, lacrosse W, soccer, softball W, swimming, tennis, track and field, volleyball W. **Intramural:** Basketball, field hockey, football (tackle), golf, lacrosse, racquetball, rugby M, soccer, softball, table tennis, tennis, volleyball, weight lifting, wrestling M. **Team name:** Bobcats.

Student services. Campus ministries, career counseling, student employment services, health services, minority student services, on-campus daycare, personal counseling, placement for graduates, veterans' counselor. **Physically disabled:** Services for visually, speech, hearing impaired.

Contact. E-mail: fsuadmissions@frostburg.edu
Phone: (301) 687-4201 Fax: (301) 687-7074
Trish Gregory, Director of Admissions, Frostburg State University, 101 Braddock Road, Frostburg, MD 21532-1099

Goucher College
Baltimore, Maryland — **CB member**
www.goucher.edu — **CB code: 5257**

- Private 4-year liberal arts college
- Residential campus in small city

- 1,325 degree-seeking undergraduates: 2% part-time, 66% women, 4% African American, 3% Asian American, 3% Hispanic American, 1% international
- 831 degree-seeking graduate students
- 67% of applicants admitted
- SAT or ACT with writing, application essay required
- 64% graduate within 6 years; 26% enter graduate study

General. Founded in 1885. Regionally accredited. **Degrees:** 274 bachelor's awarded; master's offered. **ROTC:** Army. **Location:** 8 miles from downtown. **Calendar:** Semester. **Full-time faculty:** 112 total; 91% have terminal degrees, 14% minority, 63% women. **Part-time faculty:** 78 total; 45% have terminal degrees, 9% minority, 65% women. **Class size:** 76% < 20, 22% 20-39, 1% 40-49, less than 1% 50-99. **Special facilities:** Politics center, dance studio, pilates studio, computerized scientific visualization lab, nuclear magnetic resonance spectrometer, black box theater.

Freshman class profile. 2,976 applied, 1,991 admitted, 340 enrolled.

Mid 50% test scores			
SAT verbal:	560-670	Rank in top quarter:	63%
SAT math:	540-640	Rank in top tenth:	26%
ACT:	23-27	End year in good standing:	83%
GPA 3.50 or higher:	24%	Return as sophomores:	83%
GPA 3.0-3.49:	36%	Out-of-state:	76%
GPA 2.0-2.99:	40%	Live on campus:	97%
		International:	1%

Basis for selection. Record in traditional college-preparatory program, secondary school record, and recommendations most important. Interview recommended. **Homeschooled:** Statement describing homeschool structure and mission, transcript of courses and grades, state high school equivalency certificate, letter of recommendation (nonparent) required.

High school preparation. 16 units required; 20 recommended. Required and recommended units include English 4, mathematics 3-4, social studies 3, science 2-3, foreign language 2-4 and academic electives 2.

2005-2006 Annual costs. Tuition/fees: $27,525. Room/board: $8,700. Books/supplies: $800. Personal expenses: $800.

2004-2005 Financial aid. Need-based: 293 full-time freshmen applied for aid; 229 were judged to have need; 229 of these received aid. Average need met was 81%. Average scholarship/grant was $13,722; average loan $3,607. 74% of total undergraduate aid awarded as scholarships/grants, 26% as loans/jobs. **Non-need-based:** Awarded to 500 full-time undergraduates, including 174 freshmen. Scholarships awarded for academics, art, leadership, music/drama.

Application procedures. Admission: Closing date 2/1 (postmark date). $40 fee, may be waived for applicants with need. Application may be submitted online. Admission notification 4/1. Must reply by 5/1. **Financial aid:** Closing date 2/15. FAFSA, CSS PROFILE required. Applicants notified by 4/1; must reply by 5/1 or within 2 week(s) of notification.

Academics. Students required to complete an off-campus experience through an internship, study abroad, or an independent project. **Special study options:** Combined bachelor's/graduate degree, cross-registration, distance learning, double major, dual enrollment of high school students, independent study, internships, student-designed major, study abroad, teacher certification program, Washington semester. Teachers Institute, post-baccalaureate premedical program, master's level distance learning, 3-2 engineering program with Johns Hopkins University, 4-1 BA/MA with Monterey Institute of International Studies. Study abroad programs at the Sorbonne in Paris, University of Salamanca in Spain, Hebrew University in Israel, Russian Summer Institute at Odessa State University in Moscow, Oxford University in England, Glasgow School of Art in Scotland, Honduras Institute of Marine Studies in Roatan, University of East Anglia in England, Middlesex University in London, Syracuse University in Florence, Denmark International Study Program Copenhagen. **Credit/placement by examination:** AP, CLEP, IB, institutional tests. 30 credit hours maximum toward bachelor's degree. **Support services:** Learning center, reduced course load, study skills assistance, tutoring, writing center.

Majors. Area/ethnic studies: American, women's. **Biology:** General. **Business:** Business admin. **Communications:** Media studies. **Computer sciences:** Computer science. **Education:** Elementary, special. **English:** English lit. **Foreign languages:** French, Russian, Spanish. **History:** General. **Interdisciplinary:** Historic preservation, intercultural, peace/conflict. **Math:** General. **Philosophy/religion:** Philosophy, religion. **Physical sciences:** Chemistry, physics. **Psychology:** General. **Social sciences:** Anthropology, economics, international relations, political science, sociology. **Visual/performing arts:** Art, dance, dramatic.

Most popular majors. Business/marketing 8%, communications/journalism 9%, English 11%, psychology 15%, social sciences 8%, visual/performing arts 14%.

Computing on campus. 140 workstations in dormitories, library, computer center. Dormitories wired for high-speed internet access. Commuter students can connect to campus network. Helpline, wireless network available.

Student life. Freshman orientation: Available. Preregistration for classes offered. **Policies:** Freshmen permitted cars on campus. **Housing:** Guaranteed on-campus for freshmen. Coed dorms, single-sex dorms, special housing for disabled, apartments, substance-free housing available. $100 deposit, deadline 5/15. **Activities:** Jazz band, choral groups, dance, drama, film society, literary magazine, music ensembles, opera, radio station, student government, student newspaper, TV station, African alliance, community action program, bisexual gay and lesbian alliance, Hillel, international club, Christian fellowship, Amnesty International, environmental organization, Jubilate Deo.

Athletics. NCAA. **Intercollegiate:** Basketball, cross-country, equestrian, field hockey W, lacrosse, soccer, swimming, tennis, track and field, volleyball W. **Intramural:** Football (tackle), racquetball, soccer, softball, squash, tennis, volleyball, water polo, weight lifting. **Team name:** Gophers.

Student services. Adult student services, campus ministries, career counseling, student employment services, health services, minority student services, personal counseling, placement for graduates. **Physically disabled:** Services for visually, hearing impaired.

Contact. E-mail: admissions@goucher.edu
Phone: (410) 337-6100 Toll-free number: (800) 468-2437
Fax: (410) 337-6354
Carlton Surbeck, Director of Admissions, Goucher College, 1021 Dulaney Valley Road, Baltimore, MD 21204-2753

Griggs University
Silver Spring, Maryland
www.griggs.edu

- Private 4-year Bible college

General. Accredited by DETC.

Annual costs/financial aid. Tuition/fees (2005-2006): $7,520.

Contact. Phone: (301) 680-6570
12501 Old Columbia Pike, Silver Spring, MD 20904-6600

Hood College
Frederick, Maryland — **CB member**
www.hood.edu — **CB code: 5296**

- Private 4-year liberal arts college
- Residential campus in small city
- 1,136 degree-seeking undergraduates: 12% part-time, 75% women, 12% African American, 2% Asian American, 3% Hispanic American, 3% international
- 799 degree-seeking graduate students
- 51% of applicants admitted
- SAT or ACT (ACT writing optional), application essay required
- 66% graduate within 6 years

General. Founded in 1893. Regionally accredited. **Degrees:** 189 bachelor's awarded; master's offered. **Location:** 52 miles from Baltimore, 52 miles from Washington, DC. **Calendar:** Semester, limited summer session. **Full-time faculty:** 81 total; 99% have terminal degrees, 17% minority, 52% women. **Part-time faculty:** 121 total; 40% have terminal degrees, 2% minority, 53% women. **Class size:** 63% < 20, 36% 20-39, less than 1% 40-49, less than 1% 50-99. **Special facilities:** Psychology and preschool laboratories, observatory.

Freshman class profile. 1,852 applied, 938 admitted, 237 enrolled.

Mid 50% test scores			
SAT verbal:	510-600	Rank in top quarter:	64%
SAT math:	500-600	Rank in top tenth:	33%
ACT:	20-25	Return as sophomores:	87%
GPA 3.50 or higher:	38%	Out-of-state:	31%
GPA 3.0-3.49:	40%	Live on campus:	80%
GPA 2.0-2.99:	21%	International:	2%

Basis for selection. High school record, class rank, test scores important. Recommendations; contributions to school, family and community; essay considered. Interview recommeded. **Homeschooled:** Must interview and present bibliography of all reading materials used; two recommendations; partial portfolio of work.

High school preparation. 16 units required. Required units include English 4, mathematics 3, social studies 1, history 2, science 3 (laboratory 2), foreign language 2 and academic electives 1.

2005-2006 Annual costs. Tuition/fees: $22,335. Unlimited meal plan available. Room/board: $7,750. Books/supplies: $800. Personal expenses: $700.

2005-2006 Financial aid. Need-based: 213 full-time freshmen applied for aid; 184 were judged to have need; 182 of these received aid. Average need met was 86%. Average scholarship/grant was $16,092; average loan $3,819. 78% of total undergraduate aid awarded as scholarships/grants, 22% as loans/jobs. **Non-need-based:** Awarded to 407 full-time undergraduates, including 98 freshmen. Scholarships awarded for academics, alumni affiliation, leadership, minority status, music/drama, ROTC.

Application procedures. Admission: Priority date 2/15; no deadline. $35 fee, may be waived for applicants with need. Application may be submitted online. Admission notification on a rolling basis beginning on or about 10/15. Must reply by May 1 or within 2 week(s) if notified thereafter. Applications received after February 1 considered on a space available basis. **Financial aid:** Priority date 2/15; no closing date. FAFSA required. Applicants notified on a rolling basis starting 3/1; must reply by 5/1 or within 3 week(s) of notification.

Academics. Students in all fields may earn academic credits for internships. Opportunities available for students to earn degree in 3 years, 2 degrees in 4 years, or bachelor's and master's in 5 years. **Special study options:** Accelerated study, combined bachelor's/graduate degree, distance learning, double major, dual enrollment of high school students, honors, independent study, internships, liberal arts/career combination, semester at sea, student-designed major, study abroad, teacher certification program, Washington semester. **Credit/placement by examination:** AP, CLEP, IB, SAT, institutional tests. 30 credit hours maximum toward bachelor's degree. **Support services:** Learning center, reduced course load, remedial instruction, study skills assistance, tutoring, writing center.

Majors. Area/ethnic studies: Latin American. **Biology:** General, biochemistry. **Business:** Business admin. **Communications:** General. **Computer sciences:** Computer science, information systems. **Conservation:** Environmental studies. **Education:** Early childhood, special. **English:** English lit. **Foreign languages:** French, German, Spanish. **History:** General. **Math:** General. **Philosophy/religion:** Philosophy, religion. **Physical sciences:** Chemistry. **Psychology:** General. **Public administration:** Social work. **Social sciences:** Economics, political science, sociology. **Visual/performing arts:** Art.

Most popular majors. Biology 9%, business/marketing 8%, communications/journalism 9%, education 12%, English 10%, history 6%, psychology 12%, social sciences 12%.

Computing on campus. 252 workstations in dormitories, library, computer center, student center. Dormitories wired for high-speed internet access and linked to campus network. Commuter students can connect to campus network. Online course registration, online library, helpline, wireless network available.

Student life. Freshman orientation: Available. Preregistration for classes offered. Held 4 days before fall term. **Policies:** Students responsible for governing themselves through honor code. Freshmen permitted cars on campus. **Housing:** Guaranteed on-campus for all undergraduates. Coed dorms, single-sex dorms, special housing for disabled available. $250 fully refundable deposit, deadline 5/1. Language, special interest housing available. **Activities:** Choral groups, dance, drama, film society, literary magazine, music ensembles, musical theater, radio station, student government, student newspaper, black student union, Circle-K, Catholic campus ministry, La Union Latina, Best Buddies, intervarsity christian fellowship, international club, College Democrats, Jewish student union, College Republicans, For Goodness Sakes.

Athletics. NCAA. **Intercollegiate:** Basketball, cross-country, field hockey W, golf, lacrosse, soccer, softball W, swimming, tennis, track and field, volleyball W. **Team name:** Blazers.

Student services. Adult student services, alcohol/substance abuse counseling, campus ministries, career counseling, student employment services, financial aid counseling, health services, minority student services, personal counseling, placement for graduates, women's services. **Physically disabled:** Services for visually, speech, hearing impaired.

Contact. E-mail: admissions@hood.edu
Phone: (301) 696-3400 Toll-free number: (800) 922-1599
Fax: (301) 696-3819
Glen Thomas, Director of Admissions, Hood College, 401 Rosemont Avenue, Frederick, MD 21701-8575

Johns Hopkins University

Baltimore, Maryland — **CB member**
www.jhu.edu — **CB code: 5332**

- Private 4-year university
- Residential campus in very large city
- 4,306 degree-seeking undergraduates: 46% women, 5% African American, 22% Asian American, 6% Hispanic American, 1% Native American, 5% international
- 1,583 degree-seeking graduate students
- 35% of applicants admitted
- SAT or ACT with writing, application essay required
- 90% graduate within 6 years; 41% enter graduate study

General. Founded in 1876. Regionally accredited. Centers in Bologna and Florence, Italy and Nanjing, China. **Degrees:** 1,412 bachelor's awarded; master's, doctoral, first professional offered. **ROTC:** Army, Air Force. **Location:** 4 miles from downtown. **Calendar:** 4-1-4, limited summer session. **Full-time faculty:** 484 total; 12% minority, 23% women. **Part-time faculty:** 4 total. **Class size:** 51% < 20, 25% 20-39, 5% 40-49, 12% 50-99, 7% >100. **Special facilities:** Space telescope science institute.

Freshman class profile. 11,274 applied, 3,907 admitted, 1,133 enrolled.

Mid 50% test scores		**Rank in top tenth:**	78%
SAT verbal:	630-740	**Return as sophomores:**	96%
SAT math:	660-760	**Out-of-state:**	85%
ACT:	28-32	**Live on campus:**	99%
GPA 3.50 or higher:	71%	**International:**	6%
GPA 3.0-3.49:	27%	**Fraternities:**	21%
GPA 2.0-2.99:	2%	**Sororities:**	16%
Rank in top quarter:	96%		

Basis for selection. School achievement record most important, with emphasis on course grades related to applicant's major field of academic interest. Test scores very important. Intellectual interests and accomplishments, recommendations, personal character, extracurricular activities also significant. Students wishing to enroll in the biomedical engineering major (BME) must indicate BME as their first-choice major. SAT Subject Tests recommended. Recommend 3 SAT Subject Tests. Interview recommended. Audition required of applicants to dual degree program with Peabody Institute.

High school preparation. Recommended units include English 4, mathematics 4, social studies 4, science 4 and foreign language 4. 4 combined units recommended for social studies and history.

2006-2007 Annual costs. Tuition/fees: $34,400. Room/board: $10,622. Books/supplies: $850. Personal expenses: $800.

2005-2006 Financial aid. Need-based: 746 full-time freshmen applied for aid; 572 were judged to have need; 558 of these received aid. Average need met was 99%. Average scholarship/grant was $23,713; average loan $2,715. 76% of total undergraduate aid awarded as scholarships/grants, 24% as loans/jobs. **Non-need-based:** Awarded to 564 full-time undergraduates, including 66 freshmen. Scholarships awarded for academics, athletics, leadership, ROTC, state residency. **Additional information:** Selected students receive aid packages without loan expectation, grants to full need. Private merit aid does not reduce Hopkins grant.

Application procedures. Admission: Closing date 1/1 (postmark date). $60 fee, may be waived for applicants with need. Application may be submitted online. Admission notification 4/1. Must reply by May 1 or within 2 week(s) if notified thereafter. **Financial aid:** Priority date 2/1, closing date 2/15. FAFSA, CSS PROFILE required. Applicants notified by 4/1; must reply by 5/1 or within 2 week(s) of notification.

Academics. Special study options: Combined bachelor's/graduate degree, cross-registration, double major, dual enrollment of high school students, independent study, internships, student-designed major, study abroad, Washington semester. Combined bachelor's/master's programs. **Credit/placement by examination:** AP, CLEP, IB, institutional tests. **Support services:** Pre-admission summer program, reduced course load, study skills assistance, tutoring, writing center.

Majors. Area/ethnic studies: African-American, East Asian, Latin American, Near/Middle Eastern. **Biology:** General, biophysics, cell/histology, molecular. **Computer sciences:** General. **Engineering:** General, biomedical, chemical, civil, computer, electrical, environmental, materials, materials science, mechanical, mechanics. **English:** Creative writing, English lit. **Foreign languages:** Classics, French, German, Italian, Spanish. **History:** General, science/technology. **Interdisciplinary:** Behavioral sciences, cognitive science, neuroscience. **Liberal arts:** Arts/sciences. **Math:** General. **Philosophy/religion:** Philosophy. **Physical sciences:** Astronomy, chemistry, geology, physics. **Psychology:** General. **Public administration:** Policy analysis. **Social sciences:** General, anthropology, economics, geography, international relations, political science, sociology. **Visual/performing arts:** Art history/conservation, film/cinema.

Most popular majors. Biology 8%, engineering/engineering technologies 19%, health sciences 21%, interdisciplinary studies 6%, social sciences 16%.

Computing on campus. 140 workstations in dormitories, library, computer center. Dormitories wired for high-speed internet access and linked to campus network. Commuter students can connect to campus network. Online course registration, online library, helpline, student web hosting, wireless network available.

Student life. Freshman orientation: Mandatory. Preregistration for classes offered. 5-day extensive program held 1 week prior to start of fall semester. **Policies:** Freshmen and sophomores required to live on campus unless they live with a parent or legal guardian within commuting distance. **Housing:** Guaranteed on-campus for freshmen. Coed dorms, single-sex dorms, special housing for disabled, apartments, fraternity/sorority housing, substance-free housing available. $200 nonrefundable deposit. Substance-free and vacation housing floors available. Specific spaces accessible or modified for disabled students. **Activities:** Bands, choral groups, dance, drama, film society, literary magazine, music ensembles, musical theater, radio station, student government, student newspaper, symphony orchestra, Jewish Student Association, Catholic Community, Christian Fellowship, Black Student Union, Organizacion Latina Estudiantil, Chinese Student Association, emergency response organization, senior citizens community outreach program, College Democrats, College Republicans.

Athletics. NCAA. **Intercollegiate:** Baseball M, basketball, cross-country, diving, fencing, field hockey W, football (tackle) M, lacrosse, rowing (crew), soccer, swimming, tennis, track and field, volleyball W, water polo M, wrestling M. **Intramural:** Basketball, football (non-tackle), soccer, volleyball. **Team name:** Blue Jays.

Student services. Alcohol/substance abuse counseling, campus ministries, career counseling, student employment services, financial aid counseling, health services, minority student services, personal counseling, placement for graduates. **Physically disabled:** Services for visually, speech, hearing impaired.

Contact. E-mail: gotojhu@jhu.edu
Phone: (410) 516-8171 Fax: (410) 516-6025
John Latting, Director of Undergraduate Admissions, Johns Hopkins University, 3400 North Charles Street, 140 Garland Hall, Baltimore, MD 21218

Johns Hopkins University: Peabody Conservatory of Music

Baltimore, Maryland
www.peabody.jhu.edu — **CB code: 5532**

- Private 4-year music college
- Residential campus in very large city
- 330 degree-seeking undergraduates: 3% part-time, 44% women
- 315 degree-seeking graduate students
- SAT or ACT required

General. Founded in 1857. Regionally accredited. **Degrees:** 70 bachelor's awarded; master's, doctoral offered. **Location:** 36 miles from Washington, DC. **Calendar:** Semester. **Full-time faculty:** 67 total. **Part-time faculty:** 81 total. **Special facilities:** Concert halls.

Freshman class profile. 76 enrolled.

Basis for selection. Audition most important; secondary school record, test scores also important. Interview recommended. Audition required.

2005-2006 Annual costs. Tuition/fees: $29,215. Room/board: $9,225. Books/supplies: $625. Personal expenses: $1,000.

Financial aid. Non-need-based: Scholarships awarded for academics, music/drama.

Application procedures. Admission: Priority date 11/15; deadline 4/1 (postmark date). $55 fee, may be waived for applicants with need. Application may be submitted online. Admission notification 4/1. Must reply by 5/1. Must apply by December 15 for guarantee of scholarship consideration. **Financial aid:** Closing date 2/1. FAFSA, institutional form required. Applicants notified by 4/7; must reply by 5/1 or within 2 week(s) of notification.

Academics. Special study options: Cross-registration, double major, internships, teacher certification program. **Credit/placement by examination:** AP, CLEP, IB, institutional tests. **Support services:** Remedial instruction, tutoring.

Majors. Communications technology: Recording arts. **Education:** Music. **Visual/performing arts:** Music performance, music theory/composition, piano/organ, voice/opera.

Most popular majors. Visual/performing arts 96%.

Computing on campus. Dormitories linked to campus network. Commuter students can connect to campus network. Helpline, repair service available.

Student life. Freshman orientation: Available. **Policies:** Freshmen permitted cars on campus. **Housing:** Guaranteed on-campus for freshmen. Coed dorms, single-sex dorms available. **Activities:** Bands, choral groups, music ensembles, opera, student government, symphony orchestra.

Student services. Alcohol/substance abuse counseling, career counseling, student employment services, financial aid counseling, health services, personal counseling, placement for graduates. **Physically disabled:** Services for visually, speech, hearing impaired.

Contact. Phone: (410) 659-8110 Toll-free number: (800) 368-2521
David Lane, Director of Admissions, Johns Hopkins University: Peabody Conservatory of Music, One East Mount Vernon Place, Baltimore, MD 21202

Loyola College in Maryland

Baltimore, Maryland — **CB member**
www.loyola.edu — **CB code: 5370**

- Private 4-year business and liberal arts college affiliated with Roman Catholic Church
- Residential campus in very large city
- 3,533 degree-seeking undergraduates: 1% part-time, 58% women, 5% African American, 2% Asian American, 3% Hispanic American, 1% international
- 2,534 degree-seeking graduate students
- 47% of applicants admitted
- SAT or ACT (ACT writing optional) required
- 83% graduate within 6 years

General. Founded in 1852. Regionally accredited. **Degrees:** 766 bachelor's awarded; master's, doctoral offered. **ROTC:** Army, Air Force. **Location:** 38 miles from Washington, DC, 103 miles from Philadelphia. **Calendar:** Semester, extensive summer session. **Full-time faculty:** 305 total; 84% have terminal degrees, 8% minority, 44% women. **Part-time faculty:** 232 total; 7% minority, 44% women. **Class size:** 39% < 20, 60% 20-39, less than 1% 40-49, less than 1% 50-99.

Freshman class profile. 10,391 applied, 4,913 admitted, 898 enrolled.

Mid 50% test scores		**Rank in top quarter:**	74%
SAT verbal:	560-650	**Rank in top tenth:**	35%
SAT math:	570-660	**Return as sophomores:**	90%
ACT:	24-28	**Out-of-state:**	83%
GPA 3.50 or higher:	53%	**Live on campus:**	96%
GPA 3.0-3.49:	39%	**International:**	1%
GPA 2.0-2.99:	8%		

Basis for selection. Test scores, school record, academic qualifications most important. Extracurricular activities, recommendations, personal background, class rank also considered. Mid-year senior grades and additional SAT scores required for borderline applicants. Interview and essay recommended.

High school preparation. College-preparatory program recommended. 16 units required; 19 recommended. Required and recommended units include English 4, mathematics 3-4, history 2-3, science 3-4 and foreign language 3-4.

2005-2006 Annual costs. Tuition/fees: $30,500. Room/board: $9,215. Books/supplies: $780. Personal expenses: $990.

2005-2006 Financial aid. Need-based: 635 full-time freshmen applied for aid; 445 were judged to have need; 445 of these received aid. Average need met was 97%. Average scholarship/grant was $13,545; average loan $5,880. 73% of total undergraduate aid awarded as scholarships/grants, 27%

as loans/jobs. **Non-need-based:** Awarded to 1,131 full-time undergraduates, including 317 freshmen. Scholarships awarded for academics, athletics, minority status, ROTC.

Application procedures. Admission: Closing date 1/15 (postmark date). $50 fee, may be waived for applicants with need. Admission notification 4/1. Must reply by 5/1. **Financial aid:** Closing date 2/15. FAFSA, CSS PROFILE required. Applicants notified by 4/1; must reply by 5/1.

Academics. Service learning courses available. **Special study options:** Accelerated study, cross-registration, double major, honors, independent study, internships, teacher certification program, weekend college. **Credit/ placement by examination:** AP, CLEP, IB, institutional tests. 30 credit hours maximum toward bachelor's degree. **Support services:** Learning center, remedial instruction, study skills assistance, tutoring.

Majors. Biology: General. **Business:** General, accounting. **Communications:** General. **Computer sciences:** General. **Education:** Elementary. **Engineering:** General, electrical. **English:** Creative writing, English lit. **Foreign languages:** Classics, French, German, Latin, Spanish. **Health:** Speech pathology. **History:** General. **Math:** Applied. **Philosophy/religion:** Philosophy, religion. **Physical sciences:** Chemistry, physics. **Psychology:** General. **Social sciences:** Economics, political science, sociology. **Visual/ performing arts:** Art.

Most popular majors. Biology 6%, business/marketing 34%, communications/journalism 13%, English 6%, psychology 9%, social sciences 7%.

Computing on campus. 292 workstations in dormitories, library, computer center, student center. Dormitories wired for high-speed internet access and linked to campus network. Commuter students can connect to campus network. Helpline, student web hosting available.

Student life. Freshman orientation: Mandatory, $125 fee. Preregistration for classes offered. Must attend 1 of 4 programs offered in summer; parents invited to attend. **Housing:** Guaranteed on-campus for freshmen. Coed dorms, apartments, substance-free housing available. $500 deposit, deadline 5/1. Honors housing and special interest housing (community service, leadership, wellness) available. **Activities:** Jazz band, choral groups, dance, drama, literary magazine, music ensembles, musical theater, radio station, student government, student newspaper, campus ministries, black student association, College Republicans, Korean students association, Circle K, Amnesty International, young feminist, Jewish students association, College Democrats, evergreens for life.

Athletics. NCAA. **Intercollegiate:** Basketball, cross-country, diving, golf M, lacrosse, rowing (crew), soccer, swimming, tennis, track and field, volleyball W. **Intramural:** Baseball M, basketball, football (non-tackle), lacrosse, racquetball, rifle, soccer M, softball, squash, tennis, volleyball. **Team name:** Greyhounds.

Student services. Alcohol/substance abuse counseling, campus ministries, career counseling, student employment services, financial aid counseling, health services, minority student services, personal counseling, placement for graduates. **Physically disabled:** Services for visually, speech, hearing impaired.

Contact. Phone: (410) 617-5012 Toll-free number: (800) 221-9107
Fax: (410) 617-2176
William Bossemeyer, Dean of Admissions, Loyola College in Maryland, 4501 North Charles Street, Baltimore, MD 21210-2699

Maryland Institute College of Art

Baltimore, Maryland — **CB member**
www.mica.edu — **CB code: 5399**

- Private 4-year visual arts college
- Residential campus in very large city
- 1,497 degree-seeking undergraduates: 1% part-time, 62% women, 4% African American, 8% Asian American, 5% Hispanic American, 5% international
- 220 degree-seeking graduate students
- 45% of applicants admitted
- SAT or ACT (ACT writing optional), application essay required
- 72% graduate within 6 years; 23% enter graduate study

General. Founded in 1826. Regionally accredited. **Degrees:** 284 bachelor's awarded; master's offered. **ROTC:** Army. **Location:** 180 miles from New York City, 50 miles from Washington, DC. **Calendar:** Semester, extensive summer session. **Full-time faculty:** 118 total; 86% have terminal degrees, 49% women. **Part-time faculty:** 149 total; 86% have terminal degrees, 49% women. **Class size:** 71% < 20, 29% 20-39, less than 1% 40-49. **Special facilities:** Nature library, extensive slide library, graphics laboratory, student-run galleries, independent studios.

Freshman class profile. 2,487 applied, 1,118 admitted, 396 enrolled.

Mid 50% test scores			
SAT verbal:	540-650	Return as sophomores:	86%
SAT math:	510-620	Out-of-state:	82%
End year in good standing:	98%	Live on campus:	88%
		International:	4%

Basis for selection. Emphasis placed on artistic ability as demonstrated in the portfolio, academic achievement, test scores, GPA, and level of coursework. Essays, recommendations, interview, and extra-curricular activities also considered. Portfolio of 12-20 pieces of artwork must be submitted with application. Interview recommended. **Learning Disabled:** Students with documented learning disabilities not required to submit SAT or ACT test scores.

High school preparation. 24 units required. Required and recommended units include English 4, mathematics 2-3, social studies 4, history 3-4, science 2-3 (laboratory 1) and academic electives 6. 2 studio art required, 4 studio art recommended, 1 art history recommended.

2005-2006 Annual costs. Tuition/fees: $26,920. Room/board: $7,530. Books/supplies: $1,400. Personal expenses: $600.

2005-2006 Financial aid. Need-based: 309 full-time freshmen applied for aid; 229 were judged to have need; 229 of these received aid. Average need met was 68%. Average scholarship/grant was $9,640; average loan $2,877. 61% of total undergraduate aid awarded as scholarships/grants, 39% as loans/jobs. **Non-need-based:** Scholarships awarded for academics, art.

Application procedures. Admission: Closing date 2/15 (receipt date). $50 fee, may be waived for applicants with need. Application must be submitted on paper. Admission notification 3/15. Must reply by 5/1. **Financial aid:** Closing date 3/1. FAFSA, institutional form required. Applicants notified by 4/15; must reply by 5/2.

Academics. One-third of course work in liberal arts and two-thirds in studio art required for graduation. Minors available in academic subjects. Independent studio and study requirement sometimes met by job internships. Foundation program required in the first year. **Special study options:** Accelerated study, combined bachelor's/graduate degree, cross-registration, distance learning, double major, dual enrollment of high school students, exchange student, independent study, internships, New York semester, student-designed major, study abroad, teacher certification program. Cooperative exchange programs with Johns Hopkins University, Goucher College, Peabody Conservatory of Music, University of Baltimore, Loyola College, Notre Dame College, University of Maryland Baltimore County, Morgan State University, Baltimore Hebrew College and Towson University; 5-year BFA/ MA; 5-year BFA/MAT. **Credit/placement by examination:** AP, CLEP, IB, institutional tests. 15 credit hours maximum toward bachelor's degree. **Support services:** Learning center, pre-admission summer program, reduced course load, remedial instruction, study skills assistance, tutoring, writing center.

Majors. Education: Art. **Visual/performing arts:** Art history/ conservation, ceramics, drawing, fiber arts, graphic design, illustration, interior design, multimedia, painting, photography, printmaking, sculpture.

Most popular majors. Education 6%, visual/performing arts 94%.

Computing on campus. 305 workstations in dormitories, library, computer center, student center. Dormitories wired for high-speed internet access and linked to campus network. Helpline, student web hosting, wireless network available.

Student life. Freshman orientation: Mandatory, $95 fee. Preregistration for classes offered. **Policies:** Freshmen permitted cars on campus. **Housing:** Guaranteed on-campus for freshmen. Coed dorms, special housing for disabled, apartments available. $550 deposit, deadline 5/1. **Activities:** Choral groups, dance, drama, film society, literary magazine, student government, TV station, Amnesty International, service club, Baha'i club, Koinonia (Christian Fellowship), Korean-American student association, student voice association, urban initiative, Z-point political acitivist group.

Student services. Career counseling, student employment services, financial aid counseling, health services, minority student services, personal counseling, placement for graduates.

Contact. E-mail: admissions@mica.edu
Phone: (410) 225-2222 Fax: (410) 225-2337
Theresa Bedoya, Vice President and Dean of Admission and Financial Aid, Maryland Institute College of Art, 1300 Mount Royal Avenue, Baltimore, MD 21217-4134

McDaniel College

Westminster, Maryland **CB member**
www.mcdaniel.edu **CB code: 5898**

- Private 4-year liberal arts college
- Residential campus in large town
- 1,645 degree-seeking undergraduates: 2% part-time, 57% women, 7% African American, 2% Asian American, 2% Hispanic American, 1% Native American, 1% international
- 1,719 degree-seeking graduate students
- 79% of applicants admitted
- SAT or ACT (ACT writing optional), application essay required
- 74% graduate within 6 years

General. Founded in 1867. Regionally accredited. Wireless hot spots available in various locations on campus. **Degrees:** 352 bachelor's awarded; master's offered. **ROTC:** Army. **Location:** 30 miles from Baltimore, 60 miles from Washington, DC. **Calendar:** 4-1-4, limited summer session. **Full-time faculty:** 132 total; 83% have terminal degrees, 10% minority, 48% women. **Part-time faculty:** 72 total; 15% have terminal degrees, 7% minority, 49% women. **Class size:** 62% < 20, 37% 20-39, less than 1% 50-99. **Special facilities:** 9-hole golf course, film/video production laboratory, photography studio, audiology laboratory, human performance laboratory, graphics laboratory, physics observatory.

Freshman class profile. 2,256 applied, 1,782 admitted, 449 enrolled.

Mid 50% test scores			
SAT verbal:	490-610	Rank in top quarter:	55%
SAT math:	500-620	Rank in top tenth:	26%
ACT:	19-25	End year in good standing:	90%
GPA 3.50 or higher:	50%	Return as sophomores:	80%
GPA 3.0-3.49:	31%	Out-of-state:	35%
GPA 2.0-2.99:	19%	Live on campus:	94%
		International:	1%

Basis for selection. Class rank, interview, course work and grades, test results, personal traits, goals, motivation, recommendations by counselors, and participation in nonacademic activities considered. Test score optional for first year students who are in the top 10% of their class or who have a 3.5 cumulative GPA if their high school does not rank. Students must submit SAT or ACT scores to be considered for academic scholarship. Interview recommended. **Homeschooled:** Must submit documentation used to satisfy your state graduation requirement.

High school preparation. 19 units required; 24 recommended. Required and recommended units include English 4, mathematics 3-4, social studies 2-3, history 2-3, science 3-4 (laboratory 2-3) and foreign language 3-4.

2005-2006 Annual costs. Tuition/fees: $26,010. Room/board: $5,600. Books/supplies: $900. Personal expenses: $170.

2005-2006 Financial aid. Need-based: 369 full-time freshmen applied for aid; 284 were judged to have need; 283 of these received aid. Average need met was 95%. Average scholarship/grant was $9,330; average loan $3,892. 81% of total undergraduate aid awarded as scholarships/grants, 19% as loans/jobs. **Non-need-based:** Awarded to 536 full-time undergraduates, including 283 freshmen. Scholarships awarded for academics, ROTC.

Application procedures. Admission: Closing date 2/1 (postmark date). $50 fee, may be waived for applicants with need. Application may be submitted online. Admission notification 4/1. Must reply by May 1 or within 2 week(s) if notified thereafter. **Financial aid:** Priority date 3/1; no closing date. FAFSA, institutional form required. Applicants notified on a rolling basis starting 3/1; must reply by 5/1 or within 2 week(s) of notification.

Academics. January term offered as a two-credit period of concentrated study. May include travel, classroom study or independent study. **Special study options:** Accelerated study, double major, dual enrollment of high school students, exchange student, honors, independent study, internships, liberal arts/career combination, New York semester, semester at sea, student-designed major, study abroad, teacher certification program, United Nations semester, Washington semester. 3-2 program in engineering with Washington University (MO), 3-2 program in forestry with Duke University. **Credit/placement by examination:** AP, CLEP, IB, SAT, ACT, institutional tests. 32 credit hours maximum toward bachelor's degree. **Support services:** Learning center, reduced course load, remedial instruction, study skills assistance, tutoring, writing center.

Majors. Biology: General, biochemistry, environmental. **Business:** Business admin. **Communications:** General. **Computer sciences:** General. **Conservation:** Environmental science. **English:** English lit. **Foreign languages:** French, German, Spanish. **History:** General. **Math:** General. **Parks/recreation:** Exercise sciences. **Philosophy/religion:** Philosophy, religion. **Physical sciences:** Chemistry, physics. **Psychology:** General. **Public administration:** Social work. **Social sciences:** Economics, political science, sociology. **Visual/performing arts:** Art, art history/conservation, dramatic.

Most popular majors. Biology 7%, business/marketing 12%, communications/journalism 8%, English 6%, history 6%, psychology 10%, social sciences 19%, visual/performing arts 9%.

Computing on campus. 175 workstations in library, computer center. Dormitories wired for high-speed internet access and linked to campus network. Commuter students can connect to campus network. Online course registration, helpline, wireless network available.

Student life. Freshman orientation: Mandatory. Preregistration for classes offered. 5-day program includes awareness training about alcohol, harassment, and diversity. **Housing:** Guaranteed on-campus for freshmen. Coed dorms, single-sex dorms, special housing for disabled, apartments, substance-free housing available. $500 deposit, deadline 5/1. Honors, language houses, community service groups available. **Activities:** Bands, choral groups, drama, literary magazine, music ensembles, musical theater, radio station, student government, student newspaper, TV station, Jewish student union, Christian fellowship, Circle K, ecology club, black student union, multicultural student association, Catholic campus ministry, German club, French club, Spanish club.

Athletics. NCAA. **Intercollegiate:** Baseball M, basketball, cross-country, field hockey W, football (tackle) M, golf, lacrosse, soccer, softball W, swimming, tennis, track and field, volleyball W, wrestling M. **Intramural:** Badminton, basketball, football (tackle) M, golf, racquetball, soccer, softball, swimming, table tennis, tennis, volleyball, weight lifting. **Team name:** The Green Terror.

Student services. Career counseling, student employment services, financial aid counseling, health services, minority student services, personal counseling, placement for graduates. **Physically disabled:** Services for visually, hearing impaired. **Learning disabled:** Comprehensive services available.

Contact. E-mail: admissions@mcdaniel.edu
Phone: (410) 857-2230 Toll-free number: (800) 638-5005
Fax: (410) 857-2757
M. O'Connell, Vice President for Enrollment Management and Dean of Admissions, McDaniel College, Two College Hill, Westminster, MD 21157-4390

Morgan State University

Baltimore, Maryland **CB member**
www.morgan.edu **CB code: 5416**

- Public 4-year university and liberal arts college
- Commuter campus in very large city
- 5,676 degree-seeking undergraduates: 10% part-time, 56% women
- 663 degree-seeking graduate students
- 37% of applicants admitted
- SAT or ACT with writing required

General. Founded in 1867. Regionally accredited. **Degrees:** 833 bachelor's awarded; master's, doctoral offered. **ROTC:** Army. **Location:** 45 miles from Washington, DC, 100 miles from Philadelphia. **Calendar:** Semester, limited summer session. **Full-time faculty:** 322 total; 77% have terminal degrees, 80% minority, 37% women. **Special facilities:** Art galleries, historical and government documents collections, special collections of African American history, super computer, engineering complex.

Freshman class profile. 11,031 applied, 4,070 admitted, 1,396 enrolled.

Mid 50% test scores			
SAT verbal:	400-490	Out-of-state:	33%
SAT math:	400-500	Live on campus:	76%

Basis for selection. School achievement record and test scores most important. 820 SAT (exclusive of Writing) with 2.5 high school GPA or 900 SAT (exclusive of Writing) with 2.0 high school GPA, principal's recommendation, and parents' consent form (for minors) required. Interview and essay recommended. Audition recommended for music majors. **Homeschooled:** Need state-recognized diploma. **Learning Disabled:** Students with learning disability must provide documentation and take untimed SAT with assistance from counseling center.

High school preparation. 13 units recommended. Recommended units include English 4, mathematics 4, social studies 2, history 2, science 2 and foreign language 1.

2005-2006 Annual costs. Tuition/fees: $6,110; $13,520 out-of-state. Room/board: $6,990. Books/supplies: $721. Personal expenses: $2,369.

Application procedures. Admission: Priority date 4/15; no deadline. $25 fee, may be waived for applicants with need. Application may be submitted online. Admission notification on a rolling basis. Must reply by May 1 or within 2 week(s) if notified thereafter. **Financial aid:** Priority date 4/1; no closing date. FAFSA required. Applicants notified on a rolling basis starting 6/1; must reply within 2 week(s) of notification.

Academics. Special study options: Cooperative education, cross-registration, distance learning, double major, dual enrollment of high school students, honors, independent study, internships, liberal arts/career combination, teacher certification program, weekend college. Fulbright Program. **Credit/placement by examination:** AP, CLEP, institutional tests. 46 credit hours maximum toward bachelor's degree. Proficiency tests in general education requirements. **Support services:** Learning center, pre-admission summer program, reduced course load, remedial instruction, study skills assistance, tutoring, writing center.

Majors. Architecture: Environmental design. **Area/ethnic studies:** African-American. **Biology:** General. **Business:** General, accounting, business admin, finance, hospitality admin, marketing, public finance. **Communications:** Broadcast journalism. **Computer sciences:** General, computer science, information systems, networking. **Education:** Business, elementary, health, multi-level teacher, physical, secondary. **Engineering:** Civil, electrical, industrial, physics. **English:** Speech/rhetoric. **Family/consumer sciences:** Food/nutrition. **Health:** Predentistry, premedicine, prepharmacy, staff services technology. **History:** General. **Legal studies:** Prelaw. **Math:** General. **Physical sciences:** Chemistry, physics. **Psychology:** General. **Social sciences:** Economics, political science, sociology. **Visual/performing arts:** Dramatic, studio arts.

Most popular majors. Biology 7%, business/marketing 23%, computer/information sciences 9%, education 9%, visual/performing arts 7%.

Computing on campus. Dormitories wired for high-speed internet access and linked to campus network. Commuter students can connect to campus network. Online course registration, online library, helpline, repair service, student web hosting, wireless network available.

Student life. Freshman orientation: Available. Preregistration for classes offered. Held twice during summer for 5 days. **Housing:** Coed dorms, single-sex dorms, special housing for disabled, substance-free housing available. **Activities:** Bands, choral groups, dance, drama, film society, music ensembles, musical theater, radio station, student government, student newspaper, Council on Religious Life.

Athletics. NCAA. **Intercollegiate:** Basketball, bowling W, cheerleading M, cross-country, football (tackle) M, softball W, tennis, track and field, volleyball W. **Intramural:** Basketball, bowling, cross-country, handball, racquetball, rifle, soccer, softball, swimming, table tennis, tennis, track and field, volleyball. **Team name:** Bears.

Student services. Alcohol/substance abuse counseling, career counseling, student employment services, health services, on-campus daycare, personal counseling, placement for graduates, veterans' counselor. **Physically disabled:** Services for visually, speech, hearing impaired.

Contact. E-mail: admissions@morgan.edu
Phone: (443) 885-3000 Toll-free number: (800) 332-6674
Fax: (443) 885-8260
Edwin Johnson, Director of Admissions and Recruitment, Morgan State University, 1700 East Coldspring Lane, Baltimore, MD 21251

Mount St. Mary's University

Emmitsburg, Maryland — CB member
www.msmary.edu — CB code: 5421

- Private 4-year university and liberal arts college affiliated with Roman Catholic Church
- Residential campus in rural community
- 1,656 degree-seeking undergraduates: 10% part-time, 61% women, 7% African American, 2% Asian American, 3% Hispanic American, 1% international
- 520 degree-seeking graduate students
- 84% of applicants admitted
- SAT or ACT (ACT writing optional) required
- 68% graduate within 6 years; 26% enter graduate study

General. Founded in 1808. Regionally accredited. **Degrees:** 329 bachelor's awarded; master's, first professional offered. **ROTC:** Army. **Location:** 65 miles from Washington, DC, 50 miles from Baltimore. **Calendar:** Semester, limited summer session. **Full-time faculty:** 105 total; 90% have terminal degrees, 4% minority, 33% women. **Part-time faculty:** 100 total; 24% have terminal degrees, 3% minority, 45% women. **Class size:** 42% < 20, 58% 20-39, less than 1% 50-99. **Special facilities:** 300 acre recreation area.

Freshman class profile. 2,190 applied, 1,847 admitted, 439 enrolled.

Mid 50% test scores			
SAT verbal:	500-600	Rank in top tenth:	20%
SAT math:	500-600	End year in good standing:	93%
GPA 3.50 or higher:	29%	Return as sophomores:	84%
GPA 3.0-3.49:	36%	Out-of-state:	44%
GPA 2.0-2.99:	35%	Live on campus:	96%
Rank in top quarter:	48%	International:	1%

Basis for selection. High school record most important followed by standardized test scores, character, extracurricular activities. Interview and essay recommended. Auditions and/or portfolios are recommended for VPA majors, but not required. **Homeschooled:** Statement describing homeschool structure and mission, letter of recommendation (nonparent) required.

High school preparation. College-preparatory program required. 16 units required. Required units include English 4, mathematics 3, social studies 3, science 3 (laboratory 2), foreign language 2 and academic electives 1.

2005-2006 Annual costs. Tuition/fees: $22,900. Room/board: $8,030. Books/supplies: $800. Personal expenses: $600.

2005-2006 Financial aid. Need-based: 378 full-time freshmen applied for aid; 288 were judged to have need; 288 of these received aid. Average need met was 80%. Average scholarship/grant was $12,877; average loan $3,359. 71% of total undergraduate aid awarded as scholarships/grants, 29% as loans/jobs. **Non-need-based:** Awarded to 797 full-time undergraduates, including 231 freshmen. Scholarships awarded for academics, athletics, leadership, minority status, music/drama, ROTC.

Application procedures. Admission: No deadline. $35 fee, may be waived for applicants with need. Application may be submitted online. Admission notification on a rolling basis beginning on or about 12/1. Must reply by May 1 or within 2 week(s) if notified thereafter. **Financial aid:** Closing date 2/15. FAFSA, institutional form required. Applicants notified on a rolling basis starting 2/15; must reply by 5/1.

Academics. Liberal arts core curriculum integrated over 4 years includes: western civilization (clustered with literature and art courses), American experience, philosophy, theology, ethics, non-western cultures, mathematical science, foreign language, social science, written and oral communication. Undergraduate professional studies programs in business and criminal justice in an accelerated format offered off-campus; open to adult students only. **Special study options:** Accelerated study, combined bachelor's/graduate degree, cross-registration, double major, dual enrollment of high school students, honors, independent study, internships, liberal arts/career combination, student-designed major, study abroad, teacher certification program, Washington semester, weekend college. 3-2 with Johns Hopkins University (BS Biology, BS Nursing), 3-3 with Sacred Heart University (BS in Biology, MS in Physical Therapy), 4-2 with Sacred Heart University (BS in Biology, MS in Occupational Therapy). **Credit/placement by examination:** AP, CLEP, IB, SAT, ACT, institutional tests. 30 credit hours maximum toward bachelor's degree. **Support services:** Learning center, reduced course load, remedial instruction, study skills assistance, tutoring, writing center.

Majors. Biology: General, biochemistry. **Business:** General, accounting, information resources management. **Communications:** General. **Computer sciences:** General. **Education:** Elementary. **English:** English lit. **Foreign languages:** French, German, Spanish. **History:** General. **Math:** General. **Parks/recreation:** Sports admin. **Philosophy/religion:** Philosophy. **Physical sciences:** Chemistry. **Protective services:** Criminal justice. **Psychology:** General. **Social sciences:** General, economics, international relations, political science, sociology. **Theology:** Theology. **Visual/performing arts:** General.

Most popular majors. Business/marketing 35%, communications/journalism 7%, education 11%, social sciences 14%.

Computing on campus. 150 workstations in library, computer center. Dormitories wired for high-speed internet access and linked to campus network. Commuter students can connect to campus network. Online course registration, helpline, repair service, student web hosting, wireless network available.

Student life. Freshman orientation: Mandatory. Preregistration for classes offered. 3-day weekend in August and choice of 1 of 2 weekends in June for pre-registration. **Policies:** Freshmen permitted cars on campus. **Housing:** Guaranteed on-campus for all undergraduates. Coed dorms, special housing for disabled, apartments, substance-free housing available. Theme houses available. **Activities:** Bands, choral groups, dance, drama, literary magazine, music ensembles, musical theater, radio station, student government, student newspaper, TV station, College Democrats, College Republicans, Amnesty International, campus ministry student organization, Circle K, Heritage (people of color), commuter student association, international student association, Habitat for Humanity, students for life.

Athletics. NCAA. **Intercollegiate:** Baseball M, basketball, cross-country, golf, lacrosse, soccer, softball W, swimming W, tennis, track and field. **Intramural:** Basketball, field hockey W, football (non-tackle) M, racquetball, skiing, soccer, softball, swimming, tennis, volleyball. **Team name:** Mountaineers.

Student services. Adult student services, alcohol/substance abuse counseling, campus ministries, career counseling, student employment services, financial aid counseling, health services, minority student services, personal counseling, placement for graduates. **Physically disabled:** Services for visually, hearing impaired.

Contact. E-mail: admissions@msmary.edu
Phone: (301) 447-5214 Toll-free number: (800) 448-4347
Fax: (301) 447-5860
Stephen Neitz, Executive Director of Admissions and Financial Aid, Mount St. Mary's University, 16300 Old Emmitsburg Road, Emmitsburg, MD 21727

National Labor College

Silver Spring, Maryland
www.georgemeany.org/

- Private 4-year liberal arts college
- Small city
- 199 degree-seeking undergraduates

General. Regionally accredited. **Degrees:** 98 bachelor's awarded. **Calendar:** Trimester. **Full-time faculty:** 11 total. **Part-time faculty:** 2 total.

2006-2007 Annual costs. $150 per-credit-hour for union members affiliated with the AFL-CIO. $200 per-credit-hour for union members not affiliated with the AFL-CIO. $982 per-credit-hour for non-union members. $25 activities fee for all.

Application procedures. **Admission:** No deadline. $50 fee. Admission notification on a rolling basis.

Academics. **Credit/placement by examination:** CLEP.

Majors. **Business:** Labor relations, labor studies.

Contact. Phone: (301) 431-6400 Fax: (301) 431-5411
Eve Dauer, Registrar, National Labor College, 10000 New Hampshire Avenue, Silver Spring, MD 20904

Ner Israel Rabbinical College

Baltimore, Maryland
CB code: 0839

- Private 4-year rabbinical college for men affiliated with Jewish faith
- Very large city
- 378 degree-seeking undergraduates
- 59% of applicants admitted
- Interview required

General. Accredited by AARTS. **Degrees:** 41 bachelor's awarded; master's, doctoral, first professional offered. **Calendar:** Semester. **Full-time faculty:** 21 total.

Freshman class profile. 96 applied, 57 admitted, 57 enrolled.

Basis for selection. Interview, character, religious affiliation most important. High school record and recommendations also important.

2006-2007 Annual costs. Tuition/fees (projected): $8,000. Room/board: $6,000.

Application procedures. **Admission:** No deadline. $50 fee. Admission notification on a rolling basis.

Academics. **Credit/placement by examination:** CLEP, institutional tests.

Student life. **Policies:** Religious observance required.

Contact. Phone: (410) 484-7200
Rabbi Beryl Weisbord, Admissions Director, Ner Israel Rabbinical College, 400 Mount Wilson Lane, Baltimore, MD 21208

St. John's College

Annapolis, Maryland — **CB member**
www.stjohnscollege.edu — **CB code: 5598**

- Private 4-year liberal arts college
- Residential campus in large town
- 474 degree-seeking undergraduates: 46% women, 1% African American, 3% Asian American, 3% Hispanic American, 1% Native American, 1% international
- 91 degree-seeking graduate students
- 76% of applicants admitted
- Application essay required
- 77% graduate within 6 years; 19% enter graduate study

General. Founded in 1784. Regionally accredited. Second campus in Santa Fe, New Mexico. Students may transfer between campuses. **Degrees:** 93 bachelor's awarded; master's offered. **Location:** 35 miles from Washington, DC, 30 miles from Baltimore. **Calendar:** Semester, limited summer session. **Full-time faculty:** 68 total; 72% have terminal degrees, 6% minority, 24% women. **Part-time faculty:** 7 total; 57% have terminal degrees, 43% women. **Class size:** 94% < 20, 5% 20-39, less than 1% >100. **Special facilities:** Planetarium, boathouse, observatory.

Freshman class profile. 494 applied, 375 admitted, 149 enrolled.

Mid 50% test scores		**End year in good standing:**	90%
SAT verbal:	660-760	**Return as sophomores:**	82%
SAT math:	590-680	**Out-of-state:**	82%
Rank in top quarter:	69%	**Live on campus:**	100%
Rank in top tenth:	40%	**International:**	1%

Basis for selection. One optional and 3 required essays most important. School achievement record and teacher recommendations important. 2-day campus visit and interview recommended. SAT or ACT recommended. **Homeschooled:** Statement describing homeschool structure and mission, letter of recommendation (nonparent) required. Must submit results of PSAT, SAT, or ACT if high school diploma will not be earned.

High school preparation. College-preparatory program recommended. 5 units required. Required and recommended units include English 4, mathematics 3-4, social studies 2, history 2, science 3 (laboratory 3) and foreign language 2-4.

2006-2007 Annual costs. Tuition/fees: $34,506. Room/board: $8,270. Books/supplies: $280. Personal expenses: $750.

2005-2006 Financial aid. All financial aid based on need. Average need met was 99%. Average scholarship/grant was $19,949; average loan $3,967. 71% of total undergraduate aid awarded as scholarships/grants, 29% as loans/jobs.

Application procedures. **Admission:** Priority date 3/1; no deadline. No application fee. Application may be submitted online. Admission notification on a rolling basis. Must reply by May 1 or within 2 week(s) if notified thereafter. Early application encouraged as class generally fills by first week in May. **Financial aid:** Priority date 2/15; no closing date. FAFSA, CSS PROFILE required. Applicants notified on a rolling basis starting 1/15; must reply by 5/1.

Academics. **Special study options:** Internships. **Credit/placement by examination:** CLEP. **Support services:** Tutoring, writing center.

Majors. **Area/ethnic studies:** Western European. **Liberal arts:** Arts/sciences, humanities.

Computing on campus. 20 workstations in library, computer center. Dormitories wired for high-speed internet access and linked to campus network. Commuter students can connect to campus network.

Student life. **Freshman orientation:** Mandatory. 2-day program, after registration and prior to start of classes. **Policies:** Freshmen required to live in dormitories. **Housing:** Guaranteed on-campus for freshmen. Coed dorms, substance-free housing available. **Activities:** Choral groups, dance, drama, film society, literary magazine, music ensembles, musical theater, student government, student newspaper, Political Forum, Project Politae (campus community service organization), Pink Triangle Society, Christian Fellowship, Jewish Students Society, Student Committee on Instruction, Environmental Club, Amnesty International, Delegate Council.

Athletics. **Intramural:** Badminton, basketball, boxing M, fencing, handball, racquetball, rowing (crew), sailing, soccer, softball, squash, table tennis, tennis, track and field, volleyball.

Student services. Alcohol/substance abuse counseling, career counseling, student employment services, financial aid counseling, health services, personal counseling, placement for graduates, women's services.

Contact. E-mail: admissions@sjca.edu
Phone: (410) 626-2522 Toll-free number: (800) 727-9238
Fax: (410) 269-7916
John Christensen, Director of Admissions, St. John's College, PO Box 2800, Annapolis, MD 21404

St. Mary's College of Maryland

St. Mary's City, Maryland — **CB member**
www.smcm.edu — **CB code: 5601**

- Public 4-year liberal arts college
- Residential campus in rural community
- 1,879 degree-seeking undergraduates: 3% part-time, 57% women, 8% African American, 4% Asian American, 3% Hispanic American, 1% international
- 68% of applicants admitted
- SAT or ACT (ACT writing optional), application essay required
- 72% graduate within 6 years; 37% enter graduate study

General. Founded in 1840. Regionally accredited. **Degrees:** 465 bachelor's awarded. **Location:** 70 miles from Washington, DC. **Calendar:** Semester, limited summer session. **Full-time faculty:** 128 total; 98% have terminal degrees, 45% women. **Part-time faculty:** 81 total; 54% have terminal degrees, 48% women. **Class size:** 60% < 20, 38% 20-39, less than 1% 40-49, 1% 50-99. **Special facilities:** Archaelogical site of Historic St. Mary's City, electron microscope, marine research vessel, fresh and salt water research facilities.

Freshman class profile. 2,200 applied, 1,503 admitted, 488 enrolled.

Mid 50% test scores			
SAT verbal:	570-690	Rank in top quarter:	70%
SAT math:	560-650	Rank in top tenth:	34%
GPA 3.50 or higher:	49%	Return as sophomores:	89%
GPA 3.0-3.49:	38%	Out-of-state:	18%
GPA 2.0-2.99:	13%	Live on campus:	97%
		International:	1%

Basis for selection. High school record, SAT or ACT scores, recommendations by counselors/teachers, co-curricular resume, and essay most important. Interview recommended. Audition recommended for music and dramatic arts majors. Portfolio recommended for art majors.

High school preparation. 22 units required; 25 recommended. Required and recommended units include English 4, mathematics 3, social studies 3, science 3 (laboratory 2-3), foreign language 2 and academic electives 7.

2006-2007 Annual costs. Tuition/fees: $11,710; $21,280 out-of-state. Room/board: $8,505. Books/supplies: $1,000. Personal expenses: $1,500.

2005-2006 Financial aid. **Need-based:** 344 full-time freshmen applied for aid; 221 were judged to have need; 221 of these received aid. Average need met was 59%. Average scholarship/grant was $3,000; average loan $2,625. 64% of total undergraduate aid awarded as scholarships/grants, 36% as loans/jobs. **Non-need-based:** Awarded to 767 full-time undergraduates, including 242 freshmen. Scholarships awarded for academics, art, leadership, music/drama.

Application procedures. **Admission:** Priority date 12/1; deadline 1/15 (postmark date). $40 fee, may be waived for applicants with need. Application may be submitted online. Admission notification 4/1. Must reply by 5/1. **Financial aid:** Closing date 3/1. FAFSA required. Applicants notified by 4/1.

Academics. **Special study options:** Combined bachelor's/graduate degree, double major, dual enrollment of high school students, exchange student, honors, independent study, internships, liberal arts/career combination, student-designed major, study abroad, teacher certification program. International study programs in China, England, France, Germany, Gambia, Senegal, Thailand, and other countries; archaeological field school at historic St. Mary's City; pre-engineering 3-2 program with University of Maryland School of Engineering. **Credit/placement by examination:** AP, CLEP, IB, SAT, ACT, institutional tests. 45 credit hours maximum toward bachelor's degree. **Support services:** Reduced course load, study skills assistance, tutoring, writing center.

Majors. **Biology:** General, biochemistry. **Computer sciences:** General. **English:** English lit. **Foreign languages:** General. **History:** General. **Interdisciplinary:** Biological/physical sciences. **Math:** General. **Philosophy/religion:** Philosophy, religion. **Physical sciences:** Chemistry, physics. **Psychology:** General. **Public administration:** Policy analysis. **Social sciences:** Anthropology, economics, political science, sociology. **Visual/performing arts:** Art, dramatic.

Most popular majors. Biology 11%, English 10%, history 7%, psychology 21%, social sciences 28%, visual/performing arts 6%.

Computing on campus. 255 workstations in dormitories, library, computer center, student center. Dormitories wired for high-speed internet access and linked to campus network. Commuter students can connect to campus network. Online course registration, helpline, student web hosting, wireless network available.

Student life. **Freshman orientation:** Mandatory, $80 fee. Preregistration for classes offered. Offered in July; additional program in August. **Policies:** Freshmen permitted cars on campus. **Housing:** Guaranteed on-campus for all undergraduates. Coed dorms, single-sex dorms, special housing for disabled, apartments available. $150 deposit, deadline 5/1. Townhouses available for single students. **Activities:** Jazz band, choral groups, dance, drama, film society, literary magazine, music ensembles, musical theater, radio station, student government, student newspaper, symphony orchestra, TV station, black student union, College Republicans, College Democrats, Amnesty International, For Goodness Sake (community service), Hillel, Habitat for Humanity, Student Environmental Action Coalition, InterVarsity Christian Fellowship, St. Mary's Triangle and Rainbow Society (gay and lesbian).

Athletics. NCAA. **Intercollegiate:** Baseball M, basketball, field hockey W, lacrosse, sailing, soccer, swimming, tennis, volleyball W. **Intramural:** Basketball, bowling, cross-country, football (non-tackle), soccer, softball, swimming, tennis, volleyball, water polo. **Team name:** Seahawks.

Student services. Alcohol/substance abuse counseling, career counseling, student employment services, financial aid counseling, health services, minority student services, personal counseling, placement for graduates, veterans' counselor, women's services. **Physically disabled:** Services for visually, hearing impaired.

Contact. E-mail: admissions@smcm.edu
Phone: (240) 895-5000 Toll-free number: (800) 492-7181
Fax: (240) 895-5001
Richard Edgar, Director of Admissions, St. Mary's College of Maryland, 18952 East Fisher Road, St. Mary's City, MD 20686-3001

Salisbury University

Salisbury, Maryland — **CB member**
www.salisbury.edu — **CB code: 5403**

- Public 4-year university and liberal arts college
- Residential campus in large town
- 6,141 degree-seeking undergraduates: 6% part-time, 56% women, 9% African American, 2% Asian American, 3% Hispanic American, 1% international
- 432 degree-seeking graduate students
- 57% of applicants admitted
- SAT and SAT Subject Tests or ACT with writing required
- 73% graduate within 6 years; 30% enter graduate study

General. Founded in 1925. Regionally accredited. **Degrees:** 1,313 bachelor's awarded; master's offered. **ROTC:** Army. **Location:** 110 miles from Baltimore and Washington, DC. **Calendar:** 4-1-4, extensive summer session. **Full-time faculty:** 323 total; 82% have terminal degrees, 9% minority, 45% women. **Part-time faculty:** 171 total; 10% have terminal degrees, 4% minority, 64% women. **Class size:** 28% < 20, 61% 20-39, 7% 40-49, 3% 50-99, less than 1% >100. **Special facilities:** Arboretum, research center for Delmarva history and culture, center for conflict resolution, small business development center network, sculpture garden, museum.

Freshman class profile. 5,296 applied, 3,011 admitted, 958 enrolled.

Mid 50% test scores		GPA 2.0-2.99:	17%
SAT verbal:	520-600	Rank in top quarter:	56%
SAT math:	530-610	Rank in top tenth:	22%
ACT:	21-25	Out-of-state:	18%
GPA 3.50 or higher:	49%	Live on campus:	91%
GPA 3.0-3.49:	34%	International:	1%

Basis for selection. Level of courses, depth of subjects, GPA most important. Activities, leadership roles, artistic or athletic talents, ability to contribute to a culturally diverse community also important. Essay recommended.

High school preparation. College-preparatory program recommended. 15 units required; 21 recommended. Required and recommended units include English 4, mathematics 3-4, social studies 3, science 3-4 (laboratory 2-3), foreign language 2-3 and academic electives 3.

2005-2006 Annual costs. Tuition/fees: $6,376; $14,054 out-of-state. Room/board: $6,932. Books/supplies: $900. Personal expenses: $1,400.

2004-2005 Financial aid. Need-based: 752 full-time freshmen applied for aid; 374 were judged to have need; 374 of these received aid. Average need met was 53%. Average scholarship/grant was $4,754; average loan $2,020. 39% of total undergraduate aid awarded as scholarships/grants, 61% as loans/jobs. **Non-need-based:** Awarded to 733 full-time undergraduates, including 182 freshmen. Scholarships awarded for academics, alumni affiliation, art, leadership, state residency. **Additional information:** Job opportunities provided for almost 30% of full-time undergraduate students (over 900 jobs). Students can expect to earn $1500 per academic year by working 10 to 15 hours per week.

Application procedures. Admission: $45 fee, may be waived for applicants with need. Application must be submitted online. Admission notification 3/15. Must reply by 5/1. **Financial aid:** Priority date 2/1, closing date 3/1. FAFSA required. Applicants notified on a rolling basis starting 4/1; must reply by 5/1 or within 2 week(s) of notification.

Academics. Special study options: Accelerated study, combined bachelor's/graduate degree, cooperative education, cross-registration, distance learning, double major, dual enrollment of high school students, ESL, exchange student, external degree, honors, independent study, internships, liberal arts/career combination, student-designed major, study abroad, teacher certification program, Washington semester. **Credit/placement by examination:** AP, CLEP, IB, institutional tests. 60 credit hours maximum toward bachelor's degree. **Support services:** Learning center, study skills assistance, tutoring, writing center.

Majors. Biology: General. **Business:** Accounting, business admin, entrepreneurial studies, management information systems, marketing. **Communications:** General. **Computer sciences:** Computer science. **Education:** Early childhood, elementary, health, physical. **Foreign languages:** French, Spanish. **Health:** Athletic training, clinical lab science, environmental health, nursing (RN), respiratory therapy technology. **History:** General. **Interdisciplinary:** Peace/conflict. **Liberal arts:** Arts/sciences. **Math:** General. **Philosophy/religion:** Philosophy. **Physical sciences:** Chemistry, geology, physics. **Psychology:** General. **Public administration:** Social work. **Social sciences:** Economics, geography, political science, sociology. **Visual/performing arts:** Dramatic, music performance, studio arts.

Most popular majors. Biology 7%, business/marketing 17%, communications/journalism 10%, education 12%, health sciences 10%, history 6%, psychology 6%, social sciences 6%.

Computing on campus. 275 workstations in library, computer center, student center. Dormitories wired for high-speed internet access and linked to campus network. Commuter students can connect to campus network. Online course registration, online library, helpline, repair service, student web hosting, wireless network available.

Student life. Freshman orientation: Mandatory. Preregistration for classes offered. Orientation fee varies per program. **Policies:** Class attendance policies vary by instructor. Hazing and smoking is prohibited. **Housing:** Coed dorms, single-sex dorms, apartments, substance-free housing available. $250 deposit. Affiliated off-campus apartments, quiet/study housing available. World living/learning option-community of international and American students. **Activities:** Bands, choral groups, dance, drama, film society, literary magazine, music ensembles, musical theater, radio station, student government, student newspaper, symphony orchestra, TV station, Campus Crusade for Christ, Christian fellowship, Catholic campus ministries, reformed university fellowship, Muslim student organization, junior gospel choir, Union of African-Americans, NAACP, African-American historical & philosophical society, international student association.

Athletics. NCAA. **Intercollegiate:** Baseball M, basketball, cross-country, field hockey W, football (tackle) M, lacrosse, soccer, softball W, swimming, tennis, track and field, volleyball W. **Intramural:** Basketball, cross-country, football (non-tackle), golf, ice hockey M, lacrosse, racquetball, soccer, softball, tennis, volleyball, water polo. **Team name:** Seagulls.

Student services. Alcohol/substance abuse counseling, career counseling, student employment services, financial aid counseling, health services, minority student services, personal counseling, veterans' counselor. **Physically disabled:** Services for visually, speech, hearing impaired.

Contact. E-mail: admissions@salisbury.edu
Phone: (410) 543-6161 Toll-free number: (888) 543-0148
Fax: (410) 546-6016
Laura Thorpe, Director of Admissions, Salisbury University, 1200 Camden Avenue, Salisbury, MD 21801-6862

Sojourner-Douglass College

Baltimore, Maryland
www.sdc.edu **CB code: 0504**

- Private 4-year liberal arts college
- Very large city
- 1,000 full-time, degree-seeking undergraduates
- Interview required

General. Founded in 1980. Regionally accredited. Campus in the Bahamas. **Degrees:** 172 bachelor's awarded; master's offered. **Calendar:** Trimester. **Full-time faculty:** 57 total. **Part-time faculty:** 150 total. **Special facilities:** Learning resource center, writing lab.

Basis for selection. Essay, interview, and extracurricular activities important. Institutional placement tests used for all programs.

2005-2006 Annual costs. Tuition/fees: $6,190. Books/supplies: $800. Personal expenses: $2,800.

Application procedures. Admission: No deadline. $25 fee, may be waived for applicants with need. Admission notification on a rolling basis. **Financial aid:** Priority date 3/1; no closing date. FAFSA, institutional form required. Applicants notified on a rolling basis; must reply within 2 week(s) of notification.

Academics. Special study options: Accelerated study, cooperative education, honors, independent study, internships. **Credit/placement by examination:** CLEP. **Support services:** Learning center, remedial instruction, tutoring.

Majors. Business: Business admin, hospitality admin, management information systems. **Health:** Health care admin. **Interdisciplinary:** Gerontology. **Public administration:** Social work. **Social sciences:** General.

Computing on campus. 100 workstations in computer center.

Student life. Freshman orientation: Available. Held the Saturday before classes start in the fall. **Activities:** Student government, student newspaper, Phi Beta Sigma, Zeta Phi Beta, Sigma Beta Delta honor society, student government association, Association for the Study of African American Life and History.

Student services. Career counseling, on-campus daycare, personal counseling.

Contact. Phone: (410) 276-0306 ext. 248 Fax: (410) 675-1811
Diana Samuels, Coordinator of Admissions, Sojourner-Douglass College, 500 North Caroline Street, Baltimore, MD 21205

Towson University

Towson, Maryland **CB member**
www.towson.edu **CB code: 5404**

- Public 4-year university
- Commuter campus in large city
- 13,969 degree-seeking undergraduates: 10% part-time, 61% women, 11% African American, 4% Asian American, 2% Hispanic American, 2% international
- 2,895 degree-seeking graduate students
- 64% of applicants admitted
- SAT or ACT with writing required
- 58% graduate within 6 years

General. Founded in 1866. Regionally accredited. **Degrees:** 2,984 bachelor's awarded; master's, doctoral offered. **ROTC:** Army, Air Force. **Location:** 1.5 miles from Baltimore. **Calendar:** Semester, extensive summer session. **Full-time faculty:** 663 total; 75% have terminal degrees, 14% minority, 50% women. **Part-time faculty:** 582 total; 27% have terminal degrees, 9% minority, 51% women. **Class size:** 33% < 20, 61% 20-39, 5% 40-49, less than 1% 50-99. **Special facilities:** Planetarium, Asian art collection, theaters, concert hall, greenhouse, herbarium, observatory, animal museum.

Freshman class profile. 11,746 applied, 7,499 admitted, 2,310 enrolled.

Mid 50% test scores			
SAT verbal:	490-580	Rank in top tenth:	24%
SAT math:	510-600	Return as sophomores:	83%
ACT:	19-26	Out-of-state:	24%
GPA 3.50 or higher:	47%	Live on campus:	71%
GPA 3.0-3.49:	47%	International:	2%
GPA 2.0-2.99:	6%	Fraternities:	1%
Rank in top quarter:	54%	Sororities:	1%

Basis for selection. High school record, test scores important; class rank, recommendations, essay considered. Interview and essay recommended. Audition required of music, dance majors. **Homeschooled:** Writing samples, 3 letters of recommendation, course-work summary required.

High school preparation. 21 units required. Required and recommended units include English 4, mathematics 3-4, social studies 3, science 3 (laboratory 2-3), foreign language 2-4 and academic electives 6.

2005-2006 Annual costs. Tuition/fees: $7,096; $16,030 out-of-state. Room/board: $7,286. Books/supplies: $800. Personal expenses: $1,500.

2005-2006 Financial aid. Need-based: Average need met was 62%. Average scholarship/grant was $4,122; average loan $2,472. 45% of total undergraduate aid awarded as scholarships/grants, 55% as loans/jobs. **Non-need-based:** Scholarships awarded for academics, alumni affiliation, art, athletics, job skills, leadership, music/drama, ROTC, state residency.

Application procedures. Admission: Priority date 12/1; deadline 2/15 (postmark date). $45 fee, may be waived for applicants with need. Application may be submitted online. Admission notification on a rolling basis beginning on or about 10/1. Must reply by May 1 or within 2 week(s) if notified thereafter. **Financial aid:** Priority date 1/31; no closing date. FAFSA required. Applicants notified on a rolling basis starting 3/21; must reply within 2 week(s) of notification.

Academics. Special study options: Combined bachelor's/graduate degree, cooperative education, cross-registration, distance learning, double major, dual enrollment of high school students, ESL, exchange student, honors, independent study, internships, liberal arts/career combination, student-designed major, study abroad, teacher certification program. 3-2 engineering with University of Maryland, College Park. **Credit/placement by examination:** AP, CLEP, IB, institutional tests. 45 credit hours maximum toward bachelor's degree. Portfolio reviews, oral exams, demonstrations or written reports/papers considered for credit. **Support services:** Learning center, remedial instruction, study skills assistance, tutoring, writing center.

Majors. Area/ethnic studies: Women's. **Biology:** General, ecology. **Business:** Accounting, business admin. **Communications:** General, journalism. **Computer sciences:** General, computer science. **Conservation:** Environmental studies. **Education:** Art, early childhood, elementary, music, physical, special. **Family/consumer sciences:** Family systems. **Foreign languages:** French, German, Spanish. **Health:** Athletic training, audiology/speech pathology, health care admin, substance abuse counseling. **History:** General. **Interdisciplinary:** Biological/physical sciences, gerontology. **Legal studies:** General. **Math:** General. **Parks/recreation:** Exercise sciences, sports admin. **Physical sciences:** Chemistry, geology, physics, planetary. **Psychology:** General. **Social sciences:** General, economics, geography, political science, sociology, urban studies. **Visual/performing arts:** Art, dance, dramatic, studio arts.

Most popular majors. Business/marketing 19%, communications/journalism 9%, education 14%, health sciences 8%, psychology 8%, social sciences 10%, visual/performing arts 7%.

Computing on campus. 1,200 workstations in dormitories, library, computer center, student center. Dormitories wired for high-speed internet access and linked to campus network. Commuter students can connect to campus network. Online course registration, online library, helpline, wireless network available.

Student life. Freshman orientation: Mandatory. **Policies:** Students play active role in university governance. **Housing:** Guaranteed on-campus for freshmen. Coed dorms, special housing for disabled, apartments, substance-free housing available. $225 deposit, deadline 5/1. Honors hall, alcohol free floors, academic emphasis floors, non-traditional age area, non-smoking floors, leadership floor, special quiet floors available. **Activities:** Bands, choral groups, dance, drama, literary magazine, music ensembles, musical theater, radio station, student government, student newspaper, symphony orchestra, TV station, black student union, Jewish student association, Circle-K, student ambassadors, international club, Newman Club, Campus Crusades, Hillel, sisterhood.

Athletics. NCAA. **Intercollegiate:** Baseball M, basketball, cheerleading, cross-country, diving, field hockey W, football (tackle) M, golf M, gymnastics W, lacrosse, soccer, softball W, swimming, tennis, track and field, volleyball W. **Intramural:** Basketball, cross-country, football (non-tackle), lacrosse, racquetball, soccer, softball, tennis, triathlon, volleyball. **Team name:** Tigers.

Student services. Adult student services, alcohol/substance abuse counseling, campus ministries, career counseling, student employment services, financial aid counseling, health services, minority student services, on-campus daycare, personal counseling, placement for graduates, veterans' counselor, women's services. **Physically disabled:** Services for visually, speech, hearing impaired.

Contact. E-mail: admissions@towson.edu
Phone: (410) 704-2113 Toll-free number: (888) 486-9766
Fax: (410) 704-3030
Louise Shulack, Director of Undergraduate Admissions, Towson University, 8000 York Road, Towson, MD 21252-0001

United States Naval Academy

Annapolis, Maryland **CB member**
www.usna.edu **CB code: 5809**

- Public 4-year military college
- Residential campus in large town
- 4,422 degree-seeking undergraduates: 18% women, 6% African American, 5% Asian American, 9% Hispanic American, 2% Native American, 1% international
- 13% of applicants admitted
- SAT or ACT with writing, application essay, interview required
- 86% graduate within 6 years; 5% enter graduate study

General. Founded in 1845. Regionally accredited. Military environment and organization under student leadership with officer supervision. Professional training at US bases and with units of fleet during summer months. Graduates receive B.S. degree with a major in one of 19 disciplines, plus commission as ensign in US Navy or second lieutenant in US Marine Corps. **Degrees:** 972 bachelor's awarded. **Location:** 30 miles from Baltimore, 35 miles from Washington, DC. **Calendar:** Semester, limited summer session. **Full-time faculty:** 528 total; 63% have terminal degrees, 20% women. **Part-time faculty:** 63 total; 19% have terminal degrees, 25% women. **Class size:** 51% < 20, 49% 20-39, less than 1% 40-49. **Special facilities:** Observatory, planetarium, satellite dish, oceanographic research vessel, weather station, towing tanks, propulsion laboratory, transsonic and hypersonic sound tunnels, museum.

Freshman class profile. 11,259 applied, 1,514 admitted, 1,227 enrolled.

Mid 50% test scores			
SAT verbal:	570-680	Rank in top tenth:	54%
SAT math:	620-700	End year in good standing:	98%
GPA 3.50 or higher:	74%	Return as sophomores:	97%
GPA 3.0-3.49:	23%	Out-of-state:	95%
GPA 2.0-2.99:	3%	Live on campus:	100%
Rank in top quarter:	81%	International:	1%

Basis for selection. Test scores, school achievement record, interview, recommendations of school officials, participation in sports, school, and community activities important. Rank in top 40% of class usually required. Successful candidate must be qualified medically, pass a physical aptitude examination, and be nominated by an official source.

High school preparation. College-preparatory program recommended. Recommended units include English 4, mathematics 4, history 2, science 2 (laboratory 2) and foreign language 2. Computer skills - familiarity with the use of personal computers, including the Windows Operating System, word processing, spreadsheets, and the Internet.

2006-2007 Annual costs. First-year students pay deposit of $2,200 for initial outfitting of uniforms and other supplies. Tuition, room and board, and medical and dental care provided by United States Government. Each midshipman receives monthly salary of about $849 to cover costs of books, supplies, uniforms, laundry, and equipment, including microcomputer. Books/supplies: $1,000.

Application procedures. Admission: Closing date 1/31 (receipt date). No application fee. Application must be submitted online. Admission notification 6/25. Admission notification on a rolling basis beginning on or about 9/1. Must reply by May 1 or within 2 week(s) if notified thereafter. Nomination essential prior to consideration for appointment. Nominating authorities include President, Vice President, Secretary of Navy, members of Congress, delegates to Congress, governors of United States Territories, and resident commissioner of Puerto Rico. Applicants for presidential appointments limited by law to sons and daughters of career military personnel, active or retired. Applicants encouraged to apply to the Academy and nominating authority by May one year prior to desired admission.

Academics. Special study options: Double major, honors, independent study. Qualified students have opportunities to begin work in senior year towards a Master's degree at local graduate schools. Selected midshipmen can also engage in research with thesis, or work towards honors in their majors. **Credit/placement by examination:** AP, CLEP, institutional tests. Midshipmen take local examinations after admission for placement. AP Exam scores also used for validation of some courses. **Support services:** Learning center, remedial instruction, study skills assistance, tutoring, writing center.

Majors. Computer sciences: General, information technology. **Engineering:** General, aerospace, electrical, marine, mechanical, ocean, systems. **English:** English lit. **History:** General. **Math:** General. **Physical sciences:** General, chemistry, oceanography, physics. **Social sciences:** Econometrics, economics, political science.

Most popular majors. Computer/information sciences 10%, engineering/engineering technologies 33%, English 8%, history 11%, physical sciences 10%, social sciences 26%.

Computing on campus. PC or laptop required. Dormitories wired for high-speed internet access and linked to campus network. Online course registration, helpline, repair service available.

Student life. Freshman orientation: Mandatory. All freshmen report in late June for approximately 6 weeks of military indoctrination. **Policies:** The Naval Academy has an Honor Concept administered by the Brigade of Midshipmen. **Housing:** Guaranteed on-campus for all undergraduates. Coed dorms, substance-free housing available. Midshipmen must live on campus for all four years. **Activities:** Bands, choral groups, drama, film society, literary magazine, music ensembles, musical theater, radio station, student newspaper, Fellowship of Christian Athletes, Black Studies Club, Midshipmen Action Group, Officers' Christian Fellowship, Foreign Affairs Conference, Women's Professional Association.

Athletics. NCAA. **Intercollegiate:** Baseball M, basketball, cross-country, diving, football (tackle) M, golf M, gymnastics M, lacrosse M, rifle, rowing (crew), sailing, soccer, squash M, swimming, tennis M, track and field, volleyball W, water polo M, wrestling M. **Intramural:** Basketball, football (non-tackle), handball, racquetball, soccer, softball, weight lifting. **Team name:** Midshipmen.

Student services. Alcohol/substance abuse counseling, campus ministries, career counseling, health services, legal services, personal counseling, placement for graduates.

Contact. E-mail: webmail@usna.edu
Phone: (410) 293-4361 Fax: (410) 293-4348
Dean of Admissions, United States Naval Academy, 117 Decatur Road, Annapolis, MD 21402-5018

University of Baltimore

Baltimore, Maryland — **CB member**
www.ubalt.edu — **CB code: 5810**

- Public upper-division university
- Commuter campus in very large city

General. Founded in 1925. Regionally accredited. **Degrees:** 480 bachelor's awarded; master's, doctoral, first professional offered. **Articulation:** Agreements with all Maryland 2-year public institutions. **ROTC:** Army. **Location:** Downtown. **Calendar:** Semester, extensive summer session. **Full-time faculty:** 159 total. **Part-time faculty:** 223 total. **Special facilities:** Graphics laboratory, business center, interactive video network.

Student profile. 2,096 degree-seeking undergraduates, 1,739 graduate students. 72% entered as juniors, 18% entered as seniors. 57% transferred from two-year, 43% transferred from four-year institutions.

Out-of-state:	1%	**25 or older:**	78%

Basis for selection. College transcript required. 2.25 minimum GPA for accounting majors and 3.0 for jurisprudence, business, forensic studies and liberal arts tracks. Credit not given for grades of 1.0 in lower level general education courses or lower level business core. Admission based on transcript evaluation. Notification on rolling basis. 30-hour residency requirement. Credit will be given for grades of 1.0 for some programs and for some courses, if cumulative GPA is 2.0 or higher. Transfer accepted as sophomores, juniors, seniors.

2005-2006 Annual costs. Tuition/fees: $6,794; $18,373 out-of-state. Books/supplies: $730.

Financial aid. Additional information: Full need met for dependent students only.

Application procedures. Admission: Priority date 7/1. $45 fee, may be waived for applicants with need. Application may be submitted online. **Financial aid:** Priority date 4/1. Scholarship application deadline, March 1. FAFSA, institutional form required.

Academics. All undergraduate students take 9 hours in an upper-level core curriculum in a general humanities-based general education. **Special study options:** Accelerated study, combined bachelor's/graduate degree, cooperative education, cross-registration, distance learning, exchange student, honors, independent study, internships, student-designed major, study abroad, weekend college. **Credit/placement by examination:** CLEP, institutional tests. 30 credit hours maximum toward bachelor's degree. **Support services:** Learning center, reduced course load, remedial instruction, study skills assistance, tutoring, writing center.

Majors. Business: General, accounting, business admin, human resources, international, management information systems, managerial economics, marketing. **Communications:** General. **Computer sciences:** General. **Health:** Health care admin. **History:** General. **Legal studies:** Prelaw. **Liberal arts:** Arts/sciences. **Protective services:** Criminal justice, forensics. **Psychology:** General. **Public administration:** Human services. **Social sciences:** Political science.

Most popular majors. Business/marketing 47%, communications/journalism 6%, health sciences 9%, legal studies 6%, liberal arts 8%, social sciences 17%.

Computing on campus. 155 workstations in library, computer center. Commuter students can connect to campus network. Helpline available.

Student life. Activities: Literary magazine, student government, student newspaper, black student association, international student association, Project Hunger, Domestic Violence Advocacy Program.

Athletics. Intramural: Badminton, basketball, golf, judo, racquetball, rowing (crew), skiing, soccer W, table tennis, tennis, volleyball.

Student services. Career counseling, student employment services, health services, personal counseling, placement for graduates, veterans' counselor. **Physically disabled:** Services for visually, speech, hearing impaired.

Contact. E-mail: admissions@ubalt.edu
Phone: (410) 837-4777 Toll-free number: (877) 277-5982
Fax: (410) 837-4793
Joan Anson, Director of Admissions, University of Baltimore, 1420 North Charles Street, Baltimore, MD 21201-5779

University of Maryland: Baltimore

Baltimore, Maryland
www.umaryland.edu — **CB code: 0527**

- Public upper-division university and health science college
- Commuter campus in very large city
- 45% of applicants admitted

General. Founded in 1807. Regionally accredited. **Degrees:** 444 bachelor's awarded; master's, doctoral, first professional offered. **Articulation:** Agreements with all Maryland community colleges. **Calendar:** 4-1-4, limited summer session. **Full-time faculty:** 504 total; 97% have terminal degrees, 19% minority, 46% women. **Part-time faculty:** 137 total; 92% have terminal degrees, 19% minority, 36% women. **Special facilities:** Dental, medical, pharmacy and nursing museums; law library; health sciences library; center for health policy and health services research; center for research on aging; center for vaccine development; biotechnology institute; center for health and homeland security.

Student profile. 846 degree-seeking undergraduates, 4,534 degree-seeking graduate students. 1,468 applied as first time-transfer students, 665 admitted, 389 enrolled. 35% transferred from two-year, 65% transferred from four-year institutions.

Women:	88%	**International:**	2%
African American:	27%	**Part-time:**	27%
Asian American:	10%	**Out-of-state:**	11%
Hispanic American:	3%	**25 or older:**	53%

Basis for selection. College transcript required. Undergraduate deadlines range from February 1 to August 15 (nursing, dental hygiene, medical technology). Transfer accepted as juniors, seniors.

2005-2006 Annual costs. Tuition/fees: $7,579; $18,649 out-of-state. Books/supplies: $1,530. Personal expenses: $1,596.

Financial aid. **Need-based:** 28% of total undergraduate aid awarded as scholarships/grants, 72% as loans/jobs. **Non-need-based:** Scholarships awarded for ROTC. **Additional information:** Maryland state deadline 3/1.

Application procedures. **Admission:** $50 fee. Application may be submitted online. **Financial aid:** FAFSA required.

Academics. **Special study options:** Distance learning, double major. **Credit/placement by examination:** AP, CLEP, institutional tests. 30 credit hours maximum toward bachelor's degree. **Support services:** Learning center, pre-admission summer program, reduced course load, tutoring, writing center.

Majors. **Health:** Dental hygiene, nursing (RN), preop/surgical nursing.

Computing on campus. 100 workstations in library, computer center, student center. Dormitories wired for high-speed internet access and linked to campus network. Commuter students can connect to campus network. Online library, helpline, wireless network available.

Student life. **Housing:** Apartments available. **Activities:** Student government, Newman Center, International Student Group, African-American student association, Community Volunteer Program.

Athletics. **Intramural:** Badminton, basketball, football (non-tackle), golf, racquetball, soccer, softball, squash, tennis, volleyball.

Student services. Alcohol/substance abuse counseling, campus ministries, career counseling, services for economically disadvantaged, student employment services, financial aid counseling, health services, minority student services, on-campus daycare, personal counseling, placement for graduates, women's services. **Physically disabled:** Services for visually, speech, hearing impaired.

Contact. E-mail: gradinfo@umaryland.edu
Phone: (410) 706-7480 Fax: (410) 706-4053
Thomas Day, Director of Records and Registration, University of Maryland: Baltimore, Office of Records and Registration, Baltimore, MD 21201-1575

University of Maryland: Baltimore County

Baltimore, Maryland — **CB member**
www.umbc.edu — **CB code: 5835**

- Public 4-year university
- Residential campus in large city
- 9,244 degree-seeking undergraduates: 14% part-time, 46% women, 14% African American, 20% Asian American, 4% Hispanic American, 4% international
- 1,985 degree-seeking graduate students
- 71% of applicants admitted
- SAT or ACT (ACT writing optional), application essay required
- 55% graduate within 6 years

General. Founded in 1963. Regionally accredited. **Degrees:** 1,819 bachelor's awarded; master's, doctoral offered. **ROTC:** Army. **Location:** 5 miles from Baltimore, 35 miles from Washington, DC. **Calendar:** 4-1-4, extensive summer session. **Full-time faculty:** 458 total; 90% have terminal degrees, 15% minority, 38% women. **Part-time faculty:** 295 total; 31% have terminal degrees, 16% minority, 43% women. **Class size:** 43% < 20, 37% 20-39, 7% 40-49, 9% 50-99, 4% >100. **Special facilities:** Research telescope, greenhouse, research spectrometers, nuclear magnetic resonance machines, electron microscope facility, computer art laboratory, healthcare informatics laboratory, centers for imaging research, earth systems technology, environmental science, telecommunications research, medical institute, institutes for biotechnology, global electronic commerce, policy analysis and research.

Freshman class profile. 5,229 applied, 3,735 admitted, 1,429 enrolled.

Mid 50% test scores		**Rank in top quarter:**	59%
SAT verbal:	540-650	**Rank in top tenth:**	30%
SAT math:	570-670	**Return as sophomores:**	81%
ACT:	23-27	**Out-of-state:**	11%
GPA 3.50 or higher:	53%	**Live on campus:**	71%
GPA 3.0-3.49:	31%	**International:**	2%
GPA 2.0-2.99:	16%		

Basis for selection. High school record, test scores important. Audition required for music, dance, theater majors. Portfolio required for visual arts majors.

High school preparation. 22 units required; 23 recommended. Required and recommended units include English 4, mathematics 3-4, social studies 2, history 2, science 3 (laboratory 2), foreign language 3 and academic electives 4. Algebra I and II, and geometry required.

2005-2006 Annual costs. Tuition/fees: $8,520; $16,596 out-of-state. Room/board: $8,090.

2004-2005 Financial aid. **Need-based:** 925 full-time freshmen applied for aid; 630 were judged to have need; 630 of these received aid. Average need met was 77%. Average scholarship/grant was $4,761; average loan $3,060. 51% of total undergraduate aid awarded as scholarships/grants, 49% as loans/jobs. **Non-need-based:** Awarded to 3,587 full-time undergraduates, including 992 freshmen. Scholarships awarded for academics, art, athletics, music/drama, ROTC.

Application procedures. **Admission:** Priority date 11/1; deadline 2/1 (postmark date). $50 fee, may be waived for applicants with need. Application may be submitted online. Admission notification on a rolling basis beginning on or about 2/1. Must reply by May 1 or within 2 week(s) if notified thereafter. **Financial aid:** Priority date 2/15; no closing date. FAFSA required. Applicants notified on a rolling basis starting 3/30; must reply within 2 week(s) of notification.

Academics. **Special study options:** Combined bachelor's/graduate degree, cooperative education, cross-registration, distance learning, double major, dual enrollment of high school students, ESL, exchange student, honors, independent study, internships, liberal arts/career combination, semester at sea, student-designed major, study abroad, teacher certification program. **Credit/placement by examination:** AP, CLEP, IB, institutional tests. 60 credit hours maximum toward bachelor's degree. **Support services:** Learning center, remedial instruction, study skills assistance, tutoring, writing center.

Honors college/program. Minimum 1300 SAT (exclusive of Writing) and 3.5 GPA required. Approximately 140 students accepted each year, with average SAT of 1300 (exclusive of Writing) and 3.81 GPA. Each semester 40-50 courses offered along with non-curricular activities.

Majors. **Area/ethnic studies:** African-American, American. **Biology:** General, Biochemistry/biophysics and molecular biology, bioinformatics. **Computer sciences:** General, information systems. **Conservation:** Environmental science, environmental studies. **Engineering:** General, chemical, computer, mechanical. **English:** English lit. **Foreign languages:** General, linguistics. **Health:** Dental hygiene, EMT paramedic, health services, predentistry, premedicine, prenursing, prepharmacy, preveterinary, staff services technology. **History:** General. **Interdisciplinary:** Ancient studies. **Legal studies:** Prelaw. **Math:** General, statistics. **Philosophy/religion:** Philosophy. **Physical sciences:** Chemistry, physics. **Psychology:** General. **Public administration:** Social work. **Social sciences:** Anthropology, economics, geography, political science, sociology. **Visual/performing arts:** General, acting, dance, dramatic.

Most popular majors. Biology 11%, communication technologies 24%, engineering/engineering technologies 6%, psychology 11%, social sciences 15%, visual/performing arts 8%.

Computing on campus. 1,100 workstations in dormitories, library, computer center, student center. Dormitories wired for high-speed internet access and linked to campus network. Commuter students can connect to campus network. Online course registration, online library, helpline, repair service, student web hosting, wireless network available.

Student life. **Freshman orientation:** Mandatory, $125 fee. Held June and July. Separate program for honors college students. **Policies:** Freshmen permitted cars on campus. **Housing:** Guaranteed on-campus for freshmen. Coed dorms, special housing for disabled, apartments, substance-free housing available. $100 nonrefundable deposit, deadline 5/1. Living-learning communities. **Activities:** Bands, choral groups, dance, drama, film society, literary magazine, music ensembles, radio station, student government, student newspaper, symphony orchestra, black student union, Chinese student association, Jewish student association, Korean club, international student association, gay and lesbian organization, Progressive Action Committee, Christian Fellowship, women's union, Amnesty International.

Athletics. NCAA. **Intercollegiate:** Baseball M, basketball, cross-country, diving, field hockey W, lacrosse, soccer, softball W, swimming, tennis, track and field, volleyball W. **Intramural:** Basketball, cross-country, field hockey, football (non-tackle), golf, handball, soccer, softball, tennis, track and field, volleyball, weight lifting. **Team name:** Retrievers.

Student services. Adult student services, alcohol/substance abuse counseling, campus ministries, career counseling, services for economically disadvantaged, student employment services, financial aid counseling, health services, minority student services, on-campus daycare, personal counseling, placement for graduates, veterans' counselor, women's services. **Physically disabled:** Services for visually, hearing impaired.

Contact. E-mail: admissions@umbc.edu
Phone: (410) 455-2291 Toll-free number: (800) 862-2482
Fax: (410) 455-1094
Yvette Mozie-Ross, Assistant Provost for Enrollment Management, University of Maryland: Baltimore County, 1000 Hilltop Circle, Baltimore, MD 21250

University of Maryland: College Park

College Park, Maryland — **CB member**
www.maryland.edu — **CB code: 5814**

- Public 4-year university
- Commuter campus in large town
- 24,876 degree-seeking undergraduates: 7% part-time, 49% women, 13% African American, 14% Asian American, 6% Hispanic American, 2% international
- 9,315 degree-seeking graduate students
- 49% of applicants admitted
- SAT or ACT with writing, application essay required
- 76% graduate within 6 years

General. Founded in 1856. Regionally accredited. Research and internship opportunities at Smithsonian Institution, National Institutes for Health, NASA, US Capitol, White House, FBI, Department of Agriculture, other federal agencies. **Degrees:** 6,263 bachelor's awarded; master's, doctoral, first professional offered. **ROTC:** Army, Navy, Air Force. **Location:** 30 miles from Baltimore, 3 miles from Washington, DC. **Calendar:** Semester, extensive summer session. **Full-time faculty:** 1,508 total; 94% have terminal degrees, 17% minority, 30% women. **Part-time faculty:** 562 total; 59% have terminal degrees, 12% minority, 42% women. **Class size:** 34% < 20, 43% 20-39, 8% 40-49, 7% 50-99, 7% >100. **Special facilities:** National Archives II, astronomy observatory, engineering wind tunnel, space systems lab, nuclear reactor, performing arts center, center for young children, agricultural biotechnology, superconductivity research, institute for systems research, fire and rescue institute.

Freshman class profile. 22,428 applied, 11,002 admitted, 4,211 enrolled.

Mid 50% test scores		**Rank in top tenth:**	53%
SAT verbal:	580-670	**Return as sophomores:**	93%
SAT math:	600-700	**Out-of-state:**	34%
GPA 3.50 or higher:	80%	**Live on campus:**	92%
GPA 3.0-3.49:	16%	**International:**	1%
GPA 2.0-2.99:	4%	**Fraternities:**	13%
Rank in top quarter:	87%	**Sororities:**	14%

Basis for selection. Academic record, rigor of the high school academic program, standardized admission test scores, class rank (if available), essay, extracurricular activities, counselor recommendation, and other letters of recommendation reviewed. Applications with test scores submitted after 2/01 will be considered based on space-availability. Audition required of music majors. Portfolio recommended for architecture majors. **Homeschooled:** Statement describing homeschool structure and mission, transcript of courses and grades required. Transcript should include description of course work, books used, method of evaluation and actual grades or evaluation. Letter of recommendation required and must be from academic professional.

High school preparation. 17 units required; 18 recommended. Required and recommended units include English 4, mathematics 3-4, social studies 3, science 3 (laboratory 2) and foreign language 2. Algebra I and II, plane geometry required. Social studies units should include history.

2005-2006 Annual costs. Tuition/fees: $7,821; $20,145 out-of-state. Room/board: $8,075. Books/supplies: $909. Personal expenses: $2,022.

2004-2005 Financial aid. Need-based: 3,412 full-time freshmen applied for aid; 1,822 were judged to have need; 1,651 of these received aid. Average need met was 69%. Average scholarship/grant was $5,885; average loan $2,390. 39% of total undergraduate aid awarded as scholarships/grants, 61% as loans/jobs. **Non-need-based:** Awarded to 6,960 full-time undergraduates, including 1,909 freshmen. Scholarships awarded for academics, art, athletics, music/drama. **Additional information:** Prepaid tuition plans available through state.

Application procedures. Admission: Priority date 12/1; deadline 1/20 (receipt date). $55 fee, may be waived for applicants with need. Application may be submitted online. Admission notification 4/1. Must reply by May 1 or within 4 week(s) if notified thereafter. **Financial aid:** Priority date 2/15; no closing date. FAFSA required. Applicants notified on a rolling basis starting 4/1.

Academics. Special study options: Accelerated study, combined bachelor's/graduate degree, cooperative education, cross-registration, distance learning, double major, dual enrollment of high school students, ESL, exchange student, external degree, honors, independent study, internships, semester at sea, student-designed major, study abroad, teacher certification program. Living/learning programs: Gemstone program, Honors Humanities, First Year Learning Communities, CIVICUS program, College Park Scholars, Beyond the Classroom, Global Communities, Language House, Jiminez-Porter Writers House, University Honors (the Honors program), Hinman CEOs. **Credit/placement by examination:** AP, CLEP, IB, SAT, ACT, institutional tests. 60 credit hours maximum toward bachelor's degree. **Support services:** Learning center, pre-admission summer program, reduced course load, remedial instruction, study skills assistance, tutoring, writing center.

Majors. Agriculture: General, animal sciences, economics, food science. **Architecture:** Architecture, landscape. **Area/ethnic studies:** African-American, American, Russian/Slavic, women's. **Biology:** General, biochemistry, ecology, microbiology. **Business:** General, accounting, finance, logistics, management science, marketing. **Communications:** General, journalism. **Computer sciences:** General, information systems. **Conservation:** General. **Education:** General, art, elementary, English, foreign languages, health, kindergarten/preschool, mathematics, music, physical, science, social studies, special. **Engineering:** General, aerospace, agricultural, chemical, civil, computer, electrical, materials, mechanical. **English:** English lit. **Family/consumer sciences:** General, family/community services, food/nutrition. **Foreign languages:** Chinese, classics, French, German, Italian, Japanese, linguistics, Romance, Russian, Spanish. **Health:** Communication disorders, dietetics. **History:** General. **Legal studies:** Prelaw. **Math:** General. **Parks/recreation:** Exercise sciences. **Philosophy/religion:** Judaic, philosophy. **Physical sciences:** General, astronomy, chemistry, geology, physics. **Psychology:** General. **Social sciences:** Anthropology, criminology, economics, geography, political science, sociology. **Visual/performing arts:** Art history/conservation, dance, dramatic, music performance, studio arts.

Most popular majors. Biology 8%, business/marketing 15%, communications/journalism 7%, engineering/engineering technologies 10%, social sciences 22%.

Computing on campus. 1,431 workstations in dormitories, library, computer center, student center. Dormitories wired for high-speed internet access and linked to campus network. Commuter students can connect to campus network. Online course registration, online library, helpline, student web hosting, wireless network available.

Student life. Freshman orientation: Mandatory, $145 fee. Preregistration for classes offered. 2-day program. **Policies:** Freshmen permitted cars on campus. **Housing:** Guaranteed on-campus for freshmen. Coed dorms, single-sex dorms, special housing for disabled, apartments, fraternity/sorority housing, substance-free housing available. **Activities:** Bands, choral groups, dance, drama, film society, literary magazine, music ensembles, musical theater, opera, radio station, student government, student newspaper, symphony orchestra, TV station, Black Student Union, Asian American Student Union, Latino Student Union, Native American Student Union, MaryPIRG, international student council, Alpha Phi Omega, Habitat for Humanity.

Athletics. NCAA. **Intercollegiate:** Baseball M, basketball, cheerleading M, cross-country, equestrian, field hockey W, football (tackle) M, golf, gymnastics W, lacrosse, soccer, softball W, swimming, tennis, track and field, volleyball W, water polo W, wrestling M. **Intramural:** Badminton, basketball, football (non-tackle), golf, ice hockey W, racquetball, soccer, softball, table tennis, tennis, track and field, volleyball, wrestling M. **Team name:** Terrapins.

Student services. Adult student services, alcohol/substance abuse counseling, campus ministries, career counseling, services for economically disadvantaged, student employment services, financial aid counseling, health services, legal services, minority student services, on-campus daycare, personal counseling, placement for graduates, veterans' counselor, women's services. **Physically disabled:** Services for visually, speech, hearing impaired.

Contact. E-mail: um-admit@uga.umd.edu
Phone: (301) 314-8385 Toll-free number: (800) 422-5867
Fax: (301) 314-9693
Barbara Gill, Director of Undergraduate Admissions, University of Maryland: College Park, Mitchell Building, College Park, MD 20742-5235

University of Maryland: Eastern Shore

Princess Anne, Maryland — **CB member**
www.umes.edu — **CB code: 5400**

- Public 4-year university
- Residential campus in rural community

- 3,448 degree-seeking undergraduates: 8% part-time, 61% women, 81% African American, 1% Asian American, 1% Hispanic American, 3% international
- 422 degree-seeking graduate students
- 66% of applicants admitted
- SAT or ACT (ACT writing optional), application essay required
- 41% graduate within 6 years

General. Founded in 1886. Regionally accredited. **Degrees:** 389 bachelor's awarded; master's, doctoral offered. **Location:** 12 miles from Salisbury. **Calendar:** Semester, extensive summer session. **Full-time faculty:** 169 total; 62% have terminal degrees, 60% minority, 43% women. **Part-time faculty:** 98 total; 15% have terminal degrees, 39% minority, 57% women. **Class size:** 45% < 20, 45% 20-39, 6% 40-49, 4% 50-99, less than 1% >100. **Special facilities:** Arts and technology center, performing arts center, hydroponic greenhouse, education center.

Freshman class profile. 2,826 applied, 1,871 admitted, 1,021 enrolled.

Mid 50% test scores			
SAT verbal:	370-460	Return as sophomores:	64%
SAT math:	360-460	Out-of-state:	24%
ACT:	14-18	Live on campus:	60%
End year in good standing:	59%	International:	2%

Basis for selection. School record, class rank, and test scores most important. Interview recommended for honors program and physical therapy applicants. Audition required for music majors.

High school preparation. 20 units required. Required units include English 4, mathematics 3, social studies 3, science 2, foreign language 2 and academic electives 6.

2005-2006 Annual costs. Tuition/fees: $5,808; $11,964 out-of-state. Room/board: $6,010. Books/supplies: $1,400. Personal expenses: $1,400.

2004-2005 Financial aid. Need-based: 762 full-time freshmen applied for aid; 625 were judged to have need; 625 of these received aid. Average need met was 73%. Average scholarship/grant was $6,225; average loan $2,600. 51% of total undergraduate aid awarded as scholarships/grants, 49% as loans/jobs. **Non-need-based:** Awarded to 647 full-time undergraduates, including 134 freshmen. Scholarships awarded for academics, alumni affiliation, art, athletics, leadership, music/drama, ROTC, state residency.

Application procedures. Admission: Priority date 3/1; deadline 7/15 (postmark date). $25 fee, may be waived for applicants with need. Application may be submitted online. Admission notification on a rolling basis. **Financial aid:** Priority date 3/1, closing date 4/1. FAFSA, institutional form required. Applicants notified on a rolling basis starting 4/1.

Academics. Special study options: Accelerated study, cooperative education, cross-registration, distance learning, double major, dual enrollment of high school students, exchange student, honors, independent study, internships, liberal arts/career combination, New York semester, study abroad, teacher certification program. **Credit/placement by examination:** AP, CLEP, IB, institutional tests. 60 credit hours maximum toward bachelor's degree. **Support services:** Learning center, pre-admission summer program, reduced course load, remedial instruction, study skills assistance, tutoring, writing center.

Majors. Agriculture: General, business, poultry. **Architecture:** Architecture. **Area/ethnic studies:** African-American. **Biology:** General, ecology. **Business:** General, accounting, business admin, hotel/motel admin. **Communications:** General. **Computer sciences:** General. **Conservation:** Forestry. **Construction:** Maintenance. **Education:** General, agricultural, art, business, elementary, English, family/consumer sciences, health, mathematics, music, physical, science, social studies, special, technology/industrial arts. **Engineering:** General. **Engineering technology:** General, civil. **English:** English lit. **Family/consumer sciences:** General. **Health:** Clinical lab assistant, clinical lab science, clinical lab technology, dental hygiene, medical radiologic technology/radiation therapy, nursing (RN), physician assistant, predentistry, premedicine, prepharmacy, preveterinary. **History:** General. **Legal studies:** Prelaw. **Liberal arts:** Arts/sciences. **Math:** General. **Parks/recreation:** General, exercise sciences. **Physical sciences:** Chemistry. **Protective services:** Police science. **Public administration:** Social work. **Social sciences:** Sociology. **Transportation:** Aviation. **Visual/performing arts:** Commercial/advertising art.

Most popular majors. Biology 10%, business/marketing 21%, family/consumer sciences 10%, health sciences 7%, interdisciplinary studies 7%, security/protective services 12%, social sciences 9%.

Computing on campus. 739 workstations in dormitories, library, computer center. Dormitories linked to campus network. Commuter students can connect to campus network. Online library, helpline available.

Student life. Freshman orientation: Mandatory, $100 fee. Preregistration for classes offered. 2 day program in the Fall. **Policies:** Freshmen permitted cars on campus. **Housing:** Coed dorms, single-sex dorms, apartments, substance-free housing available. $300 fully refundable deposit, deadline 5/1. **Activities:** Bands, choral groups, dance, drama, music ensembles, radio station, student government, student newspaper, ecumenical campus ministry, NAACP, Students for Progressive Action, Phenomenal Women, Rotaract club, College Democrats of America, Students in Free Enterprise, Caribbean international club, For Sisters Only, National Student Business League.

Athletics. NCAA. **Intercollegiate:** Baseball M, basketball, bowling W, cross-country, golf M, softball W, tennis, track and field, volleyball W. **Intramural:** Basketball, bowling, soccer, softball W, swimming, table tennis, volleyball. **Team name:** Hawks.

Student services. Adult student services, career counseling, student employment services, financial aid counseling, health services, on-campus daycare, personal counseling, placement for graduates, veterans' counselor. **Physically disabled:** Services for speech, hearing impaired.

Contact. E-mail: umesadmissions@umes.edu
Phone: (410) 651-6410 Fax: (410) 651-7922
Edwina Morse, Director of Admissions and Recruitment, University of Maryland: Eastern Shore, Bird Hall, Princess Anne, MD 21853

University of Maryland: University College

Adelphi, Maryland
www.umuc.edu **CB code: 0551**

- Public 4-year university
- Commuter campus in large town
- 17,749 degree-seeking undergraduates: 85% part-time, 60% women, 33% African American, 5% Asian American, 5% Hispanic American, 1% Native American, 1% international
- 7,972 degree-seeking graduate students

General. Founded in 1947. Regionally accredited. Courses held at over 20 locations throughout Maryland, Virginia and Washington, D.C. Associate degree programs available only to active military personnel. Offers BA/BS program with 12 other universities through National University Degree Consortium. Courses offered at 100 sites in Europe and 60 sites in Asia. **Degrees:** 2,677 bachelor's, 107 associate awarded; master's, doctoral offered. **Location:** 9 miles from Washington, DC. **Calendar:** Semester, extensive summer session. **Full-time faculty:** 221 total; 63% have terminal degrees, 14% minority, 46% women. **Part-time faculty:** 1,172 total; 66% have terminal degrees, 21% minority, 40% women. **Class size:** 51% < 20, 46% 20-39, 4% 40-49.

Freshman class profile. 1,599 applied, 1,599 admitted, 974 enrolled.

Basis for selection. Open admission.

2005-2006 Annual costs. Tuition/fees: $5,670; $10,302 out-of-state.

2004-2005 Financial aid. Need-based: 49 full-time freshmen applied for aid; 48 were judged to have need; 33 of these received aid. Average need met was 18%. Average scholarship/grant was $1,639; average loan $1,284. **Non-need-based:** Scholarships awarded for academics, leadership.

Application procedures. Admission: No deadline. $30 fee. Application may be submitted online. Admission notification on a rolling basis. **Financial aid:** Priority date 6/1; no closing date. FAFSA, institutional form required. Applicants notified on a rolling basis starting 5/1; must reply within 2 week(s) of notification.

Academics. Degree programs offered primarily for adults attending part-time. No traditional freshman class. **Special study options:** Accelerated study, cooperative education, cross-registration, distance learning, double major, dual enrollment of high school students, external degree, student-designed major, teacher certification program, weekend college. **Credit/placement by examination:** AP, CLEP, IB, institutional tests. 30 credit hours maximum toward associate degree, 60 toward bachelor's. **Support services:** Tutoring, writing center.

Majors. Area/ethnic studies: Asian. **Business:** Accounting, business admin, human resources, marketing. **Communications:** General. **Computer sciences:** General, computer science, information systems. **Conservation:** General. **History:** General. **Liberal arts:** Arts/sciences. **Psychology:** General. **Social sciences:** General, criminology.

Most popular majors. Business/marketing 29%, computer/information sciences 25%, interdisciplinary studies 26%.

Computing on campus. Commuter students can connect to campus network. Online course registration, online library, helpline, student web hosting, wireless network available.

Student life. Freshman orientation: Available.

Student services. Adult student services, career counseling, veterans' counselor. **Physically disabled:** Services for visually, hearing impaired.

Contact. E-mail: umucinfo@umuc.edu
Phone: (301) 985-7000 Toll-free number: (800) 888-8682
Fax: (301) 985-7364
Jessica Sadaka, Director of Admissions, University of Maryland: University College, 3501 University Boulevard East, Adelphi, MD 20783

Villa Julie College

Stevenson, Maryland — **CB member**
www.vjc.edu — **CB code: 5856**

- Private 4-year liberal arts college
- Commuter campus in very large city
- 2,764 degree-seeking undergraduates: 17% part-time, 71% women, 15% African American, 3% Asian American, 1% Hispanic American
- 149 degree-seeking graduate students
- 70% of applicants admitted
- SAT or ACT, application essay required
- 65% graduate within 6 years; 11% enter graduate study

General. Founded in 1947. Regionally accredited. **Degrees:** 488 bachelor's, 10 associate awarded; master's offered. **ROTC:** Army. **Location:** 8 miles from Baltimore. **Calendar:** Semester, limited summer session. **Full-time faculty:** 93 total; 67% have terminal degrees, 12% minority, 63% women. **Part-time faculty:** 256 total; 9% minority, 53% women. **Class size:** 64% < 20, 36% 20-39, less than 1% 40-49.

Freshman class profile. 2,166 applied, 1,509 admitted, 542 enrolled.

Mid 50% test scores		Rank in top quarter:	42%
SAT verbal:	450-560	Rank in top tenth:	17%
SAT math:	450-560	Return as sophomores:	79%
GPA 3.50 or higher:	26%	Out-of-state:	5%
GPA 3.0-3.49:	38%	Live on campus:	58%
GPA 2.0-2.99:	36%		

Basis for selection. High school record and test scores most important. Optional interview, recommendations, essay, extracurricular activities also important. Interviews are recommended but not required.

High school preparation. College-preparatory program recommended. 17 units required. Required and recommended units include English 4, mathematics 3, social studies 2, history 1, science 3 (laboratory 2), foreign language 2 and academic electives 4.

2005-2006 Annual costs. Tuition/fees: $15,674. Room only: $6,550. Books/supplies: $1,000. Personal expenses: $200.

2004-2005 Financial aid. Need-based: 436 full-time freshmen applied for aid; 347 were judged to have need; 343 of these received aid. Average need met was 68%. Average scholarship/grant was $7,806; average loan $2,420. 66% of total undergraduate aid awarded as scholarships/grants, 34% as loans/jobs. **Non-need-based:** Awarded to 1,240 full-time undergraduates, including 399 freshmen. Scholarships awarded for academics, art, leadership, music/drama, ROTC. **Additional information:** Cooperative Education Program allows students to work in their field of study with area corporations.

Application procedures. Admission: Priority date 3/1; no deadline. $25 fee, may be waived for applicants with need. Application may be submitted online. Admission notification on a rolling basis beginning on or about 12/1. Must reply by May 1 or within 2 week(s) if notified thereafter. **Financial aid:** Priority date 2/15; no closing date. FAFSA required. Applicants notified on a rolling basis starting 3/15; must reply by 5/1 or within 2 week(s) of notification.

Academics. Advanced technology programs, forensic science program and forensic studies programs offered. Cooperative education program available to third- and fourth-year students. Career Architecture, a program for personal and professional development, is integrated into all programs. **Special study options:** Accelerated study, combined bachelor's/graduate degree, cooperative education, distance learning, double major, dual enrollment of high school students, honors, independent study, internships, liberal arts/career combination, student-designed major, study abroad, teacher certification program, Washington semester, weekend college. **Credit/placement by examination:** AP, CLEP, IB, institutional tests. 15 credit hours maximum toward associate degree, 30 toward bachelor's. **Support services:** Learning center, pre-admission summer program, reduced course load, remedial instruction, study skills assistance, tutoring, writing center.

Majors. Biology: General. **Business:** Accounting, business admin, communications. **Communications technology:** General. **Computer sciences:** General, information systems. **Education:** Early childhood, elementary. **Family/consumer sciences:** Family/community services. **Health:** Predentistry, premedicine, prepharmacy, preveterinary. **History:** Public archives. **Interdisciplinary:** Biological/physical sciences. **Legal studies:** Paralegal, prelaw. **Liberal arts:** Arts/sciences. **Physical sciences:** Chemistry. **Psychology:** General. **Science technology:** Biological. **Visual/performing arts:** Cinematography, design.

Computing on campus. 550 workstations in library, computer center, student center. Dormitories wired for high-speed internet access and linked to campus network. Commuter students can connect to campus network. Online course registration, online library, helpline, repair service, wireless network available.

Student life. Freshman orientation: Mandatory. Preregistration for classes offered. Full-day program, conducted by major, normally held during third week of June. Freshmen also attend second orientation in August, prior to start of fall semester. **Policies:** Freshmen permitted cars on campus. **Housing:** Apartments, substance-free housing available. $200 deposit, deadline 5/1. **Activities:** Jazz band, choral groups, dance, drama, literary magazine, music ensembles, student government, student newspaper, symphony orchestra, Black Student Union, Service Corps, Campus Crusade for Christ, Extreme Acts, Reformed University Fellowship, Angus Dei.

Athletics. NCAA. **Intercollegiate:** Baseball M, basketball, cheerleading, cross-country, field hockey W, golf, lacrosse, soccer, softball W, tennis, track and field, volleyball. **Intramural:** Badminton, basketball, fencing, football (tackle) M, sailing, skiing, soccer, table tennis, tennis, track and field, volleyball. **Team name:** Mustangs.

Student services. Adult student services, alcohol/substance abuse counseling, career counseling, student employment services, financial aid counseling, health services, personal counseling, placement for graduates, veterans' counselor.

Contact. E-mail: admissions@vjc.edu
Phone: (410) 486-7001 Toll-free number: (877) 468-6852
Fax: (443) 352-4440
Mark Hergan, Vice President for Enrollment Management, Villa Julie College, 1525 Greenspring Valley Road, Stevenson, MD 21153-0641

Washington Bible College

Lanham, Maryland
www.bible.edu — **CB code: 5884**

- Private 4-year Bible and seminary college affiliated with nondenominational tradition
- Commuter campus in large town
- 340 degree-seeking undergraduates
- 67% of applicants admitted
- SAT or ACT (ACT writing optional), application essay required

General. Founded in 1938. Accredited by ABHE. Northern branch in Randallstown. **Degrees:** 37 bachelor's, 2 associate awarded; master's offered. **Location:** 10 miles from Washington, DC. **Calendar:** Semester, limited summer session. **Full-time faculty:** 24 total. **Part-time faculty:** 18 total.

Freshman class profile. 127 applied, 85 admitted, 70 enrolled.

Mid 50% test scores		Out-of-state:	31%
SAT verbal:	420-580	Live on campus:	68%
SAT math:	410-550		

Basis for selection. Student's spiritual qualifications most important, followed by academic achievement, test scores, essay, recommendations. 2 references required. Interview recommended. Audition required of music majors.

High school preparation. 15 units recommended. Recommended units include English 4, mathematics 2, social studies 2, science 2 and academic electives 5. Typing recommended.

2006-2007 Annual costs. Tuition/fees (projected): $10,900. Room/board: $5,670. Books/supplies: $500. Personal expenses: $1,300.

2004-2005 Financial aid. **Need-based:** 52% of total undergraduate aid awarded as scholarships/grants, 48% as loans/jobs. **Non-need-based:** Scholarships awarded for academics, leadership.

Application procedures. **Admission:** Closing date 8/1 (receipt date). $25 fee, may be waived for applicants with need. Application may be submitted online. Admission notification on a rolling basis. Campus visit suggested. Deadline for housing deposit 30 days after acceptance. **Financial aid:** Priority date 3/1, closing date 6/1. FAFSA, institutional form required. Applicants notified on a rolling basis starting 7/1; must reply within 2 week(s) of notification.

Academics. All students major in Bible; other areas may be studied for concentrations. **Special study options:** Double major, ESL, independent study, internships, study abroad, teacher certification program. **Credit/placement by examination:** AP, CLEP. 15 credit hours maximum toward bachelor's degree. **Support services:** Reduced course load, tutoring, writing center.

Majors. **Education:** Elementary, music. **Theology:** Bible, pastoral counseling, religious ed, sacred music, theology, youth ministry. **Visual/performing arts:** Music performance, piano/organ, voice/opera.

Computing on campus. 10 workstations in library, student center. Dormitories wired for high-speed internet access and linked to campus network. Commuter students can connect to campus network. Online library, helpline, wireless network available.

Student life. **Freshman orientation:** Mandatory, $100 fee. 2-day spring and summer programs. **Policies:** Religious observance required. Freshmen permitted cars on campus. **Housing:** Guaranteed on-campus for freshmen. Single-sex dorms, apartments, substance-free housing available. $100 deposit. **Activities:** Choral groups, drama, music ensembles, student government, student newspaper, Student Missions Fellowship, Fellowship of Christian Athletes.

Athletics. NCCAA. **Intercollegiate:** Basketball, soccer M, volleyball W. **Intramural:** Basketball M, cheerleading M, football (tackle) M, racquetball, soccer M, table tennis, volleyball, weight lifting. **Team name:** Cougars.

Student services. Career counseling, student employment services, financial aid counseling, health services, personal counseling, placement for graduates, veterans' counselor.

Contact. E-mail: admissions@bible.edu
Phone: (301) 552-1400 ext. 1212 Toll-free number: (877) 793-7227 ext. 1212 Fax: (301) 552-2775
Mark Johnson, Director of Admissions, Washington Bible College, 6511 Princess Garden Parkway, Lanham, MD 20706-3599

Washington College
Chestertown, Maryland
www.washcoll.edu
CB member
CB code: 5888

- Private 4-year liberal arts college
- Residential campus in small town
- 1,292 degree-seeking undergraduates: 61% women, 4% African American, 1% Asian American, 1% Hispanic American, 3% international
- 71 degree-seeking graduate students
- 59% of applicants admitted
- SAT or ACT (ACT writing recommended), application essay required
- 68% graduate within 6 years

General. Founded in 1782. Regionally accredited. **Degrees:** 280 bachelor's awarded; master's offered. **Location:** 70 miles from Baltimore, 75 miles from Washington, DC. **Calendar:** Semester, limited summer session. **Full-time faculty:** 98 total. **Part-time faculty:** 51 total. **Class size:** 69% < 20, 28% 20-39, 2% 40-49, 1% 50-99. **Special facilities:** Center for the Study of the American Experience, center for environment and society.

Freshman class profile. 2,224 applied, 1,312 admitted, 343 enrolled.

Mid 50% test scores		**Rank in top tenth:**	30%
SAT verbal:	530-630	**Return as sophomores:**	84%
SAT math:	520-620	**Out-of-state:**	56%
ACT:	22-28	**Live on campus:**	100%
Rank in top quarter:	59%	**International:**	3%

Basis for selection. High school program and grades, class rank, test scores, recommendations important, extracurricular activities considered. Interview recommended.

High school preparation. 16 units required; 20 recommended. Required and recommended units include English 4, mathematics 3-4, social studies 3-4, science 3-4 (laboratory 2-3) and foreign language 2-4.

2005-2006 Annual costs. Tuition/fees: $28,790. Room/board: $6,200. Books/supplies: $1,500. Personal expenses: $800.

2004-2005 Financial aid. **Need-based:** 77% of total undergraduate aid awarded as scholarships/grants, 23% as loans/jobs. **Non-need-based:** Scholarships awarded for academics.

Application procedures. **Admission:** Priority date 2/15; deadline 3/1 (postmark date). $40 fee, may be waived for applicants with need. Application may be submitted online. Admission notification on a rolling basis beginning on or about 1/15. Must reply by May 1 or within 2 week(s) if notified thereafter. Applicants applying after February 15 and no later than May 30 may be wait-listed. **Financial aid:** Closing date 2/15. FAFSA, institutional form required. Applicants notified on a rolling basis starting 3/1; must reply by 5/1.

Academics. **Special study options:** Combined bachelor's/graduate degree, double major, ESL, exchange student, independent study, internships, liberal arts/career combination, student-designed major, study abroad, teacher certification program, Washington semester. **Credit/placement by examination:** AP, CLEP, IB, institutional tests. **Support services:** Learning center, reduced course load, study skills assistance, tutoring, writing center.

Majors. **Area/ethnic studies:** African, American. **Biology:** General. **Business:** General. **Computer sciences:** Computer science. **Foreign languages:** General, French, German, Spanish. **History:** General. **Interdisciplinary:** Biological/physical sciences, math/computer science, neuroscience. **Liberal arts:** Arts/sciences. **Philosophy/religion:** Philosophy. **Physical sciences:** Chemistry, physics. **Psychology:** General. **Social sciences:** Anthropology, economics, international relations, political science, sociology. **Visual/performing arts:** Art, dramatic.

Most popular majors. Biology 9%, business/marketing 13%, English 10%, natural resources/environmental science 7%, psychology 10%, social sciences 32%.

Computing on campus. 200 workstations in dormitories, library, computer center, student center. Dormitories wired for high-speed internet access and linked to campus network. Commuter students can connect to campus network. Online course registration, online library, helpline, repair service, student web hosting, wireless network available.

Student life. **Freshman orientation:** Mandatory. Preregistration for classes offered. **Policies:** Freshmen permitted cars on campus. **Housing:** Guaranteed on-campus for freshmen. Coed dorms, single-sex dorms, special housing for disabled, fraternity/sorority housing available. $200 deposit. Creative arts dorm, special interest housing for writers, language majors, international studies majors, science/math majors, community service and leadership available. **Activities:** Concert band, choral groups, dance, drama, literary magazine, music ensembles, student government, student newspaper, College Republicans, Christian Fellowship, Amnesty International, International Relations Club, Hillel, Black Student Alliance, Cleopatra's Daughters, College Democrats, Best Buddies, EROS, Newman Club, Canterbury Club.

Athletics. NCAA. **Intercollegiate:** Baseball M, basketball, equestrian, field hockey W, lacrosse, rowing (crew), rugby, sailing, soccer, softball, swimming, table tennis, tennis, volleyball W. **Intramural:** Basketball, equestrian, fencing, golf M, ice hockey M, racquetball, rugby, sailing, soccer, softball, squash, tennis, volleyball. **Team name:** Shoremen/Shorewomen.

Student services. Adult student services, alcohol/substance abuse counseling, career counseling, student employment services, financial aid counseling, health services, minority student services, personal counseling, placement for graduates, veterans' counselor. **Physically disabled:** Services for hearing impaired.

Contact. E-mail: adm.off@washcoll.edu
Phone: (410) 778-7700 Toll-free number: (800) 442-1782
Fax: (410) 778-7287
Kevin Coveney, Vice President for Admissions, Washington College, 300 Washington Avenue, Chestertown, MD 21620-1197

Yeshiva College of the Nations Capital
Silver Spring, Maryland

- Private 4-year rabbinical college for men affiliated with Jewish faith
- Residential campus
- 52 degree-seeking undergraduates

General. Accredited by AARTS. **Degrees:** 13 bachelor's awarded. **Calendar:** Continuous. **Full-time faculty:** 6 total.

2006-2007 Annual costs. Tuition/fees (projected): $7,700. Room/board: $6,000.

Academics. Credit/placement by examination: CLEP.

Majors. Philosophy/religion: Judaic. **Theology:** Talmudic.

Contact. Phone: (301) 593-2534
David Hyatt, Academic Dean, Yeshiva College of the Nations Capital, 1216 Arcola Avenue, Silver Spring, MD 20902

Massachusetts

American International College

Springfield, Massachusetts — **CB member**
www.aic.edu — **CB code: 3002**

- Private 4-year liberal arts college
- Residential campus in small city
- 1,398 degree-seeking undergraduates: 13% part-time, 59% women, 25% African American, 2% Asian American, 9% Hispanic American, 1% international
- 357 degree-seeking graduate students
- 84% of applicants admitted
- SAT or ACT with writing required
- 49% graduate within 6 years; 30% enter graduate study

General. Founded in 1885. Regionally accredited. **Degrees:** 177 bachelor's, 5 associate awarded; master's, doctoral offered. **ROTC:** Army, Air Force. **Location:** 90 miles from Boston, 20 miles from Hartford, Connecticut. **Calendar:** Semester, extensive summer session. **Full-time faculty:** 72 total; 90% have terminal degrees, 54% women. **Part-time faculty:** 87 total; 70% have terminal degrees, 42% women. **Class size:** 69% < 20, 30% 20-39, 1% 40-49. **Special facilities:** Cultural arts center, performing arts center, anatomical laboratory.

Freshman class profile. 1,333 applied, 1,118 admitted, 331 enrolled.

Mid 50% test scores			
SAT verbal:	430-520	Rank in top quarter:	25%
SAT math:	430-580	Rank in top tenth:	15%
GPA 3.50 or higher:	20%	End year in good standing:	79%
GPA 3.0-3.49:	70%	Return as sophomores:	60%
GPA 2.0-2.99:	10%	Out-of-state:	44%
		Live on campus:	64%

Basis for selection. School achievement record most important; recommendations and test scores also important. Essay and interview recommended. **Homeschooled:** Statement describing homeschool structure and mission, transcript of courses and grades, interview required. **Learning Disabled:** Wechsler Adult Intelligence Scale, interview, and diagnostic documentation required.

High school preparation. 16 units required. Required and recommended units include English 4, mathematics 2-3, social studies 2, history 2, science 2 (laboratory 1) and foreign language 2.

2006-2007 Annual costs. Tuition/fees: $21,000. Room/board: $9,270. Books/supplies: $1,000. Personal expenses: $1,200.

2005-2006 Financial aid. Need-based: 331 full-time freshmen applied for aid; 327 were judged to have need; 327 of these received aid. Average need met was 85%. Average scholarship/grant was $12,821; average loan $3,758. 63% of total undergraduate aid awarded as scholarships/grants, 37% as loans/jobs. **Non-need-based:** Awarded to 1,281 full-time undergraduates, including 369 freshmen. Scholarships awarded for academics, athletics.

Application procedures. Admission: No deadline. $25 fee, may be waived for applicants with need. Application may be submitted online. Admission notification on a rolling basis beginning on or about 11/15. Must reply by May 1 or within 2 week(s) if notified thereafter. **Financial aid:** Priority date 5/1; no closing date. FAFSA required. Applicants notified on a rolling basis starting 3/15; must reply by 5/1 or within 2 week(s) of notification.

Academics. Special study options: Accelerated study, combined bachelor's/graduate degree, cross-registration, double major, dual enrollment of high school students, ESL, honors, independent study, internships, liberal arts/career combination, study abroad, teacher certification program, weekend college. **Credit/placement by examination:** AP, CLEP, IB, institutional tests. 30 credit hours maximum toward bachelor's degree. **Support services:** Learning center, reduced course load, remedial instruction, study skills assistance, tutoring, writing center.

Majors. Biology: General, biochemistry. **Business:** General, accounting, business admin, communications, finance, hospitality admin, human resources, international, management information systems, management science, managerial economics, marketing. **Communications:** Advertising, broadcast journalism, journalism, media studies, public relations, radio/tv. **Computer sciences:** Computer science, information systems. **Education:** Early childhood, elementary, middle, secondary, special. **Foreign languages:** Spanish. **Health:** Nursing (RN), predentistry, premedicine, preveterinary. **Interdisciplinary:** Accounting/computer science, biological/physical sciences, math/computer science. **Legal studies:** Prelaw. **Liberal arts:** Arts/sciences. **Math:** General. **Parks/recreation:** General, sports admin. **Philosophy/religion:** Philosophy. **Physical sciences:** Chemistry. **Protective services:** Criminal justice, law enforcement admin, police science. **Psychology:** General. **Public administration:** General. **Social sciences:** Criminology, economics, international relations, political science, sociology.

Most popular majors. Business/marketing 33%, education 12%, health sciences 7%, liberal arts 8%, physical sciences 6%, psychology 8%, security/protective services 8%.

Computing on campus. 100 workstations in library, computer center. Dormitories wired for high-speed internet access and linked to campus network. Commuter students can connect to campus network. Online library, helpline, wireless network available.

Student life. Freshman orientation: Mandatory. Preregistration for classes offered. **Policies:** Freshmen permitted cars on campus. **Housing:** Guaranteed on-campus for all undergraduates. Coed dorms, single-sex dorms, apartments, substance-free housing available. $100 nonrefundable deposit, deadline 7/1. **Activities:** Choral groups, dance, drama, literary magazine, musical theater, radio station, student government, student newspaper, Hillel, United Protestant Fellowship, PRIDE (minority student organization), Partners.

Athletics. NCAA. **Intercollegiate:** Baseball M, basketball, cheerleading, field hockey W, football (tackle) M, golf M, ice hockey M, lacrosse, soccer, softball W, tennis, volleyball W, wrestling M. **Intramural:** Basketball, equestrian, football (non-tackle) M, skiing, soccer, softball, swimming, volleyball. **Team name:** Yellow Jackets.

Student services. Adult student services, alcohol/substance abuse counseling, campus ministries, career counseling, services for economically disadvantaged, student employment services, financial aid counseling, health services, minority student services, personal counseling, placement for graduates, veterans' counselor, women's services. **Physically disabled:** Services for visually impaired. **Learning disabled:** Comprehensive services available.

Contact. E-mail: inquiry@acad.aic.edu
Phone: (413) 205-3201 Toll-free number: (800) 242-3142
Fax: (413) 205-3051
Peter Miller, Vice President for Admission Services, American International College, 1000 State Street, Springfield, MA 01109

Amherst College

Amherst, Massachusetts — **CB member**
www.amherst.edu — **CB code: 3003**

- Private 4-year liberal arts college
- Residential campus in large town
- 1,612 degree-seeking undergraduates: 48% women, 9% African American, 13% Asian American, 6% Hispanic American, 7% international
- 19% of applicants admitted
- SAT and SAT Subject Tests or ACT (ACT writing recommended), application essay required
- 96% graduate within 6 years

General. Founded in 1821. Regionally accredited. **Degrees:** 408 bachelor's awarded. **Location:** 90 miles from Boston, 150 miles from New York City. **Calendar:** Semester. **Full-time faculty:** 190 total; 94% have terminal degrees, 16% minority, 41% women. **Part-time faculty:** 28 total; 93% have terminal degrees, 11% minority, 54% women. **Class size:** 71% < 20, 23% 20-39, 1% 40-49, 3% 50-99, less than 1% >100. **Special facilities:** Recital hall, observatory, planetarium, center for Russian culture, Dickinson homestead, natural history museum, fine arts museum.

Freshman class profile. 6,273 applied, 1,175 admitted, 431 enrolled.

Mid 50% test scores			
SAT verbal:	670-780	Rank in top tenth:	80%
SAT math:	680-780	Return as sophomores:	97%
ACT:	29-33	Out-of-state:	87%
Rank in top quarter:	95%	Live on campus:	100%
		International:	7%

Basis for selection. Grades, test scores, essays, recommendations, independent work, quality of individual's secondary school program, achievements outside of classroom most important.

High school preparation. Recommended units include English 4, mathematics 4, social studies 2, history 2, science 3 (laboratory 1) and foreign language 4.

2005-2006 Annual costs. Tuition/fees: $33,005. Room/board: $8,585. Books/supplies: $950. Personal expenses: $1,700.

2005-2006 Financial aid. All financial aid based on need. 247 full-time freshmen applied for aid; 199 were judged to have need; 199 of these received aid. Average need met was 100%. Average scholarship/grant was $29,373; average loan $1,620. 89% of total undergraduate aid awarded as scholarships/grants, 11% as loans/jobs.

Application procedures. Admission: Closing date 1/1 (postmark date). $55 fee, may be waived for applicants with need. Application may be submitted online. Admission notification 4/5. Must reply by 5/1. **Financial aid:** Priority date 2/15; no closing date. FAFSA, CSS PROFILE required. Applicants notified by 4/1; must reply by 5/1.

Academics. First-year students must choose 1 seminar from range of 20 special topics, often interdisciplinary. No core curriculum, no distribution requirements. Students select major at end of sophomore year. **Special study options:** Cross-registration, double major, exchange student, honors, independent study, student-designed major, study abroad, teacher certification program. Member of 5-college consortium. **Credit/placement by examination:** AP, CLEP, IB, institutional tests. **Support services:** Tutoring, writing center.

Majors. Area/ethnic studies: African, African-American, American, Asian, Central/Eastern European, European, Western European, women's. **Biology:** General. **Computer sciences:** Computer science. **Foreign languages:** Ancient Greek, classics, French, German, Latin, Russian, Spanish. **History:** General. **Interdisciplinary:** Math/computer science, neuroscience. **Legal studies:** General. **Math:** General. **Philosophy/religion:** Philosophy, religion. **Physical sciences:** Astronomy, chemistry, geology, physics. **Psychology:** General. **Social sciences:** Anthropology, economics, political science, sociology. **Visual/performing arts:** Dance, dramatic, studio arts.

Most popular majors. English 11%, foreign language 9%, history 9%, legal studies 6%, physical sciences 6%, psychology 9%, social sciences 19%, visual/performing arts 9%.

Computing on campus. 220 workstations in library, computer center, student center. Dormitories wired for high-speed internet access and linked to campus network. Commuter students can connect to campus network. Helpline, repair service, wireless network available.

Student life. Freshman orientation: Mandatory. 8-day orientation with events planned by student groups and cultural organizations. **Housing:** Guaranteed on-campus for all undergraduates. Coed dorms, cooperative housing, substance-free housing available. Language and other theme houses available including French/Spanish, Russian/German, Latino, African American, health and wellness house, and arts house. Men's and women's floors available to all students. **Activities:** Bands, choral groups, dance, drama, film society, literary magazine, music ensembles, musical theater, opera, radio station, student government, student newspaper, symphony orchestra, Hillel, Boltwood House (service), Christian association, Newman club, Black Student Union, Association of Asian Students, Cambodian family tutoring, LaCausa, Amherst Christian Fellowship, Korean American students association.

Athletics. NCAA. **Intercollegiate:** Baseball M, basketball, cross-country, diving, field hockey W, football (tackle) M, golf, ice hockey, lacrosse, soccer, softball W, squash, swimming, tennis, track and field, volleyball W. **Intramural:** Badminton, basketball, football (non-tackle), golf, ice hockey, soccer, softball, squash, table tennis, tennis, volleyball. **Team name:** Lord Jeffs.

Student services. Alcohol/substance abuse counseling, campus ministries, career counseling, services for economically disadvantaged, student employment services, financial aid counseling, health services, minority student services, personal counseling, placement for graduates, women's services. **Physically disabled:** Services for visually, speech, hearing impaired.

Contact. E-mail: admission@amherst.edu
Phone: (413) 542-2328 Fax: (413) 542-2040
Katie Fretwell, Director of Admission, Amherst College, PO Box 5000, Amherst, MA 01002-5000

Anna Maria College

Paxton, Massachusetts — **CB member**
www.annamaria.edu — **CB code: 3005**

- Private 4-year liberal arts college affiliated with Roman Catholic Church
- Residential campus in small town
- 713 degree-seeking undergraduates: 24% part-time, 59% women, 2% African American, 1% Asian American, 3% Hispanic American, 1% international
- 250 degree-seeking graduate students
- 90% of applicants admitted
- SAT or ACT (ACT writing recommended), application essay required
- 63% graduate within 6 years

General. Founded in 1946. Regionally accredited. BBA, MBA, BA/MA in criminal justice offered at 8 sites throughout Massachusetts. **Degrees:** 140 bachelor's, 2 associate awarded; master's offered. **ROTC:** Air Force. **Location:** 8 miles from Worcester, 40 miles from Boston. **Calendar:** Semester, limited summer session. **Full-time faculty:** 38 total; 47% have terminal degrees, 60% women. **Part-time faculty:** 132 total; 21% have terminal degrees, 43% women. **Class size:** 75% < 20, 25% 20-39. **Special facilities:** Arts building, nature trail.

Freshman class profile. 557 applied, 501 admitted, 161 enrolled.

Mid 50% test scores		**GPA 2.0-2.99:**	54%
SAT verbal:	420-510	**Rank in top quarter:**	15%
SAT math:	400-520	**Rank in top tenth:**	4%
ACT:	15-19	**Return as sophomores:**	59%
GPA 3.50 or higher:	10%	**Out-of-state:**	26%
GPA 3.0-3.49:	19%	**Live on campus:**	81%

Basis for selection. High school record most important, followed by essay, test scores, recommendations, interview, school and community activities. Audition required of music majors; portfolio required of art majors.

High school preparation. 20 units required. Required units include English 4, mathematics 3, social studies 2, history 2, science 3 (laboratory 1), foreign language 2 and academic electives 4.

2005-2006 Annual costs. Tuition/fees: $21,880. Additional tuition for music program. Room/board: $7,935. Books/supplies: $800. Personal expenses: $1,630.

2005-2006 Financial aid. Need-based: 142 full-time freshmen applied for aid; 129 were judged to have need; 129 of these received aid. Average need met was 78%. Average scholarship/grant was $11,071; average loan $2,843. 48% of total undergraduate aid awarded as scholarships/grants, 52% as loans/jobs. **Non-need-based:** Awarded to 432 full-time undergraduates, including 139 freshmen. Scholarships awarded for academics, alumni affiliation, music/drama, religious affiliation, state residency.

Application procedures. Admission: Priority date 3/1; no deadline. $40 fee, may be waived for applicants with need. Application may be submitted online. Admission notification on a rolling basis beginning on or about 12/15. Must reply by May 1 or within 2 week(s) if notified thereafter. Catholic College Common Application accepted. **Financial aid:** Priority date 3/1; no closing date. FAFSA required. Applicants notified on a rolling basis starting 4/1; must reply within 4 week(s) of notification.

Academics. Upper-division transfer program for registered nursing and fire science. **Special study options:** Accelerated study, combined bachelor's/graduate degree, cooperative education, cross-registration, double major, dual enrollment of high school students, independent study, internships, liberal arts/career combination, student-designed major, study abroad, teacher certification program, Washington semester. Member of 15-college Worcester Consortium; 3-2 engineering program with Worcester Polytechnic Institute. **Credit/placement by examination:** AP, CLEP, institutional tests. 30 credit hours maximum toward bachelor's degree. **Support services:** Learning center, reduced course load, remedial instruction, study skills assistance, tutoring, writing center.

Majors. Biology: General. **Business:** Accounting, business admin, management information systems. **Computer sciences:** General. **Education:** Art, early childhood, elementary, English, music, secondary. **Foreign languages:** Spanish. **Health:** Art therapy, health services, music therapy, nursing (RN). **History:** General. **Interdisciplinary:** Biological/physical sciences. **Legal studies:** General, paralegal. **Liberal arts:** Arts/sciences, humanities. **Philosophy/religion:** Religion. **Protective services:** Firefighting, law enforcement admin. **Psychology:** General. **Public administration:** Human services, policy analysis, social work. **Theology:** Pastoral counseling. **Visual/performing arts:** Art, graphic design, music performance, piano/organ, studio arts, voice/opera.

Most popular majors. Business/marketing 12%, health sciences 9%, liberal arts 10%, public administration/social services 13%, security/protective services 39%.

Computing on campus. 61 workstations in dormitories, library, computer center, student center. Dormitories wired for high-speed internet access and linked to campus network.

Student life. **Freshman orientation:** Mandatory. Preregistration for classes offered. **Policies:** Freshmen permitted cars on campus. **Housing:** Guaranteed on-campus for freshmen. Coed dorms, special housing for disabled, substance-free housing available. $300 fully refundable deposit, deadline 5/1. **Activities:** Bands, choral groups, drama, music ensembles, student government, Society for Peace and Justice, campus ministry, social action club.

Athletics. NCAA. **Intercollegiate:** Baseball M, basketball, cheerleading W, cross-country M, field hockey W, golf M, soccer, softball W, volleyball W. **Intramural:** Basketball, soccer, volleyball. **Team name:** Amcats.

Student services. Alcohol/substance abuse counseling, campus ministries, career counseling, student employment services, financial aid counseling, health services, minority student services, personal counseling, placement for graduates. **Physically disabled:** Services for visually, speech, hearing impaired.

Contact. E-mail: admission@annamaria.edu
Phone: (508) 849-3360 Toll-free number: (800) 344-4586
Fax: (508) 849-3362
Tim Donahue, Director of Admission, Anna Maria College, 50 Sunset Lane, Box O, Paxton, MA 01612-1198

Art Institute of Boston at Lesley University

Boston, Massachusetts
www.aiboston.edu **CB code: 3777**

- Private 4-year visual arts and liberal arts college
- Residential campus in very large city
- 565 degree-seeking undergraduates: 6% African American, 5% Asian American, 5% Hispanic American, 3% international
- 72% of applicants admitted
- SAT or ACT (ACT writing optional), application essay, interview required
- 50% graduate within 6 years

General. Regionally accredited. Part of Lesley University. **Degrees:** 422 bachelor's awarded; master's offered. **Location:** Downtown. **Calendar:** Semester, limited summer session. **Full-time faculty:** 53 total; 74% have terminal degrees, 9% minority, 64% women. **Part-time faculty:** 131 total; 29% have terminal degrees, 52% women. **Class size:** 75% < 20, 24% 20-39, less than 1% 40-49. **Special facilities:** Animation lab, clay studio, woodworking studio, print-making studio, photo lab, digital-printing lab.

Freshman class profile. 1,351 applied, 967 admitted, 267 enrolled.

Mid 50% test scores			
SAT verbal:	480-600	**Rank in top quarter:**	50%
SAT math:	460-570	**Rank in top tenth:**	23%
ACT:	19-25	**Return as sophomores:**	79%
GPA 3.50 or higher:	11%	**Out-of-state:**	51%
GPA 3.0-3.49:	42%	**Live on campus:**	88%
GPA 2.0-2.99:	46%	**International:**	1%

Basis for selection. Admission based on art portfolio, academic record, test scores, personal interview, essay, extracurricular activities, and letters of recommendation. Portfolios required.

High school preparation. 14 units recommended. Required and recommended units include English 4, mathematics 1, social studies 2, history 2, science 1, foreign language 1 and academic electives 2. 2 units studio art recommended.

2006-2007 Annual costs. Tuition/fees: $22,225. Room/board: $10,500. Books/supplies: $1,575. Personal expenses: $1,975.

2005-2006 Financial aid. **Need-based:** 234 full-time freshmen applied for aid; 189 were judged to have need; 189 of these received aid. Average need met was 70%. Average scholarship/grant was $12,741; average loan $3,507. 66% of total undergraduate aid awarded as scholarships/grants, 34% as loans/jobs. **Non-need-based:** Scholarships awarded for academics, art, leadership, minority status.

Application procedures. **Admission:** Priority date 2/15; no deadline. $40 fee, may be waived for applicants with need. Application may be submitted online. Admission notification on a rolling basis. **Financial aid:** Priority date 3/1; no closing date. FAFSA, institutional form required. Applicants notified on a rolling basis starting 3/15; must reply within 2 week(s) of notification.

Academics. **Special study options:** Accelerated study, combined bachelor's/graduate degree, cross-registration, distance learning, double major, dual enrollment of high school students, exchange student, honors, independent study, internships, liberal arts/career combination, New York semester, student-designed major, study abroad, teacher certification program. AICAD Mobility Program, NY Studio Program, Bridge Program. **Credit/placement by examination:** AP, CLEP, institutional tests. **Support services:** Learning center, pre-admission summer program, reduced course load, study skills assistance, tutoring, writing center.

Majors. **Education:** Art. **Visual/performing arts:** General, commercial photography, commercial/advertising art, drawing, graphic design, illustration, painting, photography, studio arts.

Computing on campus. 80 workstations in dormitories, library, computer center, student center. Dormitories wired for high-speed internet access and linked to campus network. Commuter students can connect to campus network. Online course registration, online library, helpline, repair service, student web hosting, wireless network available.

Student life. **Freshman orientation:** Mandatory. Program held first week before classes. **Housing:** Coed dorms, single-sex dorms, substance-free housing available. $300 deposit. Themed housing available. **Activities:** Choral groups, dance, drama, literary magazine, musical theater, student government, student newspaper, peer advisors, ski club, international student association, student gallery committee, literary journal, Prism, Women for Social Justice.

Athletics. NCAA. **Intercollegiate:** Basketball, rowing (crew), soccer, softball W, volleyball. **Team name:** Lesley Lynx.

Student services. Adult student services, alcohol/substance abuse counseling, campus ministries, career counseling, student employment services, financial aid counseling, health services, minority student services, personal counseling, placement for graduates. **Physically disabled:** Services for visually, speech, hearing impaired.

Contact. E-mail: admissions@aiboston.edu
Phone: (617) 585-6710 Toll-free number: (800) 773-0494 ext. 6710
Fax: (617) 585-6720
Alan Van Reed, Director of Admissions, Art Institute of Boston at Lesley University, 700 Beacon Street, Boston, MA 02215-2598

Assumption College

Worcester, Massachusetts **CB member**
www.assumption.edu **CB code: 3009**

- Private 4-year liberal arts college affiliated with Roman Catholic Church
- Residential campus in small city
- 2,105 degree-seeking undergraduates: 60% women, 1% African American, 2% Asian American, 2% Hispanic American
- 263 degree-seeking graduate students
- 76% of applicants admitted
- SAT or ACT (ACT writing recommended), application essay required
- 71% graduate within 6 years; 23% enter graduate study

General. Founded in 1904. Regionally accredited. Students may register for courses at 11 area colleges. Volunteer programs available: comprehensive 2-week programs in Mexico and Puerto Rico, 1-week spring break programs in various locations. **Degrees:** 457 bachelor's awarded; master's offered. **ROTC:** Army, Air Force. **Location:** 45 miles from Boston. **Calendar:** Semester, limited summer session. **Full-time faculty:** 129 total; 95% have terminal degrees, 4% minority, 36% women. **Part-time faculty:** 87 total; 54% have terminal degrees, 7% minority, 47% women. **Class size:** 42% < 20, 57% 20-39, less than 1% 40-49. **Special facilities:** French institute (academic research center for study of Francophone questions).

Freshman class profile. 3,357 applied, 2,538 admitted, 565 enrolled.

Mid 50% test scores		**Rank in top quarter:**	41%
SAT verbal:	490-580	**Rank in top tenth:**	12%
SAT math:	490-590	**End year in good standing:**	89%
ACT:	18-24	**Return as sophomores:**	84%
GPA 3.50 or higher:	30%	**Out-of-state:**	32%
GPA 3.0-3.49:	38%	**Live on campus:**	95%
GPA 2.0-2.99:	31%	**International:**	1%

Basis for selection. School achievement most important, followed by class rank in top 40%, test scores, extracurricular activities, interview, recommendations. **Homeschooled:** Statement describing homeschool structure and mission, letter of recommendation (nonparent) required.

High school preparation. 18 units required. Required units include English 4, mathematics 3, history 2, science 2, foreign language 2 and academic electives 5.

2005-2006 Annual costs. Tuition/fees: $24,095. Room/board: $8,780. Books/supplies: $700. Personal expenses: $1,130.

2005-2006 Financial aid. **Need-based:** 483 full-time freshmen applied for aid; 394 were judged to have need; 394 of these received aid. Average need met was 70%. Average scholarship/grant was $12,018; average loan $3,000. 65% of total undergraduate aid awarded as scholarships/grants, 35% as loans/jobs. **Non-need-based:** Awarded to 650 full-time undergraduates, including 187 freshmen. Scholarships awarded for academics, athletics.

Application procedures. **Admission:** Closing date 2/15 (postmark date). $50 fee, may be waived for applicants with need. Application may be submitted online. Admission notification 5/1. Admission notification on a rolling basis. Must reply by May 1 or within 2 week(s) if notified thereafter. **Financial aid:** Closing date 2/1. FAFSA required. Applicants notified on a rolling basis starting 2/15; must reply by 5/1.

Academics. **Special study options:** Combined bachelor's/graduate degree, cross-registration, double major, honors, independent study, internships, student-designed major, study abroad, teacher certification program, Washington semester. Worcester Consortium gerontology studies program; 3-2 engineering program (BA/BS) with Worcester Polytechnic Institute. **Credit/placement by examination:** AP, CLEP, IB, SAT, institutional tests. **Support services:** Learning center, study skills assistance, tutoring, writing center.

Majors. **Area/ethnic studies:** Latin American. **Biology:** General. **Business:** Accounting, business admin, international, marketing. **Communications:** Organizational. **Computer sciences:** General. **Conservation:** Environmental science. **English:** English lit. **Foreign languages:** General, classics, French, Spanish. **History:** General. **Interdisciplinary:** Global studies. **Math:** General. **Philosophy/religion:** Philosophy. **Physical sciences:** Chemistry. **Psychology:** General. **Social sciences:** Economics, political science, sociology. **Theology:** Theology. **Visual/performing arts:** General.

Most popular majors. Biology 6%, business/marketing 14%, communications/journalism 13%, English 12%, health sciences 8%, history 7%, psychology 14%, social sciences 9%.

Computing on campus. 225 workstations in dormitories, library, computer center, student center. Dormitories wired for high-speed internet access and linked to campus network. Commuter students can connect to campus network. Online course registration, online library, helpline, repair service, student web hosting, wireless network available.

Student life. **Freshman orientation:** Mandatory, $250 fee. Preregistration for classes offered. 2-day program in June. **Housing:** Guaranteed on-campus for all undergraduates. Coed dorms, single-sex dorms, special housing for disabled, substance-free housing available. Freshman dorms, substance-free dorms, living/learning center available. **Activities:** Bands, choral groups, drama, film society, literary magazine, musical theater, student government, student newspaper, TV station, ALANA Network, environmental club, College Democrats, College Republicans, Green Party club, student volunteer center, students encountering and responding to Christ, students advocating change, Alpha and Omega, Omicron Delta Kappa leadership circle.

Athletics. NCAA. **Intercollegiate:** Baseball M, basketball, cross-country, field hockey W, football (tackle) M, golf M, ice hockey M, lacrosse, rowing (crew), soccer, softball W, tennis, track and field, volleyball W. **Intramural:** Basketball, football (tackle) M, racquetball, skiing, soccer, softball, swimming, volleyball. **Team name:** Greyhounds.

Student services. Alcohol/substance abuse counseling, campus ministries, career counseling, student employment services, financial aid counseling, health services, minority student services, personal counseling, placement for graduates. **Physically disabled:** Services for visually, speech, hearing impaired.

Contact. E-mail: admiss@assumption.edu
Phone: (508) 767-7285 Toll-free number: (888) 882-7786
Fax: (508) 799-4412
Kathleen Murphy, Dean of Enrollment, Assumption College, 500 Salisbury Street, Worcester, MA 01609-1296

Atlantic Union College

South Lancaster, Massachusetts
www.atlanticuc.edu **CB code: 3010**

- Private 4-year liberal arts college affiliated with Seventh-day Adventists
- Residential campus in small town
- 470 degree-seeking undergraduates
- 20 graduate students
- SAT or ACT with writing required

General. Founded in 1882. Regionally accredited. **Degrees:** 79 bachelor's, 15 associate awarded; master's offered. **Location:** 45 miles from Boston. **Calendar:** Semester, limited summer session. **Full-time faculty:** 45 total. **Part-time faculty:** 4 total. **Class size:** 86% < 20, 14% 20-39. **Special facilities:** Music conservatory.

Basis for selection. School achievement record, interview, recommendations, test scores important. Interview recommended for non-Seventh-day Adventists. Audition required of music majors. Portfolio recommended for art majors. **Homeschooled:** Transcript from accredited high school or GED test score required.

High school preparation. 14 units required. Required and recommended units include English 4, mathematics 3, social studies 2, science 2 (laboratory 1) and foreign language 2. One unit computer science also required.

2005-2006 Annual costs. Tuition/fees: $13,420. Additional fees for nursing program. Room/board: $5,040. Books/supplies: $1,000. Personal expenses: $2,300.

Financial aid. **Non-need-based:** Scholarships awarded for academics, athletics, job skills, leadership, music/drama.

Application procedures. **Admission:** Closing date 8/1. $25 fee, may be waived for applicants with need. Application may be submitted online. Admission notification on a rolling basis. **Financial aid:** Priority date 4/1; no closing date. FAFSA, institutional form required. Applicants notified on a rolling basis starting 4/1; must reply within 2 week(s) of notification.

Academics. External degree program of directed independent study for those 25 and over. Master of education program available summer session only. **Special study options:** Accelerated study, cooperative education, cross-registration, distance learning, double major, dual enrollment of high school students, ESL, external degree, honors, independent study, internships, liberal arts/career combination, study abroad, teacher certification program. **Credit/placement by examination:** AP, CLEP, IB, institutional tests. 32 credit hours maximum toward bachelor's degree. **Support services:** Learning center, reduced course load, remedial instruction, tutoring.

Majors. **Biology:** General. **Business:** Accounting, business admin. **Computer sciences:** General, computer science. **Education:** Early childhood, elementary, secondary. **Foreign languages:** French, Spanish. **Health:** Nursing (RN). **History:** General. **Liberal arts:** Arts/sciences. **Math:** General. **Philosophy/religion:** Religion. **Psychology:** General. **Public administration:** Social work. **Theology:** Theology. **Visual/performing arts:** Interior design, music history, studio arts.

Computing on campus. 84 workstations in dormitories, library, computer center. Dormitories linked to campus network.

Student life. **Freshman orientation:** Mandatory, $100 fee. Preregistration for classes offered. Program held one week before official registration. **Policies:** Religious observance required. Freshmen permitted cars on campus. **Housing:** Single-sex dorms, apartments available. $350 deposit. **Activities:** Concert band, choral groups, drama, music ensembles, student government, student newspaper, symphony orchestra, campus community outreach, Big Brother, Adopt-A-Grandparent.

Athletics. **Intramural:** Cross-country, golf, gymnastics, racquetball, sailing, skiing, skin diving, softball, swimming, tennis, track and field, volleyball. **Team name:** Flames.

Student services. Campus ministries, career counseling, student employment services, financial aid counseling, health services, personal counseling, placement for graduates.

Contact. E-mail: rlashley@atlanticuc.edu
Phone: (978) 368-2235 Toll-free number: (800) 282-2030
Fax: (978) 368-2015
Rosita Lashley, Director of Admissions, Atlantic Union College, Main Street, South Lancaster, MA 01561

Babson College

Babson Park, Massachusetts **CB member**
www.babson.edu **CB code: 3075**

- Private 4-year business college
- Residential campus in large town
- 1,725 degree-seeking undergraduates
- 37% of applicants admitted
- SAT or ACT with writing, application essay required

General. Founded in 1919. Regionally accredited. Students start and operate own business during freshman year under Foundation Management Experience Program. **Degrees:** 424 bachelor's awarded; master's offered. **ROTC:** Army, Navy, Air Force. **Location:** 14 miles from Boston. **Calendar:** Semester, limited summer session. **Full-time faculty:** 151 total. **Part-time faculty:** 78 total. **Class size:** 23% < 20, 60% 20-39, 15% 40-49, 3% 50-99. **Special facilities:** Museum and archives, student-run businesses, entrepreneurship center, women's center.

Freshman class profile. 3,159 applied, 1,164 admitted, 420 enrolled.

Mid 50% test scores			
SAT verbal:	540-640	Out-of-state:	71%
SAT math:	580-690	Live on campus:	100%
Rank in top quarter:	83%	Fraternities:	2%
Rank in top tenth:	53%	Sororities:	2%

Basis for selection. Academic performance and level of course work (college preparation, honors, Advanced Placement) most important, followed by academic motivation, including interest in learning and willingness to challenge oneself; test scores; writing ability; involvement in cocurricular activities and/or work experience; leadership, creativity, enthusiasm. SAT Subject Tests recommended. SAT Subject Tests recommended in math. **Homeschooled:** Provide information about completed courses, schooling, testing, and diploma requirements.

High school preparation. Required and recommended units include English 4, mathematics 3-4, social studies 2-3, history 1, science 3 (laboratory 2) and foreign language 2-4. Pre-calculus strongly recommended.

2006-2007 Annual costs. Tuition/fees: $32,256. Room/board: $11,222. Books/supplies: $890.

2005-2006 Financial aid. Need-based: 83% of total undergraduate aid awarded as scholarships/grants, 17% as loans/jobs. **Non-need-based:** Scholarships awarded for academics, leadership, minority status.

Application procedures. Admission: Priority date 11/15; deadline 1/15 (postmark date). $60 fee, may be waived for applicants with need. Application must be submitted on paper. Admission notification 4/1. Must reply by 5/1. **Financial aid:** Closing date 2/15. FAFSA, CSS PROFILE required. Applicants notified by 4/1; must reply by 5/1.

Academics. Special study options: Accelerated study, combined bachelor's/graduate degree, cross-registration, exchange student, honors, independent study, internships, liberal arts/career combination, semester at sea, student-designed major, study abroad. **Credit/placement by examination:** AP, CLEP, IB, institutional tests. 64 credit hours maximum toward bachelor's degree. **Support services:** Reduced course load, study skills assistance, tutoring, writing center.

Majors. Business: General, accounting, accounting/business management, accounting/finance, auditing, business admin, communications, entrepreneurial studies, finance, international, international finance, international marketing, investments/securities, management information systems, management science, managerial economics, marketing, office management, operations, sales/distribution, small business admin, statistics. **Communications:** Advertising. **Computer sciences:** General, information systems. **Legal studies:** Prelaw.

Computing on campus. PC or laptop required. 290 workstations in dormitories, library, computer center, student center. Dormitories wired for high-speed internet access and linked to campus network. Commuter students can connect to campus network. Online course registration, online library, helpline, repair service, wireless network available.

Student life. Freshman orientation: Mandatory. Preregistration for classes offered. 3-day program preceeding the start of classes. **Policies:** First-year students required to live on campus unless commuting from home (must live within 25-mile radius of campus). Freshmen permitted cars on campus. **Housing:** Guaranteed on-campus for all undergraduates. Coed dorms, single-sex dorms, special housing for disabled, apartments, fraternity/sorority housing, substance-free housing available. $500 deposit, deadline 5/1. Cultural, nontraditional, suite style, single-sex floors, wings for women available. **Activities:** Bands, choral groups, dance, drama, literary magazine, music ensembles, musical theater, radio station, student government, student newspaper, 60 student-run organizations.

Athletics. NCAA. **Intercollegiate:** Baseball M, basketball, cross-country, diving, field hockey W, golf M, ice hockey M, lacrosse, skiing, soccer, softball W, swimming, tennis, track and field, volleyball W. **Intramural:** Basketball, football (non-tackle), ice hockey, racquetball, soccer, softball, squash, tennis, volleyball, water polo. **Team name:** Beavers.

Student services. Alcohol/substance abuse counseling, campus ministries, career counseling, student employment services, financial aid counseling, health services, personal counseling, placement for graduates. **Physically disabled:** Services for visually, speech, hearing impaired.

Contact. E-mail: ugradadmission@babson.edu
Phone: (781) 239-5522 Toll-free number: (800) 488-3696
Fax: (781) 239-4135
R. Kines, Dean of Undergraduate Admission, Babson College, Lunder Undergraduate Admission Center, Babson Park, MA 02457-0310

Bay Path College
Longmeadow, Massachusetts
www.baypath.edu **CB code: 3078**

- Private 4-year business and liberal arts college for women
- Residential campus in large town
- 1,343 degree-seeking undergraduates: 17% part-time, 100% women, 12% African American, 1% Asian American, 7% Hispanic American, 1% international
- 113 degree-seeking graduate students
- 71% of applicants admitted
- SAT or ACT with writing, application essay required
- 38% graduate within 6 years

General. Founded in 1897. Regionally accredited. Member of 8-college consortium. **Degrees:** 206 bachelor's, 126 associate awarded; master's offered. **ROTC:** Army, Air Force. **Location:** 5 miles from Springfield; 23 miles from Hartford, Connecticut. **Calendar:** Semester, limited summer session. **Full-time faculty:** 38 total; 58% have terminal degrees, 8% minority, 79% women. **Part-time faculty:** 124 total; 30% have terminal degrees, 5% minority, 55% women. **Class size:** 65% < 20, 35% 20-39, less than 1% 50-99. **Special facilities:** Academic development center, on-campus preschool, occupational therapy laboratory, business hall, career development center.

Freshman class profile. 573 applied, 404 admitted, 129 enrolled.

Mid 50% test scores			
SAT verbal:	460-560	GPA 2.0-2.99:	42%
SAT math:	440-540	Return as sophomores:	70%
ACT:	17-25	Out-of-state:	35%
GPA 3.50 or higher:	26%	Live on campus:	70%
GPA 3.0-3.49:	32%	International:	2%

Basis for selection. Admission based on applicant's high school transcript and performance, class rank, grade point average, SAT or ACT and/or TOEFL scores, letters of recommendation, and essay. Interviews recommended. **Homeschooled:** Statement describing homeschool structure and mission, transcript of courses and grades, letter of recommendation (nonparent) required. Submit certificate from town or Board of Education for proof of completion of educational plan.

High school preparation. 15 units required; 17 recommended. Required and recommended units include English 4, mathematics 3-4, social studies 2, history 1-2, science 2-3 (laboratory 2) and foreign language 2.

2005-2006 Annual costs. Tuition/fees: $20,606. Room/board: $8,756. Books/supplies: $800. Personal expenses: $900.

2005-2006 Financial aid. Need-based: Average need met was 74%. Average scholarship/grant was $10,653; average loan $3,976. 55% of total undergraduate aid awarded as scholarships/grants, 45% as loans/jobs. **Non-need-based:** Scholarships awarded for academics, state residency.

Application procedures. Admission: No deadline. $25 fee, may be waived for applicants with need. Application may be submitted online. Admission notification on a rolling basis beginning on or about 9/15. Must reply by May 1 or within 2 week(s) if notified thereafter. **Financial aid:** Priority date 3/15; no closing date. FAFSA, institutional form required. Applicants notified on a rolling basis starting 3/1; must reply within 2 week(s) of notification.

Academics. Special study options: Accelerated study, combined bachelor's/graduate degree, cooperative education, cross-registration, double major, ESL, honors, independent study, internships, study abroad, teacher certification program, Washington semester, weekend college. **Credit/placement by examination:** AP, CLEP, IB, institutional tests. **Support services:** Learning center, study skills assistance, tutoring, writing center.

Majors. Biology: General, biotechnology. **Business:** General, business admin, marketing. **Communications:** Organizational. **Education:** Early childhood, elementary. **Legal studies:** General, prelaw. **Liberal arts:** Arts/sciences. **Protective services:** Criminal justice. **Psychology:** General.

Most popular majors. Business/marketing 52%, legal studies 6%, liberal arts 21%, psychology 12%.

Computing on campus. 185 workstations in dormitories, library, computer center, student center. Dormitories wired for high-speed internet access and linked to campus network. Commuter students can connect to campus network. Online library, helpline, wireless network available.

Student life. Freshman orientation: Mandatory. Preregistration for classes offered. **Policies:** No smoking or alcohol in dormitories. Freshmen permitted cars on campus. **Housing:** Guaranteed on-campus for all undergraduates. $300 deposit, deadline 5/1. **Activities:** Choral groups, dance, drama, literary magazine, music ensembles, musical theater, radio station, student government, TV station, Interfaith Council, Habitat for Humanity, women in technology, Women of Culture, Alliance, Phi Beta Lambda.

Athletics. NCAA. **Intercollegiate:** Basketball W, cross-country W, soccer W, softball W, tennis W, volleyball W. **Team name:** Wildcats.

Student services. Adult student services, career counseling, student employment services, financial aid counseling, health services, minority student services, personal counseling, placement for graduates, women's services.

Contact. E-mail: admiss@baypath.edu
Phone: (413) 565-1000 ext. 331 Toll-free number: (800) 782-7284 ext. 331
Fax: (413) 565-1105
Lisa Casassa, Director of Admissions, Bay Path College, 588 Longmeadow Street, Longmeadow, MA 01106

Becker College

Worcester, Massachusetts — **CB member**
www.beckercollege.edu — **CB code: 3079**

- Private 4-year liberal arts college
- Residential campus in small city
- 1,739 degree-seeking undergraduates: 36% part-time, 72% women, 8% African American, 1% Asian American, 4% Hispanic American
- 71% of applicants admitted
- SAT or ACT (ACT writing optional) required
- 47% graduate within 6 years

General. Founded in 1887. Regionally accredited. Campuses in Worcester and Leicester. Member of Colleges of the Worcester Consortium. **Degrees:** 174 bachelor's, 157 associate awarded. **ROTC:** Army, Navy, Air Force. **Location:** 49 miles from Boston, 39 miles from Providence, Rhode Island. **Calendar:** Semester, limited summer session. **Full-time faculty:** 40 total. **Part-time faculty:** 40 total. **Class size:** 59% < 20, 35% 20-39, 4% 40-49, 3% 50-99. **Special facilities:** Veterinary clinic, on-site preschool and daycare facility.

Freshman class profile. 2,074 applied, 1,472 admitted, 647 enrolled.

Mid 50% test scores		**Rank in top tenth:**	8%
SAT verbal:	450-540	**End year in good standing:**	60%
SAT math:	370-420	**Return as sophomores:**	60%
ACT:	12-20	**Out-of-state:**	28%
Rank in top quarter:	40%	**Live on campus:**	66%

Basis for selection. High school record, GPA, extracurricular activities important. Recommendations, interview considered. Additional prerequisites for nursing, veterinary technology, and veterinary science programs. Essay recommended. **Homeschooled:** Official transcript from high school with which student is affiliated.

High school preparation. Required and recommended units include English 4, mathematics 3, social studies 1, history 2 and science 2. 2 math including 1 algebra, 1 chemistry with lab, 1 biology with lab required for nursing, physical therapist assistant, veterinary technician, veterinary science, kinesiology programs.

2006-2007 Annual costs. Tuition/fees: $21,080. Additional one time charge of $250 for nursing program. Room/board: $8,500. Books/supplies: $1,000. Personal expenses: $1,170.

2004-2005 Financial aid. Need-based: 282 full-time freshmen applied for aid; 270 were judged to have need; 267 of these received aid. Average need met was 33%. Average scholarship/grant was $6,355; average loan $25. 38% of total undergraduate aid awarded as scholarships/grants, 62% as loans/jobs. **Non-need-based:** Awarded to 80 full-time undergraduates, including 16 freshmen. Scholarships awarded for academics.

Application procedures. Admission: No deadline. $30 fee, may be waived for applicants with need. Application may be submitted online. Admission notification on a rolling basis. Must reply by May 1 or within 4 week(s) if notified thereafter. **Financial aid:** Priority date 3/1; no closing date. FAFSA required. Applicants notified on a rolling basis starting 2/1; must reply within 2 week(s) of notification.

Academics. Special study options: Accelerated study, combined bachelor's/graduate degree, cooperative education, cross-registration, distance learning, independent study, internships, liberal arts/career combination, study abroad, teacher certification program. Member of 15-school Colleges of Worcester consortium, cooperative education at Disney World, international exchange student program. **Credit/placement by examination:** AP, CLEP, institutional tests. 30 credit hours maximum toward associate degree, 60 toward bachelor's. **Support services:** Learning center, reduced course load, remedial instruction, study skills assistance, tutoring, writing center.

Majors. Biology: General. **Business:** Accounting, business admin, hospitality admin, human resources, marketing, tourism/travel. **Communications technology:** General. **Computer sciences:** Networking. **Education:** Early childhood, elementary. **Health:** Preveterinary. **Legal studies:** General, prelaw. **Liberal arts:** Arts/sciences. **Parks/recreation:** Exercise sciences, health/fitness, sports admin. **Protective services:** Criminal justice. **Psychology:** General. **Public administration:** Human services. **Visual/performing arts:** Commercial/advertising art, interior design.

Most popular majors. Business/marketing 40%, communications/journalism 7%, health sciences 7%, legal studies 6%, psychology 24%, security/protective services 7%.

Computing on campus. 155 workstations in dormitories, library, computer center. Dormitories wired for high-speed internet access and linked to campus network. Online library, helpline available.

Student life. Freshman orientation: Mandatory. Preregistration for classes offered. **Policies:** Freshmen permitted cars on campus. **Housing:** Guaranteed on-campus for freshmen. Coed dorms, single-sex dorms, apartments, substance-free housing available. $300 deposit. Substance-free dormitory and over-21 housing available. **Activities:** Choral groups, dance, drama, student government, student newspaper, campus community service club, international club, animal health club, business club, commuter club, early childhood education club, outdoors club, travel club, nursing club.

Athletics. NCAA. **Intercollegiate:** Baseball M, basketball, cross-country, equestrian, field hockey W, football (tackle) M, golf M, ice hockey M, lacrosse, soccer, softball W, tennis, volleyball W. **Intramural:** Badminton, basketball, soccer, table tennis, volleyball. **Team name:** Hawks.

Student services. Adult student services, alcohol/substance abuse counseling, career counseling, student employment services, financial aid counseling, health services, on-campus daycare, personal counseling, placement for graduates. **Physically disabled:** Services for visually, speech, hearing impaired.

Contact. E-mail: admissions@beckercollege.edu
Phone: (508) 791-9241 ext. 245 Toll-free number: (877) 523-2537
Fax: (508) 890-1500
Karen Schedin, Director of Admissions, Becker College, 61 Sever Street, Worcester, MA 01609

Bentley College

Waltham, Massachusetts — **CB member**
www.bentley.edu — **CB code: 3096**

- Private 4-year business college
- Residential campus in small city
- 4,220 degree-seeking undergraduates: 7% part-time, 41% women, 3% African American, 8% Asian American, 4% Hispanic American, 8% international
- 1,271 degree-seeking graduate students
- 43% of applicants admitted
- SAT or ACT with writing, application essay required
- 81% graduate within 6 years; 15% enter graduate study

General. Founded in 1917. Regionally accredited. **Degrees:** 1,019 bachelor's, 3 associate awarded; master's offered. **ROTC:** Army. **Location:** 10 miles from Boston. **Calendar:** Semester, extensive summer session. **Full-time faculty:** 270 total; 82% have terminal degrees, 14% minority, 38% women. **Part-time faculty:** 205 total; 38% have terminal degrees, 10% minority, 39% women. **Class size:** 24% < 20, 76% 20-39, less than 1% 40-49. **Special facilities:** Accounting center for electronic learning and business measurement, academic technology center, alliance for ethics and social responsibility, center for arts and sciences, center for business ethics, center for languages and international collaboration, center for marketing.

Freshman class profile. 5,802 applied, 2,516 admitted, 937 enrolled.

Mid 50% test scores			
SAT verbal:	550-630	Return as sophomores:	94%
SAT math:	600-670	Out-of-state:	52%
Rank in top quarter:	81%	Live on campus:	98%
Rank in top tenth:	39%	International:	6%

Basis for selection. Academic performance, test scores, extracurricular involvement, recommendations most important. Interviews recommended. **Homeschooled:** Statement describing homeschool structure and mission, transcript of courses and grades, letter of recommendation (nonparent) required. Interview strongly recommended.

High school preparation. 19 units recommended. Recommended units include English 4, mathematics 4, history 3, science 3 (laboratory 3), foreign language 3 and academic electives 3. 2 additional units English, math, social or lab science, foreign language or speech recommended.

2006-2007 Annual costs. Tuition/fees: $30,044. Room/board: $10,530.

2004-2005 Financial aid. Need-based: 737 full-time freshmen applied for aid; 511 were judged to have need; 511 of these received aid. Average need met was 91%. Average scholarship/grant was $16,755; average loan $3,940. 68% of total undergraduate aid awarded as scholarships/grants, 32% as loans/jobs. **Non-need-based:** Awarded to 947 full-time undergraduates, including 217 freshmen. Scholarships awarded for academics, athletics, leadership, minority status. **Additional information:** Deadlines for receipt of CSS PROFILE: early decision 12/15, early action and regular decision 2/1.

Application procedures. Admission: Closing date 2/1 (postmark date). $50 fee, may be waived for applicants with need. Application may be submitted online. Admission notification 4/1. Must reply by 5/1. **Financial aid:** Closing date 2/1. FAFSA, CSS PROFILE required. Applicants notified on a rolling basis starting 3/25.

Academics. Special study options: Accelerated study, combined bachelor's/graduate degree, cooperative education, cross-registration, distance learning, double major, honors, independent study, internships, liberal arts/career combination, student-designed major, study abroad, Washington semester. **Credit/placement by examination:** AP, CLEP, IB, SAT, ACT, institutional tests. 15 credit hours maximum toward associate degree, 30 toward bachelor's. CLEP examinations in French, German, Spanish not available to native speakers. Language exams may be taken by part-time evening students only, and require oral exam with department. **Support services:** Learning center, reduced course load, study skills assistance, tutoring, writing center.

Majors. Business: General, accounting, business admin, communications, finance, managerial economics, marketing. **Computer sciences:** General. **English:** English lit. **History:** General. **Legal studies:** Paralegal. **Liberal arts:** Arts/sciences. **Math:** General. **Philosophy/religion:** Philosophy. **Public administration:** Policy analysis.

Most popular majors. Business/marketing 89%, computer/information sciences 7%.

Computing on campus. PC or laptop required. 4,433 workstations in dormitories, library, computer center, student center. Dormitories wired for high-speed internet access and linked to campus network. Commuter students can connect to campus network. Online course registration, online library, helpline, repair service, student web hosting, wireless network available.

Student life. Freshman orientation: Available. Preregistration for classes offered. 3-day program, usually held in June; family members invited on the last day. Attendance strongly encouraged. **Policies:** Academic honesty system, minimum GPA for student leaders. **Housing:** Guaranteed on-campus for all undergraduates. Coed dorms, special housing for disabled, apartments, substance-free housing available. **Activities:** Bands, choral groups, dance, drama, radio station, student government, student newspaper, College Democrats, College Republicans, People Respecting Individuality and Diversity through Education, Christian Fellowship, Habitat for Humanity, Muslim student association, Hillel, Newman club, women's center, Model United Nations.

Athletics. NCAA. **Intercollegiate:** Baseball M, basketball, cross-country, diving, field hockey W, football (tackle) M, golf M, ice hockey M, lacrosse, soccer, softball W, swimming, tennis, track and field, volleyball W. **Intramural:** Basketball, football (non-tackle) M, soccer, softball, volleyball. **Team name:** Falcons.

Student services. Adult student services, alcohol/substance abuse counseling, campus ministries, career counseling, student employment services, financial aid counseling, health services, minority student services, personal counseling, placement for graduates, veterans' counselor, women's services. **Physically disabled:** Services for visually, speech, hearing impaired.

Contact. E-mail: ugadmission@bentley.edu
Phone: (781) 891-2244 Toll-free number: (800) 523-2354
Fax: (781) 891-3414
Kenton Rinehart, Director of Admissions, Bentley College, 175 Forest Street, Waltham, MA 02452-4705

Berklee College of Music

Boston, Massachusetts — **CB member**
www.berklee.edu — **CB code: 3107**

- Private 4-year music college
- Commuter campus in very large city
- 3,164 degree-seeking undergraduates
- 57% of applicants admitted
- SAT or ACT (ACT writing optional), application essay, interview required

General. Founded in 1945. Regionally accredited. Emphasis on contemporary musical idioms. **Degrees:** 576 bachelor's awarded. **Calendar:** Semester, extensive summer session. **Full-time faculty:** 207 total. **Part-time faculty:** 277 total. **Special facilities:** Concert performance center, synthesizer laboratories, recording studios, film scoring laboratories, media center.

Freshman class profile. 2,964 applied, 1,703 admitted, 920 enrolled.

Basis for selection. Musical training and experience, recommendations, academic record, test scores, extracurricular music activities, interview important. Auditions required. **Homeschooled:** Statement describing homeschool structure and mission, transcript of courses and grades, state high school equivalency certificate required. **Learning Disabled:** Students with disabilities should contact Special Services Coordinator.

High school preparation. Recommended units include English 4, mathematics 1, history 1, science 1 (laboratory 1) and academic electives 6. Minimum 2 years recent formal musical study on principal instrument covering standard methods/materials and/or significant practical performance experience plus knowledge of written-music fundamentals normally required of all applicants.

2005-2006 Annual costs. Tuition/fees: $25,778. Room/board: $11,690. Books/supplies: $805. Personal expenses: $2,500.

2004-2005 Financial aid. All financial aid based on need. 623 full-time freshmen applied for aid; 413 were judged to have need; 413 of these received aid. Average need met was 57%. Average scholarship/grant was $5,451; average loan $2,990. 5% of total undergraduate aid awarded as scholarships/grants, 95% as loans/jobs.

Application procedures. Admission: Priority date 11/1; deadline 2/1 (postmark date). $100 fee, may be waived for applicants with need. Application must be submitted online. Admission notification 3/31. Applicants should submit completed application materials well in advance of deadline to ensure placement in desired entry class. **Financial aid:** Priority date 3/1; no closing date. FAFSA, institutional form required. Applicants notified on a rolling basis starting 4/1; must reply within 3 week(s) of notification.

Academics. Bachelor's degree program includes 30 credits general education courses. Four-year professional diploma available (not including general education). **Special study options:** Accelerated study, cross-registration, distance learning, double major, ESL, internships, student-designed major, study abroad, teacher certification program. ProArts Consortium with Boston Architectural Center, Boston Conservatory, Emerson College, Massachusetts College of Art, School of the Museum of Fine Arts. **Credit/placement by examination:** CLEP, institutional tests. 60 credit hours maximum toward bachelor's degree. **Support services:** Learning center, preadmission summer program, tutoring.

Majors. Education: Music. **Health:** Music therapy. **Visual/performing arts:** Jazz, music management, music performance, music theory/composition, piano/organ, voice/opera.

Computing on campus. PC or laptop required. 50 workstations in dormitories, library, computer center. Dormitories wired for high-speed internet access and linked to campus network. Helpline, repair service, student web hosting, wireless network available.

Student life. Freshman orientation: Available. Series of events before and during registration week. **Housing:** Coed dorms available. $200 deposit. Residence space limited. **Activities:** Bands, choral groups, drama, music ensembles, musical theater, student government, student newspaper, black student union, Christian Fellowship, Berklee Cares, women musicians' network, Latinos association, GLBT Allies at Berklee, Korean student association, Amnesty International.

Athletics. Intramural: Basketball, football (non-tackle), ice hockey, soccer.

Student services. Career counseling, student employment services, personal counseling, veterans' counselor. **Physically disabled:** Services for visually impaired.

Contact. E-mail: admissions@berklee.edu
Phone: (617) 747-2222 Toll-free number: (800) 237-5533
Fax: (617) 747-2047
Damien Bracken, Director of Admissions/OSSE, Berklee College of Music, 1140 Boylston Street, Boston, MA 02215

Boston Architectural Center

Boston, Massachusetts
www.the-bac.edu **CB code: 1168**

- Private 6-year school of architecture, design studies and interior design
- Commuter campus in very large city
- 513 degree-seeking undergraduates: 3% part-time, 36% women, 1% African American, 2% Asian American, 5% Hispanic American
- 420 degree-seeking graduate students

General. Founded in 1889. Regionally accredited. Program offers practice-based learning with simultaneous employment in field and academic study. **Degrees:** 55 bachelor's awarded; master's offered. **Calendar:** Semester, limited summer session. **Full-time faculty:** 15 total; 40% have terminal degrees, 27% women. **Part-time faculty:** 391 total; 22% have terminal degrees, 14% minority, 22% women. **Class size:** 88% < 20, 10% 20-39, less than 1% 40-49, 2% 50-99. **Special facilities:** On-campus gallery featuring exhibits of architectural and interior design interest, CAD lab, photography studio.

Basis for selection. Open admission.

2005-2006 Annual costs. Tuition/fees: $8,624. Books/supplies: $1,480. Personal expenses: $2,950.

2005-2006 Financial aid. Need-based: Average need met was 41%. Average scholarship/grant was $4,410; average loan $2,625. 21% of total undergraduate aid awarded as scholarships/grants, 79% as loans/jobs. **Non-need-based:** Scholarships awarded for academics, art, leadership.

Application procedures. Admission: No deadline. $50 fee, may be waived for applicants with need. Application may be submitted online. Admission notification on a rolling basis. Must reply by May 1 or within 2 week(s) if notified thereafter. **Financial aid:** Priority date 4/15; no closing date. FAFSA required. Applicants notified on a rolling basis starting 3/1; must reply within 2 week(s) of notification.

Academics. Bachelor of architecture or interior design awarded after 6-year program of concurrent work and academic curriculum. Students usually transfer into program during second or third years. **Special study options:** Cross-registration, distance learning, independent study, internships, liberal arts/career combination. Member Professional Arts Consortium. **Credit/placement by examination:** AP, CLEP, institutional tests. **Support services:** Learning center, tutoring, writing center.

Majors. Architecture: Architecture, interior.

Computing on campus. 50 workstations in library, computer center. Online library, helpline, wireless network available.

Student life. Freshman orientation: Mandatory. Preregistration for classes offered. Several dates; includes writing test. **Policies:** Campus code of conduct. **Housing:** Dormitory space, when available, at Pro Arts Consortium schools. **Activities:** Student government, community design studio, Studio Q, Atelier.

Student services. Adult student services, career counseling, student employment services, financial aid counseling, minority student services, veterans' counselor. **Physically disabled:** Services for visually, speech, hearing impaired.

Contact. E-mail: admissions@the-bac.edu
Phone: (617) 585-0123 Toll-free number: (877) 585-0100
Fax: (617) 585-0121
Jeff Cutting, Director of Admissions, Boston Architectural Center, 320 Newbury Street, Boston, MA 02115-2795

Boston College

Chestnut Hill, Massachusetts **CB member**
www.bc.edu **CB code: 3083**

- Private 4-year university affiliated with Roman Catholic Church
- Residential campus in small city
- 9,019 degree-seeking undergraduates: 52% women, 6% African American, 9% Asian American, 8% Hispanic American, 2% international
- 4,736 graduate students
- 31% of applicants admitted
- SAT and SAT Subject Tests or ACT with writing, application essay required
- 89% graduate within 6 years; 22% enter graduate study

General. Founded in 1863. Regionally accredited. Independent institution in Jesuit Catholic tradition. **Degrees:** 2,341 bachelor's awarded; master's, doctoral, first professional offered. **ROTC:** Army, Navy, Air Force. **Location:** 6 miles from Boston. **Calendar:** Semester, extensive summer session. **Full-time faculty:** 662 total; 98% have terminal degrees, 12% minority, 38% women. **Part-time faculty:** 623 total. **Class size:** 38% < 20, 47% 20-39, 7% 40-49, 6% 50-99, 3% >100. **Special facilities:** Observatory, theatre arts center, chemistry center, art museum.

Freshman class profile. 23,823 applied, 7,302 admitted, 2,174 enrolled.

Mid 50% test scores		**Return as sophomores:**	96%
SAT verbal:	610-700	**Out-of-state:**	72%
SAT math:	640-720	**Live on campus:**	100%
Rank in top quarter:	95%	**International:**	3%
Rank in top tenth:	75%		

Basis for selection. Evidence of academic ability, intellectual curiosity, strength of character, motivation, creativity, energy, and promise for personal growth and development very important. Recommendations by counselors and teachers, required personal statement and extracurricular activities important. 2 SAT Subject Tests of student's choice required if SAT submitted. Portfolio recommended for studio art majors. **Learning Disabled:** May provide documentation of disability at option of applicant.

High school preparation. 20 units recommended. Recommended units include English 4, mathematics 4, social studies 2, science 4 (laboratory 4) and foreign language 2. 4 units combined between social studies and history recommended. 4 mathematics strongly recommended for School of Management applicants. 2 laboratory science (including 1 chemistry) required of nursing applicants.

2006-2007 Annual costs. Tuition/fees: $33,506. Room/board: $10,720. Books/supplies: $650. Personal expenses: $1,000.

2004-2005 Financial aid. Need-based: 1,441 full-time freshmen applied for aid; 967 were judged to have need; 967 of these received aid. Average need met was 100%. Average scholarship/grant was $19,072; average loan $3,707. 72% of total undergraduate aid awarded as scholarships/grants, 28% as loans/jobs. **Non-need-based:** Awarded to 617 full-time undergraduates, including 112 freshmen. Scholarships awarded for academics, athletics, leadership, ROTC.

Application procedures. Admission: Closing date 1/2 (postmark date). $70 fee, may be waived for applicants with need. Application may be submitted online. Admission notification 4/15. Must reply by 5/1. **Financial aid:** Priority date 2/1; no closing date. FAFSA, CSS PROFILE required. Applicants notified by 4/1; must reply by 5/1.

Academics. Special study options: Accelerated study, combined bachelor's/graduate degree, cross-registration, double major, ESL, exchange student, honors, independent study, internships, liberal arts/career combination, student-designed major, study abroad, teacher certification program, Washington semester. 3-2 program in engineering with Boston University; Tufts Medical School Early Acceptance Program. **Credit/placement by examination:** AP, CLEP, IB. 30 credit hours maximum toward bachelor's degree. **Support services:** Learning center, pre-admission summer program, reduced course load, study skills assistance, tutoring, writing center.

Majors. Area/ethnic studies: Hispanic-American/Latino/Chicano. **Biology:** General, biochemistry. **Business:** Accounting, business admin, finance, human resources, management information systems, managerial economics, operations. **Communications:** General. **Computer sciences:** General, computer science, information systems. **Education:** Early childhood, elementary, secondary. **English:** English lit. **Foreign languages:** Ancient Greek, classics, French, German, Italian, Latin, linguistics, Russian, Spanish. **Health:**

Nursing (RN). **History:** General. **Math:** General. **Philosophy/religion:** Philosophy. **Physical sciences:** Chemistry, geology, geophysics, physics. **Psychology:** General. **Social sciences:** Economics, political science, sociology. **Visual/performing arts:** Art history/conservation, dramatic, film/cinema, studio arts.

Most popular majors. Business/marketing 23%, communications/journalism 10%, education 9%, English 9%, history 7%, social sciences 15%.

Computing on campus. 1,000 workstations in library, computer center, student center. Dormitories wired for high-speed internet access and linked to campus network. Commuter students can connect to campus network. Online course registration, online library, helpline, repair service, student web hosting, wireless network available.

Student life. Freshman orientation: Mandatory, $370 fee. Preregistration for classes offered. 3-day, 2-night program; several sessions offered during summer. **Housing:** Coed dorms, single-sex dorms, special housing for disabled, substance-free housing available. $250 partly refundable deposit, deadline 5/1. Honors house, multicultural floor, 24-hour quiet living floor, social justice floor available. Apartment-style housing and townhouse-style housing available for upperclassmen. **Activities:** Bands, choral groups, dance, drama, film society, literary magazine, music ensembles, musical theater, radio station, student government, student newspaper, symphony orchestra, TV station, 4Boston, Amnesty International, Appalachia Volunteers, Asian Caucus, black student forum, Buddhist club, Hillel, Ignatian Society, Puerto Rican association.

Athletics. NCAA. **Intercollegiate:** Baseball M, basketball, cheerleading, cross-country, diving, fencing, field hockey W, football (tackle) M, golf, ice hockey, lacrosse, rowing (crew) W, sailing, skiing, soccer, softball W, swimming, tennis, track and field, volleyball W. **Intramural:** Basketball, cross-country, ice hockey, racquetball, softball, tennis, track and field, volleyball. **Team name:** Eagles.

Student services. Alcohol/substance abuse counseling, campus ministries, career counseling, services for economically disadvantaged, student employment services, financial aid counseling, health services, minority student services, personal counseling, placement for graduates, women's services. **Physically disabled:** Services for visually, speech, hearing impaired.

Contact. E-mail: ugadmis@bc.edu
Phone: (617) 552-3100 Toll-free number: (800) 360-2522
Fax: (617) 552-0798
John Mahoney, Director of Undergraduate Admission, Boston College, 140 Commonwealth Avenue, Devlin Hall 208, Chestnut Hill, MA 02467-3809

Boston Conservatory

Boston, Massachusetts — **CB member**
www.bostonconservatory.edu — **CB code: 3084**

- Private 4-year music college
- Residential campus in very large city
- 409 degree-seeking undergraduates
- 167 graduate students
- 43% of applicants admitted
- Application essay required

General. Founded in 1867. Regionally accredited. **Degrees:** 71 bachelor's awarded; master's offered. **Location:** Downtown. **Calendar:** Semester, limited summer session. **Full-time faculty:** 44 total. **Part-time faculty:** 128 total. **Class size:** 89% < 20, 9% 20-39, less than 1% 40-49, less than 1% 50-99.

Freshman class profile. 940 applied, 408 admitted, 138 enrolled.

Out-of-state:	75%	**Sororities:**	5%
Live on campus:	98%		

Basis for selection. Audition carries most weight. Academic record and artistic background strongly considered. Test scores, recommendations, personal essay, school and community activities, interview important. Audition required. Interview required of music education, composition majors.

High school preparation. Required units include English 4, mathematics 3, social studies 2, history 2, science 2 and foreign language 2.

2005-2006 Annual costs. Tuition/fees: $26,005. Room/board: $13,780. Books/supplies: $500. Personal expenses: $1,413.

Financial aid. Non-need-based: Scholarships awarded for music/drama.

Application procedures. Admission: Priority date 12/1; deadline 2/1 (postmark date). $105 fee. Admission notification 4/1. Must reply by 5/1. **Financial aid:** Closing date 2/1. FAFSA, institutional form required. Applicants notified by 4/1; must reply by 5/1.

Academics. Special study options: Cross-registration, double major, ESL, independent study, teacher certification program. **Credit/placement by examination:** CLEP, institutional tests. 75 credit hours maximum toward bachelor's degree. **Support services:** Pre-admission summer program, study skills assistance, tutoring, writing center.

Majors. Education: Music. **Visual/performing arts:** Dance, music performance, music theory/composition, piano/organ, voice/opera.

Computing on campus. 20 workstations in library. Dormitories linked to campus network. Online library available.

Student life. Freshman orientation: Mandatory, $150 fee. Week prior to registration includes college life seminar, advising, parent luncheon, school tours, city-wide tours, placements, auditions. **Housing:** Guaranteed on-campus for freshmen. Coed dorms, single-sex dorms available. $250 deposit, deadline 5/1. Graduate house. **Activities:** Literary magazine, student government, student newspaper, African American artists' association, community services association, Christian Fellowship, international student organization, environmental awareness group, peer support aides, Taiwan Chinese student association, gay and lesbian artists' association, Organizacion De Artistas Hispanos, Korean Society.

Student services. Career counseling, health services, personal counseling.

Contact. E-mail: admissions@bostonconservatory.edu
Phone: (617) 912-9153 Fax: (617) 536-3176
Zaragoza Guerra, Dean of Enrollment Services, Boston Conservatory, 8 The Fenway, Boston, MA 02215

Boston University

Boston, Massachusetts — **CB member**
www.bu.edu — **CB code: 3087**

- Private 4-year university
- Residential campus in very large city
- 16,538 degree-seeking undergraduates: 2% part-time, 59% women, 3% African American, 13% Asian American, 6% Hispanic American, 6% international
- 11,639 degree-seeking graduate students
- 57% of applicants admitted
- SAT or ACT with writing, SAT Subject Tests, application essay required
- 77% graduate within 6 years; 30% enter graduate study

General. Founded in 1839. Regionally accredited. **Degrees:** 3,551 bachelor's awarded; master's, doctoral, first professional offered. **ROTC:** Army, Navy, Air Force. **Calendar:** Semester, extensive summer session. **Full-time faculty:** 1,454 total; 85% have terminal degrees, 10% minority, 34% women. **Part-time faculty:** 984 total; 5% minority, 42% women. **Class size:** 51% < 20, 34% 20-39, 5% 40-49, 6% 50-99, 4% >100. **Special facilities:** Biodiversity station in Ecuador, dedicated management library, art galleries, planetarium, National Public Radio station, 20th century archives, professional theater/theater company, language laboratory, center for remote sensing, speech, language and hearing clinic, culinary center, communication multimedia lab.

Freshman class profile. 31,431 applied, 17,810 admitted, 4,212 enrolled.

Mid 50% test scores		**Rank in top tenth:**	58%
SAT verbal:	580-680	**End year in good standing:**	93%
SAT math:	600-690	**Return as sophomores:**	91%
ACT:	26-30	**Out-of-state:**	81%
GPA 3.50 or higher:	55%	**Live on campus:**	98%
GPA 3.0-3.49:	36%	**International:**	6%
GPA 2.0-2.99:	9%	**Fraternities:**	1%
Rank in top quarter:	87%	**Sororities:**	1%

Basis for selection. Evidence of strong academic performance in challenging college-prep curriculum most important. SAT Subject Tests in Chemistry and Math (level 2) required for accelerated medical and dental programs. Others required to submit 2 subject tests in subject areas of their choice. Interview required for accelerated medical/dental programs, all non-performance theater arts majors. Audition required for music, theater performance programs. Portfolio required of visual arts, stage management, theatrical design majors. Portfolio or audition required for College of Fine Arts.

High school preparation. 15 units required; 20 recommended. Required and recommended units include English 4, mathematics 3-4, social studies 3-4, science 3-4 (laboratory 3-4) and foreign language 2-4. Precalculus required. Social studies should include history.

2006-2007 Annual costs. Tuition/fees: $33,792. Room/board: $10,480. Books/supplies: $754. Personal expenses: $1,169.

2005-2006 Financial aid. **Need-based:** 2,708 full-time freshmen applied for aid; 2,163 were judged to have need; 2,156 of these received aid. Average need met was 90%. Average scholarship/grant was $19,149; average loan $3,593. 76% of total undergraduate aid awarded as scholarships/grants, 24% as loans/jobs. **Non-need-based:** Awarded to 4,003 full-time undergraduates, including 1,462 freshmen. Scholarships awarded for academics, alumni affiliation, art, athletics, leadership, music/drama, religious affiliation, ROTC, state residency. **Additional information:** Financial aid deadline for early decision applicants: 11/01; notification date: 2/15.

Application procedures. **Admission:** Closing date 1/1 (receipt date). $70 fee, may be waived for applicants with need. Application may be submitted online. Admission notification 4/15. Must reply by 5/1. Application deadline December 1 for accelerated medical and dental combined degree and trustee, Boston high school, Cardinal Medeiros Scholar programs. **Financial aid:** Closing date 2/15. FAFSA, CSS PROFILE required. Applicants notified on a rolling basis starting 3/15; must reply by 5/1 or within 2 week(s) of notification.

Academics. University Professors Program offers cross-disciplinary degree to academically gifted students. **Special study options:** Accelerated study, combined bachelor's/graduate degree, cooperative education, cross-registration, distance learning, double major, dual enrollment of high school students, ESL, honors, independent study, internships, liberal arts/career combination, semester at sea, student-designed major, study abroad, teacher certification program, Washington semester. Extensive opportunities for study abroad as well as internships available in South and Central America, Europe, Africa, China, Pacific Rim, Russia. Field study in marine science at Woods Hole Institute, in environmental/ecological science in Ecuador, and at Photonics Center, combined bachelor's/master's degrees, 6-year physical therapy (BS/DPT) program, 5-year occupational therapy (BS/MS) program; 7-year accelerated MD, DMD programs. **Credit/placement by examination:** AP, CLEP, IB, institutional tests. 32 credit hours maximum toward bachelor's degree. Credits assigned vary by school and college. Scores higher than minimums may result in additional credit depending on department. **Support services:** Learning center, study skills assistance, tutoring, writing center.

Majors. **Area/ethnic studies:** American, East Asian, Italian, Latin American, Russian/Slavic. **Biology:** General, biochemistry, ecology, marine, molecular. **Business:** Accounting, business admin, entrepreneurial studies, finance, hospitality admin, international, international finance, management information systems, market research, marketing, operations, organizational behavior. **Communications:** General, advertising, broadcast journalism, journalism, public relations. **Computer sciences:** General. **Conservation:** General, environmental science, environmental studies, management/policy. **Education:** General, art, bilingual, chemistry, Deaf/hearing impaired, drama/dance, early childhood, elementary, English, mathematics, music, physical, science, social studies, special. **Engineering:** General, aerospace, biomedical, computer, electrical, mechanical. **Foreign languages:** General, ancient Greek, classics, French, German, Italian, Latin, linguistics, modern Greek, Russian, Spanish. **Health:** Athletic training, communication disorders, dental lab technology. **History:** General. **Interdisciplinary:** Math/computer science, neuroscience, nutrition sciences. **Legal studies:** Legal secretary, paralegal. **Math:** General. **Parks/recreation:** Exercise sciences. **Philosophy/religion:** Philosophy, religion. **Physical sciences:** Astronomy, astrophysics, chemistry, geology, geophysics, physics, planetary. **Psychology:** General. **Social sciences:** Anthropology, archaeology, economics, geography, international relations, political science, sociology, urban studies. **Visual/performing arts:** General, acting, art history/conservation, cinematography, commercial/advertising art, directing/producing, drawing, music history, music performance, music theory/composition, painting, piano/organ, sculpture, theater design, theater history, voice/opera.

Most popular majors. Business/marketing 17%, communications/journalism 17%, engineering/engineering technologies 8%, psychology 8%, social sciences 17%.

Computing on campus. 750 workstations in dormitories, library, computer center, student center. Dormitories wired for high-speed internet access and linked to campus network. Commuter students can connect to campus network. Online course registration, online library, helpline, repair service, student web hosting, wireless network available.

Student life. **Freshman orientation:** Mandatory, $135 fee. Preregistration for classes offered. Summer program. **Policies:** Campus residents must abide by guest/visitor policy. Freshmen permitted cars on campus. **Housing:** Guaranteed on-campus for all undergraduates. Coed dorms, single-sex dorms, special housing for disabled, apartments, cooperative housing available. $650 deposit, deadline 5/1. Specialty residences or floors for students with common academic, cultural, or extracurricular interests available. **Activities:** Bands, choral groups, dance, drama, film society, literary magazine, opera, radio station, student government, student newspaper, symphony orchestra, over 400 student organizations.

Athletics. NCAA. **Intercollegiate:** Basketball, cross-country, diving, field hockey W, golf, ice hockey, lacrosse W, rowing (crew), soccer, softball W, swimming, tennis, track and field, wrestling M. **Intramural:** Basketball, football (non-tackle), ice hockey W, soccer, softball, swimming, tennis, volleyball, water polo. **Team name:** Terriers.

Student services. Adult student services, campus ministries, career counseling, student employment services, financial aid counseling, health services, minority student services, personal counseling, placement for graduates, veterans' counselor. **Physically disabled:** Services for visually, speech, hearing impaired. **Learning disabled:** Comprehensive services available.

Contact. E-mail: admissions@bu.edu
Phone: (617) 353-2300 Fax: (617) 353-9695
Kelly Walter, Director, Office of Undergraduate Admissions, Boston University, 121 Bay State Road, Boston, MA 02215

Brandeis University

Waltham, Massachusetts — **CB member**
www.brandeis.edu — **CB code: 3092**

- Private 4-year university
- Residential campus in small city
- 3,215 degree-seeking undergraduates: 56% women, 3% African American, 7% Asian American, 4% Hispanic American, 8% international
- 1,601 degree-seeking graduate students
- 38% of applicants admitted
- SAT or ACT with writing, application essay required
- 88% graduate within 6 years

General. Founded in 1948. Regionally accredited. **Degrees:** 722 bachelor's awarded; master's, doctoral offered. **ROTC:** Army, Air Force. **Location:** 10 miles from Boston. **Calendar:** Semester, limited summer session. **Full-time faculty:** 343 total; 96% have terminal degrees, 11% minority, 38% women. **Part-time faculty:** 129 total; 76% have terminal degrees, 7% minority, 54% women. **Class size:** 62% < 20, 25% 20-39, 4% 40-49, 6% 50-99, 3% >100. **Special facilities:** Basic medical sciences research center, art museum, spatial orientation laboratory, center for complex systems, astronomical observatory.

Freshman class profile. 7,343 applied, 2,794 admitted, 739 enrolled.

Mid 50% test scores			
SAT verbal:	630-720	Rank in top quarter:	96%
SAT math:	640-720	Rank in top tenth:	74%
ACT:	28-33	Return as sophomores:	94%
GPA 3.50 or higher:	84%	Out-of-state:	63%
GPA 3.0-3.49:	13%	Live on campus:	95%
GPA 2.0-2.99:	3%	International:	9%

Basis for selection. Evidence of accomplishment and development most important. School and teacher statements, test scores also important. Students taking SAT must take 2 SAT Subject Tests from 2 subject areas. Interview recommended.

High school preparation. 16 units recommended. Recommended units include English 4, mathematics 3, history 1, science 1 (laboratory 1), foreign language 3 and academic electives 4.

2005-2006 Annual costs. Tuition/fees: $32,501. Room/board: $9,050. Books/supplies: $700. Personal expenses: $1,000.

2005-2006 Financial aid. **Need-based:** 581 full-time freshmen applied for aid; 401 were judged to have need; 401 of these received aid. Average need met was 83%. Average scholarship/grant was $19,252; average loan $3,826. 75% of total undergraduate aid awarded as scholarships/grants, 25% as loans/jobs. **Non-need-based:** Awarded to 907 full-time undergraduates, including 639 freshmen. Scholarships awarded for academics.

Application procedures. **Admission:** Closing date 1/15 (receipt date). $55 fee, may be waived for applicants with need. Application may be submitted online. Admission notification 4/1. Must reply by 5/1. **Financial aid:** Priority date 1/15; no closing date. FAFSA, CSS PROFILE required. Applicants notified on a rolling basis starting 4/1.

Academics. **Special study options:** Cross-registration, double major, independent study, internships, student-designed major, study abroad, Washington semester. BA/MA in physics, history; seminars at Boston Museum of Fine Arts and seminars available through Massachusetts Bay Marine Studies Consortium, early admission to Mt. Sinai Medical School (NY) and Tufts Medical School (MA). **Credit/placement by examination:** CLEP, IB, institutional tests. **Support services:** Reduced course load, remedial instruction, study skills assistance, tutoring, writing center.

Majors. **Area/ethnic studies:** African, African-American, American, East Asian, European, Latin American, Near/Middle Eastern, women's. **Biology:** General, biochemistry. **Computer sciences:** General, computer science. **English:** American lit, creative writing, English lit. **Foreign languages:** Ancient Greek, Arabic, Biblical, Chinese, classics, comparative lit, French, German, Hebrew, Italian, Japanese, Latin, linguistics, Russian, Spanish. **Health:** Health care admin. **History:** General. **Interdisciplinary:** Global studies, neuroscience. **Math:** General. **Philosophy/religion:** Islamic, Judaic, philosophy. **Physical sciences:** Chemistry, physics. **Psychology:** General. **Social sciences:** Anthropology, economics, political science, sociology. **Visual/performing arts:** Art, dramatic.

Most popular majors. Area/ethnic studies 11%, biology 10%, English 6%, history 6%, psychology 9%, social sciences 35%, visual/performing arts 6%.

Computing on campus. 104 workstations in library, computer center, student center. Dormitories linked to campus network. Commuter students can connect to campus network. Online course registration, helpline, repair service, student web hosting, wireless network available.

Student life. **Freshman orientation:** Mandatory, $175 fee. Preregistration for classes offered. 5-day program beginning weekend before Labor Day weekend. **Housing:** Guaranteed on-campus for freshmen. Coed dorms, special housing for disabled, apartments available. $200 deposit, deadline 6/1. **Activities:** Bands, choral groups, dance, drama, film society, literary magazine, music ensembles, musical theater, radio station, student government, student newspaper, symphony orchestra, TV station, 246 recognized clubs and organizations.

Athletics. NCAA. **Intercollegiate:** Baseball M, basketball, cross-country, diving, fencing, golf M, sailing, soccer, softball W, swimming, tennis, track and field, volleyball W. **Intramural:** Basketball, equestrian, football (non-tackle) M, golf, ice hockey M, softball, squash, table tennis, tennis, volleyball, water polo, weight lifting. **Team name:** Judges.

Student services. Campus ministries, career counseling, student employment services, health services, on-campus daycare, personal counseling, placement for graduates, veterans' counselor. **Physically disabled:** Services for visually, speech, hearing impaired.

Contact. E-mail: sendinfo@brandeis.edu
Phone: (781) 736-3500 Toll-free number: (800) 622-0622
Fax: (781) 736-3536
Gil Villanueva, Dean of Admissions, Brandeis University, Office of Admissions, Waltham, MA 02454-9110

Bridgewater State College

Bridgewater, Massachusetts — **CB member**
www.bridgew.edu — **CB code: 3517**

- Public 4-year liberal arts and teachers college
- Commuter campus in large town
- 7,467 degree-seeking undergraduates: 15% part-time, 60% women, 4% African American, 1% Asian American, 2% Hispanic American, 1% international
- 1,798 graduate students
- 80% of applicants admitted
- SAT or ACT (ACT writing optional) required
- 48% graduate within 6 years

General. Founded in 1840. Regionally accredited. **Degrees:** 1,233 bachelor's awarded; master's offered. **ROTC:** Army, Air Force. **Location:** 30 miles from Boston, 35 miles from Providence, Rhode Island. **Calendar:** Semester, extensive summer session. **Full-time faculty:** 260 total. **Part-time faculty:** 230 total.

Freshman class profile. 5,446 applied, 4,369 admitted, 1,332 enrolled.

Mid 50% test scores			
SAT verbal:	460-560	Rank in top quarter:	30%
SAT math:	460-560	Rank in top tenth:	6%
ACT:	19-23	Return as sophomores:	75%
GPA 3.50 or higher:	17%	Out-of-state:	5%
GPA 3.0-3.49:	30%	Live on campus:	49%
GPA 2.0-2.99:	53%	International:	1%

Basis for selection. High school achievement most important, including weighted high school GPA and completion of 16 college preparatory courses. Test scores, essay, extracurricular activities also important. Class rank, recommendations considered. Essay recommended. **Learning Disabled:** Exemption from admissions standardized testing upon documentation of diagnostic test results. Must complete 16 required academic courses with minimum GPA 3.00 or present evidence of potential for academic success.

High school preparation. 16 units required. Required units include English 4, mathematics 3, social studies 1, history 1, science 3 (laboratory 2), foreign language 2 and academic electives 2. Foreign language units must be in same language.

2005-2006 Annual costs. Tuition/fees: $5,506; $11,646 out-of-state. Room/board: $6,614. Books/supplies: $800. Personal expenses: $1,500.

2005-2006 Financial aid. **Need-based:** 1,012 full-time freshmen applied for aid; 709 were judged to have need; 706 of these received aid. Average need met was 51%. Average scholarship/grant was $2,356; average loan $2,688. 41% of total undergraduate aid awarded as scholarships/grants, 59% as loans/jobs. **Non-need-based:** Awarded to 180 full-time undergraduates, including 43 freshmen. Scholarships awarded for academics, leadership, minority status, state residency.

Application procedures. **Admission:** Priority date 2/15; no deadline. $25 fee, may be waived for applicants with need. Application may be submitted online. Admission notification on a rolling basis beginning on or about 12/15. **Financial aid:** Priority date 3/1; no closing date. FAFSA required. Applicants notified on a rolling basis starting 4/1.

Academics. Graduate certificates available in geo-technology, information systems management, accounting, finance, marketing management, operations. Post-baccalaureate teaching certification also available. **Special study options:** Accelerated study, combined bachelor's/graduate degree, cross-registration, distance learning, double major, dual enrollment of high school students, ESL, exchange student, honors, independent study, internships, liberal arts/career combination, study abroad, teacher certification program, Washington semester. 5-year combined BS/MS management program. **Credit/placement by examination:** AP, CLEP, IB, institutional tests. **Support services:** Learning center, pre-admission summer program, reduced course load, remedial instruction, study skills assistance, tutoring, writing center.

Majors. **Architecture:** Urban/community planning. **Biology:** General, biochemistry, biomedical sciences, cellular/molecular, environmental. **Business:** Accounting, business admin, finance, international, management information systems, marketing, transportation. **Communications:** General. **Computer sciences:** Computer science. **Education:** Art, biology, drama/dance, early childhood, elementary, English, health, health occupations, music, physical, special. **English:** Creative writing, English lit. **Foreign languages:** Spanish. **Health:** Athletic training, communication disorders, kinesiotherapy. **History:** General. **Legal studies:** General. **Math:** General. **Parks/recreation:** General, exercise sciences, sports admin. **Philosophy/religion:** Ethics, philosophy. **Physical sciences:** Chemistry, geochemistry, geology, physics. **Protective services:** Criminal justice. **Psychology:** General. **Public administration:** Social work. **Social sciences:** Archaeology, economics, geography, international relations, political science, sociology, U.S. government. **Transportation:** Airline/commercial pilot, aviation management. **Visual/performing arts:** Art history/conservation, crafts, dramatic, graphic design, photography, studio arts.

Most popular majors. Business/marketing 14%, communications/journalism 7%, education 12%, English 6%, psychology 15%, security/protective services 7%, social sciences 8%.

Computing on campus. PC or laptop required. 780 workstations in library, computer center, student center. Dormitories wired for high-speed internet access and linked to campus network. Commuter students can connect to campus network. Online course registration, online library, helpline, repair service, wireless network available.

Student life. **Freshman orientation:** Mandatory, $160 fee. Preregistration for classes offered. **Housing:** Coed dorms, single-sex dorms, apartments, substance-free housing available. $150 fully refundable deposit, deadline 5/1. Quiet floor, nonsmoking floor available in residence hall. Housing available over breaks for athletes, student teachers, international students. **Activities:** Bands, choral groups, dance, drama, literary magazine, music ensembles, musical theater, radio station, student government, student newspaper, Christian Fellowship, College Democrats, Afro-American Society, international club, La Sociedad Latina, Amnesty International, Big Brothers/Big Sisters, Habitat for Humanity.

Athletics. NCAA. **Intercollegiate:** Baseball M, basketball, cross-country, diving, field hockey W, football (tackle) M, lacrosse W, soccer, softball W, swimming, tennis, track and field, volleyball W, wrestling M. **Intramural:** Basketball, football (tackle) M, lacrosse M, soccer, softball, tennis, volleyball, water polo. **Team name:** Bears.

Student services. Adult student services, campus ministries, career counseling, student employment services, financial aid counseling, health services, minority student services, on-campus daycare, personal counseling, placement for graduates, veterans' counselor, women's services. **Physically disabled:** Services for visually, speech, hearing impaired.

Contact. E-mail: admission@bridgew.edu
Phone: (508) 531-1237 Fax: (508) 531-1746
Gregg Meyer, Director of Admissions, Bridgewater State College, Gates House, Bridgewater, MA 02325

Cambridge College

Cambridge, Massachusetts
www.cambridgecollege.edu **CB code: 3612**

- Private 4-year liberal arts college
- Commuter campus in very large city
- 909 degree-seeking undergraduates: 75% part-time, 72% women
- 3,116 degree-seeking graduate students

General. Regionally accredited. **Degrees:** 111 bachelor's awarded; master's, doctoral offered. **Calendar:** Continuous, limited summer session. **Full-time faculty:** 30 total. **Part-time faculty:** 700 total.

Basis for selection. Open admission. Open admissions but 3 years work experience after high school recommended, including employment, volunteer work, training, community involvement. Placement testing may be used if applicant does not have high school degree or GED.

2005-2006 Annual costs. Tuition/fees: $9,750.

2005-2006 Financial aid. Need-based: Average scholarship/grant was $4,550; average loan $3,230. 24% of total undergraduate aid awarded as scholarships/grants, 76% as loans/jobs.

Application procedures. Admission: No deadline. $30 fee. Admission notification on a rolling basis. **Financial aid:** No deadline. FAFSA, institutional form required.

Academics. Special study options: Independent study, weekend college. **Credit/placement by examination:** CLEP. **Support services:** Writing center.

Majors. Business: Management science. **Psychology:** General. **Public administration:** Human services.

Most popular majors. Business/marketing 9%, liberal arts 42%, psychology 41%, public administration/social services 8%.

Computing on campus. Online library available.

Contact. E-mail: admit@cambridgecollege.edu
Phone: (888) 868-1002
Ezat Parnia, Executive Vice President, Cambridge College, 1000 Massachusetts Avenue, Cambridge, MA 02138

Clark University

Worcester, Massachusetts **CB member**
www.clarku.edu **CB code: 3279**

- Private 4-year university and liberal arts college
- Residential campus in small city
- 2,142 degree-seeking undergraduates: 3% part-time, 60% women, 2% African American, 4% Asian American, 2% Hispanic American, 7% international
- 809 degree-seeking graduate students
- 62% of applicants admitted
- SAT or ACT (ACT writing optional), application essay required
- 70% graduate within 6 years; 30% enter graduate study

General. Founded in 1887. Regionally accredited. Clark European Center in Luxembourg offers intensive May term including classes and field work. Courses also offered at Bermuda Biological Station. Students may also enroll in semester-long environmental science program at marine biological laboratory at Woods Hole Oceanographic Institute. **Degrees:** 472 bachelor's awarded; master's, doctoral offered. **ROTC:** Army, Navy, Air Force. **Location:** 50 miles from Boston. **Calendar:** Semester, limited summer session. **Full-time faculty:** 167 total; 98% have terminal degrees, 15% minority, 38% women. **Part-time faculty:** 96 total. **Class size:** 61% < 20, 31% 20-39, 3% 40-49, 4% 50-99, less than 1% >100. **Special facilities:** Robert Goddard exhibition, map library, rare book room, NMR research facility, observatory, electronic music facility, arboretum, crafts studio, 2 theaters, environmental education laboratory, student-run recycling center, pulsed magnetic field laboratory, Holocaust studies center.

Freshman class profile. 4,463 applied, 2,748 admitted, 560 enrolled.

Mid 50% test scores		**Rank in top quarter:**	70%
SAT verbal:	560-660	**Rank in top tenth:**	34%
SAT math:	540-650	**Return as sophomores:**	86%
ACT:	24-28	**Out-of-state:**	66%
GPA 3.50 or higher:	49%	**Live on campus:**	97%
GPA 3.0-3.49:	38%	**International:**	8%
GPA 2.0-2.99:	13%		

Basis for selection. School achievement record and courses, recommendations, test scores most important. Special talents, accomplishments, motivation, and individual circumstances, including outside activities and jobs, also important. Interview recommended. Portfolio recommended for art majors.

High school preparation. 16 units recommended. Recommended units include English 4, mathematics 3, social studies 2, history 2, science 3 (laboratory 2) and foreign language 2.

2006-2007 Annual costs. Tuition/fees: $31,465. New student contingency fee: $50. Fifth-year tuition waived for eligible undergraduates admitted to accelerated bachelor's/master's programs. Room/board: $5,900. Books/supplies: $800. Personal expenses: $700.

2005-2006 Financial aid. Need-based: 408 full-time freshmen applied for aid; 309 were judged to have need; 302 of these received aid. Average need met was 93%. Average scholarship/grant was $17,645; average loan $3,208. 73% of total undergraduate aid awarded as scholarships/grants, 27% as loans/jobs. **Non-need-based:** Awarded to 1,144 full-time undergraduates, including 306 freshmen. Scholarships awarded for academics, leadership.

Application procedures. Admission: Closing date 1/15 (postmark date). $50 fee, may be waived for applicants with need. Application may be submitted online. Admission notification 4/1. Must reply by 5/1. **Financial aid:** Closing date 2/1. FAFSA, CSS PROFILE required. Applicants notified by 3/31; must reply by 5/1 or within 2 week(s) of notification.

Academics. Interdisciplinary majors, special programs, and accelerated bachelor's/master's program with fifth-year tuition free available. **Special study options:** Combined bachelor's/graduate degree, cross-registration, double major, ESL, independent study, internships, liberal arts/career combination, student-designed major, study abroad, teacher certification program, Washington semester. 3-2 engineering programs with Columbia University (NY), Worcester Polytechnic Institute, and Washington University. **Credit/placement by examination:** AP, CLEP, IB, SAT, institutional tests. 16 credit hours maximum toward bachelor's degree. **Support services:** Reduced course load, study skills assistance, writing center.

Majors. Biology: General, biochemistry, bioinformatics, molecular. **Business:** General, business admin. **Communications:** General. **Computer sciences:** General, computer science. **Conservation:** Environmental science, environmental studies. **Foreign languages:** General, classics, comparative lit, French, Spanish. **History:** General. **Interdisciplinary:** Global studies, math/computer science, science/society. **Liberal arts:** Arts/sciences. **Math:** General. **Philosophy/religion:** Philosophy. **Physical sciences:** Chemistry, physics. **Psychology:** General. **Public administration:** General. **Social sciences:** Economics, geography, international relations, political science, sociology. **Visual/performing arts:** General, art, art history/conservation, dramatic, film/cinema, studio arts.

Most popular majors. Biology 11%, communications/journalism 7%, English 7%, psychology 17%, social sciences 29%, visual/performing arts 6%.

Computing on campus. 200 workstations in library, computer center, student center. Dormitories wired for high-speed internet access and linked to campus network. Commuter students can connect to campus network. Online course registration, online library, helpline, student web hosting, wireless network available.

Student life. Freshman orientation: Mandatory, $200 fee. Preregistration for classes offered. Program held during week prior to fall semester; includes course selection and registration. **Policies:** Freshmen permitted cars on campus. **Housing:** Guaranteed on-campus for freshmen. Coed dorms, single-sex dorms, special housing for disabled, apartments, substance-free housing available. $100 nonrefundable deposit, deadline 5/1. Some university-owned off-campus housing available. Year-round house, quiet house, other special interest houses available. All residence halls nonsmoking. **Activities:** Bands, choral groups, dance, drama, film society, literary magazine, music ensembles, musical theater, radio station, student government, student newspaper, symphony orchestra, TV station, approximately 80 student clubs and organizations.

Athletics. NCAA. **Intercollegiate:** Baseball M, basketball, cross-country, diving, field hockey W, lacrosse M, rowing (crew), soccer, softball W, swimming, tennis, volleyball W. **Intramural:** Badminton, basketball, racquetball, soccer, softball, squash, volleyball, water polo. **Team name:** Cougars.

Student services. Adult student services, alcohol/substance abuse counseling, campus ministries, career counseling, student employment services, financial aid counseling, health services, minority student services, personal counseling, placement for graduates, women's services. **Physically disabled:** Services for visually, speech, hearing impaired.

Contact. E-mail: admissions@clarku.edu
Phone: (508) 793-7431 Toll-free number: (800) 462-5275
Fax: (508) 793-8821
Harold Wingood, Dean of Admissions, Clark University, 950 Main Street, Worcester, MA 01610-1477

College of the Holy Cross

Worcester, Massachusetts — **CB member**
www.holycross.edu — **CB code: 3282**

- Private 4-year liberal arts college affiliated with Roman Catholic Church
- Residential campus in small city
- 2,777 degree-seeking undergraduates: 55% women, 4% African American, 5% Asian American, 6% Hispanic American, 1% international
- 48% of applicants admitted
- Application essay required
- 91% graduate within 6 years; 24% enter graduate study

General. Founded in 1843. Regionally accredited. College in the Jesuit tradition. **Degrees:** 646 bachelor's awarded. **ROTC:** Army, Navy, Air Force. **Location:** 45 miles from Boston. **Calendar:** Semester. **Full-time faculty:** 240 total; 92% have terminal degrees, 11% minority, 54% women. **Part-time faculty:** 57 total; 4% minority, 54% women. **Class size:** 51% < 20, 47% 20-39, 1% 40-49, 2% 50-99. **Special facilities:** Greenhouse, facilities for aquatic research.

Freshman class profile. 4,744 applied, 2,270 admitted, 723 enrolled.

Mid 50% test scores		**Return as sophomores:**	97%
SAT verbal:	620-640	**Out-of-state:**	62%
SAT math:	580-680	**Live on campus:**	100%
Rank in top quarter:	93%	**International:**	1%
Rank in top tenth:	66%		

Basis for selection. Academic record, recommendations, interview, essay, extracurricular activities important. Evidence of superior achievement in analytical reading and writing of particular importance. Advanced placement and honors courses recommended. Standardized test scores optional. Students have option to submit scores if they believe results present fuller picture of achievements and potential. Students who opt not to submit scores will not be at any disadvantage in admissions decisions. **Homeschooled:** On-campus interview highly encouraged. Applicants should submit course work samples, personal statement, and college transcripts if applicable. If homeschooling associated with particular organization or program, submit description.

High school preparation. 20 units recommended. Recommended units include English 4, mathematics 4, social studies 2, history 2, science 4, foreign language 3 and academic electives 1.

2006-2007 Annual costs. Tuition/fees: $33,313. Room/board: $9,580. Books/supplies: $700. Personal expenses: $900.

2005-2006 Financial aid. Need-based: 522 full-time freshmen applied for aid; 437 were judged to have need; 421 of these received aid. Average need met was 100%. Average scholarship/grant was $20,573; average loan $3,513. 73% of total undergraduate aid awarded as scholarships/grants, 27% as loans/jobs. **Non-need-based:** Awarded to 210 full-time undergraduates, including 101 freshmen. Scholarships awarded for academics, athletics, ROTC.

Application procedures. Admission: Closing date 1/15 (postmark date). $50 fee, may be waived for applicants with need. Application may be submitted online. Admission notification 4/1. Must reply by 5/1. **Financial aid:** Closing date 2/1. FAFSA required. CSS PROFILE required of all students applying for institutional aid. Applicants notified by 3/30; must reply by 5/1.

Academics. Students encouraged to participate in Oxford-style tutorials. 32 courses of 1 or more units required for graduation. 10 to 14 courses of 1 or more units required in major. **Special study options:** Accelerated study, cross-registration, double major, dual enrollment of high school students, honors, independent study, internships, liberal arts/career combination, semester at sea, student-designed major, study abroad, teacher certification program, Washington semester. Optional first-year living and learning program. **Credit/placement by examination:** AP, CLEP, IB. **Support services:** Tutoring, writing center.

Majors. Area/ethnic studies: Asian, German, Russian/Slavic. **Biology:** General. **Business:** Accounting. **Computer sciences:** General. **Conservation:** Environmental studies. **English:** English lit. **Foreign languages:** Classics, comparative lit, French, German, Italian, Russian, Spanish. **History:** General. **Interdisciplinary:** Medieval/Renaissance. **Math:** General. **Philosophy/religion:** Philosophy, religion. **Physical sciences:** Chemistry, physics. **Psychology:** General. **Social sciences:** Anthropology, economics, political science, sociology. **Visual/performing arts:** Art history/conservation, dramatic, studio arts.

Most popular majors. Biology 7%, English 11%, foreign language 9%, history 11%, mathematics 7%, psychology 9%, social sciences 34%.

Computing on campus. 480 workstations in dormitories, library, computer center, student center. Dormitories wired for high-speed internet access and linked to campus network. Commuter students can connect to campus network. Online library, helpline, repair service, student web hosting, wireless network available.

Student life. Freshman orientation: Available, $125 fee. 4-day program in late August. **Policies:** Responsible drinking policy for students over 21. Initiation hazing prohibited. **Housing:** Guaranteed on-campus for all undergraduates. Coed dorms, special housing for disabled, apartments, substance-free housing available. $500 nonrefundable deposit, deadline 5/1. First-year living and learning program available. **Activities:** Bands, choral groups, dance, drama, literary magazine, music ensembles, musical theater, radio station, student government, student newspaper, black student union, Purple Key Society, student program for urban development, women's forum, Latin American student organization, Asian student society, Muslim student association, Appalachia service project, Habitat for Humanity, association of bisexuals, gays and lesbians.

Athletics. NCAA. **Intercollegiate:** Baseball M, basketball, cross-country, diving, field hockey W, football (tackle) M, golf, ice hockey, lacrosse, rowing (crew), soccer, softball W, swimming, tennis, track and field, volleyball W. **Intramural:** Basketball, football (non-tackle), softball, tennis, volleyball. **Team name:** Crusaders.

Student services. Alcohol/substance abuse counseling, campus ministries, career counseling, student employment services, financial aid counseling, health services, minority student services, personal counseling, placement for graduates, women's services. **Physically disabled:** Services for visually, hearing impaired.

Contact. E-mail: admissions@holycross.edu
Phone: (508) 793-2443 Toll-free number: (800) 442-2421
Fax: (508) 793-3888
Ann McDermott, Director of Admissions, College of the Holy Cross, One College Street, Worcester, MA 01610-2395

Curry College

Milton, Massachusetts — **CB member**
www.curry.edu — **CB code: 3285**

- Private 4-year nursing and liberal arts college
- Residential campus in large town
- 2,503 degree-seeking undergraduates: 22% part-time, 57% women, 7% African American, 1% Asian American, 3% Hispanic American, 1% international
- 176 degree-seeking graduate students
- 69% of applicants admitted
- Application essay required
- 46% graduate within 6 years

General. Founded in 1879. Regionally accredited. **Degrees:** 542 bachelor's awarded; master's offered. **ROTC:** Army. **Location:** 7 miles from Boston. **Calendar:** Semester, limited summer session. **Full-time faculty:** 100 total. **Part-time faculty:** 276 total. **Class size:** 59% < 20, 39% 20-39, 2% 40-49, less than 1% 50-99.

Freshman class profile. 2,975 applied, 2,059 admitted, 600 enrolled.

Mid 50% test scores		**Rank in top tenth:**	11%
SAT verbal:	460-570	**Return as sophomores:**	69%
SAT math:	450-540	**Out-of-state:**	40%
Rank in top quarter:	40%		

Basis for selection. High school record, recommendations, extracurricular activities most important. Test scores also important. Interviews encouraged but not required. **Homeschooled:** Statement describing homeschool structure and mission, transcript of courses and grades, state high school equivalency certificate required. **Learning Disabled:** Wechsler Adult Intelligence Scale required of learning disabled applicants for admission. This replaces SAT requirement but SAT or ACT still recommended.

High school preparation. 16 units required. Required and recommended units include English 4, mathematics 3, social studies 2, science 2-3 (laboratory 2) and foreign language 2. 3 mathematics through algebra II, 1 chemistry, and 1 biology required for nursing applicants.

2006-2007 Annual costs. Tuition/fees: $24,140. PAL (Program for Advancement of Learning) students pay an additional program participation fee of up to $4,960. Room/board: $9,770. Books/supplies: $700. Personal expenses: $1,128.

2004-2005 Financial aid. Need-based: 392 full-time freshmen applied for aid; 390 were judged to have need; 389 of these received aid. Average need met was 67%. Average scholarship/grant was $10,839; average loan $2,668. 67% of total undergraduate aid awarded as scholarships/grants, 33% as loans/jobs. **Non-need-based:** Awarded to 49 full-time undergraduates, including 11 freshmen. Scholarships awarded for academics, leadership.

Application procedures. Admission: Closing date 4/1 (postmark date). $40 fee, may be waived for applicants with need. Application may be submitted online. Admission notification on a rolling basis beginning on or about 1/1. Must reply by May 1 or within 2 week(s) if notified thereafter. **Financial aid:** Priority date 3/1; no closing date. FAFSA required. Applicants notified on a rolling basis starting 3/10; must reply by 5/1 or within 2 week(s) of notification.

Academics. Special study options: Accelerated study, double major, honors, independent study, internships, student-designed major, study abroad, teacher certification program. **Credit/placement by examination:** AP, CLEP, SAT, institutional tests. 60 credit hours maximum toward bachelor's degree. **Support services:** Learning center, pre-admission summer program, reduced course load, remedial instruction, study skills assistance, tutoring, writing center.

Majors. Biology: General. **Business:** Business admin. **Communications:** General. **Computer sciences:** General. **Conservation:** Environmental science. **Education:** General, early childhood, elementary, health, special. **Health:** Nursing (RN). **Liberal arts:** Arts/sciences. **Philosophy/religion:** Philosophy. **Protective services:** Criminal justice. **Psychology:** General. **Social sciences:** Sociology. **Visual/performing arts:** Studio arts.

Most popular majors. Business/marketing 18%, communications/journalism 10%, health sciences 24%, psychology 9%, security/protective services 23%.

Computing on campus. 100 workstations in dormitories, library, computer center. Dormitories wired for high-speed internet access and linked to campus network. Commuter students can connect to campus network. Helpline, student web hosting available.

Student life. Freshman orientation: Mandatory, $150 fee. Preregistration for classes offered. Program held at end of August. **Housing:** Coed dorms, single-sex dorms, substance-free housing available. $200 nonrefundable deposit, deadline 5/1. Wellness, honors housing available. **Activities:** Choral groups, dance, drama, literary magazine, music ensembles, musical theater, radio station, student government, student newspaper, TV station, religious clubs, nursing association, international club, student activities board, community service organization, multicultural club, Martin Luther King Society, Hillel.

Athletics. NCAA. **Intercollegiate:** Baseball M, basketball, cross-country W, football (tackle) M, ice hockey M, lacrosse, soccer, softball W, tennis. **Intramural:** Basketball, cheerleading W, rugby, softball, tennis, volleyball. **Team name:** Colonels.

Student services. Adult student services, alcohol/substance abuse counseling, campus ministries, career counseling, student employment services, financial aid counseling, health services, minority student services, on-campus daycare, personal counseling, placement for graduates, veterans' counselor, women's services.

Contact. E-mail: curryadm@curry.edu
Phone: (617) 333-2210 Toll-free number: (800) 669-0686
Fax: (617) 333-2114
Jane Fidler, Dean of Admissions, Curry College, 1071 Blue Hill Avenue, Milton, MA 02186-9984

Eastern Nazarene College

Quincy, Massachusetts — **CB member**
www.enc.edu — **CB code: 3365**

- Private 4-year liberal arts college affiliated with Church of the Nazarene
- Residential campus in small city
- 1,060 degree-seeking undergraduates
- 130 graduate students
- SAT or ACT (ACT writing optional), application essay, interview required

General. Founded in 1900. Regionally accredited. Degree-completion program in business offered to professionals with equivalent of 2 years college work and professional experience. Associate degree also offered for those without prior college experience. **Degrees:** 170 bachelor's, 32 associate awarded; master's offered. **ROTC:** Army, Air Force. **Location:** 6 miles from Boston. **Calendar:** 4-1-4, limited summer session. **Full-time faculty:** 50 total. **Part-time faculty:** 5 total. **Class size:** 70% < 20, 26% 20-39, 3% 40-49, less than 1% 50-99. **Special facilities:** College-operated preschool.

Freshman class profile.

Mid 50% test scores		**Rank in top quarter:**	30%
SAT verbal:	450-600	**Rank in top tenth:**	14%
SAT math:	450-590	**Out-of-state:**	51%
ACT:	18-26	**Live on campus:**	91%

Basis for selection. Transcripts from high school(s), SAT/ACT scores, academic/character references, personal interview or essay most important. Audition required of music majors.

High school preparation. College-preparatory program recommended. Required and recommended units include English 4, mathematics 2-4, social studies 1-2, history 1-2, science 2-4 and foreign language 2-4.

2005-2006 Annual costs. Tuition/fees: $18,310. Room/board: $6,590. Books/supplies: $1,000. Personal expenses: $2,000.

2005-2006 Financial aid. Need-based: 76% of total undergraduate aid awarded as scholarships/grants, 24% as loans/jobs. **Non-need-based:** Scholarships awarded for academics, alumni affiliation, leadership, music/drama, religious affiliation, state residency. **Additional information:** Participant in Massachusetts University pre-payment plan.

Application procedures. Admission: Priority date 3/15; no deadline. No application fee. Application may be submitted online. Admission notification on a rolling basis. Must reply by May 1 or within 3 week(s) if notified thereafter. **Financial aid:** Priority date 2/28; no closing date. FAFSA, institutional form required. Applicants notified on a rolling basis starting 3/15; must reply within 2 week(s) of notification.

Academics. Special study options: Accelerated study, cross-registration, double major, dual enrollment of high school students, exchange student, honors, independent study, internships, liberal arts/career combination, semester at sea, study abroad, teacher certification program, urban semester, Washington semester. **Credit/placement by examination:** AP, CLEP, IB, institutional tests. **Support services:** Learning center, reduced course load, remedial instruction, study skills assistance, tutoring, writing center.

Majors. Biology: General, biochemistry. **Business:** General, business admin. **Communications:** General, advertising, journalism, public relations, radio/tv. **Computer sciences:** Computer science. **Education:** General, biology, chemistry, early childhood, elementary, English, history, mathematics, middle, music, physical, physics, science, social studies, special. **Engineering:** General, chemical, computer, electrical, physics. **English:** Composition, English lit. **Health:** Predentistry, premedicine, prepharmacy, preveterinary. **History:** General. **Interdisciplinary:** Biological/physical sciences. **Legal studies:** Prelaw. **Liberal arts:** Arts/sciences. **Math:** General. **Parks/recreation:** Health/fitness. **Philosophy/religion:** Religion. **Physical sciences:** Chemistry, physics. **Psychology:** General. **Public administration:** Social work. **Social sciences:** Sociology. **Theology:** Religious ed, sacred music, theology. **Visual/performing arts:** Dramatic, music performance, music theory/composition, piano/organ, theater arts management, voice/opera.

Computing on campus. 98 workstations in library, computer center. Dormitories wired for high-speed internet access and linked to campus network. Commuter students can connect to campus network. Online library, helpline, repair service available.

Student life. **Freshman orientation:** Mandatory. Preregistration for classes offered. **Policies:** No alcohol, drugs, or tobacco permitted. Religious observance required. **Housing:** Guaranteed on-campus for freshmen. Single-sex dorms, special housing for disabled, apartments available. $250 nonrefundable deposit, deadline 8/25. **Activities:** Bands, choral groups, drama, film society, music ensembles, musical theater, radio station, student government, student newspaper, TV station, MESA, Fellowship of Christian Athletes, inner-city ministry, Salvation Army student fellowships, nursing home ministry, children's ministry.

Athletics. NCAA. **Intercollegiate:** Baseball M, basketball, cross-country, soccer, softball W, tennis, volleyball W. **Intramural:** Basketball, football (non-tackle), lacrosse W, soccer, softball, volleyball. **Team name:** Crusaders.

Student services. Adult student services, alcohol/substance abuse counseling, campus ministries, career counseling, student employment services, financial aid counseling, health services, minority student services, on-campus daycare, personal counseling, placement for graduates. **Physically disabled:** Services for visually impaired.

Contact. E-mail: admissions@enc.edu
Phone: (617) 745-3711 Toll-free number: (800) 883-6288
Fax: (617) 745-3929
Dawna Williams, Director of Admissions, Eastern Nazarene College, 23 East Elm Avenue, Quincy, MA 02170-2999

Elms College

Chicopee, Massachusetts — **CB member**
www.elms.edu — **CB code: 3283**

- Private 4-year liberal arts college affiliated with Roman Catholic Church
- Residential campus in small city
- 825 degree-seeking undergraduates
- 89% of applicants admitted
- SAT or ACT (ACT writing optional), application essay required

General. Founded in 1928. Regionally accredited. **Degrees:** 166 bachelor's, 7 associate awarded; master's offered. **ROTC:** Army, Air Force. **Location:** 2 miles from Springfield, 30 miles from Hartford, Connecticut. **Calendar:** Semester, extensive summer session. **Full-time faculty:** 50 total. **Part-time faculty:** 5 total. **Class size:** 79% < 20, 21% 20-39. **Special facilities:** Rare book gallery, alumnae library (including government documents).

Freshman class profile. 447 applied, 396 admitted, 145 enrolled.

Mid 50% test scores		**ACT:**	20-24
SAT verbal:	440-570	**Out-of-state:**	29%
SAT math:	450-550	**Live on campus:**	76%

Basis for selection. Students should rank in top half of high school class. 2.5 GPA or better, minimum combined SAT score of 1000 (exclusive of Writing) recommended. Interview recommended.

High school preparation. 12 units required; 20 recommended. Required and recommended units include English 4, mathematics 2-4, social studies 1-2, history 1-2, science 2-4 (laboratory 2) and foreign language 2-4. Biology, chemistry required for nursing and medical technology applicants.

2005-2006 Annual costs. Tuition/fees: $21,515. Room/board: $8,000. Books/supplies: $525. Personal expenses: $900.

Financial aid. **Non-need-based:** Scholarships awarded for academics, alumni affiliation, leadership, state residency.

Application procedures. **Admission:** Priority date 3/1; no deadline. $30 fee, may be waived for applicants with need. Admission notification on a rolling basis. Must reply by May 1 or within 2 week(s) if notified thereafter. **Financial aid:** Priority date 3/1; no closing date. FAFSA, institutional form required. Applicants notified on a rolling basis starting 2/15; must reply by 5/1 or within 2 week(s) of notification.

Academics. **Special study options:** Cross-registration, distance learning, double major, ESL, exchange student, honors, independent study, internships, study abroad, teacher certification program, Washington semester, weekend college. **Credit/placement by examination:** AP, CLEP, IB, institutional tests. 6 credit hours maximum toward bachelor's degree. **Support services:** Learning center, pre-admission summer program, reduced course load, remedial instruction, tutoring, writing center.

Majors. **Area/ethnic studies:** American, Spanish/Iberian. **Biology:** General. **Business:** Accounting, business admin, international. **Communications:** General. **Computer sciences:** General. **Education:** General, bilingual, Deaf/hearing impaired, early childhood, elementary, English, ESL, secondary, special. **Foreign languages:** Spanish. **Health:** Audiology/speech pathology, health care admin, health services admin, predentistry, premedicine, preop/surgical nursing, preveterinary, speech pathology. **History:** General. **Interdisciplinary:** Biological/physical sciences. **Legal studies:** General, paralegal, prelaw. **Liberal arts:** Arts/sciences. **Math:** General. **Philosophy/religion:** Religion. **Physical sciences:** Chemistry. **Psychology:** General. **Public administration:** Social work. **Social sciences:** International relations, sociology. **Visual/performing arts:** Studio arts.

Computing on campus. 70 workstations in dormitories, library, computer center, student center. Dormitories wired for high-speed internet access and linked to campus network. Commuter students can connect to campus network.

Student life. **Freshman orientation:** Available, $50 fee. **Policies:** Freshmen permitted cars on campus. **Housing:** Guaranteed on-campus for all undergraduates. Coed dorms, single-sex dorms available. $50 deposit. **Activities:** Choral groups, dance, drama, literary magazine, music ensembles, student government, student newspaper, social work club, campus ministry, foreign language club, speech pathology and audiology club, Student Ambassadors organization, affirmative action committee.

Athletics. NCAA. **Intercollegiate:** Baseball M, basketball, cross-country, equestrian W, field hockey W, golf M, lacrosse W, soccer, softball W, swimming, volleyball. **Intramural:** Basketball, bowling, cross-country, field hockey W, golf, lacrosse W, racquetball, skiing, soccer, softball W, swimming, volleyball, water polo. **Team name:** Blazers.

Student services. Adult student services, career counseling, student employment services, health services, personal counseling, placement for graduates. **Physically disabled:** Services for visually, speech, hearing impaired.

Contact. E-mail: admissions@elms.edu
Phone: (413) 592-3189 Toll-free number: (800) 255-3567
Fax: (413) 594-2781
Joseph Wagner, Director of Admissions, Elms College, 291 Springfield Street, Chicopee, MA 01013

Emerson College

Boston, Massachusetts — **CB member**
www.emerson.edu — **CB code: 3367**

- Private 4-year college of communication and the arts
- Residential campus in very large city
- 3,165 degree-seeking undergraduates: 3% part-time, 56% women, 2% African American, 4% Asian American, 5% Hispanic American, 1% Native American, 3% international
- 953 degree-seeking graduate students
- 45% of applicants admitted
- SAT or ACT with writing, application essay required
- 70% graduate within 6 years; 13% enter graduate study

General. Founded in 1880. Regionally accredited. **Degrees:** 715 bachelor's awarded; master's, doctoral offered. **Location:** Downtown. **Calendar:** Semester, limited summer session. **Full-time faculty:** 143 total; 74% have terminal degrees, 13% minority, 43% women. **Part-time faculty:** 238 total; 46% have terminal degrees, 6% minority, 45% women. **Class size:** 60% < 20, 28% 20-39, 4% 40-49, 8% 50-99. **Special facilities:** 2 radio stations, 3 theaters, integrated digital newsroom, seven clinics/programs to observe speech and hearing therapy, media center, marketing research suite, film production facilities (with AVID nonlinear editing system), performance and production center.

Freshman class profile. 5,008 applied, 2,278 admitted, 721 enrolled.

Mid 50% test scores		Rank in top quarter:	83%
SAT verbal:	590-670	Rank in top tenth:	36%
SAT math:	560-650	Return as sophomores:	89%
ACT:	25-29	Out-of-state:	78%
GPA 3.50 or higher:	68%	Live on campus:	97%
GPA 3.0-3.49:	29%	International:	2%
GPA 2.0-2.99:	3%		

Basis for selection. Secondary school record, recommendations, writing competency, and personal qualities as seen in extracurricular activities, community involvement, demonstrated leadership important. Applicants for programs in performing arts must submit resume of theater-related activities and either audition, interview, or submit portfolio or essay.

High school preparation. 16 units required; 20 recommended. Required and recommended units include English 4, mathematics 3, social studies 3, science 3, foreign language 3 and academic electives 4.

2005-2006 Annual costs. Tuition/fees: $24,534. Room/board: $10,420. Books/supplies: $680. Personal expenses: $900.

2004-2005 Financial aid. **Need-based:** 539 full-time freshmen applied for aid; 397 were judged to have need; 397 of these received aid. Average need met was 76%. Average scholarship/grant was $11,814; average loan $3,545. 51% of total undergraduate aid awarded as scholarships/grants, 49% as loans/jobs. **Non-need-based:** Awarded to 702 full-time undergraduates, including 235 freshmen. Scholarships awarded for academics, music/drama. **Additional information:** Massachusetts Loan Plan available for parents of dependent undergraduates.

Application procedures. **Admission:** Closing date 1/5 (postmark date). $60 fee, may be waived for applicants with need. Application may be submitted online. Admission notification 4/1. Must reply by May 1 or within 2 week(s) if notified thereafter. **Financial aid:** Priority date 3/1; no closing date. FAFSA, CSS PROFILE required. Applicants notified on a rolling basis starting 4/1; must reply by 5/1 or within 3 week(s) of notification.

Academics. **Special study options:** Cross-registration, double major, honors, independent study, internships, liberal arts/career combination, student-designed major, study abroad, teacher certification program. Cross-registration available with Suffolk University and 6-member Boston ProArts Consortium (Berklee College of Music, Boston Architectural Center, Boston Conservatory, Massachusetts College of Art, and the School of the Museum of Fine Arts). **Credit/placement by examination:** AP, CLEP, IB, institutional tests. 32 credit hours maximum toward bachelor's degree. SAT or ACT math score may be used to waive semester course of math requirements. **Support services:** Learning center, reduced course load, study skills assistance, tutoring, writing center.

Honors college/program. Approximately 50 first-year students admitted on the basis of superior academic record, creative accomplishments, community service, demonstrated leadership. Applicants submit honors essay and graded writing sample from humanities course.

Majors. **Business:** Communications, marketing. **Communications:** General, advertising, broadcast journalism, journalism, media studies, political, public relations, publishing. **Education:** Autistic, Deaf/hearing impaired, drama/dance, speech, speech impaired. **English:** Creative writing, speech/rhetoric. **Health:** Audiology/hearing, audiology/speech pathology, communication disorders, speech pathology. **Visual/performing arts:** General, acting, cinematography, directing/producing, dramatic, film/cinema, play/screenwriting, theater arts management, theater design.

Most popular majors. Business/marketing 17%, communications/journalism 29%, English 17%, visual/performing arts 33%.

Computing on campus. 458 workstations in dormitories, library, computer center, student center. Dormitories wired for high-speed internet access and linked to campus network. Commuter students can connect to campus network. Online course registration, helpline, repair service, wireless network available.

Student life. **Freshman orientation:** Mandatory, $122 fee. Preregistration for classes offered. 4-day event preceding first day of classes. **Housing:** Coed dorms, substance-free housing available. $300 deposit, deadline 5/1. Living/learning communities available. **Activities:** Choral groups, dance, drama, film society, literary magazine, musical theater, radio station, student government, student newspaper, TV station, Hillel, Newman Club, Goodnews Fellowship, Islamic community, Alliance of Gays and Lesbians and Everyone, Latino student organization, international club, Earth Emerson, Asian Students for Intercultural Awareness, Amnesty International.

Athletics. NCAA. **Intercollegiate:** Basketball, cross-country, lacrosse, soccer, softball W, tennis, track and field W, volleyball W. **Team name:** Lions.

Student services. Adult student services, campus ministries, career counseling, student employment services, financial aid counseling, health services, minority student services, personal counseling, placement for graduates. **Physically disabled:** Services for visually, speech, hearing impaired.

Contact. E-mail: admission@emerson.edu
Phone: (617) 824-8600 Fax: (617) 824-8609
Sara Ramirez, Director of Undergraduate Admission, Emerson College, 120 Boylston Street, Boston, MA 02116-4624

Emmanuel College

Boston, Massachusetts **CB member**
www.emmanuel.edu **CB code: 3368**

- Private 4-year liberal arts college affiliated with Roman Catholic Church
- Residential campus in very large city
- 2,000 degree-seeking undergraduates: 25% part-time, 76% women, 7% African American, 4% Asian American, 4% Hispanic American, 3% international
- 200 degree-seeking graduate students
- 61% of applicants admitted
- SAT or ACT (ACT writing optional), application essay required
- 53% graduate within 6 years

General. Founded in 1919. Regionally accredited. Member of the Colleges of the Fenway Consortium, which enables cross registration with the following 5 institutions: Massachusetts College of Pharmacy & Health Services, Wentworth Institute of Technology, Simmons College, Massachusetts College of Art, Wheelock College. **Degrees:** 326 bachelor's awarded; master's offered. **ROTC:** Army. **Calendar:** Semester, limited summer session. **Full-time faculty:** 67 total; 85% have terminal degrees, 9% minority, 70% women. **Part-time faculty:** 155 total; 83% have terminal degrees, 9% minority, 43% women. **Class size:** 62% < 20, 37% 20-39, less than 1% 40-49.

Freshman class profile. 3,107 applied, 1,881 admitted, 438 enrolled.

Mid 50% test scores		Rank in top quarter:	41%
SAT verbal:	490-600	Rank in top tenth:	15%
SAT math:	470-580	End year in good standing:	83%
ACT:	20-25	Out-of-state:	37%
GPA 3.50 or higher:	45%	Live on campus:	90%
GPA 3.0-3.49:	29%	International:	1%
GPA 2.0-2.99:	26%		

Basis for selection. High school curriculum and record most important, followed by recommendations, test scores, essay, creativity, initiative. Interview recommended. **Homeschooled:** Portfolio, on-campus interview recommended.

High school preparation. 16 units recommended. Recommended units include English 4, mathematics 3, social studies 2, science 2 (laboratory 2) and foreign language 2.

2006-2007 Annual costs. Tuition/fees: $24,200. Room/board: $10,400. Books/supplies: $750. Personal expenses: $1,710.

2005-2006 Financial aid. **Need-based:** 387 full-time freshmen applied for aid; 332 were judged to have need; 332 of these received aid. Average need met was 68%. Average scholarship/grant was $10,057; average loan $3,449. 83% of total undergraduate aid awarded as scholarships/grants, 17% as loans/jobs. **Non-need-based:** Awarded to 755 full-time undergraduates, including 169 freshmen. Scholarships awarded for academics, alumni affiliation, art, leadership.

Application procedures. **Admission:** Priority date 12/1; deadline 3/1 (postmark date). $40 fee, may be waived for applicants with need. Application may be submitted online. Admission notification on a rolling basis. Notification within 3 weeks after file completion. Must reply by 5/1. **Financial aid:** Priority date 4/1; no closing date. FAFSA, institutional form required. Applicants notified on a rolling basis starting 3/15; must reply by 5/1.

Academics. Interdepartmental program allows students to concentrate in 2 departments. Internship offerings available in all areas of study. **Special study options:** Accelerated study, cross-registration, double major, exchange student, honors, independent study, internships, liberal arts/career combination, student-designed major, study abroad, teacher certification program, Washington semester. Degree completion opportunities at corporate sites. **Credit/placement by examination:** AP, CLEP, IB, SAT, institutional tests. 32 credit hours maximum toward bachelor's degree. **Support services:** Learning center, pre-admission summer program, remedial instruction, study skills assistance, tutoring, writing center.

Majors. **Area/ethnic studies:** American. **Biology:** General, biochemistry, biostatistics. **Business:** Business admin. **Communications:** General. **Conservation:** Environmental studies. **Education:** Elementary. **English:** English lit. **Foreign languages:** Spanish. **Health:** Art therapy, health services, nursing (RN), preop/surgical nursing. **History:** General. **Interdisciplinary:** Global studies. **Math:** General. **Philosophy/religion:** Religion. **Physical sciences:** Chemistry. **Psychology:** General. **Social sciences:** Political science, sociology. **Visual/performing arts:** Graphic design, painting, printmaking, studio arts.

Most popular majors. Biology 6%, business/marketing 35%, communications/journalism 7%, education 8%, health sciences 9%, psychology 7%.

Computing on campus. 115 workstations in dormitories, library. Dormitories wired for high-speed internet access and linked to campus network. Commuter students can connect to campus network. Online library, helpline, wireless network available.

Student life. **Freshman orientation:** Mandatory, $100 fee. Preregistration for classes offered. Summer and fall program. **Policies:** No alcohol permitted on campus. **Housing:** Guaranteed on-campus for all undergraduates. Coed dorms, special housing for disabled, substance-free housing available. $300 fully refundable deposit, deadline 5/1. **Activities:** Pep band, choral groups, dance, drama, literary magazine, musical theater, radio station, student government, student newspaper, symphony orchestra, black student union, College Democrats, political forum, feminist coalition, Helping Unite Emmanuel Latinos to Lead & Achieve Success, multicultural club, peace and justice club, Republican club, social awareness club, campus ministry.

Athletics. NCAA. **Intercollegiate:** Basketball, cross-country, soccer, softball W, tennis W, track and field, volleyball. **Team name:** Saints.

Student services. Adult student services, alcohol/substance abuse counseling, campus ministries, career counseling, student employment services, financial aid counseling, health services, minority student services, personal counseling, placement for graduates. **Physically disabled:** Services for visually, speech, hearing impaired.

Contact. E-mail: enroll@emmanuel.edu
Phone: (617) 735-9715 Fax: (617) 735-9877
Sandra Robbins, Dean of Enrollment Management, Emmanuel College, 400 The Fenway, Boston, MA 02115

Endicott College

Beverly, Massachusetts — **CB member**
www.endicott.edu — **CB code: 3369**

- Private 4-year liberal arts college
- Residential campus in large town
- 2,038 degree-seeking undergraduates: 9% part-time, 58% women
- 390 degree-seeking graduate students
- 47% of applicants admitted
- SAT or ACT with writing, application essay required
- 56% graduate within 6 years; 14% enter graduate study

General. Founded in 1939. Regionally accredited. **Degrees:** 402 bachelor's, 8 associate awarded; master's offered. **ROTC:** Army, Air Force. **Location:** 24 miles from Boston. **Calendar:** 4-1-4, limited summer session. **Full-time faculty:** 66 total; 59% have terminal degrees, 4% minority, 52% women. **Part-time faculty:** 80 total; 31% have terminal degrees, 60% women. **Class size:** 53% < 20, 47% 20-39.

Freshman class profile. 3,081 applied, 1,455 admitted, 502 enrolled.

Mid 50% test scores			
SAT verbal:	490-580	Rank in top tenth:	9%
SAT math:	490-580	Return as sophomores:	82%
ACT:	20-23	Out-of-state:	51%
Rank in top quarter:	36%	Live on campus:	97%
		International:	2%

Basis for selection. School achievement record and SAT/ACT scores most important. Class rank, essay, volunteer work, extracurricular activities, leadership also important. Teacher, counselor recommendations considered. Interview recommended. **Homeschooled:** Verification that curriculum has been certified by local school system or state, or GED.

High school preparation. 16 units recommended. Recommended units include English 4, mathematics 3, social studies 2, history 1, science 2 and academic electives 4. One chemistry with laboratory and algebra required for nursing and athletic training programs.

2006-2007 Annual costs. Tuition/fees: $21,374. Room/board: $10,254. Books/supplies: $600. Personal expenses: $1,000.

2005-2006 Financial aid. **Need-based:** 359 full-time freshmen applied for aid; 272 were judged to have need; 271 of these received aid. Average need met was 55%. Average scholarship/grant was $6,359; average loan $2,851. 64% of total undergraduate aid awarded as scholarships/grants, 36% as loans/jobs. **Non-need-based:** Scholarships awarded for academics, alumni affiliation, art, leadership, ROTC, state residency.

Application procedures. **Admission:** Closing date 2/15. $40 fee, may be waived for applicants with need. Application may be submitted online. Admission notification on a rolling basis beginning on or about 11/1. Must reply by May 1 or within 1 week(s) if notified thereafter. **Financial aid:** Closing date 3/15. FAFSA, institutional form required. Applicants notified on a rolling basis starting 3/15; must reply within 2 week(s) of notification.

Academics. **Special study options:** Accelerated study, combined bachelor's/graduate degree, cross-registration, distance learning, honors, independent study, internships, student-designed major, study abroad, teacher certification program. **Credit/placement by examination:** AP, CLEP, IB, SAT, institutional tests. 32 credit hours maximum toward bachelor's degree. **Support services:** Learning center, reduced course load, remedial instruction, study skills assistance, tutoring, writing center.

Majors. **Business:** Business admin, hospitality admin. **Communications:** General. **Computer sciences:** General. **Conservation:** Environmental studies. **Education:** Early childhood, elementary. **English:** English lit. **Foreign languages:** Spanish. **Health:** Art therapy, athletic training, nursing (RN). **History:** General. **Interdisciplinary:** Global studies. **Liberal arts:** Arts/sciences. **Parks/recreation:** Sports admin. **Protective services:** Criminal justice. **Psychology:** General. **Visual/performing arts:** Design, interior design.

Most popular majors. Business/marketing 33%, communications/journalism 9%, liberal arts 6%, parks/recreation 11%, psychology 13%, visual/performing arts 16%.

Computing on campus. 150 workstations in library, computer center. Dormitories wired for high-speed internet access and linked to campus network. Commuter students can connect to campus network. Online course registration, online library, helpline, repair service, wireless network available.

Student life. **Freshman orientation:** Available. Preregistration for classes offered. **Policies:** Freshmen permitted cars on campus. **Housing:** Guaranteed on-campus for freshmen. Coed dorms, single-sex dorms, special housing for disabled, apartments available. $500 deposit, deadline 5/1. Single-parent housing, suite-type, modular housing available. **Activities:** Jazz band, choral groups, dance, literary magazine, radio station, student government, student newspaper, TV station, intercultural club, Phi Theta Kappa, Endicott Volunteer Network, ALANA.

Athletics. NCAA. **Intercollegiate:** Baseball M, basketball, cross-country, equestrian, field hockey W, football (tackle) M, golf, lacrosse, soccer, softball W, tennis, volleyball. **Intramural:** Basketball, football (non-tackle), racquetball, soccer, softball, tennis, volleyball. **Team name:** Gulls.

Student services. Alcohol/substance abuse counseling, campus ministries, career counseling, financial aid counseling, health services, personal counseling.

Contact. E-mail: admissio@endicott.edu
Phone: (978) 921-1000 Toll-free number: (800) 325-1114
Fax: (978) 232-2520
Thomas Redman, Vice President for Admissions and Financial Aid, Endicott College, 376 Hale Street, Beverly, MA 01915-9985

Fitchburg State College

Fitchburg, Massachusetts — **CB member**
www.fsc.edu — **CB code: 3518**

- Public 4-year liberal arts and teachers college
- Commuter campus in large town
- 3,411 degree-seeking undergraduates: 14% part-time, 56% women, 3% African American, 2% Asian American, 3% Hispanic American, 1% international
- 929 degree-seeking graduate students
- 67% of applicants admitted
- SAT or ACT (ACT writing optional), application essay required
- 55% graduate within 6 years

General. Founded in 1894. Regionally accredited. **Degrees:** 489 bachelor's awarded; master's offered. **ROTC:** Air Force. **Location:** 50 miles from Boston, 25 miles from Worcester. **Calendar:** Semester, limited summer session. **Full-time faculty:** 166 total; 90% have terminal degrees, 13%

minority, 44% women. **Part-time faculty:** 76 total; 18% have terminal degrees, 7% minority, 53% women. **Class size:** 52% < 20, 48% 20-39. **Special facilities:** Teacher education laboratory school, 120-acre conservation area.

Freshman class profile. 3,070 applied, 2,059 admitted, 607 enrolled.

Mid 50% test scores		**GPA 2.0-2.99:**	56%
SAT verbal:	460-560	**Return as sophomores:**	78%
SAT math:	470-560	**Out-of-state:**	10%
ACT:	18-23	**Live on campus:**	66%
GPA 3.50 or higher:	15%	**Fraternities:**	1%
GPA 3.0-3.49:	29%	**Sororities:**	3%

Basis for selection. Secondary school record, test scores, essay important. Recommendations considered. Interview recommended for nursing, undeclared major, computer science, business administration, communications/media majors. **Learning Disabled:** Students with professionally diagnosed learning disabilities exempt from standardized test requirements.

High school preparation. 16 units required. Required units include English 4, mathematics 3, social studies 1, history 1, science 3 (laboratory 2), foreign language 2 and academic electives 2. Additional units of mathematics, science preferred for nursing, medical technology, computer science, business applicants.

2005-2006 Annual costs. Tuition/fees: $5,002; $11,082 out-of-state. Room/board: $6,104. Books/supplies: $600. Personal expenses: $1,500.

Financial aid. Non-need-based: Scholarships awarded for academics, alumni affiliation, leadership, state residency.

Application procedures. Admission: Priority date 1/1; no deadline. $10 fee ($40 out-of-state), may be waived for applicants with need. Application may be submitted online. Admission notification on a rolling basis beginning on or about 12/1. Must reply by May 1 or within 2 week(s) if notified thereafter. **Financial aid:** Priority date 3/1; no closing date. FAFSA, institutional form required. Applicants notified on a rolling basis starting 3/15; must reply within 2 week(s) of notification.

Academics. Many major programs include internship, practicum, or clinical experience. All degree programs require completion of 60 credits in liberal arts and sciences. **Special study options:** Cross-registration, distance learning, double major, dual enrollment of high school students, honors, independent study, internships, liberal arts/career combination, student-designed major, study abroad, teacher certification program. **Credit/placement by examination:** AP, CLEP, institutional tests. 60 credit hours maximum toward bachelor's degree. **Support services:** Learning center, pre-admission summer program, reduced course load, remedial instruction, study skills assistance, tutoring, writing center.

Majors. Biology: General. **Business:** Accounting, business admin, finance, international, marketing. **Communications:** General. **Computer sciences:** General, computer science. **Education:** Biology, early childhood, elementary, English, history, mathematics, middle, secondary, special, technology/industrial arts. **Engineering:** Electrical. **Engineering technology:** Architectural, construction, electrical, energy systems, manufacturing. **English:** English lit, technical writing. **Health:** Nursing (RN). **History:** General. **Liberal arts:** Arts/sciences. **Math:** General. **Parks/recreation:** Exercise sciences, sports admin. **Psychology:** General. **Public administration:** Human services. **Social sciences:** Economics, geography, political science, sociology. **Visual/performing arts:** Cinematography, design, dramatic, graphic design, photography, theater design.

Most popular majors. Business/marketing 18%, computer/information sciences 6%, education 14%, health sciences 8%, liberal arts 8%, psychology 6%, visual/performing arts 15%.

Computing on campus. 150 workstations in dormitories, library, computer center, student center. Dormitories wired for high-speed internet access and linked to campus network. Commuter students can connect to campus network. Helpline, wireless network available.

Student life. Freshman orientation: Mandatory. Preregistration for classes offered. Testing, academic advising, registration for classes key components of program. **Policies:** Students subject to responsibilities outlined in student code of conduct and good neighbor policy. Freshmen permitted cars on campus. **Housing:** Coed dorms, special housing for disabled, apartments, substance-free housing available. $150 nonrefundable deposit, deadline 5/1. Substance-free housing and quiet halls available. **Activities:** Bands, choral groups, dance, drama, literary magazine, radio station, student government, student newspaper, Christian Fellowship, Amnesty International, black student union, Latin American student organization, international student union, MassPIRG, legal association, rescue squad.

Athletics. NCAA. **Intercollegiate:** Baseball M, basketball, cross-country, field hockey W, football (tackle) M, ice hockey M, soccer, softball W, track and field. **Intramural:** Basketball, bowling, football (non-tackle), racquetball, soccer, softball, volleyball. **Team name:** Falcons.

Student services. Alcohol/substance abuse counseling, career counseling, services for economically disadvantaged, student employment services, financial aid counseling, health services, on-campus daycare, personal counseling. **Physically disabled:** Services for visually, speech, hearing impaired. **Learning disabled:** Comprehensive services available.

Contact. E-mail: admissions@fsc.edu
Phone: (978) 665-3144 Toll-free number: (800) 705-9692
Fax: (978) 665-4540
Director of Admissions, Fitchburg State College, 160 Pearl Street, Fitchburg, MA 01420-2697

Framingham State College

Framingham, Massachusetts — **CB member**
www.framingham.edu — **CB code: 3519**

- Public 4-year liberal arts and teachers college
- Residential campus in small city
- 3,460 degree-seeking undergraduates: 13% part-time, 67% women, 3% African American, 3% Asian American, 3% Hispanic American, 1% international
- 919 degree-seeking graduate students
- 64% of applicants admitted
- SAT or ACT with writing required
- 42% graduate within 6 years; 15% enter graduate study

General. Founded in 1839. Regionally accredited. **Degrees:** 658 bachelor's awarded; master's offered. **ROTC:** Army. **Location:** 20 miles from Boston. **Calendar:** Semester, extensive summer session. **Full-time faculty:** 167 total; 85% have terminal degrees, 5% minority, 55% women. **Part-time faculty:** 67 total; 40% have terminal degrees, 13% minority, 52% women. **Class size:** 31% < 20, 65% 20-39, 2% 40-49, 1% 50-99. **Special facilities:** Greenhouse, early childhood demonstration lab, education curriculum library, learning center.

Freshman class profile. 3,955 applied, 2,518 admitted, 670 enrolled.

Mid 50% test scores		**Rank in top quarter:**	31%
SAT verbal:	480-560	**Rank in top tenth:**	8%
SAT math:	480-560	**End year in good standing:**	96%
GPA 3.50 or higher:	20%	**Return as sophomores:**	75%
GPA 3.0-3.49:	28%	**Out-of-state:**	8%
GPA 2.0-2.99:	52%	**Live on campus:**	75%

Basis for selection. Strength of high school curriculum, weighted high school GPA, class rank, test scores most important. Some attention given to organized and volunteer activities, recommendations and special talents. Consideration given to students whose educational opportunities have been limited due to economic disadvantage. Admission standards policy of Massachusetts Board of Higher Education requires minimum of 16 college-preparatory courses with weighted GPA of 3.0. Students with lower GPA may qualify based on sliding scale combining SAT scores with GPA. Essay recommended. Portfolio required of studio art majors. **Homeschooled:** Students may be required to submit results of additional nationally normed tests, such as SAT Subject Tests. **Learning Disabled:** Students with diagnosed learning disability must submit individualized educational plan/504 plan along with all psychoeducational testing current within last 3 years.

High school preparation. 16 units required; 20 recommended. Required and recommended units include English 4, mathematics 3-4, social studies 1, history 1-2, science 3-4 (laboratory 2-3), foreign language 2-4 and academic electives 2. Math must include algebra I, algebra II, and geometry. Additional unit of math strongly recommended for computer science, math, pre-engineering, and science majors. Additional units of biology, chemistry, physics recommended for science majors. Foreign language must be 2 units of same language. All units must be college preparatory level.

2005-2006 Annual costs. Tuition/fees: $4,999; $11,079 out-of-state. Fees include mandatory laptop purchase by new students. New England Regional tuition rate $1456. Room/board: $6,157. Books/supplies: $700. Personal expenses: $1,200.

2004-2005 Financial aid. Need-based: 495 full-time freshmen applied for aid; 345 were judged to have need; 345 of these received aid. Average need met was 80%. Average scholarship/grant was $3,512; average loan $2,112. 46% of total undergraduate aid awarded as scholarships/grants, 54% as loans/jobs. **Non-need-based:** Awarded to 75 full-time undergraduates, including 33 freshmen. Scholarships awarded for academics.

Four-Year Colleges

Application procedures. Admission: Priority date 2/15; deadline 5/1 (postmark date). $25 fee ($40 out-of-state), may be waived for applicants with need. Application may be submitted online. Admission notification on a rolling basis beginning on or about 1/15. Must reply by May 1 or within 2 week(s) if notified thereafter. Late applications may be considered. Some majors and on-campus housing may be filled by priority filing date of 2/15. Application fee waiver available to in-state students who submit College Board fee waiver. **Financial aid:** Priority date 3/1; no closing date. FAFSA required. Applicants notified on a rolling basis starting 4/15; must reply by 5/1 or within 2 week(s) of notification.

Academics. Special study options: Cross-registration, distance learning, double major, honors, independent study, internships, liberal arts/career combination, study abroad, teacher certification program, Washington semester. Pre-engineering program in conjunction with University of Massachusetts at Amherst, University of Massachusetts at Dartmouth, University of Massachusetts at Lowell. **Credit/placement by examination:** AP, CLEP, IB, institutional tests. 54 credit hours maximum toward bachelor's degree. **Support services:** Learning center, reduced course load, study skills assistance, tutoring, writing center.

Majors. Agriculture: Food science. **Biology:** General. **Business:** General. **Communications:** General. **Computer sciences:** General. **Education:** Biology, chemistry, early childhood, elementary, English, family/consumer sciences, foreign languages, geography, health, history, mathematics, secondary, social science. **English:** English lit. **Family/consumer sciences:** General, clothing/textiles, food/nutrition. **Foreign languages:** General. **Health:** Nursing (RN). **History:** General. **Liberal arts:** Arts/sciences. **Math:** General. **Physical sciences:** Chemistry. **Psychology:** General. **Social sciences:** Economics, geography, political science, sociology. **Visual/performing arts:** Art.

Most popular majors. Business/marketing 17%, communication technologies 9%, education 6%, English 8%, family/consumer sciences 8%, psychology 11%, social sciences 15%.

Computing on campus. PC or laptop required. 200 workstations in dormitories, library, computer center, student center. Dormitories wired for high-speed internet access and linked to campus network. Commuter students can connect to campus network. Online course registration, online library, helpline, wireless network available.

Student life. Freshman orientation: Mandatory. Preregistration for classes offered. 1-day orientation offered in June, followed up by additional day in late August or early September. **Policies:** Freshmen permitted cars on campus. **Housing:** Coed dorms, single-sex dorms, substance-free housing available. $150 nonrefundable deposit, deadline 5/1. **Activities:** Choral groups, dance, drama, literary magazine, musical theater, radio station, student government, student newspaper, active sociologists, Hispanic student club, black student union, Christian Fellowship, Hillel, Newman Association, student union activities board, MASSPIRG, international student union.

Athletics. NCAA. **Intercollegiate:** Baseball M, basketball, cross-country, field hockey W, football (tackle) M, ice hockey M, lacrosse W, soccer, softball W, volleyball W. **Intramural:** Basketball, football (non-tackle) M, golf, softball, volleyball, weight lifting. **Team name:** Rams.

Student services. Adult student services, alcohol/substance abuse counseling, campus ministries, career counseling, services for economically disadvantaged, student employment services, financial aid counseling, health services, minority student services, personal counseling, placement for graduates, veterans' counselor, women's services. **Physically disabled:** Services for visually, hearing impaired.

Contact. E-mail: admiss@frc.mass.edu
Phone: (508) 626-4500 Fax: (508) 626-4017
Elizabeth Canella, Dean of Enrollment Management, Framingham State College, 100 State Street, Framingham, MA 01701-9101

Franklin W. Olin College of Engineering

Needham, Massachusetts
www.olin.edu **CB code: 2824**

- Private 4-year engineering college
- Residential campus in large town
- 279 degree-seeking undergraduates: 42% women, 3% African American, 10% Asian American, 4% Hispanic American, 1% international
- 23% of applicants admitted
- SAT or ACT with writing, SAT Subject Tests, application essay required

General. Regionally accredited. **Location:** 14 miles from Boston. **Calendar:** Semester. **Full-time faculty:** 29 total; 14% minority, 34% women. **Part-time faculty:** 3 total; 100% have terminal degrees, 67% women. **Class size:** 35% < 20, 62% 20-39, 2% 40-49.

Freshman class profile. 546 applied, 123 admitted, 77 enrolled.

Mid 50% test scores			
SAT verbal:	710-770	Rank in top tenth:	94%
SAT math:	710-800	Return as sophomores:	97%
ACT:	31-34	Out-of-state:	86%
Rank in top quarter:	100%	Live on campus:	100%

Basis for selection. Secondary school achievement, course rigor, test scores, personal character most important; creativity, entrepreneurial spirit also very important. Cultural, economic, geographic diversity encouraged. After a review of all applications, group of applicants chosen as candidates. Candidates attend 1 of 2 weekends on campus to participate in design project, individual interviews, and team exercises. Incoming class selected from this group. 3 SAT Subject Tests required, including math and science.

High school preparation. Required units include English 4, mathematics 4, social studies 2, history 2, science 3 (laboratory 3) and foreign language 2. Recommend highest level of math and science courses available.

2005-2006 Annual costs. Tuition/fees: $150. Every admitted student receives 4-year full-tuition scholarship. Room/board: $10,870. Books/supplies: $750. Personal expenses: $1,500.

2005-2006 Financial aid. Need-based: 81% of total undergraduate aid awarded as scholarships/grants, 19% as loans/jobs. **Non-need-based:** Scholarships awarded for academics, leadership. **Additional information:** No financial aid forms necessary.

Application procedures. Admission: Closing date 1/7 (postmark date). $60 fee, may be waived for applicants with need. Application may be submitted online. Admission notification 3/21. Must reply by 5/1. **Financial aid:** Closing date 4/16. FAFSA required. Applicants notified by 3/1; must reply by 5/1.

Academics. Special study options: Combined bachelor's/graduate degree, cross-registration, exchange student, independent study, internships, liberal arts/career combination, student-designed major, study abroad. **Credit/placement by examination:** AP, CLEP, institutional tests. **Support services:** Tutoring, writing center.

Majors. Engineering: General, electrical, mechanical.

Computing on campus. PC or laptop required. Dormitories wired for high-speed internet access and linked to campus network. Commuter students can connect to campus network. Online course registration, online library, helpline, repair service, student web hosting, wireless network available.

Student life. Freshman orientation: Available. **Policies:** All students sign honor code that addresses personal and academic integrity. Freshmen permitted cars on campus. **Housing:** Guaranteed on-campus for all undergraduates. Coed dorms available. **Activities:** Jazz band, choral groups, dance, drama, film society, music ensembles, musical theater, student government, student newspaper, symphony orchestra, Christian club, Support, Encourage and Recognize Volunteerism, international club, Korean club, political caucus, martial arts club.

Athletics. Intramural: Basketball, football (non-tackle), ice hockey, racquetball, soccer, softball, squash, tennis, volleyball.

Student services. Alcohol/substance abuse counseling, campus ministries, career counseling, financial aid counseling, health services, personal counseling, placement for graduates, women's services.

Contact. E-mail: info@olin.edu
Phone: (781) 292-2222 Fax: (781) 292-2210
Duncan Murdoch, Dean of Admission, Franklin W. Olin College of Engineering, Olin Way, Needham, MA 02492-1245

Gordon College

Wenham, Massachusetts **CB member**
www.gordon.edu **CB code: 3417**

- Private 4-year liberal arts college affiliated with nondenominational tradition
- Residential campus in small town
- 1,584 degree-seeking undergraduates: 2% part-time, 63% women, 1% African American, 2% Asian American, 3% Hispanic American, 2% international
- 43 degree-seeking graduate students

- 84% of applicants admitted
- SAT or ACT with writing, application essay, interview required
- 74% graduate within 6 years; 20% enter graduate study

General. Founded in 1889. Regionally accredited. **Degrees:** 376 bachelor's awarded; master's offered. **ROTC:** Army, Air Force. **Location:** 25 miles from Boston. **Calendar:** Semester. **Full-time faculty:** 93 total; 86% have terminal degrees, 11% minority, 30% women. **Part-time faculty:** 52 total; 2% minority, 56% women. **Class size:** 65% < 20, 25% 20-39, 4% 40-49, 4% 50-99, 1% >100. **Special facilities:** Christian studies center, international office for Christians in the Visual Arts, electron microscope, gene sequencing machine, Shakespearean folios, center for balance and mobility.

Freshman class profile. 1,098 applied, 921 admitted, 414 enrolled.

Mid 50% test scores		**End year in good standing:**	93%
SAT verbal:	550-670	**Return as sophomores:**	85%
SAT math:	540-650	**Out-of-state:**	77%
ACT:	23-29	**Live on campus:**	99%
Rank in top quarter:	69%	**International:**	2%
Rank in top tenth:	33%		

Basis for selection. High school course selection and grades, rank in class, essay of Christian commitment, test scores, references, interview important. School and community activities considered. SAT Subject Tests not required but may be used for placement. Audition required of music majors. Portfolio required of visual art majors. **Homeschooled:** Transcript of courses and grades, interview, letter of recommendation (nonparent) required. Information regarding course of study, including description of curriculum and reading list, required. **Learning Disabled:** Students with diagnosed learning disability may submit documentation with application, as well as any learning plans used through high school.

High school preparation. 20 units required; 25 recommended. Required and recommended units include English 4, mathematics 2-3, social studies 2-3, science 2-3 (laboratory 1-3), foreign language 2-4 and academic electives 5. Academic profile should include AP, honors, or accelerated courses.

2006-2007 Annual costs. Tuition/fees: $24,278. Room/board: $6,640. Books/supplies: $800. Personal expenses: $1,000.

2005-2006 Financial aid. Need-based: Average need met was 71%. Average scholarship/grant was $10,938; average loan $3,057. 61% of total undergraduate aid awarded as scholarships/grants, 39% as loans/jobs. **Non-need-based:** Scholarships awarded for academics, alumni affiliation, leadership, minority status, music/drama, religious affiliation.

Application procedures. Admission: Priority date 3/1; no deadline. $50 fee, may be waived for applicants with need. Application may be submitted online. Admission notification on a rolling basis beginning on or about 12/15. Must reply by May 1 or within 2 week(s) if notified thereafter. Must submit deposit by May 1. **Financial aid:** Closing date 3/1. FAFSA, CSS PROFILE required. Applicants notified on a rolling basis starting 4/15; must reply by 5/1 or within 2 week(s) of notification.

Academics. Study abroad in England, France, Israel, Italy, Egypt, Russia, China, Canada, Kenya. Extensive domestic programs include marine biology, film studies in Hollywood. Great Books Honors Program in Jerusalem and Athens. **Special study options:** Cooperative education, cross-registration, double major, honors, independent study, internships, liberal arts/career combination, student-designed major, study abroad, teacher certification program, urban semester, Washington semester. Gordon-in-Boston; Orvieto; Oregon Extension; LaVida Wilderness Expedition; Co-op programs: arts, business, computer science, education, engineering, health professions, humanities, natural science, social/behaviorial science. **Credit/placement by examination:** AP, CLEP, IB, SAT, institutional tests. **Support services:** Learning center, reduced course load, remedial instruction, study skills assistance, tutoring, writing center.

Majors. Biology: General, exercise physiology. **Business:** Accounting, business admin, finance. **Communications:** General. **Computer sciences:** Computer science. **Education:** Early childhood, elementary, middle, music, secondary, special. **English:** English lit. **Foreign languages:** General, French, German, Spanish. **History:** General. **Math:** General. **Parks/recreation:** General. **Philosophy/religion:** Christian, philosophy. **Physical sciences:** Chemistry, physics. **Psychology:** General. **Public administration:** Social work. **Social sciences:** Economics, international relations, political science, sociology. **Theology:** Youth ministry. **Visual/performing arts:** Art, dramatic, music performance.

Most popular majors. Biology 6%, business/marketing 10%, education 13%, English 12%, history 6%, philosophy/religious studies 6%, psychology 8%, social sciences 10%.

Computing on campus. 125 workstations in dormitories, library, computer center, student center. Dormitories wired for high-speed internet access and linked to campus network. Commuter students can connect to campus network. Online library, helpline, wireless network available.

Student life. Freshman orientation: Mandatory. Preregistration for classes offered. 4-day program prior to fall semester. **Policies:** No alcohol or smoking allowed. Religious observance required. Freshmen permitted cars on campus. **Housing:** Guaranteed on-campus for freshmen. Coed dorms, single-sex dorms, special housing for disabled, apartments, substance-free housing available. International hall, mentoring hall, theme houses. **Activities:** Bands, choral groups, drama, literary magazine, music ensembles, musical theater, student government, student newspaper, symphony orchestra, Society for New Politics, Advocates for Cultural Diversity, Christians for Social Action, fellowship group for children of missionaries, ministry to deaf persons, outreach service, short-term mission trips, Amnesty International, ALANA.

Athletics. NCAA. **Intercollegiate:** Baseball M, basketball, cross-country, field hockey W, golf, lacrosse, soccer, softball W, swimming, tennis, track and field, volleyball W. **Intramural:** Basketball, football (non-tackle), racquetball, soccer, softball, table tennis, track and field, volleyball. **Team name:** Fighting Scots.

Student services. Alcohol/substance abuse counseling, campus ministries, career counseling, student employment services, financial aid counseling, health services, minority student services, personal counseling, placement for graduates. **Physically disabled:** Services for visually, speech, hearing impaired.

Contact. E-mail: admissions@gordon.edu
Phone: (978) 867-4218 Toll-free number: (866) 464-6736
Fax: (978) 867-4682
Nancy Mering, Director of Admissions, Gordon College, 255 Grapevine Road, Wenham, MA 01984-1813

Hampshire College

Amherst, Massachusetts — **CB member**
www.hampshire.edu — **CB code: 3447**

- Private 4-year liberal arts college
- Residential campus in large town
- 1,362 degree-seeking undergraduates: 59% women, 3% African American, 4% Asian American, 4% Hispanic American, 3% international
- 64% of applicants admitted
- Application essay required
- 71% graduate within 6 years; 5% enter graduate study

General. Founded in 1965. Regionally accredited. Students design individual concentrations of study, test theory with off-campus study and community service, and complete original research and projects. **Degrees:** 310 bachelor's awarded. **ROTC:** Army. **Location:** 90 miles from Boston, 20 miles from Springfield. **Calendar:** 4-1-4. **Full-time faculty:** 94 total; 87% have terminal degrees, 17% minority, 53% women. **Part-time faculty:** 43 total; 79% have terminal degrees, 12% minority, 46% women. **Class size:** 68% < 20, 31% 20-39, less than 1% 40-49. **Special facilities:** Bioshelter (integrated greenhouse/aquaculture facility), farm center, electronic music production studio, extensive film and photography facilities, fabrication center, National Yiddish book center, museum of picturebook art.

Freshman class profile. 2,243 applied, 1,441 admitted, 399 enrolled.

Mid 50% test scores		**Rank in top quarter:**	63%
SAT verbal:	600-710	**Rank in top tenth:**	28%
SAT math:	560-660	**Return as sophomores:**	82%
ACT:	24-30	**Out-of-state:**	81%
GPA 3.50 or higher:	45%	**Live on campus:**	100%
GPA 3.0-3.49:	37%	**International:**	3%
GPA 2.0-2.99:	17%		

Basis for selection. Criteria include desire to do rigorous independent work, school record, academic writing samples, recommendations, school and community activities. Interview recommended.

High school preparation. 18 units recommended. Recommended units include English 4, mathematics 3, social studies 2, history 2, science 3 (laboratory 3), foreign language 3 and academic electives 1.

2006-2007 Annual costs. Tuition/fees: $34,605. Room/board: $9,030. Books/supplies: $500. Personal expenses: $500.

2005-2006 Financial aid. Need-based: 242 full-time freshmen applied for aid; 209 were judged to have need; 208 of these received aid. Average

need met was 87%. Average scholarship/grant was $21,000; average loan $2,625. 79% of total undergraduate aid awarded as scholarships/grants, 21% as loans/jobs. **Non-need-based:** Awarded to 428 full-time undergraduates, including 195 freshmen. Scholarships awarded for academics, leadership, minority status.

Application procedures. **Admission:** Priority date 11/15; deadline 1/15 (receipt date). $55 fee, may be waived for applicants with need. Application may be submitted online. Admission notification 4/1. Must reply by May 1 or within 2 week(s) if notified thereafter. **Financial aid:** Closing date 2/1. FAFSA, institutional form, CSS PROFILE required. Applicants notified by 4/1; must reply by 5/1.

Academics. All students pursue individualized program of study. Requirements for graduation not based on credit, but on completion of division one courses in all 5 schools, an independent concentration consisting of combination of courses, independent project work, year-long thesis. **Special study options:** Accelerated study, cross-registration, exchange student, independent study, internships, student-designed major, study abroad, teacher certification program. Member 5-college consortium; may take classes at other member institutions. **Credit/placement by examination:** AP, CLEP, IB. **Support services:** Writing center.

Majors. **Agriculture:** Animal sciences. **Architecture:** Environmental design. **Area/ethnic studies:** African-American, American, Asian, Asian-American, Hispanic-American/Latino/Chicano, Latin American, women's. **Biology:** General. **Business:** General, international. **Communications:** General, journalism. **Computer sciences:** General, computer graphics, computer science. **Conservation:** Environmental studies. **Education:** General, early childhood, elementary, secondary. **English:** American lit, British lit. **Family/consumer sciences:** Family studies, food/nutrition. **Foreign languages:** Comparative lit, linguistics. **Health:** Predentistry, premedicine, preveterinary. **History:** General. **Interdisciplinary:** Behavioral sciences, biological/physical sciences, biopsychology, global studies, math/computer science, natural sciences, neuroscience, nutrition sciences, peace/conflict, science/society. **Legal studies:** General. **Liberal arts:** Arts/sciences. **Math:** General. **Philosophy/religion:** Judaic, philosophy, religion. **Physical sciences:** Chemistry, geology, physics. **Psychology:** General. **Social sciences:** General, anthropology, demography, economics, political science, sociology, urban studies. **Visual/performing arts:** General, art, art history/conservation, cinematography, dance, design, dramatic, drawing, film/cinema, multimedia, painting, photography, play/screenwriting, sculpture, studio arts.

Most popular majors. Area/ethnic studies 9%, English 10%, history 6%, social sciences 12%, visual/performing arts 33%.

Computing on campus. 186 workstations in library, computer center, student center. Dormitories wired for high-speed internet access and linked to campus network. Commuter students can connect to campus network. Online course registration, helpline, student web hosting, wireless network available.

Student life. **Freshman orientation:** Mandatory, $140 fee. Preregistration for classes offered. Program held during week immediately before matriculation. **Policies:** Freshmen permitted cars on campus. **Housing:** Guaranteed on-campus for freshmen. Coed dorms, special housing for disabled, apartments available. $200 nonrefundable deposit, deadline 5/1. **Activities:** Jazz band, choral groups, dance, drama, film society, music ensembles, student government, student newspaper, forum of international students, Excaliber, Jewish students, poetry club.

Student services. Career counseling, financial aid counseling, health services, minority student services, on-campus daycare, personal counseling, women's services. **Physically disabled:** Services for visually, hearing impaired.

Contact. E-mail: admissions@hampshire.edu
Phone: (413) 559-5471 Toll-free number: (877) 937-4267
Fax: (413) 559-5631
Karen Parker, Director of Admissions, Hampshire College, 893 West Street, Amherst, MA 01002-9988

Harvard College

Cambridge, Massachusetts
www.college.harvard.edu **CB code: 3434**

- Private 4-year university
- Residential campus in small city
- 6,613 degree-seeking undergraduates: 49% women
- 12,290 degree-seeking graduate students
- 9% of applicants admitted
- SAT or ACT with writing, SAT Subject Tests, application essay, interview required
- 98% graduate within 6 years

General. Founded in 1636. Regionally accredited. Harvard College is the undergraduate program within Harvard University, part of the faculty of arts and sciences, and offers programs in liberal arts. **Degrees:** 1,689 bachelor's awarded; master's, doctoral, first professional offered. **ROTC:** Army, Navy, Air Force. **Location:** 3 miles from Boston. **Calendar:** Semester, extensive summer session. **Full-time faculty:** 1,555 total; 12% minority, 29% women. **Part-time faculty:** 404 total; 10% minority, 37% women. **Special facilities:** Museum of Scandinavian and Germanic art; experimental forest in New York state; center for study of Italian Renaissance in Florence, Italy; center for Byzantine studies in Washington, DC; Smithsonian astrophysical observatory.

Freshman class profile. 22,796 applied, 2,102 admitted, 1,640 enrolled.

Mid 50% test scores			
SAT verbal:	700-790	End year in good standing:	99%
SAT math:	700-790	Return as sophomores:	98%
ACT:	30-34	Out-of-state:	86%
Rank in top quarter:	100%	Live on campus:	100%
Rank in top tenth:	95%	International:	9%

Basis for selection. Secondary school record most important; character, creative ability in some discipline or activity, leadership, liveliness of mind, demonstrated stamina and ability to carry out a demanding college program, and strong sense of social responsibility important. Any 3 SAT Subject Tests required. Interview with an alumnus/alumna required of all applicants if possible; documentation of special talents encouraged.

High school preparation. Recommended units include English 4, mathematics 4, social studies 3, history 2, science 4 and foreign language 4. Applicants encouraged to take rigorous courses and make the most of any opportunities for enrichment.

2006-2007 Annual costs. Tuition/fees: $33,709. Room/board: $9,946. Books/supplies: $950. Personal expenses: $1,620.

2005-2006 Financial aid. All financial aid based on need. 1,034 full-time freshmen applied for aid; 852 were judged to have need; 852 of these received aid. Average need met was 100%. Average scholarship/grant was $30,162; average loan $1,560. 91% of total undergraduate aid awarded as scholarships/grants, 9% as loans/jobs. **Additional information:** Institution meets full need of all admitted students.

Application procedures. **Admission:** Closing date 1/1 (postmark date). $65 fee, may be waived for applicants with need. Application may be submitted online. Admission notification 4/1. Must reply by 5/1. Early action candidates encouraged to apply by October 15. **Financial aid:** Closing date 2/1. FAFSA, CSS PROFILE required. Applicants notified by 4/1; must reply by 5/1 or within 2 week(s) of notification.

Academics. Require 12 one-term courses for completion of major and 32 one-term courses for graduation. **Special study options:** Accelerated study, cross-registration, double major, exchange student, honors, independent study, internships, student-designed major, study abroad, teacher certification program. **Credit/placement by examination:** AP, CLEP, IB, institutional tests. SAT Subject Test policy varies depending on subject matter and score. Sophomore standing available on basis of 4 AP exams with qualifying scores, or on basis of IB scores. Students with fewer than 4 AP qualifying scores eligible for placement in more challenging courses. **Support services:** Learning center, tutoring, writing center.

Majors. **Architecture:** Urban/community planning. **Area/ethnic studies:** African, African-American, American, Asian, Asian-American, Central Asian, Central/Eastern European, Chinese, East Asian, European, Japanese, Latin American, Near/Middle Eastern, Russian/Slavic, Scandinavian, South Asian, Southeast Asian, Western European, women's. **Biology:** General, biochemistry, biophysics, cell/histology, evolutionary, molecular. **Business:** General, managerial economics. **Computer sciences:** Computer science. **Conservation:** Environmental science. **Engineering:** Science. **English:** English lit. **Foreign languages:** General, ancient Greek, Celtic, Chinese, classics, comparative lit, German, Japanese, Latin, linguistics, Romance, Russian, Sanskrit, Slavic, South Asian. **Health:** Premedicine. **History:** General, American, European, science/technology. **Liberal arts:** Arts/sciences. **Math:** General, applied, statistics. **Philosophy/religion:** Philosophy, religion. **Physical sciences:** General, astronomy, chemistry, geochemistry, geology, geophysics, molecular physics, physics. **Psychology:** General. **Social sciences:** General, anthropology, archaeology, economics, political science, sociology. **Visual/performing arts:** General, art, music theory/composition.

Most popular majors. Biology 11%, English 7%, history 11%, psychology 7%, social sciences 38%.

Computing on campus. 605 workstations in dormitories, library, computer center. Dormitories wired for high-speed internet access and linked to campus network. Commuter students can connect to campus network. Online course registration, helpline, repair service available.

Student life. **Freshman orientation:** Mandatory. Week-long program in early September. **Policies:** Freshmen permitted cars on campus. **Housing:** Guaranteed on-campus for all undergraduates. Coed dorms, special housing for disabled, apartments available. All freshmen live together. Other students and some faculty members reside in 13 on-campus houses, self-contained communities offering seminars and tutorials. **Activities:** Bands, choral groups, dance, drama, film society, literary magazine, music ensembles, musical theater, opera, radio station, student government, student newspaper, symphony orchestra, TV station, over 320 official clubs available.

Athletics. NCAA. **Intercollegiate:** Baseball M, basketball, cross-country, diving, fencing, field hockey W, football (tackle) M, golf, ice hockey, lacrosse, rowing (crew), sailing, skiing, soccer, softball W, squash, swimming, tennis, track and field, volleyball, water polo, wrestling M. **Intramural:** Badminton, basketball, cross-country, equestrian, fencing, field hockey W, football (tackle) M, gymnastics W, ice hockey, rowing (crew), rugby, sailing, skiing, soccer, softball, squash, swimming, table tennis, tennis, track and field, volleyball, wrestling M. **Team name:** Crimson.

Student services. Alcohol/substance abuse counseling, campus ministries, career counseling, services for economically disadvantaged, student employment services, financial aid counseling, health services, on-campus daycare, personal counseling, placement for graduates. **Physically disabled:** Services for visually, speech, hearing impaired.

Contact. E-mail: college@fas.harvard.edu
Phone: (617) 495-1551 Fax: (617) 495-8821
Tom Dingman, Dean of Freshmen, Harvard College, Byerly Hall, 8 Garden Street, Cambridge, MA 02138

Hebrew College

Newton Centre, Massachusetts — **CB member**
www.hebrewcollege.edu — **CB code: 3435**

- Private 4-year rabbinical college affiliated with Jewish faith
- Commuter campus in small city
- 4 degree-seeking undergraduates: 25% part-time, 50% women, 25% international
- 125 degree-seeking graduate students
- 67% of applicants admitted
- Application essay, interview required

General. Founded in 1921. Regionally accredited. Institution features Jewish studies in a transdenominational setting which includes both Jews (of all denominations) and non-Jews. **Degrees:** 5 bachelor's awarded; master's offered. **Location:** 4 miles from Boston. **Calendar:** Semester, limited summer session. **Full-time faculty:** 19 total; 68% have terminal degrees, 16% women. **Part-time faculty:** 23 total; 61% have terminal degrees, 48% women. **Special facilities:** Museum of Judaic items, Judaic book library.

Freshman class profile. 3 applied, 2 admitted, 2 enrolled.

Basis for selection. Interview, recommendations, school record important. Audition may be required in some cases. Interview required but may be conducted over telephone if student lives at a distance.

2005-2006 Annual costs. Tuition/fees: $23,450. Books/supplies: $800. Personal expenses: $500.

Financial aid. **Non-need-based:** Scholarships awarded for academics.

Application procedures. **Admission:** Priority date 12/30; no deadline. $50 fee, may be waived for applicants with need. Application must be submitted on paper. Admission notification on a rolling basis. Must reply by May 1 or within 3 week(s) if notified thereafter. **Financial aid:** Priority date 5/1; no closing date. FAFSA, institutional form required. Applicants notified on a rolling basis starting 7/1; must reply within 3 week(s) of notification.

Academics. Cross-registration available at 6 local colleges. **Special study options:** Accelerated study, combined bachelor's/graduate degree, cross-registration, distance learning, dual enrollment of high school students, independent study, internships, student-designed major, teacher certification program. **Credit/placement by examination:** AP, CLEP.

Majors. **Philosophy/religion:** Judaic. **Theology:** Religious ed.

Computing on campus. 5 workstations in computer center.

Student life. **Freshman orientation:** Mandatory. Preregistration for classes offered. **Policies:** Freshmen permitted cars on campus. **Activities:** Choral groups.

Student services. Career counseling, financial aid counseling, personal counseling.

Contact. E-mail: admissions@hebrewcollege.edu
Phone: (617) 559-8619 Toll-free number: (800) 866-4814 ext. 8619
Fax: (617) 559-8601
Kate Nachman, Admissions Manager, Hebrew College, 160 Herrick Road, Newton Centre, MA 02459

Hellenic College/Holy Cross

Brookline, Massachusetts — **CB member**
www.hchc.edu — **CB code: 3449**

- Private 4-year liberal arts and seminary college affiliated with Eastern Orthodox Church
- Residential campus in large town
- 84 degree-seeking undergraduates: 39% women
- 107 degree-seeking graduate students
- 92% of applicants admitted
- SAT or ACT (ACT writing optional), application essay, interview required

General. Founded in 1937. Regionally accredited. **Degrees:** 21 bachelor's awarded; master's, first professional offered. **Location:** 5 miles from downtown Boston. **Calendar:** Semester, limited summer session. **Full-time faculty:** 13 total; 46% women. **Part-time faculty:** 19 total; 53% women. **Class size:** 49% < 20, 51% 20-39.

Freshman class profile. 37 applied, 34 admitted, 20 enrolled.

Mid 50% test scores			
SAT verbal:	390-600	Return as sophomores:	13%
SAT math:	470-660	Out-of-state:	80%
End year in good standing:	90%	Live on campus:	95%

Basis for selection. High school achievement, GPA, 2 recommendations from instructors, test scores very important, school and community activities also important. For religious studies majors, 2 letters from clergy important if members of Orthodox Christian Church.

High school preparation. 15 units required. Required units include English 4, mathematics 2, social studies 2, history 2, science 3 and foreign language 2.

2005-2006 Annual costs. Tuition/fees: $15,775. Room/board: $9,260. Books/supplies: $750. Personal expenses: $1,500.

2004-2005 Financial aid. All financial aid based on need. 24 full-time freshmen applied for aid; 24 were judged to have need; 24 of these received aid. Average need met was 45%. Average scholarship/grant was $12,000; average loan $2,625. 76% of total undergraduate aid awarded as scholarships/grants, 24% as loans/jobs.

Application procedures. **Admission:** Priority date 5/1; deadline 8/15 (receipt date). $50 fee, may be waived for applicants with need. Admission notification on a rolling basis. Students who apply by 12/01 are eligible to have application fee waived and receive priority consideration for scholarships; early applications are encouraged. **Financial aid:** Closing date 4/1. FAFSA, institutional form required. Applicants notified on a rolling basis starting 10/1; must reply within 2 week(s) of notification.

Academics. **Special study options:** Cross-registration, exchange student, independent study, internships, liberal arts/career combination, study abroad. **Credit/placement by examination:** AP, CLEP, IB, institutional tests. Credit granted varies by degree program. **Support services:** Tutoring.

Majors. **Education:** Elementary. **Family/consumer sciences:** Family studies. **Foreign languages:** Classics. **Liberal arts:** Arts/sciences. **Psychology:** General. **Theology:** Theology.

Most popular majors. Education 20%, foreign language 10%, liberal arts 30%, philosophy/religious studies 40%.

Student life. **Freshman orientation:** Available. **Policies:** Religious observance required for some students. Freshmen permitted cars on campus. **Housing:** Single-sex dorms, apartments available. $200 nonrefundable deposit. **Activities:** Choral groups, dance, drama, music ensembles, student government, several Orthodox groups, campus ministry, prison ministry, missions group.

Athletics. **Intramural:** Basketball, football (tackle) M, soccer M, table tennis, tennis, volleyball.

Student services. Campus ministries, career counseling, student employment services, financial aid counseling, health services, personal counseling, placement for graduates.

Contact. E-mail: admissions@hchc.edu
Phone: (617) 850-1260 Toll-free number: (866) 424-2338
Fax: (617) 850-1460
Sonia Daly, Director of Admissions and Records, Hellenic College/Holy Cross, 50 Goddard Avenue, Brookline, MA 02445

Lasell College

Newton, Massachusetts **CB member**
www.lasell.edu **CB code: 3481**

- Private 4-year business and liberal arts college
- Residential campus in small city
- 1,207 degree-seeking undergraduates: 1% part-time, 69% women, 6% African American, 3% Asian American, 6% Hispanic American, 3% international
- 37 degree-seeking graduate students
- 67% of applicants admitted
- SAT or ACT (ACT writing optional) required
- 63% graduate within 6 years; 10% enter graduate study

General. Founded in 1851. Regionally accredited. **Degrees:** 188 bachelor's awarded; master's offered. **Location:** 8 miles from Boston. **Calendar:** Semester. **Full-time faculty:** 56 total; 46% have terminal degrees, 64% women. **Part-time faculty:** 107 total; 8% have terminal degrees, 49% women. **Class size:** 32% < 20, 68% 20-39.

Freshman class profile. 2,652 applied, 1,787 admitted, 374 enrolled.

Mid 50% test scores		**Rank in top quarter:**	14%
SAT verbal:	450-530	**Rank in top tenth:**	3%
SAT math:	440-520	**Return as sophomores:**	73%
ACT:	20-21	**Out-of-state:**	51%
GPA 3.50 or higher:	7%	**Live on campus:**	93%
GPA 3.0-3.49:	20%	**International:**	2%
GPA 2.0-2.99:	69%		

Basis for selection. Academic GPA, curriculum, class rank, interview, recommendations, extracurricular activities, and standardized test scores considered.

High school preparation. College-preparatory program recommended. 15 units required; 21 recommended. Required and recommended units include English 4, mathematics 3-4, social studies 2-3, history 2-3, science 2-3 (laboratory 2) and foreign language 2.

2006-2007 Annual costs. Tuition/fees: $20,900. Room/board: $9,200. Books/supplies: $1,000. Personal expenses: $2,000.

2005-2006 Financial aid. Need-based: 337 full-time freshmen applied for aid; 295 were judged to have need; 295 of these received aid. Average need met was 68%. Average scholarship/grant was $12,200; average loan $2,500. 68% of total undergraduate aid awarded as scholarships/grants, 32% as loans/jobs. **Non-need-based:** Awarded to 225 full-time undergraduates, including 65 freshmen. Scholarships awarded for academics, alumni affiliation, leadership.

Application procedures. Admission: Priority date 3/15; no deadline. $40 fee, may be waived for applicants with need. Application may be submitted online. Admission notification on a rolling basis beginning on or about 12/15. Must reply by May 1 or within 2 week(s) if notified thereafter. **Financial aid:** Priority date 3/1; no closing date. FAFSA, institutional form required. Applicants notified on a rolling basis starting 2/15; must reply by 5/1 or within 2 week(s) of notification.

Academics. Special study options: Double major, honors, independent study, internships, liberal arts/career combination, semester at sea, student-designed major, study abroad, teacher certification program. **Credit/placement by examination:** AP, CLEP, IB, institutional tests. **Support services:** Learning center, reduced course load, study skills assistance, tutoring.

Majors. Biology: Exercise physiology. **Business:** Accounting, accounting/business management, accounting/finance, business admin, fashion, finance, hospitality admin, hotel/motel admin, international, management information systems, marketing, restaurant/food services, tourism/travel. **Communications:** General. **Computer sciences:** General, computer science. **Education:** Early childhood, elementary, English, history, mathematics, physical, secondary. **Family/consumer sciences:** Child development, fashion consultant. **Health:** Athletic training, health care admin, health services. **History:** General. **Legal studies:** General. **Liberal arts:** Humanities. **Parks/recreation:** Exercise sciences, health/fitness, sports admin. **Protective services:** Law enforcement admin. **Psychology:** General. **Public administration:** Human services. **Social sciences:** General, sociology. **Visual/performing arts:** Fashion design, graphic design.

Most popular majors. Business/marketing 43%, education 15%, social sciences 7%, visual/performing arts 13%.

Computing on campus. 150 workstations in dormitories, library, computer center, student center. Dormitories wired for high-speed internet access and linked to campus network. Commuter students can connect to campus network. Online course registration, online library, helpline, wireless network available.

Student life. Freshman orientation: Available. Preregistration for classes offered. **Policies:** Freshmen permitted cars on campus. **Housing:** Coed dorms, single-sex dorms, substance-free housing available. $400 nonrefundable deposit, deadline 5/1. Community service, wellness houses. **Activities:** Jazz band, choral groups, dance, drama, literary magazine, music ensembles, musical theater, radio station, student government, student newspaper, TV station.

Athletics. NCAA. **Intercollegiate:** Basketball, cross-country, field hockey W, lacrosse, soccer, softball W, volleyball. **Intramural:** Basketball, football (non-tackle), soccer, volleyball. **Team name:** Lasers.

Student services. Alcohol/substance abuse counseling, career counseling, student employment services, financial aid counseling, health services, personal counseling, placement for graduates.

Contact. E-mail: info@lasell.edu
Phone: (617) 243-2225 Toll-free number: (888) 527-3554
Fax: (617) 243-2380
James Tweed, Director of Undergraduate Admission, Lasell College, 1844 Commonwealth Avenue, Newton, MA 02466

Lesley University

Cambridge, Massachusetts **CB member**
www.lesley.edu/lc **CB code: 3483**

- Private 4-year liberal arts and teachers college
- Residential campus in very large city
- 1,079 degree-seeking undergraduates: 12% part-time, 79% women, 6% African American, 5% Asian American, 5% Hispanic American, 3% international
- 5,540 degree-seeking graduate students
- 72% of applicants admitted
- SAT or ACT with writing, application essay, interview required
- 50% graduate within 6 years; 32% enter graduate study

General. Founded in 1909. Regionally accredited. Lesley University includes 2 undergraduate colleges, Lesley College and The Art Institute of Boston. Main campus in Cambridge, with graduate degree programs offered online and at more than 150 locations in 23 states. **Degrees:** 422 bachelor's, 2 associate awarded; master's, doctoral offered. **Calendar:** Semester, limited summer session. **Full-time faculty:** 53 total; 74% have terminal degrees, 9% minority, 64% women. **Part-time faculty:** 131 total; 29% have terminal degrees, 52% women. **Class size:** 75% < 20, 24% 20-39, less than 1% 40-49. **Special facilities:** Center for teaching resources, media production facility, fine arts studios.

Freshman class profile. 1,351 applied, 967 admitted, 267 enrolled.

Mid 50% test scores		**Rank in top quarter:**	50%
SAT verbal:	480-600	**Rank in top tenth:**	23%
SAT math:	460-570	**End year in good standing:**	89%
ACT:	19-25	**Return as sophomores:**	79%
GPA 3.50 or higher:	11%	**Out-of-state:**	51%
GPA 3.0-3.49:	42%	**Live on campus:**	88%
GPA 2.0-2.99:	46%	**International:**	1%

Basis for selection. Primary focus given to academic record, both grades and challenging courses. Test scores, recommendations, interview, community service, leadership experience also considered.

High school preparation. 18 units required; 20 recommended. Required and recommended units include English 4, mathematics 3-4, social studies 1-2, history 1-2, science 3-4 (laboratory 2), foreign language 2 and academic electives 4.

2006-2007 Annual costs. Tuition/fees: $24,450. Room/board: $10,500. Books/supplies: $700. Personal expenses: $1,925.

2005-2006 Financial aid. **Need-based:** 234 full-time freshmen applied for aid; 189 were judged to have need; 189 of these received aid. Average need met was 70%. Average scholarship/grant was $12,741; average loan $3,507. 66% of total undergraduate aid awarded as scholarships/grants, 34% as loans/jobs. **Non-need-based:** Scholarships awarded for academics, alumni affiliation, art, leadership, minority status, state residency.

Application procedures. **Admission:** Priority date 3/1; no deadline. $40 fee, may be waived for applicants with need. Application may be submitted online. Admission notification on a rolling basis beginning on or about 12/1. Must reply by May 1 or within 2 week(s) if notified thereafter. **Financial aid:** Priority date 3/1; no closing date. FAFSA, institutional form required. Applicants notified on a rolling basis starting 3/15.

Academics. Students complete between 450 and 650 hours of significant internship experience which begins freshman year. **Special study options:** Accelerated study, combined bachelor's/graduate degree, cross-registration, distance learning, double major, exchange student, honors, independent study, internships, liberal arts/career combination, New York semester, student-designed major, study abroad, teacher certification program, Washington semester. **Credit/placement by examination:** AP, CLEP, IB, SAT, ACT, institutional tests. 16 credit hours maximum toward bachelor's degree. **Support services:** Learning center, pre-admission summer program, reduced course load, study skills assistance, tutoring, writing center.

Majors. **Area/ethnic studies:** American. **Biology:** General. **Business:** Business admin. **Communications technology:** General. **Conservation:** Environmental studies. **Education:** General, art, early childhood, early childhood special, elementary, English, kindergarten/preschool, mathematics, middle, science, secondary, social studies, special. **Family/consumer sciences:** Child development, family studies. **Health:** Art therapy, health services. **Interdisciplinary:** Global studies, natural sciences. **Liberal arts:** Arts/sciences. **Math:** General. **Social sciences:** General. **Visual/performing arts:** Art, studio arts.

Most popular majors. Business/marketing 22%, education 7%, liberal arts 33%, psychology 10%, visual/performing arts 20%.

Computing on campus. 195 workstations in dormitories, library, computer center, student center. Dormitories wired for high-speed internet access and linked to campus network. Commuter students can connect to campus network. Online course registration, online library, helpline, wireless network available.

Student life. **Freshman orientation:** Mandatory. Begins 1 week prior to start of classes. **Housing:** Guaranteed on-campus for all undergraduates. Coed dorms, single-sex dorms, substance-free housing available. $300 fully refundable deposit. Themed housing. **Activities:** Choral groups, dance, drama, film society, literary magazine, musical theater, student government, student newspaper, Women for Social Justice, Hillel, Third Wave Women's Group, Prism, Students For a Free Tibet, ALANA, Christian Fellowship.

Athletics. NCAA. **Intercollegiate:** Basketball, rowing (crew), soccer, softball W, volleyball. **Team name:** Lynx.

Student services. Adult student services, alcohol/substance abuse counseling, campus ministries, career counseling, student employment services, financial aid counseling, health services, minority student services, personal counseling, placement for graduates. **Physically disabled:** Services for visually, speech, hearing impaired. **Learning disabled:** Comprehensive services available.

Contact. E-mail: ugadm@lesley.edu
Phone: (617) 349-8800 Toll-free number: (800) 999-1959 ext. 8800
Fax: (617) 349-8810
Deb Kocar, Director of Admissions, Lesley University, 29 Everett Street, Cambridge, MA 02138-2790

Massachusetts College of Art

Boston, Massachusetts — **CB member**
www.massart.edu — **CB code: 3516**

- Public 4-year visual arts college
- Residential campus in very large city
- 1,549 degree-seeking undergraduates: 12% part-time, 63% women, 4% African American, 5% Asian American, 5% Hispanic American, 1% Native American, 3% international
- 129 degree-seeking graduate students
- 61% of applicants admitted
- SAT or ACT with writing, application essay required
- 62% graduate within 6 years

General. Founded in 1873. Regionally accredited. **Degrees:** 285 bachelor's awarded; master's offered. **Calendar:** Semester, extensive summer session. **Full-time faculty:** 75 total. **Part-time faculty:** 115 total. **Class size:** 76% < 20, 24% 20-39, less than 1% 40-49. **Special facilities:** 7 art galleries, foundry, glass furnaces, ceramic kilns, video and film studios, performance and studio spaces, Polaroid 20X24 camera.

Freshman class profile. 1,210 applied, 735 admitted, 265 enrolled.

Mid 50% test scores		**Return as sophomores:**	83%
SAT verbal:	520-630	**Out-of-state:**	30%
SAT math:	480-580	**Live on campus:**	70%
Rank in top quarter:	41%	**International:**	2%
Rank in top tenth:	20%		

Basis for selection. Emphasis on portfolio, academic record, essay, test scores, recommendations. Minimum GPA 3.0. For GPA between 2.0 and 2.9, SAT/ACT scores considered in combination with GPA on sliding scale. Applicants must meet Massachusetts public college admission standards. Portfolio of at least 15 pieces of artwork required, presented as 35 mm 2x2 slides. Work may also be submitted on VHS videotape or digital media. **Homeschooled:** General college preparatory program required for degree-seeking students. **Learning Disabled:** Testing may be waived for applicants with professionally certified learning disabilities.

High school preparation. 17 units required. Required units include English 4, mathematics 2, social studies 2, history 2, science 2 (laboratory 1), foreign language 2 and academic electives 2. At least 2 additional academic units of computer science, humanities, or visual and performing arts also required.

2005-2006 Annual costs. Tuition/fees: $6,850; $16,060 out-of-state. Out-of-state students pay required fees of $8960. Room/board: $9,800. Books/supplies: $2,000. Personal expenses: $1,150.

2005-2006 Financial aid. **Need-based:** 216 full-time freshmen applied for aid; 161 were judged to have need; 161 of these received aid. Average scholarship/grant was $5,189; average loan $2,654. 45% of total undergraduate aid awarded as scholarships/grants, 55% as loans/jobs. **Non-need-based:** Awarded to 165 full-time undergraduates, including 50 freshmen. Scholarships awarded for academics, art, leadership, minority status. **Additional information:** Tuition waiver available to Vietnam veterans.

Application procedures. **Admission:** Closing date 2/1. $30 fee ($65 out-of-state), may be waived for applicants with need. Admission notification 4/20. Must reply by May 1 or within 3 week(s) if notified thereafter. **Financial aid:** Priority date 3/15; no closing date. FAFSA required. Applicants notified on a rolling basis starting 3/15; must reply within 3 week(s) of notification.

Academics. Three-year certificates available. **Special study options:** Cross-registration, double major, exchange student, independent study, internships, liberal arts/career combination, student-designed major, study abroad. Member of American Independent Colleges of Art and Design (AICAD), College Academic Program Sharing (CAPS), Colleges of the Fenway, and Pro Arts Consortium. Exchange programs available in Holland, England, Germany, Ireland, Italy, France. Study abroad available in Spain, Greece, China, Mexico. **Credit/placement by examination:** CLEP, IB, institutional tests. **Support services:** Pre-admission summer program, reduced course load, remedial instruction, tutoring.

Majors. **Architecture:** Environmental design. **Education:** Art. **Visual/performing arts:** Art history/conservation, ceramics, cinematography, commercial/advertising art, design, fashion design, fiber arts, film/cinema, industrial design, metal/jewelry, multimedia, painting, photography, printmaking, sculpture, studio arts.

Most popular majors. Education 6%, visual/performing arts 94%.

Computing on campus. 250 workstations in library, computer center.

Student life. **Housing:** Coed dorms available. $300 deposit. Additional housing also available in Simmons College dorm. **Activities:** Dance, drama, film society, music ensembles, radio station, student government, student newspaper, TV station, minority student organization, gay/lesbian organization, student-run design firm, international student organization, nontraditional student organization.

Athletics. NCAA. **Intramural:** Basketball, ice hockey, soccer, softball W, table tennis, volleyball.

Student services. Adult student services, career counseling, student employment services, health services, personal counseling, placement for graduates, veterans' counselor. **Physically disabled:** Services for visually, hearing impaired.

Contact. E-mail: admissions@massart.edu
Phone: (617) 879-7222 Fax: (617) 879-7250
Kay Ransdell, Dean of Admissions and Enrollment Management, Massachusetts College of Art, 621 Huntington Avenue, Boston, MA 02115-5882

Massachusetts College of Liberal Arts

North Adams, Massachusetts **CB member**
www.mcla.mass.edu **CB code: 3521**

- Public 4-year liberal arts college
- Residential campus in large town
- 1,430 degree-seeking undergraduates
- 419 graduate students
- 75% of applicants admitted
- SAT or ACT (ACT writing optional), application essay required

General. Founded in 1894. Regionally accredited. **Degrees:** 289 bachelor's awarded; master's offered. **Location:** 50 miles from Albany, New York, 120 miles from Boston. **Calendar:** Semester, limited summer session. **Full-time faculty:** 81 total. **Part-time faculty:** 40 total. **Special facilities:** Multimedia computer laboratory.

Freshman class profile. 1,043 applied, 779 admitted, 270 enrolled.

Mid 50% test scores		Out-of-state:	26%
SAT verbal:	480-600	Live on campus:	83%
SAT math:	450-560		

Basis for selection. Secondary school record most important; test scores, essay also important; recommendations, extracurricular activities considered. Interview recommended.

High school preparation. 16 units required. Required units include English 4, mathematics 3, history 2, science 3 (laboratory 2), foreign language 2 and academic electives 2.

2005-2006 Annual costs. Tuition/fees: $5,617; $14,562 out-of-state. Room/board: $6,681. Books/supplies: $700. Personal expenses: $1,300.

Financial aid. Non-need-based: Scholarships awarded for academics, alumni affiliation, art, leadership, minority status, music/drama.

Application procedures. Admission: No deadline. $25 fee, may be waived for applicants with need. Application may be submitted online. Admission notification on a rolling basis beginning on or about 1/1. Must reply by May 1 or within 3 week(s) if notified thereafter. **Financial aid:** Priority date 4/1; no closing date. FAFSA, institutional form required. Applicants notified on a rolling basis starting 4/1; must reply within 2 week(s) of notification.

Academics. Special study options: Cross-registration, distance learning, double major, dual enrollment of high school students, exchange student, honors, independent study, internships, liberal arts/career combination, student-designed major, study abroad, teacher certification program, Washington semester. **Credit/placement by examination:** AP, CLEP, IB, institutional tests. **Support services:** Learning center, pre-admission summer program, reduced course load, remedial instruction, tutoring, writing center.

Majors. Biology: General. **Business:** Accounting, business admin, communications, finance, management science. **Communications:** Broadcast journalism, journalism, public relations. **Computer sciences:** General, information systems, programming. **Conservation:** Environmental studies. **Education:** General. **English:** Creative writing. **Foreign languages:** Comparative lit. **Health:** Clinical lab technology. **History:** General. **Liberal arts:** Arts/sciences. **Math:** General. **Philosophy/religion:** Philosophy. **Physical sciences:** Chemistry, physics. **Psychology:** General. **Public administration:** Social work. **Social sciences:** Sociology. **Visual/performing arts:** General, art history/conservation, dramatic, studio arts.

Computing on campus. 125 workstations in dormitories, library, computer center. Dormitories linked to campus network. Helpline available.

Student life. Freshman orientation: Mandatory, $75 fee. **Housing:** Guaranteed on-campus for all undergraduates. Coed dorms, special housing for disabled, apartments available. $150 deposit. **Activities:** Bands, choral groups, dance, drama, literary magazine, music ensembles, radio station, student government, student newspaper, TV station, interfaith association, Campus Christian Fellowship, Jewish student organization, Newman Club, Gay and Lesbian Allied student society, multicultural society.

Athletics. NCAA. **Intercollegiate:** Baseball M, basketball, cross-country, golf M, ice hockey M, soccer, softball W, tennis W, volleyball W. **Intramural:** Basketball, ice hockey M, soccer, softball, swimming, tennis, volleyball, water polo M. **Team name:** Mohawks.

Student services. Adult student services, career counseling, student employment services, health services, on-campus daycare, personal counseling, placement for graduates, veterans' counselor, women's services. **Physically disabled:** Services for visually, hearing impaired.

Contact. E-mail: admissions@mcla.edu
Phone: (413) 662-5410 Toll-free number: (800) 292-6632
Fax: (413) 662-5179
Steve King, Dean of Enrollment Management, Massachusetts College of Liberal Arts, 375 Church Street, North Adams, MA 01247

Massachusetts College of Pharmacy and Health Sciences

Boston, Massachusetts **CB member**
www.mcphs.edu **CB code: 3512**

- Private 4-year health science and pharmacy college
- Commuter campus in very large city
- 1,854 degree-seeking undergraduates: 5% part-time, 68% women
- 1,010 degree-seeking graduate students
- 76% of applicants admitted
- SAT or ACT with writing, application essay required
- 77% graduate within 6 years

General. Founded in 1823. Regionally accredited. Member of Fenway College Consortium, 14-college library consortium, Worcester Consortium, and Manchester Area College Consortium. Students have access to Harvard Medical School library. Accelerated PharmD program available at Worcester campus and Manchester campus; physician assistant program offered at Boston and Manchester campuses. **Degrees:** 99 bachelor's, 13 associate awarded; master's, doctoral, first professional offered. **Calendar:** Semester, limited summer session. **Full-time faculty:** 157 total; 86% have terminal degrees, 61% women. **Part-time faculty:** 5 total; 80% have terminal degrees, 60% women. **Class size:** 29% < 20, 56% 20-39, 3% 40-49, 5% 50-99, 8% >100. **Special facilities:** Pharmacy practice lab, dental hygiene clinic, patient assessment lab, nursing skills and technology lab.

Freshman class profile. 1,200 applied, 917 admitted, 409 enrolled.

Mid 50% test scores		GPA 2.0-2.99:	17%
SAT verbal:	490-530	Rank in top quarter:	64%
SAT math:	570-620	Rank in top tenth:	28%
ACT:	20-25	Return as sophomores:	88%
GPA 3.50 or higher:	41%	Out-of-state:	48%
GPA 3.0-3.49:	42%	Live on campus:	81%

Basis for selection. School academic record, class rank most important, emphasis on math and science courses. Test scores, essays, counselor's recommendation also very important. Student's interest, aptitude for pharmacy and allied health fields considered. Interview required for premedical and health sciences. **Homeschooled:** Require documentation of curriculum and program of study; equivalency exam.

High school preparation. 18 units recommended. Recommended units include English 4, mathematics 3, social studies 1, history 1, science 2 (laboratory 2) and academic electives 5. Additional units of advanced mathematics and science (especially chemistry) strongly recommended.

2005-2006 Annual costs. Tuition/fees: $21,050. Room/board: $11,220. Books/supplies: $750. Personal expenses: $2,000.

2005-2006 Financial aid. Need-based: 377 full-time freshmen applied for aid; 336 were judged to have need; 334 of these received aid. Average need met was 48%. Average scholarship/grant was $8,227; average loan $4,666. 24% of total undergraduate aid awarded as scholarships/grants, 76% as loans/jobs. **Non-need-based:** Awarded to 177 full-time undergraduates, including 73 freshmen. Scholarships awarded for academics.

Application procedures. Admission: Closing date 2/1 (postmark date). $70 fee, may be waived for applicants with need. Application may be submitted online. Admission notification on a rolling basis beginning on or about 1/10. Within 30 days of offer of acceptance. **Financial aid:** Priority date 3/15; no closing date. FAFSA required. Applicants notified on a rolling basis.

Academics. Academic success seminars/workshops, peer mentors. **Special study options:** Accelerated study, combined bachelor's/graduate degree, cross-registration, distance learning, dual enrollment of high school students, independent study, internships, liberal arts/career combination. **Credit/**

placement by examination: AP, CLEP, IB, SAT, ACT, institutional tests. 6 credit hours maximum toward bachelor's degree. CLEP exams must be taken before student's first semester of enrollment in order for credit to be granted. **Support services:** Learning center, reduced course load, study skills assistance, tutoring, writing center.

Majors. Health: Dental hygiene, health services, medical radiologic technology/radiation therapy, nuclear medical technology, nursing (RN), premedicine, radiologic technology/medical imaging. **Physical sciences:** Chemistry.

Computing on campus. 360 workstations in dormitories, library, computer center, student center. Dormitories wired for high-speed internet access and linked to campus network. Commuter students can connect to campus network. Online library, helpline, wireless network available.

Student life. Freshman orientation: Mandatory, $100 fee. Preregistration for classes offered. 2-day overnight program in summer; 1-day freshman parent orientation. **Housing:** Guaranteed on-campus for freshmen. Coed dorms, substance-free housing available. $250 deposit, deadline 5/1. Women only floors available. **Activities:** Choral groups, dance, drama, musical theater, student government, student newspaper, symphony orchestra, Academy of Student Pharmacists, Kappa Psi fraternity, Vietnamese student association, student American dental hygienist association, black student union, physician assistant society, Academy of Students of Health Systems Pharmacy, campus activities board, student government association, Indian student organization.

Athletics. Intramural: Baseball, basketball, bowling, cross-country, field hockey W, football (non-tackle), racquetball, soccer, softball, squash, table tennis, tennis, volleyball, water polo. **Team name:** Cardinals.

Student services. Adult student services, alcohol/substance abuse counseling, career counseling, student employment services, financial aid counseling, health services, minority student services, personal counseling, placement for graduates, veterans' counselor, women's services. **Physically disabled:** Services for visually, speech, hearing impaired.

Contact. E-mail: admissions@mcphs.edu
Phone: (617) 732-2850 Toll-free number: (800) 225-5506
Fax: (617) 732-2118
William Dunfey, Executive Director of Admissions, Massachusetts College of Pharmacy and Health Sciences, 179 Longwood Avenue, Boston, MA 02115-5896

Massachusetts Institute of Technology

Cambridge, Massachusetts — **CB member**
www.mit.edu — **CB code: 3514**

- Private 4-year university
- Residential campus in small city
- 4,053 degree-seeking undergraduates: 1% part-time, 43% women, 6% African American, 27% Asian American, 11% Hispanic American, 2% Native American, 8% international
- 5,977 degree-seeking graduate students
- 14% of applicants admitted
- SAT or ACT (ACT writing optional), SAT Subject Tests, application essay required
- 94% graduate within 6 years; 47% enter graduate study

General. Founded in 1861. Regionally accredited. **Degrees:** 1,220 bachelor's awarded; master's, doctoral offered. **ROTC:** Army, Navy, Air Force. **Location:** One mile from Boston. **Calendar:** 4-1-4, limited summer session. **Full-time faculty:** 1,177 total; 96% have terminal degrees, 13% minority, 22% women. **Part-time faculty:** 377 total; 88% have terminal degrees, 6% minority, 22% women. **Special facilities:** Research library with collections of historical scientific books, manuscripts, instruments, art works, museum of science and technology, visual arts center, laboratories for artificial intelligence and computer science, energy and environment, information and decision systems, manufacturing and productivity, nuclear science, microsystems technology, magnet laboratory, media laboratory.

Freshman class profile. 10,440 applied, 1,494 admitted, 996 enrolled.

Mid 50% test scores		**Return as sophomores:**	98%
SAT verbal:	690-770	**Out-of-state:**	89%
SAT math:	740-800	**Live on campus:**	100%
ACT:	31-34	**International:**	9%
Rank in top quarter:	100%	**Fraternities:**	50%
Rank in top tenth:	97%	**Sororities:**	26%
End year in good standing:	99%		

Basis for selection. Grades, quality of academic program, test scores, personal accomplishments, creativity, leadership, love of learning most important. Class rank, recommendations also important. Non-native English speakers have the option of taking TOEFL and SAT Subject Tests in math and science. Others must take SAT or ACT and SAT Subject Tests in math and science. Interviews strongly recommended. **Homeschooled:** Letter of recommendation (nonparent) required. Information about applicant's participation in activities with peers recommended.

High school preparation. Recommended units include English 4, mathematics 4, social studies 2, science 4 and foreign language 2.

2006-2007 Annual costs. Tuition/fees: $33,600. Room/board: $9,950. Books/supplies: $1,100. Personal expenses: $1,700.

2004-2005 Financial aid. All financial aid based on need. 872 full-time freshmen applied for aid; 712 were judged to have need; 712 of these received aid. Average need met was 100%. Average scholarship/grant was $25,666; average loan $3,321. 83% of total undergraduate aid awarded as scholarships/grants, 17% as loans/jobs.

Application procedures. Admission: Closing date 1/1 (postmark date). $65 fee, may be waived for applicants with need. Application may be submitted online. Admission notification 3/25. Must reply by May 1 or within 2 week(s) if notified thereafter. **Financial aid:** Closing date 3/1. FAFSA, CSS PROFILE required. Applicants notified by 4/1; must reply by 5/1.

Academics. Special study options: Combined bachelor's/graduate degree, cooperative education, cross-registration, internships, study abroad, teacher certification program. Undergraduate research opportunities program; independent activities period; alternative freshman programs; cross-registration with Harvard University, Wellesley College, Massachusetts College of Art, School of the Museum of Fine Arts. **Credit/placement by examination:** AP, CLEP, IB, institutional tests. **Support services:** Learning center, pre-admission summer program, study skills assistance, tutoring, writing center.

Majors. Architecture: Architecture, urban/community planning. **Biology:** General. **Business:** General. **Communications:** Media studies. **Computer sciences:** Computer science. **Engineering:** Aerospace, chemical, civil, electrical, environmental, materials, mechanical, nuclear, ocean. **English:** Creative writing, English lit. **Foreign languages:** General, linguistics. **History:** General. **Interdisciplinary:** Math/computer science, science/society. **Liberal arts:** Arts/sciences. **Math:** General. **Philosophy/religion:** Philosophy. **Physical sciences:** Chemistry, geology, physics. **Social sciences:** Anthropology, economics, political science.

Most popular majors. Biology 10%, business/marketing 9%, computer/information sciences 17%, engineering/engineering technologies 32%, mathematics 8%, physical sciences 9%.

Computing on campus. 1,100 workstations in dormitories, library, computer center, student center. Dormitories wired for high-speed internet access and linked to campus network. Commuter students can connect to campus network. Online course registration, online library, helpline, repair service, student web hosting, wireless network available.

Student life. Freshman orientation: Mandatory. Held last 2 weeks of August. **Policies:** Many undergraduate buildings designated smoke-free. **Housing:** Guaranteed on-campus for freshmen. Coed dorms, single-sex dorms, special housing for disabled, apartments, cooperative housing, fraternity/sorority housing, substance-free housing available. Pets allowed in dorm rooms. Independent living group housing, apartments for students with dependent children available. **Activities:** Bands, choral groups, dance, drama, film society, literary magazine, music ensembles, musical theater, radio station, student government, student newspaper, symphony orchestra, TV station, over 300 recognized organizations.

Athletics. NCAA. **Intercollegiate:** Baseball M, basketball, cross-country, diving, fencing, field hockey W, football (tackle) M, golf M, gymnastics, ice hockey W, lacrosse, rifle, rowing (crew), sailing, skiing, soccer, softball W, squash M, swimming, tennis, track and field, volleyball, water polo M, wrestling M. **Intramural:** Badminton, basketball, bowling, cross-country, football (non-tackle), ice hockey, rugby, soccer, softball, squash, table tennis, tennis, triathlon W, volleyball, water polo. **Team name:** Engineers.

Student services. Alcohol/substance abuse counseling, campus ministries, career counseling, student employment services, financial aid counseling, health services, on-campus daycare, personal counseling, placement for graduates. **Physically disabled:** Services for visually, speech, hearing impaired.

Contact. E-mail: admissions@mit.edu
Phone: (617) 253-4791 Fax: (617) 258-8304
Marilee Jones, Dean of Admissions, Massachusetts Institute of Technology, 77 Massachusetts Avenue, Rm 3-108, Cambridge, MA 02139-4307

Massachusetts Maritime Academy

Buzzards Bay, Massachusetts CB member
www.maritime.edu CB code: 3515

- Public 4-year military and maritime college
- Residential campus in large town
- 951 degree-seeking undergraduates: 3% part-time, 11% women
- 18 degree-seeking graduate students
- 68% of applicants admitted
- SAT or ACT (ACT writing optional), application essay required
- 61% graduate within 6 years; 3% enter graduate study

General. Founded in 1891. Regionally accredited. **Degrees:** 155 bachelor's awarded; master's offered. **ROTC:** Army, Navy, Air Force. **Location:** 55 miles from Boston, 50 miles from Providence, Rhode Island. **Calendar:** 2 semesters and 8-week winter sea term. Limited summer session. **Full-time faculty:** 60 total. **Part-time faculty:** 20 total. **Special facilities:** 540' training ship enterprise, slow-speed diesel simulator, video full-function bridge navigation simulator, commercial fishing simulator, spill management simulator, cargo handling simulator, hands-on aquaculture center.

Freshman class profile. 901 applied, 614 admitted, 326 enrolled.

Mid 50% test scores			
SAT verbal:	470-570	End year in good standing:	88%
SAT math:	480-590	Return as sophomores:	78%
ACT:	20-24	Live on campus:	100%
		International:	1%

Basis for selection. School achievement record, test scores, extracurricular accomplishments most important. Character and personality emphasized, leadership potential desirable. Interview recommended.

High school preparation. College-preparatory program required. 18 units required. Required units include English 4, mathematics 3, social studies 2, history 2, science 3 (laboratory 2) and foreign language 2. Math units must include 2 algebra, 1 plane geometry. Science units must include 1 chemistry, or two courses with a lab. Physics recommended.

2005-2006 Annual costs. Tuition/fees: $5,107; $15,912 out-of-state. Semester at Sea cost $2,929. Room/board: $6,464. Books/supplies: $800. Personal expenses: $1,200.

2004-2005 Financial aid. Need-based: 245 full-time freshmen applied for aid; 161 were judged to have need; 161 of these received aid. Average need met was 45%. Average scholarship/grant was $1,030; average loan $2,625. 40% of total undergraduate aid awarded as scholarships/grants, 60% as loans/jobs. **Non-need-based:** Awarded to 386 full-time undergraduates, including 169 freshmen. Scholarships awarded for academics, leadership.

Application procedures. Admission: No deadline. $50 fee, may be waived for applicants with need. Application may be submitted online. Admission notification on a rolling basis beginning on or about 11/15. Must reply by May 1 or within 1 week(s) if notified thereafter. **Financial aid:** Priority date 4/30; no closing date. FAFSA, institutional form required. Applicants notified on a rolling basis starting 3/1.

Academics. Technical and practical training for third assistant engineer and third mate licenses. Graduates may apply for commissions in U.S. Navy, Coast Guard, Marine Reserve, Army, or Air Force. **Special study options:** Combined bachelor's/graduate degree, cooperative education, double major, internships, liberal arts/career combination, semester at sea. **Credit/placement by examination:** AP, CLEP, IB, institutional tests. 6 credit hours maximum toward bachelor's degree. **Support services:** Learning center, pre-admission summer program, reduced course load, study skills assistance, tutoring.

Majors. Business: Transportation. **Engineering:** General. **Engineering technology:** Industrial management. **Transportation:** Marine science/Merchant Marine.

Computing on campus. PC or laptop required. 70 workstations in dormitories, library, computer center. Dormitories wired for high-speed internet access and linked to campus network. Commuter students can connect to campus network. Helpline, wireless network available.

Student life. Freshman orientation: Mandatory, $400 fee. Preregistration for classes offered. Held last 2 weeks of August, paramilitary style orientation. **Policies:** No mandatory military obligation. Freshmen permitted cars on campus. **Housing:** Guaranteed on-campus for all undergraduates. Coed dorms available. All majors required to live on campus. **Activities:** Bands, drama, literary magazine, music ensembles, student government, student newspaper, Newman Club, marine careers group, Association of Industrial Plant Engineers.

Athletics. NCAA. **Intercollegiate:** Baseball M, cross-country, football (tackle) M, lacrosse M, rifle, rowing (crew), sailing, soccer M, softball W, volleyball W. **Intramural:** Basketball, boxing M, cross-country, football (tackle) M, ice hockey, racquetball, rifle, sailing, soccer, softball, swimming, table tennis, tennis, volleyball, water polo, wrestling M. **Team name:** Buccaneers.

Student services. Adult student services, alcohol/substance abuse counseling, campus ministries, career counseling, student employment services, financial aid counseling, health services, personal counseling, placement for graduates, veterans' counselor, women's services. **Learning disabled:** Comprehensive services available.

Contact. E-mail: admissions@maritime.edu
Phone: (508) 830-5000 ext. 1102 Toll-free number: (800) 544-3411
Fax: (508) 830-5077
Roy Fulgueras, Director of Admissions, Massachusetts Maritime Academy, 101 Academy Drive, Buzzards Bay, MA 02532-1803

Merrimack College

North Andover, Massachusetts CB member
www.merrimack.edu CB code: 3525

- Private 4-year business and liberal arts college affiliated with Roman Catholic Church
- Residential campus in large town
- 2,113 degree-seeking undergraduates: 8% part-time, 54% women, 1% African American, 1% Asian American, 2% Hispanic American, 1% international
- 17 degree-seeking graduate students
- 71% of applicants admitted
- SAT or ACT with writing, application essay required
- 71% graduate within 6 years; 17% enter graduate study

General. Founded in 1947. Regionally accredited. Associated with Augustinian Friars. Associate degree and M.Ed programs offered through continuing education division only. **Degrees:** 524 bachelor's, 10 associate awarded; master's offered. **ROTC:** Air Force. **Location:** 25 miles from Boston. **Calendar:** Semester, limited summer session. **Full-time faculty:** 143 total; 78% have terminal degrees, 8% minority, 41% women. **Part-time faculty:** 80 total; 36% have terminal degrees, 9% minority, 48% women. **Class size:** 57% < 20, 42% 20-39, 1% 40-49, less than 1% 50-99. **Special facilities:** Urban resource institute, astronomy dome and telescope, arts center, library gallery.

Freshman class profile. 3,413 applied, 2,436 admitted, 556 enrolled.

Mid 50% test scores			
SAT verbal:	500-570	Rank in top quarter:	47%
SAT math:	510-580	Rank in top tenth:	19%
ACT:	19-22	End year in good standing:	91%
GPA 3.50 or higher:	20%	Return as sophomores:	79%
GPA 3.0-3.49:	65%	Out-of-state:	22%
GPA 2.0-2.99:	15%	Live on campus:	90%
		International:	1%

Basis for selection. School achievement record, course selection, test scores, class rank, essay, recommendations important. Interview recommended. **Homeschooled:** State certificate of completion, list of coursework, interview required.

High school preparation. College-preparatory program required. 20 units required; 26 recommended. Required and recommended units include English 4, mathematics 3-4, social studies 1-2, history 1-2, science 3-4 (laboratory 3-4), foreign language 2-3 and academic electives 3. Mathematics must include algebra I and II and plane geometry. 1 additional mathematics and 3 science, including physics, required of mathematics, science, engineering, and computer science applicants.

2006-2007 Annual costs. Tuition/fees: $27,070. Room/board: $10,705. Books/supplies: $800. Personal expenses: $625.

2005-2006 Financial aid. Need-based: 440 full-time freshmen applied for aid; 405 were judged to have need; 405 of these received aid. Average need met was 70%. Average scholarship/grant was $13,000; average loan $3,625. 75% of total undergraduate aid awarded as scholarships/grants, 25% as loans/jobs. **Non-need-based:** Awarded to 661 full-time undergraduates, including 120 freshmen. Scholarships awarded for academics, athletics, leadership, minority status, music/drama, religious affiliation. **Additional information:** Accept the Challenge program provides tuition for students from Lawrence who meet program criteria.

Application procedures. Admission: Closing date 2/1 (postmark date). $50 fee, may be waived for applicants with need. Application may be submitted online. Admission notification 4/1. Admission notification on a rolling basis. Must reply by May 1 or within 2 week(s) if notified thereafter.

Financial aid: Closing date 2/1. FAFSA required. Applicants notified by 3/15; must reply by 5/1 or within 2 week(s) of notification.

Academics. First-year seminars in civilization, inquiry, and conversation required. **Special study options:** Accelerated study, cooperative education, cross-registration, double major, dual enrollment of high school students, ESL, independent study, internships, liberal arts/career combination, student-designed major, study abroad, teacher certification program, Washington semester. 5-year combined BA/BS program. **Credit/placement by examination:** AP, CLEP, IB, institutional tests. No established limits. **Support services:** Learning center, reduced course load, remedial instruction, study skills assistance, tutoring, writing center.

Majors. Biology: General, biochemistry. **Business:** Business admin. **Communications:** General. **Computer sciences:** Computer science. **Conservation:** Environmental science. **Engineering:** General, civil, computer, electrical. **English:** English lit. **Foreign languages:** French, Romance, Spanish. **Health:** Athletic training, health services. **History:** General. **Liberal arts:** Arts/sciences. **Math:** General. **Philosophy/religion:** Philosophy, religion. **Physical sciences:** Chemistry, physics. **Psychology:** General. **Social sciences:** Economics, political science, sociology. **Visual/performing arts:** Studio arts.

Most popular majors. Business/marketing 47%, psychology 8%, social sciences 13%.

Computing on campus. 250 workstations in dormitories, library, computer center, student center. Dormitories wired for high-speed internet access and linked to campus network. Commuter students can connect to campus network. Online course registration, helpline, repair service, wireless network available.

Student life. Freshman orientation: Mandatory, $150 fee. Preregistration for classes offered. 2-day June orientation, 3-day August pre-class orientation. **Policies:** All residence halls drug-free. **Housing:** Guaranteed on-campus for freshmen. Coed dorms, special housing for disabled, apartments, cooperative housing, substance-free housing available. Townhouses for upperclassmen, international house, wellness house available. Applications accepted from groups of students for theme housing in townhouses. **Activities:** Bands, dance, drama, film society, literary magazine, music ensembles, musical theater, student government, student newspaper, TV station, student tutoring group, community service organizations, campus ministry, College Democrats, College Republicans, Society Organized Against Racism (SOAR), Brothers and Sisters United, international student organization.

Athletics. NCAA. **Intercollegiate:** Baseball M, basketball, cross-country, field hockey W, football (tackle) M, ice hockey M, lacrosse, soccer, softball W, tennis, volleyball W. **Intramural:** Basketball, ice hockey M, soccer, softball, volleyball. **Team name:** Warriors.

Student services. Adult student services, alcohol/substance abuse counseling, campus ministries, career counseling, student employment services, financial aid counseling, health services, minority student services, personal counseling, placement for graduates.

Contact. E-mail: admission@merrimack.edu
Phone: (978) 837-5100 Fax: (978) 837-5133
Director of Admission, Merrimack College, 315 Turnpike Street, North Andover, MA 01845

Montserrat College of Art

Beverly, Massachusetts — **CB member**
www.montserrat.edu — **CB code: 9101**

- Private 4-year visual arts college
- Residential campus in small city
- 299 degree-seeking undergraduates: 7% part-time, 63% women, 1% African American, 2% Asian American, 2% Hispanic American
- 85% of applicants admitted
- SAT or ACT (ACT writing optional), application essay, interview required
- 49% graduate within 6 years

General. Founded in 1970. Regionally accredited. **Degrees:** 77 bachelor's awarded. **ROTC:** Air Force. **Location:** 20 miles from Boston. **Calendar:** Semester, limited summer session. **Full-time faculty:** 26 total; 12% have terminal degrees, 4% minority, 58% women. **Part-time faculty:** 37 total; 3% minority, 51% women. **Class size:** 92% < 20, 8% 20-39. **Special facilities:** Computer design laboratory, photography, printmaking and sculpture facilities, alumni gallery, studio gallery.

Freshman class profile. 326 applied, 276 admitted, 75 enrolled.

Mid 50% test scores			
SAT verbal:	420-640	GPA 3.0-3.49:	33%
SAT math:	370-590	GPA 2.0-2.99:	53%
ACT:	18-22	Return as sophomores:	51%
GPA 3.50 or higher:	10%	Out-of-state:	50%
		Live on campus:	94%

Basis for selection. Visual art portfolio most important. High school record, interview, artist statement, letters of recommendation, test scores required of BFA applicants. If personal visit impractical, portfolio in slide form may be sent to college; telephone interview will be conducted. SAT or ACT scores not required of diploma applicants. **Learning Disabled:** Official documentation of disability is required if accommodation is requested.

High school preparation. Recommended units include English 4, social studies 2 and history 2. Visual arts courses including drawing recommended.

2005-2006 Annual costs. Tuition/fees: $20,679. Room/board: $5,300. Books/supplies: $900. Personal expenses: $900.

2005-2006 Financial aid. Need-based: 74 full-time freshmen applied for aid; 55 were judged to have need; 55 of these received aid. Average need met was 26%. Average scholarship/grant was $4,717; average loan $2,928. 29% of total undergraduate aid awarded as scholarships/grants, 71% as loans/jobs. **Non-need-based:** Scholarships awarded for academics, art.

Application procedures. Admission: Priority date 3/1; no deadline. $40 fee, may be waived for applicants with need. Admission notification on a rolling basis beginning on or about 12/20. Must reply by May 1 or within 3 week(s) if notified thereafter. **Financial aid:** Closing date 3/1. FAFSA, institutional form required. Applicants notified on a rolling basis starting 12/20; must reply within 2 week(s) of notification.

Academics. In addition to frequent class critiques, each student's work reviewed annually by faculty panel in semester-end evaluations. **Special study options:** Cross-registration, dual enrollment of high school students, exchange student, independent study, internships, New York semester, student-designed major, study abroad, teacher certification program. Association of Independent Colleges of Art and Design (AICAD) mobility, summer program in Trieste. Northeast Consortium of colleges and universities in Massachusetts (NECCU) Registration Consortium. **Credit/placement by examination:** AP, CLEP, IB, institutional tests. **Support services:** Pre-admission summer program, reduced course load, study skills assistance, tutoring, writing center.

Majors. Visual/performing arts: Art, commercial/advertising art, design, drawing, painting, photography, printmaking, sculpture, studio arts.

Computing on campus. 158 workstations in library, computer center. Commuter students can connect to campus network. Online library available.

Student life. Freshman orientation: Mandatory, $50 fee. Preregistration for classes offered. **Policies:** Freshmen permitted cars on campus. **Housing:** Special housing for disabled, apartments, substance-free housing available. $275 nonrefundable deposit, deadline 5/1. Coed buildings with single-sex apartments available. **Activities:** Literary magazine, music ensembles, student government.

Student services. Adult student services, career counseling, student employment services, financial aid counseling, personal counseling, placement for graduates. **Physically disabled:** Services for visually, speech, hearing impaired.

Contact. E-mail: admiss@montserrat.edu
Phone: (978) 921-4242 ext. 1153 Toll-free number: (800) 836-0487
Fax: (978) 921-4241
Jessica Sarin-Perry, Dean of Admissions and Enrollment Management, Montserrat College of Art, 23 Essex Street, Beverly, MA 01915

Mount Holyoke College

South Hadley, Massachusetts — **CB member**
www.mtholyoke.edu — **CB code: 3529**

- Private 4-year liberal arts college for women
- Residential campus in large town
- 2,064 degree-seeking undergraduates: 2% part-time, 100% women, 4% African American, 12% Asian American, 5% Hispanic American, 1% Native American, 14% international
- 2 degree-seeking graduate students
- 52% of applicants admitted

- Application essay required
- 80% graduate within 6 years; 21% enter graduate study

General. Founded in 1837. Regionally accredited. Member of 5-college consortium with Amherst College, Hampshire College, Smith College, and University of Massachusetts at Amherst. **Degrees:** 553 bachelor's awarded; master's offered. **ROTC:** Army, Air Force. **Location:** 10 miles from Springfield, 90 miles from Boston. **Calendar:** Semester. **Full-time faculty:** 207 total; 94% have terminal degrees, 24% minority, 50% women. **Part-time faculty:** 34 total; 50% have terminal degrees, 38% minority, 71% women. **Class size:** 69% < 20, 24% 20-39, 4% 40-49, 4% 50-99. **Special facilities:** Nuclear accelerator, nuclear magnetic resonance equipment, electron microscope, bronze-casting foundry, solar greenhouse, Japanese meditation garden and tea house, equestrian center, language learning center with satellite communication and interactive video, child study center, environmental literacy center, leadership center, center for global initiatives, greenhouse and botanical garden.

Freshman class profile. 2,924 applied, 1,530 admitted, 504 enrolled.

Mid 50% test scores			
SAT verbal:	620-710	**Rank in top quarter:**	80%
SAT math:	610-690	**Rank in top tenth:**	51%
ACT:	27-30	**End year in good standing:**	94%
GPA 3.50 or higher:	67%	**Return as sophomores:**	94%
GPA 3.0-3.49:	27%	**Out-of-state:**	80%
GPA 2.0-2.99:	6%	**Live on campus:**	100%
		International:	16%

Basis for selection. School record most important, followed by special talents, particular goals, evidence of determination. Submission of standardized test scores optional. Applicants who do not submit test scores not disadvantaged in admission process. Personal interview on campus recommended if candidate lives within 200 miles of college, or with alumna admissions representative if applicant resides outside of area. **Homeschooled:** Detailed outline of study and 5 SAT Subject Tests recommended.

High school preparation. Recommended units include English 4, mathematics 3, history 3, science 3 (laboratory 3), foreign language 3 and academic electives 1. History requirement includes U.S. and world history. Either 4 units of one foreign language, or 2 units of one and 3 units of a second foreign language recommended. 1 art recommended.

2006-2007 Annual costs. Tuition/fees: $34,256. Room/board: $10,040.

2005-2006 Financial aid. Need-based: 370 full-time freshmen applied for aid; 285 were judged to have need; 285 of these received aid. Average need met was 100%. Average scholarship/grant was $24,079; average loan $2,659. 77% of total undergraduate aid awarded as scholarships/grants, 23% as loans/jobs. **Non-need-based:** Scholarships awarded for academics, leadership. **Additional information:** Parent loan plans include MASSPLAN, Achievers and PLUS. 10-month payment plan offered.

Application procedures. Admission: Closing date 1/15 (postmark date). $60 fee, may be waived for applicants with need. Application may be submitted online. Admission notification 4/1. Must reply by 5/1. **Financial aid:** Priority date 1/15, closing date 2/1. FAFSA, CSS PROFILE required. Applicants notified by 3/25; must reply by 5/1.

Academics. Honor system and self-scheduled examinations practiced. All students must complete minor. **Special study options:** Combined bachelor's/graduate degree, cooperative education, cross-registration, double major, exchange student, independent study, internships, liberal arts/career combination, semester at sea, student-designed major, study abroad, teacher certification program, Washington semester. Community-based learning courses. **Credit/placement by examination:** AP, CLEP, IB, institutional tests. 32 credit hours maximum toward bachelor's degree. **Support services:** Reduced course load, study skills assistance, tutoring, writing center.

Majors. Architecture: Architecture. **Area/ethnic studies:** African-American, American, Asian, European, German, Latin American, Russian/Slavic, women's. **Biology:** General, biochemistry. **Computer sciences:** Computer science. **Conservation:** Environmental studies. **Education:** General. **Foreign languages:** Ancient Greek, classics, French, Italian, Latin, Romance, Spanish. **History:** General. **Interdisciplinary:** Ancient studies, medieval/Renaissance, neuroscience. **Math:** General, statistics. **Philosophy/religion:** Philosophy, religion. **Physical sciences:** Astronomy, chemistry, geology, physics. **Psychology:** General. **Social sciences:** Anthropology, economics, geography, international relations, political science, sociology. **Visual/performing arts:** Art, dance, dramatic.

Most popular majors. Area/ethnic studies 7%, biology 11%, English 6%, interdisciplinary studies 7%, psychology 11%, social sciences 27%, visual/performing arts 6%.

Computing on campus. 561 workstations in dormitories, library, computer center, student center. Dormitories wired for high-speed internet access and linked to campus network. Commuter students can connect to campus network. Online course registration, online library, helpline, repair service, student web hosting, wireless network available.

Student life. Freshman orientation: Mandatory. Preregistration for classes offered. Program held week before start of classes. Specific orientation programs for international students, women of color. **Policies:** Smoke-free campus. Freshmen permitted cars on campus. **Housing:** Guaranteed on-campus for all undergraduates. Special housing for disabled, apartments available. $200 nonrefundable deposit, deadline 5/15. Kosher/halal kitchen available; special accommodations by need. **Activities:** Jazz band, choral groups, dance, drama, film society, literary magazine, music ensembles, musical theater, radio station, student government, student newspaper, symphony orchestra, approximately 140 student organizations, 10 religious organizations.

Athletics. NCAA. **Intercollegiate:** Basketball W, cross-country W, diving W, equestrian W, field hockey W, golf W, lacrosse W, rowing (crew) W, soccer W, squash W, swimming W, tennis W, track and field W, volleyball W. **Team name:** Lyons.

Student services. Adult student services, alcohol/substance abuse counseling, campus ministries, career counseling, student employment services, financial aid counseling, health services, minority student services, personal counseling, placement for graduates, women's services. **Physically disabled:** Services for visually, speech, hearing impaired.

Contact. E-mail: admission@mtholyoke.edu
Phone: (413) 538-2023 Fax: (413) 538-2409
Diane Anci, Dean of Admission, Mount Holyoke College, 50 College Street, South Hadley, MA 01075-1488

Mount Ida College

Newton, Massachusetts — **CB member**
www.mountida.edu — **CB code: 3530**

- Private 4-year liberal arts college
- Residential campus in small city
- 1,290 degree-seeking undergraduates
- 84% of applicants admitted
- SAT or ACT required

General. Founded in 1899. Regionally accredited. **Degrees:** 147 bachelor's, 55 associate awarded. **Location:** 8 miles from Boston. **Calendar:** Semester, limited summer session. **Full-time faculty:** 61 total. **Part-time faculty:** 87 total. **Class size:** 65% < 20, 34% 20-39, less than 1% 40-49, less than 1% 50-99. **Special facilities:** Communications laboratory, darkroom, blueprint making facility, veterinary kennel and operating facility, technical electricity laboratory, television laboratory, dental laboratory.

Freshman class profile. 1,903 applied, 1,604 admitted, 393 enrolled.

Mid 50% test scores			
		ACT:	16-21
SAT verbal:	400-510	**Out-of-state:**	45%
SAT math:	390-500	**Live on campus:**	80%

Basis for selection. Special requirements for science applicants and students interested in Learning Opportunities Program. Minimum 2.0 GPA required for admission to all bachelor's degree programs, except interior design, which requires 2.5 GPA. Veterinary science students must have some science background. Prefer art students to have art background. Portfolio recommended for art, interior design, fashion illustration majors. Interviews required for dental hygiene majors. Essay or personal statement strongly recommended. Interview and campus visit strongly recommended and may be required for certain programs.

High school preparation. 16 units recommended. Recommended units include English 4, mathematics 4, social studies 4 and science 4. 4 mathematics, 2 physical science strongly recommended for science majors.

2006-2007 Annual costs. Tuition/fees: $20,450. Room/board: $10,225. Books/supplies: $800. Personal expenses: $525.

2005-2006 Financial aid. Need-based: 34% of total undergraduate aid awarded as scholarships/grants, 66% as loans/jobs.

Application procedures. Admission: No deadline. $35 fee, may be waived for applicants with need. Application may be submitted online. Admission notification on a rolling basis beginning on or about 10/1. **Financial aid:** Priority date 5/1; no closing date. FAFSA, institutional form required. Applicants notified on a rolling basis starting 3/1; must reply within 3 week(s) of notification.

Academics. Professionally intensive courses of study coupled with liberal arts requirements. **Special study options:** ESL, honors, independent study, internships, student-designed major, study abroad, teacher certification program. Affiliation with Tufts Veterinary School and Tufts University

School of Dental Medicine. **Credit/placement by examination:** CLEP, institutional tests. 12 credit hours maximum toward bachelor's degree. **Support services:** Learning center, reduced course load, remedial instruction, study skills assistance, tutoring.

Majors. Agriculture: Animal sciences, equestrian studies. **Business:** Business admin, fashion, hospitality admin, sales/distribution, tourism promotion. **Communications:** Journalism. **Communications technology:** Radio/tv. **Education:** General, early childhood. **Health:** Veterinary technology/assistant. **Legal studies:** General. **Liberal arts:** Arts/sciences. **Personal/culinary services:** Mortuary science. **Protective services:** Criminal justice. **Public administration:** General. **Visual/performing arts:** Art, commercial/advertising art, fashion design, interior design.

Computing on campus. 100 workstations in library, computer center. Dormitories wired for high-speed internet access and linked to campus network. Online library available.

Student life. Freshman orientation: Available. Preregistration for classes offered. Held in July. Students able to make housing selections. Orientation activities also held prior to first day of class in late-August. **Policies:** Freshmen permitted cars on campus. **Housing:** Guaranteed on-campus for freshmen. Coed dorms, single-sex dorms, special housing for disabled, substance-free housing available. $350 deposit. **Activities:** Choral groups, dance, drama, literary magazine, musical theater, radio station, student government, student newspaper, TV station, Black Student Achievement Coalition, Foundation for Non-Violent Action, commuter council, career club, gay/lesbian/bisexual student group.

Athletics. NCAA. **Intercollegiate:** Basketball, cross-country, equestrian W, football (tackle) M, lacrosse M, soccer, softball W, volleyball. **Intramural:** Badminton, basketball, equestrian W, field hockey W, ice hockey, lacrosse M, rugby M, skiing M, soccer, softball, swimming M, tennis, volleyball. **Team name:** Mustangs.

Student services. Adult student services, alcohol/substance abuse counseling, career counseling, student employment services, financial aid counseling, health services, personal counseling, placement for graduates.

Contact. E-mail: admissions@mountida.edu
Phone: (617) 928-4535 Fax: (617) 928-4507
Elizabeth Storinge, Dean of Admissions, Mount Ida College, 777 Dedham Street, Newton, MA 02459

New England Conservatory of Music

Boston, Massachusetts — **CB member**
www.newenglandconservatory.edu — **CB code: 3659**

- Private 4-year music college
- Commuter campus in very large city
- 404 degree-seeking undergraduates
- 30% of applicants admitted
- Application essay required

General. Founded in 1867. Regionally accredited. In close proximity to Symphony Hall. Faculty includes members of Boston Symphony Orchestra. **Degrees:** 87 bachelor's awarded; master's, doctoral offered. **Location:** 2 miles from downtown. **Calendar:** Semester, limited summer session. **Full-time faculty:** 83 total. **Part-time faculty:** 126 total. **Class size:** 76% < 20, 23% 20-39, 1% 40-49. **Special facilities:** Listening library of 46,384 recordings.

Freshman class profile. 968 applied, 292 admitted, 84 enrolled.

Out-of-state:	81%	Live on campus:	97%

Basis for selection. Audition most important, followed by test scores, recommendations, essay, high school record. Accepted students permitted to postpone admission one-half year. Live or taped auditions required. **Homeschooled:** Must provide curriculum overview.

2006-2007 Annual costs. Tuition/fees (projected): $29,300. On-campus residents pay $335 health fee. Room/board: $16,239. Books/supplies: $700. Personal expenses: $2,386.

2004-2005 Financial aid. Need-based: 59% of total undergraduate aid awarded as scholarships/grants, 41% as loans/jobs. **Non-need-based:** Scholarships awarded for music/drama.

Application procedures. Admission: Priority date 12/1; no deadline. $100 fee. Application may be submitted online. Admission notification on a rolling basis beginning on or about 4/1. Must reply by May 1 or within 4 week(s) if notified thereafter. **Financial aid:** Priority date 12/1, closing date 2/1. FAFSA, institutional form required. Applicants notified on a rolling basis starting 4/1; must reply by 5/1 or within 2 week(s) of notification.

Academics. Undergraduate diploma available in lieu of bachelor's degree (performance-oriented, with fewer academic requirements). Artist's diploma (professional degree) available for particularly gifted performers. Graduate diploma also available. **Special study options:** Cross-registration, dual enrollment of high school students, ESL, independent study, internships, study abroad. 5-year double degree program with Tufts University. **Credit/placement by examination:** CLEP, IB, institutional tests. 12 credit hours maximum toward bachelor's degree. **Support services:** Tutoring, writing center.

Majors. Visual/performing arts: Jazz, music history, music performance, music theory/composition, musicology, piano/organ, stringed instruments, voice/opera.

Computing on campus. 48 workstations in dormitories, library, computer center, student center. Online library available.

Student life. Freshman orientation: Mandatory. Preregistration for classes offered. Held 5 days before start of classes. **Housing:** Guaranteed on-campus for freshmen. Coed dorms available. $500 deposit, deadline 6/15. **Activities:** Bands, choral groups, music ensembles, opera, student government, symphony orchestra, Christian Fellowship, feminist and minority student organizations.

Student services. Career counseling, student employment services, health services, personal counseling, placement for graduates. **Physically disabled:** Services for visually impaired.

Contact. E-mail: admissions@newenglandconservatory.edu
Phone: (617) 585-1101 Fax: (617) 585-1115
Thomas Novak, Director of Admissions, New England Conservatory of Music, 290 Huntington Avenue, Boston, MA 02115

New England Institute of Art

Brookline, Massachusetts
www.neia.aii.edu — **CB code: 3636**

- For-profit 4-year visual arts and technical college
- Commuter campus in very large city
- 965 full-time, degree-seeking undergraduates
- 48% of applicants admitted
- Application essay, interview required

General. Accredited by ACCSCT. **Degrees:** 28 bachelor's, 196 associate awarded. **Calendar:** Semester, extensive summer session. **Full-time faculty:** 30 total. **Part-time faculty:** 55 total. **Class size:** 79% < 20, 19% 20-39, 2% 40-49. **Special facilities:** Radio, TV, and audio production studios.

Freshman class profile. 680 applied, 328 admitted, 283 enrolled.

Out-of-state:	37%	Live on campus:	19%

Basis for selection. Essay and interview most important, followed by secondary school record. Class rank, recommendations, test scores considered. Audio production program has limited admission.

2005-2006 Annual costs. Tuition/fees: $18,300. Books/supplies: $800. Personal expenses: $2,800.

Financial aid. Non-need-based: Scholarships awarded for academics. **Additional information:** Institutional scholarships (need and non-need based) available; separate application required.

Application procedures. Admission: No deadline. $50 fee. Application may be submitted online. Admission notification on a rolling basis. **Financial aid:** Priority date 5/1; no closing date. FAFSA required. Applicants notified on a rolling basis starting 3/1.

Academics. Bachelor's degrees offered in graphic design and multimedia/web design. Non-collegiate certificates offered in web site development and digital graphic design. **Special study options:** Internships. **Credit/placement by examination:** CLEP. **Support services:** Learning center, remedial instruction, study skills assistance, tutoring.

Majors. Communications: Digital media. **Communications technology:** Graphics, photo/film/video, recording arts. **Computer sciences:** Web page design. **Visual/performing arts:** Commercial/advertising art, graphic design, illustration, multimedia.

Student life. Freshman orientation: Mandatory. Half-day program held prior to start of semester. **Policies:** Student code of conduct. **Housing:** Coed dorms available. $200 deposit. **Activities:** Drama, film society, literary magazine, radio station, student government, community service club, student leadership program.

Student services. Adult student services, alcohol/substance abuse counseling, career counseling, student employment services, financial aid counseling, personal counseling, placement for graduates.

Contact. E-mail: aineadm@aii.edu
Phone: (617) 739-1700 Toll-free number: (800) 903-4425
Fax: (617) 582-4500
Ric Jackson, Director of Admissions, New England Institute of Art, 10 Brookline Place West, Brookline, MA 02445-7295

Newbury College

Brookline, Massachusetts **CB member**
www.newbury.edu **CB code: 3639**

- Private 4-year business and liberal arts college
- Commuter campus in large city
- 1,250 degree-seeking undergraduates
- Application essay required

General. Founded in 1962. Regionally accredited. **Degrees:** 165 bachelor's, 93 associate awarded. **Location:** 3 miles from Boston. **Calendar:** Semester, limited summer session. **Full-time faculty:** 33 total. **Special facilities:** 7 culinary arts production kitchens, on-campus restaurant.

Freshman class profile.

Out-of-state:	25%	Live on campus:	35%

Basis for selection. High school GPA and interviews important. 2 letters of recommendation and essay required. SAT or ACT recommended. SAT required for scholarship consideration but not for admissions. Interview recommended. **Learning Disabled:** Students reporting learning disability should submit copy of documents stating disability.

High school preparation. Recommended units include English 3, mathematics 3 and science 2.

2005-2006 Annual costs. Tuition/fees: $17,100. Room/board: $8,600. Books/supplies: $630. Personal expenses: $1,000.

2005-2006 Financial aid. All financial aid based on need. 51% of total undergraduate aid awarded as scholarships/grants, 49% as loans/jobs.

Application procedures. Admission: Priority date 3/1; no deadline. $50 fee, may be waived for applicants with need. Application may be submitted online. Admission notification on a rolling basis beginning on or about 1/1. Must reply by May 1 or within 4 week(s) if notified thereafter. **Financial aid:** Closing date 5/1. FAFSA required. Applicants notified on a rolling basis starting 4/1; must reply within 2 week(s) of notification.

Academics. Academic enrichment program available for students entering who demonstrate need for academic support. **Special study options:** Combined bachelor's/graduate degree, cross-registration, double major, honors, independent study, internships, liberal arts/career combination, study abroad, weekend college. **Credit/placement by examination:** CLEP, IB, institutional tests. 30 credit hours maximum toward associate degree, 60 toward bachelor's. **Support services:** Learning center, remedial instruction, study skills assistance, tutoring.

Majors. Architecture: Interior. **Business:** Accounting, business admin, finance, hospitality admin, hospitality/recreation, international, international marketing, marketing. **Communications:** General. **Computer sciences:** General, computer graphics, computer science. **Health:** Facilities admin, health care admin. **Legal studies:** General, paralegal, prelaw. **Personal/culinary services:** Chef training, culinary arts, restaurant/catering. **Protective services:** Law enforcement admin. **Psychology:** General. **Visual/performing arts:** Commercial/advertising art, graphic design, interior design.

Most popular majors. Business/marketing 66%, computer/information sciences 10%, legal studies 15%.

Computing on campus. 65 workstations in library, computer center, student center. Dormitories wired for high-speed internet access. Online library, helpline available.

Student life. Freshman orientation: Mandatory. Preregistration for classes offered. Information sessions and activities held a few days before each semester. **Housing:** Guaranteed on-campus for freshmen. Coed dorms, single-sex dorms available. $350 deposit, deadline 5/1. Summer housing available. **Activities:** Jazz band, dance, drama, radio station, student government, TV station, International student organization, black student union, Latino student association, Habitat for Humanity, Innkeepers Club, Chef Society, Alpha Business Club, radio club, programming board.

Athletics. NCAA. **Intercollegiate:** Basketball, cross-country, golf, soccer M, softball W, tennis, volleyball. **Intramural:** Basketball, softball W, volleyball, weight lifting. **Team name:** Nighthawks.

Student services. Alcohol/substance abuse counseling, campus ministries, career counseling, student employment services, financial aid counseling, personal counseling, placement for graduates.

Contact. E-mail: info@newbury.edu
Phone: (617) 730-7007 Toll-free number: (800) 639-2879
Fax: (617) 731-9618
Salvadore Liberto, Admissions Director, Newbury College, 129 Fisher Avenue, Brookline, MA 02445

Nichols College

Dudley, Massachusetts **CB member**
www.nichols.edu **CB code: 3666**

- Private 4-year business and liberal arts college
- Residential campus in small town
- 1,193 degree-seeking undergraduates: 25% part-time, 41% women, 6% African American, 2% Asian American, 4% Hispanic American
- 237 degree-seeking graduate students
- 79% of applicants admitted
- SAT or ACT with writing, application essay required
- 41% graduate within 6 years

General. Founded in 1815. Regionally accredited. **Degrees:** 232 bachelor's, 25 associate awarded; master's offered. **ROTC:** Army. **Location:** 50 miles from Boston, 20 miles from Worcester. **Calendar:** Semester, limited summer session. **Full-time faculty:** 38 total; 87% have terminal degrees. **Part-time faculty:** 27 total; 15% have terminal degrees. **Special facilities:** Policy and cultural institute.

Freshman class profile. 1,261 applied, 1,000 admitted, 297 enrolled.

Mid 50% test scores			
SAT verbal:	410-500	Rank in top quarter:	25%
SAT math:	420-510	Rank in top tenth:	2%
		Return as sophomores:	64%

Basis for selection. Secondary school record most important; test scores important, followed by recommendations, essay and interview. Interview recommended.

High school preparation. 16 units required. Required and recommended units include English 4, mathematics 3-4, social studies 2, science 2-3 (laboratory 2-3), foreign language 2 and academic electives 5. 2 foreign language recommended for liberal arts majors.

2005-2006 Annual costs. Tuition/fees: $22,250. Room/board: $8,290. Books/supplies: $1,000. Personal expenses: $1,200.

2004-2005 Financial aid. Need-based: 287 full-time freshmen applied for aid; 259 were judged to have need; 252 of these received aid. Average need met was 69%. Average scholarship/grant was $10,686; average loan $5,270. 57% of total undergraduate aid awarded as scholarships/grants, 43% as loans/jobs. **Non-need-based:** Awarded to 242 full-time undergraduates, including 60 freshmen. Scholarships awarded for academics, ROTC.

Application procedures. Admission: No deadline. $25 fee, may be waived for applicants with need. Application must be submitted on paper. Admission notification on a rolling basis beginning on or about 10/1. **Financial aid:** Closing date 3/1. FAFSA required. Applicants notified on a rolling basis starting 3/15; must reply within 2 week(s) of notification.

Academics. Special study options: Combined bachelor's/graduate degree, cooperative education, distance learning, double major, independent study, internships, liberal arts/career combination, study abroad, teacher certification program, Washington semester. **Credit/placement by examination:** AP, CLEP. 30 credit hours maximum toward bachelor's degree. **Support services:** Learning center, reduced course load, remedial instruction, study skills assistance, tutoring, writing center.

Majors. Business: Accounting, business admin, communications, e-commerce, finance, human resources, management information systems, managerial economics, marketing, training/development. **Computer sciences:** Systems analysis. **Education:** Secondary. **History:** General. **Math:** General. **Parks/recreation:** Sports admin. **Protective services:** Criminal justice. **Psychology:** General. **Social sciences:** Economics.

Most popular majors. Business/marketing 90%, liberal arts 10%.

Computing on campus. 57 workstations in dormitories, library, computer center, student center. Dormitories wired for high-speed internet access and linked to campus network. Commuter students can connect to campus network. Online course registration, online library, helpline, repair service available.

Student life. Freshman orientation: Mandatory. Preregistration for classes offered. Overnight pre-college summer programs for students and parents. **Policies:** Freshmen permitted cars on campus. **Housing:** Guaranteed on-campus for all undergraduates. Coed dorms, special housing for disabled, substance-free housing available. **Activities:** Choral groups, drama, literary magazine, radio station, student government, student newspaper, TV station, campus ministry, Institute for American Values, Republican Club, Young Democrats, Bacchus, Umoja.

Athletics. NCAA. **Intercollegiate:** Baseball M, basketball, cheerleading, field hockey W, football (tackle) M, golf, ice hockey M, lacrosse, soccer, softball W, tennis. **Intramural:** Basketball, football (tackle) M, racquetball, rugby, softball M, table tennis, volleyball. **Team name:** Bison.

Student services. Campus ministries, career counseling, student employment services, financial aid counseling, health services, personal counseling, placement for graduates.

Contact. E-mail: admissions@nichols.edu
Phone: (508) 213-2203 Toll-free number: (800) 470-3379
Fax: (508) 943-9885
Diane Gillespie, Director of Admissions and Financial Aid, Nichols College, Office of Admissions, Dudley, MA 01571-5000

Northeastern University

Boston, Massachusetts — **CB member**
www.northeastern.edu — **CB code: 3667**

- Private 5-year university
- Residential campus in very large city
- 14,730 degree-seeking undergraduates: 51% women, 6% African American, 7% Asian American, 5% Hispanic American, 5% international
- 4,811 graduate students
- 47% of applicants admitted
- SAT or ACT with writing, application essay required

General. Founded in 1898. Regionally accredited. 6 undergraduate colleges, 8 graduate and professional schools, 2 part-time undergraduate divisions, several suburban campuses. **Degrees:** 2,583 bachelor's awarded; master's, doctoral, first professional offered. **ROTC:** Army, Navy, Air Force. **Calendar:** Semester, extensive summer session. **Full-time faculty:** 853 total; 88% have terminal degrees, 14% minority, 35% women. **Part-time faculty:** 404 total; 40% have terminal degrees, 11% minority, 56% women. **Class size:** 51% < 20, 30% 20-39, 10% 40-49, 7% 50-99, 2% >100. **Special facilities:** African-American institute, marine science center, center for subsurfacing sensing and imaging systems, institute of chemical and biological analysis, reseach vessel MYSIS.

Freshman class profile. 25,467 applied, 11,958 admitted, 2,831 enrolled.

Mid 50% test scores		**Rank in top tenth:**	36%
SAT verbal:	560-650	**Return as sophomores:**	90%
SAT math:	580-670	**Out-of-state:**	66%
ACT:	24-28	**Live on campus:**	95%
Rank in top quarter:	73%	**International:**	3%

Basis for selection. Academic achievement as measured by grades earned, quality of classes, test scores, class rank most important. Recommendations, personal statement, school and community activities also important. Interviews encouraged but not required. Portfolios/auditions required for art, media art and design, music technology programs. **Homeschooled:** Transcript of courses and grades required. Students should submit comprehensive outline of academic curriculum, list of textbooks, special projects and activities.

High school preparation. 17 units required. Required and recommended units include English 4, mathematics 3-4, social studies 3, history 2, science 3-4 (laboratory 2-4) and foreign language 2-4. Each department and college of university may have more specific recommendations for additional preparation.

2005-2006 Annual costs. Tuition/fees: $28,792. Room/board: $10,550. Books/supplies: $900. Personal expenses: $900.

2005-2006 Financial aid. Need-based: 2,244 full-time freshmen applied for aid; 1,770 were judged to have need; 1,763 of these received aid. Average need met was 64%. Average scholarship/grant was $13,524; average loan $3,460. 55% of total undergraduate aid awarded as scholarships/grants, 45% as loans/jobs. **Non-need-based:** Awarded to 4,093 full-time undergraduates, including 1,074 freshmen. Scholarships awarded for academics, athletics, minority status.

Application procedures. Admission: Closing date 1/15 (postmark date). $75 fee, may be waived for applicants with need. Application may be submitted online. Admission notification 4/1. Admission notification on a rolling basis beginning on or about 3/15. Must reply by May 1 or within 4 week(s) if notified thereafter. **Financial aid:** Closing date 2/15. FAFSA, CSS PROFILE required. Applicants notified on a rolling basis starting 2/15; must reply by 5/1.

Academics. Special study options: Accelerated study, combined bachelor's/graduate degree, cooperative education, cross-registration, distance learning, double major, ESL, exchange student, honors, independent study, internships, liberal arts/career combination, semester at sea, student-designed major, study abroad, teacher certification program, Washington semester. International cooperative experience. **Credit/placement by examination:** AP, CLEP, IB. **Support services:** Learning center, pre-admission summer program, reduced course load, remedial instruction, study skills assistance, tutoring, writing center.

Majors. Architecture: Architecture. **Biology:** General, biochemistry, marine. **Business:** General, accounting, entrepreneurial studies, finance, human resources, international, logistics, management information systems, management science, marketing, operations. **Communications:** General, broadcast journalism, journalism, public relations. **Computer sciences:** General, computer science. **Conservation:** Environmental studies. **Education:** General, art, early childhood, elementary, foreign languages, health, mathematics, multi-level teacher, music, physical, social studies, speech. **Engineering:** General, chemical, civil, computer, electrical, mechanical. **Engineering technology:** Computer, electrical, mechanical. **English:** British lit, speech/rhetoric. **Foreign languages:** General, French, German, Italian, linguistics, Russian, sign language interpretation, Spanish. **Health:** Athletic training, audiology/speech pathology, clinical lab science, clinical lab technology, medical records admin, nursing (RN), recreational therapy, speech pathology. **History:** General. **Interdisciplinary:** Global studies, neuroscience. **Liberal arts:** Arts/sciences. **Math:** General. **Parks/recreation:** Health/fitness. **Philosophy/religion:** Philosophy. **Physical sciences:** Chemistry, geology, physics. **Protective services:** Criminal justice, police science, security services. **Psychology:** General. **Social sciences:** General, anthropology, economics, international relations, political science, sociology. **Visual/performing arts:** General, art, art history/conservation, commercial/advertising art, design, dramatic, music history, music management, music performance, studio arts.

Most popular majors. Business/marketing 28%, communications/journalism 7%, engineering/engineering technologies 14%, health sciences 8%, security/protective services 8%, social sciences 10%.

Computing on campus. 1,993 workstations in dormitories, library, computer center, student center. Dormitories wired for high-speed internet access and linked to campus network. Commuter students can connect to campus network. Online course registration, helpline, student web hosting, wireless network available.

Student life. Freshman orientation: Mandatory, $100 fee. Preregistration for classes offered. **Policies:** Freshmen permitted cars on campus. **Housing:** Guaranteed on-campus for freshmen. Coed dorms, single-sex dorms, special housing for disabled, apartments, fraternity/sorority housing, substance-free housing available. $400 deposit, deadline 5/1. Honors, wellness, quiet, living and learning, international, college/program housing available. **Activities:** Bands, choral groups, dance, drama, literary magazine, music ensembles, musical theater, radio station, student government, student newspaper, symphony orchestra, TV station, over 200 student organizations.

Athletics. NCAA. **Intercollegiate:** Baseball M, basketball, cross-country, diving W, field hockey W, football (tackle) M, ice hockey, rowing (crew), soccer, swimming W, tennis M, track and field, volleyball W. **Intramural:** Basketball, football (tackle), ice hockey, racquetball, soccer, softball, squash, tennis, volleyball W, water polo. **Team name:** Huskies.

Student services. Alcohol/substance abuse counseling, campus ministries, career counseling, services for economically disadvantaged, student employment services, financial aid counseling, health services, legal services, minority student services, personal counseling, placement for graduates, veterans' counselor, women's services. **Physically disabled:** Services for visually, speech, hearing impaired.

Contact. E-mail: admissions@neu.edu
Phone: (617) 373-2200 Fax: (617) 373-8780
Ronne Turner, Dean of Undergraduate Admissions, Northeastern University, 360 Huntington Avenue, 150 Richards Hall, Boston, MA 02115-9959

Pine Manor College
Chestnut Hill, Massachusetts **CB member**
www.pmc.edu **CB code: 3689**

- Private 4-year liberal arts college for women
- Residential campus in very large city
- 455 degree-seeking undergraduates: 2% part-time, 100% women, 42% African American, 5% Asian American, 12% Hispanic American, 1% Native American, 9% international
- 94% of applicants admitted
- SAT or ACT, application essay required
- 39% graduate within 6 years

General. Founded in 1911. Regionally accredited. **Degrees:** 89 bachelor's, 3 associate awarded. **Location:** 5 miles from Boston. **Calendar:** Semester, limited summer session. **Full-time faculty:** 30 total; 77% have terminal degrees, 13% minority, 77% women. **Part-time faculty:** 36 total; 44% have terminal degrees, 11% minority, 72% women. **Class size:** 83% < 20, 17% 20-39. **Special facilities:** Center for inclusive leadership and social responsibility, child study center.

Freshman class profile. 387 applied, 364 admitted, 138 enrolled.

Mid 50% test scores			
SAT verbal:	370-490	Rank in top quarter:	23%
SAT math:	350-460	Rank in top tenth:	8%
ACT:	16-18	End year in good standing:	63%
GPA 3.50 or higher:	5%	Return as sophomores:	64%
GPA 3.0-3.49:	16%	Out-of-state:	26%
GPA 2.0-2.99:	58%	Live on campus:	93%
		International:	7%

Basis for selection. School achievement record most important; class rank, counselor recommendation, test scores, leadership also important; school activities considered. Rolling deadline for SAT/ACT score submission. Interview recommended. **Learning Disabled:** Students may be required to submit learning disability documentation.

High school preparation. Required units include English 4, mathematics 3, social studies 2, science 3 and foreign language 2.

2005-2006 Annual costs. Tuition/fees: $15,538. Room/board: $9,500. Books/supplies: $800. Personal expenses: $1,000.

2004-2005 Financial aid. Need-based: 161 full-time freshmen applied for aid; 158 were judged to have need; 157 of these received aid. Average need met was 75%. Average scholarship/grant was $11,413; average loan $4,189. 63% of total undergraduate aid awarded as scholarships/grants, 37% as loans/jobs. **Non-need-based:** Awarded to 35 full-time undergraduates, including 12 freshmen. Scholarships awarded for academics, alumni affiliation, leadership.

Application procedures. Admission: No deadline. $25 fee, may be waived for applicants with need. Application may be submitted online. Admission notification on a rolling basis. Must reply by May 1 or within 2 week(s) if notified thereafter. **Financial aid:** Priority date 5/1; no closing date. FAFSA required. Applicants notified on a rolling basis starting 3/1; must reply by 5/1 or within 2 week(s) of notification.

Academics. All students required to participate in internship program. All students receive comprehensive advising. **Special study options:** Cross-registration, double major, ESL, honors, independent study, internships, liberal arts/career combination, semester at sea, student-designed major, study abroad, teacher certification program, Washington semester. Students with sophomore status or higher eligible to take courses offered by Marine Studies Consortium. **Credit/placement by examination:** AP, CLEP, IB, institutional tests. 24 credit hours maximum toward bachelor's degree. **Support services:** Learning center, reduced course load, remedial instruction, study skills assistance, tutoring.

Majors. Biology: General. **Business:** Business admin. **Communications:** Media studies. **English:** English lit. **History:** General. **Liberal arts:** Arts/sciences. **Psychology:** General. **Social sciences:** Political science. **Visual/performing arts:** General.

Most popular majors. Biology 18%, business/marketing 19%, communications/journalism 9%, psychology 26%, social sciences 11%, visual/performing arts 11%.

Computing on campus. 134 workstations in dormitories, library, computer center, student center. Dormitories wired for high-speed internet access and linked to campus network. Commuter students can connect to campus network. Online course registration, helpline, repair service available.

Student life. Freshman orientation: Mandatory, $150 fee. Preregistration for classes offered. Held in June and September. **Policies:** Freshmen permitted cars on campus. **Housing:** Guaranteed on-campus for freshmen. Special housing for disabled, substance-free housing available. $250 deposit. Quiet residence halls available. **Activities:** Choral groups, dance, drama, literary magazine, radio station, student government, Ladies of Various Ebony Shades, African American, Latina, Asian, Native American and All club, Alianza Latina, Bisexuals, Gays, Lesbians and Allies in diversity, Cape Verdean student alliance, dance ensemble, student government association, student health advisory board, Imani Christian club, Camerata singers.

Athletics. NCAA. **Intercollegiate:** Basketball W, cross-country W, lacrosse W, soccer W, softball W, tennis W, volleyball W. **Team name:** Gators.

Student services. Adult student services, career counseling, services for economically disadvantaged, student employment services, financial aid counseling, health services, minority student services, personal counseling, placement for graduates, women's services. **Physically disabled:** Services for visually, hearing impaired.

Contact. E-mail: admission@pmc.edu
Phone: (617) 731-7104 Toll-free number: (800) 762-1357
Fax: (617) 731-7102
Robin Engel, Dean of Admissions and Financial Aid, Pine Manor College, 400 Heath Street, Chestnut Hill, MA 02467

Regis College
Weston, Massachusetts **CB member**
www.regiscollege.edu **CB code: 3723**

- Private 4-year liberal arts college for women affiliated with Roman Catholic Church
- Residential campus in large town
- 843 degree-seeking undergraduates: 26% part-time, 96% women, 14% African American, 7% Asian American, 10% Hispanic American, 1% international
- 460 degree-seeking graduate students
- 76% of applicants admitted
- SAT or ACT (ACT writing optional), application essay required
- 65% graduate within 6 years; 20% enter graduate study

General. Founded in 1927. Regionally accredited. College founded by Sisters of St. Joseph. **Degrees:** 234 bachelor's, 99 associate awarded; master's offered. **ROTC:** Army. **Location:** 12 miles from Boston. **Calendar:** Semester, limited summer session. **Full-time faculty:** 54 total; 80% have terminal degrees, 6% minority, 82% women. **Part-time faculty:** 63 total; 30% have terminal degrees, 2% minority, 71% women. **Class size:** 67% < 20, 29% 20-39, 4% 40-49, less than 1% 50-99. **Special facilities:** Philatelic museum, fine arts center, 2 digital imaging studios, music laboratory with electronic keyboards and computers.

Freshman class profile. 908 applied, 688 admitted, 161 enrolled.

Mid 50% test scores			
SAT verbal:	420-530	Rank in top quarter:	58%
SAT math:	410-520	Rank in top tenth:	20%
ACT:	14-20	End year in good standing:	82%
GPA 3.50 or higher:	21%	Return as sophomores:	78%
GPA 3.0-3.49:	27%	Out-of-state:	17%
GPA 2.0-2.99:	50%	Live on campus:	85%
		International:	3%

Basis for selection. All credentials within student's file reviewed. At times, interview or additional grades requested or guidance counselors spoken with. PAA accepted in lieu of SAT for students from Puerto Rico. Interview highly recommended. Portfolio recommended for art majors. **Homeschooled:** Statement describing homeschool structure and mission, transcript of courses and grades required. **Learning Disabled:** Must apprise Director of Student Disabilities of disability status and document condition to receive appropriate accommodations.

High school preparation. 16 units required. Required units include English 4, mathematics 3, social studies 2, science 2 (laboratory 1), foreign language 2 and academic electives 3.

2005-2006 Annual costs. Tuition/fees: $21,525. Room/board: $9,825.

2005-2006 Financial aid. Need-based: 150 full-time freshmen applied for aid; 139 were judged to have need; 131 of these received aid. Average need met was 66%. Average scholarship/grant was $11,396; average loan $4,351. 19% of total undergraduate aid awarded as scholarships/grants, 81% as loans/jobs. **Non-need-based:** Awarded to 326 full-time undergraduates, including 85 freshmen. Scholarships awarded for academics, alumni affiliation, leadership, minority status, religious affiliation, state residency.

Application procedures. **Admission:** No deadline. $40 fee, may be waived for applicants with need. Application may be submitted online. Admission notification on a rolling basis beginning on or about 12/1. Must reply by May 1 or within 2 week(s) if notified thereafter. Students encouraged to apply by January 1. **Financial aid:** Priority date 2/15; no closing date. FAFSA, institutional form required. Applicants notified on a rolling basis starting 3/15; must reply by 5/1.

Academics. First year seminar required. Internships required for some majors, encouraged for all; available semester, summer, school year; academic credit awarded. **Special study options:** Accelerated study, combined bachelor's/graduate degree, cross-registration, double major, exchange student, honors, independent study, internships, liberal arts/career combination, student-designed major, study abroad, teacher certification program, Washington semester. **Credit/placement by examination:** AP, CLEP, IB, institutional tests. 24 credit hours maximum toward bachelor's degree. **Support services:** Learning center, reduced course load, study skills assistance, tutoring, writing center.

Majors. **Biology:** General, biochemistry. **Business:** General. **Communications:** General, public relations. **Computer sciences:** General, computer science, information systems. **Education:** Mathematics. **English:** English lit. **Foreign languages:** Spanish. **Health:** Nursing (RN). **History:** General. **Interdisciplinary:** Museum. **Psychology:** General. **Public administration:** Social work. **Social sciences:** International relations, political science, sociology. **Visual/performing arts:** Art, dramatic.

Most popular majors. Biology 12%, business/marketing 11%, communications/journalism 7%, health sciences 35%, history 6%, psychology 6%, social sciences 8%, visual/performing arts 7%.

Computing on campus. 179 workstations in library, computer center, student center. Dormitories wired for high-speed internet access and linked to campus network. Commuter students can connect to campus network. Online course registration, online library, helpline, wireless network available.

Student life. **Freshman orientation:** Mandatory, $175 fee. Preregistration for classes offered. 2-day program in June. **Policies:** Freshmen permitted cars on campus. **Housing:** Guaranteed on-campus for all undergraduates. Substance-free housing available. $250 deposit, deadline 5/1. All residences smoke-free. Quiet floors available. **Activities:** Choral groups, dance, drama, literary magazine, music ensembles, musical theater, radio station, student government, student newspaper, Asian American organization, African American, Hispanic, Asian, and Native American organization, student organization for Latino culture, campus activities board, campus ministry association, student government association, student athletic advisory committee.

Athletics. NCAA. **Intercollegiate:** Basketball W, cross-country W, diving W, field hockey W, lacrosse W, soccer W, softball W, swimming W, tennis W, track and field W, volleyball W. **Intramural:** Basketball W, soccer W, softball W, swimming W, tennis W, volleyball W, water polo W. **Team name:** Regis Pride.

Student services. Adult student services, campus ministries, career counseling, student employment services, financial aid counseling, health services, minority student services, on-campus daycare, personal counseling, placement for graduates. **Physically disabled:** Services for visually, hearing impaired.

Contact. E-mail: admission@regiscollege.edu
Phone: (781) 768-7100 Toll-free number: (866) 438-7344
Fax: (781) 768-7071
Emily Keily, Director of Admission, Regis College, 235 Wellesley Street, Weston, MA 02493-1571

St. John's Seminary College

Brighton, Massachusetts
www.sjs.edu **CB code: 3295**

- Private 4-year liberal arts and seminary college for men affiliated with Roman Catholic Church
- Residential campus in very large city
- 165 graduate students
- Application essay, interview required

General. Founded in 1883. Regionally accredited; also accredited by ATS. **ROTC:** Army. **Location:** 5 miles from downtown Boston. **Calendar:** Semester. **Full-time faculty:** 8 total. **Part-time faculty:** 16 total. **Class size:** 100% < 20. **Special facilities:** 3 chapels.

Freshman class profile.

Out-of-state:	70%	**Live on campus:**	100%

Basis for selection. Adequate religious vocational discernment. Interviews most important, followed by school achievement record, test scores, and letters of recommendation. Applicants must be sponsored by local bishops. Otis Lennon Mental Ability Test, Iowa Silent Reading Tests required. **Homeschooled:** Applicants should consult local parish priest.

High school preparation. 18 units required. Required and recommended units include English 4, mathematics 2, social studies 2, history 2, science 2 (laboratory 2), foreign language 2-3 and academic electives 2.

2005-2006 Annual costs. Tuition/fees: $11,250. Room/board: $6,250. Books/supplies: $500. Personal expenses: $600.

Financial aid. **Non-need-based:** Scholarships awarded for state residency.

Application procedures. **Admission:** Closing date 7/15 (postmark date). No application fee. Admission notification on a rolling basis beginning on or about 5/1. **Financial aid:** No deadline. FAFSA required. Applicants notified on a rolling basis; must reply within 3 week(s) of notification.

Academics. **Special study options:** Cross-registration, double major, independent study, study abroad. **Credit/placement by examination:** CLEP, institutional tests. **Support services:** Reduced course load, tutoring.

Majors. **History:** General. **Liberal arts:** Arts/sciences. **Philosophy/religion:** Philosophy. **Psychology:** General. **Social sciences:** Sociology. **Theology:** Preministerial.

Computing on campus. 9 workstations in library, computer center. Dormitories wired for high-speed internet access. Commuter students can connect to campus network.

Student life. **Freshman orientation:** Mandatory. Preregistration for classes offered. **Policies:** Religious observance required. **Housing:** Guaranteed on-campus for all undergraduates. Students must live at seminary. **Activities:** Choral groups, drama, musical theater, student government, participation in Harvard's Model UN (representing the Vatican), Students for Pro-Life.

Athletics. **Intramural:** Basketball M, cross-country M, football (non-tackle) M, softball M, table tennis M, tennis M. **Team name:** Eagles.

Student services. Career counseling, health services, personal counseling.

Contact. E-mail: martin_grace@rcab.org
Phone: (617) 254-2610 ext. 273 Fax: (617) 787-2336
Robert Flagg, Dean of the College, Dean of Admissions, St. John's Seminary College, 127 Lake Street, Brighton, MA 02135

Salem State College

Salem, Massachusetts **CB member**
www.salemstate.edu **CB code: 3522**

- Public 4-year university
- Commuter campus in large town
- 6,687 degree-seeking undergraduates: 20% part-time, 64% women, 6% African American, 3% Asian American, 5% Hispanic American, 4% international
- 1,316 degree-seeking graduate students
- 90% of applicants admitted
- SAT or ACT (ACT writing optional) required
- 42% graduate within 6 years

General. Founded in 1854. Regionally accredited. **Degrees:** 845 bachelor's awarded; master's offered. **ROTC:** Air Force. **Location:** 20 miles from Boston. **Calendar:** Semester, extensive summer session. **Full-time faculty:** 296 total; 6% minority, 50% women. **Part-time faculty:** 372 total. **Class size:** 52% < 20, 46% 20-39, 1% 40-49, less than 1% 50-99. **Special facilities:** Media facility, center for creative and performing arts, observatories, glass blowing studio.

Freshman class profile. 4,827 applied, 4,324 admitted, 1,226 enrolled.

Mid 50% test scores			
SAT verbal:	420-530	GPA 2.0-2.99:	64%
SAT math:	420-520	Return as sophomores:	75%
ACT:	18-21	Out-of-state:	3%
GPA 3.50 or higher:	11%	Live on campus:	54%
GPA 3.0-3.49:	25%	International:	2%

Basis for selection. If high school GPA 2.0 or below, preference given to test scores. Recommendations also considered. Interview recommended. Portfolio required for art major applicants.

High school preparation. 16 units required; 18 recommended. Required and recommended units include English 4, mathematics 3, social studies 2, history 1-3, science 3 (laboratory 2), foreign language 2 and academic electives 2. Additional requirements for some programs.

2005-2006 Annual costs. Tuition/fees: $5,594; $11,734 out-of-state. New England Regional tuition and fees per year: $6049. Room/board: $6,678. Books/supplies: $800. Personal expenses: $900.

Financial aid. Non-need-based: Scholarships awarded for academics, alumni affiliation, art, leadership, music/drama, state residency. **Additional information:** Tuition waivers for qualified veterans and National Guard members. Grant assistance available for eligible adult students.

Application procedures. Admission: Priority date 3/1; no deadline. $25 fee ($40 out-of-state), may be waived for applicants with need. Admission notification on a rolling basis beginning on or about 1/3. Must reply within 30 days. **Financial aid:** Priority date 4/1; no closing date. FAFSA required. Applicants notified on a rolling basis starting 4/1; must reply within 2 week(s) of notification.

Academics. Special study options: Accelerated study, cooperative education, cross-registration, double major, ESL, exchange student, honors, independent study, internships, student-designed major, study abroad, teacher certification program. **Credit/placement by examination:** AP, CLEP, institutional tests. **Support services:** Learning center, pre-admission summer program, reduced course load, remedial instruction, tutoring, writing center.

Majors. Biology: General, biochemistry, ecology, marine. **Business:** Accounting, business admin, entrepreneurial studies, finance, human resources, international, management information systems, managerial economics, marketing, office management. **Communications:** General, advertising, journalism, media studies, public relations. **Computer sciences:** General. **Education:** General, early childhood, elementary, middle, physical. **English:** Composition, English lit, technical writing. **Foreign languages:** Comparative lit, Spanish, translation. **Health:** Athletic training, clinical lab science, nuclear medical technology, nursing (RN). **History:** General, American, European, public archives. **Interdisciplinary:** Math/computer science. **Liberal arts:** Arts/sciences. **Math:** General. **Parks/recreation:** General, exercise sciences, health/fitness, sports admin. **Physical sciences:** Chemistry, geology. **Protective services:** Fire services admin, law enforcement admin. **Psychology:** General. **Public administration:** Social work. **Social sciences:** Cartography, economics, geography, political science, sociology. **Transportation:** Aviation management. **Visual/performing arts:** Acting, art, art history/conservation, commercial/advertising art, dramatic, drawing, photography, printmaking, sculpture, theater design, theater history.

Most popular majors. Business/marketing 20%, communications/journalism 6%, education 12%, health sciences 9%, psychology 10%, security/protective services 7%, social sciences 9%.

Computing on campus. PC or laptop required. Dormitories wired for high-speed internet access and linked to campus network. Commuter students can connect to campus network. Online course registration, online library, helpline, repair service, student web hosting, wireless network available.

Student life. Freshman orientation: Mandatory, $85 fee. Preregistration for classes offered. Sessions held prior to start of semester. **Policies:** Freshmen permitted cars on campus. **Housing:** Coed dorms, single-sex dorms, special housing for disabled, cooperative housing, substance-free housing available. $200 nonrefundable deposit, deadline 8/12. Scholars-in-residence, academic achievement, townhouse apartments for juniors and seniors and students over 21 available. **Activities:** Choral groups, dance, drama, literary magazine, music ensembles, musical theater, radio station, student government, student newspaper, Hillel, women's center, international student association, political science academy, Catholic student community, African American student association, Hispanic American society, student nurses association, criminal justice academy, MASSPIRG.

Athletics. NCAA. **Intercollegiate:** Baseball M, basketball, cross-country, field hockey W, golf M, ice hockey M, lacrosse, soccer, softball W, swimming W, tennis, track and field, volleyball W. **Intramural:** Archery, badminton, baseball M, basketball, field hockey W, football (non-tackle) M, golf, gymnastics, handball, ice hockey, racquetball, soccer, softball W, swimming, table tennis, tennis, volleyball. **Team name:** Vikings.

Student services. Adult student services, alcohol/substance abuse counseling, campus ministries, career counseling, student employment services, financial aid counseling, health services, minority student services, on-campus daycare, personal counseling, placement for graduates, veterans' counselor, women's services. **Physically disabled:** Services for visually, speech, hearing impaired. **Learning disabled:** Comprehensive services available.

Contact. E-mail: admissions@salemstate.edu
Phone: (978) 542-6200 Fax: (978) 542-6893
Nate Bryant, Director of Admissions, Salem State College, 352 Lafayette Street, Salem, MA 01970-5353

School of the Museum of Fine Arts

Boston, Massachusetts
www.smfa.edu **CB code: 3794**

- Private 4-year visual arts college
- Commuter campus in very large city
- 677 degree-seeking undergraduates: 10% part-time, 66% women, 2% African American, 3% Asian American, 5% Hispanic American, 1% Native American, 6% international
- 96 degree-seeking graduate students
- 84% of applicants admitted
- Application essay required
- 53% graduate within 6 years

General. Founded in 1876. Students have access to the Museum of Fine Arts, Boston. All degree programs offered in affiliation with Tufts University, and all degree students may join sporting, musical, and other extracurricular activities offered at Tufts. **Degrees:** 77 bachelor's awarded; master's offered. **Location:** 1 mile from downtown. **Calendar:** Semester, limited summer session. **Full-time faculty:** 51 total; 67% have terminal degrees, 16% minority, 41% women. **Part-time faculty:** 129 total; 37% have terminal degrees, 7% minority, 46% women. **Class size:** 88% < 20, 11% 20-39, 1% 40-49.

Freshman class profile. 858 applied, 718 admitted, 129 enrolled.

Mid 50% test scores			
SAT verbal:	510-650	Return as sophomores:	81%
SAT math:	460-600	Out-of-state:	72%
ACT:	22-28	Live on campus:	49%
		International:	5%

Basis for selection. Portfolio, previous schooling, and quality and content of essays important; grades and test scores important for degree applicants, considered for diploma applicants. Combined-Degree program applicants must apply to the Museum School and Tufts University simultaneously. Scores accepted on a rolling basis after 02/01. Test scores not required for Diploma applicants. Portfolio required. Interview available by appointment. **Homeschooled:** Transcript of courses and grades required. Must have graduation date indicating successful completion of program; must be signed and dated by recognized record keeper, which may include outside testing agency, homeschool representative, or parent.

2005-2006 Annual costs. Tuition/fees: $24,760. Room only: $11,600. Books/supplies: $1,250. Personal expenses: $1,600.

2005-2006 Financial aid. Need-based: 124 full-time freshmen applied for aid; 118 were judged to have need; 118 of these received aid. Average need met was 43%. Average scholarship/grant was $10,521; average loan $2,553. 53% of total undergraduate aid awarded as scholarships/grants, 47% as loans/jobs. **Non-need-based:** Awarded to 52 full-time undergraduates, including 48 freshmen. Scholarships awarded for art.

Application procedures. Admission: Priority date 2/1; no deadline. $60 fee, may be waived for applicants with need. Application must be submitted on paper. Admission notification on a rolling basis beginning on or about 3/15. Must reply by May 1 or within 2 week(s) if notified thereafter. Students may apply early and request early notification of admission. **Financial aid:** Priority date 3/15; no closing date. FAFSA, institutional form required. Applicants notified on a rolling basis starting 4/15; must reply by 5/1 or within 2 week(s) of notification.

Academics. Special study options: Cross-registration, double major, ESL, exchange student, independent study, internships, liberal arts/career combination, New York semester, student-designed major, study abroad, teacher certification program. 5-year BFA/BA with Tufts University, studio art elective diploma program, optional fifth-year certificate program for diploma recipients. **Credit/placement by examination:** AP, CLEP. **Support services:** Pre-admission summer program, study skills assistance, writing center.

Majors. Communications technology: Animation/special effects. **Education:** Art. **Visual/performing arts:** Art, ceramics, cinematography, drawing, illustration, metal/jewelry, multimedia, painting, photography, printmaking, sculpture, studio arts.

Most popular majors. Visual/performing arts 98%.

Computing on campus. 127 workstations in library, computer center, student center. Dormitories wired for high-speed internet access. Wireless network available.

Student life. Freshman orientation: Mandatory, $55 fee. Preregistration for classes offered. Typically held during the last week in August, right before the beginning of the semester. **Policies:** Freshmen permitted cars on campus. **Housing:** Coed dorms available. $450 nonrefundable deposit, deadline 5/3. **Activities:** Film society, student government, Outloud, chess club, infrasculpture, Amnesty International, photo club, vegan cooking collective, yoga club.

Student services. Career counseling, student employment services, financial aid counseling, personal counseling, placement for graduates.

Contact. E-mail: admissions@smfa.edu
Phone: (617) 369-3626 Toll-free number: (800) 643-6078
Fax: (617) 369-4264
Susan Clain, Dean of Admissions, School of the Museum of Fine Arts, 230 The Fenway, Boston, MA 02115

Simmons College

Boston, Massachusetts **CB member**
www.simmons.edu **CB code: 3761**

- Private 4-year liberal arts college for women
- Residential campus in large city
- 1,846 degree-seeking undergraduates: 9% part-time, 100% women, 7% African American, 8% Asian American, 3% Hispanic American, 2% international
- 2,562 degree-seeking graduate students
- 64% of applicants admitted
- SAT or ACT (ACT writing optional), application essay required

General. Founded in 1899. Regionally accredited. **Degrees:** 428 bachelor's awarded; master's, doctoral offered. **ROTC:** Army. **Location:** 2 miles from downtown. **Calendar:** Semester, extensive summer session. **Full-time faculty:** 193 total; 19% minority, 70% women. **Part-time faculty:** 181 total; 9% minority, 71% women. **Class size:** 65% < 20, 27% 20-39, 3% 40-49, 5% 50-99. **Special facilities:** Audiovisual media center, dream analysis lab, physical therapy lab.

Freshman class profile. 2,303 applied, 1,469 admitted, 413 enrolled.

Mid 50% test scores		Rank in top tenth:	25%
SAT verbal:	510-610	Out-of-state:	45%
SAT math:	500-590	Live on campus:	90%
ACT:	20-25	International:	3%
Rank in top quarter:	59%		

Basis for selection. School achievement record most important. Test scores, 2 recommendations, essay, interview (if available), personal qualities also important. Interests, accomplishments considered.

High school preparation. College-preparatory program required. 19 units required; 22 recommended. Required and recommended units include English 4, mathematics 3-4, social studies 3-4, history 3, science 3 and foreign language 3-4.

2005-2006 Annual costs. Tuition/fees: $25,440. Room/board: $10,200. Books/supplies: $800. Personal expenses: $1,250.

2005-2006 Financial aid. Need-based: 340 full-time freshmen applied for aid; 301 were judged to have need; 299 of these received aid. Average need met was 60%. Average scholarship/grant was $11,751; average loan $3,018. 69% of total undergraduate aid awarded as scholarships/grants, 31% as loans/jobs. **Non-need-based:** Awarded to 344 full-time undergraduates, including 137 freshmen. Scholarships awarded for academics, alumni affiliation, leadership, minority status.

Application procedures. Admission: Priority date 2/1; deadline 4/1 (postmark date). $35 fee, may be waived for applicants with need. Application may be submitted online. Admission notification 4/15. Must reply by May 1 or within 2 week(s) if notified thereafter. **Financial aid:** Priority date 2/15, closing date 3/1. FAFSA required. Applicants notified on a rolling basis starting 3/15; must reply by 5/1 or within 4 week(s) of notification.

Academics. Special study options: Accelerated study, combined bachelor's/graduate degree, cooperative education, cross-registration, double major, dual enrollment of high school students, ESL, exchange student, honors, independent study, internships, liberal arts/career combination, semester at sea, student-designed major, study abroad, teacher certification program, Washington semester. Exchange programs with Mills College, Spellman College, Fisk University, American University, Colleges of the Fenway; double degree programs with Massachusetts College of Pharmacy and Health Sciences and Hebrew College. **Credit/placement by examination:** AP, CLEP, IB, institutional tests. 32 credit hours maximum toward bachelor's degree. **Support services:** Learning center, pre-admission summer program, reduced course load, remedial instruction, study skills assistance, tutoring, writing center.

Majors. Area/ethnic studies: African-American, East Asian, women's. **Biology:** General, biochemistry. **Business:** Business admin, finance, management information systems, sales/distribution. **Communications:** General, public relations. **Computer sciences:** General. **Conservation:** General, environmental science. **Education:** General, early childhood, elementary, ESL, middle, secondary, social studies, special. **English:** American lit, British lit. **Foreign languages:** Comparative lit, French, Spanish. **Health:** Nursing (RN), predentistry, premedicine, prepharmacy. **History:** General. **Interdisciplinary:** Biopsychology, nutrition sciences. **Math:** General. **Philosophy/religion:** Philosophy. **Physical sciences:** Chemistry, physics. **Psychology:** General. **Public administration:** Human services, policy analysis. **Social sciences:** Economics, international relations, political science, sociology. **Visual/performing arts:** Art history/conservation, arts management, commercial/advertising art, graphic design, music history, music performance.

Most popular majors. Business/marketing 6%, communications/journalism 9%, English 6%, health sciences 19%, psychology 10%, social sciences 19%, visual/performing arts 8%.

Computing on campus. 250 workstations in dormitories, library, computer center, student center. Dormitories wired for high-speed internet access and linked to campus network. Commuter students can connect to campus network. Online course registration, online library, helpline, wireless network available.

Student life. Freshman orientation: Mandatory. Preregistration for classes offered. **Housing:** Guaranteed on-campus for all undergraduates. Special housing for disabled available. $250 fully refundable deposit, deadline 5/1. Special interest housing available. **Activities:** Choral groups, dance, drama, film society, literary magazine, student government, student newspaper, Asian club, African American club, Hispanic club, international student club, Christian Fellowship, Hillel, Amnesty International, Society Organized Against Racism, Feminist Union, gay and lesbian student association.

Athletics. NCAA. **Intercollegiate:** Basketball W, diving W, field hockey W, rowing (crew) W, soccer W, softball W, swimming W, tennis W, track and field W, volleyball W. **Intramural:** Basketball W, diving W, softball W, tennis W, volleyball W, water polo W. **Team name:** Sharks.

Student services. Adult student services, alcohol/substance abuse counseling, campus ministries, career counseling, student employment services, financial aid counseling, health services, personal counseling, placement for graduates, veterans' counselor, women's services. **Physically disabled:** Services for visually, speech, hearing impaired.

Contact. E-mail: ugadm@simmons.edu
Phone: (617) 521-2051 Toll-free number: (800) 345-8468
Fax: (617) 521-3190
Catherine Childs-Capolupo, Director of Undergraduate Admissions, Simmons College, 300 The Fenway, Boston, MA 02115-5898

Simon's Rock College of Bard

Great Barrington, Massachusetts **CB member**
www.simons-rock.edu **CB code: 3795**

- Private 4-year liberal arts college
- Residential campus in small town
- 380 degree-seeking undergraduates
- 53% of applicants admitted
- Application essay, interview required

General. Founded in 1964. Regionally accredited. College accepts applications from students who have completed the 10th grade and are ready to begin a 4-year liberal arts education. **Degrees:** 51 bachelor's, 104 associate awarded. **Location:** 22 miles from Pittsfield, 120 miles from Boston. **Calendar:** Semester. **Full-time faculty:** 38 total. **Part-time faculty:** 30 total. **Class size:** 97% < 20, 3% 20-39. **Special facilities:** Visual and performing arts center, environmental research center.

Freshman class profile. 356 applied, 190 admitted, 145 enrolled.

Mid 50% test scores			
SAT verbal:	580-700	ACT:	22-28
SAT math:	530-690	Out-of-state:	79%
		Live on campus:	81%

Basis for selection. School achievement record, essays, recommendations (counselor and teacher), test scores, interview most important. SAT or ACT recommended. On-campus interview with parents recommended. **Learning Disabled:** Counseling is limited but available. Tutoring available. Every consideration given based on capabilities as small college.

High school preparation. 15 units recommended. Recommended units include English 2, mathematics 2, social studies 2, history 2, science 2 (laboratory 1), foreign language 2 and academic electives 2. Applicants who have completed tenth or eleventh grade should have 2 or 3 years college-preparatory curriculum respectively.

2005-2006 Annual costs. Tuition/fees: $33,364. Room/board: $8,654. Books/supplies: $2,000. Personal expenses: $225.

2004-2005 Financial aid. Need-based: 88% of total undergraduate aid awarded as scholarships/grants, 12% as loans/jobs. **Non-need-based:** Scholarships awarded for academics, alumni affiliation, leadership, state residency.

Application procedures. Admission: Closing date 6/30 (postmark date). $50 fee, may be waived for applicants with need. Admission notification on a rolling basis beginning on or about 1/15. Must reply by May 1 or within 2 week(s) if notified thereafter. **Financial aid:** Priority date 4/15; no closing date. FAFSA, CSS PROFILE required. Applicants notified on a rolling basis starting 4/15; must reply within 2 week(s) of notification.

Academics. Upper-class students may take courses at Bard College. **Special study options:** Combined bachelor's/graduate degree, cooperative education, cross-registration, dual enrollment of high school students, exchange student, independent study, internships, student-designed major, study abroad. Globalization and International Affairs, undergraduate summer research fellows program with Rockefeller University, International Human Rights Exchange. **Credit/placement by examination:** AP, CLEP, institutional tests. 10 credit hours maximum toward associate degree, 10 toward bachelor's. Credit for Advanced Placement courses determined by individual divisions. **Support services:** Reduced course load, study skills assistance, tutoring, writing center.

Majors. Area/ethnic studies: African, African-American, Asian, Central/Eastern European, Chinese, East Asian, French, German, Native American, Spanish/Iberian, women's. **Biology:** General, botany, cell/histology, ecology, endocrinology, genetics, microbiology, plant physiology. **Communications technology:** Photo/film/video. **Computer sciences:** General, computer science, programming. **Conservation:** Environmental science, environmental studies. **Engineering:** General. **English:** British lit, creative writing, English lit. **Foreign languages:** General, Arabic, Chinese, comparative lit, French, German, Germanic, Latin, linguistics, Spanish. **History:** American, Asian. **Interdisciplinary:** Behavioral sciences, cognitive science, math/computer science, natural sciences. **Legal studies:** General. **Liberal arts:** Arts/sciences. **Math:** General, analysis, statistics. **Philosophy/religion:** Buddhist, philosophy. **Physical sciences:** Chemistry, organic chemistry, physics. **Psychology:** General. **Social sciences:** General, anthropology, economics, political science, sociology. **Visual/performing arts:** General, acting, art, art history/conservation, ceramics, cinematography, dance, directing/producing, dramatic, drawing, film/cinema, jazz, music history, music performance, music theory/composition, musicology, painting, photography, play/screenwriting, printmaking, sculpture, stringed instruments, studio arts, theater history.

Computing on campus. 50 workstations in dormitories, library, computer center, student center. Dormitories wired for high-speed internet access and linked to campus network. Commuter students can connect to campus network. Online course registration, online library, helpline, repair service, student web hosting available.

Student life. Freshman orientation: Mandatory, $500 fee. Preregistration for classes offered. 1-week writing and thinking workshop prior to start of semester. **Policies:** No alcohol, drugs or weapons allowed on campus. **Housing:** Guaranteed on-campus for all undergraduates. Coed dorms, single-sex dorms, substance-free housing available. $150 deposit, deadline 4/30. Theater group residence and other group residences. **Activities:** Jazz band, choral groups, dance, drama, film society, literary magazine, music ensembles, musical theater, radio station, student government, student newspaper, multicultural student organization, Amnesty International, environmental activist network, younger scholars group, community garden, debate club, Model UN, queer/straight alliance, Spanish club, mock trial team.

Athletics. Intercollegiate: Basketball, cheerleading, cricket, cross-country, fencing, field hockey W, racquetball, soccer, swimming. **Intramural:** Archery, basketball, cheerleading, cricket, cross-country, fencing, field hockey W, racquetball, skiing, soccer, squash, swimming, tennis, volleyball.

Student services. Alcohol/substance abuse counseling, career counseling, student employment services, financial aid counseling, health services, minority student services, personal counseling, placement for graduates, women's services.

Contact. E-mail: admit@simons-rock.edu
Phone: (413) 528-7312 Toll-free number: (800) 235-7186
Fax: (413) 528-7334
Mary Davidson, Dean of Admission and Student Affairs, Simon's Rock College of Bard, 84 Alford Road, Great Barrington, MA 01230-1990

Smith College

Northampton, Massachusetts — **CB member**
www.smith.edu — **CB code: 3762**

- Private 4-year liberal arts college for women
- Residential campus in large town
- 2,635 degree-seeking undergraduates: 1% part-time, 100% women, 6% African American, 11% Asian American, 6% Hispanic American, 1% Native American, 7% international
- 447 degree-seeking graduate students
- 48% of applicants admitted
- SAT or ACT (ACT writing optional), application essay required
- 86% graduate within 6 years

General. Founded in 1871. Regionally accredited. **Degrees:** 734 bachelor's awarded; master's, doctoral offered. **ROTC:** Army, Air Force. **Location:** 35 miles from Hartford, Connecticut, 90 miles from Boston. **Calendar:** Semester. **Full-time faculty:** 288 total; 96% have terminal degrees, 14% minority, 52% women. **Part-time faculty:** 28 total; 89% have terminal degrees, 4% minority, 50% women. **Class size:** 71% < 20, 23% 20-39, 2% 40-49, 3% 50-99, less than 1% >100. **Special facilities:** Art museum, physiology and horticultural laboratories, printmaking studio, darkroom and sculpture (including bronze casting studio) facilities, dance, theater and television studios, electronic music studio, recital hall, electronics classrooms, digital design studio, animal care facilities, electron microscopes, on-campus elementary school, multimedia language lab, greenhouses, astronomy observatories.

Freshman class profile. 3,408 applied, 1,649 admitted, 615 enrolled.

Mid 50% test scores			
SAT verbal:	580-710	Rank in top tenth:	61%
SAT math:	570-670	End year in good standing:	96%
ACT:	25-31	Return as sophomores:	89%
GPA 3.50 or higher:	87%	Out-of-state:	82%
GPA 3.0-3.49:	13%	Live on campus:	100%
Rank in top quarter:	90%	International:	8%

Basis for selection. Secondary school record, including GPA and difficulty of courses, recommendations most important. Class rank, essay, school and community activities and test scores also important. SAT Subject Tests recommended. 2 SAT Subject Tests recommended. Interview strongly recommended, may be conducted off-campus by alumna. **Homeschooled:** Statement describing homeschool structure and mission, transcript of courses and grades, interview, letter of recommendation (nonparent) required. Submit portfolio including transcript and evaluation of coursework and sample of short research or analytical paper with evaluator's remarks.

High school preparation. 15 units recommended. Recommended units include English 4, mathematics 4, history 2, science 3 (laboratory 3) and foreign language 3. 3 units of 1 foreign language or 2 each of 2 languages recommended.

2006-2007 Annual costs. Tuition/fees: $32,558. Room/board: $10,880. Books/supplies: $1,620. Personal expenses: $1,550.

2005-2006 Financial aid. Need-based: 466 full-time freshmen applied for aid; 366 were judged to have need; 366 of these received aid. Average need met was 100%. Average scholarship/grant was $25,169; average loan $2,058. 81% of total undergraduate aid awarded as scholarships/grants, 19% as loans/jobs. **Non-need-based:** Awarded to 182 full-time undergraduates, including 73 freshmen. Scholarships awarded for academics, state residency. **Additional information:** Financial aid policy guarantees to meet full financial need, as calculated by college, of all admitted students. Evaluation and ratings based strictly on academic and personal qualities of each applicant, with no consideration of financial need. Full aid packages offered to most qualified students until aid budget exhausted. College need-blind for 95% to 99% of applicants.

Application procedures. Admission: Closing date 1/15 (postmark date). $60 fee, may be waived for applicants with need. Application may be submitted online. Notification by early April. Must reply by May 1 or within 2 week(s) if notified thereafter. **Financial aid:** Closing date 2/1. FAFSA, CSS PROFILE required. Applicants notified by 4/1; must reply by 5/1.

Academics. Academic Honor Code; writing course required in freshman year. **Special study options:** Accelerated study, cross-registration, double major, exchange student, honors, independent study, internships, semester at sea, student-designed major, study abroad, teacher certification program, Washington semester. Member of Five College Consortium, program in engineering and technology, engineering science program within liberal arts curriculum leading to BS degree, post-baccalaureate certificate in American studies (available to international students). **Credit/placement by examination:** AP, CLEP, IB, institutional tests. 32 credit hours maximum toward bachelor's degree. **Support services:** Learning center, study skills assistance, tutoring, writing center.

Majors. Area/ethnic studies: African-American, American, Asian, Latin American, women's. **Biology:** General, biochemistry. **Computer sciences:** Computer science. **Education:** General. **Engineering:** General, biomedical, chemical, civil, computer, electrical, environmental, mechanical, mechanics, science. **English:** English lit. **Foreign languages:** Ancient Greek, classics, comparative lit, East Asian, French, German, Italian, Latin, Portuguese, Russian, Spanish. **History:** General. **Interdisciplinary:** Ancient studies, medieval/Renaissance, neuroscience. **Math:** General. **Philosophy/religion:** Philosophy, religion. **Physical sciences:** Astronomy, astrophysics, chemistry, geology, physics. **Psychology:** General. **Social sciences:** Anthropology, economics, political science, sociology. **Visual/performing arts:** Art, art history/conservation, dance, dramatic, studio arts.

Most popular majors. Area/ethnic studies 8%, biology 9%, foreign language 9%, history 14%, psychology 11%, social sciences 16%, visual/performing arts 10%.

Computing on campus. 600 workstations in dormitories, library, computer center, student center. Dormitories wired for high-speed internet access and linked to campus network. Commuter students can connect to campus network. Online course registration, online library, helpline, repair service, student web hosting, wireless network available.

Student life. Freshman orientation: Mandatory. Program 4-5 days prior to beginning of classes. Program includes Parent Day. **Policies:** Each residence self-governed within framework of college regulations. Residents determine house responsibilities. **Housing:** Guaranteed on-campus for all undergraduates. Cooperative housing available. $300 nonrefundable deposit, deadline 5/1. French-speaking house, senior house, nontraditional age house, apartment complexes for juniors and seniors available. **Activities:** Bands, choral groups, dance, drama, literary magazine, music ensembles, musical theater, radio station, student government, student newspaper, TV station, service organizations, women's resource center, black student alliance, Asian student association, Hillel, Newman Club, Christian council, international relations club, Latina organization, Native American organization.

Athletics. NCAA. **Intercollegiate:** Basketball W, cross-country W, diving W, equestrian W, field hockey W, lacrosse W, rowing (crew) W, skiing W, soccer W, softball W, squash W, swimming W, tennis W, track and field W, volleyball W. **Intramural:** Basketball W, cross-country W, rowing (crew) W, soccer W, softball W, squash W, swimming W, tennis W, track and field W, volleyball W. **Team name:** Pioneers.

Student services. Adult student services, alcohol/substance abuse counseling, campus ministries, career counseling, services for economically disadvantaged, student employment services, financial aid counseling, health services, minority student services, on-campus daycare, personal counseling, placement for graduates, women's services. **Physically disabled:** Services for visually, speech, hearing impaired.

Contact. E-mail: admission@smith.edu
Phone: (413) 585-2500 Fax: (413) 585-2527
Debra Shaver, Director of Admission, Smith College, 7 College Lane, Northampton, MA 01063

Springfield College

Springfield, Massachusetts — **CB member**
www.spfldcol.edu — **CB code: 3763**

- Private 4-year health science and liberal arts college
- Residential campus in small city
- 2,188 degree-seeking undergraduates: 1% part-time, 48% women, 3% African American, 1% Asian American, 2% Hispanic American
- 973 degree-seeking graduate students
- 69% of applicants admitted
- SAT or ACT with writing, application essay required
- 65% graduate within 6 years

General. Founded in 1885. Regionally accredited. Adult weekend degree programs at 10 sites across the country. **Degrees:** 484 bachelor's awarded; master's, doctoral offered. **ROTC:** Army, Air Force. **Location:** 90 miles from Boston, 26 miles from Hartford, Connecticut. **Calendar:** Semester, limited summer session. **Full-time faculty:** 174 total; 78% have terminal degrees, 9% minority, 45% women. **Part-time faculty:** 168 total; 12% minority, 61% women. **Special facilities:** 81-acre campground and outdoor adventure area.

Freshman class profile. 2,326 applied, 1,610 admitted, 574 enrolled.

Mid 50% test scores		End year in good standing:	92%
SAT verbal:	460-550	Return as sophomores:	81%
SAT math:	470-570	Out-of-state:	69%
Rank in top quarter:	35%	Live on campus:	98%
Rank in top tenth:	13%		

Basis for selection. School achievement record, essay, extracurricular activities, personal references, and test scores important. Portfolio required of art majors. **Homeschooled:** Statement describing homeschool structure and mission, transcript of courses and grades, letter of recommendation (nonparent) required.

High school preparation. 16 units required. Required and recommended units include English 4, mathematics 3, social studies 2, history 1, science 3 (laboratory 2) and foreign language 3. Emphasis on science for majors in allied health fields.

2005-2006 Annual costs. Tuition/fees: $21,595. Room/board: $8,340. Books/supplies: $900. Personal expenses: $1,000.

2005-2006 Financial aid. Need-based: 62% of total undergraduate aid awarded as scholarships/grants, 38% as loans/jobs. **Additional information:** Co-operative education program available to students after freshman year.

Application procedures. Admission: Priority date 3/1; deadline 4/1 (postmark date). $50 fee, may be waived for applicants with need. Admission notification on a rolling basis beginning on or about 12/1. Must reply by May 1 or within 2 week(s) if notified thereafter. Application closing date for athletic training, physical therapy majors 12/1; closing date for physician assistant and occupational therapy majors 2/1; SAT or ACT score reports must be received by February 1. **Financial aid:** Priority date 3/15; no closing date. FAFSA, CSS PROFILE required. Applicants notified on a rolling basis starting 3/15; must reply by 5/1 or within 2 week(s) of notification.

Academics. Emphasis on practical fieldwork experiences to supplement classroom learning. **Special study options:** Combined bachelor's/graduate degree, cooperative education, cross-registration, double major, ESL, honors, independent study, internships, liberal arts/career combination, semester at sea, student-designed major, study abroad, teacher certification program. **Credit/placement by examination:** AP, CLEP, SAT, ACT, institutional tests. 30 credit hours maximum toward bachelor's degree. **Support services:** Learning center, reduced course load, study skills assistance, tutoring, writing center.

Majors. Biology: General. **Business:** Business admin. **Computer sciences:** General, computer graphics, information systems. **Conservation:** General, environmental studies. **Education:** Art, early childhood, elementary, health, physical, secondary, special. **Health:** Art therapy, athletic training, clinical lab science, clinical lab technology, EMT paramedic, health care admin, medical records admin, physician assistant, predentistry, recreational therapy. **History:** General. **Interdisciplinary:** Biological/physical sciences. **Legal studies:** Prelaw. **Liberal arts:** Arts/sciences. **Math:** General. **Parks/recreation:** Exercise sciences, facilities management, health/fitness, sports admin. **Protective services:** Law enforcement admin. **Psychology:** General. **Public administration:** Community org/advocacy, human services. **Social sciences:** Political science, sociology. **Visual/performing arts:** Art, dance.

Computing on campus. 235 workstations in dormitories, library, computer center, student center. Dormitories wired for high-speed internet access and linked to campus network. Commuter students can connect to campus network. Wireless network available.

Student life. Freshman orientation: Mandatory, $100 fee. SOAR in June to register; new student orientation immediately preceding fall semester. **Housing:** Guaranteed on-campus for all undergraduates. Coed dorms, single-sex dorms, special housing for disabled, apartments, substance-free housing available. **Activities:** Choral groups, dance, drama, literary magazine, music ensembles, musical theater, radio station, student government, student newspaper, women's group, multicultural organization, Hot Line, community volunteer program, Alpha Phi Omega, service-oriented organizations, Newman Club, Association of Christian Athletes.

Athletics. NCAA. **Intercollegiate:** Baseball M, basketball, cross-country, diving, field hockey W, football (tackle) M, golf, gymnastics, lacrosse, soccer, softball W, swimming, tennis, track and field, volleyball, wrestling M. **Intramural:** Basketball, field hockey, football (non-tackle), handball, lacrosse, racquetball, soccer, softball, swimming, tennis, track and field, volleyball, wrestling M. **Team name:** Pride.

Student services. Adult student services, alcohol/substance abuse counseling, campus ministries, career counseling, student employment services, financial aid counseling, health services, minority student services, on-campus daycare, personal counseling, placement for graduates, veterans' counselor, women's services. **Physically disabled:** Services for visually, speech, hearing impaired.

Contact. E-mail: admissions@spfldcol.edu
Phone: (413) 748-3136 Toll-free number: (800) 343-1257
Fax: (413) 748-3694
Mary DeAngelo, Director of Admissions, Springfield College, 263 Alden Street, Springfield, MA 01109

Stonehill College

Easton, Massachusetts — **CB member**
www.stonehill.edu — **CB code: 3770**

- Private 4-year liberal arts college affiliated with Roman Catholic Church
- Residential campus in large town
- 2,366 degree-seeking undergraduates: 5% part-time, 60% women, 3% African American, 3% Asian American, 3% Hispanic American, 1% international
- 12 degree-seeking graduate students
- 57% of applicants admitted
- SAT or ACT with writing, application essay required
- 83% graduate within 6 years; 30% enter graduate study

General. Founded in 1948. Regionally accredited. **Degrees:** 582 bachelor's awarded; master's offered. **ROTC:** Army. **Location:** 20 miles from Boston. **Calendar:** Semester, limited summer session. **Full-time faculty:** 132 total; 85% have terminal degrees, 8% minority, 34% women. **Part-time faculty:** 121 total; 38% have terminal degrees, 8% minority, 43% women. **Class size:** 47% < 20, 53% 20-39, less than 1% 40-49, less than 1% 50-99. **Special facilities:** Observatory.

Freshman class profile. 4,848 applied, 2,745 admitted, 619 enrolled.

Mid 50% test scores			
SAT verbal:	560-640	**Rank in top quarter:**	87%
SAT math:	570-640	**Rank in top tenth:**	48%
ACT:	23-27	**End year in good standing:**	97%
GPA 3.50 or higher:	63%	**Return as sophomores:**	90%
GPA 3.0-3.49:	29%	**Out-of-state:**	45%
GPA 2.0-2.99:	8%	**Live on campus:**	95%
		International:	1%

Basis for selection. School achievement record, class rank, test scores most important. Guidance counselor recommendation, activities, essay, campus visit also important. Other letters of recommendation also considered. **Homeschooled:** Statement describing homeschool structure and mission, transcript of courses and grades, state high school equivalency certificate required.

High school preparation. 16 units required; 20 recommended. Required and recommended units include English 4, mathematics 3-4, history 3, science 1-3 (laboratory 1-2), foreign language 2-3 and academic electives 3. Foreign language units should be in same language. 3 combined units in history, political science, social science required. Mathematics units should consist of algegra I, algebra II, and geometry. Additional units in science and mathematics recommended for science applicants. Additional math units recommended for business applicants.

2006-2007 Annual costs. Tuition/fees: $27,080. Room/board: $11,040. Books/supplies: $1,200. Personal expenses: $932.

2005-2006 Financial aid. Need-based: 519 full-time freshmen applied for aid; 398 were judged to have need; 398 of these received aid. Average need met was 82%. Average scholarship/grant was $13,594; average loan $4,798. 66% of total undergraduate aid awarded as scholarships/grants, 34% as loans/jobs. **Non-need-based:** Awarded to 735 full-time undergraduates, including 236 freshmen. Scholarships awarded for academics, athletics, leadership, minority status, music/drama, ROTC.

Application procedures. Admission: Closing date 1/15 (postmark date). $50 fee, may be waived for applicants with need. Application may be submitted online. Admission notification 4/1. Must reply by 5/1. **Financial aid:** Closing date 2/1. FAFSA, CSS PROFILE required. Applicants notified by 4/1; must reply by 5/1.

Academics. Evening technology workshops and web-based electronic portfolios are open to all students. **Special study options:** Combined bachelor's/graduate degree, cross-registration, double major, dual enrollment of high school students, honors, independent study, internships, liberal arts/career combination, New York semester, student-designed major, study abroad, teacher certification program, Washington semester. Full-time international internship sites in London, Brussels, Zaragoza, Dublin, Paris; Stonehill-Quebec exchange program; 3-2 computer engineering BA/BS program with University of Notre Dame, Indiana; Stonehill Undergraduate Research Experience (SURE) program. **Credit/placement by examination:** AP, CLEP, IB, institutional tests. 30 credit hours maximum toward bachelor's degree. **Support services:** Learning center, pre-admission summer program, reduced course load, study skills assistance, tutoring, writing center.

Majors. Area/ethnic studies: American. **Biology:** General, biochemistry. **Business:** Accounting, business admin, finance, international, marketing. **Communications:** General. **Computer sciences:** Computer science. **Education:** Early childhood, elementary. **Engineering:** Computer. **English:** English lit. **Foreign languages:** General. **Health:** Health care admin. **History:** General. **Interdisciplinary:** Gerontology, neuroscience. **Math:** General. **Philosophy/religion:** Philosophy, religion. **Physical sciences:** Chemistry. **Psychology:** General. **Public administration:** General. **Social sciences:** Criminology, economics, international relations, political science, sociology. **Visual/performing arts:** Studio arts.

Most popular majors. Biology 6%, business/marketing 22%, communications/journalism 6%, education 7%, English 7%, psychology 11%, social sciences 17%.

Computing on campus. 300 workstations in dormitories, library, computer center, student center. Dormitories wired for high-speed internet access and linked to campus network. Commuter students can connect to campus network. Online course registration, online library, helpline, student web hosting, wireless network available.

Student life. Freshman orientation: Available. Preregistration for classes offered. 2-day program in June. **Housing:** Guaranteed on-campus for all undergraduates. Coed dorms, single-sex dorms, special housing for disabled, substance-free housing available. $300 nonrefundable deposit, deadline 5/1. Special interest housing proposals considered for groups. **Activities:** Pep band, choral groups, dance, drama, film society, literary magazine, music ensembles, musical theater, radio station, student government, student newspaper, College Republicans, College Democrats, Amnesty International, BACCHUS, Into the Streets (volunteer network), Habitat for Humanity, Circle K, politics society, environmental club, campus free thought alliance club.

Athletics. NCAA. **Intercollegiate:** Baseball M, basketball, cross-country, equestrian W, field hockey W, football (tackle) M, ice hockey M, lacrosse W, soccer, softball W, tennis, track and field, volleyball W. **Intramural:** Basketball, field hockey, football (non-tackle), handball, racquetball, soccer, softball, tennis, volleyball. **Team name:** Skyhawks.

Student services. Adult student services, alcohol/substance abuse counseling, campus ministries, career counseling, services for economically disadvantaged, student employment services, financial aid counseling, health services, minority student services, personal counseling, placement for graduates, women's services. **Physically disabled:** Services for visually, speech, hearing impaired.

Contact. E-mail: admissions@stonehill.edu
Phone: (508) 565-1373 Fax: (508) 565-1545
Brian Murphy, Dean of Admissions and Enrollment, Stonehill College, 320 Washington Street, Easton, MA 02357-0100

Suffolk University

Boston, Massachusetts — **CB member**
www.suffolk.edu — **CB code: 3771**

- Private 4-year university
- Commuter campus in very large city
- 4,595 degree-seeking undergraduates: 12% part-time, 59% women, 3% African American, 7% Asian American, 4% Hispanic American, 9% international
- 3,544 degree-seeking graduate students
- 82% of applicants admitted
- SAT or ACT with writing required
- 53% graduate within 6 years; 31% enter graduate study

General. Founded in 1906. Regionally accredited. Campuses in Spain and Senegal. Branch campuses in Cape Cod, Merimack, and Franklin. **Degrees:** 807 bachelor's, 1 associate awarded; master's, doctoral, first professional offered. **ROTC:** Army. **Location:** Downtown. **Calendar:** Semester, extensive summer session. **Full-time faculty:** 280 total; 89% have terminal degrees, 12% minority, 38% women. **Part-time faculty:** 436 total; 11% have terminal degrees, 6% minority, 46% women. **Class size:** 43% < 20, 55% 20-39, 2% 40-49, less than 1% 50-99. **Special facilities:** Marine biology station, theatre, poetry center.

Freshman class profile. 6,229 applied, 5,132 admitted, 1,134 enrolled.

Mid 50% test scores		**Rank in top quarter:**	25%
SAT verbal:	460-570	**Rank in top tenth:**	10%
SAT math:	460-560	**End year in good standing:**	87%
ACT:	19-24	**Return as sophomores:**	73%
GPA 3.50 or higher:	15%	**Out-of-state:**	38%
GPA 3.0-3.49:	34%	**Live on campus:**	49%
GPA 2.0-2.99:	51%	**International:**	6%

Basis for selection. High school record including courses taken, level of study, class rank, test scores, essay important. Counselor recommendation considered. Interview recommended. Portfolio required for BFA program applicants. **Homeschooled:** Transcript of courses and grades, state high school equivalency certificate, letter of recommendation (nonparent) required. Admission Interview highly recomended.

High school preparation. 17 units required; 23 recommended. Required and recommended units include English 4, mathematics 3-4, social studies 1, history 1-2, science 2-3 (laboratory 1-2), foreign language 2-3 and academic electives 4.

2006-2007 Annual costs. Tuition/fees: $22,690. Room/board: $12,996. Books/supplies: $1,000. Personal expenses: $2,473.

2005-2006 Financial aid. Need-based: 862 full-time freshmen applied for aid; 642 were judged to have need; 641 of these received aid. Average need met was 63%. Average scholarship/grant was $6,685; average loan $3,768. 50% of total undergraduate aid awarded as scholarships/grants, 50% as loans/jobs. **Non-need-based:** Awarded to 1,039 full-time undergraduates, including 261 freshmen. Scholarships awarded for academics, alumni affiliation. **Additional information:** Foreign students may apply for institutional employment awards.

Application procedures. Admission: Priority date 3/1; no deadline. $50 fee, may be waived for applicants with need. Application may be submitted online. Admission notification on a rolling basis beginning on or about 1/14. Must reply by May 1 or within 2 week(s) if notified thereafter. Housing available on first-come first-served basis. **Financial aid:** Closing date 4/1. FAFSA, institutional form required. Applicants notified on a rolling basis starting 3/1; must reply within 2 week(s) of notification.

Academics. Special study options: Accelerated study, combined bachelor's/graduate degree, cooperative education, cross-registration, distance learning, double major, ESL, exchange student, honors, independent study, internships, liberal arts/career combination, study abroad, Washington semester. **Credit/placement by examination:** AP, CLEP, IB, SAT, ACT, institutional tests. 30 credit hours maximum toward associate degree, 30 toward bachelor's. **Support services:** Learning center, pre-admission summer program, reduced course load, remedial instruction, study skills assistance, tutoring, writing center.

Majors. Area/ethnic studies: African-American, French, German, women's. **Biology:** General, biochemistry, biomedical sciences, biophysics, environmental, marine, radiobiology. **Business:** General, accounting, business admin, entrepreneurial studies, finance, international, management information systems, marketing, office technology. **Communications:** General, advertising, broadcast journalism, journalism, media studies, organizational, political, public relations. **Communications technology:** General, radio/tv. **Computer sciences:** General, computer science, information systems. **Conservation:** Environmental science. **Education:** General. **Engineering:** Computer, electrical, environmental. **Engineering technology:** Biomedical. **English:** Creative writing, English lit. **Foreign languages:** General, French, German, Spanish. **History:** General, American, European. **Legal studies:** Paralegal, prelaw. **Liberal arts:** Arts/sciences, humanities. **Math:** General. **Philosophy/religion:** Philosophy. **Physical sciences:** General, chemistry, physics. **Protective services:** Law enforcement admin. **Psychology:** General. **Public administration:** General, policy analysis. **Social sciences:** General, criminology, economics, international economics, international relations, political science, sociology, U.S. government. **Visual/performing arts:** General, acting, art, art history/conservation, arts management, commercial/advertising art, dramatic, film/cinema, interior design, studio arts, theater history.

Most popular majors. Business/marketing 44%, communications/journalism 14%, psychology 6%, social sciences 16%.

Computing on campus. 600 workstations in dormitories, library, computer center, student center. Dormitories wired for high-speed internet access and linked to campus network. Commuter students can connect to campus network. Online course registration, online library, helpline, wireless network available.

Student life. Freshman orientation: Available, $85 fee. Preregistration for classes offered. 3-day orientation held in June and August. **Policies:** Freshmen permitted cars on campus. **Housing:** Coed dorms, substance-free housing available. $500 nonrefundable deposit, deadline 5/1. **Activities:** Jazz band, choral groups, dance, drama, literary magazine, music ensembles, musical theater, radio station, student government, student newspaper, TV station, Hillel, political science association, black student union, Hispanic association, Asian American association, international student association, Haitian American student association, service organization.

Athletics. NCAA. **Intercollegiate:** Baseball M, basketball, cross-country, golf M, ice hockey M, soccer M, softball W, tennis, volleyball W. **Intramural:** Basketball, football (non-tackle), soccer W, table tennis, volleyball. **Team name:** Rams.

Student services. Adult student services, alcohol/substance abuse counseling, campus ministries, career counseling, student employment services, financial aid counseling, health services, minority student services, personal counseling, placement for graduates, veterans' counselor, women's services. **Physically disabled:** Services for visually, speech, hearing impaired.

Contact. E-mail: admission@suffolk.edu
Phone: (617) 573-8460 Toll-free number: (800) 678-3365
Fax: (617) 742-4291
John Hamel, Director of Admissions, Suffolk University, 8 Ashburton Place, Boston, MA 02108

Tufts University

Medford, Massachusetts — **CB member**
www.tufts.edu — **CB code: 3901**

- Private 4-year university
- Residential campus in small city
- 5,048 degree-seeking undergraduates: 2% part-time, 52% women, 7% African American, 13% Asian American, 7% Hispanic American, 6% international
- 4,219 degree-seeking graduate students
- 28% of applicants admitted
- SAT or ACT with writing, SAT Subject Tests, application essay required
- 90% graduate within 6 years

General. Founded in 1852. Regionally accredited. **Degrees:** 1,240 bachelor's awarded; master's, doctoral, first professional offered. **ROTC:** Army, Navy, Air Force. **Location:** 5 miles from Boston. **Calendar:** Semester, limited summer session. **Full-time faculty:** 765 total; 39% women. **Part-time faculty:** 429 total; 44% women. **Class size:** 75% < 20, 18% 20-39, 2% 40-49, 3% 50-99, 1% >100. **Special facilities:** Computer-aided design laboratory, arts center, theater in the round, engineering project design center.

Freshman class profile. 15,536 applied, 4,398 admitted, 1,365 enrolled.

Mid 50% test scores		**Rank in top tenth:**	80%
SAT verbal:	660-740	**Return as sophomores:**	95%
SAT math:	670-740	**Out-of-state:**	78%
ACT:	28-32	**Live on campus:**	98%
Rank in top quarter:	96%	**International:**	6%

Basis for selection. School achievement record most important. School recommendation, test scores, character, personality, extracurricular participation, special talents also important. Geographical distribution, alumni relationship, minority status, socioeconomic status all considered. For applicants who submit SAT scores: 2 SAT Subject Tests required of liberal arts applicants; Math 1 or 2 and either physics or chemistry required of engineering applicants. Interview recommended.

High school preparation. Recommended units include English 4, mathematics 3, history 2, science 2 and foreign language 3. 4 math, 2 laboratory science recommended for engineering, math, and science majors.

2005-2006 Annual costs. Tuition/fees: $32,621. Room/board: $9,397. Books/supplies: $800. Personal expenses: $1,182.

2005-2006 Financial aid. All financial aid based on need. 753 full-time freshmen applied for aid; 534 were judged to have need; 534 of these received aid. Average need met was 100%. Average scholarship/grant was

$23,271; average loan $3,025. 81% of total undergraduate aid awarded as scholarships/grants, 19% as loans/jobs.

Application procedures. Admission: Closing date 1/1 (postmark date). $70 fee, may be waived for applicants with need. Application may be submitted online. Admission notification 4/1. Must reply by 5/1. **Financial aid:** Priority date 2/1, closing date 2/15. FAFSA, CSS PROFILE required. Applicants notified by 4/5; must reply by 5/1.

Academics. Special study options: Combined bachelor's/graduate degree, cross-registration, double major, exchange student, independent study, internships, liberal arts/career combination, semester at sea, student-designed major, study abroad, teacher certification program, Washington semester. Experimental college, semester exchange with Lincoln University and Swarthmore College, 3-2 programs with New England Conservatory of Music (BA/BM), School of the Museum of Fine Arts (BA/BFA) European Center in Talloires, France. **Credit/placement by examination:** AP, CLEP, IB, institutional tests. Limit 1 year of credit by acceleration. **Support services:** Learning center, study skills assistance, tutoring.

Majors. Area/ethnic studies: African-American, American, Asian, Central/Eastern European, East Asian, European, Latin American, Near/Middle Eastern, Russian/Slavic, Western European, women's. **Biology:** General, ecology. **Computer sciences:** General, computer science, information systems, programming. **Education:** Early childhood. **Engineering:** General, architectural, biomedical, chemical, civil, computer, electrical, environmental, mechanical, physics, science. **English:** American lit, British lit. **Foreign languages:** General, ancient Greek, Chinese, classics, comparative lit, French, German, Italian, Japanese, Latin, Russian, Spanish. **History:** General. **Interdisciplinary:** Math/computer science, peace/conflict. **Liberal arts:** Arts/sciences. **Math:** General, applied. **Philosophy/religion:** Philosophy, religion. **Physical sciences:** Astronomy, chemistry, geology, physics. **Psychology:** General. **Social sciences:** Anthropology, archaeology, economics, international relations, political science, sociology. **Visual/performing arts:** Art history/conservation, music history, music theory/composition, musicology, studio arts, theater history.

Most popular majors. Engineering/engineering technologies 12%, English 7%, foreign language 6%, psychology 7%, social sciences 33%, visual/performing arts 8%.

Computing on campus. 500 workstations in library, computer center. Dormitories wired for high-speed internet access and linked to campus network. Commuter students can connect to campus network. Online course registration, helpline available.

Student life. Freshman orientation: Available. Preregistration for classes offered. 3-day program prior to beginning of fall semester. **Housing:** Guaranteed on-campus for freshmen. Coed dorms, single-sex dorms, special housing for disabled, cooperative housing, fraternity/sorority housing, substance-free housing available. Culture, special interest, language houses available. **Activities:** Bands, choral groups, dance, drama, film society, literary magazine, music ensembles, musical theater, opera, radio station, student government, student newspaper, symphony orchestra, TV station, 160 student organizations.

Athletics. NCAA. **Intercollegiate:** Baseball M, basketball, cross-country, diving, fencing W, field hockey W, football (tackle) M, golf M, ice hockey M, lacrosse, rowing (crew), rugby, sailing, soccer, softball W, squash, swimming, tennis, track and field, volleyball W. **Intramural:** Basketball, fencing M, handball, racquetball, softball, squash, tennis, volleyball. **Team name:** Jumbos.

Student services. Adult student services, alcohol/substance abuse counseling, campus ministries, career counseling, services for economically disadvantaged, student employment services, financial aid counseling, health services, legal services, minority student services, on-campus daycare, personal counseling, placement for graduates, women's services. **Physically disabled:** Services for visually, speech, hearing impaired.

Contact. E-mail: admissions.inquiry@ase.tufts.edu
Phone: (617) 627-3170 Fax: (617) 627-3860
Lee Coffin, Dean of Undergraduate Admissions and Enrollment Management, Tufts University, Bendetson Hall, Medford, MA 02155-5555

University of Massachusetts Amherst

Amherst, Massachusetts **CB member**
www.umass.edu **CB code: 3917**

- Public 4-year university
- Residential campus in large town
- 18,812 degree-seeking undergraduates: 5% part-time, 50% women, 5% African American, 7% Asian American, 3% Hispanic American, 1% international
- 4,890 degree-seeking graduate students
- 80% of applicants admitted
- SAT or ACT (ACT writing recommended), application essay required
- 66% graduate within 6 years

General. Founded in 1863. Regionally accredited. **Degrees:** 4,262 bachelor's, 54 associate awarded; master's, doctoral offered. **ROTC:** Army, Air Force. **Location:** 90 miles from Boston, 30 miles from Springfield. **Calendar:** Semester, limited summer session. **Full-time faculty:** 1,148 total; 93% have terminal degrees, 16% minority, 34% women. **Part-time faculty:** 190 total; 55% have terminal degrees, 6% minority, 45% women. **Class size:** 41% < 20, 36% 20-39, 6% 40-49, 8% 50-99, 9% >100. **Special facilities:** Observatory, botanical gardens, sports arena with ice rink.

Freshman class profile. 20,205 applied, 16,240 admitted, 4,427 enrolled.

Mid 50% test scores		**Rank in top tenth:**	19%
SAT verbal:	510-620	**Return as sophomores:**	84%
SAT math:	520-630	**Out-of-state:**	21%
GPA 3.50 or higher:	42%	**Live on campus:**	95%
GPA 3.0-3.49:	41%	**Fraternities:**	2%
GPA 2.0-2.99:	17%	**Sororities:**	3%
Rank in top quarter:	51%		

Basis for selection. High school grades most important, followed by test scores, recommendations, essay, activities. Audition required of music majors and dance majors. Portfolio required of art majors. **Homeschooled:** Detailed transcript required. **Learning Disabled:** Applicants must submit diagnostic data and/or individualized educational plan. Massachusetts residents with documented learning disabilities not required to submit standardized test scores for admissions consideration.

High school preparation. 16 units required. Required units include English 4, mathematics 3, social studies 2, science 3 (laboratory 2), foreign language 2 and academic electives 2.

2005-2006 Annual costs. Tuition/fees: $9,278; $18,397 out-of-state. Room/board: $6,517. Books/supplies: $1,000. Personal expenses: $1,000.

2004-2005 Financial aid. Need-based: 2,581 full-time freshmen applied for aid; 1,785 were judged to have need; 1,681 of these received aid. Average need met was 81%. Average scholarship/grant was $6,366; average loan $1,281. 46% of total undergraduate aid awarded as scholarships/grants, 54% as loans/jobs. **Non-need-based:** Awarded to 801 full-time undergraduates, including 94 freshmen. Scholarships awarded for academics, art, athletics, music/drama, ROTC, state residency.

Application procedures. Admission: Closing date 1/15 (postmark date). $40 fee ($50 out-of-state), may be waived for applicants with need. Application may be submitted online. Admission notification on a rolling basis beginning on or about 12/15. Must reply by May 1 or within 2 week(s) if notified thereafter. **Financial aid:** Priority date 3/1; no closing date. FAFSA required. Applicants notified on a rolling basis starting 4/1.

Academics. Students may take courses at Amherst, Hampshire, Mt. Holyoke and Smith Colleges at no extra charge. **Special study options:** Accelerated study, cooperative education, cross-registration, distance learning, double major, dual enrollment of high school students, ESL, exchange student, honors, independent study, internships, liberal arts/career combination, student-designed major, study abroad, teacher certification program. University Without Walls program offers individualized degrees to working adults; residential academic programs allow first-year students to live and take classes together. **Credit/placement by examination:** AP, CLEP, IB, institutional tests. 30 credit hours maximum toward bachelor's degree. Credit awarded for International Baccalaureate scores of 4-7. **Support services:** Learning center, remedial instruction, study skills assistance, tutoring, writing center.

Honors college/program. First-year students admitted by invitation, approximately 500 freshmen admitted. Continuing students with GPA of 3.2 or above eligible to enroll. Interdisciplinary seminars, enriched honors courses, colloquia, independent study, service learning offered; honors thesis, project, or activity required.

Majors. Agriculture: Animal sciences, food science, plant sciences. **Architecture:** Environmental design, landscape. **Area/ethnic studies:** African-American, Near/Middle Eastern, Russian/Slavic, women's. **Biology:** General, Biochemistry/biophysics and molecular biology, microbiology. **Business:** Accounting, business admin, finance, hospitality admin, marketing. **Communications:** General, journalism. **Computer sciences:** Computer science. **Conservation:** Environmental science, forestry, management/policy, wildlife, wood science. **Education:** General. **Engineering:** Chemical, civil, computer, electrical, industrial, mechanical. **English:** English lit. **Family/consumer sciences:** Human nutrition. **Foreign languages:** Chinese, classics, comparative lit, French, German, Italian, Japanese, linguistics, Portuguese,

Spanish. **Health:** Clinical lab science, communication disorders, nursing (RN), predentistry, premedicine, preveterinary. **History:** General. **Interdisciplinary:** Biological/physical sciences. **Legal studies:** General. **Liberal arts:** Humanities. **Math:** General. **Parks/recreation:** Exercise sciences, sports admin. **Philosophy/religion:** Judaic, philosophy. **Physical sciences:** Astronomy, chemistry, geology, physics. **Psychology:** General. **Social sciences:** Anthropology, applied economics, economics, geography, political science, sociology. **Visual/performing arts:** Art history/conservation, dance, dramatic, interior design, studio arts.

Most popular majors. Business/marketing 14%, communications/journalism 7%, education 7%, engineering/engineering technologies 7%, psychology 6%, social sciences 13%.

Computing on campus. 450 workstations in dormitories, library, computer center, student center. Dormitories wired for high-speed internet access and linked to campus network. Commuter students can connect to campus network. Online course registration, online library, helpline, repair service, student web hosting, wireless network available.

Student life. **Freshman orientation:** Mandatory, $125 fee. Preregistration for classes offered. Program includes placement testing, registration, meeting with faculty adviser. **Policies:** Students required to live on campus through sophomore year unless living with relatives, married, or veteran of U.S. armed forces. Freshmen permitted cars on campus. **Housing:** Guaranteed on-campus for freshmen. Coed dorms, single-sex dorms, apartments, fraternity/sorority housing, substance-free housing available. Special interest housing; residential academic programs for first-year students. Gradual penalty for cancellation of housing up to $300. **Activities:** Bands, choral groups, dance, drama, film society, literary magazine, music ensembles, musical theater, opera, radio station, student government, student newspaper, symphony orchestra, TV station, 200 student organizations.

Athletics. NCAA. **Intercollegiate:** Baseball M, basketball, cheerleading, cross-country, diving, field hockey W, football (tackle) M, ice hockey M, lacrosse, rowing (crew) W, skiing, soccer, softball W, swimming, tennis W, track and field. **Intramural:** Basketball, cross-country, field hockey W, football (non-tackle), ice hockey, lacrosse W, soccer, softball, swimming, tennis, volleyball, wrestling. **Team name:** Minutemen/ Minutewomen.

Student services. Adult student services, alcohol/substance abuse counseling, career counseling, student employment services, financial aid counseling, health services, legal services, minority student services, on-campus daycare, personal counseling, placement for graduates, veterans' counselor, women's services. **Physically disabled:** Services for visually, speech, hearing impaired. **Learning disabled:** Comprehensive services available.

Contact. E-mail: mail@admissions.umass.edu
Phone: (413) 545-0222 Fax: (413) 545-4312
Kevin Kelly, Vice Chancellor for Student Affairs and Campus Life, University of Massachusetts Amherst, University Admissions Center, Amherst, MA 01003-9291

University of Massachusetts Boston

Boston, Massachusetts **CB member**
www.umb.edu **CB code: 3924**

- Public 4-year university
- Commuter campus in very large city
- 7,621 degree-seeking undergraduates: 28% part-time, 58% women, 15% African American, 12% Asian American, 7% Hispanic American, 1% Native American, 4% international
- 2,407 degree-seeking graduate students
- 60% of applicants admitted
- SAT or ACT (ACT writing optional), application essay required

General. Founded in 1964. Regionally accredited. **Degrees:** 1,578 bachelor's awarded; master's, doctoral offered. **Location:** 3 miles from downtown. **Calendar:** Semester, extensive summer session. **Full-time faculty:** 445 total; 96% have terminal degrees, 21% minority, 46% women. **Part-time faculty:** 368 total; 33% have terminal degrees, 14% minority, 57% women. **Class size:** 48% < 20, 47% 20-39, 2% 40-49, 2% 50-99, less than 1% >100. **Special facilities:** Tropical greenhouse, observatory, adaptive computer laboratory.

Freshman class profile. 3,174 applied, 1,920 admitted, 781 enrolled.

Mid 50% test scores		GPA 2.0-2.99:	52%
SAT verbal:	460-570	Return as sophomores:	71%
SAT math:	470-570	Out-of-state:	6%
GPA 3.50 or higher:	16%	International:	3%
GPA 3.0-3.49:	32%		

Basis for selection. School achievement record, range of test scores, high school GPA most important. Recommendations, essay also important. Extracurricular activities considered. Grades for college preparatory background B- or better. Interview recommended for nontraditional students.

High school preparation. 16 units required. Required units include English 4, mathematics 3, history 2, science 3 (laboratory 2), foreign language 2 and academic electives 2.

2005-2006 Annual costs. Tuition/fees: $8,265; $19,320 out-of-state.

2004-2005 Financial aid. **Need-based:** 445 full-time freshmen applied for aid; 379 were judged to have need; 370 of these received aid. Average need met was 86%. Average scholarship/grant was $6,046; average loan $2,009. 41% of total undergraduate aid awarded as scholarships/grants, 59% as loans/jobs. **Non-need-based:** Awarded to 644 full-time undergraduates, including 101 freshmen. Scholarships awarded for academics, leadership, ROTC. **Additional information:** Some Massachusetts state employees and Massachusetts Vietnam veterans eligible for tuition waiver. Some waivers available based on talent and academic excellence.

Application procedures. **Admission:** Priority date 3/1; deadline 6/1. $40 fee, may be waived for applicants with need. Application may be submitted online. Admission notification on a rolling basis. Must reply by May 1 or within 3 week(s) if notified thereafter. **Financial aid:** Priority date 3/1; no closing date. FAFSA required. Applicants notified on a rolling basis starting 4/1; must reply within 4 week(s) of notification.

Academics. Certificates available in many areas, including communication studies, computer and information sciences, technical and business writing, international relations, accounting, hydrogeology, alcohol/substance abuse, Spanish translation, management information systems. **Special study options:** Accelerated study, combined bachelor's/graduate degree, cooperative education, cross-registration, distance learning, double major, dual enrollment of high school students, ESL, exchange student, honors, independent study, internships, liberal arts/career combination, student-designed major, study abroad, teacher certification program. 2-2 programs in engineering with area institutions. **Credit/placement by examination:** AP, CLEP, SAT, ACT, institutional tests. 90 credit hours maximum toward bachelor's degree. **Support services:** Learning center, pre-admission summer program, reduced course load, remedial instruction, study skills assistance, tutoring, writing center.

Majors. **Area/ethnic studies:** African-American, American, women's. **Biology:** General, biochemistry. **Business:** Business admin, labor relations. **Computer sciences:** General. **Education:** Physical. **Engineering:** Physics. **English:** English lit. **Foreign languages:** Classics, French, German, Italian, Russian, Spanish. **Health:** Clinical lab science, nursing (RN). **History:** General. **Interdisciplinary:** Gerontology. **Legal studies:** General. **Math:** General. **Philosophy/religion:** Philosophy. **Physical sciences:** Chemistry, physics. **Protective services:** Criminal justice. **Psychology:** General. **Public administration:** General, community org/advocacy, human services. **Social sciences:** General, anthropology, economics, geography, political science, sociology. **Visual/performing arts:** Art, dramatic.

Most popular majors. Biology 6%, business/marketing 24%, English 8%, health sciences 8%, psychology 13%, social sciences 17%.

Computing on campus. 315 workstations in library, computer center, student center. Commuter students can connect to campus network. Online course registration, online library, helpline, repair service, wireless network available.

Student life. **Freshman orientation:** Mandatory, $25 fee. Preregistration for classes offered. **Policies:** Freshmen permitted cars on campus. **Housing:** Housing referral services available. **Activities:** Bands, choral groups, dance, drama, film society, literary magazine, music ensembles, radio station, student government, student newspaper, symphony orchestra, 70 organizations available.

Athletics. NCAA. **Intercollegiate:** Baseball M, basketball, cross-country, ice hockey M, lacrosse M, soccer, softball W, tennis, track and field, volleyball W. **Intramural:** Basketball, ice hockey M, racquetball, sailing, soccer, softball, squash, tennis, volleyball. **Team name:** Beacons.

Student services. Adult student services, alcohol/substance abuse counseling, campus ministries, career counseling, student employment services, health services, legal services, minority student services, on-campus daycare, personal counseling, placement for graduates, veterans' counselor. **Physically disabled:** Services for visually, speech, hearing impaired.

Contact. E-mail: undergrad@umb.edu
Phone: (617) 287-6100 Fax: (617) 287-5999
Liliana Mickle, Director of Admissions, University of Massachusetts Boston, 100 Morrissey Boulevard, Boston, MA 02125-3393

University of Massachusetts Dartmouth

North Dartmouth, Massachusetts **CB member**
www.umassd.edu **CB code: 3786**

- Public 4-year university
- Commuter campus in large town
- 7,173 degree-seeking undergraduates: 11% part-time, 50% women, 6% African American, 3% Asian American, 2% Hispanic American
- 776 degree-seeking graduate students
- 74% of applicants admitted
- SAT or ACT, application essay required
- 50% graduate within 6 years

General. Founded in 1895. Regionally accredited. **Degrees:** 1,042 bachelor's awarded; master's, doctoral offered. **ROTC:** Army. **Location:** 60 miles from Boston, 30 miles from Providence, Rhode Island. **Calendar:** Semester, extensive summer session. **Full-time faculty:** 355 total; 71% have terminal degrees, 16% minority, 36% women. **Part-time faculty:** 216 total; 9% minority, 49% women. **Class size:** 38% < 20, 46% 20-39, 8% 40-49, 6% 50-99, 2% >100. **Special facilities:** Observatory, marine research vessel, coastal marine laboratory, full art studios, Jewish culture and Portuguese studies centers, Robert F. Kennedy assassination archive.

Freshman class profile. 6,432 applied, 4,730 admitted, 1,545 enrolled.

Mid 50% test scores		**GPA 2.0-2.99:**	50%
SAT verbal:	480-570	**Rank in top quarter:**	39%
SAT math:	490-590	**Rank in top tenth:**	9%
ACT:	20-24	**Out-of-state:**	4%
GPA 3.50 or higher:	19%	**Live on campus:**	75%
GPA 3.0-3.49:	31%		

Basis for selection. High school record, test scores most important; class rank, essay, recommendations considered. Minimum high school GPA 2.0. Recommended high school GPA 3.0. Audition required for music majors; portfolio required for design majors. **Homeschooled:** State high school equivalency certificate required. Must get certification or equivalency from local high school. **Learning Disabled:** SAT scores may be waived for Massachusetts students with documented disability.

High school preparation. 16 units required. Required units include English 4, mathematics 3, social studies 1, history 1, science 3 (laboratory 2), foreign language 2 and academic electives 2. One American history unit required. Programs in science, engineering and business require additional math units. Science and engineering require physical science. 2 foreign language units must be same language.

2005-2006 Annual costs. Tuition/fees: $8,036; $17,638 out-of-state. Out-of-state students pay required fees of $9,539. Room/board: $8,268. Books/supplies: $600. Personal expenses: $1,244.

Financial aid. Non-need-based: Scholarships awarded for academics, minority status, ROTC, state residency.

Application procedures. Admission: No deadline. $35 fee ($55 out-of-state), may be waived for applicants with need. Application may be submitted online. Admission notification on a rolling basis beginning on or about 1/1. Must reply by May 1 or within 2 week(s) if notified thereafter. Competitive programs may be filled by March 1. Nursing closes by late January. Freshman applicants advised to apply before end of December and not later than March. **Financial aid:** Priority date 3/1; no closing date. FAFSA required. Applicants notified on a rolling basis starting 3/25; must reply within 3 week(s) of notification.

Academics. Alternative admissions program for academically disadvantaged Massachusetts residents; program offers special freshman curriculum and counseling support. **Special study options:** Combined bachelor's/graduate degree, cooperative education, cross-registration, distance learning, double major, dual enrollment of high school students, honors, independent study, internships, student-designed major, study abroad, teacher certification program, Washington semester. **Credit/placement by examination:** AP, CLEP, IB, SAT, ACT, institutional tests. 30 credit hours maximum toward bachelor's degree. **Support services:** Learning center, reduced course load, remedial instruction, study skills assistance, tutoring, writing center.

Majors. Biology: General. **Business:** Accounting, business admin, finance, management information systems, marketing. **Computer sciences:** General. **Education:** Art. **Engineering:** Civil, computer, electrical, mechanical, textile. **English:** English lit. **Foreign languages:** French, Portuguese, Spanish. **Health:** Clinical lab science, nursing (RN). **History:** General. **Liberal arts:** Arts/sciences. **Math:** General. **Philosophy/religion:** Philosophy. **Physical sciences:** Chemistry, physics. **Psychology:** General. **Social sciences:** Economics, political science, sociology. **Visual/performing arts:** General, art history/conservation, ceramics, commercial/advertising art, design, fiber arts, metal/jewelry, multimedia, painting, photography, sculpture, studio arts.

Most popular majors. Business/marketing 28%, engineering/engineering technologies 9%, health sciences 7%, psychology 9%, social sciences 12%, visual/performing arts 11%.

Computing on campus. 368 workstations in dormitories, library, computer center, student center. Dormitories wired for high-speed internet access and linked to campus network. Commuter students can connect to campus network. Helpline, repair service, wireless network available.

Student life. Freshman orientation: Mandatory, $200 fee. Preregistration for classes offered. 3-day, 2-night program in July and August. **Policies:** Freshmen permitted cars on campus. **Housing:** Coed dorms, special housing for disabled, apartments, substance-free housing available. $200 partly refundable deposit, deadline 5/1. Quiet substance-free, smoke-free housing, program-dedicated suites available. **Activities:** Bands, choral groups, dance, drama, literary magazine, music ensembles, musical theater, radio station, student government, student newspaper, symphony orchestra, women's center, Portuguese center, Unity House, Indian student organization, Arab student organization, Luso-American student organization, Taiwanese student organization, MassPIRG.

Athletics. NCAA. **Intercollegiate:** Baseball M, basketball, cheerleading M, cross-country, diving, equestrian W, field hockey W, football (tackle) M, golf M, ice hockey M, lacrosse, soccer, softball W, swimming, tennis, track and field, volleyball W. **Intramural:** Badminton, basketball, cross-country, football (non-tackle), sailing, soccer, softball, swimming, table tennis, tennis, volleyball. **Team name:** Corsairs.

Student services. Adult student services, alcohol/substance abuse counseling, campus ministries, career counseling, student employment services, financial aid counseling, health services, minority student services, on-campus daycare, personal counseling, placement for graduates, veterans' counselor, women's services. **Physically disabled:** Services for visually, speech, hearing impaired.

Contact. E-mail: admissions@umassd.edu
Phone: (508) 999-8605 Fax: (508) 999-8755
Steven Briggs, Director of Admissions, University of Massachusetts Dartmouth, 285 Old Westport Road, North Dartmouth, MA 02747-2300

University of Massachusetts Lowell

Lowell, Massachusetts **CB member**
www.uml.edu **CB code: 3911**

- Public 4-year university
- Commuter campus in small city
- 5,695 full-time, degree-seeking undergraduates
- 2,365 graduate students
- 63% of applicants admitted
- SAT or ACT (ACT writing optional), application essay required
- 48% graduate within 6 years

General. Founded in 1894. Regionally accredited. **Degrees:** 1,324 bachelor's, 41 associate awarded; master's, doctoral offered. **ROTC:** Air Force. **Location:** 25 miles from Boston, 45 miles from Worcester. **Calendar:** Semester, extensive summer session. **Full-time faculty:** 383 total; 18% minority, 34% women. **Part-time faculty:** 240 total; 5% minority, 45% women. **Special facilities:** Industrial history center, teaching and research laboratories in sound recording technology, digital imaging, wellness resource room.

Freshman class profile. 4,766 applied, 3,020 admitted, 1,088 enrolled.

Mid 50% test scores		**GPA 2.0-2.99:**	42%
SAT verbal:	490-580	**Return as sophomores:**	74%
SAT math:	510-610	**Out-of-state:**	8%
GPA 3.50 or higher:	23%	**International:**	1%
GPA 3.0-3.49:	35%		

Basis for selection. School record, test scores, recommendations most important. Interview recommended. Audition required of music majors.

High school preparation. 16 units required. Required units include English 4, mathematics 3, social studies 2, science 3 (laboratory 2), foreign language 2 and academic electives 2.

2005-2006 Annual costs. Tuition/fees: $8,166; $19,066 out-of-state. Room/board: $6,311. Books/supplies: $600. Personal expenses: $800.

2004-2005 Financial aid. Need-based: 745 full-time freshmen applied for aid; 486 were judged to have need; 473 of these received aid. Average

need met was 94%. Average scholarship/grant was $3,720; average loan $2,545. 41% of total undergraduate aid awarded as scholarships/grants, 59% as loans/jobs. **Non-need-based:** Awarded to 929 full-time undergraduates, including 147 freshmen. Scholarships awarded for academics, art, athletics, ROTC.

Application procedures. Admission: Priority date 7/1; no deadline. $20 fee ($35 out-of-state), may be waived for applicants with need. Application may be submitted online. Admission notification on a rolling basis beginning on or about 4/1. Must reply by May 1 or within 2 week(s) if notified thereafter. **Financial aid:** Priority date 3/1; no closing date. FAFSA required. Applicants notified on a rolling basis starting 3/25.

Academics. Special focus on applied science and technology; coursework emphasizes context and implications of each discipline. Funded research initatives available in nanotechnology, bioinformatics, advanced materials, photonics. **Special study options:** Accelerated study, combined bachelor's/graduate degree, cooperative education, cross-registration, distance learning, double major, dual enrollment of high school students, honors, internships, liberal arts/career combination, study abroad, teacher certification program. **Credit/placement by examination:** AP, CLEP, institutional tests. 30 credit hours maximum toward bachelor's degree. **Support services:** Learning center, pre-admission summer program, reduced course load, study skills assistance, tutoring, writing center.

Majors. Area/ethnic studies: American. **Biology:** General. **Business:** Business admin, entrepreneurial studies. **Computer sciences:** Computer science, information systems. **Conservation:** General, environmental science. **Education:** Health, music. **Engineering:** Chemical, civil, electrical, mechanical, polymer. **Engineering technology:** Civil, electrical, industrial. **Foreign languages:** General. **Health:** Clinical lab science, nursing (RN). **History:** General. **Liberal arts:** Arts/sciences. **Math:** General, applied. **Parks/recreation:** Exercise sciences. **Philosophy/religion:** Philosophy. **Physical sciences:** Chemistry, physics. **Protective services:** Law enforcement admin. **Psychology:** General. **Social sciences:** Economics, political science, sociology. **Visual/performing arts:** General, music performance, studio arts.

Most popular majors. Business/marketing 22%, computer/information sciences 13%, engineering/engineering technologies 12%, health sciences 8%, liberal arts 6%, psychology 7%, security/protective services 9%, visual/performing arts 8%.

Computing on campus. 4,000 workstations in dormitories, library, computer center. Dormitories linked to campus network. Commuter students can connect to campus network. Online library, helpline available.

Student life. Freshman orientation: Mandatory. Preregistration for classes offered. **Policies:** Freshmen permitted cars on campus. **Housing:** Coed dorms, single-sex dorms, special housing for disabled, apartments, cooperative housing available. $200 deposit. **Activities:** Bands, choral groups, dance, drama, film society, literary magazine, music ensembles, radio station, student government, student newspaper, symphony orchestra, Abundant Life Christian Fellowship, Chi Alpha, Latter-day Saints student association, association of students of African origin, Cambodian student association, Latin American student association, community service organization, College Democrats, College Republicans.

Athletics. NCAA. **Intercollegiate:** Baseball M, basketball, cross-country, field hockey W, football (tackle) M, golf M, ice hockey M, lacrosse M, rowing (crew), soccer, softball W, tennis, track and field, volleyball W. **Intramural:** Badminton, basketball, bowling, diving, equestrian W, ice hockey, racquetball, rowing (crew), soccer, softball, swimming, table tennis, tennis, volleyball. **Team name:** River Hawks.

Student services. Adult student services, alcohol/substance abuse counseling, campus ministries, career counseling, financial aid counseling, health services, personal counseling, placement for graduates, veterans' counselor. **Physically disabled:** Services for visually, speech, hearing impaired.

Contact. E-mail: admissions@uml.edu
Phone: (978) 934-3931 Toll-free number: (800) 410-4607
Fax: (978) 934-3086
Michael Belcher, Co-Director Admissions, University of Massachusetts Lowell, 883 Broadway Street, Room 110, Lowell, MA 01854-5104

Wellesley College

Wellesley, Massachusetts — **CB member**
www.wellesley.edu — **CB code: 3957**

- Private 4-year liberal arts college for women
- Residential campus in large town
- 2,224 degree-seeking undergraduates: 1% part-time, 100% women, 6% African American, 27% Asian American, 7% Hispanic American, 8% international
- 34% of applicants admitted
- SAT or ACT with writing, application essay required
- 93% graduate within 6 years; 22% enter graduate study

General. Founded in 1870. Regionally accredited. **Degrees:** 576 bachelor's awarded. **ROTC:** Army, Air Force. **Location:** 12 miles from Boston. **Calendar:** Semester, limited summer session. **Full-time faculty:** 227 total; 97% have terminal degrees, 22% minority, 51% women. **Part-time faculty:** 102 total; 83% have terminal degrees, 13% minority, 71% women. **Class size:** 63% < 20, 34% 20-39, 1% 40-49, 2% 50-99, less than 1% >100. **Special facilities:** Science center with X-ray diffractometer, nuclear magnetic resonance, spectrometers (NMR and microMRI), electron microscopes, argon and dye lasers, observatory with three telescopes (6-, 12-, and 24-inch), art museum, cultural center, greenhouses, botanic gardens, arboretum, media and technology center with linear editing room for video, digital-based video editing suite, plotter, film recorder, slide scanner.

Freshman class profile. 4,347 applied, 1,463 admitted, 605 enrolled.

Mid 50% test scores		End year in good standing:	98%
SAT verbal:	660-750	Return as sophomores:	94%
SAT math:	650-730	Out-of-state:	86%
ACT:	28-31	Live on campus:	100%
Rank in top quarter:	95%	International:	8%
Rank in top tenth:	77%		

Basis for selection. Rigor of secondary school record, recommendations, test scores, essay, and character/personal qualities very important. If SAT submitted, 2 SAT Subject Tests required. Interview recommended.

High school preparation. Recommended units include English 4, mathematics 4, social studies 4, history 4, science 3 (laboratory 2) and foreign language 4.

2005-2006 Annual costs. Tuition/fees: $31,348. Room/board: $9,682. Books/supplies: $800. Personal expenses: $1,200.

2005-2006 Financial aid. All financial aid based on need. 454 full-time freshmen applied for aid; 364 were judged to have need; 364 of these received aid. Average need met was 100%. Average scholarship/grant was $26,239; average loan $2,463. 87% of total undergraduate aid awarded as scholarships/grants, 13% as loans/jobs.

Application procedures. Admission: Closing date 1/15 (postmark date). $50 fee, may be waived for applicants with need. Application may be submitted online. Admission notification 4/1. Must reply by 5/1. Application fee waived for online applications. **Financial aid:** Closing date 1/15. FAFSA, institutional form, CSS PROFILE required. Applicants notified by 4/1; must reply by 5/1.

Academics. Special study options: Cross-registration, double major, dual enrollment of high school students, exchange student, honors, independent study, internships, semester at sea, student-designed major, study abroad, teacher certification program, Washington semester. **Credit/placement by examination:** AP, CLEP, IB, institutional tests. **Support services:** Learning center, reduced course load, study skills assistance, tutoring, writing center.

Majors. Architecture: Architecture. **Area/ethnic studies:** African, African-American, American, Asian, Central/Eastern European, East Asian, European, Latin American, Russian/Slavic, women's. **Biology:** General, biochemistry. **Computer sciences:** General, computer science. **Conservation:** Environmental studies. **Engineering:** General. **English:** English lit. **Foreign languages:** General, ancient Greek, Chinese, classics, comparative lit, French, German, Italian, Japanese, Latin, linguistics, Russian, Spanish. **History:** General. **Interdisciplinary:** Biological/physical sciences, classical/archaeology, medieval/Renaissance, neuroscience, peace/conflict, science/society. **Math:** General. **Philosophy/religion:** Judaic, philosophy, religion. **Physical sciences:** Astronomy, chemistry, geology, physics. **Psychology:** General. **Social sciences:** Anthropology, archaeology, economics, international relations, political science, sociology. **Visual/performing arts:** Art history/conservation, dramatic, music history, studio arts.

Most popular majors. Area/ethnic studies 9%, biology 6%, English 7%, foreign language 10%, interdisciplinary studies 6%, psychology 12%, social sciences 26%, visual/performing arts 8%.

Computing on campus. 481 workstations in dormitories, library, computer center, student center. Dormitories wired for high-speed internet access and linked to campus network. Commuter students can connect to campus network. Online course registration, online library, helpline, repair service, student web hosting, wireless network available.

Student life. Freshman orientation: Mandatory. Preregistration for classes offered. Multiday program held in late August. **Housing:** Guaranteed on-campus for all undergraduates. Special housing for disabled, apartments, cooperative housing, substance-free housing available. $300 deposit, deadline 5/1. Pets allowed in dorm rooms. French and Spanish houses available. **Activities:** Jazz band, choral groups, dance, drama, film society, literary magazine, music ensembles, radio station, student government, student newspaper, symphony orchestra, black student club, Latina student club, Asian students union, Hillel, Al-Muslimat, Intervarsity Christian Fellowship, international organization, political and legislative action organization, Best Buddies, Habitat for Humanity.

Athletics. NCAA. **Intercollegiate:** Basketball W, cross-country W, diving W, fencing W, field hockey W, golf W, lacrosse W, rowing (crew) W, soccer W, softball W, swimming W, tennis W, track and field W, volleyball W. **Intramural:** Basketball W, ice hockey W, racquetball W, rowing (crew) W, rugby W, sailing W, soccer W, table tennis W. **Team name:** Wellesley Blue.

Student services. Adult student services, alcohol/substance abuse counseling, campus ministries, career counseling, services for economically disadvantaged, student employment services, financial aid counseling, health services, minority student services, on-campus daycare, personal counseling, placement for graduates, women's services. **Physically disabled:** Services for visually, hearing impaired.

Contact. E-mail: admission@wellesley.edu
Phone: (781) 283-2270 Fax: (781) 283-3678
Jennifer Desjarlais, Dean of Admission, Wellesley College, 106 Central Street, Wellesley, MA 02481-8203

Wentworth Institute of Technology

Boston, Massachusetts — **CB member**
www.wit.edu — **CB code: 3958**

- Private 4-year engineering and technical college
- Residential campus in very large city
- 3,579 degree-seeking undergraduates: 12% part-time, 20% women, 4% African American, 5% Asian American, 3% Hispanic American, 3% international
- 60% of applicants admitted
- SAT or ACT with writing, application essay required
- 42% graduate within 6 years

General. Founded in 1904. Regionally accredited. Cooperative education program. Member of Colleges of the Fenway. **Degrees:** 501 bachelor's, 170 associate awarded. **ROTC:** Army. **Location:** 2 miles from downtown. **Calendar:** Semester, limited summer session. **Full-time faculty:** 115 total. **Part-time faculty:** 124 total. **Class size:** 36% < 20, 60% 20-39, 2% 40-49, 2% 50-99.

Freshman class profile. 3,040 applied, 1,825 admitted, 832 enrolled.

Mid 50% test scores			
SAT verbal:	470-510	Return as sophomores:	80%
SAT math:	560-600	Out-of-state:	45%
ACT:	21-25	Live on campus:	77%
End year in good standing:	90%	International:	2%

Basis for selection. School achievement record most important, followed by test scores. **Homeschooled:** Transcript of courses and grades, letter of recommendation (nonparent) required. Course content description may be requested.

High school preparation. 8 units required. Required and recommended units include English 4, mathematics 3-4, science 1-2 (laboratory 1-2). 4 units of college-preparatory mathematics, 1 unit physics recommended for many programs. Architecture program requires drafting.

2005-2006 Annual costs. Tuition/fees: $18,500. Tuition includes laptop. Room/board: $9,000. Books/supplies: $1,000. Personal expenses: $1,000.

2004-2005 Financial aid. Need-based: 852 full-time freshmen applied for aid; 568 were judged to have need; 568 of these received aid. Average need met was 40%. Average scholarship/grant was $2,163; average loan $3,076. 32% of total undergraduate aid awarded as scholarships/grants, 68% as loans/jobs. **Non-need-based:** Awarded to 1,294 full-time undergraduates, including 689 freshmen. Scholarships awarded for academics, leadership, ROTC.

Application procedures. Admission: Priority date 5/1; no deadline. $30 fee, may be waived for applicants with need. Application must be submitted on paper. Admission notification on a rolling basis beginning on or about 10/30. Must reply by May 1 or within 2 week(s) if notified thereafter. **Financial aid:** Priority date 3/1; no closing date. FAFSA required. Applicants notified on a rolling basis starting 3/15; must reply within 2 week(s) of notification.

Academics. Some bachelor's programs require 5 years. All bachelor's candidates required to complete 2 semesters full-time co-op. Architecture students enter 2-year core curriculum, must petition to enter junior year. **Special study options:** Cooperative education, cross-registration, honors, independent study, student-designed major, study abroad, weekend college. Cross-registration with Simmons College, Emmanuel College, Wheelock College, Massachusetts College of Pharmacy and Health Sciences, Massachusetts College of Art (Colleges of The Fenway). **Credit/placement by examination:** AP, CLEP, institutional tests. **Support services:** Learning center, reduced course load, study skills assistance, tutoring.

Majors. Architecture: Architecture. **Business:** Construction management. **Computer sciences:** General, computer science, information systems. **Construction:** Maintenance. **Engineering:** Electrical, mechanical. **Engineering technology:** General, architectural, civil, computer, electrical, industrial management, mechanical. **Family/consumer sciences:** Facilities/event planning. **Visual/performing arts:** Industrial design, interior design.

Most popular majors. Architecture 8%, business/marketing 6%, computer/information sciences 14%, engineering/engineering technologies 47%.

Computing on campus. 370 workstations in dormitories, library, computer center. Dormitories wired for high-speed internet access and linked to campus network. Commuter students can connect to campus network. Online course registration, helpline, wireless network available.

Student life. Freshman orientation: Mandatory. Preregistration for classes offered. Week-long session held the week before classes begin. **Housing:** Coed dorms available. $500 deposit, deadline 5/1. Apartments available for upperclassmen. **Activities:** Choral groups, drama, film society, musical theater, radio station, student government, student newspaper, honor society, society of women engineers, student association of interior design, solar-powered vehicle club, National Society of Black Engineers, Asian student association, architecture club, international student organization.

Athletics. NCAA. **Intercollegiate:** Baseball M, basketball, golf M, ice hockey M, lacrosse M, rifle, soccer, softball W, tennis, volleyball. **Team name:** Leopards.

Student services. Alcohol/substance abuse counseling, career counseling, student employment services, financial aid counseling, health services, minority student services, personal counseling, placement for graduates, women's services.

Contact. E-mail: admissions@wit.edu
Phone: (617) 989-4000 Toll-free number: (800) 556-0610
Fax: (617) 989-4010
Director of Admissions, Wentworth Institute of Technology, 550 Huntington Avenue, Boston, MA 02115

Western New England College

Springfield, Massachusetts — **CB member**
www.wnec.edu — **CB code: 3962**

- Private 4-year business college
- Residential campus in small city
- 2,828 degree-seeking undergraduates: 17% part-time, 38% women, 4% African American, 2% Asian American, 3% Hispanic American
- 887 degree-seeking graduate students
- 74% of applicants admitted
- SAT or ACT (ACT writing optional) required
- 60% graduate within 6 years; 14% enter graduate study

General. Founded in 1919. Regionally accredited. **Degrees:** 727 bachelor's awarded; master's, first professional offered. **ROTC:** Army, Air Force. **Location:** 95 miles from Boston, 20 miles from Hartford. **Calendar:** Semester, limited summer session. **Full-time faculty:** 164 total; 92% have terminal degrees, 11% minority, 35% women. **Part-time faculty:** 156 total. **Class size:** 50% < 20, 50% 20-39, less than 1% 40-49.

Freshman class profile. 4,343 applied, 3,193 admitted, 666 enrolled.

Mid 50% test scores			
SAT verbal:	480-570	GPA 2.0-2.99:	49%
SAT math:	480-600	Rank in top quarter:	32%
ACT:	20-24	Rank in top tenth:	10%
GPA 3.50 or higher:	23%	Return as sophomores:	75%
GPA 3.0-3.49:	28%	Out-of-state:	67%
		Live on campus:	91%

Basis for selection. School achievement record, test scores, recommendation most important. Interview, class rank, extracurricular activities also considered. Interview and essay recommended.

High school preparation. 10 units required; 18 recommended. Required and recommended units include English 4, mathematics 2-4, social studies 1-2, history 1-2, science 1-2 (laboratory 1-2) and foreign language 2. One American history required. Additional science and math required for certain programs.

2005-2006 Annual costs. Tuition/fees: $23,164. Room/board: $8,890. Books/supplies: $862.

2005-2006 Financial aid. **Need-based:** 618 full-time freshmen applied for aid; 493 were judged to have need; 490 of these received aid. Average need met was 70%. Average scholarship/grant was $9,868; average loan $3,321. 65% of total undergraduate aid awarded as scholarships/grants, 35% as loans/jobs. **Non-need-based:** Awarded to 293 full-time undergraduates, including 84 freshmen. Scholarships awarded for academics, ROTC.

Application procedures. **Admission:** Priority date 3/1; no deadline. $50 fee, may be waived for applicants with need. Application may be submitted online. Admission notification on a rolling basis beginning on or about 12/1. Must reply by May 1 or within 2 week(s) if notified thereafter. **Financial aid:** Priority date 4/1; no closing date. FAFSA required. Applicants notified on a rolling basis starting 3/15; must reply by 5/1 or within 2 week(s) of notification.

Academics. **Special study options:** Accelerated study, combined bachelor's/graduate degree, cross-registration, distance learning, double major, dual enrollment of high school students, honors, independent study, internships, liberal arts/career combination, student-designed major, study abroad, teacher certification program, Washington semester. 3+3 law program. Accelerated part-time degree completion (PACE). **Credit/placement by examination:** AP, CLEP, IB, institutional tests. **Support services:** Pre-admission summer program, reduced course load, study skills assistance, tutoring, writing center.

Majors. **Biology:** General, molecular. **Business:** General, accounting, business admin, finance, management information systems, marketing. **Communications:** General, advertising, media studies. **Computer sciences:** Computer science. **Education:** General. **Engineering:** Biomedical, electrical, industrial, mechanical. **English:** Creative writing, English lit. **History:** General. **Interdisciplinary:** Global studies. **Liberal arts:** Arts/sciences. **Math:** General. **Parks/recreation:** Sports admin. **Philosophy/religion:** Philosophy. **Physical sciences:** Chemistry. **Protective services:** Criminal justice. **Psychology:** General. **Public administration:** Social work. **Social sciences:** Economics, political science, sociology.

Most popular majors. Business/marketing 34%, engineering/engineering technologies 11%, psychology 8%, security/protective services 33%, social sciences 6%.

Computing on campus. 490 workstations in dormitories, library, computer center, student center. Dormitories wired for high-speed internet access and linked to campus network. Commuter students can connect to campus network. Online library, helpline, repair service, wireless network available.

Student life. **Freshman orientation:** Available. Preregistration for classes offered. Two-day program held over summer for students and parents. **Policies:** Freshmen permitted cars on campus. **Housing:** Guaranteed on-campus for freshmen. Coed dorms, special housing for disabled, apartments available. $300 nonrefundable deposit, deadline 5/1. **Activities:** Bands, choral groups, dance, drama, literary magazine, music ensembles, radio station, student government, student newspaper, United and Mutually Equal, campus ministry, Helping Hands Society, international student association.

Athletics. NCAA. **Intercollegiate:** Baseball M, basketball, bowling, cross-country, field hockey W, football (tackle) M, golf M, ice hockey M, lacrosse, soccer, softball W, swimming W, tennis, volleyball W, wrestling M. **Intramural:** Badminton, basketball, football (non-tackle), handball, soccer, softball, table tennis, volleyball, water polo. **Team name:** Golden Bears.

Student services. Adult student services, alcohol/substance abuse counseling, campus ministries, career counseling, student employment services, financial aid counseling, health services, minority student services, personal counseling, veterans' counselor. **Physically disabled:** Services for visually, hearing impaired.

Contact. E-mail: ugradmis@wnec.edu
Phone: (413) 782-1321 Toll-free number: (800) 325-1122 ext. 1321
Fax: (413) 782-1777
Charles Pollock, Vice President for Enrollment Management, Western New England College, 1215 Wilbraham Road, Springfield, MA 01119-2684

Westfield State College

Westfield, Massachusetts — **CB member**
www.wsc.ma.edu — **CB code: 3523**

- Public 4-year liberal arts and teachers college
- Residential campus in large town
- 4,488 degree-seeking undergraduates: 9% part-time, 56% women
- 330 degree-seeking graduate students
- 74% of applicants admitted
- SAT or ACT (ACT writing optional) required
- 53% graduate within 6 years

General. Founded in 1838. Regionally accredited. **Degrees:** 867 bachelor's awarded; master's offered. **ROTC:** Army, Air Force. **Location:** 10 miles from Springfield, 100 miles from Boston. **Calendar:** Semester, extensive summer session. **Full-time faculty:** 179 total; 81% have terminal degrees, 10% minority, 45% women. **Part-time faculty:** 165 total; 16% have terminal degrees, 6% minority, 50% women. **Class size:** 32% < 20, 62% 20-39, 5% 40-49, less than 1% 50-99, less than 1% >100. **Special facilities:** Electron microscope, museum of rocks and minerals.

Freshman class profile. 4,248 applied, 3,129 admitted, 1,183 enrolled.

Mid 50% test scores			
SAT verbal:	470-550	GPA 3.0-3.49:	27%
SAT math:	470-560	GPA 2.0-2.99:	58%
ACT:	20-24	Return as sophomores:	77%
GPA 3.50 or higher:	14%	Out-of-state:	7%
		Live on campus:	88%

Basis for selection. School achievement record, test scores most important; school and community activities also important; class rank, recommendations considered. Essay recommended. Audition required of music majors. Portfolio required of art majors. **Learning Disabled:** Test scores waived for students with documented learning disability.

High school preparation. College-preparatory program required. 16 units required. Required units include English 4, mathematics 3, social studies 1, history 1, science 3 (laboratory 2), foreign language 2 and academic electives 2.

2005-2006 Annual costs. Tuition/fees: $5,657; $11,737 out-of-state. New England Regional tuition and fees per year: $6142. Room/board: $5,580. Books/supplies: $800. Personal expenses: $1,263.

2004-2005 Financial aid. **Need-based:** 48% of total undergraduate aid awarded as scholarships/grants, 52% as loans/jobs. **Non-need-based:** Scholarships awarded for academics.

Application procedures. **Admission:** Closing date 3/1 (postmark date). $25 fee ($40 out-of-state), may be waived for applicants with need. Application may be submitted online. Admission notification 4/15. Admission notification on a rolling basis beginning on or about 1/1. Must reply by May 1 or within 2 week(s) if notified thereafter. **Financial aid:** Priority date 3/1; no closing date. FAFSA required. Applicants notified by 4/15.

Academics. **Special study options:** Cooperative education, cross-registration, distance learning, double major, dual enrollment of high school students, exchange student, honors, independent study, internships, student-designed major, study abroad, teacher certification program, Washington semester. **Credit/placement by examination:** AP, CLEP, institutional tests. 60 credit hours maximum toward bachelor's degree. Maximum of 3 credits awarded for AP tests in English. Students taking CLEP tests in English Composition with Essay or Freshman Composition must also submit writing portfolio; portfolio evaluated before credit can be awarded. Maximum of 3 credits awarded for composition. **Support services:** Learning center, pre-admission summer program, reduced course load, study skills assistance, tutoring, writing center.

Majors. **Architecture:** Urban/community planning. **Biology:** General. **Business:** General, accounting, business admin, finance. **Communications:** General, broadcast journalism, journalism. **Computer sciences:** General, computer science, information systems. **Conservation:** General. **Education:** General, art, biology, business, early childhood, elementary, English, health, history, mathematics, middle, music, physical, science, social studies, special, technology/industrial arts. **Health:** Athletic training. **History:** General. **Liberal arts:** Arts/sciences. **Math:** General. **Parks/recreation:** General, exercise sciences, health/fitness. **Physical sciences:** General. **Protective services:** Criminal justice. **Psychology:** General. **Public administration:** Social work. **Social sciences:** Economics, political science, sociology. **Visual/performing arts:** Art, commercial/advertising art, dramatic, jazz, music performance, music theory/composition, studio arts.

Most popular majors. Business/marketing 12%, communications/journalism 9%, education 11%, liberal arts 12%, psychology 11%, security/protective services 16%.

Computing on campus. 238 workstations in dormitories, library, computer center. Dormitories wired for high-speed internet access and linked to campus network. Commuter students can connect to campus network. Online library, helpline, student web hosting available.

Student life. **Freshman orientation:** Available. **Housing:** Guaranteed on-campus for freshmen. Coed dorms, special housing for disabled, apartments available. $100 nonrefundable deposit, deadline 6/1. Living/learning unit (academic intensive), quiet living section, all women section, designated smoking section (other housing smoke-free), movement science student section available. **Activities:** Bands, choral groups, drama, literary magazine, music ensembles, musical theater, radio station, student government, student newspaper, TV station, third world group, public interest research group, Campus Crusade, Circle K, Amnesty International, international relations club, Latino association for empowerment.

Athletics. NCAA. **Intercollegiate:** Baseball M, basketball, cheerleading, cross-country, diving W, field hockey W, football (tackle) M, soccer, softball W, swimming W, track and field, volleyball W. **Intramural:** Badminton, basketball, bowling, football (tackle), racquetball, soccer, softball, table tennis, tennis, volleyball. **Team name:** Owls.

Student services. Adult student services, alcohol/substance abuse counseling, career counseling, services for economically disadvantaged, student employment services, health services, minority student services, personal counseling, placement for graduates, veterans' counselor. **Physically disabled:** Services for visually, speech, hearing impaired. **Learning disabled:** Comprehensive services available.

Contact. E-mail: admission@wsc.ma.edu
Phone: (413) 572-5218 Toll-free number: (800) 322-8401
Fax: (413) 572-0520
Michelle Mattie, Associate Dean, Enrollment Management, Westfield State College, 577 Western Avenue, Westfield, MA 01086-1630

Wheaton College

Norton, Massachusetts — **CB member**
www.wheatoncollege.edu — **CB code: 3963**

- Private 4-year liberal arts college
- Residential campus in large town
- 1,559 degree-seeking undergraduates: 62% women, 3% African American, 3% Asian American, 4% Hispanic American, 3% international
- 44% of applicants admitted
- Application essay required
- 75% graduate within 6 years; 29% enter graduate study

General. Founded in 1834. Regionally accredited. **Degrees:** 410 bachelor's awarded. **ROTC:** Army. **Location:** 35 miles from Boston, 15 miles from Providence, Rhode Island. **Calendar:** Semester. **Full-time faculty:** 121 total; 98% have terminal degrees, 48% women. **Part-time faculty:** 40 total; 78% have terminal degrees, 55% women. **Class size:** 60% < 20, 31% 20-39, 5% 40-49, 3% 50-99, less than 1% >100. **Special facilities:** Observatory, language laboratory receiving international broadcasts via satellite.

Freshman class profile. 3,697 applied, 1,638 admitted, 466 enrolled.

Mid 50% test scores			
SAT verbal:	600-690	**Rank in top quarter:**	82%
SAT math:	580-660	**Rank in top tenth:**	56%
ACT:	26-30	**End year in good standing:**	95%
GPA 3.50 or higher:	48%	**Return as sophomores:**	86%
GPA 3.0-3.49:	36%	**Out-of-state:**	65%
GPA 2.0-2.99:	16%	**Live on campus:**	100%
		International:	3%

Basis for selection. School record, essay/writing sample, personal academic portfolio, extracurricular activities, recommendations, and interview important. Standardized testing optional. **Homeschooled:** Statement describing homeschool structure and mission, transcript of courses and grades required. **Learning Disabled:** Students who have diagnosed learning difference encouraged to submit supporting testing for review.

High school preparation. 20 units recommended. Recommended units include English 4, mathematics 4, social studies 3, history 2, science 3 (laboratory 2) and foreign language 4. English should emphasize composition skills.

2006-2007 Annual costs. Tuition/fees: $34,610. Freshmen pay one-time $50 general fee (non-refundable); all residents pay annual $120 technology fee. Room/board: $8,150. Books/supplies: $940. Personal expenses: $760.

2005-2006 Financial aid. **Need-based:** 270 full-time freshmen applied for aid; 227 were judged to have need; 227 of these received aid. Average need met was 94%. Average scholarship/grant was $19,030; average loan $3,566. 75% of total undergraduate aid awarded as scholarships/grants, 25% as loans/jobs. **Non-need-based:** Scholarships awarded for academics.

Application procedures. **Admission:** Closing date 1/15 (postmark date). $55 fee, may be waived for applicants with need. Application may be submitted online. Admission notification 4/1. Must reply by 5/1. **Financial aid:** Closing date 2/1. FAFSA, CSS PROFILE required. Applicants notified by 4/1; must reply by 5/1.

Academics. **Special study options:** Accelerated study, combined bachelor's/graduate degree, cross-registration, double major, dual enrollment of high school students, exchange student, honors, independent study, internships, liberal arts/career combination, student-designed major, study abroad, teacher certification program, Washington semester. BS in engineering with George Washington University, Dartmouth College and Worcester Polytechnic Institute; MA in communications with Emerson College; MBA in management with Clark University and University of Rochester; BFA in studio art with School of the Museum of Fine Arts (Boston); MA in religion with Andover Newton Theological School; Doctor of Optometry with New England School of Optometry. **Credit/placement by examination:** AP, CLEP, IB, institutional tests. 8 credit hours maximum toward bachelor's degree. **Support services:** Learning center, reduced course load, study skills assistance, tutoring, writing center.

Majors. **Area/ethnic studies:** American, Asian, Russian/Slavic, women's. **Biology:** General, biochemistry. **Computer sciences:** General, computer science. **Conservation:** General. **English:** Composition. **Foreign languages:** Classics, French, German, Italian, Latin, modern Greek, Russian, Spanish. **History:** General. **Interdisciplinary:** Biological/physical sciences, math/computer science. **Liberal arts:** Arts/sciences. **Math:** General. **Philosophy/religion:** Philosophy, religion. **Physical sciences:** Astronomy, chemistry, physics. **Psychology:** General. **Social sciences:** Anthropology, economics, international relations, political science, sociology. **Visual/performing arts:** Art history/conservation, studio arts.

Most popular majors. Biology 7%, English 14%, foreign language 6%, history 7%, psychology 14%, social sciences 26%, visual/performing arts 10%.

Computing on campus. 285 workstations in library, computer center. Dormitories wired for high-speed internet access and linked to campus network. Commuter students can connect to campus network. Online course registration, online library, helpline, repair service, student web hosting, wireless network available.

Student life. **Freshman orientation:** Mandatory. Preregistration for classes offered. Held 2-3 days prior to start of classes. **Policies:** Freshmen permitted cars on campus. **Housing:** Guaranteed on-campus for all undergraduates. Coed dorms, single-sex dorms, special housing for disabled, substance-free housing available. Special interest houses available: wellness, quiet, and theme. **Activities:** Bands, choral groups, dance, drama, film society, literary magazine, music ensembles, musical theater, radio station, student government, student newspaper, symphony orchestra, Amnesty International, student art league, black students association, Latino students organization, Asian students association, Hillel, College Democrats, College Republicans, Habitat for Humanity, international students association.

Athletics. NCAA. **Intercollegiate:** Baseball M, basketball, cross-country, diving, field hockey W, lacrosse, soccer, softball W, swimming, synchronized swimming W, tennis, track and field, volleyball W. **Intramural:** Badminton, basketball, soccer, softball, tennis, volleyball. **Team name:** Lyons.

Student services. Career counseling, student employment services, financial aid counseling, health services, minority student services, personal counseling, placement for graduates, women's services. **Physically disabled:** Services for visually, hearing impaired.

Contact. E-mail: admission@wheatoncollege.edu
Phone: (508) 286-8251 Toll-free number: (800) 394-6003
Fax: (508) 286-8271
Gail Berson, Vice President for Enrollment and Dean of Admission and Student Aid, Wheaton College, 26 East Main Street, Norton, MA 02766

Wheelock College

Boston, Massachusetts — **CB member**
www.wheelock.edu — **CB code: 3964**

- Private 4-year liberal arts and teachers college
- Residential campus in very large city
- 675 degree-seeking undergraduates: 6% part-time, 94% women
- 353 graduate students
- 82% of applicants admitted
- SAT or ACT (ACT writing optional), application essay required

General. Founded in 1888. Regionally accredited. **Degrees:** 81 bachelor's awarded; master's offered. **Location:** 2 miles from downtown. **Calendar:** Semester. **Full-time faculty:** 60 total. **Part-time faculty:** 145 total.

Freshman class profile. 658 applied, 538 admitted, 181 enrolled.

Mid 50% test scores			
SAT verbal:	450-560	GPA 3.0-3.49:	28%
SAT math:	430-530	GPA 2.0-2.99:	48%
ACT:	16-25	Out-of-state:	56%
GPA 3.50 or higher:	22%	Live on campus:	91%

Basis for selection. School achievement record most important. Test scores, school and community activities considered. Interview recommended.

High school preparation. 16 units required. Required units include English 4, mathematics 3, social studies 2, science 2 (laboratory 1). Child development course recommended.

2005-2006 Annual costs. Tuition/fees: $23,625. Room/board: $9,450. Books/supplies: $600. Personal expenses: $1,000.

Financial aid. **Non-need-based:** Scholarships awarded for academics, job skills, leadership, minority status.

Application procedures. **Admission:** Priority date 3/1; no deadline. $35 fee, may be waived for applicants with need. Application may be submitted online. Admission notification on a rolling basis beginning on or about 1/1. Must reply by May 1 or within 2 week(s) if notified thereafter. **Financial aid:** Closing date 3/1. FAFSA, institutional form required. Applicants notified on a rolling basis starting 3/1; must reply by 5/1.

Academics. Fieldwork throughout all 4 years supplements classwork in day care, infant and toddler behavior, museum teaching, children in health care settings, elementary education, special education, social work programs. Students choose major and professional studies concentration in early childhood care and education, elementary school education, juvenile justice, social work, or child life. **Special study options:** Combined bachelor's/graduate degree, cross-registration, double major, independent study, internships, liberal arts/career combination, study abroad, teacher certification program, Washington semester. **Credit/placement by examination:** AP, CLEP, institutional tests. 32 credit hours maximum toward bachelor's degree. **Support services:** Learning center, reduced course load, remedial instruction, study skills assistance, tutoring, writing center.

Majors. **Education:** Early childhood, elementary, special. **Family/consumer sciences:** Child care, child development. **Liberal arts:** Arts/sciences. **Public administration:** Social work. **Visual/performing arts:** General.

Computing on campus. 120 workstations in dormitories, library, computer center, student center. Dormitories wired for high-speed internet access and linked to campus network. Commuter students can connect to campus network. Online library, helpline, repair service, wireless network available.

Student life. **Freshman orientation:** Mandatory. Preregistration for classes offered. Program held week before start of classes. **Housing:** Guaranteed on-campus for freshmen. Coed dorms, single-sex dorms, cooperative housing available. $100 nonrefundable deposit, deadline 5/1. Smoke-free areas, wellness floor available. **Activities:** Choral groups, dance, drama, musical theater, student government, social work club, Students of Faith, peace and social action committee, women's center, Boston Association for the Education of Young Children, child life council, council for exceptional children, sign language club.

Athletics. NCAA. **Intercollegiate:** Basketball W, cross-country W, diving W, field hockey W, soccer W, softball W, swimming W. **Intramural:** Basketball, handball, racquetball, soccer, softball, squash, volleyball. **Team name:** Wildcats.

Student services. Alcohol/substance abuse counseling, career counseling, student employment services, financial aid counseling, health services, personal counseling, placement for graduates, women's services. **Physically disabled:** Services for visually, speech, hearing impaired.

Contact. E-mail: undergrad@wheelock.edu
Phone: (617) 879-2206 Toll-free number: (800) 734-5212
Fax: (617) 879-2449
Lynne Harding, Director of Admissions, Wheelock College, 200 The Riverway, Boston, MA 02215-4176

Williams College

Williamstown, Massachusetts — **CB member**
www.williams.edu — **CB code: 3965**

- Private 4-year liberal arts college
- Residential campus in small town
- 1,970 degree-seeking undergraduates: 51% women, 9% African American, 9% Asian American, 9% Hispanic American, 6% international
- 53 degree-seeking graduate students
- 19% of applicants admitted
- SAT or ACT with writing, SAT Subject Tests, application essay required
- 95% graduate within 6 years

General. Founded in 1793. Regionally accredited. **Degrees:** 504 bachelor's awarded; master's offered. **Location:** 35 miles from Albany, New York, 150 miles from Boston. **Calendar:** 4-1-4. **Full-time faculty:** 257 total; 98% have terminal degrees, 17% minority, 40% women. **Part-time faculty:** 55 total; 84% have terminal degrees, 11% minority, 33% women. **Class size:** 71% < 20, 21% 20-39, 5% 40-49, 3% 50-99, less than 1% >100. **Special facilities:** Performing arts center, 2,000-acre experimental forest, environmental studies center, observatory, electron-scanning microscope, transmission microscopes, studio art center, nuclear magnetic resonance imager.

Freshman class profile. 5,822 applied, 1,095 admitted, 536 enrolled.

Mid 50% test scores			
SAT verbal:	660-760	Return as sophomores:	97%
SAT math:	670-760	Out-of-state:	84%
Rank in top quarter:	97%	Live on campus:	100%
Rank in top tenth:	85%	International:	6%

Basis for selection. School achievement record, character and personal promise, test scores, essay important. College seeks diversity of social, economic, and geographic backgrounds. Leadership and accomplishment in extracurricular activities also considered.

High school preparation. College-preparatory program required. Recommended units include English 4, mathematics 4, social studies 3, science 3 (laboratory 3) and foreign language 4. Writing skills stressed. Course work should be at highest level available, especially in major interest areas.

2005-2006 Annual costs. Tuition/fees: $31,760. Room/board: $8,550. Books/supplies: $800. Personal expenses: $1,200.

2005-2006 Financial aid. All financial aid based on need. 319 full-time freshmen applied for aid; 264 were judged to have need; 264 of these received aid. Average need met was 100%. Average scholarship/grant was $29,507; average loan $2,128. 89% of total undergraduate aid awarded as scholarships/grants, 11% as loans/jobs.

Application procedures. **Admission:** Closing date 1/1 (postmark date). $60 fee, may be waived for applicants with need. Application may be submitted online. Admission notification 4/1. Must reply by May 1 or within 2 week(s) if notified thereafter. **Financial aid:** Closing date 2/15. FAFSA, CSS PROFILE required. Applicants notified by 4/1; must reply by 5/1.

Academics. **Special study options:** Accelerated study, combined bachelor's/graduate degree, cross-registration, double major, exchange student, honors, independent study, internships, New York semester, student-designed major, study abroad, teacher certification program. Preadmission summer program for premedical and science students; summer science research program; Williams in Oxford; Mystic maritime studies program; tutorials; 3-2 engineering program with Columbia University and Washington University. **Credit/placement by examination:** AP, CLEP, IB, institutional tests. **Support services:** Pre-admission summer program, study skills assistance, tutoring, writing center.

Majors. **Area/ethnic studies:** American, Asian. **Biology:** General. **Computer sciences:** Computer science. **Foreign languages:** Chinese, classics, comparative lit, French, German, Japanese, Russian, Spanish. **History:** General. **Math:** General. **Philosophy/religion:** Philosophy, religion. **Physical sciences:** Astronomy, astrophysics, chemistry, geology, physics. **Psychology:** General. **Social sciences:** Anthropology, economics, political science, sociology. **Visual/performing arts:** Art history/conservation, dramatic, studio arts.

Most popular majors. Biology 7%, English 10%, history 9%, mathematics 7%, physical sciences 9%, psychology 10%, social sciences 25%, visual/performing arts 11%.

Computing on campus. 247 workstations in library, computer center, student center. Dormitories wired for high-speed internet access and linked to campus network. Commuter students can connect to campus network. Online course registration, helpline, repair service, student web hosting, wireless network available.

Student life. **Freshman orientation:** Mandatory. **Housing:** Guaranteed on-campus for all undergraduates. Coed dorms, cooperative housing available. $200 deposit, deadline 5/1. **Activities:** Bands, choral groups, dance, drama, film society, literary magazine, music ensembles, musical theater, radio station, student government, student newspaper, symphony orchestra, black student union, Purple Key, Asian Link, VISTA (Hispanic students), Korean club, minority coalition, nonviolent alternatives committee, women's club, Hillel.

Athletics. NCAA. **Intercollegiate:** Baseball M, basketball, cross-country, diving, field hockey W, football (tackle) M, golf, ice hockey, lacrosse, rowing (crew), skiing, soccer, softball W, squash, swimming, tennis, track and field, volleyball W, wrestling M. **Intramural:** Badminton, basketball, golf W, ice hockey M, skiing, soccer, softball, volleyball, water polo. **Team name:** Ephs.

Student services. Adult student services, alcohol/substance abuse counseling, campus ministries, career counseling, services for economically disadvantaged, financial aid counseling, health services, minority student services, personal counseling, placement for graduates. **Physically disabled:** Services for visually, hearing impaired.

Contact. E-mail: admission@williams.edu
Phone: (413) 597-2211 Fax: (413) 597-4052
Richard Nesbitt, Director of Admissions, Williams College, 33 Stetson Court, Williamstown, MA 01267

Worcester Polytechnic Institute

Worcester, Massachusetts — **CB member**
www.wpi.edu — **CB code: 3969**

- Private 4-year university
- Residential campus in small city
- 2,838 degree-seeking undergraduates: 1% part-time, 25% women, 2% African American, 6% Asian American, 4% Hispanic American, 5% international
- 837 degree-seeking graduate students
- 85% of applicants admitted
- SAT or ACT (ACT writing optional), application essay required
- 74% graduate within 6 years

General. Founded in 1865. Regionally accredited. Off-campus project sites include General Electric and Gillette Corporation, University of Massachusetts Medical Center, Tufts School of Veterinary Medicine. Foreign project centers include universities or research facilities in Puerto Rico, England, Italy, Thailand, Hong Kong, the Netherlands, Costa Rica, Australia, Denmark, Ireland, Spain, France, Switzerland. **Degrees:** 615 bachelor's awarded; master's, doctoral offered. **ROTC:** Army, Navy, Air Force. **Location:** 35 miles from Boston. **Calendar:** Quarter, limited summer session. **Full-time faculty:** 232 total; 96% have terminal degrees, 15% minority, 21% women. **Part-time faculty:** 85 total; 74% have terminal degrees, 11% minority, 22% women. **Class size:** 70% < 20, 24% 20-39, 2% 40-49, 4% 50-99, less than 1% >100. **Special facilities:** Nuclear reactor, computer-aided design and manufacturing laboratories, robotics laboratory, center for holographic studies and laser technology, hydraulics laboratory, wind tunnel, design laboratory, bioprocessing laboratory.

Freshman class profile. 3,314 applied, 2,806 admitted, 733 enrolled.

Mid 50% test scores		**Rank in top tenth:**	46%
SAT verbal:	560-670	**Return as sophomores:**	92%
SAT math:	620-710	**Out-of-state:**	48%
ACT:	24-29	**Live on campus:**	98%
GPA 3.50 or higher:	65%	**International:**	7%
GPA 3.0-3.49:	29%	**Fraternities:**	38%
GPA 2.0-2.99:	6%	**Sororities:**	28%
Rank in top quarter:	77%		

Basis for selection. High school record most important. Test scores, extracurricular activities, recommendations important. No specific rank or grade average required; motivation, creativity, and initiative important. SAT and SAT Subject Tests or ACT recommended. SAT Subject Tests recommended in math and science of student's choosing; scores only used if they benefit applicant. Interviews offered, but not required. **Homeschooled:** Transcript of courses and grades, interview required. Please submit as much relevant support material as possible and outside recommendations.

High school preparation. 10 units required. Required and recommended units include English 4, mathematics 4, social studies 2, history 1, science 2-4 (laboratory 2) and foreign language 2. Mathematics requirement should include trigonometry and pre-calculus analytic geometry. Science should include physics, chemistry, or biology.

2005-2006 Annual costs. Tuition/fees: $31,590. Room/board: $9,460. Books/supplies: $735. Personal expenses: $1,145.

2004-2005 Financial aid. Need-based: 695 full-time freshmen applied for aid; 559 were judged to have need; 555 of these received aid. Average need met was 76%. Average scholarship/grant was $17,390; average loan $4,558. 75% of total undergraduate aid awarded as scholarships/grants, 25% as loans/jobs. **Non-need-based:** Awarded to 679 full-time undergraduates, including 299 freshmen. Scholarships awarded for academics, minority status, ROTC.

Application procedures. Admission: Closing date 2/1 (postmark date). $60 fee, may be waived for applicants with need. Application may be submitted online. Admission notification 4/1. Must reply by May 1 or within 2 week(s) if notified thereafter. Second early action closing date: 1/01; notification date: 2/01. **Financial aid:** Closing date 2/1. FAFSA required. Parents' and student's prior-year federal tax returns and W-2 statements required. Applicants notified by 4/1; must reply by 5/1.

Academics. Programs student-designed, stress projects and individualized study combining classroom and professional experience. **Special study options:** Accelerated study, combined bachelor's/graduate degree, cooperative education, cross-registration, double major, dual enrollment of high school students, ESL, exchange student, independent study, internships, liberal arts/career combination, student-designed major, study abroad, teacher certification program, Washington semester. International scholars program, 3-2 BS/BA liberal arts programs with any Worcester Consortium college and selected other colleges. Accelerated 3-4 BS/DVM with Tufts University. 5-year BS/MS and BS/MBA programs. **Credit/placement by examination:** AP, CLEP, IB, institutional tests. 3 credit hours maximum toward bachelor's degree. **Support services:** Reduced course load, study skills assistance, tutoring, writing center.

Majors. Biology: General, biochemistry, biotechnology. **Business:** Business admin, management information systems, management science, operations. **Computer sciences:** Computer science, web page design. **Engineering:** Aerospace, biomedical, chemical, civil, electrical, environmental, industrial, manufacturing, mechanical, physics, systems. **Engineering technology:** Industrial management. **English:** Technical writing. **Health:** Predentistry, premedicine, preveterinary. **Interdisciplinary:** Biological/physical sciences, global studies, science/society. **Legal studies:** Prelaw. **Liberal arts:** Humanities. **Math:** General, applied. **Physical sciences:** Chemistry, physics. **Social sciences:** General, economics.

Most popular majors. Biology 11%, business/marketing 6%, computer/information sciences 15%, engineering/engineering technologies 61%.

Computing on campus. 1,000 workstations in dormitories, library, computer center. Dormitories wired for high-speed internet access and linked to campus network. Commuter students can connect to campus network. Online course registration, online library, helpline, repair service, student web hosting, wireless network available.

Student life. Freshman orientation: Available, $200 fee. Preregistration for classes offered. Program held in late August. **Policies:** Freshmen permitted cars on campus. **Housing:** Guaranteed on-campus for freshmen. Coed dorms, special housing for disabled, apartments, fraternity/sorority housing, substance-free housing available. $500 nonrefundable deposit, deadline 5/1. **Activities:** Bands, choral groups, dance, drama, film society, literary magazine, music ensembles, musical theater, radio station, student government, student newspaper, symphony orchestra, African American cultural society, volunteer tutoring group, Big Brother/Big Sister, World House, European student association, Asian society, Hispanic student association, women's awareness group, students for social awareness, Amnesty International.

Athletics. NCAA. **Intercollegiate:** Baseball M, basketball, cross-country, field hockey W, football (tackle) M, rowing (crew), soccer, softball W, swimming, track and field, volleyball W, wrestling M. **Intramural:** Basketball, bowling, cross-country, fencing, football (non-tackle) M, racquetball, soccer, softball, swimming, table tennis, volleyball, water polo M, wrestling M. **Team name:** Engineers.

Student services. Adult student services, alcohol/substance abuse counseling, campus ministries, career counseling, student employment services, financial aid counseling, health services, minority student services, personal counseling, placement for graduates, veterans' counselor, women's services. **Physically disabled:** Services for visually, speech, hearing impaired. **Learning disabled:** Comprehensive services available.

Contact. E-mail: admissions@wpi.edu
Phone: (508) 831-5286 Fax: (508) 831-5875
Edward Connor, Director of Admission, Worcester Polytechnic Institute, 100 Institute Road, Worcester, MA 01609-2280

Worcester State College

Worcester, Massachusetts — **CB member**
www.worcester.edu — **CB code: 3524**

- Public 4-year liberal arts and teachers college
- Commuter campus in small city

- 3,964 degree-seeking undergraduates: 19% part-time, 59% women, 4% African American, 3% Asian American, 4% Hispanic American, 3% international
- 443 degree-seeking graduate students
- 59% of applicants admitted

General. Founded in 1874. Regionally accredited. **Degrees:** 705 bachelor's awarded; master's offered. **ROTC:** Army, Navy, Air Force. **Location:** 40 miles from Boston, 65 miles from Hartford, Connecticut. **Calendar:** Semester, extensive summer session. **Full-time faculty:** 167 total; 76% have terminal degrees, 16% minority, 52% women. **Part-time faculty:** 233 total; 7% minority, 55% women. **Class size:** 51% < 20, 49% 20-39, less than 1% 40-49, less than 1% 50-99. **Special facilities:** Photographic labs; multimedia classrooms with satellite connectivity; speech, language and hearing clinic.

Freshman class profile. 3,113 applied, 1,841 admitted, 648 enrolled.

Mid 50% test scores			
SAT verbal:	450-550	GPA 3.0-3.49:	29%
SAT math:	460-550	GPA 2.0-2.99:	51%
ACT:	17-22	Return as sophomores:	75%
GPA 3.50 or higher:	20%	Out-of-state:	4%
		Live on campus:	51%

Basis for selection. Secondary school record most important; test scores important; extracurricular activities considered. Interview and personal essay recommended for academically weak. **Homeschooled:** Student must submit documentation that home school plan meets district curriculum standards. **Learning Disabled:** SAT waiver available for students with learning disabilties with IEP plan.

High school preparation. 16 units required. Required units include English 4, mathematics 3, social studies 1, history 1, science 3 (laboratory 2), foreign language 2 and academic electives 2. History unit must be US history.

2005-2006 Annual costs. Tuition/fees: $5,079; $11,159 out-of-state. Room/board: $7,420. Books/supplies: $984. Personal expenses: $1,200.

2004-2005 Financial aid. Need-based: 477 full-time freshmen applied for aid; 317 were judged to have need; 305 of these received aid. Average need met was 75%. Average scholarship/grant was $1,717; average loan $1,022. 69% of total undergraduate aid awarded as scholarships/grants, 31% as loans/jobs. **Non-need-based:** Awarded to 262 full-time undergraduates, including 94 freshmen. Scholarships awarded for academics, alumni affiliation. **Additional information:** Veterans, Native Americans and those certified by Massachusetts Rehabilitation Commission and Massachusetts Commission for the Blind considered for tuition waivers while funds available. Tuition also waived for needy Massachusetts residents and in-state National Guard members.

Application procedures. Admission: Priority date 3/15; deadline 6/1 (receipt date). $20 fee, may be waived for applicants with need. Application may be submitted online. Admission notification 6/15. Admission notification on a rolling basis beginning on or about 12/15. Must reply by May 1 or within 4 week(s) if notified thereafter. **Financial aid:** Priority date 3/1; no closing date. FAFSA, institutional form required. Applicants notified on a rolling basis starting 3/1; must reply within 2 week(s) of notification.

Academics. Special study options: Combined bachelor's/graduate degree, cooperative education, cross-registration, distance learning, double major, dual enrollment of high school students, ESL, exchange student, honors, independent study, internships, liberal arts/career combination, study abroad, teacher certification program, urban semester, Washington semester. Foreign exchange student program, evening college program in chemistry. **Credit/placement by examination:** AP, CLEP, institutional tests. 30 credit hours maximum toward bachelor's degree. **Support services:** Learning center, pre-admission summer program, reduced course load, remedial instruction, study skills assistance, tutoring, writing center.

Majors. Biology: General, biotechnology. **Business:** Business admin. **Communications:** Media studies. **Communications technology:** General. **Computer sciences:** General. **Education:** Elementary, kindergarten/preschool. **Foreign languages:** Spanish. **Health:** Communication disorders, health services, nursing (RN), preop/surgical nursing. **History:** General. **Interdisciplinary:** Biological/physical sciences. **Legal studies:** Prelaw. **Math:** General. **Physical sciences:** Chemistry. **Protective services:** Criminal justice. **Psychology:** General. **Social sciences:** Economics, geography, sociology, urban studies.

Most popular majors. Business/marketing 20%, education 7%, health sciences 17%, psychology 17%.

Computing on campus. PC or laptop required. 102 workstations in dormitories, library, computer center, student center. Dormitories linked to campus network. Commuter students can connect to campus network. Online course registration, helpline, wireless network available.

Student life. Freshman orientation: Available. Programs held in the spring. **Policies:** Freshmen permitted cars on campus. **Housing:** Coed dorms, single-sex dorms, special housing for disabled available. $150 nonrefundable deposit, deadline 3/15. **Activities:** Bands, choral groups, dance, drama, music ensembles, radio station, student government, student newspaper, TV station, Newman Society, student events committee, yearbook, Student Voice, Third World Alliance, campus ambassadors, Bacchus Pen Delta.

Athletics. NCAA. **Intercollegiate:** Baseball M, basketball, cheerleading, cross-country, field hockey W, football (tackle) M, golf M, ice hockey M, lacrosse W, rowing (crew), soccer, softball W, tennis, track and field, volleyball W. **Intramural:** Baseball M, basketball, cross-country, equestrian W, football (tackle) M, golf M, ice hockey M, rowing (crew), soccer, softball W, tennis, track and field, volleyball W. **Team name:** Lancers.

Student services. Alcohol/substance abuse counseling, campus ministries, career counseling, student employment services, financial aid counseling, health services, personal counseling, placement for graduates, veterans' counselor, women's services. **Physically disabled:** Services for visually, speech, hearing impaired.

Contact. E-mail: admissions@worcester.edu
Phone: (508) 929-8040 Toll-free number: (866) 972-2255
Fax: (508) 929-8183
Jay Tierney, Admissions Director, Worcester State College, 486 Chandler Street, Worcester, MA 01602-2597

Michigan

Adrian College

Adrian, Michigan
www.adrian.edu
CB member
CB code: 1001

- Private 4-year liberal arts college affiliated with United Methodist Church
- Residential campus in large town
- 971 degree-seeking undergraduates: 4% part-time, 52% women
- 80% of applicants admitted
- SAT or ACT (ACT writing optional) required

General. Founded in 1859. Regionally accredited. **Degrees:** 176 bachelor's, 1 associate awarded. **Location:** 75 miles from Detroit, 30 miles from Toledo, Ohio. **Calendar:** Semester, limited summer session. **Full-time faculty:** 66 total; 71% have terminal degrees, 11% minority, 41% women. **Part-time faculty:** 53 total; 21% have terminal degrees, 8% minority, 62% women. **Class size:** 77% < 20, 22% 20-39, less than 1% 40-49, less than 1% 50-99. **Special facilities:** Observatory, planetarium, arboretum, solar greenhouse, human anatomy laboratory, writing laboratory, educational curriculum center.

Freshman class profile. 1,116 applied, 891 admitted, 267 enrolled.

Mid 50% test scores			
ACT:	18-24	Live on campus:	77%
Out-of-state:	18%	Fraternities:	29%
		Sororities:	29%

Basis for selection. School achievement most important, followed by test scores. Applicants should rank in top half of high school class. School recommendations and extracurricular activities considered. ACT preferred. **Homeschooled:** Must have transcript approved by school district.

High school preparation. College-preparatory program recommended. 16 units recommended. Recommended units include English 4, mathematics 3, social studies 1, history 1, science 2 (laboratory 1), foreign language 2 and academic electives 2.

2005-2006 Annual costs. Tuition/fees: $18,630. Room/board: $6,170. Books/supplies: $400. Personal expenses: $928.

2005-2006 Financial aid. Need-based: 291 full-time freshmen applied for aid; 242 were judged to have need; 242 of these received aid. Average need met was 99.61%. Average scholarship/grant was $10,709; average loan $3,845. 63% of total undergraduate aid awarded as scholarships/grants, 37% as loans/jobs. **Non-need-based:** Scholarships awarded for academics, alumni affiliation, art, music/drama, religious affiliation.

Application procedures. Admission: Priority date 3/15; deadline 8/15 (receipt date). No application fee. Application may be submitted online. Admission notification on a rolling basis beginning on or about 9/1. Must reply by May 1 or within 2 week(s) if notified thereafter. **Financial aid:** Closing date 3/15. FAFSA required. Applicants notified on a rolling basis starting 3/15; must reply by 5/1 or within 2 week(s) of notification.

Academics. Special study options: Combined bachelor's/graduate degree, cooperative education, cross-registration, double major, dual enrollment of high school students, ESL, exchange student, honors, independent study, internships, liberal arts/career combination, student-designed major, study abroad, teacher certification program, Washington semester. Philadelphia semester, bilingual multicultural program, exchange programs with Urban Life Center (Chicago), American College (London, England). **Credit/placement by examination:** AP, CLEP, IB, institutional tests. 15 credit hours maximum toward associate degree, 30 toward bachelor's. **Support services:** Learning center, pre-admission summer program, reduced course load, remedial instruction, study skills assistance, tutoring, writing center.

Majors. Biology: General. **Business:** Accounting, business admin, international, international marketing, management science, marketing. **Communications:** General, journalism. **Conservation:** General. **Education:** General, art, elementary, health, multi-level teacher, music, physical, secondary, social science. **English:** English lit. **Foreign languages:** French, German, Spanish. **Health:** Predentistry, premedicine, prepharmacy, preveterinary. **History:** General. **Legal studies:** Prelaw. **Math:** General. **Parks/recreation:** Exercise sciences, health/fitness. **Philosophy/religion:** Philosophy, religion. **Physical sciences:** Chemistry, physics, planetary. **Protective services:** Criminal justice. **Psychology:** General. **Public administration:** Social work. **Social sciences:** General, economics, international relations, political science, sociology. **Theology:** Preministerial. **Visual/performing arts:** Art, arts management, dramatic, interior design, music performance.

Most popular majors. Biology 7%, business/marketing 20%, communications/journalism 9%, education 8%, English 12%, health sciences 7%, visual/performing arts 11%.

Computing on campus. 170 workstations in library, computer center, student center. Dormitories wired for high-speed internet access and linked to campus network. Commuter students can connect to campus network. Online course registration, online library, helpline, student web hosting, wireless network available.

Student life. Freshman orientation: Mandatory. Preregistration for classes offered. 2-day program; 5 sessions offered in June. **Policies:** Freshmen permitted cars on campus. **Housing:** Guaranteed on-campus for all undergraduates. Coed dorms, special housing for disabled, apartments, fraternity/sorority housing, substance-free housing available. $50 deposit, deadline 7/1. Freshmen, sophomores, and juniors required to live on campus unless living with family. **Activities:** Bands, choral groups, dance, drama, literary magazine, music ensembles, musical theater, radio station, student government, student newspaper, symphony orchestra, Wesley Fellowship, international club, Circle K, Religious Life Council, Habitat for Humanity, African-American Leaders Promoting Higher Achievement (ALPHA), Leaders in College Service (LINCS), Catholic student organization.

Athletics. NCAA. **Intercollegiate:** Baseball M, basketball, cross-country, field hockey W, football (tackle) M, golf, lacrosse, soccer, softball W, tennis, track and field, volleyball W. **Intramural:** Basketball, lacrosse, racquetball, soccer, softball, tennis, volleyball. **Team name:** Bulldogs.

Student services. Adult student services, alcohol/substance abuse counseling, campus ministries, career counseling, student employment services, financial aid counseling, health services, minority student services, personal counseling, placement for graduates. **Physically disabled:** Services for visually, speech, hearing impaired.

Contact. E-mail: admissions@adrian.edu
Phone: (517) 265-5161 ext. 4326 Toll-free number: (800) 877-2246
Fax: (517) 264-3878
Carolyn Quinlan, Director of Admissions, Adrian College, 110 South Madison Street, Adrian, MI 49221-2575

Albion College

Albion, Michigan
www.albion.edu
CB member
CB code: 1007

- Private 4-year liberal arts college affiliated with United Methodist Church
- Residential campus in large town
- 1,953 degree-seeking undergraduates: 1% part-time, 56% women, 4% African American, 2% Asian American, 1% Hispanic American, 1% Native American, 1% international
- 82% of applicants admitted
- SAT or ACT (ACT writing optional), application essay required
- 72% graduate within 6 years

General. Founded in 1835. Regionally accredited. **Degrees:** 341 bachelor's awarded. **Location:** 35 miles from Lansing, 45 miles from Ann Arbor. **Calendar:** Semester, limited summer session. **Full-time faculty:** 139 total; 91% have terminal degrees, 9% minority, 37% women. **Part-time faculty:** 36 total; 31% have terminal degrees, 11% minority, 56% women. **Class size:** 73% < 20, 25% 20-39, 2% 40-49, less than 1% 50-99. **Special facilities:** 144-acre nature center, observatory, institute for public service, equestrian center and facility.

Freshman class profile. 1,946 applied, 1,593 admitted, 574 enrolled.

Mid 50% test scores			
SAT verbal:	510-640	Rank in top tenth:	34%
SAT math:	520-660	Return as sophomores:	86%
ACT:	22-27	Out-of-state:	10%
Rank in top quarter:	61%	Live on campus:	99%
		International:	2%

Basis for selection. Admission based on school achievement record, ACT/SAT test scores, recommendations from counselor or principal. Interview recommended. Audition recommended of music and theater majors.

High school preparation. 15 units required; 17 recommended. Required and recommended units include English 4, mathematics 3, social studies 3, history 3, science 3 (laboratory 1), foreign language 3 and academic electives 3.

2006-2007 Annual costs. Tuition/fees: $26,122. Room/board: $7,408. Books/supplies: $650. Personal expenses: $350.

2005-2006 Financial aid. Need-based: 442 full-time freshmen applied for aid; 355 were judged to have need; 355 of these received aid. Average need met was 97%. Average scholarship/grant was $16,890; average loan $3,297. 80% of total undergraduate aid awarded as scholarships/grants, 20% as loans/jobs. **Non-need-based:** Awarded to 1,695 full-time undergraduates, including 536 freshmen. Scholarships awarded for academics, alumni affiliation, art, leadership, minority status, music/drama, religious affiliation, state residency.

Application procedures. Admission: Priority date 4/1; deadline 7/1 (postmark date). $20 fee, may be waived for applicants with need. Application may be submitted online. Admission notification on a rolling basis beginning on or about 11/1. Must reply by May 1 or within 2 week(s) if notified thereafter. **Financial aid:** Priority date 2/15; no closing date. FAFSA required. Applicants notified on a rolling basis starting 3/15; must reply by 5/1 or within 2 week(s) of notification.

Academics. Special study options: Combined bachelor's/graduate degree, double major, dual enrollment of high school students, honors, independent study, internships, liberal arts/career combination, New York semester, semester at sea, student-designed major, study abroad, teacher certification program, urban semester, Washington semester. Environmental Institute, Ford Institute for Public Service, Gerstacker Liberal Arts Program in Professional Management. **Credit/placement by examination:** AP, CLEP, IB, institutional tests. **Support services:** Learning center, reduced course load, study skills assistance, tutoring, writing center.

Majors. Area/ethnic studies: American. **Biology:** General, biochemistry. **Business:** General, accounting, business admin. **Communications:** General. **Computer sciences:** General, computer science. **Conservation:** General, environmental science, environmental studies. **Education:** Art, biology, chemistry, English, foreign languages, French, German, history, mathematics, music, physical, physics, science, social studies, Spanish. **English:** Speech/rhetoric. **Foreign languages:** Chinese, French, German, Spanish. **Health:** Predentistry, premedicine, preveterinary. **History:** General. **Interdisciplinary:** Behavioral sciences, biological/physical sciences, math/computer science, natural sciences, neuroscience. **Legal studies:** Prelaw. **Math:** General. **Philosophy/religion:** Philosophy, religion. **Physical sciences:** Chemistry, geology, physics. **Psychology:** General. **Public administration:** Policy analysis. **Social sciences:** Anthropology, economics, international relations, political science, sociology. **Visual/performing arts:** General, art, art history/conservation, dramatic, music performance, studio arts.

Most popular majors. Biology 9%, business/marketing 7%, communications/journalism 7%, English 8%, history 6%, physical sciences 9%, psychology 11%, social sciences 20%, visual/performing arts 9%.

Computing on campus. 257 workstations in dormitories, library, computer center, student center. Dormitories wired for high-speed internet access and linked to campus network. Commuter students can connect to campus network. Online course registration, online library, helpline, repair service, wireless network available.

Student life. Freshman orientation: Mandatory. Preregistration for classes offered. **Policies:** Freshmen permitted cars on campus. **Housing:** Guaranteed on-campus for all undergraduates. Coed dorms, single-sex dorms, special housing for disabled, apartments, cooperative housing, fraternity/sorority housing available. Special interest annexes available. **Activities:** Bands, choral groups, dance, drama, literary magazine, music ensembles, musical theater, radio station, student government, student newspaper, symphony orchestra, TV station, 110 campus organizations.

Athletics. NCAA. **Intercollegiate:** Baseball M, basketball, cheerleading M, cross-country, diving, equestrian, football (tackle) M, golf, soccer, softball W, swimming, tennis, track and field, volleyball W. **Intramural:** Badminton, baseball M, basketball, bowling, diving, field hockey W, football (non-tackle), football (tackle) M, golf, ice hockey M, lacrosse, racquetball, rugby M, soccer, softball, swimming, tennis, track and field, volleyball. **Team name:** Britons.

Student services. Alcohol/substance abuse counseling, campus ministries, career counseling, services for economically disadvantaged, student employment services, financial aid counseling, health services, minority student services, personal counseling, placement for graduates, women's services. **Physically disabled:** Services for visually, hearing impaired.

Contact. E-mail: admissions@albion.edu
Phone: (517) 629-0321 Toll-free number: (800) 858-6770
Fax: (517) 629-0569
Doug Kellar, Associate Vice President for Enrollment, Albion College, 611 East Porter Street, Albion, MI 49224-1831

Alma College

Alma, Michigan — **CB member**
www.alma.edu — **CB code: 1010**

- Private 4-year liberal arts college affiliated with Presbyterian Church (USA)
- Residential campus in small town
- 1,242 degree-seeking undergraduates: 1% part-time, 58% women, 2% African American, 1% Asian American, 2% Hispanic American, 1% Native American, 1% international
- 81% of applicants admitted
- SAT or ACT (ACT writing optional) required
- 71% graduate within 6 years; 36% enter graduate study

General. Founded in 1886. Regionally accredited. **Degrees:** 232 bachelor's awarded. **ROTC:** Army. **Location:** 50 miles from Lansing, 45 miles from Saginaw. **Calendar:** 4-4-1 semester system. Limited summer session. **Full-time faculty:** 82 total; 88% have terminal degrees, 6% minority, 34% women. **Part-time faculty:** 37 total; 22% have terminal degrees, 46% women. **Class size:** 59% < 20, 37% 20-39, 2% 40-49, 2% 50-99. **Special facilities:** Planetarium, performing arts center, climbing wall.

Freshman class profile. 1,471 applied, 1,189 admitted, 336 enrolled.

Mid 50% test scores		**Rank in top quarter:**	62%
SAT verbal:	520-670	**Rank in top tenth:**	32%
SAT math:	510-650	**End year in good standing:**	92%
ACT:	21-27	**Return as sophomores:**	80%
GPA 3.50 or higher:	52%	**Out-of-state:**	4%
GPA 3.0-3.49:	32%	**Live on campus:**	98%
GPA 2.0-2.99:	16%	**International:**	1%

Basis for selection. Applicant should be in top half of class, have 3.0 high school GPA, or ACT composite score of 22, or combined SAT score of 1030 (exclusive of Writing). Cocurricular activities considered. Portfolio recommended for art majors. Interview recommended for all, strongly recommended for academically weak and those whose grades and test scores show discrepancies. **Homeschooled:** Must provide written statement describing anticipated impact of liberal arts education on candidate's personal and professional future.

High school preparation. 16 units required. Required and recommended units include English 4, mathematics 4, social studies 4, science 4 and foreign language 2.

2006-2007 Annual costs. Tuition/fees: $22,380. Room/board: $7,774. Books/supplies: $700. Personal expenses: $700.

2005-2006 Financial aid. Need-based: 336 full-time freshmen applied for aid; 257 were judged to have need; 257 of these received aid. Average need met was 86%. Average scholarship/grant was $15,322; average loan $4,613. 74% of total undergraduate aid awarded as scholarships/grants, 26% as loans/jobs. **Non-need-based:** Awarded to 405 full-time undergraduates, including 114 freshmen. Scholarships awarded for academics, alumni affiliation, art, music/drama. **Additional information:** Auditions required for music, drama, dance scholarship candidates. Portfolios required for art scholarship candidates.

Application procedures. Admission: Priority date 3/1; no deadline. $25 fee, may be waived for applicants with need. Application may be submitted online. Admission notification on a rolling basis beginning on or about 9/1. Must reply by May 1 or within 2 week(s) if notified thereafter. **Financial aid:** No deadline. FAFSA required. Applicants notified on a rolling basis starting 3/1; must reply within 3 week(s) of notification.

Academics. One-month spring term provides special opportunities for study in United States or overseas. Students required to complete 2 spring terms. **Special study options:** Combined bachelor's/graduate degree, double major, dual enrollment of high school students, exchange student, honors, independent study, internships, New York semester, student-designed major, study abroad, teacher certification program, urban semester, Washington semester. Pre-engineering 3-2 programs with University of Michigan, Michigan Technological University; pre-occupational therapy 3-2 program with Washington University (MO). **Credit/placement by examination:** AP, CLEP, IB, ACT, institutional tests. 32 credit hours maximum toward bachelor's degree. **Support services:** Pre-admission summer program, reduced course load, remedial instruction, study skills assistance, tutoring, writing center.

Majors. Biology: General, biochemistry. **Business:** Accounting, business admin, finance, international, marketing. **Communications:** Media studies. **Computer sciences:** Computer science. **Education:** General, elementary, secondary. **English:** English lit. **Foreign languages:** French, German, Spanish. **Health:** Medical illustrating, predentistry, premedicine, preveterinary.

History: General. **Interdisciplinary:** Biological/physical sciences, gerontology. **Legal studies:** Prelaw. **Liberal arts:** Arts/sciences, humanities. **Math:** General. **Parks/recreation:** Exercise sciences. **Philosophy/religion:** Philosophy, religion. **Physical sciences:** Chemistry, physics. **Psychology:** General. **Social sciences:** Anthropology, economics, political science, sociology. **Theology:** Preministerial. **Visual/performing arts:** General, art, art history/conservation, dance, design, dramatic, graphic design, music performance, studio arts.

Most popular majors. Biology 13%, business/marketing 16%, education 7%, health sciences 10%, history 9%, social sciences 9%, visual/performing arts 10%.

Computing on campus. 266 workstations in dormitories, library, computer center. Dormitories wired for high-speed internet access and linked to campus network. Commuter students can connect to campus network. Online library, helpline, student web hosting, wireless network available.

Student life. Freshman orientation: Mandatory, $300 fee. Preregistration for classes offered. 1-week session begins last weekend of August and runs to Labor Day weekend. **Policies:** Freshmen permitted cars on campus. **Housing:** Guaranteed on-campus for all undergraduates. Coed dorms, single-sex dorms, apartments, fraternity/sorority housing, substance-free housing available. $100 partly refundable deposit, deadline 5/15. Academic theme houses available. **Activities:** Bands, choral groups, dance, drama, literary magazine, music ensembles, radio station, student government, student newspaper, symphony orchestra, College Republicans/College Democrats, Amnesty International, Big Brothers/Big Sisters, Catholic student organization, Habitat for Humanity, international club, Model United Nations, Students Against Sweatshops, Students Offering Service, Trinity Bible Fellowship.

Athletics. NCAA. **Intercollegiate:** Baseball M, basketball, cross-country, diving, football (tackle) M, golf, soccer, softball W, swimming, tennis, track and field, volleyball W. **Intramural:** Basketball, football (non-tackle), soccer, softball, tennis, volleyball. **Team name:** Scots.

Student services. Alcohol/substance abuse counseling, campus ministries, career counseling, student employment services, financial aid counseling, health services, personal counseling. **Physically disabled:** Services for visually, hearing impaired.

Contact. E-mail: admissions@alma.edu
Phone: (989) 463-7139 Toll-free number: (800) 321-2562
Fax: (989) 463-7057
Karen Klumpp, Vice President for Enrollment, Alma College, 614 West Superior Street, Alma, MI 48801-1599

Andrews University

Berrien Springs, Michigan
www.andrews.edu **CB code: 1030**

- Private 4-year university affiliated with Seventh-day Adventists
- Residential campus in small town
- 1,571 degree-seeking undergraduates: 7% part-time, 56% women, 20% African American, 8% Asian American, 11% Hispanic American, 12% international
- 1,323 degree-seeking graduate students
- 40% of applicants admitted
- SAT or ACT (ACT writing optional), application essay required
- 49% graduate within 6 years

General. Founded in 1874. Regionally accredited. **Degrees:** 293 bachelor's, 5 associate awarded; master's, doctoral, first professional offered. **Location:** 10 miles from St. Joseph-Benton Harbor, 25 miles from South Bend, Indiana. **Calendar:** Semester, limited summer session. **Full-time faculty:** 220 total; 71% have terminal degrees, 26% minority, 31% women. **Part-time faculty:** 82 total; 28% have terminal degrees, 16% minority, 35% women. **Class size:** 64% < 20, 25% 20-39, 4% 40-49, 5% 50-99, 1% >100. **Special facilities:** Natural history museum, archaeology museum, performing arts center, arboretum.

Freshman class profile. 1,324 applied, 527 admitted, 305 enrolled.

Mid 50% test scores		Rank in top tenth:	14%
SAT verbal:	470-590	Return as sophomores:	78%
SAT math:	450-580	Out-of-state:	72%
ACT:	20-26	Live on campus:	81%
Rank in top quarter:	38%	International:	11%

Basis for selection. School achievement record, test scores, recommendations important. ACT preferred, SAT accepted. Interview recommended. Audition recommended for music majors. Portfolios recommended for architecture, art majors and homeschoolers. **Homeschooled:** Portfolio required. **Learning Disabled:** Must advise student services of learning disability prior to admission interview and testing.

High school preparation. 13 units required; 15 recommended. Required and recommended units include English 3-4, mathematics 2-3, social studies 1, history 2, science 2 and academic electives 3. Additional 1 unit chemistry, 1 unit physics, 1 unit computer recommended.

2005-2006 Annual costs. Tuition/fees: $16,506. Room/board: $5,280. Books/supplies: $1,000. Personal expenses: $600.

2004-2005 Financial aid. Need-based: 323 full-time freshmen applied for aid; 214 were judged to have need; 214 of these received aid. Average need met was 99%. Average scholarship/grant was $6,291; average loan $2,553. 50% of total undergraduate aid awarded as scholarships/grants, 50% as loans/jobs. **Non-need-based:** Awarded to 1,374 full-time undergraduates, including 321 freshmen. Scholarships awarded for academics, alumni affiliation, leadership, music/drama, religious affiliation.

Application procedures. Admission: No deadline. $30 fee. Application must be submitted on paper. Admission notification on a rolling basis beginning on or about 1/1. **Financial aid:** Priority date 3/31; no closing date. FAFSA, institutional form required. Applicants notified on a rolling basis starting 3/15.

Academics. Special study options: Accelerated study, combined bachelor's/graduate degree, cooperative education, distance learning, double major, dual enrollment of high school students, ESL, honors, internships, student-designed major, study abroad, teacher certification program. **Credit/placement by examination:** AP, CLEP, IB, institutional tests. 32 credit hours maximum toward associate degree, 32 toward bachelor's. DANTES (for nontraditional students). **Support services:** Learning center, pre-admission summer program, reduced course load, remedial instruction, study skills assistance, tutoring, writing center.

Majors. Agriculture: Animal sciences, business, horticulture. **Architecture:** Architecture. **Biology:** General, biochemistry, biophysics, botany, molecular, zoology. **Business:** Accounting, business admin, entrepreneurial studies, finance, managerial economics, nonprofit/public, training/development. **Communications:** General, journalism, public relations. **Communications technology:** General. **Computer sciences:** General, information systems. **Conservation:** Environmental science. **Education:** Elementary, mathematics, secondary, social science, social studies. **Engineering:** General, electrical, industrial, mechanical. **Engineering technology:** Aerospace, automotive, electrical, mechanical. **Family/consumer sciences:** Family studies, food/nutrition. **Foreign languages:** French, Spanish. **Health:** Audiology/speech pathology, clinical lab science, dietetics, nursing (RN). **History:** General. **Interdisciplinary:** Biological/physical sciences, neuroscience. **Math:** General. **Mechanic/repair:** Aircraft. **Philosophy/religion:** Religion. **Physical sciences:** Chemistry, physics. **Psychology:** General. **Public administration:** Social work. **Social sciences:** General, anthropology, economics, international economic development, political science, sociology. **Theology:** Religious ed, sacred music, theology, youth ministry. **Transportation:** Aviation. **Visual/performing arts:** General, art, art history/conservation, ceramics, commercial/advertising art, design, graphic design, multimedia, music performance, painting, photography, printmaking, studio arts.

Computing on campus. 130 workstations in dormitories, library, computer center. Dormitories wired for high-speed internet access and linked to campus network. Commuter students can connect to campus network. Online course registration, online library, helpline, student web hosting, wireless network available.

Student life. Freshman orientation: Mandatory, $50 fee. Preregistration for classes offered. Held the week before fall registration. **Policies:** Students expected to abide by ethical and moral standards of the university, which are mission-driven as published in official documents. Resident students required to stay in dorm until age 22. Religious observance required. Freshmen permitted cars on campus. **Housing:** Guaranteed on-campus for all undergraduates. Single-sex dorms, apartments, substance-free housing available. $100 deposit. **Activities:** Concert band, choral groups, drama, music ensembles, musical theater, radio station, student government, student newspaper, symphony orchestra, Christian Youth Action.

Athletics. Intramural: Badminton, basketball, field hockey, football (non-tackle), soccer, softball, triathlon, volleyball.

Student services. Campus ministries, career counseling, student employment services, financial aid counseling, health services, on-campus daycare, personal counseling, placement for graduates, veterans' counselor. **Physically disabled:** Services for visually, speech, hearing impaired.

Contact. E-mail: enroll@andrews.edu
Phone: (800) 253-2874 Toll-free number: (800) 253-2874
Fax: (269) 471-3228
Stephen Payne, Vice President for Enrollment Management, Andrews University, Berrien Springs, MI 49104

Aquinas College
Grand Rapids, Michigan
www.aquinas.edu **CB code: 1018**

- Private 4-year liberal arts college affiliated with Roman Catholic Church
- Residential campus in small city
- 1,782 degree-seeking undergraduates: 18% part-time, 65% women, 4% African American, 2% Asian American, 4% Hispanic American
- 411 degree-seeking graduate students
- 86% of applicants admitted
- SAT or ACT (ACT writing optional) required
- 49% graduate within 6 years; 13% enter graduate study

General. Founded in 1886. Regionally accredited. **Degrees:** 381 bachelor's, 2 associate awarded; master's offered. **Location:** 140 miles from Detroit, 180 miles from Chicago. **Calendar:** Semester, extensive summer session. **Full-time faculty:** 94 total; 66% have terminal degrees, 8% minority, 46% women. **Part-time faculty:** 105 total; 28% have terminal degrees, 6% minority, 52% women. **Class size:** 64% < 20, 35% 20-39, less than 1% 40-49, less than 1% 50-99. **Special facilities:** Greenhouse, astronomy tower, nature trails, community theater.

Freshman class profile. 1,646 applied, 1,409 admitted, 363 enrolled.

Mid 50% test scores		**Rank in top tenth:**	17%
ACT:	19-25	**End year in good standing:**	88%
GPA 3.50 or higher:	47%	**Return as sophomores:**	79%
GPA 3.0-3.49:	31%	**Out-of-state:**	6%
GPA 2.0-2.99:	22%	**Live on campus:**	83%
Rank in top quarter:	41%	**International:**	1%

Basis for selection. GED not accepted. 2.5 high school GPA in academic subjects. Test scores important. ACT recommended. Interview required for applicants with above average test scores but less than 2.5 high school GPA in academic subjects, recommended for others. Audition recommended for music majors. Portfolio recommended for art majors. **Homeschooled:** Transcript of courses and grades required. **Learning Disabled:** Make appointment with Academic Achievement Center to express needed accommodations prior to enrollment.

High school preparation. 15 units required. Required units include English 4, mathematics 4, social studies 4 and science 3.

2006-2007 Annual costs. Tuition/fees: $19,000. Room/board: $6,174. Books/supplies: $695. Personal expenses: $685.

2005-2006 Financial aid. Need-based: 334 full-time freshmen applied for aid; 279 were judged to have need; 279 of these received aid. Average need met was 89%. Average scholarship/grant was $12,518; average loan $1,928. 86% of total undergraduate aid awarded as scholarships/grants, 14% as loans/jobs. **Non-need-based:** Scholarships awarded for academics, alumni affiliation, art, athletics, leadership, religious affiliation.

Application procedures. Admission: No deadline. No application fee. Application may be submitted online. Admission notification on a rolling basis beginning on or about 8/1. **Financial aid:** Priority date 2/15; no closing date. FAFSA required. Applicants notified on a rolling basis starting 4/1; must reply within 2 week(s) of notification.

Academics. Special study options: Accelerated study, cooperative education, cross-registration, distance learning, double major, dual enrollment of high school students, exchange student, honors, independent study, internships, liberal arts/career combination, student-designed major, study abroad, teacher certification program. **Credit/placement by examination:** AP, CLEP, institutional tests. 30 credit hours maximum toward bachelor's degree. **Support services:** Learning center, remedial instruction, study skills assistance, tutoring, writing center.

Majors. Biology: General. **Business:** Accounting, business admin, communications, international. **Communications:** General. **Computer sciences:** General. **Conservation:** Environmental science, environmental studies. **Education:** General, art, elementary, learning disabled, music, physical, reading, science, social science, special. **English:** English lit. **Foreign languages:** French, German, Japanese, Spanish. **Health:** Athletic training. **History:** General. **Legal studies:** Prelaw. **Liberal arts:** Arts/sciences. **Math:** General. **Parks/recreation:** General, health/fitness, sports admin. **Philosophy/religion:** Philosophy, religion. **Physical sciences:** Chemistry, physics. **Protective services:** Fire safety technology. **Psychology:** General. **Public administration:** Community org/advocacy. **Social sciences:** General, economics, geography, international relations, political science, sociology, urban studies. **Theology:** Sacred music. **Visual/performing arts:** Art, art history/conservation, arts management, theater arts management.

Most popular majors. Business/marketing 21%, communications/journalism 6%, education 22%, psychology 6%, social sciences 9%.

Computing on campus. 155 workstations in dormitories, library, computer center, student center. Dormitories wired for high-speed internet access and linked to campus network. Commuter students can connect to campus network. Online library, helpline, wireless network available.

Student life. Freshman orientation: Mandatory, $100 fee. Preregistration for classes offered. 3 days during week before fall classes begin. Includes start of common freshman class. **Policies:** Students serve on administrative and faculty committees. Freshmen permitted cars on campus. **Housing:** Guaranteed on-campus for freshmen. Coed dorms, apartments, substance-free housing available. $100 deposit, deadline 8/15. Project/theme houses. **Activities:** Jazz band, choral groups, drama, literary magazine, music ensembles, radio station, student government, student newspaper, community action volunteers, minority and international student unions, campus ministry, social action commission, community senate, Bible Study, College Democrats, College Republicans, Catholic studies club, Habitat for Humanity.

Athletics. NAIA. **Intercollegiate:** Baseball M, basketball, cross-country, golf, soccer, softball W, tennis, track and field, volleyball W. **Intramural:** Basketball, bowling, fencing M, golf, ice hockey M, skiing, soccer, softball, tennis, volleyball. **Team name:** Saints.

Student services. Adult student services, alcohol/substance abuse counseling, campus ministries, career counseling, student employment services, financial aid counseling, health services, minority student services, personal counseling, placement for graduates, veterans' counselor, women's services. **Physically disabled:** Services for visually, speech, hearing impaired.

Contact. E-mail: admissions@aquinas.edu
Phone: (616) 632-2900 Toll-free number: (800) 678-9593
Fax: (616) 732-4469
Paula Meehan, Dean of Admissions, Aquinas College, 1607 Robinson Road Southeast, Grand Rapids, MI 49506-1799

Ave Maria College
Ypsilanti, Michigan
www.avemaria.edu **CB code: 3840**

- Private 4-year liberal arts college
- Residential campus

General. Calendar: Semester.

Annual costs/financial aid. Tuition/fees (2005-2006): $12,600. Room/board: $6,138.

Contact. Phone: (734) 337-4525
300 West Forest Avenue, Ypsilanti, MI 48197

Baker College of Auburn Hills
Auburn Hills, Michigan
www.baker.edu **CB code: 1457**

- Private 4-year business and technical college
- Commuter campus in small city
- 3,517 degree-seeking undergraduates

General. Founded in 1990. Regionally accredited. Part of multicampus system specializing in career education. **Degrees:** 132 bachelor's, 278 associate awarded. **Location:** 30 miles from Detroit. **Calendar:** Quarter, limited summer session. **Full-time faculty:** 11 total. **Part-time faculty:** 144 total. **Class size:** 45% < 20, 55% 20-39.

Freshman class profile. 795 enrolled.

Basis for selection. Open admission. Specific entrance requirements for allied health programs and bachelor of business leadership degree program. Interview recommended.

2006-2007 Annual costs. Tuition/fees (projected): $8,100. Books/supplies: $1,000.

Financial aid. **Non-need-based:** Scholarships awarded for academics, alumni affiliation.

Application procedures. **Admission:** No deadline. $20 fee, may be waived for applicants with need. Application may be submitted online. Admission notification on a rolling basis. **Financial aid:** Priority date 2/21, closing date 9/1. FAFSA, institutional form required. Applicants notified on a rolling basis starting 4/1.

Academics. 2+2 system allows students to begin required courses in major while completing associate degree. **Special study options:** Accelerated study, combined bachelor's/graduate degree, distance learning, double major, dual enrollment of high school students, independent study, internships, liberal arts/career combination, teacher certification program. **Credit/placement by examination:** AP, CLEP, IB, institutional tests. 48 credit hours maximum toward associate degree, 96 toward bachelor's. **Support services:** Learning center, reduced course load, remedial instruction, study skills assistance, tutoring, writing center.

Majors. **Business:** General, accounting, business admin, management science. **Education:** General, elementary, middle, multi-level teacher, secondary.

Computing on campus. 131 workstations in library, computer center, student center. Commuter students can connect to campus network. Helpline available.

Student life. **Freshman orientation:** Mandatory. **Activities:** Accounting club, management club, interior design society, society of automotive engineers, marketing club.

Student services. Career counseling, student employment services, financial aid counseling, personal counseling, placement for graduates, veterans' counselor. **Physically disabled:** Services for visually, hearing impaired.

Contact. Phone: (248) 340-0600 Toll-free number: (888) 429-0410
Fax: (248) 340-0600
Jan Bohlen, Vice President for Admissions, Baker College of Auburn Hills, 1500 University Drive, Auburn Hills, MI 48326

Baker College of Cadillac

Cadillac, Michigan
www.baker.edu **CB code: 1381**

- Private 4-year business and health science college
- Commuter campus in large town
- 1,559 undergraduates

General. Founded in 1911. Regionally accredited. Part of multicampus system specializing in career education. **Degrees:** 24 bachelor's, 155 associate awarded. **Location:** 90 miles from Grand Rapids, 45 miles from Traverse City. **Calendar:** Quarter, limited summer session. **Full-time faculty:** 4 total. **Part-time faculty:** 101 total. **Class size:** 68% < 20, 31% 20-39, 1% 40-49. **Special facilities:** Mock operating room, massage therapy room.

Basis for selection. Open admission. Some allied health programs require health appraisal. Interview recommended.

2005-2006 Annual costs. Tuition/fees: $7,875. Books/supplies: $1,000.

Financial aid. **Non-need-based:** Scholarships awarded for academics.

Application procedures. **Admission:** No deadline. $20 fee, may be waived for applicants with need. Admission notification on a rolling basis beginning on or about 10/1. **Financial aid:** Priority date 2/21; no closing date. FAFSA, institutional form required. Applicants notified on a rolling basis starting 5/1.

Academics. **Special study options:** Accelerated study, combined bachelor's/graduate degree, cooperative education, distance learning, double major, dual enrollment of high school students, external degree, independent study, internships, liberal arts/career combination, weekend college. 2+2 bachelor's degree and bachelor of business leadership degree. **Credit/placement by examination:** AP, CLEP, IB, institutional tests. 48 credit hours maximum toward associate degree, 96 toward bachelor's. **Support services:** Learning center, reduced course load, remedial instruction, study skills assistance, tutoring, writing center.

Majors. **Business:** Accounting, business admin, human resources, office management. **Computer sciences:** Computer science. **Public administration:** Human services.

Computing on campus. 154 workstations in library, computer center. Commuter students can connect to campus network. Online library, helpline, repair service available.

Student life. **Freshman orientation:** Mandatory. Preregistration for classes offered. **Policies:** Freshmen permitted cars on campus. **Activities:** Student activities group, professional student organizations.

Student services. Career counseling, student employment services, financial aid counseling, personal counseling, placement for graduates, veterans' counselor. **Physically disabled:** Services for visually, hearing impaired.

Contact. E-mail: tisdal_m@cadillac.baker.edu
Phone: (231) 876-3100 Toll-free number: (888) 313-3463
Fax: (231) 775-8505
Mike Tisdale, Director of Admissions, Baker College of Cadillac, 9600 East 13th Street, Cadillac, MI 49601

Baker College of Clinton Township

Clinton Township, Michigan
www.baker.edu **CB code: 1386**

- Private 4-year business and technical college
- Commuter campus in very large city
- 5,103 degree-seeking undergraduates

General. Founded in 1911. Regionally accredited. Part of multicampus system specializing in career education. **Degrees:** 137 bachelor's, 312 associate awarded. **Location:** 15 miles from Detroit. **Calendar:** Quarter, limited summer session. **Full-time faculty:** 17 total. **Part-time faculty:** 191 total. **Class size:** 25% < 20, 74% 20-39, less than 1% 40-49.

Basis for selection. Open admission, but selective for some programs. Physical exam may be required for some programs. Interview recommended. **Learning Disabled:** Students must complete special needs intake form signed by a professional.

High school preparation. Recommended units include English 4, mathematics 4, social studies 2, science 3 and foreign language 4.

2006-2007 Annual costs. Tuition/fees (projected): $8,100. Books/supplies: $1,000. Personal expenses: $2,000.

Financial aid. **Non-need-based:** Scholarships awarded for academics, minority status.

Application procedures. **Admission:** Priority date 9/1; no deadline. $20 fee, may be waived for applicants with need. Application may be submitted online. Admission notification on a rolling basis. **Financial aid:** Priority date 2/21, closing date 9/1. FAFSA, institutional form required. Applicants notified on a rolling basis starting 4/1.

Academics. 2+2 system allows students to begin required courses in major while completing associate degree. **Special study options:** Accelerated study, combined bachelor's/graduate degree, cooperative education, distance learning, double major, dual enrollment of high school students, external degree, independent study, internships, teacher certification program. **Credit/placement by examination:** AP, CLEP, IB, institutional tests. 48 credit hours maximum toward associate degree, 96 toward bachelor's. **Support services:** Learning center, reduced course load, remedial instruction, study skills assistance, tutoring, writing center.

Majors. **Business:** Accounting, administrative services, business admin, human resources, management science, office management. **Computer sciences:** General, computer science. **Health:** Health care admin, nursing (RN), office admin. **Public administration:** Human services.

Computing on campus. 108 workstations in library, computer center. Commuter students can connect to campus network. Helpline available.

Student life. **Freshman orientation:** Mandatory. Preregistration for classes offered.

Student services. Adult student services, career counseling, student employment services, financial aid counseling, personal counseling, placement for graduates, veterans' counselor. **Physically disabled:** Services for visually, hearing impaired.

Contact. E-mail: adm_mc@baker.edu
Phone: (586) 790-9580 Toll-free number: (888) 272-2842
Fax: (586) 791-6610
Annette Looser, Director of Admissions, Baker College of Clinton Township, 34401 Gratiot Avenue, Clinton Township, MI 48035

Baker College of Flint

Flint, Michigan
www.baker.edu **CB code: 0806**

- Private 4-year business and technical college
- Commuter campus in large city
- 3,466 full-time, degree-seeking undergraduates

General. Founded in 1911. Regionally accredited. Corporate services division offers degree-granting programs on campus and/or at work site, coordinated with corporate training and professional development programs. Part of multicampus system specializing in career education. **Degrees:** 147 bachelor's, 451 associate awarded; master's offered. **Location:** 10 miles from downtown, 60 miles from Detroit. **Calendar:** Quarter, limited summer session. **Full-time faculty:** 40 total. **Part-time faculty:** 304 total.

Freshman class profile. 1,535 enrolled.

Out-of-state:	2%	**Live on campus:**	5%

Basis for selection. Open admission, but selective for some programs. Health applicants must have health appraisal. Occupational therapy applicants must present minimum of 1 year biology, 1 year chemistry/physics, 2 years mathematics including algebra or equivalent. All health programs require 2.0 GPA for entrance to professional classes. Class size may be limited. Trucking programs require drug screening prior to enrollment acceptance. Interview recommended.

2006-2007 Annual costs. Tuition/fees (projected): $8,100. Additional fees vary with program. Room only: $2,500. Books/supplies: $900.

Financial aid. Non-need-based: Scholarships awarded for academics, minority status.

Application procedures. Admission: Priority date 9/1; no deadline. $20 fee, may be waived for applicants with need. Admission notification on a rolling basis. **Financial aid:** Priority date 2/21, closing date 9/1. FAFSA, institutional form required. Applicants notified on a rolling basis starting 4/1.

Academics. 2+2 system allows students to begin required courses in major while completing associate degree. Calendar based on 10-week quarters. **Special study options:** Accelerated study, combined bachelor's/graduate degree, cooperative education, distance learning, double major, dual enrollment of high school students, external degree, independent study, internships. **Credit/placement by examination:** AP, CLEP, IB, institutional tests. 48 credit hours maximum toward associate degree, 96 toward bachelor's. **Support services:** Learning center, reduced course load, remedial instruction, study skills assistance, tutoring, writing center.

Majors. Business: Accounting, business admin, management information systems, office management, operations. **Computer sciences:** General. **Engineering:** Mechanical. **Engineering technology:** Electrical. **Health:** Health care admin, medical records admin, nursing (RN). **Transportation:** Aviation management. **Visual/performing arts:** Commercial/advertising art, interior design.

Most popular majors. Business/marketing 65%, health sciences 25%.

Computing on campus. 300 workstations in library, computer center. Commuter students can connect to campus network. Helpline available.

Student life. Freshman orientation: Mandatory. Preregistration for classes offered. **Policies:** Freshmen permitted cars on campus. **Housing:** Coed dorms available. $50 deposit, deadline 9/20. **Activities:** Literary magazine, National Association of Accountants, American Marketing Association, Interior Design Society, travel club, environmental club, physical therapy assistant club, medical assistants student organization, Health Information Management Association, graphic communications club, Society of Manufacturing Engineers student chapter.

Student services. Career counseling, student employment services, on-campus daycare, personal counseling, placement for graduates, veterans' counselor. **Physically disabled:** Services for visually, hearing impaired.

Contact. E-mail: adm-fl@baker.edu
Phone: (810) 766-4000 Toll-free number: (800) 964-4299
Fax: (810) 766-4293
Troy Crowe, Vice President of Admissions, Baker College of Flint, 1050 West Bristol Road, Flint, MI 48507

Baker College of Jackson

Jackson, Michigan
www.baker.edu **CB code: 1887**

- Private 4-year business and technical college
- Commuter campus in small city
- 1,625 undergraduates

General. Founded in 1994. Regionally accredited. Part of multicampus system specializing in career education. **Degrees:** 53 bachelor's, 136 associate awarded. **Location:** 40 miles from Lansing, 40 miles from Ann Arbor. **Calendar:** Quarter, limited summer session. **Full-time faculty:** 5 total. **Part-time faculty:** 93 total.

Basis for selection. Open admission, but selective for some programs. Physical exam may be required for allied health programs. All health programs require specific GPA. Interview recommended.

2006-2007 Annual costs. Tuition/fees (projected): $8,100. Books/supplies: $975.

Financial aid. Non-need-based: Scholarships awarded for academics, minority status.

Application procedures. Admission: No deadline. $20 fee, may be waived for applicants with need. Application may be submitted online. Admission notification on a rolling basis. **Financial aid:** Priority date 2/21, closing date 9/1. FAFSA, institutional form required. Applicants notified on a rolling basis starting 4/1.

Academics. 2+2 system allows students to begin required courses in major while completing associate degree. **Special study options:** Accelerated study, cooperative education, distance learning, double major, dual enrollment of high school students, external degree, independent study, internships. **Credit/placement by examination:** AP, CLEP, IB, institutional tests. 48 credit hours maximum toward associate degree, 96 toward bachelor's. **Support services:** Learning center, reduced course load, remedial instruction, study skills assistance, tutoring, writing center.

Majors. Business: General, accounting.

Computing on campus. 114 workstations in library, computer center. Commuter students can connect to campus network. Helpline available.

Student life. Freshman orientation: Mandatory. Preregistration for classes offered. **Activities:** Student government.

Student services. Career counseling, student employment services, personal counseling, placement for graduates, veterans' counselor. **Physically disabled:** Services for visually, hearing impaired.

Contact. E-mail: kelli.stepka@baker.edu
Phone: (517) 788-7800 Toll-free number: (888) 343-3683
Fax: (517) 789-7331
Kelli Stepka, Director of Admissions, Baker College of Jackson, 2800 Springport Road, Jackson, MI 49202

Baker College of Muskegon

Muskegon, Michigan
www.baker.edu **CB code: 1527**

- Private 4-year business and technical college
- Commuter campus in small city
- 4,744 undergraduates

General. Founded in 1888. Regionally accredited. Part of multicampus system specializing in career education. All associate degree programs include internship, co-op or clinical affiliation experience. **Degrees:** 122 bachelor's, 419 associate awarded. **Location:** 40 miles from Grand Rapids. **Calendar:** Quarter, limited summer session. **Full-time faculty:** 17 total. **Part-time faculty:** 169 total. **Class size:** 38% < 20, 57% 20-39, 3% 40-49, 2% 50-99. **Special facilities:** Restaurant run by culinary and food and beverage management students.

Basis for selection. Open admission, but selective for some programs. 2.75 GPA required for admission to occupational therapy assisting, physical therapist assisting, veterinary technician, surgical technology, teacher preparation. Class size may be limited in some programs. Physical examination, background check required for some programs. Interview recommended. **Homeschooled:** Basic skills placement assessments in math, language arts, and reading part of orientation/registration process. **Learning Disabled:** Learning disability must be documented and presented to counseling staff before registering for classes.

2006-2007 Annual costs. Tuition/fees (projected): $8,100. Room only: $2,500. Books/supplies: $975. Personal expenses: $2,000.

Financial aid. Non-need-based: Scholarships awarded for academics, minority status.

Application procedures. Admission: Priority date 9/1; no deadline. $20 fee, may be waived for applicants with need. Application may be submitted online. Admission notification on a rolling basis. **Financial aid:** Priority date 2/21; no closing date. FAFSA, institutional form required. Applicants notified on a rolling basis starting 4/1.

Academics. 2-2 system allows students to begin required courses in major while completing associate degree. Maximum number of credits awarded for prior work and/or life experiences, 48 for associate and 144 for bachelor. **Special study options:** Accelerated study, combined bachelor's/graduate degree, cooperative education, distance learning, double major, dual enrollment of high school students, external degree, independent study, internships, liberal arts/career combination, teacher certification program. Accelerated bachelor of business administration offered in weekend delivery format. **Credit/placement by examination:** AP, CLEP, IB, institutional tests. 48 credit hours maximum toward associate degree, 144 toward bachelor's. **Support services:** Learning center, reduced course load, remedial instruction, study skills assistance, tutoring.

Majors. Business: Accounting, accounting/business management, administrative services, business admin, human resources, management science, marketing, office management, restaurant/food services. **Computer sciences:** General, computer science, information systems, systems analysis. **Education:** Elementary, kindergarten/preschool, middle, multi-level teacher, secondary. **Engineering technology:** Industrial management. **Health:** Health care admin. **Personal/culinary services:** General, culinary arts, restaurant/catering. **Public administration:** Human services. **Transportation:** Aviation management.

Computing on campus. 180 workstations in dormitories, library, computer center. Dormitories wired for high-speed internet access and linked to campus network. Commuter students can connect to campus network. Online course registration, online library, helpline, wireless network available.

Student life. Freshman orientation: Mandatory. Preregistration for classes offered. 3-4 hour session prior to start of quarter, includes COMPASS testing, registration, academic advising. **Policies:** No drug or alcohol use permitted anywhere on campus or in residence halls. Freshmen permitted cars on campus. **Housing:** Coed dorms, special housing for disabled, apartments available. $50 deposit, deadline 9/1. **Activities:** Student government, travel club, rehab club, residence hall association, culinary arts club, human resource management club.

Athletics. Intramural: Bowling.

Student services. Adult student services, career counseling, student employment services, financial aid counseling, personal counseling, placement for graduates, veterans' counselor. **Physically disabled:** Services for visually, hearing impaired.

Contact. E-mail: kathy.jacobson@baker.edu
Phone: (231) 777-5200 Toll-free number: (800) 937-0337
Fax: (231) 777-5201
Kathy Jacobson, Vice President and Director of Admissions, Baker College of Muskegon, 1903 Marquette Avenue, Muskegon, MI 49442

Baker College of Owosso

Owosso, Michigan
www.baker.edu **CB code: 5270**

- Private 4-year business and technical college
- Commuter campus in large town
- 2,823 undergraduates

General. Founded in 1911. Regionally accredited. Part of multicampus system, with affiliated graduate school, specializing in career education. Master's degree available at Flint campus. **Degrees:** 63 bachelor's, 269 associate awarded. **Location:** 30 miles from Lansing, 300 miles from Flint. **Calendar:** Quarter, limited summer session. **Full-time faculty:** 8 total. **Part-time faculty:** 146 total.

Freshman class profile.

Out-of-state:	3%	**Live on campus:**	30%

Basis for selection. Open admission. Limited enrollment for medical programs.

2006-2007 Annual costs. Tuition/fees (projected): $8,100. Room only: $2,500. Books/supplies: $900.

Financial aid. Non-need-based: Scholarships awarded for academics, minority status.

Application procedures. Admission: Priority date 9/1; no deadline. $20 fee, may be waived for applicants with need. Application may be submitted online. Admission notification on a rolling basis. **Financial aid:** Priority date 2/21, closing date 9/1. FAFSA, institutional form required. Applicants notified on a rolling basis starting 4/1.

Academics. 2+2 system allows students to begin required courses in major while completing associate degree. **Special study options:** Accelerated study, cooperative education, distance learning, double major, dual enrollment of high school students, external degree, independent study, internships. **Credit/placement by examination:** AP, CLEP, IB, institutional tests. 48 credit hours maximum toward associate degree, 96 toward bachelor's. **Support services:** Learning center, reduced course load, remedial instruction, study skills assistance, tutoring, writing center.

Majors. Business: Accounting, administrative services, business admin, human resources, management information systems, marketing, office management. **Communications technology:** Graphics. **Computer sciences:** General, computer graphics, computer science. **Education:** Elementary, middle, multi-level teacher, secondary. **Health:** Health care admin. **Public administration:** Human services.

Computing on campus. 226 workstations in dormitories, library, computer center. Dormitories wired for high-speed internet access. Commuter students can connect to campus network. Online library, helpline available.

Student life. Freshman orientation: Mandatory. Preregistration for classes offered. **Policies:** Freshmen permitted cars on campus. **Housing:** Guaranteed on-campus for freshmen. Coed dorms available. $50 deposit. **Activities:** Student newspaper, accounting club, MLT club, interior design club, radiology club, graphics club.

Athletics. Intramural: Basketball, volleyball.

Student services. Adult student services, career counseling, services for economically disadvantaged, student employment services, financial aid counseling, on-campus daycare, personal counseling, placement for graduates, veterans' counselor. **Physically disabled:** Services for visually, speech, hearing impaired.

Contact. E-mail: michael.konopacke@baker.edu
Phone: (989) 729-3350 Toll-free number: (800) 879-3797
Fax: (989) 729-3359
Michael Konopacke, Director of Admissions, Baker College of Owosso, 1020 South Washington Street, Owosso, MI 48867

Baker College of Port Huron

Port Huron, Michigan
www.baker.edu **CB code: 1413**

- Private 4-year business and technical college
- Commuter campus in large town
- 1,578 undergraduates

General. Founded in 1911. Regionally accredited. Part of multicampus system specializing in career education. **Degrees:** 75 bachelor's, 144 associate awarded; master's offered. **Location:** 60 miles from Detroit. **Calendar:** Quarter, limited summer session. **Full-time faculty:** 12 total. **Part-time faculty:** 114 total. **Class size:** 58% < 20, 37% 20-39, 1% 40-49, 4% 50-99. **Special facilities:** Dental hygiene clinic.

Basis for selection. Open admission, but selective for some programs. Specific entrance requirements for health and human services programs. Interview recommended.

2006-2007 Annual costs. Tuition/fees (projected): $8,100. Books/supplies: $1,000. Personal expenses: $2,000.

Financial aid. All financial aid based on need.

Application procedures. Admission: Priority date 9/1; no deadline. $20 fee, may be waived for applicants with need. Application may be submitted online. Admission notification on a rolling basis. **Financial aid:** Priority date 2/21; no closing date. FAFSA, institutional form required. Applicants notified on a rolling basis starting 4/1.

Academics. 2+2 system allows students to begin required courses in major while completing associate degree. Accelerated BBA available. **Special**

study options: Accelerated study, combined bachelor's/graduate degree, cooperative education, distance learning, double major, dual enrollment of high school students, external degree, independent study, internships, liberal arts/career combination. **Credit/placement by examination:** AP, CLEP, IB, institutional tests. 48 credit hours maximum toward associate degree, 96 toward bachelor's. **Support services:** Learning center, reduced course load, remedial instruction, study skills assistance, tutoring, writing center.

Majors. Business: General, accounting, administrative services, business admin, human resources, international, management information systems, marketing, office management. **Computer sciences:** General, computer science, information systems. **Health:** Health care admin.

Computing on campus. 229 workstations in library, computer center. Commuter students can connect to campus network. Online course registration, helpline available.

Student life. Freshman orientation: Mandatory. Preregistration for classes offered. **Activities:** Dental hygiene society.

Student services. Adult student services, career counseling, student employment services, personal counseling, placement for graduates, veterans' counselor. **Physically disabled:** Services for visually, hearing impaired.

Contact. E-mail: daniel.kenny@baker.edu
Phone: (810) 985-7000 Toll-free number: (888) 262-2442
Fax: (810) 985-7066
Dan Kenny, Vice President of Admissions, Baker College of Port Huron, 3403 Lapeer Road, Port Huron, MI 48060-2597

Calvin College

Grand Rapids, Michigan — **CB member**
www.calvin.edu — **CB code: 1095**

- Private 4-year liberal arts college affiliated with Christian Reformed Church
- Residential campus in large city
- 4,040 degree-seeking undergraduates: 2% part-time, 54% women, 1% African American, 3% Asian American, 1% Hispanic American, 7% international
- 37 degree-seeking graduate students
- 98% of applicants admitted
- SAT or ACT (ACT writing optional), application essay required
- 71% graduate within 6 years; 16% enter graduate study

General. Founded in 1876. Regionally accredited. **Degrees:** 913 bachelor's awarded; master's offered. **ROTC:** Army. **Location:** 150 miles from Detroit, 150 miles from Chicago. **Calendar:** 4-1-4, limited summer session. **Full-time faculty:** 309 total; 82% have terminal degrees, 7% minority, 29% women. **Part-time faculty:** 89 total; 22% have terminal degrees, 8% minority, 58% women. **Class size:** 39% < 20, 58% 20-39, 2% 40-49, 1% 50-99. **Special facilities:** Ecosystem preserve and interpretive center, electron microscope, rhetoric center, observatory.

Freshman class profile. 2,156 applied, 2,104 admitted, 1,007 enrolled.

Mid 50% test scores			
SAT verbal:	540-660	Rank in top quarter:	54%
SAT math:	550-670	Rank in top tenth:	26%
ACT:	23-28	End year in good standing:	96%
GPA 3.50 or higher:	64%	Return as sophomores:	88%
GPA 3.0-3.49:	24%	Out-of-state:	44%
GPA 2.0-2.99:	12%	Live on campus:	97%
		International:	5%

Basis for selection. Genuine interest in Christian goals of college, 2.5 high school GPA required. Recommendation, personal statement important. ACT composite score above 20 or SAT Verbal above 470 and SAT Math above 470 recommended. GED accepted only for those age 19 years or over. SAT Subject Tests recommended. **Homeschooled:** Provide some form of transcript with grades.

High school preparation. 12 units required; 17 recommended. Required and recommended units include English 3-4, mathematics 3, social studies 2-3, science 2 (laboratory 1), foreign language 2 and academic electives 3. Mathematics must include algebra and geometry.

2005-2006 Annual costs. Tuition/fees: $19,150. Room/board: $6,585. Books/supplies: $680. Personal expenses: $875.

2005-2006 Financial aid. Need-based: 831 full-time freshmen applied for aid; 628 were judged to have need; 628 of these received aid. Average need met was 83%. Average scholarship/grant was $9,200; average loan $4,000. 62% of total undergraduate aid awarded as scholarships/grants, 38% as loans/jobs. **Non-need-based:** Awarded to 1,613 full-time undergraduates, including 476 freshmen. Scholarships awarded for academics, alumni affiliation, art, leadership, minority status, music/drama, religious affiliation, state residency.

Application procedures. Admission: Closing date 8/15 (postmark date). $35 fee, may be waived for applicants with need. Application may be submitted online. Admission notification on a rolling basis beginning on or about 11/1. Must reply by May 1 or within 4 week(s) if notified thereafter. **Financial aid:** Priority date 2/15; no closing date. FAFSA, institutional form required. Applicants notified on a rolling basis starting 3/15.

Academics. Importance of faith perspective in all disciplines and cocurricular activities emphasized. **Special study options:** Accelerated study, combined bachelor's/graduate degree, double major, dual enrollment of high school students, honors, independent study, internships, student-designed major, study abroad, teacher certification program, urban semester, Washington semester. Overseas programs with Central College, January interim exchange with other colleges, academically-based service-learning. **Credit/placement by examination:** AP, CLEP, IB, institutional tests. **Support services:** Learning center, reduced course load, remedial instruction, study skills assistance, tutoring, writing center.

Majors. Area/ethnic studies: Asian. **Biology:** General, biochemistry, biotechnology. **Business:** General, accounting, business admin, communications, management information systems. **Communications:** General, digital media, media studies. **Computer sciences:** General, computer science, information systems, networking, programming. **Conservation:** Environmental science. **Education:** General, art, bilingual, biology, chemistry, Deaf/hearing impaired, early childhood, elementary, English, French, German, history, mathematics, mentally handicapped, middle, music, physical, physics, reading, secondary, social studies, Spanish, special, speech impaired. **Engineering:** General, chemical, civil, electrical, mechanical. **English:** English lit, speech/rhetoric. **Foreign languages:** Ancient Greek, Biblical, classics, Dutch/Flemish, French, German, Latin, modern Greek, Spanish. **Health:** Athletic training, audiology/speech pathology, communication disorders, predentistry, premedicine, preop/surgical nursing, prepharmacy, preveterinary, recreational therapy, speech pathology. **History:** General, American, European. **Interdisciplinary:** Biological/physical sciences, classical/archaeology, natural sciences. **Legal studies:** Prelaw. **Liberal arts:** Arts/sciences. **Math:** General. **Parks/recreation:** General, exercise sciences, health/fitness. **Philosophy/religion:** Philosophy, religion. **Physical sciences:** Chemistry, geology, physics. **Psychology:** General. **Public administration:** General, social work. **Social sciences:** General, economics, geography, international economic development, international relations, political science, sociology. **Theology:** Bible, sacred music. **Visual/performing arts:** General, art, art history/conservation, conducting, dramatic, film/cinema, music history, music performance, music theory/composition, piano/organ, studio arts, voice/opera.

Most popular majors. Business/marketing 11%, education 11%, engineering/engineering technologies 7%, English 7%, foreign language 7%, health sciences 9%, psychology 6%, social sciences 7%, visual/performing arts 6%.

Computing on campus. 737 workstations in dormitories, library, computer center. Dormitories wired for high-speed internet access and linked to campus network. Commuter students can connect to campus network. Online course registration, online library, helpline, student web hosting, wireless network available.

Student life. Freshman orientation: Mandatory, $75 fee. 2-day program held in summer. **Policies:** Strong emphasis on student leadership and service. Religious observance strongly expected and encouraged. Freshmen permitted cars on campus. **Housing:** Guaranteed on-campus for freshmen. Single-sex dorms, apartments, substance-free housing available. $50 deposit, deadline 5/1. Project Neighborhood houses available. First- and second-year students (under 21) not living at home required to live in residence halls. **Activities:** Bands, choral groups, dance, drama, film society, literary magazine, music ensembles, musical theater, radio station, student government, student newspaper, symphony orchestra, Amnesty International, Campus Crusade for Christ, Environmental Stewardship, Republicans Club, InterVarsity Christian Fellowship, Liberals and Democrats, Young Life, Social Justice, Korean Christian Fellowship.

Athletics. NCAA. **Intercollegiate:** Baseball M, basketball, cross-country, diving, golf, soccer, softball W, swimming, tennis, track and field, volleyball W. **Intramural:** Badminton, basketball, cross-country, golf, racquetball, soccer, softball, swimming, tennis, track and field, volleyball, water polo. **Team name:** Knights.

Student services. Adult student services, alcohol/substance abuse counseling, campus ministries, career counseling, student employment services, financial aid counseling, health services, minority student services, personal counseling, placement for graduates. **Physically disabled:** Services for visually, speech, hearing impaired.

Contact. E-mail: admissions@calvin.edu
Phone: (616) 526-6106 Toll-free number: (800) 688-0122
Fax: (616) 526-6777
Dale Kuiper, Director of Admissions, Calvin College, 3201 Burton Street SE, Grand Rapids, MI 49546

Central Michigan University

Mount Pleasant, Michigan
www.cmich.edu
CB member
CB code: 1106

- Public 4-year university
- Commuter campus in large town
- 19,715 degree-seeking undergraduates: 11% part-time, 57% women, 6% African American, 1% Asian American, 2% Hispanic American, 1% Native American, 1% international
- 6,473 degree-seeking graduate students
- 75% of applicants admitted
- ACT (writing optional) required
- 55% graduate within 6 years

General. Founded in 1892. Regionally accredited. **Degrees:** 3,555 bachelor's awarded; master's, doctoral offered. **ROTC:** Army. **Location:** 70 miles from Lansing. **Calendar:** Semester, limited summer session. **Full-time faculty:** 704 total; 82% have terminal degrees, 15% minority, 39% women. **Part-time faculty:** 391 total; 24% have terminal degrees, 10% minority, 42% women. **Class size:** 31% < 20, 46% 20-39, 12% 40-49, 8% 50-99, 3% >100. **Special facilities:** Center for clinical care and education, English language institute, center for applied research and rural studies, center for professional and personal ethics, Michigan services for children and young adults who are deaf-blind, psychological training and consultation center, language learning center, biological station, conservation genetics lab, water research center, museum of cultural and natural history, historical library, 255-acre natural woodland.

Freshman class profile. 13,550 applied, 10,198 admitted, 3,718 enrolled.

Mid 50% test scores		**Rank in top tenth:**	15%
SAT verbal:	450-570	**End year in good standing:**	75%
SAT math:	450-580	**Return as sophomores:**	77%
ACT:	19-24	**Out-of-state:**	2%
GPA 3.50 or higher:	36%	**Live on campus:**	94%
GPA 3.0-3.49:	39%	**International:**	1%
GPA 2.0-2.99:	25%	**Fraternities:**	5%
Rank in top quarter:	38%	**Sororities:**	3%

Basis for selection. School achievement record, test scores, recommendations important. Interview and essay recommended. Audition required for music majors.

High school preparation. 19 units recommended. Recommended units include English 4, mathematics 4, social studies 2, history 2, science 3, foreign language 2 and academic electives 2. 1-2 units computer literacy or fine and performing arts recommended.

2005-2006 Annual costs. Tuition/fees: $6,390; $14,850 out-of-state. Room/board: $6,376. Books/supplies: $750. Personal expenses: $1,240.

2005-2006 Financial aid. Need-based: 2,900 full-time freshmen applied for aid; 1,961 were judged to have need; 1,947 of these received aid. Average need met was 99%. Average scholarship/grant was $4,784; average loan $3,605. 36% of total undergraduate aid awarded as scholarships/grants, 64% as loans/jobs. **Non-need-based:** Awarded to 2,605 full-time undergraduates, including 973 freshmen. Scholarships awarded for academics, alumni affiliation, art, athletics, leadership, minority status, music/drama, ROTC, state residency. **Additional information:** Tuition waiver for Native American students qualifying under state program criteria.

Application procedures. Admission: No deadline. $35 fee, may be waived for applicants with need. Application may be submitted online. Admission notification on a rolling basis. Must reply by May 1 or within 2 week(s) if notified thereafter. **Financial aid:** Priority date 3/21; no closing date. FAFSA required. Applicants notified on a rolling basis starting 4/1.

Academics. Special study options: Accelerated study, combined bachelor's/graduate degree, cooperative education, distance learning, double major, dual enrollment of high school students, ESL, external degree, honors, independent study, internships, semester at sea, student-designed major, study abroad, teacher certification program, Washington semester. Leadership institute, preprofessional studies. **Credit/placement by examination:** AP, CLEP, IB, ACT, institutional tests. **Support services:** Learning center, pre-admission summer program, reduced course load, remedial instruction, study skills assistance, tutoring, writing center.

Honors college/program. Freshmen applicants must have 3.75 GPA or 3.5 GPA and ACT of 24. Transfer or current students must have 3.5 college GPA.

Majors. Architecture: Interior. **Area/ethnic studies:** European, women's. **Biology:** General, bacteriology, microbiology. **Business:** General, accounting, actuarial science, business admin, entrepreneurial studies, fashion, finance, financial planning, hospitality admin, human resources, international, logistics, management information systems, marketing, purchasing. **Communications:** Advertising, journalism, photojournalism, public relations. **Computer sciences:** General, information systems. **Conservation:** General, environmental science, environmental studies. **Education:** Business, emotionally handicapped, English, health, mentally handicapped, music, physical, science, technology/industrial arts. **Engineering:** Electrical, manufacturing, mechanical. **Engineering technology:** Automotive, computer, construction, electrical, manufacturing, mechanical. **English:** Creative writing, English lit, speech/rhetoric. **Family/consumer sciences:** Child development, family systems, institutional food production. **Foreign languages:** French, German, Spanish. **Health:** Athletic training, audiology/speech pathology, clinical lab science, dietetics, facilities admin, recreational therapy. **History:** General. **Interdisciplinary:** Neuroscience. **Legal studies:** Court reporting. **Liberal arts:** Arts/sciences. **Math:** General, statistics. **Parks/recreation:** General, facilities management, sports admin. **Philosophy/religion:** Philosophy, religion. **Physical sciences:** General, astronomy, chemistry, geology, meteorology, oceanography, physics. **Psychology:** General. **Public administration:** Community org/advocacy, social work. **Social sciences:** General, anthropology, economics, geography, international relations, political science, sociology. **Visual/performing arts:** Art, dramatic, graphic design, music theory/composition.

Most popular majors. Business/marketing 27%, education 11%, health sciences 6%, social sciences 8%.

Computing on campus. 1,585 workstations in dormitories, library, computer center, student center. Dormitories wired for high-speed internet access and linked to campus network. Commuter students can connect to campus network. Online course registration, online library, helpline, repair service, student web hosting, wireless network available.

Student life. Freshman orientation: Mandatory, $125 fee. Preregistration for classes offered. One-day sessions; morning refreshments and lunch provided. **Policies:** Freshmen permitted cars on campus. **Housing:** Guaranteed on-campus for freshmen. Coed dorms, single-sex dorms, special housing for disabled, apartments, fraternity/sorority housing, substance-free housing available. $500 fully refundable deposit, deadline 5/20. Residential colleges for health professions, science and technology, language, school of music, school of business, honors, leadership, international students. Some alcohol- and smoke-free halls offered. **Activities:** Bands, choral groups, dance, drama, film society, literary magazine, music ensembles, musical theater, radio station, student government, student newspaper, TV station, Asian cultural organization, Hispanic student organization, North American Indian student organization, organization for black unity, gay/lesbian/bisexual club, College Republicans, University Democrats, Baha'i club, Campus Crusade for Christ, Fellowship of Christian Athletes.

Athletics. NCAA. **Intercollegiate:** Baseball M, basketball, cross-country, field hockey W, football (tackle) M, gymnastics W, soccer W, softball W, track and field, volleyball W, wrestling M. **Intramural:** Basketball, football (non-tackle), golf, racquetball, soccer, softball, table tennis, tennis, volleyball, wrestling M. **Team name:** Chippewas.

Student services. Alcohol/substance abuse counseling, career counseling, student employment services, health services, minority student services, personal counseling, placement for graduates, veterans' counselor. **Physically disabled:** Services for visually, speech, hearing impaired.

Contact. E-mail: cmuadmit@cmich.edu
Phone: (989) 774-3076 Toll-free number: (888) 292-5366
Fax: (989) 774-7267
Betty Wagner, Director of Admissions, Central Michigan University, Admissions Office, Mount Pleasant, MI 48859

Cleary University

Howell, Michigan
www.cleary.edu
CB code: 1123

- Private 4-year university and business college
- Commuter campus in small city
- 490 degree-seeking undergraduates: 19% part-time, 62% women, 7% African American, 1% Asian American, 1% Hispanic American, 1% Native American
- 34 graduate students
- SAT or ACT (ACT writing optional) required

General. Founded in 1883. Regionally accredited. Campuses in Howell and Ann Arbor; extension sites throughout Southeastern Michigan. **Degrees:** 179 bachelor's, 58 associate awarded; master's offered. **Location:** 55 miles from Detroit, 27 miles from Ann Arbor. **Calendar:** Quarter, limited summer session. **Full-time faculty:** 12 total; 50% have terminal degrees. **Part-time faculty:** 94 total; 15% have terminal degrees. **Class size:** 93% < 20, 7% 20-39. **Special facilities:** Nature trails.

Basis for selection. 2.0 minimum GPA, high school/GED most important. Minimum composite ACT 20 or minimum total SAT of 1000 (exclusive of Writing) recommended. Regular, special, guest, dual, provisional, transfer, and international admissions available. Applicants with below 2.0 GPA may be accepted if probable success in chosen program indicated.

High school preparation. College-preparatory program recommended. 24 units recommended. Recommended units include English 4, mathematics 2, social studies 2, history 2, science 2 and academic electives 12.

2006-2007 Annual costs. Tuition/fees: $12,825. Tuition prices guaranteed if student enrolled continuously. Tuition includes all books and fees.

2004-2005 Financial aid. Need-based: Average need met was 41%. Average scholarship/grant was $1,234; average loan $1,130. 34% of total undergraduate aid awarded as scholarships/grants, 66% as loans/jobs. **Non-need-based:** Scholarships awarded for academics. **Additional information:** Filing electronically preferred; paper applications available. Tuition guarantee based on continuous enrollment. Essay and recommendations required for scholarship consideration.

Application procedures. Admission: Closing date 8/15 (postmark date). $25 fee, may be waived for applicants with need. Application may be submitted online. Admission notification on a rolling basis. **Financial aid:** Priority date 3/15, closing date 8/15. FAFSA required. Applicants notified on a rolling basis; must reply within 2 week(s) of notification.

Academics. Compressed academic calendar reduces time to degree completion. First-time college students can complete bachelor's degree in 3 1/2 years and adults with previous college experience can complete degree in just over 1 year. **Special study options:** Accelerated study, combined bachelor's/graduate degree, cooperative education, distance learning, dual enrollment of high school students, independent study, internships. **Credit/placement by examination:** AP, CLEP, institutional tests. 22 credit hours maximum toward bachelor's degree. **Support services:** Pre-admission summer program, reduced course load, remedial instruction, study skills assistance, tutoring.

Majors. Business: Accounting, business admin, e-commerce, entrepreneurial studies, financial planning, human resources, management information systems, marketing, nonprofit/public, public finance. **Computer sciences:** Security.

Computing on campus. 60 workstations in computer center, student center. Commuter students can connect to campus network. Online library, helpline, wireless network available.

Student life. Freshman orientation: Mandatory, $270 fee. Preregistration for classes offered. **Policies:** Freshmen permitted cars on campus. **Activities:** Rotaract, automotive alley, Michigan quality council, quality improvement network, economic club.

Student services. Adult student services, career counseling, student employment services, financial aid counseling, placement for graduates.

Contact. E-mail: admissions@cleary.edu
Phone: (800) 686-1883 ext. 2249 Toll-free
number: (800) 686-1883 ext. 2249 Fax: (517) 552-7805
Carrie Bonofiglio, Director of Admissions, Cleary University, 3750 Cleary Drive, Howell, MI 48843

College for Creative Studies

Detroit, Michigan — **CB member**
www.ccscad.edu — **CB code: 1035**

- Private 4-year visual arts college
- Commuter campus in very large city
- 1,270 degree-seeking undergraduates
- 60% of applicants admitted
- SAT or ACT (ACT writing optional) required

General. Founded in 1926. Regionally accredited. **Degrees:** 192 bachelor's awarded. **Location:** 4 miles from downtown. **Calendar:** Semester, limited summer session. **Full-time faculty:** 45 total; 60% have terminal degrees, 13% minority, 24% women. **Part-time faculty:** 159 total; 1% minority, 42% women. **Special facilities:** Extensive studio space, art gallery for student exhibitions, foundry, computer studios, wood shop, metals shop, glassblowing studio, ceramic studio, fiber studio.

Freshman class profile. 598 applied, 358 admitted, 207 enrolled.

Mid 50% test scores		Out-of-state:	23%
ACT:	17-24	Live on campus:	37%

Basis for selection. Art portfolio, test scores, and high school record important. Minimum 2.5 high school GPA for applicants. ACT/SAT scores required. Portfolio required.

High school preparation. 13 units recommended. Recommended units include English 4, mathematics 3, social studies 2, science 2 and foreign language 2. College-preparatory program recommended, art courses highly recommended.

2005-2006 Annual costs. Tuition/fees: $23,116. Room only: $3,900. Books/supplies: $2,500. Personal expenses: $1,800.

2004-2005 Financial aid. Need-based: 26% of total undergraduate aid awarded as scholarships/grants, 74% as loans/jobs. **Non-need-based:** Scholarships awarded for academics, art.

Application procedures. Admission: Priority date 3/1; deadline 8/1 (postmark date). $35 fee, may be waived for applicants with need. Application may be submitted online. Admission notification on a rolling basis beginning on or about 9/1. Must reply by May 1 or within 3 week(s) if notified thereafter. **Financial aid:** Priority date 2/21; no closing date. FAFSA required. Applicants notified on a rolling basis starting 3/15; must reply within 3 week(s) of notification.

Academics. Special study options: Cooperative education, cross-registration, double major, dual enrollment of high school students, exchange student, independent study, internships, New York semester, study abroad, teacher certification program. Advanced students may petition for 1 semester in New York studio space. **Credit/placement by examination:** CLEP, IB. 6 credit hours maximum toward bachelor's degree. **Support services:** Learning center, pre-admission summer program, reduced course load, remedial instruction, study skills assistance, tutoring, writing center.

Majors. Business: Transportation. **Communications:** Digital media. **Communications technology:** Animation/special effects. **Production:** Furniture. **Visual/performing arts:** Ceramics, cinematography, commercial photography, commercial/advertising art, crafts, design, drawing, fiber arts, graphic design, illustration, industrial design, interior design, metal/jewelry, multimedia, painting, photography, printmaking, sculpture, studio arts.

Computing on campus. 400 workstations in library, computer center. Dormitories wired for high-speed internet access and linked to campus network. Commuter students can connect to campus network. Online library, student web hosting available.

Student life. Freshman orientation: Mandatory. Preregistration for classes offered. **Policies:** Freshmen permitted cars on campus. **Housing:** Apartments available. $200 deposit, deadline 5/1. Furnished, college-owned apartments available. **Activities:** Student government, black student club, women artists club, industrial design students club.

Student services. Alcohol/substance abuse counseling, career counseling, student employment services, financial aid counseling, minority student services, personal counseling, placement for graduates. **Physically disabled:** Services for hearing impaired.

Contact. E-mail: admissions@ccsad.edu
Phone: (313) 664-7425 Toll-free number: (800) 952-2787
Fax: (313) 872-2739
Julie Hingelberg, Dean of Enrollment Services, College for Creative Studies, 201 East Kirby, Detroit, MI 48202-4034

Concordia University

Ann Arbor, Michigan
www.cuaa.edu — **CB code: 1094**

- Private 4-year liberal arts and teachers college affiliated with Lutheran Church - Missouri Synod
- Residential campus in small city
- 535 degree-seeking undergraduates: 7% part-time, 56% women, 10% African American, 1% Asian American, 2% Hispanic American, 1% Native American, 1% international
- 41 degree-seeking graduate students
- 82% of applicants admitted
- SAT and SAT Subject Tests or ACT (ACT writing optional) required
- 52% graduate within 6 years

General. Founded in 1962. Regionally accredited. Accelerated degree program for mature students. **Degrees:** 86 bachelor's, 1 associate awarded; master's offered. **ROTC:** Army, Air Force. **Location:** 35 miles from Detroit. **Calendar:** Semester, limited summer session. **Full-time faculty:** 35 total; 69% have terminal degrees, 6% minority, 43% women. **Part-time faculty:** 50 total; 16% minority, 58% women. **Class size:** 78% < 20, 19% 20-39, 1% 40-49, 2% 50-99. **Special facilities:** Chapel, Earhart Manor (Michigan historic landmark).

Freshman class profile. 550 applied, 451 admitted, 115 enrolled.

Mid 50% test scores		**GPA 2.0-2.99:**	28%
SAT verbal:	470-630	**Return as sophomores:**	65%
SAT math:	510-640	**Out-of-state:**	24%
ACT:	19-26	**Live on campus:**	95%
GPA 3.50 or higher:	42%	**International:**	2%
GPA 3.0-3.49:	29%		

Basis for selection. School achievement record most important. Test scores and rank in top half of class also important. Interview and essay recommended. Audition recommended for music majors. Portfolio recommended for art majors. **Homeschooled:** Transcript of courses and grades required. Essay required. **Learning Disabled:** Require an explanation of the disability and written recommended accommodations from an appropriate professional.

High school preparation. 20 units recommended. Recommended units include English 4, mathematics 3, social studies 2, science 2 (laboratory 2) and foreign language 2.

2005-2006 Annual costs. Tuition/fees: $18,205. Room/board: $6,948. Books/supplies: $600. Personal expenses: $1,175.

2005-2006 Financial aid. Need-based: 108 full-time freshmen applied for aid; 93 were judged to have need; 93 of these received aid. Average need met was 86%. Average scholarship/grant was $12,076; average loan $4,427. 62% of total undergraduate aid awarded as scholarships/grants, 38% as loans/jobs. **Non-need-based:** Awarded to 239 full-time undergraduates, including 52 freshmen. Scholarships awarded for academics, alumni affiliation, art, athletics, leadership, music/drama, religious affiliation.

Application procedures. Admission: No deadline. $25 fee, may be waived for applicants with need. Application may be submitted online. Admission notification on a rolling basis. **Financial aid:** Closing date 3/1. FAFSA, institutional form required. Applicants notified on a rolling basis starting 3/1; must reply within 3 week(s) of notification.

Academics. Special study options: Accelerated study, cross-registration, distance learning, double major, dual enrollment of high school students, exchange student, independent study, internships, liberal arts/career combination, student-designed major, study abroad, teacher certification program, weekend college. **Credit/placement by examination:** AP, CLEP, IB, institutional tests. No limit on credit by examination. **Support services:** Learning center, reduced course load, study skills assistance, tutoring, writing center.

Majors. Biology: General. **Business:** Business admin. **Communications:** General, journalism, organizational. **Computer sciences:** General. **Education:** Art, biology, chemistry, early childhood, elementary, English, history, mathematics, music, physical, psychology, science, secondary, social studies, Spanish, speech. **English:** English lit. **Family/consumer sciences:** Family studies. **Foreign languages:** Ancient Greek, Biblical, Spanish. **Health:** Premedicine. **History:** General. **Interdisciplinary:** Biological/physical sciences. **Legal studies:** Prelaw. **Math:** General. **Parks/recreation:** Health/fitness. **Philosophy/religion:** Philosophy, religion. **Physical sciences:** Chemistry, physics. **Protective services:** Law enforcement admin. **Psychology:** General. **Social sciences:** General. **Theology:** Preministerial, religious ed, sacred music. **Visual/performing arts:** Art, theater arts management.

Most popular majors. Business/marketing 13%, education 25%, family/consumer sciences 6%, health sciences 6%, security/protective services 9%, theological studies 11%.

Computing on campus. 65 workstations in dormitories, library, computer center, student center. Dormitories wired for high-speed internet access and linked to campus network. Commuter students can connect to campus network. Online library, helpline, repair service, student web hosting, wireless network available.

Student life. Freshman orientation: Mandatory. Preregistration for classes offered. 3-day program includes academic, social, and orientation events. **Policies:** Freshmen permitted cars on campus. **Housing:** Guaranteed on-campus for all undergraduates. Single-sex dorms, apartments, substance-free housing available. $100 nonrefundable deposit, deadline 8/15. Students must live on campus (or with family member) until attaining junior status or 21 years of age. **Activities:** Bands, choral groups, dance, drama, music ensembles, musical theater, student government, student newspaper, several religious and community service groups.

Athletics. NAIA, NCCAA. **Intercollegiate:** Baseball M, basketball, cross-country, golf M, soccer, softball W, volleyball W. **Intramural:** Badminton, basketball, football (non-tackle), soccer, softball, table tennis, volleyball. **Team name:** Cardinals.

Student services. Adult student services, alcohol/substance abuse counseling, campus ministries, career counseling, student employment services, financial aid counseling, health services, on-campus daycare, personal counseling, placement for graduates, women's services. **Physically disabled:** Services for visually, speech, hearing impaired.

Contact. E-mail: admissions@cuaa.edu
Phone: (734) 995-7322 Toll-free number: (800) 253-0680
Fax: (734) 995-4610
Gary Neumann, Director of Admissions, Concordia University, 4090 Geddes Road, Ann Arbor, MI 48105

Cornerstone University

Grand Rapids, Michigan
www.cornerstone.edu **CB code: 1253**

- Private 4-year university and liberal arts college affiliated with Baptist faith
- Residential campus in large city
- 2,105 degree-seeking undergraduates: 17% part-time, 62% women, 18% African American, 1% Asian American, 3% Hispanic American, 1% international
- 380 degree-seeking graduate students
- 76% of applicants admitted
- SAT or ACT (ACT writing optional), application essay required
- 56% graduate within 6 years; 7% enter graduate study

General. Founded in 1941. Regionally accredited. **Degrees:** 273 bachelor's, 51 associate awarded; master's, first professional offered. **Location:** 4 miles from downtown. **Calendar:** Semester, limited summer session. **Full-time faculty:** 76 total; 49% have terminal degrees, 4% minority, 24% women. **Part-time faculty:** 64 total; 3% have terminal degrees, 3% minority, 36% women. **Class size:** 53% < 20, 41% 20-39, 2% 40-49, 2% 50-99, 1% >100. **Special facilities:** Center for the study of antiquities.

Freshman class profile. 1,122 applied, 854 admitted, 355 enrolled.

Mid 50% test scores		**Rank in top quarter:**	42%
SAT verbal:	460-590	**Rank in top tenth:**	17%
SAT math:	490-590	**End year in good standing:**	91%
ACT:	20-26	**Return as sophomores:**	78%
GPA 3.50 or higher:	47%	**Out-of-state:**	21%
GPA 3.0-3.49:	33%	**Live on campus:**	55%
GPA 2.0-2.99:	20%		

Basis for selection. Statement of Christian commitment, pastoral reference, 2.5 high school GPA, and ACT score of 19. Students with lower scores and GPA may be admitted conditionally. Interview recommended. Audition required for music majors. **Homeschooled:** Statement describing homeschool structure and mission, transcript of courses and grades, letter of recommendation (nonparent) required.

High school preparation. College-preparatory program recommended. Recommended units include English 4, mathematics 3, social studies 2, history 2, science 2 (laboratory 1), foreign language 2 and academic electives 4.

2005-2006 Annual costs. Tuition/fees: $15,550. Tuition includes laptop computer. Room/board: $5,800. Books/supplies: $950. Personal expenses: $1,232.

2004-2005 Financial aid. Need-based: 269 full-time freshmen applied for aid; 223 were judged to have need; 223 of these received aid. Average need met was 88%. Average scholarship/grant was $7,852; average loan $3,160. 49% of total undergraduate aid awarded as scholarships/grants, 51% as loans/jobs. **Non-need-based:** Awarded to 1,112 full-time undergraduates, including 286 freshmen. Scholarships awarded for academics, athletics, leadership, music/drama, state residency. **Additional information:** Audition required for music scholarship applicants.

Application procedures. Admission: No deadline. $25 fee, may be waived for applicants with need. Application may be submitted online. Admission notification on a rolling basis. **Financial aid:** Priority date 3/1; no

closing date. FAFSA required. Applicants notified on a rolling basis starting 3/15; must reply within 2 week(s) of notification.

Academics. All students must complete internship in major field. Core curriculum. **Special study options:** Accelerated study, distance learning, double major, dual enrollment of high school students, ESL, honors, independent study, internships, liberal arts/career combination, study abroad, teacher certification program, urban semester, Washington semester, weekend college. **Credit/placement by examination:** AP, CLEP, IB, ACT, institutional tests. 30 credit hours maximum toward bachelor's degree. **Support services:** Learning center, reduced course load, remedial instruction, study skills assistance, tutoring, writing center.

Honors college/program. Requires 28 ACT; 12 admitted annually.

Majors. Biology: General, environmental. **Business:** Accounting, business admin, international, management information systems, management science, marketing. **Communications:** General, digital media, media studies, organizational, public relations. **Computer sciences:** General, computer science, information systems. **Education:** Biology, early childhood, elementary, English, history, mathematics, music, physical, science, secondary, social science, social studies, voc/tech. **English:** Creative writing, English lit, speech/rhetoric. **Family/consumer sciences:** Family systems, work/family studies. **Foreign languages:** Biblical, linguistics. **Health:** Health services, predentistry, premedicine, preveterinary. **History:** General. **Legal studies:** Prelaw. **Math:** General. **Parks/recreation:** Exercise sciences, sports admin. **Philosophy/religion:** Philosophy, religion. **Psychology:** General. **Public administration:** Social work. **Social sciences:** General, political science, sociology. **Theology:** Bible, pastoral counseling, preministerial, religious ed, youth ministry. **Transportation:** Airline/commercial pilot. **Visual/performing arts:** Music performance, music theory/composition.

Most popular majors. Business/marketing 41%, education 27%, psychology 7%, theological studies 8%.

Computing on campus. PC or laptop required. 117 workstations in dormitories, library, computer center, student center. Dormitories wired for high-speed internet access and linked to campus network. Commuter students can connect to campus network. Online course registration, online library, helpline, repair service, wireless network available.

Student life. Freshman orientation: Mandatory. Preregistration for classes offered. Four-day program held prior to start of Fall classes. **Policies:** Dry campus; curfew enforced; chapel attendance required. Religious observance required. Freshmen permitted cars on campus. **Housing:** Guaranteed on-campus for all undergraduates. Single-sex dorms, apartments, substance-free housing available. $150 fully refundable deposit. Students under 21 with fewer than 63 credit hours must live on campus unless living with immediate family. **Activities:** Bands, choral groups, drama, literary magazine, music ensembles, musical theater, radio station, student government, student newspaper, symphony orchestra, student ministries, student outreach committee, Young Republicans, cross-cultural ministries, social committee, fine arts committee, literature club.

Athletics. NAIA. **Intercollegiate:** Basketball, cross-country, golf M, soccer, softball W, track and field, volleyball W. **Intramural:** Basketball, football (non-tackle), ice hockey M, racquetball, soccer, softball, volleyball. **Team name:** Golden Eagles.

Student services. Adult student services, alcohol/substance abuse counseling, campus ministries, career counseling, student employment services, financial aid counseling, health services, personal counseling, placement for graduates, veterans' counselor. **Physically disabled:** Services for visually, hearing impaired.

Contact. E-mail: admissions@cornerstone.edu
Phone: (616) 222-1426 Toll-free number: (800) 787-9778
Fax: (616) 222-1418
Brent Rudin, Associate Dean of Marketing and Admissions, Cornerstone University, 1001 East Beltline NE, Grand Rapids, MI 49525

Davenport University

Grand Rapids, Michigan
www.davenport.edu **CB code: 1183**

- Private 4-year business and health science college
- Commuter campus in small city
- 11,733 degree-seeking undergraduates: 74% part-time, 76% women, 24% African American, 1% Asian American, 4% Hispanic American
- 738 degree-seeking graduate students

General. Founded in 1866. Regionally accredited. Campuses in Alma, Bad Axe, Battle Creek, Bay City, Caro, Dearborn, Flint, Gaylord, Holland, Kalamazoo, Lansing, Lapeer, Midland, Oxford, Romeo, Saginaw, South Bend/Mishawaka, Traverse City, Warren, Merrillville and South Bend, Indiana. **Degrees:** 1,260 bachelor's, 693 associate awarded; master's offered. **Location:** 150 miles from Detroit, 175 miles from Chicago. **Calendar:** Semester, limited summer session. **Full-time faculty:** 129 total; 18% have terminal degrees, 9% minority, 52% women. **Part-time faculty:** 953 total; 7% have terminal degrees, 12% minority, 51% women. **Class size:** 87% < 20, 13% 20-39, less than 1% 40-49, less than 1% 50-99.

Freshman class profile. 1,231 applied, 1,231 admitted, 1,231 enrolled.

Basis for selection. Open admission. ASSET testing required of all first time degree-seeking students for placement purposes. Interview recommended.

High school preparation. Required and recommended units include English 6, mathematics 6-9 and social studies 9.

2005-2006 Annual costs. Tuition/fees: $11,070.

2004-2005 Financial aid. Need-based: 509 full-time freshmen applied for aid; 481 were judged to have need; 463 of these received aid. Average need met was 50%. Average scholarship/grant was $3,781; average loan $2,486. 45% of total undergraduate aid awarded as scholarships/grants, 55% as loans/jobs. **Non-need-based:** Awarded to 1,180 full-time undergraduates, including 335 freshmen. Scholarships awarded for academics, alumni affiliation, athletics, leadership.

Application procedures. Admission: No deadline. $25 fee. Application may be submitted online. Admission notification on a rolling basis beginning on or about 9/1. **Financial aid:** Priority date 3/15; no closing date. FAFSA required. Applicants notified on a rolling basis starting 3/1; must reply within 2 week(s) of notification.

Academics. Special study options: Accelerated study, distance learning, dual enrollment of high school students, ESL, independent study, internships, student-designed major, study abroad. **Credit/placement by examination:** AP, CLEP, IB, institutional tests. **Support services:** Learning center, remedial instruction, tutoring, writing center.

Majors. Business: General, accounting, business admin, entrepreneurial studies, finance, international, marketing, office management, operations. **Computer sciences:** Networking, security, systems analysis, vendor certification, webmaster. **Health:** Health care admin, management/clinical assistant, nursing (RN). **Legal studies:** Paralegal.

Most popular majors. Business/marketing 79%, computer/information sciences 15%.

Computing on campus. 2,705 workstations in library, computer center, student center. Dormitories wired for high-speed internet access. Online course registration, online library, wireless network available.

Student life. Freshman orientation: Mandatory. Preregistration for classes offered. **Policies:** Freshmen permitted cars on campus. **Housing:** Coed dorms, substance-free housing available. **Activities:** Minority student association.

Athletics. NAIA. **Intercollegiate:** Basketball, golf, ice hockey M. **Intramural:** Basketball, soccer, volleyball. **Team name:** Panthers.

Student services. Career counseling, student employment services, financial aid counseling, placement for graduates.

Contact. E-mail: gradmiss@davenport.edu
Phone: (616) 698-7111 Toll-free number: (866) 383-3548
Lynnae Selberg, Director of Career and Education Advising, Davenport University, 6191 Kraft Avenue, Grand Rapids, MI 49512

Eastern Michigan University

Ypsilanti, Michigan **CB member**
www.emich.edu **CB code: 1201**

- Public 4-year university
- Residential campus in small city
- 18,165 degree-seeking undergraduates: 29% part-time, 60% women, 18% African American, 2% Asian American, 2% Hispanic American, 1% Native American, 1% international
- 3,687 degree-seeking graduate students
- 79% of applicants admitted
- SAT or ACT (ACT writing recommended) required
- 38% graduate within 6 years

General. Founded in 1849. Regionally accredited. **Degrees:** 2,923 bachelor's awarded; master's, doctoral offered. **ROTC:** Army, Navy, Air Force.

Location: 7 miles from Ann Arbor, 35 miles from Detroit. **Calendar:** Semester, limited summer session. **Full-time faculty:** 769 total; 73% have terminal degrees, 18% minority, 48% women. **Part-time faculty:** 427 total; 9% minority, 58% women. **Class size:** 38% < 20, 49% 20-39, 5% 40-49, 7% 50-99, less than 1% >100. **Special facilities:** Research center, corporate education center, observatory, laser laboratory, textiles research and training institute, man-made lake.

Freshman class profile. 10,151 applied, 8,041 admitted, 2,386 enrolled.

Mid 50% test scores		**Rank in top quarter:**	35%
SAT verbal:	450-570	**Rank in top tenth:**	12%
SAT math:	450-570	**Return as sophomores:**	73%
ACT:	18-24	**Out-of-state:**	15%
GPA 3.50 or higher:	22%	**Live on campus:**	60%
GPA 3.0-3.49:	33%	**International:**	1%
GPA 2.0-2.99:	45%		

Basis for selection. School achievement record and test scores important. Grades and test results combined to predict academic success. MELAB (Michigan English Language Assessment Battery) accepted in place of TOEFL with minimum score 72 for unconditional acceptance. Essay recommended. Audition required of music majors. Portfolio required of art majors.

High school preparation. College-preparatory program recommended. 16 units recommended. Recommended units include English 4, mathematics 3, social studies 2, science 2 (laboratory 1) and foreign language 2. 2 units fine arts and 1 computer literacy also recommended.

2005-2006 Annual costs. Tuition/fees: $6,508; $17,863 out-of-state. Room/board: $6,356. Books/supplies: $900. Personal expenses: $1,080.

2004-2005 Financial aid. Need-based: 1,791 full-time freshmen applied for aid; 1,305 were judged to have need; 1,254 of these received aid. Average need met was 62%. Average scholarship/grant was $3,471; average loan $3,088. 32% of total undergraduate aid awarded as scholarships/grants, 68% as loans/jobs. **Non-need-based:** Awarded to 3,519 full-time undergraduates, including 1,106 freshmen. Scholarships awarded for academics, alumni affiliation, art, athletics, leadership, music/drama, ROTC, state residency.

Application procedures. Admission: Priority date 2/15; no deadline. $30 fee, may be waived for applicants with need. Application may be submitted online. Admission notification on a rolling basis beginning on or about 10/1. **Financial aid:** Priority date 3/15; no closing date. FAFSA required. Applicants notified on a rolling basis starting 3/15.

Academics. Special study options: Accelerated study, combined bachelor's/graduate degree, cooperative education, distance learning, double major, dual enrollment of high school students, ESL, honors, independent study, internships, student-designed major, study abroad, teacher certification program, Washington semester, weekend college. Dual enrollment program requires students to apply for admission to EMU. **Credit/placement by examination:** AP, CLEP, IB, SAT, ACT, institutional tests. 30 credit hours maximum toward bachelor's degree. **Support services:** Learning center, reduced course load, remedial instruction, tutoring, writing center.

Honors college/program. Admission based on high school GPA, test scores, letters of recommendation. Approximately 250 freshmen per year admitted; reduced class size emphasizing student-professor interaction.

Majors. Architecture: Urban/community planning. **Area/ethnic studies:** African-American, women's. **Biology:** General, biochemistry, toxicology. **Business:** General, accounting, actuarial science, business admin, construction management, fashion, finance, hospitality admin, international, labor studies, managerial economics, marketing, office management. **Communications:** Journalism, public relations. **Communications technology:** General, radio/tv. **Computer sciences:** General, information systems. **Education:** Art, biology, business, chemistry, computer, Deaf/hearing impaired, elementary, emotionally handicapped, English, French, German, history, mathematics, mentally handicapped, music, physical, physically handicapped, physics, reading, sales/marketing, science, social science, social studies, Spanish, speech impaired, technology/industrial arts, visually handicapped. **Engineering:** Computer, manufacturing, polymer. **Engineering technology:** CAD/CADD, electrical, industrial, industrial management, manufacturing, mechanical, mechanical drafting. **English:** Composition, English lit, speech/rhetoric. **Family/consumer sciences:** Facilities/event planning. **Foreign languages:** French, German, Germanic, Japanese, linguistics, Romance, Spanish. **Health:** Athletic training, clinical lab science, dietetics, health care admin, music therapy, nursing (RN), recreational therapy. **History:** General. **Interdisciplinary:** Biological/physical sciences. **Legal studies:** Paralegal. **Math:** General, statistics. **Parks/recreation:** Facilities management, health/fitness. **Philosophy/religion:** Philosophy. **Physical sciences:** Chemistry, geology, geophysics, physics. **Psychology:** General. **Public administration:** General, social work. **Social sciences:** General, anthropology, criminology, economics, geography, political science, sociology. **Transportation:** Airline/commercial pilot, aviation management. **Visual/performing arts:** Art, art history/conservation, arts management, dance, dramatic, interior design, music pedagogy, music performance, voice/opera.

Most popular majors. Business/marketing 20%, communications/journalism 6%, education 25%, health sciences 7%, social sciences 7%, visual/performing arts 6%.

Computing on campus. 1,500 workstations in dormitories, library, computer center, student center. Dormitories linked to campus network. Commuter students can connect to campus network. Helpline, student web hosting available.

Student life. Freshman orientation: Mandatory, $150 fee. Preregistration for classes offered. 4-day orientation held Saturday through Tuesday. **Policies:** Freshmen permitted cars on campus. **Housing:** Coed dorms, special housing for disabled, apartments, fraternity/sorority housing, substance-free housing available. $200 deposit, deadline 5/1. Over 21 floors providing freshman housing, honors halls, in-hall academic services available. All non-commuting freshmen must live on campus. **Activities:** Bands, choral groups, dance, drama, film society, literary magazine, music ensembles, musical theater, radio station, student government, student newspaper, symphony orchestra, TV station, 10 honor societies, over 140 student organizations.

Athletics. NCAA. **Intercollegiate:** Baseball M, basketball, cross-country, diving, football (tackle) M, golf, gymnastics W, rowing (crew) W, soccer W, softball W, swimming, tennis W, track and field, volleyball W, wrestling M. **Intramural:** Badminton, basketball, bowling, cross-country, football (non-tackle), golf, racquetball, soccer, softball, swimming, table tennis, tennis, track and field, volleyball, weight lifting. **Team name:** Eagles.

Student services. Adult student services, alcohol/substance abuse counseling, campus ministries, career counseling, student employment services, health services, minority student services, on-campus daycare, personal counseling, placement for graduates, veterans' counselor, women's services. **Physically disabled:** Services for visually, speech, hearing impaired.

Contact. E-mail: admissions@emich.edu
Phone: (734) 487-3060 Toll-free number: (800) 468-6368
Fax: (734) 487-6559
Judy Tatum, Director of Admissions, Eastern Michigan University, 400 Pierce Hall, Ypsilanti, MI 48197

Ferris State University
Big Rapids, Michigan
www.ferris.edu **CB code: 1222**

- Public 4-year university
- Residential campus in large town
- 11,051 degree-seeking undergraduates: 20% part-time, 47% women, 6% African American, 2% Asian American, 1% Hispanic American, 1% Native American, 1% international
- 1,110 graduate students
- 47% of applicants admitted
- SAT or ACT (ACT writing optional) required
- 35% graduate within 6 years

General. Founded in 1884. Regionally accredited. **Degrees:** 1,403 bachelor's, 843 associate awarded; master's, first professional offered. **ROTC:** Army. **Location:** 55 miles from Grand Rapids. **Calendar:** Semester, limited summer session. **Full-time faculty:** 545 total; 51% have terminal degrees, 9% minority, 37% women. **Part-time faculty:** 278 total; 22% have terminal degrees, 4% minority, 52% women. **Class size:** 50% < 20, 46% 20-39, less than 1% 40-49, 2% 50-99, less than 1% >100. **Special facilities:** Wildlife museum, Jim Crow museum.

Freshman class profile. 12,877 applied, 6,021 admitted, 2,417 enrolled.

Mid 50% test scores		**GPA 2.0-2.99:**	42%
ACT:	18-23	**Return as sophomores:**	70%
GPA 3.50 or higher:	30%	**Out-of-state:**	1%
GPA 3.0-3.49:	28%	**International:**	1%

Basis for selection. School achievement record most important. 3.0 GPA in mathematics, biology, and chemistry required of some allied health applicants. General admission requirements: 2.35 or higher GPA (49 or higher GED score) or 16 or higher ACT composite score or 800 or higher SAT Verbal and Math score. Students meeting minimum ACT or SAT composite standard must have at least 2.0 high school GPA (44 GED score). Students meeting the minimum GPA standard must have at least 15 ACT composite score or 750 SAT Verbal and Math score. Many specialized programs have higher GPA/ACT requirement, some with ACT Math and ACT Reading requirements as well. ACT and SAT scores used for admissions purposes for marginal applicants. Interview recommended. Portfolio recommended of visual communication majors. **Learning Disabled:** Students with learning disabilities should submit documentation from professional psychologist or social worker to Disabilities Services Office.

High school preparation. 24 units recommended. Recommended units include English 4, mathematics 4, social studies 2, history 2, science 4 (laboratory 2), foreign language 3 and academic electives 3. 2 units in fine arts and 1 unit in computer literacy recommended.

2005-2006 Annual costs. Tuition/fees: $6,856; $13,596 out-of-state. Midwest Compact states of Illinois, Indiana, Kansas, Minnesota, Missouri, Nebraska, Ohio, and Wisconsin pay discounted tuition. Room/board: $6,816. Books/supplies: $1,000. Personal expenses: $784.

2004-2005 Financial aid. Need-based: 1,780 full-time freshmen applied for aid; 1,561 were judged to have need; 1,235 of these received aid. Average need met was 75%. Average scholarship/grant was $3,000; average loan $1,800. 33% of total undergraduate aid awarded as scholarships/grants, 67% as loans/jobs. **Non-need-based:** Awarded to 1,622 full-time undergraduates, including 577 freshmen. Scholarships awarded for academics, alumni affiliation, art, athletics, leadership, minority status, music/drama, religious affiliation, ROTC.

Application procedures. Admission: Closing date 8/4 (postmark date). $30 fee, may be waived for applicants with need. Application may be submitted online. Admission notification on a rolling basis beginning on or about 7/1. **Financial aid:** Priority date 3/1; no closing date. FAFSA required. Applicants notified on a rolling basis starting 3/1; must reply within 2 week(s) of notification.

Academics. Special study options: Accelerated study, combined bachelor's/graduate degree, cooperative education, cross-registration, distance learning, double major, dual enrollment of high school students, exchange student, external degree, honors, independent study, internships, liberal arts/career combination, study abroad, teacher certification program. **Credit/placement by examination:** AP, CLEP, SAT, ACT, institutional tests. **Support services:** Learning center, remedial instruction, study skills assistance, tutoring, writing center.

Majors. Biology: General, biochemistry, biotechnology, environmental. **Business:** Accounting, accounting/finance, business admin, construction management, e-commerce, entrepreneurial studies, finance, hospitality admin, hospitality/recreation, hotel/motel admin, human resources, international, marketing, operations. **Communications:** General, advertising, public relations. **Communications technology:** Animation/special effects, graphic/printing, printing management, radio/tv. **Education:** Biology, business, chemistry, elementary, English, family/consumer sciences, health, history, mathematics, secondary, social studies, voc/tech. **Engineering technology:** Automotive, electrical, energy systems, environmental, industrial, manufacturing, mechanical, plastics, quality control, surveying, telecommunications. **English:** Composition, speech/rhetoric, technical writing. **Health:** Clinical lab science, health care admin, medical records admin, nuclear medical technology, nursing (RN). **History:** General. **Math:** General, applied, statistics. **Mechanic/repair:** Heavy equipment. **Parks/recreation:** Facilities management. **Physical sciences:** Chemistry. **Production:** Furniture, welding. **Protective services:** Police science. **Psychology:** General. **Public administration:** General, social work. **Social sciences:** Sociology. **Visual/performing arts:** Art history/conservation, commercial/advertising art, design, graphic design, industrial design, interior design, metal/jewelry, music management, painting, photography, sculpture, studio arts.

Most popular majors. Business/marketing 24%, education 9%, engineering/engineering technologies 17%, health sciences 7%, security/protective services 9%, visual/performing arts 10%.

Computing on campus. 1,610 workstations in dormitories, library, computer center, student center. Dormitories wired for high-speed internet access and linked to campus network. Commuter students can connect to campus network. Online course registration, online library, helpline, repair service, wireless network available.

Student life. Freshman orientation: Mandatory. Preregistration for classes offered. **Policies:** All students sign Bulldog Values ethics statement during orientation. Freshmen permitted cars on campus. **Housing:** Guaranteed on-campus for all undergraduates. Coed dorms, special housing for disabled, apartments, substance-free housing available. $200 nonrefundable deposit, deadline 5/31. Honors hall available. **Activities:** Bands, choral groups, dance, drama, literary magazine, music ensembles, radio station, student government, student newspaper, symphony orchestra, TV station, Alpha Omega Co-ed Christian Fraternity, Circle K, Diverse Sexuality and Gender Alliance, gospel choir, Habitat for Humanity, Indian students association, international student organization, Muslim student organization, National Organization for Women, Red Cross student chapter.

Athletics. NCAA. **Intercollegiate:** Basketball, cheerleading, cross-country, football (tackle) M, golf, ice hockey M, soccer W, softball W, tennis, track and field, volleyball W. **Intramural:** Badminton, basketball, football (non-tackle) M, golf, handball, ice hockey M, racquetball, softball, swimming, table tennis, tennis, volleyball, water polo M. **Team name:** Bulldogs.

Student services. Adult student services, alcohol/substance abuse counseling, campus ministries, career counseling, student employment services, financial aid counseling, health services, minority student services, on-campus daycare, personal counseling, placement for graduates, veterans' counselor. **Physically disabled:** Services for visually, speech, hearing impaired.

Contact. E-mail: admissions@ferris.edu
Phone: (231) 591-2100 Toll-free number: (800) 433-7747
Fax: (231) 591-3944
Ronnie Higgs, Assistant Vice President Student Affairs/Dean, Enrollment Services, Ferris State University, 1201 S. State Street, CSS 201, Big Rapids, MI 49307-2714

Finlandia University

Hancock, Michigan
www.finlandia.edu **CB code: 1743**

- Private 4-year university and liberal arts college affiliated with Evangelical Lutheran Church in America
- Commuter campus in small town
- 548 degree-seeking undergraduates: 14% part-time, 66% women, 1% African American, 1% Native American, 5% international
- 95% of applicants admitted
- SAT or ACT (ACT writing optional), application essay required
- 56% graduate within 6 years

General. Founded in 1896. Regionally accredited. **Degrees:** 49 bachelor's, 49 associate awarded. **ROTC:** Army, Navy, Air Force. **Location:** 100 miles from Marquette, 220 miles from Green Bay, Wisconsin. **Calendar:** Semester, limited summer session. **Full-time faculty:** 39 total; 26% have terminal degrees, 3% minority, 77% women. **Part-time faculty:** 2 total; 50% women. **Class size:** 69% < 20, 28% 20-39, 2% 40-49, less than 1% 50-99. **Special facilities:** Finnish archives.

Freshman class profile. 502 applied, 477 admitted, 330 enrolled.

End year in good standing:	90%	**Out-of-state:**	5%
Return as sophomores:	72%	**Live on campus:**	37%

Basis for selection. 1 high school unit of algebra and 1 of chemistry with grade of 3.0, and 2.5 cumulative high school GPA required for nursing. 1 high school unit of algebra and 1 of biology with grade of 3.0, and 3.0 cumulative high school GPA required for physical therapist assistant. Cumulative GPA of 2.25 required of all other programs. If GPA below 2.0, special consideration given in determining admission. Student may obtain admission into academic warning program based on placement test results. Nursing applicants should apply by March 15, physical therapy assistant applicants by April 15. **Homeschooled:** Placement tests required. **Learning Disabled:** Must submit IEP test results.

High school preparation. Recommended units include English 4 and mathematics 2.

2006-2007 Annual costs. Tuition/fees (projected): $15,434. Room/board: $5,314. Books/supplies: $1,300. Personal expenses: $100.

2004-2005 Financial aid. Need-based: 92 full-time freshmen applied for aid; 84 were judged to have need; 84 of these received aid. 56% of total undergraduate aid awarded as scholarships/grants, 44% as loans/jobs. **Non-need-based:** Scholarships awarded for academics, leadership. **Additional information:** Work/study program; up to $2,800 per year.

Application procedures. Admission: Priority date 5/1; deadline 8/23 (postmark date). $30 fee, may be waived for applicants with need. Application may be submitted online. Admission notification on a rolling basis. **Financial aid:** Priority date 3/1, closing date 8/1. FAFSA, institutional form required. Applicants notified on a rolling basis starting 3/1.

Academics. Special study options: Cooperative education, cross-registration, distance learning, double major, dual enrollment of high school students, ESL, independent study, internships, liberal arts/career combination, student-designed major, study abroad, teacher certification program. **Credit/placement by examination:** AP, CLEP, IB, institutional tests. 18 credit hours maximum toward associate degree, 30 toward bachelor's. **Support services:** Learning center, remedial instruction, study skills assistance, tutoring, writing center.

Majors. Business: General, accounting, business admin, fashion, international, international marketing, marketing. **Education:** Elementary. **Health:** Nursing (RN). **Liberal arts:** Arts/sciences. **Public administration:** Human services. **Visual/performing arts:** Art, ceramics, commercial/advertising art, design, drawing, fashion design, fiber arts, graphic design, illustration, interior design, painting, studio arts.

Most popular majors. Business/marketing 21%, education 34%, liberal arts 13%, psychology 23%, visual/performing arts 9%.

Computing on campus. 80 workstations in dormitories, library, computer center. Dormitories wired for high-speed internet access and linked to campus network. Online library, helpline available.

Student life. **Freshman orientation:** Mandatory. Preregistration for classes offered. Held in August. **Policies:** Freshmen permitted cars on campus. **Housing:** Guaranteed on-campus for all undergraduates. Coed dorms, special housing for disabled, substance-free housing available. $100 deposit, deadline 8/20. **Activities:** Pep band, choral groups, drama, literary magazine, music ensembles, musical theater, student government, student newspaper, religious life committee, servant leadership program, local agency volunteer programs.

Athletics. NCAA. **Intercollegiate:** Baseball M, basketball, cheerleading, cross-country, ice hockey, skiing, soccer, softball W, volleyball W. **Intramural:** Baseball, basketball, bowling, football (non-tackle), golf, skiing, softball, swimming, table tennis, tennis, volleyball. **Team name:** Lions.

Student services. Adult student services, alcohol/substance abuse counseling, campus ministries, career counseling, services for economically disadvantaged, student employment services, financial aid counseling, health services, personal counseling, placement for graduates. **Learning disabled:** Comprehensive services available.

Contact. E-mail: admissions@finlandia.edu
Phone: (906) 487-7274 Toll-free number: (877) 202-5491
Fax: (906) 487-7383
Ben Larson, Dean of Enrollment Management and Student Development, Finlandia University, 601 Quincy Street, Hancock, MI 49930-1882

Grace Bible College

Grand Rapids, Michigan
www.gbcol.edu **CB code: 0809**

- Private 4-year Bible and liberal arts college affiliated with Grace Gospel Fellowship
- Residential campus in small city
- 160 degree-seeking undergraduates: 6% part-time, 48% women, 2% African American, 1% Asian American, 1% Hispanic American, 2% Native American, 1% international
- 64% of applicants admitted
- SAT or ACT (ACT writing optional) required
- 50% graduate within 6 years

General. Founded in 1945. Regionally accredited; also accredited by ABHE. **Degrees:** 25 bachelor's, 15 associate awarded. **ROTC:** Army. **Location:** 50 miles from Kalamazoo. **Calendar:** Semester. **Full-time faculty:** 8 total; 25% have terminal degrees, 25% women. **Part-time faculty:** 25 total; 12% have terminal degrees, 8% minority, 48% women. **Class size:** 84% < 20, 12% 20-39, 2% 40-49, 2% 50-99. **Special facilities:** College-operated Schoolhouse Recording studio.

Freshman class profile. 133 applied, 85 admitted, 33 enrolled.

Mid 50% test scores		**Rank in top quarter:**	35%
SAT verbal:	560-600	**Rank in top tenth:**	15%
SAT math:	490-550	**End year in good standing:**	91%
ACT:	17-23	**Return as sophomores:**	61%
GPA 3.50 or higher:	48%	**Out-of-state:**	28%
GPA 3.0-3.49:	31%	**Live on campus:**	70%
GPA 2.0-2.99:	18%		

Basis for selection. Evidence of personal salvation through Jesus Christ important. High school GPA of 2.5, average ACT composite of 20, and rank in top half of class for regular admission. Probationary admission for those in third quarter of class. Interview may be recommended.

High school preparation. 11 units recommended.

2005-2006 Annual costs. Tuition/fees: $10,950. Room/board: $6,860. Books/supplies: $496. Personal expenses: $884.

2004-2005 Financial aid. **Need-based:** 46% of total undergraduate aid awarded as scholarships/grants, 54% as loans/jobs. **Non-need-based:** Scholarships awarded for academics, music/drama, religious affiliation.

Application procedures. **Admission:** Closing date 6/1 (receipt date). No application fee. Admission notification on a rolling basis. Must reply by May 1 or within 4 week(s) if notified thereafter. **Financial aid:** Priority date 3/1; no closing date. FAFSA required. Applicants notified on a rolling basis starting 5/15; must reply within 2 week(s) of notification.

Academics. All students major in Bible and theology in addition to degree major. **Special study options:** Combined bachelor's/graduate degree, cross-registration, double major, dual enrollment of high school students, independent study, internships, liberal arts/career combination. **Credit/placement by examination:** AP, CLEP, institutional tests. **Support services:** Reduced course load, remedial instruction, tutoring, writing center.

Majors. **Business:** General, accounting, business admin, international, management science, marketing. **Communications:** Digital media. **Communications technology:** Photo/film/video, recording arts. **Computer sciences:** General, information technology, web page design. **Education:** Early childhood, elementary, music, secondary. **Liberal arts:** Arts/sciences. **Public administration:** Human services. **Theology:** Bible, missionary, pastoral counseling, religious ed, sacred music, theology, youth ministry.

Most popular majors. Business/marketing 8%, communication technologies 16%, education 24%, public administration/social services 8%, theological studies 16%, visual/performing arts 20%.

Computing on campus. 25 workstations in library, computer center. Dormitories wired for high-speed internet access and linked to campus network. Helpline, wireless network available.

Student life. **Freshman orientation:** Mandatory. Freshmen meet for 3 days prior to start of fall semester. **Policies:** Religious observance required. Freshmen permitted cars on campus. **Housing:** Guaranteed on-campus for freshmen. Single-sex dorms, apartments, substance-free housing available. $100 deposit, deadline 5/1. **Activities:** Jazz band, choral groups, drama, music ensembles, student government, Christian ministry organization, missionary fellowship.

Athletics. NCCAA. **Intercollegiate:** Basketball, soccer M, volleyball W. **Intramural:** Basketball M, bowling, golf, handball, racquetball, skiing, table tennis, tennis, volleyball. **Team name:** Tigers.

Student services. Campus ministries, career counseling, student employment services, financial aid counseling, health services, personal counseling, placement for graduates.

Contact. E-mail: gbc@gbcol.edu
Phone: (616) 538-2330 Toll-free number: (800) 968-1887
Fax: (616) 538-0599
Kevin Gilliam, Enrollment Director, Grace Bible College, PO Box 910, Grand Rapids, MI 49509

Grand Valley State University

Allendale, Michigan **CB member**
www.gvsu.edu **CB code: 1258**

- Public 4-year university
- Residential campus in small town
- 18,715 degree-seeking undergraduates: 12% part-time, 61% women, 5% African American, 3% Asian American, 3% Hispanic American, 1% Native American, 1% international
- 3,063 degree-seeking graduate students
- 68% of applicants admitted
- SAT or ACT (ACT writing optional) required
- 53% graduate within 6 years; 38% enter graduate study

General. Founded in 1960. Regionally accredited. **Degrees:** 2,944 bachelor's awarded; master's offered. **Location:** 12 miles from Grand Rapids. **Calendar:** Semester, extensive summer session. **Full-time faculty:** 910 total; 60% have terminal degrees, 14% minority, 45% women. **Part-time faculty:** 460 total; 53% women. **Class size:** 26% < 20, 58% 20-39, 9% 40-49, 4% 50-99, 1% >100. **Special facilities:** Cross-country fitness trail, recital hall, two Great Lakes research vessels, water resources research institute, center for presidential studies.

Freshman class profile. 13,255 applied, 9,055 admitted, 3,412 enrolled.

Mid 50% test scores		**Rank in top tenth:**	22%
ACT:	21-26	**Return as sophomores:**	82%
GPA 3.50 or higher:	54%	**Out-of-state:**	4%
GPA 3.0-3.49:	42%	**Live on campus:**	78%
GPA 2.0-2.99:	4%	**Fraternities:**	4%
Rank in top quarter:	55%	**Sororities:**	3%

Basis for selection. Admission based on secondary school grades as well as courses, personal and academic data submitted on application and ACT or SAT results. Audition required of music majors. Portfolio required of art majors. Interviews and essays required of some.

High school preparation. 20 units recommended. Recommended units include English 4, mathematics 4, social studies 3, science 4 (laboratory 2), foreign language 2 and academic electives 1. Math should include 2 algebra. English should include 1 composition. Also recommend 2 fine arts and computer literacy.

2005-2006 Annual costs. Tuition/fees: $6,220; $12,510 out-of-state. Junior and Senior in-state students pay $6448 per year or $281 per-credit-hour. Junior and senior out-of-state students pay $12,932 per year or $550 per-credit-hour. Room/board: $6,360. Books/supplies: $600. Personal expenses: $450.

2005-2006 Financial aid. Need-based: 3,092 full-time freshmen applied for aid; 2,009 were judged to have need; 2,009 of these received aid. Average need met was 100%. Average scholarship/grant was $4,190; average loan $2,638. 33% of total undergraduate aid awarded as scholarships/grants, 67% as loans/jobs. **Non-need-based:** Awarded to 4,592 full-time undergraduates, including 3,269 freshmen. Scholarships awarded for academics, alumni affiliation, art, athletics, minority status, music/drama, state residency. **Additional information:** College traditionally funds 100% of each student's demonstrated need.

Application procedures. Admission: Priority date 2/1; deadline 5/1 (receipt date). $30 fee, may be waived for applicants with need. Application may be submitted online. Admission notification on a rolling basis beginning on or about 9/1. Must reply by 5/1. Application closing date February 1 for campus housing, scholarships. **Financial aid:** Priority date 2/15; no closing date. FAFSA required. Applicants notified on a rolling basis starting 4/15; must reply within 3 week(s) of notification.

Academics. Special study options: Combined bachelor's/graduate degree, cooperative education, cross-registration, distance learning, double major, dual enrollment of high school students, ESL, exchange student, honors, independent study, internships, liberal arts/career combination, student-designed major, study abroad, teacher certification program, Washington semester. Undergraduates may take graduate level classes as seniors; co-op programs in education, engineering, health professions. **Credit/placement by examination:** AP, CLEP, IB, institutional tests. 32 credit hours maximum toward bachelor's degree. **Support services:** Learning center, preadmission summer program, remedial instruction, study skills assistance, tutoring, writing center.

Honors college/program. 3.5 GPA and 28 ACT required.

Majors. Architecture: Urban/community planning. **Area/ethnic studies:** Russian/Slavic. **Biology:** General, biochemistry, cellular/molecular. **Business:** Accounting, business admin, finance, human resources, international, management science, managerial economics, marketing, tourism promotion, tourism/travel. **Communications:** General, advertising, broadcast journalism, journalism, public relations. **Computer sciences:** General, computer science, information systems, programming. **Conservation:** Management/policy. **Education:** Music, physical, science, special. **Engineering:** Electrical, manufacturing, mechanical. **English:** Creative writing, technical writing. **Foreign languages:** Ancient Greek, classics, French, German, Latin, Spanish. **Health:** Clinical lab science, nursing (RN), occupational health, predentistry, premedicine, prepharmacy, preveterinary. **History:** General. **Interdisciplinary:** Behavioral sciences, biological/physical sciences, biopsychology. **Legal studies:** General. **Liberal arts:** Arts/sciences. **Math:** General, statistics. **Parks/recreation:** General, health/fitness. **Philosophy/religion:** Philosophy. **Physical sciences:** Chemistry, geochemistry, geology, physics. **Protective services:** Law enforcement admin, security services. **Psychology:** General. **Public administration:** General, social work. **Social sciences:** General, anthropology, economics, geography, international relations, political science, sociology. **Visual/performing arts:** Art, ceramics, commercial/advertising art, dramatic, metal/jewelry, painting, photography, printmaking, sculpture, studio arts.

Most popular majors. Business/marketing 19%, English 9%, health sciences 14%, psychology 8%, security/protective services 7%, social sciences 8%.

Computing on campus. 1,700 workstations in dormitories, library, computer center, student center. Dormitories wired for high-speed internet access and linked to campus network. Commuter students can connect to campus network. Online course registration, helpline, repair service, student web hosting, wireless network available.

Student life. Freshman orientation: Mandatory, $75 fee. Preregistration for classes offered. One day long and held for small groups on 50 possible dates through May, June, July, and August. Students register for classes for full year. **Policies:** Freshmen permitted cars on campus. **Housing:** Guaranteed on-campus for freshmen. Coed dorms, apartments, substance-free housing available. $150 deposit, deadline 2/1. Honors College, specialty, languages, engineering housing available. **Activities:** Bands, choral groups, dance, drama, film society, literary magazine, music ensembles, musical theater, radio station, student government, student newspaper, symphony orchestra, TV station, 143 registered organizations.

Athletics. NCAA. **Intercollegiate:** Baseball M, basketball, cross-country, diving, football (tackle) M, golf, soccer W, softball W, swimming, tennis, track and field, volleyball W. **Intramural:** Archery, badminton, basketball, bowling, cross-country, diving, fencing, field hockey W, football (tackle) M, golf, gymnastics, racquetball, rowing (crew), skiing, skin diving, soccer, softball, squash, swimming, table tennis, tennis, volleyball, wrestling M. **Team name:** Lakers.

Student services. Adult student services, alcohol/substance abuse counseling, campus ministries, career counseling, services for economically disadvantaged, student employment services, financial aid counseling, health services, minority student services, on-campus daycare, personal counseling, placement for graduates, women's services. **Physically disabled:** Services for visually, speech, hearing impaired.

Contact. E-mail: go2gvsu@gvsu.edu
Phone: (616) 331-2025 Toll-free number: (800) 748-0246
Fax: (616) 331-2000
Jodi Chycinski, Director of Admissions, Grand Valley State University, One Campus Drive, Allendale, MI 49401-9403

Great Lakes Christian College

Lansing, Michigan
www.glcc.edu **CB code: 7320**

- Private 4-year Bible college affiliated with Church of Christ (Christian)
- Residential campus in small city
- 160 full-time, degree-seeking undergraduates
- 92% of applicants admitted
- SAT or ACT (ACT writing optional) required

General. Founded in 1949. Accredited by ABHE. **Degrees:** 24 bachelor's, 5 associate awarded. **Location:** 90 miles from Detroit. **Calendar:** Semester, limited summer session. **Full-time faculty:** 10 total. **Part-time faculty:** 25 total.

Freshman class profile. 75 applied, 69 admitted, 59 enrolled.

GPA 3.50 or higher:	26%	**Out-of-state:**	16%
GPA 3.0-3.49:	31%	**Live on campus:**	95%
GPA 2.0-2.99:	37%	**International:**	3%

Basis for selection. Recommendations of character from applicant's minister and church leaders required. Students with high school GPA below 2.25 or ACT below 16 or SAT below 820 (exclusive of Writing) admitted on probation. Essay recommended. Interview required for accelerated ministries program. **Homeschooled:** Transcript of courses and grades required.

2005-2006 Annual costs. Tuition/fees: $8,448. Room/board: $5,200. Books/supplies: $600. Personal expenses: $1,500.

2004-2005 Financial aid. Need-based: 25 full-time freshmen applied for aid; 17 were judged to have need; 17 of these received aid. Average need met was 55%. Average scholarship/grant was $5,961; average loan $2,072. 54% of total undergraduate aid awarded as scholarships/grants, 46% as loans/jobs. **Non-need-based:** Awarded to 31 full-time undergraduates, including 8 freshmen. Scholarships awarded for academics, alumni affiliation, music/drama.

Application procedures. Admission: Priority date 8/1; no deadline. $30 fee, may be waived for applicants with need. Application may be submitted online. Admission notification on a rolling basis. **Financial aid:** Priority date 8/1; no closing date. FAFSA, institutional form required. Applicants notified on a rolling basis starting 5/1; must reply within 3 week(s) of notification.

Academics. Special study options: Accelerated study, cross-registration, double major, dual enrollment of high school students, internships. 18-month accelerated program in ministries for students over 25. **Credit/placement by examination:** CLEP. **Support services:** Reduced course load, tutoring.

Majors. History: General. **Theology:** Bible, religious ed, sacred music.

Computing on campus. 21 workstations in library, computer center. Dormitories wired for high-speed internet access and linked to campus network. Commuter students can connect to campus network. Online library, wireless network available.

Student life. Freshman orientation: Mandatory, $350 fee. Preregistration for classes offered. **Policies:** Regular Christian service participation required of all full-time students. Religious observance required. Freshmen permitted cars on campus. **Housing:** Single-sex dorms, apartments, substance-free housing available. $200 fully refundable deposit, deadline 6/1. **Activities:** Choral groups, drama, music ensembles, student government.

Athletics. NCCAA. **Intercollegiate:** Baseball M, soccer, volleyball W. **Intramural:** Baseball M, basketball, soccer, volleyball. **Team name:** Crusaders.

Student services. Campus ministries, financial aid counseling, personal counseling.

Contact. E-mail: admissions@glcc.edu
Phone: (517) 321-0242 ext. 221 Toll-free number: (800) 937-4522
Fax: (517) 321-5902
Mike Klauka, Director of Admissions and Athletics, Great Lakes Christian College, 6211 West Willow Highway, Lansing, MI 48917-1231

Hillsdale College

Hillsdale, Michigan — **CB member**
www.hillsdale.edu — **CB code: 1295**

- Private 4-year liberal arts college
- Residential campus in large town
- 1,304 degree-seeking undergraduates: 3% part-time, 52% women
- 1,262 graduate students
- 82% of applicants admitted
- SAT or ACT (ACT writing optional), application essay required

General. Founded in 1844. Regionally accredited. **Degrees:** 243 bachelor's awarded. **Location:** 120 miles from Detroit, 75 miles from Ann Arbor. **Calendar:** Semester, limited summer session. **Full-time faculty:** 100 total; 86% have terminal degrees, 20% women. **Part-time faculty:** 36 total; 33% have terminal degrees, 39% women. **Class size:** 74% < 20, 24% 20-39, less than 1% 40-49, 1% 50-99. **Special facilities:** Arboretum, preschool, K-12 private academy, economics library, special collections library for first editions, 685-acre lake biological station.

Freshman class profile. 1,093 applied, 896 admitted, 373 enrolled.

Mid 50% test scores			
SAT verbal:	580-720	**Rank in top quarter:**	75%
SAT math:	540-670	**Rank in top tenth:**	39%
ACT:	24-29	**Out-of-state:**	59%
GPA 3.50 or higher:	78%	**Live on campus:**	99%
GPA 3.0-3.49:	19%	**Fraternities:**	30%
GPA 2.0-2.99:	3%	**Sororities:**	40%

Basis for selection. Minimum 3.1 GPA, class rank in top third preferred. Test scores, recommendations, interview, personal essay important. SAT Subject Tests recommended. Portfolio recommended for art majors. Audition required for music scholarship applicants. **Homeschooled:** Transcript of courses and grades required.

High school preparation. College-preparatory program recommended. 16 units recommended. Recommended units include English 4, mathematics 4, social studies 1, history 2, science 3 (laboratory 1) and foreign language 2.

2005-2006 Annual costs. Tuition/fees: $17,310. Room/board: $6,850. Books/supplies: $800. Personal expenses: $500.

2004-2005 Financial aid. Need-based: 315 full-time freshmen applied for aid; 300 were judged to have need; 300 of these received aid. Average need met was 75%. Average scholarship/grant was $8,500; average loan $2,500. 40% of total undergraduate aid awarded as scholarships/grants, 60% as loans/jobs. **Non-need-based:** Awarded to 1,155 full-time undergraduates, including 300 freshmen. Scholarships awarded for academics, alumni affiliation, art, athletics, leadership, music/drama, state residency. **Additional information:** Campus employment available.

Application procedures. Admission: Priority date 11/15; deadline 2/15 (postmark date). $35 fee. Application may be submitted online. Admission notification on a rolling basis beginning on or about 12/15. Must reply by May 1 or within 2 week(s) if notified thereafter. **Financial aid:** Priority date 3/1; no closing date. FAFSA, institutional form required. Required for returning students only. Applicants notified on a rolling basis starting 2/1; must reply by 5/1 or within 3 week(s) of notification.

Academics. Highly qualified students may study at Oxford University, England for a semester or for a summer. Summer business program at Regents College, London, England as well as study abroad programs in France, Germany and Spain. **Special study options:** Accelerated study, double major, dual enrollment of high school students, honors, independent study, internships, study abroad, teacher certification program, Washington semester. **Credit/placement by examination:** AP, CLEP, IB, SAT, ACT, institutional tests. **Support services:** Reduced course load, study skills assistance, tutoring, writing center.

Majors. Area/ethnic studies: American, European. **Biology:** General. **Business:** General, accounting, business admin, finance, international marketing, marketing. **Communications:** General, journalism. **Computer sciences:** Computer science. **Education:** General, early childhood, elementary, multi-level teacher, physical, secondary. **English:** English lit, speech/rhetoric. **Foreign languages:** Classics, comparative lit, French, German, Spanish. **Health:** Predentistry, premedicine, prenursing, prepharmacy, preveterinary. **History:** General. **Interdisciplinary:** Math/computer science. **Legal studies:** Prelaw. **Liberal arts:** Arts/sciences. **Math:** General, computational. **Philosophy/religion:** Christian, philosophy, religion. **Physical sciences:** Chemistry, physics. **Psychology:** General. **Social sciences:** Economics, political science, sociology. **Theology:** Preministerial. **Visual/performing arts:** Art, dramatic.

Most popular majors. Biology 7%, business/marketing 18%, education 12%, English 8%, history 12%, philosophy/religious studies 7%, social sciences 10%.

Computing on campus. 200 workstations in library, computer center, student center. Dormitories wired for high-speed internet access and linked to campus network. Commuter students can connect to campus network. Online library, helpline, repair service, wireless network available.

Student life. Freshman orientation: Mandatory. Preregistration for classes offered. 3-day program in the fall. **Policies:** Freshmen permitted cars on campus. **Housing:** Guaranteed on-campus for all undergraduates. Single-sex dorms, apartments, fraternity/sorority housing, substance-free housing available. $200 nonrefundable deposit, deadline 5/1. **Activities:** Bands, choral groups, dance, drama, literary magazine, music ensembles, musical theater, student government, student newspaper, symphony orchestra, Catholic student council, Varsity H-Club, international relations club, student federation, enterprising leaders, Intervarsity Christian Fellowship, Fellowship of Christian Athletes, College Republicans, Young Life, Praxis, Charis.

Athletics. NCAA. **Intercollegiate:** Baseball M, basketball, cross-country, diving W, equestrian W, football (tackle) M, softball W, swimming W, track and field, volleyball W. **Intramural:** Basketball, football (non-tackle), handball, racquetball, soccer, softball, squash, swimming, table tennis, tennis, track and field, volleyball, water polo. **Team name:** Chargers.

Student services. Campus ministries, career counseling, student employment services, financial aid counseling, health services, personal counseling, placement for graduates. **Physically disabled:** Services for visually impaired.

Contact. E-mail: admissions@hillsdale.edu
Phone: (517) 607-2327 Fax: (517) 607-2223
Jeffrey Lantis, Director of Admissions, Hillsdale College, 33 East College Street, Hillsdale, MI 49242

Hope College

Holland, Michigan — **CB member**
www.hope.edu — **CB code: 1301**

- Private 4-year liberal arts college affiliated with Reformed Church in America
- Residential campus in small city
- 3,070 degree-seeking undergraduates: 2% part-time, 61% women, 2% African American, 2% Asian American, 2% Hispanic American, 1% international
- 77% of applicants admitted
- SAT or ACT (ACT writing optional), application essay required
- 75% graduate within 6 years; 27% enter graduate study

General. Founded in 1862. Regionally accredited. **Degrees:** 652 bachelor's awarded. **ROTC:** Army. **Location:** 30 miles from Grand Rapids, 160 miles from Chicago. **Calendar:** Semester, limited summer session. **Full-time faculty:** 215 total; 78% have terminal degrees, 12% minority, 42% women. **Part-time faculty:** 107 total; 27% have terminal degrees, 6% minority, 47% women. **Class size:** 54% < 20, 44% 20-39, less than 1% 40-49,

2% 50-99. **Special facilities:** Museum, Pelletron particle accelerator, biological field station, electron microscopes, laser research, cadaver lab.

Freshman class profile. 2,674 applied, 2,071 admitted, 760 enrolled.

Mid 50% test scores		Return as sophomores:	90%
SAT verbal:	550-680	Out-of-state:	33%
SAT math:	560-680	Live on campus:	98%
ACT:	23-29	International:	1%
Rank in top quarter:	61%	Fraternities:	9%
Rank in top tenth:	34%	Sororities:	9%
End year in good standing:	96%		

Basis for selection. High school achievement record, recommendations, activities, and test scores considered. Class rank in top half preferred. Interview recommended. Auditions required for scholarship consideration in music, theater, dance programs. Portfolio required for scholarship consideration in art programs. **Homeschooled:** Paper of at least 3 pages from final 2 years of home schooling, list of non-textbooks read in last 2 years of home schooling, letter of recommendation from adult outside of family required.

High school preparation. Required and recommended units include English 4, mathematics 2-3, social studies 2, history 1, science 1-3 (laboratory 1-2), foreign language 2 and academic electives 5.

2006-2007 Annual costs. Tuition/fees: $22,570. Room/board: $6,982. Books/supplies: $640. Personal expenses: $1,040.

2004-2005 Financial aid. All financial aid based on need. 630 full-time freshmen applied for aid; 471 were judged to have need; 471 of these received aid. Average need met was 86%. Average scholarship/grant was $14,114; average loan $3,367. 69% of total undergraduate aid awarded as scholarships/grants, 31% as loans/jobs.

Application procedures. Admission: Priority date 3/1; no deadline. $35 fee, may be waived for applicants with need. Application must be submitted on paper. Admission notification on a rolling basis beginning on or about 12/15. Must reply by May 1 or within 2 week(s) if notified thereafter. **Financial aid:** Priority date 3/1; no closing date. FAFSA, institutional form required. Applicants notified on a rolling basis starting 3/20; must reply by 5/1 or within 2 week(s) of notification.

Academics. Extensive undergraduate scientific research opportunities available. All fine arts divisions nationally accredited. **Special study options:** Double major, ESL, independent study, internships, liberal arts/career combination, New York semester, student-designed major, study abroad, teacher certification program, urban semester, Washington semester. Internships in Chicago, New York City, Washington DC, and Philadelphia. **Credit/placement by examination:** AP, CLEP, IB, institutional tests. 32 credit hours maximum toward bachelor's degree. **Support services:** Reduced course load, study skills assistance, tutoring, writing center.

Majors. Area/ethnic studies: Japanese. **Biology:** General, biochemistry. **Business:** Accounting, business admin. **Communications:** General. **Computer sciences:** General. **Conservation:** Environmental science. **Education:** Elementary, emotionally handicapped, Latin, learning disabled, music, physical, secondary. **Engineering:** General, physics. **Foreign languages:** Biblical, classics, French, German, Latin, Spanish. **Health:** Athletic training, nursing (RN). **History:** General. **Interdisciplinary:** Biological/physical sciences. **Math:** General. **Parks/recreation:** Exercise sciences. **Philosophy/religion:** Philosophy, religion. **Physical sciences:** Chemistry, geochemistry, geology, geophysics, physics. **Psychology:** General. **Public administration:** Social work. **Social sciences:** General, economics, political science, sociology. **Visual/performing arts:** Art history/conservation, dance, dramatic, jazz, music performance, piano/organ, stringed instruments, studio arts, voice/opera.

Most popular majors. Business/marketing 14%, education 18%, foreign language 6%, psychology 9%, social sciences 7%.

Computing on campus. 300 workstations in dormitories, library, computer center, student center. Dormitories wired for high-speed internet access and linked to campus network. Commuter students can connect to campus network. Online library, helpline, wireless network available.

Student life. Freshman orientation: Mandatory. Preregistration for classes offered. 3-day orientation for students and parents begins Friday before school starts. **Policies:** Visitors of opposite gender not allowed after 2 a.m. No alcohol allowed on campus. Freshmen permitted cars on campus. **Housing:** Guaranteed on-campus for all undergraduates. Coed dorms, single-sex dorms, apartments, fraternity/sorority housing, substance-free housing available. $300 nonrefundable deposit, deadline 5/1. Cottages (houses on or near campus), theme housing available. **Activities:** Bands, choral groups, dance, drama, literary magazine, music ensembles, musical theater, radio station, student government, student newspaper, symphony orchestra, TV station, Ministry of Christ's People, Fellowship of Christian Athletes, Inter-Varsity Christian Fellowship, Fellowship of Christian Students, College Republicans and Democrats, international relations club, Higher Horizons, black student union, Hispanic students organization, Catholic student union.

Athletics. NCAA. **Intercollegiate:** Baseball M, basketball, cheerleading, cross-country, diving, football (tackle) M, golf, soccer, softball W, swimming, tennis, track and field, volleyball W. **Intramural:** Badminton, basketball, bowling, football (non-tackle), racquetball, soccer, softball, table tennis, track and field, volleyball, water polo M. **Team name:** Flying Dutchmen, Flying Dutch.

Student services. Adult student services, alcohol/substance abuse counseling, campus ministries, career counseling, student employment services, financial aid counseling, health services, minority student services, personal counseling, placement for graduates, women's services. **Physically disabled:** Services for visually, hearing impaired.

Contact. E-mail: admissions@hope.edu
Phone: (616) 395-7850 Toll-free number: (800) 968-7850
Fax: (616) 395-7130
James Bekkering, Vice President for Admissions, Hope College, 69 East 10th Street, Holland, MI 49422-9000

International Academy of Design and Technology: Detroit

Troy, Michigan
www.iadtdetroit.com/

- For-profit 4-year art and technical college
- Small city

General. Accredited by ACICS. **Calendar:** Semester.

Annual costs/financial aid. Tuition/fees (projected): $16,620.

Contact. Phone: (248) 457-2700
1850 Research Drive, Troy, MI 48083

Kalamazoo College

Kalamazoo, Michigan — **CB member**
www.kzoo.edu — **CB code: 1365**

- Private 4-year liberal arts college
- Residential campus in small city
- 1,226 degree-seeking undergraduates: 57% women, 3% African American, 5% Asian American, 2% Hispanic American
- 68% of applicants admitted
- SAT or ACT with writing, application essay required
- 80% graduate within 6 years

General. Founded in 1833. Regionally accredited. Study abroad centers in Kenya, Senegal, Ecuador, Spain, France, Germany, Mexico, and China. **Degrees:** 271 bachelor's awarded. **ROTC:** Army. **Location:** 140 miles from Detroit, 140 miles from Chicago. **Calendar:** Quarter. **Full-time faculty:** 100 total; 85% have terminal degrees, 15% minority, 48% women. **Part-time faculty:** 14 total; 36% have terminal degrees, 14% minority, 64% women. **Class size:** 68% < 20, 29% 20-39, 3% 40-49. **Special facilities:** 3 theaters, rare books collection, Dow Science Center.

Freshman class profile. 1,669 applied, 1,133 admitted, 367 enrolled.

Mid 50% test scores		GPA 2.0-2.99:	5%
SAT verbal:	610-710	Rank in top quarter:	77%
SAT math:	600-690	Rank in top tenth:	43%
ACT:	26-31	Return as sophomores:	88%
GPA 3.50 or higher:	68%	Out-of-state:	28%
GPA 3.0-3.49:	27%	Live on campus:	100%

Basis for selection. Curriculum, grades, essay, recommendations, and special accomplishments influence decision. Interview recommended. **Homeschooled:** Interview required.

High school preparation. 17 units required. Required and recommended units include English 4, mathematics 3, social studies 2, history 2, science 3 and foreign language 3.

2006-2007 Annual costs. Tuition/fees: $27,144. Room/board: $6,915. Books/supplies: $750. Personal expenses: $828.

2005-2006 Financial aid. Need-based: 237 full-time freshmen applied for aid; 179 were judged to have need; 179 of these received aid. Average

scholarship/grant was $15,100; average loan $4,100. 69% of total undergraduate aid awarded as scholarships/grants, 31% as loans/jobs. **Non-need-based:** Awarded to 1,074 full-time undergraduates, including 304 freshmen. Scholarships awarded for academics, alumni affiliation. **Additional information:** Paid career development internship and senior project experiences available on campus.

Application procedures. **Admission:** Closing date 2/15 (receipt date). $35 fee, may be waived for applicants with need. Application must be submitted on paper. Admission notification 4/1. Must reply by 5/1. **Financial aid:** Priority date 2/15; no closing date. FAFSA, institutional form required. Applicants notified on a rolling basis starting 3/21; must reply by 5/1.

Academics. Most students participate in career internships and study abroad. College subsidizes most study abroad expenses. Students complete senior individualized project and portfolio as part of graduation requirements. **Special study options:** Cross-registration, double major, dual enrollment of high school students, exchange student, independent study, internships, New York semester, study abroad, urban semester. **Credit/placement by examination:** AP, CLEP, IB. 18 credit hours maximum toward bachelor's degree. **Support services:** Learning center, reduced course load, study skills assistance, tutoring, writing center.

Majors. **Biology:** General. **Computer sciences:** General. **Family/consumer sciences:** Family studies. **Foreign languages:** Classics, French, German, Spanish. **Health:** Predentistry, premedicine, preveterinary. **History:** General. **Legal studies:** Prelaw. **Math:** General. **Philosophy/religion:** Philosophy, religion. **Physical sciences:** Chemistry, physics. **Psychology:** General. **Social sciences:** Anthropology, economics, political science, sociology. **Visual/performing arts:** Art, art history/conservation, dramatic.

Most popular majors. Biology 14%, English 12%, foreign language 6%, history 6%, physical sciences 8%, psychology 9%, public administration/social services 27%.

Computing on campus. 130 workstations in computer center, student center. Dormitories linked to campus network. Commuter students can connect to campus network. Helpline available.

Student life. **Freshman orientation:** Mandatory. **Housing:** Guaranteed on-campus for all undergraduates. Coed dorms available. $350 deposit, deadline 5/1. Special-interest housing available. **Activities:** Bands, choral groups, dance, drama, literary magazine, music ensembles, musical theater, radio station, student government, student newspaper, symphony orchestra, Jewish and Christian interest groups, international student and African American student organizations, college forum, women's equity coalition, volunteer bureau, environmental organization, film society, Habitat for Humanity, Amnesty International, coalition on racial diversity.

Athletics. NCAA. **Intercollegiate:** Baseball M, basketball, cross-country, diving, football (tackle) M, golf, soccer, softball W, swimming, tennis, volleyball W. **Intramural:** Basketball, golf, gymnastics W, handball, racquetball, rugby, skiing, soccer, softball, squash, table tennis, tennis, track and field, volleyball, water polo.

Student services. Alcohol/substance abuse counseling, career counseling, student employment services, health services, personal counseling, placement for graduates, women's services.

Contact. E-mail: admission@kzoo.edu
Phone: (269) 337-7166 Toll-free number: (800) 253-3602
Fax: (269) 337-7390
John Carroll, Director of Admission, Kalamazoo College, 1200 Academy Street, Kalamazoo, MI 49006-3295

Kendall College of Art and Design of Ferris State University

Grand Rapids, Michigan
www.kcad.edu **CB code: 1376**

- Public 4-year visual arts college
- Commuter campus in large city
- 758 degree-seeking undergraduates: 60% women
- 30 graduate students
- 83% of applicants admitted
- ACT (writing optional), SAT Subject Tests, application essay required

General. Founded in 1928. Regionally accredited. **Degrees:** 140 bachelor's awarded; master's offered. **Location:** 175 miles from Detroit, 160 miles from Chicago. **Calendar:** Semester, limited summer session. **Full-time faculty:** 46 total; 6% have terminal degrees, 4% minority. **Part-time faculty:** 83 total; 4% have terminal degrees, 4% minority. **Special facilities:** 35,000-title slide collection.

Freshman class profile. 335 applied, 277 admitted, 194 enrolled.

Basis for selection. High school GPA, statement of purpose/essay, ACT or SAT test scores, and portfolio considered in admission process. Portfolio required. **Learning Disabled:** Highly recommended that students with learning disabilities meet College Counselor to discuss education needs/assistance to help achieve learning success.

2005-2006 Annual costs. Tuition/fees: $11,925; $17,910 out-of-state. Studio art courses: $460 per-credit-hour in-state and $690 out-of-state. General education courses: $265 per-credit-hour in-state and $398 out-of-state. Books/supplies: $1,926. Personal expenses: $864.

2005-2006 Financial aid. All financial aid based on need.

Application procedures. **Admission:** Priority date 6/1; no deadline. $30 fee, may be waived for applicants with need. Application must be submitted on paper. Admission notification on a rolling basis. **Financial aid:** Closing date 2/15. FAFSA required. Applicants notified on a rolling basis starting 4/15; must reply within 4 week(s) of notification.

Academics. For bachelor's degree, 42-54 credits in major required, depending on specified major. **Special study options:** Combined bachelor's/graduate degree, double major, dual enrollment of high school students, exchange student, independent study, internships, liberal arts/career combination, New York semester, study abroad, teacher certification program. Continuing Studies (non-credit). **Credit/placement by examination:** AP, CLEP, institutional tests. 30 credit hours maximum toward bachelor's degree. **Support services:** Reduced course load, study skills assistance, tutoring, writing center.

Majors. **Education:** Art. **Production:** Furniture. **Visual/performing arts:** Art history/conservation, commercial/advertising art, design, drawing, graphic design, illustration, industrial design, interior design, metal/jewelry, multimedia, painting, photography, printmaking, sculpture, studio arts.

Computing on campus. 200 workstations in library, computer center. Commuter students can connect to campus network. Online course registration, online library available.

Student life. **Freshman orientation:** Available. Preregistration for classes offered. Held 2 weeks before classes begin. **Housing:** Apartments available. **Activities:** Student government, American Society of Interior Designers, Industrial Design Society of America, American Society of Illustrators, Grand Rapids Furniture Design Association.

Student services. Adult student services, career counseling, student employment services, financial aid counseling, personal counseling, placement for graduates, veterans' counselor. **Physically disabled:** Services for hearing impaired.

Contact. E-mail: brittons@ferris.edu
Phone: (616) 451-2787 Toll-free number: (800) 676-2787
Fax: (616) 831-9689
Sandy Britton, Director of Enrollment Management, Kendall College of Art and Design of Ferris State University, 17 Fountain Street NW, Grand Rapids, MI 49503-3002

Kettering University

Flint, Michigan **CB member**
www.kettering.edu **CB code: 1246**

- Private 5-year university and engineering college
- Residential campus in small city
- 2,411 degree-seeking undergraduates: 15% women, 5% African American, 5% Asian American, 2% Hispanic American, 2% international
- 525 degree-seeking graduate students
- 73% of applicants admitted
- SAT or ACT (ACT writing optional) required

General. Founded in 1919. Regionally accredited. Formerly GMI Engineering and Management Institute. All students required to participate in paid professional cooperative work experiences typically beginning freshman year. Students alternate 11-week terms of full-time study on campus with 12-week terms of full-time work experience with their co-op employer, generally located near home. **Degrees:** 441 bachelor's awarded; master's offered. **Location:** 70 miles from Detroit. **Calendar:** Semester, extensive summer session. **Full-time faculty:** 140 total; 91% have terminal degrees, 22% minority, 20% women. **Part-time faculty:** 17 total; 18% have terminal degrees, 6% minority, 18% women. **Class size:** 35% < 20, 48% 20-39, 11% 40-49, 5% 50-99. **Special facilities:** Computer-integrated manufacturing laboratory, GM-PACE e-design and e-manufacturing studio, acoustics laboratory, Richard P. Scharchburg Archives, polymer optimization center, engine test center, SAE vehicle development laboratory, mechatronics laboratory, biomedical laboratories on campus and at nearby medical center, Ford design simulation studio, crash study lab, fuel cell research center.

Freshman class profile. 2,127 applied, 1,555 admitted, 495 enrolled.

Mid 50% test scores			
SAT verbal:	550-630	Rank in top quarter:	62%
SAT math:	600-690	Rank in top tenth:	31%
ACT:	23-28	Return as sophomores:	87%
GPA 3.50 or higher:	56%	Out-of-state:	32%
GPA 3.0-3.49:	40%	Live on campus:	99%
GPA 2.0-2.99:	4%	International:	2%

Basis for selection. GED not accepted. Strength of preparation, performance in school, test scores, and nonscholastic activities and achievements. Accepted students encouraged to confirm enrollment plans early so co-op employment search process can begin. SAT Subject Tests (especially math level II, chemistry, and physics), while not required, helpful when presented. Interview not required but recommended, especially if there are special circumstances. **Homeschooled:** Laboratory science experience very important and may need to be documented.

High school preparation. 16 units required; 22 recommended. Required and recommended units include English 3-4, mathematics 4, social studies 4, history 2, science 2-4 (laboratory 2), foreign language 2 and academic electives 5. At least 1 unit of either chemistry or physics with laboratory required. Both chemistry and physics strongly recommended. Algebra I and II, geometry and trigonometry required. Drafting or CAD recommended, especially for those considering engineering.

2005-2006 Annual costs. Tuition/fees: $23,898. Room/board: $5,440. Books/supplies: $1,000.

2005-2006 Financial aid. **Need-based:** 493 full-time freshmen applied for aid; 442 were judged to have need; 442 of these received aid. Average need met was 48%. Average scholarship/grant was $4,376; average loan $2,594. 40% of total undergraduate aid awarded as scholarships/grants, 60% as loans/jobs. **Non-need-based:** Awarded to 1,682 full-time undergraduates, including 409 freshmen. Scholarships awarded for academics, alumni affiliation, leadership, minority status, state residency. **Additional information:** All undergraduate students participate in paid professional co-op work experience in industry that typically begins in freshman year. Total student earnings over 4.5-year program typically range from $40,000 to $65,000.

Application procedures. **Admission:** No deadline. $35 fee, may be waived for applicants with need. Application may be submitted online. Admission notification on a rolling basis beginning on or about 9/1. Must reply by May 1 or within 2 week(s) if notified thereafter. **Financial aid:** Priority date 2/14; no closing date. FAFSA, institutional form required. Applicants notified on a rolling basis starting 2/6; must reply within 2 week(s) of notification.

Academics. **Special study options:** Accelerated study, combined bachelor's/graduate degree, cooperative education, distance learning, double major, dual enrollment of high school students, independent study, study abroad. Paid professional co-op experience in industry required of all undergraduates. Co-op typically begins in first year. Each 24-week semester divided into 11 weeks of classes and 12 weeks of co-op. **Credit/placement by examination:** AP, CLEP, IB, institutional tests. **Support services:** Learning center, study skills assistance, tutoring, writing center.

Majors. **Biology:** Biochemistry. **Business:** General, accounting, accounting/finance, business admin, management information systems, marketing, operations. **Computer sciences:** Computer science, LAN/WAN management, networking. **Engineering:** General, computer, electrical, industrial, manufacturing, mechanical. **Engineering technology:** Industrial management. **Math:** Applied, computational, statistics. **Physical sciences:** Chemistry, physics.

Most popular majors. Business/marketing 8%, engineering/engineering technologies 85%.

Computing on campus. 450 workstations in dormitories, library, computer center, student center. Dormitories wired for high-speed internet access and linked to campus network. Commuter students can connect to campus network. Online library, helpline, student web hosting, wireless network available.

Student life. **Freshman orientation:** Mandatory, $150 fee. 4-day orientation required of all new students beginning Thursday before start of school; includes placement testing, team building. **Policies:** Grade requirement to be eligible to join or maintain active membership in Greek letter organizations. Freshmen permitted cars on campus. **Housing:** Guaranteed on-campus for freshmen. Coed dorms, apartments, fraternity/sorority housing available. $100 fully refundable deposit, deadline 6/1. Freshmen required to live in residence hall. Approximately 35 percent of upperclass students live in campus village apartments and about 35 percent live in fraternity and sorority housing. **Activities:** Jazz band, choral groups, drama, literary magazine, music ensembles, radio station, student government, student newspaper, international club, Intervarsity Christian Fellowship, Christians in Action, Society of Automotive Engineers, Society of Women Engineers, National Society of Black Engineers, National Society of Hispanic Engineers, Habitat for Humanity Club, Asian American Association.

Athletics. **Intramural:** Basketball, bowling, cross-country, football (non-tackle), golf, handball, ice hockey, lacrosse, racquetball, rugby, skin diving, soccer, softball, squash, swimming, table tennis, tennis, track and field, volleyball, water polo. **Team name:** Bulldogs.

Student services. Alcohol/substance abuse counseling, campus ministries, career counseling, student employment services, financial aid counseling, health services, minority student services, personal counseling, placement for graduates, veterans' counselor, women's services. **Physically disabled:** Services for visually, speech, hearing impaired.

Contact. E-mail: admissions@kettering.edu
Phone: (810) 762-7865 Toll-free number: (800) 955-4464 ext. 7865
Fax: (810) 762-9837
Barbara Sosin, Director of Admissions, Kettering University, 1700 West Third Avenue, Flint, MI 48504-4898

Lake Superior State University

Sault Ste. Marie, Michigan
www.lssu.edu **CB code: 1421**

- Public 4-year university
- Residential campus in small city
- 2,753 degree-seeking undergraduates: 16% part-time, 51% women, 1% African American, 1% Asian American, 1% Hispanic American, 9% Native American, 11% international
- 85% of applicants admitted
- SAT or ACT (ACT writing recommended) required
- 39% graduate within 6 years

General. Founded in 1946. Regionally accredited. **Degrees:** 514 bachelor's, 104 associate awarded; master's offered. **Location:** 3 miles from Sault Ste. Marie, Canada. **Calendar:** Semester, limited summer session. **Full-time faculty:** 111 total; 66% have terminal degrees, 5% minority, 41% women. **Part-time faculty:** 97 total; 10% minority, 54% women. **Class size:** 40% < 20, 45% 20-39, 7% 40-49, 7% 50-99, less than 1% >100. **Special facilities:** Aquatic research laboratory with fish hatchery and toxicology lab, planetarium, natural science museum, 200-acre biology station, robotics laboratory, indoor rifle range, indoor ice arena.

Freshman class profile. 1,566 applied, 1,328 admitted, 546 enrolled.

Mid 50% test scores			
SAT verbal:	420-560	Rank in top tenth:	9%
SAT math:	460-590	Return as sophomores:	61%
ACT:	18-23	Out-of-state:	4%
Rank in top quarter:	28%	Live on campus:	64%

Basis for selection. School achievement and test scores most important. Recommendations considered when applicant's academic record marginal. **Learning Disabled:** Students with learning disabilities referred to coordinator for Resource Center for Students with Disabilities.

High school preparation. 18 units recommended. Recommended units include English 4, mathematics 3, social studies 2, history 1, science 3 (laboratory 3) and foreign language 2. Specific academic units required vary by college program.

2005-2006 Annual costs. Tuition/fees: $6,308; $12,296 out-of-state. Residents of Ontario, Canada pay in-state rates. Residents of Kansas, Minnesota, Missouri, Nebraska and North Dakota are eligible for the Midwest Consortium agreement rate. Room/board: $6,536. Books/supplies: $850. Personal expenses: $1,397.

2004-2005 Financial aid. **Need-based:** Average need met was 78%. Average scholarship/grant was $3,338; average loan $3,164. 19% of total undergraduate aid awarded as scholarships/grants, 81% as loans/jobs. **Non-need-based:** Awarded to 316 full-time undergraduates, including 96 freshmen. Scholarships awarded for academics, alumni affiliation, athletics.

Application procedures. **Admission:** No deadline. $20 fee, may be waived for applicants with need. Application may be submitted online. Admission notification on a rolling basis beginning on or about 9/15. **Financial aid:** Priority date 2/21; no closing date. FAFSA required. Applicants notified on a rolling basis starting 11/1; must reply within 3 week(s) of notification.

Academics. **Special study options:** Combined bachelor's/graduate degree, cooperative education, distance learning, double major, dual enrollment of high school students, honors, independent study, internships, student-designed major, study abroad, teacher certification program. **Credit/placement by examination:** AP, CLEP, ACT, institutional tests. 30 credit hours maximum toward associate degree, 30 toward bachelor's. **Support services:** Learning center, tutoring, writing center.

Majors. **Biology:** General. **Business:** General, accounting, business admin, managerial economics. **Conservation:** General, fisheries, management/policy, wildlife. **Education:** Elementary, multi-level teacher. **Engineering:** Computer, electrical, mechanical. **Engineering technology:** Electrical, environmental, industrial management. **Family/consumer sciences:** Child care. **Health:** Clinical lab science, nursing (RN), recreational therapy. **History:** General. **Interdisciplinary:** Math/computer science. **Legal studies:** Paralegal. **Math:** General. **Parks/recreation:** Exercise sciences, facilities management. **Physical sciences:** Chemistry, geology. **Protective services:** Fire safety technology. **Psychology:** General. **Public administration:** Human services. **Social sciences:** General, political science, sociology. **Visual/performing arts:** Studio arts.

Most popular majors. Business/marketing 19%, computer/information sciences 12%, education 9%, health sciences 7%, security/protective services 22%.

Computing on campus. 450 workstations in library, computer center. Dormitories wired for high-speed internet access and linked to campus network. Commuter students can connect to campus network. Online course registration, online library, helpline, wireless network available.

Student life. **Freshman orientation:** Mandatory, $125 fee. Preregistration for classes offered. One-day program held during the summer; 4 dates available. **Policies:** Freshmen permitted cars on campus. **Housing:** Guaranteed on-campus for freshmen. Coed dorms, single-sex dorms, apartments, fraternity/sorority housing, substance-free housing available. $300 partly refundable deposit, deadline 6/15. **Activities:** Pep band, choral groups, dance, drama, music ensembles, radio station, student government, student newspaper, Campus Crusade for Christ, HIS House Christian Fellowship, Newman Center, Anchor House Christian Fellowship, Native American Students' Council, political science club, environmental awareness club, professional organizations.

Athletics. NCAA. **Intercollegiate:** Basketball, cross-country, ice hockey M, softball W, tennis, track and field, volleyball W. **Intramural:** Badminton, basketball, boxing, football (non-tackle) M, handball, ice hockey, racquetball, soccer, softball, tennis, track and field, volleyball, water polo, wrestling M. **Team name:** Lakers.

Student services. Adult student services, alcohol/substance abuse counseling, campus ministries, career counseling, services for economically disadvantaged, student employment services, financial aid counseling, health services, minority student services, on-campus daycare, personal counseling, placement for graduates, veterans' counselor. **Physically disabled:** Services for visually, speech, hearing impaired.

Contact. E-mail: admissions@lssu.edu
Phone: (906) 635-2231 Toll-free number: (888) 800-5778
Fax: (906) 635-6696
Susan Camp, Director of Admissions, Lake Superior State University, 650 West Easterday Avenue, Sault Ste. Marie, MI 49783-1699

Lawrence Technological University

Southfield, Michigan — **CB member**
www.ltu.edu — **CB code: 1399**

- Private 4-year university
- Commuter campus in small city
- 2,482 degree-seeking undergraduates: 36% part-time, 23% women, 12% African American, 3% Asian American, 2% Hispanic American, 2% international
- 1,243 degree-seeking graduate students
- 76% of applicants admitted
- SAT or ACT (ACT writing recommended) required
- 46% graduate within 6 years

General. Founded in 1932. Regionally accredited. **Degrees:** 435 bachelor's, 36 associate awarded; master's, doctoral offered. **ROTC:** Army, Navy, Air Force. **Location:** 20 miles from Detroit. **Calendar:** Semester, extensive summer session. **Full-time faculty:** 113 total; 76% have terminal degrees, 15% minority, 24% women. **Part-time faculty:** 276 total; 42% have terminal degrees, 25% minority, 25% women. **Class size:** 72% < 20, 26% 20-39, less than 1% 40-49, 1% 50-99. **Special facilities:** Frank Lloyd Wright designed residence for academic study.

Freshman class profile. 1,298 applied, 990 admitted, 372 enrolled.

Mid 50% test scores		**Rank in top tenth:**	20%
SAT verbal:	430-640	**End year in good standing:**	62%
SAT math:	490-630	**Return as sophomores:**	69%
ACT:	20-26	**Out-of-state:**	2%
GPA 3.50 or higher:	34%	**Live on campus:**	33%
GPA 3.0-3.49:	30%	**Fraternities:**	2%
GPA 2.0-2.99:	35%	**Sororities:**	4%
Rank in top quarter:	41%		

Basis for selection. School achievement record important. Minimum 2.0 GPA in English, mathematics, natural sciences, social studies. Minimum 2.5 GPA in 4 academic areas combined. Minimum 2.0 GPA for industrial management, humanities (natural science courses excluded), and associate degree programs. SAT Subject Tests recommended. Interview and essay recommended. **Homeschooled:** Transcript of courses and grades, letter of recommendation (nonparent) required. **Learning Disabled:** Contact Academic Achievement Center Director.

High school preparation. 12 units required. Required and recommended units include English 4, mathematics 3-4, social studies 3, history 2, science 2-4 (laboratory 2). Programs in engineering, architecture, chemistry, computer science, and mathematics require 2 algebra, 1 geometry, .5 trigonometry, 1 physics. One chemistry required for all but architecture. Programs in business, industrial management, and humanities require 1.5 algebra, 1 laboratory science. Remedial courses available for any deficiencies.

2006-2007 Annual costs. Tuition/fees (projected): $19,306. Room/board: $7,537. Books/supplies: $1,206. Personal expenses: $1,900.

2004-2005 Financial aid. **Need-based:** 269 full-time freshmen applied for aid; 189 were judged to have need; 189 of these received aid. Average need met was 78%. Average scholarship/grant was $7,317; average loan $2,696. 46% of total undergraduate aid awarded as scholarships/grants, 54% as loans/jobs. **Non-need-based:** Awarded to 862 full-time undergraduates, including 206 freshmen. Scholarships awarded for academics, alumni affiliation, job skills, minority status, ROTC, state residency. **Additional information:** State deadline for Michigan Competitive Scholarship and Michigan Tuition Grant 3/1.

Application procedures. **Admission:** No deadline. $30 fee, may be waived for applicants with need. Application may be submitted online. Admission notification on a rolling basis. **Financial aid:** Priority date 4/1; no closing date. FAFSA required. Applicants notified on a rolling basis starting 3/1; must reply within 2 week(s) of notification.

Academics. **Special study options:** Combined bachelor's/graduate degree, cooperative education, cross-registration, distance learning, double major, dual enrollment of high school students, ESL, honors, independent study, internships, liberal arts/career combination, study abroad, weekend college. **Credit/placement by examination:** AP, CLEP, IB, institutional tests. **Support services:** Learning center, pre-admission summer program, reduced course load, remedial instruction, study skills assistance, tutoring, writing center.

Majors. **Architecture:** Architecture, environmental design, interior. **Biology:** Biochemistry. **Business:** Business admin, construction management. **Communications technology:** General. **Computer sciences:** Computer science, information technology. **Engineering:** Biomedical, civil, computer, electrical, mechanical. **Engineering technology:** General, architectural drafting, industrial, industrial management. **Interdisciplinary:** Math/computer science. **Liberal arts:** Humanities. **Math:** General. **Physical sciences:** Chemistry, physics. **Psychology:** General. **Visual/performing arts:** Illustration.

Most popular majors. Architecture 26%, computer/information sciences 10%, engineering/engineering technologies 54%.

Computing on campus. PC or laptop required. 150 workstations in dormitories, library, computer center. Dormitories wired for high-speed internet access and linked to campus network. Commuter students can connect to campus network. Online course registration, online library, helpline, repair service, student web hosting, wireless network available.

Student life. **Freshman orientation:** Mandatory. Preregistration for classes offered. **Policies:** Freshmen permitted cars on campus. **Housing:** Special housing for disabled, apartments, substance-free housing available. $200 deposit. **Activities:** Literary magazine, music ensembles, student government, student newspaper, Society of Women Engineers, international students organization, Students Against Drunk Driving, Society of Automotive Engineers, Architecture Students Association, Campus Crusade for Christ.

Athletics. Intramural: Badminton, basketball, bowling, football (non-tackle) M, golf, racquetball, skiing, soccer, softball, table tennis, volleyball. **Team name:** Blue Devils.

Student services. Alcohol/substance abuse counseling, career counseling, services for economically disadvantaged, student employment services, financial aid counseling, personal counseling, placement for graduates, veterans' counselor. **Physically disabled:** Services for visually, speech, hearing impaired.

Contact. E-mail: admissions@ltu.edu
Phone: (248) 204-3160 Toll-free number: (800) 225-5588
Fax: (248) 204-3188
Jane Rohrback, Director of Admissions, Lawrence Technological University, 21000 West Ten Mile Road, Southfield, MI 48075-1058

Madonna University

Livonia, Michigan
www.madonna.edu **CB code: 1437**

- Private 4-year university and liberal arts college affiliated with Roman Catholic Church
- Commuter campus in small city
- 3,073 degree-seeking undergraduates: 46% part-time, 77% women, 14% African American, 2% Asian American, 3% Hispanic American, 3% international
- 932 graduate students
- 86% of applicants admitted
- SAT or ACT (ACT writing optional), application essay required

General. Founded in 1947. Regionally accredited. **Degrees:** 510 bachelor's, 7 associate awarded; master's offered. **Location:** 18 miles from Detroit, 20 miles from Ann Arbor. **Calendar:** Semester, limited summer session. **Full-time faculty:** 127 total; 57% have terminal degrees, 6% minority, 59% women. **Part-time faculty:** 273 total; 17% have terminal degrees, 17% minority, 64% women. **Class size:** 66% < 20, 30% 20-39, 3% 40-49, 1% 50-99.

Freshman class profile. 573 applied, 490 admitted, 200 enrolled.

Mid 50% test scores		**GPA 2.0-2.99:**	21%
ACT:	22-26	**Out-of-state:**	2%
GPA 3.50 or higher:	51%	**Live on campus:**	9%
GPA 3.0-3.49:	27%	**International:**	2%

Basis for selection. Cumulative high school GPA and curriculum most important. Majors in sciences, allied health and nursing, and mathematics require specific high school subjects. ACT test results important. Some majors require letters of recommendation. ACT preferred. Interview recommended.

High school preparation. College-preparatory program recommended. 19 units required. Required and recommended units include English 3-4, mathematics 2-3, social studies 3, history 3, science 3 (laboratory 1) and foreign language 2. 1 biology, 1 chemistry, 1 algebra required for nursing applicants; biology, 1 chemistry, 2 algebra required for medical and radiologic technology program applicants.

2005-2006 Annual costs. Tuition/fees: $10,400. Nursing students pay $385 per credit hour. Non-resident aliens pay $2,500 deposit. Room/board: $5,768. Books/supplies: $760. Personal expenses: $890.

2004-2005 Financial aid. Need-based: 110 full-time freshmen applied for aid; 85 were judged to have need; 85 of these received aid. Average need met was 52%. Average scholarship/grant was $3,945; average loan $1,883. 37% of total undergraduate aid awarded as scholarships/grants, 63% as loans/jobs. **Non-need-based:** Awarded to 363 full-time undergraduates, including 122 freshmen. Scholarships awarded for academics, alumni affiliation, art, athletics, minority status, music/drama, religious affiliation, state residency.

Application procedures. Admission: Priority date 9/1; no deadline. $25 fee, may be waived for applicants with need. Application may be submitted online. Admission notification on a rolling basis. **Financial aid:** Priority date 2/21; no closing date. FAFSA required. Applicants notified on a rolling basis starting 4/1; must reply by 9/1 or within 2 week(s) of notification.

Academics. Special study options: Cooperative education, cross-registration, distance learning, double major, dual enrollment of high school students, ESL, independent study, internships, liberal arts/career combination, student-designed major, study abroad, teacher certification program, weekend college. **Credit/placement by examination:** AP, CLEP, IB, institutional tests. 30 credit hours maximum toward associate degree, 60 toward bachelor's. **Support services:** Learning center, pre-admission summer program, reduced course load, remedial instruction, study skills assistance, tutoring, writing center.

Majors. Biology: General, biochemistry. **Business:** Accounting, business admin, hospitality admin, human resources, international, management information systems, management science, marketing, selling, special products marketing. **Communications:** Journalism, media studies, public relations. **Computer sciences:** General, computer science. **Education:** General, art, early childhood, elementary, learning disabled, mathematics, music, science, secondary, social studies, special, trade/industrial. **Engineering technology:** Occupational safety. **English:** English lit, speech/rhetoric, technical writing. **Family/consumer sciences:** General, aging, child development, food/nutrition, merchandising. **Foreign languages:** American Sign Language, French, Polish, Spanish. **Health:** Clinical lab science, clinical lab technology, dietetics, health care admin, health services, nursing (RN), predentistry, premedicine, prepharmacy, preveterinary. **History:** General. **Interdisciplinary:** Biological/physical sciences, gerontology, natural sciences. **Legal studies:** Legal secretary, prelaw. **Math:** General. **Philosophy/religion:** Philosophy, religion. **Physical sciences:** Chemistry. **Protective services:** Criminal justice, firefighting. **Psychology:** General. **Public administration:** Social work. **Science technology:** Radiologic. **Social sciences:** Sociology. **Theology:** Pastoral counseling, theology. **Visual/performing arts:** Art, music management.

Most popular majors. Business/marketing 16%, English 8%, health sciences 15%, psychology 7%, security/protective services 10%.

Computing on campus. 90 workstations in dormitories, library, computer center. Dormitories wired for high-speed internet access and linked to campus network. Commuter students can connect to campus network. Online course registration, online library, helpline, wireless network available.

Student life. Freshman orientation: Mandatory. Preregistration for classes offered. All day orientation in April, May, and June; evening orientation in January, May, July and August. **Policies:** Use of alcohol or drugs prohibited on campus; all buildings are smoke free; sexual assault, harassment policies in place. Freshmen permitted cars on campus. **Housing:** Single-sex dorms, substance-free housing available. $75 deposit, deadline 9/1. **Activities:** Choral groups, music ensembles, radio station, student government, student newspaper, TV station, campus ministry, social work student association, gerontology association, student-faculty academic clubs, athletic club, nursing student association, multicultural student association, business professional association, student teacher association.

Athletics. NAIA. **Intercollegiate:** Baseball M, basketball, cross-country, golf, soccer, softball W, volleyball W. **Team name:** Crusaders.

Student services. Alcohol/substance abuse counseling, campus ministries, career counseling, services for economically disadvantaged, student employment services, financial aid counseling, health services, minority student services, personal counseling, placement for graduates, women's services. **Physically disabled:** Services for visually, speech, hearing impaired.

Contact. E-mail: muinfo@madonna.edu
Phone: (734) 432-5339 Fax: (734) 432-5424
Michael Quattro, Coordinator of Undergraduate Admission, Madonna University, 36600 Schoolcraft Road, Livonia, MI 48150

Marygrove College

Detroit, Michigan
www.marygrove.edu **CB code: 1452**

- Private 4-year liberal arts college affiliated with Roman Catholic Church
- Commuter campus in very large city
- 677 degree-seeking undergraduates: 42% part-time, 77% women, 64% African American, 1% Hispanic American, 3% international
- 2,859 degree-seeking graduate students
- 42% of applicants admitted
- ACT (writing recommended), application essay required

General. Founded in 1905. Regionally accredited. **Degrees:** 101 bachelor's, 13 associate awarded; master's offered. **Location:** 6 miles from downtown. **Calendar:** Semester, limited summer session. **Full-time faculty:** 65 total; 68% have terminal degrees, 28% minority, 60% women. **Part-time faculty:** 6 total; 83% women. **Class size:** 84% < 20, 15% 20-39, less than 1% 40-49, less than 1% 50-99.

Freshman class profile. 412 applied, 173 admitted, 80 enrolled.

Mid 50% test scores		**Return as sophomores:**	74%
ACT:	16-20	**Live on campus:**	43%
End year in good standing:	71%	**International:**	1%

Basis for selection. School achievement record and test scores most important. Audition required of music, theater, dance majors. Portfolio required of art majors. Interview required of older applicants and academically weak applicants.

High school preparation. 16 units recommended. Recommended units include English 4, mathematics 2, social studies 2, science 2 and foreign language 2. One computer science recommended.

2005-2006 Annual costs. Tuition/fees: $13,110. Room/board: $6,200. Books/supplies: $1,040. Personal expenses: $2,200.

2005-2006 Financial aid. All financial aid based on need. 38% of total undergraduate aid awarded as scholarships/grants, 62% as loans/jobs.

Application procedures. Admission: Closing date 3/15 (postmark date). $25 fee, may be waived for applicants with need. Application may be submitted online. Admission notification on a rolling basis. Must reply by 5/1. **Financial aid:** Priority date 3/15; no closing date. FAFSA, institutional form required. Applicants notified on a rolling basis starting 5/15; must reply within 2 week(s) of notification.

Academics. Special study options: Cooperative education, cross-registration, distance learning, double major, honors, independent study, internships, student-designed major, study abroad, teacher certification program. **Credit/placement by examination:** AP, CLEP, ACT, institutional tests. 16 credit hours maximum toward associate degree, 32 toward bachelor's. Credit awarded for score of 3 or higher on AP exam. Credit hours awarded determined by faculty. **Support services:** Learning center, pre-admission summer program, reduced course load, remedial instruction, study skills assistance, tutoring, writing center.

Majors. Biology: General. **Business:** General, accounting, business admin, international. **Computer sciences:** General. **Conservation:** Environmental science. **Education:** General, early childhood, special. **English:** English lit. **Health:** Art therapy. **History:** General. **Interdisciplinary:** Natural sciences. **Math:** General. **Philosophy/religion:** Religion. **Physical sciences:** Chemistry. **Psychology:** General. **Public administration:** Social work. **Social sciences:** General, political science. **Visual/performing arts:** Art, dance, music performance, music theory/composition, studio arts.

Computing on campus. 50 workstations in library, computer center. Dormitories linked to campus network. Online course registration, helpline available.

Student life. Freshman orientation: Mandatory. Preregistration for classes offered. 2-day weekday program; students spend night in dorms. **Policies:** Freshmen permitted cars on campus. **Housing:** Coed dorms available. $250 nonrefundable deposit, deadline 8/1. **Activities:** Choral groups, dance, music ensembles, student government, business club, black social worker club, Soulful Expressions ensemble gospel choir, art club.

Athletics. USCAA. **Intercollegiate:** Basketball. **Team name:** Mustangs.

Student services. Campus ministries, career counseling, student employment services, financial aid counseling, health services, on-campus daycare, personal counseling, placement for graduates.

Contact. E-mail: info@marygrove.edu
Phone: (313) 927-1240 Toll-free number: (866) 313-1927
Fax: (313) 927-1345
John Ambrose, Director of Admissions, Marygrove College, 8425 West McNichols Road, Detroit, MI 48221

Michigan Jewish Institute

Oak Park, Michigan
www.mji.edu **CB code: 1505**

- Private 4-year business and liberal arts college affiliated with Jewish faith
- Commuter campus in very large city
- 325 degree-seeking undergraduates

General. Accredited by ACICS. **Degrees:** 10 bachelor's awarded. **Calendar:** Semester, limited summer session. **Full-time faculty:** 3 total. **Part-time faculty:** 7 total. **Special facilities:** Synagogue available on West Bloomfield campus.

Basis for selection. Open admission, but selective for some programs. Interview, character and personal qualities most important; school record, recommendations, essay, and talent or ability important.

High school preparation. Recommended units include English 3, mathematics 3, social studies 1, history 2, science 3 and foreign language 2. Computer literacy strongly recommended.

2005-2006 Annual costs. Tuition/fees: $9,600. Books/supplies: $1,215. Personal expenses: $1,060.

Application procedures. Admission: No deadline. $50 fee. Application must be submitted on paper. Admission notification on a rolling basis.

Academics. Special study options: Accelerated study, cooperative education, double major, dual enrollment of high school students, ESL, independent study, internships, liberal arts/career combination, study abroad, weekend college. **Credit/placement by examination:** AP, CLEP, IB, institutional tests. **Support services:** Learning center, reduced course load, remedial instruction, study skills assistance, tutoring.

Majors. Business: Business admin. **Computer sciences:** General. **Philosophy/religion:** Judaic.

Computing on campus. PC or laptop required. 8 workstations in library, computer center. Online library, helpline, wireless network available.

Student life. Freshman orientation: Available. Preregistration for classes offered. **Policies:** Freshmen permitted cars on campus.

Student services. Adult student services, alcohol/substance abuse counseling, campus ministries, career counseling, student employment services, financial aid counseling, personal counseling.

Contact. E-mail: info@mji.edu
Phone: (248) 414-6900 ext. 12 Fax: (248) 414-6907
Fran Herman, Registrar, Michigan Jewish Institute, 25401 Coolidge Highway, Oak Park, MI 48237

Michigan State University

East Lansing, Michigan **CB member**
www.msu.edu **CB code: 1465**

- Public 4-year university
- Residential campus in small city
- 35,330 degree-seeking undergraduates: 9% part-time, 54% women, 9% African American, 5% Asian American, 3% Hispanic American, 1% Native American, 3% international
- 8,250 degree-seeking graduate students
- 76% of applicants admitted
- SAT or ACT with writing, application essay required
- 71% graduate within 6 years; 20% enter graduate study

General. Founded in 1855. Regionally accredited. **Degrees:** 7,733 bachelor's awarded; master's, doctoral, first professional offered. **ROTC:** Army, Air Force. **Location:** 3 miles from Lansing, 80 miles from Detroit. **Calendar:** Semester, extensive summer session. **Full-time faculty:** 2,411 total; 94% have terminal degrees, 19% minority, 34% women. **Part-time faculty:** 351 total; 62% have terminal degrees, 12% minority, 55% women. **Class size:** 21% <20, 48% 20-39, 8% 40-49, 11% 50-99, 12% >100. **Special facilities:** Planetarium, botanical garden, center for environmental toxicology, superconducting cyclotron laboratory, pesticide research center, experimental farms, 2 museums, center for performing arts, 2 golf courses, agricultural and livestock pavilion, children's garden.

Freshman class profile. 21,844 applied, 16,686 admitted, 7,485 enrolled.

Mid 50% test scores		**Rank in top tenth:**	26%
SAT verbal:	490-620	**Return as sophomores:**	91%
SAT math:	520-650	**Out-of-state:**	12%
ACT:	22-27	**Live on campus:**	96%
Rank in top quarter:	64%	**International:**	3%

Basis for selection. Emphasis on grades and test scores, supplemented by class rank, principal and counselor recommendations, leadership qualities; quality of curriculum. Audition required of music majors. **Homeschooled:** Submit grades, even if from parent. List or provide information on curriculum and be prepared to answer questions. Test scores have stronger emphasis; transcript required.

High school preparation. 14 units required. Required units include English 4, mathematics 3, social studies 3, science 2 and foreign language 2.

2005-2006 Annual costs. Tuition/fees: $7,880; $19,632 out-of-state. Room/board: $6,228. Books/supplies: $1,206. Personal expenses: $1,526.

2005-2006 Financial aid. All financial aid based on need. 4,934 full-time freshmen applied for aid; 3,090 were judged to have need; 3,088 of these received aid. Average need met was 78%. Average scholarship/grant was $4,322; average loan $2,748. 43% of total undergraduate aid awarded as scholarships/grants, 57% as loans/jobs.

Application procedures. Admission: No deadline. $35 fee, may be waived for applicants with need. Application may be submitted online. Admission notification on a rolling basis. Must reply by May 1 or within 4 week(s) if notified thereafter. Although Common Application accepted, use of internal application preferred. Early Action by invitation only. **Financial aid:** Priority date 3/1; no closing date. FAFSA required. Applicants notified on a rolling basis starting 3/15; must reply within 4 week(s) of notification.

Academics. Special study options: Accelerated study, cooperative education, distance learning, double major, dual enrollment of high school students, ESL, exchange student, honors, independent study, internships, liberal arts/career combination, student-designed major, study abroad, teacher certification program, weekend college. **Credit/placement by examination:** AP, CLEP, IB, SAT, ACT, institutional tests. **Support services:** Learning center, pre-admission summer program, reduced course load, remedial instruction, study skills assistance, tutoring, writing center.

Honors college/program. Selection criteria include test scores and class rank. Number admitted varies.

Majors. Agriculture: Animal sciences, business, communications, economics, food science, horticultural science, soil science. **Architecture:** Interior, landscape, urban/community planning. **Area/ethnic studies:** African-American, American, women's. **Biology:** General, bacteriology, biochemistry, Biochemistry/biophysics and molecular biology, botany, entomology, environmental, microbiology, physiology, plant pathology, zoology. **Business:** Accounting, business admin, construction management, finance, hospitality admin, human resources, logistics, marketing, operations. **Communications:** General, advertising, journalism, radio/tv. **Computer sciences:** General, information systems. **Conservation:** Environmental science, environmental studies, forestry, wildlife. **Education:** General, art, Deaf/hearing impaired, elementary, family/consumer sciences, learning disabled, music, physical, special. **Engineering:** General, agricultural, biomedical, chemical, civil, computer, electrical, materials science, mechanical. **English:** English lit, technical writing. **Family/consumer sciences:** General, child development, family/community services. **Foreign languages:** French, German, linguistics, Russian, Spanish. **Health:** Audiology/speech pathology, clinical lab science, community health services, dietetics, marriage/family therapy, music therapy, nurse practitioner, nursing (RN), premedicine, veterinary technology/assistant. **History:** General. **Interdisciplinary:** Biological/physical sciences, global studies, nutrition sciences, science/society. **Legal studies:** Prelaw. **Liberal arts:** Humanities. **Math:** General, applied, computational, statistics. **Parks/recreation:** General, exercise sciences, facilities management. **Philosophy/religion:** Philosophy. **Physical sciences:** General, astrophysics, chemical physics, chemistry, geology, geophysics, physics. **Protective services:** Criminal justice, law enforcement admin. **Psychology:** General. **Public administration:** General, social work. **Social sciences:** General, anthropology, applied economics, economics, geography, international relations, political science, sociology. **Visual/performing arts:** Art, art history/conservation, dramatic, fashion design, interior design, jazz, music pedagogy, music performance, music theory/composition.

Most popular majors. Biology 8%, business/marketing 19%, communications/journalism 14%, engineering/engineering technologies 7%, social sciences 10%.

Computing on campus. PC or laptop required. 2,000 workstations in dormitories, library, computer center, student center. Dormitories wired for high-speed internet access and linked to campus network. Commuter students can connect to campus network. Online course registration, helpline, repair service, student web hosting available.

Student life. Freshman orientation: Mandatory, $175 fee. Preregistration for classes offered. Freshmen attend day-and-a-half session in summer; includes placement tests. **Housing:** Guaranteed on-campus for freshmen. Coed dorms, single-sex dorms, special housing for disabled, apartments, cooperative housing, fraternity/sorority housing, substance-free housing available. $25 fully refundable deposit, deadline 5/1. Freshmen required to live in college housing unless age 21, married, veteran, residing with parents or legal guardian, or registered for under 7 credits. **Activities:** Bands, choral groups, dance, drama, film society, music ensembles, musical theater, opera, radio station, student government, student newspaper, symphony orchestra, TV station, over 500 academic, athletic, social, religious, and political organizations.

Athletics. NCAA. **Intercollegiate:** Baseball M, basketball, cheerleading, cross-country, diving, field hockey W, football (tackle) M, golf, gymnastics, ice hockey M, rowing (crew) W, soccer, softball W, swimming, tennis, track and field, volleyball W, wrestling M. **Intramural:** Archery, baseball M, basketball, cross-country, fencing, football (non-tackle) M, golf, gymnastics, ice hockey, lacrosse M, racquetball, rowing (crew) M, rugby, sailing, skiing, soccer, softball, squash, swimming, tennis, track and field, volleyball, water polo, wrestling M. **Team name:** Spartans.

Student services. Adult student services, alcohol/substance abuse counseling, career counseling, student employment services, financial aid counseling, health services, legal services, minority student services, on-campus daycare, personal counseling, placement for graduates, veterans' counselor, women's services. **Physically disabled:** Services for visually, speech, hearing impaired. **Learning disabled:** Comprehensive services available.

Contact. E-mail: admis@msu.edu
Phone: (517) 355-8332 Fax: (517) 353-1647
Pamela Horne, Assistant to the Provost for Enrollment Management and Director of Admissions, Michigan State University, 250 Administration Building, East Lansing, MI 48824-1046

Michigan Technological University

Houghton, Michigan
www.mtu.edu **CB code: 1464**

- Public 4-year university
- Residential campus in small town
- 5,516 degree-seeking undergraduates: 7% part-time, 21% women, 2% African American, 1% Asian American, 1% Hispanic American, 1% Native American, 4% international
- 877 degree-seeking graduate students
- 85% of applicants admitted
- SAT or ACT (ACT writing optional) required
- 59% graduate within 6 years; 15% enter graduate study

General. Founded in 1885. Regionally accredited. **Degrees:** 1,048 bachelor's, 28 associate awarded; master's, doctoral offered. **ROTC:** Army, Air Force. **Location:** 210 miles from Green Bay, Wisconsin, 325 miles from Milwaukee. **Calendar:** Semester, limited summer session. **Full-time faculty:** 343 total; 83% have terminal degrees, 16% minority, 24% women. **Part-time faculty:** 46 total; 37% have terminal degrees, 6% minority, 44% women. **Class size:** 43% < 20, 37% 20-39, 8% 40-49, 10% 50-99, 2% >100. **Special facilities:** Mineral museum, performing arts center, forestry center and research forest, cosmic ray observatory, x-ray fluorescence spectrometer, process simulation and control center, remote sensing institute, computer-aided engineering lab, microfabrication lab, subsurface visualization lab.

Freshman class profile. 3,928 applied, 3,326 admitted, 1,327 enrolled.

Mid 50% test scores		Rank in top quarter:	56%
SAT verbal:	530-660	Rank in top tenth:	25%
SAT math:	580-700	End year in good standing:	80%
ACT:	22-28	Return as sophomores:	81%
GPA 3.50 or higher:	55%	Out-of-state:	27%
GPA 3.0-3.49:	31%	Live on campus:	90%
GPA 2.0-2.99:	14%	International:	2%

Basis for selection. School record, class rank, test scores very important. Rank in top quarter of class preferred for engineering programs. Rank in top third to top half of class preferred for other bachelor's programs. Rank in top half of class preferred for associate degree programs. SAT or ACT scores must be received 30 days prior to start of term. Essay recommended. Interview recommended for borderline applicants. **Homeschooled:** ACT required.

High school preparation. 15 units required. Required and recommended units include English 3-4, mathematics 3-4, social studies 3, history 1, science 2-3, foreign language 2 and academic electives 1. Course requirements vary depending on curriculum. Units recommended but not required for non-engineering majors.

2005-2006 Annual costs. Tuition/fees: $8,194; $19,384 out-of-state. Room/board: $6,375. Books/supplies: $1,000. Personal expenses: $1,013.

2005-2006 Financial aid. Need-based: 1,104 full-time freshmen applied for aid; 700 were judged to have need; 699 of these received aid. Average need met was 82%. Average scholarship/grant was $5,829; average loan $3,712. 44% of total undergraduate aid awarded as scholarships/grants, 56% as loans/jobs. **Non-need-based:** Awarded to 2,733 full-time undergraduates, including 819 freshmen. Scholarships awarded for academics, alumni affiliation, athletics, leadership, minority status, ROTC, state residency.

Application procedures. Admission: Priority date 1/15; no deadline. $40 fee, may be waived for applicants with need. Application may be submitted online. Notification within 3 weeks of acceptance. Must reply by May 1 or within 2 week(s) if notified thereafter. **Financial aid:** Priority date 2/18; no closing date. FAFSA required. Applicants notified on a rolling basis starting 3/1; must reply within 4 week(s) of notification.

Academics. Special study options: Cooperative education, distance learning, double major, dual enrollment of high school students, ESL, exchange student, honors, independent study, internships, semester at sea, study abroad, teacher certification program. Dual enrollment programs with Northwestern Michigan College, Delta College, Oakland Community College, Adrian College, Albion College, Augsburg College (MN), College of St. Scholastica

(MN), Mount Senario College, Lansing Community College, Olivet College, Northland College, University of Wisconsin-Superior. **Credit/placement by examination:** AP, CLEP, IB, SAT, ACT, institutional tests. **Support services:** Learning center, reduced course load, remedial instruction, study skills assistance, tutoring, writing center.

Majors. Biology: General, bioinformatics. **Business:** Business admin, construction management. **Communications:** General. **Communications technology:** Recording arts. **Computer sciences:** General, networking, system admin. **Conservation:** Environmental science, forestry, wildlife. **Engineering:** General, biomedical, chemical, civil, computer, electrical, environmental, geological, materials, mechanical, software, surveying. **Engineering technology:** Electrical, mechanical. **Health:** Clinical lab science. **History:** General. **Liberal arts:** Arts/sciences. **Math:** General. **Physical sciences:** Chemistry, geology, geophysics, physics. **Psychology:** General. **Social sciences:** General, economics. **Visual/performing arts:** Theater design.

Most popular majors. Business/marketing 9%, engineering/engineering technologies 68%.

Computing on campus. 1,300 workstations in dormitories, library, computer center, student center. Dormitories wired for high-speed internet access and linked to campus network. Commuter students can connect to campus network. Online course registration, online library, helpline, student web hosting, wireless network available.

Student life. Freshman orientation: Mandatory, $150 fee. Preregistration for classes offered. Week-long program before start of classes. **Policies:** Students must abide by rights and responsibilities policy on alcohol and illegal drugs; sexual assault policy; academic integrity policy. Freshmen permitted cars on campus. **Housing:** Guaranteed on-campus for freshmen. Coed dorms, special housing for disabled, apartments, fraternity/sorority housing, substance-free housing available. **Activities:** Bands, choral groups, dance, drama, film society, literary magazine, music ensembles, musical theater, opera, radio station, student government, student newspaper, symphony orchestra, numerous academic, professional, ethnic, cultural, governing, honor society, media, religious service, special interest, sports organizations.

Athletics. NCAA. **Intercollegiate:** Basketball, cross-country, football (tackle) M, ice hockey M, skiing, tennis, track and field, volleyball W. **Intramural:** Badminton, basketball, bowling, cross-country, football (non-tackle), golf, ice hockey, racquetball, rifle, soccer, softball, swimming, table tennis, tennis, volleyball, water polo, wrestling. **Team name:** Huskies.

Student services. Alcohol/substance abuse counseling, career counseling, student employment services, financial aid counseling, health services, minority student services, on-campus daycare, personal counseling, placement for graduates, veterans' counselor, women's services. **Physically disabled:** Services for visually, speech, hearing impaired.

Contact. E-mail: mtu4u@mtu.edu
Phone: (906) 487-2335 Toll-free number: (888) 688-1885
Fax: (906) 487-2125
Allison Carter, Director of Undergraduate Recruitment, Michigan Technological University, 1400 Townsend Drive, Houghton, MI 49931-1295

Northern Michigan University

Marquette, Michigan — **CB member**
www.nmu.edu — **CB code: 1560**

- Public 4-year university
- Residential campus in large town
- 8,500 degree-seeking undergraduates: 8% part-time, 53% women, 2% African American, 1% Asian American, 1% Hispanic American, 2% Native American
- 452 degree-seeking graduate students
- 84% of applicants admitted
- SAT or ACT (ACT writing optional) required
- 47% graduate within 6 years

General. Founded in 1899. Regionally accredited. **Degrees:** 1,200 bachelor's, 137 associate awarded; master's offered. **ROTC:** Army. **Location:** 300 miles from Milwaukee, 380 miles from Chicago. **Calendar:** Semester, limited summer session. **Full-time faculty:** 305 total; 61% have terminal degrees, 6% minority, 39% women. **Part-time faculty:** 125 total. **Class size:** 37% < 20, 47% 20-39, 7% 40-49, 7% 50-99, 2% >100. **Special facilities:** Olympic education center; center for teaching and learning science and mathematics, art museum, art and design studios, observatory with 12.5 F:6 Newtonian telescope, 120-acre nature preserve.

Freshman class profile. 4,772 applied, 3,995 admitted, 1,406 enrolled.

Mid 50% test scores		**GPA 2.0-2.99:**	43%
ACT:	20-25	**Return as sophomores:**	73%
GPA 3.50 or higher:	25%	**Out-of-state:**	26%
GPA 3.0-3.49:	23%	**Live on campus:**	71%

Basis for selection. High school record, test scores most important. Recommendations and essay considered. Students who do not fulfill normal requirements for admission may be conditionally admitted for freshman probation and college transition programs. Some certificate, diploma, and associate degree programs do not require test scores. Essay recommended. Audition recommended for music, drama majors. Portfolio recommended for art majors. Interview, extracurricular activities, talent/ability, character/personal qualities considered for borderline students.

High school preparation. College-preparatory program recommended. 12 units required. Required and recommended units include English 4, mathematics 3, social studies 2, history 2, science 2 and foreign language 3. 2 fine arts and 1 computer literacy also recommended.

2005-2006 Annual costs. Tuition/fees: $5,958; $9,702 out-of-state. Includes one-time athletic fee. All full-time students provided with IBM ThinkPad or Apple iBook with software as part of tuition and fees. Room/board: $6,013. Books/supplies: $645. Personal expenses: $979.

2004-2005 Financial aid. Need-based: 1,467 full-time freshmen applied for aid; 887 were judged to have need; 879 of these received aid. Average need met was 80%. Average scholarship/grant was $3,856; average loan $2,941. 39% of total undergraduate aid awarded as scholarships/grants, 61% as loans/jobs. **Non-need-based:** Awarded to 296 full-time undergraduates, including 17 freshmen. Scholarships awarded for academics, alumni affiliation, art, athletics, leadership, minority status, music/drama, religious affiliation, ROTC, state residency. **Additional information:** Audition or portfolio required for music, drama, and art scholarship applicants. Alumni Dependent Tuition Program gives resident tuition rates to nonresident dependents of NMU alumni who received master's, baccalaureate, or associate degree; renewable.

Application procedures. Admission: Priority date 8/1; no deadline. $30 fee, may be waived for applicants with need. Application may be submitted online. Admission notification on a rolling basis beginning on or about 9/1. **Financial aid:** Priority date 3/1; no closing date. FAFSA required. Applicants notified on a rolling basis starting 4/1; must reply within 2 week(s) of notification.

Academics. Special study options: Combined bachelor's/graduate degree, distance learning, double major, dual enrollment of high school students, exchange student, honors, independent study, internships, liberal arts/career combination, student-designed major, study abroad, teacher certification program, Washington semester, weekend college. **Credit/placement by examination:** AP, CLEP, IB, ACT, institutional tests. 32 credit hours maximum toward bachelor's degree. **Support services:** Learning center, preadmission summer program, reduced course load, remedial instruction, study skills assistance, tutoring, writing center.

Honors college/program. Limited to 50 students, honors college requires 3.5 GPA and 27 ACT or equivalent.

Majors. Biology: General, bacteriology, biochemistry, botany, ecology, microbiology, physiology, zoology. **Business:** General, accounting, administrative services, business admin, entrepreneurial studies, finance, financial planning, hospitality admin, management information systems, management science, marketing, small business admin, tourism/travel. **Communications:** General, broadcast journalism, journalism, media studies, public relations, radio/tv. **Computer sciences:** General, computer graphics, computer science, networking, programming. **Conservation:** General, environmental studies, land use planning. **Construction:** Maintenance. **Education:** General, adult/continuing, art, biology, business, chemistry, computer, early childhood, elementary, English, family/consumer sciences, foreign languages, French, geography, health, history, learning disabled, mathematics, mentally handicapped, middle, music, physical, physics, school counseling, science, secondary, social science, social studies, Spanish, special, speech, technology/industrial arts. **Engineering:** Industrial, mechanical, mechanics. **Engineering technology:** Construction, drafting, electrical, manufacturing, water quality. **English:** Creative writing, English lit, speech/rhetoric, technical writing. **Family/consumer sciences:** Family studies, family/community services, food/nutrition, human nutrition. **Foreign languages:** French, Spanish. **Health:** Athletic training, clinical lab science, communication disorders, cytotechnology, dietetics, histologic technology, nursing (RN), predentistry, premedicine, prepharmacy, preveterinary, speech pathology. **History:** General. **Interdisciplinary:** Biological/physical sciences. **Legal studies:** Prelaw. **Liberal arts:** Arts/sciences. **Math:** General, applied. **Parks/recreation:** General, exercise sciences, facilities management, health/fitness, sports admin. **Personal/culinary services:** Culinary arts. **Philosophy/religion:** Philosophy. **Physical sciences:** Chemistry, hydrology, physics, planetary. **Protective services:**

Criminal justice, police science. **Psychology:** General. **Public administration:** General, social work. **Social sciences:** General, economics, geography, international relations, political science, sociology. **Visual/performing arts:** Art, ceramics, cinematography, commercial/advertising art, design, dramatic, drawing, fiber arts, metal/jewelry, music history, painting, photography, printmaking, sculpture.

Most popular majors. Biology 6%, business/marketing 16%, education 17%, health sciences 8%, social sciences 8%, visual/performing arts 7%.

Computing on campus. PC or laptop required. 7,100 workstations in dormitories, library, computer center, student center. Dormitories wired for high-speed internet access and linked to campus network. Commuter students can connect to campus network. Online course registration, online library, helpline, repair service, student web hosting, wireless network available.

Student life. Freshman orientation: Mandatory, $75 fee. Preregistration for classes offered. 3-day program for students and parents. **Policies:** Freshmen permitted cars on campus. **Housing:** Guaranteed on-campus for all undergraduates. Coed dorms, special housing for disabled, apartments, substance-free housing available. $125 deposit. **Activities:** Bands, choral groups, dance, drama, film society, literary magazine, music ensembles, musical theater, radio station, student government, student newspaper, symphony orchestra, TV station, campus ministries, Young Democrats, College Republicans, student social work organization, Gonzo Media, Amnesty International.

Athletics. NCAA. **Intercollegiate:** Basketball, cheerleading, cross-country W, football (tackle) M, golf M, ice hockey M, skiing, soccer W, swimming W, track and field W, volleyball W. **Intramural:** Basketball, field hockey W, football (tackle), ice hockey, lacrosse M, racquetball, soccer, softball, table tennis, volleyball. **Team name:** Wildcats.

Student services. Adult student services, campus ministries, career counseling, student employment services, financial aid counseling, health services, minority student services, personal counseling, placement for graduates, veterans' counselor. **Physically disabled:** Services for visually, hearing impaired.

Contact. E-mail: admiss@nmu.edu
Phone: (906) 227-2650 Toll-free number: (800) 682-9797
Fax: (906) 227-4747
Gerri Daniels, Director of Admissions, Northern Michigan University, 1401 Presque Isle Avenue, Marquette, MI 49855

Northwood University

Midland, Michigan
www.northwood.edu **CB code: 1568**

- Private 4-year university and business college
- Residential campus in large town
- 1,924 degree-seeking undergraduates: 2% part-time, 35% women, 13% African American, 2% Asian American, 2% Hispanic American, 9% international
- 311 degree-seeking graduate students
- 85% of applicants admitted
- SAT or ACT (ACT writing optional), application essay required

General. Founded in 1959. Regionally accredited. Specialty university offering only business degrees in management; 3 residential campuses in Michigan, Florida, and Texas; 44 program centers; Margaret Chase Smith Library Center in Maine. **Degrees:** 434 bachelor's, 218 associate awarded; master's offered. **Location:** 125 miles from Detroit, 25 miles from Saginaw. **Calendar:** Quarter, extensive summer session. **Full-time faculty:** 46 total; 28% have terminal degrees, 6% minority, 39% women. **Part-time faculty:** 31 total; 3% have terminal degrees, 10% minority, 36% women. **Class size:** 34% < 20, 54% 20-39, 8% 40-49, 4% 50-99, less than 1% >100. **Special facilities:** Creativity center, university-operated hotel.

Freshman class profile. 1,638 applied, 1,391 admitted, 505 enrolled.

Mid 50% test scores			
SAT verbal:	420-520	Rank in top quarter:	24%
SAT math:	440-530	Rank in top tenth:	7%
ACT:	18-23	End year in good standing:	74%
GPA 3.50 or higher:	23%	Return as sophomores:	72%
GPA 3.0-3.49:	29%	Out-of-state:	15%
GPA 2.0-2.99:	45%	Live on campus:	87%
		International:	2%

Basis for selection. Minimum GPA of 2.0 and strong interest in business or related field. Test scores considered. Students with lower GPA admitted on probation. Interview recommended. **Homeschooled:** Transcript of courses and grades required.

High school preparation. 16 units recommended. Recommended units include English 4, mathematics 3, social studies 3, science 2 (laboratory 1) and foreign language 3.

2005-2006 Annual costs. Tuition/fees: $15,183. Room/board: $6,696.

2005-2006 Financial aid. Need-based: 398 full-time freshmen applied for aid; 327 were judged to have need; 327 of these received aid. Average need met was 99%. Average scholarship/grant was $5,948; average loan $2,452. 58% of total undergraduate aid awarded as scholarships/grants, 42% as loans/jobs. **Non-need-based:** Awarded to 1,034 full-time undergraduates, including 199 freshmen. Scholarships awarded for academics, alumni affiliation, athletics, minority status.

Application procedures. Admission: No deadline. $25 fee, may be waived for applicants with need. Application may be submitted online. Admission notification on a rolling basis. **Financial aid:** No deadline. FAFSA required. Applicants notified on a rolling basis starting 3/1.

Academics. Special study options: Accelerated study, combined bachelor's/graduate degree, distance learning, double major, dual enrollment of high school students, ESL, external degree, honors, independent study, internships, study abroad, weekend college. **Credit/placement by examination:** AP, CLEP, IB, SAT, ACT, institutional tests. 12 credit hours maximum toward associate degree, 12 toward bachelor's. **Support services:** Learning center, reduced course load, remedial instruction, study skills assistance, tutoring, writing center.

Majors. Business: Accounting, banking/financial services, business admin, entrepreneurial studies, fashion, hotel/motel admin, international, management information systems, managerial economics, marketing, vehicle parts marketing. **Communications:** Advertising. **Computer sciences:** General. **Parks/recreation:** Sports admin.

Most popular majors. Business/marketing 79%, communications/journalism 8%, parks/recreation 10%.

Computing on campus. 215 workstations in dormitories, library, computer center. Dormitories wired for high-speed internet access and linked to campus network. Commuter students can connect to campus network. Online course registration, online library, helpline, student web hosting, wireless network available.

Student life. Freshman orientation: Mandatory. Preregistration for classes offered. 2-day programs held in early August and early September. **Policies:** Freshmen permitted cars on campus. **Housing:** Guaranteed on-campus for freshmen. Single-sex dorms, apartments, substance-free housing available. $100 partly refundable deposit. **Activities:** Jazz band, choral groups, dance, drama, student government, student newspaper, Business Professionals of America, American Marketing Association, Ambassador club, Rotaract, law club, International Business Association, Minority Business Women, American Advertising Federation, The Church Reloaded, diversity club.

Athletics. NCAA. **Intercollegiate:** Baseball M, basketball, cheerleading, cross-country, football (tackle) M, golf, soccer, softball W, tennis, track and field, volleyball W. **Intramural:** Badminton, basketball, field hockey, football (non-tackle) M, soccer, tennis, volleyball. **Team name:** Timberwolves.

Student services. Adult student services, alcohol/substance abuse counseling, career counseling, student employment services, financial aid counseling, health services, minority student services, personal counseling, placement for graduates, veterans' counselor. **Physically disabled:** Services for visually, speech, hearing impaired.

Contact. E-mail: miadmit@northwood.edu
Phone: (989) 837-4273 Toll-free number: (800) 457-7878
Fax: (989) 837-4490
Daniel Toland, Dean of Admissions, Northwood University, 4000 Whiting Drive, Midland, MI 48640

Oakland University

Rochester, Michigan **CB member**
www.oakland.edu **CB code: 1497**

- Public 4-year university
- Commuter campus in small city
- 12,945 degree-seeking undergraduates: 25% part-time, 62% women, 9% African American, 4% Asian American, 2% Hispanic American, 1% international
- 3,707 degree-seeking graduate students
- 82% of applicants admitted
- 45% graduate within 6 years; 20% enter graduate study

General. Founded in 1957. Regionally accredited. **Degrees:** 2,012 bachelor's awarded; master's, doctoral offered. **ROTC:** Air Force. **Location:** 30 miles from Detroit. **Calendar:** Semester, limited summer session. **Full-time faculty:** 449 total; 92% have terminal degrees, 23% minority, 40% women. **Part-time faculty:** 441 total; 30% have terminal degrees, 12% minority, 56% women. **Class size:** 31% < 20, 43% 20-39, 9% 40-49, 15% 50-99, 2% >100. **Special facilities:** Theater, music pavilion, engineering and science research laboratories, robotics laboratory, CAD-CAM laboratory, historic house, lean learning center, product development and manufacturing center.

Freshman class profile. 5,948 applied, 4,890 admitted, 2,213 enrolled.

Mid 50% test scores		**Rank in top quarter:**	38%
ACT:	19-24	**End year in good standing:**	80%
GPA 3.50 or higher:	29%	**Return as sophomores:**	71%
GPA 3.0-3.49:	31%	**Out-of-state:**	1%
GPA 2.0-2.99:	39%	**Live on campus:**	31%

Basis for selection. Admission based on 2.5 high school GPA in academic subjects, school and community activities, recommendations. Applicants with minimum 2.0 GPA may be admitted to summer program. Engineering, business, education, nursing, and physical therapy programs require higher GPA. SAT or ACT recommended. Except for homeschooled students, ACT scores used only for placement and scholarship purposes. Audition required of music majors. **Homeschooled:** 25 ACT Composite score.

High school preparation. Required and recommended units include English 4, mathematics 3, social studies 3, science 3 and foreign language 2. Recommend fine arts, computing.

2005-2006 Annual costs. Tuition/fees: $5,856; $13,056 out-of-state. Room/board: $6,080. Books/supplies: $1,035. Personal expenses: $1,500.

2004-2005 Financial aid. **Need-based:** 1,059 full-time freshmen applied for aid; 688 were judged to have need; 654 of these received aid. Average need met was 87.7%. Average scholarship/grant was $3,451; average loan $2,224. 41% of total undergraduate aid awarded as scholarships/grants, 59% as loans/jobs. **Non-need-based:** Awarded to 1,462 full-time undergraduates, including 671 freshmen. Scholarships awarded for academics, art, athletics, leadership, music/drama, state residency.

Application procedures. **Admission:** No deadline. $40 fee, may be waived for applicants with need. Application may be submitted online. Admission notification on a rolling basis. **Financial aid:** Priority date 2/15; no closing date. FAFSA required. Applicants notified on a rolling basis starting 3/15.

Academics. **Special study options:** Accelerated study, cooperative education, distance learning, double major, ESL, honors, independent study, internships, student-designed major, study abroad, teacher certification program. **Credit/placement by examination:** AP, CLEP, IB, ACT, institutional tests. 60 credit hours maximum toward bachelor's degree. **Support services:** Learning center, pre-admission summer program, reduced course load, remedial instruction, study skills assistance, tutoring, writing center.

Majors. **Area/ethnic studies:** African, East Asian, Latin American, Slavic, South Asian, women's. **Biology:** General, biochemistry, biophysics. **Business:** General, accounting, finance, management information systems, managerial economics, marketing, training/development. **Communications:** General, journalism. **Computer sciences:** General. **Education:** Elementary, music. **Engineering:** Computer, electrical, mechanical, physics, systems. **English:** English lit. **Foreign languages:** General, French, German, linguistics, Spanish. **Health:** Clinical lab science, environmental health, nursing (RN), occupational health. **History:** General. **Liberal arts:** Arts/sciences. **Math:** General, statistics. **Philosophy/religion:** Philosophy. **Physical sciences:** Chemistry, physics. **Psychology:** General. **Public administration:** General. **Social sciences:** General, anthropology, economics, political science, sociology. **Visual/performing arts:** General, art history/conservation, music performance, music theory/composition, piano/organ, studio arts, theater design, voice/opera.

Most popular majors. Business/marketing 22%, communications/journalism 10%, education 15%, engineering/engineering technologies 7%, health sciences 8%, psychology 6%, social sciences 8%.

Computing on campus. 713 workstations in dormitories, library, computer center, student center. Dormitories linked to campus network. Commuter students can connect to campus network. Online course registration, online library, helpline, student web hosting, wireless network available.

Student life. **Freshman orientation:** Mandatory. Preregistration for classes offered. Held on weekdays from end of June through mid-July. 1.5-day program requires overnight stay in residence halls. Condensed 1-day orientation available. **Policies:** Freshmen permitted cars on campus. **Housing:** Guaranteed on-campus for freshmen. Coed dorms, special housing for disabled, apartments, fraternity/sorority housing, substance-free housing available. $100 nonrefundable deposit, deadline 9/1. Freshmen must live on campus unless living with family. Residence halls easily accessible to handicapped persons. Living/learning communities available. **Activities:** Bands, choral groups, dance, drama, film society, literary magazine, music ensembles, musical theater, radio station, student government, student newspaper, symphony orchestra, TV station, Association of Black Students, Indian student association, Asian American association, College Democrats, College Republicans, Campus Crusade for Christ, Hillel, Muslim student association, international student friendship, Gay/Straight Alliance.

Athletics. NCAA. **Intercollegiate:** Baseball M, basketball, cross-country, diving, golf, soccer, softball W, swimming, tennis W, track and field, volleyball W. **Intramural:** Badminton, basketball, football (non-tackle), racquetball, soccer, softball, table tennis, triathlon, volleyball. **Team name:** Golden Grizzlies.

Student services. Alcohol/substance abuse counseling, campus ministries, career counseling, student employment services, financial aid counseling, health services, minority student services, on-campus daycare, personal counseling, placement for graduates. **Physically disabled:** Services for visually, speech, hearing impaired.

Contact. E-mail: ouinfo@oakland.edu
Phone: (248) 370-3360 Toll-free number: (800) 625-8648
Fax: (248) 370-4462
Eleanor Reynolds, Interim Assistant Vice President Student Affairs,
Oakland University, 101 North Foundation Hall, Rochester, MI 48309-4401

Olivet College

Olivet, Michigan — **CB member**
www.olivetcollege.edu — **CB code: 1595**

- Private 4-year liberal arts college affiliated with Congregational Christian Churches and United Church of Christ
- Residential campus in rural community
- 1,020 degree-seeking undergraduates
- SAT or ACT (ACT writing recommended) required

General. Founded in 1844. Regionally accredited. Olivet Plan degree program includes service learning experience, portfolio assessment measuring 6 essential competencies, senior experience, professional mentoring, and 3 1/2 week intensive learning term. **Degrees:** 132 bachelor's awarded; master's offered. **Location:** 30 miles from Lansing, 120 miles from Detroit. **Calendar:** Semester, limited summer session. **Full-time faculty:** 34 total; 71% have terminal degrees, 18% minority, 41% women. **Part-time faculty:** 33 total; 24% have terminal degrees, 3% minority, 46% women. **Class size:** 63% < 20, 35% 20-39, 1% 40-49, less than 1% 50-99. **Special facilities:** Observatory/planetarium, dynamic ecology laboratory, office of multicultural affairs, character education resource center, women's resource center, biological preserve.

Freshman class profile.

Mid 50% test scores		**Out-of-state:**	8%
ACT:	14-19	**Live on campus:**	82%
Rank in top quarter:	38%	**Fraternities:**	10%
Rank in top tenth:	25%	**Sororities:**	10%

Basis for selection. Minimum 2.6 high school GPA most important. Test scores, school achievement record, recommendations for those below 2.6 GPA important. Interview recommended. Portfolio recommended for art majors.

High school preparation. 14 units required; 19 recommended. Required and recommended units include English 4, mathematics 3-4, social studies 2-3, science 3-4 (laboratory 1-2) and foreign language 2.

2006-2007 Annual costs. Tuition/fees: $17,584. Room/board: $6,060. Books/supplies: $690. Personal expenses: $698.

2005-2006 Financial aid. All financial aid based on need.

Application procedures. **Admission:** No deadline. $25 fee, may be waived for applicants with need. Application may be submitted online. Admission notification on a rolling basis beginning on or about 11/1. **Financial aid:** No deadline. FAFSA required. Applicants notified on a rolling basis starting 2/1; must reply within 3 week(s) of notification.

Academics. **Special study options:** Combined bachelor's/graduate degree, cooperative education, double major, dual enrollment of high school students, honors, independent study, internships, liberal arts/career combination, student-designed major, teacher certification program. **Credit/**

placement by examination: AP, CLEP, institutional tests. **Support services:** Learning center, remedial instruction, tutoring, writing center.

Majors. **Biology:** General, biochemistry. **Business:** General, accounting, accounting/finance, business admin, finance, insurance, international, managerial economics, statistics. **Communications:** General, journalism, media studies. **Computer sciences:** Computer science. **Conservation:** Environmental science. **Education:** General, art, biology, business, chemistry, elementary, English, health, history, middle, multi-level teacher, music, physical, science, secondary, social science, social studies. **Health:** Athletic training, predentistry, premedicine. **History:** General. **Interdisciplinary:** Biological/physical sciences, natural sciences. **Legal studies:** Prelaw. **Liberal arts:** Arts/sciences, humanities. **Math:** General. **Parks/recreation:** General, health/fitness, sports admin. **Physical sciences:** General, chemistry, organic chemistry. **Protective services:** Law enforcement admin, police science. **Psychology:** General. **Social sciences:** General, anthropology, economics, geography, sociology. **Visual/performing arts:** General, art, commercial/advertising art, music performance, studio arts, theater arts management, voice/opera.

Computing on campus. 60 workstations in dormitories, library, computer center, student center. Dormitories wired for high-speed internet access and linked to campus network. Commuter students can connect to campus network. Online course registration, helpline, repair service, student web hosting, wireless network available.

Student life. **Freshman orientation:** Mandatory, $75 fee. Preregistration for classes offered. **Policies:** Freshmen permitted cars on campus. **Housing:** Guaranteed on-campus for all undergraduates. Coed dorms, single-sex dorms, apartments, fraternity/sorority housing, substance-free housing available. International, African American, and honors houses, wellness floor available. **Activities:** Bands, choral groups, drama, literary magazine, music ensembles, musical theater, radio station, student government, student newspaper, symphony orchestra, Phi Kappa Delta, Psi Chi, international club, Earth Bound, black student union, N.O.W., campus media board, Students Organizing Community Service.

Athletics. NCAA. **Intercollegiate:** Baseball M, basketball, cross-country, diving, football (tackle) M, golf, soccer, softball W, swimming, tennis W, track and field, volleyball W, wrestling M. **Intramural:** Basketball, cheerleading, football (non-tackle) M, weight lifting M. **Team name:** Comets.

Student services. Adult student services, alcohol/substance abuse counseling, campus ministries, career counseling, services for economically disadvantaged, student employment services, financial aid counseling, health services, minority student services, personal counseling, placement for graduates, women's services. **Physically disabled:** Services for visually, speech, hearing impaired.

Contact. E-mail: admissions@olivetcollege.edu
Phone: (269) 749-7635 Toll-free number: (800) 456-7189
Fax: (269) 749-6617
Thomas Shaw, Vice President for Enrollment Management, Olivet College, 320 South Main Street, Olivet, MI 49076

Reformed Bible College

Grand Rapids, Michigan
www.reformed.edu **CB code: 1672**

- Private 4-year Bible college affiliated with Reformed Presbyterian tradition
- Commuter campus in large city
- 262 degree-seeking undergraduates: 16% part-time, 57% women, 3% African American, 3% Asian American, 3% Hispanic American, 9% international
- 4 degree-seeking graduate students
- 61% of applicants admitted
- SAT or ACT (ACT writing optional), application essay required
- 42% graduate within 6 years

General. Founded in 1939. Regionally accredited; also accredited by ABHE. **Degrees:** 59 bachelor's, 5 associate awarded. **Location:** 7 miles from downtown, 180 miles from Chicago. **Calendar:** Semester, limited summer session. **Full-time faculty:** 12 total; 50% have terminal degrees, 33% women. **Part-time faculty:** 14 total; 36% have terminal degrees, 14% minority, 36% women. **Class size:** 64% < 20, 36% 20-39.

Freshman class profile. 233 applied, 142 admitted, 49 enrolled.

Mid 50% test scores			
SAT verbal:	370-640	Rank in top quarter:	17%
SAT math:	390-570	Rank in top tenth:	3%
ACT:	19-23	Return as sophomores:	62%
GPA 3.50 or higher:	22%	Out-of-state:	9%
GPA 3.0-3.49:	32%	Live on campus:	45%
GPA 2.0-2.99:	37%	International:	10%

Basis for selection. Secondary school record, test scores important. Applicants with 2.0 - 2.5 GPA evaluated individually and admitted on conditional acceptance. Interview required for borderline applicants. **Homeschooled:** Transcript of courses and grades required.

2006-2007 Annual costs. Tuition/fees (projected): $12,340. Room/board: $5,300. Books/supplies: $500. Personal expenses: $1,300.

2004-2005 Financial aid. **Need-based:** 42 full-time freshmen applied for aid; 38 were judged to have need; 37 of these received aid. Average need met was 64%. Average scholarship/grant was $5,921; average loan $2,588. 58% of total undergraduate aid awarded as scholarships/grants, 42% as loans/jobs. **Non-need-based:** Awarded to 37 full-time undergraduates, including 11 freshmen. Scholarships awarded for academics, leadership, minority status.

Application procedures. **Admission:** Priority date 8/15; no deadline. $25 fee, may be waived for applicants with need. Application may be submitted online. Admission notification on a rolling basis. **Financial aid:** Priority date 3/1; no closing date. FAFSA, institutional form required. Applicants notified on a rolling basis starting 3/20; must reply within 2 week(s) of notification.

Academics. All students take 1 major in Bible/Theology, 1 major or concentration in professional ministry, and 1 or 2 minors in liberal arts. Faculty members are Calvinistic/Reformed, but present other theological perspectives. **Special study options:** Combined bachelor's/graduate degree, cooperative education, cross-registration, double major, dual enrollment of high school students, ESL, independent study, internships, liberal arts/career combination, study abroad, teacher certification program. **Credit/placement by examination:** AP, CLEP, ACT, institutional tests. **Support services:** Learning center, pre-admission summer program, reduced course load, remedial instruction, study skills assistance, tutoring, writing center.

Majors. **Business:** Accounting, business admin. **Communications:** General, journalism, radio/tv. **Computer sciences:** General. **Education:** Elementary, secondary. **Family/consumer sciences:** Child development. **Health:** Prenursing. **Interdisciplinary:** Accounting/computer science, global studies, intercultural. **Public administration:** Social work. **Theology:** Bible, missionary, preministerial, religious ed, theology, youth ministry.

Most popular majors. Education 8%, public administration/social services 19%, theological studies 70%.

Computing on campus. 54 workstations in dormitories, library, computer center. Dormitories linked to campus network. Commuter students can connect to campus network. Online library, helpline, student web hosting, wireless network available.

Student life. **Freshman orientation:** Available. Preregistration for classes offered. Held first week of fall semester. **Policies:** Smoke-free campus, alcohol and drug-free campus, standards of conduct and housing policies in accordance with school moral values. Religious observance required. Freshmen permitted cars on campus. **Housing:** Guaranteed on-campus for freshmen. Coed dorms, apartments, substance-free housing available. $100 fully refundable deposit. **Activities:** Choral groups, drama, student government, Bible studies, student activities committee.

Athletics. **Intramural:** Basketball, field hockey, football (non-tackle), soccer, softball, table tennis, volleyball.

Student services. Alcohol/substance abuse counseling, campus ministries, career counseling, student employment services, financial aid counseling, health services, minority student services, personal counseling, placement for graduates, veterans' counselor. **Physically disabled:** Services for visually impaired. **Learning disabled:** Comprehensive services available.

Contact. E-mail: admissions@reformed.edu
Phone: (616) 222-3000 Toll-free number: (800) 511-3749
Fax: (616) 222-3045
Larissa Lighthiser, Director of Admissions, Reformed Bible College, 3333 East Beltline NE, Grand Rapids, MI 49525-9749

Rochester College
Rochester Hills, Michigan
www.rc.edu **CB code: 1516**

- Private 4-year liberal arts college affiliated with Church of Christ
- Residential campus in small city
- 1,100 degree-seeking undergraduates
- ACT (writing optional), application essay required

General. Founded in 1959. Regionally accredited. **Degrees:** 278 bachelor's, 15 associate awarded. **Location:** 25 miles from Detroit. **Calendar:** Semester, limited summer session. **Full-time faculty:** 50 total. **Part-time faculty:** 95 total.

Basis for selection. ACT score and high school GPA most important. Recommendations and interview considered. **Homeschooled:** Transcript of courses and grades required.

2005-2006 Annual costs. Tuition/fees: $12,356. Room/board: $6,560. Books/supplies: $600. Personal expenses: $728.

Financial aid. Non-need-based: Scholarships awarded for academics, alumni affiliation, athletics, leadership, music/drama, state residency.

Application procedures. Admission: No deadline. $25 fee. Application may be submitted online. Admission notification on a rolling basis. **Financial aid:** Priority date 8/1; no closing date. FAFSA required. Applicants notified on a rolling basis starting 6/1; must reply within 2 week(s) of notification.

Academics. Special study options: Accelerated study, combined bachelor's/graduate degree, cross-registration, double major, dual enrollment of high school students, honors, independent study, internships, liberal arts/career combination, study abroad, teacher certification program, weekend college. **Credit/placement by examination:** AP, CLEP, IB, institutional tests. 32 credit hours maximum toward associate degree, 64 toward bachelor's. Credit awarded for successful completion of selected DANTES Subject Standardized Testing Program. **Support services:** Learning center, reduced course load, remedial instruction, study skills assistance, tutoring, writing center.

Majors. Business: Accounting, business admin, management information systems, marketing. **Communications:** General. **Computer sciences:** General. **Education:** General, early childhood, elementary, English, history, mathematics, middle, music, science, secondary. **History:** General. **Philosophy/religion:** Religion. **Psychology:** General. **Public administration:** Social work. **Theology:** Bible, theology. **Visual/performing arts:** Music performance.

Computing on campus. 32 workstations in dormitories, library, computer center. Dormitories wired for high-speed internet access and linked to campus network. Online library, helpline, student web hosting available.

Student life. Freshman orientation: Mandatory, $100 fee. Preregistration for classes offered. **Policies:** Freshmen permitted cars on campus. **Housing:** Guaranteed on-campus for freshmen. Single-sex dorms, apartments available. $180 partly refundable deposit, deadline 5/1. **Activities:** Bands, choral groups, drama, music ensembles, musical theater, opera, student government, student newspaper, service and mission organizations, student government, social clubs, departmental organizations, honor societies.

Athletics. NCCAA. **Intercollegiate:** Baseball M, basketball, soccer, softball W, volleyball W. **Intramural:** Basketball, football (non-tackle), softball, volleyball. **Team name:** Warriors.

Student services. Adult student services, alcohol/substance abuse counseling, campus ministries, career counseling, student employment services, financial aid counseling, minority student services, personal counseling, placement for graduates, veterans' counselor. **Physically disabled:** Services for visually, speech, hearing impaired.

Contact. E-mail: admissions@rc.edu
Phone: (248) 218-2031 Toll-free number: (800) 521-6010
Fax: (248) 218-2035
Kelvin Brown, Vice President for Enrollment Management, Rochester College, 800 West Avon Road, Rochester Hills, MI 48307

Sacred Heart Major Seminary
Detroit, Michigan
www.shmsonline.org **CB code: 1686**

- Private 4-year seminary college affiliated with Roman Catholic Church
- Commuter campus in very large city
- 68 degree-seeking undergraduates: 34% part-time, 31% women, 1% Asian American, 7% Hispanic American, 3% international
- 135 degree-seeking graduate students
- 100% of applicants admitted
- SAT or ACT (ACT writing optional), application essay required
- 100% graduate within 6 years; 75% enter graduate study

General. Founded in 1919. Regionally accredited. Most B.A. students candidates for priesthood. 2-year programs leading to ordination as deacon or certification in pastoral-liturgical ministry offered. Pastoral ministry courses and degree programs open to men and women. Master level courses designed for laity who wish to minister in church. **Degrees:** 11 bachelor's, 3 associate awarded; master's, first professional offered. **Location:** Within Detroit city limits. **Calendar:** Semester. **Full-time faculty:** 32 total; 75% have terminal degrees, 22% women. **Part-time faculty:** 25 total; 28% have terminal degrees, 16% women. **Class size:** 69% < 20, 19% 20-39, 9% 40-49, 3% 50-99.

Freshman class profile. 1 applied, 1 admitted, 1 enrolled.

End year in good standing:	100%	**Live on campus:**	100%
Return as sophomores:	100%		

Basis for selection. Recommendations of parish pastor, high school principal, and college counselor vital. School, community, and church-related activities viewed as important formative experiences. Religious commitment very important. Interview required for priesthood candidates.

High school preparation. Required and recommended units include English 4, mathematics 2, social studies 2, history 2, science 2 (laboratory 1), foreign language 2 and academic electives 1-2.

2006-2007 Annual costs. Tuition/fees (projected): $11,690. Room/board: $6,500. Books/supplies: $1,240. Personal expenses: $2,272.

Application procedures. Admission: Closing date 8/1 (postmark date). $30 fee. Application must be submitted on paper. Admission notification on a rolling basis. **Financial aid:** No deadline. FAFSA, institutional form required.

Academics. 30 to 40% of undergraduate course work taken at other consortium colleges. **Special study options:** Cross-registration. **Credit/placement by examination:** AP, CLEP, institutional tests. 6 credit hours maximum toward associate degree, 12 toward bachelor's. Must accumulate 15 hours at SHMS before credit is recorded. **Support services:** Learning center, reduced course load, study skills assistance, tutoring.

Majors. Liberal arts: Arts/sciences. **Philosophy/religion:** Philosophy.

Most popular majors. Liberal arts 55%, philosophy/religious studies 45%.

Computing on campus. 12 workstations in library, computer center. Online library available.

Student life. Freshman orientation: Mandatory. 3 days for seminarians, 1 day for commuters at beginning of fall term. **Policies:** Religious observance required. Freshmen permitted cars on campus. **Housing:** $110 fully refundable deposit, deadline 8/25. Guaranteed on-campus housing available to seminarians. **Activities:** Choral groups, Christian ministry program.

Athletics. Intercollegiate: Basketball M. **Intramural:** Handball M, racquetball M, soccer M, softball M, volleyball M.

Student services. Personal counseling.

Contact. Phone: (313) 883-8520 Fax: (313) 883-8530
John Lajiness, Director of Admissions and Enrollment Management, Sacred Heart Major Seminary, 2701 Chicago Boulevard, Detroit, MI 48206-1799

Saginaw Valley State University
University Center, Michigan
www.svsu.edu **CB code: 1766**

- Public 4-year university
- Commuter campus in small city
- 7,714 degree-seeking undergraduates: 22% part-time, 60% women, 7% African American, 1% Asian American, 2% Hispanic American, 3% international
- 1,640 degree-seeking graduate students
- 89% of applicants admitted
- ACT (writing optional) required
- 36% graduate within 6 years; 22% enter graduate study

General. Founded in 1963. Regionally accredited. **Degrees:** 1,084 bachelor's awarded; master's offered. **Location:** 10 miles from Bay City and Saginaw. **Calendar:** Semester, limited summer session. **Full-time faculty:** 260 total; 79% have terminal degrees, 42% women. **Part-time faculty:** 300 total. **Class size:** 27% < 20, 63% 20-39, 4% 40-49, 6% 50-99, less than 1% >100. **Special facilities:** Fine arts center, sculpture museum, observatory.

Freshman class profile. 3,796 applied, 3,392 admitted, 1,267 enrolled.

Mid 50% test scores			
ACT:	18-24	End year in good standing:	84%
GPA 3.50 or higher:	41%	Return as sophomores:	71%
GPA 3.0-3.49:	28%	Out-of-state:	1%
GPA 2.0-2.99:	31%	Live on campus:	59%
		International:	2%

Basis for selection. Minimum high school GPA of 2.5 preferred. **Homeschooled:** Required to schedule personal interview.

High school preparation. College-preparatory program recommended. Required and recommended units include English 4, mathematics 3-4, social studies 3-4, science 2-4 and foreign language 2. One unit of communications recommended.

2005-2006 Annual costs. Tuition/fees: $5,282; $11,891 out-of-state. Room/board: $6,150. Books/supplies: $800. Personal expenses: $880.

2004-2005 Financial aid. Need-based: 1,162 full-time freshmen applied for aid; 726 were judged to have need; 713 of these received aid. Average need met was 70%. Average scholarship/grant was $2,885; average loan $2,236. 39% of total undergraduate aid awarded as scholarships/grants, 61% as loans/jobs. **Non-need-based:** Awarded to 2,925 full-time undergraduates, including 1,000 freshmen. Scholarships awarded for academics, art, athletics, leadership, minority status, music/drama.

Application procedures. Admission: No deadline. $25 fee, may be waived for applicants with need. Application may be submitted online. Admission notification on a rolling basis. **Financial aid:** Priority date 2/14; no closing date. FAFSA required. Applicants notified on a rolling basis starting 3/20; must reply within 10 week(s) of notification.

Academics. Special study options: Accelerated study, combined bachelor's/graduate degree, cooperative education, distance learning, double major, dual enrollment of high school students, ESL, honors, independent study, internships, student-designed major, study abroad, teacher certification program. **Credit/placement by examination:** AP, CLEP, IB, ACT, institutional tests. 62 credit hours maximum toward bachelor's degree. **Support services:** Learning center, reduced course load, remedial instruction, study skills assistance, tutoring, writing center.

Majors. Biology: General, biochemistry. **Business:** General, accounting, business admin, finance, international, managerial economics, marketing, operations. **Communications:** General. **Computer sciences:** General, systems analysis. **Education:** Elementary, physical, special. **Engineering:** Electrical, mechanical. **English:** English lit. **Foreign languages:** French, Spanish. **Health:** Athletic training, clinical lab science, nursing (RN). **History:** General. **Interdisciplinary:** Global studies. **Math:** General, applied. **Parks/recreation:** Exercise sciences. **Physical sciences:** Chemical physics, chemistry, optics, physics. **Protective services:** Criminal justice. **Psychology:** General. **Public administration:** General, social work. **Social sciences:** Economics, political science, sociology. **Visual/performing arts:** Art, design, dramatic, studio arts.

Most popular majors. Business/marketing 14%, education 33%, engineering/engineering technologies 6%, health sciences 9%, public administration/social services 6%, security/protective services 8%.

Computing on campus. 800 workstations in library, computer center, student center. Dormitories linked to campus network. Commuter students can connect to campus network. Online course registration, online library, helpline, student web hosting, wireless network available.

Student life. Freshman orientation: Mandatory, $35 fee. Preregistration for classes offered. Day-long sessions before each semester include university placement testing, advising, and registration. **Policies:** Freshmen permitted cars on campus. **Housing:** Guaranteed on-campus for freshmen. Coed dorms, special housing for disabled, apartments, substance-free housing available. $200 partly refundable deposit. **Activities:** Bands, choral groups, dance, drama, literary magazine, music ensembles, musical theater, student government, student newspaper, over 75 campus organizations.

Athletics. NCAA. **Intercollegiate:** Baseball M, basketball, bowling M, cheerleading, cross-country, football (tackle) M, golf M, soccer, softball W, tennis W, track and field, volleyball W. **Intramural:** Badminton, basketball, football (non-tackle), golf, soccer, softball, tennis, volleyball. **Team name:** Cardinals.

Student services. Adult student services, alcohol/substance abuse counseling, career counseling, services for economically disadvantaged, student employment services, financial aid counseling, health services, legal services, minority student services, personal counseling, placement for graduates, veterans' counselor, women's services. **Physically disabled:** Services for visually, hearing impaired.

Contact. E-mail: admissions@svsu.edu
Phone: (989) 964-4200 Toll-free number: (800) 968-9500
Fax: (989) 790-0180
James Dwyer, Director of Admissions, Saginaw Valley State University, 7400 Bay Road, University Center, MI 48710

Siena Heights University

Adrian, Michigan — **CB member**
www.sienahts.edu — **CB code: 1719**

- Private 4-year university affiliated with Roman Catholic Church
- Residential campus in large town
- 876 full-time, degree-seeking undergraduates
- 281 graduate students
- 50% of applicants admitted
- SAT or ACT (ACT writing optional) required

General. Founded in 1919. Regionally accredited. Branch campuses in Benton Harbor, Battle Creek, Kalamazoo, Lansing, Southfield, Monroe, and Jackson. Monroe County Community College, Lake Michigan College, and Southfield Community Center provide off-campus upper-division degree completion. **Degrees:** 609 bachelor's, 14 associate awarded; master's offered. **Location:** 30 miles from Toledo, Ohio, 60 miles from Detroit. **Calendar:** Semester, limited summer session. **Full-time faculty:** 65 total. **Part-time faculty:** 75 total. **Special facilities:** Montessori children's house on campus.

Freshman class profile. 1,341 applied, 665 admitted, 206 enrolled.

Mid 50% test scores			
SAT verbal:	430-430	ACT:	18-20
SAT math:	400-410	Out-of-state:	15%
		Live on campus:	70%

Basis for selection. School achievement record, test scores, self-motivation, and ability to benefit from available resources most important. Interview required for art, theater, and music majors; audition required for music majors; portfolio required for art majors. Essay recommended for marginally qualified applicants. **Homeschooled:** Must complete GED for state or federal assistance.

2005-2006 Annual costs. Tuition/fees: $16,280. Room/board: $5,680. Books/supplies: $600. Personal expenses: $900.

Financial aid. Non-need-based: Scholarships awarded for academics, art, athletics, music/drama, religious affiliation.

Application procedures. Admission: No deadline. $25 fee, may be waived for applicants with need. Admission notification on a rolling basis. **Financial aid:** Priority date 3/15, closing date 8/15. FAFSA, institutional form, CSS PROFILE required. Applicants notified on a rolling basis starting 2/15.

Academics. Special study options: Combined bachelor's/graduate degree, cooperative education, double major, dual enrollment of high school students, exchange student, external degree, honors, independent study, internships, liberal arts/career combination, student-designed major, study abroad, teacher certification program, weekend college. 3-1 field experience/liberal arts in technical and nursing programs. **Credit/placement by examination:** AP, CLEP. 36 credit hours maximum toward bachelor's degree. **Support services:** Learning center, pre-admission summer program, reduced course load, remedial instruction, study skills assistance, tutoring, writing center.

Majors. Area/ethnic studies: American. **Biology:** General. **Business:** General, accounting, hospitality/recreation. **Communications:** General. **Computer sciences:** General. **Education:** Business, elementary, secondary. **English:** Creative writing. **Foreign languages:** Spanish. **Health:** Predentistry, premedicine, prepharmacy. **History:** General. **Interdisciplinary:** Natural sciences. **Legal studies:** Prelaw. **Liberal arts:** Arts/sciences. **Math:** General. **Parks/recreation:** Sports admin. **Philosophy/religion:** Philosophy, religion. **Physical sciences:** Chemistry. **Protective services:** Criminal justice. **Psychology:** General. **Public administration:** Social work. **Social sciences:** General. **Visual/performing arts:** Art, ceramics, commercial/advertising art, dramatic, drawing, metal/jewelry, painting, photography, sculpture, studio arts.

Computing on campus. 80 workstations in dormitories, library, computer center. Dormitories linked to campus network. Helpline available.

Student life. Freshman orientation: Available. Preregistration for classes offered. One-day program offered in April, May, June, July, and August.

Housing: Guaranteed on-campus for all undergraduates. Coed dorms, single-sex dorms available. $50 deposit. **Activities:** Jazz band, choral groups, dance, drama, film society, literary magazine, music ensembles, musical theater, student government, student newspaper, Campus ministry, Siena Heights African American Knowledge Association, student programming association, Greek council, Students Against Violent Environments.

Athletics. NAIA. **Intercollegiate:** Baseball M, basketball, cross-country, golf M, soccer, softball W, track and field, volleyball W. **Intramural:** Basketball, softball, volleyball.

Student services. Adult student services, career counseling, student employment services, health services, personal counseling, placement for graduates.

Contact. E-mail: admissions@sienahts.edu
Phone: (517) 264-7180 Toll-free number: (800) 521-0009 ext. 7180
Fax: (517) 264-7745
Kevin Kucera, Dean of Admissions and Enrollment Services, Siena Heights University, 1247 East Siena Heights Drive, Adrian, MI 49221-1796

Spring Arbor University

Spring Arbor, Michigan
www.arbor.edu **CB code: 1732**

- Private 4-year university and liberal arts college affiliated with Free Methodist Church of North America
- Residential campus in rural community
- 2,447 degree-seeking undergraduates: 23% part-time, 68% women
- 1,065 degree-seeking graduate students
- 75% of applicants admitted
- SAT or ACT (ACT writing optional) required
- 57% graduate within 6 years; 30% enter graduate study

General. Founded in 1873. Regionally accredited. Adult studies offers degree completion with courses and majors available at 14 off-campus sites. **Degrees:** 768 bachelor's, 5 associate awarded; master's offered. **ROTC:** Army. **Location:** 8 miles from Jackson, 45 miles from Ann Arbor. **Calendar:** Semester, limited summer session. **Full-time faculty:** 80 total; 60% have terminal degrees, 8% minority, 36% women. **Part-time faculty:** 58 total; 10% have terminal degrees, 50% women. **Class size:** 58% < 20, 34% 20-39, 4% 40-49, 4% 50-99.

Freshman class profile. 1,313 applied, 986 admitted, 318 enrolled.

Mid 50% test scores			
SAT verbal:	490-620	Rank in top quarter:	46%
SAT math:	490-590	Rank in top tenth:	20%
ACT:	19-25	Return as sophomores:	78%
GPA 3.50 or higher:	45%	Out-of-state:	14%
GPA 3.0-3.49:	29%	Live on campus:	94%
GPA 2.0-2.99:	26%	International:	2%

Basis for selection. ACT score of 20 and 2.6 GPA preferred. Letters of recommendation from high school guidance counselor also required with application, high school transcript, ACT or SAT score. Interview recommended for borderline applicants. **Homeschooled:** Require letter of recommendation from parent/teacher and 2- to 3-page paper on homeschool experience.

High school preparation. Recommended units include English 4, mathematics 2, social studies 2, science 2 and foreign language 2.

2005-2006 Annual costs. Tuition/fees: $16,666. Room/board: $5,810. Books/supplies: $625. Personal expenses: $755.

2004-2005 Financial aid. Need-based: 306 full-time freshmen applied for aid; 267 were judged to have need; 267 of these received aid. Average need met was 93%. Average scholarship/grant was $9,661; average loan $3,462. 63% of total undergraduate aid awarded as scholarships/grants, 37% as loans/jobs. **Non-need-based:** Awarded to 422 full-time undergraduates, including 134 freshmen. Scholarships awarded for academics, art, athletics.

Application procedures. Admission: Priority date 2/15; deadline 8/1 (receipt date). $30 fee, may be waived for applicants with need. Application may be submitted online. Admission notification on a rolling basis beginning on or about 9/1. **Financial aid:** Priority date 3/1; no closing date. FAFSA required. Applicants notified on a rolling basis starting 4/1; must reply within 2 week(s) of notification.

Academics. Special study options: Accelerated study, combined bachelor's/graduate degree, cross-registration, distance learning, double major, dual enrollment of high school students, ESL, honors, independent study, internships, student-designed major, study abroad, teacher certification program, Washington semester, weekend college. Environmental study semester at AuSable Trails Institute in northern Michigan, cross-cultural program. **Credit/placement by examination:** AP, CLEP, IB, SAT, ACT, institutional tests. 60 credit hours maximum toward bachelor's degree. No more than 1/3 of credits for student's major can be through credit by examination. **Support services:** Learning center, pre-admission summer program, reduced course load, remedial instruction, study skills assistance, tutoring.

Majors. Biology: General, biochemistry. **Business:** Accounting, business admin, management information systems, managerial economics, operations. **Communications:** General. **Computer sciences:** Computer science. **Education:** Art, elementary, secondary, special. **Engineering technology:** General. **English:** English lit, speech/rhetoric. **Family/consumer sciences:** Family studies. **Foreign languages:** Spanish. **Health:** Health care admin, nursing (RN). **History:** General. **Math:** General. **Parks/recreation:** General, health/fitness. **Philosophy/religion:** Christian, philosophy, religion. **Physical sciences:** Chemistry, theoretical physics. **Psychology:** General. **Public administration:** Social work. **Social sciences:** General, political science, sociology. **Theology:** Youth ministry. **Visual/performing arts:** Art, design, film/cinema.

Most popular majors. Business/marketing 35%, education 11%, family/consumer sciences 22%.

Computing on campus. 171 workstations in dormitories, library, computer center, student center. Dormitories wired for high-speed internet access and linked to campus network. Commuter students can connect to campus network. Helpline, repair service, student web hosting, wireless network available.

Student life. Freshman orientation: Mandatory. 3-day session held at beginning of September. **Policies:** Emphasis on active commitment to person and teachings of Jesus Christ. Chapel required twice weekly. Religious observance required. **Housing:** Guaranteed on-campus for freshmen. Single-sex dorms, special housing for disabled, apartments, substance-free housing available. $200 fully refundable deposit. **Activities:** Bands, choral groups, film society, music ensembles, radio station, student government, student newspaper, symphony orchestra, many religious and community organizations available.

Athletics. NAIA, NCCAA. **Intercollegiate:** Baseball M, basketball, cross-country, golf M, soccer, softball W, tennis, track and field, volleyball W. **Intramural:** Basketball, football (non-tackle) M, soccer, softball, table tennis, tennis, volleyball. **Team name:** Cougars.

Student services. Adult student services, campus ministries, career counseling, student employment services, financial aid counseling, health services, minority student services, personal counseling, placement for graduates, veterans' counselor. **Physically disabled:** Services for visually, speech, hearing impaired.

Contact. E-mail: admissions@arbor.edu
Phone: (517) 750-1200 ext. 1468 Toll-free number: (800) 968-0011
Fax: (517) 750-6620
Randy Comfort, Director of Admissions, Spring Arbor University, 106 East Main Street, Spring Arbor, MI 49283-9799

University of Detroit Mercy

Detroit, Michigan **CB member**
www.udmercy.edu **CB code: 1835**

- Private 4-year university affiliated with Roman Catholic Church
- Commuter campus in very large city
- 2,892 degree-seeking undergraduates: 33% part-time, 65% women, 31% African American, 3% Asian American, 3% Hispanic American, 1% Native American, 3% international
- 2,765 degree-seeking graduate students
- 69% of applicants admitted
- SAT or ACT (ACT writing optional) required
- 52% graduate within 6 years

General. Founded in 1991. Regionally accredited. **Degrees:** 575 bachelor's, 29 associate awarded; master's, doctoral, first professional offered. **Calendar:** Semester, extensive summer session. **Full-time faculty:** 270 total. **Part-time faculty:** 385 total. **Class size:** 61% < 20, 35% 20-39, 3% 40-49, 2% 50-99.

Freshman class profile. 2,339 applied, 1,605 admitted, 501 enrolled.

Mid 50% test scores		Rank in top tenth:	31%
SAT verbal:	470-630	Return as sophomores:	75%
SAT math:	450-600	Out-of-state:	8%
ACT:	20-26	Live on campus:	53%
Rank in top quarter:	63%	International:	1%

Basis for selection. High school GPA in college-preparatory work, test scores, counselor's recommendation considered. Interview required for University College applicants, recommended for all others.

High school preparation. 16 units required. Required and recommended units include English 4, mathematics 3-4, social studies 2, history 2, science 2-3 (laboratory 1) and academic electives 4. Study in speech, foreign language, music, art.

2005-2006 Annual costs. Tuition/fees: $22,470. Engineering and architecture students pay slightly higher tuition. Room/board: $7,328. Books/supplies: $1,342. Personal expenses: $2,732.

2005-2006 Financial aid. Need-based: Average need met was 89%. Average scholarship/grant was $18,531; average loan $3,579. 36% of total undergraduate aid awarded as scholarships/grants, 64% as loans/jobs. **Non-need-based:** Scholarships awarded for academics, alumni affiliation, athletics, leadership, minority status, music/drama, religious affiliation.

Application procedures. Admission: Closing date 7/1. $25 fee, may be waived for applicants with need. Application may be submitted online. Admission notification on a rolling basis beginning on or about 9/1. Must reply by May 1 or within 3 week(s) if notified thereafter. **Financial aid:** Priority date 3/1; no closing date. FAFSA required. Applicants notified on a rolling basis starting 3/1; must reply within 3 week(s) of notification.

Academics. Special study options: Combined bachelor's/graduate degree, cooperative education, double major, dual enrollment of high school students, ESL, honors, independent study, internships, liberal arts/career combination, study abroad, teacher certification program, Washington semester, weekend college. Bachelor's degree completion program for registered nurses, 5-year program leading to master's degree in architecture. **Credit/placement by examination:** CLEP, institutional tests. 30 credit hours maximum toward bachelor's degree. **Support services:** Learning center, reduced course load, remedial instruction, study skills assistance, tutoring, writing center.

Majors. Architecture: Architecture. **Biology:** General, biochemistry. **Business:** General, accounting, business admin, marketing. **Communications:** General, broadcast journalism, journalism, public relations. **Computer sciences:** General, computer science, systems analysis. **Education:** General, biology, chemistry, elementary, emotionally handicapped, history, mathematics, mentally handicapped, middle, reading, science, secondary, social science, social studies, special, Waldorf/Steiner teacher. **Engineering:** General, civil, computer, electrical, manufacturing, mechanical. **English:** Creative writing, English lit, speech/rhetoric, technical writing. **Health:** Dental hygiene, nursing (RN), predentistry, premedicine, substance abuse counseling. **History:** General. **Legal studies:** Paralegal, prelaw. **Liberal arts:** Arts/sciences. **Math:** General, applied. **Philosophy/religion:** Philosophy, religion. **Physical sciences:** Chemistry. **Protective services:** Criminal justice, law enforcement admin, police science. **Psychology:** General. **Public administration:** Social work. **Social sciences:** Economics, political science, sociology. **Visual/performing arts:** Dramatic.

Computing on campus. 250 workstations in dormitories, library, computer center, student center. Dormitories wired for high-speed internet access and linked to campus network. Commuter students can connect to campus network. Online library, helpline, student web hosting, wireless network available.

Student life. Freshman orientation: Available, $200 fee. Preregistration for classes offered. **Policies:** Freshmen permitted cars on campus. **Housing:** Coed dorms available. $100 deposit. International housing, intensive quiet floors, peace and justice floor, floor for women studying engineering, science, or architecture, honors floor available. **Activities:** Pep band, dance, drama, literary magazine, radio station, student government, student newspaper, American Institute of Architecture students, College Democrats, College Republicans, international student association, minority student association, NAACP, philosophy club, chemistry club, engineering societies, poet and writers forum, student environmental club.

Athletics. NCAA. **Intercollegiate:** Basketball, cheerleading, cross-country, fencing, golf, soccer, softball W, tennis W, track and field. **Intramural:** Baseball M, basketball, racquetball, soccer M, softball, table tennis, tennis, volleyball. **Team name:** Detroit Titans.

Student services. Adult student services, alcohol/substance abuse counseling, campus ministries, career counseling, student employment services, financial aid counseling, health services, on-campus daycare, personal counseling, placement for graduates, veterans' counselor.

Contact. E-mail: admissions@udmercy.edu
Phone: (313) 993-1245 Toll-free number: (800) 635-5020
Fax: (313) 993-3326
Denise Williams, Director of Admissions, University of Detroit Mercy, 4001 West McNichols Road, Detroit, MI 48221-3038

University of Michigan

Ann Arbor, Michigan — **CB member**
www.umich.edu — **CB code: 1839**

- Public 4-year university
- Residential campus in small city
- 25,282 degree-seeking undergraduates: 4% part-time, 51% women, 7% African American, 12% Asian American, 5% Hispanic American, 1% Native American, 5% international
- 14,526 degree-seeking graduate students
- 57% of applicants admitted
- SAT or ACT with writing, application essay required

General. Founded in 1817. Regionally accredited. **Degrees:** 5,923 bachelor's awarded; master's, doctoral, first professional offered. **ROTC:** Army, Navy, Air Force. **Location:** 50 miles from Detroit. **Calendar:** Trimester, limited summer session. **Full-time faculty:** 2,347 total; 91% have terminal degrees, 22% minority, 35% women. **Part-time faculty:** 589 total; 77% have terminal degrees, 15% minority, 50% women. **Class size:** 46% < 20, 34% 20-39, 4% 40-49, 10% 50-99, 6% >100. **Special facilities:** Botanical garden, museums, biological station in northern Michigan, arboretum, planetarium, laboratories, observatory, research centers and institutes, field station in the greater Yellowstone ecosystem.

Freshman class profile. 23,882 applied, 13,610 admitted, 6,113 enrolled.

Mid 50% test scores		Rank in top tenth:	90%
SAT verbal:	590-690	Out-of-state:	37%
SAT math:	630-730	Live on campus:	98%
ACT:	26-31	International:	4%
Rank in top quarter:	98%		

Basis for selection. Admissions based on school achievement record, including quality of school and courses elected, and test scores. Talents and extracurricular activities considered. Special consideration to educationally disadvantaged applicants. Audition required for music majors; portfolio required for art majors. **Homeschooled:** SAT Subject Test may be required.

High school preparation. College-preparatory program recommended. 15 units required; 18 recommended. Required and recommended units include English 4, mathematics 3-4, social studies 3, history 2, science 3-4 (laboratory 1), foreign language 2-4 and academic electives 2. Recommend 1-2 units computer literacy, 2 units fine or performing arts. Also recommend AP, honors, enriched, and accelerated courses.

2005-2006 Annual costs. Tuition/fees: $9,213; $27,601 out-of-state. Room/board: $7,374. Books/supplies: $980. Personal expenses: $2,076.

2004-2005 Financial aid. Need-based: 3,320 full-time freshmen applied for aid; 2,932 were judged to have need; 2,932 of these received aid. Average need met was 90%. Average scholarship/grant was $6,886; average loan $4,305. 32% of total undergraduate aid awarded as scholarships/grants, 68% as loans/jobs. **Non-need-based:** Awarded to 13,948 full-time undergraduates, including 4,520 freshmen. Scholarships awarded for academics, alumni affiliation, art, athletics, leadership, minority status, music/drama, religious affiliation, ROTC, state residency.

Application procedures. Admission: Closing date 2/1 (postmark date). $40 fee, may be waived for applicants with need. Application may be submitted online. Admission notification on a rolling basis. Must reply by 5/1. Students should apply early in the fall of senior year. Applications may be considered after 2/1 for school of art and design, school of music, school of natural resources, and school of nursing programs on space availability basis. **Financial aid:** Priority date 2/15, closing date 4/30. FAFSA, CSS PROFILE required. Applicants notified on a rolling basis starting 3/15; must reply within 2 week(s) of notification.

Academics. Community health nursing program involves staying on-campus from Friday through Sunday for long weekend once a month for 47-credit master's degree. Small-scale, interdisciplinary instruction programs in residence halls; freshman and sophomore seminars, unique undergraduate research, and mentoring opportunities available. **Special study options:** Accelerated study, combined bachelor's/graduate degree, cooperative education, cross-registration, distance learning, double major, dual enrollment of high school students, ESL, exchange student, honors, independent study, internships, liberal arts/career combination, student-designed major, study abroad, teacher certification program, Washington semester, weekend college. Preferred admissions program to UM graduate/professional schools, graduate business program available through branch campus, and weekend college for graduate students in public health, business administration & engineering. **Credit/placement by examination:** AP, CLEP, IB, institutional tests. 60 credit hours maximum toward bachelor's degree. Policies on credit by examination varies by exam. **Support services:** Reduced course load, study skills assistance, tutoring, writing center.

Honors college/program. 10% of each incoming freshman class admitted; grades, test scores, recommendations, and essay used in decision process.

Majors. **Architecture:** Architecture, environmental design, landscape. **Area/ethnic studies:** African, African-American, American, Asian, Caribbean, Central/Eastern European, East Asian, Hispanic-American/Latino/Chicano, Latin American, Near/Middle Eastern, Russian/Slavic, Scandinavian, South Asian, Southeast Asian, Western European, women's. **Biology:** General, biochemistry, biophysics, botany, cellular/molecular, microbiology, zoology. **Business:** Business admin, organizational behavior. **Communications:** General. **Computer sciences:** General, computer science. **Conservation:** General, environmental studies, management/policy. **Education:** Art, elementary, multi-level teacher, music, physical, secondary. **Engineering:** General, aerospace, biomedical, chemical, civil, computer, electrical, environmental, industrial, marine, materials science, mechanical, metallurgical, nuclear, physics, science. **English:** British lit, creative writing, speech/rhetoric. **Foreign languages:** Ancient Greek, Arabic, Biblical, classics, comparative lit, French, German, Hebrew, Italian, Japanese, Latin, linguistics, modern Greek, Russian, Spanish. **Health:** Athletic training, clinical lab science, dental hygiene, nursing (RN). **History:** General. **Interdisciplinary:** Ancient studies, biopsychology, classical/archaeology, medieval/Renaissance, museum, nutrition sciences. **Liberal arts:** Humanities. **Math:** General, applied, statistics. **Parks/recreation:** General, exercise sciences, sports admin. **Philosophy/religion:** Islamic, Judaic, philosophy, religion. **Physical sciences:** Astronomy, atmospheric science, chemistry, geology, oceanography, paleontology, physics. **Psychology:** General. **Social sciences:** General, anthropology, economics, geography, political science, sociology. **Visual/performing arts:** Art history/conservation, ceramics, commercial/advertising art, dance, design, dramatic, drawing, fiber arts, film/cinema, graphic design, illustration, industrial design, interior design, jazz, metal/jewelry, music history, music performance, music theory/composition, play/screenwriting, printmaking, sculpture, studio arts, theater design, theater history.

Most popular majors. Biology 6%, business/marketing 6%, engineering/engineering technologies 17%, English 6%, psychology 11%, social sciences 15%, visual/performing arts 6%.

Computing on campus. 2,600 workstations in dormitories, library, computer center, student center. Dormitories wired for high-speed internet access and linked to campus network. Commuter students can connect to campus network. Online course registration, online library, helpline, repair service, student web hosting, wireless network available.

Student life. **Freshman orientation:** Mandatory, $185 fee. Preregistration for classes offered. Students must attend 1 of several 3-day summer programs. **Policies:** Student code book in place. Freshmen permitted cars on campus. **Housing:** Guaranteed on-campus for freshmen. Coed dorms, single-sex dorms, special housing for disabled, apartments, cooperative housing, fraternity/sorority housing, substance-free housing available. **Activities:** Bands, choral groups, dance, drama, film society, literary magazine, music ensembles, musical theater, opera, radio station, student government, student newspaper, symphony orchestra, TV station, over 1,000 student organizations.

Athletics. NCAA. **Intercollegiate:** Baseball M, basketball, cross-country, diving, field hockey W, football (tackle) M, golf, gymnastics, ice hockey M, rowing (crew) W, soccer, softball W, swimming, tennis, track and field, volleyball W, water polo W, wrestling M. **Intramural:** Badminton, basketball, cross-country, diving, golf, ice hockey, racquetball, soccer, softball, swimming, table tennis, tennis, track and field, volleyball, water polo, wrestling. **Team name:** Wolverines.

Student services. Adult student services, alcohol/substance abuse counseling, career counseling, student employment services, financial aid counseling, health services, legal services, minority student services, on-campus daycare, personal counseling. **Physically disabled:** Services for visually, speech, hearing impaired.

Contact. E-mail: ugadmiss@umich.edu
Phone: (734) 764-7433 Fax: (734) 936-0740
Theodore Spencer, Director for Undergraduate Admissions Office,
University of Michigan, 1220 Student Activities Building, Ann Arbor, MI 48109-1316

University of Michigan: Dearborn

Dearborn, Michigan — **CB member**
www.umd.umich.edu — **CB code: 1861**

- Public 4-year university
- Commuter campus in small city
- 5,942 degree-seeking undergraduates: 35% part-time, 52% women, 9% African American, 6% Asian American, 3% Hispanic American, 1% Native American, 2% international
- 2,016 degree-seeking graduate students
- 71% of applicants admitted
- SAT or ACT (ACT writing optional) required
- 48% graduate within 6 years

General. Founded in 1959. Regionally accredited. **Degrees:** 1,155 bachelor's awarded; master's offered. **ROTC:** Army, Navy, Air Force. **Location:** 10 miles from Detroit. **Calendar:** Semester, limited summer session. **Full-time faculty:** 277 total; 88% have terminal degrees, 28% minority, 34% women. **Part-time faculty:** 240 total; 42% have terminal degrees, 11% minority, 38% women. **Class size:** 41% < 20, 46% 20-39, 8% 40-49, 4% 50-99, less than 1% >100. **Special facilities:** Henry Ford's Fair Lane estate, environmental study area, extensive rotating art collection in university library, engineering CAD-CAM robotics laboratory, Armenian research center.

Freshman class profile. 2,605 applied, 1,842 admitted, 840 enrolled.

Mid 50% test scores			
SAT verbal:	460-600	Rank in top quarter:	58%
SAT math:	480-630	Rank in top tenth:	27%
ACT:	21-26	End year in good standing:	90%
GPA 3.50 or higher:	49%	Return as sophomores:	82%
GPA 3.0-3.49:	32%	Out-of-state:	1%
GPA 2.0-2.99:	19%	Fraternities:	3%
		Sororities:	3%

Basis for selection. Minimum 3.0 high school GPA with minimum SAT verbal and mathematics scores of 500 or ACT composite score of 22 preferred. Class rank considered. Interview recommended for applicants with high school GPA of less than 3.0 or with ACT composite score of less than 20 or combined SAT score less than 1000 (exclusive of Writing). Essay recommended for all.

High school preparation. 15 units required; 20 recommended. Required and recommended units include English 4, mathematics 4, social studies 4, history 4, science 3 (laboratory 1) and foreign language 3. 1 unit information technology and 1 unit fine and performing arts recommeded.

2005-2006 Annual costs. Tuition/fees: $7,116; $15,008 out-of-state. Books/supplies: $800. Personal expenses: $1,504.

2004-2005 Financial aid. **Need-based:** 451 full-time freshmen applied for aid; 317 were judged to have need; 311 of these received aid. Average need met was 31%. Average scholarship/grant was $3,919; average loan $1,554. 33% of total undergraduate aid awarded as scholarships/grants, 67% as loans/jobs. **Non-need-based:** Awarded to 1,201 full-time undergraduates, including 330 freshmen. Scholarships awarded for academics, alumni affiliation, athletics, job skills, leadership, minority status, ROTC.

Application procedures. **Admission:** Priority date 5/1; no deadline. $30 fee, may be waived for applicants with need. Application may be submitted online. Admission notification on a rolling basis beginning on or about 9/1. Must reply by May 1 or within 4 week(s) if notified thereafter. **Financial aid:** Priority date 2/14; no closing date. FAFSA required. Applicants notified on a rolling basis starting 3/1; must reply within 3 week(s) of notification.

Academics. **Special study options:** Accelerated study, cooperative education, cross-registration, distance learning, double major, dual enrollment of high school students, honors, independent study, internships, liberal arts/career combination, student-designed major, study abroad, teacher certification program, Washington semester. Professional development courses in education, engineering, liberal arts, and management. **Credit/placement by examination:** AP, CLEP, institutional tests. 30 credit hours maximum toward bachelor's degree. **Support services:** Learning center, pre-admission summer program, tutoring.

Majors. **Area/ethnic studies:** American. **Biology:** General, bacteriology, biochemistry, ecology. **Business:** Business admin, management science. **Communications:** General. **Computer sciences:** General, programming. **Conservation:** General, environmental studies. **Education:** General, art, business, chemistry, early childhood, foreign languages, mathematics, science, secondary, social studies. **Engineering:** General, computer, electrical, manufacturing, mechanical. **Foreign languages:** French, Spanish. **Health:** Health care admin. **History:** General. **Interdisciplinary:** Behavioral sciences. **Liberal arts:** Arts/sciences. **Math:** General. **Philosophy/religion:** Philosophy. **Physical sciences:** Chemistry, physics. **Psychology:** General. **Public administration:** General. **Social sciences:** Anthropology, economics, political science, sociology. **Visual/performing arts:** Painting.

Most popular majors. Business/marketing 23%, education 11%, engineering/engineering technologies 16%, psychology 8%, social sciences 9%.

Computing on campus. 140 workstations in library, computer center, student center. Commuter students can connect to campus network. Online course registration, helpline available.

Student life. **Freshman orientation:** Mandatory, $50 fee. **Activities:** Drama, film society, literary magazine, radio station, student government, student newspaper, TV station, Arab student union, association for African American students, Dearborn Campus Engineers, Asian American association, student activities board, professional accounting society, Muslim student association.

Athletics. NAIA. **Intercollegiate:** Basketball, ice hockey M, volleyball W. **Intramural:** Basketball, ice hockey, softball, table tennis, tennis, volleyball. **Team name:** Wolves.

Student services. Adult student services, alcohol/substance abuse counseling, career counseling, student employment services, financial aid counseling, health services, on-campus daycare, personal counseling, placement for graduates, veterans' counselor, women's services. **Physically disabled:** Services for visually, speech, hearing impaired.

Contact. E-mail: admissions@umd.umich.edu
Phone: (313) 593-5100 Fax: (313) 436-9167
Christopher Tremblay, Director of Admissions, University of Michigan: Dearborn, 4901 Evergreen Road, 1145 UC, Dearborn, MI 48128-1491

University of Michigan: Flint

Flint, Michigan — **CB member**
www.umflint.edu — **CB code: 1853**

- Public 4-year university and branch campus college
- Commuter campus in small city
- 5,481 degree-seeking undergraduates: 38% part-time, 63% women, 11% African American, 2% Asian American, 3% Hispanic American, 1% Native American, 1% international
- 728 degree-seeking graduate students
- 85% of applicants admitted
- SAT or ACT (ACT writing optional) required
- 37% graduate within 6 years

General. Founded in 1956. Regionally accredited. Institution shares many resources of entire University of Michigan system. **Degrees:** 907 bachelor's awarded; master's, first professional offered. **Location:** 60 miles from Detroit. **Calendar:** Semester, limited summer session. **Full-time faculty:** 213 total; 75% have terminal degrees, 22% minority, 58% women. **Part-time faculty:** 207 total; 27% have terminal degrees, 11% minority, 55% women. **Class size:** 36% < 20, 52% 20-39, 7% 40-49, 5% 50-99, less than 1% >100.

Freshman class profile. 1,651 applied, 1,396 admitted, 579 enrolled.

Mid 50% test scores		**Rank in top quarter:**	42%
SAT verbal:	440-540	**Rank in top tenth:**	16%
SAT math:	400-550	**End year in good standing:**	82%
ACT:	18-24	**Return as sophomores:**	80%
GPA 3.50 or higher:	31%	**Out-of-state:**	1%
GPA 3.0-3.49:	36%	**Fraternities:**	1%
GPA 2.0-2.99:	32%	**Sororities:**	1%

Basis for selection. GPA of 2.7 or higher and test scores equaling the national average automatically admitted. SAT Subject Tests recommended. Essay and interview recommended. Audition required for art and music majors.

High school preparation. 12 units required; 21 recommended. Required and recommended units include English 4, mathematics 3-4, social studies 3, history 2, science 2-4 (laboratory 2) and foreign language 2. Fine arts and computer science courses recommended.

2005-2006 Annual costs. Tuition/fees: $6,398; $12,150 out-of-state. Books/supplies: $850. Personal expenses: $1,350.

2004-2005 Financial aid. **Need-based:** 342 full-time freshmen applied for aid; 236 were judged to have need; 231 of these received aid. Average scholarship/grant was $3,674; average loan $2,800. 45% of total undergraduate aid awarded as scholarships/grants, 55% as loans/jobs. **Non-need-based:** Awarded to 616 full-time undergraduates, including 185 freshmen. Scholarships awarded for academics, art, leadership, minority status, music/drama. **Additional information:** SAT/ACT scores must be submitted for scholarship consideration.

Application procedures. **Admission:** Priority date 11/1; no deadline. $30 fee, may be waived for applicants with need. Application may be submitted online. Admission notification on a rolling basis beginning on or about 12/1. Must reply by May 1 or within 2 week(s) if notified thereafter. **Financial aid:** Priority date 3/1; no closing date. FAFSA required. Applicants notified on a rolling basis starting 3/15.

Academics. **Special study options:** Combined bachelor's/graduate degree, cooperative education, distance learning, double major, dual enrollment of high school students, honors, independent study, internships, student-designed major, study abroad, teacher certification program. **Credit/placement by examination:** AP, CLEP, institutional tests. Maximum of 3 courses may be passed by examination in Arts & Sciences, School of Management and Nursing. **Support services:** Learning center, reduced course load, remedial instruction, study skills assistance, tutoring, writing center.

Majors. **Area/ethnic studies:** African-American. **Biology:** General, biomedical sciences, ecology, molecular, wildlife. **Business:** Accounting, actuarial science, business admin, finance, marketing, operations, organizational behavior. **Communications:** General, media studies, organizational. **Computer sciences:** Computer science, information systems. **Conservation:** Environmental science. **Education:** General, art, elementary, music. **Engineering:** Science. **English:** Composition, creative writing, English lit. **Foreign languages:** French, Spanish. **Health:** Clinical lab science, health care admin, health services, medical radiologic technology/radiation therapy, nursing (RN), public health ed. **History:** General. **Liberal arts:** Arts/sciences. **Math:** General. **Philosophy/religion:** Ethics, philosophy. **Physical sciences:** Chemistry, physics. **Protective services:** Law enforcement admin. **Psychology:** General. **Public administration:** General, social work. **Social sciences:** General, anthropology, economics, political science, sociology. **Visual/performing arts:** Acting, ceramics, dance, dramatic, graphic design, music performance, painting, photography, printmaking, sculpture, studio arts, theater design, theater history.

Most popular majors. Business/marketing 16%, education 25%, health sciences 16%.

Computing on campus. 155 workstations in library, computer center, student center. Commuter students can connect to campus network. Online course registration, online library, helpline, repair service, student web hosting, wireless network available.

Student life. **Freshman orientation:** Mandatory, $60 fee. Preregistration for classes offered. 2-day program for students and parents before start of fall semester. **Policies:** Freshmen permitted cars on campus. **Activities:** Bands, choral groups, dance, drama, literary magazine, music ensembles, musical theater, student government, student newspaper, TV station, Amnesty International, College Democrats, College Republicans, Hillel student organization, InterVarsity Christian Fellowship, Muslim student association, organization for university tolerance, students defending Christian principles, students for social change, voices for women on campus.

Athletics. **Intramural:** Basketball, football (non-tackle), golf, racquetball, soccer, softball, table tennis, volleyball.

Student services. Adult student services, alcohol/substance abuse counseling, career counseling, student employment services, financial aid counseling, health services, minority student services, on-campus daycare, personal counseling, women's services. **Physically disabled:** Services for visually, speech, hearing impaired.

Contact. E-mail: admissions@list.umflint.edu
Phone: (810) 762-3300 Fax: (810) 762-3272
Kimberley Buster-Williams, Director of Admissions, University of Michigan: Flint, 303 East Kearsley Street, Flint, MI 48502-1950

Walsh College of Accountancy and Business Administration

Troy, Michigan
www.walshcollege.edu — **CB code: 0372**

- Private upper-division business college
- Commuter campus in large city

General. Founded in 1922. Regionally accredited. Bachelor degree partnership with Macomb Community College University Center. **Degrees:** 356 bachelor's awarded; master's offered. **Articulation:** Agreements with Henry

Ford CC, Oakland CC, Macomb CC, Mott CC, Schoolcraft College, Washtenaw CC, St. Clair County CC, Wayne County CC, Kellogg CC, Jackson CC, Lansing CC, Lewis College of Business. **Location:** 17 miles from Detroit. **Calendar:** Differs by program, extensive summer session. **Full-time faculty:** 14 total. **Part-time faculty:** 150 total. **Class size:** 25% < 20, 70% 20-39, 5% 40-49.

Student profile. 939 degree-seeking undergraduates, 2,116 degree-seeking graduate students. 100% entered as juniors.

Women:	57%	**Out-of-state:**	2%
Part-time:	81%	**25 or older:**	64%

Basis for selection. Open admission. College transcript required. 30 transferred credits must be in liberal arts, including course in English composition or written communication. Transfer accepted as juniors.

2006-2007 Annual costs. Tuition/fees (projected): $7,730. Books/supplies: $2,016.

Financial aid. Need-based: 79 applied for aid; 74 were judged to have need; 74 of these received aid. Average need met was 33%. 24% of total undergraduate aid awarded as scholarships/grants, 76% as loans/jobs. **Non-need-based:** Awarded to 43 undergraduates. Scholarships awarded for academics.

Application procedures. Admission: Rolling admission. $25 fee, may be waived for applicants with need. Application may be submitted online. **Financial aid:** FAFSA required.

Academics. Special study options: Accelerated study, distance learning, double major, internships. **Credit/placement by examination:** CLEP, IB. **Support services:** Reduced course load, study skills assistance, tutoring.

Majors. Business: General, accounting, business admin, finance. **Computer sciences:** General, information technology.

Most popular majors. Business/marketing 74%.

Computing on campus. 200 workstations in library, computer center. Commuter students can connect to campus network. Helpline available.

Student life. Activities: Student government, American Marketing Association, finance/economics club, National Association of Black Accountants, accounting club, Association of Information Technology Professionals, international club.

Student services. Career counseling, student employment services, financial aid counseling, placement for graduates. **Physically disabled:** Services for visually, hearing impaired.

Contact. E-mail: admissions@walshcollege.edu
Phone: (248) 689-8282 Toll-free number: (800) 925-7401
Fax: (248) 524-2520
Karen Mahaffy, Director of Admissions and Academic Advising, Walsh College of Accountancy and Business Administration, PO Box 7006, Troy, MI 48007-7006

Wayne State University

Detroit, Michigan — **CB member**
www.wayne.edu — **CB code: 1898**

- Public 4-year university
- Commuter campus in very large city
- 19,505 degree-seeking undergraduates: 40% part-time, 59% women, 33% African American, 5% Asian American, 3% Hispanic American, 4% international
- 11,076 degree-seeking graduate students
- 67% of applicants admitted
- SAT or ACT (ACT writing optional) required
- 32% graduate within 6 years

General. Founded in 1868. Regionally accredited. 5 off-campus locations and University Center at local community college. **Degrees:** 2,294 bachelor's awarded; master's, doctoral, first professional offered. **ROTC:** Air Force. **Location:** 3 miles from downtown. **Calendar:** Semester, extensive summer session. **Full-time faculty:** 1,004 total; 70% have terminal degrees, 23% minority, 39% women. **Part-time faculty:** 913 total; 18% have terminal degrees, 27% minority, 51% women. **Special facilities:** 3 theaters.

Freshman class profile. 10,128 applied, 6,789 admitted, 2,878 enrolled.

Mid 50% test scores		**End year in good standing:**	61%
ACT:	16-24	**Return as sophomores:**	72%
GPA 3.50 or higher:	28%	**Out-of-state:**	1%
GPA 3.0-3.49:	49%	**Live on campus:**	24%
GPA 2.0-2.99:	23%	**International:**	3%
Rank in top quarter:	50%	**Fraternities:**	1%
Rank in top tenth:	25%	**Sororities:**	1%

Basis for selection. High school record, test scores important. Minimum 2.75 GPA or 2.0 GPA combined with 21 ACT. Audition required of music applicants, recommended for dance and theater applicants; portfolio required for art applicants.

High school preparation. 18 units recommended. Recommended units include English 4, mathematics 4, social studies 3, science 3, foreign language 2 and academic electives 2. Computer literacy.

2005-2006 Annual costs. Tuition/fees: $6,389; $13,721 out-of-state. Room/board: $6,775. Books/supplies: $816. Personal expenses: $1,939.

2004-2005 Financial aid. Need-based: Average need met was 43%. Average scholarship/grant was $3,085; average loan $2,457. 29% of total undergraduate aid awarded as scholarships/grants, 71% as loans/jobs. **Non-need-based:** Scholarships awarded for academics, art, athletics, leadership, music/drama.

Application procedures. Admission: Closing date 8/1 (receipt date). $30 fee, may be waived for applicants with need. Application may be submitted online. Admission notification on a rolling basis. **Financial aid:** Priority date 3/1; no closing date. FAFSA required. Applicants notified on a rolling basis starting 4/15; must reply within 2 week(s) of notification.

Academics. Special study options: Accelerated study, combined bachelor's/graduate degree, cooperative education, cross-registration, distance learning, double major, dual enrollment of high school students, ESL, exchange student, honors, independent study, internships, liberal arts/career combination, study abroad, teacher certification program, weekend college. Off-campus courses for credit, city-wide adult education program. **Credit/placement by examination:** AP, CLEP, IB, institutional tests. 32 credit hours maximum toward bachelor's degree. **Support services:** Learning center, pre-admission summer program, remedial instruction, study skills assistance, tutoring, writing center.

Majors. Area/ethnic studies: African-American, American, Asian, East Asian, Hispanic-American/Latino/Chicano, Near/Middle Eastern, women's. **Biology:** General. **Business:** General, accounting, finance, logistics, management information systems, marketing, organizational behavior. **Communications:** General, broadcast journalism, journalism, public relations. **Computer sciences:** General, information systems. **Conservation:** Environmental science. **Education:** Art, elementary, English, health, mathematics, physical, science, social studies, special, speech impaired, voc/tech. **Engineering:** Chemical, civil, electrical, industrial, manufacturing, mechanical. **Engineering technology:** Computer systems, electrical, electromechanical, manufacturing, mechanical. **English:** English lit. **Family/consumer sciences:** Family studies, food/nutrition. **Foreign languages:** Classics, French, German, Italian, linguistics, Russian, Slavic, Spanish. **Health:** Clinical lab science, communication disorders, medical radiologic technology/radiation therapy, nursing (RN), pathology assistant, speech pathology. **History:** General. **Interdisciplinary:** Peace/conflict. **Math:** General. **Parks/recreation:** General. **Personal/culinary services:** Mortuary science. **Philosophy/religion:** Philosophy. **Physical sciences:** Chemistry, geology, physics. **Protective services:** Criminal justice. **Psychology:** General. **Public administration:** General, social work. **Social sciences:** Anthropology, economics, geography, international relations, political science, sociology, urban studies. **Visual/performing arts:** Art, art history/conservation, dance, dramatic, film/cinema.

Most popular majors. Business/marketing 17%, education 15%, engineering/engineering technologies 9%, health sciences 12%, psychology 7%, visual/performing arts 7%.

Computing on campus. 1,000 workstations in library. Dormitories wired for high-speed internet access and linked to campus network. Commuter students can connect to campus network. Online course registration, helpline, repair service, wireless network available.

Student life. Freshman orientation: Mandatory, $75 fee. Preregistration for classes offered. **Policies:** Freshmen permitted cars on campus. **Housing:** Coed dorms, special housing for disabled, apartments, fraternity/sorority housing, substance-free housing available. $150 partly refundable deposit. **Activities:** Bands, choral groups, dance, drama, film society, literary magazine, music ensembles, musical theater, opera, student government, student newspaper, symphony orchestra, Indian student association, Golden Key honor society, Campus Crusade for Christ, friendship association of Chinese students.

Athletics. NCAA. **Intercollegiate:** Baseball M, basketball, cross-country, diving, fencing, football (tackle) M, golf M, ice hockey, softball W, swimming, tennis, volleyball W. **Intramural:** Badminton, basketball, bowling, football (non-tackle), football (tackle), racquetball, soccer, softball, tennis, volleyball. **Team name:** Warriors.

Student services. Adult student services, alcohol/substance abuse counseling, campus ministries, career counseling, services for economically disadvantaged, student employment services, financial aid counseling, health services, legal services, minority student services, on-campus daycare, personal counseling, placement for graduates, veterans' counselor, women's services. **Physically disabled:** Services for visually, speech, hearing impaired.

Contact. E-mail: admissions@wayne.edu
Phone: (313) 577-3577 Toll-free number: (877) 978-4636
Fax: (313) 577-7536
Susan Zwieg, Director of University Admissions, Wayne State University, 42 West Warren, Detroit, MI 48202

Western Michigan University

Kalamazoo, Michigan — **CB member**
www.wmich.edu — **CB code: 1902**

- Public 4-year university
- Residential campus in small city
- 21,287 degree-seeking undergraduates: 12% part-time, 51% women, 6% African American, 2% Hispanic American, 2% Native American, 2% international
- 4,187 degree-seeking graduate students
- 85% of applicants admitted
- SAT or ACT (ACT writing optional) required
- 55% graduate within 6 years

General. Founded in 1903. Regionally accredited. **Degrees:** 4,291 bachelor's awarded; master's, doctoral offered. **ROTC:** Army. **Location:** 140 miles from Detroit, 140 miles from Chicago. **Calendar:** Semester, extensive summer session. **Full-time faculty:** 932 total; 80% have terminal degrees, 13% minority, 38% women. **Part-time faculty:** 538 total; 52% women. **Class size:** 41% < 20, 38% 20-39, 9% 40-49, 8% 50-99, 4% >100. **Special facilities:** Van de Graaff particle accelerator, pilot plant for manufacturing and printing of paper and fiber recovery, aviation flight simulators, business technology park.

Freshman class profile. 12,928 applied, 11,045 admitted, 3,751 enrolled.

Mid 50% test scores		**End year in good standing:**	75%
ACT:	20-25	**Return as sophomores:**	73%
GPA 3.50 or higher:	32%	**Out-of-state:**	8%
GPA 3.0-3.49:	38%	**Live on campus:**	72%
GPA 2.0-2.99:	30%	**International:**	1%
Rank in top quarter:	33%	**Fraternities:**	2%
Rank in top tenth:	13%	**Sororities:**	4%

Basis for selection. School achievement record, test scores most important. Trend of grades and number of solid high school academic subjects completed considered; students not meeting college-preparatory program requirements may be admitted conditionally if they meet other admission requirements. Interview recommended. Audition required for dance, music, and theater applicants. Portfolio required for some art applicants.

High school preparation. Required and recommended units include English 4, mathematics 3-4, social studies 2, history 1, science 2 (laboratory 1), foreign language 1-2 and academic electives 2.

2005-2006 Annual costs. Tuition/fees: $6,478; $15,856 out-of-state. Room/board: $6,651.

2004-2005 Financial aid. Need-based: 2,950 full-time freshmen applied for aid; 2,100 were judged to have need; 2,100 of these received aid. Average need met was 68%. Average scholarship/grant was $4,200; average loan $2,500. 36% of total undergraduate aid awarded as scholarships/grants, 64% as loans/jobs. **Non-need-based:** Awarded to 2,520 full-time undergraduates, including 340 freshmen. Scholarships awarded for academics, art, athletics, minority status, music/drama, ROTC, state residency.

Application procedures. Admission: No deadline. $35 fee, may be waived for applicants with need. Application may be submitted online. Admission notification on a rolling basis beginning on or about 9/15. **Financial aid:** Priority date 3/15; no closing date. FAFSA required. Applicants notified on a rolling basis starting 3/15.

Academics. Special study options: Accelerated study, cooperative education, cross-registration, distance learning, double major, dual enrollment of high school students, ESL, exchange student, honors, independent study, internships, student-designed major, study abroad, teacher certification program, weekend college. **Credit/placement by examination:** AP, CLEP, IB, SAT, ACT, institutional tests. Maximum semester hours of credit by examination which may be counted toward degree varies by department. Credit by examination may not be used to satisfy minimum residency requirement of 30 semester hours. **Support services:** Learning center, pre-admission summer program, reduced course load, remedial instruction, study skills assistance, tutoring, writing center.

Honors college/program. GPA (usually 3.6 or higher) and ACT (usually 25 or better) most important. Academic essay, college cocurricular and community activities, and 2 recommendations from faculty also required. Academic program includes freshman/sophomore course clusters (3 courses in each group, at least 3 credits each), junior and senior seminars, honors thesis. Each year, Honors College receives about 800 applications for about 270 available positions.

Majors. Area/ethnic studies: African, Asian, European, Latin American, Russian/Slavic, women's. **Biology:** General, biochemistry, Biochemistry/biophysics and molecular biology, biomedical sciences. **Business:** General, accounting, business admin, finance, financial planning, human resources, information resources management, logistics, management science, marketing, nonprofit/public, real estate, travel services. **Communications:** General, journalism, media studies, public relations. **Computer sciences:** General, applications programming, computer science. **Conservation:** Environmental science, environmental studies, wood science. **Education:** Art, biology, chemistry, elementary, emotionally handicapped, English, family/consumer sciences, foreign languages, French, geography, German, health, history, Latin, mathematics, mentally handicapped, music, physical, physics, sales/marketing, science, secondary, social science, Spanish, technology/industrial arts. **Engineering:** General, aerospace, chemical, civil, computer, electrical, industrial, mechanical, structural. **Engineering technology:** Aerospace, automotive, construction, industrial, industrial management, plastics. **English:** Composition, creative writing, English lit. **Family/consumer sciences:** Child development, clothing/textiles, family systems, institutional food production. **Foreign languages:** French, German, Latin, Spanish. **Health:** Audiology/speech pathology, community health services, health services, music therapy, nursing (RN). **History:** General, public archives. **Interdisciplinary:** Global studies. **Math:** General, applied, statistics. **Mechanic/repair:** Avionics. **Parks/recreation:** General, exercise sciences. **Philosophy/religion:** Philosophy, religion. **Physical sciences:** Chemistry, geochemistry, geology, geophysics, hydrology, physics. **Protective services:** Criminal justice. **Psychology:** General. **Public administration:** General, social work. **Social sciences:** General, anthropology, economics, geography, international relations, political science, sociology, U.S. government. **Transportation:** Airline/commercial pilot, aviation management. **Visual/performing arts:** Acting, art, art history/conservation, dance, dramatic, graphic design, industrial design, interior design, jazz, music performance, music theory/composition, theater design.

Most popular majors. Business/marketing 24%, communications/journalism 7%, education 20%.

Computing on campus. 2,000 workstations in dormitories, library, computer center, student center. Dormitories wired for high-speed internet access and linked to campus network. Commuter students can connect to campus network. Online course registration, helpline, repair service, student web hosting, wireless network available.

Student life. Freshman orientation: Mandatory, $125 fee. Preregistration for classes offered. 2-day program in June; includes session for parents. **Policies:** Freshmen permitted cars on campus. **Housing:** Guaranteed on-campus for freshmen. Coed dorms, single-sex dorms, special housing for disabled, apartments, fraternity/sorority housing, substance-free housing available. $500 partly refundable deposit. Themed halls available, including: community service, health and wellness, honors, arts and athletics, first year initiative, upperclass students, diversity. **Activities:** Bands, choral groups, dance, drama, literary magazine, music ensembles, musical theater, opera, radio station, student government, student newspaper, symphony orchestra, nearly 300 organizations.

Athletics. NCAA. **Intercollegiate:** Baseball M, basketball, cross-country W, football (tackle) M, golf W, gymnastics W, ice hockey M, soccer, softball W, tennis, track and field W, volleyball W. **Intramural:** Badminton, basketball, bowling, equestrian, fencing, football (tackle), golf M, ice hockey, lacrosse, racquetball, rugby, sailing, skiing, soccer, softball, swimming, table tennis, tennis, volleyball. **Team name:** Broncos.

Student services. Adult student services, alcohol/substance abuse counseling, campus ministries, career counseling, student employment services, financial aid counseling, health services, minority student services, on-campus daycare, personal counseling, placement for graduates, veterans' counselor, women's services. **Physically disabled:** Services for visually, speech, hearing impaired.

Contact. E-mail: www.ask-wmu@wmich.edu
Phone: (269) 387-2000 Toll-free number: (800) 400-4968
Fax: (269) 387-2096
Pamela Liberacki, Associate Director of Admissions, Western Michigan University, 1903 West Michigan Avenue, Kalamazoo, MI 49008-5211

Yeshiva Beth Yehuda-Yeshiva Gedolah of Greater Detroit

Oak Park, Michigan

CB code: 7010

- Private 5-year rabbinical college for men affiliated with Jewish faith
- Residential campus in large town
- 41 degree-seeking undergraduates
- 83% of applicants admitted
- Interview required

General. Accredited by AARTS. **Calendar:** Semester. **Full-time faculty:** 6 total. **Part-time faculty:** 8 total.

Freshman class profile. 23 applied, 19 admitted, 19 enrolled.

Basis for selection. GED not accepted. Qualifications include independent comprehension of basic Talmudic text and completion of 150 folios of Talmud with commentary of Rashi, completion of Pentateuch and substantial parts of Prophets and Hagiography, ability to read and write classical Hebrew, working knowledge of Aramaic language of Talmud, and Yiddish.

2006-2007 Annual costs. Tuition/fees (projected): $8,000. Room/board: $3,300. Books/supplies: $500. Personal expenses: $500.

Application procedures. **Admission:** No deadline. No application fee. **Financial aid:** Closing date 8/1. Applicants notified on a rolling basis.

Academics. **Special study options:** Independent study. **Credit/placement by examination:** CLEP. **Support services:** Tutoring.

Majors. **Theology:** Talmudic.

Student life. **Housing:** Guaranteed on-campus for all undergraduates.

Student services. Adult student services, career counseling, health services, on-campus daycare, personal counseling, placement for graduates.

Contact. Phone: (248) 968-3360 Fax: (248) 968-8613
Yeshiva Beth Yehuda-Yeshiva Gedolah of Greater Detroit, 24600 Greenfield Road, Oak Park, MI 48237

Minnesota

Art Institutes International Minnesota

Minneapolis, Minnesota
www.aim.artinstitutes.edu **CB code: 2332**

- For-profit 4-year culinary school and visual arts college
- Commuter campus in very large city
- 1,594 degree-seeking undergraduates: 44% part-time, 54% women
- Application essay, interview required

General. Accredited by ACICS. **Degrees:** 131 bachelor's, 95 associate awarded. **Location:** Downtown. **Calendar:** Quarter, extensive summer session. **Full-time faculty:** 48 total; 29% women. **Part-time faculty:** 70 total; 61% women. **Special facilities:** Student-run dining lab, school run gallery.

Basis for selection. Open admission. School tour required prior to admission. **Learning Disabled:** Notify Dean of Student Affairs.

2005-2006 Annual costs. Tuition/fees: $16,380. Full-program tuition varies. Starter kits for most programs $550-850; lab fee for culinary arts program $300 per quarter; lab fee for photography program $25 per quarter. Books/supplies: $1,649. Personal expenses: $2,880.

Application procedures. Admission: No deadline. $50 fee. Application may be submitted online. Admission notification on a rolling basis. **Financial aid:** FAFSA required.

Academics. Special study options: Cooperative education, distance learning, internships. **Credit/placement by examination:** AP, CLEP. **Support services:** Learning center, remedial instruction, tutoring.

Majors. Communications: Advertising, digital media, photojournalism. **Communications technology:** Animation/special effects, graphics. **Computer sciences:** Computer graphics, webmaster. **Personal/culinary services:** Restaurant/catering. **Visual/performing arts:** Commercial/advertising art, graphic design, interior design, multimedia.

Computing on campus. 212 workstations in library, computer center. Dormitories wired for high-speed internet access. Student web hosting available.

Student life. Freshman orientation: Mandatory. Preregistration for classes offered. **Policies:** Freshmen permitted cars on campus. **Housing:** Apartments, substance-free housing available. $250 deposit. **Activities:** Student government.

Student services. Alcohol/substance abuse counseling, career counseling, student employment services, financial aid counseling, personal counseling, placement for graduates. **Physically disabled:** Services for hearing impaired.

Contact. E-mail: aimadm@aii.edu
Phone: (612) 332-3361 Toll-free number: (800) 777-3643
Fax: (612) 332-3934
Russ Gill, Director of Admissions, Art Institutes International Minnesota, 15 South Ninth Street, Minneapolis, MN 55402

Augsburg College

Minneapolis, Minnesota **CB member**
www.augsburg.edu **CB code: 6014**

- Private 4-year liberal arts college affiliated with Evangelical Lutheran Church in America
- Residential campus in large city
- 2,668 degree-seeking undergraduates: 18% part-time, 57% women, 5% African American, 3% Asian American, 2% Hispanic American, 1% Native American, 2% international
- 674 degree-seeking graduate students
- 76% of applicants admitted
- SAT and SAT Subject Tests or ACT (ACT writing optional), application essay required
- 55% graduate within 6 years; 25% enter graduate study

General. Founded in 1869. Regionally accredited. **Degrees:** 512 bachelor's awarded; master's offered. **ROTC:** Army, Navy, Air Force. **Location:** 5 miles from downtown. **Calendar:** Differs by program, extensive summer session. **Full-time faculty:** 158 total; 85% have terminal degrees, 7% minority, 48% women. **Part-time faculty:** 222 total. **Class size:** 63% < 20, 36% 20-39, less than 1% 40-49, less than 1% 50-99. **Special facilities:** Center for atmospheric research.

Freshman class profile. 996 applied, 758 admitted, 335 enrolled.

Mid 50% test scores		**Rank in top quarter:**	36%
SAT verbal:	490-610	**Rank in top tenth:**	16%
SAT math:	490-610	**End year in good standing:**	97%
ACT:	20-25	**Return as sophomores:**	78%
GPA 3.50 or higher:	40%	**Out-of-state:**	15%
GPA 3.0-3.49:	30%	**Live on campus:**	88%
GPA 2.0-2.99:	29%	**International:**	2%

Basis for selection. School achievement record, class rank in top half, test scores, essays and recommendations very important; extracurricular activities important. Interview recommended.

High school preparation. College-preparatory program recommended. 15 units required. Required and recommended units include English 4, mathematics 3, social studies 2-4, history 2, science 3 and foreign language 2.

2005-2006 Annual costs. Tuition/fees: $21,958. Room/board: $6,340. Books/supplies: $1,000. Personal expenses: $1,670.

2004-2005 Financial aid. Need-based: 248 full-time freshmen applied for aid; 201 were judged to have need; 199 of these received aid. Average need met was 74%. Average scholarship/grant was $11,877; average loan $3,212. 20% of total undergraduate aid awarded as scholarships/grants, 80% as loans/jobs. **Non-need-based:** Awarded to 456 full-time undergraduates, including 108 freshmen. Scholarships awarded for academics, alumni affiliation, leadership, minority status, music/drama, religious affiliation.

Application procedures. Admission: Priority date 5/1; deadline 8/1 (receipt date). $25 fee, may be waived for applicants with need. Application may be submitted online. Admission notification on a rolling basis. **Financial aid:** Priority date 4/15, closing date 8/1. FAFSA required. Applicants notified on a rolling basis starting 3/1; must reply within 3 week(s) of notification.

Academics. Special study options: Cooperative education, cross-registration, double major, dual enrollment of high school students, ESL, honors, independent study, internships, liberal arts/career combination, student-designed major, study abroad, teacher certification program, urban semester, weekend college. Metro-urban studies internship program; global education program in Central America, Mexico, Namibia and Norway. **Credit/placement by examination:** AP, CLEP, IB, institutional tests. 1 credit hours maximum toward bachelor's degree. **Support services:** Learning center, reduced course load, remedial instruction, study skills assistance, tutoring.

Majors. Area/ethnic studies: Central/Eastern European, East Asian, Native American, Scandinavian, women's. **Biology:** General. **Business:** Accounting, accounting/business management, business admin, finance, international, management information systems, marketing. **Communications:** General, media studies, organizational. **Computer sciences:** Computer science. **Education:** General, biology, early childhood, elementary, emotionally handicapped, health, music, physical, secondary. **Engineering:** General. **English:** English lit. **Foreign languages:** French, German, Scandinavian, Spanish. **Health:** Clinical lab science, music therapy, nursing (RN). **History:** General. **Interdisciplinary:** Medieval/Renaissance. **Liberal arts:** Arts/sciences. **Math:** General. **Philosophy/religion:** Philosophy, religion. **Physical sciences:** Chemistry, physics. **Psychology:** General. **Public administration:** Social work. **Social sciences:** General, applied economics, economics, international relations, political science, sociology, urban studies. **Theology:** Youth ministry. **Visual/performing arts:** Art history/conservation, dramatic, film/cinema, music management, music performance, studio arts, theater history.

Most popular majors. Business/marketing 32%, communications/journalism 6%, education 13%, health sciences 6%, social sciences 8%, visual/performing arts 6%.

Computing on campus. 260 workstations in dormitories, library, computer center, student center. Dormitories wired for high-speed internet access and linked to campus network. Commuter students can connect to campus network. Online course registration, online library, helpline, student web hosting, wireless network available.

Student life. Freshman orientation: Available, $100 fee. Preregistration for classes offered. Students attend in June or July; lasts Friday through Saturday morning. **Policies:** Freshmen permitted cars on campus. **Housing:** Guaranteed on-campus for freshmen. Coed dorms, special housing for disabled, apartments, substance-free housing available. $200 nonrefundable deposit. **Activities:** Bands, choral groups, drama, literary magazine, music ensembles, radio station, student government, student newspaper, symphony orchestra, Religious Life Commission, Fellowship of Christian Athletes, Black Student Union, Intertribal Student Union, Minnesota Public Interest Research Group, Global Awareness Community, International Association for Business Communication.

Athletics. NCAA. **Intercollegiate:** Baseball M, basketball, cross-country, football (tackle) M, golf, ice hockey, soccer, softball W, swimming W, tennis, track and field, volleyball W, wrestling M. **Intramural:** Basketball, softball, tennis, volleyball. **Team name:** Auggies.

Student services. Adult student services, alcohol/substance abuse counseling, campus ministries, career counseling, student employment services, financial aid counseling, health services, minority student services, personal counseling, placement for graduates. **Physically disabled:** Services for visually, speech, hearing impaired.

Contact. E-mail: admissions@augsburg.edu
Phone: (612) 330-1001 Toll-free number: (800) 788-5678
Fax: (612) 330-1590
Carrie Carroll, Director of Admissions, Augsburg College, 2211 Riverside Avenue, Minneapolis, MN 55454

Bemidji State University

Bemidji, Minnesota
www.bemidjistate.edu **CB code: 6676**

- Public 4-year university
- Residential campus in large town
- 4,396 degree-seeking undergraduates: 27% part-time, 54% women
- 437 degree-seeking graduate students
- 73% of applicants admitted
- ACT (writing recommended) required
- 41% graduate within 6 years

General. Founded in 1919. Regionally accredited. Arrowhead University Center located on Minnesota's Mesabi Iron Range offers several degree programs. **Degrees:** 873 bachelor's, 61 associate awarded; master's offered. **Location:** 150 miles from Duluth, 230 miles from Minneapolis-St. Paul. **Calendar:** Semester, extensive summer session. **Full-time faculty:** 246 total; 73% have terminal degrees, 4% minority, 41% women. **Class size:** 58% < 20, 34% 20-39, 5% 40-49, 2% 50-99, 1% >100. **Special facilities:** Freshwater aquatics laboratory, center for research and innovation.

Freshman class profile. 1,700 applied, 1,235 admitted, 633 enrolled.

Mid 50% test scores			
ACT:	20-24	Return as sophomores:	72%
Rank in top quarter:	50%	Out-of-state:	2%
Rank in top tenth:	10%	Live on campus:	75%

Basis for selection. Rank in top half of class or test scores above 50th percentile preferred. ACT scores considered for applicants in bottom half of class. Composite score of 21 or higher preferred. Interview recommended. Audition recommended for music applicants; portfolio recommended for art applicants. **Learning Disabled:** Students encouraged to identify themselves to Office of Disabilities to be appraised of services available.

High school preparation. 16 units required. Required and recommended units include English 4, mathematics 3, social studies 3, history 1, science 3 (laboratory 1), foreign language 2 and academic electives 1. 1 unit of art, music, world culture required.

2005-2006 Annual costs. Tuition/fees: $6,016; $6,016 out-of-state. Room/board: $5,166. Books/supplies: $800. Personal expenses: $1,245.

2005-2006 Financial aid. Need-based: 465 full-time freshmen applied for aid; 316 were judged to have need; 315 of these received aid. Average need met was 75%. Average scholarship/grant was $4,677; average loan $2,666. 47% of total undergraduate aid awarded as scholarships/grants, 53% as loans/jobs. **Non-need-based:** Awarded to 1,811 full-time undergraduates, including 383 freshmen. Scholarships awarded for academics, alumni affiliation, art, music/drama.

Application procedures. Admission: Priority date 8/15; no deadline. $20 fee. Application may be submitted online. Admission notification on a rolling basis. **Financial aid:** Priority date 5/15; no closing date. FAFSA, institutional form required. Applicants notified on a rolling basis starting 5/15.

Academics. Special study options: Accelerated study, combined bachelor's/graduate degree, cooperative education, distance learning, double major, dual enrollment of high school students, ESL, external degree, honors, independent study, internships, liberal arts/career combination, study abroad, teacher certification program. Exchange program with other Minnesota state universities, Euro-spring semester, Sino-summer semester. **Credit/placement by examination:** AP, CLEP, institutional tests. Department defined number of hours of credit by examination may be counted towards degree. **Support services:** Learning center, pre-admission summer program, reduced course load, remedial instruction, study skills assistance, tutoring, writing center.

Majors. Area/ethnic studies: Native American. **Biology:** General, marine. **Business:** Accounting, business admin. **Communications:** Journalism. **Computer sciences:** General, computer science. **Conservation:** General. **Education:** General, elementary, voc/tech. **Engineering:** Physics. **Foreign languages:** German, Spanish. **Health:** Clinical lab science, preop/surgical nursing. **History:** General. **Liberal arts:** Arts/sciences. **Math:** General. **Parks/recreation:** Health/fitness. **Philosophy/religion:** Philosophy. **Physical sciences:** Chemistry, geology, physics. **Protective services:** Criminal justice. **Psychology:** General. **Public administration:** Community org/advocacy, social work. **Social sciences:** General, economics, geography, political science, sociology. **Visual/performing arts:** Art, commercial/advertising art, dramatic.

Most popular majors. Business/marketing 13%, communications/journalism 6%, education 18%, engineering/engineering technologies 15%, health sciences 7%, psychology 6%, security/protective services 6%.

Computing on campus. 800 workstations in dormitories, library, computer center, student center. Dormitories wired for high-speed internet access and linked to campus network. Commuter students can connect to campus network. Online course registration, online library, helpline, repair service, student web hosting available.

Student life. Freshman orientation: Available, $25 fee. Preregistration for classes offered. One-day orientation for students and parents. **Policies:** Zero tolerance for discrimination, racism, sexual violence, illegal activities. Freshmen permitted cars on campus. **Housing:** Coed dorms, single-sex dorms, substance-free housing available. $100 deposit. Single parents hall (includes child care facilities), quiet floors, hall/dorm for students older than average age. **Activities:** Bands, choral groups, dance, drama, film society, literary magazine, music ensembles, musical theater, opera, radio station, student government, student newspaper, symphony orchestra, TV station, Newman Center, Lutheran center, Young Republicans, Young Democrats, social service organizations, international students club, veterans club, campus ministry, Council of Indian Students, Black Student Coalition.

Athletics. NCAA. **Intercollegiate:** Baseball M, basketball, cross-country, football (tackle) M, golf, ice hockey, soccer W, softball W, tennis W, track and field, volleyball W. **Intramural:** Badminton, baseball, basketball, field hockey, football (non-tackle), golf, ice hockey, racquetball, skiing, soccer, softball, table tennis, tennis, triathlon, volleyball, weight lifting M, wrestling M. **Team name:** Beavers.

Student services. Alcohol/substance abuse counseling, campus ministries, career counseling, services for economically disadvantaged, student employment services, financial aid counseling, health services, minority student services, on-campus daycare, personal counseling, placement for graduates, women's services. **Physically disabled:** Services for visually, speech, hearing impaired.

Contact. E-mail: admissions@bemidjistate.edu
Phone: (218) 755-2040 Toll-free number: (800) 475-2001
Fax: (218) 755-2074
Russ Kreager, Director of Admissions, Bemidji State University, 1500 Birchmont Drive Northeast, D-102, Bemidji, MN 56601

Bethany Lutheran College

Mankato, Minnesota
www.blc.edu **CB code: 6035**

- Private 4-year liberal arts college affiliated with Evangelical Lutheran Synod
- Residential campus in large town
- 565 degree-seeking undergraduates: 7% part-time, 54% women
- 84% of applicants admitted
- SAT or ACT (ACT writing recommended), application essay required

General. Founded in 1927. Regionally accredited. **Degrees:** 45 bachelor's awarded. **ROTC:** Army. **Location:** 80 miles from Minneapolis-St. Paul. **Calendar:** Semester. **Full-time faculty:** 38 total; 76% have terminal degrees, 21% women. **Part-time faculty:** 23 total; 44% have terminal degrees, 52% women. **Class size:** 81% < 20, 17% 20-39, 1% 40-49, 1% 50-99.

Freshman class profile. 346 applied, 290 admitted, 143 enrolled.

Mid 50% test scores			
ACT:	20-26	Rank in top quarter:	35%
GPA 3.50 or higher:	47%	Rank in top tenth:	12%
GPA 3.0-3.49:	31%	Out-of-state:	30%
GPA 2.0-2.99:	22%	Live on campus:	92%

Basis for selection. College-prep GPA, overall GPA, test scores most important. **Learning Disabled:** Students with learning disabilities must meet with head of tutorial program.

High school preparation. Recommended units include English 4, mathematics 3, social studies 3, history 3, science 3 (laboratory 1) and foreign language 2.

2006-2007 Annual costs. Tuition/fees: $16,508. Room/board: $5,278. Books/supplies: $800. Personal expenses: $1,000.

2004-2005 Financial aid. Need-based: 148 full-time freshmen applied for aid; 135 were judged to have need; 135 of these received aid. Average need met was 86.19%. Average scholarship/grant was $9,512; average loan $3,384. 67% of total undergraduate aid awarded as scholarships/grants, 33% as loans/jobs. **Non-need-based:** Awarded to 129 full-time undergraduates, including 37 freshmen. Scholarships awarded for academics, art, athletics, music/drama.

Application procedures. Admission: Closing date 8/15 (postmark date). No application fee. Application may be submitted online. Admission notification on a rolling basis beginning on or about 9/1. **Financial aid:** Priority date 4/15; no closing date. FAFSA, institutional form required. Applicants notified on a rolling basis starting 3/1; must reply within 2 week(s) of notification.

Academics. Special study options: Cross-registration, double major, dual enrollment of high school students, independent study, internships, teacher certification program. **Credit/placement by examination:** AP, CLEP, IB, SAT, ACT, institutional tests. 15 credit hours maximum toward associate degree, 15 toward bachelor's. **Support services:** Learning center, reduced course load, remedial instruction, tutoring.

Majors. Biology: Biomedical sciences. **Business:** Business admin. **Communications:** General. **Education:** Elementary. **English:** English lit. **History:** General. **Liberal arts:** Arts/sciences. **Physical sciences:** General, chemistry. **Psychology:** General. **Social sciences:** General. **Theology:** Sacred music. **Visual/performing arts:** Dramatic, studio arts.

Most popular majors. Biology 9%, business/marketing 16%, communications/journalism 36%, education 9%, liberal arts 13%, visual/performing arts 7%.

Computing on campus. 100 workstations in dormitories, library, computer center, student center. Dormitories wired for high-speed internet access and linked to campus network. Commuter students can connect to campus network. Helpline, repair service, student web hosting, wireless network available.

Student life. Freshman orientation: Mandatory. Preregistration for classes offered. **Policies:** Freshmen and sophomores not living with family required to live on campus. Freshmen permitted cars on campus. **Housing:** Guaranteed on-campus for all undergraduates. Single-sex dorms, apartments, substance-free housing available. **Activities:** Bands, choral groups, drama, literary magazine, music ensembles, musical theater, student government, student newspaper, TV station, spiritual life committee, Lutherans for Life, student senate, Lambda Pi Eta, scholastic leadership society.

Athletics. NCCAA. **Intercollegiate:** Baseball M, basketball, golf, soccer, softball W, tennis, volleyball W. **Intramural:** Baseball M, basketball, soccer, softball, tennis, volleyball. **Team name:** Vikings.

Student services. Campus ministries, career counseling, financial aid counseling, minority student services, personal counseling.

Contact. E-mail: admiss@blc.edu
Phone: (507) 344-7331 Toll-free number: (800) 944-3066
Fax: (507) 344-7376
Don Westphal, Dean of Admissions, Bethany Lutheran College, 700 Luther Drive, Mankato, MN 56001-4490

Bethel University

Saint Paul, Minnesota — **CB member**
www.bethel.edu — **CB code: 6038**

- Private 4-year liberal arts college affiliated with Baptist General Conference
- Residential campus in large city
- 3,172 degree-seeking undergraduates: 10% part-time, 62% women, 3% African American, 3% Asian American, 2% Hispanic American
- 660 graduate students
- 87% of applicants admitted
- SAT or ACT (ACT writing optional), application essay required
- 74% graduate within 6 years

General. Founded in 1871. Regionally accredited. **Degrees:** 817 bachelor's, 5 associate awarded; master's, doctoral offered. **ROTC:** Army, Air Force. **Location:** 10 miles from Minneapolis-St. Paul. **Calendar:** 4-1-4, limited summer session. **Full-time faculty:** 175 total; 74% have terminal degrees, 6% minority, 43% women. **Part-time faculty:** 131 total; 25% have terminal degrees, 7% minority, 60% women. **Class size:** 50% < 20, 40% 20-39, 5% 40-49, 3% 50-99, 1% >100.

Freshman class profile. 1,636 applied, 1,427 admitted, 731 enrolled.

Mid 50% test scores			
SAT verbal:	520-670	Rank in top tenth:	32%
SAT math:	520-630	End year in good standing:	82%
ACT:	22-28	Return as sophomores:	84%
Rank in top quarter:	63%	Out-of-state:	26%
		Live on campus:	99%

Basis for selection. Rank in top half of class, 92 PSAT, 21 ACT, or 920 SAT (exclusive of Writing). Applicant must make personal statement regarding Christian commitment and agree to live in accordance with college's lifestyle. 2 recommendations required. PSAT/NMSQT may be submitted in place of SAT or ACT. Interview recommended for art, drama, and music applicants; audition recommended for music applicants; portfolio recommended for art applicants. **Homeschooled:** Transcript of courses and grades required.

High school preparation. College-preparatory program recommended. 19 units recommended. Recommended units include English 4, mathematics 3, social studies 4, history 3, science 3 and foreign language 2.

2005-2006 Annual costs. Tuition/fees: $21,300. Room/board: $6,800. Books/supplies: $840. Personal expenses: $1,160.

2005-2006 Financial aid. Need-based: 568 full-time freshmen applied for aid; 462 were judged to have need; 462 of these received aid. Average need met was 79%. Average scholarship/grant was $9,817; average loan $3,979. 58% of total undergraduate aid awarded as scholarships/grants, 42% as loans/jobs. **Non-need-based:** Scholarships awarded for academics, alumni affiliation, art, job skills, leadership, music/drama, religious affiliation.

Application procedures. Admission: Priority date 12/1; deadline 3/1 (postmark date). $25 fee. Application may be submitted online. Admission notification 4/1. Must reply by May 1 or within 4 week(s) if notified thereafter. **Financial aid:** Priority date 4/15; no closing date. FAFSA, institutional form required. Applicants notified on a rolling basis starting 3/1; must reply by 5/1 or within 3 week(s) of notification.

Academics. Special study options: Accelerated study, combined bachelor's/graduate degree, double major, exchange student, honors, independent study, internships, New York semester, student-designed major, study abroad, teacher certification program, urban semester, Washington semester. 3-2 pre-engineering with University of Minnesota, Case Western Reserve, Washington University, American Studies Program, Washington DC Au Sable Inst. Environmental Studies Program, Urban Studies-Chicago, Los Angeles Film Studies Center. **Credit/placement by examination:** AP, CLEP, institutional tests. 32 credit hours maximum toward associate degree, 32 toward bachelor's. **Support services:** Learning center, reduced course load, study skills assistance, tutoring, writing center.

Majors. Biology: General, Biochemistry/biophysics and molecular biology. **Business:** Business admin. **Communications:** General, journalism, media studies. **Computer sciences:** General. **Conservation:** Environmental science, environmental studies. **Education:** Art, biology, business, chemistry, early childhood, elementary, English, ESL, French, health, kindergarten/preschool, mathematics, music, physical, physics, social studies, Spanish. **Engineering:** Science. **English:** Composition, English lit. **Foreign languages:** French, Spanish. **Health:** Athletic training, community health services, nursing (RN). **History:** General. **Interdisciplinary:** Peace/conflict. **Math:** General. **Parks/recreation:** Health/fitness. **Philosophy/religion:** Philosophy. **Physical sciences:** Chemistry, physics. **Psychology:** General. **Public administration:** Social work. **Social sciences:** General, economics, international relations, political science. **Theology:** Bible, sacred music, youth ministry. **Visual/performing arts:** Art, dramatic, music performance.

Most popular majors. Business/marketing 24%, communications/journalism 6%, education 15%, health sciences 14%, theological studies 6%.

Computing on campus. 300 workstations in dormitories, library, computer center. Dormitories wired for high-speed internet access and linked to

campus network. Commuter students can connect to campus network. Online course registration, helpline, wireless network available.

Student life. Freshman orientation: Mandatory. Preregistration for classes offered. 2 days prior to the start of classes. **Policies:** High moral standards stressed. Use of tobacco and alcohol prohibited. **Housing:** Guaranteed on-campus for freshmen. Coed dorms, special housing for disabled, apartments, substance-free housing available. $150 fully refundable deposit. **Activities:** Bands, choral groups, dance, drama, literary magazine, music ensembles, musical theater, radio station, student government, student newspaper, symphony orchestra, TV station, campus and community ministries, United Cultures of Bethel, administrative fellowship groups, College Republicans, Habitat for Humanity, dormitory discipleship programs.

Athletics. NCAA. **Intercollegiate:** Baseball M, basketball, cross-country, football (tackle) M, golf M, ice hockey, soccer, softball W, tennis, track and field, volleyball W. **Intramural:** Badminton, basketball, football (non-tackle), golf, racquetball, softball, table tennis, tennis, track and field, volleyball. **Team name:** Royals.

Student services. Adult student services, alcohol/substance abuse counseling, campus ministries, career counseling, student employment services, financial aid counseling, health services, minority student services, personal counseling, placement for graduates. **Physically disabled:** Services for visually, hearing impaired.

Contact. E-mail: BUadmissions-cas@bethel.edu
Phone: (651) 638-6242 Toll-free number: (800) 255-8706 ext. 6242
Fax: (651) 635-1490
Jay Fedje, Director of Admissions, Bethel University, 3900 Bethel Drive, Saint Paul, MN 55112-6999

Brown College
Mendota Heights, Minnesota
www.browncollege.edu **CB code: 1210**

- For-profit 4-year business, liberal arts and technical college
- Commuter campus in small city
- 1,760 degree-seeking undergraduates: 49% women
- Interview required
- 72% graduate within 6 years

General. Founded in 1946. Accredited by ACCSCT. **Degrees:** 52 bachelor's, 1,090 associate awarded. **Location:** 14 miles from Minneapolis-St. Paul. **Calendar:** Quarter, extensive summer session. **Full-time faculty:** 78 total; 28% women. **Part-time faculty:** 44 total; 36% women.

Freshman class profile. 352 enrolled.

Basis for selection. Open admission. ACCUPLACER Test Required in lieu of other tests. **Learning Disabled:** IEP's and/or other requests for ADA-level Accomodations accepted. Eligible students must complete brief Application for Auxiliary Aid and return with any supporting documentation available well in advance of enrollment.

High school preparation. Recommended units include English 4, mathematics 2 and science 1.

2005-2006 Annual costs. Tuition/fees: $18,540. Books/supplies: $2,000. Personal expenses: $1,600.

Financial aid. Non-need-based: Scholarships awarded for academics.

Application procedures. Admission: No deadline. $50 fee. Application may be submitted online. Admission notification on a rolling basis beginning on or about 1/1. **Financial aid:** Priority date 7/1; no closing date. FAFSA, institutional form required. Applicants notified on a rolling basis starting 1/1; must reply within 2 week(s) of notification.

Academics. Special study options: Cooperative education, internships, liberal arts/career combination. **Credit/placement by examination:** AP, CLEP, institutional tests. **Support services:** Learning center, reduced course load, remedial instruction, study skills assistance, tutoring, writing center.

Majors. Business: General. **Communications:** General. **Communications technology:** Graphics. **Computer sciences:** Information systems, information technology. **Protective services:** Criminal justice. **Visual/performing arts:** Design.

Computing on campus. 231 workstations in library, computer center, student center. Commuter students can connect to campus network. Online course registration, online library, helpline, repair service available.

Student life. Freshman orientation: Mandatory. **Policies:** Freshmen permitted cars on campus. **Housing:** Apartments available. **Activities:** Radio station, student government, student senate, Campus Crusade for Christ, minority students club.

Athletics. Intramural: Football (non-tackle) M.

Student services. Adult student services, career counseling, student employment services, financial aid counseling, placement for graduates.

Contact. E-mail: info@browncollege.edu
Phone: (651) 905-3240 Toll-free number: (800) 627-6966 ext. 240
Fax: (651) 905-3540
Lee Kurimay, Vice President, Admissions, Brown College, 1440 Northland Drive, Mendota Heights, MN 55120

Capella University
Minneapolis, Minnesota
www.capellauniversity.edu **CB code: 3829**

- For-profit 4-year virtual university
- Very large city
- 2,358 degree-seeking undergraduates

General. Regionally accredited. Over 600 courses and 70 degree programs and specializations offered online. **Degrees:** 225 bachelor's awarded; master's, doctoral offered. **Calendar:** Quarter, limited summer session. **Full-time faculty:** 15 total. **Part-time faculty:** 138 total.

Basis for selection. Applicants must be at least 24 years of age unless in military or unless they enter with 90 college level credits from previous institution. Bachelor's programs are completion programs for students who have associate's degree or at least 90 quarter credits of undergraduate coursework completed.

2005-2006 Annual costs. Tuition/fees: $13,050. Costs vary by program. Books/supplies: $1,000.

Application procedures. Admission: No deadline. $50 fee. Application may be submitted online. Admission notification on a rolling basis.

Academics. Special study options: Combined bachelor's/graduate degree. **Credit/placement by examination:** CLEP, IB. **Support services:** Learning center.

Majors. Business: General, e-commerce, human resources, organizational behavior. **Computer sciences:** General, computer graphics, information systems, information technology, LAN/WAN management, security, web page design. **Engineering technology:** Quality control.

Computing on campus. PC or laptop required.

Contact. E-mail: info@capella.edu
Phone: (888) 227-3552
Capella University, 222 South Sixth Street, 9th Floor, Minneapolis, MN 55402

Carleton College
Northfield, Minnesota **CB member**
www.carleton.edu **CB code: 6081**

- Private 4-year liberal arts college
- Residential campus in large town
- 1,936 degree-seeking undergraduates: 52% women, 6% African American, 10% Asian American, 5% Hispanic American, 1% Native American, 6% international
- 29% of applicants admitted
- SAT or ACT with writing, application essay required
- 87% graduate within 6 years; 20% enter graduate study

General. Founded in 1866. Regionally accredited. Interest in sustainability initiatives - green roofs, eco-building class, eco house built by students, 1.65 megawatt wind turbine. **Degrees:** 500 bachelor's awarded. **Location:** 35 miles from Minneapolis-St. Paul. **Calendar:** Trimester. **Full-time faculty:** 198 total; 95% have terminal degrees, 22% minority, 42% women. **Part-time faculty:** 18 total; 67% have terminal degrees, 17% minority, 50% women. **Class size:** 66% < 20, 32% 20-39, 2% 40-49, less than 1% 50-99. **Special facilities:** 955 acre arboretum, 35 acre virgin prairie, greenhouse, observatory, scanning and transmission electron microscope, refractor and reflector telescopes, nuclear magnet resonance spectrometer, teaching and learning center.

Freshman class profile. 5,036 applied, 1,471 admitted, 542 enrolled.

Mid 50% test scores		End year in good standing:	99%
SAT verbal:	660-760	Return as sophomores:	97%
SAT math:	660-740	Out-of-state:	73%
ACT:	27-32	Live on campus:	100%
Rank in top quarter:	91%	International:	5%
Rank in top tenth:	71%		

Basis for selection. School achievement record and recommendations most important. Test scores, extracurricular school and community activities also important. SAT Subject Tests recommended. Interview recommended. **Learning Disabled:** Untimed standardized tests and GED accepted.

High school preparation. Recommended units include English 4, mathematics 3, social studies 3, science 3 (laboratory 1) and foreign language 3. 3 units distributed between history and social sciences recommended.

2006-2007 Annual costs. Tuition/fees: $34,272. Room/board: $8,592. Books/supplies: $600.

2004-2005 Financial aid. Need-based: 414 full-time freshmen applied for aid; 368 were judged to have need; 368 of these received aid. Average need met was 100%. Average scholarship/grant was $21,611; average loan $2,730. 73% of total undergraduate aid awarded as scholarships/grants, 27% as loans/jobs. **Non-need-based:** Awarded to 343 full-time undergraduates, including 109 freshmen. Scholarships awarded for academics. **Additional information:** Full financial need of all admitted applicants met through combination of work, loans, grants.

Application procedures. Admission: Closing date 1/15 (postmark date). $30 fee, may be waived for applicants with need. Application may be submitted online. Admission notification 4/15. Must reply by May 1 or within 2 week(s) if notified thereafter. **Financial aid:** Closing date 2/15. FAFSA, CSS PROFILE required. Applicants notified by 4/1; must reply by 5/1 or within 2 week(s) of notification.

Academics. 15-20 freshman seminars offered, enrollment limited to 15 students each. **Special study options:** Accelerated study, cross-registration, double major, dual enrollment of high school students, independent study, internships, student-designed major, study abroad, teacher certification program, urban semester. **Credit/placement by examination:** AP, CLEP, IB, institutional tests. 36 credit hours maximum toward bachelor's degree. **Support services:** Learning center, tutoring, writing center.

Majors. Area/ethnic studies: African, African-American, American, Asian, Latin American, Russian/Slavic, women's. **Biology:** General. **Computer sciences:** Computer science. **Foreign languages:** Ancient Greek, classics, French, German, Hebrew, Latin, Romance, Russian, Spanish. **History:** General. **Interdisciplinary:** Math/computer science. **Math:** General. **Philosophy/religion:** Philosophy, religion. **Physical sciences:** Chemistry, geology, physics. **Psychology:** General. **Social sciences:** Anthropology, economics, international relations, political science, sociology. **Visual/performing arts:** Art history/conservation, studio arts.

Most popular majors. Area/ethnic studies 6%, biology 11%, English 6%, foreign language 7%, physical sciences 8%, psychology 8%, social sciences 27%, visual/performing arts 9%.

Computing on campus. 247 workstations in library, computer center. Dormitories wired for high-speed internet access and linked to campus network. Online course registration, online library, helpline, wireless network available.

Student life. Freshman orientation: Mandatory. Preregistration for classes offered. 4 days prior to start of fall classes. **Housing:** Guaranteed on-campus for all undergraduates. Coed dorms, special housing for disabled, apartments, substance-free housing available. 25 college-owned houses within 2 blocks of campus, some coeducational, with varying board options. Several for special interest groups. **Activities:** Bands, choral groups, dance, drama, film society, literary magazine, music ensembles, musical theater, radio station, student government, student newspaper, symphony orchestra, 132 registered student organizations.

Athletics. NCAA. **Intercollegiate:** Baseball M, basketball, cross-country, diving, football (tackle) M, golf, soccer, softball W, swimming, synchronized swimming W, tennis, track and field, volleyball W, wrestling M. **Intramural:** Badminton, basketball, ice hockey, racquetball, soccer, softball, table tennis, tennis, volleyball. **Team name:** Knights.

Student services. Alcohol/substance abuse counseling, campus ministries, career counseling, student employment services, financial aid counseling, health services, minority student services, personal counseling, placement for graduates, women's services. **Physically disabled:** Services for visually, hearing impaired.

Contact. E-mail: admissions@acs.carleton.edu
Phone: (507) 646-4190 Toll-free number: (800) 995-2275
Fax: (507) 646-4526
Paul Thiboutot, Dean of Admissions, Carleton College, 100 South College Street, Northfield, MN 55057

College of St. Benedict

St. Joseph, Minnesota — **CB member**
www.csbsju.edu — **CB code: 6104**

- Private 4-year liberal arts college for women affiliated with Roman Catholic Church
- Residential campus in small town
- 1,992 degree-seeking undergraduates: 100% women, 1% African American, 3% Asian American, 1% Hispanic American, 4% international
- 86% of applicants admitted
- SAT or ACT (ACT writing optional), application essay required
- 77% graduate within 6 years; 16% enter graduate study

General. Founded in 1887. Regionally accredited. Coeducational academic and campus life shared with St. John's University in nearby Collegeville. Access to all St. John's University facilities. **Degrees:** 504 bachelor's awarded. **ROTC:** Army. **Location:** 10 miles from St. Cloud, 70 miles from Minneapolis-St. Paul. **Calendar:** Semester. **Full-time faculty:** 148 total; 83% have terminal degrees, 8% minority, 57% women. **Part-time faculty:** 22 total; 41% have terminal degrees, 46% women. **Class size:** 47% < 20, 52% 20-39, less than 1% 40-49, less than 1% 50-99. **Special facilities:** Fine arts complex, arboretum, museum, manuscript library, pottery kiln, observatory, nature preserve.

Freshman class profile. 1,472 applied, 1,267 admitted, 576 enrolled.

Mid 50% test scores		Rank in top quarter:	79%
SAT verbal:	520-630	Rank in top tenth:	44%
SAT math:	520-640	End year in good standing:	97%
ACT:	23-27	Return as sophomores:	88%
GPA 3.50 or higher:	82%	Out-of-state:	13%
GPA 3.0-3.49:	17%	Live on campus:	99%
GPA 2.0-2.99:	1%	International:	3%

Basis for selection. Course selection, scholastic achievement, GPA, essay, test scores most important. Extracurricular involvement, high school rank and recommendation also important. Students who have completed the application process by 12/01 will receive notification of their scholarship award on 12/20. Interview recommended for conditionally accepted/academically weak applicants. **Homeschooled:** Applicants not required to have high school diploma but are required to provide appropriate documentation of college preparatory curriculum.

High school preparation. 17 units recommended. Recommended units include English 4, mathematics 3, social studies 2, science 2 (laboratory 2), foreign language 2 and academic electives 4.

2005-2006 Annual costs. Tuition/fees: $23,454. Room/board: $6,637. Books/supplies: $800. Personal expenses: $700.

2005-2006 Financial aid. Need-based: 474 full-time freshmen applied for aid; 393 were judged to have need; 393 of these received aid. Average need met was 94%. Average scholarship/grant was $14,435; average loan $5,107. 57% of total undergraduate aid awarded as scholarships/grants, 43% as loans/jobs. **Non-need-based:** Awarded to 1,794 full-time undergraduates, including 539 freshmen. Scholarships awarded for academics, art, leadership, minority status, music/drama, ROTC.

Application procedures. Admission: Priority date 12/1; no deadline. No application fee. Application may be submitted online. Admission notification on a rolling basis beginning on or about 10/1. Non-refundable enrollment deposit due May 1. **Financial aid:** Priority date 3/15; no closing date. FAFSA, institutional form required. Applicants notified on a rolling basis starting 3/15.

Academics. Special study options: Accelerated study, combined bachelor's/graduate degree, cross-registration, double major, dual enrollment of high school students, ESL, honors, independent study, internships, liberal arts/career combination, student-designed major, study abroad, teacher certification program. Cross registration with St. Cloud State University. **Credit/placement by examination:** AP, CLEP, IB, institutional tests. **Support services:** Study skills assistance, tutoring, writing center.

Majors. Biology: General, biochemistry. **Business:** Accounting, business admin. **Computer sciences:** Computer science. **Conservation:** Environmental studies. **Education:** General, art, elementary. **English:** Speech/rhetoric. **Foreign languages:** Classics, French, German, Spanish. **Health:** Nursing

(RN), predentistry, premedicine, prepharmacy, preveterinary. **History:** General. **Interdisciplinary:** Biological/physical sciences, math/computer science, medieval/Renaissance, natural sciences, nutrition sciences, peace/conflict. **Legal studies:** Prelaw. **Liberal arts:** Arts/sciences, humanities. **Math:** General. **Philosophy/religion:** Philosophy. **Physical sciences:** Chemistry, physics. **Psychology:** General. **Public administration:** Social work. **Social sciences:** General, economics, political science, sociology. **Theology:** Preministerial, religious ed, theology. **Visual/performing arts:** Art, art history/conservation, dramatic.

Most popular majors. Biology 10%, business/marketing 12%, education 8%, English 16%, health sciences 9%, psychology 11%, social sciences 8%.

Computing on campus. 604 workstations in dormitories, library, computer center, student center. Dormitories wired for high-speed internet access and linked to campus network. Commuter students can connect to campus network. Online course registration, helpline, student web hosting available.

Student life. Freshman orientation: Mandatory. Preregistration for classes offered. Summer orientation is 1 day; parents attend with students. Fall orientation begins the evening of move-in day and concludes with Convocation the first day of classes. **Policies:** Freshmen and sophomores are required to live on campus. Freshmen permitted cars on campus. **Housing:** Guaranteed on-campus for freshmen. Special housing for disabled, apartments, substance-free housing available. Health and wellness floor, service learning/social justice floor, global initiative group, environmental living group. **Activities:** Bands, choral groups, dance, drama, literary magazine, music ensembles, musical theater, opera, radio station, student government, student newspaper, symphony orchestra, volunteers in services to others, College Republicans, College Democrats, joints events council, Asia club, student coalition for global solidarity, students in free enterprise, Magis, cultural fusion club, Outdoor Leadership Center.

Athletics. NCAA. **Intercollegiate:** Basketball W, cross-country W, diving W, golf W, ice hockey W, skiing W, soccer W, softball W, swimming W, tennis W, track and field W, volleyball W. **Intramural:** Basketball W, racquetball W, soccer W, softball W, volleyball W. **Team name:** Blazers.

Student services. Alcohol/substance abuse counseling, campus ministries, career counseling, student employment services, financial aid counseling, health services, personal counseling, placement for graduates, women's services. **Physically disabled:** Services for hearing impaired.

Contact. E-mail: admissions@csbsju.edu
Phone: (320) 363-2196 Toll-free number: (800) 544-1489
Fax: (320) 363-2750
Mary Milbert, Dean of Admission, College of St. Benedict, PO Box 7155, Collegeville, MN 56321-7155

Freshman class profile. 1,475 applied, 1,157 admitted, 413 enrolled.

Mid 50% test scores			
SAT verbal:	520-660	Rank in top quarter:	75%
SAT math:	500-650	Rank in top tenth:	34%
ACT:	22-27	Return as sophomores:	81%
GPA 3.50 or higher:	69%	Out-of-state:	15%
GPA 3.0-3.49:	25%	Live on campus:	79%
GPA 2.0-2.99:	4%	International:	2%

Basis for selection. School achievement record with rank in top half of class and test scores important. Extracurricular and community involvement also considered. Recommendations important. Interview recommended for all applicants, required for marginal students. Audition recommended for music students; portfolio recommended for art students. Essay recommended for marginal students.

High school preparation. 15 units recommended. Recommended units include English 4, mathematics 3, social studies 2, science 2 and foreign language 4.

2005-2006 Annual costs. Tuition/fees: $21,310. Room/board: $6,120. Books/supplies: $625. Personal expenses: $400.

2005-2006 Financial aid. Need-based: Average need met was 78%. Average scholarship/grant was $7,991; average loan $3,710. 50% of total undergraduate aid awarded as scholarships/grants, 50% as loans/jobs. **Non-need-based:** Scholarships awarded for academics, leadership. **Additional information:** Audition required for music scholarships.

Application procedures. Admission: No deadline. No application fee. Students must be accepted by 02/01 to be eligible to compete in merit scholarship competition. **Financial aid:** Priority date 4/15; no closing date. FAFSA, institutional form required. Applicants notified on a rolling basis starting 3/30; must reply within 2 week(s) of notification.

Academics. Special study options: Combined bachelor's/graduate degree, cross-registration, double major, dual enrollment of high school students, exchange student, honors, independent study, internships, liberal arts/career combination, student-designed major, study abroad, teacher certification program, Washington semester, weekend college. Cooperative program in fashion merchandising with Fashion Institute of Technology in New York City and Fashion Institute of Design in Los Angeles, academic year of study in New York City, exchange program with other Carondolet Colleges, internship program includes over 500 sites in Twin Cities area. **Credit/placement by examination:** AP, CLEP, IB, institutional tests. 32 credit hours maximum toward bachelor's degree. **Support services:** Learning center, reduced course load, tutoring, writing center.

Majors. Area/ethnic studies: Women's. **Biology:** General, biochemistry. **Business:** Accounting, business admin, fashion, international, management information systems, sales/distribution. **Communications:** General. **Computer sciences:** General, information systems. **Education:** General, art, business, early childhood, elementary, English, family/consumer sciences, foreign languages, mathematics, middle, music, physical, secondary. **Family/consumer sciences:** General, food/nutrition. **Foreign languages:** French, sign language interpretation, Spanish. **Health:** Clinical lab science, medical records admin, nursing (RN), predentistry, premedicine, prepharmacy, preveterinary, respiratory therapy technology. **History:** General. **Legal studies:** Prelaw. **Liberal arts:** Library science. **Math:** General. **Philosophy/religion:** Philosophy. **Physical sciences:** Chemistry, physics. **Psychology:** General. **Public administration:** Social work. **Social sciences:** General, economics, international relations, political science, sociology. **Theology:** Theology. **Visual/performing arts:** Art history/conservation, dramatic, fashion design, music performance, studio arts.

Most popular majors. Business/marketing 17%, education 9%, English 6%, health sciences 25%, public administration/social services 6%.

Computing on campus. 350 workstations in dormitories, library, computer center, student center. Dormitories wired for high-speed internet access and linked to campus network. Commuter students can connect to campus network. Helpline available.

Student life. Freshman orientation: Mandatory. **Policies:** Freshmen permitted cars on campus. **Housing:** Guaranteed on-campus for freshmen. Apartments available. Apartments for student-parents. **Activities:** Choral groups, dance, drama, literary magazine, music ensembles, musical theater, student government, student newspaper, Volunteers in Action, Campus Ministry, League of Women Voters, Minnesota Public Interest Research Group, Women of Color, international student club, clubs for majors, women's issues groups.

Athletics. NCAA. **Intercollegiate:** Basketball W, cross-country W, diving W, ice hockey W, soccer W, softball W, swimming W, tennis W, track and field W, volleyball W. **Intramural:** Basketball W, football (non-tackle) W, golf W, racquetball W, soccer W, softball W, tennis W, volleyball W. **Team name:** Wildcats.

College of St. Catherine

St. Paul, Minnesota — **CB member**
www.stkate.edu — **CB code: 6105**

- Private 4-year liberal arts college for women affiliated with Roman Catholic Church
- Commuter campus in large city
- 3,511 degree-seeking undergraduates: 33% part-time, 97% women, 8% African American, 7% Asian American, 3% Hispanic American, 2% international
- 1,302 degree-seeking graduate students
- 78% of applicants admitted
- SAT or ACT (ACT writing optional) required
- 58% graduate within 6 years

General. Founded in 1905. Regionally accredited. Men may attend classes through cross-registration. Traditional day, weekend and graduate programs offered on St. Paul campus. 2-year associate's program in various health professions at Minneapolis campus. **Degrees:** 518 bachelor's, 219 associate awarded; master's, doctoral offered. **ROTC:** Air Force. **Location:** 6 miles from downtown. **Calendar:** Differs by program, extensive summer session. **Full-time faculty:** 246 total; 7% minority, 79% women. **Part-time faculty:** 237 total; 5% minority, 78% women. **Class size:** 75% < 20, 22% 20-39, 1% 40-49, 2% 50-99. **Special facilities:** Center for women's research, observatory.

Student services. Adult student services, campus ministries, career counseling, student employment services, financial aid counseling, health services, minority student services, on-campus daycare, personal counseling, placement for graduates, women's services. **Physically disabled:** Services for visually, speech, hearing impaired.

Contact. E-mail: admissions@stkate.edu
Phone: (651) 690-6505 Toll-free number: (800) 656-5283
Fax: (651) 690-8824
Cal Mosley, Assistant Director of Admissions, College of St. Catherine, 2004 Randolph Avenue, St. Paul, MN 55105

College of St. Scholastica

Duluth, Minnesota — **CB member**
www.css.edu — **CB code: 6107**

- Private 4-year liberal arts college affiliated with Roman Catholic Church
- Residential campus in small city
- 1,986 degree-seeking undergraduates: 5% part-time, 72% women, 1% African American, 2% Asian American, 1% Hispanic American, 2% Native American, 3% international
- 441 degree-seeking graduate students
- 87% of applicants admitted
- SAT or ACT (ACT writing optional) required
- 62% graduate within 6 years; 29% enter graduate study

General. Founded in 1912. Regionally accredited. **Degrees:** 568 bachelor's awarded; master's, first professional offered. **ROTC:** Air Force. **Location:** 2 miles from downtown, 150 miles from Minneapolis-St. Paul. **Calendar:** Semester, limited summer session. **Full-time faculty:** 142 total; 56% have terminal degrees, 6% minority, 61% women. **Part-time faculty:** 110 total; 19% have terminal degrees, 4% minority, 69% women. **Class size:** 50% < 20, 43% 20-39, 2% 40-49, 4% 50-99, 1% >100. **Special facilities:** Wellness center with Climbing Wall.

Freshman class profile. 1,459 applied, 1,268 admitted, 490 enrolled.

Mid 50% test scores		**Rank in top quarter:**	54%
SAT verbal:	490-600	**Rank in top tenth:**	25%
SAT math:	520-620	**End year in good standing:**	86%
ACT:	21-26	**Return as sophomores:**	77%
GPA 3.50 or higher:	58%	**Out-of-state:**	10%
GPA 3.0-3.49:	28%	**Live on campus:**	84%
GPA 2.0-2.99:	14%	**International:**	4%

Basis for selection. School achievement record and test scores most important. Interview recommended.

High school preparation. Recommended units include English 4, mathematics 2, social studies 3, history 3, science 3 and foreign language 3.

2005-2006 Annual costs. Tuition/fees: $22,240. Room/board: $6,216. Books/supplies: $850. Personal expenses: $932.

2005-2006 Financial aid. Need-based: 429 full-time freshmen applied for aid; 376 were judged to have need; 374 of these received aid. Average need met was 80%. Average scholarship/grant was $4,877; average loan $3,368. 59% of total undergraduate aid awarded as scholarships/grants, 41% as loans/jobs. **Non-need-based:** Awarded to 1,628 full-time undergraduates, including 450 freshmen. Scholarships awarded for academics, alumni affiliation, religious affiliation, ROTC.

Application procedures. Admission: No deadline. $25 fee, may be waived for applicants with need. Application may be submitted online. Admission notification on a rolling basis beginning on or about 9/1. Must reply by May 1 or within 4 week(s) if notified thereafter. **Financial aid:** Priority date 3/15; no closing date. FAFSA, institutional form required. Applicants notified on a rolling basis starting 3/1; must reply by 5/1 or within 2 week(s) of notification.

Academics. Special study options: Accelerated study, combined bachelor's/graduate degree, cross-registration, distance learning, double major, dual enrollment of high school students, external degree, honors, independent study, internships, liberal arts/career combination, student-designed major, study abroad, teacher certification program, Washington semester. **Credit/placement by examination:** AP, CLEP, IB, institutional tests. 96 credit hours maximum toward bachelor's degree. All external credit meeting score expectations will be accepted; last 32 semester hours must be completed in residence. **Support services:** Pre-admission summer program, reduced course load, study skills assistance, tutoring, writing center.

Honors college/program. Should meet 2 of the following: top 15% of high school class, 26 ACT or 1100 (exclusive of Writing) SAT, GPA of 3.5; others may apply by contacting the honors director. Students must complete 20 honors credits, at least 8 of which are upper-level credits.

Majors. Biology: General, biochemistry, exercise physiology. **Business:** Accounting, business admin, marketing, organizational behavior. **Communications:** General, advertising. **Computer sciences:** General. **Education:** Elementary, school librarian, social studies. **English:** English lit. **Health:** Health services, medical records admin, nursing (RN). **History:** General. **Interdisciplinary:** Global studies. **Liberal arts:** Arts/sciences, humanities. **Math:** General. **Philosophy/religion:** Religion. **Physical sciences:** Chemistry. **Psychology:** General. **Public administration:** Social work. **Social sciences:** General, applied economics. **Visual/performing arts:** Music performance.

Most popular majors. Biology 6%, business/marketing 30%, computer/information sciences 9%, health sciences 29%, social sciences 7%.

Computing on campus. 183 workstations in dormitories, library, computer center, student center. Dormitories wired for high-speed internet access and linked to campus network. Commuter students can connect to campus network. Online library, helpline, student web hosting, wireless network available.

Student life. Freshman orientation: Mandatory. Preregistration for classes offered. Combines academic advising with social activities. **Policies:** Freshmen permitted cars on campus. **Housing:** Guaranteed on-campus for freshmen. Coed dorms, special housing for disabled, apartments, substance-free housing available. $150 deposit, deadline 5/1. Quiet or study wing; apartments for students with dependent children. **Activities:** Bands, choral groups, dance, drama, literary magazine, music ensembles, student government, student newspaper, TV station, Circle-K, InterVarsity Christian Fellowship, international club, Booshkeginiin (American Indian student organization), Benedictine Friends, volunteers involved through action, Amnesty International, Kaleidoscope multicultural club, Habitat for Humanity, United for Africa.

Athletics. NAIA, NCAA. **Intercollegiate:** Baseball M, basketball, cross-country, ice hockey M, soccer, softball W, tennis, track and field, volleyball W. **Intramural:** Badminton, basketball, bowling, football (non-tackle), volleyball. **Team name:** Saints.

Student services. Adult student services, alcohol/substance abuse counseling, campus ministries, career counseling, student employment services, financial aid counseling, health services, minority student services, personal counseling, placement for graduates, veterans' counselor, women's services. **Physically disabled:** Services for visually, hearing impaired.

Contact. E-mail: admissions@css.edu
Phone: (218) 723-6046 Toll-free number: (800) 249-6412
Fax: (218) 723-5991
Brian Dalton, Vice President for Enrollment Management, College of St. Scholastica, 1200 Kenwood Avenue, Duluth, MN 55811-4199

College of Visual Arts

St. Paul, Minnesota
www.cva.edu — **CB code: 6147**

- Private 4-year visual arts college
- Commuter campus in large city
- 190 degree-seeking undergraduates: 8% part-time, 60% women
- SAT or ACT (ACT writing optional), application essay required
- 29% graduate within 6 years

General. Founded in 1924. Regionally accredited. **Degrees:** 47 bachelor's awarded. **Calendar:** Semester, limited summer session. **Full-time faculty:** 10 total. **Part-time faculty:** 50 total. **Special facilities:** Photography facilities, sculpture studio, printmaking studio, drawing studio, painting studio.

Freshman class profile. 61 admitted, 42 enrolled.

Mid 50% test scores		**Return as sophomores:**	60%
ACT:	18-24	**Out-of-state:**	20%
End year in good standing:	87%		

Basis for selection. Personal statement, test scores, transcript and portfolio very important. Portfolio required. **Learning Disabled:** Documentation of disabilities required.

High school preparation. Recommended units include English 4, mathematics 4, social studies 4, science 6 and foreign language 2. 2 years art preferred.

2005-2006 Annual costs. Tuition/fees: $18,040. Books/supplies: $2,071. Personal expenses: $1,868.

2005-2006 Financial aid. **Need-based:** Average need met was 36%. Average scholarship/grant was $4,766; average loan $2,113. 26% of total undergraduate aid awarded as scholarships/grants, 74% as loans/jobs. **Non-need-based:** Scholarships awarded for academics, art.

Application procedures. **Admission:** Priority date 3/1; no deadline. $40 fee, may be waived for applicants with need. Application may be submitted online. Admission notification on a rolling basis. Must reply by May 1 or within 2 week(s) if notified thereafter. **Financial aid:** Priority date 4/15, closing date 6/1. FAFSA, institutional form required. Applicants notified on a rolling basis starting 1/1; must reply within 2 week(s) of notification.

Academics. **Special study options:** Honors, independent study, internships, study abroad. **Credit/placement by examination:** AP, CLEP. **Support services:** Learning center, remedial instruction, study skills assistance, tutoring, writing center.

Majors. **Visual/performing arts:** Commercial/advertising art, design, drawing, illustration, painting, photography, printmaking, sculpture, studio arts.

Computing on campus. 52 workstations in library, computer center. Online library available.

Student life. **Freshman orientation:** Mandatory. Preregistration for classes offered. **Policies:** Freshmen permitted cars on campus. **Housing:** Housing coordinator and roommate matching services. **Activities:** Student government.

Student services. Career counseling, financial aid counseling, personal counseling, placement for graduates.

Contact. E-mail: info@cva.edu
Phone: (651) 224-3416 Toll-free number: (800) 224-1536
Fax: (651) 224-8854
Jane Nordhorn, Director of Admissions, College of Visual Arts, 344 Summit Avenue, St. Paul, MN 55102-2199

Concordia College: Moorhead

Moorhead, Minnesota — **CB member**
www.concordiacollege.edu — **CB code: 6113**

- Private 4-year liberal arts college affiliated with Evangelical Lutheran Church in America
- Residential campus in small city
- 2,686 degree-seeking undergraduates: 1% part-time, 63% women, 1% African American, 2% Asian American, 1% Hispanic American, 4% international
- 5 degree-seeking graduate students
- 83% of applicants admitted
- SAT or ACT (ACT writing optional) required
- 63% graduate within 6 years

General. Founded in 1891. Regionally accredited. **Degrees:** 625 bachelor's awarded; master's offered. **ROTC:** Army, Air Force. **Location:** 234 miles from Minneapolis-St. Paul, 1 mile from Fargo, North Dakota. **Calendar:** Semester, limited summer session. **Full-time faculty:** 190 total; 73% have terminal degrees, 7% minority, 46% women. **Part-time faculty:** 62 total; 16% have terminal degrees, 3% minority. **Class size:** 45% < 20, 50% 20-39, 3% 40-49, 2% 50-99. **Special facilities:** Observatory, microparticle accelerator, language villages, television production studio, biology research facility, nursing lab.

Freshman class profile. 2,645 applied, 2,206 admitted, 796 enrolled.

Mid 50% test scores			
SAT verbal:	500-620	Rank in top tenth:	30%
SAT math:	490-620	Return as sophomores:	79%
ACT:	21-27	Out-of-state:	28%
Rank in top quarter:	59%	Live on campus:	92%
		International:	3%

Basis for selection. Academic record (types of courses and grades) most important, followed by test scores and recommendations. Interview recommended.

High school preparation. 15 units required; 17 recommended. Required and recommended units include English 4, mathematics 3, social studies 3, science 3, foreign language 2 and academic electives 2. Computer science and exposure to fine arts recommended.

2005-2006 Annual costs. Tuition/fees: $19,520. Room/board: $4,990. Books/supplies: $700. Personal expenses: $900.

2004-2005 Financial aid. All financial aid based on need. 668 full-time freshmen applied for aid; 547 were judged to have need; 547 of these received aid. Average need met was 93%. Average scholarship/grant was $9,972; average loan $4,794. 89% of total undergraduate aid awarded as scholarships/grants, 11% as loans/jobs. **Additional information:** Students in ACCORD program (age 25 and older) may apply for tuition reductions for first 4 courses.

Application procedures. **Admission:** No deadline. $20 fee, may be waived for applicants with need. Application may be submitted online. Admission notification on a rolling basis beginning on or about 7/1. **Financial aid:** Priority date 4/15; no closing date. FAFSA, institutional form required. Applicants notified on a rolling basis starting 2/15.

Academics. **Special study options:** Accelerated study, cooperative education, cross-registration, double major, dual enrollment of high school students, exchange student, honors, independent study, internships, liberal arts/career combination, semester at sea, study abroad, teacher certification program, urban semester, Washington semester. Urban studies program in Chicago, Lutheran Consortium with Dar es Salaam University in Tanzania; master of science in nursing offered through consortium with Minnesota State University Moorhead and North Dakota State University. **Credit/placement by examination:** AP, CLEP, IB, SAT, ACT, institutional tests. 20 credit hours maximum toward bachelor's degree. **Support services:** Learning center, reduced course load, study skills assistance, tutoring, writing center.

Majors. **Area/ethnic studies:** French, German, Russian/Slavic, Scandinavian, Spanish/Iberian. **Biology:** General. **Business:** General, accounting, business admin, international, office management. **Communications:** General, advertising, broadcast journalism, journalism, media studies, public relations. **Computer sciences:** Computer science. **Conservation:** Environmental studies. **Education:** General, art, biology, business, chemistry, elementary, English, French, German, health, history, Latin, mathematics, music, physical, physics, science, secondary, social science, social studies, Spanish, speech. **English:** American lit, British lit, composition, creative writing. **Family/consumer sciences:** General, clothing/textiles, family studies, food/nutrition. **Foreign languages:** Classics, French, German, Latin, Russian, Scandinavian, Spanish. **Health:** Clinical lab science, facilities admin, health care admin, nursing (RN), predentistry, premedicine, prepharmacy, preveterinary. **History:** General. **Interdisciplinary:** Math/computer science. **Legal studies:** Prelaw. **Liberal arts:** Arts/sciences. **Math:** General, applied. **Parks/recreation:** Exercise sciences, health/fitness. **Philosophy/religion:** Philosophy, religion. **Physical sciences:** Chemistry, physics. **Psychology:** General. **Public administration:** Social work. **Social sciences:** Economics, international relations, political science, sociology. **Theology:** Theology. **Visual/performing arts:** Art, art history/conservation, conducting, dramatic, music performance, piano/organ, studio arts, voice/opera.

Most popular majors. Biology 8%, business/marketing 20%, education 20%, English 7%, foreign language 9%, psychology 7%, visual/performing arts 7%.

Computing on campus. 400 workstations in dormitories, library, computer center, student center. Dormitories wired for high-speed internet access and linked to campus network. Commuter students can connect to campus network. Online library, repair service, student web hosting available.

Student life. **Freshman orientation:** Mandatory. Preregistration for classes offered. 4-day program one week prior to fall semester. **Policies:** Freshmen permitted cars on campus. **Housing:** Guaranteed on-campus for freshmen. Single-sex dorms, apartments, substance-free housing available. $200 deposit. Students studying Spanish, French, or German have opportunity to live with native speakers in campus apartments. **Activities:** Bands, choral groups, dance, drama, film society, literary magazine, music ensembles, musical theater, radio station, student government, student newspaper, symphony orchestra, TV station, 80 clubs and organizations.

Athletics. NCAA. **Intercollegiate:** Baseball M, basketball, cross-country, diving W, football (tackle) M, golf, ice hockey, soccer, softball W, swimming W, tennis, track and field, volleyball W, wrestling M. **Intramural:** Badminton, baseball M, basketball, bowling, cross-country, football (non-tackle), golf, ice hockey, racquetball, rugby, skiing, soccer, softball, swimming, table tennis, tennis, track and field, volleyball, weight lifting. **Team name:** Cobbers.

Student services. Adult student services, alcohol/substance abuse counseling, campus ministries, career counseling, student employment services, financial aid counseling, health services, minority student services, on-campus daycare, personal counseling, placement for graduates. **Physically disabled:** Services for visually, speech, hearing impaired.

Contact. E-mail: admissions@cord.edu
Phone: (218) 299-3004 Toll-free number: (800) 699-9897
Fax: (218) 299-4720
Lee Johnson, Admissions Director, Concordia College: Moorhead, 901 Eighth Street South, Moorhead, MN 56562-9981

Concordia University: St. Paul

St. Paul, Minnesota **CB member**
www.csp.edu **CB code: 6114**

- Private 4-year university affiliated with Lutheran Church - Missouri Synod
- Commuter campus in large city
- 1,594 degree-seeking undergraduates: 9% part-time, 61% women, 7% African American, 5% Asian American, 2% Hispanic American
- 333 degree-seeking graduate students
- 64% of applicants admitted
- ACT (writing optional) required
- 42% graduate within 6 years

General. Founded in 1893. Regionally accredited. **Degrees:** 543 bachelor's, 5 associate awarded; master's offered. **ROTC:** Army, Navy, Air Force. **Calendar:** Semester, limited summer session. **Full-time faculty:** 82 total; 66% have terminal degrees, 5% minority, 40% women. **Part-time faculty:** 385 total; 6% minority, 46% women. **Class size:** 81% < 20, 18% 20-39, less than 1% 40-49.

Freshman class profile. 651 applied, 415 admitted, 165 enrolled.

Mid 50% test scores			
SAT verbal:	390-630	Rank in top quarter:	33%
SAT math:	430-600	Rank in top tenth:	16%
ACT:	18-25	End year in good standing:	83%
GPA 3.50 or higher:	39%	Return as sophomores:	74%
GPA 3.0-3.49:	22%	Out-of-state:	26%
GPA 2.0-2.99:	35%	Live on campus:	85%

Basis for selection. School record, test scores, recommendations important. Interview recommended.

High school preparation. 15 units required; 16 recommended. Required and recommended units include English 4, mathematics 2, social studies 1, history 1, science 2 (laboratory 2) and foreign language 1. 2 units of fine arts, 1 unit of health/physical education.

2006-2007 Annual costs. Tuition/fees: $22,378. Room/board: $6,596. Books/supplies: $600. Personal expenses: $900.

2005-2006 Financial aid. Need-based: 163 full-time freshmen applied for aid; 140 were judged to have need; 140 of these received aid. Average need met was 78%. Average scholarship/grant was $13,391; average loan $2,748. 49% of total undergraduate aid awarded as scholarships/grants, 51% as loans/jobs. **Non-need-based:** Awarded to 128 full-time undergraduates, including 31 freshmen. Scholarships awarded for academics, art, athletics, minority status, music/drama, religious affiliation. **Additional information:** Church districts and local congregations are major sources of aid for church-vocation students.

Application procedures. Admission: Priority date 5/1; deadline 8/1 (receipt date). $30 fee, may be waived for applicants with need. Application may be submitted online. Admission notification on a rolling basis. **Financial aid:** Priority date 5/1; no closing date. FAFSA, institutional form required. Applicants notified on a rolling basis starting 3/1; must reply within 3 week(s) of notification.

Academics. Special study options: Accelerated study, cross-registration, distance learning, double major, dual enrollment of high school students, exchange student, honors, independent study, internships, study abroad, teacher certification program. **Credit/placement by examination:** AP, CLEP, IB, institutional tests. **Support services:** Learning center, reduced course load, study skills assistance, tutoring, writing center.

Majors. Biology: General. **Business:** Accounting, business admin, finance, management information systems, marketing, organizational behavior. **Communications:** Media studies. **Conservation:** Environmental science. **Education:** Art, bilingual, biology, chemistry, early childhood, elementary, English, ESL, health, history, kindergarten/preschool, mathematics, middle, music, physical, science, secondary, social studies. **English:** English lit. **Family/consumer sciences:** Child care. **History:** General. **Interdisciplinary:** Biological/physical sciences. **Math:** General. **Parks/recreation:** Exercise sciences, health/fitness. **Protective services:** Criminal justice, law enforcement admin. **Psychology:** General. **Public administration:** Human services, youth services. **Social sciences:** Sociology. **Theology:** Bible, missionary, religious ed, sacred music, theology. **Visual/performing arts:** Art, dramatic, studio arts.

Most popular majors. Business/marketing 56%, education 11%, family/consumer sciences 6%, security/protective services 6%.

Computing on campus. PC or laptop required. Dormitories wired for high-speed internet access and linked to campus network. Commuter students can connect to campus network. Helpline, repair service, wireless network available.

Student life. Freshman orientation: Mandatory. 3-day program provides information about student life, support services, social programs, employment opportunities, and technology training. **Policies:** Freshmen permitted cars on campus. **Housing:** Guaranteed on-campus for freshmen. Coed dorms, single-sex dorms, special housing for disabled, apartments, substance-free housing available. $125 deposit. **Activities:** Bands, choral groups, dance, drama, music ensembles, musical theater, student government, student newspaper, TV station, Fellowship of Christian Athletes, Lutherans for Life, Southeast Asian student association, United Minds of Joint Action, student senate, mission society.

Athletics. NCAA. **Intercollegiate:** Baseball M, basketball, cross-country, football (tackle) M, golf, soccer W, softball W, track and field, volleyball W. **Intramural:** Basketball, bowling, football (non-tackle), racquetball, skiing, soccer, softball, table tennis, volleyball. **Team name:** Golden Bears.

Student services. Adult student services, alcohol/substance abuse counseling, campus ministries, career counseling, services for economically disadvantaged, student employment services, financial aid counseling, health services, minority student services, on-campus daycare, personal counseling, placement for graduates. **Physically disabled:** Services for visually, speech, hearing impaired.

Contact. E-mail: admiss@csp.edu
Phone: (651) 641-8230 Toll-free number: (800) 333-4705
Fax: (651) 603-6320
Scott Morrell, VP for University Admission & Marketing, Concordia University: St. Paul, 275 Syndicate Street North, St. Paul, MN 55104-5494

Crossroads College

Rochester, Minnesota
www.crossroadscollege.edu **CB code: 6412**

- Private 4-year Bible college affiliated with Christian Church
- Residential campus in small city
- 165 degree-seeking undergraduates
- SAT or ACT (ACT writing optional), application essay required

General. Founded in 1913. Accredited by ABHE. **Degrees:** 20 bachelor's, 15 associate awarded. **Location:** 85 miles from Minneapolis-St. Paul. **Calendar:** Semester. **Full-time faculty:** 12 total. **Part-time faculty:** 13 total. **Class size:** 79% < 20, 16% 20-39, 2% 40-49, 4% 50-99. **Special facilities:** 38-acre wooded area with nature trails, pond.

Freshman class profile. 26 enrolled.

Mid 50% test scores		Out-of-state:	31%
ACT:	17-23	Live on campus:	92%
Rank in top quarter:	58%		

Basis for selection. High school rank, experience, aptitude for Christian ministry, character references, and personal statement of goals considered. High school GPA, rank and ACT/SAT scores determine number of credit hours a student may take during first semester if accepted. Interview recommended. **Learning Disabled:** Provide Vice President of Student Development with verification of learning disability.

2006-2007 Annual costs. Tuition/fees (projected): $9,530. Room only: $3,400. Books/supplies: $600. Personal expenses: $1,500.

2004-2005 Financial aid. Need-based: 57% of total undergraduate aid awarded as scholarships/grants, 43% as loans/jobs. **Non-need-based:** Scholarships awarded for academics, leadership, music/drama, religious affiliation.

Application procedures. Admission: Closing date 8/15 (receipt date). $30 fee. Admission notification on a rolling basis. **Financial aid:** Priority date 4/1; no closing date. FAFSA, institutional form required. Applicants notified on a rolling basis starting 2/1; must reply within 4 week(s) of notification.

Academics. Minors in religious music, counseling psychology, biblical and classical languages, missions, youth ministries. **Special study options:** Double major, independent study, internships, liberal arts/career combination, student-designed major. **Credit/placement by examination:** AP, CLEP, institutional tests. 30 credit hours maximum toward bachelor's degree. **Support services:** Reduced course load, remedial instruction, study skills assistance, tutoring, writing center.

Majors. Psychology: Counseling. **Theology:** Missionary, religious ed, sacred music, theology, youth ministry.

Computing on campus. 17 workstations in library, computer center. Dormitories wired for high-speed internet access. Wireless network available.

Student life. Freshman orientation: Mandatory. Preregistration for classes offered. 2-day session with some placement testing in August; 1-day session in January. **Policies:** Attendance required at weekly Chapel and Spiritual Formation Group meetings; Field Service participation required. Religious observance required. Freshmen permitted cars on campus. **Housing:** Guaranteed on-campus for freshmen. Single-sex dorms, apartments, substance-free housing available. **Activities:** Choral groups, drama, music ensembles, student government, student newspaper, Christians outdoors, ambassadors [missions-minded] group, international students fellowship.

Athletics. Intercollegiate: Baseball M, basketball, golf M, soccer M, softball W, tennis, volleyball. **Intramural:** Bowling, golf, ice hockey, racquetball, skiing, soccer W, swimming, table tennis, tennis, volleyball. **Team name:** Knights.

Student services. Campus ministries, career counseling, student employment services, financial aid counseling, personal counseling, placement for graduates, veterans' counselor.

Contact. E-mail: admissions@crossroads.edu
Phone: (507) 288-4563 ext. 313 Toll-free number: (800) 456-7651
Fax: (507) 288-9046
Scott Klaehn, Director of Admissions, Crossroads College, 920 Mayowood Road SW, Rochester, MN 55902

Crown College
St. Bonifacius, Minnesota
www.crown.edu **CB code: 6639**

- Private 4-year Bible and liberal arts college affiliated with Christian and Missionary Alliance
- Residential campus in small town
- 1,054 degree-seeking undergraduates: 24% part-time, 59% women, 3% African American, 6% Asian American, 2% Hispanic American, 1% Native American
- 99 degree-seeking graduate students
- 71% of applicants admitted
- SAT or ACT (ACT writing optional), application essay required
- 48% graduate within 6 years

General. Founded in 1916. Regionally accredited; also accredited by ABHE. **Degrees:** 155 bachelor's, 23 associate awarded; master's offered. **Location:** 25 miles from Minneapolis-St. Paul. **Calendar:** Semester, limited summer session. **Full-time faculty:** 39 total; 59% have terminal degrees, 8% minority, 15% women. **Part-time faculty:** 25 total; 8% have terminal degrees, 52% women. **Class size:** 69% < 20, 28% 20-39, 3% 40-49.

Freshman class profile. 435 applied, 311 admitted, 170 enrolled.

Mid 50% test scores		**Rank in top quarter:**	28%
SAT verbal:	490-620	**Rank in top tenth:**	13%
SAT math:	440-610	**Return as sophomores:**	72%
ACT:	19-24	**Out-of-state:**	30%
GPA 3.50 or higher:	40%	**Live on campus:**	80%
GPA 3.0-3.49:	23%	**International:**	1%
GPA 2.0-2.99:	32%		

Basis for selection. Applicants must profess personal faith in Jesus Christ. Pastor's and general recommendations very important, academic records and test scores important. **Learning Disabled:** Applicant should meet with director of academic support.

High school preparation. Recommended units include English 4, mathematics 3, social studies 3, science 3 and foreign language 2.

2006-2007 Annual costs. Tuition/fees (projected): $17,054. Room/board: $6,654. Books/supplies: $1,400. Personal expenses: $2,120.

2005-2006 Financial aid. Need-based: 151 full-time freshmen applied for aid; 137 were judged to have need; 137 of these received aid. Average need met was 57%. Average scholarship/grant was $4,036; average loan $3,193. 45% of total undergraduate aid awarded as scholarships/grants, 55% as loans/jobs. **Non-need-based:** Awarded to 524 full-time undergraduates, including 141 freshmen. Scholarships awarded for academics, alumni affiliation, leadership, minority status, music/drama, religious affiliation.

Application procedures. Admission: Closing date 8/18 (postmark date). $35 fee, may be waived for applicants with need. Application may be submitted online. Admission notification on a rolling basis. **Financial aid:** Priority date 4/1, closing date 8/1. FAFSA, institutional form required. Applicants notified on a rolling basis starting 4/1; must reply within 4 week(s) of notification.

Academics. Special study options: Accelerated study, distance learning, double major, dual enrollment of high school students, ESL, honors, independent study, internships, liberal arts/career combination, study abroad, teacher certification program, weekend college. 2-2 with nonaccredited Bible colleges. **Credit/placement by examination:** AP, CLEP, IB, ACT, institutional tests. 30 credit hours maximum toward associate degree, 30 toward bachelor's. **Support services:** Learning center, reduced course load, remedial instruction, study skills assistance, tutoring, writing center.

Majors. Biology: General. **Business:** General, business admin. **Computer sciences:** General, information systems, information technology. **Education:** Early childhood, elementary, English, history, music, secondary, social studies. **English:** English lit. **Foreign languages:** Linguistics. **History:** General. **Liberal arts:** Arts/sciences. **Parks/recreation:** Sports admin. **Physical sciences:** General. **Psychology:** General. **Public administration:** Youth services. **Theology:** Bible, missionary, pastoral counseling, religious ed, theology, youth ministry. **Visual/performing arts:** Music performance.

Most popular majors. Business/marketing 18%, education 12%, family/consumer sciences 9%, psychology 7%, theological studies 35%.

Computing on campus. PC or laptop required. 60 workstations in library, computer center. Dormitories wired for high-speed internet access and linked to campus network. Commuter students can connect to campus network. Online library, helpline, wireless network available.

Student life. Freshman orientation: Available. Preregistration for classes offered. 2-day orientation porgram at the beginning of the spring semester. **Policies:** Religious observance required. Freshmen permitted cars on campus. **Housing:** Guaranteed on-campus for all undergraduates. Single-sex dorms, special housing for disabled, apartments, substance-free housing available. $50 fully refundable deposit. **Activities:** Bands, choral groups, drama, literary magazine, music ensembles, musical theater, student government, student newspaper, Christian service groups, mission support groups, Student Missionary Society, ethnic clubs, activity planning group, student family association, Intercultural Experiences, College Republicans, Missionary Cabinet.

Athletics. NCAA, NCCAA. **Intercollegiate:** Baseball M, basketball, cross-country, football (tackle) M, golf, soccer, softball W, volleyball W. **Intramural:** Basketball, volleyball. **Team name:** The Storm.

Student services. Adult student services, campus ministries, career counseling, student employment services, financial aid counseling, health services, personal counseling, placement for graduates. **Physically disabled:** Services for visually impaired.

Contact. E-mail: info@crown.edu
Phone: (952) 446-4142 Toll-free number: (800) 682-7696
Fax: (952) 446-4149
Mitch Fisk, Director of Admissions, Crown College, 8700 College View Drive, St. Bonifacius, MN 55375-9001

Devry University: Edina
Edina, Minnesota
www.devry.edu

- For-profit 4-year university
- Commuter campus
- 45 degree-seeking undergraduates: 64% part-time, 33% women, 9% African American, 2% Asian American, 2% Native American
- 49 graduate students

General. Degrees: 3 bachelor's awarded; master's offered. **Calendar:** Semester. **Part-time faculty:** 22 total; 14% minority, 41% women.

Basis for selection. Interview importatn, Academic GPA and recommendations considered.

Application procedures. Admission: No deadline. $50 fee. Admission notification on a rolling basis.

Academics. Credit/placement by examination: CLEP.

Contact. Phone: (877) 733-3879
Devry University: Edina, 7700 France Avenue South, Suite 575, Edina, MN 55435

Globe College

Oakdale, Minnesota
www.globecollege.com **CB code: 2296**

- For-profit 4-year business and health science college
- Commuter campus in large town
- 848 degree-seeking undergraduates
- Interview required

General. Accredited by ACICS. **Degrees:** 16 bachelor's, 125 associate awarded; master's offered. **Location:** 8 miles from Minneapolis-St. Paul. **Calendar:** Quarter, extensive summer session. **Full-time faculty:** 25 total. **Part-time faculty:** 35 total. **Class size:** 87% < 20, 13% 20-39.

Basis for selection. Open admission. **Learning Disabled:** Interview with Dean of Students.

2005-2006 Annual costs. Tuition/fees: $14,850. Books/supplies: $900.

Application procedures. Admission: No deadline. $50 fee. Application may be submitted online. Admission notification on a rolling basis. **Financial aid:** No deadline. FAFSA, institutional form required. Applicants notified on a rolling basis starting 5/1.

Academics. Special study options: Distance learning, independent study, internships, liberal arts/career combination. **Credit/placement by examination:** CLEP, institutional tests. **Support services:** Reduced course load, study skills assistance, tutoring, writing center.

Majors. Business: Accounting, business admin. **Computer sciences:** General, information technology, LAN/WAN management, security, system admin, web page design. **Engineering technology:** Computer, computer hardware, computer systems, software. **Legal studies:** Paralegal.

Computing on campus. 173 workstations in library, computer center. Commuter students can connect to campus network. Online library, helpline, repair service, wireless network available.

Student life. Freshman orientation: Mandatory. 4-hour orientation held prior to each quarter. **Policies:** Freshmen permitted cars on campus. **Activities:** Student government, student newspaper.

Student services. Career counseling, services for economically disadvantaged, student employment services, financial aid counseling, placement for graduates.

Contact. E-mail: admissions@globecollege.com
Phone: (651) 730-5100 Toll-free number: (800) 231-0660
Fax: (651) 730-5151
Christina Hilpipre, Director of Admissions, Globe College, 7166 10th Street North, Oakdale, MN 55128-5939

Gustavus Adolphus College

St. Peter, Minnesota **CB member**
www.gustavus.edu **CB code: 6253**

- Private 4-year liberal arts college affiliated with Evangelical Lutheran Church in America
- Residential campus in small town
- 2,545 degree-seeking undergraduates: 57% women, 1% African American, 4% Asian American, 2% Hispanic American, 1% international
- 79% of applicants admitted
- SAT or ACT (ACT writing optional), application essay required
- 80.6% graduate within 6 years; 39% enter graduate study

General. Founded in 1862. Regionally accredited. **Degrees:** 580 bachelor's awarded. **ROTC:** Army. **Location:** 65 miles from Minneapolis-St. Paul. **Calendar:** 4-1-4, limited summer session. **Full-time faculty:** 187 total. **Part-time faculty:** 88 total. **Class size:** 56% < 20, 37% 20-39, 4% 40-49, 3% 50-99, less than 1% >100. **Special facilities:** Aboretum with walking and skiing paths, theme gardens, native woods and prairies; art musuem.

Freshman class profile. 2,689 applied, 2,135 admitted, 705 enrolled.

Mid 50% test scores			
SAT verbal:	570-670	Rank in top tenth:	41%
SAT math:	560-680	Return as sophomores:	88%
ACT:	23-28	Out-of-state:	18%
Rank in top quarter:	71%	Live on campus:	100%
		International:	1%

Basis for selection. School achievement record, test scores, recommendations, interview, essay or personal statement, school and community activities most important. Special consideration given to children of alumni and minority applicants.

High school preparation. 17 units required; 22 recommended. Required and recommended units include English 4, mathematics 3-4, social studies 2, history 2, science 2-3 (laboratory 2-3), foreign language 2-3 and academic electives 2.

2005-2006 Annual costs. Tuition/fees: $24,735. Room/board: $6,055. Books/supplies: $800. Personal expenses: $1,000.

Financial aid. Non-need-based: Scholarships awarded for academics, alumni affiliation, music/drama, ROTC.

Application procedures. Admission: Closing date 4/1 (postmark date). No application fee. Application may be submitted online. Admission notification 4/15. Admission notification on a rolling basis beginning on or about 11/20. Must reply by May 1 or within 2 week(s) if notified thereafter. **Financial aid:** Priority date 2/15, closing date 4/15. FAFSA, institutional form required. CSS PROFILE required of students desiring a financial aid award before March 1 of their applicant year. Applicants notified on a rolling basis starting 3/1; must reply by 5/1 or within 2 week(s) of notification.

Academics. Special study options: Cooperative education, cross-registration, double major, dual enrollment of high school students, exchange student, honors, independent study, internships, liberal arts/career combination, student-designed major, study abroad, teacher certification program, Washington semester. **Credit/placement by examination:** AP, CLEP, IB, institutional tests. **Support services:** Reduced course load, study skills assistance, tutoring, writing center.

Majors. Area/ethnic studies: Japanese, Russian/Slavic, Scandinavian, women's. **Biology:** General, biochemistry. **Business:** General, accounting, international. **Communications:** General. **Computer sciences:** General, computer science. **Conservation:** General, environmental studies. **Education:** General, elementary, secondary. **Foreign languages:** Classics, French, German, Japanese, Russian, Scandinavian, Spanish. **Health:** Athletic training, nursing (RN), predentistry, premedicine, preveterinary. **History:** General. **Legal studies:** Prelaw. **Math:** General. **Parks/recreation:** Health/fitness. **Philosophy/religion:** Philosophy, religion. **Physical sciences:** Chemistry, geology, physics. **Protective services:** Criminal justice. **Psychology:** General. **Social sciences:** Anthropology, economics, geography, political science, sociology. **Theology:** Sacred music. **Visual/performing arts:** Art, art history/conservation, dance, dramatic, music performance.

Most popular majors. Biology 8%, business/marketing 12%, communications/journalism 6%, education 7%, physical sciences 6%, psychology 7%, social sciences 18%, visual/performing arts 8%.

Computing on campus. 441 workstations in dormitories, library, computer center, student center. Dormitories wired for high-speed internet access and linked to campus network. Commuter students can connect to campus network. Online course registration, online library, helpline, repair service, student web hosting available.

Student life. Freshman orientation: Mandatory, $100 fee. Preregistration for classes offered. One day in summer for class registration. Other orientation activities 3 days prior to beginning of classes. **Housing:** Guaranteed on-campus for all undergraduates. Coed dorms, special housing for disabled, apartments available. $300 deposit, deadline 5/1. **Activities:** Bands, choral groups, dance, drama, literary magazine, music ensembles, musical theater, radio station, student government, student newspaper, symphony orchestra, TV station, 29 musical organizations, 10 religious groups, 9 service organizations, 7 club sports, 31 intramural activities, student media and 30 other special interest groups.

Athletics. NCAA. **Intercollegiate:** Baseball M, basketball, cross-country, diving, football (tackle) M, golf, gymnastics W, ice hockey, skiing, soccer, softball W, swimming, tennis, track and field, volleyball W. **Intramural:** Badminton, basketball, football (non-tackle) M, golf, handball, ice hockey, lacrosse M, racquetball, rugby, skiing, soccer, softball, swimming, table tennis, tennis, volleyball. **Team name:** Gusties.

Student services. Alcohol/substance abuse counseling, campus ministries, career counseling, student employment services, financial aid counseling, health services, minority student services, personal counseling, placement for graduates, women's services. **Physically disabled:** Services for visually, hearing impaired.

Contact. E-mail: admission@gustavus.edu
Phone: (507) 933-7676 Toll-free number: (800) 487-8288
Fax: (507) 933-7474
Mark Anderson, Dean of Admissions, Gustavus Adolphus College, 800 West College Avenue, St. Peter, MN 56082

Hamline University

St. Paul, Minnesota **CB member**
www.hamline.edu **CB code: 6265**

- Private 4-year university and liberal arts college affiliated with United Methodist Church
- Residential campus in very large city
- 1,944 degree-seeking undergraduates: 2% part-time, 60% women, 3% African American, 6% Asian American, 2% Hispanic American, 1% Native American, 3% international
- 2,217 degree-seeking graduate students
- 78% of applicants admitted
- SAT or ACT (ACT writing optional), application essay required
- 68% graduate within 6 years

General. Founded in 1854. Regionally accredited. **Degrees:** 432 bachelor's awarded; master's, doctoral, first professional offered. **ROTC:** Air Force. **Location:** 5 miles from downtown. **Calendar:** 4-1-4, extensive summer session. **Full-time faculty:** 110 total; 91% have terminal degrees, 16% minority, 52% women. **Part-time faculty:** 112 total; 12% minority, 53% women. **Class size:** 51% < 20, 38% 20-39, 6% 40-49, 6% 50-99. **Special facilities:** Music hall.

Freshman class profile. 1,806 applied, 1,417 admitted, 461 enrolled.

Mid 50% test scores			
SAT verbal:	560-670	**Rank in top quarter:**	51%
SAT math:	530-640	**Rank in top tenth:**	27%
ACT:	21-27	**Return as sophomores:**	84%
GPA 3.50 or higher:	53%	**Out-of-state:**	18%
GPA 3.0-3.49:	29%	**Live on campus:**	86%
GPA 2.0-2.99:	18%	**International:**	3%

Basis for selection. Class rank, high school GPA, and selection of college-preparatory courses of primary importance. Test scores, extracurricular activities, recommendations of teacher and guidance counselor also emphasized. ACT writing exam preferred but not required. Interview recommended.

High school preparation. 20 units recommended. Recommended units include English 4, mathematics 3, social studies 4, science 3 (laboratory 3), foreign language 2 and academic electives 4.

2006-2007 Annual costs. Tuition/fees: $24,076. Room/board: $7,280. Books/supplies: $1,325.

2005-2006 Financial aid. Need-based: 443 full-time freshmen applied for aid; 354 were judged to have need; 354 of these received aid. Average need met was 77%. Average scholarship/grant was $7,413; average loan $517. 67% of total undergraduate aid awarded as scholarships/grants, 33% as loans/jobs. **Non-need-based:** Awarded to 1,355 full-time undergraduates, including 318 freshmen. Scholarships awarded for academics, alumni affiliation, art, job skills, leadership, minority status, music/drama, religious affiliation, state residency.

Application procedures. Admission: No deadline. No application fee. Application may be submitted online. Admission notification on a rolling basis beginning on or about 1/1. Must reply by May 1 or within 2 week(s) if notified thereafter. **Financial aid:** Priority date 3/1; no closing date. FAFSA, institutional form required. Applicants notified on a rolling basis starting 3/1; must reply within 2 week(s) of notification.

Academics. Intensive fall semester course for conditionally-admitted students. **Special study options:** Combined bachelor's/graduate degree, cross-registration, double major, ESL, exchange student, honors, independent study, internships, student-designed major, study abroad, teacher certification program, urban semester, Washington semester. **Credit/placement by examination:** AP, CLEP, IB. **Support services:** Learning center, study skills assistance, tutoring, writing center.

Majors. Area/ethnic studies: Asian, East Asian, European, Latin American, South Asian, Southeast Asian, women's. **Biology:** General, biochemistry. **Business:** Business admin, international. **Communications:** General. **Conservation:** Environmental studies. **Education:** General, art, elementary, ESL, health, music, physical, science, secondary. **English:** English lit. **Foreign languages:** French, German, Spanish. **Health:** Athletic training, predentistry, premedicine, preveterinary. **History:** General. **Interdisciplinary:** Peace/conflict. **Legal studies:** General, paralegal. **Math:** General. **Parks/recreation:** Exercise sciences, health/fitness. **Philosophy/religion:** Philosophy, religion. **Physical sciences:** Chemistry, physics. **Protective services:** Criminal justice. **Psychology:** General. **Social sciences:** General, anthropology, criminology, economics, international relations, political science, sociology. **Visual/performing arts:** General, art history/conservation, dramatic, music performance, music theory/composition, studio arts.

Most popular majors. Business/marketing 8%, English 6%, legal studies 6%, psychology 11%, security/protective services 7%, social sciences 25%.

Computing on campus. 200 workstations in library, computer center. Dormitories wired for high-speed internet access and linked to campus network. Commuter students can connect to campus network. Online course registration, online library, helpline, repair service, wireless network available.

Student life. Freshman orientation: Mandatory, $150 fee. 3 days immediately before classes begin. **Policies:** Freshmen permitted cars on campus. **Housing:** Guaranteed on-campus for all undergraduates. Coed dorms, special housing for disabled, apartments, fraternity/sorority housing, substance-free housing available. $50 partly refundable deposit, deadline 5/1. Black Student Alliance House, Hmong Student Association House, Spanish Language House, residence halls organized around area of interest such as arts, weekends on campus, GLBT, social justice. **Activities:** Bands, choral groups, dance, drama, literary magazine, music ensembles, musical theater, radio station, student government, student newspaper, symphony orchestra, TV station, PRIDE Black Student Alliance, MPIRG, Intervarsity Christian Fellowship, Habitat for Humanity, Asian student association, Spectrum GLBT organization, Hand in Hand mentoring program, MAMADADA Art League, Native American Student Association, Anthropological Society.

Athletics. NCAA. **Intercollegiate:** Baseball M, basketball, cross-country, diving, football (tackle) M, gymnastics W, ice hockey, soccer, softball W, swimming, tennis, track and field, volleyball W. **Intramural:** Basketball, bowling, football (non-tackle), golf M, lacrosse M, racquetball, skiing, softball, table tennis, tennis, volleyball, water polo. **Team name:** Pipers.

Student services. Alcohol/substance abuse counseling, campus ministries, career counseling, student employment services, financial aid counseling, health services, minority student services, personal counseling, placement for graduates, women's services. **Physically disabled:** Services for visually, speech, hearing impaired.

Contact. E-mail: cla-admis@hamline.edu
Phone: (651) 523-2207 Toll-free number: (800) 753-9753
Fax: (651) 523-2458
Steven Bjork, Associate Vice President for Admission and Career Services, Hamline University, 1536 Hewitt Avenue, St. Paul, MN 55104-1284

Macalester College

St. Paul, Minnesota **CB member**
www.macalester.edu **CB code: 6390**

- Private 4-year liberal arts college affiliated with Presbyterian Church (USA)
- Residential campus in large city
- 1,843 degree-seeking undergraduates: 1% part-time, 58% women, 4% African American, 7% Asian American, 4% Hispanic American, 1% Native American, 12% international
- 44% of applicants admitted
- SAT or ACT (ACT writing optional), application essay required
- 85% graduate within 6 years; 61% enter graduate study

General. Founded in 1874. Regionally accredited. International program integrates symposia, foreign language study, and foreign student enrollment. **Degrees:** 460 bachelor's awarded. **ROTC:** Navy, Air Force. **Location:** 5 miles from Minneapolis-St. Paul. **Calendar:** Semester. **Full-time faculty:** 151 total; 92% have terminal degrees, 17% minority, 44% women. **Part-time faculty:** 72 total; 58% have terminal degrees, 22% minority, 56% women. **Class size:** 69% < 20, 28% 20-39, 2% 40-49, 1% 50-99. **Special facilities:** Observatory with DT-M 16 inch F/8 cassegrain telescope, 250-acre nature preserve, nuclear accelerator, computer modeling facilities, laser spectroscopy laboratory, x-ray diffractometer and a nuclear magnetic spectrometer, fully equipped animal operant chamber, international research center, econometrics lab.

Freshman class profile. 4,317 applied, 1,893 admitted, 491 enrolled.

Mid 50% test scores			
SAT verbal:	630-740	End year in good standing:	98%
SAT math:	630-710	Return as sophomores:	94%
ACT:	28-32	Out-of-state:	66%
Rank in top quarter:	94%	Live on campus:	100%
Rank in top tenth:	65%	International:	10%

Basis for selection. Test scores and curriculum most important. Leadership potential and extracurricular involvements also important, with special attention given to service to others. Interview recommended.

High school preparation. Recommended units include English 4, mathematics 3, social studies 3, science 3 (laboratory 3) and foreign language 3. Honors, AP, or IB level courses recommended.

2006-2007 Annual costs. Tuition/fees: $31,038. Room/board: $7,982. Books/supplies: $850. Personal expenses: $830.

2005-2006 Financial aid. Need-based: 377 full-time freshmen applied for aid; 348 were judged to have need; 348 of these received aid. Average need met was 100%. Average scholarship/grant was $20,455; average loan $2,896. 76% of total undergraduate aid awarded as scholarships/grants, 24% as loans/jobs. **Non-need-based:** Awarded to 107 full-time undergraduates, including 30 freshmen. Scholarships awarded for academics, minority status. **Additional information:** College meets full need for all admitted students. Minnesota Self Loan available to qualified students.

Application procedures. Admission: Closing date 1/15 (postmark date). $40 fee, may be waived for applicants with need. Application may be submitted online. Admission notification 4/1. Must reply by 5/1. **Financial aid:** Priority date 2/8, closing date 4/15. FAFSA, CSS PROFILE required. Applicants notified by 4/1; must reply by 5/1 or within 1 week(s) of notification.

Academics. Special study options: Cross-registration, double major, honors, independent study, internships, student-designed major, study abroad, teacher certification program, urban semester, Washington semester. BA/masters in architecture with Washington University of St. Louis, BA/BS in engineering with Washington University of St. Louis and with the University of Minnesota, BA/BS in nursing with Rush University in Chicago. **Credit/placement by examination:** AP, CLEP, institutional tests. **Support services:** Learning center, remedial instruction, study skills assistance, tutoring.

Majors. Area/ethnic studies: African, American, Asian, Central/Eastern European, German, Latin American, Russian/Slavic, women's. **Biology:** General. **Communications:** General. **Computer sciences:** General. **Conservation:** Environmental studies. **Foreign languages:** Classics, French, linguistics, Russian, Spanish. **History:** General. **Interdisciplinary:** Neuroscience. **Liberal arts:** Arts/sciences. **Math:** General. **Philosophy/religion:** Philosophy, religion. **Physical sciences:** Chemistry, geology, physics. **Psychology:** General. **Social sciences:** Anthropology, economics, geography, international relations, political science, sociology, urban studies. **Visual/performing arts:** Art history/conservation, dramatic, studio arts.

Most popular majors. Biology 7%, English 7%, foreign language 7%, interdisciplinary studies 9%, philosophy/religious studies 6%, physical sciences 8%, psychology 8%, social sciences 26%.

Computing on campus. 360 workstations in dormitories, library, computer center, student center. Dormitories wired for high-speed internet access and linked to campus network. Commuter students can connect to campus network. Online library, helpline, repair service, student web hosting, wireless network available.

Student life. Freshman orientation: Mandatory. Preregistration for classes offered. 5 days prior to classes in September. **Housing:** Guaranteed on-campus for freshmen. Coed dorms, apartments, cooperative housing available. $300 nonrefundable deposit, deadline 5/1. 6 language houses (French, German, Russian, Spanish, Japanese, Chinese), Jewish cultural house, vegetarian co-op housing available. 2-year residency requirement for first-year students, single-sex floors within coed dorms. **Activities:** Bands, choral groups, dance, drama, literary magazine, music ensembles, radio station, student government, student newspaper, symphony orchestra, Voices of Tamani, production studio, theater club, Asian Student Alliance, GOP club, Adelante!, Habitat for Humanity, Model United Nations, Amnesty International, council for religious understanding.

Athletics. NCAA. **Intercollegiate:** Baseball M, basketball, cross-country, diving, football (tackle) M, golf, soccer, softball W, swimming, tennis, track and field, volleyball W, water polo W. **Intramural:** Badminton, basketball, bowling, football (non-tackle) M, racquetball, soccer, softball, table tennis, tennis, volleyball, water polo. **Team name:** Fighting Scots.

Student services. Alcohol/substance abuse counseling, campus ministries, career counseling, student employment services, financial aid counseling, health services, minority student services, personal counseling, placement for graduates. **Physically disabled:** Services for visually, speech, hearing impaired.

Contact. E-mail: admissions@macalester.edu
Phone: (651) 696-6357 Toll-free number: (800) 231-7974
Fax: (651) 696-6724
Lorne Robinson, Dean of Admissions and Financial Aid, Macalester College, 1600 Grand Avenue, St. Paul, MN 55105-1899

Martin Luther College
New Ulm, Minnesota
www.mlc-wels.edu **CB code: 6435**

- Private 4-year college of theology and education affiliated with Wisconsin Evangelical Lutheran Synod
- Residential campus in large town
- 815 degree-seeking undergraduates: 2% part-time, 51% women, 1% international
- 80% of applicants admitted
- ACT (writing optional) required

General. Founded in 1995. Regionally accredited. Offers programs of study in early childhood education and staff ministry. **Degrees:** 210 bachelor's awarded. **Location:** 90 miles from Minneapolis-St. Paul. **Calendar:** Semester, limited summer session. **Full-time faculty:** 59 total; 48% have terminal degrees, 12% women. **Part-time faculty:** 18 total; 39% have terminal degrees, 39% women. **Class size:** 44% < 20, 53% 20-39, 2% 40-49, less than 1% 50-99, less than 1% >100.

Freshman class profile. 249 applied, 200 admitted, 149 enrolled.

Mid 50% test scores			
ACT:	23-27	Rank in top quarter:	47%
GPA 3.50 or higher:	66%	Rank in top tenth:	24%
GPA 3.0-3.49:	24%	Return as sophomores:	79%
GPA 2.0-2.99:	10%	Out-of-state:	89%
		Live on campus:	100%

Basis for selection. Primarily pastor's letter of recommendation, high school transcript, and test scores required. Rating provided by student's high school considered.

High school preparation. 14 units required. Required units include English 4, mathematics 3, social studies 2, science 3 and academic electives 2. 5 units in foreign language required for pastoral program.

2005-2006 Annual costs. Tuition/fees: $8,925. Room/board: $3,475. Books/supplies: $800. Personal expenses: $1,150.

2004-2005 Financial aid. Need-based: 177 full-time freshmen applied for aid; 144 were judged to have need; 144 of these received aid. Average need met was 52%. Average scholarship/grant was $3,900; average loan $3,400. 59% of total undergraduate aid awarded as scholarships/grants, 41% as loans/jobs. **Non-need-based:** Awarded to 920 full-time undergraduates, including 194 freshmen. Scholarships awarded for academics, alumni affiliation, leadership, music/drama, religious affiliation.

Application procedures. Admission: Closing date 4/15 (postmark date). $25 fee, may be waived for applicants with need. Admission notification on a rolling basis beginning on or about 9/15. Must reply by May 1 or within 2 week(s) if notified thereafter. **Financial aid:** Closing date 4/15. FAFSA, institutional form required. Applicants notified by 4/1; must reply by 8/15.

Academics. Special study options: Double major, ESL, independent study, internships, teacher certification program. **Credit/placement by examination:** AP, CLEP, ACT. **Support services:** Learning center, reduced course load, remedial instruction, study skills assistance, tutoring.

Majors. Education: Early childhood, elementary, multi-level teacher. **Theology:** Theology.

Computing on campus. 129 workstations in dormitories, library, computer center. Dormitories linked to campus network. Helpline, repair service available.

Student life. Freshman orientation: Mandatory, $20 fee. **Policies:** Religious observance required. Freshmen permitted cars on campus. **Housing:** Guaranteed on-campus for freshmen. Single-sex dorms available. $100 nonrefundable deposit, deadline 5/1. **Activities:** Bands, choral groups, dance, drama, literary magazine, music ensembles, musical theater, student government.

Athletics. NAIA, NCAA. **Intercollegiate:** Baseball M, basketball, cross-country, football (tackle) M, golf M, soccer, softball W, tennis, track and field, volleyball W. **Intramural:** Badminton, basketball, bowling, football (tackle) M, soccer, softball, tennis, volleyball. **Team name:** Knights.

Student services. Campus ministries, student employment services, financial aid counseling, health services, personal counseling.

Contact. E-mail: mlcadmit@mlc-wels.edu
Phone: (507) 354-8221 Fax: (507) 354-8225
Ronald Brutlag, Director of Admissions, Martin Luther College, 1995 Luther Court, New Ulm, MN 56073-3965

Metropolitan State University

St. Paul, Minnesota
www.metrostate.edu **CB code: 1245**

- Public 4-year university
- Commuter campus in very large city
- 5,452 degree-seeking undergraduates: 64% part-time, 61% women, 10% African American, 8% Asian American, 2% Hispanic American, 1% Native American, 2% international
- 474 degree-seeking graduate students
- 81% of applicants admitted
- SAT or ACT required

General. Founded in 1971. Regionally accredited. Commuter institution that primarily serves working adults. **Degrees:** 1,175 bachelor's awarded; master's offered. **Calendar:** Semester, extensive summer session. **Full-time faculty:** 123 total; 81% have terminal degrees, 22% minority, 52% women. **Part-time faculty:** 368 total; 21% have terminal degrees, 15% minority, 45% women. **Class size:** 35% < 20, 65% 20-39, less than 1% 40-49, less than 1% 50-99.

Freshman class profile. 541 applied, 438 admitted, 193 enrolled.

Mid 50% test scores		**Rank in top tenth:**	8%
ACT:	16-24	**Out-of-state:**	2%
Rank in top quarter:	24%		

Basis for selection. School achievement record and test scores most important. ACT or SAT at or above national median or high school rank in upper half of class. Interview and essays only used as part of the appeals process if admission was denied.

High school preparation. 16 units required. Required units include English 4, mathematics 3, social studies 3, science 3 (laboratory 1) and academic electives 3. 3 years of electives from language, world culture, or arts.

2005-2006 Annual costs. Tuition/fees: $4,682; $9,111 out-of-state. Books/supplies: $1,500. Personal expenses: $1,976.

2004-2005 Financial aid. Need-based: 49 full-time freshmen applied for aid; 46 were judged to have need; 44 of these received aid. Average need met was 36%. Average scholarship/grant was $2,013; average loan $2,564. 21% of total undergraduate aid awarded as scholarships/grants, 79% as loans/jobs. **Non-need-based:** Awarded to 163 full-time undergraduates, including 4 freshmen. Scholarships awarded for academics, leadership, minority status, state residency.

Application procedures. Admission: Closing date 6/15. $20 fee, may be waived for applicants with need. Application may be submitted online. Admission notification on a rolling basis. **Financial aid:** Priority date 5/1; no closing date. FAFSA required. Applicants notified on a rolling basis starting 5/1; must reply within 2 week(s) of notification.

Academics. Special study options: Cross-registration, distance learning, double major, external degree, independent study, internships, liberal arts/career combination, student-designed major, weekend college. **Credit/placement by examination:** AP, CLEP, IB, institutional tests. 90 credit hours maximum toward bachelor's degree. **Support services:** Learning center, study skills assistance, tutoring, writing center.

Majors. Area/ethnic studies: Women's. **Biology:** General. **Business:** Accounting, business admin, finance, hospitality admin, human resources, international, management information systems, marketing, operations, sales/distribution. **Communications:** General, advertising. **Computer sciences:** Computer science, information systems, security, systems analysis. **Education:** Kindergarten/preschool. **English:** Composition, English lit, technical writing. **Health:** Nursing (RN), substance abuse counseling. **History:** General. **Liberal arts:** Arts/sciences. **Math:** Applied. **Personal/culinary services:** Chef training. **Philosophy/religion:** Philosophy. **Protective services:** Criminal justice, police science. **Psychology:** General. **Public administration:** Human services, social work. **Social sciences:** General, economics. **Visual/performing arts:** Dramatic, play/screenwriting.

Most popular majors. Business/marketing 32%, computer/information sciences 8%, interdisciplinary studies 15%, psychology 8%, public administration/social services 7%, security/protective services 7%.

Computing on campus. 950 workstations in library, computer center. Commuter students can connect to campus network. Online course registration, helpline, wireless network available.

Student life. Freshman orientation: Mandatory, $10 fee. Preregistration for classes offered. Orientation sessions of 3-1/2 hours are held several times each semester. **Policies:** Annual registration required of all student organizations. **Activities:** Drama, literary magazine, student government, student newspaper, Asian student organization, Lavender Bridge, African-American student association, graduate student advisory committee, international student organization, Voice of Indian Council for Educational Success, social work student association, psychology club, Muslim student association, Urban Teachers Student Program Organization.

Student services. Adult student services, career counseling, minority student services, personal counseling, women's services. **Physically disabled:** Services for visually, speech, hearing impaired.

Contact. E-mail: admissionsmetro@metrostate.edu
Phone: (651) 793-1300 Fax: (651) 793-1310
Monir Johnson, Admissions Director, Metropolitan State University, 700 East Seventh Street, St. Paul, MN 55106-5000

Minneapolis College of Art and Design

Minneapolis, Minnesota **CB member**
www.mcad.edu **CB code: 6411**

- Private 4-year visual arts college
- Residential campus in very large city
- 656 degree-seeking undergraduates: 5% part-time, 49% women
- 47 degree-seeking graduate students
- 77% of applicants admitted
- SAT or ACT, application essay required
- 137% graduate within 6 years

General. Founded in 1886. Regionally accredited. **Degrees:** 121 bachelor's awarded; master's offered. **Calendar:** Semester, limited summer session. **Full-time faculty:** 38 total; 100% have terminal degrees, 42% women. **Part-time faculty:** 67 total; 48% women. **Class size:** 80% < 20, 18% 20-39, 2% 40-49. **Special facilities:** Art and design galleries.

Freshman class profile. 332 applied, 254 admitted, 190 enrolled.

Return as sophomores:	96%	**Live on campus:**	81%
Out-of-state:	60%		

Basis for selection. Bachelor of Fine Arts applicants required to submit a portfolio of creative work. For all students, academic record and test scores reviewed. Level of interest and motivation determined through personal statement of interest, letter of recommendation and essay required. Tests not required for applicants who have been out of high school for a semester or more. Interview recommended.

High school preparation. Recommended units include English 4, social studies 4 and history 4.

2005-2006 Annual costs. Tuition/fees: $25,040. Room/board: $4,290. Books/supplies: $2,200. Personal expenses: $1,000.

2004-2005 Financial aid. Need-based: 108 full-time freshmen applied for aid; 92 were judged to have need; 91 of these received aid. Average need met was 49%. Average scholarship/grant was $7,922; average loan $2,674. 42% of total undergraduate aid awarded as scholarships/grants, 58% as loans/jobs. **Non-need-based:** Awarded to 84 full-time undergraduates, including 22 freshmen. Scholarships awarded for academics, alumni affiliation, art.

Application procedures. Admission: No deadline. $35 fee, may be waived for applicants with need. Application may be submitted online. Admission notification on a rolling basis. Must reply by May 1 or within 4 week(s) if notified thereafter. **Financial aid:** Priority date 3/15; no closing date. FAFSA required. Applicants notified on a rolling basis starting 4/1; must reply by 5/1 or within 2 week(s) of notification.

Academics. Special study options: Combined bachelor's/graduate degree, cooperative education, cross-registration, distance learning, exchange student, independent study, internships, New York semester, study abroad. **Credit/placement by examination:** AP, CLEP, IB. **Support services:** Learning center, reduced course load, study skills assistance, tutoring, writing center.

Majors. Communications technology: Animation/special effects. **Production:** Furniture. **Visual/performing arts:** General, cinematography, commercial/advertising art, design, drawing, illustration, multimedia, painting, photography, printmaking, sculpture, studio arts.

Most popular majors. Visual/performing arts 90%.

Computing on campus. 120 workstations in library, computer center, student center. Dormitories wired for high-speed internet access and linked to campus network. Online library, helpline, student web hosting, wireless network available.

Student life. Freshman orientation: Mandatory. Preregistration for classes offered. 3 days in fall including 1 day for parents. **Policies:** Freshmen permitted cars on campus. **Housing:** Coed dorms, apartments available. $175 deposit, deadline 5/1. **Activities:** Film society, radio station, student government.

Student services. Alcohol/substance abuse counseling, career counseling, student employment services, financial aid counseling, personal counseling.

Contact. E-mail: admissions@mcad.edu
Phone: (612) 874-3760 Toll-free number: (800) 874-6223
Fax: (612) 874-3701
William Mullen, Director of Admissions & Recruitment, Minneapolis College of Art and Design, 2501 Stevens Avenue South, Minneapolis, MN 55404

Minnesota School of Business

Richfield, Minnesota
www.msbcollege.edu **CB code: 3313**

- For-profit 4-year business and technical college
- Commuter campus in very large city
- 941 degree-seeking undergraduates: 54% part-time, 57% women, 12% African American, 17% Asian American, 2% Hispanic American, 1% Native American
- 1 degree-seeking graduate students
- Interview required
- 42% graduate within 6 years

General. Accredited by ACICS. **Degrees:** 32 bachelor's, 120 associate awarded; master's offered. **Calendar:** Quarter. **Full-time faculty:** 15 total. **Part-time faculty:** 60 total. **Class size:** 96% < 20, 4% 20-39.

Freshman class profile.

End year in good standing:	65%	**Out-of-state:**	1%

Basis for selection. Standardized test scores most important. Interview also important. SAT or ACT recommended. Scores are used to exempt applicants from entrance exam. **Learning Disabled:** Students with learning disabilities are allowed 90 minutes for exams while all other students are allowed 60 minutes.

2005-2006 Annual costs. Tuition/fees: $14,900. Books/supplies: $1,500. Personal expenses: $2,178.

2004-2005 Financial aid. Need-based: 31 full-time freshmen applied for aid; 28 were judged to have need; 22 of these received aid. Average need met was 5%. Average scholarship/grant was $395; average loan $721. 97% of total undergraduate aid awarded as scholarships/grants, 3% as loans/jobs.

Application procedures. Admission: No deadline. $50 fee. Admission notification on a rolling basis. **Financial aid:** No deadline. FAFSA, institutional form required. Applicants notified on a rolling basis starting 7/1; must reply within 2 week(s) of notification.

Academics. Special study options: Distance learning, liberal arts/career combination. **Credit/placement by examination:** CLEP. **Support services:** Tutoring, writing center.

Majors. Business: Accounting, business admin. **Computer sciences:** Information technology. **Health:** Nursing (RN).

Most popular majors. Business/marketing 82%, computer/information sciences 28%.

Computing on campus. 12 workstations in library, computer center. Online library, helpline available.

Student life. Freshman orientation: Mandatory.

Student services. Student employment services, financial aid counseling, placement for graduates.

Contact. E-mail: pmurray@msbcollege.edu
Phone: (612) 861-2000 Toll-free number: (800) 752-4223
Fax: (612) 861-5548
Patricia Murray, Director of Admissions, Minnesota School of Business, 1401 West 76 Street, Suite 500, Richfield, MN 55423

Minnesota State University: Mankato

Mankato, Minnesota **CB member**
www.mnsu.edu **CB code: 6677**

- Public 4-year university
- Commuter campus in large town
- 12,241 degree-seeking undergraduates: 8% part-time, 52% women, 2% African American, 2% Asian American, 1% Hispanic American, 3% international
- 1,351 graduate students
- 90% of applicants admitted
- ACT (writing optional) required
- 48% graduate within 6 years

General. Founded in 1867. Regionally accredited. **Degrees:** 1,974 bachelor's, 121 associate awarded; master's offered. **ROTC:** Army. **Location:** 85 miles from Minneapolis-St. Paul. **Calendar:** Semester, extensive summer session. **Full-time faculty:** 491 total; 79% have terminal degrees, 7% minority, 44% women. **Part-time faculty:** 226 total; 7% have terminal degrees, 1% minority, 48% women. **Class size:** 35% < 20, 47% 20-39, 7% 40-49, 7% 50-99, 3% >100. **Special facilities:** 2 observatories, ropes course.

Freshman class profile. 5,605 applied, 5,035 admitted, 2,257 enrolled.

Mid 50% test scores		**Return as sophomores:**	76%
ACT:	19-24	**Out-of-state:**	15%
Rank in top quarter:	27%	**Live on campus:**	81%
Rank in top tenth:	8%	**International:**	1%

Basis for selection. Rank in top 50% of high school class or equivalent, most important. College preparatory courses also reviewed. ACT is used only when admission cannot be achieved using high school rank and college preparatory courses. Test scores due fifth class day of fall semester. ACT used only when admission cannot be achieved using high school rank and college preparatory courses. Essays and/or recommendations used only for contract/admission review by faculty committees. **Homeschooled:** Must submit standardized test results in lieu of rank/record.

High school preparation. College-preparatory program required. 16 units required. Required units include English 4, mathematics 3, social studies 2, history 1, science 3 (laboratory 3) and foreign language 2. One year world culture course or arts course.

2005-2006 Annual costs. Tuition/fees: $5,402; $10,750 out-of-state. Room/board: $4,770. Books/supplies: $820. Personal expenses: $2,600.

2005-2006 Financial aid. All financial aid based on need. 1,831 full-time freshmen applied for aid; 1,117 were judged to have need; 1,098 of these received aid. Average need met was 77%. Average scholarship/grant was $3,750; average loan $3,280. 33% of total undergraduate aid awarded as scholarships/grants, 67% as loans/jobs.

Application procedures. Admission: $20 fee. Application may be submitted online. Admission notification on a rolling basis. **Financial aid:** Priority date 3/15; no closing date. FAFSA required. Applicants notified on a rolling basis starting 3/30; must reply within 2 week(s) of notification.

Academics. Special study options: Combined bachelor's/graduate degree, cross-registration, distance learning, double major, dual enrollment of high school students, ESL, exchange student, external degree, honors, independent study, internships, semester at sea, student-designed major, study abroad, teacher certification program. **Credit/placement by examination:** AP, CLEP, IB, institutional tests. **Support services:** Learning center, reduced course load, remedial instruction, study skills assistance, tutoring, writing center.

Majors. Agriculture: Food science, plant sciences. **Architecture:** Urban/community planning. **Area/ethnic studies:** French, German, Scandinavian, women's. **Biology:** General, anatomy, bacteriology, biochemistry, biotechnology, botany, ecology, genetics, toxicology, zoology. **Business:** General, accounting, banking/financial services, business admin, finance, financial planning, human resources, insurance, international, investments/securities, management information systems, management science, operations. **Communications:** General, journalism, media studies, public relations. **Computer sciences:** General, computer science, information systems. **Conservation:** General, environmental studies. **Construction:** Maintenance. **Education:** General, art, biology, business, chemistry, computer, curriculum, drama/dance, elementary, English, family/consumer sciences, foreign languages, French, German, health, health occupations, history, mathematics, middle, music, physical, physics, school counseling, science, secondary, social science, social studies, Spanish, speech, speech impaired, technology/industrial arts, voc/tech. **Engineering:** General, civil, computer, electrical, mechanical. **Engineering technology:** Automotive, computer, electrical, manufacturing, mechanical. **English:** Creative writing, speech/rhetoric, technical writing. **Family/consumer sciences:** General, clothing/textiles, family studies, family/community services, food/nutrition, housing. **Foreign languages:** General, French, German, Spanish. **Health:** Athletic training, clinical lab assistant, clinical lab science, clinical lab technology, communication disorders, cytotechnology, dental hygiene, health care admin, licensed practical nurse, nursing (RN), predentistry, premedicine, preop/surgical nursing, prepharmacy, preveterinary, recreational therapy. **History:** General. **Interdisciplinary:** Biological/physical sciences. **Legal studies:** Prelaw. **Liberal arts:** Arts/sciences. **Math:** General. **Mechanic/repair:** Automotive. **Parks/recreation:** General, exercise sciences, facilities management, health/fitness, sports admin. **Philosophy/religion:** Philosophy. **Physical sciences:** Astronomy, chemistry, physics. **Protective services:** Corrections, law enforcement admin, police science. **Psychology:** General. **Public administration:** Human services, social work. **Social sciences:** Anthropology, criminology, economics, geography, international relations, political science, sociology, urban studies. **Transportation:** Aviation management. **Visual/performing arts:** General, art, art history/conservation, ceramics, commercial/advertising art, dramatic, drawing, fiber arts, interior design, music management, music performance, music theory/composition, painting, piano/organ, sculpture, studio arts, theater design, voice/opera.

Most popular majors. Business/marketing 19%, education 14%, engineering/engineering technologies 6%, health sciences 12%, social sciences 7%.

Computing on campus. 900 workstations in dormitories, library, computer center, student center. Dormitories wired for high-speed internet access and linked to campus network. Commuter students can connect to campus network. Online course registration, online library, helpline, repair service, student web hosting, wireless network available.

Student life. **Freshman orientation:** Mandatory, $65 fee. Preregistration for classes offered. Includes overnight stay. **Policies:** Freshmen permitted cars on campus. **Housing:** Guaranteed on-campus for freshmen. Coed dorms, special housing for disabled available. $250 partly refundable deposit. **Activities:** Bands, choral groups, dance, drama, literary magazine, music ensembles, musical theater, radio station, student government, student newspaper, symphony orchestra, Hmong Student Association, American Indian Student Association, Chicano LatinoAM Student Association, Lutheran Campus Ministry, Campus Lutheran Chapel, Fellowship of Christian Athletes, InterVarsity, MSU Pagan Organization, St. Thomas More Newman Center.

Athletics. NCAA. **Intercollegiate:** Baseball M, basketball, bowling W, cheerleading, cross-country, diving, football (tackle) M, golf, ice hockey, soccer W, softball W, swimming, tennis, track and field, volleyball W, wrestling M. **Intramural:** Archery, basketball, bowling, fencing, football (non-tackle), golf, ice hockey, racquetball, rugby, skiing, soccer, softball, swimming, table tennis, tennis, track and field, triathlon, volleyball, wrestling M. **Team name:** Mavericks.

Student services. Adult student services, alcohol/substance abuse counseling, campus ministries, career counseling, services for economically disadvantaged, student employment services, financial aid counseling, health services, legal services, minority student services, on-campus daycare, personal counseling, placement for graduates, veterans' counselor, women's services. **Physically disabled:** Services for visually, speech, hearing impaired.

Contact. E-mail: admissions@mnsu.edu
Phone: (507) 389-1822 Toll-free number: (800) 722-0544
Fax: (507) 389-1511
Walt Wolff, Director of Admissions, Minnesota State University: Mankato, 122 Taylor Center, Mankato, MN 56001

Minnesota State University: Moorhead

Moorhead, Minnesota
www.mnstate.edu **CB code: 6678**

- Public 4-year university
- Residential campus in small city
- 6,881 degree-seeking undergraduates: 11% part-time, 59% women
- SAT or ACT (ACT writing recommended) required

General. Founded in 1885. Regionally accredited. **Degrees:** 1,283 bachelor's, 50 associate awarded; master's offered. **ROTC:** Army, Air Force. **Location:** 240 miles from Minneapolis-St. Paul. **Calendar:** Semester, limited summer session. **Full-time faculty:** 305 total. **Part-time faculty:** 45 total. **Special facilities:** Planetarium, biology museum.

Freshman class profile.

Mid 50% test scores		Rank in top quarter:	31%
ACT:	18-24	Rank in top tenth:	10%

Basis for selection. Applicants must rank in top half of class or have minimum ACT composite score of 21 or equivalent scores on SAT or PSAT/NMSQT. Some applicants not meeting requirements will be admitted to transitional college program. Applicants must also fulfill minimum requirements of secondary course work. Students not meeting automatic admission standards may apply through alternative admissions program, New Center. **Learning Disabled:** Contact Office of Disability Services to make sure appropriate accommodations can be provided.

High school preparation. 16 units required. Required units include English 4, mathematics 3, social studies 3, science 3 (laboratory 1) and academic electives 3. One unit fine arts, .5 computer science recommended.

2005-2006 Annual costs. Tuition/fees: $5,225. Out-of-state students pay same rate as in-state. Room/board: $4,974. Books/supplies: $800. Personal expenses: $2,206.

Financial aid. **Non-need-based:** Scholarships awarded for academics, athletics, state residency.

Application procedures. **Admission:** Closing date 8/1 (postmark date). $20 fee. Application may be submitted online. Admission notification on a rolling basis. **Financial aid:** Priority date 3/1; no closing date. FAFSA, institutional form required. Applicants notified on a rolling basis starting 5/1; must reply within 2 week(s) of notification.

Academics. **Special study options:** Cross-registration, distance learning, double major, dual enrollment of high school students, exchange student, external degree, honors, independent study, internships, student-designed major, study abroad, teacher certification program. Reciprocal bachelor's degree programs with North Dakota State University. **Credit/placement by examination:** CLEP, institutional tests. 12 credit hours maximum toward bachelor's degree. **Support services:** Pre-admission summer program, reduced course load, remedial instruction, study skills assistance, tutoring, writing center.

Majors. **Area/ethnic studies:** American, East Asian. **Biology:** General. **Business:** Accounting, business admin, finance, international, management information systems, marketing. **Communications:** Media studies. **Computer sciences:** General, computer science. **Education:** Art, biology, chemistry, elementary, English, health, kindergarten/preschool, mathematics, music, physical, physics, science, social studies, Spanish, special, speech. **Engineering technology:** Construction, industrial. **English:** English lit, speech/rhetoric. **Foreign languages:** Spanish. **Health:** Athletic training, audiology/speech pathology, clinical lab science, community health services, health care admin, nurse practitioner, predentistry, premedicine, prepharmacy, preveterinary. **History:** General. **Interdisciplinary:** Gerontology. **Legal studies:** General, paralegal. **Math:** General. **Parks/recreation:** Exercise sciences, health/fitness. **Philosophy/religion:** Philosophy. **Physical sciences:** Chemistry, physics. **Protective services:** Criminal justice. **Psychology:** General. **Public administration:** Social work. **Social sciences:** Anthropology, economics, political science, sociology. **Visual/performing arts:** Art, commercial/advertising art, dramatic, music management, music performance.

Computing on campus. 791 workstations in dormitories, library, computer center. Dormitories linked to campus network. Commuter students can connect to campus network. Online course registration, online library, helpline, repair service, student web hosting, wireless network available.

Student life. **Freshman orientation:** Available, $50 fee. Preregistration for classes offered. **Policies:** Freshmen permitted cars on campus. **Housing:** Coed dorms, single-sex dorms, special housing for disabled, apartments, fraternity/sorority housing available. $350 deposit. **Activities:** Bands, choral groups, dance, drama, literary magazine, music ensembles, musical theater, radio station, student government, student newspaper, symphony orchestra, TV station, 125 student clubs, including Spurs, Circle-K, Newman Club, United Campus Ministry, Spanish Club, Habitat for Humanity, Amnesty International, Model United Nations, United Campus Ministry, Volunteer Visions.

Athletics. NCAA. **Intercollegiate:** Basketball, cross-country, diving W, football (tackle) M, golf W, soccer W, softball W, swimming W, tennis W, track and field, volleyball W, wrestling M. **Intramural:** Badminton, basketball, golf, ice hockey M, lacrosse M, racquetball, rugby, soccer, softball, swimming, tennis, track and field, volleyball, water polo, wrestling M. **Team name:** Dragons.

Student services. Adult student services, alcohol/substance abuse counseling, career counseling, student employment services, financial aid counseling, health services, minority student services, on-campus daycare, personal counseling, placement for graduates, veterans' counselor, women's services. **Physically disabled:** Services for visually, speech, hearing impaired.

Contact. E-mail: dragon@mnstate.edu
Phone: (218) 477-2161 Toll-free number: (800) 593-7246
Fax: (218) 477-4374
Gina Monson, Director of Admissions, Minnesota State University: Moorhead, Owens Hall, Moorhead, MN 56563

National American University: St. Paul

Bloomington, Minnesota
www.national.edu **CB code: 5358**

- For-profit 4-year branch campus and business college
- Commuter campus in very large city
- 270 degree-seeking undergraduates

General. Founded in 1974. Regionally accredited. Campuses in Bloomington/ Mall of America, Brooklyn Center and Roseville. **Degrees:** 40 bachelor's, 15 associate awarded; master's offered. **Calendar:** Quarter, extensive summer session. **Full-time faculty:** 5 total. **Part-time faculty:** 65 total. **Class size:** 95% < 20, 5% 20-39.

Basis for selection. Open admission.

2005-2006 Annual costs. Tuition/fees: $13,365. Online courses: $225 per-credit-hour. Books/supplies: $1,000.

Financial aid. Non-need-based: Scholarships awarded for academics.

Application procedures. Admission: No deadline. $25 fee. Admission notification on a rolling basis. **Financial aid:** Priority date 8/21; no closing date. FAFSA required. Applicants notified on a rolling basis.

Academics. Special study options: Accelerated study, distance learning, double major, independent study, internships. **Credit/placement by examination:** AP, CLEP, IB, institutional tests. **Support services:** Reduced course load, tutoring.

Majors. Business: General, accounting, business admin, hospitality admin, international, management information systems, marketing. **Computer sciences:** General, programming.

Computing on campus. 112 workstations in library, computer center. Online library available.

Student life. Freshman orientation: Mandatory. Preregistration for classes offered. **Activities:** Student government, student business club, Southeast Asian student organization, student government, international student organizations.

Athletics. Team name: Mavericks.

Student services. Career counseling, student employment services, placement for graduates.

Contact. E-mail: mmottl@national.edu
Phone: (952) 883-0439 Toll-free number: (866) 628-6387
Fax: (952) 883-0439
Matthew Mottl, Regional Director of Admissions, National American University: St. Paul, Mall of America West 112 West Market, Bloomington, MN 55425

North Central University

Minneapolis, Minnesota
www.northcentral.edu **CB code: 0051**

- Private 4-year university and Bible college affiliated with Assemblies of God
- Residential campus in large city
- 1,217 degree-seeking undergraduates: 7% part-time, 57% women
- 98% of applicants admitted
- SAT or ACT (ACT writing optional), application essay required
- 45% graduate within 6 years

General. Founded in 1930. Regionally accredited. **Degrees:** 183 bachelor's, 8 associate awarded. **ROTC:** Army, Air Force. **Location:** One mile from downtown. **Calendar:** Semester, limited summer session. **Full-time faculty:** 40 total; 45% have terminal degrees, 12% minority, 38% women. **Part-time faculty:** 66 total; 14% minority, 41% women. **Class size:** 52% < 20, 34% 20-39, 10% 40-49, 3% 50-99, less than 1% >100. **Special facilities:** Recording studio, youth and leadership center, word and worship center, children's literature library.

Freshman class profile. 422 applied, 414 admitted, 239 enrolled.

Mid 50% test scores		**Rank in top quarter:**	11%
SAT verbal:	480-630	**Rank in top tenth:**	2%
ACT:	18-24	**End year in good standing:**	87%
GPA 3.50 or higher:	38%	**Return as sophomores:**	75%
GPA 3.0-3.49:	35%	**Out-of-state:**	60%
GPA 2.0-2.99:	26%	**Live on campus:**	92%

Basis for selection. School achievement record, essay and pastor's recommendation most important. Conditional admission available for students not in good standing at previous institution. Applicants with GPA below 2.2 or ACT scores below 18 may be admitted provisionally. Interview recommended. Audition required for music students. **Homeschooled:** Must meet their state's requirements for graduation.

High school preparation. 9 units required. Required units include English 3, mathematics 1, social studies 2, history 1, science 1 and foreign language 1.

2005-2006 Annual costs. Tuition/fees: $12,166. Room/board: $4,480. Books/supplies: $600.

2004-2005 Financial aid. Need-based: 62% of total undergraduate aid awarded as scholarships/grants, 38% as loans/jobs. **Non-need-based:** Scholarships awarded for academics, music/drama.

Application procedures. Admission: Closing date 6/1 (postmark date). $25 fee, may be waived for applicants with need. Application may be submitted online. Admission notification on a rolling basis. **Financial aid:** Priority date 4/1, closing date 5/1. FAFSA, institutional form required. Applicants notified on a rolling basis starting 3/15; must reply within 2 week(s) of notification.

Academics. Special study options: Distance learning, double major, exchange student, independent study, internships, liberal arts/career combination, student-designed major, study abroad, teacher certification program, weekend college. **Credit/placement by examination:** AP, CLEP, SAT, ACT. **Support services:** Learning center, pre-admission summer program, reduced course load, remedial instruction, study skills assistance, tutoring, writing center.

Majors. Business: Accounting, business admin. **Communications:** Journalism, media studies. **Education:** Elementary, ESL, secondary. **English:** English lit. **Foreign languages:** Arabic, Chinese, sign language interpretation, Spanish. **Philosophy/religion:** Christian, religion. **Psychology:** General. **Theology:** Bible, missionary, pastoral counseling, religious ed, sacred music, theology, youth ministry. **Visual/performing arts:** Dramatic, music performance.

Most popular majors. Area/ethnic studies 7%, business/marketing 14%, education 7%, psychology 10%, theological studies 32%, visual/performing arts 8%.

Computing on campus. 80 workstations in dormitories, library, computer center, student center. Dormitories wired for high-speed internet access and linked to campus network.

Student life. Freshman orientation: Mandatory, $115 fee. Preregistration for classes offered. **Policies:** No smoking, drinking, or pre-marital sex permitted. Religious observance required. **Housing:** Guaranteed on-campus for freshmen. Single-sex dorms, apartments, substance-free housing available. $150 partly refundable deposit, deadline 6/1. Honor dormitories available. **Activities:** Bands, choral groups, dance, drama, literary magazine, music ensembles, musical theater, radio station, student government, student newspaper, TV station, Apartment Student Connection, commuter student fellowship, deaf culture ministry fellowship, Psi Chi, Delta Kappa, leadership council, Mu Kappa North, One in Heart, Silver and Gold, student senate.

Athletics. NCAA. **Intercollegiate:** Baseball M, basketball, cross-country, golf M, soccer, softball W, track and field, volleyball W. **Intramural:** Football (non-tackle). **Team name:** Rams.

Student services. Campus ministries, career counseling, student employment services, financial aid counseling, health services, personal counseling, placement for graduates, women's services. **Physically disabled:** Services for visually, speech, hearing impaired.

Contact. E-mail: admissions@northcentral.edu
Phone: (612) 343-4460 Toll-free number: (800) 289-6222
Fax: (612) 343-4146
Joe Kessler, Director of Admissions, North Central University, 910 Elliot Avenue, Minneapolis, MN 55404

Northwestern College

Saint Paul, Minnesota
www.nwc.edu **CB code: 6489**

- Private 4-year Bible and liberal arts college affiliated with nondenominational tradition
- Residential campus in large city
- 1,760 degree-seeking undergraduates: 2% part-time, 60% women, 2% African American, 4% Asian American, 2% Hispanic American, 1% international
- 18 degree-seeking graduate students
- 98% of applicants admitted
- SAT or ACT (ACT writing optional), application essay required
- 59% graduate within 6 years; 14% enter graduate study

General. Founded in 1902. Regionally accredited. All students entering as freshmen are required to complete a second major in Bible (30 credits). Transfer students meet the Bible requirement on a proportional basis. **Degrees:** 514 bachelor's, 13 associate awarded; master's offered. **ROTC:** Army, Air Force. **Location:** 9 miles from Minneapolis-St. Paul. **Calendar:** Semester, limited summer session. **Full-time faculty:** 85 total; 67% have terminal degrees, 7% minority, 34% women. **Part-time faculty:** 80 total; 22% have terminal degrees, 10% minority, 44% women. **Class size:** 46% < 20, 41% 20-39, 7% 40-49, 4% 50-99, 2% >100.

Freshman class profile. 918 applied, 904 admitted, 469 enrolled.

Mid 50% test scores			
SAT verbal:	500-660	GPA 2.0-2.99:	16%
SAT math:	500-610	Rank in top quarter:	51%
ACT:	21-26	Rank in top tenth:	26%
GPA 3.50 or higher:	58%	End year in good standing:	89%
GPA 3.0-3.49:	26%	Return as sophomores:	79%
		Out-of-state:	33%

Basis for selection. Evidence that student will benefit from the education and contribute to the community important. School record, recommendations, test scores, essay, character, and religious affiliation very important. Audition required for music students. Portfolio recommended for art students. Interview recommended for borderline students.

High school preparation. 16 units recommended. Recommended units include English 4, mathematics 3, social studies 3, science 3, foreign language 2 and academic electives 1.

2005-2006 Annual costs. Tuition/fees: $19,100. Room/board: $6,120. Books/supplies: $600. Personal expenses: $1,900.

2004-2005 Financial aid. Need-based: 403 full-time freshmen applied for aid; 341 were judged to have need; 338 of these received aid. Average need met was 68%. Average scholarship/grant was $10,539; average loan $3,569. 57% of total undergraduate aid awarded as scholarships/grants, 43% as loans/jobs. **Non-need-based:** Awarded to 1,358 full-time undergraduates, including 356 freshmen. Scholarships awarded for academics, alumni affiliation, leadership, music/drama.

Application procedures. Admission: Priority date 6/1; deadline 7/1 (receipt date). $30 fee, may be waived for applicants with need. Application may be submitted online. Admission notification on a rolling basis beginning on or about 10/1. **Financial aid:** Priority date 3/1, closing date 6/1. FAFSA, institutional form required. Applicants notified on a rolling basis starting 3/1; must reply within 2 week(s) of notification.

Academics. Special study options: Combined bachelor's/graduate degree, distance learning, double major, exchange student, honors, independent study, internships, liberal arts/career combination, student-designed major, study abroad, teacher certification program, Washington semester. **Credit/placement by examination:** AP, CLEP, IB, ACT, institutional tests. 32 credit hours maximum toward associate degree, 32 toward bachelor's. **Support services:** Learning center, reduced course load, remedial instruction, study skills assistance, tutoring.

Majors. Biology: General. **Business:** Accounting, business admin, finance, international, management information systems, marketing. **Communications:** General, digital media, journalism, public relations, radio/tv. **Education:** Art, early childhood, elementary, English, ESL, mathematics, music, physical, social studies. **English:** Creative writing, English lit, technical writing. **History:** General. **Math:** General. **Parks/recreation:** Exercise sciences, health/fitness. **Protective services:** Criminal justice. **Psychology:** General. **Social sciences:** General. **Theology:** Bible, missionary, preministerial, religious ed, youth ministry. **Visual/performing arts:** Dramatic, graphic design, music performance, music theory/composition, piano/organ, stringed instruments, studio arts, voice/opera.

Most popular majors. Business/marketing 25%, communications/journalism 9%, education 15%, psychology 15%, theological studies 16%, visual/performing arts 7%.

Computing on campus. PC or laptop required. 100 workstations in library, computer center, student center. Dormitories wired for high-speed internet access and linked to campus network. Commuter students can connect to campus network. Online course registration, online library, helpline, wireless network available.

Student life. Freshman orientation: Mandatory. Preregistration for classes offered. Summer registration/orientation: 6 one-day events during summer. General orientation: 4 days prior to start of classes. Multicultural orientation: 4 days prior to general orientation. **Policies:** Religious observance required. **Housing:** Guaranteed on-campus for freshmen. Coed dorms, single-sex dorms, special housing for disabled, apartments, substance-free housing available. **Activities:** Bands, choral groups, drama, literary magazine, music ensembles, musical theater, opera, radio station, student government, student newspaper, symphony orchestra, Student Missionary Fellowship, worship group, transfer organization, Guardian Angels, Mu Kappa, organization for students of color, Young Republicans.

Athletics. NCAA, NCCAA. **Intercollegiate:** Baseball M, basketball, cheerleading M, cross-country, football (tackle) M, golf M, soccer, softball W, tennis, track and field, volleyball W. **Intramural:** Basketball, football (non-tackle), softball, volleyball. **Team name:** Eagles.

Student services. Adult student services, campus ministries, career counseling, student employment services, financial aid counseling, health services, minority student services, personal counseling, placement for graduates.

Contact. E-mail: admissions@nwc.edu
Phone: (651) 631-5111 Toll-free number: (800) 827-6827
Fax: (651) 631-5680
Kenneth Faffler, Director of Admissions, Northwestern College, 3003 Snelling Avenue North, Saint Paul, MN 55113

Oak Hills Christian College

Bemidji, Minnesota
www.oakhills.edu **CB code: 7247**

- Private 4-year Bible college affiliated with interdenominational tradition
- Residential campus in large town
- 165 degree-seeking undergraduates: 8% part-time, 42% women, 1% African American, 1% Asian American, 1% Hispanic American, 3% Native American, 1% international
- 66% of applicants admitted
- ACT (writing optional), application essay required
- 45% graduate within 6 years

General. Founded in 1946. Accredited by ABHE. **Degrees:** 18 bachelor's, 6 associate awarded. **Location:** 4 miles from Bemidji, 230 miles from Minneapolis-St. Paul. **Calendar:** Semester. **Full-time faculty:** 9 total; 33% have terminal degrees, 11% minority, 33% women. **Part-time faculty:** 1 total; 100% women. **Class size:** 57% < 20, 34% 20-39, 2% 40-49, 6% 50-99, 2% >100. **Special facilities:** American Indian Resource Center.

Freshman class profile. 79 applied, 52 admitted, 42 enrolled.

Mid 50% test scores			
ACT:	17-23	Rank in top tenth:	11%
GPA 3.50 or higher:	37%	End year in good standing:	71%
GPA 3.0-3.49:	17%	Return as sophomores:	63%
GPA 2.0-2.99:	40%	Out-of-state:	36%
Rank in top quarter:	26%	Live on campus:	91%

Basis for selection. Applicants must have high school GPA of 2.0 or above and/or ACT score of 18 or above to be eligible for consideration. Applicants not meeting minimum requirements considered on individual basis. SAT/ACT scores must be received at latest 4 weeks after first day of classes. Not required if student has 1 year of college credit or if 2 years out of high school. **Homeschooled:** Transcript of courses and grades, letter of recommendation (nonparent) required. **Learning Disabled:** All special education or diagnostic (IEP) records required. Interview may be requested.

2005-2006 Annual costs. Tuition/fees: $11,590. Room/board: $4,320. Books/supplies: $710. Personal expenses: $2,775.

2004-2005 Financial aid. Need-based: 41 full-time freshmen applied for aid; 39 were judged to have need; 39 of these received aid. Average need met was 59%. Average scholarship/grant was $6,080; average loan $2,436. 66% of total undergraduate aid awarded as scholarships/grants, 34% as loans/jobs. **Non-need-based:** Awarded to 8 full-time undergraduates, including 2 freshmen. Scholarships awarded for academics, alumni affiliation.

Application procedures. Admission: No deadline. $25 fee, may be waived for applicants with need. Application may be submitted online. Admission notification on a rolling basis. **Financial aid:** No deadline. FAFSA, institutional form required. Applicants notified on a rolling basis starting 3/1.

Academics. Special study options: Combined bachelor's/graduate degree, cooperative education, double major, honors, independent study, internships, study abroad. **Credit/placement by examination:** AP, CLEP, ACT. **Support services:** Remedial instruction, study skills assistance, tutoring, writing center.

Majors. Psychology: General. **Theology:** Bible, missionary, sacred music.

Computing on campus. 12 workstations in library, computer center. Dormitories wired for high-speed internet access and linked to campus network. Online library available.

Student life. Freshman orientation: Mandatory. Preregistration for classes offered. Held first weekend of school year. **Policies:** Mandatory chapel, no alcohol, illegal drugs, gambling, or smoking on campus. Religious observance required. Freshmen permitted cars on campus. **Housing:** Guaranteed on-campus for freshmen. Single-sex dorms, special housing for disabled, apartments, substance-free housing available. $20 fully refundable deposit. Apartments for students with dependent children. **Activities:** Choral groups, drama, music ensembles, student government, student newspaper, married students group, students older than average group, women's group, engaged couples group, many outreach programs, single student cell groups.

Athletics. Intercollegiate: Basketball, volleyball W. **Intramural:** Basketball, football (non-tackle), golf, racquetball, soccer, softball, table tennis, volleyball. **Team name:** Wolfpack.

Student services. Adult student services, campus ministries, career counseling, student employment services, financial aid counseling, health services, minority student services, personal counseling, placement for graduates. **Physically disabled:** Services for visually, speech, hearing impaired.

Contact. E-mail: admissions@oakhills.edu
Phone: (218) 751-8671 ext. 1285 Toll-free number: (888) 751-8670
Fax: (218) 751-8825
Dan Hovestol, Admissions Director, Oak Hills Christian College, 1600 Oak Hills Road, SW, Bemidji, MN 56601

Pillsbury Baptist Bible College

Owatonna, Minnesota
www.pillsbury.edu/ **CB code: 0260**

- Private 4-year Bible college
- 182 degree-seeking undergraduates
- ACT (writing optional), application essay required

General. Accredited by ABHE. **Degrees:** 23 bachelor's, 1 associate awarded. **Calendar:** Semester. **Full-time faculty:** 17 total. **Part-time faculty:** 7 total.

Freshman class profile. 51 enrolled.

Mid 50% test scores	ACT:	18-24

Basis for selection. Must demonstrate personal relationship with Jesus Christ and a Christian lifestyle; high school record, achievements and abilities important; ACT, statement, reference from pastor and teacher required. **Homeschooled:** GED may be required.

High school preparation. Recommended units include English 4, mathematics 3, social studies 3, science 3 and foreign language 2. Foreign language units should be in same language.

2005-2006 Annual costs. Tuition/fees: $7,638. Room/board: $3,884.

Application procedures. Admission: No deadline. $25 fee. **Financial aid:** Priority date 4/15; no closing date.

Academics. Credit/placement by examination: CLEP.

Majors. Business: Accounting, business admin. **Education:** Elementary, mathematics, physical, secondary. **Theology:** Bible, pastoral counseling, youth ministry. **Visual/performing arts:** Graphic design.

Student life. Freshman orientation: Available. **Activities:** Student government.

Athletics. NCCAA. **Intercollegiate:** Baseball M, basketball, golf, soccer M, softball W, volleyball W.

Contact. E-mail: admissions@pillsbury.edu
Phone: (507) 451-2710 Toll-free number: (800) 747-4557
Steve Seidler, Director of Admissions, Pillsbury Baptist Bible College, 315 South Grove Avenue, Owatonna, MN 55060

St. Cloud State University

St. Cloud, Minnesota
www.stcloudstate.edu **CB code: 6679**

- Public 4-year university
- Commuter campus in small city
- 13,120 degree-seeking undergraduates: 13% part-time, 53% women
- 1,478 degree-seeking graduate students
- 78% of applicants admitted
- SAT or ACT (ACT writing optional) required
- 43% graduate within 6 years

General. Founded in 1869. Regionally accredited. **Degrees:** 2,379 bachelor's, 109 associate awarded; master's offered. **ROTC:** Army. **Location:** 80 miles from Minneapolis - St. Paul. **Calendar:** Semester, limited summer session. **Full-time faculty:** 650 total; 80% have terminal degrees, 18% minority, 41% women. **Part-time faculty:** 211 total; 12% have terminal degrees, 8% minority, 53% women. **Class size:** 36% < 20, 53% 20-39, 5% 40-49, 4% 50-99, 2% >100. **Special facilities:** Anthropology museum, greenhouse, aquarium, planetarium, nature preserve, observatory, GIS cartographic center, aviation facilities, weather labs, National Hockey Center, AVID editing equipment, safe driving track.

Freshman class profile. 5,912 applied, 4,622 admitted, 2,152 enrolled.

Mid 50% test scores		Return as sophomores:	71%
ACT:	19-24	Out-of-state:	12%
Rank in top quarter:	29%	Live on campus:	74%
Rank in top tenth:	7%	International:	2%

Basis for selection. Rank in top half of high school class or minimum 25 ACT, 1000 SAT (exclusive of Writing), or 100 PSAT/NMSQT. Division of General Studies may accept applicants ranked between 33rd and 50th percentiles in high school class.

High school preparation. 17 units required. Required units include English 4, mathematics 3, social studies 3, history 1, science 3 (laboratory 1) and foreign language 2. 1 unit fine arts or humanites required.

2005-2006 Annual costs. Tuition/fees: $5,322; $10,894 out-of-state. Room/board: $4,688.

2005-2006 Financial aid. Need-based: 1,545 full-time freshmen applied for aid; 1,046 were judged to have need; 1,046 of these received aid. Average need met was 94%. Average scholarship/grant was $3,971; average loan $3,874. 33% of total undergraduate aid awarded as scholarships/grants, 67% as loans/jobs. **Non-need-based:** Awarded to 958 full-time undergraduates, including 344 freshmen. Scholarships awarded for academics, art, athletics, leadership, music/drama.

Application procedures. Admission: Priority date 5/1; deadline 6/1 (receipt date). $20 fee, may be waived for applicants with need. Application may be submitted online. Admission notification on a rolling basis beginning on or about 9/15. Early application recommended for those who want to live on-campus. **Financial aid:** Closing date 6/30. FAFSA, institutional form required. Applicants notified on a rolling basis starting 6/3.

Academics. Special study options: Accelerated study, cooperative education, cross-registration, distance learning, double major, dual enrollment of high school students, ESL, honors, independent study, internships, student-designed major, study abroad, teacher certification program. **Credit/**

placement by examination: AP, CLEP, IB, institutional tests. **Support services:** Learning center, pre-admission summer program, remedial instruction, study skills assistance, tutoring, writing center.

Honors college/program. Essay required, must be in top 15% of high school class with strong college preparatory curriculum and corresponding test scores.

Majors. **Architecture:** Urban/community planning. **Area/ethnic studies:** American, East Asian, Latin American. **Biology:** General, bacteriology, biotechnology, botany, environmental, marine. **Business:** General, accounting, business admin, finance, human resources, insurance, international, marketing, real estate, tourism/travel. **Communications:** General, advertising, broadcast journalism, journalism, media studies, public relations, radio/tv. **Communications technology:** Photo/film/video. **Computer sciences:** General, computer science. **Conservation:** General, wildlife. **Education:** Art, biology, chemistry, drama/dance, driver/safety, early childhood, elementary, English, foreign languages, history, instructional media, mathematics, multi-level teacher, music, physical, physics, psychology, reading, science, secondary, social science, social studies, Spanish, special, speech, technology/industrial arts. **Engineering:** General, aerospace, biomedical, chemical, civil, computer, electrical, industrial, manufacturing, mechanical. **Engineering technology:** General, electrical, manufacturing, mechanical, surveying. **English:** American lit, British lit, composition, English lit, speech/rhetoric. **Family/consumer sciences:** Work/family studies. **Foreign languages:** Comparative lit, French, German, linguistics, Spanish. **Health:** Audiology/speech pathology, clinical lab science, communication disorders, nuclear medical technology, nursing (RN), predentistry, premedicine, prepharmacy, preveterinary, recreational therapy, substance abuse counseling. **History:** General. **Interdisciplinary:** Behavioral sciences, gerontology, natural sciences. **Legal studies:** Prelaw. **Liberal arts:** Arts/sciences, library science. **Math:** General, statistics. **Parks/recreation:** Exercise sciences, health/fitness. **Philosophy/religion:** Philosophy. **Physical sciences:** General, atmospheric science, chemistry, geology, hydrology, physics, planetary. **Protective services:** Law enforcement admin. **Psychology:** General. **Public administration:** General, policy analysis, social work. **Science technology:** Biological. **Social sciences:** General, anthropology, criminology, economics, geography, international relations, political science, sociology, urban studies. **Transportation:** Air traffic control, airline/commercial pilot, aviation management, flight instructor. **Visual/performing arts:** Acting, art, art history/conservation, ceramics, dramatic, drawing, film/cinema, jazz, music history, painting, piano/organ, printmaking, sculpture, stringed instruments, studio arts, voice/opera.

Most popular majors. Business/marketing 23%, education 18%, social sciences 9%.

Computing on campus. Dormitories wired for high-speed internet access and linked to campus network. Commuter students can connect to campus network. Online course registration, online library, helpline, repair service, student web hosting, wireless network available.

Student life. **Freshman orientation:** Mandatory. Preregistration for classes offered. Includes assistance with fall term registration. **Policies:** Freshmen permitted cars on campus. **Housing:** Coed dorms available. $100 fully refundable deposit, deadline 4/9. **Activities:** Concert band, choral groups, dance, drama, music ensembles, musical theater, opera, radio station, student government, student newspaper, symphony orchestra, TV station, more than 240 clubs and departmental organizations.

Athletics. NCAA. **Intercollegiate:** Baseball M, basketball, cross-country, diving, football (tackle) M, golf, ice hockey, skiing W, soccer W, softball W, swimming, tennis, track and field, volleyball W, wrestling M. **Intramural:** Basketball, football (non-tackle), golf, soccer, softball, volleyball, water polo. **Team name:** Huskies.

Student services. Adult student services, alcohol/substance abuse counseling, career counseling, student employment services, financial aid counseling, health services, minority student services, on-campus daycare, personal counseling, placement for graduates, veterans' counselor, women's services. **Physically disabled:** Services for visually, speech, hearing impaired.

Contact. E-mail: scsu4u@stcloudstate.edu
Phone: (320) 308-2244 Toll-free number: (877) 654-7278
Fax: (320) 308-2243
Pat Krueger, Associate Director for Admission, St. Cloud State University, 720 Fourth Avenue South, St. Cloud, MN 56301-4498

St. John's University

Collegeville, Minnesota — **CB member**
www.csbsju.edu — **CB code: 6624**

- Private 4-year university and liberal arts college for men affiliated with Roman Catholic Church
- Residential campus in rural community
- 1,842 degree-seeking undergraduates: 1% African American, 2% Asian American, 1% Hispanic American, 4% international
- 121 degree-seeking graduate students
- 87% of applicants admitted
- SAT or ACT (ACT writing optional), application essay required
- 78% graduate within 6 years; 21% enter graduate study

General. Founded in 1857. Regionally accredited. Coeducational academic and campus life shared with Saint Benedict in St. Joseph, MN. **Degrees:** 424 bachelor's awarded; master's, first professional offered. **ROTC:** Army. **Location:** 70 miles from Minneapolis-St. Paul, 15 miles from St. Cloud. **Calendar:** Semester. **Full-time faculty:** 147 total; 88% have terminal degrees, 10% minority, 29% women. **Part-time faculty:** 29 total; 34% have terminal degrees, 31% women. **Class size:** 47% < 20, 52% 20-39, less than 1% 40-49, less than 1% 50-99. **Special facilities:** Observatory, ecumenical center, Hill museum and manuscript library, liturgical press, nature preserve, arboretum, natural history museum, pottery kiln.

Freshman class profile. 1,167 applied, 1,017 admitted, 447 enrolled.

Mid 50% test scores			
SAT verbal:	530-660	Rank in top quarter:	51%
SAT math:	540-650	Rank in top tenth:	22%
ACT:	23-28	End year in good standing:	97%
GPA 3.50 or higher:	56%	Return as sophomores:	87%
GPA 3.0-3.49:	38%	Out-of-state:	15%
GPA 2.0-2.99:	6%	Live on campus:	99%
		International:	4%

Basis for selection. Course selection, scholastic achievement, GPA, test scores and essay most important. Extracurricular involvement, high school rank, and recommendation also important. Students who have completed the application process by 12/01 will receive notification of their scholarship award on 12/20. Interview recommended for academically weak/conditionally accepted students. **Homeschooled:** Applicants not required to have high school diploma but are required to provide appropriate documentation of college preparatory curriculum.

High school preparation. 17 units recommended. Recommended units include English 4, mathematics 3, social studies 2, science 2 (laboratory 2), foreign language 2 and academic electives 4.

2005-2006 Annual costs. Tuition/fees: $23,474. Room/board: $6,275. Books/supplies: $800. Personal expenses: $700.

2005-2006 Financial aid. **Need-based:** 339 full-time freshmen applied for aid; 271 were judged to have need; 271 of these received aid. Average need met was 92%. Average scholarship/grant was $14,142; average loan $3,875. 60% of total undergraduate aid awarded as scholarships/grants, 40% as loans/jobs. **Non-need-based:** Awarded to 1,563 full-time undergraduates, including 411 freshmen. Scholarships awarded for academics, art, leadership, minority status, music/drama, ROTC.

Application procedures. **Admission:** Priority date 12/1; no deadline. No application fee. Application may be submitted online. Admission notification on a rolling basis beginning on or about 10/1. A non-refundable enrollment deposit of $300 is due by May 1st. **Financial aid:** Priority date 3/15; no closing date. FAFSA, institutional form required. Applicants notified on a rolling basis starting 3/15; must reply by 5/1 or within 3 week(s) of notification.

Academics. **Special study options:** Accelerated study, combined bachelor's/graduate degree, cross-registration, double major, dual enrollment of high school students, honors, independent study, internships, liberal arts/career combination, student-designed major, study abroad, teacher certification program. 3-2 program in engineering with University of Minnesota, 3-1 program in dentistry with University of Minnesota, cross registration with St. Cloud State University. **Credit/placement by examination:** AP, CLEP, IB, institutional tests. **Support services:** Study skills assistance, tutoring, writing center.

Majors. **Biology:** General, biochemistry. **Business:** Accounting, business admin. **Computer sciences:** Computer science. **Conservation:** Environmental science. **Education:** General, art, elementary. **English:** Speech/rhetoric. **Foreign languages:** Classics, French, German, Spanish. **Health:** Nursing (RN), predentistry, premedicine, prepharmacy, preveterinary. **History:** General. **Interdisciplinary:** Biological/physical sciences, math/computer science, medieval/Renaissance, natural sciences, nutrition sciences, peace/conflict. **Legal studies:** Prelaw. **Liberal arts:** Arts/sciences, humanities. **Math:** General. **Philosophy/religion:** Philosophy. **Physical sciences:** Chemistry, physics. **Psychology:** General. **Public administration:** Social work. **Social sciences:** General, economics, political science, sociology. **Theology:** Preministerial, religious ed, theology. **Visual/performing arts:** Art, art history/conservation, dramatic.

Most popular majors. Biology 11%, business/marketing 19%, computer/information sciences 6%, English 12%, social sciences 22%.

Computing on campus. 604 workstations in dormitories, library, computer center, student center. Dormitories wired for high-speed internet access and linked to campus network. Commuter students can connect to campus network. Online course registration, helpline, student web hosting available.

Student life. Freshman orientation: Mandatory. Preregistration for classes offered. One day summer session for students and parents. **Policies:** Freshmen permitted cars on campus. **Housing:** Guaranteed on-campus for freshmen. Special housing for disabled, apartments, substance-free housing available. Earth-sheltered, solar-heated apartments available to upperclassmen; health/wellness floor and other special interest groups available, such as ROTC and international students. Freshmen and sophomores are required to live on campus. **Activities:** Bands, choral groups, dance, drama, literary magazine, music ensembles, musical theater, opera, radio station, student government, student newspaper, symphony orchestra, volunteers in service to others, Magis, College Republicans, College Democrats, joint events council, Asia club, student coalition for global solidarity, cultural fusion club, outdoor leadership center, students in free enterprise.

Athletics. NCAA. **Intercollegiate:** Baseball M, basketball M, cross-country M, diving M, football (tackle) M, golf M, ice hockey M, skiing M, soccer M, swimming M, tennis M, track and field M, wrestling M. **Intramural:** Basketball M, football (tackle) M, ice hockey M, racquetball M, soccer M, softball M, table tennis M, tennis M, volleyball M, water polo M. **Team name:** Johnnies.

Student services. Alcohol/substance abuse counseling, campus ministries, career counseling, student employment services, financial aid counseling, health services, minority student services, personal counseling, placement for graduates. **Physically disabled:** Services for hearing impaired.

Contact. E-mail: admissions@csbsju.edu
Phone: (320) 363-2196 Toll-free number: (800) 544-1489
Fax: (320) 363-2750
Mary Milbert, Dean of Admissions, St. John's University, PO Box 7155, Collegeville, MN 56321-7155

St. Mary's University of Minnesota

Winona, Minnesota — **CB member**
www.smumn.edu — **CB code: 6632**

- Private 4-year university affiliated with Roman Catholic Church
- Residential campus in large town
- 1,635 degree-seeking undergraduates: 22% part-time, 52% women, 4% African American, 2% Asian American, 2% Hispanic American, 1% international
- 3,378 degree-seeking graduate students
- 83% of applicants admitted
- SAT or ACT (ACT writing optional), application essay required

General. Founded in 1912. Regionally accredited. **Degrees:** 369 bachelor's awarded; master's, doctoral offered. **ROTC:** Army. **Location:** 110 miles from Minneapolis-St. Paul, 45 miles from Rochester. **Calendar:** Semester, limited summer session. **Full-time faculty:** 101 total; 80% have terminal degrees, 1% minority, 40% women. **Part-time faculty:** 460 total; 34% have terminal degrees, 3% minority, 49% women. **Class size:** 56% < 20, 44% 20-39, less than 1% 40-49. **Special facilities:** Woodland and stream, nature preserve, observatory.

Freshman class profile. 1,048 applied, 873 admitted, 311 enrolled.

Mid 50% test scores		Rank in top quarter:	47%
SAT verbal:	520-630	Rank in top tenth:	19%
SAT math:	500-650	Return as sophomores:	75%
ACT:	19-25	Out-of-state:	35%
GPA 3.50 or higher:	39%	Live on campus:	96%
GPA 3.0-3.49:	26%	International:	1%
GPA 2.0-2.99:	34%		

Basis for selection. Minimum 2.5 GPA, upper half of class, 50th percentile on standardized tests, essay, college prep coursework required. Recommendations, interview, school and community activities considered. Interview recommended for academically marginal students.

High school preparation. 18 units required. Required and recommended units include English 4, mathematics 3, social studies 2, science 3 (laboratory 2), foreign language 2 and academic electives 6.

2005-2006 Annual costs. Tuition/fees: $19,149. Room/board: $5,720. Books/supplies: $1,056. Personal expenses: $800.

2005-2006 Financial aid. Need-based: 250 full-time freshmen applied for aid; 213 were judged to have need; 213 of these received aid. Average need met was 94%. Average scholarship/grant was $8,350; average loan $4,375. 55% of total undergraduate aid awarded as scholarships/grants, 45% as loans/jobs. **Non-need-based:** Scholarships awarded for academics, art, leadership, music/drama.

Application procedures. Admission: Priority date 4/1; deadline 5/1 (postmark date). $25 fee, may be waived for applicants with need. Application may be submitted online. Admission notification on a rolling basis beginning on or about 9/1. Must reply by May 1 or within 3 week(s) if notified thereafter. **Financial aid:** Priority date 3/15; no closing date. FAFSA required. Applicants notified on a rolling basis starting 3/5; must reply within 3 week(s) of notification.

Academics. Special study options: Cooperative education, cross-registration, double major, dual enrollment of high school students, ESL, honors, independent study, internships, student-designed major, study abroad, teacher certification program, urban semester, Washington semester. **Credit/placement by examination:** AP, CLEP, IB, SAT, ACT, institutional tests. 8 credits per area allowed. **Support services:** Learning center, reduced course load, remedial instruction, study skills assistance, tutoring, writing center.

Majors. Biology: General, biophysics, environmental. **Business:** Accounting, business admin, human resources, international, management science, marketing. **Communications:** Journalism, public relations. **Communications technology:** General, desktop publishing. **Computer sciences:** Computer science, information systems. **Education:** Biology, chemistry, early childhood, English, foreign languages, French, mathematics, music, physics, science, social science, social studies, Spanish. **Engineering:** Physics. **Engineering technology:** Industrial. **English:** English lit, technical writing. **Foreign languages:** French, Spanish. **Health:** Clinical lab science, cytotechnology, health care admin, nuclear medical technology. **History:** General. **Interdisciplinary:** Math/computer science. **Math:** General. **Philosophy/religion:** Philosophy. **Physical sciences:** Chemistry, molecular physics, physics. **Protective services:** Criminal justice, law enforcement admin, police science. **Psychology:** General. **Public administration:** General, human services. **Social sciences:** General, political science, sociology. **Theology:** Pastoral counseling, preministerial, theology. **Visual/performing arts:** Commercial/advertising art, dramatic, music management, music performance, studio arts, voice/opera.

Most popular majors. Biology 6%, business/marketing 33%, communications/journalism 6%, computer/information sciences 7%, education 6%, security/protective services 6%, visual/performing arts 7%.

Computing on campus. 365 workstations in dormitories, library, computer center, student center. Dormitories wired for high-speed internet access and linked to campus network. Commuter students can connect to campus network. Online course registration, online library, helpline, repair service, student web hosting available.

Student life. Freshman orientation: Mandatory. Preregistration for classes offered. Held during summer prior to fall enrollment. **Policies:** Freshmen permitted cars on campus. **Housing:** Guaranteed on-campus for all undergraduates. Coed dorms, single-sex dorms, special housing for disabled, apartments available. $200 deposit, deadline 4/1. **Activities:** Bands, choral groups, dance, drama, literary magazine, music ensembles, musical theater, radio station, student government, student newspaper, Big and Little Pals, college democrats, college republicans, Collegians for Life, Community of Women, InsideOut Christian Fellowship, international student association, LaSallian Collegians, liturgical ministers.

Athletics. NCAA. **Intercollegiate:** Baseball M, basketball, cross-country, diving, golf, ice hockey, soccer, softball W, swimming, tennis, track and field, volleyball W. **Intramural:** Basketball, golf, ice hockey M, racquetball, soccer, softball, tennis, volleyball. **Team name:** Cardinals.

Student services. Alcohol/substance abuse counseling, campus ministries, career counseling, student employment services, financial aid counseling, health services, personal counseling, placement for graduates. **Physically disabled:** Services for visually, hearing impaired.

Contact. E-mail: admissions@smumn.edu
Phone: (507) 457-1600 Toll-free number: (800) 635-5987
Fax: (507) 457-1722
Anthony Piscitiello, Vice President for Admissions, St. Mary's University of Minnesota, 700 Terrace Heights, #2, Winona, MN 55987-1399

St. Olaf College

Northfield, Minnesota — **CB member**
www.stolaf.edu — **CB code: 6638**

- Private 4-year liberal arts college affiliated with Evangelical Lutheran Church in America
- Residential campus in large town

- 3,007 degree-seeking undergraduates: 58% women, 1% African American, 5% Asian American, 1% Hispanic American, 1% international
- 73% of applicants admitted
- SAT or ACT (ACT writing optional), application essay required
- 84% graduate within 6 years; 29% enter graduate study

General. Founded in 1874. Regionally accredited. **Degrees:** 689 bachelor's awarded. **Location:** 35 miles from Minneapolis-St. Paul. **Calendar:** 4-1-4, limited summer session. **Full-time faculty:** 196 total; 93% have terminal degrees, 6% minority, 42% women. **Part-time faculty:** 135 total; 60% have terminal degrees, 4% minority, 50% women. **Class size:** 47% < 20, 48% 20-39, less than 1% 40-49, 4% 50-99, less than 1% >100. **Special facilities:** Norwegian-American Historical Society Archives; natural habitat includes 5 wetland areas, 45-acre native prairie grasses and bluebird trail of 70 houses.

Freshman class profile. 2,991 applied, 2,183 admitted, 764 enrolled.

Mid 50% test scores			
SAT verbal:	590-700	Rank in top quarter:	76%
SAT math:	580-690	Rank in top tenth:	49%
ACT:	25-30	End year in good standing:	98%
GPA 3.50 or higher:	66%	Return as sophomores:	92%
GPA 3.0-3.49:	24%	Out-of-state:	42%
GPA 2.0-2.99:	10%	Live on campus:	100%
		International:	1%

Basis for selection. School achievement most important, followed by essay and test scores. Interview recommended. Audition required for music students. **Learning Disabled:** Personal interview recommended. Untimed standardized tests accepted.

High school preparation. 14 units required; 24 recommended. Required and recommended units include English 4, mathematics 2-4, social studies 1-2, history 1-2, science 2-4 (laboratory 1-2), foreign language 2-4 and academic electives 2-4.

2006-2007 Annual costs. Tuition/fees: $28,200. Room/board: $7,400. Books/supplies: $950. Personal expenses: $700.

2005-2006 Financial aid. Need-based: 577 full-time freshmen applied for aid; 475 were judged to have need; 475 of these received aid. Average need met was 100%. Average scholarship/grant was $15,103; average loan $4,343. 72% of total undergraduate aid awarded as scholarships/grants, 28% as loans/jobs. **Non-need-based:** Awarded to 1,279 full-time undergraduates, including 343 freshmen. Scholarships awarded for academics, leadership, music/drama. **Additional information:** Limited number of music lesson fee waivers available for music majors, awarded on audition basis only.

Application procedures. Admission: Priority date 2/1; no deadline. $35 fee, may be waived for applicants with need. Application may be submitted online. Admission notification on a rolling basis beginning on or about 12/1. Must reply by May 1 or within 2 week(s) if notified thereafter. **Financial aid:** Priority date 12/1, closing date 2/1. FAFSA, CSS PROFILE required. Applicants notified on a rolling basis starting 3/1; must reply by 5/1 or within 2 week(s) of notification.

Academics. Students may propose self-designed integrative majors. **Special study options:** Cross-registration, double major, dual enrollment of high school students, independent study, internships, student-designed major, study abroad, teacher certification program, urban semester, Washington semester. Great Conversation: 5-semester program emphasizing reading, writing, and outside-of-the-classroom discussion available to 70 incoming students each year; BA/BS in engineering with Washington University (MO), University of Minnesota, Minneapolis; center for experiential learning; center for integrative studies; joint law degree with Columbia University. **Credit/placement by examination:** AP, CLEP, IB, institutional tests. 5 credit hours maximum toward bachelor's degree. **Support services:** Learning center, study skills assistance, tutoring, writing center.

Majors. Area/ethnic studies: American, Asian, Latin American, Russian/Slavic, women's. **Biology:** General. **Computer sciences:** Computer science. **Conservation:** Environmental studies. **Education:** Music, social studies. **English:** English lit. **Family/consumer sciences:** Family studies. **Foreign languages:** Ancient Greek, classics, French, German, Latin, Norwegian, Russian, Spanish. **Health:** Nursing (RN). **History:** General. **Interdisciplinary:** Ancient studies, medieval/Renaissance. **Liberal arts:** Arts/sciences. **Math:** General. **Parks/recreation:** Exercise sciences. **Philosophy/religion:** Philosophy, religion. **Physical sciences:** Chemistry, physics. **Psychology:** General. **Public administration:** Social work. **Social sciences:** Economics, political science, sociology. **Theology:** Sacred music. **Visual/performing arts:** Art, art history/conservation, dance, dramatic, music performance, music theory/composition.

Most popular majors. Area/ethnic studies 7%, biology 8%, English 10%, mathematics 7%, physical sciences 6%, psychology 9%, social sciences 13%, visual/performing arts 13%.

Computing on campus. 804 workstations in dormitories, library, computer center, student center. Dormitories wired for high-speed internet access and linked to campus network. Commuter students can connect to campus network. Helpline, wireless network available.

Student life. Freshman orientation: Mandatory. Held 5 days before start of fall classes. **Policies:** Alcohol not permitted on campus. **Housing:** Guaranteed on-campus for all undergraduates. Coed dorms, special housing for disabled, substance-free housing available. $300 nonrefundable deposit, deadline 5/1. Honor houses, language houses, quiet halls, first-year only dorms. **Activities:** Bands, choral groups, dance, drama, film society, literary magazine, music ensembles, musical theater, opera, radio station, student government, student newspaper, symphony orchestra, TV station, 117 registered student organizations.

Athletics. NCAA. **Intercollegiate:** Baseball M, basketball, cross-country, diving, football (tackle) M, golf, ice hockey, skiing, soccer, softball W, swimming, tennis, track and field, volleyball W, wrestling M. **Intramural:** Badminton, basketball, diving, field hockey M, football (tackle), ice hockey M, lacrosse, racquetball, rowing (crew), rugby, skiing, soccer, softball, swimming, synchronized swimming, table tennis, tennis, volleyball, water polo. **Team name:** Oles.

Student services. Alcohol/substance abuse counseling, campus ministries, career counseling, student employment services, financial aid counseling, health services, minority student services, personal counseling. **Physically disabled:** Services for visually, hearing impaired.

Contact. E-mail: admissions@stolaf.edu
Phone: (507) 646-3025 Toll-free number: (800) 800-3025
Fax: (507) 646-3832
Michael Kyle, Director of Admissions, St. Olaf College, 1520 St. Olaf Avenue, Northfield, MN 55057

Southwest Minnesota State University

Marshall, Minnesota
www.southwest.msus.edu **CB code: 6703**

- Public 4-year liberal arts and technical college
- Residential campus in large town
- 2,640 degree-seeking undergraduates: 13% part-time, 55% women, 4% African American, 1% Asian American, 2% Hispanic American, 1% Native American, 8% international
- 521 degree-seeking graduate students
- 76% of applicants admitted
- SAT or ACT (ACT writing optional) required

General. Founded in 1963. Regionally accredited. **Degrees:** 435 bachelor's, 7 associate awarded; master's offered. **Location:** 150 miles from Minneapolis-St. Paul. **Calendar:** Semester, limited summer session. **Full-time faculty:** 127 total. **Part-time faculty:** 103 total. **Special facilities:** Natural history museum, anthropology museum, planetarium.

Freshman class profile. 1,750 applied, 1,327 admitted, 568 enrolled.

Mid 50% test scores		Out-of-state:	16%
ACT:	18-24	Live on campus:	60%
Return as sophomores:	66%	International:	12%

Basis for selection. Class rank in top half of class or SAT combined score of 970 (exclusive of Writing) or ACT composite score of 21. Provisional admission may be granted to students who rank in top two-thirds of class or have ACT composite score of 19 or SAT combined score of 890. GED students must submit ACT. PSAT/NMSQT may be submitted in place of SAT or ACT. Interview recommended for academically weak students; audition recommended for music students.

High school preparation. 15 units required. Required units include English 4, mathematics 3, social studies 3, history 1, science 3 and foreign language 2. Social studies units must include American history and geography.

2005-2006 Annual costs. Tuition/fees: $5,855. Participates in pilot project allowing one tuition rate for in-state and out-of-state. Room/board: $5,120. Books/supplies: $800. Personal expenses: $1,000.

2005-2006 Financial aid. Need-based: 62% of total undergraduate aid awarded as scholarships/grants, 38% as loans/jobs. **Non-need-based:** Scholarships awarded for academics, art, athletics, leadership, minority status, music/drama, state residency.

Application procedures. Admission: No deadline. $20 fee. Application may be submitted online. Admission notification on a rolling basis.

Financial aid: Priority date 4/1; no closing date. FAFSA, institutional form required. Applicants notified on a rolling basis starting 5/15.

Academics. Special study options: Accelerated study, cooperative education, cross-registration, distance learning, double major, dual enrollment of high school students, ESL, exchange student, external degree, honors, independent study, internships, student-designed major, study abroad, teacher certification program. 2+2 bachelor's programs with Ridgewater College, Central Lakes College, Worthington College, and Riverland Community College. **Credit/placement by examination:** CLEP, institutional tests. 36 credit hours maximum toward associate degree, 36 toward bachelor's. **Support services:** Learning center, reduced course load, remedial instruction, study skills assistance, tutoring, writing center.

Majors. Agriculture: Agribusiness operations, agronomy. **Biology:** General, cell/histology, ecology. **Business:** Accounting, business admin, finance. **Communications:** General, broadcast journalism, public relations. **Computer sciences:** General. **Education:** Art, biology, chemistry, drama/dance, early childhood, elementary, health, mathematics, music, physical, science, speech. **English:** Creative writing, speech/rhetoric. **Foreign languages:** Spanish. **History:** General. **Liberal arts:** Arts/sciences. **Math:** General. **Parks/recreation:** Health/fitness. **Philosophy/religion:** Philosophy. **Physical sciences:** Chemistry. **Protective services:** Fire services admin, law enforcement admin. **Psychology:** General. **Public administration:** General, social work. **Social sciences:** Political science, sociology. **Visual/performing arts:** Art, dramatic.

Computing on campus. 300 workstations in dormitories, library, computer center. Dormitories wired for high-speed internet access and linked to campus network. Commuter students can connect to campus network. Online course registration, online library, helpline, repair service, student web hosting available.

Student life. Freshman orientation: Available, $45 fee. Preregistration for classes offered. **Housing:** Coed dorms, single-sex dorms, special housing for disabled available. **Activities:** Bands, choral groups, dance, drama, film society, literary magazine, music ensembles, musical theater, radio station, student government, student newspaper, symphony orchestra, TV station, Black Student Union, international student organization, Inter-Varsity Christian Fellowship, Lutheran Student Commission, student activities committee, Republican Speakers Club, Young DFL, non-traditional students organization.

Athletics. NAIA. **Intercollegiate:** Baseball M, basketball, football (tackle) M, golf W, soccer W, softball W, tennis W, volleyball W, wrestling M. **Intramural:** Basketball, ice hockey M, racquetball, skiing, softball, tennis, track and field, volleyball, wrestling M. **Team name:** Mustangs.

Student services. Adult student services, campus ministries, career counseling, student employment services, financial aid counseling, health services, minority student services, on-campus daycare, personal counseling, placement for graduates, veterans' counselor. **Physically disabled:** Services for visually, speech, hearing impaired.

Contact. E-mail: shearerr@southwest.msus.edu
Phone: (507) 537-6286 Toll-free number: (800) 642-0684
Fax: (507) 537-7154
Richard Shearer, Enrollment Services Director, Southwest Minnesota State University, 1501 State Street, Marshall, MN 56258-1598

University of Minnesota: Crookston

Crookston, Minnesota
www.UMCrookston.edu **CB code: 6893**

- Public 4-year branch campus college
- Residential campus in small town
- 1,053 degree-seeking undergraduates: 19% part-time, 44% women, 4% African American, 1% Asian American, 2% Hispanic American, 1% Native American, 3% international
- 92% of applicants admitted
- SAT or ACT (ACT writing optional) required
- 36% graduate within 6 years

General. Founded in 1965. Regionally accredited. Eeach student and faculty member issued laptop computer. **Degrees:** 203 bachelor's, 21 associate awarded. **ROTC:** Air Force. **Location:** 25 miles from Grand Forks, North Dakota, 75 miles from Fargo, North Dakota. **Calendar:** Semester, limited summer session. **Full-time faculty:** 53 total; 49% have terminal degrees, 8% minority, 34% women. **Part-time faculty:** 51 total; 20% have terminal degrees, 2% minority, 35% women. **Class size:** 50% < 20, 39% 20-39, 7% 40-49, 4% 50-99. **Special facilities:** 85-acre Red River Valley Natural History Area (containing prairie, marshes, and forests); teaching and outreach center.

Freshman class profile. 408 applied, 376 admitted, 198 enrolled.

Mid 50% test scores		Rank in top tenth:	13%
SAT verbal:	380-600	Out-of-state:	30%
SAT math:	410-570	Live on campus:	78%
ACT:	18-24	International:	2%
Rank in top quarter:	32%		

Basis for selection. High school class rank and ACT test scores most important. **Learning Disabled:** Students encouraged to contact Disability Services early in the admissions process to insure availability of appropriate services.

High school preparation. College-preparatory program recommended. Recommended units include English 4, mathematics 3, social studies 2, science 3 and foreign language 2.

2005-2006 Annual costs. Tuition/fees: $8,119; $8,119 out-of-state. Laptop computer included in fees. Room/board: $5,038. Books/supplies: $700. Personal expenses: $800.

2004-2005 Financial aid. Need-based: 179 full-time freshmen applied for aid; 152 were judged to have need; 151 of these received aid. Average need met was 80%. Average scholarship/grant was $4,802; average loan $5,917. 37% of total undergraduate aid awarded as scholarships/grants, 63% as loans/jobs. **Non-need-based:** Awarded to 228 full-time undergraduates, including 72 freshmen. Scholarships awarded for academics, athletics, leadership, minority status, ROTC, state residency. **Additional information:** Tuition guarantee plan available to all students who apply for it.

Application procedures. Admission: Priority date 2/1; deadline 8/15 (postmark date). $25 fee, may be waived for applicants with need. Application may be submitted online. Admission notification on a rolling basis beginning on or about 9/15. **Financial aid:** Priority date 3/1; no closing date. FAFSA required. Applicants notified on a rolling basis starting 3/15; must reply within 3 week(s) of notification.

Academics. 10-week applied internship for all programs. **Special study options:** Cross-registration, distance learning, double major, dual enrollment of high school students, independent study, internships, student-designed major, study abroad. **Credit/placement by examination:** AP, CLEP, IB. 12 credit hours maximum toward associate degree. 4 to 8 credits may be awarded for CLEP General Examinations, depending on percentile rank. **Support services:** Learning center, pre-admission summer program, reduced course load, remedial instruction, study skills assistance, tutoring.

Majors. Agriculture: Agribusiness operations, agronomy, animal sciences, business, equestrian studies, equine science, farm/ranch, greenhouse operations, horticultural science, horticulture, power machinery, soil science, turf management. **Business:** Accounting, business admin, hospitality/recreation, hotel/motel admin, information resources management, management information systems, marketing, resort management, restaurant/food services. **Computer sciences:** Information systems, LAN/WAN management, system admin, web page design. **Conservation:** General, water/wetlands/marine, wildlife. **Education:** Agricultural, early childhood. **English:** Technical writing. **Health:** Health care admin, health services. **Parks/recreation:** Facilities management, sports admin. **Personal/culinary services:** Restaurant/catering. **Transportation:** Aviation management.

Most popular majors. Agriculture 26%, business/marketing 30%, education 6%, engineering/engineering technologies 8%, natural resources/environmental science 15%.

Computing on campus. PC or laptop required. 1,250 workstations in dormitories, library, computer center, student center. Dormitories wired for high-speed internet access and linked to campus network. Commuter students can connect to campus network. Online course registration, online library, helpline, repair service, student web hosting, wireless network available.

Student life. Freshman orientation: Mandatory, $30 fee. Preregistration for classes offered. Held immediately prior to start of fall semester. **Policies:** Freshmen permitted cars on campus. **Housing:** Coed dorms, apartments, substance-free housing available. $50 deposit, deadline 8/1. **Activities:** Bands, choral groups, drama, musical theater, student government, campus ministry club, multicultural club, UMC Ambassadors, Students in Free Enterprise, Wildlife Society Chapter, Collegiate FFA, flying club, Habitat for Humanity, Rodeo Association, Student Athletic Advisory Committee.

Athletics. NCAA. **Intercollegiate:** Baseball M, basketball, cheerleading, equestrian W, football (tackle) M, golf, ice hockey M, soccer W, softball W, tennis W, volleyball W. **Intramural:** Basketball, bowling, racquetball, tennis, volleyball. **Team name:** Golden Eagles.

Student services. Adult student services, alcohol/substance abuse counseling, campus ministries, career counseling, student employment services,

financial aid counseling, health services, minority student services, on-campus daycare, personal counseling, placement for graduates, veterans' counselor. **Physically disabled:** Services for visually, hearing impaired.

Contact. E-mail: info@UMCrookston.edu
Phone: (218) 281-8569 Toll-free number: (800) 862-6466
Fax: (218) 281-8050 ext. 369
Mary Feller, Director of Admissions, University of Minnesota: Crookston, 2900 University Avenue, Crookston, MN 56716-5001

University of Minnesota: Duluth

Duluth, Minnesota
www.d.umn.edu **CB code: 6873**

- Public 4-year university
- Residential campus in small city
- 8,995 degree-seeking undergraduates: 12% part-time, 49% women
- 1,000 graduate students
- 79% of applicants admitted
- ACT with writing required
- 48% graduate within 6 years

General. Founded in 1947. Regionally accredited. **Degrees:** 1,632 bachelor's awarded; master's offered. **ROTC:** Air Force. **Location:** 130 miles from Minneapolis-St. Paul. **Calendar:** Semester, extensive summer session. **Full-time faculty:** 406 total; 77% have terminal degrees, 17% minority, 41% women. **Part-time faculty:** 109 total; 36% have terminal degrees, 8% minority, 53% women. **Class size:** 43% < 20, 42% 20-39, 5% 40-49, 6% 50-99, 4% >100. **Special facilities:** Planetarium.

Freshman class profile. 6,989 applied, 5,522 admitted, 2,158 enrolled.

Mid 50% test scores		Return as sophomores:	75%
ACT:	20-25	Out-of-state:	12%
Rank in top quarter:	61%	Live on campus:	65%
Rank in top tenth:	15%	International:	1%

Basis for selection. Students at or above 65th percentile of high school class automatically admitted. Test scores required. Students ranking between the 40th and 64th are selectively admitted based on test scores and academic preparation. Essays may be part of an appeals process. Audition required for music students.

High school preparation. 14 units required. Required units include English 4, mathematics 3, social studies 2, science 3 and foreign language 2. Third year of science can be either physical or biological; mathematics sequence includes algebra, geometry and higher algebra.

2005-2006 Annual costs. Tuition/fees: $8,512; $19,619 out-of-state. Room/board: $5,544. Books/supplies: $1,144. Personal expenses: $1,600.

2005-2006 Financial aid. Need-based: 1,722 full-time freshmen applied for aid; 1,093 were judged to have need; 1,081 of these received aid. Average need met was 60%. Average scholarship/grant was $5,438; average loan $2,811. 27% of total undergraduate aid awarded as scholarships/grants, 73% as loans/jobs. **Non-need-based:** Scholarships awarded for academics, athletics, ROTC.

Application procedures. Admission: Priority date 2/1; deadline 8/1. $35 fee. Application may be submitted online. Admission notification on a rolling basis beginning on or about 10/1. Applications are accepted on a space available basis after 2/01. **Financial aid:** Priority date 3/31; no closing date. FAFSA required. Applicants notified on a rolling basis starting 3/1; must reply within 2 week(s) of notification.

Academics. Special study options: Cross-registration, distance learning, double major, dual enrollment of high school students, independent study, internships, student-designed major, study abroad, teacher certification program. **Credit/placement by examination:** AP, CLEP, IB, institutional tests. **Support services:** Learning center, reduced course load, remedial instruction, study skills assistance, tutoring, writing center.

Majors. Area/ethnic studies: Native American, women's. **Biology:** General, biochemistry, cell/histology, molecular. **Business:** Accounting, business admin. **Communications:** General. **Computer sciences:** Computer science. **Conservation:** Environmental studies. **Education:** Art, early childhood, elementary, English, French, German, health, mathematics, music, physical, science, social studies, Spanish. **Engineering:** Chemical, computer, electrical, mechanical. **Foreign languages:** French, German, Spanish. **Health:** Communication disorders, health care admin, predentistry, prepharmacy, preveterinary. **History:** General. **Legal studies:** Prelaw. **Math:** General, statistics. **Parks/recreation:** General, exercise sciences. **Philosophy/religion:** Philosophy. **Physical sciences:** Chemistry, geology, physics. **Psychology:** General. **Social sciences:** Anthropology, criminology, economics, geography, political science, sociology, urban studies. **Visual/performing arts:** Art, art history/conservation, commercial/advertising art, dramatic, jazz, music pedagogy, music performance, studio arts, theater design.

Most popular majors. Biology 22%, business/marketing 26%, computer/information sciences 6%, education 14%, psychology 7%, visual/performing arts 6%.

Computing on campus. PC or laptop required. 575 workstations in dormitories, library, computer center, student center. Dormitories wired for high-speed internet access and linked to campus network. Commuter students can connect to campus network. Online course registration, online library, helpline, repair service, student web hosting, wireless network available.

Student life. Freshman orientation: Mandatory, $40 fee. **Policies:** Freshmen permitted cars on campus. **Housing:** Coed dorms, single-sex dorms, apartments available. $200 deposit, deadline 4/15. Housing facilities are fully accessible to persons with physical disabilities. **Activities:** Bands, choral groups, dance, drama, music ensembles, musical theater, radio station, student government, student newspaper, symphony orchestra, Intervarsity Christian Fellowship, MN Public Interest Research Group, Anishinabe club (American Indian students), black student association, Circle-K, Hispanic organization, international club, Southeast Asian association, Students Engaged in Rewarding Volunteer Experiences.

Athletics. NCAA. **Intercollegiate:** Baseball M, basketball, cross-country, football (tackle) M, ice hockey, soccer W, softball W, tennis, track and field, volleyball W. **Intramural:** Archery, basketball, bowling, cross-country, golf, ice hockey, lacrosse, rugby, skiing, soccer, softball, swimming, tennis, track and field, volleyball. **Team name:** Bulldogs.

Student services. Campus ministries, career counseling, student employment services, financial aid counseling, health services, minority student services, on-campus daycare, personal counseling, placement for graduates, veterans' counselor, women's services. **Physically disabled:** Services for visually, speech, hearing impaired.

Contact. E-mail: umdadmis@d.umn.edu
Phone: (218) 726-7171 Toll-free number: (800) 232-1339
Fax: (218) 726-7040
Beth Esselstrom, Director of Admissions, University of Minnesota: Duluth, 1117 University Drive, Duluth, MN 55812-3000

University of Minnesota: Morris

Morris, Minnesota
www.morris.umn.edu **CB code: 6890**

- Public 4-year university and liberal arts college
- Residential campus in small town
- 1,530 degree-seeking undergraduates: 3% part-time, 59% women, 2% African American, 3% Asian American, 1% Hispanic American, 9% Native American, 1% international
- 82% of applicants admitted
- SAT or ACT with writing required
- 59% graduate within 6 years; 36% enter graduate study

General. Founded in 1959. Regionally accredited. **Degrees:** 342 bachelor's awarded. **Location:** 150 miles from Minneapolis-St. Paul, 100 miles from Fargo, North Dakota. **Calendar:** Semester, limited summer session. **Full-time faculty:** 121 total; 93% have terminal degrees, 16% minority, 43% women. **Part-time faculty:** 55 total; 22% have terminal degrees, 7% minority, 54% women. **Class size:** 69% < 20, 25% 20-39, 3% 40-49, 3% 50-99. **Special facilities:** Tropical conservatory, prairie gate press, historical center, experiment station, USDA soil laboratory, center for small towns, theatres, observatory.

Freshman class profile. 1,097 applied, 901 admitted, 388 enrolled.

Mid 50% test scores		Rank in top tenth:	32%
SAT verbal:	520-640	Return as sophomores:	86%
SAT math:	510-650	Out-of-state:	13%
ACT:	23-28	Live on campus:	98%
Rank in top quarter:	60%	International:	1%

Basis for selection. Admission based on four primary factors: high school performance, ACT/SAT scores, extra-curricular involvement/leadership experience/honors. Interview recommended. Audition required for music students receiving scholarships. **Homeschooled:** Submit porfolio of works studied.

High school preparation. 17 units recommended. Recommended units include English 4, mathematics 3, social studies 4, history 4, science 3 (laboratory 2) and foreign language 2. Science units must include 1 biological science and 1 physical science.

2005-2006 Annual costs. Tuition/fees: $9,722; $9,722 out-of-state. Tuition is the same for all students, both In-state and out-of-state, except for Wisconsin students who pay a lower rate due to reciprocity agreement. Room/board: $5,750. Books/supplies: $600. Personal expenses: $1,200.

2005-2006 Financial aid. Need-based: Average need met was 83%. Average scholarship/grant was $6,613; average loan $6,423. 54% of total undergraduate aid awarded as scholarships/grants, 46% as loans/jobs. **Non-need-based:** Scholarships awarded for academics, alumni affiliation, leadership, minority status, music/drama. **Additional information:** Land-grant program waiving tuition for Native Americans.

Application procedures. Admission: Priority date 12/1; deadline 3/15 (postmark date). $35 fee, may be waived for applicants with need. Application may be submitted online. Admission notification 4/1. Must reply by May 1 or within 2 week(s) if notified thereafter. **Financial aid:** Priority date 3/1; no closing date. FAFSA required. Applicants notified on a rolling basis starting 3/1; must reply within 3 week(s) of notification.

Academics. Academic opportunities that allow students to assist faculty in research or teaching endeavors and receive a stipend or expense allowances include: The Undergraduate Research Opportunities Program, The Morris Academic Partnership, The Minority Mentorship Program, The Morris Administrative Internship, and The Student Internship Program. **Special study options:** Cooperative education, distance learning, double major, exchange student, honors, independent study, internships, liberal arts/career combination, New York semester, semester at sea, student-designed major, study abroad, teacher certification program, United Nations semester, urban semester, Washington semester. **Credit/placement by examination:** AP, CLEP, IB, ACT, institutional tests. No limit for credit by exam, but the credit awarded does not count as resident credit; must have 30 resident credits. **Support services:** Learning center, reduced course load, study skills assistance, tutoring, writing center.

Majors. Area/ethnic studies: European, Latin American, women's. **Biology:** General. **Business:** Management science. **Communications:** General. **Computer sciences:** Computer science. **Education:** Elementary. **Foreign languages:** French, German, Spanish. **History:** General. **Liberal arts:** Humanities. **Math:** General, statistics. **Philosophy/religion:** Philosophy. **Physical sciences:** Chemistry, geology, physics. **Psychology:** General. **Public administration:** Social work. **Social sciences:** Anthropology, economics, political science, sociology. **Visual/performing arts:** Art history/conservation, dramatic, music performance, studio arts.

Most popular majors. Biology 8%, business/marketing 7%, education 8%, English 11%, history 7%, public administration/social services 7%, social sciences 17%, visual/performing arts 6%.

Computing on campus. 220 workstations in dormitories, library, computer center, student center. Dormitories wired for high-speed internet access and linked to campus network. Commuter students can connect to campus network. Online course registration, online library, helpline, repair service, wireless network available.

Student life. Freshman orientation: Mandatory. Preregistration for classes offered. Held 4 days prior to fall semester. **Policies:** Freshmen permitted cars on campus. **Housing:** Guaranteed on-campus for all undergraduates. Coed dorms, special housing for disabled, substance-free housing available. $200 deposit, deadline 8/1. **Activities:** Bands, choral groups, dance, drama, film society, literary magazine, music ensembles, musical theater, radio station, student government, student newspaper, symphony orchestra, TV station, Amnesty International, Big Friend/Little Friend, Campus Aglow Outreach, E-Quality, Habitat for Humanity, Intervarsity Christian Fellowship, Minnesota Public Interest Research Group (MPIRG), Morris Campus Student Association (MCSA), Positive Spirituality, Women of Color Association.

Athletics. NCAA. **Intercollegiate:** Baseball M, basketball, cross-country W, diving W, football (tackle) M, golf, soccer, softball W, swimming W, tennis, track and field, volleyball W. **Intramural:** Baseball, basketball, bowling, field hockey, football (non-tackle), ice hockey, softball, triathlon, volleyball. **Team name:** Cougars.

Student services. Alcohol/substance abuse counseling, career counseling, student employment services, financial aid counseling, health services, minority student services, personal counseling, placement for graduates, veterans' counselor, women's services. **Physically disabled:** Services for visually, speech, hearing impaired. **Learning disabled:** Comprehensive services available.

Contact. E-mail: admissions@morris.umn.edu
Phone: (320) 589-6035 Toll-free number: (888) 866-3382
Fax: (320) 589-1673
Jaime Moquin, Director of Admissions, University of Minnesota: Morris, 600 East 4th Street, Morris, MN 56267

University of Minnesota: Twin Cities

Minneapolis, Minnesota — **CB member**
www.umn.edu/tc — **CB code: 6874**

- Public 4-year university
- Residential campus in very large city
- 28,957 degree-seeking undergraduates: 10% part-time, 53% women, 5% African American, 9% Asian American, 2% Hispanic American, 1% Native American, 2% international
- 17,582 degree-seeking graduate students
- 71% of applicants admitted
- SAT or ACT with writing required
- 61% graduate within 6 years

General. Founded in 1851. Regionally accredited. Campuses in Minneapolis and St. Paul. **Degrees:** 6,088 bachelor's awarded; master's, doctoral, first professional offered. **ROTC:** Army, Navy, Air Force. **Location:** Main campus less than a mile from downtown. **Calendar:** Semester, extensive summer session. **Full-time faculty:** 1,680 total; 69% have terminal degrees, 13% minority, 31% women. **Part-time faculty:** 253 total; 51% have terminal degrees, 5% minority, 26% women. **Class size:** 41% < 20, 38% 20-39, 5% 40-49, 9% 50-99, 6% >100. **Special facilities:** West Bank Arts Quarter, natural history museum, art museum, gallery, showboat, rehabilitation museum, arboretum, concert hall.

Freshman class profile. 20,641 applied, 14,708 admitted, 5,305 enrolled.

Mid 50% test scores			
SAT verbal:	540-660	Rank in top tenth:	34%
SAT math:	570-690	Return as sophomores:	87%
ACT:	23-28	Out-of-state:	33%
Rank in top quarter:	74%	Live on campus:	78%
		International:	1%

Basis for selection. Successful completion of a college preparatory curriculum, high school rank percentile, grade point average, ACT or SAT scores, and strength of curriculum very important. Writing tests required. Results considered as secondary admission factor.

High school preparation. 16 units required. Required units include English 4, mathematics 3, social studies 3, history 1, science 3 and foreign language 2. 1 year of visual and/or performing arts also required. Management, biological sciences, and technology applicants require a fourth year of mathematics and 3 years of science including 1 year each of biological science, chemistry, and physics.

2005-2006 Annual costs. Tuition/fees: $8,622; $20,252 out-of-state. Room/board: $6,722.

2005-2006 Financial aid. Need-based: 4,095 full-time freshmen applied for aid; 2,598 were judged to have need; 2,518 of these received aid. Average need met was 85%. Average scholarship/grant was $6,842; average loan $6,058. 41% of total undergraduate aid awarded as scholarships/grants, 59% as loans/jobs. **Non-need-based:** Awarded to 5,330 full-time undergraduates, including 1,518 freshmen. Scholarships awarded for academics, art, athletics, job skills, leadership, minority status, music/drama, ROTC, state residency.

Application procedures. Admission: Priority date 12/15; no deadline. $45 fee, may be waived for applicants with need. Application may be submitted online. Admission notification on a rolling basis. Must reply by May 1 or within 2 week(s) if notified thereafter. **Financial aid:** Priority date 1/15; no closing date. FAFSA required. Applicants notified on a rolling basis starting 2/15.

Academics. Four year graduation guarantee offered. **Special study options:** Accelerated study, combined bachelor's/graduate degree, cooperative education, cross-registration, distance learning, double major, dual enrollment of high school students, ESL, exchange student, external degree, honors, independent study, internships, liberal arts/career combination, student-designed major, study abroad, teacher certification program. Qualified undergraduates may take graduate-level classes. **Credit/placement by examination:** AP, CLEP, IB, institutional tests. **Support services:** Learning center, pre-admission summer program, reduced course load, remedial instruction, study skills assistance, tutoring, writing center.

Majors. Agriculture: Animal sciences, business, economics, food science. **Architecture:** Architecture, environmental design, landscape. **Area/ethnic**

studies: African, African-American, American, East Asian, European, Hispanic-American/Latino/Chicano, Latin American, Native American, Near/Middle Eastern, Russian/Slavic, women's. **Biology:** General, bacteriology, biochemistry, biostatistics, cell/histology, ecology. **Business:** Accounting, actuarial science, business admin, human resources, insurance, international, labor relations, logistics, management information systems, marketing, sales/distribution. **Communications:** Journalism. **Computer sciences:** Computer science, networking. **Conservation:** General, fisheries, forest resources, forestry, wildlife. **Construction:** Maintenance. **Education:** Agricultural, art, business, early childhood, elementary, foundations, mathematics, music, physical, sales/marketing, technology/industrial arts. **Engineering:** Aerospace, agricultural, chemical, civil, computer, electrical, geological, materials, materials science, mechanical. **English:** Speech/rhetoric. **Family/consumer sciences:** General, clothing/textiles, family studies, food/nutrition, housing. **Foreign languages:** General, ancient Greek, Chinese, classics, comparative lit, French, German, Hebrew, Italian, Japanese, Latin, linguistics, Portuguese, Russian, Scandinavian, Spanish. **Health:** Audiology/speech pathology, dental hygiene, music therapy, nurse anesthetist, nursing (RN), predentistry, premedicine, prepharmacy, preveterinary. **History:** General. **Interdisciplinary:** Biological/physical sciences, nutrition sciences. **Legal studies:** Prelaw. **Liberal arts:** Arts/sciences. **Math:** General, statistics. **Parks/recreation:** General. **Personal/culinary services:** Mortuary science. **Philosophy/religion:** Judaic, philosophy, religion. **Physical sciences:** Astronomy, astrophysics, chemistry, geology, geophysics, physics. **Psychology:** General. **Social sciences:** Anthropology, applied economics, criminology, econometrics, economics, geography, international relations, political science, sociology, urban studies. **Visual/performing arts:** Art history/conservation, commercial/advertising art, dance, design, dramatic, fashion design, film/cinema, interior design, music performance.

Most popular majors. Biology 6%, business/marketing 9%, engineering/engineering technologies 12%, English 6%, psychology 7%, social sciences 12%, visual/performing arts 6%.

Computing on campus. Dormitories wired for high-speed internet access and linked to campus network. Commuter students can connect to campus network. Online course registration, online library, helpline, repair service, student web hosting, wireless network available.

Student life. Freshman orientation: Mandatory. **Policies:** Freshmen permitted cars on campus. **Housing:** Guaranteed on-campus for freshmen. Coed dorms, special housing for disabled, apartments, cooperative housing, fraternity/sorority housing, substance-free housing available. $100 fully refundable deposit, deadline 5/1. Honors housing available. 24 living and learning communities. **Activities:** Bands, choral groups, dance, drama, film society, literary magazine, music ensembles, musical theater, opera, radio station, student government, student newspaper, symphony orchestra, TV station, 600 student-run organizations.

Athletics. NCAA. **Intercollegiate:** Baseball, basketball, cheerleading, cross-country, diving, football (tackle), golf, gymnastics, ice hockey, rowing (crew) W, soccer W, softball W, swimming, tennis, track and field, volleyball W, wrestling M. **Intramural:** Badminton, baseball, basketball, bowling, fencing, football (tackle) M, golf, gymnastics, handball, ice hockey, judo, lacrosse, racquetball, rugby, sailing, skiing, soccer, softball, squash, swimming, synchronized swimming, tennis, volleyball, water polo, wrestling M. **Team name:** Gophers.

Student services. Adult student services, alcohol/substance abuse counseling, campus ministries, career counseling, services for economically disadvantaged, student employment services, financial aid counseling, health services, legal services, minority student services, on-campus daycare, personal counseling, placement for graduates, veterans' counselor, women's services. **Physically disabled:** Services for visually, speech, hearing impaired.

Contact. Phone: (612) 625-2008 Toll-free number: (800) 752-1000
Fax: (612) 626-1693
Waybe Sigler, Director of Admissions, University of Minnesota: Twin Cities, 240 Williamson Hall, 231 Pillsbury Drive Southeast, Minneapolis, MN 55455-0115

University of St. Thomas

St. Paul, Minnesota — **CB member**
www.stthomas.edu — **CB code: 6110**

- Private 4-year university and liberal arts college affiliated with Roman Catholic Church
- Commuter campus in very large city
- 5,442 degree-seeking undergraduates: 6% part-time, 50% women, 3% African American, 5% Asian American, 2% Hispanic American, 1% Native American, 1% international
- 4,958 degree-seeking graduate students
- 91% of applicants admitted
- SAT or ACT (ACT writing optional), application essay required

General. Founded in 1885. Regionally accredited. **Degrees:** 1,025 bachelor's awarded; master's, doctoral, first professional offered. **ROTC:** Army, Navy, Air Force. **Location:** 5 miles from downtown. **Calendar:** 4-1-4, limited summer session. **Full-time faculty:** 384 total; 87% have terminal degrees, 11% minority, 38% women. **Part-time faculty:** 381 total; 32% have terminal degrees, 6% minority, 40% women. **Class size:** 35% < 20, 60% 20-39, 2% 40-49, 2% 50-99, less than 1% >100.

Freshman class profile. 4,189 applied, 3,832 admitted, 1,326 enrolled.

Mid 50% test scores			
SAT verbal:	540-660	Rank in top quarter:	53%
SAT math:	530-650	Rank in top tenth:	22%
ACT:	22-27	Out-of-state:	19%
		Live on campus:	92%

Basis for selection. Admissions decision by formula using a combination of high school rank and standardized test scores. Applicants who don't meet these conditions are given individual review. Interview recommended. **Homeschooled:** Submit course descriptions.

High school preparation. Required and recommended units include English 4, mathematics 3-4, social studies 2, science 2, foreign language 4 and academic electives 2. Some departments may require 3 units social studies (includes 1 geography), 1 US history, 1 unit visual or performing arts.

2006-2007 Annual costs. Tuition/fees: $24,808. Room/board: $6,932. Books/supplies: $1,000. Personal expenses: $1,300.

2005-2006 Financial aid. Need-based: 891 full-time freshmen applied for aid; 632 were judged to have need; 632 of these received aid. Average need met was 78%. Average scholarship/grant was $10,124; average loan $2,763. 54% of total undergraduate aid awarded as scholarships/grants, 46% as loans/jobs. **Non-need-based:** Awarded to 936 full-time undergraduates, including 380 freshmen. Scholarships awarded for academics, music/drama, ROTC.

Application procedures. Admission: No deadline. No application fee. Application may be submitted online. Applications accepted until class is full; reviewed starting 10/01. **Financial aid:** Priority date 4/1; no closing date. FAFSA required. Applicants notified on a rolling basis starting 3/1; must reply within 3 week(s) of notification.

Academics. Special study options: Cross-registration, double major, exchange student, honors, independent study, internships, student-designed major, study abroad, teacher certification program, urban semester, Washington semester. Renaissance Program in which students major in a liberal arts area, take career-oriented classes as a minor, and after graduation can take additional undergraduate business courses free of charge. **Credit/placement by examination:** AP, CLEP, IB, institutional tests. Typically credit by exam can be used for only 1/8 of a student's courses. CLEP credit awarded if student scores at 50th percentile or above for those examinations that have been approved by the department in which the subject is usually taught. **Support services:** Learning center, reduced course load, study skills assistance, tutoring, writing center.

Majors. Area/ethnic studies: East Asian, Russian/Slavic, women's. **Biology:** General, biochemistry. **Business:** Accounting, business admin, entrepreneurial studies, finance, human resources, international, marketing, operations, real estate. **Communications:** General, broadcast journalism, journalism. **Computer sciences:** General. **Conservation:** Environmental studies. **Education:** Biology, chemistry, elementary, English, foreign languages, French, German, health, mathematics, middle, music, physical, physics, science, secondary, social studies, Spanish. **Engineering:** Electrical, mechanical, systems. **English:** Creative writing, English lit. **Family/consumer sciences:** General, clothing/textiles, food/nutrition. **Foreign languages:** Ancient Greek, French, German, Japanese, Latin, Russian, Spanish. **Health:** Clinical/medical social work, nursing (RN), predentistry, preveterinary, public health ed. **History:** General. **Interdisciplinary:** Ancient studies, peace/conflict. **Liberal arts:** Arts/sciences. **Math:** General. **Parks/recreation:** Health/fitness. **Philosophy/religion:** Philosophy, religion. **Physical sciences:** Chemistry, geology, physics. **Psychology:** General. **Public administration:** General, social work. **Social sciences:** General, anthropology, criminology, econometrics, economics, geography, international relations, political science, sociology. **Visual/performing arts:** Art history/conservation, dramatic, music performance, studio arts.

Most popular majors. Biology 6%, business/marketing 40%, communications/journalism 7%, philosophy/religious studies 6%, psychology 6%, social sciences 9%.

Computing on campus. 843 workstations in dormitories, library, computer center, student center. Dormitories wired for high-speed internet access and linked to campus network. Commuter students can connect to campus network. Online course registration, helpline, student web hosting available.

Student life. **Freshman orientation:** Mandatory. Preregistration for classes offered. Held 2 days over summer; students and parents can stay overnight in the dorms. Separate programs for students and parents. **Policies:** Freshmen permitted cars on campus. **Housing:** Single-sex dorms, apartments available. $200 fully refundable deposit, deadline 5/1. Chemical-free lifestyle, women in science house, first year experience houses, Catholic women's and Catholic men's communities. **Activities:** Bands, choral groups, dance, drama, literary magazine, music ensembles, student government, student newspaper, Globally Minded Student Association, campus ministry, Volunteers in Action, HANA (Hispanic, African American, Native American, Asian American), Student Coalition for Social Justice, African Nations Students Association, Fellowship of Christian Athletes, St. Paul's Outreach student organization, theology club, Black Empowerment Student Alliance.

Athletics. NCAA. **Intercollegiate:** Baseball M, basketball, cross-country, football (tackle) M, golf, ice hockey, soccer, softball W, swimming, tennis, track and field, volleyball W. **Intramural:** Basketball, football (non-tackle), racquetball, soccer, softball, tennis, volleyball. **Team name:** Tommies.

Student services. Adult student services, alcohol/substance abuse counseling, campus ministries, career counseling, student employment services, financial aid counseling, health services, minority student services, on-campus daycare, personal counseling, veterans' counselor, women's services. **Physically disabled:** Services for visually, speech, hearing impaired. **Learning disabled:** Comprehensive services available.

Contact. E-mail: admissions@stthomas.edu
Phone: (651) 962-6150 Toll-free number: (800) 328-6819 ext. 26150
Fax: (651) 962-6160
Marla Friederichs, Associate Vice President for Enrollment Management, University of St. Thomas, 2115 Summit Avenue, 32F, St. Paul, MN 55455-0115

Walden University

Minneapolis, Minnesota
www.waldenu.edu

- For-profit upper-division virtual college
- Large city

General. Undergraduate and graduate degrees offered via online education. At the undergraduate level, only upper level degree completions offered. Academic offices located in Minneapolis, MN and administrative offices located in Baltimore, MD. **Degrees:** 33 bachelor's awarded; master's, doctoral offered. **Calendar:** Differs by program, extensive summer session. **Full-time faculty:** 20 total. **Part-time faculty:** 600 total.

Student profile. 1,229 degree-seeking undergraduates, 20,932 degree-seeking graduate students.

Women:	61%	**Hispanic American:**	30%
African American:	2%	**Part-time:**	96%

Application procedures. **Admission:** $50 fee. Application may be submitted online.

Academics. **Special study options:** Distance learning, double major, student-designed major. **Credit/placement by examination:** CLEP.

Majors. **Business:** Business admin.

Computing on campus. PC or laptop required.

Student life. **Activities:** Student newspaper.

Student services. Financial aid counseling, veterans' counselor. **Learning disabled:** Comprehensive services available.

Contact. Phone: (866) 492-5336 Toll-free number: (800) 444-6795
Walden University, 155 Fifth Avenue South, Minneapolis, MN 55401

Winona State University

Winona, Minnesota
www.winona.edu **CB code: 6680**

- Public 4-year university
- Residential campus in large town
- 7,447 degree-seeking undergraduates
- 80% of applicants admitted
- SAT and SAT Subject Tests or ACT (ACT writing optional) required

General. Founded in 1858. Regionally accredited. 4-year graduation guarantee. **Degrees:** 1,348 bachelor's, 43 associate awarded; master's offered. **ROTC:** Army. **Location:** 90 miles from Minneapolis-St. Paul. **Calendar:** Semester, extensive summer session. **Full-time faculty:** 320 total. **Part-time faculty:** 140 total. **Class size:** 32% < 20, 53% 20-39, 7% 40-49, 7% 50-99, less than 1% >100. **Special facilities:** Library/media center with 1400 connections for laptops.

Freshman class profile. 5,405 applied, 4,316 admitted, 1,721 enrolled.

Mid 50% test scores		**Out-of-state:**	40%
SAT verbal:	460-580	**Live on campus:**	90%
SAT math:	500-610	**Fraternities:**	2%
ACT:	20-24	**Sororities:**	2%

Basis for selection. 16 units of college prep high school courses and rank in top half of class or SAT combined score of 1000 (exclusive of Writing) or ACT composite score of 21 required for regular admission. Interview required for academically marginal students.

High school preparation. 16 units required. Required units include English 4, mathematics 3, social studies 2, history 1, science 3 (laboratory 3), foreign language 2 and academic electives 1. One English unit may be speech.

2005-2006 Annual costs. Tuition/fees: $5,661; $9,607 out-of-state. Fees include mandatory laptop lease for full-time students. Room/board: $5,470. Books/supplies: $500. Personal expenses: $600.

2004-2005 Financial aid. **Need-based:** 34% of total undergraduate aid awarded as scholarships/grants, 66% as loans/jobs. **Non-need-based:** Scholarships awarded for academics, alumni affiliation, art, athletics, leadership, minority status, music/drama.

Application procedures. **Admission:** Closing date 7/30 (postmark date). $20 fee, may be waived for applicants with need. Application may be submitted online. Admission notification on a rolling basis. **Financial aid:** Priority date 3/1; no closing date. FAFSA required. Applicants notified on a rolling basis starting 3/1; must reply within 2 week(s) of notification.

Academics. **Special study options:** Accelerated study, cross-registration, distance learning, double major, dual enrollment of high school students, exchange student, external degree, honors, independent study, internships, student-designed major, study abroad, teacher certification program. **Credit/placement by examination:** AP, CLEP, IB, institutional tests. **Support services:** Learning center, reduced course load, study skills assistance, tutoring, writing center.

Majors. **Biology:** General, cell/histology, molecular. **Business:** General, accounting, administrative services, business admin, finance, hospitality admin, human resources, labor relations, management information systems, management science, managerial economics, market research, marketing, office management, office/clerical, operations. **Communications:** General, advertising, broadcast journalism, journalism, media studies, photojournalism, public relations. **Communications technology:** General. **Computer sciences:** General, applications programming, computer science, data processing, information systems, information technology, programming, systems analysis. **Conservation:** General, environmental studies. **Education:** General, art, bilingual, biology, business, chemistry, curriculum, drama/dance, early childhood, elementary, emotionally handicapped, English, foreign languages, French, German, health, health occupations, history, learning disabled, mathematics, mentally handicapped, middle, multi-level teacher, multiple handicapped, music, physical, physically handicapped, physics, reading, science, secondary, social science, social studies, Spanish, special, speech. **Engineering:** General, chemical, materials, materials science, mechanical, mechanics, polymer. **English:** Composition, speech/rhetoric. **Foreign languages:** General, French, German, Spanish. **Health:** Athletic training, clinical lab technology, cytotechnology, health care admin, nursing (RN), predentistry, premedicine, preop/surgical nursing, prepharmacy, preveterinary, public health ed, recreational therapy. **History:** General. **Interdisciplinary:** Biological/physical sciences, math/computer science. **Legal studies:** General, legal secretary, paralegal, prelaw. **Liberal arts:** Arts/sciences. **Math:** General, applied, statistics. **Parks/recreation:** General, exercise sciences, facilities management, health/fitness, sports admin. **Physical sciences:** Chemistry, geology, physics, planetary, polymer chemistry, theoretical physics. **Protective services:** Corrections, criminal justice, law enforcement admin, police science, security services. **Psychology:** General. **Public administration:** General, community org/advocacy, human services, policy analysis, social work. **Social sciences:** General, criminology, economics, political science, sociology, urban studies. **Visual/performing arts:** General, art, commercial/advertising art, design, dramatic, music management, music performance, studio arts.

Computing on campus. PC or laptop required. 1,400 workstations in dormitories, library, computer center, student center. Dormitories wired for high-speed internet access and linked to campus network. Commuter students can connect to campus network. Online course registration, helpline, repair service, student web hosting available.

Student life. **Freshman orientation:** Available, $25 fee. Preregistration for classes offered. **Policies:** Freshmen permitted cars on campus. **Housing:** Guaranteed on-campus for freshmen. Coed dorms, single-sex dorms, special housing for disabled, apartments available. $150 deposit, deadline 2/4. Residence hall with classrooms and faculty offices. **Activities:** Bands, choral groups, dance, drama, literary magazine, music ensembles, musical theater, opera, radio station, student government, student newspaper, symphony orchestra, TV station, over 130 organizations including religious, political, international, ethnic, and fraternal clubs.

Athletics. NCAA. **Intercollegiate:** Baseball M, basketball, cross-country, football (tackle) M, golf, gymnastics W, soccer W, softball W, tennis, track and field W, volleyball W. **Intramural:** Archery, badminton, baseball M, basketball, bowling, cross-country, diving, equestrian, fencing, field hockey, golf, gymnastics W, handball, ice hockey, racquetball, rifle, rugby, skiing, soccer, softball, swimming, table tennis, tennis, track and field, volleyball, wrestling M. **Team name:** Warriors.

Student services. Adult student services, alcohol/substance abuse counseling, campus ministries, career counseling, services for economically disadvantaged, student employment services, financial aid counseling, health services, legal services, minority student services, on-campus daycare, personal counseling, placement for graduates, veterans' counselor, women's services. **Physically disabled:** Services for visually, speech, hearing impaired.

Contact. E-mail: admissions@winona.edu
Phone: (507) 457-5100 Toll-free number: (800) 342-5978
Fax: (507) 457-5620
Carl Strange, Director of Admissions, Winona State University, Office of Admissions, Winona, MN 55987

Mississippi

Alcorn State University

Alcorn State, Mississippi **CB member**
www.alcorn.edu **CB code: 1008**

- Public 4-year university and agricultural college
- Residential campus in rural community
- 2,962 degree-seeking undergraduates: 10% part-time, 63% women, 92% African American, 2% international
- 582 degree-seeking graduate students
- 68% of applicants admitted
- SAT or ACT, application essay, interview required
- 44% graduate within 6 years

General. Founded in 1871. Regionally accredited. School of Nursing is located in Natchez. **Degrees:** 397 bachelor's, 28 associate awarded; master's offered. **ROTC:** Army. **Location:** 40 miles from Natchez, 45 miles from Vicksburg. **Calendar:** Semester, limited summer session. **Full-time faculty:** 175 total; 64% have terminal degrees, 78% minority, 38% women. **Part-time faculty:** 34 total; 47% have terminal degrees, 76% minority, 65% women. **Class size:** 51% < 20, 37% 20-39, 5% 40-49, 6% 50-99. **Special facilities:** Nature trails, lakes.

Freshman class profile. 2,335 applied, 1,581 admitted, 497 enrolled.

Mid 50% test scores		Return as sophomores:	74%
ACT:	16-19	Out-of-state:	26%
GPA 3.50 or higher:	22%	Live on campus:	76%
GPA 3.0-3.49:	25%	International:	2%
GPA 2.0-2.99:	45%		

Basis for selection. Test scores, school achievement record important; specific academic units considered. Test score requirements depend upon high school GPA. Audition required for music majors.

High school preparation. College-preparatory program required. 15.5 units required. Required and recommended units include English 4, mathematics 3, social studies 3, science 3 (laboratory 2), foreign language 1 and academic electives 2. One advanced elective must be in foreign language or world geography. Half unit in computer application also required.

2005-2006 Annual costs. Tuition/fees: $3,919; $8,887 out-of-state. Room/board: $4,272. Books/supplies: $1,320. Personal expenses: $2,200.

2004-2005 Financial aid. Need-based: 552 full-time freshmen applied for aid; 448 were judged to have need; 386 of these received aid. Average need met was 70%. Average scholarship/grant was $5,250; average loan $2,625. 41% of total undergraduate aid awarded as scholarships/grants, 59% as loans/jobs. **Non-need-based:** Awarded to 1,410 full-time undergraduates, including 374 freshmen. Scholarships awarded for academics, athletics, ROTC.

Application procedures. Admission: No deadline. No application fee. Application must be submitted on paper. Admission notification on a rolling basis. **Financial aid:** Priority date 4/1; no closing date. FAFSA, institutional form required. Applicants notified on a rolling basis starting 4/1; must reply within 4 week(s) of notification.

Academics. Special study options: Accelerated study, cooperative education, distance learning, double major, honors, independent study, internships, liberal arts/career combination, teacher certification program. **Credit/placement by examination:** CLEP, SAT, ACT, institutional tests. 15 credit hours maximum toward associate degree, 30 toward bachelor's. Student must earn 12 hours at Alcorn State University before credit by examination may be recorded on the student's transript. **Support services:** Learning center, pre-admission summer program, reduced course load, remedial instruction, tutoring.

Majors. Agriculture: General, animal sciences, business, economics. **Biology:** General. **Business:** Accounting, administrative services, business admin. **Communications:** Media studies. **Computer sciences:** General. **Education:** Elementary, music, physical, secondary, special, technology/industrial arts. **Engineering technology:** Industrial. **English:** English lit. **Family/consumer sciences:** General, child development, food/nutrition. **Health:** Clinical lab science, health services, nursing (RN), physical therapy assistant. **History:** General. **Liberal arts:** Arts/sciences. **Math:** General. **Parks/recreation:** General. **Physical sciences:** Chemistry. **Protective services:** Criminal justice. **Psychology:** General. **Social sciences:** Economics, political science, sociology. **Visual/performing arts:** Music performance.

Most popular majors. Biology 8%, business/marketing 10%, education 10%, engineering/engineering technologies 6%, health sciences 11%, liberal arts 21%, security/protective services 8%, social sciences 8%.

Computing on campus. 500 workstations in library, computer center, student center. Dormitories wired for high-speed internet access and linked to campus network. Commuter students can connect to campus network. Online course registration, helpline available.

Student life. Freshman orientation: Mandatory. Preregistration for classes offered. Entrance and placement exams given. **Policies:** Freshmen permitted cars on campus. **Housing:** Guaranteed on-campus for all undergraduates. Single-sex dorms available. $75 deposit. **Activities:** Bands, choral groups, dance, drama, music ensembles, radio station, student government, student newspaper, TV station, Baptist Student Union, Wesley Foundation, NAACP, Black History Month Society, Young Women's Christian Association, Adventist Youth Society.

Athletics. NCAA. **Intercollegiate:** Baseball M, basketball, bowling W, cross-country, football (tackle) M, golf, soccer W, softball W, tennis, track and field, volleyball W. **Intramural:** Basketball, football (non-tackle) M, gymnastics, softball W, swimming, table tennis, tennis, track and field, volleyball, wrestling. **Team name:** Braves.

Student services. Career counseling, student employment services, health services, on-campus daycare, personal counseling, placement for graduates, veterans' counselor.

Contact. E-mail: ebarnes@lorman.alcorn.edu
Phone: (601) 877-6147 Toll-free number: (800) 222-6790
Fax: (601) 877-6347
Emanuel Barnes, Director of Admissions and Recruiting, Alcorn State University, 1000 ASU Drive #300, Alcorn State, MS 39096-7500

Belhaven College

Jackson, Mississippi
www.belhaven.edu **CB code: 1055**

- Private 4-year liberal arts college affiliated with Presbyterian Church (USA)
- Commuter campus in large city
- 2,228 degree-seeking undergraduates: 3% part-time, 68% women, 39% African American, 3% Hispanic American, 1% Native American, 1% international
- 342 graduate students
- 58% of applicants admitted
- SAT or ACT (ACT writing optional), application essay required

General. Founded in 1883. Regionally accredited. **Degrees:** 389 bachelor's, 43 associate awarded; master's offered. **Location:** 188 miles from New Orleans, 200 miles from Memphis, Tennessee. **Calendar:** Differs by program. **Full-time faculty:** 58 total. **Part-time faculty:** 291 total. **Class size:** 72% < 20, 22% 20-39, 5% 40-49, less than 1% 50-99.

Freshman class profile. 746 applied, 431 admitted, 206 enrolled.

Mid 50% test scores		Return as sophomores:	85%
SAT verbal:	470-590	Out-of-state:	59%
SAT math:	480-810	Live on campus:	62%
ACT:	19-27		

Basis for selection. Test scores, school record, recommendations, and character important. ACT and SAT scores used for placement in math and English. Interview recommended for art, dance, music, and theater majors; portfolio recommended for art majors. Audition required for dance, music, and theater majors.

High school preparation. 16 units required. Required and recommended units include English 4, mathematics 2, social studies 1, science 1, foreign language 2 and academic electives 8. One computer science course recommended.

2006-2007 Annual costs. Tuition/fees (projected): $14,774. Room/board: $5,704. Books/supplies: $1,400.

2005-2006 Financial aid. **Need-based:** 27% of total undergraduate aid awarded as scholarships/grants, 73% as loans/jobs. **Non-need-based:** Scholarships awarded for academics, art, athletics, leadership, minority status, music/drama, state residency.

Application procedures. **Admission:** Priority date 12/15; no deadline. $25 fee, may be waived for applicants with need. Application may be submitted online. Admission notification on a rolling basis. Accepted applicants must reply within 30 days after acceptance. **Financial aid:** Priority date 3/1; no closing date. FAFSA required. Applicants notified on a rolling basis starting 2/1; must reply within 4 week(s) of notification.

Academics. **Special study options:** Accelerated study, double major, dual enrollment of high school students, ESL, honors, independent study, internships, student-designed major, study abroad, teacher certification program, weekend college. **Credit/placement by examination:** AP, CLEP, IB, SAT, ACT, institutional tests. 30 credit hours maximum toward bachelor's degree. **Support services:** Learning center, pre-admission summer program, reduced course load, remedial instruction, study skills assistance, tutoring, writing center.

Majors. **Biology:** General. **Business:** Accounting, business admin, international. **Communications:** General. **Computer sciences:** Computer science, information systems. **Education:** Elementary. **English:** Creative writing, English lit. **Health:** Athletic training. **History:** General. **Interdisciplinary:** Math/computer science. **Legal studies:** Prelaw. **Liberal arts:** Humanities. **Math:** General. **Parks/recreation:** Exercise sciences, sports admin. **Philosophy/religion:** Philosophy, religion. **Physical sciences:** Chemistry. **Psychology:** General. **Public administration:** Social work. **Social sciences:** Political science. **Theology:** Bible, sacred music. **Visual/performing arts:** Art, dance, dramatic, music performance.

Most popular majors. Business/marketing 52%, education 7%, parks/recreation 8%, psychology 8%.

Computing on campus. 40 workstations in library, computer center. Dormitories wired for high-speed internet access and linked to campus network. Commuter students can connect to campus network. Online library available.

Student life. **Freshman orientation:** Mandatory. Held 5 days before fall classes begin. **Policies:** Freshmen permitted cars on campus. **Housing:** Guaranteed on-campus for all undergraduates. Single-sex dorms, substance-free housing available. $100 deposit, deadline 6/1. **Activities:** Pep band, choral groups, dance, drama, literary magazine, music ensembles, musical theater, student government, student newspaper, Black Student Association, Baptist Student Union, Fellowship of Christian Athletes, Reformed University Fellowship, Student Missions Fellowship, Highland Players.

Athletics. NAIA. **Intercollegiate:** Baseball M, basketball, cross-country, football (tackle) M, golf, soccer, softball W, tennis, volleyball W. **Intramural:** Basketball, football (non-tackle), soccer W, softball, volleyball, weight lifting W. **Team name:** Blazers.

Student services. Adult student services, campus ministries, career counseling, student employment services, financial aid counseling, health services, personal counseling.

Contact. E-mail: admission@belhaven.edu
Phone: (601) 968-5940 Toll-free number: (800) 960-5940
Fax: (601) 968-9998
Suzanne Sullivan, Director of Admissions, Belhaven College, 1500 Peachtree Street, Jackson, MS 39202

Blue Mountain College
Blue Mountain, Mississippi
www.bmc.edu **CB code: 1066**

- Private 4-year liberal arts college affiliated with Southern Baptist Convention
- Commuter campus in rural community
- 344 degree-seeking undergraduates: 18% part-time, 76% women, 14% African American
- 54% of applicants admitted
- SAT or ACT (ACT writing optional) required
- 44% graduate within 6 years; 20% enter graduate study

General. Founded in 1873. Regionally accredited. Men admitted to church-related programs. **Degrees:** 94 bachelor's awarded. **Location:** 69 miles from Memphis, Tennessee. **Calendar:** Semester, limited summer session. **Full-time faculty:** 24 total; 50% have terminal degrees, 50% women. **Part-time faculty:** 12 total; 33% have terminal degrees, 67% women. **Class size:** 75% < 20, 23% 20-39, less than 1% 40-49, less than 1% 50-99.

Freshman class profile. 169 applied, 92 admitted, 45 enrolled.

Mid 50% test scores		**Rank in top tenth:**	30%
ACT:	17-23	**End year in good standing:**	79%
GPA 3.50 or higher:	40%	**Return as sophomores:**	58%
GPA 3.0-3.49:	22%	**Out-of-state:**	27%
GPA 2.0-2.99:	34%	**Live on campus:**	71%
Rank in top quarter:	58%		

Basis for selection. High school record, test scores, and individual motivation considered. Interview required for ministerial majors; audition required for music majors.

High school preparation. 15 units recommended. Recommended units include English 4, mathematics 3, social studies 1, history 2, science 3 (laboratory 2) and foreign language 2.

2005-2006 Annual costs. Tuition/fees: $7,860. Room/board: $3,654. Books/supplies: $550. Personal expenses: $792.

2005-2006 Financial aid. **Need-based:** 36 full-time freshmen applied for aid; 28 were judged to have need; 28 of these received aid. Average need met was 82%. Average scholarship/grant was $2,225; average loan $2,673. 32% of total undergraduate aid awarded as scholarships/grants, 68% as loans/jobs. **Non-need-based:** Awarded to 249 full-time undergraduates, including 37 freshmen. Scholarships awarded for academics, alumni affiliation, athletics, religious affiliation, state residency.

Application procedures. **Admission:** No deadline. $10 fee, may be waived for applicants with need. Application may be submitted online. Admission notification on a rolling basis beginning on or about 10/1. **Financial aid:** Priority date 6/1, closing date 8/1. FAFSA, institutional form required. Applicants notified on a rolling basis starting 5/1; must reply within 2 week(s) of notification.

Academics. Coordinated academic program for men preparing for church-related vocations. **Special study options:** Accelerated study, combined bachelor's/graduate degree, double major, honors, internships, teacher certification program. **Credit/placement by examination:** AP, CLEP, institutional tests. 30 credit hours maximum toward bachelor's degree. **Support services:** Learning center, reduced course load, remedial instruction.

Majors. **Biology:** General. **Business:** General, business admin. **Education:** Biology, chemistry, elementary, English, foreign languages, mathematics, middle, music, science, social science, Spanish. **English:** Speech/rhetoric. **Foreign languages:** Spanish. **Health:** Clinical lab technology, predentistry, premedicine, prepharmacy, preveterinary. **History:** General. **Legal studies:** Prelaw. **Math:** General. **Physical sciences:** Chemistry. **Psychology:** General. **Social sciences:** General. **Theology:** Bible, theology. **Visual/performing arts:** Dramatic, piano/organ, voice/opera.

Most popular majors. Education 49%, philosophy/religious studies 12%, psychology 6%, social sciences 10%, visual/performing arts 6%.

Computing on campus. 60 workstations in dormitories, library, computer center. Dormitories wired for high-speed internet access and linked to campus network. Online library, helpline, repair service available.

Student life. **Freshman orientation:** Mandatory, $50 fee. Preregistration for classes offered. Held the week prior to the opening of the fall semester; designed to provide opportunities for learning methods that support college success. **Policies:** Smoking and alcoholic beverages forbidden. Freshmen permitted cars on campus. **Housing:** Single-sex dorms available. $50 fully refundable deposit. Single women must live in dormitory if not living with family. **Activities:** Choral groups, drama, literary magazine, music ensembles, musical theater, student government, Alpha Psi Omega, Baptist Student Union, Cap and Gown Honor Society, Mississippi Association of Educators student chapter, psychology club, Society of Mathematicians and Scientists, Vivace club.

Athletics. NAIA. **Intercollegiate:** Basketball W, tennis W. **Intramural:** Basketball W, softball W, swimming W, table tennis W, tennis W, track and field W, volleyball W. **Team name:** Toppers.

Student services. Health services, personal counseling, placement for graduates. **Physically disabled:** Services for visually, hearing impaired.

Contact. E-mail: admissions@bmc.edu
Phone: (662) 685-4771 ext. 166 Toll-free number: (800) 235-0136
Fax: (662) 685-4776
Maria Teel, Director of Admissions, Blue Mountain College, PO Box 160, Blue Mountain, MS 38610-0160

Delta State University

Cleveland, Mississippi **CB member**
www.deltastate.edu **CB code: 1163**

- Public 4-year university
- Commuter campus in large town
- 3,258 degree-seeking undergraduates: 15% part-time, 60% women, 39% African American, 1% Asian American, 1% Hispanic American
- 707 degree-seeking graduate students
- 91% of applicants admitted
- SAT or ACT (ACT writing optional) required
- 50% graduate within 6 years

General. Founded in 1924. Regionally accredited. **Degrees:** 584 bachelor's awarded; master's, doctoral offered. **Location:** 40 miles from Greenville, 110 miles from Memphis, Tennessee. **Calendar:** Semester, extensive summer session. **Full-time faculty:** 165 total; 64% have terminal degrees, 10% minority, 50% women. **Part-time faculty:** 109 total; 49% have terminal degrees, 12% minority, 46% women. **Special facilities:** Planetarium, airport.

Freshman class profile. 439 applied, 398 admitted, 395 enrolled.

GPA 3.50 or higher:	21%	**Rank in top quarter:**	49%
GPA 3.0-3.49:	34%	**Return as sophomores:**	71%
GPA 2.0-2.99:	36%	**Out-of-state:**	14%

Basis for selection. Combination of college preparatory curriculum, test scores, class rank. Mississippi residents must take ACT for admission. Interview required for art, music majors. Audition recommended for music majors; portfolio recommended for art majors.

High school preparation. 15 units required. Required units include English 4, mathematics 3, social studies 3, science 3 (laboratory 2), foreign language 1 and academic electives 1. Require .5 unit in computer applications.

2005-2006 Annual costs. Tuition/fees: $3,761; $8,947 out-of-state. Room/board: $4,248. Books/supplies: $700.

2004-2005 Financial aid. Need-based: 34% of total undergraduate aid awarded as scholarships/grants, 66% as loans/jobs. **Non-need-based:** Scholarships awarded for academics, alumni affiliation, art, athletics, leadership, music/drama, religious affiliation, ROTC, state residency.

Application procedures. Admission: Priority date 5/1; deadline 8/1 (receipt date). $15 fee. Application may be submitted online. Admission notification on a rolling basis beginning on or about 5/15. **Financial aid:** Priority date 3/1; no closing date. FAFSA, institutional form required. Applicants notified on a rolling basis starting 4/1; must reply within 2 week(s) of notification.

Academics. Special study options: Cooperative education, distance learning, double major, dual enrollment of high school students, honors, independent study, internships, teacher certification program, weekend college. **Credit/placement by examination:** AP, CLEP, SAT, ACT, institutional tests. 30 credit hours maximum toward bachelor's degree. **Support services:** Learning center, pre-admission summer program, remedial instruction, study skills assistance, tutoring, writing center.

Majors. Biology: General. **Business:** General, accounting, business admin, finance, hospitality admin, insurance, management information systems, marketing, office management. **Communications:** Journalism. **Education:** Business, elementary, English, mathematics, music, physical, social science, special. **English:** English lit. **Family/consumer sciences:** General. **Foreign languages:** General. **Health:** Athletic training, audiology/speech pathology, nursing (RN). **History:** General. **Interdisciplinary:** Biological/physical sciences. **Math:** General. **Physical sciences:** Chemistry. **Protective services:** Criminal justice. **Psychology:** General. **Public administration:** Social work. **Social sciences:** General, political science. **Transportation:** Airline/commercial pilot, aviation. **Visual/performing arts:** General.

Most popular majors. Business/marketing 31%, education 24%, health sciences 7%, visual/performing arts 6%.

Computing on campus. 293 workstations in library, computer center. Dormitories wired for high-speed internet access and linked to campus network. Commuter students can connect to campus network. Online course registration, student web hosting available.

Student life. Freshman orientation: Available, $35 fee. Preregistration for classes offered. Orientation provides opportunity for academic advisement and pre-registration. **Policies:** Freshmen permitted cars on campus. **Housing:** Guaranteed on-campus for all undergraduates. Single-sex dorms, apartments available. $50 deposit. **Activities:** Bands, choral groups, drama, literary magazine, music ensembles, musical theater, opera, student government, student newspaper, symphony orchestra, several religious, ethnic, social, political organizations available on campus.

Athletics. NCAA. **Intercollegiate:** Baseball M, basketball, cross-country W, diving, football (tackle) M, golf M, soccer, softball W, swimming, tennis. **Intramural:** Archery, badminton, basketball, bowling, cross-country, diving, football (non-tackle), golf, racquetball, rifle, soccer, softball, swimming, table tennis, tennis, triathlon, volleyball. **Team name:** Statesmen; Lady Statesmen.

Student services. Career counseling, student employment services, health services, on-campus daycare, personal counseling, placement for graduates. **Physically disabled:** Services for speech, hearing impaired.

Contact. E-mail: dheslep@deltastate.edu
Phone: (662) 846-4655 Fax: (662) 846-4684
Debbie Heslep, Associate Dean of Enrollment Mgt, Delta State University, Kent Wyatt Hall Rm 117, Cleveland, MS 38733

Jackson State University

Jackson, Mississippi **CB member**
www.jsums.edu **CB code: 1341**

- Public 4-year university
- Commuter campus in small city
- 6,637 degree-seeking undergraduates: 14% part-time, 63% women
- 1,752 degree-seeking graduate students
- 39% of applicants admitted

General. Founded in 1877. Regionally accredited. **Degrees:** 812 bachelor's awarded; master's, doctoral offered. **ROTC:** Army. **Location:** 210 miles from Memphis, Tennessee, 190 miles from New Orleans. **Calendar:** Semester, extensive summer session. **Full-time faculty:** 380 total; 72% have terminal degrees, 83% minority, 44% women. **Part-time faculty:** 57 total; 40% have terminal degrees, 86% minority, 54% women. **Special facilities:** National research center, science observatory, academic research and computing center.

Freshman class profile. 11,448 applied, 4,485 admitted, 1,159 enrolled.

Mid 50% test scores		**Live on campus:**	41%
ACT:	16-20	**International:**	1%
Out-of-state:	33%		

Basis for selection. Test scores and high school transcript important. Audition recommended for music majors.

High school preparation. 15 units required. Required units include English 4, mathematics 3, social studies 3, science 3, foreign language 2 and academic electives 2.

2005-2006 Annual costs. Tuition/fees: $3,964; $8,872 out-of-state. Room/board: $4,994. Books/supplies: $800. Personal expenses: $2,250.

2004-2005 Financial aid. All financial aid based on need. 46% of total undergraduate aid awarded as scholarships/grants, 54% as loans/jobs.

Application procedures. Admission: Priority date 8/1; no deadline. No application fee. Application may be submitted online. Admission notification on a rolling basis beginning on or about 1/1. **Financial aid:** Priority date 4/1, closing date 8/1. FAFSA required. Applicants notified on a rolling basis starting 8/1.

Academics. Special study options: Cooperative education, distance learning, double major, dual enrollment of high school students, exchange student, honors, independent study, internships, study abroad, teacher certification program, weekend college. **Credit/placement by examination:** AP, CLEP. 30 credit hours maximum toward bachelor's degree. **Support services:** Learning center, pre-admission summer program, reduced course load, remedial instruction, study skills assistance, tutoring, writing center.

Majors. Biology: General. **Business:** Accounting, banking/financial services, business admin, finance, marketing, office management. **Communications:** Media studies. **Communications technology:** General. **Computer sciences:** General. **Education:** Business, elementary, instructional media, physical, social science, special. **Engineering:** Civil, computer, electrical. **Engineering technology:** Industrial. **English:** British lit, speech/rhetoric. **Foreign languages:** General, linguistics. **Health:** Health care admin, predentistry, premedicine. **History:** General. **Legal studies:** Prelaw. **Math:** General. **Physical sciences:** Atmospheric science, chemistry, physics. **Protective services:** Criminal justice. **Psychology:** General. **Public administration:**

Social work. **Social sciences:** General, economics, political science, sociology, urban studies. **Visual/performing arts:** General, music performance.

Most popular majors. Biology 9%, business/marketing 19%, education 19%, psychology 6%, security/protective services 7%, social sciences 6%.

Computing on campus. Dormitories wired for high-speed internet access and linked to campus network. Commuter students can connect to campus network. Online course registration, helpline, wireless network available.

Student life. Freshman orientation: Available. **Housing:** Single-sex dorms available. $25 deposit. **Activities:** Bands, choral groups, dance, drama, film society, literary magazine, music ensembles, opera, radio station, student government, student newspaper, symphony orchestra, TV station, Church of God in Christ (COGIC) club, NAACP, Alpha Phi Omega.

Athletics. NCAA. **Intercollegiate:** Baseball M, basketball, bowling, cross-country, football (tackle) M, golf, rifle, soccer W, softball W, tennis, track and field, volleyball W. **Intramural:** Basketball, rifle, swimming, tennis, volleyball. **Team name:** JSU Tigers.

Student services. Adult student services, career counseling, student employment services, financial aid counseling, health services, on-campus daycare, personal counseling, placement for graduates, veterans' counselor. **Physically disabled:** Services for visually, speech, hearing impaired.

Contact. E-mail: admappl@jsums.edu
Phone: (601) 979-2100 Toll-free number: (800) 848-6917
Fax: (601) 979-2237
Stephanie Chatman, Director of Admissions and Financial Aid, Jackson State University, 1400 JR Lynch Street, Jackson, MS 39217

Magnolia Bible College

Kosciusko, Mississippi — **CB member**
www.magnolia.edu — **CB code: 0162**

- Private 4-year Bible college affiliated with Church of Christ
- Commuter campus in small town
- 24 degree-seeking undergraduates: 17% part-time, 12% women

General. Founded in 1976. Regionally accredited. **Degrees:** 2 bachelor's awarded. **Location:** 70 miles from Jackson. **Calendar:** Semester, limited summer session. **Full-time faculty:** 3 total. **Part-time faculty:** 4 total. **Class size:** 100% < 20. **Special facilities:** Restoration artifacts collection, preaching laboratory.

Freshman class profile. 13 applied, 10 admitted, 1 enrolled.

ACT:	-15	**GPA 2.0-2.99:**	100%

Basis for selection. Open admission. Recommendations, religious commitment and personal character very important. ACT recommended. Students encouraged to take ACT by end of first semester. Audition and portfolio recommended. **Homeschooled:** Complete junior year of high school with B average and score of 20 on ACT. Need transcript and letter of readiness from group leader or official.

2006-2007 Annual costs. Tuition/fees (projected): $6,090. Reduced tuition for Attala County residents: $1,950 full-time, $65 per credit hour, $90 required fees. Room only: $1,500. Books/supplies: $400. Personal expenses: $1,000.

2004-2005 Financial aid. Need-based: 1 full-time freshmen applied for aid; 1 were judged to have need; 1 of these received aid. 95% of total undergraduate aid awarded as scholarships/grants, 5% as loans/jobs. **Non-need-based:** Scholarships awarded for academics, leadership, religious affiliation.

Application procedures. Admission: No deadline. No application fee. Admission notification on a rolling basis. **Financial aid:** Priority date 8/1; no closing date. FAFSA, institutional form required. Applicants notified on a rolling basis starting 4/15; must reply within 4 week(s) of notification.

Academics. Credit/placement by examination: AP, CLEP, ACT, institutional tests. 30 credit hours maximum toward bachelor's degree. **Support services:** Remedial instruction, writing center.

Majors. Theology: Bible, missionary, pastoral counseling, religious ed, sacred music, theology.

Computing on campus. 3 workstations in library, computer center.

Student life. Freshman orientation: Mandatory. **Policies:** Religious observance required. Freshmen permitted cars on campus. **Housing:** Single-sex dorms, apartments available. $100 deposit, deadline 8/1. Women students housed with families in area. **Activities:** Student government.

Student services. Personal counseling, placement for graduates.

Contact. E-mail: mbcadmissions@hotmail.com
Phone: (662) 289-2896 ext. 106 Toll-free number: (800) 748-8655
Fax: (662) 289-1850
Allen Coker, Director of Admissions, Magnolia Bible College, PO Box 1109, Kosciusko, MS 39090

Millsaps College

Jackson, Mississippi — **CB member**
www.millsaps.edu — **CB code: 1471**

- Private 4-year business and liberal arts college affiliated with United Methodist Church
- Residential campus in large city
- 1,065 degree-seeking undergraduates: 3% part-time, 49% women, 12% African American, 3% Asian American, 1% Hispanic American, 1% international
- 69 degree-seeking graduate students
- 82% of applicants admitted
- SAT or ACT (ACT writing optional), application essay required
- 71% graduate within 6 years; 54% enter graduate study

General. Founded in 1890. Regionally accredited. **Degrees:** 276 bachelor's awarded; master's offered. **ROTC:** Army. **Location:** 190 miles from New Orleans, 210 miles from Memphis, Tennessee. **Calendar:** Semester, limited summer session. **Full-time faculty:** 92 total; 97% have terminal degrees, 8% minority, 45% women. **Part-time faculty:** 5 total; 60% have terminal degrees, 40% women. **Class size:** 64% < 20, 36% 20-39. **Special facilities:** Observatory, x-ray machine, earthquake seismograph, nuclear magnetic resonance spectrometer, biocultural reserve and archaeological site in Yucatan, Mexico.

Freshman class profile. 1,008 applied, 829 admitted, 258 enrolled.

Mid 50% test scores		**Rank in top tenth:**	38%
SAT verbal:	540-680	**End year in good standing:**	87%
SAT math:	540-650	**Return as sophomores:**	83%
ACT:	23-30	**Out-of-state:**	60%
GPA 3.50 or higher:	67%	**Live on campus:**	98%
GPA 3.0-3.49:	18%	**International:**	1%
GPA 2.0-2.99:	15%	**Fraternities:**	62%
Rank in top quarter:	63%	**Sororities:**	58%

Basis for selection. Test scores, GPA in academic courses, recommendations, essays, and school and community activities are important. Advanced credit is awarded for A-Levels, International Baccalaureate, and some other systems. TOEFL is accepted for foreign language students. Auditions and portfolios are recommended. **Homeschooled:** Statement describing homeschool structure and mission, transcript of courses and grades, letter of recommendation (nonparent) required. **Learning Disabled:** There are no special admissions requirements, and students are not asked to identify disabilities during the admissions process. All accepted students are notified that if they need disabilities assistance, they should contact the Director of Services for Students with Disabilities to obtain forms to be completed by their healthcare providers.

High school preparation. 14 units required; 20 recommended. Required and recommended units include English 4, mathematics 3-4, social studies 2, history 2, science 3-4 (laboratory 1) and foreign language 2.

2006-2007 Annual costs. Tuition/fees: $22,032. Room/board: $7,956. Books/supplies: $1,000. Personal expenses: $1,000.

2005-2006 Financial aid. Need-based: 207 full-time freshmen applied for aid; 156 were judged to have need; 156 of these received aid. Average need met was 85%. Average scholarship/grant was $14,618; average loan $3,544. 71% of total undergraduate aid awarded as scholarships/grants, 29% as loans/jobs. **Non-need-based:** Awarded to 508 full-time undergraduates, including 139 freshmen. Scholarships awarded for academics, art, leadership, music/drama, religious affiliation.

Application procedures. Admission: Priority date 12/1; deadline 6/1 (postmark date). $25 fee, may be waived for applicants with need. Application may be submitted online. Admission notification on a rolling basis beginning on or about 11/1. Must reply by May 1 or within 2 week(s) if notified thereafter. **Financial aid:** Priority date 3/1; no closing date. FAFSA, institutional form required. Applicants notified on a rolling basis starting 3/15; must reply by 5/1 or within 2 week(s) of notification.

Academics. **Special study options:** Accelerated study, combined bachelor's/graduate degree, double major, honors, independent study, internships, liberal arts/career combination, New York semester, semester at sea, student-designed major, study abroad, teacher certification program, United Nations semester, urban semester, Washington semester. Foreign exchange programs in conjunction with University of Ulster and Queens University in Northern Ireland, Kansai Gaidai University in Osaka, Japan, and Université Catholique de Lille in France; pre-professional programs in dentistry, engineering, law, medicine, ministry and social work. **Credit/placement by examination:** AP, CLEP, IB, institutional tests. 28 credit hours maximum toward bachelor's degree. Limited to two courses in any discipline and seven courses overall. **Support services:** Pre-admission summer program, reduced course load, study skills assistance, tutoring, writing center.

Majors. **Area/ethnic studies:** European. **Biology:** General. **Business:** Accounting, business admin. **Computer sciences:** Computer science. **Education:** Elementary. **English:** English lit. **Foreign languages:** Classics, French, German, Spanish. **History:** General. **Math:** General. **Philosophy/religion:** Philosophy, religion. **Physical sciences:** Chemistry, geology, physics. **Psychology:** General. **Social sciences:** Anthropology, economics, political science, sociology. **Visual/performing arts:** Art, dramatic, music performance.

Most popular majors. Biology 8%, business/marketing 16%, English 8%, history 6%, physical sciences 9%, psychology 14%, social sciences 16%.

Computing on campus. 135 workstations in dormitories, library, computer center, student center. Dormitories wired for high-speed internet access and linked to campus network. Commuter students can connect to campus network. Online library, helpline, student web hosting, wireless network available.

Student life. **Freshman orientation:** Mandatory. Preregistration for classes offered. 3 days before classes start, emphasizes wellness education, interpersonal skills development, and the mission of the College and the community. Includes initial 8 days of educational and social activities and 8-week Foundations program held once weekly to explore student issues and involvement in campus activities. **Policies:** Students required to live on campus through sophomore year. Students with family in the area may be exempted from the policy. Freshmen permitted cars on campus. **Housing:** Guaranteed on-campus for freshmen. Coed dorms, single-sex dorms, fraternity/sorority housing, substance-free housing available. **Activities:** Choral groups, dance, drama, film society, literary magazine, music ensembles, musical theater, student government, student newspaper, Circle K, Campus Ministry Team, Black Student Association, Habitat for Humanity, Catholic Campus Ministry, Fellowship of Christian Athletes, Millsaps College Republicans, Young Democrats, Multicultural Affairs Diversity Group, E.A.R.T.H. (environmental service club).

Athletics. NCAA. **Intercollegiate:** Baseball M, basketball, cheerleading, cross-country, football (tackle) M, golf, soccer, softball W, tennis, volleyball W. **Intramural:** Basketball, football (non-tackle), handball, racquetball, soccer, softball, table tennis, tennis, volleyball, weight lifting. **Team name:** Millsaps Majors, Lady Majors.

Student services. Adult student services, alcohol/substance abuse counseling, campus ministries, career counseling, student employment services, financial aid counseling, health services, minority student services, personal counseling, placement for graduates.

Contact. E-mail: admissions@millsaps.edu
Phone: (601) 974-1050 Toll-free number: (800) 352-1050
Fax: (601) 974-1059
Mathew Cox, Dean of Enrollment Management, Millsaps College, 1701 North State Street, Jackson, MS 39210-0001

Mississippi College

Clinton, Mississippi
www.mc.edu **CB code: 1477**

- Private 4-year university affiliated with Southern Baptist Convention
- Residential campus in large city
- 2,543 degree-seeking undergraduates: 13% part-time, 59% women, 21% African American, 1% Asian American, 1% Hispanic American, 2% international
- 1,311 degree-seeking graduate students
- 57% of applicants admitted
- SAT or ACT (ACT writing optional), application essay required
- 66% graduate within 6 years

General. Founded in 1826. Regionally accredited. **Degrees:** 510 bachelor's awarded; master's, first professional offered. **ROTC:** Army. **Location:** 10 miles from Jackson. **Calendar:** Semester, limited summer session. **Full-time faculty:** 161 total; 73% have terminal degrees, 4% minority, 44% women. **Part-time faculty:** 147 total; 43% have terminal degrees, 49% women. **Class size:** 48% < 20, 41% 20-39, 10% 40-49, 1% 50-99.

Freshman class profile. 2,038 applied, 1,164 admitted, 396 enrolled.

Mid 50% test scores		**Rank in top tenth:**	27%
ACT:	20-26	**Return as sophomores:**	73%
GPA 3.50 or higher:	50%	**Out-of-state:**	36%
GPA 3.0-3.49:	23%	**Live on campus:**	93%
GPA 2.0-2.99:	25%	**International:**	7%
Rank in top quarter:	56%		

Basis for selection. ACT/SAT scores most important, followed by high school record. Recommendations considered in marginal cases. For placement purposes, provisional admission if ACT score is less than 18. Admission and advising affects course load and course selection. Audition recommended for music majors; portfolio recommended for art majors. **Homeschooled:** Transcript of courses and grades required. Personal interview with an admissions representative required.

High school preparation. 22 units recommended. Recommended units include English 4, mathematics 3, social studies 3, history 1, science 4 (laboratory 1), foreign language 1 and academic electives 5. 2 units of advanced electives and .5 unit of computer applications recommended.

2006-2007 Annual costs. Tuition/fees (projected): $12,288. Room/board: $5,894. Books/supplies: $900. Personal expenses: $1,575.

2005-2006 Financial aid. **Need-based:** 309 full-time freshmen applied for aid; 163 were judged to have need; 163 of these received aid. Average need met was 80%. Average scholarship/grant was $10,652; average loan $3,681. 50% of total undergraduate aid awarded as scholarships/grants, 50% as loans/jobs. **Non-need-based:** Awarded to 907 full-time undergraduates, including 202 freshmen. Scholarships awarded for academics, alumni affiliation, art, leadership, music/drama, religious affiliation. **Additional information:** Student reply date for institutional scholarships: May 1.

Application procedures. **Admission:** No deadline. $25 fee, may be waived for applicants with need. Admission notification on a rolling basis. Either SAT or ACT may be substituted for TOEFL scores for foreign students. **Financial aid:** Priority date 3/1; no closing date. FAFSA required. Applicants notified on a rolling basis starting 3/1; must reply by 5/1.

Academics. **Special study options:** Accelerated study, combined bachelor's/graduate degree, double major, dual enrollment of high school students, ESL, honors, independent study, internships, study abroad, teacher certification program. Academic remediation, workstudy program, learning disabilities services available. **Credit/placement by examination:** AP, CLEP, IB, institutional tests. 30 credit hours maximum toward bachelor's degree. **Support services:** Reduced course load, remedial instruction, study skills assistance, tutoring, writing center.

Majors. **Biology:** General, biochemistry. **Business:** Accounting, business admin, communications, marketing. **Communications:** General, journalism, public relations. **Computer sciences:** General, computer science. **Education:** Art, biology, business, chemistry, computer, elementary, English, French, history, mathematics, music, physics, science, secondary, social science, social studies, Spanish, special, speech. **Engineering:** Physics. **Foreign languages:** General, French, Spanish. **Health:** Nursing (RN). **History:** General. **Legal studies:** Paralegal, prelaw. **Math:** General. **Philosophy/religion:** Religion. **Physical sciences:** Chemistry, molecular physics, physics. **Protective services:** Law enforcement admin. **Psychology:** General. **Public administration:** Social work. **Social sciences:** General, political science, sociology. **Theology:** Sacred music. **Visual/performing arts:** Art, commercial/advertising art, interior design, music performance, music theory/composition, piano/organ, voice/opera.

Most popular majors. Biology 22%, business/marketing 16%, education 13%, health sciences 13%, psychology 6%.

Computing on campus. 207 workstations in dormitories, library, computer center. Dormitories wired for high-speed internet access and linked to campus network. Commuter students can connect to campus network. Helpline available.

Student life. **Freshman orientation:** Available, $50 fee. Preregistration for classes offered. Held on a Friday and Saturday in July. **Policies:** No alcohol policy. Freshmen permitted cars on campus. **Housing:** Single-sex dorms, special housing for disabled available. $100 fully refundable deposit, deadline 7/15. **Activities:** Bands, choral groups, drama, literary magazine, music ensembles, musical theater, opera, radio station, student government, student newspaper, Baptist student union, Civitan, Circle-K, Rotoract,

Young Democrats, Young Republicans, Black Student Association, 5 women's social/service clubs, Reformed University Fellowship, Habitat for Humanity.

Athletics. NCAA. **Intercollegiate:** Baseball M, basketball, cross-country, football (tackle) M, golf, soccer, softball W, tennis, track and field, volleyball W. **Intramural:** Basketball, football (non-tackle), soccer, softball, tennis, volleyball. **Team name:** Choctaws.

Student services. Campus ministries, career counseling, student employment services, financial aid counseling, health services, personal counseling, placement for graduates. **Physically disabled:** Services for visually, speech, hearing impaired.

Contact. E-mail: enrollment-services@mc.edu
Phone: (601) 925-3800 Toll-free number: (800) 738-1236
Fax: (601) 925-3950
Chad Phillips, Director of Admissions, Mississippi College, PO Box 4026, Clinton, MS 39058

Mississippi State University

Mississippi State, Mississippi — **CB member**
www.msstate.edu — **CB code: 1480**

- Public 4-year university
- Commuter campus in large town
- 12,261 degree-seeking undergraduates: 10% part-time, 48% women
- 3,546 degree-seeking graduate students
- 69% of applicants admitted
- SAT or ACT (ACT writing optional) required
- 56% graduate within 6 years

General. Founded in 1878. Regionally accredited. Branches include Vicksburg Center for graduate studies in engineering, the Meridian Campus, and the Stennis Space Center on Gulf Coast. **Degrees:** 2,636 bachelor's awarded; master's, doctoral, first professional offered. **ROTC:** Army, Air Force. **Location:** 125 miles from Jackson. **Calendar:** Semester, extensive summer session. **Full-time faculty:** 974 total; 83% have terminal degrees, 15% minority, 32% women. **Part-time faculty:** 165 total; 41% have terminal degrees, 12% minority, 56% women. **Class size:** 40% < 20, 39% 20-39, 9% 40-49, 8% 50-99, 3% >100. **Special facilities:** Observatory, solar energy laboratory, student-operated florist, music museum, climatology laboratory, arboretum, engineering research center for computational field simulation, flight research laboratory, forest products laboratory, center for advanced vehicular systems.

Freshman class profile. 5,778 applied, 3,982 admitted, 1,966 enrolled.

Mid 50% test scores			
ACT:	19-27	**Return as sophomores:**	80%
GPA 3.50 or higher:	35%	**Out-of-state:**	23%
GPA 3.0-3.49:	28%	**Live on campus:**	98%
GPA 2.0-2.99:	35%	**International:**	1%
Rank in top quarter:	55%	**Fraternities:**	13%
Rank in top tenth:	26%	**Sororities:**	16%

Basis for selection. Admission based on ACT score, GPA, class rank. Open admission for summer only; successful completion of summer developmental program results in regular admission for fall term. Some requirements may vary by department, so student should contact the appropriate department to ensure that requirements are met. Full admission is granted to high school graduates with a minimum of a 3.2 GPA in the required high school units regardless of test scores. Audition, portfolio required. Interview recommended for architecture, professional golf management, and veterinary medicine students.

High school preparation. 15 units required; 18 recommended. Required and recommended units include English 4, mathematics 3-4, social studies 1-2, history 2, science 3-4 (laboratory 2), foreign language 1 and academic electives 2. World Geography 1 recommended.

2005-2006 Annual costs. Tuition/fees: $4,312; $9,769 out-of-state. Room/board: $5,859. Books/supplies: $900. Personal expenses: $1,828.

2004-2005 Financial aid. All financial aid based on need. 1,240 full-time freshmen applied for aid; 1,054 were judged to have need; 1,017 of these received aid. Average need met was 63%. Average scholarship/grant was $3,665; average loan $2,651. 39% of total undergraduate aid awarded as scholarships/grants, 61% as loans/jobs. **Additional information:** No institutional closing date for FAFSA.

Application procedures. Admission: Priority date 2/1; no deadline. $25 fee, may be waived for applicants with need. Application may be submitted online. Admission notification on a rolling basis beginning on or about 7/1. Program-specific reply date for accepted applicants to architecture and professional golf management programs: March 1. **Financial aid:** Priority date 4/1; no closing date. FAFSA required. Applicants notified on a rolling basis starting 12/1; must reply by 5/1.

Academics. Special study options: Accelerated study, combined bachelor's/graduate degree, cooperative education, cross-registration, distance learning, double major, dual enrollment of high school students, ESL, exchange student, honors, independent study, internships, liberal arts/career combination, student-designed major, study abroad, teacher certification program, Washington semester, weekend college. **Credit/placement by examination:** AP, CLEP, IB, SAT, ACT, institutional tests. 32 credit hours maximum toward bachelor's degree. Maximum of 25% of any curriculum may be earned by examination. **Support services:** Learning center, pre-admission summer program, reduced course load, remedial instruction, study skills assistance, tutoring.

Majors. Agriculture: Agribusiness operations, agronomy, animal sciences, economics, food science, horticultural science, landscaping, plant protection, poultry. **Architecture:** Architecture, landscape. **Biology:** General, bacteriology, biochemistry. **Business:** Accounting, business admin, construction management, finance, insurance, management information systems, managerial economics, marketing, operations, real estate. **Communications:** General. **Computer sciences:** General. **Conservation:** Forestry, wildlife, wood science. **Education:** Agricultural, business, computer, elementary, music, physical, secondary, special, voc/tech. **Engineering:** Aerospace, agricultural, biomedical, chemical, civil, computer, electrical, industrial, mechanical, software. **Engineering technology:** Manufacturing. **Family/consumer sciences:** General. **Foreign languages:** General. **Health:** Clinical lab science. **History:** General. **Interdisciplinary:** Biological/physical sciences. **Liberal arts:** Arts/sciences. **Math:** General. **Philosophy/religion:** Philosophy. **Physical sciences:** Chemistry, geology, physics. **Psychology:** General. **Public administration:** Social work. **Social sciences:** Anthropology, economics, political science, sociology. **Visual/performing arts:** General.

Most popular majors. Agriculture 6%, business/marketing 26%, education 15%, engineering/engineering technologies 14%, interdisciplinary studies 6%.

Computing on campus. 2,000 workstations in dormitories, library, computer center. Dormitories wired for high-speed internet access and linked to campus network. Commuter students can connect to campus network. Online course registration, online library, helpline, repair service, student web hosting, wireless network available.

Student life. Freshman orientation: Available, $65 fee. Preregistration for classes offered. 2-day program for freshmen and a 1-day program for transfer students. Held three times during the summer and prior to the beginning of each semester. Orientation program fees as well as the parents' fees vary for freshman and transfer students. **Policies:** Freshmen permitted cars on campus. **Housing:** Guaranteed on-campus for freshmen. Coed dorms, single-sex dorms, special housing for disabled, apartments, fraternity/sorority housing, substance-free housing available. $25 nonrefundable deposit. Honors housing, housing for first year students, graduate student housing available. **Activities:** Bands, choral groups, dance, drama, literary magazine, music ensembles, musical theater, radio station, student government, student newspaper, symphony orchestra, TV station, more than 300 organizations on campus.

Athletics. NCAA. **Intercollegiate:** Baseball M, basketball, cross-country, football (tackle) M, golf, soccer W, softball W, tennis, track and field, volleyball W. **Intramural:** Badminton, basketball, football (non-tackle), golf, racquetball, soccer, softball, table tennis, tennis, volleyball, water polo. **Team name:** Bulldogs.

Student services. Adult student services, alcohol/substance abuse counseling, campus ministries, career counseling, services for economically disadvantaged, student employment services, financial aid counseling, health services, minority student services, on-campus daycare, personal counseling, placement for graduates, veterans' counselor. **Physically disabled:** Services for visually, speech, hearing impaired.

Contact. E-mail: admit@admissions.msstate.edu
Phone: (662) 325-2224 Fax: (662) 325-7360
Diane Wolfe, Director of Admissions, Mississippi State University, Box 6305, Mississippi State, MS 39762

Mississippi University for Women

Columbus, Mississippi — **CB member**
www.muw.edu — **CB code: 1481**

- Public 4-year university and liberal arts college
- Commuter campus in large town

General. Founded in 1884. Regionally accredited. **Location:** 120 miles from Birmingham, Alabama, 160 miles from Memphis, Tennessee. **Calendar:** Semester.

Annual costs/financial aid. Tuition/fees (2005-2006): $3,691; $8,915 out-of-state. Room/board: $4,260. Books/supplies: $800. Personal expenses: $2,671. Need-based financial aid available to full-time and part-time students.

Contact. Phone: (662) 329-7106
Director of Admissions, Box W-1613, Columbus, MS 39701

Mississippi Valley State University

Itta Bena, Mississippi — **CB member**
www.mvsu.edu — **CB code: 1482**

- Public 4-year university and liberal arts college
- Commuter campus in small town
- 2,713 degree-seeking undergraduates: 11% part-time, 69% women, 94% African American
- 417 degree-seeking graduate students
- 40% graduate within 6 years

General. Founded in 1946. Regionally accredited. **Degrees:** 346 bachelor's awarded; master's offered. **ROTC:** Army. **Location:** 100 miles from Jackson, 130 miles from Memphis, Tennessee. **Calendar:** Semester, extensive summer session. **Full-time faculty:** 117 total; 61% have terminal degrees, 83% minority, 44% women. **Part-time faculty:** 66 total; 23% have terminal degrees, 85% minority, 64% women. **Class size:** 47% < 20, 42% 20-39, 4% 40-49, 6% 50-99, less than 1% >100.

Freshman class profile.

Mid 50% test scores		**Return as sophomores:**	59%
ACT:	15-18		

Basis for selection. High school curriculum and test scores very important. Audition required for music education majors. Interview required of some students, but recommended for all students.

High school preparation. 16 units required; 18 recommended. Required and recommended units include English 4, mathematics 3, social studies 3, science 3 (laboratory 2), foreign language 1 and academic electives 2. Mathematics requirement includes algebra I and II and geometry. Social sciences must include US government and US history. Sciences must be chosen from introductory and advanced biology, physics, and chemistry. Advanced science or mathematics may be substituted for a foreign language.

2005-2006 Annual costs. Tuition/fees: $4,024; $9,283 out-of-state. Room/board: $3,946.

Financial aid. Non-need-based: Scholarships awarded for academics, athletics, minority status, ROTC.

Application procedures. Admission: Priority date 8/1; deadline 8/17 (receipt date). No application fee. Admission notification on a rolling basis. **Financial aid:** Closing date 4/1. FAFSA, institutional form required. Applicants notified on a rolling basis starting 8/15; must reply within 2 week(s) of notification.

Academics. Special study options: Cooperative education, double major, dual enrollment of high school students, honors, independent study, internships, teacher certification program. **Credit/placement by examination:** AP, CLEP. 30 credit hours maximum toward bachelor's degree. **Support services:** Learning center, pre-admission summer program, reduced course load, remedial instruction, study skills assistance, tutoring, writing center.

Majors. Biology: General. **Business:** Accounting, business admin, office management. **Communications:** General. **Computer sciences:** General. **Education:** Biology, early childhood, elementary, English, mathematics, music, physical, social science. **Engineering:** General. **English:** English lit, speech/rhetoric. **Health:** Environmental health. **History:** General. **Math:** General. **Physical sciences:** Chemistry. **Protective services:** Criminal justice. **Public administration:** General, social work. **Social sciences:** Political science, sociology. **Visual/performing arts:** Music management, studio arts.

Most popular majors. Business/marketing 10%, education 28%, history 9%, public administration/social services 18%, security/protective services 9%.

Computing on campus. 600 workstations in dormitories, library, computer center. Dormitories wired for high-speed internet access and linked to campus network. Commuter students can connect to campus network. Online course registration, online library available.

Student life. Freshman orientation: Mandatory. Preregistration for classes offered. **Policies:** Freshmen permitted cars on campus. **Housing:** Single-sex dorms, apartments available. $50 deposit, deadline 7/31. **Activities:** Bands, choral groups, dance, drama, music ensembles, radio station, student government, student newspaper, numerous honor societies, political, social, religious organizations, prelaw club.

Athletics. NCAA. **Intercollegiate:** Baseball M, basketball, bowling, cross-country, football (tackle) M, golf, soccer W, softball W, tennis, track and field, volleyball W. **Intramural:** Baseball M, basketball, bowling, cross-country, softball W, swimming, tennis, volleyball. **Team name:** Delta Devils (M), Devilettes (W).

Student services. Adult student services, career counseling, student employment services, financial aid counseling, health services, on-campus daycare, personal counseling, placement for graduates, veterans' counselor.

Contact. E-mail: nbtaylor@mvsu.edu
Phone: (662) 254-3437 Fax: (662) 254-6709
Nora Taylor, Director of Admissions and Recruitment, Mississippi Valley State University, 14000 Highway 82 West, Itta Bena, MS 38941-1400

Rust College

Holly Springs, Mississippi
www.rustcollege.edu — **CB code: 1669**

- Private 4-year liberal arts college affiliated with United Methodist Church
- Residential campus in small town
- 935 degree-seeking undergraduates: 13% part-time, 62% women, 93% African American, 6% international
- 26% of applicants admitted
- ACT required

General. Founded in 1866. Regionally accredited. **Degrees:** 89 bachelor's, 13 associate awarded. **Location:** 35 miles from Memphis, Tennessee. **Calendar:** Semester, limited summer session. **Full-time faculty:** 45 total; 44% have terminal degrees, 53% minority, 38% women. **Part-time faculty:** 5 total; 80% minority, 40% women. **Class size:** 59% < 20, 19% 20-39, 4% 40-49, 12% 50-99, 5% >100. **Special facilities:** Histories, religious, poetry, speech writing books for ministers and ministerial students, Inuit and African art collections, international artifacts collection.

Freshman class profile. 6,135 applied, 1,585 admitted, 349 enrolled.

Mid 50% test scores		**Out-of-state:**	54%
ACT:	14-18	**International:**	5%
Return as sophomores:	54%		

Basis for selection. School achievement record and recommendations most important. Test scores also important.

High school preparation. 19 units required. Required units include English 4, mathematics 3, social studies 3, science 3 and academic electives 6.

2005-2006 Annual costs. Tuition/fees: $6,200. Room/board: $2,750. Books/supplies: $500. Personal expenses: $1,450.

2005-2006 Financial aid. Need-based: 255 full-time freshmen applied for aid; 255 were judged to have need; 255 of these received aid. Average need met was 59%. Average scholarship/grant was $6,139; average loan $1,793. 63% of total undergraduate aid awarded as scholarships/grants, 37% as loans/jobs. **Non-need-based:** Awarded to 571 full-time undergraduates, including 203 freshmen. Scholarships awarded for academics, leadership, music/drama, religious affiliation, state residency.

Application procedures. Admission: Priority date 5/15; no deadline. $10 fee, may be waived for applicants with need. Admission notification on a rolling basis. Must reply by May 1 or within 2 week(s) if notified thereafter. **Financial aid:** Closing date 5/1. FAFSA, institutional form required. Applicants notified on a rolling basis starting 5/1; must reply within 2 week(s) of notification.

Academics. Special study options: Double major, honors, independent study, internships, liberal arts/career combination, study abroad, teacher certification program. Nursing and medical technology cooperative program with other institutions. **Credit/placement by examination:** CLEP, institutional tests. 12 credit hours maximum toward associate degree, 12 toward bachelor's. **Support services:** Learning center, pre-admission summer program, reduced course load, remedial instruction, study skills assistance, tutoring, writing center.

Majors. Biology: General. **Business:** Business admin. **Communications:** Broadcast journalism, journalism. **Computer sciences:** Computer science. **Education:** Biology, business, elementary, English, mathematics, social science. **Family/consumer sciences:** Child care. **Math:** General. **Physical sciences:** Chemistry. **Public administration:** Social work. **Social sciences:** General, political science, sociology.

Computing on campus. 220 workstations in dormitories, library, computer center. Dormitories wired for high-speed internet access and linked to campus network. Commuter students can connect to campus network.

Student life. Freshman orientation: Mandatory. Orientation and assessment program begins 1 week prior to registration. **Policies:** Freshmen permitted cars on campus. **Housing:** Guaranteed on-campus for all undergraduates. Single-sex dorms, apartments available. $50 deposit. **Activities:** Bands, choral groups, dance, drama, music ensembles, radio station, student government, student newspaper, TV station, Methodist Student Movement, Baptist Student Union, Catholic Student Association, pre-law club, NAACP, social work club, Sunday School Association, international student association, All Saints Student Movement.

Athletics. NCAA. **Intercollegiate:** Baseball M, basketball, cheerleading, cross-country, soccer M, softball W, tennis, track and field, volleyball. **Intramural:** Badminton, baseball, basketball, bowling, cheerleading, cross-country, football (non-tackle), soccer, softball, swimming, table tennis, tennis, track and field, volleyball, weight lifting. **Team name:** Bearcats.

Student services. Adult student services, career counseling, student employment services, health services, minority student services, on-campus daycare, personal counseling, placement for graduates, veterans' counselor.

Contact. E-mail: jbmcdonald@rustcollege.edu
Phone: (662) 252-8000 ext. 4059 Toll-free number: (888) 886-8492 ext. 4059 Fax: (662) 252-8895
Johnny McDonald, Director of Enrollment Services, Rust College, 150 Rust Avenue, Holly Springs, MS 38635-2328

Southeastern Baptist College

Laurel, Mississippi
www.southeasternbaptist.edu **CB code: 1781**

- Private 4-year Bible college affiliated with Baptist Missionary Association of America
- Commuter campus in large town

General. Founded in 1949. Accredited by ABHE. **Location:** 90 miles from Jackson. **Calendar:** Semester.

Annual costs/financial aid. Tuition/fees (2005-2006): $4,200. Room: $1,050. Books/supplies: $300. Personal expenses: $350.

Contact. Phone: (601) 426-6346
Academic Dean, 4229 Highway 15 North, Laurel, MS 39440

Tougaloo College

Tougaloo, Mississippi **CB member**
www.tougaloo.edu **CB code: 1807**

- Private 4-year liberal arts college affiliated with United Christian Mission Society and United Church of Christ
- Residential campus in large city
- 934 degree-seeking undergraduates: 4% part-time, 69% women, 99% African American, 1% international
- 96% of applicants admitted
- SAT or ACT (ACT writing optional) required
- 42% graduate within 6 years

General. Founded in 1869. Regionally accredited. Cooperative program with Brown University provides exchange of financial resources and students. Exchange opportunities available between New York and Boston universities in pre-med and other areas. **Degrees:** 107 bachelor's, 3 associate awarded. **ROTC:** Army, Navy. **Calendar:** Semester, limited summer session. **Full-time faculty:** 80 total; 49% have terminal degrees, 72% minority, 55% women. **Part-time faculty:** 25 total; 36% have terminal degrees, 100% minority, 64% women. **Class size:** 68% < 20, 30% 20-39, 2% 40-49, less than 1% 50-99. **Special facilities:** Largest collection of civil rights legal documents in state, East and West African art and artifacts, collection of Mississippi Civil Rights original prints.

Freshman class profile. 1,152 applied, 1,105 admitted, 209 enrolled.

Mid 50% test scores			
SAT verbal:	370-530	Return as sophomores:	67%
SAT math:	360-520	Out-of-state:	24%
ACT:	15-21	Live on campus:	78%

Basis for selection. Transcript, test scores important. Minimum 3.0 GPA and ACT composite score of 18 required of applicants in junior year of high school. Audition required for music majors. Portfolio recommended for art majors.

High school preparation. 16 units required. Required and recommended units include English 3, mathematics 2, social studies 2, science 2, foreign language 2 and academic electives 9.

2005-2006 Annual costs. Tuition/fees: $9,035. Room/board: $6,220. Books/supplies: $500. Personal expenses: $800.

2005-2006 Financial aid. Need-based: Average need met was 90%. Average scholarship/grant was $2,025. 56% of total undergraduate aid awarded as scholarships/grants, 44% as loans/jobs. **Non-need-based:** Scholarships awarded for academics, athletics, ROTC.

Application procedures. Admission: Priority date 4/15; no deadline. $25 fee. Admission notification on a rolling basis. **Financial aid:** Priority date 4/15; no closing date. FAFSA, institutional form required. Applicants notified on a rolling basis starting 5/1; must reply within 2 week(s) of notification.

Academics. Special study options: Accelerated study, cooperative education, cross-registration, double major, exchange student, honors, independent study, internships, liberal arts/career combination, New York semester, student-designed major, study abroad, teacher certification program, Washington semester, weekend college. 3-2 program in pre-engineering and physical sciences with Brown University, Georgia Institute of Technology, University of Mississippi, University of Wisconsin Madison, Tuskegee Institute, Washington University St. Louis, Howard University, University of Memphis, Florida A&M. **Credit/placement by examination:** CLEP, IB, SAT, ACT, institutional tests. 12 credit hours maximum toward bachelor's degree. **Support services:** Learning center, pre-admission summer program, reduced course load, remedial instruction, study skills assistance, tutoring, writing center.

Majors. Biology: General. **Communications:** Media studies. **Education:** General, elementary, health, secondary. **English:** English lit. **History:** General. **Interdisciplinary:** Math/computer science. **Liberal arts:** Arts/sciences. **Math:** General. **Physical sciences:** Chemistry, physics. **Psychology:** General. **Social sciences:** Economics, political science, sociology. **Visual/performing arts:** Art.

Most popular majors. Biology 12%, education 9%, English 12%, physical sciences 9%, psychology 6%, social sciences 35%.

Computing on campus. Dormitories linked to campus network. Commuter students can connect to campus network. Helpline, repair service available.

Student life. Freshman orientation: Mandatory. Preregistration for classes offered. **Policies:** Freshmen permitted cars on campus. **Housing:** Single-sex dorms, substance-free housing available. $50 deposit. **Activities:** Choral groups, dance, drama, music ensembles, radio station, student government, student newspaper, Baptist student union, biology club, Afro-American studies group, College Republicans, foreign students club, French club, pre-health club, prelaw club, honor societies, human services clubs.

Athletics. NAIA. **Intercollegiate:** Baseball M, basketball, cross-country, golf, tennis. **Intramural:** Badminton, baseball M, basketball, cheerleading, cross-country M, football (non-tackle) M, golf, soccer M, softball, tennis, track and field, volleyball. **Team name:** Bulldogs.

Student services. Adult student services, campus ministries, career counseling, student employment services, financial aid counseling, health services, personal counseling, placement for graduates, veterans' counselor.

Contact. E-mail: info@tougaloo.edu
Phone: (601) 977-7765 Toll-free number: (888) 424-2566
Junoesque Jacobs, Director of Admissions, Tougaloo College, 500 West County Line Road, Tougaloo, MS 39174

University of Mississippi

University, Mississippi **CB member**
www.olemiss.edu **CB code: 1840**

- Public 4-year university
- Residential campus in large town

- 12,117 degree-seeking undergraduates: 8% part-time, 53% women, 13% African American, 1% Asian American, 1% Hispanic American, 1% international
- 2,425 degree-seeking graduate students
- 73% of applicants admitted
- 56% graduate within 6 years

General. Founded in 1844. Regionally accredited. **Degrees:** 2,153 bachelor's awarded; master's, doctoral, first professional offered. **ROTC:** Army, Navy, Air Force. **Location:** 75 miles from Memphis, Tennessee. **Calendar:** Semester, extensive summer session. **Full-time faculty:** 622 total; 35% women. **Part-time faculty:** 224 total; 57% women. **Class size:** 44% < 20, 34% 20-39, 7% 40-49, 12% 50-99, 3% >100. **Special facilities:** Accredited teaching museum, William Faulkner home and grounds, Southern culture center, National Center for Physical Acoustics, 2 super computers, National Center for the Development of Natural Products, National School Food Service Management Institute, water and wetland resources center.

Freshman class profile. 6,763 applied, 4,942 admitted, 2,192 enrolled.

Mid 50% test scores		**GPA 3.0-3.49:**	28%
SAT verbal:	480-580	**GPA 2.0-2.99:**	31%
SAT math:	490-600	**Rank in top quarter:**	47%
ACT:	20-26	**Return as sophomores:**	81%
GPA 3.50 or higher:	40%	**International:**	1%

Basis for selection. School achievement record and test scores important. SAT or ACT may be required for students with core GPA of under 3.2. Essay required for Croff Institute for International Studies, honors college; audition required for music, theater majors. Portfolio recommended for art majors.

High school preparation. 15 units required. Required and recommended units include English 4, mathematics 3-4, social studies 1-2, history 2, science 3-4 (laboratory 3), foreign language 1-2 and academic electives 1. Mathematics units must include algebra and 2 higher courses. Social sciences units must include U.S. history and U.S. government. Academic electives must include 1 year world geography and fourth year math or science.

2005-2006 Annual costs. Tuition/fees: $4,320; $9,744 out-of-state. Room/board: $4,698. Books/supplies: $750. Personal expenses: $2,000.

2004-2005 Financial aid. **Need-based:** 1,325 full-time freshmen applied for aid; 809 were judged to have need; 792 of these received aid. Average need met was 53%. Average scholarship/grant was $3,875; average loan $2,448. 41% of total undergraduate aid awarded as scholarships/grants, 59% as loans/jobs. **Non-need-based:** Awarded to 6,389 full-time undergraduates, including 1,445 freshmen. Scholarships awarded for academics, alumni affiliation, art, athletics, leadership, minority status, music/drama, ROTC, state residency.

Application procedures. **Admission:** Priority date 6/15; deadline 7/20 (postmark date). $25 fee ($40 out-of-state), may be waived for applicants with need. Application may be submitted online. Admission notification on a rolling basis beginning on or about 10/1. **Financial aid:** Priority date 3/15; no closing date. FAFSA required. Applicants notified on a rolling basis starting 4/1; must reply within 3 week(s) of notification.

Academics. **Special study options:** Accelerated study, cooperative education, distance learning, double major, ESL, exchange student, honors, independent study, internships, study abroad, teacher certification program. **Credit/placement by examination:** AP, CLEP, IB, institutional tests. 63 credit hours maximum toward bachelor's degree. Student must earn 12 hours in residence before any credit-by-examination hours are recorded on transcript. **Support services:** Learning center, reduced course load, remedial instruction, study skills assistance, tutoring, writing center.

Honors college/program. Requires test scores, transcript, essays, and recommendations. 120 students admitted each fall. Unique courses which meet general education requirements taught by senior/master faculty. Senior thesis required.

Majors. **Area/ethnic studies:** African-American. **Biology:** General. **Business:** Accounting, business admin, finance, insurance, management information systems, managerial economics, marketing, real estate. **Communications:** Journalism. **Computer sciences:** General. **Education:** Biology, elementary, English, foreign languages, mathematics, music, school counseling, science, social studies, special. **Engineering:** General, chemical, civil, electrical, geological, mechanical. **English:** English lit. **Family/consumer sciences:** General. **Foreign languages:** Classics, French, German, linguistics, Spanish. **Health:** Audiology/speech pathology, clinical lab science. **History:** General. **Legal studies:** Paralegal. **Liberal arts:** Arts/sciences. **Math:** General. **Parks/recreation:** Exercise sciences, facilities management. **Philosophy/religion:** Philosophy. **Physical sciences:** Chemistry, geology, physics. **Protective services:** Forensics. **Psychology:** General. **Public administration:** General, policy analysis, social work. **Social sciences:** Anthropology, economics, international relations, political science, sociology. **Visual/performing arts:** General, art history/conservation, dramatic.

Most popular majors. Business/marketing 30%, education 11%, health sciences 6%, social sciences 7%.

Computing on campus. 500 workstations in dormitories, library, computer center. Dormitories linked to campus network. Commuter students can connect to campus network. Online course registration, helpline available.

Student life. **Freshman orientation:** Mandatory. Preregistration for classes offered. 2 days in June, additional session immediately before beginning of term. **Policies:** Freshmen permitted cars on campus. **Housing:** Guaranteed on-campus for freshmen. Single-sex dorms, special housing for disabled, apartments, fraternity/sorority housing available. Intensive study floors available to honors and other students. Special interest, graduate/older students, substance-free, environmental interest housing available. **Activities:** Bands, choral groups, dance, drama, music ensembles, musical theater, radio station, student government, student newspaper, symphony orchestra, TV station, Black Student Union, Students for Environmental Awareness, Mortar Board, Habitat for Humanity, Students Envisioning Equality through Diversity.

Athletics. NCAA. **Intercollegiate:** Baseball M, basketball, cheerleading, cross-country, fencing, football (tackle) M, golf, lacrosse M, racquetball M, rifle W, rugby M, skiing M, soccer, softball W, tennis, track and field, volleyball W. **Intramural:** Badminton, basketball, bowling, football (tackle), golf, handball, rifle, soccer, softball, swimming, table tennis, tennis, track and field, volleyball, water polo. **Team name:** Rebels.

Student services. Adult student services, alcohol/substance abuse counseling, campus ministries, career counseling, student employment services, financial aid counseling, health services, legal services, minority student services, personal counseling, placement for graduates, veterans' counselor, women's services. **Physically disabled:** Services for visually, speech, hearing impaired.

Contact. E-mail: admissions@olemiss.edu
Phone: (662) 915-7226 Toll-free number: (800) 653-6477
Fax: (662) 915-5869
Charlotte Fant, Director of Admissions and Registrar, University of Mississippi, 145 Martindale, University, MS 38677-1848

University of Mississippi Medical Center
Jackson, Mississippi
www.umc.edu **CB code: 0358**

- Public upper-division university and health science college
- Commuter campus in large city
- 46% of applicants admitted

General. Founded in 1955. Regionally accredited. **Degrees:** 206 bachelor's awarded; master's, doctoral, first professional offered. **Location:** 200 miles from Memphis, Tennessee, 200 miles from New Orleans. **Calendar:** Quarter, limited summer session. **Full-time faculty:** 683 total; 80% have terminal degrees, 40% women. **Part-time faculty:** 161 total; 94% have terminal degrees, 44% women.

Student profile. 557 degree-seeking undergraduates, 1,470 graduate students. 1,562 applied as first time-transfer students, 722 admitted, 603 enrolled.

Out-of-state:	1%	**25 or older:**	80%
Live on campus:	3%		

Basis for selection. College transcript required. Competitive admission to health science programs based on grades, recommendations, test scores, interviews. Transfer accepted as sophomores, juniors.

2005-2006 Annual costs. Tuition/fees: $3,531; $7,391 out-of-state. Tuition and fees quoted are for nursing program. Required fees vary per program. Room only: $2,412. Books/supplies: $1,596. Personal expenses: $1,500.

Financial aid. All financial aid based on need.

Application procedures. **Admission:** Deadline 2/11. $10 fee. Admission notification 4/11. Must reply by 5/11. Application closing dates and reply dates vary by program. **Financial aid:** FAFSA, institutional form required.

Academics. Includes schools of medicine, nursing, health-related professions, and dentistry, graduate programs in medical and clinical health sciences, and 623-bed teaching hospital. Certificate programs in emergency medical technology and radiologic technology and clinical nuclear medicine offered. **Special study options:** Liberal arts/career combination. **Credit/placement by examination:** CLEP. **Support services:** Pre-admission summer program, study skills assistance, tutoring.

Majors. Health: Clinical lab science, cytotechnology, dental hygiene, medical records admin.

Computing on campus. 75 workstations in library, computer center. Online library available.

Student life. Housing: Single-sex dorms, apartments available. $75 deposit. **Activities:** Student government, student newspaper, University Christian Fellowship, Catholic Student Organization.

Athletics. Intramural: Baseball, basketball, football (tackle) M, golf, soccer, softball, table tennis.

Student services. Alcohol/substance abuse counseling, campus ministries, career counseling, financial aid counseling, health services, minority student services, personal counseling. **Physically disabled:** Services for speech, hearing impaired.

Contact. Phone: (601) 984-1080
Barbara Westerfield, Registrar, University of Mississippi Medical Center, 2500 North State Street, Jackson, MS 39216

University of Southern Mississippi

Hattiesburg, Mississippi **CB member**
www.usm.edu **CB code: 1479**

- Public 4-year university
- Residential campus in small city
- 12,468 degree-seeking undergraduates: 14% part-time, 61% women, 28% African American, 1% Asian American, 1% Hispanic American, 1% international
- 2,562 degree-seeking graduate students
- 61% of applicants admitted
- SAT or ACT (ACT writing optional) required
- 46% graduate within 6 years

General. Founded in 1910. Regionally accredited. Dual campus with main campus in Hattiesburg and nonresidential, nontraditional campus, in Long Beach, and other sites along Mississippi Gulf Coast. **Degrees:** 2,300 bachelor's awarded; master's, doctoral offered. **ROTC:** Army, Air Force. **Location:** 85 miles from Jackson, 120 miles from New Orleans. **Calendar:** Semester, extensive summer session. **Full-time faculty:** 714 total; 79% have terminal degrees, 11% minority, 41% women. **Part-time faculty:** 133 total; 44% have terminal degrees, 10% minority, 62% women. **Class size:** 51% < 20, 34% 20-39, 5% 40-49, 7% 50-99, 3% >100. **Special facilities:** Marine education center, aquarium.

Freshman class profile. 5,153 applied, 3,151 admitted, 1,346 enrolled.

Mid 50% test scores		**Rank in top tenth:**	19%
SAT verbal:	460-580	**End year in good standing:**	78%
SAT math:	480-570	**Return as sophomores:**	75%
ACT:	18-24	**Out-of-state:**	25%
GPA 3.50 or higher:	28%	**Live on campus:**	72%
GPA 3.0-3.49:	29%	**International:**	1%
GPA 2.0-2.99:	41%	**Fraternities:**	20%
Rank in top quarter:	47%	**Sororities:**	17%

Basis for selection. School achievement record and test scores considered. Applicants who do not meet stated criteria may be required to participate in screening process that will include diagnostic test.

High school preparation. 16 units required; 18 recommended. Required and recommended units include English 4, mathematics 3, social studies 1, history 2, science 3 (laboratory 3), foreign language 2 and academic electives 2. Mathematics must include algebra I and II, geometry or higher mathematics. Social sciences must include US government, US history, world history, and economics or geography. Sciences must be chosen from introductory and advanced biology, physics, and chemistry. 2 units world geography, or additional science or mathematics may be substituted for 1 foreign language. 2 units of electives and .5 units of computer applications required.

2005-2006 Annual costs. Tuition/fees: $4,310; $9,740 out-of-state. Room/board: $4,818. Books/supplies: $800. Personal expenses: $2,700.

2004-2005 Financial aid. Need-based: 1,227 full-time freshmen applied for aid; 982 were judged to have need; 965 of these received aid. Average need met was 77%. Average scholarship/grant was $3,296; average loan $2,851. 41% of total undergraduate aid awarded as scholarships/grants, 59% as loans/jobs. **Non-need-based:** Awarded to 4,076 full-time undergraduates, including 800 freshmen.

Application procedures. Admission: No deadline. No application fee. Application may be submitted online. Admission notification on a rolling basis. **Financial aid:** Priority date 3/15; no closing date. FAFSA, institutional form required. Applicants notified on a rolling basis starting 4/1; must reply within 4 week(s) of notification.

Academics. Special study options: Accelerated study, combined bachelor's/graduate degree, cooperative education, distance learning, double major, dual enrollment of high school students, ESL, honors, internships, study abroad, teacher certification program. **Credit/placement by examination:** AP, CLEP, SAT, ACT, institutional tests. 30 credit hours maximum toward bachelor's degree. **Support services:** Learning center, pre-admission summer program, reduced course load, remedial instruction, study skills assistance, tutoring, writing center.

Honors college/program. Requires an ACT score of 24 or equivalent and essay.

Majors. Architecture: Interior, urban/community planning. **Area/ethnic studies:** American. **Biology:** General, marine. **Business:** Accounting, business admin, finance, human resources, management information systems, managerial economics, marketing. **Communications:** General, advertising, broadcast journalism, journalism. **Computer sciences:** General, data processing. **Education:** Business, Deaf/hearing impaired, elementary, music, physical, school counseling, special, technology/industrial arts. **Engineering technology:** Architectural, electrical, plastics. **Family/consumer sciences:** General, clothing/textiles, family studies, food/nutrition. **Foreign languages:** General. **Health:** Audiology/hearing, audiology/speech pathology, clinical lab science, nursing (RN). **History:** General. **Interdisciplinary:** Museum. **Legal studies:** Paralegal. **Liberal arts:** Library science. **Math:** General. **Parks/recreation:** General, health/fitness. **Personal/culinary services:** Mortuary science. **Philosophy/religion:** Philosophy. **Physical sciences:** Chemistry, geology, physics, polymer chemistry. **Protective services:** Criminal justice. **Psychology:** General. **Public administration:** Social work. **Social sciences:** Anthropology, geography, political science, sociology. **Visual/performing arts:** General, dance, dramatic.

Most popular majors. Business/marketing 20%, education 11%, health sciences 10%, parks/recreation 6%, psychology 7%.

Computing on campus. 484 workstations in dormitories, library, computer center, student center. Dormitories wired for high-speed internet access and linked to campus network. Commuter students can connect to campus network. Online course registration, online library, helpline, repair service, student web hosting, wireless network available.

Student life. Freshman orientation: Available. Preregistration for classes offered. **Policies:** Freshmen permitted cars on campus. **Housing:** Single-sex dorms, special housing for disabled, apartments, fraternity/sorority housing available. Freshmen who reside in area may live at home. All freshmen who request campus housing required to live in freshman dormitories. **Activities:** Bands, choral groups, dance, drama, film society, literary magazine, music ensembles, musical theater, opera, radio station, student government, student newspaper, symphony orchestra, honor societies, service and religious organizations, Young Republicans, Young Democrats.

Athletics. NCAA. **Intercollegiate:** Baseball M, basketball, cross-country, football (tackle) M, golf, rugby M, soccer W, softball W, tennis, track and field, volleyball W. **Intramural:** Badminton, basketball, bowling, golf, racquetball, soccer, softball, squash, swimming, table tennis, tennis, track and field, volleyball. **Team name:** Golden Eagles.

Student services. Adult student services, career counseling, student employment services, health services, minority student services, on-campus daycare, personal counseling, placement for graduates, veterans' counselor, women's services. **Physically disabled:** Services for visually, speech, hearing impaired. **Learning disabled:** Comprehensive services available.

Contact. E-mail: admissions@usm.edu
Phone: (601) 266-5000 Fax: (601) 266-5148
Kristi Motter, Director of Recruitment/Operations, University of Southern Mississippi, 118 College Drive #5166, Hattiesburg, MS 39406-0001

Wesley College

Florence, Mississippi
www.wesleycollege.edu **CB code: 1923**

- Private 4-year Bible college affiliated with Congregational Methodist Church
- Residential campus in small town

- 86 degree-seeking undergraduates: 26% part-time, 31% women, 38% African American, 1% Asian American, 1% Hispanic American, 1% international
- 67% of applicants admitted
- SAT or ACT (ACT writing optional), application essay required
- 32% graduate within 6 years; 41% enter graduate study

General. Founded in 1972. Accredited by ABHE. **Degrees:** 17 bachelor's awarded. **Location:** 12 miles from Jackson. **Calendar:** Semester, limited summer session. **Full-time faculty:** 5 total; 40% have terminal degrees, 20% women. **Part-time faculty:** 14 total; 21% have terminal degrees, 14% minority, 29% women. **Class size:** 82% < 20, 18% 20-39.

Freshman class profile. 27 applied, 18 admitted, 12 enrolled.

Rank in top quarter:	12%	**Return as sophomores:**	42%
Rank in top tenth:	2%	**Out-of-state:**	46%
End year in good standing:	68%	**Live on campus:**	92%

Basis for selection. Test scores, school achievement record, essay important. **Homeschooled:** Must have certified diploma, GED, or meet minimum ACT/SAT scores as specified in current college catalog. **Learning Disabled:** Copies of previous diagnostic records requested.

High school preparation. College-preparatory program recommended. 15 units required. Required units include English 4, mathematics 2, social studies 4, science 3 and academic electives 2.

2005-2006 Annual costs. Tuition/fees: $6,620. Room/board: $2,960. Books/supplies: $700. Personal expenses: $650.

2004-2005 Financial aid. **Need-based:** 16 full-time freshmen applied for aid; 15 were judged to have need; 15 of these received aid. Average need met was 65%. Average scholarship/grant was $3,165; average loan $2,625. 42% of total undergraduate aid awarded as scholarships/grants, 58% as loans/jobs. **Non-need-based:** Awarded to 21 full-time undergraduates, including 7 freshmen. Scholarships awarded for academics, alumni affiliation, leadership, religious affiliation.

Application procedures. **Admission:** Priority date 7/1; deadline 8/1 (receipt date). $20 fee. Application may be submitted online. Admission notification on a rolling basis. Must reply by May 1 or within 4 week(s) if notified thereafter. **Financial aid:** Closing date 5/14. FAFSA required. Applicants notified on a rolling basis starting 7/1; must reply within 2 week(s) of notification.

Academics. **Special study options:** Distance learning, double major, dual enrollment of high school students, independent study, internships. **Credit/placement by examination:** AP, CLEP, institutional tests. 15 credit hours maximum toward associate degree, 15 toward bachelor's. **Support services:** Learning center, reduced course load, remedial instruction, study skills assistance, tutoring.

Majors. **Philosophy/religion:** Religion. **Theology:** Bible, missionary, pastoral counseling, religious ed, theology, youth ministry.

Most popular majors. Theological studies 99%.

Computing on campus. 4 workstations in library, student center. Dormitories wired for high-speed internet access. Wireless network available.

Student life. **Freshman orientation:** Mandatory. Preregistration for classes offered. **Policies:** Religious observance required. Freshmen permitted cars on campus. **Housing:** Single-sex dorms, apartments, substance-free housing available. $50 partly refundable deposit, deadline 8/1. **Activities:** Choral groups, drama, music ensembles, student government, missionary prayer band, ministerial partnership, Christian service program.

Athletics. NCCAA. **Intercollegiate:** Basketball M. **Intramural:** Basketball, table tennis, volleyball, weight lifting. **Team name:** Warriors.

Student services. Campus ministries, career counseling, student employment services, financial aid counseling, personal counseling.

Contact. E-mail: admissions@wesleycollege.edu
Phone: (601) 845-1355 Toll-free number: (800) 748-9972
Fax: (601) 845-2266
Charity Nielsen, Director of Admissions, Wesley College, PO Box 1070, Florence, MS 39073-0070

William Carey College

Hattiesburg, Mississippi
www.wmcarey.edu **CB code: 1907**

- Private 4-year liberal arts college affiliated with Baptist faith
- Commuter campus in small city
- 1,840 degree-seeking undergraduates
- SAT or ACT (ACT writing optional) required

General. Founded in 1906. Regionally accredited. **Degrees:** 432 bachelor's awarded; master's offered. **ROTC:** Army, Air Force. **Location:** 98 miles from New Orleans. **Calendar:** Trimester, extensive summer session. **Full-time faculty:** 93 total; 66% have terminal degrees, 2% minority, 53% women. **Part-time faculty:** 92 total; 45% have terminal degrees, 6% minority, 61% women. **Class size:** 61% < 20, 38% 20-39, 1% 40-49, less than 1% 50-99. **Special facilities:** Center for study of the life and work of William Carey.

Freshman class profile. 309 applied, 306 admitted, 164 enrolled.

Mid 50% test scores		**Return as sophomores:**	57%
SAT verbal:	370-600	**Out-of-state:**	23%
SAT math:	470-600	**Live on campus:**	82%
ACT:	19-25	**Fraternities:**	1%
End year in good standing:	93%	**Sororities:**	1%

Basis for selection. Open admission, but selective for some programs. ACT of 18 or SAT of 870 required. **Homeschooled:** Transcript of courses and grades required.

High school preparation. 16 units required. Required units include English 4, mathematics 3, social studies 2 and science 3.

2005-2006 Annual costs. Tuition/fees: $8,415. Room/board: $3,465. Books/supplies: $1,221. Personal expenses: $688.

2004-2005 Financial aid. **Need-based:** 16% of total undergraduate aid awarded as scholarships/grants, 84% as loans/jobs. **Non-need-based:** Scholarships awarded for academics, alumni affiliation, art, athletics, music/drama, religious affiliation.

Application procedures. **Admission:** Priority date 7/12; no deadline. $20 fee. Application may be submitted online. Admission notification on a rolling basis. Admissions application priority date: 30 days prior to beginning of term. **Financial aid:** Priority date 4/1, closing date 9/1. FAFSA required. Applicants notified on a rolling basis starting 6/1; must reply within 2 week(s) of notification.

Academics. **Special study options:** Accelerated study, cross-registration, distance learning, double major, dual enrollment of high school students, honors, independent study, internships, study abroad, teacher certification program. **Credit/placement by examination:** AP, CLEP, IB, SAT, ACT, institutional tests. 30 credit hours maximum toward bachelor's degree. **Support services:** Reduced course load, remedial instruction, study skills assistance, tutoring.

Majors. **Biology:** General. **Business:** Business admin. **Communications:** General, journalism. **Education:** Art, biology, drama/dance, elementary, English, mathematics, music, physical, social science, speech. **English:** English lit. **Health:** Health services, music therapy, nursing (RN). **History:** General. **Math:** General. **Parks/recreation:** Health/fitness. **Physical sciences:** Chemistry. **Psychology:** General. **Social sciences:** General. **Theology:** Bible, sacred music. **Visual/performing arts:** Art, dramatic, music performance, studio arts.

Most popular majors. Business/marketing 11%, education 18%, health sciences 20%, liberal arts 15%, psychology 13%.

Computing on campus. 50 workstations in library, computer center. Dormitories wired for high-speed internet access. Helpline available.

Student life. **Freshman orientation:** Mandatory. Preregistration for classes offered. Orientation for new students is held at a published date and time prior to the start of the fall term. **Policies:** Religious observance required. Freshmen permitted cars on campus. **Housing:** Guaranteed on-campus for freshmen. Single-sex dorms, apartments, substance-free housing available. $100 fully refundable deposit. **Activities:** Jazz band, choral groups, dance, drama, music ensembles, musical theater, student government, student newspaper, Baptist student union, Afro-American club, psychology club, Fellowship of Christian Athletes, honorary organizations, Church Related Vocations Fellowship, science society, student nurses association, student government association, music, therapy association,.

Athletics. NAIA. **Intercollegiate:** Baseball M, basketball, golf, soccer, softball W. **Intramural:** Basketball, football (non-tackle) M, football (tackle), soccer, softball, tennis, volleyball. **Team name:** Crusaders.

Student services. Adult student services, alcohol/substance abuse counseling, campus ministries, career counseling, services for economically disadvantaged, student employment services, financial aid counseling, personal counseling, placement for graduates, veterans' counselor. **Physically disabled:** Services for visually impaired.

Contact. E-mail: admissions@wmcarey.edu
Phone: (601) 318-6103 Toll-free number: (800) 962-5991
Fax: (601) 318-6765
William Curry, Director of Admissions/Financial Aid, William Carey College, 498 Tuscan Avenue, Hattiesburg, MS 39401-5499

Missouri

Avila University
Kansas City, Missouri
www.avila.edu **CB code: 6109**

- Private 4-year university and liberal arts college affiliated with Roman Catholic Church
- Commuter campus in very large city
- 1,118 degree-seeking undergraduates: 22% part-time, 67% women, 17% African American, 2% Asian American, 5% Hispanic American, 1% Native American, 2% international
- 483 graduate students
- 56% of applicants admitted
- SAT or ACT (ACT writing optional) required
- 41% graduate within 6 years

General. Founded in 1916. Regionally accredited. Campus connected with local network and student-operated, closed circuit cable television stations. **Degrees:** 201 bachelor's awarded; master's offered. **ROTC:** Army. **Calendar:** Semester, extensive summer session. **Full-time faculty:** 64 total; 69% have terminal degrees, 5% minority, 62% women. **Part-time faculty:** 135 total; 27% have terminal degrees, 4% minority, 54% women. **Class size:** 68% < 20, 32% 20-39. **Special facilities:** Theater, radiological laboratory, 30 off-campus medical-clinical learning sites, campus media production facilities, nursing learning resource center, photography lab.

Freshman class profile. 898 applied, 505 admitted, 165 enrolled.

Mid 50% test scores			
SAT verbal:	440-610	Return as sophomores:	71%
SAT math:	460-610	Out-of-state:	34%
ACT:	19-24	Live on campus:	71%
		International:	3%

Basis for selection. Unconditional acceptance for applicants with minimum GPA of 2.5 and ACT composite of 20 or higher. Others may be considered. ACT/SAT not required if student has been out of high school 1 year or more. Use ACT subscores for placement in math and English. Audition recommended for drama, music students. **Homeschooled:** SAT or ACT and home school transcripts required. GED may be requested.

High school preparation. 16 units recommended. Recommended units include English 4, mathematics 3, social studies 3, history 2, science 2 (laboratory 1) and foreign language 2. One fine arts also recommended.

2006-2007 Annual costs. Tuition/fees (projected): $18,000. Room/board: $5,400. Books/supplies: $800. Personal expenses: $2,200.

2005-2006 Financial aid. Need-based: Average need met was 19%. Average scholarship/grant was $5,598; average loan $3,712. 54% of total undergraduate aid awarded as scholarships/grants, 46% as loans/jobs. **Non-need-based:** Scholarships awarded for academics, alumni affiliation, art, athletics, music/drama, religious affiliation. **Additional information:** Financial aid adjusted for increases in tuition based on need.

Application procedures. Admission: No deadline. No application fee. Application may be submitted online. Admission notification on a rolling basis. **Financial aid:** Priority date 4/1; no closing date. FAFSA, institutional form required. Applicants notified on a rolling basis starting 2/1; must reply within 3 week(s) of notification.

Academics. Outcome-based core curriculum; interdisciplinary course work at junior level required; unique senior experience bridges transition from college to community. **Special study options:** Accelerated study, combined bachelor's/graduate degree, cooperative education, cross-registration, distance learning, double major, dual enrollment of high school students, ESL, exchange student, independent study, internships, liberal arts/career combination, study abroad, teacher certification program, Washington semester, weekend college. **Credit/placement by examination:** AP, CLEP, IB, SAT, ACT, institutional tests. 32 credit hours maximum toward bachelor's degree. **Support services:** Learning center, reduced course load, remedial instruction, study skills assistance, tutoring, writing center.

Majors. Biology: General. **Business:** General, accounting, business admin, finance, international, marketing. **Communications:** General. **Computer sciences:** General. **Education:** Elementary, middle, special. **English:** English lit. **Health:** Facilities admin, nursing (RN). **History:** General. **Interdisciplinary:** Biological/physical sciences. **Legal studies:** Paralegal. **Philosophy/religion:** Religion. **Physical sciences:** Chemistry. **Psychology:** General. **Public administration:** Social work. **Social sciences:** Political science, sociology. **Visual/performing arts:** Dramatic, music performance, studio arts.

Most popular majors. Biology 6%, business/marketing 35%, communications/journalism 9%, education 12%, health sciences 10%, psychology 13%.

Computing on campus. 126 workstations in dormitories, library, computer center. Dormitories wired for high-speed internet access and linked to campus network. Commuter students can connect to campus network. Online library, helpline available.

Student life. Freshman orientation: Mandatory. Preregistration for classes offered. Held 3 days prior to first day of classes; programs available for freshmen-adult transfer students and friends/family of new students. **Policies:** First-time, first-year students not living at home with parents/guardians required to live on campus through sophomore year. Freshmen permitted cars on campus. **Housing:** Guaranteed on-campus for freshmen. Coed dorms, substance-free housing available. $50 deposit. Single-sex floors available. **Activities:** Choral groups, dance, drama, literary magazine, musical theater, student government, student newspaper, student nurses association, psychology club, Black Student Union, premedical club, English club, education club, association of radiological science, social work association, National Association of Masters in Psychology, Society of Life Scientists.

Athletics. NAIA. **Intercollegiate:** Baseball M, basketball, cheerleading W, football (tackle) M, golf W, soccer, softball W, volleyball W. **Intramural:** Basketball, bowling, football (tackle), soccer, softball, table tennis, tennis, volleyball. **Team name:** Eagles.

Student services. Adult student services, alcohol/substance abuse counseling, campus ministries, career counseling, student employment services, financial aid counseling, health services, on-campus daycare, personal counseling, placement for graduates, veterans' counselor, women's services. **Physically disabled:** Services for visually, speech, hearing impaired.

Contact. E-mail: admission@avila.edu
Phone: (816) 501-2400 Toll-free number: (800) 462-8452
Fax: (816) 501-2453
Patricia Harper, Director of Admission, Avila University, 11901 Wornall Road, Kansas City, MO 64145-1698

Baptist Bible College
Springfield, Missouri
www.baptist.edu **CB code: 0991**

- Private 4-year Bible and seminary college affiliated with Baptist Bible Fellowship
- Residential campus in small city
- 616 degree-seeking undergraduates: 12% part-time, 44% women, 1% African American, 1% Asian American, 3% Hispanic American, 1% Native American

General. Founded in 1950. Candidate for regional accreditation; also accredited by ABHE. **Degrees:** 103 bachelor's, 7 associate awarded; master's offered. **Location:** 180 miles from Kansas City, 225 miles from St. Louis. **Calendar:** Semester, limited summer session. **Full-time faculty:** 40 total. **Part-time faculty:** 16 total.

Freshman class profile.

Out-of-state:	71%	Live on campus:	69%

Basis for selection. Open admission. Pastoral recommendation required.

2006-2007 Annual costs. Tuition/fees (projected): $13,060. Room/board: $5,300. Books/supplies: $800. Personal expenses: $2,164.

2004-2005 Financial aid. Need-based: 42% of total undergraduate aid awarded as scholarships/grants, 58% as loans/jobs.

Application procedures. Admission: Priority date 8/1; no deadline. $40 fee. Application may be submitted online. Admission notification on a rolling basis. **Financial aid:** Closing date 5/1. FAFSA, institutional form required. Applicants notified on a rolling basis; must reply within 2 week(s) of notification.

Academics. Special study options: Distance learning. **Credit/placement by examination:** AP, CLEP. **Support services:** Reduced course load, remedial instruction, study skills assistance, tutoring.

Majors. **Business:** Administrative services. **Education:** Elementary, music. **Philosophy/religion:** Religion. **Theology:** Missionary, pastoral counseling, religious ed, sacred music, theology.

Computing on campus. 70 workstations in library, computer center, student center. Dormitories wired for high-speed internet access and linked to campus network. Online library, helpline, repair service available.

Student life. **Freshman orientation:** Mandatory. Preregistration for classes offered. **Policies:** Religious observance required. Freshmen permitted cars on campus. **Housing:** Guaranteed on-campus for freshmen. Single-sex dorms, apartments available. **Activities:** Concert band, choral groups, drama, music ensembles, radio station, student government.

Athletics. NCCAA. **Intercollegiate:** Basketball, soccer, track and field W, volleyball W. **Intramural:** Basketball, soccer M, softball, table tennis, volleyball. **Team name:** Patriots.

Student services. Campus ministries, career counseling, financial aid counseling, health services, on-campus daycare, personal counseling, veterans' counselor.

Contact. Phone: (417) 268-6013 Toll-free number: (800) 228-5754
Fax: (417) 268-6694
Terry Allcorn, Director of Admissions, Baptist Bible College, 628 East Kearney Street, Springfield, MO 65803

Calvary Bible College and Theological Seminary

Kansas City, Missouri
www.calvary.edu **CB code: 6331**

- Private 4-year Bible and seminary college affiliated with nondenominational tradition
- Residential campus in large city
- 281 degree-seeking undergraduates: 20% part-time, 43% women, 3% African American, 1% Asian American, 2% Hispanic American, 1% international
- 60 graduate students
- 47% graduate within 6 years

General. Founded in 1932. Regionally accredited; also accredited by ABHE. **Degrees:** 50 bachelor's, 9 associate awarded; master's, first professional offered. **Location:** 20 miles from Kansas City. **Calendar:** Semester, limited summer session. **Full-time faculty:** 14 total; 29% have terminal degrees, 21% women. **Part-time faculty:** 20 total; 20% have terminal degrees, 5% minority, 35% women.

Freshman class profile. 40 enrolled.

Mid 50% test scores			
SAT verbal:	440-670	Return as sophomores:	73%
SAT math:	260-570	Out-of-state:	65%
ACT:	18-28	Live on campus:	83%

Basis for selection. Open admission. Christian character stressed along with academic preparation. Pastor's and personal reference forms required. School achievement record and test scores considered. Applicants are required to submit a written Personal Testimony/Confirmation and Statement of Faith. Audition required for music students. **Homeschooled:** Transcripts are required in compliance with state's home-school policies. **Learning Disabled:** Students should contact the Director of Admissions.

2005-2006 Annual costs. Tuition/fees: $6,936. Room/board: $3,900. Books/supplies: $600.

2004-2005 Financial aid. **Need-based:** 87% of total undergraduate aid awarded as scholarships/grants, 13% as loans/jobs. **Non-need-based:** Scholarships awarded for academics, alumni affiliation, religious affiliation.

Application procedures. **Admission:** Closing date 7/15 (receipt date). $25 fee, may be waived for applicants with need. **Financial aid:** Priority date 3/1, closing date 4/1. FAFSA, institutional form required. Applicants notified on a rolling basis starting 4/1.

Academics. Each student carries major in Bible and theology and second major in a professional area. These majors prepare students for vocational and/or volunteer involvement in Christian ministry. **Special study options:** Distance learning, double major, dual enrollment of high school students, independent study, internships, student-designed major, teacher certification program. **Credit/placement by examination:** AP, CLEP, IB, institutional tests. **Support services:** Learning center, reduced course load, remedial instruction, study skills assistance, tutoring.

Majors. **Business:** Organizational behavior. **Communications:** Broadcast journalism, media studies. **Education:** Elementary, music, secondary. **Social sciences:** Urban studies. **Theology:** Bible, missionary, pastoral counseling, religious ed, sacred music, theology, youth ministry. **Visual/performing arts:** Music performance, piano/organ, voice/opera.

Most popular majors. Business/marketing 18%, education 18%, theological studies 60%.

Computing on campus. 23 workstations in library, student center. Dormitories wired for high-speed internet access. Repair service, wireless network available.

Student life. **Freshman orientation:** Mandatory, $50 fee. **Policies:** Weekly Christian ministry, chapel and church attendance required. Single students required to live in college housing unless living with parents or at least 23 years of age. Religious observance required. Freshmen permitted cars on campus. **Housing:** Guaranteed on-campus for all undergraduates. Single-sex dorms, apartments available. Duplexes available for married students. **Activities:** Choral groups, drama, music ensembles, radio station, student government, Christian Ministry, Missionary Prayer Fellowship, short-term missions.

Athletics. NCCAA. **Intercollegiate:** Basketball, soccer M, volleyball W. **Intramural:** Basketball, bowling, cheerleading W, golf, racquetball, softball, table tennis, tennis, volleyball. **Team name:** Warriors.

Student services. Alcohol/substance abuse counseling, campus ministries, student employment services, financial aid counseling, health services, personal counseling, placement for graduates, veterans' counselor, women's services.

Contact. E-mail: admissions@calvary.edu
Phone: (816) 326-3960 Toll-free number: (800) 326-3960
Fax: (816) 331-4474
Robert Reinsch, Director of Admissions and Financial Aid, Calvary Bible College and Theological Seminary, 15800 Calvary Road, Kansas City, MO 64147

Central Bible College

Springfield, Missouri
www.cbcag.edu **CB code: 6085**

- Private 4-year Bible college affiliated with Assemblies of God
- Residential campus in small city
- 741 degree-seeking undergraduates
- Application essay required

General. Founded in 1922. Accredited by ABHE. **Degrees:** 126 bachelor's, 10 associate awarded. **Location:** 210 miles from St. Louis. **Calendar:** Semester, extensive summer session. **Full-time faculty:** 40 total. **Part-time faculty:** 35 total.

Freshman class profile.

Mid 50% test scores			
SAT verbal:	400-620	SAT math:	410-600
		ACT:	18-24

Basis for selection. Special consideration given to members of Assemblies of God and all applicants who rank in top half of graduating class who meet entrance requirements. Interview recommended for all students; audition recommended for music students.

High school preparation. Strong background in English, mathematics and science recommended. Computer literacy course recommended.

2005-2006 Annual costs. Tuition/fees: $9,774. Room/board: $4,720. Books/supplies: $550. Personal expenses: $1,000.

Application procedures. **Admission:** Priority date 8/15; no deadline. $25 fee, may be waived for applicants with need. Admission notification on a rolling basis. **Financial aid:** Priority date 5/1; no closing date. FAFSA required. Applicants notified on a rolling basis starting 5/15; must reply within 3 week(s) of notification.

Academics. **Special study options:** Accelerated study, cooperative education, cross-registration, double major, independent study, internships. **Credit/placement by examination:** CLEP, institutional tests. 24 credit hours maximum toward bachelor's degree. **Support services:** Reduced course load, remedial instruction, tutoring.

Majors. **Theology:** Bible, missionary, religious ed, sacred music, theology.

Computing on campus. 20 workstations in library, computer center.

Student life. **Freshman orientation:** Mandatory, $150 fee. Preregistration for classes offered. **Policies:** Religious observance required. **Housing:** Single-sex dorms, apartments available. **Activities:** Concert band, choral groups, drama, music ensembles, radio station, student government, student newspaper.

Athletics. NCCAA. **Intercollegiate:** Basketball M, volleyball W. **Intramural:** Basketball M, softball.

Student services. Student employment services, health services, personal counseling, placement for graduates, veterans' counselor.

Contact. E-mail: info@cbcag.edu
Phone: (417) 833-2551 ext. 1184 Toll-free number: (800) 831-4222
Fax: (417) 833-5141
Bill Davis, Registrar, Central Bible College, 3000 North Grant Avenue, Springfield, MO 65803-1069

Central Christian College of the Bible

Moberly, Missouri
www.cccb.edu **CB code: 6145**

- Private 4-year Bible college affiliated with Christian Church
- Residential campus in large town
- 517 degree-seeking undergraduates
- ACT (writing recommended), application essay required

General. Founded in 1957. Accredited by ABHE. Every full-time student receives a full-tuition scholarship. **Degrees:** 35 bachelor's, 12 associate awarded. **Location:** 35 miles from Columbia. **Calendar:** Semester, limited summer session. **Full-time faculty:** 9 total; 78% have terminal degrees, 11% minority. **Part-time faculty:** 18 total; 6% have terminal degrees, 6% women. **Special facilities:** 71,000 volume library with computer lab and foreign language lab.

Basis for selection. High school transcript, ACT/SAT scores and references very important. Students with GPA below 2.0 assigned reduced course load.

High school preparation. 15 units recommended. Recommended units include English 2, mathematics 2, social studies 1 and science 2.

2005-2006 Annual costs. Full-time students receive full scholarship. Room and board $5,000. Required fees $750. Books/supplies: $750. Personal expenses: $3,846.

Application procedures. **Admission:** No deadline. No application fee. Application may be submitted online. Admission notification on a rolling basis beginning on or about 12/1. Admitted applicants must reply within 6 weeks of notification. **Financial aid:** Priority date 3/15, closing date 4/1. FAFSA required. Applicants notified by 5/15; must reply within 2 week(s) of notification.

Academics. **Special study options:** Dual enrollment of high school students, internships. **Credit/placement by examination:** CLEP. 6 credit hours maximum toward bachelor's degree. **Support services:** Reduced course load, study skills assistance, tutoring.

Majors. **Philosophy/religion:** Religion. **Theology:** Pastoral counseling, religious ed, sacred music, theology.

Computing on campus. 30 workstations in library, student center. Dormitories wired for high-speed internet access and linked to campus network. Commuter students can connect to campus network. Wireless network available.

Student life. **Freshman orientation:** Mandatory. Preregistration for classes offered. **Policies:** Religious observance required. Freshmen permitted cars on campus. **Housing:** Guaranteed on-campus for all undergraduates. Single-sex dorms, substance-free housing available. **Activities:** Choral groups, music ensembles, student government, Harvesters missions group, Gospel choir, international students group.

Athletics. NCCAA. **Intercollegiate:** Basketball, soccer M, volleyball W. **Intramural:** Basketball, bowling, softball, table tennis, tennis, volleyball. **Team name:** Heralds.

Student services. Campus ministries, career counseling, financial aid counseling, personal counseling, placement for graduates, veterans' counselor.

Contact. E-mail: admissions2@cccb.edu
Phone: (888) 263-3900 Toll-free number: (888) 263-3900
Fax: (888) 263-3936
Tracy Roach, Director of Admission, Central Christian College of the Bible, 911 East Urbandale Drive, Moberly, MO 65270-1997

Central Methodist University

Fayette, Missouri
www.cmc.edu **CB code: 6089**

- Private 4-year liberal arts college affiliated with United Methodist Church
- Residential campus in small town
- 818 degree-seeking undergraduates
- SAT or ACT (ACT writing recommended) required

General. Founded in 1854. Regionally accredited. **Degrees:** 145 bachelor's, 4 associate awarded; master's offered. **ROTC:** Army, Air Force. **Location:** 150 miles from St. Louis, 125 miles from Kansas City. **Calendar:** Semester, limited summer session. **Full-time faculty:** 57 total. **Part-time faculty:** 16 total. **Class size:** 67% < 20, 29% 20-39, 2% 40-49, 2% 50-99. **Special facilities:** Observatory and laboratory, natural history museum, 225-seat theater, conservatory of music.

Freshman class profile.

Mid 50% test scores			
SAT verbal:	530-640	Rank in top quarter:	33%
SAT math:	450-500	Rank in top tenth:	8%
ACT:	18-23	Out-of-state:	8%
		Live on campus:	95%

Basis for selection. Rank in upper half of class or above-average test scores important. Minimum high school cumulative GPA of 2.0 and minimum 18 ACT score required. Interview required for nursing applicants; audition recommended for drama, music students.

High school preparation. 20 units recommended. Recommended units include English 4, mathematics 3, social studies 2, science 2 and foreign language 2. 2 humanities recommended.

2005-2006 Annual costs. Tuition/fees: $15,200. Room/board: $5,360. Books/supplies: $650. Personal expenses: $2,250.

2005-2006 Financial aid. **Need-based:** 171 full-time freshmen applied for aid; 146 were judged to have need; 146 of these received aid. Average need met was 72%. Average scholarship/grant was $4,662; average loan $2,625. 48% of total undergraduate aid awarded as scholarships/grants, 52% as loans/jobs. **Non-need-based:** Awarded to 641 full-time undergraduates, including 151 freshmen. Scholarships awarded for academics, alumni affiliation, athletics, music/drama, religious affiliation.

Application procedures. **Admission:** No deadline. $20 fee, may be waived for applicants with need. Application may be submitted online. Admission notification on a rolling basis beginning on or about 10/1. Must reply by May 1 or within 4 week(s) if notified thereafter. **Financial aid:** Priority date 3/15; no closing date. FAFSA required. Applicants notified on a rolling basis starting 1/30; must reply within 2 week(s) of notification.

Academics. Curriculum offers liberal arts foundation with intensive concentration in special area. Nursing students required to have computer. **Special study options:** Accelerated study, distance learning, double major, dual enrollment of high school students, honors, independent study, internships, liberal arts/career combination, student-designed major, study abroad, teacher certification program. 3-year bachelor's degree, 2-week January travel program. **Credit/placement by examination:** CLEP, institutional tests. 32 credit hours maximum toward associate degree, 32 toward bachelor's. **Support services:** Learning center, pre-admission summer program, reduced course load, remedial instruction, tutoring.

Majors. **Biology:** General. **Business:** Accounting, business admin, management information systems, management science. **Communications:** General. **Computer sciences:** Computer science. **Conservation:** General. **Education:** Biology, chemistry, early childhood, elementary, foreign languages, middle, music, physical, physics, science, secondary, social science. **Foreign languages:** French, Spanish. **Health:** Athletic training, nursing (RN), nursing admin, preop/surgical nursing. **History:** General. **Math:** General. **Parks/recreation:** Facilities management. **Philosophy/religion:** Philosophy, religion. **Physical sciences:** Chemistry, physics. **Protective services:** Criminal justice. **Psychology:** General. **Public administration:** General, human services. **Social sciences:** Economics, political science, sociology. **Visual/performing arts:** Dramatic, music performance.

Most popular majors. Biology 11%, business/marketing 16%, education 22%, health sciences 13%, interdisciplinary studies 6%.

Computing on campus. 200 workstations in dormitories, library, computer center. Commuter students can connect to campus network. Online library, helpline available.

Student life. **Freshman orientation:** Available, $35 fee. Preregistration for classes offered. **Policies:** Freshmen permitted cars on campus. **Housing:** Guaranteed on-campus for all undergraduates. Coed dorms, single-sex dorms, apartments available. $200 deposit, deadline 5/1. **Activities:** Bands, choral groups, drama, literary magazine, music ensembles, musical theater, radio station, student government, student newspaper, symphony orchestra, TV station, Alpha Phi Omega, prelaw club; religious, service, business, music organizations.

Athletics. NAIA. **Intercollegiate:** Baseball M, basketball, cross-country, football (tackle) M, golf, soccer, softball W, track and field, volleyball W. **Intramural:** Basketball, football (tackle) M, golf, racquetball, soccer, softball, tennis, track and field, volleyball. **Team name:** Eagles.

Student services. Alcohol/substance abuse counseling, campus ministries, career counseling, student employment services, financial aid counseling, health services, personal counseling, placement for graduates.

Contact. E-mail: admissions@cmc.edu
Phone: (660) 248-6251 Toll-free number: (888) 262-1854
Fax: (660) 248-1872
Edward Lamm, Director of Admissions, Central Methodist University, 411 Central Methodist Square, Fayette, MO 65248-1198

Central Missouri State University

Warrensburg, Missouri
www.cmsu.edu **CB code: 6090**

- Public 4-year university
- Commuter campus in large town
- 8,254 degree-seeking undergraduates: 14% part-time, 56% women, 7% African American, 1% Asian American, 2% Hispanic American, 1% Native American, 2% international
- 1,474 degree-seeking graduate students
- 85% of applicants admitted
- ACT (writing optional) required
- 50% graduate within 6 years

General. Founded in 1871. Regionally accredited. Extensive international exchange program. **Degrees:** 1,643 bachelor's, 20 associate awarded; master's offered. **ROTC:** Army, Air Force. **Location:** 50 miles from Kansas City. **Calendar:** Semester, extensive summer session. **Full-time faculty:** 439 total; 75% have terminal degrees, 11% minority, 40% women. **Part-time faculty:** 266 total; 19% have terminal degrees, 6% minority, 49% women. **Class size:** 46% < 20, 45% 20-39, 6% 40-49, 2% 50-99, less than 1% >100. **Special facilities:** Airport, 260-acre farm, museum, children's literature collection, musical instruments collection, child development lab, advanced technology library.

Freshman class profile. 3,619 applied, 3,066 admitted, 1,575 enrolled.

Mid 50% test scores		**Out-of-state:**	4%
ACT:	19-24	**Live on campus:**	82%
Rank in top quarter:	40%	**International:**	4%
Rank in top tenth:	14%	**Fraternities:**	22%
End year in good standing:	92%	**Sororities:**	17%
Return as sophomores:	71%		

Basis for selection. Applicant must be in top two-thirds of high school class, complete 16-unit core curriculum and have minimum ACT score of 20. TOEFL required for international students. Essay required for some programs; audition recommended for music students. **Homeschooled:** Recommend ACT, GED, or equivalent.

High school preparation. College-preparatory program required. 16 units required. Required and recommended units include English 4, mathematics 3, social studies 3, science 2 (laboratory 1), foreign language 2 and academic electives 3. One fine/performing arts required.

2005-2006 Annual costs. Tuition/fees: $5,550; $10,680 out-of-state. Room/board: $5,180. Books/supplies: $500. Personal expenses: $1,400.

2004-2005 Financial aid. Need-based: 1,172 full-time freshmen applied for aid; 812 were judged to have need; 790 of these received aid. Average need met was 77%. Average scholarship/grant was $1,631; average loan $1,258. 38% of total undergraduate aid awarded as scholarships/grants, 62% as loans/jobs. **Non-need-based:** Awarded to 4,835 full-time undergraduates, including 1,200 freshmen. Scholarships awarded for academics, alumni affiliation, art, athletics, leadership, minority status, music/drama, ROTC, state residency.

Application procedures. Admission: Priority date 6/1; no deadline. $30 fee, may be waived for applicants with need. Application may be submitted online. Admission notification on a rolling basis beginning on or about 8/1. **Financial aid:** Priority date 3/1; no closing date. FAFSA required. Applicants notified on a rolling basis starting 3/1; must reply within 2 week(s) of notification.

Academics. Online services and resources include library, technical support, writing center and bookstore. **Special study options:** Combined bachelor's/graduate degree, cooperative education, cross-registration, distance learning, double major, dual enrollment of high school students, ESL, honors, internships, liberal arts/career combination, student-designed major, study abroad, teacher certification program, weekend college. Engineering program with University of Missouri (Columbia, Rolla) and University of Indiana. **Credit/placement by examination:** AP, CLEP, IB, ACT, institutional tests. 15 credit hours maximum toward associate degree, 30 toward bachelor's. **Support services:** Learning center, remedial instruction, study skills assistance, tutoring, writing center.

Honors college/program. Minimum ACT score of 25; 319 freshmen admitted; requires 48 credit hours.

Majors. Agriculture: General, business, economics. **Biology:** General. **Business:** Accounting, actuarial science, business admin, finance, hotel/motel admin, human resources, management information systems, marketing, office management, tourism promotion. **Communications:** General, broadcast journalism, journalism, public relations. **Communications technology:** Graphic/printing. **Computer sciences:** General, data processing. **Education:** Agricultural, art, biology, business, chemistry, elementary, English, family/consumer sciences, foreign languages, French, German, mathematics, middle, music, physical, physics, science, secondary, social studies, Spanish, special, speech, technology/industrial arts. **Engineering technology:** Aerospace, architectural, construction, drafting, electrical, industrial. **English:** Speech/rhetoric. **Family/consumer sciences:** General, child development, clothing/textiles, family studies. **Foreign languages:** French, German, Spanish. **Health:** Nursing (RN), speech pathology. **History:** General. **Math:** General. **Parks/recreation:** General, facilities management. **Physical sciences:** Chemistry, geology, physics, planetary. **Protective services:** Law enforcement admin. **Psychology:** General. **Public administration:** Social work. **Social sciences:** Economics, geography, political science, sociology. **Visual/performing arts:** Art, commercial/advertising art, dramatic, interior design, photography, studio arts.

Most popular majors. Business/marketing 20%, education 22%, engineering/engineering technologies 8%, security/protective services 9%, visual/performing arts 6%.

Computing on campus. 1,600 workstations in dormitories, library, computer center, student center. Dormitories wired for high-speed internet access and linked to campus network. Commuter students can connect to campus network. Online course registration, online library, helpline, student web hosting, wireless network available.

Student life. Freshman orientation: Mandatory. Preregistration for classes offered. 8 one-day sessions in early summer. **Policies:** Freshmen permitted cars on campus. **Housing:** Guaranteed on-campus for all undergraduates. Coed dorms, single-sex dorms, special housing for disabled, apartments, fraternity/sorority housing, substance-free housing available. $100 nonrefundable deposit, deadline 6/1. Honors hall, economy suites. **Activities:** Bands, choral groups, dance, drama, film society, literary magazine, music ensembles, musical theater, opera, radio station, student government, student newspaper, symphony orchestra, TV station, Association of Black Collegiates, international student organizations, nontraditional student association, student ambassadors, religious organizations, College Republicans, College Democrats, United Students for Equal Access, Student Government Association.

Athletics. NCAA. **Intercollegiate:** Baseball M, basketball, bowling W, cross-country, football (tackle) M, golf M, soccer W, softball W, track and field, volleyball W, wrestling M. **Intramural:** Archery M, badminton M, basketball, bowling, cross-country, diving, football (tackle), golf, racquetball, rifle, rugby M, soccer, softball, swimming, table tennis, tennis, track and field, volleyball, water polo, weight lifting M, wrestling M. **Team name:** Mules (M), Jennies (W).

Student services. Adult student services, alcohol/substance abuse counseling, campus ministries, career counseling, student employment services, financial aid counseling, health services, minority student services, on-campus daycare, personal counseling, placement for graduates, veterans' counselor, women's services. **Physically disabled:** Services for visually, speech, hearing impaired.

Contact. E-mail: admit@cmsuvmb.cmsu.edu
Phone: (660) 543-4290 Toll-free number: (800) 729-2678
Fax: (660) 543-8517
Matt Melvin, Director of Enrollment Management, Central Missouri State University, WDE 1401, Warrensburg, MO 64093

College of the Ozarks

Point Lookout, Missouri
www.cofo.edu **CB code: 6713**

- Private 4-year liberal arts college affiliated with Presbyterian Church (USA)
- Residential campus in small town
- 1,332 degree-seeking undergraduates: 2% part-time, 55% women
- 12% of applicants admitted
- SAT or ACT (ACT writing optional), interview required
- 52% graduate within 6 years; 15% enter graduate study

General. Founded in 1906. Regionally accredited. College of the Ozarks charges no tuition; students work at a campus job rather than pay tuition. **Degrees:** 251 bachelor's awarded. **ROTC:** Army. **Location:** 2 miles from Branson, 45 miles from Springfield. **Calendar:** Semester. **Full-time faculty:** 74 total; 58% have terminal degrees, 1% minority, 31% women. **Part-time faculty:** 32 total; 19% have terminal degrees, 3% minority, 28% women. **Class size:** 55% < 20, 42% 20-39, 2% 40-49, 2% 50-99. **Special facilities:** Museum, greenhouses.

Freshman class profile. 2,385 applied, 285 admitted, 242 enrolled.

Mid 50% test scores		**Rank in top tenth:**	13%
ACT:	19-24	**End year in good standing:**	80%
GPA 3.50 or higher:	47%	**Return as sophomores:**	86%
GPA 3.0-3.49:	39%	**Out-of-state:**	37%
GPA 2.0-2.99:	14%	**Live on campus:**	99%
Rank in top quarter:	39%		

Basis for selection. High school record, financial need, test scores, class rank, recommendations, activities and interview important. Academic interest and growth, development of intellectual skills considered. TOEFL for non-native English speakers. ACT recommended. Audition recommended for music students; portfolio recommended for art students. **Homeschooled:** We do not accept pass grades. Candidates must present a transcript with a letter or percentage grade.

High school preparation. College-preparatory program recommended. 24 units recommended. Recommended units include English 4, mathematics 3, social studies 3, science 2 (laboratory 1) and foreign language 2. Public speaking, visual and performing arts recommended.

2006-2007 Annual costs. Cost of full-time tuition met through a combination of institutional work program and federal, state, and institutional funding. Required fees: $280. Full-time students participating in the work program work 15 hours per week for 16 weeks and one 40-hour work week per semester. Part-time students (commuters only) and full-time students not participating in the work program pay $295 per credit hour for tuition and an additional $280 per year as required fees. Room/board: $4,100. Books/supplies: $800. Personal expenses: $330.

2005-2006 Financial aid. Need-based: Average need met was 84%. Average scholarship/grant was $12,527. 83% of total undergraduate aid awarded as scholarships/grants, 17% as loans/jobs. **Non-need-based:** Scholarships awarded for academics, art, athletics, leadership, music/drama, ROTC, state residency.

Application procedures. Admission: Priority date 2/15; deadline 3/15 (receipt date). No application fee. Application may be submitted online. Admission notification on a rolling basis beginning on or about 2/1. Must reply by May 1 or within 2 week(s) if notified thereafter. **Financial aid:** Priority date 2/15; no closing date. FAFSA required. Applicants notified by 7/1.

Academics. Curriculum offers liberal arts foundation with intensive concentration in special areas. **Special study options:** Accelerated study, combined bachelor's/graduate degree, double major, dual enrollment of high school students, honors, independent study, internships, liberal arts/career combination, student-designed major, teacher certification program. Aviation technology (flight ratings), 3-2 engineering program, interdisciplinary programs, paraprofessional counseling certificate, pre-professional programs, dietetics program. **Credit/placement by examination:** AP, CLEP, IB, ACT, institutional tests. **Support services:** Learning center, reduced course load, remedial instruction, study skills assistance, tutoring, writing center.

Majors. Agriculture: Agribusiness operations, agronomy, animal sciences, business, horticultural science, horticulture. **Biology:** General. **Business:** Accounting, business admin, hotel/motel admin, international, managerial economics, marketing, restaurant/food services. **Communications:** General, broadcast journalism, journalism, public relations. **Communications technology:** Graphic/printing. **Computer sciences:** General, computer science. **Conservation:** Wildlife. **Education:** Art, biology, business, chemistry, elementary, English, family/consumer sciences, foreign languages, French, German, history, mathematics, music, physical, science, secondary, social studies, Spanish, technology/industrial arts. **English:** English lit. **Family/consumer sciences:** General, child care, clothing/textiles, food/nutrition. **Foreign languages:** French, Spanish. **Health:** Dietetics. **History:** General. **Legal studies:** Prelaw. **Math:** General. **Mechanic/repair:** Avionics. **Parks/recreation:** Facilities management, health/fitness. **Philosophy/religion:** Philosophy, religion. **Physical sciences:** Chemistry. **Protective services:** Corrections, forensics, police science. **Psychology:** General. **Public administration:** Social work. **Social sciences:** Political science, sociology. **Transportation:** Aviation. **Visual/performing arts:** Acting, art, dramatic, music management, studio arts, theater design.

Most popular majors. Agriculture 8%, business/marketing 18%, communications/journalism 6%, education 18%, security/protective services 6%.

Computing on campus. 160 workstations in dormitories, library. Dormitories wired for high-speed internet access and linked to campus network. Commuter students can connect to campus network. Online course registration, online library available.

Student life. Freshman orientation: Mandatory. Preregistration for classes offered. 10-day program. **Policies:** Convocations and chapel attendance required for some students. All full-time students must live in residence halls unless they meet one of the following criteria: 21 years of age or older, married, living with parents, or veteran of armed services. Religious observance required. Freshmen permitted cars on campus. **Housing:** Guaranteed on-campus for all undergraduates. Single-sex dorms, substance-free housing available. $50 fully refundable deposit. **Activities:** Bands, choral groups, drama, film society, literary magazine, music ensembles, musical theater, radio station, student government, student newspaper, Baptist Student Union, fire department, InterVarsity Christian Fellowship, wilderness activities club, Aggie club, Flying Falcons, business undergraduate society, Bonner Organization, College Republicans, College Democrats.

Athletics. NAIA. **Intercollegiate:** Baseball M, basketball, volleyball W. **Intramural:** Basketball, fencing, football (non-tackle) M, soccer, softball, swimming, tennis, volleyball. **Team name:** Bobcats.

Student services. Campus ministries, career counseling, student employment services, financial aid counseling, health services, on-campus daycare, personal counseling, placement for graduates, veterans' counselor.

Contact. E-mail: admiss4@cofo.edu
Phone: (417) 334-6411 ext. 4218 Toll-free number: (800) 222-0525
Fax: (417) 335-2618
Marci Linson, Dean of Admissions, College of the Ozarks, PO Box 17, Point Lookout, MO 65726-0017

Columbia College

Columbia, Missouri
www.ccis.edu **CB code: 6095**

- Private 4-year liberal arts college affiliated with Christian Church (Disciples of Christ)
- Commuter campus in small city
- 943 degree-seeking undergraduates: 20% part-time, 59% women
- 140 degree-seeking graduate students
- 62% of applicants admitted
- SAT or ACT (ACT writing optional) required
- 37% graduate within 6 years

General. Founded in 1851. Regionally accredited. Programs for adult students offered on campus and at 30 teaching locations in United States and Cuba. **Degrees:** 135 bachelor's, 17 associate awarded; master's offered. **ROTC:** Army, Navy, Air Force. **Location:** 120 miles from Kansas City, 120 miles from St. Louis. **Calendar:** Semester, extensive summer session. **Full-time faculty:** 56 total; 86% have terminal degrees, 7% minority, 43% women. **Part-time faculty:** 26 total; 27% have terminal degrees, 12% minority, 50% women. **Class size:** 63% < 20, 37% 20-39.

Freshman class profile. 819 applied, 509 admitted, 163 enrolled.

Mid 50% test scores			
SAT verbal:	510-600	Rank in top quarter:	28%
SAT math:	470-600	Rank in top tenth:	6%
ACT:	19-24	Return as sophomores:	57%
GPA 3.50 or higher:	34%	Out-of-state:	10%
GPA 3.0-3.49:	23%	Live on campus:	69%
GPA 2.0-2.99:	38%	International:	12%

Basis for selection. School achievement, class rank, test scores most important. Non-native English speaking applicants are required to submit TOEFL scores. ACT recommended. Audition required for music students; portfolio required for art students. Interview recommended for academically weak students. **Homeschooled:** GED is required; ACT strongly recommended.

High school preparation. 11 units recommended. Recommended units include English 4, mathematics 3, social studies 2 and science 2.

2006-2007 Annual costs. Tuition/fees: $12,414. Room/board: $5,164. Books/supplies: $600. Personal expenses: $900.

2005-2006 Financial aid. Need-based: 145 full-time freshmen applied for aid; 90 were judged to have need; 87 of these received aid. Average need met was 72%. Average scholarship/grant was $6,092; average loan $2,839. 44% of total undergraduate aid awarded as scholarships/grants, 56% as loans/jobs. **Non-need-based:** Awarded to 511 full-time undergraduates, including 99 freshmen. Scholarships awarded for academics, alumni affiliation, art, athletics, leadership, music/drama, religious affiliation, ROTC, state residency.

Application procedures. Admission: No deadline. $25 fee, may be waived for applicants with need. Application may be submitted online. Admission notification on a rolling basis beginning on or about 3/15. **Financial aid:** Priority date 3/15; no closing date. FAFSA, institutional form required. Applicants notified on a rolling basis starting 3/1; must reply within 2 week(s) of notification.

Academics. Evening degree program available based on 8-week ongoing terms. **Special study options:** Accelerated study, cooperative education, cross-registration, distance learning, double major, dual enrollment of high school students, ESL, honors, independent study, internships, student-designed major, study abroad, teacher certification program. **Credit/placement by examination:** AP, CLEP, IB, SAT, ACT, institutional tests. 6 credit hours maximum toward associate degree, 12 toward bachelor's. **Support services:** Learning center, reduced course load, remedial instruction, study skills assistance, tutoring, writing center.

Honors college/program. High school GPA of 3.5 or greater, ACT in 78th percentile or higher required for admission.

Majors. Area/ethnic studies: American. **Biology:** General. **Business:** Accounting, business admin, finance, international, management science, marketing. **Computer sciences:** General, computer science. **Conservation:** Environmental studies. **History:** General. **Liberal arts:** Arts/sciences. **Math:** General. **Philosophy/religion:** Philosophy, religion. **Physical sciences:** Chemistry. **Protective services:** Forensics, law enforcement admin. **Psychology:** General. **Social sciences:** Political science, sociology. **Visual/performing arts:** Art, ceramics, drawing, painting, photography, printmaking, studio arts.

Most popular majors. Business/marketing 49%, liberal arts 15%, psychology 10%, security/protective services 13%.

Computing on campus. 150 workstations in dormitories, library, computer center, student center. Dormitories wired for high-speed internet access and linked to campus network. Commuter students can connect to campus network. Online course registration, online library, helpline, student web hosting, wireless network available.

Student life. Freshman orientation: Mandatory, $25 fee. Preregistration for classes offered. Held weekend before classes start. **Policies:** Alcohol and illegal drugs forbidden on campus. Freshmen permitted cars on campus. **Housing:** Guaranteed on-campus for freshmen. Coed dorms, single-sex dorms, apartments, substance-free housing available. $100 fully refundable deposit. **Activities:** Choral groups, drama, literary magazine, student government, student newspaper, Black student associaton, Students in Free Enterprise, Student Leaders Advocating Teaching Excellence, Partners in Education, criminal justice association, Habitat for Humanity.

Athletics. NAIA. **Intercollegiate:** Basketball, soccer M, softball W, volleyball W. **Intramural:** Basketball, soccer, softball, table tennis, tennis, volleyball. **Team name:** Cougars.

Student services. Adult student services, alcohol/substance abuse counseling, career counseling, services for economically disadvantaged, student employment services, financial aid counseling, health services, personal counseling, placement for graduates, veterans' counselor.

Contact. E-mail: admissions@ccis.edu
Phone: (573) 875-7352 Toll-free number: (800) 231-2391 ext. 7352
Fax: (573) 875-7506
Regina Morin, Director of Admissions, Columbia College, 1001 Rogers Street, Columbia, MO 65216

Conception Seminary College
Conception, Missouri
www.conceptionabbey.org **CB code: 6112**

- Private 4-year seminary college for men affiliated with Roman Catholic Church
- Residential campus in rural community
- 112 degree-seeking undergraduates
- ACT, application essay required

General. Founded in 1883. Regionally accredited. Operated by Benedictine Monks of Conception Abbey, for both independent seminary students and candidates affiliated with sponsoring diocese. Women may enroll on part-time basis. **Degrees:** 28 bachelor's awarded. **Location:** 100 miles from Kansas City, 45 miles from St. Joseph. **Calendar:** Semester. **Full-time faculty:** 14 total. **Part-time faculty:** 5 total. **Class size:** 81% < 20, 19% 20-39. **Special facilities:** Basilica.

Freshman class profile. 17 enrolled.

Mid 50% test scores			
		ACT:	16-26
SAT verbal:	200-590	Out-of-state:	71%
SAT math:	200-450	Live on campus:	100%

Basis for selection. ACT composite scores tend to count more heavily than high school grades. Class rank considered. Applicants must be sponsored. Interview recommended.

High school preparation. 16 units required. Required units include English 4, social studies 4 and science 4.

2005-2006 Annual costs. Tuition/fees: $12,298. Room/board: $7,200. Books/supplies: $450. Personal expenses: $800.

Financial aid. Non-need-based: Scholarships awarded for academics.

Application procedures. Admission: Priority date 6/1; deadline 7/31 (receipt date). No application fee. Application may be submitted online. Admission notification on a rolling basis beginning on or about 2/1. Must reply by 8/10. Foreign applications require written certification of financial, ecclesiastical sponsorship. **Financial aid:** No deadline. FAFSA required. Applicants notified on a rolling basis starting 8/1; must reply by 8/20.

Academics. Curriculum combines liberal arts and pre-theology training to accommodate varying degrees of vocational commitment. **Special study options:** ESL, independent study. **Credit/placement by examination:** CLEP, institutional tests. 12 credit hours maximum toward bachelor's degree. **Support services:** Learning center, reduced course load, remedial instruction, tutoring.

Majors. Liberal arts: Arts/sciences.

Computing on campus. 15 workstations in library, computer center. Dormitories wired for high-speed internet access and linked to campus network. Online library, helpline, repair service available.

Student life. Freshman orientation: Mandatory. Preregistration for classes offered. **Policies:** Religious observance required. Freshmen permitted cars on campus. **Housing:** Guaranteed on-campus for all undergraduates. Substance-free housing available. $50 deposit. **Activities:** Choral groups, drama, music ensembles, musical theater, student government, student newspaper, apostolic work, mission club, social concerns, community council, Inner-Life.

Athletics. Intercollegiate: Basketball M, soccer M. **Intramural:** Football (non-tackle) M, racquetball M, softball M, swimming M, table tennis M, tennis M, track and field M, volleyball M, weight lifting M. **Team name:** Blue Knights.

Student services. Adult student services, alcohol/substance abuse counseling, campus ministries, career counseling, financial aid counseling, health services, personal counseling.

Contact. E-mail: vocations@conception.edu
Phone: (660) 944-2886 Fax: (660) 944-2829
Vincent Casper, Director of Admissions, Conception Seminary College, Box 502, Conception, MO 64433-0502

Culver-Stockton College
Canton, Missouri **CB member**
www.culver.edu **CB code: 6123**

- Private 4-year liberal arts college affiliated with Christian Church (Disciples of Christ)
- Residential campus in small town
- 840 degree-seeking undergraduates: 9% part-time, 58% women, 7% African American, 3% Hispanic American, 1% international
- 76% of applicants admitted
- SAT or ACT (ACT writing optional) required
- 55% graduate within 6 years; 12% enter graduate study

General. Founded in 1853. Regionally accredited. **Degrees:** 172 bachelor's awarded. **Location:** 130 miles from St. Louis, 20 miles from Quincy, Illinois. **Calendar:** Semester, limited summer session. **Full-time faculty:** 44 total; 68% have terminal degrees, 7% minority, 32% women. **Part-time faculty:** 45 total; 13% have terminal degrees, 58% women. **Class size:** 62% < 20, 34% 20-39, 2% 40-49, 2% 50-99.

Freshman class profile. 959 applied, 727 admitted, 155 enrolled.

Mid 50% test scores		End year in good standing:	92%
ACT:	18-26	Return as sophomores:	68%
GPA 3.50 or higher:	38%	Out-of-state:	51%
GPA 3.0-3.49:	34%	Live on campus:	94%
GPA 2.0-2.99:	28%	Fraternities:	12%
Rank in top quarter:	37%	Sororities:	24%
Rank in top tenth:	16%		

Basis for selection. Secondary school record, class rank, test scores most important; extracurricular activities, talent, personal qualities considered. **Learning Disabled:** Must request accommodations and submit appropriate documentation.

High school preparation. 15 units required. Required and recommended units include English 4, mathematics 2, social studies 3 and science 4.

2006-2007 Annual costs. Tuition/fees (projected): $15,450. Room/board: $6,546. Books/supplies: $700. Personal expenses: $502.

2005-2006 Financial aid. Need-based: 153 full-time freshmen applied for aid; 141 were judged to have need; 141 of these received aid. Average need met was 74%. Average scholarship/grant was $9,537; average loan $2,899. 59% of total undergraduate aid awarded as scholarships/grants, 41% as loans/jobs. **Non-need-based:** Scholarships awarded for academics, alumni affiliation, art, athletics, job skills, leadership, music/drama, religious affiliation, state residency. **Additional information:** Interview required for scholarships, audition required for music students, portfolio required for art students.

Application procedures. Admission: Priority date 5/1; no deadline. $25 fee, may be waived for applicants with need. Application may be submitted online. Admission notification on a rolling basis. **Financial aid:** Priority date 4/1, closing date 6/15. FAFSA required. Applicants notified on a rolling basis starting 2/15; must reply within 2 week(s) of notification.

Academics. Special study options: Combined bachelor's/graduate degree, distance learning, double major, dual enrollment of high school students, honors, independent study, internships, liberal arts/career combination, semester at sea, student-designed major, study abroad, teacher certification program, Washington semester. **Credit/placement by examination:** AP, CLEP, IB, ACT. 94 credit hours maximum toward bachelor's degree. **Support services:** Learning center, reduced course load, study skills assistance, tutoring, writing center.

Majors. Biology: General. **Business:** Accounting, business admin, finance, management information systems. **Communications:** Journalism. **Education:** General, art, elementary, music, physical, speech. **English:** English lit. **Health:** Athletic training, nursing (RN). **History:** General. **Math:** General. **Parks/recreation:** Facilities management. **Philosophy/religion:** Religion. **Protective services:** Law enforcement admin. **Psychology:** General. **Visual/performing arts:** Art, arts management, dramatic.

Most popular majors. Business/marketing 24%, education 11%, health sciences 18%, social sciences 9%, visual/performing arts 9%.

Computing on campus. 100 workstations in dormitories, library, computer center, student center. Dormitories wired for high-speed internet access and linked to campus network. Commuter students can connect to campus network. Online library, helpline, repair service, student web hosting, wireless network available.

Student life. Freshman orientation: Mandatory. Preregistration for classes offered. 4 one-day sessions each summer for students and parents. **Policies:** Students have voting representation on faculty committees. Freshmen permitted cars on campus. **Housing:** Guaranteed on-campus for all undergraduates. Coed dorms, single-sex dorms, fraternity/sorority housing, substance-free housing available. $100 fully refundable deposit, deadline 8/15. All students under age 21 required to live on campus unless living with parents. **Activities:** Bands, choral groups, dance, drama, literary magazine, music ensembles, radio station, student government, student newspaper, Christian Fellowship Group, Disciples on Campus, Students in Missouri Assisting Rural and Urban Transportation (SMART), Student Government Association, Volunteers Out in Community Environments Serving (VOICES).

Athletics. NAIA. **Intercollegiate:** Baseball M, basketball, cheerleading, football (tackle) M, golf, soccer, softball W, volleyball W. **Intramural:** Basketball, football (non-tackle), racquetball, soccer, softball, table tennis, tennis, volleyball. **Team name:** Wildcats.

Student services. Adult student services, alcohol/substance abuse counseling, campus ministries, career counseling, student employment services, financial aid counseling, personal counseling, placement for graduates, veterans' counselor.

Contact. E-mail: enrollment@culver.edu
Phone: (573) 288-6331 Toll-free number: (800) 537-1883
Fax: (573) 288-6618
Betty Smith, Director of Enrollment Services, Culver-Stockton College, One College Hill, Canton, MO 63435-1299

Deaconess College of Nursing
St. Louis, Missouri
www.deaconess.edu **CB code: 3139**

- For-profit 4-year nursing college affiliated with United Church of Christ
- Commuter campus in very large city
- 580 degree-seeking undergraduates
- 136 graduate students
- 32% of applicants admitted
- Application essay required

General. Founded in 1889. Regionally accredited. Affiliated with Fontbonne College. General education requirements offered on both campuses. **Degrees:** 120 bachelor's, 76 associate awarded. **Calendar:** Semester, limited summer session. **Full-time faculty:** 30 total. **Part-time faculty:** 50 total. **Special facilities:** Hospital, archives.

Freshman class profile. 200 applied, 65 admitted, 42 enrolled.

Mid 50% test scores		Live on campus:	47%
ACT:	32-45		

Basis for selection. High school GPA of 2.5, rank in top third of class, ACT scores, personal statement important. Interview and reference may be considered. SAT or ACT recommended.

High school preparation. Required units include English 4, mathematics 3 and science 3.

2005-2006 Annual costs. Tuition/fees: $13,900. Students enrolled in web-based program pay $465 per credit-hour. Room/board: $4,800. Books/supplies: $1,100. Personal expenses: $1,140.

Financial aid. Non-need-based: Scholarships awarded for academics.

Application procedures. Admission: Closing date 4/15. $50 fee, may be waived for applicants with need. Admission notification on a rolling basis. **Financial aid:** No deadline. FAFSA, institutional form required. Applicants notified on a rolling basis starting 4/1; must reply within 2 week(s) of notification.

Academics. Special study options: Cross-registration, liberal arts/career combination. **Credit/placement by examination:** CLEP, institutional tests. 30 credit hours maximum toward bachelor's degree. **Support services:** Learning center, reduced course load, remedial instruction, tutoring.

Majors. Health: Nursing (RN).

Computing on campus. 20 workstations in computer center.

Student life. Freshman orientation: Mandatory. **Housing:** Single-sex dorms available. $50 deposit. **Activities:** Choral groups, student government, National Student Nurse Association.

Student services. Health services, on-campus daycare, personal counseling.

Contact. E-mail: lisa.mancini@deaconess.edu
Phone: (314) 768-7528 Toll-free number: (800) 942-3410
Fax: (314) 768-5673
Michelle McGrail, Dean of Enrollment and Student Services, Deaconess College of Nursing, 6150 Oakland Avenue, St. Louis, MO 63139

DeVry University: Kansas City

Kansas City, Missouri
www.kc.devry.edu
CB code: 6092

- For-profit 4-year university
- Commuter campus in large city
- 1,097 degree-seeking undergraduates: 26% part-time, 48% women
- 132 graduate students
- Interview required
- 33% graduate within 6 years

General. Founded in 1931. Regionally accredited. **Degrees:** 408 bachelor's, 58 associate awarded; master's offered. **Location:** 15 miles from downtown. **Calendar:** Semester, extensive summer session. **Full-time faculty:** 49 total; 4% minority, 26% women. **Part-time faculty:** 39 total; 10% minority, 33% women.

Freshman class profile. 198 enrolled.

Return as sophomores:	45%	**International:**	1%

Basis for selection. Applicants must have high school diploma or equivalant degree from accredited postsecondary institution, and be at least 17 years of age on the first day of classes. New students may enter at beginning of any semester. SAT or ACT recommended. CPT also accepted.

High school preparation. College-preparatory program recommended. Required units include mathematics 1. Math unit must be algebra or higher.

2005-2006 Annual costs. Tuition/fees: $12,140. Books/supplies: $1,100. Personal expenses: $1,816.

2004-2005 Financial aid. All financial aid based on need. 222 full-time freshmen applied for aid; 210 were judged to have need; 207 of these received aid. Average need met was 43%. Average scholarship/grant was $4,763; average loan $6,080. 18% of total undergraduate aid awarded as scholarships/grants, 82% as loans/jobs.

Application procedures. Admission: No deadline. $50 fee. Application may be submitted online. Admission notification on a rolling basis. **Financial aid:** No deadline. FAFSA required. Applicants notified on a rolling basis.

Academics. Special study options: Accelerated study, cooperative education, distance learning, weekend college. **Credit/placement by examination:** CLEP, institutional tests. **Support services:** Learning center, remedial instruction, tutoring.

Majors. Biology: Bioinformatics. **Business:** General, business admin. **Computer sciences:** General, networking, systems analysis. **Engineering technology:** Biomedical, computer, electrical.

Most popular majors. Business/marketing 26%, computer/information sciences 59%, engineering/engineering technologies 15%.

Computing on campus. 1,300 workstations in library, computer center. Online course registration, online library, helpline available.

Student life. Freshman orientation: Mandatory. **Policies:** Freshmen permitted cars on campus. **Housing:** Private apartments, student-plan housing, private rooms available. **Activities:** Student government, student newspaper, Association of Information Technology Professionals, Campus Crusade for Christ, Institute for Electrical & Electronics Engineers, Phi Beta Lambda, Tau Alpha Pi, professional certification club, drama club, Gamma Beta Phi.

Athletics. Intramural: Volleyball.

Student services. Career counseling, student employment services, financial aid counseling, placement for graduates, veterans' counselor. **Physically disabled:** Services for visually, hearing impaired.

Contact. E-mail: ssmeed@kc.devry.edu
Phone: (816) 941-2810 Toll-free number: (800) 821-3766
Fax: (816) 941-0896
Shane Smeed, Director of Admissions, DeVry University: Kansas City, 11224 Holmes Street, Kansas City, MO 64131-3626

Drury University

Springfield, Missouri
www.drury.edu
CB member
CB code: 6169

- Private 4-year university and liberal arts college affiliated with United Church of Christ and Christian Church (Disciples of Christ)
- Residential campus in large city
- 1,577 degree-seeking undergraduates: 2% part-time, 56% women, 1% African American, 2% Asian American, 2% Hispanic American, 1% Native American, 4% international
- 358 degree-seeking graduate students
- 78% of applicants admitted
- SAT or ACT (ACT writing optional) required
- 63% graduate within 6 years; 33% enter graduate study

General. Founded in 1873. Regionally accredited. **Degrees:** 308 bachelor's awarded; master's offered. **ROTC:** Army. **Location:** 220 miles from St. Louis, 170 miles from Kansas City. **Calendar:** Semester, limited summer session. **Full-time faculty:** 123 total; 89% have terminal degrees, 6% minority, 40% women. **Part-time faculty:** 62 total; 16% have terminal degrees, 8% minority, 42% women. **Class size:** 62% < 20, 35% 20-39, 1% 40-49, 1% 50-99. **Special facilities:** Science center, greenhouse, astronomical observation station, electronic music lab.

Freshman class profile. 1,106 applied, 858 admitted, 378 enrolled.

Mid 50% test scores		**Rank in top tenth:**	38%
SAT verbal:	530-640	**Return as sophomores:**	78%
SAT math:	520-650	**Out-of-state:**	22%
ACT:	23-28	**Live on campus:**	80%
GPA 3.50 or higher:	73%	**International:**	3%
GPA 3.0-3.49:	18%	**Fraternities:**	27%
GPA 2.0-2.99:	9%	**Sororities:**	24%
Rank in top quarter:	67%		

Basis for selection. School achievement record, test scores, reference from high school counselor, essay important. Interview recommended for all students. Audition recommended for music, theater students; portfolio recommended for architecture, art students.

High school preparation. College-preparatory program recommended. 12 units required. Required and recommended units include English 4, mathematics 3-4, social studies 3, science 3 and foreign language 2.

2006-2007 Annual costs. Tuition/fees: $15,387. Room/board: $5,790. Books/supplies: $1,000. Personal expenses: $1,500.

2004-2005 Financial aid. Need-based: 354 full-time freshmen applied for aid; 339 were judged to have need; 339 of these received aid. Average need met was 84%. Average scholarship/grant was $6,102; average loan $3,962. 33% of total undergraduate aid awarded as scholarships/grants, 67% as loans/jobs. **Non-need-based:** Awarded to 1,604 full-time undergraduates, including 423 freshmen. Scholarships awarded for academics, alumni affiliation, art, athletics, job skills, leadership, minority status, music/drama, religious affiliation.

Application procedures. Admission: Priority date 3/1; deadline 3/15 (postmark date). $25 fee, may be waived for applicants with need. Application may be submitted online. Admission notification on a rolling basis beginning on or about 10/1. Must reply by May 1 or within 3 week(s) if notified thereafter. Application fee is waived if applicant visits campus. **Financial aid:** Closing date 3/15. FAFSA, institutional form required. Applicants notified on a rolling basis starting 3/30; must reply within 2 week(s) of notification.

Academics. Offers a unique general education curriculum, Global Persepctives 21, which leads to a minor in global studies for each student. **Special study options:** Accelerated study, combined bachelor's/graduate degree, cooperative education, distance learning, double major, dual enrollment of high school students, ESL, honors, independent study, internships, liberal arts/career combination, student-designed major, study abroad, teacher certification program, Washington semester. Living-learning communities, leadership/community service communities, Drury Center in Volos, Greece. **Credit/placement by examination:** AP, CLEP, IB, institutional tests. **Support services:** Pre-admission summer program, reduced course load, remedial instruction, study skills assistance, tutoring, writing center.

Majors. Architecture: Architecture. **Biology:** General. **Business:** General, accounting, business admin, international, management information systems. **Communications:** General, advertising, broadcast journalism, journalism, public relations. **Computer sciences:** General, computer science, information systems. **Conservation:** Environmental science, environmental studies. **Education:** General, elementary, music, physical, secondary. **English:** Creative writing. **Foreign languages:** French, German, Spanish. **Health:** Predentistry, premedicine, preop/surgical nursing, preveterinary. **History:** General. **Liberal arts:** Arts/sciences. **Math:** General. **Parks/recreation:** Exercise sciences. **Philosophy/religion:** Philosophy. **Physical sciences:** Chemistry. **Psychology:** General. **Social sciences:** Criminology, economics, political science, sociology. **Visual/performing arts:** General, art, art history/conservation, arts management, commercial/advertising art, design, dramatic, jazz, music management, music performance, music theory/composition, piano/organ, studio arts, voice/opera.

Most popular majors. Architecture 7%, biology 13%, business/marketing 18%, communications/journalism 10%, education 6%, psychology 8%, social sciences 8%, visual/performing arts 8%.

Computing on campus. 323 workstations in dormitories, library, computer center, student center. Dormitories wired for high-speed internet access and linked to campus network. Commuter students can connect to campus network. Online course registration, online library, helpline, repair service, student web hosting, wireless network available.

Student life. **Freshman orientation:** Mandatory, $14 fee. Preregistration for classes offered. 4 days. Includes parent orientation session. Registration for classes occurs separately, in late June. **Policies:** Freshmen permitted cars on campus. **Housing:** Guaranteed on-campus for freshmen. Coed dorms, single-sex dorms, apartments, fraternity/sorority housing available. $200 fully refundable deposit, deadline 6/1. Living-learning communities, themed housing, leadership/service communities available. **Activities:** Bands, choral groups, dance, drama, film society, literary magazine, music ensembles, musical theater, opera, radio station, student government, student newspaper, symphony orchestra, TV station, 60 student organizations, including Alliance of Minority Minds, international student organization, Young Republicans, College Democrats, student government association, Student Union Board, Mortar Board, Environmental Club, Habitat for Humanity, Students in Free Enterprise.

Athletics. NCAA. **Intercollegiate:** Baseball M, basketball, cheerleading, cross-country, diving, golf, soccer, swimming, tennis, volleyball W. **Intramural:** Basketball, bowling, football (non-tackle) M, golf M, racquetball, soccer, softball, tennis. **Team name:** Panthers.

Student services. Adult student services, alcohol/substance abuse counseling, campus ministries, career counseling, services for economically disadvantaged, student employment services, financial aid counseling, health services, minority student services, personal counseling, placement for graduates, veterans' counselor, women's services. **Physically disabled:** Services for visually, speech, hearing impaired.

Contact. E-mail: druryad@drury.edu
Phone: (417) 873-7205 Toll-free number: (800) 922-2274
Fax: (417) 866-3873
Chip Parker, Director of Admission, Drury University, 900 North Benton Avenue, Springfield, MO 65802

Evangel University

Springfield, Missouri
www.evangel.edu **CB code: 6198**

- Private 4-year liberal arts college affiliated with Assemblies of God
- Residential campus in small city
- 1,941 degree-seeking undergraduates
- 75 graduate students
- 81% of applicants admitted
- SAT or ACT with writing required

General. Founded in 1955. Regionally accredited. **Degrees:** 408 bachelor's, 3 associate awarded; master's offered. **ROTC:** Army. **Location:** 170 miles from Kansas City, 212 miles from St. Louis. **Calendar:** Semester, limited summer session. **Full-time faculty:** 103 total. **Part-time faculty:** 23 total. **Class size:** 65% < 20, 26% 20-39, 7% 40-49, 3% 50-99.

Freshman class profile. 881 applied, 713 admitted, 423 enrolled.

Mid 50% test scores		Out-of-state:	45%
ACT:	19-25	Live on campus:	84%

Basis for selection. Minimum 2.0 high school GPA, acceptance of college's moral and religious standards, acceptable ACT or SAT scores, rank in top half of graduating class. Statement of Christian faith required. Audition required for music, sport students. Essay and portfolio recommended. **Homeschooled:** Admissions based upon ACT/SAT scores and letters of recommendation.

High school preparation. Recommended units include English 3, mathematics 2, social studies 2 and science 1.

2005-2006 Annual costs. Tuition/fees: $12,790. Room/board: $4,620. Books/supplies: $1,000. Personal expenses: $1,750.

2004-2005 Financial aid. All financial aid based on need. 38% of total undergraduate aid awarded as scholarships/grants, 62% as loans/jobs.

Application procedures. **Admission:** Closing date 8/1 (receipt date). $25 fee. Application may be submitted online. Admission notification on a rolling basis. **Financial aid:** Priority date 3/1, closing date 6/1. FAFSA required. Applicants notified on a rolling basis starting 4/1; must reply within 3 week(s) of notification.

Academics. **Special study options:** Cross-registration, double major, dual enrollment of high school students, internships, liberal arts/career combination, study abroad, teacher certification program, Washington semester. **Credit/placement by examination:** AP, CLEP, IB, institutional tests. 30 credit hours maximum toward associate degree, 30 toward bachelor's. **Support services:** Learning center, reduced course load, remedial instruction, study skills assistance, tutoring, writing center.

Majors. **Biology:** General. **Business:** General, accounting, business admin. **Communications:** General, broadcast journalism, journalism. **Communications technology:** General. **Computer sciences:** General. **Education:** General, art, business, early childhood, elementary, English, foreign languages, mathematics, middle, music, physical, science, secondary, social studies, special. **English:** Speech/rhetoric. **Foreign languages:** Spanish. **Health:** Clinical lab technology, predentistry, premedicine, preveterinary. **History:** General. **Legal studies:** Prelaw. **Math:** General. **Physical sciences:** Chemistry. **Protective services:** Criminal justice. **Psychology:** General. **Public administration:** Social work. **Social sciences:** General, criminology, political science, sociology. **Theology:** Bible, missionary, sacred music. **Visual/performing arts:** Dramatic, music performance, studio arts.

Most popular majors. Business/marketing 6%, communications/journalism 12%, education 13%, philosophy/religious studies 10%, psychology 9%, social sciences 6%.

Computing on campus. 305 workstations in dormitories, library, computer center, student center. Dormitories wired for high-speed internet access and linked to campus network.

Student life. **Freshman orientation:** Mandatory. Preregistration for classes offered. **Policies:** Freshmen permitted cars on campus. **Housing:** Guaranteed on-campus for freshmen. Coed dorms, single-sex dorms, apartments, substance-free housing available. $200 deposit, deadline 8/1. **Activities:** Bands, choral groups, drama, literary magazine, music ensembles, radio station, student government, student newspaper, symphony orchestra, TV station, international students club, honor fraternities, student ministries.

Athletics. NAIA. **Intercollegiate:** Baseball M, basketball, cross-country, football (tackle) M, golf, softball W, tennis, track and field, volleyball W. **Intramural:** Basketball, football (non-tackle), soccer, softball, volleyball W. **Team name:** Crusaders.

Student services. Career counseling, student employment services, financial aid counseling, health services, on-campus daycare, personal counseling, placement for graduates, veterans' counselor. **Physically disabled:** Services for visually, hearing impaired.

Contact. E-mail: admission@evangel.edu
Phone: (417) 865-2811 Toll-free number: (800) 382-6435
Fax: (417) 520-054
Charity Waltner, Director of Admissions, Evangel University, 1111 North Glenstone, Springfield, MO 65802

Fontbonne University

St. Louis, Missouri **CB member**
www.fontbonne.edu **CB code: 6216**

- Private 4-year liberal arts college affiliated with Roman Catholic Church
- Commuter campus in very large city
- 2,005 degree-seeking undergraduates: 23% part-time, 76% women, 32% African American, 1% Asian American, 1% Hispanic American
- 713 degree-seeking graduate students
- 74% of applicants admitted
- SAT or ACT (ACT writing recommended) required

General. Founded in 1923. Regionally accredited. **Degrees:** 362 bachelor's awarded; master's offered. **Location:** 6 miles from downtown St. Louis. **Calendar:** Semester, limited summer session. **Full-time faculty:** 72

total; 68% have terminal degrees, 10% minority, 69% women. **Part-time faculty:** 300 total; 35% have terminal degrees, 8% minority, 65% women. **Class size:** 81% < 20, 19% 20-39. **Special facilities:** Speech and hearing clinic.

Freshman class profile. 618 applied, 456 admitted, 185 enrolled.

Mid 50% test scores		**Return as sophomores:**	51%
ACT:	19-24	**Out-of-state:**	11%
Rank in top quarter:	31%	**Live on campus:**	46%
Rank in top tenth:	12%	**International:**	1%

Basis for selection. High school GPA, class rank, test scores considered. Recommendations may be requested. Essay and interview recommended. Audition required for theater students; portfolio required for art students.

High school preparation. 16 units required. Required units include English 4, mathematics 3, social studies 3, science 3 (laboratory 1) and academic electives 3. Core electives 3 units. Must include foreign language and 1 unit visual or performing arts.

2005-2006 Annual costs. Tuition/fees: $16,320. Room/board: $6,298. Books/supplies: $650. Personal expenses: $1,300.

2005-2006 Financial aid. Need-based: 38% of total undergraduate aid awarded as scholarships/grants, 62% as loans/jobs. **Non-need-based:** Scholarships awarded for academics, alumni affiliation, art, leadership, minority status, music/drama, religious affiliation, state residency.

Application procedures. Admission: Priority date 1/15; deadline 8/1. $25 fee, may be waived for applicants with need. Application may be submitted online. Admission notification on a rolling basis. Must reply by May 1 or within 3 week(s) if notified thereafter. **Financial aid:** Priority date 4/1; no closing date. FAFSA, institutional form required. Applicants notified on a rolling basis starting 2/1; must reply within 2 week(s) of notification.

Academics. Special study options: Accelerated study, cooperative education, cross-registration, distance learning, double major, dual enrollment of high school students, ESL, exchange student, honors, independent study, internships, liberal arts/career combination, student-designed major, study abroad, teacher certification program, weekend college. 3-2 program in social work or engineering with Washington University. **Credit/placement by examination:** AP, CLEP, institutional tests. **Support services:** Learning center, reduced course load, remedial instruction, study skills assistance, tutoring, writing center.

Majors. Biology: General, biotechnology. **Business:** Business admin, organizational behavior. **Communications:** General, advertising. **Computer sciences:** General. **Education:** General, computer, Deaf/hearing impaired, early childhood, elementary, family/consumer sciences, middle, special. **English:** English lit. **Family/consumer sciences:** Clothing/textiles. **Health:** Dietetics, speech pathology. **History:** General. **Legal studies:** Prelaw. **Liberal arts:** Arts/sciences. **Math:** General. **Psychology:** General. **Public administration:** Human services. **Visual/performing arts:** Art, dramatic, studio arts.

Most popular majors. Business/marketing 51%, education 20%, visual/performing arts 6%.

Computing on campus. 110 workstations in dormitories, library, computer center. Dormitories wired for high-speed internet access and linked to campus network. Commuter students can connect to campus network. Online course registration, online library, helpline, repair service, wireless network available.

Student life. Freshman orientation: Mandatory, $75 fee. Preregistration for classes offered. Held during week prior to classes; includes community service, meeting with faculty and social activities. **Policies:** Freshmen permitted cars on campus. **Housing:** Coed dorms, apartments, substance-free housing available. $75 deposit. Apartment style residence halls available. **Activities:** Choral groups, dance, drama, literary magazine, music ensembles, musical theater, radio station, student government, student newspaper, Fontbonne in Service and Humility, Go Deep (Spiritual Book Study), international students association, Pro-life Organization, Straights and Gays for Equality, Students for the Enhancement of Black Awareness.

Athletics. NCAA. **Intercollegiate:** Baseball M, basketball, bowling W, cross-country, golf, soccer, softball W, tennis, volleyball W. **Intramural:** Badminton, basketball, bowling M, football (non-tackle), soccer, softball, table tennis, tennis, volleyball. **Team name:** Griffins.

Student services. Adult student services, alcohol/substance abuse counseling, campus ministries, career counseling, student employment services, financial aid counseling, health services, minority student services, personal counseling, placement for graduates. **Physically disabled:** Services for speech, hearing impaired.

Contact. E-mail: fcadmission@fontbonne.edu
Phone: (314) 889-1400 Toll-free number: (800) 205-5862
Fax: (314) 719-8021
Peggy Musen, Associate Dean for Enrollment Management, Fontbonne University, 6800 Wydown Boulevard, St. Louis, MO 63105

Global University
Springfield, Missouri
www.globaluniversity.edu **CB code: 4916**

- Private 4-year Bible and seminary college affiliated with Assemblies of God
- Commuter campus in small city
- 3,776 degree-seeking undergraduates

General. Founded in 1948. Accredited by DETC. Correspondence institution. All course work completed via distance education. **Degrees:** 206 bachelor's, 15 associate awarded; master's, first professional offered. **Location:** 200 miles to St. Louis, 170 miles to Kansas City. **Calendar:** Continuous, extensive summer session. **Full-time faculty:** 52 total; 29% have terminal degrees, 27% women. **Part-time faculty:** 400 total.

Basis for selection. Open admission.

2005-2006 Annual costs. Tuition/fees: $2,700. Quoted tuition is for U.S. students. Tuition for international students varies by country. Books/supplies: $600.

Application procedures. Admission: No deadline. $35 fee. Application may be submitted online. Admission notification on a rolling basis.

Academics. Special study options: Distance learning, external degree, independent study. **Credit/placement by examination:** CLEP. 16 credit hours maximum toward associate degree, 32 toward bachelor's. **Support services:** Study skills assistance.

Majors. Theology: Bible, missionary, pastoral counseling, religious ed, theology.

Computing on campus. Online library available.

Contact. E-mail: info@globaluniversity.edu
Phone: (417) 862-9533 Toll-free number: (800) 443-1083
Fax: (417) 862-0863
Lynne Kroh, Assistant Dean of Student Affairs, Global University, 1211 South Glenstone Avenue, Springfield, MO 65804

Grantham University
Kansas City, Missouri
www.grantham.edu **CB code: 2244**

- For-profit 4-year virtual university
- Small city
- 7,800 undergraduates

General. Founded in 1951. Accredited by DETC. Applications accepted on a continuous basis throughout the year. **Degrees:** 55 bachelor's, 75 associate awarded; master's offered. **Location:** Located in Kansas City. **Calendar:** Continuous. **Part-time faculty:** 60 total.

Basis for selection. Open admission. High school diploma, GED, or equivalent required. Basic computer skills and use of computer with Windows, Internet access, e-mail account, printer also required. Applicants must have Internet access.

2006-2007 Annual costs. Tuition/fees: $6,978. Tuition includes required textbooks, software and shipping (within U.S.).

Financial aid. Additional information: Defense Activity for Non Traditional Education Support (DANTES) and some employer reimbursement programs available. Department of Defense tuition assistance.

Application procedures. Admission: No deadline. No application fee. Application may be submitted online. Admission notification on a rolling basis. **Financial aid:** No deadline.

Academics. Special study options: Accelerated study, combined bachelor's/graduate degree, distance learning, independent study. **Credit/placement by examination:** CLEP, IB.

Majors. Business: Business admin, management information systems. **Computer sciences:** General, applications programming, computer science, data processing, information systems, information technology, LAN/WAN management, systems analysis. **Engineering:** Computer, electrical, software. **Engineering technology:** Computer, electrical, software. **Protective services:** Law enforcement admin.

Computing on campus. PC or laptop required.

Student life. **Freshman orientation:** Mandatory.

Student services. Adult student services, financial aid counseling, veterans' counselor.

Contact. E-mail: admissions@grantham.edu
Phone: (800) 955-2527 Toll-free number: (800) 955-2527
Fax: (816) 448-3796
DeAnn Wandler, Director of Admissions, Grantham University, 7200 NW 86th Street, Suite M, Kansas City, MO 64153

Hannibal-LaGrange College

Hannibal, Missouri
www.hlg.edu **CB code: 6266**

- Private 4-year liberal arts college affiliated with Southern Baptist Convention
- Commuter campus in large town
- 952 degree-seeking undergraduates: 8% part-time, 66% women
- SAT or ACT (ACT writing optional) required
- 53% graduate within 6 years; 27% enter graduate study

General. Founded in 1858. Regionally accredited. Christian environment. **Degrees:** 172 bachelor's, 34 associate awarded. **Location:** 100 miles from St. Louis. **Calendar:** Semester, limited summer session. **Full-time faculty:** 59 total; 32% have terminal degrees, 2% minority, 49% women. **Part-time faculty:** 59 total; 8% have terminal degrees, 5% minority, 54% women. **Class size:** 75% < 20, 24% 20-39, 1% 40-49. **Special facilities:** Nature trail, fine arts theatre, mission center.

Freshman class profile. 119 enrolled.

Mid 50% test scores		Rank in top quarter:	36%
ACT:	18-26	Rank in top tenth:	20%

Basis for selection. Most applicants admitted. Test scores important. 20 or above ACT composite required. Applicants with 16-19 ACT composite admitted provisionally. ACT administered on campus on registration day. Applications without English Composition 1 and college algebra must submit ACT scores and take mathematics placement exam. **Homeschooled:** Transcript of courses and ACT score.

High school preparation. College-preparatory program recommended. Recommended units include English 2, mathematics 1, history 3, science 1 (laboratory 1).

2005-2006 Annual costs. Tuition/fees: $11,780. Room/board: $4,610. Books/supplies: $910. Personal expenses: $2,061.

2005-2006 Financial aid. **Non-need-based:** Scholarships awarded for academics, art, athletics, music/drama, religious affiliation. **Additional information:** Work-study opportunities vary according to on- and off-campus needs.

Application procedures. **Admission:** Closing date 8/26. $25 fee, may be waived for applicants with need. Application may be submitted online. Admission notification on a rolling basis beginning on or about 9/1. **Financial aid:** Closing date 7/1. FAFSA, institutional form required. Applicants notified on a rolling basis; must reply by 8/31.

Academics. **Special study options:** Accelerated study, cooperative education, distance learning, double major, dual enrollment of high school students, honors, independent study, internships, study abroad, teacher certification program, weekend college. **Credit/placement by examination:** AP, CLEP, SAT, ACT, institutional tests. 30 credit hours maximum toward bachelor's degree. No more than 8 credit hours in one discipline. **Support services:** Reduced course load, remedial instruction, study skills assistance, tutoring.

Honors college/program. Minimum ACT-25, essay. Additional 21 hours plus research project, must maintain requirements for eligibility each semester.

Majors. **Biology:** General. **Business:** General, accounting, business admin, marketing, organizational behavior. **Communications:** General. **Computer sciences:** General. **Education:** General, art, business, early childhood, elementary, English, mathematics, music, physical, science, secondary, social studies. **English:** English lit. **Health:** Nursing (RN). **History:** General. **Liberal arts:** Arts/sciences. **Math:** General. **Parks/recreation:** Facilities management. **Philosophy/religion:** Christian. **Protective services:** Law enforcement admin. **Psychology:** General. **Public administration:** Human services. **Theology:** Bible, religious ed, sacred music. **Visual/performing arts:** Art, dramatic, music performance, piano/organ, studio arts, voice/opera.

Most popular majors. Business/marketing 12%, education 23%, legal studies 6%.

Computing on campus. 89 workstations in library, computer center. Dormitories linked to campus network. Commuter students can connect to campus network. Online library, repair service available.

Student life. **Freshman orientation:** Mandatory. Conducted 2 days before classes begin. **Policies:** Religious observance required. Freshmen permitted cars on campus. **Housing:** Single-sex dorms, special housing for disabled, apartments, substance-free housing available. $100 deposit. **Activities:** Choral groups, drama, music ensembles, student government, student newspaper, Christian Ministry Vocations Fellowship, Democratic club, Fellowship of Christian Athletes, Phi Beta Delta (men's service), Phi Beta Lambda, Gatekeepers (mentoring), Students for Life, Natures Investigation Circulus, Missouri State Teachers Association, Republican club, art club, science club.

Athletics. NAIA, NCCAA. **Intercollegiate:** Baseball M, basketball, golf M, soccer, softball W, volleyball W. **Intramural:** Baseball M, basketball, racquetball, softball, table tennis, tennis, volleyball, weight lifting. **Team name:** Trojans.

Student services. Campus ministries, career counseling, student employment services, health services, personal counseling, placement for graduates. **Physically disabled:** Services for visually, hearing impaired.

Contact. E-mail: admissio@hlg.edu
Phone: (573) 221-3113 Toll-free number: (800) 454-1119
Fax: (573) 221-6594
Ray Carty, Vice President of Enrollment Management, Hannibal-LaGrange College, 2800 Palmyra Road, Hannibal, MO 63401

Harris-Stowe State University

St. Louis, Missouri
www.hssu.edu **CB code: 6269**

- Public 4-year business and teachers college
- Commuter campus in large city
- 1,496 degree-seeking undergraduates
- SAT or ACT (ACT writing optional) required

General. Founded in 1857. Regionally accredited. **Degrees:** 133 bachelor's awarded. **ROTC:** Army, Air Force. **Location:** Midtown. **Calendar:** Semester, limited summer session. **Full-time faculty:** 58 total. **Part-time faculty:** 96 total. **Class size:** 81% < 20, 19% 20-39.

Freshman class profile. 240 enrolled.

Mid 50% test scores		Rank in top quarter:	28%
ACT:	15-19	Rank in top tenth:	13%

Basis for selection. ACT composite score of 21, or combined ACT composite percentile rank and high school class percentile rank greater than or equal to 100. Full-time, first-year freshmen must meet Missouri High School Core Curriculum requirements. Applicants with scores below 18 on any section of the ACT or below 440 on any section of the SAT must take Harris-Stowe's institutional placement test.

High school preparation. Required and recommended units include English 4, mathematics 3, social studies 3, science 2 (laboratory 1), foreign language 2 and academic electives 3. One visual/performing arts required. History must be American history, including one semester of American government. Electives must be from above list.

2005-2006 Annual costs. Tuition/fees: $4,650; $8,869 out-of-state. Books/supplies: $600. Personal expenses: $1,700.

2005-2006 Financial aid. **Need-based:** 53% of total undergraduate aid awarded as scholarships/grants, 47% as loans/jobs. **Non-need-based:** Scholarships awarded for academics, athletics, music/drama, state residency.

Application procedures. **Admission:** No deadline. $15 fee. Admission notification on a rolling basis. **Financial aid:** Priority date 4/1; no closing date. FAFSA, institutional form required. Must reply within 3 week(s) of notification.

Academics. Special study options: Cooperative education, ESL, internships, student-designed major, teacher certification program. **Credit/placement by examination:** CLEP, institutional tests. **Support services:** Learning center, pre-admission summer program, reduced course load, remedial instruction, study skills assistance, tutoring, writing center.

Majors. Business: General, accounting, business admin, hospitality admin, marketing. **Computer sciences:** General, information systems, networking. **Education:** Early childhood, elementary, middle, multi-level teacher, secondary. **Health:** Health services admin. **Protective services:** Juvenile corrections, law enforcement admin. **Public administration:** General. **Social sciences:** Urban studies.

Most popular majors. Business/marketing 32%, computer/information sciences 14%, education 27%, interdisciplinary studies 22%.

Computing on campus. 205 workstations in library, computer center. Commuter students can connect to campus network.

Student life. Freshman orientation: Mandatory. Program directed by counseling staff during semester. **Policies:** Freshmen permitted cars on campus. **Housing:** Coed dorms available. **Activities:** Choral groups, drama, literary magazine, music ensembles, student government, student newspaper, African American Studies Society, international student association, multicultural council, 100 Strong, Organization for Cultrual Progress, Student Ambassadors.

Athletics. NAIA. **Intercollegiate:** Baseball M, basketball, cheerleading M, soccer, softball W, track and field W, volleyball W. **Intramural:** Basketball, tennis, volleyball. **Team name:** Hornets.

Student services. Career counseling, student employment services, financial aid counseling, health services, personal counseling, placement for graduates, veterans' counselor.

Contact. E-mail: admissions@hssu.edu
Phone: (314) 340-3300 Fax: (314) 340-3555
Lashanda Boone, Director of Admissions, Harris-Stowe State University, 3026 Laclede Avenue, St. Louis, MO 63103-2199

Hickey College
St. Louis, Missouri
www.hickeycollege.edu **CB code: 2308**

- For-profit 4-year business and technical college
- Commuter campus in very large city
- 500 undergraduates

General. Founded in 1933. Accredited by ACICS. **Degrees:** 130 associate awarded. **Location:** 15 miles from downtown. **Calendar:** Semester. **Full-time faculty:** 11 total. **Part-time faculty:** 6 total.

Basis for selection. Open admission, but selective for some programs. Test required for paralegal applicants.

2005-2006 Annual costs. Tuition/fees: $11,120. Room/board: $5,320. Books/supplies: $1,000.

Application procedures. Admission: No deadline. $50 fee. Admission notification on a rolling basis. **Financial aid:** No deadline. FAFSA required. Applicants notified on a rolling basis.

Academics. Credit/placement by examination: CLEP.

Majors. Business: Management science.

Computing on campus. 134 workstations in library, computer center.

Student life. Housing: Apartments available.

Student services. Placement for graduates.

Contact. E-mail: admin@hickeycollege.edu
Phone: (314) 434-2212 Toll-free number: (800) 777-1544
Fax: (314) 434-1974
Michelle Hayes, Admissions Manager, Hickey College, 940 West Port Plaza, St. Louis, MO 63146

ITT Technical Institute: Arnold
Arnold, Missouri
www.itt-tech.edu **CB code: 2691**

- For-profit 4-year technical college
- Commuter campus in large town

General. Accredited by ACICS. **Calendar:** Quarter.

Annual costs/financial aid. Tuition varies by program, $260-$368 per credit hour. Books/supplies: $3,100.

Contact. Phone: (636) 464-6600
Director of Recruitment, 1930 Meyer Drury Drive, Arnold, MO 63010

ITT Technical Institute: Earth City
Earth City, Missouri
www.itt-tech.edu **CB code: 1216**

- For-profit 4-year technical college
- Commuter campus in large city

General. Founded in 1936. Accredited by ACICS. **Location:** 15 miles from St. Louis. **Calendar:** Quarter.

Annual costs/financial aid. Tuition varies by program, $260-$368 per credit hour.

Contact. Phone: (314) 298-7800
Director of Recruitment, 13505 Lakefront Drive, Earth City, MO 63045

Jewish Hospital College of Nursing and Allied Health
St. Louis, Missouri
www.barnesjewishcollege.edu **CB code: 6329**

- Private 4-year health science and nursing college
- Commuter campus in large city
- 810 degree-seeking undergraduates
- 67% of applicants admitted
- SAT or ACT (ACT writing recommended) required

General. Regionally accredited. Affiliated with Barnes-Jewish Hospital, and Washington University Medical Center. **Degrees:** 54 bachelor's, 158 associate awarded; master's offered. **Location:** Downtown. **Calendar:** Semester. **Full-time faculty:** 40 total; 50% have terminal degrees, 95% women. **Part-time faculty:** 15 total; 13% have terminal degrees, 67% women. **Class size:** 20% < 20, 50% 20-39, 25% 40-49, 5% 50-99.

Freshman class profile. 39 applied, 26 admitted, 17 enrolled.

Mid 50% test scores		**Out-of-state:**	1%
ACT:	4-9	**Live on campus:**	1%

Basis for selection. High school or college level algebra, biology, chemistry are prerequisites. 2.75 GPA for undergraduate programs.

High school preparation. Recommended units include mathematics 4, science 4 (laboratory 4).

Application procedures. Admission: Priority date 12/1; deadline 3/1 (postmark date). $25 fee. Application must be submitted on paper. Admission notification 3/10. Admission notification on a rolling basis beginning on or about 12/10. Must reply by 5/1.

Academics. Special study options: Combined bachelor's/graduate degree, liberal arts/career combination. **Credit/placement by examination:** AP, CLEP, IB, institutional tests. **Support services:** Tutoring, writing center.

Majors. Health: Clinical lab technology, cytotechnology, nursing (RN), radiologic technology/medical imaging.

Computing on campus. 60 workstations in dormitories, library, computer center, student center. Dormitories wired for high-speed internet access and linked to campus network. Commuter students can connect to campus network. Helpline available.

Student life. Freshman orientation: Available. **Policies:** Freshmen permitted cars on campus. **Housing:** Coed dorms, substance-free housing available. $150 deposit, deadline 5/1.

Contact. E-mail: jhcollegeinquiry@bjc.org
Phone: (314) 454-7057 Toll-free number: (800) 832-9009
Fax: (314) 454-5239
Christie Schneider, Chief Admissions Officer, Jewish Hospital College of Nursing and Allied Health, 306 South Kingshighway Boulevard, St. Louis, MO 63110-1091

Kansas City Art Institute

Kansas City, Missouri
www.kcai.edu **CB code: 6330**

- Private 4-year visual arts college
- Commuter campus in large city
- 582 degree-seeking undergraduates: 1% part-time, 56% women, 4% African American, 4% Asian American, 6% Hispanic American, 1% Native American, 3% international
- 74% of applicants admitted
- SAT or ACT with writing, application essay required
- 60% graduate within 6 years

General. Founded in 1885. Regionally accredited. **Degrees:** 105 bachelor's awarded. **Location:** 250 miles from St. Louis, 500 miles from Denver. **Calendar:** Semester, limited summer session. **Full-time faculty:** 46 total; 83% have terminal degrees, 44% women. **Part-time faculty:** 48 total; 83% have terminal degrees, 2% minority, 50% women. **Class size:** 73% < 20, 27% 20-39. **Special facilities:** Foundry, arboretum.

Freshman class profile. 435 applied, 321 admitted, 112 enrolled.

Mid 50% test scores		**Rank in top quarter:**	33%
SAT verbal:	480-630	**Rank in top tenth:**	12%
SAT math:	450-580	**End year in good standing:**	90%
ACT:	19-24	**Return as sophomores:**	70%
GPA 3.50 or higher:	35%	**Out-of-state:**	75%
GPA 3.0-3.49:	33%	**Live on campus:**	90%
GPA 2.0-2.99:	28%		

Basis for selection. Portfolio, academic record, recommendations, test scores, personal interview important. Acceptable level of studio proficiency required prior to consideration of other credentials.

High school preparation. College-preparatory program recommended. 20 units recommended. Recommended units include English 4, mathematics 3, social studies 3, science 3 and academic electives 3. 4 fine arts electives recommended.

2005-2006 Annual costs. Tuition/fees: $22,392. Room/board: $7,150. Books/supplies: $1,500. Personal expenses: $2,000.

2005-2006 Financial aid. Need-based: Average need met was 65%. Average scholarship/grant was $12,432; average loan $4,250. 55% of total undergraduate aid awarded as scholarships/grants, 45% as loans/jobs. **Non-need-based:** Scholarships awarded for academics, art. **Additional information:** February 15 and March 15 priority application dates for merit scholarships; deadline July 1.

Application procedures. Admission: No deadline. $35 fee, may be waived for applicants with need. Application may be submitted online. Admission notification on a rolling basis beginning on or about 9/1. Must reply by May 1 or within 2 week(s) if notified thereafter. **Financial aid:** Priority date 3/15; no closing date. FAFSA required. Applicants notified on a rolling basis starting 4/1; must reply within 2 week(s) of notification.

Academics. Special study options: Double major, exchange student, independent study, internships, study abroad. **Credit/placement by examination:** AP, CLEP. 15 credit hours maximum toward bachelor's degree. **Support services:** Learning center, reduced course load, remedial instruction, study skills assistance, tutoring.

Majors. English: Creative writing. **Visual/performing arts:** Art history/conservation, ceramics, cinematography, fiber arts, graphic design, painting, photography, printmaking, sculpture.

Computing on campus. 50 workstations in library, computer center. Dormitories wired for high-speed internet access and linked to campus network. Commuter students can connect to campus network. Online course registration, online library, helpline available.

Student life. Freshman orientation: Mandatory. Preregistration for classes offered. 3-day program held prior to start of academic year. **Policies:** Freshmen permitted cars on campus. **Housing:** Guaranteed on-campus for freshmen. Coed dorms, apartments, substance-free housing available. $125 nonrefundable deposit, deadline 5/1. **Activities:** Film society, student government.

Student services. Adult student services, career counseling, student employment services, financial aid counseling, minority student services, personal counseling, placement for graduates, veterans' counselor. **Physically disabled:** Services for visually, hearing impaired. **Learning disabled:** Comprehensive services available.

Contact. E-mail: admiss@kcai.edu
Phone: (816) 474-5224 Toll-free number: (800) 522-5224
Fax: (816) 802-3309
Larry Stone, Vice President for Enrollment Management, Kansas City Art Institute, 4415 Warwick Boulevard, Kansas City, MO 64111-1762

Kansas City College of Legal Studies

Kansas City, Missouri
www.metropolitancollege.edu **CB code: 3050**

- Private 4-year branch campus and technical college
- Commuter campus in very large city
- 108 degree-seeking undergraduates
- Interview required

General. Accredited by ACCSCT. **Degrees:** 8 bachelor's, 21 associate awarded. **Calendar:** Trimester, extensive summer session. **Full-time faculty:** 4 total. **Part-time faculty:** 13 total.

Basis for selection. Admission requires (1) an acceptable score on the national Wonderlic Test (contact Admissions for scores) or 19 on ACT or comparable SAT and (2) a satisfactory score on a keyboarding test which is 30 wpm net for Paralegals and 40 wpm net for Court Reporters. A language usage test will be used for placement purposes. Transfer students may not transfer more than 75% of credits into any associate or bachelor degree program.

2005-2006 Annual costs. Tuition/fees: $6,534. Quoted tuition is for bachelor's degree in court reporting. Estimated cost of books $260. Tuition for associate paralegal program $6,593 per academic year; estimated cost of books $1,050. Books/supplies: $1,000.

2005-2006 Financial aid. All financial aid based on need.

Application procedures. Admission: No deadline. $50 fee. **Financial aid:** No deadline. FAFSA, institutional form required.

Academics. Special study options: Accelerated study, internships. **Credit/placement by examination:** CLEP.

Majors. Legal studies: Court reporting.

Computing on campus. 35 workstations in computer center.

Student life. Freshman orientation: Mandatory. Preregistration for classes offered. **Policies:** Freshmen permitted cars on campus.

Contact. E-mail: kccadmissions@hotmail.com
Phone: (816) 444-2232 Fax: (816) 444-3142
Heidi Mattingly, Admissions Director, Kansas City College of Legal Studies, 800 East 101st Terrace, Suite 100, Kansas City, MO 64131

Lester L. Cox College of Nursing and Health Sciences

Springfield, Missouri
www.coxcollege.edu **CB code: 3932**

- Private 4-year health science and nursing college
- Commuter campus in small city
- 592 degree-seeking undergraduates

General. Regionally accredited. **Degrees:** 27 bachelor's, 163 associate awarded. **Calendar:** Semester, limited summer session. **Full-time faculty:** 21 total. **Part-time faculty:** 26 total. **Special facilities:** Nursing resource center.

Basis for selection. Open admission, but selective for some programs. Students considered for matriculation based on rankings, which are determined by selection criteria. TOEFL required of non-native English speakers and all international applicants. ACT or SAT scores required for early decision candidates. If ACT or SAT scores are less than 5 years old, student may be exempt from pre-entrance placement testing. **Homeschooled:** Applicants must submit official transcript from a state accredited institution or official GED or high school equivalency score report.

High school preparation. Recommended units include English 4, mathematics 2 and science 2. Early Decision candidates must achieve grade of C or better in biology, chemistry, 4 units English, 2 units math, including algebra.

2005-2006 Annual costs. Tuition/fees: $9,267. Educational fee of $35 per credit hour. Room only: $2,000. Books/supplies: $1,200.

Application procedures. Admission: Closing date 8/1 (receipt date). $30 fee, may be waived for applicants with need. Application must be submitted on paper. Admission notification on a rolling basis. **Financial aid:** Priority date 3/1; no closing date.

Academics. Special study options: Accelerated study. **Credit/placement by examination:** CLEP, SAT, ACT, institutional tests. 6 credit hours maximum toward associate degree, 6 toward bachelor's. **Support services:** Remedial instruction, study skills assistance, tutoring, writing center.

Majors. Health: Nursing (RN).

Computing on campus. 34 workstations in dormitories, library, computer center.

Student life. Freshman orientation: Available. **Policies:** Freshmen permitted cars on campus. **Housing:** Coed dorms available. $100 deposit. **Activities:** Student government, National Student Nurses Association, student council, residence hall council, Christian Fellowship.

Student services. Financial aid counseling.

Contact. E-mail: admissions@coxcollege.edu
Phone: (417) 269-3068 Toll-free number: (866) 898-5355
Fax: (417) 269-3586
Stacy Danaher, Director of Admission, Lester L. Cox College of Nursing and Health Sciences, 1423 North Jefferson Avenue, Springfield, MO 65802

Lincoln University
Jefferson City, Missouri
www.lincolnu.edu **CB code: 6366**

- Public 4-year university and liberal arts college
- Commuter campus in small city
- 2,543 degree-seeking undergraduates: 21% part-time, 60% women, 46% African American, 1% Asian American, 2% Hispanic American, 5% international
- 188 degree-seeking graduate students
- 30% graduate within 6 years

General. Founded in 1866. Regionally accredited. 1890 land-grant institution, founded in 1866 through the cooperative efforts of the enlisted men and officers of the 62nd Colored Infantries to meet the educational and social needs of freed African Americans. **Degrees:** 304 bachelor's, 103 associate awarded; master's offered. **ROTC:** Army, Navy, Air Force. **Location:** 132 miles from St. Louis, 157 miles from Kansas City. **Calendar:** Semester, limited summer session. **Full-time faculty:** 127 total; 61% have terminal degrees, 32% minority, 49% women. **Part-time faculty:** 93 total; 29% minority, 46% women. **Class size:** 57% < 20, 38% 20-39, 4% 40-49, 1% 50-99, less than 1% >100. **Special facilities:** Ethnic studies center and archives, 3 research farms, agriculture and extension information center.

Freshman class profile. 1,487 applied, 1,405 admitted, 632 enrolled.

Mid 50% test scores		**Rank in top tenth:**	5%
ACT:	14-19	**Return as sophomores:**	54%
GPA 3.50 or higher:	8%	**Out-of-state:**	19%
GPA 3.0-3.49:	15%	**Live on campus:**	66%
GPA 2.0-2.99:	58%	**International:**	1%
Rank in top quarter:	17%		

Basis for selection. Open admission, but selective for some programs and for out-of-state students. Selective admission criteria for Nursing and Education programs. Audition required for sacred music and music education students. **Homeschooled:** Must submit a transcript with the parent's notarized signature, demonstrating completion of the Missouri Minimum Core Curriculum.

High school preparation. 16 units recommended. Recommended units include English 4, mathematics 3, social studies 3, science 2 (laboratory 1) and academic electives 3. 1 visual or performing arts required.

2005-2006 Annual costs. Tuition/fees: $4,602; $8,249 out-of-state. Room/board: $3,790. Books/supplies: $950. Personal expenses: $166.

Financial aid. Non-need-based: Scholarships awarded for academics, athletics, ROTC, state residency.

Application procedures. Admission: Closing date 7/1 (postmark date). $17 fee. Application must be submitted on paper. Admission notification on a rolling basis. **Financial aid:** Priority date 3/1; no closing date. FAFSA required. Applicants notified on a rolling basis starting 2/1; must reply within 2 week(s) of notification.

Academics. Special study options: Accelerated study, double major, dual enrollment of high school students, exchange student, honors, independent study, internships, teacher certification program. Intersession courses. **Credit/placement by examination:** AP, CLEP, institutional tests. 15 credit hours maximum toward associate degree, 30 toward bachelor's. Students may take department examinations at the discretion of the individual departments. A maximum of 20 hours of credit can be earned in this manner. **Support services:** Learning center, pre-admission summer program, reduced course load, remedial instruction, study skills assistance, tutoring, writing center.

Majors. Agriculture: General, business. **Biology:** General. **Business:** Accounting, administrative services, business admin, managerial economics, marketing. **Communications:** Journalism. **Computer sciences:** Information systems. **Education:** Art, biology, business, chemistry, elementary, English, mathematics, middle, music, physical, physics, social science, special. **Engineering technology:** Civil, mechanical. **English:** English lit. **Family/consumer sciences:** Food/nutrition. **Foreign languages:** Spanish. **Health:** Clinical lab science, nursing (RN). **History:** General. **Liberal arts:** Arts/sciences. **Math:** General. **Physical sciences:** Chemistry, physics. **Protective services:** Law enforcement admin. **Psychology:** General. **Public administration:** General. **Social sciences:** Political science, sociology. **Theology:** Sacred music. **Visual/performing arts:** Studio arts.

Most popular majors. Business/marketing 27%, communications/journalism 8%, computer/information sciences 10%, education 13%, liberal arts 10%, security/protective services 10%.

Computing on campus. 141 workstations in dormitories, library, computer center, student center. Dormitories wired for high-speed internet access and linked to campus network. Online library, helpline, repair service available.

Student life. Freshman orientation: Mandatory. Preregistration for classes offered. One session is held in July, and a second session is held the week prior to the start of fall classes. Both last one week. **Policies:** Unmarried freshmen and sophomores under 21 years of age, whose primary domicile is beyond a 60-mile radius of the university, are required to live in residence halls for four consecutive semesters. Armed Forces veterans and any student who has established a primary domicile one year prior to entering the University are exempted from this policy. Freshmen permitted cars on campus. **Housing:** Guaranteed on-campus for freshmen. Coed dorms, single-sex dorms, substance-free housing available. $125 fully refundable deposit, deadline 7/1. Housing for honors students available. **Activities:** Bands, choral groups, dance, drama, literary magazine, music ensembles, radio station, student government, student newspaper, TV station, Baptist Student Center, Interfaith Campus Ministries, College Republicans, College Democrats, Barrier Breakers, Wesley Foundation, Kathleen McGuire Newman Center.

Athletics. NCAA. **Intercollegiate:** Baseball M, basketball, cheerleading M, cross-country W, football (tackle) M, golf M, softball W, tennis W, track and field. **Intramural:** Basketball, bowling. **Team name:** Blue Tigers.

Student services. Campus ministries, career counseling, services for economically disadvantaged, financial aid counseling, health services, personal counseling, veterans' counselor. **Physically disabled:** Services for visually, speech, hearing impaired.

Contact. E-mail: enroll@lincolnu.edu
Phone: (573) 681-5599 Toll-free number: (800) 521-5052
Fax: (573) 681-5889
Mohammed Khaleel, Director of Admissions and Records, Lincoln University, 820 Chestnut Street/B-7 Young Hall, Jefferson City, MO 65102

Lindenwood University
St. Charles, Missouri
www.lindenwood.edu **CB code: 6367**

- Private 4-year university and liberal arts college affiliated with Presbyterian Church (USA)
- Residential campus in very large city
- 5,258 degree-seeking undergraduates: 4% part-time, 57% women, 12% African American, 1% Asian American, 1% Hispanic American, 7% international
- 3,275 degree-seeking graduate students
- 43% of applicants admitted
- SAT or ACT (ACT writing recommended) required
- 46% graduate within 6 years; 14% enter graduate study

General. Founded in 1827. Regionally accredited. Evening school students attend in accelerated quarter terms. Coaching for Character programs available. **Degrees:** 872 bachelor's awarded; master's offered. **ROTC:** Army. **Location:** 20 miles from St. Louis. **Calendar:** 4-1-4, limited summer session. **Full-time faculty:** 210 total; 55% have terminal degrees, 9% minority,

46% women. **Part-time faculty:** 321 total; 42% have terminal degrees, 8% minority, 44% women. **Class size:** 60% < 20, 35% 20-39, 5% 40-49, less than 1% 50-99. **Special facilities:** Greenhouse, wetlands program facility, sucess center.

Freshman class profile. 2,906 applied, 1,249 admitted, 821 enrolled.

Mid 50% test scores		**Out-of-state:**	21%
ACT:	19-26	**Live on campus:**	89%
Rank in top quarter:	39%	**International:**	8%
Rank in top tenth:	14%	**Fraternities:**	1%
End year in good standing:	83%	**Sororities:**	1%
Return as sophomores:	69%		

Basis for selection. Admissions criteria include high school GPA, standardized test scores, character, citizenship, and leadership. International students must provide TOEFL results or other proof of English language proficiency. Essay recommended. Interview recommended for scholarship students; audition recommended for music and theater students; portfolio recommended for art students. **Homeschooled:** Transcript of courses and grades required. Satisfactory ACT/SAT scores required.

High school preparation. College-preparatory program recommended. 16 units recommended. Recommended units include English 4, mathematics 3, social studies 3, science 3 and foreign language 2.

2006-2007 Annual costs. Tuition/fees (projected): $12,240. Room/board: $6,000. Books/supplies: $2,900.

2005-2006 Financial aid. Need-based: 61% of total undergraduate aid awarded as scholarships/grants, 39% as loans/jobs. **Non-need-based:** Scholarships awarded for academics, alumni affiliation, art, athletics, job skills, leadership, music/drama, ROTC.

Application procedures. Admission: No deadline. $30 fee, may be waived for applicants with need. Application may be submitted online. Admission notification on a rolling basis beginning on or about 9/1. **Financial aid:** Priority date 4/1; no closing date. FAFSA required. Applicants notified on a rolling basis; must reply within 2 week(s) of notification.

Academics. Special program for working adults offers 9 credit hours per term. Freshman seminars also available. **Special study options:** Accelerated study, combined bachelor's/graduate degree, cooperative education, cross-registration, distance learning, double major, dual enrollment of high school students, exchange student, external degree, honors, independent study, internships, liberal arts/career combination, student-designed major, study abroad, teacher certification program. Bachelor of engineering with Washington University, 3-2 Lindenwood University/University of Missouri Columbia dual degree program in engineering and math or computer sciences, 2-2 program in engineering. **Credit/placement by examination:** AP, CLEP, IB, SAT, ACT, institutional tests. **Support services:** Learning center, reduced course load, study skills assistance, tutoring, writing center.

Majors. Agriculture: Business. **Area/ethnic studies:** American. **Biology:** General, environmental. **Business:** General, accounting, business admin, communications, finance, hospitality admin, human resources, international, management information systems, marketing, retailing. **Communications:** General, advertising, digital media, media studies, organizational. **Computer sciences:** General, computer science, information technology. **Conservation:** Environmental science. **Education:** General, art, biology, business, chemistry, early childhood, early childhood special, elementary, French, health, history, middle, physical, physics, science, social science, social studies, Spanish, technology/industrial arts, trade/industrial. **English:** Creative writing, English lit. **Foreign languages:** French, Spanish. **Health:** Athletic training, clinical lab science, health care admin, predentistry, premedicine, prenursing, preveterinary. **History:** General. **Interdisciplinary:** Gerontology. **Legal studies:** Prelaw. **Math:** General. **Parks/recreation:** Sports admin. **Personal/culinary services:** Funeral direction, mortuary science. **Philosophy/religion:** Christian, philosophy, religion. **Physical sciences:** Chemistry. **Protective services:** Criminal justice, fire services admin. **Psychology:** General. **Public administration:** General, human services, social work. **Social sciences:** International relations, political science, sociology. **Theology:** Pastoral counseling, youth ministry. **Visual/performing arts:** General, acting, art, art history/conservation, arts management, dance, directing/producing, dramatic, fashion design, multimedia, music performance, music theory/composition, studio arts, theater arts management, theater design.

Most popular majors. Business/marketing 44%, communications/journalism 7%, education 15%, social sciences 7%, visual/performing arts 7%.

Computing on campus. 153 workstations in library, computer center, student center. Dormitories wired for high-speed internet access and linked to campus network. Commuter students can connect to campus network. Online library, helpline, wireless network available.

Student life. Freshman orientation: Mandatory. Preregistration for classes offered. **Policies:** Zero tolerance for illegal substances. Freshmen permitted cars on campus. **Housing:** Guaranteed on-campus for all undergraduates. Single-sex dorms, apartments, fraternity/sorority housing, substance-free housing available. $300 nonrefundable deposit. Housing for single parents with children available. **Activities:** Bands, choral groups, dance, drama, film society, literary magazine, music ensembles, musical theater, radio station, student government, student newspaper, symphony orchestra, TV station, Campus Crusade For Christ, intercultural club, American Humanics, Circle K, Reform Campus Fellowship, Lewis & Clark Historical Society, Eastern Debating Society, Christian Life Group, Fellowship of Christian Athletes, student government association.

Athletics. NAIA. **Intercollegiate:** Baseball M, basketball, bowling, cheerleading, cross-country, diving, field hockey W, football (tackle) M, golf, rifle, soccer, softball W, swimming, tennis, track and field, volleyball, wrestling M. **Intramural:** Basketball, bowling, football (non-tackle), soccer, softball, swimming, table tennis, tennis, volleyball, water polo. **Team name:** Lions.

Student services. Adult student services, campus ministries, career counseling, student employment services, financial aid counseling, placement for graduates, veterans' counselor. **Physically disabled:** Services for visually, hearing impaired.

Contact. E-mail: admissions@lindenwood.edu
Phone: (636) 949-4949 Fax: (636) 949-4989
Joe Parisi, ASSOCIATE DEAN OF ADMISSIONS, Lindenwood University, 209 South Kingshighway, St. Charles, MO 63301-1695

Maryville University of Saint Louis

St. Louis, Missouri — CB member
www.maryville.edu — CB code: 6399

- Private 4-year university
- Commuter campus in very large city
- 2,532 degree-seeking undergraduates: 36% part-time, 75% women, 6% African American, 1% Asian American, 1% Hispanic American, 1% international
- 564 graduate students
- 73% of applicants admitted
- SAT or ACT (ACT writing optional) required

General. Founded in 1872. Regionally accredited. **Degrees:** 564 bachelor's awarded; master's, doctoral offered. **ROTC:** Army. **Location:** 20 miles from downtown St. Louis. **Calendar:** Semester, limited summer session. **Full-time faculty:** 99 total. **Part-time faculty:** 244 total. **Class size:** 69% < 20, 30% 20-39, less than 1% 40-49, less than 1% 50-99. **Special facilities:** Conference center, observatory, auditorium, outdoor walking trails, videoconferencing center, teaching laboratory, clinical laboratories, communications laboratory, multi-media classrooms, outdoor swimming pool.

Freshman class profile. 1,357 applied, 984 admitted, 335 enrolled.

Mid 50% test scores		**Return as sophomores:**	77%
ACT:	21-27	**Out-of-state:**	26%
Rank in top quarter:	53%	**Live on campus:**	60%
Rank in top tenth:	22%	**International:**	1%

Basis for selection. School record most important. Recommendations and extracurricular activities considered. ACT or SAT very important. Interview and 20 hours observation in clinical setting required for physical therapy students. Audition required for music therapy students; portfolio required for art education, graphic design, interior design, and studio art majors. **Homeschooled:** Increased weight placed on ACT or SAT scores.

High school preparation. College-preparatory program required. 22 units required. Required and recommended units include English 4, mathematics 3, social studies 2, science 2, foreign language 3 and academic electives 8. Applicants for actuarial science, art, education, interior design, clinical laboratory science, nursing, occupational therapy, and physical therapy must meet other specific requirements.

2005-2006 Annual costs. Tuition/fees: $17,320. Room/board: $7,350. Books/supplies: $1,030. Personal expenses: $1,500.

2005-2006 Financial aid. Need-based: 58% of total undergraduate aid awarded as scholarships/grants, 42% as loans/jobs. **Non-need-based:** Scholarships awarded for academics, art, leadership, minority status, religious affiliation, state residency.

Application procedures. Admission: Closing date 8/15. $25 fee, may be waived for applicants with need. Application may be submitted online. Admission notification on a rolling basis. Must reply by May 1 or within 4 week(s) if notified thereafter. **Financial aid:** Priority date 3/1; no closing date. FAFSA, institutional form required. Applicants notified on a rolling basis starting 2/1; must reply by 5/1 or within 2 week(s) of notification.

Academics. Special study options: Accelerated study, combined bachelor's/graduate degree, cooperative education, cross-registration, distance learning, double major, dual enrollment of high school students, ESL, honors, independent study, internships, liberal arts/career combination, semester at sea, student-designed major, study abroad, teacher certification program, Washington semester, weekend college. Prior learning assessment. **Credit/placement by examination:** AP, CLEP, IB, ACT, institutional tests. 30 credit hours maximum toward bachelor's degree. **Support services:** Learning center, reduced course load, study skills assistance, tutoring, writing center.

Honors college/program. Entering freshmen with ACT of 27 or above or high school GPA of 3.5 or above are invited to join the Bascom Honors Program. Existing students may apply directly if they have GPA of 3.5 or higher. Over 200 students currently enrolled.

Majors. Biology: General, biomedical sciences. **Business:** General, accounting, accounting technology, actuarial science, business admin, e-commerce, management information systems, marketing. **Communications:** Media studies. **Computer sciences:** Computer science. **Conservation:** Environmental science, environmental studies. **Education:** Art, biology, chemistry, early childhood, elementary, English, history, mathematics, middle, music, secondary. **English:** English lit. **Health:** Clinical lab science, community health services, music therapy, nursing (RN), predentistry, premedicine, vocational rehab counseling. **History:** General. **Interdisciplinary:** Biological/physical sciences. **Legal studies:** Paralegal, prelaw. **Liberal arts:** Arts/sciences. **Math:** General, applied. **Physical sciences:** Chemistry. **Psychology:** General. **Social sciences:** Criminology, sociology. **Visual/performing arts:** Graphic design, interior design, studio arts.

Most popular majors. Business/marketing 39%, health sciences 21%, psychology 9%, visual/performing arts 9%.

Computing on campus. 400 workstations in dormitories, library, computer center, student center. Dormitories wired for high-speed internet access and linked to campus network. Commuter students can connect to campus network. Online course registration, online library, helpline, student web hosting, wireless network available.

Student life. Freshman orientation: Available. Preregistration for classes offered. 3-day program prior to start of classes. **Policies:** Freshmen permitted cars on campus. **Housing:** Guaranteed on-campus for all undergraduates. Coed dorms, apartments, substance-free housing available. $150 fully refundable deposit, deadline 5/1. **Activities:** Jazz band, choral groups, dance, drama, literary magazine, music ensembles, student government, student newspaper, wide variety of student academic majors clubs, Fellowship of Christian Athletes, Baptist student union, Campus Crusade for Christ, Roman Catholic student community, international club, Ujima, community service club, student environmental action coalition.

Athletics. NCAA. **Intercollegiate:** Baseball M, basketball, cross-country, golf, soccer, softball W, tennis, track and field, volleyball W. **Intramural:** Basketball, bowling, cheerleading, football (non-tackle), soccer, softball, table tennis, volleyball. **Team name:** Saints.

Student services. Adult student services, alcohol/substance abuse counseling, campus ministries, career counseling, student employment services, financial aid counseling, health services, minority student services, personal counseling, placement for graduates, veterans' counselor. **Physically disabled:** Services for visually, speech, hearing impaired.

Contact. E-mail: admissions@maryville.edu
Phone: (314) 529-9350 Toll-free number: (800) 627-9855 ext. 9350
Fax: (314) 529-9927
Lynn Jackson, Director of Admissions, Maryville University of Saint Louis, 13550 Conway Road, St. Louis, MO 63141-7299

Missouri Baptist University

St. Louis, Missouri
www.mobap.edu **CB code: 2258**

- Private 4-year university and liberal arts college affiliated with Southern Baptist Convention
- Commuter campus in very large city
- 1,425 degree-seeking undergraduates: 19% part-time, 58% women
- 781 degree-seeking graduate students
- 52% of applicants admitted
- 57% graduate within 6 years

General. Founded in 1963. Regionally accredited. **Degrees:** 255 bachelor's, 4 associate awarded; master's offered. **ROTC:** Army. **Location:** 10 miles from downtown. **Calendar:** Semester, limited summer session. **Full-time faculty:** 60 total. **Part-time faculty:** 120 total.

Freshman class profile. 551 applied, 288 admitted, 221 enrolled.

Mid 50% test scores		**ACT:**	17-23
SAT verbal:	390-490	**Return as sophomores:**	66%
SAT math:	420-510		

Basis for selection. Minimum 2.0 high school GPA. Minimum score of 20 is required for ACT and/or a minimum score of 950 (exclusive of Writing) on SAT. Final class rank must be in the upper 50 percent of the graduating class. Applicants with high school GPA below 2.0 may be admitted on a probational status. Interview and/or essay required for academically weak students; audition required for music majors. **Learning Disabled:** To qualify for services, students must self-identify to the Special Needs Access Office, provide current written documentation of a disability from a qualified professional or agency, and request accommodations from the university. Documentation must meet Missouri Baptist University's documentation criteria, indicate a substantial limitation in the education environment, and be completed at least six weeks prior to the start of the semester or class.

High school preparation. 22 units required. Required and recommended units include English 4, mathematics 3, social studies 2, history 1, science 2 (laboratory 1), foreign language 2 and academic electives 3. One visual and performing arts required.

2005-2006 Annual costs. Tuition/fees: $13,830. Room/board: $6,000.

Financial aid. Non-need-based: Scholarships awarded for academics, alumni affiliation, athletics, leadership, music/drama, religious affiliation.

Application procedures. Admission: No deadline. $25 fee, may be waived for applicants with need. Admission notification on a rolling basis beginning on or about 11/18. **Financial aid:** Priority date 4/1; no closing date. FAFSA, institutional form required. Applicants notified on a rolling basis starting 4/15; must reply within 2 week(s) of notification.

Academics. Special study options: Accelerated study, combined bachelor's/graduate degree, cooperative education, cross-registration, distance learning, double major, dual enrollment of high school students, independent study, internships, liberal arts/career combination, student-designed major, study abroad, teacher certification program. **Credit/placement by examination:** AP, CLEP, institutional tests. 45 credit hours maximum toward bachelor's degree. No single source may account for more than 30 of the 45 credit-hour maximum. **Support services:** Reduced course load, remedial instruction, study skills assistance, tutoring, writing center.

Majors. Biology: General. **Business:** Accounting, business admin, marketing, operations. **Communications:** General. **Computer sciences:** General. **Education:** Business, early childhood, elementary, health, middle, music, physical, science. **English:** English lit. **Family/consumer sciences:** Family studies. **Health:** Athletic training. **History:** General. **Math:** General. **Parks/recreation:** Sports admin. **Philosophy/religion:** Religion. **Physical sciences:** Chemistry. **Protective services:** Criminal justice. **Psychology:** General. **Public administration:** Human services. **Social sciences:** General. **Theology:** Religious ed, sacred music, theology. **Visual/performing arts:** Music performance.

Most popular majors. Business/marketing 17%, education 31%, philosophy/religious studies 7%, psychology 10%.

Computing on campus. Dormitories wired for high-speed internet access and linked to campus network. Commuter students can connect to campus network. Online library, helpline, wireless network available.

Student life. Freshman orientation: Mandatory. Program begins with welcome weekend activities. Students also enroll for 1-credt-hour required course for first semester. **Policies:** Religious observance required. Freshmen permitted cars on campus. **Housing:** Single-sex dorms, apartments, substance-free housing available. $200 deposit, deadline 7/1. **Activities:** Bands, choral groups, drama, literary magazine, music ensembles, musical theater, opera, radio station, student government, student newspaper, Baptist Student Union, Fellowship of Christian Athletes, Student Mission, state teachers association, Ministerial Alliance, international club, human services club, science club, computer club, College Music Educators National Conference, Students in Free Enterprise.

Athletics. NAIA. **Intercollegiate:** Baseball M, basketball, bowling, cheerleading, cross-country, golf, lacrosse W, soccer, softball W, tennis W, track and field, volleyball, wrestling M. **Intramural:** Basketball, softball, volleyball. **Team name:** Spartans.

Student services. Adult student services, campus ministries, career counseling, student employment services, financial aid counseling, personal counseling, placement for graduates, veterans' counselor. **Physically disabled:** Services for visually, hearing impaired.

Contact. E-mail: admissions@mobap.edu
Phone: (314) 392-2290 Toll-free number: (877) 434-1115
Fax: (314) 392-2292
Terry Cruse, Director of Admissions, Missouri Baptist University, One College Park Drive, St. Louis, MO 63141-8698

Missouri Southern State University

Joplin, Missouri
www.mssu.edu **CB code: 6322**

- Public 4-year university and liberal arts college
- Commuter campus in large town
- 4,842 degree-seeking undergraduates: 22% part-time, 59% women, 3% African American, 1% Asian American, 2% Hispanic American, 2% Native American, 2% international
- 99% of applicants admitted
- SAT or ACT (ACT writing optional) required
- 32% graduate within 6 years

General. Founded in 1937. Regionally accredited. Extension courses offered in Lamar, Monett, Nevada (evening only), limited weekend courses. Television and online courses offered. **Degrees:** 706 bachelor's, 124 associate awarded; master's offered. **Location:** 138 miles from Kansas City, 126 miles from Tulsa, Oklahoma. **Calendar:** Semester, extensive summer session. **Full-time faculty:** 206 total; 64% have terminal degrees, 8% minority, 38% women. **Part-time faculty:** 102 total; 19% have terminal degrees, 7% minority, 51% women. **Class size:** 47% < 20, 47% 20-39, 4% 40-49, 2% 50-99, less than 1% >100. **Special facilities:** Biology pond, crime lab, art gallery, child development center, small business development center, indoor "livefire" firearms range, performing arts center, greenhouse, law library, cyber coffee shop, international trade and quality center, graduate center.

Freshman class profile. 1,576 applied, 1,560 admitted, 897 enrolled.

Mid 50% test scores		**Out-of-state:**	17%
ACT:	19-24	**Live on campus:**	30%
Rank in top quarter:	43%	**Fraternities:**	1%
Rank in top tenth:	17%	**Sororities:**	1%
Return as sophomores:	64%		

Basis for selection. Minimum 18 ACT or rank in upper 50% of class. Must score in the 75th percentile on the Michigan Test for English as foreign language or score 535 on the TOEFL paper-based test or minimum of 200 on the TOEFL computer-based test. ACT recommended. **Learning Disabled:** Contact the Coordinator for Disability Services.

High school preparation. 16 units required. Required and recommended units include English 4, mathematics 3, social studies 3, science 2 (laboratory 1), foreign language 2 and academic electives 3. One unit from visual arts, music, dance or theater.

2005-2006 Annual costs. Tuition/fees: $3,916; $7,666 out-of-state. Room/board: $4,770. Books/supplies: $600. Personal expenses: $1,500.

2005-2006 Financial aid. Need-based: 11% of total undergraduate aid awarded as scholarships/grants, 89% as loans/jobs. **Non-need-based:** Scholarships awarded for academics, alumni affiliation, art, athletics, job skills, leadership, minority status, music/drama, state residency.

Application procedures. Admission: Priority date 8/1; no deadline. $15 fee, may be waived for applicants with need. Application may be submitted online. Admission notification on a rolling basis beginning on or about 9/1. Must reply by 9/1. **Financial aid:** Priority date 2/15; no closing date. FAFSA required. Applicants notified on a rolling basis starting 2/15; must reply within 3 week(s) of notification.

Academics. Special study options: Accelerated study, cooperative education, distance learning, double major, dual enrollment of high school students, ESL, exchange student, honors, independent study, internships, liberal arts/career combination, study abroad, teacher certification program, weekend college. **Credit/placement by examination:** AP, CLEP, IB, SAT, ACT, institutional tests. **Support services:** Learning center, reduced course load, remedial instruction, study skills assistance, tutoring, writing center.

Honors college/program. Entrance by invitation. Approximately 50 students admitted each year. Application closing date March 1. Require 28 ACT or 3.5 GPA.

Majors. Biology: General, bacteriology, biochemistry, biotechnology, conservation, ecology, genetics, marine. **Business:** General, accounting, finance, financial planning, international, management science, marketing, operations. **Communications:** General, media studies. **Computer sciences:** General, computer science, information systems, programming. **Conservation:** General, management/policy. **Education:** General, art, biology, business, chemistry, early childhood, elementary, English, ESL, foreign languages, French, German, health, history, mathematics, middle, multi-level teacher, music, physical, physics, reading, science, secondary, social science, Spanish, special, speech, technology/industrial arts. **Engineering:** Industrial. **Engineering technology:** CAD/CADD, drafting. **English:** Creative writing, English lit, technical writing. **Foreign languages:** French, German, Spanish. **Health:** Environmental health, nursing (RN), predentistry, premedicine, prepharmacy, preveterinary. **History:** General. **Math:** General, computational. **Parks/recreation:** Health/fitness. **Physical sciences:** Chemistry, physics. **Protective services:** Forensics, law enforcement admin. **Psychology:** General. **Social sciences:** General, international relations, political science, sociology. **Visual/performing arts:** Dramatic, studio arts.

Most popular majors. Business/marketing 24%, education 21%, health sciences 8%, security/protective services 8%.

Computing on campus. 529 workstations in library, computer center, student center. Dormitories wired for high-speed internet access and linked to campus network. Commuter students can connect to campus network. Online library, helpline, repair service, student web hosting, wireless network available.

Student life. Freshman orientation: Mandatory, $30 fee. Preregistration for classes offered. One-day introduction to campus and enrollment process during summer, plus 8-week course. Additional 8-week career/life-planning course available after completion of orientation class. **Policies:** Freshmen permitted cars on campus. **Housing:** Guaranteed on-campus for freshmen. Coed dorms, single-sex dorms, special housing for disabled, apartments, substance-free housing available. $150 fully refundable deposit. Freshmen must live in residence halls if space is available, unless married, residing with relatives, or excused by the Coordinator of Student Housing. **Activities:** Bands, choral groups, dance, drama, film society, literary magazine, music ensembles, musical theater, radio station, student government, student newspaper, symphony orchestra, TV station, over 90 clubs and organizations available.

Athletics. NCAA. **Intercollegiate:** Baseball M, basketball, cheerleading, cross-country, football (tackle) M, golf M, soccer, softball W, tennis W, track and field, volleyball W. **Intramural:** Basketball, football (non-tackle), golf, racquetball, soccer, softball, table tennis, tennis, volleyball. **Team name:** Lions, Lady Lions.

Student services. Adult student services, career counseling, services for economically disadvantaged, student employment services, financial aid counseling, health services, on-campus daycare, personal counseling, placement for graduates, veterans' counselor. **Physically disabled:** Services for visually, hearing impaired. **Learning disabled:** Comprehensive services available.

Contact. E-mail: admissions@mssu.edu
Phone: (417) 625-9378 Toll-free number: (866) 818-6778
Fax: (417) 659-4429
Derek Skaggs, Director of Enrollment Services, Missouri Southern State University, 3950 East Newman Road, Joplin, MO 64801-1595

Missouri State University

Springfield, Missouri
www.smsu.edu **CB code: 6665**

- Public 4-year university
- Commuter campus in small city
- 14,463 degree-seeking undergraduates: 13% part-time, 56% women
- 2,330 degree-seeking graduate students
- 77% of applicants admitted
- SAT or ACT (ACT writing optional) required

General. Founded in 1906. Regionally accredited. **Degrees:** 2,546 bachelor's awarded; master's, doctoral offered. **ROTC:** Army. **Location:** 180 miles from Kansas City, 200 miles from St. Louis. **Calendar:** Semester, extensive summer session. **Full-time faculty:** 726 total; 80% have terminal degrees, 8% minority, 40% women. **Part-time faculty:** 252 total; 20% have terminal degrees, 2% minority, 51% women. **Class size:** 44% < 20, 41% 20-39, 8% 40-49, 5% 50-99, 2% >100. **Special facilities:** Observatory, 125-acre agriculture research and demonstration center, summer tent theater, archaeological research center, social research center.

Freshman class profile. 6,866 applied, 5,257 admitted, 2,621 enrolled.

Rank in top quarter:	47%	**International:**	1%
Rank in top tenth:	20%	**Fraternities:**	3%
Out-of-state:	7%	**Sororities:**	4%
Live on campus:	80%		

Basis for selection. 16-unit high school core curriculum required. Applicant must have 107 or higher on selection index (sum of high school class rank percentile and test score percentile) for fall 2005, spring 2006, and summer 2006 admission.

High school preparation. Required units include English 4, mathematics 3, social studies 3, science 2 (laboratory 1) and academic electives 3. 1 visual/performing arts required. Academic electives must include foreign language.

2005-2006 Annual costs. Tuition/fees: $5,454; $10,374 out-of-state. Room/board: $4,980. Books/supplies: $800. Personal expenses: $3,352.

2005-2006 Financial aid. Need-based: Average need met was 62%. Average scholarship/grant was $4,595; average loan $2,708. 38% of total undergraduate aid awarded as scholarships/grants, 62% as loans/jobs. **Non-need-based:** Scholarships awarded for academics, alumni affiliation, art, athletics, job skills, leadership, minority status, music/drama, ROTC, state residency. **Additional information:** Extensive scholarship program offered to freshmen and transfer students. Out-of-state fee stipends available. Student employment service available to assist students in securing employment on campus and in community.

Application procedures. Admission: Priority date 3/1; deadline 7/20 (postmark date). $30 fee, may be waived for applicants with need. Application may be submitted online. Admission notification on a rolling basis. **Financial aid:** Priority date 3/30; no closing date. FAFSA required. Applicants notified on a rolling basis starting 4/15.

Academics. Special study options: Accelerated study, combined bachelor's/graduate degree, cooperative education, distance learning, double major, dual enrollment of high school students, ESL, exchange student, honors, independent study, internships, student-designed major, study abroad, teacher certification program. London semester. **Credit/placement by examination:** AP, CLEP, IB, SAT, ACT, institutional tests. Some deparments have departmental credit by examination options. **Support services:** Learning center, preadmission summer program, study skills assistance, tutoring, writing center.

Honors college/program. Minimum score of 27 on ACT or 1220 (exclusive of Writing) on SAT and rank in top 10th percentile of class required. Approximately 250 to 300 freshmen enroll each year. Program includes freshman honors seminar, honors general education courses, departmental honors courses, senior project, senior honors seminar.

Majors. Agriculture: Agronomy, animal sciences, business, horticultural science. **Architecture:** Urban/community planning. **Biology:** General, cell/histology. **Business:** General, accounting, business admin, finance, insurance, management information systems, marketing. **Communications:** General, broadcast journalism, journalism. **Computer sciences:** General. **Conservation:** Wildlife. **Education:** Agricultural, art, biology, business, chemistry, early childhood, elementary, English, family/consumer sciences, French, German, history, Latin, mathematics, middle, music, physical, physics, science, Spanish, special, technology/industrial arts. **Engineering:** Physics. **Engineering technology:** Construction, drafting, electrical, industrial management. **English:** Technical writing. **Family/consumer sciences:** Clothing/textiles, family studies, housing. **Foreign languages:** French, German, Latin, Spanish. **Health:** Athletic training, audiology/speech pathology, clinical lab science, medical radiologic technology/radiation therapy, preop/surgical nursing, respiratory therapy technology. **History:** General. **Interdisciplinary:** Ancient studies, gerontology. **Math:** General. **Military:** General. **Parks/recreation:** General. **Philosophy/religion:** Philosophy, religion. **Physical sciences:** Chemistry, geology, physics. **Protective services:** Criminal justice. **Psychology:** General. **Public administration:** General, social work. **Social sciences:** Anthropology, cartography, economics, geography, political science, sociology. **Visual/performing arts:** Art, dance, design, dramatic, music performance.

Most popular majors. Business/marketing 34%, communications/journalism 8%, education 16%, social sciences 6%.

Computing on campus. 1,800 workstations in dormitories, library, computer center, student center. Dormitories wired for high-speed internet access and linked to campus network. Commuter students can connect to campus network. Online library, helpline, student web hosting, wireless network available.

Student life. Freshman orientation: Mandatory, $40 fee. Preregistration for classes offered. 2-day student orientation, advisement and registration (SOAR) program during summer. One-credit "Introduction to University Life" course required during first semester. **Policies:** Freshmen permitted cars on campus. **Housing:** Guaranteed on-campus for freshmen. Coed dorms, single-sex dorms, special housing for disabled, apartments, fraternity/sorority housing, substance-free housing available. $100 deposit, deadline 7/1. Graduate, nontraditional, upper-class, honor, transfer student housing also available. **Activities:** Bands, choral groups, dance, drama, film society, literary magazine, music ensembles, musical theater, radio station, student government, student newspaper, symphony orchestra, TV station, over 250 student organizations available.

Athletics. NCAA. **Intercollegiate:** Baseball M, basketball, cross-country, field hockey W, football (tackle) M, golf, soccer, softball W, swimming, tennis, track and field, volleyball W. **Intramural:** Basketball, bowling, football (non-tackle), golf, racquetball, soccer, softball, table tennis, tennis, track and field, volleyball, weight lifting. **Team name:** Bears.

Student services. Adult student services, campus ministries, career counseling, services for economically disadvantaged, student employment services, financial aid counseling, health services, legal services, minority student services, on-campus daycare, personal counseling, placement for graduates, veterans' counselor. **Physically disabled:** Services for visually, speech, hearing impaired.

Contact. E-mail: info@missouristate.edu/apply
Phone: (417) 836-5517 Toll-free number: (800) 492-7900
Fax: (417) 836-6334
Donald Simpson, Director of Admissions, Missouri State University, 901 South National Avenue, Springfield, MO 65804-0094

Missouri Technical School

St. Louis, Missouri
www.motech.edu **CB code: 2383**

- For-profit 4-year engineering and technical college
- Commuter campus in very large city
- 201 degree-seeking undergraduates
- Interview required

General. Founded in 1932. Accredited by ACCSCT. **Degrees:** 9 bachelor's, 21 associate awarded. **Location:** 20 miles from downtown. **Calendar:** Semester, extensive summer session. **Full-time faculty:** 6 total; 83% have terminal degrees. **Part-time faculty:** 9 total.

Basis for selection. Test scores and interview most important. Minimum ACT score of 20 required. TOEFL required for international students. Internal admissions test or ACT score of 20 or higher needed for admission.

High school preparation. Math and science courses recommended.

2005-2006 Annual costs. Costs for calendar year: lab fees $95 per term, apartment assistance housing $4800. Books/supplies: $800.

Financial aid. All financial aid based on need.

Application procedures. Admission: No deadline. $100 fee. Application may be submitted online. Admission notification on a rolling basis. **Financial aid:** No deadline. FAFSA, institutional form required. Applicants notified on a rolling basis.

Academics. Special study options: Accelerated study, double major, independent study, internships. **Credit/placement by examination:** CLEP, IB, institutional tests. **Support services:** Reduced course load, remedial instruction, study skills assistance, tutoring.

Majors. Computer sciences: Computer graphics, computer science, information systems, LAN/WAN management, programming, systems analysis. **Engineering:** Computer, electrical, software. **Engineering technology:** Electrical. **Health:** Substance abuse counseling.

Computing on campus. 120 workstations in library, computer center, student center. Commuter students can connect to campus network. Helpline, repair service available.

Student life. Freshman orientation: Mandatory. Preregistration for classes offered. Held for 2 hours on Saturday before the term starts. **Policies:** Freshmen permitted cars on campus. **Housing:** Single-sex dorms, substance-free housing available. $175 nonrefundable deposit. Apartment housing available, must be applied for. **Activities:** Student government, student newspaper.

Student services. Adult student services, alcohol/substance abuse counseling, career counseling, student employment services, financial aid counseling, placement for graduates. **Physically disabled:** Services for visually, hearing impaired.

Contact. E-mail: bob@motech.edu
Phone: (314) 569-3600 Toll-free number: (800) 280-3600
Fax: (314) 569-1167
Robert Honaker, Director of Admissions, Missouri Technical School, 1167 Corporate Lake Drive, St. Louis, MO 63132-1716

Missouri Valley College
Marshall, Missouri
www.moval.edu **CB code: 6413**

- Private 4-year liberal arts college affiliated with Presbyterian Church (USA)
- Residential campus in large town
- 1,405 degree-seeking undergraduates
- SAT or ACT (ACT writing optional) required

General. Founded in 1889. Regionally accredited. **Degrees:** 198 bachelor's, 5 associate awarded. **ROTC:** Army. **Location:** 75 miles from Kansas City. **Calendar:** Semester, limited summer session. **Full-time faculty:** 69 total. **Part-time faculty:** 50 total. **Class size:** 45% < 20, 54% 20-39, less than 1% 40-49, less than 1% 50-99.

Freshman class profile.

Rank in top quarter:	19%	**International:**	9%
Rank in top tenth:	6%	**Fraternities:**	25%
Out-of-state:	40%	**Sororities:**	25%
Live on campus:	90%		

Basis for selection. Interview, recommendations, high school record, test scores important; extracurricular activities, personal attributes also important; class rank considered. Essay recommended for academically weak students. Audition recommended for drama majors; portfolio recommended for art majors. **Homeschooled:** A GED in addition to an acceptable ACT/SAT score is sufficient.

High school preparation. Recommended units include English 4, mathematics 3, social studies 1, history 3, science 3 and foreign language 1.

2006-2007 Annual costs. Tuition/fees: $15,250. Room/board: $5,650. Books/supplies: $1,300. Personal expenses: $2,900.

Financial aid. Non-need-based: Scholarships awarded for academics, state residency.

Application procedures. Admission: Priority date 3/1; no deadline. $15 fee, may be waived for applicants with need. Application may be submitted online. Admission notification on a rolling basis. Must reply by May 1 or within 4 week(s) if notified thereafter. **Financial aid:** Priority date 3/1; no closing date. FAFSA required. Applicants notified on a rolling basis starting 2/1; must reply within 6 week(s) of notification.

Academics. Special study options: Combined bachelor's/graduate degree, double major, dual enrollment of high school students, ESL, external degree, independent study, internships, liberal arts/career combination, student-designed major, teacher certification program. **Credit/placement by examination:** AP, CLEP, SAT, ACT, institutional tests. 30 credit hours maximum toward bachelor's degree. **Support services:** Learning center, reduced course load, remedial instruction, study skills assistance, tutoring, writing center.

Majors. Biology: General. **Business:** Accounting, business admin. **Communications:** Media studies. **Computer sciences:** General. **Education:** Elementary, multiple handicapped, physical, secondary, social studies, special. **Health:** Athletic training, substance abuse counseling. **History:** General. **Interdisciplinary:** Biological/physical sciences. **Liberal arts:** Arts/sciences. **Math:** General. **Parks/recreation:** Exercise sciences, facilities management. **Protective services:** Law enforcement admin. **Psychology:** General. **Public administration:** General. **Social sciences:** Economics, political science, sociology. **Visual/performing arts:** Art, dramatic.

Computing on campus. 172 workstations in library, computer center, student center. Dormitories wired for high-speed internet access and linked to campus network. Commuter students can connect to campus network. Online library, helpline, repair service available.

Student life. Freshman orientation: Available. Preregistration for classes offered. **Policies:** Freshmen permitted cars on campus. **Housing:** Guaranteed on-campus for all undergraduates. Single-sex dorms, apartments, fraternity/sorority housing available. $500 deposit, deadline 8/1. **Activities:** Bands, choral groups, dance, drama, film society, literary magazine, music ensembles, musical theater, radio station, student government, student newspaper, symphony orchestra, TV station, international student organization, American Humanics, minority student union, Fellowship of Christian Athletes, student council for exceptional children.

Athletics. NAIA. **Intercollegiate:** Baseball M, basketball, cheerleading, cross-country, football (tackle) M, golf, rodeo, soccer, softball W, tennis, track and field, volleyball, wrestling. **Intramural:** Badminton, baseball M, basketball, bowling, cross-country, football (non-tackle), soccer, softball, table tennis, track and field, volleyball, weight lifting. **Team name:** Vikings.

Student services. Alcohol/substance abuse counseling, campus ministries, career counseling, student employment services, financial aid counseling, health services, placement for graduates, veterans' counselor.

Contact. E-mail: admissions@moval.edu
Phone: (660) 831-4114 Fax: (660) 831-4233
Jacqueline Burton, Director of Admissions, Missouri Valley College, 500 East College Street, Marshall, MO 65340

Missouri Western State University
St. Joseph, Missouri
www.missouriwestern.edu **CB code: 6625**

- Public 4-year business and liberal arts college
- Commuter campus in small city
- 4,769 degree-seeking undergraduates

General. Founded in 1915. Regionally accredited. **Degrees:** 6,544 bachelor's, 64 associate awarded. **ROTC:** Army. **Location:** 48 miles from Kansas City. **Calendar:** Semester, extensive summer session. **Full-time faculty:** 180 total. **Part-time faculty:** 125 total. **Class size:** 40% < 20, 53% 20-39, 3% 40-49, 4% 50-99, less than 1% >100. **Special facilities:** Biology nature study area, planetarium.

Freshman class profile.

Mid 50% test scores		**Out-of-state:**	6%
ACT:	16-22	**Live on campus:**	46%

Basis for selection. Open admission, but selective for some programs. School record, test scores, interview, recommendations important for education, nursing, mathematics, computer science, social work applicants. Special talents important for music, art applicants. High school units mandated by state law may vary by program. Interview required for education, nursing, social work programs. Portfolio recommended for art majors, audition recommended for music majors.

2005-2006 Annual costs. Tuition/fees: $4,778; $8,408 out-of-state. Room/board: $4,400. Books/supplies: $600. Personal expenses: $1,500.

2005-2006 Financial aid. Need-based: 46% of total undergraduate aid awarded as scholarships/grants, 54% as loans/jobs. **Non-need-based:** Scholarships awarded for academics, alumni affiliation, art, athletics, job skills, leadership, minority status, music/drama, state residency.

Application procedures. Admission: Priority date 7/15; deadline 8/15. $15 fee, may be waived for applicants with need. Application may be submitted online. Admission notification on a rolling basis. **Financial aid:** Closing date 3/1. FAFSA, institutional form required. Applicants notified on a rolling basis starting 4/5; must reply within 3 week(s) of notification.

Academics. Special study options: Combined bachelor's/graduate degree, distance learning, double major, dual enrollment of high school students, honors, internships, liberal arts/career combination, teacher certification program, weekend college. **Credit/placement by examination:** AP, CLEP, institutional tests. 30 credit hours maximum toward associate degree, 30 toward bachelor's. **Support services:** Learning center, pre-admission summer program, reduced course load, remedial instruction, study skills assistance, tutoring, writing center.

Majors. Biology: General, biochemistry. **Business:** Accounting, business admin, finance, marketing. **Communications:** General. **Computer sciences:** General, information systems. **Education:** Art, elementary, English, French, middle, music, Spanish. **Engineering technology:** Computer, construction, electrical. **English:** Speech/rhetoric. **Foreign languages:** French, Spanish. **Health:** Clinical lab technology, nursing (RN). **History:** General. **Interdisciplinary:** Natural sciences. **Liberal arts:** Arts/sciences. **Math:** General. **Parks/recreation:** Facilities management, health/fitness. **Physical sciences:** Chemistry. **Protective services:** Criminal justice. **Psychology:** General. **Public administration:** Social work. **Social sciences:** Economics, political science. **Visual/performing arts:** Art, graphic design.

Most popular majors. Business/marketing 19%, education 12%, health sciences 9%, parks/recreation 9%, security/protective services 15%.

Computing on campus. 300 workstations in dormitories, library, computer center, student center. Dormitories linked to campus network. Commuter students can connect to campus network. Online course registration available.

Student life. **Freshman orientation:** Available, $100 fee. Preregistration for classes offered. **Policies:** Freshmen permitted cars on campus. **Housing:** Coed dorms, apartments, fraternity/sorority housing available. $100 deposit. **Activities:** Bands, choral groups, dance, drama, music ensembles, musical theater, student government, student newspaper, symphony orchestra, over 70 organizations.

Athletics. NCAA. **Intercollegiate:** Baseball M, basketball, football (tackle) M, golf, soccer W, softball W, tennis W, volleyball W, wrestling M. **Intramural:** Archery, badminton, baseball M, basketball, bowling, golf, handball, racquetball, rugby M, soccer M, softball, table tennis, tennis, volleyball. **Team name:** Griffons.

Student services. Adult student services, alcohol/substance abuse counseling, career counseling, student employment services, financial aid counseling, health services, minority student services, on-campus daycare, personal counseling, placement for graduates, veterans' counselor.

Contact. E-mail: admissions@mwsc.edu
Phone: (816) 271-4200 Toll-free number: (800) 662-7041
Fax: (816) 271-5833
Howard McCauley, Director of Admissions, Missouri Western State University, 4525 Downs Drive, St. Joseph, MO 64507

National American University: Kansas City

Independence, Missouri
www.national.edu **CB code: 5357**

- For-profit 4-year university
- Commuter campus in large city
- 330 undergraduates
- Interview required

General. Founded in 1941. Regionally accredited. **Degrees:** 37 bachelor's, 11 associate awarded. **Location:** 8 miles from downtown. **Calendar:** Quarter, extensive summer session. **Full-time faculty:** 2 total. **Part-time faculty:** 36 total.

Basis for selection. Open admission.

2005-2006 Annual costs. Technology fees vary by program.

Financial aid. All financial aid based on need.

Application procedures. **Admission:** No deadline. $25 fee. Application may be submitted online. Admission notification on a rolling basis. **Financial aid:** No deadline. FAFSA, institutional form required. Applicants notified on a rolling basis starting 6/4.

Academics. **Special study options:** Accelerated study, distance learning, double major, independent study, internships, liberal arts/career combination. **Credit/placement by examination:** CLEP, institutional tests. **Support services:** Learning center, study skills assistance, tutoring.

Majors. **Business:** Accounting, business admin, management information systems, marketing. **Computer sciences:** Information systems. **Health:** Nursing (RN). **Legal studies:** Paralegal.

Computing on campus. 50 workstations in computer center. Online library available.

Student life. **Freshman orientation:** Mandatory. Preregistration for classes offered. **Activities:** Student government, student newspaper.

Athletics. **Team name:** Mavericks.

Student services. Adult student services, career counseling, student employment services, financial aid counseling, placement for graduates.

Contact. E-mail: msmith2@national.edu
Phone: (866) 628-1288 Fax: (816) 412-7705
Marcus Smith, Director of Admissions, National American University: Kansas City, 3620 Arrowhead Avenue, Independence, MO 64057

Northwest Missouri State University

Maryville, Missouri
www.nwmissouri.edu **CB code: 6488**

- Public 4-year university
- Residential campus in large town
- 5,269 degree-seeking undergraduates: 11% part-time, 56% women
- 561 degree-seeking graduate students
- 45% of applicants admitted
- SAT or ACT (ACT writing optional) required

General. Founded in 1905. Regionally accredited. **Degrees:** 1,029 bachelor's, 40 associate awarded; master's offered. **ROTC:** Army. **Calendar:** Trimester, extensive summer session. **Full-time faculty:** 244 total; 66% have terminal degrees, 10% minority, 42% women. **Part-time faculty:** 44 total; 27% have terminal degrees, 7% minority, 54% women. **Special facilities:** Campus is state-recognized arboretum.

Freshman class profile. 3,655 applied, 1,647 admitted, 1,264 enrolled.

GPA 3.50 or higher:	48%	**Live on campus:**	91%
GPA 3.0-3.49:	35%	**International:**	1%
GPA 2.0-2.99:	17%	**Fraternities:**	30%
Rank in top quarter:	44%	**Sororities:**	18%
Rank in top tenth:	16%		

Basis for selection. School achievement record and test scores most important. Index based on class rank and national test. Audition recommended for dramatic arts and music students; portfolio recommended for art students. **Homeschooled:** Transcript of courses and grades, state high school equivalency certificate required. Must provide ACT scores.

High school preparation. College-preparatory program required. 16 units required. Required units include English 4, mathematics 3, science 2 (laboratory 1) and academic electives 4. One fine arts required. Foreign language and additional math and science highly recommended.

2006-2007 Annual costs. Tuition/fees (projected): $5,910; $9,960 out-of-state. New student fee of $75. Primary textbooks included in tuition. Room/board: $5,792. Books/supplies: $500. Personal expenses: $1,400.

2004-2005 Financial aid. **Need-based:** 35% of total undergraduate aid awarded as scholarships/grants, 65% as loans/jobs. **Non-need-based:** Scholarships awarded for academics, alumni affiliation, art, athletics, job skills, leadership, minority status, music/drama, state residency.

Application procedures. **Admission:** No deadline. $25 fee, may be waived for applicants with need. Application may be submitted online. Admission notification on a rolling basis beginning on or about 9/1. **Financial aid:** Priority date 4/1; no closing date. FAFSA required. Applicants notified on a rolling basis starting 3/15; must reply within 2 week(s) of notification.

Academics. Laptop computers issued to every on campus resident student. **Special study options:** Accelerated study, combined bachelor's/graduate degree, cross-registration, double major, dual enrollment of high school students, ESL, exchange student, independent study, internships, liberal arts/career combination, study abroad, teacher certification program, Washington semester. **Credit/placement by examination:** AP, CLEP, SAT, ACT, institutional tests. **Support services:** Learning center, reduced course load, remedial instruction, study skills assistance, tutoring, writing center.

Majors. **Agriculture:** Agronomy, animal sciences, business, farm/ranch, horticultural science. **Area/ethnic studies:** Pacific. **Biology:** General, botany, molecular, zoology. **Business:** General, accounting, finance, human resources, international, international marketing, managerial economics. **Communications:** General, broadcast journalism, journalism, public relations. **Computer sciences:** General, computer science, information systems. **Conservation:** Wildlife. **Education:** Agricultural, art, biology, business, chemistry, curriculum, early childhood, elementary, English, family/consumer sciences, foreign languages, French, health, learning disabled, mathematics, mentally handicapped, middle, music, physical, physics, social science, Spanish, special. **Family/consumer sciences:** Family studies, food/nutrition. **Foreign languages:** French, Spanish. **Health:** Clinical lab science, preveterinary. **History:** General. **Interdisciplinary:** Biopsychology. **Legal studies:** General. **Liberal arts:** Arts/sciences, humanities. **Math:** General, statistics. **Parks/recreation:** General. **Philosophy/religion:** Philosophy. **Physical sciences:** Chemistry, geology, physics. **Psychology:** General. **Public administration:** General. **Social sciences:** Economics, geography, political science, sociology. **Visual/performing arts:** Art, dramatic.

Most popular majors. Agriculture 6%, business/marketing 23%, communications/journalism 11%, education 23%, psychology 8%, social sciences 7%.

Computing on campus. 4,000 workstations in dormitories, library, computer center, student center. Dormitories wired for high-speed internet access and linked to campus network. Commuter students can connect to campus network. Online course registration, online library, helpline, repair service, student web hosting, wireless network available.

Student life. **Freshman orientation:** Mandatory, $75 fee. Preregistration for classes offered. 4-day program. **Policies:** All campus locations are alcohol and smoke free: housing, classroom buildings, labs, etc. Freshmen permitted cars on campus. **Housing:** Guaranteed on-campus for freshmen. Coed dorms, single-sex dorms, special housing for disabled, apartments, fraternity/sorority housing, substance-free housing available. $150 partly refundable deposit. **Activities:** Bands, choral groups, dance, drama, film society, literary magazine, music ensembles, musical theater, radio station, student government, student newspaper, TV station, Wesley Center, Young Democrats, Pan-Hellenic council, Newman Center, College Republicans, Peer Education, Volunteer Center, Alliance of Black Collegians, International Stundent Organization.

Athletics. NCAA. **Intercollegiate:** Baseball M, basketball, cross-country, football (tackle) M, soccer W, softball W, tennis, track and field, volleyball W. **Intramural:** Badminton, basketball, bowling, cross-country, football (non-tackle), golf, racquetball, skiing, soccer, softball, swimming, table tennis, tennis, track and field, volleyball. **Team name:** Bearcats.

Student services. Adult student services, alcohol/substance abuse counseling, campus ministries, career counseling, services for economically disadvantaged, student employment services, financial aid counseling, health services, minority student services, on-campus daycare, personal counseling, placement for graduates, veterans' counselor. **Physically disabled:** Services for visually, speech, hearing impaired.

Contact. E-mail: admissions@mail.nwmissouri.edu
Phone: (660) 562-1562 Toll-free number: (800) 633-1175
Fax: (660) 562-1121
Beverly Schenkel, Dean of Enrollment Management, Northwest Missouri State University, 800 University Drive, Maryville, MO 64468-6001

Ozark Christian College

Joplin, Missouri
www.occ.edu **CB code: 6542**

- Private 4-year Bible college affiliated with nondenominational tradition
- Residential campus in large town
- 827 degree-seeking undergraduates: 12% part-time, 45% women, 1% African American, 3% Hispanic American, 2% Native American, 3% international
- SAT or ACT (ACT writing optional), application essay required
- 33% graduate within 6 years

General. Founded in 1942. Accredited by ABHE. **Degrees:** 112 bachelor's, 9 associate awarded. **Location:** 70 miles from Springfield, 100 miles from Tulsa, Oklahoma. **Calendar:** Semester, limited summer session. **Full-time faculty:** 32 total; 19% have terminal degrees, 3% minority, 16% women. **Part-time faculty:** 37 total; 11% have terminal degrees, 3% minority, 19% women. **Class size:** 51% < 20, 30% 20-39, 10% 40-49, 8% 50-99, less than 1% >100.

Freshman class profile.

Return as sophomores:	69%	**International:**	2%
Live on campus:	90%		

Basis for selection. Secondary school record, test scores, essay important. 2 references required. Audition required for music ministry students. **Homeschooled:** Transcript of courses and grades required. Provide notarized transcript of grades signed by student and parents.

High school preparation. 15 units recommended. Recommended units include English 3, mathematics 2, social studies 1, history 1, science 2 and academic electives 6.

2005-2006 Annual costs. Tuition/fees: $7,040. Room/board: $4,050. Books/supplies: $800. Personal expenses: $1,500.

2005-2006 Financial aid. **Need-based:** 47% of total undergraduate aid awarded as scholarships/grants, 53% as loans/jobs. **Non-need-based:** Scholarships awarded for academics, leadership.

Application procedures. **Admission:** Closing date 8/5 (receipt date). $30 fee. Application may be submitted online. Admission notification on a rolling basis. Applicant must submit high school transcript through first half of senior year. **Financial aid:** Priority date 4/1; no closing date. FAFSA required. Applicants notified on a rolling basis starting 6/1; must reply within 4 week(s) of notification.

Academics. **Special study options:** Combined bachelor's/graduate degree, distance learning, double major, independent study, internships, liberal arts/career combination. 5-year bachelor's degree program in theology, cooperative program with Missouri Southern State College for certification in elementary and secondary education as well as nursing. **Credit/placement by examination:** CLEP, ACT, institutional tests. **Support services:** Learning center, study skills assistance, tutoring.

Majors. **Theology:** Bible, missionary, religious ed, sacred music, theology.

Computing on campus. 23 workstations in library, computer center, student center. Dormitories wired for high-speed internet access and linked to campus network. Commuter students can connect to campus network. Online library, helpline, repair service, wireless network available.

Student life. **Freshman orientation:** Mandatory. **Policies:** Freshmen permitted cars on campus. **Housing:** Guaranteed on-campus for all undergraduates. Single-sex dorms, substance-free housing available. $90 nonrefundable deposit, deadline 8/5. **Activities:** Choral groups, drama, music ensembles, musical theater, radio station, student government.

Athletics. NCCAA. **Intercollegiate:** Basketball, soccer M, volleyball W. **Intramural:** Basketball, racquetball, volleyball. **Team name:** Ambassadors.

Student services. Adult student services, career counseling, student employment services, financial aid counseling, health services, personal counseling, placement for graduates, veterans' counselor. **Physically disabled:** Services for hearing impaired.

Contact. E-mail: occadmin@occ.edu
Phone: (417) 624-2518 Fax: (417) 624-0090
Troy B. Nelson, Director of Enrollment Growth, Ozark Christian College, 1111 North Main Street, Joplin, MO 64801

Park University

Parkville, Missouri
www.park.edu **CB code: 6574**

- Private 4-year university
- Commuter campus in small town
- 11,857 degree-seeking undergraduates: 92% part-time, 48% women, 22% African American, 3% Asian American, 16% Hispanic American, 1% Native American, 2% international
- 565 degree-seeking graduate students
- 74% of applicants admitted
- 43% graduate within 6 years

General. Founded in 1875. Regionally accredited. MetroPark School for adult education in Kansas City offers bachelor's degree. School for Extended Learning (SEL) offers degree programs in 20 states around U.S. serving approximately 24,000 each year. Six bachelors and three master's degrees offered on line as well as extensive coursework for other programs. **Degrees:** 2,496 bachelor's, 53 associate awarded; master's offered. **ROTC:** Army. **Location:** 12 miles from downtown Kansas City. **Calendar:** Semester, extensive summer session. **Full-time faculty:** 107 total; 59% have terminal degrees, 9% minority, 47% women. **Part-time faculty:** 769 total; 30% women. **Special facilities:** 700 acres of woodland.

Freshman class profile. 352 applied, 260 admitted, 142 enrolled.

Mid 50% test scores		**Return as sophomores:**	66%
ACT:	18-23	**Out-of-state:**	15%
Rank in top quarter:	38%	**Live on campus:**	35%
Rank in top tenth:	12%	**International:**	21%

Basis for selection. GPA (minimum 2.0), followed by test scores and rank in top half of class important. Exceptions considered on individual merit. Students with 3.0 GPA not required to submit SAT/ACT for admission; however, institutional placement test must be substituted. Entering freshmen with GPA of 2.0 to 3.0 must either be in top half of graduating class or submit satisfactory SAT/ACT scores. Interview recommended for academically weak students; audition recommended for music and theater students; portfolio recommended for art students.

High school preparation. College-preparatory program recommended. 19 units recommended. Recommended units include English 3, mathematics 2, social studies 3, history 1, science 2 (laboratory 1), foreign language 2 and academic electives 6.

2005-2006 Annual costs. Tuition/fees: $6,870. Tuition varies by program and hours taken. Room/board: $5,180. Books/supplies: $1,200. Personal expenses: $1,745.

2004-2005 Financial aid. **Need-based:** 134 full-time freshmen applied for aid; 124 were judged to have need; 124 of these received aid. Average need met was 76%. Average scholarship/grant was $1,910; average loan $2,590. 35% of total undergraduate aid awarded as scholarships/grants, 65% as loans/jobs. **Non-need-based:** Awarded to 11,029 full-time undergraduates, including 21 freshmen. Scholarships awarded for academics, alumni affiliation, art, athletics, job skills, leadership, minority status, music/drama, religious affiliation, ROTC.

Four-Year Colleges

Application procedures. Admission: Priority date 4/15; deadline 8/1. $25 fee, may be waived for applicants with need. Application may be submitted online. Admission notification on a rolling basis. **Financial aid:** Priority date 4/1, closing date 8/1. FAFSA, institutional form required. Applicants notified on a rolling basis starting 4/1.

Academics. Special study options: Accelerated study, cross-registration, distance learning, double major, dual enrollment of high school students, ESL, honors, independent study, internships, student-designed major, study abroad, teacher certification program, Washington semester, weekend college. **Credit/placement by examination:** AP, CLEP, ACT, institutional tests. **Support services:** Learning center, reduced course load, remedial instruction, study skills assistance, tutoring, writing center.

Majors. Biology: General. **Business:** Accounting, accounting/business management, business admin, logistics, management information systems, managerial economics, marketing. **Communications:** General. **Computer sciences:** General, computer science. **Education:** Early childhood, elementary. **English:** English lit. **Family/consumer sciences:** Child development. **Foreign languages:** Spanish. **Health:** Athletic training. **History:** General. **Interdisciplinary:** Math/computer science, natural sciences. **Legal studies:** General. **Liberal arts:** Arts/sciences. **Math:** General. **Physical sciences:** Chemistry. **Protective services:** Fire services admin, law enforcement admin. **Psychology:** General. **Public administration:** General, social work. **Social sciences:** Economics, geography, political science, sociology. **Transportation:** Aviation management. **Visual/performing arts:** Dramatic, graphic design, interior design, studio arts.

Most popular majors. Business/marketing 64%, psychology 15%, security/protective services 7%.

Computing on campus. 570 workstations in dormitories, library, computer center, student center. Dormitories linked to campus network. Commuter students can connect to campus network. Online course registration available.

Student life. Freshman orientation: Mandatory. Preregistration for classes offered. **Policies:** Freshmen permitted cars on campus. **Housing:** Guaranteed on-campus for freshmen. Coed dorms, apartments available. $100 deposit. **Activities:** Choral groups, drama, literary magazine, radio station, student government, student newspaper, symphony orchestra, service organizations, Christian Fellowship, World Student Union, Brothers and Sisters United, accounting society, Latin American student organization, marketing club, honors club, non-traditional student organization.

Athletics. NAIA. **Intercollegiate:** Baseball M, basketball, cross-country, golf W, soccer, softball W, track and field, volleyball. **Intramural:** Basketball, soccer, softball, volleyball. **Team name:** Pirates.

Student services. Career counseling, student employment services, financial aid counseling, health services, on-campus daycare, personal counseling, placement for graduates, veterans' counselor. **Physically disabled:** Services for visually, speech, hearing impaired.

Contact. E-mail: admissions@park.edu
Phone: (816) 584-6214 Toll-free number: (800) 745-7275
Fax: (816) 741-4462
Cathy Colapietro, Director of Admissions and Student Financial Services, Park University, 8700 River Park Drive, Parkville, MO 64152

Ranken Technical College

St. Louis, Missouri
www.ranken.edu **CB code: 7028**

- Private 4-year technical college
- Commuter campus in very large city
- 1,617 degree-seeking undergraduates: 35% part-time, 5% women
- Interview required

General. Founded in 1907. Regionally accredited. **Degrees:** 8 bachelor's, 304 associate awarded. **Location:** 3 miles from downtown. **Calendar:** Semester, limited summer session. **Full-time faculty:** 70 total; 9% minority, 11% women. **Part-time faculty:** 26 total; 8% women.

Freshman class profile. 1,065 enrolled.

Out-of-state:	40%	Live on campus:	1%

Basis for selection. Open admission. Institutional placement test and counseling session required. **Learning Disabled:** We have facilities available to students with special accomodations needs with appropriate documentation.

2006-2007 Annual costs. Tuition/fees: $10,670. Book and tool costs vary by program. Books/supplies: $1,700. Personal expenses: $1,774.

Application procedures. Admission: No deadline. $25 fee, may be waived for applicants with need. Application may be submitted online. Admission notification on a rolling basis. Interview and tour recommended for new applicants. **Financial aid:** No deadline. FAFSA required. Applicants notified on a rolling basis starting 4/1.

Academics. Ranken now offers the federally-funded TRIO Student Support Services program for students who are first-generation college students, low-income, or have a disability or academic need. **Special study options:** Combined bachelor's/graduate degree, cooperative education, distance learning, dual enrollment of high school students, internships. **Credit/placement by examination:** AP, CLEP, IB, institutional tests. **Support services:** Learning center, pre-admission summer program, reduced course load, remedial instruction, study skills assistance, tutoring.

Computing on campus. Commuter students can connect to campus network. Online course registration, online library, repair service, wireless network available.

Student life. Freshman orientation: Mandatory. **Policies:** Freshmen permitted cars on campus. **Housing:** Apartments available. **Activities:** Student government, student newspaper, women's support program, Phi Theta Kappa.

Student services. Adult student services, alcohol/substance abuse counseling, career counseling, services for economically disadvantaged, student employment services, financial aid counseling, minority student services, personal counseling, placement for graduates, veterans' counselor, women's services. **Physically disabled:** Services for visually, speech, hearing impaired.

Contact. E-mail: admissions@ranken.edu
Phone: (314) 371-0236 Toll-free number: (866) 472-6536
Fax: (314) 371-0241
Elizabeth Keserauskis, Director of Admissions, Ranken Technical College, 4431 Finney Avenue, St. Louis, MO 63113

Research College of Nursing

Kansas City, Missouri
www.researchcollege.edu **CB code: 6612**

- For-profit 4-year nursing college affiliated with Roman Catholic Church
- Residential campus in very large city
- 246 degree-seeking undergraduates: 1% part-time, 86% women
- 41 graduate students
- 64% of applicants admitted
- SAT or ACT required

General. Founded in 1905. Regionally accredited. Natural science, social science and liberal arts courses taken at Rockhurst University. Students have access to facilities, organizations, sports and activities on both campuses-.The undergraduate Bachelor of Science in Nursing is awarded jointly by Research College of Nursing and Rockhurst University. **Degrees:** 76 bachelor's awarded; master's offered. **ROTC:** Army. **Location:** 5 miles from downtown. **Calendar:** Semester, limited summer session. **Full-time faculty:** 30 total; 23% have terminal degrees, 3% minority, 100% women. **Part-time faculty:** 3 total. **Special facilities:** Medical library, 532-bed research medical center.

Freshman class profile. 192 applied, 123 admitted, 48 enrolled.

Mid 50% test scores		Out-of-state:	25%
ACT:	22-26	Live on campus:	77%

Basis for selection. Academic record, high school GPA, rank in top half of class, counselor's recommendation, test scores very important. ACT score of 20 required. Interview, high school activities considered. Interview recommended for all; strongly recommended for applicants with ACT scores below 20.

High school preparation. College-preparatory program recommended. 18 units recommended. Recommended units include English 4, mathematics 3, social studies 3, science 4 and foreign language 2. Visual or performing arts also recommended. Mathematics should include algebra II, science should include chemistry.

2005-2006 Annual costs. Tuition/fees: $19,600. Room/board: $6,100. Books/supplies: $720. Personal expenses: $915.

2005-2006 Financial aid. Need-based: 42% of total undergraduate aid awarded as scholarships/grants, 58% as loans/jobs. **Additional information:** Financial aid handled by Rockhurst University for freshmen and sophomores.

Application procedures. Admission: Priority date 3/1; no deadline. $20 fee, may be waived for applicants with need. Admission notification on a rolling basis beginning on or about 10/1. Must reply by May 1 or within 4 week(s) if notified thereafter. **Financial aid:** Priority date 3/15; no closing date. FAFSA, institutional form required. Applicants notified on a rolling basis starting 3/15.

Academics. Students admitted into nursing program in freshman year guaranteed place in upper-division nursing courses if academic requirements maintained. **Special study options:** Accelerated study, cross-registration, double major, dual enrollment of high school students, exchange student, honors, independent study, study abroad. **Credit/placement by examination:** CLEP, institutional tests. 32 credit hours maximum toward bachelor's degree. **Support services:** Learning center, reduced course load, tutoring.

Majors. Health: Nursing (RN).

Computing on campus. 300 workstations in dormitories, library, computer center. Commuter students can connect to campus network. Helpline available.

Student life. Freshman orientation: Mandatory, $50 fee. Preregistration for classes offered. **Housing:** Guaranteed on-campus for freshmen. Coed dorms, single-sex dorms, apartments, fraternity/sorority housing available. Freshman nursing students not living at home must live on Rockhurst College campus. All other undergraduates may choose to live on Research College campus or at Rockhurst College. **Activities:** Choral groups, drama, music ensembles, musical theater, radio station, student government, student newspaper, Alpha Phi Omega, Black Student Union, campus ministry, Young Republicans, Young Democrats, Missouri Student Nurses Association, National Student Nurses Association, Rockhurst Organization of Collegiate Women.

Athletics. NCAA. **Intercollegiate:** Baseball M, basketball, cross-country, golf, soccer, tennis, volleyball W. **Intramural:** Basketball, golf, lacrosse, racquetball, rugby, soccer, table tennis, volleyball.

Student services. Campus ministries, career counseling, student employment services, financial aid counseling, health services, on-campus daycare, personal counseling, placement for graduates, veterans' counselor.

Contact. E-mail: jo.hoglund@researchcollege.edu
Phone: (816) 995-2812 Toll-free number: (866) 855-0296
Fax: (816) 995-2813
Leslie Mendenhall, Director of Transfer and Graduate Recruitment, Research College of Nursing, 2525 East Meyer Boulevard, Kansas City, MO 64132-1199

Rockhurst University

Kansas City, Missouri — **CB member**
www.rockhurst.edu — **CB code: 6611**

- Private 4-year business and liberal arts college affiliated with Roman Catholic Church
- Residential campus in very large city
- 1,385 degree-seeking undergraduates: 12% part-time, 57% women, 7% African American, 2% Asian American, 5% Hispanic American, 1% Native American, 1% international
- 835 degree-seeking graduate students
- 74% of applicants admitted
- SAT or ACT (ACT writing optional) required
- 61% graduate within 6 years; 30% enter graduate study

General. Founded in 1910. Regionally accredited. College in the Jesuit tradition. **Degrees:** 372 bachelor's awarded; master's, doctoral offered. **ROTC:** Army. **Location:** 5 miles from downtown. **Calendar:** Semester, limited summer session. **Full-time faculty:** 127 total; 84% have terminal degrees, 6% minority, 44% women. **Part-time faculty:** 91 total; 32% have terminal degrees, 1% minority, 43% women. **Class size:** 40% < 20, 56% 20-39, less than 1% 40-49, 2% 50-99, less than 1% >100. **Special facilities:** Science center.

Freshman class profile. 1,775 applied, 1,314 admitted, 371 enrolled.

Mid 50% test scores			
SAT verbal:	530-640	Rank in top quarter:	65%
SAT math:	530-640	Rank in top tenth:	31%
ACT:	21-27	End year in good standing:	95%
GPA 3.50 or higher:	62%	Return as sophomores:	89%
GPA 3.0-3.49:	26%	Out-of-state:	62%
GPA 2.0-2.99:	12%	Live on campus:	90%
		International:	1%

Basis for selection. High school GPA, class rank, test scores, recommendations most important; school and community activities considered. Interviews recommended for all students. Essay or personal statement may be required or requested.

High school preparation. 16 units recommended. Recommended units include English 4, mathematics 3, science 3 (laboratory 1) and academic electives 4. Recommend 3 units in foreign language and/or social studies.

2005-2006 Annual costs. Tuition/fees: $19,480. Room/board: $6,100. Books/supplies: $1,400. Personal expenses: $1,300.

2004-2005 Financial aid. Need-based: 303 full-time freshmen applied for aid; 272 were judged to have need; 272 of these received aid. Average need met was 100%. Average scholarship/grant was $5,850; average loan $2,319. 70% of total undergraduate aid awarded as scholarships/grants, 30% as loans/jobs. **Non-need-based:** Awarded to 1,140 full-time undergraduates, including 325 freshmen. Scholarships awarded for academics, alumni affiliation, art, athletics, leadership, music/drama, ROTC. **Additional information:** Auditions, portfolios required for some scholarships.

Application procedures. Admission: Priority date 1/15; deadline 6/30 (receipt date). $25 fee, may be waived for applicants with need. Application may be submitted online. Admission notification on a rolling basis beginning on or about 9/15. Must reply by May 1 or within 2 week(s) if notified thereafter. **Financial aid:** Priority date 3/1, closing date 6/1. FAFSA required. Applicants notified on a rolling basis starting 1/30; must reply within 4 week(s) of notification.

Academics. Core curriculum based on 7 "modes of inquiry," different ways people approach reality to seek truth including artistic, literary, historical, scientific-causal, scientific-relational, philosophical, and theological. **Special study options:** Accelerated study, combined bachelor's/graduate degree, cooperative education, cross-registration, double major, dual enrollment of high school students, exchange student, honors, independent study, internships, New York semester, study abroad, teacher certification program, Washington semester. **Credit/placement by examination:** AP, CLEP, IB, SAT, ACT, institutional tests. 32 credit hours maximum toward bachelor's degree. **Support services:** Learning center, study skills assistance, tutoring, writing center.

Majors. Biology: General, biochemistry, bioinformatics. **Business:** Business admin, communications, nonprofit/public. **Communications:** General, organizational, public relations. **Computer sciences:** General, information systems, systems analysis. **Education:** Elementary, secondary. **English:** English lit. **Foreign languages:** French, Spanish. **Health:** Clinical lab science, nursing (RN), speech pathology. **History:** General. **Interdisciplinary:** Global studies. **Liberal arts:** Arts/sciences. **Math:** General. **Philosophy/religion:** Philosophy, religion. **Physical sciences:** Chemistry, physics. **Psychology:** General. **Public administration:** Community org/advocacy. **Social sciences:** General, economics, international relations, political science, sociology.

Most popular majors. Business/marketing 31%, health sciences 19%, psychology 11%, social sciences 9%.

Computing on campus. 500 workstations in dormitories, library, computer center, student center. Dormitories wired for high-speed internet access and linked to campus network. Commuter students can connect to campus network. Online course registration, online library, helpline, student web hosting, wireless network available.

Student life. Freshman orientation: Mandatory, $70 fee. Preregistration for classes offered. Programs held 4 days before fall semester begins. Includes participation in first of many community service projects. **Policies:** Full-time unmarried freshmen and sophomores must live on campus if not living with family. Freshmen permitted cars on campus. **Housing:** Coed dorms, single-sex dorms, special housing for disabled, apartments, substance-free housing available. $200 deposit. Theme houses and student townhouse available. **Activities:** Choral groups, dance, drama, literary magazine, musical theater, student government, student newspaper, Alpha Phi Omega, Black Student Union, campus ministry, Multicultural Affairs Office, American Humanics, Appalachian Service Project, Peace of the World, Amnesty International, student alumni association.

Athletics. NCAA. **Intercollegiate:** Baseball M, basketball, golf, soccer, softball W, tennis, volleyball W. **Intramural:** Baseball M, basketball, cross-country, football (tackle) M, golf, handball M, racquetball, soccer, softball, table tennis, volleyball, wrestling M. **Team name:** Hawks.

Student services. Adult student services, alcohol/substance abuse counseling, campus ministries, career counseling, student employment services, financial aid counseling, health services, personal counseling, placement for graduates, veterans' counselor.

Contact. E-mail: admission@rockhurst.edu
Phone: (816) 501-4100 Toll-free number: (800) 842-6776
Fax: (816) 501-4241
Lane Ramey, Director of Freshman Admissions, Rockhurst University, 1100 Rockhurst Road, Kansas City, MO 64110-2561

St. Louis Christian College

Florissant, Missouri
www.slcconline.edu **CB code: 0334**

- Private 4-year Bible college affiliated with Christian Church
- Residential campus in small city
- 261 degree-seeking undergraduates: 19% part-time, 45% women, 32% African American, 3% Hispanic American, 1% Native American, 1% international
- ACT (writing optional), application essay required

General. Founded in 1956. Candidate for regional accreditation; also accredited by ABHE. Christian Churches/Churches of Christ affiliation. Students highly involved in service and field education. **Degrees:** 34 bachelor's, 8 associate awarded. **Location:** 15 miles from downtown St. Louis. **Calendar:** Semester, limited summer session. **Full-time faculty:** 10 total. **Part-time faculty:** 15 total.

Freshman class profile.

Mid 50% test scores			
ACT:	20-26	Out-of-state:	54%
Return as sophomores:	69%	Live on campus:	73%

Basis for selection. ACT score, high school class rank, and GPA very important. English and Math placement based on ACT subscores or ACCUPLACER tests. Interview recommended for all. Audition required for religious music students. **Homeschooled:** ACT required, GED recommended.

High school preparation. Recommended units include English 4, mathematics 3, social studies 3, science 3, foreign language 2 and academic electives 4.

2005-2006 Annual costs. Full-time residential students receive full scholarships for tuition; required fees are $900 annually. Full-time commuter students pay $125 per-credit-hour; required fees, $900. Room/board: $5,000. Books/supplies: $800. Personal expenses: $600.

2005-2006 Financial aid. Need-based: 50% of total undergraduate aid awarded as scholarships/grants, 50% as loans/jobs. **Non-need-based:** Scholarships awarded for academics, alumni affiliation, leadership, music/drama, religious affiliation.

Application procedures. Admission: Priority date 1/15; deadline 8/1 (receipt date). $15 fee, may be waived for applicants with need. Admission notification on a rolling basis beginning on or about 10/1. **Financial aid:** Closing date 8/1. FAFSA, institutional form required. Applicants notified on a rolling basis starting 7/20; must reply within 2 week(s) of notification.

Academics. Preparation for ministries in preaching, education, youth work, mission fields, music, worship and pre-seminary education. **Special study options:** Cross-registration, internships. **Credit/placement by examination:** CLEP, ACT, institutional tests. 30 credit hours maximum toward associate degree, 30 toward bachelor's. **Support services:** Remedial instruction, tutoring, writing center.

Majors. Education: General. **Theology:** Bible, missionary, religious ed, sacred music, theology.

Computing on campus. 13 workstations in library, computer center. Dormitories linked to campus network.

Student life. Freshman orientation: Mandatory, $250 fee. Preregistration for classes offered. Held weekend before first day of class. **Policies:** Students involved in evangelistic activities of area churches. Religious observance required. Freshmen permitted cars on campus. **Housing:** Guaranteed on-campus for all undergraduates. Single-sex dorms, apartments available. $100 deposit, deadline 8/10. **Activities:** Choral groups, drama, music ensembles, student government, missions interest group, ministry teams.

Athletics. NCCAA. **Intercollegiate:** Baseball M, basketball M, volleyball W. **Intramural:** Baseball M, basketball, softball, tennis, volleyball. **Team name:** Soldiers.

Student services. Adult student services, campus ministries, career counseling, student employment services, personal counseling. **Physically disabled:** Services for visually, hearing impaired.

Contact. E-mail: admissions@slcconline.edu
Phone: (314) 837-6777 Toll-free number: (800) 877-7522
Fax: (314) 837-8291
Amy Gall, Director of Admissions, St. Louis Christian College, 1360 Grandview Drive, Florissant, MO 63033

St. Louis University

St. Louis, Missouri **CB member**
www.slu.edu **CB code: 6629**

- Private 4-year university affiliated with Roman Catholic Church
- Residential campus in very large city
- 7,081 degree-seeking undergraduates: 8% part-time, 57% women, 8% African American, 5% Asian American, 3% Hispanic American, 2% international
- 4,311 degree-seeking graduate students
- 78% of applicants admitted
- SAT or ACT (ACT writing optional), application essay required
- 75% graduate within 6 years; 30% enter graduate study

General. Founded in 1818. Regionally accredited. College in the Jesuit tradition. Institution maintains campus with extensive facilities in Madrid, Spain. **Degrees:** 1,710 bachelor's awarded; master's, doctoral, first professional offered. **ROTC:** Army, Air Force. **Location:** Midtown. **Calendar:** Semester, extensive summer session. **Full-time faculty:** 616 total; 92% have terminal degrees, 11% minority, 40% women. **Part-time faculty:** 478 total; 9% have terminal degrees, 8% minority, 48% women. **Class size:** 48% < 20, 41% 20-39, 5% 40-49, 5% 50-99, 2% >100. **Special facilities:** Vatican manuscripts microfilm library, art museums, biological station, entrepreneurial studies center, earthquake research center, supersonic wind tunnel, water tunnel, shock tube, flight simulators, airport.

Freshman class profile. 8,105 applied, 6,310 admitted, 1,521 enrolled.

Mid 50% test scores			
SAT verbal:	550-650	Rank in top quarter:	66%
SAT math:	550-670	Rank in top tenth:	36%
ACT:	24-29	Return as sophomores:	86%
GPA 3.50 or higher:	69%	Out-of-state:	62%
GPA 3.0-3.49:	22%	Live on campus:	87%
GPA 2.0-2.99:	9%	International:	1%

Basis for selection. Secondary school record, standardized test scores important; recommendations, essay, extracurricular activities, character/personal qualities, volunteer work considered. Admission of international students is granted mainly on the basis of their past academic performances, not on their TOEFL scores. However, for non-native English speakers, a 525 TOEFL or its equivalent is necessary to begin full-time academic work. Audition recommended for music majors; portfolio recommended for art majors. **Homeschooled:** Appplicants are strongly recommended to present 5 academic courses each semester for all four years. These should include 4 years of English, 4 years of mathematics (Algebra I and II, and Geometry), 3 years each of foreign language, natural science, social science and academic electives.

High school preparation. 20 units required. Required units include English 4, mathematics 4, social studies 3, science 3, foreign language 2 and academic electives 3.

2005-2006 Annual costs. Tuition/fees: $24,760. Room/board: $8,200. Books/supplies: $1,040. Personal expenses: $1,050.

2005-2006 Financial aid. Need-based: Average need met was 64%. Average scholarship/grant was $13,434; average loan $3,450. 59% of total undergraduate aid awarded as scholarships/grants, 41% as loans/jobs. **Non-need-based:** Scholarships awarded for academics, art, athletics, leadership, music/drama, religious affiliation, ROTC. **Additional information:** Physical therapy scholarship candidates must apply by December 1.

Application procedures. Admission: Closing date 8/1 (receipt date). $25 fee, may be waived for applicants with need. Application may be submitted online. Admission notification on a rolling basis beginning on or about 10/1. Must reply by 5/1. **Financial aid:** Priority date 3/1; no closing date. FAFSA required. Applicants notified on a rolling basis starting 3/1; must reply by 5/1 or within 4 week(s) of notification.

Academics. Special study options: Accelerated study, combined bachelor's/graduate degree, cooperative education, cross-registration, distance learning, double major, dual enrollment of high school students, ESL, honors, independent study, internships, liberal arts/career combination, student-designed major, study abroad, teacher certification program. **Credit/placement by examination:** AP, CLEP, IB, SAT, ACT, institutional tests.

30 credit hours maximum toward bachelor's degree. **Support services:** Pre-admission summer program, reduced course load, study skills assistance, tutoring, writing center.

Majors. Area/ethnic studies: American, women's. **Biology:** General, biochemistry. **Business:** Business admin, human resources, management information systems, organizational behavior. **Communications:** General. **Computer sciences:** General, information technology. **Conservation:** Environmental science. **Education:** General, multi-level teacher. **Engineering:** Aerospace, biomedical, electrical, mechanical. **Engineering technology:** Aerospace, industrial management. **English:** English lit. **Family/consumer sciences:** Food/nutrition. **Foreign languages:** General, classics, French, German, modern Greek, Russian, Spanish. **Health:** Audiology/speech pathology, clinical lab science, medical records admin, nuclear medical technology, nursing (RN). **History:** General. **Liberal arts:** Humanities. **Math:** General, applied. **Parks/recreation:** Exercise sciences. **Philosophy/religion:** Philosophy. **Physical sciences:** Atmospheric science, chemistry, geology, geophysics, physics. **Protective services:** Corrections, law enforcement admin. **Psychology:** General. **Public administration:** Social work. **Social sciences:** General, economics, international relations, political science, sociology, urban studies. **Theology:** Theology. **Transportation:** Airline/commercial pilot, aviation management. **Visual/performing arts:** Art history/conservation, dramatic, studio arts.

Most popular majors. Business/marketing 27%, communications/journalism 6%, health sciences 14%, psychology 8%, social sciences 6%.

Computing on campus. 1,350 workstations in dormitories, library, computer center, student center. Dormitories wired for high-speed internet access and linked to campus network. Commuter students can connect to campus network. Online course registration, online library, helpline, student web hosting, wireless network available.

Student life. Freshman orientation: Available. Preregistration for classes offered. 2-day program offered 7 times during summer. **Policies:** Freshmen permitted cars on campus. **Housing:** Coed dorms, single-sex dorms, apartments, substance-free housing available. $300 partly refundable deposit, deadline 5/1. Language houses (Spanish, French, and German). **Activities:** Bands, choral groups, dance, drama, film society, literary magazine, music ensembles, musical theater, radio station, student government, student newspaper, TV station, Black Student Alliance, Young Democrats, College Republicans, international student federation, student activities board, Muslim Student Association, Alpha Phi Omega Fraternity, Amnesty International, St. Louis University Community Action Project, Interfaith Council.

Athletics. NCAA. **Intercollegiate:** Baseball M, basketball, cross-country, diving, field hockey W, golf, soccer, softball W, swimming, tennis, volleyball W. **Intramural:** Badminton, basketball, bowling, football (non-tackle), handball, racquetball, soccer, softball, squash, swimming, table tennis, tennis, triathlon, volleyball, water polo M. **Team name:** Billikens.

Student services. Adult student services, alcohol/substance abuse counseling, campus ministries, career counseling, services for economically disadvantaged, student employment services, financial aid counseling, health services, minority student services, personal counseling, placement for graduates, veterans' counselor, women's services. **Physically disabled:** Services for visually, speech, hearing impaired.

Contact. E-mail: admitme@slu.edu
Phone: (314) 977-2500 Toll-free number: (800) 758-3678
Fax: (314) 977-7136
Kalith Smith, Director, St. Louis University, 221 North Grand Boulevard, St. Louis, MO 63103-2097

St. Luke's College

Kansas City, Missouri
www.saintlukescollege.edu **CB code: 7127**

- Private upper-division nursing college affiliated with Episcopal Church
- Commuter campus in large city
- Application essay, interview required

General. Founded in 1903. Regionally accredited. **Degrees:** 48 bachelor's awarded. **Calendar:** Semester, limited summer session. **Full-time faculty:** 16 total; 25% have terminal degrees, 88% women. **Special facilities:** Simulated clinical settings for nursing students.

Student profile. 113 degree-seeking undergraduates. 53 applied as first time-transfer students. 100% entered as juniors.

Women:	96%	**Hispanic American:**	2%
African American:	6%	**Part-time:**	10%
Asian American:	4%	**25 or older:**	54%

Basis for selection. High school transcript, college transcript, application essay, interview required. Recommendations required. Health care-related work and community service considered. Transfer accepted as juniors.

2005-2006 Annual costs. Tuition/fees: $9,520. Books/supplies: $600.

Application procedures. Admission: Deadline 12/31. $35 fee. Admission notification 3/1. **Financial aid:** FAFSA, institutional form required.

Academics. Special study options: Combined bachelor's/graduate degree. **Credit/placement by examination:** AP, CLEP. **Support services:** Learning center, pre-admission summer program, study skills assistance, tutoring.

Majors. Health: Nursing (RN).

Computing on campus. 30 workstations in computer center. Helpline available.

Student life. Activities: Student government.

Student services. Career counseling, financial aid counseling, health services, personal counseling.

Contact. E-mail: slc-admissions@saint-lukes.org
Phone: (816) 932-2367 Fax: (816) 932-9064
Jeff Gannon, Director of Admissions & Financial Aid, St. Luke's College, 8320 Ward Parkway, Suite 300, Kansas City, MO 64114

Southeast Missouri State University

Cape Girardeau, Missouri **CB member**
www.semo.edu **CB code: 6655**

- Public 4-year university
- Commuter campus in large town
- 8,380 degree-seeking undergraduates: 19% part-time, 59% women
- 768 degree-seeking graduate students
- 89% of applicants admitted
- ACT (writing optional) required
- 51% graduate within 6 years

General. Founded in 1873. Regionally accredited. **Degrees:** 1,481 bachelor's, 27 associate awarded; master's offered. **ROTC:** Air Force. **Location:** 120 miles from St. Louis. **Calendar:** Semester, extensive summer session. **Full-time faculty:** 390 total. **Part-time faculty:** 130 total. **Class size:** 40% < 20, 57% 20-39, 2% 40-49, less than 1% 50-99, less than 1% >100. **Special facilities:** Museum, demonstration farm, NASA Educator Resource Center.

Freshman class profile. 4,060 applied, 3,619 admitted, 1,679 enrolled.

Mid 50% test scores		**End year in good standing:**	71%
ACT:	19-24	**Return as sophomores:**	70%
GPA 3.50 or higher:	42%	**Out-of-state:**	12%
GPA 3.0-3.49:	26%	**Live on campus:**	60%
GPA 2.0-2.99:	31%	**International:**	1%
Rank in top quarter:	35%	**Fraternities:**	17%
Rank in top tenth:	15%	**Sororities:**	12%

Basis for selection. Standard test scores, academic GPA, rigor of secondary school records very important. Nontraditional students may take the ASSET. Audition required for music and theater majors.

High school preparation. 17 units required; 21 recommended. Required and recommended units include English 4, mathematics 3-4, social studies 2, history 1, science 3-4 (laboratory 1), foreign language 2 and academic electives 3. 1 visual performing arts required. Of social studies requirements, 0.5 units must be in American government.

2005-2006 Annual costs. Tuition/fees: $5,145; $9,000 out-of-state. Room/board: $5,321. Books/supplies: $400. Personal expenses: $1,937.

2004-2005 Financial aid. Need-based: 1,058 full-time freshmen applied for aid; 755 were judged to have need; 753 of these received aid. Average need met was 66%. Average scholarship/grant was $3,986; average loan $2,690. 39% of total undergraduate aid awarded as scholarships/grants, 61% as loans/jobs. **Non-need-based:** Awarded to 1,180 full-time undergraduates, including 387 freshmen. Scholarships awarded for academics, alumni affiliation, art, athletics, job skills, leadership, minority status, music/drama, ROTC, state residency.

Application procedures. **Admission:** No deadline. $20 fee, may be waived for applicants with need. Application may be submitted online. Admission notification on a rolling basis beginning on or about 10/1. **Financial aid:** Priority date 3/1; no closing date. FAFSA required. Applicants notified on a rolling basis starting 4/1; must reply by 4/1 or within 3 week(s) of notification.

Academics. **Special study options:** Accelerated study, distance learning, double major, dual enrollment of high school students, ESL, honors, independent study, internships, liberal arts/career combination, student-designed major, study abroad, teacher certification program. **Credit/placement by examination:** AP, CLEP, ACT, institutional tests. 30 credit hours maximum toward associate degree, 30 toward bachelor's. Departmental exams offered. **Support services:** Learning center, pre-admission summer program, reduced course load, remedial instruction, study skills assistance, tutoring, writing center.

Majors. **Agriculture:** Agribusiness operations, business. **Biology:** General. **Business:** Accounting, administrative services, business admin, finance, marketing, office management. **Communications:** General. **Computer sciences:** General, programming. **Conservation:** Environmental studies. **Education:** Art, business, early childhood, elementary, English, family/consumer sciences, foreign languages, kindergarten/preschool, mathematics, middle, music, physical, science, social studies, special, speech, technology/industrial arts. **Engineering:** Physics. **Engineering technology:** Construction, industrial. **English:** English lit, speech/rhetoric. **Family/consumer sciences:** General. **Foreign languages:** French, German, Spanish. **Health:** Clinical lab science, communication disorders, nursing (RN). **History:** General. **Liberal arts:** Humanities. **Math:** General. **Parks/recreation:** General, health/fitness, sports admin. **Philosophy/religion:** Philosophy. **Physical sciences:** Chemistry, geology, physics. **Protective services:** Corrections. **Psychology:** General. **Public administration:** Social work. **Social sciences:** Anthropology, economics, geography, political science, sociology. **Visual/performing arts:** General, art, dramatic.

Most popular majors. Business/marketing 18%, communications/journalism 7%, education 20%, engineering/engineering technologies 6%, liberal arts 9%.

Computing on campus. 1,022 workstations in dormitories, library, computer center, student center. Dormitories wired for high-speed internet access and linked to campus network. Online course registration, online library, helpline, student web hosting, wireless network available.

Student life. **Freshman orientation:** Mandatory, $50 fee. Preregistration for classes offered. One-day program offered many times throughout the semester. **Policies:** Freshmen permitted cars on campus. **Housing:** Coed dorms, fraternity/sorority housing available. $150 partly refundable deposit. Apartments for students with dependents. **Activities:** Bands, choral groups, dance, drama, literary magazine, music ensembles, musical theater, opera, radio station, student government, student newspaper, symphony orchestra, Baptist Student Union, Lutheran Student Fellowship, Association of Black Collegians, United Methodist Campus Ministry/Wesley House, Greek Life, College Republicans, College Democrats, Friends Without Borders, Indian Subcontinent Student Association, student activities council, alumni association.

Athletics. NCAA. **Intercollegiate:** Baseball M, basketball, cheerleading, cross-country, football (tackle) M, golf M, gymnastics W, soccer W, softball W, tennis W, track and field, volleyball W. **Intramural:** Badminton, basketball, football (non-tackle), golf, racquetball, soccer, softball, swimming, table tennis, tennis, track and field, volleyball. **Team name:** Redhawks.

Student services. Adult student services, alcohol/substance abuse counseling, campus ministries, career counseling, services for economically disadvantaged, student employment services, financial aid counseling, health services, minority student services, on-campus daycare, personal counseling, placement for graduates, veterans' counselor. **Physically disabled:** Services for visually, speech, hearing impaired.

Contact. E-mail: admissions@semo.edu
Phone: (573) 651-2590 Fax: (573) 651-5936
Deborah Below, Director, Southeast Missouri State University, One University Plaza, Cape Girardeau, MO 63701

Southwest Baptist University

Bolivar, Missouri
www.sbuniv.edu **CB code: 6664**

- Private 4-year university affiliated with Southern Baptist Convention
- Residential campus in small town
- 2,358 degree-seeking undergraduates: 25% part-time, 67% women, 3% African American, 1% Asian American, 1% Hispanic American, 1% Native American, 1% international
- 411 degree-seeking graduate students
- 85% of applicants admitted
- SAT or ACT (ACT writing optional) required
- 44% graduate within 6 years

General. Founded in 1878. Regionally accredited. **Degrees:** 345 bachelor's, 111 associate awarded; master's, doctoral offered. **ROTC:** Army. **Location:** 25 miles from Springfield, 120 miles from Kansas City. **Calendar:** 4-1-4, extensive summer session. **Full-time faculty:** 105 total; 64% have terminal degrees, 2% minority, 41% women. **Part-time faculty:** 141 total; 26% have terminal degrees, 53% women. **Class size:** 63% < 20, 31% 20-39, 4% 40-49, 2% 50-99.

Freshman class profile. 720 applied, 614 admitted, 364 enrolled.

Mid 50% test scores		**Rank in top quarter:**	43%
SAT verbal:	460-600	**Rank in top tenth:**	20%
SAT math:	470-590	**End year in good standing:**	84%
ACT:	20-26	**Return as sophomores:**	68%
GPA 3.50 or higher:	52%	**Out-of-state:**	31%
GPA 3.0-3.49:	23%	**Live on campus:**	92%
GPA 2.0-2.99:	22%	**International:**	1%

Basis for selection. Must present proof of graduation from an accredited or approved high school or present an acceptable secondary certificate. Additionally, students must meet 2 of 3 three qualifiers: 2.50 GPA, 21 ACT or 990 SAT score (exclusive of Writing), top 50% high school class rank. Interview required for conditionally admitted applicants, recommended for all. Audition recommended for music, speech, and theater students.

High school preparation. 13 units recommended. Recommended units include English 4, mathematics 3, social studies 2, science 2 and academic electives 2. 2 additional units of foreign language or computer science or 2 units of English, math, social studies or natural sciences recommended.

2006-2007 Annual costs. Tuition/fees (projected): $14,100. Room/board: $4,200. Books/supplies: $1,000. Personal expenses: $1,000.

2005-2006 Financial aid. **Need-based:** 334 full-time freshmen applied for aid; 262 were judged to have need; 261 of these received aid. Average need met was 72%. Average scholarship/grant was $3,866; average loan $3,641. 24% of total undergraduate aid awarded as scholarships/grants, 76% as loans/jobs. **Non-need-based:** Awarded to 1,591 full-time undergraduates, including 394 freshmen. Scholarships awarded for academics, art, athletics, minority status, music/drama, state residency.

Application procedures. **Admission:** No deadline. $30 fee, may be waived for applicants with need. Application may be submitted online. Admission notification on a rolling basis beginning on or about 9/1. **Financial aid:** Priority date 3/15; no closing date. FAFSA, institutional form required. Applicants notified on a rolling basis starting 3/1; must reply within 2 week(s) of notification.

Academics. **Special study options:** Cooperative education, distance learning, double major, dual enrollment of high school students, honors, independent study, internships, study abroad, teacher certification program, Washington semester. **Credit/placement by examination:** AP, CLEP, IB, institutional tests. 16 credit hours maximum toward associate degree, 32 toward bachelor's. **Support services:** Learning center, reduced course load, remedial instruction, study skills assistance, tutoring, writing center.

Majors. **Biology:** General. **Business:** Accounting, business admin. **Communications:** General. **Computer sciences:** General, computer science. **Education:** Art, biology, chemistry, elementary, English, health, middle, music, physical, science, social science. **Engineering technology:** Occupational safety. **English:** English lit. **Foreign languages:** Spanish. **Health:** Athletic training, clinical lab science, nursing (RN). **History:** General. **Math:** General. **Parks/recreation:** General, health/fitness, sports admin. **Physical sciences:** Chemistry. **Protective services:** Corrections, police science. **Psychology:** General. **Public administration:** Human services. **Social sciences:** Political science, sociology. **Theology:** Bible, missionary, pastoral counseling, religious ed, sacred music, theology. **Visual/performing arts:** Art, commercial/advertising art, dramatic.

Most popular majors. Business/marketing 11%, education 20%, health sciences 7%, psychology 16%, theological studies 9%.

Computing on campus. 261 workstations in dormitories, library, computer center, student center. Dormitories linked to campus network. Commuter students can connect to campus network. Online library, helpline, wireless network available.

Student life. **Freshman orientation:** Available. Preregistration for classes offered. 5 days prior to start of the fall semester. **Policies:** Religious observance required. Freshmen permitted cars on campus. **Housing:** Guaranteed on-campus for freshmen. Single-sex dorms, apartments, substance-free housing available. $100 partly refundable deposit. **Activities:** Bands, choral groups, drama, music ensembles, opera, student government, student newspaper, symphony orchestra, university missions, student government association, Habitat for Humanity, Christian service organization, theatrical Evangelism and mission, small group ministries, international student association, students in free enterprise, discipleship-now teams.

Athletics. NCAA. **Intercollegiate:** Baseball M, basketball, cheerleading, cross-country, football (tackle) M, golf M, soccer W, softball W, tennis, track and field, volleyball W. **Intramural:** Basketball, football (non-tackle), soccer, softball, table tennis, volleyball. **Team name:** Bearcats.

Student services. Campus ministries, career counseling, student employment services, financial aid counseling, health services, personal counseling, placement for graduates.

Contact. E-mail: dcrowder@sbuniv.edu
Phone: (417) 328-1810 Toll-free number: (800) 526-5859
Fax: (417) 328-1514
Darren Crowder, Director of Admissions, Southwest Baptist University, 1600 University Avenue, Bolivar, MO 65613-2597

Stephens College

Columbia, Missouri — **CB member**
www.stephens.edu — **CB code: 6683**

- Private 4-year liberal arts college for women
- Residential campus in small city
- 734 degree-seeking undergraduates: 22% part-time, 97% women, 8% African American, 2% Asian American, 3% Hispanic American, 1% Native American, 1% international
- 72 degree-seeking graduate students
- 79% of applicants admitted
- SAT or ACT (ACT writing optional), application essay required
- 50% graduate within 6 years

General. Founded in 1833. Regionally accredited. **Degrees:** 111 bachelor's, 1 associate awarded; master's offered. **ROTC:** Army, Navy, Air Force. **Location:** 125 miles from St. Louis and Kansas City. **Calendar:** Semester, limited summer session. **Full-time faculty:** 45 total; 44% have terminal degrees, 2% minority, 60% women. **Part-time faculty:** 28 total; 4% minority, 64% women. **Class size:** 76% < 20, 24% 20-39. **Special facilities:** Professional-level theater, private elementary school and child study center, 60-horse stables, historic senior hall, 8,000+ garments in historical costume collection.

Freshman class profile. 526 applied, 414 admitted, 203 enrolled.

Mid 50% test scores		Rank in top quarter:	47%
SAT verbal:	540-610	Rank in top tenth:	15%
SAT math:	480-580	End year in good standing:	87%
ACT:	21-26	Return as sophomores:	74%
GPA 3.50 or higher:	46%	Out-of-state:	49%
GPA 3.0-3.49:	33%	Live on campus:	95%
GPA 2.0-2.99:	21%	Sororities:	7%

Basis for selection. School achievement record most important, followed by test scores. Interview recommended for all students; audition mandatory for dance, recommended for theater, musical theater students.

High school preparation. 12 units recommended. Recommended units include English 4, mathematics 2, social studies 2, science 2 and foreign language 2.

2005-2006 Annual costs. Tuition/fees: $19,300. Room/board: $7,630. Books/supplies: $750. Personal expenses: $1,925.

2005-2006 Financial aid. Need-based: 139 full-time freshmen applied for aid; 119 were judged to have need; 119 of these received aid. Average need met was 74%. Average scholarship/grant was $6,604; average loan $3,452. 76% of total undergraduate aid awarded as scholarships/grants, 24% as loans/jobs. **Non-need-based:** Awarded to 459 full-time undergraduates, including 121 freshmen. Scholarships awarded for academics, alumni affiliation, athletics, leadership.

Application procedures. Admission: No deadline. $25 fee, may be waived for applicants with need. Application may be submitted online. Admission notification on a rolling basis beginning on or about 9/1. **Financial aid:** Priority date 3/15; no closing date. FAFSA required. Applicants notified on a rolling basis starting 3/1; must reply within 2 week(s) of notification.

Academics. Special study options: Accelerated study, combined bachelor's/graduate degree, cross-registration, distance learning, double major, dual enrollment of high school students, external degree, honors, independent study, internships, liberal arts/career combination, semester at sea, student-designed major, study abroad, teacher certification program, Washington semester. Cambridge (England) program; Japanese exchange program; summer seminar in Japan; fashion tours in New York, Florence and Paris; science research in Costa Rica; 3-2 occupational therapy program in biology with Washington University in St. Louis. **Credit/placement by examination:** AP, CLEP, IB. 10 credit hours maximum toward associate degree, 10 toward bachelor's. **Support services:** Learning center, tutoring, writing center.

Majors. Agriculture: Equine science. **Biology:** General. **Business:** Accounting, business admin, fashion, marketing. **Communications:** General, advertising, broadcast journalism, journalism, public relations. **Education:** General, early childhood, elementary. **English:** Creative writing. **Family/consumer sciences:** Clothing/textiles. **Health:** Medical records admin. **Legal studies:** Prelaw. **Liberal arts:** Arts/sciences. **Psychology:** General. **Visual/performing arts:** General, commercial/advertising art, dance, dramatic, fashion design.

Most popular majors. Health sciences 7%, interdisciplinary studies 13%, visual/performing arts 41%.

Computing on campus. 85 workstations in dormitories, library, computer center. Dormitories linked to campus network. Commuter students can connect to campus network. Online library, repair service, wireless network available.

Student life. Freshman orientation: Mandatory. Preregistration for classes offered. Typically held third week of August; one week prior to classes beginning. Registration held mid-June on campus with academic advisor. **Policies:** Freshmen permitted cars on campus. **Housing:** Guaranteed on-campus for all undergraduates. Apartments available. $100 deposit. Pets allowed in dorm rooms. Freshman academic residence hall available. **Activities:** Choral groups, dance, drama, literary magazine, music ensembles, musical theater, radio station, student government, student newspaper, TV station, more than 45 clubs and organizations.

Athletics. NAIA. **Intercollegiate:** Basketball W, swimming W, tennis W, volleyball W. **Intramural:** Equestrian W. **Team name:** Stars.

Student services. Adult student services, career counseling, student employment services, financial aid counseling, health services, personal counseling, placement for graduates, women's services.

Contact. E-mail: apply@stephens.edu
Phone: (573) 876-7207 Toll-free number: (800) 876-7207
Fax: (573) 876-7237
David Adams, Dean of Enrollment Management, Stephens College, 1200 East Broadway, Box 2121, Columbia, MO 65215

Truman State University

Kirksville, Missouri — **CB member**
www.admissions.truman.edu — **CB code: 6483**

- Public 4-year university and liberal arts college
- Residential campus in large town
- 5,474 degree-seeking undergraduates: 2% part-time, 58% women, 4% African American, 2% Asian American, 2% Hispanic American, 3% international
- 208 degree-seeking graduate students
- 82% of applicants admitted
- SAT or ACT (ACT writing optional), application essay required
- 66% graduate within 6 years; 47% enter graduate study

General. Founded in 1867. Regionally accredited. **Degrees:** 1,215 bachelor's awarded; master's offered. **ROTC:** Army. **Location:** 220 miles from St. Louis, 150 miles from Kansas City. **Calendar:** Semester, extensive summer session. **Full-time faculty:** 353 total; 83% have terminal degrees, 10% minority, 39% women. **Part-time faculty:** 25 total; 20% have terminal degrees, 8% minority, 64% women. **Class size:** 33% < 20, 62% 20-39, 3% 40-49, 2% 50-99, less than 1% >100. **Special facilities:** Observatory, greenhouse, local history museum, farm, human performance laboratory, speech and hearing clinic, biofeedback laboratory, IR and NMR instrumentation, independent learning center for nursing.

Freshman class profile. 4,912 applied, 4,035 admitted, 1,444 enrolled.

Mid 50% test scores			
SAT verbal:	570-670	Rank in top tenth:	48%
SAT math:	560-660	End year in good standing:	96%
ACT:	25-30	Return as sophomores:	86%
GPA 3.50 or higher:	82%	Out-of-state:	24%
GPA 3.0-3.49:	17%	Live on campus:	91%
GPA 2.0-2.99:	1%	International:	2%
Rank in top quarter:	80%	Fraternities:	31%
		Sororities:	16%

Basis for selection. High school performance (class rank, GPA, college preparatory curriculum), test scores, essay most important; special ability, talent and achievement considered. Admission for out-of-state students more competitive. TOEFL required for non-native speakers. Portfolio recommended for fine arts students. Audition required for music students.

High school preparation. College-preparatory program required. 16 units required; 17 recommended. Required and recommended units include English 4, mathematics 3-4, social studies 3, science 3 (laboratory 2) and foreign language 2. One fine arts required.

2005-2006 Annual costs. Tuition/fees: $5,862; $10,042 out-of-state. Room/board: $5,380. Books/supplies: $900. Personal expenses: $2,500.

2005-2006 Financial aid. **Need-based:** 891 full-time freshmen applied for aid; 534 were judged to have need; 534 of these received aid. Average need met was 81%. Average scholarship/grant was $2,906; average loan $3,110. 30% of total undergraduate aid awarded as scholarships/grants, 70% as loans/jobs. **Non-need-based:** Awarded to 4,383 full-time undergraduates, including 1,511 freshmen. Scholarships awarded for academics, alumni affiliation, art, athletics, leadership, music/drama, ROTC, state residency. **Additional information:** Out-of-state students whose parents work in Missouri may deduct $1 for every dollar paid in Missouri income taxes from out-of-state tuition.

Application procedures. **Admission:** Priority date 11/15; deadline 3/1 (postmark date). No application fee. Application may be submitted online. Admission notification on a rolling basis beginning on or about 12/15. Must reply by May 1 or within 3 week(s) if notified thereafter. **Financial aid:** Priority date 4/1; no closing date. FAFSA required. Applicants notified on a rolling basis starting 3/1; must reply within 4 week(s) of notification.

Academics. **Special study options:** Combined bachelor's/graduate degree, double major, dual enrollment of high school students, exchange student, honors, independent study, internships, semester at sea, student-designed major, study abroad, teacher certification program, Washington semester. **Credit/placement by examination:** AP, CLEP, IB, institutional tests. **Support services:** Tutoring, writing center.

Majors. **Agriculture:** Agronomy, animal sciences, economics, equestrian studies. **Biology:** General. **Business:** Accounting, business admin. **Communications:** Journalism. **Computer sciences:** General. **Education:** Speech impaired. **English:** Speech/rhetoric. **Foreign languages:** Classics, French, German, Russian, Spanish. **Health:** Communication disorders, nursing (RN), predentistry, premedicine, prepharmacy, preveterinary. **History:** General. **Legal studies:** Prelaw. **Math:** General, applied. **Parks/recreation:** Exercise sciences, health/fitness. **Philosophy/religion:** Ethics, logic. **Physical sciences:** Chemistry, physics. **Protective services:** Criminal justice. **Psychology:** General. **Social sciences:** Economics, political science, sociology. **Visual/performing arts:** Art, art history/conservation, commercial/advertising art, dramatic, music performance, studio arts.

Most popular majors. Biology 10%, business/marketing 20%, communications/journalism 6%, English 8%, parks/recreation 8%, psychology 9%, social sciences 7%, visual/performing arts 8%.

Computing on campus. 870 workstations in dormitories, library, computer center, student center. Dormitories wired for high-speed internet access and linked to campus network. Commuter students can connect to campus network. Online library, helpline, student web hosting, wireless network available.

Student life. **Freshman orientation:** Mandatory, $250 fee. Preregistration for classes offered. Program begins week before beginning of the fall semester. Class component continues to meet each week of fall semester. **Policies:** Freshmen permitted cars on campus. **Housing:** Coed dorms, single-sex dorms, special housing for disabled, apartments, fraternity/sorority housing, substance-free housing available. $75 partly refundable deposit, deadline 5/1. Smoke-free residence halls and apartments, international roommate options, quiet floors, faculty advisers in residence halls available. **Activities:** Bands, choral groups, dance, drama, literary magazine, music ensembles, musical theater, radio station, student government, student newspaper, symphony orchestra, TV station, Alpha Phi Omega, Association of Black Collegians, College Republicans, Campus Christian Fellowship, Amnesty International, Blue Key, Cardinal Key, Circle-K, College Democrats, Baptist Student Union.

Athletics. NCAA. **Intercollegiate:** Baseball M, basketball, cross-country, football (tackle) M, golf, soccer, softball W, swimming, tennis, track and field, volleyball W, wrestling M. **Intramural:** Badminton, basketball, bowling, cross-country, football (non-tackle), golf, handball, racquetball, soccer, softball, swimming, table tennis, tennis, track and field, volleyball. **Team name:** Bulldogs.

Student services. Career counseling, services for economically disadvantaged, student employment services, financial aid counseling, health services, minority student services, personal counseling, placement for graduates, veterans' counselor, women's services. **Physically disabled:** Services for visually, speech, hearing impaired.

Contact. E-mail: admissions@truman.edu
Phone: (660) 785-4114 Toll-free number: (800) 892-7792
Fax: (660) 785-7456
Brad Chambers, Co-Director of Admissions, Truman State University, McClain Hall 205, Kirksville, MO 63501-9980

University of Missouri: Columbia

Columbia, Missouri — **CB member**
www.missouri.edu — **CB code: 6875**

- Public 4-year university
- Residential campus in small city
- 21,046 degree-seeking undergraduates: 5% part-time, 52% women, 6% African American, 3% Asian American, 2% Hispanic American, 1% Native American, 1% international
- 6,066 degree-seeking graduate students
- 83% of applicants admitted
- SAT or ACT (ACT writing optional) required
- 66% graduate within 6 years

General. Founded in 1839. Regionally accredited. Students with same academic interest are housed in same residence hall and enrolled in 3 classes together. **Degrees:** 4,259 bachelor's awarded; master's, doctoral, first professional offered. **ROTC:** Army, Navy, Air Force. **Location:** 125 miles from Kansas City, 125 miles from St. Louis. **Calendar:** Semester, limited summer session. **Full-time faculty:** 1,066 total; 90% have terminal degrees, 18% minority, 34% women. **Part-time faculty:** 83 total; 76% have terminal degrees, 7% minority, 32% women. **Class size:** 43% < 20, 39% 20-39, 4% 40-49, 7% 50-99, 7% >100. **Special facilities:** Museums, observatory, research nuclear reactor, Freedom of Information Center, Food for 21st Century program, engineering experiment station, center for research in social behavior, equine center, university research farms, child development laboratory, daily city newspaper production, nightly newscasts, Black culture center, medical research center, new recreation center, Life Sciences Center.

Freshman class profile. 12,404 applied, 10,262 admitted, 4,764 enrolled.

Mid 50% test scores			
SAT verbal:	540-660	Return as sophomores:	84%
SAT math:	540-650	Out-of-state:	21%
ACT:	23-28	Live on campus:	68%
Rank in top quarter:	57%	International:	1%
Rank in top tenth:	27%	Fraternities:	12%
		Sororities:	9%

Basis for selection. Admission based on required core courses and combination of high school rank and test scores. Individual programs may have additional requirements. Trial summer admission open to Missouri residents. Students must complete mathematics and English with C or better to continue enrollment on probation in fall. ACT is preferred.

High school preparation. 17 units required. Required units include English 4, mathematics 4, social studies 3, science 3 (laboratory 1), foreign language 2 and academic electives 1. Mathematics units must include algebra I and higher. 1fine arts unit required.

2005-2006 Annual costs. Tuition/fees: $7,745; $17,522 out-of-state. Room/board: $6,245. Books/supplies: $920. Personal expenses: $1,340.

2005-2006 Financial aid. **Need-based:** 3,303 full-time freshmen applied for aid; 2,072 were judged to have need; 2,058 of these received aid. Average need met was 89%. Average scholarship/grant was $6,005; average loan $3,609. 41% of total undergraduate aid awarded as scholarships/grants, 59% as loans/jobs. **Non-need-based:** Awarded to 5,974 full-time undergraduates, including 1,701 freshmen. Scholarships awarded for academics, alumni affiliation, art, athletics, leadership, minority status, music/drama, ROTC, state residency. **Additional information:** Scholarship available for international students based on success during 1st semester.

Application procedures. **Admission:** Priority date 5/1; no deadline. $35 fee, may be waived for applicants with need. Application may be submitted online. Admission notification on a rolling basis. Must reply by May 1 or within 4 week(s) if notified thereafter. **Financial aid:** Priority date 3/1; no closing date. FAFSA required. Applicants notified on a rolling basis starting 4/1; must reply within 4 week(s) of notification.

Academics. Pre-physical therapy and physical therapy programs open only to Missouri residents. Guaranteed admission to School of Law with ACT composite 30 or higher, and maintenance of 3.3 GPA. Early admission to School of Medicine with ACT composite 30 or higher, maintenance of 3.4 GPA, and required interview. Early admission to School of Nursing with 29 ACT composite and rank in top 10% of high school class. Project for Excellence in Teaching offered. **Special study options:** Accelerated study, combined bachelor's/graduate degree, cooperative education, cross-registration, distance learning, double major, dual enrollment of high school students, ESL, exchange student, external degree, honors, independent study, internships, student-designed major, study abroad, teacher certification program, Washington semester. Evening college. **Credit/placement by examination:** AP, CLEP, IB, institutional tests. Credit by examination policy varies by school/college. **Support services:** Learning center, pre-admission summer program, reduced course load, study skills assistance, tutoring, writing center.

Majors. Agriculture: General, animal sciences, business, communications, economics, food science, plant sciences, soil science. **Area/ethnic studies:** African-American, East Asian, European, Latin American, Russian/Slavic, South Asian, women's. **Biology:** General, biochemistry, conservation, microbiology. **Business:** General, accounting, banking/financial services, business admin, hotel/motel admin, international, marketing, real estate, restaurant/food services, travel services. **Communications:** General, advertising, broadcast journalism, journalism, photojournalism, radio/tv. **Computer sciences:** General, computer science. **Conservation:** Fisheries, forestry, wildlife. **Education:** General, agricultural, art, biology, business, chemistry, early childhood, elementary, English, foreign languages, mathematics, middle, multiple handicapped, music, physics, science, secondary, social studies, Spanish, voc/tech. **Engineering:** Agricultural, biomedical, chemical, civil, computer, electrical, industrial, mechanical. **English:** English lit. **Family/consumer sciences:** Clothing/textiles, family resources, family studies, food/nutrition, housing, human nutrition. **Foreign languages:** Classics, East Asian, French, German, linguistics, Russian, South Asian, Spanish. **Health:** Audiology/speech pathology, dietetics, health services admin, medical radiologic technology/radiation therapy, nuclear medical technology, nursing (RN), premedicine, prepharmacy, preveterinary, radiologic technology/medical imaging, respiratory therapy technology, sonography. **History:** General. **Interdisciplinary:** Behavioral sciences, nutrition sciences, peace/conflict. **Math:** General, statistics. **Military:** General. **Parks/recreation:** General, exercise sciences. **Philosophy/religion:** Philosophy, religion. **Physical sciences:** Atmospheric science, chemistry, geology, physics. **Psychology:** General. **Public administration:** Social work. **Social sciences:** Anthropology, archaeology, economics, geography, political science, sociology. **Visual/performing arts:** Art, dramatic.

Most popular majors. Business/marketing 18%, communications/journalism 12%, education 6%, engineering/engineering technologies 7%, family/consumer sciences 6%, health sciences 7%, social sciences 6%.

Computing on campus. 1,615 workstations in dormitories, library, computer center, student center. Dormitories wired for high-speed internet access and linked to campus network. Commuter students can connect to campus network. Online course registration, online library, helpline, repair service, student web hosting, wireless network available.

Student life. Freshman orientation: Available. Preregistration for classes offered. Nineteen 2-day sessions during summer; parents invited. **Policies:** Alcohol-free and smoke-free campus buildings, residence halls, and Greek housing. Freshmen permitted cars on campus. **Housing:** Guaranteed on-campus for freshmen. Coed dorms, single-sex dorms, apartments, fraternity/sorority housing, substance-free housing available. $300 fully refundable deposit, deadline 4/1. Specialized living/learning communities and freshman interest groups in residence halls for fine arts, French, Spanish, women in engineering, men in engineering, wellness and service, journalism, service learning, first-time college students, international studies, nursing, law, graduate/professional students. Freshmen required to live on campus. **Activities:** Bands, choral groups, dance, drama, film society, literary magazine, music ensembles, musical theater, opera, radio station, student government, student newspaper, symphony orchestra, TV station, Over 518 clubs available.

Athletics. NCAA. **Intercollegiate:** Baseball M, basketball, cross-country, diving, football (tackle) M, golf, gymnastics W, soccer W, softball W, swimming, tennis W, track and field, volleyball W, wrestling M. **Intramural:** Basketball, bowling, football (non-tackle), golf, soccer, softball, volleyball. **Team name:** Tigers.

Student services. Alcohol/substance abuse counseling, campus ministries, career counseling, services for economically disadvantaged, student employment services, financial aid counseling, health services, legal services, minority student services, on-campus daycare, personal counseling, placement for graduates, veterans' counselor, women's services. **Physically disabled:** Services for visually, speech, hearing impaired.

Contact. E-mail: mu4u@missouri.edu
Phone: (573) 882-7786 Toll-free number: (800) 225-6075
Fax: (573) 882-7887
Barbara Rupp, Director of Admissions, University of Missouri: Columbia, 230 Jesse Hall, Columbia, MO 65211

University of Missouri: Kansas City

Kansas City, Missouri **CB member**
www.umkc.edu **CB code: 6872**

- Public 4-year university
- Commuter campus in large city
- 7,070 degree-seeking undergraduates: 20% part-time, 59% women, 15% African American, 6% Asian American, 4% Hispanic American, 1% Native American, 3% international
- 4,634 degree-seeking graduate students
- 75% of applicants admitted
- SAT or ACT (ACT writing optional) required
- 45% graduate within 6 years

General. Founded in 1929. Regionally accredited. **Degrees:** 1,393 bachelor's awarded; master's, doctoral, first professional offered. **ROTC:** Army, Air Force. **Location:** 500 miles from Chicago, 250 miles from St. Louis. **Calendar:** Semester, extensive summer session. **Full-time faculty:** 641 total; 75% have terminal degrees, 17% minority, 41% women. **Part-time faculty:** 414 total; 31% have terminal degrees, 11% minority, 47% women. **Class size:** 53% < 20, 35% 20-39, 6% 40-49, 5% 50-99, 1% >100. **Special facilities:** Observatory, science and technology library, theater, music conservatory, miniature toy museum.

Freshman class profile. 3,018 applied, 2,254 admitted, 1,028 enrolled.

Mid 50% test scores		**Rank in top tenth:**	30%
SAT verbal:	510-650	**Return as sophomores:**	71%
SAT math:	500-700	**Out-of-state:**	20%
ACT:	21-27	**Live on campus:**	40%
GPA 3.50 or higher:	42%	**International:**	2%
GPA 3.0-3.49:	27%	**Fraternities:**	13%
GPA 2.0-2.99:	30%	**Sororities:**	20%
Rank in top quarter:	55%		

Basis for selection. Admission based on class rank, test scores, and high school course requirements. Admission is very selective to combined arts and sciences/medical, moderately selective to pharmacy program. Interview required for dentistry, medicine, and pharmacy applicants; audition required for dance and music applicants. Portfolio recommended. **Homeschooled:** Applicants submit a transcript of the home-school work as well as ACT or SAT score.

High school preparation. 17 units required. Required units include English 4, mathematics 4, social studies 3, science 3 (laboratory 1) and foreign language 2. 1 fine arts required.

2005-2006 Annual costs. Tuition/fees: $7,394; $17,171 out-of-state. Room/board: $6,670. Books/supplies: $946. Personal expenses: $3,640.

2005-2006 Financial aid. Need-based: 950 full-time freshmen applied for aid; 642 were judged to have need; 642 of these received aid. Average need met was 56%. Average scholarship/grant was $6,941; average loan $3,666. 32% of total undergraduate aid awarded as scholarships/grants, 68% as loans/jobs. **Non-need-based:** Awarded to 2,075 full-time undergraduates, including 616 freshmen. Scholarships awarded for academics, alumni affiliation, art, athletics, leadership, minority status, music/drama, state residency.

Application procedures. Admission: Priority date 4/1; no deadline. $35 fee, may be waived for applicants with need. Application may be submitted online. Admission notification on a rolling basis. Architecture, dentistry, medicine and pharmacy programs have separate application deadlines and specific admissions requirements. **Financial aid:** Priority date 3/1; no closing date. FAFSA required. Applicants notified on a rolling basis starting 4/1; must reply within 2 week(s) of notification.

Academics. Special study options: Accelerated study, combined bachelor's/graduate degree, cooperative education, distance learning, double major, dual enrollment of high school students, ESL, honors, independent study, internships, study abroad, teacher certification program. **Credit/placement by examination:** AP, CLEP, IB, institutional tests. 30 credit hours maximum toward bachelor's degree. **Support services:** Learning center, reduced course load, study skills assistance, tutoring, writing center.

Majors. **Architecture:** Urban/community planning. **Area/ethnic studies:** American. **Biology:** General. **Business:** General, accounting. **Communications:** General, journalism, media studies. **Computer sciences:** General, information systems. **Conservation:** Environmental studies. **Education:** General, elementary, middle, music, secondary. **Engineering:** Civil, electrical, mechanical. **English:** English lit. **Foreign languages:** French, German, Spanish. **Health:** Clinical lab science, dental hygiene, music therapy, nursing (RN). **History:** General. **Liberal arts:** Arts/sciences. **Math:** General, statistics. **Philosophy/religion:** Philosophy. **Physical sciences:** Chemistry, geology, physics. **Protective services:** Law enforcement admin. **Psychology:** General. **Social sciences:** Economics, geography, political science, sociology, urban studies. **Visual/performing arts:** Art, art history/conservation, dance, dramatic, jazz, music performance, music theory/composition, studio arts.

Most popular majors. Business/marketing 13%, education 9%, health sciences 7%, liberal arts 21%, psychology 6%, social sciences 7%, visual/performing arts 7%.

Computing on campus. 680 workstations in dormitories, library, computer center, student center. Dormitories wired for high-speed internet access and linked to campus network. Commuter students can connect to campus network. Online course registration, online library, helpline, student web hosting, wireless network available.

Student life. **Freshman orientation:** Mandatory, $40 fee. Preregistration for classes offered. Several 1-day orientations during summer. **Policies:** Freshmen permitted cars on campus. **Housing:** Coed dorms, fraternity/sorority housing, substance-free housing available. $300 partly refundable deposit, deadline 3/15. University owned houses are available. **Activities:** Bands, choral groups, dance, drama, literary magazine, music ensembles, opera, radio station, student government, student newspaper, symphony orchestra, over 200 religious, political, ethnic, and social service organizations.

Athletics. NCAA. **Intercollegiate:** Basketball, cheerleading, cross-country, golf, rifle, soccer M, softball W, tennis, track and field, volleyball W. **Intramural:** Badminton, basketball, football (tackle), golf, handball, racquetball, soccer, softball, squash, swimming, table tennis, tennis, track and field, volleyball, water polo, weight lifting. **Team name:** Roos.

Student services. Adult student services, alcohol/substance abuse counseling, campus ministries, career counseling, student employment services, financial aid counseling, health services, minority student services, on-campus daycare, personal counseling, placement for graduates, veterans' counselor, women's services. **Physically disabled:** Services for visually, speech, hearing impaired.

Contact. E-mail: admit@umkc.edu
Phone: (816) 235-1111 Toll-free number: (800) 775-8652
Fax: (816) 235-5544
Jennifer DeHaemers, Director of Admissions, University of Missouri: Kansas City, 5100 Rockhill Road, AC120, Kansas City, MO 64110-2499

University of Missouri: Rolla

Rolla, Missouri — **CB member**
www.umr.edu — **CB code: 6876**

- Public 4-year university and engineering college
- Residential campus in large town
- 4,220 degree-seeking undergraduates: 8% part-time, 22% women, 4% African American, 2% Asian American, 2% Hispanic American, 2% international
- 1,266 degree-seeking graduate students
- SAT or ACT (ACT writing optional) required
- 64% graduate within 6 years

General. Founded in 1870. Regionally accredited. **Degrees:** 731 bachelor's awarded; master's, doctoral offered. **ROTC:** Army, Navy, Air Force. **Location:** 90 miles from St. Louis, 100 miles from Springfield. **Calendar:** Semester, extensive summer session. **Full-time faculty:** 309 total; 92% have terminal degrees, 22% minority, 12% women. **Part-time faculty:** 91 total; 64% have terminal degrees, 4% minority, 23% women. **Class size:** 45% < 20, 41% 20-39, 8% 40-49, 6% 50-99, less than 1% >100. **Special facilities:** Computerized manufacturing system, nuclear reactor, observatory, experimental mine, museum of rocks, minerals, and gemstones, centers for environmental research, virtual reality laboratory, student design team center, wind tunnel.

Freshman class profile. 884 enrolled.

Mid 50% test scores			
SAT verbal:	540-660	Return as sophomores:	87%
SAT math:	590-690	Out-of-state:	21%
ACT:	24-30	Live on campus:	95%
Rank in top quarter:	71%	International:	2%
Rank in top tenth:	41%	Fraternities:	30%
		Sororities:	27%

Basis for selection. Admissions based on secondary school record, class rank, and standardized test scores. Recommendations considered. ACT or SAT score percentage, plus high school class rank percentile should equal 120 (minimum). Exceptions may be made on an individual basis. Campus visit and personal statement encouraged. **Homeschooled:** Transcript of courses and grades required. Must submit a standardized test score. **Learning Disabled:** Should submit voluntary declaration of disability to receive accommodation.

High school preparation. 17 units required. Required units include English 4, mathematics 4, social studies 3, science 3 (laboratory 1), foreign language 2 and academic electives 1. One fine arts required. Foreign language units must be in same language.

2005-2006 Annual costs. Tuition/fees: $7,536; $17,313 out-of-state. Room/board: $5,840. Books/supplies: $875. Personal expenses: $2,007.

2004-2005 Financial aid. **Need-based:** 720 full-time freshmen applied for aid; 510 were judged to have need; 500 of these received aid. Average need met was 87%. Average scholarship/grant was $6,700; average loan $2,970. 70% of total undergraduate aid awarded as scholarships/grants, 30% as loans/jobs. **Non-need-based:** Awarded to 1,760 full-time undergraduates, including 570 freshmen. Scholarships awarded for academics, alumni affiliation, athletics, job skills, leadership, minority status, music/drama, religious affiliation, ROTC, state residency.

Application procedures. **Admission:** Priority date 12/1; deadline 7/1 (postmark date). $35 fee, may be waived for applicants with need. Application may be submitted online. Admission notification on a rolling basis beginning on or about 10/1. Must reply by May 1 or within 3 week(s) if notified thereafter. **Financial aid:** Priority date 3/1; no closing date. FAFSA required. Applicants notified on a rolling basis; must reply within 3 week(s) of notification.

Academics. **Special study options:** Accelerated study, combined bachelor's/graduate degree, cooperative education, distance learning, double major, dual enrollment of high school students, ESL, honors, independent study, internships, liberal arts/career combination, student-designed major, study abroad, teacher certification program. **Credit/placement by examination:** AP, CLEP, IB, institutional tests. **Support services:** Learning center, pre-admission summer program, reduced course load, study skills assistance, tutoring, writing center.

Majors. **Biology:** General, biochemistry, biophysics. **Business:** General, business admin, management information systems. **Computer sciences:** General, computer science, information systems, information technology. **Engineering:** Aerospace, architectural, ceramic, chemical, civil, computer, electrical, environmental, geological, mechanical, mechanics, metallurgical, mining, nuclear, petroleum, polymer. **Engineering technology:** Industrial management. **English:** Technical writing. **Health:** Predentistry, premedicine. **History:** General. **Legal studies:** Prelaw. **Math:** Applied. **Philosophy/religion:** Philosophy. **Physical sciences:** Chemistry, geochemistry, geology, geophysics, physics. **Psychology:** General. **Social sciences:** Economics.

Most popular majors. Computer/information sciences 11%, engineering/engineering technologies 67%.

Computing on campus. 812 workstations in dormitories, library, computer center. Dormitories wired for high-speed internet access and linked to campus network. Commuter students can connect to campus network. Online course registration, online library, helpline, repair service, student web hosting, wireless network available.

Student life. **Freshman orientation:** Mandatory, $135 fee. Preregistration for classes offered. Program includes meetings with advisers and placement testing. **Policies:** Freshmen permitted cars on campus. **Housing:** Guaranteed on-campus for freshmen. Coed dorms, special housing for disabled, apartments, cooperative housing, fraternity/sorority housing, substance-free housing available. $160 deposit, deadline 6/1. Special accommodations for disabled students in co-ed dormitories. **Activities:** Bands, choral groups, dance, drama, literary magazine, music ensembles, musical theater, radio station, student government, student newspaper, symphony orchestra, Over 200 student groups avaliable.

Athletics. NCAA. **Intercollegiate:** Baseball M, basketball, cheerleading, cross-country, football (tackle) M, soccer, softball W, swimming M, track and field. **Intramural:** Badminton, basketball, bowling, cross-country, football (non-tackle), golf, racquetball, soccer, softball, swimming, table tennis, tennis, track and field, volleyball, weight lifting. **Team name:** Miners.

Student services. Adult student services, alcohol/substance abuse counseling, campus ministries, career counseling, student employment services, financial aid counseling, health services, legal services, minority student services, personal counseling, placement for graduates, women's services. **Physically disabled:** Services for visually, speech, hearing impaired. **Learning disabled:** Comprehensive services available.

Contact. E-mail: admissions@umr.edu
Phone: (573) 341-4164 Toll-free number: (800) 522-0938
Fax: (573) 341-4082
Lynn Stichnote, Director of Admissions, University of Missouri: Rolla, 106 Parker Hall, Rolla, MO 65409

University of Missouri: St. Louis

St. Louis, Missouri — **CB member**
www.umsl.edu — **CB code: 6889**

- Public 4-year university
- Commuter campus in very large city
- 9,150 degree-seeking undergraduates: 37% part-time, 59% women, 17% African American, 3% Asian American, 2% Hispanic American, 2% international
- 2,843 degree-seeking graduate students
- 52% of applicants admitted
- SAT or ACT (ACT writing optional) required
- 45% graduate within 6 years; 14% enter graduate study

General. Founded in 1963. Regionally accredited. **Degrees:** 1,902 bachelor's awarded; master's, doctoral, first professional offered. **ROTC:** Army, Air Force. **Location:** 7 miles from downtown. **Calendar:** Semester, extensive summer session. **Full-time faculty:** 371 total; 81% have terminal degrees, 24% minority, 46% women. **Part-time faculty:** 322 total; 27% have terminal degrees, 13% minority, 54% women. **Class size:** 43% < 20, 40% 20-39, 8% 40-49, 7% 50-99, 2% >100. **Special facilities:** Mercantile library, observatory, 3 art galleries, performing arts center.

Freshman class profile. 2,207 applied, 1,151 admitted, 532 enrolled.

Mid 50% test scores			
SAT verbal:	460-640	Rank in top tenth:	21%
SAT math:	490-610	Return as sophomores:	73%
ACT:	21-26	Out-of-state:	9%
Rank in top quarter:	50%	International:	4%

Basis for selection. Class rank, test scores and high school course requirements most important. Audition required for music majors; portfolio required for art majors. **Homeschooled:** ACT scores are key factor in determining admission. Students should strive for score of 24 or higher.

High school preparation. 17 units required. Required units include English 4, mathematics 4, social studies 3, science 3 (laboratory 1) and foreign language 2. 1 fine art required.

2005-2006 Annual costs. Tuition/fees: $7,618; $17,395 out-of-state. Room/board: $6,428. Books/supplies: $880.

2005-2006 Financial aid. Need-based: 340 full-time freshmen applied for aid; 263 were judged to have need; 259 of these received aid. Average need met was 64%. Average scholarship/grant was $5,836; average loan $2,595. 26% of total undergraduate aid awarded as scholarships/grants, 74% as loans/jobs. **Non-need-based:** Awarded to 814 full-time undergraduates, including 156 freshmen. Scholarships awarded for academics, alumni affiliation, art, athletics, music/drama, ROTC, state residency.

Application procedures. Admission: Closing date 8/25. $35 fee, may be waived for applicants with need. Application may be submitted online. Admission notification on a rolling basis beginning on or about 10/1. **Financial aid:** Priority date 4/1; no closing date. FAFSA required. Applicants notified on a rolling basis starting 4/1; must reply within 2 week(s) of notification.

Academics. Special study options: Accelerated study, cooperative education, cross-registration, distance learning, double major, dual enrollment of high school students, ESL, exchange student, honors, independent study, internships, liberal arts/career combination, student-designed major, study abroad, teacher certification program. **Credit/placement by examination:** AP, CLEP, IB, SAT, ACT, institutional tests. 30 credit hours maximum toward bachelor's degree. **Support services:** Learning center, study skills assistance, tutoring, writing center.

Honors college/program. Selection based on scores, class rank, extracurricular activities, test scores, 2 recommendations, essay, interview with Dean. Approximately 50 freshmen admitted each fall. Academic program includes honors classes.

Majors. Biology: General. **Business:** Accounting, business admin, finance, international, logistics, management information systems, marketing, operations, organizational behavior. **Communications:** General. **Computer sciences:** General. **Education:** General, early childhood, elementary, music, physical, secondary, special. **Engineering:** Civil, electrical, mechanical. **English:** English lit. **Foreign languages:** French, German, Spanish. **History:** General. **Liberal arts:** Arts/sciences. **Math:** General, applied. **Philosophy/religion:** Philosophy. **Physical sciences:** Chemistry, physics. **Psychology:** General. **Public administration:** General, social work. **Social sciences:** Anthropology, criminology, economics, political science, sociology. **Visual/performing arts:** Art history/conservation.

Most popular majors. Business/marketing 28%, communications/journalism 8%, education 15%, health sciences 8%, psychology 7%, social sciences 11%.

Computing on campus. 1,120 workstations in dormitories, library, computer center, student center. Dormitories wired for high-speed internet access and linked to campus network. Commuter students can connect to campus network. Online course registration, online library, helpline, student web hosting, wireless network available.

Student life. Freshman orientation: Available. Preregistration for classes offered. **Policies:** Freshmen permitted cars on campus. **Housing:** Guaranteed on-campus for all undergraduates. Coed dorms, special housing for disabled, apartments, fraternity/sorority housing, substance-free housing available. Housing available for students 21 and older in residence halls and condominiums. **Activities:** Bands, choral groups, dance, drama, film society, literary magazine, music ensembles, musical theater, opera, student government, student newspaper, Associated Black Collegians, international student organization, Spanish club, Alpha Phi Omega, Amnesty International, Pan-Hellenic Council, College Republicans, Catholic Students at Newman Center, Campus Crusade for Christ, life group.

Athletics. NCAA. **Intercollegiate:** Baseball M, basketball, golf, ice hockey M, soccer, softball W, tennis, volleyball W. **Intramural:** Badminton, basketball, bowling, cheerleading, cross-country, football (tackle), golf, racquetball, soccer, softball, swimming, table tennis, tennis, volleyball, weight lifting. **Team name:** Rivermen/Riverwomen.

Student services. Adult student services, alcohol/substance abuse counseling, campus ministries, career counseling, services for economically disadvantaged, student employment services, financial aid counseling, health services, minority student services, on-campus daycare, personal counseling, placement for graduates, veterans' counselor, women's services. **Physically disabled:** Services for visually, speech, hearing impaired.

Contact. E-mail: admissions@umsl.edu
Phone: (314) 516-5451 Toll-free number: (888) GO2-UMSL
Fax: (314) 516-5310
John Kundel, Associate Vice Provost, University of Missouri: St. Louis, One University Boulevard, St. Louis, MO 63121-4400

Washington University in St. Louis

St. Louis, Missouri — **CB member**
www.wustl.edu — **CB code: 6929**

- Private 4-year university
- Residential campus in large city
- 6,495 degree-seeking undergraduates: 6% part-time, 51% women, 9% African American, 10% Asian American, 3% Hispanic American, 4% international
- 5,708 degree-seeking graduate students
- 19% of applicants admitted
- SAT or ACT with writing, application essay required
- 91% graduate within 6 years

General. Founded in 1853. Regionally accredited. **Degrees:** 1,529 bachelor's awarded; master's, doctoral, first professional offered. **ROTC:** Army, Air Force. **Location:** 7 miles from downtown. **Calendar:** Semester, extensive summer session. **Full-time faculty:** 850 total; 99% have terminal degrees, 31% women. **Part-time faculty:** 231 total; 44% women. **Class size:** 73% < 20, 16% 20-39, 3% 40-49, 6% 50-99, 2% >100. **Special facilities:** Research center, 59-acre medical campus, observatory, plant growth facility, international writer's center, planetarium, business/economics experimental lab, lab science building, outdoor research center, theater.

Freshman class profile. 21,515 applied, 4,044 admitted, 1,388 enrolled.

Mid 50% test scores		Out-of-state:	90%
SAT verbal:	670-750	Live on campus:	99%
SAT math:	690-770	International:	5%
ACT:	30-33	Fraternities:	25%
Return as sophomores:	96%	Sororities:	25%

Basis for selection. Rigor of high school curriculum and academic performance, GPA, test scores, extracurricular activities, essay, and recommendations very important. Interview recommended. Counselor and teacher recommendations required of all applicants. Portfolio optional for students applying to the school of art and architecture. **Homeschooled:** Letter of recommendation (nonparent) required.

High school preparation. 20 units recommended. Recommended units include English 4, mathematics 4, social studies 4, history 4, science 4 (laboratory 4) and foreign language 2.

2006-2007 Annual costs. Tuition/fees: $33,788. Room/board: $10,452. Books/supplies: $1,100. Personal expenses: $1,770.

2005-2006 Financial aid. Need-based: 915 full-time freshmen applied for aid; 547 were judged to have need; 534 of these received aid. Average need met was 100%. Average scholarship/grant was $21,653; average loan $4,461. 78% of total undergraduate aid awarded as scholarships/grants, 22% as loans/jobs. **Non-need-based:** Awarded to 984 full-time undergraduates, including 306 freshmen. Scholarships awarded for academics, ROTC.

Application procedures. Admission: Closing date 1/15. $55 fee, may be waived for applicants with need. Application may be submitted online. Admission notification 4/1. Must reply by 5/1. **Financial aid:** Closing date 2/15. FAFSA, CSS PROFILE required. Applicants notified by 4/1; must reply by 5/1.

Academics. Special study options: Accelerated study, combined bachelor's/graduate degree, cooperative education, cross-registration, double major, dual enrollment of high school students, ESL, exchange student, independent study, internships, liberal arts/career combination, student-designed major, study abroad, teacher certification program, Washington semester. University Scholars Program. **Credit/placement by examination:** AP, CLEP, IB, institutional tests. **Support services:** Learning center, pre-admission summer program, reduced course load, study skills assistance, tutoring, writing center.

Majors. Architecture: Architecture, technology. **Area/ethnic studies:** African, African-American, American, Asian, East Asian, European, German, Latin American, Near/Middle Eastern, Russian/Slavic, women's. **Biology:** General, biochemistry, biophysics. **Business:** General, accounting, business admin, entrepreneurial studies, finance, human resources, international, international finance, managerial economics, marketing, operations. **Communications:** Advertising, journalism. **Computer sciences:** General, computer science, data processing, information systems. **Conservation:** General, environmental studies. **Education:** General, art, biology, chemistry, drama/dance, elementary, English, foundations, French, German, history, mathematics, middle, physics, science, secondary, social science, social studies, Spanish. **Engineering:** General, aerospace, biomedical, chemical, civil, computer, electrical, mechanical, science, systems. **Engineering technology:** Architectural, biomedical, civil. **English:** American lit, British lit, English lit. **Foreign languages:** General, ancient Greek, Arabic, Chinese, classics, comparative lit, French, German, Germanic, Hebrew, Italian, Japanese, Latin, Spanish. **Health:** Predentistry, premedicine, prepharmacy, preveterinary. **History:** General. **Interdisciplinary:** Ancient studies, biological/physical sciences, biopsychology, math/computer science, neuroscience, science/society, systems science. **Legal studies:** Prelaw. **Liberal arts:** Arts/sciences, humanities. **Math:** General, applied, statistics. **Philosophy/religion:** Islamic, Judaic, philosophy, religion. **Physical sciences:** Chemistry, geology, physics, planetary. **Psychology:** General. **Social sciences:** General, anthropology, archaeology, economics, international relations, political science. **Visual/performing arts:** General, art, art history/conservation, ceramics, commercial/advertising art, dance, design, dramatic, drawing, fashion design, film/cinema, graphic design, illustration, music history, music theory/composition, painting, photography, printmaking, sculpture, studio arts, theater history, voice/opera.

Most popular majors. Biology 8%, business/marketing 11%, computer/information sciences 6%, engineering/engineering technologies 14%, psychology 12%, social sciences 14%, visual/performing arts 9%.

Computing on campus. 2,500 workstations in dormitories, library, computer center, student center. Dormitories wired for high-speed internet access and linked to campus network. Commuter students can connect to campus network. Online course registration, online library, helpline, repair service, student web hosting, wireless network available.

Student life. Freshman orientation: Mandatory. Preregistration for classes offered. **Housing:** Guaranteed on-campus for freshmen. Coed dorms, apartments, cooperative housing, fraternity/sorority housing, substance-free housing available. $250 deposit, deadline 5/1. Special interest suites, single-sex floors in coed buildings, transfer housing, small group housing available. **Activities:** Bands, choral groups, dance, drama, film society, literary magazine, music ensembles, musical theater, opera, radio station, student government, student newspaper, symphony orchestra, TV station, approximately 200 clubs and organizations available.

Athletics. NCAA. **Intercollegiate:** Baseball M, basketball, cross-country, diving, football (tackle) M, soccer, softball W, swimming, tennis, track and field, volleyball W. **Intramural:** Badminton, basketball, bowling, cross-country, football (non-tackle), golf, racquetball, soccer, softball, swimming, table tennis, tennis, track and field, volleyball. **Team name:** Bears.

Student services. Adult student services, alcohol/substance abuse counseling, campus ministries, career counseling, student employment services, financial aid counseling, health services, minority student services, on-campus daycare, personal counseling, placement for graduates, veterans' counselor, women's services. **Physically disabled:** Services for visually, speech, hearing impaired.

Contact. E-mail: admissions@wustl.edu
Phone: (314) 935-6000 Toll-free number: (800) 638-0700
Fax: (314) 935-4290
Nanette Tarbouni, Director of Admissions, Washington University in St. Louis, Campus Box 1089, One Brookings Drive, St. Louis, MO 63130-4899

Webster University

St. Louis, Missouri — **CB member**
www.webster.edu — **CB code: 6933**

- Private 4-year university
- Commuter campus in large city
- 3,407 degree-seeking undergraduates: 26% part-time, 60% women, 12% African American, 1% Asian American, 2% Hispanic American, 3% international
- 3,652 degree-seeking graduate students
- 55% of applicants admitted
- SAT or ACT (ACT writing recommended), application essay required
- 57% graduate within 6 years; 10% enter graduate study

General. Founded in 1915. Regionally accredited. In addition to programs offered at its five St. Louis area campuses, Webster University offers undergraduate degrees at extended campus locations in California and Florida as well as its international campuses in Vienna, Austria; Leiden, The Netherlands; Geneva, Switzerland; Cha-am, Thailand; and London, England. **Degrees:** 839 bachelor's awarded; master's, doctoral offered. **ROTC:** Army, Air Force. **Location:** 12 miles from St. Louis. **Calendar:** Semester, limited summer session. **Full-time faculty:** 172 total; 80% have terminal degrees, 8% minority, 43% women. **Part-time faculty:** 635 total; 28% have terminal degrees, 8% minority, 43% women. **Class size:** 84% < 20, 13% 20-39, less than 1% 40-49. **Special facilities:** Performing arts theater.

Freshman class profile. 1,468 applied, 807 admitted, 804 enrolled.

Mid 50% test scores		End year in good standing:	95%
SAT verbal:	530-620	Return as sophomores:	81%
SAT math:	500-620	Out-of-state:	33%
ACT:	21-27	Live on campus:	45%
Rank in top quarter:	48%	International:	5%
Rank in top tenth:	23%		

Basis for selection. School achievement record, test scores important. Rank in top half of class recommended. Recommendation, essay, resume of activities required. Interview recommended for all students. Audition required for dance, music, music theater, and theater students; portfolio required for art and film students. **Homeschooled:** Transcripts, ACT or SATscores, recommendations from community leader or employer must be submitted.

High school preparation. 19 units recommended. Recommended units include English 4, mathematics 3, social studies 3, science 3 (laboratory 2), foreign language 2 and academic electives 4. 1 unit fine arts also recommended.

2005-2006 Annual costs. Tuition/fees: $17,210. Tuition $20,390 for theater conservatory students. Room/board: $7,070. Books/supplies: $1,000. Personal expenses: $1,500.

2004-2005 Financial aid. Need-based: 408 full-time freshmen applied for aid; 332 were judged to have need; 332 of these received aid. Average

scholarship/grant was $4,866; average loan $2,525. 56% of total undergraduate aid awarded as scholarships/grants, 44% as loans/jobs. **Non-need-based:** Awarded to 1,596 full-time undergraduates, including 392 freshmen. Scholarships awarded for academics, art, music/drama.

Application procedures. Admission: Priority date 3/1; deadline 6/1. $25 fee, may be waived for applicants with need. Application must be submitted on paper. Admission notification on a rolling basis beginning on or about 9/1. Must reply by May 1 or within 4 week(s) if notified thereafter. **Financial aid:** Priority date 4/1; no closing date. FAFSA, institutional form required. Applicants notified on a rolling basis starting 2/9; must reply within 2 week(s) of notification.

Academics. Professional Actors Equity theater company in residence for theater program. Internships and practicums available in most areas. **Special study options:** Accelerated study, combined bachelor's/graduate degree, cooperative education, cross-registration, distance learning, double major, dual enrollment of high school students, ESL, exchange student, independent study, internships, liberal arts/career combination, student-designed major, study abroad, teacher certification program. Certificate programs and combination bachelor's/master's degree in many subject areas, student leadership development program, individualized majors. **Credit/placement by examination:** AP, CLEP, IB. 64 credit hours maximum toward bachelor's degree. **Support services:** Learning center, reduced course load, remedial instruction, study skills assistance, tutoring, writing center.

Majors. Area/ethnic studies: American. **Biology:** General. **Business:** General, accounting, accounting/finance, business admin, finance, international, managerial economics, marketing. **Communications:** General, advertising, broadcast journalism, digital media, journalism, public relations. **Computer sciences:** Computer science. **Education:** General, music. **English:** English lit. **Foreign languages:** General, French, German, Spanish. **Health:** Nursing (RN). **History:** General. **Legal studies:** General, paralegal. **Liberal arts:** Arts/sciences, humanities. **Math:** General. **Philosophy/religion:** Ethics, philosophy, religion. **Psychology:** General. **Social sciences:** General, anthropology, economics, international relations, political science, sociology. **Visual/performing arts:** Acting, art, art history/conservation, cinematography, dance, directing/producing, dramatic, film/cinema, music theory/composition, photography, studio arts, theater design.

Most popular majors. Business/marketing 34%, communications/journalism 13%, computer/information sciences 9%, social sciences 6%, visual/performing arts 11%.

Computing on campus. 453 workstations in dormitories, library, computer center, student center. Dormitories wired for high-speed internet access and linked to campus network. Online course registration, online library, helpline, student web hosting, wireless network available.

Student life. Freshman orientation: Available. **Policies:** Freshmen permitted cars on campus. **Housing:** Guaranteed on-campus for freshmen. Coed dorms, apartments available. $150 deposit, deadline 4/1. **Activities:** Jazz band, choral groups, dance, drama, film society, literary magazine, music ensembles, musical theater, opera, radio station, student government, student newspaper, symphony orchestra, TV station, animal rights network, Baptist Student Union, Campus Crusade for Christ, colleges against cancer, Habitat for Humanity, international student association, Muslim student association, peer education zeitgeist, Rock the Vote, Webster pride association.

Athletics. NCAA. **Intercollegiate:** Baseball M, basketball, cross-country W, golf M, soccer, softball W, swimming, tennis, volleyball W. **Intramural:** Bowling, soccer, table tennis, volleyball M. **Team name:** Gorloks.

Student services. Alcohol/substance abuse counseling, campus ministries, career counseling, student employment services, financial aid counseling, health services, minority student services, personal counseling, placement for graduates, women's services. **Physically disabled:** Services for visually, speech, hearing impaired.

Contact. E-mail: admit@webster.edu
Phone: (314) 968-6991 Toll-free number: (800) 753-6765
Fax: (314) 968-7115
Niel DeVasto, Director of Undergraduate Admissions, Webster University, 470 East Lockwood Avenue, St. Louis, MO 63119-3194

Westminster College

Fulton, Missouri — **CB member**
www.westminster-mo.edu — **CB code: 6937**

- Private 4-year liberal arts college affiliated with Presbyterian Church (USA)
- Residential campus in large town
- 891 degree-seeking undergraduates: 42% women, 4% African American, 1% Asian American, 2% Hispanic American, 2% Native American, 9% international
- 79% of applicants admitted
- SAT or ACT (ACT writing optional) required
- 61% graduate within 6 years; 24% enter graduate study

General. Founded in 1851. Regionally accredited. **Degrees:** 158 bachelor's awarded. **ROTC:** Army, Navy, Air Force. **Location:** 100 miles from St. Louis, 22 miles from Columbia. **Calendar:** Semester, limited summer session. **Full-time faculty:** 58 total; 72% have terminal degrees, 10% minority, 36% women. **Part-time faculty:** 24 total; 33% have terminal degrees, 4% minority, 38% women. **Class size:** 54% < 20, 46% 20-39. **Special facilities:** Winston Churchill Memorial and Library, 12th century church built by Christopher Wren in London was moved and re-built on the Westminster College campus.

Freshman class profile. 1,155 applied, 908 admitted, 270 enrolled.

Mid 50% test scores		Rank in top tenth:	14%
SAT verbal:	460-600	End year in good standing:	73%
SAT math:	490-630	Return as sophomores:	75%
ACT:	22-27	Out-of-state:	28%
GPA 3.50 or higher:	52%	Live on campus:	97%
GPA 3.0-3.49:	31%	International:	14%
GPA 2.0-2.99:	17%	Fraternities:	60%
Rank in top quarter:	35%	Sororities:	40%

Basis for selection. High school achievement (including class rank, involvement, ACT scores, curriculum, GPA) and recommendations most important. Interview recommended for borderline students, required for students with learning disabilities. **Learning Disabled:** Direct application to LD program; interview required.

High school preparation. 16 units required. Required and recommended units include English 4, mathematics 3, social studies 2, science 2 (laboratory 2), foreign language 2 and academic electives 2. Pre-med and pre-dental students should have at least 3 lab science, 1 advanced math.

2006-2007 Annual costs. Tuition/fees (projected): $15,030. Room/board: $6,140. Books/supplies: $800.

2005-2006 Financial aid. Need-based: 235 full-time freshmen applied for aid; 183 were judged to have need; 183 of these received aid. Average need met was 87%. Average scholarship/grant was $10,896; average loan $3,358. 86% of total undergraduate aid awarded as scholarships/grants, 14% as loans/jobs. **Non-need-based:** Awarded to 360 full-time undergraduates, including 132 freshmen. Scholarships awarded for academics, alumni affiliation, leadership, minority status, music/drama, state residency.

Application procedures. Admission: Priority date 2/1; no deadline. No application fee. Application may be submitted online. Admission notification on a rolling basis beginning on or about 10/1. Must reply by May 1 or within 3 week(s) if notified thereafter. Learning Disabilities Program applicants must have completed applications credentials and personal interview prior to April 1, including untimed SAT or ACT results. **Financial aid:** Priority date 2/15; no closing date. FAFSA required. Applicants notified on a rolling basis starting 2/28; must reply within 3 week(s) of notification.

Academics. First-year seminar fosters communication, critical thinking and study skills. **Special study options:** Combined bachelor's/graduate degree, cooperative education, cross-registration, double major, dual enrollment of high school students, exchange student, honors, independent study, internships, liberal arts/career combination, New York semester, student-designed major, study abroad, teacher certification program, urban semester, Washington semester. **Credit/placement by examination:** AP, CLEP, IB, institutional tests. 30 credit hours maximum toward bachelor's degree. **Support services:** Learning center, reduced course load, remedial instruction, study skills assistance, tutoring, writing center.

Majors. Biology: General. **Business:** Accounting, business admin, management information systems. **Communications:** Advertising, journalism, media studies. **Computer sciences:** General. **Conservation:** General, environmental science, environmental studies. **Education:** Elementary, middle, physical, secondary. **English:** English lit. **Foreign languages:** French, Spanish. **Health:** Athletic training. **History:** General. **Math:** General. **Philosophy/religion:** Philosophy, religion. **Physical sciences:** Chemistry, physics. **Psychology:** General. **Social sciences:** Anthropology, economics, international relations, political science, sociology.

Most popular majors. Biology 8%, business/marketing 25%, computer/information sciences 9%, education 11%, psychology 8%, social sciences 6%.

Computing on campus. 200 workstations in library, computer center. Dormitories wired for high-speed internet access and linked to campus network. Commuter students can connect to campus network. Online course registration, online library, helpline, student web hosting, wireless network available.

Student life. **Freshman orientation:** Mandatory. Preregistration for classes offered. Held three days before classes start. **Policies:** Freshmen permitted cars on campus. **Housing:** Guaranteed on-campus for freshmen. Coed dorms, single-sex dorms, apartments, fraternity/sorority housing available. **Activities:** Jazz band, choral groups, dance, drama, literary magazine, music ensembles, musical theater, student government, student newspaper, Young Democrats, Young Republicans, Big Brother-Big Sister program, Model United Nations, Environmentally Concerned Students, Chapel Leadership Council, Habitat For Humanity, International Club, Fellowship of Christian Athletes.

Athletics. NCAA. **Intercollegiate:** Baseball M, basketball, cross-country W, football (tackle) M, golf, soccer, softball W, tennis, volleyball W. **Intramural:** Basketball, softball, volleyball. **Team name:** Blue Jays.

Student services. Alcohol/substance abuse counseling, campus ministries, career counseling, student employment services, financial aid counseling, health services, minority student services, personal counseling, placement for graduates, women's services. **Learning disabled:** Comprehensive services available.

Contact. E-mail: admissions@westminster-mo.edu
Phone: (573) 592-5251 Toll-free number: (800) 475-3361
Fax: (573) 592-5255
Patrick Kirby, Vice President and Dean of Enrollment Services, Westminster College, 501 Westminster Avenue, Fulton, MO 65251-1299

William Jewell College

Liberty, Missouri — **CB member**
www.jewell.edu — **CB code: 6941**

- Private 4-year liberal arts college affiliated with Baptist faith
- Residential campus in large town
- 1,331 degree-seeking undergraduates: 3% part-time, 59% women
- 64% of applicants admitted
- SAT or ACT (ACT writing recommended) required

General. Founded in 1849. Regionally accredited. Campus in Harlaxton, England. **Degrees:** 291 bachelor's awarded. **Location:** 14 miles from downtown Kansas City. **Calendar:** Semester, limited summer session. **Full-time faculty:** 76 total; 86% have terminal degrees, 5% minority, 51% women. **Part-time faculty:** 79 total; 47% women. **Class size:** 74% < 20, 24% 20-39, 1% 40-49, 1% 50-99. **Special facilities:** Observatory.

Freshman class profile. 1,681 applied, 1,084 admitted, 304 enrolled.

Mid 50% test scores			
SAT verbal:	490-630	Rank in top quarter:	65%
SAT math:	480-650	Rank in top tenth:	33%
ACT:	23-28	Return as sophomores:	81%
GPA 3.50 or higher:	70%	Live on campus:	79%
GPA 3.0-3.49:	21%	Fraternities:	40%
GPA 2.0-2.99:	9%	Sororities:	30%

Basis for selection. Admissions based on secondary school record. Class rank, standardized test scores, and essay also important. Audition required for music and theater students.

High school preparation. Recommended units include English 4, mathematics 3, social studies 3, science 3 (laboratory 1), foreign language 2 and academic electives 4. One fine arts recommended.

2005-2006 Annual costs. Tuition/fees: $18,500. Room/board: $5,350. Books/supplies: $650. Personal expenses: $1,800.

2005-2006 Financial aid. **Need-based:** 249 full-time freshmen applied for aid; 170 were judged to have need; 170 of these received aid. Average scholarship/grant was $12,773; average loan $3,777. 58% of total undergraduate aid awarded as scholarships/grants, 42% as loans/jobs. **Non-need-based:** Awarded to 743 full-time undergraduates, including 193 freshmen. Scholarships awarded for academics, alumni affiliation, art, athletics, job skills, music/drama, religious affiliation.

Application procedures. **Admission:** Priority date 12/1; deadline 8/15. $25 fee, may be waived for applicants with need. Admission notification on a rolling basis beginning on or about 9/1. Must reply by May 1 or within 2 week(s) if notified thereafter. **Financial aid:** Priority date 3/1; no closing date. FAFSA required. Applicants notified on a rolling basis starting 1/31.

Academics. Interdisciplinary core curriculum required. **Special study options:** Accelerated study, cooperative education, double major, dual enrollment of high school students, honors, independent study, internships, liberal arts/career combination, student-designed major, study abroad, teacher certification program, weekend college. Pryor Leadership Studies. **Credit/placement by examination:** AP, CLEP, IB, SAT, ACT, institutional tests. No limit to credit by examination, but student must complete 30 hours in residence. **Support services:** Study skills assistance, tutoring, writing center.

Honors college/program. Oxbridge Honors Program allows students to study their major subject using tutorial mode of instruction used at Oxford and Cambridge. Minimum 3.8 GPA, ACT score of 28 required for admission.

Majors. **Area/ethnic studies:** Japanese. **Biology:** General, biochemistry, molecular. **Business:** Accounting, business admin, international, managerial economics. **Communications:** General, broadcast journalism, organizational, radio/tv. **Computer sciences:** General, computer science, information systems. **Education:** Elementary, music. **English:** English lit, speech/rhetoric. **Foreign languages:** French, Spanish. **Health:** Clinical lab science, nursing (RN). **History:** General. **Interdisciplinary:** Math/computer science. **Math:** General. **Philosophy/religion:** Philosophy, religion. **Physical sciences:** Chemistry, physics. **Psychology:** General. **Social sciences:** International relations, political science. **Theology:** Sacred music. **Visual/performing arts:** Art, dramatic, music performance, music theory/composition.

Most popular majors. Biology 6%, business/marketing 25%, communications/journalism 6%, education 7%, health sciences 18%, history 6%, psychology 9%, visual/performing arts 6%.

Computing on campus. 120 workstations in library, computer center. Dormitories wired for high-speed internet access and linked to campus network. Commuter students can connect to campus network. Student web hosting available.

Student life. **Freshman orientation:** Mandatory. Preregistration for classes offered. **Policies:** Freshmen permitted cars on campus. **Housing:** Guaranteed on-campus for all undergraduates. Coed dorms, single-sex dorms, special housing for disabled, fraternity/sorority housing available. $100 nonrefundable deposit, deadline 5/1. Off-campus houses utilized as residence halls available. **Activities:** Bands, choral groups, dance, drama, music ensembles, musical theater, opera, radio station, student government, student newspaper, symphony orchestra, Young Democrats, College Republicans, Christian Student Ministries, UNITY, Amnesty International, Fellowship of Christian Athletes.

Athletics. NAIA. **Intercollegiate:** Baseball M, basketball, cheerleading, cross-country, football (tackle) M, golf, soccer, softball W, tennis, track and field, volleyball W. **Intramural:** Basketball, football (non-tackle), golf, racquetball, soccer, softball, tennis, volleyball. **Team name:** Cardinals.

Student services. Adult student services, campus ministries, career counseling, student employment services, financial aid counseling, health services, personal counseling, placement for graduates.

Contact. E-mail: admission@william.jewell.edu
Phone: (816) 781-7700 ext. 5137 Toll-free number: (800) 753-7009
Fax: (816) 415-5040
Dean of Enrollment Development, William Jewell College, 500 College Hill, Liberty, MO 64068

William Woods University

Fulton, Missouri — **CB member**
www.williamwoods.edu — **CB code: 6944**

- Private 4-year university and liberal arts college affiliated with Christian Church (Disciples of Christ)
- Residential campus in large town
- 1,118 degree-seeking undergraduates: 28% part-time, 75% women, 3% African American, 2% Hispanic American, 1% Native American, 4% international
- 1,874 degree-seeking graduate students
- 68% of applicants admitted
- SAT or ACT (ACT writing optional) required
- 48% graduate within 6 years

General. Founded in 1870. Regionally accredited. Students may enroll in courses offered at 4 other mid-Missouri colleges and universities. Qualified students may complete bachelor's degree in 3 years through Century Scholars program. **Degrees:** 272 bachelor's, 14 associate awarded; master's offered. **ROTC:** Army, Navy, Air Force. **Location:** 100 miles from St. Louis, 30 miles from Columbia. **Calendar:** Semester, limited summer session. **Full-time faculty:** 50 total; 50% have terminal degrees, 4% minority, 52% women. **Part-time faculty:** 64 total; 2% have terminal degrees, 11% minority, 58%

women. **Class size:** 81% < 20, 18% 20-39, less than 1% 40-49, less than 1% 50-99. **Special facilities:** Equestrian studies facilities, observatory, broadcasting laboratory, computer laboratories, model courtroom, ASL interpreting laboratories.

Freshman class profile. 792 applied, 540 admitted, 258 enrolled.

Mid 50% test scores		**Rank in top tenth:**	15%
SAT verbal:	460-580	**Return as sophomores:**	76%
SAT math:	420-570	**Out-of-state:**	37%
ACT:	19-25	**Live on campus:**	78%
GPA 3.50 or higher:	43%	**International:**	8%
GPA 3.0-3.49:	31%	**Fraternities:**	29%
GPA 2.0-2.99:	26%	**Sororities:**	43%
Rank in top quarter:	40%		

Basis for selection. Secondary school record, class rank, test scores most important; extracurricular activities, 2 academic references also important; interview considered. Interview recommended for all students. Audition required for performing arts students; portfolio required for visual arts students. **Homeschooled:** Letter of recommendation (nonparent) required. GED required; ACT/SAT should be submitted.

High school preparation. 16 units required; 20 recommended. Required and recommended units include English 4, mathematics 3, social studies 2, history 3, science 3 (laboratory 3) and foreign language 2.

2005-2006 Annual costs. Tuition/fees: $15,070. Commuter students pay additional $50 fee per year. Room/board: $5,900. Books/supplies: $1,000. Personal expenses: $2,700.

2005-2006 Financial aid. Need-based: 194 full-time freshmen applied for aid; 142 were judged to have need; 142 of these received aid. Average need met was 77%. Average scholarship/grant was $9,626; average loan $3,035. 62% of total undergraduate aid awarded as scholarships/grants, 38% as loans/jobs. **Non-need-based:** Awarded to 389 full-time undergraduates, including 122 freshmen. Scholarships awarded for academics, alumni affiliation, art, athletics, leadership, music/drama, religious affiliation.

Application procedures. Admission: Priority date 3/1; no deadline. $25 fee, may be waived for applicants with need. Application may be submitted online. Admission notification on a rolling basis. Must reply by May 1 or within 3 week(s) if notified thereafter. **Financial aid:** Priority date 3/1; no closing date. FAFSA, institutional form required. Applicants notified on a rolling basis starting 3/15; must reply within 2 week(s) of notification.

Academics. ASL interpreting available. **Special study options:** Accelerated study, combined bachelor's/graduate degree, cross-registration, double major, dual enrollment of high school students, honors, independent study, internships, liberal arts/career combination, New York semester, student-designed major, study abroad, teacher certification program, Washington semester. Hollywood semester. **Credit/placement by examination:** AP, CLEP, IB, SAT, ACT, institutional tests. 30 credit hours maximum toward bachelor's degree. **Support services:** Reduced course load, study skills assistance, tutoring, writing center.

Majors. Agriculture: Equestrian studies. **Biology:** General. **Business:** Accounting, business admin, international, management information systems, managerial economics. **Communications:** General, advertising, broadcast journalism, journalism, public relations. **Computer sciences:** General. **Education:** General, art, elementary, English, mathematics, middle, physical, science, secondary, social science, special. **English:** Composition. **Foreign languages:** American Sign Language, Spanish. **Health:** Athletic training. **History:** General. **Legal studies:** General, paralegal. **Math:** General. **Parks/recreation:** Sports admin. **Psychology:** General. **Public administration:** Social work. **Social sciences:** Political science. **Visual/performing arts:** Art, design, dramatic, graphic design, studio arts.

Most popular majors. Agriculture 11%, business/marketing 45%, computer/information sciences 12%, education 8%, visual/performing arts 6%.

Computing on campus. 135 workstations in dormitories, library, computer center, student center. Dormitories wired for high-speed internet access and linked to campus network. Online course registration, online library, helpline, repair service, wireless network available.

Student life. Freshman orientation: Mandatory. Preregistration for classes offered. 7 days prior to start of fall term. **Policies:** Students under age 23 must reside on campus unless married or living with parent or guardian. Freshmen permitted cars on campus. **Housing:** Guaranteed on-campus for all undergraduates. Coed dorms, single-sex dorms, special housing for disabled, apartments, fraternity/sorority housing, substance-free housing available. $250 deposit. No-smoking halls, senior housing, single rooms, independent housing, upper-class halls and apartments available. **Activities:** Choral groups, dance, drama, literary magazine, musical theater, radio station, student government, student newspaper, Big Brothers/Big Sisters, campus activities board, Association of Christian Ecumenical Students, community action network, international club, Jesters, Students for Social Work, departmental clubs.

Athletics. NAIA. **Intercollegiate:** Baseball M, basketball W, cross-country, golf, soccer, softball W, track and field, volleyball. **Intramural:** Badminton, baseball M, basketball, equestrian, football (non-tackle), softball, table tennis, tennis, volleyball, weight lifting. **Team name:** Owls.

Student services. Adult student services, alcohol/substance abuse counseling, campus ministries, career counseling, financial aid counseling, health services, personal counseling. **Physically disabled:** Services for visually, speech, hearing impaired.

Contact. E-mail: admissions@williamwoods.edu
Phone: (573) 592-4221 Toll-free number: (800) 995-3159
Fax: (573) 592-1146
Jimmy Clay, Executive Director of Enrollment Services, William Woods University, One University Avenue, Fulton, MO 65251-2388

Montana

Carroll College

Helena, Montana **CB member**
www.carroll.edu **CB code: 4041**

- Private 4-year liberal arts college affiliated with Roman Catholic Church
- Residential campus in large town
- 1,317 degree-seeking undergraduates: 7% part-time, 57% women, 1% Asian American, 1% Hispanic American, 1% Native American, 1% international
- 79% of applicants admitted
- SAT or ACT required
- 61% graduate within 6 years

General. Founded in 1909. Regionally accredited. **Degrees:** 229 bachelor's, 1 associate awarded. **ROTC:** Army. **Location:** 90 miles from Great Falls, 240 miles from Billings. **Calendar:** Semester, limited summer session. **Full-time faculty:** 80 total; 70% have terminal degrees, 2% minority, 36% women. **Part-time faculty:** 54 total; 13% have terminal degrees, 2% minority, 46% women. **Class size:** 62% < 20, 33% 20-39, 4% 40-49, 1% 50-99, less than 1% >100. **Special facilities:** Observatory, seismograph station, engineering lab, nursing lab.

Freshman class profile. 1,048 applied, 827 admitted, 304 enrolled.

Mid 50% test scores		**GPA 2.0-2.99:**	20%
SAT verbal:	480-590	**Rank in top quarter:**	44%
SAT math:	480-600	**Rank in top tenth:**	22%
ACT:	21-26	**Return as sophomores:**	79%
GPA 3.50 or higher:	48%	**Out-of-state:**	45%
GPA 3.0-3.49:	31%	**Live on campus:**	92%

Basis for selection. School achievement record, test scores, recommendations most important. SAT Subject Tests required of home schooled and nonaccredited high school graduates. Personal statement required. Interview recommended for academically weak students.

High school preparation. College-preparatory program recommended. 17 units recommended. Recommended units include English 4, mathematics 3, social studies 1, history 2, science 2 (laboratory 1), foreign language 2 and academic electives 2. 1 technology unit recommended.

2005-2006 Annual costs. Tuition/fees: $17,078. Room/board: $6,246. Books/supplies: $700. Personal expenses: $1,600.

2005-2006 Financial aid. Need-based: 300 full-time freshmen applied for aid; 203 were judged to have need; 203 of these received aid. Average need met was 81%. Average scholarship/grant was $9,394; average loan $4,617. 63% of total undergraduate aid awarded as scholarships/grants, 37% as loans/jobs. **Non-need-based:** Awarded to 539 full-time undergraduates, including 140 freshmen. Scholarships awarded for academics, athletics, leadership, music/drama, religious affiliation, ROTC.

Application procedures. Admission: Priority date 3/1; deadline 6/1 (receipt date). $35 fee. Application may be submitted online. Admission notification on a rolling basis beginning on or about 9/1. Must reply by May 1 or within 2 week(s) if notified thereafter. **Financial aid:** Priority date 3/1; no closing date. FAFSA required. Applicants notified on a rolling basis starting 3/1; must reply within 4 week(s) of notification.

Academics. Special study options: Accelerated study, cooperative education, double major, dual enrollment of high school students, ESL, exchange student, honors, independent study, internships, liberal arts/career combination, student-designed major, study abroad, teacher certification program. 3-2 engineering program with Notre Dame, Columbia University (NY), USC, Gonzaga University (WA), Montana State University-Bozeman, Montana Tech; complete Civil Engineering program ABATE. **Credit/placement by examination:** AP, CLEP, IB, institutional tests. 9 credit hours maximum toward associate degree, 18 toward bachelor's. **Support services:** Learning center, pre-admission summer program, reduced course load, study skills assistance, tutoring, writing center.

Majors. Biology: General. **Business:** Accounting, business admin, finance, managerial economics. **Communications:** General, public relations. **Conservation:** Environmental studies. **Education:** Elementary, ESL, physical, secondary. **Engineering:** Civil, software. **English:** Creative writing. **Foreign languages:** Biblical, French, Spanish. **Health:** Nursing (RN), predentistry, premedicine, prepharmacy, preveterinary. **History:** General. **Interdisciplinary:** Biological/physical sciences. **Math:** General. **Parks/recreation:** Health/fitness, sports admin. **Philosophy/religion:** Philosophy. **Physical sciences:** Chemistry, physics. **Psychology:** General. **Public administration:** General. **Social sciences:** General, international relations, political science, sociology. **Theology:** Pastoral counseling. **Visual/performing arts:** Dramatic.

Most popular majors. Biology 10%, business/marketing 21%, education 14%, health sciences 9%, psychology 8%, social sciences 10%.

Computing on campus. 85 workstations in dormitories, library, computer center, student center. Dormitories wired for high-speed internet access and linked to campus network. Online course registration, helpline available.

Student life. Freshman orientation: Mandatory, $100 fee. Preregistration for classes offered. 4-day program. Fee includes cost of meals, entertainment, and various activities. **Policies:** Freshmen and sophomores required to live on campus. Freshmen permitted cars on campus. **Housing:** Guaranteed on-campus for freshmen. Coed dorms, single-sex dorms, apartments, substance-free housing available. $100 partly refundable deposit, deadline 7/1. **Activities:** Pep band, choral groups, dance, drama, literary magazine, music ensembles, musical theater, radio station, student government, student newspaper, symphony orchestra, College Democrats, Circle K, cultural exchange club, Into the Streets service organization, peer mentors, social work club, sociology club, student community outreach experience, Young Republicans.

Athletics. NAIA. **Intercollegiate:** Basketball, football (tackle) M, golf, soccer W, swimming, volleyball W. **Intramural:** Badminton, basketball, bowling, cross-country, golf, handball, racquetball, skiing, soccer, softball, swimming, table tennis, volleyball, water polo. **Team name:** Saints.

Student services. Adult student services, alcohol/substance abuse counseling, campus ministries, career counseling, student employment services, financial aid counseling, health services, personal counseling, placement for graduates, veterans' counselor.

Contact. E-mail: enroll@carroll.edu
Phone: (406) 447-4384 Toll-free number: (800) 992-3648
Fax: (406) 447-4533
Cynthia Thornquist, Director of Admissions and Enrollment, Carroll College, 1601 North Benton Avenue, Helena, MT 59625

Montana State University: Billings

Billings, Montana **CB member**
www.msubillings.edu **CB code: 4298**

- Public 4-year university and technical college
- Commuter campus in small city
- 4,337 degree-seeking undergraduates: 27% part-time, 64% women, 1% African American, 1% Asian American, 3% Hispanic American, 5% Native American, 1% international
- 361 degree-seeking graduate students
- 96% of applicants admitted
- SAT or ACT (ACT writing recommended) required

General. Founded in 1927. Regionally accredited. College of Technology offers training and retraining for employment by combining academics and vocational opportunities. **Degrees:** 525 bachelor's, 162 associate awarded; master's offered. **Location:** 224 miles from Helena, 560 miles from Denver. **Calendar:** Semester, limited summer session. **Full-time faculty:** 156 total; 83% have terminal degrees, 2% minority, 40% women. **Part-time faculty:** 101 total; 2% minority, 54% women. **Class size:** 47% < 20, 43% 20-39, 4% 40-49, 4% 50-99, less than 1% >100. **Special facilities:** Biological station, center for business enterprise, Montana Center for Disabilities, special education learning center, center for gerontological studies, small business institute, urban institute, public radio, center for applied economic research.

Freshman class profile. 949 applied, 911 admitted, 602 enrolled.

Mid 50% test scores		**Rank in top quarter:**	30%
SAT verbal:	450-550	**Rank in top tenth:**	10%
SAT math:	460-570	**End year in good standing:**	59%
ACT:	19-23	**Return as sophomores:**	63%
GPA 3.50 or higher:	30%	**Out-of-state:**	7%
GPA 3.0-3.49:	34%	**Live on campus:**	27%
GPA 2.0-2.99:	33%	**International:**	1%

Basis for selection. Applicants out of high school within the last 3 years must meet one of the following requirements: (1) minimum GPA of 2.5, or

(2) composite score of 22 on ACT or 1030 (exclusive of Writing) on SAT, or (3) rank in upper half of graduating class. **Homeschooled:** Applicants may be admitted based on GED or ACT COMPASS scores.

High school preparation. Required units include English 4, mathematics 3, social studies 3, science 2 (laboratory 2). 2 years foreign language, computer science, visual and performing arts, or vocational education also recommended.

2005-2006 Annual costs. Tuition/fees: $4,856; $13,000 out-of-state. Room/board: $3,920. Books/supplies: $900. Personal expenses: $1,570.

2004-2005 Financial aid. Need-based: 617 full-time freshmen applied for aid; 493 were judged to have need; 468 of these received aid. Average need met was 54%. Average scholarship/grant was $4,086; average loan $2,414. 41% of total undergraduate aid awarded as scholarships/grants, 59% as loans/jobs. **Non-need-based:** Awarded to 1,057 full-time undergraduates, including 313 freshmen. Scholarships awarded for academics, alumni affiliation, art, athletics, job skills, leadership, minority status, music/drama, state residency. **Additional information:** Veterans and honors fee waivers offered.

Application procedures. Admission: Priority date 7/1; no deadline. $30 fee. Application must be submitted on paper. Admission notification on a rolling basis. **Financial aid:** Priority date 3/1; no closing date. FAFSA required. Applicants notified on a rolling basis starting 5/1; must reply within 3 week(s) of notification.

Academics. Full degree programs and many courses designed for working professionals. **Special study options:** Accelerated study, combined bachelor's/graduate degree, cooperative education, cross-registration, distance learning, double major, dual enrollment of high school students, ESL, external degree, honors, independent study, internships, study abroad, teacher certification program, weekend college. Evening College, with extensive online programs and courses. **Credit/placement by examination:** AP, CLEP, SAT, ACT. **Support services:** Learning center, reduced course load, remedial instruction, study skills assistance, tutoring, writing center.

Majors. Biology: General. **Business:** General. **Communications:** General, media studies, public relations. **Conservation:** Environmental studies. **Education:** General, art, biology, chemistry, curriculum, elementary, English, foreign languages, health, history, mathematics, music, physical, physics, science, secondary, social science, social studies, Spanish, special. **English:** English lit. **Foreign languages:** Spanish. **Health:** Athletic training, health care admin, vocational rehab counseling. **History:** General. **Liberal arts:** Arts/sciences. **Math:** General. **Parks/recreation:** Health/fitness, sports admin. **Physical sciences:** Chemistry. **Psychology:** General. **Public administration:** Human services. **Social sciences:** Sociology. **Visual/performing arts:** Art, dramatic, music performance.

Most popular majors. Business/marketing 18%, communications/journalism 6%, education 30%, liberal arts 18%, psychology 8%.

Computing on campus. 850 workstations in dormitories, library, computer center. Dormitories wired for high-speed internet access and linked to campus network. Online course registration, online library, helpline, student web hosting, wireless network available.

Student life. Freshman orientation: Mandatory, $65 fee. Preregistration for classes offered. One-day orientations held throughout summer. **Policies:** Freshmen permitted cars on campus. **Housing:** Coed dorms, single-sex dorms, special housing for disabled, apartments, substance-free housing available. $75 fully refundable deposit. **Activities:** Bands, choral groups, dance, drama, literary magazine, music ensembles, musical theater, radio station, student government, student newspaper, more than 50 student groups available.

Athletics. NCAA. **Intercollegiate:** Baseball M, basketball, cheerleading, cross-country, golf, soccer, softball W, tennis, volleyball W. **Intramural:** Archery, basketball, cross-country, golf, racquetball, skiing, softball, swimming, table tennis, tennis, volleyball. **Team name:** Yellowjackets.

Student services. Adult student services, alcohol/substance abuse counseling, campus ministries, career counseling, services for economically disadvantaged, student employment services, financial aid counseling, health services, legal services, minority student services, on-campus daycare, personal counseling, placement for graduates, veterans' counselor. **Physically disabled:** Services for visually, speech, hearing impaired.

Contact. E-mail: cjohannes@msubillings.edu
Phone: (406) 657-2158 Toll-free number: (800) 656-6782
Fax: (406) 657-2051
Cheri Johannes, Director of Admissions, Montana State University: Billings, 1500 University Drive, Billings, MT 59101-0298

Montana State University: Bozeman

Bozeman, Montana — **CB member**
www.montana.edu — **CB code: 4488**

- Public 4-year university
- Residential campus in large town
- 10,771 degree-seeking undergraduates: 14% part-time, 47% women, 1% Asian American, 1% Hispanic American, 2% Native American, 1% international
- 1,173 degree-seeking graduate students
- 74% of applicants admitted
- SAT or ACT (ACT writing optional) required
- 46% graduate within 6 years

General. Founded in 1893. Regionally accredited. **Degrees:** 1,805 bachelor's awarded; master's, doctoral offered. **ROTC:** Army, Air Force. **Location:** 139 miles from Billings. **Calendar:** Semester, limited summer session. **Full-time faculty:** 553 total; 2% minority, 34% women. **Part-time faculty:** 275 total; 2% minority, 52% women. **Class size:** 32% < 20, 39% 20-39, 14% 40-49, 10% 50-99, 6% >100. **Special facilities:** Museum of the Rockies, agricultural bioscience center, wind tunnel, electron microscope, center for biofilm engineering, planetarium, telecommunication center, geographic information and analysis center, thermal biology institute, rural dwellers center, center for excellence, center for entrepreneurship.

Freshman class profile. 5,124 applied, 3,784 admitted, 2,236 enrolled.

Mid 50% test scores		**Rank in top tenth:**	17%
SAT verbal:	490-610	**End year in good standing:**	91%
SAT math:	500-630	**Return as sophomores:**	71%
ACT:	20-26	**Out-of-state:**	34%
GPA 3.50 or higher:	41%	**Live on campus:**	84%
GPA 3.0-3.49:	32%	**International:**	1%
GPA 2.0-2.99:	26%	**Fraternities:**	3%
Rank in top quarter:	41%	**Sororities:**	3%

Basis for selection. Minimum 2.5 GPA or ACT composite score of 22 or SAT equivalent, or rank in top half of graduating class required. Completion of state college-preparatory requirements important. Students may use SAT/ACT math scores for placement or take departmental exam. Students with ACT English score of at least 27 or SAT verbal score of at least 640 can waive freshman composition. Varies by program. **Homeschooled:** GED required.

High school preparation. College-preparatory program required. 14 units required. Required units include English 4, mathematics 3, social studies 3, science 2 (laboratory 2). 4 mathematics recommended for science majors. Substitutions for foreign language requirement possible. 2 years chosen from the following: foreign language (preferably 2 years), computer science, visual and performing arts, or approved vocational education units.

2005-2006 Annual costs. Tuition/fees: $5,220; $14,859 out-of-state. Additional $1,338 annually in health insurance required of uninsured students. Room/board: $6,156. Books/supplies: $980. Personal expenses: $2,550.

2004-2005 Financial aid. Need-based: 1,774 full-time freshmen applied for aid; 1,092 were judged to have need; 1,057 of these received aid. Average need met was 54%. Average scholarship/grant was $3,939; average loan $3,302. 41% of total undergraduate aid awarded as scholarships/grants, 59% as loans/jobs. **Non-need-based:** Awarded to 1,562 full-time undergraduates, including 562 freshmen. Scholarships awarded for academics, alumni affiliation, art, athletics, job skills, leadership, minority status, music/drama, ROTC, state residency.

Application procedures. Admission: No deadline. $30 fee. Application may be submitted online. Admission notification on a rolling basis. **Financial aid:** Priority date 3/1; no closing date. FAFSA required. Applicants notified on a rolling basis starting 4/1; must reply within 3 week(s) of notification.

Academics. Special study options: Combined bachelor's/graduate degree, cross-registration, distance learning, double major, ESL, exchange student, honors, independent study, internships, student-designed major, study abroad, teacher certification program. Combined bachelor's/master's programs in environmental design/architecture and construction engineering technology/construction engineering management. **Credit/placement by examination:** AP, CLEP, IB, SAT, ACT, institutional tests. No more than 30 semester credits earned by correspondence, extension, or continuing education counted toward bachelor's degree. **Support services:** Learning center, remedial instruction, study skills assistance, tutoring, writing center.

Majors. Agriculture: Animal sciences, business, horticultural science, plant sciences, range science. **Architecture:** Environmental design. **Biology:** General, bacteriology, biotechnology. **Business:** General. **Computer sciences:**

Computer science. **Conservation:** General, management/policy. **Education:** Agricultural, elementary, music, secondary, technology/industrial arts. **Engineering:** Chemical, civil, computer, electrical, mechanical. **Engineering technology:** Construction. **Family/consumer sciences:** General. **Foreign languages:** General. **Health:** Nursing (RN). **History:** General. **Math:** General. **Parks/recreation:** Sports admin. **Philosophy/religion:** Philosophy. **Physical sciences:** Chemistry, physics, planetary. **Psychology:** General. **Social sciences:** Anthropology, economics, political science, sociology. **Visual/performing arts:** Art, cinematography.

Most popular majors. Biology 6%, business/marketing 13%, education 9%, engineering/engineering technologies 15%, health sciences 8%, social sciences 6%, visual/performing arts 10%.

Computing on campus. 850 workstations in dormitories, library, computer center. Dormitories linked to campus network. Commuter students can connect to campus network. Online course registration, helpline, wireless network available.

Student life. Freshman orientation: Mandatory, $65 fee. Preregistration for classes offered. **Policies:** Freshmen permitted cars on campus. **Housing:** Guaranteed on-campus for freshmen. Coed dorms, single-sex dorms, apartments, fraternity/sorority housing, substance-free housing available. $200 nonrefundable deposit. Nonsmoking, students over traditional age, wellness floors available. **Activities:** Bands, choral groups, dance, drama, film society, literary magazine, music ensembles, musical theater, radio station, student government, student newspaper, TV station, campus service organizations, campus ministry, Circle-K, Native American club, international coordinating council, black student union, Campus Crusade for Christ, Intervarsity Christian Fellowship.

Athletics. NCAA. **Intercollegiate:** Basketball, cheerleading, cross-country, football (tackle) M, golf W, rodeo, skiing, tennis, track and field, volleyball W. **Intramural:** Archery, badminton, basketball, bowling, cross-country, golf, gymnastics, handball, racquetball, rodeo, skiing, soccer, softball, swimming, table tennis, tennis, track and field, volleyball, water polo, weight lifting, wrestling M. **Team name:** Bobcats.

Student services. Adult student services, alcohol/substance abuse counseling, campus ministries, career counseling, student employment services, financial aid counseling, health services, legal services, minority student services, on-campus daycare, personal counseling, placement for graduates, veterans' counselor, women's services. **Physically disabled:** Services for visually, speech, hearing impaired.

Contact. E-mail: admissions@montana.edu
Phone: (406) 994-2452 Toll-free number: (888) 678-2287
Fax: (406) 994-1923
Ronda Russell, Director of New Student Services, Montana State University: Bozeman, PO Box 172190, Bozeman, MT 59717-2190

Montana State University: Northern

Havre, Montana
www.msun.edu **CB code: 4538**

- Public 4-year university and liberal arts college
- Commuter campus in large town

General. Founded in 1929. Regionally accredited. **Location:** 100 miles from Great Falls. **Calendar:** Semester.

Annual costs/financial aid. Tuition/fees (2005-2006): $4,466; $13,438 out-of-state. Room/board: $4,880. Books/supplies: $800. Personal expenses: $558. Need-based financial aid available to full-time and part-time students.

Contact. Phone: (406) 265-3704
Director of Admissions, Box 7751, Havre, MT 59501

Montana Tech of the University of Montana

Butte, Montana
www.mtech.edu **CB code: 4487**

- Public 4-year engineering and technical college
- Commuter campus in large town
- 1,894 degree-seeking undergraduates: 10% part-time, 43% women, 1% African American, 1% Asian American, 1% Hispanic American, 1% Native American, 3% international
- 88 degree-seeking graduate students
- 99% of applicants admitted
- 40% graduate within 6 years

General. Founded in 1893. Regionally accredited. **Degrees:** 287 bachelor's, 97 associate awarded; master's offered. **ROTC:** Army. **Location:** 82 miles from Bozeman, 65 miles from Helena. **Calendar:** Semester, limited summer session. **Full-time faculty:** 110 total; 54% have terminal degrees, 26% women. **Part-time faculty:** 39 total; 13% have terminal degrees, 41% women. **Class size:** 65% < 20, 23% 20-39, 7% 40-49, 5% 50-99, less than 1% >100. **Special facilities:** Mineral museum, earthquake studies office.

Freshman class profile. 404 applied, 400 admitted, 394 enrolled.

Mid 50% test scores		Rank in top quarter:	50%
SAT verbal:	470-600	End year in good standing:	86%
SAT math:	490-630	Return as sophomores:	67%
ACT:	21-27	Out-of-state:	7%
GPA 3.0-3.49:	68%	International:	2%
GPA 2.0-2.99:	28%		

Basis for selection. 22 ACT, 1030 SAT (exclusive of Writing), 2.5 high school GPA, or ranking in top half of class required. SAT or ACT recommended.

High school preparation. 14 units required. Required and recommended units include English 4, mathematics 3, social studies 3, science 2-4 (laboratory 2). 2 additional units required from foreign language, computer science, visual or performing arts, or vocational instruction.

2005-2006 Annual costs. Tuition/fees: $5,123; $14,114 out-of-state. Room/board: $5,356. Books/supplies: $700. Personal expenses: $1,500.

2004-2005 Financial aid. All financial aid based on need. 250 full-time freshmen applied for aid; 225 were judged to have need; 200 of these received aid. Average need met was 75%. Average scholarship/grant was $2,000; average loan $2,500. 42% of total undergraduate aid awarded as scholarships/grants, 58% as loans/jobs.

Application procedures. Admission: Priority date 3/1; no deadline. $30 fee, may be waived for applicants with need. Application may be submitted online. Admission notification on a rolling basis. **Financial aid:** Priority date 3/1; no closing date. FAFSA, institutional form required. Applicants notified on a rolling basis starting 4/1; must reply within 2 week(s) of notification.

Academics. Special study options: Combined bachelor's/graduate degree, cooperative education, distance learning, double major, dual enrollment of high school students, independent study, internships, liberal arts/career combination, student-designed major, teacher certification program. 3-2 liberal arts-engineering program with Carroll College, dual enrollment agreement with Flathead Valley Community College. **Credit/placement by examination:** AP, CLEP, IB, SAT, ACT, institutional tests. 10 credit hours maximum toward associate degree, 30 toward bachelor's. **Support services:** Learning center, pre-admission summer program, reduced course load, study skills assistance, tutoring.

Majors. Biology: General. **Business:** General, accounting, business admin, marketing. **Communications:** General. **Communications technology:** General. **Computer sciences:** General, applications programming, computer science, information systems, information technology, programming, systems analysis. **Engineering:** General, civil, computer, electrical, environmental, geological, materials, materials science, mechanical, metallurgical, mining, petroleum, science, software. **English:** Technical writing. **Health:** Medical informatics, nursing (RN), occupational health, predentistry, premedicine, prepharmacy, preveterinary. **Interdisciplinary:** Biological/physical sciences, science/society. **Legal studies:** Prelaw. **Liberal arts:** Arts/sciences. **Math:** General, applied, statistics. **Physical sciences:** Chemistry. **Production:** Welding.

Computing on campus. 500 workstations in dormitories, library, computer center, student center. Dormitories wired for high-speed internet access and linked to campus network. Commuter students can connect to campus network. Online course registration, online library, student web hosting, wireless network available.

Student life. Freshman orientation: Mandatory. Preregistration for classes offered. Held several days before semester start. **Policies:** Freshmen permitted cars on campus. **Housing:** Guaranteed on-campus for freshmen. Coed dorms, special housing for disabled, apartments, substance-free housing available. $100 deposit. **Activities:** Pep band, choral groups, music ensembles, radio station, student government, student newspaper, symphony orchestra, Baptist Student Union, international club, Circle-K, Baha'i Club, Prospectors, American Indian Science and Engineering Society, Students in Engineering Programs, Abundant Campus Life Ministry, Newman Club.

Athletics. NAIA. **Intercollegiate:** Basketball, football (tackle) M, golf, volleyball W. **Intramural:** Basketball, football (non-tackle), handball, racquetball, softball, swimming, volleyball, weight lifting. **Team name:** Orediggers.

Student services. Adult student services, alcohol/substance abuse counseling, campus ministries, career counseling, student employment services, financial aid counseling, health services, minority student services, personal counseling, placement for graduates, veterans' counselor, women's services. **Physically disabled:** Services for visually, hearing impaired.

Contact. E-mail: admissions@mtech.edu
Phone: (406) 496-4178 Toll-free number: (800) 445-8324
Fax: (406) 496-4710
Tony Campeau, Director of Admissions, Montana Tech of the University of Montana, 1300 West Park Street, Butte, MT 59701-8997

Rocky Mountain College
Billings, Montana
www.rocky.edu **CB code: 4660**

- Private 4-year liberal arts college affiliated with United Church of Christ, United Methodist Church, and United Presbyterian Church
- Commuter campus in small city
- 924 degree-seeking undergraduates: 4% part-time, 55% women, 1% African American, 2% Asian American, 2% Hispanic American, 7% Native American, 5% international
- 45 degree-seeking graduate students
- 78% of applicants admitted
- SAT or ACT with writing required
- 39% graduate within 6 years; 22% enter graduate study

General. Founded in 1878. Regionally accredited. **Degrees:** 157 bachelor's, 2 associate awarded; master's offered. **Calendar:** Semester, limited summer session. **Full-time faculty:** 53 total; 62% have terminal degrees, 2% minority, 38% women. **Part-time faculty:** 60 total; 22% have terminal degrees, 5% minority, 50% women. **Class size:** 69% < 20, 28% 20-39, 2% 40-49, 1% 50-99. **Special facilities:** Geology library, rock climbing wall, outdoor recreation center, flight school, equestrian facilities.

Freshman class profile. 728 applied, 565 admitted, 218 enrolled.

Mid 50% test scores		**Rank in top quarter:**	40%
SAT verbal:	450-580	**Rank in top tenth:**	15%
SAT math:	460-590	**End year in good standing:**	80%
ACT:	19-25	**Return as sophomores:**	72%
GPA 3.50 or higher:	43%	**Out-of-state:**	41%
GPA 3.0-3.49:	35%	**Live on campus:**	89%
GPA 2.0-2.99:	21%	**International:**	5%

Basis for selection. 2.50 GPA or ACT score of 21 or comparable SAT meets requirement for regular admission. Essay recommended for all students. Interview recommended for academically weak students; audition recommended for music, theater students; portfolio recommended for art students. **Homeschooled:** Applicants must either have GED or pass ACT based on college entrance standards.

High school preparation. 13 units required. Required and recommended units include English 4, mathematics 2-3, social studies 2, history 2, science 2 (laboratory 1) and foreign language 1-2.

2005-2006 Annual costs. Tuition/fees: $15,325. Room/board: $5,480. Books/supplies: $900. Personal expenses: $1,000.

2005-2006 Financial aid. Need-based: 196 full-time freshmen applied for aid; 149 were judged to have need; 149 of these received aid. Average need met was 73%. Average scholarship/grant was $9,195; average loan $1,701. 61% of total undergraduate aid awarded as scholarships/grants, 39% as loans/jobs. **Non-need-based:** Awarded to 238 full-time undergraduates, including 100 freshmen. Scholarships awarded for academics, alumni affiliation, art, athletics, leadership, minority status, music/drama, religious affiliation, state residency.

Application procedures. Admission: Priority date 3/1; no deadline. $25 fee, may be waived for applicants with need. Application may be submitted online. Admission notification on a rolling basis beginning on or about 9/1. Must reply by May 1 or within 4 week(s) if notified thereafter. Students who make their decision by Dec. 31 receive priority placement in housing and class selection. **Financial aid:** Priority date 3/1; no closing date. FAFSA, institutional form required. Applicants notified on a rolling basis starting 2/1; must reply within 4 week(s) of notification.

Academics. Special study options: Accelerated study, combined bachelor's/graduate degree, distance learning, double major, dual enrollment of high school students, honors, independent study, internships, student-designed major, study abroad, teacher certification program. 3-2 program in occupational therapy, degree completion program, master's in physician assistant studies. **Credit/placement by examination:** AP, CLEP, IB, SAT, ACT, institutional tests. 15 credit hours maximum toward associate degree, 31 toward bachelor's. **Support services:** Learning center, pre-admission summer program, reduced course load, remedial instruction, study skills assistance, tutoring.

Majors. Agriculture: Business, equestrian studies. **Biology:** General. **Business:** Accounting, business admin, management science. **Communications:** General. **Computer sciences:** Computer science, information technology. **Conservation:** Environmental science, environmental studies. **Education:** General, art, biology, drama/dance, elementary, English, history, mathematics, middle, multi-level teacher, music, physical, secondary, social studies. **English:** English lit. **Health:** Athletic training, physician assistant. **History:** General. **Math:** General. **Parks/recreation:** Exercise sciences, health/fitness. **Physical sciences:** Chemistry, geology. **Psychology:** General. **Social sciences:** Economics, political science, sociology. **Transportation:** Airline/commercial pilot, aviation management. **Visual/performing arts:** Art, dramatic, music performance, theater design.

Most popular majors. Biology 9%, business/marketing 18%, education 11%, health sciences 10%, psychology 7%, trade and industry 6%, visual/performing arts 8%.

Computing on campus. 104 workstations in dormitories, library, computer center, student center. Dormitories wired for high-speed internet access and linked to campus network. Commuter students can connect to campus network. Online course registration, helpline, wireless network available.

Student life. Freshman orientation: Mandatory. Preregistration for classes offered. Held during the 4 days before classes start. Placement, validation, registration/advising, activities. Smaller sessions held over the summer. **Policies:** Freshmen permitted cars on campus. **Housing:** Guaranteed on-campus for freshmen. Coed dorms, apartments available. $150 deposit. Suites available. **Activities:** Bands, choral groups, drama, literary magazine, music ensembles, student government, student newspaper, Newman Club, intervarsity, American Indian science & engineering society, American Indian cultural association, health occupation groups, business club, precision flying team, ski club, equestrian club, Sojourner's club.

Athletics. NAIA. **Intercollegiate:** Basketball, cheerleading, football (tackle) M, golf, skiing, soccer W, volleyball W. **Intramural:** Basketball, football (tackle) M, golf, handball, racquetball, skiing, soccer, softball, swimming, table tennis, tennis, volleyball. **Team name:** Battlin' Bears.

Student services. Adult student services, alcohol/substance abuse counseling, campus ministries, career counseling, student employment services, financial aid counseling, health services, on-campus daycare, personal counseling, placement for graduates. **Physically disabled:** Services for visually, speech, hearing impaired.

Contact. E-mail: admissions@rocky.edu
Phone: (406) 657-1026 Toll-free number: (800) 877-6259
Fax: (406) 657-1189
Bonnie Knapp, Director of Admissions, Rocky Mountain College, 1511 Poly Drive, Billings, MT 59102-1796

Salish Kootenai College
Pablo, Montana
www.skc.edu **CB code: 0898**

- Private 4-year liberal arts college
- Commuter campus in rural community
- 1,148 undergraduates

General. Founded in 1977. Regionally accredited. Native American cultural heritage. **Degrees:** 25 bachelor's, 107 associate awarded. **Location:** 55 miles from Missoula, 65 miles from Kalispell. **Calendar:** Quarter, limited summer session. **Full-time faculty:** 72 total; 61% have terminal degrees, 33% minority, 47% women. **Part-time faculty:** 40 total; 12% have terminal degrees, 52% minority, 58% women.

Basis for selection. Open admission, but selective for some programs. Special requirements for highway construction worker training, social work, dental assisting technology and nursing. Highway construction worker training program has special application which includes drug testing. Third-year applicants to social work program must complete special application which includes background check. Dental assisting technology has special application.

2006-2007 Annual costs. Tuition/fees (projected): $789; $23,170 out-of-state. Books/supplies: $750. Personal expenses: $1,800.

2004-2005 Financial aid. Need-based: 344 full-time freshmen applied for aid; 178 were judged to have need; 166 of these received aid. Average need met was 54%. Average scholarship/grant was $4,817; average loan

$2,126. 83% of total undergraduate aid awarded as scholarships/grants, 17% as loans/jobs. **Non-need-based:** Awarded to 39 full-time undergraduates, including 12 freshmen.

Application procedures. Admission: Priority date 7/1; no deadline. No application fee. Admission notification on a rolling basis. **Financial aid:** Priority date 3/31; no closing date. FAFSA required. Applicants notified on a rolling basis starting 7/15; must reply within 6 week(s) of notification.

Academics. Special study options: Cooperative education, distance learning, double major, dual enrollment of high school students, independent study, internships. **Credit/placement by examination:** CLEP, institutional tests. **Support services:** Learning center, remedial instruction, tutoring.

Majors. Business: Administrative services. **Computer sciences:** General. **Conservation:** General. **Health:** Nursing (RN). **Public administration:** Social work.

Most popular majors. Business/marketing 16%, computer/information sciences 8%, health sciences 20%, natural resources/environmental science 12%, public administration/social services 44%.

Computing on campus. 42 workstations in library, computer center. Helpline, wireless network available.

Student life. Freshman orientation: Mandatory. Preregistration for classes offered. Held prior to registration day; one-half to one-day session. **Policies:** Freshmen permitted cars on campus. **Housing:** Special housing for disabled, apartments available. Housing costs based on income. **Activities:** Student government, student newspaper, TV station.

Athletics. Intercollegiate: Basketball. **Intramural:** Basketball, skiing, softball, volleyball. **Team name:** Bison.

Student services. Career counseling, student employment services, on-campus daycare, personal counseling, placement for graduates, veterans' counselor. **Physically disabled:** Services for visually, speech, hearing impaired.

Contact. E-mail: jackie_moran@skc.edu
Phone: (406) 275-4866 Fax: (406) 275-4801
Jackie Moran, Admissions, Salish Kootenai College, Box 70, Pablo, MT 59855

University of Great Falls

Great Falls, Montana
www.ugf.edu **CB code: 4058**

- Private 4-year university and liberal arts college affiliated with Roman Catholic Church
- Residential campus in small city
- 656 degree-seeking undergraduates: 26% part-time, 64% women, 3% African American, 2% Asian American, 5% Hispanic American, 4% Native American, 2% international
- 105 degree-seeking graduate students
- 79% of applicants admitted
- Application essay required

General. Founded in 1932. Regionally accredited. **Degrees:** 159 bachelor's, 11 associate awarded; master's offered. **Location:** 600 miles from Seattle, 370 miles from Spokane, Washington. **Calendar:** Semester, limited summer session. **Full-time faculty:** 33 total; 61% have terminal degrees, 6% minority, 30% women. **Part-time faculty:** 50 total; 24% have terminal degrees, 2% minority, 46% women. **Class size:** 84% < 20, 16% 20-39. **Special facilities:** Herbarium, business incubator.

Freshman class profile. 242 applied, 192 admitted, 122 enrolled.

Mid 50% test scores			
SAT verbal:	410-540	GPA 2.0-2.99:	40%
SAT math:	380-520	End year in good standing:	41%
ACT:	19-24	Return as sophomores:	42%
GPA 3.50 or higher:	16%	Out-of-state:	33%
GPA 3.0-3.49:	38%	Live on campus:	76%
		International:	2%

Basis for selection. High school record and character most important. ACT/SAT scores may be considered when making scholarship decisions. SAT or ACT, SAT Subject Tests recommended. Interview recommended. **Homeschooled:** Transcript of courses and grades required. Applicants should submit SAT/ACT test scores, bibliography of school literature and essay describing and evaluating preparation for university-level work.

High school preparation. College-preparatory program recommended. 20 units required; 22 recommended. Required and recommended units include English 4, mathematics 3, social studies 1-2, history 3, science 3 (laboratory 1) and academic electives 5.

2006-2007 Annual costs. Tuition/fees (projected): $15,250. Room/board: $5,500. Books/supplies: $900. Personal expenses: $750.

2005-2006 Financial aid. Need-based: Average need met was 46%. Average scholarship/grant was $3,410; average loan $2,704. 36% of total undergraduate aid awarded as scholarships/grants, 64% as loans/jobs. **Non-need-based:** Scholarships awarded for academics, art, athletics, job skills, leadership, minority status, music/drama, religious affiliation, state residency.

Application procedures. Admission: Priority date 5/5; deadline 9/1 (postmark date). $35 fee, may be waived for applicants with need. Application may be submitted online. Admission notification on a rolling basis. Admission granted with 6th semester transcripts. **Financial aid:** Priority date 5/1; no closing date. FAFSA required. Applicants notified on a rolling basis starting 2/1; must reply within 2 week(s) of notification.

Academics. Trio Title IV Student Support Services program available to eligible students. **Special study options:** Combined bachelor's/graduate degree, cooperative education, cross-registration, distance learning, double major, dual enrollment of high school students, independent study, internships, liberal arts/career combination, teacher certification program. **Credit/placement by examination:** AP, CLEP, IB, SAT, ACT, institutional tests. 30 credit hours maximum toward associate degree, 30 toward bachelor's. **Support services:** Learning center, pre-admission summer program, reduced course load, remedial instruction, study skills assistance, tutoring, writing center.

Majors. Biology: General, botany. **Business:** Accounting, accounting/business management, business admin. **Computer sciences:** General, applications programming, computer graphics, computer science, data processing, LAN/WAN management, networking, programming, security, system admin, systems analysis. **Education:** Art, biology, chemistry, early childhood, elementary, English, gifted/talented, health, history, kindergarten/preschool, mathematics, middle, physical, psychology, reading, science, secondary, social science, social studies, special. **Health:** Preveterinary, substance abuse counseling. **History:** General. **Legal studies:** Paralegal. **Math:** General. **Parks/recreation:** Health/fitness. **Philosophy/religion:** Religion. **Physical sciences:** Chemistry. **Protective services:** Corrections, criminal justice, forensics, juvenile corrections, police science. **Psychology:** General. **Social sciences:** General, political science, sociology. **Visual/performing arts:** Art.

Most popular majors. Education 24%, psychology 21%, public administration/social services 9%, security/protective services 7%.

Computing on campus. 120 workstations in dormitories, library, computer center, student center. Dormitories wired for high-speed internet access and linked to campus network. Commuter students can connect to campus network. Online course registration, online library, helpline, repair service, student web hosting, wireless network available.

Student life. Freshman orientation: Mandatory, $75 fee. Preregistration for classes offered. Programs held 3 days prior to fall and spring semesters; includes float trip down Missouri River. **Policies:** No drugs, alcohol, firearms or weapons allowed on campus. Freshmen permitted cars on campus. **Housing:** Guaranteed on-campus for freshmen. Coed dorms, special housing for disabled, apartments, substance-free housing available. $150 fully refundable deposit, deadline 8/15. **Activities:** Bands, choral groups, drama, literary magazine, music ensembles, musical theater, radio station, student government, student newspaper, symphony orchestra, campus ministry, United Tribes Club, Americorps, drama club, art club, Students In Free Enterprise, international law and justice club, medical science club, student Montana education association, paralegal club.

Athletics. NAIA. **Intercollegiate:** Basketball, cross-country, golf, soccer W, softball W, volleyball W, wrestling M. **Intramural:** Baseball, basketball, bowling, cheerleading, football (non-tackle), softball, tennis, volleyball. **Team name:** Argonauts.

Student services. Adult student services, alcohol/substance abuse counseling, campus ministries, career counseling, services for economically disadvantaged, student employment services, financial aid counseling, health services, minority student services, on-campus daycare, personal counseling, placement for graduates, veterans' counselor, women's services. **Physically disabled:** Services for visually, hearing impaired.

Contact. E-mail: enroll@ugf.edu
Phone: (406) 791-5200 Toll-free number: (800) 856-9544
Fax: (406) 791-5209
Paula Highlander, Assistant Director of Admissions, University of Great Falls, 1301 20th Street South, Great Falls, MT 59405

University of Montana: Missoula

Missoula, Montana **CB member**
www.umt.edu **CB code: 4489**

- Public 4-year university and liberal arts college
- Residential campus in small city
- 10,125 degree-seeking undergraduates
- 83% of applicants admitted
- SAT or ACT (ACT writing optional) required

General. Founded in 1893. Regionally accredited. 2-year technical college within campus available. **Degrees:** 1,709 bachelor's, 222 associate awarded; master's, doctoral, first professional offered. **ROTC:** Army. **Location:** 210 miles from Spokane, Washington. **Calendar:** Semester, extensive summer session. **Full-time faculty:** 547 total. **Part-time faculty:** 187 total. **Class size:** 45% < 20, 36% 20-39, 6% 40-49, 8% 50-99, 5% >100. **Special facilities:** Performing arts, radio and television building, 3 art galleries, wildlife museum, 29,000-acre experimental forest, biological research station, bureau of business and economic research, geology field camp, HIV research lab, environmental studies laboratory, center for people and forests, primate colony, forensics lab.

Freshman class profile. 5,802 applied, 4,827 admitted, 1,864 enrolled.

Mid 50% test scores			
SAT verbal:	510-590	Rank in top tenth:	14%
SAT math:	490-580	Out-of-state:	27%
ACT:	20-25	Live on campus:	69%
Rank in top quarter:	34%	Fraternities:	6%
		Sororities:	5%

Basis for selection. Minimum 2.5 GPA, ACT composite score of 22, combined SAT score of 1030 (exclusive of Writing), or rank in top half of graduating class required. Extracurricular activities important. TOEFL or Michigan Test and statement of intent and personal contribution required for international students. SAT/ACT not required for nontraditional students or international students.

High school preparation. 14 units required. Required and recommended units include English 4, mathematics 3, social studies 3, history 1-2, science 2 (laboratory 2), foreign language 2 and academic electives 2. Computer science, visual and performing arts, and/or vocational education.

2005-2006 Annual costs. Tuition/fees: $4,703; $13,419 out-of-state. Room/board: $5,646. Books/supplies: $800. Personal expenses: $3,248.

2005-2006 Financial aid. **Need-based:** 29% of total undergraduate aid awarded as scholarships/grants, 71% as loans/jobs. **Non-need-based:** Scholarships awarded for academics, art, athletics, leadership, music/drama, ROTC, state residency.

Application procedures. **Admission:** Priority date 3/1; no deadline. $30 fee. Admission notification on a rolling basis beginning on or about 9/15. **Financial aid:** Priority date 3/1; no closing date. FAFSA, institutional form, CSS PROFILE required. Applicants notified on a rolling basis starting 4/1; must reply by 8/1 or within 4 week(s) of notification.

Academics. **Special study options:** Combined bachelor's/graduate degree, cooperative education, cross-registration, distance learning, double major, ESL, exchange student, honors, independent study, internships, study abroad, teacher certification program. English language institute, combined programs with other institutions for bachelor in nursing and master in public administration with Montana State University - Bozeman. **Credit/placement by examination:** AP, CLEP, institutional tests. 10 credit hours maximum toward associate degree. Credit hours awarded determined by academic department. **Support services:** Learning center, pre-admission summer program, reduced course load, remedial instruction, study skills assistance, tutoring, writing center.

Honors college/program. ACT composite 27 or SAT 1150 (exclusive of Writing) required. 250 admitted. Students take honors sections of the curriculum, participate in volunteer service, and complete 7 specific honors courses.

Majors. **Architecture:** Urban/community planning. **Area/ethnic studies:** Asian, Native American, women's. **Biology:** General, bacteriology, botany, cellular/molecular, zoology. **Business:** General, business admin, finance, international, management information systems, marketing. **Communications:** General, broadcast journalism, journalism. **Computer sciences:** Computer science. **Conservation:** General, forestry, wildlife. **Education:** General, art, biology, business, elementary, English, mathematics, music, physical, secondary. **English:** Speech/rhetoric. **Foreign languages:** Classics, French, German, Japanese, Latin, Russian, Spanish. **Health:** Athletic training, clinical lab science. **History:** General. **Interdisciplinary:** Math/computer science. **Liberal arts:** Arts/sciences. **Math:** General. **Parks/recreation:** Exercise sciences, facilities management, health/fitness. **Philosophy/religion:** Philosophy. **Physical sciences:** Chemistry, geology, physics. **Psychology:** General. **Public administration:** Social work. **Social sciences:** Anthropology, cartography, criminology, economics, geography, international relations, political science, sociology. **Visual/performing arts:** General, art, art history/conservation, dance, dramatic, music performance, music theory/composition.

Computing on campus. 1,800 workstations in dormitories, library, computer center, student center. Dormitories wired for high-speed internet access and linked to campus network. Commuter students can connect to campus network. Online course registration, online library, helpline, repair service, wireless network available.

Student life. **Freshman orientation:** Mandatory, $45 fee. Preregistration for classes offered. 3-day summer session which includes parent track. **Policies:** Freshmen permitted cars on campus. **Housing:** Guaranteed on-campus for freshmen. Coed dorms, single-sex dorms, special housing for disabled, apartments, fraternity/sorority housing available. $120 deposit, deadline 3/1. Honors floors, international floors, quiet floors, activity dorms, personal development housing available. **Activities:** Bands, choral groups, dance, drama, literary magazine, music ensembles, musical theater, opera, radio station, student government, student newspaper, symphony orchestra, TV station, Associated Students of University of Montana, University of Montana Advocates, Mortar Board, Spurs, Circle-K, forestry student association, honors student association, Kyi-Yo (Native American organization), environmental action club, American Indian Business Leaders.

Athletics. NCAA. **Intercollegiate:** Basketball, cheerleading, cross-country, football (tackle) M, golf W, rodeo, soccer W, tennis, track and field, volleyball W. **Intramural:** Badminton, baseball M, basketball, football (tackle), golf, handball, racquetball, soccer, softball, swimming, table tennis, tennis, track and field, triathlon, volleyball. **Team name:** Grizzlies.

Student services. Adult student services, alcohol/substance abuse counseling, campus ministries, career counseling, services for economically disadvantaged, student employment services, financial aid counseling, health services, legal services, minority student services, on-campus daycare, personal counseling, placement for graduates, veterans' counselor, women's services. **Physically disabled:** Services for visually, speech, hearing impaired.

Contact. E-mail: admiss@selway.umt.edu
Phone: (406) 243-6266 Toll-free number: (800) 462-8636
Fax: (406) 243-5711
Jed Liston, Assistant Vice President for Enrollment Services, University of Montana: Missoula, Lommasson Center 103, Missoula, MT 59812

University of Montana: Western

Dillon, Montana **CB member**
www.umwestern.edu **CB code: 4945**

- Public 4-year liberal arts and teachers college
- Residential campus in small town
- 1,346 degree-seeking undergraduates: 18% part-time, 59% women
- SAT or ACT required

General. Founded in 1893. Regionally accredited. Offer classes in block scheduling system. **Degrees:** 131 bachelor's, 34 associate awarded. **Location:** 65 miles from Butte. **Calendar:** Semester, extensive summer session. **Full-time faculty:** 50 total; 74% have terminal degrees, 8% minority, 44% women. **Part-time faculty:** 21 total; 62% women. **Class size:** 67% < 20, 33% 20-39, less than 1% 40-49, less than 1% 50-99. **Special facilities:** Outdoor education center, wildlife exhibit, office simulation center.

Freshman class profile.

Mid 50% test scores		Rank in top quarter:	18%
SAT verbal:	410-510	Rank in top tenth:	5%
SAT math:	430-520	Out-of-state:	32%
ACT:	16-22	Live on campus:	88%

Basis for selection. School record, class rank, test scores most important.

High school preparation. 16 units recommended. Recommended units include English 4, mathematics 3, social studies 3, science 2 (laboratory 2) and academic electives 4. Vocational education, computer education, foreign language, visual or performing arts recommended.

2005-2006 Annual costs. Tuition/fees: $3,939; $11,915 out-of-state. Room/board: $4,740. Books/supplies: $750. Personal expenses: $2,000.

2005-2006 Financial aid. Need-based: Average need met was 16%. Average scholarship/grant was $2,210; average loan $2,394. 54% of total undergraduate aid awarded as scholarships/grants, 46% as loans/jobs. **Non-need-based:** Scholarships awarded for academics, alumni affiliation, art, athletics, job skills, leadership, minority status, music/drama, state residency. **Additional information:** Tuition and/or fee waiver for veterans and Native Americans.

Application procedures. Admission: Priority date 7/1; no deadline. $30 fee. Application may be submitted online. Admission notification on a rolling basis. **Financial aid:** Priority date 3/1; no closing date. FAFSA required. Applicants notified on a rolling basis starting 3/1; must reply within 2 week(s) of notification.

Academics. Special study options: Cooperative education, distance learning, double major, dual enrollment of high school students, honors, independent study, internships, liberal arts/career combination, teacher certification program. **Credit/placement by examination:** AP, CLEP, institutional tests. 30 credit hours maximum toward associate degree, 30 toward bachelor's. **Support services:** Learning center, reduced course load, remedial instruction, study skills assistance, tutoring.

Majors. Biology: General. **Business:** General, communications, tourism/travel. **Conservation:** General, environmental studies, wildlife. **Education:** General, art, biology, business, chemistry, early childhood, elementary, English, health, history, mathematics, multi-level teacher, music, physical, school librarian, science, secondary, social studies, technology/industrial arts. **Liberal arts:** Arts/sciences. **Math:** Applied. **Physical sciences:** Chemistry, geology. **Social sciences:** General. **Visual/performing arts:** General, art, dramatic.

Most popular majors. Business/marketing 20%, education 58%, natural resources/environmental science 7%.

Computing on campus. 125 workstations in dormitories, library, computer center. Dormitories linked to campus network. Commuter students can connect to campus network. Online course registration available.

Student life. Freshman orientation: Mandatory, $50 fee. Preregistration for classes offered. **Policies:** Freshmen permitted cars on campus. **Housing:** Guaranteed on-campus for freshmen. Coed dorms, single-sex dorms, special housing for disabled, apartments, substance-free housing available. $100 deposit. Students with fewer than 30 credits not living with family required to live in dormitory. Transfer students under 21 with fewer than 30 credits not living with parents required to live on campus. **Activities:** Choral groups, drama, literary magazine, music ensembles, radio station, student government, student newspaper, admissions volunteers, Chi Alpha-Christian fellowship, outdoor club, Polynesian club, rodeo club, IT club.

Athletics. NAIA. **Intercollegiate:** Basketball, equestrian, football (tackle) M, golf, rodeo, volleyball W. **Intramural:** Basketball, golf, racquetball, skiing, soccer, softball, table tennis, tennis, volleyball. **Team name:** Bulldogs.

Student services. Alcohol/substance abuse counseling, career counseling, student employment services, financial aid counseling, legal services, on-campus daycare, personal counseling, placement for graduates, veterans' counselor. **Physically disabled:** Services for visually, speech, hearing impaired.

Contact. E-mail: admissions@umwestern.edu
Phone: (406) 683-7331 Toll-free number: (866) 869-6668
Fax: (406) 683-7493
Eric Murray, Dean of Students, University of Montana: Western, 710 South Atlantic Street, Dillon, MT 59725

Nebraska

Bellevue University
Bellevue, Nebraska
www.bellevue.edu **CB code: 6053**

- Private 4-year university and business college
- Commuter campus in large city
- 4,125 degree-seeking undergraduates: 32% part-time, 49% women, 10% African American, 2% Asian American, 6% Hispanic American, 1% Native American, 6% international
- 1,482 degree-seeking graduate students
- 34% graduate within 6 years

General. Founded in 1965. Regionally accredited. Satellite operations throughout tri-state area. Focus on adult learners and non-traditional students. Evening classes offered on trimester calendar. **Degrees:** 1,563 bachelor's awarded; master's offered. **ROTC:** Army, Air Force. **Calendar:** Differs by program, extensive summer session. **Full-time faculty:** 72 total; 51% have terminal degrees, 10% minority, 36% women. **Part-time faculty:** 326 total; 21% have terminal degrees, 5% minority, 39% women. **Class size:** 72% < 20, 28% 20-39.

Freshman class profile.

Out-of-state:	28%	International:	32%

Basis for selection. Open admission, but selective for some programs. Students dismissed from another institution for academic or disciplinary reasons will be accepted for admission after 1 year has lapsed since dismissal from that institution. Admission to Professional Studies program requires 60 transfer credit hours from accredited institution. Michigan English Language Assessment Battery used for placement after arrival. IELT also accepted. **Homeschooled:** Students should submit official verification of completion.

High school preparation. Recommended units include English 3, mathematics 3, social studies 3, history 3, science 3 (laboratory 1), foreign language 3 and academic electives 3.

2006-2007 Annual costs. Tuition/fees: $5,345. Books/supplies: $1,000. Personal expenses: $1,800.

2004-2005 Financial aid. Need-based: 77 full-time freshmen applied for aid; 77 were judged to have need; 77 of these received aid. Average scholarship/grant was $2,554; average loan $2,003. 14% of total undergraduate aid awarded as scholarships/grants, 86% as loans/jobs. **Non-need-based:** Awarded to 597 full-time undergraduates, including 32 freshmen. Scholarships awarded for academics, athletics.

Application procedures. Admission: No deadline. $50 fee, may be waived for applicants with need. Application may be submitted online. Admission notification on a rolling basis. **Financial aid:** Priority date 4/15; no closing date. FAFSA, institutional form required. Applicants notified on a rolling basis starting 4/15; must reply within 2 week(s) of notification.

Academics. All degree programs also available through evening division. Language lab, self-study course support. **Special study options:** Accelerated study, cross-registration, distance learning, double major, dual enrollment of high school students, ESL, independent study, internships, liberal arts/career combination, weekend college. **Credit/placement by examination:** AP, CLEP, IB, institutional tests. Credit awarded for computer proficiency testing in Microsoft applications. **Support services:** Learning center, remedial instruction, study skills assistance, tutoring, writing center.

Majors. Biology: General. **Business:** General, accounting, business admin, e-commerce, human resources, management information systems, marketing. **Communications:** General, public relations. **Computer sciences:** General, information systems, information technology, web page design. **Conservation:** General, environmental science. **Education:** Biology, history, physical. **Health:** Health care admin, premedicine, prenursing, prepharmacy, substance abuse counseling. **Legal studies:** Prelaw. **Liberal arts:** Arts/sciences. **Parks/recreation:** Sports admin. **Protective services:** Law enforcement admin. **Psychology:** General. **Public administration:** General, human services. **Social sciences:** General, sociology. **Visual/performing arts:** Art, art history/conservation, arts management, commercial/advertising art, studio arts.

Most popular majors. Business/marketing 57%, computer/information sciences 9%, health sciences 10%, security/protective services 10%.

Computing on campus. 538 workstations in library, computer center. Commuter students can connect to campus network. Online course registration, online library, helpline, wireless network available.

Student life. Freshman orientation: Available. Preregistration for classes offered. One day program typically held the beginning week of fall term. **Policies:** No alcohol at any student events. Any event must be coordinated through the Student Activities Office. Freshmen permitted cars on campus. **Housing:** Apartments available. **Activities:** Student government, Alpha Chi, Campus Crusade for Christ, computer graphic design club, Delta Epsilon Chi, economics club, institute of management accountants, international club, multicultural student organization, student advisory council, toastmasters.

Athletics. NAIA. **Intercollegiate:** Baseball M, basketball M, soccer, softball W, volleyball W. **Team name:** Bruins.

Student services. Career counseling, student employment services, financial aid counseling, personal counseling, placement for graduates, veterans' counselor. **Physically disabled:** Services for visually, speech, hearing impaired.

Contact. E-mail: info@bellevue.edu
Phone: (402) 293-2000 Toll-free number: (800) 756-7920
Fax: (402) 293-3730
Nicholas Baker, Undergraduate Admissions Manager, Bellevue University, 1000 Galvin Road South, Bellevue, NE 68005-3098

Chadron State College
Chadron, Nebraska
www.csc.edu **CB code: 6466**

- Public 4-year business, liberal arts and teachers college
- Residential campus in small town
- 1,994 degree-seeking undergraduates: 16% part-time, 57% women, 2% African American, 1% Asian American, 2% Hispanic American, 2% Native American, 1% international
- 321 degree-seeking graduate students
- 40% graduate within 6 years

General. Founded in 1911. Regionally accredited. Off-campus classes offered at Scottsbluff, Alliance, Sidney, and throughout western Nebraska and eastern Wyoming. **Degrees:** 380 bachelor's awarded; master's offered. **ROTC:** Army. **Location:** 100 miles from Scottsbluff, 100 miles from Rapid City, South Dakota. **Calendar:** Semester, limited summer session. **Full-time faculty:** 101 total; 57% have terminal degrees, 4% minority, 36% women. **Part-time faculty:** 9 total; 22% have terminal degrees, 11% minority, 33% women. **Class size:** 65% < 20, 30% 20-39, 4% 40-49, less than 1% 50-99. **Special facilities:** Planetarium, herbarium, geological museum.

Freshman class profile. 326 enrolled.

Mid 50% test scores		Rank in top tenth:	11%
ACT:	17-24	Return as sophomores:	70%
GPA 3.50 or higher:	31%	Out-of-state:	29%
GPA 3.0-3.49:	22%	Live on campus:	90%
GPA 2.0-2.99:	28%	International:	1%
Rank in top quarter:	26%		

Basis for selection. Open admission, but selective for some programs. Test scores must be submitted for placement, but no minimum score required. Audition recommended for music program.

High school preparation. 12 units recommended. Recommended units include English 4, mathematics 3, social studies 3, science 2 (laboratory 2). Units in visual or performing arts, computer literacy, or foreign language recommended.

2005-2006 Annual costs. Tuition/fees: $3,672; $6,604 out-of-state. Room/board: $4,074. Books/supplies: $600. Personal expenses: $972.

Financial aid. Non-need-based: Scholarships awarded for academics, alumni affiliation, art, athletics, leadership, minority status, music/drama, state residency.

Application procedures. Admission: No deadline. $15 fee. Application may be submitted online. Admission notification on a rolling basis. **Financial aid:** Priority date 6/1; no closing date. FAFSA, institutional form required. Applicants notified on a rolling basis starting 4/1; must reply within 2 week(s) of notification.

Academics. **Special study options:** Accelerated study, combined bachelor's/graduate degree, cooperative education, distance learning, double major, dual enrollment of high school students, honors, independent study, internships, student-designed major, study abroad, teacher certification program. **Credit/placement by examination:** AP, CLEP, SAT, ACT, institutional tests. 65 credit hours maximum toward bachelor's degree. **Support services:** Learning center, pre-admission summer program, reduced course load, remedial instruction, study skills assistance, tutoring, writing center.

Majors. **Agriculture:** Range science. **Biology:** General. **Business:** Accounting, business admin, finance, management information systems, management science, office management. **Computer sciences:** Information systems. **Education:** Art, biology, business, chemistry, drama/dance, elementary, English, family/consumer sciences, history, mathematics, middle, music, physical, physics, science, secondary, social science, Spanish, technology/industrial arts, trade/industrial. **English:** Speech/rhetoric. **Family/consumer sciences:** General. **Foreign languages:** Spanish. **History:** General. **Legal studies:** General, prelaw. **Liberal arts:** Arts/sciences, library science. **Math:** General. **Parks/recreation:** General. **Physical sciences:** Chemistry. **Psychology:** General. **Public administration:** Social work. **Social sciences:** General, sociology. **Visual/performing arts:** Art, dramatic.

Most popular majors. Biology 11%, business/marketing 20%, education 27%, security/protective services 8%.

Computing on campus. 120 workstations in dormitories, library, computer center, student center. Dormitories wired for high-speed internet access and linked to campus network. Commuter students can connect to campus network. Online course registration, online library, helpline, wireless network available.

Student life. **Freshman orientation:** Available, $50 fee. Preregistration for classes offered. Four or five 2-day weekend orientations held prior to start of fall term. **Policies:** Freshmen permitted cars on campus. **Housing:** Guaranteed on-campus for freshmen. Coed dorms, single-sex dorms, special housing for disabled, apartments, substance-free housing available. $100 nonrefundable deposit, deadline 6/1. **Activities:** Bands, choral groups, dance, drama, music ensembles, musical theater, student government, student newspaper, Circle-K, international club, student education association, multicultural club, Intervarsity Christian Fellowship, White Buffalo Club.

Athletics. NCAA. **Intercollegiate:** Basketball, football (tackle) M, golf W, track and field, volleyball W, wrestling M. **Intramural:** Archery, badminton, basketball, bowling, golf, racquetball, rugby M, softball, track and field, volleyball, wrestling M. **Team name:** Eagles.

Student services. Adult student services, alcohol/substance abuse counseling, career counseling, services for economically disadvantaged, student employment services, financial aid counseling, health services, on-campus daycare, personal counseling, placement for graduates, veterans' counselor. **Physically disabled:** Services for visually, speech, hearing impaired.

Contact. E-mail: inquire@cscl.csc.edu
Phone: (308) 432-6263 Toll-free number: (800) 242-3766
Fax: (308) 432-6229
Tena Gould, Director of Admissions, Chadron State College, 1000 Main Street, Chadron, NE 69337

Clarkson College
Omaha, Nebraska
www.clarksoncollege.edu **CB code: 2250**

- Private 4-year health science college affiliated with Episcopal Church
- Commuter campus in large city
- 640 degree-seeking undergraduates
- 114 graduate students
- Application essay required

General. Founded in 1888. Regionally accredited. Some undergrad and all graduate programs offered through distance learning. Open to all students of all religions. **Degrees:** 74 bachelor's, 39 associate awarded; master's offered. **ROTC:** Army, Air Force. **Location:** 50 miles from Lincoln, 132 miles from Des Moines. **Calendar:** Semester, extensive summer session. **Full-time faculty:** 42 total. **Class size:** 71% < 20, 16% 20-39, 5% 40-49, 8% 50-99. **Special facilities:** Health care clinical facilities for professional education (more than 180 clinical sites) Fully energized radiologic technology lab on campus.

Freshman class profile. 607 applied, 217 admitted, 98 enrolled.

Mid 50% test scores			
ACT:	19-23	Out-of-state:	79%
		Live on campus:	80%

Basis for selection. Open admission, but selective for some programs. GPA, class rank, test scores, essay important. ACT recommended. **Home-schooled:** Must take GED and submit ACT scores. Essay required. Transcript or portfolio recommended.

High school preparation. 9 units required. Required and recommended units include English 3-4, mathematics 2-4, social studies 2-3, history 2, science 2-4 (laboratory 1-2) and foreign language 2.

2005-2006 Annual costs. Tuition/fees: $10,932. Distance learning fee: $33 per credit-hour. Room only: $4,200. Books/supplies: $600. Personal expenses: $1,500.

Financial aid. **Non-need-based:** Scholarships awarded for academics, alumni affiliation, minority status, religious affiliation.

Application procedures. **Admission:** Closing date 7/25 (receipt date). $25 fee. Admission notification on a rolling basis. Must reply by May 1 or within 4 week(s) if notified thereafter. **Financial aid:** Priority date 4/1; no closing date. FAFSA, institutional form required. Applicants notified on a rolling basis starting 4/13; must reply within 3 week(s) of notification.

Academics. **Special study options:** Accelerated study, combined bachelor's/graduate degree, cooperative education, cross-registration, distance learning, double major, dual enrollment of high school students, external degree, independent study, internships, study abroad. **Credit/placement by examination:** CLEP, institutional tests. 40 credit hours maximum toward associate degree, 88 toward bachelor's. Unlimited number of hours of credit by examination may be counted toward degree if residency requirement of 40 hours is met. **Support services:** Learning center, reduced course load, study skills assistance, tutoring, writing center.

Majors. **Business:** General, business admin. **Health:** Health care admin, medical radiologic technology/radiation therapy, nursing (RN), preop/surgical nursing, radiologic technology/medical imaging.

Computing on campus. 60 workstations in dormitories, library, computer center. Dormitories wired for high-speed internet access. Commuter students can connect to campus network. Online library, helpline, repair service available.

Student life. **Freshman orientation:** Mandatory. Preregistration for classes offered. One day program held on Friday before classes begin. **Policies:** Freshmen permitted cars on campus. **Housing:** Guaranteed on-campus for freshmen. Coed dorms, apartments available. $250 deposit. Board plan not available, kitchens located in each apartment. **Activities:** Student government, student newspaper, Christian Fellowship, Red Cross, National Student Nurses Association, Fellows club, Ambassador club, student leadership council.

Athletics. **Intercollegiate:** Skiing M.

Student services. Adult student services, alcohol/substance abuse counseling, career counseling, student employment services, financial aid counseling, health services, minority student services, on-campus daycare, personal counseling, placement for graduates. **Physically disabled:** Services for visually, hearing impaired.

Contact. E-mail: admiss@clarksoncollege.edu
Phone: (402) 552-3041 Toll-free number: (800) 647-5500
Fax: (402) 552-6057
Sara Bonney, Director of Admission, Clarkson College, 101 South 42nd Street, Omaha, NE 68131-2739

College of Saint Mary
Omaha, Nebraska
www.csm.edu **CB code: 6106**

- Private 4-year nursing and liberal arts college for women affiliated with Roman Catholic Church
- Commuter campus in very large city
- 917 degree-seeking undergraduates: 30% part-time, 100% women, 7% African American, 1% Asian American, 3% Hispanic American, 1% Native American, 1% international
- 16 degree-seeking graduate students
- 56% of applicants admitted
- SAT or ACT (ACT writing optional) required
- 46% graduate within 6 years

General. Founded in 1923. Regionally accredited. Weekend accelerated programs in Omaha and Lincoln. **Degrees:** 112 bachelor's, 97 associate awarded; master's offered. **ROTC:** Army, Air Force. **Location:** 10 miles from Omaha. **Calendar:** Semester, limited summer session. **Full-time faculty:** 54 total; 43% have terminal degrees, 7% minority, 80% women. **Part-time faculty:** 114 total; 17% have terminal degrees, 3% minority, 71% women. **Class size:** 76% < 20, 22% 20-39, 1% 40-49, less than 1% 50-99.

Freshman class profile. 417 applied, 233 admitted, 79 enrolled.

Mid 50% test scores		**Rank in top tenth:**	11%
ACT:	18-23	**End year in good standing:**	76%
GPA 3.50 or higher:	37%	**Return as sophomores:**	71%
GPA 3.0-3.49:	40%	**Out-of-state:**	14%
GPA 2.0-2.99:	22%	**Live on campus:**	59%
Rank in top quarter:	46%		

Basis for selection. Test scores, secondary school record, class rank important. Recommendations considered. **Homeschooled:** Must take ACT exam and submit scores.

High school preparation. Required and recommended units include English 4, mathematics 2-3, social studies 2 and science 2-3. Chemistry and biology required of nursing, occupational therapy and preprofessional studies students.

2005-2006 Annual costs. Tuition/fees: $18,038. Room/board: $5,900.

2005-2006 Financial aid. Need-based: Average need met was 51%. Average scholarship/grant was $8,717; average loan $3,488. 49% of total undergraduate aid awarded as scholarships/grants, 51% as loans/jobs. **Non-need-based:** Scholarships awarded for academics, athletics, music/drama.

Application procedures. Admission: No deadline. $30 fee, may be waived for applicants with need. Application may be submitted online. Admission notification on a rolling basis. **Financial aid:** Priority date 3/1; no closing date. FAFSA required. Applicants notified on a rolling basis starting 3/1; must reply within 2 week(s) of notification.

Academics. Special study options: Accelerated study, combined bachelor's/graduate degree, cooperative education, cross-registration, distance learning, double major, exchange student, independent study, internships, liberal arts/career combination, student-designed major, teacher certification program, weekend college. **Credit/placement by examination:** AP, CLEP, IB, institutional tests. 30% of program may be earned through credit by examination. **Support services:** Learning center, reduced course load, remedial instruction, study skills assistance, tutoring, writing center.

Majors. Biology: General. **Business:** Business admin. **Computer sciences:** General. **Education:** Biology, chemistry, computer, early childhood, elementary, English, mathematics, middle, reading, science, secondary, social science, special. **Health:** Clinical lab technology, medical records admin, nursing (RN), predentistry, premedicine, prepharmacy, preveterinary. **Legal studies:** Paralegal. **Liberal arts:** Arts/sciences. **Math:** General. **Physical sciences:** General, chemistry. **Psychology:** General. **Public administration:** Human services. **Theology:** Theology. **Visual/performing arts:** Studio arts.

Most popular majors. Business/marketing 22%, computer/information sciences 6%, education 15%, English 6%, health sciences 21%, legal studies 11%, public administration/social services 6%.

Computing on campus. 90 workstations in dormitories, library, computer center. Dormitories wired for high-speed internet access and linked to campus network. Online course registration, online library available.

Student life. Freshman orientation: Available. Preregistration for classes offered. One day summer program. **Policies:** Freshmen permitted cars on campus. **Housing:** Guaranteed on-campus for freshmen. $125 deposit, deadline 8/1. Residence hall for single mothers with children. **Activities:** Choral groups, student government, FLAMES, do unto others board, residence hall council, Golden S, student nurse association, student senate, campus activities board, occupational therapy club, student education association of Nebraska, business student association.

Athletics. NAIA. **Intercollegiate:** Basketball W, cheerleading M, cross-country W, soccer W, softball W, volleyball W. **Team name:** Flames.

Student services. Adult student services, alcohol/substance abuse counseling, campus ministries, career counseling, services for economically disadvantaged, student employment services, financial aid counseling, health services, minority student services, on-campus daycare, personal counseling, placement for graduates, veterans' counselor, women's services. **Physically disabled:** Services for visually, speech, hearing impaired.

Contact. E-mail: enroll@csm.edu
Phone: (402) 399-2405 Toll-free number: (800) 926-5534
Fax: (402) 399-2412
Lori Werth, Vice President of Enrollment Management, College of Saint Mary, 7000 Mercy Road, Omaha, NE 68106

Concordia University
Seward, Nebraska
www.cune.edu **CB code: 6116**

- Private 4-year university and teachers college affiliated with Lutheran Church - Missouri Synod
- Residential campus in small town
- 1,123 degree-seeking undergraduates: 3% part-time, 55% women, 1% African American, 1% Asian American, 2% Hispanic American
- 160 degree-seeking graduate students
- 88% of applicants admitted
- SAT or ACT (ACT writing recommended) required
- 61% graduate within 6 years

General. Founded in 1894. Regionally accredited. Christ-centered environment. **Degrees:** 379 bachelor's awarded; master's offered. **ROTC:** Army, Air Force. **Location:** 25 miles from Lincoln, 75 miles from Omaha. **Calendar:** Semester, limited summer session. **Full-time faculty:** 56 total; 93% have terminal degrees, 30% women. **Part-time faculty:** 70 total; 24% have terminal degrees, 1% minority, 47% women. **Class size:** 52% < 20, 43% 20-39, 4% 40-49, less than 1% 50-99. **Special facilities:** Natural history museum, observatory, arboretum.

Freshman class profile. 778 applied, 687 admitted, 291 enrolled.

Mid 50% test scores		**GPA 2.0-2.99:**	21%
SAT verbal:	420-610	**Rank in top quarter:**	60%
SAT math:	430-580	**Rank in top tenth:**	24%
ACT:	20-27	**Out-of-state:**	65%
GPA 3.50 or higher:	53%	**Live on campus:**	97%
GPA 3.0-3.49:	25%		

Basis for selection. 2.5 high school GPA and rank in top half of class very important. Students with GPA below 2.5 or ACT scores between 15-18 remanded to admission committee for decision. Audition required for drama, music, and speech programs; portfolio required for art program.

High school preparation. 16 units required. Required units include English 4, mathematics 3, social studies 3, science 2 and foreign language 2. One unit each in music, art, and physical education recommended.

2006-2007 Annual costs. Tuition/fees (projected): $18,800. Room/board: $4,970. Books/supplies: $700. Personal expenses: $1,200.

2005-2006 Financial aid. Need-based: Average need met was 93%. Average scholarship/grant was $3,893; average loan $2,503. 74% of total undergraduate aid awarded as scholarships/grants, 26% as loans/jobs. **Non-need-based:** Scholarships awarded for academics, athletics, religious affiliation.

Application procedures. Admission: Priority date 7/1; deadline 8/1 (receipt date). $25 fee, may be waived for applicants with need. Application may be submitted online. Admission notification on a rolling basis beginning on or about 6/1. Must reply by May 1 or within 4 week(s) if notified thereafter. Early application encouraged because of limited housing availability. Campus visit required for conditionally admitted students. **Financial aid:** Priority date 3/1, closing date 5/1. FAFSA, institutional form required. Applicants notified on a rolling basis starting 3/1; must reply within 4 week(s) of notification.

Academics. Curriculum for degree completion program for bachelor of arts in organizational management contains 16 modules taken sequentially one night a week for 18 months. Summer term offering hybrid online and face to face instruction. **Special study options:** Accelerated study, combined bachelor's/graduate degree, cooperative education, distance learning, double major, dual enrollment of high school students, ESL, exchange student, honors, independent study, internships, liberal arts/career combination, study abroad, teacher certification program. India semester, China summer school, Slovakia semester, Indonesia. **Credit/placement by examination:** AP, CLEP, IB, institutional tests. **Support services:** Learning center, reduced course load, study skills assistance, tutoring, writing center.

Majors. Biology: General. **Business:** Accounting, business admin, management information systems. **Communications:** General. **Computer sciences:** Computer science. **Education:** General, art, biology, business, chemistry, computer, early childhood, elementary, English, ESL, family/consumer sciences, geography, health, history, mathematics, middle, multi-level teacher, music, physical, physics, science, secondary, social science, Spanish, special, speech, technology/industrial arts. **Foreign languages:** Spanish. **Health:** Predentistry, premedicine, prenursing, prepharmacy, preveterinary. **History:** General. **Interdisciplinary:** Behavioral sciences, natural sciences. **Legal studies:** Prelaw. **Math:** General. **Parks/recreation:** Exercise sciences, health/fitness, sports admin. **Physical sciences:** General, chemistry. **Psychology:** General. **Social sciences:** General, geography. **Theology:**

Preministerial, religious ed, sacred music, theology, youth ministry. **Visual/performing arts:** Commercial/advertising art, dramatic, piano/organ, voice/opera.

Most popular majors. Business/marketing 12%, education 30%, philosophy/religious studies 38%.

Computing on campus. 170 workstations in dormitories, library, computer center, student center. Dormitories wired for high-speed internet access and linked to campus network. Commuter students can connect to campus network. Online course registration, online library, helpline, student web hosting available.

Student life. **Freshman orientation:** Mandatory. Preregistration for classes offered. 3 days before classes start. Includes community service events and community building. **Policies:** College responsibly maintains Christian standards of conduct among its students, faculty and staff. Freshmen permitted cars on campus. **Housing:** Guaranteed on-campus for freshmen. Single-sex dorms, special housing for disabled, apartments, substance-free housing available. $100 deposit, deadline 8/24. **Activities:** Bands, choral groups, drama, literary magazine, music ensembles, musical theater, student government, student newspaper, symphony orchestra, student worship committee, Circle K, Clowns for Christ, Concordia Youth Ministry, Ambassadors for Christ, Multicultural Awareness Club, Peers and Leaders Serving.

Athletics. NAIA. **Intercollegiate:** Baseball M, basketball, cross-country, football (tackle) M, golf, soccer, softball W, tennis, track and field, volleyball W. **Intramural:** Basketball, bowling, football (non-tackle), racquetball, soccer, softball, table tennis, tennis, track and field, volleyball. **Team name:** Bulldogs.

Student services. Adult student services, alcohol/substance abuse counseling, campus ministries, career counseling, services for economically disadvantaged, student employment services, financial aid counseling, health services, minority student services, personal counseling, placement for graduates. **Physically disabled:** Services for visually, speech, hearing impaired.

Contact. E-mail: admiss@seward.cune.edu
Phone: (402) 643-7233 Toll-free number: (800) 535-5494 ext. 7233
Fax: (402) 643-4073
Chad Thies, Director of Admission, Concordia University, 800 North Columbia Avenue, Seward, NE 68434-9989

Creighton University

Omaha, Nebraska **CB member**
www.creighton.edu **CB code: 6121**

- Private 4-year university affiliated with Roman Catholic Church
- Residential campus in large city
- 3,904 degree-seeking undergraduates: 7% part-time, 60% women, 3% African American, 7% Asian American, 4% Hispanic American, 1% Native American, 1% international
- 2,802 degree-seeking graduate students
- 87% of applicants admitted
- SAT or ACT (ACT writing optional), application essay required

General. Founded in 1878. Regionally accredited. College in the Jesuit tradition. **Degrees:** 792 bachelor's awarded; master's, doctoral, first professional offered. **ROTC:** Army, Air Force. **Calendar:** Semester, extensive summer session. **Full-time faculty:** 475 total; 85% have terminal degrees, 12% minority, 39% women. **Part-time faculty:** 174 total; 27% have terminal degrees, 10% minority, 52% women. **Class size:** 46% < 20, 43% 20-39, 6% 40-49, 4% 50-99, less than 1% >100. **Special facilities:** Performing arts center.

Freshman class profile. 3,435 applied, 2,985 admitted, 971 enrolled.

Mid 50% test scores			
SAT verbal:	530-660	Rank in top quarter:	73%
SAT math:	540-660	Rank in top tenth:	40%
ACT:	23-29	Out-of-state:	62%
GPA 3.50 or higher:	74%	Live on campus:	90%
GPA 3.0-3.49:	19%	Fraternities:	24%
GPA 2.0-2.99:	7%	Sororities:	34%

Basis for selection. School record, type of school, test scores, letters of recommendation important, class rank considered. Applicants may elect to submit personal statement detailing qualifications not reflected in credentials. **Homeschooled:** GED required.

High school preparation. College-preparatory program recommended. 16 units recommended. Recommended units include English 4, mathematics 3, social studies 1, history 1, science 2, foreign language 2 and academic electives 3.

2005-2006 Annual costs. Tuition/fees: $22,382. Room/board: $7,540. Books/supplies: $1,000. Personal expenses: $1,400.

2005-2006 Financial aid. **Need-based:** 766 full-time freshmen applied for aid; 598 were judged to have need; 578 of these received aid. Average need met was 91%. Average scholarship/grant was $15,096; average loan $5,188. 65% of total undergraduate aid awarded as scholarships/grants, 35% as loans/jobs. **Non-need-based:** Awarded to 2,813 full-time undergraduates, including 838 freshmen. Scholarships awarded for academics, alumni affiliation, art, athletics, leadership, minority status, music/drama, ROTC. **Additional information:** For academic scholarship consideration, student must be admitted by January 1 of fall matriculation.

Application procedures. **Admission:** Priority date 1/1; deadline 8/1 (postmark date). $40 fee, may be waived for applicants with need. Application may be submitted online. Admission notification on a rolling basis beginning on or about 9/1. Must reply by May 1 or within 2 week(s) if notified thereafter. Preferred reply date May 1. Students notified of admission after May 1 should reply as soon as possible. March 1 is priority deadline for scholarship purposes for international students. **Financial aid:** Priority date 4/1; no closing date. FAFSA, institutional form required. Applicants notified on a rolling basis starting 3/15; must reply by 5/1 or within 4 week(s) of notification.

Academics. Sequences of courses offered in preengineering, predentistry, prelaw, premedicine, prepharmacy, prephysical therapy, preveterinary. Institution's students given admissions preference into all of university's professional schools. Core curriculum required (61 semester hours from 5 areas: cultures, ideas and civilizations; theology, philosophy and ethics; natural science; social and behavioral sciences; skills). **Special study options:** Accelerated study, combined bachelor's/graduate degree, cross-registration, distance learning, double major, dual enrollment of high school students, ESL, exchange student, honors, independent study, internships, liberal arts/career combination, study abroad, teacher certification program, Washington semester. 3-2 program in engineering with University of Detroit Mercy; study abroad opportunities at 110 partner institutions in 40 countries. **Credit/placement by examination:** AP, CLEP, IB, SAT, ACT, institutional tests. CLEP Subject Examinations must be taken with essay where applicable. **Support services:** Learning center, pre-admission summer program, reduced course load, remedial instruction, study skills assistance, tutoring, writing center.

Majors. **Area/ethnic studies:** American, Native American. **Biology:** General. **Business:** Accounting, communications, finance, international, management information systems, marketing. **Communications:** General, journalism, organizational. **Computer sciences:** Computer science, programming. **Conservation:** Environmental science. **Education:** Chemistry, elementary, Latin. **Foreign languages:** Ancient Greek, classics, French, German, Latin, Spanish. **Health:** EMT paramedic, health care admin, nursing (RN). **History:** General. **Interdisciplinary:** Peace/conflict. **Legal studies:** Prelaw. **Math:** General, applied. **Parks/recreation:** Exercise sciences. **Philosophy/religion:** Philosophy. **Physical sciences:** Atmospheric science, chemistry, physics. **Psychology:** General. **Public administration:** Social work. **Social sciences:** Anthropology, economics, international relations, political science, sociology. **Theology:** Theology. **Visual/performing arts:** Art, arts management, commercial/advertising art, dramatic.

Most popular majors. Biology 8%, business/marketing 21%, communications/journalism 6%, health sciences 26%, psychology 6%.

Computing on campus. 520 workstations in dormitories, library, computer center, student center. Dormitories wired for high-speed internet access and linked to campus network. Commuter students can connect to campus network. Online course registration, online library, helpline, repair service, student web hosting, wireless network available.

Student life. **Freshman orientation:** Mandatory. Preregistration for classes offered. Welcome week first week of fall semester. **Policies:** Freshmen permitted cars on campus. **Housing:** Guaranteed on-campus for all undergraduates. Coed dorms, single-sex dorms, special housing for disabled, apartments available. $100 deposit, deadline 5/1. **Activities:** Bands, choral groups, dance, drama, literary magazine, music ensembles, musical theater, radio station, student government, student newspaper, symphony orchestra, TV station, campus ministry, world hunger awareness group, Afro-American students association, international relations club, women's resource center, community service center, Christian life community, Young Democrats, Young Republican.

Athletics. NCAA. **Intercollegiate:** Baseball M, basketball, cross-country, golf, rowing (crew) W, soccer, softball W, tennis, volleyball W. **Intramural:** Badminton, basketball, bowling, football (non-tackle), golf, racquetball, soccer, softball, tennis, volleyball. **Team name:** Bluejays.

Student services. Adult student services, alcohol/substance abuse counseling, campus ministries, career counseling, services for economically disadvantaged, student employment services, financial aid counseling, health services, minority student services, on-campus daycare, personal counseling, placement for graduates, veterans' counselor, women's services. **Physically disabled:** Services for visually, speech, hearing impaired. **Learning disabled:** Comprehensive services available.

Contact. E-mail: admissions@creighton.edu
Phone: (402) 280-2703 Toll-free number: (800) 282-5835
Fax: (402) 280-2685
Mary Chase, Director of Admissions, Creighton University, 2500 California Plaza, Omaha, NE 68178-0001

Dana College

Blair, Nebraska — **CB member**
www.dana.edu — **CB code: 6157**

- Private 4-year liberal arts college affiliated with Evangelical Lutheran Church in America
- Residential campus in small town
- 667 degree-seeking undergraduates: 2% part-time, 45% women, 5% African American, 1% Asian American, 3% Hispanic American, 1% Native American, 1% international
- 76% of applicants admitted
- SAT or ACT (ACT writing optional) required
- 57% graduate within 6 years; 13% enter graduate study

General. Founded in 1884. Regionally accredited. **Degrees:** 116 bachelor's awarded. **ROTC:** Army, Air Force. **Location:** 20 miles from Omaha. **Calendar:** 4-1-4, limited summer session. **Full-time faculty:** 42 total; 69% have terminal degrees, 5% minority, 60% women. **Part-time faculty:** 33 total; 12% have terminal degrees, 3% minority, 39% women. **Class size:** 67% < 20, 30% 20-39, 1% 40-49, 2% 50-99. **Special facilities:** Fine arts center, Danish heritage room, Danish immigrant archives.

Freshman class profile. 901 applied, 686 admitted, 208 enrolled.

Mid 50% test scores			
SAT verbal:	420-540	Rank in top quarter:	35%
SAT math:	430-520	Rank in top tenth:	10%
ACT:	19-24	End year in good standing:	82%
GPA 3.50 or higher:	42%	Return as sophomores:	58%
GPA 3.0-3.49:	29%	Out-of-state:	40%
GPA 2.0-2.99:	29%	Live on campus:	96%

Basis for selection. 2.0 cumulative GPA in college preparatory courses, standardized test scores important. Recommendations by school officials considered. **Homeschooled:** Transcript of courses and grades required. ACT composite of 18 or above or combined SAT score of 860 or above (exclusive of Writing), a signed parental transcript, plus one of the following: transcript from high school or college where courses were taken, GED score of 500 or above, portfolio of representative work.

High school preparation. 16 units recommended. Recommended units include English 4, mathematics 3, social studies 4, science 3 (laboratory 2) and foreign language 2.

2005-2006 Annual costs. Tuition/fees: $17,450. Room/board: $5,320. Books/supplies: $750. Personal expenses: $1,150.

2005-2006 Financial aid. Need-based: 202 full-time freshmen applied for aid; 174 were judged to have need; 174 of these received aid. Average need met was 89%. Average scholarship/grant was $4,678; average loan $3,412. 43% of total undergraduate aid awarded as scholarships/grants, 57% as loans/jobs. **Non-need-based:** Awarded to 855 full-time undergraduates, including 293 freshmen. Scholarships awarded for academics, alumni affiliation, art, athletics, leadership, music/drama, religious affiliation, ROTC, state residency. **Additional information:** Auditions recommended for music and drama scholarship applicants. Portfolios recommended for art, graphic design, and cheerleading/dance scholarship applicants.

Application procedures. Admission: No deadline. No application fee. Application may be submitted online. Admission notification on a rolling basis. **Financial aid:** Priority date 3/15; no closing date. FAFSA, institutional form required. Applicants notified on a rolling basis starting 3/1; must reply within 3 week(s) of notification.

Academics. Special study options: Cross-registration, double major, dual enrollment of high school students, ESL, honors, independent study, internships, liberal arts/career combination, New York semester, semester at sea, student-designed major, study abroad, teacher certification program, United Nations semester, urban semester. **Credit/placement by examination:** AP, CLEP, IB, SAT, ACT, institutional tests. 30 credit hours maximum toward bachelor's degree. **Support services:** Learning center, reduced course load, remedial instruction, study skills assistance, tutoring.

Majors. Biology: General. **Business:** Accounting, business admin, management information systems. **Communications:** General, organizational. **Communications technology:** Animation/special effects. **Computer sciences:** Computer science, web page design. **Conservation:** General, environmental studies. **Education:** General, art, biology, business, chemistry, drama/dance, elementary, English, foreign languages, German, history, mathematics, multi-level teacher, music, physical, science, secondary, social science, social studies, Spanish, special, speech. **English:** English lit. **Foreign languages:** German, Spanish. **Health:** Clinical lab technology, predentistry, premedicine, prepharmacy, preveterinary. **History:** General. **Legal studies:** Prelaw. **Liberal arts:** Arts/sciences. **Math:** General. **Parks/recreation:** Health/fitness, sports admin. **Philosophy/religion:** Religion. **Physical sciences:** Chemistry. **Protective services:** Law enforcement admin. **Psychology:** General. **Public administration:** Social work. **Social sciences:** General, sociology. **Visual/performing arts:** Art, commercial/advertising art.

Computing on campus. 110 workstations in dormitories, library, computer center. Dormitories wired for high-speed internet access and linked to campus network. Commuter students can connect to campus network. Online library, student web hosting, wireless network available.

Student life. Freshman orientation: Mandatory. Preregistration for classes offered. **Policies:** Freshmen permitted cars on campus. **Housing:** Guaranteed on-campus for all undergraduates. Coed dorms, single-sex dorms, apartments, substance-free housing available. $100 deposit. **Activities:** Bands, choral groups, dance, drama, film society, literary magazine, music ensembles, musical theater, radio station, student government, student newspaper, TV station, Fellowship of Christian Athletes, social awareness organization, campus ministry, student activities board, German club, Help Our People Expand, communication club.

Athletics. NAIA. **Intercollegiate:** Baseball M, basketball, cross-country, football (tackle) M, golf W, soccer, softball W, track and field, volleyball W, wrestling M. **Intramural:** Basketball, bowling, handball, soccer, softball, swimming, table tennis, tennis, volleyball. **Team name:** Vikings.

Student services. Adult student services, alcohol/substance abuse counseling, campus ministries, career counseling, student employment services, financial aid counseling, health services, personal counseling, placement for graduates, veterans' counselor. **Physically disabled:** Services for visually, hearing impaired.

Contact. E-mail: admissions@dana.edu
Phone: (402) 426-7222 Toll-free number: (800) 444-3262 ext. 1
Fax: (402) 426-7386
James Lynes, Dean of Enrollment, Dana College, 2848 College Drive, Blair, NE 68008-1099

Doane College

Crete, Nebraska — **CB member**
www.doane.edu — **CB code: 6165**

- Private 4-year liberal arts college affiliated with United Church of Christ
- Residential campus in small town
- 1,590 degree-seeking undergraduates: 15% part-time, 49% women
- 658 degree-seeking graduate students
- 80% of applicants admitted
- 64% graduate within 6 years

General. Founded in 1872. Regionally accredited. Campuses also in Lincoln and Grand Island. **Degrees:** 371 bachelor's awarded; master's offered. **ROTC:** Army, Air Force. **Location:** 25 miles from Lincoln, 75 miles from Omaha. **Calendar:** 4-1-4, limited summer session. **Full-time faculty:** 80 total; 56% have terminal degrees, 4% minority, 40% women. **Part-time faculty:** 55 total; 7% have terminal degrees, 2% minority, 56% women. **Class size:** 77% < 20, 23% 20-39. **Special facilities:** Arboretum, open-air theater, observatory, all-American rose test garden, ropes challenge course, fitness trail.

Freshman class profile. 1,144 applied, 919 admitted, 263 enrolled.

Mid 50% test scores			
ACT:	20-26	Return as sophomores:	71%
Rank in top quarter:	51%	Out-of-state:	21%
Rank in top tenth:	22%	Live on campus:	98%

Basis for selection. Academic and personal record, recommendations, test scores important. Class rank considered. SAT or ACT recommended.

Interview required for academically marginal students; audition required for drama, music programs and forensics; portfolio required for art program.

High school preparation. College-preparatory program recommended. Recommended units include English 4, mathematics 3, social studies 3 and science 4.

2005-2006 Annual costs. Tuition/fees: $17,536. Room/board: $4,922. Books/supplies: $700. Personal expenses: $1,030.

2005-2006 Financial aid. **Need-based:** 295 full-time freshmen applied for aid; 253 were judged to have need; 253 of these received aid. Average need met was 97%. Average scholarship/grant was $10,211; average loan $3,000. 55% of total undergraduate aid awarded as scholarships/grants, 45% as loans/jobs. **Non-need-based:** Scholarships awarded for academics, art, athletics, leadership, music/drama, religious affiliation.

Application procedures. **Admission:** No deadline. $15 fee, may be waived for applicants with need. Application may be submitted online. Admission notification on a rolling basis beginning on or about 3/1. **Financial aid:** Priority date 3/1; no closing date. FAFSA, institutional form required. Applicants notified on a rolling basis starting 2/1; must reply within 2 week(s) of notification.

Academics. Midwest Institute for International Students prepares students to meet English language requirement for admission to Doane and other American colleges. **Special study options:** Accelerated study, combined bachelor's/graduate degree, cooperative education, cross-registration, double major, dual enrollment of high school students, ESL, exchange student, external degree, honors, independent study, internships, liberal arts/career combination, student-designed major, study abroad, teacher certification program. 3-2 programs in engineering with Washington University, Columbia University, 3-2 program in environmental and forestry studies with Duke University. **Credit/placement by examination:** AP, CLEP, IB, ACT, institutional tests. 36 credit hours maximum toward bachelor's degree. International students who successfully complete Midwest Institute ESL program may be admitted without TOEFL scores. **Support services:** Learning center, reduced course load, remedial instruction, study skills assistance, tutoring, writing center.

Majors. **Biology:** General. **Communications:** General, journalism, media studies, organizational. **Computer sciences:** General, computer science, information systems. **Conservation:** Environmental studies. **Education:** Elementary, physical, special. **English:** Speech/rhetoric. **Foreign languages:** French, German, Spanish. **History:** General. **Math:** General. **Philosophy/religion:** Philosophy, religion. **Physical sciences:** Chemistry, physics. **Psychology:** General. **Public administration:** General, human services. **Social sciences:** General, economics, international relations, political science, sociology. **Visual/performing arts:** Art, commercial/advertising art, dramatic.

Computing on campus. 400 workstations in dormitories, library, computer center, student center. Dormitories wired for high-speed internet access and linked to campus network. Commuter students can connect to campus network. Online course registration, online library, helpline, student web hosting, wireless network available.

Student life. **Freshman orientation:** Available. Preregistration for classes offered. **Policies:** Freshmen permitted cars on campus. **Housing:** Guaranteed on-campus for freshmen. Coed dorms, single-sex dorms, apartments available. $200 partly refundable deposit. Unmarried students under 22 not living with parents expected to live on campus. **Activities:** Bands, choral groups, dance, drama, film society, literary magazine, music ensembles, musical theater, radio station, student government, student newspaper, TV station, student education association, Doane speakers, Club Internationale, Fellowship of Christian Athletes, campus ministry, American Minority Student Alliance, College Republicans, Young Democrats.

Athletics. NAIA. **Intercollegiate:** Baseball M, basketball, bowling, cross-country, football (tackle) M, golf, soccer, softball W, tennis, track and field, volleyball W. **Intramural:** Basketball, football (tackle) M, golf, softball, swimming, tennis, volleyball. **Team name:** Tigers.

Student services. Adult student services, campus ministries, career counseling, student employment services, financial aid counseling, health services, personal counseling, placement for graduates, veterans' counselor.

Contact. E-mail: admissions@doane.edu
Phone: (402) 826-8222 Toll-free number: (800) 333-6263
Fax: (402) 826-8600
Dan Kunzman, Dean of Admission, Doane College, 1014 Boswell Avenue, Crete, NE 68333

Grace University
Omaha, Nebraska
www.graceu.edu **CB code: 6248**

- Private 4-year university and Bible college affiliated with interdenominational tradition
- Residential campus in very large city
- 360 degree-seeking undergraduates: 30% part-time, 59% women, 6% African American, 1% Asian American, 1% Hispanic American
- 80 graduate students
- 97% of applicants admitted
- ACT with writing, application essay required

General. Founded in 1943. Regionally accredited; also accredited by ABHE. **Degrees:** 77 bachelor's, 7 associate awarded; master's offered. **Calendar:** Semester, limited summer session. **Full-time faculty:** 21 total. **Part-time faculty:** 37 total.

Freshman class profile. 226 applied, 219 admitted, 76 enrolled.

Mid 50% test scores		SAT math:	390-540
SAT verbal:	410-650	ACT:	19-25

Basis for selection. School achievement record, religious affiliation/commitment, test scores, recommendations, and student profile important. ACT offered during registration for students who have not submitted score prior to enrollment. Conditional admission for students who have not taken SAT/ACT. Audition required for music programs. **Homeschooled:** ACT score of 20 or GED required.

High school preparation. Those admitted to teacher education program must have 4 units of language arts, 2 units of mathematics, 2 units of sciences, 2 units of social sciences.

2005-2006 Annual costs. Tuition/fees: $11,980. Room/board: $5,400.

Financial aid. **Non-need-based:** Scholarships awarded for academics, alumni affiliation, music/drama, religious affiliation.

Application procedures. **Admission:** No deadline. $35 fee, may be waived for applicants with need. Application may be submitted online. Admission notification on a rolling basis. **Financial aid:** Priority date 2/1; no closing date. FAFSA, institutional form required. Applicants notified on a rolling basis starting 4/15; must reply within 2 week(s) of notification.

Academics. **Special study options:** Accelerated study, double major, dual enrollment of high school students, ESL, independent study, internships, liberal arts/career combination, study abroad, teacher certification program. Adult degree completion program. **Credit/placement by examination:** AP, CLEP, ACT. 15 credit hours maximum toward bachelor's degree. Prior work/life experience limited to adult degree completion program. **Support services:** Learning center, reduced course load, study skills assistance, tutoring.

Majors. **Business:** Management science. **Communications:** Broadcast journalism, journalism. **Education:** Music. **Family/consumer sciences:** Family studies. **Health:** Nursing (RN). **Liberal arts:** Arts/sciences. **Theology:** Bible, missionary, religious ed, sacred music, theology.

Computing on campus. 35 workstations in library, computer center. Dormitories wired for high-speed internet access and linked to campus network. Commuter students can connect to campus network. Online course registration, online library available.

Student life. **Freshman orientation:** Mandatory. Preregistration for classes offered. Held weekly throughout semester. **Policies:** Religious observance required. Freshmen permitted cars on campus. **Housing:** Guaranteed on-campus for freshmen. Single-sex dorms, apartments, substance-free housing available. **Activities:** Concert band, choral groups, drama, music ensembles, student government, student newspaper.

Athletics. NCCAA. **Intercollegiate:** Basketball, soccer M, volleyball W. **Intramural:** Basketball M, volleyball W. **Team name:** Royals.

Student services. Career counseling, student employment services, financial aid counseling, health services, personal counseling, placement for graduates.

Contact. E-mail: admissions@graceuniversity.edu
Phone: (800) 383-1422 Toll-free number: (800) 383-1422
Fax: (402) 341-9587
Diane Lee, Director of Admissions, Grace University, 1311 South Ninth Street, Omaha, NE 68108

Hastings College

Hastings, Nebraska — **CB member**
www.hastings.edu — **CB code: 6270**

- Private 4-year liberal arts college affiliated with Presbyterian Church (USA)
- Residential campus in large town
- 1,114 degree-seeking undergraduates: 1% part-time, 48% women, 3% African American, 1% Asian American, 2% Hispanic American, 1% international
- 44 degree-seeking graduate students
- 79% of applicants admitted
- SAT or ACT (ACT writing optional) required
- 62% graduate within 6 years; 24% enter graduate study

General. Founded in 1882. Regionally accredited. Vocation and Values program asks the campus community to explore how faith intersects with vocation. **Degrees:** 221 bachelor's awarded; master's offered. **Location:** 90 miles from Lincoln, 150 miles from Omaha. **Calendar:** 4-1-4, limited summer session. **Full-time faculty:** 79 total; 71% have terminal degrees, 33% women. **Part-time faculty:** 42 total; 12% have terminal degrees, 2% minority, 62% women. **Class size:** 66% < 20, 33% 20-39, less than 1% 40-49, less than 1% 50-99. **Special facilities:** Glass blowing studio, observatory, 18 private music studios, communications center.

Freshman class profile. 1,413 applied, 1,115 admitted, 311 enrolled.

Mid 50% test scores		**End year in good standing:**	86%
SAT verbal:	460-600	**Return as sophomores:**	78%
SAT math:	490-590	**Out-of-state:**	20%
ACT:	20-26	**Live on campus:**	95%
Rank in top quarter:	37%	**Fraternities:**	19%
Rank in top tenth:	14%	**Sororities:**	39%

Basis for selection. Academic achievement record most important; counselor recommendations, test scores, class ranking also important. Placement interview strongly recommended for all applicants; interview required for allied health program; audition required for forensics, music, theater programs; portfolio required for art program. **Homeschooled:** ACT or SAT scores, satisfactory completion of high school graduation equivalency required. **Learning Disabled:** Interview recommended.

High school preparation. Required and recommended units include English 3-4, mathematics 3-4, social studies 4, history 3-4, science 3-4 (laboratory 1) and foreign language 2.

2005-2006 Annual costs. Tuition/fees: $17,268. Room/board: $4,950. Books/supplies: $680. Personal expenses: $2,172.

2005-2006 Financial aid. **Need-based:** 284 full-time freshmen applied for aid; 239 were judged to have need; 238 of these received aid. Average need met was 76%. Average scholarship/grant was $9,643; average loan $3,695. 63% of total undergraduate aid awarded as scholarships/grants, 37% as loans/jobs. **Non-need-based:** Awarded to 590 full-time undergraduates, including 178 freshmen. Scholarships awarded for academics, art, athletics, leadership, music/drama.

Application procedures. **Admission:** No deadline. $20 fee, may be waived for applicants with need. Application may be submitted online. Admission notification on a rolling basis beginning on or about 10/15. **Financial aid:** No deadline. FAFSA, institutional form required. Applicants notified on a rolling basis starting 2/15; must reply within 2 week(s) of notification.

Academics. College offers 4-year liberal arts program of required courses in arts and humanities, math and science, communications, and other areas. **Special study options:** Combined bachelor's/graduate degree, double major, exchange student, independent study, internships, student-designed major, study abroad, teacher certification program, urban semester. 3-2 engineering programs with Columbia University, Georgia Institute of Technology, and Washington University, Missouri; International exchange program with colleges in England, Holland, Germany and Ireland; BA-BSN program with Creighton University. **Credit/placement by examination:** AP, CLEP, IB. 20 credit hours maximum toward bachelor's degree. All credit by examinations subject to approval of department. **Support services:** Learning center, reduced course load, study skills assistance, tutoring, writing center.

Majors. **Biology:** General. **Business:** Accounting, business admin, human resources, marketing. **Communications:** General, advertising, broadcast journalism, journalism, media studies, public relations, radio/tv. **Communications technology:** General. **Computer sciences:** General, computer science. **Education:** General, art, biology, business, chemistry, drama/dance, early childhood, elementary, English, foreign languages, history, mathematics, music, physical, physics, science, secondary, social science, social studies, special, speech. **English:** Creative writing, English lit, speech/rhetoric. **Foreign languages:** General, German, Spanish. **Health:** Health care admin, predentistry, premedicine, preveterinary. **History:** General. **Interdisciplinary:** Biopsychology. **Legal studies:** Prelaw. **Liberal arts:** Arts/sciences. **Math:** General. **Parks/recreation:** Exercise sciences, facilities management, health/fitness, sports admin. **Philosophy/religion:** Philosophy, religion. **Physical sciences:** Chemistry, physics. **Protective services:** Corrections. **Psychology:** General. **Public administration:** General, human services. **Social sciences:** Economics, international relations, political science, sociology. **Visual/performing arts:** Art, art history/conservation, dramatic, music history, music pedagogy, music performance, piano/organ, stringed instruments, voice/opera.

Most popular majors. Business/marketing 17%, communications/journalism 6%, education 22%, interdisciplinary studies 9%, psychology 12%, social sciences 7%, visual/performing arts 8%.

Computing on campus. 181 workstations in library, computer center, student center. Dormitories wired for high-speed internet access and linked to campus network. Commuter students can connect to campus network. Wireless network available.

Student life. **Freshman orientation:** Mandatory. Preregistration for classes offered. Weekend-long program, prior to the first day of class. Includes community service project. **Policies:** Alcohol not permitted on campus except in apartments for students of legal age; smoking forbidden in campus buildings. Freshmen permitted cars on campus. **Housing:** Guaranteed on-campus for all undergraduates. Coed dorms, single-sex dorms, apartments available. $200 partly refundable deposit, deadline 8/1. Honors housing and other campus houses; apartments available to upperclass students. **Activities:** Bands, choral groups, drama, literary magazine, music ensembles, musical theater, radio station, student government, student newspaper, symphony orchestra, TV station, Fellowship of Christian Athletes, student health advisory council, religious programs committee, Religion in Life Committee, Multicultural Student Union, Peer HIV Education Organization, College Democrats, College Republicans, Habitat for Humanity, gay/straight alliance.

Athletics. NAIA. **Intercollegiate:** Baseball M, basketball, cheerleading M, cross-country, football (tackle) M, golf, soccer, softball W, tennis, track and field, volleyball W. **Intramural:** Basketball, bowling, football (non-tackle), racquetball, softball, table tennis, volleyball. **Team name:** Broncos.

Student services. Adult student services, campus ministries, career counseling, student employment services, financial aid counseling, health services, minority student services, personal counseling, placement for graduates. **Physically disabled:** Services for hearing impaired.

Contact. E-mail: mmolliconi@hastings.edu
Phone: (402) 461-7403 Toll-free number: (800) 532-7642
Fax: (402) 461-7490
Mary Molliconi, Director of Admissions, Hastings College, 710 N Turner Avenue, Hastings, NE 68901-7621

ITT Technical Institute: Omaha

Omaha, Nebraska
www.itt-tech.edu — **CB code: 2740**

- For-profit 4-year technical college
- Commuter campus in large city

General. Accredited by ACICS. **Calendar:** Quarter.

Annual costs/financial aid. Tuition varies by program, $260-$368 per credit hour.

Contact. Phone: (402) 331-2900
Director of Recruitment, 9814 M Street, Omaha, NE 68127

Midland Lutheran College

Fremont, Nebraska
www.mlc.edu — **CB code: 6406**

- Private 4-year liberal arts college affiliated with Evangelical Lutheran Church in America
- Residential campus in large town
- 909 degree-seeking undergraduates: 2% part-time, 55% women
- 86% of applicants admitted
- ACT (writing optional) required
- 49% graduate within 6 years

General. Founded in 1883. Regionally accredited. **Degrees:** 196 bachelor's awarded. **Location:** 35 miles from Omaha, 52 miles from Lincoln.

Calendar: 4-1-4, limited summer session. **Full-time faculty:** 61 total. **Part-time faculty:** 27 total. **Class size:** 49% < 20, 47% 20-39, 3% 40-49, 2% 50-99. **Special facilities:** Planetarium/observatory, arboretum.

Freshman class profile. 898 applied, 768 admitted, 252 enrolled.

Mid 50% test scores		**Rank in top tenth:**	9%
ACT:	19-24	**Out-of-state:**	21%
Rank in top quarter:	14%	**Live on campus:**	80%

Basis for selection. School achievement record, test scores, recommendation by school official, rank in top half of class reviewed. Applicants with lesser qualifications considered by review of test scores and personal educational objectives. Interview recommended for all students; audition recommended for drama, music programs.

High school preparation. College-preparatory program recommended. 12 units recommended. Recommended units include English 4, mathematics 2, social studies 2, history 1, science 2 and foreign language 1.

2006-2007 Annual costs. Tuition/fees (projected): $19,510. Room/board: $4,950. Books/supplies: $800. Personal expenses: $1,430.

2004-2005 Financial aid. Need-based: 246 full-time freshmen applied for aid; 222 were judged to have need; 222 of these received aid. Average need met was 89%. Average scholarship/grant was $9,746; average loan $4,991. 33% of total undergraduate aid awarded as scholarships/grants, 67% as loans/jobs. **Non-need-based:** Awarded to 133 full-time undergraduates, including 28 freshmen. Scholarships awarded for academics, alumni affiliation, art, athletics, leadership, minority status, music/drama, religious affiliation.

Application procedures. Admission: No deadline. $30 fee, may be waived for applicants with need. Application may be submitted online. Admission notification on a rolling basis beginning on or about 10/1. **Financial aid:** Priority date 5/1; no closing date. FAFSA required. Applicants notified on a rolling basis starting 3/1; must reply within 4 week(s) of notification.

Academics. Special study options: Accelerated study, distance learning, double major, dual enrollment of high school students, independent study, internships, liberal arts/career combination, student-designed major, study abroad, teacher certification program. **Credit/placement by examination:** AP, CLEP, ACT, institutional tests. 32 credit hours maximum toward associate degree, 32 toward bachelor's. **Support services:** Learning center, reduced course load, study skills assistance, tutoring.

Majors. Area/ethnic studies: American. **Biology:** General. **Business:** General, accounting, business admin, management information systems, office management. **Communications:** General, journalism, public relations. **Computer sciences:** General, computer science, programming. **Conservation:** General. **Education:** General, art, biology, business, chemistry, early childhood, elementary, English, German, history, mathematics, middle, multi-level teacher, music, physical, science, secondary, social science, social studies, Spanish, speech. **Foreign languages:** Spanish. **Health:** Athletic training, predentistry, premedicine, preop/surgical nursing, prepharmacy, preveterinary, respiratory therapy technology. **History:** General. **Legal studies:** Paralegal, prelaw. **Liberal arts:** Arts/sciences. **Math:** General. **Philosophy/religion:** Religion. **Physical sciences:** Chemistry. **Psychology:** General. **Public administration:** Human services. **Social sciences:** General, criminology, economics, sociology. **Visual/performing arts:** Art, commercial/advertising art, dramatic, studio arts.

Most popular majors. Business/marketing 32%, communications/journalism 8%, education 27%, health sciences 20%, social sciences 10%.

Computing on campus. 190 workstations in library, computer center, student center. Dormitories wired for high-speed internet access and linked to campus network. Online library, helpline, wireless network available.

Student life. Freshman orientation: Mandatory. Preregistration for classes offered. **Policies:** Freshmen permitted cars on campus. **Housing:** Guaranteed on-campus for freshmen. Coed dorms, single-sex dorms, special housing for disabled, substance-free housing available. $100 deposit, deadline 8/1. **Activities:** Bands, choral groups, dance, drama, literary magazine, music ensembles, musical theater, student government, student newspaper, Fellowship of Christian Athletes, Circle K, Religious Life Council.

Athletics. NAIA. **Intercollegiate:** Baseball M, basketball, cross-country, football (tackle) M, golf, soccer W, softball W, tennis, track and field, volleyball W. **Intramural:** Basketball, bowling, field hockey W, handball, racquetball, soccer M, softball, swimming, tennis, track and field, volleyball. **Team name:** Warriors.

Student services. Career counseling, student employment services, health services, personal counseling, placement for graduates.

Contact. E-mail: admissions@mlc.edu
Phone: (402) 941-6501 Toll-free number: (800) 642-8382
Fax: (402) 721-0250
Todd Hansen, Associate Vice President for Admissions, Midland Lutheran College, 900 North Clarkson, Fremont, NE 68025

Nebraska Christian College
Norfolk, Nebraska
www.nechristian.edu **CB code: 1332**

- Private 4-year Bible college affiliated with Christian Church/Churches of Christ
- Residential campus in large town
- 146 degree-seeking undergraduates: 8% part-time, 45% women
- ACT with writing required

General. Founded in 1944. Accredited by ABHE. **Degrees:** 23 bachelor's, 16 associate awarded. **Location:** 110 miles from Omaha. **Calendar:** Semester. **Full-time faculty:** 13 total. **Part-time faculty:** 5 total.

Freshman class profile.

Rank in top quarter:	19%	**Out-of-state:**	45%
Rank in top tenth:	17%		

Basis for selection. Christian commitment and references very important; high school transcript or GED required. Transcript of any previous college work required.

2005-2006 Annual costs. Tuition/fees: $6,700. Room/board: $3,900. Books/supplies: $600. Personal expenses: $1,900.

Financial aid. Non-need-based: Scholarships awarded for academics, leadership.

Application procedures. Admission: Closing date 9/1. $25 fee. Application may be submitted online. Admission notification on a rolling basis. **Financial aid:** Priority date 6/1; no closing date. FAFSA, institutional form required. Applicants notified on a rolling basis starting 5/5.

Academics. Special study options: Double major, independent study, internships. **Credit/placement by examination:** CLEP.

Majors. Theology: Bible, missionary, religious ed, sacred music, theology.

Computing on campus. Dormitories wired for high-speed internet access.

Student life. Freshman orientation: Available. **Policies:** Religious observance required. Freshmen permitted cars on campus. **Housing:** Single-sex dorms, apartments available. $100 deposit. **Activities:** Choral groups, drama, music ensembles, student government.

Athletics. NCCAA. **Intercollegiate:** Basketball, soccer M, volleyball W. **Intramural:** Basketball M, football (non-tackle), soccer, volleyball. **Team name:** Parsons.

Student services. Adult student services, career counseling, student employment services, financial aid counseling, health services, personal counseling, placement for graduates.

Contact. E-mail: admissions@nechristian.edu
Phone: (402) 379-5000 Fax: (402) 379-5100
Michael Sander, Director of Admissions, Nebraska Christian College, 1800 Syracuse Avenue, Norfolk, NE 68701

Nebraska Methodist College of Nursing and Allied Health
Omaha, Nebraska
www.methodistcollege.edu **CB code: 6510**

- Private 4-year health science and nursing college affiliated with United Methodist Church
- Commuter campus in large city
- 454 degree-seeking undergraduates: 27% part-time, 91% women, 2% African American, 1% Asian American
- 64 degree-seeking graduate students
- 50% of applicants admitted

- SAT or ACT (ACT writing recommended), application essay, interview required
- 70% graduate within 6 years

General. Founded in 1891. Regionally accredited. Health care classes offered at Josie Harper campus. **Degrees:** 49 bachelor's, 15 associate awarded; master's offered. **ROTC:** Army. **Location:** 120 miles from Des Moines, Iowa, 180 miles from Kansas City, Missouri. **Calendar:** Semester, limited summer session. **Full-time faculty:** 50 total. **Part-time faculty:** 40 total. **Class size:** 34% < 20, 59% 20-39, 7% 40-49. **Special facilities:** Human cadaver lab.

Freshman class profile. 119 applied, 60 admitted, 40 enrolled.

Mid 50% test scores		**Rank in top tenth:**	15%
ACT:	20-22	**End year in good standing:**	76%
GPA 3.50 or higher:	55%	**Return as sophomores:**	84%
GPA 3.0-3.49:	30%	**Out-of-state:**	5%
GPA 2.0-2.99:	15%	**Live on campus:**	80%
Rank in top quarter:	30%		

Basis for selection. School achievement, test scores most important. Personal statement, interview important. Recommendations, school and community activities considered. **Homeschooled:** Transcript of courses and grades, state high school equivalency certificate required. Submit portfolio demonstrating range and depth of academic ability.

High school preparation. 10 units required. Required units include English 4, mathematics 2, social studies 2, science 2 (laboratory 2). Chemistry, biology and algebra required.

2005-2006 Annual costs. Tuition/fees: $11,160. Room/board: $4,213. Books/supplies: $900. Personal expenses: $1,242.

2004-2005 Financial aid. Need-based: 11 full-time freshmen applied for aid; 9 were judged to have need; 9 of these received aid. Average need met was 47%. Average scholarship/grant was $3,243; average loan $2,844. 36% of total undergraduate aid awarded as scholarships/grants, 64% as loans/jobs. **Non-need-based:** Scholarships awarded for academics, leadership, religious affiliation, ROTC.

Application procedures. Admission: Priority date 1/1; deadline 4/1 (receipt date). $25 fee. Application may be submitted online. Admission notification on a rolling basis beginning on or about 1/15. Must reply by 5/15. Application deadlines vary by program. **Financial aid:** Priority date 5/1; no closing date. FAFSA, institutional form required. Applicants notified on a rolling basis starting 3/1; must reply by 5/1 or within 4 week(s) of notification.

Academics. Peer tutoring available for most courses. **Special study options:** Accelerated study, distance learning, independent study, internships. **Credit/placement by examination:** AP, CLEP, institutional tests. 9 credit hours maximum toward associate degree, 9 toward bachelor's. Credit by examination considered on an indivdual basis. **Support services:** Learning center, reduced course load, remedial instruction, study skills assistance, tutoring, writing center.

Majors. Health: Cardiovascular technology, nursing (RN), radiologic technology/medical imaging, respiratory therapy technology, sonography.

Computing on campus. 75 workstations in dormitories, library, computer center. Helpline available.

Student life. Freshman orientation: Mandatory. Preregistration for classes offered. One-day event for students and parents. **Policies:** Freshmen permitted cars on campus. **Housing:** Guaranteed on-campus for freshmen. Coed dorms available. $50 deposit, deadline 6/1. **Activities:** Student government, student nurse association (state and national), allied health student association, College Ambassadors, minority student organization, Pathfinders, residence hall council.

Student services. Adult student services, alcohol/substance abuse counseling, campus ministries, career counseling, student employment services, financial aid counseling, health services, minority student services, personal counseling, placement for graduates, veterans' counselor.

Contact. E-mail: admissions@methodistcollege.edu
Phone: (402) 354-7200 Toll-free number: (800) 335-5510
Fax: (402) 354-7020
Deann Sterner, Director of Admissions, Nebraska Methodist College of Nursing and Allied Health, The Josie Harper Campus, Omaha, NE 68114

Nebraska Wesleyan University

Lincoln, Nebraska
www.nebrwesleyan.edu **CB code: 6470**

- Private 4-year liberal arts college affiliated with United Methodist Church
- Residential campus in small city
- 1,801 degree-seeking undergraduates: 12% part-time, 58% women
- 174 degree-seeking graduate students
- 84% of applicants admitted
- SAT or ACT (ACT writing optional) required
- 69% graduate within 6 years

General. Founded in 1887. Regionally accredited. Non-traditional programs on accelerated semesters. **Degrees:** 394 bachelor's awarded; master's offered. **ROTC:** Army, Air Force. **Location:** 55 miles from Omaha, 200 miles from Kansas City, Missouri. **Calendar:** Semester, limited summer session. **Full-time faculty:** 102 total; 80% have terminal degrees, 2% minority, 49% women. **Part-time faculty:** 123 total; 54% women. **Class size:** 54% < 20, 43% 20-39, less than 1% 40-49, 3% 50-99. **Special facilities:** Planetarium, laboratory theatre, greenhouse, herbarium, nuclear magnetic resonance laboratory, sleep laboratory.

Freshman class profile. 1,508 applied, 1,262 admitted, 406 enrolled.

Mid 50% test scores		**Out-of-state:**	10%
ACT:	21-26	**Live on campus:**	91%
Rank in top quarter:	57%	**Fraternities:**	26%
Rank in top tenth:	22%	**Sororities:**	26%
Return as sophomores:	82%		

Basis for selection. Students who rank in the top half of their graduating class or achieve ACT composite score of 20 or an SAT combined score of 950 (exclusive of Writing) invited to apply for admissions. Campus visit recommended for all students; audition required for drama, music scholarships; portfolio required for art scholarships.

High school preparation. College-preparatory program recommended. Recommended units include English 4, mathematics 3, social studies 3, science 3 and foreign language 2. 3 years of social studies and/or history recommended.

2005-2006 Annual costs. Tuition/fees: $18,530. Room/board: $5,020. Books/supplies: $800. Personal expenses: $1,800.

2005-2006 Financial aid. Need-based: 350 full-time freshmen applied for aid; 286 were judged to have need; 286 of these received aid. Average need met was 71%. Average scholarship/grant was $9,836; average loan $3,709. 66% of total undergraduate aid awarded as scholarships/grants, 34% as loans/jobs. **Non-need-based:** Awarded to 469 full-time undergraduates, including 141 freshmen. Scholarships awarded for academics, art, music/drama, religious affiliation.

Application procedures. Admission: Closing date 8/15 (postmark date). $20 fee, may be waived for applicants with need. Application may be submitted online. Admission notification on a rolling basis beginning on or about 1/15. Must reply by May 1 or within 4 week(s) if notified thereafter. **Financial aid:** No deadline. FAFSA required. Applicants notified on a rolling basis starting 3/15; must reply within 4 week(s) of notification.

Academics. Special study options: Combined bachelor's/graduate degree, double major, dual enrollment of high school students, exchange student, independent study, internships, liberal arts/career combination, semester at sea, study abroad, teacher certification program, United Nations semester, urban semester, Washington semester. 3-2 engineering with Washington University or Columbia University; Capitol Hill Internship Program; Urban Life Center (Chicago); summer research fellowships in the natural sciences; faculty led international study tours. **Credit/placement by examination:** AP, CLEP, IB, institutional tests. Unlimited number of hours of credit by examination may be counted toward degree. **Support services:** Reduced course load, study skills assistance, tutoring, writing center.

Majors. Area/ethnic studies: Women's. **Biology:** General, biochemistry, Biochemistry/biophysics and molecular biology. **Business:** Accounting, business admin, international. **Communications:** General, political. **Computer sciences:** Computer science, information systems. **Education:** Elementary, English, middle, music, physical, science, social science, special. **English:** Speech/rhetoric. **Foreign languages:** French, German, Spanish. **Health:** Athletic training, nursing (RN). **History:** General. **Interdisciplinary:** Biopsychology, global studies. **Math:** General. **Parks/recreation:** Exercise sciences, health/fitness, sports admin. **Philosophy/religion:** Philosophy, religion.

Physical sciences: Chemistry, physics. **Psychology:** General. **Public administration:** Social work. **Social sciences:** Economics, political science, sociology. **Visual/performing arts:** Art, dramatic, music performance, studio arts.

Most popular majors. Biology 8%, business/marketing 17%, education 14%, English 6%, health sciences 10%, parks/recreation 10%, psychology 10%, social sciences 6%.

Computing on campus. 360 workstations in dormitories, library, computer center, student center. Dormitories wired for high-speed internet access and linked to campus network. Commuter students can connect to campus network. Online course registration, online library, helpline, repair service, student web hosting, wireless network available.

Student life. **Freshman orientation:** Mandatory. Preregistration for classes offered. Summer 1-day registration sessions in June; 4-day orientation program before fall classes begin. **Policies:** Freshmen permitted cars on campus. **Housing:** Guaranteed on-campus for freshmen. Coed dorms, single-sex dorms, apartments, fraternity/sorority housing available. $100 deposit, deadline 5/1. Residence hall suites and townhomes. **Activities:** Bands, choral groups, drama, literary magazine, music ensembles, musical theater, opera, student government, student newspaper, Wesleyan Student Fellowship, Fellowship of Christian Athletes, Rainbow Club, College Republicans, Young Democrats, Nebraskans for Peace, International Relations Organization, Circle-K, Environmental Action.

Athletics. NAIA, NCAA. **Intercollegiate:** Baseball M, basketball, cross-country, football (tackle) M, golf, soccer, softball W, tennis, track and field, volleyball W. **Intramural:** Basketball, football (non-tackle), racquetball, soccer, softball, volleyball. **Team name:** Prairie Wolves.

Student services. Adult student services, campus ministries, career counseling, student employment services, financial aid counseling, health services, minority student services, personal counseling, placement for graduates, women's services. **Physically disabled:** Services for visually, speech, hearing impaired.

Contact. E-mail: admissions@nebrwesleyan.edu
Phone: (402) 465-2218 Toll-free number: (800) 541-3818
Fax: (402) 465-2179
Patricia Karthauser, Vice President for Enrollment and Marketing, Nebraska Wesleyan University, 5000 St. Paul Avenue, Lincoln, NE 68504

Peru State College

Peru, Nebraska
www.peru.edu **CB code: 6468**

- Public 4-year liberal arts and teachers college
- Residential campus in rural community
- 1,600 degree-seeking undergraduates
- 200 graduate students

General. Founded in 1867. Regionally accredited. Offers degree completion programs in nearby communities: Community college technical graduates can complete bachelor's degree in Omaha or Lincoln. Elementary school teacher certification courses offered at Offutt Air Force Base. **Degrees:** 240 bachelor's awarded; master's offered. **Location:** 64 miles from Omaha, 67 miles from Lincoln. **Calendar:** Semester, limited summer session. **Full-time faculty:** 40 total; 85% have terminal degrees, 28% women. **Part-time faculty:** 61 total.

Freshman class profile.

Out-of-state:	7%	**Live on campus:**	75%

Basis for selection. Open admission, but selective for out-of-state students. Out-of-state applicants must rank in top half of graduating class or have ACT score of 14 or SAT score of 560 (exclusive of Writing), and 2.0 GPA.

High school preparation. 16 units recommended. Recommended units include English 4, mathematics 2, social studies 3, science 2 and foreign language 1.

2005-2006 Annual costs. Tuition/fees: $3,639; $6,571 out-of-state. Room/board: $4,296. Books/supplies: $600. Personal expenses: $1,000.

Financial aid. All financial aid based on need.

Application procedures. **Admission:** Priority date 2/1; no deadline. $10 fee, may be waived for applicants with need. Application may be submitted online. Admission notification on a rolling basis beginning on or about 9/1. **Financial aid:** Priority date 3/1; no closing date. FAFSA, institutional form required. Applicants notified on a rolling basis starting 3/1; must reply within 2 week(s) of notification.

Academics. **Special study options:** Cooperative education, cross-registration, distance learning, double major, dual enrollment of high school students, honors, independent study, internships, liberal arts/career combination, study abroad, teacher certification program. **Credit/placement by examination:** CLEP. 16 credit hours maximum toward bachelor's degree. **Support services:** Learning center, reduced course load, remedial instruction, study skills assistance, tutoring.

Majors. **Biology:** Plant physiology. **Business:** Business admin, office technology. **Computer sciences:** General, computer science, programming. **Education:** General, art, biology, computer, early childhood, elementary, English, history, mathematics, middle, music, physical, physics, science, secondary, social science, special, speech, voc/tech. **Interdisciplinary:** Natural sciences. **Math:** General. **Protective services:** Law enforcement admin. **Psychology:** General. **Social sciences:** General, sociology. **Visual/performing arts:** Art.

Most popular majors. Business/marketing 38%, education 47%, psychology 6%.

Computing on campus. 140 workstations in dormitories, library, computer center, student center. Dormitories linked to campus network.

Student life. **Freshman orientation:** Mandatory. Preregistration for classes offered. 5 different 1-day sessions in June, July, August. **Policies:** Freshmen permitted cars on campus. **Housing:** Guaranteed on-campus for freshmen. Coed dorms, single-sex dorms, apartments, substance-free housing available. $100 deposit. **Activities:** Bands, choral groups, drama, literary magazine, music ensembles, musical theater, student government, student newspaper, TV station, Fellowship of Christian Athletes, multicultural committee, Phi Beta Lambda, Peru Players, Women's Athletic Association, Ambassadors.

Athletics. NAIA. **Intercollegiate:** Baseball M, basketball, football (tackle) M, softball W, volleyball W. **Intramural:** Basketball, soccer, softball, swimming, table tennis, tennis, volleyball, water polo M. **Team name:** Bobcats.

Student services. Adult student services, alcohol/substance abuse counseling, campus ministries, career counseling, student employment services, financial aid counseling, health services, on-campus daycare, personal counseling, placement for graduates, veterans' counselor. **Physically disabled:** Services for visually, hearing impaired.

Contact. E-mail: admissions@oakmail.peru.edu
Phone: (402) 872-2221 Toll-free number: (800) 742-4412
Fax: (402) 872-2296
Micki Willis, Director of Recruitment and Admissions, Peru State College, Box 10, Peru, NE 68421-0010

Union College

Lincoln, Nebraska
www.ucollege.edu **CB code: 6865**

- Private 4-year liberal arts college affiliated with Seventh-day Adventists
- Residential campus in small city
- 845 degree-seeking undergraduates: 11% part-time, 56% women
- 45 degree-seeking graduate students
- 43% of applicants admitted
- SAT or ACT (ACT writing optional), application essay required
- 54% graduate within 6 years

General. Founded in 1889. Regionally accredited. **Degrees:** 199 bachelor's, 11 associate awarded; master's offered. **Location:** 50 miles from Omaha. **Calendar:** Semester, limited summer session. **Full-time faculty:** 60 total; 48% have terminal degrees, 13% minority, 35% women. **Part-time faculty:** 36 total; 11% have terminal degrees, 8% minority, 64% women. **Class size:** 70% < 20, 24% 20-39, 1% 40-49, 4% 50-99.

Freshman class profile. 635 applied, 271 admitted, 180 enrolled.

Mid 50% test scores		**End year in good standing:**	71%
ACT:	19-25	**Return as sophomores:**	71%
GPA 3.50 or higher:	46%	**Out-of-state:**	83%
GPA 3.0-3.49:	40%	**Live on campus:**	89%
GPA 2.0-2.99:	14%		

Basis for selection. School achievement record and 3 references (including 1 from pastor) very important. Interview recommended for all students;

audition recommended for music program; portfolio recommended for art program. **Homeschooled:** Letter of recommendation (nonparent) required.

High school preparation. College-preparatory program recommended. 20 units required. Required and recommended units include English 3-4, mathematics 2-3, social studies 1, history 1, science 2-3 (laboratory 1), foreign language 1 and academic electives 3. 2 algebra, 1 geometry, trigonometry recommended for mathematics and science-related programs. Physics and chemistry recommended for nursing, biology, chemistry, physics, engineering, medical technology, premedicine, and predental programs.

2006-2007 Annual costs. Tuition/fees (projected): $15,160. Room/board: $4,973. Books/supplies: $950. Personal expenses: $1,200.

2004-2005 Financial aid. Need-based: Average need met was 84%. Average scholarship/grant was $7,838; average loan $3,788. 58% of total undergraduate aid awarded as scholarships/grants, 42% as loans/jobs. **Non-need-based:** Scholarships awarded for academics. **Additional information:** Special institutional grants offered to all freshmen and sophomores demonstrating exceptional financial need.

Application procedures. Admission: No deadline. No application fee. Application may be submitted online. Admission notification on a rolling basis. **Financial aid:** Priority date 5/1; no closing date. FAFSA required. Applicants notified on a rolling basis starting 4/15; must reply by 5/2 or within 3 week(s) of notification.

Academics. Special study options: Cross-registration, double major, dual enrollment of high school students, ESL, honors, independent study, internships, student-designed major, study abroad, teacher certification program. **Credit/placement by examination:** AP, CLEP, IB, ACT, institutional tests. **Support services:** Learning center, reduced course load, remedial instruction, study skills assistance, tutoring, writing center.

Majors. Biology: General, biochemistry. **Business:** Accounting, business admin, finance, international finance, management science. **Communications:** Journalism, public relations. **Computer sciences:** Computer science, information systems, systems analysis. **Education:** General, elementary, secondary. **English:** Creative writing, English lit, speech/rhetoric. **Foreign languages:** French, German, Spanish. **History:** General. **Math:** General. **Parks/recreation:** Health/fitness, sports admin. **Philosophy/religion:** Religion. **Physical sciences:** Chemistry, physics. **Psychology:** General. **Public administration:** Social work. **Social sciences:** General. **Theology:** Pastoral counseling, religious ed, theology. **Visual/performing arts:** Commercial/advertising art, music performance, studio arts.

Most popular majors. Biology 8%, business/marketing 12%, communications/journalism 6%, education 6%, health sciences 26%, philosophy/religious studies 8%, psychology 7%, visual/performing arts 9%.

Computing on campus. 60 workstations in dormitories, library, computer center, student center. Dormitories wired for high-speed internet access and linked to campus network. Commuter students can connect to campus network. Online library, helpline, student web hosting, wireless network available.

Student life. Freshman orientation: Available. Preregistration for classes offered. **Policies:** Religious observance required. Freshmen permitted cars on campus. **Housing:** Guaranteed on-campus for all undergraduates. Single-sex dorms, apartments available. **Activities:** Concert band, choral groups, drama, literary magazine, music ensembles, student government, student newspaper, Collegiate Adventists for Better Living, Union for Christ, Union for Kids.

Athletics. Intercollegiate: Basketball. **Intramural:** Badminton, baseball M, basketball, golf, gymnastics, racquetball, soccer, softball, tennis, volleyball. **Team name:** Warriors and Lady Warriors.

Student services. Campus ministries, career counseling, student employment services, financial aid counseling, health services, minority student services, personal counseling, placement for graduates. **Physically disabled:** Services for visually, speech, hearing impaired.

Contact. E-mail: ucenroll@ucollege.edu
Phone: (402) 486-2504 Toll-free number: (800) 228-4600
Fax: (402) 486-2895
Huda McClelland, Director of Admission, Union College, 3800 South 48th Street, Lincoln, NE 68506-4300

University of Nebraska - Kearney

Kearney, Nebraska
www.unk.edu **CB code: 6467**

- Public 4-year university
- Residential campus in large town
- 5,346 degree-seeking undergraduates: 9% part-time, 55% women, 1% African American, 1% Asian American, 3% Hispanic American, 7% international
- 1,064 degree-seeking graduate students
- 84% of applicants admitted
- SAT and SAT Subject Tests or ACT (ACT writing optional) required
- 55% graduate within 6 years

General. Founded in 1903. Regionally accredited. **Degrees:** 1,006 bachelor's awarded; master's offered. **Location:** 180 miles from Omaha. **Calendar:** Semester, extensive summer session. **Full-time faculty:** 306 total; 73% have terminal degrees, 7% minority, 44% women. **Part-time faculty:** 74 total; 27% have terminal degrees, 3% minority, 54% women. **Special facilities:** Nebraska state art collection, state arboretum, planetarium.

Freshman class profile. 2,443 applied, 2,057 admitted, 1,062 enrolled.

Mid 50% test scores		Return as sophomores:	84%
SAT verbal:	410-600	Out-of-state:	6%
SAT math:	430-570	Live on campus:	85%
ACT:	20-25	International:	8%
Rank in top quarter:	37%	Fraternities:	13%
Rank in top tenth:	13%	Sororities:	15%

Basis for selection. Test scores, school achievement record most important. Applicants who show promise of academic success, but do not meet admission requirements, may be admitted on conditional basis.

High school preparation. 16 units required. Required units include English 4, mathematics 3, social studies 3, science 2, foreign language 2 and academic electives 1.

2005-2006 Annual costs. Tuition/fees: $4,393; $8,233 out-of-state. Room/board: $5,460. Books/supplies: $720. Personal expenses: $2,204.

2004-2005 Financial aid. Need-based: 924 full-time freshmen applied for aid; 690 were judged to have need; 683 of these received aid. Average need met was 78%. Average scholarship/grant was $4,668; average loan $2,472. 50% of total undergraduate aid awarded as scholarships/grants, 50% as loans/jobs. **Non-need-based:** Awarded to 2,825 full-time undergraduates, including 199 freshmen. Scholarships awarded for academics, athletics, state residency.

Application procedures. Admission: Priority date 8/1; no deadline. $45 fee. Admission notification on a rolling basis beginning on or about 10/1. **Financial aid:** Priority date 4/1; no closing date. FAFSA, institutional form required. Applicants notified on a rolling basis starting 3/15; must reply within 3 week(s) of notification.

Academics. Special study options: Accelerated study, cross-registration, distance learning, double major, dual enrollment of high school students, ESL, exchange student, honors, independent study, internships, study abroad, teacher certification program. International student exchange program with Sapporo University and Kansai Gaidai, Japan; Nebraska semester abroad. **Credit/placement by examination:** CLEP, SAT, ACT, institutional tests. 45 credit hours maximum toward bachelor's degree. **Support services:** Learning center, study skills assistance, tutoring, writing center.

Majors. Agriculture: Business. **Biology:** General. **Business:** Actuarial science, business admin, office management, office/clerical, tourism/travel. **Communications:** General, advertising, broadcast journalism, journalism. **Computer sciences:** General, information systems, networking. **Education:** General, art, biology, business, chemistry, early childhood, elementary, English, ESL, family/consumer sciences, foreign languages, French, German, health, history, learning disabled, mathematics, mentally handicapped, middle, multiple handicapped, music, physical, physically handicapped, physics, science, secondary, social science, special, speech, speech impaired, technology/industrial arts, trade/industrial. **English:** Speech/rhetoric. **Family/consumer sciences:** General, business, clothing/textiles, family studies, food/nutrition, housing. **Foreign languages:** French, German, Spanish, translation. **Health:** Medical radiologic technology/radiation therapy, respiratory therapy technology, speech pathology. **History:** General. **Liberal arts:** Arts/sciences. **Math:** General, statistics. **Parks/recreation:** Facilities management, sports admin. **Physical sciences:** Chemistry, physics, planetary. **Protective services:** Criminal justice, police science. **Psychology:** General. **Public administration:** Social work. **Social sciences:** General, economics, geography, international relations, political science, sociology. **Transportation:** Aviation. **Visual/performing arts:** General, art, art history/conservation, commercial/advertising art, dramatic, music performance, studio arts.

Most popular majors. Business/marketing 25%, education 23%.

Computing on campus. 411 workstations in dormitories, library, computer center, student center. Dormitories linked to campus network. Commuter students can connect to campus network. Online course registration, helpline available.

Student life. **Freshman orientation:** Available. **Housing:** Guaranteed on-campus for freshmen. Coed dorms, single-sex dorms, apartments, fraternity/sorority housing available. Honors residence hall available. **Activities:** Bands, choral groups, dance, drama, music ensembles, musical theater, radio station, student government, student newspaper, symphony orchestra, TV station, Young Republicans, Young Democrats, Alpha Phi Omega, Fellowship of Christian Athletes, international student association, People of Color.

Athletics. NCAA. **Intercollegiate:** Baseball M, basketball, cross-country, diving W, football (tackle) M, golf, softball W, swimming W, tennis, track and field, volleyball W, wrestling M. **Intramural:** Archery, basketball, bowling, cross-country, diving, golf, racquetball, soccer, softball, swimming, table tennis, tennis, track and field, volleyball, water polo, wrestling M.

Student services. Career counseling, student employment services, health services, personal counseling, placement for graduates, veterans' counselor. **Physically disabled:** Services for visually, hearing impaired.

Contact. E-mail: admissionsug@unk.edu
Phone: (308) 865-8526 Toll-free number: (800) 532-7639
Fax: (308) 865-8987
Lee Amm, Assistant Director of Admissions, University of Nebraska - Kearney, 905 West 25th, Kearney, NE 68849

University of Nebraska - Lincoln

Lincoln, Nebraska — **CB member**
www.unl.edu — **CB code: 6877**

- Public 4-year university
- Residential campus in small city
- 17,037 degree-seeking undergraduates: 7% part-time, 47% women, 2% African American, 3% Asian American, 3% Hispanic American, 1% Native American, 3% international
- 3,896 degree-seeking graduate students
- 75% of applicants admitted
- SAT and SAT Subject Tests or ACT (ACT writing optional) required
- 63% graduate within 6 years

General. Founded in 1869. Regionally accredited. Nebraska's only land-grant university. Research opportunities impacting state's economic development available to students. **Degrees:** 3,267 bachelor's, 4 associate awarded; master's, doctoral, first professional offered. **ROTC:** Army, Navy, Air Force. **Location:** 50 miles from Omaha. **Calendar:** Semester, extensive summer session. **Full-time faculty:** 1,048 total; 94% have terminal degrees, 15% minority, 26% women. **Part-time faculty:** 10 total; 80% have terminal degrees, 20% minority, 30% women. **Class size:** 37% < 20, 44% 20-39, 6% 40-49, 7% 50-99, 6% >100. **Special facilities:** State museum, planetarium, center for performing arts, arboretum, center for Asian Culture, center for Great Plains studies, center for biomaterials and genetic research.

Freshman class profile. 7,474 applied, 5,633 admitted, 3,560 enrolled.

Mid 50% test scores			
SAT verbal:	530-660	Return as sophomores:	84%
SAT math:	540-670	Out-of-state:	22%
ACT:	22-28	Live on campus:	79%
Rank in top quarter:	54%	International:	1%
Rank in top tenth:	27%	Fraternities:	21%
		Sororities:	26%

Basis for selection. Students must meet minimum requirements of ACT composite score of 20 or higher, SAT combined score of 950 (exclusive of writing) or rank in top half of class. Audition required for music program. **Homeschooled:** Statement describing homeschool structure and mission, transcript of courses and grades required.

High school preparation. 16 units required. Required and recommended units include English 4, mathematics 4, social studies 3, history 1, science 3 (laboratory 1) and foreign language 2. English must include significant reading and writing. Mathematics must include algebra I and II, geometry, and 1 unit of higher level math. 2 units of foreign language must be in same language. At least 1 unit of social studies should be American and/or world history and 1 additional unit should be history, American government, and/or geography. College of Engineering & Technology requires 1 unit of pre-calculus/trigonometry, 1 unit of physics and 1 unit of chemistry. Architecture requires 1/2 unit of trigonometry or pre-calculus for pre-architecture.

2005-2006 Annual costs. Tuition/fees: $5,540; $14,450 out-of-state. Reciprocity agreement for selected programs with University of Missouri-Columbia, Kansas State University, University of South Dakota. Room/board: $5,861. Books/supplies: $880. Personal expenses: $2,670.

2004-2005 Financial aid. **Need-based:** 2,222 full-time freshmen applied for aid; 1,531 were judged to have need; 1,505 of these received aid. Average need met was 88%. Average scholarship/grant was $5,512; average loan $3,066. 46% of total undergraduate aid awarded as scholarships/grants, 54% as loans/jobs. **Non-need-based:** Awarded to 1,591 full-time undergraduates, including 649 freshmen. Scholarships awarded for academics, alumni affiliation, art, athletics, leadership, minority status, music/drama, state residency.

Application procedures. **Admission:** Priority date 1/15; deadline 5/1 (receipt date). $45 fee, may be waived for applicants with need. Application may be submitted online. Admission notification on a rolling basis beginning on or about 9/1. Must reply by 5/1. **Financial aid:** Priority date 4/15; no closing date. FAFSA required. Applicants notified on a rolling basis starting 4/15.

Academics. Comprehensive Education Program (CEP) is required of all entering students. Master of architecture professional degree available. **Special study options:** Accelerated study, combined bachelor's/graduate degree, cooperative education, cross-registration, distance learning, double major, dual enrollment of high school students, ESL, exchange student, external degree, honors, independent study, internships, liberal arts/career combination, student-designed major, study abroad, teacher certification program. **Credit/placement by examination:** AP, CLEP, IB, SAT, ACT, institutional tests. Individual colleges have different policies. **Support services:** Learning center, pre-admission summer program, reduced course load, remedial instruction, study skills assistance, tutoring, writing center.

Honors college/program. Formal application required. Acceptance based on evaluation of the student's potential by the faculty committee.

Majors. **Agriculture:** General, agronomy, animal sciences, business, communications, economics, food science, horticultural science, landscaping, mechanization, plant protection, range science, soil science. **Architecture:** Architecture, interior. **Area/ethnic studies:** Latin American, regional, Western European, women's. **Biology:** General, biochemistry. **Business:** Accounting, actuarial science, business admin, finance, international, management science, managerial economics, marketing, office management. **Communications:** General, advertising, broadcast journalism, journalism. **Computer sciences:** General. **Conservation:** General, environmental studies, management/policy. **Education:** Agricultural, art, biology, business, chemistry, computer, Deaf/hearing impaired, elementary, English, ESL, foreign languages, French, German, health, history, mathematics, middle, multi-level teacher, music, physical, physics, reading, sales/marketing, science, social science, Spanish, technology/industrial arts, trade/industrial. **Engineering:** Agricultural, architectural, biomedical, chemical, civil, computer, electrical, industrial, mechanical. **Engineering technology:** Construction, electrical, industrial. **English:** English lit. **Family/consumer sciences:** Clothing/textiles, food/nutrition, housing. **Foreign languages:** Ancient Greek, classics, French, German, Latin, Russian, Spanish. **Health:** Athletic training, community health services, predentistry, premedicine, prepharmacy, preveterinary, speech pathology, veterinary technology/assistant. **History:** General. **Interdisciplinary:** Medieval/Renaissance. **Legal studies:** General. **Liberal arts:** Arts/sciences, humanities. **Math:** General. **Parks/recreation:** Exercise sciences. **Philosophy/religion:** Philosophy. **Physical sciences:** Atmospheric science, chemistry, geology, hydrology, physics. **Psychology:** General. **Social sciences:** Anthropology, economics, geography, international relations, political science, sociology. **Visual/performing arts:** Art history/conservation, dance, dramatic, film/cinema, studio arts.

Most popular majors. Agriculture 7%, business/marketing 22%, communication technologies 8%, education 9%, engineering/engineering technologies 12%, family/consumer sciences 6%, social sciences 6%.

Computing on campus. 650 workstations in dormitories, library, computer center, student center. Dormitories wired for high-speed internet access and linked to campus network. Commuter students can connect to campus network. Online course registration, online library, helpline, student web hosting available.

Student life. **Freshman orientation:** Available. Preregistration for classes offered. Day-long program conducted from mid-June to mid-July. **Policies:** No smoking allowed in University buildings. No alcohol on campus. Freshmen permitted cars on campus. **Housing:** Guaranteed on-campus for freshmen. Coed dorms, single-sex dorms, special housing for disabled, apartments, cooperative housing, fraternity/sorority housing, substance-free housing available. $400 partly refundable deposit, deadline 5/1. Pets allowed in dorm rooms. Special interest floors available. Freshmen required to live on campus if not living with parents or close relatives. **Activities:** Bands, choral groups, dance, drama, film society, literary magazine, music ensembles, musical theater, opera, radio station, student government, student newspaper, symphony orchestra, TV station, Afrikaan People's Union, University of Nebraska Inter-Tribal Exchange, Mexican-American student association, adult student network, Ecology Now, student foundation, student-alumni association, UNL Entrepreneurial Society.

Athletics. NCAA. **Intercollegiate:** Baseball M, basketball, bowling W, cross-country, diving W, football (tackle) M, golf, gymnastics, rifle W, rodeo, rowing (crew), soccer W, softball W, swimming W, tennis, track and field, volleyball W, wrestling M. **Intramural:** Football (non-tackle), soccer, softball, tennis, track and field, volleyball, water polo, wrestling M. **Team name:** Cornhuskers.

Student services. Adult student services, alcohol/substance abuse counseling, campus ministries, career counseling, student employment services, financial aid counseling, health services, legal services, minority student services, on-campus daycare, personal counseling, placement for graduates, veterans' counselor, women's services. **Physically disabled:** Services for visually, speech, hearing impaired.

Contact. E-mail: admissions@unl.edu
Phone: (402) 472-2023 Toll-free number: (800) 742-8800
Fax: (402) 472-0670
Alan Cerveny, Dean of Admissions, University of Nebraska - Lincoln, 313 N 13th, Van Brunt Visitors Center, Lincoln, NE 68588-0256

University of Nebraska - Omaha

Omaha, Nebraska — **CB member**
www.unomaha.edu — **CB code: 6420**

- Public 4-year university
- Commuter campus in large city
- 11,039 degree-seeking undergraduates: 23% part-time, 54% women, 6% African American, 3% Asian American, 3% Hispanic American, 2% international
- 2,469 degree-seeking graduate students
- 89% of applicants admitted
- SAT or ACT (ACT writing optional) required
- 39% graduate within 6 years; 18% enter graduate study

General. Founded in 1908. Regionally accredited. Cooperative classes at Offutt Air Force Base, Cooperative programs with UNMC medical center. **Degrees:** 1,648 bachelor's awarded; master's, doctoral offered. **ROTC:** Army, Air Force. **Location:** 160 miles from Kansas City, Missouri. **Calendar:** Semester, extensive summer session. **Full-time faculty:** 482 total; 85% have terminal degrees, 17% minority, 41% women. **Part-time faculty:** 360 total; 22% have terminal degrees, 14% minority, 50% women. **Class size:** 38% < 20, 41% 20-39, 8% 40-49, 11% 50-99, 2% >100. **Special facilities:** Outdoor venture center, climbing wall, nature preserve, planetarium, Nebraska Book Arts Center.

Freshman class profile. 3,732 applied, 3,310 admitted, 1,758 enrolled.

Mid 50% test scores		**Rank in top tenth:**	13%
SAT verbal:	490-620	**End year in good standing:**	76%
SAT math:	490-600	**Return as sophomores:**	75%
ACT:	20-25	**Out-of-state:**	8%
GPA 3.50 or higher:	41%	**Live on campus:**	27%
GPA 3.0-3.49:	29%	**International:**	1%
GPA 2.0-2.99:	29%	**Fraternities:**	5%
Rank in top quarter:	35%	**Sororities:**	4%

Basis for selection. School achievement record, test scores important. Must have ACT score of 20, comparable SAT score or class rank in upper half of graduating class. Admitted for special talent consideration on case by case basis. Open admission for non-degree applicants and non-traditional adult freshman applicants. Audition required for music program. **Homeschooled:** Applicants must submit official GED scores verifying successful completion of the GED. An ACT composite score of 25+ may be substituted in lieu of the GED score.

High school preparation. 16 units required. Required units include English 4, mathematics 3, social studies 1, history 2, science 3 (laboratory 1), foreign language 2 and academic electives 1. Specific course requirements for programs in business administration, human resources and family services for College of Engineering and Technology.

2005-2006 Annual costs. Tuition/fees: $4,825; $12,872 out-of-state. Room/board: $4,340. Books/supplies: $750. Personal expenses: $1,940.

2005-2006 Financial aid. Need-based: 41% of total undergraduate aid awarded as scholarships/grants, 59% as loans/jobs. **Non-need-based:** Scholarships awarded for academics, alumni affiliation, art, athletics, leadership, minority status, music/drama, ROTC, state residency.

Application procedures. Admission: Closing date 8/1 (postmark date). $45 fee. Application may be submitted online. Admission notification on a rolling basis. **Financial aid:** Priority date 3/1; no closing date. FAFSA required. Applicants notified on a rolling basis starting 4/15; must reply within 2 week(s) of notification.

Academics. Associate degree program available on Omaha campus through University of Nebraska-Lincoln in construction, drafting and design technology, electronic technology, fire control and safety technology, fire protection, manufacturing technology. On-line courses in aviation studies also available. **Special study options:** Combined bachelor's/graduate degree, cooperative education, cross-registration, distance learning, double major, dual enrollment of high school students, ESL, exchange student, honors, independent study, internships, student-designed major, study abroad, teacher certification program. **Credit/placement by examination:** AP, CLEP, ACT, institutional tests. 30 credit hours maximum toward bachelor's degree. CLEP exams in American History and Western Civilization must be accompanied by essay. **Support services:** Reduced course load, study skills assistance, tutoring, writing center.

Majors. Area/ethnic studies: African-American, Latin American, women's. **Biology:** General, biotechnology. **Business:** General, accounting, banking/financial services, finance, management information systems, managerial economics, market research, marketing, real estate. **Communications:** General, broadcast journalism, journalism. **Computer sciences:** Computer science. **Conservation:** Environmental studies. **Education:** Elementary, music, physical, secondary, speech impaired. **Engineering:** Architectural, chemical, civil, computer, electrical, physics. **Engineering technology:** Construction, industrial, manufacturing. **English:** Creative writing, English lit, speech/rhetoric. **Family/consumer sciences:** General, communication, family resources. **Foreign languages:** French, German, Spanish. **Health:** Community health services. **History:** General. **Interdisciplinary:** Gerontology, global studies, natural sciences. **Liberal arts:** Library science. **Math:** General. **Parks/recreation:** General. **Philosophy/religion:** Philosophy, religion. **Physical sciences:** Chemistry, geology, physics. **Protective services:** Criminal justice. **Psychology:** General. **Public administration:** Social work. **Social sciences:** Geography, political science, sociology. **Transportation:** Aviation, aviation management. **Visual/performing arts:** Art, art history/conservation, dramatic, music performance, music theory/composition, piano/organ, stringed instruments, studio arts, voice/opera.

Most popular majors. Business/marketing 31%, communications/journalism 6%, education 13%, security/protective services 10%.

Computing on campus. 2,100 workstations in library, computer center, student center. Dormitories wired for high-speed internet access and linked to campus network. Commuter students can connect to campus network. Online course registration, online library, helpline, student web hosting, wireless network available.

Student life. Freshman orientation: Mandatory. Preregistration for classes offered. Held every week April 15 thru August 1st. **Policies:** Freshmen permitted cars on campus. **Housing:** Coed dorms, substance-free housing available. $250 partly refundable deposit. **Activities:** Bands, choral groups, dance, drama, film society, literary magazine, music ensembles, musical theater, opera, radio station, student government, student newspaper, symphony orchestra, TV station, American multi-cultural students, Catholic campus ministry, chapter summary Bible study, student government legislative & public relations, Campus Crusade for Christ, Campus Ministry International, Honor Societies, Greek letter organizations, EDGE/Focus.

Athletics. NCAA. **Intercollegiate:** Baseball M, basketball, cross-country W, football (tackle) M, golf W, ice hockey M, soccer W, softball W, swimming W, tennis W, track and field W, volleyball W, wrestling M. **Intramural:** Badminton, basketball, bowling, golf, gymnastics, handball, racquetball, soccer, softball, squash, swimming, tennis, volleyball, wrestling M. **Team name:** Mavericks.

Student services. Adult student services, alcohol/substance abuse counseling, campus ministries, career counseling, services for economically disadvantaged, student employment services, financial aid counseling, health services, minority student services, on-campus daycare, personal counseling, placement for graduates, veterans' counselor, women's services. **Physically disabled:** Services for visually, speech, hearing impaired.

Contact. E-mail: unoadm@unomaha.edu
Phone: (402) 554-2393 Toll-free number: (800) 858-8648
Fax: (402) 554-3472
Jolene Adams, Director of Admissions, University of Nebraska - Omaha, 6001 Dodge Street, Omaha, NE 68182-0005

University of Nebraska Medical Center

Omaha, Nebraska
www.unmc.edu — **CB code: 6896**

- Public upper-division health science college
- Commuter campus in very large city
- 30% of applicants admitted

General. Founded in 1869. Regionally accredited. Students admitted at sophomore level or higher. **Degrees:** 463 bachelor's awarded; master's, doctoral, first professional offered. **ROTC:** Army, Air Force. **Calendar:** Semester, limited summer session. **Full-time faculty:** 771 total; 16% minority, 38% women. **Part-time faculty:** 231 total; 10% minority, 48% women.

Student profile. 846 degree-seeking undergraduates, 1,680 degree-seeking graduate students. 3,984 applied as first time-transfer students, 1,178 admitted, 1,025 enrolled. 16% entered as juniors, 12% entered as seniors. 5% transferred from two-year, 95% transferred from four-year institutions.

Women:	90%	**International:**	1%
African American:	1%	**Part-time:**	8%
Asian American:	1%	**Out-of-state:**	9%
Hispanic American:	2%	**25 or older:**	72%

Basis for selection. College transcript required. Admissions requirements, application procedures, and closing dates vary by program. Health professions program applicants must have completed prerequisite courses at another institution. Transfer accepted as sophomores, juniors, seniors.

2005-2006 Annual costs. Tuition/fees: $4,895; $13,805 out-of-state. Nursing program is $191 per-credit-hour for in-state and $559 per-credit-hour for out-of-state. Books/supplies: $900. Personal expenses: $1,500.

Financial aid. Need-based: 30% of total undergraduate aid awarded as scholarships/grants, 70% as loans/jobs. **Additional information:** Parental data collected from applicants for certain types of aid.

Application procedures. Admission: $45 fee, may be waived for applicants with need. **Financial aid:** Priority date 4/1. FAFSA, institutional form required.

Academics. Post-baccalaureate certificates available in cytotechnology and clinical nutrition education. **Special study options:** Combined bachelor's/graduate degree, distance learning, honors. **Credit/placement by examination:** CLEP, IB, institutional tests. 24 credit hours maximum toward bachelor's degree.

Majors. Health: Clinical lab science, dental hygiene, medical radiologic technology/radiation therapy, nuclear medical technology, nursing (RN), radiologic technology/medical imaging, sonography.

Computing on campus. 108 workstations in library, computer center, student center. Commuter students can connect to campus network. Online library, helpline, repair service, wireless network available.

Student life. Activities: Student government, Committee on Minority Concerns, American Academy of Physician Assistants, Religious Life Council, Christian Fellowship, Student Association for Rural Health, student services council, student professional organizations.

Student services. Alcohol/substance abuse counseling, career counseling, student employment services, financial aid counseling, health services, minority student services, on-campus daycare, personal counseling, veterans' counselor. **Physically disabled:** Services for hearing impaired.

Contact. E-mail: ttonjes@unmc.edu
Phone: (402) 559-6468 Toll-free number: (800) 626-8431 ext. 96468
Fax: (402) 559-6796
University of Nebraska Medical Center, 984230 Nebraska Medical Center, Omaha, NE 68198-4230

Wayne State College

Wayne, Nebraska
www.wsc.edu
CB member
CB code: 6469

- Public 4-year liberal arts and teachers college
- Residential campus in small town
- 2,706 degree-seeking undergraduates: 8% part-time, 56% women, 3% African American, 1% Asian American, 2% Hispanic American, 1% Native American, 1% international
- 541 degree-seeking graduate students
- 46% graduate within 6 years

General. Founded in 1909. Regionally accredited. Campus is state arboretum. **Degrees:** 552 bachelor's awarded; master's offered. **ROTC:** Army. **Location:** 45 miles from Sioux City, Iowa. **Calendar:** Semester, extensive summer session. **Full-time faculty:** 126 total; 75% have terminal degrees, 3% minority, 46% women. **Part-time faculty:** 79 total; 9% have terminal degrees, 4% minority, 71% women. **Class size:** 43% < 20, 50% 20-39, 6% 40-49, 1% 50-99. **Special facilities:** Planetarium, outdoor amphitheater.

Freshman class profile. 1,202 applied, 1,202 admitted, 593 enrolled.

Mid 50% test scores		**Rank in top tenth:**	13%
ACT:	18-25	**Return as sophomores:**	67%
GPA 3.50 or higher:	46%	**Out-of-state:**	13%
GPA 3.0-3.49:	29%	**Live on campus:**	93%
GPA 2.0-2.99:	24%	**International:**	1%
Rank in top quarter:	33%		

Basis for selection. Open admission.

High school preparation. College-preparatory program recommended. 12 units recommended. Recommended units include English 4, mathematics 3, social studies 3 and science 2.

2005-2006 Annual costs. Tuition/fees: $3,803; $6,735 out-of-state. Room/board: $4,230. Books/supplies: $900. Personal expenses: $900.

2005-2006 Financial aid. Need-based: 500 full-time freshmen applied for aid; 351 were judged to have need; 346 of these received aid. Average need met was 32%. Average scholarship/grant was $1,479; average loan $1,516. 37% of total undergraduate aid awarded as scholarships/grants, 63% as loans/jobs. **Non-need-based:** Awarded to 468 full-time undergraduates, including 119 freshmen. Scholarships awarded for academics, alumni affiliation, art, athletics, leadership, minority status, music/drama, religious affiliation, state residency.

Application procedures. Admission: No deadline. $30 fee, may be waived for applicants with need. Application may be submitted online. Admission notification on a rolling basis. **Financial aid:** Priority date 5/1; no closing date. FAFSA required. Applicants notified on a rolling basis starting 3/15; must reply within 3 week(s) of notification.

Academics. Special study options: Cooperative education, distance learning, double major, dual enrollment of high school students, honors, independent study, internships, student-designed major, teacher certification program. **Credit/placement by examination:** AP, CLEP, institutional tests. **Support services:** Learning center, reduced course load, study skills assistance, tutoring, writing center.

Majors. Biology: General. **Business:** Business admin. **Communications:** General, journalism, media studies. **Computer sciences:** General, information systems. **Education:** Art, biology, business, chemistry, drama/dance, early childhood, elementary, English, family/consumer sciences, foreign languages, geography, history, mathematics, middle, music, physical, psychology, social science, special, speech, technology/industrial arts. **Engineering technology:** General. **English:** English lit. **Family/consumer sciences:** General, food/nutrition. **Foreign languages:** General, Spanish. **Health:** Athletic training. **History:** General. **Math:** General. **Parks/recreation:** Exercise sciences, health/fitness, sports admin. **Physical sciences:** Chemistry. **Protective services:** Criminal justice. **Psychology:** General. **Social sciences:** General, geography, political science, sociology. **Visual/performing arts:** Art, dramatic, graphic design.

Most popular majors. Business/marketing 25%, education 25%, parks/recreation 7%, psychology 9%.

Computing on campus. 365 workstations in library, computer center, student center. Dormitories wired for high-speed internet access and linked to campus network. Commuter students can connect to campus network. Online course registration, helpline available.

Student life. Freshman orientation: Available, $75 fee. Preregistration for classes offered. **Policies:** Freshmen permitted cars on campus. **Housing:** Guaranteed on-campus for freshmen. Coed dorms, single-sex dorms, substance-free housing available. $75 deposit. **Activities:** Bands, choral groups, dance, drama, literary magazine, music ensembles, musical theater, radio station, student government, student newspaper, TV station.

Athletics. NCAA. **Intercollegiate:** Baseball M, basketball, cross-country, football (tackle) M, golf, soccer W, softball W, track and field, volleyball W. **Intramural:** Archery, badminton, basketball, bowling, cross-country, football (non-tackle) M, golf, gymnastics, handball, racquetball, soccer, softball, swimming, table tennis, tennis, track and field, volleyball, weight lifting M, wrestling M. **Team name:** Wildcats.

Student services. Alcohol/substance abuse counseling, campus ministries, career counseling, services for economically disadvantaged, student employment services, financial aid counseling, health services, minority student services, personal counseling, placement for graduates, veterans' counselor. **Physically disabled:** Services for visually, speech, hearing impaired.

Contact. E-mail: admit1@wsc.edu
Phone: (402) 375-7234 Toll-free number: (800) 228-9972
Fax: (402) 375-7204
R Morris, Director of Admissions, Wayne State College, 1111 Main Street, Wayne, NE 68787

York College
York, Nebraska
www.york.edu **CB code: 6984**

- Private 4-year liberal arts and teachers college affiliated with Church of Christ
- Residential campus in small town
- 443 degree-seeking undergraduates: 7% part-time, 51% women, 5% African American, 2% Asian American, 4% Hispanic American, 2% international
- 99% of applicants admitted
- SAT or ACT (ACT writing optional) required
- 36% graduate within 6 years

General. Founded in 1956. Regionally accredited. **Degrees:** 74 bachelor's, 17 associate awarded. **ROTC:** Army, Navy, Air Force. **Location:** 50 miles from Lincoln. **Calendar:** Semester, limited summer session. **Full-time faculty:** 33 total; 42% have terminal degrees, 27% women. **Part-time faculty:** 25 total; 12% have terminal degrees, 52% women. **Class size:** 77% < 20, 21% 20-39, 2% 40-49, less than 1% 50-99.

Freshman class profile. 206 applied, 203 admitted, 119 enrolled.

Mid 50% test scores			
SAT verbal:	450-590	Rank in top tenth:	12%
SAT math:	360-650	End year in good standing:	85%
ACT:	17-27	Return as sophomores:	70%
GPA 3.50 or higher:	35%	Out-of-state:	63%
GPA 3.0-3.49:	26%	Live on campus:	94%
GPA 2.0-2.99:	36%	International:	6%
Rank in top quarter:	26%	Fraternities:	67%
		Sororities:	75%

Basis for selection. ACT/SAT test scores, high school GPA, class rank of graduating class, and recommendation letters (both educational and private) very important. Essay recommended but not required.

High school preparation. 15 units required; 21 recommended. Required and recommended units include English 3-4, mathematics 2-4, social studies 1-4, history 1-4, science 2-4 and foreign language 3.

2005-2006 Annual costs. Tuition/fees: $12,430. Room/board: $3,900. Books/supplies: $700. Personal expenses: $1,600.

2004-2005 Financial aid. **Need-based:** 117 full-time freshmen applied for aid; 106 were judged to have need; 106 of these received aid. Average need met was 61%. Average scholarship/grant was $6,215; average loan $5,917. 54% of total undergraduate aid awarded as scholarships/grants, 46% as loans/jobs. **Non-need-based:** Awarded to 224 full-time undergraduates, including 77 freshmen. Scholarships awarded for academics, alumni affiliation, athletics, leadership, music/drama.

Application procedures. **Admission:** Priority date 3/31; deadline 8/31. $20 fee, may be waived for applicants with need. Admission notification on a rolling basis. Must reply by 9/5. **Financial aid:** Priority date 4/30; no closing date. FAFSA required. Applicants notified on a rolling basis starting 3/1; must reply within 4 week(s) of notification.

Academics. **Special study options:** Accelerated study, double major, dual enrollment of high school students, honors, independent study, internships, teacher certification program. **Credit/placement by examination:** AP, CLEP, IB, SAT, ACT, institutional tests. 12 credit hours maximum toward associate degree, 32 toward bachelor's. **Support services:** Learning center, reduced course load, remedial instruction, study skills assistance, tutoring.

Majors. **Biology:** General. **Business:** Accounting, business admin, human resources. **Communications:** General. **Education:** General, art, biology, business, drama/dance, elementary, English, history, mathematics, middle, multi-level teacher, music, physical, reading, secondary, social science, special, speech. **English:** English lit. **History:** General. **Math:** General. **Philosophy/religion:** Religion. **Physical sciences:** Chemistry. **Psychology:** General. **Theology:** Bible, religious ed. **Visual/performing arts:** Voice/opera.

Most popular majors. Biology 11%, business/marketing 16%, communications/journalism 8%, education 37%, English 6%, history 6%, liberal arts 6%, psychology 8%.

Computing on campus. 57 workstations in dormitories, library, computer center. Dormitories wired for high-speed internet access and linked to campus network. Online library, helpline available.

Student life. **Freshman orientation:** Mandatory. Preregistration for classes offered. **Policies:** Students expected to conform to Christian norms. Freshmen permitted cars on campus. **Housing:** Guaranteed on-campus for all undergraduates. Single-sex dorms, apartments, substance-free housing available. $75 deposit, deadline 8/31. Unmarried, full-time students under 21 required to live on campus or with relatives or staff off campus. **Activities:** Choral groups, drama, music ensembles, musical theater, student government, student newspaper, service clubs, LST, MAP, Chi Rho, spiritual life committee, campus ministries, marksmen, PBL.

Athletics. NAIA. **Intercollegiate:** Baseball M, basketball, cross-country, golf, soccer, softball W, track and field, volleyball W, wrestling M. **Intramural:** Basketball, cross-country, football (non-tackle), soccer, softball, table tennis, track and field, volleyball. **Team name:** Panthers.

Student services. Adult student services, campus ministries, career counseling, student employment services, financial aid counseling, health services, personal counseling, placement for graduates, veterans' counselor.

Contact. E-mail: enroll@york.edu
Phone: (402) 363-5627 Toll-free number: (800) 950-9675
Fax: (402) 363-5623
Tod Martin, Director of Admissions, York College, 1125 East 8th Street, York, NE 68467

Nevada

Art Institute of Las Vegas
Henderson, Nevada
www.ailv.artinstitutes.edu **CB code: 3141**

- For-profit 4-year culinary school and visual arts college
- Commuter campus in very large city
- 1,041 degree-seeking undergraduates

General. Accredited by ACCSCT. **Degrees:** 61 bachelor's, 37 associate awarded. **Location:** 10 miles from Las Vegas. **Calendar:** Quarter, extensive summer session. **Full-time faculty:** 14 total. **Part-time faculty:** 60 total. **Class size:** 72% < 20, 26% 20-39, less than 1% 40-49, less than 1% 50-99. **Special facilities:** Student-run restaurant.

Basis for selection. Open admission. Applicants for GAD program must have GPA of 2.5. Applicants for both GAD and MAA must present acceptable portfolios. **Homeschooled:** Institution must be recognized by state or national department of education.

Financial aid. Non-need-based: Scholarships awarded for academics, state residency.

Application procedures. Admission: No deadline. $50 fee, may be waived for applicants with need. Application must be submitted on paper. Admission notification on a rolling basis. **Financial aid:** No deadline. Applicants notified on a rolling basis.

Academics. Special study options: Distance learning, independent study, internships. **Credit/placement by examination:** AP, CLEP, IB, institutional tests. 28 credit hours maximum toward associate degree, 48 toward bachelor's. **Support services:** Learning center, reduced course load, remedial instruction, study skills assistance, tutoring.

Majors. Personal/culinary services: Chef training.

Computing on campus. 42 workstations in library, computer center. Dormitories wired for high-speed internet access. Commuter students can connect to campus network. Online course registration, online library, student web hosting available.

Student life. Freshman orientation: Mandatory. Preregistration for classes offered. Held Thursday before start of classes. **Policies:** Freshmen permitted cars on campus. **Housing:** Coed dorms, substance-free housing available.

Student services. Alcohol/substance abuse counseling, career counseling, services for economically disadvantaged, student employment services, financial aid counseling, personal counseling, placement for graduates. **Physically disabled:** Services for visually, speech, hearing impaired. **Learning disabled:** Comprehensive services available.

Contact. Phone: (702) 369-9944
Suzanne Noel, Director of Admissions, Art Institute of Las Vegas, 2350 Corporate Circle, Henderson, NV 89074

DeVry University: Las Vegas
Henderson, Nevada
www.devry.edu/locations/campuses/loc_henderson.jsp

- For-profit 4-year university
- Commuter campus
- 89 degree-seeking undergraduates: 38% part-time, 40% women, 13% African American, 13% Asian American, 17% Hispanic American
- 33 graduate students

General. Degrees: 4 bachelor's awarded; master's offered. **Calendar:** Semester. **Part-time faculty:** 31 total; 26% minority, 29% women.

Freshman class profile. 17 enrolled.

Basis for selection. Academic record and interview most important.

2005-2006 Annual costs. Tuition/fees: $11,900. Books/supplies: $1,250. Personal expenses: $1,950.

Financial aid. Non-need-based: Scholarships awarded for academics.

Application procedures. Admission: No deadline. $50 fee. Admission notification on a rolling basis. **Financial aid:** No deadline. FAFSA required. Applicants notified on a rolling basis.

Academics. Special study options: Accelerated study, cooperative education, distance learning. **Credit/placement by examination:** CLEP.

Contact. Phone: (702) 933-9700
DeVry University: Las Vegas, 2490 Paseo Verde Parkway, Suite 150, Henderson, NV 89074

Great Basin College
Elko, Nevada
www.gbcnv.edu **CB code: 4293**

- Public 4-year community and teachers college
- Commuter campus in large town
- 1,695 degree-seeking undergraduates
- Application essay, interview required

General. Founded in 1967. Regionally accredited. **Degrees:** 45 bachelor's, 143 associate awarded. **Location:** 280 miles from Reno, 220 miles from Salt Lake City. **Calendar:** Semester, limited summer session. **Full-time faculty:** 55 total. **Part-time faculty:** 150 total.

Freshman class profile.

Out-of-state:	5%	**Live on campus:**	3%

Basis for selection. Open admission, but selective for some programs. Nursing applicants selected on basis of point system. Points given for courses completed, grades, current work experience in health field, certifications, letters of recommendation, and scores obtained on required entrance exam which measures math and reading comprehension skills. Application/selection process for formal admission to last 2 years of bachelor degree programs. Placement test required for some English and math courses. Interview and essay required for last 2 years of bachelor degree programs.

2005-2006 Annual costs. Tuition/fees: $1,643; $6,558 out-of-state. Tuition shown is for lower-division classes. Reduced tuition for non-residents who are within 50 miles of Nevada border. Out-of-state residents pay additional fees which are included in tuition. Books/supplies: $800. Personal expenses: $1,200.

Application procedures. Admission: No deadline. $10 fee. Application may be submitted online. Admission notification on a rolling basis. **Financial aid:** Priority date 6/1; no closing date. FAFSA required. Applicants notified on a rolling basis starting 7/1.

Academics. Special study options: Cooperative education, distance learning, dual enrollment of high school students, ESL, independent study, liberal arts/career combination, teacher certification program. **Credit/placement by examination:** AP, CLEP, institutional tests. 15 credit hours maximum toward associate degree, 30 toward bachelor's. **Support services:** Learning center, reduced course load, remedial instruction, study skills assistance, tutoring, writing center.

Majors. Agriculture: Business. **Business:** Business admin. **Education:** Agricultural, biology, elementary, history, mathematics, science, secondary, social science, trade/industrial. **Engineering:** Surveying. **Health:** Nursing (RN). **Interdisciplinary:** Cultural resource management. **Liberal arts:** Arts/sciences. **Social sciences:** General.

Computing on campus. 200 workstations in dormitories, library, computer center. Dormitories linked to campus network. Commuter students can connect to campus network. Online course registration, online library, helpline, wireless network available.

Student life. Freshman orientation: Mandatory, $26 fee. Preregistration for classes offered. **Policies:** Freshmen permitted cars on campus. **Housing:** Coed dorms, apartments, substance-free housing available. **Activities:** Choral groups, drama, musical theater, student government, vocational clubs, nursing club, rodeo, intramural sports, student ambassadors.

Athletics. Intramural: Rodeo, table tennis, volleyball.

Student services. Adult student services, career counseling, services for economically disadvantaged, student employment services, financial aid counseling, minority student services, on-campus daycare, personal counseling, placement for graduates, veterans' counselor. **Physically disabled:** Services for visually, speech, hearing impaired.

Contact. E-mail: admissions@gbcnv.edu
Phone: (775) 753-2311 Fax: (775) 738-8771
Julie Byrnes, Director of Enrollment Management, Great Basin College, 1500 College Parkway, Elko, NV 89801

International Academy of Design and Technology: Henderson

Henderson, Nevada
www.iadtvegas.com

- For-profit 3-year visual arts and technical college
- Very large city
- 410 degree-seeking undergraduates

General. Accredited by ACICS. **Location:** 10 miles from Las Vegas. **Calendar:** Quarter. **Part-time faculty:** 20 total.

Basis for selection. Open admission.

Application procedures. Admission: No deadline. $50 fee.

Academics. Credit/placement by examination: CLEP.

Majors. Visual/performing arts: Fashion design, graphic design, interior design.

Contact. E-mail: vegas_web@iadtvegas.com
Phone: (702) 990-0150 Toll-free number: (866) 400-4238
Mary Ameln, Director of Education, International Academy of Design and Technology: Henderson, 2495 Village View Drive, Henderson, NV 89074

ITT Technical Institute: Henderson

Henderson, Nevada
www.itt-tech.edu **CB code: 2710**

- For-profit 4-year technical college
- Commuter campus in small city

General. Accredited by ACICS. **Calendar:** Quarter.

Annual costs/financial aid. Tuition varies by program, $260-$368 per credit hour.

Contact. Phone: (702) 558-5404
Director of Recruitment, 168 North Gibson Road, Henderson, NV 89014

Morrison University

Reno, Nevada
www.morrison.neumont.edu **CB code: 2114**

- For-profit 4-year university and business college
- Commuter campus in small city
- 65 degree-seeking undergraduates: 9% part-time, 58% women
- 19 degree-seeking graduate students
- Interview required

General. Founded in 1902. Accredited by ACICS. **Degrees:** 6 bachelor's, 8 associate awarded; master's offered. **Location:** Half mile from downtown. **Calendar:** Quarter, extensive summer session. **Full-time faculty:** 3 total; 67% women. **Part-time faculty:** 18 total; 39% have terminal degrees, 11% minority, 44% women. **Class size:** 91% < 20, 9% 20-39.

Freshman class profile.

Out-of-state:	3%	**Live on campus:**	2%

Basis for selection. Open admission.

2005-2006 Annual costs. Books/supplies: $825. Personal expenses: $1,800.

Application procedures. Admission: No deadline. $25 fee, may be waived for applicants with need. Application may be submitted online. Admission notification on a rolling basis. **Financial aid:** No deadline. FAFSA required. Applicants notified on a rolling basis starting 7/1.

Academics. Special study options: Accelerated study, combined bachelor's/graduate degree, cooperative education, double major, dual enrollment of high school students, independent study, internships, liberal arts/career combination, weekend college. **Credit/placement by examination:** CLEP, IB. 9 credit hours maximum toward associate degree, 9 toward bachelor's. Students may take challenge exam for credit within first week of class start. **Support services:** Learning center, reduced course load, remedial instruction, study skills assistance, tutoring, writing center.

Majors. Business: Accounting, business admin, management information systems, office management.

Computing on campus. 62 workstations in library, computer center.

Student life. Freshman orientation: Mandatory. Preregistration for classes offered. **Policies:** Dress code, appropriate conduct policy, zero tolerance for alcohol and drug use while in school. Freshmen permitted cars on campus. **Activities:** Student government, student newspaper.

Student services. Adult student services, alcohol/substance abuse counseling, career counseling, student employment services, financial aid counseling, personal counseling, placement for graduates, veterans' counselor.

Contact. E-mail: ctiminsky@morrison.neumont.edu
Phone: (775) 850-0700 ext. 101 Fax: (775) 850-0711
Charles Timinsky, Director of Enrollment, Morrison University, 10315 Professional Circle, #201, Reno, NV 89521

Sierra Nevada College

Incline Village, Nevada **CB member**
www.sierranevada.edu **CB code: 4757**

- Private 4-year liberal arts college
- Residential campus in small town
- 329 degree-seeking undergraduates: 13% part-time, 49% women
- 176 graduate students
- 66% of applicants admitted
- SAT or ACT with writing, application essay required

General. Founded in 1969. Regionally accredited. **Degrees:** 58 bachelor's awarded; master's offered. **ROTC:** Army. **Location:** 35 miles from Reno. **Calendar:** Semester, limited summer session. **Full-time faculty:** 15 total; 100% have terminal degrees, 7% minority, 40% women. **Part-time faculty:** 55 total; 18% have terminal degrees, 4% minority, 56% women. **Class size:** 84% < 20, 16% 20-39. **Special facilities:** Observatory, entertainment technology lab.

Freshman class profile. 359 applied, 237 admitted, 64 enrolled.

Mid 50% test scores			
SAT verbal:	440-630	**Rank in top quarter:**	35%
SAT math:	440-600	**Rank in top tenth:**	10%
ACT:	18-26	**Out-of-state:**	71%
		Live on campus:	90%

Basis for selection. Motivation as evidenced in personal interview and/or autobiographical statement very important. Applicants with GPA below 2.0 may be admitted provisionally, upon review by faculty admission committee. Interview recommended. **Homeschooled:** Submit any course plans or transcripts along with any home schooling plans that are available.

High school preparation. Recommended units include English 4, mathematics 3, social studies 2, history 2, science 2 and foreign language 2.

2005-2006 Annual costs. Tuition/fees: $19,650. Room/board: $7,450. Books/supplies: $750. Personal expenses: $2,035.

2005-2006 Financial aid. Need-based: Average need met was 75%. Average scholarship/grant was $6,050. 37% of total undergraduate aid awarded as scholarships/grants, 63% as loans/jobs. **Non-need-based:** Scholarships awarded for academics, art, athletics.

Application procedures. Admission: Priority date 2/15; no deadline. No application fee. Application may be submitted online. Admission notification on a rolling basis beginning on or about 12/1. Must reply by May 1 or within 3 week(s) if notified thereafter. **Financial aid:** Closing date 4/1. FAFSA, institutional form required. Applicants notified on a rolling basis starting 8/15; must reply by 5/1 or within 4 week(s) of notification.

Academics. Special study options: Combined bachelor's/graduate degree, double major, honors, independent study, internships, liberal arts/career combination, study abroad, teacher certification program. **Credit/placement by examination:** AP, CLEP, IB, institutional tests. 30 credit hours maximum toward bachelor's degree. **Support services:** Preadmission summer program, remedial instruction, study skills assistance, tutoring, writing center.

Majors. Biology: General, ecology. **Business:** Business admin, hospitality admin, resort management. **Computer sciences:** General, computer science. **Conservation:** Environmental science, management/policy. **English:**

English lit. **Health:** Premedicine, prenursing, prepharmacy. **Interdisciplinary:** Global studies. **Liberal arts:** Arts/sciences. **Psychology:** General. **Visual/performing arts:** General, ceramics, drawing, painting, printmaking, sculpture, studio arts.

Most popular majors. Business/marketing 31%, English 9%, liberal arts 12%, psychology 7%, visual/performing arts 24%.

Computing on campus. PC or laptop required. 30 workstations in dormitories, library, computer center, student center. Dormitories wired for high-speed internet access and linked to campus network. Commuter students can connect to campus network. Online library, helpline, repair service, wireless network available.

Student life. Freshman orientation: Mandatory. Preregistration for classes offered. Week-long program; 4 sessions held in June, July, and August. **Policies:** Freshmen permitted cars on campus. **Housing:** Guaranteed on-campus for all undergraduates. Coed dorms, substance-free housing available. $200 deposit, deadline 5/1. Students must live on campus for 2 years unless married or over 21. **Activities:** Jazz band, choral groups, drama, literary magazine, music ensembles, musical theater, student government, student newspaper, recycling club, Christian club, Amnesty International.

Athletics. NCAA. **Intercollegiate:** Equestrian, skiing. **Intramural:** Basketball W, bowling, fencing, skiing, soccer, softball, volleyball M. **Team name:** Eagles.

Student services. Alcohol/substance abuse counseling, career counseling, student employment services, financial aid counseling, health services, personal counseling, placement for graduates, veterans' counselor.

Contact. E-mail: admissions@sierranevada.edu
Phone: (775) 831-1314 Fax: (775) 831-6223
Pat Coleman, Dean of Admission, Sierra Nevada College, 999 Tahoe Boulevard, Incline Village, NV 89451-4269

University of Nevada: Las Vegas

Las Vegas, Nevada — **CB member**
www.unlv.edu — **CB code: 4861**

- Public 4-year university
- Commuter campus in very large city
- 21,004 degree-seeking undergraduates: 26% part-time, 56% women, 8% African American, 14% Asian American, 11% Hispanic American, 1% Native American, 4% international
- 4,519 degree-seeking graduate students
- 81% of applicants admitted
- 41% graduate within 6 years

General. Founded in 1957. Regionally accredited. Credit courses available at Nellis Air Force Base. **Degrees:** 3,079 bachelor's awarded; master's, doctoral, first professional offered. **ROTC:** Army, Air Force. **Location:** 268 miles from Los Angeles, 290 miles from Phoenix, Arizona. **Calendar:** Semester, limited summer session. **Full-time faculty:** 810 total; 88% have terminal degrees, 18% minority, 33% women. **Part-time faculty:** 732 total. **Class size:** 29% < 20, 50% 20-39, 6% 40-49, 12% 50-99, 2% >100. **Special facilities:** National supercomputing center for energy and environment, natural history museum, arboretum, 3 theaters, concert hall, international gaming institute, professional practice school for teachers.

Freshman class profile. 6,952 applied, 5,663 admitted, 3,048 enrolled.

Mid 50% test scores			
SAT verbal:	440-560	Rank in top tenth:	18%
SAT math:	450-580	Return as sophomores:	72%
ACT:	18-24	Out-of-state:	23%
GPA 3.50 or higher:	28%	Live on campus:	26%
GPA 3.0-3.49:	41%	International:	1%
GPA 2.0-2.99:	30%	Fraternities:	8%
Rank in top quarter:	44%	Sororities:	6%

Basis for selection. GED not accepted. Secondary school record most important, 2.55 minimum GPA in core courses required. Recommendations, personal essay and test scores considered for students applying through Alternate Criteria program. ACT/SAT required for English and math course placement. SAT/ACT required for students appealing admission through alternate criteria and for placement into English/math courses. Audition recommended for music, theater arts programs; portfolio recommended for art program. **Homeschooled:** Transcript of courses and grades, letter of recommendation (nonparent) required. Students must submit personal statement, 2 letters of recommendation, ACT/SAT test scores.

High school preparation. 13 units required. Required units include English 4, mathematics 3, social studies 3, science 3 (laboratory 2). Algebra or higher level math required.

2005-2006 Annual costs. Tuition/fees: $3,060; $12,527 out-of-state. Reduced tuition rate for out-of-state students who live within 50 miles of Nevada border and for those who reside in Western Undergraduate Exchange states. Room/board: $8,373. Books/supplies: $850. Personal expenses: $1,800.

2005-2006 Financial aid. Need-based: 2,505 full-time freshmen applied for aid; 1,448 were judged to have need; 1,428 of these received aid. Average need met was 65%. Average scholarship/grant was $2,909; average loan $2,619. 32% of total undergraduate aid awarded as scholarships/grants, 68% as loans/jobs. **Non-need-based:** Awarded to 6,350 full-time undergraduates, including 2,274 freshmen. Scholarships awarded for academics, alumni affiliation, art, athletics, job skills, leadership, minority status, music/drama, state residency. **Additional information:** Tuition reduction for state residents through consortium programs and for out-of-state students graduating from high schools in designated counties bordering Nevada, for military dependents residing in-state, and for dependents of children of alumni not residing in-state.

Application procedures. Admission: Closing date 2/1 (receipt date). $60 fee. Application may be submitted online. Admission notification on a rolling basis beginning on or about 11/1. **Financial aid:** Priority date 2/1; no closing date. FAFSA, institutional form required. Applicants notified on a rolling basis starting 4/1; must reply within 2 week(s) of notification.

Academics. Curriculum encourages innovative and interdisciplinary approaches to instruction. **Special study options:** Accelerated study, cooperative education, distance learning, double major, dual enrollment of high school students, ESL, exchange student, honors, independent study, internships, student-designed major, study abroad, teacher certification program. 2+2 culinary arts program with Community College of Southern Nevada. **Credit/placement by examination:** AP, CLEP, IB, SAT, ACT, institutional tests. 30 credit hours maximum toward bachelor's degree. **Support services:** Learning center, pre-admission summer program, remedial instruction, study skills assistance, tutoring, writing center.

Honors college/program. Honors College applicants must complete the honors application, letters of recommendation, test scores, personal statements, and essay response.

Majors. Architecture: Architecture, interior, landscape, urban/community planning. **Area/ethnic studies:** Asian, Latin American, women's. **Biology:** General. **Business:** Accounting, finance, hospitality admin, human resources, international marketing, management information systems, managerial economics, marketing, real estate. **Communications:** General. **Computer sciences:** Computer science. **Conservation:** General, environmental studies, management/policy. **Education:** Adult/continuing, computer, curriculum, early childhood, elementary, health, physical, secondary, special. **Engineering:** Civil, computer, electrical, mechanical, software. **Engineering technology:** Construction. **Foreign languages:** French, German, Spanish. **Health:** Athletic training, clinical lab science, health care admin, medical radiologic technology/radiation therapy, nuclear medical technology, nursing (RN), physics/radiologic health. **History:** General. **Interdisciplinary:** Nutrition sciences. **Liberal arts:** Arts/sciences. **Math:** General, applied. **Parks/recreation:** General, exercise sciences, health/fitness. **Personal/culinary services:** Culinary arts. **Philosophy/religion:** Philosophy. **Physical sciences:** Chemistry, geology, physics. **Psychology:** General. **Public administration:** Social work. **Social sciences:** Anthropology, political science, sociology. **Visual/performing arts:** Art, dance, dramatic, film/cinema, jazz, studio arts.

Most popular majors. Business/marketing 31%, communications/journalism 7%, education 12%, health sciences 6%, psychology 7%, social sciences 6%, visual/performing arts 6%.

Computing on campus. 250 workstations in dormitories, library, computer center, student center. Dormitories wired for high-speed internet access and linked to campus network. Commuter students can connect to campus network. Online course registration, online library, helpline, wireless network available.

Student life. Freshman orientation: Available, $90 fee. Two-day program. **Policies:** First-year residential, upper-class and Tonopah living/learning programs place students with others at similar levels and integrate classroom knowledge with life experience. Freshmen permitted cars on campus. **Housing:** Guaranteed on-campus for freshmen. Coed dorms, single-sex dorms, substance-free housing available. $125 partly refundable deposit. All-female, study intensive floors available; handicapped accessible suites in all complexes. **Activities:** Bands, choral groups, dance, drama, literary magazine, music ensembles, musical theater, opera, radio station, student government, student newspaper, TV station, Young Democrats/Republicans, international student organization, Rebel Christian Fellowship, Hillel, ethnic student council, student organization of Latinos, black student association, Latter-day Saints student organization, Hawaii club.

Athletics. NCAA. **Intercollegiate:** Baseball M, basketball, cheerleading, cross-country W, diving, football (tackle) M, golf, soccer, softball W, swimming, tennis, track and field W, volleyball W. **Intramural:** Badminton, basketball, bowling, cross-country, diving W, football (tackle) M, golf, racquetball, soccer, softball, swimming, table tennis, tennis, track and field, volleyball. **Team name:** Rebels.

Student services. Adult student services, alcohol/substance abuse counseling, campus ministries, career counseling, services for economically disadvantaged, student employment services, financial aid counseling, health services, minority student services, on-campus daycare, personal counseling, placement for graduates, veterans' counselor, women's services. **Physically disabled:** Services for visually, speech, hearing impaired. **Learning disabled:** Comprehensive services available.

Contact. Phone: (702) 774-8658 Fax: (702) 774-8008
Stephanie Brown, Executive Director of Enrollment Management, University of Nevada: Las Vegas, 4505 Maryland Parkway Box 451021, Las Vegas, NV 89154-1021

University of Nevada: Reno

Reno, Nevada — **CB member**
www.unr.edu — **CB code: 4844**

- Public 4-year university
- Commuter campus in small city
- 12,404 degree-seeking undergraduates: 17% part-time, 55% women, 2% African American, 7% Asian American, 7% Hispanic American, 1% Native American, 2% international
- 2,547 degree-seeking graduate students
- 86% of applicants admitted
- 49% graduate within 6 years

General. Founded in 1874. Regionally accredited. **Degrees:** 1,815 bachelor's awarded; master's, doctoral, first professional offered. **ROTC:** Army. **Location:** 225 miles from San Francisco, 460 miles from Las Vegas. **Calendar:** Semester, extensive summer session. **Full-time faculty:** 555 total; 74% have terminal degrees, 12% minority, 40% women. **Part-time faculty:** 485 total; 35% have terminal degrees, 11% minority, 48% women. **Class size:** 37% < 20, 46% 20-39, 5% 40-49, 8% 50-99, 5% >100. **Special facilities:** Mineral museum, planetarium, arboretum, disability resource center, ethnic student resource center, internship center.

Freshman class profile. 4,793 applied, 4,138 admitted, 2,432 enrolled.

Mid 50% test scores		**End year in good standing:**	72%
SAT verbal:	470-580	**Return as sophomores:**	75%
SAT math:	480-590	**Out-of-state:**	17%
ACT:	20-25	**Live on campus:**	51%
GPA 3.50 or higher:	40%	**International:**	1%
GPA 3.0-3.49:	41%	**Fraternities:**	12%
GPA 2.0-2.99:	19%	**Sororities:**	10%

Basis for selection. GED not accepted. Secondary school record most important. All students applying for scholarships must submit test scores. Interview recommended for nursing program; audition recommended for music program; portfolio recommended for fine arts program.

High school preparation. 13 units required. Required units include English 4, mathematics 3, social studies 3, science 3 (laboratory 2).

2005-2006 Annual costs. Tuition/fees: $3,270; $12,737 out-of-state. Reduced tuition rate for out-of-state students who live within 50 miles of Nevada border. Room/board: $7,785. Books/supplies: $1,000. Personal expenses: $3,395.

2004-2005 Financial aid. All financial aid based on need. 1,018 full-time freshmen applied for aid; 669 were judged to have need; 654 of these received aid. Average need met was 47%. Average scholarship/grant was $4,238; average loan $2,465. 49% of total undergraduate aid awarded as scholarships/grants, 51% as loans/jobs. **Additional information:** Reduced out-of-state tuition available for children of alumni and for non-residents from some neighboring counties in California.

Application procedures. Admission: Priority date 3/1; no deadline. $60 fee, may be waived for applicants with need. Application may be submitted online. Admission notification on a rolling basis. **Financial aid:** Priority date 2/1; no closing date. Applicants notified on a rolling basis starting 4/1; must reply within 2 week(s) of notification.

Academics. Special study options: Distance learning, double major, dual enrollment of high school students, ESL, exchange student, honors, independent study, internships, study abroad, teacher certification program. **Credit/placement by examination:** AP, CLEP, SAT, ACT, institutional tests. 60 credit hours maximum toward bachelor's degree. **Support services:** Remedial instruction, study skills assistance, tutoring, writing center.

Majors. Agriculture: Animal sciences, economics. **Area/ethnic studies:** Women's. **Biology:** General, biochemistry, biotechnology. **Business:** General, accounting, finance, international, logistics, management information systems, managerial economics, marketing. **Communications:** General, journalism. **Computer sciences:** General, computer science, information technology. **Conservation:** General, forestry, management/policy, wildlife. **Education:** Agricultural, art, biology, business, chemistry, drama/dance, early childhood, elementary, English, family/consumer sciences, foreign languages, French, German, health, history, mathematics, music, physical, physics, science, secondary, social science, social studies, Spanish, special, speech, technology/industrial arts, trade/industrial. **Engineering:** Chemical, civil, electrical, environmental, geological, materials, mechanical, metallurgical, mining, physics, water resource. **Engineering technology:** Construction. **English:** English lit. **Family/consumer sciences:** Child development, family studies, food/nutrition. **Foreign languages:** French, German, Spanish. **Health:** Audiology/speech pathology, nursing (RN), premedicine, preveterinary, speech pathology. **History:** General. **Math:** General. **Parks/recreation:** General. **Philosophy/religion:** Philosophy. **Physical sciences:** Chemistry, geology, geophysics, hydrology, physics. **Psychology:** General. **Public administration:** Social work. **Social sciences:** Anthropology, applied economics, criminology, economics, geography, international relations, political science, sociology. **Visual/performing arts:** Art, art history/conservation, dramatic, interior design, music performance.

Most popular majors. Biology 6%, business/marketing 14%, communications/journalism 6%, education 11%, engineering/engineering technologies 8%, health sciences 9%, liberal arts 7%, psychology 6%, social sciences 8%.

Computing on campus. 500 workstations in dormitories, library, computer center, student center. Dormitories wired for high-speed internet access and linked to campus network. Commuter students can connect to campus network. Online course registration, online library, helpline, student web hosting, wireless network available.

Student life. Freshman orientation: Mandatory, $95 fee. Preregistration for classes offered. Sessions held before each semester. Family members welcome. **Policies:** Freshmen permitted cars on campus. **Housing:** Coed dorms, single-sex dorms, special housing for disabled, apartments, substance-free housing available. $300 partly refundable deposit. Special interest floors (fitness, arts and culture, stereo limitation, alcohol prohibition, honors) available. **Activities:** Bands, choral groups, dance, drama, literary magazine, music ensembles, musical theater, opera, radio station, student government, student newspaper, Intervarsity Christian Fellowship, black student union, American Indian organization, Asian American Alliance, Chinese students association, Young Republicans, Young Democrats, Hillel, MEXA.

Athletics. NCAA. **Intercollegiate:** Baseball M, basketball, cheerleading, cross-country W, diving W, football (tackle) M, golf, rifle, skiing, soccer W, softball W, swimming W, tennis, track and field W, volleyball W. **Intramural:** Badminton, basketball, bowling, cross-country, diving, football (non-tackle), golf, handball M, racquetball, skiing, soccer, softball, swimming, table tennis, tennis, track and field, volleyball, water polo, weight lifting. **Team name:** Wolf Pack.

Student services. Adult student services, alcohol/substance abuse counseling, career counseling, services for economically disadvantaged, student employment services, financial aid counseling, health services, legal services, minority student services, on-campus daycare, personal counseling, placement for graduates, veterans' counselor, women's services. **Physically disabled:** Services for visually, speech, hearing impaired.

Contact. E-mail: asknevada@unr.edu
Phone: (775) 784-4700 Toll-free number: (866) 263-8232
Fax: (775) 784-4283
Melisa Choroszy, Assistant Vice President, Enrollment Services, University of Nevada: Reno, Mail Stop 120, Reno, NV 89557

New Hampshire

Chester College of New England

Chester, New Hampshire
www.chestercollege.edu
CB member
CB code: 3977

- Private 4-year visual arts college
- Residential campus in rural community
- 218 degree-seeking undergraduates: 14% part-time, 58% women
- 48% of applicants admitted
- Application essay, interview required

General. Founded in 1965. Regionally accredited. **Degrees:** 19 bachelor's, 2 associate awarded. **Location:** 10 miles from Manchester, 50 miles from Boston. **Calendar:** Semester, limited summer session. **Full-time faculty:** 10 total. **Part-time faculty:** 15 total. **Class size:** 93% < 20, 6% 20-39, 1% 40-49.

Freshman class profile. 290 applied, 140 admitted, 82 enrolled.

Mid 50% test scores			
SAT verbal:	440-610	Return as sophomores:	93%
SAT math:	390-550	Out-of-state:	14%
ACT:	14-21	Live on campus:	26%

Basis for selection. High school achievement record, recommendations important; SAT/ACT scores considered; portfolio strongly recommended; interview required. **Homeschooled:** Students may be required to complete an essay under examination conditions. SAT scores required.

High school preparation. Recommended units include English 4, mathematics 2, social studies 1, history 1 and science 2.

2006-2007 Annual costs. Tuition/fees (projected): $14,700. Lab fees vary per student; average cost $600. Room/board: $7,600. Books/supplies: $1,100. Personal expenses: $1,000.

2004-2005 Financial aid. Need-based: 10% of total undergraduate aid awarded as scholarships/grants, 90% as loans/jobs. **Non-need-based:** Scholarships awarded for academics, art, state residency.

Application procedures. Admission: No deadline. $35 fee, may be waived for applicants with need. Application may be submitted online. Admission notification on a rolling basis beginning on or about 1/15. Must reply by May 1 or within 2 week(s) if notified thereafter. **Financial aid:** Priority date 3/15; no closing date. FAFSA required. Applicants notified on a rolling basis starting 12/1; must reply within 2 week(s) of notification.

Academics. Special study options: Double major, independent study, internships, teacher certification program. Art education certification. **Credit/placement by examination:** CLEP, institutional tests. 30 credit hours maximum toward associate degree, 60 toward bachelor's. **Support services:** Reduced course load, remedial instruction, study skills assistance, tutoring.

Majors. Computer sciences: Web page design. **English:** Creative writing. **Visual/performing arts:** Art, graphic design, photography, studio arts.

Computing on campus. 42 workstations in library, computer center, student center. Dormitories wired for high-speed internet access. Online library available.

Student life. Freshman orientation: Mandatory, $90 fee. Preregistration for classes offered. 3-day orientation. **Policies:** Freshmen permitted cars on campus. **Housing:** Guaranteed on-campus for all undergraduates. Coed dorms available. $200 deposit, deadline 8/15. **Activities:** Drama, literary magazine, student government.

Athletics. Intramural: Basketball, football (non-tackle), soccer, softball, table tennis, volleyball.

Student services. Career counseling, financial aid counseling, placement for graduates.

Contact. E-mail: admissions@chestercollege.edu
Phone: (603) 887-7400 Toll-free number: (800) 974-6372
Fax: (603) 887-1777
Sarah Vogell, Director of Admissions, Chester College of New England, 40 Chester Street, Chester, NH 03036

Colby-Sawyer College

New London, New Hampshire
www.colby-sawyer.edu
CB member
CB code: 3281

- Private 4-year liberal arts college
- Residential campus in small town
- 964 degree-seeking undergraduates: 1% part-time, 64% women, 1% African American, 1% Asian American, 1% international
- 90% of applicants admitted
- SAT or ACT with writing, application essay required

General. Founded in 1837. Regionally accredited. **Degrees:** 183 bachelor's, 5 associate awarded. **ROTC:** Army, Air Force. **Location:** 30 miles from Hanover, 35 miles from Concord. **Calendar:** Semester. **Full-time faculty:** 57 total. **Part-time faculty:** 68 total. **Class size:** 59% < 20, 41% 20-39, less than 1% 40-49. **Special facilities:** Fine arts center, laboratory school (preschool, K-3), library learning center, conservatory and greenhouse, Curtis Ivey Science Center.

Freshman class profile. 1,474 applied, 1,328 admitted, 282 enrolled.

Mid 50% test scores			
SAT verbal:	460-550	Return as sophomores:	79%
SAT math:	460-550	Out-of-state:	70%
ACT:	19-24	Live on campus:	99%
		International:	1%

Basis for selection. High school transcript most important. Test scores, recommendations, school and community activities, essay also considered. Interviews highly recommended, but not required. Portfolio recommended for art program.

High school preparation. 15 units required. Required units include English 4, mathematics 3, social studies 3, science 2 (laboratory 2) and foreign language 2. Nursing applicants strongly encouraged to have 3 years of college-preparatory lab sciences, including biology and chemistry.

2006-2007 Annual costs. Tuition/fees (projected): $26,350. Room/board: $9,900. Books/supplies: $750. Personal expenses: $1,000.

2004-2005 Financial aid. Need-based: 231 full-time freshmen applied for aid; 176 were judged to have need; 176 of these received aid. Average need met was 88%. Average scholarship/grant was $8,500; average loan $2,500. 70% of total undergraduate aid awarded as scholarships/grants, 30% as loans/jobs. **Non-need-based:** Awarded to 393 full-time undergraduates, including 184 freshmen. Scholarships awarded for academics, alumni affiliation, art, leadership, music/drama.

Application procedures. Admission: No deadline. $45 fee, may be waived for applicants with need. Application may be submitted online. Admission notification on a rolling basis beginning on or about 12/15. Must reply by 5/1. **Financial aid:** Priority date 2/15; no closing date. FAFSA, institutional form required. Applicants notified on a rolling basis starting 3/1; must reply by 5/1 or within 2 week(s) of notification.

Academics. Liberal arts and experiential education integrated. Internships or senior research projects required in all major programs. **Special study options:** Accelerated study, cross-registration, double major, dual enrollment of high school students, ESL, exchange student, honors, independent study, internships, semester at sea, student-designed major, study abroad, teacher certification program, Washington semester. **Credit/placement by examination:** AP, CLEP, IB, institutional tests. 30 credit hours maximum toward associate degree, 60 toward bachelor's. **Support services:** Learning center, reduced course load, study skills assistance, tutoring.

Majors. Biology: General. **Business:** Business admin. **Communications:** Media studies. **Conservation:** Environmental studies. **Education:** Art, early childhood, English, social studies. **English:** English lit. **Health:** Athletic training, nursing (RN). **Parks/recreation:** Exercise sciences, sports admin. **Psychology:** General. **Visual/performing arts:** Art, graphic design, studio arts.

Most popular majors. Business/marketing 15%, communications/journalism 9%, education 10%, health sciences 7%, parks/recreation 14%, psychology 21%, visual/performing arts 13%.

Computing on campus. 189 workstations in library, computer center. Dormitories wired for high-speed internet access and linked to campus network. Commuter students can connect to campus network. Online library available.

Student life. Freshman orientation: Mandatory. Preregistration for classes offered. Three days immediately preceeding beginning of fall semester. **Policies:** Freshmen permitted cars on campus. **Housing:** Guaranteed on-campus for all undergraduates. Coed dorms, single-sex dorms, special housing for disabled, substance-free housing available. **Activities:** Choral groups, dance, drama, literary magazine, musical theater, radio station, student government, student newspaper, Community service club, Safe Zones, SAVE (Sexual Assault and Violence Education), cross cultural club, Christian Fellowship.

Athletics. NCAA. **Intercollegiate:** Baseball M, basketball, diving, equestrian, lacrosse W, skiing, soccer, swimming, tennis, track and field, volleyball W. **Intramural:** Basketball, football (non-tackle), golf, soccer, volleyball. **Team name:** Chargers.

Student services. Alcohol/substance abuse counseling, career counseling, student employment services, financial aid counseling, health services, personal counseling. **Physically disabled:** Services for visually, hearing impaired.

Contact. E-mail: csadmiss@colby-sawyer.edu
Phone: (603) 526-3700 Toll-free number: (800) 272-1015
Fax: (603) 526-3452
Richard Ellis, Admissions Director, Colby-Sawyer College, 541 Main Street, New London, NH 03257-7835

Daniel Webster College

Nashua, New Hampshire **CB member**
www.dwc.edu **CB code: 3648**

- Private 4-year business and technical college
- Residential campus in small city
- 540 degree-seeking undergraduates
- SAT or ACT (ACT writing optional) required

General. Founded in 1965. Regionally accredited. **Degrees:** 211 bachelor's, 19 associate awarded; master's offered. **ROTC:** Army, Air Force. **Location:** 17 miles from Manchester, 35 miles from Boston. **Calendar:** Semester, limited summer session. **Full-time faculty:** 34 total; 47% have terminal degrees, 6% minority, 26% women. **Part-time faculty:** 27 total; 67% have terminal degrees, 30% women. **Class size:** 77% < 20, 23% 20-39. **Special facilities:** On-campus flight center, 35 aircraft including powered gliders, aerobatic planes, 3 flight simulators, air-traffic-control simulation system.

Freshman class profile.

Mid 50% test scores			
SAT verbal:	470-570	ACT:	19-24
SAT math:	480-610	Out-of-state:	65%
		Live on campus:	85%

Basis for selection. High school transcript, recommendations, test scores most important. Interview recommended; essay and extracurricular activities also considered. TOEFL scores considered for non-native speakers of English. Interviews recommended, essays optional.

High school preparation. 16 units required. Required and recommended units include English 4, mathematics 3-4, social studies 2, history 2, science 3 (laboratory 2) and foreign language 2. One computer science recommended.

2005-2006 Annual costs. Tuition/fees: $22,955. Room/board: $8,450. Books/supplies: $800. Personal expenses: $1,500.

Financial aid. Non-need-based: Scholarships awarded for academics, leadership.

Application procedures. Admission: No deadline. $35 fee, may be waived for applicants with need. Application may be submitted online. Admission notification on a rolling basis. Must reply by May 1 or within 2 week(s) if notified thereafter. **Financial aid:** Priority date 3/1; no closing date. FAFSA, institutional form required. Applicants notified on a rolling basis starting 3/15; must reply within 2 week(s) of notification.

Academics. Credit granted for pilot licenses. Flight students must have FAA Class II physical examination. Flight operations majors must pass FAA written examinations and flight tests to earn pilot ratings. **Special study options:** Accelerated study, cooperative education, cross-registration, distance learning, double major, dual enrollment of high school students, independent study, internships, liberal arts/career combination, study abroad, Washington semester. **Credit/placement by examination:** CLEP, IB, institutional tests. 30 credit hours maximum toward associate degree, 30 toward bachelor's. **Support services:** Learning center, study skills assistance, tutoring, writing center.

Majors. Business: General, management information systems. **Computer sciences:** General, computer science, information systems. **Engineering:** Aerospace, mechanical. **Parks/recreation:** Sports admin. **Social sciences:** General. **Transportation:** Air traffic control, aviation, aviation management.

Most popular majors. Business/marketing 73%, computer/information sciences 7%, trade and industry 18%.

Computing on campus. 150 workstations in dormitories, library, computer center. Dormitories linked to campus network. Helpline available.

Student life. Freshman orientation: Mandatory, $250 fee. 4-day program. **Policies:** Freshmen permitted cars on campus. **Housing:** Guaranteed on-campus for all undergraduates. Coed dorms, single-sex dorms, apartments available. $400 deposit, deadline 5/1. Townhouses attained by merit. Suites for 4 to 7 students available. **Activities:** Jazz band, choral groups, drama, film society, student government, student newspaper, Campus Crusade for Christ.

Athletics. NCAA. **Intercollegiate:** Baseball M, basketball, cross-country, golf, ice hockey, lacrosse M, soccer, softball W, volleyball W. **Intramural:** Basketball, ice hockey, skiing, soccer, softball, tennis, volleyball, weight lifting. **Team name:** Eagles.

Student services. Adult student services, alcohol/substance abuse counseling, career counseling, student employment services, financial aid counseling, health services, personal counseling, placement for graduates, veterans' counselor.

Contact. E-mail: admissions@dwc.edu
Phone: (603) 577-6600 Toll-free number: (800) 325-6876
Fax: (603) 577-6001
Sean Ryan, Director of Admissions, Daniel Webster College, 20 University Drive, Nashua, NH 03063

Dartmouth College

Hanover, New Hampshire **CB member**
www.dartmouth.edu **CB code: 3351**

- Private 4-year university and liberal arts college
- Residential campus in large town
- 3,991 degree-seeking undergraduates: 50% women, 7% African American, 14% Asian American, 6% Hispanic American, 3% Native American, 5% international
- 1,642 degree-seeking graduate students
- 17% of applicants admitted
- SAT or ACT with writing, SAT Subject Tests, application essay required
- 94% graduate within 6 years; 25% enter graduate study

General. Founded in 1769. Regionally accredited. **Degrees:** 1,109 bachelor's awarded; master's, doctoral, first professional offered. **ROTC:** Army. **Location:** 130 miles from Boston. **Calendar:** Quarter, extensive summer session. **Full-time faculty:** 505 total; 93% have terminal degrees, 14% minority. **Part-time faculty:** 120 total; 64% have terminal degrees, 6% minority. **Class size:** 64% < 20, 22% 20-39, 5% 40-49, 8% 50-99, 1% >100. **Special facilities:** Art museum; observatory; centers for humanities, social sciences, physical science, performing arts, ethics, life science, computation.

Freshman class profile. 12,756 applied, 2,171 admitted, 1,074 enrolled.

Mid 50% test scores			
SAT verbal:	670-770	GPA 2.0-2.99:	3%
SAT math:	680-780	Rank in top tenth:	87%
ACT:	29-34	Return as sophomores:	98%
GPA 3.50 or higher:	80%	Out-of-state:	97%
GPA 3.0-3.49:	16%	Live on campus:	100%
		International:	5%

Basis for selection. Evidence of intellectual capability, motivation, and personal integrity of primary importance. Talent, accomplishment, and involvement in nonacademic areas also evaluated. 2 SAT Subject Tests of student's choice required. Interview optional.

High school preparation. Recommended units include English 4, mathematics 4, social studies 3, science 3 and foreign language 3. Strongest academic program available to applicant recommended.

2006-2007 Annual costs. Tuition/fees: $33,612. Room/board: $9,976. Books/supplies: $1,122. Personal expenses: $1,264.

2004-2005 Financial aid. All financial aid based on need. 656 full-time freshmen applied for aid; 520 were judged to have need; 520 of these received aid. Average need met was 100%. Average scholarship/grant was $26,838; average loan $3,138. 81% of total undergraduate aid awarded as scholarships/grants, 19% as loans/jobs.

Application procedures. **Admission:** Closing date 1/1 (postmark date). $70 fee, may be waived for applicants with need. Application may be submitted online. Admission notification 4/10. Must reply by 5/1. **Financial aid:** Closing date 2/1. FAFSA, CSS PROFILE required. Applicants notified by 4/2; must reply by 5/1.

Academics. Undergraduate research encouraged. **Special study options:** Combined bachelor's/graduate degree, double major, exchange student, honors, independent study, internships, semester at sea, student-designed major, study abroad, teacher certification program, Washington semester. Williams Mystic Seaport Maritime Studies program, study at Eugene O'Neill National Theater Institute, Twelve College Exchange, University of California-San Diego exchange program, McGill University exchange program, exchange programs with over 50 foreign universities, special academic programs in Washington, DC and Tucson, AZ. **Credit/placement by examination:** AP, CLEP, IB, SAT, ACT, institutional tests. **Support services:** Learning center, study skills assistance, tutoring, writing center.

Majors. **Area/ethnic studies:** African, African-American, Asian, Caribbean, German, Hispanic-American/Latino/Chicano, Latin American, Native American, Near/Middle Eastern, Russian/Slavic, Spanish/Iberian, women's. **Biology:** General, biochemistry, Biochemistry/biophysics and molecular biology, cell/histology, ecology, evolutionary, genetics, molecular. **Computer sciences:** Computer science. **Conservation:** General, environmental studies. **Engineering:** Biomedical, physics, science. **Foreign languages:** Arabic, Chinese, classics, comparative lit, French, German, Hebrew, Italian, Japanese, linguistics, Russian, South Asian, Spanish. **History:** General. **Interdisciplinary:** Ancient studies, classical/archaeology, neuroscience. **Math:** General. **Philosophy/religion:** Philosophy, religion. **Physical sciences:** Astronomy, chemistry, physics, planetary. **Psychology:** General. **Social sciences:** Anthropology, economics, geography, political science, sociology. **Visual/performing arts:** Art history/conservation, dramatic, film/cinema, studio arts.

Most popular majors. Biology 6%, English 7%, history 10%, psychology 8%, social sciences 29%, visual/performing arts 7%.

Computing on campus. PC or laptop required. Dormitories wired for high-speed internet access and linked to campus network. Commuter students can connect to campus network. Online course registration, online library, helpline, repair service, student web hosting, wireless network available.

Student life. **Freshman orientation:** Mandatory. Held week before fall classes begin; freshmen trips led by Dartmouth outing club. **Housing:** Guaranteed on-campus for freshmen. Coed dorms, apartments, cooperative housing, fraternity/sorority housing, substance-free housing available. Academic affinity housing, faculty-in-residence programs, special interest housing available. **Activities:** Bands, choral groups, dance, drama, film society, literary magazine, music ensembles, musical theater, opera, radio station, student government, student newspaper, symphony orchestra, TV station, community and service programs, religious groups, and political and ethnic organizations available.

Athletics. NCAA. **Intercollegiate:** Baseball M, basketball, cross-country, diving, equestrian, field hockey W, football (tackle) M, golf, ice hockey, lacrosse, rowing (crew), sailing, skiing, soccer, softball W, squash, swimming, tennis, track and field, volleyball W. **Intramural:** Baseball M, basketball, bowling, cross-country, football (non-tackle), golf, handball, ice hockey, lacrosse, racquetball, skiing, soccer, softball, squash, swimming, table tennis, tennis, track and field, volleyball, water polo, wrestling M. **Team name:** Big Green.

Student services. Alcohol/substance abuse counseling, campus ministries, career counseling, student employment services, financial aid counseling, health services, minority student services, on-campus daycare, personal counseling, placement for graduates, women's services. **Physically disabled:** Services for visually, speech, hearing impaired.

Contact. E-mail: admissions.office@dartmouth.edu
Phone: (603) 646-2875 Fax: (603) 646-1216
Karl Furstenberg, Dean of Admissions and Financial Aid, Dartmouth College, 6016 McNutt Hall, Hanover, NH 03755

Franklin Pierce College

Rindge, New Hampshire — **CB member**
www.fpc.edu — **CB code: 3395**

- Private 4-year liberal arts college
- Residential campus in small town
- 1,615 degree-seeking undergraduates: 1% part-time, 49% women, 4% African American, 1% Asian American, 2% Hispanic American, 2% international
- 74% of applicants admitted
- SAT or ACT with writing, application essay required
- 50% graduate within 6 years

General. Founded in 1962. Regionally accredited. 6 satellite campuses offer continuing education sequence of 8-week sessions. Associate, bachelor's, MBA, MPT degrees offered through graduate and professional studies division campuses in Concord, Keene, Lebanon, Nashua, Portsmouth, and Salem. **Degrees:** 262 bachelor's awarded. **ROTC:** Army, Air Force. **Location:** 20 miles from Keene, 60 miles from Boston. **Calendar:** Semester, limited summer session. **Full-time faculty:** 74 total; 74% have terminal degrees, 7% minority, 35% women. **Part-time faculty:** 76 total; 25% have terminal degrees, 8% minority, 42% women. **Class size:** 65% < 20, 33% 20-39, 1% 50-99, less than 1% >100. **Special facilities:** Graphics workshop, colonial archaeological dig site, glass blowing studio, ceramic kiln, black box theater.

Freshman class profile. 4,068 applied, 3,021 admitted, 507 enrolled.

Mid 50% test scores		**Rank in top quarter:**	21%
SAT verbal:	440-540	**Rank in top tenth:**	1%
SAT math:	430-530	**Return as sophomores:**	66%
GPA 3.50 or higher:	10%	**Out-of-state:**	83%
GPA 3.0-3.49:	26%	**Live on campus:**	94%
GPA 2.0-2.99:	61%	**International:**	2%

Basis for selection. School achievement record, difficulty of course work, recommendations and school involvement primary considerations. Test scores also important. Interview recommended for all.

High school preparation. 16 units required. Required units include English 4, mathematics 3, social studies 3, science 2 (laboratory 2) and academic electives 4.

2005-2006 Annual costs. Tuition/fees: $23,710. Room/board: $7,990. Books/supplies: $850. Personal expenses: $1,094.

2005-2006 Financial aid. **Need-based:** 398 full-time freshmen applied for aid; 345 were judged to have need; 345 of these received aid. Average need met was 64%. Average scholarship/grant was $12,044; average loan $2,875. 56% of total undergraduate aid awarded as scholarships/grants, 44% as loans/jobs. **Non-need-based:** Awarded to 447 full-time undergraduates, including 141 freshmen. Scholarships awarded for academics, alumni affiliation, athletics, leadership, minority status, music/drama.

Application procedures. **Admission:** No deadline. No application fee. Application may be submitted online. Admission notification on a rolling basis beginning on or about 10/15. Must reply by May 1 or within 2 week(s) if notified thereafter. **Financial aid:** Priority date 3/1; no closing date. FAFSA required. Applicants notified on a rolling basis starting 4/1; must reply within 2 week(s) of notification.

Academics. Most courses in 42-credit core curriculum, "The Individual and Community," are interdisciplinary and team-taught. **Special study options:** Distance learning, double major, dual enrollment of high school students, ESL, exchange student, honors, independent study, internships, student-designed major, study abroad, teacher certification program, Washington semester. Walk Across Europe, Arcadia Study Abroad. **Credit/placement by examination:** AP, CLEP, IB, institutional tests. 30 credit hours maximum toward bachelor's degree. **Support services:** Learning center, reduced course load, remedial instruction, study skills assistance, tutoring, writing center.

Majors. **Area/ethnic studies:** American. **Biology:** General. **Business:** General, accounting, accounting/finance, business admin, finance, management information systems, marketing. **Communications:** General, advertising, broadcast journalism, journalism, media studies, radio/tv. **Computer sciences:** General, computer graphics, computer science, information systems, information technology, networking. **Conservation:** General, environmental science, environmental studies. **Education:** General. **Health:** Predentistry, premedicine, preveterinary. **History:** General. **Liberal arts:** Arts/sciences. **Math:** General. **Parks/recreation:** Facilities management, sports admin. **Protective services:** Criminal justice. **Psychology:** General. **Public administration:** Social work. **Social sciences:** General, anthropology, archaeology, political science, sociology. **Visual/performing arts:** General, acting, art, art history/conservation, arts management, commercial/advertising art, dance, design, dramatic, music management, music performance, music theory/composition, studio arts, theater design.

Most popular majors. Area/ethnic studies 6%, business/marketing 15%, communications/journalism 13%, English 8%, security/protective services 6%, social sciences 6%, visual/performing arts 17%.

Computing on campus. 109 workstations in dormitories, library, computer center. Dormitories wired for high-speed internet access and linked to campus network. Commuter students can connect to campus network. Online library, helpline, repair service available.

Student life. Freshman orientation: Mandatory. Preregistration for classes offered. Held immediately prior to start of semester;includes placement testing. **Policies:** Freshmen permitted cars on campus. **Housing:** Guaranteed on-campus for all undergraduates. Coed dorms, special housing for disabled, apartments available. $200 nonrefundable deposit, deadline 6/20. College-owned townhouses within 1 mile of campus available. **Activities:** Choral groups, dance, drama, literary magazine, music ensembles, musical theater, radio station, student government, student newspaper, TV station, student senate, law club, business club, Black Student Alliance, Pierce Pals, outing club, environmental awareness club, Emergency Medical Services club, education club.

Athletics. NCAA. **Intercollegiate:** Baseball M, basketball, cross-country, field hockey W, golf, ice hockey M, lacrosse, rowing (crew), soccer, softball W, tennis, volleyball W. **Intramural:** Baseball M, basketball, cross-country, field hockey W, football (non-tackle), golf, ice hockey M, lacrosse, sailing, skiing, soccer, softball, table tennis, tennis, volleyball. **Team name:** Ravens.

Student services. Alcohol/substance abuse counseling, campus ministries, career counseling, student employment services, financial aid counseling, health services, personal counseling, placement for graduates. **Physically disabled:** Services for hearing impaired.

Contact. E-mail: admissions@fpc.edu
Phone: (603) 899-4050 Toll-free number: (800) 437-0048
Fax: (603) 899-4394
Lucy Shonk, Dean of Admissions, Franklin Pierce College, 20 College Road, Rindge, NH 03461-0060

Granite State College

Concord, New Hampshire
www.granite.edu **CB code: 0458**

- Public 4-year liberal arts college
- Commuter campus in large town
- 1,105 degree-seeking undergraduates: 59% part-time, 77% women, 1% African American, 1% Asian American, 1% Hispanic American, 1% Native American
- 128 degree-seeking graduate students
- Application essay required

General. Founded in 1972. Regionally accredited. Classes held in local communities at 40 different sites. Master's courses provided at some sites for continuing education of teachers and management professionals. Statewide Special Education post-baccalaureate certificate program. **Degrees:** 237 bachelor's, 140 associate awarded. **ROTC:** Army. **Calendar:** Trimester, limited summer session. **Part-time faculty:** 139 total; 60% women. **Class size:** 91% < 20, 9% 20-39.

Basis for selection. For all applicants who have not earned degree from regionally accredited college within past 5 years, admission based on skills assessment.

2005-2006 Annual costs. Tuition/fees: $6,045; $6,645 out-of-state. Books/supplies: $800.

2004-2005 Financial aid. Need-based: 31% of total undergraduate aid awarded as scholarships/grants, 69% as loans/jobs.

Application procedures. Admission: No deadline. $45 fee. Application must be submitted on paper. Admission notification on a rolling basis. **Financial aid:** No deadline. Applicants notified on a rolling basis.

Academics. Special study options: Accelerated study, cross-registration, distance learning, double major, independent study, internships, liberal arts/career combination, student-designed major. Post-baccalaureate graduate certificate program in special education. **Credit/placement by examination:** CLEP, institutional tests. 32 credit hours maximum toward associate degree, 64 toward bachelor's. Exams must support degree program. **Support services:** Reduced course load, remedial instruction, study skills assistance.

Majors. Business: Management science. **Computer sciences:** General. **Education:** Early childhood. **Interdisciplinary:** Behavioral sciences. **Liberal arts:** Arts/sciences. **Protective services:** Criminal justice, law enforcement admin.

Most popular majors. Business/marketing 23%, interdisciplinary studies 26%, liberal arts 45%.

Computing on campus. 128 workstations in computer center. Online library, wireless network available.

Student life. Policies: Freshmen permitted cars on campus. **Activities:** Alumni/Learner Association.

Student services. Adult student services, career counseling, financial aid counseling, veterans' counselor.

Contact. E-mail: ruth.nawn@granite.edu
Phone: (603) 228-3000 ext. 339 Toll-free number: (888) 228-3000 ext. 339
Fax: (603) 513-1387
Ruth Nawn, Associate Director of Admissions, Granite State College, 8 Old Suncook Road, Concord, NH 03301-7317

Hesser College

Manchester, New Hampshire
www.hesser.edu **CB code: 3452**

- For-profit 4-year business and junior college
- Residential campus in small city

General. Founded in 1900. Regionally accredited. **Location:** 50 miles from Boston. **Calendar:** Semester.

Annual costs/financial aid. Tuition/fees (2005-2006): $12,365. Room/board: $6,600. Books/supplies: $1,200. Personal expenses: $550. Need-based financial aid available to full-time and part-time students.

Contact. Phone: (603) 668-6660 ext. 2110
Director of Admissions, 3 Sundial Avenue, Manchester, NH 03103

Keene State College

Keene, New Hampshire **CB member**
www.keene.edu **CB code: 3472**

- Public 4-year liberal arts and teachers college
- Residential campus in large town
- 4,370 degree-seeking undergraduates: 5% part-time, 57% women, 1% Asian American, 1% Hispanic American, 1% international
- 90 degree-seeking graduate students
- 76% of applicants admitted
- SAT or ACT with writing, application essay required
- 54% graduate within 6 years; 18% enter graduate study

General. Founded in 1909. Regionally accredited. **Degrees:** 855 bachelor's, 49 associate awarded; master's offered. **ROTC:** Air Force. **Location:** 52 miles from Concord, 85 miles from Boston. **Calendar:** Semester, extensive summer session. **Full-time faculty:** 187 total. **Part-time faculty:** 203 total. **Class size:** 59% < 20, 34% 20-39, 2% 40-49, 4% 50-99, less than 1% >100. **Special facilities:** Theater complex, child development center, college-owned camp, 400-acre preserve.

Freshman class profile. 3,527 applied, 2,693 admitted, 1,008 enrolled.

Mid 50% test scores			
SAT verbal:	450-550	Rank in top quarter:	21%
SAT math:	450-550	Rank in top tenth:	4%
GPA 3.50 or higher:	11%	Return as sophomores:	77%
GPA 3.0-3.49:	35%	Out-of-state:	53%
GPA 2.0-2.99:	53%	Live on campus:	92%
		International:	1%

Basis for selection. High school record, class rank, recommendations, SAT scores most important. Preference to state residents. TOEFL score of 500 required for non-native speakers of English. SAT tests not required of students applying only for admission to 2-year technology program. Interview recommended for all; audition required for music education and music performance programs; portfolio required for art program. **Homeschooled:** Academic preparation for home-schooled students must include at least the 14 academic courses required of all students. SAT scores required. **Learning Disabled:** Documented proof of disability required for some services.

High school preparation. 14 units required. Required units include English 4, mathematics 3, social studies 2, science 3 and academic electives 2.

2005-2006 Annual costs. Tuition/fees: $7,352; $14,192 out-of-state. New England Regional tuition is 150% of in-state public institution tuition. Room/board: $6,484. Books/supplies: $600. Personal expenses: $750.

2004-2005 Financial aid. Need-based: 906 full-time freshmen applied for aid; 639 were judged to have need; 620 of these received aid. Average need met was 70%. Average scholarship/grant was $4,458; average loan $2,934. 39% of total undergraduate aid awarded as scholarships/grants, 61% as loans/jobs. **Non-need-based:** Awarded to 876 full-time undergraduates, including 237 freshmen. Scholarships awarded for academics, alumni affiliation, art, music/drama.

Application procedures. Admission: Closing date 4/1 (postmark date). $35 fee, may be waived for applicants with need. Application may be submitted online. Admission notification on a rolling basis beginning on or about 12/1. Must reply by 5/1. **Financial aid:** Closing date 3/1. FAFSA required. Applicants notified on a rolling basis; must reply within 4 week(s) of notification.

Academics. Special study options: Cooperative education, double major, ESL, exchange student, honors, independent study, internships, liberal arts/career combination, semester at sea, student-designed major, study abroad, teacher certification program, United Nations semester, Washington semester. 3-2 engineering program with Clarkson University, 2-2 engineering program with University of New Hampshire. **Credit/placement by examination:** AP, CLEP. 30 credit hours maximum toward associate degree, 60 toward bachelor's. **Support services:** Learning center, pre-admission summer program, reduced course load, study skills assistance, tutoring, writing center.

Majors. Architecture: Technology. **Area/ethnic studies:** American. **Biology:** General. **Business:** General. **Communications:** General, journalism. **Computer sciences:** General. **Conservation:** Environmental science, environmental studies. **Education:** General, early childhood, elementary, English, foreign languages, French, mathematics, middle, music, physical, science, secondary, social studies, Spanish, special, technology/industrial arts, trade/industrial. **Engineering technology:** Electrical, occupational safety. **English:** English lit. **Foreign languages:** French, Spanish. **Health:** Athletic training, dietetics. **History:** General. **Interdisciplinary:** Biological/physical sciences, math/computer science. **Math:** General, applied. **Parks/recreation:** Health/fitness. **Philosophy/religion:** Philosophy. **Physical sciences:** Chemical physics, chemistry, geology. **Psychology:** General. **Social sciences:** General, economics, geography, sociology. **Visual/performing arts:** Art, commercial/advertising art, dance, dramatic, film/cinema, graphic design, music history, music performance, music theory/composition, studio arts, theater design.

Most popular majors. Business/marketing 7%, communications/journalism 9%, education 19%, engineering/engineering technologies 10%, psychology 14%, social sciences 11%, visual/performing arts 10%.

Computing on campus. 500 workstations in dormitories, library, computer center, student center. Dormitories wired for high-speed internet access and linked to campus network. Commuter students can connect to campus network. Online course registration, online library, helpline, repair service, student web hosting, wireless network available.

Student life. Freshman orientation: Mandatory, $75 fee. Preregistration for classes offered. Held Friday/Saturday in June. Parents invited. **Policies:** Freshmen permitted cars on campus. **Housing:** Coed dorms, single-sex dorms, apartments, fraternity/sorority housing, substance-free housing available. $100 nonrefundable deposit, deadline 5/1. Leadership and music housing available. **Activities:** Bands, choral groups, dance, drama, film society, literary magazine, music ensembles, musical theater, radio station, student government, student newspaper, symphony orchestra, TV station, Habitat for Humanity, Amnesty International, student government, campus ecology, civil liberties union, international friends club, student volunteer organization, environmental outing club, KSC Pride, Circle K.

Athletics. NCAA. **Intercollegiate:** Baseball M, basketball, cheerleading, cross-country, diving, field hockey W, lacrosse, soccer, softball W, swimming, track and field, volleyball W. **Intramural:** Badminton, basketball, cross-country, football (non-tackle), racquetball, soccer, softball, tennis, track and field, volleyball, water polo. **Team name:** Owls.

Student services. Adult student services, alcohol/substance abuse counseling, campus ministries, career counseling, student employment services, financial aid counseling, health services, minority student services, on-campus daycare, personal counseling, placement for graduates, veterans' counselor. **Physically disabled:** Services for visually, hearing impaired.

Contact. E-mail: admissions@keene.edu
Phone: (603) 358-2276 Toll-free number: (800) 572-1909
Fax: (603) 358-2767
Margaret Richmond, Director of Admissions, Keene State College, 229 Main Street, Keene, NH 03435-2604

Magdalen College

Warner, New Hampshire
www.magdalen.edu **CB code: 3562**

- Private 4-year liberal arts college affiliated with Roman Catholic Church
- Residential campus in small town
- 71 degree-seeking undergraduates: 1% part-time, 54% women, 1% African American, 4% Asian American, 14% Hispanic American, 4% international
- 78% of applicants admitted
- SAT or ACT (ACT writing recommended), application essay, interview required

General. Degrees: 18 bachelor's awarded. **Location:** 20 miles from Concord. **Calendar:** Semester. **Full-time faculty:** 7 total. **Part-time faculty:** 2 total. **Special facilities:** Observatory.

Freshman class profile. 49 applied, 38 admitted, 29 enrolled.

Mid 50% test scores			
SAT verbal:	510-670	Return as sophomores:	90%
SAT math:	390-570	Out-of-state:	86%
ACT:	21-24	Live on campus:	100%
End year in good standing:	95%	International:	7%

Basis for selection. Campus visit required. High school transcripts reviewed.

High school preparation. 24 units recommended. Recommended units include English 4, mathematics 4, social studies 3, history 2, science 3, foreign language 2 and academic electives 6.

2006-2007 Annual costs. Tuition/fees: $10,750. Room/board: $6,500. Books/supplies: $300. Personal expenses: $200.

Financial aid. All financial aid based on need.

Application procedures. Admission: Closing date 5/1 (postmark date). $35 fee. Must reply by May 1 or within 4 week(s) if notified thereafter. **Financial aid:** Closing date 6/30. Institutional form required. Applicants notified by 7/1; must reply by 7/1 or within 4 week(s) of notification.

Academics. Classical curriculum taught in Socratic seminar classes. Catholic instruction in church teachings and morality. **Special study options:** Study abroad. **Credit/placement by examination:** CLEP. **Support services:** Learning center, remedial instruction, study skills assistance, tutoring.

Majors. Liberal arts: Arts/sciences.

Computing on campus. 10 workstations in dormitories, library. Online library available.

Student life. Freshman orientation: Mandatory. Freshmen Welcome Weekend held 2 days in early Spetember. **Policies:** Dress code for class. Required attendance at meals. Curfews in dormitories. No-cut policy for class. Campus service required. Sunday mass required for Catholic students. Religious observance required. **Housing:** Guaranteed on-campus for all undergraduates. Single-sex dorms, substance-free housing available. $500 nonrefundable deposit, deadline 6/15. **Activities:** Choral groups, drama, music ensembles, musical theater, campus service organization, college choir.

Athletics. Intramural: Basketball, soccer, volleyball.

Student services. Campus ministries, financial aid counseling, personal counseling.

Contact. E-mail: admissions@magdalen.edu
Phone: (603) 456-2656 Toll-free number: (877) 498-1723
Justin Fout, Admissions Counselor, Magdalen College, 511 Kearsarge Mountain Road, Warner, NH 03278

New England College

Henniker, New Hampshire
www.nec.edu **CB code: 3657**

- Private 4-year liberal arts and teachers college
- Residential campus in small town
- 1,008 degree-seeking undergraduates: 6% part-time, 52% women, 2% African American, 2% Asian American, 2% Hispanic American, 3% international
- 339 degree-seeking graduate students
- 83% of applicants admitted
- Application essay required
- 49% graduate within 6 years; 21% enter graduate study

General. Founded in 1946. Regionally accredited. Cross-registration with other 4-year institutions available through New Hampshire College and University Council. **Degrees:** 141 bachelor's awarded; master's offered. **ROTC:** Army, Air Force. **Location:** 18 miles from Concord. **Calendar:** Semester, limited summer session. **Full-time faculty:** 57 total; 63% have terminal degrees, 4% minority, 49% women. **Part-time faculty:** 95 total; 19% have terminal degrees, 1% minority, 50% women. **Class size:** 68% < 20, 31% 20-39, less than 1% 40-49, less than 1% 50-99. **Special facilities:** Center for educational innovation.

Freshman class profile. 1,817 applied, 1,512 admitted, 356 enrolled.

Mid 50% test scores		**Rank in top tenth:**	9%
SAT verbal:	400-500	**End year in good standing:**	73%
SAT math:	390-490	**Return as sophomores:**	63%
GPA 3.50 or higher:	6%	**Out-of-state:**	68%
GPA 3.0-3.49:	17%	**Live on campus:**	92%
GPA 2.0-2.99:	61%	**Fraternities:**	5%
Rank in top quarter:	29%	**Sororities:**	3%

Basis for selection. School achievement record most important, followed by recommendations, essay or personal statement, evidence of leadership and extracurricular activities. TOEFL required for non-native speakers of English. SAT/ACT considered if submitted. Interview recommended for all; portfolio recommended for art program.

High school preparation. College-preparatory program recommended. 12 units required. Required and recommended units include English 4, mathematics 2-3, social studies 2, science 2-3 (laboratory 1-2) and foreign language 2.

2005-2006 Annual costs. Tuition/fees: $23,010. Room/board: $8,456. Books/supplies: $600. Personal expenses: $1,200.

2005-2006 Financial aid. Need-based: 281 full-time freshmen applied for aid; 251 were judged to have need; 249 of these received aid. Average need met was 83%. Average scholarship/grant was $11,375; average loan $6,810. 60% of total undergraduate aid awarded as scholarships/grants, 40% as loans/jobs. **Non-need-based:** Scholarships awarded for academics, alumni affiliation, art, job skills, leadership, music/drama.

Application procedures. Admission: No deadline. $30 fee, may be waived for applicants with need. Application may be submitted online. Admission notification on a rolling basis beginning on or about 11/1. **Financial aid:** Priority date 4/1; no closing date. FAFSA, institutional form required. Applicants notified on a rolling basis starting 1/12; must reply within 2 week(s) of notification.

Academics. Special study options: Combined bachelor's/graduate degree, cross-registration, distance learning, double major, dual enrollment of high school students, ESL, exchange student, external degree, honors, independent study, internships, liberal arts/career combination, semester at sea, student-designed major, study abroad, teacher certification program, Washington semester. Exchange program with Regent's College, London, American University of Paris, 18 colleges in Quebec, Canada, University of the Sunshine Coast, Australia. **Credit/placement by examination:** AP, CLEP, IB, institutional tests. 21 credit hours maximum toward bachelor's degree. **Support services:** Learning center, reduced course load, remedial instruction, study skills assistance, tutoring, writing center.

Majors. Biology: General. **Business:** Accounting, business admin, entrepreneurial studies, finance, human resources, management information systems, marketing. **Communications:** General, advertising, public relations. **Computer sciences:** General. **Conservation:** Environmental science. **Education:** Art, biology, elementary, English, learning disabled, mathematics, physical, science, secondary, social science, social studies, special. **Engineering:** Civil. **English:** Creative writing, English lit. **Foreign languages:** Comparative lit. **Health:** Health care admin, premedicine. **History:** General. **Legal studies:** Prelaw. **Liberal arts:** Arts/sciences. **Math:** General. **Parks/recreation:** General, exercise sciences, facilities management, sports admin. **Philosophy/religion:** Philosophy. **Protective services:** Criminal justice. **Psychology:** General. **Social sciences:** Political science, sociology. **Visual/performing arts:** Art, art history/conservation, dramatic, photography.

Most popular majors. Business/marketing 29%, communications/journalism 7%, parks/recreation 11%, psychology 13%, security/protective services 7%, social sciences 7%, visual/performing arts 7%.

Computing on campus. 148 workstations in library, computer center, student center. Dormitories wired for high-speed internet access and linked to campus network. Commuter students can connect to campus network. Online course registration, online library, helpline, wireless network available.

Student life. Freshman orientation: Available. Preregistration for classes offered. 3 days prior to first day of classes and 2 mid-summer options. **Policies:** Freshmen permitted cars on campus. **Housing:** Guaranteed on-campus for all undergraduates. Coed dorms, apartments, fraternity/sorority housing, substance-free housing available. $100 nonrefundable deposit. Resident freshmen and sophomores required to live in college housing. Quiet study options, special interest housing available. **Activities:** Choral groups, dance, drama, literary magazine, radio station, student government, student newspaper, international student association, Hillel, Servcorps, Environmental Action Committee, Womyn's Network, International Diplomacy Council, Adventure Bound, T.E.A.C.H.

Athletics. NCAA. **Intercollegiate:** Baseball M, basketball, cross-country, field hockey W, ice hockey, lacrosse, soccer, softball W. **Intramural:** Baseball M, basketball, ice hockey, soccer, softball, table tennis, tennis, volleyball. **Team name:** Pilgrims.

Student services. Adult student services, alcohol/substance abuse counseling, career counseling, student employment services, financial aid counseling, health services, personal counseling, placement for graduates, veterans' counselor.

Contact. E-mail: admission@nec.edu
Phone: (603) 428-2223 Toll-free number: (800) 521-7642
Fax: (603) 428-3155
Paul Miller, Director of Admissions and Financial Aid, New England College, 26 Bridge Street, Henniker, NH 03242

Plymouth State University

Plymouth, New Hampshire — **CB member**
www.plymouth.edu — **CB code: 3690**

- Public 4-year university and teachers college
- Residential campus in small town
- 4,081 degree-seeking undergraduates: 3% part-time, 49% women, 1% African American, 1% Asian American, 1% Hispanic American, 1% international
- 549 degree-seeking graduate students
- 77% of applicants admitted
- SAT or ACT with writing, application essay required
- 49% graduate within 6 years; 16% enter graduate study

General. Founded in 1871. Regionally accredited. **Degrees:** 745 bachelor's, 2 associate awarded; master's offered. **ROTC:** Army, Air Force. **Location:** 60 miles from Manchester, 115 miles from Boston. **Calendar:** Semester, limited summer session. **Full-time faculty:** 170 total; 86% have terminal degrees, 5% minority. **Part-time faculty:** 260 total; 25% have terminal degrees, 2% minority. **Class size:** 46% < 20, 48% 20-39, 4% 40-49, 2% 50-99, less than 1% >100. **Special facilities:** Planetarium, cultural arts center, child development and family center, geographic information systems lab, meteorology institute, center for the environment, climbing wall, ropes course.

Freshman class profile. 3,655 applied, 2,818 admitted, 1,003 enrolled.

Mid 50% test scores		**Rank in top quarter:**	16%
SAT verbal:	430-530	**Rank in top tenth:**	4%
SAT math:	430-540	**End year in good standing:**	82%
ACT:	17-20	**Return as sophomores:**	76%
GPA 3.50 or higher:	9%	**Out-of-state:**	43%
GPA 3.0-3.49:	27%	**Live on campus:**	94%
GPA 2.0-2.99:	61%	**International:**	1%

Basis for selection. Decision is made by committee, based on school achievement record most important followed by test scores, recommendations, essay and extracurricular activites. TOEFL is also accepted. SAT/ACT not required for resident or non-resident aliens. Audition required for music and theater programs. Portfolio required for art program. **Homeschooled:** Transcript of any work attempted in secondary school, SAT or ACT, GED or home school diploma, outline of home school curriculum required.

High school preparation. College-preparatory program required. 13 units required; 18 recommended. Required and recommended units include English 4, mathematics 3, social studies 2-3, history 1-2, science 2-3 (laboratory 1) and foreign language 2.

2005-2006 Annual costs. Tuition/fees: $7,028; $13,868 out-of-state. New England Regional tuition is 150% of in-state public institution tuition. Room/board: $6,780. Books/supplies: $700. Personal expenses: $1,002.

2004-2005 Financial aid. Need-based: 904 full-time freshmen applied for aid; 638 were judged to have need; 623 of these received aid. Average need met was 57%. Average scholarship/grant was $4,274; average loan $2,554. 34% of total undergraduate aid awarded as scholarships/grants, 66% as loans/jobs. **Non-need-based:** Awarded to 1,029 full-time undergraduates, including 309 freshmen. Scholarships awarded for academics, minority status, music/drama.

Application procedures. Admission: Closing date 4/1 (postmark date). $35 fee, may be waived for applicants with need. Application may be submitted online. Admission notification on a rolling basis beginning on or

about 11/1. Must reply by 5/1. **Financial aid:** Priority date 3/1; no closing date. FAFSA required. Applicants notified on a rolling basis starting 3/1; must reply by 5/1.

Academics. Special study options: Distance learning, double major, exchange student, honors, independent study, internships, student-designed major, study abroad, teacher certification program. **Credit/placement by examination:** AP, CLEP, institutional tests. 30 credit hours maximum toward bachelor's degree. **Support services:** Study skills assistance, tutoring, writing center.

Majors. Architecture: Urban/community planning. **Biology:** General, biotechnology, environmental. **Business:** General, accounting, business admin, marketing. **Communications:** General. **Computer sciences:** Computer science, information technology. **Conservation:** Environmental studies. **Education:** Art, early childhood, elementary, music. **English:** English lit. **Foreign languages:** French, Spanish. **Health:** Athletic training, public health ed. **History:** General. **Liberal arts:** Humanities. **Math:** General. **Parks/recreation:** Health/fitness. **Philosophy/religion:** Philosophy. **Physical sciences:** Atmospheric science, chemistry. **Protective services:** Criminal justice. **Psychology:** General. **Public administration:** General, social work. **Social sciences:** General, applied economics, geography, political science. **Visual/performing arts:** Art, commercial/advertising art, dramatic, studio arts.

Most popular majors. Business/marketing 17%, communications/journalism 8%, education 21%, parks/recreation 9%, psychology 7%, visual/performing arts 9%.

Computing on campus. 500 workstations in dormitories, library, computer center, student center. Dormitories wired for high-speed internet access and linked to campus network. Commuter students can connect to campus network. Online course registration, online library, helpline, repair service, student web hosting, wireless network available.

Student life. Freshman orientation: Mandatory, $75 fee. Preregistration for classes offered. Program involves introduction to campus, academic advising, peer group meetings. 5 sessions in June, one session in September, one session in January. **Policies:** Freshmen permitted cars on campus. **Housing:** Guaranteed on-campus for freshmen. Coed dorms, apartments, fraternity/sorority housing, substance-free housing available. $90 partly refundable deposit, deadline 5/1. Wellness housing, substance-free housing, music/theater/dance housing, honors housing, special interest housing, and community service housing available. **Activities:** Bands, choral groups, dance, drama, film society, literary magazine, music ensembles, musical theater, radio station, student government, student newspaper, Chi Alpha Christian Fellowship, International Student Association, multicultural student organization, Nicaragua Club, PSC Volunteers, social work club, health and wellness club, Peer Educators, Alternative Spring Break.

Athletics. NCAA. **Intercollegiate:** Baseball M, basketball, cheerleading M, diving W, field hockey W, football (tackle) M, ice hockey, lacrosse, skiing, soccer, softball W, swimming W, tennis W, volleyball W, wrestling M. **Intramural:** Basketball, bowling, cross-country, football (non-tackle), golf, racquetball, soccer, softball, table tennis, tennis, triathlon, volleyball. **Team name:** Panthers.

Student services. Alcohol/substance abuse counseling, campus ministries, career counseling, student employment services, financial aid counseling, health services, on-campus daycare, personal counseling, placement for graduates, veterans' counselor, women's services. **Physically disabled:** Services for visually, hearing impaired.

Contact. E-mail: plymouthadmit@plymouth.edu
Phone: (603) 535-2237 Toll-free number: (800) 842-6900
Fax: (603) 535-2714
Eugene Fahey, Senior Associate Director of Admission, Plymouth State University, 17 High Street MSC 52, Plymouth, NH 03264-1595

Rivier College

Nashua, New Hampshire — **CB member**
www.rivier.edu — **CB code: 3728**

- Private 4-year liberal arts college affiliated with Roman Catholic Church
- Commuter campus in small city
- 1,380 degree-seeking undergraduates: 39% part-time, 79% women
- 447 degree-seeking graduate students
- 72% of applicants admitted
- SAT or ACT with writing, application essay required
- 62% graduate within 6 years

General. Founded in 1933. Regionally accredited. Founded in 1933 by the Sisters of the Presentation of May. **Degrees:** 206 bachelor's, 125 associate awarded; master's offered. **ROTC:** Air Force. **Location:** 19 miles from Manchester, 45 miles from Boston. **Calendar:** Semester, limited summer session. **Full-time faculty:** 71 total; 69% have terminal degrees, 61% women. **Part-time faculty:** 109 total; 13% have terminal degrees, 2% minority, 73% women. **Class size:** 61% < 20, 36% 20-39, 3% 40-49, less than 1% 50-99. **Special facilities:** Center for peace and social justice, early childhood center/laboratory school.

Freshman class profile. 1,132 applied, 813 admitted, 324 enrolled.

End year in good standing:	88%	**Out-of-state:**	45%
Return as sophomores:	76%	**Live on campus:**	68%

Basis for selection. High school academic record (course selection, course level, grades), test scores, extracurricular activities, application essay, and letters of recommendation considered. SAT or ACT required of all applicants under age 24 unless student is transferring 12 or more college credits to Rivier. Interview recommended for all; portfolio required for art programs.

High school preparation. 16 units recommended. Recommended units include English 4, mathematics 3, social studies 2, history 1, science 1 (laboratory 1), foreign language 2 and academic electives 3. Nursing program applicants must have completed chemistry and algebra.

2005-2006 Annual costs. Tuition/fees: $20,380. Room/board: $7,564. Books/supplies: $800. Personal expenses: $1,500.

2004-2005 Financial aid. Need-based: 202 full-time freshmen applied for aid; 186 were judged to have need; 186 of these received aid. Average need met was 74%. Average scholarship/grant was $9,479; average loan $5,313. 47% of total undergraduate aid awarded as scholarships/grants, 53% as loans/jobs. **Non-need-based:** Awarded to 91 full-time undergraduates, including 30 freshmen. Scholarships awarded for academics, alumni affiliation, minority status.

Application procedures. Admission: Priority date 3/1; no deadline. $25 fee, may be waived for applicants with need. Application may be submitted online. Admission notification on a rolling basis beginning on or about 12/1. **Financial aid:** Priority date 2/1; no closing date. FAFSA required. Applicants notified on a rolling basis starting 3/1; must reply by 5/1 or within 2 week(s) of notification.

Academics. Formal programs for learning disabled students not offered, but college staffs an Office of Special Needs Services with a part-time learning disabilities specialist. **Special study options:** Cross-registration, double major, ESL, honors, independent study, internships, liberal arts/career combination, study abroad, teacher certification program. **Credit/placement by examination:** AP, CLEP, institutional tests. **Support services:** Learning center, reduced course load, study skills assistance, tutoring, writing center.

Honors college/program. Honors program limited to 15 students per class. Special application and interview required. Scholarship available to all participants. SAT 1200 plus (exclusive of Writing), top 20% of high school class. Honors classes will fulfill some core requirements.

Majors. Biology: General. **Business:** Business admin, management information systems, management science. **Communications:** General, broadcast journalism, journalism, public relations. **Computer sciences:** Computer science. **Education:** General, biology, early childhood, elementary, English, foreign languages, history, mathematics, science, secondary, social science, social studies, Spanish. **Foreign languages:** Spanish. **Health:** Nursing (RN), predentistry, premedicine, preop/surgical nursing, preveterinary. **History:** General. **Interdisciplinary:** Math/computer science. **Legal studies:** Prelaw. **Liberal arts:** Arts/sciences. **Math:** General. **Psychology:** General. **Social sciences:** General, political science, sociology. **Visual/performing arts:** Commercial/advertising art, design, drawing, painting, photography, studio arts.

Most popular majors. Business/marketing 10%, education 29%, health sciences 22%, psychology 8%.

Computing on campus. 100 workstations in dormitories, library, computer center. Dormitories linked to campus network. Commuter students can connect to campus network. Helpline, repair service, wireless network available.

Student life. Freshman orientation: Mandatory, $100 fee. Preregistration for classes offered. 2-day June freshman orientation includes academic advising and registration, social activities. Parallel program for parents. Students spend night on-campus. **Policies:** Freshmen permitted cars on campus. **Housing:** Guaranteed on-campus for all undergraduates. Coed dorms, substance-free housing available. $100 deposit, deadline 5/1. **Activities:** Choral groups, dance, drama, student government, student newspaper, campus ministry, REACT (Rivier Environmental Activists), Amnesty International, international club, Chinese Student Association, America Reads, Americorps, Habitat for Humanity, Model United Nations.

Athletics. NCAA. **Intercollegiate:** Baseball M, basketball, cross-country, golf M, soccer, softball W, volleyball. **Intramural:** Basketball, soccer, softball, table tennis, tennis, volleyball, weight lifting. **Team name:** Raiders.

Student services. Adult student services, alcohol/substance abuse counseling, campus ministries, career counseling, student employment services, financial aid counseling, health services, minority student services, on-campus daycare, personal counseling, placement for graduates.

Contact. E-mail: rivadmit@rivier.edu
Phone: (603) 897-8507 Toll-free number: (800) 447-4843
Fax: (603) 891-1799
David Boisvert, Director of Undergraduate Admissions, Rivier College, 420 Main Street, Nashua, NH 03060-5086

St. Anselm College

Manchester, New Hampshire — **CB member**
www.anselm.edu — **CB code: 3748**

- Private 4-year nursing and liberal arts college affiliated with Roman Catholic Church
- Residential campus in small city
- 1,952 degree-seeking undergraduates: 1% part-time, 58% women, 1% African American, 1% Asian American, 1% Hispanic American, 1% international
- 73% of applicants admitted
- SAT or ACT (ACT writing optional), application essay required
- 75% graduate within 6 years

General. Founded in 1889. Regionally accredited. Administered by Order of St. Benedict. **Degrees:** 403 bachelor's awarded. **ROTC:** Army, Air Force. **Location:** 50 miles from Boston. **Calendar:** Semester, limited summer session. **Full-time faculty:** 131 total; 92% have terminal degrees, 5% minority, 40% women. **Part-time faculty:** 46 total; 41% have terminal degrees, 52% women. **Class size:** 52% < 20, 44% 20-39, 3% 50-99, 1% >100. **Special facilities:** Observatory, New Hampshire Institute of Politics, ice arena.

Freshman class profile. 3,258 applied, 2,366 admitted, 519 enrolled.

Mid 50% test scores			
SAT verbal:	510-600	Rank in top quarter:	45%
SAT math:	510-600	Rank in top tenth:	15%
ACT:	21-26	Return as sophomores:	82%
GPA 3.50 or higher:	14%	Out-of-state:	80%
GPA 3.0-3.49:	47%	Live on campus:	93%
GPA 2.0-2.99:	39%	International:	1%

Basis for selection. School achievement record and character most important, followed by test scores, 2 recommendations, essay. SAT Subject Tests recommended. Interview recommended. **Homeschooled:** Statement describing homeschool structure and mission, interview, letter of recommendation (nonparent) required.

High school preparation. College-preparatory program required. 16 units required. Required and recommended units include English 4, mathematics 3-4, social studies 2, science 3-4 (laboratory 3), foreign language 2-4 and academic electives 2.

2005-2006 Annual costs. Tuition/fees: $25,140. Room/board: $9,070. Books/supplies: $800.

2005-2006 Financial aid. Need-based: 64% of total undergraduate aid awarded as scholarships/grants, 36% as loans/jobs. **Non-need-based:** Scholarships awarded for academics, athletics, state residency.

Application procedures. Admission: Priority date 3/1; no deadline. $55 fee, may be waived for applicants with need. Application may be submitted online. Admission notification on a rolling basis beginning on or about 1/1. Must reply by May 1 or within 2 week(s) if notified thereafter. **Financial aid:** Priority date 3/1; no closing date. FAFSA, CSS PROFILE required. Applicants notified on a rolling basis starting 3/10; must reply by 5/1.

Academics. 4-semester humanities program required of all students. Special studies certificates in addition to major concentrations available in fine arts (visual arts, theater, music), international studies, communications, human relations and work, French, Spanish, German, Latin, Greek, Russian area studies, Latin American studies, Asian studies, Catholic studies, medieval studies, public policy studies. **Special study options:** Cross-registration, dual enrollment of high school students, exchange student, honors, independent study, internships, liberal arts/career combination, New York semester, study abroad, teacher certification program, Washington semester. Member New Hampshire College and University Council. **Credit/placement by examination:** AP, CLEP, IB, institutional tests. 30 credit hours maximum toward bachelor's degree. **Support services:** Learning center, reduced course load, study skills assistance, tutoring, writing center.

Majors. Biology: General, biochemistry. **Business:** General, accounting, finance, managerial economics. **Computer sciences:** Computer science. **Conservation:** Environmental science. **Engineering:** General, physics. **English:** English lit. **Foreign languages:** Classics, French, Spanish. **Health:** Nursing (RN), predentistry, premedicine. **History:** General. **Interdisciplinary:** Biological/physical sciences, math/computer science. **Legal studies:** Prelaw. **Liberal arts:** Arts/sciences. **Math:** General. **Philosophy/religion:** Philosophy. **Physical sciences:** Chemistry, physics. **Protective services:** Criminal justice. **Psychology:** General. **Social sciences:** Economics, international relations, political science, sociology. **Theology:** Theology. **Visual/performing arts:** Art.

Most popular majors. Business/marketing 26%, English 7%, health sciences 7%, history 6%, psychology 9%, security/protective services 10%, social sciences 16%.

Computing on campus. 400 workstations in dormitories, library, computer center, student center. Dormitories wired for high-speed internet access and linked to campus network. Commuter students can connect to campus network. Online library, helpline, repair service available.

Student life. Freshman orientation: Available, $25 fee. 3 days prior to Fall semester. **Policies:** Intervisitation allowed on weeknights and weekends during designated hours. Freshmen permitted cars on campus. **Housing:** Guaranteed on-campus for all undergraduates. Single-sex dorms, special housing for disabled, apartments, substance-free housing available. $200 nonrefundable deposit, deadline 5/1. **Activities:** Jazz band, choral groups, dance, drama, literary magazine, radio station, student government, student newspaper, TV station, Knights of Columbus, Political Union, King Edward Society, Center for Volunteers, El Club Hispanico, Club Simon Bolivar, Celtic Society, Spring Break Alternative, Red Key Society, Alpine Club, Ski Club.

Athletics. NCAA. **Intercollegiate:** Baseball M, basketball, cross-country, field hockey W, football (tackle) M, golf, ice hockey, lacrosse, skiing, soccer, softball W, tennis, volleyball W. **Intramural:** Basketball, handball, ice hockey, racquetball, skiing, soccer, softball, table tennis, tennis, volleyball. **Team name:** Hawks.

Student services. Alcohol/substance abuse counseling, campus ministries, career counseling, student employment services, financial aid counseling, health services, minority student services, personal counseling, placement for graduates, veterans' counselor. **Physically disabled:** Services for visually impaired.

Contact. E-mail: admission@anselm.edu
Phone: (603) 641-7500 Toll-free number: (888) 426-7356
Fax: (603) 641-7550
Nancy Davis Griffin, Director of Admission, St. Anselm College, 100 Saint Anselm Drive, Manchester, NH 03102-1310

Southern New Hampshire University

Manchester, New Hampshire — **CB member**
www.snhu.edu — **CB code: 3649**

- Private 4-year university
- Residential campus in small city
- 1,706 degree-seeking undergraduates: 3% part-time, 55% women, 1% African American, 2% Asian American, 1% Hispanic American, 4% international
- 1,841 graduate students
- 72% of applicants admitted
- SAT or ACT with writing, application essay required
- 52% graduate within 6 years

General. Founded in 1932. Regionally accredited. Continuing Education Centers in Manchester, Nashua, Salem, Portsmouth, Laconia (NH) and Brunswick (ME). Graduate School of Business locations in Concord, Laconia, Nashua, Portmouth, Salem, Brunswick (ME), Athens, Greece, Dubai, and Puerto Rico. Approximately 3,000 students enrolled in continuing education courses. **Degrees:** 304 bachelor's, 67 associate awarded; master's, doctoral offered. **ROTC:** Army, Air Force. **Location:** 55 miles from Boston. **Calendar:** Semester, extensive summer session. **Full-time faculty:** 126 total; 63% have terminal degrees, 11% minority, 39% women. **Part-time faculty:** 249 total; 34% women. **Class size:** 50% < 20, 50% 20-39, less than 1% 40-49. **Special facilities:** Culinary institute, center for financial studies.

Freshman class profile. 2,295 applied, 1,644 admitted, 479 enrolled.

Mid 50% test scores		Rank in top quarter:	26%
SAT verbal:	450-540	Rank in top tenth:	6%
SAT math:	460-560	Return as sophomores:	71%
GPA 3.50 or higher:	17%	Out-of-state:	61%
GPA 3.0-3.49:	34%	Live on campus:	87%
GPA 2.0-2.99:	48%	International:	1%

Basis for selection. School achievement, recommendations, personal statement, SAT scores, class rank most important. Extracurricular activities and personal interview considered. Students with technical-vocational background also considered for culinary arts program. Interview recommended.

High school preparation. Recommended units include English 4, mathematics 3, social studies 2, history 2, science 3 (laboratory 2) and foreign language 2.

2005-2006 Annual costs. Tuition/fees: $20,514. Room/board: $8,250. Books/supplies: $850. Personal expenses: $900.

2005-2006 Financial aid. Need-based: 368 full-time freshmen applied for aid; 315 were judged to have need; 315 of these received aid. Average need met was 70%. Average scholarship/grant was $9,740; average loan $2,572. 57% of total undergraduate aid awarded as scholarships/grants, 43% as loans/jobs. **Non-need-based:** Awarded to 1,497 full-time undergraduates, including 373 freshmen. Scholarships awarded for academics, alumni affiliation, athletics, leadership, state residency.

Application procedures. Admission: Priority date 3/15; no deadline. $35 fee, may be waived for applicants with need. Application may be submitted online. Admission notification on a rolling basis. Must reply by May 1 or within 2 week(s) if notified thereafter. **Financial aid:** Priority date 3/15; no closing date. FAFSA required. Applicants notified on a rolling basis starting 3/1; must reply within 3 week(s) of notification.

Academics. Students enrolling in School of Business required to purchase laptop computer. **Special study options:** Accelerated study, combined bachelor's/graduate degree, cooperative education, distance learning, double major, ESL, honors, independent study, internships, study abroad, teacher certification program, United Nations semester, weekend college. Three-year honors program in business administration. **Credit/placement by examination:** AP, CLEP, IB. **Support services:** Learning center, reduced course load, remedial instruction, study skills assistance, tutoring.

Majors. Area/ethnic studies: American. **Business:** General, accounting, business admin, finance, hospitality admin, international, management information systems, managerial economics, sales/distribution, tourism/travel. **Communications:** General, advertising, digital media. **Computer sciences:** Information technology. **Education:** Business, early childhood, elementary, English, ESL, sales/marketing, secondary, social studies. **English:** Creative writing, English lit. **History:** General. **Liberal arts:** Arts/sciences. **Parks/recreation:** Sports admin. **Psychology:** General. **Social sciences:** General, economics, political science. **Visual/performing arts:** Graphic design.

Most popular majors. Business/marketing 72%, personal/culinary services 16%.

Computing on campus. 557 workstations in library, computer center. Dormitories wired for high-speed internet access and linked to campus network. Online course registration, helpline, wireless network available.

Student life. Freshman orientation: Mandatory, $110 fee. 4 days prior to arrival of upperclassmen. **Policies:** Freshmen permitted cars on campus. **Housing:** Guaranteed on-campus for all undergraduates. Coed dorms, special housing for disabled, apartments, substance-free housing available. $200 deposit, deadline 5/1. Townhouses, single-sex areas in residence halls available. **Activities:** Choral groups, dance, drama, musical theater, radio station, student government, student newspaper, over 40 clubs and organizations available.

Athletics. NCAA. **Intercollegiate:** Baseball M, basketball, cheerleading, cross-country, golf M, ice hockey M, lacrosse, soccer, softball W, tennis, volleyball W. **Intramural:** Basketball, football (tackle), racquetball, soccer, softball, tennis, volleyball. **Team name:** Penmen.

Student services. Adult student services, alcohol/substance abuse counseling, campus ministries, career counseling, student employment services, financial aid counseling, health services, personal counseling, placement for graduates, veterans' counselor. **Physically disabled:** Services for visually, speech, hearing impaired.

Contact. E-mail: admission@snhu.edu
Phone: (603) 645-9611 Toll-free number: (800) 642-4968
Fax: (603) 645-9693
Steve Soba, Director of Admission, Southern New Hampshire University, 2500 North River Road, Manchester, NH 03106-1045

Thomas More College of Liberal Arts

Merrimack, New Hampshire
www.thomasmorecollege.edu **CB code: 3892**

- Private 4-year liberal arts college affiliated with Roman Catholic Church
- Residential campus in large town
- 86 degree-seeking undergraduates: 1% part-time, 50% women
- 95% of applicants admitted
- Application essay required

General. Founded in 1978. Regionally accredited. Semester in Rome for second-semester sophomores. **Degrees:** 15 bachelor's awarded. **Location:** 45 miles from Boston. **Calendar:** Semester. **Full-time faculty:** 5 total; 100% have terminal degrees, 20% women. **Part-time faculty:** 5 total; 40% have terminal degrees, 60% women. **Class size:** 80% < 20, 10% 20-39, 10% 50-99.

Freshman class profile. 37 applied, 35 admitted, 19 enrolled.

Return as sophomores:	60%	Live on campus:	85%
Out-of-state:	84%	International:	5%

Basis for selection. Evidence of student's desire to learn important. Complete application includes essay, 2 academic letters of recommendation, high school transcript, and SAT or ACT scores. Interviews and/or visits are strongly recommended. SAT or ACT recommended. Interviews recommended.

High school preparation. 17 units required. Required units include English 4, mathematics 3, social studies 2, history 2, science 2 (laboratory 2) and foreign language 2. Recommended languages: Latin, French, German. Recommended electives: music, art.

2005-2006 Annual costs. Tuition/fees: $10,650. Room/board: $8,000. Books/supplies: $600. Personal expenses: $100.

2005-2006 Financial aid. Need-based: 18 full-time freshmen applied for aid; 9 were judged to have need; 9 of these received aid. Average need met was 70%. Average scholarship/grant was $4,564; average loan $2,438. 50% of total undergraduate aid awarded as scholarships/grants, 50% as loans/jobs. **Non-need-based:** Awarded to 47 full-time undergraduates, including 11 freshmen. Scholarships awarded for academics.

Application procedures. Admission: No deadline. No application fee. Admission notification on a rolling basis beginning on or about 1/1. **Financial aid:** Priority date 5/1; no closing date. FAFSA required. Applicants notified on a rolling basis starting 5/15; must reply within 2 week(s) of notification.

Academics. Each student, regardless of major, takes a 6-hour humanities course every semester throughout the four years: philosophy, literature, politics, history, theology taught by faculty from various disciplines. **Special study options:** Study abroad. Sophomore semester in Rome. **Credit/placement by examination:** AP, CLEP. **Support services:** Tutoring.

Majors. Biology: General. **English:** English lit. **Philosophy/religion:** Philosophy. **Social sciences:** Political science.

Computing on campus. 5 workstations in library.

Student life. Freshman orientation: Mandatory. **Policies:** Students are responsible, in main part, for care of campus. Freshmen permitted cars on campus. **Housing:** Guaranteed on-campus for all undergraduates. Single-sex dorms available. **Activities:** Choral groups.

Student services. Campus ministries, career counseling, financial aid counseling, personal counseling.

Contact. E-mail: admissions@thomasmorecollege.edu
Phone: (603) 880-8308 Toll-free number: (800) 880-8308
Fax: (603) 880-9280
Joanne Geiger, Director of Admissions, Thomas More College of Liberal Arts, Six Manchester Street, Merrimack, NH 03054-4818

University of New Hampshire

Durham, New Hampshire **CB member**
www.unh.edu **CB code: 3918**

- Public 4-year university
- Residential campus in small town

- 11,063 degree-seeking undergraduates: 2% part-time, 57% women, 1% African American, 2% Asian American, 2% Hispanic American, 1% international
- 2,481 degree-seeking graduate students
- 72% of applicants admitted
- SAT or ACT with writing, application essay required
- 73% graduate within 6 years

General. Founded in 1866. Regionally accredited. **Degrees:** 2,293 bachelor's, 186 associate awarded; master's, doctoral offered. **ROTC:** Army, Air Force. **Location:** 50 miles from Boston, 50 miles from Portland, Maine. **Calendar:** Semester, extensive summer session. **Full-time faculty:** 694 total; 7% have terminal degrees, 8% minority, 36% women. **Part-time faculty:** 268 total; 13% have terminal degrees, 1% minority, 62% women. **Class size:** 46% < 20, 33% 20-39, 6% 40-49, 9% 50-99, 6% >100. **Special facilities:** Journalism laboratory, optical observatory, marine research laboratory, experiential learning center, child development center, art galleries, agricultural and equine facilities, electron microscope, sawmill.

Freshman class profile. 12,310 applied, 8,804 admitted, 1,622 enrolled.

Mid 50% test scores		**Return as sophomores:**	86%
SAT verbal:	510-610	**Out-of-state:**	46%
SAT math:	520-620	**Live on campus:**	96%
Rank in top quarter:	61%	**Fraternities:**	4%
Rank in top tenth:	20%	**Sororities:**	5%
End year in good standing:	90%		

Basis for selection. School achievement record most important, followed by course selection, class rank, recommendations, test scores. Cocurricular activities, character/leadership considered. SAT Subject Tests can satisfy a foreign language requirement for students in a BA program. Audition required for music programs. **Homeschooled:** Supporting documents include GED scores, transcripts, education plans, syllabi, SAT or ACT scores, home-school association information.

High school preparation. College-preparatory program required. 18 units recommended. Recommended units include English 4, mathematics 4, social studies 3, science 4 (laboratory 4) and foreign language 3. Additional requirements determined by intended major.

2005-2006 Annual costs. Tuition/fees: $9,778; $21,498 out-of-state. New England Regional Student Program tuition 175% of in-state public institution tuition. Students in following majors pay differential per academic year: engineering, computer science, business-economics-hospitality management (Whittemore School). Room/board: $7,032. Books/supplies: $1,400. Personal expenses: $1,924.

2004-2005 Financial aid. **Need-based:** 1,961 full-time freshmen applied for aid; 1,487 were judged to have need; 1,459 of these received aid. Average need met was 82%. Average scholarship/grant was $2,708; average loan $2,345. 43% of total undergraduate aid awarded as scholarships/grants, 57% as loans/jobs. **Non-need-based:** Awarded to 2,681 full-time undergraduates, including 724 freshmen. Scholarships awarded for academics, art, athletics, leadership, music/drama, ROTC.

Application procedures. **Admission:** Closing date 2/1 (postmark date). $45 fee ($60 out-of-state), may be waived for applicants with need. Application may be submitted online. Admission notification 4/15. Must reply by 5/1. **Financial aid:** Priority date 3/1; no closing date. FAFSA required. Applicants notified on a rolling basis starting 3/1.

Academics. General education requirement has 8 components. Students admitted as freshmen or as freshmen transfers must complete 4 writing intensive courses. **Special study options:** Cross-registration, double major, ESL, exchange student, honors, independent study, internships, semester at sea, student-designed major, study abroad, teacher certification program, Washington semester. Undergraduate research opportunities, International Undergraduate Opportunities Program. **Credit/placement by examination:** AP, CLEP, IB, institutional tests. 32 credit hours maximum toward associate degree, 64 toward bachelor's. **Support services:** Learning center, reduced course load, study skills assistance, tutoring, writing center.

Majors. **Agriculture:** Agronomy, animal sciences, business, dairy, dairy husbandry, equestrian studies, food science, horticultural science, plant sciences. **Architecture:** Urban/community planning. **Area/ethnic studies:** European, French, Western European, women's. **Biology:** General, bacteriology, biochemistry, microbiology, plant molecular, plant physiology, zoology. **Business:** General, accounting, business admin, entrepreneurial studies, finance, hospitality admin, hotel/motel admin, tourism/travel. **Communications:** General, digital media, journalism, media studies. **Computer sciences:** General, computer science. **Conservation:** General, economics, environmental science, environmental studies, forestry, wildlife. **Education:** Art, English, mathematics, music, science. **Engineering:** General, chemical, civil, computer, electrical, environmental, materials, materials science, mechanical, ocean. **English:** British lit, English lit. **Family/consumer sciences:** Child development, family studies, family/community services, food/nutrition, human nutrition. **Foreign languages:** Ancient Greek, classics, French, German, Latin, linguistics, modern Greek, Russian, Spanish. **Health:** Athletic training, clinical lab science, clinical lab technology, clinical nutrition, communication disorders, dietetics, health care admin, nursing (RN), recreational therapy, speech pathology. **History:** General. **Interdisciplinary:** Global studies, natural sciences. **Liberal arts:** Humanities. **Math:** General, applied. **Parks/recreation:** General, exercise sciences. **Personal/culinary services:** Restaurant/catering. **Philosophy/religion:** Philosophy. **Physical sciences:** Chemistry, geology, physics. **Psychology:** General. **Public administration:** Social work. **Social sciences:** Anthropology, criminology, economics, geography, international relations, political science, sociology. **Visual/performing arts:** Art history/conservation, dramatic, music history, music performance, music theory/composition, studio arts.

Most popular majors. Biology 6%, business/marketing 15%, English 8%, health sciences 8%, psychology 8%, social sciences 13%.

Computing on campus. 345 workstations in library, computer center, student center. Dormitories wired for high-speed internet access and linked to campus network. Commuter students can connect to campus network. Online course registration, online library, helpline, repair service, student web hosting available.

Student life. **Freshman orientation:** Available. Preregistration for classes offered. June: course selection and registration. Fall: academic and social expectations, resource information. Minority student orientation offered. **Housing:** Guaranteed on-campus for freshmen. Coed dorms, single-sex dorms, apartments, fraternity/sorority housing, substance-free housing available. $200 partly refundable deposit, deadline 5/1. Substance free housing, 14 theme housing options available. **Activities:** Bands, choral groups, dance, drama, film society, literary magazine, music ensembles, musical theater, radio station, student government, student newspaper, symphony orchestra, TV station, Hillel, Diversity Support Coalition, honor societies, governance organizations, media and publications, hall councils, arts and entertainment groups, special interest groups, political and world affairs groups, religious groups.

Athletics. NCAA. **Intercollegiate:** Basketball, cross-country, diving, field hockey W, football (tackle) M, gymnastics W, ice hockey, lacrosse W, rowing (crew) W, skiing, soccer, swimming, tennis, track and field, volleyball W. **Intramural:** Basketball, field hockey W, football (non-tackle), ice hockey, racquetball, soccer, softball, table tennis, tennis, volleyball. **Team name:** Wildcats.

Student services. Adult student services, alcohol/substance abuse counseling, campus ministries, career counseling, services for economically disadvantaged, student employment services, financial aid counseling, health services, legal services, minority student services, on-campus daycare, personal counseling, placement for graduates, veterans' counselor, women's services. **Physically disabled:** Services for visually, speech, hearing impaired.

Contact. E-mail: admissions@unh.edu
Phone: (603) 862-1360 Fax: (603) 862-0077
Robert McGann, Director of Admissions, University of New Hampshire, Grant House, 4 Garrison Avenue, Durham, NH 03824

University of New Hampshire at Manchester

Manchester, New Hampshire — **CB member**
www.unhm.unh.edu — **CB code: 2094**

- Public 4-year university and liberal arts college
- Commuter campus in small city
- 779 degree-seeking undergraduates: 29% part-time, 59% women, 2% African American, 2% Asian American, 3% Hispanic American, 1% international
- SAT or ACT (ACT writing optional), application essay required

General. Founded in 1985. Regionally accredited. **Degrees:** 141 bachelor's, 41 associate awarded; master's offered. **ROTC:** Army, Air Force. **Location:** 55 miles from Boston, 35 miles from Concord. **Calendar:** Semester, limited summer session. **Full-time faculty:** 28 total. **Part-time faculty:** 60 total.

Freshman class profile.

Mid 50% test scores		**ACT:**	18-23
SAT verbal:	450-550	**Out-of-state:**	1%
SAT math:	450-550		

Basis for selection. Achievement in high school college preparatory program most important. SAT scores should be consistent with achievement. Recommendation, essay, interview very helpful for students of moderate achievement or in nontraditional cases. Non-native speakers of English must submit TOEFL scores. Test scores not required for applicants out of high school 3 or more years. Interview recommended for college transition program. **Homeschooled:** Encourage GED, SAT, syllabus of curriculum; diploma from home-school association if available.

High school preparation. Required and recommended units include English 4, mathematics 3-4, social studies 2, science 3-4 (laboratory 3) and foreign language 2-3.

2005-2006 Annual costs. Tuition/fees: $7,103; $17,753 out-of-state. New England Regional Student tuition is 150% of in-state public institution tuition. Books/supplies: $700. Personal expenses: $2,020.

Financial aid. Non-need-based: Scholarships awarded for academics, state residency.

Application procedures. Admission: Priority date 4/1; deadline 6/15. $35 fee ($50 out-of-state), may be waived for applicants with need. Admission notification on a rolling basis. Must reply by May 1 or within 3 week(s) if notified thereafter. **Financial aid:** Closing date 5/1. FAFSA required. Applicants notified on a rolling basis starting 4/1; must reply within 2 week(s) of notification.

Academics. Special study options: Cross-registration, double major, ESL, exchange student, external degree, independent study, internships, semester at sea, student-designed major, study abroad, teacher certification program, Washington semester. **Credit/placement by examination:** AP, CLEP, IB, institutional tests. 48 credit hours maximum toward associate degree, 64 toward bachelor's. ACT, PEP exams accepted to RN Baccalaureate program. **Support services:** Learning center, reduced course load, remedial instruction, study skills assistance, tutoring.

Majors. Business: Business admin. **Communications:** General. **Computer sciences:** General. **Engineering technology:** Electrical. **Foreign languages:** Sign language interpretation. **Health:** Nursing (RN). **History:** General. **Liberal arts:** Arts/sciences. **Psychology:** General.

Computing on campus. 37 workstations in library, computer center. Helpline available.

Student life. Freshman orientation: Mandatory, $30 fee. Preregistration for classes offered. 3-day (or evening) program held in June, August, and January. June attendees able to preregister for fall courses. **Housing:** Students may reside in dormitories at New Hampshire Technical Institute: Concord. Contact admissions office for other housing possibilities. **Activities:** Student government, student newspaper.

Athletics. Team name: Wildcats.

Student services. Career counseling. **Physically disabled:** Services for visually, speech, hearing impaired.

Contact. E-mail: unhm.admissions@unh.edu
Phone: (603) 641-4150 Fax: (603) 641-4125
Miho Bean, Associate Director of Admissions, University of New Hampshire at Manchester, 400 Commercial Street, Manchester, NH 03101-1113

New Jersey

Berkeley College

West Paterson, New Jersey
www.berkeleycollege.edu
CB member
CB code: 2061

- For-profit 4-year business college
- Commuter campus in large town
- 2,406 degree-seeking undergraduates: 15% part-time, 73% women, 17% African American, 5% Asian American, 34% Hispanic American, 2% international
- 84% of applicants admitted
- 50% graduate within 6 years

General. Founded in 1931. Regionally accredited. Branch campuses in Paramus and Woodbridge, NJ. **Degrees:** 185 bachelor's, 326 associate awarded. **Location:** 20 miles from New York City. **Calendar:** Quarter, extensive summer session. **Full-time faculty:** 51 total. **Part-time faculty:** 93 total.

Freshman class profile. 1,955 applied, 1,645 admitted, 871 enrolled.

Return as sophomores:	55%	**Live on campus:**	6%
Out-of-state:	3%	**International:**	2%

Basis for selection. Class rank, high school record, interview most important. Passing grade on school entrance/placement exam required. Interviews strongly recommended.

2006-2007 Annual costs. Tuition/fees: $17,700. Room/board: $9,000. Books/supplies: $1,200.

Financial aid. Non-need-based: Scholarships awarded for academics, alumni affiliation. **Additional information:** Alumni scholarship examination given in November and December. Full and partial scholarships awarded.

Application procedures. Admission: No deadline. $50 fee. Application may be submitted online. Admission notification on a rolling basis. Admitted applicants must reply within 2 weeks of notification. **Financial aid:** No deadline. FAFSA required. Applicants notified on a rolling basis starting 3/1; must reply within 6 week(s) of notification.

Academics. Special study options: Accelerated study, distance learning, internships, New York semester, study abroad. **Credit/placement by examination:** AP, CLEP, SAT, ACT, institutional tests. **Support services:** Learning center, remedial instruction, study skills assistance, tutoring, writing center.

Majors. Business: General, accounting, business admin, fashion, international, marketing, office management.

Computing on campus. 358 workstations in library, computer center, student center. Dormitories linked to campus network. Commuter students can connect to campus network. Online library, helpline, wireless network available.

Student life. Freshman orientation: Mandatory. **Policies:** Freshmen permitted cars on campus. **Housing:** Coed dorms available. $400 partly refundable deposit. **Activities:** Choral groups, literary magazine, student government, Phi Beta Lambda, paralegal club, interior design club, athletic club, fashion and marketing club, Phi Theta Kappa.

Athletics. Team name: Bulldogs.

Student services. Adult student services, alcohol/substance abuse counseling, career counseling, student employment services, financial aid counseling, on-campus daycare, personal counseling, placement for graduates.

Contact. E-mail: admissions@berkeleycollege.edu
Phone: (973) 278-5400 ext. 1210 Toll-free number: (800) 446-5400
Fax: (973) 278-9141
Dave Bertone, Director for High School Admissions, Berkeley College, 44 Rifle Camp Road, West Paterson, NJ 07424-0440

Beth Medrash Govoha

Lakewood, New Jersey
CB code: 2166

- Private 4-year rabbinical college for men affiliated with Jewish faith
- Large town
- 2,034 degree-seeking undergraduates

General. Founded in 1943. Accredited by AARTS. Ordination available. **Degrees:** 391 bachelor's awarded; master's offered. **Calendar:** Semester. **Full-time faculty:** 130 total. **Part-time faculty:** 20 total.

2005-2006 Annual costs. Tuition/fees: $10,056. Room/board: $3,912. Books/supplies: $450.

Application procedures. Admission: Closing date 8/25. $125 fee, may be waived for applicants with need. **Financial aid:** No deadline.

Academics. Credit/placement by examination: CLEP.

Majors. Theology: Talmudic.

Contact. Phone: (732) 367-1060 Fax: (732) 367-7487
Rabbi Yaakov Pollak, Director of Admissions, Beth Medrash Govoha, 617 Sixth Street, Lakewood, NJ 08701

Bloomfield College

Bloomfield, New Jersey
www.bloomfield.edu
CB member
CB code: 2044

- Private 4-year liberal arts college affiliated with Presbyterian Church (USA)
- Commuter campus in large town
- 2,181 degree-seeking undergraduates: 21% part-time, 69% women, 53% African American, 4% Asian American, 18% Hispanic American, 2% international
- 47% of applicants admitted
- SAT or ACT (ACT writing optional), application essay required

General. Founded in 1868. Regionally accredited. Bloomfield College is organized into seven divisions: Business and Computer Information Systems, Creative Arts and Technology, Humanities, Natural Science and Mathematics, Nursing, and Social and Behavioral Sciences, and Education. **Degrees:** 243 bachelor's awarded. **ROTC:** Army. **Location:** 7 miles from Newark, 15 miles from New York City. **Calendar:** Semester, limited summer session. **Full-time faculty:** 62 total; 77% have terminal degrees, 27% minority, 63% women. **Part-time faculty:** 220 total; 14% have terminal degrees, 36% minority, 52% women. **Class size:** 77% < 20, 22% 20-39, less than 1% 40-49, less than 1% 50-99, less than 1% >100. **Special facilities:** Art gallery; technology and multimedia center.

Freshman class profile. 2,531 applied, 1,179 admitted, 413 enrolled.

Mid 50% test scores		**Rank in top tenth:**	1%
SAT verbal:	380-470	**End year in good standing:**	100%
SAT math:	390-480	**Return as sophomores:**	65%
GPA 3.50 or higher:	8%	**Out-of-state:**	6%
GPA 3.0-3.49:	26%	**Live on campus:**	34%
GPA 2.0-2.99:	63%	**International:**	1%
Rank in top quarter:	11%		

Basis for selection. Acceptance for regular admission requires SAT combined score equal to 900 (exclusive of Writing) and a minimum high school GPA of 2.70. Interviews are not required but strongly recommended. Essays must be a self-recommendation or a reflection on previous educational experiences. A recent graded term paper can be substituted for an essay. **Homeschooled:** Transcript of courses and grades, state high school equivalency certificate, interview, letter of recommendation (nonparent) required. Applicants must submit SAT scores and an official transcript with information about the organization that performed the accreditation/conversion. **Learning Disabled:** Students must meet regular admission requirements, and should ask for special accommodations for SAT testing.

High school preparation. College-preparatory program required. 14 units required.

2005-2006 Annual costs. Tuition/fees: $15,100. Room/board: $7,400. Books/supplies: $500. Personal expenses: $1,496.

2005-2006 Financial aid. Need-based: 398 full-time freshmen applied for aid; 357 were judged to have need; 353 of these received aid. Average

need met was 70%. Average scholarship/grant was $12,071; average loan $2,838. 66% of total undergraduate aid awarded as scholarships/grants, 34% as loans/jobs. **Non-need-based:** Awarded to 421 full-time undergraduates, including 129 freshmen. Scholarships awarded for academics, alumni affiliation, athletics, leadership, religious affiliation.

Application procedures. Admission: Priority date 3/14; deadline 7/1 (postmark date). $35 fee, may be waived for applicants with need. Application may be submitted online. Admission notification on a rolling basis beginning on or about 10/1. **Financial aid:** Priority date 3/15, closing date 10/1. FAFSA required. Applicants notified on a rolling basis starting 3/15; must reply by 3/15 or within 2 week(s) of notification.

Academics. Special study options: Accelerated study, cooperative education, distance learning, double major, dual enrollment of high school students, ESL, honors, independent study, internships, liberal arts/career combination, student-designed major, study abroad, teacher certification program, weekend college. Four-year clinical laboratory science program and allied health technologies major offered in conjunction with University of Medicine and Dentistry of New Jersey. Joint BS/MS in Computer Information Systems program offered with NJIT. Institute for Technology and Professional Studies offers special programs in advanced technology, allied health, computer classes, and special programs for teachers. **Credit/placement by examination:** AP, CLEP. 16 credit hours maximum toward bachelor's degree. A maximum of 16 course units may be earned through CLEP examinations, portfolio assessment, and nursing assessment. **Support services:** Learning center, pre-admission summer program, reduced course load, remedial instruction, study skills assistance, tutoring.

Majors. Biology: General. **Business:** Accounting, business admin, human resources, marketing. **Communications:** General. **Computer sciences:** General, networking. **Education:** General, special. **English:** English lit. **Health:** Clinical lab science, nursing (RN). **History:** General. **Math:** General, applied. **Philosophy/religion:** Philosophy, religion. **Physical sciences:** Chemistry. **Psychology:** General. **Social sciences:** Economics, political science, sociology. **Visual/performing arts:** General.

Most popular majors. Biology 7%, business/marketing 28%, education 6%, health sciences 10%, mathematics 8%, psychology 14%, social sciences 16%, visual/performing arts 9%.

Computing on campus. 191 workstations in dormitories, library, computer center, student center. Dormitories wired for high-speed internet access and linked to campus network. Commuter students can connect to campus network. Online library, helpline, student web hosting, wireless network available.

Student life. Freshman orientation: Mandatory, $100 fee. Preregistration for classes offered. Conducted in August. **Policies:** Bloomfield College has adopted a Statement of Shared Values, addressing student conduct and standards for behavior. Freshmen permitted cars on campus. **Housing:** Coed dorms, fraternity/sorority housing, substance-free housing available. $50 deposit, deadline 3/1. Theme housing based on academic interest available. **Activities:** Choral groups, dance, drama, film society, literary magazine, musical theater, radio station, student government, African Student Association, Association of Latin American Students, Haitian Student Association, Lambda Theta Alpha, Phi Beta Sigma, Lambda Sigma Upsilon, B.C. Bible Study, Gospel Choir, Muslim Student Association.

Athletics. NCAA. **Intercollegiate:** Baseball M, basketball, cross-country, soccer, softball W, tennis M, volleyball W. **Intramural:** Basketball, soccer, volleyball. **Team name:** Deacons.

Student services. Adult student services, alcohol/substance abuse counseling, campus ministries, career counseling, student employment services, financial aid counseling, health services, personal counseling, placement for graduates. **Physically disabled:** Services for visually, speech, hearing impaired. **Learning disabled:** Comprehensive services available.

Contact. E-mail: admission@bloomfield.edu
Phone: (973) 748-9000 ext. 230 Toll-free number: (800) 848-4555
Fax: (973) 748-0916
Lourdes Mangual De Delgado, Vice President for Enrollment Management and Dean of Admissions, Bloomfield College, One Park Place, Bloomfield, NJ 07003-9981

Caldwell College

Caldwell, New Jersey
www.caldwell.edu

CB member
CB code: 2072

- Private 4-year liberal arts college affiliated with Roman Catholic Church
- Commuter campus in large town
- 1,550 degree-seeking undergraduates: 32% part-time, 66% women, 16% African American, 2% Asian American, 11% Hispanic American, 5% international
- 290 degree-seeking graduate students
- 78% of applicants admitted
- SAT or ACT with writing, application essay required
- 47% graduate within 6 years

General. Founded in 1939. Regionally accredited. Caldwell College offers affiliation programs with institutions such as New York University, Columbia University, Temple University, UMDNJ and others where students earn a bachelor's degree, typically in biology, and a professional degree from the affiliated school. **Degrees:** 322 bachelor's awarded; master's offered. **ROTC:** Army. **Location:** 20 miles from New York City. **Calendar:** Semester, limited summer session. **Full-time faculty:** 83 total. **Part-time faculty:** 101 total. **Class size:** 79% < 20, 21% 20-39.

Freshman class profile. 1,234 applied, 960 admitted, 298 enrolled.

Mid 50% test scores		**Return as sophomores:**	73%
SAT verbal:	430-530	**Out-of-state:**	8%
SAT math:	420-540	**Live on campus:**	44%
End year in good standing:	85%	**International:**	10%

Basis for selection. Class rank in top half, school achievement record, test scores, interview, extracurricular activities very important. Counselor's recommendation, volunteer work important. Essay, interview recommended for all, audition required for music programs, portfolio required for art programs.

High school preparation. 16 units required. Required units include English 4, mathematics 2, history 1, science 2 (laboratory 1), foreign language 2 and academic electives 5.

2005-2006 Annual costs. Tuition/fees: $18,900. Room/board: $7,650. Books/supplies: $900. Personal expenses: $1,000.

2005-2006 Financial aid. Need-based: 275 full-time freshmen applied for aid; 270 were judged to have need; 270 of these received aid. Average need met was 75%. Average scholarship/grant was $7,300; average loan $3,800. 69% of total undergraduate aid awarded as scholarships/grants, 31% as loans/jobs. **Non-need-based:** Awarded to 852 full-time undergraduates, including 212 freshmen. Scholarships awarded for academics, alumni affiliation, art, athletics, leadership, music/drama, religious affiliation.

Application procedures. Admission: Priority date 12/1; no deadline. $40 fee, may be waived for applicants with need. Application may be submitted online. Admission notification on a rolling basis beginning on or about 12/31. Must reply by May 1 or within 2 week(s) if notified thereafter. **Financial aid:** Priority date 4/15; no closing date. FAFSA, institutional form required. Applicants notified on a rolling basis starting 3/1; must reply within 4 week(s) of notification.

Academics. Special study options: Accelerated study, combined bachelor's/graduate degree, cooperative education, distance learning, double major, ESL, external degree, honors, independent study, internships, liberal arts/career combination, student-designed major, study abroad, teacher certification program, Washington semester, weekend college. **Credit/placement by examination:** AP, CLEP, IB, institutional tests. 30 credit hours maximum toward bachelor's degree. Credit by exam only available during first year (30 credits) of matriculation. Credit toward major dependent on departmental approval. Prior Learning Assessment (PLA) for adult students who must attend PLA workshop. **Support services:** Learning center, pre-admission summer program, remedial instruction, study skills assistance, tutoring, writing center.

Majors. Biology: General. **Business:** Accounting, business admin, international, management science, marketing. **Communications:** General. **Computer sciences:** General, computer science. **Education:** Elementary. **English:** English lit. **Foreign languages:** French, Spanish. **Health:** Clinical lab technology. **History:** General. **Math:** General. **Physical sciences:** Chemistry. **Protective services:** Criminal justice. **Psychology:** General. **Social sciences:** General, political science, sociology. **Theology:** Theology. **Visual/performing arts:** Art, studio arts.

Most popular majors. Business/marketing 17%, education 15%, English 8%, psychology 20%, security/protective services 10%.

Computing on campus. 204 workstations in dormitories, library, computer center, student center. Dormitories wired for high-speed internet access and linked to campus network. Commuter students can connect to campus network. Online course registration, online library, helpline, student web hosting available.

Student life. Freshman orientation: Mandatory, $100 fee. Preregistration for classes offered. Held Sunday and Monday prior to beginning of classes in August. **Policies:** Freshmen permitted cars on campus. **Housing:** Guaranteed on-campus for all undergraduates. Coed dorms, substance-free housing available. $200 nonrefundable deposit, deadline 5/1. **Activities:** Jazz band, choral groups, drama, literary magazine, music ensembles, musical theater, student government, student newspaper, Circle-K, campus ministry, Black students cooperative union, Latin American student association, international student organization, Portuguese club, Irish club.

Athletics. NCAA. **Intercollegiate:** Baseball M, basketball, cross-country W, golf M, soccer, softball W, tennis. **Intramural:** Basketball, football (non-tackle), soccer, softball, volleyball. **Team name:** Cougars.

Student services. Adult student services, alcohol/substance abuse counseling, campus ministries, career counseling, services for economically disadvantaged, student employment services, financial aid counseling, health services, minority student services, personal counseling, placement for graduates, women's services. **Physically disabled:** Services for visually, hearing impaired.

Contact. E-mail: admissions@caldwell.edu
Phone: (973) 618-3500 Toll-free number: (888) 864-9516
Fax: (973) 618-3600
Kathryn Reilly, Director of Admissions, Caldwell College, 9 Ryerson Avenue, Caldwell, NJ 07006-6195

Centenary College

Hackettstown, New Jersey — **CB member**
www.centenarycollege.edu — **CB code: 2080**

- Private 4-year liberal arts college affiliated with United Methodist Church
- Residential campus in large town
- 1,887 degree-seeking undergraduates: 14% part-time, 64% women
- 585 degree-seeking graduate students
- 75% of applicants admitted
- SAT or ACT, application essay required
- 32% graduate within 6 years

General. Founded in 1867. Regionally accredited. Laptop computers provided to all full-time students. **Degrees:** 322 bachelor's, 51 associate awarded; master's offered. **Location:** 55 miles from New York City. **Calendar:** Semester, limited summer session. **Full-time faculty:** 63 total; 6% have terminal degrees. **Part-time faculty:** 241 total. **Class size:** 60% < 20, 39% 20-39, 1% 40-49. **Special facilities:** Textile laboratory, equestrian center, theater.

Freshman class profile. 693 applied, 523 admitted, 266 enrolled.

Mid 50% test scores			
SAT verbal:	400-520	Rank in top quarter:	18%
SAT math:	420-520	Rank in top tenth:	3%
ACT:	16-17	Return as sophomores:	73%
GPA 3.50 or higher:	8%	Out-of-state:	16%
GPA 3.0-3.49:	16%	Live on campus:	87%
GPA 2.0-2.99:	69%	Sororities:	1%

Basis for selection. School achievement record, standardized test scores most important. Interview, recommendations, community activities also strongly considered. Interviews required for academically marginal students with special needs; recommended for others. Portfolio required for art and design, graphic arts majors. **Homeschooled:** State high school equivalency certificate required. **Learning Disabled:** Interview with Director of Services, documentation of psycho-education evaluation and IEP required for supportive services programs.

High school preparation. 16 units required. Required and recommended units include English 4, mathematics 3-4, social studies 2, history 2, science 2-4 and foreign language 2. Major-related courses on high school level recommended.

2005-2006 Annual costs. Tuition/fees: $21,085. Additional fees required for equine majors and for comprehensive learning support program. Room/board: $7,900. Books/supplies: $660. Personal expenses: $600.

2005-2006 Financial aid. Need-based: 243 full-time freshmen applied for aid; 214 were judged to have need; 211 of these received aid. Average need met was 70%. Average scholarship/grant was $12,945; average loan $3,414. 61% of total undergraduate aid awarded as scholarships/grants, 39% as loans/jobs. **Non-need-based:** Awarded to 198 full-time undergraduates, including 51 freshmen. Scholarships awarded for academics, alumni affiliation, art, leadership, state residency.

Application procedures. Admission: Priority date 8/1; no deadline. $50 fee, may be waived for applicants with need. Application may be submitted online. Admission notification on a rolling basis beginning on or about 9/15. Must reply by May 1 or within 4 week(s) if notified thereafter. **Financial aid:** Priority date 4/15; no closing date. FAFSA required. Applicants notified on a rolling basis starting 3/1.

Academics. Core curriculum required. Educational program balances career and liberal arts. **Special study options:** Accelerated study, cross-registration, distance learning, double major, honors, independent study, internships, liberal arts/career combination, student-designed major, study abroad, teacher certification program, weekend college. **Credit/placement by examination:** AP, CLEP, IB. 15 credit hours maximum toward associate degree, 30 toward bachelor's. **Support services:** Learning center, pre-admission summer program, reduced course load, remedial instruction, study skills assistance, tutoring.

Majors. Agriculture: Equestrian studies. **Biology:** General. **Business:** Accounting, business admin. **Communications:** General. **Computer sciences:** General. **History:** General. **Math:** General. **Protective services:** Criminal justice. **Psychology:** General. **Social sciences:** Political science, sociology. **Visual/performing arts:** Commercial/advertising art, dramatic, fashion design.

Most popular majors. Agriculture 9%, business/marketing 54%, English 7%, psychology 9%, social sciences 11%.

Computing on campus. Dormitories wired for high-speed internet access and linked to campus network. Commuter students can connect to campus network. Helpline, repair service, wireless network available.

Student life. Freshman orientation: Mandatory. Preregistration for classes offered. 3-day orientation prior to start of classes. **Policies:** Freshmen permitted cars on campus. **Housing:** Coed dorms, single-sex dorms, special housing for disabled, apartments available. $150 deposit, deadline 7/1. **Activities:** Choral groups, drama, literary magazine, musical theater, radio station, student government, student newspaper, TV station, art guild, student activities committee, service groups, fashion group, academic clubs, professional and honor societies, special interest clubs, Students in Free Enterprise.

Athletics. NCAA. **Intercollegiate:** Baseball M, basketball, cross-country, equestrian, golf, lacrosse, soccer, softball W, volleyball W, wrestling M. **Intramural:** Basketball M, equestrian M. **Team name:** Cyclones.

Student services. Alcohol/substance abuse counseling, campus ministries, career counseling, services for economically disadvantaged, student employment services, financial aid counseling, health services, personal counseling, placement for graduates. **Learning disabled:** Comprehensive services available.

Contact. E-mail: admissions@centenarycollege.edu
Phone: (908) 852-1400 ext. 2217 Toll-free number: (800) 236-8679
Fax: (908) 852-3454
Diane Finnan, Vice President for Enrollment Management, Centenary College, 400 Jefferson Street, Hackettstown, NJ 07840-9989

The College of New Jersey

Ewing, New Jersey
www.tcnj.edu — **CB code: 2519**

- Public 4-year liberal arts college
- Residential campus in large town
- 5,836 degree-seeking undergraduates: 2% part-time, 58% women, 6% African American, 5% Asian American, 7% Hispanic American
- 749 degree-seeking graduate students
- 45% of applicants admitted
- SAT or ACT (ACT writing optional), application essay required
- 81% graduate within 6 years; 28% enter graduate study

General. Founded in 1855. Regionally accredited. **Degrees:** 1,415 bachelor's awarded; master's offered. **ROTC:** Army, Air Force. **Location:** 6 miles from Trenton. **Calendar:** Semester, limited summer session. **Full-time faculty:** 341 total; 86% have terminal degrees, 23% minority, 46% women. **Part-time faculty:** 364 total; 17% have terminal degrees, 7% minority, 53% women. **Class size:** 47% < 20, 50% 20-39, 3% 40-49, less than 1% 50-99. **Special facilities:** Concert hall, observatory, electron microscopy lab, nuclear magnetic resonance laboratory, greenhouse.

Freshman class profile. 7,300 applied, 3,289 admitted, 1,236 enrolled.

Mid 50% test scores			
SAT verbal:	570-670	Rank in top tenth:	68%
SAT math:	600-700	Return as sophomores:	95%
Rank in top quarter:	94%	Out-of-state:	5%
		Live on campus:	96%

Basis for selection. Standardized test scores, high school rank and choice of curriculum very important. Extracurricular service, activities and community involvement are considered. Audition required for music; portfolio required for art. **Homeschooled:** Statement describing homeschool structure and mission, transcript of courses and grades, state high school equivalency certificate, letter of recommendation (nonparent) required.

High school preparation. College-preparatory program required. 18 units required; 20 recommended. Required and recommended units include English 4, mathematics 3, social studies 2-3, science 3 (laboratory 2-3) and foreign language 2-3.

2005-2006 Annual costs. Tuition/fees: $9,707; $14,970 out-of-state. Room/board: $8,458.

2005-2006 Financial aid. Need-based: 428 full-time freshmen applied for aid; 428 were judged to have need; 404 of these received aid. Average need met was 51%. Average scholarship/grant was $12,033; average loan $5,337. 49% of total undergraduate aid awarded as scholarships/grants, 51% as loans/jobs. **Non-need-based:** Awarded to 3,282 full-time undergraduates, including 846 freshmen. Scholarships awarded for academics, art, minority status, music/drama, ROTC, state residency. **Additional information:** Merit scholarships available to New Jersey high school graduates based on academic distinction. Limited number of scholarships available to out-of-state students who demonstrate exceptional academic achievement in high school and on SAT.

Application procedures. Admission: Closing date 2/15 (postmark date). $50 fee, may be waived for applicants with need. Application may be submitted online. Admission notification on a rolling basis beginning on or about 12/15. Must reply by May 1 or within 2 week(s) if notified thereafter. **Financial aid:** Priority date 3/1, closing date 10/1. FAFSA required. Applicants notified on a rolling basis starting 7/15; must reply within 2 week(s) of notification.

Academics. Special study options: Combined bachelor's/graduate degree, cross-registration, double major, dual enrollment of high school students, exchange student, honors, independent study, internships, liberal arts/career combination, semester at sea, student-designed major, study abroad, teacher certification program. **Credit/placement by examination:** AP, CLEP, IB, SAT, institutional tests. 30 credit hours maximum toward bachelor's degree. **Support services:** Learning center, pre-admission summer program, reduced course load, remedial instruction, study skills assistance, tutoring, writing center.

Majors. Area/ethnic studies: Women's. **Biology:** General. **Business:** General, accounting, business admin, finance, international, marketing. **Communications:** General, journalism. **Computer sciences:** General. **Education:** Art, biology, chemistry, Deaf/hearing impaired, early childhood, elementary, English, foreign languages, health, history, mathematics, middle, physical, physics, social science, social studies, Spanish, special, speech, technology/industrial arts. **Engineering:** General, computer, electrical, mechanical, science. **English:** English lit, speech/rhetoric. **Foreign languages:** Spanish. **Health:** Nursing (RN), preop/surgical nursing. **History:** General. **Math:** General, statistics. **Philosophy/religion:** Philosophy. **Physical sciences:** Chemistry, physics. **Protective services:** Law enforcement admin. **Psychology:** General. **Public administration:** General. **Social sciences:** Criminology, economics, international relations, political science, sociology. **Visual/performing arts:** General, art, commercial/advertising art, multimedia, studio arts.

Most popular majors. Biology 6%, business/marketing 20%, education 26%, English 12%, psychology 6%, visual/performing arts 6%.

Computing on campus. 581 workstations in dormitories, library, computer center, student center. Dormitories wired for high-speed internet access and linked to campus network. Commuter students can connect to campus network. Online course registration, online library, helpline, repair service, student web hosting, wireless network available.

Student life. Freshman orientation: Mandatory. Preregistration for classes offered. 4-part orientation program including June advisement week, summer readings, welcome week, college seminar. **Housing:** Guaranteed on-campus for freshmen. Coed dorms, single-sex dorms, special housing for disabled, apartments, substance-free housing available. $100 nonrefundable deposit, deadline 6/6. Pets allowed in dorm rooms. Housing for transfer students available. **Activities:** Bands, choral groups, dance, drama, literary magazine, music ensembles, musical theater, opera, radio station, student government, student newspaper, symphony orchestra, Black Student Union, Catholic Campus Ministry, Amnesty International, Circle K, EOF Alliance, Friendship Day Committee, Islamic Society, Outreach Association, Students Acting for the Environment, Jewish Student Union.

Athletics. NCAA. **Intercollegiate:** Baseball M, basketball, cross-country, diving, field hockey W, football (tackle) M, golf M, lacrosse W, soccer, softball W, swimming, tennis, track and field, wrestling M. **Intramural:** Basketball, bowling, fencing, field hockey, football (non-tackle), golf M, ice hockey M, lacrosse M, racquetball, rugby, skiing, soccer, softball, swimming, tennis, volleyball, water polo. **Team name:** Lions.

Student services. Adult student services, alcohol/substance abuse counseling, campus ministries, career counseling, services for economically disadvantaged, student employment services, financial aid counseling, health services, minority student services, on-campus daycare, personal counseling, placement for graduates, veterans' counselor, women's services. **Physically disabled:** Services for visually, speech, hearing impaired.

Contact. E-mail: admiss@vm.tcnj.edu
Phone: (609) 771-2131 Toll-free number: (800) 624-0967
Fax: (609) 637-5174
Lisa Angeloni, Dean of Admissions, The College of New Jersey, Box 7718, Ewing, NJ 08628

College of St. Elizabeth

Morristown, New Jersey — **CB member**
www.cse.edu — **CB code: 2090**

- Private 4-year liberal arts college for women affiliated with Roman Catholic Church
- Residential campus in large town
- 1,073 degree-seeking undergraduates: 38% part-time, 95% women, 16% African American, 6% Asian American, 15% Hispanic American, 4% international
- 421 degree-seeking graduate students
- 79% of applicants admitted
- SAT or ACT (ACT writing optional), application essay required
- 58% graduate within 6 years

General. Founded in 1899. Regionally accredited. Men admitted to adult undergraduate programs and master's programs. An accelerated coed baccalaureate program with majors in business, communication, nursing and psychology for adults over age 23 with classes evenings and on Saturdays. **Degrees:** 263 bachelor's awarded; master's offered. **Location:** 40 miles from New York City. **Calendar:** Semester, limited summer session. **Full-time faculty:** 65 total; 82% have terminal degrees, 5% minority, 65% women. **Part-time faculty:** 113 total; 35% have terminal degrees, 11% minority, 64% women. **Class size:** 83% < 20, 17% 20-39. **Special facilities:** Library of rare books and manuscripts, Greek theater, Shakespeare garden, Holocaust Education Resource Center, Center for Catholic Women's History, Center for Theological and Spiritual Development.

Freshman class profile. 422 applied, 335 admitted, 130 enrolled.

Mid 50% test scores		**Return as sophomores:**	78%
SAT verbal:	400-530	**Out-of-state:**	2%
SAT math:	390-530	**Live on campus:**	78%
Rank in top quarter:	44%	**International:**	6%
Rank in top tenth:	16%		

Basis for selection. School achievement record and recommendations most important, followed by test scores, class rank; interview recommended. **Homeschooled:** Letter of recommendation (nonparent) required. Applicants processed on an individual basis. Must provide approved curriculum guide.

High school preparation. College-preparatory program required. 16 units required; 23 recommended. Required and recommended units include English 3-4, mathematics 2-3, history 1-3, science 1-2 (laboratory 1-2), foreign language 2 and academic electives 7.

2005-2006 Annual costs. Tuition/fees: $19,440. Room/board: $8,975. Books/supplies: $800. Personal expenses: $650.

2004-2005 Financial aid. Need-based: 161 full-time freshmen applied for aid; 135 were judged to have need; 133 of these received aid. Average need met was 79%. Average scholarship/grant was $15,112; average loan $2,512. 71% of total undergraduate aid awarded as scholarships/grants, 29% as loans/jobs. **Non-need-based:** Awarded to 180 full-time undergraduates, including 80 freshmen. Scholarships awarded for academics, alumni affiliation, art, leadership, state residency.

Application procedures. Admission: Priority date 3/1; deadline 8/15 (receipt date). $35 fee, may be waived for applicants with need. Application may be submitted online. Admission notification on a rolling basis beginning on or about 11/15. Must reply by May 1 or within 2 week(s) if notified thereafter. **Financial aid:** Priority date 3/1; no closing date. FAFSA required. Applicants notified on a rolling basis starting 11/15; must reply by 5/1 or within 2 week(s) of notification.

Academics. Distance learning courses available. Students with 60 undergradute credits may take an accelerated program in Business or Communication on Saturdays and complete a bachelors in two years. **Special study options:** Accelerated study, combined bachelor's/graduate degree, cross-registration, distance learning, double major, dual enrollment of high school students, ESL, exchange student, honors, independent study, internships, liberal arts/career combination, student-designed major, study abroad, teacher certification program, United Nations semester, weekend college. **Credit/placement by examination:** AP, CLEP, IB. 30 credit hours maximum toward bachelor's degree. Credit for prior work and/or life experience offered via portfolio. **Support services:** Learning center, pre-admission summer program, reduced course load, remedial instruction, study skills assistance, tutoring.

Majors. Area/ethnic studies: American. **Biology:** General, biochemistry, toxicology. **Business:** Business admin. **Communications:** General. **Computer sciences:** General, computer science. **Education:** Elementary, special. **Family/consumer sciences:** Food/nutrition. **Foreign languages:** Spanish. **Health:** Clinical lab science, cytotechnology, preop/surgical nursing. **History:** General. **Math:** General. **Philosophy/religion:** Philosophy. **Physical sciences:** Chemistry. **Protective services:** Criminal justice. **Psychology:** General. **Social sciences:** Economics, sociology. **Visual/performing arts:** Art.

Most popular majors. Business/marketing 21%, communications/journalism 17%, education 12%, psychology 14%.

Computing on campus. 152 workstations in dormitories, library, computer center. Dormitories wired for high-speed internet access and linked to campus network. Commuter students can connect to campus network. Helpline available.

Student life. Freshman orientation: Mandatory, $200 fee. Preregistration for classes offered. Comprehensive program held before start of classes for Women's College students. **Policies:** Freshmen permitted cars on campus. **Housing:** Guaranteed on-campus for all undergraduates. $200 nonrefundable deposit. **Activities:** Choral groups, drama, literary magazine, music ensembles, student government, student newspaper, campus ministry, volunteer services center, international/intercultural club, Latin Roots, Students Take Action Committee, foreign language club, American Chemical Society Affiliates, psychology club, sociology club.

Athletics. NCAA. **Intercollegiate:** Basketball W, equestrian W, soccer W, softball W, swimming W, tennis W, volleyball W. **Intramural:** Volleyball W. **Team name:** Eagles.

Student services. Adult student services, alcohol/substance abuse counseling, campus ministries, career counseling, services for economically disadvantaged, student employment services, financial aid counseling, health services, minority student services, personal counseling, placement for graduates, women's services. **Physically disabled:** Services for visually, speech, hearing impaired.

Contact. E-mail: apply@cse.edu
Phone: (973) 290-4700 Toll-free number: (800) 210-7900
Fax: (973) 290-4710
Donna Tatarka, Dean of Admission, College of St. Elizabeth, 2 Convent Road, Morristown, NJ 07960-6989

DeVry University: North Brunswick

North Brunswick, New Jersey
www.nj.devry.edu **CB code: 2113**

- For-profit 4-year university
- Commuter campus in small city
- 1,491 degree-seeking undergraduates: 23% part-time, 39% women
- Interview required

General. Founded in 1996. Regionally accredited. **Degrees:** 277 bachelor's, 326 associate awarded. **Location:** 30 miles from New York City. **Calendar:** Semester, extensive summer session. **Full-time faculty:** 80 total. **Part-time faculty:** 93 total.

Freshman class profile. 315 enrolled.

Basis for selection. Applicants must have high school diploma or equivalent, degree from an accredited postsecondary institution, or submit acceptable test scores and be at least 17 years of age on the first day of classes. New students may enter at beginning of any semester. SAT or ACT recommended. CPT also accepted.

High school preparation. Required units include mathematics 1. Math unit must be algebra or higher.

2005-2006 Annual costs. Tuition/fees: $12,240. Books/supplies: $1,100. Personal expenses: $1,816.

Financial aid. All financial aid based on need.

Application procedures. Admission: No deadline. $50 fee. Application may be submitted online. Admission notification on a rolling basis. **Financial aid:** No deadline. FAFSA required. Applicants notified on a rolling basis.

Academics. Special study options: Accelerated study, cooperative education, distance learning, weekend college. **Credit/placement by examination:** CLEP, institutional tests. **Support services:** Learning center, remedial instruction, tutoring.

Majors. Business: General. **Computer sciences:** Networking, systems analysis. **Engineering technology:** Electrical.

Most popular majors. Computer/information sciences 81%, engineering/engineering technologies 19%.

Computing on campus. 575 workstations in library, computer center. Online course registration, online library, helpline available.

Student life. Freshman orientation: Mandatory. **Policies:** Freshmen permitted cars on campus. **Activities:** Student government, Phi Theta Kappa, Golden Key, Institution of Electrical and Electronics Engineers, cultural exchange club, chess club, art club, Crusade for Christ.

Student services. Career counseling, student employment services, financial aid counseling, on-campus daycare, placement for graduates, veterans' counselor. **Physically disabled:** Services for visually, hearing impaired.

Contact. E-mail: admissions@devry.edu
Phone: (732) 435-4850 Toll-free number: (800) 333-3879
Fax: (732) 435-4850
Gerald Wargo, Director of Admissions, DeVry University: North Brunswick, 630 US Highway One, North Brunswick, NJ 08902-3362

Drew University

Madison, New Jersey **CB member**
www.drew.edu **CB code: 2193**

- Private 4-year university and liberal arts college affiliated with United Methodist Church
- Residential campus in large town
- 1,561 degree-seeking undergraduates: 2% part-time, 58% women, 3% African American, 6% Asian American, 6% Hispanic American, 1% international
- 982 degree-seeking graduate students
- 77% of applicants admitted
- 73% graduate within 6 years; 22% enter graduate study

General. Founded in 1867. Regionally accredited. **Degrees:** 323 bachelor's awarded; master's, doctoral, first professional offered. **Location:** 30 miles from New York City. **Calendar:** Semester, limited summer session. **Full-time faculty:** 148 total; 94% have terminal degrees, 17% minority, 48% women. **Part-time faculty:** 85 total. **Class size:** 63% < 20, 32% 20-39, 3% 40-49, 2% 50-99. **Special facilities:** Theater, 80-acre forest preserve, arboretum, photography gallery, observatory, research greenhouse, laser holography laboratory, center for the arts, music hall.

Freshman class profile. 3,802 applied, 2,941 admitted, 391 enrolled.

Mid 50% test scores		Rank in top quarter:	66%
SAT verbal:	550-660	Rank in top tenth:	36%
SAT math:	540-650	End year in good standing:	91%
ACT:	24-27	Return as sophomores:	84%
GPA 3.50 or higher:	40%	Out-of-state:	46%
GPA 3.0-3.49:	36%	Live on campus:	91%
GPA 2.0-2.99:	23%	International:	1%

Basis for selection. School achievement record most important; test scores also important. Interview recommended. **Homeschooled:** Statement describing homeschool structure and mission, transcript of courses and grades required.

High school preparation. Recommended units include English 4, mathematics 3, social studies 2, history 2, science 2, foreign language 2 and academic electives 3.

2005-2006 Annual costs. Tuition/fees: $31,286. Room/board: $8,412. Books/supplies: $1,090. Personal expenses: $2,438.

2004-2005 Financial aid. **Need-based:** 302 full-time freshmen applied for aid; 225 were judged to have need; 223 of these received aid. Average need met was 83%. Average scholarship/grant was $17,024; average loan $3,536. 77% of total undergraduate aid awarded as scholarships/grants, 23% as loans/jobs. **Non-need-based:** Awarded to 551 full-time undergraduates, including 181 freshmen. Scholarships awarded for academics, art, minority status, music/drama.

Application procedures. **Admission:** Closing date 2/15. $50 fee, may be waived for applicants with need. Application may be submitted online. Applicants notified by third week in March. Must reply by 5/1. **Financial aid:** Closing date 2/15. FAFSA, CSS PROFILE required. Applicants notified by 3/31; must reply by 5/1.

Academics. RISE program enables students to conduct scientific research with retired scientists. **Special study options:** Accelerated study, combined bachelor's/graduate degree, cross-registration, double major, exchange student, independent study, internships, New York semester, student-designed major, study abroad, teacher certification program, United Nations semester, Washington semester. Art, theater, Wall Street semesters in New York City, semesters in Brussels and London, summer semester in South Africa, 7-year dual degree (BA/MD) with UMDNJ-New Jersey Medical School, 5-year dual degree (BA/BS) with Columbia University and Washington University (St. Louis), month-long international seminars in January and May. **Credit/placement by examination:** AP, CLEP, IB, institutional tests. 32 credit hours maximum toward bachelor's degree. **Support services:** Learning center, pre-admission summer program, reduced course load, tutoring, writing center.

Majors. **Area/ethnic studies:** African, women's. **Biology:** General, biochemistry. **Computer sciences:** Computer science. **English:** English lit. **Foreign languages:** Chinese, classics, French, German, Spanish. **History:** General. **Interdisciplinary:** Behavioral sciences. **Math:** General. **Philosophy/religion:** Philosophy, religion. **Physical sciences:** Chemistry, physics. **Psychology:** General. **Social sciences:** Anthropology, economics, political science, sociology. **Visual/performing arts:** Art, art history/conservation, dramatic.

Most popular majors. Biology 6%, English 9%, foreign language 8%, interdisciplinary studies 7%, psychology 11%, social sciences 34%, visual/performing arts 10%.

Computing on campus. PC or laptop required. 2,500 workstations in library, computer center. Dormitories wired for high-speed internet access and linked to campus network. Commuter students can connect to campus network. Online course registration, online library, helpline, repair service, wireless network available.

Student life. **Freshman orientation:** Mandatory, $250 fee. Preregistration for classes offered. Week before start of fall semester. **Housing:** Guaranteed on-campus for all undergraduates. Coed dorms, special housing for disabled, substance-free housing available. Theme houses available. **Activities:** Choral groups, dance, drama, film society, literary magazine, music ensembles, radio station, student government, student newspaper, symphony orchestra, TV station, Amnesty International, Ariel (Hispanic student organization), College Democrats, College Republicans, Kuumba (Pan-African student organization), Inter-Varsity Christian Fellowship, Jewish Student Organization/Hillel, Drew Environmental Action League, SAVE (Students Against Violence Everywhere), The Alliance (gay, lesbian, and bisexual student group).

Athletics. NCAA. **Intercollegiate:** Baseball M, basketball, cross-country, equestrian, fencing, field hockey W, lacrosse, soccer, softball W, swimming, tennis. **Intramural:** Basketball, football (non-tackle), racquetball, soccer, softball, squash, table tennis, volleyball. **Team name:** Rangers.

Student services. Adult student services, alcohol/substance abuse counseling, campus ministries, career counseling, services for economically disadvantaged, student employment services, financial aid counseling, health services, minority student services, on-campus daycare, personal counseling, placement for graduates, women's services. **Physically disabled:** Services for visually, hearing impaired.

Contact. E-mail: cadm@drew.edu
Phone: (973) 408-3739 Fax: (973) 408-3068
Mary Beth Carey, Dean of College Admissions and Financial Assistance, Drew University, 36 Madison Avenue, Madison, NJ 07940-1493

Fairleigh Dickinson University: College at Florham

Madison, New Jersey
www.fdu.edu **CB code: 2262**

- Private 4-year business and liberal arts college
- Residential campus in large town
- 2,495 degree-seeking undergraduates: 8% part-time, 52% women, 8% African American, 3% Asian American, 7% Hispanic American, 2% international
- 864 degree-seeking graduate students
- 72% of applicants admitted
- SAT and SAT Subject Tests or ACT (ACT writing optional) required
- 52% graduate within 6 years

General. Regionally accredited. Additional campus at Wroxton College, England. non-governmental organization (NGO), status with United Nations affords students participatory opportunities. **Degrees:** 461 bachelor's, 1 associate awarded; master's offered. **ROTC:** Army, Air Force. **Location:** 27 miles from New York City. **Calendar:** Semester, extensive summer session. **Full-time faculty:** 113 total. **Part-time faculty:** 220 total. **Special facilities:** ITV multimedia classrooms, web-lab, center for students with learning disabilities, theaters, fitness center, art gallery.

Freshman class profile. 2,829 applied, 2,030 admitted, 616 enrolled.

Mid 50% test scores		**Out-of-state:**	18%
SAT verbal:	480-570	**Live on campus:**	82%
SAT math:	460-570	**International:**	1%
Rank in top quarter:	28%	**Fraternities:**	12%
Rank in top tenth:	10%	**Sororities:**	20%
Return as sophomores:	80%		

Basis for selection. GPA, class rank, difficulty of high school curriculum most important; test scores. **Homeschooled:** Applicant must take SAT or ACT. **Learning Disabled:** Separate application along with admissions application.

High school preparation. College-preparatory program required. 16 units required. Required and recommended units include English 4, mathematics 3, social studies 2, history 2, science 2-3 (laboratory 2-3), foreign language 2 and academic electives 3.

2005-2006 Annual costs. Tuition/fees: $24,904. Room/board: $9,008.

2004-2005 Financial aid. **Need-based:** 480 full-time freshmen applied for aid; 420 were judged to have need; 420 of these received aid. Average scholarship/grant was $10,712; average loan $2,467. 60% of total undergraduate aid awarded as scholarships/grants, 40% as loans/jobs. **Non-need-based:** Awarded to 1,487 full-time undergraduates, including 466 freshmen. Scholarships awarded for academics, alumni affiliation, leadership.

Application procedures. **Admission:** Priority date 3/15; no deadline. $40 fee, may be waived for applicants with need. Admission notification on a rolling basis beginning on or about 10/15. Must reply by May 1 or within 2 week(s) if notified thereafter. **Financial aid:** Priority date 2/15; no closing date. FAFSA required. Applicants notified on a rolling basis starting 4/1; must reply by 5/1 or within 2 week(s) of notification.

Academics. **Special study options:** Accelerated study, combined bachelor's/graduate degree, cooperative education, distance learning, double major, external degree, honors, independent study, internships, liberal arts/career combination, study abroad, teacher certification program, Washington semester, weekend college. **Credit/placement by examination:** CLEP, IB, institutional tests. 33 credit hours maximum toward bachelor's degree. **Support services:** Learning center, remedial instruction, study skills assistance, tutoring, writing center.

Majors. **Biology:** General, marine. **Business:** Accounting, business admin, hospitality admin, managerial economics, marketing, sales/distribution. **Communications:** General. **Computer sciences:** General. **English:** Creative writing, English lit. **Foreign languages:** French, Spanish. **Health:** Clinical lab science, health services, medical radiologic technology/radiation therapy, nursing (RN). **History:** General. **Liberal arts:** Humanities. **Math:** General. **Philosophy/religion:** Philosophy. **Physical sciences:** Chemistry. **Psychology:** General. **Social sciences:** Economics, political science, sociology. **Visual/performing arts:** General, cinematography, dramatic.

Most popular majors. History 29%, liberal arts 13%, psychology 16%, social sciences 8%, visual/performing arts 11%.

Computing on campus. 350 workstations in dormitories, library, computer center. Dormitories wired for high-speed internet access and linked to campus network. Commuter students can connect to campus network. Online library, helpline, student web hosting, wireless network available.

Student life. **Freshman orientation:** Mandatory. Preregistration for classes offered. **Housing:** Guaranteed on-campus for freshmen. Coed dorms, special housing for disabled, apartments available. $350 partly refundable deposit, deadline 5/1. All residence halls are non-smoking. **Activities:** Choral groups, dance, drama, film society, literary magazine, music ensembles, musical theater, radio station, student government, student newspaper.

Athletics. NCAA. **Intercollegiate:** Baseball M, basketball, cross-country, field hockey W, football (tackle) M, golf M, lacrosse, soccer, softball W, swimming, tennis, volleyball W. **Intramural:** Basketball, bowling, football (tackle) M, racquetball, soccer, softball. **Team name:** Devils.

Student services. Adult student services, alcohol/substance abuse counseling, campus ministries, career counseling, services for economically disadvantaged, student employment services, financial aid counseling, health services, minority student services, personal counseling, placement for graduates. **Learning disabled:** Comprehensive services available.

Contact. E-mail: globaleducation@fdu.edu
Phone: (800) 338-8803 Toll-free number: (800) 338-8803
Fax: (973) 443-8088
Bernetta Millonde, University Director of Admissions, Fairleigh Dickinson University: College at Florham, 285 Madison Avenue, Madison, NJ 07940

Fairleigh Dickinson University: Metropolitan Campus

Teaneck, New Jersey
www.fdu.edu **CB code: 2263**

- Private 4-year university
- Commuter campus in large town
- 3,284 degree-seeking undergraduates: 36% part-time, 58% women, 19% African American, 6% Asian American, 17% Hispanic American, 7% international
- 2,469 degree-seeking graduate students
- 65% of applicants admitted
- SAT and SAT Subject Tests or ACT (ACT writing optional) required
- 40% graduate within 6 years

General. Founded in 1942. Regionally accredited. Additional campus at Wroxton College, England. non-governmental organization status with United Nations affords students participatory opportunities. **Degrees:** 545 bachelor's, 46 associate awarded; master's, doctoral offered. **ROTC:** Army, Air Force. **Location:** 13 miles from New York City. **Calendar:** Semester, extensive summer session. **Full-time faculty:** 182 total. **Part-time faculty:** 379 total. **Special facilities:** Computer labs, ITV multimedia classrooms, photonics lab, center for students with learning disabilities, theater, art galleries, fitness center, center for psychological services, Web lab, marine biology lab.

Freshman class profile. 2,775 applied, 1,792 admitted, 499 enrolled.

Mid 50% test scores		Return as sophomores:	76%
SAT verbal:	440-540	Out-of-state:	24%
SAT math:	450-550	Live on campus:	25%
Rank in top quarter:	31%	International:	4%
Rank in top tenth:	11%		

Basis for selection. Rigor of secondary school record and GPA most important. Recommendations, standardized test scores, extracurricular activities are important. **Learning Disabled:** Regional Center for College Students with Learning Disabilities requires separate application. Must also apply to university admissions.

High school preparation. 16 units required. Required and recommended units include English 4, mathematics 3, social studies 2, history 2, science 2-3 (laboratory 2-3), foreign language 2 and academic electives 3.

2005-2006 Annual costs. Tuition/fees: $23,144. Room/board: $9,482.

2004-2005 Financial aid. Need-based: 350 full-time freshmen applied for aid; 332 were judged to have need; 332 of these received aid. Average scholarship/grant was $10,390; average loan $2,367. 63% of total undergraduate aid awarded as scholarships/grants, 37% as loans/jobs. **Non-need-based:** Awarded to 1,105 full-time undergraduates, including 264 freshmen. Scholarships awarded for academics, alumni affiliation, art, athletics, leadership, state residency.

Application procedures. Admission: Priority date 3/15; no deadline. $40 fee, may be waived for applicants with need. Application may be submitted online. Admission notification on a rolling basis beginning on or about 11/15. Must reply by May 1 or within 2 week(s) if notified thereafter. **Financial aid:** Priority date 2/15; no closing date. FAFSA required. Applicants notified on a rolling basis starting 4/1; must reply by 5/1 or within 2 week(s) of notification.

Academics. Core curriculum consists of 4 interdisciplinary courses. Marine biology majors spend 1 summer in Hilo, Hawaii, and 1 summer at Shoals Laboratory, Maine. FDU also offers University Honors Program and Global Scholars Program. **Special study options:** Accelerated study, combined bachelor's/graduate degree, cooperative education, distance learning, double major, ESL, honors, independent study, internships, liberal arts/career combination, student-designed major, study abroad, teacher certification program, weekend college. **Credit/placement by examination:** AP, CLEP, IB, institutional tests. 30 credit hours maximum toward associate degree, 33 toward bachelor's. Maximum of 32 semester hours of credit by examination may be counted toward degree from College of Business. **Support services:** Learning center, pre-admission summer program, reduced course load, remedial instruction, study skills assistance, tutoring, writing center.

Majors. Biology: General, biochemistry, marine. **Business:** Accounting, business admin, hospitality admin, managerial economics, marketing, sales/distribution. **Communications:** General. **Computer sciences:** General, information technology. **Conservation:** General. **Engineering:** Electrical. **Engineering technology:** Civil, construction, electrical, mechanical. **English:** English lit. **Foreign languages:** French, Spanish. **Health:** Clinical lab science, health services, medical radiologic technology/radiation therapy, nursing (RN). **History:** General. **Interdisciplinary:** Biological/physical sciences. **Liberal arts:** Humanities. **Math:** General. **Philosophy/religion:** Philosophy. **Physical sciences:** Chemistry. **Protective services:** Criminal justice. **Psychology:** General. **Social sciences:** Economics, international relations, political science, sociology. **Visual/performing arts:** General, dramatic.

Computing on campus. 350 workstations in dormitories, library, computer center. Dormitories wired for high-speed internet access and linked to campus network. Commuter students can connect to campus network. Online library, helpline, student web hosting, wireless network available.

Student life. Freshman orientation: Mandatory. Preregistration for classes offered. **Policies:** Freshmen permitted cars on campus. **Housing:** Coed dorms, single-sex dorms, special housing for disabled, apartments available. $350 partly refundable deposit, deadline 5/1. Honors and Global scholar housing. **Activities:** Concert band, choral groups, dance, drama, literary magazine, radio station, student government, student newspaper, TV station.

Athletics. NCAA. **Intercollegiate:** Baseball M, basketball, bowling W, cross-country, fencing W, football (tackle) M, golf M, soccer, softball W, swimming M, tennis, track and field, volleyball W. **Intramural:** Baseball M, basketball, bowling, cheerleading, golf M, racquetball, skiing, softball, table tennis, tennis, volleyball. **Team name:** Knights.

Student services. Adult student services, alcohol/substance abuse counseling, campus ministries, career counseling, services for economically disadvantaged, student employment services, financial aid counseling, health services, personal counseling, placement for graduates. **Learning disabled:** Comprehensive services available.

Contact. E-mail: globaleducation@fdu.edu
Phone: (201) 692-2553 Toll-free number: (800) 338-8803
Fax: (201) 692-7319
Bernetta Millonde, University Director of Admissions, Fairleigh Dickinson University: Metropolitan Campus, 1000 River Road, H-DH3-10, Teaneck, NJ 07666-1996

Felician College

Lodi, New Jersey
www.felician.edu **CB code: 2321**

- Private 4-year liberal arts college affiliated with Roman Catholic Church
- Commuter campus in large city
- 1,464 degree-seeking undergraduates: 22% part-time, 75% women, 12% African American, 7% Asian American, 17% Hispanic American
- 255 degree-seeking graduate students
- 87% of applicants admitted
- SAT or ACT (ACT writing optional) required
- 39% graduate within 6 years

General. Founded in 1942. Regionally accredited. Additional campus in Rutherford. All programs spread through both campuses. **Degrees:** 513 bachelor's, 24 associate awarded; master's offered. **Location:** 12 miles from New York City. **Calendar:** Semester, limited summer session. **Full-time faculty:** 83 total; 13% minority, 55% women. **Part-time faculty:** 65 total. **Class size:** 79% < 20, 20% 20-39, less than 1% 40-49. **Special facilities:** Nursing skills laboratory, performance and theater facilities.

Freshman class profile. 1,250 applied, 1,090 admitted, 262 enrolled.

Mid 50% test scores		Return as sophomores:	62%
SAT verbal:	410-500	Out-of-state:	7%
SAT math:	400-510		

Basis for selection. School achievement record, test scores most important. Interview, school and community activities, recommendations of high school counselor considered. Interview recommended for all; portfolio recommended for art programs.

High school preparation. 19 units recommended. Recommended units include English 4, mathematics 3, social studies 3, science 3 and academic electives 6. Biology, chemistry, algebra required for nursing and medical laboratory technology applicants.

2005-2006 Annual costs. Tuition/fees: $18,600. Room/board: $7,950. Books/supplies: $2,000. Personal expenses: $1,500.

2004-2005 Financial aid. Need-based: 213 full-time freshmen applied for aid; 119 were judged to have need; 119 of these received aid. Average need met was 85%. Average scholarship/grant was $6,000; average loan $3,500. 58% of total undergraduate aid awarded as scholarships/grants, 42% as loans/jobs. **Non-need-based:** Awarded to 549 full-time undergraduates, including 144 freshmen. Scholarships awarded for academics, alumni affiliation, athletics, religious affiliation.

Application procedures. Admission: No deadline. $30 fee, may be waived for applicants with need. Application may be submitted online. Admission notification on a rolling basis beginning on or about 3/15. Must reply by May 1 or within 2 week(s) if notified thereafter. **Financial aid:** Priority date 6/1; no closing date. FAFSA, institutional form required. Applicants notified on a rolling basis starting 4/1; must reply within 2 week(s) of notification.

Academics. Post-baccalaureate certification available in elementary and secondary education. **Special study options:** Accelerated study, combined bachelor's/graduate degree, cooperative education, cross-registration, distance learning, double major, dual enrollment of high school students, ESL, honors, independent study, internships, liberal arts/career combination, student-designed major, study abroad, teacher certification program, weekend college. **Credit/placement by examination:** AP, CLEP, IB, institutional tests. 15 credit hours maximum toward associate degree, 30 toward bachelor's. **Support services:** Learning center, writing center.

Majors. Biology: General, toxicology. **Business:** Accounting, business admin, marketing. **Communications:** General, broadcast journalism, digital media, journalism. **Computer sciences:** General, computer science. **Education:** Early childhood, early childhood special, elementary, mathematics. **Health:** Cytotechnology, health services, nuclear medical technology, nursing (RN), nursing admin, respiratory therapy technology. **History:** General. **Interdisciplinary:** Natural sciences. **Liberal arts:** Humanities. **Math:** General. **Philosophy/religion:** Philosophy, religion. **Psychology:** General. **Social sciences:** Sociology. **Visual/performing arts:** Art, studio arts.

Most popular majors. Business/marketing 43%, education 30%, psychology 12%.

Computing on campus. 140 workstations in dormitories, library, computer center. Dormitories wired for high-speed internet access and linked to campus network. Commuter students can connect to campus network. Online library, repair service available.

Student life. Freshman orientation: Mandatory. 3 summer programs available. **Policies:** No drugs or alcohol on campus. Freshmen permitted cars on campus. **Housing:** Guaranteed on-campus for freshmen. Coed dorms, single-sex dorms, special housing for disabled available. $200 deposit. **Activities:** Choral groups, drama, literary magazine, student government, Angelicum Club, history club, international club, RCIA (Latino), Kappa Sigma Xi, Aspiring Authors, Students in Free Enterprise, Kappa Gamma Pi (honorary society).

Athletics. NAIA, NCAA. **Intercollegiate:** Baseball M, basketball, cross-country, golf M, soccer, softball W, track and field, volleyball W. **Intramural:** Basketball M, bowling. **Team name:** Golden Falcons.

Student services. Campus ministries, financial aid counseling, health services. **Learning disabled:** Comprehensive services available.

Contact. E-mail: admissions@inet.felician.edu
Phone: (201) 559-6131 Fax: (201) 559-6188
Cara Gibbons, Director of Undergraduate Admissions, Felician College, 262 South Main Street, Lodi, NJ 07644-2198

Georgian Court University

Lakewood, New Jersey — **CB member**
www.georgian.edu — **CB code: 2274**

- Private 4-year university and liberal arts college for women affiliated with Roman Catholic Church
- Commuter campus in large town
- 1,740 degree-seeking undergraduates: 24% part-time, 92% women, 6% African American, 2% Asian American, 6% Hispanic American, 1% international
- 813 degree-seeking graduate students
- 75% of applicants admitted
- SAT or ACT (ACT writing optional) required
- 49% graduate within 6 years

General. Founded in 1908. Regionally accredited. Evening and graduate divisions coeducational. **Degrees:** 382 bachelor's awarded; master's offered. **Location:** 60 miles from New York City and Philadelphia. **Calendar:** Semester, limited summer session. **Full-time faculty:** 110 total; 84% have terminal degrees, 9% minority, 61% women. **Part-time faculty:** 188 total; 26% have terminal degrees, 6% minority, 50% women. **Class size:** 73% < 20, 27% 20-39, less than 1% 40-49. **Special facilities:** Arboretum, NASA Education Resource Center.

Freshman class profile. 532 applied, 397 admitted, 188 enrolled.

Mid 50% test scores		Rank in top tenth:	11%
SAT verbal:	420-530	End year in good standing:	97%
SAT math:	410-520	Return as sophomores:	84%
GPA 3.50 or higher:	27%	Out-of-state:	7%
GPA 3.0-3.49:	45%	Live on campus:	57%
GPA 2.0-2.99:	26%	International:	1%
Rank in top quarter:	42%		

Basis for selection. The completed high school program is reviewed for rigor of courses and grades received. Students should be completing a program of 16 academic units with grades of 2.5 or higher. Standardized test scores are required, either SAT or ACT. An ACT or 18 or higher or SAT score (CR+M) 860 or higher is required for regular acceptance. Students not meeting the criteria are referred to a faculty committee for review. **Homeschooled:** Statement describing homeschool structure and mission required.

High school preparation. 16 units required. Required units include English 4, mathematics 2, history 1, (laboratory 1), foreign language 2 and academic electives 6.

2005-2006 Annual costs. Tuition/fees: $19,100. Room/board: $7,600. Books/supplies: $1,000. Personal expenses: $2,000.

2004-2005 Financial aid. Need-based: Average need met was 56%. Average scholarship/grant was $10,036; average loan $2,920. 53% of total undergraduate aid awarded as scholarships/grants, 47% as loans/jobs. **Non-need-based:** Awarded to 213 full-time undergraduates, including 71 freshmen. Scholarships awarded for academics, alumni affiliation, art, athletics, leadership, minority status, music/drama, religious affiliation.

Application procedures. Admission: Closing date 8/1 (receipt date). $40 fee, may be waived for applicants with need. Application may be submitted online. Admission notification on a rolling basis beginning on or about 10/1. Must reply by May 1 or within 2 week(s) if notified thereafter. **Financial aid:** Priority date 3/1; no closing date. FAFSA, institutional form required. Applicants notified on a rolling basis starting 2/1; must reply within 2 week(s) of notification.

Academics. Special study options: Accelerated study, combined bachelor's/graduate degree, distance learning, double major, dual enrollment of high school students, ESL, independent study, internships, liberal arts/career combination, study abroad, teacher certification program. **Credit/placement by examination:** AP, CLEP, institutional tests. 30 credit hours maximum toward bachelor's degree. **Support services:** Learning center, reduced course load, remedial instruction, study skills assistance, tutoring.

Majors. Biology: General, biochemistry. **Business:** Accounting, business admin. **Communications:** General. **Computer sciences:** General. **Education:** Elementary, special. **English:** English lit. **Foreign languages:** Spanish. **History:** General. **Interdisciplinary:** Natural sciences. **Liberal arts:** Arts/sciences, humanities. **Math:** General. **Philosophy/religion:** Religion. **Physical sciences:** Chemistry, physics. **Protective services:** Law enforcement admin. **Psychology:** General. **Public administration:** Social work. **Social sciences:** Sociology. **Visual/performing arts:** Art, art history/conservation, studio arts.

Most popular majors. Business/marketing 12%, education 35%, English 6%, liberal arts 8%, psychology 14%.

Computing on campus. 180 workstations in dormitories, library, computer center. Dormitories wired for high-speed internet access and linked to campus network. Commuter students can connect to campus network. Online course registration, online library, helpline, wireless network available.

Student life. **Freshman orientation:** Available. Held the weekend before classes begin. Includes academic, educational, social programs. Cost: $50 spring semester, $100 fall semester. **Policies:** Freshmen permitted cars on campus. **Housing:** Guaranteed on-campus for all undergraduates. Substance-free housing available. $250 deposit, deadline 5/1. **Activities:** Bands, choral groups, literary magazine, music ensembles, student government, student newspaper, Council for Exceptional Children, Sisters United, Re-Entry Women's Club, Campus Ministry, Alliance Francaise de Georgian Court College, Circle K, Court Keys, Amnesty International, Safe Zone.

Athletics. NCAA. **Intercollegiate:** Basketball W, cross-country W, lacrosse W, soccer W, softball W, tennis W, volleyball W. **Team name:** Lions.

Student services. Campus ministries, career counseling, financial aid counseling, health services, personal counseling. **Physically disabled:** Services for visually, speech, hearing impaired.

Contact. E-mail: admissions@georgian.edu
Phone: (732) 364-2200 ext. 2760 Toll-free number: (800) 458-8422
Fax: (732) 987-2000
Kathie DeBona, Director of Admissions, Georgian Court University, 900 Lakewood Avenue, Lakewood, NJ 08701-2697

Kean University

Union, New Jersey — **CB member**
www.kean.edu — **CB code: 2517**

- Public 4-year university and liberal arts college
- Commuter campus in small city
- 9,612 degree-seeking undergraduates: 22% part-time, 63% women, 21% African American, 6% Asian American, 20% Hispanic American, 2% international
- 1,957 degree-seeking graduate students
- 71% of applicants admitted
- SAT or ACT (ACT writing optional), application essay required
- 45% graduate within 6 years

General. Founded in 1855. Regionally accredited. **Degrees:** 1,802 bachelor's awarded; master's offered. **ROTC:** Army, Air Force. **Location:** 12 miles from New York City. **Calendar:** Semester, limited summer session. **Full-time faculty:** 382 total; 87% have terminal degrees, 26% minority, 46% women. **Part-time faculty:** 778 total; 23% minority, 50% women. **Class size:** 45% < 20, 55% 20-39, less than 1% 40-49.

Freshman class profile. 4,289 applied, 3,039 admitted, 1,432 enrolled.

Mid 50% test scores		**Rank in top quarter:**	22%
SAT verbal:	430-510	**Rank in top tenth:**	7%
SAT math:	430-530	**Return as sophomores:**	77%
GPA 3.50 or higher:	13%	**Out-of-state:**	2%
GPA 3.0-3.49:	31%	**Live on campus:**	34%
GPA 2.0-2.99:	53%	**International:**	1%

Basis for selection. High school GPA at or above 2.50, test scores, counselor recommendations important. Consideration given to military service, work, personal life experiences. Non-U.S. educated applicants are evaluated based upon academic record in home country. If needed, applicants are advised of specific additional requirements, i.e. external evaluations.

High school preparation. 16 units required. Required and recommended units include English 4, mathematics 3-4, social studies 2, history 2, science 2 (laboratory 2), foreign language 2 and academic electives 5.

2005-2006 Annual costs. Tuition/fees: $7,507; $10,139 out-of-state. Room/board: $8,374.

2005-2006 Financial aid. **Need-based:** 1,167 full-time freshmen applied for aid; 841 were judged to have need; 806 of these received aid. Average need met was 54%. Average scholarship/grant was $6,091; average loan $2,688. 53% of total undergraduate aid awarded as scholarships/grants, 47% as loans/jobs. **Non-need-based:** Awarded to 116 full-time undergraduates, including 59 freshmen. Scholarships awarded for academics, alumni affiliation, art, leadership, music/drama.

Application procedures. **Admission:** Priority date 5/1; deadline 5/31 (postmark date). $50 fee, may be waived for applicants with need. Application may be submitted online. Admission notification on a rolling basis beginning on or about 11/1. Must reply by May 1 or within 2 week(s) if notified thereafter. **Financial aid:** Priority date 3/15; no closing date. FAFSA required. Applicants notified on a rolling basis starting 3/15; must reply by 5/1.

Academics. **Special study options:** Accelerated study, combined bachelor's/graduate degree, cooperative education, cross-registration, distance learning, double major, dual enrollment of high school students, ESL, honors, independent study, internships, liberal arts/career combination, study abroad, teacher certification program, Washington semester, weekend college. 2-year bachelor's degree program for RNs, foreign transfer programs, Travelearn. **Credit/placement by examination:** AP, CLEP, IB, SAT, institutional tests. 46 credit hours maximum toward bachelor's degree. **Support services:** Learning center, pre-admission summer program, reduced course load, remedial instruction, study skills assistance, tutoring, writing center.

Majors. **Biology:** General. **Business:** Accounting, business admin, finance, marketing. **Communications:** General. **Communications technology:** Printing management. **Computer sciences:** General, networking. **Education:** Elementary, kindergarten/preschool, music, physical, special, speech, technology/industrial arts. **Engineering technology:** Electrical, manufacturing. **English:** English lit. **Foreign languages:** Spanish. **Health:** Clinical lab science, medical records admin. **History:** General. **Liberal arts:** Arts/sciences. **Math:** General. **Parks/recreation:** Facilities management. **Physical sciences:** Chemistry, geology. **Protective services:** Law enforcement admin. **Psychology:** General. **Public administration:** General, social work. **Social sciences:** Economics, political science, sociology. **Visual/performing arts:** Art, art history/conservation, design, dramatic, industrial design, interior design, studio arts.

Most popular majors. Business/marketing 24%, education 22%, psychology 9%.

Computing on campus. 1,650 workstations in dormitories, library, computer center, student center. Dormitories wired for high-speed internet access and linked to campus network. Commuter students can connect to campus network. Online course registration, helpline, repair service, student web hosting available.

Student life. **Freshman orientation:** Mandatory. Preregistration for classes offered. One-on-one tour of campus, group tours, one credit freshman seminar. **Housing:** Coed dorms, special housing for disabled, apartments, substance-free housing available. $100 nonrefundable deposit, deadline 5/1. **Activities:** Jazz band, choral groups, dance, drama, literary magazine, music ensembles, musical theater, radio station, student government, student newspaper, TV station, Association of Latin American Students, Intervarsity Christian Fellowship, Il Circolo Italiano, Students for Solidarity and Justice, African students association, Jewish culture club, Circle K International, Muslim student association, political science student association, Korean student association.

Athletics. NCAA. **Intercollegiate:** Baseball M, basketball, cross-country, field hockey W, football (tackle) M, lacrosse, soccer, softball W, tennis W, track and field, volleyball W. **Intramural:** Basketball, cheerleading, skiing, softball, swimming, table tennis, tennis, volleyball, weight lifting. **Team name:** Cougars.

Student services. Adult student services, alcohol/substance abuse counseling, campus ministries, career counseling, services for economically disadvantaged, student employment services, financial aid counseling, health services, minority student services, on-campus daycare, personal counseling, placement for graduates, veterans' counselor, women's services. **Physically disabled:** Services for visually, speech, hearing impaired. **Learning disabled:** Comprehensive services available.

Contact. E-mail: admitme@kean.edu
Phone: (908) 737-7100 Fax: (908) 737-7105
Audley Bridges, Director of Admissions, Kean University, 1000 Morris Avenue, Union, NJ 07083-0411

Monmouth University

West Long Branch, New Jersey — **CB member**
www.monmouth.edu — **CB code: 2416**

- Private 4-year university
- Residential campus in small town
- 4,513 degree-seeking undergraduates: 9% part-time, 58% women, 4% African American, 2% Asian American, 4% Hispanic American
- 1,621 degree-seeking graduate students
- 69% of applicants admitted
- SAT or ACT with writing required
- 55% graduate within 6 years

General. Founded in 1933. Regionally accredited. **Degrees:** 904 bachelor's, 6 associate awarded; master's offered. **ROTC:** Air Force. **Location:** 50 miles from New York City, 75 miles from Philadelphia. **Calendar:** Semester, limited summer session. **Full-time faculty:** 246 total; 77% have terminal degrees, 18% minority, 52% women. **Part-time faculty:** 267 total; 19% have terminal degrees, 4% minority, 46% women. **Class size:** 42% < 20, 58% 20-39, less than 1% 40-49, less than 1% 50-99. **Special facilities:** Multi-media communications center with TV and radio station, sculpture garden, ice house-gallery, theater.

Freshman class profile. 5,089 applied, 3,504 admitted, 943 enrolled.

Mid 50% test scores		**Rank in top quarter:**	33%
SAT verbal:	490-570	**Rank in top tenth:**	11%
SAT math:	500-590	**End year in good standing:**	95%
ACT:	20-26	**Return as sophomores:**	75%
GPA 3.50 or higher:	23%	**Out-of-state:**	12%
GPA 3.0-3.49:	40%	**Live on campus:**	80%
GPA 2.0-2.99:	37%		

Basis for selection. Minimum 950 SAT (exclusive of Writing) and 2.25 high school GPA required for consideration for admission. Resume of activities including community involvement and leadership positions required; audition recommended for music programs; portfolio recommended for art programs. **Homeschooled:** State high school equivalency certificate required.

High school preparation. College-preparatory program required. 16 units required; 20 recommended. Required and recommended units include English 4, mathematics 3, social studies 2, history 2, science 2 (laboratory 1), foreign language 2 and academic electives 5.

2005-2006 Annual costs. Tuition/fees: $20,684. Room/board: $8,092. Books/supplies: $900. Personal expenses: $1,830.

2004-2005 Financial aid. **Need-based:** 764 full-time freshmen applied for aid; 763 were judged to have need; 763 of these received aid. Average need met was 78%. Average scholarship/grant was $9,050; average loan $3,012. 35% of total undergraduate aid awarded as scholarships/grants, 65% as loans/jobs. **Non-need-based:** Awarded to 3,159 full-time undergraduates, including 1,008 freshmen. Scholarships awarded for academics, alumni affiliation, art, athletics, leadership.

Application procedures. **Admission:** Priority date 12/15; deadline 3/1 (receipt date). $35 fee, may be waived for applicants with need. Application may be submitted online. Admission notification 4/1. Must reply by 5/1. **Financial aid:** No deadline. FAFSA required. Applicants notified on a rolling basis starting 2/1; must reply within 2 week(s) of notification.

Academics. **Special study options:** Accelerated study, combined bachelor's/graduate degree, cooperative education, cross-registration, double major, dual enrollment of high school students, honors, independent study, internships, liberal arts/career combination, student-designed major, study abroad, teacher certification program, Washington semester. **Credit/placement by examination:** AP, CLEP, IB, institutional tests. 30 credit hours maximum toward bachelor's degree. AP credit awarded only for institutional course equivalents. **Support services:** Learning center, reduced course load, remedial instruction, study skills assistance, tutoring, writing center.

Majors. **Biology:** General, environmental. **Business:** Accounting, business admin, finance, international, managerial economics, marketing. **Communications:** General. **Computer sciences:** General. **Education:** General. **Engineering:** Software. **English:** English lit. **Foreign languages:** General. **Health:** Clinical lab science, nursing (RN). **History:** General. **Math:** General. **Physical sciences:** Chemistry. **Protective services:** Criminal justice. **Psychology:** General. **Public administration:** Social work. **Social sciences:** General, anthropology, political science. **Visual/performing arts:** Art, studio arts.

Most popular majors. Business/marketing 29%, communications/journalism 17%, education 18%, psychology 7%, visual/performing arts 6%.

Computing on campus. 698 workstations in dormitories, library, computer center, student center. Dormitories wired for high-speed internet access and linked to campus network. Commuter students can connect to campus network. Online library, helpline, student web hosting, wireless network available.

Student life. **Freshman orientation:** Mandatory, $100 fee. Preregistration for classes offered. 3-day program held weekend before upperclassmen return in the fall. **Policies:** No one may associate with a fraternity or sorority who has not successfully completed at least 12 credit hours at Monmouth University. Students must have a minimum 2.2 cumulative GPA and be registered full-time. Transfer students taking 12 or more credits may also associate. Freshmen permitted cars on campus. **Housing:** Coed dorms, apartments, substance-free housing available. $150 deposit. **Activities:** Bands, choral groups, dance, drama, literary magazine, music ensembles, musical theater, radio station, student government, student newspaper, TV station, Hillel, Christian Ambassadors, Catholic center, African-American student union, Latin American club, international club, Circle K, Rotaract Club, alternative lifestyles clubs (including gay, lesbian, bisexual), H.O.P.E. (environmental issues).

Athletics. NCAA. **Intercollegiate:** Baseball M, basketball, cross-country, field hockey W, football (tackle) M, golf, lacrosse W, sailing, soccer, softball W, tennis, track and field. **Intramural:** Badminton, basketball, football (non-tackle), soccer, softball, tennis, volleyball, water polo. **Team name:** Hawks.

Student services. Adult student services, alcohol/substance abuse counseling, campus ministries, career counseling, services for economically disadvantaged, student employment services, financial aid counseling, health services, legal services, personal counseling, placement for graduates, veterans' counselor, women's services. **Physically disabled:** Services for visually, speech, hearing impaired.

Contact. E-mail: admission@monmouth.edu
Phone: (732) 571-3456 Toll-free number: (800) 543-9671
Fax: (732) 263-5166
Lauren Cifelli, Director of Undergraduate Admission, Monmouth University, 400 Cedar Avenue, West Long Branch, NJ 07764-1898

Montclair State University

Upper Montclair, New Jersey — **CB member**
www.montclair.edu — **CB code: 2520**

- Public 4-year university
- Residential campus in large town
- 12,007 degree-seeking undergraduates: 18% part-time, 61% women, 10% African American, 6% Asian American, 17% Hispanic American, 3% international
- 2,451 degree-seeking graduate students
- 54% of applicants admitted
- SAT required
- 58% graduate within 6 years

General. Founded in 1908. Regionally accredited. Includes Institute for the Humanities, Institute for the Advancement of Philosophy for Children, Institute for Critical Thinking, New Jersey School of Conservation in Stokes State Forest, Branchville, and Center for Continuing Education. **Degrees:** 2,211 bachelor's awarded; master's, doctoral offered. **Location:** 14 miles from New York City. **Calendar:** Semester, limited summer session. **Full-time faculty:** 477 total; 94% have terminal degrees, 24% minority, 44% women. **Part-time faculty:** 695 total; 7% have terminal degrees, 12% minority, 55% women. **Class size:** 201% < 20, 581% 20-39, 13% 40-49, 13% 50-99, 2% >100.

Freshman class profile. 8,877 applied, 4,783 admitted, 1,944 enrolled.

Mid 50% test scores		**Return as sophomores:**	82%
SAT verbal:	470-560	**Out-of-state:**	3%
SAT math:	490-570	**Live on campus:**	53%
Rank in top quarter:	47%	**International:**	2%
Rank in top tenth:	18%		

Basis for selection. School achievement record most important. Extracurricular activities, test scores, community activities also important. Consideration given to disadvantaged applicants. Interview required for art, music, music therapy, speech, theater, and dance programs; audition required for dance, music, speech, theater programs; portfolio required for art programs.

High school preparation. 16 units required. Required units include English 4, mathematics 3, social studies 2, science 2 (laboratory 2), foreign language 2 and academic electives 3. 4 mathematics (including trigonometry) required of computer science majors. Algebra II required for business administration majors. 3 additional units in English, social studies, science, mathematics, or foreign language required.

2005-2006 Annual costs. Tuition/fees: $7,570; $12,018 out-of-state. Room/board: $8,618. Books/supplies: $800. Personal expenses: $1,500.

2005-2006 Financial aid. **Need-based:** 1,152 full-time freshmen applied for aid; 939 were judged to have need; 804 of these received aid. Average need met was 53%. Average scholarship/grant was $5,603; average loan $2,760. 49% of total undergraduate aid awarded as scholarships/grants, 51% as loans/jobs. **Non-need-based:** Awarded to 814 full-time undergraduates, including 166 freshmen. Scholarships awarded for academics, alumni affiliation, art, leadership, minority status, music/drama, religious affiliation, ROTC, state residency.

Application procedures. **Admission:** Closing date 3/1 (postmark date). $55 fee, may be waived for applicants with need. Application may be submitted online. Admission notification on a rolling basis beginning on or about 10/1. Must reply by 5/1. Immediate decision process available to seniors at some local high schools. **Financial aid:** Priority date 3/1; no closing date. FAFSA required. Applicants notified on a rolling basis starting 4/1; must reply within 2 week(s) of notification.

Academics. **Special study options:** Combined bachelor's/graduate degree, cooperative education, double major, ESL, honors, independent study, internships, study abroad, teacher certification program, Washington semester. Joint admission with UMDNJ. **Credit/placement by examination:** AP, CLEP, institutional tests. 24 credit hours maximum toward bachelor's degree. **Support services:** Learning center, pre-admission summer program, reduced course load, remedial instruction, tutoring.

Honors college/program. Admission to Honors Program as freshman requires applicant to meet 2 of following criteria; rank in top 10 percent in high school class; score of at least 600 on either verbal or math SAT; combined SAT of at least 1200 (exclusive of Writing); unusual ability in creative arts or exceptional leadership or other extraordinary accomplishment.

Majors. **Area/ethnic studies:** Women's. **Biology:** General, biochemistry, molecular. **Business:** Business admin. **Communications:** Broadcast journalism, organizational. **Computer sciences:** General. **Education:** Business, health, physical, technology/industrial arts. **Family/consumer sciences:** General. **Foreign languages:** Classics, French, Italian, Latin, linguistics, Spanish. **Health:** Health services, music therapy. **History:** General. **Interdisciplinary:** Peace/conflict. **Liberal arts:** Arts/sciences. **Math:** General. **Parks/recreation:** Facilities management. **Philosophy/religion:** Philosophy, religion. **Physical sciences:** Chemistry, geology, physics. **Psychology:** General. **Social sciences:** Anthropology, economics, geography, political science, sociology. **Visual/performing arts:** Art, dance, dramatic, music performance, studio arts.

Most popular majors. Biology 6%, business/marketing 22%, English 7%, family/consumer sciences 12%, interdisciplinary studies 6%, psychology 11%, social sciences 7%, visual/performing arts 7%.

Computing on campus. 500 workstations in dormitories, library, computer center. Dormitories wired for high-speed internet access and linked to campus network. Commuter students can connect to campus network. Helpline available.

Student life. **Freshman orientation:** Mandatory, $100 fee. Preregistration for classes offered. **Policies:** Freshmen permitted cars on campus. **Housing:** Guaranteed on-campus for freshmen. Coed dorms, single-sex dorms, special housing for disabled, apartments available. $125 deposit, deadline 5/1. International students may request assignment to the international cluster apartments. **Activities:** Concert band, choral groups, drama, radio station, student government, student newspaper, Newman Center, African-American, Latin American, Jewish, and Arab student organizations, conservation club, Players, college life union board, student intramural and leisure council.

Athletics. NCAA. **Intercollegiate:** Baseball M, basketball, cross-country, diving, field hockey W, football (tackle) M, golf, lacrosse, soccer, softball W, swimming, tennis, track and field, volleyball W, wrestling M. **Intramural:** Baseball M, basketball, bowling, football (tackle) M, softball, tennis, volleyball. **Team name:** Red Hawks.

Student services. Adult student services, alcohol/substance abuse counseling, campus ministries, career counseling, services for economically disadvantaged, student employment services, financial aid counseling, health services, on-campus daycare, personal counseling, placement for graduates, veterans' counselor, women's services. **Physically disabled:** Services for visually impaired.

Contact. E-mail: undergraduate.admissions@mail.montclair.edu
Phone: (973) 655-4444 Toll-free number: (800) 331-9205
Fax: (973) 655-7700
Dennis Craig, Director of Admissions, Montclair State University, One Normal Avenue, Upper Montclair, NJ 07043-1624

New Jersey City University

Jersey City, New Jersey — **CB member**
www.njcu.edu — **CB code: 2516**

- Public 4-year liberal arts college
- Commuter campus in small city
- 5,949 degree-seeking undergraduates: 30% part-time, 63% women, 20% African American, 8% Asian American, 33% Hispanic American, 1% international
- 1,015 degree-seeking graduate students
- 54% of applicants admitted
- SAT or ACT, application essay required
- 37% graduate within 6 years

General. Founded in 1927. Regionally accredited. **Degrees:** 879 bachelor's awarded; master's offered. **Location:** 5 miles from New York City. **Calendar:** Semester, extensive summer session. **Full-time faculty:** 251 total; 79% have terminal degrees. **Part-time faculty:** 273 total. **Class size:** 59% < 20, 40% 20-39, less than 1% 40-49, less than 1% 50-99. **Special facilities:** School for multihandicapped children, performing arts center, computer technology center, cooperative education center, catalyst teaching center, media studies center.

Freshman class profile. 2,719 applied, 1,467 admitted, 690 enrolled.

Mid 50% test scores		**Live on campus:**	5%
SAT verbal:	400-500	**International:**	1%
SAT math:	410-500	**Fraternities:**	1%
Return as sophomores:	74%	**Sororities:**	1%
Out-of-state:	1%		

Basis for selection. High school courses, grades, class rank, and test scores most important, followed by essay or personal statement. Special program for educationally disadvantaged applicants available with above criteria. Interview recommended for all; audition required for music programs; portfolio recommended for art programs.

High school preparation. College-preparatory program required. Required and recommended units include English 4, mathematics 4, social studies 4, science 4 (laboratory 2-3) and foreign language 2.

2005-2006 Annual costs. Tuition/fees: $7,040; $12,080 out-of-state. Room/board: $7,306. Books/supplies: $1,600. Personal expenses: $1,600.

2004-2005 Financial aid. All financial aid based on need. 570 full-time freshmen applied for aid; 503 were judged to have need; 479 of these received aid. Average need met was 68%. Average scholarship/grant was $6,020; average loan $2,412. 64% of total undergraduate aid awarded as scholarships/grants, 36% as loans/jobs.

Application procedures. **Admission:** Closing date 4/1. $35 fee, may be waived for applicants with need. Admission notification on a rolling basis beginning on or about 1/1. Must reply by May 1 or within 3 week(s) if notified thereafter. **Financial aid:** FAFSA required. Applicants notified by 5/4.

Academics. Cooperative education placement offered in all majors. Professional diploma in school psychology offered. **Special study options:** Cooperative education, distance learning, double major, dual enrollment of high school students, ESL, honors, independent study, internships, liberal arts/career combination, study abroad, teacher certification program, Washington semester, weekend college. **Credit/placement by examination:** AP, CLEP, IB, institutional tests. 30 credit hours maximum toward bachelor's degree. **Support services:** Learning center, pre-admission summer program, reduced course load, remedial instruction, tutoring, writing center.

Majors. **Biology:** General. **Business:** Business admin. **Communications:** General. **Computer sciences:** General. **Education:** Early childhood, elementary, reading, special. **Foreign languages:** Spanish. **History:** General. **Math:** General. **Philosophy/religion:** Philosophy. **Physical sciences:** Chemistry, geology, physics. **Protective services:** Security services. **Psychology:** General. **Social sciences:** Economics, political science, sociology. **Visual/performing arts:** Art, studio arts.

Most popular majors. Business/marketing 26%, computer/information sciences 6%, education 6%, English 6%, psychology 12%, security/protective services 9%, social sciences 8%.

Computing on campus. 1,400 workstations in dormitories, library, computer center, student center. Dormitories wired for high-speed internet access and linked to campus network. Commuter students can connect to campus network. Online library, helpline available.

Student life. **Freshman orientation:** Mandatory. **Policies:** Freshmen permitted cars on campus. **Housing:** Coed dorms available. $150 deposit, deadline 8/13. **Activities:** Bands, choral groups, dance, drama, film society, music ensembles, musical theater, opera, radio station, student government, student newspaper, symphony orchestra, Campus Christian fellowship, Black Freedom Society, Latin Power Association, international student association, Africana Journal.

Athletics. NCAA. **Intercollegiate:** Baseball M, basketball, bowling W, cross-country, soccer, softball W, track and field, volleyball. **Intramural:** Basketball, bowling, golf, racquetball, soccer, softball, swimming, table tennis, tennis, volleyball, weight lifting. **Team name:** Gothic Knights.

Student services. Career counseling, student employment services, health services, on-campus daycare, personal counseling, placement for graduates, veterans' counselor, women's services. **Physically disabled:** Services for visually, speech, hearing impaired.

Contact. E-mail: admissions@njcu.edu
Phone: (201) 200-3234 Toll-free number: (888) 441-6528
Jason Hand, Director of Admissions, New Jersey City University, 2039 Kennedy Boulevard, Jersey City, NJ 07305-1597

New Jersey Institute of Technology

Newark, New Jersey **CB member**
www.njit.edu **CB code: 2513**

- Public 4-year university
- Residential campus in very large city
- 4,909 degree-seeking undergraduates: 18% part-time, 19% women, 11% African American, 21% Asian American, 13% Hispanic American, 6% international
- 2,629 degree-seeking graduate students
- 71% of applicants admitted
- SAT or ACT with writing required
- 56% graduate within 6 years

General. Founded in 1881. Regionally accredited. **Degrees:** 925 bachelor's awarded; master's, doctoral offered. **ROTC:** Army, Air Force. **Location:** 10 miles from New York City. **Calendar:** Semester, extensive summer session. **Full-time faculty:** 416 total; 100% have terminal degrees, 20% minority, 14% women. **Part-time faculty:** 238 total; 10% minority, 15% women. **Class size:** 43% < 20, 49% 20-39, 4% 40-49, 3% 50-99, less than 1% >100. **Special facilities:** Computer chip manufacturing laboratory, multi-lifecycle engineering center, numerous government and industry-sponsored research laboratories, hazardous waste management research center, "factory floor" manufacturing center, observatory.

Freshman class profile. 2,562 applied, 1,831 admitted, 762 enrolled.

Mid 50% test scores			
SAT verbal:	470-590	Out-of-state:	5%
SAT math:	540-650	Live on campus:	50%
Rank in top quarter:	50%	International:	5%
Rank in top tenth:	24%	Fraternities:	9%
Return as sophomores:	82%	Sororities:	4%

Basis for selection. Class rank, test scores, secondary school record including grades and curriculum (e.g., types of mathematics courses) most important. Grades in mathematics and science very important, especially for engineering, engineering science and computer science applicants. Essay and interview required for honors college; interview and portfolio required for architecture programs. Interview required for conditional admission, educational opportunity program.

High school preparation. 16 units required. Required and recommended units include English 4, mathematics 4, social studies 1, history 1, science 2, foreign language 2 and academic electives 2. 3 mathematics required of management majors and science, technology and society majors. One laboratory science required for management majors.

2005-2006 Annual costs. Tuition/fees: $9,822; $16,026 out-of-state. Room/board: $8,958. Books/supplies: $1,200. Personal expenses: $1,100.

2004-2005 Financial aid. Need-based: 666 full-time freshmen applied for aid; 398 were judged to have need; 398 of these received aid. Average need met was 87%. Average scholarship/grant was $4,678; average loan $2,929. 62% of total undergraduate aid awarded as scholarships/grants, 38% as loans/jobs. **Non-need-based:** Awarded to 1,514 full-time undergraduates, including 602 freshmen. Scholarships awarded for academics, alumni affiliation, art, leadership, minority status, music/drama, ROTC, state residency. **Additional information:** Extensive co-op program for all majors.

Application procedures. Admission: Closing date 4/1. $35 fee, may be waived for applicants with need. Application may be submitted online. Admission notification on a rolling basis beginning on or about 11/15. Must reply by May 1 or within 2 week(s) if notified thereafter. **Financial aid:** Priority date 3/15, closing date 5/15. FAFSA required. Applicants notified on a rolling basis starting 3/1; must reply within 2 week(s) of notification.

Academics. All freshmen given personal computers for their use while at NJIT. Numerous research opportunities available. **Special study options:** Accelerated study, combined bachelor's/graduate degree, cooperative education, cross-registration, distance learning, double major, ESL, honors, independent study, internships, study abroad. Environmental Scholars Program, Educational Opportunity Program, Career Advancement Plan (CAP), University Research Experience (URE). **Credit/placement by examination:** AP, CLEP, SAT, institutional tests. **Support services:** Learning center, pre-admission summer program, reduced course load, remedial instruction, study skills assistance, tutoring.

Majors. Architecture: Architecture. **Biology:** General. **Business:** Business admin. **Computer sciences:** General, information systems, information technology. **Conservation:** Environmental science. **Engineering:** Biomedical, chemical, civil, computer, electrical, environmental, geological, industrial, manufacturing, mechanical, science. **Engineering technology:** General. **English:** Technical writing. **History:** General. **Interdisciplinary:** Science/society. **Math:** Applied. **Physical sciences:** Chemistry, physics.

Most popular majors. Architecture 9%, business/marketing 9%, computer/information sciences 30%, engineering/engineering technologies 47%.

Computing on campus. PC or laptop required. 1,500 workstations in dormitories, library, computer center, student center. Dormitories wired for high-speed internet access and linked to campus network. Commuter students can connect to campus network. Online course registration, online library, helpline, repair service, student web hosting, wireless network available.

Student life. Freshman orientation: Mandatory. **Policies:** Freshmen permitted cars on campus. **Housing:** Coed dorms available. $100 nonrefundable deposit, deadline 6/2. **Activities:** Dance, drama, literary magazine, radio station, student government, student newspaper, Arab student association, Black student engineers association, Caribbean student association, Chinese student association, Hispanic students in technology association, Intervarsity Christian Federation, Polish student association, Islamic student association, women engineers club.

Athletics. NCAA. **Intercollegiate:** Baseball M, basketball, cross-country, fencing, soccer, swimming, tennis, volleyball. **Intramural:** Badminton, basketball, bowling, cricket, fencing, racquetball, soccer, swimming, table tennis, tennis, track and field, volleyball, weight lifting. **Team name:** Highlanders.

Student services. Alcohol/substance abuse counseling, career counseling, student employment services, health services, on-campus daycare, personal counseling, placement for graduates, veterans' counselor, women's services. **Physically disabled:** Services for visually, speech, hearing impaired.

Contact. E-mail: admissions@njit.edu
Phone: (973) 596-3300 Toll-free number: (800) 925-6548
Fax: (973) 596-3461
Kathy Kelly, Director of Admissions, New Jersey Institute of Technology, University Heights, Newark, NJ 07102

Princeton University

Princeton, New Jersey **CB member**
www.princeton.edu **CB code: 2672**

- Private 4-year university
- Residential campus in large town
- 4,710 degree-seeking undergraduates: 9% African American, 13% Asian American, 7% Hispanic American, 1% Native American, 9% international
- 1,999 graduate students
- 11% of applicants admitted
- SAT or ACT with writing, SAT Subject Tests, application essay required

General. Founded in 1746. Regionally accredited. **Degrees:** 1,122 bachelor's awarded; master's, doctoral offered. **ROTC:** Army, Air Force. **Location:** 50 miles from New York City, 45 miles from Philadelphia. **Calendar:** Semester. **Full-time faculty:** 800 total. **Part-time faculty:** 250 total. **Class size:** 74% < 20, 13% 20-39, 2% 40-49, 8% 50-99, 3% >100. **Special facilities:** Art museum with permanent collection, museum of natural history, center for energy and environmental studies, plasma physics laboratory.

Freshman class profile. 16,529 applied, 1,826 admitted, 1,230 enrolled.

Mid 50% test scores			
SAT verbal:	680-770	Return as sophomores:	98%
SAT math:	690-790	Out-of-state:	84%
Rank in top quarter:	99%	Live on campus:	100%
Rank in top tenth:	94%	International:	9%

Basis for selection. GED not accepted. School achievement record and recommendations of guidance counselor and 2 teachers very important. Test scores and essays also required of each applicant reviewed. Three SAT Subject Tests required. Interview recommended for all; audition recommended for music programs; portfolio recommended for creative writing, dance (video), visual arts programs. **Homeschooled:** Statement describing homeschool structure and mission required.

High school preparation. Recommended units include English 4, mathematics 4, social studies 2, history 2, science 3 and foreign language 4. One unit physics or chemistry (preferably both) and 4 mathematics urged for prospective engineering majors.

2006-2007 Annual costs. Tuition/fees: $33,000. Room/board: $9,200. Books/supplies: $990. Personal expenses: $2,039.

2004-2005 Financial aid. All financial aid based on need. 715 full-time freshmen applied for aid; 608 were judged to have need; 608 of these received aid. Average need met was 100%. Average scholarship/grant was $26,121. 96% of total undergraduate aid awarded as scholarships/grants, 4% as loans/jobs. **Additional information:** All aid is need based; all aid is grant money (no loans); meets full demonstrated need.

Application procedures. Admission: Closing date 1/1 (postmark date). $65 fee, may be waived for applicants with need. Application may be submitted online. Admission notification 4/1. Must reply by 5/1. **Financial aid:** Priority date 2/1; no closing date. FAFSA, institutional form required. Applicants notified by 4/1; must reply by 5/1.

Academics. Independent project in junior year and senior thesis required for graduation. **Special study options:** Cross-registration, independent study, student-designed major, study abroad, teacher certification program. Field study opportunities. **Credit/placement by examination:** AP, CLEP, IB, institutional tests. **Support services:** Learning center, pre-admission summer program, study skills assistance, tutoring, writing center.

Majors. Architecture: Architecture. **Area/ethnic studies:** East Asian, Near/Middle Eastern. **Biology:** Ecology, molecular. **Engineering:** Chemical, civil, computer, electrical, mechanical, operations research. **English:** English lit. **Foreign languages:** Classics, comparative lit, German, Italian, Slavic, Spanish. **History:** General. **Math:** General. **Philosophy/religion:** Philosophy, religion. **Physical sciences:** Astrophysics, chemistry, geology, physics. **Psychology:** General. **Public administration:** General. **Social sciences:** Anthropology, economics, political science, sociology. **Visual/performing arts:** Art history/conservation.

Most popular majors. Biology 6%, engineering/engineering technologies 16%, English 8%, psychology 6%, security/protective services 8%, social sciences 36%.

Computing on campus. 500 workstations in dormitories, library, computer center, student center. Dormitories wired for high-speed internet access and linked to campus network. Commuter students can connect to campus network. Online course registration, online library, helpline, repair service, student web hosting, wireless network available.

Student life. Freshman orientation: Mandatory. **Housing:** Guaranteed on-campus for all undergraduates. Coed dorms, single-sex dorms, special housing for disabled available. Residential colleges for freshmen and sophomores. Kosher dining facilities available. **Activities:** Bands, choral groups, dance, drama, literary magazine, music ensembles, musical theater, opera, radio station, student government, student newspaper, symphony orchestra, over 200 student organizations available.

Athletics. NCAA. **Intercollegiate:** Baseball M, basketball, cross-country, diving, fencing, field hockey W, football (tackle), golf, ice hockey, lacrosse, rowing (crew), soccer, softball W, squash, swimming, tennis, track and field, volleyball, water polo, wrestling M. **Intramural:** Badminton, basketball, bowling, golf, ice hockey, soccer, softball, tennis, water polo. **Team name:** Tigers.

Student services. Alcohol/substance abuse counseling, campus ministries, career counseling, student employment services, financial aid counseling, health services, minority student services, personal counseling, placement for graduates, women's services. **Physically disabled:** Services for visually, speech, hearing impaired.

Contact. E-mail: uaoffice@Princeton.edu
Phone: (609) 258-3060 Fax: (609) 258-6743
Janet Rapelye, Dean of Admission, Princeton University, Box 430, Princeton, NJ 08544-0430

Rabbi Jacob Joseph School
Edison, New Jersey

- Private 4-year rabbinical college

General. Accredited by AARTS.

Annual costs/financial aid. Comprehensive fee (2005-2006): $11,350.

Contact. Phone: (732) 985-6533
One Plainfield Avenue, Edison, NJ 08817

Rabbinical College of America
Morristown, New Jersey
CB code: 1546

- Private 4-year rabbinical college for men affiliated with Jewish faith
- Residential campus in large town
- 286 degree-seeking undergraduates
- 100% of applicants admitted

General. Founded in 1956. Accredited by AARTS. Affiliate of world-wide Lubavitch movement. **Degrees:** 76 bachelor's awarded. **Location:** One mile from downtown, 35 miles from New York City. **Calendar:** Semester, extensive summer session. **Full-time faculty:** 15 total.

Freshman class profile. 31 applied, 31 admitted, 31 enrolled.

Basis for selection. Applicants must demonstrate interest, ability, and perseverance necessary for successful completion of required courses. Recommendation required, preferably from local rabbi. Interview recommended.

2006-2007 Annual costs. Tuition/fees: $8,700. Room/board: $6,600.

Application procedures. Admission: Closing date 9/1. $150 fee. Admission notification on a rolling basis. **Financial aid:** Priority date 10/20; no closing date. Applicants notified on a rolling basis starting 10/31.

Academics. New Direction program for young Jewish men with little or no Jewish education. Program ranges from basics of Judaism to Talmud and Chassidic philosophy. **Special study options:** Internships. **Credit/placement by examination:** CLEP. **Support services:** Pre-admission summer program, remedial instruction.

Majors. Philosophy/religion: Judaic, religion.

Student life. Policies: Religious observance required. **Housing:** Guaranteed on-campus for all undergraduates. Apartments available. **Activities:** Student newspaper, community activities.

Student services. Personal counseling.

Contact. Phone: (973) 267-9404 Fax: (973) 267-5208
Israel Teitelbaum, Registrar, Rabbinical College of America, 226 Sussex Avenue, CN 1996, Morristown, NJ 07962-1996

Ramapo College of New Jersey
Mahwah, New Jersey — **CB member**
www.ramapo.edu — **CB code: 2884**

- Public 4-year liberal arts college
- Residential campus in large town
- 4,860 degree-seeking undergraduates: 14% part-time, 60% women, 7% African American, 4% Asian American, 8% Hispanic American, 3% international
- 226 degree-seeking graduate students
- 41% of applicants admitted
- SAT, application essay required
- 59% graduate within 6 years

General. Founded in 1969. Regionally accredited. **Degrees:** 1,046 bachelor's awarded; master's offered. **ROTC:** Air Force. **Location:** 35 miles from New York City. **Calendar:** Semester, extensive summer session. **Full-time faculty:** 187 total; 91% have terminal degrees, 20% minority, 42% women. **Part-time faculty:** 246 total. **Class size:** 38% < 20, 61% 20-39, less than 1% 40-49, less than 1% 50-99. **Special facilities:** International telecommunications center, electron microscope, Holocaust center, performing arts center, arts and lecture series, international and intercultural education office, environmental studies/alternate energy center.

Freshman class profile. 4,507 applied, 1,860 admitted, 748 enrolled.

Mid 50% test scores		**Rank in top quarter:**	80%
SAT verbal:	540-620	**Rank in top tenth:**	31%
SAT math:	550-640	**Return as sophomores:**	89%
GPA 3.50 or higher:	56%	**Out-of-state:**	3%
GPA 3.0-3.49:	36%	**Live on campus:**	89%
GPA 2.0-2.99:	8%	**International:**	3%

Basis for selection. School achievement record, test scores most important. Applicants should rank in top 25 percent of high school class. Ramapo College uses ESL or TOEFL assessment to determine English language proficiency. Certain majors have additional entrance requirements.

High school preparation. 18 units required. Required and recommended units include English 4, mathematics 3, social studies 3, science 3 (laboratory 3), foreign language 2 and academic electives 3. Science units must include 3 units of lab.

2005-2006 Annual costs. Tuition/fees: $8,791; $13,708 out-of-state. Room/board: $9,464. Books/supplies: $1,000. Personal expenses: $1,500.

2004-2005 Financial aid. **Need-based:** 574 full-time freshmen applied for aid; 391 were judged to have need; 367 of these received aid. Average need met was 86%. Average scholarship/grant was $8,904; average loan $2,579. 47% of total undergraduate aid awarded as scholarships/grants, 53% as loans/jobs. **Non-need-based:** Awarded to 1,347 full-time undergraduates, including 310 freshmen. Scholarships awarded for academics, state residency.

Application procedures. **Admission:** Closing date 3/1. $55 fee, may be waived for applicants with need. Application may be submitted online. Admission notification on a rolling basis beginning on or about 11/15. Must reply by 5/1. **Financial aid:** Priority date 3/1; no closing date. FAFSA required. Applicants notified on a rolling basis starting 4/1; must reply by 5/1 or within 2 week(s) of notification.

Academics. Programs in liberal arts and sciences as well as in business and other professional studies offered within liberal arts context. Thematic learning communities present curriculum of traditional majors and innovative programs in interdisciplinary fashion. **Special study options:** Accelerated study, combined bachelor's/graduate degree, cooperative education, double major, dual enrollment of high school students, ESL, exchange student, external degree, honors, independent study, internships, liberal arts/career combination, student-designed major, study abroad, teacher certification program. **Credit/placement by examination:** AP, CLEP, IB, SAT. 75 credit hours maximum toward bachelor's degree. **Support services:** Learning center, pre-admission summer program, reduced course load, remedial instruction, study skills assistance, tutoring, writing center.

Majors. **Area/ethnic studies:** American. **Biology:** General, biochemistry, bioinformatics. **Business:** Accounting, business admin, international. **Communications:** General. **Computer sciences:** General, information systems. **Conservation:** Environmental science, environmental studies. **Foreign languages:** Comparative lit, Spanish. **Health:** Clinical lab science, health services, nursing (RN). **History:** General. **Interdisciplinary:** Biological/physical sciences, global studies. **Legal studies:** General. **Liberal arts:** Arts/sciences. **Math:** General. **Physical sciences:** Chemistry, physics. **Psychology:** General. **Public administration:** Social work. **Social sciences:** Economics, political science, sociology. **Visual/performing arts:** General, dramatic, multimedia.

Most popular majors. Biology 25%, business/marketing 18%, English 13%, social sciences 14%, visual/performing arts 11%.

Computing on campus. 605 workstations in dormitories, library, computer center. Dormitories wired for high-speed internet access and linked to campus network. Commuter students can connect to campus network. Online course registration, online library, helpline, repair service, student web hosting, wireless network available.

Student life. **Freshman orientation:** Mandatory, $130 fee. Preregistration for classes offered. **Policies:** Freshmen permitted cars on campus. **Housing:** Guaranteed on-campus for freshmen. Coed dorms, special housing for disabled, apartments, cooperative housing, substance-free housing available. $200 deposit, deadline 5/1. **Activities:** Choral groups, dance, drama, film society, literary magazine, music ensembles, musical theater, radio station, student government, student newspaper, TV station, Organization for African Unity, Organization of Latin Unity, Hillel, international student organization, Ramapo Pride, women's center, veterans' association, resident student association, returning adult students organization, Future Educators of America at Ramapo (FEAR).

Athletics. NCAA. **Intercollegiate:** Baseball M, basketball, cheerleading M, cross-country, field hockey W, soccer, softball W, tennis, track and field, volleyball. **Intramural:** Basketball, bowling, softball, swimming, tennis, track and field, volleyball. **Team name:** Roadrunners.

Student services. Adult student services, alcohol/substance abuse counseling, campus ministries, career counseling, services for economically disadvantaged, student employment services, financial aid counseling, health services, minority student services, personal counseling, placement for graduates, veterans' counselor, women's services. **Physically disabled:** Services for visually, speech, hearing impaired. **Learning disabled:** Comprehensive services available.

Contact. E-mail: admissions@ramapo.edu
Phone: (201) 684-7300 Toll-free number: (800) 972-6276
Fax: (201) 684-7964
Nancy Jaeger, Director of Admissions, Ramapo College of New Jersey, 505 Ramapo Valley Road, Mahwah, NJ 07430-1680

Richard Stockton College of New Jersey

Pomona, New Jersey — **CB member**
www.stockton.edu — **CB code: 2889**

- Public 4-year liberal arts college
- Residential campus in large town
- 6,371 degree-seeking undergraduates: 12% part-time, 58% women, 8% African American, 4% Asian American, 6% Hispanic American
- 340 degree-seeking graduate students
- 52% of applicants admitted
- SAT or ACT (ACT writing optional), application essay required
- 63% graduate within 6 years

General. Founded in 1969. Regionally accredited. Preceptorial advising, opportunities for specialized research, extensive Washington internship available. **Degrees:** 1,639 bachelor's awarded; master's offered. **Location:** 12 miles from Atlantic City, 50 miles from Philadelphia. **Calendar:** Semester, extensive summer session. **Full-time faculty:** 227 total. **Part-time faculty:** 234 total. **Class size:** 29% < 20, 64% 20-39, 4% 40-49, 2% 50-99, less than 1% >100. **Special facilities:** 400-acre outdoor research laboratory with arboretum, forestry nursery, ecologic succession plots and study preserve, child care center, interdisciplinary natural sciences laboratory, observatory, Holocaust center, geothermal plant, 7-acre marine science field station, ITV classroom, performing arts theater, hospital located on college grounds.

Freshman class profile. 3,448 applied, 1,777 admitted, 812 enrolled.

Mid 50% test scores			
SAT verbal:	510-590	GPA 2.0-2.99:	23%
SAT math:	520-610	Rank in top quarter:	56%
ACT:	21-26	Rank in top tenth:	15%
GPA 3.50 or higher:	46%	Return as sophomores:	83%
GPA 3.0-3.49:	28%	Out-of-state:	3%
		Live on campus:	86%

Basis for selection. Secondary school record, class rank, test scores most important; essay, recommendations, extracurricular activities also important; interview, work experience considered. **Homeschooled:** Statement describing homeschool structure and mission, transcript of courses and grades required.

High school preparation. College-preparatory program required. 16 units required. Required units include English 4, mathematics 3, social studies 2, science 2 (laboratory 2) and academic electives 5.

2005-2006 Annual costs. Tuition/fees: $7,870; $11,055 out-of-state. Room/board: $8,109. Books/supplies: $900. Personal expenses: $1,115.

2005-2006 Financial aid. **Need-based:** 645 full-time freshmen applied for aid; 461 were judged to have need; 445 of these received aid. Average need met was 62%. Average scholarship/grant was $6,512; average loan $3,042. 37% of total undergraduate aid awarded as scholarships/grants, 63% as loans/jobs. **Non-need-based:** Awarded to 834 full-time undergraduates, including 219 freshmen. Scholarships awarded for academics, art, leadership, minority status, music/drama, state residency.

Application procedures. **Admission:** Priority date 2/1; deadline 5/1 (postmark date). $50 fee, may be waived for applicants with need. Application may be submitted online. Admission notification on a rolling basis beginning on or about 11/1. Must reply by May 1 or within 2 week(s) if notified thereafter. **Financial aid:** Priority date 3/1; no closing date. FAFSA required. Applicants notified on a rolling basis starting 4/1; must reply within 2 week(s) of notification.

Academics. **Special study options:** Combined bachelor's/graduate degree, cross-registration, distance learning, double major, dual enrollment of high school students, honors, independent study, internships, liberal arts/career combination, semester at sea, student-designed major, study abroad, teacher certification program, Washington semester. Dual degree bachelor's program in engineering with Rutgers University and New Jersey Institute of Technology. **Credit/placement by examination:** AP, CLEP, IB, SAT, ACT, institutional tests. 32 credit hours maximum toward bachelor's degree. **Support services:** Learning center, pre-admission summer program, reduced course load, remedial instruction, study skills assistance, tutoring, writing center.

Majors. **Biology:** General, biochemistry, marine. **Communications:** General. **Computer sciences:** Information systems. **Conservation:** Environmental studies. **Education:** Multi-level teacher. **English:** English lit. **Foreign**

languages: General. **Health:** Audiology/speech pathology, nursing (RN). **History:** General. **Liberal arts:** Arts/sciences. **Math:** General. **Philosophy/religion:** Philosophy. **Physical sciences:** Chemistry, geology, physics. **Psychology:** General. **Public administration:** Social work. **Social sciences:** Criminology, economics, political science, sociology. **Visual/performing arts:** General.

Most popular majors. Biology 8%, business/marketing 17%, education 11%, psychology 12%, social sciences 16%.

Computing on campus. 3,375 workstations in dormitories, library, computer center, student center. Dormitories wired for high-speed internet access and linked to campus network. Commuter students can connect to campus network. Online course registration, online library, helpline, student web hosting, wireless network available.

Student life. Freshman orientation: Available, $50 fee. Preregistration for classes offered. Program includes parents' sessions. **Policies:** Freshmen permitted cars on campus. **Housing:** Guaranteed on-campus for freshmen. Coed dorms, special housing for disabled, substance-free housing available. $150 deposit, deadline 5/1. Academic units available. Wellness (substance free) housing. **Activities:** Bands, choral groups, dance, drama, literary magazine, music ensembles, musical theater, radio station, student government, student newspaper, TV station, Books Without Borders, Unified Black Students Society, Christian Fellowship, Jewish Student Union, Campus Religious Council, Circle K International, CHANGE, Amnesty International, Coalition for Women's Rights, Certified Peer Educators.

Athletics. NCAA. **Intercollegiate:** Baseball M, basketball, cheerleading, cross-country, field hockey W, lacrosse M, rowing (crew) W, soccer, softball W, tennis W, track and field, volleyball W. **Intramural:** Basketball, football (non-tackle), soccer, softball, volleyball. **Team name:** Ospreys.

Student services. Adult student services, alcohol/substance abuse counseling, campus ministries, career counseling, student employment services, health services, on-campus daycare, personal counseling, placement for graduates, veterans' counselor. **Physically disabled:** Services for visually, speech, hearing impaired. **Learning disabled:** Comprehensive services available.

Contact. E-mail: admissions@stockton.edu
Phone: (609) 652-4261 Fax: (609) 748-5541
Sal Catalfamo, Dean of Enrollment Management, Richard Stockton College of New Jersey, Jim Leeds Road, Pomona, NJ 08240-0195

Rider University

Lawrenceville, New Jersey — **CB member**
www.rider.edu — **CB code: 2758**

- Private 4-year university
- Residential campus in large town
- 4,139 degree-seeking undergraduates: 13% part-time, 59% women, 9% African American, 3% Asian American, 5% Hispanic American, 2% international
- 923 degree-seeking graduate students
- 81% of applicants admitted
- SAT or ACT (ACT writing recommended), application essay required
- 55% graduate within 6 years; 16% enter graduate study

General. Founded in 1865. Regionally accredited. Westminster Choir College, in Princeton, is one of the institution's 4 colleges. **Degrees:** 851 bachelor's, 4 associate awarded; master's offered. **ROTC:** Army. **Location:** 5 miles from Princeton, 3 miles from Trenton. **Calendar:** Semester, extensive summer session. **Full-time faculty:** 234 total; 96% have terminal degrees, 13% minority, 39% women. **Part-time faculty:** 267 total; 47% have terminal degrees, 14% minority, 58% women. **Class size:** 47% < 20, 47% 20-39, 4% 40-49, 2% 50-99, less than 1% >100. **Special facilities:** Cross-country trail, Holocaust/genocide center.

Freshman class profile. 4,463 applied, 3,629 admitted, 948 enrolled.

Mid 50% test scores			
SAT verbal:	470-570	Rank in top quarter:	34%
SAT math:	480-580	Rank in top tenth:	10%
ACT:	20-24	Return as sophomores:	78%
GPA 3.50 or higher:	23%	Live on campus:	80%
GPA 3.0-3.49:	37%	International:	1%
GPA 2.0-2.99:	39%	Fraternities:	10%
		Sororities:	12%

Basis for selection. High school curriculum most important, followed by GPA, test scores. Extracurricular activities, interview considered. TOEFL required for international applicants. Interview recommended for all; audition required for music program with Westminster Choir College.

High school preparation. College-preparatory program required. 16 units required. Required and recommended units include English 4, mathematics 3-4, social studies 2, history 2, science 4 (laboratory 2) and foreign language 2. Algebra I and II and geometry required for business administration, science, mathematics majors.

2005-2006 Annual costs. Tuition/fees: $23,470. Room/board: $8,840. Books/supplies: $1,000. Personal expenses: $2,000.

2004-2005 Financial aid. Need-based: 808 full-time freshmen applied for aid; 666 were judged to have need; 666 of these received aid. Average need met was 70%. Average scholarship/grant was $12,707; average loan $3,214. 54% of total undergraduate aid awarded as scholarships/grants, 46% as loans/jobs. **Non-need-based:** Awarded to 1,137 full-time undergraduates, including 294 freshmen. Scholarships awarded for academics, alumni affiliation, art, athletics, minority status, music/drama, state residency.

Application procedures. Admission: No deadline. $45 fee, may be waived for applicants with need. Application may be submitted online. Admission notification on a rolling basis beginning on or about 12/1. Must reply by May 1 or within 4 week(s) if notified thereafter. Notification of admission decision sent within 3-4 weeks of receiving application. **Financial aid:** Priority date 3/1, closing date 6/1. FAFSA required. Applicants notified on a rolling basis starting 4/15.

Academics. Special study options: Accelerated study, cross-registration, double major, ESL, honors, independent study, internships, liberal arts/career combination, study abroad, teacher certification program, weekend college. **Credit/placement by examination:** AP, CLEP, SAT, institutional tests. Policy varies by major. 30 hours of credit by general examination may be counted toward degree. No limit for subject examinations. Not acceptable for last 30 credits of degree program. 4-8 AP courses (24 credits) required for sophomore standing. **Support services:** Learning center, reduced course load, remedial instruction, study skills assistance, tutoring, writing center.

Majors. Area/ethnic studies: American. **Biology:** General, biochemistry, marine. **Business:** Accounting, actuarial science, business admin, finance, human resources, international, management science, managerial economics, marketing, office management. **Communications:** General, advertising, journalism. **Computer sciences:** General. **Conservation:** Environmental science. **Education:** Business, elementary, music. **English:** English lit. **Foreign languages:** French, German, Russian, Spanish. **History:** General. **Interdisciplinary:** Biopsychology, global studies, intercultural. **Liberal arts:** Arts/sciences. **Math:** General. **Physical sciences:** Chemistry, oceanography, physics. **Psychology:** General. **Public administration:** Human services. **Social sciences:** Economics, political science, sociology. **Visual/performing arts:** Music theory/composition, piano/organ, studio arts, voice/opera.

Most popular majors. Business/marketing 32%, computer/information sciences 6%, education 18%, liberal arts 6%, psychology 8%.

Computing on campus. 590 workstations in dormitories, library, computer center, student center. Dormitories wired for high-speed internet access and linked to campus network. Commuter students can connect to campus network. Online course registration, online library, helpline, student web hosting, wireless network available.

Student life. Freshman orientation: Mandatory, $200 fee. Preregistration for classes offered. **Policies:** Freshmen permitted cars on campus. **Housing:** Guaranteed on-campus for all undergraduates. Coed dorms, single-sex dorms, special housing for disabled, apartments, fraternity/sorority housing, substance-free housing available. $200 partly refundable deposit, deadline 5/1. Wellness, quiet, science, freshman experience, learning community, faculty-in-residence options, suites available. **Activities:** Bands, choral groups, dance, drama, film society, literary magazine, music ensembles, musical theater, opera, radio station, student government, student newspaper, symphony orchestra, TV station, student entertainment council, residence hall hssociation, finance board, Asian Students at Rider, Interfraternity council, hunger & homelessness Awareness, College Republicans, Catholic Campus Ministry, National Model United Nations, Latin American student organization.

Athletics. NCAA. **Intercollegiate:** Baseball M, basketball, cheerleading, cross-country, diving, field hockey W, golf M, soccer, softball W, swimming, tennis, track and field, volleyball W, wrestling M. **Intramural:** Basketball, football (non-tackle), ice hockey M, lacrosse, soccer, softball, track and field, volleyball. **Team name:** Broncs.

Student services. Adult student services, alcohol/substance abuse counseling, campus ministries, career counseling, student employment services, financial aid counseling, health services, minority student services, personal counseling, placement for graduates, veterans' counselor. **Physically disabled:** Services for visually, speech, hearing impaired.

Contact. E-mail: admissions@rider.edu
Phone: (609) 896-5042 Toll-free number: (800) 257-9026
Fax: (609) 895-6645
Laurie Kennedy-Rotondo, Director of Undergraduate Admissions, Rider University, 2083 Lawrenceville Road, Lawrenceville, NJ 08648-3099

Rowan University

Glassboro, New Jersey
www.rowan.edu
CB member
CB code: 2515

- Public 4-year university and liberal arts college
- Commuter campus in large town
- 8,065 degree-seeking undergraduates: 11% part-time, 54% women, 9% African American, 3% Asian American, 7% Hispanic American
- 997 degree-seeking graduate students
- 47% of applicants admitted
- SAT or ACT (ACT writing optional), interview required
- 63% graduate within 6 years

General. Founded in 1923. Regionally accredited. Camden campus offers general education courses and major programs in elementary education, business administration, law/justice, and sociology. **Degrees:** 1,703 bachelor's awarded; master's, doctoral offered. **ROTC:** Army. **Location:** 20 miles from Philadelphia. **Calendar:** Semester, extensive summer session. **Full-time faculty:** 436 total; 82% have terminal degrees, 22% minority, 42% women. **Part-time faculty:** 450 total; 19% have terminal degrees, 8% minority, 44% women. **Class size:** 42% < 20, 58% 20-39, less than 1% 40-49, less than 1% 50-99, less than 1% >100. **Special facilities:** Observatory, glass-blowing museum, on-campus early childhood demonstration center, animal penthouse, greenhouse for biological studies, concert hall.

Freshman class profile. 7,303 applied, 3,396 admitted, 1,247 enrolled.

Mid 50% test scores			
SAT verbal:	510-600	Rank in top quarter:	55%
SAT math:	510-620	Rank in top tenth:	10%
GPA 3.50 or higher:	55%	Return as sophomores:	87%
GPA 3.0-3.49:	35%	Out-of-state:	3%
GPA 2.0-2.99:	10%	Live on campus:	78%

Basis for selection. School achievement record and test scores most important, followed by recommendations. Special admissions program for in-state disadvantaged and minority students. Audition required for music, theater programs; portfolio interview required for art program.

High school preparation. 16 units required. Required units include English 4, mathematics 3, social studies 2, science 2 (laboratory 2) and academic electives 5.

2005-2006 Annual costs. Tuition/fees: $8,606; $14,900 out-of-state. Room/board: $8,242. Books/supplies: $800.

2004-2005 Financial aid. **Need-based:** 1,143 full-time freshmen applied for aid; 1,098 were judged to have need; 1,022 of these received aid. Average need met was 66%. Average scholarship/grant was $5,722; average loan $3,252. 37% of total undergraduate aid awarded as scholarships/grants, 63% as loans/jobs. **Non-need-based:** Awarded to 3,154 full-time undergraduates, including 646 freshmen. Scholarships awarded for academics, alumni affiliation, leadership, minority status, music/drama, ROTC.

Application procedures. **Admission:** Priority date 1/31; deadline 3/15 (postmark date). $50 fee, may be waived for applicants with need. Admission notification 4/15. Admission notification on a rolling basis beginning on or about 11/1. Must reply by 5/1. **Financial aid:** Closing date 3/15. FAFSA required. Applicants notified on a rolling basis starting 5/1; must reply within 2 week(s) of notification.

Academics. **Special study options:** Cross-registration, double major, honors, independent study, semester at sea, study abroad, teacher certification program. Cross-registration with Drexel University, Temple University, Rutgers-the State University of New Jersey, New Jersey Institute of Technology; combination programs with University of Medicine and Dentistry of New Jersey, Philadelphia College of Pharmacy and Science. **Credit/placement by examination:** AP, CLEP, institutional tests. 30 credit hours maximum toward bachelor's degree. **Support services:** Learning center, pre-admission summer program, reduced course load, remedial instruction, study skills assistance, tutoring, writing center.

Majors. **Area/ethnic studies:** African-American, American, women's. **Biology:** General, bacteriology, biochemistry, botany, cell/histology, zoology. **Business:** General, accounting, finance, human resources, labor relations, management information systems, management science, marketing. **Communications:** General, advertising, broadcast journalism, journalism, public relations. **Communications technology:** General. **Computer sciences:** General, computer science, data processing. **Conservation:** Wildlife. **Education:** General, art, early childhood, elementary, English, health, middle, music, physical, secondary, special. **Engineering:** General, chemical, civil, electrical, materials, mechanical. **English:** American lit, British lit, composition. **Foreign languages:** General, Spanish. **Health:** Athletic training, predentistry, premedicine, prepharmacy, preveterinary. **History:** General. **Legal studies:** Prelaw. **Liberal arts:** Arts/sciences. **Math:** General. **Parks/recreation:** Health/fitness, sports admin. **Philosophy/religion:** Philosophy, religion. **Physical sciences:** Chemistry, physics. **Protective services:** Criminal justice, police science. **Psychology:** General. **Social sciences:** General, anthropology, economics, geography, political science, sociology. **Visual/performing arts:** General, art, art history/conservation, ceramics, commercial/advertising art, dance, dramatic, drawing, fiber arts, film/cinema, jazz, metal/jewelry, music performance, music theory/composition, painting, photography, printmaking, sculpture, studio arts, theater design, theater history.

Most popular majors. Business/marketing 15%, communications/journalism 15%, education 21%, security/protective services 8%, social sciences 7%, visual/performing arts 6%.

Computing on campus. 600 workstations in dormitories, library, computer center. Dormitories wired for high-speed internet access and linked to campus network. Commuter students can connect to campus network. Online course registration, helpline, repair service, student web hosting available.

Student life. **Freshman orientation:** Available. Preregistration for classes offered. Overnight program for freshmen and their families during summer. **Housing:** Guaranteed on-campus for freshmen. Coed dorms, special housing for disabled, apartments available. $200 deposit, deadline 5/1. Unmarried students under age 21 not living with parent/guardian required to live in college housing for freshman and sophomore years. **Activities:** Bands, choral groups, dance, drama, film society, literary magazine, music ensembles, musical theater, opera, radio station, student government, student newspaper, symphony orchestra, TV station, over 150 clubs and student organizations.

Athletics. NCAA. **Intercollegiate:** Baseball M, basketball, cheerleading, cross-country, diving, field hockey W, football (tackle) M, lacrosse W, soccer, softball W, swimming, tennis, track and field, volleyball W, wrestling M. **Intramural:** Archery, basketball, bowling, football (non-tackle), golf, handball, racquetball, soccer W, softball, volleyball. **Team name:** Profs.

Student services. Adult student services, alcohol/substance abuse counseling, campus ministries, career counseling, student employment services, financial aid counseling, health services, legal services, minority student services, on-campus daycare, personal counseling, placement for graduates, veterans' counselor, women's services. **Physically disabled:** Services for visually, speech, hearing impaired.

Contact. E-mail: admissions@rowan.edu
Phone: (856) 256-4200 Toll-free number: (800) 447-1165
Fax: (856) 256-4430
Marvin Sills, Director of Admissions, Rowan University, Savitz Hall, 201 Mullica Hill Road, Glassboro, NJ 08028

Rutgers, The State University of New Jersey: Camden Regional Campus

Camden, New Jersey
www.rutgers.edu
CB member

- Public 4-year university
- Commuter campus in small city
- 3,774 degree-seeking undergraduates: 22% part-time, 58% women, 15% African American, 8% Asian American, 6% Hispanic American, 1% international
- 1,390 degree-seeking graduate students
- 53% of applicants admitted
- SAT or ACT with writing required
- 54% graduate within 6 years

General. Founded in 1927. Regionally accredited. Undergraduate schools: Camden College of Arts and Sciences, University College-Camden, School of Business-Camden. Graduate degrees available at School of Business. Graduate schools: Graduate School-Camden, School of Law-Camden. **Degrees:** 831 bachelor's awarded; master's, first professional offered. **ROTC:** Army, Air Force. **Location:** One mile from Philadelphia. **Calendar:** Semester, extensive summer session. **Full-time faculty:** 229 total; 99% have terminal degrees, 17% minority, 37% women. **Part-time faculty:** 172 total; 99% have terminal degrees, 14% minority, 43% women. **Class size:** 43% < 20,

42% 20-39, 6% 40-49, 6% 50-99, 2% >100. **Special facilities:** Fine arts center.

Freshman class profile. 6,153 applied, 3,284 admitted, 353 enrolled.

Mid 50% test scores		Return as sophomores:	84%
SAT verbal:	500-600	Out-of-state:	7%
SAT math:	520-610	Live on campus:	44%
Rank in top quarter:	64%	International:	1%
Rank in top tenth:	2%		

Basis for selection. School achievement record (including grades, rank, strength of program, honors) and test scores most important. Extracurricular activities, talent, disadvantaged status considered. SAT Subject Tests required for applicants who will not have diploma from accredited high school by entrance date. May also be required of GED holders. SAT/ACT scores should be submitted by December of senior year.

High school preparation. 16 units required. Required and recommended units include English 4, mathematics 3-4, science 2, foreign language 2 and academic electives 5. Mathematics requirement includes algebra I and II and geometry. 4 mathematics, 1 chemistry, 1 physics required for engineering applicants.

2005-2006 Annual costs. Tuition/fees: $9,028; $16,626 out-of-state. Room/board: $8,078. Books/supplies: $733. Personal expenses: $1,453.

2005-2006 Financial aid. **Need-based:** 295 full-time freshmen applied for aid; 207 were judged to have need; 206 of these received aid. Average need met was 74%. Average scholarship/grant was $7,404; average loan $2,773. 45% of total undergraduate aid awarded as scholarships/grants, 55% as loans/jobs. **Non-need-based:** Awarded to 863 full-time undergraduates, including 199 freshmen. Scholarships awarded for academics, alumni affiliation, art, athletics, minority status, music/drama, religious affiliation, ROTC, state residency.

Application procedures. **Admission:** Priority date 12/1; no deadline. $50 fee, may be waived for applicants with need. Application may be submitted online. Admission notification on a rolling basis beginning on or about 2/28. Must reply by May 1 or within 2 week(s) if notified thereafter. May apply to up to 3 Rutgers colleges with 1 application. Students applying by December 1 notified by February 28. **Financial aid:** Priority date 3/15; no closing date. FAFSA required. Applicants notified on a rolling basis starting 2/1; must reply within 2 week(s) of notification.

Academics. **Special study options:** Accelerated study, combined bachelor's/graduate degree, cooperative education, cross-registration, distance learning, double major, dual enrollment of high school students, ESL, exchange student, honors, independent study, internships, liberal arts/career combination, student-designed major, study abroad, teacher certification program. 8-year BA/MD with University of Medicine and Dentistry of New Jersey; 5-year BA or BS/MA in Criminal Justice with School of Criminal Justice-Newark; 2+2 BS and 2+3 dual bachelor's degree transfer programs with School of Engineering; BA in Political Science/MPA; BA in Economics/MPA; BA/MS in Biology; BA/MS in Chemistry; BA/MA in English; BA/MA in History; BA/MA in Liberal Studies; BA/MS in Mathematics; articulated Bachelor's/Dentistry program with University of Medicine and Dentistry of New Jersey. **Credit/placement by examination:** AP, CLEP, IB, institutional tests. No more than 8 credits given for elementary or intermediate levels of any foreign language. Graduating seniors may take no more than one examination in their final term. **Support services:** Learning center, preadmission summer program, reduced course load, remedial instruction, study skills assistance, tutoring, writing center.

Majors. **Area/ethnic studies:** African-American. **Biology:** General, biomedical sciences. **Business:** Accounting, business admin, finance, hospitality admin, marketing. **Computer sciences:** Computer science. **Engineering:** Biomedical, ceramic, chemical, civil, electrical, mechanical, science. **Foreign languages:** French, German, Spanish. **Health:** Nursing (RN), predentistry, premedicine. **History:** General. **Interdisciplinary:** Biological/physical sciences. **Legal studies:** Prelaw. **Liberal arts:** Arts/sciences. **Math:** General. **Philosophy/religion:** Philosophy. **Physical sciences:** Chemistry, physics. **Protective services:** Criminal justice. **Psychology:** General. **Public administration:** Social work. **Social sciences:** Economics, political science, sociology, urban studies. **Visual/performing arts:** Art, dramatic.

Most popular majors. Business/marketing 27%, English 6%, science technologies 16%, security/protective services 7%, social sciences 14%.

Computing on campus. 187 workstations in dormitories, library, computer center, student center. Dormitories linked to campus network. Commuter students can connect to campus network. Helpline, repair service available.

Student life. **Freshman orientation:** Available. **Housing:** Coed dorms, special housing for disabled, apartments available. **Activities:** Drama, literary magazine, radio station, student government, student newspaper, accounting society, forensics society, political science association, Black student union, Latin American students organization, physics society, Jewish student union, marketing association, psychology club.

Athletics. NCAA. **Intercollegiate:** Baseball M, basketball, cross-country, golf M, rowing (crew) W, soccer, softball W, track and field, volleyball W. **Intramural:** Badminton, basketball, football (tackle) M, handball, racquetball, soccer, softball, squash, volleyball. **Team name:** Scarlet Raptors.

Student services. Career counseling, student employment services, health services, on-campus daycare, personal counseling, placement for graduates, veterans' counselor. **Physically disabled:** Services for visually, speech, hearing impaired.

Contact. Phone: (856) 225-6104 Fax: (856) 225-6498
Deborah Bowles, Director of Admissions, Rutgers, The State University of New Jersey: Camden Regional Campus, 406 Penn Street, Camden, NJ 08102

Rutgers, The State University of New Jersey: New Brunswick Regional Campus

Piscataway, New Jersey — **CB member**
www.rutgers.edu — **CB code: 2765**

- Public 4-year university
- Residential campus in large town
- 26,172 degree-seeking undergraduates: 7% part-time, 51% women, 9% African American, 22% Asian American, 8% Hispanic American, 2% international
- 6,691 degree-seeking graduate students
- 61% of applicants admitted
- SAT or ACT with writing required
- 71% graduate within 6 years

General. Founded in 1969. Regionally accredited. Undergraduate schools include Douglass College, Livingston College, Rutgers College, University College-New Brunswick, Cook College, School of Engineering, Mason Gross School of the Arts, Edward J. Bloustein School of Planning and Public Policy, College of Nursing, College of Pharmacy, School of Business-New Brunswick, School of Communication, Information and Library Studies. Graduate degrees also available at Mason Gross School of the Arts, Edward J. Bloustein School of Planning and Public Policy, College of Pharmacy, School of Communication, Information and Library Studies. **Degrees:** 5,948 bachelor's awarded; master's, doctoral, first professional offered. **ROTC:** Army, Air Force. **Location:** 33 miles from New York City. **Calendar:** Semester, extensive summer session. **Full-time faculty:** 1,535 total; 99% have terminal degrees, 16% minority, 32% women. **Part-time faculty:** 689 total; 95% have terminal degrees, 15% minority, 46% women. **Class size:** 42% < 20, 33% 20-39, 6% 40-49, 10% 50-99, 9% >100. **Special facilities:** Geology museum, ecological preserve, 2 theaters, center for urban policy research, institute for health, health care policy and aging research, journalism resources institute, laboratory for computer science research, center for mathematics, science and computer education.

Freshman class profile. 25,462 applied, 15,437 admitted, 5,245 enrolled.

Mid 50% test scores		Rank in top tenth:	36%
SAT verbal:	530-630	Return as sophomores:	89%
SAT math:	560-670	Out-of-state:	10%
Rank in top quarter:	78%	Live on campus:	84%

Basis for selection. School achievement record (including grades, rank, strength of program, honors, AP) and test scores most important. Extracurricular activities, leadership talent, minority, disadvantaged status considered. State residents with educationally and economically disadvantaged backgrounds given consideration through state Educational Opportunity Fund (EOF) program. SAT Subject Tests required of applicants who, by expected date of entrance, will not have diploma from accredited high school. May also be required of GED holders. Recommended that SAT/ACT be submitted by December of senior year. Interview, audition, portfolio review required for Mason Gross School of the Arts.

High school preparation. College-preparatory program required. 16 units required. Required and recommended units include English 4, mathematics 3-4, science 2, foreign language 2 and academic electives 5. Mathematics requirement includes algebra I and II and geometry. 4 mathematics, 1 chemistry, 1 physics required for engineering program. One biology, 1 chemistry required for nursing program. 5-9 academic electives required, depending on college.

2005-2006 Annual costs. Tuition/fees: $9,108; $16,706 out-of-state. Tuition and fees may vary by program. Room/board: $8,578. Books/supplies: $733. Personal expenses: $1,453.

2005-2006 Financial aid. Need-based: 4,016 full-time freshmen applied for aid; 2,751 were judged to have need; 2,691 of these received aid. Average need met was 69%. Average scholarship/grant was $8,579; average loan $3,010. 47% of total undergraduate aid awarded as scholarships/grants, 53% as loans/jobs. **Non-need-based:** Awarded to 11,241 full-time undergraduates, including 2,802 freshmen. Scholarships awarded for academics, alumni affiliation, art, athletics, leadership, minority status, music/drama, religious affiliation, state residency.

Application procedures. Admission: Priority date 12/1; no deadline. $50 fee, may be waived for applicants with need. Application may be submitted online. Admission notification on a rolling basis beginning on or about 2/28. Must reply by May 1 or within 2 week(s) if notified thereafter. May apply to up to 3 Rutgers colleges with 1 application. Applications received by December 1 will be answered by February 28. **Financial aid:** Priority date 3/15; no closing date. FAFSA required. Applicants notified on a rolling basis starting 2/1; must reply within 2 week(s) of notification.

Academics. Special study options: Accelerated study, combined bachelor's/graduate degree, cooperative education, cross-registration, distance learning, double major, dual enrollment of high school students, ESL, exchange student, honors, independent study, internships, liberal arts/career combination, student-designed major, study abroad, teacher certification program, Washington semester. Washington semester; 8-year BA or BS/MD with University of Medicine and Dentistry of New Jersey 5-year BA/MBA; 5-year dual degrees in liberal arts and engineering; 5-year BA or BS/MPP with Edward J. Bloustein School of Planning and Public Policy; 5-year BA or BS/MA in Criminal Justice with School of Criminal Justice in Newark; 6-year BA in biology/MS in physician assistant; 5-year BA or BS/M.Ed. offered in conjunction with the Graduate School of Education; dual admission to Newark School of Law; BA or BS/MPH with Edward J. Bloustein School of Planning and Public Policy; articulated Bachelor's/Dentistry program with the University of Medicine and Dentistry of New Jersey. **Credit/placement by examination:** AP, CLEP, IB, institutional tests. 30 credit hours maximum toward bachelor's degree. **Support services:** Learning center, pre-admission summer program, reduced course load, remedial instruction, study skills assistance, tutoring, writing center.

Majors. Agriculture: Animal sciences, food science, plant sciences. **Architecture:** Environmental design, urban/community planning. **Area/ethnic studies:** African, African-American, American, Caribbean, Central/Eastern European, East Asian, Hispanic-American/Latino/Chicano, Latin American, Near/Middle Eastern, Russian/Slavic, women's. **Biology:** General, bacteriology, biochemistry, biometrics, cell/histology, genetics, marine, molecular. **Business:** Accounting, business admin, finance, labor relations, management information systems, management science, marketing. **Communications:** General, journalism. **Computer sciences:** Computer science. **Conservation:** General, environmental studies, management/policy. **Engineering:** Biomedical, ceramic, chemical, civil, electrical, environmental, mechanical, science. **Foreign languages:** Chinese, classics, comparative lit, French, German, Italian, linguistics, Portuguese, Russian, Spanish. **Health:** Clinical lab technology, nursing (RN), physician assistant, predentistry, premedicine. **History:** General. **Interdisciplinary:** Medieval/Renaissance, nutrition sciences. **Legal studies:** Prelaw. **Math:** General, statistics. **Parks/recreation:** Exercise sciences. **Philosophy/religion:** Judaic, philosophy, religion. **Physical sciences:** Atmospheric science, chemistry, geology, physics. **Protective services:** Law enforcement admin. **Psychology:** General. **Public administration:** Social work. **Science technology:** Biological. **Social sciences:** Anthropology, economics, geography, political science, sociology, urban studies. **Visual/performing arts:** Art, art history/conservation, dance, dramatic.

Most popular majors. Biology 8%, business/marketing 7%, communications/journalism 8%, engineering/engineering technologies 7%, psychology 10%, social sciences 20%.

Computing on campus. 1,450 workstations in dormitories, library, computer center, student center. Dormitories linked to campus network. Commuter students can connect to campus network. Helpline, repair service available.

Student life. Freshman orientation: Available. **Housing:** Guaranteed on-campus for freshmen. Coed dorms, single-sex dorms, special housing for disabled, apartments, cooperative housing, fraternity/sorority housing available. $100 deposit, deadline 6/15. Cooperative housing at Cook College only. Special interest housing, language and cultural houses, substance-free house, math/science/engineering house for women, first-year residence, transfer center, residence for single mothers and children available. **Activities:** Bands, choral groups, dance, drama, film society, literary magazine, music ensembles, opera, radio station, student government, student newspaper, symphony orchestra, TV station, 400 organizations available.

Athletics. NCAA. **Intercollegiate:** Baseball M, basketball, cross-country, diving, fencing, field hockey W, football (tackle) M, golf, gymnastics W, lacrosse, rowing (crew), soccer, softball W, swimming, tennis, track and field, volleyball W, wrestling M. **Intramural:** Badminton, basketball, bowling, cross-country, golf, racquetball, soccer, softball, squash, swimming, table tennis, tennis, track and field, volleyball, water polo, wrestling M. **Team name:** Scarlet Knights.

Student services. Adult student services, career counseling, student employment services, health services, on-campus daycare, personal counseling, placement for graduates, veterans' counselor. **Physically disabled:** Services for visually, speech, hearing impaired.

Contact. Phone: (732) 932-4636 Fax: (732) 445-0237
Diane Harris, Associate Director of Undergraduate Admissions, Rutgers, The State University of New Jersey: New Brunswick Regional Campus, 65 Davidson Road, Room 202, Piscataway, NJ 08854-8097

Rutgers, The State University of New Jersey: Newark Regional Campus

Newark, New Jersey
www.rutgers.edu

- Public 4-year university
- Commuter campus in large city
- 5,963 degree-seeking undergraduates: 18% part-time, 58% women, 21% African American, 23% Asian American, 18% Hispanic American, 2% international
- 3,424 degree-seeking graduate students
- 47% of applicants admitted
- SAT or ACT with writing required
- 54% graduate within 6 years

General. Founded in 1930. Regionally accredited. Undergraduate schools: College of Nursing, Newark College of Arts and Sciences, University College-Newark, School of Management. **Degrees:** 1,164 bachelor's awarded; master's, doctoral, first professional offered. **ROTC:** Army, Air Force. **Location:** 10 miles from New York City. **Calendar:** Semester, extensive summer session. **Full-time faculty:** 422 total; 95% have terminal degrees, 15% minority, 39% women. **Part-time faculty:** 231 total; 99% have terminal degrees, 15% minority, 43% women. **Class size:** 40% < 20, 34% 20-39, 14% 40-49, 9% 50-99, 3% >100. **Special facilities:** Biology learning center, jazz institute, animal behavior institute, center for molecular and behavioral neuroscience, center for negotiation and conflict resolution.

Freshman class profile. 9,927 applied, 4,653 admitted, 704 enrolled.

Mid 50% test scores		**Return as sophomores:**	86%
SAT verbal:	490-590	**Out-of-state:**	6%
SAT math:	500-620	**Live on campus:**	42%
Rank in top quarter:	70%	**International:**	2%
Rank in top tenth:	35%		

Basis for selection. School achievement record and test scores most important. Extracurricular activities, leadership talent, minority, disadvantaged status considered. State residents with educational and economically disadvantaged backgrounds given consideration through state Educational Opportunity Fund (EOF) program. SAT Subject Tests required of applicants who, by expected date of entrance, will not have diploma from accredited high school. May also be required of GED holders. SAT/ACT scores should be submitted by December of senior year.

High school preparation. College-preparatory program required. 16 units required. Required and recommended units include English 4, mathematics 3-4, science 2, foreign language 2 and academic electives 5. Mathematics requirement includes algebra I, II and geometry. 4 mathematics, 1 chemistry, 1 physics required for engineering program. One biology, 1 chemistry required for nursing program. Foreign language recommended.

2005-2006 Annual costs. Tuition/fees: $8,812; $16,411 out-of-state. Room/board: $9,110. Books/supplies: $733. Personal expenses: $1,453.

2005-2006 Financial aid. Need-based: 549 full-time freshmen applied for aid; 439 were judged to have need; 426 of these received aid. Average need met was 81%. Average scholarship/grant was $8,210; average loan $2,927. 55% of total undergraduate aid awarded as scholarships/grants, 45% as loans/jobs. **Non-need-based:** Awarded to 1,331 full-time undergraduates, including 228 freshmen. Scholarships awarded for academics, alumni affiliation, art, athletics, leadership, minority status, music/drama, religious affiliation, state residency.

Application procedures. Admission: Priority date 12/1; no deadline. $50 fee, may be waived for applicants with need. Application may be submitted online. Admission notification on a rolling basis beginning on or about 2/28. Must reply by May 1 or within 2 week(s) if notified thereafter. May apply to up to 3 Rutgers colleges with 1 application. Applications completed by December 1 will be answered by February 28. **Financial aid:**

Priority date 3/15; no closing date. FAFSA required. Applicants notified on a rolling basis starting 2/1; must reply within 2 week(s) of notification.

Academics. **Special study options:** Accelerated study, combined bachelor's/graduate degree, cooperative education, cross-registration, distance learning, double major, dual enrollment of high school students, ESL, honors, independent study, liberal arts/career combination, student-designed major, study abroad, teacher certification program, Washington semester. 8-year BA/MD with University of Medicine and Dentistry of New Jersey, 5-year BA or BS/MA in criminal justice, 2-2 and 2-3 in engineering, dual admission to School of Law, 5-year BA/MBA, industrial engineering program with New Jersey Institute of Technology, Bachelor's/Dentistry program with Universtiy of Medicine and Dentistry of New Jersey. **Credit/placement by examination:** AP, CLEP, IB, institutional tests. 24 credit hours maximum toward bachelor's degree. **Support services:** Learning center, preadmission summer program, reduced course load, remedial instruction, study skills assistance, tutoring, writing center.

Majors. **Area/ethnic studies:** African, African-American, American, Caribbean, Hispanic-American/Latino/Chicano, women's. **Biology:** General, botany, zoology. **Business:** Accounting, business admin, finance, marketing. **Communications:** Journalism. **Computer sciences:** Computer science, information systems. **Conservation:** General. **Engineering:** Biomedical, ceramic, chemical, civil, electrical, mechanical. **Foreign languages:** French, Spanish. **Health:** Clinical lab science, clinical lab technology, nursing (RN), predentistry, premedicine. **History:** General. **Interdisciplinary:** Science/society. **Legal studies:** Prelaw. **Math:** General, applied. **Philosophy/religion:** Philosophy. **Physical sciences:** Chemistry, geology, physics. **Protective services:** Criminal justice. **Psychology:** General. **Public administration:** Social work. **Social sciences:** Anthropology, economics, political science, sociology. **Visual/performing arts:** Art, dramatic.

Most popular majors. Biology 8%, business/marketing 28%, computer/information sciences 9%, health sciences 11%, psychology 9%, security/protective services 9%, social sciences 8%.

Computing on campus. 450 workstations in dormitories, library, computer center. Dormitories linked to campus network. Commuter students can connect to campus network. Helpline, repair service available.

Student life. **Freshman orientation:** Available. **Housing:** Coed dorms, special housing for disabled, apartments, fraternity/sorority housing available. $100 deposit. **Activities:** Choral groups, drama, radio station, student government, student newspaper, Black Organization of Students, Puerto Rican and Latin American student organizations, political, religious, and service organizations.

Athletics. NCAA. **Intercollegiate:** Baseball M, basketball, soccer, softball W, tennis, volleyball. **Intramural:** Basketball, racquetball, soccer, tennis, volleyball. **Team name:** Scarlet Raiders.

Student services. Career counseling, student employment services, health services, personal counseling, placement for graduates, veterans' counselor. **Physically disabled:** Services for visually, speech, hearing impaired.

Contact. Phone: (973) 353-5205 Fax: (973) 353-1440
Bruce Neimeyer, Director of Admissions at Newark, Rutgers, The State University of New Jersey: Newark Regional Campus, 249 University Avenue, Newark, NJ 07102-1896

St. Peter's College

Jersey City, New Jersey — **CB member**
www.spc.edu — **CB code: 2806**

- Private 4-year liberal arts college affiliated with Roman Catholic Church
- Commuter campus in small city
- 2,095 degree-seeking undergraduates: 14% part-time, 52% women, 22% African American, 7% Asian American, 24% Hispanic American, 3% international
- 664 degree-seeking graduate students
- 69% of applicants admitted
- SAT or ACT (ACT writing optional), application essay required
- 43% graduate within 6 years

General. Founded in 1872. Regionally accredited. Affiliated with Jesuit order. Extensive evening program on main campus, at branch locations at Englewood Cliffs and South Amboy for adult learners, and other locations throughout metropolitan area. **Degrees:** 383 bachelor's, 31 associate awarded; master's offered. **ROTC:** Army, Air Force. **Location:** 3 miles from New York City. **Calendar:** Semester, extensive summer session. **Full-time faculty:** 104 total; 82% have terminal degrees, 10% minority, 41% women. **Part-time faculty:** 207 total; 29% have terminal degrees, 23% minority, 31% women. **Class size:** 67% < 20, 33% 20-39.

Freshman class profile. 2,863 applied, 1,966 admitted, 507 enrolled.

Mid 50% test scores			
SAT verbal:	420-520	GPA 2.0-2.99:	37%
SAT math:	440-530	Out-of-state:	19%
GPA 3.50 or higher:	30%	Live on campus:	53%
GPA 3.0-3.49:	32%	International:	1%

Basis for selection. Admissions decision based on (in rank order) school achievement record, test scores, essay, letters of recommendation, class activities. Interview recommended.

High school preparation. 16 units required; 19 recommended. Required and recommended units include English 4, mathematics 3-4, history 2-3, science 2-3 (laboratory 1), foreign language 2 and academic electives 3.

2005-2006 Annual costs. Tuition/fees: $21,465. Room/board: $8,770. Books/supplies: $700. Personal expenses: $600.

2004-2005 Financial aid. **Need-based:** 79% of total undergraduate aid awarded as scholarships/grants, 21% as loans/jobs. **Non-need-based:** Scholarships awarded for academics, athletics. **Additional information:** Cooperative education internships available in all majors, with average salaries exceeding $5,200.

Application procedures. **Admission:** Priority date 4/1; no deadline. , may be waived for applicants with need. No application fee. Admission notification on a rolling basis beginning on or about 11/1. Must reply by May 1 or within 2 week(s) if notified thereafter. **Financial aid:** Priority date 3/15; no closing date. FAFSA required. Applicants notified on a rolling basis starting 2/15; must reply by 5/1 or within 2 week(s) of notification.

Academics. Joint Pre-Med/MD program with UMDNJ, joint Pre-Law/Law program with Seton Hall University. **Special study options:** Accelerated study, combined bachelor's/graduate degree, cooperative education, double major, dual enrollment of high school students, exchange student, honors, independent study, internships, liberal arts/career combination, student-designed major, study abroad, teacher certification program, Washington semester. Joint degree in clinical laboratory sciences with University of Medicine and Dentistry of New Jersey. **Credit/placement by examination:** AP, CLEP, institutional tests. 30 credit hours maximum toward bachelor's degree. **Support services:** Learning center, pre-admission summer program, reduced course load, remedial instruction, study skills assistance, tutoring, writing center.

Majors. **Area/ethnic studies:** American. **Biology:** General, biochemistry, toxicology. **Business:** Accounting, actuarial science, banking/financial services, business admin, international, management information systems, managerial economics. **Communications:** General. **Computer sciences:** General, computer science, information systems, programming. **Education:** Elementary. **Foreign languages:** General, classics, Spanish. **Health:** Clinical lab science, cytotechnology, nursing (RN). **History:** General. **Interdisciplinary:** Biological/physical sciences. **Math:** General. **Philosophy/religion:** Philosophy, religion. **Physical sciences:** Chemistry, physics. **Psychology:** General. **Public administration:** Policy analysis. **Social sciences:** General, economics, political science, sociology, urban studies. **Visual/performing arts:** Studio arts.

Most popular majors. Business/marketing 40%, computer/information sciences 6%, education 9%, security/protective services 7%.

Computing on campus. 225 workstations in dormitories, library, computer center, student center. Dormitories wired for high-speed internet access and linked to campus network. Commuter students can connect to campus network. Online library, helpline, wireless network available.

Student life. **Freshman orientation:** Mandatory, $200 fee. Preregistration for classes offered. 3-day sessions held throughout July. Program features academic advising, social activities, and introduction to community service. **Housing:** Guaranteed on-campus for all undergraduates. Coed dorms, special housing for disabled, apartments available. $200 deposit, deadline 5/1. **Activities:** Choral groups, drama, literary magazine, radio station, student government, student newspaper, Alpha Phi Omega, Emmaus Spiritual Retreats, Circle K, Young Republicans, Hispanic culture club, Irish American club, Asian American Student Union, Black Action Committee, Indo-Pak culture club, International club.

Athletics. NCAA. **Intercollegiate:** Baseball M, basketball, bowling, cheerleading, cross-country, diving, football (tackle) M, golf M, soccer, softball W, swimming, tennis, track and field, volleyball W. **Intramural:** Baseball M, basketball, bowling, racquetball, soccer, softball, swimming, table tennis, tennis, volleyball, water polo. **Team name:** Peacocks/Peahens.

Student services. Adult student services, alcohol/substance abuse counseling, campus ministries, career counseling, services for economically disadvantaged, student employment services, financial aid counseling, health services, minority student services, personal counseling, placement for graduates, veterans' counselor. **Physically disabled:** Services for visually, speech, hearing impaired.

Contact. E-mail: admissions@spc.edu
Phone: (201) 915-9213 Toll-free number: (888) 772-9933
Fax: (201) 432-5860
Giuseppe Giglio, Director of Admission, St. Peter's College, 2641 Kennedy Boulevard, Jersey City, NJ 07306

Seton Hall University

South Orange, New Jersey — **CB member**
www.shu.edu — **CB code: 2811**

- Private 4-year university affiliated with Roman Catholic Church
- Residential campus in large town
- 5,093 degree-seeking undergraduates: 6% part-time, 53% women, 11% African American, 7% Asian American, 9% Hispanic American, 1% international
- 3,826 degree-seeking graduate students
- 84% of applicants admitted
- SAT or ACT with writing, application essay required
- 56% graduate within 6 years

General. Founded in 1856. Regionally accredited. Immaculate Conception Seminary and school of theology located on campus. Off-campus sites for nursing and education. **Degrees:** 1,027 bachelor's awarded; master's, doctoral, first professional offered. **ROTC:** Army. **Location:** 14 miles from New York City. **Calendar:** Semester, extensive summer session. **Full-time faculty:** 441 total; 90% have terminal degrees, 15% minority, 46% women. **Part-time faculty:** 485 total; 14% minority, 44% women. **Class size:** 50% < 20, 48% 20-39, 1% 40-49, 1% 50-99, less than 1% >100. **Special facilities:** Museum, computer graphics and communications laboratories, educational media center, nursing demonstration room, art center, recreation center, music laboratories, special collections center.

Freshman class profile. 4,982 applied, 4,160 admitted, 1,120 enrolled.

Mid 50% test scores			
SAT verbal:	500-610	Rank in top quarter:	51%
SAT math:	510-610	Rank in top tenth:	25%
GPA 3.50 or higher:	36%	Return as sophomores:	83%
GPA 3.0-3.49:	38%	Out-of-state:	30%
GPA 2.0-2.99:	26%	Live on campus:	75%
		International:	1%

Basis for selection. School achievement record, test scores, recommendations, essay most important. Extracurricular activities, volunteer work, work experience important. Class rank, interview, talent/ability, character/personal qualities considered. Students who reside in Puerto Rico may submit SAT or TOEFL score along with PAA score; either ACT with Writing or SAT required, but not used in admission decisions. Interview strongly recommended. Audition required for music majors. **Homeschooled:** Statement describing homeschool structure and mission required. Must submit GED and SAT scores.

High school preparation. College-preparatory program required. 16 units required. Required units include English 4, mathematics 3, social studies 2, science 1 (laboratory 1), foreign language 2 and academic electives 4. Nursing majors must have an additional 2 units in science (biology and chemistry).

2005-2006 Annual costs. Tuition/fees: $23,760. Required fees include lease of laptop computer. Room/board: $10,162. Books/supplies: $950. Personal expenses: $1,476.

2004-2005 Financial aid. **Need-based:** 1,080 full-time freshmen applied for aid; 930 were judged to have need; 906 of these received aid. Average need met was 74%. Average scholarship/grant was $5,179; average loan $2,533. 53% of total undergraduate aid awarded as scholarships/grants, 47% as loans/jobs. **Non-need-based:** Awarded to 2,587 full-time undergraduates, including 815 freshmen. Scholarships awarded for academics, alumni affiliation, athletics, leadership, minority status, ROTC, state residency.

Application procedures. **Admission:** Priority date 3/1; no deadline. $55 fee, may be waived for applicants with need. Application may be submitted online. Admission notification on a rolling basis beginning on or about 12/1. Must reply by May 1 or within 4 week(s) if notified thereafter. **Financial aid:** Priority date 2/15; no closing date. FAFSA required. Applicants notified on a rolling basis starting 3/1; must reply by 5/1 or within 4 week(s) of notification.

Academics. **Special study options:** Accelerated study, combined bachelor's/graduate degree, cooperative education, cross-registration, distance learning, double major, dual enrollment of high school students, ESL, honors, independent study, internships, liberal arts/career combination, study abroad, teacher certification program, Washington semester. **Credit/placement by examination:** AP, CLEP, IB, SAT, institutional tests. 30 credit hours maximum toward bachelor's degree. **Support services:** Pre-admission summer program, reduced course load, remedial instruction, study skills assistance, tutoring, writing center.

Majors. **Area/ethnic studies:** African-American, Asian. **Biology:** General, biochemistry. **Business:** Accounting, business admin, finance, labor relations, management information systems, managerial economics, marketing. **Communications:** General. **Computer sciences:** General. **Education:** Art, early childhood, elementary, health, secondary, special. **Foreign languages:** General, classics, French, Italian, Spanish. **History:** General. **Liberal arts:** Arts/sciences. **Math:** General. **Parks/recreation:** Sports admin. **Philosophy/religion:** Philosophy, religion. **Physical sciences:** Chemistry, physics. **Protective services:** Criminal justice. **Psychology:** General. **Public administration:** Social work. **Social sciences:** Anthropology, economics, international relations, political science, sociology. **Theology:** Religious ed, sacred music. **Visual/performing arts:** General, art history/conservation, commercial/advertising art, music history, music performance, theater arts management.

Most popular majors. Business/marketing 21%, communications/journalism 13%, education 7%, health sciences 16%, psychology 6%, social sciences 8%.

Computing on campus. PC or laptop required. 350 workstations in dormitories, library, computer center, student center. Dormitories wired for high-speed internet access and linked to campus network. Online course registration, online library, helpline, repair service, student web hosting, wireless network available.

Student life. **Freshman orientation:** Mandatory, $225 fee. Preregistration for classes offered. 2-day program held at various times from June through July. **Policies:** 1.8 GPA housing requirement. **Housing:** Coed dorms, special housing for disabled, apartments, substance-free housing available. $250 fully refundable deposit, deadline 5/1. **Activities:** Pep band, choral groups, drama, radio station, student government, student newspaper, TV station, Adelante, Black students union, international students organization, community service organizations, campus ministry, Puerto Rican Institute, Amnesty International, Student Ambassadors.

Athletics. NCAA. **Intercollegiate:** Baseball M, basketball, cross-country, golf M, soccer, softball W, swimming, tennis W, track and field, volleyball W. **Intramural:** Basketball, football (non-tackle), racquetball, soccer, softball, tennis, volleyball. **Team name:** Pirates.

Student services. Alcohol/substance abuse counseling, campus ministries, career counseling, services for economically disadvantaged, student employment services, financial aid counseling, health services, minority student services, personal counseling, placement for graduates. **Physically disabled:** Services for visually, speech, hearing impaired.

Contact. E-mail: thehall@shu.edu
Phone: (973) 761-9332 Toll-free number: (800) 843-4255
Fax: (973) 275-2040
Robert Herr, Director of Admission, Seton Hall University, 400 South Orange Avenue, South Orange, NJ 07079-2680

Stevens Institute of Technology

Hoboken, New Jersey — **CB member**
www.stevens.edu — **CB code: 2819**

- Private 4-year university and engineering college
- Residential campus in small city
- 1,786 degree-seeking undergraduates: 25% women, 5% African American, 13% Asian American, 9% Hispanic American, 5% international
- 2,707 degree-seeking graduate students
- 47% of applicants admitted
- SAT or ACT (ACT writing optional), application essay, interview required
- 72% graduate within 6 years; 12% enter graduate study

General. Founded in 1870. Regionally accredited. **Degrees:** 367 bachelor's awarded; master's, doctoral offered. **ROTC:** Army, Air Force. **Location:** One mile from New York City. **Calendar:** Semester, extensive summer session. **Full-time faculty:** 210 total; 84% have terminal degrees, 20% minority, 17% women. **Part-time faculty:** 121 total; 19% women. **Class size:** 45% < 20, 43% 20-39, 6% 40-49, 4% 50-99, 3% >100. **Special facilities:** Laboratory for coastal, ocean and naval engineering, environmental laboratory, design and manufacturing institute, advanced telecommunications institute, center for product lifecycle management, materials institute, geoenvironmental laboratory, optical communications lab, management lab, quantum cascade laser, center for mass spectrometry, center for microchemical systems, computer visualization laboratory.

Freshman class profile. 2,418 applied, 1,131 admitted, 484 enrolled.

Mid 50% test scores		Return as sophomores:	88%
SAT verbal:	560-660	Out-of-state:	39%
SAT math:	620-710	Live on campus:	88%
Rank in top quarter:	81%	Fraternities:	26%
Rank in top tenth:	49%	Sororities:	21%
End year in good standing:	98%		

Basis for selection. GED not accepted. Admissions committee meets to review applicant's file once official transcript and standardized test scores have been received and interview requirement has been completed. Other information submitted (essay, recommendations, etc.) is considered as well. SAT Subject Tests required for accelerated premed, predentistry, or prelaw programs and recommended for all others. Students who live outside a 250-mile radius and are unable to visit campus may schedule a phone interview. Additional interview with departmental committee required of applicants to accelerated premed, predentistry, and prelaw programs. **Homeschooled:** Letter of recommendation (nonparent) required.

High school preparation. 16 units required. Required and recommended units include English 4, mathematics 4, social studies 2, history 2, science 3-4 (laboratory 3-4), foreign language 2 and academic electives 4. Business, engineering, computer science, and applied science programs require 2 algebra, 1 geometry, 1 pre-calculus or calculus, 1 chemistry, 1 physics, 1 biology. Electives: computer science, economics, AP courses.

2005-2006 Annual costs. Tuition/fees: $31,835. Room/board: $9,500. Books/supplies: $900. Personal expenses: $750.

2005-2006 Financial aid. Need-based: 430 full-time freshmen applied for aid; 350 were judged to have need; 350 of these received aid. Average need met was 86%. Average scholarship/grant was $14,530; average loan $3,546. 73% of total undergraduate aid awarded as scholarships/grants, 27% as loans/jobs. **Non-need-based:** Awarded to 1,182 full-time undergraduates, including 324 freshmen. Scholarships awarded for academics, leadership, music/drama, ROTC.

Application procedures. Admission: Priority date 11/15; deadline 2/15 (postmark date). $55 fee, may be waived for applicants with need. Application may be submitted online. Admission notification on a rolling basis beginning on or about 3/15. Must reply by May 1 or within 2 week(s) if notified thereafter. **Financial aid:** Priority date 2/15; no closing date. FAFSA required. Applicants notified on a rolling basis starting 3/30; must reply by 5/1.

Academics. Special study options: Accelerated study, combined bachelor's/graduate degree, cooperative education, cross-registration, distance learning, double major, dual enrollment of high school students, honors, independent study, internships, study abroad. 4-year bachelor's/master's programs in all disciplines; dual enrollment program with New York University. **Credit/placement by examination:** AP, CLEP, IB, SAT. **Support services:** Preadmission summer program, reduced course load, remedial instruction, study skills assistance, tutoring, writing center.

Majors. Biology: Biochemistry. **Business:** Business admin, management information systems. **Computer sciences:** General, networking, security. **Engineering:** General, biomedical, chemical, civil, computer, electrical, environmental, materials, materials science, mechanical, physics. **Engineering technology:** Industrial management. **History:** General. **Interdisciplinary:** Math/computer science. **Liberal arts:** Arts/sciences. **Math:** Applied. **Physical sciences:** Chemistry, physics.

Most popular majors. Business/marketing 10%, computer/information sciences 18%, engineering/engineering technologies 66%.

Computing on campus. PC or laptop required. 484 workstations in dormitories, library, computer center, student center. Dormitories wired for high-speed internet access and linked to campus network. Commuter students can connect to campus network. Online course registration, online library, helpline, repair service, student web hosting, wireless network available.

Student life. Freshman orientation: Mandatory, $400 fee. Preregistration for classes offered. 3 day mandatory freshman orientation, during which students travel into New York City for baseball games, museum trips, group activities and seminars on adjusting to college life. **Policies:** Honor system observed. **Housing:** Guaranteed on-campus for all undergraduates. Coed dorms, single-sex dorms, apartments, fraternity/sorority housing, substance-free housing available. $350 nonrefundable deposit, deadline 6/15. Freshmen not living at home must live on campus. **Activities:** Bands, choral groups, dance, drama, literary magazine, music ensembles, musical theater, radio station, student government, student newspaper, TV station, over 70 organizations.

Athletics. NCAA. **Intercollegiate:** Baseball M, basketball, cross-country, equestrian W, fencing, field hockey W, golf, lacrosse, soccer, swimming, tennis, track and field, volleyball, wrestling M. **Intramural:** Archery, badminton, basketball, cricket, football (non-tackle), lacrosse M, racquetball, soccer, softball, squash, tennis, volleyball. **Team name:** Ducks.

Student services. Alcohol/substance abuse counseling, campus ministries, career counseling, services for economically disadvantaged, student employment services, financial aid counseling, health services, minority student services, personal counseling, placement for graduates, veterans' counselor, women's services. **Physically disabled:** Services for visually, speech, hearing impaired.

Contact. E-mail: admissions@stevens.edu
Phone: (201) 216-5194 Toll-free number: (800) 458-5323
Fax: (201) 216-8348
Daniel Gallagher, Dean of University Admissions, Stevens Institute of Technology, Castle Point on Hudson, Hoboken, NJ 07030

Talmudical Academy of New Jersey

Adelphia, New Jersey

CB code: 0686

- Private 4-year rabbinical college for men affiliated with Jewish faith
- Large town

General. Founded in 1967. Accredited by AARTS. **Calendar:** Semester.

Annual costs/financial aid. Tuition/fees (2005-2006): $8,000.

Contact. Phone: (732) 431-1600
Registrar and Admissions Director, Route 524, PO Box 7, Adelphia, NJ 07710

Thomas Edison State College

Trenton, New Jersey — **CB member**
www.tesc.edu — **CB code: 0682**

- Public 4-year liberal arts college
- Small city
- 10,904 degree-seeking undergraduates: 100% part-time, 44% women, 12% African American, 2% Asian American, 6% Hispanic American, 1% Native American, 2% international
- 320 degree-seeking graduate students

General. Founded in 1972. Regionally accredited. Provides flexibility to complete degree, including credit by examination, assessment of experiential learning, guided study, online courses, e-pack courses and credit for corporate and military training. **Degrees:** 1,799 bachelor's, 261 associate awarded; master's offered. **Location:** 45 miles from Philadelphia, 76 miles from New York City. **Calendar:** Continuous.

Basis for selection. Open admission, but selective for some programs. Applicants should be at least 21 years old. Certain programs in health professions limited to persons holding appropriate certification. Admission to bachelor's degree nursing program limited to registered nurses (RNs) currently licensed in the USA.

2005-2006 Annual costs. Tuition/fees: $3,780; $5,400 out-of-state.

2005-2006 Financial aid. Need-based: 22% of total undergraduate aid awarded as scholarships/grants, 78% as loans/jobs. **Additional information:** Financial aid applications should be received two months before each new term begins.

Application procedures. Admission: No deadline. $75 fee. Application may be submitted online. Admission notification on a rolling basis. **Financial aid:** No deadline. FAFSA, institutional form required. Applicants notified on a rolling basis.

Academics. Special study options: Distance learning, external degree, independent study. Joint degree program with the University of Medicine and Dentistry of New Jersey for Bachelor of Science in Health Sciences. **Credit/placement by examination:** AP, CLEP. 60 credit hours maximum toward associate degree, 120 toward bachelor's.

Majors. Agriculture: Horticulture. **Biology:** General. **Business:** Accounting, banking/financial services, business admin, entrepreneurial studies, finance, hotel/motel admin, human resources, insurance, international, labor relations, logistics, marketing, office management, operations, organizational behavior, purchasing, real estate, retailing, transportation. **Communications:** General, advertising, journalism. **Computer sciences:** Computer science. **Conservation:** Environmental science, environmental studies, forestry. **Engineering technology:** Architectural drafting, biomedical, civil, computer systems, construction, electrical, manufacturing, mechanical, nuclear, surveying. **English:** English lit. **Family/consumer sciences:** Child care. **Foreign languages:** General. **Health:** Clinical lab science, cytotechnology, dental hygiene, facilities admin, health services, health services admin, medical radiologic technology/radiation therapy, mental health services, nuclear medical technology, nursing (RN), perfusion technology, public health ed, radiation protection, respiratory therapy technology, veterinary technology/assistant. **History:** General. **Interdisciplinary:** Gerontology, natural sciences. **Legal studies:** Paralegal. **Liberal arts:** Arts/sciences, humanities. **Math:** General. **Mechanic/repair:** Aircraft. **Parks/recreation:** General. **Philosophy/religion:** Philosophy, religion. **Physical sciences:** Chemistry, physics. **Protective services:** Fire safety technology, law enforcement admin. **Psychology:** General. **Public administration:** General, community org/advocacy, human services. **Social sciences:** General, anthropology, economics, political science, sociology. **Transportation:** Air traffic control, airline/commercial pilot, aviation. **Visual/performing arts:** Art, dramatic, photography.

Most popular majors. Business/marketing 13%, engineering/engineering technologies 18%, liberal arts 32%, social sciences 6%.

Computing on campus. Commuter students can connect to campus network. Online library, wireless network available.

Student services. Adult student services, financial aid counseling, veterans' counselor. **Physically disabled:** Services for visually, hearing impaired.

Contact. E-mail: admissions@tesc.edu
Phone: (888) 442-8372 Toll-free number: (888) 442-8372
Fax: (609) 984-8447
Renee San Giacomo, Director of Admissions, Thomas Edison State College, 101 West State Street, Trenton, NJ 08608-1176

University of Medicine and Dentistry of New Jersey: School of Health Related Professions

Newark, New Jersey
www.shrp.umdj.edu **CB code: 0598**

- Public upper-division health science college
- Commuter campus in large city
- Application essay, interview required

General. Founded in 1976. Regionally accredited. Courses offered through videoconferencing in Newark, Scotch Plains, and Stratford. **Degrees:** 8 bachelor's, 4 associate awarded; master's, doctoral offered. **Location:** 15 miles from New York City. **Calendar:** Semester, limited summer session. **Full-time faculty:** 110 total. **Part-time faculty:** 20 total. **Special facilities:** Accelerators.

Student profile. 600 degree-seeking undergraduates.

Out-of-state:	3%	**25 or older:**	67%

Basis for selection. Open admission. College transcript, application essay, interview required. Admission requirements vary per program; transfer applicants evaluated by faculty and associate dean. Minimum GPA and interview most important; health-related experience and letters of recommendation also important. Qualified minority, disabled and disadvantaged students encouraged to apply. Application procedures and closing dates vary per program. Transfer accepted as sophomores, juniors, seniors.

2005-2006 Annual costs. Tuition/fees: $7,160; $10,490 out-of-state. Fees are 50% higher for out-of-state students. Books/supplies: $1,000.

Application procedures. Admission: Rolling admission. $50 fee. Application may be submitted online. **Financial aid:** Priority date 5/4. Notification of awards on rolling basis; students must reply within 3 weeks of notification. FAFSA, institutional form required.

Academics. Special study options: Accelerated study, combined bachelor's/graduate degree, cross-registration, distance learning, double major, dual enrollment of high school students, independent study, internships, liberal arts/career combination. **Credit/placement by examination:** CLEP, IB, institutional tests. Maximum of half of graduation requirement credits for professional component may be earned by examination.

Majors. Biology: Toxicology. **Health:** Clinical lab science, cytotechnology, dental hygiene, health services, medical radiologic technology/radiation therapy, nuclear medical technology, physician assistant, respiratory therapy technology, sonography.

Computing on campus. 50 workstations in library, computer center. Commuter students can connect to campus network. Online course registration, online library, helpline, repair service available.

Student life. Activities: Student professional organizations (by allied health specialty).

Student services. Adult student services, career counseling, student employment services, health services, on-campus daycare, personal counseling, placement for graduates, veterans' counselor.

Contact. E-mail: shrpadm@umdnj.edu
Phone: (973) 972-5454 Fax: (973) 972-7463
Brian Lewis, Assistant Dean for Enrollment Services, University of Medicine and Dentistry of New Jersey: School of Health Related Professions, 65 Bergen Street, Newark, NJ 07107-3001

University of Medicine and Dentistry of New Jersey: School of Nursing

Newark, New Jersey
CB code: 0769

- Public 4-year nursing college
- Commuter campus in large city
- 530 degree-seeking undergraduates

General. Founded in 1992. Regionally accredited. All undergraduate programs are joint degree programs: general education courses are taught by joint degree partner, while nursing content is taught by UMDNJ. All courses meet on campus of joint partner. **Degrees:** 164 bachelor's, 137 associate awarded; master's, doctoral offered. **Location:** 10 miles from New York City. **Calendar:** Semester, extensive summer session.

Basis for selection. Each program has established criteria for admissions. Minimum GPA and interview most important. Nursing and health related experiences and letters of recommendation also important. Qualified minority, handicapped, and disadvantaged students encouraged to apply. Essay, interview recommended.

High school preparation. Specific high school course requirements vary by program.

2005-2006 Annual costs. All undergraduate degree programs are joint degree programs: associate degree with Middlesex County College, bachelor's degrees with Ramapo College and Rowan University. Tuition is determined by joint degree partner. Books/supplies: $775.

Application procedures. Admission: No deadline. $30 fee. Admission notification on a rolling basis. Closing date varies for each program. **Financial aid:** Priority date 3/1; no closing date. Applicants notified on a rolling basis.

Academics. Special study options: Accelerated study, double major, independent study. 3 joint degree programs: AS in nursing with Middlesex County College and BSN with Ramapo College of NJ and New Jersey Institute of Technology, MS in nursing transition option for registered nurses. **Credit/placement by examination:** CLEP. **Support services:** Reduced course load, tutoring.

Majors. Health: Nursing assistant.

Computing on campus. 10 workstations in computer center.

Student life. Activities: Student government, student newspaper, Student professional organizations by nursing specialty.

Student services. Adult student services, career counseling, student employment services, health services, on-campus daycare, personal counseling, placement for graduates, veterans' counselor. **Physically disabled:** Services for visually, hearing impaired.

Contact. Phone: (973) 972-5336 Fax: (973) 972-7453
Lesley Perry, Director of Admissions, University of Medicine and Dentistry of New Jersey: School of Nursing, 65 Bergen Street, Room 1126, Newark, NJ 07101

Westminster Choir College of Rider University

Princeton, New Jersey
www.rider.edu/284.htm **CB code: 2974**

- Private 4-year music college
- Residential campus in small town
- 324 degree-seeking undergraduates
- 119 graduate students
- SAT or ACT, application essay required

General. Founded in 1926. Regionally accredited. All students perform for 3 years in Symphonic Choir with major orchestras such as New York Philharmonic and Philadelphia Orchestra. Most students receive Bachelor of Music degree. **Degrees:** 42 bachelor's awarded; master's offered. **Location:** 50 miles from New York City and Philadelphia. **Calendar:** Semester, limited summer session. **Full-time faculty:** 35 total. **Part-time faculty:** 50 total. **Special facilities:** 21 pipe organs, 120 pianos, 400,000-volume choral library, Organ Historical Society archives, 9,000 recordings, voice resource center.

Freshman class profile. 88 enrolled.

Out-of-state:	80%	**Live on campus:**	98%

Basis for selection. Music audition on instrument for which applying most important. School achievement record and test scores also considered. Audition required; interview recommended.

High school preparation. 16 units required. Required and recommended units include English 4, social studies 2, science 5 and foreign language 2. 2 music units required. Background in choral music expected and music theory recommended.

2006-2007 Annual costs. Tuition/fees (projected): $23,470. Room/board: $9,200. Books/supplies: $500. Personal expenses: $700.

Financial aid. Additional information: Approximately 130 churches employ students for weekend positions as organists, directors, and soloists. Average earnings are $2,000 to $3,000 per year.

Application procedures. Admission: Priority date 5/1; no deadline. $40 fee, may be waived for applicants with need. Admission notification on a rolling basis. **Financial aid:** Priority date 3/1; no closing date. FAFSA required. Applicants notified on a rolling basis starting 4/1; must reply within 2 week(s) of notification.

Academics. 75% music, 25% liberal arts required for Bachelor of Music. All students study voice and keyboard and sing in choirs. Bachelor of Arts students study 50% music, 50% liberal arts. Master of Music degree awarded. **Special study options:** Double major, dual enrollment of high school students, independent study, internships, study abroad, teacher certification program. Cooperative program with Princeton University. **Credit/placement by examination:** CLEP, institutional tests. **Support services:** Learning center, pre-admission summer program, reduced course load, remedial instruction, tutoring.

Majors. Education: Music. **Theology:** Sacred music. **Visual/performing arts:** Music theory/composition, piano/organ, voice/opera.

Computing on campus. 58 workstations in library, computer center.

Student life. Housing: Guaranteed on-campus for all undergraduates. Coed dorms, single-sex dorms available. **Activities:** Choral groups, drama, music ensembles, musical theater, opera, radio station, student government, student newspaper, symphony orchestra, composers' guild, Music Educators National Conference, Black and Hispanic Alliance, Christian Life Fellowship.

Athletics. NCAA. **Intramural:** Baseball M, basketball, cross-country, field hockey W, golf M, soccer, softball W, swimming, tennis, track and field, volleyball, wrestling M.

Student services. Career counseling, student employment services, health services, personal counseling, placement for graduates.

Contact. E-mail: wccadmission@rider.edu
Phone: (609) 921-7144 Toll-free number: (800) 96-CHOIR
Fax: (609) 921-2538
Katherine Shields, Associate Director of Admissions, Westminster Choir College of Rider University, 101 Walnut Lane, Princeton, NJ 08540-3899

William Paterson University of New Jersey

Wayne, New Jersey **CB member**
www.wpunj.edu **CB code: 2518**

- Public 4-year university and liberal arts college
- Commuter campus in large town
- 9,037 degree-seeking undergraduates: 18% part-time, 58% women, 13% African American, 6% Asian American, 17% Hispanic American, 1% international
- 894 degree-seeking graduate students
- 67% of applicants admitted
- SAT or ACT (ACT writing optional), application essay required
- 48% graduate within 6 years

General. Founded in 1855. Regionally accredited. **Degrees:** 1,608 bachelor's awarded; master's offered. **ROTC:** Air Force. **Location:** 20 miles from New York City. **Calendar:** Semester, limited summer session. **Full-time faculty:** 372 total; 90% have terminal degrees, 33% minority, 45% women. **Part-time faculty:** 699 total; 15% minority, 47% women. **Class size:** 44% < 20, 53% 20-39, 2% 40-49, less than 1% 50-99, less than 1% >100. **Special facilities:** 5 Silicon Graphics Iris workstations; satellite uplink and downlink capabilities; 2 theaters, fully wireless college of business and education center.

Freshman class profile. 5,380 applied, 3,592 admitted, 1,421 enrolled.

Mid 50% test scores		**Return as sophomores:**	77%
SAT verbal:	450-540	**Out-of-state:**	2%
SAT math:	450-550	**Live on campus:**	42%
Rank in top quarter:	30%	**International:**	1%
Rank in top tenth:	12%		

Basis for selection. School record and test score most important; recommendations also important; class rank and essay considered. Audition required for music programs; portfolio required for art programs.

High school preparation. 16 units required. Required units include English 4, mathematics 3, social studies 2, science 2 (laboratory 2) and academic electives 5. Advanced math, literature, foreign language, social sciences required for academic electives.

2005-2006 Annual costs. Tuition/fees: $8,740; $13,856 out-of-state. Room/board: $9,060. Books/supplies: $800. Personal expenses: $1,500.

2005-2006 Financial aid. Need-based: 1,015 full-time freshmen applied for aid; 746 were judged to have need; 710 of these received aid. Average need met was 82%. Average scholarship/grant was $6,412; average loan $2,584. 50% of total undergraduate aid awarded as scholarships/grants, 50% as loans/jobs. **Non-need-based:** Awarded to 1,157 full-time undergraduates, including 356 freshmen. Scholarships awarded for academics, alumni affiliation, minority status, music/drama.

Application procedures. Admission: Priority date 4/1; deadline 5/1. $50 fee, may be waived for applicants with need. Application may be submitted online. Admission notification on a rolling basis beginning on or about 10/1. Must reply by May 1 or within 2 week(s) if notified thereafter. **Financial aid:** Closing date 4/1. FAFSA required. Applicants notified on a rolling basis starting 3/1; must reply within 2 week(s) of notification.

Academics. Honors programs available in biopsychology, humanities, cognitive science, life science and environmental ethics, music, nursing, performing and literary arts. **Special study options:** Accelerated study, cross-registration, distance learning, double major, dual enrollment of high school students, ESL, exchange student, honors, independent study, internships, study abroad, teacher certification program, Washington semester. Cluster courses (program that provides opportunities for students and faculty to study and learn together in courses grouped in interdisciplinary clusters of three), international exchange program. **Credit/placement by examination:** AP, CLEP, SAT, ACT, institutional tests. 90 credit hours maximum toward bachelor's degree. **Support services:** Learning center, pre-admission summer program, reduced course load, remedial instruction, study skills assistance, tutoring, writing center.

Majors. Area/ethnic studies: African, African-American, Caribbean, French, Latin American, women's. **Biology:** General, biotechnology. **Business:** Accounting, business admin, finance, international finance, managerial economics. **Communications:** General. **Computer sciences:** General, computer science. **Conservation:** General, environmental science. **Education:** Elementary, health, mathematics, music, physical, special. **Foreign languages:** French, Spanish. **Health:** Nursing (RN), public health nursing, speech pathology. **History:** General. **Math:** General. **Parks/recreation:** Exercise sciences. **Philosophy/religion:** Philosophy. **Physical sciences:** Chemistry. **Psychology:**

General. **Social sciences:** Anthropology, economics, geography, political science, sociology. **Visual/performing arts:** Art, jazz, music management, music performance.

Most popular majors. Business/marketing 17%, communications/journalism 15%, education 9%, English 7%, psychology 11%, social sciences 17%, visual/performing arts 8%.

Computing on campus. 700 workstations in dormitories, library, computer center. Dormitories wired for high-speed internet access and linked to campus network. Commuter students can connect to campus network. Online course registration, online library, helpline available.

Student life. Freshman orientation: Mandatory. 2-day program held twice in the early summer. Freshmen and parents are invited and may stay overnight for nominal fee. **Housing:** Coed dorms, special housing for disabled, apartments available. $150 deposit, deadline 4/1. Academic interest housing, 21-or-older dorm, apartment-style housing (for groups of students who are 21 or older, or who are 20 with 52 or more credits) available. Floor for women available in one residence hall. **Activities:** Dance, drama, film society, literary magazine, musical theater, radio station, student government, student newspaper, TV station, Black student association, Christian Fellowship Club, Jewish student association, Feminist Collective, Organization of Latin American Students, Catholic campus ministry, United Asian Americans, Coalition of Lesbians, Gays & Friends.

Athletics. NCAA. **Intercollegiate:** Baseball M, basketball, cross-country, field hockey W, football (tackle) M, soccer, softball W, swimming, tennis W, track and field, volleyball W. **Intramural:** Basketball, field hockey W, soccer W, softball, tennis, volleyball. **Team name:** Pioneers.

Student services. Adult student services, alcohol/substance abuse counseling, campus ministries, career counseling, services for economically disadvantaged, student employment services, financial aid counseling, health services, legal services, minority student services, on-campus daycare, personal counseling, placement for graduates, veterans' counselor, women's services. **Physically disabled:** Services for visually, speech, hearing impaired.

Contact. E-mail: admissions@wpunj.edu
Phone: (973) 720-2125 Toll-free number: (877) 978-3923
Fax: (973) 720-2910
Jonathan McCoy, Director of Admissions, William Paterson University of New Jersey, 300 Pompton Road, Wayne, NJ 07470

New Mexico

College of Santa Fe

Santa Fe, New Mexico
www.csf.edu
CB member
CB code: 4676

- Private 4-year liberal arts college
- Residential campus in small city
- 1,225 degree-seeking undergraduates: 49% part-time, 58% women
- 293 degree-seeking graduate students
- 73% of applicants admitted
- SAT or ACT with writing, application essay, interview required
- 40% graduate within 6 years

General. Founded in 1947. Regionally accredited. **Degrees:** 304 bachelor's, 6 associate awarded; master's offered. **ROTC:** Air Force. **Location:** 60 miles from Albuquerque. **Calendar:** Semester, limited summer session. **Full-time faculty:** 76 total; 79% have terminal degrees, 14% minority, 36% women. **Part-time faculty:** 199 total; 12% minority, 46% women. **Class size:** 88% < 20, 12% 20-39, less than 1% 50-99. **Special facilities:** Theater center, art history center, photographic arts center, film production facility, contemporary music facility, creative writing center.

Freshman class profile. 598 applied, 437 admitted, 129 enrolled.

Mid 50% test scores			
SAT verbal:	520-630	GPA 2.0-2.99:	40%
SAT math:	470-570	Rank in top quarter:	30%
ACT:	18-25	Rank in top tenth:	9%
GPA 3.50 or higher:	27%	Return as sophomores:	75%
GPA 3.0-3.49:	33%	Out-of-state:	82%
		Live on campus:	95%

Basis for selection. Admissions based on secondary school record, interview, talent, ability, character, and personal qualities. Class rank, recommendations, standardized test scores, essay, and volunteer work also important.

High school preparation. 18 units required. Required and recommended units include English 4, mathematics 2-3, social studies 2, history 2, science 2-3 (laboratory 2), foreign language 2 and academic electives 6.

2005-2006 Annual costs. Tuition/fees: $22,276. Room/board: $6,702. Books/supplies: $840. Personal expenses: $1,226.

2005-2006 Financial aid. Need-based: Average need met was 77%. Average scholarship/grant was $7,782; average loan $3,661. 59% of total undergraduate aid awarded as scholarships/grants, 41% as loans/jobs. **Non-need-based:** Scholarships awarded for academics, alumni affiliation, art, athletics, leadership, minority status, music/drama.

Application procedures. Admission: Priority date 3/15; no deadline. $35 fee, may be waived for applicants with need. Application may be submitted online. Admission notification on a rolling basis beginning on or about 1/15. Preferred that student replies by May 1. **Financial aid:** Priority date 3/15; no closing date. FAFSA required. Applicants notified on a rolling basis starting 3/1; must reply by 5/1 or within 2 week(s) of notification.

Academics. Special study options: Accelerated study, cooperative education, distance learning, double major, dual enrollment of high school students, exchange student, independent study, internships, New York semester, semester at sea, student-designed major, study abroad, teacher certification program. Evening curriculum for adults, London semester, Lasallian Consortium for Study Abroad. **Credit/placement by examination:** AP, CLEP, institutional tests. 24 credit hours maximum toward associate degree, 48 toward bachelor's. **Support services:** Learning center, reduced course load, remedial instruction, study skills assistance, tutoring, writing center.

Majors. Area/ethnic studies: Regional. **Biology:** Conservation. **Business:** General, accounting, international, management information systems. **Communications:** General. **Computer sciences:** Computer science, information technology. **Conservation:** Environmental science, management/policy. **Education:** Elementary, secondary. **English:** Creative writing, English lit, technical writing. **Health:** Art therapy. **Interdisciplinary:** Intercultural. **Liberal arts:** Humanities. **Philosophy/religion:** Religion. **Protective services:** Law enforcement admin. **Psychology:** General, counseling. **Public administration:** General. **Social sciences:** Political science. **Visual/performing arts:** Acting, art history/conservation, arts management, directing/producing, dramatic, film/cinema, multimedia, painting, photography, sculpture, studio arts, theater arts management, theater design.

Most popular majors. Business/marketing 22%, computer/information sciences 11%, education 13%, psychology 10%, visual/performing arts 24%.

Computing on campus. 74 workstations in library, computer center. Dormitories wired for high-speed internet access and linked to campus network. Online library, helpline, student web hosting, wireless network available.

Student life. Freshman orientation: Mandatory. Preregistration for classes offered. 4-day program involves meetings with faculty advisors, social activities, club sign-ups, off-campus trips to learn more about the community. **Policies:** Freshmen permitted cars on campus. **Housing:** Guaranteed on-campus for freshmen. Coed dorms, single-sex dorms, special housing for disabled, apartments, substance-free housing available. Separate quiet floors, substance-free floors, smoking floors available. **Activities:** Choral groups, dance, drama, literary magazine, music ensembles, musical theater, student government, student newspaper, TV station, Amnesty International, bowling club, student writers association, Crafty Progressives, anime club, Soo Bak Do, rugby club, composting club, Sierra Club, outdoor recreation program.

Athletics. NAIA. **Intercollegiate:** Tennis. **Intramural:** Basketball, racquetball, soccer, volleyball. **Team name:** Spin.

Student services. Adult student services, alcohol/substance abuse counseling, campus ministries, career counseling, student employment services, financial aid counseling, health services, personal counseling, placement for graduates, veterans' counselor, women's services. **Physically disabled:** Services for visually, speech, hearing impaired. **Learning disabled:** Comprehensive services available.

Contact. E-mail: admissions@csf.edu
Phone: (505) 473-6133 Toll-free number: (800) 456-2673
Fax: (505) 473-6129
Jeff Miller, Dean of Enrollment, College of Santa Fe, 1600 Saint Michael's Drive, Santa Fe, NM 87505-7634

College of the Southwest

Hobbs, New Mexico
www.csw.edu
CB code: 4116

- Private 4-year liberal arts and teachers college
- Commuter campus in large town
- 504 degree-seeking undergraduates: 22% part-time, 60% women
- 82 degree-seeking graduate students
- 50% of applicants admitted
- SAT or ACT with writing required

General. Founded in 1956. Regionally accredited. **Degrees:** 122 bachelor's awarded; master's offered. **Location:** 110 miles from Lubbock, Texas. **Calendar:** Semester, extensive summer session. **Full-time faculty:** 30 total. **Part-time faculty:** 60 total. **Class size:** 83% < 20, 16% 20-39, less than 1% 50-99.

Freshman class profile. 2,015 applied, 998 admitted, 75 enrolled.

Mid 50% test scores			
SAT verbal:	400-510	Rank in top quarter:	45%
SAT math:	410-560	Rank in top tenth:	14%
ACT:	15-20	End year in good standing:	90%
GPA 3.50 or higher:	41%	Return as sophomores:	53%
GPA 3.0-3.49:	37%	Out-of-state:	50%
GPA 2.0-2.99:	22%	Live on campus:	89%
		International:	3%

Basis for selection. Applicants must meet 2 of 3 criteria: ACT composite score of 19 or SAT combined score of 910(exclusive of Writing); cumulative high school GPA of 2.0; top half of graduating class. **Homeschooled:** Statement describing homeschool structure and mission, transcript of courses and grades, state high school equivalency certificate required. **Learning Disabled:** Students with special needs required to submit diagnostic test results in which special need was evaluated during last 3 years, Individual Education Plan (IEP), and other supporting documentation.

2006-2007 Annual costs. Tuition/fees (projected): $10,500. Room/board: $5,400. Books/supplies: $800. Personal expenses: $750.

2005-2006 Financial aid. Need-based: 72 full-time freshmen applied for aid; 60 were judged to have need; 60 of these received aid. Average need met was 76%. Average scholarship/grant was $5,166; average loan $2,465. 45% of total undergraduate aid awarded as scholarships/grants, 55%

as loans/jobs. **Non-need-based:** Scholarships awarded for academics, alumni affiliation, athletics, leadership, music/drama, religious affiliation, state residency.

Application procedures. Admission: No deadline. $25 fee. Application may be submitted online. Admission notification on a rolling basis beginning on or about 7/1. **Financial aid:** Priority date 4/1, closing date 6/1. FAFSA, institutional form required. Applicants notified on a rolling basis starting 4/1; must reply within 2 week(s) of notification.

Academics. 6 hours religious studies, 3 hours economics required of all students. **Special study options:** Combined bachelor's/graduate degree, cooperative education, distance learning, double major, internships, teacher certification program. Internet program for criminal justice degree only. **Credit/placement by examination:** AP, CLEP, IB, SAT, ACT. 45 credit hours maximum toward bachelor's degree. **Support services:** Reduced course load, remedial instruction, study skills assistance, tutoring.

Majors. Biology: General. **Business:** Accounting, business admin, management information systems, marketing. **Computer sciences:** Computer science. **Conservation:** General, environmental studies. **Education:** Bilingual, elementary, English, mathematics, physical, sales/marketing, science, secondary, social science, special. **History:** General. **Liberal arts:** Arts/sciences, humanities. **Math:** General. **Protective services:** Criminal justice. **Psychology:** General. **Social sciences:** General. **Visual/performing arts:** Dramatic, studio arts.

Most popular majors. Business/marketing 13%, education 37%, psychology 16%, security/protective services 14%.

Computing on campus. 35 workstations in library, computer center. Dormitories wired for high-speed internet access and linked to campus network. Commuter students can connect to campus network. Online library, helpline available.

Student life. Freshman orientation: Mandatory. Preregistration for classes offered. Held 1 week prior to beginning of classes. **Policies:** Freshmen permitted cars on campus. **Housing:** Single-sex dorms, apartments, substance-free housing available. $150 fully refundable deposit. **Activities:** Choral groups, drama, literary magazine, music ensembles, student government, student newspaper, accounting, teaching, and game clubs, Students in Free Enterprise, Alpha Phi Omega, Southwest Cultural Pride Club, Sigma Tau Delta, CSW Alumni Association.

Athletics. NAIA. **Intercollegiate:** Baseball M, cross-country, golf, rodeo, soccer, softball W, track and field, volleyball W. **Intramural:** Badminton, basketball, football (tackle) M, racquetball, soccer W, table tennis, volleyball W. **Team name:** Mustangs.

Student services. Campus ministries, student employment services, financial aid counseling, personal counseling, placement for graduates, veterans' counselor.

Contact. E-mail: admissions@csw.edu
Phone: (505) 392-6563 Toll-free number: (800) 530-4400 ext. 1007
Fax: (505) 392-6006
Karen Workentin, Dean of Admissions, College of the Southwest, 6610 Lovington Highway, Hobbs, NM 88240

Eastern New Mexico University

Portales, New Mexico
www.enmu.edu **CB code: 4299**

- Public 4-year university
- Residential campus in large town
- 3,043 degree-seeking undergraduates: 18% part-time, 56% women, 7% African American, 1% Asian American, 30% Hispanic American, 3% Native American, 1% international
- 588 degree-seeking graduate students
- 65% of applicants admitted
- SAT or ACT (ACT writing optional) required
- 35% graduate within 6 years

General. Founded in 1927. Regionally accredited. **Degrees:** 449 bachelor's, 5 associate awarded; master's offered. **Location:** 225 miles from Albuquerque; 120 miles from Lubbock, Texas. **Calendar:** Semester, extensive summer session. **Full-time faculty:** 149 total; 78% have terminal degrees, 13% minority, 44% women. **Part-time faculty:** 114 total; 19% have terminal degrees, 10% minority, 50% women. **Class size:** 52% < 20, 36% 20-39, 8% 40-49, 4% 50-99, less than 1% >100. **Special facilities:** Natural history museum, mineral museum, scanning and transmission electron microscopes.

Freshman class profile. 1,804 applied, 1,167 admitted, 567 enrolled.

Mid 50% test scores		**Rank in top quarter:**	34%
SAT verbal:	390-540	**Rank in top tenth:**	12%
SAT math:	380-550	**Return as sophomores:**	58%
ACT:	16-22	**Out-of-state:**	23%
GPA 3.50 or higher:	29%	**Live on campus:**	69%
GPA 3.0-3.49:	36%	**International:**	1%
GPA 2.0-2.99:	33%		

Basis for selection. Test scores, school record, recommendations important. Students not meeting regular admission standards may be admitted on probation. **Homeschooled:** Transcript of courses and grades required.

High school preparation. 14 units recommended. Recommended units include English 4, mathematics 3, social studies 2, science 4 and foreign language 1.

2005-2006 Annual costs. Tuition/fees: $2,784; $8,340 out-of-state. Room/board: $4,480.

2005-2006 Financial aid. Need-based: 361 full-time freshmen applied for aid; 359 were judged to have need; 359 of these received aid. Average need met was 36%. Average scholarship/grant was $3,034; average loan $2,753. 41% of total undergraduate aid awarded as scholarships/grants, 59% as loans/jobs. **Non-need-based:** Awarded to 1,171 full-time undergraduates, including 403 freshmen. Scholarships awarded for academics, alumni affiliation, art, athletics, leadership, music/drama, state residency. **Additional information:** Not all merit scholarships are need-based.

Application procedures. Admission: Priority date 8/15; no deadline. No application fee. Application may be submitted online. Admission notification on a rolling basis. **Financial aid:** Priority date 3/1; no closing date. FAFSA required. Applicants notified by 4/1; must reply within 3 week(s) of notification.

Academics. Special study options: Accelerated study, cooperative education, distance learning, double major, dual enrollment of high school students, exchange student, honors, independent study, internships, student-designed major, study abroad, teacher certification program. **Credit/placement by examination:** AP, CLEP, ACT, institutional tests. 32 credit hours maximum toward associate degree, 50 toward bachelor's. **Support services:** Learning center, pre-admission summer program, remedial instruction, tutoring.

Majors. Agriculture: Agribusiness operations. **Biology:** General. **Business:** Accounting, business admin, finance, human resources, management information systems, managerial economics, marketing. **Communications:** General, broadcast journalism, journalism. **Computer sciences:** General, computer science. **Conservation:** Wildlife. **Education:** Agricultural, business, early childhood, elementary, music, physical, sales/marketing, special. **Engineering technology:** General. **English:** Speech/rhetoric. **Family/consumer sciences:** General. **Foreign languages:** Spanish. **Health:** Audiology/speech pathology, clinical lab science, nursing (RN). **History:** General. **Liberal arts:** Arts/sciences. **Math:** General. **Parks/recreation:** Health/fitness. **Philosophy/religion:** Religion. **Physical sciences:** Chemistry, geology, physics. **Protective services:** Criminal justice. **Psychology:** General. **Public administration:** Social work. **Social sciences:** General, anthropology, political science, sociology. **Visual/performing arts:** Art, dramatic.

Most popular majors. Business/marketing 17%, education 22%, liberal arts 11%, visual/performing arts 6%.

Computing on campus. 493 workstations in dormitories, library, computer center. Dormitories linked to campus network. Commuter students can connect to campus network. Repair service available.

Student life. Freshman orientation: Mandatory, $60 fee. Preregistration for classes offered. **Policies:** Freshmen permitted cars on campus. **Housing:** Guaranteed on-campus for freshmen. Coed dorms, single-sex dorms, special housing for disabled, apartments, fraternity/sorority housing available. $150 fully refundable deposit. **Activities:** Bands, choral groups, dance, drama, film society, literary magazine, music ensembles, musical theater, radio station, student government, student newspaper, symphony orchestra, TV station, several religious, political, honorary, and service organization.

Athletics. NCAA. **Intercollegiate:** Baseball M, basketball, cross-country, football (tackle) M, rodeo, soccer, softball W, tennis W, track and field, volleyball W. **Intramural:** Badminton, basketball, cross-country, football (tackle) M, golf, racquetball, soccer, softball, tennis, volleyball. **Team name:** Greyhounds.

Student services. Adult student services, career counseling, student employment services, financial aid counseling, health services, minority student services, on-campus daycare, personal counseling, placement for graduates, veterans' counselor. **Physically disabled:** Services for visually, speech, hearing impaired.

Contact. Phone: (505) 562-2178 Toll-free number: (800) 367-3668
Fax: (505) 562-2566
Donna Kittrell, Director of Enrollment Services, Eastern New Mexico University, Station Seven, Portales, NM 88130

Institute of American Indian Arts
Santa Fe, New Mexico
www.iaiancad.org **CB code: 0180**

- Public 4-year visual arts and junior college
- Residential campus in small city
- 203 degree-seeking undergraduates: 19% part-time, 52% women
- 38% of applicants admitted
- Application essay required

General. Founded in 1962. Regionally accredited. Dedicated to providing education in fine arts and cultural studies to American Indians and Alaska Natives. **Degrees:** 15 bachelor's, 24 associate awarded. **Location:** 60 miles from Albuquerque. **Calendar:** Semester. **Full-time faculty:** 19 total. **Part-time faculty:** 19 total.

Freshman class profile. 112 applied, 43 admitted, 43 enrolled.

Basis for selection. Academic achievement, 2.25 high school GPA, art interest important. Art portfolio evaluated for potential. Handwritten statement of educational intention required. Quality of art portfolio most important. Spring term application priority date November 15. Portfolio required; interview recommended.

2005-2006 Annual costs. Tuition/fees: $2,490. Room/board: $4,536. Books/supplies: $1,850. Personal expenses: $2,400.

Financial aid. Additional information: For American Indian and Alaskan natives, financial aid available through Tribe or Native Corporation in which student is enrolled.

Application procedures. Admission: Closing date 8/4. $5 fee. Application may be submitted online. Admission notification on a rolling basis beginning on or about 5/1. Must reply by May 1 or within 1 week(s) if notified thereafter. **Financial aid:** Priority date 3/15; no closing date. FAFSA, institutional form required. Applicants notified on a rolling basis starting 5/1.

Academics. Most courses emphasize American Indian perspective. **Special study options:** Cross-registration, double major, exchange student, independent study, internships. **Credit/placement by examination:** CLEP, SAT, ACT, institutional tests. **Support services:** Learning center, remedial instruction, study skills assistance, tutoring.

Majors. English: Creative writing. **Interdisciplinary:** Museum. **Visual/performing arts:** Studio arts.

Computing on campus. 3 workstations in dormitories, library, computer center. Dormitories linked to campus network.

Student life. Freshman orientation: Mandatory. Preregistration for classes offered. Freshmen class orientation conducted each semester one week before registration. **Policies:** Freshmen permitted cars on campus. **Housing:** Guaranteed on-campus for freshmen. Coed dorms available. $150 deposit. Student housing provided on College of Santa Fe campus. **Activities:** Literary magazine, student government, student newspaper, TV station, student senate, Pow-Wow Club, traditional dance club, museum club, photography club, theater club, Campus Cleanup club.

Athletics. Intramural: Badminton, basketball, bowling, skiing, softball, swimming, table tennis, tennis, volleyball.

Student services. Alcohol/substance abuse counseling, career counseling, student employment services, financial aid counseling, personal counseling, placement for graduates.

Contact. E-mail: admissions@iaiancad.org
Phone: (505) 424-2332 Toll-free number: (800) 804-6422
Fax: (505) 424-4500
Ramus Suina, Director of Admissions/Dean of Students, Institute of American Indian Arts, 83 Avan Nu Po Road, Santa Fe, NM 87508-1300

International Institute of the Americas
Albuquerque, New Mexico
www.iia.edu

- Private 4-year business and health science college
- Commuter campus in large city
- 232 degree-seeking undergraduates: 3% African American, 67% Hispanic American, 13% Native American
- Interview required

General. Accredited by ACICS. 4 campuses in Arizona (Phoenix, West Valley, Mesa, Tucson) and 1 in New Mexico (Albuquerque). **Degrees:** 2 bachelor's, 18 associate awarded. **Calendar:** Continuous, extensive summer session. **Full-time faculty:** 14 total. **Part-time faculty:** 12 total. **Special facilities:** Child activity center.

Basis for selection. Open admission. Must have high school diploma or GED (earned prior to graduation from program of study) or pass CPAT entrance exam.

2006-2007 Annual costs. Tuition/fees (projected): $10,050.

Application procedures. Admission: No deadline. $200 fee. Application must be submitted on paper. Admission notification on a rolling basis. **Financial aid:** No deadline. FAFSA, institutional form required.

Academics. Special study options: Distance learning, liberal arts/career combination. **Credit/placement by examination:** CLEP.

Majors. Business: Business admin.

Computing on campus. Commuter students can connect to campus network. Online library available.

Student life. Freshman orientation: Mandatory.

Student services. Career counseling, financial aid counseling, on-campus daycare, placement for graduates.

Contact. Phone: (505) 880-2877 Toll-free number: (888) 744-6340
Fax: (505) 352-0199
John Pechota, Director of Admissions, International Institute of the Americas, 4201 Central Avenue NW, Suite J, Albuquerque, NM 87105

ITT Technical Institute: Albuquerque
Albuquerque, New Mexico
www.itt-tech.edu **CB code: 2690**

- For-profit 4-year technical college
- Commuter campus in large city

General. Accredited by ACICS. **Calendar:** Quarter.

Annual costs/financial aid. Tuition varies by program, $260-$368 per credit hour.

Contact. Phone: (505) 828-1114
Director of Recruitment, 5100 Masthead Street Northeast, Albuquerque, NM 87109

Metropolitan College of Court Reporting
Albuquerque, New Mexico
www.metropolitancollege.edu **CB code: 3069**

- For-profit 4-year college of court reporting
- Large city
- 100 undergraduates

General. Accredited by ACCSCT. **Degrees:** 2 bachelor's, 54 associate awarded. **Calendar:** Continuous. **Full-time faculty:** 20 total.

Basis for selection. Interview very important.

2005-2006 Annual costs. 33-month court reporter bachelor's degree program tuition $19,000.; 2-year paralegal associate's degree program tuition $10,989 without books, $12,989 with books.

Application procedures. Admission: No deadline. $50 fee. Admission notification on a rolling basis.

Academics. Credit/placement by examination: CLEP.

Majors. Business: Business admin.

Contact. E-mail: swilliams@metropolitancollege.edu
Phone: (505) 888-3400 Fax: (505) 254-3738
Sarah Williams, Director of Admissions, Metropolitan College of Court Reporting, 8100 Mountain Road N.E., Suite 200, Albuquerque, NM 87110

National American University
Albuquerque, New Mexico
www.national.edu **CB code: 5360**

- For-profit 4-year business college
- Large city
- 600 degree-seeking undergraduates

General. Founded in 1941. Regionally accredited. Free tutoring. **Degrees:** 155 bachelor's, 80 associate awarded. **ROTC:** Navy, Air Force. **Calendar:** Quarter. **Part-time faculty:** 60 total.

Basis for selection. Open admission.

2005-2006 Annual costs. Tuition/fees: $7,365. Books/supplies: $675.

Application procedures. **Admission:** No deadline. $25 fee. Admission notification on a rolling basis. **Financial aid:** No deadline. Institutional form required. Applicants notified on a rolling basis.

Academics. **Special study options:** Distance learning, independent study. **Credit/placement by examination:** CLEP. 45 credit hours maximum toward associate degree, 95 toward bachelor's. **Support services:** Tutoring.

Majors. **Business:** Accounting, business admin, management information systems.

Most popular majors. Business/marketing 82%, computer/information sciences 18%.

Computing on campus. 15 workstations in library, computer center.

Student life. **Activities:** Choral groups, literary magazine, music ensembles, TV station.

Student services. Adult student services, career counseling, student employment services, placement for graduates, veterans' counselor.

Contact. Phone: (505) 265-7517 Fax: (505) 265-7542
Nancy Pointer-Meason, Director of Admissions, National American University, 4775 Indian School Road Northeast, Suite 200, Albuquerque, NM 87110

New Mexico Highlands University
Las Vegas, New Mexico **CB member**
www.nmhu.edu **CB code: 4532**

- Public 4-year university
- Commuter campus in large town
- 1,784 degree-seeking undergraduates: 31% part-time, 61% women, 4% African American, 1% Asian American, 58% Hispanic American, 9% Native American
- 1,092 degree-seeking graduate students

General. Founded in 1893. Regionally accredited. **Degrees:** 332 bachelor's awarded; master's offered. **Location:** 68 miles from Santa Fe, 120 miles from Albuquerque. **Calendar:** Semester, limited summer session. **Full-time faculty:** 74 total. **Part-time faculty:** 37 total. **Class size:** 73% < 20, 24% 20-39, 2% 40-49, less than 1% 50-99.

Freshman class profile. 828 applied, 828 admitted, 236 enrolled.

Mid 50% test scores			
SAT verbal:	370-480	**GPA 2.0-2.99:**	43%
SAT math:	380-480	**Rank in top quarter:**	14%
ACT:	16-20	**Rank in top tenth:**	5%
GPA 3.50 or higher:	27%	**End year in good standing:**	76%
GPA 3.0-3.49:	25%	**Return as sophomores:**	54%
		Out-of-state:	12%

Basis for selection. Open admission. All tests used for placement purposes. If student has not taken ACT, he or she must take COMPASS.

2005-2006 Annual costs. Tuition/fees: $2,300; $3,440 out-of-state. Room/board: $4,298. Books/supplies: $700. Personal expenses: $1,494.

2005-2006 Financial aid. **Need-based:** 238 full-time freshmen applied for aid; 211 were judged to have need; 209 of these received aid. Average need met was 68%. Average scholarship/grant was $4,766; average loan $1,339. 42% of total undergraduate aid awarded as scholarships/grants, 58% as loans/jobs. **Non-need-based:** Scholarships awarded for academics, athletics, leadership, minority status, music/drama, state residency. **Additional information:** Work study funds available on no-need basis to state residents.

Application procedures. **Admission:** No deadline. $15 fee, may be waived for applicants with need. Application may be submitted online. Admission notification on a rolling basis. **Financial aid:** Closing date 3/1. FAFSA required. Applicants notified on a rolling basis starting 5/15; must reply within 2 week(s) of notification.

Academics. **Special study options:** Combined bachelor's/graduate degree, distance learning, double major, dual enrollment of high school students, ESL, honors, independent study, internships, liberal arts/career combination, teacher certification program. **Credit/placement by examination:** AP, CLEP, institutional tests. As approved by appropriate department. **Support services:** Learning center, pre-admission summer program, reduced course load, remedial instruction, study skills assistance, tutoring, writing center.

Majors. **Biology:** General. **Business:** Accounting, business admin, finance, management information systems. **Communications:** General. **Computer sciences:** General, information systems. **Conservation:** Environmental studies, management/policy. **Education:** Elementary, physical, science, special. **Engineering:** General. **English:** English lit. **Foreign languages:** Spanish. **Health:** Clinical/medical social work. **History:** General. **Math:** General. **Parks/recreation:** Facilities management. **Physical sciences:** Chemistry, geology, physics. **Protective services:** Criminal justice. **Psychology:** General. **Social sciences:** Political science. **Visual/performing arts:** General, cinematography, design.

Most popular majors. Business/marketing 20%, education 27%, health sciences 28%, social sciences 8%.

Computing on campus. 250 workstations in dormitories, library, computer center, student center. Dormitories wired for high-speed internet access and linked to campus network. Commuter students can connect to campus network. Online course registration, online library, repair service available.

Student life. **Freshman orientation:** Mandatory. Preregistration for classes offered. **Policies:** Freshmen permitted cars on campus. **Housing:** Guaranteed on-campus for freshmen. Coed dorms, single-sex dorms, apartments available. $100 deposit, deadline 8/15. **Activities:** Bands, choral groups, dance, drama, film society, music ensembles, musical theater, radio station, student government, student newspaper, TV station, social work club, international student club, several ethnic and religious groups.

Athletics. NAIA, NCAA. **Intercollegiate:** Baseball M, basketball, cross-country, football (tackle) M, soccer W, softball W, track and field W, volleyball W, wrestling M. **Intramural:** Baseball M, basketball, golf, handball, racquetball, rifle, rugby, skiing, softball, swimming, table tennis, tennis, track and field. **Team name:** Cowboys, Cowgirls.

Student services. Adult student services, career counseling, student employment services, financial aid counseling, health services, minority student services, on-campus daycare, personal counseling, placement for graduates, veterans' counselor. **Physically disabled:** Services for visually impaired.

Contact. E-mail: admissions@nmhu.edu
Phone: (505) 454-3434 Toll-free number: (877) 338-6648
Fax: (505) 454-3552
John Coca, Director of Admissions, New Mexico Highlands University, Box 9000, Las Vegas, NM 87701

New Mexico Institute of Mining and Technology
Socorro, New Mexico **CB member**
www.nmt.edu **CB code: 4533**

- Public 4-year engineering and liberal arts college
- Residential campus in small town
- 1,184 degree-seeking undergraduates: 5% part-time, 27% women, 1% African American, 3% Asian American, 20% Hispanic American, 3% Native American, 3% international
- 364 degree-seeking graduate students
- 81% of applicants admitted
- SAT or ACT (ACT writing optional) required

General. Founded in 1889. Regionally accredited. Employment of students in research facilities central to programs. **Degrees:** 177 bachelor's, 14 associate awarded; master's, doctoral offered. **Location:** 75 miles from Albuquerque. **Calendar:** Semester, limited summer session. **Full-time faculty:** 125 total; 99% have terminal degrees, 17% minority, 20% women. **Part-time faculty:** 22 total; 9% have terminal degrees, 9% minority, 36% women. **Class size:** 58% < 20, 34% 20-39, 2% 40-49, 4% 50-99, less than

1% >100. **Special facilities:** Experimental mine, mineral museum, laboratory for atmospheric physics and chemistry, energetic materials research, seismic research network, scanning electron microscope, scanning transmission electron microscope, transmission electron microscope, New Mexico Bureau of Geology, observatory.

Freshman class profile. 428 applied, 346 admitted, 281 enrolled.

Mid 50% test scores			
SAT verbal:	560-670	GPA 2.0-2.99:	11%
SAT math:	570-680	Rank in top quarter:	71%
ACT:	24-29	Rank in top tenth:	41%
GPA 3.50 or higher:	59%	Return as sophomores:	68%
GPA 3.0-3.49:	30%	Out-of-state:	22%
		International:	1%

Basis for selection. Test scores and high school GPA very important. Interview considered. 2.5 minimum high school GPA required. Minimum test scores of 21 ACT or SAT 970 (exclusive of Writing) also required. ACT recommended. New writing components of SAT and ACT accepted but not crucial to admission. Interview recommended. **Homeschooled:** Must supply documentation of courses completed.

High school preparation. College-preparatory program recommended. 15 units required; 18 recommended. Required and recommended units include English 4, mathematics 3-4, social studies 2-3, history 1, science 2-4 (laboratory 2-3), foreign language 2 and academic electives 3.

2005-2006 Annual costs. Tuition/fees: $3,643; $10,463 out-of-state. Room/board: $4,836. Books/supplies: $800. Personal expenses: $1,635.

2005-2006 Financial aid. Need-based: Average need met was 94%. Average scholarship/grant was $4,444; average loan $3,470. 45% of total undergraduate aid awarded as scholarships/grants, 55% as loans/jobs. **Non-need-based:** Scholarships awarded for academics, alumni affiliation, minority status, state residency. **Additional information:** Campus research projects offer student employment based on merit.

Application procedures. Admission: Priority date 3/1; deadline 8/1. $15 fee, may be waived for applicants with need. Application may be submitted online. Admission notification on a rolling basis beginning on or about 3/1. Must reply by May 1 or within 2 week(s) if notified thereafter. **Financial aid:** Priority date 6/1; no closing date. FAFSA, institutional form required. Applicants notified on a rolling basis starting 6/1; must reply within 2 week(s) of notification.

Academics. Special study options: Accelerated study, cooperative education, distance learning, double major, dual enrollment of high school students, exchange student, independent study, internships, student-designed major, teacher certification program. **Credit/placement by examination:** AP, CLEP, institutional tests. No limit to number of credits. Must have permission of instructor. **Support services:** Pre-admission summer program, reduced course load, study skills assistance, tutoring, writing center.

Majors. Biology: General, biochemistry. **Business:** Business admin. **Computer sciences:** General, computer science, information technology. **Conservation:** General, environmental studies. **Engineering:** General, chemical, civil, electrical, environmental, materials, mechanical, metallurgical, mining, petroleum. **English:** Technical writing. **Math:** General, applied. **Physical sciences:** Astrophysics, atmospheric physics, chemistry, geology, geophysics, physics. **Psychology:** General.

Most popular majors. Biology 8%, computer/information sciences 12%, engineering/engineering technologies 41%, mathematics 10%, physical sciences 21%.

Computing on campus. 225 workstations in dormitories, library, computer center, student center. Dormitories wired for high-speed internet access and linked to campus network. Commuter students can connect to campus network. Helpline, student web hosting, wireless network available.

Student life. Freshman orientation: Available, $40 fee. Preregistration for classes offered. 2-day event held weekend before classes start. **Policies:** Freshmen permitted cars on campus. **Housing:** Coed dorms, single-sex dorms, apartments, substance-free housing available. $100 fully refundable deposit. Students living on-campus must purchase meal plan. **Activities:** Bands, choral groups, dance, drama, film society, music ensembles, musical theater, radio station, student government, student newspaper, many organizations available.

Athletics. Intramural: Badminton, basketball, fencing, golf, racquetball, rifle, rugby, soccer, softball, table tennis, tennis, volleyball.

Student services. Adult student services, career counseling, student employment services, health services, on-campus daycare, personal counseling, placement for graduates. **Physically disabled:** Services for visually, hearing impaired.

Contact. E-mail: admission@admin.nmt.edu
Phone: (505) 835-5424 Toll-free number: (800) 428-8324
Fax: (505) 835-5989
Mike Kloeppel, Director of Admission, New Mexico Institute of Mining and Technology, 801 Leroy Place, Socorro, NM 87801

New Mexico State University

Las Cruces, New Mexico — **CB member**
www.nmsu.edu — **CB code: 4531**

- Public 4-year university
- Commuter campus in small city
- 11,929 degree-seeking undergraduates: 15% part-time, 56% women, 3% African American, 1% Asian American, 45% Hispanic American, 3% Native American, 1% international
- 2,993 degree-seeking graduate students
- 81% of applicants admitted
- SAT or ACT with writing required
- 42% graduate within 6 years

General. Founded in 1888. Regionally accredited. Arts/cultural events, art gallery, bookstore, chapel, food service, health services, language labs, library, performing arts, arts center, sports/fitness center. **Degrees:** 2,122 bachelor's, 26 associate awarded; master's, doctoral offered. **ROTC:** Army, Air Force. **Location:** 42 miles from El Paso, Texas. **Calendar:** Semester, extensive summer session. **Full-time faculty:** 667 total; 82% have terminal degrees, 19% minority, 37% women. **Part-time faculty:** 166 total; 28% have terminal degrees, 8% minority, 58% women. **Class size:** 45% < 20, 37% 20-39, 7% 40-49, 9% 50-99, 3% >100. **Special facilities:** Observatory, horse farm, rodeo grounds, electron microscope, CRAY supercomputer, sports medicine training clinic.

Freshman class profile. 5,522 applied, 4,482 admitted, 2,019 enrolled.

Mid 50% test scores		Return as sophomores:	70%
ACT:	18-24	Out-of-state:	20%
Rank in top quarter:	49%	Live on campus:	27%
Rank in top tenth:	20%	International:	1%

Basis for selection. School achievement record, test scores most important.

High school preparation. 10 units required. Required units include English 4, mathematics 3, science 2 (laboratory 2) and foreign language 1. English must include at least 2 units of composition, 1 of which must be at junior or senior level. Mathematics must be from algebra I, algebra II, geometry, trigonometry or advanced mathematics. Will accept 1 unit of foreign language or fine arts.

2005-2006 Annual costs. Tuition/fees: $3,918; $13,206 out-of-state. Room/board: $5,332. Books/supplies: $817. Personal expenses: $3,310.

2005-2006 Financial aid. Need-based: 1,471 full-time freshmen applied for aid; 1,198 were judged to have need; 1,160 of these received aid. Average need met was 61%. Average scholarship/grant was $6,203; average loan $2,698. 52% of total undergraduate aid awarded as scholarships/grants, 48% as loans/jobs. **Non-need-based:** Scholarships awarded for academics, alumni affiliation, athletics, leadership, minority status, state residency.

Application procedures. Admission: No deadline. $15 fee. Application may be submitted online. Admission notification on a rolling basis. **Financial aid:** Priority date 3/1; no closing date. FAFSA, institutional form required. Applicants notified on a rolling basis starting 4/1; must reply within 4 week(s) of notification.

Academics. Special study options: Accelerated study, cooperative education, cross-registration, distance learning, double major, exchange student, honors, independent study, internships, student-designed major, study abroad, teacher certification program, weekend college. **Credit/placement by examination:** AP, CLEP, institutional tests. 30 credit hours maximum toward bachelor's degree. **Support services:** Learning center, reduced course load, study skills assistance, tutoring, writing center.

Majors. Agriculture: General, agribusiness operations, agronomy, animal sciences, horticultural science, range science, soil science. **Architecture:** Urban/community planning. **Biology:** General, bacteriology, biochemistry, microbiology, plant pathology. **Business:** General, accounting, business admin, finance, hospitality admin, international, management science, marketing, tourism promotion, tourism/travel. **Communications:** Journalism. **Computer sciences:** General, information systems, information technology. **Conservation:** Environmental studies, wildlife. **Education:** Agricultural, early childhood, elementary, family/consumer sciences, music, physical, secondary, special, speech impaired. **Engineering:** Chemical, civil, electrical, industrial, mechanical, physics. **Engineering technology:** General, surveying. **English:** English lit. **Family/consumer sciences:** Clothing/textiles, family studies, food/nutrition. **Foreign languages:** General. **Health:** Athletic training, environmental health, nursing (RN), public health ed. **History:** General. **Math:** General. **Parks/recreation:** Facilities management. **Philosophy/religion:** Philosophy. **Physical sciences:** Chemistry, geology, physics. **Protective services:** Criminal justice. **Psychology:** General. **Public administration:** Community org/advocacy, social work. **Social sciences:** Anthropology, economics, geography, political science, sociology. **Visual/performing arts:** General, dance, dramatic, music performance, studio arts.

Most popular majors. Business/marketing 21%, education 13%, engineering/engineering technologies 13%.

Computing on campus. 563 workstations in library, computer center, student center. Dormitories wired for high-speed internet access and linked to campus network. Commuter students can connect to campus network. Online course registration, online library, helpline, repair service, student web hosting available.

Student life. Freshman orientation: Available. Preregistration for classes offered. **Policies:** Freshmen permitted cars on campus. **Housing:** Coed dorms, single-sex dorms, special housing for disabled, apartments, fraternity/sorority housing, substance-free housing available. $100 deposit, deadline 7/1. Upper division dorms available. **Activities:** Bands, choral groups, dance, drama, literary magazine, music ensembles, musical theater, opera, radio station, student government, student newspaper, symphony orchestra, TV station, Baptist Student Union, Catholic Center, Presbyterian Campus Ministry, Young Democrats, College Republicans, Black Allied Student Association, Movimiento Estudiantil Chicano de Azatlan, United Native American Organization.

Athletics. NCAA. **Intercollegiate:** Baseball M, basketball, cross-country, equestrian, football (tackle) M, golf, softball W, swimming W, tennis, track and field W, volleyball W. **Intramural:** Archery, badminton, basketball, cheerleading, football (non-tackle), football (tackle), golf, racquetball, soccer, softball, tennis, volleyball, water polo, weight lifting, wrestling M. **Team name:** Aggies.

Student services. Adult student services, alcohol/substance abuse counseling, career counseling, student employment services, health services, personal counseling, placement for graduates, veterans' counselor. **Physically disabled:** Services for visually, speech, hearing impaired.

Contact. E-mail: admissions@nmsu.edu
Phone: (505) 646-3121 Toll-free number: (800) 662-6678
Fax: (505) 646-6330
Angela Mora-Riley, Director of Admissions, New Mexico State University, Box 30001, MSC 3A, Las Cruces, NM 88003-8001

Northern New Mexico College

Espanola, New Mexico
www.nnmcc.edu **CB code: 0425**

- Public 4-year community and teachers college
- Commuter campus in small town
- 2,200 undergraduates

General. Founded in 1909. Regionally accredited. Serves community of El Rito, attendance centers in Tierra Amarilla. **Degrees:** 110 associate awarded. **Location:** 24 miles from Santa Fe. **Calendar:** Semester, limited summer session. **Full-time faculty:** 45 total. **Part-time faculty:** 150 total.

Freshman class profile.

Out-of-state:	1%	**Live on campus:**	1%

Basis for selection. Open admission, but selective for some programs and for out-of-state students. Nursing, radiography, barbering, and cosmetology programs require separate applications subsequent to admission. 2-year nursing program requires 2.5 GPA and preadmission test. Limited number of out-of-state applicants considered. No admission tests. Tests administered before or after admission for course placement purposes only, except for those admitted under ability to benefit.

2005-2006 Annual costs. Tuition/fees: $958; $2,374 out-of-state. Upper division courses are $90 per-credit-hour for in-state students and $367 per-credit-hour for out-of-state students. Room/board: $3,528. Books/supplies: $600. Personal expenses: $1,740.

Financial aid. All financial aid based on need.

Application procedures. Admission: No deadline. No application fee. Admission notification on a rolling basis. **Financial aid:** Priority date 3/1; no closing date. FAFSA required. Applicants notified on a rolling basis starting 6/1; must reply within 2 week(s) of notification.

Academics. Special study options: Distance learning, dual enrollment of high school students, internships, liberal arts/career combination, teacher certification program. **Credit/placement by examination:** AP, CLEP, institutional tests. 15 credit hours maximum toward associate degree. **Support services:** Learning center, remedial instruction, study skills assistance, tutoring, writing center.

Computing on campus. 24 workstations in library, computer center. Commuter students can connect to campus network.

Student life. Housing: Single-sex dorms available. **Activities:** Choral groups, drama, music ensembles, student government, Phi Theta Kappa.

Athletics. Intramural: Basketball, softball.

Student services. Career counseling, student employment services, personal counseling, placement for graduates, veterans' counselor. **Physically disabled:** Services for visually, speech, hearing impaired.

Contact. E-mail: tina@nnm.cc.nm.us
Phone: (505) 747-2112 Fax: (505) 747-2180
Michael Costello, Dean of Student Services, Northern New Mexico College, 921 Paseo de Onate, Espanola, NM 87532

St. John's College

Santa Fe, New Mexico **CB member**
www.stjohnscollege.edu **CB code: 4737**

- Private 4-year liberal arts college
- Residential campus in small city
- 435 degree-seeking undergraduates: 1% part-time, 46% women, 1% African American, 2% Asian American, 6% Hispanic American, 2% international
- 98 degree-seeking graduate students
- 83% of applicants admitted
- Application essay required
- 67% graduate within 6 years; 78% enter graduate study

General. Founded in 1964. Regionally accredited. Second campus in Annapolis, MD, where students may transfer during their 4 years. **Degrees:** 78 bachelor's awarded; master's offered. **Location:** 60 miles from Albuquerque. **Calendar:** Semester, limited summer session. **Full-time faculty:** 70 total. **Part-time faculty:** 1 total. **Class size:** 95% < 20, 2% 20-39, 2% 40-49. **Special facilities:** Search and rescue center, Ptolemy stone, forest with hiking trails.

Freshman class profile. 318 applied, 265 admitted, 117 enrolled.

Mid 50% test scores		**Rank in top tenth:**	17%
SAT verbal:	650-750	**Return as sophomores:**	76%
SAT math:	580-670	**Out-of-state:**	92%
ACT:	28-31	**Live on campus:**	99%
Rank in top quarter:	54%	**International:**	1%

Basis for selection. 3 essays describing educational and personal background and goals most important along with 2 letters of reference from teachers; secondary school reference from counselor or other school official also requested. High school achievement record considered. SAT or ACT required of early admission or home schooled applicants. Due to college's unusual curriculum and learning methods, interview and 3-day campus visit to observe classes strongly encouraged. **Homeschooled:** Statement describing homeschool structure and mission, transcript of courses and grades, letter of recommendation (nonparent) required. **Learning Disabled:** Campus visit required.

High school preparation. 21 units recommended. Required and recommended units include English 4, mathematics 3-4, social studies 2, history 2, science 3 (laboratory 3) and foreign language 2-3. Mathematics requirement includes 2 algebra, 1 geometry. Precalculus or trigonometry recommended.

2006-2007 Annual costs. Tuition/fees (projected): $34,506. Room/board: $8,270. Books/supplies: $275. Personal expenses: $900.

2005-2006 Financial aid. Need-based: 86 full-time freshmen applied for aid; 81 were judged to have need; 81 of these received aid. Average need met was 95%. Average scholarship/grant was $18,063; average loan $3,187. 74% of total undergraduate aid awarded as scholarships/grants, 26% as loans/jobs. **Non-need-based:** Awarded to 26 full-time undergraduates,

including 13 freshmen. Scholarships awarded for state residency. **Additional information:** 100% of need met for most of those qualified to receive aid. Families receive individual attention in determining need fairly. Independent students must submit parental data. Financial aid information also required of noncustodial parent in cases of separation or divorce. Aid awarded first-come, first-served until institutional money exhausted. Apply early by February 15; after April 1 aid difficult to obtain.

Application procedures. Admission: Priority date 3/1; no deadline. No application fee. Application may be submitted online. Admission notification on a rolling basis beginning on or about 9/1. Must reply by May 1 or within 2 week(s) if notified thereafter. Early application encouraged, but no formal plan. **Financial aid:** Priority date 2/15; no closing date. FAFSA, CSS PROFILE required. Applicants notified on a rolling basis starting 12/1; must reply by 5/1 or within 2 week(s) of notification.

Academics. Special study options: Internships, weekend college. Great Books Program. **Credit/placement by examination:** CLEP. **Support services:** Tutoring, writing center.

Majors. Liberal arts: Arts/sciences.

Computing on campus. 20 workstations in library, computer center. Dormitories wired for high-speed internet access and linked to campus network. Commuter students can connect to campus network. Helpline available.

Student life. Freshman orientation: Mandatory. 4-day program held twice a year. Includes on-campus service day, student acitivties fair, numerous community meals and formal welcoming ceremony. **Policies:** Freshmen permitted cars on campus. **Housing:** Guaranteed on-campus for freshmen. Coed dorms, single-sex dorms, special housing for disabled, apartments available. $300 deposit, deadline 6/15. Single-sex suites, nonsmoking, nondrinking dorms available. **Activities:** Jazz band, choral groups, dance, drama, film society, literary magazine, music ensembles, student government, student newspaper, Amnesty International, adult literacy, historic church restoration, Koran study group, women's literature group, peer counseling, community farm, soup kitchen, Beneficial Farm, Open Hands.

Athletics. Intercollegiate: Fencing. **Intramural:** Badminton, basketball, cross-country, fencing, racquetball, skiing, soccer, softball, squash, swimming, table tennis, tennis, volleyball, weight lifting.

Student services. Career counseling, student employment services, financial aid counseling, health services, personal counseling, placement for graduates.

Contact. E-mail: admissions@sjcsf.edu
Phone: (505) 984-6060 Toll-free number: (800) 331-5232
Fax: (505) 984-6162
Lawernce Clendenin, Director of Admissions, St. John's College, 1160 Camino Cruz Blanca, Santa Fe, NM 87505-4599

University of New Mexico

Albuquerque, New Mexico — **CB member**
www.unm.edu — **CB code: 4845**

- Public 4-year university
- Commuter campus in very large city
- 18,330 degree-seeking undergraduates: 20% part-time, 58% women, 3% African American, 3% Asian American, 35% Hispanic American, 6% Native American, 1% international
- 5,920 degree-seeking graduate students
- 74% of applicants admitted
- SAT or ACT (ACT writing recommended) required
- 40% graduate within 6 years

General. Founded in 1889. Regionally accredited. Branch campuses in Valencia County, Los Alamos, Gallup, and Taos. Graduate centers in Los Alamos and Santa Fe. **Degrees:** 3,074 bachelor's, 11 associate awarded; master's, doctoral, first professional offered. **ROTC:** Army, Navy, Air Force. **Location:** 2 miles from downtown. **Calendar:** Semester, limited summer session. **Full-time faculty:** 885 total; 86% have terminal degrees, 22% minority, 59% women. **Part-time faculty:** 526 total; 43% have terminal degrees, 16% minority, 53% women. **Class size:** 40% < 20, 41% 20-39, 6% 40-49, 10% 50-99, 4% >100. **Special facilities:** 5 museums, observatory, meteoritics institute, arboretum, teaching hospital, major research facilities in ceramics, optoelectronics, space nuclear power, and high power devices and systems, institute of lithography, Latin American institute, bureau of business and economic research.

Freshman class profile. 7,134 applied, 5,254 admitted, 3,095 enrolled.

Mid 50% test scores			
SAT verbal:	480-600	GPA 2.0-2.99:	26%
SAT math:	470-600	Rank in top quarter:	48%
ACT:	19-24	Rank in top tenth:	21%
GPA 3.50 or higher:	42%	Return as sophomores:	76%
GPA 3.0-3.49:	32%	Out-of-state:	11%
		International:	1%

Basis for selection. School achievement record (high school GPA of 2.25 required in college-preparatory units) most important. Test scores, class rank second. Essays, recommendations considered. Test of English as a Foreign Language (TOEFL) or International English Language Testing System (IELTS) or University of Cambridge Examinations Certificate of Proficiency in English (CPE) or Certificate of Advanced English (CAE) required of non-native speakers of English. Essay considered if student appeal denied. **Homeschooled:** Applicants must either pass GED, submit SAT Subject Test scores, or have 2.25 minimum high school GPA and complete 13 college prep academic units. **Learning Disabled:** Student who is not admissable according to numerical admissions and self-discloses disability can be admitted after being approved by Special Admissions Committee.

High school preparation. 13 units required. Required units include English 4, mathematics 3, social studies 1, history 1, science 2 (laboratory 1) and foreign language 2. Foreign language requirements must be in same language. One science must be laboratory in biology, chemistry or physics. Mathematics must be algebra I, geometry, algebra II, trigonometry or higher.

2005-2006 Annual costs. Tuition/fees: $4,109; $13,438 out-of-state. Room/board: $6,518. Books/supplies: $792. Personal expenses: $1,562.

Financial aid. Non-need-based: Scholarships awarded for academics, alumni affiliation, art, athletics, job skills, leadership, minority status, music/drama, religious affiliation, ROTC, state residency. **Additional information:** Regent scholarship program has priority date of December 1. UNM scholars program has deadline of February 1.

Application procedures. Admission: Closing date 6/15 (postmark date). $20 fee, may be waived for applicants with need. Application may be submitted online. Admission notification on a rolling basis. Must enroll by start of semester applied for. **Financial aid:** Priority date 3/1; no closing date. FAFSA required. Applicants notified on a rolling basis starting 4/15.

Academics. Special study options: Accelerated study, combined bachelor's/graduate degree, cooperative education, distance learning, double major, dual enrollment of high school students, ESL, exchange student, honors, independent study, internships, semester at sea, student-designed major, study abroad, teacher certification program, Washington semester, weekend college. **Credit/placement by examination:** AP, CLEP, IB, SAT, ACT, institutional tests. 30 credit hours maximum toward bachelor's degree. **Support services:** Learning center, reduced course load, remedial instruction, tutoring.

Majors. Architecture: Architecture, environmental design. **Area/ethnic studies:** African-American, American, Asian, European, Latin American, Native American, Russian/Slavic, women's. **Biology:** General, biochemistry. **Business:** Business admin. **Communications:** Journalism. **Computer sciences:** General. **Conservation:** Environmental science. **Education:** Art, early childhood, elementary, health, music, physical, secondary, special, technology/industrial arts. **Engineering:** Chemical, civil, computer, electrical, mechanical, nuclear, science. **English:** Speech/rhetoric. **Family/consumer sciences:** General, family studies, food/nutrition. **Foreign languages:** General, classics, comparative lit, French, German, linguistics, Portuguese, Russian, sign language interpretation, Spanish. **Health:** Audiology/speech pathology, clinical lab technology, dental hygiene, EMT paramedic, medical radiologic technology/radiation therapy, nursing (RN), physician assistant. **History:** General. **Liberal arts:** Arts/sciences, humanities. **Math:** General, statistics. **Parks/recreation:** General. **Philosophy/religion:** Philosophy, religion. **Physical sciences:** Astrophysics, chemistry, geology, physics. **Protective services:** Corrections. **Psychology:** General. **Public administration:** Community org/advocacy. **Social sciences:** Anthropology, economics, geography, political science, sociology. **Visual/performing arts:** Art, art history/conservation, dance, dramatic, film/cinema, music performance, theater design.

Most popular majors. Biology 7%, business/marketing 16%, education 12%, engineering/engineering technologies 6%, health sciences 8%, liberal arts 7%, psychology 7%, social sciences 7%.

Computing on campus. 459 workstations in dormitories, library, computer center, student center. Dormitories wired for high-speed internet access and linked to campus network. Commuter students can connect to campus network. Online course registration, online library, helpline, student web hosting, wireless network available.

Student life. Freshman orientation: Mandatory, $30 fee. 2-day sessions held June-August and January. **Policies:** Freshmen permitted cars on campus. **Housing:** Coed dorms, special housing for disabled, apartments, fraternity/

sorority housing, substance-free housing available. $300 partly refundable deposit. Special living options include graduate and senior housing, academic floors, scholar's wing, Global Learning Center, Freshman Living Learning Community, and outdoors/wellness units. Computer science and engineering unit also available. **Activities:** Bands, choral groups, dance, drama, film society, literary magazine, music ensembles, musical theater, opera, radio station, student government, student newspaper, symphony orchestra, TV station, Panhellenic Council, RAZA En Accion, Black Student Union, KIVA Club, Del Otro Lado, NMPIRG, Hillel, Campus Crusade for Christ, Progressive Student Alliance, International Center.

Athletics. NCAA. **Intercollegiate:** Baseball M, basketball, cross-country, diving W, football (tackle) M, golf, skiing, soccer, softball W, swimming W, tennis, track and field, volleyball W. **Intramural:** Archery, badminton, basketball, bowling, cross-country, fencing, football (non-tackle), football (tackle) M, golf, racquetball, skiing, soccer, softball, swimming, table tennis, tennis, triathlon, volleyball, water polo. **Team name:** Lobos.

Student services. Adult student services, alcohol/substance abuse counseling, campus ministries, career counseling, services for economically disadvantaged, student employment services, financial aid counseling, health services, legal services, minority student services, on-campus daycare, personal counseling, placement for graduates, veterans' counselor, women's services. **Physically disabled:** Services for visually, speech, hearing impaired.

Contact. E-mail: apply@unm.edu
Phone: (505) 277-2446 Toll-free number: (800) 225-5866
Fax: (505) 277-6686
Terry Babbitt, Interim Director of Admissions, University of New Mexico, Office of Admissions, Albuquerque, NM 87196-4895

Western New Mexico University

Silver City, New Mexico **CB member**
www.wnmu.edu **CB code: 4535**

- Public 4-year university
- Commuter campus in large town
- 1,857 degree-seeking undergraduates: 24% part-time, 65% women, 3% African American, 48% Hispanic American, 3% Native American, 1% international
- 493 degree-seeking graduate students
- 20% graduate within 6 years

General. Founded in 1893. Regionally accredited. **Degrees:** 147 bachelor's, 105 associate awarded; master's offered. **Location:** 155 miles from El Paso, Texas; 193 miles from Tucson, Arizona. **Calendar:** Semester, extensive summer session. **Full-time faculty:** 93 total; 91% have terminal degrees. **Part-time faculty:** 240 total. **Class size:** 81% < 20, 18% 20-39, less than 1% 40-49, less than 1% 50-99. **Special facilities:** Museum specializing in Native American cultures, fine arts center and gallery, amphitheater.

Freshman class profile. 1,983 applied, 1,983 admitted, 629 enrolled.

Mid 50% test scores			
SAT verbal:	410-550	Out-of-state:	13%
SAT math:	410-580	Live on campus:	50%
ACT:	15-21	International:	2%

Basis for selection. Open admission. Regular admission requires 21 or better sub-score for ACT/SAT equivalent in math, English, and social science or completion of COMPASS placement exam in corresponding areas where the ACT/SAT sub-score was less. All other students admitted conditionally for one semester. COMPASS test used for placement. **Homeschooled:** State high school equivalency certificate required. If state high school equivalency certificate not received, student must take GED.

High school preparation. Recommended units include English 4, mathematics 3, social studies 2, history 1 and science 2.

2005-2006 Annual costs. Tuition/fees: $2,863; $9,565 out-of-state. Room/board: $4,460. Books/supplies: $810. Personal expenses: $2,060.

2004-2005 Financial aid. Need-based: 243 full-time freshmen applied for aid; 243 were judged to have need; 243 of these received aid. Average need met was 64%. Average scholarship/grant was $3,221; average loan $2,526. 50% of total undergraduate aid awarded as scholarships/grants, 50% as loans/jobs. **Non-need-based:** Awarded to 342 full-time undergraduates, including 77 freshmen. Scholarships awarded for academics, athletics, state residency.

Application procedures. Admission: Priority date 8/1; no deadline. No application fee. Application may be submitted online. Admission notification on a rolling basis. **Financial aid:** Closing date 4/1. FAFSA, institutional form required. Applicants notified on a rolling basis starting 4/1; must reply within 2 week(s) of notification.

Academics. Special study options: Cooperative education, distance learning, double major, dual enrollment of high school students, honors, independent study, internships, liberal arts/career combination, teacher certification program. **Credit/placement by examination:** AP, CLEP, IB. 12 credit hours maximum toward associate degree, 32 toward bachelor's. **Support services:** Learning center, remedial instruction, study skills assistance, tutoring, writing center.

Majors. Area/ethnic studies: Hispanic-American/Latino/Chicano. **Biology:** General, botany, zoology. **Business:** General, accounting, business admin, managerial economics, marketing, operations. **Computer sciences:** General. **Conservation:** Wildlife. **Education:** General, art, biology, business, chemistry, elementary, ESL, health, mathematics, middle, music, physical, science, secondary, social science, social studies, Spanish, special, technology/industrial arts, voc/tech. **Foreign languages:** Spanish. **Health:** Clinical lab technology. **History:** General. **Liberal arts:** Arts/sciences. **Math:** General. **Physical sciences:** Chemistry. **Protective services:** Criminal justice, law enforcement admin. **Psychology:** General. **Public administration:** Social work. **Social sciences:** General, sociology. **Visual/performing arts:** Studio arts.

Most popular majors. Business/marketing 23%, education 19%, liberal arts 15%, psychology 6%, security/protective services 7%, social sciences 7%.

Computing on campus. 150 workstations in dormitories, library, computer center. Dormitories linked to campus network. Commuter students can connect to campus network. Online course registration, online library, helpline available.

Student life. Freshman orientation: Available, $10 fee. Preregistration for classes offered. 2-day sessions held once a month from late May through mid-August. **Policies:** Freshmen permitted cars on campus. **Housing:** Guaranteed on-campus for all undergraduates. Coed dorms, single-sex dorms, special housing for disabled, apartments available. $75 deposit. First-time students whose permanent homes are outside tri-county area and who register as full-time students under the age of 21 with less than 32 credit hours are required to reside on campus. Mandatory meal plan for those who live in residence halls. **Activities:** Bands, choral groups, drama, music ensembles, musical theater, student government, student newspaper, symphony orchestra, Baptist Student Union, Society for the Advancement of Management, St. Francis Newman Club, Chicano Student Organization, United Campus Ministry, criminal justice, Native American Club.

Athletics. NCAA. **Intercollegiate:** Basketball, cross-country, football (tackle) M, golf, softball W, tennis, volleyball W. **Intramural:** Basketball, racquetball, softball, swimming, tennis, volleyball. **Team name:** Mustangs.

Student services. Campus ministries, career counseling, student employment services, financial aid counseling, health services, minority student services, on-campus daycare, personal counseling, placement for graduates. **Physically disabled:** Services for visually, speech, hearing impaired.

Contact. E-mail: tresslerd@wnmu.edu
Phone: (505) 538-6106 Toll-free number: (800) 872-9668
Fax: (505) 538-6127
Laurie Romero-Jones, Director of Admissions, Western New Mexico University, Castorena 106, Silver City, NM 88062

New York

Adelphi University

Garden City, New York
www.adelphi.edu
CB member
CB code: 2003

- Private 4-year university
- Commuter campus in large town
- 4,718 degree-seeking undergraduates: 16% part-time, 72% women, 13% African American, 5% Asian American, 8% Hispanic American, 3% international
- 3,070 degree-seeking graduate students
- 68% of applicants admitted
- SAT or ACT with writing, application essay required
- 54% graduate within 6 years; 41% enter graduate study

General. Founded in 1896. Regionally accredited. **Degrees:** 1,007 bachelor's, 6 associate awarded; master's, doctoral offered. **ROTC:** Army, Air Force. **Location:** 20 miles from New York City. **Calendar:** Semester, limited summer session. **Full-time faculty:** 258 total; 90% have terminal degrees, 18% minority, 51% women. **Part-time faculty:** 600 total; 11% minority, 60% women. **Class size:** 41% < 20, 49% 20-39, 7% 40-49, 3% 50-99. **Special facilities:** Theater, speech and hearing center, science library, observatory, day care facility, arboretum.

Freshman class profile. 5,197 applied, 3,545 admitted, 770 enrolled.

Mid 50% test scores		**Rank in top quarter:**	58%
SAT verbal:	490-600	**Rank in top tenth:**	23%
SAT math:	510-620	**End year in good standing:**	91%
ACT:	21-25	**Return as sophomores:**	82%
GPA 3.50 or higher:	37%	**Out-of-state:**	13%
GPA 3.0-3.49:	34%	**Live on campus:**	45%
GPA 2.0-2.99:	28%	**International:**	5%

Basis for selection. 2.5 cumulative high school GPA and SAT combined score of 900 (exclusive of Writing) or higher very important. Rank in top third of class, school and community activities also important. References important. SAT scores accepted on rolling basis. SAT recommended for General Studies entrants, not required for Adult Baccalaureate Learning Experience (ABLE). Applicants to dance, drama, music, or art require audition and portfolio review, education majors must have 2.75 minimum GPA. Interview required for honors college applicants. **Homeschooled:** State high school equivalency certificate required. GED required if not receiving diploma from accredited high school or academy. **Learning Disabled:** Interview required. Fee-based learning disability program where students receive academic and counseling support, requires admission; SAT recommended. Accommodations for learning disabled students not in program without cost, including accommodative testing, scribes, academic assistance.

High school preparation. 16 units recommended. Recommended units include English 4, mathematics 3, science 3 and foreign language 2. 4 additional units recommended in either social studies, history, English, math, science or foreign language.

2006-2007 Annual costs. Tuition/fees: $20,900. Tuition, fees, and per-credit-hour charges for upper-division nursing, social work, and education programs are slightly higher. Room/board: $9,500. Books/supplies: $1,000. Personal expenses: $1,200.

2004-2005 Financial aid. **Need-based:** 693 full-time freshmen applied for aid; 590 were judged to have need; 590 of these received aid. Average need met was 29.3%. Average scholarship/grant was $4,958; average loan $3,240. 52% of total undergraduate aid awarded as scholarships/grants, 48% as loans/jobs. **Non-need-based:** Awarded to 2,351 full-time undergraduates, including 599 freshmen. Scholarships awarded for academics, alumni affiliation, art, athletics, job skills, leadership, minority status, music/drama, religious affiliation.

Application procedures. **Admission:** No deadline. $35 fee, may be waived for applicants with need. Application may be submitted online. Admission notification on a rolling basis beginning on or about 10/1. **Financial aid:** Priority date 3/1; no closing date. FAFSA required. Applicants notified on a rolling basis starting 3/1.

Academics. **Special study options:** Accelerated study, combined bachelor's/graduate degree, cross-registration, distance learning, double major, dual enrollment of high school students, ESL, honors, independent study, internships, liberal arts/career combination, student-designed major, study abroad, teacher certification program, Washington semester, weekend college. Learning disabled program combining matriculation with support services, ABLE for adults 21 and over, 1-year intensive general studies program for freshmen with HS records/SAT scores that do not meet school standards; students who successfully complete program invited to enroll in other school programs in their sophomore year. **Credit/placement by examination:** AP, CLEP, IB. 30 credit hours maximum toward bachelor's degree. **Support services:** Learning center, pre-admission summer program, reduced course load, study skills assistance, tutoring, writing center.

Honors college/program. SAT, 3.5 GPA, evidence of academic or creative writing and interview required. 60-80 freshmen admitted.

Majors. **Area/ethnic studies:** Latin American. **Biology:** General, biochemistry. **Business:** Accounting, business admin, finance. **Communications:** Journalism, media studies. **Computer sciences:** General, information systems. **Conservation:** Environmental studies. **Education:** Art, health, physical, secondary. **English:** English lit. **Foreign languages:** French, Spanish. **Health:** Audiology/speech pathology, nursing (RN). **History:** General. **Interdisciplinary:** Global studies. **Liberal arts:** Humanities. **Math:** General. **Philosophy/religion:** Philosophy. **Physical sciences:** Chemistry, physics. **Protective services:** Law enforcement admin. **Psychology:** General. **Public administration:** Social work. **Social sciences:** General, anthropology, economics, political science, sociology. **Visual/performing arts:** Art history/conservation, dance, dramatic, studio arts.

Most popular majors. Business/marketing 20%, education 7%, health sciences 15%, psychology 8%, social sciences 18%, visual/performing arts 7%.

Computing on campus. 598 workstations in dormitories, library, computer center, student center. Dormitories wired for high-speed internet access and linked to campus network. Commuter students can connect to campus network. Online course registration, online library, helpline, repair service, student web hosting, wireless network available.

Student life. **Freshman orientation:** Mandatory, $240 fee. Preregistration for classes offered. 3-day orientation held on Garden City campus. **Policies:** Freshmen permitted cars on campus. **Housing:** Coed dorms, special housing for disabled, substance-free housing available. $100 fully refundable deposit, deadline 5/4. Special housing available for students in honors college, performing arts, and Excel Program. **Activities:** Bands, choral groups, dance, drama, film society, literary magazine, music ensembles, radio station, student government, student newspaper, symphony orchestra, nearly 80 clubs and organizations.

Athletics. NCAA. **Intercollegiate:** Baseball M, basketball, bowling W, cross-country, golf M, lacrosse, soccer, softball W, swimming, tennis, track and field, volleyball W. **Intramural:** Badminton, basketball, football (non-tackle), racquetball, soccer, volleyball. **Team name:** Panthers.

Student services. Adult student services, alcohol/substance abuse counseling, campus ministries, career counseling, student employment services, financial aid counseling, health services, minority student services, on-campus daycare, personal counseling, placement for graduates, veterans' counselor. **Physically disabled:** Services for visually, speech, hearing impaired. **Learning disabled:** Comprehensive services available.

Contact. E-mail: admissions@adelphi.edu
Phone: (516) 877-3050 Toll-free number: (800) 233-5744
Fax: (516) 877-3039
Christine Murphy, Director of Admissions, Adelphi University, One South Avenue, Levermore 110, Garden City, NY 11530-0701

Albany College of Pharmacy

Albany, New York
www.acp.edu
CB code: 2013

- Private 6-year health science and pharmacy college
- Residential campus in small city
- 855 degree-seeking undergraduates: 56% women, 1% African American, 10% Asian American, 1% Hispanic American, 8% international
- 282 graduate students
- 58% of applicants admitted
- SAT or ACT (ACT writing recommended) required

General. Founded in 1881. Regionally accredited. **Degrees:** 4 bachelor's awarded; first professional offered. **ROTC:** Army, Navy, Air Force. **Location:** 200 miles from New York City. **Calendar:** Semester, limited summer session. **Full-time faculty:** 69 total. **Part-time faculty:** 9 total. **Class size:**

77% 20-39, 15% 50-99, 8% >100. **Special facilities:** Turn-of-the-century antique pharmacy, virtual reality pharmacy.

Freshman class profile. 1,014 applied, 590 admitted, 261 enrolled.

Mid 50% test scores			
SAT verbal:	520-600	Rank in top tenth:	43%
SAT math:	560-640	Return as sophomores:	76%
ACT:	22-26	Out-of-state:	19%
Rank in top quarter:	83%	Live on campus:	99%

Basis for selection. High school record, test scores, essay, letters of recommendation, New York State Regents Examinations considered. Special emphasis on science and mathematics grades.

High school preparation. College-preparatory program required. 17 units required. Required and recommended units include English 4, mathematics 4, social studies 1 and science 3-4. Chemistry and precalculus required.

2005-2006 Annual costs. Tuition/fees: $20,370. Fees include mandatory laptop purchase. Room/board: $6,100.

2005-2006 Financial aid. **Need-based:** 212 full-time freshmen applied for aid; 168 were judged to have need; 166 of these received aid. Average need met was 52%. Average scholarship/grant was $5,875; average loan $3,423. **Non-need-based:** Scholarships awarded for academics.

Application procedures. **Admission:** Closing date 2/1. $75 fee. Application must be submitted online. Admission notification on a rolling basis. **Financial aid:** Priority date 2/1; no closing date. FAFSA required.

Academics. **Special study options:** Accelerated study, combined bachelor's/graduate degree, cross-registration, independent study. Externships. **Credit/placement by examination:** AP, CLEP. 30 credit hours maximum toward bachelor's degree. **Support services:** Study skills assistance, tutoring, writing center.

Majors. **Engineering technology:** Biomedical. **Health:** Clinical lab science, cytotechnology, physician assistant, predentistry, premedicine, preveterinary. **Legal studies:** Prelaw.

Computing on campus. PC or laptop required. 100 workstations in library, computer center. Dormitories wired for high-speed internet access and linked to campus network. Commuter students can connect to campus network. Online library, helpline, repair service, wireless network available.

Student life. **Freshman orientation:** Mandatory, $145 fee. Usually held over first weekend prior to class start. **Policies:** College observes honor code. Residency required in first 2 years of study except for students living within 30-mile radius of campus. Freshmen permitted cars on campus. **Housing:** Guaranteed on-campus for freshmen. Coed dorms, substance-free housing available. $100 deposit, deadline 4/1. **Activities:** Jazz band, choral groups, literary magazine, student government, student newspaper, Student American Pharmaceutical Association, American Chemical Society, international club.

Athletics. **Intercollegiate:** Basketball, soccer. **Intramural:** Basketball, football (non-tackle), volleyball. **Team name:** Panthers.

Student services. Alcohol/substance abuse counseling, campus ministries, career counseling, student employment services, financial aid counseling, health services, minority student services, personal counseling, placement for graduates.

Contact. E-mail: admissions@acp.edu
Phone: (518) 694-7221 Toll-free number: (888) 203-8010
Fax: (518) 694-7322
Carly Connors, Director of Admissions, Albany College of Pharmacy, 106 New Scotland Avenue, Albany, NY 12208

Alfred University

Alfred, New York — **CB member**
www.alfred.edu — **CB code: 2005**

- Private 4-year university
- Residential campus in rural community
- 1,905 degree-seeking undergraduates: 2% part-time, 49% women
- 258 degree-seeking graduate students
- 77% of applicants admitted
- SAT or ACT (ACT writing optional), application essay required
- 62% graduate within 6 years; 28% enter graduate study

General. Founded in 1836. Regionally accredited. **Degrees:** 430 bachelor's awarded; master's, doctoral offered. **ROTC:** Army. **Location:** 75 miles from Rochester, 65 miles from Elmira. **Calendar:** Semester, limited summer session. **Full-time faculty:** 165 total; 91% have terminal degrees, 38% women. **Part-time faculty:** 40 total; 18% have terminal degrees, 45% women. **Class size:** 64% < 20, 31% 20-39, 3% 40-49, 2% 50-99, less than 1% >100. **Special facilities:** Observatory, carillon, 3 art galleries, library of ceramics, ceramics museum.

Freshman class profile. 2,134 applied, 1,640 admitted, 429 enrolled.

Mid 50% test scores			
SAT verbal:	500-620	Rank in top tenth:	19%
SAT math:	520-610	Return as sophomores:	78.6%
ACT:	22-27	Out-of-state:	30%
Rank in top quarter:	48%	Live on campus:	95%

Basis for selection. Rigor of high school curriculum, grades, class rank, standardized ACT or SAT test results, extracurricular involvement, letters of recommendation all factors. International students may submit TOEFL in lieu of SAT or ACT. Interview recommended. Portfolio required for students seeking admission to School of Art & Design. **Homeschooled:** Advise students to document courses taken and provide reading list. SAT or ACT mandatory and relied on heavily.

High school preparation. College-preparatory program required. 16 units required. Required units include English 4, mathematics 2, social studies 2, science 2 (laboratory 2). 3-4 math for business college, 2-3 math for liberal arts and science college, 2 math for art and design college, 4 math for engineering school.

2005-2006 Annual costs. Tuition/fees: $20,860. Reported cost information is for programs whose source of institutional control is private (nonprofit). Cost of public programs at Alfred, such as those offered by the New York State College of Ceramics (SUNY), may vary by program. Room/board: $9,600. Books/supplies: $700. Personal expenses: $350.

2004-2005 Financial aid. **Need-based:** 452 full-time freshmen applied for aid; 406 were judged to have need; 406 of these received aid. Average need met was 94%. Average scholarship/grant was $14,574; average loan $4,146. 72% of total undergraduate aid awarded as scholarships/grants, 28% as loans/jobs. **Non-need-based:** Awarded to 1,062 full-time undergraduates, including 321 freshmen. Scholarships awarded for academics, art, leadership, music/drama.

Application procedures. **Admission:** Priority date 2/1; no deadline. $40 fee, may be waived for applicants with need. Application may be submitted online. Admission notification on a rolling basis beginning on or about 11/15. Must reply by May 1 or within 2 week(s) if notified thereafter. **Financial aid:** Priority date 2/1; no closing date. FAFSA, institutional form required. Applicants notified on a rolling basis starting 2/15; must reply by 5/1 or within 2 week(s) of notification.

Academics. Credit hours required for graduation vary from 120-138 depending on program. Credit hours required for major also vary by program. Preadmission summer program for students enrolling through Opportunity Programs (EOP or HEOP). **Special study options:** Combined bachelor's/graduate degree, cooperative education, cross-registration, double major, ESL, exchange student, honors, independent study, internships, liberal arts/career combination, New York semester, semester at sea, student-designed major, study abroad, teacher certification program, United Nations semester, Washington semester. **Credit/placement by examination:** AP, CLEP, IB, SAT, ACT, institutional tests. **Support services:** Reduced course load, study skills assistance, tutoring, writing center.

Majors. **Biology:** General. **Business:** Accounting, business admin, finance, marketing. **Communications:** General. **Conservation:** Environmental studies. **Education:** Elementary. **Engineering:** Ceramic, electrical, materials, materials science, mechanical. **Foreign languages:** French, German, Spanish. **Health:** Athletic training, clinical lab technology, predentistry, premedicine, preveterinary. **History:** General. **Interdisciplinary:** Biological/physical sciences, gerontology, intercultural, natural sciences. **Liberal arts:** Arts/sciences. **Math:** General. **Philosophy/religion:** Philosophy. **Physical sciences:** Chemistry, geology, physics. **Protective services:** Criminal justice. **Psychology:** General. **Public administration:** General. **Social sciences:** Economics, political science, sociology. **Visual/performing arts:** Art, dramatic, studio arts.

Most popular majors. Business/marketing 13%, education 6%, engineering/engineering technologies 12%, psychology 8%, social sciences 6%, visual/performing arts 28%.

Computing on campus. 450 workstations in dormitories, library, computer center, student center. Dormitories wired for high-speed internet access and linked to campus network. Commuter students can connect to campus network. Online course registration, online library, helpline, student web hosting, wireless network available.

Student life. Freshman orientation: Mandatory. Preregistration for classes offered. Begins 4 days before classes start. Combination of academic and nonacademic activities. **Policies:** Students must abide by Alfred University Code of Honor. Policies against hazing and sexual harassment. Freshmen permitted cars on campus. **Housing:** Guaranteed on-campus for freshmen. Coed dorms, apartments, substance-free housing available. $300 nonrefundable deposit, deadline 5/1. Theme housing available (e.g., Honors, Language House, Outdoor Sports). All students required to live in residence halls 4 semesters. Students in poor academic standing required to live on campus. Exceptions granted for married students, students 23 and older, students living with parents/legal guardian and commuting from home, students with dependents, and veterans. **Activities:** Bands, choral groups, dance, drama, film society, literary magazine, music ensembles, musical theater, radio station, student government, student newspaper, symphony orchestra, TV station, Hillel, Brothers and Sisters in Christ, Spectrum, Student Volunteers for Community Action, Alpha Phi Omega, Habitat for Humanity, Christian fellowship, women's issues coalition.

Athletics. NCAA. **Intercollegiate:** Basketball, cross-country, diving, equestrian, football (tackle) M, lacrosse, skiing, soccer, softball W, swimming, tennis, track and field, volleyball W. **Intramural:** Basketball, football (non-tackle), lacrosse M, racquetball, skiing, soccer, softball, squash, tennis, volleyball. **Team name:** Saxons.

Student services. Alcohol/substance abuse counseling, campus ministries, career counseling, services for economically disadvantaged, student employment services, financial aid counseling, health services, minority student services, personal counseling, placement for graduates, women's services. **Physically disabled:** Services for visually, speech, hearing impaired.

Contact. E-mail: admissions@alfred.edu
Phone: (607) 871-2115 Toll-free number: (800) 541-9229
Fax: (607) 871-2198
Jeremy Spencer, Director of Admissions, Alfred University, Alumni Hall, Alfred, NY 14802-1205

Bard College

Annandale-on-Hudson, New York — **CB member**
www.bard.edu — **CB code: 2037**

- Private 4-year liberal arts college affiliated with Episcopal Church
- Residential campus in small town
- 1,555 degree-seeking undergraduates: 3% part-time, 57% women, 2% African American, 4% Asian American, 4% Hispanic American, 8% international
- 273 degree-seeking graduate students
- 32% of applicants admitted
- Application essay required
- 72% graduate within 6 years

General. Founded in 1860. Regionally accredited. Writing-intensive, multidisciplinary programs. Extensive programs in languages, human rights and globalization and international affairs. Unique collaboration with The Rockefeller University. **Degrees:** 330 bachelor's awarded; master's, doctoral offered. **Location:** 90 miles from New York City, 50 miles from Albany. **Calendar:** Semester. **Full-time faculty:** 130 total; 79% have terminal degrees, 18% minority, 45% women. **Part-time faculty:** 100 total; 58% have terminal degrees, 16% minority, 49% women. **Class size:** 75% < 20, 25% 20-39, less than 1% 40-49. **Special facilities:** Ecology field station contiguous to Hudson River Estuary Preserves, curatorial studies and art center, museum of late 20th-century art, archaeological field school, economics institute, center for studies in decorative arts, design and culture, performance hall.

Freshman class profile. 4,142 applied, 1,325 admitted, 515 enrolled.

Mid 50% test scores			
SAT verbal:	640-720	**Rank in top tenth:**	63%
SAT math:	580-690	**End year in good standing:**	88%
GPA 3.50 or higher:	56%	**Return as sophomores:**	88%
GPA 3.0-3.49:	43%	**Out-of-state:**	72%
GPA 2.0-2.99:	1%	**Live on campus:**	99%
Rank in top quarter:	85%	**International:**	8%

Basis for selection. School transcripts and achievement record, rigor of high school program, essays, academic recommendations, talents and dedication to activities, a love of learning, and personal ambition important. Campus tour and information session recommended. Tape or CD, brief musical autobiography, and audition required of music applicants.

High school preparation. Recommended units include English 4, mathematics 4, social studies 4, history 4, science 4 and foreign language 4.

2005-2006 Annual costs. Tuition/fees: $32,490. Room/board: $9,310. Books/supplies: $1,000. Personal expenses: $1,500.

2005-2006 Financial aid. Need-based: 359 full-time freshmen applied for aid; 289 were judged to have need; 289 of these received aid. Average need met was 87%. Average scholarship/grant was $24,046; average loan $1,614. 76% of total undergraduate aid awarded as scholarships/grants, 24% as loans/jobs. **Non-need-based:** Awarded to 67 full-time undergraduates, including 33 freshmen. Scholarships awarded for academics. **Additional information:** Excellence and Equal Cost Program for students who graduate in top 10 of public high school class lowers fees to levels equivalent to those at home state university or college.

Application procedures. Admission: Closing date 1/15 (receipt date). $50 fee, may be waived for applicants with need. Application must be submitted on paper. Admission notification 4/1. Must reply by May 1 or within 2 week(s) if notified thereafter. Applicants may be admitted through early action, regular procedure, or Immediate Decision Plan, which gives next-day decision after day-long program and individual interview. Sessions scheduled in early fall. **Financial aid:** Priority date 2/1, closing date 2/15. FAFSA, CSS PROFILE required. Applicants notified by 4/1; must reply by 5/1.

Academics. Strong tradition of independent study and tutorial work with faculty member. **Special study options:** Accelerated study, combined bachelor's/graduate degree, cross-registration, double major, exchange student, independent study, internships, liberal arts/career combination, New York semester, student-designed major, study abroad, Washington semester. Intensive language studies in Italy, Germany, France, Mexico, Russia, China, program in International Education. **Credit/placement by examination:** AP, CLEP, IB, institutional tests. **Support services:** Learning center, reduced course load, remedial instruction, study skills assistance, tutoring, writing center.

Majors. Area/ethnic studies: African, African-American, American, Asian, Central/Eastern European, European, French, German, Italian, Latin American, Russian/Slavic, Spanish/Iberian, Western European. **Biology:** General, biochemistry, bioinformatics, cell/histology, ecology, environmental, microbiology, molecular. **Computer sciences:** Computer science. **English:** American lit, British lit, composition, creative writing, English lit. **Foreign languages:** General, ancient Greek, Chinese, classics, comparative lit, French, German, Italian, Japanese, Latin, Romance, Russian, Sanskrit, Spanish, translation. **Health:** Predentistry, premedicine, prepharmacy, preveterinary. **History:** General, American, Asian, European. **Interdisciplinary:** Global studies, intercultural, medieval/Renaissance, neuroscience. **Legal studies:** Prelaw. **Liberal arts:** Arts/sciences. **Math:** General. **Philosophy/religion:** Judaic, philosophy, religion. **Physical sciences:** Chemistry, physics. **Psychology:** General. **Social sciences:** General, anthropology, archaeology, economics, international relations, political science, sociology. **Visual/performing arts:** General, acting, art, art history/conservation, cinematography, conducting, dance, directing/producing, dramatic, drawing, film/cinema, jazz, multimedia, music history, music performance, music theory/composition, painting, photography, piano/organ, play/screenwriting, printmaking, sculpture, stringed instruments, studio arts, theater history, voice/opera.

Most popular majors. English 15%, psychology 6%, social sciences 15%, visual/performing arts 38%.

Computing on campus. 425 workstations in library, computer center, student center. Dormitories wired for high-speed internet access and linked to campus network. Commuter students can connect to campus network. Online course registration, online library, helpline, student web hosting, wireless network available.

Student life. Freshman orientation: Mandatory, $550 fee. 3-week writing-intensive Workshop in Language and Thinking held on campus in August immediately prior to fall semester; coincides with Bard Music Festival. **Policies:** All Bard students are members of the student government association, a democratic forum that allocates funds, takes action on campus issues, and provides student representation on administrative and faculty committees. Freshmen permitted cars on campus. **Housing:** Guaranteed on-campus for freshmen. Coed dorms, single-sex dorms, cooperative housing available. $500 nonrefundable deposit, deadline 5/1. Pets allowed in dorm rooms. **Activities:** Bands, choral groups, dance, drama, film society, literary magazine, music ensembles, musical theater, opera, radio station, student government, student newspaper, symphony orchestra, over 120 organizations available.

Athletics. NCAA. **Intercollegiate:** Basketball, cross-country, soccer, squash, tennis, volleyball. **Intramural:** Badminton, basketball, bowling, golf, soccer, softball, table tennis, tennis, volleyball. **Team name:** Raptors.

Student services. Adult student services, alcohol/substance abuse counseling, campus ministries, career counseling, services for economically disadvantaged, student employment services, financial aid counseling, health services, legal services, minority student services, personal counseling, placement for graduates, women's services. **Physically disabled:** Services for visually, hearing impaired.

Contact. E-mail: admissions@bard.edu
Phone: (845) 758-7472 Fax: (845) 758-5208
Mary Backlund, Director of Admission, Bard College, 30 Campus Road, Annandale-on-Hudson, NY 12504-5000

Barnard College

New York, New York
www.barnard.edu
CB member
CB code: 2038

- Private 4-year liberal arts college for women
- Residential campus in very large city
- 2,356 degree-seeking undergraduates: 3% part-time, 100% women, 5% African American, 17% Asian American, 7% Hispanic American, 3% international
- 27% of applicants admitted
- SAT and SAT Subject Tests or ACT (ACT writing recommended), application essay required
- 89% graduate within 6 years; 23% enter graduate study

General. Founded in 1889. Regionally accredited. Cross-registration and shared facilities with Columbia University. Students receive Columbia University degrees. **Degrees:** 585 bachelor's awarded. **Calendar:** Semester. **Full-time faculty:** 193 total; 94% have terminal degrees, 15% minority, 58% women. **Part-time faculty:** 126 total; 71% have terminal degrees, 5% minority, 72% women. **Class size:** 67% < 20, 22% 20-39, 4% 40-49, 6% 50-99, 2% >100. **Special facilities:** Center for toddler development, center for research on women, theater, dance studios, access to 3600-acre nature preserve in upstate New York, greenhouse, access to geological observatory.

Freshman class profile. 4,431 applied, 1,216 admitted, 571 enrolled.

Mid 50% test scores			
SAT verbal:	650-740	Rank in top tenth:	83%
SAT math:	640-710	End year in good standing:	99%
ACT:	27-30	Return as sophomores:	95%
GPA 3.50 or higher:	96%	Out-of-state:	67%
GPA 3.0-3.49:	4%	Live on campus:	98%
Rank in top quarter:	99%	International:	2%

Basis for selection. High school record most important. Depth and difficulty of high school program considered. Test scores, recommendations, involvement in school and community activities, special talents, skills considered. Interview recommended.

High school preparation. 16 units recommended. Recommended units include English 4, mathematics 3, history 3, science 3 (laboratory 2) and foreign language 3. Additional units in social sciences, art, music also recommended.

2005-2006 Annual costs. Tuition/fees: $30,676. Room/board: $11,126. Books/supplies: $1,050. Personal expenses: $1,250.

2005-2006 Financial aid. All financial aid based on need. 329 full-time freshmen applied for aid; 241 were judged to have need; 241 of these received aid. Average need met was 100%. Average scholarship/grant was $25,413; average loan $2,376. 83% of total undergraduate aid awarded as scholarships/grants, 17% as loans/jobs.

Application procedures. Admission: Closing date 1/1 (postmark date). $45 fee, may be waived for applicants with need. Application must be submitted on paper. Admission notification 4/1. Must reply by 5/1. **Financial aid:** Closing date 2/1. FAFSA, institutional form, CSS PROFILE required. Applicants notified by 4/1; must reply by 5/1.

Academics. Interdisciplinary first year seminar mandatory. Coursework in global cultures, which may also fulfill other degree requirements, is mandatory. **Special study options:** Accelerated study, combined bachelor's/graduate degree, cross-registration, double major, dual enrollment of high school students, exchange student, honors, independent study, internships, liberal arts/career combination, student-designed major, study abroad, teacher certification program. Independent scholars program, BA/BS in engineering and applied science. **Credit/placement by examination:** AP, CLEP, IB, institutional tests. 30 credit hours maximum toward bachelor's degree. **Support services:** Pre-admission summer program, tutoring, writing center.

Majors. Architecture: Architecture, history/criticism. **Area/ethnic studies:** African, American, Asian, European, French, German, Latin American, Near/Middle Eastern, Russian/Slavic, Slavic, Spanish/Iberian, women's. **Biology:** General, biochemistry, biophysics, environmental. **Computer sciences:** General, computer science. **Conservation:** Environmental science, environmental studies. **Engineering:** Physics. **English:** English lit. **Foreign languages:** Ancient Greek, classics, comparative lit, French, German, Italian, Latin, linguistics, modern Greek, Russian, Spanish. **History:** General. **Interdisciplinary:** Ancient studies, biopsychology, medieval/Renaissance. **Math:** General, applied, statistics. **Philosophy/religion:** Philosophy, religion. **Physical sciences:** Astronomy, astrophysics, chemical physics, chemistry, geology, physics. **Psychology:** General. **Social sciences:** Anthropology, economics, geography, political science, sociology, urban studies. **Visual/performing arts:** General, art history/conservation, dance, dramatic, film/cinema, jazz.

Most popular majors. Area/ethnic studies 8%, English 13%, psychology 13%, social sciences 26%, visual/performing arts 11%.

Computing on campus. 208 workstations in dormitories, library, computer center, student center. Dormitories wired for high-speed internet access and linked to campus network. Commuter students can connect to campus network. Online course registration, online library, helpline, repair service, wireless network available.

Student life. Freshman orientation: Mandatory, $275 fee. 8-day program. **Policies:** Freshmen permitted cars on campus. **Housing:** Guaranteed on-campus for all undergraduates. Special housing for disabled, apartments, substance-free housing available. $400 nonrefundable deposit, deadline 5/1. Coed dorms available through Columbia University. **Activities:** Bands, choral groups, dance, drama, film society, literary magazine, music ensembles, musical theater, opera, radio station, student government, student newspaper, symphony orchestra, TV station, more than 100 organizations.

Athletics. NCAA. **Intercollegiate:** Archery W, basketball W, cross-country W, diving W, fencing W, field hockey W, golf W, lacrosse W, rowing (crew) W, soccer W, softball W, swimming W, tennis W, track and field W, volleyball W. **Intramural:** Archery W, badminton W, basketball W, bowling W, cross-country W, fencing W, racquetball W, sailing W, soccer W, softball W, swimming W, tennis W, volleyball W. **Team name:** Lions.

Student services. Alcohol/substance abuse counseling, career counseling, student employment services, financial aid counseling, health services, personal counseling, placement for graduates, women's services. **Physically disabled:** Services for visually, speech, hearing impaired.

Contact. E-mail: admissions@barnard.edu
Phone: (212) 854-2014 Fax: (212) 854-6220
Jennifer Fondiller, Dean of Admissions, Barnard College, 3009 Broadway, New York, NY 10027-6598

Beis Medrash Heichal Dovid

Far Rockaway, New York

- Private 4-year rabbinical college for men
- Large city

General. Accredited by AARTS. **Calendar:** Continuous.

Annual costs/financial aid. Tuition/fees (2005-2006): $6,000.

Contact. Phone: (718) 868-2300
Registrar, 257 Beach 17th Street, Far Rockaway, NY 11691

Berkeley College

White Plains, New York
www.berkeleycollege.edu
CB code: 2064

- For-profit 4-year business college
- Commuter campus in small city
- 608 degree-seeking undergraduates: 7% part-time, 72% women, 26% African American, 3% Asian American, 21% Hispanic American, 6% international
- 610 graduate students
- 50% graduate within 6 years

General. Founded in 1945. Regionally accredited. **Degrees:** 81 bachelor's, 54 associate awarded. **Location:** 28 miles from New York City. **Calendar:** Quarter, extensive summer session. **Full-time faculty:** 17 total. **Part-time faculty:** 25 total. **Special facilities:** Access to Manhattanville College facilities.

Freshman class profile.

Return as sophomores:	55%	Live on campus:	25%
Out-of-state:	12%	International:	6%

Basis for selection. Class rank, high school record, interview most important. Passing grade on school entrance examination required. SAT/ACT considered if submitted. Interviews strongly recommended.

2006-2007 Annual costs. Tuition/fees: $17,700. Part-time students pay $75 administrative fee per quarter. Room/board: $9,000. Books/supplies: $1,200.

Financial aid. Non-need-based: Scholarships awarded for academics, alumni affiliation. **Additional information:** Alumni scholarship examination given in November and December. Full and partial scholarships awarded.

Application procedures. Admission: No deadline. $50 fee. Application may be submitted online. Admission notification on a rolling basis. Admitted applicants must reply within 2 weeks of notification. **Financial aid:** No deadline. FAFSA required. Applicants notified on a rolling basis starting 3/1; must reply within 6 week(s) of notification.

Academics. Special study options: Accelerated study, cooperative education, distance learning, ESL, internships, New York semester, study abroad. **Credit/placement by examination:** AP, CLEP, SAT, ACT, institutional tests. **Support services:** Learning center, remedial instruction, study skills assistance, tutoring.

Majors. Business: General, accounting, business admin, e-commerce, fashion, international, marketing, office management.

Computing on campus. 150 workstations in library, computer center. Dormitories linked to campus network. Commuter students can connect to campus network. Online library, helpline, wireless network available.

Student life. Freshman orientation: Mandatory. **Policies:** Freshmen permitted cars on campus. **Housing:** Coed dorms available. $400 partly refundable deposit. **Activities:** Student government, student newspaper, accounting club, Berkeley club, Phi Beta Lambda, Phi Theta Kappa, international club, fashion club, paralegal club.

Athletics. Intramural: Basketball, softball, volleyball. **Team name:** Bulldogs.

Student services. Adult student services, career counseling, student employment services, financial aid counseling, personal counseling, placement for graduates.

Contact. E-mail: admissions@berkeleycollege.edu
Phone: (914) 694-1122 Toll-free number: (800) 446-5400
Fax: (914) 328-9469
Kimberly Satriale, Director, High School Admissions, Berkeley College, 99 Church Street, White Plains, NY 10601

Berkeley College of New York City
New York, New York
www.berkeleycollege.edu **CB code: 0954**

- For-profit 4-year business college
- Commuter campus in very large city
- 2,307 degree-seeking undergraduates: 8% part-time, 70% women, 23% African American, 5% Asian American, 23% Hispanic American, 15% international
- 2,321 graduate students
- 73% of applicants admitted
- 50% graduate within 6 years

General. Founded in 1936. Regionally accredited. **Degrees:** 308 bachelor's, 140 associate awarded. **Location:** Midtown Manhattan. **Calendar:** Quarter, extensive summer session. **Full-time faculty:** 40 total. **Part-time faculty:** 100 total.

Freshman class profile. 2,279 applied, 1,675 admitted, 639 enrolled.

Return as sophomores:	48%	**International:**	9%
Out-of-state:	8%		

Basis for selection. High school record and interview most important. Institutional entrance tests required of all applicants. SAT or ACT accepted in lieu of institutional entrance exam. Interviews strongly recommended.

2006-2007 Annual costs. Tuition/fees: $17,700. Part-time students pay $75 administrative fee per quarter. Books/supplies: $1,200.

Financial aid. Non-need-based: Scholarships awarded for academics, alumni affiliation. **Additional information:** Alumni scholarship examination given in November and December. Full and partial scholarships awarded.

Application procedures. Admission: No deadline. $50 fee. Application may be submitted online. Admission notification on a rolling basis. Admitted applicants must reply within 2 weeks of notification. **Financial aid:** No deadline. FAFSA required. Applicants notified on a rolling basis starting 3/1; must reply within 6 week(s) of notification.

Academics. Special study options: Accelerated study, distance learning, ESL, internships, study abroad. **Credit/placement by examination:** AP, CLEP, SAT, ACT, institutional tests. **Support services:** Learning center, remedial instruction, study skills assistance, tutoring, writing center.

Majors. Business: General, accounting, business admin, fashion, international, marketing, office management.

Computing on campus. 200 workstations in library, computer center. Commuter students can connect to campus network. Online library, wireless network available.

Student life. Freshman orientation: Mandatory. **Policies:** Freshmen permitted cars on campus. **Housing:** $400 partly refundable deposit. **Activities:** Student government, international club, multicultural club, fashion club, accounting club, paralegal club, student government.

Athletics. Team name: Bulldogs.

Student services. Adult student services, alcohol/substance abuse counseling, career counseling, student employment services, financial aid counseling, personal counseling, placement for graduates.

Contact. E-mail: admissions@berkeleycollege.edu
Phone: (212) 986-4343 Toll-free number: (800) 446-5400
Fax: (212) 818-1079
Stuart Siegman, Director of High School Admissions, Berkeley College of New York City, 3 East 43rd Street, New York, NY 10017

Beth Hamedrash Shaarei Yosher Institute
Brooklyn, New York
CB code: 0731

- Private 5-year rabbinical college for men affiliated with Jewish faith
- Very large city

General. Founded in 1962. Accredited by AARTS. **Calendar:** Semester.

Annual costs/financial aid. Tuition/fees (2005-2006): $6,010. Personal expenses: $1,600.

Contact. Phone: (718) 854-2290
Director of Student Financial Aid, 4102-10 16th Avenue, Brooklyn, NY 11204

Beth Hatalmud Rabbinical College
Brooklyn, New York
CB code: 7317

- Private 4-year rabbinical college for men affiliated with Jewish faith
- Very large city

General. Founded in 1950. Accredited by AARTS. **Calendar:** Semester.

Annual costs/financial aid. Tuition/fees (2005-2006): $5,000.

Contact. Phone: (718) 259-2525
Director of Admissions, 2127 82nd Street, Brooklyn, NY 11214

Boricua College
New York, New York
www.boricuacollege.edu **CB code: 2901**

- Private 4-year liberal arts college
- Commuter campus in very large city
- 1,200 full-time, degree-seeking undergraduates
- Application essay, interview required

General. Founded in 1974. Regionally accredited. 2 additional campuses in Brooklyn. **Degrees:** 144 bachelor's, 186 associate awarded; master's offered. **Calendar:** Trimester, limited summer session. **Full-time faculty:** 52 total. **Part-time faculty:** 80 total.

Basis for selection. Entrance examination, academic record, interview, 2 letters of recommendation, working knowledge of English and Spanish important. Foreign students not admitted. Institutional tests required for admissions and placement.

2005-2006 Annual costs. Tuition/fees: $7,300. Books/supplies: $450. Personal expenses: $844.

Application procedures. **Admission:** No deadline. $25 fee. Admission notification on a rolling basis. **Financial aid:** No deadline. Applicants notified on a rolling basis; must reply within 3 week(s) of notification.

Academics. Curriculum comprised of 5 courses per semester: 3 applied studies courses (individualized instruction, colloquium, experiential), 1 theoretical, and 1 cultural class. **Special study options:** Accelerated study, independent study, internships. **Credit/placement by examination:** CLEP, institutional tests. 30 credit hours maximum toward bachelor's degree. **Support services:** Tutoring.

Majors. **Area/ethnic studies:** Latin American. **Business:** Business admin. **Education:** Elementary. **Liberal arts:** Arts/sciences. **Public administration:** Human services.

Student life. **Activities:** Choral groups, dance, drama, opera, student government, student newspaper.

Student services. Career counseling, student employment services, personal counseling, placement for graduates.

Contact. Phone: (212) 694-1000
Abraham Cruz, Director of Admissions, Boricua College, 3755 Broadway, New York, NY 10032

Briarcliffe College

Bethpage, New York
www.briarcliffe.edu
CB code: 3108

- For-profit 4-year business and technical college
- Commuter campus in large town
- 3,009 degree-seeking undergraduates: 21% part-time, 51% women, 14% African American, 1% Asian American, 9% Hispanic American
- 85% of applicants admitted

General. Founded in 1966. Regionally accredited. 4-year BFA program with concentration in graphic design available. **Degrees:** 364 bachelor's, 552 associate awarded. **Location:** 20 miles from New York City. **Calendar:** Semester, extensive summer session. **Full-time faculty:** 50 total; 20% have terminal degrees, 14% minority, 38% women. **Part-time faculty:** 197 total; 2% have terminal degrees, 11% minority, 36% women. **Class size:** 60% < 20, 39% 20-39, less than 1% 40-49.

Freshman class profile. 947 applied, 805 admitted, 596 enrolled.

Basis for selection. School achievement record important, recommendations suggested. Interviews recommended. **Homeschooled:** Not accepted.

High school preparation. Recommended units include English 4, mathematics 2, social studies 4 and science 1.

2005-2006 Annual costs. Tuition/fees: $14,696. Additional costs for technical, graphic design and digital photography programs.

Financial aid. **Non-need-based:** Scholarships awarded for academics.

Application procedures. **Admission:** No deadline. $35 fee. Application may be submitted online. Admission notification on a rolling basis. **Financial aid:** No deadline. FAFSA, institutional form required. Applicants notified on a rolling basis.

Academics. **Special study options:** Cooperative education, independent study, internships, study abroad. **Credit/placement by examination:** CLEP, institutional tests. 15 credit hours maximum toward associate degree, 15 toward bachelor's. **Support services:** Learning center, reduced course load, remedial instruction, study skills assistance, tutoring.

Majors. **Business:** Accounting, business admin. **Computer sciences:** Networking, programming. **Visual/performing arts:** General.

Computing on campus. 400 workstations in library, computer center. Commuter students can connect to campus network. Online library available.

Student life. **Freshman orientation:** Mandatory. Preregistration for classes offered. **Policies:** Freshmen permitted cars on campus. **Housing:** Single-sex dorms available. **Activities:** Student government, student newspaper.

Athletics. NJCAA, USCAA. **Intercollegiate:** Baseball M, basketball W, bowling, cross-country, lacrosse M, soccer W, softball W. **Team name:** Seahawks.

Student services. Career counseling, student employment services, financial aid counseling, placement for graduates.

Contact. E-mail: info@bcl.edu
Phone: (516) 918-3600 Fax: (516) 470-6020
Terry Donohue, Vice President of Admissions, Briarcliffe College, 1055 Stewart Avenue, Bethpage, NY 11714

Canisius College

Buffalo, New York
www.canisius.edu
CB member
CB code: 2073

- Private 4-year liberal arts and teachers college affiliated with Roman Catholic Church
- Residential campus in large city
- 3,395 degree-seeking undergraduates: 3% part-time, 56% women, 6% African American, 2% Asian American, 2% Hispanic American, 3% international
- 1,386 degree-seeking graduate students
- 72% of applicants admitted
- SAT or ACT (ACT writing optional) required
- 67% graduate within 6 years

General. Founded in 1870. Regionally accredited. Campus connected by underground tunnel system, rapid transit stations near campus. **Degrees:** 792 bachelor's awarded; master's offered. **ROTC:** Army. **Calendar:** Semester, limited summer session. **Full-time faculty:** 215 total; 94% have terminal degrees, 6% minority, 32% women. **Part-time faculty:** 316 total. **Class size:** 351% < 20, 356% 20-39, 31% 40-49, 10% 50-99. **Special facilities:** Mini-planetarium, seismograph station, rare book room, digital media lab, human performance lab, animal care unit.

Freshman class profile. 4,114 applied, 2,962 admitted, 775 enrolled.

Mid 50% test scores		**Rank in top quarter:**	51%
SAT verbal:	470-630	**Rank in top tenth:**	22%
SAT math:	480-650	**Return as sophomores:**	84%
ACT:	20-28	**Out-of-state:**	10%
GPA 3.50 or higher:	52%	**Live on campus:**	69%
GPA 3.0-3.49:	29%	**International:**	3%
GPA 2.0-2.99:	19%		

Basis for selection. GED not accepted. Primary emphasis placed on strength of academic record, achievement, class rank and SAT/ACT scores. Essays, recommendations important. Extracurricular activities, alumni affiliation. Interview and essay recommended.

High school preparation. College-preparatory program recommended. 23 units recommended. Recommended units include English 4, mathematics 3, social studies 4, science 3 (laboratory 2), foreign language 3 and academic electives 4.

2005-2006 Annual costs. Tuition/fees: $23,297. Room/board: $8,960.

2005-2006 Financial aid. **Need-based:** 696 full-time freshmen applied for aid; 621 were judged to have need; 619 of these received aid. Average need met was 84%. Average scholarship/grant was $14,812; average loan $2,996. 71% of total undergraduate aid awarded as scholarships/grants, 29% as loans/jobs. **Non-need-based:** Awarded to 1,374 full-time undergraduates, including 297 freshmen. Scholarships awarded for academics, alumni affiliation, art, athletics, job skills, music/drama, religious affiliation, ROTC.

Application procedures. **Admission:** Priority date 3/1; deadline 5/1. $40 fee, may be waived for applicants with need. Application may be submitted online. Admission notification on a rolling basis beginning on or about 12/15. Must reply by 5/1. Must reply by May 1 or within 2 week(s) if notified thereafter. **Financial aid:** Priority date 2/15; no closing date. FAFSA, institutional form required. Applicants notified on a rolling basis starting 3/1; must reply within 2 week(s) of notification.

Academics. Pre-professional programs include pre-engineering, prelaw, premedical, predentistry, preveterinary medicine, prepharmacy. **Special study options:** Combined bachelor's/graduate degree, cross-registration, distance learning, double major, dual enrollment of high school students, honors, independent study, internships, study abroad, teacher certification program. Early assurance for medical and dental school with SUNY Buffalo Medical and Dental Schools (New York state residents only), and the Upstate Medical School at Syracuse; 7-year joint degree programs with SUNY Buffalo Dental School, the Ohio College of Podiatric Medicine, the New York College of Podiatric Medicine and SUNY State College of Optometry in NYC;

AS/BS with Fashion Institute of Technology. **Credit/placement by examination:** AP, CLEP, IB, SAT, ACT, institutional tests. 30 credit hours maximum toward bachelor's degree. **Support services:** Learning center, pre-admission summer program, reduced course load, remedial instruction, study skills assistance, tutoring, writing center.

Majors. Area/ethnic studies: European. **Biology:** General, biochemistry, bioinformatics. **Business:** Accounting, accounting technology, entrepreneurial studies, finance, international, management information systems, management science, marketing. **Communications:** General, digital media. **Computer sciences:** Computer science. **Conservation:** Environmental science. **Education:** Early childhood, early childhood special, elementary, physical, secondary. **English:** English lit. **Foreign languages:** French, Germanic, Spanish. **Health:** Athletic training, clinical lab science. **History:** General. **Liberal arts:** Arts/sciences, humanities. **Philosophy/religion:** Philosophy, religion. **Physical sciences:** Chemistry, physics. **Protective services:** Criminal justice. **Psychology:** General. **Social sciences:** Anthropology, economics, international relations, political science, sociology, urban studies. **Visual/performing arts:** Art history/conservation.

Most popular majors. Biology 7%, business/marketing 25%, communications/journalism 12%, education 25%, psychology 10%, social sciences 8%.

Computing on campus. 500 workstations in dormitories, library, computer center, student center. Dormitories wired for high-speed internet access and linked to campus network. Commuter students can connect to campus network. Online course registration, online library, helpline, repair service, student web hosting, wireless network available.

Student life. Freshman orientation: Mandatory, $125 fee. Preregistration for classes offered. Program includes testing, advisement, registration, introduction to student services. **Policies:** Religious observance required. Freshmen permitted cars on campus. **Housing:** Coed dorms, special housing for disabled, apartments, substance-free housing available. $200 partly refundable deposit, deadline 5/1. Themed housing; science; honors; townhouses. **Activities:** Bands, choral groups, dance, drama, film society, literary magazine, music ensembles, musical theater, radio station, student government, student newspaper, campus ministry, political science association, ethnic and social service organizations, international affairs society, social justice club, Circle K, Global Horizons, German club, Italian club, Little Theater.

Athletics. NCAA. **Intercollegiate:** Baseball M, basketball, cross-country, golf M, ice hockey M, lacrosse, soccer, softball W, swimming, synchronized swimming W, volleyball W. **Intramural:** Cheerleading, golf M, rowing (crew) W, rugby. **Team name:** Golden Griffins.

Student services. Adult student services, alcohol/substance abuse counseling, campus ministries, career counseling, services for economically disadvantaged, student employment services, financial aid counseling, health services, minority student services, personal counseling, placement for graduates, veterans' counselor. **Physically disabled:** Services for visually, speech, hearing impaired. **Learning disabled:** Comprehensive services available.

Contact. E-mail: admissions@canisius.edu
Phone: (716) 888-2200 Toll-free number: (800) 843-1517
Fax: (716) 888-3230
Jill Atkinson, Co-Director of Admissions, Canisius College, 2001 Main Street, Buffalo, NY 14208-1098

Cazenovia College

Cazenovia, New York
www.cazenovia.edu **CB code: 2078**

- Private 4-year liberal arts college
- Residential campus in small town
- 919 degree-seeking undergraduates: 12% part-time, 79% women, 3% African American, 1% Asian American, 2% Hispanic American, 1% Native American
- 82% of applicants admitted
- 40% graduate within 6 years

General. Founded in 1824. Regionally accredited. Preprofessional programs grounded in the liberal arts. **Degrees:** 166 bachelor's, 14 associate awarded. **ROTC:** Army, Air Force. **Location:** 20 miles from Syracuse. **Calendar:** Semester, limited summer session. **Full-time faculty:** 49 total; 63% have terminal degrees, 4% minority, 63% women. **Part-time faculty:** 90 total; 67% women. **Special facilities:** 160-acre farm and equine center, theater, state-of-the-art art & design facility.

Freshman class profile. 1,286 applied, 1,059 admitted, 285 enrolled.

Mid 50% test scores		**GPA 2.0-2.99:**	31%
SAT verbal:	440-560	**Rank in top quarter:**	29%
SAT math:	440-540	**Rank in top tenth:**	9%
ACT:	18-23	**Return as sophomores:**	74%
GPA 3.50 or higher:	33%	**Out-of-state:**	21%
GPA 3.0-3.49:	33%	**Live on campus:**	96%

Basis for selection. School achievement record, test scores, interview, recommendations, school activities considered. Minimum 2.0 high school GPA recommended. SAT or ACT recommended. Interview, essay recommended for all; portfolio recommended for art, graphic and interior design, photography programs.

High school preparation. College-preparatory program recommended. 16 units recommended. Recommended units include English 4, mathematics 2, social studies 4 and science 2. Art courses recommended for art and design majors.

2006-2007 Annual costs. Tuition/fees (projected): $20,180. Room/board: $8,445. Books/supplies: $900. Personal expenses: $500.

2005-2006 Financial aid. Need-based: 265 full-time freshmen applied for aid; 234 were judged to have need; 234 of these received aid. Average need met was 70%. Average scholarship/grant was $8,500; average loan $2,626. 65% of total undergraduate aid awarded as scholarships/grants, 35% as loans/jobs. **Non-need-based:** Awarded to 126 full-time undergraduates, including 50 freshmen. Scholarships awarded for academics.

Application procedures. Admission: Priority date 3/1; no deadline. $30 fee, may be waived for applicants with need. Application may be submitted online. Admission notification on a rolling basis beginning on or about 11/1. Must reply by May 1 or within 2 week(s) if notified thereafter. **Financial aid:** Priority date 3/15; no closing date. FAFSA required. Applicants notified on a rolling basis starting 11/1; must reply by 5/1 or within 2 week(s) of notification.

Academics. Management and supervision, purchasing management and equine certificate programs offered through continuing education office. **Special study options:** Combined bachelor's/graduate degree, honors, independent study, internships, student-designed major, study abroad, teacher certification program, Washington semester. Fall term of sophomore and junior years offered in London. **Credit/placement by examination:** AP, CLEP, IB, institutional tests. **Support services:** Learning center, pre-admission summer program, reduced course load, remedial instruction, study skills assistance, tutoring, writing center.

Majors. Business: Accounting, business admin, fashion. **Communications:** General. **Conservation:** Environmental studies. **Education:** Early childhood, special. **Liberal arts:** Arts/sciences. **Protective services:** Criminal justice. **Psychology:** General. **Public administration:** Human services. **Social sciences:** General. **Visual/performing arts:** Design, fashion design, interior design, studio arts.

Most popular majors. Business/marketing 30%, liberal arts 8%, psychology 7%, public administration/social services 11%, visual/performing arts 34%.

Computing on campus. 120 workstations in dormitories, library, computer center. Dormitories wired for high-speed internet access and linked to campus network. Commuter students can connect to campus network. Online library, helpline, wireless network available.

Student life. Freshman orientation: Mandatory, $135 fee. Preregistration for classes offered. 4 days prior to fall semester. **Policies:** Freshmen permitted cars on campus. **Housing:** Guaranteed on-campus for freshmen. Coed dorms, single-sex dorms available. $200 deposit, deadline 5/1. **Activities:** Jazz band, choral groups, dance, drama, film society, literary magazine, music ensembles, musical theater, radio station, student government, student newspaper, human services club, overseas travel club, campus ministry clubs, Young Democrats, Young Republicans, Cazventures outdoor club, Certified Peer Educators, You Are Not Alone (YANA), Student Organization of Ethnic Diversity.

Athletics. NCAA. **Intercollegiate:** Baseball M, basketball, cheerleading, cross-country, equestrian, golf M, lacrosse, rowing (crew), soccer, softball W, volleyball W. **Intramural:** Basketball, bowling, equestrian, football (non-tackle), racquetball, rowing (crew), skiing, soccer, softball, swimming, table tennis, tennis, volleyball, weight lifting. **Team name:** Wildcats.

Student services. Adult student services, alcohol/substance abuse counseling, campus ministries, career counseling, student employment services, financial aid counseling, health services, personal counseling, placement for graduates. **Physically disabled:** Services for visually, speech, hearing impaired.

Contact. E-mail: admission@cazenovia.edu
Phone: (315) 655-7208 Toll-free number: (800) 654-3210
Fax: (315) 655-4860
Robert Croot, VP for Enrollment Management and Dean for Admissions and Financial Aid, Cazenovia College, 3 Sullivan Street, Cazenovia, NY 13035

Central Yeshiva Tomchei Tmimim-Lubavitch

Brooklyn, New York

CB code: 0549

- Private 4-year rabbinical college for men affiliated with Jewish faith
- Very large city

General. Accredited by AARTS. **Calendar:** Continuous.

Annual costs/financial aid. Tuition/fees (2005-2006): $4,800.

Contact. Phone: (718) 859-7600
841-853 Ocean Parkway, Brooklyn, NY 11230

City University of New York: Baruch College

New York, New York **CB member**
www.baruch.cuny.edu **CB code: 2034**

- Public 4-year business and liberal arts college
- Commuter campus in very large city
- 12,617 degree-seeking undergraduates: 23% part-time, 55% women, 13% African American, 28% Asian American, 17% Hispanic American, 11% international
- 2,893 degree-seeking graduate students
- 33% of applicants admitted
- SAT or ACT (ACT writing optional) required
- 59% graduate within 6 years

General. Founded in 1919. Regionally accredited. **Degrees:** 2,639 bachelor's awarded; master's offered. **ROTC:** Army. **Calendar:** Semester, extensive summer session. **Full-time faculty:** 473 total; 22% minority, 36% women. **Part-time faculty:** 452 total; 19% minority, 37% women. **Class size:** 26% < 20, 56% 20-39, 5% 40-49, 10% 50-99, 2% >100. **Special facilities:** Performing arts center (black box theater, gallery, various theaters and recital halls).

Freshman class profile. 14,917 applied, 4,962 admitted, 1,641 enrolled.

Mid 50% test scores		**Rank in top tenth:**	23%
SAT verbal:	460-570	**End year in good standing:**	90%
SAT math:	530-630	**Return as sophomores:**	88%
GPA 3.50 or higher:	22%	**Out-of-state:**	3%
GPA 3.0-3.49:	38%	**International:**	8%
GPA 2.0-2.99:	37%	**Fraternities:**	1%
Rank in top quarter:	56%	**Sororities:**	1%

Basis for selection. Overall high school performance and 82 average or combined SAT score of 1200 required. **Homeschooled:** 1200 SAT required.

High school preparation. 16 units required. Required and recommended units include English 4, mathematics 3-4, social studies 4, science 2 (laboratory 2), foreign language 2-3 and academic electives 1.

2005-2006 Annual costs. Tuition/fees: $4,318; $11,118 out-of-state. Books/supplies: $879. Personal expenses: $2,710.

2005-2006 Financial aid. Need-based: 1,471 full-time freshmen applied for aid; 1,240 were judged to have need; 1,211 of these received aid. Average need met was 67%. Average scholarship/grant was $4,800; average loan $2,300. 81% of total undergraduate aid awarded as scholarships/grants, 19% as loans/jobs. **Non-need-based:** Awarded to 1,345 full-time undergraduates, including 295 freshmen. Scholarships awarded for academics, alumni affiliation, state residency.

Application procedures. Admission: Closing date 2/1 (postmark date). $65 fee. Application may be submitted online. Admission notification on a rolling basis beginning on or about 2/1. Must reply by May 1 or within 2 week(s) if notified thereafter. **Financial aid:** Priority date 3/15, closing date 4/30. FAFSA required. Applicants notified on a rolling basis starting 4/1; must reply by 6/1 or within 6 week(s) of notification.

Academics. 120 credit hours required for BA/BS degrees, 124 for BBA. Optional humanities seminar examining 2 or more disciplines in arts and sciences; joint business/liberal arts and science majors; programs in arts administration, management of musical enterprise, real estate, and metropolitan development. **Special study options:** Accelerated study, combined bachelor's/graduate degree, cross-registration, distance learning, double major, ESL, exchange student, honors, independent study, internships, liberal arts/career combination, student-designed major, study abroad. **Credit/placement by examination:** AP, CLEP, IB, institutional tests. 21 credit hours maximum toward bachelor's degree. No more than 21 credits through AP and/or college courses taken in high school. **Support services:** Learning center, pre-admission summer program, reduced course load, study skills assistance, tutoring, writing center.

Honors college/program. Applicants must have high standardized test scores (1300+ on the SAT, exclusive of Writing) and high school averages (90+). Leadership potential and community involvement sought. Applicants must supply teacher recommendations and essay.

Majors. Architecture: Urban/community planning. **Biology:** General. **Business:** General, accounting, actuarial science, business admin, communications, finance, human resources, labor relations, management information systems, managerial economics, operations, real estate, sales/distribution. **Communications:** General, advertising, journalism. **Computer sciences:** General, computer science, information systems. **Engineering:** Operations research. **English:** American lit, British lit, creative writing. **Foreign languages:** Comparative lit, Spanish. **History:** General. **Interdisciplinary:** Biological/physical sciences. **Liberal arts:** Arts/sciences. **Math:** General, statistics. **Philosophy/religion:** Philosophy. **Psychology:** General. **Public administration:** General. **Social sciences:** Economics, political science, sociology. **Visual/performing arts:** Arts management, design, music management.

Most popular majors. Business/marketing 76%, computer/information sciences 7%.

Computing on campus. 1,300 workstations in library, computer center, student center. Online course registration, online library, helpline, wireless network available.

Student life. Freshman orientation: Mandatory. Half day-long, on-campus session offered on multiple days. **Activities:** Choral groups, dance, drama, literary magazine, musical theater, radio station, student government, student newspaper, Hillel, National Association of Black Accountants, Golden Key, International Honor Society, Asian student association, Muslim student association, United International Student Body, Model United Nations, Pre-Law Society, Caribbean student association.

Athletics. NCAA. **Intercollegiate:** Baseball M, basketball, cheerleading M, cross-country, soccer M, softball W, swimming, tennis, volleyball, weight lifting. **Intramural:** Badminton, basketball, racquetball, table tennis, volleyball. **Team name:** Bearcats.

Student services. Adult student services, alcohol/substance abuse counseling, campus ministries, career counseling, student employment services, financial aid counseling, health services, legal services, personal counseling, placement for graduates, veterans' counselor. **Physically disabled:** Services for visually, speech, hearing impaired.

Contact. E-mail: admissions@baruch.cuny.edu
Phone: (646) 312-1400 Fax: (646) 312-1361
James Murphy, Vice President for Enrollment Management Services, City University of New York: Baruch College, One Bernard Baruch Way, Box H-0720, New York, NY 10010-5585

City University of New York: Brooklyn College

Brooklyn, New York
www.brooklyn.cuny.edu **CB code: 2046**

- Public 4-year liberal arts college
- Commuter campus in very large city
- 11,068 degree-seeking undergraduates: 27% part-time, 60% women, 28% African American, 11% Asian American, 12% Hispanic American, 7% international
- 3,437 degree-seeking graduate students
- 46% of applicants admitted
- SAT or ACT required
- 39% graduate within 6 years

General. Founded in 1930. Regionally accredited. **Degrees:** 1,688 bachelor's awarded; master's offered. **Location:** 10 miles from Manhattan. **Calendar:** Semester, extensive summer session. **Full-time faculty:** 517 total;

90% have terminal degrees, 26% minority, 40% women. **Part-time faculty:** 586 total; 36% have terminal degrees, 26% minority, 48% women. **Class size:** 41% < 20, 50% 20-39, 5% 40-49, 4% 50-99, less than 1% >100. **Special facilities:** Astronomical observatory, greenhouse, library cafe, applied sciences institute, institute for the humanities, infant study center, Brooklyn Center for the Performing Arts, art museum, particle accelerator.

Freshman class profile. 13,494 applied, 6,273 admitted, 1,413 enrolled.

Mid 50% test scores			
SAT verbal:	450-570	Rank in top tenth:	14%
SAT math:	490-590	Return as sophomores:	76%
GPA 3.50 or higher:	17%	Out-of-state:	1%
GPA 3.0-3.49:	23%	International:	6%
GPA 2.0-2.99:	54%	Fraternities:	1%
Rank in top quarter:	42%	Sororities:	1%

Basis for selection. Students accepted based on SAT scores and academic average. Essay required for BA/MD, CHC and Scholars, interview recommended for scholars program. Audition required for music conservatory, theater programs; portfolio required for fine arts program.

High school preparation. 21 units recommended. Recommended units include English 4, mathematics 3, social studies 4, science 3, foreign language 3 and academic electives 4.

2005-2006 Annual costs. Tuition/fees: $4,375; $11,175 out-of-state. Books/supplies: $800. Personal expenses: $2,000.

2005-2006 Financial aid. **Need-based:** 1,196 full-time freshmen applied for aid; 1,065 were judged to have need; 1,065 of these received aid. Average need met was 99%. Average scholarship/grant was $3,300; average loan $2,050. 60% of total undergraduate aid awarded as scholarships/grants, 40% as loans/jobs. **Non-need-based:** Scholarships awarded for academics, art, leadership, music/drama, state residency.

Application procedures. **Admission:** $65 fee. Admission notification on a rolling basis beginning on or about 1/15. **Financial aid:** Priority date 4/1; no closing date. FAFSA required. Applicants notified by 5/1; Applicants notified on a rolling basis starting 5/1.

Academics. **Special study options:** Accelerated study, combined bachelor's/graduate degree, cooperative education, cross-registration, distance learning, double major, dual enrollment of high school students, ESL, exchange student, honors, independent study, internships, liberal arts/career combination, study abroad, teacher certification program, Washington semester, weekend college. **Credit/placement by examination:** AP, CLEP, IB, institutional tests. 35 credit hours maximum toward bachelor's degree. **Support services:** Learning center, pre-admission summer program, reduced course load, study skills assistance, tutoring, writing center.

Majors. **Area/ethnic studies:** African-American, American, Caribbean, Hispanic-American/Latino/Chicano, Latin American, women's. **Biology:** General. **Business:** Accounting, business admin. **Communications:** General, broadcast journalism, journalism, radio/tv. **Communications technology:** Radio/tv. **Computer sciences:** General. **Conservation:** Environmental studies. **Education:** General, art, bilingual, biology, chemistry, early childhood, elementary, English, French, kindergarten/preschool, mathematics, music, physical, physics, social studies, Spanish, special, speech, speech impaired. **English:** Creative writing, English lit, speech/rhetoric. **Family/consumer sciences:** Food/nutrition. **Foreign languages:** Classics, comparative lit, French, Italian, linguistics, Russian, Spanish. **Health:** Audiology/speech pathology, speech pathology. **History:** General. **Interdisciplinary:** Biological/physical sciences, math/computer science. **Math:** General, algebra, computational. **Parks/recreation:** Health/fitness. **Philosophy/religion:** Judaic, philosophy, religion. **Physical sciences:** Chemistry, geology, physics. **Psychology:** General. **Public administration:** Community org/advocacy. **Social sciences:** Anthropology, economics, political science, sociology. **Visual/performing arts:** Acting, art, art history/conservation, cinematography, dramatic, film/cinema, music performance, music theory/composition, play/screenwriting.

Most popular majors. Business/marketing 30%, computer/information sciences 7%, education 8%, health sciences 6%, psychology 13%, social sciences 8%, visual/performing arts 7%.

Computing on campus. 2,000 workstations in library, computer center, student center. Online library, wireless network available.

Student life. **Freshman orientation:** Available. **Activities:** Concert band, choral groups, dance, drama, film society, literary magazine, music ensembles, musical theater, opera, radio station, student government, student newspaper, symphony orchestra, TV station, Hillel, Newman Club, student Christian association, Alpha Phi Omega, Christian fellowship, Islamic society, Caribbean student union, accounting society, lesbian/gay/bisexual/transgender alliance.

Athletics. NCAA. **Intercollegiate:** Basketball, cross-country, soccer M, softball W, tennis, track and field, volleyball. **Intramural:** Badminton W, basketball, racquetball, soccer M, softball W, tennis, track and field, volleyball. **Team name:** Bridges.

Student services. Adult student services, alcohol/substance abuse counseling, campus ministries, career counseling, services for economically disadvantaged, student employment services, financial aid counseling, health services, on-campus daycare, personal counseling, placement for graduates, veterans' counselor, women's services. **Physically disabled:** Services for visually, speech, hearing impaired. **Learning disabled:** Comprehensive services available.

Contact. E-mail: adminqry@brooklyn.cuny.edu
Phone: (718) 951-5001 Fax: (718) 951-4506
Marianne Booufall-Tynan, Director of Admissions, City University of New York: Brooklyn College, 2900 Bedford Avenue, Brooklyn, NY 11210

City University of New York: City College

New York, New York **CB member**
www.ccny.cuny.edu **CB code: 2083**

- Public 4-year university
- Commuter campus in very large city
- 9,264 degree-seeking undergraduates
- 97% of applicants admitted
- SAT or ACT required

General. Founded in 1847. Regionally accredited. **Degrees:** 1,184 bachelor's awarded; master's, doctoral offered. **Calendar:** Semester, extensive summer session. **Full-time faculty:** 521 total. **Part-time faculty:** 597 total. **Class size:** 46% < 20, 49% 20-39, 3% 40-49, 2% 50-99, less than 1% >100. **Special facilities:** Planetarium, weather station, ultra-fast laser spectroscopy laboratory, microwave laboratory, computer-aided design facilities, slide library, darkroom facilities, sonic music arts facility.

Freshman class profile. 12,141 applied, 11,766 admitted, 1,326 enrolled.

Mid 50% test scores		Rank in top quarter:	17%
SAT verbal:	420-560	Rank in top tenth:	14%
SAT math:	460-610	Out-of-state:	15%

Basis for selection. Academic average and number of academic units achieved in high school, SAT, or GED score of 325 or better important. Units recommended for admission must be acquired before graduation from any CUNY senior college. SAT section test scores of 450 or 20 ACT on math and verbal exempts student from taking placement exam. Interview required for biomedical education, audition required for music program; portfolio required for electronic design and multimedia. **Homeschooled:** Applicants must obtain GED or diploma through regionally accredited program.

High school preparation. 16 units recommended. Recommended units include English 4, mathematics 2, social studies 4, science 2 (laboratory 2) and foreign language 2. One unit of art or music recommended. For science and engineering students, 3 units of mathematics required.

2005-2006 Annual costs. Tuition/fees: $4,277; $11,077 out-of-state. Books/supplies: $832. Personal expenses: $2,679.

2005-2006 Financial aid. All financial aid based on need. 62% of total undergraduate aid awarded as scholarships/grants, 38% as loans/jobs.

Application procedures. **Admission:** Priority date 3/15; no deadline. $65 fee. Application may be submitted online. Admission notification on a rolling basis beginning on or about 1/15. **Financial aid:** Priority date 4/1; no closing date. FAFSA required. Applicants notified on a rolling basis starting 4/15.

Academics. **Special study options:** Accelerated study, combined bachelor's/graduate degree, cooperative education, cross-registration, dual enrollment of high school students, ESL, exchange student, honors, independent study, internships, liberal arts/career combination, study abroad, teacher certification program. Center for Worker Education, doctoral degrees through CUNY Graduate Center. **Credit/placement by examination:** AP, CLEP, IB, institutional tests. **Support services:** Learning center, pre-admission summer program, reduced course load, tutoring, writing center.

Majors. **Architecture:** Architecture. **Area/ethnic studies:** African-American, Asian, Caribbean, Latin American. **Biology:** General, biochemistry. **Business:** General. **Communications:** General, advertising, journalism, public relations. **Computer sciences:** Computer science. **Education:** Art, bilingual, biology, chemistry, early childhood, elementary, English, foreign languages, French, history, mathematics, music, physics, science, secondary, social studies, Spanish. **Engineering:** Biomedical, chemical, civil, computer, electrical, mechanical. **Foreign languages:** General, comparative lit, French, Spanish. **Health:** Physician assistant, premedicine, prepharmacy, preveterinary. **History:** General. **Interdisciplinary:** Global studies. **Legal studies:** Prelaw. **Math:** General. **Philosophy/religion:** Judaic, philosophy. **Physical sciences:** Chemistry, geology, physics, planetary. **Psychology:** General. **Social sciences:** Anthropology, economics, international relations, political science, sociology. **Visual/performing arts:** General, art, art history/conservation, cinematography, commercial/advertising art, dramatic, film/cinema, graphic design, jazz, music performance, music theory/composition, studio arts.

Computing on campus. 4,000 workstations in library, computer center, student center. Commuter students can connect to campus network. Online library, helpline, wireless network available.

Student life. **Freshman orientation:** Mandatory. Full-day program, including registration, held in spring and summer. **Housing:** Housing office available. **Activities:** Jazz band, choral groups, dance, drama, film society, music ensembles, musical theater, radio station, student government, student newspaper, numerous religious, political, ethnic, and social service organizations.

Athletics. NCAA. **Intercollegiate:** Baseball M, basketball, cross-country, fencing, lacrosse M, soccer, tennis, track and field, volleyball. **Intramural:** Badminton M, basketball, fencing, soccer M, softball W, swimming, tennis, track and field, volleyball. **Team name:** Beavers.

Student services. Campus ministries, career counseling, student employment services, financial aid counseling, health services, on-campus daycare, personal counseling, placement for graduates, veterans' counselor. **Physically disabled:** Services for visually, speech, hearing impaired. **Learning disabled:** Comprehensive services available.

Contact. E-mail: admissions@ccny.cuny.edu
Phone: (212) 650-6977 Fax: (212) 650-6417
Joseph Fatozzi, Director of Admissions, City University of New York: City College, 160 Convent Avenue, New York, NY 10031

City University of New York: College of Staten Island

Staten Island, New York — **CB member**
www.csi.cuny.edu — **CB code: 2778**

- Public 4-year liberal arts college
- Commuter campus in very large city
- 10,598 degree-seeking undergraduates: 31% part-time, 60% women, 9% African American, 7% Asian American, 10% Hispanic American, 4% international
- 1,055 degree-seeking graduate students
- 99% of applicants admitted
- 52% graduate within 6 years

General. Founded in 1955. Regionally accredited. **Degrees:** 1,024 bachelor's, 692 associate awarded; master's, doctoral offered. **Location:** 10 miles from downtown Manhattan. **Calendar:** Semester, extensive summer session. **Full-time faculty:** 330 total; 87% have terminal degrees, 22% minority, 44% women. **Part-time faculty:** 512 total; 27% have terminal degrees, 12% minority, 49% women. **Class size:** 30% < 20, 54% 20-39, 13% 40-49, 3% 50-99, less than 1% >100. **Special facilities:** Astrophysical observatory, archives & special collections, artificial intelligence laboratory.

Freshman class profile. 7,393 applied, 7,333 admitted, 2,198 enrolled.

Mid 50% test scores		**GPA 2.0-2.99:**	54%
SAT verbal:	460-560	**End year in good standing:**	72%
SAT math:	490-570	**Return as sophomores:**	81%
GPA 3.50 or higher:	19%	**Out-of-state:**	1%
GPA 3.0-3.49:	27%	**International:**	4%

Basis for selection. High school record and GPA most important. Open admission for associate degree-seeking students. SAT or ACT recommended. Audition required for music programs; portfolio recommended for art programs.

High school preparation. 16 units required. Required units include English 4, mathematics 3, social studies 4, science 2, foreign language 2 and academic electives 1.

2005-2006 Annual costs. Tuition/fees: $4,326; $11,126 out-of-state. Books/supplies: $832. Personal expenses: $1,659.

2005-2006 Financial aid. **Need-based:** 1,490 full-time freshmen applied for aid; 1,053 were judged to have need; 1,017 of these received aid. Average need met was 59%. Average scholarship/grant was $5,087; average loan $2,526. 72% of total undergraduate aid awarded as scholarships/grants, 28% as loans/jobs. **Non-need-based:** Awarded to 759 full-time undergraduates, including 408 freshmen. Scholarships awarded for academics, art, athletics, job skills, leadership, minority status, music/drama, state residency.

Application procedures. **Admission:** Priority date 3/15; no deadline. $65 fee, may be waived for applicants with need. Application may be submitted online. Admission notification on a rolling basis beginning on or about 12/15. **Financial aid:** Closing date 3/31. FAFSA required. Applicants notified on a rolling basis starting 6/30.

Academics. **Special study options:** Combined bachelor's/graduate degree, cooperative education, cross-registration, distance learning, double major, ESL, honors, independent study, internships, liberal arts/career combination, student-designed major, study abroad, teacher certification program, weekend college. Cross-registration at any CUNY. **Credit/placement by examination:** AP, CLEP, IB, SAT, ACT, institutional tests. 30 credit hours maximum toward associate degree, 30 toward bachelor's. **Support services:** Learning center, pre-admission summer program, remedial instruction, study skills assistance, tutoring.

Majors. **Area/ethnic studies:** African-American, American, women's. **Biology:** General, biochemistry. **Business:** General, accounting. **Communications:** General. **Computer sciences:** General, information systems. **Education:** Biology, chemistry, elementary, English, mathematics, Spanish. **Engineering:** General. **English:** English lit. **Foreign languages:** Spanish. **Health:** Nursing (RN), physician assistant. **History:** General. **Liberal arts:** Arts/sciences. **Math:** General. **Philosophy/religion:** Philosophy. **Physical sciences:** Chemistry, physics. **Psychology:** General. **Public administration:** Social work. **Social sciences:** Economics, international relations, political science. **Visual/performing arts:** Cinematography, dramatic.

Most popular majors. Business/marketing 27%, computer/information sciences 9%, English 6%, health sciences 6%, liberal arts 7%, psychology 10%, trade and industry 11%.

Computing on campus. 1,095 workstations in library, computer center, student center. Commuter students can connect to campus network. Online course registration, online library, helpline, student web hosting, wireless network available.

Student life. **Freshman orientation:** Mandatory. Scheduled at beginning of each semester before or during testing, advisement, and registration. **Policies:** Freshmen permitted cars on campus. **Activities:** Jazz band, choral groups, dance, drama, film society, literary magazine, music ensembles, radio station, student government, student newspaper, Muslim student association, Nigerian student association, Middle Eastern club, international affairs club, Israel club, Hillel, Colleges Against Cancer, Cardinal Newman Society, Project FYI (Fresh Youth Involvement).

Athletics. NCAA. **Intercollegiate:** Badminton M, baseball M, basketball, diving W, soccer, softball W, swimming, table tennis W, tennis, volleyball W. **Intramural:** Badminton, football (non-tackle), handball, racquetball, softball, table tennis, tennis. **Team name:** Dolphins.

Student services. Adult student services, alcohol/substance abuse counseling, campus ministries, career counseling, services for economically disadvantaged, student employment services, financial aid counseling, health services, minority student services, on-campus daycare, personal counseling, placement for graduates, veterans' counselor, women's services. **Physically disabled:** Services for visually, hearing impaired.

Contact. E-mail: admissions@mail.cuny.csi.edu
Phone: (718) 982-2010 Fax: (718) 982-2500
Mary Reilly, Director of Recruitment and Admissions, City University of New York: College of Staten Island, 2800 Victory Boulevard 2A-104, Staten Island, NY 10314

City University of New York: Hunter College

New York, New York — **CB member**
www.hunter.cuny.edu — **CB code: 2301**

- Public 4-year liberal arts college
- Commuter campus in very large city
- 14,357 degree-seeking undergraduates: 28% part-time, 69% women, 15% African American, 17% Asian American, 20% Hispanic American, 7% international
- 4,057 degree-seeking graduate students
- 35% of applicants admitted
- SAT or ACT required
- 37% graduate within 6 years

General. Founded in 1870. Regionally accredited. **Degrees:** 2,295 bachelor's awarded; master's offered. **Calendar:** Semester, limited summer session. **Full-time faculty:** 633 total; 87% have terminal degrees, 26% minority, 51% women. **Part-time faculty:** 802 total; 36% have terminal degrees, 18% minority, 56% women. **Class size:** 36% < 20, 51% 20-39, 5% 40-49, 6% 50-99, 1% >100. **Special facilities:** Mathematics learning center, theater, on-campus elementary and secondary schools.

Freshman class profile. 20,985 applied, 7,443 admitted, 1,837 enrolled.

Mid 50% test scores		Rank in top quarter:	50%
SAT verbal:	480-580	Rank in top tenth:	19%
SAT math:	500-590	Return as sophomores:	82%
GPA 3.50 or higher:	20%	Out-of-state:	4%
GPA 3.0-3.49:	29%	International:	4%
GPA 2.0-2.99:	46%		

Basis for selection. Requirements vary by program. Indexing formula using weighted averages, high school academic units, and SAT scores used for admission to some programs. SAT or ACT not required, but recommended, of first-time freshmen who graduated high school more than a year preceding admission.

High school preparation. 16 units recommended. Required and recommended units include English 2-4, mathematics 2-3, social studies 4, science 1-2 (laboratory 1), foreign language 2 and academic electives 1. 1 fine art or performing art recommended.

2005-2006 Annual costs. Tuition/fees: $4,347; $11,147 out-of-state. Dormitory availability very limited. Room only: $3,129. Books/supplies: $832.

2004-2005 Financial aid. **Need-based:** 1,476 full-time freshmen applied for aid; 1,213 were judged to have need; 1,180 of these received aid. Average need met was 68%. Average scholarship/grant was $5,921; average loan $2,322. 74% of total undergraduate aid awarded as scholarships/grants, 26% as loans/jobs. **Non-need-based:** Awarded to 621 full-time undergraduates, including 785 freshmen. Scholarships awarded for academics.

Application procedures. **Admission:** Closing date 3/15 (postmark date). $65 fee, may be waived for applicants with need. Admission notification on a rolling basis beginning on or about 1/15. **Financial aid:** Priority date 5/1; no closing date. FAFSA required. Applicants notified on a rolling basis starting 5/15.

Academics. **Special study options:** Accelerated study, combined bachelor's/graduate degree, cross-registration, distance learning, double major, dual enrollment of high school students, exchange student, honors, independent study, internships, liberal arts/career combination, student-designed major, study abroad, teacher certification program. BA/MA/MS programs in anthropology, biology/EOPS, economics, English, history, math, music, physics, social research (MS). **Credit/placement by examination:** AP, CLEP, IB, institutional tests. 30 credit hours maximum toward bachelor's degree. **Support services:** Learning center, reduced course load, remedial instruction, study skills assistance, tutoring, writing center.

Majors. **Area/ethnic studies:** African-American, Latin American, Near/Middle Eastern, women's. **Biology:** General, pharmacology. **Business:** Accounting. **Communications:** Media studies. **Computer sciences:** General. **Education:** General, art, biology, chemistry, drama/dance, early childhood, elementary, English, foreign languages, French, geography, German, health, history, Latin, mathematics, music, physical, physics, secondary, social studies, Spanish. **English:** British lit, creative writing, English lit. **Family/consumer sciences:** Food/nutrition. **Foreign languages:** General, ancient Greek, Chinese, classics, comparative lit, French, German, Hebrew, Italian, Latin, Romance, Russian, Spanish. **Health:** Adult health nursing, clinical lab science, clinical lab technology, maternal/child health nursing, nurse practitioner, nursing (RN), pediatric nursing, psychiatric nursing, public health nursing, speech pathology. **History:** General. **Liberal arts:** Humanities. **Math:** General, statistics. **Philosophy/religion:** Judaic, philosophy, religion. **Physical sciences:** Chemistry, physics. **Psychology:** General. **Social sciences:** Anthropology, archaeology, economics, geography, international relations, political science, sociology, urban studies. **Visual/performing arts:** Art history/conservation, cinematography, dance, dramatic, film/cinema, music performance, music theory/composition, studio arts.

Most popular majors. Business/marketing 6%, communications/journalism 7%, English 15%, health sciences 6%, psychology 11%, social sciences 24%, visual/performing arts 9%.

Computing on campus. 750 workstations in dormitories, library, computer center, student center. Commuter students can connect to campus network. Online course registration, online library, helpline, repair service, student web hosting, wireless network available.

Student life. **Freshman orientation:** Available. Preregistration for classes offered. **Housing:** Coed dorms, substance-free housing available. **Activities:** Bands, choral groups, dance, drama, film society, literary magazine, music ensembles, musical theater, radio station, student government, student newspaper, symphony orchestra, TV station, over 100 political, ethnic, social, and religious organizations.

Athletics. NCAA. **Intercollegiate:** Basketball, cross-country, fencing, football (non-tackle) W, soccer M, softball W, swimming W, tennis, track and field, volleyball, wrestling M. **Intramural:** Basketball, bowling, football (non-tackle), racquetball, swimming, table tennis, tennis, volleyball. **Team name:** Hawks.

Student services. Adult student services, alcohol/substance abuse counseling, campus ministries, career counseling, services for economically disadvantaged, student employment services, financial aid counseling, health services, legal services, minority student services, on-campus daycare, personal counseling, placement for graduates, veterans' counselor, women's services. **Physically disabled:** Services for visually, speech, hearing impaired.

Contact. E-mail: admissions@hunter.cuny.edu
Phone: (212) 772-4490
William Zlata, Director of Admissions, City University of New York: Hunter College, 695 Park Avenue, New York, NY 10021

City University of New York: John Jay College of Criminal Justice

New York, New York
www.jjay.cuny.edu **CB code: 2115**

- Public 4-year college of criminal justice and public safety
- Commuter campus in very large city
- 12,278 degree-seeking undergraduates: 24% part-time, 60% women, 24% African American, 6% Asian American, 38% Hispanic American, 4% international
- 1,676 degree-seeking graduate students
- 82% of applicants admitted
- SAT and SAT Subject Tests or ACT with writing required
- 36% graduate within 6 years; 29% enter graduate study

General. Founded in 1964. Regionally accredited. **Degrees:** 1,522 bachelor's, 125 associate awarded; master's offered. **Calendar:** Semester, limited summer session. **Full-time faculty:** 341 total; 78% have terminal degrees, 25% minority, 43% women. **Part-time faculty:** 628 total; 30% minority, 45% women. **Class size:** 20% < 20, 74% 20-39, 6% 40-49, less than 1% 50-99, less than 1% >100. **Special facilities:** Security laboratory, fire science laboratory, explosion-proof toxicology research laboratory.

Freshman class profile. 8,383 applied, 6,853 admitted, 2,704 enrolled.

Mid 50% test scores		GPA 2.0-2.99:	63%
SAT verbal:	420-520	Return as sophomores:	73%
SAT math:	420-520	Out-of-state:	7%
GPA 3.0-3.49:	16%	International:	4%

Basis for selection. Admission to associate degree programs requires minimum SAT score of 900 (exclusive of Writing), high school average of 72, or GED score of 300. Admission to baccalaureate degree program requires minimum SAT score from 960 to 1020 or minimum high school average of 80 and minimum of 12 academic units with a total of 4 units in English and mathematics with at least 1 unit in each discipline. **Homeschooled:** Applicants must have diploma issued by local registered high school.

High school preparation. 16 units required. Required and recommended units include English 4, mathematics 3, social studies 4, (laboratory 2), foreign language 2 and academic electives 4. One unit in fine arts required.

2005-2006 Annual costs. Tuition/fees: $4,278; $11,078 out-of-state. Books/supplies: $875. Personal expenses: $3,550.

2004-2005 Financial aid. **Need-based:** 2,400 full-time freshmen applied for aid; 2,400 were judged to have need; 2,226 of these received aid. Average need met was 85%. Average scholarship/grant was $2,770. 66% of total undergraduate aid awarded as scholarships/grants, 34% as loans/jobs. **Non-need-based:** Scholarships awarded for academics, state residency.

Application procedures. **Admission:** Closing date 5/1. $65 fee, may be waived for applicants with need. Application may be submitted online. Admission notification on a rolling basis beginning on or about 1/15. Centralized application processing allows students to apply to 6 academic programs within CUNY system at same time. Admissions to John Jay on space-available basis. **Financial aid:** No deadline. FAFSA required. Applicants notified on a rolling basis starting 7/15; must reply within 2 week(s) of notification.

Academics. Degree requirements and curriculum combine professional education with the liberal arts. **Special study options:** Combined bachelor's/graduate degree, cooperative education, cross-registration, distance learning, dual enrollment of high school students, ESL, exchange student, honors, independent study, internships, liberal arts/career combination, student-designed major, study abroad, weekend college. **Credit/placement by examination:** AP, CLEP, institutional tests. 32 credit hours maximum toward associate degree, 32 toward bachelor's. **Support services:** Learning center, pre-admission summer program, reduced course load, remedial instruction, tutoring, writing center.

Majors. **Computer sciences:** General. **Physical sciences:** General. **Protective services:** Law enforcement admin. **Psychology:** General. **Public administration:** General, community org/advocacy. **Social sciences:** Criminology, political science.

Most popular majors. Psychology 26%, security/protective services 53%, social sciences 16%.

Computing on campus. 1,500 workstations in library, computer center. Commuter students can connect to campus network. Online course registration, helpline available.

Student life. **Freshman orientation:** Available. Preregistration for classes offered. **Policies:** Students represented on college committees. **Activities:** Choral groups, dance, drama, musical theater, radio station, student government, student newspaper, Law Society, Irish club, Students against War and Racism, Haitian club, Christian Seekers Fellowship Club, Jewish Students Society, Newman Club, Betances Society, Black Student Society, ethnic organizations.

Athletics. NCAA. **Intercollegiate:** Baseball M, basketball, cross-country, diving W, rifle, soccer, softball W, swimming W, tennis, volleyball W. **Intramural:** Basketball, rifle, soccer M, swimming. **Team name:** Bloodhounds.

Student services. Adult student services, alcohol/substance abuse counseling, career counseling, services for economically disadvantaged, student employment services, financial aid counseling, health services, on-campus daycare, personal counseling, placement for graduates, veterans' counselor, women's services. **Physically disabled:** Services for visually, speech, hearing impaired.

Contact. E-mail: admiss@jjay.cuny.edu
Phone: (212) 237-8865 Fax: (212) 237-8777
Sandra Palleja, Dean of Admissions and Registration, City University of New York: John Jay College of Criminal Justice, 445 West 59th Street, New York, NY 10019

City University of New York: Lehman College

Bronx, New York — **CB member**
www.lehman.cuny.edu — **CB code: 2312**

- Public 4-year liberal arts college
- Commuter campus in very large city
- 7,805 degree-seeking undergraduates: 35% part-time, 72% women, 34% African American, 4% Asian American, 47% Hispanic American, 5% international
- 1,674 degree-seeking graduate students
- 35% of applicants admitted
- SAT or ACT (ACT writing optional) required
- 34% graduate within 6 years

General. Founded in 1931. Regionally accredited. **Degrees:** 1,187 bachelor's awarded; master's offered. **ROTC:** Army. **Location:** 8 miles from Manhattan. **Calendar:** Semester, limited summer session. **Full-time faculty:** 337 total; 83% have terminal degrees, 54% minority, 45% women. **Part-time faculty:** 443 total; 30% have terminal degrees, 27% minority, 55% women. **Class size:** 40% < 20, 58% 20-39, less than 1% 40-49, less than 1% 50-99. **Special facilities:** 2,500-seat performing arts center theater.

Freshman class profile. 10,193 applied, 3,535 admitted, 804 enrolled.

Mid 50% test scores			
SAT verbal:	380-480	Return as sophomores:	74%
SAT math:	380-480	Out-of-state:	1%
End year in good standing:	77%	International:	8%

Basis for selection. High school record, GPA, and college preparatory courses most important. Tests are used to exempt students from placement tests.

High school preparation. 12 units required; 16 recommended. Required and recommended units include English 4, mathematics 2-3, social studies 1, history 1-2, science 2-3 (laboratory 1) and foreign language 2.

2005-2006 Annual costs. Tuition/fees: $4,288; $11,088 out-of-state. Books/supplies: $798. Personal expenses: $1,656.

2004-2005 Financial aid. All financial aid based on need. 777 full-time freshmen applied for aid; 775 were judged to have need; 773 of these received aid. Average need met was 72%. Average scholarship/grant was $1,609; average loan $1,202. 78% of total undergraduate aid awarded as scholarships/grants, 22% as loans/jobs.

Application procedures. **Admission:** Priority date 2/15; deadline 8/15. $50 fee. Application may be submitted online. Admission notification on a rolling basis. **Financial aid:** No deadline. FAFSA required. Applicants notified on a rolling basis starting 3/1.

Academics. **Special study options:** Accelerated study, cooperative education, cross-registration, distance learning, double major, dual enrollment of high school students, ESL, exchange student, honors, independent study, internships, student-designed major, study abroad, teacher certification program, Washington semester, weekend college. Bilingual liberal arts (first 2 years may be taken in Spanish), professional writing concentration, 3-2 engineering program with City College. **Credit/placement by examination:** AP, CLEP, IB, institutional tests. 30 credit hours maximum toward bachelor's degree. **Support services:** Learning center, pre-admission summer program, reduced course load, remedial instruction, study skills assistance, tutoring, writing center.

Honors college/program. Criteria for selection include high school academic record, SAT/ACT scores, essay, 2 letters of recommendation and interview.

Majors. **Area/ethnic studies:** African-American, American, Hispanic-American/Latino/Chicano, Latin American, regional. **Biology:** General, biochemistry. **Business:** Accounting, business admin. **Communications:** General, media studies. **Computer sciences:** General, computer graphics, information systems. **Education:** Business, health, mathematics, physical. **Family/consumer sciences:** General, food/nutrition. **Foreign languages:** Ancient Greek, comparative lit, French, German, Hebrew, Italian, Latin, linguistics, Russian, Spanish. **Health:** Audiology/speech pathology, health care admin, health services, nursing (RN), speech pathology. **History:** General. **Interdisciplinary:** Biological/physical sciences. **Liberal arts:** Arts/sciences. **Math:** General. **Philosophy/religion:** Judaic, philosophy. **Physical sciences:** Chemistry, geology, physics. **Psychology:** General. **Public administration:** Social work. **Social sciences:** Anthropology, economics, geography, political science, sociology. **Visual/performing arts:** Art, art history/conservation, dance, dramatic, music performance, music theory/composition, studio arts, theater arts management.

Most popular majors. Business/marketing 11%, computer/information sciences 9%, education 9%, health sciences 16%, psychology 8%, public administration/social services 11%, social sciences 23%.

Computing on campus. 53 workstations in library, computer center, student center. Commuter students can connect to campus network. Online library, helpline, repair service, student web hosting, wireless network available.

Student life. **Freshman orientation:** Mandatory. Preregistration for classes offered. **Policies:** Freshmen permitted cars on campus. **Activities:** Bands, choral groups, dance, drama, film society, literary magazine, music ensembles, musical theater, opera, radio station, student government, student newspaper, symphony orchestra, TV station, various religious, political, ethnic, and social service organizations.

Athletics. NCAA. **Intercollegiate:** Baseball M, basketball, cross-country, diving, soccer M, softball W, swimming, tennis, track and field, volleyball, water polo M. **Intramural:** Badminton, basketball, soccer M, softball, swimming, tennis, volleyball. **Team name:** Lightning.

Student services. Adult student services, campus ministries, career counseling, services for economically disadvantaged, student employment services, financial aid counseling, health services, on-campus daycare, personal counseling, placement for graduates, veterans' counselor, women's services. **Physically disabled:** Services for visually, speech, hearing impaired.

Contact. E-mail: enroll@lehman.cuny.edu
Phone: (718) 960-8706 Fax: (718) 960-8712
Clarence Wilkes, Director of Admissions, City University of New York: Lehman College, 250 Bedford Park Boulevard West, Bronx, NY 10468

City University of New York: Medgar Evers College

Brooklyn, New York **CB member**
www.mec.cuny.edu **CB code: 2460**

- Public 4-year liberal arts college
- Commuter campus in very large city
- 4,841 degree-seeking undergraduates: 35% part-time, 77% women, 88% African American, 1% Asian American, 4% Hispanic American, 4% international

General. Founded in 1969. Regionally accredited. **Degrees:** 265 bachelor's, 270 associate awarded. **Calendar:** Semester, extensive summer session. **Full-time faculty:** 150 total. **Part-time faculty:** 190 total. **Class size:** 8% < 20, 68% 20-39, 21% 40-49, 2% 50-99.

Freshman class profile. 787 enrolled.

Mid 50% test scores		**Rank in top quarter:**	24%
SAT verbal:	340-440	**End year in good standing:**	67%
SAT math:	340-430	**Return as sophomores:**	52%
GPA 3.0-3.49:	15%	**International:**	3%
GPA 2.0-2.99:	30%	**Fraternities:**	1%

Basis for selection. Open admission, but selective for some programs. Special requirements for nursing and baccalaureate programs with school record, class rank, and test scores considered. Discretionary policy admits 25 students each semester without high school diplomas. Must be 21 years old, legal residents of New York City.

High school preparation. 15 units recommended. Recommended units include English 4, mathematics 3, history 2, science 2 and academic electives 4.

2005-2006 Annual costs. Tuition/fees: $4,250; $11,050 out-of-state. Books/supplies: $500. Personal expenses: $232.

2005-2006 Financial aid. **Need-based:** 89% of total undergraduate aid awarded as scholarships/grants, 11% as loans/jobs.

Application procedures. **Admission:** Priority date 7/5; no deadline. $65 fee, may be waived for applicants with need. Application may be submitted online. Admission notification on a rolling basis. **Financial aid:** No deadline. FAFSA required. Applicants notified on a rolling basis; must reply by 3/5 or within 2 week(s) of notification.

Academics. **Special study options:** Combined bachelor's/graduate degree, cross-registration, distance learning, ESL, honors, independent study, internships, liberal arts/career combination, study abroad, teacher certification program. 2-year bachelor's program in nursing for RNs. **Credit/placement by examination:** AP, CLEP, IB, institutional tests. 15 credit hours maximum toward associate degree, 30 toward bachelor's. **Support services:** Learning center, pre-admission summer program, reduced course load, remedial instruction, tutoring.

Majors. **Biology:** General. **Business:** General, accounting. **Computer sciences:** Information systems. **Conservation:** Environmental science. **Education:** Early childhood, elementary, special. **English:** English lit. **Health:** Nursing (RN). **Liberal arts:** Arts/sciences. **Math:** General. **Psychology:** General. **Public administration:** General.

Most popular majors. Biology 8%, business/marketing 24%, psychology 19%.

Computing on campus. 450 workstations in library, computer center, student center.

Student life. **Freshman orientation:** Available. Preregistration for classes offered. **Policies:** Freshmen permitted cars on campus. **Activities:** Choral groups, dance, drama, literary magazine, radio station, student government, student newspaper, TV station, numerous religious, political, ethnic, and social service clubs.

Athletics. NCAA. **Intercollegiate:** Basketball, cross-country, soccer, softball W, track and field, volleyball. **Intramural:** Basketball, bowling, cheerleading W, soccer M, swimming, track and field W. **Team name:** Cougar.

Student services. Career counseling, student employment services, financial aid counseling, health services, on-campus daycare, personal counseling, placement for graduates, veterans' counselor, women's services. **Physically disabled:** Services for visually, speech, hearing impaired.

Contact. E-mail: enroll@mec.cuny.edu
Phone: (718) 270-6021 Fax: (718) 270-6411
Warren Heusner, Director of Enrollment Management, City University of New York: Medgar Evers College, 1665 Bedford Avenue, Brooklyn, NY 11225-2201

City University of New York: New York City College of Technology

Brooklyn, New York **CB member**
www.citytech.cuny.edu **CB code: 2550**

- Public 4-year technical college
- Commuter campus in very large city
- 11,795 degree-seeking undergraduates: 40% part-time, 49% women, 40% African American, 15% Asian American, 30% Hispanic American, 3% international
- 7% graduate within 6 years

General. Founded in 1946. Regionally accredited. **Degrees:** 528 bachelor's, 918 associate awarded. **Calendar:** Semester, extensive summer session. **Full-time faculty:** 306 total; 87% have terminal degrees, 28% minority, 41% women. **Part-time faculty:** 579 total; 62% have terminal degrees, 36% minority, 38% women. **Class size:** 31% < 20, 69% 20-39. **Special facilities:** Ophthalmic dispensing and dental clinics, laboratory kitchens and dining room.

Freshman class profile. 2,499 enrolled.

Mid 50% test scores		**Rank in top tenth:**	6%
SAT verbal:	410-420	**Return as sophomores:**	77%
SAT math:	480-510	**Out-of-state:**	1%
Rank in top quarter:	19%	**International:**	2%

Basis for selection. Open admission, but selective for some programs.

High school preparation. 16 units recommended. Recommended units include English 4, mathematics 3, social studies 4, science 2 (laboratory 2), foreign language 2 and academic electives 1.

2005-2006 Annual costs. Tuition/fees: $4,287; $11,087 out-of-state. Books/supplies: $759. Personal expenses: $2,414.

2005-2006 Financial aid. **Need-based:** 74% of total undergraduate aid awarded as scholarships/grants, 26% as loans/jobs. **Non-need-based:** Scholarships awarded for state residency. **Additional information:** Foreign students applying for aid must have resided in New York for at least a year.

Application procedures. **Admission:** Priority date 3/15; no deadline. $65 fee, may be waived for applicants with need. Application may be submitted online. Admission notification on a rolling basis. **Financial aid:** Priority date 5/15; no closing date. FAFSA required.

Academics. Students in health science programs work under supervision with patients in clinical settings. Industry standard facilities used in hospitality management program. **Special study options:** Distance learning, dual enrollment of high school students, ESL, honors, independent study, internships, study abroad, teacher certification program, weekend college. Bridge programs to higher education or careers in engineering technology, alternate format program for those out of high school 5 years with or without diploma. **Credit/placement by examination:** AP, CLEP, IB, institutional tests. 30 credit hours maximum toward associate degree. **Support services:** Learning center, pre-admission summer program, remedial instruction, study skills assistance, tutoring, writing center.

Majors. **Business:** Hospitality admin, tourism/travel. **Communications technology:** Graphic/printing. **Computer sciences:** General. **Construction:** Maintenance. **Education:** Technology/industrial arts. **Engineering technology:** Architectural, electromechanical, telecommunications. **Health:** Health services admin. **Legal studies:** Paralegal. **Math:** Applied. **Public administration:** Human services. **Visual/performing arts:** Commercial/advertising art, theater design.

Most popular majors. Business/marketing 13%, computer/information sciences 36%, engineering/engineering technologies 12%, legal studies 8%, public administration/social services 14%, visual/performing arts 12%.

Computing on campus. Online course registration, online library, helpline, student web hosting, wireless network available.

Student life. **Freshman orientation:** Available. **Housing:** Some housing available at nearby university. **Activities:** Drama, musical theater, student government, student newspaper, full range of student clubs.

Athletics. NCAA. **Intercollegiate:** Basketball, cross-country, soccer M, softball W, tennis, volleyball. **Intramural:** Badminton, basketball, cross-country, handball, softball, table tennis, track and field, volleyball, weight lifting. **Team name:** Yellow Jackets.

Student services. Adult student services, career counseling, services for economically disadvantaged, student employment services, financial aid counseling, health services, minority student services, on-campus daycare, personal counseling, placement for graduates. **Physically disabled:** Services for visually, speech, hearing impaired.

Contact. E-mail: admissions@citytech.cuny.edu
Phone: (718) 260-5500 Fax: (718) 260-5504
Joseph Lento, Director of Admissions, City University of New York: New York City College of Technology, 300 Jay Street Namm G17, Brooklyn, NY 11201

City University of New York: Queens College

Flushing, New York — **CB member**
www.qc.cuny.edu — **CB code: 2750**

- Public 4-year liberal arts college
- Commuter campus in very large city
- 12,320 degree-seeking undergraduates: 28% part-time, 61% women, 9% African American, 18% Asian American, 17% Hispanic American, 8% international
- 4,011 degree-seeking graduate students
- 43% of applicants admitted
- SAT or ACT (ACT writing optional) required
- 53% graduate within 6 years; 20% enter graduate study

General. Founded in 1937. Regionally accredited. **Degrees:** 2,151 bachelor's awarded; master's offered. **ROTC:** Army, Navy. **Location:** 17 miles from Manhattan. **Calendar:** Semester, extensive summer session. **Full-time faculty:** 575 total; 86% have terminal degrees, 20% minority, 42% women. **Part-time faculty:** 716 total; 36% have terminal degrees, 20% minority, 50% women. **Special facilities:** Louis Armstrong archives; center for performing arts; speech, language, and learning center; biology of natural systems center; environmental teaching and research center; Byzantine and modern Greek studies center; labor resource center; Italian American institute; Jewish studies center; center for democratic values and social change; worker education extension center.

Freshman class profile. 12,023 applied, 5,217 admitted, 1,509 enrolled.

Mid 50% test scores		End year in good standing:	85%
SAT verbal:	440-550	Return as sophomores:	86%
SAT math:	480-580	Out-of-state:	1%
GPA 3.50 or higher:	16%	International:	9%
GPA 3.0-3.49:	62%	Fraternities:	1%
GPA 2.0-2.99:	22%	Sororities:	1%

Basis for selection. Admission based on variety of factors including high school grades, strength of academic program, and test scores. Successful candidates will have chosen well-rounded program of study and attained at least B+ average. SAT Subject Tests recommended. SAT and SAT Subject Test required of scholarship and honors college applicants. Essay and interview recommended for scholarship, honors program; audition recommended for music, performance; portfolio recommended for bachelor of fine arts. Other criteria considered for appeals. **Learning Disabled:** Untimed SAT/ACT accepted.

High school preparation. 16 units required; 17 recommended. Required and recommended units include English 4, mathematics 3, social studies 4, science 2-3 (laboratory 2-3) and foreign language 3.

2005-2006 Annual costs. Tuition/fees: $4,375; $11,175 out-of-state. Books/supplies: $879. Personal expenses: $1,690.

2005-2006 Financial aid. **Need-based:** Average need met was 77%. Average scholarship/grant was $1,250; average loan $2,625. 65% of total undergraduate aid awarded as scholarships/grants, 35% as loans/jobs. **Non-need-based:** Scholarships awarded for academics, athletics, music/drama, state residency.

Application procedures. **Admission:** Priority date 1/1; no deadline. $65 fee, may be waived for applicants with need. Application may be submitted online. Admission notification on a rolling basis beginning on or about 2/1. Must reply by 5/1. **Financial aid:** Priority date 2/1; no closing date. FAFSA, institutional form required. Applicants notified on a rolling basis starting 3/1; must reply within 3 week(s) of notification.

Academics. Required core liberal arts curriculum includes courses in the humanities, physical and biological sciences, scientific methodology and quantitative reasoning, social sciences, and pre-industrial/non-western civilization. **Special study options:** Accelerated study, combined bachelor's/graduate degree, cooperative education, cross-registration, distance learning, double major, dual enrollment of high school students, ESL, honors, independent study, internships, liberal arts/career combination, New York semester, student-designed major, study abroad, teacher certification program, weekend college. Albany semester, New York University internship, visiting student program at Fashion Institute of Technology. **Credit/placement by examination:** AP, CLEP, SAT. **Support services:** Learning center, pre-admission summer program, study skills assistance, tutoring, writing center.

Honors college/program. 40 students, average SAT of 1300 (exclusive of Writing) or higher, high school average 95.0 or higher, required to submit SAT Subject Test scores, interview required.

Majors. **Area/ethnic studies:** African, American, East Asian, Latin American, women's. **Biology:** General, biochemistry. **Business:** Accounting, actuarial science, finance, international, labor studies. **Communications:** Media studies. **Computer sciences:** Computer science. **Conservation:** Environmental science, environmental studies. **Education:** Art, early childhood, elementary, family/consumer sciences, music, physical. **English:** English lit. **Family/consumer sciences:** General. **Foreign languages:** Ancient Greek, comparative lit, French, German, Hebrew, Italian, Latin, linguistics, Russian, Spanish. **Health:** Communication disorders. **History:** General. **Math:** General. **Philosophy/religion:** Judaic, philosophy, religion. **Physical sciences:** Chemistry, geology, physics. **Psychology:** General. **Social sciences:** Anthropology, economics, political science, sociology, urban studies. **Visual/performing arts:** Art history/conservation, dance, dramatic, film/cinema, music performance, music theory/composition, studio arts.

Most popular majors. Business/marketing 15%, computer/information sciences 6%, English 7%, psychology 13%, social sciences 25%.

Computing on campus. 2,000 workstations in library, computer center, student center. Commuter students can connect to campus network. Online course registration, online library, helpline, student web hosting, wireless network available.

Student life. **Freshman orientation:** Mandatory. Preregistration for classes offered. Held in June, July, August. **Policies:** Students found guilty of any form of academic dishonesty, such as plagiarism or cheating on an examination, are subject to discipline, including suspension or dismissal from the college. Freshmen permitted cars on campus. **Activities:** Bands, choral groups, dance, drama, film society, literary magazine, music ensembles, musical theater, radio station, student government, student newspaper, symphony orchestra, TV station, Catholic, Protestant, Hindu, Jewish, Greek Orthodox, Muslim, African American, Asian, Bangladeshi, Guyanese, Haitian, Hispanic, Italian, Irish, lesbian, and gay student organizations; honor societies; various clubs; political student associations.

Athletics. NAIA, NCAA. **Intercollegiate:** Baseball M, basketball, bowling W, fencing W, golf M, soccer W, softball W, swimming, tennis, volleyball, water polo. **Intramural:** Baseball M, basketball, fencing M, ice hockey M, racquetball, soccer, softball, tennis, volleyball, water polo. **Team name:** Knights.

Student services. Adult student services, alcohol/substance abuse counseling, career counseling, student employment services, financial aid counseling, health services, minority student services, on-campus daycare, personal counseling, placement for graduates, veterans' counselor, women's services. **Physically disabled:** Services for visually, speech, hearing impaired.

Contact. E-mail: vincent@qc1.qc.edu
Phone: (718) 997-5600 Fax: (718) 997-5617
Vincent Angrisani, Executive Director of Admissions, City University of New York: Queens College, 65-30 Kissena Boulevard, Jefferson 117, Flushing, NY 11367-1597

City University of New York: York College

Jamaica, New York — **CB member**
www.york.cuny.edu — **CB code: 2992**

- Public 4-year liberal arts college
- Commuter campus in very large city
- 5,753 degree-seeking undergraduates: 33% part-time, 68% women, 48% African American, 10% Asian American, 15% Hispanic American
- SAT or ACT (ACT writing optional) required

General. Founded in 1966. Regionally accredited. **Degrees:** 823 bachelor's awarded. **Location:** 14 miles from midtown Manhattan. **Calendar:**

Semester, limited summer session. **Full-time faculty:** 170 total. **Part-time faculty:** 270 total. **Special facilities:** Theater, cardio-pneumo-simulator.

Freshman class profile. 776 enrolled.

End year in good standing:	80.26%	**Out-of-state:**	22%
Return as sophomores:	69%		

Basis for selection. 75 average with 15 high school academic units basic admission requirement; allowance made for higher average or test scores. Units recommended for admission must be acquired before graduation from any CUNY senior college. Admission requirements for CUNY senior colleges will be automatically satisfied with completion of our core requirement. Interview required for occupational therapy, nursing, physician assistant, and social work or for appeal.

High school preparation. 15 units required. Required and recommended units include English 3, mathematics 2, social studies 1, history 2, science 2 (laboratory 2), foreign language 1 and academic electives 2.

2005-2006 Annual costs. Tuition/fees: $4,260; $11,060 out-of-state. Books/supplies: $832. Personal expenses: $3,481.

2004-2005 Financial aid. Need-based: 619 full-time freshmen applied for aid; 552 were judged to have need; 538 of these received aid. Average need met was 32%. Average scholarship/grant was $3,017; average loan $1,791. 87% of total undergraduate aid awarded as scholarships/grants, 13% as loans/jobs. **Non-need-based:** Awarded to 93 full-time undergraduates, including 74 freshmen.

Application procedures. Admission: Priority date 12/15; no deadline. $50 fee. Application may be submitted online. Admission notification on a rolling basis. Centralized application processing allows students to apply to 6 schools within CUNY system at same time. **Financial aid:** Priority date 5/1; no closing date. FAFSA required. Applicants notified on a rolling basis starting 3/1.

Academics. Special study options: Cooperative education, double major, dual enrollment of high school students, ESL, honors, independent study, internships, teacher certification program. Co-op programs in business, computer science, health professions. **Credit/placement by examination:** AP, CLEP, IB, institutional tests. 16 credit hours maximum toward bachelor's degree. Students with SAT/ACT scores exempt from CUNY skills assessment tests. **Support services:** Learning center, pre-admission summer program, remedial instruction, study skills assistance, tutoring, writing center.

Majors. Area/ethnic studies: African-American. **Biology:** General, biotechnology. **Business:** Accounting, business admin, management information systems, marketing. **Education:** Health, physical. **English:** Speech/rhetoric. **Foreign languages:** French, Spanish. **Health:** Clinical lab technology, environmental health, nursing (RN). **History:** General. **Interdisciplinary:** Gerontology. **Liberal arts:** Arts/sciences. **Math:** General. **Philosophy/religion:** Philosophy. **Physical sciences:** Chemistry, geology, physics. **Psychology:** General. **Public administration:** Social work. **Social sciences:** Anthropology, economics, political science, sociology. **Visual/performing arts:** Art history/conservation, dramatic.

Most popular majors. Business/marketing 29%, education 7%, engineering/engineering technologies 10%, health sciences 9%, psychology 14%, public administration/social services 6%, social sciences 8%.

Computing on campus. 530 workstations in library, computer center.

Student life. Freshman orientation: Available. Preregistration for classes offered. **Activities:** Jazz band, choral groups, drama, film society, literary magazine, student government, student newspaper, TV station, 48 organizations.

Athletics. NCAA. **Intercollegiate:** Basketball, cheerleading, cross-country, soccer, softball W, swimming, tennis, track and field, volleyball, weight lifting. **Intramural:** Badminton, basketball, soccer M, softball W, swimming, table tennis, tennis, track and field, volleyball, weight lifting. **Team name:** Cardinals.

Student services. Adult student services, campus ministries, career counseling, student employment services, financial aid counseling, health services, on-campus daycare, personal counseling, placement for graduates, veterans' counselor. **Physically disabled:** Services for visually, speech, hearing impaired.

Contact. E-mail: admissions@york.cuny.edu
Phone: (718) 262-2165 Fax: (718) 262-2601
Richard Stuckhardt, Director of Admissions/Enrollment, City University of New York: York College, 94-20 Guy R. Brewer Boulevard, Jamaica, NY 11451-9989

Clarkson University

Potsdam, New York **CB member**
www.clarkson.edu **CB code: 2084**

- Private 4-year university
- Residential campus in large town
- 2,624 degree-seeking undergraduates: 24% women, 2% African American, 2% Asian American, 2% Hispanic American, 2% international
- 393 degree-seeking graduate students
- 86% of applicants admitted
- SAT or ACT (ACT writing optional), application essay required
- 74% graduate within 6 years; 26% enter graduate study

General. Founded in 1896. Regionally accredited. **Degrees:** 637 bachelor's awarded; master's, doctoral offered. **ROTC:** Army, Air Force. **Location:** 140 miles from Syracuse, 70 miles from Watertown. **Calendar:** Semester, extensive summer session. **Full-time faculty:** 170 total; 92% have terminal degrees, 12% minority, 19% women. **Part-time faculty:** 22 total; 27% have terminal degrees, 54% women. **Class size:** 32% < 20, 36% 20-39, 8% 40-49, 17% 50-99, 7% >100. **Special facilities:** Center for Advanced Materials Processing (CAMP) with multidisciplinary engineering labs.

Freshman class profile. 2,405 applied, 2,073 admitted, 630 enrolled.

Mid 50% test scores		**Rank in top quarter:**	69%
SAT verbal:	520-620	**Rank in top tenth:**	35%
SAT math:	580-670	**Return as sophomores:**	86%
ACT:	22-28	**Out-of-state:**	27%
GPA 3.50 or higher:	63%	**Live on campus:**	93%
GPA 3.0-3.49:	28%	**International:**	2%
GPA 2.0-2.99:	8%		

Basis for selection. School achievement record, test scores, recommendations, school and community involvement important. SAT Subject Tests recommended. Applicants whose TOEFL score falls below minimum required for admission can enter Clarkson Intensive English Program to study English as a Second Language in preparation for full-time study in a degree program. Interview recommended. **Homeschooled:** Transcript of courses and grades required. **Learning Disabled:** Documented information on disabilities necessary.

High school preparation. 16 units required. Required and recommended units include English 4, mathematics 3-4 and science 2-3.

2006-2007 Annual costs. Tuition/fees: $27,090. Room/board: $9,648. Books/supplies: $1,000. Personal expenses: $1,970.

2005-2006 Financial aid. Need-based: Average need met was 87%. Average scholarship/grant was $13,588; average loan $2,926. 65% of total undergraduate aid awarded as scholarships/grants, 35% as loans/jobs. **Non-need-based:** Scholarships awarded for academics, alumni affiliation, leadership, minority status, ROTC.

Application procedures. Admission: Priority date 2/1; deadline 3/15 (postmark date). $50 fee, may be waived for applicants with need. Application may be submitted online. Admission notification on a rolling basis beginning on or about 2/1. Must reply by May 1 or within 2 week(s) if notified thereafter. Candidates encouraged to submit completed application between October 1 and March 1 of their final year in secondary school. **Financial aid:** Priority date 3/1; no closing date. FAFSA, institutional form required. Applicants notified on a rolling basis starting 3/23; must reply by 5/1 or within 2 week(s) of notification.

Academics. 3-year B.S. degree option. Students must be in top 10 percent of their high school class. Students apply Advanced Placement credits and/or work on special projects during the summer. **Special study options:** Accelerated study, combined bachelor's/graduate degree, cooperative education, cross-registration, double major, dual enrollment of high school students, ESL, honors, independent study, liberal arts/career combination, student-designed major, study abroad. 3-2 agreements with SUNY Albany, SUNY Brockport, SUNY Buffalo, Daniel Webster College, SUNY Cortland, SUNY Fredonia, SUNY Geneseo, Hartwick College, Houghton College, Ithaca College, Juniata College, Keene State College, LeMoyne College, Manhattanville College, New England College, SUNY Oneonta, SUNY Oswego, SUNY Plattsburgh, SUNY Potsdam, Roberts Wesleyan College, Siena College, Skidmore College, St. Bonaventure U, St. John Fisher College, St. Lawrence U, St. Michael's College, St. Rose College. **Credit/placement by examination:** AP, CLEP. **Support services:** Pre-admission summer program, study skills assistance, tutoring, writing center.

Honors college/program. Applicants must graduate in top 10% of high school class, have SAT scores of 1350 (exclusive of Writing) or above, or have outstanding academic record or leadership. Students take 1 honors course per semester that brings viewpoints of different disciplines to bear on a contemporary, open-ended problem or challenge. Students must earn a minimum of 24 hours in honors classes and graduate with minimum 3.25 GPA.

Majors. **Biology:** General, molecular, toxicology. **Business:** Business admin, e-commerce, finance, information resources management, management information systems, marketing, operations. **Communications:** General, digital media. **Computer sciences:** General, computer science. **Conservation:** Environmental studies. **Engineering:** General, aerospace, chemical, civil, computer, electrical, environmental, mechanical, software. **English:** Technical writing. **Health:** Environmental health, occupational health, predentistry, premedicine, preveterinary. **History:** General. **Legal studies:** Prelaw. **Liberal arts:** Arts/sciences. **Math:** General, applied, statistics. **Physical sciences:** Chemistry, physics. **Psychology:** General. **Social sciences:** General, political science, sociology.

Most popular majors. Biology 6%, business/marketing 19%, engineering/engineering technologies 47%, interdisciplinary studies 12%.

Computing on campus. PC or laptop required. 400 workstations in library, computer center. Dormitories wired for high-speed internet access and linked to campus network. Helpline, repair service, student web hosting, wireless network available.

Student life. **Freshman orientation:** Available. Students meet housemates, classmates, advisers. Optional pre-orientation outing club trips; $125 charge for students who participate. **Policies:** Freshmen permitted cars on campus. **Housing:** Guaranteed on-campus for freshmen. Coed dorms, single-sex dorms, special housing for disabled, apartments, fraternity/sorority housing, substance-free housing available. Theme housing available. **Activities:** Bands, choral groups, drama, literary magazine, musical theater, radio station, student government, student newspaper, symphony orchestra, TV station, Inter-Varsity Christian Fellowship, American Indian science and engineering society, Black engineers society, Hispanic professional engineers society, women engineers society, special interest clubs, international student organization.

Athletics. NCAA. **Intercollegiate:** Baseball M, basketball, cross-country, diving, golf M, ice hockey, lacrosse, skiing, soccer, swimming, tennis, volleyball W. **Intramural:** Basketball, football (tackle) M, ice hockey, racquetball, rowing (crew) M, soccer, softball, swimming, volleyball. **Team name:** Golden Knights.

Student services. Alcohol/substance abuse counseling, career counseling, services for economically disadvantaged, student employment services, financial aid counseling, health services, minority student services, personal counseling, placement for graduates, veterans' counselor, women's services. **Physically disabled:** Services for visually, speech, hearing impaired. **Learning disabled:** Comprehensive services available.

Contact. E-mail: admission@clarkson.edu
Phone: (315) 268-6479 Toll-free number: (800) 527-6577
Fax: (315) 268-7647
Brian Grant, Director of Admission, Clarkson University, Holcroft House, Potsdam, NY 13699-5605

Colgate University

Hamilton, New York — **CB member**
www.colgate.edu — **CB code: 2086**

- Private 4-year liberal arts college
- Residential campus in small town
- 2,743 degree-seeking undergraduates: 51% women, 4% African American, 6% Asian American, 4% Hispanic American, 1% Native American, 5% international
- 3 degree-seeking graduate students
- 27% of applicants admitted
- SAT or ACT (ACT writing optional), application essay required
- 91% graduate within 6 years; 15% enter graduate study

General. Founded in 1819. Regionally accredited. **Degrees:** 690 bachelor's awarded; master's offered. **ROTC:** Army. **Location:** 38 miles from Syracuse, 25 miles from Utica. **Calendar:** Semester. **Full-time faculty:** 245 total; 97% have terminal degrees, 18% minority, 38% women. **Part-time faculty:** 70 total; 64% have terminal degrees, 21% minority, 57% women. **Class size:** 61% < 20, 37% 20-39, less than 1% 40-49, 1% 50-99, less than 1% >100. **Special facilities:** Anthropology museum, center for learning, teaching, and research, cable TV station, life sciences complex, geology/fossil collection, observatory, electron microscopes, laser lab, weather lab, geographic information system, center for outreach, volunteerism, and education.

Freshman class profile. 8,008 applied, 2,168 admitted, 729 enrolled.

Mid 50% test scores			
SAT verbal:	630-710	Rank in top quarter:	90%
SAT math:	650-720	Rank in top tenth:	68%
ACT:	29-32	End year in good standing:	96%
GPA 3.50 or higher:	61%	Return as sophomores:	92%
GPA 3.0-3.49:	34%	Out-of-state:	71%
GPA 2.0-2.99:	5%	Live on campus:	100%
		International:	5%

Basis for selection. School achievement record of primary importance. Teacher/counselor recommendations, test scores, and major talent or personal accomplishment considered. Disadvantaged, nontraditional, and minority applicants given special consideration. **Homeschooled:** Statement describing homeschool structure and mission, transcript of courses and grades, letter of recommendation (nonparent) required. **Learning Disabled:** Optional self-disclosure of disabiilties in admissions process.

High school preparation. 16 units required; 20 recommended. Required and recommended units include English 4, mathematics 3-4, social studies 2, history 1-3, science 3-4 (laboratory 2-3) and foreign language 3-4. Foreign language units should be in 1 language.

2005-2006 Annual costs. Tuition/fees: $33,105. Room/board: $8,065. Books/supplies: $880. Personal expenses: $860.

2005-2006 Financial aid. **Need-based:** 272 full-time freshmen applied for aid; 219 were judged to have need; 219 of these received aid. Average need met was 100%. Average scholarship/grant was $27,326; average loan $2,571. 86% of total undergraduate aid awarded as scholarships/grants, 14% as loans/jobs. **Non-need-based:** Awarded to 70 full-time undergraduates, including 37 freshmen. Scholarships awarded for athletics.

Application procedures. **Admission:** Closing date 1/15 (postmark date). $55 fee, may be waived for applicants with need. Application may be submitted online. Admission notification 4/1. Must reply by May 1 or within 2 week(s) if notified thereafter. **Financial aid:** Closing date 1/15. FAFSA, CSS PROFILE required. Applicants notified by 4/1; must reply by 5/1 or within 2 week(s) of notification.

Academics. **Special study options:** Combined bachelor's/graduate degree, cross-registration, double major, honors, independent study, internships, semester at sea, student-designed major, study abroad, teacher certification program, urban semester, Washington semester. 3-4 architecture program with Washington University (MO), 3-2 program in engineering with Columbia University, Rensselaer Polytechnic Institute, and Washington University; Early Assurance Medical School program with American University. **Credit/placement by examination:** AP, CLEP, IB, SAT, institutional tests. **Support services:** Learning center, pre-admission summer program, reduced course load, study skills assistance, tutoring, writing center.

Majors. **Area/ethnic studies:** African, African-American, Asian, Latin American, Native American, Russian/Slavic, women's. **Biology:** General, biochemistry, molecular. **Computer sciences:** General, computer science. **Conservation:** General, environmental studies. **Education:** General. **Foreign languages:** Classics, French, German, Japanese, Latin, modern Greek, Russian, Spanish. **Health:** Predentistry, premedicine, preveterinary. **History:** General. **Interdisciplinary:** Biological/physical sciences, math/computer science, natural sciences, neuroscience, peace/conflict. **Liberal arts:** Arts/sciences. **Math:** General. **Philosophy/religion:** Philosophy, religion. **Physical sciences:** Astronomy, astrophysics, chemistry, geology, physics. **Psychology:** General. **Social sciences:** General, anthropology, economics, geography, international economic development, international relations, political science, sociology. **Visual/performing arts:** Art, art history/conservation, dramatic, studio arts.

Most popular majors. Area/ethnic studies 19%, English 8%, foreign language 7%, social sciences 29%.

Computing on campus. 848 workstations in dormitories, library, computer center, student center. Dormitories wired for high-speed internet access and linked to campus network. Commuter students can connect to campus network. Online course registration, helpline, repair service, student web hosting, wireless network available.

Student life. **Freshman orientation:** Mandatory. Preregistration for classes offered. 4-day program held 4 days before first day of classes. **Policies:** All students required to read, sign, and abide by Academic Honor Code. Freshmen permitted cars on campus. **Housing:** Guaranteed on-campus for all undergraduates. Coed dorms, special housing for disabled, apartments, fraternity/sorority housing, substance-free housing available. $500 nonrefundable deposit, deadline 5/1. Shared interest housing available. **Activities:** Bands, choral groups, dance, drama, film society, literary magazine, music ensembles, musical theater, radio station, student government, student newspaper, symphony orchestra, TV station, over 125 campus organizations.

Athletics. NCAA. **Intercollegiate:** Basketball, cheerleading, cross-country, diving, field hockey W, football (tackle) M, golf M, ice hockey, lacrosse, rowing (crew), soccer, softball W, swimming, tennis, track and field, volleyball W. **Intramural:** Basketball, bowling, football (non-tackle), golf, ice hockey, racquetball, rifle, soccer, softball, squash, table tennis, tennis, volleyball. **Team name:** Raiders.

Student services. Alcohol/substance abuse counseling, campus ministries, career counseling, services for economically disadvantaged, student employment services, financial aid counseling, health services, minority student services, personal counseling, placement for graduates, women's services. **Physically disabled:** Services for visually, hearing impaired.

Contact. E-mail: admission@mail.colgate.edu
Phone: (315) 228-7401 Fax: (315) 228-7544
Gary Ross, Dean of Admission, Colgate University, 13 Oak Drive, Hamilton, NY 13346-1383

College of Mount St. Vincent

Riverdale, New York — **CB member**
www.mountsaintvincent.edu — **CB code: 2088**

- Private 4-year liberal arts college affiliated with Roman Catholic Church
- Residential campus in very large city
- 1,423 degree-seeking undergraduates: 12% part-time, 74% women
- 321 degree-seeking graduate students
- 69% of applicants admitted
- SAT or ACT, application essay required

General. Founded in 1847. Regionally accredited. Cross-registration with Manhattan College. Dual certification in elementary and special education and secondary and special education. 5-year program for master of science in education. **Degrees:** 210 bachelor's, 2 associate awarded; master's offered. **ROTC:** Air Force. **Location:** 12 miles from midtown Manhattan. **Calendar:** Semester, limited summer session. **Full-time faculty:** 77 total; 6% minority, 54% women. **Part-time faculty:** 84 total; 17% have terminal degrees, 17% minority, 52% women. **Class size:** 42% < 20, 56% 20-39, 2% 40-49, less than 1% 50-99. **Special facilities:** NMR spectrometer, computer graphics and animation center, computer classrooms, new forensic science equipment.

Freshman class profile. 1,907 applied, 1,309 admitted, 345 enrolled.

Mid 50% test scores			
SAT verbal:	460-550	GPA 3.0-3.49:	30%
SAT math:	450-530	GPA 2.0-2.99:	48%
GPA 3.50 or higher:	16%	Out-of-state:	19%
		Live on campus:	68%

Basis for selection. School achievement record (rank in top half of class, 3.0 high school GPA) most important, test scores and recommendations important, school and community activities considered. Interview recommended. **Learning Disabled:** Must submit IEP or other certification to receive service.

High school preparation. College-preparatory program required. 16 units required; 20 recommended. Required and recommended units include English 4, mathematics 2-3, social studies 2-3, science 2-3 and foreign language 2-3. 3 mathematics for nursing, science, and mathematics majors, 3 science with lab for nursing and science majors.

2006-2007 Annual costs. Tuition/fees (projected): $21,400. Room/board: $8,350. Books/supplies: $850. Personal expenses: $900.

2005-2006 Financial aid. All financial aid based on need. 333 full-time freshmen applied for aid; 288 were judged to have need; 288 of these received aid. Average need met was 74%. Average scholarship/grant was $8,553; average loan $2,500. 65% of total undergraduate aid awarded as scholarships/grants, 35% as loans/jobs.

Application procedures. Admission: No deadline. $35 fee, may be waived for applicants with need. Application may be submitted online. Admission notification on a rolling basis beginning on or about 2/1. Must reply by May 1 or within 3 week(s) if notified thereafter. **Financial aid:** Priority date 3/1; no closing date. FAFSA required. Applicants notified on a rolling basis starting 3/1; must reply by 5/1 or within 3 week(s) of notification.

Academics. Special study options: Accelerated study, combined bachelor's/graduate degree, cross-registration, double major, honors, independent study, internships, liberal arts/career combination, study abroad, teacher certification program. 3-2 occupational therapy program with Columbia University, 3-2 physical therapy with New York Medical College. **Credit/placement by examination:** AP, CLEP, IB, institutional tests. 18 credit hours maximum toward bachelor's degree. **Support services:** Learning center, preadmission summer program, reduced course load, remedial instruction, study skills assistance, tutoring, writing center.

Majors. Biology: General, biochemistry. **Business:** General, business admin. **Communications:** General. **Computer sciences:** General. **Education:** Physical, special. **Foreign languages:** General, French, Spanish. **Health:** Preop/surgical nursing. **History:** General. **Liberal arts:** Arts/sciences. **Math:** General. **Philosophy/religion:** Philosophy, religion. **Physical sciences:** Chemistry, physics. **Psychology:** General. **Social sciences:** Economics, sociology, urban studies.

Most popular majors. Biology 6%, business/marketing 18%, communications/journalism 12%, health sciences 34%, liberal arts 8%, psychology 11%.

Computing on campus. 194 workstations in library, computer center. Dormitories wired for high-speed internet access and linked to campus network. Commuter students can connect to campus network. Online course registration, online library, helpline, repair service, wireless network available.

Student life. Freshman orientation: Mandatory, $125 fee. 3 days with overnight for all freshmen; parent participation overnight optional. **Housing:** Guaranteed on-campus for all undergraduates. Coed dorms, single-sex dorms, special housing for disabled available. $200 nonrefundable deposit, deadline 5/1. **Activities:** Choral groups, dance, drama, literary magazine, musical theater, radio station, student government, student newspaper, TV station, Culturally Aware Students of Today, international students association, Latino club, campus ministry team, student nurses association, Circle-K, Student Action for Viable Earth, Black student union, pep club, communications club.

Athletics. NCAA. **Intercollegiate:** Baseball M, basketball, cross-country, lacrosse, soccer, softball W, swimming W, tennis, track and field W, volleyball. **Intramural:** Basketball, soccer, softball, volleyball, water polo M. **Team name:** Dolphins.

Student services. Adult student services, career counseling, student employment services, health services, personal counseling, placement for graduates. **Physically disabled:** Services for visually, hearing impaired.

Contact. E-mail: admissions.office@mountsaintvincent.edu
Phone: (718) 405-3267 Toll-free number: (800) 665-2678
Fax: (718) 549-7945
Timothy Nash, Dean of Admission and Financial Aid, College of Mount St. Vincent, 6301 Riverdale Avenue, Riverdale, NY 10471-1093

College of New Rochelle

New Rochelle, New York — **CB member**
www.cnr.edu — **CB code: 2089**

- Private 4-year nursing and liberal arts college for women affiliated with Roman Catholic Church
- Residential campus in small city
- 1,041 degree-seeking undergraduates: 32% part-time, 96% women, 38% African American, 6% Asian American, 13% Hispanic American, 1% international
- 904 degree-seeking graduate students
- 50% of applicants admitted
- SAT or ACT (ACT writing optional) required
- 46% graduate within 6 years

General. Founded in 1904. Regionally accredited. **Degrees:** 244 bachelor's awarded; master's offered. **ROTC:** Army. **Location:** 14 miles from New York City. **Calendar:** Semester, limited summer session. **Full-time faculty:** 85 total. **Part-time faculty:** 134 total. **Class size:** 75% < 20, 24% 20-39, less than 1% 40-49. **Special facilities:** Art galleries, 2 learning skills centers (including 1 for nursing), electron microscope, institute for entrepreneurial studies, computer graphics laboratory, model classroom, rare book collections of James Joyce, Thomas More, and Ursuline Order.

Freshman class profile. 1,430 applied, 710 admitted, 195 enrolled.

Mid 50% test scores			
SAT verbal:	440-530	Rank in top tenth:	15%
SAT math:	440-530	Return as sophomores:	71%
ACT:	16-22	Out-of-state:	18%
Rank in top quarter:	46%	Live on campus:	93%

Basis for selection. Admissions based on secondary school record. Class rank and standardized test scores also important. Essay, interview recommended; portfolio required for art program.

High school preparation. 16 units required. Required and recommended units include English 4, mathematics 3, social studies 3, science 3 (laboratory 2) and foreign language 2. Biology, chemistry, 3 mathematics required for nursing and physical therapy.

2005-2006 Annual costs. Tuition/fees: $20,596. Tuition for incoming students includes required laptop for each student. Room/board: $7,880. Books/supplies: $600. Personal expenses: $1,000.

2004-2005 Financial aid. **Need-based:** 136 full-time freshmen applied for aid; 122 were judged to have need; 122 of these received aid. Average need met was 100%. Average scholarship/grant was $11,882; average loan $8,626. 54% of total undergraduate aid awarded as scholarships/grants, 46% as loans/jobs. **Non-need-based:** Awarded to 546 full-time undergraduates, including 101 freshmen. Scholarships awarded for academics, art, leadership.

Application procedures. **Admission:** No deadline. $20 fee, may be waived for applicants with need. Admission notification on a rolling basis beginning on or about 11/1. Must reply by May 1 or within 3 week(s) if notified thereafter. **Financial aid:** Priority date 9/1; no closing date. FAFSA, institutional form required. Applicants notified on a rolling basis starting 1/1; must reply within 1 week(s) of notification.

Academics. **Special study options:** Accelerated study, combined bachelor's/graduate degree, cooperative education, cross-registration, double major, exchange student, honors, independent study, internships, liberal arts/career combination, student-designed major, study abroad, teacher certification program, United Nations semester, Washington semester. Preprofessional programs in law, medicine, health. **Credit/placement by examination:** AP, CLEP, institutional tests. 15 credit hours maximum toward bachelor's degree. **Support services:** Learning center, pre-admission summer program, reduced course load, remedial instruction, study skills assistance, tutoring, writing center.

Majors. **Area/ethnic studies:** American, women's. **Biology:** General. **Business:** General. **Communications:** Broadcast journalism, media studies. **Conservation:** Environmental studies. **Education:** General, art, elementary, special. **English:** English lit. **Foreign languages:** Classics, French, Latin, Spanish. **Health:** Art therapy, nursing (RN). **History:** General. **Interdisciplinary:** Biological/physical sciences, global studies. **Legal studies:** Prelaw. **Math:** General. **Philosophy/religion:** Philosophy, religion. **Physical sciences:** Chemistry. **Psychology:** General. **Public administration:** Social work. **Social sciences:** Economics, political science, sociology. **Visual/performing arts:** Art history/conservation, studio arts.

Most popular majors. Communications/journalism 7%, health sciences 56%, psychology 12%.

Computing on campus. 223 workstations in dormitories, library, computer center. Dormitories wired for high-speed internet access and linked to campus network. Commuter students can connect to campus network. Online course registration, online library, helpline, wireless network available.

Student life. **Freshman orientation:** Available. Preregistration for classes offered. **Policies:** Commuter students may park cars in parking lots on campus. Resident students must park cars on the street. **Housing:** Guaranteed on-campus for all undergraduates. $100 deposit. **Activities:** Choral groups, dance, drama, film society, literary magazine, musical theater, student government, student newspaper, TV station, community services, campus ministry, international and ethnic student organizations, theater and musical theater, professional clubs.

Athletics. NCAA. **Intercollegiate:** Basketball W, cross-country W, softball W, swimming W, tennis W, volleyball W. **Team name:** Blue Angels.

Student services. Adult student services, alcohol/substance abuse counseling, campus ministries, career counseling, services for economically disadvantaged, student employment services, financial aid counseling, health services, personal counseling, placement for graduates, women's services. **Physically disabled:** Services for visually, speech impaired.

Contact. E-mail: admission@cnr.edu
Phone: (914) 654-5452 Toll-free number: (800) 933-5923
Fax: (914) 654-5464
Stephanie Decker, Director of Admissions, College of New Rochelle, 29 Castle Place, New Rochelle, NY 10805-2339

College of Saint Rose

Albany, New York — **CB member**
www.strose.edu — **CB code: 2091**

- Private 4-year liberal arts and teachers college affiliated with Roman Catholic Church
- Commuter campus in small city
- 3,005 degree-seeking undergraduates: 7% part-time, 73% women, 2% African American, 1% Asian American, 3% Hispanic American
- 1,995 degree-seeking graduate students
- 71% of applicants admitted
- SAT or ACT (ACT writing optional) required
- 65% graduate within 6 years

General. Founded in 1920. Regionally accredited. **Degrees:** 596 bachelor's awarded; master's offered. **ROTC:** Army, Navy, Air Force. **Location:** 140 miles from New York City. **Calendar:** Semester, limited summer session. **Full-time faculty:** 175 total; 77% have terminal degrees, 11% minority, 57% women. **Part-time faculty:** 306 total; 6% minority, 60% women. **Special facilities:** Communications studio, speech and hearing clinic.

Freshman class profile. 3,133 applied, 2,218 admitted, 598 enrolled.

Mid 50% test scores			
SAT verbal:	490-580	GPA 2.0-2.99:	35%
SAT math:	480-580	Rank in top quarter:	39%
ACT:	21-25	Rank in top tenth:	12%
GPA 3.50 or higher:	31%	Return as sophomores:	85%
GPA 3.0-3.49:	34%	Out-of-state:	11%
		Live on campus:	81%

Basis for selection. School achievement record, test scores, recommendations most important. School and community involvement and interview also considered. Music applicants must read music, play at least 1 instrument, and pass audition using standard repertoire as guide. Art applicants must submit portfolio.

High school preparation. Required and recommended units include English 4, mathematics 3-4, social studies 4, history 4, science 3-4 (laboratory 2-3), foreign language 3-4 and academic electives 4.

2005-2006 Annual costs. Tuition/fees: $17,954. Room/board: $7,730. Books/supplies: $1,000. Personal expenses: $1,500.

2004-2005 Financial aid. **Need-based:** 510 full-time freshmen applied for aid; 441 were judged to have need; 440 of these received aid. Average need met was 59%. Average scholarship/grant was $3,520; average loan $1,278. 57% of total undergraduate aid awarded as scholarships/grants, 43% as loans/jobs. **Non-need-based:** Awarded to 263 full-time undergraduates, including 64 freshmen. Scholarships awarded for academics, alumni affiliation, art, athletics, minority status, music/drama.

Application procedures. **Admission:** Priority date 12/1; deadline 2/1 (receipt date). $35 fee, may be waived for applicants with need. Application may be submitted online. Admission notification on a rolling basis beginning on or about 10/1. Must reply by 5/1. **Financial aid:** Priority date 3/1, closing date 10/1. FAFSA required. Applicants notified on a rolling basis starting 3/15; must reply by 5/1 or within 2 week(s) of notification.

Academics. **Special study options:** Accelerated study, combined bachelor's/graduate degree, cross-registration, double major, independent study, internships, study abroad, teacher certification program. **Credit/placement by examination:** CLEP, IB, institutional tests. 15 credit hours maximum toward bachelor's degree. **Support services:** Learning center, pre-admission summer program, reduced course load, remedial instruction, study skills assistance, tutoring, writing center.

Majors. **Area/ethnic studies:** American, women's. **Biology:** General, biochemistry, cell/histology. **Business:** Accounting, business admin. **Computer sciences:** General. **Conservation:** Environmental studies. **Education:** Art, biology, chemistry, elementary, English, mathematics, music, secondary, social studies, Spanish, trade/industrial. **English:** English lit. **Foreign languages:** Spanish. **Health:** Audiology/speech pathology, clinical lab science. **History:** General. **Liberal arts:** Arts/sciences. **Math:** General. **Philosophy/religion:** Religion. **Physical sciences:** Chemistry. **Protective services:** Law enforcement admin. **Psychology:** General. **Public administration:** Social work. **Social sciences:** Political science, sociology. **Visual/performing arts:** Commercial/advertising art, music performance.

Most popular majors. Business/marketing 10%, communication technologies 9%, education 48%, visual/performing arts 8%.

Computing on campus. Dormitories wired for high-speed internet access and linked to campus network. Commuter students can connect to campus network. Helpline available.

Student life. **Freshman orientation:** Mandatory, $125 fee. Two-part orientation: 2-day overnight summer program and week-long program that begins 2 days prior to start of fall classes. **Housing:** Guaranteed on-campus for freshmen. Coed dorms, single-sex dorms, apartments available. $150 nonrefundable deposit, deadline 5/1. **Activities:** Jazz band, choral groups, dance, drama, literary magazine, music ensembles, student government, student newspaper, many religious, ethnic, political, and social service organizations available.

Athletics. NCAA. **Intercollegiate:** Baseball M, basketball, cross-country, golf M, soccer, softball W, swimming, tennis W, volleyball W. **Intramural:** Basketball, soccer, volleyball. **Team name:** Golden Knights.

Student services. Adult student services, alcohol/substance abuse counseling, campus ministries, career counseling, services for economically disadvantaged, student employment services, financial aid counseling, health services, legal services, minority student services, personal counseling, placement for graduates. **Physically disabled:** Services for visually, speech, hearing impaired.

Contact. E-mail: admit@strose.edu
Phone: (518) 454-5111 Toll-free number: (800) 637-8556
Fax: (518) 454-2013
Mary Grondahl, Associate Vice President for Enrollment Planning and Undergraduate Admissions, College of Saint Rose, 432 Western Avenue, Albany, NY 12203

Columbia University: Columbia College

New York, New York **CB member**
www.college.columbia.edu **CB code: 2116**

- Private 4-year university and liberal arts college
- Residential campus in very large city
- 4,225 degree-seeking undergraduates: 52% women, 9% African American, 13% Asian American, 9% Hispanic American, 6% international
- 11% of applicants admitted
- SAT or ACT with writing, SAT Subject Tests, application essay required
- 94% graduate within 6 years

General. Founded in 1754. Regionally accredited. **Degrees:** 970 bachelor's awarded. **ROTC:** Army, Navy, Air Force. **Location:** 3 miles from midtown Manhattan. **Calendar:** Semester, extensive summer session. **Full-time faculty:** 727 total; 15% minority, 32% women. **Class size:** 58% < 20, 26% 20-39, 4% 40-49, 9% 50-99, 4% >100. **Special facilities:** Art and architecture galleries; geological observatory; theaters.

Freshman class profile. 15,793 applied, 1,693 admitted, 1,024 enrolled.

Mid 50% test scores		**Rank in top quarter:**	97%
SAT verbal:	670-770	**Rank in top tenth:**	86%
SAT math:	660-760	**End year in good standing:**	98%
ACT:	27-32	**Return as sophomores:**	98%
GPA 3.50 or higher:	85%	**Out-of-state:**	76%
GPA 3.0-3.49:	12%	**Live on campus:**	99%
GPA 2.0-2.99:	3%	**International:**	6%

Basis for selection. School achievement record most important. Test scores, recommendations, essay, extracurricular activities also important. TOEFL required of all non-native speakers. Interview recommended for all; audition required for Juilliard program.

High school preparation. Recommended units include English 4, mathematics 4, history 4, science 4 (laboratory 4), foreign language 4 and academic electives 4. All (except English and foreign language) are 3-4 recommended.

2005-2006 Annual costs. Tuition/fees: $33,246. Room/board: $9,338. Books/supplies: $1,000. Personal expenses: $1,060.

2005-2006 Financial aid. All financial aid based on need. 622 full-time freshmen applied for aid; 546 were judged to have need; 546 of these received aid. Average need met was 100%. Average scholarship/grant was $25,440; average loan $3,257. 80% of total undergraduate aid awarded as scholarships/grants, 20% as loans/jobs.

Application procedures. Admission: Closing date 1/2 (receipt date). $65 fee, may be waived for applicants with need. Application may be submitted online. Admission notification 4/4. Must reply by May 1 or within 2 week(s) if notified thereafter. **Financial aid:** Closing date 2/10. FAFSA, institutional form, CSS PROFILE required. Applicants notified by 4/1; must reply by 5/1.

Academics. Special study options: Combined bachelor's/graduate degree, cross-registration, double major, ESL, exchange student, honors, independent study, internships, liberal arts/career combination, student-designed major, study abroad, teacher certification program. Combined 3-2 program with engineering. **Credit/placement by examination:** AP, CLEP, IB, institutional tests. 16 credit hours maximum toward bachelor's degree. **Support services:** Tutoring.

Majors. Architecture: Architecture. **Area/ethnic studies:** African, African-American, American, Asian, Asian-American, Central/Eastern European, Chinese, East Asian, European, French, German, Hispanic-American/Latino/Chicano, Italian, Japanese, Korean, Latin American, Near/Middle Eastern, Polish, regional, Russian/Slavic, Slavic, Spanish/Iberian, women's. **Biology:** General, biochemistry, biophysics, ecology, environmental, evolutionary. **Computer sciences:** Computer science. **Conservation:** General, environmental science. **Education:** General. **English:** American lit, British lit, creative writing, English lit. **Foreign languages:** Ancient Greek, Biblical, Chinese, classics, comparative lit, East Asian, French, German, Germanic, Italian, Japanese, Korean, Latin, linguistics, modern Greek, Russian, Slavic, Spanish. **History:** General. **Interdisciplinary:** Ancient studies, classical/archaeology, intercultural, medieval/Renaissance, neuroscience. **Math:** General, applied, statistics. **Philosophy/religion:** Philosophy, religion. **Physical sciences:** Astronomy, astrophysics, chemical physics, chemistry, geochemistry, geology, geophysics, physics, planetary. **Psychology:** General. **Social sciences:** Anthropology, archaeology, economics, political science, sociology, urban studies. **Visual/performing arts:** General, art history/conservation, dance, dramatic, film/cinema, jazz, studio arts, theater history.

Most popular majors. English 14%, foreign language 8%, history 9%, social sciences 28%, visual/performing arts 9%.

Computing on campus. 150 workstations in dormitories, library, computer center, student center. Dormitories wired for high-speed internet access and linked to campus network. Commuter students can connect to campus network. Helpline available.

Student life. Freshman orientation: Mandatory, $300 fee. Preregistration for classes offered. One week prgoram ending on Labor Day. **Housing:** Guaranteed on-campus for all undergraduates. Coed dorms, special housing for disabled, fraternity/sorority housing available. $250 deposit, deadline 5/1. Freshmen required to live on campus. Special interest (group) housing available; single-sex first-year floor available. **Activities:** Bands, choral groups, dance, drama, film society, literary magazine, music ensembles, musical theater, opera, radio station, student government, student newspaper, symphony orchestra, TV station, African-American, Hispanic, Asian-American, Gay/Lesbian student organizations, community service groups, religious groups of all denominations.

Athletics. NCAA. **Intercollegiate:** Archery W, baseball M, basketball, cross-country, diving, fencing, field hockey W, football (tackle) M, golf, lacrosse W, rowing (crew), soccer, softball W, swimming, tennis, track and field, volleyball W, wrestling M. **Intramural:** Basketball, football (non-tackle), racquetball, soccer, softball, squash, tennis, volleyball. **Team name:** Lions.

Student services. Alcohol/substance abuse counseling, campus ministries, career counseling, services for economically disadvantaged, student employment services, financial aid counseling, health services, minority student services, personal counseling, placement for graduates, women's services. **Physically disabled:** Services for visually, speech, hearing impaired.

Contact. E-mail: ugrad-admiss@columbia.edu
Phone: (212) 854-2522 Fax: (212) 854-1209
Jessica Marinaccio, Director of Undergraduate Admissions, Columbia University: Columbia College, 1130 Amsterdam Avenue MC2807, New York, NY 10027

Columbia University: Fu Foundation School of Engineering and Applied Science

New York, New York
www.engineering.columbia.edu **CB code: 2111**

- Private 4-year engineering college
- Residential campus in very large city
- 1,430 degree-seeking undergraduates: 27% women, 3% African American, 32% Asian American, 6% Hispanic American, 12% international
- 1,204 graduate students
- 27% of applicants admitted
- SAT or ACT with writing, SAT Subject Tests, application essay required
- 88% graduate within 6 years

General. Founded in 1864. Regionally accredited. **Degrees:** 340 bachelor's awarded; master's, doctoral offered. **ROTC:** Army, Navy, Air Force. **Calendar:** Semester, limited summer session. **Full-time faculty:** 142 total; 20% minority, 8% women. **Class size:** 46% < 20, 31% 20-39, 6% 40-49, 12% 50-99, 5% >100. **Special facilities:** Interactive graphics laboratory, telecommunications research center, plasma laboratory, materials laboratory, astronomical observatory; cinemas, theaters, art and architecture galleries.

Freshman class profile. 2,332 applied, 624 admitted, 315 enrolled.

Mid 50% test scores		Rank in top tenth:	91%
SAT verbal:	660-750	End year in good standing:	99%
SAT math:	740-800	Return as sophomores:	98%
ACT:	30-33	Out-of-state:	73%
GPA 3.50 or higher:	90%	Live on campus:	99%
GPA 3.0-3.49:	10%	International:	14%
Rank in top quarter:	99%		

Basis for selection. Strong school achievement record most important. 2 recommendations with 1 from mathematics teacher, test scores important. Personal qualities also important, with attention given to essay, personal history, and extracurricular distinction. Tests should be taken by end of junior year or December of senior year. 2 SAT Subject Tests required, Math Levels 1 or 2, and either physics or chemistry. Interview recommended.

High school preparation. Recommended units include English 4, mathematics 4, history 4, science 4 (laboratory 4), foreign language 3 and academic electives 4. Mathematics units should include calculus. Lab, History/Social Science, Academic Electives are all 3 or 4 recommended.

2005-2006 Annual costs. Tuition/fees: $33,246. Room/board: $9,338. Books/supplies: $1,000. Personal expenses: $1,060.

2005-2006 Financial aid. All financial aid based on need. 208 full-time freshmen applied for aid; 187 were judged to have need; 187 of these received aid. Average need met was 100%. Average scholarship/grant was $24,180; average loan $3,375. 91% of total undergraduate aid awarded as scholarships/grants, 9% as loans/jobs.

Application procedures. Admission: Closing date 1/2 (receipt date). $65 fee, may be waived for applicants with need. Application may be submitted online. Admission notification 4/4. Must reply by May 1 or within 2 week(s) if notified thereafter. **Financial aid:** Closing date 2/10. FAFSA, institutional form, CSS PROFILE required. Applicants notified by 4/1; must reply by 5/1.

Academics. Specialized engineering study generally begins in third year; however, entering students usually have defined interests. **Special study options:** Combined bachelor's/graduate degree, cross-registration, independent study, internships, liberal arts/career combination, study abroad, teacher certification program. 3-2 programs with over 90 liberal arts colleges around the country. **Credit/placement by examination:** AP, CLEP, IB, institutional tests. **Support services:** Tutoring.

Majors. Computer sciences: Computer science. **Engineering:** Biomedical, chemical, civil, computer, electrical, environmental, geological, materials, materials science, mechanical, mechanics, metallurgical, mining, operations research. **Engineering technology:** Industrial management. **Math:** Applied.

Most popular majors. Computer/information sciences 11%, engineering/engineering technologies 63%, social sciences 17%.

Computing on campus. 150 workstations in dormitories, library, computer center, student center. Dormitories wired for high-speed internet access and linked to campus network. Commuter students can connect to campus network. Online course registration, helpline, student web hosting, wireless network available.

Student life. Freshman orientation: Mandatory, $300 fee. Preregistration for classes offered. One week program ending on Labor Day. **Housing:** Guaranteed on-campus for all undergraduates. Coed dorms, special housing for disabled, apartments, fraternity/sorority housing available. $250 deposit, deadline 5/1. Freshmen required to live on-campus. Single-sex first-year floor available. **Activities:** Bands, choral groups, dance, drama, film society, literary magazine, music ensembles, musical theater, opera, radio station, student government, student newspaper, symphony orchestra, TV station, 150 student organizations available.

Athletics. NCAA. **Intercollegiate:** Archery W, baseball M, basketball, cross-country, diving, fencing, field hockey W, football (tackle) M, golf, lacrosse W, rowing (crew), soccer, softball W, swimming, tennis, track and field, volleyball W, wrestling M. **Intramural:** Basketball, racquetball, soccer, softball, squash, tennis, volleyball. **Team name:** Lions.

Student services. Alcohol/substance abuse counseling, campus ministries, career counseling, services for economically disadvantaged, student employment services, financial aid counseling, health services, minority student services, personal counseling, placement for graduates, women's services. **Physically disabled:** Services for visually, speech, hearing impaired.

Contact. E-mail: ugrad-admiss@columbia.edu
Phone: (212) 854-2522 Fax: (212) 854-1209
Jessica Marinaccio, Director of Undergraduate Admissions, Columbia University: Fu Foundation School of Engineering and Applied Science, 1130 Amsterdam Avenue, MC2807, New York, NY 10027

Columbia University: School of General Studies

New York, New York
www.gs.columbia.edu **CB code: 2095**

- Private 4-year university and liberal arts college
- Commuter campus in very large city
- 1,146 degree-seeking undergraduates: 44% part-time, 50% women, 6% African American, 11% Asian American, 8% Hispanic American, 1% Native American, 9% international
- 48% of applicants admitted
- SAT or ACT (ACT writing optional), application essay required

General. Founded in 1947. Regionally accredited. Liberal arts division of university for nontraditional students whose undergraduate study has been interrupted or postponed for at least 1 year. Postbaccalaureate premedical program offered. **Degrees:** 244 bachelor's awarded; first professional offered. **ROTC:** Army, Air Force. **Calendar:** Semester, extensive summer session. **Full-time faculty:** 727 total; 99% have terminal degrees, 15% minority, 32% women. **Special facilities:** Biosphere, earth observatory.

Freshman class profile. 254 applied, 121 admitted, 63 enrolled.

Basis for selection. Maturity and varied backgrounds of students considered. Aptitude and motivation important together with academic performance and test scores. Interview requested when needed.

2005-2006 Annual costs. Tuition/fees: $31,765. Institutionally managed double-occupancy apartments available starting at $600/month. Books/supplies: $2,000. Personal expenses: $1,850.

2004-2005 Financial aid. All financial aid based on need. 48% of total undergraduate aid awarded as scholarships/grants, 52% as loans/jobs.

Application procedures. Admission: Priority date 3/1; deadline 6/1 (postmark date). $65 fee. Application may be submitted online. 4 to 6 weeks after receipt of application. Must reply by May 1 or within 2 week(s) if notified thereafter. Nonbinding early action deadline of March 1; students must notify school of enrollment plans within 2 weeks of receiving offer of admission. **Financial aid:** Priority date 4/15, closing date 6/1. FAFSA, institutional form required. Applicants notified on a rolling basis; must reply within 2 week(s) of notification.

Academics. Special study options: Accelerated study, cross-registration, double major, dual enrollment of high school students, ESL, exchange student, honors, independent study, internships, student-designed major, study abroad, teacher certification program. Combined degree program with Jewish Theological Seminary. **Credit/placement by examination:** AP, CLEP, institutional tests. 30 credit hours maximum toward bachelor's degree. **Support services:** Learning center, pre-admission summer program, reduced course load, remedial instruction, study skills assistance, tutoring, writing center.

Majors. Architecture: Architecture. **Area/ethnic studies:** African, African-American, American, Asian, East Asian, Hispanic-American/Latino/Chicano, Latin American, Near/Middle Eastern, Russian/Slavic, women's. **Biology:** General, evolutionary. **Computer sciences:** General, computer science. **Conservation:** General, environmental studies. **English:** British lit, creative writing. **Foreign languages:** Classics, comparative lit, French, German, Italian, Portuguese, Russian, Spanish. **Health:** Premedicine. **History:** General. **Math:** General, applied, statistics. **Philosophy/religion:** Philosophy, religion. **Physical sciences:** Astronomy, astrophysics, chemistry, geochemistry, geology, geophysics, oceanography, physics. **Psychology:** General. **Public administration:** Human services. **Social sciences:** Economics, political science, sociology, urban studies. **Visual/performing arts:** General, art history/conservation, dance, dramatic, film/cinema, music performance, musicology, painting, sculpture, voice/opera.

Most popular majors. English 18%, history 8%, liberal arts 11%, philosophy/religious studies 6%, psychology 7%, social sciences 29%.

Computing on campus. 347 workstations in dormitories, library, computer center, student center. Dormitories wired for high-speed internet access and linked to campus network. Commuter students can connect to campus network. Online course registration, online library, helpline, repair service, student web hosting, wireless network available.

Student life. Freshman orientation: Mandatory, $75 fee. Preregistration for classes offered. Generally held 1 week before classes start. Academic planning session (held prior to beginning of semester) required of all new students. **Housing:** Coed dorms, single-sex dorms, special housing for disabled, apartments, fraternity/sorority housing available. $400 nonrefundable deposit. Limited on-campus housing available. Off-campus housing registry provides listings of Columbia-affiliated apartments. **Activities:** Bands, choral groups, dance, drama, film society, literary magazine, music ensembles, musical theater, opera, radio station, student government, student newspaper, symphony orchestra, TV station, many religious, political, and ethnic organizations.

Athletics. NCAA. **Intercollegiate:** Baseball M, basketball, cross-country, diving, fencing, field hockey W, football (tackle) M, golf M, lacrosse W, rowing (crew), soccer, softball W, swimming, tennis, track and field, volleyball W, wrestling M. **Intramural:** Baseball M, basketball, boxing, cricket M, diving, fencing, lacrosse, racquetball, skiing, soccer, softball, squash, swimming, tennis, volleyball. **Team name:** Lions.

Student services. Adult student services, alcohol/substance abuse counseling, campus ministries, career counseling, student employment services, financial aid counseling, health services, minority student services, personal counseling, placement for graduates, women's services. **Physically disabled:** Services for visually impaired. **Learning disabled:** Comprehensive services available.

Contact. E-mail: gsdegree@columbia.edu
Phone: (212) 854-2772 Toll-free number: (800) 895-1169
Fax: (212) 854-6316
Curtis Rodgers, Dean of Admissions, Columbia University: School of General Studies, 408 Lewisohn Hall, Mail Code 4101, 2970 Broadway, New York, NY 10027

Columbia University: School of Nursing

New York, New York
www.nursing.hs.columbia.edu **CB code: 2142**

- Private upper-division university and nursing college
- Commuter campus in very large city

General. Founded in 1892. Regionally accredited. Located on the Columbia University Medical Center campus. **Degrees:** 155 bachelor's awarded; master's, doctoral offered. **Calendar:** Semester, limited summer session. **Full-time faculty:** 35 total. **Part-time faculty:** 80 total. **Special facilities:** Technology Learning Center (practice laboratory for nursing students), clinical sites for hands-on experience.

Student profile. 2 degree-seeking undergraduates, 501 graduate students. 100% entered as juniors.

2005-2006 Annual costs. Tuition/fees: $28,390. Room only: $4,600. Books/supplies: $1,800. Personal expenses: $1,200.

Application procedures. Admission: Rolling admission. $75 fee. Application may be submitted online. **Financial aid:** FAFSA required.

Academics. Special study options: Accelerated study, combined bachelor's/graduate degree, cross-registration, double major, dual enrollment of high school students, independent study, liberal arts/career combination. **Credit/placement by examination:** AP, CLEP, IB, institutional tests. **Support services:** Learning center, reduced course load, study skills assistance, tutoring.

Majors. Health: Nursing (RN), preop/surgical nursing.

Computing on campus. 50 workstations in dormitories, library, computer center. Dormitories wired for high-speed internet access and linked to campus network. Commuter students can connect to campus network. Online library, helpline, repair service, wireless network available.

Student life. Housing: Coed dorms, special housing for disabled, apartments available. **Activities:** Choral groups, dance, drama, musical theater, student government, student newspaper, various religious, political, ethnic, social service organizations.

Student services. Adult student services, career counseling, student employment services, health services, on-campus daycare, personal counseling, placement for graduates, veterans' counselor. **Physically disabled:** Services for visually, speech, hearing impaired.

Contact. E-mail: nursing@columbia.edu
Phone: (212) 305-5756 Toll-free number: (800) 899-8895
Fax: (212) 305-3680
Columbia University: School of Nursing, 630 West 168th Street, New York, NY 10032

Concordia College

Bronxville, New York **CB member**
www.concordia-ny.edu **CB code: 2096**

- Private 4-year liberal arts college affiliated with Lutheran Church - Missouri Synod
- Residential campus in small town
- 533 degree-seeking undergraduates: 2% part-time, 53% women
- 66% of applicants admitted
- SAT or ACT with writing, application essay required

General. Founded in 1881. Regionally accredited. Christian principles central to program of study. **Degrees:** 124 bachelor's, 3 associate awarded. **Location:** 14 miles from New York City. **Calendar:** Semester, limited summer session. **Full-time faculty:** 35 total. **Part-time faculty:** 50 total. **Class size:** 62% < 20, 37% 20-39, 1% 40-49. **Special facilities:** Electric-piano laboratory, distance learning classroom.

Freshman class profile. 688 applied, 455 admitted, 142 enrolled.

Mid 50% test scores		**Rank in top quarter:**	25%
SAT verbal:	420-540	**Rank in top tenth:**	11%
SAT math:	410-530	**Out-of-state:**	6%
ACT:	17-19	**Live on campus:**	65%
GPA 3.50 or higher:	11%	**Fraternities:**	14%
GPA 3.0-3.49:	22%	**Sororities:**	9%
GPA 2.0-2.99:	57%		

Basis for selection. Test scores, school achievement record, interview important; community and church involvement considered. Interview required for some, recommended for others; audition required for music program. **Homeschooled:** Show explanation of all course work studied and grades obtained. **Learning Disabled:** Students required to meet with learning specialist and submit most recent psychological assessment.

High school preparation. 15 units recommended. Recommended units include English 4, mathematics 3, social studies 2, science 2 (laboratory 2) and foreign language 2.

2005-2006 Annual costs. Tuition/fees: $19,800. Room/board: $7,940. Books/supplies: $900. Personal expenses: $1,500.

Financial aid. Non-need-based: Scholarships awarded for academics, athletics, leadership, music/drama.

Application procedures. Admission: Closing date 3/15 (postmark date). $40 fee, may be waived for applicants with need. Application may be submitted online. Admission notification on a rolling basis beginning on or about 12/1. Must reply by May 1 or within 4 week(s) if notified thereafter. **Financial aid:** Priority date 4/1; no closing date. FAFSA required. Applicants notified on a rolling basis starting 4/1; must reply by 5/1 or within 3 week(s) of notification.

Academics. Special study options: Combined bachelor's/graduate degree, cooperative education, cross-registration, distance learning, double major, ESL, exchange student, honors, independent study, internships, liberal arts/career combination, student-designed major, study abroad, teacher certification program. **Credit/placement by examination:** AP, CLEP, IB, institutional tests. 30 credit hours maximum toward associate degree, 30 toward bachelor's. **Support services:** Reduced course load, remedial instruction, study skills assistance, tutoring, writing center.

Majors. Biology: General, ecology. **Business:** General, accounting, business admin, finance, international. **Education:** General, elementary. **Health:** Premedicine. **History:** General. **Interdisciplinary:** Behavioral sciences. **Legal studies:** Prelaw. **Liberal arts:** Arts/sciences. **Math:** General. **Philosophy/religion:** Religion. **Physical sciences:** Geology. **Psychology:** General. **Public administration:** Social work. **Social sciences:** General. **Theology:** Religious ed, sacred music.

Most popular majors. Biology 8%, business/marketing 24%, education 11%, English 6%, liberal arts 16%, social sciences 21%.

Computing on campus. 30 workstations in library, computer center. Dormitories wired for high-speed internet access and linked to campus network. Commuter students can connect to campus network. Online course registration, online library, helpline, repair service, wireless network available.

Student life. Freshman orientation: Mandatory. Preregistration for classes offered. Held at beginning of semester with adviser. **Housing:** Guaranteed on-campus for all undergraduates. Single-sex dorms available. $300 nonrefundable deposit, deadline 5/1. **Activities:** Jazz band, choral groups, drama, music ensembles, musical theater, student government, student newspaper,

Christian service organizations, Campus Christian ministries, Afro-Latino American club, social work club, Prayer Partners, environmental club, In His Name, Lutheran Women League, Rotaract club.

Athletics. NCAA. **Intercollegiate:** Baseball M, basketball, cross-country, soccer, softball W, tennis, volleyball. **Intramural:** Basketball, football (non-tackle), softball W, squash, tennis, volleyball. **Team name:** Clippers.

Student services. Adult student services, alcohol/substance abuse counseling, campus ministries, career counseling, student employment services, financial aid counseling, health services, minority student services, personal counseling, placement for graduates. **Learning disabled:** Comprehensive services available.

Contact. E-mail: admission@concordia-ny.edu
Phone: (914) 337-9300 ext. 2155 Toll-free number: (800) 937-2655
Fax: (914) 395-4636
Donna Hoyt, Director of Admission, Concordia College, 171 White Plains Road, Bronxville, NY 10708

Cooper Union for the Advancement of Science and Art

New York, New York — **CB member**
www.cooper.edu — **CB code: 2097**

- Private 4-year visual arts and engineering college
- Commuter campus in very large city
- 929 degree-seeking undergraduates: 36% women, 5% African American, 20% Asian American, 9% Hispanic American, 12% international
- 54 degree-seeking graduate students
- 13% of applicants admitted
- SAT or ACT with writing, application essay required
- 79% graduate within 6 years; 45% enter graduate study

General. Founded in 1859. Regionally accredited. Full-tuition scholarship school of architecture, art, and engineering. **Degrees:** 223 bachelor's awarded; master's offered. **Calendar:** Semester, limited summer session. **Full-time faculty:** 52 total. **Part-time faculty:** 163 total. **Class size:** 65% < 20, 32% 20-39, 3% 40-49.

Freshman class profile. 2,301 applied, 308 admitted, 228 enrolled.

Mid 50% test scores			
SAT verbal:	610-690	Rank in top tenth:	85%
SAT math:	600-760	End year in good standing:	91%
GPA 3.50 or higher:	50%	Return as sophomores:	97%
GPA 3.0-3.49:	35%	Out-of-state:	40%
GPA 2.0-2.99:	15%	Live on campus:	80%
Rank in top quarter:	98%	International:	9%

Basis for selection. Engineering applicants reviewed on high school record and program, essays, SAT, and required SAT Subject Test scores in physics or chemistry and mathematics. Art and architecture applicants selected on basis of home test, high school record and program, SAT. All international students must apply from an address in United States. Institutional exams required for art and architecture students. Portfolios required for art applicants. **Homeschooled:** Statement describing homeschool structure and mission required. Must present proof of high school graduation certification (national) or equivalent.

High school preparation. 16 units required; 18 recommended. Required and recommended units include English 4, mathematics 1-4, social studies 1-4, history 1, science 1-4 (laboratory 3) and academic electives 8. One science required for architecture and art. 2 science and 4 mathematics required for engineering including physics, chemistry, and precalculus; calculus preferred. One mathematics required for art, 3 mathematics for architecture including trigonometry or precalculus. 18 units recommended for engineering.

2006-2007 Annual costs. Tuition/fees: $31,500. Every student admitted receives full tuition scholarship, covering tuition only, for duration of enrollment. Room only: $9,360. Books/supplies: $1,800. Personal expenses: $1,575.

2004-2005 Financial aid. Need-based: Average need met was 90%. Average scholarship/grant was $3,323; average loan $1,848. 63% of total undergraduate aid awarded as scholarships/grants, 37% as loans/jobs. **Non-need-based:** Scholarships awarded for academics. **Additional information:** All students receive full-tuition scholarships. Students able to document need receive financial aid package that may include combination of grants, loans, work-study, internships.

Application procedures. Admission: Closing date 1/1 (receipt date). $50 fee, may be waived for applicants with need. Application may be submitted online. Admission notification 4/1. Must reply by 5/1. Regular application closing date for architecture January 1, for fine arts January 10, for engineering February 1. **Financial aid:** Priority date 4/15, closing date 6/1. FAFSA, CSS PROFILE required. Applicants notified by 6/1; must reply by 6/30 or within 2 week(s) of notification.

Academics. Engineering tutorials and engineering mentor program available. All freshman engineering majors required to prove or acquire computer literacy. 128 credit hours required for graduation in art program, 135 in engineering, and 160 in architecture. **Special study options:** Combined bachelor's/graduate degree, cross-registration, exchange student, honors, independent study, internships, student-designed major, study abroad. **Credit/placement by examination:** AP, CLEP, institutional tests. **Support services:** Tutoring, writing center.

Majors. Architecture: Architecture. **Engineering:** General, chemical, civil, electrical, mechanical. **Visual/performing arts:** Graphic design, studio arts.

Most popular majors. Architecture 14%, engineering/engineering technologies 57%, visual/performing arts 29%.

Computing on campus. 650 workstations in dormitories, library, computer center. Dormitories linked to campus network. Commuter students can connect to campus network. Online library, helpline, repair service, student web hosting, wireless network available.

Student life. Freshman orientation: Available, $100 fee. 1.5 days at Cooper; 1.5 days away at camp. **Policies:** Freshmen permitted cars on campus. **Housing:** Coed dorms available. $500 partly refundable deposit, deadline 6/1. Limited shared studio apartments available on first-come first-serve basis for freshmen. **Activities:** Bands, choral groups, drama, film society, literary magazine, music ensembles, student government, student newspaper, symphony orchestra, 90 registered clubs.

Athletics. Intercollegiate: Basketball, bowling, equestrian W, lacrosse M, soccer M, tennis, volleyball M. **Intramural:** Badminton, baseball M, basketball, bowling, cross-country M, fencing, golf, soccer, softball, table tennis, tennis, volleyball. **Team name:** Pioneers.

Student services. Alcohol/substance abuse counseling, career counseling, student employment services, financial aid counseling, minority student services, personal counseling, placement for graduates. **Physically disabled:** Services for visually, hearing impaired.

Contact. E-mail: admissions@cooper.edu
Phone: (212) 353-4120 Fax: (212) 353-4342
Mitchell Lipton, Dean of Admissions and Records/Registrar, Cooper Union for the Advancement of Science and Art, 30 Cooper Square, Suite 300, New York, NY 10003-7183

Cornell University

Ithaca, New York — **CB member**
www.cornell.edu — **CB code: 2098**

- Private 4-year university
- Residential campus in large town
- 13,474 degree-seeking undergraduates: 50% women, 5% African American, 16% Asian American, 5% Hispanic American, 8% international
- 5,898 degree-seeking graduate students
- 27% of applicants admitted
- SAT or ACT with writing, SAT Subject Tests, application essay required
- 92% graduate within 6 years; 34% enter graduate study

General. Founded in 1865. Regionally accredited. 7 undergraduate colleges: agriculture and life sciences; architecture, art, and planning; arts and sciences; engineering; hotel administration; human ecology; industrial and labor relations. 6 graduate/professional colleges. **Degrees:** 3,474 bachelor's awarded; master's, doctoral, first professional offered. **ROTC:** Army, Navy, Air Force. **Location:** 60 miles from Syracuse. **Calendar:** Semester, extensive summer session. **Full-time faculty:** 1,675 total; 92% have terminal degrees, 14% minority, 29% women. **Part-time faculty:** 169 total; 69% have terminal degrees, 9% minority, 36% women. **Class size:** 44% < 20, 27% 20-39, 7% 40-49, 14% 50-99, 8% >100. **Special facilities:** Africana studies/research center, particle accelerator, biotechnology institute, supercomputer, national research centers, center for performing arts, observatory, marine laboratory, plantations, ornithology laboratory.

Freshman class profile. 24,452 applied, 6,621 admitted, 3,108 enrolled.

Mid 50% test scores			
SAT verbal:	630-720	End year in good standing:	96%
SAT math:	660-760	Return as sophomores:	96%
ACT:	28-32	Out-of-state:	64%
Rank in top quarter:	96%	Live on campus:	99%
Rank in top tenth:	80%	International:	8%

Basis for selection. School achievement record (difficulty of courses, grades earned), test scores, preparation and background for specific programs especially important. Essays, recommendations considered. Minority status considered. SAT Subject Test requirements vary by college and dependent upon version of SAT/ACT submitted. Interview required for architecture, hotel administration programs; portfolio required for art, architecture programs. **Homeschooled:** Well documented coursework required.

High school preparation. 16 units required. Required and recommended units include English 4, mathematics 3, social studies 3, history 3, science 3 (laboratory 3) and foreign language 3. Requirements vary by college.

2006-2007 Annual costs. Tuition/fees: $32,981. Tuition amounts listed are for Endowed/Private colleges only: Architecture, Art & Planning; Arts & Sciences; Engineering; Hotel Administration. Contract/State college amounts differ and vary by program. Room/board: $10,726. Books/supplies: $680. Personal expenses: $1,380.

2005-2006 Financial aid. All financial aid based on need. 1,967 full-time freshmen applied for aid; 1,499 were judged to have need; 1,499 of these received aid. Average need met was 100%. Average scholarship/grant was $21,000; average loan $6,300. 70% of total undergraduate aid awarded as scholarships/grants, 30% as loans/jobs.

Application procedures. Admission: Closing date 1/1 (receipt date). $65 fee, may be waived for applicants with need. Application may be submitted online. Must reply by May 1 or within 2 week(s) if notified thereafter. Notification on rolling basis and dates vary by program/college. **Financial aid:** Closing date 2/11. FAFSA, institutional form, CSS PROFILE required. Applicants notified by 4/1; must reply by 5/1 or within 2 week(s) of notification.

Academics. Cornell/Hughes Scholars program for independent research in neurobiology, physiology, genetics and development, and biochemistry (molecular and cell biology), Cornell in Rome program for studies in architecture and fine arts, undergraduate research opportunities in traditional majors as well as in many interdisciplinary fields including American Indian studies, cognitive studies, agriculture, food and society, FALCON language programs. **Special study options:** Accelerated study, combined bachelor's/graduate degree, cooperative education, cross-registration, distance learning, double major, ESL, exchange student, honors, independent study, internships, liberal arts/career combination, New York semester, semester at sea, student-designed major, study abroad, teacher certification program, urban semester, Washington semester. **Credit/placement by examination:** AP, CLEP, IB, SAT, institutional tests. **Support services:** Learning center, pre-admission summer program, reduced course load, study skills assistance, tutoring, writing center.

Majors. Agriculture: Agribusiness operations, agronomy, animal sciences, business, crop production, economics, education services, food science, horticultural science, international, ornamental horticulture, plant breeding, plant protection, plant sciences, soil science. **Architecture:** Architecture, environmental design, history/criticism, interior, landscape, urban/community planning. **Area/ethnic studies:** African-American, American, Asian, gay/lesbian, German, Hispanic-American/Latino/Chicano, Latin American, Near/Middle Eastern, Russian/Slavic, women's. **Biology:** General, animal genetics, animal physiology, bacteriology, biochemistry, biometrics, botany, ecology, entomology, molecular, plant genetics, plant pathology. **Business:** General, hospitality admin, hotel/motel admin, human resources, labor relations, organizational behavior, restaurant/food services. **Communications:** General. **Computer sciences:** General. **Conservation:** General, environmental science. **Education:** General, adult/continuing, secondary. **Engineering:** General, aerospace, agricultural, biomedical, chemical, civil, electrical, environmental, materials, materials science, mechanical, mechanics, nuclear, operations research, physics, systems. **English:** British lit, creative writing, English lit. **Family/consumer sciences:** General, consumer economics, family resources, family studies, food/nutrition, housing, textile science. **Foreign languages:** Classics, comparative lit, East Asian, French, German, Italian, linguistics, Romance, Russian, Semitic, Slavic, Spanish. **Health:** Premedicine, preveterinary. **History:** General, science/technology. **Interdisciplinary:** Historic preservation, medieval/Renaissance, neuroscience, nutrition sciences, science/society. **Legal studies:** Prelaw. **Liberal arts:** Arts/sciences. **Math:** General, applied, statistics. **Philosophy/religion:** Philosophy, religion. **Physical sciences:** Astronomy, atmospheric science, chemistry, geology, meteorology, physics. **Psychology:** General. **Public administration:** Community org/advocacy, policy analysis. **Social sciences:** Anthropology, archaeology, economics, international relations, political science, sociology, U.S. government. **Visual/performing arts:** General, art, art history/conservation, commercial/advertising art, dance, dramatic, fiber arts, film/cinema, music theory/composition, musicology, studio arts.

Most popular majors. Agriculture 12%, biology 12%, business/marketing 12%, engineering/engineering technologies 18%, social sciences 12%.

Computing on campus. 2,650 workstations in dormitories, library, computer center, student center. Dormitories wired for high-speed internet access and linked to campus network. Commuter students can connect to campus network. Online course registration, online library, helpline, repair service, student web hosting, wireless network available.

Student life. Freshman orientation: Available. Preregistration for classes offered. **Policies:** Freshmen permitted cars on campus. **Housing:** Guaranteed on-campus for freshmen. Coed dorms, single-sex dorms, special housing for disabled, apartments, cooperative housing, fraternity/sorority housing, substance-free housing available. $40 deposit, deadline 5/1. Ecology house, JAM (Just About Music), language house, international living center, Ujamaa residential college (Third World house), Risley residential college (theater and expressive arts), multicultural living learning unit, Akwe:Kon (Native American and Non-native American), Latino living center, transfer center. **Activities:** Bands, choral groups, dance, drama, film society, literary magazine, music ensembles, musical theater, radio station, student government, student newspaper, symphony orchestra, Hillel, Campus Crusade for Christ, La Asociacion Latina, African, Native American, Caribbean, Vietnamese, international, and lesbian/gay/bisexual groups, debate.

Athletics. NCAA. **Intercollegiate:** Baseball M, basketball, cross-country, equestrian W, fencing W, field hockey W, football (tackle) M, golf M, gymnastics W, ice hockey, lacrosse, rowing (crew), soccer, softball W, squash, swimming, tennis, track and field, volleyball W, wrestling M. **Intramural:** Badminton, basketball, bowling, cross-country, fencing, football (non-tackle), golf, ice hockey, skiing, soccer, softball, squash, table tennis, tennis, track and field, volleyball, water polo, wrestling. **Team name:** Big Red.

Student services. Alcohol/substance abuse counseling, campus ministries, career counseling, student employment services, financial aid counseling, health services, minority student services, personal counseling, placement for graduates, veterans' counselor, women's services. **Physically disabled:** Services for visually, speech, hearing impaired.

Contact. E-mail: admissions@cornell.edu
Phone: (607) 255-5241 Fax: (607) 255-0659
Jason Locke, Director of Undergraduate Admissions, Cornell University, 410 Thurston Avenue, Ithaca, NY 14853-2488

Culinary Institute of America

Hyde Park, New York
www.ciachef.edu **CB code: 3301**

- Private 4-year culinary school
- Residential campus in large town
- 2,713 degree-seeking undergraduates
- 69% of applicants admitted
- Application essay required
- 82% graduate within 6 years

General. Founded in 1946. Candidate for regional accreditation; also accredited by ACCSCT. Curriculum devoted exclusively to culinary arts and baking and pastry arts education. Freshmen may enroll in one of 4 enrollment seasons throughout the year. All students complete 18-week paid externship program. **Degrees:** 178 bachelor's, 1,012 associate awarded. **Location:** 80 miles from New York City. **Calendar:** Continuous. **Full-time faculty:** 120 total. **Part-time faculty:** 28 total. **Special facilities:** 41 teaching kitchens and bakeshops, 5 restaurants, culinary library with over 70,000 volumes.

Freshman class profile. 903 applied, 624 admitted, 514 enrolled.

Rank in top quarter:	23%	Return as sophomores:	95%
Rank in top tenth:	6.5%	Out-of-state:	76%
End year in good standing:	92%		

Basis for selection. School achievement record, work experience (particularly in hands-on food preparation), and interview important. SAT or ACT recommended.

High school preparation. Recommended units include English 4, mathematics 3, social studies 1, history 1 and foreign language 1.

2005-2006 Annual costs. Tuition/fees: $20,775. Room/board: $6,820. Books/supplies: $975.

2004-2005 Financial aid. Need-based: 31% of total undergraduate aid awarded as scholarships/grants, 69% as loans/jobs. **Non-need-based:** Scholarships awarded for academics, alumni affiliation, job skills, leadership, minority status.

Application procedures. Admission: No deadline. $30 fee, may be waived for applicants with need. Application may be submitted online. Admission notification on a rolling basis. **Financial aid:** Closing date 2/15. FAFSA required. Applicants notified by 4/1; must reply by 5/1 or within 4 week(s) of notification.

Academics. Two-thirds of class time involves hands-on cooking, baking, table service, and dining room operations management in kitchens, bakeshops, and 5 student-staffed public restaurants. **Special study options:** Cross-registration, distance learning, internships. **Credit/placement by examination:** AP, CLEP, institutional tests. **Support services:** Learning center, reduced course load, remedial instruction, study skills assistance, tutoring, writing center.

Majors. Business: Restaurant/food services. **Personal/culinary services:** Baking.

Computing on campus. 250 workstations in dormitories, library, computer center, student center. Dormitories wired for high-speed internet access and linked to campus network. Commuter students can connect to campus network. Online library, helpline, repair service, wireless network available.

Student life. Freshman orientation: Mandatory. **Policies:** Freshmen permitted cars on campus. **Housing:** Guaranteed on-campus for freshmen. Coed dorms, special housing for disabled, substance-free housing available. Hearing impaired student housing available. **Activities:** Literary magazine, student government, student newspaper, Culinary Christian Fellowship, Black Culinarian Society, Eta Sigma Delta, Global Culinary Society, Jewish culture club, Oye Me.

Athletics. Intramural: Baseball, basketball, football (tackle), ice hockey, racquetball, soccer, softball, tennis, volleyball. **Team name:** Flames.

Student services. Alcohol/substance abuse counseling, campus ministries, career counseling, student employment services, financial aid counseling, health services, personal counseling, placement for graduates, veterans' counselor. **Physically disabled:** Services for visually, speech, hearing impaired.

Contact. E-mail: admissions@culinary.edu
Phone: (845) 452-9430 Toll-free number: (800) 285-4627
Fax: (845) 451-1068
Rachel Birchwood, Director of Admissions, Culinary Institute of America, 1946 Campus Drive, Hyde Park, NY 12538-1499

Daemen College

Amherst, New York — **CB member**
www.daemen.edu — **CB code: 2762**

- Private 4-year liberal arts college
- Residential campus in small city
- 1,440 degree-seeking undergraduates: 12% part-time, 77% women, 15% African American, 1% Asian American, 2% Hispanic American, 1% Native American, 1% international
- 672 degree-seeking graduate students
- 79% of applicants admitted
- SAT or ACT (ACT writing optional) required
- 38% graduate within 6 years

General. Founded in 1947. Regionally accredited. All professional programs require internships or field placements; service learning requirement for graduation. **Degrees:** 284 bachelor's awarded; master's, first professional offered. **ROTC:** Army. **Location:** 9 miles from downtown Buffalo. **Calendar:** Semester, limited summer session. **Full-time faculty:** 80 total; 74% have terminal degrees, 8% minority, 51% women. **Part-time faculty:** 179 total; 21% have terminal degrees, 4% minority, 65% women. **Class size:** 70% < 20, 30% 20-39, less than 1% 40-49. **Special facilities:** Natural and health science research center, video-conference center.

Freshman class profile. 1,609 applied, 1,276 admitted, 366 enrolled.

Mid 50% test scores		**Rank in top quarter:**	45%
SAT verbal:	450-550	**Rank in top tenth:**	15%
SAT math:	460-560	**End year in good standing:**	69%
ACT:	18-24	**Out-of-state:**	3%
GPA 3.50 or higher:	57%	**Live on campus:**	65%
GPA 3.0-3.49:	40%	**Fraternities:**	1%
GPA 2.0-2.99:	3%		

Basis for selection. Emphasis on academic achievement and test scores with secondary consideration given to school activities and recommendations. Work experience also considered for entry into the physician assistant program. 30 credit hour transfer limit on International Baccalaureate coursework. Applicants who have been out of high school for more than 2 years not required to submit SAT or ACT scores. Essay, interview required for physician assistant program; portfolio required for art program. **Homeschooled:** Applicants should provide evidence of equivalency of high school education by GED or attestation of equivalency by the superintendent of schools in the student's public school district of residence. This documentation needed for financial aid eligibility. **Learning Disabled:** Bring to the attention of the Admission Office the need for special accommodations and submit current medical evidence of the disability and limitations that require accommodations. Feasibility will be determined considering nature and cost of accommodation, availability of funding, and whether accommodation will impact fundamental nature of course or program, among other factors.

High school preparation. 16 units recommended. Recommended units include English 4, mathematics 4, social studies 4, science 4 (laboratory 1). All science and allied health programs require 3 mathematics and 3 science. Business program requires 3 mathematics. Foreign language programs require 3 foreign language.

2005-2006 Annual costs. Tuition/fees: $16,800. Room/board: $7,780. Books/supplies: $800. Personal expenses: $800.

2004-2005 Financial aid. Need-based: 223 full-time freshmen applied for aid; 211 were judged to have need; 211 of these received aid. Average need met was 88%. Average scholarship/grant was $7,484; average loan $3,231. 47% of total undergraduate aid awarded as scholarships/grants, 53% as loans/jobs. **Non-need-based:** Awarded to 1,094 full-time undergraduates, including 189 freshmen. Scholarships awarded for academics, alumni affiliation, art, athletics.

Application procedures. Admission: No deadline. $25 fee, may be waived for applicants with need. Application may be submitted online. Admission notification on a rolling basis beginning on or about 10/15. Must reply by May 1 or within 2 week(s) if notified thereafter. . **Financial aid:** Priority date 2/15; no closing date. FAFSA required. Applicants notified on a rolling basis starting 2/1; must reply within 2 week(s) of notification.

Academics. Special study options: Accelerated study, combined bachelor's/graduate degree, cross-registration, distance learning, double major, dual enrollment of high school students, exchange student, honors, independent study, internships, student-designed major, study abroad, teacher certification program, Washington semester, weekend college. Post-RN BS program in nursing, weekend college only for candiates of the BS, Business Administration-General Business Programs. **Credit/placement by examination:** AP, CLEP, IB, institutional tests. No limit other than residency of 30 credit hours minimum required in courses completed at school (select programs may require a higher minimum). Veterans may receive credit for military educational experiences. **Support services:** Learning center, preadmission summer program, remedial instruction, study skills assistance, tutoring, writing center.

Majors. Biology: General, biochemistry. **Business:** Accounting, business admin. **Education:** Art, biology, early childhood, elementary, English, French, mathematics, social studies, Spanish, special. **English:** English lit. **Foreign languages:** French, Spanish. **Health:** Health services, nursing (RN). **History:** General. **Interdisciplinary:** Natural sciences. **Math:** General. **Philosophy/religion:** Religion. **Psychology:** General. **Public administration:** Social work. **Social sciences:** Political science. **Visual/performing arts:** Art, graphic design, printmaking, studio arts.

Most popular majors. Biology 15%, business/marketing 11%, education 14%, health sciences 27%, psychology 9%, visual/performing arts 10%.

Computing on campus. 131 workstations in library, computer center, student center. Dormitories wired for high-speed internet access and linked to campus network. Commuter students can connect to campus network. Online library, repair service, wireless network available.

Student life. Freshman orientation: Mandatory, $105 fee. Preregistration for classes offered. Two sessions offered in July. **Policies:** Freshmen permitted cars on campus. **Housing:** Guaranteed on-campus for freshmen.

Coed dorms, substance-free housing available. $200 deposit, deadline 5/1. Coed apartment-style residence halls; some apartments are handicapped accessible. **Activities:** Choral groups, drama, literary magazine, student government, student newspaper, student government association, multicultural association, students without borders, new brighter future, Voices of Zion, Amnesty International.

Athletics. NAIA. **Intercollegiate:** Basketball, cross-country, golf M, soccer, volleyball W. **Intramural:** Basketball, football (non-tackle) M, softball. **Team name:** Wildcats.

Student services. Alcohol/substance abuse counseling, campus ministries, career counseling, student employment services, financial aid counseling, personal counseling, placement for graduates. **Physically disabled:** Services for hearing impaired.

Contact. E-mail: admissions@daemen.edu
Phone: (716) 839-8225 Toll-free number: (800) 462-7652
Fax: (716) 839-8229
Donna Shaffner, Director of Undergraduate Admissions, Daemen College, 4380 Main Street, Amherst, NY 14226-3592

Darkei Noam Rabbinical College
Brooklyn, New York
CB code: 1270

- Private 5-year rabbinical college for men affiliated with Jewish faith
- Very large city

General. Founded in 1977. Accredited by AARTS. **Calendar:** Semester.

Annual costs/financial aid. Tuition/fees (2005-2006): $5,050. Books/supplies: $300. Personal expenses: $3,000.

Contact. Phone: (718) 338-6464
Director of Admissions, 2822 Avenue J, Brooklyn, NY 11210

Davis College
Johnson City, New York
www.davisny.edu **CB code: 2233**

- Private 4-year Bible college affiliated with nondenominational tradition
- Large town
- 250 full-time, degree-seeking undergraduates
- 67% of applicants admitted
- SAT or ACT (ACT writing optional) required

General. Regionally accredited; also accredited by ABHE. **Degrees:** 60 bachelor's, 10 associate awarded. **Location:** 2 miles from Binghamton. **Calendar:** Semester, limited summer session. **Full-time faculty:** 7 total. **Part-time faculty:** 17 total.

Freshman class profile. 150 applied, 100 admitted, 80 enrolled.

Basis for selection. Pastor recommendation, high school record most important. Applicants must give evidence of personal knowledge of the Lord Jesus Christ as Savior. Applicant lifestyle consistency with biblical principles important.

2005-2006 Annual costs. Tuition/fees: $9,300. Room/board: $5,100.

Application procedures. Admission: No deadline. $25 fee. Application may be submitted online. Admission notification on a rolling basis. **Financial aid:** No deadline. FAFSA, institutional form required. Applicants notified on a rolling basis.

Academics. Credit/placement by examination: CLEP. **Support services:** Reduced course load, study skills assistance, tutoring.

Majors. Theology: Religious ed.

Computing on campus. Dormitories linked to campus network. Commuter students can connect to campus network. Wireless network available.

Student life. Policies: Freshmen permitted cars on campus.

Athletics. Intercollegiate: Basketball, soccer, volleyball W. **Intramural:** Soccer, volleyball. **Team name:** Falcons.

Contact. E-mail: admissions@davisny.edu
Phone: (607) 729-1581 ext. 406 Toll-free number: (800) 331-4137 ext. 406
Fax: (607) 729-2962
Wes Ehret, Admissions Director, Davis College, 400 Riverside Drive, Johnson City, NY 13790

DeVry Institute of Technology: New York
Long Island City, New York
www.devry.edu **CB code: 4276**

- For-profit 4-year business and technical college
- Commuter campus in very large city
- 1,264 degree-seeking undergraduates: 26% part-time, 32% women
- 106 graduate students
- Interview required
- 25% graduate within 6 years

General. Regionally accredited. **Degrees:** 215 bachelor's, 84 associate awarded; master's offered. **Calendar:** Semester, extensive summer session. **Full-time faculty:** 47 total; 34% minority, 17% women. **Part-time faculty:** 42 total; 40% minority, 12% women.

Basis for selection. Applicants must have high school diploma or equivalent, or degree from an accredited postsecondary institution. Must demonstrate proficiency in basic college-level skills through test scores and/or institutionally-administered placement examinations, and be at least 17 years of age on the first day of classes. New students may enter at beginning of any semester. Applicants may also take institution-administered admissions test.

High school preparation. College-preparatory program recommended.

2005-2006 Annual costs. Tuition/fees: $13,410. Books/supplies: $1,100. Personal expenses: $1,816.

Financial aid. All financial aid based on need.

Application procedures. Admission: No deadline. $50 fee. Application may be submitted online. Admission notification on a rolling basis. **Financial aid:** No deadline. FAFSA required. Applicants notified on a rolling basis.

Academics. Special study options: Accelerated study, cooperative education, distance learning. **Credit/placement by examination:** CLEP, institutional tests. **Support services:** Learning center, remedial instruction, tutoring.

Majors. Business: General. **Computer sciences:** Information technology, networking, systems analysis. **Engineering technology:** Biomedical, computer, electrical.

Most popular majors. Business/marketing 25%, computer/information sciences 61%, engineering/engineering technologies 14%.

Computing on campus. 394 workstations in library, computer center. Online course registration, online library, helpline available.

Student life. Freshman orientation: Mandatory. **Policies:** Freshmen permitted cars on campus. **Housing:** Private apartments, student-plan housing, private rooms available. **Activities:** Muslim Student Association, martial arts club.

Student services. Career counseling, student employment services, financial aid counseling, placement for graduates, veterans' counselor. **Physically disabled:** Services for visually, hearing impaired.

Contact. Phone: (718) 472-9933
Newton Myvett, Director of Admissions, DeVry Institute of Technology: New York, 3020 Thomson Avenue, Long Island City, NY 11101-3051

Dominican College of Blauvelt
Orangeburg, New York **CB member**
www.dc.edu **CB code: 2190**

- Private 4-year health science and liberal arts college affiliated with Roman Catholic Church
- Commuter campus in small town
- 1,386 degree-seeking undergraduates: 23% part-time, 67% women, 18% African American, 7% Asian American, 15% Hispanic American
- 123 degree-seeking graduate students
- 83% of applicants admitted

- SAT or ACT (ACT writing recommended) required
- 77% graduate within 6 years

General. Founded in 1952. Regionally accredited. **Degrees:** 264 bachelor's, 7 associate awarded; master's, doctoral offered. **Location:** 17 miles from New York City. **Calendar:** Differs by program, limited summer session. **Full-time faculty:** 60 total; 48% have terminal degrees, 5% minority, 53% women. **Part-time faculty:** 120 total; 14% have terminal degrees, 8% minority, 57% women. **Class size:** 56% < 20, 44% 20-39.

Freshman class profile. 1,228 applied, 1,014 admitted, 292 enrolled.

Mid 50% test scores			
SAT verbal:	400-490	Return as sophomores:	68%
SAT math:	400-500	Out-of-state:	26%
GPA 3.50 or higher:	12%	Live on campus:	72%
GPA 3.0-3.49:	31%		
GPA 2.0-2.99:	54%		

Basis for selection. Admissions based on secondary school record and standardized test scores. **Learning Disabled:** Students with current professional documentation of disabilities will be provided with reasonable accommodations to assure access to and full participation in mainstream of educational process.

High school preparation. 8 units recommended. Recommended units include English 2, mathematics 2, science 2 and foreign language 2.

2005-2006 Annual costs. Tuition/fees: $17,910. Room/board: $8,720. Books/supplies: $1,350. Personal expenses: $1,900.

2005-2006 Financial aid. Need-based: Average need met was 76%. Average scholarship/grant was $10,584; average loan $2,766. 55% of total undergraduate aid awarded as scholarships/grants, 45% as loans/jobs. **Non-need-based:** Scholarships awarded for academics, athletics. **Additional information:** Individual financial aid counseling available.

Application procedures. Admission: No deadline. $35 fee, may be waived for applicants with need. Application may be submitted online. Admission notification on a rolling basis. **Financial aid:** Priority date 2/15; no closing date. FAFSA, institutional form required. Applicants notified on a rolling basis starting 2/1.

Academics. Special study options: Accelerated study, combined bachelor's/graduate degree, cooperative education, distance learning, dual enrollment of high school students, honors, independent study, internships, teacher certification program, weekend college. Accelerated BSN for college graduates. **Credit/placement by examination:** AP, CLEP, IB, institutional tests. 30 credit hours maximum toward associate degree, 60 toward bachelor's. **Support services:** Learning center, remedial instruction, study skills assistance, tutoring, writing center.

Majors. Biology: General. **Business:** Accounting, business admin, finance, human resources, international, management information systems, marketing. **Computer sciences:** General. **Education:** General, biology, elementary, English, mathematics, multiple handicapped, secondary, social science, special. **English:** English lit. **Foreign languages:** Spanish. **Health:** Athletic training, health services, nursing (RN). **History:** General. **Legal studies:** Prelaw. **Liberal arts:** Humanities. **Math:** General. **Psychology:** General. **Public administration:** Social work. **Social sciences:** General.

Most popular majors. Business/marketing 18%, computer/information sciences 8%, education 8%, health sciences 29%, social sciences 13%.

Computing on campus. 40 workstations in dormitories, library, computer center. Dormitories wired for high-speed internet access and linked to campus network. Online library available.

Student life. Freshman orientation: Mandatory. **Policies:** Alcohol-free campus. Freshmen permitted cars on campus. **Housing:** Coed dorms, substance-free housing available. $200 fully refundable deposit. Local hotel accommodates overflow students. **Activities:** Choral groups, dance, drama, literary magazine, musical theater, student government, student newspaper, campus ministry, student government association, Dominicans Uniting Latinos for Cultural Education (DULCE), Helping Hands (community service).

Athletics. NAIA, NCAA. **Intercollegiate:** Baseball M, basketball, cross-country, golf M, lacrosse, soccer, softball W, volleyball W. **Intramural:** Basketball, softball, volleyball W. **Team name:** Chargers.

Student services. Alcohol/substance abuse counseling, campus ministries, career counseling, student employment services, financial aid counseling, health services, personal counseling, placement for graduates. **Physically disabled:** Services for visually, hearing impaired.

Contact. E-mail: admissions@dc.edu
Phone: (845) 359-3533 Toll-free number: (866) 432-4636
Fax: (845) 359-3150
Joyce Elbe, Director of Admissions, Dominican College of Blauvelt, 470 Western Highway, Orangeburg, NY 10962-1210

Dowling College

Oakdale, New York — **CB member**
www.dowling.edu — **CB code: 2011**

- Private 4-year liberal arts college
- Commuter campus in large town
- 3,627 degree-seeking undergraduates: 37% part-time, 61% women, 9% African American, 2% Asian American, 9% Hispanic American, 4% international
- 2,752 degree-seeking graduate students
- 87% of applicants admitted
- 34% graduate within 6 years

General. Founded in 1955. Regionally accredited. **Degrees:** 531 bachelor's awarded; master's, doctoral offered. **ROTC:** Air Force. **Location:** 50 miles from New York City. **Calendar:** Semester, extensive summer session. **Full-time faculty:** 124 total; 90% have terminal degrees, 9% minority, 34% women. **Part-time faculty:** 376 total; 31% have terminal degrees, 7% minority, 46% women. **Class size:** 66% < 20, 34% 20-39, less than 1% 40-49, less than 1% 50-99. **Special facilities:** College-operated museum.

Freshman class profile. 2,399 applied, 2,082 admitted, 465 enrolled.

Mid 50% test scores		Rank in top tenth:	6%
SAT verbal:	410-520	End year in good standing:	66%
SAT math:	410-520	Return as sophomores:	66%
GPA 3.50 or higher:	30%	Out-of-state:	5%
GPA 3.0-3.49:	18%	Live on campus:	3%
GPA 2.0-2.99:	43%	International:	4%
Rank in top quarter:	19%		

Basis for selection. Program of study, recent achievement, academic rank, school record, interview, standardized test scores, counselor's recommendation considered. SAT and SAT Subject Tests recommended.

High school preparation. College-preparatory program recommended. 16 units recommended. Recommended units include English 4, mathematics 3, social studies 3 and science 2. 4 additional units recommended.

2005-2006 Annual costs. Tuition/fees: $17,040. Room only: $5,800. Books/supplies: $1,000. Personal expenses: $1,066.

2005-2006 Financial aid. Need-based: 373 full-time freshmen applied for aid; 309 were judged to have need; 306 of these received aid. Average need met was 87%. Average scholarship/grant was $2,742; average loan $2,469. 48% of total undergraduate aid awarded as scholarships/grants, 52% as loans/jobs. **Non-need-based:** Awarded to 406 full-time undergraduates, including 116 freshmen. Scholarships awarded for academics, alumni affiliation, athletics.

Application procedures. Admission: No deadline. $25 fee, may be waived for applicants with need. Application may be submitted online. Admission notification on a rolling basis. **Financial aid:** Priority date 4/30; no closing date. FAFSA required. Applicants notified on a rolling basis starting 3/1.

Academics. Optional winter term enables students to take 2 additional courses. **Special study options:** Accelerated study, combined bachelor's/graduate degree, cooperative education, double major, ESL, honors, independent study, internships, liberal arts/career combination, student-designed major, study abroad, teacher certification program, weekend college. Federal Aviation Administration cooperative program. **Credit/placement by examination:** AP, CLEP, IB, institutional tests. 30 credit hours maximum toward bachelor's degree. **Support services:** Learning center, pre-admission summer program, reduced course load, remedial instruction, study skills assistance, tutoring.

Majors. Biology: General. **Business:** Accounting, business admin, finance, international, management information systems, marketing, tourism promotion, tourism/travel. **Computer sciences:** General, computer science. **Education:** General, art, biology, business, chemistry, elementary, English, foreign languages, mathematics, middle, multi-level teacher, music, science, secondary, social science, social studies, Spanish, special. **History:** General. **Liberal arts:** Arts/sciences. **Math:** General. **Psychology:** General. **Social sciences:** General, anthropology, economics, political science, sociology. **Transportation:** Aviation, aviation management. **Visual/performing arts:** General, art, dramatic, interior design.

Most popular majors. Business/marketing 32%, computer/information sciences 6%, education 18%, liberal arts 10%, psychology 6%, social sciences 8%.

Computing on campus. 170 workstations in library, computer center. Dormitories wired for high-speed internet access and linked to campus network. Online course registration, online library, helpline available.

Student life. **Freshman orientation:** Available. Preregistration for classes offered. **Policies:** Freshmen permitted cars on campus. **Housing:** Coed dorms available. $200 deposit. **Activities:** Jazz band, choral groups, drama, literary magazine, music ensembles, musical theater, student government, student newspaper, symphony orchestra, 23 clubs and organizations related to academics, honor societies in business, education, economics, and psychology, Circle-K, computer science, scholarship society.

Athletics. NCAA. **Intercollegiate:** Baseball M, basketball, cheerleading, cross-country W, equestrian W, golf M, lacrosse M, rowing (crew), soccer, softball W, tennis, volleyball W. **Intramural:** Basketball, bowling, soccer, softball. **Team name:** Golden Lions.

Student services. Adult student services, alcohol/substance abuse counseling, campus ministries, career counseling, services for economically disadvantaged, student employment services, financial aid counseling, health services, personal counseling, placement for graduates. **Physically disabled:** Services for visually, speech, hearing impaired.

Contact. E-mail: admissions@dowling.edu
Phone: (631) 244-3030 Toll-free number: (800) 369-5464
Fax: (631) 563-3827
Bridget Masturzo, Director of Enrollment Services/Admission & Recruitment, Dowling College, 150 Idle Hour Boulevard, Oakdale, NY 11769-1999

D'Youville College

Buffalo, New York **CB member**
www.dyc.edu **CB code: 2197**

- Private 4-year health science and teachers college
- Commuter campus in large city
- 1,330 degree-seeking undergraduates: 12% part-time, 75% women, 17% African American, 1% Asian American, 5% Hispanic American, 1% Native American, 12% international
- 1,468 degree-seeking graduate students
- 73% of applicants admitted
- SAT or ACT (ACT writing optional) required
- 41% graduate within 6 years

General. Founded in 1908. Regionally accredited. **Degrees:** 195 bachelor's awarded; master's, doctoral, first professional offered. **ROTC:** Army. **Location:** 1 mile from downtown. **Calendar:** Semester, extensive summer session. **Full-time faculty:** 107 total; 63% have terminal degrees, 10% minority, 54% women. **Part-time faculty:** 116 total; 40% have terminal degrees, 16% minority. **Class size:** 63% < 20, 34% 20-39, 3% 40-49, less than 1% 50-99. **Special facilities:** Equipment for blind and visually impaired including computer system with speech synthesizer, Braille printer, versa-Braille, and print enhancer, physical therapy gait analysis lab, professional theater, gross anatomy lab.

Freshman class profile. 1,408 applied, 1,024 admitted, 252 enrolled.

Mid 50% test scores			
SAT verbal:	440-530	GPA 2.0-2.99:	43%
SAT math:	440-540	End year in good standing:	70%
ACT:	19-23	Return as sophomores:	70%
GPA 3.50 or higher:	19%	Out-of-state:	7%
GPA 3.0-3.49:	35%	Live on campus:	40%
		International:	4%

Basis for selection. High school GPA, class rank, test scores, type of high school program important. Interview, essay, letters of recommendation optional. 3 recommendations required for physician's assistant program. Interview required for physician's assistant and chiropractic programs.

High school preparation. 16 units recommended. Recommended units include English 4, mathematics 3, social studies 3, science 3 and foreign language 3. Biology and chemistry required for nursing, occupational therapy, physical therapy, dietetics, chiropractic and physician's assistant programs. 3 years mathematics required for accounting.

2005-2006 Annual costs. Tuition/fees: $15,800. Substantial tuition reduction depending on SAT scores. Room/board: $7,800. Books/supplies: $1,000. Personal expenses: $800.

2004-2005 Financial aid. Need-based: 159 full-time freshmen applied for aid; 144 were judged to have need; 143 of these received aid. Average need met was 79%. Average scholarship/grant was $9,620; average loan $3,418. 53% of total undergraduate aid awarded as scholarships/grants, 47% as loans/jobs. **Non-need-based:** Awarded to 353 full-time undergraduates, including 29 freshmen. Scholarships awarded for academics, leadership, ROTC.

Application procedures. Admission: No deadline. $25 fee, may be waived for applicants with need. Application may be submitted online. Admission notification on a rolling basis. Must reply by May 1 or within 2 week(s) if notified thereafter. **Financial aid:** Priority date 3/1; no closing date. FAFSA required. Applicants notified on a rolling basis starting 4/1; must reply within 3 week(s) of notification.

Academics. Special study options: Accelerated study, combined bachelor's/graduate degree, cross-registration, distance learning, double major, dual enrollment of high school students, exchange student, independent study, internships, liberal arts/career combination, study abroad, teacher certification program, weekend college. Career Discovery Program for undecided students. **Credit/placement by examination:** AP, CLEP, IB, institutional tests. 15 credit hours maximum toward bachelor's degree. **Support services:** Learning center, pre-admission summer program, reduced course load, remedial instruction, study skills assistance, tutoring, writing center.

Majors. Biology: General. **Business:** General, accounting, business admin, international. **Computer sciences:** Information technology. **Education:** General, biology, business, early childhood, elementary, English, history, middle, multi-level teacher, secondary, social studies, special. **Health:** Health care admin, nursing (RN), physician assistant, predentistry, premedicine, preop/surgical nursing, prepharmacy, preveterinary. **History:** General. **Interdisciplinary:** Global studies. **Legal studies:** Prelaw. **Philosophy/religion:** Philosophy. **Psychology:** General. **Social sciences:** Sociology.

Most popular majors. Business/marketing 23%, health sciences 50%, interdisciplinary studies 9%.

Computing on campus. 100 workstations in dormitories, library, computer center, student center. Dormitories wired for high-speed internet access and linked to campus network. Commuter students can connect to campus network. Online library, helpline, repair service, student web hosting, wireless network available.

Student life. Freshman orientation: Mandatory, $25 fee. Preregistration for classes offered. Programs vary for traditional, transfer, and graduate students. **Policies:** Freshmen permitted cars on campus. **Housing:** Guaranteed on-campus for freshmen. Coed dorms, special housing for disabled, apartments, substance-free housing available. $100 deposit. Quiet floors for upper level students. **Activities:** Choral groups, drama, literary magazine, student government, student newspaper, Black Student Union, Latin American club, campus ministry, Lambda Sigma, writers club, Student Nurses Association, Asian Student Union.

Athletics. NCAA. **Intercollegiate:** Baseball M, basketball, cross-country W, golf, rowing (crew) W, soccer, softball W, volleyball. **Intramural:** Basketball, cheerleading W, cross-country, rowing (crew) W, skiing, table tennis, tennis. **Team name:** Spartans.

Student services. Adult student services, alcohol/substance abuse counseling, campus ministries, career counseling, services for economically disadvantaged, student employment services, financial aid counseling, health services, minority student services, personal counseling, placement for graduates, veterans' counselor. **Physically disabled:** Services for visually, speech, hearing impaired.

Contact. E-mail: admiss@dyc.edu
Phone: (716) 829-8000 Toll-free number: (800) 777-3921
Fax: (716) 829-7900
Ronald Dannecker, Director of Admissions, D'Youville College, 320 Porter Avenue, Buffalo, NY 14201-1084

Eastman School of Music of the University of Rochester

Rochester, New York
www.rochester.edu/eastman **CB code: 2224**

- Private 4-year music college
- Residential campus in large city
- 503 degree-seeking undergraduates
- 24% of applicants admitted
- Application essay, interview required

General. Founded in 1921. Regionally accredited. Eastman School of Music is a professional school within the University of Rochester. Eastman students may take nonmusic classes, earn a BA or BS degree, and attend social events at the University of Rochester's River Campus. Separate application required for double-degree program. **Degrees:** 87 bachelor's awarded; master's, doctoral offered. **ROTC:** Navy. **Location:** 357 miles from New York City, 80 miles from Niagara Falls. **Calendar:** Semester, limited summer session. **Full-time faculty:** 96 total. **Part-time faculty:** 65 total. **Class size:** 89% < 20, 9% 20-39, 1% 40-49, less than 1% 50-99. **Special facilities:** 4 performance halls, computers for synthesis and analysis of music, complete analog and digital recording studios, music library containing over 700,000 items.

Freshman class profile. 994 applied, 243 admitted, 130 enrolled.

Out-of-state:	75%	**Fraternities:**	7%
Live on campus:	99%	**Sororities:**	11%

Basis for selection. Proficiency in major area most important, followed by academic record, test scores, interview, recommendations. Composition majors submit portfolio of scores. SAT or ACT recommended. Institution's theory test required at fall orientation for placement only. Audition required for all; research/term paper required for theory majors; portfolio required for composition majors. Interview recommended for all, required for composition, music education, musical arts, theory majors. **Homeschooled:** SAT or ACT required.

High school preparation. 16 units required. Required units include English 4.

2006-2007 Annual costs. Tuition/fees (projected): $29,195. Room/board: $10,188. Books/supplies: $600. Personal expenses: $700.

2005-2006 Financial aid. Need-based: 50% of total undergraduate aid awarded as scholarships/grants, 50% as loans/jobs. **Non-need-based:** Scholarships awarded for academics, alumni affiliation, music/drama.

Application procedures. Admission: Closing date 12/1 (postmark date). $100 fee, may be waived for applicants with need. Application may be submitted online. Admission notification on a rolling basis beginning on or about 3/15. Must reply by May 1 or within 2 week(s) if notified thereafter. **Financial aid:** Priority date 2/1; no closing date. FAFSA, institutional form, CSS PROFILE required. Applicants notified on a rolling basis starting 3/15; must reply by 5/1 or within 2 week(s) of notification.

Academics. Arts leadership programs; orchestral studies and sacred music diploma programs. **Special study options:** Double major, ESL, internships, student-designed major, teacher certification program. **Credit/placement by examination:** AP, CLEP, institutional tests. **Support services:** Pre-admission summer program, study skills assistance, tutoring, writing center.

Majors. Education: Music. **Visual/performing arts:** Jazz, music performance, music theory/composition, piano/organ, voice/opera.

Most popular majors. Education 16%, visual/performing arts 84%.

Computing on campus. 15 workstations in dormitories, library, computer center. Dormitories wired for high-speed internet access and linked to campus network. Commuter students can connect to campus network. Online course registration, online library, helpline, wireless network available.

Student life. Freshman orientation: Mandatory. Includes mandatory placement testing. **Policies:** Freshmen permitted cars on campus. **Housing:** Guaranteed on-campus for freshmen. Coed dorms, single-sex dorms, special housing for disabled, fraternity/sorority housing, substance-free housing available. Undergraduates required to live in college housing for first three years unless released by Dean of Students. **Activities:** Bands, choral groups, literary magazine, music ensembles, opera, student government, student newspaper, symphony orchestra, International Students Association, Amnesty International, Intervarsity Christian Fellowship, Eastman Jewish Students, Lambda, Student Association, Graduate Student Association and other musical organizations.

Student services. Adult student services, alcohol/substance abuse counseling, campus ministries, career counseling, student employment services, financial aid counseling, health services, personal counseling, placement for graduates. **Physically disabled:** Services for visually, speech impaired.

Contact. E-mail: admissions@esm.rochester.edu
Phone: (585) 274-1060 Toll-free number: (800) 388-9695
Fax: (585) 232-8601
Adrian Daly, Director of Admissions, Eastman School of Music of the University of Rochester, 26 Gibbs Street, Rochester, NY 14604-2599

Elmira College

Elmira, New York — **CB member**
www.elmira.edu — **CB code: 2226**

- Private 4-year liberal arts college
- Residential campus in large town
- 1,382 degree-seeking undergraduates: 15% part-time, 71% women
- 369 graduate students
- 64% of applicants admitted
- SAT or ACT (ACT writing optional), application essay required
- 60% graduate within 6 years; 52% enter graduate study

General. Founded in 1855. Regionally accredited. **Degrees:** 325 bachelor's, 2 associate awarded; master's offered. **ROTC:** Army, Air Force. **Location:** 106 miles from Rochester, 90 miles from Syracuse. **Calendar:** 4-4-1. Limited summer session. **Full-time faculty:** 82 total; 100% have terminal degrees, 5% minority, 45% women. **Part-time faculty:** 17 total; 100% have terminal degrees, 12% minority, 29% women. **Class size:** 77% < 20, 23% 20-39. **Special facilities:** Center for Mark Twain Studies.

Freshman class profile. 1,966 applied, 1,266 admitted, 305 enrolled.

Mid 50% test scores		**Rank in top quarter:**	70%
SAT verbal:	530-630	**Rank in top tenth:**	28%
SAT math:	520-630	**End year in good standing:**	84%
ACT:	24-28	**Return as sophomores:**	84%
GPA 3.50 or higher:	40%	**Out-of-state:**	52%
GPA 3.0-3.49:	31%	**Live on campus:**	98%
GPA 2.0-2.99:	29%		

Basis for selection. School academic record primary. Test scores, recommendations, essay, character and extracurricular activities important. Interview highly recommended.

High school preparation. 16 units required. Required and recommended units include English 4, mathematics 3, social studies 3, history 1, science 3 (laboratory 2), foreign language 2 and academic electives 2. 1 additional unit of foreign language recommended for foreign language and international business programs.

2005-2006 Annual costs. Tuition/fees: $28,500. Room/board: $8,700. Books/supplies: $450. Personal expenses: $550.

2005-2006 Financial aid. Need-based: 272 full-time freshmen applied for aid; 250 were judged to have need; 250 of these received aid. Average need met was 80%. Average scholarship/grant was $17,500; average loan $4,631. 68% of total undergraduate aid awarded as scholarships/grants, 32% as loans/jobs. **Non-need-based:** Awarded to 318 full-time undergraduates, including 82 freshmen. Scholarships awarded for academics, leadership, ROTC. **Additional information:** Sibling Scholarship program provides 50% discounts on second family member's room and board, regardless of need.

Application procedures. Admission: Priority date 2/1; deadline 3/1 (postmark date). $50 fee, may be waived for applicants with need. Application may be submitted online. Admission notification on a rolling basis beginning on or about 10/15. Must reply by May 1 or within 2 week(s) if notified thereafter. **Financial aid:** Priority date 2/1, closing date 6/30. FAFSA required. Applicants notified on a rolling basis starting 2/1; must reply by 5/1 or within 2 week(s) of notification.

Academics. Mandatory writing program for all freshmen. 7.5-credit internship/community service, often done during 6-week spring term, required of all students. Off-campus study emphasized. **Special study options:** Accelerated study, combined bachelor's/graduate degree, double major, dual enrollment of high school students, ESL, exchange student, independent study, internships, liberal arts/career combination, student-designed major, study abroad, teacher certification program. Critical languages programs consortium member. **Credit/placement by examination:** AP, CLEP, IB, institutional tests. 30 credit hours maximum toward bachelor's degree. **Support services:** Reduced course load, study skills assistance, tutoring, writing center.

Majors. Area/ethnic studies: American. **Biology:** General, biochemistry. **Business:** Accounting, business admin, international, management information systems, managerial economics, marketing. **Conservation:** General, environmental studies. **Education:** Art, biology, chemistry, Deaf/hearing impaired, elementary, English, foreign languages, French, history, mathematics, middle, multi-level teacher, science, secondary, social science, social studies, Spanish, speech, speech impaired. **English:** British lit. **Foreign languages:** General, ancient Greek, classics, French, Latin, Spanish. **Health:** Audiology/speech pathology, clinical lab science, nursing (RN), predentistry, premedicine, preveterinary. **History:** General. **Legal studies:** Prelaw. **Math:** General. **Parks/recreation:** Sports admin. **Philosophy/religion:** Philosophy, religion. **Physical sciences:** Chemistry. **Protective services:** Criminal justice. **Psychology:** General. **Public administration:** Social work. **Social sciences:** General, anthropology, economics, international relations, political science, sociology. **Visual/performing arts:** Art, dramatic.

Most popular majors. Business/marketing 24%, education 26%, health sciences 9%, psychology 9%, social sciences 6%.

Computing on campus. 145 workstations in library, computer center. Dormitories wired for high-speed internet access and linked to campus network. Commuter students can connect to campus network. Wireless network available.

Student life. Freshman orientation: Mandatory, $350 fee. Preregistration for classes offered. 2-day summer registration program for testing, course registration, and get-acquainted activities. 4-day orientation program in the fall. **Policies:** Freshmen permitted cars on campus. **Housing:** Guaranteed on-campus for all undergraduates. Coed dorms, single-sex dorms, special housing for disabled, apartments, substance-free housing available. Quiet floors, tobacco- and alcohol-free floors available. All undergraduates required to live in college housing unless living with family or over the age of 25. **Activities:** Bands, choral groups, dance, drama, literary magazine, music ensembles, musical theater, radio station, student government, student newspaper, over 90 student interest groups.

Athletics. NCAA. **Intercollegiate:** Basketball, cheerleading, equestrian W, field hockey W, golf, ice hockey, lacrosse, soccer, softball W, tennis, volleyball W. **Intramural:** Badminton, basketball, bowling, football (non-tackle) M, football (tackle), handball, ice hockey, racquetball, skiing, skin diving, soccer, softball, squash, swimming, table tennis, tennis, volleyball. **Team name:** Soaring Eagles.

Student services. Alcohol/substance abuse counseling, campus ministries, career counseling, student employment services, financial aid counseling, health services, personal counseling, placement for graduates, veterans' counselor, women's services. **Physically disabled:** Services for visually, speech, hearing impaired.

Contact. E-mail: admissions@elmira.edu
Phone: (607) 735-1724 Toll-free number: (800) 935-6472
Fax: (607) 735-1718
Gary Fallis, Dean of Admissions, Elmira College, One Park Place, Elmira, NY 14901

Eugene Lang College The New School for Liberal Arts

New York, New York — **CB member**
www.lang.edu — **CB code: 2521**

- Private 4-year liberal arts college
- Commuter campus in very large city
- 985 degree-seeking undergraduates: 5% part-time, 66% women, 4% African American, 4% Asian American, 5% Hispanic American, 2% international
- 61% of applicants admitted
- SAT or ACT, application essay, interview required
- 50% graduate within 6 years

General. Founded in 1978. Regionally accredited. Students design own academic programs with advisers. Access to New York University and Cooper Union libraries, ability to select courses within The New School and Cooper Union. **Degrees:** 192 bachelor's awarded. **Calendar:** Semester, limited summer session. **Full-time faculty:** 44 total; 32% minority, 46% women. **Part-time faculty:** 72 total; 21% minority, 65% women. **Class size:** 93% < 20, 7% 20-39, less than 1% 50-99. **Special facilities:** Photography laboratories, screening rooms, art galleries.

Freshman class profile. 1,244 applied, 760 admitted, 232 enrolled.

Mid 50% test scores		Rank in top quarter:	51%
SAT verbal:	570-670	Rank in top tenth:	17%
SAT math:	530-620	Return as sophomores:	73%
GPA 3.50 or higher:	18%	Out-of-state:	71%
GPA 3.0-3.49:	47%	International:	3%
GPA 2.0-2.99:	34%		

Basis for selection. Success in college preparatory studies most important supplemented by writing ability, intellectual curiosity, interview. Extracurricular/community activities, evidence of special talents, recommendations important. Telephone interviews available to students who cannot travel to New York. Essay required for BA/BFA; audition required for jazz, BA/BFA; portfolio required for art, BA/BFA.

High school preparation. 16 units required; 18 recommended. Required and recommended units include English 4, mathematics 3, social studies 3, history 2, science 3 and foreign language 2. Honors/AP courses recommended.

2005-2006 Annual costs. Tuition/fees: $27,110. Room/board: $11,750. Books/supplies: $918. Personal expenses: $1,056.

2005-2006 Financial aid. Need-based: 157 full-time freshmen applied for aid; 128 were judged to have need; 128 of these received aid. Average need met was 88%. Average scholarship/grant was $13,312; average loan $3,339. 76% of total undergraduate aid awarded as scholarships/grants, 24% as loans/jobs. **Non-need-based:** Scholarships awarded for academics.

Application procedures. Admission: Closing date 2/1 (postmark date). $40 fee, may be waived for applicants with need. Application may be submitted online. Admission notification 4/1. Must reply by May 1 or within 3 week(s) if notified thereafter. **Financial aid:** Priority date 3/1; no closing date. FAFSA required. Applicants notified on a rolling basis starting 3/1; must reply within 4 week(s) of notification.

Academics. Students map out individual program of study within 5 broad areas of concentration. Seminars rather than lecture classes. **Special study options:** Accelerated study, combined bachelor's/graduate degree, cross-registration, distance learning, dual enrollment of high school students, ESL, exchange student, independent study, internships, student-designed major, study abroad, urban semester. **Credit/placement by examination:** CLEP, IB. **Support services:** Tutoring, writing center.

Majors. Area/ethnic studies: African-American, American, European, Hispanic-American/Latino/Chicano, Western European, women's. **Education:** Foundations. **English:** American lit, British lit, creative writing. **Foreign languages:** General, comparative lit. **History:** General. **Interdisciplinary:** Science/society. **Liberal arts:** Arts/sciences. **Psychology:** General. **Social sciences:** General, anthropology, economics, international relations, political science, sociology, urban studies. **Visual/performing arts:** General, commercial/advertising art, design, fashion design, jazz, studio arts, theater history.

Computing on campus. Dormitories wired for high-speed internet access and linked to campus network. Commuter students can connect to campus network. Online course registration, online library, helpline, student web hosting, wireless network available.

Student life. Freshman orientation: Available. Preregistration for classes offered. One week before classes begin. **Housing:** Guaranteed on-campus for freshmen. Coed dorms, special housing for disabled, apartments, substance-free housing available. $250 nonrefundable deposit, deadline 5/1. **Activities:** Concert band, choral groups, drama, literary magazine, musical theater, radio station, student government, student newspaper, Amnesty International, women's group, student union, Latino and African-American student organizations, gay/lesbian student organizations, volunteer groups.

Student services. Career counseling, student employment services, financial aid counseling, health services, minority student services, personal counseling.

Contact. E-mail: Lang@newschool.edu
Phone: (212) 229-5665 Toll-free number: (877) 528-3321
Fax: (212) 229-5355
Nicole Curvin, Director of Admissions, Eugene Lang College The New School for Liberal Arts, 65 West 11th Street (3rd floor), New York, NY 10011-8693

Excelsior College

Albany, New York — **CB member**
www.excelsior.edu — **CB code: 0759**

- Private 4-year virtual liberal arts college
- Small city
- 26,277 degree-seeking undergraduates: 100% part-time, 58% women, 16% African American, 7% Asian American, 6% Hispanic American, 1% Native American, 1% international
- 534 degree-seeking graduate students

General. Founded in 1970. Regionally accredited. Provides Internet-based courses. No residency required. Professional academic advising provided. **Degrees:** 2,333 bachelor's, 2,211 associate awarded; master's offered. **Calendar:** Continuous, extensive summer session. **Class size:** 91% < 20, 9% 20-39. **Special facilities:** Comprehensive virtual library.

Basis for selection. Open admission, but selective for some programs. Admission to nursing program open to students with certain health care background.

2005-2006 Annual costs. Students are charged a $995 enrollment fee and $250 per credit hour. Because of the nontraditional pricing, the school does not charge a set tuition based on 15 credit hours per semester.

2004-2005 Financial aid. All financial aid based on need. 3% of total undergraduate aid awarded as scholarships/grants, 97% as loans/jobs. **Additional information:** College approved for all veterans' educational benefit programs.

Application procedures. Admission: No deadline. $65 fee. Application may be submitted online. Admission notification on a rolling basis. Students may enroll at any time and are not divided into traditional classifications such as freshmen or sophomores. Applicants without high school diploma admitted as special students. **Financial aid:** Priority date 7/1; no closing date. Institutional form required. Applicants notified on a rolling basis starting 8/1; must reply within 2 week(s) of notification.

Academics. Portfolio assessment option in subject areas where proficiency or performance examinations unavailable. Failing grades not placed in student records or figured into GPA. **Special study options:** Accelerated study, combined bachelor's/graduate degree, distance learning, external degree, honors, independent study. **Credit/placement by examination:** AP, CLEP. Some degrees can be earned entirely by examination. **Support services:** Reduced course load, study skills assistance, writing center.

Majors. Biology: General. **Business:** Accounting, business admin, finance, human resources, insurance, international, management information systems, marketing, operations. **Communications:** General. **Computer sciences:** General, information systems. **Engineering technology:** General, instrumentation, nuclear. **English:** British lit. **Foreign languages:** General. **Health:** Nursing (RN), optometric assistant. **History:** General. **Liberal arts:** Arts/sciences. **Math:** General. **Philosophy/religion:** Philosophy. **Physical sciences:** Chemistry, geology, physics. **Protective services:** Law enforcement admin. **Psychology:** General. **Social sciences:** Economics, geography, political science, sociology.

Most popular majors. Business/marketing 9%, health sciences 8%, liberal arts 67%.

Computing on campus. Commuter students can connect to campus network. Online library, helpline available.

Student life. Freshman orientation: Available. Orientation conducted by mail. **Policies:** Students are kept informed of program developments through mailings, web, correspondence, and program newsletters.

Student services. Adult student services, career counseling, financial aid counseling, veterans' counselor.

Contact. E-mail: info@excelsior.edu
Phone: (518) 464-8500 Toll-free number: (888) 647-2388
Fax: (518) 464-8777
Chari Leader, Vice President for Enrollment Management, Excelsior College, 7 Columbia Circle, Albany, NY 12203-5159

Fashion Institute of Technology

New York, New York — **CB member**
www.fitnyc.edu — **CB code: 2257**

- Public 4-year visual arts and business college
- Commuter campus in very large city
- 7,540 degree-seeking undergraduates: 14% part-time, 85% women, 7% African American, 10% Asian American, 10% Hispanic American, 10% international
- 182 degree-seeking graduate students
- 42% of applicants admitted
- Application essay required

General. Founded in 1944. Regionally accredited. Specialized 2-year and 4-year programs provide professional preparation for fashion and design industries. SUNY institution. **Degrees:** 1,046 bachelor's, 1,680 associate awarded; master's offered. **Calendar:** Semester, limited summer session. **Full-time faculty:** 220 total; 54% women. **Part-time faculty:** 720 total; 50% women. **Class size:** 37% < 20, 63% 20-39. **Special facilities:** Textile and costume collection; fragrance laboratory; computer-aided design; textile, knitting, and communications facility.

Freshman class profile. 3,498 applied, 1,475 admitted, 1,026 enrolled.

GPA 3.50 or higher:	26%	**Rank in top tenth:**	14%
GPA 3.0-3.49:	44%	**Out-of-state:**	39%
GPA 2.0-2.99:	28%	**Live on campus:**	51%
Rank in top quarter:	41%	**International:**	4%

Basis for selection. Rank in class, portfolio, essay, community service, work experience, and awards and honors considered. Portfolio required for art and design.

High school preparation. Required units include English 4, mathematics 2 and social studies 3. College preparatory program recommended.

2005-2006 Annual costs. Tuition/fees: $3,444; $9,592 out-of-state. Bachelor's degree full-time tuition $4350 for state residents, $10,610 for nonresidents. Room/board: $7,066. Books/supplies: $1,400. Personal expenses: $1,050.

2005-2006 Financial aid. All financial aid based on need. 762 full-time freshmen applied for aid; 467 were judged to have need; 463 of these received aid. Average need met was 76%. Average scholarship/grant was $3,726; average loan $2,668. 54% of total undergraduate aid awarded as scholarships/grants, 46% as loans/jobs.

Application procedures. Admission: Priority date 1/1; deadline 2/15 (receipt date). $40 fee. Application may be submitted online. Admission notification 4/15. Admission notification on a rolling basis. Must reply by 5/1. **Financial aid:** Priority date 2/15; no closing date. FAFSA, institutional form required. Applicants notified on a rolling basis starting 4/15; must reply within 2 week(s) of notification.

Academics. Special study options: Distance learning, exchange student, honors, internships, study abroad. One-year visiting student program with colleges and universities throughout United States. **Credit/placement by examination:** CLEP, SAT, ACT. **Support services:** Learning center, reduced course load, remedial instruction, tutoring.

Majors. Architecture: Interior. **Business:** Fashion. **Communications:** Advertising. **Communications technology:** Animation/special effects. **Education:** Technology/industrial arts. **Family/consumer sciences:** Apparel marketing, textile manufacture. **Visual/performing arts:** Commercial/advertising art, fashion design, illustration, industrial design, interior design.

Computing on campus. 300 workstations in dormitories, library, computer center, student center. Dormitories wired for high-speed internet access and linked to campus network. Commuter students can connect to campus network. Online course registration, helpline, repair service, student web hosting, wireless network available.

Student life. Freshman orientation: Mandatory. **Housing:** Coed dorms, single-sex dorms, apartments, substance-free housing available. **Activities:** Choral groups, drama, literary magazine, radio station, student government, student newspaper, more than 60 groups and organizations available.

Athletics. NJCAA. **Intercollegiate:** Basketball M, tennis, volleyball W. **Intramural:** Basketball, tennis, volleyball.

Student services. Adult student services, career counseling, student employment services, health services, personal counseling, placement for graduates, veterans' counselor. **Physically disabled:** Services for visually, speech, hearing impaired.

Contact. E-mail: fitinfo@fitnyc.edu
Phone: (212) 217-7675 Fax: (212) 217-7481
Dolores Lombardi, Director of Admissions, Fashion Institute of Technology, Seventh Avenue at 27 Street, New York, NY 10001-5992

Five Towns College

Dix Hills, New York
www.fivetowns.edu — **CB code: 3142**

- For-profit 4-year music and liberal arts college
- Commuter campus in large town
- 1,088 degree-seeking undergraduates: 4% part-time, 39% women
- 65 degree-seeking graduate students
- 77% of applicants admitted
- SAT or ACT, application essay, interview required

General. Founded in 1972. Regionally accredited. **Degrees:** 224 bachelor's, 6 associate awarded; master's, doctoral offered. **Location:** 40 miles from New York City. **Calendar:** Semester, limited summer session. **Full-time faculty:** 45 total. **Part-time faculty:** 64 total. **Class size:** 45% < 20, 43% 20-39, 10% 40-49, 2% 50-99. **Special facilities:** 24-, 48- and 72-track recording studios with ProTools and 5.1 surround sound, Korg MIDI technology studio, professional film/video arts studio and editing labs, theatre technology lab.

Freshman class profile. 713 applied, 547 admitted, 262 enrolled.

Mid 50% test scores		**ACT:**	18-20
SAT verbal:	420-540	**Out-of-state:**	8%
SAT math:	410-530	**Live on campus:**	20%

Basis for selection. Minimum 2.5 GPA required. Applicants for music and theater programs must pass audition and demonstrate competency in music, mathematics, and English. **Learning Disabled:** Provide recent copy of individualized educational program and psychological report.

High school preparation. 18 units recommended. Recommended units include English 4, mathematics 3, social studies 3, science 2 and foreign language 2. Music harmony and other applied music classes recommended for music students.

2005-2006 Annual costs. Tuition/fees: $14,350. Room/board: $10,250. Books/supplies: $900. Personal expenses: $2,400.

2005-2006 Financial aid. Need-based: Average need met was 45%. Average scholarship/grant was $4,000; average loan $2,500. 62% of total undergraduate aid awarded as scholarships/grants, 38% as loans/jobs. **Non-need-based:** Scholarships awarded for academics, music/drama.

Application procedures. Admission: No deadline. $35 fee, may be waived for applicants with need. Admission notification on a rolling basis beginning on or about 11/1. **Financial aid:** Priority date 3/31; no closing date. FAFSA, institutional form required. Applicants notified on a rolling basis; must reply within 4 week(s) of notification.

Academics. Number of credit hours required for students in major field of study varies by program. **Special study options:** Combined bachelor's/graduate degree, cross-registration, distance learning, dual enrollment of high school students, independent study, internships, liberal arts/career combination, teacher certification program. **Credit/placement by examination:** AP, CLEP, institutional tests. **Support services:** Learning center, pre-admission summer program, reduced course load, remedial instruction, tutoring.

Majors. Business: Business admin. **Communications:** General, broadcast journalism, journalism, media studies, radio/tv. **Communications technology:** General, recording arts. **Education:** Elementary, music. **Visual/performing arts:** General, acting, cinematography, dramatic, film/cinema, jazz, music history, music management, music performance, music theory/composition, piano/organ, stringed instruments, theater design, voice/opera.

Most popular majors. Business/marketing 59%, education 18%, visual/performing arts 22%.

Computing on campus. 84 workstations in library, computer center, student center. Dormitories wired for high-speed internet access and linked to campus network. Helpline, repair service available.

Student life. Freshman orientation: Mandatory. **Housing:** Coed dorms, substance-free housing available. $250 deposit. **Activities:** Bands, choral groups, dance, drama, film society, music ensembles, musical theater, radio station, student government, student newspaper.

Athletics. Team name: Sound.

Student services. Alcohol/substance abuse counseling, career counseling, services for economically disadvantaged, student employment services, financial aid counseling, health services, personal counseling, placement for graduates. **Learning disabled:** Comprehensive services available.

Contact. E-mail: admissions@ftc.edu
Phone: (631) 424-7000 ext. 2110 Fax: (631) 656-2172
Jerry Cohen, Dean of Enrollment Services, Five Towns College, 305 North Service Road, Dix Hills, NY 11746-6055

Fordham University

Bronx, New York — **CB member**
www.fordham.edu — **CB code: 2259**

- Private 4-year university affiliated with Roman Catholic Church
- Residential campus in very large city
- 7,281 degree-seeking undergraduates: 7% part-time, 59% women, 5% African American, 6% Asian American, 12% Hispanic American, 1% international
- 6,594 degree-seeking graduate students
- 50% of applicants admitted
- SAT or ACT (ACT writing optional), application essay required
- 78% graduate within 6 years

General. Founded in 1841. Regionally accredited. Independent institution in Jesuit tradition. Rose Hill campus in Bronx, Lincoln Center campus in Manhattan. **Degrees:** 1,688 bachelor's awarded; master's, doctoral, first professional offered. **ROTC:** Army, Navy, Air Force. **Calendar:** Semester, extensive summer session. **Full-time faculty:** 654 total; 19% minority, 40% women. **Special facilities:** Environmental center in Armonk, seismic station, Fordham Hispanic Research, Third Age Center addressing issues of older population.

Freshman class profile. 15,225 applied, 7,606 admitted, 1,755 enrolled.

Mid 50% test scores		**GPA 2.0-2.99:**	6%
SAT verbal:	560-660	**Rank in top quarter:**	75%
SAT math:	560-650	**Rank in top tenth:**	39%
ACT:	24-28	**Out-of-state:**	48%
GPA 3.50 or higher:	74%	**Live on campus:**	72%
GPA 3.0-3.49:	20%	**International:**	1%

Basis for selection. School achievement record most important followed by test scores, class rank, extracurricular activities, recommendations, essay, personal characteristics. Special consideration given to children of alumni. SAT Subject Tests recommended. Interview recommended for all; audition required for dance, theater programs.

High school preparation. 22 units required; 25 recommended. Required and recommended units include English 4, mathematics 3-4, social studies 2, history 2, science 3-4, foreign language 2-3 and academic electives 6.

2005-2006 Annual costs. Tuition/fees: $27,775. Room/board: $10,895. Books/supplies: $775. Personal expenses: $1,410.

2004-2005 Financial aid. Need-based: 1,332 full-time freshmen applied for aid; 1,162 were judged to have need; 1,147 of these received aid. Average need met was 82%. Average scholarship/grant was $17,493; average loan $3,267. 83% of total undergraduate aid awarded as scholarships/grants, 17% as loans/jobs. **Non-need-based:** Awarded to 977 full-time undergraduates, including 231 freshmen. Scholarships awarded for academics, athletics, ROTC.

Application procedures. Admission: Closing date 1/15 (postmark date). $50 fee, may be waived for applicants with need. Application may be submitted online. Admission notification 4/1. Must reply by May 1 or within 2 week(s) if notified thereafter. **Financial aid:** Closing date 2/1. FAFSA, CSS PROFILE required. Applicants notified on a rolling basis starting 4/1; must reply by 5/1 or within 2 week(s) of notification.

Academics. Special study options: Combined bachelor's/graduate degree, double major, ESL, exchange student, honors, independent study, internships, student-designed major, study abroad, teacher certification program, United Nations semester. Global Program in International Business. **Credit/placement by examination:** CLEP, IB, institutional tests. 32 credit hours maximum toward bachelor's degree. Credit for CLEP examination only offered for liberal studies, adult continuing education school. **Support services:** Pre-admission summer program, tutoring, writing center.

Majors. Area/ethnic studies: African, African-American, American, Latin American, Near/Middle Eastern, Russian/Slavic, women's. **Biology:** General. **Business:** General, accounting, business admin, finance, international, management information systems, managerial economics, market research. **Communications:** General. **Computer sciences:** General. **Foreign languages:** Ancient Greek, classics, comparative lit, French, German, Italian, Latin, modern Greek, Russian, Spanish. **Health:** Predentistry, premedicine, prepharmacy, preveterinary. **History:** General. **Interdisciplinary:** Intercultural. **Legal studies:** Prelaw. **Math:** General. **Philosophy/religion:** Philosophy, religion. **Physical sciences:** Chemistry, physics. **Protective services:** Criminal justice. **Psychology:** General. **Public administration:** General, social work. **Social sciences:** Anthropology, economics, political science, sociology, urban studies. **Visual/performing arts:** Art, art history/conservation, dance, dramatic, film/cinema, photography, studio arts, theater design.

Most popular majors. Business/marketing 25%, communications/journalism 14%, English 7%, psychology 7%, public administration/social services 20%, visual/performing arts 6%.

Computing on campus. 900 workstations in dormitories, library, computer center. Dormitories wired for high-speed internet access and linked to campus network. Commuter students can connect to campus network. Online course registration, helpline, repair service available.

Student life. Freshman orientation: Mandatory, $110 fee. Comprehensive academic and social orientation 3 days prior to start of classes. **Housing:** Guaranteed on-campus for all undergraduates. Coed dorms, apartments available. $200 deposit, deadline 5/1. **Activities:** Bands, choral groups, dance, drama, film society, literary magazine, music ensembles, musical theater, radio station, student government, student newspaper, symphony orchestra, TV station, campus ministries, Rose Hill Ambassadors, international black student union, Progressive Students for Justice, Circle-K, commuter student association, Fordham University Emerging Leaders, Fordham University emergency medical services, weekend activities committee.

Athletics. NCAA. **Intercollegiate:** Baseball M, basketball, cross-country, diving, football (tackle) M, golf M, rowing (crew) W, soccer, softball W, squash M, swimming, tennis, track and field, volleyball W, water polo M.

Intramural: Basketball, football (tackle), golf W, handball, racquetball, soccer, softball, swimming, tennis, triathlon, volleyball. **Team name:** Rams.

Student services. Adult student services, alcohol/substance abuse counseling, campus ministries, career counseling, student employment services, financial aid counseling, health services, personal counseling, placement for graduates. **Physically disabled:** Services for visually, hearing impaired.

Contact. E-mail: enroll@fordham.edu
Phone: (718) 817-4000 Toll-free number: (800) 367-3426
Fax: (718) 367-9404
Peter Farrell, Director of Admissions, Fordham University, East 441 Fordham Road, Bronx, NY 10458

Globe Institute of Technology

New York, New York
www.globe.edu **CB code: 3333**

- For-profit 4-year business and technical college
- Commuter campus in very large city
- 1,712 degree-seeking undergraduates

General. Regionally accredited; also accredited by ACICS. **Degrees:** 48 bachelor's, 30 associate awarded. **ROTC:** Army, Navy, Air Force. **Calendar:** Semester, extensive summer session. **Full-time faculty:** 45 total. **Part-time faculty:** 130 total. **Class size:** 55% < 20, 40% 20-39, 5% 40-49.

Freshman class profile. 500 enrolled.

Mid 50% test scores			
SAT verbal:	500-600	SAT math:	500-600

Basis for selection. Open admission, but selective for some programs. Selective admissions to video game development program. Interviews strongly recommended. **Learning Disabled:** Student should meet with school psychologist to discuss needs.

2006-2007 Annual costs. Tuition/fees: $9,086. Room/board: $4,500. Books/supplies: $800.

Application procedures. Admission: No deadline. $50 fee, may be waived for applicants with need. Application may be submitted online. Admission notification on a rolling basis. **Financial aid:** No deadline. FAFSA, institutional form required. Applicants notified on a rolling basis.

Academics. Special study options: Combined bachelor's/graduate degree, distance learning, ESL, honors, independent study, internships, liberal arts/career combination, weekend college. Globe College of Video Game Development program admits only students in top 15% of graduating class and students with combined SAT score greater than 1350. **Credit/placement by examination:** AP, CLEP, institutional tests. 30 credit hours maximum toward associate degree, 60 toward bachelor's. **Support services:** Learning center, pre-admission summer program, reduced course load, remedial instruction, study skills assistance, tutoring, writing center.

Majors. Business: General, accounting, accounting technology, accounting/business management, accounting/finance, banking/financial services, business admin, customer service, finance, hospitality admin, hotel/motel admin, management information systems, nonprofit/public, office management, operations, resort management, restaurant/food services, small business admin, tourism/travel. **Computer sciences:** General, a.i./robotics, applications programming, computer graphics, computer science, database management, information technology, LAN/WAN management, networking, programming, security, system admin, systems analysis, vendor certification, web page design, webmaster. **Health:** Facilities admin, health care admin, office admin. **Legal studies:** Legal secretary, paralegal.

Most popular majors. Business/marketing 60%, computer/information sciences 20%, health sciences 10%, legal studies 10%.

Computing on campus. 200 workstations in library, computer center, student center. Dormitories wired for high-speed internet access. Commuter students can connect to campus network. Online course registration, online library, helpline, student web hosting, wireless network available.

Student life. Freshman orientation: Mandatory. Preregistration for classes offered. **Policies:** Freshmen permitted cars on campus. **Housing:** Guaranteed on-campus for all undergraduates. Coed dorms, apartments available. **Activities:** Dance, film society, literary magazine, student government, student newspaper, international club, Chinese club, Russian club, Latino club, Wall Street club, Carib club, film club, African club, dance club.

Athletics. NJCAA. **Intercollegiate:** Baseball M, basketball, bowling, cross-country, lacrosse M, soccer, softball W, track and field, volleyball W. **Team name:** Knights.

Student services. Adult student services, alcohol/substance abuse counseling, career counseling, services for economically disadvantaged, student employment services, financial aid counseling, minority student services, personal counseling, placement for graduates, women's services.

Contact. E-mail: admissions@globe.edu
Phone: (212) 349-4330 Toll-free number: (877) 394-5623
Fax: (212) 227-5920
Tatiana Garelik, Admission Director, Globe Institute of Technology, 291 Broadway, New York, NY 10007

Hamilton College

Clinton, New York **CB member**
www.hamilton.edu **CB code: 2286**

- Private 4-year liberal arts college
- Residential campus in small town
- 1,798 degree-seeking undergraduates: 50% women, 4% African American, 6% Asian American, 4% Hispanic American, 1% Native American, 5% international
- 36% of applicants admitted
- Application essay required
- 88% graduate within 6 years

General. Founded in 1812. Regionally accredited. **Degrees:** 423 bachelor's awarded. **ROTC:** Army, Air Force. **Location:** 10 miles from Utica, 50 miles from Syracuse. **Calendar:** Semester. **Full-time faculty:** 174 total; 95% have terminal degrees, 15% minority, 40% women. **Part-time faculty:** 32 total; 59% have terminal degrees, 9% minority, 41% women. **Class size:** 75% < 20, 21% 20-39, 3% 40-49, less than 1% 50-99. **Special facilities:** Observatory, nature preserve, electron microscope.

Freshman class profile. 4,189 applied, 1,502 admitted, 498 enrolled.

Mid 50% test scores			
SAT verbal:	630-720	Return as sophomores:	93%
SAT math:	640-720	Out-of-state:	65%
Rank in top quarter:	91%	Live on campus:	100%
Rank in top tenth:	70%	International:	5%

Basis for selection. School achievement record, rank in high school class, school and community activities, application essay, graded example of expository writing, recommendations important. Test scores and interview also considered. Some preference given children of alumni. Special consideration given students from minority groups, disadvantaged backgrounds, and certain geographic regions. Students can fulfill test requirements with SAT or ACT or 3 SAT Subject Tests or 3 AP exams or any combination of these. Interview recommended for all; audition tape recommended for music applicants; portfolio recommended for studio art applicants.

High school preparation. 16 units recommended. Recommended units include English 4, mathematics 3, social studies 3, science 3 and foreign language 3.

2005-2006 Annual costs. Tuition/fees: $33,350. Room/board: $8,310.

2005-2006 Financial aid. Need-based: 347 full-time freshmen applied for aid; 269 were judged to have need; 269 of these received aid. Average need met was 100%. Average scholarship/grant was $22,175; average loan $2,878. 86% of total undergraduate aid awarded as scholarships/grants, 14% as loans/jobs. **Non-need-based:** Awarded to 137 full-time undergraduates, including 31 freshmen. Scholarships awarded for academics, leadership, state residency. **Additional information:** Will meet demonstrated need of all aided applicants.

Application procedures. Admission: Closing date 1/1 (postmark date). $50 fee, may be waived for applicants with need. Application may be submitted online. Admission notification 4/1. Must reply by 5/1. **Financial aid:** Closing date 1/1. FAFSA, institutional form, CSS PROFILE required. Applicants notified by 4/1; must reply by 5/1.

Academics. Sophomores may attain guaranteed early admission to one of 6 participating medical schools. Students must complete senior program or project in their concentration. May participate in Williams College Mystic Seaport Program. **Special study options:** Accelerated study, combined bachelor's/graduate degree, cross-registration, double major, ESL, independent study, internships, New York semester, student-designed major, study abroad, Washington semester. 3-2 program in engineering with Columbia University, Rensselaer Polytechnic Institute, Washington University (St. Louis); 3-3 program in law at Columbia University. **Credit/placement by examination:** AP, CLEP, IB, institutional tests. **Support services:** Learning center, pre-admission summer program, reduced course load, tutoring, writing center.

Majors. **Area/ethnic studies:** African-American, American, Asian, East Asian, Russian/Slavic, women's. **Biology:** General, biochemistry, molecular. **Communications:** General. **Computer sciences:** General. **English:** British lit, creative writing. **Foreign languages:** General, ancient Greek, Chinese, classics, comparative lit, French, German, Japanese, Latin, Russian, Spanish. **History:** General. **Interdisciplinary:** Biopsychology, neuroscience. **Liberal arts:** Arts/sciences. **Math:** General. **Philosophy/religion:** Philosophy, religion. **Physical sciences:** Chemistry, geology, physics. **Psychology:** General. **Public administration:** Policy analysis. **Social sciences:** Anthropology, archaeology, economics, international relations, political science, sociology. **Visual/performing arts:** Art history/conservation, dance, dramatic, studio arts.

Most popular majors. Biology 6%, English 9%, foreign language 10%, mathematics 6%, physical sciences 6%, psychology 6%, social sciences 35%, visual/performing arts 9%.

Computing on campus. 522 workstations in library, computer center, student center. Dormitories wired for high-speed internet access and linked to campus network. Commuter students can connect to campus network. Online course registration, online library, helpline, repair service, student web hosting, wireless network available.

Student life. **Freshman orientation:** Mandatory. One week prior to start of classes. **Policies:** Honor code covers all examinations, papers, research, and use of library. **Housing:** Guaranteed on-campus for all undergraduates. Coed dorms, special housing for disabled, apartments available. Special interest housing available including language houses and international house, quiet areas, substance-free areas. **Activities:** Bands, choral groups, dance, drama, film society, literary magazine, music ensembles, musical theater, radio station, student government, student newspaper, symphony orchestra, Newman Club, Jewish students organization, Black and Latin student union, women's center, international student association, La Vanguardia, Amnesty International, Muslim student organization, Asian cultural society.

Athletics. NCAA. **Intercollegiate:** Baseball M, basketball, cross-country, diving, field hockey W, football (tackle) M, golf M, ice hockey, lacrosse, rowing (crew), soccer, softball W, squash, swimming, tennis, track and field, volleyball W. **Intramural:** Basketball, cross-country, diving, fencing W, football (non-tackle), football (tackle) M, golf, handball, ice hockey, lacrosse, racquetball, soccer, softball, squash, swimming, tennis, volleyball. **Team name:** Continentals.

Student services. Adult student services, alcohol/substance abuse counseling, campus ministries, career counseling, student employment services, financial aid counseling, health services, minority student services, on-campus daycare, personal counseling, placement for graduates, women's services. **Physically disabled:** Services for visually, speech, hearing impaired.

Contact. E-mail: admission@hamilton.edu
Phone: (315) 859-4421 Toll-free number: (800) 843-2655
Fax: (315) 859-4457
Monica Inzer, Dean of Admissions and Financial Aid, Hamilton College, 198 College Hill Road, Clinton, NY 13323-1293

Hartwick College

Oneonta, New York — **CB member**
www.hartwick.edu — **CB code: 2288**

- Private 4-year liberal arts college
- Residential campus in large town
- 1,444 degree-seeking undergraduates: 3% part-time, 57% women, 5% African American, 1% Asian American, 4% Hispanic American, 1% Native American, 4% international
- 87% of applicants admitted
- Application essay required
- 55% graduate within 6 years; 23% enter graduate study

General. Founded in 1797. Regionally accredited. Additional campus for recreation, research, student residences. **Degrees:** 289 bachelor's awarded. **ROTC:** Army, Air Force. **Location:** 68 miles from Binghamton, 75 miles from Albany. **Calendar:** Semester, limited summer session. **Full-time faculty:** 108 total; 94% have terminal degrees, 6% minority, 39% women. **Part-time faculty:** 61 total; 46% women. **Class size:** 64% < 20, 35% 20-39, less than 1% 40-49, less than 1% 50-99. **Special facilities:** Environmental field station, museum, Native American artifact and library collections, tissue culture laboratory, electron microscope, 16-inch telescope, observatory, nuclear magnetic resonance spectrometer, fine and performing arts center.

Freshman class profile. 2,211 applied, 1,928 admitted, 409 enrolled.

Mid 50% test scores		**Return as sophomores:**	76%
SAT verbal:	520-620	**Out-of-state:**	39%
SAT math:	510-620	**Live on campus:**	99%
Rank in top tenth:	24%	**International:**	4%

Basis for selection. School achievement record, class rank, personal qualities, extracurricular activities, and recommendations considered. Test scores optional. Early action applicants must submit scores by Jan. 1. Interview recommended for all; audition required for music program; portfolio recommended for art program. **Homeschooled:** Letter of recommendation (nonparent) required. Must meet all stated application requirements and submit SAT or ACT test score. At least 3 SAT Subject Tests strongly recommended. Transcripts should be submitted with course description and/or syllabi.

High school preparation. 19 units recommended. Recommended units include English 4, mathematics 3, social studies 2, history 2, science 3 (laboratory 2) and foreign language 3.

2006-2007 Annual costs. Tuition/fees: $29,605. New students (freshmen and transfers) must purchase laptop from the college; cost of computer ($1,575) is included in required fees for 2006/2007: $2,155. Room/board: $7,910. Books/supplies: $700. Personal expenses: $400.

2005-2006 Financial aid. **Need-based:** 350 full-time freshmen applied for aid; 310 were judged to have need; 310 of these received aid. Average need met was 82%. Average scholarship/grant was $9,065; average loan $3,861. 67% of total undergraduate aid awarded as scholarships/grants, 33% as loans/jobs. **Non-need-based:** Awarded to 1,077 full-time undergraduates, including 357 freshmen. Scholarships awarded for academics, alumni affiliation, athletics, leadership, state residency.

Application procedures. **Admission:** Closing date 2/15. $35 fee, may be waived for applicants with need. Application may be submitted online. Admission notification 3/15. Must reply by May 1 or within 2 week(s) if notified thereafter. **Financial aid:** Priority date 2/15; no closing date. FAFSA, institutional form required. Applicants notified on a rolling basis starting 2/16; must reply by 5/1 or within 2 week(s) of notification.

Academics. Curriculum XXI includes first year seminar, core requirements and contemporary issues seminar. Senior thesis required. First-year students provided with notebook-sized personal computer. **Special study options:** Accelerated study, combined bachelor's/graduate degree, cross-registration, double major, exchange student, honors, independent study, internships, liberal arts/career combination, student-designed major, study abroad, teacher certification program, urban semester, Washington semester. Off-campus January term in Thailand, Germany, France, China, Hungary, Ireland, Mexico; Philadelphia Urban Semester; Boston Semester; Outward Bound, NOLS programs; cooperative program in law with Albany Law School; study abroad programs in 15 countries including Kenya, China, Japan, India; 3-2 engineering with Clarkson University, Columbia University. **Credit/placement by examination:** AP, CLEP, IB, institutional tests. **Support services:** Reduced course load, study skills assistance, tutoring, writing center.

Majors. **Biology:** General, biochemistry. **Business:** Accounting, business admin. **Computer sciences:** General, information systems. **Education:** Music. **English:** English lit. **Foreign languages:** French, German, Spanish. **Health:** Clinical lab science, nursing (RN). **History:** General. **Liberal arts:** Arts/sciences. **Math:** General. **Philosophy/religion:** Philosophy, religion. **Physical sciences:** Chemistry, geology, physics. **Psychology:** General. **Social sciences:** Anthropology, economics, political science, sociology. **Visual/performing arts:** Art, art history/conservation, dramatic.

Most popular majors. Biology 7%, business/marketing 18%, English 6%, health sciences 6%, history 6%, psychology 11%, social sciences 22%, visual/performing arts 12%.

Computing on campus. PC or laptop required. 56 workstations in library, computer center. Dormitories wired for high-speed internet access and linked to campus network. Commuter students can connect to campus network. Online library, helpline, repair service, student web hosting, wireless network available.

Student life. **Freshman orientation:** Mandatory, $300 fee. Preregistration for classes offered. Summer registration/parent orientation; 4-day pre-semester in residence program. **Policies:** Freshmen permitted cars on campus. **Housing:** Guaranteed on-campus for freshmen. Coed dorms, single-sex dorms, special housing for disabled, apartments, fraternity/sorority housing, substance-free housing available. Special interest housing, housing at environmental campus available. **Activities:** Bands, choral groups, dance, drama, literary magazine, music ensembles, musical theater, radio station, student government, student newspaper, TV station, over 60 academic and social organizations available.

Athletics. NCAA. **Intercollegiate:** Baseball M, basketball, cross-country, diving, equestrian W, field hockey W, football (tackle) M, golf M, lacrosse, soccer, softball W, swimming, tennis, track and field, volleyball W, water polo W. **Intramural:** Archery, badminton, basketball, cross-country, equestrian, football (tackle), golf, racquetball, soccer, softball W, squash, swimming, table tennis, tennis, track and field, volleyball, water polo. **Team name:** Hawks.

Student services. Alcohol/substance abuse counseling, campus ministries, career counseling, student employment services, financial aid counseling, health services, personal counseling, placement for graduates. **Physically disabled:** Services for visually, hearing impaired.

Contact. E-mail: admissions@hartwick.edu
Phone: (607) 431-4150 Toll-free number: (888) 427-8942
Fax: (607) 431-4154
Jacqueline Gregory, Director of Admissions, Hartwick College, Box 4022, Oneonta, NY 13820-4022

Hilbert College
Hamburg, New York
www.hilbert.edu **CB code: 2334**

- Private 4-year liberal arts college affiliated with Roman Catholic Church
- Commuter campus in large town
- 1,059 degree-seeking undergraduates: 22% part-time, 63% women, 4% African American, 1% Asian American, 2% Hispanic American, 2% Native American
- 94% of applicants admitted
- 48% graduate within 6 years; 10% enter graduate study

General. Founded in 1957. Regionally accredited. Affiliated with Franciscan Sisters of St. Joseph. Legal assistant program approved by American Bar Association. **Degrees:** 249 bachelor's, 32 associate awarded. **ROTC:** Army. **Location:** 10 miles from Buffalo. **Calendar:** Semester, limited summer session. **Full-time faculty:** 43 total; 49% have terminal degrees, 44% women. **Part-time faculty:** 58 total; 29% have terminal degrees, 7% minority, 40% women. **Class size:** 72% < 20, 28% 20-39. **Special facilities:** Comprehensive law library.

Freshman class profile. 423 applied, 399 admitted, 165 enrolled.

Mid 50% test scores			
SAT verbal:	370-530	Rank in top quarter:	14%
SAT math:	390-540	Rank in top tenth:	4%
ACT:	18-23	End year in good standing:	70%
GPA 3.50 or higher:	15%	Return as sophomores:	79%
GPA 3.0-3.49:	27%	Out-of-state:	2%
GPA 2.0-2.99:	52%	Live on campus:	30%

Basis for selection. School achievement record and course selection important. Candidates must meet minimum academic criteria including high school GPA, class rank, and test scores. SAT or ACT recommended. Essay, interview recommended. **Homeschooled:** Transcript of courses and grades, state high school equivalency certificate required. **Learning Disabled:** Separate statement directly to academic services required.

High school preparation. 17 units required; 19 recommended. Required and recommended units include English 4, mathematics 2-3, social studies 2-3, history 2, science 2-3 (laboratory 1), foreign language 1 and academic electives 4.

2005-2006 Annual costs. Tuition/fees: $14,900. Room/board: $5,580. Books/supplies: $700. Personal expenses: $800.

2005-2006 Financial aid. Need-based: Average need met was 73%. Average scholarship/grant was $8,466; average loan $3,560. 53% of total undergraduate aid awarded as scholarships/grants, 47% as loans/jobs. **Non-need-based:** Scholarships awarded for academics, leadership, minority status, state residency.

Application procedures. Admission: Priority date 6/30; deadline 9/1 (receipt date). $20 fee, may be waived for applicants with need. Application may be submitted online. Admission notification on a rolling basis beginning on or about 6/30. **Financial aid:** Priority date 3/1; no closing date. FAFSA required. Applicants notified on a rolling basis starting 3/15; must reply within 2 week(s) of notification.

Academics. Special study options: Combined bachelor's/graduate degree, cooperative education, cross-registration, dual enrollment of high school students, honors, independent study, internships, study abroad, Washington semester. Member of Western New York consortium. **Credit/placement by examination:** AP, CLEP, IB, SAT, institutional tests. 18 credit hours maximum toward associate degree, 32 toward bachelor's. **Support services:** Learning center, reduced course load, tutoring, writing center.

Majors. Business: Accounting, business admin, finance. **Legal studies:** Paralegal. **Liberal arts:** Arts/sciences. **Protective services:** Criminal justice. **Psychology:** General. **Public administration:** Human services.

Computing on campus. 146 workstations in dormitories, library, computer center, student center. Dormitories wired for high-speed internet access. Online course registration, wireless network available.

Student life. Freshman orientation: Mandatory, $20 fee. Two 1-day programs. **Policies:** Freshmen permitted cars on campus. **Housing:** Guaranteed on-campus for all undergraduates. Coed dorms, apartments available. $50 nonrefundable deposit, deadline 8/1. **Activities:** Choral groups, drama, literary magazine, student government, student newspaper, SADD, wellness club, human service association, psychology club, great expectations, criminal justice club, accounting and business club, students in free enterprise, campus ministry club.

Athletics. NCAA. **Intercollegiate:** Baseball M, basketball, cross-country, golf, soccer, softball W, volleyball. **Intramural:** Basketball, football (non-tackle), soccer, softball, table tennis, volleyball. **Team name:** Hawks.

Student services. Adult student services, alcohol/substance abuse counseling, campus ministries, career counseling, student employment services, financial aid counseling, personal counseling, placement for graduates, veterans' counselor. **Physically disabled:** Services for visually, hearing impaired.

Contact. E-mail: admissions@hilbert.edu
Phone: (716) 649-7900 ext. 211 Toll-free number: (800) 649-8003
Fax: (716) 649-0702
Harry Gong, Director of Admissions, Hilbert College, 5200 South Park Avenue, Hamburg, NY 14075-1597

Hobart and William Smith Colleges
Geneva, New York **CB member**
www.hws.edu **CB code: 2294**

- Private 4-year liberal arts college
- Residential campus in large town
- 1,855 degree-seeking undergraduates: 54% women, 3% African American, 2% Asian American, 4% Hispanic American, 2% international
- 15 degree-seeking graduate students
- 65% of applicants admitted
- SAT or ACT (ACT writing recommended), application essay required
- 69% graduate within 6 years; 31% enter graduate study

General. Founded in 1822. Regionally accredited. Hobart (1822) and William Smith (1908) are coordinate colleges. All classes coeducational but one faculty, one President, one Board of Trustees, one campus; residences both coed and single sex. Separate deans, student governments, athletic departments due to separate founding. **Degrees:** 491 bachelor's awarded; master's offered. **Location:** 50 miles from Syracuse, 40 miles from Rochester. **Calendar:** Semester. **Full-time faculty:** 156 total; 94% have terminal degrees, 13% minority, 41% women. **Part-time faculty:** 29 total; 97% have terminal degrees, 17% minority, 55% women. **Class size:** 66% < 20, 32% 20-39, 2% 40-49, less than 1% 50-99. **Special facilities:** 70-foot research vessel, 100-acre nature preserve, Finger Lakes Institute.

Freshman class profile. 3,410 applied, 2,209 admitted, 545 enrolled.

Mid 50% test scores			
SAT verbal:	530-640	Rank in top tenth:	33%
SAT math:	540-630	End year in good standing:	85%
GPA 3.50 or higher:	31%	Return as sophomores:	85%
GPA 3.0-3.49:	38%	Out-of-state:	60%
GPA 2.0-2.99:	31%	Live on campus:	100%
Rank in top quarter:	67%	International:	1%

Basis for selection. Secondary school record, school and community activities, recommendations, and test scores important. Interview and talent considered. Economically and educationally disadvantaged New York State students may apply through Higher Education Opportunity Program. Interview recommended for all. Candidates for arts scholars program must submit portfolio or audition on campus. **Homeschooled:** Interview required.

High school preparation. 20 units required. Required and recommended units include English 4, mathematics 3, social studies 2-3, history 2, science 3 (laboratory 2), foreign language 2-3 and academic electives 2-4. Mathematics must include algebra, geometry, and trigonometry sequence.

2005-2006 Annual costs. Tuition/fees: $32,737. Room/board: $8,386. Books/supplies: $850. Personal expenses: $600.

2005-2006 Financial aid. Need-based: Average need met was 90%. Average scholarship/grant was $22,193; average loan $2,394. 79% of total undergraduate aid awarded as scholarships/grants, 21% as loans/jobs. **Non-need-based:** Scholarships awarded for academics, art, leadership, music/drama.

Application procedures. Admission: Closing date 2/1 (postmark date). $45 fee, may be waived for applicants with need. Application may be submitted online. Admission notification 4/1. Must reply by 5/1. **Financial aid:** Closing date 2/1. FAFSA, CSS PROFILE required. Applicants notified by 4/1; must reply by 5/1 or within 2 week(s) of notification.

Academics. All students must complete a major and a minor or a second major, 1 of which must be interdisciplinary. **Special study options:** Combined bachelor's/graduate degree, cross-registration, double major, ESL, exchange student, honors, independent study, internships, New York semester, semester at sea, student-designed major, study abroad, teacher certification program, United Nations semester, urban semester, Washington semester. Architecture and urban studies program in New York City and Los Angeles, combined degree program in architecture with Washington University, Missouri, in engineering with Dartmouth College, Rensselaer Polytechnic Institute, and Columbia University, study abroad programs in nearly 30 countries. **Credit/placement by examination:** AP, CLEP, IB, institutional tests. Credit by examination counted toward degree limited to equivalent of 7 courses. **Support services:** Learning center, pre-admission summer program, reduced course load, study skills assistance, tutoring, writing center.

Majors. Architecture: Architecture. **Area/ethnic studies:** African, African-American, American, Asian, European, gay/lesbian, Hispanic-American/Latino/Chicano, Latin American, Russian/Slavic, women's. **Biology:** General, biochemistry. **Communications:** Media studies. **Computer sciences:** General, computer science. **Conservation:** Environmental studies. **Foreign languages:** Chinese, classics, comparative lit, French, Japanese, Latin, Russian, Spanish. **Health:** Predentistry, premedicine, preveterinary. **History:** General. **Interdisciplinary:** Math/computer science. **Math:** General. **Philosophy/religion:** Philosophy, religion. **Physical sciences:** Chemistry, geology, physics. **Psychology:** General. **Public administration:** Policy analysis. **Social sciences:** Anthropology, economics, international relations, political science, sociology, urban studies. **Visual/performing arts:** Art history/conservation, dance, dramatic, studio arts.

Most popular majors. Area/ethnic studies 7%, English 10%, history 9%, physical sciences 7%, psychology 7%, social sciences 19%, visual/performing arts 6%.

Computing on campus. 150 workstations in library, computer center. Dormitories wired for high-speed internet access and linked to campus network. Commuter students can connect to campus network. Online course registration, online library, helpline, repair service, student web hosting, wireless network available.

Student life. Freshman orientation: Mandatory. Preregistration for classes offered. 3-day program. **Policies:** Freshmen permitted cars on campus. **Housing:** Guaranteed on-campus for all undergraduates. Coed dorms, single-sex dorms, apartments, cooperative housing, fraternity/sorority housing, substance-free housing available. Theme residences, upperclassmen townhouses available. Undergraduates not residing in college housing live in own apartments off campus. Extensive residential education program. **Activities:** Bands, choral groups, dance, drama, film society, literary magazine, music ensembles, musical theater, radio station, student government, student newspaper, symphony orchestra, Service Network, Literary Corps, international students club, denominational clubs, African-American Student Coalition, political educational network, Pan-African-Latin Organization, Pride Network, Big Brothers/Big Sisters, Latin American Student Organization.

Athletics. NCAA. **Intercollegiate:** Basketball, cross-country, diving W, field hockey W, football (tackle) M, golf, ice hockey M, lacrosse, rowing (crew), sailing, soccer, squash, swimming W, tennis. **Intramural:** Archery, badminton, basketball, bowling, cross-country, diving M, equestrian, fencing, football (non-tackle), golf, gymnastics M, ice hockey, lacrosse, racquetball, rowing (crew), rugby, skiing, soccer M, softball, squash, swimming, table tennis M, tennis, track and field M, volleyball, water polo M. **Team name:** Statesmen (Hobart); Herons (William Smith).

Student services. Adult student services, alcohol/substance abuse counseling, campus ministries, career counseling, services for economically disadvantaged, student employment services, financial aid counseling, health services, legal services, minority student services, personal counseling, placement for graduates, women's services. **Physically disabled:** Services for visually, speech, hearing impaired.

Contact. E-mail: admissions@hws.edu
Phone: (315) 781-3622 Toll-free number: (800) 852-2256
Fax: (315) 781-3914
John Young, Director of Admissions, Hobart and William Smith Colleges, 629 South Main Street, Geneva, NY 14456

Hofstra University

Hempstead, New York — **CB member**
www.hofstra.edu — **CB code: 2295**

- Private 4-year university
- Residential campus in large city
- 8,701 degree-seeking undergraduates: 9% part-time, 53% women, 9% African American, 5% Asian American, 8% Hispanic American, 2% international
- 3,765 degree-seeking graduate students
- 62% of applicants admitted
- Application essay required
- 55% graduate within 6 years; 27% enter graduate study

General. Founded in 1935. Regionally accredited. **Degrees:** 1,822 bachelor's awarded; master's, doctoral, first professional offered. **ROTC:** Army. **Location:** 25 miles from New York City. **Calendar:** 4-1-4, extensive summer session. **Full-time faculty:** 527 total; 90% have terminal degrees, 15% minority, 40% women. **Part-time faculty:** 719 total; 32% have terminal degrees, 8% minority, 50% women. **Class size:** 45% < 20, 48% 20-39, 3% 40-49, 3% 50-99, less than 1% >100. **Special facilities:** Financial trading room, comprehensive media production facility, career center, writing center, Linux Beowolf cluster, digital language lab, technology, science and engineering labs, rooftop observatory, 7 theaters, assessment centers for child observation and counseling, child care institute, cultural center, museum, arboretum, bird sanctuary.

Freshman class profile. 15,981 applied, 9,953 admitted, 1,774 enrolled.

Mid 50% test scores			
SAT verbal:	520-620	Rank in top quarter:	47%
SAT math:	540-620	Rank in top tenth:	24%
ACT:	21-26	End year in good standing:	87%
GPA 3.50 or higher:	34%	Return as sophomores:	78%
GPA 3.0-3.49:	31%	Out-of-state:	46%
GPA 2.0-2.99:	34%	Live on campus:	73%
		International:	1%

Basis for selection. Secondary school record, standardized test scores (SAT or ACT), personal essay and letters of recommendation most important. SAT Subject Tests recommended. Standardized test not required for admission to Saturday College, PALS, and School for University Studies. Interview required of HEOP, special studies, and academic learning skills applicants. Audition recommended for music, theater programs; portfolio recommended for fine arts program. **Homeschooled:** Transcript of courses and grades required. Must provide at least 2 recommendations, including 1 from primary instructor or person who has primary responsibility for assessing applicant's academic performance. School required to certify completion of secondary school for all enrolled students prior to graduation. **Learning Disabled:** Students may apply to the Program for Academic Learning Skills. Application includes copy of psychological testing, WAISR or WISC.

High school preparation. 16 units required. Required and recommended units include English 4, mathematics 3-4, social studies 3-4, science 3-4 (laboratory 1-2) and foreign language 2-3. Social studies includes history; 4 mathematics, 1 chemistry, and 1 physics required for engineering.

2005-2006 Annual costs. Tuition/fees: $23,130. Room/board: $9,500. Books/supplies: $1,000. Personal expenses: $1,150.

2005-2006 Financial aid. Need-based: 1,400 full-time freshmen applied for aid; 1,110 were judged to have need; 1,090 of these received aid. Average need met was 55%. Average scholarship/grant was $10,100; average loan $3,025. 47% of total undergraduate aid awarded as scholarships/grants, 53% as loans/jobs. **Non-need-based:** Awarded to 1,705 full-time undergraduates, including 535 freshmen. Scholarships awarded for academics, art, athletics, leadership, music/drama, ROTC, state residency. **Additional information:** Special financial aid funds may be available for applicants with special talents, those with superior academic ability, minority applicants, and low/middle income applicants.

Application procedures. Admission: No deadline. $50 fee, may be waived for applicants with need. Application may be submitted online. Admission notification on a rolling basis beginning on or about 2/1. Must reply by May 1 or within 2 week(s) if notified thereafter. **Financial aid:** Priority date 2/15; no closing date. FAFSA required. Applicants notified on a rolling basis starting 3/15; must reply within 2 week(s) of notification.

Academics. **Special study options:** Accelerated study, combined bachelor's/graduate degree, cross-registration, double major, dual enrollment of high school students, ESL, external degree, honors, independent study, internships, liberal arts/career combination, student-designed major, study abroad, teacher certification program, Washington semester, weekend college. **Credit/placement by examination:** AP, CLEP, IB, institutional tests. 30 credit hours maximum toward bachelor's degree. **Support services:** Learning center, pre-admission summer program, reduced course load, study skills assistance, tutoring, writing center.

Honors college/program. Students invited to join when applying for admission. Typically only top 8% of all applicants offered invitation. During first year, students enroll in small multidisciplinary courses. After first year, students choose from wide range of honors-level courses in all academic areas of study.

Majors. **Area/ethnic studies:** African, American, Asian, Caribbean, Hispanic-American/Latino/Chicano, Latin American. **Biology:** General, biochemistry. **Business:** General, accounting, actuarial science, business admin, entrepreneurial studies, finance, international, labor studies, management information systems, managerial economics, marketing. **Communications:** General, broadcast journalism, journalism, media studies, public relations, radio/tv. **Computer sciences:** Computer science. **Conservation:** Environmental studies. **Education:** Art, biology, business, chemistry, early childhood, elementary, English, foreign languages, French, German, health, mathematics, multi-level teacher, music, physical, physics, science, secondary, social studies, Spanish. **Engineering:** Biomedical, civil, computer, electrical, environmental, industrial, manufacturing, mechanical, science. **English:** British lit, creative writing, English lit. **Foreign languages:** Classics, comparative lit, French, German, Hebrew, Italian, Latin, linguistics, Russian, Spanish. **Health:** Athletic training, audiology/speech pathology, community health, physician assistant, predentistry, premedicine, preveterinary. **History:** General. **Interdisciplinary:** Math/computer science, natural sciences. **Legal studies:** Prelaw. **Liberal arts:** Arts/sciences, humanities. **Math:** General, applied. **Philosophy/religion:** Judaic, philosophy. **Physical sciences:** Chemistry, geology, physics. **Psychology:** General. **Social sciences:** General, anthropology, econometrics, economics, geography, political science, sociology. **Visual/performing arts:** Acting, art history/conservation, ceramics, dance, directing/producing, dramatic, jazz, metal/jewelry, music history, music management, music performance, music theory/composition, painting, photography, studio arts.

Most popular majors. Business/marketing 34%, communications/journalism 15%, education 9%, psychology 12%, social sciences 7%.

Computing on campus. 1,601 workstations in library, computer center. Dormitories wired for high-speed internet access and linked to campus network. Commuter students can connect to campus network. Online course registration, online library, helpline, repair service, student web hosting, wireless network available.

Student life. **Freshman orientation:** Available, $100 fee. Preregistration for classes offered. 3-day program in which students invited to live on campus. **Policies:** Freshmen permitted cars on campus. **Housing:** Guaranteed on-campus for freshmen. Coed dorms, single-sex dorms, special housing for disabled, apartments available. $300 nonrefundable deposit, deadline 5/1. Honors housing, living-learning centers, and quiet floors available. **Activities:** Bands, choral groups, dance, drama, film society, literary magazine, music ensembles, musical theater, opera, radio station, student government, student newspaper, symphony orchestra, TV station, Christian InterVarsity Fellowship, Hillel, Muslim student association, Karma, Mitrah Mommas, Iranian Jews, Newman club, African people's organization, Hellenic society.

Athletics. NCAA. **Intercollegiate:** Baseball M, basketball, cross-country, field hockey W, football (tackle) M, golf, lacrosse, soccer, softball W, tennis, volleyball W, wrestling M. **Intramural:** Badminton, basketball, football (non-tackle) W, football (tackle), soccer, softball, table tennis, tennis, volleyball, weight lifting. **Team name:** Pride.

Student services. Adult student services, alcohol/substance abuse counseling, campus ministries, career counseling, student employment services, financial aid counseling, health services, minority student services, on-campus daycare, personal counseling, placement for graduates. **Physically disabled:** Services for visually, speech, hearing impaired. **Learning disabled:** Comprehensive services available.

Contact. E-mail: admitme@hofstra.edu
Phone: (516) 463-6700 Toll-free number: (800) 463-7872
Fax: (516) 463-5100
Jessica Eads, Dean of Undergraduate Admissions Operations, Hofstra University, Admissions Center, 100 Hofstra University, Hempstead, NY 11549

Holy Trinity Orthodox Seminary

Jordanville, New York
www.hts.edu **CB code: 2298**

- Private 5-year seminary college for men affiliated with Russian Orthodox Church
- Residential campus in rural community
- 20 degree-seeking undergraduates: 5% Hispanic American, 60% international
- 79% of applicants admitted
- Application essay required

General. Founded in 1948. Regionally accredited. **Degrees:** 11 bachelor's awarded. **Location:** 20 miles from Utica. **Calendar:** Semester, limited summer session. **Full-time faculty:** 6 total; 17% have terminal degrees, 17% women. **Part-time faculty:** 13 total; 8% have terminal degrees, 8% women. **Special facilities:** Museum of Russian history, archives, icon painting studio.

Freshman class profile. 14 applied, 11 admitted, 7 enrolled.

Out-of-state:	50%	Live on campus:	100%

Basis for selection. Orthodoxy/Orthodox baptism, knowledge of Russian, entrance exam required. Recommendation from spiritual father or parish priest important. **Homeschooled:** Letter of recommendation (nonparent) required.

2005-2006 Annual costs. Tuition/fees: $2,000.

Application procedures. **Admission:** Closing date 5/1 (postmark date). No application fee.

Academics. **Special study options:** Distance learning. **Credit/placement by examination:** CLEP, institutional tests. **Support services:** Remedial instruction, tutoring.

Majors. **Theology:** Theology.

Computing on campus. 7 workstations in computer center.

Student life. **Freshman orientation:** Mandatory. **Policies:** Religious observance required. Freshmen permitted cars on campus. **Housing:** Guaranteed on-campus for all undergraduates. Substance-free housing available. **Activities:** Choral groups, student newspaper.

Contact. E-mail: info@hts.edu
Phone: (315) 858-0945
Dc. Vladimir Tsurikov, Assistant Dean, Holy Trinity Orthodox Seminary, Box 36, Jordanville, NY 13361

Houghton College

Houghton, New York **CB member**
www.houghton.edu **CB code: 2299**

- Private 4-year liberal arts college affiliated with Wesleyan Church
- Residential campus in rural community
- 1,368 degree-seeking undergraduates: 3% part-time, 67% women, 3% African American, 1% Asian American, 1% Hispanic American, 3% international
- 13 degree-seeking graduate students
- 77% of applicants admitted
- SAT or ACT (ACT writing optional), application essay required
- 65% graduate within 6 years; 42% enter graduate study

General. Founded in 1883. Regionally accredited. All students receive laptop computer and printer as part of tuition. Extension campuses in suburban Buffalo and in Adirondack Park. School of Music accredited by National Association of Schools of Music. **Degrees:** 405 bachelor's, 4 associate awarded; master's offered. **ROTC:** Army. **Location:** 60 miles from Buffalo, 70 miles from Rochester. **Calendar:** Semester, limited summer session. **Full-time faculty:** 83 total; 81% have terminal degrees, 6% minority, 22% women. **Part-time faculty:** 21 total; 14% have terminal degrees, 62% women. **Class size:** 64% < 20, 32% 20-39, 1% 40-49, 2% 50-99. **Special facilities:** Equestrian center with indoor riding ring, initiatives course, downhill and cross-country skiing facilities, ropes course.

Freshman class profile. 1,176 applied, 908 admitted, 322 enrolled.

Mid 50% test scores		Rank in top quarter:	68%
SAT verbal:	530-660	Rank in top tenth:	32%
SAT math:	520-630	End year in good standing:	94%
ACT:	24-28	Return as sophomores:	84%
GPA 3.50 or higher:	66%	Out-of-state:	38%
GPA 3.0-3.49:	25%	Live on campus:	96%
GPA 2.0-2.99:	9%	International:	4%

Basis for selection. Class rank, GPA, test scores, pastor's recommendation, essays required. Interview recommended for all; audition required for music program; portfolio recommended for art program. **Homeschooled:** Applicants should take SAT or ACT.

High school preparation. College-preparatory program recommended. 16 units recommended. Recommended units include English 4, mathematics 3, social studies 1, history 2, science 2 (laboratory 2) and foreign language 2. Mathematics should include 1 algebra, 1 geometry.

2006-2007 Annual costs. Tuition/fees: $20,400. Tuition includes laptop computer, printer, fees. Room/board: $6,680. Books/supplies: $750. Personal expenses: $750.

2004-2005 Financial aid. Need-based: 319 full-time freshmen applied for aid; 299 were judged to have need; 299 of these received aid. Average need met was 75%. Average scholarship/grant was $11,337; average loan $3,306. 51% of total undergraduate aid awarded as scholarships/grants, 49% as loans/jobs. **Non-need-based:** Awarded to 267 full-time undergraduates, including 44 freshmen. Scholarships awarded for academics, alumni affiliation, art, athletics, music/drama, religious affiliation, ROTC, state residency.

Application procedures. Admission: No deadline. $40 fee, may be waived for applicants with need. Application may be submitted online. Admission notification on a rolling basis beginning on or about 1/1. Must reply by May 1 or within 4 week(s) if notified thereafter. **Financial aid:** Priority date 3/1; no closing date. FAFSA required. Applicants notified on a rolling basis starting 3/15; must reply by 5/1 or within 4 week(s) of notification.

Academics. Special study options: Cross-registration, double major, exchange student, honors, independent study, internships, liberal arts/career combination, study abroad, teacher certification program, Washington semester. **Credit/placement by examination:** AP, CLEP, IB, SAT, ACT. 16 credit hours maximum toward associate degree, 32 toward bachelor's. **Support services:** Learning center, reduced course load, study skills assistance, tutoring, writing center.

Majors. Biology: General, environmental. **Business:** General, accounting, business admin. **Communications:** General. **Computer sciences:** Computer science, information technology. **Education:** General, biology, chemistry, elementary, English, foreign languages, French, mathematics, music, physical, physics, secondary, social science, social studies, Spanish. **English:** English lit. **Foreign languages:** French, Spanish. **Health:** Predentistry, premedicine, preveterinary. **History:** General. **Interdisciplinary:** Natural sciences. **Math:** General. **Parks/recreation:** General, health/fitness. **Philosophy/religion:** Philosophy, religion. **Physical sciences:** Chemistry, physics. **Psychology:** General. **Social sciences:** International relations, political science, sociology. **Theology:** Bible, theology. **Visual/performing arts:** Art, music performance, music theory/composition, piano/organ, stringed instruments, studio arts, voice/opera.

Most popular majors. Biology 7%, business/marketing 27%, education 15%, English 8%, psychology 7%, theological studies 7%, visual/performing arts 6%.

Computing on campus. PC or laptop required. 8 workstations in dormitories, library, computer center, student center. Dormitories wired for high-speed internet access and linked to campus network. Commuter students can connect to campus network. Helpline, repair service, wireless network available.

Student life. Freshman orientation: Mandatory. Preregistration for classes offered. 2-day event held spring semester prior to fall start. **Policies:** Drinking of alcoholic beverages and smoking on or off campus prohibited. Religious observance required. Freshmen permitted cars on campus. **Housing:** Guaranteed on-campus for freshmen. Single-sex dorms, special housing for disabled, apartments, substance-free housing available. $300 nonrefundable deposit, deadline 5/1. Townhouses and apartments available. **Activities:** Bands, choral groups, drama, literary magazine, music ensembles, musical theater, opera, student government, student newspaper, symphony orchestra, Allegany County Outreach, World Missions Fellowship, Habitat for Humanity, Youth for Christ, fellowship of Christian athletes, cross-cultural student society.

Athletics. NAIA. **Intercollegiate:** Basketball, cross-country, field hockey W, soccer, track and field, volleyball W. **Intramural:** Basketball, equestrian, football (non-tackle) M, racquetball, soccer, volleyball, water polo. **Team name:** Highlanders.

Student services. Campus ministries, career counseling, student employment services, financial aid counseling, health services, personal counseling, placement for graduates.

Contact. E-mail: admission@houghton.edu
Phone: (585) 567-9353 Toll-free number: (800) 777-2556
Fax: (585) 567-9522
Timothy Fuller, Vice President for Enrollment Management, Houghton College, One Willard Avenue/Box 128, Houghton, NY 14744-0128

Iona College

New Rochelle, New York — **CB member**
www.iona.edu — **CB code: 2324**

- Private 4-year business and liberal arts college affiliated with Roman Catholic Church
- Commuter campus in small city
- 3,327 degree-seeking undergraduates: 6% part-time, 54% women, 7% African American, 2% Asian American, 11% Hispanic American, 2% international
- 812 degree-seeking graduate students
- 67% of applicants admitted
- SAT or ACT (ACT writing optional), application essay required
- 56% graduate within 6 years; 67% enter graduate study

General. Founded in 1940. Regionally accredited. Independent institution in Roman Catholic, Christian Brothers tradition. **Degrees:** 649 bachelor's awarded; master's offered. **ROTC:** Army, Air Force. **Location:** 20 miles from New York City. **Calendar:** Semester, extensive summer session. **Full-time faculty:** 176 total; 92% have terminal degrees, 9% minority, 35% women. **Part-time faculty:** 197 total; 41% have terminal degrees, 9% minority, 41% women. **Class size:** 43% < 20, 56% 20-39, 1% 40-49. **Special facilities:** Extensive Irish and rare books collection.

Freshman class profile. 4,802 applied, 3,217 admitted, 779 enrolled.

Mid 50% test scores		Rank in top quarter:	51%
SAT verbal:	510-610	Rank in top tenth:	29%
SAT math:	520-610	Return as sophomores:	80%
GPA 3.50 or higher:	28%	Out-of-state:	25%
GPA 3.0-3.49:	32%	Live on campus:	63%
GPA 2.0-2.99:	40%	International:	2%

Basis for selection. High school curriculum and GPA most important, followed by test scores, recommendations, interview, extracurricular activities, essays, grade trends. Interviews recommended. **Homeschooled:** Transcript of courses and grades, interview required.

High school preparation. 16 units required; 20 recommended. Required and recommended units include English 4, mathematics 3-4, social studies 1, history 1-2, science 2-3 (laboratory 2), foreign language 2 and academic electives 1-2.

2006-2007 Annual costs. Tuition/fees: $23,218. Room/board: $9,998. Books/supplies: $700. Personal expenses: $1,250.

2005-2006 Financial aid. Need-based: 763 full-time freshmen applied for aid; 613 were judged to have need; 608 of these received aid. Average need met was 19%. Average scholarship/grant was $3,788; average loan $2,367. 51% of total undergraduate aid awarded as scholarships/grants, 49% as loans/jobs. **Non-need-based:** Awarded to 2,999 full-time undergraduates, including 794 freshmen. Scholarships awarded for academics, alumni affiliation, athletics, ROTC.

Application procedures. Admission: Closing date 2/15 (postmark date). $50 fee, may be waived for applicants with need. Application may be submitted online. Admission notification 3/20. Must reply by 5/1. **Financial aid:** Closing date 2/15. FAFSA, institutional form required. Applicants notified on a rolling basis starting 12/20; must reply by 5/1 or within 2 week(s) of notification.

Academics. Special study options: Accelerated study, combined bachelor's/graduate degree, distance learning, double major, dual enrollment of high school students, honors, independent study, internships, liberal arts/career combination, study abroad, teacher certification program, weekend college. **Credit/placement by examination:** AP, CLEP, SAT, ACT. 60 credit hours maximum toward bachelor's degree. **Support services:** Learning center, pre-admission summer program, reduced course load, tutoring, writing center.

Majors. Biology: General, biochemistry. **Business:** Accounting, business admin, finance, international, management information systems, marketing. **Communications:** General, advertising, journalism, media studies, public relations. **Computer sciences:** Computer science. **Education:** General, biology, early childhood, elementary, English, French, mathematics, multi-level teacher, secondary, social studies, Spanish. **English:** English lit. **Foreign languages:** French, Italian, Spanish. **Health:** Audiology/speech pathology, clinical lab science, health care admin. **History:** General. **Interdisciplinary:** Global studies. **Liberal arts:** Arts/sciences. **Math:** General, applied. **Philosophy/religion:** Philosophy, religion. **Physical sciences:** Chemistry, physics. **Protective services:** Law enforcement admin. **Psychology:** General. **Public administration:** Social work. **Social sciences:** Economics, political science, sociology. **Visual/performing arts:** Dramatic.

Most popular majors. Business/marketing 38%, communications/journalism 13%, education 10%, psychology 9%, security/protective services 7%.

Computing on campus. 500 workstations in dormitories, library, computer center, student center. Dormitories wired for high-speed internet access and linked to campus network. Commuter students can connect to campus network. Online course registration, online library, helpline, repair service, wireless network available.

Student life. Freshman orientation: Mandatory, $25 fee. Preregistration for classes offered. **Policies:** Active campus ministry. **Housing:** Coed dorms, special housing for disabled, apartments available. $500 nonrefundable deposit, deadline 5/1. Honors program student housing available. **Activities:** Pep band, choral groups, dance, drama, film society, literary magazine, musical theater, radio station, student government, student newspaper, TV station, Big Brothers, Big Sisters, Special Olympics, Circle-K, People's Club, Gaelic Society, Campus Ministries, Council of Multicultural Leaders, Latin American Student Organization, Italian club, Spanish club.

Athletics. NCAA. **Intercollegiate:** Baseball M, basketball, cross-country, diving, football (tackle) M, golf M, lacrosse W, rowing (crew), rugby W, soccer, softball W, swimming, track and field, volleyball W, water polo. **Intramural:** Basketball, football (tackle) M, soccer, softball, table tennis, volleyball. **Team name:** Gaels.

Student services. Adult student services, alcohol/substance abuse counseling, campus ministries, career counseling, student employment services, financial aid counseling, health services, personal counseling, placement for graduates. **Physically disabled:** Services for speech impaired.

Contact. E-mail: icad@iona.edu
Phone: (914) 633-2502 Toll-free number: (800) 231-4662
Fax: (914) 633-2182
Thomas Weede, Director of Admissions, Iona College, 715 North Avenue, New Rochelle, NY 10801-1890

Ithaca College

Ithaca, New York **CB member**
www.ithaca.edu **CB code: 2325**

- Private 4-year health science and liberal arts college
- Residential campus in large town
- 5,997 degree-seeking undergraduates: 1% part-time, 55% women, 3% African American, 3% Asian American, 3% Hispanic American, 3% international
- 304 degree-seeking graduate students
- 76% of applicants admitted
- SAT or ACT with writing, application essay required
- 73% graduate within 6 years; 30% enter graduate study

General. Founded in 1892. Regionally accredited. **Degrees:** 1,585 bachelor's awarded; master's, doctoral offered. **ROTC:** Army, Air Force. **Location:** 250 miles from New York City, 60 miles from Syracuse. **Calendar:** Semester, extensive summer session. **Full-time faculty:** 442 total; 92% have terminal degrees, 8% minority, 44% women. **Part-time faculty:** 214 total; 64% have terminal degrees, 8% minority, 56% women. **Class size:** 61% < 20, 34% 20-39, 2% 40-49, 2% 50-99, less than 1% >100. **Special facilities:** Digital audio/video labs, photography labs, cinematography postproduction studio, film animation lab, lighting studio, physical therapy and occupational therapy clinics, speech and hearing clinic, exercise science labs, greenhouse, tissue culture laboratory, simulated trading room, recording and electroacoustic music studio, observatory, wellness clinic.

Freshman class profile. 10,421 applied, 7,869 admitted, 1,680 enrolled.

Mid 50% test scores		**Return as sophomores:**	86%
SAT verbal:	540-640	**Out-of-state:**	57%
SAT math:	540-640	**Live on campus:**	99%
Rank in top quarter:	64%	**International:**	2%
Rank in top tenth:	29%	**Fraternities:**	1%
End year in good standing:	95%	**Sororities:**	1%

Basis for selection. School achievement record, test scores most important. School and community activities, accomplishments, special talents, interview also important. Audition required for music, theater arts programs; portfolio recommended for BFA program. **Homeschooled:** Applicants encouraged to provide in-depth information regarding academic preparation.

High school preparation. 16 units required. Required units include English 4, mathematics 3, social studies 3, science 3, foreign language 2 and academic electives 1.

2006-2007 Annual costs. Tuition/fees: $26,832. Room/board: $10,314. Books/supplies: $968. Personal expenses: $1,302.

2005-2006 Financial aid. Need-based: 1,358 full-time freshmen applied for aid; 1,250 were judged to have need; 1,248 of these received aid. Average need met was 89%. Average scholarship/grant was $8,133; average loan $6,768. 66% of total undergraduate aid awarded as scholarships/grants, 34% as loans/jobs. **Non-need-based:** Awarded to 1,411 full-time undergraduates, including 443 freshmen. Scholarships awarded for academics, alumni affiliation, leadership, music/drama, ROTC.

Application procedures. Admission: Closing date 2/1. $55 fee, may be waived for applicants with need. Application may be submitted online. Admission notification on a rolling basis beginning on or about 1/10. Must reply by May 1 or within 2 week(s) if notified thereafter. **Financial aid:** Priority date 2/1; no closing date. FAFSA required. CSS PROFILE required of early decision applicants; deadline November 1. Applicants notified on a rolling basis starting 2/15.

Academics. Over 50 minors available. **Special study options:** Accelerated study, combined bachelor's/graduate degree, cross-registration, distance learning, double major, dual enrollment of high school students, honors, independent study, internships, liberal arts/career combination, student-designed major, study abroad, teacher certification program, Washington semester. London Center (England), Los Angeles program, Walkabout Down Under program (Australia), study opportunities in over 50 countries. **Credit/placement by examination:** AP, CLEP, IB, institutional tests. 90 credit hours maximum toward bachelor's degree. **Support services:** Study skills assistance, tutoring, writing center.

Majors. Biology: General, biochemistry. **Business:** General, accounting, business admin, finance, international, managerial economics, market research, marketing. **Communications:** General, broadcast journalism, journalism, media studies, organizational, radio/tv. **Communications technology:** Recording arts. **Computer sciences:** General, computer science, information systems, information technology, programming. **Conservation:** General, environmental studies. **Education:** Art, biology, chemistry, Deaf/hearing impaired, English, foreign languages, French, German, health, history, mathematics, multi-level teacher, music, physical, physics, science, secondary, social studies, Spanish, speech impaired. **English:** Composition, creative writing, speech/rhetoric. **Foreign languages:** General, French, German, Italian, Spanish. **Health:** Athletic training, audiology/speech pathology, predentistry, premedicine, preveterinary, public health ed, recreational therapy. **History:** General. **Interdisciplinary:** Gerontology, nutrition sciences. **Legal studies:** General, prelaw. **Liberal arts:** Arts/sciences. **Math:** General. **Parks/recreation:** General, exercise sciences, health/fitness, sports admin. **Philosophy/religion:** Philosophy. **Physical sciences:** Chemistry, physics. **Psychology:** General. **Social sciences:** General, anthropology, applied economics, economics, political science, sociology. **Visual/performing arts:** General, acting, art, art history/conservation, arts management, cinematography, dance, dramatic, film/cinema, jazz, music performance, music theory/composition, photography, studio arts, theater arts management, theater design.

Most popular majors. Business/marketing 12%, communications/journalism 19%, education 6%, English 7%, health sciences 12%, social sciences 9%, visual/performing arts 16%.

Computing on campus. 640 workstations in library, computer center. Dormitories wired for high-speed internet access and linked to campus network. Commuter students can connect to campus network. Online course registration, online library, helpline, repair service, student web hosting, wireless network available.

Student life. Freshman orientation: Available, $185 fee. Preregistration for classes offered. 2.5 days in summer and 4 days before school highlighted by placement tests and registration. Separate parent orientation program offered in summer. **Policies:** Freshmen permitted cars on campus. **Housing:** Guaranteed on-campus for all undergraduates. Coed dorms, single-sex dorms, special housing for disabled, apartments, fraternity/sorority housing, substance-free housing available. First year students only, quiet study residence halls, music honor fraternity housing, smoke-free buildings and floors, co-ed by door buildings, honors floor, several freshmen seminar groups housed together, H.O.M.E. Program (Housing Offering a Multicultural Experience) available. **Activities:** Bands, choral groups, dance, drama, film society, literary magazine, music ensembles, musical theater, opera, radio station, student government, student newspaper, symphony orchestra, TV station, Jewish, Christian, Catholic, Muslim, and Christian Science organizations; African-Latino society; Amnesty International; BiGayla; community service network; Habitat for Humanity, Sex and Gender Education, Asia Society, Friends of Israel.

Athletics. NCAA. **Intercollegiate:** Baseball M, basketball, cross-country, diving, field hockey W, football (tackle) M, gymnastics W, lacrosse, rowing (crew), soccer, softball W, swimming, tennis, track and field, volleyball W, wrestling M. **Intramural:** Basketball, bowling, golf, ice hockey M, rowing (crew), rugby W, skiing, soccer, softball, tennis, volleyball. **Team name:** Bombers.

Student services. Adult student services, alcohol/substance abuse counseling, campus ministries, career counseling, student employment services, financial aid counseling, health services, minority student services, personal counseling, placement for graduates, veterans' counselor. **Physically disabled:** Services for visually, speech, hearing impaired.

Contact. E-mail: admission@ithaca.edu
Phone: (607) 274-3124 Toll-free number: (800) 429-4274
Fax: (607) 274-1900
Paula Mitchell, Director of Admissions, Ithaca College, 100 Job Hall, Ithaca, NY 14850-7020

Jewish Theological Seminary of America

New York, New York
www.jtsa.edu **CB code: 2339**

- Private 4-year university and seminary college affiliated with Jewish faith
- Residential campus in very large city
- 201 degree-seeking undergraduates
- SAT or ACT (ACT writing optional) required

General. Founded in 1886. Regionally accredited. **Degrees:** 42 bachelor's awarded; master's, doctoral, first professional offered. **Calendar:** Semester, extensive summer session. **Full-time faculty:** 59 total. **Part-time faculty:** 62 total. **Special facilities:** Jewish museum containing a large and comprehensive permanent collection of over 27,000 objects (paintings, sculptures, works on paper, artifacts, etc.), library containing largest collection of Hebraica and Judaica outside of Israel.

Freshman class profile. 52 enrolled.

Out-of-state:	80%	**Live on campus:**	95%

Basis for selection. School achievement record, interest in Jewish studies, test scores, recommendations important; leadership potential considered. Interview recommended for residents in the New York area (within 100 mile radius).

High school preparation. Recommended units include English 4, mathematics 4, social studies 3, history 3, science 3 and foreign language 4.

2006-2007 Annual costs. Tuition/fees: $13,420. Costs quoted paid to school only; separate costs assessed for dual-degree enrollment at Columbia University/Barnard College.

Application procedures. Admission: Closing date 2/15. $65 fee. **Financial aid:** Closing date 3/1.

Academics. Special study options: Distance learning, double major, dual enrollment of high school students, honors, independent study, internships, liberal arts/career combination, student-designed major, study abroad. Joint program with Columbia University; double degree program with Barnard College. **Credit/placement by examination:** AP, CLEP, institutional tests. 6 credit hours maximum toward bachelor's degree. **Support services:** Preadmission summer program, remedial instruction, tutoring, writing center.

Majors. Foreign languages: General. **Philosophy/religion:** Judaic. **Theology:** Sacred music. **Visual/performing arts:** Music performance, music theory/composition.

Computing on campus. 50 workstations in dormitories, library, computer center. Dormitories wired for high-speed internet access and linked to campus network. Commuter students can connect to campus network.

Student life. Freshman orientation: Mandatory. **Policies:** Student life centers around supportive Jewish community. Undergraduates enrolled in joint degree programs with Barnard and Columbia participate in their extracurricular activities. **Housing:** $450 deposit, deadline 5/15. Women undergraduates enrolled in double degree program with Barnard may live in Barnard dormitories. **Activities:** Bands, choral groups, dance, drama, literary magazine, music ensembles, musical theater, radio station, student government, student newspaper, symphony orchestra, TV station, community service organization.

Athletics. Intramural: Basketball, bowling, field hockey W, lacrosse M, softball, volleyball.

Student services. Career counseling, student employment services, health services, personal counseling, placement for graduates.

Contact. E-mail: lcadmissions@jtsa.edu
Phone: (212) 678-8832 Fax: (212) 678-8947
Reina Cohen, Director of Admissions, Jewish Theological Seminary of America, 3080 Broadway, New York, NY 10027

Juilliard School

New York, New York
www.juilliard.edu **CB code: 2340**

- Private 4-year music and performing arts college
- Commuter campus in very large city
- 478 degree-seeking undergraduates: 48% women, 12% African American, 13% Asian American, 4% Hispanic American, 20% international
- 327 degree-seeking graduate students
- 5% of applicants admitted
- Application essay, interview required
- 81% graduate within 6 years

General. Founded in 1905. Regionally accredited. **Degrees:** 102 bachelor's awarded; master's, doctoral offered. **Calendar:** Semester. **Full-time faculty:** 114 total; 11% minority, 40% women. **Part-time faculty:** 154 total; 11% minority, 28% women. **Class size:** 92% < 20, 7% 20-39, less than 1% 50-99. **Special facilities:** Media center, over 100 practice rooms with over 200 pianos, scenery and costume shops, 15 2-story rehearsal studios, 5 theaters, 2 recital halls.

Freshman class profile. 2,523 applied, 136 admitted, 96 enrolled.

Return as sophomores:	94%	**Live on campus:**	100%
Out-of-state:	84%	**International:**	8%

Basis for selection. Quality of performance at audition most important. Foreign students given English proficiency examination at time of audition or may present TOEFL. Audition required.

High school preparation. Extensive previous study in major field of dance, drama, or music required.

2006-2007 Annual costs. Tuition/fees: $25,610. Room/board: $10,095. Books/supplies: $3,720.

2005-2006 Financial aid. Need-based: 91 full-time freshmen applied for aid; 72 were judged to have need; 72 of these received aid. Average need met was 85%. Average scholarship/grant was $17,493; average loan $4,429. 75% of total undergraduate aid awarded as scholarships/grants, 25% as loans/jobs. **Non-need-based:** Awarded to 21 full-time undergraduates, including 1 freshmen. Scholarships awarded for music/drama.

Application procedures. Admission: Closing date 12/1. $100 fee, may be waived for applicants with need. Admission notification 4/1. Must reply by 5/1. Auditions held in March. Drama auditions in January and Febuary, application closing date December 1; notification by April 1, or 1 month after audition. **Financial aid:** Closing date 3/1. FAFSA, institutional form required. Applicants notified on a rolling basis starting 4/1; must reply by 5/1 or within 2 week(s) of notification.

Academics. 3-year diploma program available in performing arts. **Special study options:** Accelerated study, cooperative education, cross-registration, exchange student, liberal arts/career combination, study abroad. Eligible students can enroll in courses at Barnard and Columbia to fulfill liberal arts elective requirements. **Credit/placement by examination:** AP, CLEP, institutional tests. **Support services:** Tutoring.

Majors. Visual/performing arts: General, dance, dramatic, jazz, music performance, music theory/composition, piano/organ, stringed instruments.

Computing on campus. 65 workstations in dormitories, library, computer center. Dormitories wired for high-speed internet access. Online library, wireless network available.

Student life. **Freshman orientation:** Mandatory, $200 fee. **Policies:** Freshmen permitted cars on campus. **Housing:** Guaranteed on-campus for freshmen. Coed dorms available. Single sex floor, quiet floor, substance-free floor available. **Activities:** Jazz band, choral groups, dance, drama, music ensembles, opera, student newspaper, symphony orchestra, ArtREACH, Korea Campus Crusade for Christ, Christian fellowship, Artists Inspired, The Forum.

Student services. Adult student services, career counseling, student employment services, financial aid counseling, health services, minority student services, personal counseling, placement for graduates.

Contact. E-mail: admissions@juilliard.edu
Phone: (212) 799-5000 ext. 223 Fax: (212) 724-0263
Lee Cioppa, Associate Dean for Admissions, Juilliard School, 60 Lincoln Center Plaza, New York, NY 10023-6588

Kehilath Yakov Rabbinical Seminary
Brooklyn, New York
CB code: 0619

- Private 4-year rabbinical college for men affiliated with Jewish faith
- Very large city

General. Accredited by AARTS. **Calendar:** Continuous.

Annual costs/financial aid. Tuition/fees (2005-2006): $4,500.

Contact. Phone: (718) 963-3940
206 Wilson Street, Brooklyn, NY 11211

Keuka College
Keuka Park, New York
www.keuka.edu
CB member
CB code: 2350

- Private 4-year liberal arts college affiliated with American Baptist Churches in the USA
- Residential campus in rural community
- 939 degree-seeking undergraduates: 1% part-time, 70% women, 5% African American, 1% Asian American, 2% Hispanic American, 1% Native American
- 100 degree-seeking graduate students
- 81% of applicants admitted
- SAT or ACT (ACT writing optional), application essay required
- 49% graduate within 6 years; 20% enter graduate study

General. Founded in 1890. Regionally accredited. All students must complete 1 field period or internship each year, every 30 credit hours (experiential education). **Degrees:** 258 bachelor's awarded; master's offered. **Location:** 50 miles from Rochester, 60 miles from Syracuse. **Calendar:** 4-1-4, limited summer session. **Full-time faculty:** 57 total; 88% have terminal degrees, 4% minority, 56% women. **Part-time faculty:** 43 total; 26% have terminal degrees, 2% minority, 58% women. **Class size:** 55% < 20, 43% 20-39, 2% 50-99.

Freshman class profile. 818 applied, 659 admitted, 268 enrolled.

Mid 50% test scores			
SAT verbal:	420-530	Rank in top quarter:	27%
SAT math:	440-540	Rank in top tenth:	9%
GPA 3.50 or higher:	14%	Return as sophomores:	73%
GPA 3.0-3.49:	44%	Out-of-state:	9%
GPA 2.0-2.99:	40%	Live on campus:	96%

Basis for selection. Overall GPA, extracurricular activities, community service, leadership experience, letter of recommendation, quality of essay, SAT/ACT scores considered by committee. Interview recommended for all, required for some.

High school preparation. 18 units recommended. Recommended units include English 4, mathematics 3, social studies 3, history 2, science 3 (laboratory 2) and foreign language 3.

2005-2006 Annual costs. Tuition/fees: $18,360. Room/board: $7,980. Books/supplies: $800. Personal expenses: $1,000.

2005-2006 Financial aid. **Need-based:** 267 full-time freshmen applied for aid; 245 were judged to have need; 245 of these received aid. Average need met was 84%. Average scholarship/grant was $12,809; average loan $5,345. 58% of total undergraduate aid awarded as scholarships/grants, 42% as loans/jobs. **Non-need-based:** Awarded to 182 full-time undergraduates, including 59 freshmen. Scholarships awarded for academics, alumni affiliation, leadership, minority status, religious affiliation.

Application procedures. **Admission:** No deadline. $30 fee, may be waived for applicants with need. Application may be submitted online. Admission notification on a rolling basis beginning on or about 9/1. Must reply by 5/1. **Financial aid:** Priority date 3/15; no closing date. FAFSA required. Applicants notified on a rolling basis starting 3/1; must reply by 5/1 or within 2 week(s) of notification.

Academics. Field Period enables students to spend 4 weeks a year participating in an internship or international travel, or undertaking an independent project. **Special study options:** Accelerated study, cooperative education, cross-registration, double major, dual enrollment of high school students, independent study, internships, student-designed major, study abroad, teacher certification program, Washington semester. Albany semester; 3-1 in clinical science with New York Chiropractic College. **Credit/placement by examination:** AP, CLEP, institutional tests. 12 credit hours maximum toward bachelor's degree. **Support services:** Learning center, reduced course load, remedial instruction, study skills assistance, tutoring, writing center.

Majors. **Biology:** General, biochemistry. **Business:** Accounting, business admin, sales/distribution. **Communications:** General. **Conservation:** General. **Education:** Biology, early childhood, English, mathematics, social studies, special. **Foreign languages:** American Sign Language. **Health:** Clinical lab science, nursing (RN). **Legal studies:** Prelaw. **Liberal arts:** Arts/sciences. **Math:** General. **Protective services:** Law enforcement admin. **Psychology:** General. **Public administration:** Social work. **Social sciences:** General, criminology, sociology.

Most popular majors. Business/marketing 21%, education 18%, health sciences 25%, security/protective services 8%, social sciences 10%.

Computing on campus. 62 workstations in dormitories, library, computer center. Dormitories wired for high-speed internet access and linked to campus network. Helpline available.

Student life. **Freshman orientation:** Mandatory, $150 fee. Preregistration for classes offered. 2-session summer program. **Policies:** No smoking allowed in any campus building, including residence halls. Freshmen permitted cars on campus. **Housing:** Guaranteed on-campus for all undergraduates. Coed dorms, single-sex dorms, special housing for disabled, cooperative housing available. $150 deposit. Leadership, wellness, management, and theme housing. **Activities:** Choral groups, dance, drama, film society, literary magazine, musical theater, radio station, student government, student newspaper, campus ministries, international club, social work club, Keuka Leaders club, Keuka Circle (community service), Newman Club, minority support group, political action coalition, Student Nurse Association.

Athletics. NCAA. **Intercollegiate:** Baseball M, basketball, cross-country, golf M, lacrosse, soccer, softball W, synchronized swimming W, tennis, volleyball W. **Intramural:** Badminton, basketball, lacrosse M, rowing (crew), skiing, soccer, softball, table tennis, tennis, volleyball, water polo. **Team name:** Storm.

Student services. Adult student services, alcohol/substance abuse counseling, campus ministries, career counseling, student employment services, financial aid counseling, health services, minority student services, personal counseling, placement for graduates, women's services. **Physically disabled:** Services for visually, speech, hearing impaired.

Contact. E-mail: admissions@mail.keuka.edu
Phone: (315) 279-5254 Toll-free number: (800) 335-3852
Fax: (315) 279-5386
Carolanne Marquis, Vice President of College Advancement and Enrollment, Keuka College, Wagner House, Keuka Park, NY 14478-0098

King's College
New York, New York
www.tkc.edu
CB code: 2871

- Private 4-year liberal arts college affiliated with nondenominational tradition
- Residential campus in very large city
- 213 degree-seeking undergraduates: 9% part-time, 63% women
- 57% of applicants admitted
- SAT or ACT (ACT writing recommended), interview required

General. Regionally accredited. **Degrees:** 15 bachelor's, 4 associate awarded. **Calendar:** Semester. **Full-time faculty:** 12 total; 92% have terminal degrees, 8% women. **Part-time faculty:** 11 total; 91% have terminal degrees, 36% women. **Class size:** 61% < 20, 29% 20-39, 8% 40-49, 2% 50-99.

Freshman class profile. 348 applied, 197 admitted, 81 enrolled.

Mid 50% test scores			
SAT verbal:	570-670	Rank in top quarter:	80%
SAT math:	520-640	Rank in top tenth:	48%
ACT:	23-27	Return as sophomores:	78%
GPA 3.50 or higher:	73%	Out-of-state:	62%
GPA 3.0-3.49:	23%	Live on campus:	95%
GPA 2.0-2.99:	4%	International:	7%

Basis for selection. Admissions decisions based on combination of academic preparedness and leadership giftedness, primarily assessed through transcript, SAT or ACT scores, and interview. Short answer personal statements required in online application. **Learning Disabled:** Documentation requested of any learning disabilities that will require special accommodation.

High school preparation. Required units include English 4, mathematics 4, social studies 2, history 2, science 4 and foreign language 2.

2006-2007 Annual costs. Tuition/fees: $18,940. Room only: $7,980. Books/supplies: $1,000. Personal expenses: $1,250.

2005-2006 Financial aid. Need-based: 74 full-time freshmen applied for aid; 59 were judged to have need; 59 of these received aid. Average need met was 73%. Average scholarship/grant was $12,916. 85% of total undergraduate aid awarded as scholarships/grants, 15% as loans/jobs. **Non-need-based:** Awarded to 43 full-time undergraduates, including 21 freshmen. Scholarships awarded for academics, leadership. **Additional information:** School does not participate in Title IV federal financial aid; students must file PROFILE and/or TAP application for institutional aid consideration.

Application procedures. Admission: Priority date 11/15; deadline 2/1 (postmark date). $30 fee, may be waived for applicants with need. Application may be submitted online. Admission notification 3/8. Must reply by May 1 or within 3 week(s) if notified thereafter. **Financial aid:** Priority date 12/15, closing date 3/1. CSS PROFILE required. Applicants notified by 3/15; must reply by 5/1.

Academics. Special study options: ESL, independent study, internships, study abroad. **Credit/placement by examination:** CLEP, IB. **Support services:** Learning center, reduced course load, study skills assistance, tutoring, writing center.

Majors. Business: Business admin. **Education:** Elementary.

Most popular majors. Business/marketing 80%, education 7%.

Computing on campus. PC or laptop required. Dormitories wired for high-speed internet access and linked to campus network. Commuter students can connect to campus network. Online course registration, online library, repair service, wireless network available.

Student life. Freshman orientation: Available. Held in fall 1 week prior to classes. **Policies:** 3 required religion courses. No alcoholic beverages/drug usage permitted. **Housing:** Apartments available. $400 fully refundable deposit, deadline 6/15. **Activities:** Choral groups, dance, drama, literary magazine, student government, student newspaper, Praise of Worship (Christian chorus), model UN, C.S. Lewis society.

Contact. E-mail: info@tkc.edu
Phone: (212) 659-7200 ext. 3611
Brian Bell, Vice President of Enrollment Management, King's College, 350 5th Avenue, 15th Floor, New York, NY 10118

Laboratory Institute of Merchandising

New York, New York — **CB member**
www.limcollege.edu — **CB code: 2380**

- For-profit 4-year college of fashion business
- Commuter campus in very large city
- 792 degree-seeking undergraduates: 2% part-time, 95% women, 8% African American, 6% Asian American, 15% Hispanic American, 1% international
- 66% of applicants admitted
- SAT or ACT, application essay, interview required
- 45% graduate within 6 years

General. Founded in 1939. Regionally accredited. Freshmen and sophomores participate in 3-credit, 5-week work project. Seniors participate in 16-week full-semester co-op. Curriculum also includes weekly field trips into fashion industry and guest lecturer series featuring fashion professionals. **Degrees:** 128 bachelor's, 40 associate awarded. **Calendar:** Semester, limited summer session. **Full-time faculty:** 14 total; 29% have terminal degrees, 14% minority, 50% women. **Part-time faculty:** 76 total; 16% have terminal degrees, 10% minority, 51% women.

Freshman class profile. 514 applied, 337 admitted, 197 enrolled.

Mid 50% test scores			
SAT verbal:	430-520	Rank in top quarter:	19%
SAT math:	410-500	Rank in top tenth:	11%
ACT:	17-19	End year in good standing:	80%
GPA 3.50 or higher:	12%	Return as sophomores:	80%
GPA 3.0-3.49:	26%	Out-of-state:	42%
GPA 2.0-2.99:	58%	Live on campus:	38%

Basis for selection. Interview, high school transcript, SAT/ACT score, letters of recommendation and college transcripts important.

High school preparation. College-preparatory program recommended.

2005-2006 Annual costs. Tuition/fees: $17,050. Room only: $10,000. Books/supplies: $1,000. Personal expenses: $2,000.

2004-2005 Financial aid. All financial aid based on need. 55% of total undergraduate aid awarded as scholarships/grants, 45% as loans/jobs.

Application procedures. Admission: No deadline. $40 fee, may be waived for applicants with need. Admission notification on a rolling basis. **Financial aid:** Priority date 4/15; no closing date. FAFSA, institutional form required. Applicants notified on a rolling basis; must reply within 2 week(s) of notification.

Academics. Associate degree program distributed among liberal arts, business, and professional courses, including 2 work projects of 3 credits and 5 weeks each. Bachelor's degree programs distributed among liberal arts, business, and professional courses with a semester-long, 13-credit cooperative work project. **Special study options:** Combined bachelor's/graduate degree, cooperative education, independent study, internships, study abroad. 3-credit class held winter/summer in France, England, Germany, Spain, Italy, or China. **Credit/placement by examination:** AP, CLEP, institutional tests. **Support services:** Learning center, reduced course load, remedial instruction, study skills assistance, tutoring, writing center.

Majors. Business: Apparel, fashion, management science.

Computing on campus. 204 workstations in library, computer center, student center. Commuter students can connect to campus network. Online library, helpline available.

Student life. Freshman orientation: Mandatory. **Housing:** Coed dorms available. Affiliated with local YW-YMHA and Educational Housing Inc. in which traditional residence life experience available. **Activities:** Film society, student government, cultures club.

Student services. Alcohol/substance abuse counseling, career counseling, student employment services, financial aid counseling, personal counseling, placement for graduates.

Contact. E-mail: admissions@limcollege.edu
Phone: (212) 752-1530 ext. 289 Toll-free number: (800) 677-1323
Fax: (212) 750-3432
Kristina Gibson, Director of Admissions, Laboratory Institute of Merchandising, 12 East 53rd Street, New York, NY 10022

Le Moyne College

Syracuse, New York — **CB member**
www.lemoyne.edu — **CB code: 2366**

- Private 4-year liberal arts college affiliated with Roman Catholic Church
- Residential campus in small city
- 2,436 degree-seeking undergraduates: 6% part-time, 61% women, 5% African American, 2% Asian American, 4% Hispanic American, 1% Native American, 1% international
- 597 degree-seeking graduate students
- 72% of applicants admitted
- SAT or ACT (ACT writing optional), application essay required
- 71% graduate within 6 years; 29% enter graduate study

General. Founded in 1946. Regionally accredited. College in Jesuit tradition. **Degrees:** 537 bachelor's awarded; master's offered. **ROTC:** Army, Air Force. **Location:** 2 miles from downtown. **Calendar:** Semester, extensive summer session. **Full-time faculty:** 154 total; 92% have terminal degrees, 17% minority, 42% women. **Part-time faculty:** 170 total; 34% have terminal degrees, 4% minority, 40% women. **Class size:** 37% < 20, 61% 20-39, less than 1% 40-49, less than 1% 50-99. **Special facilities:** Performing arts center.

Freshman class profile. 2,946 applied, 2,133 admitted, 520 enrolled.

Mid 50% test scores		**Rank in top quarter:**	52%
SAT verbal:	500-600	**Rank in top tenth:**	23%
SAT math:	510-610	**End year in good standing:**	92%
ACT:	21-26	**Return as sophomores:**	87%
GPA 3.50 or higher:	48%	**Out-of-state:**	8%
GPA 3.0-3.49:	31%	**Live on campus:**	91%
GPA 2.0-2.99:	21%	**International:**	1%

Basis for selection. High school courses and performance most important; class rank, test scores, recommendations, essay, interview, extracurricular activities also important. Students from underrepresented populations encouraged. February 1 priority date by which SAT scores must be received for fall term admission. Interview recommended. **Homeschooled:** Statement describing homeschool structure and mission, transcript of courses and grades, interview, letter of recommendation (nonparent) required. **Learning Disabled:** Interview strongly recommended.

High school preparation. 17 units required. Required and recommended units include English 4, mathematics 3-4, social studies 4, science 3-4 (laboratory 3) and foreign language 3. 4 mathematics required for science and mathematics majors.

2006-2007 Annual costs. Tuition/fees: $22,580. Room/board: $8,620. Books/supplies: $600. Personal expenses: $1,130.

2004-2005 Financial aid. Need-based: 389 full-time freshmen applied for aid; 389 were judged to have need; 389 of these received aid. Average need met was 88%. Average scholarship/grant was $14,765; average loan $3,286. 67% of total undergraduate aid awarded as scholarships/grants, 33% as loans/jobs. **Non-need-based:** Awarded to 1,339 full-time undergraduates, including 319 freshmen. Scholarships awarded for academics, alumni affiliation, athletics, leadership, minority status, ROTC. **Additional information:** Parent loan program at low interest, monthly payment plans and alternative loans for students.

Application procedures. Admission: Priority date 2/1; no deadline. $35 fee, may be waived for applicants with need. Application may be submitted online. Admission notification on a rolling basis beginning on or about 1/1. **Financial aid:** Priority date 2/1; no closing date. FAFSA, institutional form required. Applicants notified by 3/15; must reply by 5/1 or within 2 week(s) of notification.

Academics. Academic accommodations and services for students with documented disabilities. **Special study options:** Accelerated study, combined bachelor's/graduate degree, double major, honors, independent study, internships, liberal arts/career combination, semester at sea, study abroad, teacher certification program, Washington semester. Physician assistant program leading to certification, certificate of advanced studies in educational leadership. **Credit/placement by examination:** AP, CLEP, IB. **Support services:** Learning center, remedial instruction, study skills assistance, tutoring, writing center.

Majors. Biology: General, biochemistry. **Business:** General, accounting, business admin, finance, human resources, labor relations, management information systems, management science, managerial economics, marketing. **Communications:** General. **English:** English lit. **Foreign languages:** French, Spanish. **Health:** Nursing (RN), predentistry, premedicine, preveterinary. **History:** General. **Interdisciplinary:** Biological/physical sciences, peace/conflict. **Legal studies:** Prelaw. **Math:** General. **Philosophy/religion:** Philosophy, religion. **Physical sciences:** Chemistry, physics. **Psychology:** General. **Social sciences:** Criminology, economics, international relations, political science, sociology. **Visual/performing arts:** Dramatic.

Most popular majors. Biology 9%, business/marketing 35%, English 10%, history 7%, psychology 17%, social sciences 13%.

Computing on campus. 325 workstations in dormitories, library, computer center. Dormitories wired for high-speed internet access and linked to campus network. Commuter students can connect to campus network. Online course registration, online library, helpline, repair service, student web hosting, wireless network available.

Student life. Freshman orientation: Mandatory, $150 fee. Preregistration for classes offered. 4 summer orientation sessions of 2 days each and one fall orientation. **Policies:** Freshmen permitted cars on campus. **Housing:** Guaranteed on-campus for all undergraduates. Coed dorms, single-sex dorms, special housing for disabled, apartments, substance-free housing available. $300 deposit, deadline 5/1. Living/learning communities available. **Activities:** Bands, choral groups, dance, drama, literary magazine, music ensembles, musical theater, radio station, student government, student newspaper, international club, Amnesty International, Habitat for Humanity, Democrats Club, Republican Club, Gaelic Society, El Progreso, Pride in Our Work Ethnicity and Race (POWER), Muslim student association.

Athletics. NCAA. **Intercollegiate:** Baseball M, basketball, cross-country, diving, golf M, lacrosse, soccer, softball W, swimming, tennis, volleyball W. **Intramural:** Basketball, cross-country, football (non-tackle) M, racquetball, soccer, softball, volleyball. **Team name:** Dolphins.

Student services. Adult student services, alcohol/substance abuse counseling, campus ministries, career counseling, student employment services, financial aid counseling, health services, minority student services, personal counseling, placement for graduates. **Physically disabled:** Services for visually, speech, hearing impaired.

Contact. E-mail: admission@lemoyne.edu
Phone: (315) 445-4300 Toll-free number: (800) 333-4733
Fax: (315) 445-4711
Dennis Nicholson, Director of Admission, Le Moyne College, 1419 Salt Springs Road, Syracuse, NY 13214-1301

Long Island University: Brooklyn Campus

Brooklyn, New York **CB member**
www.liu.edu **CB code: 2369**

- Private 4-year university and branch campus college
- Commuter campus in very large city
- 5,297 degree-seeking undergraduates: 17% part-time, 72% women, 40% African American, 15% Asian American, 12% Hispanic American, 2% international
- 2,735 degree-seeking graduate students
- 61% of applicants admitted
- 19% graduate within 6 years

General. Founded in 1926. Regionally accredited. **Degrees:** 509 bachelor's, 47 associate awarded; master's, doctoral, first professional offered. **ROTC:** Army. **Calendar:** Semester, extensive summer session. **Full-time faculty:** 259 total; 29% minority, 52% women. **Part-time faculty:** 695 total.

Freshman class profile. 5,068 applied, 3,110 admitted, 1,045 enrolled.

Mid 50% test scores		**GPA 2.0-2.99:**	49%
SAT verbal:	400-520	**Return as sophomores:**	67%
SAT math:	410-560	**Out-of-state:**	18%
GPA 3.50 or higher:	10%	**International:**	1%
GPA 3.0-3.49:	24%		

Basis for selection. ACT or SAT required for admission to computer science, molecular biology, nursing, pharmacy, pre-athletic training, pre-occupational therapy, and pre-physician assistant majors. Interview, audition, and/or personal statement may be required for particular programs.

High school preparation. 16 units recommended. Recommended units include English 4, mathematics 2, social studies 3 and academic electives 4. Academic electives include any electives from fields of foreign languages, social studies, mathematics or natural science. Other electives include 3 credits of any studies except physical education and military science that lead to graduation from accredited high school.

2005-2006 Annual costs. Tuition/fees: $23,230. Room/board: $7,860.

Application procedures. Admission: Priority date 6/1; no deadline. $30 fee, may be waived for applicants with need. Application may be submitted online. Admission notification on a rolling basis. **Financial aid:** No deadline. FAFSA required. Applicants notified on a rolling basis.

Academics. Special study options: Combined bachelor's/graduate degree, cooperative education, double major, ESL, honors, independent study, internships, student-designed major, study abroad, teacher certification program, United Nations semester, weekend college. **Credit/placement by examination:** AP, CLEP, IB, institutional tests. **Support services:** Learning center, pre-admission summer program, reduced course load, remedial instruction, study skills assistance, tutoring, writing center.

Majors. Biology: General, biochemistry. **Business:** Accounting, business admin, finance, sales/distribution. **Communications:** General, journalism.

Computer sciences: General. **Education:** Art, biology, chemistry, elementary, English, mathematics, music, physical, Spanish, speech impaired. **Engineering:** Operations research. **English:** English lit, speech/rhetoric. **Foreign languages:** General. **Health:** Audiology/speech pathology, clinical lab science, community health, cytotechnology, nursing (RN), physician assistant. **History:** General. **Liberal arts:** Arts/sciences, humanities. **Math:** General. **Parks/recreation:** Exercise sciences. **Philosophy/religion:** Philosophy. **Physical sciences:** Chemistry. **Psychology:** General. **Public administration:** Social work. **Social sciences:** General, economics, political science, sociology. **Visual/performing arts:** General, commercial/advertising art, dance, music performance, studio arts.

Most popular majors. Business/marketing 15%, communications/journalism 11%, health sciences 28%, psychology 11%, social sciences 11%.

Computing on campus. 600 workstations in dormitories, library, computer center. Dormitories wired for high-speed internet access and linked to campus network. Online library, wireless network available.

Student life. **Freshman orientation:** Available. **Housing:** Coed dorms available. $150 fully refundable deposit. **Activities:** Jazz band, choral groups, dance, drama, literary magazine, music ensembles, musical theater, radio station, student government, student newspaper, TV station.

Athletics. NCAA. **Intercollegiate:** Baseball M, basketball, cross-country, golf, lacrosse W, soccer, softball W, tennis W, track and field, volleyball W. **Team name:** Blackbirds.

Student services. Campus ministries, career counseling, student employment services, financial aid counseling, health services, personal counseling, placement for graduates. **Physically disabled:** Services for visually, speech, hearing impaired.

Contact. E-mail: attend@liu.edu
Phone: (718) 488-1011 Toll-free number: (800) 548-7526
Fax: (718) 797-2399
Kristin Cohen, Dean of Admissions and Enrollment Management, Long Island University: Brooklyn Campus, 1 University Plaza, Brooklyn, NY 11201

Long Island University: C. W. Post Campus

Brookville, New York — **CB member**
www.liu.edu — **CB code: 2070**

- Private 4-year university and branch campus college
- Commuter campus in small town
- 5,149 degree-seeking undergraduates: 13% part-time, 61% women, 10% African American, 3% Asian American, 8% Hispanic American, 3% international
- 3,270 degree-seeking graduate students
- 78% of applicants admitted
- Application essay required
- 36% graduate within 6 years

General. Founded in 1954. Regionally accredited. **Degrees:** 869 bachelor's awarded; master's, doctoral offered. **ROTC:** Army. **Location:** 25 miles from New York City. **Calendar:** Semester, extensive summer session. **Full-time faculty:** 355 total; 16% minority, 44% women. **Part-time faculty:** 810 total.

Freshman class profile. 5,162 applied, 4,006 admitted, 1,042 enrolled.

Mid 50% test scores		**GPA 3.0-3.49:**	30%
SAT verbal:	450-540	**GPA 2.0-2.99:**	48%
SAT math:	450-550	**Return as sophomores:**	74%
ACT:	17-23	**Out-of-state:**	13%
GPA 3.50 or higher:	17%	**International:**	2%

Basis for selection. SAT or ACT recommended. Audition required for dance, music, and theater programs; interview recommended for communication arts, dance, and theater/film programs; portfolio required for art programs.

High school preparation. 16 units recommended. Recommended units include English 4, mathematics 3, social studies 4, science 3 (laboratory 3) and foreign language 2.

2005-2006 Annual costs. Tuition/fees: $23,230. Room/board: $9,020.

Application procedures. **Admission:** No deadline. $30 fee, may be waived for applicants with need. Application may be submitted online. Admission notification on a rolling basis. **Financial aid:** Priority date 3/1; no closing date. FAFSA, CSS PROFILE required. Applicants notified on a rolling basis starting 3/1; must reply by 5/1.

Academics. **Special study options:** Accelerated study, combined bachelor's/graduate degree, cooperative education, cross-registration, double major, dual enrollment of high school students, ESL, honors, independent study, internships, student-designed major, study abroad, teacher certification program, United Nations semester, Washington semester, weekend college. **Credit/placement by examination:** AP, CLEP, IB, institutional tests. **Support services:** Learning center, pre-admission summer program, reduced course load, remedial instruction, study skills assistance, tutoring, writing center.

Majors. **Biology:** General, biomedical sciences, cell/histology. **Business:** Accounting, business admin. **Communications:** Advertising, journalism. **Communications technology:** Radio/tv. **Computer sciences:** Information systems, information technology. **Education:** Art, biology, chemistry, elementary, English, foreign languages, French, health, kindergarten/preschool, mathematics, music, physical, social studies, Spanish. **English:** English lit. **Foreign languages:** General, French, Italian, Spanish. **Health:** Art therapy, audiology/speech pathology, facilities admin, marriage/family therapy, medical radiologic technology/radiation therapy, medical records admin, nursing (RN). **History:** General. **Liberal arts:** Arts/sciences. **Math:** General, applied. **Philosophy/religion:** Philosophy. **Physical sciences:** Chemistry, geology, physics. **Protective services:** Forensics, law enforcement admin. **Psychology:** General. **Public administration:** General, social work. **Social sciences:** Economics, geography, international relations, political science, sociology. **Visual/performing arts:** Art history/conservation, arts management, cinematography, commercial/advertising art, dance, dramatic, music performance, photography, studio arts.

Most popular majors. Business/marketing 19%, communications/journalism 7%, education 25%, psychology 8%, security/protective services 9%, visual/performing arts 12%.

Computing on campus. Dormitories wired for high-speed internet access and linked to campus network. Commuter students can connect to campus network. Repair service, wireless network available.

Student life. **Freshman orientation:** Available, $95 fee. Preregistration for classes offered. 2-day sessions for freshmen held in July and August prior to start of fall classes. **Policies:** Freshmen permitted cars on campus. **Housing:** Guaranteed on-campus for freshmen. Coed dorms, single-sex dorms available. $300 fully refundable deposit, deadline 5/1. 24-hour intensified study housing available. **Activities:** Bands, choral groups, dance, drama, film society, literary magazine, music ensembles, musical theater, radio station, student government, student newspaper, TV station.

Athletics. NCAA. **Intercollegiate:** Baseball M, basketball, cross-country, field hockey W, football (tackle) M, lacrosse, soccer, softball W, swimming W, tennis W, track and field, volleyball W. **Team name:** Pioneers.

Student services. Adult student services, alcohol/substance abuse counseling, campus ministries, career counseling, student employment services, financial aid counseling, health services, personal counseling, placement for graduates, veterans' counselor. **Physically disabled:** Services for visually, speech, hearing impaired. **Learning disabled:** Comprehensive services available.

Contact. E-mail: enroll@cwpost.liu.edu
Phone: (516) 299-2900 Toll-free number: (800) 548-7526
Fax: (516) 299-2137
Gary Bergman, Associate Provost, Enrollment Services, Long Island University: C. W. Post Campus, 720 Northern Boulevard, Brookville, NY 11548-1300

Machzikei Hadath Rabbinical College

Brooklyn, New York
CB code: 0726

- Private 5-year seminary college for men affiliated with Jewish faith
- Commuter campus in very large city
- 117 degree-seeking undergraduates
- 100% of applicants admitted
- Interview required

General. Founded in 1956. Accredited by AARTS. First Talmudic degree and ordination available. **Degrees:** 18 bachelor's awarded; first professional offered. **Calendar:** Semester. **Full-time faculty:** 8 total. **Part-time faculty:** 3 total.

Freshman class profile. 23 applied, 23 admitted, 23 enrolled.

Basis for selection. Interview most important. Essay recommended.

2006-2007 Annual costs. Tuition/fees (projected): $6,100. Room/board: $1,800.

Application procedures. **Admission:** Priority date 6/1; deadline 7/1. $150 fee, may be waived for applicants with need. Admission notification on a rolling basis. **Financial aid:** No deadline. Applicants notified on a rolling basis.

Academics. **Special study options:** Independent study, study abroad. **Credit/placement by examination:** CLEP. **Support services:** Pre-admission summer program, remedial instruction.

Majors. **Theology:** Talmudic.

Student life. **Policies:** Religious observance required.

Contact. Phone: (718) 854-8777 ext. 23 Fax: (718) 851-1265
Rabbi A.M. Leizerowitz, Director of Admissions, Machzikei Hadath Rabbinical College, 5407 16th Avenue, Brooklyn, NY 11204

Manhattan College

Riverdale, New York — **CB member**
www.manhattan.edu — **CB code: 2395**

- Private 4-year engineering and liberal arts college affiliated with Roman Catholic Church
- Residential campus in very large city
- 3,026 degree-seeking undergraduates: 5% part-time, 50% women
- 399 degree-seeking graduate students
- 57% of applicants admitted
- SAT or ACT with writing, interview required

General. Founded in 1853. Regionally accredited. Independent institution in the Roman Catholic tradition sponsored by De La Salle Christian Brothers. **Degrees:** 620 bachelor's awarded; master's offered. **ROTC:** Army, Air Force. **Location:** 10 miles from midtown Manhattan. **Calendar:** Semester, extensive summer session. **Full-time faculty:** 195 total. **Part-time faculty:** 255 total. **Class size:** 52% < 20, 48% 20-39, less than 1% 40-49. **Special facilities:** Plant morphogenesis laboratory.

Freshman class profile. 4,712 applied, 2,708 admitted, 701 enrolled.

Mid 50% test scores		Out-of-state:	37%
SAT verbal:	510-600	Live on campus:	79%
SAT math:	520-620	Fraternities:	2%
Return as sophomores:	84%	Sororities:	3%

Basis for selection. School achievement record and test scores most important. Essay, recommendations, and extracurricular acivities also reviewed. Interview recommended.

High school preparation. 16 units required. Required and recommended units include English 4, mathematics 3-4, social studies 3, science 3 and foreign language 2-3. 4 mathematics, 4 science (including precalculus, chemistry, and physics) recommended of engineering majors and most science majors.

2006-2007 Annual costs. Tuition/fees: $21,550. Program fees range from $1,000 to $1,900 depending on program. Room/board: $8,800. Books/supplies: $750. Personal expenses: $1,000.

Financial aid. All financial aid based on need.

Application procedures. **Admission:** Closing date 3/1. $50 fee, may be waived for applicants with need. Application may be submitted online. Admission notification on a rolling basis beginning on or about 12/15. Must reply by 5/1. **Financial aid:** Priority date 2/15, closing date 4/15. FAFSA required. Applicants notified on a rolling basis starting 1/1; must reply by 5/1.

Academics. **Special study options:** Accelerated study, combined bachelor's/graduate degree, cooperative education, cross-registration, distance learning, double major, ESL, exchange student, honors, independent study, internships, study abroad, teacher certification program, Washington semester. **Credit/placement by examination:** AP, CLEP, institutional tests. 30 credit hours maximum toward bachelor's degree. **Support services:** Learning center, reduced course load, remedial instruction, study skills assistance, tutoring, writing center.

Majors. **Biology:** General, biochemistry. **Business:** General, accounting, finance, international, management information systems, managerial economics, statistics. **Communications:** General, broadcast journalism, journalism. **Computer sciences:** General, computer science, information systems. **Education:** General, biology, chemistry, computer, early childhood, elementary, English, foreign languages, French, health, history, mathematics, middle, physical, physics, science, secondary, social science, social studies, Spanish, special. **Engineering:** Chemical, civil, electrical, environmental, mechanical. **English:** Composition. **Foreign languages:** French, Spanish. **Health:** Nuclear medical technology, predentistry, premedicine, preveterinary. **History:** General. **Interdisciplinary:** Peace/conflict. **Legal studies:** Prelaw. **Math:** General. **Philosophy/religion:** Philosophy, religion. **Physical sciences:** Chemistry, physics. **Psychology:** General. **Social sciences:** Economics, sociology.

Computing on campus. 320 workstations in library, computer center, student center. Dormitories wired for high-speed internet access and linked to campus network. Commuter students can connect to campus network. Online course registration, online library, helpline, repair service available.

Student life. **Freshman orientation:** Mandatory. **Housing:** Guaranteed on-campus for all undergraduates. Coed dorms available. $700 deposit, deadline 5/1. **Activities:** Bands, choral groups, dance, drama, literary magazine, music ensembles, musical theater, radio station, student government, student newspaper, TV station, campus ministry, African American club, Caribbean society, Chinese student association, Circle-K, Gaelic society, Young Conservatives, Democrats, Republicans, multicultural student union.

Athletics. NCAA. **Intercollegiate:** Baseball M, basketball, cheerleading, cross-country, golf M, lacrosse, soccer, softball W, swimming W, tennis, track and field, volleyball W. **Intramural:** Baseball M, basketball, cross-country, soccer, softball, track and field, volleyball. **Team name:** Jaspers.

Student services. Alcohol/substance abuse counseling, campus ministries, career counseling, student employment services, financial aid counseling, health services, personal counseling, placement for graduates, veterans' counselor. **Physically disabled:** Services for visually, hearing impaired.

Contact. E-mail: admit@manhattan.edu
Phone: (718) 862-7200 Toll-free number: (800) 622-9235
Fax: (718) 862-8019
William Bissett, Assistant VP for Enrollment Management, Manhattan College, 4513 Manhattan College Parkway, Riverdale, NY 10471

Manhattan School of Music

New York, New York
www.msmnyc.edu — **CB code: 2396**

- Private 4-year music college
- Residential campus in very large city
- 416 degree-seeking undergraduates: 2% part-time, 50% women
- 474 degree-seeking graduate students
- 32% of applicants admitted
- Application essay required

General. Founded in 1917. Regionally accredited. **Degrees:** 90 bachelor's awarded; master's, doctoral offered. **Calendar:** Semester. **Full-time faculty:** 75 total; 25% have terminal degrees, 9% minority, 37% women. **Part-time faculty:** 305 total; 23% have terminal degrees, 17% minority, 43% women. **Class size:** 89% < 20, 5% 20-39, less than 1% 50-99, 6% >100. **Special facilities:** 1,000-seat concert hall, 3 recital halls, 2 electronic music studios, recording studio, performance library.

Freshman class profile. 863 applied, 279 admitted, 99 enrolled.

Out-of-state:	68%	Live on campus:	99%

Basis for selection. Audition, availability of space in specific performance area, and academic record most important. SAT or ACT recommended. Audition required. **Homeschooled:** Statement describing homeschool structure and mission, transcript of courses and grades required. GED accepted, but if no GED, SAT or ACT required.

High school preparation. College-preparatory program recommended. Recommended units include English 4, mathematics 3, social studies 4, history 4, science 3 and foreign language 4. Extensive music training required.

2005-2006 Annual costs. Tuition/fees: $26,460. Health fee of $1,875 is required unless already insured. Room/board: $12,250. Books/supplies: $1,000. Personal expenses: $1,500.

2004-2005 Financial aid. **Need-based:** 56% of total undergraduate aid awarded as scholarships/grants, 44% as loans/jobs. **Non-need-based:** Scholarships awarded for academics, alumni affiliation, leadership, music/drama.

Application procedures. **Admission:** Closing date 12/1 (receipt date). $100 fee, may be waived for applicants with need. Application must be submitted online. Admission notification 4/1. Must reply by May 1 or within 2 week(s) if notified thereafter. **Financial aid:** Closing date 3/1. FAFSA, institutional form, CSS PROFILE required. Applicants notified by 4/1; must reply by 5/1 or within 2 week(s) of notification.

Academics. **Special study options:** Cross-registration, ESL, study abroad. **Credit/placement by examination:** AP, CLEP, institutional tests. 60 credit hours maximum toward bachelor's degree. **Support services:** Reduced course load, remedial instruction, tutoring.

Majors. **Visual/performing arts:** Music performance, music theory/composition.

Computing on campus. 14 workstations in computer center. Dormitories wired for high-speed internet access.

Student life. **Freshman orientation:** Mandatory. Preregistration for classes offered. Held 1-2 weeks before classes start. **Policies:** Undergraduate students required to live in residence hall for first 2 years. First-year transfer students required to live in residence hall. Alcohol only allowed for those over 21 and only in designated areas. **Housing:** Guaranteed on-campus for freshmen. Coed dorms available. $500 nonrefundable deposit, deadline 6/15. **Activities:** Bands, choral groups, music ensembles, musical theater, opera, student government, symphony orchestra, Pan-African Student Union, international student association, Korean student association, resident community council, student council, politics discussion group, gay, lesbian and transgender club, Parallel Motion (a cappella choir), American music production.

Student services. Career counseling, student employment services, financial aid counseling. **Physically disabled:** Services for visually impaired.

Contact. E-mail: admission@msmnyc.edu
Phone: (212) 749-2802 ext. 4501 Fax: (212) 749-3025
Amy Anderson, Assistant Dean for Admission and Financial Aid, Manhattan School of Music, 120 Claremont Avenue, New York, NY 10027-4698

Manhattanville College

Purchase, New York — **CB member**
www.manhattanville.edu — **CB code: 2397**

- Private 4-year liberal arts and teachers college
- Residential campus in small town
- 1,713 degree-seeking undergraduates: 4% part-time, 69% women, 7% African American, 4% Asian American, 18% Hispanic American, 1% Native American, 3% international
- 1,009 graduate students
- 60% of applicants admitted
- SAT or ACT, application essay required
- 58% graduate within 6 years; 21% enter graduate study

General. Founded in 1841. Regionally accredited. Strong relationship with United Nations. **Degrees:** 360 bachelor's awarded; master's offered. **Location:** 25 miles from New York City. **Calendar:** Semester, extensive summer session. **Full-time faculty:** 90 total; 96% have terminal degrees, 13% minority, 51% women. **Part-time faculty:** 208 total; 7% minority, 60% women. **Class size:** 75% < 20, 24% 20-39, less than 1% 40-49. **Special facilities:** Photography laboratory, observatory, environmental biology laboratory, TV production studio.

Freshman class profile. 3,184 applied, 1,900 admitted, 642 enrolled.

Mid 50% test scores			
SAT verbal:	490-610	Rank in top tenth:	21%
SAT math:	490-610	End year in good standing:	74%
ACT:	19-24	Return as sophomores:	74%
Rank in top quarter:	47%	International:	4%

Basis for selection. School achievement record, recommendations, test scores or samples of academic work most important. Essay, school and community activities. Interview strongly recommended. Portfolio required for fine arts program; audition recommended for dance, music and theater programs.

High school preparation. 16 units required. Required units include English 4, mathematics 3, social studies 2, science 2 and academic electives 5.

2006-2007 Annual costs. Tuition/fees: $28,000. Room/board: $11,550. Books/supplies: $800. Personal expenses: $1,550.

2004-2005 Financial aid. **Need-based:** 391 full-time freshmen applied for aid; 340 were judged to have need; 338 of these received aid. Average need met was 81%. Average scholarship/grant was $11,137; average loan $3,132. **Non-need-based:** Awarded to 1,345 full-time undergraduates, including 399 freshmen. Scholarships awarded for academics, art, music/drama. **Additional information:** Upper level students may earn additional money and academic credit through internship program.

Application procedures. **Admission:** Closing date 3/1 (postmark date). $55 fee, may be waived for applicants with need. Application may be submitted online. Admission notification on a rolling basis beginning on or about 1/2. Must reply by May 1 or within 2 week(s) if notified thereafter. **Financial aid:** Closing date 3/1. FAFSA required. Applicants notified on a rolling basis starting 2/1; must reply by 5/1 or within 2 week(s) of notification.

Academics. Students must complete portfolio before graduation, which is individualized academic plan and profile. **Special study options:** Accelerated study, combined bachelor's/graduate degree, cooperative education, cross-registration, distance learning, double major, dual enrollment of high school students, ESL, exchange student, external degree, honors, independent study, internships, liberal arts/career combination, New York semester, student-designed major, study abroad, teacher certification program, Washington semester, weekend college. Study abroad programs in Oxford, Paris, Tokyo, Osaka, Madrid, Seville, Florence, Rome, Berlin, Galway and the world capitals program in Jerusalem, Santiago, Brussels, Buenos Aires, Prague, Moscow, and South Africa. **Credit/placement by examination:** AP, CLEP, IB, institutional tests. Up to 60 transfer credits allowed: up to 30 AP credits, up to 18 IB credits, no CLEP limit. **Support services:** Learning center, reduced course load, remedial instruction, study skills assistance, tutoring, writing center.

Majors. **Area/ethnic studies:** American, Asian, French. **Biology:** General, biochemistry. **Business:** Business admin, finance. **Communications:** General. **Computer sciences:** General. **Education:** General. **Foreign languages:** Romance. **History:** General. **Interdisciplinary:** Neuroscience. **Liberal arts:** Arts/sciences. **Math:** General. **Philosophy/religion:** Philosophy, religion. **Physical sciences:** Chemistry, physics. **Psychology:** General. **Social sciences:** Economics, political science, sociology. **Visual/performing arts:** Art history/conservation, dance, dramatic.

Most popular majors. Business/marketing 17%, communications/journalism 6%, education 9%, history 7%, psychology 15%, social sciences 13%, visual/performing arts 15%.

Computing on campus. 267 workstations in dormitories, library, computer center. Dormitories wired for high-speed internet access and linked to campus network. Commuter students can connect to campus network. Online course registration, online library, helpline, repair service, student web hosting, wireless network available.

Student life. **Freshman orientation:** Mandatory. **Policies:** Freshmen permitted cars on campus. **Housing:** Coed dorms, substance-free housing available. $325 deposit, deadline 5/1. **Activities:** Bands, choral groups, dance, drama, film society, literary magazine, music ensembles, musical theater, opera, radio station, student government, student newspaper, symphony orchestra, TV station, campus ministry, language and culture clubs, international students club, Students Organized Against Racism, Model United Nations, women's resource center, gay/straight coalition, political science association, multicultural advisory board, Black Student Union.

Athletics. NCAA. **Intercollegiate:** Baseball M, basketball, cheerleading M, field hockey W, golf M, ice hockey, lacrosse, soccer, softball W, tennis. **Intramural:** Basketball. **Team name:** Valiants.

Student services. Adult student services, alcohol/substance abuse counseling, campus ministries, career counseling, student employment services, financial aid counseling, health services, personal counseling, placement for graduates. **Physically disabled:** Services for visually, speech, hearing impaired. **Learning disabled:** Comprehensive services available.

Contact. E-mail: admissions@mville.edu
Phone: (914) 323-5464 Toll-free number: (800) 328-4553
Fax: (914) 694-1732
Erica Padilla, Director of Admissions, Manhattanville College, 2900 Purchase Street, Purchase, NY 10577

Mannes College The New School for Music

New York, New York
www.mannes.edu — **CB code: 2398**

- Private 4-year music college
- Commuter campus in very large city
- 208 degree-seeking undergraduates: 10% part-time, 56% women, 2% African American, 5% Asian American, 5% Hispanic American, 32% international
- 89 degree-seeking graduate students
- 29% of applicants admitted
- 57% graduate within 6 years

General. Founded in 1916. Regionally accredited. Division of the New School University. **Degrees:** 31 bachelor's awarded; master's offered. **Calendar:** Semester, limited summer session. **Full-time faculty:** 5 total; 20% women. **Part-time faculty:** 251 total; 17% minority, 48% women. **Class size:** 89% < 20, 11% 20-39. **Special facilities:** 2 concert halls.

Freshman class profile. 371 applied, 109 admitted, 38 enrolled.

GPA 3.50 or higher:	39%	**Return as sophomores:**	89%
GPA 3.0-3.49:	28%	**Out-of-state:**	58%
GPA 2.0-2.99:	28%	**International:**	18%

Basis for selection. In order of importance: specific talent for major as evidenced by audition in major instrument or evaluation of previous accomplishment for composers and theory majors, general musicianship skills (ear, theory, etc.), academic record. Institutionally designed entrance examination, including major audition. Written examinations in music theory, dictation, ear training, and English usage. Audition required, essay recommended. Placement exams and interviews required for all Bachelor of Music, Bachelor of Science, Undergraduate Diploma, and Master of Music applicants. If applicant does not complete all sessions, application incomplete and will not be considered for acceptance. Tapes may be submitted for advisory opinion.

High school preparation. Required and recommended units include English 4, mathematics 4, social studies 2, science 2 (laboratory 2) and foreign language 2.

2005-2006 Annual costs. Tuition/fees: $26,070. Room/board: $11,750. Books/supplies: $900. Personal expenses: $1,550.

2005-2006 Financial aid. Need-based: Average need met was 57%. Average scholarship/grant was $3,116; average loan $2,625. 49% of total undergraduate aid awarded as scholarships/grants, 51% as loans/jobs. **Non-need-based:** Scholarships awarded for academics, music/drama. **Additional information:** Closing date for scholarship applications 2 weeks prior to audition date.

Application procedures. Admission: Closing date 12/1 (postmark date). $100 fee. Admission notification on a rolling basis beginning on or about 4/15. Must reply by May 1 or within 4 week(s) if notified thereafter. **Financial aid:** Priority date 3/1; no closing date. FAFSA required. Applicants notified on a rolling basis starting 3/1; must reply within 4 week(s) of notification.

Academics. Special study options: Cross-registration, double major, ESL. **Credit/placement by examination:** CLEP, institutional tests. **Support services:** Remedial instruction, tutoring.

Majors. Visual/performing arts: Conducting, music performance, music theory/composition, piano/organ, stringed instruments, studio arts, voice/opera.

Computing on campus. 7 workstations in computer center. Dormitories wired for high-speed internet access and linked to campus network. Commuter students can connect to campus network. Online course registration, helpline, student web hosting, wireless network available.

Student life. Freshman orientation: Available. **Policies:** Freshmen permitted cars on campus. **Housing:** Coed dorms, special housing for disabled, apartments available. $250 deposit, deadline 6/1. **Activities:** Choral groups, music ensembles, opera, symphony orchestra.

Student services. Student employment services, health services, personal counseling.

Contact. E-mail: mannesadmissions@newschool.edu
Phone: (212) 580-0210 ext. 4862 Toll-free number: (800) 292-3040
Allison Scola, Associate Director of Admissions, Mannes College The New School for Music, 150 West 85th Street, New York, NY 10024

Marist College

Poughkeepsie, New York — **CB member**
www.marist.edu — **CB code: 2400**

- Private 4-year liberal arts college
- Residential campus in small city
- 4,851 degree-seeking undergraduates: 9% part-time, 57% women, 3% African American, 2% Asian American, 6% Hispanic American
- 805 degree-seeking graduate students
- 50% of applicants admitted
- SAT or ACT with writing, application essay required
- 76% graduate within 6 years; 26% enter graduate study

General. Founded in 1929. Regionally accredited. Substantial internship opportunities for all majors. Students participate in community service program. **Degrees:** 1,084 bachelor's awarded; master's offered. **ROTC:** Army. **Location:** 75 miles from New York City, 75 miles from Albany. **Calendar:** Semester, limited summer session. **Full-time faculty:** 201 total; 83% have terminal degrees, 11% minority, 43% women. **Part-time faculty:** 395 total; 10% minority, 45% women. **Class size:** 48% < 20, 52% 20-39, less than 1% 40-49, less than 1% 50-99. **Special facilities:** Bureau of economic research, laboratory for environmental studies, management studies center, institute for public opinion, on-campus arboretum, online journalism laboratory.

Freshman class profile. 7,077 applied, 3,513 admitted, 1,014 enrolled.

Mid 50% test scores		**GPA 2.0-2.99:**	14%
SAT verbal:	540-620	**Rank in top quarter:**	67%
SAT math:	550-640	**Rank in top tenth:**	29%
ACT:	24-28	**Return as sophomores:**	89%
GPA 3.50 or higher:	46%	**Out-of-state:**	48%
GPA 3.0-3.49:	40%	**Live on campus:**	95%

Basis for selection. Secondary school achievement record, rank in top third of class primary consideration. Test scores, recommendations, activities, personal and leadership qualities also important. Campus visits and information sessions with counselors strongly recommended. **Homeschooled:** Transcript of courses and grades, letter of recommendation (nonparent) required.

High school preparation. 17 units required. Required and recommended units include English 4, mathematics 3-4, social studies 2, history 1, science 3-4 (laboratory 2-3), foreign language 2-3 and academic electives 2. One American history required. 4 units mathematics recommended for computer science and physical science majors, 2 units social studies required, 2 units social science recommended.

2005-2006 Annual costs. Tuition/fees: $21,202. Room/board: $9,364. Books/supplies: $1,170. Personal expenses: $115.

2005-2006 Financial aid. Need-based: 858 full-time freshmen applied for aid; 625 were judged to have need; 624 of these received aid. Average need met was 78%. Average scholarship/grant was $10,971; average loan $3,565. 55% of total undergraduate aid awarded as scholarships/grants, 45% as loans/jobs. **Non-need-based:** Awarded to 2,387 full-time undergraduates, including 748 freshmen. Scholarships awarded for academics, athletics, music/drama, state residency.

Application procedures. Admission: Closing date 2/15 (postmark date). $40 fee, may be waived for applicants with need. Application may be submitted online. Admission notification 3/15. Must reply by 5/1. **Financial aid:** Priority date 2/15, closing date 5/1. FAFSA, institutional form required. Applicants notified on a rolling basis starting 3/15; must reply by 5/1 or within 2 week(s) of notification.

Academics. Paralegal certificates offered. **Special study options:** Accelerated study, combined bachelor's/graduate degree, cooperative education, cross-registration, distance learning, double major, dual enrollment of high school students, ESL, honors, independent study, internships, liberal arts/career combination, semester at sea, study abroad, teacher certification program, United Nations semester, Washington semester, weekend college. Undergraduates may take graduate classes. Cooperative education in arts, business, computer science, education, humanities, natural science, social/behavioral science, technologies. **Credit/placement by examination:** AP, CLEP, IB, SAT, ACT, institutional tests. ACT-PEP accepted on individual basis. **Support services:** Learning center, reduced course load, study skills assistance, tutoring, writing center.

Majors. Area/ethnic studies: American. **Biology:** General, biochemistry, biomedical sciences. **Business:** Accounting, business admin, fashion. **Communications:** Advertising, digital media, journalism, organizational, public relations, radio/tv. **Computer sciences:** General, computer science, information systems, information technology. **Conservation:** Environmental science. **Education:** Biology, chemistry, English, French, history, mathematics, social studies, Spanish, special. **English:** English lit. **Foreign languages:** French, Spanish. **Health:** Athletic training, clinical lab science. **History:** General. **Math:** General, computational. **Philosophy/religion:** Philosophy. **Physical sciences:** Chemistry. **Protective services:** Law enforcement admin. **Psychology:** General. **Public administration:** Social work. **Social sciences:** Economics, political science. **Visual/performing arts:** Art, art history/conservation, fashion design, studio arts.

Most popular majors. Business/marketing 24%, communications/journalism 22%, education 11%, liberal arts 11%.

Computing on campus. 566 workstations in dormitories, library, computer center, student center. Dormitories wired for high-speed internet access and linked to campus network. Commuter students can connect to campus network. Online course registration, online library, helpline, repair service, student web hosting, wireless network available.

Student life. Freshman orientation: Mandatory, $90 fee. 1-day orientation in June. **Housing:** Guaranteed on-campus for freshmen. Coed dorms, special housing for disabled, apartments, substance-free housing available. $200 nonrefundable deposit, deadline 5/1. Garden apartments, townhouses, suites available. **Activities:** Bands, choral groups, dance, drama, film society, literary magazine, music ensembles, musical theater, radio station, student government, student newspaper, TV station, campus ministry, Black student union, Asian Alliance, Circle K, ARCO, community service programs, Habitat for Humanity, political science club, Marist College Council on Theatre Arts, social action clubs.

Athletics. NCAA. **Intercollegiate:** Baseball M, basketball, cross-country, diving, football (tackle) M, lacrosse, rowing (crew), soccer, softball W, swimming, tennis, track and field, volleyball W, water polo W. **Intramural:** Basketball, soccer, softball, volleyball. **Team name:** Red Foxes.

Student services. Adult student services, alcohol/substance abuse counseling, campus ministries, career counseling, student employment services, financial aid counseling, health services, personal counseling, placement for graduates, veterans' counselor. **Physically disabled:** Services for visually, hearing impaired. **Learning disabled:** Comprehensive services available.

Contact. E-mail: admissions@marist.edu
Phone: (845) 575-3226 Toll-free number: (800) 436-5483
Fax: (845) 575-3215
Jay Murray, Director of Admissions, Marist College, 3399 North Road, Poughkeepsie, NY 12601-1387

Marymount Manhattan College

New York, New York — **CB member**
www.mmm.edu — **CB code: 2405**

- Private 4-year liberal arts college
- Residential campus in very large city
- 1,908 degree-seeking undergraduates: 17% part-time, 78% women, 12% African American, 5% Asian American, 11% Hispanic American, 2% international
- 77% of applicants admitted
- SAT or ACT with writing, application essay required
- 46% graduate within 6 years; 33% enter graduate study

General. Founded in 1936. Regionally accredited. **Degrees:** 435 bachelor's, 6 associate awarded. **Calendar:** Semester, limited summer session. **Full-time faculty:** 86 total; 80% have terminal degrees, 12% minority, 58% women. **Part-time faculty:** 217 total; 34% have terminal degrees, 13% minority, 58% women. **Class size:** 74% < 20, 26% 20-39. **Special facilities:** Communications and learning center, communication arts multimedia suite, center for science education.

Freshman class profile. 2,033 applied, 1,559 admitted, 451 enrolled.

Mid 50% test scores			
SAT verbal:	490-600	GPA 2.0-2.99:	34%
SAT math:	460-570	End year in good standing:	91%
ACT:	20-25	Return as sophomores:	72%
GPA 3.50 or higher:	25%	Out-of-state:	68%
GPA 3.0-3.49:	39%	Live on campus:	82%
		International:	2%

Basis for selection. High school GPA of 3.0 and SAT verbal and math scores of 450 each recommended. Letters of recommendation from teachers and administrators, extracurricular and community activities important. Rolling deadline for SAT/ACT score receipt. Interview recommended for all; audition required for acting, dance, and theater programs; portfolio recommended for art program. **Homeschooled:** Transcript of courses and grades required. Must submit official high school transcripts if high school attended before withdrawing. **Learning Disabled:** Interview and Wechsler Delta Adult Intelligence Scale test required.

High school preparation. 16 units required. Required and recommended units include English 4, mathematics 3, social studies 3, science 2-3, foreign language 3 and academic electives 4.

2005-2006 Annual costs. Tuition/fees: $18,530. Room only: $9,520. Books/supplies: $1,000. Personal expenses: $1,500.

2005-2006 Financial aid. Need-based: Average need met was 46%. Average scholarship/grant was $3,469; average loan $2,594. 48% of total undergraduate aid awarded as scholarships/grants, 52% as loans/jobs. **Non-need-based:** Scholarships awarded for academics, art, leadership, music/drama. **Additional information:** Limited international scholarships for top applicants.

Application procedures. Admission: Priority date 3/15; no deadline. $60 fee, may be waived for applicants with need. Application may be submitted online. Admission notification on a rolling basis. Must reply by May 1 or within 2 week(s) if notified thereafter. **Financial aid:** Priority date 3/15; no closing date. FAFSA required. Applicants notified on a rolling basis starting 3/15; must reply by 5/1 or within 2 week(s) of notification.

Academics. Special study options: Accelerated study, cooperative education, cross-registration, distance learning, double major, dual enrollment of high school students, ESL, exchange student, honors, independent study, internships, liberal arts/career combination, study abroad, teacher certification program. 5-year bachelors/masters program in computer science with Polytechnic University, programs with Laboratory Institute of Merchandising, New York School of Interior Design, Deutsches Haus at New York University, China Institute, New York Institute of Finance, American Institute of Banking, Hunter College of CUNY, Martha Graham School of Dance, HEOP. **Credit/placement by examination:** AP, CLEP, IB, institutional tests. 30 credit hours maximum toward bachelor's degree. Maximum of 12 credits for language proficiency. SAT Subject used for placement if submitted. **Support services:** Learning center, reduced course load, remedial instruction, study skills assistance, tutoring, writing center.

Majors. Biology: General. **Business:** Accounting, business admin. **Communications:** General. **English:** English lit. **Health:** Audiology/speech pathology. **History:** General. **Liberal arts:** Humanities. **Psychology:** General. **Social sciences:** International relations, sociology. **Visual/performing arts:** Acting, art, dance, dramatic, studio arts.

Most popular majors. Business/marketing 12%, communications/journalism 26%, English 6%, psychology 9%, social sciences 9%, visual/performing arts 33%.

Computing on campus. 175 workstations in library, computer center, student center. Dormitories wired for high-speed internet access and linked to campus network. Commuter students can connect to campus network. Wireless network available.

Student life. Freshman orientation: Mandatory. Preregistration for classes offered. 3 days of introductions, information, activities, and social engagements. **Policies:** Freshmen permitted cars on campus. **Housing:** Coed dorms, apartments available. $500 nonrefundable deposit, deadline 5/1. **Activities:** Choral groups, dance, drama, film society, literary magazine, music ensembles, musical theater, opera, radio station, student government, student newspaper, TV station, ethnic, religious, political, women's, environmental, and cultural groups, student professional organizations, and honor societies.

Student services. Adult student services, alcohol/substance abuse counseling, campus ministries, career counseling, student employment services, financial aid counseling, health services, personal counseling, placement for graduates. **Physically disabled:** Services for speech, hearing impaired. **Learning disabled:** Comprehensive services available.

Contact. E-mail: admissions@mmm.edu
Phone: (212) 517-0430 Toll-free number: (800) 627-9668
Fax: (212) 517-0448
Jim Rogers, Dean of Admissions, Marymount Manhattan College, 221 East 71st Street, New York, NY 10021-4597

Medaille College

Buffalo, New York
www.medaille.edu — **CB code: 2422**

- Private 4-year liberal arts college
- Commuter campus in large city
- 1,718 degree-seeking undergraduates: 8% part-time, 64% women, 14% African American, 1% Asian American, 3% Hispanic American
- 1,241 degree-seeking graduate students
- 73% of applicants admitted
- SAT or ACT with writing, application essay, interview required
- 40% graduate within 6 years; 24% enter graduate study

General. Founded in 1875. Regionally accredited. All preprofessional programs require participation in at least 1 internship. Branch campuses in Amherst and Rochester. **Degrees:** 255 bachelor's, 104 associate awarded; master's offered. **ROTC:** Army. **Location:** 3 miles from downtown. **Calendar:** Semester, limited summer session. **Full-time faculty:** 91 total; 63% have terminal degrees, 13% minority, 46% women. **Part-time faculty:** 221 total; 9% have terminal degrees, 4% minority, 50% women. **Class size:** 77% < 20, 23% 20-39. **Special facilities:** New media institute.

Freshman class profile. 978 applied, 716 admitted, 209 enrolled.

Mid 50% test scores			
SAT verbal:	490-560	Rank in top quarter:	33%
SAT math:	470-540	Rank in top tenth:	12%
ACT:	17-21	End year in good standing:	80%
GPA 3.50 or higher:	22%	Return as sophomores:	70%
GPA 3.0-3.49:	30%	Live on campus:	28%
GPA 2.0-2.99:	42%	International:	1%

Basis for selection. Motivation and maturity, as well as academic record and test scores, considered.

High school preparation. 12 units required; 20 recommended. Required and recommended units include English 4, mathematics 2-3, social studies 4, history 2, science 2-3 (laboratory 2) and foreign language 2. 3 units mathematics, 3 units science recommended for veterinary technology.

2005-2006 Annual costs. Tuition/fees: $15,030. Room/board: $7,430. Books/supplies: $1,050. Personal expenses: $1,100.

2004-2005 Financial aid. Need-based: 296 full-time freshmen applied for aid; 296 were judged to have need; 296 of these received aid. Average need met was 70%. Average scholarship/grant was $4,000; average loan $3,200. 41% of total undergraduate aid awarded as scholarships/grants, 59% as loans/jobs. **Non-need-based:** Awarded to 692 full-time undergraduates, including 335 freshmen. Scholarships awarded for academics, state residency.

Application procedures. Admission: Priority date 8/1; no deadline. $25 fee, may be waived for applicants with need. Application may be submitted online. Admission notification on a rolling basis beginning on or about 10/1. Must reply by May 1 or within 4 week(s) if notified thereafter. **Financial aid:** Priority date 4/15; no closing date. FAFSA, institutional form required. Applicants notified on a rolling basis starting 5/1; must reply within 2 week(s) of notification.

Academics. Special study options: Accelerated study, combined bachelor's/graduate degree, cross-registration, double major, honors, independent study, internships, liberal arts/career combination, student-designed major, teacher certification program, weekend college. Module system for full-time evening students. **Credit/placement by examination:** AP, CLEP, IB, institutional tests. 30 credit hours maximum toward associate degree, 60 toward bachelor's. **Support services:** Learning center, reduced course load, remedial instruction, study skills assistance, tutoring.

Majors. Biology: General. **Business:** General, business admin, entrepreneurial studies, financial planning, training/development. **Communications:** Media studies. **Computer sciences:** General, programming, web page design. **Education:** General, early childhood, elementary, middle. **English:** Creative writing, English lit, technical writing. **Family/consumer sciences:** Child care. **Health:** Veterinary technology/assistant. **Interdisciplinary:** Biopsychology. **Liberal arts:** Arts/sciences. **Parks/recreation:** Sports admin. **Protective services:** Police science. **Psychology:** General. **Public administration:** Youth services. **Social sciences:** General, criminology. **Visual/performing arts:** General.

Most popular majors. Business/marketing 51%, education 11%, liberal arts 9%, security/protective services 8%.

Computing on campus. 120 workstations in dormitories, library, computer center, student center. Dormitories wired for high-speed internet access and linked to campus network.

Student life. Freshman orientation: Mandatory. Preregistration for classes offered. **Policies:** Freshmen permitted cars on campus. **Housing:** Coed dorms, single-sex dorms, apartments available. $100 deposit, deadline 9/1. **Activities:** Drama, film society, literary magazine, musical theater, radio station, student government, student newspaper, TV station, African American Student Union, child and youth services club, Student Volunteer Center, multicultural association, SADD, International Student Society, resident student council.

Athletics. NCAA. **Intercollegiate:** Baseball M, basketball, cross-country W, golf, lacrosse, soccer, softball W, volleyball. **Team name:** Mavericks.

Student services. Adult student services, career counseling, student employment services, financial aid counseling, health services, personal counseling, placement for graduates, veterans' counselor. **Physically disabled:** Services for visually, speech, hearing impaired.

Contact. E-mail: sdesing@medaille.edu
Phone: (716) 880-2200 Toll-free number: (800) 292-1582
Fax: (716) 880-2007
Greg Florczak, Director of Undergraduate Admissions, Medaille College, 18 Agassiz Circle, Buffalo, NY 14214

Medaille College: Amherst
Williamsville, New York

- Private 4-year liberal arts college

Annual costs/financial aid. Tuition/fees (2005-2006): $15,030.

Contact. Phone: (716) 631-1061
400 Essjay Road, Suite 100, Williamsville, NY 14221

Medaille College: Rochester
Rochester, New York

- Private 4-year liberal arts college

Annual costs/financial aid. Tuition/fees (2005-2006): $15,030.

Contact. Phone: (585) 272-0030
100 Corporate Woods, Suite 200, Rochester, NY 14623

Mercy College
Dobbs Ferry, New York
www.mercy.edu **CB code: 2409**

- Private 4-year liberal arts college
- Commuter campus in small town
- 5,204 degree-seeking undergraduates: 31% African American, 3% Asian American, 34% Hispanic American, 2% international
- 3,631 degree-seeking graduate students
- 42% of applicants admitted
- Interview required

General. Founded in 1950. Regionally accredited. Campuses in Dobbs Ferry, White Plains, Yorktown Heights, Bronx, Manhattan and several extension centers. **Degrees:** 1,219 bachelor's, 146 associate awarded; master's offered. **Calendar:** Semester, extensive summer session. **Full-time faculty:** 176 total; 65% have terminal degrees, 16% minority, 51% women. **Part-time faculty:** 655 total.

Freshman class profile. 2,110 applied, 888 admitted, 605 enrolled.

Return as sophomores:	61%	Live on campus:	3%
Out-of-state:	4%	International:	2%

Basis for selection. Recommendations, essay, interview (if required), and activities most important. SAT recommended. Most applicants must take placement examination to determine writing and mathematics skills; requirement may be waived under certain academic circumstances. Additional interview with program director required for applied music, nursing, occupational therapy, physical therapy, social work, veterinary technology, computer arts programs.

High school preparation. 21 units required. Required units include English 4, mathematics 3, social studies 2, history 2, science 3 (laboratory 1), foreign language 3 and academic electives 3.

2006-2007 Annual costs. Tuition/fees: $12,570. Room/board: $8,678.

Financial aid. Non-need-based: Scholarships awarded for athletics.

Application procedures. Admission: No deadline. $37 fee, may be waived for applicants with need. Application may be submitted online. Admission notification on a rolling basis. **Financial aid:** Priority date 6/1; no closing date. FAFSA required. Applicants notified on a rolling basis starting 3/1; must reply within 4 week(s) of notification.

Academics. Programs leading to provisional state certification offered in education. **Special study options:** Accelerated study, combined bachelor's/graduate degree, cooperative education, cross-registration, distance learning, double major, ESL, honors, independent study, internships, student-designed major, teacher certification program, weekend college. Program for college students with learning disabilities. **Credit/placement by examination:** AP, CLEP, SAT, institutional tests. 30 credit hours maximum toward associate degree, 30 toward bachelor's. **Support services:** Learning center, pre-admission summer program, reduced course load, remedial instruction, study skills assistance, tutoring, writing center.

Majors. Agriculture: Animal sciences. **Biology:** General. **Business:** Accounting, business admin. **Computer sciences:** General, information systems. **Education:** Early childhood, elementary, English, ESL, mathematics, middle, social studies, Spanish, special. **English:** English lit. **Foreign languages:** Spanish. **Health:** Audiology/speech pathology, clinical lab science. **History:** General. **Legal studies:** Paralegal. **Liberal arts:** Arts/sciences. **Math:** General. **Protective services:** Law enforcement admin. **Psychology:** General. **Public administration:** Social work. **Social sciences:** General, political science, sociology. **Visual/performing arts:** Commercial/advertising art, music performance.

Most popular majors. Business/marketing 21%, health sciences 15%, psychology 14%, social sciences 25%.

Computing on campus. 500 workstations in dormitories, library, computer center, student center. Dormitories wired for high-speed internet access and linked to campus network. Commuter students can connect to campus network. Online course registration, online library, helpline, repair service available.

Student life. Freshman orientation: Available. Preregistration for classes offered. **Policies:** 60% of students evening or adult students. Student services geared to commuter population with midday activities and programs. Freshmen permitted cars on campus. **Housing:** Coed dorms, substance-free housing available. $300 deposit, deadline 7/6. **Activities:** Dance, radio station, student government, student newspaper, Campus Christian Ministry, Honos Club, Impact, international friendship club, Latin American Student Association (LASA), Lyon Club, mentoring program, occupational therapy assistant club, physical therapy club, pre-health profession club.

Athletics. NCAA. **Intercollegiate:** Baseball M, basketball, cross-country, golf M, soccer, softball W, tennis M, track and field, volleyball W. **Intramural:** Badminton, baseball M, basketball. **Team name:** Flyers.

Student services. Adult student services, alcohol/substance abuse counseling, career counseling, services for economically disadvantaged, student employment services, financial aid counseling, health services, minority student services, personal counseling, placement for graduates. **Physically disabled:** Services for visually, speech, hearing impaired.

Contact. E-mail: admissions@mercy.edu
Phone: (914) 674-7324 Toll-free number: (800) 637-2946
Fax: (914) 674-7382
Kathleen Jackson, Director of Admissions, Mercy College, 555 Broadway, Dobbs Ferry, NY 10522

Mesivta Torah Vodaath Seminary

Brooklyn, New York

CB code: 0636

- Private 5-year rabbinical college for men affiliated with Jewish faith
- Very large city

General. Founded in 1918. Accredited by AARTS. **Calendar:** Semester.

Annual costs/financial aid. Tuition/fees (2005-2006): $6,000.

Contact. Phone: (718) 941-8000
Director of Admissions, 425 East Ninth Street, Brooklyn, NY 11218

Metropolitan College of New York

New York, New York **CB member**
www.metropolitan.edu **CB code: 4802**

- Private 4-year business and liberal arts college
- Commuter campus in very large city
- 1,072 degree-seeking undergraduates
- 373 graduate students
- 99% of applicants admitted
- Application essay, interview required

General. Founded in 1964. Regionally accredited. Students attend 3-semester full year with 1-month break. Off-site extensions for human services program in the Bronx, Staten Island and northeastern Queens. Students receive credit for applying studies to jobs or internship sites. **Degrees:** 311 bachelor's, 70 associate awarded; master's offered. **Calendar:** 3 full semesters a year. Extensive summer session. **Full-time faculty:** 40 total. **Part-time faculty:** 246 total. **Class size:** 73% < 20, 27% 20-39.

Freshman class profile. 208 applied, 206 admitted, 172 enrolled.

Basis for selection. Academic record, test scores, previous volunteer experience, school and community activities, professional recommendations, motivation and communication skills as demonstrated in interviews considered. SAT or ACT recommended. Combined SAT score of 1050 (exclusive of Writing) or higher can be substituted for institution-administered Test of Adult Basic Education or ACCUPLACER required for admission.

High school preparation. 16 units required. Required units include English 4, mathematics 2, social studies 2, science 1 and foreign language 4.

2005-2006 Annual costs. Tuition/fees: $14,540. Books/supplies: $1,500. Personal expenses: $726.

Financial aid. Non-need-based: Scholarships awarded for academics. **Additional information:** Limited merit scholarships.

Application procedures. Admission: Priority date 8/15; no deadline. $30 fee, may be waived for applicants with need. Application may be submitted online. Admission notification on a rolling basis beginning on or about 3/15. **Financial aid:** Priority date 8/15; no closing date. FAFSA required. Applicants notified on a rolling basis.

Academics. Class work integrated with field work. Class learning applied, documented and assessed in internship or employment setting. **Special study options:** Accelerated study, cooperative education, internships, study abroad, weekend college. **Credit/placement by examination:** CLEP, IB. 32 credit hours maximum toward bachelor's degree. **Support services:** Learning center, remedial instruction, tutoring.

Majors. Area/ethnic studies: African-American. **Business:** General, business admin, communications, managerial economics. **Communications:** General. **Education:** General. **Legal studies:** Prelaw. **Philosophy/religion:** Philosophy. **Psychology:** General. **Public administration:** Community org/advocacy, human services, social work. **Social sciences:** General, sociology, urban studies.

Computing on campus. 130 workstations in library, computer center.

Student life. Freshman orientation: Mandatory. **Activities:** Drama, student government, student newspaper, honor societies, networking club, dance committee.

Student services. Adult student services, career counseling, student employment services, financial aid counseling, personal counseling, placement for graduates, veterans' counselor. **Physically disabled:** Services for visually, hearing impaired.

Contact. Phone: (212) 343-1234 ext. 5001 Toll-free number: (800) 338-4465 Fax: (212) 343-8470
Peter Vida, Vice President of Enrollment Management, Metropolitan College of New York, 75 Varick Street, New York, NY 10013-1919

Mirrer Yeshiva Central Institute

Brooklyn, New York

CB code: 0661

- Private 4-year rabbinical college for men affiliated with Jewish faith
- Very large city

General. Accredited by AARTS. **Calendar:** Continuous.

Annual costs/financial aid. Tuition/fees (2005-2006): $4,700. Room/board: $4,000.

Contact. Phone: (718) 645-0536
Admissions Director, 1795 Ocean Parkway, Brooklyn, NY 11223

Molloy College

Rockville Centre, New York **CB member**
www.molloy.edu **CB code: 2415**

- Private 4-year liberal arts college affiliated with Roman Catholic Church
- Commuter campus in large town
- 2,589 degree-seeking undergraduates: 28% part-time, 78% women, 20% African American, 6% Asian American, 8% Hispanic American
- 785 degree-seeking graduate students
- 65% of applicants admitted
- SAT or ACT (ACT writing optional), application essay required
- 63% graduate within 6 years

General. Founded in 1955. Regionally accredited. Independent institution in Dominican tradition. **Degrees:** 406 bachelor's, 33 associate awarded; master's offered. **ROTC:** Army, Navy, Air Force. **Location:** 20 miles from

New York City. **Calendar:** 4-1-4, limited summer session. **Full-time faculty:** 147 total; 54% have terminal degrees, 12% minority, 74% women. **Part-time faculty:** 328 total; 16% have terminal degrees, 7% minority, 66% women. **Class size:** 64% < 20, 36% 20-39, less than 1% 40-49, less than 1% 50-99. **Special facilities:** Theater, weather station at Jones Beach, international business center.

Freshman class profile. 1,093 applied, 705 admitted, 294 enrolled.

Mid 50% test scores			
SAT verbal:	450-560	GPA 3.0-3.49:	44%
SAT math:	440-600	GPA 2.0-2.99:	32%
GPA 3.50 or higher:	24%	Rank in top quarter:	48%
		Rank in top tenth:	17%

Basis for selection. Secondary school achievement with particular attention to grade 11 performance most important. Test scores also important. Recommendations, school and community activities, interview considered. Audition required for music program; portfolio required for art program. **Learning Disabled:** Applicants reviewed by separate committee.

High school preparation. 19 units required. Required units include English 4, mathematics 3, social studies 4, science 3 and foreign language 3. Science, mathematics, and nursing majors must have 1 biology, 1 chemistry, and 3 mathematics.

2005-2006 Annual costs. Tuition/fees: $16,810. Books/supplies: $800. Personal expenses: $1,250.

2004-2005 Financial aid. Need-based: 290 full-time freshmen applied for aid; 238 were judged to have need; 238 of these received aid. Average need met was 65%. Average scholarship/grant was $7,518; average loan $3,583. 38% of total undergraduate aid awarded as scholarships/grants, 62% as loans/jobs. **Non-need-based:** Awarded to 371 full-time undergraduates, including 91 freshmen. Scholarships awarded for academics, art, athletics, leadership, music/drama.

Application procedures. Admission: No deadline. $30 fee, may be waived for applicants with need. Application may be submitted online. Admission notification on a rolling basis beginning on or about 12/1. **Financial aid:** Priority date 4/15, closing date 5/1. FAFSA required. Applicants notified by 3/1; Applicants notified on a rolling basis.

Academics. Special study options: Accelerated study, combined bachelor's/graduate degree, cooperative education, cross-registration, double major, ESL, honors, independent study, internships, liberal arts/career combination, student-designed major, study abroad, teacher certification program, weekend college. **Credit/placement by examination:** AP, CLEP, IB, SAT, ACT, institutional tests. 15 credit hours maximum toward associate degree, 30 toward bachelor's. **Support services:** Learning center, pre-admission summer program, reduced course load, remedial instruction, study skills assistance, tutoring, writing center.

Majors. Biology: General. **Business:** Accounting, business admin. **Communications:** General. **Computer sciences:** Computer science, information systems. **Conservation:** Environmental studies. **Education:** General, art, biology, business, elementary, English, French, history, mathematics, music, secondary, social studies, Spanish, special. **Foreign languages:** French, Spanish. **Health:** Audiology/speech pathology, health services admin, music therapy, nursing (RN), predentistry, premedicine, preop/surgical nursing, preveterinary. **History:** General. **Interdisciplinary:** Peace/conflict. **Legal studies:** Prelaw. **Math:** General. **Philosophy/religion:** Philosophy. **Protective services:** Criminal justice. **Psychology:** General. **Public administration:** Social work. **Social sciences:** Political science, sociology. **Visual/performing arts:** Art.

Most popular majors. Business/marketing 10%, education 19%, health sciences 30%, public administration/social services 6%.

Computing on campus. 250 workstations in library, computer center, student center. Commuter students can connect to campus network. Helpline, wireless network available.

Student life. Freshman orientation: Mandatory. **Policies:** Freshmen permitted cars on campus. **Activities:** Jazz band, choral groups, dance, drama, literary magazine, music ensembles, musical theater, student government, student newspaper, Students at Molloy Interested in Life and Environment, Siena Women's Center, campus ministry, business club, community service organization, African American Caribbean organization, Students for Social Change, Gaelic society, Institute for Cross Cultural and Ethnic Studies, National Student Speech Language and Hearing Association.

Athletics. NCAA. **Intercollegiate:** Baseball M, basketball, cross-country, lacrosse, soccer, softball W, tennis W, track and field, volleyball W. **Team name:** Lions.

Student services. Adult student services, alcohol/substance abuse counseling, campus ministries, career counseling, services for economically disadvantaged, student employment services, financial aid counseling, health services, personal counseling, placement for graduates, veterans' counselor. **Physically disabled:** Services for visually, hearing impaired.

Contact. E-mail: admissions@molloy.edu
Phone: (516) 678-5000 ext. 6240 Toll-free number: (888) 466-5569
Fax: (516) 256-2247
Marguerite Lane, Director of Admissions, Molloy College, PO Box 5002, Rockville Centre, NY 11570

Monroe College

Bronx, New York
www.monroecollege.edu **CB code: 2463**

- For-profit 4-year business college
- Commuter campus in very large city
- 5,866 degree-seeking undergraduates: 10% part-time, 71% women, 46% African American, 1% Asian American, 43% Hispanic American, 5% international
- 60% of applicants admitted
- Application essay, interview required
- 48% graduate within 6 years

General. Founded in 1933. Regionally accredited. Branch campus in New Rochelle offers all programs, courses, and services available at main campus. **Degrees:** 741 bachelor's, 1,239 associate awarded; master's offered. **ROTC:** Army. **Calendar:** Trimester, extensive summer session. **Full-time faculty:** 70 total; 40% have terminal degrees, 57% minority, 44% women. **Part-time faculty:** 160 total; 14% have terminal degrees, 71% minority, 60% women. **Class size:** 44% < 20, 55% 20-39, less than 1% 50-99.

Freshman class profile. 2,404 applied, 1,454 admitted, 1,301 enrolled.

End year in good standing:	91%	Live on campus:	25%
Return as sophomores:	69%	International:	5%
Out-of-state:	1%		

Basis for selection. Interview, school achievement record, test scores required. Modified open admissions for students who pass admissions test.

2005-2006 Annual costs. Tuition/fees: $9,760. Room/board: $6,900. Books/supplies: $900. Personal expenses: $3,720.

2004-2005 Financial aid. All financial aid based on need. Average need met was 86%. Average scholarship/grant was $7,300; average loan $3,434. 65% of total undergraduate aid awarded as scholarships/grants, 35% as loans/jobs.

Application procedures. Admission: No deadline. $35 fee. Application may be submitted online. Admission notification on a rolling basis. **Financial aid:** Closing date 3/31. FAFSA required. Applicants notified on a rolling basis starting 7/1.

Academics. Special study options: Cooperative education, distance learning, dual enrollment of high school students, honors, internships, liberal arts/career combination, study abroad, weekend college. **Credit/placement by examination:** AP, CLEP, IB. 30 credit hours maximum toward associate degree, 30 toward bachelor's. **Support services:** Learning center, pre-admission summer program, remedial instruction, tutoring, writing center.

Majors. Business: Accounting, business admin. **Computer sciences:** General. **Health:** Health services admin. **Protective services:** Law enforcement admin.

Most popular majors. Business/marketing 70%, computer/information sciences 23%.

Computing on campus. 800 workstations in dormitories, library, computer center. Dormitories wired for high-speed internet access. Helpline, wireless network available.

Student life. Freshman orientation: Mandatory. Preregistration for classes offered. **Policies:** Freshmen permitted cars on campus. **Housing:** Coed dorms available. $100 nonrefundable deposit. Assistance for foreign students in securing local housing. Student apartments available near New Rochelle campus. On-campus housing at New Rochelle campus. **Activities:** Dance, student newspaper.

Athletics. NJCAA. **Intercollegiate:** Baseball M, basketball, soccer M. **Intramural:** Basketball, softball M, volleyball. **Team name:** Mustangs.

Student services. Adult student services, career counseling, student employment services, financial aid counseling, personal counseling, placement for graduates, veterans' counselor. **Physically disabled:** Services for visually, speech, hearing impaired.

Contact. E-mail: aallen@monroecollege.edu
Phone: (718) 933-6700 Toll-free number: (800) 556-6676
Fax: (718) 364-3552
Even Jerome, Director of Admissions, Monroe College, Monroe College Way, Bronx, NY 10468

Mount St. Mary College

Newburgh, New York **CB member**
www.msmc.edu **CB code: 2423**

- Private 4-year liberal arts college
- Residential campus in large town
- 2,002 degree-seeking undergraduates: 19% part-time, 73% women, 11% African American, 3% Asian American, 9% Hispanic American
- 524 degree-seeking graduate students
- 79% of applicants admitted
- SAT or ACT with writing required
- 60% graduate within 6 years; 76% enter graduate study

General. Founded in 1954. Regionally accredited. Independent institution in Judeo-Christian tradition, founded by Dominican Sisters of Newburgh. **Degrees:** 415 bachelor's awarded; master's offered. **Location:** 58 miles from New York City. **Calendar:** Semester, limited summer session. **Full-time faculty:** 71 total; 82% have terminal degrees, 6% minority, 56% women. **Part-time faculty:** 150 total; 18% have terminal degrees, 7% minority, 53% women. **Class size:** 45% < 20, 51% 20-39, 2% 40-49, less than 1% 50-99. **Special facilities:** Elementary school on campus.

Freshman class profile. 1,625 applied, 1,285 admitted, 360 enrolled.

Mid 50% test scores			
SAT verbal:	450-550	Rank in top quarter:	27%
SAT math:	460-550	Rank in top tenth:	8%
ACT:	18-22	End year in good standing:	80%
GPA 3.50 or higher:	24%	Return as sophomores:	70%
GPA 3.0-3.49:	37%	Out-of-state:	21%
GPA 2.0-2.99:	36%	Live on campus:	71%

Basis for selection. Admissions decisions based on total admission score which weighs high school average, class rank, and test scores as well as teacher/counselor recommendations. Interview recommended for all; essay required for special consideration, recommended for all others. **Homeschooled:** Transcript of courses and grades required. **Learning Disabled:** Must include IEP with application. Must meet with Director of Counseling and Coordinator of Services for Persons with Disabilities.

High school preparation. College-preparatory program recommended. 20 units recommended. Recommended units include English 4, mathematics 3, social studies 4, science 3, foreign language 3, academic electives 3.5. Recommended mathematics sequence: algebra, geometry, trigonometry. Biology and chemistry required for nursing majors.

2005-2006 Annual costs. Tuition/fees: $16,930. Room/board: $8,320. Books/supplies: $900. Personal expenses: $800.

2005-2006 Financial aid. All financial aid based on need. 270 full-time freshmen applied for aid; 209 were judged to have need; 208 of these received aid. Average scholarship/grant was $6,569; average loan $3,334. 41% of total undergraduate aid awarded as scholarships/grants, 59% as loans/jobs.

Application procedures. Admission: Priority date 4/1; no deadline. $35 fee, may be waived for applicants with need. Application may be submitted online. Admission notification on a rolling basis beginning on or about 9/1. **Financial aid:** Closing date 2/15. FAFSA, institutional form required. Applicants notified on a rolling basis starting 4/1; must reply within 2 week(s) of notification.

Academics. Special study options: Accelerated study, combined bachelor's/graduate degree, cooperative education, cross-registration, distance learning, double major, dual enrollment of high school students, exchange student, honors, independent study, internships, liberal arts/career combination, student-designed major, study abroad, teacher certification program. **Credit/placement by examination:** AP, CLEP, IB, SAT, ACT, institutional tests. 45 credit hours maximum toward bachelor's degree. **Support services:** Learning center, pre-admission summer program, reduced course load, remedial instruction, study skills assistance, tutoring, writing center.

Majors. Biology: General. **Business:** Accounting, business admin. **Computer sciences:** General, computer science, information technology. **Education:** Elementary, multi-level teacher, science, secondary, social studies, special. **English:** English lit. **Foreign languages:** Spanish. **Health:** Clinical lab science, community health services, nursing (RN). **History:** General. **Interdisciplinary:** Natural sciences. **Legal studies:** Prelaw. **Liberal arts:** Arts/sciences. **Math:** General. **Physical sciences:** Chemistry. **Psychology:** General. **Public administration:** Community org/advocacy, human services. **Social sciences:** General, international relations, political science, sociology.

Most popular majors. Business/marketing 21%, communications/journalism 6%, English 14%, health sciences 11%, history 13%, psychology 8%, public administration/social services 6%.

Computing on campus. 325 workstations in dormitories, library, computer center, student center. Dormitories wired for high-speed internet access and linked to campus network. Commuter students can connect to campus network. Online course registration, online library, helpline, student web hosting, wireless network available.

Student life. Freshman orientation: Mandatory, $180 fee. Preregistration for classes offered. Held the weekend before classes begin. **Housing:** Coed dorms, single-sex dorms, special housing for disabled available. $450 fully refundable deposit, deadline 5/1. **Activities:** Concert band, choral groups, dance, drama, film society, literary magazine, music ensembles, musical theater, radio station, student government, student newspaper, TV station, Black student union, campus ministry, Habitat for Humanity, Big Brothers/Big Sisters, Christian fellowship, Latin student union.

Athletics. NCAA. **Intercollegiate:** Baseball M, basketball, soccer, softball W, swimming, tennis, volleyball W. **Intramural:** Baseball, basketball M, bowling, golf, soccer, softball W, swimming, table tennis, tennis, volleyball. **Team name:** Blue Knights.

Student services. Adult student services, alcohol/substance abuse counseling, campus ministries, career counseling, services for economically disadvantaged, student employment services, financial aid counseling, health services, personal counseling, placement for graduates. **Physically disabled:** Services for visually impaired.

Contact. E-mail: mtstmary@msmc.edu
Phone: (845) 569-3248 Toll-free number: (888) 937-6762
Fax: (845) 562-6762
J. Randall Ognibene, Director of Admissions, Mount St. Mary College, 330 Powell Avenue, Newburgh, NY 12550

Nazareth College of Rochester

Rochester, New York **CB member**
www.naz.edu **CB code: 2511**

- Private 4-year liberal arts college
- Residential campus in large city
- 2,013 degree-seeking undergraduates: 8% part-time, 76% women, 5% African American, 2% Asian American, 2% Hispanic American
- 1,020 degree-seeking graduate students
- 79% of applicants admitted
- SAT or ACT (ACT writing optional), application essay required
- 73% graduate within 6 years

General. Founded in 1924. Regionally accredited. **Degrees:** 467 bachelor's awarded; master's, doctoral offered. **ROTC:** Army, Air Force. **Location:** 7 miles from downtown. **Calendar:** Semester, extensive summer session. **Full-time faculty:** 135 total; 93% have terminal degrees, 13% minority, 53% women. **Part-time faculty:** 163 total; 25% have terminal degrees, 6% minority. **Class size:** 58% < 20, 42% 20-39, less than 1% 40-49. **Special facilities:** Arts center, psychology research facility, speech clinic, center for service learning, physical therapy clinic.

Freshman class profile. 1,972 applied, 1,561 admitted, 453 enrolled.

Mid 50% test scores			
SAT verbal:	520-630	Rank in top quarter:	66%
SAT math:	530-620	Rank in top tenth:	29%
ACT:	22-28	Return as sophomores:	84%
GPA 3.0-3.49:	83%	Out-of-state:	6%
GPA 2.0-2.99:	16%	Live on campus:	90%
		International:	1%

Basis for selection. School achievement record, strength of high school academic program, class rank, test scores, and recommendations are most heavily considered. Interview recommended for all; audition required for music, music education, music theater, music therapy, and theater arts programs; portfolio required for art education, studio art programs.

High school preparation. 16 units required; 20 recommended. Required and recommended units include English 4, mathematics 3-4, social studies 3-4, science 3-4 (laboratory 2-3) and foreign language 3-4.

2005-2006 Annual costs. Tuition/fees: $20,024. Room/board: $8,360. Books/supplies: $750. Personal expenses: $1,000.

2005-2006 Financial aid. Need-based: 421 full-time freshmen applied for aid; 346 were judged to have need; 346 of these received aid. Average need met was 83%. Average scholarship/grant was $11,818; average loan $3,031. 59% of total undergraduate aid awarded as scholarships/grants, 41% as loans/jobs. **Non-need-based:** Awarded to 514 full-time undergraduates, including 180 freshmen. Scholarships awarded for academics, alumni affiliation, art, minority status, music/drama, ROTC, state residency.

Application procedures. Admission: Priority date 12/15; deadline 2/15 (postmark date). $40 fee, may be waived for applicants with need. Application may be submitted online. Admission notification on a rolling basis beginning on or about 3/1. Must reply by May 1 or within 4 week(s) if notified thereafter. **Financial aid:** Priority date 12/15, closing date 5/1. FAFSA required. CSS PROFILE required of early decision applicants only. Applicants notified on a rolling basis starting 2/20; must reply by 5/1 or within 2 week(s) of notification.

Academics. Special study options: Combined bachelor's/graduate degree, cross-registration, double major, exchange student, honors, independent study, internships, liberal arts/career combination, study abroad, teacher certification program, Washington semester. 2-2 bachelor's degree completion program for registered nurses and Monroe Community College graduates. **Credit/placement by examination:** AP, CLEP, IB. 30 credit hours maximum toward bachelor's degree. **Support services:** Reduced course load, remedial instruction, study skills assistance, tutoring, writing center.

Majors. Area/ethnic studies: American. **Biology:** General, biochemistry. **Business:** General, accounting. **Communications:** General. **Computer sciences:** Information systems. **Education:** Art, business, elementary, music, secondary, special. **Foreign languages:** French, German, Italian, Spanish. **Health:** Communication disorders, music therapy, speech pathology. **History:** General. **Interdisciplinary:** Peace/conflict. **Math:** General. **Philosophy/religion:** Philosophy, religion. **Physical sciences:** Chemistry. **Psychology:** General. **Public administration:** Social work. **Social sciences:** General, anthropology, economics, political science, sociology. **Visual/performing arts:** Art, art history/conservation, dramatic, music history, music performance, music theory/composition, studio arts.

Most popular majors. Business/marketing 11%, education 8%, English 11%, health sciences 17%, history 7%, psychology 14%, social sciences 8%, visual/performing arts 6%.

Computing on campus. 150 workstations in dormitories, library, computer center. Dormitories wired for high-speed internet access and linked to campus network. Commuter students can connect to campus network. Online library, helpline, wireless network available.

Student life. Freshman orientation: Mandatory, $100 fee. Preregistration for classes offered. Orientation charge included in first-year fees. 3-day weekend program includes community service. **Policies:** Freshmen permitted cars on campus. **Housing:** Coed dorms, single-sex dorms, special housing for disabled, apartments, substance-free housing available. $100 nonrefundable deposit, deadline 5/1. Foreign language houses, special interest and collective housing available for students in various majors, quiet floor, honors floor. **Activities:** Bands, choral groups, dance, drama, music ensembles, musical theater, radio station, student government, student newspaper, symphony orchestra, Amnesty International, Campus Ministry Council, Inter-Ethnic Coalition, Undergraduate Association, Club Cervantes, French club, Italian club, Rotaract, Women's Resource Network.

Athletics. NCAA. **Intercollegiate:** Basketball, cheerleading, cross-country, diving, equestrian, field hockey W, golf, lacrosse, soccer, softball W, swimming, tennis, track and field, volleyball W. **Intramural:** Basketball, diving, racquetball, soccer, softball, swimming, tennis, volleyball. **Team name:** Golden Flyers.

Student services. Adult student services, alcohol/substance abuse counseling, campus ministries, career counseling, services for economically disadvantaged, student employment services, financial aid counseling, health services, minority student services, on-campus daycare, personal counseling, placement for graduates, women's services. **Physically disabled:** Services for visually, speech, hearing impaired.

Contact. E-mail: admissions@naz.edu
Phone: (585) 389-2860 Toll-free number: (800) 462-3944
Fax: (585) 389-2826
Thomas DaRin, Vice President for Enrollment Management, Nazareth College of Rochester, 4245 East Avenue, Rochester, NY 14618-3790

New York Institute of Technology

Old Westbury, New York
www.nyit.edu **CB code: 2561**

- Private 4-year university and health science college
- Commuter campus in large town
- 6,155 degree-seeking undergraduates: 35% part-time, 44% women, 12% African American, 9% Asian American, 10% Hispanic American, 5% international
- 4,198 degree-seeking graduate students
- 75% of applicants admitted
- SAT or ACT (ACT writing recommended), application essay required
- 45% graduate within 6 years

General. Founded in 1955. Regionally accredited. 3-campus institution: Old Westbury in Nassau County, New York City, and Islip campus in Suffolk County. **Degrees:** 928 bachelor's, 55 associate awarded; master's, doctoral, first professional offered. **ROTC:** Army, Air Force. **Location:** 15 miles from New York City. **Calendar:** Semester, extensive summer session. **Full-time faculty:** 216 total; 89% have terminal degrees, 22% minority, 29% women. **Part-time faculty:** 648 total; 19% minority, 35% women. **Class size:** 64% < 20, 32% 20-39, 2% 40-49, 1% 50-99. **Special facilities:** Center for urban/suburban studies, center for neighborhood revitalization, Parkinson's disease treatment center, center for labor and industrial relations, center for energy, environment and economics, center for teaching and learning with technology, culinary arts center, center for entrepreneurial and small business services, center for business information technologies, motion graphics laboratory.

Freshman class profile. 3,743 applied, 2,812 admitted, 915 enrolled.

Mid 50% test scores			
SAT verbal:	480-580	Out-of-state:	14%
SAT math:	530-620	Live on campus:	24%
ACT:	20-27	International:	5%
Return as sophomores:	71%	Fraternities:	2%
		Sororities:	1%

Basis for selection. 2 letters of recommendation required for 4-year nursing, occupational therapy, physical therapy, and physician assistant and all education programs. Proof of 100 hours of volunteer or work experience required for physical therapy, physician assistant, and occupational therapy programs. SAT important, minimum scores vary with program. Interview required for nursing, occupational therapy, physician assistant, physical therapy, BS/doctor of osteopathic medicine, and BS/Juris Doctor program applicants. Portfolio required for fine arts program.

High school preparation. 16 units required. Required and recommended units include English 4, mathematics 2-3, social studies 2, science 1-2 (laboratory 1) and academic electives 7. Freshmen in selected majors required to prove or acquire computer literacy.

2005-2006 Annual costs. Tuition/fees: $19,236. Room only charges apply to Manhattan campus; board charges vary on other campuses. Tuition/fee costs reported for nontechnology majors, vary for other programs. Room only: $10,804. Books/supplies: $1,200. Personal expenses: $2,550.

2004-2005 Financial aid. Need-based: 56% of total undergraduate aid awarded as scholarships/grants, 44% as loans/jobs. **Non-need-based:** Scholarships awarded for academics, athletics.

Application procedures. Admission: No deadline. $50 fee, may be waived for applicants with need. Application may be submitted online. Admission notification on a rolling basis beginning on or about 1/1. Must reply by May 1 or within 4 week(s) if notified thereafter. Application closing date for nursing, occupational therapy, physical therapy and physician assistant programs February 1. Notification to applicants to these programs sent March 1. Applicants to these programs must reply by May 1 or within 30 days if notified thereafter. No deferred admission to these programs. **Financial aid:** Priority date 3/1; no closing date. FAFSA required. Applicants notified on a rolling basis starting 3/15; must reply by 5/1 or within 2 week(s) of notification.

Academics. School focuses on career-oriented professional education, access to opportunity, applications-oriented research and service in public interest. **Special study options:** Accelerated study, combined bachelor's/graduate degree, cooperative education, cross-registration, distance learning, double major, dual enrollment of high school students, ESL, honors, independent study, internships, liberal arts/career combination, study abroad, teacher certification program, weekend college. Combined bachelor's/professional degree program in life sciences/osteopathic medicine, architectural technology/energy management, architectural technology/MBA, mechanical engineering/energy management, life sciences/physical therapy, life sciences/occupational therapy, behavioral sciences/law at Touro College Law Center. **Credit/placement by examination:** AP, CLEP, IB, institutional tests.

30 credit hours maximum toward associate degree, 60 toward bachelor's. **Support services:** Learning center, pre-admission summer program, reduced course load, remedial instruction, study skills assistance, tutoring, writing center.

Majors. Architecture: Architecture, technology. **Biology:** General. **Business:** Accounting, business admin, finance, hotel/motel admin, human resources, management information systems, marketing, restaurant/food services, tourism/travel. **Communications:** General, advertising, broadcast journalism, radio/tv. **Computer sciences:** General, computer graphics, computer science, networking. **Education:** Art, biology, business, chemistry, elementary, English, health occupations, mathematics, middle, physics, sales/marketing, science, social science, social studies, technology/industrial arts, trade/industrial, voc/tech. **Engineering:** Biomedical, computer, electrical, mechanical. **Engineering technology:** Aerospace, architectural, electrical, energy systems, environmental, manufacturing. **English:** Technical writing. **Health:** Nursing (RN), physician assistant, premedicine. **Interdisciplinary:** Nutrition sciences. **Physical sciences:** Chemistry, physics. **Protective services:** Law enforcement admin. **Psychology:** General. **Social sciences:** General, economics, political science, sociology. **Visual/performing arts:** Commercial/advertising art, interior design, studio arts.

Most popular majors. Architecture 12%, biology 6%, business/marketing 23%, communications/journalism 10%, computer/information sciences 12%, engineering/engineering technologies 10%, health sciences 7%, interdisciplinary studies 8%, visual/performing arts 6%.

Computing on campus. PC or laptop required. 740 workstations in dormitories, library, computer center, student center. Dormitories wired for high-speed internet access and linked to campus network. Commuter students can connect to campus network. Online library, helpline, student web hosting available.

Student life. Freshman orientation: Available. Preregistration for classes offered. One day at the end of August. **Policies:** Freshmen permitted cars on campus. **Housing:** Guaranteed on-campus for all undergraduates. Coed dorms, special housing for disabled, apartments available. $250 deposit. Central Islip campus fully residential, special housing for graduate, architecture students. Off-campus housing available for Manhattan campus. **Activities:** Choral groups, dance, drama, film society, literary magazine, musical theater, radio station, student government, student newspaper, TV station, American Institute of Architecture Students, biomedical society, National Society of Black Engineers, Newman Club, Christian fellowship, Jewish student union, African people's organization, Community Connection, South Asian student association, Chinese student association.

Athletics. NCAA. **Intercollegiate:** Baseball M, basketball, boxing W, cross-country, lacrosse M, soccer, softball W, track and field, volleyball W. **Intramural:** Basketball, football (non-tackle), golf, soccer, softball, swimming, tennis, track and field, volleyball, weight lifting. **Team name:** Bears.

Student services. Adult student services, campus ministries, career counseling, student employment services, financial aid counseling, health services, personal counseling, placement for graduates, veterans' counselor. **Physically disabled:** Services for hearing impaired.

Contact. E-mail: admissions@nyit.edu
Phone: (516) 686-7520 Toll-free number: (800) 345-6948
Fax: (516) 686-7613
Jacquelyn Nealon, Dean of Admissions, New York Institute of Technology, Box 8000, Old Westbury, NY 11568

New York School of Interior Design

New York, New York
www.nysid.edu **CB code: 0333**

- Private 4-year college of interior design
- Commuter campus in very large city
- 630 degree-seeking undergraduates: 73% part-time, 92% women, 3% African American, 7% Asian American, 6% Hispanic American, 7% international
- 15 degree-seeking graduate students
- 37% of applicants admitted
- Application essay required

General. Founded in 1916. **Degrees:** 14 bachelor's, 55 associate awarded; master's, first professional offered. **Location:** Upper East Side of Manhattan. **Calendar:** Semester, limited summer session. **Full-time faculty:** 2 total; 50% women. **Part-time faculty:** 77 total; 34% have terminal degrees, 5% minority, 39% women. **Class size:** 91% < 20, 9% 50-99. **Special facilities:** Gallery for architecture and interior design exhibits, lighting laboratory.

Freshman class profile. 119 applied, 44 admitted, 23 enrolled.

Basis for selection. High school transcripts, 2 letters of recommendation, essay, and portfolio in art/design. Portfolio required, interview recommended. **Homeschooled:** State high school equivalency certificate required.

High school preparation. 16 units recommended. Recommended units include English 4, mathematics 2, social studies 2, science 2 and foreign language 2. Studio art or drafting recommended.

2006-2007 Annual costs. Tuition/fees: $18,820. Books/supplies: $1,000.

2004-2005 Financial aid. All financial aid based on need. 28 full-time freshmen applied for aid; 28 were judged to have need; 28 of these received aid. Average need met was 50%. Average scholarship/grant was $5,000; average loan $2,625. 27% of total undergraduate aid awarded as scholarships/grants, 73% as loans/jobs.

Application procedures. Admission: Priority date 3/1; no deadline. $50 fee, may be waived for applicants with need. Application may be submitted online. Admission notification on a rolling basis beginning on or about 4/1. Must reply by May 1 or within 4 week(s) if notified thereafter. **Financial aid:** Priority date 5/1; no closing date. FAFSA, institutional form required. Applicants notified on a rolling basis starting 2/1; must reply within 2 week(s) of notification.

Academics. Special study options: ESL, independent study, internships, study abroad. **Credit/placement by examination:** AP, CLEP, IB, institutional tests. 17 credit hours maximum toward associate degree, 41 toward bachelor's. **Support services:** Tutoring, writing center.

Majors. Visual/performing arts: Interior design.

Computing on campus. 125 workstations in library, computer center. Commuter students can connect to campus network. Online course registration, helpline available.

Student life. Freshman orientation: Available. Preregistration for classes offered. General orientation held week before classes begin. **Activities:** Student chapter of American Society of Interior Designers (ASID).

Student services. Adult student services, career counseling, student employment services, financial aid counseling, personal counseling, placement for graduates.

Contact. E-mail: admissions@nysid.edu
Phone: (212) 472-1500 ext. 204 Toll-free number: (800) 336-9743 ext. 204
Fax: (212) 472-1867
David Sprouls, Director of Admissions, New York School of Interior Design, 170 East 70th Street, New York, NY 10021-5110

New York University

New York, New York **CB member**
www.nyu.edu **CB code: 2562**

- Private 4-year university
- Residential campus in very large city
- 20,150 degree-seeking undergraduates: 7% part-time, 61% women, 5% African American, 17% Asian American, 8% Hispanic American, 4% international
- 18,871 degree-seeking graduate students
- 37% of applicants admitted
- SAT or ACT with writing, application essay required
- 83% graduate within 6 years; 29% enter graduate study

General. Founded in 1831. Regionally accredited. School of Continuing and Professional Studies also available for adult degree and noncredit programs. **Degrees:** 4,696 bachelor's, 676 associate awarded; master's, doctoral, first professional offered. **Calendar:** Semester, extensive summer session. **Full-time faculty:** 2,043 total; 92% have terminal degrees, 39% women. **Class size:** 63% < 20, 25% 20-39, 3% 40-49, 7% 50-99, 3% >100. **Special facilities:** Study center; special academic facilities for arts, business, culture, education, international relations, language, law, media, music, public service, research, and social policy.

Freshman class profile. 34,509 applied, 12,662 admitted, 4,690 enrolled.

Mid 50% test scores			
SAT verbal:	620-710	Rank in top tenth:	68%
SAT math:	620-710	Return as sophomores:	93%
ACT:	27-31	Out-of-state:	65%
GPA 3.50 or higher:	70%	Live on campus:	86%
GPA 3.0-3.49:	28%	International:	5%
GPA 2.0-2.99:	2%	Fraternities:	3%
Rank in top quarter:	95%	Sororities:	2%

Basis for selection. School achievement record most important. Standardized test scores, activities, essay, recommendations also important. Audition and/or submission of creative materials required for applicants to either Tisch School of the Arts or art and music programs within the School of Education. SAT Subject Tests recommended. 2 SAT Subject Tests recommended for all. Candidates for Bachelor of Arts degree program in School of Continuing and Professional Studies may be required to take Comprehensive Test of Basic Skills. Audition required for dance, drama, and music programs; portfolio required for art, theater design, photography, cinema studies, film, television, radio, and dramatic writing programs. Portfolios may include writing, photography, film or other creative work.

High school preparation. College-preparatory program required. 18 units required. Required and recommended units include English 4, mathematics 3-4, history 4, science 3 (laboratory 2) and foreign language 2-3.

2005-2006 Annual costs. Tuition/fees: $31,690. Room/board: $11,480.

2005-2006 Financial aid. Need-based: 3,168 full-time freshmen applied for aid; 2,490 were judged to have need; 2,477 of these received aid. Average need met was 68%. Average scholarship/grant was $13,275; average loan $4,377. 59% of total undergraduate aid awarded as scholarships/grants, 41% as loans/jobs. **Non-need-based:** Awarded to 1,891 full-time undergraduates, including 456 freshmen. Scholarships awarded for academics. **Additional information:** Both need-based and merit scholarships available to first-time students. Range from $1,000 to $25,000.

Application procedures. Admission: Closing date 1/15 (postmark date). $65 fee, may be waived for applicants with need. Application may be submitted online. Admission notification 4/1. Must reply by 5/1. Must reply by May 1 or within 3 week(s) if notified thereafter. **Financial aid:** Closing date 2/15. FAFSA required. Applicants notified on a rolling basis starting 4/1; must reply by 5/1.

Academics. Special study options: Accelerated study, combined bachelor's/graduate degree, cooperative education, cross-registration, distance learning, double major, ESL, exchange student, honors, independent study, internships, liberal arts/career combination, student-designed major, study abroad, teacher certification program, Washington semester, weekend college. Exchange program with several historically black colleges including Spelman, Bennett, Morehouse, and Tougaloo; 3-2 engineering program with Stevens Institute of Technology, New Jersey. **Credit/placement by examination:** AP, CLEP, IB. 32 credit hours maximum toward bachelor's degree. 8 to 32 hours of credit may be awarded for International Baccalaureate. **Support services:** Learning center, pre-admission summer program, reduced course load, study skills assistance, tutoring, writing center.

Majors. Area/ethnic studies: African-American, East Asian, European, Latin American, Near/Middle Eastern, women's. **Biology:** General, biochemistry. **Business:** General, accounting, actuarial science, business admin, finance, hospitality admin, international, managerial economics, organizational behavior, real estate. **Communications:** General, digital media, journalism, radio/tv. **Communications technology:** General. **Computer sciences:** General, computer science, information systems. **Education:** Art, biology, business, chemistry, early childhood, elementary, English, foreign languages, French, German, health, mathematics, music, physics, science, social studies, Spanish, special, speech impaired. **English:** American lit, British lit, speech/rhetoric. **Family/consumer sciences:** Food/nutrition. **Foreign languages:** General, ancient Greek, classics, comparative lit, French, German, Hebrew, Italian, Latin, linguistics, modern Greek, Russian, Spanish. **Health:** Health care admin, health services, nursing (RN), predentistry, premedicine. **History:** General. **Interdisciplinary:** Medieval/Renaissance, neuroscience. **Legal studies:** Prelaw. **Liberal arts:** Arts/sciences. **Math:** General, applied, statistics. **Parks/recreation:** Sports admin. **Philosophy/religion:** Judaic, philosophy, religion. **Physical sciences:** Chemistry, physics. **Psychology:** General. **Public administration:** General, social work. **Social sciences:** General, anthropology, economics, international relations, political science, sociology, urban studies. **Visual/performing arts:** General, cinematography, dance, dramatic, film/cinema, music management, music performance, music theory/composition, photography, piano/organ, play/screenwriting, studio arts, voice/opera.

Computing on campus. 2,500 workstations in dormitories, library, computer center, student center. Dormitories wired for high-speed internet access and linked to campus network. Commuter students can connect to campus network. Online course registration, online library, helpline, repair service, student web hosting, wireless network available.

Student life. Freshman orientation: Available. Preregistration for classes offered. Each undergraduate college handles own orientation. Charge and program determined and vary by school. **Housing:** Guaranteed on-campus for all undergraduates. Coed dorms, special housing for disabled, apartments, fraternity/sorority housing, substance-free housing available. $200 deposit, deadline 5/1. All freshmen who request housing on admissions application and meet all deadlines guaranteed 4 years of housing. First Year Residential Experience program available for new students. **Activities:** Bands, choral groups, dance, drama, film society, literary magazine, music ensembles, musical theater, opera, radio station, student government, student newspaper, symphony orchestra, TV station, over 350 clubs and organizations available.

Athletics. NCAA. **Intercollegiate:** Basketball, cheerleading, cross-country, diving, fencing, golf M, soccer, swimming, tennis, track and field, volleyball, wrestling M. **Intramural:** Badminton, basketball, bowling, football (non-tackle), soccer, softball, squash, tennis, volleyball, weight lifting. **Team name:** Violets.

Student services. Adult student services, alcohol/substance abuse counseling, campus ministries, career counseling, services for economically disadvantaged, student employment services, financial aid counseling, health services, minority student services, personal counseling, placement for graduates, women's services. **Physically disabled:** Services for visually, speech, hearing impaired.

Contact. E-mail: admissions@nyu.edu
Phone: (212) 998-4500 Fax: (212) 995-4902
Barbara Hall, Associate Provost for Admissions and Finanical Aid, New York University, 22 Washington Square North, New York, NY 10011-9108

Niagara University

Niagara University, New York — **CB member**
www.niagara.edu — **CB code: 2558**

- Private 4-year university affiliated with Roman Catholic Church
- Residential campus in small city
- 2,912 degree-seeking undergraduates: 4% part-time, 61% women, 4% African American, 1% Asian American, 1% Hispanic American, 1% Native American, 5% international
- 911 degree-seeking graduate students
- 79% of applicants admitted
- SAT or ACT (ACT writing optional) required
- 63% graduate within 6 years; 43% enter graduate study

General. Founded in 1856. Regionally accredited. Independent institution in the Vincentian tradition. **Degrees:** 551 bachelor's, 3 associate awarded; master's offered. **ROTC:** Army. **Location:** 20 miles from Buffalo, 90 miles from Toronto, Canada. **Calendar:** Semester, extensive summer session. **Full-time faculty:** 137 total; 93% have terminal degrees, 10% minority, 36% women. **Part-time faculty:** 197 total; 5% minority, 58% women. **Class size:** 42% < 20, 47% 20-39, 10% 40-49. **Special facilities:** Theater, fine arts museum.

Freshman class profile. 3,246 applied, 2,555 admitted, 735 enrolled.

Mid 50% test scores			
SAT verbal:	480-570	Rank in top quarter:	40%
SAT math:	470-580	Rank in top tenth:	14%
ACT:	19-25	End year in good standing:	96%
GPA 3.50 or higher:	43%	Return as sophomores:	82%
GPA 3.0-3.49:	30%	Out-of-state:	9%
GPA 2.0-2.99:	27%	Live on campus:	74%
		International:	3%

Basis for selection. School achievement record, class rank, test scores most important. School recommendation also important. Character, personality, and extracurricular activities considered. Alumni relationship also considered. Interview, essay recommended for all; audition recommended for theater program.

High school preparation. 16 units required. Required units include English 4, mathematics 2, social studies 2, science 2, foreign language 2 and academic electives 4. 3 units science (biology, chemistry mandatory, physics recommended) for math, science, nursing applicants. 2 units foreign language required of all except business applicants. 3 units mathematics required for mathematics, biology, business, biochemistry, chemistry, computer and information sciences, natural sciences, and nursing applicants. 3 units social studies required for prospective social studies majors.

2005-2006 Annual costs. Tuition/fees: $19,925. Room/board: $8,450. Books/supplies: $700. Personal expenses: $650.

2005-2006 Financial aid. Need-based: 657 full-time freshmen applied for aid; 532 were judged to have need; 520 of these received aid. Average

need met was 86%. Average scholarship/grant was $10,446; average loan $3,660. 70% of total undergraduate aid awarded as scholarships/grants, 30% as loans/jobs. **Non-need-based:** Awarded to 1,227 full-time undergraduates, including 298 freshmen. Scholarships awarded for academics, athletics, music/drama, ROTC. **Additional information:** Opportunity program available for academically and economically disadvantaged students.

Application procedures. Admission: Closing date 8/1. $30 fee, may be waived for applicants with need. Application may be submitted online. Admission notification on a rolling basis. Must reply by May 1 or within 4 week(s) if notified thereafter. **Financial aid:** Priority date 2/15; no closing date. FAFSA required. Applicants notified on a rolling basis starting 3/1; must reply within 3 week(s) of notification.

Academics. Academic exploration program for students undecided about their choice of major. **Special study options:** Accelerated study, combined bachelor's/graduate degree, cooperative education, cross-registration, double major, dual enrollment of high school students, ESL, exchange student, honors, independent study, internships, liberal arts/career combination, New York semester, study abroad, teacher certification program, Washington semester. **Credit/placement by examination:** AP, CLEP, institutional tests. 15 credit hours maximum toward associate degree, 15 toward bachelor's. **Support services:** Learning center, pre-admission summer program, reduced course load, remedial instruction, study skills assistance, tutoring, writing center.

Majors. Biology: General, biochemistry. **Business:** General, accounting, hospitality admin, hotel/motel admin, human resources, international, logistics, marketing, restaurant/food services, tourism/travel. **Communications:** General. **Computer sciences:** General, computer science, information systems. **Education:** General, biology, business, chemistry, early childhood, elementary, English, French, mathematics, secondary, social studies, Spanish, special. **Foreign languages:** French, Spanish. **Health:** Predentistry, premedicine, preveterinary. **History:** General. **Legal studies:** Prelaw. **Liberal arts:** Arts/sciences. **Math:** General. **Philosophy/religion:** Philosophy, religion. **Physical sciences:** Chemistry. **Protective services:** Criminal justice. **Psychology:** General. **Public administration:** Social work. **Science technology:** Biological. **Social sciences:** General, criminology, political science, sociology. **Transportation:** General. **Visual/performing arts:** Dramatic.

Most popular majors. Business/marketing 33%, education 23%, psychology 7%, security/protective services 8%.

Computing on campus. 150 workstations in dormitories, library, computer center, student center. Dormitories wired for high-speed internet access and linked to campus network. Online course registration, online library, helpline, repair service available.

Student life. Freshman orientation: Available. Preregistration for classes offered. **Policies:** Freshmen permitted cars on campus. **Housing:** Guaranteed on-campus for all undergraduates. Coed dorms, apartments, substance-free housing available. $100 deposit, deadline 5/1. Freshmen not within reasonable commuting distance required to live on campus for two years. **Activities:** Pep band, choral groups, dance, drama, musical theater, radio station, student government, student newspaper, ethnic awareness society, Knights of Columbus, community action program, Muscular Dystrophy Association, foreign student council, St. Vincent DePaul Society, Black Student Union, campus ministry.

Athletics. NCAA. **Intercollegiate:** Baseball M, basketball, cross-country, diving, golf M, ice hockey, lacrosse, soccer, softball W, swimming, tennis, volleyball W. **Intramural:** Baseball M, basketball, bowling, golf, racquetball, skiing, softball, volleyball W, water polo. **Team name:** Purple Eagles.

Student services. Adult student services, alcohol/substance abuse counseling, campus ministries, career counseling, services for economically disadvantaged, student employment services, financial aid counseling, health services, minority student services, personal counseling, placement for graduates, veterans' counselor.

Contact. E-mail: admissions@niagara.edu
Phone: (716) 286-8700 Fax: (716) 286-8733
Harry Gong, Director of Admissions, Niagara University, Niagara University, NY 14109

Nyack College
Nyack, New York
www.nyack.edu **CB code: 2560**

- Private 4-year liberal arts college affiliated with Christian and Missionary Alliance
- Residential campus in large town
- 1,976 degree-seeking undergraduates
- Application essay required

General. Founded in 1882. Regionally accredited. Extension center in Manhattan. Adult Degree Completion Program offers accelerated study option for adult students, with classes held throughout the New York metropolitan and lower Hudson Valley regions, Washington, D.C., and Dayton, OH. **Degrees:** 480 bachelor's, 27 associate awarded; master's, first professional offered. **Location:** 25 miles from New York City. **Calendar:** Differs by program, limited summer session. **Full-time faculty:** 102 total. **Part-time faculty:** 136 total. **Class size:** 64% < 20, 28% 20-39, 6% 40-49, 2% 50-99.

Freshman class profile.

Mid 50% test scores		**ACT:**	17-23
SAT verbal:	410-540	**Live on campus:**	63%
SAT math:	410-530		

Basis for selection. Applicants must have Christian commitment and sign agreement to abide by community life standards. Academic record, class rank, and test scores most important. Pastor's recommendation required for students applying to traditional undergraduate program. Interview recommended for those with unsatisfactory recommendations or academic concerns; audition required for music program. **Learning Disabled:** Students should inform their admissions counselors.

High school preparation. 16 units required. Required and recommended units include English 4, foreign language 2 and academic electives 4. Recommend 3 units in any combination of mathematics and science and 3 in any combination of history and social science.

2006-2007 Annual costs. Tuition/fees: $16,300. Room/board: $7,600. Books/supplies: $750. Personal expenses: $1,810.

2004-2005 Financial aid. Need-based: 54% of total undergraduate aid awarded as scholarships/grants, 46% as loans/jobs. **Non-need-based:** Scholarships awarded for academics, alumni affiliation, art, athletics, leadership, minority status, music/drama, religious affiliation, state residency.

Application procedures. Admission: No deadline. $25 fee, may be waived for applicants with need. Application may be submitted online. Admission notification on a rolling basis. **Financial aid:** Priority date 3/1; no closing date. FAFSA required. Applicants notified on a rolling basis starting 3/1; must reply by 4/1 or within 4 week(s) of notification.

Academics. Special study options: Accelerated study, distance learning, double major, ESL, honors, independent study, internships, liberal arts/career combination, study abroad, teacher certification program, Washington semester. Adult degree completion program. **Credit/placement by examination:** AP, CLEP, institutional tests. 30 credit hours maximum toward bachelor's degree. **Support services:** Learning center, pre-admission summer program, reduced course load, remedial instruction, study skills assistance, tutoring, writing center.

Majors. Business: Accounting, business admin. **Communications:** General. **Computer sciences:** General. **Education:** Elementary, ESL, music. **English:** English lit. **History:** General. **Liberal arts:** Arts/sciences. **Math:** General. **Philosophy/religion:** Philosophy, religion. **Psychology:** General. **Public administration:** Social work. **Social sciences:** General. **Theology:** Religious ed, sacred music, theology. **Visual/performing arts:** Music performance, music theory/composition.

Computing on campus. 180 workstations in dormitories, library, computer center, student center. Online library, wireless network available.

Student life. Freshman orientation: Mandatory, $100 fee. Preregistration for classes offered. Usually 4 days the week prior to classes starting. **Policies:** Alcohol, tobacco, and narcotic drug use and possession prohibited on and off campus. Religious observance required. Freshmen permitted cars on campus. **Housing:** Single-sex dorms, apartments, substance-free housing available. $150 deposit. **Activities:** Choral groups, drama, literary magazine, music ensembles, musical theater, radio station, student government, student newspaper, symphony orchestra, African American Association of Cultural Exchange, Missions Committee, drama ensemble, Association of Latin American Students, ANSR (Asian Student Organization), ACTS (mime and interpretive dance group), business club, WNYK Radio, Student Chapter of Music Educators National Conference.

Athletics. NCAA, NCCAA. **Intercollegiate:** Baseball M, basketball, cheerleading, cross-country, golf M, soccer, softball W, volleyball W. **Team name:** Warriors.

Student services. Adult student services, alcohol/substance abuse counseling, campus ministries, career counseling, services for economically disadvantaged, student employment services, financial aid counseling, health services, personal counseling, placement for graduates. **Physically disabled:** Services for visually, hearing impaired.

Contact. E-mail: admissions@nyack.edu
Phone: (845) 358-1710 ext. 350 Toll-free number: (800) 336-9225
Fax: (845) 358-3047
Bethany Ilsley, Director of Admissions, Nyack College, 1 South Boulevard, Nyack, NY 10960-3698

Ohr Somayach Tanenbaum Education Center

Monsey, New York

CB code: 3357

- Private 5-year rabbinical college for men affiliated with Jewish faith
- Residential campus in large town

General. Founded in 1979. Accredited by AARTS. **Location:** Half a mile from Spring Valley, 33 miles from New York City. **Calendar:** Semester.

Annual costs/financial aid. Comprehensive fee (2005-2006): $10,500. Books/supplies: $300. Personal expenses: $725.

Contact. Phone: (845) 425-1370
Dean of Students, 244 Route 306, Monsey, NY 10952

Pace University

New York, New York
www.pace.edu

CB member
CB code: 2635

- Private 4-year university
- Commuter campus in very large city
- 5,021 degree-seeking undergraduates: 13% part-time, 64% women, 11% African American, 15% Asian American, 13% Hispanic American, 5% international
- 3,418 degree-seeking graduate students
- 75% of applicants admitted
- SAT or ACT (ACT writing optional), application essay required
- 61% graduate within 6 years

General. Founded in 1906. Regionally accredited. Five colleges of university located on New York City campus: Dyson College of Arts and Sciences, Lienhard School of Nursing, School of Education, Lubin School of Business, and Seidenberg School of Computer Science and Information Systems. School of Law and Lubin Graduate Center located in White Plains. **Degrees:** 1,083 bachelor's, 9 associate awarded; master's, doctoral, first professional offered. **ROTC:** Army. **Calendar:** Semester, limited summer session. **Full-time faculty:** 478 total; 87% have terminal degrees, 16% minority, 43% women. **Part-time faculty:** 760 total; 35% have terminal degrees, 17% minority, 50% women. **Class size:** 43% < 20, 51% 20-39, 5% 40-49, 1% 50-99, less than 1% >100. **Special facilities:** Center for the arts, laboratory theater, communication center, language center.

Freshman class profile. 5,762 applied, 4,324 admitted, 984 enrolled.

Mid 50% test scores		**Rank in top tenth:**	19%
SAT verbal:	490-580	**End year in good standing:**	71%
SAT math:	490-600	**Return as sophomores:**	76%
ACT:	20-26	**Out-of-state:**	37%
GPA 3.50 or higher:	34%	**Live on campus:**	61%
GPA 3.0-3.49:	34%	**International:**	4%
GPA 2.0-2.99:	31%	**Fraternities:**	2%
Rank in top quarter:	47%	**Sororities:**	2%

Basis for selection. 85 high school GPA, rank in top half of class, test scores, recommendations, personal statement important. Extracurricular activities also considered. Non-native speakers of English required to take TOEFL. Official scores must be sent directly to school. Notarized copies not acceptable. Interviews strongly recommended; audition required for dance, dramatic arts, theater; portfolio recommended for art programs. Applicants to Lienhard School of Nursing must be certified in CPR. **Learning Disabled:** Diagnostic tests recommended.

High school preparation. 16 units required; 20 recommended. Required and recommended units include English 4, mathematics 3-4, social studies 1, history 2-3, science 2 (laboratory 2), foreign language 2-3 and academic electives 2-3.

2005-2006 Annual costs. Tuition/fees: $25,384. Room/board: $8,940. Books/supplies: $800. Personal expenses: $1,330.

2005-2006 Financial aid. Need-based: Average need met was 53%. Average scholarship/grant was $13,153; average loan $3,054. 61% of total undergraduate aid awarded as scholarships/grants, 39% as loans/jobs. **Non-need-based:** Scholarships awarded for academics, athletics.

Application procedures. Admission: Closing date 3/1 (postmark date). $45 fee, may be waived for applicants with need. Application may be submitted online. Admission notification on a rolling basis beginning on or about 12/15. Must reply by May 1 or within 2 week(s) if notified thereafter. **Financial aid:** Priority date 2/15; no closing date. FAFSA required. Applicants notified on a rolling basis starting 2/28; must reply by 5/1 or within 2 week(s) of notification.

Academics. Adult undergraduate degrees in liberal/general studies, business and computer science. **Special study options:** Accelerated study, combined bachelor's/graduate degree, cooperative education, cross-registration, distance learning, double major, dual enrollment of high school students, ESL, honors, independent study, internships, study abroad, teacher certification program. Evening and freshman studies programs, pre-freshman summer program. **Credit/placement by examination:** AP, CLEP, IB, institutional tests. 30 credit hours maximum toward associate degree, 96 toward bachelor's. **Support services:** Learning center, reduced course load, remedial instruction, study skills assistance, tutoring, writing center.

Majors. Area/ethnic studies: Women's. **Biology:** General, biochemistry. **Business:** General, accounting, business admin, entrepreneurial studies, finance, hotel/motel admin, human resources, international, international marketing, management science, marketing, nonprofit/public. **Communications:** General, advertising. **Computer sciences:** General, computer science, data processing, information systems, systems analysis. **Conservation:** Environmental studies. **Education:** Biology, business, chemistry, early childhood, elementary, English, French, history, mathematics, physics, science, social studies, Spanish, speech impaired. **English:** English lit, speech/rhetoric. **Foreign languages:** General, French, Spanish. **Health:** Clinical lab science, communication disorders, nursing (RN), physician assistant, speech pathology. **History:** General. **Liberal arts:** Arts/sciences. **Math:** General. **Physical sciences:** Chemistry, geology, physics. **Protective services:** Forensics, law enforcement admin. **Psychology:** General. **Social sciences:** General, economics, political science. **Visual/performing arts:** Art, art history/conservation, dramatic.

Most popular majors. Business/marketing 44%, communications/journalism 8%, computer/information sciences 13%, health sciences 7%, psychology 6%.

Computing on campus. 250 workstations in library, computer center. Dormitories linked to campus network. Commuter students can connect to campus network. Online library, helpline, wireless network available.

Student life. Freshman orientation: Available. Preregistration for classes offered. Held during summer for small groups (strongly recommended); held in the fall before school starts for large groups. **Housing:** Coed dorms, apartments available. $400 nonrefundable deposit, deadline 5/1. **Activities:** Choral groups, dance, drama, film society, literary magazine, musical theater, radio station, student government, student newspaper, TV station, collegiate Italian American organization, Asian cultural society, international student organization, Jewish student association, Pace Christian Fellowship, Caribbean student association, Arab student association, African students association, Sabor Latino.

Athletics. NCAA. **Intercollegiate:** Baseball M, basketball, cross-country, equestrian, football (tackle) M, golf, lacrosse M, soccer W, softball W, swimming, tennis, track and field, volleyball W. **Intramural:** Basketball, football (tackle) M, soccer, softball, volleyball. **Team name:** Setters.

Student services. Adult student services, career counseling, student employment services, health services, personal counseling, placement for graduates, veterans' counselor. **Physically disabled:** Services for visually, speech, hearing impaired.

Contact. E-mail: infoctr@pace.edu
Phone: (212) 346-1323 Toll-free number: (800) 874-7223
Fax: (212) 346-1040
Joanna Broda, Director of Admission, Pace University, 1 Pace Plaza, New York, NY 10038

Pace University: Pleasantville/Briarcliff

Pleasantville, New York
www.pace.edu

CB code: 2685

- Private 4-year university
- Commuter campus in small town

General. Regionally accredited. **Location:** 7 miles from White Plains, 30 miles from New York City. **Calendar:** Semester.

Annual costs/financial aid. Tuition/fees (2005-2006): $25,384. Room/board: $8,940. Books/supplies: $800. Personal expenses: $1,330. Need-based financial aid available to full-time and part-time students.

Contact. Phone: (914) 773-3746
Director of Admission, 861 Bedford Road, Pleasantville, NY 10570

Parsons The New School for Design

New York, New York
www.parsons.edu **CB code: 2638**

- Private 4-year visual arts college
- Commuter campus in very large city
- 3,072 degree-seeking undergraduates: 7% part-time, 79% women, 3% African American, 17% Asian American, 6% Hispanic American, 33% international
- 430 degree-seeking graduate students
- 47% of applicants admitted
- SAT or ACT required
- 66% graduate within 6 years

General. Founded in 1896. Regionally accredited. Division of the New School University. **Degrees:** 472 bachelor's, 244 associate awarded; master's offered. **Calendar:** Semester, extensive summer session. **Full-time faculty:** 72 total; 26% minority, 51% women. **Part-time faculty:** 879 total; 19% minority, 50% women. **Class size:** 71% < 20, 29% 20-39.

Freshman class profile. 2,106 applied, 992 admitted, 482 enrolled.

Mid 50% test scores		**Rank in top quarter:**	49%
SAT verbal:	520-620	**Rank in top tenth:**	13%
SAT math:	460-600	**Return as sophomores:**	85%
GPA 3.50 or higher:	29%	**Out-of-state:**	57%
GPA 3.0-3.49:	36%	**International:**	30%
GPA 2.0-2.99:	32%		

Basis for selection. Portfolio and home examination most important, followed by school achievement record and test scores. Activities, leadership, motivation considered. Applicants required to complete home examination of 4 specific art and design problems as supplement to portfolio. Portfolio required, essay recommended for all; interview required for those geographically close.

High school preparation. As much art as possible also recommended.

2005-2006 Annual costs. Tuition/fees: $29,180. Room/board: $11,750. Books/supplies: $2,050. Personal expenses: $1,550.

2005-2006 Financial aid. **Need-based:** 291 full-time freshmen applied for aid; 209 were judged to have need; 206 of these received aid. Average need met was 58%. Average scholarship/grant was $8,812; average loan $2,287. 74% of total undergraduate aid awarded as scholarships/grants, 26% as loans/jobs. **Non-need-based:** Awarded to 767 full-time undergraduates, including 212 freshmen. Scholarships awarded for academics, music/drama.

Application procedures. **Admission:** Closing date 3/1. $50 fee, may be waived for applicants with need. Admission notification on a rolling basis. Must reply by May 1 or within 4 week(s) if notified thereafter. **Financial aid:** Priority date 3/1; no closing date. FAFSA required. Applicants notified on a rolling basis starting 3/1; must reply within 4 week(s) of notification.

Academics. **Special study options:** Accelerated study, cooperative education, cross-registration, distance learning, dual enrollment of high school students, ESL, exchange student, independent study, internships, liberal arts/career combination, student-designed major, study abroad, teacher certification program. Five-year combined BA/BFA, New York Studio Program. **Credit/placement by examination:** CLEP, IB, institutional tests. **Support services:** Pre-admission summer program, remedial instruction, tutoring.

Majors. **Architecture:** Architecture, environmental design, interior, landscape. **Business:** Fashion. **Visual/performing arts:** Art, ceramics, commercial photography, commercial/advertising art, design, drawing, fashion design, fiber arts, interior design, metal/jewelry, painting, photography, sculpture, studio arts.

Most popular majors. Business/marketing 14%, physical sciences 6%, visual/performing arts 81%.

Computing on campus. 705 workstations in library, computer center. Dormitories wired for high-speed internet access and linked to campus network. Commuter students can connect to campus network. Online course registration, helpline, student web hosting, wireless network available.

Student life. **Freshman orientation:** Mandatory. Orientation to the school, programs, services, and New York City. **Policies:** Freshmen permitted cars on campus. **Housing:** Coed dorms, special housing for disabled, apartments available. $250 deposit, deadline 5/1. **Activities:** Bands, dance, drama, film society, literary magazine, music ensembles, musical theater, radio station, student government.

Student services. Alcohol/substance abuse counseling, career counseling, services for economically disadvantaged, student employment services, financial aid counseling, health services, minority student services, personal counseling, placement for graduates.

Contact. E-mail: parsadm@newschool.edu
Phone: (212) 229-8910 Toll-free number: (877) 528-3321
Fax: (212) 229-5166
Heather Ward, Associate Dean of Enrollment Management, Parsons The New School for Design, 66 Fifth Avenue, New York, NY 10011

Paul Smith's College

Paul Smiths, New York
www.paulsmiths.edu **CB code: 2640**

- Private 4-year liberal arts college
- Residential campus in rural community
- 841 degree-seeking undergraduates: 2% part-time, 32% women, 2% African American, 1% Asian American, 2% Hispanic American
- 84% of applicants admitted

General. Founded in 1937. Regionally accredited. Hands-on experience in major, internship programs within college, and externships with leading companies. **Degrees:** 73 bachelor's, 173 associate awarded. **Location:** 150 miles from Albany, 20 miles from Lake Placid. **Calendar:** Semester, limited summer session. **Full-time faculty:** 56 total; 30% have terminal degrees, 2% minority, 34% women. **Class size:** 60% < 20, 31% 20-39, 5% 40-49, 4% 50-99. **Special facilities:** Sugar maple plantation, sawmill, hotel, restaurant, 14,200-acre forest.

Freshman class profile. 1,026 applied, 866 admitted, 446 enrolled.

End year in good standing:	62%	**Out-of-state:**	40%
Return as sophomores:	62%	**Live on campus:**	97%

Basis for selection. High school background most important. Interview recommended. **Homeschooled:** Statement describing homeschool structure and mission, transcript of courses and grades, interview, letter of recommendation (nonparent) required.

High school preparation. 8 units required. Required and recommended units include English 4, mathematics 2, science 2 (laboratory 1-2) and foreign language 2. High school subject requirements vary according to program.

2006-2007 Annual costs. Tuition/fees (projected): $16,770. Program fees range from $600 to $1,700 depending on program. Room/board: $7,060. Books/supplies: $1,000. Personal expenses: $1,250.

2005-2006 Financial aid. **Need-based:** 301 full-time freshmen applied for aid; 280 were judged to have need; 280 of these received aid. Average need met was 69%. Average scholarship/grant was $7,316; average loan $3,227. 54% of total undergraduate aid awarded as scholarships/grants, 46% as loans/jobs. **Non-need-based:** Awarded to 125 full-time undergraduates, including 45 freshmen. Scholarships awarded for academics. **Additional information:** Merit aid only for international students; no financial aid application required.

Application procedures. **Admission:** Priority date 3/15; no deadline. $30 fee, may be waived for applicants with need. Application may be submitted online. Admission notification on a rolling basis beginning on or about 10/1. Must reply by May 1 or within 3 week(s) if notified thereafter. **Financial aid:** Priority date 3/31; no closing date. FAFSA required. Applicants notified on a rolling basis starting 3/5; must reply within 4 week(s) of notification.

Academics. Students in hotel and restaurant management and culinary arts spend 1 semester in college's hotel, restaurant. **Special study options:** Combined bachelor's/graduate degree, double major, honors, independent study, internships, liberal arts/career combination. **Credit/placement by examination:** AP, CLEP, institutional tests. 15 credit hours maximum toward associate degree, 15 toward bachelor's. **Support services:** Learning center, reduced course load, remedial instruction, tutoring.

Majors. **Biology:** General. **Business:** General, business admin, entrepreneurial studies, hospitality admin, hospitality/recreation, hotel/motel admin, resort management, restaurant/food services, tourism promotion, tourism/

travel. **Conservation:** General, environmental science, fisheries, forest management, forest resources, forest sciences, forestry, management/policy, wildlife. **Health:** Predentistry, premedicine, preveterinary. **Interdisciplinary:** Biological/physical sciences. **Liberal arts:** Arts/sciences. **Parks/recreation:** General, facilities management. **Personal/culinary services:** Chef training, culinary arts, restaurant/catering.

Most popular majors. Business/marketing 17%, natural resources/environmental science 41%, parks/recreation 12%, personal/culinary services 27%.

Computing on campus. 140 workstations in dormitories, library, computer center. Dormitories wired for high-speed internet access and linked to campus network. Commuter students can connect to campus network. Helpline, student web hosting available.

Student life. **Freshman orientation:** Mandatory, $100 fee. Preregistration for classes offered. **Policies:** Freshmen permitted cars on campus. **Housing:** Guaranteed on-campus for all undergraduates. Coed dorms, single-sex dorms, substance-free housing available. $100 deposit. Pets allowed in dorm rooms. **Activities:** Choral groups, literary magazine, radio station, student government, student newspaper, Phi Theta Kappa, Students Against Driving Drunk, Adirondack Experience Club, international students club, campus fellowship club, environmental club.

Athletics. NAIA. **Intercollegiate:** Basketball, cross-country, rugby, soccer, volleyball W. **Intramural:** Basketball, cheerleading, ice hockey M, rugby, skiing, soccer, softball, volleyball, water polo. **Team name:** Bobcats.

Student services. Adult student services, alcohol/substance abuse counseling, campus ministries, career counseling, services for economically disadvantaged, student employment services, financial aid counseling, health services, personal counseling, placement for graduates, veterans' counselor. **Physically disabled:** Services for visually, hearing impaired.

Contact. E-mail: admiss@paulsmiths.edu
Phone: (518) 327-6227 Toll-free number: (800) 421-2605
Fax: (518) 327-6016
Melik Khoury, VP of Enrollment Management, Paul Smith's College, PO Box 265, Routes 30 & 86, Paul Smiths, NY 12970-0265

Polytechnic University

Brooklyn, New York — **CB member**
www.poly.edu — **CB code: 2668**

- Private 4-year university
- Commuter campus in very large city
- 1,494 degree-seeking undergraduates: 4% part-time, 18% women, 12% African American, 32% Asian American, 11% Hispanic American, 8% international
- 1,122 degree-seeking graduate students
- 69% of applicants admitted
- SAT or ACT, application essay required
- 46% graduate within 6 years; 22% enter graduate study

General. Founded in 1854. Regionally accredited. **Degrees:** 275 bachelor's awarded; master's, doctoral offered. **ROTC:** Army. **Location:** 2 miles from New York City. **Calendar:** Semester, extensive summer session. **Full-time faculty:** 126 total; 91% have terminal degrees, 22% minority, 16% women. **Part-time faculty:** 140 total; 38% have terminal degrees, 15% minority, 16% women. **Class size:** 40% < 20, 42% 20-39, 8% 40-49, 9% 50-99, less than 1% >100. **Special facilities:** Library of science and technology, center for advanced technology in telecommunications, institute of imaging sciences, center for construction management technology, transportation research institute, wireless research institute, urban infrastructure institute.

Freshman class profile. 1,240 applied, 860 admitted, 304 enrolled.

Mid 50% test scores		**Rank in top tenth:**	43%
SAT verbal:	500-610	**End year in good standing:**	75%
SAT math:	570-680	**Return as sophomores:**	81%
GPA 3.50 or higher:	39%	**Out-of-state:**	7%
GPA 3.0-3.49:	33%	**Live on campus:**	23%
GPA 2.0-2.99:	27%	**International:**	8%
Rank in top quarter:	68%	**Fraternities:**	1%

Basis for selection. School achievement record, class rank, test scores, recommendations required. Special emphasis on mathematics and science areas. Interview recommended.

High school preparation. 12 units required. Required and recommended units include English 4, mathematics 4, social studies 3, science 4, foreign language 2 and academic electives 2. Requirements include 1 chemistry, pre-calculus, calculus.

2005-2006 Annual costs. Tuition/fees: $28,650. Room/board: $8,500. Books/supplies: $1,000. Personal expenses: $1,576.

2004-2005 Financial aid. **Need-based:** 324 full-time freshmen applied for aid; 274 were judged to have need; 274 of these received aid. Average need met was 91%. Average scholarship/grant was $7,346; average loan $5,275. 62% of total undergraduate aid awarded as scholarships/grants, 38% as loans/jobs. **Non-need-based:** Awarded to 1,137 full-time undergraduates, including 273 freshmen. Scholarships awarded for academics.

Application procedures. **Admission:** Priority date 2/1; no deadline. $60 fee, may be waived for applicants with need. Application may be submitted online. Admission notification on a rolling basis beginning on or about 2/1. Must reply by May 1 or within 4 week(s) if notified thereafter. **Financial aid:** Priority date 3/1; no closing date. FAFSA, institutional form, CSS PROFILE required. Applicants notified on a rolling basis starting 3/15; must reply within 2 week(s) of notification.

Academics. **Special study options:** Accelerated study, combined bachelor's/graduate degree, cooperative education, distance learning, double major, honors, internships, study abroad. Joint master's degree program in dental materials science with New York University. **Credit/placement by examination:** AP, CLEP, IB, institutional tests. 16 credit hours maximum toward bachelor's degree. Students with outstanding record or specialized competence may establish 16 credits maximum toward baccalaureate degree by passing comprehensive examinations. Each department determines courses in which examination available and examination format. **Support services:** Learning center, pre-admission summer program, remedial instruction, study skills assistance, tutoring, writing center.

Honors college/program. Students selected for Honors College must have superior high school academic records and interview with member of Honors College Faculty Governing Board.

Majors. **Biology:** Molecular biochemistry. **Business:** Construction management, management information systems. **Communications:** Journalism. **Computer sciences:** General, computer science. **Engineering:** Chemical, civil, computer, electrical, mechanical. **Liberal arts:** Arts/sciences. **Math:** General. **Physical sciences:** Chemistry, physics.

Most popular majors. Business/marketing 9%, computer/information sciences 26%, engineering/engineering technologies 58%.

Computing on campus. PC or laptop required. 104 workstations in dormitories, library, computer center, student center. Dormitories linked to campus network. Commuter students can connect to campus network. Online library, helpline, repair service, student web hosting, wireless network available.

Student life. **Freshman orientation:** Available. **Housing:** Guaranteed on-campus for freshmen. Coed dorms, fraternity/sorority housing available. $300 deposit. **Activities:** Film society, literary magazine, radio station, student government, student newspaper, Society of Women Engineers, Society of Black Engineers, Ambassador Society, ethnic and service organizations, Society of Hispanic Professional Engineers, Alpha Phi Omega service fraternity.

Athletics. NCAA. **Intercollegiate:** Baseball M, basketball, cross-country, judo, soccer, softball W, tennis, track and field, volleyball. **Intramural:** Basketball, bowling, football (non-tackle), golf, handball M, ice hockey M, racquetball, skiing, soccer, softball W, table tennis, track and field, volleyball, weight lifting. **Team name:** Blue Jays.

Student services. Career counseling, student employment services, placement for graduates.

Contact. E-mail: uadmit@poly.edu
Phone: (718) 260-3100 Toll-free number: (800) 765-9832
Fax: (718) 260-3446
Kathleen Davis, Associate Dean of Admissions, Polytechnic University, 6 Metrotech Center, Brooklyn, NY 11201-2999

Pratt Institute

Brooklyn, New York — **CB member**
www.pratt.edu — **CB code: 2669**

- Private 4-year university and visual arts college
- Residential campus in very large city
- 3,070 degree-seeking undergraduates: 5% part-time, 59% women, 8% African American, 12% Asian American, 9% Hispanic American, 9% international

- 1,584 degree-seeking graduate students
- 52% of applicants admitted
- SAT or ACT (ACT writing optional), application essay required

General. Founded in 1887. Regionally accredited. Additional campus located in Manhattan with associate degree programs, bachelor's degree in construction management program, and various graduate programs. **Degrees:** 525 bachelor's, 32 associate awarded; master's offered. **Location:** 2 miles from Manhattan. **Calendar:** Semester, extensive summer session. **Full-time faculty:** 121 total; 46% have terminal degrees, 8% minority, 36% women. **Part-time faculty:** 776 total; 15% minority, 41% women. **Class size:** 88% < 20, 11% 20-39, less than 1% 40-49, less than 1% 50-99. **Special facilities:** Wood and metal workshops, ceramics kiln studios and casting foundry, digital arts labs, printmaking workshop, fine arts center, center for community development.

Freshman class profile. 3,794 applied, 1,962 admitted, 625 enrolled.

Mid 50% test scores		GPA 2.0-2.99:	25%
SAT verbal:	450-670	Out-of-state:	56%
SAT math:	460-660	Live on campus:	84%
GPA 3.50 or higher:	44%	International:	6%
GPA 3.0-3.49:	31%		

Basis for selection. Admissions committee considers overall academic record which includes academic performance, portfolio, curriculum, test scores, recommendation, and essay. SAT Subject Tests Level I recommended for applicants to architecture program. Interview required for architecture, art and design applicants living within 100-mile radius; recommended for others. Letter of recommendation required for all applicants. Portfolio required for architecture, art and design programs.

High school preparation. 16 units recommended. Recommended units include English 4, mathematics 3, social studies 2 and science 2. 4 mathematics required for architecture and construction management applicants.

2006-2007 Annual costs. Tuition/fees: $29,230. Room/board: $8,752. Books/supplies: $3,000. Personal expenses: $650.

2005-2006 Financial aid. Need-based: 517 full-time freshmen applied for aid; 442 were judged to have need; 442 of these received aid. Average need met was 65%. Average scholarship/grant was $8,115; average loan $4,661. 63% of total undergraduate aid awarded as scholarships/grants, 37% as loans/jobs. **Non-need-based:** Awarded to 1,455 full-time undergraduates, including 374 freshmen. Scholarships awarded for academics, art.

Application procedures. Admission: $40 fee, may be waived for applicants with need. Application may be submitted online. Admission notification on a rolling basis beginning on or about 11/1. Must reply by May 1 or within 2 week(s) if notified thereafter. 2 regular admission deadlines: January 1 and February 1. **Financial aid:** Closing date 2/1. FAFSA, institutional form required. Applicants notified on a rolling basis starting 4/15.

Academics. Special study options: Combined bachelor's/graduate degree, ESL, exchange student, independent study, internships, liberal arts/career combination, study abroad, teacher certification program. **Credit/placement by examination:** CLEP, institutional tests. **Support services:** Learning center, pre-admission summer program, reduced course load, study skills assistance, tutoring, writing center.

Majors. Architecture: Architecture. **Business:** Construction management. **Computer sciences:** Computer graphics. **Construction:** Site management. **Education:** Art. **English:** Creative writing. **Visual/performing arts:** General, art, art history/conservation, ceramics, cinematography, commercial/advertising art, drawing, fashion design, graphic design, illustration, industrial design, interior design, metal/jewelry, painting, photography, printmaking, sculpture, studio arts.

Most popular majors. Architecture 15%, visual/performing arts 74%.

Computing on campus. 250 workstations in dormitories, library, computer center, student center. Dormitories wired for high-speed internet access and linked to campus network. Commuter students can connect to campus network. Helpline, repair service, student web hosting, wireless network available.

Student life. Freshman orientation: Available. Preregistration for classes offered. **Policies:** Freshmen permitted cars on campus. **Housing:** Guaranteed on-campus for freshmen. Coed dorms, special housing for disabled, apartments, substance-free housing available. $300 deposit, deadline 5/1. **Activities:** Jazz band, dance, drama, film society, literary magazine, musical theater, radio station, student government, student newspaper, Christian Fellowship, Jewish student union, Muslim student association, Asian student organization, The Agenda, Korean student association, environmental resource group, Gay/Lesbian at Pratt, New York Public Interest Research Group, Pratt Projects (socially conscious project design and creation).

Athletics. NCAA. **Intercollegiate:** Basketball M, cross-country, soccer, tennis, track and field, volleyball W. **Intramural:** Badminton, basketball, field hockey W, football (non-tackle) M, weight lifting. **Team name:** Cannoneers.

Student services. Alcohol/substance abuse counseling, campus ministries, career counseling, student employment services, financial aid counseling, health services, personal counseling, placement for graduates, veterans' counselor. **Physically disabled:** Services for visually, speech, hearing impaired.

Contact. E-mail: admissions@pratt.edu
Phone: (718) 636-3514 Toll-free number: (800) 331-0834
Fax: (718) 636-3670
Heidi Metcalf, Director of Admissions, Pratt Institute, 200 Willoughby Avenue, Brooklyn, NY 11205

Rabbinical Academy Mesivta Rabbi Chaim Berlin

Brooklyn, New York

CB code: 0719

- Private 4-year rabbinical college for men affiliated with Jewish faith
- Very large city
- 149 degree-seeking undergraduates

General. Accredited by AARTS. **Degrees:** 26 bachelor's awarded; master's, doctoral offered. **Calendar:** Continuous. **Full-time faculty:** 12 total. **Part-time faculty:** 3 total.

2006-2007 Annual costs. Tuition/fees: $7,543.

Application procedures. Admission: No deadline. No application fee.

Academics. Credit/placement by examination: CLEP.

Majors. Theology: Talmudic.

Contact. Phone: (718) 377-0777
Eli Rabinowitz, Admissions Director, Rabbinical Academy Mesivta Rabbi Chaim Berlin, 1605 Coney Island Avenue, Brooklyn, NY 11230

Rabbinical College Beth Shraga

Monsey, New York

- Private 4-year rabbinical college for men affiliated with Jewish faith
- Commuter campus in large town

General. Calendar: Continuous.

Annual costs/financial aid. Tuition/fees: $7,500.

Contact. Phone: (845) 356-1980
Admissions Director, P.O. Box 412, Monsey, NY 10952

Rabbinical College Bobover Yeshiva B'nei Zion

Brooklyn, New York

CB code: 7011

- Private 5-year rabbinical college for men affiliated with Jewish faith
- Very large city

General. Accredited by AARTS. **Calendar:** Continuous.

Annual costs/financial aid. Tuition/fees (2005-2006): $4,500. Books/supplies: $400. Personal expenses: $500.

Contact. Phone: (718) 438-2018
Director, 1577 48th Street, Brooklyn, NY 11219

Rabbinical College Ch'san Sofer of New York

Brooklyn, New York

CB code: 0714

- Private 4-year rabbinical college for men affiliated with Jewish faith
- Very large city

General. Founded in 1940. Accredited by AARTS. **Calendar:** Semester.

Annual costs/financial aid. Tuition/fees (2005-2006): $5,500.

Contact. Phone: (718) 236-1171
Dean of the College, 1876 50th Street, Brooklyn, NY 11204

Rabbinical College of Long Island
Long Beach, New York
CB code: 0675

- Private 4-year rabbinical and teachers college for men affiliated with Jewish faith
- Large town
- 123 degree-seeking undergraduates
- Interview required

General. Founded in 1965. Accredited by AARTS. Ordination and First Talmudic degree available. **Calendar:** Trimester. **Full-time faculty:** 4 total. **Part-time faculty:** 2 total.

Freshman class profile. 33 enrolled.

Basis for selection. Religious commitment, interview, and recommendations most important.

2006-2007 Annual costs. Tuition/fees (projected): $7,800.

Application procedures. Admission: No deadline. No application fee. Admission notification on a rolling basis.

Academics. Credit/placement by examination: CLEP.

Student life. Policies: Religious observance required.

Contact. Phone: (516) 431-7414
Rabbi Chaim Hoberman, Director of Admissions, Rabbinical College of Long Island, 205 West Beech Street, Long Beach, NY 11561

Rabbinical College of Ohr Shimon Yisroel
Brooklyn, New York

- Private 4-year rabbinical college

General. Accredited by AARTS.

Academics. Credit/placement by examination: CLEP.

Contact. Phone: (718) 855-4092
Rabbinical College of Ohr Shimon Yisroel, 215-217 Hewes Street, Brooklyn, NY 11211

Rabbinical Seminary Adas Yereim
Brooklyn, New York
CB code: 0666

- Private 4-year rabbinical college for men affiliated with Jewish faith
- Very large city

General. Founded in 1961. Accredited by AARTS. **Calendar:** Semester.

Annual costs/financial aid. Tuition/fees (2005-2006): $4,800.

Contact. Phone: (718) 388-1751
Director of Finances, 185 Wilson Street, Brooklyn, NY 11211

Rabbinical Seminary of America
Flushing, New York
CB code: 2776

- Private 5-year seminary college for men affiliated with Jewish faith
- Very large city

General. Founded in 1933. Accredited by AARTS. **Calendar:** Semester.

Annual costs/financial aid. Tuition/fees (2005-2006): $6,000.

Contact. Phone: (718) 268-4700
Registrar, 76-01 147th St., Flushing, NY 11367

Rensselaer Polytechnic Institute
Troy, New York **CB member**
www.rpi.edu **CB code: 2757**

- Private 4-year university
- Residential campus in small city
- 4,921 degree-seeking undergraduates: 24% women, 4% African American, 11% Asian American, 5% Hispanic American, 3% international
- 2,220 degree-seeking graduate students
- 78% of applicants admitted
- SAT or ACT with writing, application essay required
- 81% graduate within 6 years

General. Founded in 1824. Regionally accredited. **Degrees:** 1,173 bachelor's awarded; master's, doctoral offered. **ROTC:** Army, Navy, Air Force. **Location:** 10 miles from Albany, 150 miles from New York City. **Calendar:** Semester, extensive summer session. **Full-time faculty:** 400 total; 98% have terminal degrees, 22% minority, 20% women. **Part-time faculty:** 81 total; 95% have terminal degrees, 15% minority, 24% women. **Class size:** 42% < 20, 41% 20-39, 7% 40-49, 10% 50-99, less than 1% >100. **Special facilities:** Center for terahertz research, nanoscale science and engineering center, linear accelerator laboratory, observatory, incubator center, fresh water institute, lighting research center, social and behavioral research laboratory, center for biotechnology and interdisciplinary studies.

Freshman class profile. 5,574 applied, 4,340 admitted, 1,240 enrolled.

Mid 50% test scores			
SAT verbal:	580-690	Return as sophomores:	92%
SAT math:	640-730	Out-of-state:	58%
ACT:	24-28	Live on campus:	98%
Rank in top quarter:	95%	International:	2%
Rank in top tenth:	61%	Fraternities:	33%
		Sororities:	12%

Basis for selection. School achievement record important, test scores and essay required, activities considered. ACT or SAT and SAT Subject Tests in math and science required of all accelerated program applicants. Portfolio required for electronic arts, highly recommended for architecture.

High school preparation. 15 units required. Required and recommended units include English 4, mathematics 4, social studies 2-3 and science 3-4. Physics and chemistry preferred. Mathematics through precalculus. Additional units should include any combination of science, foreign language, social sciences. Advanced Placement or honors courses preferred.

2005-2006 Annual costs. Tuition/fees: $31,875. Room/board: $9,431. Books/supplies: $1,722.

2005-2006 Financial aid. Need-based: 1,079 full-time freshmen applied for aid; 926 were judged to have need; 926 of these received aid. Average need met was 93%. Average scholarship/grant was $22,133; average loan $6,000. 72% of total undergraduate aid awarded as scholarships/grants, 28% as loans/jobs. **Non-need-based:** Awarded to 1,708 full-time undergraduates, including 534 freshmen. Scholarships awarded for academics, alumni affiliation, art, athletics, leadership, minority status, music/drama, ROTC.

Application procedures. Admission: Closing date 1/1 (postmark date). $70 fee, may be waived for applicants with need. Application may be submitted online. Admission notification 3/20. Must reply by 5/1. **Financial aid:** Closing date 2/15. FAFSA required. Applicants notified by 3/25.

Academics. Special study options: Accelerated study, combined bachelor's/graduate degree, cooperative education, cross-registration, distance learning, double major, dual enrollment of high school students, ESL, exchange student, honors, independent study, internships, liberal arts/career combination, student-designed major, study abroad. BS/MD with Albany Medical College; BS/JD with Columbia University and Albany Law School. **Credit/placement by examination:** AP, CLEP, IB. **Support services:** Learning center, pre-admission summer program, reduced course load, study skills assistance, tutoring, writing center.

Majors. Architecture: Architecture. **Biology:** General, biochemistry, biophysics. **Business:** Business admin. **Communications:** General, digital media. **Computer sciences:** General, computer science, information technology. **Conservation:** Environmental science. **Education:** Mathematics, science. **Engineering:** General, aerospace, biomedical, chemical, civil, computer, electrical, environmental, industrial, materials, mechanical, mechanics, nuclear, physics, science, systems. **Engineering technology:** Industrial management. **Foreign languages:** German. **Health:** Predentistry, premedicine. **Interdisciplinary:** Biological/physical sciences, science/society. **Legal studies:** Prelaw. **Liberal arts:** Arts/sciences. **Math:** General. **Philosophy/religion:** Philosophy. **Physical sciences:** Chemistry, geology, hydrology, physics.

Psychology: General. **Social sciences:** Economics. **Visual/performing arts:** Studio arts.

Most popular majors. Business/marketing 9%, computer/information sciences 19%, engineering/engineering technologies 50%.

Computing on campus. PC or laptop required. 3,115 workstations in dormitories, library, computer center, student center. Dormitories wired for high-speed internet access and linked to campus network. Commuter students can connect to campus network. Online course registration, online library, helpline, repair service, student web hosting, wireless network available.

Student life. Freshman orientation: Mandatory, $150 fee. Preregistration for classes offered. Held over 2-day period in July or August. **Housing:** Guaranteed on-campus for freshmen. Coed dorms, special housing for disabled, apartments, fraternity/sorority housing available. College housing required for all freshmen unless student lives within 50-mile radius of campus with parent(s) or legal guardian(s). **Activities:** Bands, choral groups, dance, drama, film society, literary magazine, music ensembles, musical theater, radio station, student government, student newspaper, symphony orchestra, TV station, student-run union; 160 athletic, service, media, multicultural, performing arts, visual arts, religious clubs and organizations.

Athletics. NCAA. **Intercollegiate:** Baseball M, basketball, cross-country, diving, field hockey W, football (tackle) M, golf M, ice hockey, lacrosse, soccer, softball W, swimming, tennis, track and field. **Intramural:** Baseball, basketball, bowling, football (non-tackle), golf, ice hockey, racquetball, soccer, softball, swimming, table tennis, track and field, volleyball, water polo. **Team name:** Redhawks, Engineers.

Student services. Alcohol/substance abuse counseling, campus ministries, career counseling, services for economically disadvantaged, student employment services, financial aid counseling, health services, legal services, minority student services, personal counseling, placement for graduates, women's services. **Physically disabled:** Services for visually, speech, hearing impaired. **Learning disabled:** Comprehensive services available.

Contact. E-mail: admissions@rpi.edu
Phone: (518) 276-6216 Fax: (518) 276-4072
Karen Long, Dean of Enrollment Management, Rensselaer Polytechnic Institute, 110 Eighth Street, Troy, NY 12180-3590

Roberts Wesleyan College

Rochester, New York — **CB member**
www.roberts.edu — **CB code: 2759**

- Private 4-year liberal arts college affiliated with Free Methodist Church of North America
- Residential campus in large city
- 1,408 degree-seeking undergraduates: 10% part-time, 69% women, 8% African American, 1% Asian American, 3% Hispanic American, 2% international
- 502 degree-seeking graduate students
- 87% of applicants admitted
- SAT or ACT (ACT writing recommended), application essay required
- 57% graduate within 6 years; 40% enter graduate study

General. Founded in 1866. Regionally accredited. **Degrees:** 321 bachelor's awarded; master's offered. **ROTC:** Army, Air Force. **Location:** 8 miles from downtown. **Calendar:** Semester, limited summer session. **Full-time faculty:** 91 total; 63% have terminal degrees. **Part-time faculty:** 10 total; 20% have terminal degrees. **Class size:** 68% < 20, 29% 20-39, 3% 40-49, less than 1% 50-99.

Freshman class profile. 614 applied, 532 admitted, 228 enrolled.

Mid 50% test scores		Rank in top tenth:	23%
SAT verbal:	490-610	Return as sophomores:	80%
SAT math:	490-600	Out-of-state:	14%
ACT:	19-26	Live on campus:	81%
Rank in top quarter:	50%	International:	1%

Basis for selection. Rank in top 30% of high school class, 2.9 GPA, recommendations, test scores, and interview important. Students expected to recognize Christian perspectives and values college upholds. Audition required for music program; portfolio required for art education, studio art. **Homeschooled:** Transcript of courses and grades, state high school equivalency certificate, letter of recommendation (nonparent) required. Strongly recommend applicants visit.

High school preparation. 12 units required. Required and recommended units include English 4, mathematics 2-4, social studies 2-3, history 3, science 4 (laboratory 3) and foreign language 3. Biology and chemistry required of nursing applicants.

2006-2007 Annual costs. Tuition/fees: $20,002. Room/board: $7,448. Books/supplies: $700. Personal expenses: $1,350.

2004-2005 Financial aid. Need-based: 227 full-time freshmen applied for aid; 210 were judged to have need; 210 of these received aid. Average need met was 24%. Average scholarship/grant was $11,153; average loan $4,020. 60% of total undergraduate aid awarded as scholarships/grants, 40% as loans/jobs. **Non-need-based:** Awarded to 231 full-time undergraduates, including 54 freshmen. Scholarships awarded for academics, alumni affiliation, art, athletics, music/drama, religious affiliation, ROTC, state residency. **Additional information:** Dollars for Scholars offer matching grants of up to $750.

Application procedures. Admission: Priority date 2/1; deadline 8/15 (postmark date). $35 fee, may be waived for applicants with need. Application may be submitted online. Admission notification on a rolling basis. Must reply by May 1 or within 2 week(s) if notified thereafter. **Financial aid:** Priority date 3/15; no closing date. FAFSA required. Applicants notified on a rolling basis starting 3/15; must reply by 5/1 or within 2 week(s) of notification.

Academics. Special study options: Cross-registration, distance learning, double major, dual enrollment of high school students, ESL, honors, independent study, internships, liberal arts/career combination, study abroad, teacher certification program, Washington semester. **Credit/placement by examination:** AP, CLEP, IB. 30 credit hours maximum toward bachelor's degree. **Support services:** Learning center, reduced course load, remedial instruction, study skills assistance, tutoring.

Majors. Biology: General, biochemistry. **Business:** General, accounting, business admin, human resources, marketing. **Communications:** General. **Computer sciences:** General, computer science. **Education:** Art, biology, chemistry, elementary, English, history, mathematics, music, physics, science, social science, social studies, special. **English:** English lit. **Health:** Nursing (RN), preop/surgical nursing. **History:** General. **Interdisciplinary:** Biological/physical sciences. **Liberal arts:** Arts/sciences, humanities. **Math:** General. **Philosophy/religion:** Religion. **Physical sciences:** Chemistry, physics. **Protective services:** Law enforcement admin. **Psychology:** General. **Public administration:** Social work. **Social sciences:** General, sociology. **Theology:** Theology. **Visual/performing arts:** Commercial/advertising art, piano/organ, studio arts, voice/opera.

Most popular majors. Business/marketing 27%, education 23%, health sciences 13%, psychology 6%.

Computing on campus. 144 workstations in library, computer center. Dormitories wired for high-speed internet access and linked to campus network. Commuter students can connect to campus network. Online library, helpline, wireless network available.

Student life. Freshman orientation: Mandatory. Preregistration for classes offered. **Policies:** Religious observance required. Freshmen permitted cars on campus. **Housing:** Guaranteed on-campus for freshmen. Single-sex dorms, special housing for disabled, apartments, substance-free housing available. $100 fully refundable deposit, deadline 5/1. **Activities:** Bands, choral groups, drama, music ensembles, musical theater, opera, radio station, student government, student newspaper, symphony orchestra, outreach service, committee on ministries, international club, mission trips.

Athletics. NAIA, NCCAA. **Intercollegiate:** Basketball, cheerleading W, cross-country, golf, soccer, tennis, track and field, volleyball W. **Intramural:** Basketball, cross-country, racquetball, softball, table tennis, tennis, track and field, volleyball. **Team name:** Raiders.

Student services. Adult student services, alcohol/substance abuse counseling, campus ministries, career counseling, student employment services, financial aid counseling, health services, personal counseling, placement for graduates, veterans' counselor. **Physically disabled:** Services for visually, hearing impaired.

Contact. E-mail: admissions@roberts.edu
Phone: (585) 594-6400 Toll-free number: (800) 777-4792
Fax: (585) 594-6371
Linda Hoffman, Vice President for Admissions and Marketing, Roberts Wesleyan College, 2301 Westside Drive, Rochester, NY 14624-1997

Rochester Institute of Technology

Rochester, New York — **CB member**
www.rit.edu — **CB code: 2760**

- Private 4-year university
- Residential campus in large city

- 12,423 degree-seeking undergraduates: 8% part-time, 30% women
- 2,267 graduate students
- 69% of applicants admitted
- SAT or ACT (ACT writing optional), application essay required
- 64% graduate within 6 years; 10% enter graduate study

General. Founded in 1829. Regionally accredited. University comprises 8 colleges, including National Technical Institute for the Deaf. **Degrees:** 2,265 bachelor's, 356 associate awarded; master's, doctoral offered. **ROTC:** Army, Navy, Air Force. **Location:** 5 miles from downtown, 70 miles from Buffalo. **Calendar:** Quarter, extensive summer session. **Full-time faculty:** 798 total; 80% have terminal degrees, 16% minority, 29% women. **Part-time faculty:** 406 total; 29% women. **Class size:** 44% < 20, 39% 20-39, 11% 40-49, 6% 50-99, less than 1% >100. **Special facilities:** More than 100 photography darkrooms, Sunday 2000 web press, computer chip manufacturing facility, two OC3 level connections to Internet and Internet2 with 20,000 network connections, computer-controlled observatory, package testing facility, Silicon Graphics computer animation lab, RIT Inn (hotel).

Freshman class profile. 9,384 applied, 6,519 admitted, 2,217 enrolled.

Mid 50% test scores			
SAT verbal:	540-640	Return as sophomores:	90%
SAT math:	570-670	Out-of-state:	50%
ACT:	23-28	Live on campus:	95%
Rank in top quarter:	59%	Fraternities:	5%
Rank in top tenth:	28%	Sororities:	5%

Basis for selection. Primary emphasis on high school grades in required courses, which vary by major. SAT or ACT given considerable weight. Class rank important. Candidates allowed to apply for up to 3 majors. ACT preferred for applicants to National Technical Institute for the Deaf. Interview recommended for all; portfolio required for art, crafts, and design programs. **Homeschooled:** Applicants should provide state certification of graduation if available.

High school preparation. 22 units required. Required and recommended units include English 4, mathematics 2-3, social studies 4, science 2-3 (laboratory 1-2), foreign language 2 and academic electives 10. Units required for social studies may be met with history courses.

2005-2006 Annual costs. Tuition/fees: $23,619. Room/board: $8,451. Books/supplies: $600. Personal expenses: $600.

2004-2005 Financial aid. **Need-based:** 1,975 full-time freshmen applied for aid; 1,690 were judged to have need; 1,690 of these received aid. Average need met was 90%. Average scholarship/grant was $10,600; average loan $4,500. 67% of total undergraduate aid awarded as scholarships/grants, 33% as loans/jobs. **Non-need-based:** Awarded to 3,400 full-time undergraduates, including 815 freshmen. Scholarships awarded for academics, art, leadership, ROTC. **Additional information:** Most juniors and seniors participate in a cooperative education program, earning an average $5,000 per year through paid employment in jobs related to major.

Application procedures. **Admission:** Priority date 2/1; no deadline. $50 fee, may be waived for applicants with need. Application may be submitted online. Admission notification on a rolling basis beginning on or about 3/1. Must reply by May 1 or within 2 week(s) if notified thereafter. Applications received after March 15 will be processed if space available. **Financial aid:** Priority date 3/1; no closing date. FAFSA required. Applicants notified on a rolling basis starting 3/15; must reply by 5/1 or within 2 week(s) of notification.

Academics. **Special study options:** Accelerated study, combined bachelor's/graduate degree, cooperative education, cross-registration, distance learning, double major, ESL, exchange student, honors, independent study, internships, liberal arts/career combination, student-designed major, study abroad, teacher certification program, weekend college. England semester, Japan semester, summer program in Croatia. **Credit/placement by examination:** AP, CLEP, IB, SAT, ACT, institutional tests. 45 credit hours maximum toward associate degree, 135 toward bachelor's. **Support services:** Learning center, pre-admission summer program, reduced course load, study skills assistance, tutoring, writing center.

Majors. **Biology:** General, biochemistry, bioinformatics, biomedical sciences, biotechnology. **Business:** General, accounting, accounting/business management, business admin, finance, hospitality admin, hotel/motel admin, international, management information systems, market research, marketing, resort management, restaurant/food services, special products marketing, statistics, tourism promotion, tourism/travel, travel services. **Communications:** General, advertising, digital media, photojournalism, public relations. **Communications technology:** Animation/special effects, graphics, photo/film/video, printing management. **Computer sciences:** General, computer graphics, computer science, database management, information technology, LAN/WAN management, networking, security, system admin, systems analysis, web page design, webmaster. **Engineering:** Aerospace, biomedical, computer, electrical, industrial, manufacturing, mechanical, polymer, software, systems. **Engineering technology:** Civil, computer, electrical, electromechanical, environmental, manufacturing, mechanical, occupational safety, telecommunications. **Family/consumer sciences:** Food/nutrition, human nutrition. **Foreign languages:** American Sign Language, sign language interpretation. **Health:** Medical illustrating, physician assistant, predentistry, premedicine, prepharmacy, preveterinary, sonography. **Interdisciplinary:** Biopsychology, math/computer science. **Legal studies:** Prelaw. **Math:** Applied, computational, probability, statistics. **Personal/culinary services:** Restaurant/catering. **Physical sciences:** Chemistry, physics, polymer chemistry. **Production:** Furniture, woodworking. **Protective services:** Law enforcement admin. **Psychology:** General. **Public administration:** Policy analysis. **Social sciences:** Economics, international relations. **Visual/performing arts:** Ceramics, cinematography, commercial photography, commercial/advertising art, crafts, design, graphic design, illustration, industrial design, interior design, metal/jewelry, multimedia, painting, photography, printmaking, sculpture, studio arts.

Most popular majors. Business/marketing 14%, computer/information sciences 20%, engineering/engineering technologies 23%, interdisciplinary studies 9%, visual/performing arts 19%.

Computing on campus. 2,000 workstations in dormitories, library, computer center. Dormitories wired for high-speed internet access and linked to campus network. Commuter students can connect to campus network. Online course registration, online library, helpline, repair service, student web hosting, wireless network available.

Student life. **Freshman orientation:** Mandatory, $165 fee. Preregistration for classes offered. Orientation in September prior to start of classes. **Policies:** Alcohol prohibited in campus residence halls. Freshmen permitted cars on campus. **Housing:** Guaranteed on-campus for freshmen. Coed dorms, special housing for disabled, apartments, fraternity/sorority housing, substance-free housing available. $200 nonrefundable deposit, deadline 5/1. Special interest houses for students in selected majors or groups, single-sex floors within coed dorms, special honors program floor available. **Activities:** Bands, choral groups, dance, drama, film society, literary magazine, music ensembles, musical theater, radio station, student government, student newspaper, Asian Cultural Society, Intervarsity Christian Fellowship, Latin American student association, Native American student association, Society of Women Engineers, Society of Hispanic Engineers, National Society of Black Engineers, Emerging Black Artists, Feminist Action, Catholic Newman Network.

Athletics. NCAA. **Intercollegiate:** Baseball M, basketball, cheerleading, cross-country, diving, ice hockey, lacrosse, rowing (crew), soccer, softball W, swimming, tennis, track and field, volleyball W, wrestling M. **Intramural:** Badminton, basketball M, football (non-tackle) M, golf, ice hockey, racquetball, soccer, softball, table tennis, tennis, volleyball. **Team name:** Tigers.

Student services. Adult student services, alcohol/substance abuse counseling, campus ministries, career counseling, services for economically disadvantaged, student employment services, financial aid counseling, health services, legal services, minority student services, on-campus daycare, personal counseling, placement for graduates, veterans' counselor, women's services. **Physically disabled:** Services for visually, speech, hearing impaired. **Learning disabled:** Comprehensive services available.

Contact. E-mail: admissions@rit.edu
Phone: (585) 475-6631 Fax: (585) 475-7424
Daniel Shelley, Executive Director of Undergraduate Admissions, Rochester Institute of Technology, 60 Lomb Memorial Drive, Rochester, NY 14623-5604

Russell Sage College

Troy, New York — **CB member**
www.sage.edu/rsc — **CB code: 2764**

- Private 4-year comprehensive college for women
- Residential campus in small city
- 801 degree-seeking undergraduates: 5% part-time, 100% women, 4% African American, 2% Asian American, 3% Hispanic American
- 81% of applicants admitted
- SAT or ACT (ACT writing optional), application essay required
- 62% graduate within 6 years; 58% enter graduate study

General. Founded in 1916. Regionally accredited. **Degrees:** 236 bachelor's awarded. **ROTC:** Army, Navy, Air Force. **Location:** 10 miles from Albany, 150 miles from New York City. **Calendar:** Semester, extensive summer session. **Full-time faculty:** 61 total; 87% have terminal degrees, 7% minority, 61% women. **Part-time faculty:** 34 total; 32% have terminal degrees, 76% women. **Class size:** 58% < 20, 40% 20-39, 2% 40-49. **Special facilities:** Center for women's studies, New York State Theater Institute, INVEST nanotechnology business incubator.

Freshman class profile. 394 applied, 321 admitted, 117 enrolled.

Mid 50% test scores			
SAT verbal:	490-620	Rank in top quarter:	67%
SAT math:	480-590	Rank in top tenth:	30%
ACT:	21-25	End year in good standing:	87%
GPA 3.50 or higher:	52%	Return as sophomores:	79%
GPA 3.0-3.49:	30%	Out-of-state:	13%
GPA 2.0-2.99:	18%	Live on campus:	81%

Basis for selection. High school record, standardized test scores most important. Recommendations of school officials, intended major, school and community activities considered. Results from SAT or ACT examinations optional for applicants whose secondary school rank is in top 20% of graduating class. Interview recommended. **Homeschooled:** Statement describing homeschool structure and mission, transcript of courses and grades, interview, letter of recommendation (nonparent) required. **Learning Disabled:** Students seeking accommodations are required to present a recent evaluation of their disability conducted by a licensed professional.

High school preparation. 16 units required. Required and recommended units include English 4, mathematics 3, social studies 4, science 3 and foreign language 2-3. Nursing program applicants must have 6 units in mathematics/science combination including chemistry. Physical and occupational therapy students must have 4 years of math/science.

2006-2007 Annual costs. Tuition/fees: $24,720. Room/board: $8,370. Books/supplies: $900. Personal expenses: $1,100.

2005-2006 Financial aid. Need-based: 116 full-time freshmen applied for aid; 110 were judged to have need; 110 of these received aid. Average scholarship/grant was $4,480; average loan $8,835. 63% of total undergraduate aid awarded as scholarships/grants, 37% as loans/jobs. **Non-need-based:** Awarded to 444 full-time undergraduates, including 64 freshmen. Scholarships awarded for academics, alumni affiliation.

Application procedures. Admission: Priority date 3/1; no deadline. $30 fee, may be waived for applicants with need. Application may be submitted online. Admission notification on a rolling basis beginning on or about 12/15. Must reply by May 1 or within 2 week(s) if notified thereafter. **Financial aid:** Priority date 3/1; no closing date. FAFSA required. Applicants notified on a rolling basis starting 3/15; must reply by 5/1 or within 2 week(s) of notification.

Academics. All students complete internship, field experience, or clinical experience. All students engage in service learning through 2 required courses: Women in the World (first year) and Women Changing the World (senior year). **Special study options:** Accelerated study, combined bachelor's/graduate degree, cross-registration, distance learning, double major, exchange student, honors, independent study, internships, liberal arts/career combination, student-designed major, study abroad, teacher certification program. Early College for high school juniors; combined bachelor's/master's, bachelor's/doctoral programs with Sage Graduate School. **Credit/placement by examination:** AP, CLEP, IB, SAT, ACT, institutional tests. 60 credit hours maximum toward bachelor's degree. **Support services:** Learning center, pre-admission summer program, reduced course load, remedial instruction, tutoring, writing center.

Majors. Biology: General, biochemistry. **Business:** Business admin. **Communications:** Media studies. **Education:** Elementary. **English:** English lit. **Foreign languages:** Spanish. **Health:** Art therapy, athletic training, nursing (RN), recreational therapy. **History:** General. **Interdisciplinary:** Biopsychology, global studies, nutrition sciences. **Math:** General. **Physical sciences:** Chemistry. **Protective services:** Criminal justice, forensics. **Psychology:** General. **Public administration:** Human services. **Social sciences:** Political science, sociology. **Visual/performing arts:** Dramatic.

Most popular majors. Biology 11%, English 11%, health sciences 17%, interdisciplinary studies 10%, psychology 16%, security/protective services 8%, visual/performing arts 6%.

Computing on campus. 154 workstations in library, computer center, student center. Dormitories wired for high-speed internet access and linked to campus network. Commuter students can connect to campus network. Online course registration, online library, helpline, wireless network available.

Student life. Freshman orientation: Mandatory, $150 fee. Preregistration for classes offered. New students may receive academic advising and register for classes (summer, fall, spring) beginning March 1st each year. One-day acquaintance session in June, 2-day orientation in September. **Policies:** Zero tolerance for drugs, harassment, or violence on campus. **Housing:** Guaranteed on-campus for all undergraduates. Substance-free housing available. $100 nonrefundable deposit, deadline 5/1. Special houses available for honor students and students interested in language/international awareness activities. Over-21 residence hall available for seniors. 19th-century brownstone residences available. **Activities:** Choral groups, dance, drama, literary magazine, music ensembles, musical theater, student government, student newspaper, BLSA (Black & Latin Student Alliance), GALA (Gay & Lesbian Alliance), Fellowship of Christian Athletes, Hillel, Newman Community, Rotaract Club, Sage Votes.

Athletics. NCAA. **Intercollegiate:** Basketball W, soccer W, softball W, tennis W, volleyball W. **Team name:** Gators.

Student services. Adult student services, alcohol/substance abuse counseling, campus ministries, career counseling, services for economically disadvantaged, student employment services, financial aid counseling, health services, minority student services, personal counseling, placement for graduates, women's services.

Contact. E-mail: rscadm@sage.edu
Phone: (518) 244-2217 Toll-free number: (888) 837-9724
Fax: (518) 244-6880
Kathy Rusch, Director of Admission, RSC, Russell Sage College, 45 Ferry Street, Troy, NY 12180-4115

Sage College of Albany

Albany, New York
www.sage.edu **CB code: 2343**

- Private 4-year college of applied and professional studies
- Commuter campus in small city
- 941 degree-seeking undergraduates: 34% part-time, 72% women, 9% African American, 2% Asian American, 3% Hispanic American
- 28% of applicants admitted
- SAT or ACT (ACT writing optional), application essay required

General. Founded in 1957. Regionally accredited. **Degrees:** 182 bachelor's, 101 associate awarded. **ROTC:** Army, Air Force. **Location:** 150 miles from New York City. **Calendar:** Semester, extensive summer session. **Full-time faculty:** 37 total; 65% have terminal degrees, 5% minority, 54% women. **Part-time faculty:** 51 total; 12% have terminal degrees, 33% women. **Class size:** 70% < 20, 30% 20-39. **Special facilities:** Interior design studios.

Freshman class profile. 348 applied, 99 admitted, 88 enrolled.

Mid 50% test scores			
SAT verbal:	460-570	Rank in top quarter:	22%
SAT math:	460-540	Rank in top tenth:	1%
ACT:	17-21	End year in good standing:	80%
GPA 3.50 or higher:	16%	Return as sophomores:	73%
GPA 3.0-3.49:	29%	Out-of-state:	10%
GPA 2.0-2.99:	54%	Live on campus:	80%

Basis for selection. Recommendation of high school guidance counselor or teacher and academic record considered for all applicants. Applications reviewed on individual basis. Interview recommended for all; portfolio required for art and design programs. **Homeschooled:** Statement describing homeschool structure and mission, transcript of courses and grades, interview, letter of recommendation (nonparent) required. **Learning Disabled:** Students seeking accomodations required to present recent evaluation of disability conducted by licensed professional.

High school preparation. 16 units required. Required and recommended units include English 4, mathematics 2-3, social studies 4, science 2-3 and foreign language 2.

2006-2007 Annual costs. Tuition/fees (projected): $17,670. Room/board: $8,370. Books/supplies: $900. Personal expenses: $1,100.

2005-2006 Financial aid. Need-based: 84 full-time freshmen applied for aid; 80 were judged to have need; 80 of these received aid. Average scholarship/grant was $5,185; average loan $8,900. 58% of total undergraduate aid awarded as scholarships/grants, 42% as loans/jobs. **Non-need-based:** Scholarships awarded for academics, art, leadership.

Application procedures. Admission: No deadline. $30 fee, may be waived for applicants with need. Application may be submitted online. Admission notification on a rolling basis beginning on or about 11/1. Must reply by May 1 or within 2 week(s) if notified thereafter. **Financial aid:** Priority date 3/1; no closing date. FAFSA required. Applicants notified on a rolling basis starting 3/15; must reply within 2 week(s) of notification.

Academics. 4 programs in fine arts (photography, graphic design, interior design, and fine arts) accredited by National Association of Schools of Art and Design. Transfer-friendly "two plus two" curriculum; joint degrees in clinical biology and cytotechnology with Albany College of Pharmacy. **Special study options:** Combined bachelor's/graduate degree, cross-registration, distance learning, double major, honors, independent study, internships, liberal arts/career combination, student-designed major, study abroad, weekend college. **Credit/placement by examination:** AP, CLEP, IB, institutional tests. 30 credit hours maximum toward associate degree. **Support services:** Learning center, pre-admission summer program, reduced course load, remedial instruction, study skills assistance, tutoring, writing center.

Majors. Business: Accounting, business admin. **Communications:** Digital media. **Computer sciences:** General, system admin. **Education:** Physical. **Health:** Cytotechnology. **Legal studies:** General, paralegal. **Liberal arts:** Arts/sciences. **Protective services:** Law enforcement admin. **Psychology:** General. **Social sciences:** General. **Visual/performing arts:** Graphic design, illustration, interior design, studio arts.

Most popular majors. Business/marketing 28%, computer/information sciences 10%, education 6%, interdisciplinary studies 14%, liberal arts 6%, visual/performing arts 12%.

Computing on campus. 165 workstations in library, computer center. Dormitories wired for high-speed internet access and linked to campus network. Commuter students can connect to campus network. Online course registration, online library, helpline, wireless network available.

Student life. Freshman orientation: Mandatory, $125 fee. Preregistration for classes offered. New students may receive academic advising and register for classes (summer, fall, spring) beginning March 1st each year. One-day acquaintance session in June, 2-day orientation in September. **Policies:** Zero tolerance for drugs, harassment or violence on campus. Freshmen permitted cars on campus. **Housing:** Guaranteed on-campus for freshmen. Coed dorms, apartments, substance-free housing available. $100 nonrefundable deposit, deadline 5/1. Apartment-style suites available on adjacent campus. **Activities:** Literary magazine, student government, student newspaper, ALDANA (African American, Latino, Desi's, Asian, Native American Alliance), Sage Votes.

Athletics. Intramural: Badminton, basketball, football (non-tackle), soccer, volleyball.

Student services. Adult student services, alcohol/substance abuse counseling, campus ministries, career counseling, services for economically disadvantaged, student employment services, financial aid counseling, health services, minority student services, personal counseling, placement for graduates, veterans' counselor.

Contact. E-mail: scaadm@sage.adm
Phone: (518) 292-1730 Toll-free number: (888) 837-9724
Fax: (518) 292-1912
Amanda Lanoue, Director of Admission, SCA, Sage College of Albany, 140 New Scotland Avenue, Albany, NY 12208

St. Bonaventure University

St. Bonaventure, New York **CB member**
www.sbu.edu **CB code: 2793**

- Private 4-year university affiliated with Roman Catholic Church
- Residential campus in large town
- 2,072 degree-seeking undergraduates: 2% part-time, 49% women
- 447 degree-seeking graduate students
- 86% of applicants admitted
- SAT or ACT (ACT writing recommended) required
- 68% graduate within 6 years; 40% enter graduate study

General. Founded in 1858. Regionally accredited. Independent institution in Franciscan tradition. **Degrees:** 422 bachelor's awarded; master's offered. **ROTC:** Army. **Location:** 75 miles from Buffalo. **Calendar:** Semester, limited summer session. **Full-time faculty:** 153 total; 79% have terminal degrees, 6% minority, 30% women. **Part-time faculty:** 54 total; 4% minority, 54% women. **Class size:** 57% < 20, 40% 20-39, 3% 40-49. **Special facilities:** Observatory, digital media laboratory, permanent art collection, retreat facility, rare books collection.

Freshman class profile. 1,730 applied, 1,490 admitted, 477 enrolled.

Mid 50% test scores		**Rank in top quarter:**	31%
SAT verbal:	480-570	**Rank in top tenth:**	11%
SAT math:	470-570	**End year in good standing:**	8%
ACT:	19-24	**Return as sophomores:**	76%
GPA 3.50 or higher:	20%	**Out-of-state:**	26%
GPA 3.0-3.49:	53%	**Live on campus:**	91%
GPA 2.0-2.99:	26%	**International:**	1%

Basis for selection. Interview, high school GPA and curriculum most important. Recommendation, class rank, test scores, extracurricular activities also considered. Essay recommended for all. **Homeschooled:** Statement describing homeschool structure and mission, transcript of courses and grades, letter of recommendation (nonparent) required. Course syllabus, book titles, and all course evaluations required to be considered for admission.

High school preparation. 19 units recommended. Required and recommended units include English 4, mathematics 3, social studies 4, history 1, science 3 and foreign language 2. Science majors must have 4 science, 4 mathematics. Business majors need 4 mathematics. Recommend 3 science lab.

2005-2006 Annual costs. Tuition/fees: $21,450. Room/board: $7,335. Books/supplies: $700. Personal expenses: $650.

Financial aid. Non-need-based: Scholarships awarded for academics, art, athletics, leadership, minority status, music/drama, religious affiliation, ROTC, state residency.

Application procedures. Admission: Priority date 2/1; deadline 4/30 (postmark date). $30 fee, may be waived for applicants with need. Application may be submitted online. Admission notification on a rolling basis beginning on or about 10/1. Must reply by May 1 or within 1 week(s) if notified thereafter. Applications considered until housing is closed. **Financial aid:** Priority date 2/1; no closing date. FAFSA, institutional form required. Applicants notified on a rolling basis starting 4/1; must reply by 5/1 or within 3 week(s) of notification.

Academics. Special study options: Accelerated study, combined bachelor's/graduate degree, cross-registration, distance learning, double major, dual enrollment of high school students, ESL, exchange student, honors, independent study, internships, liberal arts/career combination, student-designed major, study abroad, teacher certification program, Washington semester, weekend college. **Credit/placement by examination:** AP, CLEP, IB, institutional tests. 30 credit hours maximum toward bachelor's degree. **Support services:** Learning center, pre-admission summer program, reduced course load, remedial instruction, tutoring.

Majors. Area/ethnic studies: Women's. **Biology:** General, biochemistry. **Business:** Accounting, finance, management information systems, management science. **Communications:** Journalism, media studies. **Computer sciences:** General, computer science. **Conservation:** General. **Education:** Elementary, physical. **English:** British lit. **Foreign languages:** Classics, French, Latin, Spanish. **History:** General. **Math:** General. **Philosophy/religion:** Philosophy. **Physical sciences:** Chemistry, physics. **Psychology:** General. **Social sciences:** General, political science, sociology. **Theology:** Theology. **Visual/performing arts:** General.

Most popular majors. Business/marketing 29%, communications/journalism 18%, education 14%, psychology 6%, social sciences 15%.

Computing on campus. 282 workstations in dormitories, library, computer center, student center. Dormitories wired for high-speed internet access and linked to campus network. Commuter students can connect to campus network. Online course registration, online library, helpline, repair service, student web hosting, wireless network available.

Student life. Freshman orientation: Mandatory, $150 fee. Preregistration for classes offered. 2-day session held in July. **Policies:** Freshmen permitted cars on campus. **Housing:** Guaranteed on-campus for freshmen. Coed dorms, single-sex dorms, special housing for disabled, apartments available. $200 nonrefundable deposit, deadline 5/1. Students must live on campus until they are seniors or 21 years old unless they live within commuting distance. **Activities:** Bands, choral groups, dance, drama, literary magazine, music ensembles, radio station, student government, student newspaper, TV station, campus ministry, drop-in center, Big Brother-Big Sister Youth Program, program to aid elderly, Knights of Columbus, Irish society, social action projects, World Hunger, black student union.

Athletics. NCAA. **Intercollegiate:** Baseball M, basketball, cross-country, diving, golf M, lacrosse W, soccer, softball W, swimming, tennis. **Intramural:** Basketball, bowling, football (non-tackle) M, golf, racquetball, skiing, soccer, softball, swimming, table tennis, tennis, volleyball, water polo M. **Team name:** Bonnies.

Student services. Alcohol/substance abuse counseling, campus ministries, career counseling, services for economically disadvantaged, student employment services, financial aid counseling, health services, personal counseling, placement for graduates, veterans' counselor.

Contact. E-mail: admissions@sbu.edu
Phone: (716) 375-2400 Toll-free number: (800) 462-5050
Fax: (716) 375-2005
James DiRisio, Director of Admissions, St. Bonaventure University, Route 417, St. Bonaventure, NY 14778-2284

St. Francis College

Brooklyn Heights, New York **CB member**
www.stfranciscollege.edu **CB code: 2796**

- Private 4-year liberal arts college affiliated with Roman Catholic Church
- Commuter campus in very large city
- 2,299 degree-seeking undergraduates: 12% part-time, 54% women, 20% African American, 2% Asian American, 16% Hispanic American, 9% international
- 92% of applicants admitted
- SAT, application essay required
- 54% graduate within 6 years

General. Founded in 1884. Regionally accredited. **Degrees:** 415 bachelor's, 26 associate awarded; master's offered. **ROTC:** Army, Air Force. **Calendar:** Semester, limited summer session. **Full-time faculty:** 71 total; 79% have terminal degrees, 14% minority, 45% women. **Part-time faculty:** 143 total; 44% have terminal degrees, 15% minority, 34% women. **Class size:** 50% < 20, 42% 20-39, 7% 40-49, 1% 50-99. **Special facilities:** Television production and editing facility with 3 Ikegami cameras and 17 Mac G5 digital editing stations.

Freshman class profile. 1,566 applied, 1,438 admitted, 505 enrolled.

Mid 50% test scores			
SAT verbal:	410-530	GPA 3.0-3.49:	56%
SAT math:	410-540	GPA 2.0-2.99:	18%
GPA 3.50 or higher:	25%	Return as sophomores:	76%
		International:	6%

Basis for selection. Academic achievement, test scores, counselor's recommendation, school and community activities, interview important. Degree-seeking students who do not meet criteria may be admitted after review and assessment of their educational background. Interview required of academically weak applicants. **Homeschooled:** Statement describing homeschool structure and mission, state high school equivalency certificate required.

High school preparation. 18.5 units recommended. Recommended units include English 4, mathematics 3, social studies 4, science 2, academic electives 4.5. 1 unit of art and/or music required. Applicants seeking BS should have completed 11th year high school mathematics or its equivalent.

2005-2006 Annual costs. Tuition/fees: $12,890. Books/supplies: $790. Personal expenses: $1,106.

2005-2006 Financial aid. Need-based: 467 full-time freshmen applied for aid; 388 were judged to have need; 388 of these received aid. Average scholarship/grant was $3,523. **Non-need-based:** Scholarships awarded for academics, athletics.

Application procedures. Admission: Priority date 4/3; no deadline. $35 fee, may be waived for applicants with need. Application may be submitted online. Admission notification on a rolling basis. Must reply by May 1 or within 2 week(s) if notified thereafter. **Financial aid:** Priority date 2/15; no closing date. FAFSA required. Applicants notified on a rolling basis starting 3/15; must reply within 2 week(s) of notification.

Academics. Special study options: Accelerated study, combined bachelor's/graduate degree, cooperative education, cross-registration, double major, dual enrollment of high school students, ESL, exchange student, honors, independent study, internships, student-designed major, study abroad, teacher certification program, Washington semester. Accelerated biomedical science program with New York College of Podiatric Medicine, medical technology program with St. Vincent's Catholic Medical Centers of New York and New York Methodist Hospital, joint affiliation program with St. Vincent's Catholic Medical Centers of New York in radiologic sciences, 7-year cooperative program with the New York University College of Dentistry, combined BA/MS in computer science with Polytechnic University. **Credit/placement by examination:** AP, CLEP, IB, institutional tests. 30 credit hours maximum toward associate degree, 96 toward bachelor's. **Support services:** Learning center, pre-admission summer program, remedial instruction, study skills assistance, tutoring, writing center.

Majors. Biology: General, biomedical sciences. **Business:** Accounting, business admin. **Communications:** General. **Computer sciences:** Information technology. **Education:** Biology, chemistry, elementary, English, mathematics, physical, social studies, visually handicapped. **English:** English lit. **Foreign languages:** Spanish. **Health:** Clinical lab science, medical radiologic technology/radiation therapy, physician assistant. **History:** General. **Liberal arts:** Arts/sciences. **Math:** General. **Philosophy/religion:** Philosophy, religion. **Physical sciences:** Chemistry. **Protective services:** Criminal justice. **Psychology:** General. **Social sciences:** Economics, political science, sociology. **Transportation:** Aviation.

Most popular majors. Business/marketing 21%, communications/journalism 9%, computer/information sciences 9%, education 6%, liberal arts 13%, psychology 9%, social sciences 7%.

Computing on campus. 138 workstations in library, computer center, student center. Commuter students can connect to campus network. Helpline, wireless network available.

Student life. Freshman orientation: Mandatory. Preregistration for classes offered. **Housing:** Students may apply for housing at Polytechnic University, approximately 10-minute walk from college. **Activities:** Choral groups, dance, drama, literary magazine, student government, student newspaper, Latin American Society, Haitian Alliance, Caribbean student association, Christian club, Arab-American Society, French club, College Republicans, History and Political Science Society, Italian Historical Society, Model United Nations.

Athletics. NCAA. **Intercollegiate:** Baseball M, basketball, cross-country, diving, soccer M, softball W, swimming, tennis, track and field, volleyball W, water polo. **Intramural:** Basketball, football (tackle) M, soccer M, softball, volleyball. **Team name:** Terriers.

Student services. Adult student services, campus ministries, career counseling, services for economically disadvantaged, student employment services, financial aid counseling, health services, personal counseling, placement for graduates, veterans' counselor. **Physically disabled:** Services for visually, speech, hearing impaired.

Contact. E-mail: admissions@stfranciscollege.edu
Phone: (718) 489-5200 Fax: (718) 802-0453
Bro. George Larkin, Dean of Admissions, St. Francis College, 180 Remsen Street, Brooklyn Heights, NY 11201-9902

St. John Fisher College

Rochester, New York **CB member**
www.sjfc.edu **CB code: 2798**

- Private 4-year liberal arts college affiliated with Roman Catholic Church
- Residential campus in large town
- 2,631 degree-seeking undergraduates: 7% part-time, 58% women, 3% African American, 2% Asian American, 3% Hispanic American
- 742 degree-seeking graduate students
- 65% of applicants admitted
- SAT or ACT (ACT writing optional) required
- 62% graduate within 6 years; 35% enter graduate study

General. Founded in 1948. Regionally accredited. **Degrees:** 617 bachelor's awarded; master's offered. **ROTC:** Army, Air Force. **Location:** 6 miles from downtown. **Calendar:** Semester, extensive summer session. **Full-time faculty:** 152 total; 73% have terminal degrees, 10% minority, 43% women. **Part-time faculty:** 153 total; 5% minority, 54% women. **Class size:** 45% < 20, 50% 20-39, 3% 40-49, 2% 50-99, less than 1% >100. **Special facilities:** 2 electron microscopes, language laboratory, cyber cafe.

Freshman class profile. 2,753 applied, 1,795 admitted, 553 enrolled.

Mid 50% test scores			
SAT verbal:	490-580	Rank in top quarter:	53%
SAT math:	500-600	Rank in top tenth:	15%
ACT:	21-25	End year in good standing:	92%
GPA 3.50 or higher:	48%	Return as sophomores:	84%
GPA 3.0-3.49:	36%	Out-of-state:	2%
GPA 2.0-2.99:	16%	Live on campus:	90%

Basis for selection. Academic factors considered include high school GPA, strength of curriculum, class rank, and standardized test results. Extracurricular involvements, letters of recommendation, and personal interview also considered. Interview recommended for all. **Homeschooled:** Letter of recommendation (nonparent) required.

High school preparation. 16 units required. Required and recommended units include English 4, mathematics 3, social studies 4, science 3 and foreign language 3. 4 mathematics courses required for programs needing college calculus.

2005-2006 Annual costs. Tuition/fees: $19,560. Room/board: $8,300. Books/supplies: $700. Personal expenses: $600.

2004-2005 Financial aid. Need-based: 502 full-time freshmen applied for aid; 443 were judged to have need; 443 of these received aid. Average need met was 84%. Average scholarship/grant was $11,728; average loan $4,433. 56% of total undergraduate aid awarded as scholarships/grants, 44%

as loans/jobs. **Non-need-based:** Awarded to 1,609 full-time undergraduates, including 391 freshmen. Scholarships awarded for academics.

Application procedures. Admission: Priority date 12/1; no deadline. $30 fee, may be waived for applicants with need. Application may be submitted online. Admission notification on a rolling basis beginning on or about 10/1. Must reply by May 1 or within 3 week(s) if notified thereafter. **Financial aid:** Priority date 2/15; no closing date. FAFSA required. Applicants notified on a rolling basis starting 3/21; must reply by 5/1 or within 3 week(s) of notification.

Academics. All entering freshmen participate in one of the integrative learning communities as part of first year experience. Experiential learning opportunities integrated into undergraduate programs. **Special study options:** Accelerated study, cross-registration, distance learning, double major, honors, independent study, internships, liberal arts/career combination, student-designed major, study abroad, teacher certification program, Washington semester, weekend college. 3-4 optometry program with Pennsylvania College of Optometry, 2-2 environmental science and forestry program with SUNY, 3-2 preengineering program with Clarkson University, SUNY Buffalo, Manhattan College, 2-2 preengineering program with University of Detroit Mercy, 4-2 preengineering program with Columbia University, University of Detroit. **Credit/placement by examination:** AP, CLEP, IB, institutional tests. 66 credit hours maximum toward bachelor's degree. **Support services:** Reduced course load, remedial instruction, study skills assistance, tutoring, writing center.

Majors. Area/ethnic studies: American. **Biology:** General. **Business:** Accounting, business admin, finance, human resources, international, management information systems, management science, marketing. **Communications:** General, broadcast journalism, journalism. **Computer sciences:** General, computer science. **Education:** General, biology, chemistry, elementary, English, foreign languages, French, German, history, mathematics, physics, science, secondary, social science, social studies, Spanish, special. **Foreign languages:** French, Spanish. **Health:** Nursing (RN), preop/surgical nursing. **History:** General. **Liberal arts:** Arts/sciences. **Math:** General. **Parks/recreation:** Sports admin. **Philosophy/religion:** Philosophy, religion. **Physical sciences:** Chemistry, physics. **Psychology:** General. **Social sciences:** Anthropology, economics, political science, sociology.

Most popular majors. Business/marketing 23%, communications/journalism 11%, education 24%, history 6%, psychology 8%, social sciences 6%.

Computing on campus. 260 workstations in library, computer center. Dormitories wired for high-speed internet access and linked to campus network. Commuter students can connect to campus network. Online course registration, online library, helpline, student web hosting, wireless network available.

Student life. Freshman orientation: Mandatory. Preregistration for classes offered. Held weekend prior to classes. 3-day program for new traditional undergraduates. Transfer students encouraged to choose from 3-day orientation or shorter half-day program. Great Beginnings day-long course registration in May for freshmen entering in fall, including full day of activities for parents. **Policies:** All housing smoke-free. Freshmen permitted cars on campus. **Housing:** Guaranteed on-campus for freshmen. Coed dorms, single-sex dorms available. $300 nonrefundable deposit. All residence halls accessible to students with disabilities. **Activities:** Choral groups, dance, drama, literary magazine, musical theater, radio station, student government, student newspaper, TV station, Campus ministry, Circle K, Latino student union, Black student union, Fisher Players, gospel choir, resident student association, commuter council, student activities board, Fisher Pride.

Athletics. NCAA. **Intercollegiate:** Baseball M, basketball, football (tackle) M, golf M, lacrosse, soccer, softball W, tennis, volleyball W. **Intramural:** Basketball, football (non-tackle) M, soccer, softball, volleyball. **Team name:** Cardinals.

Student services. Adult student services, campus ministries, career counseling, services for economically disadvantaged, student employment services, financial aid counseling, health services, on-campus daycare, personal counseling, placement for graduates, veterans' counselor. **Physically disabled:** Services for visually, hearing impaired.

Contact. E-mail: admissions@sjfc.edu
Phone: (585) 385-8064 Toll-free number: (800) 444-4640
Fax: (585) 385-8386
Stacy Ledermann, Director of Freshman Admissions, St. John Fisher College, 3690 East Avenue, Rochester, NY 14618-3597

St. John's University

Queens, New York — **CB member**
www.stjohns.edu — **CB code: 2799**

- Private 4-year university affiliated with Roman Catholic Church
- Commuter campus in very large city
- 12,340 degree-seeking undergraduates: 5% part-time, 58% women, 17% African American, 16% Asian American, 15% Hispanic American, 3% international
- 4,712 degree-seeking graduate students
- 63% of applicants admitted
- SAT or ACT (ACT writing recommended) required
- 64% graduate within 6 years; 18% enter graduate study

General. Founded in 1870. Regionally accredited. Branch campuses in Staten Island, Manhattan, and Oakdale; graduate center in Rome, Italy. **Degrees:** 2,165 bachelor's, 91 associate awarded; master's, doctoral, first professional offered. **ROTC:** Army. **Location:** 10 miles from midtown Manhattan. **Calendar:** Semester, extensive summer session. **Full-time faculty:** 599 total; 91% have terminal degrees, 19% minority, 36% women. **Part-time faculty:** 829 total; 36% have terminal degrees, 15% minority, 39% women. **Class size:** 35% < 20, 48% 20-39, 9% 40-49, 7% 50-99, less than 1% >100. **Special facilities:** Speech and hearing clinic, instructional media center and health education resources center.

Freshman class profile. 20,669 applied, 12,980 admitted, 3,159 enrolled.

Mid 50% test scores		**Rank in top tenth:**	18%
SAT verbal:	470-580	**End year in good standing:**	82%
SAT math:	470-600	**Return as sophomores:**	79%
GPA 3.50 or higher:	35%	**Out-of-state:**	21%
GPA 3.0-3.49:	26%	**Live on campus:**	42%
GPA 2.0-2.99:	37%	**International:**	3%
Rank in top quarter:	43%		

Basis for selection. School achievement record, standardized test scores, counselor/teacher recommendations, honor awards, extracurricular activities, personal essay used in admissions decisions. SAT not required if student has graduated or if time elapsed is more than 1 year prior to term of admission. Interview, personal statement, essay recommended for all; portfolio required for creative photography, fine art, graphic design, illlustration programs. **Homeschooled:** Statement describing homeschool structure and mission, state high school equivalency certificate required.

High school preparation. College-preparatory program required. 16 units required. Required and recommended units include English 4, mathematics 3, history 2, science 2 (laboratory 2), foreign language 2 and academic electives 1. Additional math/sciences classes highly recommended or required for certain majors.

2005-2006 Annual costs. Tuition/fees: $23,370. Tuition may vary by program and class year. Room/board: $11,000. Books/supplies: $1,000. Personal expenses: $2,700.

2004-2005 Financial aid. Need-based: 2,723 full-time freshmen applied for aid; 2,506 were judged to have need; 2,506 of these received aid. Average need met was 71%. Average scholarship/grant was $8,753; average loan $3,290. 57% of total undergraduate aid awarded as scholarships/grants, 43% as loans/jobs. **Non-need-based:** Awarded to 6,960 full-time undergraduates, including 2,480 freshmen. Scholarships awarded for academics, alumni affiliation, art, athletics, leadership, music/drama, religious affiliation, ROTC.

Application procedures. Admission: No deadline. $30 fee, may be waived for applicants with need. Application may be submitted online. Admission notification on a rolling basis. Must reply by May 1 or within 2 week(s) if notified thereafter. Application closing date for pharmacy students February 1. **Financial aid:** Priority date 2/1; no closing date. FAFSA required. Applicants notified on a rolling basis starting 3/15; must reply within 2 week(s) of notification.

Academics. Special study options: Accelerated study, combined bachelor's/graduate degree, cross-registration, distance learning, double major, dual enrollment of high school students, ESL, honors, independent study, internships, liberal arts/career combination, study abroad, teacher certification program, weekend college. **Credit/placement by examination:** AP, CLEP, IB, institutional tests. Students must complete at least 50 percent of major courses and at least 30 credits on campus. **Support services:** Learning center, preadmission summer program, reduced course load, study skills assistance, tutoring, writing center.

Majors. Area/ethnic studies: Asian. **Biology:** General, toxicology. **Business:** Accounting, actuarial science, business admin, finance, hospitality admin, insurance, management information systems, marketing. **Communications:** General, advertising, journalism. **Communications technology:** Photo/film/video. **Computer sciences:** General. **Conservation:** Environmental studies. **Education:** Elementary, English, mathematics, physics, social studies, Spanish, special. **Engineering technology:** Telecommunications. **English:** English lit, speech/rhetoric. **Foreign languages:** French, Italian, Spanish. **Health:**

Audiology/speech pathology, clinical lab science, health care admin, pathology assistant, physician assistant. **History:** General. **Legal studies:** General. **Liberal arts:** Arts/sciences. **Math:** General. **Parks/recreation:** Sports admin. **Personal/culinary services:** Mortuary science. **Philosophy/religion:** Philosophy. **Physical sciences:** General, chemistry, physics. **Protective services:** Law enforcement admin. **Psychology:** General. **Public administration:** General, human services. **Social sciences:** General, anthropology, economics, political science, sociology. **Theology:** Theology. **Visual/performing arts:** Graphic design, illustration, photography, studio arts.

Most popular majors. Business/marketing 26%, communications/journalism 10%, computer/information sciences 6%, education 8%, health sciences 6%, legal studies 6%, psychology 6%, security/protective services 7%.

Computing on campus. PC or laptop required. 9,903 workstations in dormitories, library, computer center, student center. Dormitories wired for high-speed internet access and linked to campus network. Commuter students can connect to campus network. Online course registration, online library, helpline, repair service, student web hosting, wireless network available.

Student life. **Freshman orientation:** Mandatory, $125 fee. 2-day orientation program includes academic dean's conference, social activities, summer reading program. **Policies:** Freshmen permitted cars on campus. **Housing:** Coed dorms available. $500 nonrefundable deposit. Limited apartment housing available on Staten Island campus. **Activities:** Bands, choral groups, dance, drama, film society, literary magazine, musical theater, radio station, student government, student newspaper, TV station, over 180 organizations on all campuses.

Athletics. NCAA. **Intercollegiate:** Baseball M, basketball, cross-country W, fencing, golf, lacrosse M, soccer, softball W, tennis, track and field W, volleyball W. **Intramural:** Basketball, cheerleading, football (tackle), racquetball, soccer, softball, table tennis, track and field, volleyball, weight lifting. **Team name:** Red Storm.

Student services. Adult student services, alcohol/substance abuse counseling, campus ministries, career counseling, student employment services, financial aid counseling, health services, minority student services, personal counseling, placement for graduates, veterans' counselor. **Physically disabled:** Services for visually, speech, hearing impaired.

Contact. E-mail: admissions@stjohns.edu
Phone: (718) 990-2000 Toll-free number: (888) 978-56467
Fax: (718) 990-2096
Matthew Whelan, Director of Admissions, St. John's University, 8000 Utopia Parkway, Queens, NY 11439

St. Joseph's College

Brooklyn, New York — **CB member**
www.sjcny.edu — **CB code: 2802**

- Private 4-year liberal arts and teachers college
- Commuter campus in very large city
- 3,760 degree-seeking undergraduates: 22% part-time, 75% women
- 239 degree-seeking graduate students
- 85% of applicants admitted
- SAT or ACT with writing required

General. Founded in 1916. Regionally accredited. **Degrees:** 678 bachelor's awarded; master's offered. **Location:** 8 miles from Manhattan. **Calendar:** Semester, limited summer session. **Full-time faculty:** 120 total. **Part-time faculty:** 265 total. **Class size:** 79% < 20, 21% 20-39. **Special facilities:** On-campus laboratory preschool for children 3-6 years old, model school for prospective teachers.

Freshman class profile. 1,267 applied, 1,077 admitted, 466 enrolled.

Mid 50% test scores			
SAT verbal:	430-540	SAT math:	450-560
		ACT:	21-22

Basis for selection. High school achievement record, SAT/ACT scores, class rank, activities, recommendations important. Personal statements encouraged. Essay, interview recommended.

High school preparation. 18 units required. Required and recommended units include English 4, mathematics 3, social studies 4, science 2, foreign language 2-3 and academic electives 3. 3 units science recommended for science majors. No specific course requirements for general studies applicants.

2005-2006 Annual costs. Tuition/fees: $12,386. Books/supplies: $1,000. Personal expenses: $600.

2005-2006 Financial aid. **Need-based:** 128 full-time freshmen applied for aid; 85 were judged to have need; 85 of these received aid. Average need met was 85%. Average scholarship/grant was $10,000; average loan $2,500. 69% of total undergraduate aid awarded as scholarships/grants, 31% as loans/jobs. **Non-need-based:** Awarded to 375 full-time undergraduates, including 105 freshmen. Scholarships awarded for academics, alumni affiliation, leadership.

Application procedures. **Admission:** No deadline. $25 fee, may be waived for applicants with need. Admission notification on a rolling basis. **Financial aid:** Priority date 2/25; no closing date. FAFSA, institutional form required. Applicants notified on a rolling basis starting 4/1; must reply by 5/1 or within 2 week(s) of notification.

Academics. **Special study options:** Accelerated study, honors, independent study, internships, teacher certification program, weekend college. Accelerated biomedical program with New York College of Podiatric Medicine. **Credit/placement by examination:** AP, CLEP, institutional tests. 30 credit hours maximum toward bachelor's degree. **Support services:** Reduced course load, tutoring.

Majors. **Biology:** General. **Business:** General, accounting, business admin, human resources. **Education:** General, early childhood, elementary, mathematics, middle, science, secondary, social studies, special. **English:** Speech/rhetoric. **Foreign languages:** General. **Health:** Health care admin, prenursing. **History:** General. **Liberal arts:** Arts/sciences. **Math:** General. **Physical sciences:** Chemistry. **Psychology:** General. **Social sciences:** General, sociology.

Most popular majors. Business/marketing 14%, education 55%, English 7%, psychology 8%, social sciences 7%.

Computing on campus. 90 workstations in library, computer center.

Student life. **Freshman orientation:** Mandatory. Preregistration for classes offered. **Housing:** Housing in collaboration with Polytechnic University. **Activities:** Choral groups, dance, drama, literary magazine, musical theater, student government, student newspaper, campus ministry, Gaelic Society, Hispanic Awareness club, Heritage Gallery, Asian Awareness, Japanese Animation, Political Affairs, Student Ambassador club.

Athletics. **Intercollegiate:** Basketball, cross-country, softball W, swimming W, tennis M, volleyball. **Intramural:** Basketball, table tennis, volleyball. **Team name:** Bears.

Student services. Adult student services, campus ministries, career counseling, student employment services, financial aid counseling, personal counseling, placement for graduates.

Contact. E-mail: asinfob@sjcny.edu
Phone: (718) 636-6868 Fax: (718) 636-8303
Theresa LaRocca-Meyer, Director of Admissions, St. Joseph's College, 245 Clinton Avenue, Brooklyn, NY 11205-3688

St. Joseph's College: Suffolk Campus

Patchogue, New York
www.sjcny.edu — **CB code: 2841**

- Private 4-year branch campus and liberal arts college
- Commuter campus in large town
- 3,760 degree-seeking undergraduates: 22% part-time, 75% women, 4% African American, 1% Asian American, 6% Hispanic American
- 239 degree-seeking graduate students
- 85% of applicants admitted
- SAT or ACT (ACT writing recommended) required
- 64% graduate within 6 years; 35% enter graduate study

General. Founded in 1916. Regionally accredited. **Degrees:** 817 bachelor's awarded; master's offered. **ROTC:** Army, Air Force. **Location:** 60 miles from New York City. **Calendar:** 4-1-4, extensive summer session. **Full-time faculty:** 120 total; 52% have terminal degrees, 59% women. **Part-time faculty:** 248 total; 29% have terminal degrees, 52% women. **Class size:** 51% < 20, 49% 20-39, less than 1% 40-49, less than 1% 50-99.

Freshman class profile. 1,267 applied, 1,077 admitted, 466 enrolled.

Mid 50% test scores		Rank in top tenth:	12%
SAT verbal:	430-540	End year in good standing:	97%
SAT math:	450-560	Return as sophomores:	89%
ACT:	21-26	Fraternities:	1%
Rank in top quarter:	49%	Sororities:	2%

Basis for selection. Grades in high school academic classes, GPA and rank in class most important. Performance on standardized tests important.

Strongly factored in are letters of recommendation, personal statement and school/community activities. SAT Subject Tests recommended. Interview recommended. Essays required of scholarship candidates, strongly recommended for all others. **Homeschooled:** Transcript of courses and grades required. SAT or ACT required. Interview strongly recommended.

High school preparation. College-preparatory program required. 18 units required. Required units include English 4, mathematics 3, social studies 4, science 2 (laboratory 2), foreign language 2 and academic electives 3. Social science unit must be American history.

2005-2006 Annual costs. Tuition/fees: $12,956. Books/supplies: $1,000. Personal expenses: $600.

2005-2006 Financial aid. Need-based: 419 full-time freshmen applied for aid; 388 were judged to have need; 388 of these received aid. Average need met was 32%. Average scholarship/grant was $5,630; average loan $2,584. 59% of total undergraduate aid awarded as scholarships/grants, 41% as loans/jobs. **Non-need-based:** Awarded to 1,205 full-time undergraduates, including 273 freshmen. Scholarships awarded for academics.

Application procedures. Admission: Priority date 8/15; no deadline. $25 fee, may be waived for applicants with need. Application must be submitted on paper. Admission notification on a rolling basis. Must reply by May 1 or within 2 week(s) if notified thereafter. June 30 application closing date for child study majors. **Financial aid:** Priority date 2/25; no closing date. FAFSA, institutional form required. Must reply within 2 week(s) of notification.

Academics. Special study options: Combined bachelor's/graduate degree, distance learning, double major, honors, independent study, internships, liberal arts/career combination, study abroad, teacher certification program, weekend college. 5-year program of bachelor's from St. Joseph's College/master's in computer science from Polytechnic University. **Credit/placement by examination:** AP, CLEP, institutional tests. 30 credit hours maximum toward bachelor's degree. **Support services:** Learning center, reduced course load, study skills assistance, tutoring, writing center.

Majors. Biology: General. **Business:** Accounting, business admin. **Communications:** General. **Computer sciences:** Computer science, information technology. **Education:** General, biology, early childhood, elementary, English, history, kindergarten/preschool, mathematics, middle, science, secondary, social studies, Spanish, special. **Foreign languages:** Spanish. **Health:** Facilities admin, predentistry, premedicine, preveterinary, recreational therapy. **History:** General. **Liberal arts:** Arts/sciences. **Math:** General. **Parks/recreation:** General. **Psychology:** General. **Social sciences:** General, economics, political science, sociology.

Most popular majors. Business/marketing 19%, education 46%, English 6%, health sciences 7%, psychology 6%, social sciences 6%.

Computing on campus. 223 workstations in library, computer center. Commuter students can connect to campus network. Online course registration, online library available.

Student life. Freshman orientation: Mandatory, $50 fee. Preregistration for classes offered. 1-day orientation in August just prior to start of classes. **Policies:** 2.7 average required to run for student government. Freshmen permitted cars on campus. **Activities:** Jazz band, choral groups, dance, drama, literary magazine, music ensembles, musical theater, student government, student newspaper, student government, religious affairs committee, student volunteer services, human relations club, Students Taking an Active Role in Society, Spanish club, multicultural club.

Athletics. NCAA. **Intercollegiate:** Baseball M, basketball, cross-country, equestrian, golf M, soccer, softball W, swimming, tennis, track and field, volleyball W. **Team name:** Golden Eagles.

Student services. Alcohol/substance abuse counseling, campus ministries, career counseling, student employment services, financial aid counseling, minority student services, personal counseling, veterans' counselor. **Physically disabled:** Services for visually impaired.

Contact. E-mail: suffolkas@sjcny.edu
Phone: (631) 447-3219 Fax: (631) 447-1734
Gigi Lamens, Director of Admissions and Enrollment Planning, St. Joseph's College: Suffolk Campus, 155 West Roe Boulevard, Patchogue, NY 11772-2603

St. Lawrence University

Canton, New York
www.stlawu.edu

CB member
CB code: 2805

- Private 4-year liberal arts college
- Residential campus in small town
- 2,104 degree-seeking undergraduates: 52% women, 2% African American, 2% Asian American, 2% Hispanic American, 1% Native American, 5% international
- 102 degree-seeking graduate students
- 59% of applicants admitted
- Application essay required
- 75% graduate within 6 years; 28% enter graduate study

General. Founded in 1856. Regionally accredited. **Degrees:** 434 bachelor's awarded; master's offered. **ROTC:** Army, Air Force. **Location:** 70 miles from Ottawa, Canada. **Calendar:** Semester, limited summer session. **Full-time faculty:** 167 total; 99% have terminal degrees, 16% minority. **Part-time faculty:** 23 total; 26% minority, 65% women. **Class size:** 66% < 20, 33% 20-39, less than 1% 40-49, less than 1% 50-99, less than 1% >100.

Freshman class profile. 2,989 applied, 1,770 admitted, 537 enrolled.

Mid 50% test scores		**Rank in top tenth:**	38%
SAT verbal:	520-620	**End year in good standing:**	90%
SAT math:	530-630	**Return as sophomores:**	90%
GPA 3.50 or higher:	45%	**Out-of-state:**	50%
GPA 3.0-3.49:	38%	**Live on campus:**	99%
GPA 2.0-2.99:	17%	**International:**	7%
Rank in top quarter:	71%		

Basis for selection. Academic record most important; test scores, extracurricular activities, seriousness of purpose and intellectual promise important. Diverse student body sought. Students for whom English is not the native language must submit official TOEFL results and are encouraged to submit SAT or ACT. Interview recommended.

High school preparation. College-preparatory program required. 20 units recommended. Recommended units include English 4, mathematics 4, social studies 2, history 2, science 4 and foreign language 4.

2005-2006 Annual costs. Tuition/fees: $32,150. Room/board: $8,180. Books/supplies: $650. Personal expenses: $800.

2005-2006 Financial aid. Need-based: 415 full-time freshmen applied for aid; 372 were judged to have need; 372 of these received aid. Average need met was 95%. Average scholarship/grant was $19,303; average loan $2,878. 82% of total undergraduate aid awarded as scholarships/grants, 18% as loans/jobs. **Non-need-based:** Awarded to 881 full-time undergraduates, including 209 freshmen. Scholarships awarded for academics, alumni affiliation,athletics, minority status.

Application procedures. Admission: Closing date 2/15 (postmark date). $50 fee, may be waived for applicants with need. Application may be submitted online. Admission notification 3/31. Must reply by May 1 or within 2 week(s) if notified thereafter. **Financial aid:** Closing date 2/15. FAFSA, institutional form required. Applicants notified by 3/31; must reply by 5/1 or within 2 week(s) of notification.

Academics. Special study options: Combined bachelor's/graduate degree, cross-registration, double major, exchange student, independent study, internships, student-designed major, study abroad, teacher certification program, Washington semester. 3-2 program in engineering with Clarkson University, Columbia University, Rensselaer Polytechnic Institute, SUNY at Binghamton, University of Rochester, University of Southern California, Washington University in Missouri, and Worcester Polytechnic Institute in Massachusetts; early assurance programs in medicine with SUNY Health Science Center at Syracuse and in dentistry with Columbia University and SUNY at Buffalo; combined bachelor's/graduate degree program in business administration with Clarkson University; 14 study abroad programs in Australia, Europe, Kenya, Japan, Costa Rica, India, Canada, Trinidad and Tobago, China. **Credit/placement by examination:** AP, CLEP, IB, institutional tests. 60 credit hours maximum toward bachelor's degree. **Support services:** Preadmission summer program, reduced course load, tutoring, writing center.

Majors. Area/ethnic studies: African, Asian, Canadian. **Biology:** General, biochemistry, biophysics, neurobiology/physiology. **Computer sciences:** Computer science. **Conservation:** Environmental studies. **English:** American lit, British lit, creative writing. **Foreign languages:** General, French, German, Spanish. **History:** General. **Interdisciplinary:** Global studies, math/computer science, neuroscience. **Math:** General. **Philosophy/religion:** Philosophy, religion. **Physical sciences:** Chemistry, geology, geophysics, physics. **Psychology:** General. **Social sciences:** Anthropology, economics, political science, sociology. **Visual/performing arts:** Dramatic, studio arts.

Most popular majors. Biology 6%, English 14%, history 8%, psychology 13%, social sciences 30%, visual/performing arts 8%.

Computing on campus. 350 workstations in dormitories, library, computer center. Dormitories wired for high-speed internet access and linked to

campus network. Online course registration, helpline, repair service, student web hosting, wireless network available.

Student life. **Freshman orientation:** Mandatory. Preregistration for classes offered. Introduces students to First-Year Program, campus values, faculty advisers. **Policies:** First-Year Program requires freshmen to reside in college with academic/administrative staff. Freshmen permitted cars on campus. **Housing:** Guaranteed on-campus for all undergraduates. Coed dorms, apartments, fraternity/sorority housing, substance-free housing available. Townhouse apartments for senior leaders, theme cottages/halls, some suites available. Students can petition to have quiet or single-sex halls within dormitory. **Activities:** Choral groups, dance, drama, film society, literary magazine, music ensembles, radio station, student government, student newspaper, TV station, Thelomathesian Society (student government), Jewish student organization, Black Student Union, environmental awareness organization, Habitat for Humanity, outing club, academic honorary societies, Circle K, Model UN, Amnesty International.

Athletics. NCAA. **Intercollegiate:** Baseball M, basketball, cross-country, diving, equestrian, field hockey W, football (tackle) M, golf, ice hockey, lacrosse, rowing (crew), skiing, soccer, softball W, squash, swimming, tennis, track and field, volleyball W. **Intramural:** Basketball, equestrian, football (non-tackle) M, football (tackle) M, ice hockey, racquetball M, rugby, soccer, softball W, tennis, triathlon, volleyball. **Team name:** Saints.

Student services. Alcohol/substance abuse counseling, campus ministries, career counseling, services for economically disadvantaged, student employment services, financial aid counseling, health services, minority student services, personal counseling, placement for graduates. **Physically disabled:** Services for visually, hearing impaired.

Contact. E-mail: admissions@stlawu.edu
Phone: (315) 229-5261 Toll-free number: (800) 285-1856
Fax: (315) 229-5818
Teresa Cowdrey, Vice President and Dean of Admissions and Financial Aid, St. Lawrence University, Payson Hall, Canton, NY 13617

St. Thomas Aquinas College

Sparkill, New York — **CB member**
www.stac.edu — **CB code: 2807**

- Private 4-year liberal arts college
- Commuter campus in large town
- 1,409 degree-seeking undergraduates: 7% part-time, 56% women, 5% African American, 2% Asian American, 16% Hispanic American, 1% international
- 189 degree-seeking graduate students
- 76% of applicants admitted
- SAT or ACT (ACT writing optional) required

General. Founded in 1952. Regionally accredited. **Degrees:** 282 bachelor's, 27 associate awarded; master's offered. **ROTC:** Air Force. **Location:** 15 miles from New York City. **Calendar:** Semester, extensive summer session. **Full-time faculty:** 61 total. **Part-time faculty:** 78 total. **Class size:** 50% < 20, 48% 20-39, less than 1% 40-49, less than 1% 50-99. **Special facilities:** State-of-the-art arts, sciences and technology center, digital imaging laboratory.

Freshman class profile. 1,243 applied, 945 admitted, 327 enrolled.

Mid 50% test scores			
SAT verbal:	420-520	Rank in top tenth:	5%
SAT math:	420-520	Return as sophomores:	68%
ACT:	17-23	Out-of-state:	34%
Rank in top quarter:	15%	Live on campus:	58%

Basis for selection. School achievement record, test scores, recommendation, and interview considered. Applicants should be in top half of class and have GPA above 3.0. Essay, interview recommended for all; portfolio recommended for art program.

High school preparation. 20 units required. Required and recommended units include English 4, mathematics 3, social studies 4, history 1, science 3 (laboratory 2), foreign language 3 and academic electives 3.

2006-2007 Annual costs. Tuition/fees: $17,600. Room/board: $9,120. Books/supplies: $750. Personal expenses: $1,000.

2004-2005 Financial aid. **Need-based:** 55% of total undergraduate aid awarded as scholarships/grants, 45% as loans/jobs. **Non-need-based:** Scholarships awarded for academics, athletics.

Application procedures. **Admission:** No deadline. $30 fee. Application may be submitted online. Admission notification on a rolling basis beginning on or about 10/1. **Financial aid:** Priority date 2/15; no closing date. FAFSA required. Applicants notified on a rolling basis starting 3/1; must reply by 5/1 or within 2 week(s) of notification.

Academics. **Special study options:** Accelerated study, combined bachelor's/graduate degree, cooperative education, cross-registration, double major, dual enrollment of high school students, ESL, exchange student, honors, independent study, internships, liberal arts/career combination, study abroad, teacher certification program, Washington semester. **Credit/placement by examination:** AP, CLEP, SAT, ACT, institutional tests. 30 credit hours maximum toward bachelor's degree. **Support services:** Learning center, preadmission summer program, reduced course load, remedial instruction, study skills assistance, tutoring, writing center.

Honors college/program. Combined SAT score of 1200 (exclusive of writing) with no section below 550 and 90 high school average required. Honors candidates must complete specific curriculum.

Majors. **Biology:** General. **Business:** General, accounting, business admin, finance, international marketing, marketing. **Communications:** General, broadcast journalism, journalism. **Computer sciences:** General. **Education:** General, art, biology, chemistry, elementary, English, foreign languages, history, mathematics, multi-level teacher, physics, science, secondary, social studies, Spanish, special. **Engineering:** General. **Foreign languages:** General, French, Spanish. **Health:** Art therapy, predentistry, premedicine, prenursing, prepharmacy, preveterinary. **History:** General. **Interdisciplinary:** Biological/physical sciences, math/computer science. **Legal studies:** Prelaw. **Liberal arts:** Arts/sciences. **Math:** General, applied. **Parks/recreation:** Facilities management. **Philosophy/religion:** Philosophy, religion. **Physical sciences:** Chemistry, physics. **Psychology:** General. **Social sciences:** General. **Visual/performing arts:** Art, commercial/advertising art, graphic design, studio arts.

Computing on campus. 200 workstations in dormitories, library, computer center, student center. Dormitories wired for high-speed internet access and linked to campus network. Commuter students can connect to campus network. Online library, helpline, wireless network available.

Student life. **Freshman orientation:** Mandatory, $80 fee. Preregistration for classes offered. **Policies:** Freshmen permitted cars on campus. **Housing:** Guaranteed on-campus for freshmen. Single-sex dorms, apartments available. $250 deposit, deadline 5/1. **Activities:** Choral groups, dance, drama, literary magazine, music ensembles, musical theater, opera, radio station, student government, student newspaper, TV station, political union, business association, community service organization.

Athletics. NAIA, NCAA. **Intercollegiate:** Baseball M, basketball, cross-country, golf, lacrosse W, soccer, softball W, tennis, track and field. **Intramural:** Basketball, football (non-tackle) M, skiing, softball, tennis. **Team name:** Spartans.

Student services. Adult student services, alcohol/substance abuse counseling, campus ministries, career counseling, student employment services, financial aid counseling, health services, personal counseling, placement for graduates, veterans' counselor, women's services. **Physically disabled:** Services for visually, speech, hearing impaired. **Learning disabled:** Comprehensive services available.

Contact. E-mail: admissions@stac.edu
Phone: (845) 398-4100 Fax: (845) 359-8136
Tracey Howard-Ubelhoer, Director of Admissions, St. Thomas Aquinas College, 125 Route 340, Sparkill, NY 10976

Sarah Lawrence College

Bronxville, New York — **CB member**
www.sarahlawrence.edu — **CB code: 2810**

- Private 4-year liberal arts college
- Residential campus in small city
- 1,264 degree-seeking undergraduates: 5% part-time, 74% women, 5% African American, 4% Asian American, 4% Hispanic American, 1% Native American, 2% international
- 317 degree-seeking graduate students
- 45% of applicants admitted
- Application essay required
- 74% graduate within 6 years

General. Founded in 1926. Regionally accredited. Academic system combines small seminar courses with individual tutorials with seminar professor. Students complete independent study resulting in substantial research paper or project. Students design own educational program with advice of a don in the Oxford/Cambridge tradition. **Degrees:** 262 bachelor's awarded;

master's offered. **Location:** 15 miles from New York City. **Calendar:** Semester, limited summer session. **Full-time faculty:** 188 total; 25% minority, 49% women. **Part-time faculty:** 34 total; 21% minority, 50% women. **Class size:** 93% < 20, 4% 20-39, 2% 40-49, 1% 50-99. **Special facilities:** State-of-the-art visual arts center, student-run theatre, early childhood center, greenhouse.

Freshman class profile. 2,634 applied, 1,174 admitted, 376 enrolled.

GPA 3.50 or higher:	60%	**Return as sophomores:**	91%
GPA 3.0-3.49:	33%	**Out-of-state:**	82%
GPA 2.0-2.99:	8%	**Live on campus:**	97%
Rank in top quarter:	72%	**International:**	3%
Rank in top tenth:	33%		

Basis for selection. Student essays (one of which is a graded, analytical writing sample) and transcript most important. Letters of recommendation and extracurricular commitments also important. Interview considered. Students interested in visual art or music encouraged to submit slides, cassette tapes, or compositions. If on-campus interview not possible, applicant may arrange interview with an alumna/us or counselor. **Homeschooled:** Two personal essays, 3-5 page research/analytical paper, transcript if available or comprehensive lesson plan if no transcript available, 3 letters of recommendation (2 from teachers/instructors and 1 from counselor/program supervisor) required.

High school preparation. College-preparatory program required. Required and recommended units include English 4, mathematics 2-4, social studies 4, history 2-4, science 2-4 and foreign language 2-4.

2006-2007 Annual costs. Tuition/fees: $36,088. Room/board: $12,152. Books/supplies: $600. Personal expenses: $800.

2005-2006 Financial aid. All financial aid based on need. 229 full-time freshmen applied for aid; 187 were judged to have need; 187 of these received aid. Average need met was 92%. Average scholarship/grant was $22,392; average loan $2,258. 83% of total undergraduate aid awarded as scholarships/grants, 17% as loans/jobs.

Application procedures. **Admission:** Closing date 1/1 (postmark date). $60 fee, may be waived for applicants with need. Application may be submitted online. Admission notification 4/1. Must reply by 5/1. **Financial aid:** Closing date 2/1. FAFSA, CSS PROFILE required. Applicants notified by 4/1; must reply by 5/1.

Academics. 90% of classes are seminars with 11-12 students. Individual biweekly conferences with professors and self-designed independent study available. Students design own course of study with advisor. Although there are no formal majors, students may de facto create double major. Course work required in 3 of 4 divisions: humanities, social sciences, science and math, creative and performing arts. **Special study options:** Combined bachelor's/graduate degree, double major, exchange student, independent study, internships, student-designed major, study abroad, teacher certification program. Academic year in Oxford, Paris, Florence, Catania (Sicily),Cuba, guest year at Reed College (Oregon and its study abroad program) or guest year at Eugene Lang College of the New School (New York City); theater year in London. **Credit/placement by examination:** AP, CLEP, IB. **Support services:** Writing center.

Majors. **Area/ethnic studies:** African, African-American, American, Asian, Asian-American, East Asian, European, French, gay/lesbian, German, Hispanic-American/Latino/Chicano, Japanese, Latin American, Native American, Near/Middle Eastern, Russian/Slavic, South Asian, women's. **Biology:** General, biochemistry, marine. **Computer sciences:** General. **Conservation:** Environmental studies. **English:** American lit, British lit, creative writing, English lit. **Family/consumer sciences:** Child development. **Foreign languages:** General, classics, comparative lit, French, German, Italian, Latin, Russian, Spanish. **Health:** Predentistry, premedicine. **History:** General, American, Asian, European. **Interdisciplinary:** Biological/physical sciences, global studies, medieval/Renaissance, science/society. **Legal studies:** Prelaw. **Liberal arts:** Arts/sciences, humanities. **Math:** General. **Philosophy/religion:** Islamic, Judaic, philosophy, religion. **Physical sciences:** Analytical chemistry, astronomy, chemistry, geology, inorganic chemistry, organic chemistry, physical chemistry, physics, planetary. **Psychology:** General. **Public administration:** Policy analysis. **Social sciences:** General, anthropology, economics, international relations, political science, sociology, urban studies. **Visual/performing arts:** General, art, art history/conservation, cinematography, dance, dramatic, drawing, film/cinema, jazz, music history, music performance, music theory/composition, musicology, painting, photography, piano/organ, play/screenwriting, printmaking, sculpture, stringed instruments, studio arts, theater design, theater history, voice/opera.

Computing on campus. 110 workstations in library, computer center. Dormitories wired for high-speed internet access and linked to campus network. Commuter students can connect to campus network. Online library, helpline, student web hosting available.

Student life. **Freshman orientation:** Mandatory. 9-day program held just before fall semester. **Housing:** Guaranteed on-campus for freshmen. Coed dorms, single-sex dorms, substance-free housing available. $500 deposit, deadline 5/6. Freshmen required to live on campus unless living at home. **Activities:** Jazz band, choral groups, dance, drama, film society, literary magazine, music ensembles, musical theater, radio station, student government, student newspaper, symphony orchestra, Amnesty International, Harambe (students of African descent), Hillel, Queer Variety Coalition, international student association, Asian-Pacific Islander Coalition to Advance Diversity, Unidad (students of Latino descent), Our Time Musical Theater Troupe, outdoors club, philosophy club.

Athletics. **Intercollegiate:** Basketball M, equestrian, rowing (crew), softball W, swimming W, tennis, volleyball W. **Team name:** Gryphons.

Student services. Adult student services, alcohol/substance abuse counseling, career counseling, student employment services, financial aid counseling, health services, personal counseling, placement for graduates. **Physically disabled:** Services for visually, speech, hearing impaired.

Contact. E-mail: slcadmit@sarahlawrence.edu
Phone: (914) 395-2510 Toll-free number: (800) 888-2858
Fax: (914) 395-2515
Thyra Briggs, Dean of Enrollment, Sarah Lawrence College, One Mead Way, Bronxville, NY 10708-5999

School of Visual Arts

New York, New York **CB member**
www.schoolofvisualarts.edu **CB code: 2835**

- For-profit 4-year visual arts college
- Commuter campus in very large city
- 3,003 degree-seeking undergraduates: 4% part-time, 51% women, 4% African American, 13% Asian American, 11% Hispanic American, 11% international
- 411 degree-seeking graduate students
- 70% of applicants admitted
- SAT or ACT with writing, application essay, interview required
- 64% graduate within 6 years

General. Founded in 1947. Regionally accredited. Faculty composed entirely of working professionals. **Degrees:** 642 bachelor's awarded; master's offered. **Calendar:** Semester, extensive summer session. **Full-time faculty:** 120 total. **Part-time faculty:** 640 total. **Class size:** 70% < 20, 28% 20-39, 2% 50-99, less than 1% >100. **Special facilities:** Visual arts museum, 8 student galleries including a 9,000-square-foot gallery in the Chelsea gallery district.

Freshman class profile. 2,130 applied, 1,495 admitted, 586 enrolled.

Mid 50% test scores			
SAT verbal:	480-590	**Return as sophomores:**	87%
SAT math:	460-570	**Out-of-state:**	53%
ACT:	20-25	**Live on campus:**	66%
		International:	4%

Basis for selection. Portfolio, academic record, test scores, interview important. Character and professional recommendations also considered. Interview required but waived upon request for applicants who reside more than 250 miles from campus. Portfolio required for most art programs.

High school preparation. Recommended units include English 4, social studies 4 and history 4. 2 art courses recommended.

2005-2006 Annual costs. Tuition/fees: $21,080. Additional departmental fees vary by department. Room only: $9,300. Books/supplies: $2,500. Personal expenses: $1,600.

2005-2006 Financial aid. **Need-based:** 454 full-time freshmen applied for aid; 382 were judged to have need; 377 of these received aid. Average need met was 41%. Average scholarship/grant was $6,219; average loan $2,872. 29% of total undergraduate aid awarded as scholarships/grants, 71% as loans/jobs. **Non-need-based:** Awarded to 462 full-time undergraduates, including 97 freshmen. Scholarships awarded for art.

Application procedures. **Admission:** Priority date 2/1; no deadline. $50 fee, may be waived for applicants with need. Application may be submitted online. Admission notification on a rolling basis beginning on or about 2/1. Must reply by 5/1. Regular application closing date March 12 for film, video, animation and computer art. **Financial aid:** Priority date 2/1, closing date 3/1. FAFSA required. Applicants notified on a rolling basis starting 2/15; must reply within 4 week(s) of notification.

Academics. Curriculum designed to prepare students to graduate as working professionals in the arts. **Special study options:** Cross-registration, ESL, exchange student, honors, internships, liberal arts/career combination, study abroad, teacher certification program. **Credit/placement by examination:** AP, CLEP. 44 credit hours maximum toward bachelor's degree. **Support services:** Learning center, pre-admission summer program, reduced course load, remedial instruction, study skills assistance, tutoring, writing center.

Majors. Communications: Advertising. **Communications technology:** Animation/special effects. **Visual/performing arts:** General, art, cinematography, commercial photography, commercial/advertising art, design, drawing, film/cinema, graphic design, illustration, interior design, painting, photography, printmaking, sculpture, studio arts.

Computing on campus. 600 workstations in dormitories, library, computer center, student center. Dormitories wired for high-speed internet access and linked to campus network. Commuter students can connect to campus network. Online library, helpline, wireless network available.

Student life. Freshman orientation: Mandatory. Comprehensive 5-day program. **Housing:** Coed dorms, single-sex dorms, substance-free housing available. $800 partly refundable deposit, deadline 5/1. **Activities:** Film society, literary magazine, radio station, student government, student newspaper, Korean Christian, animal rights, international film club, Campus Crusade for Christ, political, anime film club, fine art club, multicultural organization, MFA Speakers, wrestling club.

Athletics. Intramural: Basketball, skiing, softball.

Student services. Alcohol/substance abuse counseling, career counseling, student employment services, financial aid counseling, health services, personal counseling, placement for graduates, veterans' counselor, women's services.

Contact. E-mail: admissions@sva.edu
Phone: (212) 592-2100 Toll-free number: (800) 436-4204
Rick Longo, Director of Admissions, School of Visual Arts, 209 East 23rd Street, New York, NY 10010-3994

Shor Yoshuv Rabbinical College

Lawrence, New York
www.shoryoshuv.org **CB code: 7129**

- Private 4-year rabbinical college for men affiliated with Jewish faith
- Very large city

General. Accredited by AARTS. **Calendar:** Continuous.

Annual costs/financial aid. Comprehensive fee (2005-2006): $13,000.

Contact. Phone: (516) 239-9002
Admissions Director, One Cedar Lawn Avenue, Lawrence, NY 11559

Siena College

Loudonville, New York **CB member**
www.siena.edu **CB code: 2814**

- Private 4-year liberal arts college affiliated with Roman Catholic Church
- Residential campus in large town
- 3,240 degree-seeking undergraduates: 6% part-time, 57% women, 2% African American, 3% Asian American, 4% Hispanic American, 1% international
- 61% of applicants admitted
- SAT or ACT with writing, application essay required
- 80% graduate within 6 years; 19% enter graduate study

General. Founded in 1937. Regionally accredited. Affiliated with the Franciscan Friars. **Degrees:** 769 bachelor's awarded. **ROTC:** Army, Air Force. **Location:** 2 miles from Albany. **Calendar:** Semester, limited summer session. **Full-time faculty:** 180 total; 91% have terminal degrees, 9% minority, 34% women. **Part-time faculty:** 132 total; 48% have terminal degrees, 12% minority, 42% women. **Class size:** 38% < 20, 62% 20-39. **Special facilities:** Financial technology center featuring real-time capital market trading room, state-of-the-art accounting lab, stock ticker, plasma data screens, 24 multimedia workstations.

Freshman class profile. 4,326 applied, 2,620 admitted, 763 enrolled.

Mid 50% test scores		**Rank in top quarter:**	58%
SAT verbal:	500-600	**Rank in top tenth:**	21%
SAT math:	520-620	**Return as sophomores:**	89%
ACT:	23-25	**Out-of-state:**	17%
GPA 3.50 or higher:	57%	**Live on campus:**	93%
GPA 3.0-3.49:	36%	**International:**	1%
GPA 2.0-2.99:	7%		

Basis for selection. School achievement record most important, priority given to students with challenging courses. Test scores, activities, recommendations also important. Interview required for Albany Medical School program finalists; recommended for all others. **Homeschooled:** Transcript of courses and grades required.

High school preparation. College-preparatory program required. 13 units required; 19 recommended. Required and recommended units include English 4, mathematics 3-4, social studies 1, history 2-3, science 3-4 (laboratory 3-4) and foreign language 3.

2005-2006 Annual costs. Tuition/fees: $20,275. Room/board: $7,985. Books/supplies: $875. Personal expenses: $755.

2004-2005 Financial aid. Need-based: 641 full-time freshmen applied for aid; 519 were judged to have need; 518 of these received aid. Average need met was 76%. Average scholarship/grant was $11,185; average loan $2,815. 74% of total undergraduate aid awarded as scholarships/grants, 26% as loans/jobs. **Non-need-based:** Awarded to 1,897 full-time undergraduates, including 562 freshmen. Scholarships awarded for academics, art, athletics, leadership, minority status, ROTC, state residency.

Application procedures. Admission: Closing date 3/1 (postmark date). $50 fee, may be waived for applicants with need. Application may be submitted online. Admission notification 3/15. Must reply by 5/1. **Financial aid:** Closing date 2/15. FAFSA required. Applicants notified by 4/1; must reply by 5/1.

Academics. Extensive internship program in capital district with state legislature, businesses, social agencies, libraries, and museums. **Special study options:** Accelerated study, combined bachelor's/graduate degree, cross-registration, double major, ESL, honors, independent study, internships, liberal arts/career combination, study abroad, teacher certification program, Washington semester. **Credit/placement by examination:** AP, CLEP, IB, institutional tests. 36 credit hours maximum toward bachelor's degree. 36 total credits permitted by proficiency examination, non-collegiate-sponsored instructional/experiential learning combined. **Support services:** Tutoring, writing center.

Majors. Area/ethnic studies: American. **Biology:** General, biochemistry, ecology. **Business:** Accounting, finance, marketing. **Computer sciences:** General. **English:** English lit. **Foreign languages:** Classics, French, Spanish. **History:** General. **Math:** General, applied. **Philosophy/religion:** Philosophy, religion. **Physical sciences:** Chemistry, physics. **Psychology:** General. **Public administration:** Social work. **Social sciences:** Economics, political science, sociology. **Visual/performing arts:** General.

Most popular majors. Biology 9%, business/marketing 46%, English 8%, history 7%, psychology 10%, social sciences 8%.

Computing on campus. 456 workstations in library, computer center. Dormitories wired for high-speed internet access and linked to campus network. Commuter students can connect to campus network. Online course registration, online library, helpline, wireless network available.

Student life. Freshman orientation: Mandatory, $180 fee. Preregistration for classes offered. 3-day summer program for students and parents. **Housing:** Guaranteed on-campus for freshmen. Coed dorms, special housing for disabled available. On-campus townhouses (men's and women's) available. **Activities:** Pep band, dance, drama, literary magazine, musical theater, radio station, student government, student newspaper, TV station, approximately 70 clubs and organizations.

Athletics. NCAA. **Intercollegiate:** Baseball M, basketball, cross-country, diving W, field hockey W, golf, lacrosse, soccer, softball W, swimming W, tennis, volleyball W, water polo W. **Intramural:** Basketball, football (non-tackle), golf, soccer, softball, volleyball. **Team name:** Saints.

Student services. Adult student services, alcohol/substance abuse counseling, campus ministries, career counseling, services for economically disadvantaged, student employment services, financial aid counseling, health services, minority student services, personal counseling, placement for graduates, women's services. **Physically disabled:** Services for visually, speech, hearing impaired.

Contact. E-mail: admit@siena.edu
Phone: (518) 783-2423 Toll-free number: (888) 287-4362
Fax: (518) 783-2436
Heather Renault, Director for Admissions, Siena College, 515 Loudon Road, Loudonville, NY 12211-1462

Skidmore College

Saratoga Springs, New York — **CB member**
www.skidmore.edu — **CB code: 2815**

- Private 4-year liberal arts college
- Residential campus in large town
- 2,727 degree-seeking undergraduates: 8% part-time, 61% women, 3% African American, 6% Asian American, 4% Hispanic American, 1% Native American, 1% international
- 55 degree-seeking graduate students
- 44% of applicants admitted
- SAT or ACT (ACT writing optional), application essay required
- 78% graduate within 6 years

General. Founded in 1903. Regionally accredited. **Degrees:** 578 bachelor's awarded; master's offered. **ROTC:** Army, Air Force. **Location:** 30 miles from Albany. **Calendar:** Semester, limited summer session. **Full-time faculty:** 228 total; 82% have terminal degrees, 11% minority, 54% women. **Part-time faculty:** 93 total; 37% have terminal degrees, 12% minority, 54% women. **Class size:** 67% < 20, 31% 20-39, less than 1% 40-49, 1% 50-99. **Special facilities:** Fine and performing arts facilities, equestrian center, 400 acres of woodlands and trails, teaching museum.

Freshman class profile. 6,055 applied, 2,642 admitted, 694 enrolled.

Mid 50% test scores			
SAT verbal:	580-670	Rank in top quarter:	78%
SAT math:	580-660	Rank in top tenth:	46%
ACT:	25-28	Return as sophomores:	92%
GPA 3.50 or higher:	30%	Out-of-state:	71%
GPA 3.0-3.49:	49%	Live on campus:	100%
GPA 2.0-2.99:	21%	International:	1%

Basis for selection. Rigor of school record very important. Class rank, GPA, recommendations, and test scores also important. SAT Subject Tests recommended. 2 SAT Subject Tests recommended of all applicants. Interview recommended for all.

High school preparation. 20 units recommended. Recommended units include English 4, mathematics 4, social studies 4, science 4 (laboratory 3) and foreign language 4.

2006-2007 Annual costs. Tuition/fees: $34,694. Room/board: $9,556.

2005-2006 Financial aid. Need-based: 352 full-time freshmen applied for aid; 281 were judged to have need; 281 of these received aid. Average need met was 98%. Average scholarship/grant was $23,209; average loan $2,404. 83% of total undergraduate aid awarded as scholarships/grants, 17% as loans/jobs. **Non-need-based:** Awarded to 222 full-time undergraduates, including 84 freshmen. Scholarships awarded for music/drama.

Application procedures. Admission: Closing date 1/15 (postmark date). $60 fee, may be waived for applicants with need. Application may be submitted online. Admission notification 4/1. Must reply by 5/1. Enrollment deposit required of $500 on or before May 1. **Financial aid:** Closing date 1/15. FAFSA, CSS PROFILE required. Applicants notified by 4/1; must reply by 5/1.

Academics. Interdisciplinary core curriculum with team-taught courses emphasized. Approximately 40 credit hours required in major. Students can earn bachelor's degree in self-determined major. Honors forum has own admissions requirements and academic offerings. **Special study options:** Accelerated study, combined bachelor's/graduate degree, cross-registration, distance learning, double major, dual enrollment of high school students, external degree, honors, independent study, internships, liberal arts/career combination, student-designed major, study abroad, teacher certification program, Washington semester. Early admission to Cardozo School of Law, 3+2 programs in engineering with Dartmouth College and Clarkson University, 4+1 MAT with Union College, 4+1 MBA with Clarkson University and The Graduate College at Union University. **Credit/placement by examination:** AP, CLEP, IB, SAT, ACT, institutional tests. Up to 60 hours may be counted toward degree. Maximum of 12 semester hours may be granted in credit through CLEP subject examinations. **Support services:** Preadmission summer program, study skills assistance, tutoring, writing center.

Majors. Area/ethnic studies: American, Asian, French, women's. **Biology:** General, biochemistry. **Business:** General. **Computer sciences:** General. **Conservation:** Environmental science, environmental studies. **Education:** General, elementary. **English:** English lit. **Foreign languages:** Classics, French, German, Spanish. **History:** General. **Interdisciplinary:** Neuroscience. **Liberal arts:** Arts/sciences. **Math:** General. **Parks/recreation:** Exercise sciences. **Philosophy/religion:** Philosophy, religion. **Physical sciences:** Chemistry, geology, physics. **Psychology:** General. **Public administration:** Social work. **Social sciences:** Anthropology, economics, political science, sociology. **Visual/performing arts:** Art history/conservation, dance, dramatic, studio arts.

Most popular majors. Business/marketing 12%, English 10%, foreign language 6%, liberal arts 6%, psychology 8%, social sciences 15%, visual/performing arts 19%.

Computing on campus. Dormitories wired for high-speed internet access and linked to campus network. Commuter students can connect to campus network. Online course registration, online library, helpline, student web hosting, wireless network available.

Student life. Freshman orientation: Mandatory. Programs on and off campus. Fee for off-campus programs. **Policies:** Freshmen permitted cars on campus. **Housing:** Guaranteed on-campus for freshmen. Coed dorms, single-sex dorms, special housing for disabled, apartments, substance-free housing available. Theme housing available in variety of interest areas. Townhouse clusters available for upperclassmen. **Activities:** Bands, choral groups, dance, drama, film society, literary magazine, music ensembles, musical theater, opera, radio station, student government, student newspaper, symphony orchestra, TV station, 80 clubs and organizations available.

Athletics. NCAA. **Intercollegiate:** Baseball M, basketball, diving, equestrian W, field hockey W, golf M, ice hockey M, lacrosse, rowing (crew), soccer, softball W, swimming, tennis, volleyball W. **Intramural:** Basketball, football (tackle) M, racquetball, soccer, softball, tennis, volleyball, water polo. **Team name:** Thoroughbreds.

Student services. Alcohol/substance abuse counseling, campus ministries, career counseling, services for economically disadvantaged, student employment services, financial aid counseling, health services, minority student services, on-campus daycare, personal counseling, placement for graduates, veterans' counselor. **Physically disabled:** Services for visually, speech, hearing impaired.

Contact. E-mail: admissions@skidmore.edu
Phone: (518) 580-5570 Toll-free number: (800) 867-6007
Fax: (518) 580-5584
Mary Lou Bates, Dean of Admissions and Financial Aid, Skidmore College, 815 North Broadway, Saratoga Springs, NY 12866

State University of New York at Albany

Albany, New York — **CB member**
www.albany.edu — **CB code: 2532**

- Public 4-year university
- Residential campus in small city
- 11,680 degree-seeking undergraduates: 5% part-time, 50% women, 8% African American, 6% Asian American, 7% Hispanic American, 2% international
- 4,410 degree-seeking graduate students
- 63% of applicants admitted
- SAT or ACT with writing required
- 62% graduate within 6 years

General. Founded in 1844. Regionally accredited. **Degrees:** 2,675 bachelor's awarded; master's, doctoral offered. **ROTC:** Army, Air Force. **Location:** 4 miles from downtown. **Calendar:** Semester, extensive summer session. **Full-time faculty:** 631 total; 98% have terminal degrees, 16% minority, 35% women. **Part-time faculty:** 530 total; 10% minority, 47% women. **Class size:** 25% < 20, 41% 20-39, 9% 40-49, 12% 50-99, 13% >100. **Special facilities:** Atmospheric science research center and Whiteface Mountain observation facility, microbeam analysis facility, large fine arts work areas, peptide synthesis facility, recombinant DNA sequencing laboratories, nanoscale science and engineering facilities.

Freshman class profile. 16,725 applied, 10,461 admitted, 2,560 enrolled.

Mid 50% test scores		Rank in top quarter:	31%
SAT verbal:	500-590	Rank in top tenth:	14%
SAT math:	520-610	Return as sophomores:	85%
GPA 3.50 or higher:	24%	Out-of-state:	8%
GPA 3.0-3.49:	49%	Live on campus:	98%
GPA 2.0-2.99:	27%	International:	2%

High school preparation. College-preparatory program required. 18 units required. Required and recommended units include English 4, mathematics 2-4, social studies 3, history 2, science 2-3 (laboratory 2-3), foreign language 1-3 and academic electives 4.

2005-2006 Annual costs. Tuition/fees: $5,810; $12,070 out-of-state. Room/board: $8,050. Books/supplies: $1,000. Personal expenses: $1,672.

2005-2006 Financial aid. Need-based: 2,082 full-time freshmen applied for aid; 1,387 were judged to have need; 1,371 of these received aid. Average need met was 72%. Average scholarship/grant was $4,728; average loan $3,390. 53% of total undergraduate aid awarded as scholarships/grants, 47% as loans/jobs. **Non-need-based:** Awarded to 1,088 full-time undergraduates, including 362 freshmen. Scholarships awarded for academics, athletics, state residency.

Application procedures. Admission: Priority date 1/6; deadline 3/1 (receipt date). $40 fee, may be waived for applicants with need. Application may be submitted online. Admission notification on a rolling basis beginning on or about 1/1. Must reply by May 1 or within 2 week(s) if notified thereafter. **Financial aid:** Closing date 4/15. FAFSA required. Applicants notified on a rolling basis starting 3/15; must reply by 5/1 or within 2 week(s) of notification.

Academics. Project Renaissance year-long program for first-year students offers interdisciplinary course of study, close acquaintance with faculty in program, and community living. Participation open to all freshmen on first-come, first-served basis. **Special study options:** Accelerated study, combined bachelor's/graduate degree, cross-registration, distance learning, double major, dual enrollment of high school students, ESL, honors, independent study, internships, liberal arts/career combination, student-designed major, study abroad, Washington semester. Accelerated 5-year bachelor's/master's in 40 fields, internships with New York State Legislature, 3+3 program with Albany Law School, biology/dental program with Boston University Goldman School of Dental Medicine, bachelor's/doctor of optometry with SUNY State College. **Credit/placement by examination:** AP, CLEP, IB. 60 credit hours maximum toward bachelor's degree. **Support services:** Preadmission summer program, remedial instruction, study skills assistance, tutoring, writing center.

Majors. Area/ethnic studies: African-American, Asian, Caribbean, Central/Eastern European, Chinese, East Asian, Japanese, Latin American, Russian/Slavic, women's. **Biology:** General, biochemistry, environmental, molecular. **Business:** Accounting, business admin. **Communications:** General. **Computer sciences:** General, information systems. **Education:** Biology, chemistry, English, foreign languages, French, mathematics, physics, science, secondary, social studies, Spanish. **English:** Speech/rhetoric. **Foreign languages:** Classics, French, Italian, linguistics, Russian, Spanish. **Health:** Predentistry, premedicine, prepharmacy, preveterinary. **History:** General. **Interdisciplinary:** Classical/archaeology, medieval/Renaissance. **Liberal arts:** Arts/sciences. **Math:** General, applied. **Philosophy/religion:** Judaic, philosophy, religion. **Physical sciences:** Atmospheric science, chemistry, geology, physics, planetary. **Protective services:** Criminal justice. **Psychology:** General. **Public administration:** Social work. **Social sciences:** Anthropology, economics, geography, political science, sociology, urban studies. **Visual/performing arts:** Art history/conservation, dramatic, music performance, music theory/composition, studio arts.

Most popular majors. Business/marketing 14%, communications/journalism 9%, English 9%, history 6%, psychology 14%, social sciences 24%.

Computing on campus. 500 workstations in dormitories, library, computer center. Dormitories wired for high-speed internet access and linked to campus network. Commuter students can connect to campus network. Online course registration, online library, helpline, student web hosting, wireless network available.

Student life. Freshman orientation: Mandatory, $180 fee. Preregistration for classes offered. 2 days in summer with parental participation, 2 days in fall without parental participation. **Housing:** Guaranteed on-campus for freshmen. Coed dorms, single-sex dorms, apartments, substance-free housing available. $125 fully refundable deposit. Individualized services for disabled students available, including accessible housing information. **Activities:** Bands, choral groups, dance, drama, literary magazine, music ensembles, musical theater, radio station, student government, student newspaper, symphony orchestra, over 160 student groups.

Athletics. NCAA. **Intercollegiate:** Baseball M, basketball, cross-country, field hockey W, football (tackle) M, golf W, lacrosse, rugby, soccer, softball W, tennis, track and field, volleyball W. **Intramural:** Basketball, handball, ice hockey M, racquetball, skiing, soccer, softball, squash, track and field, volleyball, wrestling M. **Team name:** Great Danes.

Student services. Alcohol/substance abuse counseling, campus ministries, career counseling, services for economically disadvantaged, student employment services, financial aid counseling, health services, legal services, minority student services, on-campus daycare, personal counseling, placement for graduates, women's services. **Physically disabled:** Services for visually, speech, hearing impaired. **Learning disabled:** Comprehensive services available.

Contact. E-mail: ugadmissions@albany.edu
Phone: (518) 442-5435 Fax: (518) 442-5383
Robert Andrea, Director of Undergraduate Admission and Recruitment, State University of New York at Albany, Office of Undergraduate Admissions, University Administration Building 101, Albany, NY 12222

State University of New York at Binghamton

Binghamton, New York **CB member**
www.binghamton.edu **CB code: 2535**

- Public 4-year university
- Residential campus in small city
- 11,065 degree-seeking undergraduates: 3% part-time, 48% women, 5% African American, 15% Asian American, 6% Hispanic American, 7% international
- 2,612 degree-seeking graduate students
- 43% of applicants admitted
- SAT or ACT with writing, application essay required
- 79% graduate within 6 years; 38% enter graduate study

General. Founded in 1946. Regionally accredited. **Degrees:** 2,702 bachelor's awarded; master's, doctoral offered. **ROTC:** Air Force. **Location:** 70 miles from Syracuse, 180 miles from New York City. **Calendar:** Semester, extensive summer session. **Full-time faculty:** 537 total; 93% have terminal degrees, 22% minority, 36% women. **Part-time faculty:** 232 total; 13% minority, 47% women. **Class size:** 41% < 20, 37% 20-39, 7% 40-49, 8% 50-99, 7% >100. **Special facilities:** 190-acre nature preserve, indoor/outdoor theater, performing arts center, multiclimate greenhouse, teaching greenhouse, sculpture foundry.

Freshman class profile. 21,658 applied, 9,285 admitted, 2,215 enrolled.

Mid 50% test scores		Rank in top tenth:	47%
SAT verbal:	560-660	Return as sophomores:	90%
SAT math:	600-690	Out-of-state:	9%
ACT:	25-29	Live on campus:	96%
GPA 3.50 or higher:	66%	International:	10%
GPA 3.0-3.49:	27%	Fraternities:	8%
GPA 2.0-2.99:	7%	Sororities:	9%
Rank in top quarter:	87%		

Basis for selection. Admission based on academic strength as measured by quality of courses, grades and grade trend, and test scores. Evidence of intellectual curiosity, interest in others, and nonacademic pursuits sought through application. Geographic and ethnic diversity considered. Audition offered for music; portfolio review offered for art. **Homeschooled:** Students encouraged to obtain documentation of equivalency from their local school boards. SAT or ACT required.

High school preparation. 16 units required. Required and recommended units include English 4, mathematics 3-4, social studies 2, history 3, science 2-3 and foreign language 3. 3 units of 1 foreign language or 2 each of 2 foreign languages required of liberal arts applicants.

2005-2006 Annual costs. Tuition/fees: $5,826; $12,086 out-of-state. Room/board: $8,152. Books/supplies: $800.

2005-2006 Financial aid. Need-based: 1,604 full-time freshmen applied for aid; 891 were judged to have need; 881 of these received aid. Average need met was 77%. Average scholarship/grant was $4,874; average loan $2,957. 37% of total undergraduate aid awarded as scholarships/grants, 63% as loans/jobs. **Non-need-based:** Awarded to 1,486 full-time undergraduates, including 341 freshmen. Scholarships awarded for academics, art, athletics, leadership, minority status, music/drama, state residency.

Application procedures. Admission: Priority date 1/15; no deadline. $40 fee, may be waived for applicants with need. Application may be submitted online. Admission notification on a rolling basis beginning on or

about 1/15. Must reply by May 1 or within 4 week(s) if notified thereafter. **Financial aid:** Priority date 3/1; no closing date. FAFSA required. CSS PROFILE required of early decision applicants only. Applicants notified on a rolling basis starting 3/15; must reply within 2 week(s) of notification.

Academics. **Special study options:** Accelerated study, combined bachelor's/graduate degree, distance learning, double major, dual enrollment of high school students, ESL, exchange student, honors, independent study, internships, liberal arts/career combination, student-designed major, study abroad, teacher certification program, Washington semester. **Credit/placement by examination:** AP, CLEP, IB, SAT, ACT. 32 credit hours maximum toward bachelor's degree. **Support services:** Learning center, pre-admission summer program, study skills assistance, tutoring, writing center.

Majors. **Area/ethnic studies:** African, African-American, Asian-American, Caribbean, Latin American. **Biology:** General, biochemistry. **Business:** Accounting, management science. **Computer sciences:** General, computer science. **Conservation:** Environmental studies. **Engineering:** Biomedical, computer, electrical, industrial, mechanical. **English:** English lit, speech/rhetoric. **Family/consumer sciences:** General. **Foreign languages:** Arabic, Biblical, classics, comparative lit, French, German, Hebrew, Italian, Latin, linguistics, Spanish. **Health:** Nursing (RN). **History:** General. **Interdisciplinary:** Global studies, medieval/Renaissance. **Math:** General. **Philosophy/religion:** Judaic, philosophy. **Physical sciences:** Chemistry, geology, physics. **Psychology:** General. **Social sciences:** Anthropology, economics, geography, political science, sociology. **Visual/performing arts:** Art, art history/conservation, dramatic, film/cinema, music performance, studio arts.

Most popular majors. Biology 8%, business/marketing 15%, engineering/engineering technologies 6%, English 10%, psychology 11%, social sciences 17%.

Computing on campus. 700 workstations in dormitories, library, computer center. Dormitories wired for high-speed internet access and linked to campus network. Commuter students can connect to campus network. Online course registration, online library, helpline, student web hosting, wireless network available.

Student life. **Freshman orientation:** Mandatory, $180 fee. Preregistration for classes offered. 2-day session held in summer. Parents invited to participate. **Housing:** Guaranteed on-campus for freshmen. Coed dorms, special housing for disabled, apartments, substance-free housing available. $200 partly refundable deposit, deadline 5/1. Special interest housing available. **Activities:** Bands, choral groups, dance, drama, film society, literary magazine, music ensembles, musical theater, opera, radio station, student government, student newspaper, symphony orchestra, TV station, religious, ethnic, minority, women's, public interest, and voluntary service organizations.

Athletics. NCAA. **Intercollegiate:** Baseball M, basketball, cross-country, diving, golf M, lacrosse, soccer, softball W, swimming, tennis, track and field, volleyball W, wrestling M. **Intramural:** Badminton, basketball, bowling, cross-country, football (non-tackle), golf, racquetball, soccer, softball, squash, table tennis, tennis, volleyball, water polo. **Team name:** Bearcats.

Student services. Adult student services, alcohol/substance abuse counseling, campus ministries, career counseling, services for economically disadvantaged, student employment services, financial aid counseling, health services, legal services, minority student services, on-campus daycare, personal counseling, placement for graduates, veterans' counselor, women's services. **Physically disabled:** Services for visually, speech, hearing impaired. **Learning disabled:** Comprehensive services available.

Contact. E-mail: admit@binghamton.edu
Phone: (607) 777-2171 Fax: (607) 777-4445
Cheryl Brown, Director of Admissions, State University of New York at Binghamton, Box 6001, Binghamton, NY 13902-6001

State University of New York at Buffalo

Buffalo, New York — **CB member**
www.buffalo.edu — **CB code: 2925**

- Public 4-year university
- Commuter campus in large city
- 17,830 degree-seeking undergraduates: 6% part-time, 46% women, 7% African American, 9% Asian American, 4% Hispanic American, 7% international
- 8,838 degree-seeking graduate students
- 57% of applicants admitted
- SAT or ACT with writing required
- 59% graduate within 6 years; 39% enter graduate study

General. Founded in 1846. Regionally accredited. **Degrees:** 3,674 bachelor's, 4 associate awarded; master's, doctoral, first professional offered. **ROTC:** Army. **Location:** 10 miles from downtown. **Calendar:** Semester, extensive summer session. **Full-time faculty:** 1,159 total; 97% have terminal degrees, 22% minority, 32% women. **Part-time faculty:** 589 total; 97% have terminal degrees, 11% minority, 44% women. **Class size:** 37% < 20, 34% 20-39, 9% 40-49, 12% 50-99, 8% >100. **Special facilities:** Center for the arts, concert hall, anthropology research museum, multidisciplinary center for earthquake engineering research, center of excellence in bioinformatics, center for computational research, poetry and rare books collection, pharmacy museum, virtual site museum, New York State center for engineering design and industrial innovation, electronic poetry center, archeological survey center, center of excellence for document analysis and recognition.

Freshman class profile. 18,391 applied, 10,466 admitted, 3,235 enrolled.

Mid 50% test scores		**Rank in top quarter:**	59%
SAT verbal:	510-600	**Rank in top tenth:**	24%
SAT math:	540-640	**Return as sophomores:**	88%
ACT:	23-28	**Out-of-state:**	6%
GPA 3.50 or higher:	22%	**Live on campus:**	73%
GPA 3.0-3.49:	42%	**International:**	7%
GPA 2.0-2.99:	35%		

Basis for selection. Freshmen evaluated based on secondary school performance, strength of curriculum, standardized test scores, and, in some cases, supplemental application. SAT Subject Test considered for placement for foreign language. Audition required for music. **Homeschooled:** Statement describing homeschool structure and mission, transcript of courses and grades, letter of recommendation (nonparent) required. If admitted, will need to submit a letter from the superintendent of the local school district, attesting to the completion of a program of home instruction meeting the requirements of Section 100.10 of the Regulations of the Commissioner of Education, or a passing score on the GED. **Learning Disabled:** Must provide documentation of disability that meets institutional standards to determine eligibility for services.

High school preparation. 17 units recommended. Recommended units include English 4, mathematics 3, social studies 4, science 3 and foreign language 3.

2005-2006 Annual costs. Tuition/fees: $6,059; $12,319 out-of-state. Room/board: $8,486. Books/supplies: $850. Personal expenses: $794.

2005-2006 Financial aid. **Need-based:** 2,432 full-time freshmen applied for aid; 1,691 were judged to have need; 1,594 of these received aid. Average need met was 80%. Average scholarship/grant was $3,310; average loan $2,253. 26% of total undergraduate aid awarded as scholarships/grants, 74% as loans/jobs. **Non-need-based:** Awarded to 3,693 full-time undergraduates, including 1,233 freshmen. Scholarships awarded for academics, athletics, minority status, music/drama, state residency.

Application procedures. **Admission:** Priority date 11/1; no deadline. $40 fee, may be waived for applicants with need. Application may be submitted online. Admission notification on a rolling basis beginning on or about 1/20. Must reply by May 1 or within 2 week(s) if notified thereafter. **Financial aid:** Priority date 3/1; no closing date. FAFSA required. Applicants notified on a rolling basis starting 2/1.

Academics. **Special study options:** Accelerated study, combined bachelor's/graduate degree, cooperative education, cross-registration, distance learning, double major, dual enrollment of high school students, ESL, exchange student, honors, independent study, internships, liberal arts/career combination, semester at sea, student-designed major, study abroad, teacher certification program, United Nations semester, Washington semester. Combined degree programs. **Credit/placement by examination:** AP, CLEP, IB, SAT, ACT, institutional tests. Maximum of 30 credits from International Baccalaureate. **Support services:** Learning center, pre-admission summer program, reduced course load, study skills assistance, tutoring, writing center.

Majors. **Architecture:** Architecture, environmental design. **Area/ethnic studies:** African-American, American, Asian, women's. **Biology:** General, biochemistry, bioinformatics, biophysics, biostatistics, biotechnology, molecular pharmacology. **Business:** Business admin. **Communications:** General, media studies. **Computer sciences:** Computer science. **Education:** Music. **Engineering:** General, aerospace, chemical, civil, computer, electrical, environmental, industrial, mechanical, physics, structural. **English:** English lit. **Foreign languages:** Classics, French, German, Italian, linguistics, Spanish. **Health:** Audiology/speech pathology, clinical lab science, nuclear medical technology, nursing (RN). **History:** General. **Liberal arts:** Humanities. **Math:** General. **Parks/recreation:** Exercise sciences. **Philosophy/religion:** Philosophy. **Physical sciences:** Chemistry, geology, physics, theoretical physics. **Psychology:** General. **Social sciences:** Anthropology, economics, geography, political science, sociology. **Visual/performing arts:** Art, art history/conservation, dance, dramatic, film/cinema, music performance, studio arts.

Most popular majors. Business/marketing 19%, communications/journalism 10%, engineering/engineering technologies 11%, liberal arts 7%, psychology 10%, social sciences 9%.

Computing on campus. 2,475 workstations in dormitories, library, computer center. Dormitories wired for high-speed internet access and linked to campus network. Commuter students can connect to campus network. Online course registration, online library, helpline, repair service, student web hosting, wireless network available.

Student life. Freshman orientation: Available, $190 fee. Preregistration for classes offered. One-and-a-half-day programs include registration. **Policies:** Freshmen permitted cars on campus. **Housing:** Guaranteed on-campus for all undergraduates. Coed dorms, special housing for disabled, apartments, substance-free housing available. $200 deposit, deadline 5/1. Honors, shared interest, academic interest, freshmen housing available. **Activities:** Bands, choral groups, dance, drama, film society, music ensembles, musical theater, radio station, student government, student newspaper, symphony orchestra, TV station, over 200 organizations available.

Athletics. NCAA. **Intercollegiate:** Baseball M, basketball, cross-country, football (tackle) M, ice hockey M, lacrosse W, rowing (crew) W, soccer, softball W, swimming, tennis, track and field, volleyball W, wrestling M. **Intramural:** Basketball, football (non-tackle), racquetball, soccer, softball, volleyball. **Team name:** Bulls.

Student services. Adult student services, alcohol/substance abuse counseling, campus ministries, career counseling, services for economically disadvantaged, student employment services, financial aid counseling, health services, legal services, minority student services, on-campus daycare, personal counseling, placement for graduates, veterans' counselor, women's services. **Physically disabled:** Services for visually, speech, hearing impaired.

Contact. E-mail: ub-admissions@buffalo.edu
Phone: (716) 645-6900 Toll-free number: (888) 822-3648
Fax: (716) 645-6411
Patricia Armstrong, Director of Admissions, State University of New York at Buffalo, 12 Capen Hall, Buffalo, NY 14260

State University of New York at Farmingdale

Farmingdale, New York — **CB member**
www.farmingdale.edu — **CB code: 2526**

- Public 4-year technical college
- Commuter campus in large town
- 5,280 degree-seeking undergraduates: 27% part-time, 42% women, 13% African American, 5% Asian American, 9% Hispanic American, 1% international
- 61% of applicants admitted
- 36% graduate within 6 years

General. Founded in 1912. Regionally accredited. **Degrees:** 454 bachelor's, 538 associate awarded. **ROTC:** Army, Air Force. **Location:** 30 miles from New York City. **Calendar:** Semester, extensive summer session. **Full-time faculty:** 153 total; 52% have terminal degrees, 13% minority, 39% women. **Part-time faculty:** 306 total; 11% have terminal degrees, 10% minority, 47% women. **Class size:** 32% < 20, 51% 20-39, 16% 40-49, 2% 50-99. **Special facilities:** CAD/CAM laboratory, fleet of single-engine & multi-engine aircraft, dental and health care laboratories, state of the art bioscience labs in affiliation with Cold Springs Harbor Research lab, manufacturing labs with plasmajet and advanced robotic technology, solar cell and hydrogen fuel cell research.

Freshman class profile. 4,115 applied, 2,517 admitted, 1,053 enrolled.

Mid 50% test scores		**GPA 2.0-2.99:**	66%
SAT verbal:	430-540	**Rank in top quarter:**	11%
SAT math:	450-550	**Rank in top tenth:**	2%
GPA 3.50 or higher:	10%	**Return as sophomores:**	74%
GPA 3.0-3.49:	22%	**Out-of-state:**	1%

Basis for selection. School achievement record of primary importance. Applicants apply to and are accepted into a specific curriculum. Requirements vary according to program. SAT required for bachelor's degree students. Interview and portfolio required for advertising art and design, visual communications programs.

High school preparation. 20.5 units required. Required and recommended units include English 4, mathematics 2-4, social studies 4, science 2-4 and foreign language 2. Requirements vary by curriculum.

2005-2006 Annual costs. Tuition/fees: $5,267; $11,527 out-of-state. Room/board: $10,244. Books/supplies: $1,050. Personal expenses: $800.

Financial aid. Non-need-based: Scholarships awarded for academics.

Application procedures. Admission: No deadline. $40 fee, may be waived for applicants with need. Application may be submitted online. Admission notification on a rolling basis beginning on or about 11/1. Must reply by May 1 or within 4 week(s) if notified thereafter. Priority given to applications received by January 15 for dental hygiene program and nursing program. **Financial aid:** Priority date 4/1; no closing date. FAFSA, institutional form required. Applicants notified on a rolling basis starting 4/1.

Academics. Special study options: Distance learning, double major, honors, internships, study abroad. **Credit/placement by examination:** AP, CLEP, institutional tests. **Support services:** Learning center, remedial instruction, study skills assistance, tutoring, writing center.

Majors. Agriculture: Horticulture. **Biology:** General. **Business:** Business admin, operations, vehicle parts marketing. **Computer sciences:** Programming. **Construction:** Maintenance. **Engineering technology:** Architectural, automotive, computer, electrical, industrial, manufacturing, mechanical. **English:** Technical writing. **Health:** Dental hygiene. **Interdisciplinary:** Science/society. **Math:** Applied. **Protective services:** Security management, security services. **Transportation:** Airline/commercial pilot, aviation management. **Visual/performing arts:** Commercial/advertising art, graphic design.

Most popular majors. Business/marketing 38%, communications/journalism 15%, computer/information sciences 16%, security/protective services 10%, trade and industry 14%.

Computing on campus. 950 workstations in library, computer center, student center. Dormitories wired for high-speed internet access and linked to campus network. Commuter students can connect to campus network. Online course registration, online library, wireless network available.

Student life. Freshman orientation: Available, $75 fee. Preregistration for classes offered. **Policies:** Freshmen permitted cars on campus. **Housing:** Coed dorms available. $100 deposit. **Activities:** Choral groups, drama, literary magazine, radio station, student government, student newspaper, African Student Association, Asian Student Alliance, Caribbean student organization, Christian Fellowship.

Athletics. NCAA. **Intercollegiate:** Baseball M, basketball, cross-country, golf M, lacrosse, soccer, softball W, track and field, volleyball W. **Intramural:** Basketball, golf, racquetball, soccer, softball, squash, swimming, tennis, volleyball, weight lifting. **Team name:** Rams.

Student services. Alcohol/substance abuse counseling, campus ministries, career counseling, services for economically disadvantaged, student employment services, financial aid counseling, health services, on-campus daycare, personal counseling, placement for graduates, veterans' counselor. **Physically disabled:** Services for visually, speech, hearing impaired.

Contact. E-mail: admissions@farmingdale.edu
Phone: (631) 420-2200 Toll-free number: (800) 432-7646
Fax: (631) 420-2633
Jim Hall, Director of Admissions, State University of New York at Farmingdale, 2350 Broad Hollow Road, Farmingdale, NY 11735-1021

State University of New York at New Paltz

New Paltz, New York — **CB member**
www.newpaltz.edu — **CB code: 2541**

- Public 4-year liberal arts college
- Residential campus in large town
- 6,169 degree-seeking undergraduates: 8% part-time, 67% women, 6% African American, 3% Asian American, 10% Hispanic American, 3% international
- 1,210 degree-seeking graduate students
- 44% of applicants admitted
- SAT or ACT (ACT writing optional) required

General. Founded in 1828. Regionally accredited. More than 16 percent of undergraduates participate in international education each academic year. **Degrees:** 1,481 bachelor's awarded; master's offered. **Location:** 65 miles from Albany, 96 miles from New York City. **Calendar:** Semester, limited summer session. **Full-time faculty:** 294 total; 16% minority, 47% women. **Part-time faculty:** 412 total; 10% minority, 56% women. **Class size:** 46% < 20, 45% 20-39, 6% 40-49, 3% 50-99, less than 1% >100. **Special facilities:** 3 theaters, recital hall, speech and hearing clinical center, music therapy training center, art museum, observatory, planetarium, theater collection, electronic classrooms.

Freshman class profile. 11,358 applied, 5,024 admitted, 1,050 enrolled.

Mid 50% test scores			
SAT verbal:	520-600	GPA 2.0-2.99:	17%
SAT math:	520-610	Rank in top quarter:	56%
GPA 3.50 or higher:	29%	Rank in top tenth:	15%
GPA 3.0-3.49:	54%	Out-of-state:	3%
		Live on campus:	92%

Basis for selection. Secondary school curriculum and achievement, standardized test scores, rank in class most important. Applicants, especially academically marginal, encouraged to send personal statements regarding academic work, recommendations from academic teachers, and any other pertinent information. Essay and recommendations encouraged for all; audition required for music, music therapy, theater arts programs; portfolio required for art education, scenography, studio art, and visual arts programs. **Homeschooled:** Must submit all data as required by NYS Commissioner of Education's regulations (Section 100.10).

High school preparation. Required and recommended units include English 4, mathematics 3-4, social studies 3-4, science 3-4 (laboratory 3-4) and foreign language 2-4.

2005-2006 Annual costs. Tuition/fees: $5,260; $11,520 out-of-state. Room/board: $7,220. Books/supplies: $1,100. Personal expenses: $250.

2004-2005 Financial aid. Need-based: 690 full-time freshmen applied for aid; 448 were judged to have need; 445 of these received aid. Average need met was 71%. Average scholarship/grant was $2,324; average loan $1,918. 54% of total undergraduate aid awarded as scholarships/grants, 46% as loans/jobs. **Non-need-based:** Awarded to 426 full-time undergraduates, including 113 freshmen. Scholarships awarded for academics, art, minority status, music/drama.

Application procedures. Admission: Closing date 4/1 (receipt date). $40 fee, may be waived for applicants with need. Application may be submitted online. Admission notification on a rolling basis beginning on or about 12/15. Must reply by May 1 or within 2 week(s) if notified thereafter. **Financial aid:** Priority date 3/15; no closing date. FAFSA required. Applicants notified on a rolling basis starting 4/1; must reply within 4 week(s) of notification.

Academics. Bachelor's degree completion program for registered nurses. **Special study options:** Combined bachelor's/graduate degree, cooperative education, cross-registration, distance learning, double major, ESL, exchange student, honors, independent study, internships, liberal arts/career combination, New York semester, student-designed major, study abroad, teacher certification program, United Nations semester. Student exchange programs in Australia, Brazil, Cuba, Czech Republic, Denmark, Ecuador, England, France, Greece, Ireland, Italy, Japan, The Netherlands, New Zealand, Spain, Uzbekistan, U.S. Virgin Islands and Zimbabwe. **Credit/placement by examination:** AP, CLEP, IB, institutional tests. 30 credit hours maximum toward bachelor's degree. **Support services:** Learning center, reduced course load, remedial instruction, study skills assistance, tutoring, writing center.

Honors college/program. Minimum 90 high school average, 1200 SAT(exclusive of writing). Limited to 20 freshmen a year. Honors seminars and honors sections in specific disciplines.

Majors. Area/ethnic studies: African-American, Asian, Latin American, women's. **Biology:** General. **Business:** Accounting, business admin, finance, international, management science. **Communications:** General, broadcast journalism, journalism, public relations. **Computer sciences:** Computer science. **Education:** Art, biology, chemistry, Deaf/hearing impaired, elementary, English, foreign languages, French, German, history, mathematics, middle, physics, science, secondary, social studies, Spanish, special, speech, speech impaired. **Engineering:** Computer, electrical. **Foreign languages:** French, German, Spanish. **Health:** Audiology/hearing, audiology/speech pathology, communication disorders, music therapy, predentistry, premedicine, preop/surgical nursing, preveterinary. **History:** General. **Interdisciplinary:** Biopsychology. **Legal studies:** Prelaw. **Liberal arts:** Arts/sciences. **Math:** General. **Philosophy/religion:** Philosophy. **Physical sciences:** Chemistry, geology, physics. **Psychology:** General. **Public administration:** Social work. **Social sciences:** Anthropology, economics, geography, international relations, political science, sociology. **Visual/performing arts:** General, art, art history/conservation, ceramics, commercial/advertising art, dramatic, jazz, metal/jewelry, music history, music performance, music theory/composition, painting, photography, piano/organ, printmaking, sculpture, studio arts, theater design, voice/opera.

Most popular majors. Business/marketing 14%, communications/journalism 7%, education 20%, English 11%, psychology 7%, social sciences 10%, visual/performing arts 11%.

Computing on campus. 600 workstations in dormitories, library, computer center, student center. Dormitories wired for high-speed internet access and linked to campus network. Commuter students can connect to campus network. Online course registration, online library, helpline, student web hosting available.

Student life. Freshman orientation: Available, $150 fee. Preregistration for classes offered. 3-day academic and transition program. **Housing:** Guaranteed on-campus for freshmen. Coed dorms, special housing for disabled, substance-free housing available. $100 partly refundable deposit, deadline 5/1. Theme housing of cultural awareness residence experience, first year interest groups, contract study hall, wellness house, 10-month halls available. **Activities:** Bands, choral groups, dance, drama, music ensembles, radio station, student government, student newspaper, symphony orchestra, TV station, Catholic campus ministry, Jewish Action Movement, Black Student Union, Habitat for Humanity, Circle K International, equestrian club, NAACP, philosophy club, Korean culture union.

Athletics. NCAA. **Intercollegiate:** Baseball M, basketball, cross-country, diving, field hockey W, lacrosse W, soccer, softball W, swimming, tennis, track and field, volleyball. **Intramural:** Basketball, cross-country, golf W, racquetball, softball, tennis, volleyball. **Team name:** Hawks.

Student services. Alcohol/substance abuse counseling, campus ministries, career counseling, services for economically disadvantaged, student employment services, financial aid counseling, health services, legal services, minority student services, on-campus daycare, personal counseling, placement for graduates, veterans' counselor, women's services. **Physically disabled:** Services for visually, speech, hearing impaired.

Contact. E-mail: admissions@newpaltz.edu
Phone: (845) 257-3200 Toll-free number: (888) 639-7589
Fax: (845) 257-3209
Kimberly Lavoie, Director of Freshmen, International Admission, State University of New York at New Paltz, 75 South Manheim Boulevard, Suite 1, New Paltz, NY 12561-2499

State University of New York at Oswego

Oswego, New York — **CB member**
www.oswego.edu — **CB code: 2543**

- Public 4-year university and liberal arts college
- Residential campus in large town
- 7,000 degree-seeking undergraduates: 6% part-time, 54% women, 4% African American, 2% Asian American, 4% Hispanic American, 1% Native American, 1% international
- 890 degree-seeking graduate students
- 56% of applicants admitted
- SAT or ACT (ACT writing optional) required
- 58% graduate within 6 years; 33% enter graduate study

General. Founded in 1861. Regionally accredited. **Degrees:** 1,345 bachelor's awarded; master's offered. **ROTC:** Army. **Location:** 35 miles from Syracuse, 65 miles from Rochester. **Calendar:** Semester, limited summer session. **Full-time faculty:** 317 total; 83% have terminal degrees, 10% minority, 40% women. **Part-time faculty:** 194 total; 25% have terminal degrees, 6% minority, 49% women. **Class size:** 39% < 20, 45% 20-39, 4% 40-49, 8% 50-99, 3% >100. **Special facilities:** Weather facsimile machine, planetarium, cross-country ski facilities, advanced technology classrooms, biological field station.

Freshman class profile. 7,565 applied, 4,228 admitted, 1,354 enrolled.

Mid 50% test scores			
SAT verbal:	500-580	Rank in top tenth:	10%
SAT math:	520-580	End year in good standing:	89%
ACT:	21-25	Return as sophomores:	78%
GPA 3.50 or higher:	30%	Out-of-state:	2%
GPA 3.0-3.49:	35%	Live on campus:	88%
GPA 2.0-2.99:	35%	International:	2%
Rank in top quarter:	50%	Fraternities:	6%
		Sororities:	5%

Basis for selection. High school GPA and curriculum most important, followed by test scores, part II of application and letters of recommendation. Special talents considered. SAT recommended. Applicants recommended to send both SAT and ACT; higher score of the two accepted. Essay and interview recommended for all; audition recommended for music; portfolio required for graphic design and fine arts (BFA). **Homeschooled:** Proof of high school graduation or GED recognized by state of residency required. **Learning Disabled:** Advised to contact Office of Learning Services and/or Disability Services with copy of IEP if applicable.

High school preparation. College-preparatory program required. 18 units required; 20 recommended. Required and recommended units include English 4, mathematics 3-4, social studies 4, science 3-4 (laboratory 2-3) and foreign language 2-4. Combined minimum of 6 units mathematics and science recommended.

2005-2006 Annual costs. Tuition/fees: $5,315; $11,575 out-of-state. Room/board: $8,340. Books/supplies: $800. Personal expenses: $838.

2004-2005 Financial aid. **Need-based:** 1,228 full-time freshmen applied for aid; 923 were judged to have need; 899 of these received aid. Average need met was 75%. Average scholarship/grant was $4,503; average loan $3,243. 38% of total undergraduate aid awarded as scholarships/grants, 62% as loans/jobs. **Non-need-based:** Awarded to 1,980 full-time undergraduates, including 602 freshmen. Scholarships awarded for academics, state residency.

Application procedures. **Admission:** Priority date 1/15; no deadline. $40 fee, may be waived for applicants with need. Application may be submitted online. Admission notification on a rolling basis beginning on or about 1/15. Must reply by May 1 or within 4 week(s) if notified thereafter. **Financial aid:** Priority date 4/1; no closing date. FAFSA required. Applicants notified on a rolling basis starting 3/1; must reply by 5/1 or within 3 week(s) of notification.

Academics. **Special study options:** Accelerated study, combined bachelor's/graduate degree, cross-registration, distance learning, double major, dual enrollment of high school students, ESL, exchange student, external degree, honors, independent study, internships, liberal arts/career combination, study abroad, teacher certification program, Washington semester. **Credit/placement by examination:** AP, CLEP, IB. 30 credit hours maximum toward bachelor's degree. **Support services:** Learning center, pre-admission summer program, reduced course load, remedial instruction, study skills assistance, tutoring, writing center.

Honors college/program. Approximately 80 freshmen enroll annually, distinct program of general education classes held in small class settings.

Majors. **Area/ethnic studies:** American, women's. **Biology:** General, zoology. **Business:** Accounting, business admin, finance, human resources, management science. **Communications:** General, broadcast journalism, journalism, public relations. **Computer sciences:** Computer science, information systems. **Education:** Agricultural, biology, business, chemistry, elementary, English, French, German, health occupations, history, mathematics, physics, science, secondary, social studies, Spanish, technology/industrial arts, trade/industrial, voc/tech. **English:** English lit. **Family/consumer sciences:** Child development. **Foreign languages:** French, German, linguistics, Spanish. **Health:** Medical radiologic technology/radiation therapy, perfusion technology, public health ed. **History:** General. **Interdisciplinary:** Cognitive science, global studies. **Legal studies:** Prelaw. **Math:** General, applied. **Philosophy/religion:** Philosophy. **Physical sciences:** Chemistry, geochemistry, geology, meteorology, physics. **Psychology:** General. **Social sciences:** Anthropology, econometrics, economics, political science, sociology. **Visual/performing arts:** Art, commercial/advertising art, dramatic.

Most popular majors. Business/marketing 19%, communications/journalism 11%, education 25%, psychology 10%, social sciences 11%, visual/performing arts 6%.

Computing on campus. 750 workstations in dormitories, library, computer center, student center. Dormitories wired for high-speed internet access and linked to campus network. Commuter students can connect to campus network. Online course registration, online library, helpline, wireless network available.

Student life. **Freshman orientation:** Mandatory, $110 fee. Preregistration for classes offered. 2-day program for incoming students and families. **Policies:** Freshmen permitted cars on campus. **Housing:** Guaranteed on-campus for all undergraduates. Coed dorms available. $100 fully refundable deposit, deadline 5/1. Pets allowed in dorm rooms. Global living and learning center, suites for upperclassmen, nontraditional student housing, first-year experience residence hall for incoming freshmen only, housing for 21 and over single suites available. **Activities:** Bands, choral groups, dance, drama, film society, literary magazine, music ensembles, musical theater, radio station, student government, student newspaper, symphony orchestra, TV station, Christian, Jewish, Catholic, and Baptist groups, black student union, Latin student union, Caribbean student association, international student association, Native American brotherhood, Students Educating Everyone About Disabilities.

Athletics. NCAA. **Intercollegiate:** Baseball M, basketball, cross-country, diving, field hockey W, golf M, ice hockey M, lacrosse, soccer, softball W, swimming, tennis, track and field, volleyball W, wrestling M. **Intramural:** Basketball, football (non-tackle), golf, lacrosse, racquetball, skiing, soccer, softball, swimming, tennis, volleyball, weight lifting M, wrestling M. **Team name:** Lakers.

Student services. Adult student services, alcohol/substance abuse counseling, career counseling, services for economically disadvantaged, student employment services, financial aid counseling, health services, minority student services, on-campus daycare, personal counseling, placement for graduates, veterans' counselor, women's services. **Physically disabled:** Services for visually, speech, hearing impaired.

Contact. E-mail: admiss@oswego.edu
Phone: (315) 312-2250 Fax: (315) 312-3260
Joseph Grant, Vice President for Student Affairs and Enrollment, State University of New York at Oswego, 229 Sheldon Hall, Oswego, NY 13126-3599

State University of New York at Purchase

Purchase, New York
www.purchase.edu **CB code: 2878**

- Public 4-year college of liberal arts and visual and performing arts
- Residential campus in large town
- 3,396 degree-seeking undergraduates: 7% part-time, 55% women, 8% African American, 4% Asian American, 10% Hispanic American, 1% international
- 138 degree-seeking graduate students
- 31% of applicants admitted
- SAT or ACT required
- 47% graduate within 6 years

General. Founded in 1967. Regionally accredited. **Degrees:** 794 bachelor's awarded; master's offered. **Location:** 25 miles from New York City, 5 miles from White Plains. **Calendar:** Semester, extensive summer session. **Full-time faculty:** 143 total; 50% have terminal degrees, 13% minority, 50% women. **Part-time faculty:** 197 total; 20% have terminal degrees, 10% minority, 41% women. **Class size:** 51% < 20, 38% 20-39, 5% 40-49, 5% 50-99, 1% >100. **Special facilities:** Performing arts center, children's center, electron microscope.

Freshman class profile. 6,946 applied, 2,142 admitted, 718 enrolled.

Mid 50% test scores		**Rank in top quarter:**	29%
SAT verbal:	510-620	**Rank in top tenth:**	9%
SAT math:	480-580	**Return as sophomores:**	78%
ACT:	20-25	**Out-of-state:**	21%
GPA 3.50 or higher:	24%	**Live on campus:**	91%
GPA 3.0-3.49:	34%	**International:**	1%
GPA 2.0-2.99:	40%		

Basis for selection. For liberal arts and sciences programs, high school achievement record or test scores important. For conservatory, performing arts and visual arts applicants, audition, interview, or portfolio most important. SAT recommended. Interview and essay required for film, theater design/technology programs; audition required for acting, dance, music programs; portfolio required for visual arts program.

2005-2006 Annual costs. Tuition/fees: $5,504; $11,764 out-of-state. Room/board: $8,446. Books/supplies: $2,300. Personal expenses: $600.

2004-2005 Financial aid. **Need-based:** 501 full-time freshmen applied for aid; 329 were judged to have need; 329 of these received aid. Average need met was 62.05%. Average scholarship/grant was $5,286; average loan $3,320. 26% of total undergraduate aid awarded as scholarships/grants, 74% as loans/jobs. **Non-need-based:** Awarded to 541 full-time undergraduates, including 179 freshmen. Scholarships awarded for academics, art, minority status, music/drama. **Additional information:** All applicants automatically considered for scholarship upon review of applications, essays, auditions, and/or portfolio.

Application procedures. **Admission:** Priority date 3/1; deadline 6/1 (postmark date). $40 fee, may be waived for applicants with need. Application may be submitted online. Must reply by May 1 or within 2 week(s) if notified thereafter. Application deadlines vary by program. Priority date of 1/30 for students applying to acting, design/technology, and film programs. **Financial aid:** Priority date 3/1; no closing date. FAFSA required. Applicants notified on a rolling basis starting 3/1; must reply within 2 week(s) of notification.

Academics. **Special study options:** Cross-registration, distance learning, double major, ESL, independent study, internships, liberal arts/career combination, student-designed major, study abroad. Conservatory master-apprentice training in dance, music, acting, film, theater design technology, visual arts. **Credit/placement by examination:** AP, CLEP, institutional tests. 30 credit hours maximum toward bachelor's degree. **Support services:** Learning center, pre-admission summer program, remedial instruction, tutoring.

Majors. **Area/ethnic studies:** Women's. **Biology:** General, ecology. **Communications:** Journalism, media studies. **Conservation:** General. **English:** American lit, British lit, creative writing. **Foreign languages:** General. **History:** General. **Interdisciplinary:** Math/computer science. **Liberal arts:** Arts/sciences. **Math:** General. **Philosophy/religion:** Philosophy. **Physical sciences:** Chemistry. **Psychology:** General. **Social sciences:** Anthropology, economics, political science, sociology. **Visual/performing arts:** Art history/

conservation, arts management, cinematography, commercial/advertising art, dance, dramatic, drawing, graphic design, music performance, music theory/composition, painting, photography, play/screenwriting, printmaking, sculpture, theater design, theater history.

Most popular majors. Liberal arts 20%, social sciences 11%, visual/performing arts 44%.

Computing on campus. 350 workstations in dormitories, library, computer center. Dormitories linked to campus network. Commuter students can connect to campus network. Online course registration, online library, helpline, repair service, wireless network available.

Student life. Freshman orientation: Mandatory, $120 fee. **Policies:** Freshmen permitted cars on campus. **Housing:** Coed dorms, special housing for disabled, apartments, substance-free housing available. $100 nonrefundable deposit. Freshman residence, wellness program, nonsmoking hall, nontraditional age hall, presidential scholars, learning community available. **Activities:** Jazz band, choral groups, dance, drama, film society, radio station, student government, student newspaper, TV station, philosophy club, chemistry society, literature club, dance club, ski club, Purchase Experimental Theatre, Organization of African People in America (OAPIA), Latinos Unidos, Gay/Lesbian/Bisexual and Transgendered Union.

Athletics. NCAA. **Intercollegiate:** Baseball M, basketball, cross-country, soccer, softball W, swimming W, tennis, volleyball. **Intramural:** Badminton, basketball, bowling, cross-country, fencing, golf, racquetball, skiing, soccer, softball, squash, swimming, table tennis, tennis, volleyball, water polo, weight lifting. **Team name:** Panthers.

Student services. Adult student services, career counseling, student employment services, health services, on-campus daycare, personal counseling, placement for graduates, veterans' counselor. **Physically disabled:** Services for visually, hearing impaired.

Contact. E-mail: admissn@purchase.edu
Phone: (914) 251-6300 Fax: (914) 251-6314
Stephanie McCaine, Director of Admissions, State University of New York at Purchase, 735 Anderson Hill Road, Purchase, NY 10577-1400

State University of New York at Stony Brook

Stony Brook, New York — **CB member**
www.stonybrook.edu — **CB code: 2548**

- Public 4-year university
- Residential campus in large town
- 14,095 degree-seeking undergraduates: 7% part-time, 49% women, 10% African American, 22% Asian American, 9% Hispanic American, 5% international
- 6,649 degree-seeking graduate students
- 51% of applicants admitted
- SAT or ACT with writing required
- 58% graduate within 6 years

General. Founded in 1957. Regionally accredited. **Degrees:** 2,941 bachelor's awarded; master's, doctoral, first professional offered. **ROTC:** Army, Air Force. **Location:** 60 miles from New York City. **Calendar:** Semester, limited summer session. **Full-time faculty:** 909 total; 97% have terminal degrees, 17% minority, 33% women. **Part-time faculty:** 479 total; 10% minority, 45% women. **Class size:** 36% < 20, 32% 20-39, 7% 40-49, 14% 50-99, 11% >100. **Special facilities:** Nuclear accelerator, natural science museum, 3-theater fine arts center, nature preserve, working arrangements with Cold Spring Harbor Laboratory and Brookhaven National Laboratory.

Freshman class profile. 18,206 applied, 9,198 admitted, 2,508 enrolled.

Mid 50% test scores		**Return as sophomores:**	87%
SAT verbal:	520-620	**Out-of-state:**	6%
SAT math:	560-660	**Live on campus:**	77%
Rank in top quarter:	69%	**International:**	5%
Rank in top tenth:	33%		

Basis for selection. High school GPA and test scores most important factors. Class rank, level of high school curriculum, interview, letters of recommendation, extracurricular activities considered. SAT Subject Tests recommended. Interview and audition required for theater programs; audition required for music programs; portfolio recommended for art programs. Essay required for admission to Honors College, Scholars for Medicine, WISE (Women in Science & Engineering) and Honors Program in Computer Science. Essay required for scholarship consideration. **Homeschooled:** Applicants required to take Regents exam through their home school district. **Learning Disabled:** Applicants required to submit documentation of learning disability. Psychological and educational evaluation also required.

High school preparation. 16 units required; 19 recommended. Required and recommended units include English 4, mathematics 3-4, social studies 4, science 3-4 and foreign language 2-3. 4 mathematics and 4 science recommended for applicants to science, engineering, and mathematics programs.

2005-2006 Annual costs. Tuition/fees: $5,575; $11,835 out-of-state. Room/board: $8,050. Books/supplies: $900. Personal expenses: $1,120.

2004-2005 Financial aid. Need-based: 1,702 full-time freshmen applied for aid; 1,232 were judged to have need; 1,210 of these received aid. Average need met was 67%. Average scholarship/grant was $5,977; average loan $2,763. 52% of total undergraduate aid awarded as scholarships/grants, 48% as loans/jobs. **Non-need-based:** Awarded to 2,129 full-time undergraduates, including 539 freshmen. Scholarships awarded for academics, athletics.

Application procedures. Admission: Priority date 12/1; no deadline. $40 fee, may be waived for applicants with need. Application must be submitted online. Admission notification on a rolling basis beginning on or about 2/1. Must reply by May 1 or within 4 week(s) if notified thereafter. **Financial aid:** Priority date 3/1; no closing date. FAFSA required. Applicants notified on a rolling basis starting 3/1; must reply by 5/1 or within 2 week(s) of notification.

Academics. Special study options: Combined bachelor's/graduate degree, cross-registration, distance learning, double major, dual enrollment of high school students, ESL, exchange student, honors, independent study, internships, New York semester, student-designed major, study abroad, teacher certification program, Washington semester. **Credit/placement by examination:** AP, CLEP, IB, institutional tests. 30 credit hours maximum toward bachelor's degree. **Support services:** Learning center, reduced course load, remedial instruction, tutoring, writing center.

Honors college/program. High grades in major subject areas, minimum cumulative high school average of 93, minimum combined SAT (exclusive of Writing) of 1250, record of advanced or college-level course work, and evidence of writing ability required.

Majors. Area/ethnic studies: African-American, American, European, women's. **Biology:** General, biochemistry, marine, pharmacology. **Business:** Business admin. **Computer sciences:** Computer science, information systems. **Conservation:** Environmental studies. **Engineering:** General, biomedical, computer hardware, electrical, mechanical. **English:** English lit. **Foreign languages:** Comparative lit, French, German, Italian, linguistics, Russian, Spanish. **Health:** Clinical lab science, cytotechnology, nursing (RN), physician assistant, respiratory therapy technology. **History:** General. **Liberal arts:** Humanities. **Math:** General, applied. **Philosophy/religion:** Philosophy, religion. **Physical sciences:** Astronomy, chemistry, geology, physics. **Psychology:** General. **Public administration:** Social work. **Social sciences:** Anthropology, economics, political science, sociology. **Visual/performing arts:** Art history/conservation, dramatic, studio arts.

Most popular majors. Biology 9%, business/marketing 9%, computer/information sciences 8%, health sciences 17%, psychology 12%, social sciences 20%.

Computing on campus. 2,300 workstations in dormitories, library, computer center, student center. Dormitories wired for high-speed internet access and linked to campus network. Commuter students can connect to campus network. Online course registration, helpline, student web hosting available.

Student life. Freshman orientation: Mandatory, $150 fee. Preregistration for classes offered. 1-day session held in June or early August. **Housing:** Coed dorms, special housing for disabled, apartments, substance-free housing available. $200 deposit, deadline 5/1. 7 living/learning centers integrate residence hall experience with academic concerns. Single sex floors in coed dorms. **Activities:** Bands, choral groups, dance, drama, film society, literary magazine, music ensembles, musical theater, opera, radio station, student government, student newspaper, symphony orchestra, Jewish, Protestant, Catholic, Islamic Society, Baha'i religious organizations, InterVarsity Christian Fellowship, international club, Chinese association, Indian student association, Pakistan club, African students association.

Athletics. NCAA. **Intercollegiate:** Baseball M, basketball, cross-country, diving, football (tackle) M, lacrosse, soccer, softball W, swimming, tennis, track and field, volleyball W. **Intramural:** Basketball, softball. **Team name:** Seawolves.

Student services. Adult student services, alcohol/substance abuse counseling, campus ministries, career counseling, services for economically disadvantaged, student employment services, financial aid counseling, health

services, minority student services, on-campus daycare, personal counseling, placement for graduates, veterans' counselor, women's services. **Physically disabled:** Services for visually, speech, hearing impaired.

Contact. E-mail: enroll@stonybrook.edu
Phone: (631) 632-6868 Toll-free number: (800) 872-7869
Fax: (631) 632-9898
Judith Burke-Berhannan, Dean of Admissions, State University of New York at Stony Brook, Stony Brook, NY 11794-1901

State University of New York College at Brockport

Brockport, New York — **CB member**
www.brockport.edu — **CB code: 2537**

- Public 4-year liberal arts college
- Residential campus in small town
- 6,852 degree-seeking undergraduates: 11% part-time, 57% women, 5% African American, 1% Asian American, 3% Hispanic American, 1% international
- 1,311 degree-seeking graduate students
- 46% of applicants admitted
- SAT or ACT (ACT writing optional) required
- 56% graduate within 6 years; 25% enter graduate study

General. Founded in 1867. Regionally accredited. **Degrees:** 1,682 bachelor's awarded; master's offered. **ROTC:** Army, Navy, Air Force. **Location:** 16 miles from Rochester. **Calendar:** Semester, limited summer session. **Full-time faculty:** 320 total; 78% have terminal degrees, 16% minority, 47% women. **Part-time faculty:** 295 total; 24% have terminal degrees, 7% minority, 51% women. **Class size:** 46% < 20, 47% 20-39, 5% 40-49, 3% 50-99, less than 1% >100. **Special facilities:** Aquaculture ponds, unidata weather information system, weather radio receiver, nuclear laboratory, high resolution germanium detector, research vessel on Lake Ontario, electron microscope, two supercomputers, Doppler radar system, hydrotherapy room, parallel supercomputer, ultramodern dance facilities including green room.

Freshman class profile. 7,816 applied, 3,625 admitted, 989 enrolled.

Mid 50% test scores			
SAT verbal:	500-600	Rank in top quarter:	49%
SAT math:	480-570	Rank in top tenth:	17%
ACT:	20-25	End year in good standing:	89%
GPA 3.50 or higher:	46%	Return as sophomores:	83%
GPA 3.0-3.49:	40%	Out-of-state:	2%
GPA 2.0-2.99:	14%	Live on campus:	89%
		International:	1%

Basis for selection. High school academic record including number of academic units, GPA, class rank, test scores important. Recommendations, essay, extracurricular activites considered. Interview required in some cases; auditions required for dance and theater acting. **Homeschooled:** Outline of courses completed at high school level, official test scores, personal essay, 2 letters of recommendation, and biography of books read during high school program required.

High school preparation. 18 units required. Required and recommended units include English 4, mathematics 3, social studies 4, science 3 (laboratory 1), foreign language 3 and academic electives 4.

2005-2006 Annual costs. Tuition/fees: $5,293; $11,553 out-of-state. Room/board: $8,062. Books/supplies: $900. Personal expenses: $2,123.

2004-2005 Financial aid. Need-based: 906 full-time freshmen applied for aid; 693 were judged to have need; 689 of these received aid. Average need met was 83%. Average scholarship/grant was $3,759; average loan $4,216. 43% of total undergraduate aid awarded as scholarships/grants, 57% as loans/jobs. **Non-need-based:** Awarded to 651 full-time undergraduates, including 180 freshmen. Scholarships awarded for academics, alumni affiliation, leadership, minority status, ROTC, state residency.

Application procedures. Admission: Priority date 2/1; no deadline. $40 fee, may be waived for applicants with need. Application may be submitted online. Admission notification on a rolling basis beginning on or about 11/15. Must reply by May 1 or within 3 week(s) if notified thereafter. **Financial aid:** Priority date 2/15; no closing date. FAFSA required. Applicants notified on a rolling basis starting 2/15; must reply within 4 week(s) of notification.

Academics. Time/credit-shortened B.S. degree, experiential learning, domestic and international internships through Delta College. 3-1-3 program allows 30 college credits to be earned during student's senior year of high school. **Special study options:** Accelerated study, combined bachelor's/graduate degree, cross-registration, distance learning, double major, dual enrollment of high school students, honors, independent study, internships, New York semester, semester at sea, student-designed major, study abroad, teacher certification program, Washington semester. **Credit/placement by examination:** AP, CLEP, IB, institutional tests. 90 credit hours maximum toward bachelor's degree. **Support services:** Learning center, preadmission summer program, reduced course load, study skills assistance, tutoring, writing center.

Honors college/program. Freshman applicants should have high school average of at least a 91 and SAT of 1150 (exclusive of Writing) or ACT of 25. The average Honors student has a 93 GPA and a 1220 SAT and/or 27 ACT.

Majors. Area/ethnic studies: African, African-American, women's. **Biology:** General, aquatic, biochemistry, biotechnology, cellular/molecular, environmental, exercise physiology. **Business:** Accounting, business admin, finance, international, international marketing. **Communications:** General, broadcast journalism, journalism, media studies. **Computer sciences:** General, computer science. **Conservation:** General, environmental science, environmental studies. **Education:** Health, physical. **English:** Creative writing, English lit. **Foreign languages:** General, French, Spanish. **Health:** Athletic training, clinical lab technology, health care admin, nursing (RN), predentistry, premedicine, preveterinary. **History:** General. **Math:** General. **Parks/recreation:** General, facilities management, sports admin. **Philosophy/religion:** Philosophy. **Physical sciences:** Atmospheric science, chemistry, geology, hydrology, meteorology, physics, planetary. **Protective services:** Police science, security management. **Psychology:** General. **Public administration:** Social work. **Science technology:** Biological. **Social sciences:** Anthropology, international relations, political science, sociology. **Visual/performing arts:** General, art, dance, dramatic, studio arts.

Most popular majors. Business/marketing 14%, communications/journalism 8%, education 12%, health sciences 10%, psychology 10%, security/protective services 8%, social sciences 6%.

Computing on campus. 750 workstations in dormitories, library, computer center, student center. Dormitories wired for high-speed internet access and linked to campus network. Commuter students can connect to campus network. Online course registration, online library, helpline, wireless network available.

Student life. Freshman orientation: Mandatory. Preregistration for classes offered. Held during a long weekend before classes begin. **Policies:** Freshmen permitted cars on campus. **Housing:** Guaranteed on-campus for freshmen. Coed dorms, special housing for disabled, substance-free housing available. $100 deposit, deadline 5/1. Special living options available include freshman first-year experience program, transfer student program, health club, scholar floors, single-sex areas, adult, 24-hour quiet. **Activities:** Choral groups, dance, drama, literary magazine, music ensembles, radio station, student government, student newspaper, TV station, Organization for Students of African Descent, Association of Latin American Students, international student association, Alpha Chi Honor Society, Caribbean club, women's center, Brockport Adult Student Organization, peer counseling, student alumni association, Native American student organization.

Athletics. NCAA. **Intercollegiate:** Baseball M, basketball, cross-country, diving, field hockey W, football (tackle) M, gymnastics W, ice hockey M, lacrosse, soccer, softball W, swimming, tennis W, track and field, volleyball W, wrestling M. **Intramural:** Badminton, basketball, bowling, football (non-tackle), racquetball, soccer, softball, table tennis, volleyball. **Team name:** Golden Eagles.

Student services. Alcohol/substance abuse counseling, campus ministries, career counseling, services for economically disadvantaged, student employment services, financial aid counseling, health services, legal services, minority student services, on-campus daycare, personal counseling, placement for graduates, veterans' counselor, women's services. **Physically disabled:** Services for visually, speech, hearing impaired.

Contact. E-mail: admit@brockport.edu
Phone: (585) 395-2751 Fax: (585) 395-5452
Bernard Valento, Director of Undergraduate Admissions, State University of New York College at Brockport, 350 New Campus Drive, Brockport, NY 14420-2915

State University of New York College at Buffalo

Buffalo, New York — **CB member**
www.buffalostate.edu — **CB code: 2533**

- Public 4-year liberal arts and teachers college
- Commuter campus in large city
- 8,722 degree-seeking undergraduates: 11% part-time, 60% women, 13% African American, 2% Asian American, 4% Hispanic American

- 1,850 degree-seeking graduate students
- 44% of applicants admitted
- SAT and SAT Subject Tests or ACT (ACT writing optional) required
- 39% graduate within 6 years; 17% enter graduate study

General. Founded in 1867. Regionally accredited. **Degrees:** 1,551 bachelor's awarded; master's offered. **ROTC:** Army. **Location:** 450 miles from New York City, 250 miles from Cleveland. **Calendar:** Semester, limited summer session. **Full-time faculty:** 399 total; 78% have terminal degrees, 17% minority, 41% women. **Part-time faculty:** 360 total; 20% have terminal degrees, 9% minority, 47% women. **Class size:** 53% < 20, 36% 20-39, 3% 40-49, 6% 50-99, 1% >100. **Special facilities:** Planetarium, performing arts center, center for environmental research and education, child care center, art center.

Freshman class profile. 8,563 applied, 3,736 admitted, 1,250 enrolled.

Mid 50% test scores			
SAT verbal:	450-540	Rank in top quarter:	25%
SAT math:	460-540	Rank in top tenth:	6%
GPA 3.50 or higher:	28%	Return as sophomores:	75%
GPA 3.0-3.49:	57%	Out-of-state:	1%
GPA 2.0-2.99:	15%	Fraternities:	1%
		Sororities:	1%

Basis for selection. High school GPA, class rank, test scores important. Recommendations, essay, interview, volunteer work, work experience and extracurricular activities also considered. Portfolio required for fine arts program.

High school preparation. 17 units recommended. Required and recommended units include English 4, mathematics 2-3, science 2-3, foreign language 3 and academic electives 4.

2005-2006 Annual costs. Tuition/fees: $5,231; $11,491 out-of-state. Room/board: $6,672. Books/supplies: $900. Personal expenses: $1,000.

2004-2005 Financial aid. All financial aid based on need. 1,242 full-time freshmen applied for aid; 1,072 were judged to have need; 759 of these received aid. Average need met was 72%. Average scholarship/grant was $3,262; average loan $3,368. 52% of total undergraduate aid awarded as scholarships/grants, 48% as loans/jobs.

Application procedures. Admission: No deadline. $40 fee, may be waived for applicants with need. Application may be submitted online. Admission notification on a rolling basis beginning on or about 12/15. Must reply by May 1 or within 4 week(s) if notified thereafter. **Financial aid:** Priority date 3/15, closing date 5/1. FAFSA required. Applicants notified on a rolling basis starting 5/1; must reply within 4 week(s) of notification.

Academics. Special study options: Cooperative education, cross-registration, distance learning, double major, dual enrollment of high school students, ESL, exchange student, honors, independent study, internships, liberal arts/career combination, New York semester, study abroad, teacher certification program, Washington semester. **Credit/placement by examination:** AP, CLEP, IB, institutional tests. 30 credit hours maximum toward bachelor's degree. **Support services:** Learning center, pre-admission summer program, reduced course load, remedial instruction, study skills assistance, tutoring.

Honors college/program. High school students must have GPA of 90 or higher (or rank within the top 10 percent of their graduating class) and SAT scores of 1100 (exclusive of Writing) or higher. Advanced Placement courses with grades of B or better, cocurricular activities, and community involvement also considered.

Majors. Architecture: Urban/community planning. **Biology:** General. **Business:** General, business admin, fashion, hospitality admin, hospitality/recreation, office management. **Communications:** General, broadcast journalism, journalism, media studies. **Computer sciences:** General, information systems, programming. **Education:** General, art, biology, business, chemistry, early childhood, elementary, emotionally handicapped, English, foreign languages, French, health occupations, mathematics, mentally handicapped, physically handicapped, physics, reading, sales/marketing, science, secondary, social studies, Spanish, technology/industrial arts, trade/industrial, voc/tech. **Engineering technology:** Electrical, electromechanical, mechanical. **English:** English lit. **Family/consumer sciences:** Clothing/textiles, food/nutrition. **Foreign languages:** French, Spanish. **Health:** Speech pathology. **History:** General. **Liberal arts:** Humanities. **Math:** General. **Parks/recreation:** Health/fitness. **Philosophy/religion:** Philosophy. **Physical sciences:** Chemistry, geology, physics, planetary. **Protective services:** Criminal justice, forensics. **Psychology:** General. **Public administration:** Social work. **Social sciences:** Anthropology, economics, geography, political science, sociology. **Visual/performing arts:** General, art history/conservation, commercial/advertising art, dramatic, fashion design, fiber arts, metal/jewelry, painting, photography, printmaking, sculpture, studio arts, theater arts management.

Most popular majors. Business/marketing 7%, communications/journalism 8%, computer/information sciences 6%, education 26%, security/protective services 6%, social sciences 6%, visual/performing arts 10%.

Computing on campus. 900 workstations in dormitories, library, computer center, student center. Dormitories wired for high-speed internet access and linked to campus network. Commuter students can connect to campus network. Online course registration, online library, helpline, repair service, wireless network available.

Student life. Freshman orientation: Mandatory, $175 fee. Preregistration for classes offered. **Policies:** Freshmen permitted cars on campus. **Housing:** Coed dorms, apartments, substance-free housing available. $100 fully refundable deposit, deadline 7/1. Apartments for students with dependent children available. **Activities:** Bands, choral groups, dance, drama, film society, literary magazine, music ensembles, radio station, student government, student newspaper, Newman Club, Amnesty International, public interest groups, African American student organization, Adelante Estudiantes, international student organization, Native American student organization, Muslim student organization, Christian fellowship groups, Caribbean student organization.

Athletics. NCAA. **Intercollegiate:** Basketball, cross-country, diving, football (tackle) M, ice hockey M, lacrosse W, soccer, softball W, swimming, tennis W, track and field, volleyball W. **Intramural:** Basketball, football (tackle) M, racquetball, soccer, softball, volleyball. **Team name:** Bengals.

Student services. Adult student services, career counseling, student employment services, health services, minority student services, on-campus daycare, personal counseling, placement for graduates, veterans' counselor. **Physically disabled:** Services for visually, speech, hearing impaired.

Contact. E-mail: admissions@buffalostate.edu
Phone: (716) 878-5519 Fax: (716) 878-6100
Lesa Loritts, Director of Admissions, State University of New York College at Buffalo, 1300 Elmwood Avenue, Moot Hall, Buffalo, NY 14222-1095

State University of New York College at Cortland

Cortland, New York — **CB member**
www.cortland.edu — **CB code: 2538**

- Public 4-year university, liberal arts and teachers college
- Residential campus in large town
- 5,871 degree-seeking undergraduates: 2% part-time, 57% women, 3% African American, 1% Asian American, 4% Hispanic American, 1% Native American, 1% international
- 1,273 degree-seeking graduate students
- 48% of applicants admitted
- SAT or ACT (ACT writing recommended) required
- 57% graduate within 6 years

General. Founded in 1868. Regionally accredited. 13 study abroad programs in 11 countries. **Degrees:** 1,204 bachelor's awarded; master's offered. **ROTC:** Army, Air Force. **Location:** 35 miles from Syracuse, 18 miles from Ithaca. **Calendar:** Semester, limited summer session. **Full-time faculty:** 334 total; 65% have terminal degrees, 10% minority, 49% women. **Part-time faculty:** 221 total; 16% have terminal degrees, 7% minority, 53% women. **Class size:** 40% < 20, 45% 20-39, 4% 40-49, 5% 50-99, 1% >100. **Special facilities:** Outdoor education centers for field work, environmental center, geological field station, nature preserve for biological research.

Freshman class profile. 9,751 applied, 4,725 admitted, 1,110 enrolled.

Mid 50% test scores		GPA 2.0-2.99:	24%
SAT verbal:	500-580	Rank in top quarter:	40%
SAT math:	490-560	Rank in top tenth:	6%
GPA 3.50 or higher:	32%	Return as sophomores:	75%
GPA 3.0-3.49:	43%		

Basis for selection. Secondary school record, standardized test scores very important. Recommendations, personal statement, extracurricular activities, talent/ability, and class rank important. Additional consideration given for interview, alumni/ae relation, geographical residence, state residency, minority status, volunteer work, and work experience. Audition required for special talent: music program; portfolio recommended for special talent: art program.

High school preparation. 20 units required; 23 recommended. Required and recommended units include English 4, mathematics 3-4, social studies 4, science 3-4 (laboratory 3) and foreign language 3-4. 2 units in math, science, or foreign language can be compensated for by 4+ units or advanced course work in another one of the three areas.

2005-2006 Annual costs. Tuition/fees: $5,341; $11,601 out-of-state. Room/board: $7,650. Books/supplies: $800. Personal expenses: $1,320.

2004-2005 Financial aid. **Need-based:** 977 full-time freshmen applied for aid; 687 were judged to have need; 671 of these received aid. Average need met was 73%. Average scholarship/grant was $3,384; average loan $2,624. 45% of total undergraduate aid awarded as scholarships/grants, 55% as loans/jobs. **Non-need-based:** Awarded to 1,158 full-time undergraduates, including 220 freshmen. Scholarships awarded for academics, leadership.

Application procedures. **Admission:** Priority date 3/1; no deadline. $40 fee, may be waived for applicants with need. Application may be submitted online. Admission notification on a rolling basis beginning on or about 1/2. Must reply by May 1 or within 4 week(s) if notified thereafter. **Financial aid:** Closing date 4/1. FAFSA required. Applicants notified on a rolling basis starting 3/1; must reply by 5/1 or within 2 week(s) of notification.

Academics. **Special study options:** Combined bachelor's/graduate degree, cooperative education, cross-registration, distance learning, double major, dual enrollment of high school students, exchange student, honors, independent study, internships, liberal arts/career combination, student-designed major, study abroad, teacher certification program, Washington semester. Students eligible to participate in more than 400 international study programs offered via SUNY. **Credit/placement by examination:** CLEP, IB, institutional tests. 30 credit hours maximum toward bachelor's degree. **Support services:** Learning center, pre-admission summer program, reduced course load, study skills assistance, tutoring, writing center.

Majors. **Area/ethnic studies:** African-American. **Biology:** General. **Business:** General, management science. **Communications:** Broadcast journalism, health, journalism, organizational, public relations. **Education:** General, biology, chemistry, Deaf/hearing impaired, elementary, English, foreign languages, French, health, mathematics, middle, physical, physics, science, secondary, social studies, Spanish, special, speech. **Foreign languages:** French, Spanish. **Health:** Audiology/speech pathology. **History:** General. **Math:** General. **Parks/recreation:** General, exercise sciences, health/fitness. **Philosophy/religion:** Philosophy. **Physical sciences:** Chemistry, geochemistry, geology, physics, planetary. **Psychology:** General. **Social sciences:** Anthropology, criminology, economics, geography, international relations, political science, sociology. **Visual/performing arts:** Studio arts.

Most popular majors. Communications/journalism 7%, education 52%, parks/recreation 10%, social sciences 12%.

Computing on campus. 832 workstations in dormitories, library, computer center, student center. Dormitories linked to campus network. Commuter students can connect to campus network. Online course registration, online library, helpline, repair service available.

Student life. **Freshman orientation:** Available, $100 fee. **Policies:** Freshmen permitted cars on campus. **Housing:** Guaranteed on-campus for all undergraduates. Coed dorms, apartments, fraternity/sorority housing available. $150 deposit, deadline 5/1. **Activities:** Bands, choral groups, dance, drama, film society, literary magazine, music ensembles, musical theater, radio station, student government, student newspaper, symphony orchestra, TV station, Amnesty International, hunger homelessness coalition, New York Public Interest Research Group, Black, Latin, Jewish, & Asian student unions, community service council, Big Brothers/Big Sisters, Adopt-a-Grandparent program.

Athletics. NCAA. **Intercollegiate:** Baseball M, basketball, cross-country, diving, field hockey W, football (non-tackle) M, football (tackle) M, golf W, gymnastics W, ice hockey, lacrosse, racquetball, soccer, softball W, swimming, tennis W, track and field, volleyball W, wrestling M. **Intramural:** Archery, badminton, basketball, bowling, football (non-tackle), golf, racquetball, soccer, softball, table tennis, tennis, volleyball, water polo, weight lifting. **Team name:** Red Dragons.

Student services. Adult student services, campus ministries, career counseling, student employment services, financial aid counseling, health services, on-campus daycare, personal counseling, placement for graduates, veterans' counselor. **Physically disabled:** Services for visually, speech, hearing impaired.

Contact. E-mail: admissions@cortland.edu
Phone: (607) 753-4712 Fax: (607) 753-5998
Mark Yacavone, Director of Admissions, State University of New York College at Cortland, PO Box 2000, Cortland, NY 13045-0900

State University of New York College at Fredonia

Fredonia, New York — **CB member**
www.fredonia.edu — **CB code: 2539**

- Public 4-year liberal arts college
- Residential campus in large town
- 5,026 degree-seeking undergraduates: 4% part-time, 58% women, 2% African American, 2% Asian American, 3% Hispanic American, 1% Native American
- 372 degree-seeking graduate students
- 55% of applicants admitted
- SAT or ACT (ACT writing optional) required
- 63% graduate within 6 years

General. Founded in 1826. Regionally accredited. **Degrees:** 1,053 bachelor's awarded; master's offered. **Location:** 45 miles from Buffalo, 50 miles from Erie, Pennsylvania. **Calendar:** Semester, limited summer session. **Full-time faculty:** 245 total; 82% have terminal degrees, 10% minority, 43% women. **Part-time faculty:** 160 total; 22% have terminal degrees, 8% minority, 47% women. **Class size:** 51% < 20, 37% 20-39, 5% 40-49, 6% 50-99, 2% >100. **Special facilities:** Arts center, communication lab, greenhouse, education and local history museums.

Freshman class profile. 5,902 applied, 3,275 admitted, 1,106 enrolled.

Mid 50% test scores		**Rank in top tenth:**	17%
SAT verbal:	520-600	**End year in good standing:**	84%
SAT math:	520-600	**Return as sophomores:**	85%
ACT:	21-26	**Out-of-state:**	1%
GPA 3.50 or higher:	49%	**Live on campus:**	89%
GPA 3.0-3.49:	39%	**Fraternities:**	10%
GPA 2.0-2.99:	12%	**Sororities:**	4%
Rank in top quarter:	45%		

Basis for selection. Academic achievement, test results, and subjects taken given priority. Counselor recommendations, resume with supporting materials important when priority credentials marginal. Essay required for all media arts programs, recommended for others. Audition required for acting, music, musical performance, musical theater, production design. Portfolio required for art, computer art, media arts. **Homeschooled:** Submit all documentation of subject areas covered.

High school preparation. 16 units required; 19 recommended. Required and recommended units include English 4, mathematics 3-4, social studies 4, science 3-4, foreign language 3 and academic electives 2.

2005-2006 Annual costs. Tuition/fees: $5,441; $11,701 out-of-state. Room/board: $7,570. Books/supplies: $1,000. Personal expenses: $729.

2005-2006 Financial aid. **Need-based:** 927 full-time freshmen applied for aid; 604 were judged to have need; 595 of these received aid. Average need met was 68%. Average scholarship/grant was $3,541; average loan $2,888. 41% of total undergraduate aid awarded as scholarships/grants, 59% as loans/jobs. **Non-need-based:** Awarded to 718 full-time undergraduates, including 271 freshmen. Scholarships awarded for academics, alumni affiliation, art, leadership, minority status, music/drama.

Application procedures. **Admission:** No deadline. $40 fee, may be waived for applicants with need. Application may be submitted online. Admission notification on a rolling basis beginning on or about 12/15. Must reply by May 1 or within 4 week(s) if notified thereafter. **Financial aid:** Priority date 1/31, closing date 5/15. FAFSA required. Applicants notified on a rolling basis starting 3/10; must reply within 4 week(s) of notification.

Academics. Extensive interdisciplinary studies degree programs offered. **Special study options:** Combined bachelor's/graduate degree, cooperative education, cross-registration, distance learning, double major, dual enrollment of high school students, ESL, exchange student, honors, independent study, internships, liberal arts/career combination, student-designed major, study abroad, teacher certification program, Washington semester. Albany semester, over 90 exchange programs within SUNY system, 13 universities in engineering. **Credit/placement by examination:** AP, CLEP, IB. 30 credit hours maximum toward bachelor's degree. **Support services:** Learning center, study skills assistance, tutoring.

Majors. **Area/ethnic studies:** American. **Biology:** General, biochemistry, biotechnology, human/medical genetics. **Business:** Accounting, business admin, communications, finance, management information systems, management science. **Communications:** General, broadcast journalism, public relations. **Computer sciences:** General. **Conservation:** Environmental studies. **Education:** General, biology, chemistry, early childhood, elementary, English, foreign languages, French, mathematics, music, physics, secondary, social studies, Spanish, speech, speech impaired. **Foreign languages:** French, Spanish. **Health:** Audiology/speech pathology, clinical lab technology, communication disorders, music therapy. **History:** General. **Legal studies:** General, prelaw. **Math:** General. **Philosophy/religion:** Philosophy. **Physical sciences:** Chemistry, geochemistry, geology, geophysics, physics, planetary. **Protective services:** Criminal justice. **Psychology:** General. **Public administration:** Social work. **Social sciences:** Economics, political science, sociology. **Visual/performing arts:** Art, art history/conservation, ceramics, commercial/advertising art, dramatic, drawing, music history, music management, music performance, music theory/composition, painting, piano/organ, printmaking, sculpture, studio arts, theater design, voice/opera.

Most popular majors. Business/marketing 12%, communications/journalism 11%, education 36%, psychology 7%, social sciences 9%, visual/performing arts 8%.

Computing on campus. 500 workstations in dormitories, library, computer center. Dormitories wired for high-speed internet access and linked to campus network. Commuter students can connect to campus network. Online course registration, online library, helpline, repair service available.

Student life. Freshman orientation: Available, $105 fee. Preregistration for classes offered. 2-day program with students and parents in late June and early July; attendance strongly recommended. **Policies:** Freshmen permitted cars on campus. **Housing:** Guaranteed on-campus for all undergraduates. Coed dorms, single-sex dorms, apartments, substance-free housing available. $50 fully refundable deposit, deadline 5/1. **Activities:** Bands, choral groups, dance, drama, literary magazine, music ensembles, musical theater, opera, radio station, student government, student newspaper, symphony orchestra, TV station, campus ministry, Newman Club, Black student union, Young Republicans, service fraternities and sororities, Jewish student union, Young Democrats, Native American Student Association, Latinos Unidos, Intervarsity Christian Fellowship.

Athletics. NCAA. **Intercollegiate:** Baseball M, basketball, cross-country, ice hockey M, lacrosse W, soccer, softball W, swimming, tennis W, track and field, volleyball W. **Intramural:** Baseball M, basketball, field hockey W, handball, ice hockey, lacrosse M, racquetball, soccer, softball, volleyball, water polo. **Team name:** Blue Devils.

Student services. Alcohol/substance abuse counseling, campus ministries, career counseling, student employment services, financial aid counseling, health services, legal services, minority student services, on-campus daycare, personal counseling, placement for graduates, veterans' counselor. **Physically disabled:** Services for speech impaired.

Contact. E-mail: admissionsinq@fredonia.edu
Phone: (716) 673-3251 Toll-free number: (800) 252-1212
Fax: (716) 673-3249
Michael Bleecher, Director of Admissions, State University of New York College at Fredonia, 178 Central Avenue, Fredonia, NY 14063-1136

State University of New York College at Geneseo

Geneseo, New York — **CB member**
www.geneseo.edu — **CB code: 2540**

- Public 4-year liberal arts college
- Residential campus in small town
- 5,292 degree-seeking undergraduates: 2% part-time, 59% women
- 155 degree-seeking graduate students
- 41% of applicants admitted
- SAT or ACT (ACT writing optional), application essay required
- 79% graduate within 6 years; 41% enter graduate study

General. Founded in 1871. Regionally accredited. **Degrees:** 1,257 bachelor's awarded; master's offered. **ROTC:** Army, Air Force. **Location:** 30 miles from Rochester. **Calendar:** Semester, limited summer session. **Full-time faculty:** 242 total; 87% have terminal degrees, 12% minority, 39% women. **Part-time faculty:** 88 total; 19% have terminal degrees, 8% minority, 47% women. **Class size:** 22% < 20, 59% 20-39, 9% 40-49, 6% 50-99, 3% >100. **Special facilities:** Nuclear accelerator, planetarium, 3 theaters, ice arena, arboretum, Olympic-size pool.

Freshman class profile. 10,448 applied, 4,317 admitted, 1,029 enrolled.

Mid 50% test scores			
SAT verbal:	600-670	Rank in top quarter:	89%
SAT math:	600-670	Rank in top tenth:	51%
ACT:	26-29	End year in good standing:	90%
GPA 3.50 or higher:	79%	Return as sophomores:	90%
GPA 3.0-3.49:	16%	Out-of-state:	1%
GPA 2.0-2.99:	5%	Live on campus:	100%
		International:	2%

Basis for selection. Rigor of high school preparation, high school GPA, class rank, test scores, school and community activities, special talent, leadership, personal essay important. Special consideration given to minority applicants, children and grandchildren of alumni. Interview recommended for all; audition required for dramatic arts, music programs; portfolio recommended for art programs. **Homeschooled:** State high school equivalency certificate required.

High school preparation. College-preparatory program recommended. 20 units recommended. Recommended units include English 4, mathematics 4, social studies 4, science 4 and foreign language 4. Music, art also recommended. 4 mathematics required for computer science and business majors.

2005-2006 Annual costs. Tuition/fees: $5,520; $11,780 out-of-state. Room/board: $7,750. Books/supplies: $800. Personal expenses: $750.

2005-2006 Financial aid. Need-based: 856 full-time freshmen applied for aid; 434 were judged to have need; 434 of these received aid. Average need met was 75%. Average scholarship/grant was $2,450; average loan $3,495. 43% of total undergraduate aid awarded as scholarships/grants, 57% as loans/jobs. **Non-need-based:** Awarded to 965 full-time undergraduates, including 245 freshmen. Scholarships awarded for academics, art, leadership, minority status, music/drama, religious affiliation, ROTC, state residency.

Application procedures. Admission: Closing date 1/15 (postmark date). $40 fee, may be waived for applicants with need. Application may be submitted online. Admission notification on a rolling basis beginning on or about 3/15. Must reply by 5/1. **Financial aid:** Closing date 2/15. FAFSA required. Applicants notified on a rolling basis starting 3/15; must reply by 5/1.

Academics. Special study options: Combined bachelor's/graduate degree, cross-registration, double major, honors, independent study, internships, study abroad, teacher certification program, Washington semester. Albany semester, 3-2 engineering, 4-1 MBA, 2-3 physical therapy, 3-4 dentistry, 3-4 optometry, 3-4 osteopathic medicine. **Credit/placement by examination:** AP, CLEP, IB, institutional tests. 30 credit hours maximum toward bachelor's degree. **Support services:** Learning center, pre-admission summer program, reduced course load, study skills assistance, tutoring, writing center.

Majors. Area/ethnic studies: African-American, American. **Biology:** General, biochemistry, biophysics. **Business:** General, accounting, business admin. **Communications:** General. **Computer sciences:** General. **Education:** Biology, chemistry, elementary, English, French, history, mathematics, physics, science, social studies, Spanish, special. **Foreign languages:** Comparative lit, French, Spanish. **Health:** Communication disorders. **History:** General. **Interdisciplinary:** Natural sciences. **Legal studies:** Prelaw. **Math:** General. **Philosophy/religion:** Philosophy. **Physical sciences:** Chemistry, geochemistry, geology, geophysics, physics. **Psychology:** General. **Social sciences:** Anthropology, economics, geography, international relations, political science, sociology. **Visual/performing arts:** Art history/conservation, dramatic, music performance, studio arts.

Most popular majors. Biology 8%, business/marketing 14%, communications/journalism 6%, education 20%, English 8%, history 6%, psychology 9%, social sciences 11%.

Computing on campus. 900 workstations in dormitories, library, computer center, student center. Dormitories wired for high-speed internet access and linked to campus network. Commuter students can connect to campus network. Online course registration, helpline, student web hosting, wireless network available.

Student life. Freshman orientation: Available, $140 fee. Preregistration for classes offered. 2 sessions, 2 days each, during July. **Policies:** Freshmen permitted cars on campus. **Housing:** Guaranteed on-campus for freshmen. Coed dorms, substance-free housing available. $150 deposit, deadline 5/1. Special interest housing available. Some fraternities/sororities have housing independent of college. **Activities:** Jazz band, choral groups, dance, drama, literary magazine, music ensembles, musical theater, radio station, student government, student newspaper, symphony orchestra, TV station, 166 organizations and clubs, interfaith center.

Athletics. NCAA. **Intercollegiate:** Basketball, cross-country, diving, equestrian W, field hockey W, ice hockey M, lacrosse, soccer, softball W, swimming, tennis W, track and field, volleyball W. **Intramural:** Badminton, basketball, football (non-tackle), golf, handball, ice hockey M, racquetball, rugby, skiing, soccer, softball, squash, swimming, table tennis, volleyball, water polo M. **Team name:** Blue Knights, Lady Knights.

Student services. Alcohol/substance abuse counseling, campus ministries, career counseling, services for economically disadvantaged, student employment services, health services, minority student services, personal counseling, placement for graduates, veterans' counselor, women's services. **Physically disabled:** Services for visually, speech, hearing impaired.

Contact. E-mail: admissions@geneseo.edu
Phone: (585) 245-5571 Toll-free number: (866) 245-5211
Fax: (585) 245-5550
Kris Shay, Director of Admissions, State University of New York College at Geneseo, 1 College Circle, Geneseo, NY 14454-1471

State University of New York College at Old Westbury

Old Westbury, New York CB member
www.oldwestbury.edu CB code: 2866

- Public 4-year university and liberal arts college
- Commuter campus in small city
- 3,215 degree-seeking undergraduates: 16% part-time, 61% women, 28% African American, 7% Asian American, 16% Hispanic American, 2% international
- 25 degree-seeking graduate students
- 59% of applicants admitted
- SAT or ACT with writing required
- 31% graduate within 6 years; 100% enter graduate study

General. Founded in 1965. Regionally accredited. Curricular focus on interdisciplinary and multicultural academic programs. **Degrees:** 654 bachelor's awarded; master's offered. **ROTC:** Army, Air Force. **Location:** 25 miles from New York City. **Calendar:** Semester, limited summer session. **Full-time faculty:** 129 total; 75% have terminal degrees, 33% minority, 56% women. **Part-time faculty:** 124 total; 25% have terminal degrees, 25% minority, 46% women. **Class size:** 35% < 20, 64% 20-39, less than 1% 40-49. **Special facilities:** Language lab, performing arts theatre, recital hall, science laboratories.

Freshman class profile. 3,267 applied, 1,941 admitted, 404 enrolled.

Mid 50% test scores			
SAT verbal:	440-520	Rank in top tenth:	4%
SAT math:	450-530	Return as sophomores:	75%
ACT:	16-21	Out-of-state:	1%
GPA 3.50 or higher:	6%	Live on campus:	69%
GPA 3.0-3.49:	18%	International:	1%
GPA 2.0-2.99:	72%	Fraternities:	1%
Rank in top quarter:	30%	Sororities:	1%

Basis for selection. High school GPA, SAT scores, letters of recommendation, interview, personal essay important. Essay and interview recommended for academically weak students.

High school preparation. 22 units required. Required units include English 4, mathematics 3, social studies 2, history 2, science 3 (laboratory 3), foreign language 2 and academic electives 3.

2005-2006 Annual costs. Tuition/fees: $5,071; $11,331 out-of-state. Room/board: $8,082. Books/supplies: $675. Personal expenses: $1,210.

2005-2006 Financial aid. Need-based: 334 full-time freshmen applied for aid; 332 were judged to have need; 296 of these received aid. Average need met was 45.05%. Average scholarship/grant was $5,645; average loan $1,661. 65% of total undergraduate aid awarded as scholarships/grants, 35% as loans/jobs. **Non-need-based:** Awarded to 23 full-time undergraduates, including 10 freshmen. Scholarships awarded for academics.

Application procedures. Admission: Priority date 12/1; no deadline. $40 fee, may be waived for applicants with need. Application may be submitted online. Admission notification on a rolling basis beginning on or about 2/15. Must reply by May 1 or within 2 week(s) if notified thereafter. **Financial aid:** Closing date 4/13. FAFSA, institutional form required. Applicants notified on a rolling basis starting 4/24; must reply within 2 week(s) of notification.

Academics. All freshmen enroll in First Year Experience program. **Special study options:** Combined bachelor's/graduate degree, cross-registration, distance learning, double major, ESL, exchange student, honors, independent study, internships, liberal arts/career combination, study abroad, teacher certification program. Minority access to research careers, minority biomedical research. **Credit/placement by examination:** AP, CLEP. 30 credit hours maximum toward bachelor's degree. Each department has own policy for accepting credit by examination in fulfillment of departmental requirements. 8 credits awarded for minimum of 2 years of active duty in any branch of military service. Veterans may also apply for credit based on specific formal courses of instruction given by military services. **Support services:** Learning center, pre-admission summer program, reduced course load, remedial instruction, study skills assistance, tutoring, writing center.

Honors college/program. Students can apply to program during second semester of freshman year. Admission based on high school transcripts, current GPA (minimum 3.2), written essay, videotape or other creative work, recommendations from teachers, and indications of community service. Alll students must retain 3.2 GPA as freshmen and sophomores; 3.3 in junior year; and 3.4 to graduate from the Honors Program.

Majors. Area/ethnic studies: American. **Biology:** General, biochemistry. **Business:** Accounting, business admin, finance, labor relations, marketing. **Communications:** General. **Computer sciences:** General, information systems. **Education:** Bilingual, biology, chemistry, early childhood, elementary, foreign languages, mathematics, middle, science, secondary, social studies, special. **English:** English lit. **Foreign languages:** Comparative lit, Spanish. **Liberal arts:** Arts/sciences, humanities. **Math:** General. **Philosophy/religion:** Philosophy. **Physical sciences:** Chemistry. **Psychology:** General. **Social sciences:** General, criminology, sociology. **Visual/performing arts:** General, art.

Most popular majors. Business/marketing 33%, communications/journalism 6%, computer/information sciences 10%, education 13%, psychology 10%, social sciences 12%.

Computing on campus. 350 workstations in library, computer center, student center. Dormitories wired for high-speed internet access. Online course registration, online library, helpline, wireless network available.

Student life. Freshman orientation: Mandatory, $100 fee. Preregistration for classes offered. All newly-admitted students required to attend. Held in summer, prior to fall term, for 3 days. **Policies:** Freshmen permitted cars on campus. **Housing:** Guaranteed on-campus for all undergraduates. Coed dorms, substance-free housing available. $50 deposit. **Activities:** Choral groups, dance, drama, film society, radio station, student government, student newspaper, TV station, Women's Center, International Student Association, Alianza Latina, African People's Organization, Big Brother/Big Sister Club, Asian Club, Access for All, Council for Unity, Shekinah Chorale.

Athletics. NCAA. **Intercollegiate:** Baseball M, basketball, cross-country, soccer M, softball W, swimming, volleyball W. **Intramural:** Badminton, cheerleading W, equestrian, football (tackle), racquetball, soccer, softball, swimming, tennis, volleyball, weight lifting. **Team name:** Panthers.

Student services. Alcohol/substance abuse counseling, campus ministries, career counseling, services for economically disadvantaged, student employment services, financial aid counseling, health services, on-campus daycare, personal counseling. **Physically disabled:** Services for visually, hearing impaired.

Contact. E-mail: enroll@oldwestbury.edu
Phone: (516) 876-3073 Fax: (516) 876-3307
Mary Marquez Bell, Vice President of Enrollment Services, State University of New York College at Old Westbury, Box 307, Old Westbury, NY 11568-0307

State University of New York College at Oneonta

Oneonta, New York CB member
www.oneonta.edu CB code: 2542

- Public 4-year liberal arts college
- Residential campus in large town
- 5,589 degree-seeking undergraduates: 2% part-time, 57% women, 3% African American, 2% Asian American, 5% Hispanic American, 1% international
- 155 degree-seeking graduate students
- 45% of applicants admitted
- SAT or ACT (ACT writing optional), application essay required
- 53% graduate within 6 years; 47% enter graduate study

General. Founded in 1887. Regionally accredited. Institutional emphasis on individual student's academic and personal development, educational technology, and service-learning. **Degrees:** 1,222 bachelor's awarded; master's offered. **Location:** 75 miles from Albany, 175 miles from New York City. **Calendar:** Semester, extensive summer session. **Full-time faculty:** 252 total; 78% have terminal degrees, 17% minority, 43% women. **Part-time faculty:** 215 total; 17% have terminal degrees, 11% minority, 50% women. **Class size:** 42% < 20, 40% 20-39, 13% 40-49, 4% 50-99, 1% >100. **Special facilities:** Observatory, biological field station in Cooperstown, volunteer center, science discovery center, college camp, children's center.

Freshman class profile. 10,900 applied, 4,950 admitted, 1,145 enrolled.

Mid 50% test scores			
SAT verbal:	510-590	Rank in top quarter:	48%
SAT math:	520-600	Rank in top tenth:	11%
ACT:	21-25	End year in good standing:	93%
GPA 3.50 or higher:	22%	Return as sophomores:	80%
GPA 3.0-3.49:	67%	Out-of-state:	2%
GPA 2.0-2.99:	10%	Live on campus:	98%
		International:	2%

Basis for selection. School achievement record, curriculum, test scores most important. Personal experiences, motivations, awards, honors and recommendations considered. Students scoring below 420 on SAT math or below 450 on SAT verbal must take placement tests. High school writing sample can be submitted in place of essay; interview recommended.

High school preparation. 16 units required. Required and recommended units include English 4, mathematics 2-3, social studies 3, science 2-3 (laboratory 2) and foreign language 2-3. 15 specific units and 1 additional unit required in math, science, or foreign language.

2005-2006 Annual costs. Tuition/fees: $5,362; $11,622 out-of-state. Room/board: $7,400. Books/supplies: $850. Personal expenses: $1,070.

2005-2006 Financial aid. **Need-based:** 974 full-time freshmen applied for aid; 659 were judged to have need; 638 of these received aid. Average need met was 58%. Average scholarship/grant was $3,697; average loan $3,434. 49% of total undergraduate aid awarded as scholarships/grants, 51% as loans/jobs. **Non-need-based:** Awarded to 1,132 full-time undergraduates, including 286 freshmen. Scholarships awarded for academics, athletics.

Application procedures. **Admission:** Priority date 2/1; no deadline. $40 fee, may be waived for applicants with need. Application may be submitted online. Admission notification on a rolling basis beginning on or about 12/1. Must reply by May 1 or within 4 week(s) if notified thereafter. **Financial aid:** Priority date 2/15; no closing date. FAFSA required. Applicants notified on a rolling basis starting 3/1; must reply within 4 week(s) of notification.

Academics. **Special study options:** Combined bachelor's/graduate degree, cross-registration, distance learning, double major, honors, independent study, internships, liberal arts/career combination, New York semester, study abroad, teacher certification program, Washington semester. 3-1 program in fashion with Fashion Institute of Technology, 3-2 program in engineering with Alfred University, Clarkson University, Georgia Insitute of Technology, Polytechnic Institute of New York, Rensselaer Polytechnic Institute, SUNY at Binghamton, SUNY Buffalo, and Syracuse University, 2-2 program in forestry with SUNY College of Environmental Science and Forestry, 2-2 programs in physical therapy, medical technology, respiratory care, and cytotechnology with SUNY Upstate Medical University, combined bachelor's/graduate degree programs in accounting and management with SUNY Binghamton, 4-1 MBA program with Rochester Institute of Technology, 2-3 option in physical therapy with SUNY Upstate Medical University, 3-1 option in fashion marketing and 2-2 option in fashion design with American Intercontinental University in London. **Credit/placement by examination:** AP, CLEP, IB. 36 credit hours maximum toward bachelor's degree. **Support services:** Learning center, pre-admission summer program, reduced course load, remedial instruction, study skills assistance, tutoring, writing center.

Majors. **Area/ethnic studies:** African-American, Hispanic-American/Latino/Chicano. **Biology:** General, biochemistry. **Business:** Accounting, fashion, managerial economics. **Communications:** General, media studies. **Communications technology:** Animation/special effects. **Computer sciences:** General, computer graphics, computer science. **Conservation:** Environmental science. **Education:** Biology, chemistry, early childhood, elementary, English, family/consumer sciences, foreign languages, French, history, mathematics, multi-level teacher, physics, science, social science, Spanish. **English:** Speech/rhetoric. **Family/consumer sciences:** General, child development, clothing/textiles, family studies, food/nutrition. **Foreign languages:** French, Spanish. **History:** General. **Interdisciplinary:** Gerontology. **Math:** General, statistics. **Philosophy/religion:** Philosophy. **Physical sciences:** Atmospheric science, chemistry, geology, hydrology, physics. **Protective services:** Criminal justice. **Psychology:** General. **Social sciences:** Anthropology, economics, geography, political science, sociology. **Visual/performing arts:** Art history/conservation, dramatic, multimedia, music management, studio arts.

Most popular majors. Business/marketing 8%, communications/journalism 11%, education 25%, family/consumer sciences 8%, social sciences 7%, visual/performing arts 18%.

Computing on campus. 700 workstations in dormitories, library, computer center, student center. Dormitories wired for high-speed internet access and linked to campus network. Commuter students can connect to campus network. Online course registration, online library, helpline, student web hosting, wireless network available.

Student life. **Freshman orientation:** Available, $100 fee. Preregistration for classes offered. Meet adviser, select courses, register for classes. **Housing:** Guaranteed on-campus for freshmen. Coed dorms, substance-free housing available. $100 fully refundable deposit, deadline 5/1. Special interest housing options and apartment-style suites available within residence halls. **Activities:** Bands, choral groups, dance, drama, film society, literary magazine, music ensembles, musical theater, opera, radio station, student government, student newspaper, symphony orchestra, TV station, service organizations, Newman Club, Asian Student Union, international students organization, Hillel, HOLA Hispanic/Latino organization, Students of Color Coalition, Center for Social Responsibility and Community, Amnesty International, Students for a Free Tibet.

Athletics. NCAA. **Intercollegiate:** Baseball M, basketball, cross-country, field hockey W, lacrosse, soccer, softball W, swimming, tennis, track and field, volleyball W, wrestling M. **Intramural:** Basketball, football (non-tackle) W, soccer, softball, volleyball. **Team name:** Red Dragons.

Student services. Adult student services, alcohol/substance abuse counseling, campus ministries, career counseling, services for economically disadvantaged, student employment services, financial aid counseling, health services, minority student services, on-campus daycare, personal counseling, placement for graduates, veterans' counselor, women's services. **Physically disabled:** Services for visually, speech, hearing impaired.

Contact. E-mail: admissions@oneonta.edu
Phone: (607) 436-2524 Toll-free number: (800) 786-9123
Fax: (607) 436-3074
Karen Brown, Director of Admissions, State University of New York College at Oneonta, Admissions, Alumni Hall, Oneonta, NY 13820-4016

State University of New York College at Plattsburgh

Plattsburgh, New York — **CB member**
www.plattsburgh.edu — **CB code: 2544**

- Public 4-year liberal arts and teachers college
- Residential campus in large town
- 5,304 degree-seeking undergraduates: 5% part-time, 58% women, 5% African American, 2% Asian American, 4% Hispanic American, 6% international
- 528 degree-seeking graduate students
- 62% of applicants admitted
- SAT or ACT (ACT writing optional) required
- 54% graduate within 6 years

General. Founded in 1889. Regionally accredited. Residential satellite campus for biotechnology and environmental science majors. **Degrees:** 1,144 bachelor's awarded; master's offered. **Location:** 60 miles from Montreal, Canada, 30 miles from Burlington, Vermont. **Calendar:** Semester, limited summer session. **Full-time faculty:** 252 total; 92% have terminal degrees, 11% minority, 38% women. **Part-time faculty:** 203 total; 21% have terminal degrees, 6% minority, 55% women. **Class size:** 42% < 20, 42% 20-39, 10% 40-49, 6% 50-99, less than 1% >100. **Special facilities:** Sculpture courtyard, museum without walls, center for art, music, and theater, wilderness tract, planetarium, electron microscope, remote sensing laboratory, NMR spectrophotometer, computer operated infrared spectrophotometer, liquid scintillation counter, auditory research labs, research institute, speech and hearing clinic, Alzheimer's disease assistance center, virtual reality simulator lab, traumatic brain injury center, center for international programs and exchanges.

Freshman class profile. 5,321 applied, 3,278 admitted, 1,040 enrolled.

Mid 50% test scores			
SAT verbal:	470-560	Rank in top quarter:	33%
SAT math:	470-560	Rank in top tenth:	9%
ACT:	18-24	Return as sophomores:	77%
GPA 3.50 or higher:	11%	Out-of-state:	5%
GPA 3.0-3.49:	33%	Live on campus:	89%
GPA 2.0-2.99:	56%	International:	6%

Basis for selection. Curriculum, high school GPA, class rank, test scores most important. Trend of grades, school and community activities, personal interview, and recommendations also considered. Equal opportunity program for academically and financially disadvantaged students. Essay and interview recommended for all; audition recommended for music, theater programs; portfolio recommended for art programs.

High school preparation. 17 units required; 21 recommended. Required and recommended units include English 4, mathematics 3-4, social studies 3, history 1-2, science 3-4, foreign language 3 and academic electives 1. Chemistry required for biochemistry, medical technology, nursing, food and nutrition programs.

2005-2006 Annual costs. Tuition/fees: $5,297; $11,557 out-of-state. Room/board: $7,206. Books/supplies: $850. Personal expenses: $1,302.

2005-2006 Financial aid. **Need-based:** 846 full-time freshmen applied for aid; 618 were judged to have need; 606 of these received aid. Average need met was 85%. Average scholarship/grant was $5,102; average loan $4,023. 41% of total undergraduate aid awarded as scholarships/grants, 59%

as loans/jobs. **Non-need-based:** Awarded to 2,250 full-time undergraduates, including 563 freshmen. Scholarships awarded for academics, alumni affiliation, art, leadership, music/drama, state residency.

Application procedures. Admission: Priority date 3/1; deadline 8/1 (receipt date). $40 fee, may be waived for applicants with need. Application may be submitted online. Admission notification on a rolling basis beginning on or about 1/15. Must reply by May 1 or within 4 week(s) if notified thereafter. **Financial aid:** Priority date 3/1; no closing date. FAFSA required. Applicants notified on a rolling basis starting 3/31; must reply within 6 week(s) of notification.

Academics. Credit for military experience, pass/fail option. **Special study options:** Combined bachelor's/graduate degree, cooperative education, cross-registration, distance learning, double major, dual enrollment of high school students, ESL, exchange student, honors, independent study, internships, liberal arts/career combination, student-designed major, study abroad, teacher certification program. Semester and academic year programs in Canada, study opportunities abroad in Argentina, Australia, Chile, Uruguay, England, 3-2 program in engineering with Clarkson University, SUNY Stony Brook and Binghamton, Syracuse University, McGill University and University of Vermont, 3-4 BA/OD with SUNY College of Optometry, 4-1 BS/MBA with Clarkson University. **Credit/placement by examination:** AP, CLEP, IB, institutional tests. 30 credit hours maximum toward bachelor's degree. **Support services:** Learning center, pre-admission summer program, reduced course load, remedial instruction, study skills assistance, tutoring, writing center.

Majors. Area/ethnic studies: Canadian, Latin American. **Biology:** General, biochemistry, biotechnology, cell/histology. **Business:** General, accounting, business admin, finance, hotel/motel admin, international, marketing, restaurant/food services, tourism/travel. **Communications:** General, journalism. **Communications technology:** General. **Computer sciences:** General, computer science. **Conservation:** General. **Education:** Biology, chemistry, computer, early childhood, elementary, English, foreign languages, French, history, mathematics, multi-level teacher, physics, science, social science, social studies, Spanish, special. **Family/consumer sciences:** Child care, family/community services, food/nutrition. **Foreign languages:** French, Spanish. **Health:** Audiology/hearing, audiology/speech pathology, clinical lab science, cytotechnology, nursing (RN), predentistry, premedicine, prepharmacy, preveterinary, speech pathology. **History:** General. **Liberal arts:** Arts/sciences. **Math:** General. **Philosophy/religion:** Philosophy. **Physical sciences:** Chemistry, geology, physics. **Protective services:** Criminal justice. **Psychology:** General. **Public administration:** Social work. **Social sciences:** Anthropology, economics, geography, political science, sociology. **Visual/performing arts:** Art, art history/conservation, dramatic, photography, studio arts.

Most popular majors. Business/marketing 19%, communications/journalism 8%, education 18%, health sciences 6%, psychology 7%, social sciences 9%.

Computing on campus. 566 workstations in dormitories, library, computer center, student center. Dormitories wired for high-speed internet access and linked to campus network. Commuter students can connect to campus network. Online course registration, online library, helpline, repair service, student web hosting, wireless network available.

Student life. Freshman orientation: Available, $75 fee. Preregistration for classes offered. 2-night stay with meals included; simultaneous program for parents; includes course selection and registration. **Policies:** Freshmen permitted cars on campus. **Housing:** Guaranteed on-campus for all undergraduates. Coed dorms, special housing for disabled, substance-free housing available. $50 deposit. Living/learning communities available. **Activities:** Bands, choral groups, drama, film society, literary magazine, music ensembles, musical theater, radio station, student government, student newspaper, symphony orchestra, TV station, Akeba, El Pueblo, Environmental Action Committee, Hillel, Inter-Varsity Christian Fellowship, Newman Association, Points of View, College Democrats, College Republicans.

Athletics. NCAA. **Intercollegiate:** Baseball M, basketball, cross-country, golf, ice hockey, lacrosse M, soccer, softball W, swimming, tennis W, track and field, volleyball W. **Intramural:** Basketball, football (tackle) M, golf, ice hockey M, lacrosse M, racquetball, rugby, soccer, softball W, tennis W, volleyball, weight lifting. **Team name:** Cardinals.

Student services. Adult student services, alcohol/substance abuse counseling, campus ministries, career counseling, services for economically disadvantaged, student employment services, financial aid counseling, health services, legal services, minority student services, on-campus daycare, personal counseling, placement for graduates, veterans' counselor, women's services. **Physically disabled:** Services for visually, speech, hearing impaired.

Contact. E-mail: admissions@plattsburgh.edu
Phone: (518) 564-2040 Toll-free number: (888) 673-0012
Fax: (518) 564-2045
Richard Higgins, Associate Vice President for Enrollment Management, State University of New York College at Plattsburgh, Kehoe Administration Building, Plattsburgh, NY 12901

State University of New York College at Potsdam

Potsdam, New York — **CB member**
www.potsdam.edu — **CB code: 2545**

- Public 4-year liberal arts and teachers college
- Residential campus in large town
- 3,570 degree-seeking undergraduates: 3% part-time, 58% women, 2% African American, 1% Asian American, 2% Hispanic American, 2% Native American, 3% international
- 696 degree-seeking graduate students
- 73% of applicants admitted
- SAT or ACT (ACT writing optional) required
- 46% graduate within 6 years; 34% enter graduate study

General. Founded in 1816. Regionally accredited. First-year students may enroll in interdisciplinary program to study art, literature, science, and sociology of the Adirondacks. Extension offers undergraduate and graduate courses with emphasis on teacher education. **Degrees:** 662 bachelor's awarded; master's offered. **ROTC:** Army, Air Force. **Location:** 150 miles from Syracuse, 80 miles from Montreal, Canada. **Calendar:** Semester, limited summer session. **Full-time faculty:** 256 total; 79% have terminal degrees, 10% minority, 41% women. **Part-time faculty:** 110 total; 21% have terminal degrees, 3% minority, 57% women. **Class size:** 59% < 20, 35% 20-39, 4% 40-49, 2% 50-99, less than 1% >100. **Special facilities:** Electronic music and recording studios, planetarium, seismographic laboratory, 24-hour computer laboratory, concert hall, music theater, anthropology museum, biology museum, teaching resource center.

Freshman class profile. 3,423 applied, 2,512 admitted, 739 enrolled.

Mid 50% test scores		**Rank in top quarter:**	36%
SAT verbal:	480-590	**Rank in top tenth:**	12%
SAT math:	480-580	**End year in good standing:**	81%
ACT:	20-26	**Return as sophomores:**	76%
GPA 3.50 or higher:	33%	**Out-of-state:**	3%
GPA 3.0-3.49:	33%	**Live on campus:**	91%
GPA 2.0-2.99:	34%	**International:**	1%

Basis for selection. Admissions decisions based on secondary school record and standardized test scores. Class rank, talent, ability, activities and community service also important. Essays and interviews required for some, but not all applicants. Auditions required for music majors. Auditions encouraged for dance and drama majors. Portfolios encouraged for art majors. **Homeschooled:** GED required.

High school preparation. 16 units required; 21 recommended. Required and recommended units include English 4, mathematics 2-4, social studies 4, science 2-4 (laboratory 1-2) and foreign language 3-4. One year of art or music required.

2005-2006 Annual costs. Tuition/fees: $5,289; $11,549 out-of-state. Music Fee $300 (annual); Concert Fee $230 (annual) for the 2005-2006 academic year. Room/board: $7,670. Books/supplies: $900. Personal expenses: $1,200.

2005-2006 Financial aid. Need-based: 660 full-time freshmen applied for aid; 489 were judged to have need; 487 of these received aid. Average need met was 80%. Average scholarship/grant was $5,992; average loan $3,314. 54% of total undergraduate aid awarded as scholarships/grants, 46% as loans/jobs. **Non-need-based:** Awarded to 1,406 full-time undergraduates, including 392 freshmen. Scholarships awarded for academics, art, leadership, minority status, music/drama, ROTC. **Additional information:** Apply early to access limited, need-based awards.

Application procedures. Admission: No deadline. $40 fee, may be waived for applicants with need. Application may be submitted online. Admission notification on a rolling basis beginning on or about 10/1. Must reply by May 1 for guaranteed enrollment. **Financial aid:** Priority date 3/1; no closing date. FAFSA required. Applicants notified on a rolling basis starting 2/1; must reply within 4 week(s) of notification.

Academics. Special study options: Combined bachelor's/graduate degree, cross-registration, distance learning, double major, dual enrollment of high school students, exchange student, honors, independent study, internships, liberal arts/career combination, student-designed major, study abroad, teacher certification program. Combined degree options in engineering with Clarkson University and SUNY Binghamton; accounting, engineering or management with SUNY Utica/Rome. **Credit/placement by examination:** AP, CLEP, IB. Credit awarded for International Baccalaureate on course-by-course evaluation. **Support services:** Learning center, pre-admission summer program, reduced course load, study skills assistance, tutoring, writing center.

Majors. **Biology:** General, biochemistry. **Business:** Business admin, labor relations, managerial economics. **Computer sciences:** General. **Education:** Biology, chemistry, elementary, English, French, mathematics, music, physics, science, social studies, Spanish. **English:** English lit, speech/rhetoric. **Foreign languages:** French, Spanish. **Interdisciplinary:** Biological/physical sciences. **Liberal arts:** Arts/sciences, humanities. **Math:** General. **Philosophy/religion:** Philosophy. **Physical sciences:** Chemistry, geology, physics. **Protective services:** Law enforcement admin. **Psychology:** General. **Social sciences:** Anthropology, archaeology, economics, political science, sociology. **Visual/performing arts:** General, art, art history/conservation, dance, dramatic, music performance.

Most popular majors. Business/marketing 9%, education 27%, English 9%, history 6%, psychology 9%, social sciences 12%, visual/performing arts 12%.

Computing on campus. 515 workstations in dormitories, library, computer center, student center. Dormitories wired for high-speed internet access and linked to campus network. Commuter students can connect to campus network. Online course registration, online library, helpline, student web hosting, wireless network available.

Student life. **Freshman orientation:** Available, $165 fee. Preregistration for classes offered. Two-day program. **Policies:** Academic honor code outlines expectations for academic honesty and integrity; code of student rights, responsibilities, and conduct can be found in student handbook. Freshmen permitted cars on campus. **Housing:** Guaranteed on-campus for all undergraduates. Coed dorms, single-sex dorms, special housing for disabled, apartments, substance-free housing available. $50 fully refundable deposit, deadline 5/1. First-year experience housing available. **Activities:** Bands, choral groups, dance, drama, literary magazine, music ensembles, musical theater, opera, radio station, student government, student newspaper, symphony orchestra, Intervarsity Christian Fellowship, SUNY Potsdam Campaign Against Hunger and Homelessness, Black Student Alliance, Potsdam Association of Native Americans, Caribbean Latin American Student Society, Politics Association, Circle K, Student Unitarian Universalists of Northern New York, Lesbian, Gay, Bisexual and Transgender Association.

Athletics. NCAA. **Intercollegiate:** Basketball, cheerleading, cross-country, equestrian W, golf M, ice hockey M, lacrosse, soccer, softball W, swimming, tennis W, volleyball W. **Intramural:** Basketball, racquetball, volleyball. **Team name:** Bears.

Student services. Adult student services, alcohol/substance abuse counseling, campus ministries, career counseling, services for economically disadvantaged, student employment services, financial aid counseling, health services, legal services, minority student services, on-campus daycare, personal counseling, placement for graduates, veterans' counselor, women's services. **Physically disabled:** Services for visually, speech, hearing impaired.

Contact. E-mail: admissions@potsdam.edu
Phone: (315) 267-2180 Toll-free number: (877) 768-7326
Fax: (315) 267-2163
Thomas Nesbitt, Director of Admissions, State University of New York College at Potsdam, 44 Pierrepont Avenue, Potsdam, NY 13676

State University of New York College of Environmental Science and Forestry

Syracuse, New York **CB member**
www.esf.edu **CB code: 2530**

- Public 4-year university
- Residential campus in small city
- 1,372 degree-seeking undergraduates: 3% part-time, 37% women, 1% African American, 2% Asian American, 3% Hispanic American, 1% Native American, 1% international
- 484 degree-seeking graduate students
- 66% of applicants admitted
- SAT or ACT (ACT writing optional), application essay required
- 63% graduate within 6 years; 36% enter graduate study

General. Founded in 1911. Regionally accredited. Associate degree programs in forestry technology and land surveying technology offered through Ranger School at Wanakena in Adirondack Mountains. Institution focus on environmental science as design, engineering, life sciences and resource management. **Degrees:** 272 bachelor's, 42 associate awarded; master's, doctoral offered. **ROTC:** Army, Air Force. **Calendar:** Semester, limited summer session. **Full-time faculty:** 117 total; 86% have terminal degrees, 12% minority, 21% women. **Part-time faculty:** 31 total; 84% have terminal degrees, 42% women. **Special facilities:** 6 regional campuses and field stations used for field study and research, 25,000-acre multi-campus forest system, ecological center, wildlife collection, semicommercial paper mill.

Freshman class profile. 921 applied, 605 admitted, 260 enrolled.

Mid 50% test scores			
SAT verbal:	520-610	Rank in top tenth:	23%
SAT math:	520-620	End year in good standing:	90%
ACT:	22-27	Return as sophomores:	81%
Rank in top quarter:	53%	Out-of-state:	15%
		Live on campus:	90%

Basis for selection. High school record most important, test scores, essay, and recommendations also important. Applicant should have strong college preparatory program with focus on mathematics and science for most programs and design background preferred for Landscape Architecture. Interview or participation in informational program recommended for all; portfolio required for some landscape architecture applicants. **Homeschooled:** Statement describing homeschool structure and mission required. If no superintendent's statement provided, student must have GED to enroll.

High school preparation. Required and recommended units include English 4, mathematics 3-4, social studies 3, history 1, science 3-4 (laboratory 3-4) and foreign language 3.

2005-2006 Annual costs. Tuition/fees: $5,032; $11,292 out-of-state. Room and board available through Syracuse University. Books/supplies: $1,050. Personal expenses: $550.

2005-2006 Financial aid. **Need-based:** Average need met was 100%. Average scholarship/grant was $4,500; average loan $4,625. 48% of total undergraduate aid awarded as scholarships/grants, 52% as loans/jobs. **Non-need-based:** Scholarships awarded for academics.

Application procedures. **Admission:** Priority date 12/1; no deadline. $40 fee, may be waived for applicants with need. Application may be submitted online. Admission notification on a rolling basis beginning on or about 1/2. Must reply by May 1 or within 4 week(s) if notified thereafter. **Financial aid:** Priority date 3/1; no closing date. FAFSA required. Applicants notified on a rolling basis starting 3/15; must reply within 2 week(s) of notification.

Academics. **Special study options:** Combined bachelor's/graduate degree, cooperative education, cross-registration, double major, ESL, honors, independent study, internships, liberal arts/career combination, study abroad, teacher certification program. **Credit/placement by examination:** AP, CLEP, IB. **Support services:** Learning center, pre-admission summer program, reduced course load, remedial instruction, study skills assistance, tutoring, writing center.

Majors. **Agriculture:** Animal sciences. **Architecture:** Environmental design, landscape, urban/community planning. **Biology:** General, bacteriology, biochemistry, biotechnology, botany, cell/histology, conservation, ecology, entomology, environmental, genetics, marine, plant pathology, plant physiology, toxicology, wildlife, zoology. **Conservation:** General, environmental science, environmental studies, fisheries, forest resources, forestry, management/policy, wildlife. **Construction:** Maintenance. **Education:** Biology, chemistry, science. **Engineering:** Chemical, civil, construction, environmental, forest, materials, mechanical. **Engineering technology:** Construction. **Health:** Predentistry, premedicine, prepharmacy, preveterinary. **Interdisciplinary:** Biological/physical sciences, natural sciences. **Legal studies:** Prelaw. **Parks/recreation:** Facilities management. **Physical sciences:** Chemistry, polymer chemistry. **Public administration:** Policy analysis. **Social sciences:** Urban studies.

Most popular majors. Architecture 13%, biology 39%, engineering/engineering technologies 19%, natural resources/environmental science 26%.

Computing on campus. 150 workstations in dormitories, library, computer center. Dormitories wired for high-speed internet access and linked to campus network. Commuter students can connect to campus network. Online course registration, online library, helpline, wireless network available.

Student life. **Freshman orientation:** Mandatory, $50 fee. Preregistration for classes offered. 4-day program prior to start of classes. **Policies:** Freshmen permitted cars on campus. **Housing:** Coed dorms, special housing for disabled, apartments, cooperative housing, fraternity/sorority housing, substance-free housing available. $350 fully refundable deposit, deadline 5/1. All on-campus housing available through Syracuse University. School located adjacent to Syracuse University. **Activities:** Bands, choral groups, dance, drama, film society, literary magazine, music ensembles, musical theater, radio station, student government, student newspaper, symphony orchestra, Undergraduate Student Association, Alpha Xi Sigma, Wildlife Society, BAOBAB

Multicultural Organization, Student Environmental Action Coalition, Woodsmen's Team, Creative Minds club.

Athletics. Intramural: Basketball, football (non-tackle), weight lifting.

Student services. Adult student services, alcohol/substance abuse counseling, campus ministries, career counseling, services for economically disadvantaged, student employment services, financial aid counseling, health services, legal services, minority student services, on-campus daycare, personal counseling, placement for graduates, veterans' counselor, women's services. **Physically disabled:** Services for visually, speech, hearing impaired. **Learning disabled:** Comprehensive services available.

Contact. E-mail: esfinfo@esf.edu
Phone: (315) 470-6600 Toll-free number: (800) 777-7373
Fax: (315) 470-6933
Susan Sanford, Director of Admissions, State University of New York College of Environmental Science and Forestry, 106 Bray Hall, Syracuse, NY 13210

State University of New York Downstate Medical Center

Brooklyn, New York
www.downstate.edu **CB code: 2534**

- Public upper-division health science and nursing college
- Commuter campus in very large city
- Application essay, interview required

General. Founded in 1858. Regionally accredited. **Degrees:** 190 bachelor's awarded; master's, doctoral, first professional offered. **Articulation:** Agreements with St. Francis College, CUNY: Medgar Evers College. **Location:** 4 miles from downtown Brooklyn, 6 miles from downtown Manhattan. **Calendar:** Semester, limited summer session. **Full-time faculty:** 720 total. **Part-time faculty:** 160 total.

Student profile. 345 degree-seeking undergraduates, 1,222 graduate students. 100% entered as juniors. 80% transferred from two-year, 20% transferred from four-year institutions.

African American:	50%	**Out-of-state:**	1%
Asian American:	7%	**Live on campus:**	20%
Hispanic American:	7%	**25 or older:**	67%

Basis for selection. College transcript, application essay, interview required. College of Medicine applicants apply through AMCAS: $65 application fee. Rolling admissions for College of Nursing and College of Health-Related Professions: $30 fee. Each program has different admission requirements. RN/BS program requires New York State Registered Nurse license. Prerequisite courses vary by program. Transfer accepted as juniors.

2005-2006 Annual costs. Tuition/fees: $4,710; $10,970 out-of-state. Room/board: $11,774. Books/supplies: $1,264.

Application procedures. Admission: Deadline 4/1. $30 fee, may be waived for applicants with need. Closing dates for applications differ, depending on program, and begin December 15. **Financial aid:** FAFSA required.

Academics. Special study options: Combined bachelor's/graduate degree, liberal arts/career combination. **Credit/placement by examination:** AP, CLEP. **Support services:** Learning center, reduced course load, tutoring.

Majors. Health: Nursing (RN), physician assistant, sonography.

Student life. Housing: Coed dorms available. **Activities:** Student government, student newspaper.

Athletics. Intramural: Basketball M.

Student services. Health services.

Contact. E-mail: admissions@downstate.edu
Phone: (718) 270-2446
State University of New York Downstate Medical Center, 450 Clarkson Avenue, Box 60, Brooklyn, NY 11203-2098

State University of New York Empire State College

Saratoga Springs, New York **CB member**
www.esc.edu **CB code: 2214**

- Public 4-year liberal arts college
- Commuter campus in large town
- 8,485 degree-seeking undergraduates: 63% part-time, 59% women, 12% African American, 1% Asian American, 6% Hispanic American, 1% Native American, 8% international
- 464 degree-seeking graduate students
- 81% of applicants admitted
- Application essay required

General. Founded in 1971. Regionally accredited. No campus or classrooms; students meet with faculty and use facilities at regional centers and units throughout state. Centers in Genesee Valley (Rochester), Long Island (Old Westbury), Metropolitan New York, Hudson Valley (Hartsdale), and Buffalo. Coordinating center at Saratoga Springs. Units in Binghamton, Ithaca, Mid-Hudson (New Paltz), Mohawk Valley (Utica-Rome), North Country (Plattsburgh), Onondaga (Syracuse), Saratoga Springs, Watertown, Lebanon, Prague and several other locations. **Degrees:** 1,914 bachelor's, 734 associate awarded; master's offered. **Calendar:** Continuous. **Full-time faculty:** 153 total; 92% have terminal degrees, 12% minority, 54% women. **Part-time faculty:** 615 total.

Freshman class profile. 1,341 applied, 1,082 admitted, 463 enrolled.

Basis for selection. 2 principal requirements are: possession of high school diploma or its equivalent, and ability of an Empire State College learning location to meet applicant's explicit and implicit educational needs and objectives. College reserves the right to deny admission based on its inability to meet an applicant's needs.

2005-2006 Annual costs. Tuition/fees: $4,575; $10,835 out-of-state. Books/supplies: $2,100. Personal expenses: $900.

2004-2005 Financial aid. Need-based: 30% of total undergraduate aid awarded as scholarships/grants, 70% as loans/jobs.

Application procedures. Admission: No deadline. No application fee. Application may be submitted online. Admission notification on a rolling basis. **Financial aid:** No deadline. FAFSA required. Applicants notified on a rolling basis; must reply within 3 week(s) of notification.

Academics. Learning contracts between faculty mentors and students lead to program completion, opportunities to obtain credit for prior college level learning. **Special study options:** Accelerated study, combined bachelor's/graduate degree, cross-registration, distance learning, double major, dual enrollment of high school students, external degree, independent study, internships, student-designed major, study abroad. **Credit/placement by examination:** AP, CLEP. 40 credit hours maximum toward associate degree, 96 toward bachelor's. **Support services:** Writing center.

Majors. Business: General, labor relations. **Education:** General. **History:** General. **Interdisciplinary:** Biological/physical sciences. **Liberal arts:** Arts/sciences. **Psychology:** General. **Public administration:** Community org/advocacy. **Social sciences:** General, economics. **Visual/performing arts:** Studio arts.

Most popular majors. Business/marketing 42%, English 7%, interdisciplinary studies 6%, physical sciences 6%, psychology 7%, public administration/social services 20%.

Computing on campus. 100 workstations in computer center, student center. Commuter students can connect to campus network. Online course registration, online library, helpline available.

Student life. Freshman orientation: Mandatory, $50 fee.

Student services. Adult student services, career counseling, student employment services, veterans' counselor.

Contact. E-mail: admissions@esc.edu
Phone: (518) 587-2100 Fax: (518) 587-9759
Jennifer Riley, Assistant Director of Admissions, State University of New York Empire State College, 111 West Avenue, Saratoga Springs, NY 12866

State University of New York Institute of Technology at Utica/Rome

Utica, New York **CB member**
www.sunyit.edu **CB code: 0755**

- Public 4-year school of information systems & engineering technologies
- Commuter campus in small city
- 1,727 degree-seeking undergraduates: 29% part-time, 44% women, 7% African American, 2% Asian American, 3% Hispanic American, 1% Native American, 1% international
- 477 degree-seeking graduate students

- 43% of applicants admitted
- SAT or ACT (ACT writing recommended), application essay required

General. Founded in 1966. Regionally accredited. **Degrees:** 457 bachelor's awarded; master's offered. **ROTC:** Army. **Location:** 50 miles from Syracuse, 90 miles from Albany. **Calendar:** Semester, limited summer session. **Full-time faculty:** 95 total; 13% minority, 35% women. **Part-time faculty:** 67 total; 9% minority, 39% women. **Class size:** 61% < 20, 36% 20-39, 2% 40-49, less than 1% 50-99.

Freshman class profile. 1,015 applied, 438 admitted, 159 enrolled.

Mid 50% test scores			
SAT verbal:	540-620	End year in good standing:	61%
SAT math:	570-630	Return as sophomores:	83%
ACT:	26-29	Out-of-state:	1%
		Live on campus:	84%

Basis for selection. GED not accepted. Students must meet minimum SAT/ACT score ranges with competitive high school averages as well as minimum high school unit requirements. **Homeschooled:** Transcript of courses and grades required. Statement from local public school superintendent that verifies home school curriculum matches NYS Regents Curriculum required.

High school preparation. 17 units required; 25 recommended. Required and recommended units include English 4, mathematics 3-4, social studies 2, history 2, science 3-4 (laboratory 3-4), foreign language 3 and academic electives 2.

2005-2006 Annual costs. Tuition/fees: $5,285; $11,545 out-of-state. Room/board: $7,290. Books/supplies: $800. Personal expenses: $1,600.

2004-2005 Financial aid. Need-based: 77 full-time freshmen applied for aid; 62 were judged to have need; 61 of these received aid. Average need met was 83%. Average scholarship/grant was $2,236; average loan $2,196. 49% of total undergraduate aid awarded as scholarships/grants, 51% as loans/jobs. **Non-need-based:** Awarded to 284 full-time undergraduates, including 45 freshmen. Scholarships awarded for academics.

Application procedures. Admission: No deadline. $50 fee, may be waived for applicants with need. Application may be submitted online. Admission notification on a rolling basis. **Financial aid:** No deadline. FAFSA required. Applicants notified on a rolling basis starting 3/17; must reply within 2 week(s) of notification.

Academics. Special study options: Accelerated study, cross-registration, distance learning, double major, ESL, independent study, internships. **Credit/placement by examination:** CLEP, IB, SAT, ACT, institutional tests. Credit awarded for International Baccalaureate varies by academic department. **Support services:** Learning center, remedial instruction, study skills assistance, tutoring, writing center.

Majors. Business: General, accounting, business admin, finance. **Communications technology:** General. **Computer sciences:** General, information systems. **Engineering technology:** Civil, computer, electrical, industrial, mechanical. **Health:** Health care admin, medical records admin, nursing (RN). **Liberal arts:** Arts/sciences. **Math:** Applied. **Psychology:** General. **Social sciences:** Sociology.

Most popular majors. Business/marketing 24%, communications/journalism 6%, computer/information sciences 17%, engineering/engineering technologies 22%, health sciences 14%, psychology 8%, social sciences 6%.

Computing on campus. 410 workstations in dormitories, library, computer center. Dormitories wired for high-speed internet access and linked to campus network. Commuter students can connect to campus network. Online course registration, online library, student web hosting available.

Student life. Freshman orientation: Mandatory. **Policies:** Freshmen permitted cars on campus. **Housing:** Guaranteed on-campus for freshmen. Coed dorms, special housing for disabled available. **Activities:** Jazz band, radio station, student government, student newspaper, TV station, Black Student Union, international student organization, Latino student association.

Athletics. NCAA. **Intercollegiate:** Baseball M, basketball, cross-country, golf M, lacrosse M, soccer, softball W, volleyball W. **Intramural:** Badminton, basketball, bowling, golf, racquetball, soccer, softball, table tennis, tennis, volleyball. **Team name:** Wildcats.

Student services. Alcohol/substance abuse counseling, campus ministries, career counseling, services for economically disadvantaged, student employment services, financial aid counseling, health services, legal services, minority student services, personal counseling, placement for graduates, veterans' counselor, women's services. **Physically disabled:** Services for visually, speech, hearing impaired.

Contact. E-mail: admissions@sunyit.edu
Phone: (315) 792-7500 Toll-free number: (866) 278-6948
Fax: (315) 792-7837
Marybeth Lyons, Director of Admissions, State University of New York Institute of Technology at Utica/Rome, Box 3050, Utica, NY 13504-3050

State University of New York Maritime College

Throggs Neck, New York — **CB member**
www.sunymaritime.edu — **CB code: 2536**

- Public 4-year maritime college
- Residential campus in very large city
- 1,150 degree-seeking undergraduates
- 70% of applicants admitted
- SAT or ACT (ACT writing optional) required

General. Founded in 1874. Regionally accredited. Graduates eligible for commission as officers in Navy, Marine Corps, Coast Guard, Air Force, and commissioned Corps of the National Oceanic and Atmospheric Administration. 3 summer semesters at sea and regiment option required for students interested in obtaining U.S. Merchant Marine Officer's License. **Degrees:** 124 bachelor's, 5 associate awarded; master's offered. **ROTC:** Army, Navy, Air Force. **Location:** 10 miles from New York City. **Calendar:** Semester, limited summer session. **Full-time faculty:** 60 total. **Part-time faculty:** 15 total. **Class size:** 55% < 20, 39% 20-39, less than 1% 40-49, 4% 50-99, less than 1% >100. **Special facilities:** 565-foot training ship, training tanker, Center for Simulated Marine Operations, bridge simulator, model basin and towing tank, CAD-CAM facilities, 2 diesel propulsion simulators, maritime museum, sailing center including several 1-ton ocean racers.

Freshman class profile. 1,097 applied, 768 admitted, 338 enrolled.

Mid 50% test scores			
SAT verbal:	490-570	Out-of-state:	28%
SAT math:	520-610	Live on campus:	98%

Basis for selection. Quality and strength of preparation, school achievement record, including first semester senior grades, class rank, test scores, extracurricular activities considered. Interview and essay recommended.

High school preparation. 12 units required. Required and recommended units include English 4, mathematics 3-4, social studies 2, science 3 (laboratory 2-3) and foreign language 3. Mathematics requirement includes algebra, geometry, trigonometry; mathematics beyond trigonometry recommended. Chemistry or physics required; both strongly recommended.

2005-2006 Annual costs. Tuition/fees: $6,380; $12,640 out-of-state. Additional required uniform charges. Room/board: $8,200. Books/supplies: $700. Personal expenses: $1,500.

2005-2006 Financial aid. Non-need-based: Scholarships awarded for academics, ROTC, state residency. **Additional information:** All cadets who are United States citizens, physically qualified for Merchant Marine license, and not yet 25 at time of enrollment are eligible to apply for Student Incentive Payment (SIP) of $3,000 per year from Maritime Administration of the Department of Transportation. Out-of-state students who elect to participate in SIP pay in-state tuition fees.

Application procedures. Admission: Priority date 12/1; no deadline. $40 fee, may be waived for applicants with need. Application may be submitted online. Admission notification on a rolling basis beginning on or about 12/1. Must reply by May 1 or within 4 week(s) if notified thereafter. **Financial aid:** Priority date 2/15; no closing date. FAFSA, institutional form required. Applicants notified on a rolling basis starting 3/1; must reply by 3/15 or within 4 week(s) of notification.

Academics. Cadets acquire technical, professional, and leadership experience on training cruises to European and domestic ports during annual summer sea terms, while preparing for U.S. Merchant Marine Officer's License. **Special study options:** Cooperative education, independent study, internships, liberal arts/career combination, semester at sea, study abroad. **Credit/placement by examination:** CLEP, IB, institutional tests. 30 credit hours maximum toward bachelor's degree. **Support services:** Learning center, pre-admission summer program, reduced course load, study skills assistance, tutoring, writing center.

Majors. Business: General, business admin. **Conservation:** General. **Engineering:** General, electrical, marine, mechanical. **Liberal arts:** Arts/sciences. **Physical sciences:** Atmospheric science, oceanography.

Computing on campus. 120 workstations in dormitories, library, computer center. Dormitories wired for high-speed internet access and linked to

campus network. Online course registration, repair service, wireless network available.

Student life. Freshman orientation: Mandatory, $830 fee. Preregistration for classes offered. All incoming freshmen and transfers who pursue U.S. Merchant Marine Officer's License required to participate in 2-week indoctrination period including 4-day orientation program and 10-day military-style physical training period. **Policies:** Maritime students organized as regiment of cadets to foster personal growth, development, leadership training, and experience. In system of increasing responsibility and privilege, first-class cadets (seniors) are regimental officers ashore. Cadet officers are in charge of operation of training ship during summer sea terms. Participation in regiment is optional for some programs. **Housing:** Guaranteed on-campus for all undergraduates. Coed dorms available. $50 deposit, deadline 5/1. Most undergraduates required to live in on-campus housing. **Activities:** Bands, music ensembles, student government, student newspaper, Newman Club, Eagle Scout Fraternity, cultural club, Afro-Caribbean club, Emerald Society, Pershing Rifles, honor guard.

Athletics. NCAA. **Intercollegiate:** Baseball M, basketball, cross-country, diving, lacrosse M, rifle, rowing (crew), sailing, soccer, softball W, swimming, tennis M, volleyball W, wrestling M. **Intramural:** Basketball, cross-country, football (tackle), racquetball, sailing, skiing, soccer, softball, squash, table tennis, tennis, volleyball, weight lifting. **Team name:** Privateers.

Student services. Alcohol/substance abuse counseling, campus ministries, career counseling, services for economically disadvantaged, financial aid counseling, health services, personal counseling, placement for graduates, veterans' counselor.

Contact. E-mail: admissions@sunymaritime.edu
Phone: (718) 409-7220 Toll-free number: (800) 654-1874
Fax: (718) 409-7465
Tara Fay, Senior Associate Director of Admissions, State University of New York Maritime College, 6 Pennyfield Avenue, Throggs Neck, NY 10465-4198

State University of New York Upstate Medical University

Syracuse, New York
www.upstate.edu **CB code: 2547**

- Public upper-division health science and nursing college
- Residential campus in small city
- 48% of applicants admitted
- Application essay, interview required

General. Founded in 1834. Regionally accredited. Undergraduate level consists of upper-division programs. Affiliated with Crouse-Irving Memorial Hospital, Veteran's Administration Medical Center, Community General Hospital of Greater Syracuse, St. Joseph's Hospital Health Center, and Hutchings Psychiatric Center. **Degrees:** 106 bachelor's awarded; master's, doctoral, first professional offered. **Articulation:** Agreements with SUNY Alfred, SUNY Canton, SUNY Cobleskill, SUNY Cortland, SUNY Delhi, SUNY Geneseo, SUNY Morrisville, SUNY Oswego, SUNY Oneonta, Cayuga CC, Columbia-Greene CC, Finger Lakes CC, Genesee CC, Jefferson CC, Mohawk Valley CC, Monroe CC, Niagara County CC, North Country CC, Onondaga CC, Sullivan CC, Tompkins Cortland CC. **Location:** 250 miles from New York City, 150 miles from Buffalo. **Calendar:** Semester, limited summer session. **Full-time faculty:** 480 total. **Part-time faculty:** 215 total. **Class size:** 87% < 20, 10% 20-39, 1% 40-49, 1% 50-99, 1% >100. **Special facilities:** Institutionally owned and operated 350-bed hospital.

Student profile. 230 degree-seeking undergraduates, 964 degree-seeking graduate students. 637 applied as first time-transfer students, 308 admitted, 203 enrolled. 100% entered as juniors. 60% transferred from two-year, 40% transferred from four-year institutions.

Women:	71%	**International:**	3%
African American:	3%	**Part-time:**	35%
Asian American:	3%	**Out-of-state:**	2%
Hispanic American:	2%	**Live on campus:**	56%

Basis for selection. High school transcript, college transcript, application essay, interview required. Evaluation of academic performance in courses required for admission. Personal interviews, recommendations, and essay also important. Applicants must complete admissions course requirements prior to admission. Final decision made at discretion of admissions committee, regardless of applicant's prior academic standing. Transfer accepted as juniors, seniors.

2005-2006 Annual costs. Tuition/fees: $4,751; $11,011 out-of-state. Room only: $3,743. Books/supplies: $800. Personal expenses: $1,160.

Financial aid. All financial aid based on need.

Application procedures. Admission: Rolling admission. $40 fee, may be waived for applicants with need. Application must be submitted on paper. Application deadline for physical therapy program March 15. Cardiovascular perfusion program completes admission process March 1, and Cytotechnology deadline March 1. Preference to New York residents. High school seniors may apply for admission 2 years prior to intended date of entry. Transfer students apply in fall 1 year prior to intended date of entry. High school seniors may apply for early admission. **Financial aid:** FAFSA required.

Academics. Special study options: Combined bachelor's/graduate degree, independent study. **Credit/placement by examination:** AP, CLEP, institutional tests. 36 credit hours maximum toward bachelor's degree. **Support services:** Reduced course load, tutoring.

Majors. Health: Clinical lab science, cytotechnology, nursing (RN), perfusion technology, respiratory therapy technology.

Computing on campus. 34 workstations in dormitories, library, computer center, student center. Dormitories wired for high-speed internet access and linked to campus network. Commuter students can connect to campus network. Helpline, student web hosting, wireless network available.

Student life. Policies: Students under 21 are required to live on campus unless they are living at home. **Housing:** Guaranteed on-campus for all undergraduates. Coed dorms, apartments available. $150 fully refundable deposit, deadline 8/1. **Activities:** Student government, campus activities governing board, Diversity in Allied Health.

Athletics. Intramural: Basketball, handball, racquetball, softball, table tennis, tennis, volleyball, water polo.

Student services. Alcohol/substance abuse counseling, career counseling, financial aid counseling, health services, minority student services, on-campus daycare, personal counseling, placement for graduates, veterans' counselor.

Contact. E-mail: admiss@upstate.edu
Phone: (315) 464-4570 Toll-free number: (800) 736-2171
Fax: (315) 464-8867
Jennifer Welch, Director of Admissions, State University of New York Upstate Medical University, 766 Irving Avenue, Syracuse, NY 13210

Syracuse University

Syracuse, New York **CB member**
www.syracuse.edu **CB code: 2823**

- Private 4-year university
- Residential campus in small city
- 11,441 degree-seeking undergraduates: 1% part-time, 56% women, 6% African American, 6% Asian American, 5% Hispanic American, 3% international
- 5,825 graduate students
- 65% of applicants admitted
- SAT or ACT with writing, application essay required
- 79% graduate within 6 years; 18% enter graduate study

General. Founded in 1870. Regionally accredited. **Degrees:** 2,403 bachelor's, 8 associate awarded; master's, doctoral, first professional offered. **ROTC:** Army, Air Force. **Location:** 140 miles from Albany, 250 miles from New York. **Calendar:** Semester, extensive summer session. **Full-time faculty:** 865 total; 88% have terminal degrees, 18% minority, 34% women. **Part-time faculty:** 526 total; 7% minority, 51% women. **Class size:** 64% < 20, 25% 20-39, 3% 40-49, 6% 50-99, 2% >100. **Special facilities:** Computing network with wireless access, center for advanced technology in computer applications and software engineering, center for science and technology, laser spectroscopy laboratory, institute for sensory research, public and community service center, undergraduate research and innovative learning center, global collaboratory multimedia classroom, several museums.

Freshman class profile. 16,260 applied, 10,514 admitted, 3,248 enrolled.

Mid 50% test scores		**Rank in top tenth:**	44%
SAT verbal:	550-650	**Out-of-state:**	60%
SAT math:	570-670	**Live on campus:**	98%
GPA 3.50 or higher:	60%	**International:**	3%
GPA 3.0-3.49:	32%	**Fraternities:**	14%
GPA 2.0-2.99:	8%	**Sororities:**	25%
Rank in top quarter:	80%		

Basis for selection. Most important: strong performance in challenging, college preparatory curriculm from accredited secondary school, strong qualitative factors, good citizenship. Other items of importance, but not strongest: secondary school counselor evaluation, 2 academic recommendations, standardized test scores. Personal characteristics, talents and interests considered. Applicants considered for alternate programs if not admitted to first choice school, and applicants request additional consideration. Interview and portfolio required for art, architecture programs; interview and audition required for drama and music programs. **Homeschooled:** Transcript of courses and grades, interview, letter of recommendation (nonparent) required. Submit detailed course descriptions/syllabus used. 2 recommendations from someone outside home required. For financial aid eligibility, letter from local school district must be submitted acknowledging that curriculum taught in home meets with school district approval, OR GED.

High school preparation. 20 units required; 21 recommended. Required and recommended units include English 4, mathematics 3, social studies 3, science 3 (laboratory 3), foreign language 2-3 and academic electives 5.

2006-2007 Annual costs. Tuition/fees: $29,965. Room/board: $10,980. Books/supplies: $1,190. Personal expenses: $1,120.

2005-2006 Financial aid. Need-based: 2,377 full-time freshmen applied for aid; 1,929 were judged to have need; 1,929 of these received aid. Average need met was 84%. Average scholarship/grant was $16,600; average loan $3,800. 70% of total undergraduate aid awarded as scholarships/grants, 30% as loans/jobs. **Non-need-based:** Awarded to 2,746 full-time undergraduates, including 623 freshmen. Scholarships awarded for academics, art, athletics, music/drama, ROTC.

Application procedures. Admission: Closing date 1/1 (postmark date). $60 fee, may be waived for applicants with need. Application may be submitted online. Admission notification on a rolling basis beginning on or about 3/15. Must reply by 5/1. **Financial aid:** Closing date 2/1. FAFSA, CSS PROFILE required. Applicants notified by 4/1; must reply by 5/1.

Academics. Special study options: Accelerated study, cooperative education, distance learning, double major, dual enrollment of high school students, ESL, honors, independent study, internships, liberal arts/career combination, student-designed major, study abroad, teacher certification program. Undergraduate research program, preprofessional programs, minors. **Credit/placement by examination:** AP, CLEP, IB, institutional tests. 30 credit hours maximum toward bachelor's degree. **Support services:** Learning center, pre-admission summer program, study skills assistance, tutoring, writing center.

Majors. Architecture: Architecture, interior. **Area/ethnic studies:** African-American, American, Latin American, Russian/Slavic, women's. **Biology:** General, biochemistry. **Business:** Accounting, business admin, entrepreneurial studies, finance, hospitality admin, marketing, retailing. **Communications:** General, advertising, broadcast journalism, journalism, public relations, radio/tv. **Computer sciences:** General, computer graphics, computer science, information systems, information technology. **Conservation:** General, environmental studies. **Education:** Art, biology, chemistry, early childhood, elementary, English, mathematics, middle, music, physical, physics, science, secondary, social studies, special. **Engineering:** General, aerospace, biomedical, chemical, civil, computer, electrical, environmental, mechanical, physics. **English:** British lit, English lit, speech/rhetoric. **Family/consumer sciences:** Clothing/textiles, consumer economics, family studies, food/nutrition. **Foreign languages:** General, classics, comparative lit, French, German, Italian, linguistics, Russian, Spanish. **Health:** Audiology/speech pathology, communication disorders, predentistry, premedicine, preveterinary. **History:** General, American. **Interdisciplinary:** Medieval/Renaissance, nutrition sciences. **Legal studies:** Prelaw. **Math:** General. **Parks/recreation:** Exercise sciences, health/fitness, sports admin. **Philosophy/religion:** Philosophy, religion. **Physical sciences:** Chemistry, geology, physics. **Psychology:** General. **Public administration:** Policy analysis, social work. **Social sciences:** Anthropology, economics, geography, international relations, political science, sociology. **Visual/performing arts:** General, acting, art history/conservation, ceramics, cinematography, commercial photography, commercial/advertising art, dramatic, fashion design, fiber arts, graphic design, illustration, industrial design, interior design, metal/jewelry, music management, music performance, music theory/composition, painting, photography, piano/organ, printmaking, sculpture, studio arts, theater design, voice/opera.

Most popular majors. Business/marketing 18%, communications/journalism 6%, English 7%, psychology 7%, social sciences 11%, visual/performing arts 15%.

Computing on campus. 1,500 workstations in dormitories, library, computer center, student center. Dormitories wired for high-speed internet access and linked to campus network. Commuter students can connect to campus network. Online course registration, online library, helpline, repair service, student web hosting, wireless network available.

Student life. Freshman orientation: Mandatory. Preregistration for classes offered. Held during opening weekend, several days prior to first day of classes. Preregistration held during summer. **Policies:** Freshmen and sophomores required to live on campus. **Housing:** Guaranteed on-campus for freshmen. Coed dorms, special housing for disabled, apartments, fraternity/sorority housing, substance-free housing available. $350 deposit, deadline 5/1. International living center, single-sex floors and wings of residence halls, numerous learning communities, interest housing available. **Activities:** Bands, choral groups, dance, drama, film society, literary magazine, music ensembles, musical theater, opera, radio station, student government, student newspaper, symphony orchestra, TV station, student association, University Union Programming Board, African-American society, Asian Students in America, student environmental action coalition, AIDS task force, student volunteer groups.

Athletics. NCAA. **Intercollegiate:** Basketball, cross-country, diving, field hockey W, football (tackle) M, lacrosse, rowing (crew), soccer, softball W, swimming, tennis W, track and field, volleyball W. **Intramural:** Badminton, basketball, cross-country, football (non-tackle), golf, handball, racquetball, soccer, softball, squash, swimming, table tennis, tennis, track and field, volleyball. **Team name:** Orange.

Student services. Adult student services, alcohol/substance abuse counseling, campus ministries, career counseling, student employment services, financial aid counseling, health services, legal services, minority student services, on-campus daycare, personal counseling, placement for graduates, veterans' counselor, women's services. **Physically disabled:** Services for visually, speech, hearing impaired.

Contact. E-mail: orange@syr.edu
Phone: (315) 443-3611
Susan Donovan, Dean of Admissions, Syracuse University, 100 Crouse-Hinds Hall, Syracuse, NY 13244

Talmudical Institute of Upstate New York

Rochester, New York

CB code: 1426

- Private 5-year rabbinical and seminary college for men affiliated with Jewish faith
- Residential campus in large city

General. Founded in 1974. Accredited by AARTS. **Calendar:** Semester.

Annual costs/financial aid. Tuition/fees (2005-2006): $4,500.

Contact. Phone: (585) 473-2810
769 Park Avenue, Rochester, NY 14607

Talmudical Seminary Oholei Torah

Brooklyn, New York

CB code: 0712

- Private 4-year rabbinical and seminary college for men affiliated with Jewish faith
- Very large city

General. Founded in 1956. Accredited by AARTS. **Calendar:** Semester.

Annual costs/financial aid. Tuition/fees (2005-2006): $5,400.

Contact. Phone: (718) 774-5215
667 Eastern Parkway, Brooklyn, NY 11213-3397

Torah Teminah Talmudical Seminary

Brooklyn, New York

CB code: 7132

- Private 4-year rabbinical and seminary college for men affiliated with Jewish faith
- Very large city

General. Accredited by AARTS. **Calendar:** Continuous.

Annual costs/financial aid. Tuition/fees (2005-2006): $7,800. Room/board: $3,000.

Contact. Phone: (718) 853-8500
555 Ocean Parkway, Brooklyn, NY 11218

Touro College
New York, New York
www.touro.edu **CB code: 2902**

- Private 4-year liberal arts college
- Commuter campus in very large city
- 12,010 degree-seeking undergraduates

General. Founded in 1970. Regionally accredited. School of General Studies provides programs for part-time and adult students. **Degrees:** 1,750 bachelor's, 659 associate awarded; master's, doctoral, first professional offered. **Calendar:** Semester, limited summer session. **Full-time faculty:** 479 total. **Part-time faculty:** 859 total.

Basis for selection. For College of Liberal Arts and Sciences, 3.0 high school GPA, SAT verbal and math scores of 500 preferred. Recommendations from high school teachers and counselors and motivation important. High school experience less important for applicants to associate degree programs who take institutional admissions test. SAT or ACT recommended. SAT or ACT required for applicants to school of Health Sciences. Essay and interview recommended for College of Liberal Arts and Sciences.

High school preparation. 16 units required; 17 recommended. Required and recommended units include English 4, mathematics 2-3, social studies 2-3, science 2-3 and foreign language 2-3. Requirements may vary by division.

2005-2006 Annual costs. Tuition/fees: $11,500. Room/board: $5,200. Books/supplies: $750. Personal expenses: $1,764.

Application procedures. Admission: No deadline. $50 fee, may be waived for applicants with need. Admission notification on a rolling basis. **Financial aid:** Priority date 5/15, closing date 6/1. FAFSA required. Applicants notified by 8/15.

Academics. Special study options: Accelerated study, combined bachelor's/graduate degree, distance learning, dual enrollment of high school students, ESL, honors, independent study, internships, liberal arts/career combination, student-designed major, study abroad, teacher certification program. **Credit/placement by examination:** AP, CLEP, institutional tests. **Support services:** Learning center, reduced course load, remedial instruction, tutoring.

Majors. Biology: General. **Business:** General, accounting, business admin, management information systems, managerial economics, marketing. **Communications:** General. **Computer sciences:** General. **Education:** Special. **English:** Speech/rhetoric. **Foreign languages:** General, Hebrew. **Health:** Communication disorders, medical records technology, physician assistant, predentistry, premedicine, prepharmacy, preveterinary. **History:** General. **Interdisciplinary:** Biological/physical sciences. **Liberal arts:** Arts/sciences. **Math:** General. **Philosophy/religion:** Judaic, philosophy. **Physical sciences:** Chemistry. **Psychology:** General. **Social sciences:** General, economics, political science, sociology.

Computing on campus. 350 workstations in library, computer center.

Student life. Freshman orientation: Available. **Housing:** Single-sex dorms available. $50 deposit. No board or meal plan available. Kitchen facilities in student housing. **Activities:** Literary magazine, student government, student newspaper, accounting and business society, biology club, debating society, Jewish Affairs Committee, foreign students association, Omicron Delta.

Student services. Adult student services, career counseling, student employment services, personal counseling, placement for graduates, veterans' counselor.

Contact. E-mail: lasadmit@adminm.touro.edu
Phone: (718) 252-7800 ext. 299 Fax: (718) 253-9455
Andre Baron, Director of Admissions, Touro College, 1602 Avenue J, Brooklyn, NY 11230

U.T.A. Mesivta-Kiryas Joel
Monroe, New York

- Private 4-year rabbinical college for men

General. Accredited by AARTS.

Contact. Phone: (845) 783-9901
9 Nickelsburg Road, #312, Monroe, NY 10950-2169

Union College
Schenectady, New York **CB member**
www.union.edu **CB code: 2920**

- Private 4-year engineering and liberal arts college
- Residential campus in small city
- 2,190 degree-seeking undergraduates: 45% women, 3% African American, 6% Asian American, 5% Hispanic American, 2% international
- 47% of applicants admitted
- SAT or ACT (ACT writing optional), application essay required
- 84% graduate within 6 years; 30% enter graduate study

General. Founded in 1795. Regionally accredited. **Degrees:** 481 bachelor's awarded. **ROTC:** Army, Navy, Air Force. **Location:** 15 miles from Albany, 175 miles from New York City. **Calendar:** Trimester, limited summer session. **Full-time faculty:** 182 total; 96% have terminal degrees, 12% minority, 37% women. **Part-time faculty:** 27 total; 70% have terminal degrees, 11% minority, 56% women. **Class size:** 69% < 20, 27% 20-39, 3% 40-49, 2% 50-99. **Special facilities:** Nott Memorial exhibition and discussion center, theater, horticultural garden, multimedia auditorium, high tech classroom/lab building, superconducting nuclear magnetic resonance spectrometer, electron scanning microscope, tandem pelletron positive ion accelerator, X-ray diffraction equipment, remote-controlled telescope.

Freshman class profile. 4,230 applied, 1,997 admitted, 581 enrolled.

Mid 50% test scores			
SAT verbal:	570-660	Rank in top quarter:	87%
SAT math:	590-690	Rank in top tenth:	62%
ACT:	25-29	End year in good standing:	99%
GPA 3.50 or higher:	57%	Return as sophomores:	91%
GPA 3.0-3.49:	33%	Out-of-state:	58%
GPA 2.0-2.99:	10%	Live on campus:	99%
		International:	2%

Basis for selection. GED not accepted. Course selection and grades closely considered along with recommendations from high school and extracurricular record. Ethnic and geographic diversity sought in student body. Candidates must submit one of the following: SAT, or 2 SAT Subject Tests, or ACT. Last acceptable test date is January of senior year. Applicants for leadership in medicine and law and public policy programs are required to submit SAT and 2 SAT Subject Tests. Applicants for these programs must complete necessary tests no later than December of senior year. Portfolio recommended for art programs. **Homeschooled:** Personal interviews required.

High school preparation. 16 units required; 24 recommended. Required and recommended units include English 4, mathematics 3-4, social studies 1-2, history 1-2, science 2-4 (laboratory 2-4) and foreign language 2-4.

2005-2006 Annual costs. Comprehensive fee: $41,595. Rebates offered to students living off-campus and/or not using a meal plan. Books/supplies: $450. Personal expenses: $805.

2004-2005 Financial aid. Need-based: 330 full-time freshmen applied for aid; 254 were judged to have need; 254 of these received aid. Average need met was 100%. Average scholarship/grant was $23,287; average loan $2,967. 81% of total undergraduate aid awarded as scholarships/grants, 19% as loans/jobs. **Non-need-based:** Awarded to 248 full-time undergraduates, including 90 freshmen. Scholarships awarded for academics, ROTC. **Additional information:** Cancellable loans given to eligible students who engage in public service work after graduation. Loans cancellable at rate of 20% for each year of service.

Application procedures. Admission: Closing date 1/15 (postmark date). $50 fee, may be waived for applicants with need. Application may be submitted online. Admission notification 4/1. Must reply by 5/1. If application filed online, supplemental graded, written essay from 11th or 12th grade required to complete application. **Financial aid:** Closing date 2/1. FAFSA, CSS PROFILE required. Applicants notified by 4/1; must reply by 5/1.

Academics. Special study options: Accelerated study, combined bachelor's/graduate degree, cross-registration, double major, dual enrollment of high school students, honors, independent study, internships, liberal arts/career combination, student-designed major, study abroad, Washington semester. **Credit/placement by examination:** AP, CLEP, IB, institutional tests. 4 credit hours maximum toward bachelor's degree. **Support services:** Study skills assistance, tutoring, writing center.

Majors. Area/ethnic studies: American. **Biology:** General, biochemistry. **Computer sciences:** General. **Engineering:** Electrical, mechanical. **English:** English lit. **Foreign languages:** General, classics. **History:** General. **Interdisciplinary:** Biological/physical sciences, neuroscience, science/

society. **Liberal arts:** Arts/sciences, humanities. **Math:** General. **Philosophy/religion:** Philosophy. **Physical sciences:** Astronomy, chemistry, geology, physics. **Psychology:** General. **Social sciences:** General, anthropology, economics, political science, sociology. **Visual/performing arts:** General.

Most popular majors. Biology 10%, engineering/engineering technologies 15%, English 6%, liberal arts 8%, psychology 10%, social sciences 28%.

Computing on campus. 511 workstations in library, computer center, student center. Dormitories wired for high-speed internet access and linked to campus network. Commuter students can connect to campus network. Online library, helpline, student web hosting, wireless network available.

Student life. Freshman orientation: Mandatory. Preregistration for classes offered. Begins Thursday and ends Sunday before classes begin. Orientation fee included in admission and security deposit. **Policies:** All students expected to live on campus during undergraduate years, provided housing available. **Housing:** Guaranteed on-campus for freshmen. Coed dorms, apartments, fraternity/sorority housing, substance-free housing available. $100 fully refundable deposit, deadline 5/1. Theme housing, Minerva Houses available. All students and faculty members have house affiliations, and each house contributes intellectual, cultural, and social events to campus. **Activities:** Bands, choral groups, dance, drama, film society, literary magazine, music ensembles, radio station, student government, student newspaper, symphony orchestra, African/Latino Alliance of Students, Asian student union, Amnesty International, Big Brothers/Big Sisters, Union Community Action Reaching Everyone (UCARE), Newman Club, Protestant campus ministry, Jewish student union.

Athletics. NCAA. **Intercollegiate:** Baseball M, basketball, cross-country, field hockey W, football (tackle) M, ice hockey, lacrosse, rowing (crew), soccer, softball W, swimming, tennis, track and field, volleyball W. **Intramural:** Basketball, football (non-tackle) M, ice hockey, lacrosse, soccer, softball, volleyball. **Team name:** Dutchmen, Dutchwomen.

Student services. Campus ministries, career counseling, student employment services, financial aid counseling, health services, minority student services, personal counseling, placement for graduates. **Physically disabled:** Services for visually, hearing impaired. **Learning disabled:** Comprehensive services available.

Contact. E-mail: admissions@union.edu
Phone: (518) 388-6112 Toll-free number: (888) 843-6688
Fax: (518) 388-6986
Dianne Crozier, Director of Admissions, Union College, Grant Hall, Schenectady, NY 12308-2311

United States Merchant Marine Academy

Kings Point, New York — **CB member**
www.usmma.edu — **CB code: 2923**

- Public 4-year engineering and military college
- Residential campus in large town
- 1,021 degree-seeking undergraduates
- 24% of applicants admitted
- SAT or ACT (ACT writing recommended), application essay required

General. Founded in 1943. Regionally accredited. Accepted applicants appointed to academy as midshipmen, USNR. **Degrees:** 218 bachelor's awarded. **Location:** 20 miles from New York City. **Calendar:** Trimester, limited summer session. **Full-time faculty:** 85 total; 41% have terminal degrees, 8% minority, 12% women. **Class size:** 46% < 20, 52% 20-39, less than 1% 40-49, 2% 50-99. **Special facilities:** US Merchant Marine Museum, computer-aided operational research facility.

Freshman class profile. 1,647 applied, 397 admitted, 285 enrolled.

Mid 50% test scores		**Rank in top quarter:**	64%
SAT verbal:	560-670	**Rank in top tenth:**	26%
SAT math:	590-660	**Out-of-state:**	86%
ACT:	25-30	**Live on campus:**	100%

Basis for selection. GED not accepted. Nomination by U.S. representatives or senators. Competitive standing determined by test scores, high school GPA, class rank, motivation, extracurricular activities, interest in academy, industry, citizenship, and recommendations from counselors, teachers, school principal. Must also meet medical requirements. Untimed test results not acceptable. Interview recommended. **Homeschooled:** Must have completed chemistry with lab or physics with lab through state-certified instructor.

High school preparation. 18 units required. Required and recommended units include English 4, mathematics 3-4, social studies 4, science 3-4 (laboratory 1-2), foreign language 2 and academic electives 8.

2005-2006 Annual costs. All midshipmen receive full tuition, room and board, and medical and dental expenses from the federal government. Total required fees $6,253 including purchase of laptop computer, color printer, and PDA for $2,960. International students pay required fees plus $8,092 (international student fee).

2004-2005 Financial aid. Need-based: 141 full-time freshmen applied for aid; 73 were judged to have need; 73 of these received aid. Average need met was 100%. Average scholarship/grant was $2,711; average loan $2,414. 33% of total undergraduate aid awarded as scholarships/grants, 67% as loans/jobs. **Non-need-based:** Awarded to 47 full-time undergraduates, including 44 freshmen. **Additional information:** Students paid by steamship companies while at sea.

Application procedures. Admission: Closing date 3/1 (postmark date). No application fee. Application may be submitted online. Admission notification on a rolling basis beginning on or about 11/1. Must reply by May 1 or within 2 week(s) if notified thereafter. **Financial aid:** Closing date 5/1. FAFSA, institutional form required. Applicants notified on a rolling basis starting 1/31.

Academics. Special study options: Honors, independent study, internships, semester at sea. Sea training on merchant vessels. **Credit/placement by examination:** CLEP, institutional tests. **Support services:** Learning center, remedial instruction, study skills assistance, tutoring.

Majors. Engineering: Marine, systems. **Engineering technology:** Industrial management. **Mechanic/repair:** Marine. **Transportation:** General, marine science/Merchant Marine.

Most popular majors. Engineering/engineering technologies 50%.

Computing on campus. PC or laptop required. 1,200 workstations in dormitories, library. Dormitories wired for high-speed internet access and linked to campus network. Helpline, repair service, wireless network available.

Student life. Freshman orientation: Mandatory. **Policies:** Freshmen permitted cars on campus. **Housing:** Guaranteed on-campus for all undergraduates. Coed dorms, substance-free housing available. Students required to live on campus. **Activities:** Bands, choral groups, drama, musical theater, student government, student newspaper, Christian Fellowship Community, Neumann Club.

Athletics. NCAA. **Intercollegiate:** Baseball M, basketball, cross-country, diving, football (non-tackle), football (tackle) M, golf, lacrosse M, rifle, rowing (crew), sailing, soccer M, softball W, swimming, tennis, track and field, volleyball W, wrestling M. **Intramural:** Badminton, basketball, bowling, cross-country, diving, football (tackle) M, golf, lacrosse M, racquetball, rifle, rowing (crew), rugby M, sailing, skiing, soccer, softball, swimming, tennis, track and field, volleyball, water polo M, wrestling M. **Team name:** Mariners.

Student services. Campus ministries, career counseling, student employment services, health services, personal counseling, placement for graduates.

Contact. E-mail: admissions@usmma.edu
Phone: (516) 773-5391 Toll-free number: (866) 546-4778
Fax: (516) 773-5390
Capt. Robert Johnson, Director of Admissions, United States Merchant Marine Academy, 300 Steamboat Road, Kings Point, NY 11024-1699

United States Military Academy

West Point, New York — **CB member**
www.usma.edu — **CB code: 2924**

- Public 4-year engineering and military college
- Residential campus in small town
- 4,231 degree-seeking undergraduates: 15% women, 6% African American, 7% Asian American, 7% Hispanic American, 1% Native American, 1% international
- 14% of applicants admitted
- SAT or ACT (ACT writing recommended), application essay required
- 86% graduate within 6 years; 2% enter graduate study

General. Founded in 1802. Regionally accredited. All cadets receive Bachelor of Science degree designed specifically to meet intellectual requirements of commissioned officer in the Army. **Degrees:** 937 bachelor's awarded. **Location:** 50 miles from New York City. **Calendar:** Semester, limited summer session. **Full-time faculty:** 604 total; 63% have terminal degrees, 10% minority, 15% women. **Class size:** 96% < 20, 4% 20-39, less than 1% 40-49. **Special facilities:** 18-hole golf course, ski slope.

Freshman class profile. 10,778 applied, 1,548 admitted, 1,199 enrolled.

Mid 50% test scores			
SAT verbal:	570-670	End year in good standing:	95%
SAT math:	600-690	Return as sophomores:	88%
ACT:	26-31	Out-of-state:	92%
Rank in top quarter:	93%	Live on campus:	100%
Rank in top tenth:	72%	International:	2%

Basis for selection. ACT/SAT, rigor of high school record, class rank, and faculty recommendations used to determine academic qualification. Demonstrated leadership potential, physical ability, medical exam and Candidate Fitness Assessment also important. Must be U.S. citizen , at least 17 but not yet 23 by July 1 of year admitted, unmarried, not pregnant, and without legal child support obligations. Naturalized citizens must provide documentation. Nomination by member of Congress required. Consideration also given to percentage of students from school who attend 4-year colleges after high school. Interview recommended.

High school preparation. 19 units recommended. Recommended units include English 4, mathematics 4, social studies 1, history 1, science 4 (laboratory 2), foreign language 2 and academic electives 3. English units should have strong emphasis on composition, grammar, literature and speech; math should include algebra, geometry, intermediate algebra, and trigonometry; U.S. history should include courses in geography, government and economics. Precalculus, calculus and basic computing course helpful.

2006-2007 Annual costs. All cadets members of U.S. Army and receive annual salary of $10,140. Tuition, room and board, medical, and dental care provided at no cost to cadets. Deposit of $2,900 required for initial uniforms, books, supplies, personal computer, and fees. First-year cadets who cannot pay deposit receive no-interest loan; payments deducted from cadet salary.

Application procedures. Admission: Closing date 2/28. No application fee. Application may be submitted online. Admission notification on a rolling basis beginning on or about 11/15. Must reply by 5/1. Candidates must notify admission office in writing of intention to apply for early action by October 25. Nomination or medical exam results not necessary to apply, but required prior to admission.

Academics. Cadets must complete minimum basic requirement of 40 academic courses. 8 semesters of physical education and 4 military science courses required. Cumulative GPA of at least 2.0 required, while meeting appropriate physical fitness and proper conduct standards. **Special study options:** Double major, exchange student, honors, independent study, study abroad, Washington semester. **Credit/placement by examination:** CLEP. **Support services:** Learning center, reduced course load, remedial instruction, study skills assistance, tutoring.

Majors. Area/ethnic studies: East Asian, Latin American, Near/Middle Eastern, Russian/Slavic, Western European. **Business:** Business admin. **Computer sciences:** General, computer science, information systems. **Engineering:** Aerospace, chemical, civil, computer, electrical, mechanical, nuclear, operations research, physics, systems. **English:** American lit, British lit. **Foreign languages:** French, German, Portuguese, Russian, Spanish. **History:** General. **Interdisciplinary:** Behavioral sciences. **Legal studies:** General. **Math:** General. **Philosophy/religion:** Philosophy. **Physical sciences:** Chemistry, physics. **Psychology:** General. **Social sciences:** General, economics, geography, political science, sociology, U.S. government.

Computing on campus. PC or laptop required. 1,000 workstations in dormitories, library, computer center. Dormitories linked to campus network. Commuter students can connect to campus network. Online library, helpline, repair service, wireless network available.

Student life. Freshman orientation: Mandatory. 6-week Cadet Basic Training in Summer prior to semester. **Policies:** Honor code. Cadets administer honor system with power to recommend dismissal. Military dress required. All cadets participate in intercollegiate, club or intramural level sport each semester. Seniors and juniors (after spring break) permitted to maintain cars. **Housing:** Guaranteed on-campus for all undergraduates. Coed dorms available. **Activities:** Pep band, choral groups, dance, drama, film society, literary magazine, music ensembles, musical theater, radio station, student government, student newspaper, TV station, more than 100 extracurricular activities.

Athletics. NCAA. **Intercollegiate:** Baseball M, basketball, cross-country, diving, football (tackle) M, golf M, gymnastics M, ice hockey M, lacrosse M, rifle, soccer, softball W, swimming, tennis, track and field, volleyball W, wrestling M. **Intramural:** Basketball, bowling, boxing M, cross-country, equestrian, football (tackle) M, golf, handball, lacrosse, racquetball, rowing (crew), skin diving, soccer, softball, swimming, tennis, track and field, volleyball M, wrestling M. **Team name:** Black Knights.

Student services. Career counseling, health services, legal services, personal counseling, placement for graduates, women's services.

Contact. E-mail: admissions@usma.edu
Phone: (845) 938-5760
COL. Michael Jones, Director of Admissions, United States Military Academy, 646 Swift Road, West Point, NY 10996-1905

United Talmudical Seminary

Brooklyn, New York

CB code: 0696

- Private 5-year rabbinical college for men affiliated with Jewish faith
- Very large city

General. Founded in 1949. Accredited by AARTS. **Calendar:** Semester.

Annual costs/financial aid. Tuition/fees (2005-2006): $6,000.

Contact. Phone: (718) 963-9260
Director of Admissions, 82 Lee Avenue, Brooklyn, NY 11211

University of Rochester

Rochester, New York — **CB member**

www.rochester.edu — **CB code: 2928**

- Private 4-year university
- Residential campus in large city
- 4,532 degree-seeking undergraduates: 2% part-time, 49% women, 5% African American, 10% Asian American, 4% Hispanic American, 4% international
- 3,444 degree-seeking graduate students
- 48% of applicants admitted
- SAT or ACT (ACT writing optional), application essay required

General. Founded in 1850. Regionally accredited. **Degrees:** 1,333 bachelor's awarded; master's, doctoral, first professional offered. **ROTC:** Army, Navy, Air Force. **Location:** 2 miles from downtown. **Calendar:** Semester, extensive summer session. **Full-time faculty:** 505 total; 88% have terminal degrees, 12% minority, 26% women. **Part-time faculty:** 263 total; 4% minority, 52% women. **Class size:** 63% < 20, 23% 20-39, 5% 40-49, 7% 50-99, 3% >100. **Special facilities:** Nuclear structure research laboratory, laser energetics laboratory, African and African-American studies institute, observatory, women's studies center, 19 electron microscopes, dental center, hospital, visual science center, optics institute.

Freshman class profile. 11,272 applied, 5,374 admitted, 997 enrolled.

Mid 50% test scores			
SAT verbal:	610-710	Rank in top quarter:	93%
SAT math:	640-710	Rank in top tenth:	76%
ACT:	26-30	Return as sophomores:	95%
		International:	5%

Basis for selection. School achievement record and test scores most important. Recommendations, personal qualities, extracurricular activities important. Alumni relationship, minority status, special talents considered. SAT Subject Tests recommended. Audition required for music programs at Eastman School of Music only.

High school preparation. College-preparatory program required. 32 units recommended.

2005-2006 Annual costs. Tuition/fees: $31,263. Room/board: $9,990. Books/supplies: $575. Personal expenses: $1,125.

2005-2006 Financial aid. Need-based: Average need met was 100%. Average scholarship/grant was $21,544; average loan $4,023. 71% of total undergraduate aid awarded as scholarships/grants, 29% as loans/jobs. **Non-need-based:** Scholarships awarded for academics, alumni affiliation, leadership, music/drama, ROTC, state residency. **Additional information:** Alternative loans and financing information available.

Application procedures. Admission: Closing date 1/15 (postmark date). $50 fee, may be waived for applicants with need. Application may be submitted online. Admission notification 4/1. Must reply by 5/1. **Financial aid:** Closing date 2/1. FAFSA, CSS PROFILE required. Applicants notified by 4/1; must reply by 5/1.

Academics. Special study options: Combined bachelor's/graduate degree, cross-registration, double major, dual enrollment of high school students, ESL, honors, independent study, internships, liberal arts/career combination, student-designed major, study abroad, teacher certification program, Washington semester. Senior Scholars Research Program allowing selected undergraduates to devote entire senior year to student-designed research project; Take Five, a 5th year tuition-free to supplement regular requirements; Rochester Curriculum (clusters); Quest (1st year course emphasizing how to learn). **Credit/placement by examination:** AP, CLEP, IB, institutional tests. **Support services:** Learning center, reduced course load, study skills assistance, tutoring, writing center.

Majors. **Area/ethnic studies:** African-American, Russian/Slavic, women's. **Biology:** General, bacteriology, biochemistry, cell/histology, ecology, embryology, molecular, molecular genetics. **Computer sciences:** General. **Conservation:** Environmental science, environmental studies. **Engineering:** General, biomedical, chemical, electrical, mechanical, science. **Foreign languages:** General, comparative lit, French, German, Japanese, linguistics, Russian, sign language interpretation, Spanish. **History:** General. **Interdisciplinary:** Biological/physical sciences. **Math:** General, applied, statistics. **Philosophy/religion:** Philosophy, religion. **Physical sciences:** Astronomy, chemistry, geology, optics, physics. **Psychology:** General. **Social sciences:** Anthropology, economics, political science. **Visual/performing arts:** Art history/conservation, film/cinema, jazz, music theory/composition, studio arts.

Most popular majors. Biology 10%, engineering/engineering technologies 8%, English 6%, health sciences 6%, psychology 12%, social sciences 22%, visual/performing arts 9%.

Computing on campus. 265 workstations in dormitories, library, computer center. Dormitories linked to campus network. Commuter students can connect to campus network. Helpline available.

Student life. **Freshman orientation:** Mandatory. Preregistration for classes offered. **Housing:** Guaranteed on-campus for freshmen. Coed dorms, single-sex dorms, special housing for disabled, apartments, fraternity/sorority housing available. Drama house, medieval house, faculty-in-residence housing, special interest housing (computer interest floor, music interest floor, international living, community service) available. **Activities:** Bands, choral groups, dance, drama, film society, literary magazine, music ensembles, musical theater, opera, radio station, student government, student newspaper, symphony orchestra, more than 170 student organizations available.

Athletics. NCAA. **Intercollegiate:** Baseball M, basketball, cross-country, field hockey W, football (tackle) M, golf, lacrosse W, soccer, softball W, squash, swimming, tennis, track and field, volleyball W. **Intramural:** Basketball, football (non-tackle) M, soccer, volleyball. **Team name:** Yellowjackets.

Student services. Adult student services, alcohol/substance abuse counseling, campus ministries, career counseling, student employment services, financial aid counseling, health services, minority student services, personal counseling, placement for graduates. **Physically disabled:** Services for visually, hearing impaired.

Contact. E-mail: admit@admissions.rochester.edu
Phone: (585) 275-3221 Toll-free number: (888) 822-2256
Fax: (585) 461-4595
Jonathan Burdick, Dean of Admissions and Financial Aid, University of Rochester, 100 Wallis Hall, Rochester, NY 14627-0251

Utica College

Utica, New York — **CB member**
www.utica.edu — **CB code: 2932**

- Private 4-year liberal arts college
- Residential campus in small city
- 2,334 degree-seeking undergraduates: 13% part-time, 58% women, 9% African American, 2% Asian American, 3% Hispanic American, 1% Native American, 1% international
- 451 degree-seeking graduate students
- 79% of applicants admitted
- Application essay required
- 57% graduate within 6 years; 39% enter graduate study

General. Founded in 1946. Regionally accredited. **Degrees:** 427 bachelor's awarded; master's, first professional offered. **ROTC:** Army, Air Force. **Location:** 50 miles from Syracuse. **Calendar:** Semester, limited summer session. **Full-time faculty:** 119 total; 92% have terminal degrees, 4% minority, 50% women. **Part-time faculty:** 167 total; 28% have terminal degrees, 1% minority, 46% women. **Class size:** 66% < 20, 34% 20-39, less than 1% 40-49, less than 1% 50-99. **Special facilities:** 7 high-tech classrooms.

Freshman class profile. 2,497 applied, 1,977 admitted, 470 enrolled.

Mid 50% test scores			
SAT verbal:	430-530	Rank in top quarter:	28%
SAT math:	440-550	Rank in top tenth:	8%
ACT:	19-24	End year in good standing:	70%
GPA 3.50 or higher:	22%	Return as sophomores:	70%
GPA 3.0-3.49:	43%	Out-of-state:	15%
GPA 2.0-2.99:	33%	Live on campus:	77%
		International:	1%

Basis for selection. Academic record, high school course of study, and rank in class most important. Extracurricular activities, essay, interview, and recommendations are also important. SAT or ACT scores required only for freshmen applying to the BS Health Studies/DPT Physical Therapy, BS Health Studies/MS Occupational Therapy, Nursing, or joint health professions programs, the Higher Education Opportunity Program (HEOP), or for academic merit scholarships. Interview recommended. **Homeschooled:** Applicants must receive their GED within their first year of attendance. **Learning Disabled:** Written evaluation required, including a discrepancy analysis completed by a licensed psychologist or certified learning disability specialist indicating the specific learning disability or disabilities.

High school preparation. 16 units required. Required units include English 4, mathematics 3, social studies 3, science 3, foreign language 2 and academic electives 1.

2005-2006 Annual costs. Tuition/fees: $22,340. Room/board: $9,056. Books/supplies: $850. Personal expenses: $706.

2005-2006 Financial aid. **Need-based:** 415 full-time freshmen applied for aid; 387 were judged to have need; 387 of these received aid. Average need met was 78%. Average scholarship/grant was $9,859. 68% of total undergraduate aid awarded as scholarships/grants, 32% as loans/jobs. **Non-need-based:** Awarded to 248 full-time undergraduates, including 58 freshmen. Scholarships awarded for academics.

Application procedures. **Admission:** No deadline. $40 fee, may be waived for applicants with need. Application may be submitted online. Admission notification on a rolling basis beginning on or about 9/1. January 15 application deadline for all joint medical programs, BS in Health Studies/MS in Occupational Therapy program, and BS in Health Studies/DPT in Physical Therapy program. February 15 application deadline for nursing program. **Financial aid:** Priority date 2/15; no closing date. FAFSA required. Applicants notified on a rolling basis starting 2/1; must reply by 5/1 or within 4 week(s) of notification.

Academics. **Special study options:** Accelerated study, combined bachelor's/graduate degree, cooperative education, cross-registration, distance learning, double major, dual enrollment of high school students, exchange student, honors, independent study, internships, liberal arts/career combination, study abroad, teacher certification program, United Nations semester, Washington semester, weekend college. BS Health Studies/MS Occupational Therapy weekend program; Economic Crime Investigation online program for transfer students. **Credit/placement by examination:** AP, CLEP, IB, SAT, institutional tests. 30 credit hours maximum toward bachelor's degree. **Support services:** Learning center, pre-admission summer program, reduced course load, remedial instruction, study skills assistance, tutoring, writing center.

Majors. **Biology:** General. **Business:** Accounting, business admin, managerial economics. **Communications:** General, journalism, public relations. **Computer sciences:** General. **Education:** Biology, business, chemistry, early childhood, elementary, English, ESL, mathematics, physics, secondary, social science, social studies, special. **English:** English lit. **Family/consumer sciences:** Child care. **Health:** Facilities admin, health services, nursing (RN), recreational therapy. **History:** General. **Liberal arts:** Arts/sciences. **Math:** General. **Philosophy/religion:** Philosophy. **Physical sciences:** Chemistry, physics. **Protective services:** Criminal justice. **Psychology:** General. **Social sciences:** Economics, international relations, political science, sociology.

Most popular majors. Business/marketing 16%, communications/journalism 9%, education 9%, health sciences 15%, psychology 12%, security/protective services 17%, social sciences 6%.

Computing on campus. 146 workstations in library, computer center, student center. Dormitories wired for high-speed internet access and linked to campus network. Helpline available.

Student life. **Freshman orientation:** Available, $50 fee. Preregistration for classes offered. Summer program for freshmen and parents held during the third week of July. **Policies:** All freshmen required to live in college residence for first 2 years, unless residing at home. Freshmen permitted cars on campus. **Housing:** Guaranteed on-campus for freshmen. Coed dorms, special housing for disabled, apartments, substance-free housing available. $200 fully refundable deposit, deadline 5/1. Separate floors for men & women available in select residence halls. **Activities:** Concert band, choral groups, dance, drama, film society, literary magazine, radio station, student government, student newspaper, Latin American Student Union, Jewish Student

Union, Young Democrats, College Republicans, Womyn's Resource Center, Circle K, The Students of African Descent Alliance, UC PRIDE--People Respecting Diversity Everywhere, Gospel Choir, Africa in Motion.

Athletics. NCAA. **Intercollegiate:** Baseball M, basketball, diving, field hockey W, football (tackle) M, golf M, ice hockey, lacrosse, soccer, softball W, swimming, tennis, volleyball W, water polo W. **Intramural:** Basketball, bowling, football (non-tackle), racquetball, soccer, softball, tennis, volleyball, water polo. **Team name:** Pioneers.

Student services. Adult student services, alcohol/substance abuse counseling, campus ministries, career counseling, services for economically disadvantaged, student employment services, financial aid counseling, health services, minority student services, personal counseling, placement for graduates, veterans' counselor, women's services. **Physically disabled:** Services for visually, speech, hearing impaired.

Contact. E-mail: admiss@utica.edu
Phone: (315) 792-3006 Toll-free number: (800) 782-8884
Fax: (315) 792-3003
Patrick Quinn, Vice President for Enrollment Management, Utica College, 1600 Burrstone Road, Utica, NY 13502-4892

Vassar College

Poughkeepsie, New York — **CB member**
www.vassar.edu — **CB code: 2956**

- Private 4-year liberal arts college
- Residential campus in small city
- 2,331 degree-seeking undergraduates: 1% part-time, 59% women, 5% African American, 9% Asian American, 6% Hispanic American, 5% international
- 29% of applicants admitted
- SAT or ACT (ACT writing recommended), SAT Subject Tests, application essay required
- 91% graduate within 6 years; 17% enter graduate study

General. Founded in 1861. Regionally accredited. **Degrees:** 670 bachelor's awarded. **Location:** 75 miles from New York City. **Calendar:** Semester, limited summer session. **Full-time faculty:** 277 total; 92% have terminal degrees, 15% minority, 46% women. **Part-time faculty:** 29 total; 52% have terminal degrees, 17% minority, 62% women. **Class size:** 68% < 20, 30% 20-39, 1% 40-49, less than 1% 50-99. **Special facilities:** Environmental nature center, observatory, electron microscope, nursery school, experimental theater, art center and geology museum, theater, intercultural center and outdoor amphitheater.

Freshman class profile. 6,314 applied, 1,803 admitted, 650 enrolled.

Mid 50% test scores			
SAT verbal:	680-730	Rank in top quarter:	94%
SAT math:	660-720	Rank in top tenth:	67%
ACT:	28-32	End year in good standing:	98%
GPA 3.50 or higher:	79%	Return as sophomores:	96%
GPA 3.0-3.49:	20%	Out-of-state:	78%
GPA 2.0-2.99:	1%	Live on campus:	99%
		International:	4%

Basis for selection. Academic credentials most important. Personal achievements, essay, and recommendations also considered carefully. Evidence that students have elected most demanding program available crucial. Disadvantaged status considered. 3 SAT Subject Tests of student's choice required. Optional interviews available with alumni.

High school preparation. 20 units recommended. Recommended units include English 4, mathematics 4, social studies 2, history 2, science 4 (laboratory 3) and foreign language 4. Advanced and accelerated courses recommended whenever possible. Minimum of 20 units recommended with additional unit in science, foreign language, and studies.

2006-2007 Annual costs. Tuition/fees: $36,030. Room/board: $8,130. Books/supplies: $860. Personal expenses: $940.

2005-2006 Financial aid. All financial aid based on need. 422 full-time freshmen applied for aid; 302 were judged to have need; 302 of these received aid. Average need met was 100%. Average scholarship/grant was $23,920; average loan $2,283. 81% of total undergraduate aid awarded as scholarships/grants, 19% as loans/jobs.

Application procedures. Admission: Closing date 1/1 (receipt date). $60 fee, may be waived for applicants with need. Application must be submitted on paper. Admission notification 4/1. Must reply by 5/1. **Financial aid:** Closing date 2/1. FAFSA, institutional form, CSS PROFILE required. Applicants notified by 3/30; must reply by 5/1.

Academics. Introductory-level college course emphasizing written and oral communication required for freshmen. Majors declared through department, interdepartmental programs, multidisciplinary programs, and independent programs. Summer research with faculty. **Special study options:** Combined bachelor's/graduate degree, cooperative education, cross-registration, double major, exchange student, independent study, internships, liberal arts/career combination, student-designed major, study abroad, teacher certification program, urban semester, Washington semester. Independently designed junior year abroad programs; exchange programs with institutions in 12-college exchange as well as Fisk University, Hampton Institute, Howard University, Morehouse College, and Spelman College; 3-2 engineering program with Dartmouth College. **Credit/placement by examination:** AP, CLEP, IB, institutional tests. 4 credit hours maximum toward bachelor's degree. **Support services:** Learning center, reduced course load, study skills assistance, tutoring, writing center.

Majors. Area/ethnic studies: African, American, Asian, Latin American, women's. **Biology:** General, biochemistry. **Communications:** Media studies. **Computer sciences:** General. **Conservation:** Environmental studies. **English:** English lit. **Foreign languages:** Ancient Greek, Chinese, French, German, Italian, Japanese, Latin, Russian, Spanish. **History:** General. **Interdisciplinary:** Ancient studies, cognitive science, medieval/Renaissance, neuroscience, science/society. **Liberal arts:** Arts/sciences. **Math:** General. **Philosophy/religion:** Judaic, philosophy, religion. **Physical sciences:** Astronomy, chemistry, geology, physics. **Psychology:** General. **Social sciences:** Anthropology, economics, geography, international relations, political science, sociology, urban studies. **Visual/performing arts:** Art, dramatic, film/cinema.

Most popular majors. English 11%, interdisciplinary studies 8%, psychology 9%, social sciences 27%, visual/performing arts 15%.

Computing on campus. 432 workstations in dormitories, library, computer center, student center. Dormitories wired for high-speed internet access and linked to campus network. Commuter students can connect to campus network. Online course registration, helpline, repair service, student web hosting, wireless network available.

Student life. Freshman orientation: Mandatory. Preregistration for classes offered. Held one week prior to start of classes. **Policies:** Freshmen permitted cars on campus. **Housing:** Guaranteed on-campus for all undergraduates. Coed dorms, single-sex dorms, special housing for disabled, apartments, cooperative housing, substance-free housing available. **Activities:** Bands, choral groups, dance, drama, film society, literary magazine, music ensembles, musical theater, opera, radio station, student government, student newspaper, symphony orchestra, TV station, Catholic Community, Jewish Union, Promoting Equality and Community Everywhere, Amnesty International, Young Socialists, Republican/Libertarian Coalition, AIDS Education Committee, Habitat for Humanity, Step Beyond (community service), African Students Union.

Athletics. NCAA. **Intercollegiate:** Baseball M, basketball, cross-country, diving, fencing, field hockey W, golf W, lacrosse, rowing (crew), soccer, squash, swimming, tennis, volleyball. **Intramural:** Badminton, basketball, bowling, golf, handball, soccer, softball, squash, tennis, volleyball, water polo. **Team name:** Brewers.

Student services. Alcohol/substance abuse counseling, campus ministries, career counseling, student employment services, financial aid counseling, health services, minority student services, on-campus daycare, personal counseling, placement for graduates, veterans' counselor, women's services. **Physically disabled:** Services for visually, speech, hearing impaired.

Contact. E-mail: admissons@vassar.edu
Phone: (845) 437-7300 Toll-free number: (800) 827-7270
Fax: (845) 437-7063
David Borus, Dean of Admission and Financial Aid, Vassar College, Box 10, 124 Raymond Avenue, Poughkeepsie, NY 12604-0077

Vaughn College of Aeronautics and Technology

Flushing, New York — **CB member**
www.vaughn.edu — **CB code: 2001**

- Private 4-year engineering and technical college
- Commuter campus in very large city
- 1,119 degree-seeking undergraduates: 25% part-time, 13% women, 19% African American, 11% Asian American, 35% Hispanic American, 4% international
- 95% of applicants admitted
- SAT or ACT (ACT writing recommended), application essay required
- 34% graduate within 6 years; 5% enter graduate study

General. Founded in 1932. Regionally accredited. Engineering technology programs accredited by the Accreditation Board for Engineering and Technology (ABET). **Degrees:** 119 bachelor's, 125 associate awarded. **ROTC:** Army, Air Force. **Location:** 5 miles from Manhattan. **Calendar:** Semester, extensive summer session. **Full-time faculty:** 43 total; 26% have terminal degrees, 26% minority, 7% women. **Part-time faculty:** 70 total; 4% have terminal degrees, 39% minority, 26% women. **Class size:** 69% < 20, 30% 20-39, less than 1% 40-49. **Special facilities:** State-of-the-art fiber optic Unix-Novell computer system, 65-foot tower overlooking LaGuardia Airport, Frasca 142 flight simulator, nondestructive testing laboratory, composite materials laboratory, computerized engine test-cell.

Freshman class profile. 328 applied, 311 admitted, 197 enrolled.

Mid 50% test scores			
SAT verbal:	470-560	GPA 2.0-2.99:	42%
SAT math:	490-590	End year in good standing:	60%
GPA 3.50 or higher:	16%	Return as sophomores:	73%
GPA 3.0-3.49:	42%	Out-of-state:	6%
		International:	2%

Basis for selection. High school transcripts or GED scores most important followed by SAT, ACT, or TOEFL. B.S. programs require strong performance in high school math and sciences courses. Open admissions to associate's degree programs. SAT or ACT with Writing exam required for all first-time, first-year applicants to BS program. Interview recommended. **Homeschooled:** Statement describing homeschool structure and mission, transcript of courses and grades, state high school equivalency certificate required. **Learning Disabled:** Presentation of documental IEP necessary.

High school preparation. 14 units required; 18 recommended. Required and recommended units include English 4, mathematics 3-4, social studies 1-4 and science 2-4. Physics recommended.

2005-2006 Annual costs. Tuition/fees: $13,680. Books/supplies: $1,050. Personal expenses: $1,950.

2005-2006 Financial aid. All financial aid based on need. 187 full-time freshmen applied for aid; 173 were judged to have need; 173 of these received aid. Average need met was 80%. Average scholarship/grant was $1,000; average loan $1,313. 69% of total undergraduate aid awarded as scholarships/grants, 31% as loans/jobs.

Application procedures. Admission: Priority date 3/1; no deadline. $45 fee, may be waived for applicants with need. Application may be submitted online. Admission notification on a rolling basis beginning on or about 2/1. **Financial aid:** Priority date 3/1; no closing date. FAFSA required. Applicants notified on a rolling basis.

Academics. Special study options: Accelerated study, distance learning, double major, independent study, internships, liberal arts/career combination. **Credit/placement by examination:** AP, CLEP, SAT, ACT, institutional tests. 30 credit hours maximum toward associate degree, 60 toward bachelor's. **Support services:** Learning center, pre-admission summer program, reduced course load, remedial instruction, study skills assistance, tutoring, writing center.

Majors. Business: General. **Engineering technology:** CAD/CADD, electrical. **Mechanic/repair:** Aircraft, aircraft powerplant, avionics, communications systems. **Transportation:** Airline/commercial pilot, aviation management.

Most popular majors. Engineering/engineering technologies 24%, trade and industry 76%.

Computing on campus. 70 workstations in library, computer center, student center. Online library, helpline, repair service, wireless network available.

Student life. Freshman orientation: Available. Preregistration for classes offered. One-day session held 2 weeks before classes begin. **Policies:** Freshmen permitted cars on campus. **Activities:** Student government, student newspaper, American Institute of Aeronautics and Astronautics, Society of Automotive Engineers, Institute of Electrical and Electronics Engineers, flying club, Women in Aviation-International.

Athletics. Intramural: Basketball, soccer. **Team name:** Warriors.

Student services. Campus ministries, career counseling, services for economically disadvantaged, student employment services, financial aid counseling, health services, minority student services, personal counseling, placement for graduates, veterans' counselor.

Contact. E-mail: admitme@vaughn.edu
Phone: (718) 429-6600 ext. 118 Toll-free number: (800) 866-6828
Fax: (718) 779-2231
Vincent Papandrea, Director of Admissions, Vaughn College of Aeronautics and Technology, 86-01 23rd Avenue, Flushing, NY 11369

Wagner College

Staten Island, New York — **CB member**
www.wagner.edu — **CB code: 2966**

- Private 4-year liberal arts college affiliated with Lutheran Church in America
- Residential campus in very large city
- 1,962 degree-seeking undergraduates: 4% part-time, 63% women, 5% African American, 2% Asian American, 5% Hispanic American, 1% international
- 325 degree-seeking graduate students
- 61% of applicants admitted
- SAT or ACT (ACT writing optional), application essay required
- 68% graduate within 6 years

General. Founded in 1883. Regionally accredited. **Degrees:** 391 bachelor's awarded; master's offered. **Calendar:** Semester, limited summer session. **Full-time faculty:** 99 total; 72% have terminal degrees, 7% minority, 46% women. **Part-time faculty:** 130 total; 7% have terminal degrees, 10% minority, 53% women. **Class size:** 59% < 20, 40% 20-39, less than 1% 40-49, less than 1% 50-99. **Special facilities:** Planetarium, electron microscopes.

Freshman class profile. 2,858 applied, 1,751 admitted, 579 enrolled.

Mid 50% test scores			
SAT verbal:	530-630	Rank in top quarter:	64%
SAT math:	530-640	Rank in top tenth:	17%
ACT:	23-27	Return as sophomores:	89%
GPA 3.50 or higher:	35%	Out-of-state:	65%
GPA 3.0-3.49:	52%	Live on campus:	82%
GPA 2.0-2.99:	13%	International:	1%

Basis for selection. School achievement, test scores, recommendations, interview, special talents, essay all considered. Interview recommended for all; audition required for music, theater programs; portfolio recommended for art programs. Interview required for Physician Assistant program.

High school preparation. 21 units required. Required units include English 4, mathematics 3, social studies 1, history 3, science 2 (laboratory 1), foreign language 2 and academic electives 6. 4 economics, arts, computers, or other elective areas of study required.

2005-2006 Annual costs. Tuition/fees: $25,350. Room/board: $7,950. Books/supplies: $701. Personal expenses: $1,219.

2005-2006 Financial aid. Need-based: 465 full-time freshmen applied for aid; 359 were judged to have need; 359 of these received aid. Average need met was 72%. Average scholarship/grant was $12,357; average loan $3,432. 55% of total undergraduate aid awarded as scholarships/grants, 45% as loans/jobs. **Non-need-based:** Awarded to 775 full-time undergraduates, including 180 freshmen. Scholarships awarded for academics, athletics, leadership, music/drama.

Application procedures. Admission: Priority date 2/15; deadline 3/1 (postmark date). $50 fee, may be waived for applicants with need. Application must be submitted on paper. Admission notification on a rolling basis beginning on or about 3/1. Must reply by May 1 or within 2 week(s) if notified thereafter. **Financial aid:** Priority date 2/15; no closing date. FAFSA, institutional form required. Applicants notified on a rolling basis starting 3/1; must reply within 3 week(s) of notification.

Academics. Special study options: Combined bachelor's/graduate degree, double major, exchange student, honors, independent study, internships, study abroad, teacher certification program, United Nations semester, Washington semester. **Credit/placement by examination:** AP, CLEP, IB, institutional tests. 9 credit hours maximum toward bachelor's degree. Up to 9 units may be awarded for credit by exam and prior experience. Each unit is equivalent to 3.3 credit hours. **Support services:** Reduced course load, tutoring, writing center.

Majors. Biology: General, bacteriology. **Business:** Accounting, business admin, finance, international, managerial economics, marketing. **Computer sciences:** Computer science. **Education:** General, early childhood, middle, secondary. **English:** English lit. **Foreign languages:** Spanish. **Health:** Nursing (RN), physician assistant, predentistry, premedicine. **History:** General. **Liberal arts:** Arts/sciences. **Math:** General. **Physical sciences:** Chemistry, physics. **Psychology:** General. **Public administration:** Policy analysis. **Social sciences:** Anthropology, political science, sociology. **Visual/performing arts:** Arts management, dramatic, music performance, studio arts, theater design.

Most popular majors. Business/marketing 25%, English 6%, health sciences 14%, psychology 11%, social sciences 11%, visual/performing arts 19%.

Computing on campus. 230 workstations in dormitories, library, computer center. Dormitories wired for high-speed internet access and linked to campus network. Commuter students can connect to campus network. Online library, helpline available.

Student life. **Freshman orientation:** Mandatory. Freshmen move on-campus 3 days prior to start of fall semester. Orientation involves academic advisement and registration, social activities, and trip to Manhattan. **Policies:** Freshmen permitted cars on campus. **Housing:** Guaranteed on-campus for all undergraduates. Coed dorms, apartments, fraternity/sorority housing, substance-free housing available. $300 nonrefundable deposit, deadline 5/1. **Activities:** Bands, choral groups, dance, drama, literary magazine, music ensembles, musical theater, radio station, student government, student newspaper, Lutheran student club, Newman Society, Hillel, national honor societies, Amnesty International, Young Democrats, Young Republicans, Nubian Society.

Athletics. NCAA. **Intercollegiate:** Baseball M, basketball, cross-country, football (tackle) M, golf, lacrosse, soccer W, softball W, swimming W, tennis, track and field, volleyball W, water polo W, wrestling M. **Intramural:** Basketball, bowling, cheerleading W, football (tackle) M, soccer, softball, table tennis, tennis, volleyball. **Team name:** Seahawks.

Student services. Alcohol/substance abuse counseling, campus ministries, career counseling, student employment services, financial aid counseling, health services, personal counseling, placement for graduates. **Physically disabled:** Services for visually, hearing impaired.

Contact. E-mail: adm@wagner.edu
Phone: (718) 390-3411 Toll-free number: (800) 221-1010
Fax: (718) 390-3105
Leigh-Ann DePascale, Director of Admissions, Wagner College, One Campus Road, Staten Island, NY 10301-4495

Webb Institute

Glen Cove, New York — **CB member**
www.webb-institute.edu — **CB code: 2970**

- Private 4-year maritime college
- Residential campus in large town
- 80 degree-seeking undergraduates: 20% women, 1% African American, 2% Asian American, 1% Hispanic American
- 30% of applicants admitted
- SAT and SAT Subject Tests, interview required
- 65% graduate within 6 years; 25% enter graduate study

General. Founded in 1889. Regionally accredited. All students participate in 2-month paid winter work program in marine industry each year. **Degrees:** 12 bachelor's awarded. **Location:** 22 miles from New York City. **Calendar:** Semester. **Full-time faculty:** 8 total; 50% have terminal degrees. **Part-time faculty:** 7 total; 100% have terminal degrees. **Class size:** 20% < 20, 80% 20-39. **Special facilities:** Adjoining nature preserve, model testing tank.

Freshman class profile. 103 applied, 31 admitted, 20 enrolled.

Mid 50% test scores			
SAT verbal:	660-700	Rank in top tenth:	70%
SAT math:	720-750	End year in good standing:	92%
GPA 3.50 or higher:	100%	Return as sophomores:	92%
Rank in top quarter:	100%	Out-of-state:	95%
		Live on campus:	100%

Basis for selection. GED not accepted. High school record, class rank, test scores, and interview most important. Character, motivation, and outside activities considered.

High school preparation. 16 units required. Required units include English 4, mathematics 4, social studies 2, science 2 (laboratory 2) and academic electives 4.

2006-2007 Annual costs. All students receive 4-year, full-tuition scholarships. Room/board: $8,340. Books/supplies: $600. Personal expenses: $600.

2005-2006 Financial aid. All financial aid based on need. 7 full-time freshmen applied for aid; 6 were judged to have need; 6 of these received aid. Average need met was 81%. Average scholarship/grant was $4,050; average loan $2,389. 30% of total undergraduate aid awarded as scholarships/grants, 70% as loans/jobs.

Application procedures. Admission: Closing date 2/15 (postmark date). $25 fee, may be waived for applicants with need. Application must be submitted on paper. Admission notification on a rolling basis beginning on or about 3/15. Must reply by May 1 or within 2 week(s) if notified thereafter. **Financial aid:** Closing date 7/1. FAFSA required. Applicants notified by 8/1; must reply within 2 week(s) of notification.

Academics. Intensive single curriculum program demands high career motivation. **Special study options:** Double major, independent study, internships. **Credit/placement by examination:** CLEP. **Support services:** Study skills assistance.

Majors. Engineering: Marine.

Computing on campus. PC or laptop required. 88 workstations in dormitories, library, computer center, student center. Dormitories wired for high-speed internet access and linked to campus network. Commuter students can connect to campus network. Repair service, wireless network available.

Student life. Freshman orientation: Mandatory. **Policies:** Freshmen permitted cars on campus. **Housing:** Guaranteed on-campus for all undergraduates. Coed dorms, single-sex dorms, substance-free housing available. $150 nonrefundable deposit. **Activities:** Choral groups, drama, student government, free membership available to local YMCA, women engineers, society of American naval engineers, WebbWomen, society of naval architects and marine engineers.

Athletics. Intercollegiate: Basketball, cross-country, sailing, soccer, tennis, track and field, volleyball. **Intramural:** Basketball, soccer, softball, volleyball.

Student services. Alcohol/substance abuse counseling, career counseling, student employment services, financial aid counseling, health services, personal counseling, placement for graduates.

Contact. E-mail: admissions@webb-institute.edu
Phone: (516) 671-2213 Toll-free number: (866) 708-9322
Fax: (516) 674-9838
Stephen Ostendorff, Director of Admissions, Webb Institute, 298 Crescent Beach Road, Glen Cove, NY 11542-1398

Wells College

Aurora, New York — **CB member**
www.wells.edu — **CB code: 2971**

- Private 4-year liberal arts college
- Residential campus in rural community
- 407 degree-seeking undergraduates: 1% part-time, 92% women, 7% African American, 3% Asian American, 4% Hispanic American, 2% international
- 65% of applicants admitted
- SAT or ACT (ACT writing optional), application essay required
- 59% graduate within 6 years; 25% enter graduate study

General. Founded in 1868. Regionally accredited. Experiential learning integrated through internship and off-campus study programs, study abroad, research with professors, and community service. **Degrees:** 88 bachelor's awarded. **ROTC:** Air Force. **Location:** 30 miles from Ithaca, 50 miles from Syracuse. **Calendar:** Semester. **Full-time faculty:** 49 total; 94% have terminal degrees, 22% minority, 55% women. **Part-time faculty:** 20 total; 50% have terminal degrees, 15% minority. **Class size:** 82% < 20, 18% 20-39, less than 1% 40-49. **Special facilities:** Book arts center, lithography presses, digital imaging laboratory, darkroom, indoor tennis courts, 9-hole golf course.

Freshman class profile. 1,036 applied, 673 admitted, 130 enrolled.

Mid 50% test scores			
SAT verbal:	520-630	Rank in top quarter:	64%
SAT math:	480-580	Rank in top tenth:	25%
ACT:	20-26	End year in good standing:	90%
GPA 3.50 or higher:	49%	Return as sophomores:	71%
GPA 3.0-3.49:	28%	Out-of-state:	41%
GPA 2.0-2.99:	23%	Live on campus:	99%
		International:	1%

Basis for selection. Academic achievement record most important. Test scores, class rank, recommendations, essay, school and community extracurricular activities also important. Evidence of leadership ability through academic and cocurricular activities also considered. Interviews highly recommended. **Homeschooled:** State high school equivalency certificate required.

Four-Year Colleges

High school preparation. College-preparatory program required. 16 units required; 23 recommended. Required and recommended units include English 4, mathematics 3-4, social studies 1-2, history 2, science 2-3 (laboratory 2-3), foreign language 2 and academic electives 2-3. Students encouraged to take 2 units of computer science, art, and music. AP and honors courses recommended.

2006-2007 Annual costs. Tuition/fees (projected): $16,680. Room/board: $7,500. Books/supplies: $700. Personal expenses: $700.

2005-2006 Financial aid. All financial aid based on need. 122 full-time freshmen applied for aid; 99 were judged to have need; 99 of these received aid. Average need met was 92%. Average scholarship/grant was $12,620; average loan $3,407. 67% of total undergraduate aid awarded as scholarships/grants, 33% as loans/jobs.

Application procedures. Admission: Priority date 12/15; deadline 3/1 (postmark date). $40 fee, may be waived for applicants with need. Application may be submitted online. Admission notification 4/1. Must reply by May 1 or within 4 week(s) if notified thereafter. **Financial aid:** Priority date 2/15; no closing date. FAFSA required. CSS PROFILE required of Early Decision candidates only. Applicants notified on a rolling basis starting 3/1; must reply by 5/1 or within 4 week(s) of notification.

Academics. Special study options: Accelerated study, combined bachelor's/graduate degree, cross-registration, double major, independent study, internships, student-designed major, study abroad, teacher certification program, Washington semester. Study abroad in France, Spain, Italy, Germany, Denmark, Great Britain, Ireland, Mexico, Sweden, Japan, Dominican Republic, Senegal; field studies in Africa, Australia, the Caribbean, Maine; cross registration with Cornell University, Ithaca College and Cayuga Community College. **Credit/placement by examination:** AP, CLEP, IB, institutional tests. 6 credit hours maximum toward bachelor's degree. **Support services:** Reduced course load, study skills assistance, tutoring, writing center.

Majors. Area/ethnic studies: African-American, American, women's. **Biology:** General, biochemistry, molecular. **Business:** General, managerial economics. **Computer sciences:** Computer science. **Conservation:** General, environmental science, environmental studies. **English:** English lit. **Foreign languages:** General, comparative lit, French, German, Spanish. **Health:** Predentistry, premedicine, preveterinary. **History:** General. **Interdisciplinary:** Global studies. **Legal studies:** Prelaw. **Liberal arts:** Humanities. **Math:** General. **Philosophy/religion:** Ethics, philosophy, religion. **Physical sciences:** Chemistry, physics. **Psychology:** General. **Public administration:** Policy analysis. **Social sciences:** Anthropology, economics, international relations, sociology, U.S. government. **Visual/performing arts:** General, art, art history/conservation, dance, dramatic, studio arts.

Most popular majors. Biology 20%, history 8%, psychology 23%, public administration/social services 7%, social sciences 16%, visual/performing arts 10%.

Computing on campus. 85 workstations in dormitories, library, computer center. Dormitories wired for high-speed internet access and linked to campus network. Commuter students can connect to campus network. Online library, repair service available.

Student life. Freshman orientation: Mandatory. Preregistration for classes offered. General introduction held over a weekend in July; 5-day orientation held before classes begin. **Policies:** Honor code governs academic and cocurricular life. Freshmen permitted cars on campus. **Housing:** Guaranteed on-campus for all undergraduates. Coed dorms, single-sex dorms, substance-free housing available. $300 nonrefundable deposit, deadline 5/1. **Activities:** Choral groups, dance, drama, literary magazine, music ensembles, student government, student newspaper, Model United Nations, Amnesty International, Christian Fellowship, Green Geese (environmental club), Collegiate, Praising our Work, Ethnicity and Race (social and cultural organization), Women in Life-Long Learning, Political Action Committee, international student association.

Athletics. NCAA. **Intercollegiate:** Cross-country, field hockey W, lacrosse W, soccer, softball W, swimming, tennis W. **Intramural:** Basketball, football (non-tackle), soccer, tennis, volleyball. **Team name:** Express.

Student services. Adult student services, campus ministries, career counseling, financial aid counseling, health services, minority student services, personal counseling, women's services.

Contact. E-mail: admissions@wells.edu
Phone: (315) 364-3264 Toll-free number: (800) 952-9355
Fax: (315) 364-3227
Susan Sloan, Director of Admissions, Wells College, 170 Main Street, Aurora, NY 13026

Yeshiva and Kolel Bais Medrash Elyon
Monsey, New York

- Private 4-year rabbinical college for men affiliated with Jewish faith
- Small city
- 17 degree-seeking undergraduates
- 67% of applicants admitted

General. Accredited by AARTS. **Calendar:** Semester. **Full-time faculty:** 3 total. **Part-time faculty:** 2 total.

Freshman class profile. 6 applied, 4 admitted, 4 enrolled.

2006-2007 Annual costs. Tuition/fees: $7,500.

Application procedures. Admission: No deadline. No application fee. Admission notification on a rolling basis.

Academics. Credit/placement by examination: CLEP.

Majors. Theology: Talmudic.

Contact. Phone: (845) 356-7064
Rabbi Israel Falk, Admissions Director, Yeshiva and Kolel Bais Medrash Elyon, 73 Main Street, Monsey, NY 10952

Yeshiva and Kollel Harbotzas Torah
Brooklyn, New York

- Private 4-year rabbinical college for men affiliated with Jewish faith
- Very large city

General. Accredited by AARTS.

Contact. Phone: (718) 692-0208
1049 East 15th Street, Brooklyn, NY 11230

Yeshiva Derech Chaim
Brooklyn, New York

CB code: 0552

- Private 5-year rabbinical college for men affiliated with Jewish faith
- Very large city
- 120 degree-seeking undergraduates
- Interview required

General. Founded in 1975. Accredited by AARTS. First and advanced Talmudic degrees available. **Degrees:** 13 bachelor's awarded; doctoral, first professional offered. **Calendar:** Semester. **Full-time faculty:** 12 total. **Part-time faculty:** 7 total.

Basis for selection. Dean interviews each applicant. Recommendations very important. Applicants without high school diplomas may be admitted on basis of national AARTS exam.

2006-2007 Annual costs. Tuition/fees (projected): $7,000. Books/supplies: $400.

Financial aid. Additional information: Financial aid interview held with each admitted student.

Application procedures. Admission: Priority date 8/20; no deadline. No application fee. Admission notification on a rolling basis. **Financial aid:** No deadline. Applicants notified on a rolling basis.

Academics. Credit/placement by examination: CLEP.

Majors. Theology: Talmudic.

Student life. Policies: Religious observance required. **Activities:** Choral groups, TV station.

Contact. Phone: (718) 438-3070
Rabbi Mordechai Rennert, Admissions Director, Yeshiva Derech Chaim, 1573 39th Street, Brooklyn, NY 11218

Yeshiva D'Monsey Rabbinical College
Monsey, New York

- Private 4-year rabbinical college for men affiliated with Jewish faith

General. Accredited by AARTS.

Academics. Credit/placement by examination: CLEP.

Contact. Phone: (845) 352-5852
Yeshiva D'Monsey Rabbinical College, 2 Roman Boulevard, Monsey, NY 10952

Yeshiva Gedolah Imrei Yosef D'Spinka
Brooklyn, New York

- Private 4-year rabbinical college for men affiliated with Jewish faith
- Very large city
- 207 degree-seeking undergraduates

General. Accredited by AARTS. **Degrees:** 43 bachelor's awarded. **Full-time faculty:** 9 total.

2006-2007 Annual costs. Tuition/fees (projected): $4,500.

Application procedures. Admission: Priority date 8/18; deadline 9/28. No application fee.

Academics. Credit/placement by examination: CLEP.

Contact. Phone: (718) 851-1600
Rabbi Rosenbaum, Admissions Director, Yeshiva Gedolah Imrei Yosef D'Spinka, 1466 56th Street, Brooklyn, NY 11219

Yeshiva Gedolah Zichron Moshe
South Fallsburg, New York
CB code: 0750

- Private 4-year rabbinical college for men affiliated with Jewish faith
- Small town

General. Founded in 1969. Accredited by AARTS. **Calendar:** Semester.

Annual costs/financial aid. Tuition/fees (2005-2006): $7,000. Books/supplies: $200. Personal expenses: $2,000.

Contact. Phone: (845) 434-5240
Dean of Admissions, Laurel Park Road, South Fallsburg, NY 12779

Yeshiva Karlin Stolin
Brooklyn, New York
CB code: 1582

- Private 4-year rabbinical college for men affiliated with Jewish faith
- Very large city

General. Accredited by AARTS.

Annual costs/financial aid. Tuition/fees (2005-2006): $6,000.

Contact. Phone: (718) 232-7800
1818 54th Street, Brooklyn, NY 11204-1545

Yeshiva Mikdash Melech
Brooklyn, New York
CB code: 1432

- Private 4-year rabbinical college for men affiliated with Jewish faith
- Residential campus in very large city
- 89 degree-seeking undergraduates: 15% part-time
- 2 degree-seeking graduate students
- 77% of applicants admitted
- Interview required

General. Accredited by AARTS. **Degrees:** 2 bachelor's awarded; master's, first professional offered. **Calendar:** Semester, extensive summer session. **Full-time faculty:** 6 total; 67% have terminal degrees. **Class size:** 100% < 20.

Freshman class profile. 78 applied, 60 admitted, 60 enrolled.

End year in good standing:	98%	**Live on campus:**	70%

Basis for selection. Recommendations, school record, test scores, and class rank considered. **Homeschooled:** Statement describing homeschool structure and mission required.

High school preparation. 3 units required; 4 recommended. Required and recommended units include English 3, mathematics 3, social studies 1, history 1, science 2 (laboratory 1), foreign language 1 and academic electives 1.

2006-2007 Annual costs. Tuition/fees (projected): $6,500. Room/board: $3,800.

2004-2005 Financial aid. Need-based: 98% of total undergraduate aid awarded as scholarships/grants, 2% as loans/jobs. **Non-need-based:** Scholarships awarded for academics, leadership, religious affiliation.

Application procedures. Admission: No deadline. No application fee. Application must be submitted on paper. Admission notification on a rolling basis. **Financial aid:** No deadline. FAFSA required. Applicants notified on a rolling basis starting 5/1.

Academics. Special study options: Independent study, study abroad. **Credit/placement by examination:** CLEP. **Support services:** Remedial instruction, tutoring.

Majors. Philosophy/religion: Judaic. **Theology:** Talmudic.

Student life. Freshman orientation: Available. Preregistration for classes offered. **Policies:** Religious observance required. **Housing:** Guaranteed on-campus for freshmen. Substance-free housing available.

Student services. Adult student services, campus ministries, financial aid counseling.

Contact. E-mail: mikdashmelech@covad.net
Phone: (718) 339-1090 Fax: (718) 998-9321
Rabbi Shmuel Beyda, Admissions Director, Yeshiva Mikdash Melech, 1326 Ocean Parkway, Brooklyn, NY 11230

Yeshiva of Nitra
Mount Kisco, New York
CB code: 7131

- Private 4-year rabbinical college for men affiliated with Jewish faith
- Small city

General. Accredited by AARTS. **Calendar:** Continuous.

Annual costs/financial aid. Tuition/fees (2005-2006): $5,000.

Contact. Phone: (718) 387-0422
Pine Bridge Road, Mount Kisco, NY 10549

Yeshiva of the Telshe Alumni
Riverdale, New York

- Private 4-year rabbinical college for men affiliated with Jewish faith
- Very large city

General. Accredited by AARTS.

Contact. Phone: (718) 601-3523
4904 Independence Avenue, Riverdale, NY 10471

Yeshiva Shaar Hatorah
Kew Gardens, New York
CB code: 0743

- Private 4-year rabbinical college for men affiliated with Jewish faith
- Very large city

General. Founded in 1976. Accredited by AARTS. **Calendar:** Semester.

Annual costs/financial aid. Comprehensive fee (2005-2006): $11,500.

Contact. Phone: (718) 846-1940
Admissions Director, 117-06 84th Avenue, Kew Gardens, NY 11418

Yeshiva Shaarei Torah of Rockland
Suffern, New York

- Private 4-year rabbinical college for men affiliated with Jewish faith
- Commuter campus in small city

General. Accredited by AARTS. **Calendar:** Semester.

Annual costs/financial aid. Tuition/fees (2005-2006): $6,000.

Contact. Phone: (845) 352-3431
Admissions Director, 91 West Carlton Road, Suffern, NY 10901

Yeshiva University
New York, New York CB member
www.yu.edu CB code: 2990

- Private 4-year university and liberal arts college
- Residential campus in very large city
- 2,927 degree-seeking undergraduates
- 3,440 graduate students
- 78% of applicants admitted
- SAT or ACT with writing, application essay, interview required
- 81% graduate within 6 years

General. Founded in 1886. Regionally accredited. Campus locations in Manhattan and the Bronx. **Degrees:** 650 bachelor's, 272 associate awarded; master's, doctoral, first professional offered. **Calendar:** Semester, limited summer session. **Full-time faculty:** 844 total; 95% have terminal degrees, 19% minority, 36% women. **Part-time faculty:** 401 total; 90% have terminal degrees, 6% minority, 42% women.

Freshman class profile. 1,875 applied, 1,466 admitted, 1,004 enrolled.

Mid 50% test scores		SAT math:	550-680
SAT verbal:	550-660		

Basis for selection. Equal weight given to high school GPA, test scores, ability and motivation as indicated in interview, school and community activities, recommendations of principal, guidance counselor, and/or employer. **Homeschooled:** Statement describing homeschool structure and mission, transcript of courses and grades, state high school equivalency certificate, interview required.

2005-2006 Annual costs. Tuition/fees: $26,100. Room/board: $7,880. Books/supplies: $1,072.

Financial aid. Additional information: Essays required of Distinguished Scholarship applicants.

Application procedures. Admission: Priority date 2/1; no deadline. $50 fee, may be waived for applicants with need. Application may be submitted online. Admission notification on a rolling basis beginning on or about 12/15. Must reply by May 1 or within 2 week(s) if notified thereafter. **Financial aid:** Priority date 4/15, closing date 5/1. FAFSA, institutional form required. Applicants notified on a rolling basis starting 4/1.

Academics. Special study options: Combined bachelor's/graduate degree, cross-registration, double major, dual enrollment of high school students, exchange student, honors, independent study, internships, student-designed major, study abroad, teacher certification program. **Credit/placement by examination:** CLEP, institutional tests. 44 credit hours maximum toward bachelor's degree. **Support services:** Reduced course load, tutoring, writing center.

Honors college/program. 1400 SAT (exclusive of Writing) or ACT equivalent, 2 nominations, interview required.

Majors. Biology: General. **Business:** Accounting, business admin. **Computer sciences:** General, computer science. **Education:** Elementary, foreign languages. **Engineering:** General. **English:** Speech/rhetoric. **Foreign languages:** Classics, French, Hebrew. **Health:** Audiology/speech pathology, premedicine. **History:** General. **Math:** General. **Philosophy/religion:** Judaic, philosophy. **Physical sciences:** Chemistry, physics. **Psychology:** General. **Social sciences:** Economics, political science, sociology.

Most popular majors. Biology 11%, business/marketing 29%, English 7%, liberal arts 13%, philosophy/religious studies 6%, psychology 15%, social sciences 8%.

Computing on campus. 350 workstations in library, computer center, student center. Dormitories wired for high-speed internet access and linked to campus network. Online library, helpline, repair service, wireless network available.

Student life. Freshman orientation: Mandatory. Held the week before classes. **Policies:** Students participate in university governance through college senates. **Housing:** Guaranteed on-campus for all undergraduates. Single-sex dorms, apartments available. $250 nonrefundable deposit, deadline 8/1. **Activities:** Jazz band, choral groups, drama, literary magazine, music ensembles, musical theater, radio station, student government, student newspaper, neighborhood social service, preprofessional, special interest, and political clubs.

Athletics. NCAA. **Intercollegiate:** Baseball M, basketball, cross-country M, fencing M, golf M, soccer M, tennis M, volleyball M, wrestling M. **Intramural:** Basketball, tennis M, volleyball W. **Team name:** Macs.

Student services. Career counseling, student employment services, health services, personal counseling, placement for graduates.

Contact. E-mail: yuadmit@yu.edu
Phone: (212) 960-5277 Fax: (212) 960-0086
Michael Kranzler, Director of Undergraduate Admissions, Yeshiva University, 500 West 185th Street, New York, NY 10033

Yeshivas Novominsk
Brooklyn, New York

- Private 4-year rabbinical college for men affiliated with Jewish faith
- Very large city

General. Accredited by AARTS.

Annual costs/financial aid. Tuition/fees (2005-2006): $6,500.

Contact. Phone: (718) 438-2727
1569 47th Street, Brooklyn, NY 11219

Yeshivath Viznitz
Monsey, New York

- Private 4-year rabbinical college for men

General. Accredited by AARTS. **Calendar:** Semester.

Annual costs/financial aid. Tuition/fees (2005-2006): $4,500.

Contact. Phone: (914) 356-1010
25 Phyllis Terrace, Monsey, NY 10952

North Carolina

Appalachian State University

Boone, North Carolina **CB member**
www.appstate.edu **CB code: 5010**

- Public 4-year university
- Residential campus in large town
- 12,619 degree-seeking undergraduates: 5% part-time, 49% women, 3% African American, 1% Asian American, 2% Hispanic American
- 1,664 degree-seeking graduate students
- 69% of applicants admitted
- SAT or ACT with writing required

General. Founded in 1899. Regionally accredited. **Degrees:** 2,663 bachelor's awarded; master's, doctoral offered. **ROTC:** Army. **Location:** 87 miles from Winston-Salem. **Calendar:** Semester, extensive summer session. **Full-time faculty:** 703 total; 98% have terminal degrees, 7% minority, 42% women. **Part-time faculty:** 295 total; 81% have terminal degrees, 6% minority, 52% women. **Class size:** 41% < 20, 44% 20-39, 8% 40-49, 6% 50-99, 1% >100. **Special facilities:** Observatory, cultural museum, visual arts center, year round outdoor adventure camp.

Freshman class profile. 9,923 applied, 6,832 admitted, 2,543 enrolled.

Mid 50% test scores			
SAT verbal:	510-610	GPA 2.0-2.99:	5%
SAT math:	530-610	Rank in top quarter:	50%
ACT:	20-25	Rank in top tenth:	16%
GPA 3.50 or higher:	70%	Return as sophomores:	86%
GPA 3.0-3.49:	25%	Out-of-state:	11%
		Live on campus:	97%

Basis for selection. Satisfactory combination of grades and test scores or class rank and test scores required. SAT preferred, ACT also accepted. Audition required for music majors; portfolio required for art majors.

High school preparation. 13 units required. Required and recommended units include English 4, mathematics 3, social studies 1, history 1, science 3 (laboratory 1) and foreign language 2. Math units should include algebra I, algebra II, and geometry.

2005-2006 Annual costs. Tuition/fees: $3,436; $13,178 out-of-state. Room/board: $5,410. Books/supplies: $500. Personal expenses: $1,200.

2005-2006 Financial aid. Need-based: 1,666 full-time freshmen applied for aid; 822 were judged to have need; 785 of these received aid. Average need met was 74%. Average scholarship/grant was $4,450; average loan $2,526. 44% of total undergraduate aid awarded as scholarships/grants, 56% as loans/jobs. **Non-need-based:** Awarded to 1,808 full-time undergraduates, including 568 freshmen. Scholarships awarded for academics, alumni affiliation, art, athletics, job skills, leadership, minority status, music/drama, religious affiliation, ROTC, state residency.

Application procedures. Admission: No deadline. $45 fee, may be waived for applicants with need. Application may be submitted online. Admission notification on a rolling basis beginning on or about 9/1. **Financial aid:** Priority date 3/15; no closing date. FAFSA required. Applicants notified on a rolling basis starting 4/1; must reply within 3 week(s) of notification.

Academics. Special study options: Cooperative education, distance learning, double major, dual enrollment of high school students, ESL, honors, independent study, internships, liberal arts/career combination, student-designed major, study abroad, teacher certification program. **Credit/placement by examination:** AP, CLEP, IB, institutional tests. **Support services:** Learning center, pre-admission summer program, remedial instruction, study skills assistance, tutoring, writing center.

Majors. Architecture: Urban/community planning. **Biology:** General, ecology. **Business:** Accounting, business admin, finance, hospitality admin, insurance, international, management information systems, marketing. **Communications:** Advertising, journalism, public relations, radio/tv. **Computer sciences:** Computer science. **Education:** Art, biology, business, chemistry, drama/dance, elementary, English, family/consumer sciences, French, health, history, kindergarten/preschool, learning disabled, mathematics, middle, music, physical, physics, social studies, Spanish, special, technology/industrial arts. **Engineering technology:** Drafting, electrical, industrial. **English:** English lit, speech/rhetoric. **Family/consumer sciences:** Child development, clothing/textiles, food/nutrition. **Foreign languages:** French, Spanish. **Health:** Athletic training, clinical lab science, communication disorders, health care admin, music therapy, nursing (RN), public health ed. **History:** General. **Liberal arts:** Arts/sciences. **Math:** General, statistics. **Parks/recreation:** Exercise sciences, facilities management. **Philosophy/religion:** Philosophy, religion. **Physical sciences:** Chemistry, geology, physics. **Protective services:** Criminal justice. **Psychology:** General. **Public administration:** Social work. **Social sciences:** Anthropology, economics, geography, political science, sociology. **Visual/performing arts:** Art, arts management, dramatic, graphic design, industrial design, interior design, music management, music performance, studio arts.

Most popular majors. Business/marketing 19%, communications/journalism 6%, education 25%, science technologies 7%, social sciences 7%, visual/performing arts 6%.

Computing on campus. 900 workstations in dormitories, library, computer center, student center. Dormitories linked to campus network. Commuter students can connect to campus network. Online course registration, helpline, repair service available.

Student life. Freshman orientation: Mandatory. Preregistration for classes offered. 2-day program throughout summer and at beginning of each semester and summer school session. **Housing:** Guaranteed on-campus for freshmen. Coed dorms, single-sex dorms, special housing for disabled, apartments, cooperative housing, substance-free housing available. $100 deposit, deadline 5/1. **Activities:** Bands, choral groups, dance, drama, film society, literary magazine, music ensembles, musical theater, opera, radio station, student government, student newspaper, symphony orchestra, TV station, Baptist student union, Methodist student union, Catholic student union, Presbyterian student union, Campus Crusade for Christ, Circle K, ACLU, Amnesty International, black student association.

Athletics. NCAA. **Intercollegiate:** Baseball M, basketball, cross-country, field hockey W, football (tackle) M, golf, soccer, softball W, tennis, track and field, volleyball W, wrestling M. **Intramural:** Archery, badminton, basketball, bowling, cross-country, fencing, field hockey W, football (tackle), golf, gymnastics, handball, racquetball, rugby M, skiing, soccer, softball, squash, swimming, table tennis, tennis, track and field, volleyball, water polo, wrestling M. **Team name:** Mountaineers.

Student services. Adult student services, campus ministries, career counseling, student employment services, financial aid counseling, health services, on-campus daycare, personal counseling, placement for graduates, veterans' counselor, women's services. **Physically disabled:** Services for visually, speech, hearing impaired. **Learning disabled:** Comprehensive services available.

Contact. E-mail: admissions@appstate.edu
Phone: (828) 262-2120 Fax: (828) 262-3296
Paul Hiatt, Director of Admissions, Appalachian State University, ASU Box 32004, Boone, NC 28608

Art Institute of Charlotte

Charlotte, North Carolina
www.aich.artinstitutes.edu **CB code: 3834**

- For-profit 4-year visual arts college
- Commuter campus in very large city
- 821 degree-seeking undergraduates
- Application essay required

General. Accredited by ACICS. **Degrees:** 154 associate awarded. **Calendar:** Quarter, extensive summer session. **Full-time faculty:** 26 total. **Part-time faculty:** 30 total.

Basis for selection. Essay and high school record most important. Standardized test scores also considered. SAT or ACT recommended. Students with a 2.0 average or lower required to take accuplacer placement test.

2006-2007 Annual costs. Tuition/fees (projected): $22,437. Annual tuition varies by program. First-time students pay an average kit fee of $850 (price may vary depending on program).

Application procedures. Admission: No deadline. No application fee. Application may be submitted online. Admission notification on a rolling basis.

Academics. Special study options: Distance learning, internships, study abroad. **Credit/placement by examination:** CLEP. **Support services:** Learning center, remedial instruction, study skills assistance, tutoring, writing center.

Majors. Business: Fashion. **Computer sciences:** Web page design. **Personal/culinary services:** Restaurant/catering. **Visual/performing arts:** Graphic design, interior design, multimedia.

Computing on campus. 200 workstations in library, computer center, student center. Commuter students can connect to campus network. Helpline, student web hosting available.

Student life. Freshman orientation: Mandatory. Preregistration for classes offered. **Policies:** Freshmen permitted cars on campus. **Housing:** Apartments available. $450 deposit.

Student services. Alcohol/substance abuse counseling, career counseling, student employment services, financial aid counseling, personal counseling, placement for graduates, veterans' counselor.

Contact. E-mail: aichadm@aii.edu
Phone: (704) 357-8020 Toll-free number: (800) 872-4417
Fax: (704) 357-1133
Jeff Bucklew, Director of Admissions, Art Institute of Charlotte, Three LakePointe Plaza, Charlotte, NC 28217

Barton College

Wilson, North Carolina — **CB member**
www.barton.edu — **CB code: 5016**

- Private 4-year liberal arts college affiliated with Christian Church (Disciples of Christ)
- Residential campus in large town
- 1,189 degree-seeking undergraduates: 23% part-time, 73% women, 23% African American, 1% Asian American, 2% Hispanic American, 2% international
- 70% of applicants admitted
- SAT or ACT (ACT writing optional) required
- 42% graduate within 6 years

General. Founded in 1902. Regionally accredited. **Degrees:** 229 bachelor's awarded. **Location:** 45 miles from Raleigh. **Calendar:** 4-1-4, limited summer session. **Full-time faculty:** 79 total; 56% have terminal degrees, 8% minority, 51% women. **Part-time faculty:** 32 total; 12% have terminal degrees, 12% minority, 59% women. **Class size:** 61% < 20, 37% 20-39, 1% 40-49, less than 1% 50-99. **Special facilities:** Greenhouse, TV and music recording studios, photo developing labs and darkroom.

Freshman class profile. 1,295 applied, 908 admitted, 247 enrolled.

Mid 50% test scores			
SAT verbal:	400-570	Rank in top quarter:	34%
SAT math:	420-590	Rank in top tenth:	13%
GPA 3.50 or higher:	24%	Return as sophomores:	60%
GPA 3.0-3.49:	31%	Out-of-state:	27%
GPA 2.0-2.99:	45%	Live on campus:	79%
		International:	2%

Basis for selection. High school GPA, test scores, strong academic course study important. Interview recommended for marginal students; portfolio recommended for art students.

High school preparation. College-preparatory program required. 13 units required. Required and recommended units include English 4, mathematics 3, social studies 3, science 2 (laboratory 1), foreign language 2 and academic electives 1. Math must include algebra. Social studies units may be filled by any social science.

2005-2006 Annual costs. Tuition/fees: $16,670. Room/board: $5,880.

2004-2005 Financial aid. Need-based: 215 full-time freshmen applied for aid; 192 were judged to have need; 192 of these received aid. Average need met was 75%. Average scholarship/grant was $4,790; average loan $2,858. 43% of total undergraduate aid awarded as scholarships/grants, 57% as loans/jobs. **Non-need-based:** Awarded to 827 full-time undergraduates, including 227 freshmen. Scholarships awarded for academics, alumni affiliation, athletics, leadership, religious affiliation, state residency.

Application procedures. Admission: No deadline. $25 fee, may be waived for applicants with need. Application may be submitted online. Admission notification on a rolling basis beginning on or about 9/1. Must reply by May 1 or within 2 week(s) if notified thereafter. **Financial aid:** Priority date 4/1; no closing date. FAFSA required. Applicants notified on a rolling basis starting 2/1; must reply within 2 week(s) of notification.

Academics. Special study options: Cooperative education, double major, ESL, honors, independent study, internships, liberal arts/career combination, study abroad, teacher certification program, weekend college. **Credit/placement by examination:** AP, CLEP, IB, SAT, ACT, institutional tests. 30 credit hours maximum toward bachelor's degree. **Support services:** Learning center, remedial instruction, tutoring, writing center.

Majors. Biology: General. **Business:** Accounting, business admin, human resources, managerial economics. **Communications:** Media studies. **Computer sciences:** General. **Conservation:** Environmental science. **Education:** Art, Deaf/hearing impaired, elementary, learning disabled, middle, physical, social studies. **English:** English lit. **Foreign languages:** Spanish. **Health:** Athletic training, nursing (RN). **History:** General. **Legal studies:** Prelaw. **Liberal arts:** Arts/sciences. **Math:** General. **Parks/recreation:** Health/fitness, sports admin. **Physical sciences:** Chemistry. **Protective services:** Criminal justice. **Psychology:** General. **Public administration:** Social work. **Social sciences:** Political science. **Visual/performing arts:** Dramatic, studio arts.

Most popular majors. Biology 6%, business/marketing 28%, education 14%, health sciences 15%, public administration/social services 8%, security/protective services 6%.

Computing on campus. 175 workstations in dormitories, library, computer center, student center. Dormitories wired for high-speed internet access and linked to campus network. Commuter students can connect to campus network. Online library, helpline available.

Student life. Freshman orientation: Mandatory. Preregistration for classes offered. **Policies:** Freshmen permitted cars on campus. **Housing:** Guaranteed on-campus for freshmen. Coed dorms, single-sex dorms, special housing for disabled, fraternity/sorority housing, substance-free housing available. $150 nonrefundable deposit, deadline 8/1. Full-time freshmen and sophomores not living with parents required to live on campus. Special permission required for students under 23 to live off-campus. **Activities:** Pep band, choral groups, drama, literary magazine, musical theater, student government, student newspaper, symphony orchestra, TV station, Black Student Awareness Association, Baptist student union, Disciple student union, sign language choir, Hamlin Society, Fellowship of Christian Athletes, Habitat for Humanity, Alpha Phi Omega.

Athletics. NCAA. **Intercollegiate:** Baseball M, basketball, cross-country, golf M, soccer, softball W, tennis, volleyball W. **Intramural:** Basketball, football (non-tackle), soccer, softball, tennis, volleyball. **Team name:** Bulldogs.

Student services. Adult student services, campus ministries, career counseling, student employment services, financial aid counseling, health services, personal counseling, placement for graduates. **Physically disabled:** Services for visually, hearing impaired.

Contact. E-mail: enroll@barton.edu
Phone: (252) 399-6317 Toll-free number: (800) 345-4973
Fax: (252) 399-6572
Amy Denton, Director of Admissions, Barton College, Box 5000, Wilson, NC 27893

Belmont Abbey College

Belmont, North Carolina — **CB member**
www.belmontabbeycollege.edu — **CB code: 5055**

- Private 4-year liberal arts college affiliated with Roman Catholic Church
- Residential campus in small town
- 857 degree-seeking undergraduates: 7% part-time, 55% women, 11% African American, 1% Asian American, 4% Hispanic American, 6% international
- 77% of applicants admitted
- SAT or ACT, interview required

General. Founded in 1876. Regionally accredited. **Degrees:** 177 bachelor's awarded. **ROTC:** Army, Navy, Air Force. **Location:** 12 miles from Charlotte. **Calendar:** Semester, limited summer session. **Full-time faculty:** 48 total; 75% have terminal degrees, 4% minority, 42% women. **Part-time faculty:** 37 total; 24% have terminal degrees, 49% women. **Class size:** 72% < 20, 27% 20-39, less than 1% 40-49, less than 1% 50-99.

Freshman class profile. 903 applied, 694 admitted, 225 enrolled.

Mid 50% test scores			
SAT verbal:	460-570	Rank in top quarter:	13%
SAT math:	460-560	Rank in top tenth:	4%
ACT:	18-23	Out-of-state:	59%
GPA 3.50 or higher:	24%	Live on campus:	89%
GPA 3.0-3.49:	29%	International:	7%
GPA 2.0-2.99:	45%	Fraternities:	20%
		Sororities:	20%

Basis for selection. GPA, class rank, high school curriculum, and test scores most important. Personal accomplishments, extracurricular activities, and letters of recommendation strongly considered.

High school preparation. 16 units required. Required and recommended units include English 4, mathematics 3-4, social studies 2, science 2, foreign language 2-3 and academic electives 3. One social science must be history. For science majors, 4 math, 1 chemistry, 1 physics, 1 additional science recommended.

2005-2006 Annual costs. Tuition/fees: $17,510. Room/board: $8,588. Books/supplies: $900. Personal expenses: $1,800.

2005-2006 Financial aid. Need-based: Average need met was 64%. Average scholarship/grant was $10,797; average loan $2,232. 66% of total undergraduate aid awarded as scholarships/grants, 34% as loans/jobs. **Non-need-based:** Scholarships awarded for academics, athletics, leadership, religious affiliation, state residency.

Application procedures. Admission: Closing date 8/1 (postmark date). $35 fee, may be waived for applicants with need. Application may be submitted online. Admission notification on a rolling basis beginning on or about 9/15. Must reply by May 1 or within 3 week(s) if notified thereafter. **Financial aid:** Priority date 4/1; no closing date. FAFSA required. Applicants notified on a rolling basis starting 3/1; must reply within 2 week(s) of notification.

Academics. Special study options: Accelerated study, cooperative education, double major, dual enrollment of high school students, honors, independent study, internships, liberal arts/career combination, study abroad, teacher certification program, weekend college. **Credit/placement by examination:** AP, CLEP, IB, institutional tests. 30 credit hours maximum toward bachelor's degree. **Support services:** Learning center, reduced course load, study skills assistance, tutoring, writing center.

Majors. Biology: General. **Business:** Accounting, business admin, international. **Computer sciences:** Programming. **Education:** General, elementary. **Health:** Predentistry, premedicine, prepharmacy, preveterinary. **History:** General. **Legal studies:** Prelaw. **Liberal arts:** Arts/sciences. **Philosophy/religion:** Philosophy, religion. **Protective services:** Criminal justice. **Psychology:** General. **Social sciences:** General, criminology, economics, political science, sociology.

Most popular majors. Business/marketing 40%, education 19%, psychology 6%.

Computing on campus. 65 workstations in library, computer center, student center. Dormitories wired for high-speed internet access and linked to campus network. Commuter students can connect to campus network. Online course registration, online library, helpline, wireless network available.

Student life. Freshman orientation: Mandatory. Preregistration for classes offered. 4 days prior to start of school. **Policies:** Freshmen permitted cars on campus. **Housing:** Guaranteed on-campus for all undergraduates. Coed dorms, single-sex dorms, special housing for disabled, apartments available. $400 deposit, deadline 8/24. 24-hour quiet (honors) dorm available. **Activities:** Choral groups, drama, literary magazine, musical theater, student government, student newspaper, campus ministry, black student union, international student association, Alpha Phi Omega.

Athletics. NCAA. **Intercollegiate:** Baseball M, basketball, cheerleading, cross-country, golf, lacrosse, soccer, softball W, tennis, volleyball W, wrestling M. **Intramural:** Basketball, bowling, cross-country, football (non-tackle) M, golf, softball, table tennis, tennis, track and field, volleyball. **Team name:** Crusaders.

Student services. Adult student services, alcohol/substance abuse counseling, campus ministries, career counseling, student employment services, financial aid counseling, health services, personal counseling, placement for graduates, veterans' counselor. **Physically disabled:** Services for visually, speech, hearing impaired.

Contact. E-mail: admissions@bac.edu
Phone: (704) 825-6665 Toll-free number: (888) 222-0110
Fax: (704) 825-6220
Michelle Lynch, Director of Admissions, Belmont Abbey College, 100 Belmont - Mt. Holly Road, Belmont, NC 28012-2795

Bennett College

Greensboro, North Carolina — **CB member**
www.bennett.edu — **CB code: 5058**

- Private 4-year liberal arts college for women affiliated with United Methodist Church
- Residential campus in small city
- 572 degree-seeking undergraduates: 1% part-time, 100% women, 95% African American, 2% Hispanic American, 1% international
- 57% of applicants admitted
- SAT or ACT, application essay required
- 37% graduate within 6 years

General. Founded in 1873. Regionally accredited. **Degrees:** 68 bachelor's awarded. **ROTC:** Army, Air Force. **Location:** 26 miles from Winston-Salem, 96 miles from Charlotte. **Calendar:** Semester, limited summer session. **Full-time faculty:** 49 total; 71% have terminal degrees, 74% minority, 59% women. **Part-time faculty:** 18 total; 22% have terminal degrees, 56% minority, 67% women. **Class size:** 74% < 20, 26% 20-39, less than 1% 40-49. **Special facilities:** Women's Leadership Institute, Carnegie Negro Library.

Freshman class profile. 939 applied, 536 admitted, 205 enrolled.

Mid 50% test scores		**GPA 2.0-2.99:**	59%
SAT verbal:	360-460	**Rank in top quarter:**	14%
SAT math:	360-430	**Rank in top tenth:**	4%
ACT:	14-19	**Return as sophomores:**	68%
GPA 3.50 or higher:	6%	**Out-of-state:**	80%
GPA 3.0-3.49:	13%	**Live on campus:**	98%

Basis for selection. School achievement record, test scores, recommendations of counselors, and applicant's personal statement important. Interview recommended for borderline students.

High school preparation. College-preparatory program required. 16 units required. Required and recommended units include English 4, mathematics 2, social studies 2, science 2 and foreign language 1-2.

2005-2006 Annual costs. Tuition/fees: $13,239. Room/board: $5,850. Books/supplies: $1,200. Personal expenses: $3,000.

2005-2006 Financial aid. Need-based: 169 full-time freshmen applied for aid; 152 were judged to have need; 150 of these received aid. Average need met was 38%. Average scholarship/grant was $6,788; average loan $2,485. 42% of total undergraduate aid awarded as scholarships/grants, 58% as loans/jobs. **Non-need-based:** Awarded to 64 full-time undergraduates, including 30 freshmen. Scholarships awarded for state residency.

Application procedures. Admission: No deadline. $30 fee, may be waived for applicants with need. Application may be submitted online. Admission notification on a rolling basis. **Financial aid:** Closing date 4/15. FAFSA, institutional form required. Applicants notified by 7/15.

Academics. Accepted students who do not meet required SAT or ACT score admitted to Academic Enrichment Program which provides tutoring, counseling and other support services. **Special study options:** Accelerated study, cooperative education, cross-registration, double major, exchange student, honors, independent study, internships, liberal arts/career combination, student-designed major, teacher certification program, Washington semester. Dual degree programs in nursing and engineering with North Carolina Agricultural and Technical State University. **Credit/placement by examination:** AP, CLEP, SAT, ACT, institutional tests. **Support services:** Learning center, pre-admission summer program, reduced course load, remedial instruction, tutoring, writing center.

Majors. Biology: General. **Business:** Accounting, business admin. **Communications:** General, journalism, media studies. **Computer sciences:** General. **Education:** Early childhood, elementary, English, mathematics, middle, music, science, special. **Family/consumer sciences:** General, clothing/textiles. **Health:** Clinical lab technology. **Liberal arts:** Arts/sciences. **Math:** General. **Physical sciences:** Chemistry. **Psychology:** General. **Public administration:** Social work. **Social sciences:** Political science, sociology. **Visual/performing arts:** General, arts management.

Most popular majors. Biology 25%, communications/journalism 13%, computer/information sciences 6%, education 7%, English 9%, interdisciplinary studies 7%, psychology 12%, social sciences 7%.

Computing on campus. 130 workstations in dormitories, library, computer center. Dormitories wired for high-speed internet access. Commuter students can connect to campus network. Online library, wireless network available.

Student life. Freshman orientation: Mandatory, $100 fee. Preregistration for classes offered. **Housing:** Guaranteed on-campus for all undergraduates. Substance-free housing available. $100 nonrefundable deposit. Students with GPA of 3.0 may reside in honor residence hall. **Activities:** Choral groups, dance, drama, film society, literary magazine, music ensembles, radio station, student government, student newspaper, TV station, Student Christian Fellowship, NAACP, social work club, Women in Communications, student teachers association, psychology club, political science club.

Athletics. NCAA. **Intercollegiate:** Basketball W, cross-country W, softball W, tennis W, track and field W, volleyball W. **Intramural:** Basketball W, softball W, swimming W, tennis W, volleyball W. **Team name:** Belles.

Student services. Campus ministries, career counseling, student employment services, financial aid counseling, health services, on-campus daycare, personal counseling, placement for graduates.

Contact. E-mail: admiss@bennett.edu
Phone: (336) 370-8624 Toll-free number: (800) 413-5323
Fax: (336) 517-2166
Ulisa Bowles, Director of Admissions, Bennett College, 900 East Washington Street, Greensboro, NC 27401-3239

Brevard College

Brevard, North Carolina CB member
www.brevard.edu CB code: 5067

- Private 4-year liberal arts college affiliated with United Methodist Church
- Residential campus in small town
- 582 degree-seeking undergraduates: 3% part-time, 46% women, 4% African American, 3% Hispanic American, 1% Native American, 3% international
- 74% of applicants admitted
- SAT or ACT (ACT writing recommended), application essay required
- 33% graduate within 6 years; 10% enter graduate study

General. Founded in 1853. Regionally accredited. **Degrees:** 107 bachelor's awarded. **Location:** 33 miles from Asheville. **Calendar:** Semester. **Full-time faculty:** 56 total; 61% have terminal degrees, 43% women. **Part-time faculty:** 28 total; 21% have terminal degrees, 39% women. **Class size:** 82% < 20, 18% 20-39. **Special facilities:** Mountain climbing wall, ropes challenge course, Appalachian center for environmental solutions, fitness appraisal lab, transformational leadership, forest institute, performing arts center, policy center, academic enrichment center.

Freshman class profile. 590 applied, 435 admitted, 148 enrolled.

Mid 50% test scores			
SAT verbal:	390-630	Rank in top quarter:	23%
SAT math:	400-620	Rank in top tenth:	10%
ACT:	15-24	End year in good standing:	78%
GPA 3.50 or higher:	26%	Return as sophomores:	61%
GPA 3.0-3.49:	28%	Out-of-state:	55%
GPA 2.0-2.99:	45%	Live on campus:	99%
		International:	6%

Basis for selection. High school record, class rank, SAT/ACT scores, references, extracurricular activities, recommendations, essay, interview, talent/ability, character/personal qualities, volunteer work important. Essay, interview recommended for all students; portfolio required for art students; audition required for music students. **Homeschooled:** Statement describing homeschool structure and mission, transcript of courses and grades required. Legal documentation from home-school agency, local school district, or State Department of Education and admissions interview required. **Learning Disabled:** Evaluation by licensed professional within past 3 years.

High school preparation. 22 units recommended. Recommended units include English 4, mathematics 3, social studies 4, history 1, science 3 (laboratory 1), foreign language 2 and academic electives 4. Math units should include 2 algebra and 1 geometry.

2005-2006 Annual costs. Tuition/fees: $15,830. Telecommunications fee $760 for on-campus residents. Part-time tuition: 1-5 $340 per credit hour; 6-11, $620 per credit hour. Room/board: $5,980. Books/supplies: $800. Personal expenses: $1,000.

2005-2006 Financial aid. Need-based: 113 full-time freshmen applied for aid; 99 were judged to have need; 99 of these received aid. Average need met was 78%. Average scholarship/grant was $10,264; average loan $2,984. 71% of total undergraduate aid awarded as scholarships/grants, 29% as loans/jobs. **Non-need-based:** Awarded to 177 full-time undergraduates, including 70 freshmen. Scholarships awarded for academics, art, athletics, job skills, leadership, music/drama, religious affiliation, state residency.

Application procedures. Admission: No deadline. $30 fee, may be waived for applicants with need. Application may be submitted online. Admission notification on a rolling basis beginning on or about 7/1. **Financial aid:** Priority date 4/15; no closing date. FAFSA required. Applicants notified on a rolling basis starting 2/1; must reply within 4 week(s) of notification.

Academics. Special study options: Double major, dual enrollment of high school students, honors, independent study, internships, student-designed major, study abroad, teacher certification program. **Credit/placement by examination:** AP, CLEP, IB, SAT, ACT, institutional tests. 92 credit hours maximum toward bachelor's degree. **Support services:** Learning center, reduced course load, remedial instruction, study skills assistance, tutoring, writing center.

Majors. Biology: Ecology. **Business:** Business admin. **Conservation:** Environmental science, environmental studies. **Education:** General, art, drama/dance, elementary, English, multi-level teacher, music, physical, science, secondary, social studies. **English:** English lit. **Health:** Health services, predentistry, premedicine, prenursing, preveterinary. **History:** General. **Interdisciplinary:** Biological/physical sciences. **Legal studies:** General. **Liberal arts:** Arts/sciences. **Math:** General. **Parks/recreation:** Exercise sciences, facilities management. **Philosophy/religion:** Religion. **Psychology:** General. **Visual/performing arts:** Art, dramatic, music performance.

Most popular majors. Business/marketing 14%, English 7%, health sciences 6%, interdisciplinary studies 9%, natural resources/environmental science 7%, parks/recreation 20%, psychology 7%, visual/performing arts 17%.

Computing on campus. 100 workstations in dormitories, library, computer center, student center. Dormitories wired for high-speed internet access and linked to campus network. Online library, helpline available.

Student life. Freshman orientation: Mandatory, $95 fee. Preregistration for classes offered. **Policies:** Freshmen permitted cars on campus. **Housing:** Guaranteed on-campus for all undergraduates. Coed dorms, single-sex dorms, substance-free housing available. All non-county or non-adjacent-county residents required to live on campus until age 21. **Activities:** Bands, choral groups, dance, drama, literary magazine, music ensembles, musical theater, opera, student government, student newspaper, recycling club, Fellowship of Christian Athletes, Omicron Delta Kappa, outing club, environmental educators, fencing club, history club, Young Politicians of America, business club, debate society.

Athletics. NAIA. **Intercollegiate:** Baseball M, basketball, cheerleading, cross-country, football (tackle) M, golf M, soccer, softball W, tennis, track and field, volleyball W. **Intramural:** Archery, badminton, basketball, bowling, cross-country, equestrian, football (tackle) M, golf, skiing, soccer, softball, swimming, tennis, track and field, volleyball. **Team name:** Tornadoes.

Student services. Alcohol/substance abuse counseling, campus ministries, career counseling, student employment services, financial aid counseling, health services, personal counseling, placement for graduates, veterans' counselor. **Physically disabled:** Services for visually impaired.

Contact. E-mail: admissions@brevard.edu
Phone: (828) 884-8300 Toll-free number: (800) 527-9090
Fax: (828) 884-3790
Joretta Nelson, Vice President for Enrollment Management, Brevard College, 400 North Broad Street, Brevard, NC 28712

Cabarrus College of Health Sciences

Concord, North Carolina
www.cabarruscollege.edu CB code: 5136

- Private 4-year health science and nursing college
- Commuter campus in small city
- 301 degree-seeking undergraduates: 31% part-time, 89% women, 7% African American, 1% Asian American, 2% Hispanic American
- 69% of applicants admitted
- Application essay required
- 59% graduate within 6 years

General. Regionally accredited. **Degrees:** 7 bachelor's, 83 associate awarded. **Location:** 25 miles from Charlotte. **Calendar:** Semester, limited summer session. **Full-time faculty:** 24 total; 96% women. **Part-time faculty:** 26 total; 19% have terminal degrees, 8% minority, 62% women. **Class size:** 67% < 20, 24% 20-39, 7% 40-49, 2% 50-99.

Freshman class profile. 36 applied, 25 admitted, 21 enrolled.

Mid 50% test scores			
SAT verbal:	460-550	GPA 3.0-3.49:	33%
SAT math:	490-550	GPA 2.0-2.99:	11%
ACT:	15-22	Rank in top quarter:	47%
GPA 3.50 or higher:	56%	Rank in top tenth:	11%

Basis for selection. School record, class rank, essay, test scores, and recommendations most important.

High school preparation. Required and recommended units include English 4, mathematics 2, science 2 (laboratory 2) and foreign language 2.

2005-2006 Annual costs. Tuition/fees: $7,400.

2004-2005 Financial aid. Need-based: 60% of total undergraduate aid awarded as scholarships/grants, 40% as loans/jobs.

Application procedures. Admission: Priority date 3/1; no deadline. $35 fee. Application may be submitted online.

Academics. Special study options: Cross-registration, distance learning, liberal arts/career combination. **Credit/placement by examination:** AP, CLEP, institutional tests. 15 credit hours maximum toward associate degree, 15 toward bachelor's. **Support services:** Learning center, pre-admission summer program, study skills assistance.

Majors. Health: Health care admin, health services admin, nursing (RN).

Computing on campus. 24 workstations in computer center, student center. Online library, wireless network available.

Student life. Freshman orientation: Mandatory. Preregistration for classes offered. 2-day orientation before start of first semester. **Policies:** Freshmen permitted cars on campus. **Activities:** Student government, student newspaper, Christian student union, association of nursing students.

Student services. Career counseling, financial aid counseling, on-campus daycare, personal counseling. **Physically disabled:** Services for hearing impaired.

Contact. E-mail: admissions@cabarruscollege.edu
Phone: (704) 783-1556 Fax: (704) 783-2077
Mark Ellison, Director of Admissions, Cabarrus College of Health Sciences, 401 Medical Park Drive, Concord, NC 28025-2405

Campbell University

Buies Creek, North Carolina — **CB member**
www.campbell.edu — **CB code: 5100**

- Private 4-year university and liberal arts college affiliated with Southern Baptist Convention
- Residential campus in small town
- 2,679 degree-seeking undergraduates: 5% part-time, 56% women, 9% African American, 5% Asian American, 3% Hispanic American, 1% Native American, 4% international
- 1,655 degree-seeking graduate students
- 61% of applicants admitted
- SAT or ACT with writing required

General. Founded in 1887. Regionally accredited. **Degrees:** 916 bachelor's, 220 associate awarded; master's, doctoral, first professional offered. **ROTC:** Army. **Location:** 30 miles from Raleigh, 30 miles from Fayetteville. **Calendar:** Semester, extensive summer session. **Full-time faculty:** 188 total; 89% have terminal degrees, 8% minority, 30% women. **Part-time faculty:** 148 total; 36% have terminal degrees, 70% women. **Class size:** 57% < 20, 28% 20-39, 5% 40-49, 10% 50-99, less than 1% >100. **Special facilities:** Geological collection, drug information center, golf course, nature trail, museum, exhibit hall, seashell collection.

Freshman class profile. 2,804 applied, 1,709 admitted, 730 enrolled.

Mid 50% test scores			
SAT verbal:	510-620	**Rank in top quarter:**	78%
SAT math:	500-630	**Rank in top tenth:**	37%
GPA 3.50 or higher:	64%	**Out-of-state:**	25%
GPA 3.0-3.49:	22%	**Live on campus:**	70%
GPA 2.0-2.99:	14%	**International:**	4%

Basis for selection. Minimum 2.7 GPA, 950 SAT (exclusive of Writing), and rank in top third of class required. Interview, essay recommended for all students; audition recommended for music programs.

High school preparation. 13 units recommended. Recommended units include English 4, mathematics 3, social studies 2, science 2 and foreign language 2. One social science should be U.S. History. Math units must include algebra I and II as well as geometry.

2005-2006 Annual costs. Tuition/fees: $15,796. Room/board: $5,341. Books/supplies: $1,000. Personal expenses: $3,334.

2005-2006 Financial aid. Need-based: 653 full-time freshmen applied for aid; 538 were judged to have need; 538 of these received aid. Average need met was 100%. Average scholarship/grant was $3,851; average loan $2,809. 49% of total undergraduate aid awarded as scholarships/grants, 51% as loans/jobs. **Non-need-based:** Scholarships awarded for academics, athletics, music/drama, religious affiliation, ROTC, state residency.

Application procedures. Admission: Closing date 9/1. $35 fee, may be waived for applicants with need. Application may be submitted online. Admission notification on a rolling basis. **Financial aid:** Priority date 3/15; no closing date. FAFSA required. Applicants notified on a rolling basis starting 4/15; must reply within 2 week(s) of notification.

Academics. Special study options: Accelerated study, combined bachelor's/graduate degree, cooperative education, distance learning, double major, dual enrollment of high school students, exchange student, honors, independent study, internships, liberal arts/career combination, study abroad, teacher certification program, Washington semester. 3-2 engineering program with North Carolina State University. **Credit/placement by examination:** AP, CLEP, IB, SAT, institutional tests. 64 credit hours maximum toward bachelor's degree. **Support services:** Reduced course load, remedial instruction, study skills assistance, tutoring, writing center.

Majors. Biology: General, biochemistry. **Business:** General, accounting, business admin, communications, financial planning, international, management information systems. **Communications:** Advertising, broadcast journalism, journalism, public relations, radio/tv. **Computer sciences:** Computer graphics, computer science, information systems. **Education:** General, biology, elementary, English, family/consumer sciences, French, history, mathematics, middle, music, physical, social studies, Spanish. **English:** British lit, English lit. **Family/consumer sciences:** General, child development, family studies. **Foreign languages:** French, Spanish. **Health:** Athletic training, predentistry, premedicine, prepharmacy, preveterinary. **History:** General. **Legal studies:** Prelaw. **Math:** General. **Parks/recreation:** Exercise sciences, facilities management, health/fitness, sports admin. **Philosophy/religion:** Religion. **Physical sciences:** Chemistry. **Protective services:** Criminal justice. **Psychology:** General. **Public administration:** General, social work. **Social sciences:** Economics, international relations, political science. **Theology:** Sacred music. **Visual/performing arts:** Commercial/advertising art, dramatic, piano/organ, studio arts, voice/opera.

Most popular majors. Business/marketing 40%, health sciences 8%, psychology 12%, social sciences 10%, visual/performing arts 6%.

Computing on campus. 250 workstations in library, computer center, student center. Dormitories wired for high-speed internet access and linked to campus network. Commuter students can connect to campus network. Helpline, wireless network available.

Student life. Freshman orientation: Mandatory, $40 fee. Preregistration for classes offered. **Policies:** Freshmen permitted cars on campus. **Housing:** Guaranteed on-campus for all undergraduates. Single-sex dorms, special housing for disabled, apartments, substance-free housing available. $100 deposit. **Activities:** Bands, choral groups, drama, literary magazine, music ensembles, musical theater, radio station, student government, student newspaper, Baptist student union, College Democrats/Republicans, Alpha Phi Omega, Fellowship of Christian Athletes, North Carolina Student Legislators, Campus Crusade, Christians in Action, Campbell Catholic Community, Baptist Young Women on a Mission, international students club.

Athletics. NCAA. **Intercollegiate:** Baseball M, basketball, cheerleading W, cross-country, golf, soccer, softball W, swimming W, tennis, track and field, volleyball W, wrestling M. **Intramural:** Basketball, football (non-tackle), soccer, softball, swimming, table tennis, tennis, triathlon, volleyball, water polo. **Team name:** Fighting Camels.

Student services. Adult student services, alcohol/substance abuse counseling, campus ministries, career counseling, student employment services, financial aid counseling, health services, personal counseling, placement for graduates, veterans' counselor.

Contact. E-mail: adm@mailcenter.campbell.edu
Phone: (910) 893-1200 ext. 1290 Toll-free number: (800) 334-4111 ext. 1290 Fax: (910) 893-1288
Peggy Mason, Director of Admissions, Campbell University, PO Box 546, Buies Creek, NC 27506

Catawba College

Salisbury, North Carolina — **CB member**
www.catawba.edu — **CB code: 5103**

- Private 4-year liberal arts college affiliated with United Church of Christ
- Residential campus in large town
- 1,256 degree-seeking undergraduates: 3% part-time, 52% women
- 32 degree-seeking graduate students

- 68% of applicants admitted
- SAT or ACT with writing, application essay required
- 45% graduate within 6 years; 13% enter graduate study

General. Founded in 1851. Regionally accredited. **Degrees:** 300 bachelor's awarded; master's offered. **ROTC:** Army. **Location:** 30 miles from Charlotte, 50 miles from Greensboro. **Calendar:** Semester, limited summer session. **Full-time faculty:** 95 total. **Part-time faculty:** 35 total. **Class size:** 59% < 20, 40% 20-39, less than 1% 40-49. **Special facilities:** Comprehensive three-manual Casavant pipe-organ, observatory, 45-acre outdoor biological laboratory, nature preserve.

Freshman class profile. 724 applied, 492 admitted, 223 enrolled.

Mid 50% test scores		**Rank in top quarter:**	39%
SAT verbal:	460-560	**Rank in top tenth:**	16%
SAT math:	480-570	**Return as sophomores:**	77%
ACT:	19-25	**Out-of-state:**	45%
GPA 3.50 or higher:	42%	**Live on campus:**	93%
GPA 3.0-3.49:	29%	**International:**	1%
GPA 2.0-2.99:	29%		

Basis for selection. School achievement record, class rank, standardized test scores, school recommendations important. Interview recommended for all students; audition recommended for drama, music programs.

High school preparation. College-preparatory program recommended. 16 units required. Required and recommended units include English 4, mathematics 2-3, social studies 3, science 2-3 (laboratory 3), foreign language 2 and academic electives 6. Required credits must be academic subjects at college preparatory level.

2005-2006 Annual costs. Tuition/fees: $18,750. Room/board: $6,250. Books/supplies: $800. Personal expenses: $1,200.

2004-2005 Financial aid. Need-based: 234 full-time freshmen applied for aid; 190 were judged to have need; 190 of these received aid. Average need met was 80%. Average scholarship/grant was $3,958; average loan $4,329. 50% of total undergraduate aid awarded as scholarships/grants, 50% as loans/jobs. **Non-need-based:** Awarded to 910 full-time undergraduates, including 190 freshmen. Scholarships awarded for academics, athletics, leadership, music/drama, state residency.

Application procedures. Admission: Priority date 3/15; no deadline. $25 fee, may be waived for applicants with need. Application may be submitted online. Admission notification on a rolling basis beginning on or about 10/1. **Financial aid:** Priority date 3/1; no closing date. FAFSA required. Applicants notified on a rolling basis starting 2/15; must reply within 2 week(s) of notification.

Academics. Special study options: Cross-registration, double major, dual enrollment of high school students, honors, independent study, internships, liberal arts/career combination, student-designed major, study abroad, teacher certification program. **Credit/placement by examination:** AP, CLEP, IB, institutional tests. 30 credit hours maximum toward bachelor's degree. **Support services:** Learning center, study skills assistance, tutoring, writing center.

Majors. Biology: General. **Business:** Accounting, business admin. **Communications:** General. **Computer sciences:** General. **Conservation:** Environmental science, environmental studies. **Education:** Elementary, gifted/talented, middle, music, physical. **English:** English lit. **Foreign languages:** French, Spanish. **Health:** Athletic training, recreational therapy. **History:** General. **Legal studies:** Prelaw. **Math:** General. **Parks/recreation:** General, health/fitness, sports admin. **Philosophy/religion:** Religion. **Physical sciences:** Chemistry. **Protective services:** Law enforcement admin. **Psychology:** General. **Social sciences:** Political science, sociology. **Visual/performing arts:** Arts management, dramatic, music performance.

Most popular majors. Business/marketing 41%, computer/information sciences 18%, education 8%.

Computing on campus. 100 workstations in dormitories, library, computer center. Dormitories wired for high-speed internet access and linked to campus network. Helpline, repair service available.

Student life. Freshman orientation: Mandatory. Orientation program week prior to start of fall classes. Optional summer orientation programs for students and parents at additional cost. **Policies:** Freshmen permitted cars on campus. **Housing:** Guaranteed on-campus for all undergraduates. Coed dorms, single-sex dorms, substance-free housing available. $200 partly refundable deposit. **Activities:** Bands, choral groups, dance, drama, literary magazine, music ensembles, musical theater, student government, student newspaper, symphony orchestra, Alpha program, Athenian society, Helen Foil Beard Society, political science association, environmental service clubs, Fellowship of Christian Athletes, multi-cultural club, Philomathean club, volunteer club.

Athletics. NCAA. **Intercollegiate:** Baseball M, basketball, cross-country, field hockey W, football (tackle) M, golf, lacrosse M, soccer, softball W, swimming W, tennis, volleyball W. **Intramural:** Basketball, cross-country, football (tackle) M, golf, handball, racquetball, soccer, softball, table tennis, tennis, volleyball.

Student services. Adult student services, alcohol/substance abuse counseling, campus ministries, career counseling, student employment services, financial aid counseling, health services, personal counseling, placement for graduates. **Physically disabled:** Services for hearing impaired.

Contact. E-mail: admission@catawba.edu
Phone: (704) 637-4402 Toll-free number: (800) 228-2922
Fax: (704) 637-4422
Russell Watjen, Vice President and Dean of Admissions, Catawba College, 2300 West Innes Street, Salisbury, NC 28144

Chowan College

Murfreesboro, North Carolina — **CB member**
www.chowan.edu — **CB code: 5107**

- Private 4-year liberal arts college affiliated with Southern Baptist Convention
- Residential campus in rural community
- 797 degree-seeking undergraduates: 5% part-time, 45% women, 38% African American, 1% Asian American, 3% Hispanic American, 1% Native American, 1% international
- 59% of applicants admitted
- SAT or ACT (ACT writing optional) required

General. Founded in 1848. Regionally accredited. **Degrees:** 117 bachelor's, 1 associate awarded. **Location:** 75 miles from Norfolk, Virginia, 130 miles from Raleigh. **Calendar:** Semester, limited summer session. **Full-time faculty:** 46 total; 52% have terminal degrees, 9% minority, 41% women. **Part-time faculty:** 20 total; 10% have terminal degrees, 10% minority, 55% women. **Class size:** 64% < 20, 33% 20-39, 2% 40-49, less than 1% 50-99. **Special facilities:** Graphic communications center.

Freshman class profile. 1,940 applied, 1,147 admitted, 293 enrolled.

Mid 50% test scores		**Rank in top tenth:**	4%
SAT verbal:	370-490	**Return as sophomores:**	49%
SAT math:	390-490	**Out-of-state:**	55%
ACT:	15-19	**Live on campus:**	84%
GPA 3.50 or higher:	6%	**International:**	2%
GPA 3.0-3.49:	19%	**Fraternities:**	11%
GPA 2.0-2.99:	66%	**Sororities:**	20%
Rank in top quarter:	19%		

Basis for selection. School achievement record most important. Essay, interview recommended for all students; audition recommended for music majors; portfolio recommended for graphic design and studio art majors.

High school preparation. College-preparatory program recommended. Recommended units include English 4, mathematics 3, social studies 2, science 2 (laboratory 2) and academic electives 7.

2005-2006 Annual costs. Tuition/fees: $14,700. 1-3 hours is $230 per credit hour, 4-7 hours is $350 per credit hour, 8-11 is $640 per credit hour. Room/board: $6,600. Books/supplies: $864. Personal expenses: $1,000.

2004-2005 Financial aid. Need-based: 191 full-time freshmen applied for aid; 175 were judged to have need; 175 of these received aid. Average need met was 58%. Average scholarship/grant was $7,520; average loan $2,461. 56% of total undergraduate aid awarded as scholarships/grants, 44% as loans/jobs. **Non-need-based:** Awarded to 118 full-time undergraduates, including 42 freshmen. Scholarships awarded for academics, athletics, leadership, music/drama, religious affiliation, state residency.

Application procedures. Admission: No deadline. $20 fee, may be waived for applicants with need. Application may be submitted online. Admission notification on a rolling basis. Must reply by May 1 or within 2 week(s) if notified thereafter. **Financial aid:** Priority date 3/1; no closing date. FAFSA required. Applicants notified on a rolling basis starting 3/1; must reply within 2 week(s) of notification.

Academics. Special study options: Distance learning, double major, dual enrollment of high school students, honors, independent study, internships, liberal arts/career combination, teacher certification program. **Credit/**

placement by examination: AP, CLEP, IB, institutional tests. 15 credit hours maximum toward associate degree, 15 toward bachelor's. **Support services:** Learning center, reduced course load, remedial instruction, study skills assistance, tutoring.

Majors. **Biology:** General. **Business:** Accounting/business management, business admin, information resources management, marketing, small business admin. **Communications technology:** Graphics. **Education:** General, elementary, English, history, music, physical, secondary. **English:** English lit. **Health:** Athletic training, predentistry, premedicine, prenursing, prepharmacy, preveterinary. **History:** General. **Liberal arts:** Arts/sciences. **Parks/recreation:** Exercise sciences, health/fitness, sports admin. **Philosophy/religion:** Religion. **Physical sciences:** General. **Protective services:** Law enforcement admin. **Psychology:** General. **Visual/performing arts:** Graphic design, music performance, studio arts.

Most popular majors. Biology 12%, business/marketing 11%, communications/journalism 12%, education 17%, history 8%, parks/recreation 7%, psychology 7%, security/protective services 10%, visual/performing arts 10%.

Computing on campus. 219 workstations in dormitories, library, computer center. Dormitories wired for high-speed internet access and linked to campus network. Online course registration, online library, helpline, repair service available.

Student life. **Freshman orientation:** Mandatory, $50 fee. Preregistration for classes offered. **Policies:** No alcohol on campus; restricted dorm visitation; academic honor code. Freshmen permitted cars on campus. **Housing:** Guaranteed on-campus for all undergraduates. Single-sex dorms, substance-free housing available. $200 partly refundable deposit, deadline 5/1. **Activities:** Bands, choral groups, drama, literary magazine, music ensembles, student government, Christian Student Union, Student National Education Association, Fellowship of Christian Athletes, Rotaract, international student association, Voices of Inspiration, College Democrats, College Republicans, history club, women's club.

Athletics. NCAA, NCCAA. **Intercollegiate:** Baseball M, basketball, cheerleading, cross-country W, diving W, football (tackle) M, golf, soccer, softball W, tennis, volleyball W. **Intramural:** Badminton, basketball, football (tackle) M, golf, handball, racquetball, skiing, soccer M, softball, swimming, table tennis, tennis, volleyball. **Team name:** Braves.

Student services. Campus ministries, career counseling, student employment services, financial aid counseling, health services, personal counseling, placement for graduates, veterans' counselor.

Contact. E-mail: admissions@chowan.edu
Phone: (252) 398-1235 Toll-free number: (800) 488-4101
Fax: (252) 398-1190
Jonathan Wirt, Vice President for Enrollment Management, Chowan College, 200 Jones Drive, Murfreesboro, NC 27855-9901

Davidson College

Davidson, North Carolina — **CB member**
www.davidson.edu — **CB code: 5150**

- Private 4-year liberal arts college affiliated with Presbyterian Church (USA)
- Residential campus in small town
- 1,678 degree-seeking undergraduates: 50% women, 6% African American, 2% Asian American, 4% Hispanic American, 3% international
- 27% of applicants admitted
- SAT or ACT (ACT writing optional), application essay required

General. Founded in 1837. Regionally accredited. **Degrees:** 451 bachelor's awarded. **ROTC:** Army, Air Force. **Location:** 19 miles from Charlotte. **Calendar:** Semester. **Full-time faculty:** 159 total; 98% have terminal degrees, 14% minority, 32% women. **Part-time faculty:** 8 total; 75% have terminal degrees, 12% minority, 62% women. **Class size:** 67% < 20, 33% 20-39, less than 1% 40-49. **Special facilities:** Laser facility, electron microscope, campus arboretum.

Freshman class profile. 4,258 applied, 1,146 admitted, 463 enrolled.

Mid 50% test scores			
SAT verbal:	640-730	**Return as sophomores:**	96%
SAT math:	640-710	**Out-of-state:**	84%
ACT:	28-31	**Live on campus:**	100%
Rank in top quarter:	96%	**International:**	3%
Rank in top tenth:	72%	**Fraternities:**	44%

Basis for selection. GED not accepted. Course selection, rigor of program, grades, recommendations, essays, test scores, class rank considered. SAT Subject Tests recommended. Campus visit strongly recommended.

High school preparation. Required and recommended units include English 4, mathematics 3-4, social studies 2-4, science 2-4 and foreign language 2-4. Foreign language units should be in same language.

2006-2007 Annual costs. Tuition/fees: $30,194. Room/board: $8,590.

2004-2005 Financial aid. **Need-based:** 262 full-time freshmen applied for aid; 165 were judged to have need; 165 of these received aid. Average need met was 100%. **Non-need-based:** Scholarships awarded for academics, art, athletics, leadership, minority status, music/drama, ROTC.

Application procedures. **Admission:** Closing date 1/2 (postmark date). $50 fee, may be waived for applicants with need. Admission notification 4/1. Must reply by 5/1. **Financial aid:** Closing date 2/15. FAFSA, CSS PROFILE required. Applicants notified by 4/1; must reply by 5/1.

Academics. 2-year interdisciplinary course in humanities available for freshmen and sophomores. Center for Special Studies supervises student-designed majors. **Special study options:** Cross-registration, double major, exchange student, honors, independent study, student-designed major, study abroad, teacher certification program, Washington semester. Visiting student program with Howard University and Morehouse College; Dean Rusk program in International Studies; Philadelphia Center Pro-School for Field Studies. **Credit/placement by examination:** AP, CLEP, IB, institutional tests. **Support services:** Tutoring, writing center.

Majors. **Biology:** General. **English:** English lit. **Foreign languages:** Classics, French, German, Spanish. **History:** General. **Math:** General. **Philosophy/religion:** Philosophy, religion. **Physical sciences:** Chemistry, physics. **Psychology:** General. **Social sciences:** Anthropology, economics, political science, sociology. **Visual/performing arts:** Art, dramatic.

Most popular majors. Biology 11%, English 11%, foreign language 9%, history 13%, philosophy/religious studies 6%, psychology 10%, social sciences 27%, visual/performing arts 6%.

Computing on campus. 142 workstations in dormitories, library, computer center, student center. Dormitories wired for high-speed internet access and linked to campus network. Commuter students can connect to campus network. Online course registration, helpline, repair service, wireless network available.

Student life. **Freshman orientation:** Mandatory, $100 fee. Preregistration for classes offered. **Policies:** Freshmen permitted cars on campus. **Housing:** Guaranteed on-campus for freshmen. Coed dorms, apartments, substance-free housing available. Substance-free, suite/apartment-style housing available. **Activities:** Bands, choral groups, dance, drama, literary magazine, music ensembles, musical theater, radio station, student government, student newspaper, symphony orchestra, black student coalition, service organizations, Amnesty International, Young Democrats, College Republicans, project life, room in the inn, Habitat for Humanity, Asia 3D, gender resource center.

Athletics. NCAA. **Intercollegiate:** Baseball M, basketball, cross-country, diving, field hockey W, football (tackle) M, golf M, lacrosse W, soccer, swimming, tennis, track and field, volleyball W, wrestling M. **Intramural:** Basketball, football (non-tackle), soccer, softball, volleyball. **Team name:** Wildcats.

Student services. Alcohol/substance abuse counseling, campus ministries, career counseling, student employment services, financial aid counseling, health services, minority student services, personal counseling, placement for graduates. **Physically disabled:** Services for visually, hearing impaired.

Contact. E-mail: admission@davidson.edu
Phone: (704) 894-2230 Toll-free number: (800) 768-0380
Fax: (704) 894-2016
Christopher Gruber, Vice President and Dean of Admission and Financial Aid, Davidson College, Box 7156, Davidson, NC 28035-7156

DeVry University: Charlotte

Charlotte, North Carolina

- For-profit 4-year university
- Commuter campus
- 67 degree-seeking undergraduates: 52% part-time, 45% women, 63% African American, 6% Asian American, 4% Hispanic American, 1% international
- 99 graduate students

General. Degrees: 4 bachelor's awarded; master's offered. **Calendar:** Semester. **Full-time faculty:** 4 total. **Part-time faculty:** 11 total; 27% minority, 36% women.

Basis for selection. Academic record considered.

2005-2006 Annual costs. Tuition/fees: $11,900. Books/supplies: $1,250. Personal expenses: $1,680.

Application procedures. Admission: No deadline. $50 fee. Admission notification on a rolling basis.

Academics. Special study options: Accelerated study, distance learning. **Credit/placement by examination:** CLEP.

Majors. Business: Business admin. **Computer sciences:** General.

Contact. Phone: (704) 362-2345
DeVry University: Charlotte, 4521 Sharon Road, Charlotte, NC 28211

Duke University

Durham, North Carolina | **CB member**
www.duke.edu | **CB code: 5156**

- Private 4-year university affiliated with United Methodist Church
- Residential campus in small city
- 6,259 degree-seeking undergraduates: 48% women, 11% African American, 14% Asian American, 7% Hispanic American, 5% international
- 7,218 degree-seeking graduate students
- 22% of applicants admitted
- SAT and SAT Subject Tests or ACT with writing, application essay required

General. Founded in 1838. Regionally accredited. Duke University Marine Laboratory, located near Beaufort, offers semester and summer programs to qualified juniors, seniors, and graduate students from any college or university. **Degrees:** 1,448 bachelor's awarded; master's, doctoral, first professional offered. **ROTC:** Army, Navy, Air Force. **Location:** 30 miles from Raleigh, 170 miles from Richmond, Virginia. **Calendar:** Semester, extensive summer session. **Full-time faculty:** 949 total; 94% have terminal degrees, 17% minority, 28% women. **Class size:** 71% < 20, 21% 20-39, 3% 40-49, 4% 50-99, 2% >100. **Special facilities:** Phytotron, marine laboratory, primate center, free electron laser, nuclear magnetic resonance machine, nuclear laboratory, institute of the arts, science research center, institute of statistics and decision sciences, institute for public policy, institute for genomic sciences and policy, center for interdisciplinary and international studies, center for teaching, learning and writing, community service center, center for geometric computing, center for black culture, women's center, art museum, center for interdisciplinary engineering, medicine, and applied sciences.

Freshman class profile. 18,090 applied, 3,995 admitted, 1,724 enrolled.

Mid 50% test scores		**Rank in top tenth:**	87%
SAT verbal:	690-770	**Out-of-state:**	85%
SAT math:	690-780	**Live on campus:**	100%
ACT:	29-34	**International:**	6%
Rank in top quarter:	97%		

Basis for selection. GED not accepted. Courses, school achievement record, school and community activities, essays, recommendations, test scores considered. Special consideration to alumni children and minority applicants. Applicants requesting alumni interview must submit Part I of application by 10/1 for Early Decision or by 12/1 for regular decision. Students using ACT for admission need to submit SAT Subject Tests or AP scores for foreign language and mathematics placement. Applicants to Arts and Sciences submitting SAT must submit 2 SAT Subject Tests. Applicants to School of Engineering submitting SAT must take SAT Subject Test in mathematics and 1 other subject. Interview recommended for all students; audition recommended for drama, music majors; portfolio recommended for art majors. **Homeschooled:** Alumni interview in student's local area recommended.

High school preparation. Recommended units include English 4, mathematics 4, social studies 4, science 4 and foreign language 4. 4 math and 1 physics or chemistry required for engineering applicants, with calculus required before enrolling.

2005-2006 Annual costs. Tuition/fees: $32,409. Room/board: $8,830. Books/supplies: $940. Personal expenses: $1,640.

2005-2006 Financial aid. Need-based: 79% of total undergraduate aid awarded as scholarships/grants, 21% as loans/jobs. **Non-need-based:** Scholarships awarded for academics, alumni affiliation, art, athletics, leadership, minority status, religious affiliation, ROTC, state residency.

Application procedures. Admission: Closing date 1/2 (postmark date). $70 fee, may be waived for applicants with need. Application may be submitted online. Admission notification 4/1. Must reply by 5/1. **Financial aid:** Closing date 2/1. FAFSA, CSS PROFILE required. Applicants notified by 4/1; must reply by 5/1 or within 4 week(s) of notification.

Academics. Comparative area studies with an emphasis in one or more areas. Special focus groups for freshmen: 20th-century America, evolution and humankind, the arts in contemporary society, medieval communities, popular culture, media and identity, 20th-century Europe, nature and human designs. **Special study options:** Accelerated study, cross-registration, distance learning, double major, exchange student, honors, independent study, internships, New York semester, semester at sea, student-designed major, study abroad, teacher certification program, Washington semester. Art program/internship in New York City, marine biology semester in Beaufort. **Credit/placement by examination:** AP, CLEP. **Support services:** Learning center, pre-admission summer program, tutoring, writing center.

Majors. Area/ethnic studies: African-American, Asian, women's. **Biology:** General, anatomy. **Computer sciences:** General. **Conservation:** General. **Engineering:** Biomedical, civil, electrical, mechanical. **English:** British lit. **Foreign languages:** Ancient Greek, classics, French, German, Italian, Latin, Russian, Spanish. **History:** General. **Interdisciplinary:** Medieval/Renaissance, neuroscience. **Math:** General. **Philosophy/religion:** Philosophy, religion. **Physical sciences:** Chemistry, geology, physics. **Psychology:** General. **Public administration:** Policy analysis. **Social sciences:** Anthropology, economics, political science, sociology. **Visual/performing arts:** Art history/conservation, design, dramatic.

Most popular majors. Biology 7%, engineering/engineering technologies 15%, psychology 9%, security/protective services 10%, social sciences 34%.

Computing on campus. 685 workstations in dormitories, library, computer center. Dormitories linked to campus network. Commuter students can connect to campus network. Online course registration, online library, helpline, repair service available.

Student life. Freshman orientation: Mandatory. Preregistration for classes offered. Held week prior to start of classes. **Policies:** Freshmen permitted cars on campus. **Housing:** Guaranteed on-campus for freshmen. Coed dorms, single-sex dorms, special housing for disabled, apartments available. Special interest housing available for students in women's studies, the arts, languages, service (Alpha Phi Omega). All first-year students live together on East Campus. Most first-year residence halls have a faculty member in residence. All sophomores must live on West Campus. **Activities:** Bands, choral groups, dance, drama, film society, literary magazine, music ensembles, musical theater, opera, radio station, student government, student newspaper, symphony orchestra, TV station, Black Student Alliance, Hillel, Newman Club, Spanish American-Latin Student Association, Volunteers for Youth, Big Brother/Big Sister, Campus Crusade for Christ, Duke Democrats, College Republicans, Habitat for Humanity.

Athletics. NCAA. **Intercollegiate:** Baseball M, basketball, cross-country, diving, fencing, field hockey W, football (tackle) M, golf, lacrosse, rowing (crew) W, soccer, swimming, tennis, track and field, volleyball W, wrestling M. **Intramural:** Badminton, baseball, basketball, football (tackle) M, golf, racquetball, soccer M, softball, squash, swimming, table tennis, tennis, volleyball. **Team name:** Blue Devils.

Student services. Adult student services, alcohol/substance abuse counseling, campus ministries, career counseling, student employment services, financial aid counseling, health services, minority student services, on-campus daycare, personal counseling, placement for graduates, veterans' counselor, women's services. **Physically disabled:** Services for visually, speech, hearing impaired.

Contact. E-mail: askduke@admiss.duke.edu
Phone: (919) 684-3214 Fax: (919) 681-8941
Christoph Guttentag, Dean of Undergraduate Admissions, Duke University, 2138 Campus Drive, Durham, NC 27708

East Carolina University

Greenville, North Carolina | **CB member**
www.ecu.edu | **CB code: 5180**

- Public 4-year university
- Residential campus in small city

- 17,593 degree-seeking undergraduates: 10% part-time, 60% women, 15% African American, 2% Asian American, 2% Hispanic American, 1% Native American
- 4,288 degree-seeking graduate students
- 74% of applicants admitted
- SAT or ACT with writing required
- 53% graduate within 6 years

General. Founded in 1907. Regionally accredited. **Degrees:** 3,065 bachelor's awarded; master's, doctoral, first professional offered. **ROTC:** Army, Air Force. **Location:** 80 miles from Raleigh. **Calendar:** Semester, extensive summer session. **Full-time faculty:** 1,096 total; 85% have terminal degrees, 9% minority, 36% women. **Part-time faculty:** 196 total; 54% have terminal degrees, 6% minority, 43% women. **Class size:** 45% < 20, 36% 20-39, 8% 40-49, 9% 50-99, 2% >100. **Special facilities:** 2 accelerators, climbing wall, ropes course, global classroom, field station, art galleries.

Freshman class profile. 11,628 applied, 8,567 admitted, 3,273 enrolled.

Mid 50% test scores		GPA 2.0-2.99:	27%
SAT verbal:	460-560	Rank in top quarter:	42%
SAT math:	480-570	Rank in top tenth:	14%
ACT:	18-22	Return as sophomores:	76%
GPA 3.50 or higher:	26%	Out-of-state:	16%
GPA 3.0-3.49:	47%	Live on campus:	84%

Basis for selection. Freshman admission decisions based on a formula that weighs class rank, high school GPA (unweighted), and standardized test scores. GED accepted for non-traditional freshmen. SAT preferred, ACT also accepted. Audition required for music programs. **Homeschooled:** Transcript of courses and grades required.

High school preparation. College-preparatory program required. 20 units required. Required units include English 4, mathematics 4, social studies 2, science 3 (laboratory 1), foreign language 2 and academic electives 4. Recommended that during senior year student take the 4th math requirement, 1 foreign language, 1 natural science, 1 English. Social studies units must include 1 U.S. history. 1 fine art recommended.

2005-2006 Annual costs. Tuition/fees: $3,627; $14,141 out-of-state. Room/board: $6,840. Books/supplies: $800. Personal expenses: $1,600.

2005-2006 Financial aid. Need-based: 2,485 full-time freshmen applied for aid; 1,401 were judged to have need; 1,401 of these received aid. Average need met was 23%. Average scholarship/grant was $8,843; average loan $5,391. 46% of total undergraduate aid awarded as scholarships/grants, 54% as loans/jobs. **Non-need-based:** Awarded to 2,033 full-time undergraduates, including 464 freshmen. Scholarships awarded for academics, alumni affiliation, art, athletics, minority status, ROTC.

Application procedures. Admission: Closing date 3/15 (postmark date). $50 fee, may be waived for applicants with need. Application may be submitted online. Admission notification on a rolling basis beginning on or about 10/1. Must reply by May 1 or within 2 week(s) if notified thereafter. Out-of-state freshman enrollment limited to 18% of incoming freshman class, and processed on space-available basis. Applications received prior to December 31 receive priority. **Financial aid:** Priority date 4/15; no closing date. FAFSA required. Applicants notified on a rolling basis starting 3/15; must reply within 3 week(s) of notification.

Academics. Special study options: Accelerated study, combined bachelor's/graduate degree, cooperative education, distance learning, double major, dual enrollment of high school students, exchange student, honors, independent study, internships, student-designed major, study abroad, teacher certification program, Washington semester. **Credit/placement by examination:** AP, CLEP, IB, SAT, institutional tests. **Support services:** Learning center, reduced course load, remedial instruction, study skills assistance, tutoring, writing center.

Majors. Architecture: Urban/community planning. **Area/ethnic studies:** Women's. **Biology:** General, biochemistry. **Business:** Accounting, accounting/business management, business admin, finance, hotel/motel admin, management information systems, marketing, office technology. **Communications:** General, broadcast journalism. **Communications technology:** Animation/special effects. **Computer sciences:** Computer science, information technology. **Education:** Art, business, drama/dance, early childhood, elementary, emotionally handicapped, English, family/consumer sciences, French, German, health, learning disabled, mathematics, mentally handicapped, middle, music, physical, sales/marketing, science, social studies, Spanish. **Engineering:** Systems. **Engineering technology:** Computer, construction, drafting, environmental, industrial, manufacturing. **English:** English lit. **Family/consumer sciences:** Child development, clothing/textiles, family studies. **Foreign languages:** French, German, Spanish. **Health:** Athletic training, audiology/speech pathology, clinical lab science, clinical nutrition, dietetics, environmental health, health services, marriage/family therapy, medical records admin, music therapy, nursing (RN), public health ed, recreational therapy, vocational rehab counseling. **History:** General, public archives. **Liberal arts:** Arts/sciences. **Math:** General. **Parks/recreation:** Exercise sciences, facilities management, sports admin. **Philosophy/religion:** Philosophy. **Physical sciences:** Chemistry, geology, physics. **Protective services:** Criminal justice. **Psychology:** General. **Public administration:** Social work. **Social sciences:** Anthropology, economics, geography, political science, sociology. **Theology:** Sacred music. **Visual/performing arts:** Acting, art, art history/conservation, ceramics, cinematography, dance, directing/producing, dramatic, drawing, fiber arts, graphic design, illustration, interior design, jazz, metal/jewelry, music performance, music theory/composition, painting, photography, piano/organ, printmaking, sculpture, stringed instruments, studio arts, voice/opera.

Most popular majors. Biology 6%, business/marketing 18%, communication technologies 8%, education 12%, health sciences 15%, social sciences 7%.

Computing on campus. 2,094 workstations in dormitories, library, computer center, student center. Dormitories wired for high-speed internet access and linked to campus network. Commuter students can connect to campus network. Online course registration, online library, helpline, repair service, student web hosting, wireless network available.

Student life. Freshman orientation: Mandatory, $100 fee. Preregistration for classes offered. 2-phase program: 1 summer session (overnight stay) and 1 session the day prior to start of classes. **Policies:** Freshmen permitted cars on campus. **Housing:** Guaranteed on-campus for freshmen. Coed dorms, single-sex dorms, fraternity/sorority housing, substance-free housing available. $200 partly refundable deposit, deadline 5/1. First-year student floor, leadership hall, extended quiet-hours floor, substance-free hall, nonsmoking floor, academic year residence halls. **Activities:** Bands, choral groups, dance, drama, film society, literary magazine, music ensembles, musical theater, opera, radio station, student government, student newspaper, symphony orchestra, 280 registered organizations.

Athletics. NCAA. **Intercollegiate:** Baseball M, basketball, cheerleading, cross-country, diving, football (tackle) M, golf, soccer, softball W, swimming, tennis, track and field, volleyball. **Intramural:** Basketball, bowling, cross-country, football (non-tackle), golf, racquetball, softball, table tennis, tennis, volleyball. **Team name:** Pirates.

Student services. Adult student services, alcohol/substance abuse counseling, campus ministries, career counseling, student employment services, financial aid counseling, health services, minority student services, personal counseling, placement for graduates, veterans' counselor. **Physically disabled:** Services for visually, speech, hearing impaired.

Contact. E-mail: admis@mail.ecu.edu
Phone: (252) 328-6640 Fax: (252) 328-6945
Thomas Powell, Director of Admissions, East Carolina University, Office of Undergraduate Admissions, Greenville, NC 27858-4353

Elizabeth City State University

Elizabeth City, North Carolina
www.ecsu.edu **CB code: 5629**

- Public 4-year liberal arts college
- Commuter campus in large town
- 2,414 degree-seeking undergraduates: 6% part-time, 65% women, 82% African American, 1% Asian American, 1% Hispanic American
- 61 degree-seeking graduate students
- 87% of applicants admitted
- SAT or ACT with writing required
- 51% graduate within 6 years

General. Founded in 1891. Regionally accredited. **Degrees:** 420 bachelor's awarded; master's offered. **ROTC:** Army. **Location:** 50 miles from Norfolk, Virginia. **Calendar:** Semester, extensive summer session. **Full-time faculty:** 135 total; 64% have terminal degrees, 52% minority, 38% women. **Part-time faculty:** 67 total; 8% have terminal degrees, 72% minority, 49% women. **Class size:** 61% < 20, 31% 20-39, 7% 40-49, less than 1% 50-99. **Special facilities:** Recording studio, radio station, boardwalk in nature preseves/wetlands, golf driving range.

Freshman class profile. 1,500 applied, 1,310 admitted, 560 enrolled.

Mid 50% test scores		Rank in top tenth:	8%
SAT verbal:	380-460	End year in good standing:	79%
SAT math:	380-460	Return as sophomores:	74%
GPA 3.50 or higher:	12%	Out-of-state:	15%
GPA 3.0-3.49:	19%	Live on campus:	79%
GPA 2.0-2.99:	60%	Fraternities:	3%
Rank in top quarter:	13%	Sororities:	6%

Basis for selection. GPA and test scores considered. Special consideration given to residents from 21 neighboring counties. All applicants for admission to any campus in the UNC system, except those exempted by current campus policies, must submit a standardized test score. The SAT is preferred, but students may also submit the ACT. **Homeschooled:** Statement describing homeschool structure and mission, transcript of courses and grades, letter of recommendation (nonparent) required. **Learning Disabled:** Important to ascertain in advance the extent of the learning diability in order to provide the available service(s).

High school preparation. 20 units required. Required units include English 4, mathematics 3, social studies 2, science 2 (laboratory 1) and foreign language 2. One additional laboratory science also required. Mathematics must include 1 algebra and 1 geometry. Social science must include 1 history.

2005-2006 Annual costs. Tuition/fees: $2,493; $10,832 out-of-state. Room/board: $4,710. Books/supplies: $670. Personal expenses: $1,200.

Financial aid. Non-need-based: Scholarships awarded for academics, athletics, minority status, ROTC, state residency.

Application procedures. Admission: Priority date 3/1; deadline 8/15. $30 fee, may be waived for applicants with need. Application may be submitted online. Admission notification on a rolling basis. **Financial aid:** Priority date 3/1, closing date 8/15. FAFSA required. Applicants notified on a rolling basis starting 6/1; must reply within 3 week(s) of notification.

Academics. Special study options: Combined bachelor's/graduate degree, cooperative education, distance learning, double major, honors, independent study, internships, liberal arts/career combination, teacher certification program, weekend college. **Credit/placement by examination:** AP, CLEP, IB, SAT. 48 credit hours maximum toward bachelor's degree. **Support services:** Learning center, pre-admission summer program, reduced course load, remedial instruction, study skills assistance, tutoring, writing center.

Majors. Biology: General. **Business:** Accounting, business admin. **Computer sciences:** Computer science. **Education:** Art, business, chemistry, elementary, English, history, learning disabled, mathematics, middle, physical, special, technology/industrial arts. **Engineering technology:** Industrial. **English:** English lit. **History:** General. **Math:** General. **Physical sciences:** Chemistry, geology, oceanography, physics. **Protective services:** Criminal justice. **Psychology:** General. **Public administration:** Social work. **Social sciences:** General, political science, sociology. **Transportation:** Aviation. **Visual/performing arts:** Music management, studio arts.

Most popular majors. Biology 7%, business/marketing 21%, computer/information sciences 8%, education 9%, psychology 7%, security/protective services 21%, social sciences 6%.

Computing on campus. 250 workstations in dormitories, library, computer center, student center. Dormitories wired for high-speed internet access and linked to campus network. Commuter students can connect to campus network. Online course registration, online library, helpline, repair service, wireless network available.

Student life. Freshman orientation: Mandatory, $100 fee. Preregistration for classes offered. Three sessions held during summer months covering 2 1/2 days each. **Policies:** Freshmen permitted cars on campus. **Housing:** Guaranteed on-campus for freshmen. Coed dorms, single-sex dorms, apartments, substance-free housing available. $100 nonrefundable deposit, deadline 8/1. College-leased housing available. **Activities:** Bands, choral groups, dance, drama, literary magazine, music ensembles, radio station, student government, student newspaper, symphony orchestra, TV station, United Campus Religious Fellowship, honor and recognition societies in education, science, dramatics, journalism, student union program.

Athletics. NCAA. **Intercollegiate:** Baseball M, basketball, bowling W, boxing W, cheerleading, cross-country, football (tackle) M, golf, softball W, tennis, track and field, volleyball W, wrestling M. **Intramural:** Baseball M, basketball, boxing, football (non-tackle) M, softball, volleyball. **Team name:** Vikings.

Student services. Alcohol/substance abuse counseling, campus ministries, career counseling, student employment services, financial aid counseling, health services, personal counseling, placement for graduates, veterans' counselor. **Physically disabled:** Services for visually, speech, hearing impaired.

Contact. E-mail: gdeese@mail.ecsu.edu
Phone: (252) 335-3305 Toll-free number: (800) 347-3278
Fax: (252) 335-3537
Grady Deese, Director of Admissions, Elizabeth City State University, 1704 Weeksville Road, Campus Box 901, Elizabeth City, NC 27909

Elon University

Elon, North Carolina — **CB member**
www.elon.edu — **CB code: 5183**

- Private 4-year university and liberal arts college affiliated with United Church of Christ
- Residential campus in large town
- 4,702 degree-seeking undergraduates: 2% part-time, 61% women, 7% African American, 1% Asian American, 1% Hispanic American, 2% international
- 254 degree-seeking graduate students
- 41% of applicants admitted
- SAT or ACT with writing, application essay required
- 76% graduate within 6 years; 15% enter graduate study

General. Founded in 1889. Regionally accredited. **Degrees:** 1,084 bachelor's awarded; master's, doctoral offered. **ROTC:** Army, Air Force. **Location:** 15 miles from Greensboro. **Calendar:** 4-1-4, extensive summer session. **Full-time faculty:** 279 total; 83% have terminal degrees, 11% minority, 45% women. **Part-time faculty:** 101 total; 38% have terminal degrees, 2% minority, 54% women. **Class size:** 46% < 20, 54% 20-39, less than 1% 40-49, less than 1% 50-99. **Special facilities:** Fine arts center, science center, academic pavilions (housing classrooms, students and faculty).

Freshman class profile. 9,065 applied, 3,743 admitted, 1,237 enrolled.

Mid 50% test scores		Rank in top tenth:	32%
SAT verbal:	560-640	Return as sophomores:	89%
SAT math:	570-650	Out-of-state:	73%
ACT:	24-28	Live on campus:	100%
GPA 3.50 or higher:	76%	International:	2%
GPA 3.0-3.49:	17%	Fraternities:	23%
GPA 2.0-2.99:	7%	Sororities:	43%
Rank in top quarter:	67%		

Basis for selection. School achievement record most important, followed by test scores. Class rank, school and community activities, personal statement, recommendations also considered. Audition required for all performing arts programs.

High school preparation. Required and recommended units include English 4, mathematics 3-4, social studies 1, history 1, science 3 (laboratory 1) and foreign language 2-3. Algebra I, II and geometry required.

2005-2006 Annual costs. Tuition/fees: $18,949. Room/board: $6,422. Books/supplies: $900. Personal expenses: $1,400.

2005-2006 Financial aid. Need-based: 734 full-time freshmen applied for aid; 441 were judged to have need; 438 of these received aid. Average need met was 68%. Average scholarship/grant was $7,332; average loan $2,768. 59% of total undergraduate aid awarded as scholarships/grants, 41% as loans/jobs. **Non-need-based:** Awarded to 1,404 full-time undergraduates, including 395 freshmen. Scholarships awarded for academics, art, athletics, leadership, music/drama, ROTC, state residency.

Application procedures. Admission: Priority date 11/1; deadline 1/10 (postmark date). $40 fee, may be waived for applicants with need. Application may be submitted online. Admission notification 12/1. Must reply by May 1 or within 1 week(s) if notified thereafter. **Financial aid:** Priority date 2/15; no closing date. FAFSA, institutional form, CSS PROFILE required. Applicants notified on a rolling basis starting 3/30.

Academics. Special study options: Accelerated study, combined bachelor's/graduate degree, cross-registration, distance learning, double major, dual enrollment of high school students, ESL, exchange student, honors, independent study, internships, liberal arts/career combination, student-designed major, study abroad, teacher certification program, Washington semester. **Credit/placement by examination:** AP, CLEP, IB, SAT, ACT, institutional tests. **Support services:** Learning center, reduced course load, remedial instruction, study skills assistance, tutoring, writing center.

Majors. Biology: General. **Business:** Accounting, business admin, finance, international, management information systems, marketing. **Communications:** General, broadcast journalism, journalism. **Computer sciences:** General, computer science, information systems. **Conservation:** General, environmental studies. **Education:** General, curriculum, elementary, health, mathematics, middle, music, physical, science, secondary, special. **Engineering:** General, chemical, computer, physics. **Engineering technology:** Environmental. **Foreign languages:** General, French, Spanish. **Health:** Athletic training, predentistry, premedicine, preveterinary. **History:** General. **Legal studies:** Prelaw. **Math:** General. **Parks/recreation:** Exercise sciences, facilities management, sports admin. **Philosophy/religion:** Philosophy, religion. **Physical sciences:** Chemistry, physics. **Protective services:** Criminal justice. **Psychology:** General. **Public administration:** General, human services. **Social sciences:** Anthropology, economics, international relations, political science, sociology. **Visual/performing arts:** Art, dance, dramatic, music performance.

Most popular majors. Business/marketing 21%, communications/journalism 20%, education 10%, psychology 6%, public administration/social services 7%.

Computing on campus. 575 workstations in dormitories, library, computer center, student center. Dormitories wired for high-speed internet access and linked to campus network. Commuter students can connect to campus network. Online course registration, online library, helpline, repair service, student web hosting, wireless network available.

Student life. Freshman orientation: Mandatory. Preregistration for classes offered. Students may attend an optional orientation during the spring of their senior high school year. Formal orientation required for all entering freshmen in August. **Policies:** Freshmen and sophomores are required to live on campus; housing is guaranteed. Freshmen permitted cars on campus. **Housing:** Guaranteed on-campus for freshmen. Coed dorms, single-sex dorms, apartments, fraternity/sorority housing, substance-free housing available. $400 partly refundable deposit, deadline 5/1. Theme suites based on academic interest. **Activities:** Bands, choral groups, dance, drama, film society, literary magazine, music ensembles, musical theater, radio station, student government, student newspaper, symphony orchestra, TV station, Intervarsity Christian Fellowship, Young Republicans, Black Cultural Society, Epsilon Sigma Alpha (service society), volunteers, Liberal Arts Forum, Hillel, Model UN, student legislature, student media, Habitat for Humanity.

Athletics. NCAA. **Intercollegiate:** Baseball M, basketball, cheerleading, cross-country, football (tackle) M, golf, soccer, softball W, tennis, track and field W, volleyball W. **Intramural:** Basketball, bowling, football (non-tackle), golf M, handball, racquetball, rugby, soccer, softball, squash, table tennis, tennis, volleyball, water polo, weight lifting. **Team name:** Phoenix.

Student services. Adult student services, alcohol/substance abuse counseling, campus ministries, career counseling, student employment services, financial aid counseling, health services, minority student services, personal counseling, placement for graduates, veterans' counselor, women's services. **Physically disabled:** Services for visually, speech, hearing impaired.

Contact. E-mail: admissions@elon.edu
Phone: (336) 278-3566 Toll-free number: (800) 334-8448
Fax: (336) 278-7699
Susan Klopman, Dean of Admissions and Financial Planning, Elon University, 2700 Campus Box, Elon, NC 27244-2010

Fayetteville State University

Fayetteville, North Carolina — **CB member**
www.uncfsu.edu — **CB code: 5212**

- Public 4-year university
- Commuter campus in small city
- 4,935 degree-seeking undergraduates
- 1,036 graduate students
- 80% of applicants admitted
- SAT or ACT with writing required

General. Founded in 1867. Regionally accredited. Courses leading to bachelor's degree also available at the Fort Bragg/Pope AFB Center, Seymour Johnson AFB, and online. **Degrees:** 698 bachelor's awarded; master's, doctoral offered. **ROTC:** Army, Air Force. **Location:** 60 miles from Raleigh. **Calendar:** Semester, limited summer session. **Full-time faculty:** 200 total. **Part-time faculty:** 40 total. **Special facilities:** Greenhouse, observatory, planetarium.

Freshman class profile. 2,318 applied, 1,853 admitted, 848 enrolled.

Mid 50% test scores			
SAT verbal:	380-460	Rank in top tenth:	5%
SAT math:	370-470	Out-of-state:	16%
Rank in top quarter:	21%	Live on campus:	74%

Basis for selection. 2.0 GPA, SAT scores, completion of 18 prescribed high school units required. All applicants, except those exempted by current campus policies, must submit a standardized test score. SAT preferred, ACT also accepted.

High school preparation. 19 units required. Required and recommended units include English 4, mathematics 3, social studies 2, history 1, science 3, foreign language 2 and academic electives 6. Foreign language units can be used as academic elective units.

2005-2006 Annual costs. Tuition/fees: $2,521; $12,257 out-of-state. Room/board: $4,120. Books/supplies: $350. Personal expenses: $750.

2004-2005 Financial aid. Need-based: 684 full-time freshmen applied for aid; 582 were judged to have need; 495 of these received aid. Average need met was 78%. Average scholarship/grant was $1,500; average loan $2,200. 51% of total undergraduate aid awarded as scholarships/grants, 49% as loans/jobs. **Non-need-based:** Awarded to 823 full-time undergraduates, including 201 freshmen. Scholarships awarded for academics, alumni affiliation, athletics, music/drama, ROTC, state residency.

Application procedures. Admission: Closing date 7/1 (postmark date). $25 fee, may be waived for applicants with need. Application may be submitted online. Admission notification on a rolling basis beginning on or about 1/15. Must reply by 7/1. **Financial aid:** Priority date 3/1, closing date 4/1. FAFSA required. Applicants notified on a rolling basis starting 4/15; must reply within 2 week(s) of notification.

Academics. Special study options: Accelerated study, combined bachelor's/graduate degree, cooperative education, distance learning, double major, dual enrollment of high school students, honors, independent study, internships, study abroad, teacher certification program, weekend college. **Credit/placement by examination:** AP, CLEP, institutional tests. 30 credit hours maximum toward bachelor's degree. **Support services:** Learning center, pre-admission summer program, remedial instruction, tutoring.

Majors. Biology: General. **Business:** Accounting, business admin, office management. **Computer sciences:** General. **Education:** Business, English, health, mathematics, middle, music, physical, secondary, social science. **English:** British lit, speech/rhetoric. **History:** General. **Math:** General. **Physical sciences:** Chemistry. **Protective services:** Criminal justice. **Psychology:** General. **Public administration:** General. **Social sciences:** General, geography, political science, sociology. **Visual/performing arts:** General, dramatic.

Most popular majors. Business/marketing 22%, education 14%, psychology 11%, security/protective services 13%, social sciences 19%.

Computing on campus. 600 workstations in dormitories, library, computer center, student center. Dormitories wired for high-speed internet access and linked to campus network. Commuter students can connect to campus network. Online course registration, online library, helpline, wireless network available.

Student life. Freshman orientation: Mandatory, $45 fee. 3 Saturdays in July and August. **Policies:** Freshmen permitted cars on campus. **Housing:** Single-sex dorms available. $125 deposit, deadline 7/1. **Activities:** Bands, choral groups, drama, music ensembles, radio station, student government, student newspaper, TV station, Baptist student union, Federation of Young Democrats, NAACP, NCNW, Honda Campus All-Stars, art guild, Illusions modeling club.

Athletics. NCAA. **Intercollegiate:** Basketball, bowling W, cross-country, football (tackle) M, golf, softball W, tennis, track and field, volleyball W. **Intramural:** Baseball M, basketball, bowling, football (tackle) M, golf, gymnastics, swimming, tennis M, volleyball. **Team name:** Broncos.

Student services. Alcohol/substance abuse counseling, career counseling, student employment services, financial aid counseling, health services, on-campus daycare, personal counseling, placement for graduates, veterans' counselor. **Physically disabled:** Services for visually impaired.

Contact. E-mail: chogan@uncfsu.edu
Phone: (910) 672-1371 Toll-free number: (800) 222-2594
Fax: (910) 672-1414
Carol Hogan, Director of Admissions, Fayetteville State University, 1200 Murchison Road, Fayetteville, NC 28301-4298

Gardner-Webb University

Boiling Springs, North Carolina
www.gardner-webb.edu

CB member
CB code: 5242

- Private 4-year university and liberal arts college affiliated with Southern Baptist Convention
- Residential campus in small town
- 2,629 degree-seeking undergraduates: 15% part-time, 66% women, 17% African American, 1% Asian American, 1% Hispanic American, 1% Native American
- 1,150 degree-seeking graduate students
- 72% of applicants admitted
- SAT or ACT (ACT writing optional) required
- 45% graduate within 6 years

General. Founded in 1905. Regionally accredited. **Degrees:** 539 bachelor's, 58 associate awarded; master's, doctoral, first professional offered. **ROTC:** Army. **Location:** 45 miles from Charlotte. **Calendar:** Semester, extensive summer session. **Full-time faculty:** 133 total. **Part-time faculty:** 188 total. **Class size:** 100% 20-39. **Special facilities:** Observatory, adventure course.

Freshman class profile. 2,042 applied, 1,465 admitted, 431 enrolled.

Mid 50% test scores			
SAT verbal:	510-570	Rank in top tenth:	22%
SAT math:	510-570	Return as sophomores:	67%
ACT:	19-24	Out-of-state:	40%
Rank in top quarter:	31%	Live on campus:	65%

Basis for selection. School achievement record most important, followed by test scores, recommendations, and school and community activities. Expected 2.4 GPA. Interview, portfolio, essay recommended for all students; audition required for music scholarships.

High school preparation. Required units include English 4, mathematics 2, social studies 2, history 1, science 2 and foreign language 2.

2005-2006 Annual costs. Tuition/fees: $16,150. $85 communication fee and $30 residence hall activity fee for resident students. Room/board: $5,540. Books/supplies: $750.

2005-2006 Financial aid. Need-based: 387 full-time freshmen applied for aid; 312 were judged to have need; 312 of these received aid. Average need met was 62%. Average scholarship/grant was $2,430; average loan $2,211. 49% of total undergraduate aid awarded as scholarships/grants, 51% as loans/jobs. **Non-need-based:** Awarded to 2,063 full-time undergraduates, including 444 freshmen. Scholarships awarded for academics, athletics, leadership, minority status, music/drama, state residency.

Application procedures. Admission: No deadline. $40 fee, may be waived for applicants with need. Application may be submitted online. Admission notification on a rolling basis. Applicants using on-call application notified within 48 hours. **Financial aid:** No deadline. FAFSA required. Applicants notified on a rolling basis starting 3/1; must reply within 2 week(s) of notification.

Academics. Special study options: Combined bachelor's/graduate degree, cooperative education, double major, dual enrollment of high school students, ESL, honors, independent study, internships, liberal arts/career combination, New York semester, study abroad, teacher certification program, Washington semester. Spring Break in New York, Fall Break in Washington. **Credit/placement by examination:** AP, CLEP, IB, institutional tests. 30 credit hours maximum toward bachelor's degree. **Support services:** Learning center, pre-admission summer program, reduced course load, remedial instruction, tutoring, writing center.

Honors college/program. Students with 1170 SAT (exclusive of Writing) and 3.8 GPA average admitted.

Majors. Biology: General. **Business:** General, accounting, business admin, international, management information systems. **Communications:** General, broadcast journalism, journalism, public relations. **Computer sciences:** General. **Education:** General, biology, chemistry, elementary, English, foreign languages, French, health, history, mathematics, middle, multi-level teacher, music, physical, science, secondary, social science, Spanish. **Foreign languages:** General, American Sign Language, French, sign language interpretation, Spanish. **Health:** Athletic training, nursing (RN). **History:** General. **Legal studies:** Prelaw. **Math:** General. **Philosophy/religion:** Religion. **Physical sciences:** Chemistry. **Psychology:** General. **Social sciences:** General, political science, sociology. **Theology:** Religious ed, youth ministry. **Visual/performing arts:** Art, music performance, piano/organ, theater history, voice/opera.

Most popular majors. Business/marketing 42%, philosophy/religious studies 7%, social sciences 27%.

Computing on campus. 150 workstations in library, computer center. Dormitories wired for high-speed internet access and linked to campus network. Commuter students can connect to campus network. Online course registration, online library, helpline, repair service, wireless network available.

Student life. Freshman orientation: Mandatory, $75 fee. Preregistration for classes offered. 3-day program typically held near the end of August. **Policies:** Limited visitation hours. Religious observance required. Freshmen permitted cars on campus. **Housing:** Guaranteed on-campus for freshmen. Single-sex dorms, apartments, substance-free housing available. $150 deposit. Honors student residence hall. **Activities:** Bands, choral groups, dance, drama, film society, literary magazine, music ensembles, musical theater, opera, radio station, student government, student newspaper, symphony orchestra, TV station, Fellowship of Christian Athletes, student volunteer corps, The Verge, outdoor explorers club, gospel choir, Campus Ministries United, FOCUS, Bible Studies, Young Republicans.

Athletics. NCAA, NCCAA. **Intercollegiate:** Baseball M, basketball, cheerleading, cross-country, football (tackle) M, golf, soccer, softball W, swimming W, tennis, track and field, volleyball W, wrestling M. **Intramural:** Badminton, baseball M, basketball, bowling, football (non-tackle), racquetball, soccer, softball, swimming, table tennis, tennis, volleyball. **Team name:** Runnin' Bulldogs.

Student services. Campus ministries, career counseling, student employment services, financial aid counseling, health services, personal counseling, placement for graduates, veterans' counselor. **Physically disabled:** Services for visually, speech, hearing impaired.

Contact. E-mail: admissions@gardner-webb.edu
Phone: (704) 406-4498 Toll-free number: (800) 253-6472
Fax: (704) 406-4488
Nathan Alexander, Director of Undergraduate Admissions and Enrollment Management, Gardner-Webb University, Box 817, Boiling Springs, NC 28017

Greensboro College

Greensboro, North Carolina
www.gborocollege.edu

CB member
CB code: 5260

- Private 4-year liberal arts college affiliated with United Methodist Church
- Residential campus in small city
- 850 degree-seeking undergraduates
- 98 graduate students
- 69% of applicants admitted
- SAT or ACT with writing, application essay required

General. Founded in 1838. Regionally accredited. **Degrees:** 148 bachelor's awarded; master's offered. **ROTC:** Army, Air Force. **Location:** 90 miles from Charlotte, 75 miles from Raleigh. **Calendar:** Semester, limited summer session. **Full-time faculty:** 61 total. **Part-time faculty:** 64 total. **Class size:** 73% < 20, 26% 20-39, less than 1% 40-49, less than 1% 50-99. **Special facilities:** Historical museum, computer writing center, computerized music laboratories.

Freshman class profile. 1,112 applied, 764 admitted, 213 enrolled.

Mid 50% test scores			
SAT verbal:	430-540	Rank in top quarter:	24%
SAT math:	440-550	Rank in top tenth:	7%
ACT:	18-24	Out-of-state:	33%
		Live on campus:	93%

Basis for selection. High school curriculum most important, followed by grades, class rank, test scores, personal statement, school and community activities, high school caliber. Recommendations, interview considered. Interview recommended for all students. Audition required for music, theater majors; portfolio required for art majors. **Homeschooled:** Interview highly recommended and SAT/ACT required.

High school preparation. Recommended units include English 4, mathematics 3, history 2, science 2 (laboratory 1) and foreign language 2. Remaining units must be selected from art, music, social science and physical education.

2005-2006 Annual costs. Tuition/fees: $18,120. Room/board: $6,920. Books/supplies: $800. Personal expenses: $900.

Financial aid. Non-need-based: Scholarships awarded for academics, alumni affiliation, art, leadership, music/drama, religious affiliation, state residency.

Application procedures. Admission: Priority date 12/15; no deadline. $35 fee, may be waived for applicants with need. Application may be submitted online. Admission notification on a rolling basis. Notification within 2 weeks of receiving complete application. Must reply by May 1 or within 4 week(s) if notified thereafter. **Financial aid:** Priority date 4/15; no closing date. FAFSA, institutional form required. Applicants notified on a rolling basis starting 2/1; must reply within 2 week(s) of notification.

Academics. Special study options: Accelerated study, cross-registration, double major, dual enrollment of high school students, ESL, honors, independent study, internships, liberal arts/career combination, student-designed major, study abroad, teacher certification program, weekend college. Academic success program, minor in ethics across the curriculum. **Credit/placement by examination:** CLEP, IB, institutional tests. 45 credit hours maximum toward bachelor's degree. **Support services:** Learning center, reduced course load, study skills assistance, tutoring, writing center.

Majors. Biology: General. **Business:** Accounting, managerial economics. **Communications:** General. **Education:** General, art, biology, drama/dance, early childhood, elementary, emotionally handicapped, English, history, learning disabled, mathematics, mentally handicapped, middle, multiple handicapped, music, physical, social studies, Spanish, special. **Foreign languages:** French, Spanish. **Health:** Athletic training. **History:** General. **Math:** General. **Parks/recreation:** Exercise sciences, health/fitness, sports admin. **Philosophy/religion:** Religion. **Physical sciences:** Chemistry. **Psychology:** General. **Social sciences:** Political science, sociology. **Visual/performing arts:** Dramatic, music performance, studio arts, theater design.

Most popular majors. Biology 9%, business/marketing 26%, education 11%, parks/recreation 9%, psychology 9%, social sciences 9%, visual/performing arts 14%.

Computing on campus. 95 workstations in dormitories, library, computer center, student center. Dormitories wired for high-speed internet access and linked to campus network. Commuter students can connect to campus network. Online library, helpline, repair service available.

Student life. Freshman orientation: Mandatory, $50 fee. Preregistration for classes offered. Three 2-day early orientations held in May, June, and July for placement testing, pre-registration and group development. Additional program in August, one week prior to start of clases. Students complete advising, registration, and placement testing. **Policies:** Freshmen permitted cars on campus. **Housing:** Guaranteed on-campus for all undergraduates. Coed dorms, single-sex dorms, apartments available. $200 deposit. All students who have earned less than 58 credit hours required to live in college housing unless married, veterans, or residing with parents. All students encouraged to do so. Theme housing available, including community service housing. **Activities:** Bands, choral groups, dance, drama, literary magazine, music ensembles, musical theater, opera, student government, student newspaper, Student Christian Fellowship, United African American Society, clown ministry, Beta Beta Beta (biology society), Student National Education Association, Model United Nations, campus activity board, international student club, Fellowship of Christian Athletes, Los Amigos, Circle K.

Athletics. NCAA. **Intercollegiate:** Baseball M, basketball, cheerleading, cross-country, football (tackle) M, golf M, lacrosse, soccer, softball W, swimming W, tennis, volleyball W. **Intramural:** Baseball M, basketball, bowling, football (non-tackle), racquetball, skiing. **Team name:** Pride.

Student services. Adult student services, alcohol/substance abuse counseling, campus ministries, career counseling, student employment services, financial aid counseling, health services, personal counseling, placement for graduates. **Physically disabled:** Services for visually, speech, hearing impaired.

Contact. E-mail: admissions@gborocollege.edu
Phone: (336) 272-7102 ext. 211 Toll-free number: (800) 346-8226
Fax: (336) 378-0154
Tim Jackson, Director of Admissions, Greensboro College, 815 West Market Street, Greensboro, NC 27401-1875

Guilford College

Greensboro, North Carolina — **CB member**
www.guilford.edu — **CB code: 5261**

- Private 4-year liberal arts college affiliated with Society of Friends (Quaker)
- Residential campus in small city
- 2,682 degree-seeking undergraduates: 16% part-time, 62% women, 23% African American, 1% Asian American, 2% Hispanic American, 1% Native American, 1% international
- 64% of applicants admitted
- SAT or ACT (ACT writing optional), application essay required
- 55% graduate within 6 years; 18% enter graduate study

General. Founded in 1837. Regionally accredited. **Degrees:** 414 bachelor's awarded. **Location:** 90 miles from Raleigh, 100 miles from Charlotte. **Calendar:** Semester, limited summer session. **Full-time faculty:** 124 total; 58% have terminal degrees, 13% minority, 42% women. **Part-time faculty:** 78 total; 50% have terminal degrees, 10% minority, 51% women. **Class size:** 55% < 20, 44% 20-39, less than 1% 40-49. **Special facilities:** Observatory, multimedia learning center for cultures and languages, telecommunications center, photography studio, outdoor sculpture studio, new computer visualization laboratory.

Freshman class profile. 2,492 applied, 1,584 admitted, 412 enrolled.

Mid 50% test scores		**Rank in top quarter:**	44%
SAT verbal:	520-640	**Rank in top tenth:**	14%
SAT math:	500-620	**End year in good standing:**	79%
ACT:	20-25	**Return as sophomores:**	72%
GPA 3.50 or higher:	22%	**Out-of-state:**	59%
GPA 3.0-3.49:	34%	**Live on campus:**	90%
GPA 2.0-2.99:	43%		

Basis for selection. School achievement record and essay most important. Test scores, interview, recommendations, interests, leadership ability also important. Minimum SAT composite score of 1000 (exclusive of Writing) or ACT score of 22 recommended. Auditions and portfolios recommended in music, theatre and art. **Homeschooled:** Transcript of courses and grades, interview, letter of recommendation (nonparent) required. Provide reason for homeschool.

High school preparation. College-preparatory program recommended. 18 units required; 20 recommended. Required and recommended units include English 4, mathematics 3, social studies 2, history 1, science 2-3, foreign language 2 and academic electives 2.

2006-2007 Annual costs. Tuition/fees (projected): $23,020. Room/board: $6,690. Books/supplies: $800. Personal expenses: $1,000.

2004-2005 Financial aid. Need-based: 339 full-time freshmen applied for aid; 263 were judged to have need; 263 of these received aid. Average need met was 95%. Average scholarship/grant was $14,250; average loan $5,096. 58% of total undergraduate aid awarded as scholarships/grants, 42% as loans/jobs. **Non-need-based:** Awarded to 1,525 full-time undergraduates, including 335 freshmen. Scholarships awarded for academics, art, job skills, leadership, minority status, music/drama, religious affiliation, state residency.

Application procedures. Admission: Priority date 1/15; deadline 2/15 (postmark date). $25 fee, may be waived for applicants with need. Application may be submitted online. Admission notification on a rolling basis beginning on or about 11/1. Must reply by May 1 or within 4 week(s) if notified thereafter. **Financial aid:** Priority date 3/1; no closing date. FAFSA required. Applicants notified on a rolling basis starting 2/15; must reply by 5/1 or within 4 week(s) of notification.

Academics. Faculty tutoring for skills development and student tutoring for course-specific help available. Assistance available for non-remedial writing, organizational/time-management skills, and students with learning disabilities. Remedial assistance and reader service for the blind available. **Special study options:** Accelerated study, combined bachelor's/graduate degree, cooperative education, cross-registration, double major, ESL, exchange student, honors, independent study, internships, liberal arts/career combination, student-designed major, study abroad, teacher certification program, Washington semester, weekend college. 3-2 degree programs available in forestry and environmental studies with Duke University, and in physician assistant training with Bowman Gray School of Medicine at Wake Forest University. Many internships, work-study programs, accelerated degree programs in business management, computer information systems, psychology, and biology, dual majors, student-designed majors, study abroad in 9 countries, and cross-registration with members of the Greater Greensboro Consortium (8 colleges/universities). **Credit/placement by examination:** AP, CLEP, IB, institutional tests. 32 credit hours maximum toward bachelor's degree. **Support services:** Learning center, pre-admission summer program, reduced course load, remedial instruction, study skills assistance, tutoring, writing center.

Majors. Area/ethnic studies: African-American, women's. **Biology:** General, biomedical sciences. **Business:** Accounting, business admin. **Computer sciences:** General, information systems. **Conservation:** Environmental studies. **Education:** Elementary, physical, secondary. **Foreign languages:** French, German, Germanic, Spanish. **Health:** Athletic training. **History:** General. **Interdisciplinary:** Peace/conflict. **Math:** General. **Parks/recreation:** Exercise sciences, health/fitness, sports admin. **Philosophy/religion:** Philosophy, religion. **Physical sciences:** Chemistry, geology, physics. **Protective services:** Criminal justice, forensics. **Psychology:** General. **Social sciences:** Economics, international relations, political science, sociology. **Visual/performing arts:** Art, dramatic.

Computing on campus. 275 workstations in dormitories, library, computer center, student center. Dormitories wired for high-speed internet access and linked to campus network. Commuter students can connect to campus network. Helpline, repair service, wireless network available.

Student life. Freshman orientation: Mandatory, $75 fee. Preregistration for classes offered. One-day event in Spring; parents invited. **Policies:** Consistent with its Quaker heritage, college promotes and encourages student involvement in community service projects. Freshmen permitted cars on campus. **Housing:** Guaranteed on-campus for freshmen. Coed dorms, single-sex dorms, apartments, substance-free housing available. $400 fully refundable deposit, deadline 5/1. Special interest housing available. Alternative houses with themes and community service project requirements. **Activities:** Jazz band, choral groups, dance, drama, film society, literary magazine, music ensembles, musical theater, radio station, student government, student newspaper, international club, African American cultural society, Amnesty International, Project Community, Community Senate, Guilford Christian Fellowship, Native American club, Hillel, Quaker Concerns, Guilford Action Network.

Athletics. NCAA. **Intercollegiate:** Baseball, basketball, cross-country, football (tackle) M, golf M, lacrosse, rugby, soccer, softball W, swimming W, tennis, volleyball W. **Intramural:** Baseball, basketball, cheerleading W, football (non-tackle), soccer, softball, table tennis, tennis, volleyball, water polo. **Team name:** Quakers.

Student services. Adult student services, alcohol/substance abuse counseling, campus ministries, career counseling, student employment services, financial aid counseling, health services, minority student services, personal counseling, placement for graduates, veterans' counselor, women's services. **Physically disabled:** Services for visually, speech, hearing impaired. **Learning disabled:** Comprehensive services available.

Contact. E-mail: admission@guilford.edu
Phone: (336) 316-2100 Toll-free number: (800) 992-7759
Fax: (336) 316-2954
B Doss, Vice President, Enrollment and Campus Life, Guilford College, Admissions, New Garden Hall, Greensboro, NC 27410-4108

2004-2005 Financial aid. Need-based: 351 full-time freshmen applied for aid; 339 were judged to have need; 339 of these received aid. Average need met was 78%. Average scholarship/grant was $4,000; average loan $2,626. 53% of total undergraduate aid awarded as scholarships/grants, 47% as loans/jobs. **Non-need-based:** Awarded to 1,285 full-time undergraduates, including 400 freshmen. Scholarships awarded for academics, alumni affiliation, art, athletics, music/drama, religious affiliation, state residency.

Application procedures. Admission: Priority date 11/1; deadline 8/15 (postmark date). $25 fee, may be waived for applicants with need. Application may be submitted online. Admission notification on a rolling basis beginning on or about 11/1. Must reply by May 1 or within 4 week(s) if notified thereafter. **Financial aid:** Priority date 3/1; no closing date. FAFSA required. Applicants notified on a rolling basis starting 4/1; must reply within 3 week(s) of notification.

Academics. Special study options: Accelerated study, combined bachelor's/graduate degree, cooperative education, cross-registration, double major, dual enrollment of high school students, ESL, honors, independent study, internships, liberal arts/career combination, student-designed major, study abroad, teacher certification program. Dual degree programs with Duke University (forestry and environmental science) and Wake Forest University School of Medicine (medical technology). **Credit/placement by examination:** AP, CLEP, IB, SAT, ACT, institutional tests. 31 credit hours maximum toward bachelor's degree. **Support services:** Learning center, pre-admission summer program, reduced course load, study skills assistance, tutoring, writing center.

Majors. Area/ethnic studies: American. **Biology:** General. **Business:** Accounting, business admin, human resources, international, management information systems, organizational behavior. **Communications:** General. **Computer sciences:** General, computer science, security. **Conservation:** Forestry. **Education:** Art, early childhood, elementary, middle, physical, secondary, special. **English:** Composition, English lit. **Foreign languages:** General, French, Spanish. **Health:** Athletic training, clinical lab science. **History:** General. **Interdisciplinary:** Global studies. **Math:** General. **Parks/recreation:** Exercise sciences, facilities management, sports admin. **Philosophy/religion:** Philosophy, religion. **Physical sciences:** Chemistry. **Protective services:** Criminal justice. **Psychology:** General. **Social sciences:** Political science, sociology. **Visual/performing arts:** Art, dramatic, interior design, theater design.

Most popular majors. Business/marketing 30%, computer/information sciences 9%, psychology 6%, social sciences 10%.

High Point University
High Point, North Carolina
www.highpoint.edu
CB member
CB code: 5293

- Private 4-year university affiliated with United Methodist Church
- Residential campus in small city
- 2,507 degree-seeking undergraduates: 7% part-time, 63% women
- 236 degree-seeking graduate students
- 67% of applicants admitted
- SAT or ACT (ACT writing optional) required
- 49% graduate within 6 years

General. Founded in 1924. Regionally accredited. **Degrees:** 548 bachelor's awarded; master's offered. **ROTC:** Army, Air Force. **Location:** 15 miles from Greensboro, 20 miles from Winston-Salem. **Calendar:** Semester, limited summer session. **Full-time faculty:** 122 total; 76% have terminal degrees, 4% minority, 36% women. **Part-time faculty:** 105 total; 22% have terminal degrees, 3% minority, 40% women. **Class size:** 77% < 20, 23% 20-39. **Special facilities:** Amphitheater.

Freshman class profile. 2,243 applied, 1,512 admitted, 456 enrolled.

Mid 50% test scores		Rank in top quarter:	36%
SAT verbal:	460-570	Rank in top tenth:	14%
SAT math:	460-560	Out-of-state:	61%
GPA 3.50 or higher:	26%	Live on campus:	85%
GPA 3.0-3.49:	30%	Fraternities:	10%
GPA 2.0-2.99:	41%	Sororities:	18%

Basis for selection. Priority given to school achievement record, test scores, and interview. Recommendations, school and community activities also considered. Students who speak English as a second language must demonstrate proficiency in English. TOEFL preferred, other instruments considered. International students may submit TOEFL in lieu of SAT or ACT, unless they wish to play on intercollegiate athletic teams in which case either SAT or ACT required. Interview strongly encouraged. Applicants asked to provide short essay answers to specific questions, but personal essays invited and considered.

High school preparation. 14 units required. Required and recommended units include English 4, mathematics 3, social studies 2, history 2, science 2 (laboratory 2), foreign language 2 and academic electives 1-2.

2006-2007 Annual costs. Tuition/fees (projected): $18,130. Room/board: $7,590.

Computing on campus. 305 workstations in library, computer center, student center. Dormitories wired for high-speed internet access and linked to campus network. Commuter students can connect to campus network. Online course registration, online library, helpline, repair service, student web hosting, wireless network available.

Student life. Freshman orientation: Mandatory. Preregistration for classes offered. **Policies:** Freshmen permitted cars on campus. **Housing:** Guaranteed on-campus for freshmen. Coed dorms, single-sex dorms, special housing for disabled, apartments, cooperative housing, fraternity/sorority housing, substance-free housing available. $250 deposit. **Activities:** Bands, choral groups, dance, drama, literary magazine, music ensembles, musical theater, radio station, student government, student newspaper, TV station, Alpha Phi Omega, black cultural awareness, Board of Stewards, College Republicans, College Democrats, Fellowship of Christian Athletes, Model United Nations, Phi Theta Kappa Alumni Association, volunteer center.

Athletics. NCAA. **Intercollegiate:** Baseball M, basketball, cheerleading, cross-country, golf, soccer, tennis, track and field, volleyball W. **Intramural:** Badminton, basketball, bowling, golf, racquetball, soccer, softball, swimming, table tennis, tennis, track and field M, volleyball, water polo. **Team name:** Panthers.

Student services. Adult student services, alcohol/substance abuse counseling, campus ministries, career counseling, student employment services, financial aid counseling, health services, personal counseling, placement for graduates, veterans' counselor.

Contact. E-mail: admiss@highpoint.edu
Phone: (336) 841-9216 Toll-free number: (800) 345-6993
Fax: (336) 888-6382
Jessie McIlrath-Carter, Director of Admissions, High Point University, 833 Montlieu Avenue, High Point, NC 27262-3598

John Wesley College
High Point, North Carolina
www.johnwesley.edu
CB code: 5348

- Private 4-year Bible college affiliated with interdenominational tradition
- Commuter campus in small city

- 140 degree-seeking undergraduates: 36% part-time, 46% women, 25% African American, 1% Asian American, 2% Hispanic American, 1% Native American
- 70% of applicants admitted
- Application essay, interview required

General. Founded in 1932. Accredited by ABHE. **Degrees:** 40 bachelor's, 2 associate awarded. **Location:** 15 miles from Greensboro, 60 miles from Charlotte. **Calendar:** Semester, limited summer session. **Full-time faculty:** 3 total; 100% have terminal degrees. **Part-time faculty:** 18 total; 39% have terminal degrees, 11% minority, 50% women. **Class size:** 98% < 20, 2% 20-39.

Freshman class profile. 23 applied, 16 admitted, 12 enrolled.

End year in good standing:	87%	**Out-of-state:**	2%
Return as sophomores:	55%		

Basis for selection. Future career in church-related vocations and motivation; religious commitment and personal statement very important. Positive personal testimony required. Finding and following God's will foremost. **Homeschooled:** Junior or higher standing, GPA 3.2 or higher, 16 or older, and recommendation from high school administrator or guidance counselor required.

High school preparation. 20 units recommended. Recommended units include English 4, mathematics 3, social studies 2, science 2 (laboratory 2).

2005-2006 Annual costs. Tuition/fees: $9,226. Room only: $1,990. Books/supplies: $1,000. Personal expenses: $2,600.

2004-2005 Financial aid. Need-based: 12 full-time freshmen applied for aid; 12 were judged to have need; 12 of these received aid. Average need met was 50%. Average scholarship/grant was $500; average loan $2,625. 30% of total undergraduate aid awarded as scholarships/grants, 70% as loans/jobs. **Non-need-based:** Awarded to 3 full-time undergraduates, including 3 freshmen. **Additional information:** Early Acceptance Scholarships, Academic Honor Scholarships, Married Student Credit and Minister/Missionary Dependent Scholarship available.

Application procedures. Admission: Closing date 8/1 (postmark date). $35 fee, may be waived for applicants with need. Application may be submitted online. Admission notification on a rolling basis. **Financial aid:** Priority date 3/15; no closing date. FAFSA required. Applicants notified on a rolling basis starting 6/1; must reply within 3 week(s) of notification.

Academics. All students major in Bible; second major optional. **Special study options:** Accelerated study, cooperative education, distance learning, double major, dual enrollment of high school students, independent study, internships, student-designed major. **Credit/placement by examination:** AP, CLEP, IB, institutional tests. 15 credit hours maximum toward associate degree, 30 toward bachelor's. **Support services:** Reduced course load, remedial instruction.

Majors. Business: Business admin. **Education:** Elementary. **Theology:** Pastoral counseling, religious ed, theology.

Most popular majors. Business/marketing 45%, philosophy/religious studies 45%.

Computing on campus. 6 workstations in library, computer center. Dormitories wired for high-speed internet access. Online library available.

Student life. Freshman orientation: Mandatory. Preregistration for classes offered. Orientation activities held 2 business days before classes begin. **Policies:** Religious observance required. Freshmen permitted cars on campus. **Housing:** Apartments, substance-free housing available. $50 nonrefundable deposit, deadline 7/15. **Activities:** Drama, literary magazine, student government, evangelistic ministries, prison ministry, gospel music team, foreign missions involvement team.

Athletics. Intramural: Basketball, bowling, golf, table tennis, volleyball.

Student services. Campus ministries, student employment services, financial aid counseling, personal counseling, veterans' counselor.

Contact. E-mail: gworkman@johnwesley.edu
Phone: (336) 889-2262 ext. 127 Fax: (336) 889-2261
Greg Workman, Admissions Officer, John Wesley College, 2314 North Centennial, High Point, NC 27265-3197

Johnson & Wales University

Charlotte, North Carolina
www.jwu.edu/charlotte/

- Private 4-year university
- Commuter campus in very large city
- 2,156 degree-seeking undergraduates: 52% women, 27% African American, 2% Asian American, 2% Hispanic American
- 74% of applicants admitted

General. Calendar: Quarter. **Full-time faculty:** 66 total. **Part-time faculty:** 9 total.

Freshman class profile. 6,226 applied, 4,623 admitted, 789 enrolled.

GPA 3.50 or higher:	15%	**Out-of-state:**	61%
GPA 3.0-3.49:	26%	**Live on campus:**	22%
GPA 2.0-2.99:	58%		

Basis for selection. Secondary school record, class rank, and interview important. SAT or ACT recommended.

High school preparation. 12 units recommended. Recommended units include English 4, mathematics 3, social studies 2 and science 3.

2006-2007 Annual costs. Tuition/fees (projected): $20,826. Room/board: $8,300. Books/supplies: $900. Personal expenses: $500.

2005-2006 Financial aid. Need-based: 726 full-time freshmen applied for aid; 655 were judged to have need; 654 of these received aid. Average need met was 63%. Average scholarship/grant was $5,513; average loan $6,361. 34% of total undergraduate aid awarded as scholarships/grants, 66% as loans/jobs. **Non-need-based:** Awarded to 1,618 full-time undergraduates, including 613 freshmen.

Application procedures. Admission: No deadline. No application fee. Admission notification on a rolling basis beginning on or about 10/1. **Financial aid:** No deadline. Applicants notified by 3/1.

Academics. Special study options: Accelerated study, cooperative education, honors, independent study, study abroad. **Credit/placement by examination:** CLEP.

Majors. Business: Restaurant/food services.

Student life. Housing: Coed dorms, special housing for disabled available. $300 deposit. **Activities:** Choral groups, dance, student government.

Contact. E-mail: admissions.clt@jwu.edu
Phone: (980) 598-1111
Johnson & Wales University, 801 West Trade Street, Charlotte, NC 28202

Johnson C. Smith University

Charlotte, North Carolina **CB member**
www.jcsu.edu **CB code: 5333**

- Private 4-year university and liberal arts college
- Residential campus in very large city
- 1,404 degree-seeking undergraduates: 5% part-time, 60% women, 99% African American
- 37% of applicants admitted
- SAT or ACT with writing required
- 36% graduate within 6 years; 22% enter graduate study

General. Founded in 1867. Regionally accredited. **Degrees:** 248 bachelor's awarded. **ROTC:** Army, Air Force. **Location:** 240 miles from Atlanta. **Calendar:** Semester, limited summer session. **Full-time faculty:** 90 total; 68% have terminal degrees, 67% minority, 42% women. **Part-time faculty:** 31 total; 32% have terminal degrees, 81% minority, 45% women. **Class size:** 62% < 20, 38% 20-39, less than 1% 40-49. **Special facilities:** Technology center.

Freshman class profile. 4,047 applied, 1,488 admitted, 444 enrolled.

Mid 50% test scores		**End year in good standing:**	85%
SAT verbal:	410-510	**Return as sophomores:**	66%
SAT math:	410-500	**Out-of-state:**	73%
ACT:	19-20	**Live on campus:**	98%

Basis for selection. High school class rank, high school GPA, SAT or ACT scores important. Applicants encouraged to submit no more than 2 letters of recommendation from guidance counselors or teachers and personal essay to support application. Interview recommended.

High school preparation. 16 units required. Required units include English 4, mathematics 2, social studies 2, science 1 and academic electives 7.

2005-2006 Annual costs. Tuition/fees: $14,399. Room/board: $5,563. Books/supplies: $1,000. Personal expenses: $2,400.

2005-2006 Financial aid. **Need-based:** 399 full-time freshmen applied for aid; 342 were judged to have need; 342 of these received aid. Average need met was 40%. Average scholarship/grant was $3,000; average loan $2,625. 37% of total undergraduate aid awarded as scholarships/grants, 63% as loans/jobs. **Non-need-based:** Awarded to 213 full-time undergraduates, including 110 freshmen. Scholarships awarded for academics, athletics, ROTC, state residency.

Application procedures. **Admission:** Priority date 8/1; no deadline. $25 fee, may be waived for applicants with need. Application may be submitted online. Admission notification on a rolling basis beginning on or about 10/1. **Financial aid:** Priority date 3/1; no closing date. FAFSA required. Applicants notified on a rolling basis starting 3/1; must reply within 2 week(s) of notification.

Academics. Requirements include 10 hours per year of community service, sophomore tests in basic communication and cognitive competencies, exit exams in major field for seniors. Freshmen who have completed liberal studies program with honors may apply to enter Honors College as sophomores. **Special study options:** Accelerated study, cooperative education, cross-registration, double major, exchange student, honors, independent study, internships, liberal arts/career combination, study abroad, teacher certification program. **Credit/placement by examination:** CLEP, institutional tests. **Support services:** Learning center, pre-admission summer program, reduced course load, study skills assistance, tutoring, writing center.

Majors. **Biology:** General. **Business:** Business admin. **Communications:** Media studies. **Computer sciences:** General, information technology. **Education:** General, elementary, English, health, mathematics, physical, secondary, social science. **Engineering:** General, computer. **English:** English lit. **Foreign languages:** French, Spanish. **Health:** Premedicine. **History:** General. **Interdisciplinary:** Biological/physical sciences, natural sciences. **Liberal arts:** Arts/sciences. **Math:** General, applied. **Parks/recreation:** Health/fitness, sports admin. **Physical sciences:** Chemistry. **Protective services:** Law enforcement admin. **Psychology:** General. **Public administration:** Social work. **Social sciences:** General, criminology, economics, political science, sociology. **Visual/performing arts:** Music management.

Most popular majors. Business/marketing 16%, communications/journalism 14%, computer/information sciences 14%, engineering/engineering technologies 7%, interdisciplinary studies 7%, liberal arts 9%, parks/recreation 7%, security/protective services 8%.

Computing on campus. PC or laptop required. 250 workstations in dormitories, library, computer center. Dormitories wired for high-speed internet access and linked to campus network. Commuter students can connect to campus network. Online course registration, online library, helpline, repair service, wireless network available.

Student life. **Freshman orientation:** Mandatory. Preregistration for classes offered. **Housing:** Guaranteed on-campus for freshmen. Coed dorms, single-sex dorms, substance-free housing available. $150 nonrefundable deposit, deadline 6/1. Honors College houses about 20 honors students (coed dorms). **Activities:** Bands, choral groups, dance, music ensembles, student government, student newspaper, Student Christian Association, Fellowship of Christian Athletes, Muslim Student Association, National Association for the Advancement of Colored People, National Association of Black Accountants, National Association of Black Engineers.

Athletics. NCAA. **Intercollegiate:** Basketball, bowling W, cheerleading M, cross-country, football (tackle) M, golf, softball W, tennis, track and field, volleyball W. **Intramural:** Basketball, softball W, tennis, track and field, volleyball W. **Team name:** Golden Bulls.

Student services. Adult student services, alcohol/substance abuse counseling, campus ministries, career counseling, services for economically disadvantaged, student employment services, financial aid counseling, health services, minority student services, personal counseling. **Physically disabled:** Services for visually, speech, hearing impaired.

Contact. E-mail: admissions@jcsu.edu
Phone: (704) 378-1010 Toll-free number: (800) 782-7303
Fax: (704) 378-1242
Jocelyn Biggs, Director of Admissions, Johnson C. Smith University, 100 Beatties Ford Road, Charlotte, NC 28216-5398

Lees-McRae College

Banner Elk, North Carolina — **CB member**
www.lmc.edu — **CB code: 5364**

- Private 4-year liberal arts college affiliated with Presbyterian Church (USA)
- Residential campus in rural community
- 874 degree-seeking undergraduates
- 72% of applicants admitted
- SAT or ACT (ACT writing optional) required

General. Founded in 1900. Regionally accredited. **Degrees:** 145 bachelor's awarded. **ROTC:** Army. **Location:** 17 miles from Boone, 55 miles from Johnson City, Tennessee. **Calendar:** Semester, limited summer session. **Full-time faculty:** 49 total. **Part-time faculty:** 26 total. **Class size:** 71% < 20, 29% 20-39. **Special facilities:** Wireless campus, biology field station, Blue Ridge Wildlife Rehabilitation Institute.

Freshman class profile. 1,003 applied, 727 admitted, 224 enrolled.

Mid 50% test scores		ACT:	19-24
SAT verbal:	450-550	Out-of-state:	50%
SAT math:	450-550	Live on campus:	96%

Basis for selection. High school record, test scores most important. Rank in top half of class preferred. Recommendations considered. Interview recommended for all students; portfolio recommended for performing arts programs. Audition required for athletic, performing arts programs.

High school preparation. 18 units required. Required and recommended units include English 4, mathematics 3, social studies 2, history 1, science 2 (laboratory 1), foreign language 2 and academic electives 6.

2006-2007 Annual costs. Tuition/fees: $18,000. Room/board: $6,000. Books/supplies: $760. Personal expenses: $2,000.

2005-2006 Financial aid. **Need-based:** 60% of total undergraduate aid awarded as scholarships/grants, 40% as loans/jobs. **Non-need-based:** Scholarships awarded for academics, alumni affiliation, athletics, leadership, minority status, music/drama, religious affiliation, state residency.

Application procedures. **Admission:** Priority date 5/1; no deadline. $25 fee, may be waived for applicants with need. Application may be submitted online. Admission notification on a rolling basis beginning on or about 6/1. Accepting and notifying applicants of acceptance status begins after completion of 6 semesters in high school. **Financial aid:** Priority date 3/15; no closing date. FAFSA required. Applicants notified on a rolling basis starting 3/1; must reply within 2 week(s) of notification.

Academics. **Special study options:** Combined bachelor's/graduate degree, double major, ESL, honors, independent study, internships, liberal arts/career combination, student-designed major, study abroad, teacher certification program. 3-2 program Environmental Science/Forestry with Duke University. **Credit/placement by examination:** CLEP, IB, institutional tests. 16 credit hours maximum toward bachelor's degree. **Support services:** Learning center, remedial instruction, study skills assistance, tutoring, writing center.

Majors. **Biology:** General. **Business:** Business admin. **Communications:** General. **Computer sciences:** Computer science, information systems. **Education:** Drama/dance, elementary, physical. **Health:** Predentistry, premedicine, preveterinary. **History:** General. **Liberal arts:** Arts/sciences. **Math:** General. **Philosophy/religion:** Religion. **Protective services:** Criminal justice. **Psychology:** General. **Social sciences:** International relations, sociology. **Visual/performing arts:** Dramatic.

Most popular majors. Biology 13%, business/marketing 17%, education 29%, psychology 10%, security/protective services 13%.

Computing on campus. 125 workstations in library, computer center, student center. Dormitories wired for high-speed internet access and linked to campus network. Commuter students can connect to campus network. Online library, helpline available.

Student life. **Freshman orientation:** Mandatory. Preregistration for classes offered. 2 summer Freshmen Experience sessions (1 required) followed by an orientation in August right before classes begin. **Policies:** Dry campus. Freshmen permitted cars on campus. **Housing:** Guaranteed on-campus for freshmen. Coed dorms, single-sex dorms available. Substance-free housing. **Activities:** Choral groups, dance, drama, music ensembles, musical theater, student government, student newspaper, Order of the Tower, student ambassadors, international club, residence hall association, student government association, sports medicine club, Phi Beta Lambda, Circle K, campus after the class hours, EMS club.

Athletics. NCAA. **Intercollegiate:** Basketball, cheerleading, cross-country, golf M, lacrosse, skiing, soccer, softball W, tennis, track and field, volleyball. **Intramural:** Basketball, cross-country, football (non-tackle), golf, skiing, soccer, softball, table tennis, tennis, volleyball. **Team name:** Bobcats.

Student services. Campus ministries, career counseling, student employment services, financial aid counseling, health services, personal counseling, veterans' counselor.

Contact. E-mail: admissions@lmc.edu
Phone: (828) 898-8723 Toll-free number: (800) 280-4562
Fax: (828) 898-8707
Walter Crutchfield, Dean of Admissions, Lees-McRae College, Box 128, Banner Elk, NC 28604

Lenoir-Rhyne College

Hickory, North Carolina **CB member**
www.lrc.edu **CB code: 5365**

- Private 4-year liberal arts college affiliated with Evangelical Lutheran Church in America
- Residential campus in large town
- 1,374 degree-seeking undergraduates
- 83% of applicants admitted
- SAT or ACT (ACT writing optional) required

General. Founded in 1891. Regionally accredited. **Degrees:** 243 bachelor's awarded; master's offered. **ROTC:** Army. **Location:** 50 miles from Charlotte, 65 miles from Winston-Salem. **Calendar:** Semester, limited summer session. **Full-time faculty:** 88 total. **Part-time faculty:** 78 total. **Class size:** 69% < 20, 30% 20-39, less than 1% 40-49, less than 1% 50-99. **Special facilities:** Observatory, multimedia classrooms, outdoor classroom.

Freshman class profile. 1,693 applied, 1,408 admitted, 330 enrolled.

Mid 50% test scores			
SAT verbal:	460-570	Rank in top quarter:	47%
SAT math:	470-590	Rank in top tenth:	18%
ACT:	18-22	Out-of-state:	26%
		Live on campus:	84%

Basis for selection. School achievement record most important. Interview recommended for all students; audition required for music majors.

High school preparation. 12 units required. Required units include English 4, mathematics 3, history 1, science 1 (laboratory 1) and foreign language 2. Chemistry required for nursing program.

2006-2007 Annual costs. Tuition/fees: $20,180. Room/board: $7,130. Books/supplies: $900. Personal expenses: $1,150.

2004-2005 Financial aid. Need-based: 70% of total undergraduate aid awarded as scholarships/grants, 30% as loans/jobs. **Non-need-based:** Scholarships awarded for academics, alumni affiliation, athletics, leadership, minority status, music/drama, religious affiliation, ROTC, state residency.

Application procedures. Admission: Priority date 12/15; deadline 8/15 (postmark date). $35 fee, may be waived for applicants with need. Application may be submitted online. Admission notification on a rolling basis beginning on or about 9/1. Must reply by May 1 or within 2 week(s) if notified thereafter. **Financial aid:** Priority date 3/15, closing date 8/15. FAFSA, institutional form required. Applicants notified on a rolling basis starting 3/15; must reply within 4 week(s) of notification.

Academics. Special program for deaf, hearing-impaired and disabled students. **Special study options:** Accelerated study, cooperative education, cross-registration, distance learning, double major, dual enrollment of high school students, ESL, exchange student, external degree, honors, independent study, internships, liberal arts/career combination, semester at sea, student-designed major, study abroad, teacher certification program, Washington semester. **Credit/placement by examination:** AP, CLEP, IB, institutional tests. **Support services:** Learning center, pre-admission summer program, remedial instruction, study skills assistance, tutoring, writing center.

Majors. Biology: General. **Business:** General, accounting, finance, international, management information systems, marketing. **Communications:** General. **Computer sciences:** General, information systems. **Conservation:** Environmental science. **Education:** Art, business, Deaf/hearing impaired, early childhood, elementary, English, foreign languages, mathematics, middle, music, physical, science, social studies. **Foreign languages:** Classics, French, German, Spanish. **Health:** Athletic training, nursing (RN), physician assistant, premedicine, prepharmacy. **History:** General. **Legal studies:** Prelaw. **Liberal arts:** Arts/sciences. **Math:** General. **Parks/recreation:** Health/fitness, sports admin. **Philosophy/religion:** Philosophy, religion. **Physical sciences:** Chemistry, physics. **Psychology:** General. **Social sciences:** General, economics, political science, sociology. **Theology:** Sacred music. **Visual/performing arts:** Dramatic, music performance.

Most popular majors. Biology 6%, business/marketing 18%, communications/journalism 6%, education 10%, health sciences 20%, parks/recreation 8%, social sciences 10%.

Computing on campus. 112 workstations in library, computer center, student center. Dormitories wired for high-speed internet access and linked to campus network. Commuter students can connect to campus network. Online library, helpline, repair service, wireless network available.

Student life. Freshman orientation: Mandatory. Preregistration for classes offered. Held 2 days before start of classes. **Policies:** Freshmen permitted cars on campus. **Housing:** Guaranteed on-campus for all undergraduates. Coed dorms, special housing for disabled, fraternity/sorority housing available. $200 deposit, deadline 5/1. **Activities:** Bands, choral groups, dance, drama, literary magazine, music ensembles, musical theater, radio station, student government, student newspaper, symphony orchestra, TV station, Alpha Lambda Delta, Chi Beta Phi, Omicron Delta Epsilon, Pi Sigma Alpha, Psi Chi, Sigma Theta Tau, Baptist Student Union, Inter-Varsity Christian Fellowship, Circle K, hearing and deaf singers.

Athletics. NCAA. **Intercollegiate:** Baseball M, basketball, cross-country, football (tackle) M, golf, soccer, softball W, swimming W, tennis W, track and field M, volleyball W. **Intramural:** Basketball, bowling, football (non-tackle), golf, gymnastics, handball, lacrosse, racquetball, skiing, soccer, softball, swimming, table tennis, volleyball, water polo. **Team name:** Bears.

Student services. Adult student services, campus ministries, career counseling, student employment services, financial aid counseling, health services, minority student services, personal counseling, veterans' counselor. **Physically disabled:** Services for hearing impaired.

Contact. E-mail: admission@lrc.edu
Phone: (828) 328-7300 Toll-free number: (800) 277-5721
Fax: (828) 328-7378
Rachel Nichols, Dean of Admissions and Financial Aid, Lenoir-Rhyne College, PO Box 7227, Hickory, NC 28603

Livingstone College

Salisbury, North Carolina **CB member**
www.livingstone.edu **CB code: 5367**

- Private 4-year liberal arts college affiliated with African Methodist Episcopal Zion Church
- Residential campus in large town
- 895 degree-seeking undergraduates: 4% part-time, 45% women, 92% African American, 1% Hispanic American, 2% international
- 93% of applicants admitted
- 34% graduate within 6 years

General. Founded in 1879. Regionally accredited. **Degrees:** 118 bachelor's awarded. **ROTC:** Army. **Location:** 44 miles from Charlotte. **Calendar:** Semester. **Full-time faculty:** 58 total; 53% have terminal degrees, 88% minority, 55% women. **Part-time faculty:** 13 total; 31% have terminal degrees, 92% minority, 31% women. **Class size:** 64% < 20, 28% 20-39, 4% 40-49, 1% 50-99, 2% >100. **Special facilities:** Center for Negro and African life, literature and international studies.

Freshman class profile. 1,526 applied, 1,419 admitted, 191 enrolled.

Mid 50% test scores			
		Return as sophomores:	61%
SAT verbal:	310-410	Out-of-state:	59%
SAT math:	320-420	Live on campus:	85%
ACT:	12-17	International:	1%

Basis for selection. School achievement record, test scores, recommendations important. College's placement test, instead of ELPT, used for advising and placement. SAT or ACT recommended. Audition required for music majors; interview recommended for academically weak students.

High school preparation. 10 units required. Required and recommended units include English 4, mathematics 3, social studies 2, history 1, science 2 and foreign language 2.

2005-2006 Annual costs. Tuition/fees: $12,174. Room/board: $5,641. Books/supplies: $800. Personal expenses: $3,000.

2004-2005 Financial aid. Need-based: 50% of total undergraduate aid awarded as scholarships/grants, 50% as loans/jobs. **Non-need-based:** Scholarships awarded for academics, alumni affiliation, athletics, leadership, music/drama, religious affiliation, ROTC, state residency.

Application procedures. Admission: Priority date 5/1; deadline 8/1 (receipt date). $25 fee, may be waived for applicants with need. Application may be submitted online. Admission notification on a rolling basis. Must reply by May 1 or within 4 week(s) if notified thereafter. **Financial aid:** Closing date 5/1. FAFSA required. Applicants notified by 5/1; must reply within 4 week(s) of notification.

Academics. Special study options: Accelerated study, cross-registration, double major, independent study, internships, teacher certification program.

Credit/placement by examination: CLEP, institutional tests. **Support services:** Learning center, reduced course load, remedial instruction, tutoring.

Majors. **Biology:** General. **Business:** Accounting, business admin. **Computer sciences:** General. **Education:** Elementary. **Engineering:** General. **English:** English lit. **Health:** Predentistry, prepharmacy. **History:** General. **Legal studies:** General. **Math:** General. **Parks/recreation:** Sports admin. **Physical sciences:** Chemistry. **Protective services:** Criminal justice. **Psychology:** General. **Public administration:** Social work. **Social sciences:** General, political science, sociology. **Theology:** Theology. **Visual/performing arts:** Dramatic.

Most popular majors. Business/marketing 24%, computer/information sciences 16%, psychology 6%, security/protective services 24%, social sciences 14%.

Computing on campus. 200 workstations in library, computer center. Dormitories wired for high-speed internet access and linked to campus network.

Student life. **Freshman orientation:** Mandatory. Preregistration for classes offered. **Policies:** Freshmen permitted cars on campus. **Housing:** Single-sex dorms, special housing for disabled, apartments available. $100 deposit. **Activities:** Bands, choral groups, dance, drama, film society, music ensembles, musical theater, radio station, student government, pre-theological union, AME Zion Council.

Athletics. NCAA. **Intercollegiate:** Basketball, bowling, cross-country, football (tackle) M, softball W, tennis, track and field, volleyball W. **Intramural:** Basketball. **Team name:** Blue Bears.

Student services. Career counseling, student employment services, health services, personal counseling, placement for graduates, veterans' counselor.

Contact. E-mail: admissions@livingstone.edu
Phone: (704) 216-6001 Toll-free number: (800) 835-3435
Fax: (704) 216-6215
Rolanda Burney, Associate Vice-President of Enrollment Management, Livingstone College, 701 West Monroe Street, Salisbury, NC 28144-5213

Mars Hill College

Mars Hill, North Carolina
www.mhc.edu
CB member
CB code: 5395

- Private 4-year liberal arts college affiliated with Baptist faith
- Residential campus in small town
- 1,308 degree-seeking undergraduates
- SAT or ACT (ACT writing optional) required

General. Founded in 1856. Regionally accredited. **Degrees:** 216 bachelor's awarded. **Location:** 17 miles from Asheville. **Calendar:** Semester, extensive summer session. **Full-time faculty:** 85 total. **Part-time faculty:** 60 total. **Special facilities:** Satellite receiver for foreign language study, Appalachian archives and artifacts museum.

Freshman class profile. 382 enrolled.

Mid 50% test scores			
SAT verbal:	450-550	**Out-of-state:**	44%
SAT math:	450-560	**Live on campus:**	80%

Basis for selection. School achievement record, test scores, school and community activities, recommendations from school officials all important. Students interested in early admission must apply as full-time students, achieve A average in courses, minimum SAT 1000 (exclusive of Writing) or ACT 22, and submit 2 recommendations from high school personnel. Audition required for music, theater programs. Essay, portfolio recommended; interview recommended for students who do not meet other admissions criteria. **Homeschooled:** Transcript of courses and grades required. **Learning Disabled:** Letter of documentation required.

High school preparation. 11 units required. Required and recommended units include English 4, mathematics 3, social studies 2, history 2, science 2 and foreign language 2. One computer science recommended.

2005-2006 Annual costs. Tuition/fees: $16,854. Room/board: $5,924. Books/supplies: $1,000. Personal expenses: $1,000.

Financial aid. **Non-need-based:** Scholarships awarded for academics, art, athletics, religious affiliation, state residency.

Application procedures. **Admission:** No deadline. $25 fee, may be waived for applicants with need. Application may be submitted online. Admission notification on a rolling basis. **Financial aid:** No deadline. FAFSA, institutional form required. Applicants notified on a rolling basis; must reply within 2 week(s) of notification.

Academics. **Special study options:** Accelerated study, cooperative education, distance learning, double major, dual enrollment of high school students, ESL, exchange student, honors, independent study, internships, student-designed major, study abroad, teacher certification program. 3-2 physician assistant, 3-1 medical technology, 2-2 allied health programs. **Credit/placement by examination:** AP, CLEP, IB, SAT, ACT, institutional tests. 32 credit hours maximum toward bachelor's degree. **Support services:** Learning center, reduced course load, remedial instruction, study skills assistance, tutoring, writing center.

Majors. **Biology:** General, botany, zoology. **Business:** General, accounting, business admin, finance, international. **Communications:** General. **Computer sciences:** Computer science. **Education:** General, art, elementary, English, middle, music, physical, secondary. **Foreign languages:** Spanish. **Health:** Athletic training, clinical lab assistant, physician assistant, predentistry, premedicine, prepharmacy, preveterinary. **History:** General. **Interdisciplinary:** Biological/physical sciences. **Legal studies:** Prelaw. **Liberal arts:** Arts/sciences. **Math:** General. **Parks/recreation:** Facilities management, health/fitness. **Philosophy/religion:** Religion. **Physical sciences:** Chemistry. **Psychology:** General. **Public administration:** Social work. **Social sciences:** Political science, sociology. **Visual/performing arts:** Art, fashion design, music performance.

Computing on campus. 180 workstations in library, computer center. Dormitories wired for high-speed internet access and linked to campus network. Commuter students can connect to campus network. Helpline, repair service, wireless network available.

Student life. **Freshman orientation:** Mandatory. Preregistration for classes offered. **Policies:** Freshmen permitted cars on campus. **Housing:** Guaranteed on-campus for all undergraduates. Single-sex dorms, special housing for disabled, apartments, fraternity/sorority housing, substance-free housing available. $100 nonrefundable deposit. College townhouses and apartments available to upperclassmen. **Activities:** Bands, choral groups, dance, drama, literary magazine, music ensembles, musical theater, radio station, student government, student newspaper, Christian Student Movement, Fellowship of Christian Athletes, Young Democrats, College Republicans, debate club, health care society, Concerned Citizens for the Environment.

Athletics. NCAA. **Intercollegiate:** Baseball M, basketball, cross-country, football (tackle) M, golf, lacrosse M, soccer, softball W, swimming W, tennis, track and field, volleyball W. **Intramural:** Badminton, basketball, football (non-tackle), soccer, softball, tennis, volleyball, water polo M. **Team name:** Lions.

Student services. Adult student services, campus ministries, career counseling, services for economically disadvantaged, student employment services, financial aid counseling, health services, personal counseling, veterans' counselor. **Learning disabled:** Comprehensive services available.

Contact. E-mail: admissions@mhc.edu
Phone: (828) 689-1201 Toll-free number: (866) 642-4968
Fax: (828) 689-1473
Mars Hill College, Blackwell Hall, Box 370, Mars Hill, NC 28754

Meredith College

Raleigh, North Carolina
www.meredith.edu
CB member
CB code: 5410

- Private 4-year liberal arts college for women
- Residential campus in large city
- 1,837 degree-seeking undergraduates: 12% part-time, 100% women, 11% African American, 2% Asian American, 2% Hispanic American, 1% international
- 130 degree-seeking graduate students
- 95% of applicants admitted
- SAT or ACT (ACT writing optional) required
- 68% graduate within 6 years; 16% enter graduate study

General. Founded in 1891. Regionally accredited. **Degrees:** 423 bachelor's awarded; master's offered. **ROTC:** Army, Air Force. **Location:** 250 miles from Washington, DC, 375 miles from Atlanta. **Calendar:** Semester, limited summer session. **Full-time faculty:** 128 total; 89% have terminal degrees, 6% minority, 66% women. **Part-time faculty:** 122 total; 30% have terminal degrees, 5% minority, 70% women. **Class size:** 71% < 20, 28% 20-39, 1% 40-49, less than 1% 50-99. **Special facilities:** Amphitheatre, child care laboratory, experimental and clinical psychology laboratories, autism laboratory, astronomy observation deck, electron microscope suite, 15 student/faculty research laboratories, greenhouse.

Freshman class profile. 1,132 applied, 1,073 admitted, 451 enrolled.

Mid 50% test scores			
SAT verbal:	470-570	GPA 2.0-2.99:	31%
SAT math:	470-560	Rank in top quarter:	47%
ACT:	20-23	Rank in top tenth:	19%
GPA 3.50 or higher:	29%	Return as sophomores:	75%
GPA 3.0-3.49:	39%	Out-of-state:	12%
		Live on campus:	92%

Basis for selection. GED not accepted. Attention is paid to the strength of the school record (courses taken, grades on academic subjects, and class rank), test scores, and recommendations. Meredith seeks to enroll qualified students of varying backgrounds, interests and talents and has a need-blind admission policy. SAT preferred. Essay and/or interview may be required of some; audition recommended for music majors; portfolio recommended for art majors. **Homeschooled:** Students should submit SAT and SAT Subject Tests (English, math, and foreign language or one of applicant's choice).

High school preparation. College-preparatory program required. 16 units required. Required units include English 4, mathematics 3, science 3 and foreign language 2. 3 units required in social studies or history. At least 1 elective required, preferably from core academic subjects.

2005-2006 Annual costs. Tuition/fees: $20,000. Tuition includes laptop computer. Room/board: $5,600.

2005-2006 Financial aid. Need-based: 376 full-time freshmen applied for aid; 310 were judged to have need; 310 of these received aid. Average need met was 70%. Average scholarship/grant was $11,719; average loan $2,773. 62% of total undergraduate aid awarded as scholarships/grants, 38% as loans/jobs. **Non-need-based:** Awarded to 271 full-time undergraduates, including 125 freshmen. Scholarships awarded for academics, art, leadership, minority status, music/drama, religious affiliation, state residency.

Application procedures. Admission: Priority date 2/15; no deadline. $40 fee, may be waived for applicants with need. Application may be submitted online. Admission notification on a rolling basis beginning on or about 11/1. Must reply by May 1 or within 2 week(s) if notified thereafter. **Financial aid:** Priority date 2/15; no closing date. FAFSA required. Applicants notified on a rolling basis starting 3/15; must reply by 5/1 or within 2 week(s) of notification.

Academics. Special study options: Accelerated study, combined bachelor's/graduate degree, cooperative education, cross-registration, double major, dual enrollment of high school students, honors, independent study, internships, liberal arts/career combination, New York semester, student-designed major, study abroad, teacher certification program, United Nations semester, Washington semester. Study Abroad includes summer programs, semester/year abroad opportunities, and individually-tailored semesters. Joint degree program (3-2) in engineering with N.C. State University. **Credit/placement by examination:** AP, CLEP, IB, institutional tests. **Support services:** Learning center, reduced course load, remedial instruction, study skills assistance, tutoring, writing center.

Majors. Area/ethnic studies: American, women's. **Biology:** General, molecular. **Business:** Accounting, business admin. **Communications:** General, media studies. **Computer sciences:** General, computer science. **Conservation:** Environmental science, environmental studies. **Education:** Art, drama/dance, music, physical. **English:** English lit. **Family/consumer sciences:** General, child development. **Foreign languages:** French, Spanish. **Health:** Dietetics, predentistry, premedicine, prepharmacy, preveterinary. **History:** General, public archives. **Interdisciplinary:** Global studies. **Math:** General. **Parks/recreation:** Exercise sciences, sports admin. **Philosophy/religion:** Religion. **Physical sciences:** Chemistry. **Psychology:** General. **Public administration:** Social work. **Social sciences:** Economics, international relations, political science, sociology, U.S. government. **Visual/performing arts:** Art, dance, dramatic, fashion design, interior design, music pedagogy, music performance, music theory/composition, piano/organ, stringed instruments, voice/opera.

Most popular majors. Business/marketing 21%, communications/journalism 8%, family/consumer sciences 6%, health sciences 7%, psychology 12%, social sciences 6%, visual/performing arts 14%.

Computing on campus. PC or laptop required. 145 workstations in dormitories, library, computer center, student center. Dormitories wired for high-speed internet access and linked to campus network. Commuter students can connect to campus network. Online course registration, online library, helpline, repair service, wireless network available.

Student life. Freshman orientation: Mandatory. Preregistration for classes offered. 4-day program before start of classes. Athletes, international students, and students with disabilities have additional orientation events that involve an extra day. **Policies:** Honor Code is a long-standing tradition that requires individual integrity and community responsibility of all students. Traditional-aged freshmen and sophomores must live on campus except if married or living with parents or other relatives by special permission. Freshmen permitted cars on campus. **Housing:** Guaranteed on-campus for freshmen. Substance-free housing available. $100 nonrefundable deposit, deadline 5/1. Pets allowed in dorm rooms. Campus housing available for all 4 years. All on-campus housing is "wellness housing.". **Activities:** Concert band, choral groups, dance, drama, literary magazine, music ensembles, musical theater, student government, student newspaper, symphony orchestra, approximately 90 clubs and organizations.

Athletics. NCAA. **Intercollegiate:** Basketball W, cross-country W, soccer W, softball W, tennis W, volleyball W. **Team name:** Angels.

Student services. Adult student services, alcohol/substance abuse counseling, campus ministries, career counseling, student employment services, financial aid counseling, health services, minority student services, personal counseling, placement for graduates. **Physically disabled:** Services for visually, speech, hearing impaired.

Contact. E-mail: admissions@meredith.edu
Phone: (919) 760-8581 Toll-free number: (800) 637-3348
Fax: (919) 760-2348
Heidi Fletcher, Director of Admissions, Meredith College, 3800 Hillsborough Street, Raleigh, NC 27607-5298

Methodist College

Fayetteville, North Carolina
www.methodist.edu **CB code: 5426**

- Private 4-year liberal arts college affiliated with United Methodist Church
- Residential campus in small city
- 1,944 degree-seeking undergraduates
- 78% of applicants admitted
- SAT or ACT (ACT writing optional) required

General. Founded in 1956. Regionally accredited. **Degrees:** 305 bachelor's, 20 associate awarded; master's offered. **ROTC:** Army, Air Force. **Location:** 5 miles from Fayetteville, 50 miles from Raleigh-Durham. **Calendar:** Semester, extensive summer session. **Full-time faculty:** 119 total. **Part-time faculty:** 90 total. **Class size:** 70% < 20, 29% 20-39, less than 1% 40-49, less than 1% 50-99, less than 1% >100. **Special facilities:** Computer-assisted English composition laboratory, psychology computer-experimental laboratory, nature trail, professional golf and tennis management center, 18-hole golf course and driving range.

Freshman class profile. 1,897 applied, 1,482 admitted, 439 enrolled.

Mid 50% test scores			
SAT verbal:	440-540	Rank in top quarter:	33%
SAT math:	450-560	Rank in top tenth:	11%
ACT:	18-22	Out-of-state:	51%
		Live on campus:	93%

Basis for selection. High school record (GPA), curriculum, test scores carefully considered. All prospective student files reviewed on individual basis. Extracurricular achievements and teacher/counselor recommendations also considered. SAT/ACT scores not required of transfer students with more than 31 semester hours of transferrable coursework or for students who are over 21 years of age. New SAT reasoning test recommended and writing section on SAT or ACT may be used to assist in boarderline admissions decisions. Essay, interview recommended for all students; audition recommended for drama, music majors; portfolio recommended for art majors. **Homeschooled:** Must provide GED or provide state-approved academic transcript and standardized test results (unless 21 years of age prior to enrollment).

High school preparation. 16 units required; 20 recommended. Required and recommended units include English 4, mathematics 3-4, social studies 2, history 1-2, science 2-3 (laboratory 1-2), foreign language 2 and academic electives 4.

2006-2007 Annual costs. Tuition/fees (projected): $19,080. Professional golf management, professional tennis management, and music students have additional fees. Room/board: $7,170. Books/supplies: $800. Personal expenses: $1,500.

2004-2005 Financial aid. Need-based: 66% of total undergraduate aid awarded as scholarships/grants, 34% as loans/jobs. **Non-need-based:** Scholarships awarded for academics, alumni affiliation, leadership, music/drama, religious affiliation, ROTC, state residency.

Application procedures. Admission: No deadline. $25 fee, may be waived for applicants with need. Application may be submitted online. Admission notification on a rolling basis beginning on or about 9/1. **Financial**

aid: Priority date 5/1, closing date 7/1. FAFSA required. Applicants notified on a rolling basis starting 3/1; must reply within 2 week(s) of notification.

Academics. Special study options: Accelerated study, double major, dual enrollment of high school students, ESL, exchange student, honors, independent study, internships, liberal arts/career combination, student-designed major, study abroad, teacher certification program, Washington semester, weekend college. **Credit/placement by examination:** AP, CLEP, IB, institutional tests. 45 credit hours maximum toward associate degree, 45 toward bachelor's. **Support services:** Learning center, reduced course load, remedial instruction, study skills assistance, tutoring, writing center.

Majors. Biology: General, cell/histology, zoology. **Business:** Accounting, business admin, hospitality admin, management information systems, marketing, tourism/travel. **Communications:** General. **Computer sciences:** General, computer science. **Education:** General, art, biology, chemistry, elementary, English, foreign languages, mathematics, middle, music, physical, secondary, social studies, special. **English:** Speech/rhetoric. **Foreign languages:** French, Spanish. **Health:** Athletic training, physician assistant, predentistry, premedicine, prepharmacy, preveterinary. **History:** General. **Legal studies:** Prelaw. **Liberal arts:** Arts/sciences. **Math:** General. **Parks/recreation:** Facilities management, sports admin. **Philosophy/religion:** Philosophy, religion. **Physical sciences:** Chemistry. **Protective services:** Criminal justice. **Psychology:** General. **Public administration:** Social work. **Social sciences:** Political science, sociology. **Theology:** Religious ed. **Visual/performing arts:** General, art, music performance, studio arts.

Most popular majors. Biology 6%, business/marketing 32%, communications/journalism 6%, education 8%, parks/recreation 11%, security/protective services 9%, social sciences 13%.

Computing on campus. 220 workstations in library, computer center. Dormitories wired for high-speed internet access and linked to campus network. Commuter students can connect to campus network. Online course registration, online library, helpline, wireless network available.

Student life. Freshman orientation: Available, $25 fee. Preregistration for classes offered. Typically held the weekend (Friday and Saturday) after July 4th. **Policies:** Freshmen permitted cars on campus. **Housing:** Guaranteed on-campus for all undergraduates. Coed dorms, single-sex dorms, apartments, substance-free housing available. $100 deposit. Health/wellness hall, first-year experience hall available. Students must live on-campus through sophomore year unless living with parents/guardians. All residence halls are non-smoking facilities. **Activities:** Bands, choral groups, dance, drama, literary magazine, music ensembles, musical theater, student government, student newspaper, symphony orchestra, FCA, Young Democrats/Republicans, African American Culture Society, SGA, Student Activities Committee, Commuting Student Organization, STARS.

Athletics. NCAA. **Intercollegiate:** Baseball M, basketball, cheerleading, cross-country, football (tackle) M, golf, lacrosse W, soccer, softball W, tennis, track and field, volleyball W. **Intramural:** Basketball, cheerleading W, football (non-tackle), golf, racquetball, soccer, softball, table tennis, tennis, volleyball. **Team name:** Monarchs.

Student services. Alcohol/substance abuse counseling, campus ministries, career counseling, student employment services, financial aid counseling, health services, personal counseling, placement for graduates, veterans' counselor, women's services. **Physically disabled:** Services for visually impaired.

Contact. E-mail: admissions@methodist.edu
Phone: (910) 630-7027 Toll-free number: (800) 488-7110
Fax: (910) 630-7285
Jamie Legg, Director of Admissions, Methodist College, 5400 Ramsey Street, Fayetteville, NC 28311-1498

Miller-Motte Technical College

Wilmington, North Carolina
www.miller-motte.com **CB code: 3342**

- For-profit 4-year technical college
- Commuter campus in small city
- 775 degree-seeking undergraduates: 6% part-time, 91% women
- Interview required

General. Accredited by ACICS. **Degrees:** 50 bachelor's, 700 associate awarded. **Location:** 145 miles from Raleigh. **Calendar:** Quarter, extensive summer session. **Full-time faculty:** 32 total; 9% have terminal degrees. **Part-time faculty:** 24 total; 4% have terminal degrees.

Basis for selection. Open admission, but selective for some programs. Minimum test score of 15 on Wonderlic test for admission, 18 for medical 19 surgical tech and 20 for MCSE.

High school preparation. 17 units recommended. Recommended units include English 4, mathematics 4, social studies 4, science 4 (laboratory 1).

2006-2007 Annual costs. Tuition/fees (projected): $12,800. Books/supplies: $900. Personal expenses: $2,250.

Financial aid. All financial aid based on need.

Application procedures. Admission: No deadline. $35 fee. Application must be submitted on paper. Admission notification on a rolling basis. **Financial aid:** No deadline. FAFSA, institutional form required.

Academics. Special study options: Distance learning, double major, internships. **Credit/placement by examination:** CLEP, institutional tests. 46 credit hours maximum toward associate degree. **Support services:** Learning center, reduced course load, remedial instruction, study skills assistance, tutoring.

Majors. Business: Business admin. **Health:** Health services.

Most popular majors. Business/marketing 50%, health sciences 50%.

Computing on campus. 120 workstations in library, computer center. Commuter students can connect to campus network. Online library, repair service, student web hosting available.

Student life. Freshman orientation: Mandatory. Preregistration for classes offered. **Activities:** Student newspaper.

Athletics. Team name: Marlin.

Student services. Career counseling, financial aid counseling, placement for graduates.

Contact. Phone: (910) 392-4660 Toll-free number: (800) 784-2110
Fax: (910) 799-6224
Meredith Kennedy, Director of Admissions, Miller-Motte Technical College, 5000 Market Street, Wilmington, NC 28405

Montreat College

Montreat, North Carolina **CB member**
www.montreat.edu **CB code: 5423**

- Private 4-year liberal arts college affiliated with Presbyterian Church (USA)
- Residential campus in small town
- 984 degree-seeking undergraduates: 2% part-time, 59% women
- 60 graduate students
- SAT, application essay required

General. Founded in 1916. Regionally accredited. Christian faculty and campus life. **Degrees:** 210 bachelor's, 112 associate awarded; master's offered. **Location:** 16 miles from Asheville. **Calendar:** Semester, limited summer session. **Full-time faculty:** 39 total. **Part-time faculty:** 31 total. **Class size:** 72% < 20, 26% 20-39, 2% 40-49.

Freshman class profile.

Mid 50% test scores		**Rank in top quarter:**	34%
SAT verbal:	450-630	**Rank in top tenth:**	8%
SAT math:	450-630	**Out-of-state:**	41%
ACT:	20-28	**Live on campus:**	100%

Basis for selection. Academic transcript, class rank, GPA, 1 teacher or counselor recommendation, test scores important. Participation in school, community, church activities considered. Interview recommended for academically weak students. **Homeschooled:** Completion of accredited program, GED, or ACT scores and official transcripts required.

High school preparation. 16 units required. Required units include English 4, mathematics 3, social studies 3, science 3, foreign language 1 and academic electives 2.

2006-2007 Annual costs. Tuition/fees: $16,182. Room/board: $5,258. Books/supplies: $930. Personal expenses: $1,804.

2005-2006 Financial aid. Need-based: 44% of total undergraduate aid awarded as scholarships/grants, 56% as loans/jobs. **Non-need-based:** Scholarships awarded for academics, alumni affiliation, art, athletics, job skills, leadership, music/drama, religious affiliation, state residency.

Application procedures. Admission: Priority date 5/15; no deadline. $15 fee, may be waived for applicants with need. Application may be submitted online. Admission notification on a rolling basis beginning on or

about 9/15. **Financial aid:** Priority date 3/15; no closing date. FAFSA, institutional form required. Applicants notified on a rolling basis starting 1/15; must reply within 2 week(s) of notification.

Academics. Teacher certification for elementary grades. **Special study options:** Accelerated study, double major, dual enrollment of high school students, independent study, internships, student-designed major, study abroad, teacher certification program, Washington semester. **Credit/placement by examination:** AP, CLEP, IB. **Support services:** Reduced course load, tutoring, writing center.

Majors. Area/ethnic studies: American. **Biology:** General. **Business:** Business admin. **Computer sciences:** General. **Conservation:** Environmental studies. **Education:** Elementary. **English:** English lit. **History:** General. **Parks/recreation:** General. **Theology:** Bible. **Visual/performing arts:** Music management, music performance.

Most popular majors. Business/marketing 75%, parks/recreation 6%.

Computing on campus. 60 workstations in library, computer center, student center. Dormitories linked to campus network.

Student life. Freshman orientation: Mandatory. Preregistration for classes offered. Welcome Week, with required and optional activities. **Policies:** Alcoholic drinks not allowed on campus. Religious observance required. Freshmen permitted cars on campus. **Housing:** Guaranteed on-campus for all undergraduates. Single-sex dorms available. $100 deposit. 351 spaces available for undergraduate students. **Activities:** Choral groups, dance, drama, music ensembles, musical theater, student government, student newspaper, Student Christian Association, missions club, Fellowship of Christian Athletes, Young Life.

Athletics. NAIA. **Intercollegiate:** Baseball M, basketball, cross-country, golf M, soccer, softball W, tennis, volleyball W. **Intramural:** Basketball, football (non-tackle) M, softball, table tennis, tennis, volleyball. **Team name:** Cavaliers.

Student services. Adult student services, alcohol/substance abuse counseling, campus ministries, career counseling, student employment services, financial aid counseling, health services, personal counseling, placement for graduates, veterans' counselor.

Contact. E-mail: admissions@montreat.edu
Phone: (828) 669-8012 ext. 3781 Toll-free number: (800) 622-6968
Fax: (828) 669-0120
Anita Darby, Director of Admissions, Montreat College, Box 1267, Montreat, NC 28757-1267

Mount Olive College

Mount Olive, North Carolina **CB member**
www.mountolivecollege.edu **CB code: 5435**

- Private 4-year liberal arts college affiliated with Free Will Baptists
- Residential campus in small town
- 2,474 degree-seeking undergraduates: 27% part-time, 62% women
- 71% of applicants admitted
- SAT or ACT (ACT writing optional) required

General. Founded in 1951. Regionally accredited. **Degrees:** 637 bachelor's, 103 associate awarded. **Location:** 13 miles from Goldsboro. **Calendar:** Differs by program, extensive summer session. **Full-time faculty:** 73 total; 80% have terminal degrees, 11% minority, 37% women. **Part-time faculty:** 168 total; 21% have terminal degrees, 16% minority, 38% women. **Class size:** 73% < 20, 26% 20-39, less than 1% 40-49, less than 1% 50-99, less than 1% >100.

Freshman class profile. 807 applied, 577 admitted, 314 enrolled.

Mid 50% test scores			
SAT verbal:	410-510	GPA 2.0-2.99:	41%
SAT math:	420-540	Rank in top quarter:	36%
ACT:	15-20	Rank in top tenth:	9%
GPA 3.50 or higher:	34%	Out-of-state:	11%
GPA 3.0-3.49:	23%	Live on campus:	22%

Basis for selection. School record, test scores, class rank important. Personal recommendations considered. Interview recommended for all students; portfolio recommended for art majors. Audition required for music majors.

High school preparation. 17 units required. Required units include English 4, mathematics 3, social studies 3, science 3 (laboratory 1) and academic electives 3.

2005-2006 Annual costs. Tuition/fees: $11,800. Room/board: $4,800. Books/supplies: $1,020. Personal expenses: $1,798.

2004-2005 Financial aid. Need-based: 360 full-time freshmen applied for aid; 198 were judged to have need; 189 of these received aid. Average need met was 69%. Average scholarship/grant was $5,669; average loan $1,755. 68% of total undergraduate aid awarded as scholarships/grants, 32% as loans/jobs. **Non-need-based:** Awarded to 508 full-time undergraduates, including 136 freshmen. Scholarships awarded for academics, art, athletics, leadership, music/drama, religious affiliation, state residency.

Application procedures. Admission: No deadline. $20 fee, may be waived for applicants with need. Application may be submitted online. Admission notification on a rolling basis beginning on or about 10/1. **Financial aid:** Priority date 3/1; no closing date. FAFSA required. Applicants notified on a rolling basis starting 2/14; must reply within 2 week(s) of notification.

Academics. Special study options: Accelerated study, cooperative education, distance learning, double major, dual enrollment of high school students, external degree, honors, independent study, internships, liberal arts/career combination, teacher certification program. Accelerated extension program at Seymour Johnson Air Force Base in Goldsboro; 55-week degree completion program in business offered in New Bern, Wilmington, and Raleigh-Research Triangle Park. **Credit/placement by examination:** AP, CLEP, institutional tests. 15 credit hours maximum toward associate degree, 30 toward bachelor's. **Support services:** Learning center, reduced course load, remedial instruction, study skills assistance, tutoring, writing center.

Majors. Biology: General. **Business:** Accounting, business admin, human resources, management information systems, organizational behavior. **Communications:** General. **Computer sciences:** General. **History:** General. **Liberal arts:** Arts/sciences. **Math:** General. **Parks/recreation:** General. **Philosophy/religion:** Religion. **Protective services:** Criminal justice. **Psychology:** General. **Visual/performing arts:** Design, studio arts.

Most popular majors. Business/marketing 55%, security/protective services 15%.

Computing on campus. 50 workstations in library, computer center. Dormitories wired for high-speed internet access and linked to campus network. Commuter students can connect to campus network. Online library, repair service, wireless network available.

Student life. Freshman orientation: Available. **Policies:** Religious observance required. **Housing:** Guaranteed on-campus for freshmen. Single-sex dorms, apartments available. $50 nonrefundable deposit, deadline 3/15. **Activities:** Bands, choral groups, literary magazine, music ensembles, student government, student newspaper, symphony orchestra, English society, political forum, recreation majors club, Fellowship of Christian Athletes, international club, Phi Beta Lambda, minority students' organization, Fellowship of Christian Students, Free Spirit.

Athletics. NCAA. **Intercollegiate:** Baseball M, basketball, cross-country, golf, soccer, softball W, tennis, volleyball. **Intramural:** Badminton, baseball M, basketball, football (tackle) M, handball, racquetball, softball, table tennis, tennis, volleyball.

Student services. Adult student services, career counseling, student employment services, health services, personal counseling, placement for graduates, veterans' counselor.

Contact. E-mail: admissions@moc.edu
Phone: (919) 658-7164 Toll-free number: (800) 653-0854
Fax: (919) 658-7180
Tim Woodard, Director of Admissions, Mount Olive College, 634 Henderson Street, Mount Olive, NC 28365

North Carolina Agricultural and Technical State University

Greensboro, North Carolina **CB member**
www.ncat.edu **CB code: 5003**

- Public 4-year agricultural and technical college
- Residential campus in small city
- 9,649 degree-seeking undergraduates: 9% part-time, 52% women, 93% African American, 1% Asian American, 1% Hispanic American
- 1,072 degree-seeking graduate students
- 84% of applicants admitted
- SAT or ACT with writing, SAT Subject Tests required

General. Founded in 1891. Regionally accredited. **Degrees:** 998 bachelor's awarded; master's, doctoral offered. **ROTC:** Army, Air Force. **Location:** 91 miles from Charlotte, 70 miles from Raleigh. **Calendar:** Semester, extensive summer session. **Full-time faculty:** 367 total. **Special facilities:** African heritage center, microelectronics center, planetarium, herbarium.

Freshman class profile. 6,502 applied, 5,461 admitted, 2,255 enrolled.

Mid 50% test scores			
SAT verbal:	390-500	GPA 2.0-2.99:	58%
SAT math:	400-510	Rank in top quarter:	11%
ACT:	15-19	Rank in top tenth:	1%
GPA 3.50 or higher:	12%	Out-of-state:	25%
GPA 3.0-3.49:	25%	Live on campus:	80%

Basis for selection. High school GPA, class rank, test scores, recommendations, course selection reviewed. SAT preferred, but ACT accepted. Audition recommended for music programs; portfolio recommended for art programs.

High school preparation. 17 units required. Required units include English 4, mathematics 4, social studies 1, history 1, science 3 (laboratory 1), foreign language 2 and academic electives 2.

2005-2006 Annual costs. Tuition/fees: $3,114; $12,556 out-of-state. Room/board: $5,254. Books/supplies: $800. Personal expenses: $1,700.

2005-2006 Financial aid. Need-based: Average need met was 50%. Average scholarship/grant was $4,181; average loan $4,457. 43% of total undergraduate aid awarded as scholarships/grants, 57% as loans/jobs. **Non-need-based:** Scholarships awarded for academics, athletics, music/drama, ROTC.

Application procedures. Admission: Priority date 6/1; no deadline. $45 fee. Admission notification on a rolling basis beginning on or about 9/15. Must reply by May 1 or within 2 week(s) if notified thereafter. **Financial aid:** Priority date 3/15; no closing date. FAFSA required. Applicants notified on a rolling basis starting 4/1; must reply within 2 week(s) of notification.

Academics. Special study options: Cooperative education, cross-registration, distance learning, double major, dual enrollment of high school students, honors, internships, study abroad, teacher certification program, weekend college. **Credit/placement by examination:** AP, CLEP, SAT, ACT, institutional tests. **Support services:** Learning center, reduced course load, remedial instruction, study skills assistance, tutoring, writing center.

Majors. Agriculture: Animal sciences, business, economics, landscaping, plant sciences. **Architecture:** Landscape. **Biology:** General. **Business:** General, accounting, business admin, finance, managerial economics, marketing, transportation. **Communications:** General, broadcast journalism, journalism, public relations. **Computer sciences:** General. **Education:** General, agricultural, biology, business, chemistry, driver/safety, early childhood, elementary, English, family/consumer sciences, foreign languages, French, history, mathematics, music, physical, physics, social science, special, speech, technology/industrial arts, trade/industrial. **Engineering:** Agricultural, architectural, chemical, civil, electrical, materials, mechanical. **Engineering technology:** Industrial management, occupational safety. **English:** Speech/rhetoric. **Family/consumer sciences:** General, clothing/textiles, family studies, family/community services, food/nutrition. **Foreign languages:** French. **Health:** Occupational health. **History:** General. **Math:** General. **Parks/recreation:** Facilities management, health/fitness. **Physical sciences:** Chemistry, physics. **Psychology:** General. **Public administration:** Social work. **Social sciences:** General, political science, sociology. **Visual/performing arts:** General, art, dramatic.

Most popular majors. Agriculture 6%, business/marketing 15%, communications/journalism 6%, engineering/engineering technologies 26%, health sciences 7%, psychology 6%, visual/performing arts 6%.

Computing on campus. 675 workstations in library, computer center. Dormitories wired for high-speed internet access and linked to campus network. Commuter students can connect to campus network. Online course registration, helpline available.

Student life. Freshman orientation: Mandatory. **Policies:** Freshmen permitted cars on campus. **Housing:** Guaranteed on-campus for freshmen. Coed dorms, single-sex dorms, apartments, substance-free housing available. $150 nonrefundable deposit. **Activities:** Bands, choral groups, dance, drama, music ensembles, radio station, student government, student newspaper, symphony orchestra, TV station.

Athletics. NCAA. **Intercollegiate:** Baseball M, basketball, bowling W, cross-country, football (tackle) M, softball W, swimming W, tennis, track and field, volleyball W, wrestling M. **Intramural:** Badminton, baseball M, basketball, bowling W, cross-country, football (tackle) M, golf, handball, racquetball, soccer, softball, swimming, table tennis, tennis, track and field, volleyball. **Team name:** Aggies.

Student services. Adult student services, career counseling, student employment services, health services, personal counseling, placement for graduates, veterans' counselor. **Physically disabled:** Services for visually, speech, hearing impaired.

Contact. E-mail: uadmit@ncat.edu
Phone: (336) 334-7946 Toll-free number: (800) 443-8964
Fax: (336) 334-7484
Lee Young, Director of Admissions and Assistant Vice Chancellor for Enrollment Management, North Carolina Agricultural and Technical State University, 1601 East Market Street - Webb Hall, Greensboro, NC 27411

North Carolina Central University

Durham, North Carolina **CB member**
www.nccu.edu **CB code: 5495**

- Public 4-year university
- Commuter campus in small city
- 5,827 degree-seeking undergraduates: 15% part-time, 66% women, 89% African American, 1% Asian American, 1% Hispanic American, 1% international
- 1,593 degree-seeking graduate students
- 77% of applicants admitted
- SAT or ACT with writing required
- 45% graduate within 6 years

General. Founded in 1910. Regionally accredited. Historically, the majority of students have been African American. **Degrees:** 795 bachelor's awarded; master's, first professional offered. **ROTC:** Army, Air Force. **Location:** 23 miles from Raleigh. **Calendar:** Semester, extensive summer session. **Full-time faculty:** 325 total; 73% have terminal degrees, 72% minority, 52% women. **Part-time faculty:** 235 total; 34% have terminal degrees, 66% minority, 58% women. **Class size:** 36% < 20, 47% 20-39, 11% 40-49, 6% 50-99, less than 1% >100. **Special facilities:** Collection of primary resources on black life and culture, art museum with works of Afro-American culture.

Freshman class profile. 3,321 applied, 2,545 admitted, 1,226 enrolled.

Mid 50% test scores			
SAT verbal:	370-480	Rank in top quarter:	16%
SAT math:	380-480	Rank in top tenth:	5%
GPA 3.50 or higher:	12%	Return as sophomores:	76%
GPA 3.0-3.49:	20%	Out-of-state:	16%
GPA 2.0-2.99:	60%	Live on campus:	80%

Basis for selection. Academic achievement, class rank, test scores important. All applicants, except those exempted by current campus policies, must submit a standardized test score. SAT preferred, ACT also accepted. Audition required for music programs. **Homeschooled:** Transcript of courses and grades, state high school equivalency certificate required.

High school preparation. 14 units required. Required units include English 4, mathematics 4, social studies 2, history 1, science 3 (laboratory 2) and foreign language 2. Social studies units must include 1 U.S. history. One foreign language, and 1 math recommended during 12th grade. Students who graduate high school in and after 2006 must have one additional math course from the following: pre-calculus, AP statistics, AP calculus, IB math level II, integrated math IV, discrete math, advanced models and functions.

2005-2006 Annual costs. Tuition/fees: $3,146; $12,890 out-of-state. Room/board: $4,528. Books/supplies: $1,500. Personal expenses: $1,575.

Financial aid. Non-need-based: Scholarships awarded for academics, alumni affiliation, athletics, minority status, music/drama, state residency. **Additional information:** Departmental grants based on need plus other available criteria.

Application procedures. Admission: Closing date 8/1. $30 fee. Application may be submitted online. Admission notification on a rolling basis. Early admission available with permission from high school principal and academic dean. **Financial aid:** Priority date 4/1; no closing date. FAFSA required. Applicants notified by 5/1; must reply within 2 week(s) of notification.

Academics. Special study options: Cooperative education, distance learning, double major, ESL, honors, independent study, internships, study abroad, teacher certification program. **Credit/placement by examination:** AP, CLEP, SAT, ACT, institutional tests. 30 credit hours maximum toward bachelor's degree. **Support services:** Learning center, remedial instruction, study skills assistance, tutoring, writing center.

Majors. **Biology:** General. **Business:** Accounting, business admin, hospitality admin. **Communications:** Media studies. **Computer sciences:** Computer science, information systems. **Conservation:** Environmental science. **Education:** Art, biology, chemistry, drama/dance, elementary, English, family/consumer sciences, French, health, history, kindergarten/preschool, mathematics, middle, music, physical, physics, Spanish. **English:** English lit. **Family/consumer sciences:** General. **Foreign languages:** French, Spanish. **Health:** Athletic training, nursing (RN), public health ed. **History:** General. **Math:** General. **Parks/recreation:** Facilities management, health/fitness. **Physical sciences:** Chemistry, physics. **Protective services:** Law enforcement admin. **Psychology:** General. **Public administration:** Social work. **Social sciences:** Geography, political science, sociology. **Visual/performing arts:** Art, dramatic, jazz.

Most popular majors. Business/marketing 18%, education 9%, family/consumer sciences 6%, health sciences 6%, psychology 7%, security/protective services 10%, social sciences 11%.

Computing on campus. 400 workstations in dormitories, library, computer center. Dormitories wired for high-speed internet access and linked to campus network. Commuter students can connect to campus network. Online course registration, online library, helpline, repair service, wireless network available.

Student life. **Freshman orientation:** Mandatory. Preregistration for classes offered. **Policies:** Freshmen permitted cars on campus. **Housing:** Coed dorms, single-sex dorms available. $100 fully refundable deposit, deadline 6/1. Coed honors dormitory available. **Activities:** Bands, choral groups, dance, drama, literary magazine, radio station, student government, student newspaper.

Athletics. NAIA, NCAA. **Intercollegiate:** Basketball, bowling, cheerleading W, cross-country, football (tackle) M, golf, softball W, tennis, track and field, volleyball W. **Team name:** Eagles.

Student services. Career counseling, student employment services, health services, on-campus daycare, personal counseling, placement for graduates, veterans' counselor.

Contact. E-mail: admissions@nccu.edu
Phone: (919) 560-6298 Toll-free number: (877) 667-7533
Fax: (919) 530-7625
Jocelyn Foy, Director of Admissions, North Carolina Central University, PO Box 19717, Durham, NC 27707

North Carolina School of the Arts

Winston-Salem, North Carolina
www.ncarts.edu **CB code: 5512**

- Public 4-year conservatory and college of visual and performing arts
- Residential campus in small city
- 720 degree-seeking undergraduates: 39% women
- 101 degree-seeking graduate students
- 42% of applicants admitted
- SAT or ACT with writing required
- 50% graduate within 6 years

General. Founded in 1963. Regionally accredited. State Conservatory with high school, undergraduate and graduate facilities. **Degrees:** 120 bachelor's awarded; master's offered. **Location:** 90 miles from Charlotte, 75 miles from Raleigh. **Calendar:** Trimester, limited summer session. **Full-time faculty:** 123 total; 39% have terminal degrees, 5% minority, 24% women. **Class size:** 84% < 20, 14% 20-39, less than 1% 40-49, 1% 50-99. **Special facilities:** Stage production shop, film village with sound and recording stages.

Freshman class profile. 744 applied, 310 admitted, 178 enrolled.

Return as sophomores:	25%	**Live on campus:**	95%
Out-of-state:	51%	**International:**	2%

Basis for selection. Talent, achievement, career potential most important. Admission heavily dependent on audition. SAT combined score of 800 (exclusive of Writing) or ACT composite score of 19, school record, recommendations important. Interview recommended for all students. Audition required for dance, drama, music programs; portfolio required for design, filmmaking, production programs.

High school preparation. 20 units required. Required and recommended units include English 4, mathematics 3, social studies 2, history 1, science 3 (laboratory 1), foreign language 2 and academic electives 4.

2005-2006 Annual costs. Tuition/fees: $4,335; $15,615 out-of-state. Required fees may vary by program. Room/board: $5,956. Books/supplies: $865. Personal expenses: $1,889.

2004-2005 Financial aid. **Need-based:** 101 full-time freshmen applied for aid; 75 were judged to have need; 75 of these received aid. Average need met was 78%. Average scholarship/grant was $5,452; average loan $2,372. 49% of total undergraduate aid awarded as scholarships/grants, 51% as loans/jobs. **Non-need-based:** Awarded to 107 full-time undergraduates, including 15 freshmen. Scholarships awarded for academics, art, leadership, minority status, music/drama, state residency.

Application procedures. **Admission:** Priority date 3/1; no deadline. $50 fee, may be waived for applicants with need. Application may be submitted online. Admission notification on a rolling basis beginning on or about 4/1. Must reply by May 1 or within 3 week(s) if notified thereafter. Application closing date dependent upon audition. Applications must be submitted at least 2 weeks before audition date. Dance, drama and filmmaking interviews begin in January and end in early March. Music and technical theater auditions begin in November and end in early March. Decisions generally are made by April 1, or about 2 weeks after audition if later than April 1. **Financial aid:** Priority date 3/1; no closing date. FAFSA required. Applicants notified on a rolling basis starting 4/1; must reply within 2 week(s) of notification.

Academics. Professional training supplemented by strong general studies curriculum, small classes 7:1 student-teacher ratio. **Special study options:** Independent study, internships. **Credit/placement by examination:** AP, CLEP. **Support services:** Remedial instruction, study skills assistance, tutoring, writing center.

Majors. **Liberal arts:** Arts/sciences. **Visual/performing arts:** Cinematography, dance, dramatic, music performance, theater design.

Computing on campus. 28 workstations in dormitories, library, student center. Dormitories wired for high-speed internet access and linked to campus network. Online course registration available.

Student life. **Freshman orientation:** Mandatory, $75 fee. Includes academic assessment. **Policies:** Freshmen permitted cars on campus. **Housing:** Guaranteed on-campus for freshmen. Coed dorms, single-sex dorms, apartments available. $200 deposit. **Activities:** Jazz band, choral groups, dance, drama, music ensembles, musical theater, opera, student government, student newspaper, symphony orchestra, spirituality committee, ADAPT-drug prevention team, C.A.R.E.-AIDS awareness and prevention team, Awareness for Gay and Lesbian Equality, Artists for Christ, Awareness of Black Arts, Minorities on the Move.

Athletics. **Team name:** Fighting Pickles.

Student services. Career counseling, student employment services, financial aid counseling, health services, personal counseling.

Contact. E-mail: admissions@ncarts.edu
Phone: (336) 770-3291 Fax: (336) 770-3370
Sheeler Lawson, Director of Admissions, North Carolina School of the Arts, 1533 South Main Street, Winston-Salem, NC 27127-2188

North Carolina State University

Raleigh, North Carolina **CB member**
www.ncsu.edu **CB code: 5496**

- Public 4-year university
- Residential campus in large city
- 20,546 degree-seeking undergraduates: 7% part-time, 42% women, 10% African American, 5% Asian American, 2% Hispanic American, 1% Native American, 1% international
- 6,431 degree-seeking graduate students
- 66% of applicants admitted
- SAT or ACT with writing required
- 71% graduate within 6 years; 30% enter graduate study

General. Founded in 1887. Regionally accredited. **Degrees:** 4,620 bachelor's, 193 associate awarded; master's, doctoral, first professional offered. **ROTC:** Army, Navy, Air Force. **Location:** 1 mile from downtown. **Calendar:** Semester, extensive summer session. **Full-time faculty:** 1,671 total; 91% have terminal degrees, 16% minority, 28% women. **Part-time faculty:** 193 total; 68% have terminal degrees, 8% minority, 40% women. **Class size:** 31% < 20, 45% 20-39, 9% 40-49, 11% 50-99, 4% >100. **Special facilities:** 2 nuclear reactors, 3 electron microscopes, phytotron, research farms, 2 campus theaters, craft center, stable isotope laboratory, teaching forest, wood products laboratory, coastal marine science laboratory, 80,000 acres of research forests and research farm lands; fiber, fabric, and garment manufacturing equipment.

Freshman class profile. 13,610 applied, 9,039 admitted, 4,253 enrolled.

Mid 50% test scores		Rank in top tenth:	36%
SAT verbal:	530-620	End year in good standing:	92%
SAT math:	560-660	Return as sophomores:	89%
ACT:	23-27	Out-of-state:	9%
GPA 3.50 or higher:	94%	Live on campus:	76%
GPA 3.0-3.49:	5%	Fraternities:	7%
GPA 2.0-2.99:	1%	Sororities:	9%
Rank in top quarter:	78%		

Basis for selection. GED not accepted. School academic record, standardized test scores important. Counselor evaluations, extracurricular activities also considered. Preference given to students with exceptionally strong high school record. Level and difficulty of courses considered. Weighted grades for advanced, honors, AP courses considered. All applicants to the UNC system, except those exempted by current campus policies, must submit standardized test scores. SAT preferred, ACT also accepted. Essay recommended for all students. Interview and portfolio required for design school applicants.

High school preparation. College-preparatory program required. 16 units required; 20 recommended. Required and recommended units include English 4, mathematics 4, social studies 1, history 1, science 3-4 (laboratory 1-2), foreign language 2 and academic electives 1-4. Science units should include 1 life or biological science, 1 physical science, and 1 laboratory science. Honors, advanced, AP and IB courses given extra weight.

2005-2006 Annual costs. Tuition/fees: $4,338; $16,536 out-of-state. Room/board: $6,851. Books/supplies: $900. Personal expenses: $1,230.

2005-2006 Financial aid. Need-based: 2,911 full-time freshmen applied for aid; 1,733 were judged to have need; 1,703 of these received aid. Average need met was 83%. Average scholarship/grant was $6,216; average loan $2,208. 65% of total undergraduate aid awarded as scholarships/grants, 35% as loans/jobs. **Non-need-based:** Awarded to 5,244 full-time undergraduates, including 2,434 freshmen. Scholarships awarded for academics, alumni affiliation, athletics, leadership, ROTC, state residency. **Additional information:** Freshman Merit Scholarships; students submitting complete admissions application by the November 1 Early Action deadline automatically considered, additional information may be required after initial review.

Application procedures. Admission: Priority date 11/1; deadline 2/1 (postmark date). $60 fee, may be waived for applicants with need. Application may be submitted online. Admission notification on a rolling basis beginning on or about 10/15. Must reply by 5/1. Students applying under regular admission to School of Design must submit application by 12/1. Selected candidates will be invited to interview. **Financial aid:** Priority date 3/1; no closing date. FAFSA, institutional form required. CSS PROFILE recommended for early scholarship consideration. Applicants notified on a rolling basis starting 3/1.

Academics. Special study options: Accelerated study, combined bachelor's/graduate degree, cooperative education, cross-registration, distance learning, double major, dual enrollment of high school students, ESL, exchange student, external degree, honors, independent study, internships, liberal arts/career combination, student-designed major, study abroad, teacher certification program. 2+2 engineering with University of North Carolina-Asheville. **Credit/placement by examination:** AP, CLEP, IB, SAT, ACT, institutional tests. **Support services:** Learning center, pre-admission summer program, reduced course load, remedial instruction, study skills assistance, tutoring, writing center.

Majors. Agriculture: Agribusiness operations, agronomy, animal sciences, education services, food science, horticultural science, mechanization, poultry. **Architecture:** Architecture, environmental design, landscape. **Biology:** General, biochemistry, botany, microbiology, zoology. **Business:** Accounting, business admin, managerial economics. **Communications:** General. **Computer sciences:** Computer science. **Conservation:** General, environmental science, forest management, management/policy, wood science. **Education:** General, agricultural, English, French, health occupations, mathematics, middle, sales/marketing, science, social studies, Spanish, technology/industrial arts. **Engineering:** General, aerospace, agricultural, biomedical, chemical, civil, computer, construction, electrical, environmental, industrial, materials, mechanical, nuclear, textile. **Engineering technology:** Environmental. **English:** English lit. **Family/consumer sciences:** Apparel marketing, clothing/textiles. **Foreign languages:** French, Spanish. **History:** General. **Interdisciplinary:** Global studies, science/society. **Liberal arts:** Arts/sciences. **Math:** General, applied, statistics. **Parks/recreation:** Facilities management, sports admin. **Philosophy/religion:** Philosophy, religion. **Physical sciences:** Atmospheric science, chemistry, geology, oceanography, physics, polymer chemistry. **Psychology:** General. **Public administration:** Social work. **Social sciences:** Anthropology, criminology, geography, political science, sociology. **Visual/performing arts:** Arts management, design, graphic design, industrial design.

Most popular majors. Agriculture 6%, biology 10%, business/marketing 14%, communications/journalism 7%, engineering/engineering technologies 24%, social sciences 7%.

Computing on campus. 2,837 workstations in dormitories, library, computer center, student center. Dormitories wired for high-speed internet access and linked to campus network. Commuter students can connect to campus network. Online course registration, helpline, repair service, student web hosting, wireless network available.

Student life. Freshman orientation: Mandatory, $100 fee. Preregistration for classes offered. 2-day academic/campus life orientation with on-line registration for first year classes. **Housing:** Guaranteed on-campus for freshmen. Coed dorms, single-sex dorms, special housing for disabled, apartments, fraternity/sorority housing available. International student dormitory, Residential Scholars Program, residence hall for students interested in computers and visual and performing arts, first year college living and learning experience. **Activities:** Bands, choral groups, dance, drama, literary magazine, music ensembles, musical theater, radio station, student government, student newspaper, symphony orchestra, Alpha Phi Omega, Baptist Student Union, Campus Crusade for Christ, Circle-K, international student board, Young Democrats, Young Republicans, Society of Afro-American Culture, YMCA.

Athletics. NCAA. **Intercollegiate:** Baseball M, basketball, cheerleading, cross-country, diving, football (tackle) M, golf, gymnastics W, rifle, soccer, softball W, swimming, tennis, track and field, volleyball W, wrestling M. **Intramural:** Archery, badminton, baseball M, basketball, bowling, cross-country, fencing, field hockey W, football (non-tackle), golf, gymnastics, handball, ice hockey M, lacrosse M, racquetball, rugby M, sailing, skiing, skin diving, soccer, softball, squash, swimming, table tennis, tennis, track and field, volleyball, wrestling M. **Team name:** Wolfpack.

Student services. Adult student services, alcohol/substance abuse counseling, campus ministries, career counseling, student employment services, financial aid counseling, health services, legal services, minority student services, personal counseling, placement for graduates, veterans' counselor, women's services. **Physically disabled:** Services for visually, speech, hearing impaired.

Contact. E-mail: undergrad_admissions@ncsu.edu
Phone: (919) 515-2434 Fax: (919) 515-5039
Thomas Griffin, Director of Undergraduate Admissions, North Carolina State University, 112 Peele Hall, Box 7103, Raleigh, NC 27695-7103

North Carolina Wesleyan College

Rocky Mount, North Carolina

www.ncwc.edu **CB code: 5501**

- Private 4-year liberal arts college affiliated with United Methodist Church
- Residential campus in small city
- 1,752 degree-seeking undergraduates: 36% part-time, 49% women, 45% African American, 1% Asian American, 3% Hispanic American, 1% Native American, 1% international
- 81% of applicants admitted
- SAT or ACT (ACT writing optional) required

General. Founded in 1956. Regionally accredited. Adult students, 22 and older, can attend classes at sites in Raleigh, Goldsboro, and Rocky Mount. **Degrees:** 391 bachelor's awarded. **Location:** 57 miles from Raleigh. **Calendar:** Semester, limited summer session. **Full-time faculty:** 53 total; 76% have terminal degrees, 6% minority, 42% women. **Part-time faculty:** 103 total; 32% have terminal degrees, 15% minority, 32% women. **Class size:** 83% < 20, 17% 20-39. **Special facilities:** Collection of art by Eastern North Carolina artists, Black Mountain archival collection, center for the performing arts.

Freshman class profile. 1,169 applied, 951 admitted, 288 enrolled.

Mid 50% test scores		Rank in top tenth:	8%
SAT verbal:	420-520	Return as sophomores:	64%
SAT math:	410-520	Out-of-state:	35%
Rank in top quarter:	18%	Live on campus:	88%

Basis for selection. High school GPA most important, followed by SAT or ACT score, rigor of high school curriculum, and recommendations. Essay, school and community activities considered. Essay, interview recommended for all students.

High school preparation. College-preparatory program recommended. Recommended units include English 4, mathematics 3, social studies 2, science 2 (laboratory 2) and foreign language 2.

2005-2006 Annual costs. Tuition/fees: $16,000. Room/board: $6,670. Books/supplies: $1,000. Personal expenses: $1,200.

2004-2005 Financial aid. Need-based: 300 full-time freshmen applied for aid; 270 were judged to have need; 270 of these received aid. Average need met was 88%. Average scholarship/grant was $14,650; average loan $2,580. 74% of total undergraduate aid awarded as scholarships/grants, 26% as loans/jobs. **Non-need-based:** Awarded to 65 full-time undergraduates, including 21 freshmen. Scholarships awarded for academics, music/drama, religious affiliation. **Additional information:** Scholarships based on GPA. Various scholarship and leadership awards available.

Application procedures. Admission: No deadline. $25 fee, may be waived for applicants with need. Application may be submitted online. Admission notification on a rolling basis. **Financial aid:** Priority date 3/1; no closing date. FAFSA required. Applicants notified on a rolling basis starting 1/1; must reply within 2 week(s) of notification.

Academics. Special study options: Accelerated study, cooperative education, cross-registration, distance learning, double major, dual enrollment of high school students, honors, independent study, internships, liberal arts/career combination, teacher certification program, weekend college. **Credit/placement by examination:** AP, CLEP, institutional tests. **Support services:** Learning center, pre-admission summer program, reduced course load, remedial instruction, study skills assistance, tutoring, writing center.

Majors. Biology: General. **Business:** Accounting, business admin. **Computer sciences:** Information systems. **Conservation:** General. **Education:** Elementary, middle, physical. **Health:** Premedicine. **History:** General. **Legal studies:** General. **Math:** General. **Philosophy/religion:** Religion. **Physical sciences:** Chemistry. **Protective services:** Criminal justice. **Psychology:** General. **Social sciences:** Anthropology, political science, sociology. **Visual/performing arts:** Dramatic.

Most popular majors. Business/marketing 51%, computer/information sciences 13%, legal studies 12%, psychology 9%.

Computing on campus. 100 workstations in dormitories, library, computer center, student center. Dormitories wired for high-speed internet access and linked to campus network. Helpline, repair service available.

Student life. Freshman orientation: Mandatory. Preregistration for classes offered. **Policies:** Freshmen permitted cars on campus. **Housing:** Guaranteed on-campus for freshmen. Coed dorms, single-sex dorms, special housing for disabled, fraternity/sorority housing, substance-free housing available. $100 fully refundable deposit, deadline 7/15. **Activities:** Choral groups, drama, literary magazine, music ensembles, student government, student newspaper, Black Student Association, Fellowship of Christian Athletes, College Republicans, Wesleyan Christian Fellowship.

Athletics. NCAA. **Intercollegiate:** Baseball M, basketball, football (tackle) M, golf M, lacrosse W, soccer, softball W, tennis, volleyball W. **Intramural:** Basketball, football (tackle) M, lacrosse M, softball, table tennis, tennis, volleyball. **Team name:** Bishops.

Student services. Adult student services, alcohol/substance abuse counseling, campus ministries, career counseling, student employment services, financial aid counseling, health services, personal counseling, placement for graduates, veterans' counselor.

Contact. E-mail: adm@ncwc.edu
Phone: (252) 985-5200 Toll-free number: (800) 488-6292
Fax: (252) 985-5295
Cecilia Summers, Director of Admissions, North Carolina Wesleyan College, 3400 North Wesleyan Boulevard, Rocky Mount, NC 27804

Peace College

Raleigh, North Carolina — **CB member**
www.peace.edu — **CB code: 5533**

- Private 4-year liberal arts college for women affiliated with Presbyterian Church (USA)
- Residential campus in large city
- 662 degree-seeking undergraduates: 2% part-time, 100% women
- 78% of applicants admitted
- SAT or ACT (ACT writing optional) required

General. Founded in 1857. Regionally accredited. **Degrees:** 92 bachelor's, 32 associate awarded. **ROTC:** Army, Navy, Air Force. **Location:** Downtown. **Calendar:** Semester, limited summer session. **Full-time faculty:** 42 total; 69% have terminal degrees, 10% minority, 69% women. **Part-time faculty:** 38 total; 47% have terminal degrees, 5% minority, 74% women. **Class size:** 65% < 20, 35% 20-39, less than 1% 50-99, less than 1% >100.

Freshman class profile. 787 applied, 614 admitted, 179 enrolled.

Mid 50% test scores		**GPA 2.0-2.99:**	30%
SAT verbal:	430-520	**Rank in top quarter:**	20%
SAT math:	420-510	**Rank in top tenth:**	10%
ACT:	15-18	**Out-of-state:**	12%
GPA 3.50 or higher:	24%	**Live on campus:**	55%
GPA 3.0-3.49:	44%		

Basis for selection. School achievement record, test scores, 2.0 GPA on college preparatory courses recommended. SAT combined score of 800 (exclusive of Writing) and above preferred or ACT of 17 minimum. Interview recommended for all students. Audition required for theatre, drama, and music majors; portfolio required for art programs.

High school preparation. College-preparatory program required. 15 units required; 17 recommended. Required and recommended units include English 4, mathematics 3-4, social studies 2, history 2, science 2-3 and foreign language 2.

2005-2006 Annual costs. Tuition/fees: $19,265. Room/board: $6,918. Books/supplies: $750. Personal expenses: $2,500.

2004-2005 Financial aid. Need-based: 208 full-time freshmen applied for aid; 174 were judged to have need; 174 of these received aid. Average need met was 75%. Average scholarship/grant was $10,450; average loan $2,240. 67% of total undergraduate aid awarded as scholarships/grants, 33% as loans/jobs. **Non-need-based:** Awarded to 285 full-time undergraduates, including 107 freshmen. Scholarships awarded for academics.

Application procedures. Admission: Priority date 4/1; no deadline. $25 fee, may be waived for applicants with need. Application may be submitted online. Admission notification on a rolling basis beginning on or about 8/1. Must reply by May 1 or within 2 week(s) if notified thereafter. Prefer early admission candidates with SAT 1100 or above, 3.5 GPA in college preparatory courses, and rank in top 25% of class. On-campus interview required. **Financial aid:** Priority date 3/15; no closing date. FAFSA required. Applicants notified on a rolling basis starting 3/1; must reply by 5/1 or within 2 week(s) of notification.

Academics. Special study options: Cross-registration, double major, dual enrollment of high school students, honors, independent study, internships, liberal arts/career combination, study abroad. **Credit/placement by examination:** AP, CLEP, institutional tests. **Support services:** Learning center, reduced course load, remedial instruction, study skills assistance, tutoring, writing center.

Majors. Biology: General. **Business:** Business admin, human resources. **Communications:** General. **English:** English lit. **Family/consumer sciences:** Child development. **Foreign languages:** Spanish. **Liberal arts:** Arts/sciences. **Psychology:** General. **Social sciences:** Political science. **Visual/performing arts:** Design, music performance.

Most popular majors. Biology 6%, business/marketing 9%, communications/journalism 25%, liberal arts 14%, psychology 16%, visual/performing arts 8%.

Computing on campus. 178 workstations in dormitories, library, computer center. Dormitories wired for high-speed internet access and linked to campus network. Commuter students can connect to campus network. Online course registration, online library, helpline, repair service, student web hosting, wireless network available.

Student life. Freshman orientation: Mandatory, $75 fee. Preregistration for classes offered. 2-day program offered prior to start of classes. **Policies:** Honor code. Religious observance required. Freshmen permitted cars on campus. **Housing:** Guaranteed on-campus for freshmen. Special housing for disabled available. $150 deposit, deadline 7/1. Freshmen and sophomores required to live on campus unless living with relatives in area. **Activities:** Choral groups, dance, drama, literary magazine, music ensembles, musical theater, opera, student government, student newspaper, Christian Association, honor societies, recreation association, Young Democrats/Republicans, Phi Theta Kappa, Student Environmental Action Coalition.

Athletics. NCAA. **Intercollegiate:** Basketball W, cross-country W, soccer W, softball W, tennis W, volleyball W. **Intramural:** Badminton W, basketball W, equestrian W, soccer W, softball W, swimming W, table tennis W, tennis W, volleyball W. **Team name:** Peace Pacers.

Student services. Adult student services, campus ministries, career counseling, student employment services, financial aid counseling, health services, personal counseling, placement for graduates.

Four-Year Colleges

Contact. E-mail: admissions@peace.edu
Phone: (919) 508-2000 Toll-free number: (800) 732-2347
Fax: (919) 508-2306
Catherine Church, Director of Admissions, Peace College, 15 East Peace Street, Raleigh, NC 27604

Pfeiffer University
Misenheimer, North Carolina CB member
www.pfeiffer.edu CB code: 5536

- Private 4-year university and liberal arts college affiliated with United Methodist Church
- Residential campus in rural community
- 1,174 degree-seeking undergraduates: 11% part-time, 59% women
- 948 graduate students
- 77% of applicants admitted
- SAT or ACT (ACT writing optional) required
- 54% graduate within 6 years

General. Founded in 1885. Regionally accredited. **Degrees:** 248 bachelor's awarded; master's offered. **ROTC:** Army. **Location:** 35 miles from Charlotte, 60 miles from Winston-Salem. **Calendar:** Semester, limited summer session. **Full-time faculty:** 65 total; 71% have terminal degrees, 14% minority, 35% women. **Part-time faculty:** 73 total. **Class size:** 71% < 20, 28% 20-39, 2% 40-49. **Special facilities:** Retreat center.

Freshman class profile. 629 applied, 487 admitted, 201 enrolled.

Mid 50% test scores			
SAT verbal:	440-540	Rank in top tenth:	13%
SAT math:	460-550	Return as sophomores:	65%
ACT:	18-22	Out-of-state:	26%
Rank in top quarter:	34%	Live on campus:	68%
		International:	2%

Basis for selection. School achievement record, class rank, recommendations, and test scores reviewed. Interview recommended for all students; audition required for music programs.

High school preparation. College-preparatory program required. 12 units required; 16 recommended. Required and recommended units include English 4, mathematics 3, social studies 2-4, history 2, science 2-3 (laboratory 1) and foreign language 2. Math should include algebra I and geometry.

2005-2006 Annual costs. Tuition/fees: $15,590. Room/board: $6,310. Books/supplies: $750. Personal expenses: $600.

2004-2005 Financial aid. Need-based: 195 full-time freshmen applied for aid; 195 were judged to have need; 158 of these received aid. Average need met was 81%. Average scholarship/grant was $9,140; average loan $2,895. 65% of total undergraduate aid awarded as scholarships/grants, 35% as loans/jobs. **Non-need-based:** Awarded to 437 full-time undergraduates, including 128 freshmen. Scholarships awarded for academics, alumni affiliation, athletics, leadership, music/drama, religious affiliation, state residency.

Application procedures. Admission: No deadline. $25 fee, may be waived for applicants with need. Application may be submitted online. Admission notification on a rolling basis. **Financial aid:** Priority date 5/1; no closing date. FAFSA required. Applicants notified on a rolling basis starting 3/1; must reply within 2 week(s) of notification.

Academics. Special study options: Accelerated study, combined bachelor's/graduate degree, cooperative education, distance learning, double major, dual enrollment of high school students, honors, independent study, internships, liberal arts/career combination, study abroad, teacher certification program, Washington semester, weekend college. **Credit/placement by examination:** AP, CLEP, IB, institutional tests. **Support services:** Learning center, reduced course load, remedial instruction, study skills assistance, tutoring.

Majors. Biology: General. **Business:** General, accounting, business admin. **Communications:** General. **Computer sciences:** General. **Conservation:** Environmental studies. **Education:** Elementary, music, physical, secondary, social science, special. **Engineering:** General. **English:** English lit. **Health:** Athletic training, health care admin, predentistry, premedicine, preveterinary. **History:** General. **Legal studies:** Prelaw. **Math:** General. **Parks/recreation:** Facilities management, sports admin. **Philosophy/religion:** Religion. **Physical sciences:** Chemistry. **Protective services:** Criminal justice, police science. **Psychology:** General. **Social sciences:** Economics, sociology. **Theology:** Missionary, religious ed, sacred music, youth ministry. **Visual/performing arts:** Arts management, dramatic.

Most popular majors. Business/marketing 37%, education 10%, security/protective services 13%.

Computing on campus. 114 workstations in library, computer center. Dormitories linked to campus network. Commuter students can connect to campus network. Repair service, wireless network available.

Student life. Freshman orientation: Available, $35 fee. **Policies:** Freshmen permitted cars on campus. **Housing:** Guaranteed on-campus for all undergraduates. Coed dorms, single-sex dorms, special housing for disabled, apartments, substance-free housing available. $150 nonrefundable deposit. Apartment-style housing with shared kitchen and bath available for older students not married. **Activities:** Bands, choral groups, dance, drama, literary magazine, music ensembles, musical theater, student government, student newspaper, religious organizations, political groups, service clubs, professional clubs, black student alliance.

Athletics. NCAA. **Intercollegiate:** Baseball M, basketball, cross-country, golf, lacrosse, soccer, softball W, swimming W, tennis, volleyball W. **Intramural:** Basketball, lacrosse, soccer, softball, table tennis, tennis, volleyball. **Team name:** Falcons.

Student services. Alcohol/substance abuse counseling, campus ministries, career counseling, student employment services, health services, personal counseling, placement for graduates, veterans' counselor.

Contact. E-mail: admiss@pfeiffer.edu
Phone: (704) 463-1360 ext. 2060 Toll-free number: (800) 338-2060
Fax: (704) 463-1363
Steve Cumming, Director of Admissions, Pfeiffer University, Box 960, Misenheimer, NC 28109

Piedmont Baptist College
Winston-Salem, North Carolina
www.pbc.edu CB code: 5555

- Private 5-year Bible and seminary college affiliated with Baptist faith
- Small city
- 239 degree-seeking undergraduates
- 26 graduate students
- ACT (writing optional), application essay required

General. Founded in 1945. Accredited by ABHE. **Degrees:** 42 bachelor's, 7 associate awarded; master's offered. **Location:** 75 miles from Charlotte, 100 miles from Raleigh. **Calendar:** Semester, extensive summer session. **Full-time faculty:** 20 total. **Part-time faculty:** 14 total. **Class size:** 77% < 20, 17% 20-39, 4% 40-49, 1% 50-99. **Special facilities:** Old Salem Moravian Settlement.

Freshman class profile.

Out-of-state:	55%	Live on campus:	45%

Basis for selection. Student's life objectives and previous academic record important. Interview recommended for all students; audition required for music program.

High school preparation. Recommended units include English 4, mathematics 1, social studies 2, science 2 and foreign language 2.

2006-2007 Annual costs. Tuition/fees: $10,600. Room/board: $5,050. Books/supplies: $500. Personal expenses: $600.

Application procedures. Admission: Priority date 7/31; no deadline. $60 fee. Application may be submitted online. Admission notification on a rolling basis beginning on or about 12/1. Must reply by May 1 or within 2 week(s) if notified thereafter. **Financial aid:** No deadline. Institutional form required. Applicants notified on a rolling basis starting 3/1.

Academics. Special study options: Accelerated study, distance learning, double major, independent study, internships, liberal arts/career combination, teacher certification program. **Credit/placement by examination:** CLEP, institutional tests. **Support services:** Learning center, reduced course load, remedial instruction, study skills assistance, tutoring.

Majors. Education: Elementary, English, music, physical. **Theology:** Bible, missionary, youth ministry.

Most popular majors. Education 33%, philosophy/religious studies 60%.

Computing on campus. 26 workstations in library, computer center. Dormitories linked to campus network. Commuter students can connect to campus network. Helpline available.

Student life. Freshman orientation: Mandatory. Preregistration for classes offered. Held 2 days prior to registration, overviews basic rules and guidelines. **Policies:** Religious observance required. Freshmen permitted cars on campus. **Housing:** Guaranteed on-campus for freshmen. Single-sex dorms, apartments available. **Activities:** Choral groups, drama, music ensembles, student government, student newspaper, missions fellowship, preachers' fellowship, youth leaders' fellowship, educators' fellowship, music fellowship.

Athletics. NCCAA. **Intercollegiate:** Basketball, soccer M, volleyball W. **Intramural:** Basketball, soccer M, softball, table tennis, volleyball. **Team name:** Conquerors.

Student services. Campus ministries, career counseling, financial aid counseling, health services, personal counseling, placement for graduates, veterans' counselor.

Contact. E-mail: admissions@pbc.edu
Phone: (336) 725-8344 ext. 2328 Toll-free number: (800) 937-5097
Fax: (336) 725-5522
Kathy Holritz, Director of Admissions, Piedmont Baptist College, 716 Franklin Street, Winston-Salem, NC 27101-5133

Queens University of Charlotte

Charlotte, North Carolina — **CB member**
www.queens.edu/admissions — **CB code: 5560**

- Private 4-year university affiliated with Presbyterian Church (USA)
- Residential campus in large city
- 1,567 degree-seeking undergraduates: 35% part-time, 77% women, 17% African American, 2% Asian American, 4% Hispanic American, 1% Native American, 5% international
- 396 degree-seeking graduate students
- 67% of applicants admitted
- SAT or ACT with writing required
- 64% graduate within 6 years; 23% enter graduate study

General. Founded in 1857. Regionally accredited. 6 credit hours of internships required to enhance job placement and career opportunities. John Belk International Program (3-week study tours in Europe and Asia), interdisciplinary core curriculum, European internship program offered. **Degrees:** 260 bachelor's, 41 associate awarded; master's offered. **ROTC:** Army, Air Force. **Calendar:** Semester, limited summer session. **Full-time faculty:** 68 total; 78% have terminal degrees, 4% minority, 63% women. **Part-time faculty:** 43 total; 44% have terminal degrees, 5% minority, 58% women. **Class size:** 62% < 20, 38% 20-39. **Special facilities:** Rare books museum, recital hall.

Freshman class profile. 1,019 applied, 678 admitted, 242 enrolled.

Mid 50% test scores		**Rank in top tenth:**	16%
SAT verbal:	480-570	**Return as sophomores:**	70%
SAT math:	490-560	**Out-of-state:**	52%
ACT:	19-24	**Live on campus:**	89%
GPA 3.50 or higher:	44%	**International:**	3%
GPA 3.0-3.49:	33%	**Fraternities:**	17%
GPA 2.0-2.99:	23%	**Sororities:**	24%
Rank in top quarter:	45%		

Basis for selection. High school courses taken, school achievement record, class rank, test scores important. Extracurricular activities, recommendations also considered. Official test scores must be received prior to admission. Interview recommended for all students. Audition required for drama, music, music therapy programs; portfolio recommended for art program.

High school preparation. Recommended units include English 4, mathematics 3, social studies 2, science 2 (laboratory 1) and foreign language 2. Chemistry recommended for nursing.

2006-2007 Annual costs. Tuition/fees (projected): $19,450. Room/board: $6,980. Books/supplies: $900. Personal expenses: $900.

2005-2006 Financial aid. Need-based: 144 full-time freshmen applied for aid; 144 were judged to have need; 144 of these received aid. Average need met was 77%. Average scholarship/grant was $12,484; average loan $2,325. 67% of total undergraduate aid awarded as scholarships/grants, 33% as loans/jobs. **Non-need-based:** Scholarships awarded for academics, art, athletics, leadership, minority status, music/drama, religious affiliation, state residency.

Application procedures. Admission: Priority date 12/1; no deadline. $40 fee, may be waived for applicants with need. Application may be submitted online. Admission notification on a rolling basis beginning on or about 10/15. Must reply by May 1 or within 3 week(s) if notified thereafter. **Financial aid:** Priority date 3/1; no closing date. FAFSA required. Applicants notified on a rolling basis starting 3/1; must reply by 5/1 or within 3 week(s) of notification.

Academics. Professional golf management offered. **Special study options:** Cross-registration, double major, dual enrollment of high school students, honors, independent study, internships, liberal arts/career combination, student-designed major, study abroad, teacher certification program, Washington semester, weekend college. Harvard Model UN. **Credit/placement by examination:** AP, CLEP, IB, institutional tests. 43 credit hours maximum toward bachelor's degree. **Support services:** Reduced course load, tutoring, writing center.

Majors. Area/ethnic studies: American, European. **Biology:** General, biochemistry, environmental. **Business:** Business admin, management information systems, marketing. **Communications:** General, journalism, organizational. **Computer sciences:** Information systems. **Education:** General, elementary. **Foreign languages:** General. **Health:** Music therapy, nursing (RN), predentistry, premedicine, preop/surgical nursing, prepharmacy, preveterinary. **History:** General. **Legal studies:** Prelaw. **Math:** General, statistics. **Philosophy/religion:** Religion. **Psychology:** General. **Social sciences:** Political science, sociology. **Visual/performing arts:** Art history/conservation, dramatic, music performance, studio arts.

Most popular majors. Business/marketing 33%, communications/journalism 15%, health sciences 10%, psychology 8%, social sciences 6%, visual/performing arts 6%.

Computing on campus. 109 workstations in dormitories, library, computer center. Dormitories wired for high-speed internet access and linked to campus network. Commuter students can connect to campus network. Online library, helpline available.

Student life. Freshman orientation: Mandatory. Preregistration for classes offered. 2-day program held at beginning of academic year. **Policies:** Freshmen permitted cars on campus. **Housing:** Guaranteed on-campus for freshmen. Coed dorms, substance-free housing available. $250 deposit, deadline 5/1. **Activities:** Pep band, choral groups, dance, drama, literary magazine, music ensembles, musical theater, student government, student newspaper, Students for Black Awareness, College Republicans, College Democrats, international club, North Carolina Student Legislature, Justinian Society (prelaw).

Athletics. NCAA. **Intercollegiate:** Basketball, cheerleading W, cross-country, golf, lacrosse, soccer, softball W, tennis, track and field, volleyball W. **Intramural:** Basketball, football (non-tackle) M, soccer, softball, table tennis, volleyball. **Team name:** Royals.

Student services. Adult student services, alcohol/substance abuse counseling, campus ministries, career counseling, student employment services, financial aid counseling, health services, personal counseling, placement for graduates. **Physically disabled:** Services for visually impaired.

Contact. E-mail: admissions@queens.edu
Phone: (704) 337-2212 Toll-free number: (800) 849-0202
Fax: (704) 337-0403
William Lee, Director of Admissions, Queens University of Charlotte, 1900 Selwyn Avenue, Charlotte, NC 28274

Roanoke Bible College

Elizabeth City, North Carolina
www.roanokebible.edu — **CB code: 5597**

- Private 4-year Bible college affiliated with Church of Christ
- Residential campus in large town
- 177 degree-seeking undergraduates: 11% part-time, 50% women
- 49% of applicants admitted
- SAT or ACT (ACT writing optional), application essay required
- 44% graduate within 6 years

General. Founded in 1948. Regionally accredited; also accredited by ABHE. **Degrees:** 29 bachelor's, 7 associate awarded. **Location:** 50 miles from Norfolk, Virginia. **Calendar:** Semester, limited summer session. **Full-time faculty:** 11 total; 27% have terminal degrees, 27% women. **Part-time faculty:** 11 total; 27% women. **Class size:** 61% < 20, 33% 20-39, 6% 40-49.

Freshman class profile. 102 applied, 50 admitted, 32 enrolled.

Mid 50% test scores		**GPA 2.0-2.99:**	42%
SAT verbal:	410-570	**Rank in top quarter:**	28%
SAT math:	300-520	**Rank in top tenth:**	8%
ACT:	18-20	**Return as sophomores:**	67%
GPA 3.50 or higher:	16%	**Out-of-state:**	69%
GPA 3.0-3.49:	42%	**Live on campus:**	100%

Basis for selection. Evidence of Christian character, school achievement record, test scores, school and community activities, recommendations important. Interview recommended if questions arise from references or academic record.

High school preparation. 20 units required. Required and recommended units include English 4, mathematics 3, social studies 2, history 2, science 3 (laboratory 2), foreign language 2 and academic electives 4.

2005-2006 Annual costs. Tuition/fees: $8,225. Room/board: $4,760. Books/supplies: $900. Personal expenses: $2,500.

2004-2005 Financial aid. Need-based: 30 full-time freshmen applied for aid; 25 were judged to have need; 25 of these received aid. Average need met was 70%. Average scholarship/grant was $4,496; average loan $2,276. 47% of total undergraduate aid awarded as scholarships/grants, 53% as loans/jobs. **Non-need-based:** Awarded to 27 full-time undergraduates, including 7 freshmen. Scholarships awarded for academics, alumni affiliation, leadership, music/drama, religious affiliation.

Application procedures. Admission: No deadline. $25 fee, may be waived for applicants with need. Application may be submitted online. Admission notification on a rolling basis beginning on or about 9/1. **Financial aid:** Priority date 3/15, closing date 5/1. FAFSA, institutional form required. Applicants notified on a rolling basis starting 4/1; must reply within 2 week(s) of notification.

Academics. Special study options: Cooperative education, distance learning, dual enrollment of high school students, independent study, internships. Semester-long mission intern class overseas. **Credit/placement by examination:** AP, CLEP, institutional tests. 8 credit hours maximum toward associate degree, 16 toward bachelor's. **Support services:** Learning center, reduced course load, remedial instruction.

Majors. Philosophy/religion: Religion. **Theology:** Bible, missionary, pastoral counseling, religious ed, theology, youth ministry.

Computing on campus. 24 workstations in dormitories, library, computer center. Dormitories linked to campus network.

Student life. Freshman orientation: Mandatory, $100 fee. **Policies:** All students have opportunity to travel in choral group throughout country. Religious observance required. Freshmen permitted cars on campus. **Housing:** Guaranteed on-campus for all undergraduates. Single-sex dorms, apartments, substance-free housing available. $50 deposit, deadline 4/1. **Activities:** Choral groups, music ensembles, musical theater, student government.

Athletics. Intercollegiate: Basketball. **Intramural:** Basketball, golf, softball, table tennis, tennis, volleyball. **Team name:** Flames.

Student services. Career counseling, student employment services, personal counseling, placement for graduates. **Physically disabled:** Services for hearing impaired.

Contact. E-mail: jaf@roanokebible.edu
Phone: (252) 334-2028 Toll-free number: (800) 722-8980
Fax: (252) 334-2071
Julie Fields, Director of Admissions and Financial Aid, Roanoke Bible College, 715 North Poindexter Street, Elizabeth City, NC 27909

St. Andrews Presbyterian College

Laurinburg, North Carolina — **CB member**
www.sapc.edu — **CB code: 5214**

- Private 4-year liberal arts college affiliated with Presbyterian Church (USA)
- Residential campus in large town
- 741 degree-seeking undergraduates: 6% part-time, 62% women, 10% African American, 3% Hispanic American, 1% Native American, 4% international
- 76% of applicants admitted
- SAT or ACT (ACT writing optional) required
- 44% graduate within 6 years

General. Founded in 1958. Regionally accredited. **Degrees:** 127 bachelor's awarded. **Location:** 40 miles from Fayetteville, 20 miles from Pinehurst. **Calendar:** Semester, limited summer session. **Full-time faculty:** 44 total; 75% have terminal degrees, 2% minority, 34% women. **Part-time faculty:** 20 total; 25% have terminal degrees, 5% minority, 55% women. **Class size:** 75% < 20, 23% 20-39, less than 1% 40-49, 1% 50-99. **Special facilities:** Psychology laboratory complex, equestrian facilities, nature preserve, electronic fine arts center.

Freshman class profile. 859 applied, 656 admitted, 191 enrolled.

Mid 50% test scores		Out-of-state:	63%
SAT verbal:	460-590	Live on campus:	99%
SAT math:	460-570	International:	1%
Return as sophomores:	67%		

Basis for selection. High school GPA, test scores, curriculum, type of high school very important. Recommendations important. Writing scores from standardized tests will not be used in Fall 2006 admission decisions. Interview required for academically weak students, recommended for all other applicants. **Homeschooled:** Standardized test scores and interview required.

High school preparation. 16 units recommended. Required and recommended units include English 4, mathematics 3, social studies 3, history 1, science 3 and foreign language 2.

2006-2007 Annual costs. Tuition/fees (projected): $18,062. Room/board: $6,694. Books/supplies: $800. Personal expenses: $1,424.

2004-2005 Financial aid. Need-based: 172 full-time freshmen applied for aid; 144 were judged to have need; 144 of these received aid. Average need met was 73%. Average scholarship/grant was $9,601; average loan $2,259. 70% of total undergraduate aid awarded as scholarships/grants, 30% as loans/jobs. **Non-need-based:** Awarded to 405 full-time undergraduates, including 131 freshmen. Scholarships awarded for academics, alumni affiliation, athletics, leadership, music/drama, religious affiliation.

Application procedures. Admission: Priority date 5/1; no deadline. $30 fee. Application may be submitted online. Admission notification on a rolling basis beginning on or about 9/1. Housing deposit fully refundable until May 1st. **Financial aid:** Priority date 5/1; no closing date. FAFSA required. Applicants notified on a rolling basis starting 10/1; must reply within 2 week(s) of notification.

Academics. Academic programs include St. Andrew's General Education. **Special study options:** Cross-registration, double major, dual enrollment of high school students, exchange student, honors, independent study, internships, liberal arts/career combination, student-designed major, study abroad, teacher certification program, Washington semester. Courses offered abroad during winter or summer in Britain, Greece, India, Switzerland, Venezuela, China, Hawaii, former Soviet Union; exchange programs with Stirling University, Scotland and Kansai Gaidai University, Japan; study at Brunnenburg Castle, Italy, and Beijing Normal College of Foreign Languages. **Credit/placement by examination:** AP, CLEP, IB. 30 credit hours maximum toward bachelor's degree. **Support services:** Reduced course load, tutoring, writing center.

Majors. Agriculture: Equestrian studies. **Area/ethnic studies:** Asian. **Biology:** General. **Business:** General, business admin, international. **Education:** Elementary, physical. **English:** Creative writing. **Health:** Athletic training, premedicine, prepharmacy, preveterinary. **History:** General. **Legal studies:** Prelaw. **Liberal arts:** Arts/sciences. **Math:** General. **Philosophy/religion:** Philosophy, religion. **Physical sciences:** Chemistry. **Psychology:** General. **Social sciences:** Political science. **Visual/performing arts:** General, art.

Most popular majors. Business/marketing 25%, education 15%, English 6%, liberal arts 7%, psychology 7%, public administration/social services 11%.

Computing on campus. 100 workstations in library, computer center, student center. Dormitories wired for high-speed internet access and linked to campus network. Online library, repair service available.

Student life. Freshman orientation: Mandatory, $100 fee. 3 days prior to start of fall term. **Policies:** Honor code enforced. Freshmen permitted cars on campus. **Housing:** Guaranteed on-campus for all undergraduates. Coed dorms, single-sex dorms, special housing for disabled, substance-free housing available. $200 deposit, deadline 8/25. **Activities:** Choral groups, dance, drama, literary magazine, musical theater, student government, student newspaper, Christian Student Fellowship, Model United Nations, black student union, women's issues group, writer's forum, world culture club, Eco-Action, student activities union.

Athletics. NCAA. **Intercollegiate:** Baseball M, basketball, cross-country, equestrian, golf, lacrosse, soccer, softball W, tennis, track and field, volleyball W. **Intramural:** Basketball, bowling, racquetball, soccer, softball W, table tennis, volleyball. **Team name:** Knights.

Student services. Adult student services, alcohol/substance abuse counseling, career counseling, student employment services, financial aid counseling, health services, personal counseling, placement for graduates, women's services. **Physically disabled:** Services for visually, speech, hearing impaired.

Contact. E-mail: admissions@sapc.edu
Phone: (910) 277-5555 Toll-free number: (800) 763-0198
Fax: (910) 277-5087
Cynthia Robinson, Director of Admission, St. Andrews Presbyterian College, 1700 Dogwood Mile, Laurinburg, NC 28352

St. Augustine's College

Raleigh, North Carolina **CB member**
www.st-aug.edu **CB code: 5596**

- Private 4-year liberal arts college affiliated with Episcopal Church
- Residential campus in large city
- 1,143 degree-seeking undergraduates
- 49% of applicants admitted
- Interview required

General. Founded in 1867. Regionally accredited. Home to historic St. Augustine's College Chapel and St. Agnes Hospital. **Degrees:** 169 bachelor's awarded. **ROTC:** Army, Air Force. **Location:** One mile from downtown. **Calendar:** Semester, limited summer session. **Full-time faculty:** 78 total. **Part-time faculty:** 34 total. **Class size:** 65% < 20, 33% 20-39, 2% 40-49, less than 1% 50-99. **Special facilities:** Archival collection tracing history of African-Americans in North Carolina and Delaney family.

Freshman class profile. 1,979 applied, 975 admitted, 262 enrolled.

Mid 50% test scores			
SAT verbal:	400-430	Rank in top tenth:	15%
SAT math:	410-430	Out-of-state:	65%
ACT:	15-17	Live on campus:	92%
Rank in top quarter:	44%	Fraternities:	6%
		Sororities:	12%

Basis for selection. High school record (GPA and rank), standardized test scores and letters of recommendation reviewed. Alumni affiliation also considered. SAT or ACT recommended. Institutionally administered Accuplacer test is used for pre- and post-testing evaluation and placement purposes. Essay recommended. Auditions and interviews required of music majors. **Learning Disabled:** Students must self-identify. ADA Coordinator will assess level of disability and arrange for student to access the needed equipment or tutorials.

High school preparation. 20 units required. Required units include English 4, mathematics 3, social studies 2, science 2 and academic electives 9. One unit of algebra required, 2 units of laboratory recommended.

2005-2006 Annual costs. Tuition/fees: $11,428. Room/board: $5,844. Books/supplies: $900. Personal expenses: $1,530.

2004-2005 Financial aid. Non-need-based: Scholarships awarded for academics, art, athletics, leadership, minority status, music/drama, religious affiliation, ROTC, state residency.

Application procedures. Admission: Closing date 8/1 (postmark date). $25 fee, may be waived for applicants with need. Application may be submitted online. Admission notification on a rolling basis beginning on or about 1/1. **Financial aid:** Closing date 3/15. FAFSA, institutional form required. Applicants notified on a rolling basis starting 5/1; must reply within 2 week(s) of notification.

Academics. Required "Learning Community" program for all new freshmen and transfers. First year program includes skills enhancement and college survival tips. Community service requirement is part of course. **Special study options:** Accelerated study, cooperative education, cross-registration, double major, dual enrollment of high school students, honors, independent study, internships, liberal arts/career combination, study abroad, teacher certification program, weekend college. **Credit/placement by examination:** CLEP, IB, institutional tests. 15 credit hours maximum toward bachelor's degree. **Support services:** Learning center, pre-admission summer program, reduced course load, remedial instruction, study skills assistance, tutoring, writing center.

Majors. Area/ethnic studies: African-American. **Biology:** General, biomedical sciences. **Business:** Accounting, business admin, management science, real estate. **Communications:** General. **Computer sciences:** General, computer science. **Education:** Biology, business, elementary, English, health occupations, mathematics, music, physical, secondary, social studies, special. **Engineering:** General. **English:** English lit. **Health:** Occupational health, premedicine. **History:** General. **Legal studies:** Prelaw. **Math:** General. **Parks/recreation:** Health/fitness, sports admin. **Philosophy/religion:** Religion. **Physical sciences:** Chemistry. **Protective services:** Criminal justice, forensics. **Psychology:** General. **Social sciences:** Political science, sociology. **Visual/performing arts:** General, art, cinematography, music performance.

Most popular majors. Business/marketing 35%, communications/journalism 7%, computer/information sciences 12%, security/protective services 10%, social sciences 14%.

Computing on campus. 250 workstations in dormitories, library, computer center. Dormitories wired for high-speed internet access and linked to campus network. Commuter students can connect to campus network. Online course registration, online library, helpline, repair service available.

Student life. Freshman orientation: Mandatory, $100 fee. Preregistration for classes offered. Several 2-day orientations are held in June, July and August with students and parents. **Policies:** Alcohol and drug-free campus. No tolerance policy. No firearm policy. No smoking policy for all campus administrative buildings. Religious observance required. **Housing:** Guaranteed on-campus for freshmen. Single-sex dorms, substance-free housing available. $150 deposit. **Activities:** Bands, choral groups, dance, drama, film society, music ensembles, musical theater, radio station, student government, student newspaper, symphony orchestra, TV station, Christian Fellowship Organization, Young Democrats of America, Falcons for the Cause, National Association for the Advancement of Colored People (NAACP), Foreign Language Club, Falcon Battalion/Army ROTC, Student Service Corps, SAC Assocation for Black Journalists, International Student Association, Latin American Students Organization.

Athletics. NCAA. **Intercollegiate:** Baseball M, basketball, bowling W, cheerleading W, cross-country, football (tackle) M, golf, softball W, tennis, track and field, volleyball W. **Intramural:** Baseball M, basketball, softball W, volleyball. **Team name:** Falcons.

Student services. Adult student services, alcohol/substance abuse counseling, campus ministries, career counseling, services for economically disadvantaged, student employment services, financial aid counseling, health services, minority student services, personal counseling, placement for graduates, veterans' counselor. **Physically disabled:** Services for visually impaired.

Contact. E-mail: admissions@st-aug.edu
Phone: (919) 516-4012 Toll-free number: (800) 948-1126
Fax: (919) 516-5805
Anthony Brooks, Dean, Enrollment Management, St. Augustine's College, 1315 Oakwood Avenue, Raleigh, NC 27610-2298

Salem College

Winston-Salem, North Carolina **CB member**
www.salem.edu **CB code: 5607**

- Private 4-year liberal arts college for women affiliated with Moravian Church in America
- Residential campus in small city
- 834 degree-seeking undergraduates: 16% part-time, 98% women, 19% African American, 1% Asian American, 3% Hispanic American, 8% international
- 196 degree-seeking graduate students
- 69% of applicants admitted
- SAT or ACT (ACT writing recommended), application essay required
- 50% graduate within 6 years; 20% enter graduate study

General. Founded in 1772. Regionally accredited. Male students age 23 and over may enroll in adult program only and may not reside at the college. **Degrees:** 189 bachelor's awarded; master's offered. **Location:** 80 miles from Charlotte, 25 miles from Greensboro. **Calendar:** 4-1-4, limited summer session. **Full-time faculty:** 57 total; 88% have terminal degrees, 10% minority, 56% women. **Part-time faculty:** 34 total; 3% have terminal degrees, 12% minority, 53% women. **Class size:** 77% < 20, 23% 20-39. **Special facilities:** Historic buildings, museums.

Freshman class profile. 387 applied, 267 admitted, 131 enrolled.

Mid 50% test scores			
SAT verbal:	500-630	Rank in top quarter:	58%
SAT math:	480-620	Rank in top tenth:	33%
ACT:	21-24	End year in good standing:	78%
GPA 3.50 or higher:	68%	Return as sophomores:	72%
GPA 3.0-3.49:	19%	Out-of-state:	49%
GPA 2.0-2.99:	13%	Live on campus:	94%
		International:	13%

Basis for selection. School achievement record, essay or personal statement, test scores important. Recommendations, interview, extracurricular and community activities, talent, minority status considered. Interview recommended for all students. Audition required for music program; portfolio recommended for art program.

High school preparation. College-preparatory program required. 16 units recommended. Recommended units include English 4, mathematics 3, social studies 2, science 3, foreign language 2 and academic electives 3. Math recommendation includes 2 algebra and 1 geometry.

2005-2006 Annual costs. Tuition/fees: $17,225. Room/board: $9,251. Books/supplies: $600. Personal expenses: $1,895.

2004-2005 Financial aid. Need-based: 140 full-time freshmen applied for aid; 111 were judged to have need; 111 of these received aid. Average need met was 100%. Average scholarship/grant was $11,077; average loan $2,625. 70% of total undergraduate aid awarded as scholarships/grants, 30% as loans/jobs. **Non-need-based:** Awarded to 132 full-time undergraduates, including 58 freshmen. Scholarships awarded for academics, alumni affiliation, art, job skills, leadership, minority status, music/drama, religious affiliation, state residency.

Application procedures. Admission: Priority date 3/1; no deadline. $30 fee, may be waived for applicants with need. Application may be submitted online. Admission notification on a rolling basis. Must reply by May 1 or within 2 week(s) if notified thereafter. **Financial aid:** Priority date 3/15; no closing date. FAFSA required. Applicants notified on a rolling basis starting 3/1; must reply by 5/1 or within 2 week(s) of notification.

Academics. Special study options: Cross-registration, double major, dual enrollment of high school students, exchange student, honors, independent study, internships, liberal arts/career combination, student-designed major, study abroad, teacher certification program, United Nations semester, Washington semester. Cooperative engineering programs with Duke University and Vanderbilt University, 3-2 medical technology program with Wake Forest University's Bowman Gray School of Medicine; various study abroad options available through Brethren Colleges of America (BCA); St. Peters, Oxford; and St. Clare's, Oxford. **Credit/placement by examination:** AP, CLEP, IB, institutional tests. A maximum of 16 courses credit awarded through CLEP exam. **Support services:** Learning center, reduced course load, study skills assistance, tutoring, writing center.

Majors. Area/ethnic studies: American. **Biology:** General. **Business:** Accounting, business admin, international. **Communications:** General. **Education:** Music. **Foreign languages:** French, German, Spanish. **Health:** Clinical lab technology. **History:** General. **Math:** General. **Philosophy/religion:** Philosophy, religion. **Physical sciences:** Chemistry. **Psychology:** General. **Social sciences:** Economics, international relations, sociology. **Visual/performing arts:** Art history/conservation, arts management, interior design, music performance, studio arts.

Most popular majors. Business/marketing 11%, communications/journalism 12%, English 11%, foreign language 8%, psychology 9%, social sciences 20%, visual/performing arts 10%.

Computing on campus. 54 workstations in library, computer center. Dormitories wired for high-speed internet access and linked to campus network. Commuter students can connect to campus network. Online library, helpline, wireless network available.

Student life. Freshman orientation: Mandatory. Preregistration for classes offered. Orientation held for approximately 3 days before the fall term begins. Separate orientation program for adult students. **Policies:** Freshmen permitted cars on campus. **Housing:** Guaranteed on-campus for freshmen. Apartments, substance-free housing available. $250 nonrefundable deposit, deadline 5/1. All full-time students under 23 years required to reside on-campus unless they reside with family within a 30 mile radius of the college. **Activities:** Marching band, choral groups, dance, drama, literary magazine, music ensembles, musical theater, student government, student newspaper, Model United Nations, ONUA (minority/diversity awareness), College Republicans, College Democrats, Green Party, international club, Catholic student association, campus activities council, Intervarsity Fellowship, Habitat for Humanity.

Athletics. NCAA. **Intercollegiate:** Basketball W, cross-country W, field hockey W, soccer W, softball W, swimming W, tennis W, volleyball W. **Intramural:** Basketball W, swimming W, volleyball W, water polo W. **Team name:** Salem Spirit.

Student services. Adult student services, campus ministries, career counseling, financial aid counseling, health services, personal counseling, placement for graduates, women's services.

Contact. E-mail: admissions@salem.edu
Phone: (336) 721-2621 Toll-free number: (800) 327-2536
Fax: (336) 917-5572
Dana Evans, Dean of Admissions and Financial Aid, Salem College, PO Box 10548, Winston-Salem, NC 27108

Shaw University

Raleigh, North Carolina — **CB member**
www.shawuniversity.edu — **CB code: 5612**

- Private 4-year university and liberal arts college affiliated with Baptist faith
- Residential campus in large city
- 2,536 degree-seeking undergraduates
- 65% of applicants admitted
- SAT or ACT (ACT writing optional), application essay required

General. Founded in 1865. Regionally accredited. Five-year program in kinesiotherapy. Center for Alternative Programs of Education degree program with 9 in-state locations. Collaborates with five other Research Triangle institutions. Affiliated with General Baptist State Convention. **Degrees:** 411 bachelor's, 7 associate awarded; master's, first professional offered. **ROTC:** Army, Air Force. **Location:** 263 miles from Washington, DC, 410 miles from Atlanta. **Calendar:** Semester, limited summer session. **Full-time faculty:** 111 total. **Part-time faculty:** 179 total. **Class size:** 70% < 20, 27% 20-39, 2% 40-49, 2% 50-99. **Special facilities:** Physical education and kinesiotherapy clinic, speech and hearing clinic, Praxis Lab.

Freshman class profile. 4,226 applied, 2,728 admitted, 601 enrolled.

Mid 50% test scores			
SAT verbal:	350-460	Rank in top quarter:	11%
SAT math:	350-450	Rank in top tenth:	3%
ACT:	14-17	Out-of-state:	53%
		Live on campus:	90%

Basis for selection. 2.0 high school GPA desired. Interview, portfolio recommended for some.

High school preparation. 18 units required. Required units include English 3, mathematics 2, social studies 2, science 2 and academic electives 9. 9 electives in English, foreign language, mathematics, science.

2006-2007 Annual costs. Tuition/fees: $10,020. Room/board: $6,410. Books/supplies: $700. Personal expenses: $1,000.

2004-2005 Financial aid. Need-based: 53% of total undergraduate aid awarded as scholarships/grants, 47% as loans/jobs. **Non-need-based:** Scholarships awarded for academics, athletics, ROTC.

Application procedures. Admission: Closing date 7/30. $25 fee, may be waived for applicants with need. Within 30 days. **Financial aid:** Closing date 3/1. FAFSA required. Applicants notified on a rolling basis starting 4/30.

Academics. Alternative education program for working students offers Saturday and evening classes. Emphasis placed on volunteerism, field experiences, and internships. **Special study options:** Accelerated study, cross-registration, distance learning, double major, dual enrollment of high school students, honors, independent study, internships, student-designed major, study abroad, teacher certification program, weekend college. **Credit/placement by examination:** CLEP, institutional tests. 30 credit hours maximum toward associate degree, 60 toward bachelor's. **Support services:** Learning center, reduced course load, study skills assistance, tutoring, writing center.

Majors. Biology: General. **Business:** Business admin, international. **Communications:** Media studies. **Computer sciences:** General, computer science. **Conservation:** General. **Education:** Elementary, English, mathematics, mentally handicapped, special. **Health:** Athletic training, audiology/speech pathology, recreational therapy. **Liberal arts:** Arts/sciences. **Math:** General. **Parks/recreation:** General, exercise sciences. **Philosophy/religion:** Religion. **Physical sciences:** Chemistry, physics. **Protective services:** Criminal justice. **Psychology:** General. **Public administration:** General, social work. **Social sciences:** International relations, sociology. **Visual/performing arts:** Dramatic.

Most popular majors. Business/marketing 29%, computer/information sciences 6%, philosophy/religious studies 9%, security/protective services 25%, social sciences 9%.

Computing on campus. 150 workstations in dormitories, library, computer center, student center. Dormitories wired for high-speed internet access and linked to campus network. Commuter students can connect to campus network. Online course registration, online library, helpline, repair service, student web hosting available.

Student life. Freshman orientation: Available. **Housing:** Single-sex dorms available. $100 deposit. **Activities:** Bands, choral groups, dance, drama, music ensembles, musical theater, radio station, student government, student newspaper, NAACP, international students organization, business, sociology, criminal justice, accounting clubs, Christian Fellowship, northern exposure, order of the eastern star.

Athletics. NCAA. **Intercollegiate:** Baseball M, basketball, bowling W, cross-country, football (tackle) M, golf M, softball W, tennis, track and field, volleyball W. **Intramural:** Basketball, tennis, volleyball. **Team name:** Bears.

Student services. Adult student services, alcohol/substance abuse counseling, campus ministries, career counseling, student employment services, financial aid counseling, health services, personal counseling, placement for graduates, veterans' counselor. **Physically disabled:** Services for visually, speech, hearing impaired.

Contact. E-mail: admissions@shawu.edu
Phone: (919) 546-8275 Toll-free number: (800) 214-6683
Fax: (919) 546-8271
Sandy Clifton, Director of Admissions, Shaw University, 118 East South Street, Raleigh, NC 27601

Southeastern Baptist Theological Seminary

Wake Forest, North Carolina
www.sebts.edu **CB code: 7050**

- Private 4-year Bible and seminary college affiliated with Southern Baptist Convention
- Small town

General. Founded in 1950. Regionally accredited. **Location:** 20 miles from Raleigh, 30 miles from Durham. **Calendar:** Semester.

Annual costs/financial aid. Tuition/fees (2005-2006): $5,990. NonSouthern Baptist Students per credit hour charge is $380.

Contact. Phone: (919) 761-2280
Director of Admissions, PO Box 1889, Wake Forest, NC 27588

University of North Carolina at Asheville

Asheville, North Carolina **CB member**
www.unca.edu **CB code: 5013**

- Public 4-year university and liberal arts college
- Commuter campus in small city
- 3,124 degree-seeking undergraduates: 12% part-time, 58% women, 2% African American, 2% Asian American, 2% Hispanic American, 1% international
- 29 degree-seeking graduate students
- 63% of applicants admitted
- SAT or ACT with writing required
- 54% graduate within 6 years; 21% enter graduate study

General. Founded in 1927. Regionally accredited. **Degrees:** 574 bachelor's awarded; master's offered. **Location:** 130 miles from Charlotte, 200 miles from Atlanta. **Calendar:** Semester, limited summer session. **Full-time faculty:** 199 total; 84% have terminal degrees, 10% minority, 40% women. **Part-time faculty:** 110 total; 34% have terminal degrees, 4% minority, 51% women. **Class size:** 52% < 20, 46% 20-39, 1% 40-49, less than 1% 50-99. **Special facilities:** Botanical gardens, Jewish studies center, arboretum, environmental quality institute, distance learning facility, music recording studio, National Environmental Modeling and Analysis Center (NEMAC), astronomical research institute, National Climatic Data Center.

Freshman class profile. 2,362 applied, 1,482 admitted, 472 enrolled.

Mid 50% test scores		**Rank in top tenth:**	25%
SAT verbal:	540-660	**End year in good standing:**	92%
SAT math:	540-640	**Return as sophomores:**	76%
ACT:	22-27	**Out-of-state:**	16%
GPA 3.50 or higher:	88%	**Live on campus:**	87%
GPA 3.0-3.49:	11%	**International:**	1%
GPA 2.0-2.99:	1%	**Fraternities:**	3%
Rank in top quarter:	68%	**Sororities:**	2%

Basis for selection. GED not accepted. High school curriculum, GPA, and class rank (top third), most important. Test scores important. Recommendations, interview, extracurricular activities that support academic achievement considered. Students expected to have completed advanced coursework. SAT preferred, ACT accepted. Essays may be submitted, but not required. Personal statements helpful. Interviews recommended. **Homeschooled:** Must document all courses taken, particularly UNC system minimum admissions requirements. For North Carolina applicants, a copy of the school's registration with the North Carolina Department of Non-Public Instruction required. **Learning Disabled:** Untimed SAT accepted.

High school preparation. 15 units required. Required and recommended units include English 4, mathematics 4, social studies 1, history 1, science 3 (laboratory 1), foreign language 2 and academic electives 4. Science units should include biology and physical science such as chemistry or physics. One unit US history, 1 unit other social studies required. Math must include algebra I, II and geometry and 1 math course with algebra II as pre-requisite.

2005-2006 Annual costs. Tuition/fees: $3,526; $13,326 out-of-state. Room/board: $5,712. Books/supplies: $850. Personal expenses: $1,541.

2004-2005 Financial aid. Need-based: 503 full-time freshmen applied for aid; 289 were judged to have need; 284 of these received aid. Average need met was 73%. Average scholarship/grant was $2,825; average loan $2,338. 46% of total undergraduate aid awarded as scholarships/grants, 54% as loans/jobs. **Non-need-based:** Awarded to 668 full-time undergraduates, including 220 freshmen. Scholarships awarded for academics, alumni affiliation, art, athletics, job skills, leadership, minority status, music/drama, state residency.

Application procedures. Admission: Priority date 11/27; deadline 3/1 (postmark date). $50 fee, may be waived for applicants with need. Application may be submitted online. Admission notification 4/2. Must reply by 5/1. **Financial aid:** Priority date 3/1; no closing date. FAFSA required. Applicants notified on a rolling basis starting 3/15.

Academics. Special study options: Cross-registration, distance learning, double major, dual enrollment of high school students, exchange student, honors, independent study, internships, liberal arts/career combination, semester at sea, student-designed major, study abroad, teacher certification program, Washington semester. **Credit/placement by examination:** AP, CLEP, IB, institutional tests. 30 credit hours maximum toward bachelor's degree. AP and CLEP exam grades required for credit are subject to change. **Support services:** Learning center, reduced course load, remedial instruction, study skills assistance, tutoring, writing center.

Majors. Area/ethnic studies: Women's. **Biology:** General. **Business:** Accounting, business admin, operations. **Communications:** Media studies. **Computer sciences:** Computer science, web page design. **Conservation:** Environmental studies. **Engineering:** General. **English:** English lit. **Foreign languages:** Classics, French, German, Spanish. **Health:** Public health ed. **History:** General. **Liberal arts:** Arts/sciences. **Math:** General. **Philosophy/religion:** Philosophy. **Physical sciences:** Atmospheric science, chemistry, physics. **Psychology:** General. **Social sciences:** Economics, political science, sociology. **Visual/performing arts:** Art, dramatic, studio arts.

Most popular majors. Biology 6%, business/marketing 13%, communications/journalism 7%, computer/information sciences 9%, English 8%, natural resources/environmental science 7%, psychology 13%, social sciences 7%, visual/performing arts 9%.

Computing on campus. 385 workstations in dormitories, library, computer center, student center. Dormitories wired for high-speed internet access and linked to campus network. Commuter students can connect to campus network. Online course registration, online library, helpline, repair service, student web hosting, wireless network available.

Student life. Freshman orientation: Mandatory, $55 fee. Preregistration for classes offered. 3-day program prior to start of classes, includes service day. **Housing:** Guaranteed on-campus for all undergraduates. Coed dorms, single-sex dorms, special housing for disabled, substance-free housing available. $125 deposit, deadline 5/1. 24-hour quiet floors available. Substance free dorms. **Activities:** Bands, choral groups, dance, drama, literary magazine, music ensembles, musical theater, radio station, student government, student newspaper, Baptist student union, international student association, InterVarsity Christian Fellowship, African American student association, Active Students for a Healthy Environment, University Ambassadors, Jewish student association, Asian Students in Asheville.

Athletics. NCAA. **Intercollegiate:** Baseball M, basketball, cheerleading, cross-country, soccer, tennis, track and field, volleyball W. **Intramural:** Badminton, basketball, football (non-tackle), golf, racquetball, soccer, softball, tennis, volleyball, water polo. **Team name:** Bulldogs.

Student services. Adult student services, alcohol/substance abuse counseling, campus ministries, career counseling, student employment services, financial aid counseling, health services, minority student services, personal counseling, placement for graduates, veterans' counselor, women's services. **Physically disabled:** Services for visually, hearing impaired.

Contact. E-mail: admissions@unca.edu
Phone: (828) 251-6481 Toll-free number: (800) 531-9842
Fax: (828) 251-6482
Scot Schaeffer, Director of Admissions and Financial Aid, University of North Carolina at Asheville, CPO#1320, UNCA, Asheville, NC 28804-8510

University of North Carolina at Chapel Hill

Chapel Hill, North Carolina **CB member**
www.unc.edu **CB code: 5816**

- Public 4-year university
- Residential campus in large town
- 16,278 degree-seeking undergraduates: 2% part-time, 58% women, 11% African American, 6% Asian American, 3% Hispanic American, 1% Native American, 1% international
- 9,236 degree-seeking graduate students
- 37% of applicants admitted
- SAT or ACT with writing, application essay required

General. Founded in 1789. Regionally accredited. Entering freshmen required to own laptop meeting university specifications, as a part of the Carolina Computing Initiative; qualified students will receive special loans or grants. **Degrees:** 3,888 bachelor's awarded; master's, doctoral, first professional offered. **ROTC:** Army, Navy, Air Force. **Location:** 8 miles from Durham, 26 miles from Raleigh. **Calendar:** Semester, extensive summer session. **Full-time faculty:** 1,300 total. **Part-time faculty:** 110 total. **Class size:** 50% < 20, 34% 20-39, 6% 40-49, 5% 50-99, 6% >100. **Special facilities:** Planetarium, observatory, art museum, arboretum, botanical garden.

Freshman class profile. 18,414 applied, 6,736 admitted, 3,751 enrolled.

Mid 50% test scores		**Rank in top tenth:**	74%
SAT verbal:	600-690	**End year in good standing:**	99%
SAT math:	610-700	**Out-of-state:**	17%
ACT:	25-31	**Live on campus:**	83%
Rank in top quarter:	95%	**International:**	1%

Basis for selection. GED not accepted. High school record, including course selection and performance, very important. Test scores, essays, activities, and recommendations also receive strong consideration. Separate consideration given to out-of-state children of alumni. SAT preferred, ACT also accepted. Audition required for drama and music programs; portfolio recommended for art program. **Homeschooled:** SAT Subject Tests recommended. Students should follow curriculum equivalent to that of high school students taking Advanced Placement and honors courses. **Learning Disabled:** Students may voluntarily supply documentation regarding disability and impact on educational experiences with application.

High school preparation. 17 units required. Required and recommended units include English 4, mathematics 3-4, social studies 2-3, science 3-4 (laboratory 1), foreign language 2-4 and academic electives 2. One social studies must be U.S. History.

2005-2006 Annual costs. Tuition/fees: $4,515; $18,313 out-of-state. Room/board: $6,590. Books/supplies: $900. Personal expenses: $1,200.

2004-2005 Financial aid. Need-based: 2,611 full-time freshmen applied for aid; 1,174 were judged to have need; 1,139 of these received aid. Average need met was 100%. Average scholarship/grant was $7,091; average loan $2,752. 64% of total undergraduate aid awarded as scholarships/grants, 36% as loans/jobs. **Non-need-based:** Awarded to 4,028 full-time undergraduates, including 1,366 freshmen. Scholarships awarded for academics, alumni affiliation, art, athletics, leadership, music/drama, religious affiliation, state residency.

Application procedures. Admission: Closing date 1/15 (postmark date). $70 fee, may be waived for applicants with need. Application may be submitted online. Notification on or about 3/31. Must reply by May 1 or within 2 week(s) if notified thereafter. **Financial aid:** Priority date 3/1; no closing date. FAFSA, CSS PROFILE required. Applicants notified on a rolling basis starting 3/15; must reply by 5/1.

Academics. At least 24 of last 30 hours of degree credit must be taken while enrolled full-time at institution. **Special study options:** Cross-registration, distance learning, double major, dual enrollment of high school students, honors, independent study, internships, student-designed major, study abroad, teacher certification program. **Credit/placement by examination:** AP, CLEP, IB, institutional tests. **Support services:** Learning center, pre-admission summer program, reduced course load, study skills assistance, tutoring, writing center.

Majors. Area/ethnic studies: African-American, American, Asian, European, Latin American, Russian/Slavic, women's. **Biology:** General, biostatistics, pathology. **Business:** Business admin, human resources. **Communications:** General, media studies. **Computer sciences:** Computer science, information systems. **Conservation:** Environmental science, environmental studies. **Education:** Early childhood, elementary, middle. **English:** English lit. **Family/consumer sciences:** Food/nutrition. **Foreign languages:** Classics, comparative lit, German, linguistics. **Health:** Clinical lab science, dental hygiene, environmental health, health care admin, medical radiologic technology/radiation therapy, nursing (RN). **History:** General. **Interdisciplinary:** Peace/conflict. **Liberal arts:** Arts/sciences. **Math:** General, applied. **Parks/recreation:** Facilities management, health/fitness. **Philosophy/religion:** Philosophy, religion. **Physical sciences:** Chemistry, geology, physics. **Psychology:** General. **Public administration:** Policy analysis. **Social sciences:** Anthropology, economics, geography, political science, sociology. **Visual/performing arts:** Art history/conservation, dramatic, music performance, studio arts.

Most popular majors. Biology 9%, business/marketing 11%, communications/journalism 17%, health sciences 7%, psychology 10%, social sciences 14%.

Computing on campus. PC or laptop required. 600 workstations in dormitories, library, computer center, student center. Dormitories wired for high-speed internet access and linked to campus network. Commuter students can connect to campus network. Online course registration, online library, helpline, repair service, student web hosting, wireless network available.

Student life. Freshman orientation: Mandatory, $146 fee. Preregistration for classes offered. 2-day summer program, 13 sessions offered. **Housing:** Coed dorms, single-sex dorms, special housing for disabled, apartments, fraternity/sorority housing, substance-free housing available. $75 deposit, deadline 5/1. Students with interests in arts, international relations, or foreign languages may live in co-ed Carmichael Residence Hall. **Activities:** Bands, choral groups, dance, drama, film society, literary magazine, music ensembles, musical theater, radio station, student government, student newspaper, symphony orchestra, TV station, APPLES, Campus Crusade for Christ, student environmental action coalition, Alpha Phi Omega, black student movement, Amnesty International Group 84, InterVarsity Christian Fellowship, Asian student association, Young Life, dance marathon.

Athletics. NCAA. **Intercollegiate:** Baseball M, basketball, cross-country, diving, fencing, field hockey W, football (tackle) M, golf, gymnastics W, lacrosse, rowing (crew) W, soccer, softball W, swimming, tennis, track and field, volleyball W, wrestling M. **Intramural:** Badminton, basketball, bowling, cross-country, football (non-tackle), handball, racquetball, soccer, softball, swimming, table tennis, tennis, track and field, triathlon, volleyball, water polo. **Team name:** Tarheels.

Student services. Alcohol/substance abuse counseling, campus ministries, career counseling, student employment services, financial aid counseling, health services, legal services, minority student services, on-campus daycare, personal counseling, placement for graduates, veterans' counselor, women's services. **Physically disabled:** Services for visually, speech, hearing impaired. **Learning disabled:** Comprehensive services available.

Contact. E-mail: uadm@email.unc.edu
Phone: (919) 966-3621 Fax: (919) 962-3045
Stephen Farmer, Assistant Provost and Director of Undergraduate Admissions, University of North Carolina at Chapel Hill, Jackson Hall CB #2200, Chapel Hill, NC 27599-2200

University of North Carolina at Charlotte

Charlotte, North Carolina **CB member**
www.uncc.edu **CB code: 5105**

- Public 4-year university
- Commuter campus in very large city
- 16,225 degree-seeking undergraduates: 16% part-time, 53% women, 15% African American, 5% Asian American, 3% Hispanic American, 1% international
- 3,097 degree-seeking graduate students
- 78% of applicants admitted
- SAT or ACT with writing required
- 47% graduate within 6 years

General. Founded in 1946. Regionally accredited. **Degrees:** 2,843 bachelor's awarded; master's, doctoral offered. **ROTC:** Army, Air Force. **Location:** 10 miles from downtown. **Calendar:** Semester, limited summer session. **Full-time faculty:** 859 total; 85% have terminal degrees, 18% minority, 39% women. **Part-time faculty:** 386 total; 26% have terminal degrees, 13% minority, 59% women. **Class size:** 39% < 20, 39% 20-39, 8% 40-49, 9% 50-99, 5% >100. **Special facilities:** Botanical and horticultural complex with controlled environment, 100-acre experimental ecological reserve, tropical rain forest conservatory, 46-acre wildlife refuge, 9,600-seat multipurpose student activity center.

Freshman class profile. 8,665 applied, 6,738 admitted, 2,890 enrolled.

Mid 50% test scores			
SAT verbal:	480-570	GPA 2.0-2.99:	9%
SAT math:	500-600	Rank in top quarter:	37%
ACT:	19-24	Rank in top tenth:	11%
GPA 3.50 or higher:	61%	Out-of-state:	11%
GPA 3.0-3.49:	30%	Live on campus:	75%
		International:	1%

Basis for selection. Overall performance in high school academic courses, senior year academic courses in progress, and SAT scores considered. SAT preferred, but ACT also accepted. Audition required for music; interview required for art, architecture, and music programs; portfolio required for art, architecture programs.

High school preparation. 16 units required. Required and recommended units include English 4, mathematics 4, social studies 2, history 1, science 3 (laboratory 1), foreign language 2 and academic electives 2. Foreign language units should be in same language. One social studies must be US history.

2005-2006 Annual costs. Tuition/fees: $3,551; $13,963 out-of-state. Room/board: $5,730. Books/supplies: $900. Personal expenses: $1,250.

2005-2006 Financial aid. Need-based: 2,019 full-time freshmen applied for aid; 1,391 were judged to have need; 1,309 of these received aid. Average need met was 60%. Average scholarship/grant was $4,191; average loan $2,574. 50% of total undergraduate aid awarded as scholarships/grants, 50% as loans/jobs. **Non-need-based:** Awarded to 2,957 full-time undergraduates, including 868 freshmen. Scholarships awarded for academics, athletics, leadership, music/drama.

Application procedures. Admission: Closing date 7/1 (postmark date). $50 fee, may be waived for applicants with need. Application may be submitted online. Admission notification on a rolling basis beginning on or about 11/1. Must reply by May 1 or within 2 week(s) if notified thereafter. **Financial aid:** Priority date 4/1; no closing date. FAFSA required. Applicants notified on a rolling basis starting 4/1; must reply within 3 week(s) of notification.

Academics. Special study options: Accelerated study, cooperative education, cross-registration, distance learning, double major, dual enrollment of high school students, ESL, honors, independent study, internships, study abroad, teacher certification program, Washington semester, weekend college. Wilderness exploration program. **Credit/placement by examination:** AP, CLEP, IB, institutional tests. 30 credit hours maximum toward bachelor's degree. **Support services:** Learning center, pre-admission summer program, reduced course load, study skills assistance, tutoring, writing center.

Majors. Architecture: Architecture. **Area/ethnic studies:** African-American. **Biology:** General. **Business:** Accounting, business admin, finance, international, management information systems, managerial economics, marketing, operations. **Communications:** General. **Computer sciences:** Computer science. **Education:** Art, chemistry, drama/dance, elementary, English, French, German, history, kindergarten/preschool, mathematics, mentally handicapped, middle, music, Spanish. **Engineering:** Civil, computer, electrical, mechanical. **Engineering technology:** Civil, electrical, mechanical. **English:** English lit. **Family/consumer sciences:** Family studies. **Foreign languages:** French, German, Spanish. **Health:** Athletic training, clinical lab science, nursing (RN). **History:** General. **Math:** General. **Parks/recreation:** Health/fitness. **Philosophy/religion:** Philosophy, religion. **Physical sciences:** Chemistry, geology, meteorology, physics. **Protective services:** Criminal justice, fire services admin. **Psychology:** General. **Public administration:** Social work. **Social sciences:** Anthropology, economics, geography, political science, sociology. **Visual/performing arts:** Art, dance, dramatic, music performance, studio arts.

Most popular majors. Business/marketing 26%, education 7%, engineering/engineering technologies 10%, psychology 8%, social sciences 8%.

Computing on campus. 1,500 workstations in dormitories, library, computer center, student center. Dormitories wired for high-speed internet access and linked to campus network. Commuter students can connect to campus network. Online course registration, online library, helpline, student web hosting available.

Student life. Freshman orientation: Available, $80 fee. Preregistration for classes offered. 2-day program for freshmen and parents. **Policies:** Freshmen permitted cars on campus. **Housing:** Coed dorms, single-sex dorms, special housing for disabled, apartments, fraternity/sorority housing, substance-free housing available. $100 deposit. Housing facilities designed specifically for disabled students in wheelchairs limited; apply early. Suite housing available. **Activities:** Bands, choral groups, dance, drama, literary magazine, music ensembles, musical theater, opera, student government, student newspaper, TV station, Campus Crusade for Christ, Hillel, College Democrats, College Republicans, feminist union, black student union, Latin American student organization, Muslim student association, Native American student organization, Asian student union.

Athletics. NCAA. **Intercollegiate:** Baseball M, basketball, cross-country, golf M, soccer, softball W, tennis, track and field, volleyball W. **Intramural:** Badminton, basketball, bowling, field hockey, football (non-tackle), golf, handball, lacrosse, racquetball, rugby, soccer, softball, swimming, table tennis, tennis, track and field, volleyball, water polo. **Team name:** Fortyniners.

Student services. Alcohol/substance abuse counseling, campus ministries, career counseling, student employment services, financial aid counseling, health services, minority student services, personal counseling, placement for graduates, veterans' counselor, women's services. **Physically disabled:** Services for visually, speech, hearing impaired.

Contact. E-mail: unccadm@email.uncc.edu
Phone: (704) 687-2213 Fax: (704) 687-6483
Craig Fulton, Director of Admissions, University of North Carolina at Charlotte, 9201 University City Boulevard, Charlotte, NC 28223-0001

University of North Carolina at Greensboro

Greensboro, North Carolina — **CB member**
www.uncg.edu — **CB code: 5913**

- Public 4-year university
- Residential campus in small city
- 12,172 degree-seeking undergraduates: 13% part-time, 68% women, 20% African American, 3% Asian American, 2% Hispanic American, 1% international
- 3,075 degree-seeking graduate students
- 60% of applicants admitted
- SAT or ACT with writing required
- 51% graduate within 6 years

General. Founded in 1891. Regionally accredited. **Degrees:** 2,044 bachelor's awarded; master's, doctoral offered. **ROTC:** Army, Air Force. **Location:** 90 miles from Raleigh. **Calendar:** Semester, extensive summer session. **Full-time faculty:** 778 total; 80% have terminal degrees, 13% minority, 52% women. **Part-time faculty:** 218 total; 44% have terminal degrees, 6% minority, 62% women. **Class size:** 42% <20, 41% 20-39, 6% 40-49, 9% 50-99, 2% >100. **Special facilities:** Observatory, Silva cello music collection, Randall Jarrell collection, women's studies collection.

Freshman class profile. 8,987 applied, 5,370 admitted, 2,424 enrolled.

Mid 50% test scores			
SAT verbal:	470-580	Rank in top quarter:	45%
SAT math:	470-580	Rank in top tenth:	16%
GPA 3.50 or higher:	53%	Return as sophomores:	78%
GPA 3.0-3.49:	37%	Out-of-state:	9%
GPA 2.0-2.99:	10%	Live on campus:	78%

Basis for selection. GED not accepted. Combined test scores and high school GPA based on academic courses most important. High school recommendations and activities considered. SAT preferred, but ACT accepted. Audition required for music program.

High school preparation. 16 units required. Required units include English 4, mathematics 3, social studies 1, history 1, science 3 (laboratory 1), foreign language 2 and academic electives 1. Social sciences must include 1 US history and 1 other history, economics, sociology or civics; 1 science unit must be a laboratory course. Math includes Algebra I and II and geometry.

2005-2006 Annual costs. Tuition/fees: $3,467; $14,735 out-of-state. Room/board: $5,614. Books/supplies: $1,314. Personal expenses: $1,676.

2005-2006 Financial aid. Need-based: 1,806 full-time freshmen applied for aid; 1,640 were judged to have need; 1,583 of these received aid. Average need met was 53%. Average scholarship/grant was $3,558; average loan $2,446. 40% of total undergraduate aid awarded as scholarships/grants, 60% as loans/jobs. **Non-need-based:** Awarded to 4,214 full-time undergraduates, including 1,102 freshmen. Scholarships awarded for academics, alumni affiliation, art, athletics, leadership, music/drama, state residency.

Application procedures. Admission: Closing date 3/1. $45 fee. Application must be submitted on paper. Admission notification on a rolling basis beginning on or about 3/1. Must reply by May 1 or within 4 week(s) if notified thereafter. **Financial aid:** Priority date 3/1; no closing date. FAFSA required. Applicants notified on a rolling basis starting 3/15; must reply within 3 week(s) of notification.

Academics. Special study options: Accelerated study, combined bachelor's/graduate degree, cross-registration, distance learning, double major, dual enrollment of high school students, honors, independent study, internships, liberal arts/career combination, student-designed major, study abroad, teacher certification program, Washington semester. Evening university. **Credit/placement by examination:** AP, CLEP, institutional tests. Up to 64 semester hours of any combination of transfer, correspondence, examination or other will be accepted. SAT Subject Test scores in some subjects may qualify for credit. **Support services:** Learning center, reduced course load, remedial instruction, study skills assistance, tutoring.

Majors. Area/ethnic studies: Women's. **Biology:** General, biochemistry. **Business:** Accounting, business admin, finance, hospitality admin, international, managerial economics. **Communications:** Media studies. **Computer sciences:** Computer science, networking. **Education:** Art, biology, Deaf/hearing impaired, drama/dance, early childhood, elementary, English, French, German, health, mathematics, middle, music, physical, social science, social studies, Spanish, special, speech. **English:** English lit, speech/rhetoric. **Family/consumer sciences:** Child development, clothing/textiles, family studies, institutional food production. **Foreign languages:** Classics, French, German, Italian, Spanish. **Health:** Audiology/speech pathology, clinical lab science, nursing (RN), public health ed. **History:** General. **Liberal arts:** Arts/sciences. **Math:** General. **Parks/recreation:** General, exercise sciences, facilities management. **Philosophy/religion:** Philosophy, religion. **Physical sciences:** Chemistry, physics. **Psychology:** General. **Public administration:** Social work. **Social sciences:** Anthropology, economics, geography, political science, sociology. **Visual/performing arts:** Art, dance, dramatic, interior design, jazz, music performance, music theory/composition, studio arts.

Most popular majors. Business/marketing 20%, education 11%, English 8%, family/consumer sciences 7%, health sciences 11%, social sciences 10%, visual/performing arts 11%.

Computing on campus. 600 workstations in dormitories, library, computer center, student center. Dormitories linked to campus network. Commuter students can connect to campus network. Online course registration, online library, helpline available.

Student life. Freshman orientation: Available. **Policies:** Freshmen permitted cars on campus. **Housing:** Coed dorms, single-sex dorms, special housing for disabled, apartments available. $150 nonrefundable deposit, deadline 5/1. Residential college (academic/residential program), International House available. **Activities:** Bands, choral groups, dance, drama, film society, literary magazine, music ensembles, musical theater, opera, radio station, student government, student newspaper, symphony orchestra, international student association, neo-black society, Environmental Awareness Foundation, political awareness club, Habitat for Humanity, Model United Nations Association, Rotaract Club, gay, lesbian and bisexual student association.

Athletics. NCAA. **Intercollegiate:** Baseball M, basketball, cross-country, golf, soccer, softball W, tennis, track and field, volleyball W, wrestling M. **Intramural:** Badminton, basketball, bowling, golf, racquetball, soccer, softball, swimming, table tennis, tennis, track and field, volleyball. **Team name:** Spartans.

Student services. Adult student services, career counseling, student employment services, health services, personal counseling, placement for graduates, veterans' counselor. **Physically disabled:** Services for visually, speech, hearing impaired.

Contact. E-mail: admissions@uncg.edu
Phone: (336) 334-5243 Fax: (336) 334-4180
Lise Keller, Director of Admissions, University of North Carolina at Greensboro, 123 Mossman Building, Greensboro, NC 27402-6166

University of North Carolina at Pembroke

Pembroke, North Carolina — **CB member**
www.uncp.edu — **CB code: 5534**

- Public 4-year university and liberal arts college
- Commuter campus in small town
- 4,454 degree-seeking undergraduates: 18% part-time, 63% women, 24% African American, 2% Asian American, 3% Hispanic American, 22% Native American, 1% international
- 532 degree-seeking graduate students
- 86% of applicants admitted
- SAT or ACT with writing required
- 35% graduate within 6 years

General. Founded in 1887. Regionally accredited. **Degrees:** 581 bachelor's awarded; master's offered. **ROTC:** Army, Air Force. **Location:** 35 miles from Fayetteville. **Calendar:** Semester, limited summer session. **Full-time faculty:** 251 total. **Part-time faculty:** 108 total. **Class size:** 45% < 20, 47% 20-39, 5% 40-49, 3% 50-99, less than 1% >100. **Special facilities:** Native American Resource Center, performing arts center.

Freshman class profile. 2,374 applied, 2,036 admitted, 984 enrolled.

Mid 50% test scores		**Rank in top quarter:**	30%
SAT verbal:	420-510	**Rank in top tenth:**	9%
SAT math:	430-520	**End year in good standing:**	58%
ACT:	16-20	**Return as sophomores:**	71%
GPA 3.50 or higher:	24%	**Out-of-state:**	1%
GPA 3.0-3.49:	25%	**Live on campus:**	63%
GPA 2.0-2.99:	51%	**International:**	1%

Basis for selection. High school record, class standing, GPA, test scores, and college preparatory courses important. Interview recommended for all students and required for some students.

High school preparation. College-preparatory program required. 14 units required. Required units include English 4, mathematics 3, social studies 1, history 1, science 3 (laboratory 1) and foreign language 2.

2005-2006 Annual costs. Tuition/fees: $2,980; $12,420 out-of-state. Room/board: $4,960. Books/supplies: $900. Personal expenses: $1,718.

2005-2006 Financial aid. Need-based: 839 full-time freshmen applied for aid; 690 were judged to have need; 666 of these received aid. Average need met was 56%. Average scholarship/grant was $4,144; average loan $2,552. 50% of total undergraduate aid awarded as scholarships/grants, 50% as loans/jobs. **Non-need-based:** Awarded to 214 full-time undergraduates, including 88 freshmen. Scholarships awarded for alumni affiliation.

Application procedures. Admission: Priority date 7/15; no deadline. $40 fee, may be waived for applicants with need. Application may be submitted online. Admission notification on a rolling basis beginning on or about 9/15. **Financial aid:** Closing date 3/15. FAFSA required. Applicants notified on a rolling basis starting 4/15; must reply within 2 week(s) of notification.

Academics. Certification on secondary teaching level in English, biology, mathematics, social studies, and science education. **Special study options:** Accelerated study, cooperative education, cross-registration, distance learning, double major, dual enrollment of high school students, ESL, exchange student, external degree, honors, independent study, internships, study abroad, teacher certification program, Washington semester. **Credit/placement by examination:** AP, CLEP, institutional tests. 30 credit hours maximum toward bachelor's degree. **Support services:** Learning center, pre-admission summer program, reduced course load, remedial instruction, tutoring, writing center.

Majors. Area/ethnic studies: American, Native American. **Biology:** General. **Business:** Accounting, business admin. **Communications:** Media studies. **Computer sciences:** Computer science. **Conservation:** Environmental science. **Education:** Art, biology, elementary, English, kindergarten/preschool, mathematics, middle, music, physical, science, social studies, special. **English:** English lit. **Foreign languages:** Spanish. **Health:** Athletic training, nursing (RN), public health ed. **History:** General. **Math:** General. **Parks/recreation:** Facilities management, health/fitness. **Physical sciences:** Chemistry, physics. **Protective services:** Criminal justice. **Psychology:** General. **Public administration:** Social work. **Social sciences:** Political science, sociology. **Visual/performing arts:** Dramatic, music performance, studio arts.

Most popular majors. Biology 8%, business/marketing 15%, communications/journalism 6%, education 17%, parks/recreation 7%, public administration/social services 6%, social sciences 13%.

Computing on campus. 380 workstations in dormitories, library, computer center, student center. Dormitories wired for high-speed internet access and linked to campus network. Commuter students can connect to campus network. Online course registration, online library, helpline, wireless network available.

Student life. Freshman orientation: Mandatory, $50 fee. **Policies:** Freshmen permitted cars on campus. **Housing:** Coed dorms, single-sex dorms, apartments available. $125 partly refundable deposit, deadline 5/1. Freshmen given preference for on-campus housing. Apartments available. **Activities:** Bands, choral groups, dance, drama, film society, literary magazine, music ensembles, musical theater, student government, student newspaper, TV station, Native American organization, African American student organization, Baptist student union, international student organization, Methodist campus ministry, Fellowship of Christian Athletes, campus association of social workers, American medical student association, criminal justice club.

Athletics. NCAA. **Intercollegiate:** Baseball M, basketball, cheerleading, cross-country, golf M, soccer, softball W, tennis W, track and field, volleyball W, wrestling M. **Intramural:** Basketball, bowling, golf M, racquetball, soccer M, softball, volleyball, water polo M, wrestling M. **Team name:** Braves.

Student services. Campus ministries, career counseling, student employment services, financial aid counseling, health services, personal counseling, veterans' counselor. **Physically disabled:** Services for visually, hearing impaired.

Contact. E-mail: admissons@papa.uncp.edu
Phone: (910) 521-6262 Toll-free number: (800) 949-8627
Fax: (910) 521-6497
Jackie Clark, Vice Chancellor for Enrollment Management, University of North Carolina at Pembroke, Box 1510, Pembroke, NC 28372

University of North Carolina at Wilmington

Wilmington, North Carolina — **CB member**
www.uncw.edu — **CB code: 5907**

- Public 4-year university
- Commuter campus in small city
- 10,249 degree-seeking undergraduates: 7% part-time, 58% women, 5% African American, 2% Asian American, 2% Hispanic American, 1% Native American
- 933 degree-seeking graduate students
- 61% of applicants admitted
- SAT or ACT with writing, application essay required
- 64% graduate within 6 years

General. Founded in 1947. Regionally accredited. **Degrees:** 2,206 bachelor's awarded; master's, doctoral offered. **Location:** 125 miles from Raleigh. **Calendar:** Semester, extensive summer session. **Full-time faculty:** 491 total; 87% have terminal degrees, 13% minority, 39% women. **Part-time faculty:** 217 total; 34% have terminal degrees, 6% minority, 52% women. **Class size:** 27% < 20, 57% 20-39, 8% 40-49, 6% 50-99, 1% >100. **Special facilities:** Wildlife preserve, research vessel for marine biology laboratory.

Freshman class profile. 8,820 applied, 5,377 admitted, 1,943 enrolled.

Mid 50% test scores			
SAT verbal:	520-600	GPA 2.0-2.99:	5%
SAT math:	540-610	Rank in top quarter:	60%
ACT:	21-25	Rank in top tenth:	21%
GPA 3.50 or higher:	68%	Return as sophomores:	83%
GPA 3.0-3.49:	27%	Out-of-state:	16%
		Live on campus:	85%

Basis for selection. High school record and standardized test scores most important. Class rank also important, as well as courses completed in high school, academic level of courses and grades received. SAT preferred, ACT also accepted.

High school preparation. College-preparatory program required. Required units include English 4, mathematics 3, social studies 2, history 1, science 3 (laboratory 1), foreign language 2 and academic electives 5.

2005-2006 Annual costs. Tuition/fees: $3,695; $13,630 out-of-state. Room/board: $6,412. Books/supplies: $1,000. Personal expenses: $700.

2005-2006 Financial aid. Need-based: 1,047 full-time freshmen applied for aid; 578 were judged to have need; 578 of these received aid. Average need met was 89%. Average scholarship/grant was $3,761; average loan $2,836. 48% of total undergraduate aid awarded as scholarships/grants, 52% as loans/jobs. **Non-need-based:** Awarded to 397 full-time undergraduates, including 64 freshmen. Scholarships awarded for academics, alumni affiliation, art, athletics, leadership, music/drama, state residency.

Application procedures. Admission: Priority date 11/1; deadline 2/1 (postmark date). $45 fee, may be waived for applicants with need. Application must be submitted on paper. Admission notification 4/1. Must reply by May 1 or within 4 week(s) if notified thereafter. **Financial aid:** Priority date 3/15; no closing date. FAFSA, institutional form required. Applicants notified on a rolling basis starting 4/1; must reply within 3 week(s) of notification.

Academics. Special study options: Accelerated study, cooperative education, distance learning, double major, ESL, exchange student, honors, independent study, internships, study abroad, teacher certification program. 2+2 engineering programs. **Credit/placement by examination:** AP, CLEP, institutional tests. **Support services:** Learning center, reduced course load, remedial instruction, tutoring, writing center.

Majors. Biology: General, marine. **Business:** Accounting, business admin, finance, management information systems, managerial economics, marketing. **Computer sciences:** Computer science. **Conservation:** Environmental science, environmental studies. **Education:** Biology, chemistry, elementary, emotionally handicapped, English, French, history, kindergarten/preschool, learning disabled, mathematics, mentally handicapped, middle, music, physical, physics, Spanish. **English:** Creative writing, English lit, speech/rhetoric. **Foreign languages:** French, Spanish. **Health:** Athletic training, clinical lab science, nursing (RN), recreational therapy. **History:** General. **Math:** General, statistics. **Parks/recreation:** Facilities management, health/fitness. **Philosophy/religion:** Philosophy, religion. **Physical sciences:** Chemistry, geology, physics. **Protective services:** Criminal justice. **Psychology:** General. **Public administration:** Social work. **Social sciences:** Anthropology, economics, geography, political science, sociology. **Visual/performing arts:** Art history/conservation, cinematography, dramatic, music performance, studio arts.

Most popular majors. Biology 9%, business/marketing 24%, communications/journalism 7%, education 10%, English 6%, health sciences 7%, psychology 7%, social sciences 11%.

Computing on campus. 804 workstations in dormitories, library, computer center, student center. Dormitories wired for high-speed internet access and linked to campus network. Commuter students can connect to campus network. Online course registration, online library, helpline, repair service, student web hosting, wireless network available.

Student life. Freshman orientation: Mandatory, $80 fee. Preregistration for classes offered. **Policies:** Freshmen permitted cars on campus. **Housing:** Coed dorms, single-sex dorms, apartments, substance-free housing available. $100 nonrefundable deposit. Honors housing. **Activities:** Bands, choral groups, dance, drama, film society, literary magazine, music ensembles, musical theater, opera, radio station, student government, student newspaper, symphony orchestra, TV station, Baptist student union, black student alliance, College Republicans, Fellowship of Christian University Students, Global Serve, Alpha Phi Omega, Young Democrats, Newman Catholic Student Center, African American-Hispanic-Asian-Native American organizations.

Athletics. NCAA. **Intercollegiate:** Baseball M, basketball, cheerleading, cross-country, diving, golf, soccer, softball W, swimming, tennis, track and field, volleyball W. **Intramural:** Badminton, basketball, cross-country, football (non-tackle), golf, soccer, softball, table tennis, volleyball. **Team name:** Seahawks.

Student services. Adult student services, alcohol/substance abuse counseling, campus ministries, career counseling, student employment services, financial aid counseling, health services, minority student services, personal counseling, placement for graduates, veterans' counselor. **Physically disabled:** Services for visually, speech, hearing impaired.

Contact. E-mail: admissions@uncw.edu
Phone: (910) 962-3243 Toll-free number: (800) 228-5571
Fax: (910) 962-3038
University of North Carolina at Wilmington, 601 South College Road, Wilmington, NC 28403-5904

Wake Forest University

Winston-Salem, North Carolina — **CB member**
www.wfu.edu — **CB code: 5885**

- Private 4-year university
- Residential campus in small city
- 4,231 degree-seeking undergraduates: 3% part-time, 51% women, 7% African American, 4% Asian American, 2% Hispanic American, 1% international
- 2,371 degree-seeking graduate students
- 39% of applicants admitted
- SAT or ACT with writing, application essay required
- 88% graduate within 6 years; 12% enter graduate study

General. Founded in 1834. Regionally accredited. Each first-year student receives an IBM ThinkPad computer and a printer, which the student keeps upon graduation. **Degrees:** 953 bachelor's awarded; master's, doctoral, first professional offered. **ROTC:** Army. **Location:** 4 miles from downtown. **Calendar:** Semester, limited summer session. **Full-time faculty:** 450 total; 90% have terminal degrees, 34% women. **Part-time faculty:** 98 total; 67% have terminal degrees, 54% women. **Class size:** 59% < 20, 35% 20-39, 4% 40-49, 3% 50-99. **Special facilities:** Anthropology museum, archaeology laboratory, laser physics laboratory, center for nanotechnology and molecular materials, biomechanics laboratory, laser and electron microscopes.

Freshman class profile. 7,484 applied, 2,882 admitted, 1,120 enrolled.

Mid 50% test scores		Rank in top tenth:	65%
SAT verbal:	620-700	Return as sophomores:	93%
SAT math:	640-710	Out-of-state:	72%
Rank in top quarter:	94%	International:	1%

Basis for selection. High school curriculum and achievement, test scores, school and community activities, essay, personal recommendations, special talents all important. Audition recommended for those competing for a Presidential scholarship (for students with special talents in music, theater, art, dance, and debate).

High school preparation. 16 units required; 20 recommended. Required and recommended units include English 4, mathematics 3-4, social studies 2-4, science 1-4 and foreign language 2-4.

2006-2007 Annual costs. Tuition/fees: $32,140. Tuition covers cost of an IBM Thinkpad computer and inkjet printer for freshmen. Room/board: $8,800. Books/supplies: $800. Personal expenses: $1,200.

2005-2006 Financial aid. Need-based: 585 full-time freshmen applied for aid; 421 were judged to have need; 418 of these received aid. Average need met was 90%. Average scholarship/grant was $17,826; average loan $5,404. 63% of total undergraduate aid awarded as scholarships/grants, 37% as loans/jobs. **Non-need-based:** Awarded to 1,645 full-time undergraduates, including 521 freshmen. Scholarships awarded for academics, alumni affiliation, art, athletics, leadership, music/drama, religious affiliation, ROTC, state residency.

Application procedures. Admission: Closing date 1/15 (receipt date). $40 fee, may be waived for applicants with need. Application may be submitted online. Admission notification 4/1. Must reply by 5/1. **Financial aid:** Priority date 2/1, closing date 3/1. FAFSA, CSS PROFILE required. Applicants notified by 4/1; must reply by 5/1 or within 4 week(s) of notification.

Academics. Language courses at all levels in Russian, Greek, Italian, Hebrew; elementary and intermediate courses in Chinese, Japanese; elementary courses in Hindi, Portuguese. **Special study options:** Combined bachelor's/graduate degree, cross-registration, double major, dual enrollment of high school students, exchange student, honors, independent study, internships, liberal arts/career combination, study abroad, teacher certification program, Washington semester. Semester in London, Venice, or Vienna and semester at universities in Dijon, Salamanca, Berlin, Moscow, Beijing, and Japan. **Credit/placement by examination:** AP, CLEP, IB, institutional tests. **Support services:** Learning center, reduced course load, study skills assistance, tutoring, writing center.

Majors. Biology: General, bacteriology. **Business:** General, accounting, finance, management science. **Communications:** General. **Computer sciences:** Computer science. **Conservation:** Forestry. **Education:** Elementary, social studies. **English:** English lit. **Foreign languages:** Ancient Greek, classics, East Asian, French, German, Latin, Russian, Spanish. **Health:** Clinical lab science. **History:** General. **Math:** General. **Parks/recreation:** Exercise sciences. **Philosophy/religion:** Philosophy, religion. **Physical sciences:** Chemistry, physics. **Psychology:** General. **Social sciences:** Anthropology, econometrics, economics, political science, sociology. **Visual/performing arts:** Art history/conservation, dramatic, music history, music performance, studio arts.

Most popular majors. Biology 7%, business/marketing 17%, communications/journalism 10%, English 7%, psychology 8%, social sciences 22%.

Computing on campus. 150 workstations in library, computer center. Dormitories wired for high-speed internet access and linked to campus network. Commuter students can connect to campus network. Online course registration, online library, helpline, repair service, student web hosting, wireless network available.

Student life. Freshman orientation: Mandatory. Preregistration for classes offered. Six days before Fall classes start. **Policies:** First- and second-year students with residential status required to live on campus. Freshmen permitted cars on campus. **Housing:** Guaranteed on-campus for all undergraduates. Coed dorms, special housing for disabled, apartments, fraternity/sorority housing, substance-free housing available. Theme housing. **Activities:** Bands, choral groups, dance, drama, film society, literary magazine, music ensembles, radio station, student government, student newspaper, symphony orchestra, TV station, black student alliance, College Democrats, College Republicans, Alpha Phi Omega, international club, InterVarsity Christian Fellowship, other interdenominational and denominational groups, Amnesty International, Habitat for Humanity, Volunteer Service Corps.

Athletics. NCAA. **Intercollegiate:** Baseball M, basketball, cheerleading, cross-country, field hockey W, football (tackle) M, golf, soccer, tennis, track and field, volleyball W. **Intramural:** Basketball, bowling, cross-country, diving, equestrian W, football (non-tackle), golf, racquetball, soccer, softball, table tennis, tennis, volleyball, water polo, wrestling M. **Team name:** Demon Deacons.

Student services. Alcohol/substance abuse counseling, campus ministries, career counseling, student employment services, financial aid counseling, health services, minority student services, personal counseling, placement for graduates. **Physically disabled:** Services for visually, speech, hearing impaired.

Contact. E-mail: admissions@wfu.edu
Phone: (336) 758-5201 Fax: (336) 758-4324
Martha Allman, Director of Admissions, Wake Forest University, PO Box 7305 Reynolda Station, Winston-Salem, NC 27109

Warren Wilson College

Asheville, North Carolina — **CB member**
www.warren-wilson.edu — **CB code: 5886**

- Private 4-year liberal arts college affiliated with Presbyterian Church (USA)
- Residential campus in small city
- 823 degree-seeking undergraduates: 1% part-time, 61% women, 1% African American, 1% Asian American, 2% Hispanic American, 3% international
- 75 degree-seeking graduate students
- 78% of applicants admitted
- SAT or ACT (ACT writing optional), application essay required
- 48% graduate within 6 years

General. Founded in 1894. Regionally accredited. **Degrees:** 153 bachelor's awarded; master's offered. **Location:** One mile from Asheville. **Calendar:** 4 consecutive 8-week terms. **Full-time faculty:** 62 total; 92% have terminal degrees, 10% minority, 47% women. **Part-time faculty:** 34 total; 41% have terminal degrees, 56% women. **Class size:** 83% < 20, 17% 20-39. **Special facilities:** 300-acre college farm, archaeological site, climbing wall, adventure challenge course, hiking trails.

Freshman class profile. 852 applied, 664 admitted, 245 enrolled.

Mid 50% test scores		Rank in top tenth:	13%
SAT verbal:	570-670	Return as sophomores:	70%
SAT math:	510-620	Out-of-state:	82%
ACT:	22-28	Live on campus:	99%
Rank in top quarter:	35%		

Basis for selection. In order of importance: high school achievement, class rank, personal statement, recommendations, test scores, school and community activities. All records of examinations taken overseas plus TOEFL required of foreign applicants. Interview, portfolio recommended. **Homeschooled:** Submit transcript listing course titles and content, partial portfolio of sample work completed (graded papers), document that serves as diploma, copy of state rules under which school was formed or is recognized.

High school preparation. Required and recommended units include English 4, mathematics 3, history 3, science 2 (laboratory 2) and foreign language 2. Math requirement includes algebra I, II and geometry. Sciences must include 2 laboratories.

2006-2007 Annual costs. Tuition/fees (projected): $20,126. All resident students required to work 15 hours per week in college's work program. $2,472 earnings credited toward tuition costs. Room/board: $6,000. Books/supplies: $700. Personal expenses: $775.

2005-2006 Financial aid. Need-based: Average need met was 69%. Average scholarship/grant was $8,805; average loan $2,581. 58% of total undergraduate aid awarded as scholarships/grants, 42% as loans/jobs. **Non-need-based:** Scholarships awarded for academics, art, job skills, leadership, religious affiliation, state residency.

Application procedures. Admission: Priority date 1/15; deadline 3/15 (receipt date). No application fee. Application may be submitted online. Admission notification on a rolling basis beginning on or about 2/1. Must reply by 5/1. **Financial aid:** Priority date 4/1; no closing date. FAFSA, institutional form required. Applicants notified on a rolling basis starting 3/1; must reply within 3 week(s) of notification.

Academics. Special study options: Cross-registration, double major, dual enrollment of high school students, ESL, exchange student, honors, independent study, internships, liberal arts/career combination, student-designed major, study abroad, teacher certification program, Washington semester. **Credit/placement by examination:** AP, CLEP, institutional tests. **Support services:** Reduced course load, study skills assistance, tutoring, writing center.

Majors. Biology: General. **Business:** Business admin. **Conservation:** General. **Education:** General, early childhood, elementary, middle, secondary.

Foreign languages: General. **Health:** Premedicine, preveterinary. **History:** General. **Liberal arts:** Arts/sciences. **Math:** General. **Parks/recreation:** General. **Philosophy/religion:** Philosophy, religion. **Physical sciences:** Chemistry. **Psychology:** General. **Public administration:** Social work. **Social sciences:** Anthropology, economics, political science, sociology. **Visual/performing arts:** Art.

Computing on campus. 91 workstations in library, computer center, student center. Dormitories wired for high-speed internet access and linked to campus network. Commuter students can connect to campus network. Online course registration, online library, helpline, wireless network available.

Student life. **Freshman orientation:** Mandatory, $200 fee. 7-day orientation (late August) includes full day community service, dinner/discussion with faculty. **Policies:** Triad program requires students to work 15 hours/week at an on-campus job and do 100 hours community service by graduation, in addition to academics. **Housing:** Guaranteed on-campus for all undergraduates. Coed dorms, single-sex dorms, apartments, cooperative housing, substance-free housing available. **Activities:** Jazz band, choral groups, dance, drama, literary magazine, music ensembles, musical theater, student government, student newspaper, Amnesty International, Emmaus (Christian student group), Interfaith, Jewish student group, Buddhist experience, international student organization, earth first, sustainable living, literary magazine.

Athletics. USCAA. **Intercollegiate:** Basketball, cross-country, soccer, swimming. **Intramural:** Basketball, football (non-tackle), soccer, table tennis, tennis, triathlon, volleyball. **Team name:** Owls.

Student services. Alcohol/substance abuse counseling, campus ministries, career counseling, student employment services, financial aid counseling, health services, minority student services, personal counseling, placement for graduates.

Contact. E-mail: admit@warren-wilson.edu
Phone: (828) 771-2073 Toll-free number: (800) 934-3536
Fax: (828) 298-1440
Richard Blomgren, Dean of Admission, Warren Wilson College, Office of Admission, Asheville, NC 28815-9000

Western Carolina University

Cullowhee, North Carolina — **CB member**
www.wcu.edu — **CB code: 5897**

- Public 4-year university
- Residential campus in small town
- 6,889 degree-seeking undergraduates: 13% part-time, 52% women, 5% African American, 1% Asian American, 1% Hispanic American, 2% Native American, 3% international
- 1,437 degree-seeking graduate students
- 75% of applicants admitted
- SAT or ACT with writing required

General. Founded in 1889. Regionally accredited. **Degrees:** 1,200 bachelor's awarded; master's, doctoral offered. **Location:** 55 miles from Asheville, 140 miles from Atlanta. **Calendar:** Semester, extensive summer session. **Full-time faculty:** 374 total; 80% have terminal degrees, 5% minority, 43% women. **Part-time faculty:** 234 total; 31% have terminal degrees, 52% women. **Class size:** 35% < 20, 58% 20-39, 6% 40-49, less than 1% 50-99, less than 1% >100. **Special facilities:** Applied technology center, fine and performing arts center, collection of historical Native American artifacts and documents, center for advancement of teaching, public policy institute.

Freshman class profile. 4,964 applied, 3,705 admitted, 1,557 enrolled.

Mid 50% test scores			
SAT verbal:	460-550	GPA 2.0-2.99:	36%
SAT math:	470-560	Rank in top quarter:	27%
ACT:	18-22	Rank in top tenth:	8%
GPA 3.50 or higher:	36%	Out-of-state:	7%
GPA 3.0-3.49:	28%	Live on campus:	96%

Basis for selection. Secondary school record, test scores, class rank most important; recommendations, extracurricular activities, special talents and abilities, volunteer efforts, and paid work experiences considered. All applicants, except those exempted by current campus policies, must submit standardized test scores. SAT preferred, ACT also accepted. Essays not required but will be considered if submitted. Auditions required for music programs and portfolios recommended for art programs. **Homeschooled:** Must submit official transcript of all work completed and meet standards equivalent to those used for applicants from approved secondary schools.

High school preparation. College-preparatory program required. 20 units required; 24 recommended. Required and recommended units include English 4, mathematics 3, social studies 2, history 1, science 3 (laboratory 3), foreign language 2 and academic electives 5-7.

2005-2006 Annual costs. Tuition/fees: $3,624; $13,060 out-of-state. Room/board: $4,900.

2004-2005 Financial aid. **Need-based:** 1,066 full-time freshmen applied for aid; 702 were judged to have need; 696 of these received aid. Average need met was 78%. Average scholarship/grant was $3,523; average loan $2,603. 43% of total undergraduate aid awarded as scholarships/grants, 57% as loans/jobs. **Non-need-based:** Awarded to 939 full-time undergraduates, including 269 freshmen. Scholarships awarded for academics, art, athletics, leadership, music/drama, state residency.

Application procedures. **Admission:** Priority date 2/1; deadline 8/1 (postmark date). $40 fee, may be waived for applicants with need. Application may be submitted online. Admission notification on a rolling basis beginning on or about 1/30. Must reply by 8/1. Housing deposit due upon receipt of student's acceptance. **Financial aid:** Priority date 3/31; no closing date. FAFSA, institutional form required. Applicants notified on a rolling basis starting 4/1.

Academics. **Special study options:** Accelerated study, cooperative education, distance learning, double major, dual enrollment of high school students, ESL, exchange student, honors, independent study, internships, student-designed major, study abroad, teacher certification program. **Credit/placement by examination:** AP, CLEP, IB, institutional tests. 45 credit hours maximum toward bachelor's degree. **Support services:** Learning center, reduced course load, study skills assistance, tutoring, writing center.

Honors college/program. First-year students who have at least one of the following are invited: 3.75 GPA in high school, top 10% of high school class, 1200 score on the SAT (exclusive of Writing), or 30 score on the ACT.

Majors. **Biology:** General. **Business:** Accounting, business admin, finance, hospitality admin, international, management information systems, marketing. **Communications:** General. **Computer sciences:** Computer science. **Conservation:** Environmental science, management/policy. **Education:** Art, elementary, English, German, kindergarten/preschool, mathematics, middle, music, physical, science, social studies, Spanish, special. **Engineering:** Electrical. **Engineering technology:** Construction, electrical, manufacturing. **English:** English lit. **Foreign languages:** German, Spanish. **Health:** Clinical lab science, communication disorders, dietetics, EMT paramedic, environmental health, medical records admin, nursing (RN), recreational therapy. **History:** General. **Liberal arts:** Arts/sciences. **Math:** General. **Parks/recreation:** Facilities management, sports admin. **Philosophy/religion:** Philosophy. **Physical sciences:** Chemistry, geology. **Protective services:** Criminal justice. **Psychology:** General. **Public administration:** General, social work. **Social sciences:** General, anthropology, geography, political science, sociology. **Visual/performing arts:** Art, dramatic, interior design, music performance, studio arts.

Most popular majors. Business/marketing 24%, education 15%, health sciences 11%, security/protective services 8%.

Computing on campus. PC or laptop required. 723 workstations in dormitories, library, computer center, student center. Dormitories wired for high-speed internet access and linked to campus network. Commuter students can connect to campus network. Online course registration, online library, helpline, repair service, student web hosting, wireless network available.

Student life. **Freshman orientation:** Mandatory, $115 fee. Preregistration for classes offered. Six 2-day orientations held in June. **Policies:** Freshmen permitted cars on campus. **Housing:** Guaranteed on-campus for freshmen. Coed dorms, single-sex dorms, special housing for disabled, apartments, fraternity/sorority housing, substance-free housing available. $100 partly refundable deposit, deadline 6/1. **Activities:** Bands, choral groups, dance, drama, film society, literary magazine, music ensembles, musical theater, radio station, student government, student newspaper, TV station, Black Students Association, forensics, College Democrats, College Republicans, international student organization, Fellowship of Christian Athletes, Interfaith Council, WCU Inspirational Choir, Black Theatre Ensemble, Project CARE.

Athletics. NCAA. **Intercollegiate:** Baseball M, basketball, cheerleading, cross-country, football (tackle) M, golf, soccer W, softball W, tennis W, track and field, volleyball W. **Intramural:** Badminton, basketball, bowling, cross-country, football (non-tackle), football (tackle), handball, racquetball, rugby, soccer, softball, swimming, table tennis, tennis, track and field, volleyball, water polo, weight lifting, wrestling M. **Team name:** Catamounts.

Student services. Alcohol/substance abuse counseling, campus ministries, career counseling, student employment services, financial aid counseling, health services, minority student services, on-campus daycare, personal counseling, placement for graduates, veterans' counselor, women's services. **Physically disabled:** Services for visually, speech, hearing impaired.

Contact. E-mail: admiss@email.wcu.edu
Phone: (828) 227-7317 Toll-free number: (877) 928-4968
Fax: (828) 227-7319
Philip Cauley, Director of Admissions, Western Carolina University, 242 HFR Administration Bldg, Cullowhee, NC 28723

Wingate University

Wingate, North Carolina — **CB member**
www.wingate.edu — **CB code: 5908**

- Private 4-year liberal arts college affiliated with Baptist faith
- Residential campus in small town
- 1,332 degree-seeking undergraduates: 2% part-time, 52% women, 11% African American, 1% Asian American, 1% Hispanic American, 1% Native American, 3% international
- 291 degree-seeking graduate students
- 84% of applicants admitted
- SAT or ACT (ACT writing optional) required
- 51% graduate within 6 years; 20% enter graduate study

General. Founded in 1896. Regionally accredited. Undergraduate degree completion program for adults offered in nearby Matthews. **Degrees:** 247 bachelor's awarded; master's, first professional offered. **ROTC:** Army, Air Force. **Location:** 25 miles from Charlotte. **Calendar:** Semester, limited summer session. **Full-time faculty:** 99 total; 94% have terminal degrees, 6% minority, 40% women. **Part-time faculty:** 53 total; 42% have terminal degrees, 8% minority, 36% women. **Class size:** 50% < 20, 49% 20-39, less than 1% 40-49, less than 1% 50-99. **Special facilities:** Outdoor recreation laboratory, 11-acre lake, performing arts center.

Freshman class profile. 1,247 applied, 1,050 admitted, 371 enrolled.

Mid 50% test scores		**Rank in top quarter:**	41%
SAT verbal:	450-560	**Rank in top tenth:**	19%
SAT math:	460-580	**End year in good standing:**	89%
ACT:	18-24	**Return as sophomores:**	72%
GPA 3.50 or higher:	47%	**Out-of-state:**	45%
GPA 3.0-3.49:	23%	**Live on campus:**	93%
GPA 2.0-2.99:	29%	**International:**	2%

Basis for selection. Decisions based on secondary school record (course selection, GPA, class rank) and test scores. Interview recommended for all students; portfolio recommended for art majors; audition required for music majors.

High school preparation. College-preparatory program recommended. 13 units recommended. Recommended units include English 4, mathematics 3, social studies 2, science 2 (laboratory 1) and foreign language 2.

2005-2006 Annual costs. Tuition/fees: $16,850. Room/board: $6,450. Books/supplies: $800. Personal expenses: $900.

2004-2005 Financial aid. Need-based: Average need met was 77%. Average scholarship/grant was $3,021; average loan $2,538. 39% of total undergraduate aid awarded as scholarships/grants, 61% as loans/jobs. **Non-need-based:** Scholarships awarded for academics, alumni affiliation, art, athletics, leadership, music/drama, religious affiliation, state residency. **Additional information:** Tuition payment plans available with no interest charges for $50 per year enrollment fee. Institutional aid may not be available after June 1.

Application procedures. Admission: Priority date 4/1; no deadline. $30 fee, may be waived for applicants with need. Application may be submitted online. Admission notification on a rolling basis beginning on or about 9/15. Must reply by May 1 or within 4 week(s) if notified thereafter. **Financial aid:** Priority date 5/1; no closing date. FAFSA required. Applicants notified on a rolling basis starting 3/1; must reply within 2 week(s) of notification.

Academics. Special study options: Combined bachelor's/graduate degree, cross-registration, double major, dual enrollment of high school students, honors, independent study, internships, study abroad, teacher certification program. **Credit/placement by examination:** AP, CLEP, IB, SAT, ACT, institutional tests. 30 credit hours maximum toward bachelor's degree. **Support services:** Learning center, reduced course load, study skills assistance, tutoring.

Majors. Area/ethnic studies: American. **Biology:** General, environmental. **Business:** Accounting, business admin, finance, marketing. **Communications:** General, broadcast journalism, journalism, public relations. **Computer sciences:** Computer science. **Education:** Art, biology, elementary, English, mathematics, middle, music, physical, reading, social studies, Spanish. **English:** English lit. **Foreign languages:** Spanish. **Health:** Athletic training, predentistry, premedicine, prepharmacy, preveterinary. **History:** General. **Interdisciplinary:** Math/computer science. **Legal studies:** Prelaw. **Liberal arts:** Arts/sciences. **Math:** General. **Parks/recreation:** Facilities management, sports admin. **Philosophy/religion:** Philosophy, religion. **Physical sciences:** Chemistry. **Psychology:** General. **Public administration:** Human services. **Social sciences:** Sociology. **Visual/performing arts:** Art, music management, music performance, piano/organ, studio arts, voice/opera.

Most popular majors. Biology 9%, business/marketing 20%, communications/journalism 21%, education 11%, liberal arts 7%, parks/recreation 10%, psychology 6%.

Computing on campus. 75 workstations in library, computer center, student center. Dormitories wired for high-speed internet access. Commuter students can connect to campus network.

Student life. Freshman orientation: Mandatory. Preregistration for classes offered. Begins 4 days before classes. **Policies:** Freshmen permitted cars on campus. **Housing:** Guaranteed on-campus for freshmen. Single-sex dorms, special housing for disabled, apartments, fraternity/sorority housing available. $300 partly refundable deposit. **Activities:** Bands, choral groups, drama, literary magazine, music ensembles, student government, student newspaper, TV station, Christian student union, minority student association, activities programming board, university and community assistance network, College Republicans, College Democrats.

Athletics. NCAA. **Intercollegiate:** Baseball M, basketball, cross-country, football (tackle) M, golf, lacrosse M, soccer, softball W, swimming, tennis, volleyball W. **Intramural:** Basketball, bowling, diving, football (tackle) M, golf, racquetball, soccer, softball, swimming, table tennis, tennis, volleyball, water polo. **Team name:** Bulldogs.

Student services. Campus ministries, career counseling, student employment services, health services, minority student services, personal counseling, placement for graduates.

Contact. E-mail: admit@wingate.edu
Phone: (704) 233-8200 Toll-free number: (800) 755-5550
Fax: (704) 233-8110
Thomas Brown, Dean of Enrollment Management, Wingate University, Campus Box 3059, Wingate, NC 28174-0157

Winston-Salem Bible College

Winston-Salem, North Carolina
www.wsbc.edu

- Private 4-year Bible college
- Residential campus
- 48 degree-seeking undergraduates

General. Accredited by ABHE. **Degrees:** 1 bachelor's, 4 associate awarded. **Full-time faculty:** 4 total. **Part-time faculty:** 12 total.

2006-2007 Annual costs. Tuition/fees: $2,430.

Application procedures. Admission: No deadline. $50 fee. Admission notification on a rolling basis. **Financial aid:** No deadline.

Academics. Credit/placement by examination: CLEP.

Student life. Freshman orientation: Available.

Contact. Phone: (336) 744-0900
Winston-Salem Bible College, Box 777, Winston-Salem, NC 27102

Winston-Salem State University

Winston-Salem, North Carolina — **CB member**
www.wssu.edu — **CB code: 5909**

- Public 4-year university and health science college
- Commuter campus in small city
- 5,128 degree-seeking undergraduates: 10% part-time, 70% women, 85% African American, 1% Asian American, 1% Hispanic American
- 263 degree-seeking graduate students
- 79% of applicants admitted
- SAT or ACT with writing required
- 44% graduate within 6 years

General. Founded in 1892. Regionally accredited. **Degrees:** 543 bachelor's awarded; master's offered. **ROTC:** Army. **Location:** 28 miles from Greensboro, 75 miles from Charlotte. **Calendar:** Semester, limited summer session. **Full-time faculty:** 234 total; 62% have terminal degrees, 67% minority, 50% women. **Part-time faculty:** 153 total; 22% have terminal degrees, 52% minority, 61% women. **Class size:** 42% < 20, 50% 20-39, 6% 40-49, 2% 50-99.

Freshman class profile. 2,889 applied, 2,286 admitted, 1,083 enrolled.

Mid 50% test scores			
SAT verbal:	400-480	Rank in top quarter:	19%
SAT math:	400-490	Rank in top tenth:	4%
ACT:	16-19	Out-of-state:	12%
		Live on campus:	82%

Basis for selection. Admissions based on secondary school record, class rank, and standardized tests scores. Extracurricular activities also important. SAT preferred. Interview recommended for all students; audition required for music program.

High school preparation. 15 units required. Required units include English 4, mathematics 4, social studies 1, history 1, science 3 and foreign language 2. Mathematics units must include or exceed algebra I, geometry and algebra II.

2005-2006 Annual costs. Tuition/fees: $2,804; $11,444 out-of-state. Room/board: $5,278. Personal expenses: $2,100.

2004-2005 Financial aid. Need-based: 761 full-time freshmen applied for aid; 744 were judged to have need; 699 of these received aid. Average need met was 71%. Average scholarship/grant was $2,878; average loan $2,499. 50% of total undergraduate aid awarded as scholarships/grants, 50% as loans/jobs. **Non-need-based:** Awarded to 423 full-time undergraduates, including 129 freshmen. Scholarships awarded for academics, athletics, ROTC, state residency.

Application procedures. Admission: Priority date 5/1; deadline 7/15. $30 fee, may be waived for applicants with need. Application may be submitted online. Admission notification on a rolling basis. **Financial aid:** Priority date 4/1, closing date 5/1. FAFSA required. Applicants notified by 5/15; must reply within 2 week(s) of notification.

Academics. Special study options: Accelerated study, cross-registration, distance learning, double major, ESL, honors, independent study, internships, liberal arts/career combination, study abroad, teacher certification program, Washington semester, weekend college. **Credit/placement by examination:** AP, CLEP, institutional tests. 36 credit hours maximum toward bachelor's degree. **Support services:** Learning center, reduced course load, remedial instruction, study skills assistance, tutoring.

Majors. Biology: General, biotechnology, molecular. **Business:** Accounting, business admin, managerial economics. **Communications:** Media studies. **Computer sciences:** Computer science, information technology. **Education:** Art, early childhood, elementary, English, mathematics, middle, music, physical, social studies, Spanish, special. **English:** English lit. **Foreign languages:** Spanish. **Health:** Clinical lab science, nursing (RN), recreational therapy, vocational rehab counseling. **History:** General. **Interdisciplinary:** Gerontology. **Liberal arts:** Arts/sciences. **Math:** General. **Parks/recreation:** Exercise sciences, sports admin. **Physical sciences:** Chemistry. **Protective services:** Criminal justice. **Psychology:** General. **Public administration:** Social work. **Social sciences:** Political science, sociology. **Visual/performing arts:** Art, music management.

Computing on campus. PC or laptop required. 500 workstations in dormitories, library, computer center, student center. Dormitories wired for high-speed internet access and linked to campus network. Commuter students can connect to campus network. Online course registration, online library, wireless network available.

Student life. Freshman orientation: Available, $100 fee. Preregistration for classes offered. Held on a summer weekend. **Housing:** Coed dorms, single-sex dorms available. $75 deposit. **Activities:** Bands, dance, drama, radio station, student government, student newspaper, TV station, student religious council.

Athletics. NCAA. **Intercollegiate:** Basketball, bowling W, cheerleading W, cross-country, football (tackle) M, golf M, softball W, tennis, track and field, volleyball W. **Intramural:** Basketball M. **Team name:** Rams.

Student services. Adult student services, career counseling, student employment services, financial aid counseling, health services, personal counseling, veterans' counselor. **Physically disabled:** Services for visually impaired.

Contact. E-mail: admissions@wssu.edu
Phone: (336) 750-2070 Toll-free number: (800) 257-4052
Fax: (336) 750-2079
X. Allen, Director of Admissions, Winston-Salem State University, 601 Martin Luther King Jr Drive, Winston-Salem, NC 27110

North Dakota

Dickinson State University
Dickinson, North Dakota
www.dsu.nodak.edu **CB code: 6477**

- Public 4-year university
- Residential campus in large town
- 2,516 degree-seeking undergraduates: 30% part-time, 58% women, 2% African American, 1% Asian American, 2% Hispanic American, 2% Native American, 6% international
- 33% graduate within 6 years

General. Founded in 1918. Regionally accredited. **Degrees:** 329 bachelor's, 72 associate awarded. **Location:** 100 miles from Bismarck, 300 miles from Billings, Montana. **Calendar:** Semester, limited summer session. **Full-time faculty:** 93 total. **Part-time faculty:** 112 total. **Special facilities:** Nature preserve.

Freshman class profile. 555 applied, 544 admitted, 376 enrolled.

Mid 50% test scores			
SAT verbal:	430-530	Rank in top quarter:	15%
SAT math:	470-590	Rank in top tenth:	5%
ACT:	18-23	Out-of-state:	38%
		International:	9%

Basis for selection. Open admission, but selective for some programs. Minimum 20 ACT composite or minimum 2.0 GPA required for nursing program.

High school preparation. College-preparatory program recommended. 13 units recommended. Recommended units include English 4, mathematics 3, social studies 3 and science 3. One algebra, 1 chemistry required for nursing program.

2005-2006 Annual costs. Tuition/fees: $4,154; $9,713 out-of-state. Tuition for Minnesota residents: $3,630. Tuition for South Dakota, Montana, Manitoba, Saskatchewan residents: $4,160. Room/board: $3,694. Books/supplies: $800. Personal expenses: $1,325.

2005-2006 Financial aid. **Need-based:** 25% of total undergraduate aid awarded as scholarships/grants, 75% as loans/jobs. **Non-need-based:** Scholarships awarded for academics, alumni affiliation, art, athletics, job skills, leadership, minority status, music/drama, religious affiliation, state residency. **Additional information:** Scholarships available to new students, priority deadline December 1.

Application procedures. **Admission:** No deadline. $35 fee. Application may be submitted online. Admission notification on a rolling basis. **Financial aid:** Priority date 3/15; no closing date. FAFSA required. Must reply within 2 week(s) of notification.

Academics. Limited evening classes available. **Special study options:** Accelerated study, combined bachelor's/graduate degree, cooperative education, distance learning, double major, dual enrollment of high school students, ESL, honors, independent study, internships, liberal arts/career combination, student-designed major, study abroad, teacher certification program. **Credit/placement by examination:** AP, CLEP, institutional tests. 8 credit hours maximum toward associate degree, 15 toward bachelor's. **Support services:** Learning center, remedial instruction, study skills assistance, tutoring.

Majors. **Agriculture:** Business. **Biology:** General. **Business:** General, accounting, administrative services, business admin, finance, management information systems, office management. **Communications:** General. **Computer sciences:** Computer science. **Education:** Art, biology, business, chemistry, computer, drama/dance, early childhood, elementary, English, foreign languages, health, history, mathematics, middle, music, physical, reading, science, secondary, social science, Spanish, speech. **English:** Creative writing. **Foreign languages:** Spanish. **Health:** Nursing (RN), predentistry, premedicine, preveterinary. **History:** General. **Interdisciplinary:** Behavioral sciences, natural sciences. **Legal studies:** Prelaw. **Liberal arts:** Arts/sciences. **Math:** General. **Parks/recreation:** Health/fitness. **Physical sciences:** Chemistry. **Psychology:** General. **Social sciences:** General, political science. **Visual/performing arts:** Art, dramatic, studio arts, theater design.

Most popular majors. Agriculture 7%, business/marketing 25%, education 22%, health sciences 6%, liberal arts 15%, psychology 6%.

Computing on campus. 213 workstations in dormitories, library, computer center, student center. Dormitories wired for high-speed internet access and linked to campus network. Commuter students can connect to campus network. Online course registration, online library, helpline, repair service, wireless network available.

Student life. **Freshman orientation:** Available, $20 fee. Preregistration for classes offered. **Policies:** Freshmen permitted cars on campus. **Housing:** Guaranteed on-campus for all undergraduates. Coed dorms, single-sex dorms, special housing for disabled, apartments, substance-free housing available. $50 deposit. **Activities:** Bands, choral groups, dance, drama, literary magazine, music ensembles, musical theater, student government.

Athletics. NAIA. **Intercollegiate:** Baseball M, basketball, cross-country, football (tackle) M, golf, rodeo, softball W, track and field, volleyball W, wrestling M. **Intramural:** Badminton, basketball, football (non-tackle), soccer, softball, squash, table tennis, tennis, volleyball, water polo. **Team name:** Blue Hawks.

Student services. Adult student services, career counseling, services for economically disadvantaged, student employment services, financial aid counseling, health services, minority student services, personal counseling, placement for graduates. **Physically disabled:** Services for visually, speech, hearing impaired.

Contact. E-mail: dsu.nodak@dsu.nodak.edu
Phone: (701) 483-2331 Toll-free number: (800) 279-4295
Fax: (701) 483-2409
Marshall Melbye, Director of Admissions and Academic Records, Dickinson State University, 291 Campus Drive, Dickinson, ND 58601-4896

Jamestown College
Jamestown, North Dakota
www.jc.edu **CB code: 6318**

- Private 4-year liberal arts college affiliated with Presbyterian Church (USA)
- Residential campus in large town
- 1,019 degree-seeking undergraduates: 6% part-time, 56% women, 1% African American, 1% Asian American, 1% Hispanic American, 1% Native American, 4% international
- 98% of applicants admitted
- 46% graduate within 6 years; 13% enter graduate study

General. Founded in 1883. Regionally accredited. **Degrees:** 190 bachelor's awarded. **Location:** 100 miles from Fargo, 100 miles from Bismarck. **Calendar:** Semester, limited summer session. **Full-time faculty:** 58 total; 52% have terminal degrees, 5% minority, 48% women. **Part-time faculty:** 20 total; 10% have terminal degrees, 45% women. **Class size:** 50% < 20, 41% 20-39, 7% 40-49, 2% 50-99, less than 1% >100.

Freshman class profile. 1,026 applied, 1,003 admitted, 281 enrolled.

Mid 50% test scores			
ACT:	19-25	Rank in top quarter:	40%
GPA 3.50 or higher:	45%	Rank in top tenth:	16%
GPA 3.0-3.49:	30%	Return as sophomores:	68%
GPA 2.0-2.99:	25%	Out-of-state:	52%
		Live on campus:	95%

Basis for selection. Applicants with minimum 2.5 high school GPA or 18 ACT or 850 SAT (exclusive of writing) generally accepted. Applications reviewed by Vice President of Academic Affairs, Vice President of Student Affairs and Director of Admissions. Applicants may be admitted on standard conditional or probationary basis. Interview recommended for all students. Audition required for music program; portfolio recommended for art program.

High school preparation. College-preparatory program recommended. Recommended units include English 4, mathematics 3, social studies 3, science 4 and foreign language 2.

2006-2007 Annual costs. Tuition/fees: $10,550. Room/board: $4,340. Books/supplies: $1,000. Personal expenses: $1,300.

2005-2006 Financial aid. **Need-based:** 280 full-time freshmen applied for aid; 222 were judged to have need; 222 of these received aid. Average need met was 67%. Average scholarship/grant was $6,165; average loan $3,193. 49% of total undergraduate aid awarded as scholarships/grants, 51% as loans/jobs. **Non-need-based:** Awarded to 365 full-time undergraduates, including 131 freshmen. Scholarships awarded for academics, alumni affiliation, art, athletics, leadership, music/drama, religious affiliation. **Additional information:** FAFSA must be received by March 15th for North Dakota residents to be considered for North Dakota state grants.

Application procedures. **Admission:** No deadline. $20 fee, may be waived for applicants with need. Application may be submitted online. Admission notification on a rolling basis. **Financial aid:** Priority date 6/1; no closing date. FAFSA required. Applicants notified on a rolling basis starting 4/1; must reply within 6 week(s) of notification.

Academics. **Special study options:** Combined bachelor's/graduate degree, cooperative education, double major, dual enrollment of high school students, honors, independent study, internships, liberal arts/career combination, student-designed major, study abroad, teacher certification program. **Credit/placement by examination:** AP, CLEP, IB, institutional tests. Unlimited number of hours of credit by examination may be counted toward degree. **Support services:** Learning center, pre-admission summer program, reduced course load, remedial instruction, study skills assistance, tutoring, writing center.

Majors. **Biology:** General, biochemistry. **Business:** Accounting, business admin, finance, financial planning, international, management information systems, managerial economics, marketing. **Communications:** General. **Computer sciences:** Computer science. **Education:** Biology, chemistry, early childhood, elementary, English, history, mathematics, music, physical, secondary, special. **English:** Composition, English lit. **Foreign languages:** French, German, Spanish. **Health:** Clinical lab science, nursing (RN), radiologic technology/medical imaging. **History:** General. **Math:** General, applied. **Parks/recreation:** Sports admin. **Philosophy/religion:** Religion. **Physical sciences:** Chemistry. **Protective services:** Criminal justice. **Psychology:** General. **Social sciences:** Political science. **Visual/performing arts:** Dramatic, music performance, studio arts.

Most popular majors. Biology 7%, business/marketing 20%, computer/information sciences 8%, education 17%, health sciences 13%, security/protective services 6%, social sciences 8%, visual/performing arts 6%.

Computing on campus. 459 workstations in dormitories, library, computer center, student center. Dormitories wired for high-speed internet access and linked to campus network. Commuter students can connect to campus network. Online course registration, online library, helpline, repair service, student web hosting, wireless network available.

Student life. **Freshman orientation:** Mandatory. 3 days prior to classes. **Policies:** Weekly chapel service available on campus. Non-alcoholic nightclub available. Freshmen permitted cars on campus. **Housing:** Guaranteed on-campus for all undergraduates. Coed dorms, special housing for disabled, substance-free housing available. $50 deposit. Campus-owned houses. **Activities:** Bands, choral groups, dance, drama, music ensembles, musical theater, student government, student newspaper, Honor societies, ministry teams, Students of Service, Fellowship of Christian Athletes, Jimmie Janes, Jimmie Ambassadors.

Athletics. NAIA. **Intercollegiate:** Baseball M, basketball, cheerleading M, cross-country, football (tackle) M, golf, soccer W, softball W, track and field, volleyball W, wrestling M. **Intramural:** Basketball, bowling, football (non-tackle), racquetball, soccer, softball, volleyball. **Team name:** Jimmies.

Student services. Alcohol/substance abuse counseling, campus ministries, career counseling, student employment services, financial aid counseling, on-campus daycare, personal counseling, placement for graduates.

Contact. E-mail: admissions@jc.edu
Phone: (701) 252-3467 ext. 2562 Toll-free number: (800) 336-2554
Fax: (701) 253-4318
Carol Schmeichel, Vice President of Student Affairs and Enrollment Management, Jamestown College, 6081 College Lane, Jamestown, ND 58405

Mayville State University

Mayville, North Dakota
www.mayvillestate.edu **CB code: 6478**

- Public 4-year business and teachers college
- Residential campus in small town
- 912 degree-seeking undergraduates: 31% part-time, 54% women, 3% African American, 2% Hispanic American, 3% Native American, 6% international
- 35% graduate within 6 years; 8% enter graduate study

General. Founded in 1889. Regionally accredited. Every student issued laptop computer. **Degrees:** 106 bachelor's, 11 associate awarded. **ROTC:** Army, Air Force. **Location:** 60 miles from Fargo, 40 miles from Grand Forks. **Calendar:** Semester, limited summer session. **Full-time faculty:** 37 total; 51% have terminal degrees, 5% minority, 32% women. **Part-time faculty:** 37 total; 14% have terminal degrees, 3% minority, 60% women. **Class size:** 59% < 20, 38% 20-39, 3% 40-49. **Special facilities:** Nature area, wellness center, business incubation technology center, head start and child development center.

Freshman class profile. 307 applied, 208 admitted, 145 enrolled.

End year in good standing:	90%	**Live on campus:**	85%
Return as sophomores:	58%	**International:**	7%
Out-of-state:	35%		

Basis for selection. Open admission, but selective for some programs. Admission to teacher education programs based on meeting GPA criteria, completion of PPST, and completion of specific prerequisites. ACT math scores used for placement. Interview recommended. **Homeschooled:** Transcript of courses and grades required. Must provide documentation equivalent to high school diploma.

High school preparation. College-preparatory program required. 17 units required; 18 recommended. Required and recommended units include English 4, mathematics 3, social studies 3, science 3 (laboratory 3) and foreign language 2. One unit of computer studies recommended.

2005-2006 Annual costs. Tuition/fees: $4,943; $10,454 out-of-state. Full-time tuition for South Dakota, Montana, Manitoba, and Saskatchewan residents: $4,125. Full-time tuition for Western Undergraduate Exchange states: $4,950. Room/board: $3,724. Books/supplies: $700. Personal expenses: $2,800.

2004-2005 Financial aid. **Need-based:** 126 full-time freshmen applied for aid; 98 were judged to have need; 93 of these received aid. Average need met was 76%. Average scholarship/grant was $2,752; average loan $2,848. 25% of total undergraduate aid awarded as scholarships/grants, 75% as loans/jobs. **Non-need-based:** Awarded to 196 full-time undergraduates, including 72 freshmen. Scholarships awarded for academics, athletics, leadership, minority status, music/drama, state residency.

Application procedures. **Admission:** No deadline. $35 fee. Application may be submitted online. Admission notification on a rolling basis beginning on or about 1/1. **Financial aid:** Priority date 4/15; no closing date. FAFSA required. Applicants notified on a rolling basis starting 5/1; must reply within 2 week(s) of notification.

Academics. **Special study options:** Accelerated study, cooperative education, distance learning, double major, dual enrollment of high school students, honors, internships, student-designed major, teacher certification program. 3-year business administration degree with Cooperative Education Internship. **Credit/placement by examination:** AP, CLEP, ACT, institutional tests. 30 credit hours maximum toward bachelor's degree. **Support services:** Learning center, pre-admission summer program, remedial instruction, study skills assistance, tutoring.

Majors. **Biology:** General. **Business:** Business admin, office management. **Computer sciences:** General. **Education:** Biology, business, chemistry, elementary, English, geography, health, history, mathematics, physical, physics, social science. **English:** English lit. **Family/consumer sciences:** Child care. **Health:** Athletic training, predentistry, premedicine, prenursing, prepharmacy, preveterinary. **Legal studies:** Prelaw. **Math:** General. **Parks/recreation:** Health/fitness. **Physical sciences:** General, chemistry. **Psychology:** General. **Social sciences:** General.

Most popular majors. Business/marketing 25%, computer/information sciences 9%, education 49%, parks/recreation 7%.

Computing on campus. PC or laptop required. Dormitories wired for high-speed internet access and linked to campus network. Commuter students can connect to campus network. Online course registration, online library, helpline, repair service, wireless network available.

Student life. **Freshman orientation:** Mandatory, $20 fee. Preregistration for classes offered. Half-day events held in June and July. **Policies:** Freshmen permitted cars on campus. **Housing:** Guaranteed on-campus for all undergraduates. Single-sex dorms, apartments, substance-free housing available. $50 nonrefundable deposit. **Activities:** Pep band, choral groups, drama, literary magazine, music ensembles, musical theater, student government, student newspaper, campus crusade, student education association, residence hall association, health and physical education club, student activities council, alumni ambassadors, minority/international student association, peer educators, social science club.

Athletics. NAIA. **Intercollegiate:** Baseball M, basketball, football (tackle) M, soccer, softball W, volleyball W. **Intramural:** Badminton, basketball, bowling, football (non-tackle), golf, ice hockey M, racquetball, softball, table tennis, tennis, track and field, volleyball, weight lifting. **Team name:** Comets.

Student services. Adult student services, career counseling, student employment services, financial aid counseling, health services, on-campus daycare, personal counseling, placement for graduates, veterans' counselor. **Physically disabled:** Services for visually, hearing impaired.

Contact. E-mail: admit@mayvillestate.edu
Phone: (701) 788-4842 Toll-free number: (800) 437-4104
Fax: (701) 788-4748
Cherine Heckman, Vice President for Enrollment Management, Mayville State University, 330 Third Street, NE, Mayville, ND 58257-1299

Medcenter One College of Nursing
Bismarck, North Dakota
www.medcenterone.com/college/nursing.htm
CB code: 7051

- Private upper-division nursing college
- Commuter campus in small city
- 78% of applicants admitted
- Application essay, interview required

General. Founded in 1988. Regionally accredited. **Degrees:** 40 bachelor's awarded. **Articulation:** Agreement with Bismarck State College. **Calendar:** Semester, limited summer session. **Full-time faculty:** 10 total; 10% minority, 100% women. **Part-time faculty:** 2 total; 100% women. **Class size:** 22% 20-39, 78% 40-49.

Student profile. 92 degree-seeking undergraduates. 77 applied as first time-transfer students, 60 admitted, 49 enrolled. 100% entered as juniors. 82% transferred from two-year, 18% transferred from four-year institutions.

Women:	85%	**Out-of-state:**	3%
Native American:	3%	**Live on campus:**	7%
Part-time:	4%	**25 or older:**	63%

Basis for selection. High school transcript, college transcript, application essay, interview required. All students must transfer with minimum 64 credits of general education prerequisites, including 5 science courses. Credits not completed at time of application must be completed prior to transfer. Overall college GPA, science GPA important. Transfer accepted as sophomores, juniors, seniors.

2005-2006 Annual costs. Tuition/fees: $9,151. Room only: $1,800. Books/supplies: $1,119. Personal expenses: $1,000.

Financial aid. Need-based: 81 applied for aid; 66 were judged to have need; 66 of these received aid. Average need met was 97%. 52% of total undergraduate aid awarded as scholarships/grants, 48% as loans/jobs. **Non-need-based:** Awarded to 28 undergraduates.

Application procedures. Admission: Priority date 11/7. $40 fee. Application must be submitted on paper. **Financial aid:** Priority date 3/1, no deadline. Applicants notified on a rolling basis starting 6/1; must reply within 2 weeks of notification. FAFSA, institutional form required.

Academics. Special study options: Internships. **Credit/placement by examination:** CLEP, institutional tests. 30 credit hours maximum toward bachelor's degree.

Majors. Health: Nursing (RN).

Computing on campus. 15 workstations in library, computer center.

Student life. Housing: Coed dorms, special housing for disabled, substance-free housing available. $50 fully refundable deposit. **Activities:** Student government, student newspaper, Student Nurse Association, Student Organization.

Student services. Financial aid counseling, health services, personal counseling, placement for graduates.

Contact. E-mail: msmith@mohs.org
Phone: (701) 323-6833 Fax: (701) 323-6289
Mary Smith, Director of Student Services, Medcenter One College of Nursing, 512 North 7th Street, Bismarck, ND 58501-4494

Minot State University
Minot, North Dakota
www.minotstateu.edu
CB code: 6479

- Public 4-year university and liberal arts college
- Commuter campus in large town
- 3,547 degree-seeking undergraduates: 30% part-time, 63% women, 2% African American, 1% Asian American, 2% Hispanic American, 3% Native American, 6% international
- 250 degree-seeking graduate students
- 85% of applicants admitted
- ACT required

General. Founded in 1913. Regionally accredited. **Degrees:** 464 bachelor's, 1 associate awarded; master's offered. **Location:** 105 miles from Bismarck, 225 miles from Grand Forks. **Calendar:** Semester, limited summer session. **Full-time faculty:** 172 total; 49% women. **Part-time faculty:** 101 total; 57% women. **Class size:** 44% < 20, 52% 20-39, 2% 40-49, 2% 50-99. **Special facilities:** Art galleries, natural history museum, North Dakota Center for Persons with Disabilities, Native American collection, observatory, Rural Crime and Justice Center.

Freshman class profile. 645 applied, 551 admitted, 471 enrolled.

Mid 50% test scores		**Return as sophomores:**	66%
ACT:	18-23	**International:**	7%

Basis for selection. Secondary school record very important; ACT/SAT test scores, no less than 16 composite on ACT; 16 composite reviewed on individual basis.

High school preparation. Recommended units include English 4, mathematics 3, social studies 3 and science 3. Science should include at least 3 units of biology, chemistry, physics, or physical science. Social science should not include consumer education, cooperative marketing, orientation to social science, or marriage/family. Math must be algebra I or above.

2005-2006 Annual costs. Tuition/fees: $4,092; $9,870 out-of-state. Full-time tuition for Minnesota residents: $3,772. Full-time tuition for South Dakota, Montana, Manitoba, Saskatchewan residents: $4,325. Room/board: $3,590.

2004-2005 Financial aid. Need-based: 138 full-time freshmen applied for aid; 122 were judged to have need; 108 of these received aid. Average need met was 59%. Average scholarship/grant was $1,199; average loan $1,764. 37% of total undergraduate aid awarded as scholarships/grants, 63% as loans/jobs. **Non-need-based:** Awarded to 1,648 full-time undergraduates, including 78 freshmen. Scholarships awarded for academics, alumni affiliation, art, athletics, minority status, music/drama, state residency. **Additional information:** Scholarship application deadline is February 15.

Application procedures. Admission: Priority date 4/1; no deadline. $35 fee. Application may be submitted online. Admission notification on a rolling basis. **Financial aid:** Priority date 3/15; no closing date. FAFSA required. Applicants notified on a rolling basis starting 5/1; must reply within 2 week(s) of notification.

Academics. Wide variety of distance courses and NCA-accredited degree programs offered. **Special study options:** Accelerated study, cooperative education, distance learning, double major, dual enrollment of high school students, external degree, honors, independent study, internships, liberal arts/career combination, student-designed major, study abroad, teacher certification program. **Credit/placement by examination:** AP, CLEP, institutional tests. **Support services:** Learning center, reduced course load, remedial instruction, study skills assistance, tutoring, writing center.

Majors. Biology: General. **Business:** Accounting, business admin, finance, international, management information systems, marketing. **Communications:** Broadcast journalism, radio/tv. **Communications technology:** General. **Computer sciences:** General. **Education:** Art, biology, business, chemistry, Deaf/hearing impaired, elementary, English, foreign languages, French, German, history, mathematics, mentally handicapped, music, physical, physics, science, social science, Spanish, speech impaired. **English:** English lit, speech/rhetoric. **Foreign languages:** French, German, Spanish. **Health:** Clinical lab science, communication disorders, medical radiologic technology/radiation therapy, nursing (RN), substance abuse counseling. **History:** General. **Liberal arts:** Arts/sciences. **Math:** General. **Parks/recreation:** Health/fitness. **Physical sciences:** Chemistry, geology, physics, planetary. **Protective services:** Criminal justice. **Psychology:** General. **Public administration:** Social work. **Social sciences:** General, economics, geography, sociology. **Visual/performing arts:** Art, music performance.

Most popular majors. Business/marketing 29%, education 20%, health sciences 17%, security/protective services 9%.

Computing on campus. 300 workstations in dormitories, library, computer center, student center. Dormitories wired for high-speed internet access and linked to campus network. Commuter students can connect to campus network. Online course registration, online library, helpline, repair service, wireless network available.

Student life. Freshman orientation: Available, $35 fee. Preregistration for classes offered. **Policies:** Freshmen permitted cars on campus. **Housing:** Coed dorms, single-sex dorms, apartments, substance-free housing available. $100 fully refundable deposit. **Activities:** Bands, choral groups, dance, drama, literary magazine, music ensembles, musical theater, opera, radio station, student government, student newspaper, symphony orchestra, TV station, disability awareness organization, Democratic Party, Republican Party, Intervarsity Christian Fellowship, Native American cultural awareness club, United Campus Ministries, Catholic student association, international awareness club, Student Education of Hard of Hearing/Deaf, National Student Speech/Hearing Association.

Athletics. NAIA. **Intercollegiate:** Baseball M, basketball, cheerleading W, cross-country, football (tackle) M, golf, softball W, track and field, volleyball W. **Intramural:** Basketball, bowling, racquetball, softball, track and field, volleyball. **Team name:** Beavers.

Student services. Adult student services, campus ministries, career counseling, services for economically disadvantaged, student employment services, financial aid counseling, health services, minority student services, personal counseling, placement for graduates, veterans' counselor, women's services. **Physically disabled:** Services for visually, speech, hearing impaired.

Contact. E-mail: askmsu@minotstateu.edu
Phone: (701) 858-3350 Toll-free number: (800) 777-0750
Fax: (701) 839-6933
Lisa Johnson, Division of Records, Minot State University, 500 University Avenue West, Minot, ND 58707-5002

North Dakota State University

Fargo, North Dakota **CB member**
www.ndsu.edu **CB code: 6474**

- Public 4-year university
- Residential campus in small city
- 10,496 degree-seeking undergraduates: 10% part-time, 45% women
- 1,440 degree-seeking graduate students
- 84% of applicants admitted
- SAT or ACT (ACT writing optional) required
- 55% graduate within 6 years; 19% enter graduate study

General. Founded in 1890. Regionally accredited. **Degrees:** 1,676 bachelor's awarded; master's, doctoral, first professional offered. **ROTC:** Army, Air Force. **Location:** 250 miles from Minneapolis-St. Paul. **Calendar:** Semester, limited summer session. **Full-time faculty:** 525 total; 84% have terminal degrees, 28% women. **Part-time faculty:** 91 total; 33% have terminal degrees, 44% women. **Class size:** 38% < 20, 41% 20-39, 6% 40-49, 10% 50-99, 5% >100. **Special facilities:** Fine arts center, regional studies institute, biotechnology institute, group decision center, engineering computer center, center for writers, wellness center, technology park, downtown campus for art and architecture.

Freshman class profile. 4,007 applied, 3,346 admitted, 2,021 enrolled.

Mid 50% test scores		**Rank in top tenth:**	18%
ACT:	20-26	**Return as sophomores:**	77%
GPA 3.50 or higher:	48%	**Out-of-state:**	52%
GPA 3.0-3.49:	31%	**Live on campus:**	92%
GPA 2.0-2.99:	21%	**Fraternities:**	4%
Rank in top quarter:	43%	**Sororities:**	2%

Basis for selection. All applicants must have completed college preparatory program in high school. Admission based on overall performance in high school, performance in college preparatory courses and standardized test scores. Admission to nursing, veterinary technology, architecture, pharmacy, electrical engineering, mechanical engineering programs based on academic record and test scores. Each non-Native speaker is evaluated on an individual basis. Educational record and speaking ability evaluated. ACT/SAT required for admission except for students who have completed 24 semester/36 quarter credits of college work, a technical college degree, military service (case-by-case basis), or who are older than 25 years of age. Campus visit recommended for all students. Audition required for music programs. **Homeschooled:** Applicants advised to work with local school district for issuance of a Certificate of Graduation. **Learning Disabled:** No need to disclose disability until after admission decision is made.

High school preparation. College-preparatory program required. 13 units required. Required units include English 4, mathematics 3, social studies 3, science 3 (laboratory 3).

2005-2006 Annual costs. Tuition/fees: $5,264; $12,545 out-of-state. Tuition for Minnesota residents: $4,756. Tuition for South Dakota, Montana, Manitoba, Saskatchewan residents: $6,540. Room/board: $5,130. Books/supplies: $650. Personal expenses: $2,230.

2004-2005 Financial aid. Need-based: Average need met was 75%. Average scholarship/grant was $3,154; average loan $2,958. 26% of total undergraduate aid awarded as scholarships/grants, 74% as loans/jobs. **Non-need-based:** Scholarships awarded for academics, alumni affiliation, art, athletics, leadership, minority status, music/drama, ROTC, state residency.

Application procedures. Admission: Closing date 8/15 (receipt date). $35 fee. Application may be submitted online. Admission notification on a rolling basis. **Financial aid:** Closing date 3/15. FAFSA required. Applicants notified on a rolling basis starting 3/15.

Academics. Special study options: Combined bachelor's/graduate degree, cooperative education, cross-registration, distance learning, double major, dual enrollment of high school students, ESL, honors, independent study, internships, student-designed major, study abroad, teacher certification program. Tri-college, collaborative enrollment (ND University System). **Credit/placement by examination:** AP, CLEP, IB, ACT, institutional tests. 17 credit hours maximum toward bachelor's degree. **Support services:** Reduced course load, remedial instruction, study skills assistance, tutoring, writing center.

Majors. Agriculture: General, agribusiness operations, animal sciences, crop production, economics, equestrian studies, food science, horticultural science, mechanization, plant protection, plant sciences, soil science, turf management. **Architecture:** Architecture, environmental design, landscape. **Biology:** General, Biochemistry/biophysics and molecular biology, biotechnology, botany, microbiology, zoology. **Business:** Accounting, actuarial science, business admin, construction management, hospitality admin, management information systems. **Communications:** Media studies. **Computer sciences:** Computer science. **Conservation:** Management/policy. **Education:** Agricultural, biology, chemistry, computer, elementary, English, family/consumer sciences, French, German, health, history, mathematics, music, physical, physics, science, social science, social studies, Spanish, speech. **Engineering:** Aerospace, agricultural, civil, computer, construction, electrical, industrial, manufacturing, mechanical, physics. **English:** English lit, speech/rhetoric. **Family/consumer sciences:** Clothing/textiles, facilities/event planning, family studies. **Foreign languages:** Classics, French, Spanish. **Health:** Athletic training, clinical lab science, dietetics, nursing (RN), preveterinary, radiologic technology/medical imaging, respiratory therapy technology, veterinary technology/assistant. **History:** General. **Interdisciplinary:** Global studies. **Legal studies:** Prelaw. **Liberal arts:** Arts/sciences, humanities. **Math:** General, statistics. **Parks/recreation:** General, sports admin. **Philosophy/religion:** Philosophy. **Physical sciences:** Chemistry, geology, physics. **Protective services:** Criminal justice. **Psychology:** General. **Social sciences:** General, anthropology, economics, political science, sociology. **Transportation:** Aviation management. **Visual/performing arts:** Art, dramatic, interior design.

Most popular majors. Agriculture 6%, architecture 7%, biology 6%, business/marketing 15%, engineering/engineering technologies 16%, health sciences 11%, natural resources/environmental science 6%.

Computing on campus. 500 workstations in dormitories, library, computer center, student center. Dormitories wired for high-speed internet access. Online course registration, online library, helpline, repair service, student web hosting, wireless network available.

Student life. Freshman orientation: Available, $10 fee. Offered in July or August and day before classes. **Policies:** No alcoholic beverages allowed on campus, code of student conduct. Freshmen permitted cars on campus. **Housing:** Guaranteed on-campus for all undergraduates. Coed dorms, single-sex dorms, apartments, fraternity/sorority housing, substance-free housing available. $50 deposit. Freshmen under 19 not living with parent or guardian must live on campus. Housing is handicap accessible. Designated floors for engineering and architecture students. Learning communities. Wellness floors. **Activities:** Bands, choral groups, dance, drama, music ensembles, radio station, student government, student newspaper, Newman Center (Catholic), Lutheran Student Fellowship, United Campus Ministry, College Republicans, College Democrats, Circle-K, Mortar Board, international student association, Black Student Alliance, Native American student association.

Athletics. NCAA. **Intercollegiate:** Baseball M, basketball, cross-country, football (tackle) M, golf, soccer W, softball W, track and field, volleyball W, wrestling M. **Intramural:** Basketball, football (non-tackle), softball, volleyball. **Team name:** Bison.

Student services. Adult student services, alcohol/substance abuse counseling, campus ministries, career counseling, services for economically disadvantaged, student employment services, financial aid counseling, health services, minority student services, on-campus daycare, personal counseling, veterans' counselor. **Physically disabled:** Services for visually, speech, hearing impaired. **Learning disabled:** Comprehensive services available.

Contact. E-mail: ndsu.admission@ndsu.edu
Phone: (701) 231-8643 Toll-free number: (800) 488-6378
Fax: (701) 231-8802
Catherine Haugen, Dean of Enrollment Management, North Dakota State University, Ceres Hall 124, Fargo, ND 58105-5454

Trinity Bible College

Ellendale, North Dakota
www.trinitybiblecollege.edu **CB code: 0356**

- Private 4-year Bible college affiliated with Assemblies of God
- Residential campus in rural community

Four-Year Colleges

- 290 degree-seeking undergraduates: 10% part-time, 50% women
- 38% of applicants admitted
- ACT (writing optional), application essay required
- 44% graduate within 6 years; 5% enter graduate study

General. Founded in 1948. Regionally accredited; also accredited by ABHE. **Degrees:** 44 bachelor's, 13 associate awarded. **Location:** 60 miles from Jamestown, 38 miles from Aberdeen. **Calendar:** Semester, limited summer session. **Full-time faculty:** 30 total. **Part-time faculty:** 10 total. **Class size:** 77% < 20, 17% 20-39, 3% 40-49, 3% 50-99. **Special facilities:** Pentecostal heritage collection of rare and out-of-print works, teacher education laboratory.

Freshman class profile. 169 applied, 64 admitted, 64 enrolled.

Mid 50% test scores			
SAT verbal:	240-540	End year in good standing:	67%
SAT math:	260-520	Return as sophomores:	76%
ACT:	16-23	Out-of-state:	70%
		Live on campus:	85%

Basis for selection. Applicants must have ACT composite score of 14 and high school GPA of 2.0 to be admitted. References, school record, evidence of Christian testimony and lifestyle very important. Interview recommended. **Homeschooled:** Minimum ACT scores of 14 (English), 15 (math) required.

2005-2006 Annual costs. Tuition/fees: $11,158. Room/board: $4,370. Books/supplies: $700. Personal expenses: $1,636.

2005-2006 Financial aid. Need-based: Average scholarship/grant was $5,895; average loan $3,255. 41% of total undergraduate aid awarded as scholarships/grants, 59% as loans/jobs. **Non-need-based:** Scholarships awarded for academics, alumni affiliation, art, leadership, music/drama, religious affiliation.

Application procedures. Admission: No deadline. $25 fee, may be waived for applicants with need. Admission notification on a rolling basis. **Financial aid:** Priority date 3/1, closing date 9/1. FAFSA required. Applicants notified on a rolling basis starting 3/1; must reply within 3 week(s) of notification.

Academics. All students major or minor in Biblical studies in conjunction with another major or minor of their choice. **Special study options:** Distance learning, double major, dual enrollment of high school students, independent study, internships, liberal arts/career combination, teacher certification program. **Credit/placement by examination:** CLEP, IB, SAT, ACT, institutional tests. 30 credit hours maximum toward associate degree, 30 toward bachelor's. **Support services:** Learning center, reduced course load, remedial instruction, tutoring.

Majors. Business: General, administrative services. **Education:** Elementary. **Philosophy/religion:** Religion. **Theology:** Bible, missionary, religious ed, theology. **Visual/performing arts:** Dramatic.

Computing on campus. 30 workstations in dormitories, library, computer center. Dormitories wired for high-speed internet access and linked to campus network. Online library, helpline, wireless network available.

Student life. Freshman orientation: Mandatory. Preregistration for classes offered. **Policies:** Religious observance required. Freshmen permitted cars on campus. **Housing:** Single-sex dorms, apartments, substance-free housing available. $150 deposit, deadline 8/31. **Activities:** Bands, choral groups, drama, music ensembles, radio station, student government, missions, photography, ministry clubs.

Athletics. NCCAA. **Intercollegiate:** Basketball, football (tackle) M. **Intramural:** Basketball, football (tackle) M, volleyball. **Team name:** Lions.

Student services. Campus ministries, career counseling, student employment services, financial aid counseling, personal counseling, placement for graduates, veterans' counselor.

Contact. E-mail: admissions@trinitybiblecollege.edu
Phone: (701) 349-3621 Toll-free number: (888) 822-2329
Fax: (701) 349-5786
Steve Tvedt, Vice President of College Relations, Trinity Bible College, 50 South Sixth Avenue, Ellendale, ND 58436-7150

University of Mary

Bismarck, North Dakota
www.umary.edu **CB code: 6428**

- Private 4-year university affiliated with Roman Catholic Church
- Residential campus in small city
- 2,102 degree-seeking undergraduates: 7% part-time, 62% women, 2% African American, 1% Asian American, 2% Hispanic American, 4% Native American, 1% international
- 552 degree-seeking graduate students
- 86% of applicants admitted
- SAT or ACT (ACT writing optional) required
- 57% graduate within 6 years; 17% enter graduate study

General. Founded in 1959. Regionally accredited. Butler Center offers evening classes. Branch for accelerated programs located in Fargo. Extensive leadership development program. **Degrees:** 506 bachelor's, 2 associate awarded; master's, doctoral offered. **Location:** 6 miles from downtown. **Calendar:** Semester, limited summer session. **Full-time faculty:** 100 total; 35% have terminal degrees, 1% minority, 50% women. **Part-time faculty:** 249 total; 13% have terminal degrees, 6% minority, 43% women. **Class size:** 63% < 20, 26% 20-39, 5% 40-49, 6% 50-99, less than 1% >100. **Special facilities:** Fitness center, climbing wall.

Freshman class profile. 1,040 applied, 897 admitted, 392 enrolled.

Mid 50% test scores			
ACT:	20-23	Rank in top tenth:	16%
GPA 3.50 or higher:	48%	End year in good standing:	91%
GPA 3.0-3.49:	32%	Return as sophomores:	71%
GPA 2.0-2.99:	20%	Out-of-state:	45%
Rank in top quarter:	44%	Live on campus:	87%

Basis for selection. Automatic acceptance for applicants in top half of class with 2.5 GPA and 19 ACT. Applicants not meeting these standards may be admitted with specific conditions for enrollment. Audition required for music program; interview recommended for academically weak students.

High school preparation. College-preparatory program recommended. Recommended units include English 4, mathematics 3, social studies 4 and science 3.

2006-2007 Annual costs. Tuition/fees (projected): $11,324. Room/board: $4,050. Books/supplies: $800. Personal expenses: $920.

2004-2005 Financial aid. Need-based: 50% of total undergraduate aid awarded as scholarships/grants, 50% as loans/jobs. **Non-need-based:** Scholarships awarded for academics, athletics, leadership, state residency.

Application procedures. Admission: No deadline. $25 fee, may be waived for applicants with need. Application may be submitted online. Admission notification on a rolling basis. Must reply by May 1 or within 4 week(s) if notified thereafter. **Financial aid:** Priority date 3/15; no closing date. FAFSA required. Applicants notified on a rolling basis starting 4/1; must reply within 2 week(s) of notification.

Academics. Special study options: Accelerated study, combined bachelor's/graduate degree, cooperative education, distance learning, double major, dual enrollment of high school students, external degree, independent study, internships, liberal arts/career combination, study abroad, teacher certification program, weekend college. **Credit/placement by examination:** AP, CLEP, IB, institutional tests. 32 credit hours maximum toward associate degree, 96 toward bachelor's. **Support services:** Learning center, reduced course load, remedial instruction, study skills assistance, tutoring.

Majors. Biology: General. **Business:** Accounting, business admin, communications, management science. **Communications:** General. **Computer sciences:** Information systems. **Education:** Biology, early childhood, elementary, English, history, mathematics, mentally handicapped, music, physical, social science. **English:** English lit. **Health:** Athletic training, clinical lab science, medical radiologic technology/radiation therapy, nursing (RN), respiratory therapy technology, substance abuse counseling. **Math:** General. **Parks/recreation:** Exercise sciences. **Philosophy/religion:** Religion. **Protective services:** Criminal justice. **Psychology:** General. **Public administration:** Social work. **Social sciences:** General. **Theology:** Theology. **Visual/performing arts:** Music performance.

Most popular majors. Business/marketing 39%, education 20%, health sciences 16%, liberal arts 7%.

Computing on campus. 235 workstations in dormitories, library, computer center. Dormitories wired for high-speed internet access and linked to campus network. Commuter students can connect to campus network. Online course registration, online library, student web hosting available.

Student life. Freshman orientation: Mandatory. Preregistration for classes offered. 2-day orientation for freshmen at beginning of fall term. **Policies:** Freshmen permitted cars on campus. **Housing:** Guaranteed on-campus for freshmen. Single-sex dorms, apartments, substance-free housing available.

$100 fully refundable deposit. **Activities:** Bands, choral groups, drama, literary magazine, music ensembles, musical theater, radio station, student government, student newspaper, symphony orchestra, TV station, campus ministry, Spurs, Circle-K, student nurses association, Young Democrats, College Republicans, student education association, social work club, music educators national conference.

Athletics. NCAA. **Intercollegiate:** Baseball M, basketball, cross-country, football (tackle) M, golf, soccer, softball W, tennis, track and field, volleyball W, wrestling M. **Intramural:** Badminton, basketball, bowling, football (non-tackle), golf, racquetball, soccer, softball, swimming, table tennis, tennis, volleyball, weight lifting. **Team name:** Marauders.

Student services. Adult student services, campus ministries, career counseling, services for economically disadvantaged, student employment services, financial aid counseling, health services, minority student services, personal counseling, placement for graduates, veterans' counselor. **Physically disabled:** Services for hearing impaired.

Contact. E-mail: marauder@umary.edu
Phone: (701) 355-8030 Toll-free number: (800) 288-6279
Fax: (701) 255-7687
Dave Heringer, Vice President for Enrollment Services, University of Mary, 7500 University Drive, Bismarck, ND 58504-9652

University of North Dakota

Grand Forks, North Dakota
www.und.edu **CB code: 6878**

- Public 4-year university
- Residential campus in small city
- 10,498 degree-seeking undergraduates: 11% part-time, 46% women, 1% African American, 1% Asian American, 1% Hispanic American, 3% Native American
- 2,456 degree-seeking graduate students
- 73% of applicants admitted
- SAT or ACT (ACT writing optional) required
- 54% graduate within 6 years; 8% enter graduate study

General. Founded in 1883. Regionally accredited. **Degrees:** 1,757 bachelor's awarded; master's, doctoral, first professional offered. **ROTC:** Army, Air Force. **Location:** 320 miles from Minneapolis-St. Paul, 150 miles from Winnipeg, Canada. **Calendar:** Semester, extensive summer session. **Full-time faculty:** 668 total; 15% minority, 36% women. **Part-time faculty:** 157 total; 7% minority, 41% women. **Class size:** 36% < 20, 48% 20-39, 6% 40-49, 6% 50-99, 4% >100. **Special facilities:** US Weather Bureau observation station, atmospherium, institute for remote sensing, energy research center, fine arts center, aerospace sciences center, pilot and ATC training, CRAY supercomputer, art museum, international student center, Rural Technology Center, technology incubator, arena, technology park, writing center, theatre, recital hall, Center of Excellence in Neuroscience-Medical School.

Freshman class profile. 3,749 applied, 2,725 admitted, 1,884 enrolled.

Mid 50% test scores		**Return as sophomores:**	75%
ACT:	21-26	**Out-of-state:**	54%
Rank in top quarter:	38%	**Live on campus:**	87%
Rank in top tenth:	16%	**Fraternities:**	9%
End year in good standing:	85%	**Sororities:**	8%

Basis for selection. High school record and test scores most important. **Homeschooled:** Transcript of courses and grades required.

High school preparation. 13 units required. Required and recommended units include English 4, mathematics 3, social studies 3, science 3 (laboratory 3) and foreign language 1. Mathematics must be algebra I and above.

2005-2006 Annual costs. Tuition/fees: $5,327; $12,659 out-of-state. Tuition for South Dakota, Montana, Saskatchewan, Manitoba residents: $7521. Room/board: $4,787. Books/supplies: $700. Personal expenses: $2,080.

2005-2006 Financial aid. **Need-based:** Average need met was 83%. Average scholarship/grant was $2,967; average loan $3,309. 30% of total undergraduate aid awarded as scholarships/grants, 70% as loans/jobs. **Non-need-based:** Scholarships awarded for academics, alumni affiliation, art, athletics, job skills, leadership, minority status, music/drama, ROTC, state residency.

Application procedures. **Admission:** Closing date 7/1 (postmark date). $35 fee. Application may be submitted online. Admission notification on a rolling basis beginning on or about 9/1. **Financial aid:** Priority date 3/15; no closing date. FAFSA required. Applicants notified on a rolling basis starting 5/15; must reply within 4 week(s) of notification.

Academics. Core of General Education Requirements (GER) in English composition, social sciences, arts, humanities, math, science and technology. **Special study options:** Accelerated study, combined bachelor's/graduate degree, cooperative education, cross-registration, distance learning, double major, dual enrollment of high school students, ESL, exchange student, external degree, honors, independent study, internships, liberal arts/career combination, semester at sea, student-designed major, study abroad, teacher certification program, weekend college. **Credit/placement by examination:** AP, CLEP, IB, ACT, institutional tests. **Support services:** Learning center, pre-admission summer program, reduced course load, remedial instruction, study skills assistance, tutoring, writing center.

Majors. **Area/ethnic studies:** Native American. **Biology:** General. **Business:** General, accounting, accounting/finance, finance, management information systems, managerial economics, marketing. **Communications:** General. **Computer sciences:** General. **Education:** Art, business, elementary, mathematics, middle, music, physical, sales/marketing, science. **Engineering:** Chemical, civil, electrical, environmental, mechanical. **Engineering technology:** Occupational safety. **English:** English lit. **Family/consumer sciences:** Food/nutrition. **Foreign languages:** General, French, German, Scandinavian, Spanish. **Health:** Audiology/speech pathology, clinical lab science, cytotechnology, nursing (RN). **History:** General. **Math:** General. **Parks/recreation:** Facilities management. **Philosophy/religion:** Philosophy, religion. **Physical sciences:** Atmospheric science, chemistry, geology, physics. **Protective services:** Criminal justice, forensics. **Psychology:** General. **Public administration:** General, social work. **Social sciences:** General, anthropology, economics, geography, political science, sociology. **Transportation:** Air traffic control, airline/commercial pilot, aviation, aviation management. **Visual/performing arts:** General, art, dramatic, music performance.

Computing on campus. 1,100 workstations in dormitories, library, computer center, student center. Dormitories wired for high-speed internet access and linked to campus network. Commuter students can connect to campus network. Online course registration, online library, helpline, student web hosting, wireless network available.

Student life. **Freshman orientation:** Available, $15 fee. Preregistration for classes offered. Held weekends before school opens in August. **Policies:** Freshmen permitted cars on campus. **Housing:** Guaranteed on-campus for freshmen. Coed dorms, single-sex dorms, special housing for disabled, apartments, fraternity/sorority housing available. $250 partly refundable deposit, deadline 5/1. **Activities:** Bands, choral groups, dance, drama, film society, literary magazine, music ensembles, musical theater, opera, radio station, student government, student newspaper, symphony orchestra, TV station, over 230 organizations available.

Athletics. NCAA. **Intercollegiate:** Baseball M, basketball, cross-country, diving, football (tackle) M, golf, ice hockey, soccer W, softball W, swimming, tennis W, track and field, volleyball W. **Intramural:** Badminton, basketball, cross-country, golf, ice hockey, racquetball, soccer W, softball W, swimming, tennis W, track and field, volleyball W. **Team name:** Fighting Sioux.

Student services. Adult student services, alcohol/substance abuse counseling, campus ministries, career counseling, services for economically disadvantaged, student employment services, financial aid counseling, health services, legal services, minority student services, on-campus daycare, personal counseling, placement for graduates, veterans' counselor, women's services. **Physically disabled:** Services for visually, speech, hearing impaired.

Contact. E-mail: enrollment_services@mail.und.nodak.edu
Phone: (701) 777-3821 Toll-free number: (800) 225-5863
Fax: (701) 777-2721
Heidi Kippenhan, Director, University of North Dakota, PO Box 8357, Grand Forks, ND 58202

Valley City State University

Valley City, North Dakota
www.vcsu.edu **CB code: 6480**

- Public 4-year liberal arts and teachers college
- Residential campus in small town
- 1,011 degree-seeking undergraduates: 23% part-time, 52% women, 2% African American, 1% Hispanic American, 2% Native American, 5% international
- 22 degree-seeking graduate students
- 94% of applicants admitted
- SAT or ACT (ACT writing optional) required
- 45% graduate within 6 years

General. Founded in 1889. Regionally accredited. **Degrees:** 158 bachelor's awarded; master's offered. **Location:** 60 miles from Fargo. **Calendar:** Semester, limited summer session. **Full-time faculty:** 55 total; 36% have terminal degrees, 51% women. **Part-time faculty:** 22 total; 14% have terminal degrees, 36% women. **Special facilities:** Planetarium, medicine wheel.

Freshman class profile. 256 applied, 240 admitted, 176 enrolled.

Mid 50% test scores		**Rank in top tenth:**	6%
SAT verbal:	450-580	**Return as sophomores:**	64%
SAT math:	450-570	**Out-of-state:**	28%
ACT:	18-23	**Live on campus:**	85%
GPA 3.50 or higher:	27%	**International:**	6%
GPA 3.0-3.49:	28%	**Fraternities:**	2%
GPA 2.0-2.99:	41%	**Sororities:**	3%
Rank in top quarter:	22%		

Basis for selection. School achievement record and test scores important. All new students required to submit ACT or SAT before first day of fall term but no minimum standard required.

High school preparation. College-preparatory program required. 13 units required. Required and recommended units include English 4, mathematics 3, social studies 3, science 3 (laboratory 3) and foreign language 2.

2005-2006 Annual costs. Tuition/fees: $4,932; $10,656 out-of-state. Room/board: $3,535. Books/supplies: $700.

2004-2005 Financial aid. Need-based: Average need met was 74%. Average scholarship/grant was $2,933; average loan $2,924. 39% of total undergraduate aid awarded as scholarships/grants, 61% as loans/jobs. **Non-need-based:** Scholarships awarded for academics, alumni affiliation, athletics, leadership, minority status, music/drama.

Application procedures. Admission: No deadline. $35 fee. Application may be submitted online. Admission notification on a rolling basis beginning on or about 11/1. **Financial aid:** Priority date 3/15; no closing date. FAFSA required. Applicants notified on a rolling basis starting 1/15; must reply within 2 week(s) of notification.

Academics. Special study options: Combined bachelor's/graduate degree, cooperative education, distance learning, double major, dual enrollment of high school students, internships, liberal arts/career combination, student-designed major, teacher certification program. **Credit/placement by examination:** AP, CLEP, SAT, ACT. **Support services:** Reduced course load, study skills assistance, tutoring.

Majors. Biology: General. **Business:** Business admin, human resources, office management. **Computer sciences:** General. **Education:** Art, biology, business, chemistry, elementary, English, health, history, instructional media, mathematics, music, physical, science, secondary, social science, Spanish, technology/industrial arts, trade/industrial, voc/tech. **Foreign languages:** Spanish. **Health:** Predentistry, premedicine, prenursing, prepharmacy, preveterinary. **History:** General. **Legal studies:** Prelaw. **Liberal arts:** Arts/sciences. **Math:** General. **Parks/recreation:** Health/fitness. **Physical sciences:** Chemistry. **Psychology:** General. **Social sciences:** General. **Visual/performing arts:** Art.

Most popular majors. Business/marketing 24%, computer/information sciences 9%, education 51%.

Computing on campus. PC or laptop required. 925 workstations in dormitories, library, computer center, student center. Dormitories wired for high-speed internet access and linked to campus network. Commuter students can connect to campus network. Online course registration, online library, helpline, repair service, student web hosting, wireless network available.

Student life. Freshman orientation: Available, $10 fee. 2 days in June. **Policies:** Freshmen permitted cars on campus. **Housing:** Guaranteed on-campus for all undergraduates. Coed dorms, single-sex dorms, special housing for disabled, apartments, fraternity/sorority housing, substance-free housing available. $50 deposit. **Activities:** Bands, choral groups, drama, music ensembles, student government, student newspaper, inter-residence hall council, inter-fraternity/sorority council, inter-varsity Christian fellowship, Music Educators National Conference, Student National Education Association, Newman Club, Association of Information Technology Professionals, Faith Lutheran student club, international student club.

Athletics. NAIA. **Intercollegiate:** Baseball M, basketball, cheerleading M, football (tackle) M, softball W, volleyball W. **Intramural:** Basketball, bowling, cross-country, football (non-tackle), golf, ice hockey, racquetball, softball, track and field, volleyball. **Team name:** Vikings.

Student services. Career counseling, student employment services, health services, on-campus daycare, personal counseling, placement for graduates, veterans' counselor.

Contact. E-mail: enrollment.services@vcsu.edu
Phone: (701) 845-7101 Toll-free number: (800) 532-8641
Fax: (701) 845-7299
Dan Klein, Director of Admissions, Valley City State University, 101 College Street Southwest, Valley City, ND 58072-4098

Ohio

Allegheny Wesleyan College

Salem, Ohio
www.awc.edu **CB code: 4120**

- Private 4-year Bible college
- Residential campus
- 64 degree-seeking undergraduates

General. Accredited by ABHE. **Degrees:** 6 bachelor's awarded. **Calendar:** Semester. **Full-time faculty:** 17 total.

Basis for selection. Open admission.

2006-2007 Annual costs. Tuition/fees: $4,700. Room/board: $3,200.

Application procedures. Admission: Priority date 4/15; no deadline. $35 fee. Admission notification on a rolling basis.

Academics. Credit/placement by examination: CLEP.

Majors. Theology: Theology.

Student life. Housing: Coed dorms available.

Contact. Phone: (330) 337-6403
Jeanne Zvaritch, Director of Admissions, Allegheny Wesleyan College, 2161 Woodside Road, Salem, OH 44460-9598

Antioch College

Yellow Springs, Ohio **CB member**
www.antioch-college.edu **CB code: 1017**

- Private 4-year liberal arts college
- Residential campus in small town
- 380 degree-seeking undergraduates: 58% women, 4% African American, 1% Asian American, 3% Hispanic American, 1% Native American
- 6 graduate students
- 51% of applicants admitted
- Application essay required
- 50% graduate within 6 years

General. Founded in 1852. Regionally accredited. **Degrees:** 60 bachelor's awarded. **Location:** 18 miles from Dayton, 60 miles from Cincinnati. **Calendar:** Trimester, extensive summer session. **Full-time faculty:** 51 total; 65% have terminal degrees, 4% minority, 51% women. **Part-time faculty:** 17 total; 18% have terminal degrees, 18% minority, 59% women. **Class size:** 91% < 20, 9% 20-39. **Special facilities:** 1,000-acre nature preserve.

Freshman class profile. 368 applied, 187 admitted, 53 enrolled.

Mid 50% test scores		**GPA 2.0-2.99:**	32%
SAT verbal:	600-710	**Rank in top quarter:**	39%
SAT math:	520-630	**Rank in top tenth:**	13%
GPA 3.50 or higher:	32%	**Out-of-state:**	61%
GPA 3.0-3.49:	36%	**Live on campus:**	100%

Basis for selection. School achievement record and test scores considered equally with personal qualities (independence, creativity, initiative) as demonstrated by interview, essay, and references. All enrolled students are required to pass basic writing and math skills assessment upon entrance. Students not passing these assessments are required to take designated courses to strengthen their skills during the first term of enrollment. Interview recommended.

High school preparation. College-preparatory program recommended. 29 units recommended. Required and recommended units include English 4, mathematics 4, social studies 4, history 4, science 4 (laboratory 3), foreign language 4 and academic electives 2.

2006-2007 Annual costs. Tuition/fees: $27,212. Room/board: $7,004. Books/supplies: $700. Personal expenses: $1,500.

2005-2006 Financial aid. Need-based: Average need met was 100%. Average scholarship/grant was $11,898; average loan $2,852. 66% of total undergraduate aid awarded as scholarships/grants, 34% as loans/jobs. **Non-need-based:** Scholarships awarded for academics, art, leadership, music/drama. **Additional information:** Middle Income Assistance Program provides interest-free loans to students who qualify for little or no financial aid. If student maintains constant enrollment and graduates within normal time frame, loan forgiven at commencement.

Application procedures. Admission: Priority date 2/1; no deadline. No application fee. Application may be submitted online. Admission notification on a rolling basis beginning on or about 4/1. Must reply by May 1 or within 3 week(s) if notified thereafter. **Financial aid:** Priority date 2/1; no closing date. FAFSA, institutional form required. Applicants notified on a rolling basis starting 3/1; must reply by 5/1.

Academics. Students receive narrative evaluations instead of grades. **Special study options:** Accelerated study, cooperative education, cross-registration, double major, dual enrollment of high school students, independent study, internships, student-designed major, study abroad. All students alternate on-campus study with minimum of five 3-month cooperative education job assignments across the United States and/or abroad. **Credit/placement by examination:** AP, CLEP, IB, institutional tests. **Support services:** Learning center, remedial instruction, study skills assistance, tutoring, writing center.

Majors. Area/ethnic studies: African, African-American, American, Asian, women's. **Biology:** General, biomedical sciences. **Business:** Business admin. **Communications:** General. **Conservation:** General, environmental studies. **English:** English lit. **Foreign languages:** General, French, German, Japanese, linguistics, Spanish. **History:** General. **Interdisciplinary:** Math/computer science, peace/conflict. **Liberal arts:** Arts/sciences. **Math:** General. **Philosophy/religion:** Philosophy, religion. **Physical sciences:** Chemistry, geology, physics. **Social sciences:** General, economics, international relations, political science. **Visual/performing arts:** General, cinematography, dance, dramatic, photography, studio arts.

Computing on campus. 60 workstations in dormitories, library, computer center, student center. Helpline, wireless network available.

Student life. Freshman orientation: Mandatory. Held before new students are required to register. **Policies:** Students participate in government of college. **Housing:** Guaranteed on-campus for all undergraduates. Coed dorms, special housing for disabled available. Living/learning dormitory units available for students studying foreign languages. Substance-free housing available. **Activities:** Choral groups, dance, drama, literary magazine, music ensembles, radio station, student government, student newspaper, Third World Alliance, Womyn's Center, various food co-ops, alternative library, organic garden, Undoing Racism, music co-ops.

Athletics. Intramural: Badminton, basketball, bowling, fencing, handball, racquetball, soccer, softball, squash, swimming, tennis, track and field, volleyball.

Student services. Alcohol/substance abuse counseling, career counseling, student employment services, financial aid counseling, health services, minority student services, personal counseling, veterans' counselor.

Contact. E-mail: admissions@antioch-college.edu
Phone: (937) 769-1100 Toll-free number: (800) 543-9436
Fax: (937) 769-1111
Michael Thorp, Dean of Admission and Financial Aid, Antioch College, 795 Livermore Street, Yellow Springs, OH 45387

Antioch University McGregor

Yellow Springs, Ohio
www.mcgregor.edu **CB code: 4527**

- Private 4-year branch campus and liberal arts college
- Commuter campus in small town
- 152 degree-seeking undergraduates

General. Founded in 1988. Regionally accredited. **Degrees:** 49 bachelor's awarded; master's offered. **Location:** 18 miles from Dayton. **Calendar:** Quarter, limited summer session. **Full-time faculty:** 57 total. **Part-time faculty:** 63 total. **Special facilities:** Nature reserve.

Basis for selection. Applicants must be over 21. Recommendations and motivation most important.

2005-2006 Annual costs. Tuition/fees: $9,666. Books/supplies: $1,500.

2004-2005 Financial aid. Need-based: 41% of total undergraduate aid awarded as scholarships/grants, 59% as loans/jobs.

Application procedures. **Admission:** Priority date 6/1; deadline 11/1. $45 fee. Admission notification on a rolling basis. **Financial aid:** No deadline. Applicants notified on a rolling basis.

Academics. **Special study options:** Double major, independent study, student-designed major, weekend college. **Credit/placement by examination:** CLEP. 45 credit hours maximum toward bachelor's degree. **Support services:** Reduced course load.

Majors. **Liberal arts:** Arts/sciences, humanities. **Math:** General.

Computing on campus. 35 workstations in library, computer center. Commuter students can connect to campus network.

Student life. **Freshman orientation:** Mandatory, $25 fee. **Activities:** Radio station.

Student services. Adult student services.

Contact. E-mail: admiss@mcgregor.edu
Phone: (937) 769-1818 Fax: (937) 769-1805
Oscar Robinson, Executive Director of Operations and Registrar, Antioch University McGregor, 800 Livermore Street, Yellow Springs, OH 45387

Art Academy of Cincinnati

Cincinnati, Ohio
www.artacademy.edu **CB code: 1002**

- Private 4-year visual arts college
- Commuter campus in large city
- 176 degree-seeking undergraduates
- 26% of applicants admitted
- SAT or ACT (ACT writing optional), application essay required

General. Founded in 1869. Regionally accredited. Attached to Cincinnati Art Museum. Some shared facilities. **Degrees:** 43 bachelor's awarded; master's offered. **Location:** One mile from downtown. **Calendar:** Semester, limited summer session. **Full-time faculty:** 17 total. **Part-time faculty:** 30 total.

Freshman class profile. 205 applied, 54 admitted, 54 enrolled.

Mid 50% test scores		Out-of-state:	24%
ACT:	18-24		

Basis for selection. Academic background, portfolio, and interview very important. Portfolio required for all; interview required for those within 150 miles of campus.

High school preparation. 12 units recommended. Recommended units include English 4, mathematics 3, social studies 1 and science 2. 3-4 units art recommended.

2005-2006 Annual costs. Tuition/fees: $18,850. Books/supplies: $1,200. Personal expenses: $590.

Financial aid. **Non-need-based:** Scholarships awarded for academics, alumni affiliation, art. **Additional information:** 40 annual scholarships awarded to entering and transfer students and 50 to continuing students based on spring portfolio competition.

Application procedures. **Admission:** Priority date 3/1; deadline 6/30 (postmark date). $25 fee. Admission notification on a rolling basis. **Financial aid:** Priority date 4/1; no closing date. FAFSA required. Applicants notified on a rolling basis starting 3/1.

Academics. **Special study options:** Cross-registration, exchange student, independent study, internships, student-designed major, study abroad. **Credit/placement by examination:** CLEP, institutional tests. **Support services:** Tutoring.

Majors. **Visual/performing arts:** Art history/conservation, commercial/advertising art, drawing, illustration, painting, photography, printmaking, sculpture, studio arts.

Computing on campus. 40 workstations in computer center.

Student life. **Freshman orientation:** Mandatory. Preregistration for classes offered. Held 2 days before school begins, includes introductions to staff and faculty. **Policies:** Freshmen permitted cars on campus. **Activities:** Film society.

Student services. Career counseling, student employment services, financial aid counseling, health services, personal counseling, placement for graduates, veterans' counselor. **Physically disabled:** Services for hearing impaired.

Contact. E-mail: admissions@artacademy.edu
Phone: (513) 721-5205 Toll-free number: (800) 323-5692
Fax: (513) 562-8778
Mary Jane Zumwalde, Director of Admissions, Art Academy of Cincinnati, 1125 St. Gregory Street, Cincinnati, OH 45202-1700

Ashland University

Ashland, Ohio **CB member**
www.ashland.edu **CB code: 1021**

- Private 4-year university and liberal arts college affiliated with Brethren Church
- Residential campus in large town
- 2,741 degree-seeking undergraduates: 8% part-time, 59% women, 8% African American, 2% Hispanic American, 1% international
- 2,562 degree-seeking graduate students
- 91% of applicants admitted
- SAT or ACT (ACT writing optional), application essay required

General. Founded in 1878. Regionally accredited. **Degrees:** 509 bachelor's, 6 associate awarded; master's, doctoral, first professional offered. **ROTC:** Air Force. **Location:** 60 miles from Cleveland, 80 miles from Columbus. **Calendar:** Semester, limited summer session. **Full-time faculty:** 231 total; 86% have terminal degrees, 6% minority, 41% women. **Part-time faculty:** 362 total; 27% have terminal degrees, 5% minority, 51% women. **Class size:** 61% < 20, 42% 20-39, less than 1% 50-99. **Special facilities:** Center for public affairs, center for business and economic research, convocation center, numismatic center.

Freshman class profile. 1,950 applied, 1,780 admitted, 550 enrolled.

Mid 50% test scores		Live on campus:	98%
SAT verbal:	470-590	International:	1%
SAT math:	470-590	Fraternities:	9%
ACT:	20-25	Sororities:	24%
Out-of-state:	8%		

Basis for selection. School achievement record most important; test scores also important. Counselor's recommendation considered. Interview recommended for all; audition recommended for music, theater programs; portfolio recommended for art.

High school preparation. College-preparatory program recommended. Required and recommended units include English 3-4, mathematics 2-3, social studies 2-3, history 1, science 2-3, foreign language 2 and academic electives 1.

2005-2006 Annual costs. Tuition/fees: $19,853. Room/board: $7,314. Books/supplies: $800. Personal expenses: $1,461.

2005-2006 Financial aid. **Need-based:** 534 full-time freshmen applied for aid; 430 were judged to have need; 430 of these received aid. Average need met was 90%. Average scholarship/grant was $11,729; average loan $3,192. 57% of total undergraduate aid awarded as scholarships/grants, 43% as loans/jobs. **Non-need-based:** Awarded to 437 full-time undergraduates, including 104 freshmen. Scholarships awarded for academics, alumni affiliation, art, athletics, job skills, leadership, minority status, music/drama, religious affiliation.

Application procedures. **Admission:** No deadline. , may be waived for applicants with need. No application fee. Application may be submitted online. Admission notification on a rolling basis beginning on or about 9/15. Must reply by May 1 or within 4 week(s) if notified thereafter. **Financial aid:** Priority date 3/15; no closing date. FAFSA, institutional form required. Applicants notified on a rolling basis starting 3/15; must reply within 3 week(s) of notification.

Academics. **Special study options:** Combined bachelor's/graduate degree, double major, ESL, honors, independent study, internships, student-designed major, study abroad, teacher certification program, Washington semester, weekend college. Pre-MBA courses for graduated nonbusiness majors, bachelor's degree completion program for RNs. **Credit/placement by examination:** AP, CLEP, IB, institutional tests. 32 credit hours maximum toward associate degree, 32 toward bachelor's. **Support services:** Learning center, study skills assistance, tutoring, writing center.

Majors. **Area/ethnic studies:** American. **Biology:** General. **Business:** General, accounting, business admin, finance, franchise operations, management information systems, marketing, purchasing. **Communications:** General, journalism, radio/tv. **Computer sciences:** Computer science.

Conservation: Environmental science. **Education:** Art, biology, business, chemistry, drama/dance, early childhood, English, family/consumer sciences, French, kindergarten/preschool, mathematics, middle, music, physical, science, social studies, Spanish, special. **English:** Creative writing, English lit. **Family/consumer sciences:** Family systems, food/nutrition. **Foreign languages:** French, Spanish. **Health:** Athletic training, nursing admin, recreational therapy. **History:** General. **Legal studies:** Prelaw. **Liberal arts:** Arts/sciences. **Math:** General. **Parks/recreation:** General, facilities management, sports admin. **Philosophy/religion:** Philosophy, religion. **Physical sciences:** Chemistry, geology, physics, planetary. **Protective services:** Law enforcement admin. **Psychology:** General. **Public administration:** Social work. **Social sciences:** Economics, political science, sociology. **Theology:** Bible, missionary, religious ed. **Visual/performing arts:** Commercial/advertising art, dramatic, music performance, music theory/composition, studio arts.

Most popular majors. Business/marketing 19%, communications/journalism 6%, education 36%, health sciences 6%, social sciences 7%.

Computing on campus. 488 workstations in dormitories, library, computer center, student center. Dormitories wired for high-speed internet access and linked to campus network. Commuter students can connect to campus network. Helpline, wireless network available.

Student life. Freshman orientation: Mandatory. Preregistration for classes offered. **Policies:** Dry campus. Freshmen permitted cars on campus. **Housing:** Guaranteed on-campus for all undergraduates. Coed dorms, single-sex dorms, apartments, fraternity/sorority housing available. $100 deposit, deadline 5/1. Scholar hall available. Apartments available to seniors. **Activities:** Bands, choral groups, dance, drama, literary magazine, music ensembles, musical theater, radio station, student government, student newspaper, symphony orchestra, TV station, Christian Fellowship, Newman Club, Fellowship of Christian Athletes, international club, Black Student Union, campus activities board, community care, adventure club, Republican/Democratic club.

Athletics. NCAA. **Intercollegiate:** Baseball M, basketball, cross-country, diving, football (tackle) M, golf, soccer, softball W, swimming, tennis W, track and field, volleyball W, wrestling M. **Intramural:** Badminton, basketball, bowling, cross-country, football (non-tackle), golf, racquetball, soccer, softball, swimming, table tennis, tennis, volleyball, wrestling M. **Team name:** Eagles.

Student services. Adult student services, alcohol/substance abuse counseling, campus ministries, career counseling, student employment services, financial aid counseling, health services, minority student services, personal counseling, veterans' counselor. **Physically disabled:** Services for visually, speech, hearing impaired.

Contact. E-mail: enrollme@ashland.edu
Phone: (419) 289-5052 Toll-free number: (800) 882-1548
Fax: (419) 289-5999
Tom Mansperger, Director of Admissions, Ashland University, 401 College Avenue, Ashland, OH 44805-9981

Baldwin-Wallace College

Berea, Ohio — **CB member**
www.bw.edu — **CB code: 1050**

- Private 4-year liberal arts college affiliated with United Methodist Church
- Residential campus in large town
- 3,493 degree-seeking undergraduates: 15% part-time, 59% women, 5% African American, 1% Asian American, 1% Hispanic American, 1% international
- 741 degree-seeking graduate students
- 79% of applicants admitted
- SAT or ACT (ACT writing optional), application essay required
- 67% graduate within 6 years; 19% enter graduate study

General. Founded in 1845. Regionally accredited. **Degrees:** 748 bachelor's awarded; master's offered. **ROTC:** Air Force. **Location:** 15 miles from Cleveland. **Calendar:** Semester, limited summer session. **Full-time faculty:** 162 total; 80% have terminal degrees, 9% minority, 39% women. **Part-time faculty:** 190 total; 26% have terminal degrees, 7% minority, 48% women. **Class size:** 49% < 20, 51% 20-39, less than 1% 40-49, less than 1% 50-99. **Special facilities:** Observatory, 2 art galleries, 2 theaters, conservatory of music, 2 dance studios, cybercafe, arboretum, Lyceum Square (historical site).

Freshman class profile. 2,366 applied, 1,870 admitted, 599 enrolled.

Mid 50% test scores			
SAT verbal:	500-610	Rank in top tenth:	28%
SAT math:	500-620	End year in good standing:	96%
ACT:	21-26	Return as sophomores:	82%
GPA 3.50 or higher:	54%	Out-of-state:	14%
GPA 3.0-3.49:	32%	Live on campus:	79%
GPA 2.0-2.99:	14%	International:	1%
Rank in top quarter:	29%	Fraternities:	5%
		Sororities:	14%

Basis for selection. Academic achievement (preferably 3.2 GPA) and class rank (preferably top 30%) most important. Test scores used to support data from high school record. 23 ACT, 550 SAT verbal, 550 SAT math recommended. Applicants must be graduates of accredited secondary school. Interview recommended for all; audition required for music, music education, music theater, and music therapy programs; portfolio recommended for art program. **Homeschooled:** Statement describing homeschool structure and mission, transcript of courses and grades, letter of recommendation (nonparent) required.

High school preparation. 15 units required; 19 recommended. Required and recommended units include English 4, mathematics 3-4, social studies 2, history 1, science 3 (laboratory 2), foreign language 2 and academic electives 3. Some flexibility in choice of subjects permitted.

2005-2006 Annual costs. Tuition/fees: $20,518. Conservatory tuition is higher. Room/board: $6,738.

2005-2006 Financial aid. Need-based: 576 full-time freshmen applied for aid; 473 were judged to have need; 473 of these received aid. Average need met was 88%. Average scholarship/grant was $11,837; average loan $2,875. 68% of total undergraduate aid awarded as scholarships/grants, 32% as loans/jobs. **Non-need-based:** Awarded to 1,097 full-time undergraduates, including 350 freshmen. Scholarships awarded for academics, alumni affiliation, art, leadership, minority status, music/drama, religious affiliation, state residency.

Application procedures. Admission: Priority date 5/1; no deadline. $25 fee, may be waived for applicants with need. Application may be submitted online. Admission notification on a rolling basis beginning on or about 10/1. Must reply by May 1 or within 3 week(s) if notified thereafter. **Financial aid:** Priority date 5/1, closing date 9/1. FAFSA required. Applicants notified on a rolling basis starting 2/14.

Academics. Weekend classes limited to non-traditional students. **Special study options:** Accelerated study, combined bachelor's/graduate degree, cross-registration, distance learning, double major, dual enrollment of high school students, exchange student, honors, independent study, internships, liberal arts/career combination, student-designed major, study abroad, teacher certification program, United Nations semester, urban semester, Washington semester, weekend college. BS program in allied health fields with 3 local community colleges; 3-2 in engineering with Case Western Reserve University, Columbia University (NY), Washington University (MO); 3-2 in social work with Case Western Reserve University; 4-1 joint BS/MS program in management science with Case Western Reserve University; 3-1 or 4-1 medical technology program with local hospitals; 3-2 MBA programs in Accounting & Human Resources. **Credit/placement by examination:** AP, CLEP, IB, SAT, ACT, institutional tests. **Support services:** Learning center, reduced course load, remedial instruction, study skills assistance, tutoring, writing center.

Majors. Biology: General, exercise physiology. **Business:** Accounting, business admin, finance, human resources, marketing, small business admin. **Communications:** General, media studies, public relations. **Computer sciences:** Computer science, networking, systems analysis, webmaster. **Education:** General, early childhood, learning disabled, middle, music, physics, science. **Engineering:** General. **English:** English lit. **Foreign languages:** French, German, Spanish. **Health:** Athletic training, communication disorders, music therapy. **History:** General. **Interdisciplinary:** Global studies, neuroscience. **Math:** General. **Parks/recreation:** Health/fitness, sports admin. **Philosophy/religion:** Philosophy, religion. **Physical sciences:** Chemistry, physics. **Protective services:** Criminal justice. **Psychology:** General. **Social sciences:** Econometrics, economics, political science, sociology. **Visual/performing arts:** Art, art history/conservation, arts management, film/cinema, music history, music performance, music theory/composition, piano/organ, studio arts.

Most popular majors. Business/marketing 28%, education 14%, psychology 9%, visual/performing arts 8%.

Computing on campus. 533 workstations in dormitories, library, computer center, student center. Dormitories wired for high-speed internet access and linked to campus network. Commuter students can connect to campus network. Online course registration, online library, helpline, student web hosting, wireless network available.

Student life. Freshman orientation: Available. Preregistration for classes offered. Weekend program includes games, seminars, dances. **Housing:** Coed dorms, single-sex dorms, special housing for disabled, apartments, fraternity/sorority housing, substance-free housing available. Wellness halls, Sprout Houses (for single mothers and children), Carmel living and learning center, honors and freshman only housing available. **Activities:** Bands, choral groups, dance, drama, literary magazine, music ensembles, musical theater, opera, radio station, student government, student newspaper, symphony orchestra, TV station, Campus Crusade for Christ, Hillel, Newman Student Organization, College Democrats, College Republicans, Black Student Alliance, Hispanic American Student Association, Middle Eastern Student Alliance, Certified Peer Educators, Habitat for Humanity.

Athletics. NCAA. **Intercollegiate:** Baseball M, basketball, cross-country, diving, football (tackle) M, golf, soccer, softball W, swimming, tennis, track and field, volleyball W, wrestling M. **Intramural:** Badminton, basketball, football (non-tackle) M, football (tackle) M, golf, racquetball, softball, tennis, volleyball, wrestling M. **Team name:** Yellow Jackets.

Student services. Adult student services, alcohol/substance abuse counseling, campus ministries, career counseling, student employment services, financial aid counseling, health services, minority student services, personal counseling. **Physically disabled:** Services for visually, speech, hearing impaired.

Contact. E-mail: admission@bw.edu
Phone: (440) 826-2222 Toll-free number: (877) 292-7759
Fax: (440) 826-3830
Susan Dileno, Dean of Admission & Financial Aid, Baldwin-Wallace College, 275 Eastland Road, Berea, OH 44017-2088

Bluffton University

Bluffton, Ohio
www.bluffton.edu **CB code: 1067**

- Private 4-year liberal arts college affiliated with Mennonite Church
- Residential campus in small town
- 1,046 degree-seeking undergraduates: 5% part-time, 57% women
- 109 degree-seeking graduate students
- 71% of applicants admitted
- SAT or ACT (ACT writing optional) required
- 56% graduate within 6 years

General. Founded in 1899. Regionally accredited. Christian faith, values, and service to others in the Anabaptist, peace church tradition. **Degrees:** 242 bachelor's awarded; master's offered. **Location:** 15 miles from Lima, 75 miles from Toledo. **Calendar:** Semester, limited summer session. **Full-time faculty:** 67 total; 72% have terminal degrees, 8% minority, 31% women. **Part-time faculty:** 47 total; 23% have terminal degrees, 4% minority, 49% women. **Class size:** 51% < 20, 39% 20-39, 9% 40-49, less than 1% 50-99. **Special facilities:** Mennonite historical library, nature preserve.

Freshman class profile. 1,074 applied, 765 admitted, 230 enrolled.

Mid 50% test scores		**Rank in top quarter:**	42%
SAT verbal:	490-590	**Rank in top tenth:**	14%
SAT math:	480-560	**End year in good standing:**	91%
ACT:	19-24	**Return as sophomores:**	70%
GPA 3.50 or higher:	46%	**Out-of-state:**	13%
GPA 3.0-3.49:	36%	**Live on campus:**	100%
GPA 2.0-2.99:	18%	**International:**	1%

Basis for selection. Class rank, school achievement record, and test scores very important. Campus visit and interview strongly recommended. Essay required for academically weak students; audition and portfolio required for scholarships in music and art. **Homeschooled:** Interview required.

High school preparation. College-preparatory program recommended. 16 units recommended. Recommended units include English 4, mathematics 3, social studies 3, science 3 and foreign language 3.

2006-2007 Annual costs. Tuition/fees (projected): $20,570. Room/board: $7,082. Books/supplies: $1,000. Personal expenses: $1,200.

2005-2006 Financial aid. Need-based: 220 full-time freshmen applied for aid; 207 were judged to have need; 207 of these received aid. Average need met was 95.9%. Average scholarship/grant was $13,712; average loan $3,820. 54% of total undergraduate aid awarded as scholarships/grants, 46% as loans/jobs. **Non-need-based:** Awarded to 166 full-time undergraduates, including 40 freshmen. Scholarships awarded for academics, art, job skills, leadership, minority status, music/drama, state residency. **Additional information:** Tuition Equalization Scholarship Program guarantees qualified students nonrepayable financial aid that is at a minimum the difference between Bluffton University tuition and the average tuition at the 3 Ohio public universities with highest tuition. Requirements: minimum 23 ACT or 1050 SAT and rank in top 25% of high school class or 3.0 GPA.

Application procedures. Admission: Priority date 5/31; deadline 8/20 (receipt date). $20 fee, may be waived for applicants with need. Application may be submitted online. Admission notification on a rolling basis beginning on or about 6/1. **Financial aid:** Priority date 5/1, closing date 10/1. FAFSA required. Applicants notified on a rolling basis starting 3/1; must reply within 3 week(s) of notification.

Academics. Special study options: Accelerated study, double major, dual enrollment of high school students, honors, independent study, internships, liberal arts/career combination, student-designed major, study abroad, teacher certification program, Washington semester. Degree-completion program for working adults 25 years and older. **Credit/placement by examination:** AP, CLEP, SAT, ACT, institutional tests. 20 credit hours maximum toward bachelor's degree. **Support services:** Learning center, remedial instruction, tutoring, writing center.

Majors. Biology: General. **Business:** Accounting, business admin, management information systems, organizational behavior. **Communications:** General. **Computer sciences:** Computer science, information systems, information technology. **Education:** Art, biology, business, chemistry, early childhood, elementary, English, family/consumer sciences, health, history, kindergarten/preschool, mathematics, mentally handicapped, middle, music, physical, physics, science, secondary, social studies, special. **English:** English lit. **Family/consumer sciences:** General, clothing/textiles, food/nutrition. **Foreign languages:** Spanish. **Health:** Premedicine. **History:** General. **Interdisciplinary:** Peace/conflict. **Math:** General. **Parks/recreation:** Facilities management, health/fitness, sports admin. **Philosophy/religion:** Religion. **Physical sciences:** Chemistry, physics. **Protective services:** Criminal justice. **Psychology:** General. **Public administration:** Social work. **Social sciences:** General, economics, sociology. **Theology:** Youth ministry. **Visual/performing arts:** Art.

Most popular majors. Business/marketing 44%, education 21%, parks/recreation 6%.

Computing on campus. 125 workstations in dormitories, library, computer center, student center. Dormitories wired for high-speed internet access and linked to campus network. Commuter students can connect to campus network. Online course registration, online library, helpline, repair service, student web hosting, wireless network available.

Student life. Freshman orientation: Mandatory. Preregistration for classes offered. Fall orientation begins friday before classes and continues through first week of classes. Summer orientation is a one-day event held over the summer; students can choose one of four dates. **Policies:** No alcoholic beverages or tobacco allowed on campus. Honor system applies to all student activities. Students should feel comfortable with emphasis on faith and values. Voluntary chapel service once each week. Freshmen permitted cars on campus. **Housing:** Guaranteed on-campus for all undergraduates. Coed dorms, single-sex dorms, substance-free housing available. All traditional undergraduate students required to live on campus or commute from home. **Activities:** Bands, choral groups, dance, drama, literary magazine, music ensembles, musical theater, radio station, student government, student newspaper, departmental clubs, Brothers and Sisters in Christ, peace club, Habitat for Humanity, Fellowship of Christian Athletes, international connection, African American student organization, peer awareness leaders, College Republicans, Young Democrats.

Athletics. NCAA. **Intercollegiate:** Baseball M, basketball, cheerleading M, cross-country, football (tackle) M, soccer, softball W, tennis, track and field, volleyball W. **Intramural:** Basketball, bowling, football (non-tackle), softball, volleyball. **Team name:** Beavers.

Student services. Campus ministries, career counseling, student employment services, financial aid counseling, health services, minority student services, personal counseling, placement for graduates. **Physically disabled:** Services for visually, hearing impaired. **Learning disabled:** Comprehensive services available.

Contact. E-mail: admissions@bluffton.edu
Phone: (419) 358-3257 Toll-free number: (800) 488-3257
Fax: (419) 358-3081
Chris Jebsen, Director of Admissions, Bluffton University, 1 University Drive, Bluffton, OH 45817-2104

Bowling Green State University

Bowling Green, Ohio **CB member**
www.bgsu.edu **CB code: 1069**

- Public 4-year university
- Residential campus in large town

- 15,846 degree-seeking undergraduates: 6% part-time, 55% women, 8% African American, 1% Asian American, 3% Hispanic American, 1% Native American, 1% international
- 2,474 degree-seeking graduate students
- 90% of applicants admitted
- SAT and SAT Subject Tests or ACT (ACT writing optional) required
- 60% graduate within 6 years

General. Founded in 1910. Regionally accredited. **Degrees:** 2,960 bachelor's awarded; master's, doctoral offered. **ROTC:** Army, Air Force. **Location:** 23 miles from Toledo. **Calendar:** Semester, limited summer session. **Full-time faculty:** 851 total; 77% have terminal degrees, 15% minority, 44% women. **Part-time faculty:** 196 total; 6% minority, 52% women. **Class size:** 36% < 20, 52% 20-39, 6% 40-49, 5% 50-99, 1% >100. **Special facilities:** Planetarium, film theater, sound recording archives, popular culture library, marine biology laboratory, educational memorabilia center.

Freshman class profile. 11,168 applied, 10,058 admitted, 3,603 enrolled.

Mid 50% test scores		**GPA 2.0-2.99:**	33%
SAT verbal:	460-570	**End year in good standing:**	81%
SAT math:	460-570	**Return as sophomores:**	79.1%
ACT:	19-24	**Out-of-state:**	12%
GPA 3.50 or higher:	32%	**Live on campus:**	91%
GPA 3.0-3.49:	35%	**International:**	1%

Basis for selection. Admissions decision based on high school sixth semester GPA and ACT or SAT test scores. Interview recommended for all; audition required for music; portfolio required for art programs. Essays required for honors program.

High school preparation. College-preparatory program recommended. Recommended units include English 4, mathematics 3, social studies 3, science 3 (laboratory 2) and foreign language 2. One unit visual/performing arts.

2005-2006 Annual costs. Tuition/fees: $8,560; $15,868 out-of-state. Room/board: $6,434. Books/supplies: $1,140.

2004-2005 Financial aid. Need-based: 3,145 full-time freshmen applied for aid; 2,441 were judged to have need; 2,431 of these received aid. Average need met was 50%. Average scholarship/grant was $3,571; average loan $2,751. 33% of total undergraduate aid awarded as scholarships/grants, 67% as loans/jobs. **Non-need-based:** Awarded to 5,193 full-time undergraduates, including 1,721 freshmen. Scholarships awarded for academics, alumni affiliation, art, athletics, leadership, minority status, music/drama, ROTC, state residency.

Application procedures. Admission: Priority date 2/1; deadline 7/15 (postmark date). $35 fee, may be waived for applicants with need. Application may be submitted online. Admission notification on a rolling basis beginning on or about 10/1. Must reply by 5/1. **Financial aid:** No deadline. FAFSA required. Applicants notified on a rolling basis starting 4/15; must reply within 3 week(s) of notification.

Academics. Evening degree programs and career counseling offered for adults in the greater community. **Special study options:** Accelerated study, combined bachelor's/graduate degree, cooperative education, cross-registration, distance learning, double major, dual enrollment of high school students, exchange student, honors, independent study, internships, liberal arts/career combination, student-designed major, study abroad, teacher certification program, Washington semester. **Credit/placement by examination:** AP, CLEP, SAT, ACT, institutional tests. 30 hours toward bachelor's degree through portfolio program. **Support services:** Learning center, preadmission summer program, reduced course load, remedial instruction, study skills assistance, tutoring, writing center.

Majors. Architecture: Environmental design, interior. **Area/ethnic studies:** African, American, Asian, women's. **Biology:** General, bacteriology. **Business:** General, accounting, auditing, fashion, finance, hospitality admin, human resources, international, logistics, management information systems, managerial economics, operations, tourism promotion. **Communications:** Broadcast journalism, journalism, public relations. **Computer sciences:** General. **Conservation:** Management/policy. **Education:** General, art, biology, business, Deaf/hearing impaired, drama/dance, English, foreign languages, health, kindergarten/preschool, mathematics, middle, music, physical, sales/marketing, science, social studies, special, voc/tech. **Engineering technology:** Construction, electrical, industrial, mechanical, quality control. **English:** Creative writing, English lit, speech/rhetoric, technical writing. **Family/consumer sciences:** Aging, child development, family studies, food/nutrition. **Foreign languages:** Classics, French, German, Russian, Spanish. **Health:** Athletic training, clinical lab science, communication disorders, dietetics, environmental health, health care admin, nursing (RN). **History:** General. **Interdisciplinary:** Gerontology, neuroscience. **Legal studies:** Prelaw. **Liberal arts:** Arts/sciences. **Math:** General, applied, statistics. **Parks/recreation:** General, sports admin. **Philosophy/religion:** Philosophy. **Physical sciences:** Chemistry, geology, physics. **Protective services:** Criminal justice. **Psychology:** General. **Public administration:** General, social work. **Social sciences:** Economics, geography, international relations, political science, sociology. **Transportation:** Aviation management. **Visual/performing arts:** Acting, art, art history/conservation, cinematography, crafts, design, dramatic, film/cinema, jazz, music performance, music theory/composition, musicology, photography, piano/organ, theater design, voice/opera.

Most popular majors. Business/marketing 17%, education 26%, English 6%, health sciences 6%, visual/performing arts 8%.

Computing on campus. 1,314 workstations in dormitories, library, computer center, student center. Dormitories wired for high-speed internet access and linked to campus network. Commuter students can connect to campus network. Online course registration, helpline, repair service available.

Student life. Freshman orientation: Available. Preregistration for classes offered. Normally held in summer. **Policies:** Freshmen permitted cars on campus. **Housing:** Guaranteed on-campus for freshmen. Coed dorms, fraternity/sorority housing, substance-free housing available. $200 deposit, deadline 5/1. No-alcohol wings, nonsmoking areas, residential housing communities. **Activities:** Bands, choral groups, dance, drama, film society, literary magazine, music ensembles, musical theater, radio station, student government, student newspaper, symphony orchestra, TV station, Active Christians Today, African Peoples Association, Asian Communities, United Latino Student Union, World Student Association, Women's Group, College Democrats, College Republicans, Habitat for Humanity, Environmental Action Group.

Athletics. NCAA. **Intercollegiate:** Baseball M, basketball, cross-country, diving, football (tackle) M, golf, gymnastics W, ice hockey M, soccer, softball W, swimming, tennis, track and field, volleyball W. **Intramural:** Basketball, cross-country, football (non-tackle), golf, handball, ice hockey, racquetball, soccer, softball, swimming, tennis, track and field, volleyball. **Team name:** Falcons.

Student services. Adult student services, alcohol/substance abuse counseling, career counseling, services for economically disadvantaged, student employment services, financial aid counseling, health services, legal services, minority student services, personal counseling, placement for graduates, veterans' counselor, women's services. **Physically disabled:** Services for visually, speech, hearing impaired.

Contact. E-mail: admissions@bgnet.bgsu.edu
Phone: (419) 372-2478 Toll-free number: (866) 246-6732
Fax: (419) 372-6955
Gary Swegan, Director of Admissions, Bowling Green State University, 110 McFall Center, Bowling Green, OH 43403-0085

Capital University

Columbus, Ohio — **CB member**
www.capital.edu — **CB code: 1099**

- Private 4-year university affiliated with Evangelical Lutheran Church in America
- Residential campus in very large city
- 2,751 degree-seeking undergraduates: 19% part-time, 64% women, 12% African American, 2% Asian American, 1% Hispanic American, 1% international
- 1,027 degree-seeking graduate students
- 78% of applicants admitted
- SAT or ACT (ACT writing optional) required
- 58% graduate within 6 years

General. Founded in 1830. Regionally accredited. **Degrees:** 590 bachelor's awarded; master's, first professional offered. **ROTC:** Army, Air Force. **Location:** 3 miles from downtown. **Calendar:** Semester, limited summer session. **Full-time faculty:** 218 total; 69% have terminal degrees, 12% minority, 46% women. **Part-time faculty:** 242 total. **Class size:** 68% < 20, 31% 20-39, less than 1% 40-49, less than 1% 50-99.

Freshman class profile. 3,023 applied, 2,356 admitted, 602 enrolled.

Mid 50% test scores		**GPA 2.0-2.99:**	19%
SAT verbal:	490-600	**Rank in top quarter:**	50%
SAT math:	480-600	**Rank in top tenth:**	23%
ACT:	21-26	**Return as sophomores:**	76%
GPA 3.50 or higher:	47%	**Out-of-state:**	9%
GPA 3.0-3.49:	34%	**Live on campus:**	75%

Basis for selection. Academic achievement in a college-preparatory curriculum most important. Recommendations, test scores, and extracurricular activities considered. Interview recommended for all; audition required for music program; portfolio recommended for art, art therapy programs. **Homeschooled:** Statement describing homeschool structure and mission, transcript of courses and grades, letter of recommendation (nonparent) required.

High school preparation. College-preparatory program recommended. 18 units recommended. Recommended units include English 4, mathematics 3, social studies 3, science 3 (laboratory 2), foreign language 2 and academic electives 1. Chemistry and algebra II for nursing applicants. One fine arts recommended.

2005-2006 Annual costs. Tuition/fees: $24,100. Room/board: $6,344. Books/supplies: $1,000. Personal expenses: $1,724.

2004-2005 Financial aid. **Need-based:** 573 full-time freshmen applied for aid; 515 were judged to have need; 515 of these received aid. Average need met was 81%. Average scholarship/grant was $15,032; average loan $3,514. 69% of total undergraduate aid awarded as scholarships/grants, 31% as loans/jobs. **Non-need-based:** Awarded to 558 full-time undergraduates, including 159 freshmen. Scholarships awarded for academics, alumni affiliation, art, minority status, music/drama, religious affiliation, ROTC, state residency.

Application procedures. **Admission:** Priority date 4/15; no deadline. $25 fee, may be waived for applicants with need. Application may be submitted online. Admission notification on a rolling basis beginning on or about 9/15. Must reply by May 1 or within 2 week(s) if notified thereafter. **Financial aid:** Priority date 2/28; no closing date. FAFSA required. Applicants notified on a rolling basis starting 3/1; must reply by 5/1.

Academics. Teacher certification for learning disabilities and reading. Paralegal certification available from law school. **Special study options:** Cooperative education, cross-registration, double major, ESL, exchange student, honors, independent study, internships, liberal arts/career combination, student-designed major, study abroad, teacher certification program, Washington semester. Dual degree engineering bachelor program with Washington University, St. Louis, and Case Western Reserve, 3-2 occupational therapy bachelor program with Washington University, St. Louis. **Credit/placement by examination:** AP, CLEP, SAT, ACT, institutional tests. 27 credit hours maximum toward bachelor's degree. **Support services:** Learning center, reduced course load, remedial instruction, study skills assistance, tutoring, writing center.

Majors. **Biology:** General, biochemistry. **Business:** General, accounting, business admin. **Communications:** General, broadcast journalism, public relations. **Computer sciences:** General, computer science. **Conservation:** Environmental studies. **Education:** General, early childhood, elementary, middle, music, physical, secondary. **English:** Technical writing. **Foreign languages:** French, Spanish. **Health:** Art therapy, athletic training, occupational health, predentistry, premedicine, preop/surgical nursing, prepharmacy. **History:** General. **Legal studies:** Prelaw. **Liberal arts:** Arts/sciences. **Math:** General. **Parks/recreation:** Health/fitness. **Philosophy/religion:** Philosophy, religion. **Physical sciences:** Chemistry. **Psychology:** General. **Public administration:** General, social work. **Social sciences:** Criminology, economics, international relations, political science, sociology. **Theology:** Religious ed. **Visual/performing arts:** Art, jazz, music management, music performance, music theory/composition, piano/organ, studio arts, voice/opera.

Most popular majors. Business/marketing 11%, communications/journalism 8%, education 15%, health sciences 13%, interdisciplinary studies 13%, public administration/social services 11%, social sciences 12%.

Computing on campus. 105 workstations in dormitories, library, computer center, student center. Dormitories wired for high-speed internet access and linked to campus network. Commuter students can connect to campus network. Online library, helpline available.

Student life. **Freshman orientation:** Mandatory. One-day program in summer, 5-day program before start of classes. **Policies:** Freshmen permitted cars on campus. **Housing:** Guaranteed on-campus for freshmen. Coed dorms, special housing for disabled, apartments, substance-free housing available. $100 nonrefundable deposit, deadline 5/1. **Activities:** Bands, choral groups, dance, drama, literary magazine, music ensembles, musical theater, radio station, student government, student newspaper, symphony orchestra, TV station, Black Student Union, Young Republicans, Campus Democrats, Circle-K, Ebony Brotherhood Association, international student association, Capateers (volunteers), Habitat for Humanity, university programming.

Athletics. NCAA. **Intercollegiate:** Baseball M, basketball, cross-country, football (tackle) M, golf, soccer, softball W, tennis, track and field, volleyball W. **Intramural:** Basketball, soccer, softball, tennis, volleyball. **Team name:** Crusaders.

Student services. Campus ministries, career counseling, student employment services, financial aid counseling, health services, minority student services, personal counseling, placement for graduates, veterans' counselor.

Contact. E-mail: admissions@capital.edu
Phone: (614) 236-6101 Toll-free number: (866) 544-6175
Fax: (614) 236-6926
Kimberly Ebbrecht, Director of Admission, Capital University, One College and Main, Columbus, OH 43209-2394

Case Western Reserve University

Cleveland, Ohio — **CB member**
www.case.edu — **CB code: 1105**

- Private 4-year university
- Residential campus in very large city
- 3,824 degree-seeking undergraduates: 4% part-time, 40% women, 5% African American, 15% Asian American, 2% Hispanic American, 4% international
- 5,312 degree-seeking graduate students
- 68% of applicants admitted
- SAT or ACT with writing, application essay required
- 77% graduate within 6 years; 41% enter graduate study

General. Founded in 1826. Regionally accredited. **Degrees:** 705 bachelor's awarded; master's, doctoral, first professional offered. **ROTC:** Army, Air Force. **Location:** 4 miles from downtown. **Calendar:** Semester, limited summer session. **Full-time faculty:** 687 total; 92% have terminal degrees, 17% minority, 36% women. **Part-time faculty:** 166 total; 60% have terminal degrees, 4% minority, 46% women. **Class size:** 59% < 20, 23% 20-39, 6% 40-49, 8% 50-99, 4% >100. **Special facilities:** Biology field station, observatory, interdisciplinary research centers, art museum, natural history museum, historical society, botanical garden.

Freshman class profile. 7,181 applied, 4,916 admitted, 1,162 enrolled.

Mid 50% test scores			
SAT verbal:	600-700	Return as sophomores:	92%
SAT math:	640-740	Out-of-state:	47%
ACT:	27-31	Live on campus:	94%
Rank in top quarter:	91%	International:	2%
Rank in top tenth:	63%	Fraternities:	33%
		Sororities:	26%

Basis for selection. School achievement record and test scores most important. School and community activities, essays, recommendations, and interview also considered. Special consideration to applicants from culturally, educationally, or economically disadvantaged backgrounds. IELTS, AP International English test, or TOEFL required for all international students. Interview recommended for all; audition required for music, music education programs; portfolio required for art education program. Writing sample required. **Homeschooled:** Transcript of courses and grades required. Applicants encouraged to take at least 3 SAT Subject Tests in addition to SAT or ACT and to submit at least 2 letters from outside instructors or employers. Interview strongly recommended.

High school preparation. 16 units required. Required and recommended units include English 4, mathematics 3-4, social studies 3-4, science 3 (laboratory 1-2) and foreign language 2-3. 2 units laboratory science recommended generally. 4 mathematics, 1 chemistry and physics recommended for engineering. 2 laboratory science (1 chemistry) recommended for science, mathematics and premedical.

2006-2007 Annual costs. Tuition/fees (projected): $31,738. Tuition varies for first-year and continuing students. $400 technology fee for resident students only. Room/board: $9,280. Books/supplies: $1,040. Personal expenses: $1,350.

2005-2006 Financial aid. **Need-based:** 991 full-time freshmen applied for aid; 812 were judged to have need; 809 of these received aid. Average need met was 96%. Average scholarship/grant was $20,783; average loan $4,836. 74% of total undergraduate aid awarded as scholarships/grants, 26% as loans/jobs. **Non-need-based:** Awarded to 2,995 full-time undergraduates, including 979 freshmen. Scholarships awarded for academics, art, leadership, music/drama.

Application procedures. **Admission:** Closing date 1/15 (postmark date). $35 fee, may be waived for applicants with need. Application may be submitted online. Admission notification 4/1. Must reply by 5/1. **Financial aid:** Priority date 2/1; no closing date. FAFSA, institutional form required. Applicants notified on a rolling basis starting 2/15; must reply by 5/1 or within 2 week(s) of notification.

Academics. Preprofessional Scholars Program gives talented undergraduates conditional acceptances to our graduate schools of medicine, dentistry, law, and social work. Most programs allow students to pursue combined bachelor's/master's. **Special study options:** Accelerated study, combined bachelor's/graduate degree, cooperative education, cross-registration, double major, dual enrollment of high school students, ESL, exchange student, honors, independent study, internships, liberal arts/career combination, student-designed major, study abroad, teacher certification program, Washington semester. Exchange program with Fisk University; 3-2 binary program in engineering, biochemistry, and astronomy. **Credit/placement by examination:** AP, CLEP, IB, institutional tests. **Support services:** Learning center, pre-admission summer program, reduced course load, study skills assistance, tutoring, writing center.

Majors. **Area/ethnic studies:** American, Asian, French, German, Japanese, women's. **Biology:** General, biochemistry, evolutionary. **Business:** Accounting, business admin. **Computer sciences:** General, computer science. **Conservation:** Environmental studies. **Education:** Art, music. **Engineering:** General, aerospace, biomedical, chemical, civil, computer, electrical, materials, materials science, mechanical, physics, polymer, science, systems. **English:** English lit. **Family/consumer sciences:** Human nutrition. **Foreign languages:** Classics, comparative lit, French, German, Spanish. **Health:** Communication disorders, dietetics, nursing (RN). **History:** General, science/technology. **Interdisciplinary:** Cognitive science, gerontology, natural sciences, nutrition sciences. **Math:** General, applied, statistics. **Philosophy/religion:** Philosophy, religion. **Physical sciences:** Astronomy, chemistry, geology, physics. **Psychology:** General. **Social sciences:** Anthropology, economics, international relations, political science, sociology. **Visual/performing arts:** Art history/conservation, dramatic.

Most popular majors. Biology 12%, business/marketing 8%, engineering/engineering technologies 27%, physical sciences 6%, psychology 9%, social sciences 12%.

Computing on campus. 353 workstations in library, computer center. Dormitories wired for high-speed internet access and linked to campus network. Commuter students can connect to campus network. Online course registration, online library, helpline, repair service, student web hosting, wireless network available.

Student life. **Freshman orientation:** Mandatory, $400 fee. Preregistration for classes offered. 3-day orientation includes placement exams and special programs for parents. **Policies:** Freshmen permitted cars on campus. **Housing:** Guaranteed on-campus for freshmen. Coed dorms, apartments, fraternity/sorority housing, substance-free housing available. Secured female-only floor available. Special-interest housing available. **Activities:** Bands, choral groups, dance, drama, film society, literary magazine, music ensembles, musical theater, radio station, student government, student newspaper, symphony orchestra, University Christian Movement, Catholic Campus Ministry, Hillel Foundation, African-American Society, International Club, College Democrats, College Republicans, Habitat for Humanity, Model United Nations.

Athletics. NCAA. **Intercollegiate:** Baseball M, basketball, cross-country, football (tackle) M, soccer, softball W, swimming, tennis, track and field, volleyball W, wrestling M. **Intramural:** Badminton, basketball, bowling, cross-country, football (non-tackle), football (tackle) M, golf, racquetball, soccer, softball, squash, swimming, table tennis, tennis, track and field, volleyball, water polo, weight lifting, wrestling M. **Team name:** Spartans.

Student services. Adult student services, alcohol/substance abuse counseling, campus ministries, career counseling, student employment services, financial aid counseling, health services, legal services, minority student services, personal counseling, placement for graduates, veterans' counselor, women's services. **Physically disabled:** Services for visually, speech, hearing impaired.

Contact. E-mail: admission@case.edu
Phone: (216) 368-4450 Fax: (216) 368-5111
Elizabeth Woyczynski, Director of Undergraduate Admission, Case Western Reserve University, Tomlinson Hall, Cleveland, OH 44106-7055

Cedarville University

Cedarville, Ohio
www.cedarville.edu **CB code: 1151**

- Private 4-year university and liberal arts college affiliated with Baptist faith
- Residential campus in small town
- 3,028 degree-seeking undergraduates: 3% part-time, 56% women, 2% African American, 1% Asian American, 2% Hispanic American
- 11 degree-seeking graduate students
- 83% of applicants admitted
- SAT or ACT (ACT writing recommended), application essay required
- 71% graduate within 6 years; 20% enter graduate study

General. Founded in 1887. Regionally accredited. **Degrees:** 603 bachelor's awarded; master's offered. **ROTC:** Army, Air Force. **Location:** 12 miles from Springfield, 20 miles from Dayton. **Calendar:** Semester, limited summer session. **Full-time faculty:** 208 total; 64% have terminal degrees, 7% minority, 29% women. **Part-time faculty:** 51 total; 6% have terminal degrees, 4% minority, 51% women. **Class size:** 58% < 20, 31% 20-39, 3% 40-49, 5% 50-99, 2% >100.

Freshman class profile. 2,017 applied, 1,679 admitted, 763 enrolled.

Mid 50% test scores			
SAT verbal:	540-650	Rank in top quarter:	63%
SAT math:	520-640	Rank in top tenth:	34%
ACT:	22-28	End year in good standing:	92%
GPA 3.50 or higher:	68%	Return as sophomores:	81%
GPA 3.0-3.49:	26%	Out-of-state:	64%
GPA 2.0-2.99:	6%	Live on campus:	98%

Basis for selection. Clear testimony of personal faith in Jesus Christ, evidence of consistent Christian lifestyle, above-average academic performance (academic records, class rank, test scores), personal references considered. Applications reviewed on a rolling basis. Audition required for music majors; interview recommended for academically marginal students. **Learning Disabled:** Students encouraged to contact Coordinator of Disabilities Services.

High school preparation. College-preparatory program recommended. Recommended units include English 4, mathematics 4, social studies 3, science 3 (laboratory 3) and foreign language 3. Additional mathematics and science recommended for nursing, science, engineering, and mathematics applicants.

2006-2007 Annual costs. Tuition/fees (projected): $17,120. Room/board: $5,010. Books/supplies: $800. Personal expenses: $1,050.

2005-2006 Financial aid. **Need-based:** Average need met was 24%. Average scholarship/grant was $1,422; average loan $2,723. 35% of total undergraduate aid awarded as scholarships/grants, 65% as loans/jobs. **Non-need-based:** Scholarships awarded for academics, alumni affiliation, athletics, leadership, minority status, music/drama, ROTC, state residency.

Application procedures. **Admission:** Priority date 3/1; no deadline. $30 fee, may be waived for applicants with need. Application may be submitted online. Admission notification on a rolling basis beginning on or about 8/1. Must reply by May 1 or within 2 week(s) if notified thereafter. **Financial aid:** Priority date 3/1; no closing date. FAFSA required. Applicants notified on a rolling basis starting 3/1; must reply within 4 week(s) of notification.

Academics. **Special study options:** Accelerated study, distance learning, double major, dual enrollment of high school students, honors, independent study, internships, liberal arts/career combination, student-designed major, study abroad, teacher certification program, Washington semester. **Credit/placement by examination:** AP, CLEP, IB, SAT, ACT, institutional tests. 40 credit hours maximum toward bachelor's degree. **Support services:** Reduced course load, remedial instruction, study skills assistance, tutoring, writing center.

Majors. **Area/ethnic studies:** American. **Biology:** General. **Business:** Accounting, administrative services, business admin, finance, international, management information systems, marketing. **Communications:** General, radio/tv. **Communications technology:** General. **Computer sciences:** General, computer science. **Education:** Biology, early childhood, English, health, mathematics, middle, music, physical, physics, science, social studies, Spanish, special. **Engineering:** Electrical, mechanical. **English:** English lit, technical writing. **Foreign languages:** Spanish. **Health:** Athletic training, clinical lab science, nursing (RN), predentistry, premedicine, preveterinary. **History:** General. **Interdisciplinary:** Global studies. **Legal studies:** Prelaw. **Math:** General. **Parks/recreation:** Exercise sciences, health/fitness, sports admin. **Philosophy/religion:** Philosophy. **Physical sciences:** Chemistry, physics. **Protective services:** Law enforcement admin. **Psychology:** General. **Public administration:** General, social work. **Social sciences:** Political science, sociology. **Theology:** Missionary, pastoral counseling, religious ed, sacred music, theology, youth ministry. **Visual/performing arts:** Dramatic, graphic design, music pedagogy, music performance, music theory/composition, studio arts.

Most popular majors. Business/marketing 16%, communications/journalism 7%, education 17%, engineering/engineering technologies 6%, health sciences 9%, psychology 7%, theological studies 10%.

Computing on campus. 1,800 workstations in dormitories, library, student center. Dormitories linked to campus network. Commuter students can connect to campus network. Online course registration, helpline, repair service available.

Student life. **Freshman orientation:** Mandatory, $105 fee. **Policies:** Immorality and use of alcohol, tobacco, and drugs prohibited. Religious observance required. Freshmen permitted cars on campus. **Housing:** Guaranteed on-campus for all undergraduates. Single-sex dorms, apartments available. $250 partly refundable deposit, deadline 5/1. **Activities:** Bands, choral groups, drama, music ensembles, musical theater, radio station, student government, student newspaper, symphony orchestra, Christian ministries, College Republicans, emergency medical squad, earth stewardship organization, fellowship for world missions, Students for Social Justice, society for technical communicators, Society of Automotive Engineers International.

Athletics. NAIA, NCCAA. **Intercollegiate:** Baseball M, basketball, cross-country, golf M, soccer, softball W, tennis, track and field, volleyball W. **Intramural:** Badminton, basketball, bowling, football (non-tackle), golf, racquetball, soccer, softball, table tennis, tennis, volleyball. **Team name:** Yellow Jackets.

Student services. Campus ministries, career counseling, student employment services, financial aid counseling, health services, personal counseling, placement for graduates, veterans' counselor. **Physically disabled:** Services for visually impaired.

Contact. E-mail: admissions@cedarville.edu
Phone: (937) 766-7700 Toll-free number: (800) 233-2784
Fax: (937) 766-7575
Roscoe Smith, Director of Admissions, Cedarville University, 251 North Main Street, Cedarville, OH 45314

Central State University

Wilberforce, Ohio — **CB member**
www.centralstate.edu — **CB code: 1107**

- Public 4-year university and liberal arts college
- Residential campus in rural community
- 1,589 degree-seeking undergraduates: 9% part-time, 49% women, 87% African American, 1% Hispanic American, 1% international
- 6 degree-seeking graduate students
- 38% of applicants admitted
- SAT or ACT required

General. Founded in 1887. Regionally accredited. Ohio's only public historically black university. **Degrees:** 147 bachelor's awarded; master's offered. **ROTC:** Army, Air Force. **Location:** 18 miles from Dayton. **Calendar:** Semester, limited summer session. **Full-time faculty:** 94 total; 66% have terminal degrees, 71% minority, 35% women. **Part-time faculty:** 68 total; 44% women. **Class size:** 59% < 20, 36% 20-39, 3% 40-49, 1% 50-99. **Special facilities:** Afro-American museum, hydraulics laboratory, computer numerically controlled equipment for machining and robotic welding, business incubator.

Freshman class profile. 4,563 applied, 1,745 admitted, 346 enrolled.

End year in good standing:	40%	**Out-of-state:**	35%
Return as sophomores:	47%	**Live on campus:**	86%

Basis for selection. Out-of-state residents must have 2.5 high school GPA and ACT score of 19. Ohio residents must have 2.0 high school GPA and ACT score of 15. Applicants may appeal decision. Interview recommended. **Homeschooled:** Transcript of courses and grades, state high school equivalency certificate required. Ohio students need ONGP test results.

High school preparation. College-preparatory program recommended. 16 units recommended. Recommended units include English 4, mathematics 3, social studies 3, science 3 and foreign language 2.

2005-2006 Annual costs. Tuition/fees: $4,994; $10,814 out-of-state. Room/board: $6,982. Books/supplies: $840. Personal expenses: $933.

2004-2005 Financial aid. Need-based: 51% of total undergraduate aid awarded as scholarships/grants, 49% as loans/jobs. **Non-need-based:** Scholarships awarded for academics, alumni affiliation, art, athletics, leadership, music/drama, religious affiliation, ROTC.

Application procedures. Admission: No deadline. $20 fee, may be waived for applicants with need. Application may be submitted online. Admission notification on a rolling basis. **Financial aid:** Priority date 2/15; no closing date. FAFSA, institutional form required. Applicants notified on a rolling basis starting 5/1.

Academics. Special study options: Combined bachelor's/graduate degree, cooperative education, cross-registration, double major, honors, independent study, internships, study abroad, teacher certification program. **Credit/placement by examination:** CLEP, SAT, ACT, institutional tests. 45 credit hours maximum toward bachelor's degree. **Support services:** Learning center, pre-admission summer program, reduced course load, tutoring, writing center.

Majors. Biology: General. **Business:** General, accounting. **Communications:** Broadcast journalism, radio/tv. **Computer sciences:** Computer science. **Education:** Art, early childhood, health, middle, multi-level teacher, secondary, special. **Engineering:** Manufacturing, water resource. **Engineering technology:** Industrial. **English:** English lit. **History:** General. **Math:** General. **Parks/recreation:** General. **Physical sciences:** Chemistry, geology. **Psychology:** General. **Public administration:** Social work. **Social sciences:** Economics, political science, sociology. **Visual/performing arts:** Art, jazz, music performance.

Most popular majors. Business/marketing 31%, communications/journalism 10%, education 11%, engineering/engineering technologies 8%, psychology 10%, social sciences 10%.

Computing on campus. 350 workstations in library, computer center, student center. Dormitories wired for high-speed internet access and linked to campus network. Online course registration, online library, helpline, wireless network available.

Student life. Freshman orientation: Mandatory, $125 fee. Preregistration for classes offered. **Policies:** Freshmen permitted cars on campus. **Housing:** Guaranteed on-campus for freshmen. Coed dorms, single-sex dorms available. $195 nonrefundable deposit, deadline 8/1. **Activities:** Bands, choral groups, dance, drama, music ensembles, radio station, student government, student newspaper, TV station, Interfaith campus ministry.

Athletics. NCAA. **Intercollegiate:** Basketball, cross-country, football (tackle) M, golf, tennis, track and field, volleyball. **Intramural:** Basketball, cross-country, football (non-tackle) M, racquetball, tennis. **Team name:** Marauders.

Student services. Alcohol/substance abuse counseling, campus ministries, career counseling, services for economically disadvantaged, student employment services, financial aid counseling, health services, on-campus daycare, personal counseling, placement for graduates.

Contact. E-mail: admissions@centralstate.edu
Phone: (937) 376-6348 Toll-free number: (800) 388-2781
Fax: (937) 376-6648
Cleveland James, Director of Admissions, Central State University, PO Box 1004, Wilberforce, OH 45384-1004

Cincinnati Christian University

Cincinnati, Ohio
www.ccuniversity.edu — **CB code: 1091**

- Private 4-year university affiliated with Church of Christ/Christian Church
- Residential campus in very large city
- 765 degree-seeking undergraduates: 12% part-time, 44% women, 11% African American, 2% international
- 231 degree-seeking graduate students
- 79% of applicants admitted
- SAT or ACT (ACT writing optional) required

General. Founded in 1924. Regionally accredited; also accredited by ABHE. Member of Greater Cincinnati Consortium of Colleges and Universities. **Degrees:** 112 bachelor's, 7 associate awarded; master's, first professional offered. **Location:** 10 miles from downtown. **Calendar:** Semester, limited summer session. **Full-time faculty:** 29 total; 48% have terminal degrees, 7% minority, 28% women. **Part-time faculty:** 41 total; 17% have terminal degrees, 2% minority, 29% women. **Class size:** 64% < 20, 25% 20-39, 5% 40-49, 6% 50-99.

Freshman class profile. 391 applied, 309 admitted, 160 enrolled.

Mid 50% test scores		**GPA 2.0-2.99:**	44%
SAT verbal:	430-540	**Rank in top quarter:**	31%
SAT math:	440-590	**Rank in top tenth:**	14%
ACT:	18-25	**Out-of-state:**	44%
GPA 3.50 or higher:	31%	**Live on campus:**	82%
GPA 3.0-3.49:	24%	**International:**	1%

Basis for selection. High school academic record and standardized test scores important. Minimum 2.5 GPA, 17 ACT composite/SAT equivalent for unconditional admission. Applicants age 25 or older can substitute English proficiency test and essay for SAT/ACT requirement. Audition required for music programs. **Homeschooled:** State high school equivalency certificate required.

2006-2007 Annual costs. Tuition/fees (projected): $10,010. Room/board: $5,660. Books/supplies: $800. Personal expenses: $1,950.

2005-2006 Financial aid. **Need-based:** 138 full-time freshmen applied for aid; 132 were judged to have need; 110 of these received aid. Average need met was 78%. Average scholarship/grant was $1,220; average loan $2,625.

Application procedures. **Admission:** Closing date 7/1 (postmark date). $35 fee, may be waived for applicants with need. Application may be submitted online. Admission notification on a rolling basis. **Financial aid:** Priority date 3/1, closing date 7/15. FAFSA required. Applicants notified by 4/5; must reply by 6/5 or within 2 week(s) of notification.

Academics. **Special study options:** Cross-registration, distance learning, double major, independent study, internships, teacher certification program. Adult degree completion program. **Credit/placement by examination:** AP, CLEP, IB. 15 credit hours maximum toward associate degree, 30 toward bachelor's. **Support services:** Learning center, reduced course load, remedial instruction, study skills assistance, tutoring, writing center.

Majors. **Computer sciences:** Data processing, information technology, LAN/WAN management, programming. **Education:** Early childhood, elementary, middle, secondary, special. **Philosophy/religion:** Christian. **Psychology:** General. **Theology:** Bible, missionary, religious ed, sacred music.

Most popular majors. Education 14%, theological studies 81%.

Computing on campus. 57 workstations in dormitories, library, computer center, student center. Dormitories wired for high-speed internet access and linked to campus network. Online library, helpline, repair service, wireless network available.

Student life. **Freshman orientation:** Mandatory. Preregistration for classes offered. **Policies:** Freshmen permitted cars on campus. **Housing:** Guaranteed on-campus for all undergraduates. Single-sex dorms, substance-free housing available. $75 fully refundable deposit. **Activities:** Concert band, choral groups, drama, music ensembles, student government, student newspaper, Price Hill Party outreach to community kids.

Athletics. NCCAA. **Intercollegiate:** Baseball M, basketball, golf M, soccer, volleyball W. **Intramural:** Basketball, cheerleading, football (tackle) M, soccer, track and field, volleyball. **Team name:** Eagles.

Student services. Career counseling, student employment services, financial aid counseling, health services, personal counseling. **Physically disabled:** Services for hearing impaired.

Contact. E-mail: cbcadmission@ccuniversity.edu
Phone: (513) 244-8141 Toll-free number: (800) 949-4228
Fax: (513) 244-8140
Sam Myers, Director of Recruitment and Enrollment, Cincinnati Christian University, 2700 Glenway Avenue, Cincinnati, OH 45204-3200

Cincinnati College of Mortuary Science

Cincinnati, Ohio
www.ccms.edu **CB code: 0945**

- Private 4-year school of mortuary science
- Commuter campus in large city
- 140 degree-seeking undergraduates: 46% women

General. Founded in 1882. Regionally accredited. Program of study contingent on licensing requirements of state in which student will practice. **Degrees:** 49 bachelor's, 94 associate awarded. **Location:** 3 miles from downtown. **Calendar:** Quarter. **Full-time faculty:** 10 total. **Class size:** 100% 50-99.

Basis for selection. Open admission.

High school preparation. 15 units recommended. Recommended units include English 3, mathematics 1, social studies 2 and science 2.

2005-2006 Annual costs. Tuition/fees: $13,275. Books/supplies: $2,500.

Financial aid. All financial aid based on need.

Application procedures. **Admission:** No deadline. $25 fee. Application may be submitted online. Admission notification on a rolling basis. **Financial aid:** Priority date 7/1; no closing date. FAFSA required. Applicants notified on a rolling basis starting 3/1; must reply within 2 week(s) of notification.

Academics. **Special study options:** Internships. **Credit/placement by examination:** AP, CLEP, institutional tests. 41 credit hours maximum toward associate degree, 56 toward bachelor's. **Support services:** Reduced course load, tutoring.

Majors. **Personal/culinary services:** Mortuary science.

Student life. **Freshman orientation:** Mandatory. Preregistration for classes offered. **Housing:** Some housing available in local funeral homes.

Student services. Career counseling, student employment services, personal counseling, veterans' counselor. **Physically disabled:** Services for hearing impaired.

Contact. Phone: (513) 761-2020 Fax: (513) 761-3333
Patsy Leon, Financial Aid/Admissions Officer, Cincinnati College of Mortuary Science, 645 West North Bend Road, Cincinnati, OH 45224-1428

Circleville Bible College

Circleville, Ohio
www.biblecollege.edu **CB code: 1088**

- Private 4-year Bible college affiliated with Churches of Christ in Christian Union
- Residential campus in large town
- 423 degree-seeking undergraduates
- 50% of applicants admitted
- SAT or ACT (ACT writing optional), application essay required

General. Founded in 1948. Candidate for regional accreditation; also accredited by ABHE. **Degrees:** 99 bachelor's, 3 associate awarded. **Location:** 25 miles from Columbus. **Calendar:** Semester, limited summer session. **Full-time faculty:** 10 total. **Part-time faculty:** 30 total. **Class size:** 74% < 20, 26% 20-39.

Freshman class profile. 141 applied, 70 admitted, 47 enrolled.

Mid 50% test scores		**Out-of-state:**	15%
ACT:	15-22	**Live on campus:**	37%

Basis for selection. Positive Christian testimony, potential for Christian service, sound academic performance, and personal character references important. Students without SAT or ACT may be admitted conditionally but must meet test requirement at earliest opportunity. Interview recommended for all; audition required for music majors.

High school preparation. 15 units recommended. Recommended units include English 4, mathematics 3, social studies 3, science 3 and foreign language 2.

2005-2006 Annual costs. Tuition/fees: $9,504. Room/board: $5,884. Books/supplies: $500. Personal expenses: $1,506.

Financial aid. All financial aid based on need. **Additional information:** Religious affiliation tuition discount.

Application procedures. **Admission:** Priority date 3/1; deadline 7/1. $25 fee, may be waived for applicants with need. Application may be submitted online. Admission notification on a rolling basis. Must reply by May 1 or within 2 week(s) if notified thereafter. **Financial aid:** Priority date 4/17; no closing date. FAFSA, institutional form, CSS PROFILE required. Applicants notified on a rolling basis starting 5/1; must reply within 2 week(s) of notification.

Academics. Every student is required to complete minimum of 30 hours in Bible and theology courses. **Special study options:** Accelerated study, combined bachelor's/graduate degree, double major, dual enrollment of high school students, independent study, internships, liberal arts/career combination, student-designed major, study abroad. **Credit/placement by examination:** CLEP, institutional tests. **Support services:** Reduced course load, remedial instruction, study skills assistance, tutoring, writing center.

Majors. **Business:** General, accounting, accounting/business management, business admin. **Education:** General, early childhood, elementary, music, secondary. **Philosophy/religion:** Religion. **Psychology:** General. **Theology:** Missionary, pastoral counseling, religious ed, sacred music, theology, youth ministry.

Most popular majors. Education 7%, psychology 9%.

Computing on campus. 58 workstations in dormitories, library, computer center. Dormitories wired for high-speed internet access and linked to campus network. Online library, repair service, wireless network available.

Student life. **Freshman orientation:** Mandatory. Preregistration for classes offered. Held Sunday through Wednesday before classes start. **Policies:** Curfew of 11:30 pm (Monday-Thursday), 1:00am (Friday), 12:00 am (Saturday-Sunday); dress code. Religious observance required. Freshmen permitted cars on campus. **Housing:** Guaranteed on-campus for freshmen. Single-sex dorms, apartments available. $50 deposit, deadline 8/1. **Activities:** Choral groups, drama, music ensembles, student government, Ministerial Association, Prison Ministries, S.H.I.N.E., World Gospel Mission Student Involvement, summer camp ministries.

Athletics. NCCAA. **Intercollegiate:** Baseball M, basketball, volleyball W. **Intramural:** Basketball, golf, soccer, table tennis, volleyball. **Team name:** Crusaders.

Student services. Adult student services, campus ministries, career counseling, student employment services, financial aid counseling, health services, minority student services, personal counseling, veterans' counselor. **Physically disabled:** Services for visually impaired.

Contact. E-mail: enroll@biblecollege.edu
Phone: (740) 477-7701 Toll-free number: (800) 701-0222
Fax: (740) 477-7755
Tina Allen, Enrollment Office Coordinator, Circleville Bible College, 1476 Lancaster Pike, Circleville, OH 43113

Cleveland Institute of Art

Cleveland, Ohio — **CB member**
www.cia.edu — **CB code: 1152**

- Private 4-year visual arts college
- Commuter campus in very large city
- 536 degree-seeking undergraduates: 5% part-time, 51% women, 5% African American, 3% Asian American, 2% Hispanic American, 2% international
- 8 degree-seeking graduate students
- 69% of applicants admitted
- SAT or ACT (ACT writing optional), application essay required
- 64% graduate within 6 years

General. Founded in 1882. Regionally accredited. **Degrees:** 109 bachelor's awarded; master's offered. **ROTC:** Army. **Location:** 5 miles from downtown. **Calendar:** Semester. **Full-time faculty:** 47 total; 81% have terminal degrees, 8% minority, 45% women. **Part-time faculty:** 54 total; 46% have terminal degrees, 7% minority, 39% women. **Class size:** 75% < 20, 25% 20-39. **Special facilities:** Individual studio spaces, woodshop, metalshop.

Freshman class profile. 382 applied, 263 admitted, 93 enrolled.

Mid 50% test scores			
SAT verbal:	500-630	Rank in top quarter:	12%
SAT math:	440-550	Rank in top tenth:	3%
ACT:	19-25	End year in good standing:	73%
GPA 3.50 or higher:	28%	Return as sophomores:	78%
GPA 3.0-3.49:	29%	Out-of-state:	26%
GPA 2.0-2.99:	43%	Live on campus:	70%

Basis for selection. Portfolio of 12 to 20 pieces, high school transcripts, statement of purpose, test scores, and 2 letters of recommendation required. Interview strongly recommended. **Homeschooled:** Transcript of courses and grades, state high school equivalency certificate, letter of recommendation (nonparent) required. GED required.

High school preparation. 20 units recommended. Recommended units include English 4, mathematics 3, social studies 3, science 3 and academic electives 6. 2 years of art recommended.

2005-2006 Annual costs. Tuition/fees: $27,017. Room/board: $9,136. Books/supplies: $1,200. Personal expenses: $1,800.

2004-2005 Financial aid. Need-based: 84 full-time freshmen applied for aid; 79 were judged to have need; 77 of these received aid. Average need met was 51%. Average scholarship/grant was $9,338; average loan $3,704. 51% of total undergraduate aid awarded as scholarships/grants, 49% as loans/jobs. **Non-need-based:** Awarded to 142 full-time undergraduates, including 23 freshmen. Scholarships awarded for academics, art.

Application procedures. Admission: Priority date 7/1; no deadline. $30 fee, may be waived for applicants with need. Application may be submitted online. Admission notification on a rolling basis beginning on or about 10/1. Must reply by May 1 or within 2 week(s) if notified thereafter. **Financial aid:** Priority date 3/15; no closing date. FAFSA, institutional form required. Applicants notified on a rolling basis starting 3/16; must reply within 4 week(s) of notification.

Academics. Special study options: Combined bachelor's/graduate degree, cooperative education, cross-registration, exchange student, honors, independent study, internships, New York semester, study abroad. Study for up to 2 semesters at any Alliance of Independent Colleges of Art and Design. **Credit/placement by examination:** AP, CLEP, IB. 129 credit hours maximum toward bachelor's degree. **Support services:** Reduced course load, remedial instruction, study skills assistance, tutoring, writing center.

Majors. Health: Medical illustrating. **Visual/performing arts:** Ceramics, commercial/advertising art, drawing, fiber arts, illustration, industrial design, interior design, metal/jewelry, painting, photography, printmaking, sculpture.

Computing on campus. 303 workstations in library, computer center. Dormitories wired for high-speed internet access and linked to campus network. Commuter students can connect to campus network. Online library, wireless network available.

Student life. Freshman orientation: Mandatory, $130 fee. Preregistration for classes offered. Orientation in two parts: summer program for students/parents and fall orientation for students only. **Housing:** Guaranteed on-campus for freshmen. Coed dorms, apartments, fraternity/sorority housing available. $150 nonrefundable deposit, deadline 7/15. **Activities:** Student government, student newspaper, student artist association, student leadership council, nature and hiking club, student activities program board, student independent exhibition committee, gay/lesbian association, Artists for Christ, ghost hunting club, survey student gallery.

Student services. Alcohol/substance abuse counseling, campus ministries, student employment services, financial aid counseling, health services, personal counseling.

Contact. E-mail: admiss@cia.edu
Phone: (216) 421-7418 Toll-free number: (800) 223-4700
Fax: (216) 754-3634
Corey Thrush, Director of Admissions, Cleveland Institute of Art, 11141 East Boulevard, Cleveland, OH 44106

Cleveland Institute of Music

Cleveland, Ohio
www.cim.edu — **CB code: 1124**

- Private 4-year music college
- Residential campus in very large city
- 207 degree-seeking undergraduates: 57% women
- 180 graduate students
- 34% of applicants admitted
- SAT or ACT, application essay required
- 56% graduate within 6 years

General. Founded in 1920. Regionally accredited. **Degrees:** 34 bachelor's awarded; master's, doctoral offered. **Location:** 2 miles from downtown. **Calendar:** Semester, limited summer session. **Full-time faculty:** 30 total. **Part-time faculty:** 70 total. **Special facilities:** Electronic music studios, audio recording facilities, large records, tapes, CD library, technology learning center.

Freshman class profile. 447 applied, 151 admitted, 53 enrolled.

Return as sophomores:	95%	Live on campus:	100%
Out-of-state:	77%		

Basis for selection. Audition most important. Interviews, test scores, high school record, and letters of recommendation also reviewed. Incoming students must have scholastic and musical skills prerequisite to entering highly intensive, professionally oriented program. Institutional examinations including sight singing, keyboard harmony, general musicianship required. Audition required; interview recommended. **Homeschooled:** Transcript of courses and grades required.

High school preparation. 16 units recommended. Recommended units include English 4, mathematics 3, social studies 3, science 3 and foreign language 3.

2005-2006 Annual costs. Tuition/fees: $26,870. Room/board: $8,726. Books/supplies: $900. Personal expenses: $900.

Application procedures. Admission: Closing date 12/1. $100 fee. Application may be submitted online. Admission notification 4/1. Must reply by 5/1. **Financial aid:** Priority date 2/15; no closing date. FAFSA, institutional form required. Applicants notified on a rolling basis starting 4/1; must reply by 5/1 or within 2 week(s) of notification.

Academics. Special study options: Cross-registration, double major, ESL, independent study, study abroad, teacher certification program. **Credit/placement by examination:** AP, CLEP, IB, SAT, ACT, institutional tests.

Support services: Learning center, reduced course load, remedial instruction, study skills assistance, tutoring, writing center.

Majors. Communications technology: Recording arts. **Visual/performing arts:** Music performance, music theory/composition, voice/opera.

Computing on campus. 36 workstations in dormitories, library, computer center, student center. Dormitories wired for high-speed internet access and linked to campus network. Helpline, repair service, wireless network available.

Student life. Freshman orientation: Mandatory. Held before the start of classes. **Policies:** Library priviliges available through Case Western Reserve University. Freshmen permitted cars on campus. **Housing:** Coed dorms, substance-free housing available. **Activities:** Jazz band, choral groups, dance, drama, music ensembles, opera, student government, student newspaper, symphony orchestra, most student activities, athletics and student services available through Case Western Reserve University.

Student services. Alcohol/substance abuse counseling, career counseling, student employment services, financial aid counseling, health services, personal counseling, placement for graduates, veterans' counselor.

Contact. E-mail: cimadmission@po.cwru.edu
Phone: (216) 795-3107 Fax: (216) 795-3161
William Fay, Director of Admissions, Cleveland Institute of Music, 11021 East Boulevard, Cleveland, OH 44106

Cleveland State University

Cleveland, Ohio — **CB member**
www.csuohio.edu — **CB code: 1221**

- Public 4-year university
- Commuter campus in very large city
- 9,155 degree-seeking undergraduates: 28% part-time, 55% women, 22% African American, 3% Asian American, 3% Hispanic American, 2% international
- 4,761 degree-seeking graduate students

General. Founded in 1964. Regionally accredited. **Degrees:** 1,690 bachelor's awarded; master's, doctoral, first professional offered. **ROTC:** Army, Navy. **Calendar:** Semester, extensive summer session. **Full-time faculty:** 575 total; 86% have terminal degrees, 18% minority, 36% women. **Part-time faculty:** 422 total; 17% have terminal degrees, 17% minority, 47% women. **Class size:** 40% < 20, 44% 20-39, 6% 40-49, 8% 50-99, 2% >100.

Freshman class profile. 3,153 applied, 2,520 admitted, 1,079 enrolled.

Mid 50% test scores		**Rank in top tenth:**	9%
SAT verbal:	410-550	**Return as sophomores:**	61%
SAT math:	410-570	**Out-of-state:**	6%
ACT:	16-22	**Live on campus:**	22%
GPA 3.50 or higher:	15%	**International:**	2%
GPA 3.0-3.49:	23%	**Fraternities:**	3%
GPA 2.0-2.99:	50%	**Sororities:**	3%
Rank in top quarter:	29%		

Basis for selection. Open admission, but selective for some programs and for out-of-state students. Special requirements for education and engineering programs. SAT/ACT must be submitted for counseling purposes, but scores not considered in admission decisions. Audition required for music majors.

High school preparation. 16 units recommended. Recommended units include English 4, mathematics 3, social studies 3, science 3 (laboratory 1) and foreign language 2. 1 art recommended.

2005-2006 Annual costs. Tuition/fees: $7,344; $13,056 out-of-state. Room/board: $6,809. Books/supplies: $800. Personal expenses: $3,776.

2005-2006 Financial aid. Need-based: 829 full-time freshmen applied for aid; 736 were judged to have need; 715 of these received aid. Average need met was 43%. Average scholarship/grant was $5,200; average loan $2,699. 36% of total undergraduate aid awarded as scholarships/grants, 64% as loans/jobs. **Non-need-based:** Awarded to 918 full-time undergraduates, including 158 freshmen. Scholarships awarded for academics, alumni affiliation, art, athletics, leadership, minority status, music/drama, religious affiliation, ROTC, state residency.

Application procedures. Admission: Priority date 7/15; deadline 8/15. $30 fee, may be waived for applicants with need. Application may be submitted online. Admission notification on a rolling basis beginning on or about 9/1. **Financial aid:** Priority date 2/15; no closing date. FAFSA required. Applicants notified on a rolling basis starting 3/15; must reply within 4 week(s) of notification.

Academics. Special study options: Accelerated study, cooperative education, cross-registration, distance learning, double major, dual enrollment of high school students, ESL, exchange student, honors, internships, student-designed major, study abroad, teacher certification program. **Credit/placement by examination:** AP, CLEP, IB, institutional tests. 90 credit hours maximum toward bachelor's degree. Unlimited AP exam credits accepted. **Support services:** Learning center, reduced course load, remedial instruction, study skills assistance, tutoring, writing center.

Majors. Area/ethnic studies: French, German, Italian, Spanish/Iberian, women's. **Business:** Accounting, finance, international, labor relations, management information systems, managerial economics, marketing, statistics. **Communications:** General. **Computer sciences:** General. **Conservation:** General, environmental studies. **Education:** Early childhood, elementary, physical, special. **Engineering:** Chemical, civil, electrical, mechanical. **Engineering technology:** Electrical. **Foreign languages:** French, German, linguistics, Spanish. **Health:** Audiology/hearing, nursing (RN). **History:** General. **Liberal arts:** Arts/sciences. **Math:** General. **Philosophy/religion:** Philosophy, religion. **Physical sciences:** Chemistry, geology, physics. **Psychology:** General. **Public administration:** Social work. **Social sciences:** General, anthropology, economics, political science, sociology, urban studies. **Visual/performing arts:** Art, dramatic.

Most popular majors. Business/marketing 21%, communications/journalism 9%, education 12%, engineering/engineering technologies 6%, health sciences 8%, psychology 8%, social sciences 12%.

Computing on campus. 711 workstations in dormitories, library, computer center, student center. Dormitories wired for high-speed internet access and linked to campus network. Online library, helpline available.

Student life. Freshman orientation: Available, $25 fee. Preregistration for classes offered. All-day program during summer. **Policies:** Freshmen permitted cars on campus. **Housing:** Coed dorms available. **Activities:** Bands, choral groups, dance, drama, film society, literary magazine, music ensembles, musical theater, opera, radio station, student government, student newspaper, symphony orchestra, Newman Center, Los Latinos Unidos, Hillel, University Christian Movement, Organization for Afro-American Unity, Lutheran campus ministry, international students organization, NAACP, environmental action group, College Democrats and Republicans.

Athletics. NCAA. **Intercollegiate:** Baseball M, basketball, cross-country W, diving, fencing, golf, soccer, softball W, swimming, tennis, track and field W, volleyball W, wrestling M. **Intramural:** Badminton, basketball, bowling, cross-country, fencing, field hockey W, golf, handball, racquetball, rowing (crew), sailing, soccer, swimming, table tennis, tennis W, track and field, volleyball, water polo, wrestling M. **Team name:** Vikings.

Student services. Adult student services, career counseling, student employment services, health services, personal counseling, placement for graduates, veterans' counselor. **Physically disabled:** Services for visually, speech, hearing impaired. **Learning disabled:** Comprehensive services available.

Contact. E-mail: admissions@csuohio.edu
Phone: (216) 687-2100 Toll-free number: (800) 278-6446
Fax: (216) 687-9210
Bonnie Jones, Undergraduate Admissions Director, Cleveland State University, 1806 East 22th Street, Cleveland, OH 44115-2403

College of Mount St. Joseph

Cincinnati, Ohio — **CB member**
www.msj.edu — **CB code: 1129**

- Private 4-year liberal arts college affiliated with Roman Catholic Church
- Commuter campus in very large city
- 1,881 degree-seeking undergraduates: 29% part-time, 69% women, 10% African American, 1% Hispanic American
- 280 degree-seeking graduate students
- 73% of applicants admitted
- SAT or ACT (ACT writing recommended) required
- 69% graduate within 6 years; 17% enter graduate study

General. Founded in 1920. Regionally accredited. Project EXCEL supports students with learning disabilities. **Degrees:** 330 bachelor's, 11 associate awarded; master's, doctoral offered. **ROTC:** Army, Air Force. **Location:** 7 miles from downtown Cincinnati. **Calendar:** Semester, extensive summer session. **Full-time faculty:** 124 total; 53% have terminal degrees, 6% minority, 67% women. **Part-time faculty:** 109 total; 20% have terminal degrees, 5% minority, 55% women. **Class size:** 61% < 20, 38% 20-39, less than 1% 40-49. **Special facilities:** Sports complex, learning center, career center, studio, art gallery, chapel, health sciences suite.

Freshman class profile. 1,087 applied, 793 admitted, 315 enrolled.

Mid 50% test scores			
SAT verbal:	440-560	Rank in top quarter:	36%
SAT math:	430-540	Rank in top tenth:	13%
ACT:	18-23	End year in good standing:	90%
GPA 3.50 or higher:	31%	Return as sophomores:	78%
GPA 3.0-3.49:	36%	Out-of-state:	13%
GPA 2.0-2.99:	32%	Live on campus:	54%

Basis for selection. Criteria for admission include college prep high school curriculum, strong grade point average, standardized test scores, evidence of leadership and extracurricular involvement, and personal background. Essays, recommendations and interviews may be required for some students. Audition required for music programs. Portfolio recommended for art programs. **Homeschooled:** Transcripts are required along with any documentation from the state or national home schooling accreditation agency. **Learning Disabled:** Students can apply for Project EXCEL, which helps students with learning disabilities.

High school preparation. 13 units required; 23 recommended. Required and recommended units include English 4, mathematics 2-4, social studies 1-2, history 1-2, science 2-4 (laboratory 1-2), foreign language 2 and academic electives 1. Mathematics must include a minimum of 1 year each of algebra and geometry. 1 fine arts required. May substitute 2 additional credits from other subjects in place of foreign language.

2005-2006 Annual costs. Tuition/fees: $18,790. Room/board: $6,070. Books/supplies: $800. Personal expenses: $600.

2005-2006 Financial aid. Need-based: 274 full-time freshmen applied for aid; 250 were judged to have need; 250 of these received aid. Average need met was 90%. Average scholarship/grant was $8,787; average loan $3,730. 48% of total undergraduate aid awarded as scholarships/grants, 52% as loans/jobs. **Non-need-based:** Awarded to 585 full-time undergraduates, including 205 freshmen. Scholarships awarded for academics, art, leadership, music/drama, ROTC, state residency. **Additional information:** College offers financial aid to full and part-time students. Unlimited, renewable merit-based scholarships are offered.

Application procedures. Admission: Priority date 4/1; deadline 8/15 (postmark date). $25 fee, may be waived for applicants with need. Application may be submitted online. Admission notification on a rolling basis beginning on or about 10/1. Must reply by May 1 or within 4 week(s) if notified thereafter. Admitted applicants must reply within 30 days. **Financial aid:** Priority date 3/1; no closing date. FAFSA required. Applicants notified on a rolling basis starting 2/15; must reply by 5/1 or within 4 week(s) of notification.

Academics. Special study options: Accelerated study, cooperative education, cross-registration, distance learning, double major, honors, independent study, internships, liberal arts/career combination, study abroad, teacher certification program. **Credit/placement by examination:** AP, CLEP, IB, SAT, ACT, institutional tests. 32 credit hours maximum toward associate degree, 64 toward bachelor's. **Support services:** Learning center, reduced course load, remedial instruction, study skills assistance, tutoring, writing center.

Majors. Biology: General, biochemistry. **Business:** Accounting, business admin. **Communications:** General. **Computer sciences:** General. **Education:** Art, early childhood, middle, special. **English:** English lit. **Health:** Athletic training, nursing (RN). **History:** General. **Interdisciplinary:** Natural sciences. **Legal studies:** Paralegal. **Liberal arts:** Arts/sciences. **Math:** General. **Philosophy/religion:** Religion. **Physical sciences:** Chemistry. **Psychology:** General. **Public administration:** Social work. **Social sciences:** Criminology, sociology. **Theology:** Pastoral counseling, religious ed. **Visual/performing arts:** Art, graphic design, interior design, studio arts.

Most popular majors. Business/marketing 14%, communications/journalism 6%, education 12%, health sciences 23%, liberal arts 7%, visual/performing arts 11%.

Computing on campus. PC or laptop required. 201 workstations in library, computer center, student center. Commuter students can connect to campus network. Online course registration, online library, helpline, repair service, student web hosting, wireless network available.

Student life. Freshman orientation: Mandatory, $150 fee. Preregistration for classes offered. Summer session includes an overnight stay and welcome weekend consisting of service learning event and river cruise. Three summer session dates to choose from. **Policies:** Smoke-free buildings. All freshman and sophomore students under age 21 and unmarried who live outside of a 35 mile radius of the college are required to live on campus and participate in a meal program. Freshmen permitted cars on campus. **Housing:** Guaranteed on-campus for freshmen. Coed dorms available. $100 fully refundable deposit, deadline 8/15. **Activities:** Bands, choral groups, dance, drama, literary magazine, music ensembles, musical theater, student government, student newspaper, Student Council for Exceptional Children, Circle K, Campus Ministry, Black Student Union, Alpha Phi Omega service organization, Environmental Awareness Club, Young Democrats, Respect Life, Student Law Club.

Athletics. NCAA. **Intercollegiate:** Baseball M, basketball, cheerleading M, cross-country, football (tackle) M, golf, lacrosse M, soccer, softball W, tennis, track and field, volleyball W, wrestling M. **Intramural:** Basketball, football (non-tackle), racquetball, soccer, softball, tennis, volleyball. **Team name:** Lions.

Student services. Adult student services, alcohol/substance abuse counseling, campus ministries, career counseling, services for economically disadvantaged, student employment services, financial aid counseling, health services, minority student services, on-campus daycare, personal counseling, placement for graduates, veterans' counselor, women's services. **Physically disabled:** Services for visually, speech, hearing impaired. **Learning disabled:** Comprehensive services available.

Contact. E-mail: admissions@mail.msj.edu
Phone: (513) 244-4531 Toll-free number: (800) 654-9314
Fax: (513) 244-4629
Peggy Minnich, Director of Admission, College of Mount St. Joseph, 5701 Delhi Road, Cincinnati, OH 45233-1670

College of Wooster

Wooster, Ohio **CB member**
www.wooster.edu **CB code: 1134**

- Private 4-year liberal arts college
- Residential campus in large town
- 1,810 degree-seeking undergraduates: 53% women, 4% African American, 2% Asian American, 2% Hispanic American, 5% international
- 75% of applicants admitted
- SAT or ACT with writing, application essay required
- 75% graduate within 6 years

General. Founded in 1866. Regionally accredited. **Degrees:** 435 bachelor's awarded. **Location:** 55 miles from Cleveland, 30 miles from Akron. **Calendar:** Semester, limited summer session. **Full-time faculty:** 133 total; 98% have terminal degrees, 7% minority, 41% women. **Part-time faculty:** 58 total; 74% have terminal degrees, 3% minority, 55% women. **Class size:** 69% < 20, 28% 20-39, 3% 40-49, less than 1% 50-99, less than 1% >100. **Special facilities:** Museum.

Freshman class profile. 2,542 applied, 1,900 admitted, 537 enrolled.

Mid 50% test scores			
SAT verbal:	560-680	Rank in top tenth:	32%
SAT math:	550-660	Return as sophomores:	88%
ACT:	23-28	Out-of-state:	59%
GPA 3.50 or higher:	58%	Live on campus:	100%
GPA 3.0-3.49:	28%	International:	3%
GPA 2.0-2.99:	14%	Fraternities:	11%
Rank in top quarter:	66%	Sororities:	13%

Basis for selection. Course pattern and academic performance most important. Recommendations, extracurricular activities, class rank, test scores, interview considered. Interview recommended for all; audition recommended for music; portfolio recommended for art programs.

High school preparation. Required and recommended units include English 4, mathematics 3-4, social studies 3-4, science 3-4, foreign language 2-3 and academic electives 2. Mathematics recommendation includes 2 algebra.

2006-2007 Annual costs. Tuition/fees: $30,060. Room/board: $7,520. Books/supplies: $810. Personal expenses: $600.

2005-2006 Financial aid. Need-based: 406 full-time freshmen applied for aid; 313 were judged to have need; 313 of these received aid. Average need met was 92%. Average scholarship/grant was $17,281; average loan $5,564. 77% of total undergraduate aid awarded as scholarships/grants, 23% as loans/jobs. **Non-need-based:** Awarded to 651 full-time undergraduates, including 270 freshmen. Scholarships awarded for academics, minority status, music/drama, religious affiliation, state residency.

Application procedures. Admission: Closing date 2/15. $40 fee. Application may be submitted online. Admission notification 4/1. Must reply by May 1 or within 2 week(s) if notified thereafter. **Financial aid:** Priority date 2/15; no closing date. FAFSA, institutional form, CSS PROFILE required. Applicants notified by 3/15; must reply by 5/1 or within 4 week(s) of notification.

Academics. Centers in 6 cities for urban internships in social sciences. **Special study options:** Combined bachelor's/graduate degree, double major, exchange student, independent study, internships, New York semester, student-designed major, study abroad, teacher certification program, United Nations semester, urban semester, Washington semester. **Credit/placement by examination:** AP, CLEP, IB, institutional tests. **Support services:** Learning center, tutoring, writing center.

Majors. Area/ethnic studies: African, African-American, East Asian, Latin American, Near/Middle Eastern, Russian/Slavic, South Asian, Western European, women's. **Biology:** General, biochemistry, Biochemistry/biophysics and molecular biology, molecular. **Business:** Managerial economics. **Communications:** General. **Computer sciences:** General. **Education:** Music. **English:** American lit, British lit. **Foreign languages:** General, classics, comparative lit, French, German, Italian, Latin, modern Greek, Spanish. **Health:** Audiology/speech pathology, music therapy. **History:** General. **Math:** General. **Philosophy/religion:** Philosophy, religion. **Physical sciences:** Chemical physics, chemistry, geology, molecular physics, physics. **Psychology:** General. **Public administration:** Social work. **Social sciences:** Anthropology, archaeology, economics, international relations, political science, sociology, urban studies. **Visual/performing arts:** Art history/conservation, dance, dramatic, music history, music performance, music theory/composition, studio arts.

Most popular majors. Biology 8%, communications/journalism 6%, English 9%, history 11%, philosophy/religious studies 7%, physical sciences 8%, psychology 6%, social sciences 22%, visual/performing arts 8%.

Computing on campus. 275 workstations in dormitories, library, computer center, student center. Dormitories wired for high-speed internet access and linked to campus network. Commuter students can connect to campus network. Online library, helpline, repair service, student web hosting available.

Student life. Freshman orientation: Mandatory. Held during 3 days prior to start of semester. **Policies:** Freshmen permitted cars on campus. **Housing:** Guaranteed on-campus for all undergraduates. Coed dorms, single-sex dorms, fraternity/sorority housing available. Special housing for students participating in volunteer activities. **Activities:** Bands, choral groups, dance, drama, film society, literary magazine, music ensembles, musical theater, radio station, student government, student newspaper, symphony orchestra, variety of religious, ethnic, and social service organizations available.

Athletics. NCAA. **Intercollegiate:** Baseball M, basketball, cross-country, diving, field hockey W, football (tackle) M, golf M, lacrosse, soccer, softball W, swimming, tennis, track and field, volleyball W. **Intramural:** Badminton, basketball, bowling, football (non-tackle), golf, racquetball, soccer, softball, swimming, tennis, volleyball, water polo M. **Team name:** Fighting Scots.

Student services. Alcohol/substance abuse counseling, campus ministries, career counseling, student employment services, financial aid counseling, health services, minority student services, personal counseling, placement for graduates. **Physically disabled:** Services for visually impaired.

Contact. E-mail: admissions@wooster.edu
Phone: (330) 263-2322 Toll-free number: (800) 877-9905
Fax: (330) 263-2621
Derek Gueldenzoph, Dean of Admissions, College of Wooster, 847 College Avenue, Wooster, OH 44691-2363

Columbus College of Art and Design

Columbus, Ohio
www.ccad.edu **CB code: 1085**

- Private 4-year visual arts college
- Residential campus in very large city
- 1,308 degree-seeking undergraduates: 4% part-time, 51% women, 7% African American, 2% Asian American, 3% Hispanic American, 7% international
- 61% of applicants admitted
- SAT or ACT (ACT writing optional), application essay required
- 55% graduate within 6 years

General. Founded in 1879. Regionally accredited. Campus adjacent to Columbus Museum of Art. **Degrees:** 316 bachelor's awarded. **Location:** Downtown. **Calendar:** Semester, extensive summer session. **Full-time faculty:** 76 total; 62% have terminal degrees, 10% minority, 36% women. **Part-time faculty:** 105 total; 24% have terminal degrees, 9% minority, 40% women. **Class size:** 55% < 20, 44% 20-39, less than 1% 40-49. **Special facilities:** Student exhibition hall.

Freshman class profile. 910 applied, 551 admitted, 207 enrolled.

Mid 50% test scores		**Rank in top quarter:**	27%
SAT verbal:	460-590	**Rank in top tenth:**	3%
SAT math:	430-540	**End year in good standing:**	85%
ACT:	18-23	**Return as sophomores:**	85%
GPA 3.50 or higher:	17%	**Out-of-state:**	18%
GPA 3.0-3.49:	28%	**Live on campus:**	69%
GPA 2.0-2.99:	55%	**International:**	5%

Basis for selection. Portfolio and minimum high school GPA of 2.0 important. Portfolio required; interview recommended.

High school preparation. Recommended units include English 4, mathematics 2, science 2 and foreign language 2. Four units art recommended.

2005-2006 Annual costs. Tuition/fees: $20,278. Room/board: $6,450. Books/supplies: $3,000. Personal expenses: $1,300.

2004-2005 Financial aid. Need-based: 179 full-time freshmen applied for aid; 135 were judged to have need; 133 of these received aid. Average need met was 62%. Average scholarship/grant was $9,998; average loan $3,361. 61% of total undergraduate aid awarded as scholarships/grants, 39% as loans/jobs. **Non-need-based:** Awarded to 289 full-time undergraduates, including 51 freshmen. Scholarships awarded for academics, art, ROTC, state residency.

Application procedures. Admission: No deadline. $25 fee, may be waived for applicants with need. Application may be submitted online. Admission notification on a rolling basis. **Financial aid:** Priority date 3/2, closing date 6/3. FAFSA required. Applicants notified on a rolling basis starting 3/15; must reply within 2 week(s) of notification.

Academics. Special study options: Accelerated study, cooperative education, cross-registration, double major, ESL, independent study, internships, New York semester, study abroad. **Credit/placement by examination:** AP, CLEP. **Support services:** Learning center, reduced course load, remedial instruction, study skills assistance, tutoring.

Majors. Communications: Advertising, public relations. **Visual/performing arts:** Fashion design, illustration, industrial design, interior design, photography, studio arts.

Computing on campus. 226 workstations in library, computer center, student center. Dormitories linked to campus network. Commuter students can connect to campus network. Online library, helpline, repair service available.

Student life. Freshman orientation: Mandatory. 3 days before first day of classes. **Housing:** Guaranteed on-campus for freshmen. Coed dorms, apartments, substance-free housing available. $200 fully refundable deposit, deadline 6/1. **Activities:** Literary magazine, student government, student newspaper, student Bible study, student spirituality group, gay/lesbian/bisexual group.

Athletics. Intramural: Basketball M, soccer M, volleyball.

Student services. Adult student services, career counseling, student employment services, financial aid counseling, personal counseling, placement for graduates.

Contact. E-mail: admissions@ccad.edu
Phone: (614) 224-9101 ext. 3261 Fax: (614) 232-8344
Thomas Green, Director of Admissions, Columbus College of Art and Design, 107 North Ninth Street, Columbus, OH 43215-3875

David N. Myers University

Cleveland, Ohio
www.myers.edu **CB code: 1178**

- Private 4-year university
- Commuter campus in very large city
- 927 degree-seeking undergraduates
- SAT or ACT with writing required

General. Founded in 1848. Regionally accredited. **Degrees:** 158 bachelor's, 13 associate awarded; master's offered. **Location:** Downtown. **Calendar:** Semester, extensive summer session. **Full-time faculty:** 20 total. **Part-time faculty:** 85 total.

Basis for selection. High school GPA, test scores very important. Students with GPA below 2.5 and ACT below 18 must take college placement exams. Interview recommended for all; essay required for external degree programs.

High school preparation. 21 units required. Required units include English 4, mathematics 3, social studies 3, history 2, science 3 (laboratory 1), foreign language 2 and academic electives 3.

2005-2006 Annual costs. Tuition/fees: $12,300. Books/supplies: $800. Personal expenses: $2,596.

Financial aid. Non-need-based: Scholarships awarded for academics, state residency.

Application procedures. Admission: No deadline. $25 fee. Admission notification on a rolling basis beginning on or about 4/1. **Financial aid:** Priority date 4/30; no closing date. FAFSA required. Applicants notified on a rolling basis starting 5/1; must reply within 4 week(s) of notification.

Academics. Special study options: Accelerated study, combined bachelor's/graduate degree, cooperative education, cross-registration, distance learning, double major, dual enrollment of high school students, external degree, independent study, internships, liberal arts/career combination, student-designed major, weekend college. **Credit/placement by examination:** CLEP, institutional tests. **Support services:** Learning center, pre-admission summer program, remedial instruction, tutoring.

Majors. Business: General, accounting, administrative services, business admin, finance, human resources, management information systems, management science, managerial economics, marketing, office management, officetechnology. **Computer sciences:** Information systems. **Engineering technology:** Industrial management. **Health:** Health care admin. **Legal studies:** Legal secretary, paralegal. **Liberal arts:** Arts/sciences. **Public administration:** General, human services.

Computing on campus. Commuter students can connect to campus network.

Student life. Freshman orientation: Available. **Activities:** Choral groups, student government, student newspaper, paralegal association, marketing club, administrative management society, Students in Free Enterprise.

Athletics. Team name: Mustangs.

Student services. Career counseling, student employment services, health services, personal counseling, placement for graduates, veterans' counselor.

Contact. E-mail: Admissions@myers.edu
Phone: (216) 432-8992 Toll-free number: (877) 366-9377
Fax: (216) 361-9274
Ron Brown, Vice President for Enrollment Management, David N. Myers University, 3921 Chester Avenue, Cleveland, OH 44114

Defiance College

Defiance, Ohio — **CB member**
www.defiance.edu — **CB code: 1162**

- Private 4-year liberal arts college affiliated with United Church of Christ
- Residential campus in large town
- 827 degree-seeking undergraduates
- 103 degree-seeking graduate students
- 69% of applicants admitted
- SAT or ACT (ACT writing optional) required
- 45% graduate within 6 years

General. Founded in 1850. Regionally accredited. **Degrees:** 197 bachelor's, 6 associate awarded; master's offered. **Location:** 55 miles from Toledo, 45 miles from Fort Wayne, Indiana. **Calendar:** Semester, extensive summer session. **Full-time faculty:** 38 total; 63% have terminal degrees, 3% minority, 40% women. **Part-time faculty:** 48 total; 8% have terminal degrees, 6% minority, 40% women. **Class size:** 68% < 20, 32% 20-39, less than 1% 40-49, less than 1% 50-99. **Special facilities:** McMaster School for Advancing Humanity, Thoreau Wildlife Sanctuary.

Freshman class profile. 975 applied, 677 admitted, 244 enrolled.

Mid 50% test scores			
SAT verbal:	430-510	**ACT:**	18-24
SAT math:	400-520	**Return as sophomores:**	56%

Basis for selection. School achievement record, test scores, college preparatory curriculum important. Minimum 2.25 high school GPA, 18 ACT composite or 850 SAT combined score (exclusive of Writing). Essay and interview recommended.

High school preparation. 15 units recommended. Recommended units include English 4, mathematics 3, social studies 2, history 1, science 3 and foreign language 2. One unit fine arts and 1 unit of computer proficiency recommended.

2006-2007 Annual costs. Tuition/fees (projected): $19,750. Room/board: $6,170. Books/supplies: $800. Personal expenses: $1,800.

Financial aid. Non-need-based: Scholarships awarded for academics, leadership.

Application procedures. Admission: No deadline. $25 fee, may be waived for applicants with need. Application may be submitted online. Admission notification on a rolling basis beginning on or about 9/1. Must reply by May 1 or within 4 week(s) if notified thereafter. **Financial aid:** Priority date 3/1; no closing date. FAFSA required. Applicants notified on a rolling basis starting 3/15; must reply within 3 week(s) of notification.

Academics. Evening sessions available in many areas. Weekend college program for non-traditional students to pursue a bachelor's or master's degree in several business majors. All academic programs include a service component. **Special study options:** Accelerated study, cooperative education, cross-registration, distance learning, double major, dual enrollment of high school students, exchange student, honors, independent study, internships, liberal arts/career combination, student-designed major, study abroad, teacher certification program, weekend college. **Credit/placement by examination:** AP, CLEP, IB, institutional tests. 15 credit hours maximum toward associate degree, 30 toward bachelor's. **Support services:** Learning center, reduced course load, remedial instruction, study skills assistance, tutoring, writing center.

Majors. Biology: General. **Business:** General, accounting, banking/financial services, business admin, finance, financial planning, human resources, management information systems, market research, marketing, office management, public finance. **Communications:** General, journalism, public relations. **Computer sciences:** General, computer science. **Conservation:** General, environmental studies. **Education:** General, art, biology, business, chemistry, early childhood, elementary, English, health, history, mathematics, middle, multi-level teacher, physical, science, secondary, social science, social studies, speech. **English:** Speech/rhetoric. **Health:** Athletic training, clinical lab technology, predentistry, premedicine, preveterinary. **History:** General. **Interdisciplinary:** Biological/physical sciences, math/computer science, natural sciences. **Legal studies:** Prelaw. **Liberal arts:** Arts/sciences. **Math:** General. **Parks/recreation:** Health/fitness, sports admin. **Philosophy/religion:** Philosophy, religion. **Physical sciences:** Chemistry. **Protective services:** Forensics. **Psychology:** General. **Public administration:** Social work. **Social sciences:** General, criminology. **Theology:** Religious ed. **Visual/performing arts:** Art, commercial/advertising art.

Computing on campus. 200 workstations in dormitories, library, computer center, student center. Dormitories wired for high-speed internet access and linked to campus network. Commuter students can connect to campus network. Online library, helpline, wireless network available.

Student life. Freshman orientation: Mandatory. Preregistration for classes offered. One day sessions held in May, June and August. **Policies:** Students must live and take meals on campus unless they are seniors, married, veterans, or living with parents or close relatives within approved commuting distance. Freshmen permitted cars on campus. **Housing:** Guaranteed on-campus for freshmen. Single-sex dorms, apartments, substance-free housing available. ADA compliant rooms available in each hall. Service floors available. **Activities:** Concert band, choral groups, dance, drama, literary magazine, student government, student newspaper, American Marketing Association, Black Action Student Association, Campus Activities Board, Criminal Justice Society, Fellowship of Christian Athletes, Fraternities/Sororities, Student Ecology Club, Habitat for Humanity.

Athletics. NCAA. **Intercollegiate:** Baseball M, basketball, cross-country, football (tackle) M, golf, soccer, softball W, tennis, track and field, volleyball W. **Intramural:** Basketball, bowling, football (non-tackle), racquetball, soccer, softball, table tennis, volleyball. **Team name:** Yellow Jackets.

Student services. Adult student services, alcohol/substance abuse counseling, campus ministries, career counseling, student employment services, financial aid counseling, health services, minority student services, personal counseling, placement for graduates. **Physically disabled:** Services for hearing impaired.

Contact. E-mail: admissions@defiance.edu
Phone: (419) 783-2359 Toll-free number: (800) 520-4632
Fax: (419) 783-2468
William Nunn, Dean of Enrollment Management, Defiance College, 701 North Clinton Street, Defiance, OH 43512-1695

Denison University

Granville, Ohio **CB member**
www.denison.edu **CB code: 1164**

- Private 4-year liberal arts college
- Residential campus in small town
- 2,296 degree-seeking undergraduates: 56% women, 5% African American, 3% Asian American, 3% Hispanic American, 5% international
- 39% of applicants admitted
- SAT or ACT with writing, application essay required
- 79% graduate within 6 years; 20% enter graduate study

General. Founded in 1831. Regionally accredited. **Degrees:** 529 bachelor's awarded. **ROTC:** Army. **Location:** 27 miles from Columbus. **Calendar:** Semester. **Full-time faculty:** 183 total; 97% have terminal degrees, 12% minority, 45% women. **Part-time faculty:** 15 total; 100% have terminal degrees, 13% minority, 40% women. **Class size:** 62% < 20, 38% 20-39, less than 1% 50-99. **Special facilities:** Field research station in 350-acre biological reserve, high resolution spectrometer lab, nuclear magnetic resonance spectrometer, planetarium, economics computer lab, harmonic systems lab, digital media lab, fine and performing arts MIX lab (intermedia experimental lab), geographic Information systems lab.

Freshman class profile. 5,144 applied, 1,997 admitted, 622 enrolled.

Mid 50% test scores			
SAT verbal:	570-660	Rank in top quarter:	80%
SAT math:	580-670	Rank in top tenth:	54%
ACT:	25-29	Return as sophomores:	90%
GPA 3.50 or higher:	61%	Out-of-state:	62%
GPA 3.0-3.49:	29%	Live on campus:	100%
GPA 2.0-2.99:	10%	International:	5%

Basis for selection. Academic record, test scores, recommendations, talent and ability, character and personal qualities most important. School and community activities, essay and personal potential also important. Interview recommended for all; audition required for visual and performing arts program; portfolio recommended for studio art programs.

High school preparation. 19 units required. Required units include English 4, mathematics 4, social studies 2, history 1, science 4, foreign language 3 and academic electives 1. 1 unit fine arts recommended.

2006-2007 Annual costs. Tuition/fees: $30,660. Room/board: $8,560. Books/supplies: $600. Personal expenses: $1,200.

2005-2006 Financial aid. Need-based: 374 full-time freshmen applied for aid; 286 were judged to have need; 286 of these received aid. Average need met was 93%. Average scholarship/grant was $24,545; average loan $4,182. 61% of total undergraduate aid awarded as scholarships/grants, 39% as loans/jobs. **Non-need-based:** Awarded to 2,086 full-time undergraduates, including 540 freshmen. Scholarships awarded for academics, leadership, music/drama, state residency.

Application procedures. Admission: Priority date 12/15; deadline 1/15 (postmark date). $40 fee, may be waived for applicants with need. Application may be submitted online. Admission notification 4/1. Must reply by May 1 or within 2 week(s) if notified thereafter. **Financial aid:** Priority date 2/15; no closing date. FAFSA required. Applicants notified by 3/30; must reply by 5/1 or within 2 week(s) of notification.

Academics. Extensive honors curriculum. All students must complete a course in minority or women's studies. Computer-based laboratories for teaching mathematics and economics. Generous resources to support student involvement in faculty research. Service-Learning courses incorporate community-based experience as their subject matter. The Organizational Studies Program is designed to help students connect college study with career aspirations in such fields as finance, marketing and private and non-profit management. **Special study options:** Double major, dual enrollment of high school students, honors, independent study, internships, New York semester, semester at sea, student-designed major, study abroad, teacher certification program, Washington semester. **Credit/placement by examination:** AP, CLEP, IB, institutional tests. 16 credit hours maximum toward bachelor's degree. **Support services:** Learning center, reduced course load, study skills assistance, tutoring, writing center.

Majors. Area/ethnic studies: African-American, East Asian, gay/lesbian, Latin American, Western European, women's. **Biology:** General, biochemistry. **Business:** Organizational behavior. **Communications:** General, digital media. **Computer sciences:** General. **Conservation:** General. **Education:** General, physical. **English:** British lit. **Foreign languages:** Classics, French, German, Spanish. **History:** General. **Math:** General. **Philosophy/religion:** Philosophy, religion. **Physical sciences:** Chemistry, geology, physics. **Psychology:** General. **Social sciences:** Anthropology, economics, political science, sociology. **Visual/performing arts:** Art history/conservation, dance, dramatic, film/cinema, studio arts.

Most popular majors. Biology 9%, communications/journalism 12%, English 8%, foreign language 6%, history 6%, psychology 9%, social sciences 23%, visual/performing arts 9%.

Computing on campus. 1,237 workstations in dormitories, library, computer center, student center. Dormitories wired for high-speed internet access and linked to campus network. Commuter students can connect to campus network. Online library, helpline, student web hosting, wireless network available.

Student life. Freshman orientation: Available, $175 fee. Preregistration for classes offered. 2-day optional orientation in June; 4-day program in August. **Policies:** Freshmen permitted cars on campus. **Housing:** Guaranteed on-campus for all undergraduates. Coed dorms, single-sex dorms, apartments, substance-free housing available. 3 student-constructed buildings using alternative energy resources accommodate 12 students. Apartment-style housing for high-GPA upper division students. **Activities:** Bands, choral groups, dance, drama, film society, literary magazine, music ensembles, musical theater, radio station, student government, student newspaper, symphony orchestra, TV station, over 130 organizations available.

Athletics. NCAA. **Intercollegiate:** Baseball M, basketball, cross-country, diving, field hockey W, football (tackle) M, golf M, lacrosse, soccer, softball W, swimming, tennis, track and field, volleyball W. **Intramural:** Basketball, equestrian, football (non-tackle), golf, ice hockey M, lacrosse M, racquetball, rifle, rugby, skiing, soccer, softball, squash, tennis, volleyball, water polo, wrestling M. **Team name:** Big Red.

Student services. Alcohol/substance abuse counseling, campus ministries, career counseling, student employment services, financial aid counseling, health services, minority student services, personal counseling, placement for graduates.

Contact. E-mail: admissions@denison.edu
Phone: (740) 587-6276 Toll-free number: (800) 336-4766
Fax: (740) 587-6306
Perry Robinson, VP and Director of Admissions, Denison University, Box H, Granville, OH 43023

DeVry University: Columbus

Columbus, Ohio **CB member**
www.devrycols.edu **CB code: 1605**

- For-profit 4-year university
- Commuter campus in very large city
- 2,418 degree-seeking undergraduates: 32% part-time, 38% women
- 220 graduate students
- Interview required
- 39% graduate within 6 years

General. Founded in 1952. Regionally accredited. **Degrees:** 562 bachelor's, 85 associate awarded; master's offered. **ROTC:** Army. **Location:** 5 miles from downtown. **Calendar:** Semester, extensive summer session. **Full-time faculty:** 60 total; 8% minority, 25% women. **Part-time faculty:** 56 total; 16% minority, 23% women.

Freshman class profile. 467 enrolled.

Return as sophomores:	46%	International:	1%

Basis for selection. Applicants must have high school diploma or equivalent, demonstrate proficiency in basic college-level skills through SAT or ACT scores or institution-administered placement examinations, and be 17 years of age. New students may enter at beginning of any semester. SAT or ACT recommended. CPT also accepted.

High school preparation. College-preparatory program recommended. Required units include mathematics 1. Math unit must be algebra or higher.

2005-2006 Annual costs. Tuition/fees: $12,140. Books/supplies: $1,100. Personal expenses: $1,816.

2004-2005 Financial aid. All financial aid based on need. 567 full-time freshmen applied for aid; 530 were judged to have need; 530 of these received aid. Average need met was 44%. Average scholarship/grant was $4,775; average loan $5,251. 24% of total undergraduate aid awarded as scholarships/grants, 76% as loans/jobs.

Application procedures. Admission: No deadline. $50 fee. Application may be submitted online. Admission notification on a rolling basis.

Financial aid: No deadline. FAFSA required. Applicants notified on a rolling basis.

Academics. Special study options: Accelerated study, cooperative education, distance learning. **Credit/placement by examination:** CLEP, institutional tests. **Support services:** Learning center, tutoring.

Majors. Biology: Biomedical sciences. **Business:** Business admin, human resources, management information systems, operations. **Computer sciences:** Information systems, information technology, networking. **Engineering technology:** Biomedical, computer, electrical.

Most popular majors. Business/marketing 34%, computer/information sciences 35%, engineering/engineering technologies 31%.

Computing on campus. 408 workstations in library, computer center, student center. Online course registration, online library, helpline available.

Student life. Freshman orientation: Mandatory. **Policies:** Freshmen permitted cars on campus. **Housing:** Private apartments, student-plan housing, private rooms available. **Activities:** Student government, student newspaper, Devry student association, Tau Alpha Pi, DeVry Christian Alliance, Asian American student association, Future Accounting Society, Institute of Electrical and Electronics Engineers, Association of IT Professionals, minority student union.

Athletics. Intramural: Basketball, soccer, volleyball.

Student services. Career counseling, student employment services, financial aid counseling, placement for graduates, veterans' counselor. **Physically disabled:** Services for visually, hearing impaired.

Contact. E-mail: admissions@devry.edu
Phone: (614) 253-1525 Toll-free number: (800) 426-2206
Fax: (614) 253-0843
Bill Holtry, Deam of Admissions, DeVry University: Columbus, 1350 Alum Creek Drive, Columbus, OH 43209-2705

Franciscan University of Steubenville

Steubenville, Ohio — **CB member**
www.franciscan.edu — **CB code: 1133**

- Private 4-year university affiliated with Roman Catholic Church
- Residential campus in large town
- 1,902 degree-seeking undergraduates: 5% part-time, 61% women, 1% Asian American, 3% Hispanic American, 1% international
- 393 degree-seeking graduate students
- 81% of applicants admitted
- SAT or ACT (ACT writing optional), application essay required

General. Founded in 1946. Regionally accredited. **Degrees:** 425 bachelor's, 31 associate awarded; master's offered. **Location:** 40 miles from Pittsburgh. **Calendar:** Semester, limited summer session. **Full-time faculty:** 104 total. **Part-time faculty:** 101 total. **Class size:** 48% < 20, 44% 20-39, 7% 40-49, 2% 50-99. **Special facilities:** Replica of Portiuncula (St. Mary of the Angels) Chapel as rebuilt by St. Francis of Assisi in 1207 and Tomb of the Unborn Child.

Freshman class profile. 1,047 applied, 847 admitted, 400 enrolled.

Mid 50% test scores		**Rank in top tenth:**	28%
SAT verbal:	520-660	**Return as sophomores:**	85%
SAT math:	50-620	**Out-of-state:**	79%
ACT:	21-27	**Live on campus:**	83%
Rank in top quarter:	51%	**International:**	1%

Basis for selection. Admission requirements include minimum 2.4 high school GPA, recommendations, interview when available, combined SAT score of 1000 (exclusive of Writing) or ACT composite of 21. Interview recommended. **Homeschooled:** Applicants should contact Admissions Office for requirements.

High school preparation. 15 units required. Required and recommended units include English 4, mathematics 3, social studies 2, history 2, science 3, foreign language 3 and academic electives 1. 10 units in 4 of the following fields: English, foreign language, social science, mathematics, natural sciences. Remaining 5 units may be in other subjects counted toward graduation. Majors in chemistry, engineering science, or mathematics should have 2 units algebra and 2 units geometry/trigonometry.

2005-2006 Annual costs. Tuition/fees: $16,450. Room/board: $5,550. Books/supplies: $800. Personal expenses: $1,200.

2005-2006 Financial aid. Need-based: 58% of total undergraduate aid awarded as scholarships/grants, 42% as loans/jobs. **Non-need-based:** Scholarships awarded for academics, leadership, religious affiliation.

Application procedures. Admission: Closing date 5/1 (postmark date). $20 fee, may be waived for applicants with need. Application may be submitted online. Admission notification on a rolling basis. Must reply by 6/1. **Financial aid:** No deadline. FAFSA required. Applicants notified on a rolling basis starting 3/15; must reply within 3 week(s) of notification.

Academics. Students encouraged to spend 1 semester of sophomore year in study abroad program in Gaming, Austria. **Special study options:** Accelerated study, combined bachelor's/graduate degree, distance learning, double major, honors, independent study, internships, liberal arts/career combination, study abroad, teacher certification program. **Credit/placement by examination:** AP, CLEP, IB, institutional tests. 30 credit hours maximum toward associate degree, 30 toward bachelor's. **Support services:** Learning center, reduced course load, study skills assistance, tutoring, writing center.

Honors college/program. 1180 SAT (exclusive of Writing) and/or 26 ACT, 3.4 high school GPA, and a series of essays required. 40 freshmen admitted. Academic program consists of a great books seminar sequence.

Majors. Biology: General. **Business:** Accounting, business admin. **Communications:** General. **Computer sciences:** General, computer science. **Education:** Elementary. **Engineering:** Science. **English:** English lit. **Foreign languages:** Classics, French, German, Spanish. **Health:** Mental health services, nursing (RN). **History:** General. **Legal studies:** General. **Liberal arts:** Humanities. **Math:** General. **Philosophy/religion:** Philosophy. **Physical sciences:** Chemistry. **Psychology:** General. **Public administration:** Social work. **Social sciences:** Anthropology, economics, political science, sociology. **Theology:** Religious ed, theology.

Most popular majors. Business/marketing 12%, education 9%, English 7%, health sciences 12%, philosophy/religious studies 29%, social sciences 7%.

Computing on campus. 126 workstations in library, computer center. Commuter students can connect to campus network. Online library, helpline available.

Student life. Freshman orientation: Mandatory, $150 fee. Preregistration for classes offered. Held weekend before fall classes begin, from Friday morning to Sunday afternoon. **Housing:** Guaranteed on-campus for freshmen. Single-sex dorms available. $150 deposit. Household groups of 10-20 students in residence halls may develop distinctive environment for their group within the context of Christian and Franciscan perspective. **Activities:** Choral groups, drama, literary magazine, music ensembles, radio station, student government, student newspaper, campus ministry, International Student Organization, Human Life Concerns (pro-life), Works of Mercy Program, leadership development.

Athletics. Intramural: Basketball, bowling, football (non-tackle), golf, racquetball, soccer, softball, tennis, volleyball, weight lifting, wrestling M. **Team name:** Barons.

Student services. Adult student services, campus ministries, career counseling, student employment services, financial aid counseling, health services, personal counseling, veterans' counselor. **Physically disabled:** Services for visually, speech, hearing impaired.

Contact. E-mail: admissions@franciscan.edu
Phone: (740) 283-6226 Toll-free number: (800) 783-6220
Fax: (740) 284-5456
Margaret Weber, Director of Admissions, Franciscan University of Steubenville, 1235 University Boulevard, Steubenville, OH 43952-1763

Franklin University

Columbus, Ohio
www.franklin.edu — **CB code: 1229**

- Private 4-year university and business college
- Commuter campus in very large city
- 6,027 degree-seeking undergraduates: 66% part-time, 55% women, 20% African American, 2% Asian American, 3% Hispanic American, 1% Native American, 4% international
- 872 graduate students

General. Founded in 1902. Regionally accredited. Credit courses offered at suburban campuses and online. **Degrees:** 1,219 bachelor's, 76 associate awarded; master's offered. **ROTC:** Army. **Location:** Downtown Columbus. **Calendar:** Trimester, extensive summer session. **Full-time faculty:** 32 total; 69% have terminal degrees, 12% minority, 38% women. **Part-time faculty:** 552 total; 19% have terminal degrees, 29% minority, 42% women.

Class size: 75% < 20, 24% 20-39, less than 1% 40-49. **Special facilities:** Student learning center.

Freshman class profile. 444 applied, 444 admitted, 179 enrolled.

Return as sophomores:	66%	**International:**	6%
Out-of-state:	24%		

Basis for selection. Open admission. Selective admission for international (nonresident alien) students. Admission tests not required but considered for placement if submitted.

High school preparation. Recommended units include mathematics 3.

2005-2006 Annual costs. Tuition/fees: $7,320. Books/supplies: $750. Personal expenses: $2,150.

2005-2006 Financial aid. Need-based: 48 full-time freshmen applied for aid; 45 were judged to have need; 44 of these received aid. Average scholarship/grant was $5,847; average loan $2,706. 35% of total undergraduate aid awarded as scholarships/grants, 65% as loans/jobs. **Non-need-based:** Awarded to 1,145 full-time undergraduates, including 43 freshmen. Scholarships awarded for academics, leadership, minority status.

Application procedures. Admission: No deadline. No application fee. Application may be submitted online. Admission notification on a rolling basis. **Financial aid:** Priority date 6/15; no closing date. FAFSA required. Applicants notified on a rolling basis; must reply within 2 week(s) of notification.

Academics. Accelerated 6-week course offerings in addition to 12- and 15-week formats. **Special study options:** Accelerated study, combined bachelor's/graduate degree, cooperative education, cross-registration, distance learning, double major, dual enrollment of high school students, ESL, independent study, internships, study abroad, weekend college. **Credit/placement by examination:** AP, CLEP, institutional tests. 32 credit hours maximum toward associate degree, 84 toward bachelor's. **Support services:** Learning center, reduced course load, remedial instruction, study skills assistance, tutoring, writing center.

Majors. Business: General, accounting, finance, human resources, management information systems, management science, marketing, operations. **Communications:** Digital media. **Computer sciences:** General. **Health:** Health care admin.

Most popular majors. Business/marketing 78%, computer/information sciences 15%.

Computing on campus. 370 workstations in library, computer center, student center. Commuter students can connect to campus network. Online course registration, online library, helpline, wireless network available.

Student life. Freshman orientation: Available. **Activities:** International student association.

Student services. Adult student services, career counseling, financial aid counseling, veterans' counselor. **Physically disabled:** Services for visually, speech, hearing impaired.

Contact. E-mail: info@franklin.edu
Phone: (614) 797-4700 Toll-free number: (877) 341-6300
Fax: (614) 224-8027
Tracy Austin, Chief Student Officer, Franklin University, 201 South Grant Avenue, Columbus, OH 43215-5399

God's Bible School and College

Cincinnati, Ohio
www.gbs.edu **CB code: 1238**

- Private 4-year Bible college affiliated with interdenominational tradition
- Residential campus in large city
- 271 degree-seeking undergraduates
- 98% of applicants admitted
- SAT required

General. Founded in 1900. Accredited by ABHE. **Degrees:** 33 bachelor's, 15 associate awarded. **Location:** One mile from downtown. **Calendar:** Semester. **Full-time faculty:** 13 total; 62% have terminal degrees. **Part-time faculty:** 12 total; 8% have terminal degrees.

Freshman class profile. 60 applied, 59 admitted, 53 enrolled.

Rank in top quarter:	39%	**Live on campus:**	83%
Out-of-state:	53%	**International:**	9%

Basis for selection. Three references recommended (two required), HS diploma/GED, SAT scores.

High school preparation. 17 units recommended. Recommended units include English 3, mathematics 2, social studies 2 and science 2.

2006-2007 Annual costs. Tuition/fees (projected): $4,860. Room/board: $3,300. Books/supplies: $550. Personal expenses: $2,400.

2004-2005 Financial aid. Non-need-based: Scholarships awarded for academics, leadership, music/drama, religious affiliation. **Additional information:** Institutional work scholarships available.

Application procedures. Admission: No deadline. $25 fee. Application must be submitted on paper. Admission notification on a rolling basis. **Financial aid:** Priority date 4/30, closing date 8/1. FAFSA required. Applicants notified on a rolling basis.

Academics. Special study options: Distance learning, double major, independent study, internships, liberal arts/career combination. **Credit/placement by examination:** CLEP, SAT, institutional tests. **Support services:** Learning center.

Majors. Education: Elementary, music. **Theology:** Missionary, religious ed, sacred music, theology, youth ministry.

Computing on campus. Dormitories wired for high-speed internet access. Wireless network available.

Student life. Freshman orientation: Mandatory. Preregistration for classes offered. Takes place the week before classes begin, lasting for several days. **Policies:** Students agree to follow all rules, policies and regulations by matriculating. Please contact the Office of Student Affairs for specific information. Religious observance required. Freshmen permitted cars on campus. **Housing:** Guaranteed on-campus for freshmen. Single-sex dorms, substance-free housing available. **Activities:** Choral groups, music ensembles, student government, student newspaper, symphony orchestra.

Athletics. Intramural: Basketball, volleyball.

Student services. Campus ministries, student employment services, financial aid counseling, health services, personal counseling, placement for graduates, veterans' counselor.

Contact. E-mail: lprofitt@gbs.edu
Phone: (513) 721-7944 ext. 205 Toll-free number: (800) 486-4637 ext. 205
Fax: (513) 721-1357
Lisa Profitt, Director of Admissions and Financial Aid, God's Bible School and College, 1810 Young Street, Cincinnati, OH 45202

Heidelberg College

Tiffin, Ohio **CB member**
www.heidelberg.edu **CB code: 1292**

- Private 4-year liberal arts college affiliated with United Church of Christ
- Residential campus in large town
- 1,101 degree-seeking undergraduates: 3% part-time, 48% women, 4% African American, 1% Asian American, 1% Hispanic American, 2% international
- 205 degree-seeking graduate students
- 75% of applicants admitted
- SAT or ACT (ACT writing optional) required
- 60% graduate within 6 years

General. Founded in 1850. Regionally accredited. Freshman-level credit courses and graduate education course work offered at Sapporo, Japan campus. **Degrees:** 167 bachelor's awarded; master's offered. **ROTC:** Army, Air Force. **Location:** 52 miles from Toledo, 80 miles from Cleveland. **Calendar:** Semester, limited summer session. **Full-time faculty:** 55 total; 80% have terminal degrees, 9% minority, 46% women. **Part-time faculty:** 85 total; 24% have terminal degrees, 5% minority, 45% women. **Class size:** 59% < 20, 37% 20-39, 3% 40-49, 1% 50-99. **Special facilities:** National Center for Water Quality Research, cadaver laboratory, infant psychology laboratory, four wooded lots for science research, archaeology laboratory, historic and military archaeology center.

Freshman class profile. 1,830 applied, 1,370 admitted, 328 enrolled.

Mid 50% test scores			
SAT verbal:	450-570	Rank in top quarter:	34%
SAT math:	450-580	Rank in top tenth:	14%
ACT:	19-24	Out-of-state:	6%
GPA 3.50 or higher:	33%	Live on campus:	90%
GPA 3.0-3.49:	32%	International:	2%
GPA 2.0-2.99:	35%	Fraternities:	11%
		Sororities:	18%

Basis for selection. School achievement record is most important, followed by test scores. Special talents, community activities, and leadership qualities also considered. Audition required for music; interview recommended for academically weak students.

High school preparation. 21 units recommended. Recommended units include English 4, mathematics 4, social studies 3, science 3, foreign language 2 and academic electives 4.

2005-2006 Annual costs. Tuition/fees: $16,134. Room/board: $7,108. Books/supplies: $1,000. Personal expenses: $500.

2005-2006 Financial aid. **Need-based:** 290 full-time freshmen applied for aid; 266 were judged to have need; 266 of these received aid. Average need met was 83%. Average scholarship/grant was $10,739; average loan $3,564. 65% of total undergraduate aid awarded as scholarships/grants, 35% as loans/jobs. **Non-need-based:** Awarded to 78 full-time undergraduates, including 26 freshmen. Scholarships awarded for academics, music/drama, religious affiliation, state residency.

Application procedures. **Admission:** Priority date 1/1; deadline 8/1 (receipt date). $25 fee, may be waived for applicants with need. Application may be submitted online. Admission notification on a rolling basis beginning on or about 9/1. Must reply by May 1 or within 2 week(s) if notified thereafter. **Financial aid:** Priority date 3/1; no closing date. FAFSA required. Applicants notified on a rolling basis starting 3/15; must reply within 2 week(s) of notification.

Academics. **Special study options:** Accelerated study, cooperative education, cross-registration, double major, dual enrollment of high school students, exchange student, honors, independent study, internships, liberal arts/career combination, semester at sea, student-designed major, study abroad, teacher certification program, Washington semester, weekend college. **Credit/placement by examination:** AP, CLEP, IB, institutional tests. 30 credit hours maximum toward bachelor's degree. **Support services:** Learning center, reduced course load, study skills assistance, tutoring, writing center.

Majors. **Biology:** General, environmental. **Business:** Accounting, business admin, management science. **Communications:** General, public relations. **Computer sciences:** General, computer science. **Conservation:** Management/policy. **Education:** Music, physical. **English:** English lit. **Foreign languages:** German, Spanish. **Health:** Athletic training, health care admin, predentistry, premedicine, prenursing, preveterinary. **History:** General. **Interdisciplinary:** Biological/physical sciences. **Legal studies:** Prelaw. **Math:** General. **Parks/recreation:** Sports admin. **Philosophy/religion:** Religion. **Physical sciences:** Chemistry, physics. **Psychology:** General. **Public administration:** General. **Social sciences:** General, anthropology, economics, political science. **Visual/performing arts:** Music management, music performance, music theory/composition.

Most popular majors. Biology 6%, business/marketing 28%, communications/journalism 11%, education 17%, psychology 9%, social sciences 6%.

Computing on campus. 125 workstations in dormitories, library, computer center, student center. Dormitories wired for high-speed internet access and linked to campus network. Helpline, repair service, wireless network available.

Student life. **Freshman orientation:** Mandatory. 5 different 2-day summer sessions to choose from. **Housing:** Guaranteed on-campus for all undergraduates. Coed dorms, single-sex dorms, special housing for disabled, apartments, cooperative housing, substance-free housing available. $250 fully refundable deposit, deadline 8/1. Undergraduate specialty houses by major, interest, service groups available. **Activities:** Bands, choral groups, dance, drama, film society, literary magazine, music ensembles, musical theater, opera, radio station, student government, student newspaper, symphony orchestra, TV station, Black Student Union, Young Democrats, Young Republicans, Circle-K, religious organizations, World Student Union, Beta Beta Beta, political science organization.

Athletics. NCAA. **Intercollegiate:** Baseball M, basketball, cross-country, football (tackle) M, golf M, soccer, softball W, tennis, track and field, volleyball W, wrestling M. **Intramural:** Archery, baseball M, basketball, bowling, golf, lacrosse, soccer, softball, table tennis, volleyball. **Team name:** Student Princes.

Student services. Adult student services, campus ministries, career counseling, student employment services, financial aid counseling, health services, minority student services, personal counseling, placement for graduates, women's services. **Physically disabled:** Services for visually, hearing impaired.

Contact. E-mail: adminfo@heidelberg.edu
Phone: (419) 448-2330 Toll-free number: (800) 434-3352
Fax: (419) 448-2334
Lindsay Sooy, Director of Admission, Heidelberg College, 310 East Market Street, Tiffin, OH 44883-2462

Hiram College

Hiram, Ohio — **CB member**
www.hiram.edu — **CB code: 1297**

- Private 4-year liberal arts college affiliated with Christian Church (Disciples of Christ)
- Residential campus in rural community
- 1,086 degree-seeking undergraduates: 19% part-time, 57% women
- 17 degree-seeking graduate students
- 85% of applicants admitted
- SAT or ACT (ACT writing optional), application essay required
- 66% graduate within 6 years

General. Founded in 1850. Regionally accredited. Affiliated with John Cabot International University in Rome, Italy, Shoals Marine Laboratory in New Hampshire, Institute of European Studies, and Institute for Asian Studies. Exchange programs with Kansai University of Foreign Studies in Osaka, Japan, and Bosphorus University in Turkey. **Degrees:** 230 bachelor's awarded. **Location:** 35 miles from Cleveland. **Calendar:** Semester, limited summer session. **Full-time faculty:** 74 total. **Part-time faculty:** 45 total. **Class size:** 88% < 20, 12% 20-39, less than 1% 40-49. **Special facilities:** 2 nature/science field research stations, observatory, center for literature and medicine.

Freshman class profile. 832 applied, 710 admitted, 215 enrolled.

Mid 50% test scores			
SAT verbal:	480-630	GPA 2.0-2.99:	24%
SAT math:	490-620	Rank in top quarter:	52%
ACT:	20-26	Rank in top tenth:	24%
GPA 3.50 or higher:	48%	Return as sophomores:	80%
GPA 3.0-3.49:	28%	Out-of-state:	23%
		Live on campus:	96%

Basis for selection. School record, test scores, counselor and teacher recommendations emphasized. Extracurricular participation, alumni relationship considered. Interview required for scholarship candidates or academically marginal applicants; recommended for all others.

High school preparation. 20 units required; 21 recommended. Required and recommended units include English 4, mathematics 3, social studies 3, history 1, science 3 (laboratory 2), foreign language 2-3 and academic electives 2. One course in fine arts recommended.

2005-2006 Annual costs. Tuition/fees: $24,180. Room/board: $7,610.

Financial aid. **Non-need-based:** Scholarships awarded for academics, alumni affiliation, art, leadership, minority status, music/drama, religious affiliation, state residency.

Application procedures. **Admission:** Priority date 2/15; deadline 4/15 (postmark date). $35 fee, may be waived for applicants with need. Application may be submitted online. Admission notification on a rolling basis beginning on or about 10/1. Must reply by May 1 or within 2 week(s) if notified thereafter. **Financial aid:** Priority date 3/1; no closing date. FAFSA required. Applicants notified on a rolling basis starting 2/15; must reply by 5/1 or within 2 week(s) of notification.

Academics. Prelaw, premed and preveterinary programs offered. **Special study options:** Accelerated study, combined bachelor's/graduate degree, cross-registration, double major, dual enrollment of high school students, ESL, exchange student, independent study, internships, student-designed major, study abroad, teacher certification program, Washington semester, weekend college. **Credit/placement by examination:** AP, CLEP, IB, institutional tests. 60 credit hours maximum toward bachelor's degree. **Support services:** Reduced course load, study skills assistance, tutoring, writing center.

Majors. **Biology:** General, biochemistry, biomedical sciences. **Business:** Accounting/finance, business admin. **Communications:** General. **Computer sciences:** General, computer science. **Conservation:** Environmental studies. **Education:** General, elementary. **English:** Creative writing, English lit. **Foreign languages:** Classics, French, German, Spanish. **History:** General. **Interdisciplinary:** Math/computer science. **Legal studies:** Prelaw.

Math: General. **Philosophy/religion:** Philosophy, religion. **Physical sciences:** Chemistry, physics. **Psychology:** General. **Social sciences:** General, economics, political science, sociology. **Visual/performing arts:** Art history/conservation, dramatic, studio arts.

Most popular majors. Biology 11%, business/marketing 36%, computer/information sciences 6%, education 16%, English 6%, health sciences 6%, psychology 9%, visual/performing arts 8%.

Computing on campus. 100 workstations in dormitories, library, computer center, student center. Dormitories wired for high-speed internet access and linked to campus network. Commuter students can connect to campus network. Online course registration, online library, helpline, student web hosting, wireless network available.

Student life. **Freshman orientation:** Mandatory, $240 fee. Preregistration for classes offered. Several orientation sessions held throughout late spring and summer. **Policies:** Freshmen permitted cars on campus. **Housing:** Guaranteed on-campus for all undergraduates. Coed dorms, single-sex dorms, substance-free housing available. $100 nonrefundable deposit, deadline 5/1. Dormitories include 24-hour and 12-hour quiet floors. **Activities:** Bands, choral groups, dance, drama, literary magazine, music ensembles, musical theater, radio station, student government, student newspaper, TV station, African-American Students United, environmental awareness club, Christian Fellowship, Network for Progressive Action, conservative student forum, Model United Nations, volunteer association, international organization, Intercultural Forum, Newman Club, Islamic Society.

Athletics. NCAA. **Intercollegiate:** Baseball M, basketball, cross-country, diving, football (tackle) M, golf, soccer, softball W, swimming, tennis, track and field, volleyball W. **Intramural:** Archery, basketball, football (non-tackle), soccer, softball, tennis, volleyball, water polo. **Team name:** Terriers.

Student services. Campus ministries, career counseling, student employment services, health services, minority student services, personal counseling, placement for graduates, veterans' counselor.

Contact. E-mail: admission@hiram.edu
Phone: (330) 569-5169 Toll-free number: (800) 362-5280
Fax: (330) 569-5944
James Barrett, Executive Director of Admission, Hiram College, Teachout Price Hall, Hiram, OH 44234

John Carroll University

University Heights, Ohio — **CB member**
www.jcu.edu — **CB code: 1342**

- Private 4-year university affiliated with Roman Catholic Church
- Residential campus in large town
- 3,242 degree-seeking undergraduates: 2% part-time, 53% women, 4% African American, 2% Asian American, 2% Hispanic American
- 636 degree-seeking graduate students
- 85% of applicants admitted
- SAT or ACT (ACT writing recommended), application essay required
- 74% graduate within 6 years; 25% enter graduate study

General. Founded in 1886. Regionally accredited. College in the Jesuit tradition. **Degrees:** 743 bachelor's awarded; master's offered. **ROTC:** Army. **Location:** 10 miles from Cleveland. **Calendar:** Semester, extensive summer session. **Full-time faculty:** 222 total; 92% have terminal degrees, 10% minority, 36% women. **Part-time faculty:** 169 total; 40% have terminal degrees, 7% minority, 48% women. **Class size:** 40% < 20, 60% 20-39, less than 1% 50-99. **Special facilities:** Science and technology center containing research facility.

Freshman class profile. 3,057 applied, 2,604 admitted, 786 enrolled.

Mid 50% test scores		**Rank in top quarter:**	58%
SAT verbal:	530-630	**Rank in top tenth:**	28%
SAT math:	530-630	**Return as sophomores:**	85%
ACT:	21-26	**Out-of-state:**	32%
GPA 3.50 or higher:	52%	**Live on campus:**	89%
GPA 3.0-3.49:	29%	**Fraternities:**	19%
GPA 2.0-2.99:	19%	**Sororities:**	20%

Basis for selection. Strength of high school curriculum, high school academic record, test scores, recommendations, extracurricular activities, essay most important. Interview highly recommended. **Homeschooled:** Interview is recommended. Extra emphasis placed on standardized testing.

High school preparation. 16 units required; 21 recommended. Required and recommended units include English 4, mathematics 3-4, social studies 2-4, science 2-3 (laboratory 2-3), foreign language 2-3 and academic electives 3. Two units must be distributed between social studies and/or history; 4 recommended.

2005-2006 Annual costs. Tuition/fees: $23,630. Room/board: $7,526. Books/supplies: $1,000. Personal expenses: $750.

2005-2006 Financial aid. **Need-based:** 687 full-time freshmen applied for aid; 562 were judged to have need; 562 of these received aid. Average need met was 86%. Average scholarship/grant was $13,404; average loan $3,896. 72% of total undergraduate aid awarded as scholarships/grants, 28% as loans/jobs. **Non-need-based:** Awarded to 402 full-time undergraduates, including 113 freshmen. Scholarships awarded for academics, ROTC, state residency. **Additional information:** Institutional form for need analysis required from upperclassmen and transfer students only.

Application procedures. **Admission:** Closing date 2/1 (postmark date). $25 fee, may be waived for applicants with need. Application may be submitted online. Admission notification on a rolling basis. Must reply by May 1 or within 4 week(s) if notified thereafter. **Financial aid:** Priority date 3/1; no closing date. FAFSA required. Applicants notified on a rolling basis starting 3/1; must reply by 5/1 or within 4 week(s) of notification.

Academics. Online course registration available for second semester freshmen. **Special study options:** Accelerated study, combined bachelor's/graduate degree, cooperative education, cross-registration, double major, dual enrollment of high school students, exchange student, honors, independent study, internships, liberal arts/career combination, student-designed major, study abroad, teacher certification program, Washington semester. **Credit/placement by examination:** AP, CLEP, IB, institutional tests. 30 credit hours maximum toward bachelor's degree. **Support services:** Learning center, reduced course load, study skills assistance, tutoring, writing center.

Majors. **Biology:** General. **Business:** Accounting, business admin, finance, logistics. **Communications:** General. **Computer sciences:** General, computer science. **Conservation:** Environmental studies. **Education:** Elementary, physical. **Engineering:** Physics. **English:** English lit. **Foreign languages:** Ancient Greek, comparative lit, French, German, Latin, Spanish. **Health:** Predentistry, premedicine, preveterinary. **History:** General. **Interdisciplinary:** Gerontology. **Legal studies:** Prelaw. **Liberal arts:** Arts/sciences. **Math:** General. **Philosophy/religion:** Philosophy, religion. **Physical sciences:** Chemistry, physics. **Psychology:** General. **Social sciences:** Economics, political science, sociology. **Visual/performing arts:** Art history/conservation.

Most popular majors. Biology 9%, business/marketing 31%, communications/journalism 15%, education 12%, psychology 7%, social sciences 7%.

Computing on campus. 200 workstations in dormitories, library, computer center, student center. Dormitories wired for high-speed internet access and linked to campus network. Commuter students can connect to campus network. Online library, helpline, repair service, student web hosting, wireless network available.

Student life. **Freshman orientation:** Mandatory, $235 fee. 2 day, one overnight for parents and students. Students take placement tests. **Housing:** Guaranteed on-campus for all undergraduates. Coed dorms, single-sex dorms, substance-free housing available. $100 nonrefundable deposit, deadline 5/1. Suite style housing available. **Activities:** Bands, choral groups, dance, drama, film society, literary magazine, music ensembles, musical theater, radio station, student government, student newspaper, campus ministry, Black United Students Association, Young Republicans, international students club, Christian Life Community, Young Democrats, Christmas in April, Project Gold, science organization.

Athletics. NCAA. **Intercollegiate:** Baseball M, basketball, cross-country, diving, football (tackle) M, golf, ice hockey M, soccer, softball W, swimming, tennis, track and field, volleyball W, wrestling M. **Intramural:** Basketball, football (non-tackle), racquetball, softball, swimming, volleyball, water polo. **Team name:** Blue Streaks.

Student services. Adult student services, alcohol/substance abuse counseling, campus ministries, career counseling, student employment services, financial aid counseling, health services, minority student services, personal counseling, placement for graduates. **Physically disabled:** Services for visually, speech, hearing impaired.

Contact. E-mail: admission@jcu.edu
Phone: (216) 397-4294 Fax: (216) 397-4981
Thomas Fanning, Interim Dean of Enrollment Services, John Carroll University, 20700 North Park Boulevard, University Heights, OH 44118-4581

Kent State University

Kent, Ohio — **CB member**
www.kent.edu — **CB code: 1367**

- Public 4-year university
- Residential campus in large town
- 18,365 degree-seeking undergraduates: 15% part-time, 60% women, 8% African American, 1% Asian American, 1% Hispanic American, 1% international
- 4,328 degree-seeking graduate students
- 94% of applicants admitted
- SAT or ACT (ACT writing optional) required
- 46% graduate within 6 years

General. Founded in 1910. Regionally accredited. **Degrees:** 3,740 bachelor's awarded; master's, doctoral offered. **ROTC:** Army, Air Force. **Location:** 50 miles from Cleveland, 11 miles from Akron. **Calendar:** Semester, extensive summer session. **Full-time faculty:** 841 total; 70% have terminal degrees, 15% minority, 48% women. **Part-time faculty:** 614 total; 10% have terminal degrees, 10% minority, 54% women. **Class size:** 52% < 20, 37% 20-39, 3% 40-49, 5% 50-99, 3% >100. **Special facilities:** 287-acre airport, liquid crystal institute, fashion museum, planetarium, ice arena, 18-hole golf course.

Freshman class profile. 10,774 applied, 10,074 admitted, 3,814 enrolled.

Mid 50% test scores			
SAT verbal:	450-570	Rank in top tenth:	12%
SAT math:	450-570	End year in good standing:	73%
ACT:	19-24	Return as sophomores:	72%
GPA 3.50 or higher:	27%	Out-of-state:	12%
GPA 3.0-3.49:	35%	Live on campus:	78%
GPA 2.0-2.99:	37%	International:	1%
Rank in top quarter:	33%	Fraternities:	4%
		Sororities:	4%

Basis for selection. Academic record, course work, test scores important. Varying criteria for nursing, education, flight, fashion design and merchandising, architecture, interior design, journalism and mass communication, 6-year medical program, music, dance, and honors college applicants. Interview required for 6-year medical program, recommended for all others. Audition required for dance, music, and musical theater students.

High school preparation. 16 units recommended. Recommended units include English 4, mathematics 3, social studies 3, science 3 (laboratory 2) and foreign language 2. One fine arts or third unit of foreign language recommended.

2005-2006 Annual costs. Tuition/fees: $7,954; $15,386 out-of-state. Room/board: $6,640. Books/supplies: $990.

2005-2006 Financial aid. Need-based: 3,002 full-time freshmen applied for aid; 2,368 were judged to have need; 2,368 of these received aid. Average need met was 55%. Average scholarship/grant was $4,868; average loan $3,233. 35% of total undergraduate aid awarded as scholarships/grants, 65% as loans/jobs. **Non-need-based:** Awarded to 2,122 full-time undergraduates, including 684 freshmen. Scholarships awarded for academics, alumni affiliation, art, athletics, leadership, minority status, music/drama, ROTC, state residency. **Additional information:** Participant in U.S. Department of Education's Quality Assurance Program and Experimental Sites Program.

Application procedures. Admission: Priority date 3/15; deadline 5/1 (postmark date). $30 fee, may be waived for applicants with need. Application may be submitted online. Admission notification on a rolling basis beginning on or about 10/1. **Financial aid:** Priority date 3/1; no closing date. FAFSA required. Applicants notified by 3/15; must reply within 2 week(s) of notification.

Academics. Special study options: Accelerated study, combined bachelor's/graduate degree, cooperative education, cross-registration, distance learning, double major, dual enrollment of high school students, ESL, exchange student, external degree, honors, independent study, internships, liberal arts/career combination, student-designed major, study abroad, teacher certification program, Washington semester, weekend college. BS/MD. **Credit/placement by examination:** AP, CLEP, IB, institutional tests. 30 credit hours maximum toward bachelor's degree. **Support services:** Learning center, pre-admission summer program, reduced course load, remedial instruction, study skills assistance, tutoring, writing center.

Honors college/program. Approximately 250 incoming freshman admitted; high school class rank within top 10 percentile; 3.5 GPA or higher; 25 ACT composite (1140 SAT exclusive of Writing); small interactive classes (20 maximum); eight courses culminating with thesis project, portfolio, or course; two study abroad programs.

Majors. Architecture: Architecture. **Area/ethnic studies:** African-American, American, Latin American, Russian/Slavic. **Biology:** General, biotechnology, botany, zoology. **Business:** Accounting, business admin, fashion, finance, management information systems, management science, managerial economics, marketing. **Communications:** Advertising, broadcast journalism, digital media, journalism, photojournalism, public relations, radio/tv. **Computer sciences:** Systems analysis. **Conservation:** General. **Education:** General, art, business, chemistry, early childhood, health, mathematics, middle, music, physical, science, social studies, special, technology/industrial arts, trade/industrial. **Engineering:** General, industrial. **English:** English lit, speech/rhetoric. **Family/consumer sciences:** Family studies, food/nutrition. **Foreign languages:** French, German, Latin, Russian, sign language interpretation, Spanish. **Health:** Athletic training, audiology/speech pathology, clinical lab science, nursing (RN), predentistry, premedicine, preveterinary. **History:** General. **Interdisciplinary:** Peace/conflict. **Legal studies:** Paralegal. **Liberal arts:** Arts/sciences, humanities. **Math:** General, applied. **Parks/recreation:** Facilities management. **Philosophy/religion:** Philosophy. **Physical sciences:** Chemistry, geology, physics. **Protective services:** Criminal justice. **Psychology:** General. **Social sciences:** Anthropology, geography, international relations, political science, sociology. **Transportation:** Aviation. **Visual/performing arts:** Art history/conservation, commercial/advertising art, crafts, dance, dramatic, fashion design, interior design, painting.

Most popular majors. Business/marketing 20%, communications/journalism 6%, education 14%, English 7%, health sciences 7%, psychology 6%, visual/performing arts 6%.

Computing on campus. 2,100 workstations in dormitories, library, computer center, student center. Dormitories wired for high-speed internet access and linked to campus network. Commuter students can connect to campus network. Online course registration, online library, helpline, repair service, student web hosting, wireless network available.

Student life. Freshman orientation: Mandatory, $100 fee. Preregistration for classes offered. **Policies:** Freshmen permitted cars on campus. **Housing:** Guaranteed on-campus for freshmen. Coed dorms, single-sex dorms, special housing for disabled, apartments, fraternity/sorority housing available. $200 deposit, deadline 6/4. Single undergraduate students must live in college housing first 4 semesters with some exemptions granted. Learning communities available. **Activities:** Bands, choral groups, dance, drama, film society, literary magazine, music ensembles, musical theater, opera, radio station, student government, student newspaper, TV station, social service, political and religious organizations available.

Athletics. NCAA. **Intercollegiate:** Baseball M, basketball, cross-country, field hockey W, football (tackle) M, golf, gymnastics W, soccer W, softball W, track and field, volleyball W, wrestling M. **Intramural:** Badminton, basketball, bowling, football (non-tackle), golf, racquetball, soccer, softball, table tennis, tennis, water polo, wrestling M. **Team name:** Golden Flashes.

Student services. Adult student services, alcohol/substance abuse counseling, campus ministries, career counseling, services for economically disadvantaged, student employment services, financial aid counseling, health services, legal services, minority student services, personal counseling, placement for graduates, veterans' counselor, women's services. **Physically disabled:** Services for visually, speech, hearing impaired.

Contact. E-mail: admissions@kent.edu
Phone: (330) 672-2444 Toll-free number: (800) 988-5368
Fax: (330) 672-2499
Nancy DellaVecchia, Director of Admissions, Kent State University, PO Box 5190, Kent, OH 44242-0001

Kenyon College

Gambier, Ohio — **CB member**
www.kenyon.edu — **CB code: 1370**

- Private 4-year liberal arts college
- Residential campus in rural community
- 1,629 degree-seeking undergraduates: 53% women
- 36% of applicants admitted
- SAT or ACT (ACT writing optional), application essay required
- 92% graduate within 6 years

General. Founded in 1824. Regionally accredited. **Degrees:** 389 bachelor's awarded. **Location:** 50 miles from Columbus. **Calendar:** Semester. **Full-time faculty:** 151 total; 99% have terminal degrees, 15% minority, 39% women. **Part-time faculty:** 35 total; 63% have terminal degrees, 17% minority, 49% women. **Class size:** 64% < 20, 32% 20-39, 3% 40-49, less than 1% 50-99, less than 1% >100. **Special facilities:** Observatory, environmental center and nature preserve.

Freshman class profile. 3,929 applied, 1,420 admitted, 454 enrolled.

Mid 50% test scores			
SAT verbal:	610-700	Rank in top quarter:	91%
SAT math:	630-730	Rank in top tenth:	57%
ACT:	28-31	End year in good standing:	98%
GPA 3.50 or higher:	77%	Return as sophomores:	92%
GPA 3.0-3.49:	20%	Out-of-state:	79%
GPA 2.0-2.99:	3%	Live on campus:	100%
		International:	2%

Basis for selection. Secondary school record and personal character most important followed by test scores, class rank, recommendations, essay, talent, activities and interview. Alumni relationship, ethnicity, geographical residence and work experience considered. Non-native speakers of English required to submit TOEFL results. **Homeschooled:** Provide complete curriculum with texts and books used.

High school preparation. 21 units required; 23 recommended. Required and recommended units include English 4, mathematics 3-4, social studies 1-2, history 1, science 3-4 (laboratory 3), foreign language 3-4 and academic electives 4. 2 science laboratory required, 3 recommended. 1 fine arts recommended.

2006-2007 Annual costs. Tuition/fees: $36,050. Room/board: $5,900. Books/supplies: $1,150. Personal expenses: $830.

2005-2006 Financial aid. **Need-based:** 227 full-time freshmen applied for aid; 205 were judged to have need; 205 of these received aid. Average need met was 98%. Average scholarship/grant was $22,525; average loan $2,140. 84% of total undergraduate aid awarded as scholarships/grants, 16% as loans/jobs. **Non-need-based:** Scholarships awarded for academics, leadership, minority status.

Application procedures. **Admission:** Closing date 2/1 (postmark date). $45 fee, may be waived for applicants with need. Application may be submitted online. Admission notification 4/1. Must reply by 5/1. **Financial aid:** Closing date 2/15. FAFSA, CSS PROFILE required. Applicants notified by 4/1; must reply by 5/1.

Academics. **Special study options:** Accelerated study, combined bachelor's/graduate degree, double major, exchange student, honors, independent study, internships, liberal arts/career combination, New York semester, student-designed major, study abroad, urban semester, Washington semester. Cooperative 3-2 or 4-1 masters and teacher certification program with Bank Street College of Education; 3-2 engineering program with Case Western Reserve, Rensselaer Polytechnic Institute and Washington University; 3-2 enviormental studies program with Duke University. **Credit/placement by examination:** CLEP, IB, SAT, ACT, institutional tests. Credit determined for AP, IB or School Articulation Program (SCAP) counts toward 16 units required for graduation. No diversification requirements may be satisfied with AP credit. **Support services:** Study skills assistance, tutoring, writing center.

Majors. **Area/ethnic studies:** American. **Biology:** General, biochemistry, molecular. **Foreign languages:** General, ancient Greek, classics, French, German, Latin, Spanish. **History:** General. **Interdisciplinary:** Neuroscience. **Math:** General. **Philosophy/religion:** Philosophy, religion. **Physical sciences:** Chemistry, physics. **Psychology:** General. **Social sciences:** Anthropology, economics, international relations, political science, sociology. **Visual/performing arts:** Art, art history/conservation, dance, dramatic, studio arts.

Most popular majors. Biology 6%, English 19%, foreign language 6%, history 8%, interdisciplinary studies 10%, psychology 9%, social sciences 20%, visual/performing arts 14%.

Computing on campus. 530 workstations in dormitories, library, computer center. Dormitories wired for high-speed internet access and linked to campus network. Commuter students can connect to campus network. Online library, helpline, repair service, student web hosting, wireless network available.

Student life. **Freshman orientation:** Mandatory. Held 4 days prior to start of classes. **Policies:** Freshmen permitted cars on campus. **Housing:** Guaranteed on-campus for all undergraduates. Coed dorms, single-sex dorms, apartments available. $350 deposit, deadline 5/1. Special accomodations can be made for married, international and disabled students. Fraternity and sorority housing is available in room blocks only. There is substance free, wellness and community service and social group halls on campus. **Activities:** Bands, choral groups, dance, drama, film society, literary magazine, music ensembles, musical theater, opera, radio station, student government, student newspaper, symphony orchestra, Black Student Union, Christian Fellowship, Hillel, Asian Student Alliance, Associacion de Estudiantes Latino Americanos y de Naciones Tropicales Exoticas, Archon Society (community service organization), Allied Sexual Orientations, Amnesty International, Zen meditation group, political affairs club.

Athletics. NCAA. **Intercollegiate:** Baseball M, basketball, cross-country, diving, field hockey W, football (tackle) M, golf M, lacrosse, soccer, softball W, swimming, tennis, track and field, volleyball W. **Intramural:** Basketball, football (non-tackle), golf, racquetball, rugby, soccer, softball, tennis, volleyball, water polo. **Team name:** Lords/Ladies.

Student services. Alcohol/substance abuse counseling, campus ministries, career counseling, student employment services, financial aid counseling, health services, minority student services, personal counseling, placement for graduates, women's services. **Physically disabled:** Services for visually, hearing impaired.

Contact. Phone: (740) 427-5776 Toll-free number: (800) 848-2468
Fax: (740) 427-5770
Jennifer Britz, Dean of Admissions, Kenyon College, Ransom Hall, Gambier, OH 43022

Lake Erie College

Painesville, Ohio — **CB member**
www.lec.edu — **CB code: 1391**

- Private 4-year liberal arts college
- Residential campus in large town
- 654 degree-seeking undergraduates: 14% part-time, 73% women, 7% African American, 1% Asian American, 2% Hispanic American
- 112 degree-seeking graduate students
- 76% of applicants admitted
- SAT or ACT required
- 42% graduate within 6 years

General. Founded in 1856. Regionally accredited. **Degrees:** 153 bachelor's awarded; master's offered. **Location:** 30 miles from Cleveland. **Calendar:** Semester, limited summer session. **Full-time faculty:** 34 total; 76% have terminal degrees, 6% minority, 50% women. **Part-time faculty:** 59 total; 22% have terminal degrees, 5% minority, 49% women. **Class size:** 82% < 20, 18% 20-39. **Special facilities:** Equestrian center.

Freshman class profile. 532 applied, 404 admitted, 117 enrolled.

Mid 50% test scores			
SAT verbal:	430-550	Rank in top quarter:	29%
SAT math:	420-530	Rank in top tenth:	15%
ACT:	17-20	Return as sophomores:	64%
GPA 3.50 or higher:	26%	Out-of-state:	32%
GPA 3.0-3.49:	26%	Live on campus:	70%
GPA 2.0-2.99:	47%	Sororities:	8%

Basis for selection. School achievement record, test scores, and interview strongly considered. Special consideration of test scores for some applicants. **Homeschooled:** Statement describing homeschool structure and mission, transcript of courses and grades required. **Learning Disabled:** Documentation of learning disability required.

High school preparation. College-preparatory program recommended. Recommended units include English 4, mathematics 3, social studies 3, science 3 (laboratory 2) and foreign language 2. 1 fine arts and 1 physical education or health recommended.

2005-2006 Annual costs. Tuition/fees: $21,390. Equestrian fee $800 per course. Room/board: $6,334. Books/supplies: $850. Personal expenses: $1,304.

2004-2005 Financial aid. **Need-based:** 52% of total undergraduate aid awarded as scholarships/grants, 48% as loans/jobs. **Non-need-based:** Scholarships awarded for academics, art, leadership, music/drama, state residency. **Additional information:** Twins' scholarship, sibling discount.

Application procedures. **Admission:** No deadline. $25 fee, may be waived for applicants with need. Application may be submitted online. Admission notification on a rolling basis. **Financial aid:** Priority date 5/1; no closing date. FAFSA required. Applicants notified on a rolling basis; must reply within 2 week(s) of notification.

Academics. **Special study options:** Accelerated study, cross-registration, double major, honors, independent study, internships, liberal arts/career combination, student-designed major, study abroad, teacher certification program, weekend college. **Credit/placement by examination:** AP, CLEP, IB, SAT, ACT, institutional tests. 32 credit hours maximum toward bachelor's degree. **Support services:** Learning center, reduced course load, study skills assistance, tutoring, writing center.

Majors. **Agriculture:** Animal breeding, equestrian studies, equine science, farm/ranch. **Biology:** General. **Business:** Accounting, business admin, international. **Communications:** General. **Conservation:** General, environmental studies. **Education:** General, curriculum, elementary, reading, secondary. **Foreign languages:** General, French, German, Italian, Spanish. **History:** General. **Legal studies:** Paralegal, prelaw. **Math:** General. **Physical sciences:** Chemistry. **Protective services:** Law enforcement admin. **Psychology:** General. **Social sciences:** General, sociology. **Visual/performing arts:** General, dance, studio arts, theater arts management.

Most popular majors. Agriculture 10%, biology 7%, business/marketing 17%, communications/journalism 7%, education 22%, interdisciplinary studies 8%, psychology 6%, social sciences 10%.

Computing on campus. 112 workstations in dormitories, library, computer center, student center. Dormitories wired for high-speed internet access and linked to campus network. Commuter students can connect to campus network. Online course registration, online library, helpline, repair service, wireless network available.

Student life. **Freshman orientation:** Mandatory, $150 fee. Preregistration for classes offered. 2-day program during summer. **Policies:** Freshmen permitted cars on campus. **Housing:** Guaranteed on-campus for freshmen. Coed dorms, single-sex dorms, substance-free housing available. $150 nonrefundable deposit. Residence halls equipped with laundry and kitchen areas available. **Activities:** Choral groups, dance, drama, literary magazine, music ensembles, radio station, student government, student newspaper, honor, academic, and athletic associations; foreign language clubs; professional organizations; equestrian clubs; Student Activities Council.

Athletics. NCAA. **Intercollegiate:** Baseball M, basketball, cross-country, equestrian, golf M, soccer, softball W, volleyball W. **Team name:** Storm.

Student services. Career counseling, student employment services, financial aid counseling, placement for graduates. **Physically disabled:** Services for visually impaired.

Contact. E-mail: admissions@lec.edu
Phone: (440) 375-7050 Toll-free number: (800) 916-0904
Fax: (440) 375-7005
Jennifer Calhoun, Director of Admissions, Lake Erie College, 391 West Washington Street, Painesville, OH 44077-3389

Laura and Alvin Siegal College of Judaic Studies

Beachwood, Ohio
www.siegalcollege.edu **CB code: 1190**

- Private 4-year liberal arts and teachers college affiliated with Jewish faith
- Commuter campus in large town
- 12 degree-seeking undergraduates
- 139 graduate students
- Application essay, interview required

General. Founded in 1963. Regionally accredited. College specializes in Judaic and Hebrew studies and teacher education. **Degrees:** 3 bachelor's awarded; master's offered. **Location:** 10 miles from Cleveland. **Calendar:** Semester, extensive summer session. **Full-time faculty:** 10 total. **Part-time faculty:** 18 total.

Basis for selection. Interview and 2 recommendations most important. Essay important; high school record and community activities considered.

High school preparation. Graduation from Hebrew high school or good background in Hebrew language and Judaic subjects.

2006-2007 Annual costs. Tuition/fees (projected): $15,775. Books/supplies: $500.

Application procedures. **Admission:** No deadline. $50 fee. Admission notification on a rolling basis. **Financial aid:** No deadline. Institutional form required. Applicants notified on a rolling basis.

Academics. Continuing education program in Judaic and Hebrew studies. **Special study options:** Cross-registration, distance learning, independent study, internships. **Credit/placement by examination:** AP, CLEP, IB. 45 credit hours maximum toward bachelor's degree. **Support services:** Reduced course load, study skills assistance.

Majors. **Foreign languages:** General, Hebrew. **Philosophy/religion:** Judaic. **Theology:** Bible, religious ed.

Most popular majors. Philosophy/religious studies 50%.

Computing on campus. 8 workstations in library. Online course registration, online library available.

Student life. **Freshman orientation:** Available. Preregistration for classes offered.

Student services. Adult student services, career counseling. **Physically disabled:** Services for hearing impaired.

Contact. E-mail: admissions@siegalcollege.edu
Phone: (216) 464-4050 Toll-free number: (888) 336-2257
Fax: (216) 464-5827
Ruth Kronick, Director of Admissions, Laura and Alvin Siegal College of Judaic Studies, 26500 Shaker Boulevard, Beachwood, OH 44122

Lourdes College

Sylvania, Ohio **CB member**
www.lourdes.edu **CB code: 1427**

- Private 4-year liberal arts college affiliated with Roman Catholic Church
- Commuter campus in large town
- 1,526 degree-seeking undergraduates: 45% part-time, 84% women, 14% African American, 1% Asian American, 2% Hispanic American, 1% Native American
- 116 degree-seeking graduate students
- 41% of applicants admitted
- 31% graduate within 6 years

General. Founded in 1958. Regionally accredited. **Degrees:** 171 bachelor's, 30 associate awarded; master's offered. **ROTC:** Army, Air Force. **Location:** 10 miles from Toledo. **Calendar:** Semester, limited summer session. **Full-time faculty:** 65 total; 43% have terminal degrees, 5% minority, 72% women. **Part-time faculty:** 111 total; 14% have terminal degrees, 6% minority, 64% women. **Class size:** 65% < 20, 35% 20-39, less than 1% 40-49. **Special facilities:** Planetarium.

Freshman class profile. 314 applied, 129 admitted, 129 enrolled.

Mid 50% test scores		**GPA 2.0-2.99:**	49%
SAT verbal:	410-560	**Rank in top quarter:**	26%
SAT math:	430-580	**Rank in top tenth:**	4%
ACT:	17-21	**End year in good standing:**	83%
GPA 3.50 or higher:	20%	**Return as sophomores:**	72%
GPA 3.0-3.49:	29%	**Out-of-state:**	7%

Basis for selection. High school or previous college GPA and ACT or SAT scores considered for most students. Special admission available for freshmen with low GPA and high test scores or low test scores (ACT 15 - 18) and high GPA. Standardized test scores are not required for students out of high school five years or longer.

2005-2006 Annual costs. Tuition/fees: $12,270. Books/supplies: $624. Personal expenses: $3,240.

2004-2005 Financial aid. **Need-based:** 58 full-time freshmen applied for aid; 52 were judged to have need; 52 of these received aid. Average scholarship/grant was $4,652; average loan $2,572. 35% of total undergraduate aid awarded as scholarships/grants, 65% as loans/jobs. **Non-need-based:** Awarded to 535 full-time undergraduates, including 52 freshmen. Scholarships awarded for academics, art, minority status, music/drama, state residency.

Application procedures. **Admission:** Priority date 8/28; no deadline. $25 fee, may be waived for applicants with need. Application may be submitted online. Admission notification on a rolling basis. **Financial aid:** Priority date 3/1; no closing date. FAFSA required. Applicants notified on a rolling basis starting 3/1; must reply within 4 week(s) of notification.

Academics. **Special study options:** Accelerated study, cooperative education, distance learning, double major, dual enrollment of high school students, independent study, internships, liberal arts/career combination, student-designed major, teacher certification program, weekend college. **Credit/placement by examination:** AP, CLEP, SAT, ACT, institutional tests. 15 credit hours maximum toward associate degree, 30 toward bachelor's. **Support services:** Learning center, reduced course load, remedial instruction, study skills assistance, tutoring, writing center.

Majors. **Biology:** General. **Business:** Accounting/finance, business admin, human resources, market research, marketing. **Conservation:** Environmental science. **Education:** Early childhood, middle, secondary. **English:** English lit. **Health:** Health care admin, nursing (RN). **History:** General. **Philosophy/religion:** Religion. **Protective services:** Criminal justice. **Psychology:**

General. **Public administration:** Social work. **Social sciences:** Sociology. **Visual/performing arts:** Art, art history/conservation.

Most popular majors. Business/marketing 27%, education 13%, health sciences 26%, interdisciplinary studies 11%.

Computing on campus. 147 workstations in library, computer center, student center. Helpline, wireless network available.

Student life. Freshman orientation: Mandatory. Preregistration for classes offered. **Policies:** Freshmen permitted cars on campus. **Activities:** Choral groups, film society, literary magazine, student government, student government association, campus ministry, Pi Alpha Theta (history), Sigma Theta Tau International (nursing), Kappa Gamma Pi (Catholic college graduate honor aociety), Phi Alpha (social work), Theta Alpha Kappa (theologians and students in religious studies), Sigma Phi Omega (gerontology), Zeta Delta Chi community service organization.

Student services. Adult student services, alcohol/substance abuse counseling, campus ministries, career counseling, services for economically disadvantaged, student employment services, financial aid counseling, personal counseling. **Physically disabled:** Services for visually, speech, hearing impaired.

Contact. E-mail: lcadmits@lourdes.edu
Phone: (419) 885-5291 ext. 3682 Toll-free number: (800) 878-3210 ext. 3682 Fax: (419) 882-3987
Amy Mergen, Director of Admissions, Lourdes College, 6832 Convent Boulevard, Sylvania, OH 43560-2898

Malone College

Canton, Ohio
www.malone.edu **CB code: 1439**

- Private 4-year liberal arts college affiliated with Evangelical Friends Church-Eastern Region
- Residential campus in small city
- 1,842 degree-seeking undergraduates: 9% part-time, 61% women, 6% African American, 1% Hispanic American, 1% international
- 354 degree-seeking graduate students
- 81% of applicants admitted
- SAT or ACT (ACT writing optional), application essay required
- 57% graduate within 6 years; 21% enter graduate study

General. Founded in 1892. Regionally accredited. Interdenominational Christian environment. **Degrees:** 461 bachelor's awarded; master's offered. **ROTC:** Army, Air Force. **Location:** 55 miles from Cleveland. **Calendar:** Semester, limited summer session. **Full-time faculty:** 104 total; 70% have terminal degrees, 5% minority, 41% women. **Part-time faculty:** 98 total; 17% have terminal degrees, 4% minority, 50% women. **Class size:** 56% < 20, 35% 20-39, 7% 40-49, 2% 50-99. **Special facilities:** Child development center.

Freshman class profile. 1,036 applied, 839 admitted, 361 enrolled.

Mid 50% test scores			
SAT verbal:	470-590	Rank in top quarter:	47%
SAT math:	450-580	Rank in top tenth:	19%
ACT:	19-25	End year in good standing:	91%
GPA 3.50 or higher:	44%	Return as sophomores:	75%
GPA 3.0-3.49:	28%	Out-of-state:	13%
GPA 2.0-2.99:	28%	Live on campus:	84%
		International:	2%

Basis for selection. High school record, test scores and recommendations most important. Interview also considered and encouraged. Audition required for music programs. **Homeschooled:** Must have high school diploma, transcript, and ACT or SAT. **Learning Disabled:** Students disclosing learning disabilities must interview with Director of Disability Support Services.

High school preparation. College-preparatory program required. 18 units required. Required units include English 4, mathematics 3, social studies 2, history 1, science 3 (laboratory 1), foreign language 2 and academic electives 2. One fine arts recommended.

2005-2006 Annual costs. Tuition/fees: $16,790. Room/board: $6,250. Books/supplies: $900. Personal expenses: $1,200.

2005-2006 Financial aid. Need-based: 334 full-time freshmen applied for aid; 293 were judged to have need; 293 of these received aid. Average need met was 70%. Average scholarship/grant was $9,703; average loan $3,167. 52% of total undergraduate aid awarded as scholarships/grants, 48% as loans/jobs. **Non-need-based:** Awarded to 1,462 full-time undergraduates, including 348 freshmen. Scholarships awarded for academics, alumni affiliation, athletics, leadership, music/drama, religious affiliation. **Additional information:** Prepayment discounts and deferred payments are available for students in the adult degree-completion programs.

Application procedures. Admission: Closing date 7/1 (postmark date). $20 fee, may be waived for applicants with need. Application may be submitted online. Admission notification on a rolling basis beginning on or about 9/1. **Financial aid:** Priority date 3/1, closing date 7/31. FAFSA required. Applicants notified on a rolling basis starting 3/1; must reply within 2 week(s) of notification.

Academics. Core requirements for General Education include 60-62 hours of courses focusing on four components: Stewardship under God, Stewardship and Skills, Stewardship and the Sciences, and Stewardship and Society. **Special study options:** Accelerated study, cooperative education, cross-registration, distance learning, double major, dual enrollment of high school students, exchange student, honors, independent study, internships, student-designed major, study abroad, teacher certification program, Washington semester, weekend college. 2 degree-completion programs for adult students in management, nursing; American Studies Program (Washington, D.C.), Australia Studies Centre (Sydney), China Studies Program (Shanghai), Latin American Studies Program (San Jose, Costa Rica), Middle East Studies Program (Cairo, Egypt), Russian Studies Program, Ugandan Studies Program, Los Angeles Film Studies Center, Contemporary Music Center (Martha's Vineyard), study abroad in Guatemala, Kenya or Costa Rica. **Credit/placement by examination:** AP, CLEP, IB, SAT, ACT, institutional tests. 62 credit hours maximum toward bachelor's degree. External credit by exam limit is 20, excluding AP credit for which an additional 30 credits are available. Other credits available by in house exams. **Support services:** Reduced course load, remedial instruction, study skills assistance, tutoring, writing center.

Majors. Biology: General. **Business:** Accounting, business admin. **Communications:** General, journalism, public relations, radio/tv. **Communications technology:** Recording arts. **Computer sciences:** Computer science. **Education:** Art, early childhood, English, health, learning disabled, middle, music, physical, science, social studies, Spanish. **English:** English lit. **Foreign languages:** Spanish. **Health:** Clinical lab science, nursing (RN), public health ed. **History:** General. **Liberal arts:** Arts/sciences. **Math:** General. **Parks/recreation:** General, exercise sciences, health/fitness. **Philosophy/religion:** Philosophy. **Physical sciences:** Chemistry. **Psychology:** General. **Public administration:** Social work. **Social sciences:** Political science. **Theology:** Bible, pastoral counseling, sacred music, theology, youth ministry. **Visual/performing arts:** Dramatic, studio arts.

Most popular majors. Business/marketing 46%, education 18%, health sciences 10%.

Computing on campus. 200 workstations in dormitories, library, computer center, student center. Dormitories wired for high-speed internet access and linked to campus network. Online library, helpline, repair service, student web hosting, wireless network available.

Student life. Freshman orientation: Mandatory. Preregistration for classes offered. 5 days prior to start of semester, some on-campus events, community service, relationship-building activities. **Policies:** Christian institution with a conservative campus lifestyle. Religious observance required. Freshmen permitted cars on campus. **Housing:** Single-sex dorms, substance-free housing available. $50 nonrefundable deposit. Full-time students required to live on campus unless 22 or older, holding senior status, married or commuting from home. Exceptions considered. **Activities:** Bands, choral groups, dance, drama, literary magazine, music ensembles, musical theater, radio station, student government, student newspaper, Campus Crusade for Christ, Habitat for Humanity, Helping Hands, Multicultural Student Union, Nurses Christian Fellowship, Rotoract, Spiritual Life Committee, Students in Action, Unity Under Christ, Fellowship of Christian Athletes.

Athletics. NAIA, NCCAA. **Intercollegiate:** Baseball M, basketball, cheerleading, cross-country, football (tackle) M, golf, soccer, softball W, tennis, track and field, volleyball W. **Intramural:** Badminton, basketball, bowling, cross-country, football (non-tackle), football (tackle) M, racquetball, skiing, soccer, softball, table tennis, tennis, volleyball, weight lifting. **Team name:** Pioneers.

Student services. Adult student services, campus ministries, career counseling, student employment services, financial aid counseling, health services, minority student services, personal counseling, placement for graduates. **Physically disabled:** Services for visually, speech, hearing impaired.

Contact. E-mail: admissions@malone.edu
Phone: (330) 471-8100 ext. 8145 Toll-free number: (800) 521-1146
Fax: (330) 471-8149
John Russell, Director of Admissions, Malone College, 515 25th Street Northwest, Canton, OH 44709-3897

Marietta College

Marietta, Ohio **CB member**
www.marietta.edu **CB code: 1444**

- Private 4-year liberal arts college
- Residential campus in large town
- 1,344 degree-seeking undergraduates: 5% part-time, 51% women
- 117 degree-seeking graduate students
- 78% of applicants admitted
- SAT or ACT (ACT writing optional), application essay required
- 56% graduate within 6 years

General. Founded in 1835. Regionally accredited. **Degrees:** 296 bachelor's awarded; master's offered. **Location:** 120 miles from Columbus, 110 miles from Pittsburgh. **Calendar:** Semester, limited summer session. **Full-time faculty:** 91 total; 80% have terminal degrees, 4% minority, 37% women. **Part-time faculty:** 49 total; 18% have terminal degrees, 2% minority, 51% women. **Class size:** 72% < 20, 20% 20-39, less than 1% 40-49, less than 1% 50-99. **Special facilities:** Observatory, center for leadership development, greenhouse, cadaver lab, extensive fossil collection, many historically important documents from the beginning of the old Northwest Territory.

Freshman class profile. 2,237 applied, 1,748 admitted, 392 enrolled.

Mid 50% test scores			
SAT verbal:	480-600	Rank in top tenth:	20%
SAT math:	470-600	End year in good standing:	82%
ACT:	20-26	Return as sophomores:	73%
GPA 3.50 or higher:	41%	Out-of-state:	38%
GPA 3.0-3.49:	32%	Live on campus:	98%
GPA 2.0-2.99:	26%	International:	4%
Rank in top quarter:	47%	Fraternities:	17%
		Sororities:	20%

Basis for selection. High school curriculum, GPA, test scores most important. Recommendations and essay important. TOEFL used for admission and ESL placement. Interview recommended for all. Portfolio recommended for arts programs. **Homeschooled:** Statement describing homeschool structure and mission, transcript of courses and grades, letter of recommendation (nonparent) required. Chronicle of study and standardized test scores required.

High school preparation. College-preparatory program required. 16 units required. Required units include English 4, mathematics 3, social studies 2, history 2, science 3 (laboratory 2), foreign language 2 and academic electives 1.

2005-2006 Annual costs. Tuition/fees: $22,655. Room/board: $6,445. Books/supplies: $635. Personal expenses: $580.

2005-2006 Financial aid. Need-based: Average need met was 90%. Average scholarship/grant was $13,852; average loan $3,219. 70% of total undergraduate aid awarded as scholarships/grants, 30% as loans/jobs. **Non-need-based:** Awarded to 201 full-time undergraduates, including 48 freshmen. Scholarships awarded for academics, alumni affiliation, art, leadership, minority status, music/drama, state residency. **Additional information:** Auditions for music and theater required for competitive scholarships.

Application procedures. Admission: Priority date 3/1; deadline 5/1 (postmark date). $25 fee, may be waived for applicants with need. Application may be submitted online. Admission notification on a rolling basis beginning on or about 9/1. Must reply by May 1 or within 2 week(s) if notified thereafter. **Financial aid:** Priority date 3/1, closing date 4/15. FAFSA, institutional form required. Applicants notified on a rolling basis starting 3/1; must reply by 5/1 or within 2 week(s) of notification.

Academics. Early Alert Program whereby professors can contact the Academic Resource Center to assist those students demonstrating need for additional academic support. **Special study options:** Combined bachelor's/graduate degree, double major, dual enrollment of high school students, ESL, exchange student, honors, independent study, internships, liberal arts/career combination, student-designed major, study abroad, teacher certification program, Washington semester. Leadership program, investigative studies. **Credit/placement by examination:** AP, CLEP, IB, SAT, ACT, institutional tests. 36 credit hours maximum toward bachelor's degree. **Support services:** Reduced course load, remedial instruction, study skills assistance, tutoring, writing center.

Majors. Biology: General, biochemistry. **Business:** Accounting, communications, finance, human resources, international, management information systems, marketing. **Communications:** General, advertising, broadcast journalism, journalism, organizational, public relations, radio/tv. **Computer sciences:** General, computer science, information systems. **Conservation:** Environmental science, environmental studies. **Education:** General, early childhood, elementary, middle, multi-level teacher, secondary. **Engineering:** Petroleum. **English:** English lit. **Foreign languages:** Spanish. **Health:** Athletic training. **History:** General. **Math:** General. **Physical sciences:** Chemistry, geology, physics. **Psychology:** General. **Social sciences:** Economics, political science. **Visual/performing arts:** Commercial/advertising art, dramatic, studio arts.

Most popular majors. Business/marketing 26%, communications/journalism 9%, health sciences 7%, visual/performing arts 9%.

Computing on campus. 350 workstations in dormitories, library, computer center, student center. Dormitories wired for high-speed internet access and linked to campus network. Commuter students can connect to campus network. Online library, helpline, repair service, wireless network available.

Student life. Freshman orientation: Mandatory, $225 fee. Preregistration for classes offered. Four-and-one-half day program. Culminating event is either white water rafting trip or dinner theatre production. **Policies:** Student code of conduct, judicial system, no alcohol policy for students under age of 21. Freshmen permitted cars on campus. **Housing:** Guaranteed on-campus for all undergraduates. Coed dorms, single-sex dorms, special housing for disabled, apartments, fraternity/sorority housing, substance-free housing available. $200 deposit, deadline 5/1. Special interest theme housing. **Activities:** Bands, choral groups, dance, drama, film society, literary magazine, music ensembles, musical theater, radio station, student government, student newspaper, TV station, InterVarsity Christian Fellowship, Circle K, MC Democrats, MC Republicans, Habitat for Humanity, Feminist Majority Leadership, coalition for social change, American International association, Charles Sumner Harrison organization, student global aids campaign.

Athletics. NCAA. **Intercollegiate:** Baseball M, basketball, cross-country, football (tackle) M, rowing (crew), soccer, softball W, tennis, track and field, volleyball W. **Intramural:** Badminton, baseball M, basketball, bowling, cross-country, football (non-tackle), handball, racquetball, rowing (crew), soccer, softball, tennis, volleyball. **Team name:** Pioneers.

Student services. Adult student services, alcohol/substance abuse counseling, career counseling, student employment services, financial aid counseling, health services, minority student services, personal counseling, placement for graduates, women's services. **Physically disabled:** Services for hearing impaired.

Contact. Phone: (740) 376-4600 Toll-free number: (800) 331-7896
Fax: (740) 376-8888
Marke Vickers, Director of Admission, Marietta College, 215 Fifth Street, Marietta, OH 45750-4005

MedCentral College of Nursing

Mansfield, Ohio
www.medcentral.edu **CB code: 3935**

- Private 4-year nursing college
- Commuter campus in small city
- 360 degree-seeking undergraduates: 18% part-time, 85% women, 1% African American, 1% Hispanic American
- SAT or ACT (ACT writing recommended) required

General. Regionally accredited. General electives taken at the Ohio State University-Mansfield. **Degrees:** 45 bachelor's awarded. **Location:** 60 miles from Cleveland, 60 miles from Columbus. **Calendar:** Quarter, extensive summer session. **Full-time faculty:** 7 total. **Part-time faculty:** 1 total.

Freshman class profile.

Mid 50% test scores			
ACT:	18-28	Rank in top quarter:	80%
GPA 3.50 or higher:	29%	Rank in top tenth:	5%
GPA 3.0-3.49:	61%	End year in good standing:	86%
GPA 2.0-2.99:	10%	Live on campus:	16%

Basis for selection. High school record and standardized test scores most important. **Homeschooled:** Transcript of courses and grades required. Require ACT/SAT.

High school preparation. 17 units required; 20 recommended. Required and recommended units include English 4, mathematics 3-4, social studies 2, history 1, science 3-4 (laboratory 2), foreign language 1 and academic electives 2.

2006-2007 Annual costs. Tuition/fees (projected): $9,750. Room only: $4,800. Books/supplies: $181. Personal expenses: $1,980.

Financial aid. Non-need-based: Scholarships awarded for academics, leadership.

Application procedures. Admission: Priority date 5/1; deadline 8/1 (postmark date). $40 fee, may be waived for applicants with need. Application must be submitted on paper. Admission notification on a rolling basis beginning on or about 10/1. Must reply by 8/5. Must reply by May 1 or within 2 week(s) if notified thereafter. **Financial aid:** Priority date 4/2, closing date 9/15. FAFSA, institutional form required. Applicants notified on a rolling basis starting 9/1; must reply by 5/1.

Academics. Special study options: Accelerated study, independent study. **Credit/placement by examination:** AP, CLEP, SAT, ACT, institutional tests. **Support services:** Learning center, remedial instruction, study skills assistance, tutoring, writing center.

Majors. Health: Nursing (RN).

Computing on campus. 150 workstations in library, computer center. Dormitories wired for high-speed internet access. Online library, wireless network available.

Student life. Freshman orientation: Mandatory. **Policies:** Freshmen permitted cars on campus. **Housing:** Guaranteed on-campus for freshmen. Apartments, substance-free housing available. $100 nonrefundable deposit, deadline 6/15. **Activities:** Student government, National Student Nurses Association.

Student services. Adult student services, alcohol/substance abuse counseling, campus ministries, career counseling, student employment services, financial aid counseling, personal counseling.

Contact. E-mail: admissions@medcentral.edu
Phone: (419) 520-2600 Toll-free number: (877) 645-4360
Fax: (419) 520-2662
Christopher Harris, Executive Director for Enrollment and Student Affairs, MedCentral College of Nursing, 335 Glessner Avenue, Mansfield, OH 44903-2265

Mercy College of Northwest Ohio

Toledo, Ohio
www.mercycollege.edu

- Private 4-year health science and nursing college affiliated with Roman Catholic Church
- Commuter campus in large city
- 741 degree-seeking undergraduates: 47% part-time, 86% women, 7% African American, 1% Asian American, 4% Hispanic American, 1% Native American
- 54% of applicants admitted
- 52% graduate within 6 years

General. Degrees: 27 bachelor's, 120 associate awarded. **Calendar:** Semester, limited summer session. **Full-time faculty:** 48 total; 25% have terminal degrees, 2% minority, 88% women. **Part-time faculty:** 28 total; 11% have terminal degrees, 14% minority, 61% women.

Freshman class profile. 297 applied, 161 admitted, 89 enrolled.

Basis for selection. Students are reviewed by Admission, Progression and Graduation Committee. Students must have a minimum GPA of a 2.3 to be admitted. Admission to programs of study may have higher GPA and specific course grade requirements. SAT or ACT recommended.

High school preparation. Required units include English 3, mathematics 2, social studies 2, science 2 (laboratory 2).

2005-2006 Annual costs. Tuition/fees: $8,614. Actual cost is based on credit hours taken - 12 or more credits $255/ credit hour, less than 12 credit hours $282/credit hour. Books/supplies: $1,000.

2005-2006 Financial aid. All financial aid based on need. 30% of total undergraduate aid awarded as scholarships/grants, 70% as loans/jobs.

Application procedures. Admission: Priority date 1/31; no deadline. $25 fee, may be waived for applicants with need. Application must be submitted on paper. Admission notification on a rolling basis. **Financial aid:** No deadline. FAFSA required. Applicants notified on a rolling basis starting 4/15; must reply within 4 week(s) of notification.

Academics. Special study options: Combined bachelor's/graduate degree, distance learning, double major, independent study. **Credit/placement by examination:** AP, CLEP, ACT, institutional tests. **Support services:** Learning center, reduced course load, remedial instruction, study skills assistance, tutoring, writing center.

Majors. Health: Health care admin, nursing (RN).

Computing on campus. 24 workstations in library, computer center, student center. Online course registration, online library available.

Student life. Freshman orientation: Mandatory. Preregistration for classes offered. **Policies:** Freshmen permitted cars on campus. **Housing:** Apartments available. $100 fully refundable deposit. **Activities:** Student government, student newspaper.

Student services. Adult student services, alcohol/substance abuse counseling, campus ministries, career counseling, services for economically disadvantaged, student employment services, financial aid counseling, personal counseling. **Physically disabled:** Services for visually, hearing impaired.

Contact. E-mail: admissions@mercycollege.edu
Phone: (419) 251-1313 Toll-free number: (888) 806-3729
Fax: (419) 251-1462
Shelly McCoy-Grissom, Chief Admissions Officer, Mercy College of Northwest Ohio, 2221 Madison Avenue, Toledo, OH 43624

Miami University: Oxford Campus

Oxford, Ohio **CB member**
www.muohio.edu **CB code: 1463**

- Public 4-year university
- Residential campus in small town
- 14,582 degree-seeking undergraduates: 2% part-time, 53% women, 3% African American, 3% Asian American, 2% Hispanic American, 1% Native American, 1% international
- 1,294 degree-seeking graduate students
- SAT or ACT with writing required
- 80% graduate within 6 years

General. Founded in 1809. Regionally accredited. Associate degree programs and certificates offered at branch campuses in Hamilton and Middletown with degrees conferred by main (Oxford) campus. **Degrees:** 4,100 bachelor's, 280 associate awarded; master's, doctoral offered. **ROTC:** Army, Navy, Air Force. **Location:** 35 miles from Cincinnati, 46 miles from Dayton. **Calendar:** Semester, extensive summer session. **Full-time faculty:** 842 total; 90% have terminal degrees, 13% minority, 38% women. **Part-time faculty:** 356 total; 36% have terminal degrees, 8% minority, 45% women. **Class size:** 35% < 20, 49% 20-39, 7% 40-49, 6% 50-99, 3% >100. **Special facilities:** Art museum, museum-home of William Holmes McGuffey, zoology museum.

Freshman class profile. 3,162 enrolled.

Mid 50% test scores			
SAT verbal:	560-650	Rank in top quarter:	79%
SAT math:	580-670	Rank in top tenth:	41%
ACT:	25-29	Return as sophomores:	89%
GPA 3.50 or higher:	71%	Out-of-state:	32%
GPA 3.0-3.49:	26%	Live on campus:	98%
GPA 2.0-2.99:	3%	International:	1%

Basis for selection. Admission based upon academic performance, test scores, secondary school experience, community activities, and recommendations from the high school. Diversity of student body, applicant's special abilities, talents and achievements also considered. Essay recommended for all; audition required for music, theater programs; portfolio required for art, architecture programs. **Homeschooled:** Students who have not earned the GED may present credentials which demonstrate levels of academic achievement, ability, and performance equivalent to that of high school graduates. Applicants may be requested to submit samples of work in various areas.

High school preparation. 16 units recommended. Recommended units include English 4, mathematics 3, social studies 3, science 3, foreign language 2 and academic electives 1. One fine or performing arts also required.

2005-2006 Annual costs. Tuition/fees: $21,487; $21,507 out-of-state. All full-time, in-state students receive scholarships between $10,000 and $11,200 for the academic year, resulting in net tuition of $9,877 to $8,677. Room/board: $7,610. Books/supplies: $805. Personal expenses: $3,010.

2005-2006 Financial aid. Need-based: 2,178 full-time freshmen applied for aid; 1,466 were judged to have need; 1,455 of these received aid. Average need met was 78%. Average scholarship/grant was $3,056; average loan $2,790. 38% of total undergraduate aid awarded as scholarships/grants, 62% as loans/jobs. **Non-need-based:** Awarded to 11,312 full-time undergraduates, including 2,563 freshmen. Scholarships awarded for academics, art, athletics, leadership, minority status, music/drama, state residency.

Application procedures. Admission: Priority date 12/1; deadline 1/31 (postmark date). $45 fee, may be waived for applicants with need. Application may be submitted online. Admission notification 3/15. Must reply by

May 1 or within 2 week(s) if notified thereafter. **Financial aid:** Priority date 2/15; no closing date. FAFSA required. Applicants notified on a rolling basis starting 3/31; must reply by 5/1 or within 3 week(s) of notification.

Academics. **Special study options:** Combined bachelor's/graduate degree, cooperative education, cross-registration, double major, exchange student, honors, independent study, internships, liberal arts/career combination, student-designed major, study abroad, teacher certification program, Washington semester. Undergraduate associates, undergraduate research program, science and engineering research semester, 3-1 medical technology with regional hospitals, 3-2 engineering with Case Western Reserve University and Columbia University, 3-2 forestry/environmental studies with Duke University, 3-1 arts/professional BA/MA awarded after completing junior year and first year of graduate school. **Credit/placement by examination:** AP, CLEP, IB, institutional tests. **Support services:** Learning center, preadmission summer program, study skills assistance, tutoring.

Majors. **Architecture:** Interior, urban/community planning. **Area/ethnic studies:** African-American, American, Italian, women's. **Biology:** General, bacteriology, biochemistry, botany, zoology. **Business:** General, accounting, business admin, finance, human resources, management information systems, management science, managerial economics, marketing, operations, organizational behavior, purchasing, sales/distribution. **Communications:** General, journalism, media studies, public relations. **Computer sciences:** Systems analysis. **Conservation:** Environmental science, environmental studies, forestry, wood science. **Education:** Art, biology, chemistry, early childhood, elementary, English, French, German, health, kindergarten/preschool, Latin, mathematics, middle, music, physical, physics, science, social studies, Spanish, special, speech. **Engineering:** General, chemical, computer, electrical, manufacturing, mechanical, physics. **Engineering technology:** General, industrial management. **English:** American lit, British lit, creative writing, English lit, speech/rhetoric, technical writing. **Family/consumer sciences:** Family studies, food/nutrition, housing. **Foreign languages:** Ancient Greek, classics, comparative lit, French, German, Latin, linguistics, Russian, Spanish. **Health:** Athletic training, audiology/speech pathology, clinical lab science, dietetics, nursing (RN), predentistry, premedicine, speech pathology. **History:** General. **Legal studies:** Prelaw. **Math:** General, statistics. **Parks/recreation:** Exercise sciences, health/fitness, sports admin. **Philosophy/religion:** Philosophy, religion. **Physical sciences:** Chemistry, geology, physics. **Psychology:** General. **Public administration:** General, social work. **Social sciences:** Anthropology, economics, geography, international relations, political science, sociology. **Visual/performing arts:** Art, art history/conservation, commercial/advertising art, dramatic, music performance.

Most popular majors. Biology 7%, business/marketing 30%, education 10%, psychology 6%, social sciences 10%.

Computing on campus. 1,000 workstations in dormitories, library, computer center, student center. Dormitories wired for high-speed internet access and linked to campus network. Commuter students can connect to campus network. Online course registration, helpline, repair service, student web hosting available.

Student life. **Freshman orientation:** Available, $55 fee. Preregistration for classes offered. Held 2 days during June and July. **Housing:** Guaranteed on-campus for freshmen. Coed dorms, single-sex dorms, special housing for disabled, apartments, fraternity/sorority housing available. $250 deposit, deadline 5/1. All first-year students live in first-year student halls. Special arrangements include sorority suites in residence halls and an international hall. **Activities:** Bands, choral groups, dance, drama, film society, literary magazine, music ensembles, musical theater, opera, radio station, student government, student newspaper, symphony orchestra, TV station, Miami Service Network, minority affairs council, United Campus Ministries, Black student association, Miami student foundation, Association of International Students.

Athletics. NCAA. **Intercollegiate:** Baseball M, basketball, cross-country, diving, field hockey W, football (tackle) M, golf M, ice hockey M, soccer W, softball W, swimming, tennis W, track and field, volleyball W. **Intramural:** Archery, badminton, basketball, boxing M, cross-country, equestrian, field hockey W, football (tackle) M, golf, gymnastics, handball, ice hockey, lacrosse M, racquetball, rifle, rugby M, sailing, skiing, soccer, softball, squash, swimming, table tennis, tennis, track and field, volleyball, water polo, wrestling M. **Team name:** Red Hawks.

Student services. Alcohol/substance abuse counseling, campus ministries, career counseling, services for economically disadvantaged, student employment services, financial aid counseling, health services, legal services, minority student services, on-campus daycare, personal counseling, placement for graduates, veterans' counselor, women's services. **Physically disabled:** Services for visually, speech, hearing impaired.

Contact. E-mail: admission@muohio.edu
Phone: (513) 529-2531 Fax: (513) 529-1550
Ann Larson, Interim Director of Admissions, Miami University: Oxford Campus, 301 South Campus Avenue, Oxford, OH 45056-3434

Mount Carmel College of Nursing

Columbus, Ohio
www.mccn.edu **CB code: 1502**

- Private 4-year nursing college
- Very large city
- 582 degree-seeking undergraduates: 18% part-time, 92% women, 9% African American, 3% Asian American, 1% Hispanic American
- 28 degree-seeking graduate students
- 54% of applicants admitted

General. Regionally accredited. **Degrees:** 111 bachelor's awarded; master's offered. **Calendar:** Semester. **Full-time faculty:** 32 total. **Part-time faculty:** 24 total.

Freshman class profile. 155 applied, 84 admitted, 60 enrolled.

Basis for selection. High school record and standardized test score most important.

2005-2006 Annual costs. Tuition/fees: $6,052.

2005-2006 Financial aid. **Need-based:** 35% of total undergraduate aid awarded as scholarships/grants, 65% as loans/jobs.

Application procedures. **Admission:** Priority date 2/1; no deadline. $30 fee. **Financial aid:** Priority date 4/1; no closing date. FAFSA, institutional form required. Applicants notified on a rolling basis.

Academics. **Credit/placement by examination:** CLEP.

Majors. **Health:** Nursing (RN).

Contact. E-mail: mccnadmissions@mchs.com
Phone: (614) 234-5800 Toll-free number: (800) 556-6942
Fax: (614) 234-2875
Merchel Menefield, Director of Admissions and Recruitment, Mount Carmel College of Nursing, 127 South Davis Avenue, Columbus, OH 43222-1589

Mount Union College

Alliance, Ohio **CB member**
www.muc.edu **CB code: 1492**

- Private 4-year liberal arts college affiliated with United Methodist Church
- Residential campus in large town
- 2,005 degree-seeking undergraduates: 1% part-time, 51% women, 4% African American, 1% Hispanic American, 2% international
- 80% of applicants admitted
- SAT or ACT (ACT writing optional), application essay required
- 61% graduate within 6 years; 26% enter graduate study

General. Founded in 1846. Regionally accredited. **Degrees:** 434 bachelor's awarded. **ROTC:** Army, Air Force. **Location:** 55 miles from Cleveland, 75 miles from Pittsburgh. **Calendar:** Semester, limited summer session. **Full-time faculty:** 123 total; 80% have terminal degrees, 10% minority, 32% women. **Part-time faculty:** 103 total; 13% have terminal degrees, 43% women. **Class size:** 57% < 20, 41% 20-39, 1% 40-49, less than 1% 50-99, less than 1% >100. **Special facilities:** 2 astronomical observatories, 109-acre nature center for ecological studies, bird observatory, scanning electron microscope facility, wellness center.

Freshman class profile. 1,768 applied, 1,414 admitted, 503 enrolled.

Mid 50% test scores		**Rank in top quarter:**	41%
SAT verbal:	460-560	**Rank in top tenth:**	14%
SAT math:	450-570	**Return as sophomores:**	75%
ACT:	20-25	**Out-of-state:**	9%
GPA 3.50 or higher:	32%	**Live on campus:**	92%
GPA 3.0-3.49:	36%	**International:**	1%
GPA 2.0-2.99:	32%		

Basis for selection. Class rank, rigor of secondary school record, standardized test scores, academic GPA very impotant. Rolling deadline for SAT, ACT scores. Essay is required and interview recommended for all. Audition recommended for communications, music, and theater programs. Portfolio recommended for art and communications programs.

High school preparation. College-preparatory program recommended. 18 units recommended. Recommended units include English 4, mathematics 3, social studies 3, science 3 (laboratory 2), foreign language 2 and academic electives 1. May substitute social studies credits with history credits.

2005-2006 Annual costs. Tuition/fees: $19,850. Room/board: $5,990.

2004-2005 Financial aid. **Need-based:** 496 full-time freshmen applied for aid; 451 were judged to have need; 451 of these received aid. Average need met was 78%. Average scholarship/grant was $11,041; average loan $4,104. 69% of total undergraduate aid awarded as scholarships/grants, 31% as loans/jobs. **Non-need-based:** Awarded to 448 full-time undergraduates, including 144 freshmen. Scholarships awarded for academics, alumni affiliation, art, job skills, leadership, music/drama, religious affiliation, ROTC, state residency.

Application procedures. **Admission:** Priority date 3/1; no deadline. No application fee. Admission notification on a rolling basis beginning on or about 10/1. **Financial aid:** Priority date 4/1; no closing date. FAFSA, institutional form required. Applicants notified on a rolling basis starting 3/15; must reply within 4 week(s) of notification.

Academics. All freshmen must take the Liberal Arts Experience course. **Special study options:** Accelerated study, cooperative education, double major, ESL, honors, independent study, internships, student-designed major, study abroad, teacher certification program. **Credit/placement by examination:** AP, CLEP, IB, institutional tests. 15 credit hours maximum toward bachelor's degree. **Support services:** Learning center, study skills assistance, tutoring, writing center.

Majors. **Area/ethnic studies:** American. **Biology:** General, biochemistry, environmental. **Business:** Accounting, business admin, international. **Communications:** General, digital media, media studies. **Computer sciences:** General, computer science. **Education:** Early childhood, health, middle, music, physical. **English:** British lit, technical writing. **Foreign languages:** French, German, Japanese, Spanish. **Health:** Athletic training. **History:** General. **Interdisciplinary:** Behavioral sciences, global studies. **Math:** General. **Parks/recreation:** Exercise sciences, sports admin. **Philosophy/religion:** Philosophy, religion. **Physical sciences:** Astronomy, chemistry, geology, physics. **Psychology:** General. **Social sciences:** Economics, international relations, political science, sociology. **Visual/performing arts:** Art, design, dramatic, music performance.

Most popular majors. Business/marketing 17%, communications/journalism 6%, computer/information sciences 6%, education 24%, parks/recreation 9%, psychology 6%, social sciences 8%.

Computing on campus. 220 workstations in dormitories, library, computer center, student center. Dormitories wired for high-speed internet access and linked to campus network. Commuter students can connect to campus network. Online course registration, online library, helpline, student web hosting, wireless network available.

Student life. **Freshman orientation:** Available. Preregistration for classes offered. 2-day summer orientation includes program for parents. Fall orientation held week before registration for students only. **Policies:** Freshmen permitted cars on campus. **Housing:** Guaranteed on-campus for all undergraduates. Coed dorms, single-sex dorms, special housing for disabled, fraternity/sorority housing, substance-free housing available. Small single-sex college-owned residential homes converted to college housing available. **Activities:** Bands, choral groups, dance, drama, literary magazine, music ensembles, musical theater, radio station, student government, student newspaper, academic clubs, academic honoraries, religious clubs, service organizations, Alpha Phi Omega, Black Student Union, Association of International Students, Association of Women Students, Religious Life Council, student activities council.

Athletics. NCAA. **Intercollegiate:** Baseball M, basketball, cheerleading, cross-country, diving, football (tackle) M, golf, soccer, softball W, swimming, tennis, track and field, volleyball W, wrestling M. **Intramural:** Badminton, basketball, bowling, diving, football (non-tackle), golf, gymnastics, racquetball, soccer, softball, swimming, tennis, volleyball, water polo, weight lifting. **Team name:** Purple Raiders.

Student services. Adult student services, alcohol/substance abuse counseling, campus ministries, career counseling, student employment services, financial aid counseling, health services, minority student services, personal counseling, placement for graduates. **Physically disabled:** Services for visually impaired.

Contact. E-mail: admissn@muc.edu
Phone: (330) 823-2590 Toll-free number: (800) 334-6682
Fax: (330) 823-5097
Vince Heslop, Director of Enrollment Technology, Mount Union College, 1972 Clark Avenue, Alliance, OH 44601-3993

Mount Vernon Nazarene University

Mount Vernon, Ohio
www.mvnu.edu **CB code: 1531**

- Private 4-year university affiliated with Church of the Nazarene
- Residential campus in large town
- 2,037 degree-seeking undergraduates: 6% part-time, 59% women, 4% African American, 1% Asian American, 1% Hispanic American, 1% international
- 337 degree-seeking graduate students
- 80% of applicants admitted
- SAT or ACT (ACT writing optional), application essay required
- 48% graduate within 6 years; 16% enter graduate study

General. Founded in 1964. Regionally accredited. Several opportunities for students to participate in service learning or mission trips. During the academic year, students may participate in one of the following trips: Frankfurt, Hungary, Venezuela, Belize, Benin, Africa, Romania, or several out-of-state USA trips. **Degrees:** 459 bachelor's, 13 associate awarded; master's offered. **Location:** 45 miles from Columbus. **Calendar:** 4-1-4, limited summer session. **Full-time faculty:** 88 total; 62% have terminal degrees, 8% minority, 28% women. **Part-time faculty:** 138 total; 25% have terminal degrees, 1% minority, 41% women. **Class size:** 61% < 20, 30% 20-39, 5% 40-49, 4% 50-99. **Special facilities:** 70-acre biological research area and nature center, weather station.

Freshman class profile. 741 applied, 595 admitted, 380 enrolled.

Mid 50% test scores			
SAT verbal:	480-580	Rank in top quarter:	48%
SAT math:	450-580	Rank in top tenth:	17%
ACT:	20-25	End year in good standing:	88%
GPA 3.50 or higher:	44%	Return as sophomores:	78%
GPA 3.0-3.49:	29%	Out-of-state:	16%
GPA 2.0-2.99:	26%	Live on campus:	95%

Basis for selection. High school record, ACT or SAT scores, recommendations important. Interview recommended. **Homeschooled:** Transcript of courses and grades, letter of recommendation (nonparent) required. Family members cannot complete either the academic or character references. An employer can complete the academic reference. Students who participate in an accredited program must provide a transcript from the accrediting agency; otherwise they must provide a list of classes completed.

High school preparation. 21 units recommended. Recommended units include English 4, mathematics 3, social studies 3, science 3 (laboratory 3), foreign language 3 and academic electives 7.

2006-2007 Annual costs. Tuition/fees (projected): $16,876. Room/board: $5,090. Books/supplies: $900. Personal expenses: $970.

2005-2006 Financial aid. **Need-based:** 380 full-time freshmen applied for aid; 319 were judged to have need; 319 of these received aid. Average need met was 78%. Average scholarship/grant was $7,600; average loan $3,228. 51% of total undergraduate aid awarded as scholarships/grants, 49% as loans/jobs. **Non-need-based:** Awarded to 245 full-time undergraduates, including 91 freshmen. Scholarships awarded for academics, athletics, leadership, minority status, music/drama, religious affiliation, state residency.

Application procedures. **Admission:** Priority date 4/15; deadline 5/1 (receipt date). $25 fee, may be waived for applicants with need. Application may be submitted online. Admission notification on a rolling basis beginning on or about 9/1. **Financial aid:** Priority date 3/15; no closing date. FAFSA, institutional form required. Applicants notified on a rolling basis starting 2/15; must reply within 2 week(s) of notification.

Academics. Off-campus January term offers unique educational opportunities, including urban and international studies. **Special study options:** Combined bachelor's/graduate degree, cooperative education, cross-registration, distance learning, double major, dual enrollment of high school students, honors, independent study, internships, liberal arts/career combination, study abroad, teacher certification program, Washington semester. Cooperative prenursing program with Capital University, cooperative preengineering program with Olivet Nazarene University, cooperative preoccupational therapy/physician's assistant program with Chatham College. **Credit/placement by examination:** AP, CLEP, IB, SAT, ACT, institutional tests. 30 credit hours maximum toward associate degree, 30 toward bachelor's. **Support services:** Study skills assistance.

Majors. **Area/ethnic studies:** American, East Asian, Near/Middle Eastern, Russian/Slavic. **Biology:** General. **Business:** Accounting, business admin, finance, international, management information systems, marketing, office management. **Communications:** General, broadcast journalism, journalism. **Communications technology:** Graphics. **Computer sciences:** General, computer science. **Conservation:** General. **Education:** General, art, biology, business, chemistry, early childhood, elementary, English, family/consumer sciences, health, mathematics, middle, music, physical, physics, science, secondary, social studies, Spanish. **English:** English lit, technical writing. **Family/consumer sciences:** General. **Foreign languages:** Spanish. **Health:** Clinical lab science, predentistry, premedicine, prenursing, prepharmacy, preveterinary. **History:** General. **Math:** General. **Parks/recreation:** Exercise sciences, health/fitness, sports admin. **Philosophy/religion:** Philosophy, religion. **Physical sciences:** Chemistry, physics. **Protective services:** Criminal justice. **Psychology:** General. **Public administration:** Social work. **Social sciences:** Sociology. **Theology:** Religious ed, sacred music, youth ministry. **Visual/performing arts:** Art, design, dramatic, music performance.

Most popular majors. Business/marketing 59%, education 9%.

Computing on campus. 217 workstations in dormitories, library, computer center, student center. Dormitories wired for high-speed internet access and linked to campus network. Commuter students can connect to campus network. Online course registration, online library, helpline, wireless network available.

Student life. Freshman orientation: Mandatory, $25 fee. Preregistration for classes offered. Sessions held in June, July, and August. **Policies:** Students expected to comply with university's published lifestyle guidelines. Religious observance required. Freshmen permitted cars on campus. **Housing:** Guaranteed on-campus for freshmen. Single-sex dorms, special housing for disabled, apartments, substance-free housing available. $100 fully refundable deposit, deadline 5/1. **Activities:** Bands, choral groups, drama, music ensembles, musical theater, radio station, student government, student newspaper, community service & ministry organization, Students in Free Enterprise, Fellowship of Christian Athletes, Young Republicans Club, multicultural club, Association of Men, Association of Women, Association of Computing Machinery, American Sign Language Club, Students with Concern.

Athletics. NAIA, NCCAA. **Intercollegiate:** Baseball M, basketball, cheerleading, cross-country, golf M, soccer, softball W, volleyball W. **Intramural:** Basketball, bowling, football (non-tackle), soccer, softball, volleyball. **Team name:** Cougars.

Student services. Adult student services, alcohol/substance abuse counseling, campus ministries, career counseling, student employment services, financial aid counseling, health services, minority student services, personal counseling, placement for graduates. **Physically disabled:** Services for visually, speech, hearing impaired.

Contact. E-mail: admissions@mvnu.edu
Phone: (740) 392-6868 ext. 4510 Toll-free number: (866) 462-6868
Fax: (740) 393-0511
Tim Eades, Director of Admissions and Recruitment, Mount Vernon Nazarene University, 800 Martinsburg Road, Mount Vernon, OH 43050

Muskingum College

New Concord, Ohio — **CB member**
www.muskingum.edu — **CB code: 1496**

- Private 4-year liberal arts college affiliated with Presbyterian Church (USA)
- Residential campus in small town
- 1,639 degree-seeking undergraduates: 4% part-time, 50% women, 4% African American, 1% Asian American, 1% Hispanic American, 2% international
- 536 degree-seeking graduate students
- 80% of applicants admitted
- SAT or ACT (ACT writing optional) required

General. Founded in 1837. Regionally accredited. **Degrees:** 264 bachelor's awarded; master's offered. **Location:** 70 miles from Columbus, 125 miles from Pittsburgh. **Calendar:** Semester, limited summer session. **Full-time faculty:** 94 total. **Part-time faculty:** 38 total. **Special facilities:** Biology station.

Freshman class profile. 1,756 applied, 1,401 admitted, 434 enrolled.

Mid 50% test scores		**Out-of-state:**	8%
SAT verbal:	460-580	**Live on campus:**	92%
SAT math:	440-570	**International:**	2%
ACT:	19-24	**Fraternities:**	25%
Return as sophomores:	69%	**Sororities:**	35%

Basis for selection. School achievement record most important. Test scores, recommendations, extracurricular activities, interview considered. Special consideration to children of alumni. Essay and interview recommended for all; audition recommended for music programs; portfolio recommended for art programs.

High school preparation. 12 units required; 15 recommended. Required and recommended units include English 4, mathematics 2-3, social studies 2-3, science 2-3 and foreign language 2.

2006-2007 Annual costs. Tuition/fees (projected): $17,195. Room/board: $6,740. Books/supplies: $1,000. Personal expenses: $900.

2005-2006 Financial aid. Need-based: 73% of total undergraduate aid awarded as scholarships/grants, 27% as loans/jobs. **Non-need-based:** Scholarships awarded for academics, alumni affiliation, art, minority status, music/drama, religious affiliation, state residency. **Additional information:** Scholarship priority date 02/01.

Application procedures. Admission: Closing date 8/1. No application fee. Admission notification on a rolling basis beginning on or about 10/1. Must reply by May 1 or within 2 week(s) if notified thereafter. Application deadline of March 1 for PLUS program. **Financial aid:** Priority date 3/15, closing date 8/1. FAFSA, institutional form required. Applicants notified on a rolling basis starting 3/1; must reply by 5/1 or within 2 week(s) of notification.

Academics. Special study options: Accelerated study, double major, dual enrollment of high school students, ESL, exchange student, independent study, internships, liberal arts/career combination, student-designed major, study abroad, teacher certification program, United Nations semester, Washington semester. **Credit/placement by examination:** AP, CLEP, SAT, ACT, institutional tests. **Support services:** Learning center, pre-admission summer program, reduced course load, study skills assistance, tutoring.

Majors. Biology: General, molecular. **Business:** General, accounting, international marketing, managerial economics. **Communications:** Journalism. **Computer sciences:** General, computer science. **Conservation:** General. **Education:** Early childhood, elementary, secondary, special. **Engineering:** General, mechanics. **Foreign languages:** French, German, Spanish. **Health:** Clinical lab technology, predentistry, premedicine, prenursing, preveterinary. **History:** General. **Interdisciplinary:** Neuroscience. **Legal studies:** Prelaw. **Math:** General. **Philosophy/religion:** Philosophy, religion. **Physical sciences:** Chemistry, geology, physics, planetary. **Psychology:** General. **Social sciences:** Economics, international relations, political science, sociology. **Theology:** Religious ed, theology. **Visual/performing arts:** Art, dramatic.

Computing on campus. PC or laptop required. 76 workstations in dormitories, library, computer center.

Student life. Freshman orientation: Mandatory. **Housing:** Coed dorms, single-sex dorms, apartments, fraternity/sorority housing available. $150 deposit, deadline 5/1. **Activities:** Bands, choral groups, drama, literary magazine, music ensembles, musical theater, radio station, student government, student newspaper, symphony orchestra, TV station, Christian Fellowship, Fellowship of Christian Athletes, international student organization, political awareness program, SADD, Habitat for Humanity, Young Democrats, Young Republicans.

Athletics. NCAA. **Intercollegiate:** Baseball M, basketball, cross-country, football (tackle) M, golf, soccer, softball W, tennis, track and field, volleyball W, wrestling M. **Intramural:** Basketball, cross-country, golf, lacrosse, racquetball, rugby, softball, table tennis M, tennis, track and field, volleyball, wrestling M.

Student services. Career counseling, student employment services, health services, on-campus daycare, personal counseling, placement for graduates.

Contact. E-mail: adminfo@muskingum.edu
Phone: (740) 826-8137 Toll-free number: (800) 752-6082
Fax: (740) 826-8100
Beth DaLonzo, Director of Admissions, Muskingum College, 163 Stormont Street, New Concord, OH 43762-1160

Notre Dame College

Cleveland, Ohio — **CB member**
www.notredamecollege.edu — **CB code: 1566**

- Private 4-year liberal arts college affiliated with Roman Catholic Church
- Commuter campus in very large city

General. Founded in 1922. Regionally accredited. **Location:** 10 miles from downtown Cleveland. **Calendar:** Semester.

Annual costs/financial aid. Tuition/fees (2005-2006): $19,220. $300 per-credit-hour for Teacher Education Evening Licensure students. Room/board: $6,648. Books/supplies: $1,278. Personal expenses: $808. Need-based financial aid available for full-time students.

Contact. Phone: (216) 381-1680 ext. 5355
Director of Admissions, 4545 College Road, Cleveland, OH 44121-4293

Oberlin College

Oberlin, Ohio — **CB member**
www.oberlin.edu — **CB code: 1587**

- Private 4-year music and liberal arts college
- Residential campus in small town
- 2,845 degree-seeking undergraduates: 3% part-time, 56% women, 5% African American, 8% Asian American, 5% Hispanic American, 1% Native American, 6% international
- 19 degree-seeking graduate students
- 34% of applicants admitted
- SAT or ACT with writing required
- 81% graduate within 6 years

General. Founded in 1833. Regionally accredited. **Degrees:** 632 bachelor's awarded; master's offered. **Location:** 34 miles from Cleveland. **Calendar:** 4-1-4. **Full-time faculty:** 266 total; 16% minority, 37% women. **Class size:** 68% < 20, 27% 20-39, 2% 40-49, 3% 50-99, less than 1% >100. **Special facilities:** Art museum, observatory, bog, environmental studies building, arboretum.

Freshman class profile. 6,587 applied, 2,235 admitted, 741 enrolled.

Mid 50% test scores			
SAT verbal:	640-730	Rank in top tenth:	67%
SAT math:	610-710	Return as sophomores:	92%
ACT:	26-31	Out-of-state:	90%
Rank in top quarter:	85%	Live on campus:	100%
		International:	6%

Basis for selection. For college of arts and sciences: school achievement record, test scores, school and community leadership activities, recommendations, and interview important. Special consideration to applicants from minority and first generation college families and to foreign applicants. For conservatory: audition most important factor; admission extremely selective. TOEFL required if English not first language. SAT Subject Tests recommended. Interview required for early admission candidates; recommended for all others. Audition required of applicants to conservatory; essay required of applicants to college of arts and sciences. **Homeschooled:** Interview, SAT Subject Tests, detailed portfolio required.

High school preparation. Required units include English 4, mathematics 4, social studies 3, science 3 and foreign language 3.

2006-2007 Annual costs. Tuition/fees: $34,426. Room/board: $8,720. Books/supplies: $761. Personal expenses: $978.

2005-2006 Financial aid. Need-based: 491 full-time freshmen applied for aid; 411 were judged to have need; 411 of these received aid. Average need met was 100%. Average scholarship/grant was $17,202; average loan $3,890. 79% of total undergraduate aid awarded as scholarships/grants, 21% as loans/jobs. **Non-need-based:** Awarded to 1,154 full-time undergraduates, including 374 freshmen. Scholarships awarded for academics, leadership, music/drama, state residency.

Application procedures. Admission: Closing date 1/15 (postmark date). $35 fee, may be waived for applicants with need. Application may be submitted online. Admission notification 4/1. Must reply by May 1 or within 2 week(s) if notified thereafter. Application closing date for Conservatory of Music, February 15; application fee $100. **Financial aid:** Closing date 1/15. FAFSA, institutional form, CSS PROFILE required. Applicants notified by 4/1; must reply by 5/1 or within 2 week(s) of notification.

Academics. No core curriculum. Students required to take 9 credit hours in each academic division (Humanities, Social Sciences, and Math and Natural Science) and 9 hours related to cultural diversity. **Special study options:** Cross-registration, double major, dual enrollment of high school students, exchange student, honors, independent study, internships, liberal arts/career combination, New York semester, student-designed major, study abroad, teacher certification program, urban semester, Washington semester. 5 year double degree program with Music Conservatory and Liberal Arts College, 3-2 engineering. **Credit/placement by examination:** AP, CLEP, IB, institutional tests. 30 credit hours maximum toward bachelor's degree. **Support services:** Learning center, remedial instruction, study skills assistance, tutoring, writing center.

Majors. Area/ethnic studies: African, African-American, American, East Asian, Latin American, Russian/Slavic, women's. **Biology:** General, biochemistry. **Computer sciences:** General. **Conservation:** Environmental studies. **Education:** Music. **English:** Creative writing. **Foreign languages:** Ancient Greek, classics, comparative lit, French, German, Latin, Russian, Spanish. **Health:** Predentistry, premedicine, preveterinary. **History:** General. **Interdisciplinary:** Neuroscience. **Legal studies:** Prelaw. **Math:** General. **Philosophy/religion:** Judaic, philosophy, religion. **Physical sciences:** Chemistry, geology, physics. **Psychology:** General. **Social sciences:** Anthropology, economics, political science, sociology. **Visual/performing arts:** Art history/conservation, conducting, dance, dramatic, film/cinema, jazz, music history, music theory/composition, piano/organ, stringed instruments, studio arts, voice/opera.

Most popular majors. Area/ethnic studies 7%, biology 9%, English 12%, social sciences 16%, visual/performing arts 29%.

Computing on campus. 340 workstations in dormitories, library, computer center. Dormitories wired for high-speed internet access and linked to campus network. Commuter students can connect to campus network. Online course registration, helpline, repair service, wireless network available.

Student life. Freshman orientation: Mandatory. Preregistration for classes offered. Held week prior to fall classes. Includes day of service. **Policies:** Students agree to follow honor code. Freshmen permitted cars on campus. **Housing:** Guaranteed on-campus for all undergraduates. Coed dorms, single-sex dorms, cooperative housing, substance-free housing available. **Activities:** Bands, choral groups, dance, drama, film society, literary magazine, music ensembles, musical theater, opera, radio station, student government, student newspaper, symphony orchestra, religious, political, inter-cultural, ethnic, social service, and gay/lesbian/bisexual organizations.

Athletics. NCAA. **Intercollegiate:** Baseball M, basketball, cross-country, diving, field hockey W, football (tackle) M, golf, lacrosse, soccer, softball W, swimming, tennis, track and field, volleyball W. **Intramural:** Baseball M, basketball, bowling, football (non-tackle), handball, racquetball, rugby M, skin diving, soccer, softball, squash, table tennis, tennis, track and field, volleyball, weight lifting. **Team name:** Yeomen.

Student services. Alcohol/substance abuse counseling, campus ministries, career counseling, services for economically disadvantaged, student employment services, financial aid counseling, health services, minority student services, personal counseling, placement for graduates, women's services. **Physically disabled:** Services for visually, speech, hearing impaired.

Contact. E-mail: college.admissions@oberlin.edu
Phone: (440) 775-8411 Toll-free number: (800) 622-6243
Fax: (440) 775-6905
Debra Chermonte, Dean of Admissions and Financial Aid, Oberlin College, Carnegie Building, 101 North Professor Street, Oberlin, OH 44074

Ohio Dominican University

Columbus, Ohio — **CB member**
www.ohiodominican.edu — **CB code: 1131**

- Private 4-year university and liberal arts college affiliated with Roman Catholic Church
- Commuter campus in very large city
- 2,185 degree-seeking undergraduates: 26% part-time, 62% women, 22% African American, 1% Asian American, 1% Hispanic American
- 383 degree-seeking graduate students
- 72% of applicants admitted
- SAT or ACT with writing, application essay required
- 48% graduate within 6 years

General. Founded in 1911. Regionally accredited. **Degrees:** 377 bachelor's, 92 associate awarded; master's offered. **ROTC:** Army. **Location:** 4 miles from downtown. **Calendar:** Semester, limited summer session. **Full-time faculty:** 66 total; 86% have terminal degrees, 9% minority, 54% women. **Part-time faculty:** 135 total; 36% have terminal degrees, 12% minority, 48% women. **Class size:** 52% < 20, 47% 20-39, less than 1% 40-49.

Freshman class profile. 1,902 applied, 1,372 admitted, 381 enrolled.

Mid 50% test scores			
ACT:	18-22	Rank in top quarter:	33%
GPA 3.50 or higher:	26%	Rank in top tenth:	13%
GPA 3.0-3.49:	30%	Return as sophomores:	62%
GPA 2.0-2.99:	44%	Out-of-state:	1%
		Live on campus:	80%

Basis for selection. High school GPA, curriculum most important, followed by class rank, test scores, interview, recommendations, and activities. Interview required for in-state applicants; recommended for out-of-state.

High school preparation. College-preparatory program recommended. 16 units recommended. Recommended units include English 4, mathematics 3, social studies 3, science 3 and foreign language 3.

2005-2006 Annual costs. Tuition/fees: $19,484. Room/board: $6,800. Books/supplies: $800. Personal expenses: $1,500.

Financial aid. **Non-need-based:** Scholarships awarded for academics, athletics, state residency.

Application procedures. **Admission:** Priority date 4/1; no deadline. $25 fee. Application may be submitted online. Admission notification on a rolling basis beginning on or about 9/1. **Financial aid:** Priority date 4/1; no closing date. FAFSA required. Applicants notified on a rolling basis starting 3/1; must reply within 2 week(s) of notification.

Academics. **Special study options:** Cross-registration, distance learning, double major, dual enrollment of high school students, honors, independent study, internships, study abroad, teacher certification program, Washington semester, weekend college. **Credit/placement by examination:** AP, CLEP, IB, ACT, institutional tests. No limit on credit hours by examination, but residency requirement must be met. **Support services:** Learning center, reduced course load, remedial instruction, study skills assistance, tutoring.

Majors. **Biology:** General. **Business:** Accounting, business admin, communications, international, management information systems. **Communications:** General, public relations. **Computer sciences:** Computer science, information systems. **Education:** Art, biology, chemistry, elementary, English, ESL, instructional media, mathematics, middle, multiple handicapped, physics, school librarian, science, secondary, social studies, special. **History:** General. **Liberal arts:** Arts/sciences. **Math:** General. **Philosophy/religion:** Philosophy. **Physical sciences:** Chemistry. **Protective services:** Criminal justice. **Psychology:** General. **Public administration:** Social work. **Social sciences:** Economics, political science, sociology. **Visual/performing arts:** Art, graphic design.

Most popular majors. Business/marketing 43%, education 22%, liberal arts 7%, social sciences 9%.

Computing on campus. 330 workstations in dormitories, library, computer center. Dormitories wired for high-speed internet access and linked to campus network. Commuter students can connect to campus network. Online course registration, online library, helpline, student web hosting available.

Student life. **Freshman orientation:** Mandatory, $100 fee. Preregistration for classes offered. **Policies:** Freshmen permitted cars on campus. **Housing:** Coed dorms available. $100 deposit, deadline 7/6. **Activities:** Pep band, choral groups, drama, literary magazine, radio station, student government, student newspaper, campus ministry, Black Student Union, American international membership club, resident student association, commuter student association, social work club, Pallete Club, psychology club.

Athletics. NAIA. **Intercollegiate:** Baseball M, basketball, cheerleading, football (tackle) M, golf, soccer, softball W, tennis, volleyball W. **Intramural:** Badminton, basketball, golf, soccer, table tennis, tennis. **Team name:** Panthers.

Student services. Adult student services, campus ministries, career counseling, student employment services, financial aid counseling, health services, personal counseling, placement for graduates, veterans' counselor.

Contact. E-mail: admissions@ohiodominican.edu
Phone: (614) 251-4500 Toll-free number: (800) 955-6446
Fax: (614) 251-0156
Nicole Evans, Associate Director of Admissions, Ohio Dominican University, 1216 Sunbury Road, Columbus, OH 43219

Ohio Northern University

Ada, Ohio — **CB member**
www.onu.edu — **CB code: 1591**

- Private 4-year university affiliated with United Methodist Church
- Residential campus in small town
- 2,541 degree-seeking undergraduates: 1% part-time, 46% women, 2% African American, 1% Asian American, 1% Hispanic American
- 944 graduate students
- 80% of applicants admitted
- SAT or ACT (ACT writing optional) required
- 64% graduate within 6 years; 25% enter graduate study

General. Founded in 1871. Regionally accredited. **Degrees:** 406 bachelor's awarded; master's, first professional offered. **ROTC:** Army, Air Force. **Location:** 15 miles from Lima, 75 miles from Columbus. **Calendar:** Quarter, limited summer session. **Full-time faculty:** 205 total; 82% have terminal degrees, 7% minority, 32% women. **Part-time faculty:** 77 total; 32% have terminal degrees, 4% minority, 46% women. **Class size:** 50% < 20, 45% 20-39, 2% 40-49, 3% 50-99, less than 1% >100. **Special facilities:** Nature center, drug information center (College of Pharmacy), pharmacy museum.

Freshman class profile. 3,371 applied, 2,698 admitted, 809 enrolled.

Mid 50% test scores			
SAT verbal:	530-630	Rank in top quarter:	66%
SAT math:	530-650	Rank in top tenth:	38%
ACT:	23-28	Return as sophomores:	82%
GPA 3.50 or higher:	64%	Out-of-state:	15%
GPA 3.0-3.49:	21%	Live on campus:	97%
GPA 2.0-2.99:	14%	Fraternities:	15%
		Sororities:	15%

Basis for selection. Minimum ACT score of 20; secondary school record very important. Colleges of Pharmacy and Engineering have higher test score credentials for consideration. GPA, class rank, test scores, college prep curriculum, extracurricular activities are considered in admission decisions. Essay and interview recommended for all; audition recommended for music, performing arts programs; portfolio recommended for art program.

High school preparation. 16 units required; 22 recommended. Required and recommended units include English 4, mathematics 2-4, social studies 2-3, history 2, science 2-3 (laboratory 2), foreign language 2 and academic electives 4. 4 units mathematics and science required for engineering and pharmacy applicants.

2005-2006 Annual costs. Tuition/fees: $27,045. Tuition and fees for engineering $28,680; pharmacy $30,180. Room/board: $6,720. Books/supplies: $900. Personal expenses: $1,400.

2005-2006 Financial aid. **Need-based:** Average need met was 96%. Average scholarship/grant was $13,681; average loan $3,991. 68% of total undergraduate aid awarded as scholarships/grants, 32% as loans/jobs. **Non-need-based:** Scholarships awarded for academics, alumni affiliation, art, leadership, music/drama, ROTC, state residency.

Application procedures. **Admission:** Priority date 12/1; deadline 8/15 (postmark date). $30 fee, may be waived for applicants with need. Application may be submitted online. Admission notification on a rolling basis. Must reply by 5/1. Priority date for scholarship eligibility is December 1. First review for completed pharmacy applications begins November 1 of senior year. **Financial aid:** Priority date 4/15, closing date 6/1. FAFSA, institutional form required. Applicants notified on a rolling basis starting 2/15; must reply within 2 week(s) of notification.

Academics. Pharmacy students are admitted directly to 6-year PharmD. program. **Special study options:** Combined bachelor's/graduate degree, cooperative education, distance learning, double major, dual enrollment of high school students, exchange student, honors, independent study, internships, liberal arts/career combination, study abroad, teacher certification program, Washington semester. **Credit/placement by examination:** AP, CLEP, IB, SAT, ACT, institutional tests. 45 credit hours maximum toward bachelor's degree. **Support services:** Pre-admission summer program, reduced course load, remedial instruction, study skills assistance, tutoring, writing center.

Majors. **Biology:** General, biochemistry, exercise physiology, molecular. **Business:** Accounting, business admin, international, management science. **Communications:** General, broadcast journalism, journalism, organizational, public relations. **Computer sciences:** Computer graphics. **Conservation:** General, environmental studies. **Education:** General, biology, chemistry, early childhood, elementary, English, foreign languages, French, health, history, mathematics, middle, music, physical, physics, science, secondary, social studies, Spanish, technology/industrial arts. **Engineering:** General, civil, computer, electrical, mechanical. **Engineering technology:** Industrial. **English:** Composition, creative writing, English lit, technical writing. **Foreign languages:** French, German, Germanic, Spanish. **Health:** Athletic training, physician assistant, predentistry, premedicine, preveterinary. **History:** General. **Liberal arts:** Arts/sciences. **Math:** General, statistics. **Parks/recreation:** Exercise sciences, health/fitness, sports admin. **Philosophy/religion:** Philosophy, religion. **Physical sciences:** Astronomy, chemistry, physics. **Protective services:** Criminal justice, forensics, law enforcement admin, police science. **Psychology:** General. **Social sciences:** General, international relations, political science, sociology. **Visual/performing arts:** Art, commercial/advertising art, dramatic, music management, music performance, music theory/composition, studio arts.

Most popular majors. Biology 6%, business/marketing 15%, education 12%, engineering/engineering technologies 21%, health sciences 11%.

Computing on campus. 550 workstations in dormitories, library, computer center. Dormitories wired for high-speed internet access and linked to

campus network. Commuter students can connect to campus network. Online course registration, online library, helpline, wireless network available.

Student life. **Freshman orientation:** Mandatory. Preregistration for classes offered. 4 separate 1-day orientations in June and July, each is on Friday beginning at 8 am and concluding around 5 pm. **Policies:** All students must reside on campus until 135 credit hours are reached. No smoking in residence halls. Freshmen permitted cars on campus. **Housing:** Guaranteed on-campus for freshmen. Coed dorms, single-sex dorms, special housing for disabled, apartments, fraternity/sorority housing, substance-free housing available. $200 fully refundable deposit, deadline 8/1. Honors residence halls available. **Activities:** Bands, choral groups, dance, drama, literary magazine, music ensembles, musical theater, opera, radio station, student government, student newspaper, symphony orchestra, TV station, Christian Legal Society, Fellowship of Christian Athletes, University Religious Association Council, Black Student Union, Amnesty International, College Republicans, Black Law Student Association, international club, Habitat for Humanity, World Student Organization.

Athletics. NCAA. **Intercollegiate:** Baseball M, basketball, cross-country, diving, football (tackle) M, golf, soccer, softball W, swimming, tennis, track and field, volleyball W, wrestling M. **Intramural:** Badminton, basketball, bowling, football (non-tackle) M, racquetball, soccer, softball, swimming, table tennis M, tennis, track and field, volleyball, wrestling M. **Team name:** Polar Bears.

Student services. Alcohol/substance abuse counseling, campus ministries, career counseling, student employment services, financial aid counseling, health services, legal services, minority student services, personal counseling, placement for graduates. **Physically disabled:** Services for visually, speech, hearing impaired.

Contact. E-mail: admissions-ug@onu.edu
Phone: (419) 772-2260 Toll-free number: (888) 408-4668
Fax: (419) 772-2313
Jeff Dittman, Director of Admissions, Ohio Northern University, 525 South Main Street, Ada, OH 45810-1599

Ohio State University: Columbus Campus

Columbus, Ohio — **CB member**
www.osu.edu — **CB code: 1592**

- Public 4-year university
- Residential campus in very large city
- 36,029 degree-seeking undergraduates: 7% part-time, 47% women, 8% African American, 5% Asian American, 3% Hispanic American, 3% international
- 13,093 degree-seeking graduate students
- 74% of applicants admitted
- SAT or ACT with writing, application essay required
- 68% graduate within 6 years

General. Founded in 1870. Regionally accredited. Additional campuses in Wooster, Marion, Lima, Newark, Mansfield. **Degrees:** 8,508 bachelor's, 340 associate awarded; master's, doctoral, first professional offered. **ROTC:** Army, Navy, Air Force. **Location:** 2 miles from downtown. **Calendar:** Quarter, extensive summer session. **Full-time faculty:** 2,872 total; 99% have terminal degrees, 18% minority, 29% women. **Part-time faculty:** 1,023 total; 12% minority, 47% women. **Class size:** 43% < 20, 34% 20-39, 7% 40-49, 10% 50-99, 6% >100. **Special facilities:** Radio telescope, theater, dance notation bureau, extension center for educational research, biological science laboratory on Lake Erie, campus airport, environmental studies center, research vessel on Lake Erie, nuclear research reactor, supercomputer facility, arts center, cultural center, public service and public policy institute, polar research center, health policy studies center, mapping center, materials research center.

Freshman class profile. 17,566 applied, 12,945 admitted, 5,954 enrolled.

Mid 50% test scores			
SAT verbal:	530-640	Rank in top tenth:	39%
SAT math:	550-660	Return as sophomores:	90%
ACT:	24-28	Out-of-state:	12%
Rank in top quarter:	76%	Live on campus:	90%
		International:	1%

Basis for selection. Secondary school record, class rank, test scores most important. Audition required for dance, music programs; portfolio required for art programs. **Homeschooled:** May be required to provide GED.

High school preparation. College-preparatory program required. Required and recommended units include English 4, mathematics 3-4, social studies 2-3, science 2-3 (laboratory 2-3), foreign language 2-3 and academic electives 1. 1 visual or performing arts required.

2005-2006 Annual costs. Tuition/fees: $8,082; $19,305 out-of-state. Room/board: $7,770. Books/supplies: $1,080. Personal expenses: $3,474.

2004-2005 Financial aid. **Need-based:** 4,783 full-time freshmen applied for aid; 3,264 were judged to have need; 3,262 of these received aid. Average need met was 71.6%. Average scholarship/grant was $7,095; average loan $2,761. 45% of total undergraduate aid awarded as scholarships/grants, 55% as loans/jobs. **Non-need-based:** Awarded to 6,842 full-time undergraduates, including 2,048 freshmen. Scholarships awarded for academics, alumni affiliation, art, athletics, job skills, leadership, minority status, music/drama, ROTC, state residency.

Application procedures. **Admission:** Closing date 2/1 (postmark date). $40 fee, may be waived for applicants with need. Application may be submitted online. Admission notification on a rolling basis beginning on or about 12/1. Must reply by May 1 or within 4 week(s) if notified thereafter. **Financial aid:** Priority date 3/1; no closing date. FAFSA required. Applicants notified by 4/5; must reply by 5/1 or within 4 week(s) of notification.

Academics. **Special study options:** Accelerated study, combined bachelor's/graduate degree, cooperative education, cross-registration, distance learning, double major, dual enrollment of high school students, ESL, exchange student, honors, independent study, internships, liberal arts/career combination, semester at sea, student-designed major, study abroad, teacher certification program, Washington semester. **Credit/placement by examination:** AP, CLEP, IB, SAT, ACT, institutional tests. 45 credit hours maximum toward bachelor's degree. **Support services:** Learning center, pre-admission summer program, reduced course load, remedial instruction, study skills assistance, tutoring, writing center.

Majors. **Agriculture:** Agronomy, animal sciences, business, communications, economics, food processing, food science, landscaping, plant protection, plant sciences, turf management. **Architecture:** Architecture, environmental design, interior, landscape. **Area/ethnic studies:** African, African-American, Central/Eastern European, East Asian, Latin American, Near/Middle Eastern, Russian/Slavic, Western European, women's. **Biology:** General, biochemistry, botany, ecology, entomology, genetics, microbiology, molecular genetics, zoology. **Business:** General, accounting, actuarial science, fashion, finance, hospitality admin, hospitality/recreation, human resources, insurance, international, logistics, management information systems, managerial economics, marketing, operations, real estate, transportation. **Communications:** General, journalism, public relations. **Computer sciences:** General, computer science, information systems. **Conservation:** General, fisheries, forestry, management/policy, wildlife. **Education:** Agricultural, art, music, physical, special, technology/industrial arts, trade/industrial. **Engineering:** Aerospace, agricultural, ceramic, chemical, civil, computer, electrical, industrial, materials, materials science, mechanical, metallurgical, physics, systems. **Engineering technology:** Construction, surveying. **English:** Composition. **Family/consumer sciences:** General, clothing/textiles, family resources, family studies, family/community services, food/nutrition. **Foreign languages:** Arabic, Chinese, classics, comparative lit, French, German, Hebrew, Italian, Japanese, Latin, linguistics, modern Greek, Portuguese, Russian, Spanish. **Health:** Audiology/hearing, audiology/speech pathology, clinical lab science, dental hygiene, dietetics, medical radiologic technology/radiation therapy, medical records admin, perfusion technology, respiratory therapy technology. **History:** General. **Interdisciplinary:** Ancient studies, medieval/Renaissance, nutrition sciences, peace/conflict. **Liberal arts:** Arts/sciences. **Math:** General. **Parks/recreation:** Exercise sciences, facilities management, health/fitness, sports admin. **Philosophy/religion:** Islamic, Judaic, philosophy, religion. **Physical sciences:** Astronomy, chemistry, geology, geophysics, physics. **Production:** Welding. **Psychology:** General. **Public administration:** Social work. **Social sciences:** General, anthropology, criminology, economics, geography, international relations, political science, sociology, urban studies. **Transportation:** Aviation. **Visual/performing arts:** Art, art history/conservation, ceramics, dance, design, dramatic, drawing, industrial design, interior design, jazz, music history, music performance, music theory/composition, painting, photography, piano/organ, printmaking, sculpture, studio arts, voice/opera.

Most popular majors. Business/marketing 16%, engineering/engineering technologies 9%, family/consumer sciences 10%, psychology 6%, social sciences 13%.

Computing on campus. 800 workstations in dormitories, library, computer center, student center. Dormitories wired for high-speed internet access and linked to campus network. Commuter students can connect to campus network. Online course registration, online library, helpline, repair service, student web hosting, wireless network available.

Student life. **Freshman orientation:** Mandatory, $50 fee. Preregistration for classes offered. 27 2-day programs throughout the summer (June-August) prior to enrollment. **Policies:** Freshmen permitted cars on campus. **Housing:** Guaranteed on-campus for freshmen. Coed dorms, special housing for disabled, apartments, cooperative housing, substance-free housing available. $250 partly refundable deposit. **Activities:** Bands, choral groups, dance, drama, film society, literary magazine, music ensembles, musical theater, opera, radio station, student government, student newspaper, symphony orchestra, TV station, Afrikan Student Union, Asian American association, Bisexual Gay and Lesbian Alliance, Campus Crusade for Christ, university-wide council of Hispanic Organizations.

Athletics. NCAA. **Intercollegiate:** Baseball M, basketball, cheerleading, cross-country, diving, fencing, field hockey W, football (tackle) M, golf, gymnastics, ice hockey, lacrosse, rifle, rowing (crew) W, soccer, softball W, swimming, synchronized swimming W, tennis, track and field, volleyball, wrestling M. **Intramural:** Archery, badminton, baseball M, basketball, bowling, diving, equestrian, fencing, football (non-tackle), golf, gymnastics, handball, ice hockey, lacrosse, racquetball, rifle, rowing (crew), rugby, sailing, skiing, soccer, softball, squash, swimming, table tennis, tennis, track and field, volleyball, water polo, wrestling. **Team name:** Buckeyes.

Student services. Adult student services, alcohol/substance abuse counseling, campus ministries, career counseling, student employment services, financial aid counseling, health services, legal services, minority student services, on-campus daycare, personal counseling, placement for graduates, veterans' counselor, women's services. **Physically disabled:** Services for visually, speech, hearing impaired.

Contact. E-mail: askabuckeye@osu.edu
Phone: (614) 292-3980 Fax: (614) 292-4818
Mabel Freeman, Assistant Vice President for Undergraduate Admissions and First Year Experience, Ohio State University: Columbus Campus, 110 Enarson Hall, Columbus, OH 43210

Ohio State University: Lima Campus

Lima, Ohio
www.lima.ohio-state.edu **CB code: 1541**

- Public 4-year branch campus college
- Commuter campus in large town
- 965 degree-seeking undergraduates: 13% part-time, 55% women, 3% African American, 1% Asian American, 1% Hispanic American
- 77 degree-seeking graduate students
- Application essay required

General. Founded in 1960. Regionally accredited. Branch campus of Ohio State University; all degrees awarded through main campus. **Degrees:** 89 bachelor's, 32 associate awarded; master's offered. **ROTC:** Army, Navy, Air Force. **Location:** 90 miles from Columbus. **Calendar:** Quarter, limited summer session. **Full-time faculty:** 38 total; 97% have terminal degrees, 10% minority, 34% women. **Part-time faculty:** 39 total; 15% minority, 56% women. **Class size:** 57% < 20, 35% 20-39, 4% 40-49, 4% 50-99. **Special facilities:** Greenhouse, nature trails, dinosaur museum.

Freshman class profile. 720 applied, 716 admitted, 273 enrolled.

Mid 50% test scores			
SAT verbal:	390-540	ACT:	18-24
SAT math:	450-600	Rank in top quarter:	31%
		Rank in top tenth:	5%

Basis for selection. Open admission, but selective for out-of-state students. SAT/ACT required for out-of-state students.

High school preparation. Required and recommended units include English 4, mathematics 3-4, social studies 2-3, science 2-3 (laboratory 2), foreign language 2-3 and academic electives 1. One visual or performing arts also recommended.

2005-2006 Annual costs. Tuition/fees: $5,310; $16,533 out-of-state. Personal expenses: $3,069.

2005-2006 Financial aid. Need-based: 222 full-time freshmen applied for aid; 165 were judged to have need; 165 of these received aid. Average need met was 52%. Average scholarship/grant was $3,156; average loan $2,700. 32% of total undergraduate aid awarded as scholarships/grants, 68% as loans/jobs. **Non-need-based:** Awarded to 56 full-time undergraduates, including 20 freshmen. Scholarships awarded for academics.

Application procedures. Admission: Closing date 7/1. $40 fee, may be waived for applicants with need. Application may be submitted online. Admission notification on a rolling basis beginning on or about 12/1. **Financial aid:** Priority date 3/1; no closing date. FAFSA required. Applicants notified on a rolling basis starting 5/1; must reply within 4 week(s) of notification.

Academics. Students often leave campus after 1-3 years and complete bachelor's degree on Columbus campus. **Special study options:** Accelerated study, cooperative education, cross-registration, distance learning, double major, dual enrollment of high school students, ESL, exchange student, honors, independent study, internships, liberal arts/career combination, student-designed major, study abroad, teacher certification program. **Credit/placement by examination:** AP, CLEP, institutional tests. 45 credit hours maximum toward associate degree. **Support services:** Learning center, remedial instruction, tutoring, writing center.

Majors. Biology: General. **Business:** General, financial planning, hospitality admin. **Education:** General. **Health:** Health services. **History:** General. **Math:** General. **Psychology:** General.

Computing on campus. 104 workstations in library, computer center. Commuter students can connect to campus network. Online course registration, online library, helpline available.

Student life. Freshman orientation: Available. Orientation services available throughout year, days and evenings. **Activities:** Choral groups, drama, musical theater, student newspaper, Bible club, multicultural club.

Athletics. Intramural: Baseball M, basketball, bowling, golf M, soccer, softball, volleyball. **Team name:** Barons.

Student services. Adult student services, career counseling, student employment services, financial aid counseling, on-campus daycare, personal counseling, placement for graduates. **Physically disabled:** Services for visually, speech, hearing impaired.

Contact. E-mail: admissions@lima.ohio-state.edu
Phone: (419) 995-8396 Fax: (419) 995-8483
Garlene Smithson, Director of Enrollment Services, Ohio State University: Lima Campus, 4240 Campus Drive, Lima, OH 45804-3596

Ohio State University: Mansfield Campus

Mansfield, Ohio
www.mansfield.ohio-state.edu **CB code: 0744**

- Public 4-year branch campus college
- Commuter campus in small city
- 1,209 degree-seeking undergraduates: 20% part-time, 60% women, 5% African American, 2% Asian American, 1% Hispanic American, 1% Native American
- 97 degree-seeking graduate students
- Application essay required

General. Founded in 1958. Regionally accredited. Branch campus of Ohio State University; all degrees awarded through main campus. **Degrees:** 74 bachelor's, 55 associate awarded; master's offered. **ROTC:** Army, Navy, Air Force. **Location:** 67 miles from Columbus. **Calendar:** Quarter, limited summer session. **Full-time faculty:** 48 total; 98% have terminal degrees, 8% minority, 29% women. **Part-time faculty:** 41 total; 10% minority, 61% women. **Class size:** 55% < 20, 38% 20-39, 3% 40-49, 3% 50-99. **Special facilities:** Archives and reading room, educational enrichment laboratory, language laboratory, elementary education suite.

Freshman class profile. 979 applied, 976 admitted, 438 enrolled.

Mid 50% test scores			
SAT verbal:	450-560	Rank in top quarter:	26%
SAT math:	440-580	Rank in top tenth:	9%
ACT:	18-23	Live on campus:	30%

Basis for selection. Open admission, but selective for out-of-state students. Out-of-state applicants evaluated on basis of GPA, class rank, principal/counselor recommendations and test scores (either SAT or ACT with ACT Writing). SAT/ACT required for out-of-state students.

High school preparation. Required and recommended units include English 4, mathematics 3-4, social studies 2-3, science 2-3 (laboratory 2-3), foreign language 2-3 and academic electives 1. One unit of visual or performing arts recommended.

2005-2006 Annual costs. Tuition/fees: $5,310; $16,533 out-of-state. Books/supplies: $990. Personal expenses: $3,069.

2005-2006 Financial aid. Need-based: 325 full-time freshmen applied for aid; 254 were judged to have need; 253 of these received aid. Average need met was 54%. Average scholarship/grant was $3,891; average loan $2,725. 38% of total undergraduate aid awarded as scholarships/grants, 62% as loans/jobs. **Non-need-based:** Awarded to 89 full-time undergraduates, including 49 freshmen. Scholarships awarded for academics.

Application procedures. Admission: Closing date 7/1. $40 fee, may be waived for applicants with need. Application may be submitted online. Admission notification on a rolling basis beginning on or about 10/1. **Financial aid:** Priority date 3/1; no closing date. FAFSA required. Applicants notified on a rolling basis starting 5/1; must reply within 4 week(s) of notification.

Academics. Students often leave campus after 1-3 years and complete bachelor's degree on Columbus campus. **Special study options:** Accelerated study, cooperative education, cross-registration, distance learning, double major, dual enrollment of high school students, ESL, external degree, honors, independent study, internships, liberal arts/career combination, student-designed major, study abroad, teacher certification program. **Credit/placement by examination:** AP, CLEP, institutional tests. 45 credit hours maximum toward associate degree. **Support services:** Learning center, remedial instruction, tutoring, writing center.

Majors. Business: Business admin. **Education:** Elementary. **History:** General. **Psychology:** General.

Computing on campus. 103 workstations in library, computer center, student center. Commuter students can connect to campus network. Online course registration, online library, helpline available.

Student life. Freshman orientation: Mandatory. Preregistration for classes offered. **Policies:** Freshmen permitted cars on campus. **Housing:** Coed dorms available. **Activities:** Choral groups, dance, drama, musical theater, student government, student newspaper, black culture club.

Athletics. Intramural: Basketball, bowling, golf, softball, table tennis, tennis, volleyball.

Student services. Adult student services, career counseling, student employment services, financial aid counseling, personal counseling, placement for graduates. **Physically disabled:** Services for visually, speech, hearing impaired.

Contact. E-mail: admissions@mansfield.ohio-state.edu
Phone: (419) 755-4226 Fax: (419) 755-4241
Henry Thomas, Coordinator of Admissions and Financial Aid, Ohio State University: Mansfield Campus, 1680 University Drive, Mansfield, OH 44906

Ohio State University: Marion Campus

Marion, Ohio
www.marion.ohio-state.edu **CB code: 0752**

- Public 4-year branch campus college
- Commuter campus in large town
- 1,299 degree-seeking undergraduates: 14% part-time, 58% women, 4% African American, 3% Asian American, 2% Hispanic American
- 79 degree-seeking graduate students
- Application essay required

General. Founded in 1958. Regionally accredited. Branch campus of Ohio State University; all degrees awarded through main campus. **Degrees:** 97 bachelor's, 138 associate awarded; master's offered. **ROTC:** Army, Navy, Air Force. **Location:** 44 miles from Columbus. **Calendar:** Quarter, limited summer session. **Full-time faculty:** 35 total; 97% have terminal degrees, 14% minority, 34% women. **Part-time faculty:** 73 total; 7% minority, 55% women. **Class size:** 45% < 20, 46% 20-39, 6% 40-49, 2% 50-99.

Freshman class profile. 751 applied, 748 admitted, 409 enrolled.

Mid 50% test scores			
SAT verbal:	460-540	ACT:	18-23
SAT math:	460-550	Rank in top quarter:	28%
		Rank in top tenth:	6%

Basis for selection. Open admission, but selective for out-of-state students. Out-of-state students evaluated on basis of GPA class rank, principal/counselor recommendation, and SAT/ACT scores. SAT/ACT required for all for placement and required for out-of-state students for admissions.

High school preparation. Required and recommended units include English 4, mathematics 3-4, social studies 2-3, science 2-3 (laboratory 2-3), foreign language 2-3 and academic electives 1. One unit of visual or performing arts recommended.

2005-2006 Annual costs. Tuition/fees: $5,310; $16,533 out-of-state. Books/supplies: $600. Personal expenses: $3,069.

2005-2006 Financial aid. Need-based: 308 full-time freshmen applied for aid; 251 were judged to have need; 250 of these received aid. Average need met was 59%. Average scholarship/grant was $3,583; average loan $2,963. 37% of total undergraduate aid awarded as scholarships/grants, 63% as loans/jobs. **Non-need-based:** Awarded to 98 full-time undergraduates, including 47 freshmen. Scholarships awarded for academics.

Application procedures. Admission: Closing date 7/1 (postmark date). $40 fee, may be waived for applicants with need. Application may be submitted online. Admission notification on a rolling basis beginning on or about 10/1. **Financial aid:** Priority date 3/1; no closing date. FAFSA required. Applicants notified on a rolling basis starting 5/1; must reply within 4 week(s) of notification.

Academics. Students often leave campus after 1-3 years and complete bachelor's degree on Columbus campus. **Special study options:** Cooperative education, distance learning, double major, dual enrollment of high school students, honors, independent study, internships, student-designed major, teacher certification program, weekend college. **Credit/placement by examination:** AP, CLEP, SAT, ACT, institutional tests. 45 credit hours maximum toward associate degree. **Support services:** Learning center, reduced course load, remedial instruction, tutoring, writing center.

Majors. Business: Business admin. **Education:** Elementary. **History:** General. **Psychology:** General.

Computing on campus. 174 workstations in library, computer center. Commuter students can connect to campus network. Online course registration, online library, helpline available.

Student life. Freshman orientation: Mandatory. Preregistration for classes offered. **Policies:** Freshmen permitted cars on campus. **Activities:** Choral groups, student government, student newspaper, campus Christian group, nontraditional student group, foreign language club.

Athletics. Intercollegiate: Basketball W, golf, volleyball W. **Intramural:** Basketball, softball, volleyball. **Team name:** Scarlet Wave.

Student services. Career counseling, student employment services, legal services, on-campus daycare, personal counseling, placement for graduates. **Physically disabled:** Services for visually, speech, hearing impaired.

Contact. E-mail: moreau.1@osu.edu
Phone: (740) 389-6786 ext. 6242 Fax: (740) 386-2439
Matt Moreau, Coordinator of Admissions, Ohio State University: Marion Campus, 1465 Mount Vernon Avenue, Marion, OH 43302

Ohio State University: Newark Campus

Newark, Ohio
www.newark.osu.edu **CB code: 0824**

- Public 4-year branch campus college
- Commuter campus in large town
- 1,952 degree-seeking undergraduates: 13% part-time, 55% women, 7% African American, 1% Asian American, 1% Hispanic American, 1% Native American
- 95 degree-seeking graduate students

General. Founded in 1957. Regionally accredited. Branch campus of Ohio State University; all degrees awarded through main campus. **Degrees:** 124 bachelor's, 115 associate awarded; master's offered. **ROTC:** Army, Navy, Air Force. **Location:** 28 miles from Columbus. **Calendar:** Quarter, limited summer session. **Full-time faculty:** 50 total; 98% have terminal degrees, 12% minority, 30% women. **Part-time faculty:** 85 total; 8% minority, 55% women. **Class size:** 40% < 20, 49% 20-39, 9% 40-49, 3% 50-99. **Special facilities:** Mathematics laboratory, writing laboratory.

Freshman class profile. 1,526 applied, 1,516 admitted, 779 enrolled.

Mid 50% test scores			
SAT verbal:	440-550	Rank in top quarter:	18%
SAT math:	450-560	Rank in top tenth:	7%
ACT:	18-22	Live on campus:	18%

Basis for selection. Open admission, but selective for out-of-state students. Admission for out-of-state applicants based on college preparatory curriculum and rank in class. SAT/ACT required for out-of-state students for admissions.

High school preparation. Required and recommended units include English 4, mathematics 3-4, social studies 2-3, science 2-3 (laboratory 2-3), foreign language 2-3 and academic electives 1. One unit of visual or performing arts recommended.

2005-2006 Annual costs. Tuition/fees: $5,310; $16,533 out-of-state. Books/supplies: $750. Personal expenses: $3,069.

2005-2006 Financial aid. Need-based: 596 full-time freshmen applied for aid; 429 were judged to have need; 428 of these received aid. Average need met was 50%. Average scholarship/grant was $3,650; average loan $2,766. 34% of total undergraduate aid awarded as scholarships/grants, 66% as loans/jobs. **Non-need-based:** Awarded to 35 full-time undergraduates, including 15 freshmen. Scholarships awarded for academics.

Application procedures. **Admission:** Closing date 7/1 (postmark date). $40 fee, may be waived for applicants with need. Application may be submitted online. Admission notification on a rolling basis beginning on or about 12/1. **Financial aid:** Priority date 3/1; no closing date. FAFSA required. Applicants notified on a rolling basis starting 5/1; must reply within 4 week(s) of notification.

Academics. Students often leave campus after 1-3 years and complete bachelor's degree on Columbus campus. **Special study options:** Cooperative education, cross-registration, distance learning, double major, dual enrollment of high school students, ESL, honors, independent study, internships, student-designed major, teacher certification program, weekend college. **Credit/placement by examination:** AP, CLEP, institutional tests. 45 credit hours maximum toward associate degree. **Support services:** Learning center, remedial instruction, tutoring, writing center.

Majors. **Business:** Business admin. **Education:** General. **Psychology:** General.

Computing on campus. 36 workstations in library, computer center, student center. Commuter students can connect to campus network. Online course registration, online library, helpline available.

Student life. **Freshman orientation:** Mandatory. Preregistration for classes offered. **Policies:** Freshmen permitted cars on campus. **Housing:** Apartments available. University-owned student apartments within 2-minute walk from campus. **Activities:** Choral groups, drama, student government, campus ministry, support groups, minority organization.

Athletics. **Intercollegiate:** Baseball M, basketball, cross-country, golf M, softball W, volleyball. **Intramural:** Badminton, baseball M, basketball, soccer W, softball, table tennis, tennis, volleyball. **Team name:** Titans.

Student services. Adult student services, career counseling, student employment services, financial aid counseling, on-campus daycare, personal counseling, placement for graduates. **Physically disabled:** Services for visually, speech, hearing impaired.

Contact. E-mail: donahue.5@osu.edu
Phone: (740) 366-3333 Fax: (740) 364-9645
Ann Donahue, Coordinator of Admissions, Ohio State University: Newark Campus, 1179 University Drive, Newark, OH 43055

Ohio University

Athens, Ohio **CB member**
www.ohio.edu **CB code: 1593**

- Public 4-year university
- Residential campus in large town
- 17,042 degree-seeking undergraduates: 6% part-time, 53% women, 4% African American, 1% Asian American, 1% Hispanic American, 1% international
- 3,204 degree-seeking graduate students
- 89% of applicants admitted
- SAT or ACT with writing required
- 71% graduate within 6 years; 26% enter graduate study

General. Founded in 1804. Regionally accredited. **Degrees:** 4,222 bachelor's, 509 associate awarded; master's, doctoral, first professional offered. **ROTC:** Army, Air Force. **Location:** 75 miles from Columbus. **Calendar:** Quarter, extensive summer session. **Full-time faculty:** 875 total; 89% have terminal degrees, 17% minority, 36% women. **Part-time faculty:** 320 total; 61% have terminal degrees, 6% minority, 44% women. **Class size:** 45% < 20, 39% 20-39, 6% 40-49, 6% 50-99, 4% >100. **Special facilities:** University airport, nuclear accelerator, biotechnology research center, greenhouse, cartography center, meteorology center, contemporary history institute, art museum.

Freshman class profile. 12,367 applied, 11,027 admitted, 4,191 enrolled.

Mid 50% test scores		**Rank in top tenth:**	16%
SAT verbal:	490-600	**End year in good standing:**	84%
SAT math:	490-600	**Return as sophomores:**	81%
ACT:	21-25	**Out-of-state:**	8%
GPA 3.50 or higher:	47%	**Live on campus:**	96%
GPA 3.0-3.49:	42%	**Fraternities:**	14%
GPA 2.0-2.99:	11%	**Sororities:**	15%
Rank in top quarter:	42%		

Basis for selection. High school record as represented by rank in class, GPA, and curriculum completed most important. Secondary criteria test scores and recommendation. Rank in top third of class preferred. Audition required for dance and music programs.

High school preparation. 16 units required. Required units include English 4, mathematics 3, social studies 3, science 3 and foreign language 2. One unit visual or performing art recommended.

2005-2006 Annual costs. Tuition/fees: $8,235; $17,199 out-of-state. Room/board: $8,745. Books/supplies: $840. Personal expenses: $891.

2005-2006 Financial aid. **Need-based:** 3,589 full-time freshmen applied for aid; 2,187 were judged to have need; 2,141 of these received aid. Average need met was 48%. Average scholarship/grant was $4,046; average loan $2,658. 31% of total undergraduate aid awarded as scholarships/grants, 69% as loans/jobs. **Non-need-based:** Awarded to 4,784 full-time undergraduates, including 2,008 freshmen. Scholarships awarded for academics, art, athletics, minority status, music/drama, religious affiliation, ROTC.

Application procedures. **Admission:** Closing date 2/1 (receipt date). $45 fee, may be waived for applicants with need. Application may be submitted online. Admission notification on a rolling basis beginning on or about 10/1. Must reply by 5/1. **Financial aid:** Priority date 3/15, closing date 4/1. FAFSA required. Applicants notified on a rolling basis starting 4/1; must reply within 3 week(s) of notification.

Academics. **Special study options:** Accelerated study, combined bachelor's/graduate degree, cooperative education, cross-registration, distance learning, double major, dual enrollment of high school students, ESL, external degree, honors, independent study, internships, liberal arts/career combination, student-designed major, study abroad, teacher certification program. **Credit/placement by examination:** AP, CLEP, IB, institutional tests. Sophomore standing available by earning 45 quarter hours of credit based on AP scores. **Support services:** Learning center, pre-admission summer program, remedial instruction, study skills assistance, tutoring, writing center.

Honors college/program. Honors Tutorial College application deadline December 15, interview required.

Majors. **Area/ethnic studies:** African, African-American, Asian, European, Latin American, women's. **Biology:** General, botany, cellular/molecular, microbiology, wildlife, zoology. **Business:** General, accounting, actuarial science, business admin, finance, human resources, international, management information systems, management science, managerial economics, marketing. **Communications:** General, broadcast journalism, digital media, health, journalism, organizational, photojournalism, radio/tv. **Computer sciences:** General, computer science, information technology. **Education:** Art, early childhood, elementary, English, family/consumer sciences, French, German, middle, physical, reading, science, secondary, social studies, Spanish, special. **Engineering:** Chemical, civil, electrical, industrial, mechanical. **Engineering technology:** Industrial. **English:** Creative writing, English lit. **Family/consumer sciences:** Child development, clothing/textiles, family resources, family studies, food/nutrition, housing, institutional food production. **Foreign languages:** Ancient Greek, classics, French, German, Latin, linguistics, Russian, Spanish. **Health:** Athletic training, audiology/speech pathology, community health services, dietetics, environmental health, health care admin, nursing (RN), occupational health. **History:** General. **Math:** General, applied. **Parks/recreation:** General, exercise sciences, health/fitness. **Philosophy/religion:** Philosophy. **Physical sciences:** Astrophysics, atmospheric science, chemistry, geology, physics. **Psychology:** General. **Public administration:** Social work. **Social sciences:** Anthropology, cartography, criminology, economics, geography, political science, sociology, urban studies. **Transportation:** Aviation, aviation management. **Visual/performing arts:** General, acting, art, art history/conservation, ceramics, cinematography, dance, dramatic, graphic design, music history, music performance, music theory/composition, painting, photography, piano/organ, play/screenwriting, printmaking, sculpture, theater arts management, voice/opera.

Most popular majors. Business/marketing 13%, communications/journalism 17%, education 13%, family/consumer sciences 7%, liberal arts 7%, parks/recreation 6%, social sciences 8%.

Computing on campus. 6,100 workstations in dormitories, library, computer center. Dormitories wired for high-speed internet access and linked to campus network. Commuter students can connect to campus network. Online course registration, helpline, repair service, student web hosting, wireless network available.

Student life. **Freshman orientation:** Mandatory. Preregistration for classes offered. Weekends in summer. **Housing:** Guaranteed on-campus for freshmen. Coed dorms, single-sex dorms, special housing for disabled, apartments, cooperative housing, fraternity/sorority housing, substance-free housing available. $200 nonrefundable deposit, deadline 5/1. International, intensive-study residence halls available. **Activities:** Bands, choral groups, dance, drama, film society, literary magazine, music ensembles, musical theater, opera, radio station, student government, student newspaper, symphony orchestra, TV station, over 300 professional, religious, ethnic, political, and social service organizations.

Athletics. NCAA. **Intercollegiate:** Baseball M, basketball, cross-country, diving, field hockey W, football (tackle) M, golf, lacrosse W, soccer W, softball W, swimming, track and field, volleyball W, wrestling M. **Intramural:** Baseball M, basketball, bowling, cross-country, football (non-tackle), golf, racquetball, soccer, softball, swimming, table tennis, tennis. **Team name:** Bobcats.

Student services. Adult student services, alcohol/substance abuse counseling, career counseling, services for economically disadvantaged, student employment services, financial aid counseling, health services, legal services, minority student services, personal counseling, placement for graduates, veterans' counselor. **Physically disabled:** Services for visually, hearing impaired.

Contact. E-mail: admissions@ohio.edu
Phone: (740) 593-4100 Fax: (740) 593-0560
David Garcia, Director, Ohio University, 120 Chubb Hall, Athens, OH 45701-2979

Ohio University: Chillicothe Campus

Chillicothe, Ohio
http://oucweb.chillicothe.ohiou.edu **CB code: 0775**

- Public 4-year branch campus college
- Commuter campus in large town
- 1,692 undergraduates
- 34 graduate students

General. Founded in 1946. Regionally accredited. Bachelor's programs in management, elementary education, criminal justice, nursing, technical and applied studies and self-designed major. Degree granted by Ohio University main campus. **Degrees:** 134 associate awarded; master's offered. **Location:** 45 miles from Columbus. **Calendar:** Quarter, limited summer session. **Full-time faculty:** 40 total. **Part-time faculty:** 70 total.

Freshman class profile. 444 applied, 401 admitted, 307 enrolled.

Basis for selection. Open admission, but selective for some programs. Business, communications, education, and engineering colleges require high school GPA and ACT/SAT test scores. **Homeschooled:** Passing scores on Ohio graduation test or GED required.

High school preparation. Recommended units include English 4, mathematics 3, social studies 3, science 3 and foreign language 2. College-preparatory program strongly recommended including 1 visual or performing art.

2005-2006 Annual costs. Tuition/fees: $4,323; $8,646 out-of-state. Books/supplies: $848.

Application procedures. Admission: No deadline. $20 fee, may be waived for applicants with need. Application may be submitted online. Admission notification on a rolling basis. **Financial aid:** No deadline. FAFSA required. Applicants notified on a rolling basis.

Academics. Special study options: Distance learning, double major, dual enrollment of high school students, external degree, independent study, internships, student-designed major, study abroad, teacher certification program. **Credit/placement by examination:** AP, CLEP, institutional tests. **Support services:** Learning center, pre-admission summer program, remedial instruction, study skills assistance, tutoring, writing center.

Majors. Business: Business admin. **Communications:** Organizational. **Education:** Early childhood, middle. **Engineering technology:** Environmental. **Health:** Nursing (RN), nursing admin. **Protective services:** Criminal justice.

Computing on campus. 275 workstations in library, computer center, student center. Commuter students can connect to campus network. Online course registration, online library, helpline, student web hosting, wireless network available.

Student life. Freshman orientation: Available. Preregistration for classes offered. One-day session conducted prior to fall, winter and spring quarters. **Policies:** Freshmen permitted cars on campus. **Activities:** Drama, student government, student newspaper, National Communication Association, Ross County Association of Future Teachers, anime club, nursing student club, student programming club, human services association, law enforcement association, psychology club.

Athletics. Team name: Hilltoppers.

Student services. Adult student services, career counseling, services for economically disadvantaged, student employment services, financial aid counseling, personal counseling. **Physically disabled:** Services for visually, hearing impaired.

Contact. E-mail: diekroge@ohio.edu
Phone: (740) 774-7240 Toll-free number: (877) 462-6824 ext. 240
Fax: (740) 774-7295
Douglas Hennig, Coordinator of Enrollment Services, Ohio University: Chillicothe Campus, 101 University Drive, PO Box 629, Chillicothe, OH 45601

Ohio University: Eastern Campus

St. Clairsville, Ohio
www.eastern.ohiou.edu **CB code: 0828**

- Public 4-year branch campus college
- Commuter campus in small town
- 777 degree-seeking undergraduates
- 31 graduate students

General. Founded in 1957. Regionally accredited. **Degrees:** 17 associate awarded; master's offered. **Location:** 15 miles from downtown. **Calendar:** Quarter, limited summer session. **Full-time faculty:** 30 total; 77% have terminal degrees, 23% women. **Part-time faculty:** 40 total. **Special facilities:** Primeval oak forest laboratory, Great Western School (Little Red Schoolhouse).

Freshman class profile. 279 applied, 277 admitted, 140 enrolled.

Return as sophomores:	57%	**Out-of-state:**	3%

Basis for selection. Open admission, but selective for some programs. Special requirements for education, business, communication programs. SAT/ACT scores required for admission to education program.

High school preparation. Recommended units include English 4, mathematics 4, social studies 3, science 3 and foreign language 2.

2005-2006 Annual costs. Tuition/fees: $4,323; $8,646 out-of-state.

2004-2005 Financial aid. Need-based: 46% of total undergraduate aid awarded as scholarships/grants, 54% as loans/jobs. **Non-need-based:** Scholarships awarded for academics, alumni affiliation, minority status.

Application procedures. Admission: No deadline. $25 fee, may be waived for applicants with need. Admission notification on a rolling basis. **Financial aid:** Priority date 3/15; no closing date. FAFSA required. Applicants notified by 5/15.

Academics. Several degree programs offered through cross-registration with main campus. **Special study options:** Accelerated study, cooperative education, cross-registration, distance learning, double major, dual enrollment of high school students, external degree, independent study, internships, student-designed major, teacher certification program. **Credit/placement by examination:** CLEP, institutional tests. **Support services:** Learning center, reduced course load, remedial instruction, study skills assistance, tutoring, writing center.

Majors. Education: Elementary. **Liberal arts:** Arts/sciences.

Computing on campus. 11 workstations in library, computer center. Online course registration available.

Student life. Freshman orientation: Available. Preregistration for classes offered. **Activities:** Drama.

Athletics. Intercollegiate: Basketball, golf M, volleyball W. **Intramural:** Basketball. **Team name:** Panthers.

Student services. Adult student services, career counseling, on-campus daycare, personal counseling.

Contact. Phone: (740) 695-1720 Fax: (740) 695-7077
Kevin Chenoweth, Student Services Manager, Ohio University: Eastern Campus, 45425 National Road West, St. Clairsville, OH 43950

Ohio University: Lancaster Campus

Lancaster, Ohio
www.lancaster.ohiou.edu **CB code: 0826**

- Public 4-year branch campus college
- Large town
- 1,705 degree-seeking undergraduates

General. Founded in 1968. Regionally accredited. Some bachelor's and master's degrees available, awarded through Athens campus. **Degrees:** 72 associate awarded; master's offered. **ROTC:** Army, Navy, Air Force. **Location:** 30 miles from Columbus. **Calendar:** Quarter, extensive summer session. **Full-time faculty:** 31 total. **Part-time faculty:** 70 total.

Basis for selection. Open admission, but selective for some programs. Special requirements for business, education, engineering and communication programs. International students must take English fluency test through Ohio Program of Intensive English. ACT or SAT scores used in admission decisions to colleges of education, engineering.

2005-2006 Annual costs. Tuition/fees: $4,323; $8,646 out-of-state. Books/supplies: $500.

Financial aid. Additional information: Scholarship application deadline April 1.

Application procedures. Admission: No deadline. $20 fee, may be waived for applicants with need. Admission notification on a rolling basis. **Financial aid:** Priority date 2/15; no closing date. FAFSA required. Applicants notified on a rolling basis; must reply within 2 week(s) of notification.

Academics. Special study options: Cross-registration, double major, independent study, internships, student-designed major. **Credit/placement by examination:** CLEP, institutional tests. **Support services:** Learning center, remedial instruction, tutoring.

Computing on campus. 98 workstations in library, computer center. Online course registration, online library, helpline, student web hosting available.

Student life. Freshman orientation: Available. **Activities:** Choral groups, drama, student government, outdoor club, Young Democrats, Young Republicans, Christian Fellowship, adult support group.

Athletics. Intercollegiate: Baseball M, basketball, golf, softball W, tennis. **Intramural:** Skiing, table tennis, volleyball. **Team name:** Cougars.

Student services. Career counseling, student employment services, financial aid counseling, on-campus daycare, placement for graduates, veterans' counselor. **Physically disabled:** Services for visually, speech, hearing impaired.

Contact. Phone: (740) 654-6711 ext. 215 Toll-free number: (888) 446-4468 Fax: (740) 687-9497
Pat Fox, Coordinator Enrollment Management, Ohio University: Lancaster Campus, 1570 Granville Pike, Lancaster, OH 43130

Ohio University: Southern Campus at Ironton

Ironton, Ohio
www.southern.ohiou.edu **CB code: 1912**

- Public 4-year branch campus college
- Commuter campus in large town
- 2,000 degree-seeking undergraduates

General. Founded in 1956. Regionally accredited. Student body reflects both traditional (40%) and non-traditional (60%) students who commute to all classes from 3-state area (OH, KY, WV). **Degrees:** 129 associate awarded; master's offered. **Location:** 20 miles from Huntington, West Virginia. **Calendar:** Quarter. **Full-time faculty:** 30 total. **Part-time faculty:** 115 total. **Special facilities:** Microwave link with main campus and other regional campuses.

Basis for selection. Open admission. Nursing applicants must have associate degree or diploma.

2005-2006 Annual costs. Tuition/fees: $4,146; $5,868 out-of-state. Books/supplies: $600.

Application procedures. Admission: No deadline. $20 fee, may be waived for applicants with need. Admission notification on a rolling basis. **Financial aid:** No deadline. FAFSA required. Applicants notified on a rolling basis.

Academics. Special study options: Dual enrollment of high school students, student-designed major, teacher certification program. **Credit/placement by examination:** CLEP, institutional tests. **Support services:** Learning center, tutoring.

Majors. Business: Business admin. **Education:** Elementary. **Health:** Nursing (RN). **Protective services:** Criminal justice.

Student life. Freshman orientation: Available. Preregistration for classes offered. **Activities:** Literary magazine, music ensembles, radio station, student government, student newspaper, Los Amigos Internacionales Club, Travel and Tourism Club.

Athletics. Intercollegiate: Equestrian.

Student services. Career counseling, personal counseling, placement for graduates, veterans' counselor.

Contact. E-mail: askousc@mail.southern.ohiou.edu
Phone: (740) 533-4600 Toll-free number: (800) 626-0513
Fax: (740) 533-4632
Kim Lawson, Director of Enrollment Services, Ohio University: Southern Campus at Ironton, 1804 Liberty Avenue, Ironton, OH 45638

Ohio University: Zanesville Campus

Zanesville, Ohio
www.zanesville.ohiou.edu **CB code: 0846**

- Public 4-year branch campus college
- Commuter campus in large town
- 1,748 degree-seeking undergraduates: 37% part-time, 71% women
- 56 degree-seeking graduate students

General. Founded in 1946. Regionally accredited. **Degrees:** 102 associate awarded; master's offered. **Location:** 55 miles from Columbus. **Calendar:** Quarter, limited summer session. **Full-time faculty:** 33 total. **Part-time faculty:** 74 total.

Basis for selection. Open admission, but selective for some programs. Nursing admissions based on National League for Nursing test scores, high school GPA, and class rank. Admission to Colleges of Business, Engineering, and Communication based on high school rank and ACT scores. Essay, audition, and portfolio recommended for all; interview recommended for nursing program.

High school preparation. Recommended units include English 4, mathematics 3, social studies 3, science 3 and foreign language 2. One year of visual or performing arts recommended.

2005-2006 Annual costs. Tuition/fees: $4,323; $8,646 out-of-state. Books/supplies: $1,000. Personal expenses: $879.

Application procedures. Admission: No deadline. $20 fee, may be waived for applicants with need. Application may be submitted online. Admission notification on a rolling basis beginning on or about 1/1. **Financial aid:** Priority date 3/15; no closing date. FAFSA required. Applicants notified on a rolling basis starting 4/15; must reply within 2 week(s) of notification.

Academics. Special study options: Cross-registration, double major, dual enrollment of high school students, independent study, student-designed major, study abroad, teacher certification program. **Credit/placement by examination:** AP, CLEP, institutional tests. **Support services:** Learning center, reduced course load, remedial instruction, tutoring.

Majors. Business: General. **Communications:** Health, organizational. **Education:** Early childhood, middle. **Public administration:** Human services.

Computing on campus. 50 workstations in library, computer center. Commuter students can connect to campus network. Online course registration, online library, wireless network available.

Student life. Freshman orientation: Mandatory. Preregistration for classes offered. **Activities:** Literary magazine, radio station, student government, cultural events committee, student nursing association.

Athletics. Intercollegiate: Baseball M, basketball, golf, tennis, volleyball W. **Intramural:** Badminton, basketball, bowling, golf, skiing, table tennis, tennis, volleyball. **Team name:** Tracers.

Student services. Campus ministries, career counseling, student employment services, personal counseling, placement for graduates, veterans' counselor.

Contact. E-mail: ouzservices@ohio.edu
Phone: (740) 588-1439 Fax: (740) 588-1444
Monica Jones, Director of Student Services, Ohio University: Zanesville Campus, 1425 Newark Road, Zanesville, OH 43701

Ohio Wesleyan University

Delaware, Ohio **CB member**
http://web.owu.edu **CB code: 1594**

- Private 4-year liberal arts college affiliated with United Methodist Church
- Residential campus in large town
- 1,956 degree-seeking undergraduates: 1% part-time, 52% women, 5% African American, 2% Asian American, 1% Hispanic American, 8% international
- 75% of applicants admitted
- SAT or ACT (ACT writing optional), application essay required
- 68% graduate within 6 years; 33% enter graduate study

General. Founded in 1842. Regionally accredited. **Degrees:** 400 bachelor's awarded. **ROTC:** Army, Air Force. **Location:** 20 miles from Columbus. **Calendar:** Semester, limited summer session. **Full-time faculty:** 130 total; 100% have terminal degrees, 8% minority, 37% women. **Part-time faculty:** 61 total; 41% have terminal degrees, 10% minority, 48% women. **Class size:** 58% < 20, 38% 20-39, 4% 40-49, less than 1% 50-99. **Special facilities:** Art museum, 2 observatories, US Department of Agriculture laboratories, 2 nature field study preserves, science center; fine arts facilities.

Freshman class profile. 2,929 applied, 2,187 admitted, 595 enrolled.

Mid 50% test scores		**Rank in top tenth:**	30%
SAT verbal:	550-660	**End year in good standing:**	80%
SAT math:	570-660	**Return as sophomores:**	81%
ACT:	24-29	**Out-of-state:**	43%
GPA 3.50 or higher:	38%	**Live on campus:**	96%
GPA 3.0-3.49:	30%	**International:**	8%
GPA 2.0-2.99:	31%	**Fraternities:**	24%
Rank in top quarter:	52%	**Sororities:**	18%

Basis for selection. Secondary school record (level of challenge and success) most important, followed by class rank, recommendations, test scores, essay, extracurricular activities, general aptitude, character, volunteerism, alumni affiliation. Special consideration given to music and theater talent. TOEFL required of non-native speakers of English. Interview recommended for all. Audition required for music programs. Portfolio recommended for art programs. Essay required of all applicants. **Homeschooled:** Statement describing homeschool structure and mission, state high school equivalency certificate, letter of recommendation (nonparent) required.

High school preparation. 16 units required. Required and recommended units include English 4, mathematics 3-4, social studies 3-4, science 3-4 and foreign language 3-4.

2006-2007 Annual costs. Tuition/fees: $30,290. Room/board: $7,790.

2005-2006 Financial aid. Need-based: 420 full-time freshmen applied for aid; 351 were judged to have need; 351 of these received aid. Average need met was 85%. Average scholarship/grant was $15,595; average loan $3,245. 76% of total undergraduate aid awarded as scholarships/grants, 24% as loans/jobs. **Non-need-based:** Awarded to 840 full-time undergraduates, including 239 freshmen. Scholarships awarded for academics, alumni affiliation, art, leadership, minority status, music/drama, religious affiliation, state residency.

Application procedures. Admission: Priority date 3/1; deadline 5/1 (postmark date). $35 fee, may be waived for applicants with need. Application may be submitted online. Admission notification on a rolling basis beginning on or about 10/1. Must reply by May 1 or within 2 week(s) if notified thereafter. **Financial aid:** Priority date 3/1, closing date 5/1. FAFSA, institutional form required. Applicants notified on a rolling basis starting 2/15; must reply by 5/1 or within 2 week(s) of notification.

Academics. Students assigned to academic adviser during freshman year. Students encouraged to have consistent contact with advisers. Mentoring relationships with advisers encouraged. **Special study options:** Double major, dual enrollment of high school students, exchange student, honors, independent study, internships, New York semester, student-designed major, study abroad, teacher certification program, United Nations semester, urban semester, Washington semester. 3-2 engineering programs with Washington University (MO), Case Western Reserve University, California Institute of Technology (CA), Rensselaer Polytechnic Institute (NY), Alfred College of Ceramics (NY), and Polytechnic Institute of New York. **Credit/placement by examination:** AP, CLEP, IB, SAT, ACT, institutional tests. International Baccalaureate credit is given for specific performance levels on the higher exams. Students may receive exemption from certain requirements for test scores on the SAT, SAT Subject Tests or ACT. **Support services:** Learning center, study skills assistance, tutoring, writing center.

Majors. Area/ethnic studies: African-American, East Asian, women's. **Biology:** General, bacteriology, biochemistry, botany, genetics, microbiology, zoology. **Business:** Accounting, international, managerial economics. **Communications:** Broadcast journalism, journalism. **Computer sciences:** General, computer science. **Conservation:** Environmental studies. **Education:** General, art, biology, chemistry, drama/dance, early childhood, elementary, foreign languages, French, German, health, kindergarten/preschool, Latin, mathematics, middle, multi-level teacher, music, physical, physics, science, secondary, social science, social studies, Spanish. **English:** American lit, British lit, composition, creative writing, English lit. **Foreign languages:** Biblical, classics, comparative lit, French, German, Latin, Spanish. **Health:** Predentistry, premedicine, preveterinary. **History:** General. **Interdisciplinary:** Ancient studies, medieval/Renaissance, neuroscience. **Legal studies:** Prelaw. **Liberal arts:** Arts/sciences. **Math:** General, statistics. **Philosophy/religion:** Philosophy, religion. **Physical sciences:** Astronomy, chemistry, geology, physics. **Psychology:** General. **Social sciences:** Anthropology, economics, geography, international relations, political science, sociology, U.S. government, urban studies. **Theology:** Preministerial. **Visual/performing arts:** Art history/conservation, dance, dramatic, music performance, studio arts.

Most popular majors. Biology 14%, business/marketing 14%, psychology 11%, social sciences 18%, visual/performing arts 7%.

Computing on campus. 300 workstations in dormitories, library, computer center, student center. Dormitories wired for high-speed internet access and linked to campus network. Commuter students can connect to campus network. Online library, helpline, repair service, student web hosting, wireless network available.

Student life. Freshman orientation: Mandatory. Preregistration for classes offered. 2 day session held in June and week before classes begin in August. **Housing:** Guaranteed on-campus for all undergraduates. Coed dorms, single-sex dorms, apartments, fraternity/sorority housing, substance-free housing available. $300 nonrefundable deposit, deadline 5/1. Theme housing (unavailable to freshmen) for groups of 10-15 available. **Activities:** Bands, choral groups, dance, drama, literary magazine, music ensembles, musical theater, opera, radio station, student government, student newspaper, symphony orchestra, B'nai B'rith Hillel Chapter, Christian Fellowship, Young Democrats, College Republicans, Student Union on Black Awareness, Sisters United, Tauheed, Gay, Lesbian, Bisexual and Transgender Center, women's resource center, Habitat for Humanity.

Athletics. NCAA. **Intercollegiate:** Baseball M, basketball, cross-country, diving, field hockey W, football (tackle) M, golf M, lacrosse, sailing, soccer, softball W, swimming, tennis, track and field, volleyball W. **Intramural:** Badminton, basketball, equestrian, football (tackle) M, golf, handball, lacrosse, racquetball, soccer, softball, squash, swimming, tennis, track and field, volleyball, water polo. **Team name:** Battling Bishops.

Student services. Alcohol/substance abuse counseling, campus ministries, career counseling, student employment services, financial aid counseling, health services, minority student services, on-campus daycare, personal counseling.

Contact. E-mail: owuadmit@owu.edu
Phone: (740) 368-3020 Toll-free number: (800) 922-8953
Fax: (740) 368-3314
Carol DelPropost, Assistant Vice President of Admission and Financial Aid, Ohio Wesleyan University, 75 South Sandusky Street, Delaware, OH 43015-2398

Otterbein College

Westerville, Ohio **CB member**
www.otterbein.edu **CB code: 1597**

- Private 4-year liberal arts college affiliated with United Methodist Church
- Residential campus in large town
- 2,724 degree-seeking undergraduates: 17% part-time, 65% women
- 370 graduate students
- 50% of applicants admitted
- SAT or ACT (ACT writing optional) required
- 61% graduate within 6 years

General. Founded in 1847. Regionally accredited. **Degrees:** 470 bachelor's awarded; master's offered. **ROTC:** Army, Air Force. **Location:** 12 miles from Columbus. **Calendar:** Quarter, limited summer session. **Full-time faculty:** 152 total; 95% have terminal degrees, 11% minority, 52% women. **Part-time faculty:** 119 total. **Special facilities:** Observatory, 3 performance stages, stables.

Freshman class profile. 2,708 applied, 1,346 admitted, 630 enrolled.

Basis for selection. School achievement record most important; test scores also important. Recommendations, essay, interview, and extracurricular activities considered. Students applying between May 1 and June 1 accepted on space-available basis. Visit recommended for all; audition required for music and theater programs; portfolio recommended for visual art program. Essays required for scholarships. **Homeschooled:** Statement describing homeschool structure and mission, transcript of courses and grades required. Submit written documentation of successful completion of college preparatory high school equivalency. Transcripts from cooperating school district preferred. **Learning Disabled:** Students with diagnosed learning disabilities recommended to send documentation with admission application.

High school preparation. Recommended units include English 4, mathematics 3, social studies 3, science 3 and foreign language 2. One unit in fine arts recommended.

2005-2006 Annual costs. Tuition/fees: $22,518. Room/board: $6,468. Books/supplies: $700. Personal expenses: $1,017.

Financial aid. Non-need-based: Scholarships awarded for academics, alumni affiliation, art, leadership, minority status, music/drama, state residency.

Application procedures. Admission: Priority date 2/1; no deadline. $25 fee, may be waived for applicants with need. Application may be submitted online. Admission notification on a rolling basis beginning on or about 10/1. Must reply by May 1 or within 4 week(s) if notified thereafter. **Financial aid:** Priority date 4/1; no closing date. FAFSA, CSS PROFILE required. Applicants notified on a rolling basis starting 2/15; must reply by 5/1.

Academics. Special study options: Accelerated study, combined bachelor's/graduate degree, cross-registration, double major, dual enrollment of high school students, exchange student, honors, independent study, internships, liberal arts/career combination, semester at sea, student-designed major, study abroad, teacher certification program, Washington semester, weekend college. BA/BS in engineering with Washington University (MO) or Case Western Reserve University. **Credit/placement by examination:** AP, CLEP, institutional tests. 60 credit hours maximum toward bachelor's degree. **Support services:** Learning center, reduced course load, remedial instruction, study skills assistance, tutoring, writing center.

Honors college/program. Presidential Scholars must be in top 10% of high school class and have minimum composite ACT score of 25.

Majors. Agriculture: Equestrian studies. **Biology:** General, biochemistry, molecular. **Business:** General, accounting, business admin, finance, managerial economics. **Communications:** General, broadcast journalism, journalism, organizational, public relations. **Computer sciences:** Computer science. **Conservation:** General, environmental studies, management/policy. **Education:** General, art, biology, chemistry, early childhood, elementary, English, foreign languages, French, health, history, mathematics, middle, multi-level teacher, music, physical, physics, science, secondary, social studies, Spanish, special. **English:** Composition, creative writing, English lit. **Foreign languages:** French, Spanish. **Health:** Athletic training, nursing (RN), predentistry, premedicine, prepharmacy, preveterinary. **History:** General. **Legal studies:** Prelaw. **Math:** General. **Parks/recreation:** Health/fitness, sports admin. **Philosophy/religion:** Philosophy, religion. **Physical sciences:** Chemistry, physics. **Psychology:** General. **Social sciences:** Economics, international relations, political science, sociology. **Visual/performing arts:** General, acting, art, dramatic, music history, music performance, music theory/composition, theater design.

Most popular majors. Business/marketing 9%, communications/journalism 11%, education 11%, health sciences 6%, psychology 6%.

Computing on campus. 124 workstations in dormitories, library, computer center. Dormitories wired for high-speed internet access and linked to campus network. Commuter students can connect to campus network. Online course registration, helpline, wireless network available.

Student life. Freshman orientation: Mandatory. Preregistration for classes offered. One-day orientation held in July or August. **Policies:** Freshmen permitted cars on campus. **Housing:** Guaranteed on-campus for freshmen. Coed dorms, single-sex dorms, apartments, fraternity/sorority housing available. Theme housing available. **Activities:** Bands, choral groups, dance, drama, literary magazine, music ensembles, musical theater, opera, radio station, student government, student newspaper, symphony orchestra, TV station, Fellowship of Christian Athletes, Christian support group, Afro-American student union, Asian American student union, international students association, Religious Life Council.

Athletics. NCAA. **Intercollegiate:** Baseball M, basketball, cross-country, equestrian, football (tackle) M, golf, soccer, softball W, tennis, track and field, volleyball W. **Intramural:** Basketball, bowling, football (non-tackle) M, handball, racquetball, soccer, softball, volleyball. **Team name:** Cardinals.

Student services. Adult student services, campus ministries, career counseling, student employment services, financial aid counseling, health services, minority student services, personal counseling, placement for graduates. **Physically disabled:** Services for visually, hearing impaired.

Contact. E-mail: uotterb@otterbein.edu
Phone: (614) 823-1500 Toll-free number: (800) 488-8144
Fax: (614) 823-1200
Cass Johnson, Director of Admission, Otterbein College, One Otterbein College, Westerville, OH 43081

Pontifical College Josephinum

Columbus, Ohio
www.pcj.edu **CB code: 1348**

- Private 4-year liberal arts and seminary college for men affiliated with Roman Catholic Church
- Residential campus in very large city
- 76 degree-seeking undergraduates: 1% Asian American, 3% Hispanic American, 4% international
- 59 degree-seeking graduate students
- 80% of applicants admitted
- SAT or ACT (ACT writing optional), application essay, interview required
- 60% graduate within 6 years; 95% enter graduate study

General. Founded in 1892. Regionally accredited; also accredited by ATS. **Degrees:** 19 bachelor's awarded; master's, first professional offered. **Calendar:** Semester. **Full-time faculty:** 10 total; 60% have terminal degrees, 10% minority, 40% women. **Part-time faculty:** 14 total; 50% have terminal degrees, 7% minority, 43% women. **Class size:** 84% < 20, 16% 20-39.

Freshman class profile. 5 applied, 4 admitted, 4 enrolled.

End year in good standing:	85%	**Out-of-state:**	33%
Return as sophomores:	84%	**Live on campus:**	100%

Basis for selection. School achievement record, recommendations from pastor and director of vocations required.

High school preparation. 10 units required; 18 recommended. Required and recommended units include English 4, mathematics 2-4, social studies 2-4, science 1-4 and foreign language 1-2.

2005-2006 Annual costs. Tuition/fees: $14,635. Room/board: $7,000. Books/supplies: $350. Personal expenses: $2,500.

2004-2005 Financial aid. All financial aid based on need. 9 full-time freshmen applied for aid; 4 were judged to have need; 4 of these received aid. Average need met was 82%. Average scholarship/grant was $1,000; average loan $2,625. 70% of total undergraduate aid awarded as scholarships/grants, 30% as loans/jobs.

Application procedures. Admission: Priority date 8/1; no deadline. $25 fee, may be waived for applicants with need. Application must be submitted on paper. Admission notification on a rolling basis beginning on or about 5/1. **Financial aid:** Priority date 9/2; no closing date. FAFSA, institutional form required. Applicants notified on a rolling basis starting 8/15; must reply within 2 week(s) of notification.

Academics. Students participate in supervised field experience and clinical pastoral education. **Special study options:** Double major, ESL, honors, independent study. **Credit/placement by examination:** AP, CLEP, institutional tests. 30 credit hours maximum toward bachelor's degree. **Support services:** Learning center, reduced course load, remedial instruction, tutoring, writing center.

Majors. Area/ethnic studies: Hispanic-American/Latino/Chicano, Latin American. **English:** English lit. **History:** General. **Liberal arts:** Arts/sciences, humanities. **Philosophy/religion:** Philosophy, religion.

Most popular majors. English 8%, philosophy/religious studies 76%.

Computing on campus. 16 workstations in library, computer center. Dormitories wired for high-speed internet access and linked to campus network. Online library available.

Student life. Freshman orientation: Mandatory. **Policies:** Daily chapel, evening prayer. Religious observance required. Freshmen permitted cars on campus. **Activities:** Choral groups, music ensembles, student government, Latin American Studies Organization.

Athletics. Intramural: Basketball M, soccer M, softball M.

Student services. Career counseling, health services, personal counseling.

Contact. Phone: (614) 985-2241 Toll-free number: (888) 252-5812
Fax: (614) 885-2307
Perry Cahall, DIrector of Admissions, Pontifical College Josephinum, 7625 North High Street, Columbus, OH 43235-1499

Rabbinical College of Telshe
Wickliffe, Ohio
CB code: 1660

- Private 4-year rabbinical and teachers college for men affiliated with Jewish faith
- Small city
- 36 degree-seeking undergraduates
- 100% of applicants admitted

General. Founded in 1941. Accredited by AARTS. **Degrees:** 5 bachelor's awarded; master's, doctoral offered. **Calendar:** Semester. **Full-time faculty:** 9 total. **Part-time faculty:** 12 total.

Freshman class profile. 19 applied, 19 admitted, 19 enrolled.

Basis for selection. Personal interview and religious commitment most important.

2006-2007 Annual costs. Tuition/fees (projected): $6,800. Room/board: $3,300. Books/supplies: $300. Personal expenses: $1,000.

Application procedures. Admission: Closing date 8/15. $100 fee.

Academics. Credit/placement by examination: CLEP.

Majors. Theology: Talmudic.

Student life. Freshman orientation: Mandatory. Preregistration for classes offered.

Contact. Phone: (440) 943-5300 Fax: (440) 943-5303
Rabbi Abraham Matitia, Registrar, Rabbinical College of Telshe, 28400 Euclid Avenue, Wickliffe, OH 44092-2584

Shawnee State University
Portsmouth, Ohio
www.shawnee.edu
CB code: 1790

- Public 4-year university
- Commuter campus in large town
- 3,017 degree-seeking undergraduates: 14% part-time, 59% women, 3% African American, 1% Native American, 1% international

General. Founded in 1986. Regionally accredited. **Degrees:** 337 bachelor's, 204 associate awarded. **Location:** 90 miles from Columbus, 90 miles from Cincinnati. **Calendar:** Quarter, extensive summer session. **Full-time faculty:** 138 total; 54% have terminal degrees, 5% minority, 41% women. **Part-time faculty:** 160 total; 2% minority, 47% women. **Class size:** 60% < 20, 35% 20-39, 2% 40-49, 3% 50-99. **Special facilities:** Fine arts center, planetarium.

Freshman class profile. 2,917 applied, 2,917 admitted, 870 enrolled.

Mid 50% test scores		**Out-of-state:**	8%
ACT:	17-23	**Live on campus:**	21%
Rank in top quarter:	34%	**International:**	2%
Rank in top tenth:	15%	**Fraternities:**	6%
Return as sophomores:	64%	**Sororities:**	7%

Basis for selection. Open admission, but selective for some programs. For admission to allied health programs: ACT required, interview recommended. **Homeschooled:** GED is required.

High school preparation. 16 units recommended. Recommended units include English 4, mathematics 3, social studies 3, science 3 and foreign language 2. Algebra, biology, chemistry required for allied health programs.

2005-2006 Annual costs. Tuition/fees: $5,508; $9,396 out-of-state. Room/board: $6,729. Books/supplies: $1,800. Personal expenses: $2,072.

Financial aid. Non-need-based: Scholarships awarded for academics. **Additional information:** ACT recommended for scholarship applicants.

Application procedures. Admission: No deadline. No application fee. Application may be submitted online. Admission notification on a rolling basis. Applicants to allied health programs advised to apply by February 1. **Financial aid:** Priority date 6/15; no closing date. FAFSA, institutional form required. Applicants notified on a rolling basis starting 5/1; must reply within 4 week(s) of notification.

Academics. Special study options: Cross-registration, double major, dual enrollment of high school students, honors, independent study, internships, student-designed major, study abroad, teacher certification program, Washington semester. **Credit/placement by examination:** AP, CLEP, institutional tests. SAT or ACT may be used in lieu of university-developed placement test. **Support services:** Learning center, pre-admission summer program, reduced course load, remedial instruction, study skills assistance, tutoring, writing center.

Majors. Biology: General. **Business:** Business admin, management information systems. **Education:** General, biology, chemistry, early childhood, history, kindergarten/preschool, mathematics, multi-level teacher, science, social science. **Engineering technology:** Computer, electrical, environmental, plastics. **Health:** Athletic training, nursing (RN), premedicine, prepharmacy, preveterinary. **History:** General. **Math:** General. **Parks/recreation:** Health/fitness, sports admin. **Physical sciences:** Atmospheric science, chemistry. **Psychology:** General. **Social sciences:** General, international relations, sociology. **Visual/performing arts:** General, ceramics, drawing, painting, photography, studio arts.

Most popular majors. Biology 6%, business/marketing 26%, education 12%, engineering/engineering technologies 6%, health sciences 6%, psychology 9%, social sciences 15%.

Computing on campus. 620 workstations in library, computer center, student center. Dormitories wired for high-speed internet access. Commuter students can connect to campus network. Online course registration, helpline, wireless network available.

Student life. Freshman orientation: Mandatory. Preregistration for classes offered. Various 1-day programs held throughout the summer. **Policies:** Freshmen permitted cars on campus. **Housing:** Coed dorms available. $35 nonrefundable deposit, deadline 6/30. **Activities:** Choral groups, drama, literary magazine, music ensembles, musical theater, student government, student newspaper, campus ministry, Health Executives and Administrators Learning Society, student programming board.

Athletics. NAIA. **Intercollegiate:** Baseball M, basketball, cross-country, golf M, soccer, softball W, tennis W, volleyball W. **Intramural:** Basketball, bowling, golf, racquetball, softball M, swimming, table tennis, tennis, volleyball. **Team name:** Bears.

Student services. Alcohol/substance abuse counseling, career counseling, services for economically disadvantaged, student employment services, financial aid counseling, health services, on-campus daycare, personal counseling, placement for graduates, veterans' counselor. **Physically disabled:** Services for visually, speech, hearing impaired.

Contact. E-mail: to_ssu@shawnee.edu
Phone: (740) 351-4778 Toll-free number: (800) 959-2778
Fax: (740) 351-3111
Bob Trusz, Director of Admissions, Shawnee State University, 940 Second Street, Portsmouth, OH 45662

Tiffin University
Tiffin, Ohio
www.tiffin.edu
CB member
CB code: 1817

- Private 4-year university and business college
- Residential campus in large town
- 1,180 degree-seeking undergraduates: 7% part-time, 52% women, 16% African American, 2% Hispanic American, 2% international
- 370 degree-seeking graduate students
- 73% of applicants admitted
- SAT or ACT (ACT writing optional) required
- 31% graduate within 6 years

General. Founded in 1888. Regionally accredited. Emphasis on business and criminal justice studies. Off-campus courses offered in Lima, Lorain, Columbus, Elyria and online. **Degrees:** 218 bachelor's, 5 associate awarded; master's offered. **ROTC:** Army. **Location:** 50 miles from Toledo, 90 miles from Columbus. **Calendar:** Semester, limited summer session. **Full-time faculty:** 51 total; 71% have terminal degrees, 16% minority, 33% women. **Part-time faculty:** 82 total; 21% have terminal degrees, 8% minority, 45% women. **Class size:** 66% < 20, 30% 20-39, 3% 40-49.

Freshman class profile. 1,563 applied, 1,138 admitted, 284 enrolled.

Mid 50% test scores		Return as sophomores:	60%
SAT verbal:	380-520	Out-of-state:	15%
SAT math:	430-540	Live on campus:	93%
ACT:	18-22	International:	2%
GPA 3.50 or higher:	25%	Fraternities:	1%
GPA 3.0-3.49:	29%	Sororities:	2%
GPA 2.0-2.99:	44%		

Basis for selection. Test scores, GPA very important. Students below 2.0 GPA may be admitted conditionally into Learning Assistance Program. Interview required for academically weak applicants.

High school preparation. Required units include English 4, mathematics 3, social studies 3 and science 3.

2006-2007 Annual costs. Tuition/fees (projected): $15,870. Room/board: $6,775. Books/supplies: $1,200. Personal expenses: $2,200.

2005-2006 Financial aid. Need-based: 269 full-time freshmen applied for aid; 242 were judged to have need; 242 of these received aid. Average need met was 11%. Average scholarship/grant was $4,397; average loan $2,467. 47% of total undergraduate aid awarded as scholarships/grants, 53% as loans/jobs. **Non-need-based:** Awarded to 1,086 full-time undergraduates, including 279 freshmen. Scholarships awarded for academics, alumni affiliation, athletics, leadership, music/drama, state residency.

Application procedures. Admission: No deadline. $20 fee. Application may be submitted online. Admission notification on a rolling basis beginning on or about 9/1. **Financial aid:** Priority date 1/1; no closing date. FAFSA required. Applicants notified on a rolling basis starting 2/15; must reply within 2 week(s) of notification.

Academics. Special study options: Accelerated study, combined bachelor's/graduate degree, cross-registration, distance learning, double major, dual enrollment of high school students, ESL, honors, independent study, internships, study abroad, teacher certification program, Washington semester. **Credit/placement by examination:** AP, CLEP, IB, SAT, ACT, institutional tests. 15 credit hours maximum toward associate degree, 30 toward bachelor's. **Support services:** Learning center, pre-admission summer program, reduced course load, remedial instruction, study skills assistance, tutoring.

Majors. Business: Accounting, business admin, finance, hospitality admin, human resources, international, logistics, marketing, nonprofit/public. **Communications:** General. **Computer sciences:** Information systems. **Education:** General. **English:** English lit. **Liberal arts:** Arts/sciences. **Parks/recreation:** Sports admin. **Protective services:** Corrections, law enforcement admin. **Psychology:** General. **Social sciences:** International relations. **Visual/performing arts:** Arts management.

Most popular majors. Business/marketing 60%, parks/recreation 9%, psychology 10%, security/protective services 16%.

Computing on campus. 80 workstations in library, computer center, student center. Dormitories wired for high-speed internet access and linked to campus network. Commuter students can connect to campus network. Online course registration, online library, helpline, wireless network available.

Student life. Freshman orientation: Available, $25 fee. Preregistration for classes offered. Three-part program; first part occurs on a Saturday in April or May, or on a Friday in June; second part is a weekend in late July; third part occurs during first weekend of classes. **Policies:** Lower-division residential students required to be on meal plan. All undergraduates complete 26 hours of co-curricular credit. Freshmen permitted cars on campus. **Housing:** Guaranteed on-campus for freshmen. Coed dorms, special housing for disabled, apartments, fraternity/sorority housing available. Leadership Hall/Living Learning Community. **Activities:** Bands, choral groups, dance, drama, literary magazine, music ensembles, musical theater, student government, student newspaper, Black United Students, Chamber of Fools, world student organization, Greek council, Campus Crusade for Christ, Delta Sigma Kappa, gospel choir, Habitat for Humanity.

Athletics. NAIA, NCAA. **Intercollegiate:** Baseball M, basketball, cross-country, football (tackle) M, golf, soccer, softball, squash W, tennis, track and field, volleyball W. **Team name:** Dragons.

Student services. Adult student services, career counseling, student employment services, financial aid counseling, personal counseling, placement for graduates, veterans' counselor.

Contact. E-mail: admissions@tiffin.edu
Phone: (419) 447-6443 Toll-free number: (800) 968-6446 ext. 3423
Fax: (419) 443-5006
Cam Cruickshank, Vice President for Admissions & Student Affairs, Tiffin University, 155 Miami Street, Tiffin, OH 44883

Tri-State Bible College

South Point, Ohio
www.tsbc.edu

- Private 4-year Bible college
- Commuter campus in small town

General. Accredited by ABHE. **Calendar:** Semester.

Annual costs/financial aid. Tuition/fees (2005-2006): $5,390.

Contact. Phone: (740) 377-2520
506 Margaret Street, South Point, OH 45680

Union Institute & University

Cincinnati, Ohio
www.tui.edu **CB code: 0732**

- Private 4-year university and liberal arts college
- Commuter campus in very large city
- 1,122 degree-seeking undergraduates: 40% part-time, 68% women, 24% African American, 1% Asian American, 8% Hispanic American, 1% Native American
- 1,257 degree-seeking graduate students
- Application essay, interview required

General. Founded in 1964. Regionally accredited. Additional campus in Montpelier, VT; academic centers in Brattleboro, VT; North Miami Beach, FL; Los Angeles and Sacramento, CA. Many courses available through distance (internet-based) learning. Serves adult learners through individualized programs, carried out through faculty-mentored independent study and research. **Degrees:** 455 bachelor's awarded; master's, doctoral offered. **Location:** 2 miles from downtown. **Calendar:** Differs by program, extensive summer session. **Full-time faculty:** 52 total. **Part-time faculty:** 127 total.

Freshman class profile. 29 enrolled.

Basis for selection. Essay, interview, and transcripts from previously attended colleges most important. Maturity and evidence of ability to engage in self-directed learning is also key. Programs designed for adult learners; majority are over age 25.

2005-2006 Annual costs. Tuition/fees: $11,120. Books/supplies: $1,000. Personal expenses: $80.

2004-2005 Financial aid. Need-based: 36% of total undergraduate aid awarded as scholarships/grants, 64% as loans/jobs. **Non-need-based:** Scholarships awarded for academics, state residency.

Application procedures. Admission: No deadline. $35 fee. Application may be submitted online. Admission notification on a rolling basis. **Financial aid:** No deadline. FAFSA, institutional form required. Must reply within 4 week(s) of notification.

Academics. Individual tutorial-based courses. **Special study options:** Distance learning, double major, external degree, independent study, student-designed major, weekend college. **Credit/placement by examination:** CLEP. 32 credit hours maximum toward bachelor's degree. **Support services:** Learning center, study skills assistance, writing center.

Majors. Biology: General. **Business:** General, business admin, management information systems, organizational behavior, training/development. **Communications:** General. **Computer sciences:** General, information systems. **Education:** General, early childhood, elementary, ESL, special. **Health:** Health services, maternal/child health, substance abuse counseling. **History:** General. **Liberal arts:** Arts/sciences, humanities. **Protective services:** Criminal justice, law enforcement admin. **Psychology:** General. **Public administration:** General, social work. **Social sciences:** General, sociology. **Visual/performing arts:** General.

Most popular majors. Business/marketing 15%, education 18%, liberal arts 17%, psychology 8%, security/protective services 26%.

Computing on campus. 49 workstations in library, computer center. Commuter students can connect to campus network. Online course registration, online library, helpline available.

Student life. Freshman orientation: Available. Preregistration for classes offered. **Policies:** Programs for working adults. Freshmen permitted cars on campus.

Student services. Adult student services, financial aid counseling. **Physically disabled:** Services for visually, speech, hearing impaired.

Contact. E-mail: admissions@tui.edu
Phone: (513) 861-6400 Toll-free number: (800) 486-3116
Fax: (513) 861-3218
Carolyn Turner, Admissions Director, Union Institute & University, 440 East McMillan Street, Cincinnati, OH 45206-1925

University of Akron

Akron, Ohio — **CB member**
www.uakron.edu — **CB code: 1829**

- Public 4-year university
- Commuter campus in small city
- 16,288 degree-seeking undergraduates: 24% part-time, 52% women, 15% African American, 2% Asian American, 1% Hispanic American, 1% international
- 3,902 degree-seeking graduate students
- 82% of applicants admitted
- SAT or ACT (ACT writing optional) required
- 35% graduate within 6 years

General. Founded in 1870. Regionally accredited. **Degrees:** 2,271 bachelor's, 460 associate awarded; master's, doctoral, first professional offered. **ROTC:** Army, Air Force. **Location:** 40 miles from Cleveland. **Calendar:** Semester, limited summer session. **Full-time faculty:** 701 total; 85% have terminal degrees, 16% minority, 41% women. **Part-time faculty:** 773 total; 28% have terminal degrees, 8% minority, 53% women. **Class size:** 44% < 20, 46% 20-39, 4% 40-49, 5% 50-99, 1% >100. **Special facilities:** Performing arts hall.

Freshman class profile. 8,810 applied, 7,267 admitted, 3,082 enrolled.

Mid 50% test scores		**GPA 2.0-2.99:**	43%
SAT verbal:	440-570	**Rank in top quarter:**	18%
SAT math:	440-590	**Rank in top tenth:**	12%
ACT:	17-24	**Return as sophomores:**	64%
GPA 3.50 or higher:	25%	**Out-of-state:**	3%
GPA 3.0-3.49:	26%	**Live on campus:**	48%

Basis for selection. Open admissions to Summit College and Wayne College; all other component colleges of university select on basis of some or all of the following criteria: college prep curriculum, GPA, test scores, class rank, activities, leadership, recommendations, essays, portfolios, and auditions. Conditional admission possible for applicants with GPA less than 2.3 or test scores lower than 16 ACT/650 SAT (exclusive of Writing). Essay, interview required for honors program; audition required for dance, music programs. **Homeschooled:** Students required to obtain letter of exemption from school district.

High school preparation. 15 units recommended. Recommended units include English 4, mathematics 3, social studies 3, science 3 and foreign language 2.

2005-2006 Annual costs. Tuition/fees: $7,958; $16,682 out-of-state. Room/board: $7,208. Books/supplies: $900. Personal expenses: $1,646.

2005-2006 Financial aid. Need-based: 2,300 full-time freshmen applied for aid; 1,847 were judged to have need; 1,847 of these received aid. Average need met was 47%. Average scholarship/grant was $4,513; average loan $2,519. 40% of total undergraduate aid awarded as scholarships/grants, 60% as loans/jobs. **Non-need-based:** Awarded to 4,159 full-time undergraduates, including 1,270 freshmen. Scholarships awarded for academics, art, athletics, leadership, minority status, music/drama, ROTC, state residency.

Application procedures. Admission: Closing date 8/1. $30 fee. Application may be submitted online. Admission notification on a rolling basis. Students who apply by February 1 eligible for March orientation. **Financial aid:** Priority date 2/1; no closing date. FAFSA, institutional form required. Applicants notified on a rolling basis starting 4/15; must reply within 2 week(s) of notification.

Academics. Special study options: Accelerated study, combined bachelor's/graduate degree, cooperative education, distance learning, double major, ESL, honors, independent study, internships, student-designed major, study abroad, teacher certification program, weekend college. Undergraduates may take graduate level classes. Co-op Programs: Arts, Business, Computer Science, Engineering, Family & Consumer Sciences, Humanities, Natural Science, Technologies. **Credit/placement by examination:** AP, CLEP, IB, SAT, ACT, institutional tests. 38 credit hours maximum toward associate degree, 38 toward bachelor's. **Support services:** Learning center, reduced course load, remedial instruction, study skills assistance, tutoring, writing center.

Honors college/program. Must have 2 out of 3 of following criteria: high school GPA 3.50; high school class rank in highest 10%; 27 ACT or 1200 SAT (exclusive of Writing). Some students with other unique qualifications may be admitted.

Majors. Architecture: Urban/community planning. **Biology:** General, animal physiology, bacteriology, botany, ecology, zoology. **Business:** General, accounting, finance, hotel/motel admin, human resources, insurance, international, management information systems, marketing. **Communications:** Media studies. **Computer sciences:** General, systems analysis. **Education:** General, art, business, drama/dance, elementary, English, family/consumer sciences, French, health, mathematics, middle, music, physical, science, social studies, Spanish, voc/tech. **Engineering:** General, biomedical, chemical, civil, computer, electrical, mechanical, polymer. **Engineering technology:** Construction, electrical, industrial, mechanical. **English:** English lit, speech/rhetoric. **Family/consumer sciences:** General, child development, clothing/textiles, family systems, housing. **Foreign languages:** Classics, French, Spanish. **Health:** Athletic training, audiology/speech pathology, dietetics, nursing (RN). **History:** General. **Liberal arts:** Arts/sciences, humanities. **Math:** General, statistics. **Military:** General. **Parks/recreation:** Exercise sciences, sports admin. **Philosophy/religion:** Philosophy. **Physical sciences:** Chemistry, geology, geophysics, physics, polymer chemistry. **Protective services:** Corrections, law enforcement admin. **Psychology:** General. **Public administration:** Social work. **Social sciences:** General, cartography, economics, geography, sociology, U.S. government. **Visual/performing arts:** Art, art history/conservation, ceramics, dance, metal/jewelry, music history, music performance, music theory/composition, musicology, photography, piano/organ, printmaking, sculpture, studio arts, voice/opera.

Most popular majors. Business/marketing 21%, communications/journalism 7%, education 17%, engineering/engineering technologies 9%, health sciences 11%.

Computing on campus. 2,900 workstations in dormitories, library, student center. Dormitories wired for high-speed internet access and linked to campus network. Commuter students can connect to campus network. Online course registration, online library, helpline, repair service, student web hosting, wireless network available.

Student life. Freshman orientation: Mandatory, $50 fee. Preregistration for classes offered. One-day program. **Policies:** Freshmen permitted cars on campus. **Housing:** Coed dorms, single-sex dorms, special housing for disabled, fraternity/sorority housing, substance-free housing available. $150 nonrefundable deposit, deadline 2/1. Honors housing available. **Activities:** Bands, choral groups, dance, drama, music ensembles, musical theater, radio station, student government, student newspaper, symphony orchestra, TV station, Akron Chinese Christian Fellwship, Campus Focus, Campus Habitat for Humanity, Christian Zips, College Democrats, College Republicans, Indian Students Association, Intervarsity Christian Fellowship, University Bible Fellowship, Chinese Student Organization.

Athletics. NCAA. **Intercollegiate:** Baseball M, basketball, cheerleading, cross-country, football (tackle) M, golf M, rifle, soccer, softball W, swimming W, tennis, track and field, volleyball W. **Intramural:** Badminton, basketball, bowling, cross-country, golf, racquetball, skiing, soccer, softball, swimming, table tennis, track and field, volleyball W, wrestling M. **Team name:** Zips.

Student services. Adult student services, alcohol/substance abuse counseling, career counseling, student employment services, financial aid counseling, health services, minority student services, on-campus daycare, personal counseling, placement for graduates, veterans' counselor, women's services. **Physically disabled:** Services for visually, speech, hearing impaired.

Contact. E-mail: admissions@uakron.edu
Phone: (330) 972-7077 Toll-free number: (800) 655-4884
Fax: (330) 972-7022
Diane Raybuck, Director of Admissions, University of Akron, 277 East Buchtel Common, Akron, OH 44325-2001

University of Cincinnati

Cincinnati, Ohio — **CB member**
www.uc.edu — **CB code: 1833**

- Public 4-year university
- Commuter campus in large city
- 18,860 degree-seeking undergraduates: 15% part-time, 50% women, 14% African American, 3% Asian American, 2% Hispanic American, 1% international
- 7,785 degree-seeking graduate students
- 76% of applicants admitted

- SAT or ACT with writing, application essay required
- 50% graduate within 6 years

General. Founded in 1819. Regionally accredited. **Degrees:** 2,938 bachelor's, 202 associate awarded; master's, doctoral, first professional offered. **ROTC:** Army, Air Force. **Location:** 2 miles from downtown. **Calendar:** Quarter, extensive summer session. **Full-time faculty:** 1,200 total; 67% have terminal degrees, 18% minority, 38% women. **Part-time faculty:** 41 total; 24% have terminal degrees, 10% minority, 56% women. **Class size:** 47% < 20, 42% 20-39, 5% 40-49, 4% 50-99, 2% >100. **Special facilities:** Observatory.

Freshman class profile. 11,813 applied, 8,975 admitted, 3,138 enrolled.

Mid 50% test scores			
SAT verbal:	500-620	Rank in top quarter:	48%
SAT math:	500-640	Rank in top tenth:	19%
ACT:	21-27	Return as sophomores:	79%
GPA 3.50 or higher:	44%	Out-of-state:	10%
GPA 3.0-3.49:	32%	Live on campus:	46%
GPA 2.0-2.99:	24%	International:	1%

Basis for selection. Secondary school record, test scores most important; recommendations considered. Interview required for music programs; audition required for dance, music programs. **Homeschooled:** Transcript of courses and grades required. Release for home schooling from local Board of Education required.

High school preparation. 16 units required. Required and recommended units include English 4, mathematics 3-4, social studies 2, history 1, science 2-3, foreign language 2 and academic electives 3. Specific requirements may vary for each college.

2005-2006 Annual costs. Tuition/fees: $8,883; $22,635 out-of-state. Room/board: $7,485. Books/supplies: $815. Personal expenses: $3,474.

2005-2006 Financial aid. Need-based: 2,921 full-time freshmen applied for aid; 2,322 were judged to have need; 2,273 of these received aid. Average need met was 63%. Average scholarship/grant was $5,393; average loan $3,408. 43% of total undergraduate aid awarded as scholarships/grants, 57% as loans/jobs. **Non-need-based:** Awarded to 5,273 full-time undergraduates, including 1,622 freshmen. Scholarships awarded for academics, alumni affiliation, art, athletics, leadership, minority status, music/drama, ROTC, state residency.

Application procedures. Admission: Priority date 1/15; deadline 9/1 (postmark date). $40 fee, may be waived for applicants with need. Application may be submitted online. Admission notification on a rolling basis beginning on or about 10/1. **Financial aid:** No deadline. FAFSA required. Applicants notified on a rolling basis starting 3/10; must reply within 2 week(s) of notification.

Academics. Some engineering programs require students to acquire personal computers. **Special study options:** Accelerated study, combined bachelor's/graduate degree, cooperative education, distance learning, double major, ESL, honors, independent study, internships, liberal arts/career combination, study abroad, teacher certification program, Washington semester, weekend college. Learning at Large (students earn college credit without attending regularly scheduled classes). **Credit/placement by examination:** AP, CLEP, institutional tests. **Support services:** Pre-admission summer program, remedial instruction, study skills assistance, tutoring, writing center.

Majors. Architecture: Architecture, urban/community planning. **Area/ethnic studies:** African-American, Asian, French, German, Latin American, Spanish/Iberian. **Biology:** General. **Business:** Accounting, business admin, finance, management information systems, management science, operations, real estate. **Communications:** General. **Computer sciences:** General. **Education:** Art, early childhood, elementary, health, music, secondary. **Engineering:** General, aerospace, chemical, civil, computer, electrical, mechanical, mechanics, metallurgical, nuclear. **English:** British lit. **Family/consumer sciences:** Food/nutrition. **Foreign languages:** Classics, comparative lit, French, German, Latin, linguistics, Spanish. **Health:** Audiology/speech pathology, clinical lab science, health care admin, nuclear medical technology, nursing (RN), predentistry, premedicine, prepharmacy, preveterinary. **History:** General. **Liberal arts:** Arts/sciences. **Math:** General. **Philosophy/religion:** Judaic, philosophy. **Physical sciences:** Chemistry, geology, physics. **Protective services:** Criminal justice. **Psychology:** General. **Public administration:** Social work. **Social sciences:** Anthropology, economics, geography, international relations, political science, sociology, urban studies. **Visual/performing arts:** Art history/conservation, commercial/advertising art, conducting, dance, dramatic, fashion design, industrial design, interior design, jazz, music history, music performance, music theory/composition, piano/organ, studio arts, theater design, voice/opera.

Most popular majors. Business/marketing 22%, education 6%, engineering/engineering technologies 14%, English 9%, health sciences 7%, security/protective services 6%, social sciences 7%, visual/performing arts 10%.

Computing on campus. 560 workstations in library, computer center. Dormitories linked to campus network. Commuter students can connect to campus network. Online course registration, helpline, repair service, wireless network available.

Student life. Freshman orientation: Available. Preregistration for classes offered. **Policies:** Freshmen permitted cars on campus. **Housing:** Guaranteed on-campus for freshmen. Coed dorms, single-sex dorms, fraternity/sorority housing available. **Activities:** Bands, choral groups, dance, drama, film society, music ensembles, musical theater, opera, radio station, student government, student newspaper, symphony orchestra, Women's Initiative Network, College Democrats, College Republicans.

Athletics. NCAA. **Intercollegiate:** Baseball M, basketball, cross-country, diving, football (tackle) M, golf, rowing (crew) W, soccer, swimming, tennis, track and field, volleyball W. **Intramural:** Archery W, badminton, baseball M, basketball, bowling, diving, golf, gymnastics W, handball, racquetball, soccer, softball, squash, swimming, table tennis, tennis, track and field, volleyball, wrestling M. **Team name:** Bearcats.

Student services. Adult student services, alcohol/substance abuse counseling, campus ministries, career counseling, services for economically disadvantaged, student employment services, financial aid counseling, health services, legal services, minority student services, on-campus daycare, personal counseling, placement for graduates, veterans' counselor, women's services. **Physically disabled:** Services for visually, speech, hearing impaired.

Contact. E-mail: admissions@uc.edu
Phone: (513) 556-1100 Toll-free number: (800) 827-8728
Fax: (513) 556-1105
Thomas Canepa, Assistant Vice President, Admissions, University of Cincinnati, PO Box 210091, Cincinnati, OH 45221-0091

University of Dayton

Dayton, Ohio — **CB member**
www.udayton.edu — **CB code: 1834**

- Private 4-year university affiliated with Roman Catholic Church
- Residential campus in small city
- 7,270 degree-seeking undergraduates: 5% part-time, 49% women, 4% African American, 1% Asian American, 2% Hispanic American
- 2,867 degree-seeking graduate students
- 80% of applicants admitted
- SAT or ACT (ACT writing optional) required
- 79% graduate within 6 years

General. Founded in 1850. Regionally accredited. **Degrees:** 1,423 bachelor's awarded; master's, doctoral, first professional offered. **ROTC:** Army, Air Force. **Location:** 2 miles from downtown, 50 miles from Cincinnati. **Calendar:** Semester, extensive summer session. **Full-time faculty:** 395 total; 89% have terminal degrees, 13% minority, 26% women. **Part-time faculty:** 428 total. **Class size:** 43% < 20, 49% 20-39, 4% 40-49, 3% 50-99, less than 1% >100. **Special facilities:** Research institute, portfolio management center, learning-teaching center, information sciences center, student-operated stores and coffee bars.

Freshman class profile. 8,675 applied, 6,899 admitted, 1,981 enrolled.

Mid 50% test scores			
SAT verbal:	520-620	Rank in top tenth:	24%
SAT math:	540-650	Return as sophomores:	86%
ACT:	23-28	Out-of-state:	40%
Rank in top quarter:	50%	Live on campus:	96%

Basis for selection. Considered factors include selection of courses in preparation for college, grade record and pattern in high school, class rank, results of SAT or ACT, character, and record of leadership and service. Will review PAA if presented. Essay, interview recommended for all; audition required for all music programs. **Homeschooled:** Transcript of courses and grades required. Description of courses taken required, including bibliography of texts used for instruction. Examples of projects, homework or writing samples helpful. **Learning Disabled:** Prefer that applicant provides documentation explaining disability for assessment.

High school preparation. College-preparatory program recommended. 16 units recommended. Recommended units include English 4, mathematics 3, social studies 3, science 2 and academic electives 4. 2 units of foreign language required for admission to the College of Arts and Sciences.

2005-2006 Annual costs. Tuition/fees: $22,045. All incoming students required to purchase a computer from the university. Foreign students pay additional $55 per month for health and accident insurance. Engineering majors required to pay additional $620 per semester in fees. Room/board: $6,780. Books/supplies: $800. Personal expenses: $1,170.

2004-2005 Financial aid. Need-based: 1,442 full-time freshmen applied for aid; 1,094 were judged to have need; 1,092 of these received aid. Average need met was 94%. Average scholarship/grant was $9,185; average loan $3,145. 67% of total undergraduate aid awarded as scholarships/grants, 33% as loans/jobs. **Non-need-based:** Awarded to 6,126 full-time undergraduates, including 1,751 freshmen. Scholarships awarded for academics, alumni affiliation, art, athletics, leadership, music/drama, ROTC, state residency.

Application procedures. Admission: Priority date 1/1; no deadline. No application fee. Application must be submitted online. Admission notification on a rolling basis beginning on or about 10/31. **Financial aid:** Priority date 3/31; no closing date. FAFSA required. Applicants notified on a rolling basis starting 2/25.

Academics. Special study options: Accelerated study, combined bachelor's/graduate degree, cooperative education, cross-registration, distance learning, double major, dual enrollment of high school students, ESL, exchange student, honors, independent study, internships, liberal arts/career combination, semester at sea, student-designed major, study abroad, teacher certification program, Washington semester. Domestic exchange program with other Marianist institutions; student-designed major in general studies only. **Credit/placement by examination:** AP, CLEP, IB, SAT, ACT, institutional tests. 24 credit hours maximum toward bachelor's degree. **Support services:** Learning center, pre-admission summer program, reduced course load, remedial instruction, study skills assistance, tutoring, writing center.

Majors. Area/ethnic studies: American. **Biology:** General, biochemistry, environmental. **Business:** General, accounting, business admin, entrepreneurial studies, finance, international, management information systems, managerial economics, marketing, operations. **Communications:** General, digital media, journalism, media studies, public relations. **Computer sciences:** General, computer science. **Conservation:** Environmental science. **Education:** Art, early childhood, foreign languages, French, German, middle, multi-level teacher, music, physical, secondary, Spanish, special. **Engineering:** Chemical, civil, computer, electrical, mechanical. **Engineering technology:** General, computer, electrical, industrial, manufacturing, mechanical. **English:** English lit. **Family/consumer sciences:** Food/nutrition. **Foreign languages:** French, German, Spanish. **Health:** Dietetics, music therapy, predentistry, premedicine. **History:** General. **Interdisciplinary:** Global studies. **Legal studies:** Prelaw. **Math:** General. **Parks/recreation:** Exercise sciences, facilities management, sports admin. **Philosophy/religion:** Philosophy, religion. **Physical sciences:** General, chemistry, geology, physics. **Protective services:** Criminal justice. **Psychology:** General. **Social sciences:** Econometrics, economics, political science, sociology. **Visual/performing arts:** Art history/conservation, design, dramatic, music performance, music theory/composition, photography, studio arts.

Most popular majors. Business/marketing 23%, communications/journalism 10%, education 13%, engineering/engineering technologies 15%, social sciences 6%.

Computing on campus. PC or laptop required. Dormitories wired for high-speed internet access and linked to campus network. Commuter students can connect to campus network. Online course registration, online library, helpline, repair service, student web hosting, wireless network available.

Student life. Freshman orientation: Mandatory, $115 fee. Preregistration for classes offered. 2-3 days preceding the first day of classes. Virtual orientation also available online. **Housing:** Guaranteed on-campus for freshmen. Coed dorms, single-sex dorms, special housing for disabled, apartments, fraternity/sorority housing, substance-free housing available. $400 nonrefundable deposit, deadline 5/1. University-owned houses available. **Activities:** Bands, choral groups, dance, drama, literary magazine, music ensembles, musical theater, opera, radio station, student government, student newspaper, symphony orchestra, TV station, More than 170 student organizations available.

Athletics. NCAA. **Intercollegiate:** Baseball M, basketball, cheerleading, cross-country, football (tackle) M, golf, rowing (crew) W, soccer, softball W, tennis, track and field W, volleyball W. **Intramural:** Basketball, football (non-tackle), racquetball, soccer, softball W, tennis, volleyball. **Team name:** Flyers.

Student services. Adult student services, alcohol/substance abuse counseling, campus ministries, career counseling, services for economically disadvantaged, student employment services, financial aid counseling, health services, minority student services, on-campus daycare, personal counseling, placement for graduates, women's services. **Physically disabled:** Services for visually, speech, hearing impaired. **Learning disabled:** Comprehensive services available.

Contact. E-mail: admission@udayton.edu
Phone: (937) 229-4411 Toll-free number: (800) 837-7433
Fax: (937) 229-4729
Robert Durkle, Director of Admission, University of Dayton, 300 College Park, Dayton, OH 45469-1300

University of Findlay

Findlay, Ohio
www.findlay.edu **CB code: 1223**

- Private 4-year university and liberal arts college affiliated with Church of God
- Residential campus in large town
- 3,034 degree-seeking undergraduates: 13% part-time, 60% women, 3% African American, 1% Asian American, 1% Hispanic American, 4% international
- 898 degree-seeking graduate students
- 70% of applicants admitted
- SAT or ACT (ACT writing optional) required
- 55% graduate within 6 years

General. Founded in 1882. Regionally accredited. **Degrees:** 598 bachelor's, 101 associate awarded; master's offered. **ROTC:** Army, Air Force. **Location:** 45 miles from Toledo, 90 miles from Columbus. **Calendar:** Semester, limited summer session. **Full-time faculty:** 168 total. **Part-time faculty:** 188 total. **Class size:** 61% < 20, 33% 20-39, 4% 40-49, 2% 50-99. **Special facilities:** Planetarium, 2 equestrian farms, cadaver lab, environmental resource training center, fitness and recreation complex, outdoor sports complex.

Freshman class profile. 2,485 applied, 1,744 admitted, 646 enrolled.

Mid 50% test scores		**Rank in top tenth:**	21%
SAT verbal:	470-580	**End year in good standing:**	87%
SAT math:	470-580	**Return as sophomores:**	74%
ACT:	20-25	**Out-of-state:**	21%
GPA 3.50 or higher:	49%	**Live on campus:**	65%
GPA 3.0-3.49:	28%	**Fraternities:**	2%
GPA 2.0-2.99:	22%	**Sororities:**	2%
Rank in top quarter:	50%		

Basis for selection. Admissions based on school achievement record, curriculum, class rank, and recommendations. Essay required for special admissions program only; interview recommended for foundations program (special admissions program). **Homeschooled:** Statement describing home-school structure and mission, state high school equivalency certificate, letter of recommendation (nonparent) required. Greater weight placed on standardized entrance exam scores for admission. Evaluation of GED if taken. **Learning Disabled:** Strongly encourage interview or campus visit.

High school preparation. College-preparatory program recommended. 16 units recommended. Recommended units include English 4, mathematics 2, social studies 2, history 1, science 4, foreign language 2 and academic electives 1. One fine arts unit recommended. Additional 1 math and 1 science for preveterinary and environmental programs.

2005-2006 Annual costs. Tuition/fees: $21,746. Pre-Veterinary and equestrian majors pay additional costs during first 2 years. Room/board: $7,492. Books/supplies: $700. Personal expenses: $650.

2004-2005 Financial aid. Need-based: 412 full-time freshmen applied for aid; 410 were judged to have need; 410 of these received aid. Average need met was 75%. Average scholarship/grant was $9,828; average loan $2,600. 35% of total undergraduate aid awarded as scholarships/grants, 65% as loans/jobs. **Non-need-based:** Awarded to 2,400 full-time undergraduates, including 513 freshmen. Scholarships awarded for academics, alumni affiliation, athletics, music/drama, state residency.

Application procedures. Admission: Closing date 6/1 (receipt date). No application fee. Application may be submitted online. Admission notification on a rolling basis beginning on or about 9/1. Must reply by May 1 or within 4 week(s) if notified thereafter. Part-time applicants may be admitted year round to any of the six different program start dates. **Financial aid:** Priority date 3/1, closing date 8/1. FAFSA required. Applicants notified on a rolling basis starting 3/1; must reply within 2 week(s) of notification.

Academics. Special study options: Accelerated study, combined bachelor's/graduate degree, cooperative education, distance learning, double major, dual enrollment of high school students, ESL, external degree, honors, independent study, internships, liberal arts/career combination, semester at sea, student-designed major, study abroad, teacher certification program, Washington semester, weekend college. BS in nursing with Mount Carmel College of

Nursing and Lourdes College, 3-1 BA prgram with Art Institute Consortium. **Credit/placement by examination:** AP, CLEP, institutional tests. 15 credit hours maximum toward associate degree, 30 toward bachelor's. **Support services:** Learning center, reduced course load, remedial instruction, study skills assistance, tutoring, writing center.

Majors. **Agriculture:** Equestrian studies, farm/ranch. **Biology:** General. **Business:** General, accounting, business admin, entrepreneurial studies, finance, hospitality admin, hospitality/recreation, human resources, international, marketing. **Communications:** General, journalism, public relations. **Computer sciences:** General, computer science, systems analysis. **Education:** General, art, bilingual, biology, curriculum, developmentally delayed, drama/dance, driver/safety, early childhood, early childhood special, emotionally handicapped, English, ESL, evaluation, foreign languages, foundations, geography, health, history, kindergarten/preschool, learning disabled, mathematics, mentally handicapped, middle, multi-level teacher, multicultural, multiple handicapped, physical, psychology, reading, science, secondary, social science, social studies, Spanish, special, speech, testing/assessment. **Engineering technology:** Hazardous materials. **English:** Creative writing, English lit. **Foreign languages:** Japanese, Spanish. **Health:** Athletic training, environmental health, health care admin, nuclear medical technology, occupational health, physician assistant, premedicine, prenursing, preveterinary. **History:** General. **Legal studies:** Prelaw. **Math:** General. **Parks/recreation:** Exercise sciences, health/fitness, sports admin. **Philosophy/religion:** Philosophy, religion. **Protective services:** Law enforcement admin. **Psychology:** General. **Public administration:** Social work. **Social sciences:** General, economics, political science, sociology. **Theology:** Theology. **Visual/performing arts:** Art, commercial/advertising art, dramatic, theater design.

Most popular majors. Agriculture 6%, business/marketing 32%, computer/information sciences 7%, education 25%, health sciences 16%.

Computing on campus. 400 workstations in dormitories, library, computer center, student center. Dormitories wired for high-speed internet access and linked to campus network. Commuter students can connect to campus network. Online course registration, online library, helpline, repair service, student web hosting, wireless network available.

Student life. **Freshman orientation:** Mandatory, $100 fee. Preregistration for classes offered. One-day registrations for students and orientation for parents during summer. 2-day orientation for students 2 days before classes begin. **Policies:** All freshmen, sophomores, and juniors under the age of 22 required to live on-campus. Freshmen permitted cars on campus. **Housing:** Guaranteed on-campus for freshmen. Coed dorms, single-sex dorms, special housing for disabled, apartments, fraternity/sorority housing, substance-free housing available. $100 deposit, deadline 8/1. Honors house and special interest houses. **Activities:** Bands, choral groups, drama, literary magazine, music ensembles, musical theater, radio station, student government, student newspaper, symphony orchestra, TV station, Circle-K, Black Student Union, wilderness club, Campus Compact, College Democrats, College Republicans, Fellowship of Christian Athletes, Habitat for Humanity, international club, student government association.

Athletics. NCAA. **Intercollegiate:** Baseball M, basketball, cheerleading, cross-country, diving, equestrian, football (tackle) M, golf, soccer, softball W, swimming, tennis, track and field, volleyball W, wrestling M. **Intramural:** Basketball, bowling, football (non-tackle), golf, skiing, soccer, softball, table tennis, tennis, volleyball, water polo. **Team name:** Oilers.

Student services. Adult student services, alcohol/substance abuse counseling, campus ministries, career counseling, services for economically disadvantaged, student employment services, financial aid counseling, health services, minority student services, personal counseling, placement for graduates, veterans' counselor, women's services. **Physically disabled:** Services for visually, speech, hearing impaired.

Contact. E-mail: admissions@findlay.edu
Phone: (419) 434-4540 Toll-free number: (800) 548-0932
Fax: (419) 434-4898
Randall Langston, Director of Undergraduate Admissions, University of Findlay, 1000 North Main Street, Findlay, OH 45840-3695

University of Rio Grande

Rio Grande, Ohio
www.rio.edu **CB code: 1663**

- Private 4-year community and liberal arts college
- Commuter campus in rural community
- 1,811 degree-seeking undergraduates: 19% part-time, 63% women, 3% African American, 1% Asian American, 1% Hispanic American
- 235 degree-seeking graduate students
- 34% graduate within 6 years

General. Founded in 1876. Regionally accredited. Institution is both public and private. First 2 years are state subsidized, second 2 years are private. Affiliated with Rio Grande Community College. **Degrees:** 168 bachelor's, 155 associate awarded; master's offered. **ROTC:** Army. **Location:** 12 miles from Gallipolis. **Calendar:** Semester, limited summer session. **Full-time faculty:** 88 total; 43% have terminal degrees, 7% minority, 41% women. **Part-time faculty:** 180 total; 2% have terminal degrees, 60% women. **Class size:** 76% < 20, 22% 20-39, 1% 40-49, 1% 50-99. **Special facilities:** Early childhood care center, museum.

Freshman class profile. 712 enrolled.

End year in good standing:	66%	**Out-of-state:**	5%
Return as sophomores:	55%	**Live on campus:**	37%

Basis for selection. Open admission, but selective for some programs. ACT required for nursing, medical laboratory technician, and education programs. Deferred admission for students demonstrating need for remedial work. Acceptance to Education department occurs at end of sophomore year. Early application recommended for nursing program. SAT, ACT scores not generally used in admission decisions but required with application. ACT preferred. Scores used in decisions for nursing, medical laboratory technician, education, social work, honors programs. Audition required for music program; interview recommended for education, medical laboratory technologies, music, nursing, psychology, social work programs.

High school preparation. College-preparatory program recommended. 21 units recommended. Recommended units include English 4, mathematics 3, social studies 2, history 2, science 3 (laboratory 2), foreign language 2 and academic electives 9. Chemistry, algebra, biology required for nursing applicants.

2005-2006 Annual costs. Tuition/fees: $572; $13,322 out-of-district; $14,402 out-of-state. West Virginia residents pay $9,120 per year for the first two years only. Room/board: $6,404. Books/supplies: $1,000. Personal expenses: $1,571.

2004-2005 Financial aid. **Need-based:** 50% of total undergraduate aid awarded as scholarships/grants, 50% as loans/jobs. **Non-need-based:** Scholarships awarded for academics, alumni affiliation, athletics, leadership, music/drama, state residency.

Application procedures. **Admission:** No deadline. $15 fee, may be waived for applicants with need. Admission notification on a rolling basis. **Financial aid:** Priority date 3/15; no closing date. FAFSA, institutional form required. Applicants notified on a rolling basis starting 1/15; must reply within 3 week(s) of notification.

Academics. **Special study options:** Accelerated study, combined bachelor's/graduate degree, cooperative education, distance learning, double major, dual enrollment of high school students, ESL, honors, independent study, internships, liberal arts/career combination, student-designed major, study abroad, teacher certification program. **Credit/placement by examination:** CLEP, institutional tests. **Support services:** Learning center, pre-admission summer program, reduced course load, remedial instruction, tutoring.

Majors. **Area/ethnic studies:** American. **Biology:** General. **Business:** Accounting, business admin, finance, human resources, international, managerial economics, marketing, real estate. **Communications:** General, journalism, public relations. **Computer sciences:** General, computer science. **Conservation:** General, wildlife. **Education:** General, art, biology, business, chemistry, early childhood, elementary, English, health, history, mathematics, middle, multi-level teacher, music, physical, physics, reading, science, secondary, social science, special, speech. **Health:** Clinical lab science, health care admin, nursing (RN), premedicine. **History:** General. **Legal studies:** Prelaw. **Math:** General. **Parks/recreation:** Sports admin. **Physical sciences:** Chemistry, physics. **Psychology:** General. **Public administration:** Social work. **Social sciences:** General, economics. **Theology:** Preministerial. **Visual/performing arts:** General, art, music management, studio arts.

Most popular majors. Business/marketing 27%, education 22%, health sciences 11%.

Computing on campus. 300 workstations in library, computer center, student center. Dormitories wired for high-speed internet access and linked to campus network. Online course registration, online library, student web hosting, wireless network available.

Student life. **Freshman orientation:** Available, $40 fee. Preregistration for classes offered. Offered 4 times during the summer. **Policies:** Freshmen permitted cars on campus. **Housing:** Guaranteed on-campus for all undergraduates. Coed dorms, single-sex dorms, special housing for disabled, substance-free housing available. Private housing owned and operated by university available to responsible students. **Activities:** Bands, choral groups, dance, drama, literary magazine, music ensembles, musical theater, radio station, student government, student newspaper, TV station, international student organization, Valley Artist Services, Handicapped Coalition, Young

Republicans, Rio Christian Fellowship, Student Ambassadors, Students in Free Enterprise.

Athletics. NAIA. **Intercollegiate:** Baseball M, basketball, cheerleading, cross-country, soccer, softball W, track and field, volleyball W. **Intramural:** Archery, badminton, basketball, equestrian, handball, racquetball, softball, swimming, tennis, water polo, wrestling M. **Team name:** Redmen.

Student services. Career counseling, student employment services, financial aid counseling, health services, on-campus daycare, personal counseling, placement for graduates, veterans' counselor. **Physically disabled:** Services for visually, speech, hearing impaired.

Contact. E-mail: jmabe@rio.edu
Phone: (740) 245-7206 Toll-free number: (800) 282-7201
Fax: (740) 245-7260
Barry Dorsey, President, University of Rio Grande, 218 North College Avenue, Rio Grande, OH 45674

University of Toledo

Toledo, Ohio — **CB member**
www.utoledo.edu — **CB code: 1845**

- Public 4-year university
- Commuter campus in large city
- 15,288 degree-seeking undergraduates: 16% part-time, 49% women, 13% African American, 2% Asian American, 3% Hispanic American, 1% international
- 2,876 degree-seeking graduate students
- 43% graduate within 6 years

General. Founded in 1872. Regionally accredited. **Degrees:** 2,775 bachelor's, 240 associate awarded; master's, doctoral, first professional offered. **ROTC:** Army, Air Force. **Location:** 6 miles from downtown. **Calendar:** Semester, extensive summer session. **Full-time faculty:** 776 total; 75% have terminal degrees, 17% minority, 34% women. **Part-time faculty:** 404 total; 24% have terminal degrees, 10% minority, 51% women. **Special facilities:** 2 observatories, ion accelerator, arboretum, planetarium, linear laser and nuclear physics laboratory, art museum, Lake Erie Research Center.

Freshman class profile. 8,126 applied, 7,769 admitted, 3,160 enrolled.

Mid 50% test scores			
SAT verbal:	450-570	Out-of-state:	3%
SAT math:	450-590	Live on campus:	47%
ACT:	18-24	International:	1%
Rank in top quarter:	36%	Fraternities:	3%
Rank in top tenth:	16%	Sororities:	1%

Basis for selection. Open admission, but selective for some programs and for out-of-state students. Out-of-state students need 2.0 GPA and 21 ACT or 980 SAT. Applicants to BS program in engineering need 3.0 GPA and 22 ACT or 1020 SAT. For admission to premedicine, predentistry, or preveterinary programs, 3.0 GPA and 25 ACT or 1130 SAT required. Applicants to computer science-engineering program need 3.0 GPA and 25 ACT or 1130 SAT, engineering technology 2.0 GPA and 21 ACT or 980 SAT, business college 2.25 GPA or 25 ACT or 1130 SAT. All SAT scores exclusive of Writing. SAT/ACT scores required for admission for out-of-state applicants and for applicants to selective programs. Audition required for music program. **Homeschooled:** Official recognized transcript required. **Learning Disabled:** Registering with the Office of Accessibility recommended.

High school preparation. College-preparatory program recommended. 16 units recommended. Recommended units include history 1, (laboratory 1) and foreign language 2. 4 math and chemistry required of engineering applicants.

2005-2006 Annual costs. Tuition/fees: $7,521; $16,333 out-of-state. Room/board: $8,312. Books/supplies: $690. Personal expenses: $2,204.

2005-2006 Financial aid. Need-based: 2,300 full-time freshmen applied for aid; 1,728 were judged to have need; 1,703 of these received aid. Average need met was 51%. Average scholarship/grant was $5,043; average loan $2,890. 42% of total undergraduate aid awarded as scholarships/grants, 58% as loans/jobs. **Non-need-based:** Awarded to 1,018 full-time undergraduates, including 343 freshmen. Scholarships awarded for academics, art, athletics, leadership, minority status, music/drama, ROTC, state residency. **Additional information:** March priority date for federal aid. Students encouraged to apply as early as December for priority consideration for institutional aid.

Application procedures. Admission: No deadline. $40 fee, may be waived for applicants with need. Application may be submitted online. Admission notification on a rolling basis beginning on or about 10/1. Freshman applicants desiring on-campus housing encouraged to apply early. **Financial aid:** Priority date 4/1; no closing date. FAFSA required. Applicants notified on a rolling basis starting 3/31; must reply within 4 week(s) of notification.

Academics. Special study options: Accelerated study, combined bachelor's/graduate degree, cooperative education, cross-registration, distance learning, double major, dual enrollment of high school students, ESL, exchange student, external degree, honors, independent study, internships, liberal arts/career combination, student-designed major, study abroad, teacher certification program, weekend college. **Credit/placement by examination:** AP, CLEP, institutional tests. 30 credit hours maximum toward associate degree, 30 toward bachelor's. **Support services:** Learning center, pre-admission summer program, reduced course load, remedial instruction, tutoring.

Majors. Area/ethnic studies: African-American, American, Asian, European, Latin American, Near/Middle Eastern, women's. **Biology:** General. **Business:** General, accounting, business admin, entrepreneurial studies, finance, human resources, international, logistics, management information systems, management science, market research, marketing, operations, organizational behavior. **Communications:** General. **Computer sciences:** Information systems. **Conservation:** Environmental studies. **Education:** General, art, business, English, French, German, health, kindergarten/preschool, mathematics, music, physical, science, secondary, social studies, Spanish, speech impaired, trade/industrial. **Engineering:** General, biomedical, chemical, civil, computer, electrical, industrial, mechanical. **Engineering technology:** Civil, electromechanical, mechanical. **English:** English lit. **Foreign languages:** French, German, linguistics, Spanish. **Health:** Facilities admin, medical records admin, nursing (RN), predentistry, premedicine, preveterinary, public health ed, recreational therapy, respiratory therapy technology. **History:** General. **Interdisciplinary:** Medieval/Renaissance. **Legal studies:** Paralegal, prelaw. **Liberal arts:** Arts/sciences, humanities. **Math:** General. **Parks/recreation:** General, exercise sciences, health/fitness. **Philosophy/religion:** Philosophy, religion. **Physical sciences:** Astronomy, chemistry, geology, physics. **Protective services:** Criminal justice. **Psychology:** General. **Public administration:** Social work. **Social sciences:** Anthropology, economics, geography, international relations, political science, sociology, urban studies. **Visual/performing arts:** Art, art history/conservation, dramatic, film/cinema, studio arts.

Most popular majors. Business/marketing 22%, education 13%, engineering/engineering technologies 17%, health sciences 11%.

Computing on campus. 2,800 workstations in dormitories, library, computer center, student center. Dormitories linked to campus network. Commuter students can connect to campus network. Online course registration, online library, helpline, repair service, wireless network available.

Student life. Freshman orientation: Available, $22 fee. **Housing:** Coed dorms, single-sex dorms, special housing for disabled, fraternity/sorority housing available. $200 fully refundable deposit. **Activities:** Bands, choral groups, dance, drama, film society, music ensembles, musical theater, opera, radio station, student government, student newspaper, symphony orchestra, black student union, Campus Crusade for Christ, Hillel, Latino student union, University YMCA, gay and lesbian student union, international student association, Habitat for Humanity, Toledo Campus Ministry Fellowship.

Athletics. NCAA. **Intercollegiate:** Baseball M, basketball, cross-country, diving W, football (tackle) M, golf, soccer W, softball W, swimming W, tennis, track and field W, volleyball W. **Intramural:** Badminton, basketball, bowling M, diving W, fencing, golf, racquetball, soccer, softball, swimming W, table tennis, tennis, track and field W, volleyball, weight lifting. **Team name:** Rockets.

Student services. Adult student services, alcohol/substance abuse counseling, campus ministries, career counseling, services for economically disadvantaged, student employment services, financial aid counseling, health services, legal services, minority student services, on-campus daycare, personal counseling, placement for graduates, veterans' counselor, women's services. **Physically disabled:** Services for visually, speech, hearing impaired.

Contact. E-mail: enroll@utnet.utoledo.edu
Phone: (419) 530-8700 Toll-free number: (800) 586-5336
Fax: (419) 530-4504
Jennifer Kwiatkowski, Director of Freshman Admission, University of Toledo, 2801 West Bancroft Street, Toledo, OH 43606-3398

Urbana University

Urbana, Ohio
www.urbana.edu — **CB code: 1847**

- Private 4-year liberal arts college
- Commuter campus in large town
- 1,443 degree-seeking undergraduates
- SAT or ACT (ACT writing optional), application essay required

General. Founded in 1850. Regionally accredited. Branch sites in Bellefontaine, Piqua, Dayton, Springfield, London. **Degrees:** 229 bachelor's, 51 associate awarded; master's offered. **Location:** 42 miles from Columbus, 49 miles from Dayton. **Calendar:** Semester, limited summer session. **Full-time faculty:** 52 total. **Part-time faculty:** 70 total. **Special facilities:** Johnny Appleseed museum, rare books collection.

Freshman class profile.

Mid 50% test scores			
ACT:	18-21	Out-of-state:	1%
		Live on campus:	50%

Basis for selection. School achievement record, class rank, GPA, test scores, extra-curricular activities and honors important. Recommendations and interviews are required for some applicants. Special consideration given to children of alumni. For regular admission, composite score of 18 on ACT or equivalent on SAT required.

High school preparation. 15 units recommended. Required and recommended units include English 4, mathematics 2, social studies 2, science 2, foreign language 1 and academic electives 2.

2005-2006 Annual costs. Tuition/fees: $15,050. Room/board: $6,010. Books/supplies: $1,000. Personal expenses: $666.

2005-2006 Financial aid. Need-based: Average need met was 35%. Average scholarship/grant was $1,809; average loan $2,625. 23% of total undergraduate aid awarded as scholarships/grants, 77% as loans/jobs. **Non-need-based:** Scholarships awarded for academics, alumni affiliation, athletics, music/drama.

Application procedures. Admission: No deadline. $25 fee. Application may be submitted online. Admission notification on a rolling basis. **Financial aid:** Closing date 4/1. FAFSA required. Applicants notified on a rolling basis starting 3/1; must reply within 4 week(s) of notification.

Academics. Special study options: Accelerated study, cooperative education, cross-registration, double major, honors, independent study, internships, liberal arts/career combination, student-designed major, teacher certification program. Opportunity to study in Poland for one semester. **Credit/placement by examination:** AP, CLEP, institutional tests. 15 credit hours maximum toward associate degree, 15 toward bachelor's. **Support services:** Learning center, reduced course load, remedial instruction, tutoring, writing center.

Majors. Business: General, accounting, communications, human resources, marketing. **Communications:** General. **Computer sciences:** Information systems. **Education:** General, biology, elementary, English, mathematics, middle, science, secondary, social studies, special. **Health:** Athletic training, health services, predentistry, premedicine. **History:** General. **Interdisciplinary:** Biological/physical sciences. **Legal studies:** Prelaw. **Liberal arts:** Arts/sciences. **Math:** General. **Parks/recreation:** Sports admin. **Philosophy/religion:** Philosophy. **Protective services:** Criminal justice, law enforcement admin. **Psychology:** General. **Public administration:** Community org/advocacy. **Social sciences:** General, political science, sociology.

Computing on campus. 69 workstations in dormitories, library, computer center. Dormitories wired for high-speed internet access. Online library, repair service available.

Student life. Freshman orientation: Mandatory. Held the weekend before fall classes. **Policies:** Freshmen permitted cars on campus. **Housing:** Guaranteed on-campus for freshmen. Coed dorms, single-sex dorms available. $125 deposit, deadline 8/23. **Activities:** Bands, choral groups, drama, literary magazine, music ensembles, musical theater, student government, student newspaper, American Association of University Women, Association for Information Technology Professionals student chapter, business club, children's literature club, Gay/Straight Alliance, Habitat for Humanity, Johnny Appleseed Club, science club, Sports Medicine Association, Student Ambassadors.

Athletics. NAIA. **Intercollegiate:** Baseball M, basketball, football (tackle) M, golf M, soccer, softball W, volleyball W. **Intramural:** Basketball, racquetball, swimming, synchronized swimming W, table tennis, volleyball, water polo. **Team name:** Blue Knights.

Student services. Adult student services, alcohol/substance abuse counseling, career counseling, student employment services, financial aid counseling, health services, personal counseling, placement for graduates, veterans' counselor.

Contact. E-mail: admiss@urbana.edu
Phone: (937) 484-1356 Toll-free number: (800) 787-2262 ext. 1356
Fax: (937) 484-1389
Paula Brown, Director of Admissions, Urbana University, 579 College Way, Urbana, OH 43078

Ursuline College

Pepper Pike, Ohio
www.ursuline.edu
CB member
CB code: 1848

- Private 4-year liberal arts college for women affiliated with Roman Catholic Church
- Commuter campus in small town
- 1,118 degree-seeking undergraduates: 33% part-time, 93% women, 26% African American, 1% Asian American, 2% Hispanic American, 1% international
- 339 degree-seeking graduate students
- 65% of applicants admitted
- SAT or ACT (ACT writing optional), application essay required
- 47% graduate within 6 years

General. Founded in 1871. Regionally accredited. Primarily women's college, but some men admitted. **Degrees:** 240 bachelor's awarded; master's offered. **ROTC:** Army. **Location:** 10 miles from Cleveland. **Calendar:** Semester, limited summer session. **Full-time faculty:** 72 total; 62% have terminal degrees, 3% minority, 81% women. **Part-time faculty:** 90 total; 49% have terminal degrees, 4% minority, 52% women. **Class size:** 83% < 20, 17% 20-39.

Freshman class profile. 439 applied, 286 admitted, 141 enrolled.

Mid 50% test scores			
SAT verbal:	420-540	Rank in top quarter:	51%
SAT math:	440-550	Rank in top tenth:	40%
ACT:	17-23	End year in good standing:	62%
GPA 3.50 or higher:	36%	Return as sophomores:	65%
GPA 3.0-3.49:	34%	Out-of-state:	1%
GPA 2.0-2.99:	29%	Live on campus:	65%

Basis for selection. Secondary school record, recommendations, standardized test scores and essay are very important. Community activities considered. Interview recommended for all. **Homeschooled:** Transcript of courses and grades, letter of recommendation (nonparent) required. Official transcript from accrediting agency needed.

High school preparation. 17 units recommended. Recommended units include English 4, mathematics 3, social studies 3, science 3 (laboratory 2) and foreign language 2. One fine or performing arts recommended. Nursing students should have chemistry.

2005-2006 Annual costs. Tuition/fees: $19,090. Room/board: $6,366. Books/supplies: $900. Personal expenses: $600.

2004-2005 Financial aid. Need-based: 130 full-time freshmen applied for aid; 122 were judged to have need; 122 of these received aid. Average need met was 86%. Average scholarship/grant was $8,412; average loan $3,171. 40% of total undergraduate aid awarded as scholarships/grants, 60% as loans/jobs. **Non-need-based:** Awarded to 198 full-time undergraduates, including 181 freshmen. Scholarships awarded for academics, art, athletics, leadership, religious affiliation, ROTC.

Application procedures. Admission: No deadline. $25 fee, may be waived for applicants with need. Application may be submitted online. Admission notification on a rolling basis. Applicants notified within 3 weeks of application. Must reply by May 1 or within 4 week(s) if notified thereafter. **Financial aid:** Priority date 3/15; no closing date. FAFSA, institutional form required. Applicants notified on a rolling basis starting 3/1; must reply within 2 week(s) of notification.

Academics. Special study options: Accelerated study, combined bachelor's/graduate degree, cooperative education, cross-registration, distance learning, double major, independent study, internships, liberal arts/career combination, New York semester, teacher certification program, weekend college. Optional junior year program in fashion merchandising or design at Fashion Institute of Technology in New York City for enrichment electives only. **Credit/placement by examination:** AP, CLEP, institutional tests. 43 credit hours maximum toward bachelor's degree. **Support services:** Learning center, reduced course load, remedial instruction, study skills assistance, tutoring, writing center.

Majors. Area/ethnic studies: American. **Biology:** General, biomedical sciences, biotechnology, environmental. **Business:** Accounting, business admin, fashion, human resources, management information systems, marketing. **Communications:** Public relations. **Conservation:** Environmental studies. **Education:** Art, early childhood, English, mathematics, middle, science, social studies, special. **English:** English lit. **Family/consumer sciences:** Work/family studies. **Health:** Facilities admin, health care admin, health services, nursing (RN), prenursing, preop/surgical nursing. **History:** General. **Interdisciplinary:** Historic preservation. **Legal studies:** Paralegal. **Liberal arts:**

Humanities. **Math:** General. **Philosophy/religion:** Christian, philosophy. **Psychology:** General. **Public administration:** Social work. **Social sciences:** Sociology. **Visual/performing arts:** Art history/conservation, fashion design, graphic design, interior design, studio arts.

Most popular majors. Business/marketing 27%, education 15%, health sciences 29%, visual/performing arts 8%.

Computing on campus. 72 workstations in dormitories, library, computer center, student center. Dormitories wired for high-speed internet access and linked to campus network. Online library, wireless network available.

Student life. **Freshman orientation:** Available. Preregistration for classes offered. Three-day program offered prior to the start of fall semester. **Policies:** Freshmen permitted cars on campus. **Housing:** $100 fully refundable deposit. **Activities:** Choral groups, drama, literary magazine, student government, student nurses, education association, campus service and spiritual life committees, ethnic groups, public relations society.

Athletics. NAIA. **Intercollegiate:** Basketball W, cross-country W, golf W, soccer W, softball W, tennis W, volleyball W. **Team name:** Arrows.

Student services. Adult student services, campus ministries, career counseling, student employment services, financial aid counseling, health services, minority student services, personal counseling. **Physically disabled:** Services for visually, speech, hearing impaired.

Contact. E-mail: admission@ursuline.edu
Phone: (440) 449-4203 Toll-free number: (888) 877-8546
Fax: (440) 684-6138
Sarah Sundermeier, Director of Admissions, Ursuline College, 2550 Lander Road, Pepper Pike, OH 44124-4398

Walsh University

North Canton, Ohio — **CB member**
www.walsh.edu — **CB code: 1926**

- Private 4-year university and liberal arts college affiliated with Roman Catholic Church
- Residential campus in small city
- 1,859 degree-seeking undergraduates: 24% part-time, 64% women
- 324 degree-seeking graduate students
- 80% of applicants admitted
- SAT or ACT (ACT writing optional) required
- 54% graduate within 6 years; 21% enter graduate study

General. Founded in 1958. Regionally accredited. **Degrees:** 322 bachelor's, 3 associate awarded; master's offered. **Location:** 20 miles from Akron, 60 miles from Cleveland. **Calendar:** Semester, limited summer session. **Full-time faculty:** 82 total; 79% have terminal degrees, 7% minority, 51% women. **Part-time faculty:** 107 total; 16% have terminal degrees, 51% women. **Class size:** 70% < 20, 29% 20-39, less than 1% 40-49. **Special facilities:** Bioinformatics laboratory, prayer garden, Hoover Museum (vacuum cleaners), dance pavilion.

Freshman class profile. 1,179 applied, 946 admitted, 447 enrolled.

Mid 50% test scores		**Rank in top quarter:**	41%
SAT verbal:	450-560	**Rank in top tenth:**	15%
SAT math:	460-560	**End year in good standing:**	85%
ACT:	19-24	**Return as sophomores:**	78%
GPA 3.50 or higher:	38%	**Out-of-state:**	4%
GPA 3.0-3.49:	32%	**Live on campus:**	77%
GPA 2.0-2.99:	30%	**International:**	1%

Basis for selection. Secondary school record and standardized test scores very important; class rank, recommendations, essay, and character important. Essay, interview recommended for all.

High school preparation. 16 units recommended. Recommended units include English 4, mathematics 3, social studies 3, science 3, foreign language 2 and academic electives 1. Algebra, biology, and chemistry required for nursing applicants.

2006-2007 Annual costs. Tuition/fees (projected): $17,570. Room/board: $7,130. Books/supplies: $1,000. Personal expenses: $775.

2005-2006 Financial aid. **Need-based:** Average need met was 81%. Average scholarship/grant was $6,722; average loan $2,117. 50% of total undergraduate aid awarded as scholarships/grants, 50% as loans/jobs. **Non-need-based:** Scholarships awarded for academics, alumni affiliation, athletics, music/drama, religious affiliation, state residency.

Application procedures. **Admission:** Closing date 8/15 (postmark date). $25 fee, may be waived for applicants with need. Application may be submitted online. Admission notification on a rolling basis beginning on or about 10/1. Must reply by 8/15. **Financial aid:** Priority date 3/15; no closing date. FAFSA, institutional form required. Applicants notified on a rolling basis starting 3/15; must reply within 4 week(s) of notification.

Academics. Accelerated degree completion program for adults with evening and weekend classes, multiple locations. Structured first semester available for selected students. **Special study options:** Accelerated study, combined bachelor's/graduate degree, cross-registration, double major, dual enrollment of high school students, ESL, exchange student, external degree, honors, independent study, internships, liberal arts/career combination, study abroad, teacher certification program, Washington semester. CCSA Consortium for Study Abroad. **Credit/placement by examination:** AP, CLEP, institutional tests. 45 credit hours maximum toward bachelor's degree. **Support services:** Learning center, reduced course load, remedial instruction, study skills assistance, tutoring, writing center.

Honors college/program. 3.75 high school GPA, 27 ACT or 1200 SAT (exclusive of Writing), writing sample and interview required. Special English and History courses, upper-level seminar and thesis courses.

Majors. **Biology:** General. **Business:** General, accounting, business admin, finance, management information systems, marketing. **Communications:** General. **Computer sciences:** General. **Education:** Early childhood, elementary, emotionally handicapped, English, mathematics, mentally handicapped, middle, multiple handicapped, physical, reading, science, secondary, social science, social studies. **Foreign languages:** French, Spanish. **Health:** Clinical lab science, nursing (RN), predentistry, premedicine, preveterinary. **History:** General. **Interdisciplinary:** Biological/physical sciences, natural sciences. **Legal studies:** Prelaw. **Math:** General. **Philosophy/religion:** Philosophy, religion. **Physical sciences:** Chemistry. **Psychology:** General. **Social sciences:** Political science, sociology. **Theology:** Theology.

Most popular majors. Biology 7%, business/marketing 36%, communications/journalism 6%, education 23%, health sciences 10%.

Computing on campus. 262 workstations in dormitories, library, computer center. Dormitories wired for high-speed internet access and linked to campus network. Online library, helpline, repair service, wireless network available.

Student life. **Freshman orientation:** Mandatory, $200 fee. Preregistration for classes offered. Occurs weekend before classes begin in August. **Policies:** All full-time undergraduate students 23 and younger must live on campus (some exceptions permitted). Freshmen permitted cars on campus. **Housing:** Guaranteed on-campus for all undergraduates. Coed dorms, special housing for disabled, apartments, substance-free housing available. $200 deposit, deadline 8/15. Pets allowed in dorm rooms. Apartment-style residence hall with kitchens; quiet, themed floors for first-year students. **Activities:** Pep band, choral groups, dance, drama, literary magazine, music ensembles, radio station, student government, student newspaper, student campus ministry, Circle-K, Black Student Union, international club, Habitat for Humanity, Institute for Justice and Peace, commuter commission, major-related clubs.

Athletics. NAIA. **Intercollegiate:** Baseball M, basketball, cheerleading, cross-country, football (tackle) M, golf, soccer, softball W, synchronized swimming W, tennis, track and field, volleyball W. **Intramural:** Basketball, bowling, football (non-tackle), golf, soccer, softball, swimming, table tennis, tennis, volleyball. **Team name:** Cavaliers.

Student services. Adult student services, alcohol/substance abuse counseling, campus ministries, career counseling, student employment services, financial aid counseling, health services, minority student services, personal counseling, placement for graduates, veterans' counselor. **Physically disabled:** Services for visually, speech impaired.

Contact. E-mail: admissions@walsh.edu
Phone: (330) 490-7172 Toll-free number: (800) 362-9846
Fax: (330) 490-7165
Brett Freshour, Dean of Enrollment Management, Walsh University, 2020 East Maple Street, North Canton, OH 44720-3396

Wilberforce University

Wilberforce, Ohio — **CB member**
www.wilberforce.edu — **CB code: 1906**

- Private 4-year liberal arts college affiliated with African Methodist Episcopal Church
- Residential campus in rural community

General. Founded in 1856. Regionally accredited. **Location:** 18 miles from Dayton. **Calendar:** Semester.

Annual costs/financial aid. Tuition/fees (2005-2006): $10,780. Room/board: $5,320. Books/supplies: $1,000. Personal expenses: $1,500. Need-based financial aid available to full-time and part-time students.

Contact. Phone: (937) 708-5721
Director of Admissions, 1055 North Bickett Road, Wilberforce, OH 45384-1001

Wilmington College

Wilmington, Ohio — **CB member**
www.wilmington.edu — **CB code: 1909**

- Private 4-year liberal arts college affiliated with Society of Friends (Quaker)
- Residential campus in large town
- 1,723 degree-seeking undergraduates: 20% part-time, 54% women
- 41 graduate students
- 98% of applicants admitted
- SAT or ACT (ACT writing optional) required

General. Founded in 1870. Regionally accredited. Affiliated with Wilmington Yearly Meeting of the Religious Society of Friends. Branch campuses in Cincinnati and other locations. BA in business offered at Cincinnati branch and Wilmington evening program. **Degrees:** 339 bachelor's awarded; master's offered. **Location:** 50 miles from Cincinnati, 60 miles from Columbus. **Calendar:** Semester, limited summer session. **Full-time faculty:** 71 total; 69% have terminal degrees, 1% minority, 58% women. **Part-time faculty:** 26 total; 4% have terminal degrees, 15% minority, 54% women. **Class size:** 71% < 20, 27% 20-39, 2% 40-49. **Special facilities:** Greenhouse, herbarium, observatory, electron microscope, live animal area, sports medicine center, Peace Resource Center containing Hiroshima/Nagasaki Memorial collection.

Freshman class profile. 1,409 applied, 1,381 admitted, 389 enrolled.

Mid 50% test scores			
SAT verbal:	430-530	GPA 2.0-2.99:	33%
SAT math:	440-550	Rank in top quarter:	39%
ACT:	19-23	Rank in top tenth:	9%
GPA 3.50 or higher:	39%	Return as sophomores:	73%
GPA 3.0-3.49:	28%	Out-of-state:	5%
		Live on campus:	67%

Basis for selection. Previous academic record, test scores, counselor recommendation, and interview important. Essay, interview recommended for all.

High school preparation. 16 units required. Required and recommended units include English 4, mathematics 2, social studies 2, science 2 (laboratory 2), foreign language 2 and academic electives 4. 6 art units recommended.

2005-2006 Annual costs. Tuition/fees: $19,752. 1-6 hours $385 per-credit-hour. Room/board: $7,054. Books/supplies: $1,000. Personal expenses: $450.

Financial aid. Non-need-based: Scholarships awarded for academics, alumni affiliation, religious affiliation, state residency.

Application procedures. Admission: No deadline. $25 fee, may be waived for applicants with need. Application may be submitted online. Admission notification on a rolling basis beginning on or about 9/1. Online application does not require application fee. **Financial aid:** Priority date 3/31, closing date 6/1. FAFSA required. Applicants notified on a rolling basis starting 3/1; must reply by 5/1 or within 2 week(s) of notification.

Academics. Special study options: Accelerated study, cross-registration, double major, dual enrollment of high school students, honors, independent study, internships, liberal arts/career combination, student-designed major, study abroad, teacher certification program, Washington semester, weekend college. **Credit/placement by examination:** AP, CLEP, IB, SAT, ACT, institutional tests. 30 credit hours maximum toward bachelor's degree. **Support services:** Learning center, reduced course load, remedial instruction, study skills assistance, tutoring, writing center.

Majors. Agriculture: Agribusiness operations, agronomy, animal sciences, business, equine science, farm/ranch, production. **Biology:** General, bacteriology, biochemistry, environmental. **Business:** Accounting, business admin, management science, marketing, sales/distribution. **Communications:** General, journalism, media studies, public relations. **Computer sciences:** General, computer science. **Education:** General, agricultural, biology, chemistry, early childhood, elementary, English, health, history, mathematics, middle, multi-level teacher, physical, science, secondary, social science, social studies. **Foreign languages:** Spanish. **History:** General. **Legal studies:** Prelaw. **Liberal arts:** Arts/sciences. **Math:** General. **Parks/recreation:** Sports admin. **Physical sciences:** Astronomy, chemistry, geology, planetary. **Protective services:** Criminal justice. **Psychology:** General. **Public administration:** Social work. **Social sciences:** General, economics, political science, sociology. **Visual/performing arts:** Art, commercial/advertising art, dramatic.

Most popular majors. Agriculture 6%, business/marketing 31%, communications/journalism 6%, education 22%, social sciences 6%.

Computing on campus. 156 workstations in library, computer center. Dormitories wired for high-speed internet access and linked to campus network. Commuter students can connect to campus network. Online course registration, helpline, student web hosting available.

Student life. Freshman orientation: Mandatory. Held 3 days prior to start of fall semester. **Policies:** Freshmen permitted cars on campus. **Housing:** Guaranteed on-campus for all undergraduates. Coed dorms, single-sex dorms, apartments, fraternity/sorority housing available. $50 nonrefundable deposit, deadline 8/15. Living/learning units available. **Activities:** Concert band, choral groups, drama, literary magazine, music ensembles, musical theater, student government, student newspaper, social service, international, education, and agriculture clubs, Christian Students, Young Friends (Quaker-Christian group), Catholic campus ministry, sports medicine association.

Athletics. NCAA. **Intercollegiate:** Baseball M, basketball, cheerleading, cross-country, football (tackle), golf, soccer, softball W, swimming, tennis, track and field, volleyball W, wrestling M. **Intramural:** Basketball, football (non-tackle), racquetball, soccer, softball, squash, table tennis, tennis, volleyball, weight lifting. **Team name:** Quakers.

Student services. Adult student services, alcohol/substance abuse counseling, campus ministries, career counseling, student employment services, financial aid counseling, health services, minority student services, personal counseling, placement for graduates, veterans' counselor.

Contact. E-mail: admissions@wilmington.edu
Phone: (800) 341-9318 ext. 260 Fax: (937) 382-7077
Tina Garland, Director of Admission, Wilmington College, Box 1325 Pyle Center, Wilmington, OH 45177

Wittenberg University

Springfield, Ohio — **CB member**
www.wittenberg.edu — **CB code: 1922**

- Private 4-year liberal arts college affiliated with Evangelical Lutheran Church in America
- Residential campus in small city
- 1,880 degree-seeking undergraduates: 1% part-time, 57% women, 6% African American, 1% Asian American, 1% Hispanic American, 2% international
- 5 degree-seeking graduate students
- 85% of applicants admitted
- SAT or ACT (ACT writing recommended), application essay required
- 65% graduate within 6 years

General. Founded in 1845. Regionally accredited. **Degrees:** 407 bachelor's awarded; master's offered. **ROTC:** Army, Air Force. **Location:** 25 miles from Dayton, 45 miles from Columbus. **Calendar:** Semester, limited summer session. **Full-time faculty:** 148 total; 89% have terminal degrees, 6% minority, 39% women. **Part-time faculty:** 54 total; 33% have terminal degrees, 7% minority, 48% women. **Class size:** 62% < 20, 37% 20-39, less than 1% 40-49, less than 1% 50-99, less than 1% >100. **Special facilities:** Observatory, East Asian art collection, Martin Luther library collection, humanities and technology center.

Freshman class profile. 2,479 applied, 2,102 admitted, 496 enrolled.

Mid 50% test scores			
SAT verbal:	520-630	Rank in top quarter:	56%
SAT math:	500-620	Rank in top tenth:	27%
ACT:	21-27	Return as sophomores:	78%
GPA 3.50 or higher:	52%	Out-of-state:	29%
GPA 3.0-3.49:	29%	Live on campus:	96%
GPA 2.0-2.99:	19%	International:	1%

Basis for selection. GED not accepted. In order of importance: school achievement record, courses taken, school attended, trend in work, test scores, counselor recommendation, extracurricular activities, and interview. Special consideration for children of alumni, minorities, Lutherans, residents of Clark County, and international students. SAT Subject Tests recommended. Math and foreign language placement tests required. Interview recommended for all; portfolio required for art program; audition recommended for dance, music, theater programs. **Homeschooled:** On-campus interview.

High school preparation. Required and recommended units include English 4, mathematics 3-4, history 2-3, science 3-4 (laboratory 2) and foreign language 3.

2005-2006 Annual costs. Tuition/fees: $27,542. Room/board: $7,054. Books/supplies: $800. Personal expenses: $1,000.

2005-2006 Financial aid. All financial aid based on need. 427 full-time freshmen applied for aid; 357 were judged to have need; 356 of these received aid. Average need met was 92%. Average scholarship/grant was $18,312; average loan $3,046. 73% of total undergraduate aid awarded as scholarships/grants, 27% as loans/jobs. **Additional information:** Auditions required from applicants for music, theater, and dance scholarships. Portfolio required of applicants for art scholarships.

Application procedures. Admission: Closing date 3/15 (postmark date). $40 fee, may be waived for applicants with need. Application may be submitted online. Admission notification on a rolling basis. Must reply by May 1 or within 2 week(s) if notified thereafter. **Financial aid:** Priority date 3/15; no closing date. FAFSA required. Applicants notified on a rolling basis starting 2/15; must reply by 5/1 or within 2 week(s) of notification.

Academics. Special study options: Combined bachelor's/graduate degree, cross-registration, double major, dual enrollment of high school students, honors, independent study, internships, liberal arts/career combination, student-designed major, study abroad, teacher certification program, urban semester, Washington semester, weekend college. Semester programs with Duke University (marine biology), School of Visual Arts in New York, Camarillo Hospital in California, National Institutes of Health in Washington, D.C., Washington University (MO) (occupational therapy), Johns Hopkins Nursing Program; 3-2 engineering with Washington University (MO), Case Western University. **Credit/placement by examination:** AP, CLEP, IB, institutional tests. **Support services:** Learning center, pre-admission summer program, reduced course load, study skills assistance, tutoring, writing center.

Majors. Area/ethnic studies: American, East Asian, European, Russian/Slavic. **Biology:** General, biochemistry, molecular. **Business:** General, business admin, managerial economics, marketing. **Communications:** General. **Computer sciences:** Computer science. **Conservation:** Environmental studies. **Education:** General, elementary. **English:** English lit. **Foreign languages:** French, German, Spanish. **History:** General. **Interdisciplinary:** Biological/physical sciences, biopsychology, global studies, math/computer science. **Liberal arts:** Arts/sciences. **Math:** General. **Philosophy/religion:** Philosophy, religion. **Physical sciences:** General, chemistry, geology, physics. **Psychology:** General. **Social sciences:** General, economics, geography, political science, sociology, urban studies. **Visual/performing arts:** General, art.

Most popular majors. Biology 11%, business/marketing 16%, education 13%, English 8%, psychology 10%, social sciences 12%.

Computing on campus. 900 workstations in dormitories, library, computer center, student center. Dormitories wired for high-speed internet access and linked to campus network. Commuter students can connect to campus network. Online course registration, online library, helpline, student web hosting, wireless network available.

Student life. Freshman orientation: Mandatory. Preregistration for classes offered. Pre-orientation days offered 3 times during the summer. Full orientation held 3 days before the beginning of fall classes. **Policies:** Freshmen permitted cars on campus. **Housing:** Guaranteed on-campus for all undergraduates. Coed dorms, single-sex dorms, apartments, fraternity/sorority housing, substance-free housing available. $400 fully refundable deposit, deadline 7/1. Substance-free residence hall, honors residence hall, special theme halls available. **Activities:** Bands, choral groups, dance, drama, literary magazine, music ensembles, musical theater, opera, radio station, student government, student newspaper, symphony orchestra, Newman Club, Concerned Black Students, Community Volunteer Service, Weaver Chapel Association, Project Woman, International student organization, East Asian Studies Club, Hillel, Amnesty International, Habitat for Humanity.

Athletics. NCAA. **Intercollegiate:** Baseball M, basketball, cheerleading, cross-country, diving, field hockey W, football (tackle) M, golf, lacrosse, soccer, softball W, swimming, tennis, track and field, volleyball W. **Intramural:** Badminton, basketball, bowling, cricket M, diving, fencing, football (non-tackle), golf, gymnastics, handball M, ice hockey M, judo, racquetball, rugby, sailing, skiing, skin diving, soccer, softball, squash, swimming, table tennis, tennis, track and field, volleyball, water polo M, weight lifting. **Team name:** Tigers.

Student services. Adult student services, alcohol/substance abuse counseling, campus ministries, career counseling, student employment services, financial aid counseling, health services, minority student services, personal counseling, placement for graduates, veterans' counselor, women's services.

Contact. E-mail: admission@wittenberg.edu
Phone: (937) 327-6314 Toll-free number: (800) 677-7558 ext. 6314
Fax: (937) 327-6379
Kurt Schmidt, Dean of Admission, Wittenberg University, Ward Street and North Wittenberg, Springfield, OH 45501-0720

Wright State University

Dayton, Ohio — CB member
www.wright.edu — CB code: 1179

- Public 4-year university
- Commuter campus in small city
- 11,785 degree-seeking undergraduates: 12% part-time, 56% women, 12% African American, 2% Asian American, 1% Hispanic American, 1% international
- 3,458 degree-seeking graduate students
- SAT or ACT (ACT writing optional) required

General. Founded in 1964. Regionally accredited. **Degrees:** 2,035 bachelor's, 79 associate awarded; master's, doctoral, first professional offered. **ROTC:** Army, Air Force. **Location:** 10 miles from downtown. **Calendar:** Quarter, extensive summer session. **Full-time faculty:** 731 total; 14% minority, 39% women. **Part-time faculty:** 104 total; 16% minority, 60% women. **Class size:** 49% < 20, 41% 20-39, 4% 40-49, 5% 50-99, 1% >100. **Special facilities:** Biological preserve, disabled-accessible garden of the senses, museum of contemporary art.

Freshman class profile. 5,497 applied, 4,763 admitted, 2,336 enrolled.

Mid 50% test scores		Rank in top tenth:	15%
SAT verbal:	440-560	Return as sophomores:	73%
SAT math:	430-570	Out-of-state:	3%
ACT:	18-23	Live on campus:	60%
GPA 3.50 or higher:	29%	International:	1%
GPA 3.0-3.49:	27%	Fraternities:	5%
GPA 2.0-2.99:	40%	Sororities:	3%
Rank in top quarter:	35%		

Basis for selection. Open admission, but selective for some programs. Liberal admission policy. College-preparatory curriculum, 2.0 minimum GPA required. Test scores important for selected programs. Audition required for acting, dance, directing/stage management, music programs; portfolio required for art, art education programs.

High school preparation. 15 units required. Required units include English 4, mathematics 3, social studies 3, (laboratory 3) and foreign language 2. Mathematics requirement includes 2 algebra. Art, music or theater recommended. Students not meeting course recommendations must make up deficiency prior to admission to program.

2005-2006 Annual costs. Tuition/fees: $6,864; $13,239 out-of-state. Room/board: $6,750.

2004-2005 Financial aid. Need-based: 2,208 full-time freshmen applied for aid; 1,736 were judged to have need; 1,736 of these received aid. Average need met was 60%. Average scholarship/grant was $3,982; average loan $2,301. 38% of total undergraduate aid awarded as scholarships/grants, 62% as loans/jobs. **Non-need-based:** Awarded to 4,587 full-time undergraduates, including 1,454 freshmen. Scholarships awarded for academics, alumni affiliation, art, athletics, job skills, leadership, minority status, music/drama, ROTC. **Additional information:** Academic scholarship applications must be submitted by February 1.

Application procedures. Admission: No deadline. $30 fee. Application may be submitted online. Admission notification on a rolling basis beginning on or about 10/1. Application by January recommended for students desiring on-campus housing. **Financial aid:** Priority date 3/1; no closing date. FAFSA required. Applicants notified on a rolling basis starting 2/15; must reply within 2 week(s) of notification.

Academics. Special study options: Cooperative education, cross-registration, distance learning, double major, ESL, honors, independent study, internships, student-designed major, study abroad, teacher certification program. **Credit/placement by examination:** AP, CLEP, institutional tests. **Support services:** Learning center, pre-admission summer program, reduced course load, remedial instruction, tutoring, writing center.

Majors. Area/ethnic studies: African-American, women's. **Biology:** General, anatomy, biochemistry, pharmacology/toxicology. **Business:** Accounting, business admin, human resources, management information systems, management science, managerial economics, marketing, statistics. **Communications:** General, media studies, organizational. **Computer sciences:** General, computer science, information systems. **Education:** Art, business, early childhood, elementary, English, foreign languages, learning disabled, mathematics, mentally handicapped, multiple handicapped, music, physical, science, social studies. **Engineering:** General, biomedical, computer, electrical, materials, mechanical, physics, science, systems. **Engineering technology:** Biomedical, environmental. **Foreign languages:** General, classics, French, German, Latin, linguistics, modern Greek, Spanish. **Health:** Adult health nursing, clinical lab science, environmental health, nursing (RN), predentistry, premedicine, prepharmacy, preveterinary, vocational rehab counseling. **History:** General. **Interdisciplinary:** Systems science. **Legal studies:** Prelaw. **Liberal arts:** Arts/sciences. **Math:** General, applied, statistics. **Military:** General. **Philosophy/religion:** Philosophy, religion. **Physical sciences:** Chemistry, geology, physics. **Protective services:** Police science. **Psychology:** General. **Public administration:** General, social work. **Social sciences:** Anthropology, criminology, economics, geography, international relations, political science, sociology, urban studies. **Visual/performing arts:** Art, art history/conservation, arts management, dance, dramatic, drawing, film/cinema, music history, music performance, music theory/composition, photography, theater design.

Most popular majors. Business/marketing 20%, communications/journalism 6%, education 21%, engineering/engineering technologies 6%, health sciences 9%, psychology 9%, social sciences 8%.

Computing on campus. 600 workstations in dormitories, library, computer center, student center. Dormitories wired for high-speed internet access. Commuter students can connect to campus network. Online course registration, online library, helpline, student web hosting, wireless network available.

Student life. Freshman orientation: Available. Preregistration for classes offered. **Policies:** Freshmen permitted cars on campus. **Housing:** Coed dorms, special housing for disabled, apartments available. Honors dorm available. **Activities:** Bands, choral groups, dance, drama, literary magazine, music ensembles, musical theater, opera, radio station, student government, student newspaper, symphony orchestra, TV station, Black Student Union, Baptist Student Union, Student Association for Escorts (SAFE), College Students for Special Wish, Fellowship of Christian Students, Circle-K, Model United Nations, Campus Crusade for Christ, Ohio College Democrats, Jewish Student Union.

Athletics. NCAA. **Intercollegiate:** Baseball M, basketball, cheerleading, cross-country, diving, golf M, soccer, softball W, swimming, tennis, track and field W, volleyball W. **Intramural:** Archery, baseball M, basketball, cricket M, cross-country, football (tackle), golf, handball, lacrosse M, soccer, softball, squash, tennis, volleyball W. **Team name:** Raiders.

Student services. Adult student services, campus ministries, career counseling, student employment services, financial aid counseling, health services, legal services, minority student services, personal counseling, placement for graduates, veterans' counselor, women's services. **Physically disabled:** Services for visually, speech, hearing impaired.

Contact. E-mail: admissions@wright.edu
Phone: (937) 775-5700 Toll-free number: (800) 247-1770
Fax: (937) 775-5795
Cathy Davis, Director of Admissions, Wright State University, 3640 Colonel Glenn Highway, Dayton, OH 45435

Xavier University

Cincinnati, Ohio — **CB member**
www.xavier.edu — **CB code: 1965**

- Private 4-year university affiliated with Roman Catholic Church
- Residential campus in large city
- 3,729 degree-seeking undergraduates: 11% part-time, 56% women, 11% African American, 2% Asian American, 2% Hispanic American, 1% international
- 2,446 degree-seeking graduate students
- 66% of applicants admitted
- SAT or ACT (ACT writing optional), application essay required
- 75% graduate within 6 years; 27% enter graduate study

General. Founded in 1831. Regionally accredited. **Degrees:** 861 bachelor's, 25 associate awarded; master's, doctoral offered. **ROTC:** Army, Air Force. **Location:** 5 miles from downtown. **Calendar:** Semester, limited summer session. **Full-time faculty:** 294 total; 80% have terminal degrees, 18% minority, 46% women. **Part-time faculty:** 304 total; 21% have terminal degrees, 7% minority, 50% women. **Class size:** 50% < 20, 48% 20-39, 1% 40-49, less than 1% 50-99.

Freshman class profile. 5,468 applied, 3,612 admitted, 765 enrolled.

Mid 50% test scores			
SAT verbal:	540-640	Rank in top quarter:	62%
SAT math:	540-640	Rank in top tenth:	30%
ACT:	23-28	End year in good standing:	94%
GPA 3.50 or higher:	63%	Return as sophomores:	89%
GPA 3.0-3.49:	26%	Out-of-state:	49%
GPA 2.0-2.99:	11%	Live on campus:	90%
		International:	1%

Basis for selection. Previous academic performance, standardized test scores, rank in class, essay, and recommendations are all considered. Tests are required of all students. Interview recommended for all. **Homeschooled:** Statement describing homeschool structure and mission, transcript of courses and grades, interview required.

High school preparation. College-preparatory program recommended. 21 units recommended. Recommended units include English 4, mathematics 3, social studies 3, science 3, foreign language 2 and academic electives 5. 1 health/physical education recommended.

2005-2006 Annual costs. Tuition/fees: $22,430. Room/board: $8,310. Books/supplies: $950. Personal expenses: $1,200.

2005-2006 Financial aid. Need-based: 612 full-time freshmen applied for aid; 440 were judged to have need; 440 of these received aid. Average need met was 79%. Average scholarship/grant was $10,809; average loan $3,447. 61% of total undergraduate aid awarded as scholarships/grants, 39% as loans/jobs. **Non-need-based:** Awarded to 1,404 full-time undergraduates, including 352 freshmen. Scholarships awarded for academics, alumni affiliation, art, athletics, job skills, minority status, music/drama, ROTC.

Application procedures. Admission: Closing date 2/1 (postmark date). $35 fee, may be waived for applicants with need. Application may be submitted online. Admission notification 3/15. Must reply by 5/1. Must reply by May 1 or within 2 week(s) if notified thereafter. **Financial aid:** Priority date 2/15; no closing date. FAFSA required. Applicants notified on a rolling basis starting 3/1; must reply by 5/1.

Academics. Strong emphasis on ethics and values in core curriculum. **Special study options:** Combined bachelor's/graduate degree, cooperative education, cross-registration, double major, dual enrollment of high school students, ESL, honors, independent study, internships, study abroad, teacher certification program, urban semester, Washington semester, weekend college. Cooperative science-engineering program (physics and chemistry) with University of Cincinnati, forestry program and environmental management programs with Duke University, Service Learning Semester. **Credit/placement by examination:** AP, CLEP, IB, SAT, ACT, institutional tests. 30 credit hours maximum toward associate degree. No limit on credit by examination for bachelor's degree. **Support services:** Learning center, preadmission summer program, reduced course load, remedial instruction, study skills assistance, tutoring, writing center.

Majors. Biology: General. **Business:** General, accounting, business admin, entrepreneurial studies, finance, human resources, international, management information systems, managerial economics, marketing. **Communications:** Advertising, organizational, public relations, radio/tv. **Computer sciences:** Computer science. **Conservation:** Management/policy. **Education:** General, biology, chemistry, early childhood, elementary, middle, Montessori teacher, music, physics, special. **English:** English lit. **Foreign languages:** Classics, French, German, Spanish. **Health:** Athletic training, clinical lab science, nursing (RN). **History:** General. **Interdisciplinary:** Natural sciences. **Liberal arts:** Arts/sciences. **Math:** General. **Parks/recreation:** Sports admin. **Philosophy/religion:** Philosophy. **Physical sciences:** Chemistry, physics. **Protective services:** Criminal justice. **Psychology:** General. **Public administration:** Social work. **Social sciences:** Economics, international relations, political science, sociology. **Theology:** Theology. **Visual/performing arts:** Studio arts.

Most popular majors. Business/marketing 26%, communications/journalism 9%, education 6%, liberal arts 14%, psychology 6%.

Computing on campus. 276 workstations in dormitories, library, student center. Dormitories wired for high-speed internet access and linked to campus network. Commuter students can connect to campus network. Online course registration, online library, helpline, student web hosting, wireless network available.

Student life. Freshman orientation: Mandatory, $175 fee. Preregistration for classes offered. 4-day program for new students and their families. **Policies:** Responsible computer use, campus alcohol policy, standards for off-campus living. Freshmen permitted cars on campus. **Housing:** Guaranteed on-campus for freshmen. Coed dorms, apartments, substance-free housing available. $200 nonrefundable deposit, deadline 5/1. Special interest/theme housing available. **Activities:** Bands, choral groups, dance, drama, literary magazine, music ensembles, musical theater, opera, radio station, student government, student newspaper, TV station, Black student association, International student society, center for peace and justice, Amnesty International, College Republicans, College Democrats, Earth Bread, Earthcare, Voices of Solidarity, Student Organization of Latinos.

Athletics. NCAA. **Intercollegiate:** Baseball M, basketball, cross-country, golf, soccer, swimming, tennis, track and field, volleyball W. **Intramural:** Basketball, bowling, football (non-tackle), golf, handball, racquetball, soccer, softball, tennis, volleyball. **Team name:** Musketeers.

Student services. Adult student services, alcohol/substance abuse counseling, campus ministries, career counseling, services for economically disadvantaged, student employment services, financial aid counseling, health services, minority student services, personal counseling, placement for graduates, veterans' counselor. **Physically disabled:** Services for visually, speech, hearing impaired. **Learning disabled:** Comprehensive services available.

Contact. E-mail: xuadmit@xavier.edu
Phone: (513) 745-3301 Toll-free number: (877) 982-3648
Fax: (513) 745-4319
Marc Camille, Dean of Admission, Xavier University, 3800 Victory Parkway, Cincinnati, OH 45207-5311

Youngstown State University

Youngstown, Ohio
www.ysu.edu **CB code: 1975**

- Public 4-year university
- Commuter campus in small city
- 11,501 degree-seeking undergraduates: 20% part-time, 56% women, 12% African American, 1% Asian American, 2% Hispanic American, 1% international
- 959 degree-seeking graduate students
- 37% graduate within 6 years

General. Founded in 1908. Regionally accredited. **Degrees:** 1,537 bachelor's, 173 associate awarded; master's, doctoral offered. **ROTC:** Army, Air Force. **Location:** 60 miles from Cleveland, 60 miles from Pittsburgh. **Calendar:** Semester, limited summer session. **Full-time faculty:** 427 total; 82% have terminal degrees, 14% minority, 37% women. **Part-time faculty:** 552 total; 20% have terminal degrees, 5% minority, 52% women. **Class size:** 38% <20, 50% 20-39, 6% 40-49, 5% 50-99, 2% >100. **Special facilities:** Planetarium, historic preservation center, art museum.

Freshman class profile. 4,019 applied, 3,994 admitted, 2,258 enrolled.

Mid 50% test scores		**Rank in top tenth:**	9%
SAT verbal:	430-550	**End year in good standing:**	79%
SAT math:	410-550	**Return as sophomores:**	71%
ACT:	17-23	**Out-of-state:**	10%
GPA 3.50 or higher:	21%	**Live on campus:**	23%
GPA 3.0-3.49:	22%	**Fraternities:**	3%
GPA 2.0-2.99:	44%	**Sororities:**	3%
Rank in top quarter:	25%		

Basis for selection. Open admission, but selective for some programs and for out-of-state students. Out-of-state applicants must be in top two-thirds of class, or have ACT composite score of 17 or combined SAT of 820. Open admission policy for Ohio residents and Mercer and Lawrence County, Pennsylvania residents. Selective admission to nursing, engineering and some other programs. Interview required for BS/MD program; audition required for music, BFA theater programs. **Homeschooled:** Students conditionally admitted if high school GPA is below 2.00 and composite ACT score (or SAT equivalent) is 17 or below. Official transcript showing documentation of grades 9-12 coursework completed and date of completion required. A copy of academic assessment (i.e. Iowa Basic Skills Test, California Achievement Test, etc.) reports submitted to the appropriate superintendent of school pursuant to Section 3301-34-04 of the Ohio Administrative Code also required. Curriculum outline, detailing course content, textbooks used, and any other relevant information regarding coursework must be submitted.

High school preparation. 16 units recommended. Recommended units include English 4, mathematics 3, social studies 3, science 2 (laboratory 1) and foreign language 2. 1 fine and performing arts recommended. Recommended coursework should include English composition; algebra I and II, geometry; laboratory science; and US history and government.

2005-2006 Annual costs. Tuition/fees: $6,333; $11,541 out-of-state. Residents of any out-of-state area within 100 miles of campus are charged $8,804.88 yearly tuition. Per credit hour charge is $366.87. Room/board: $6,280. Books/supplies: $1,014. Personal expenses: $576.

2004-2005 Financial aid. Need-based: 29% of total undergraduate aid awarded as scholarships/grants, 71% as loans/jobs. **Non-need-based:** Scholarships awarded for academics, alumni affiliation, athletics, ROTC, state residency.

Application procedures. Admission: Priority date 2/15; deadline 8/15. $30 fee, may be waived for applicants with need. Application may be submitted online. Admission notification on a rolling basis. Students who apply by February 15 are eligible for early registration and orientation. **Financial aid:** Priority date 2/15; no closing date. FAFSA, institutional form required. Applicants notified on a rolling basis starting 5/30.

Academics. Special study options: Accelerated study, combined bachelor's/graduate degree, cooperative education, cross-registration, distance learning, double major, ESL, exchange student, honors, internships, student-designed major, study abroad, teacher certification program, urban semester, Washington semester, weekend college. Off-campus study with Lorain County Community College. **Credit/placement by examination:** AP, CLEP, IB, institutional tests. In select CLEP and AP tests, higher grade may make student eligible for more credits. **Support services:** Learning center, pre-admission summer program, reduced course load, remedial instruction, study skills assistance, tutoring, writing center.

Majors. Area/ethnic studies: African-American, American. **Biology:** General. **Business:** General, accounting, apparel, banking/financial services, business admin, fashion, finance, financial planning, hospitality admin, hospitality/recreation, human resources, management information systems, managerial economics, marketing, merchandising, office management, operations, public finance, purchasing, retailing, sales/distribution, selling, tourism promotion, tourism/travel. **Communications:** General, advertising, journalism, public relations, radio/tv. **Computer sciences:** General, computer science, information systems, information technology, programming. **Conservation:** General, environmental science. **Education:** General, art, autistic, biology, business, chemistry, computer, drama/dance, early childhood, elementary, emotionally handicapped, English, family/consumer sciences, foreign languages, French, health, health occupations, history, kindergarten/preschool, learning disabled, mathematics, mentally handicapped, middle, multi-level teacher, multiple handicapped, music, physical, physics, science, secondary, social science, social studies, Spanish, special, speech. **Engineering:** General, chemical, civil, computer, electrical, industrial, materials, mechanical, structural. **Engineering technology:** General, civil, electrical, mechanical. **English:** English lit, speech/rhetoric, technical writing. **Family/consumer sciences:** General, clothing/textiles, family studies, family/community services, food/nutrition, work/family studies. **Foreign languages:** General, French, German, Italian, Spanish. **Health:** Athletic training, clinical lab science, community health, community health services, dietetics, facilities admin, nursing (RN), predentistry, premedicine, prepharmacy, preveterinary, public health ed, respiratory therapy technology. **History:** General. **Legal studies:** Prelaw. **Math:** General. **Parks/recreation:** Exercise sciences, health/fitness, sports admin. **Philosophy/religion:** Philosophy, religion. **Physical sciences:** General, astronomy, chemistry, geology, physics, planetary. **Protective services:** Corrections, criminal justice, forensics, law enforcement admin, security services. **Psychology:** General. **Public administration:** General, social work. **Social sciences:** General, anthropology, econometrics, economics, geography, international economics, political science, sociology. **Visual/performing arts:** General, acting, art, art history/conservation, commercial/advertising art, dramatic, jazz, music history, music performance, music theory/composition, painting, photography, piano/organ, printmaking, stringed instruments, studio arts, theater design, voice/opera.

Most popular majors. Business/marketing 17%, education 23%, engineering/engineering technologies 8%, health sciences 8%.

Computing on campus. 1,619 workstations in dormitories, library, student center. Dormitories wired for high-speed internet access and linked to campus network. Commuter students can connect to campus network. Online course registration, online library, helpline, repair service, student web hosting, wireless network available.

Student life. Freshman orientation: Available, $50 fee. Orientation held in June, July, and August. **Policies:** Freshmen permitted cars on campus. **Housing:** Guaranteed on-campus for all undergraduates. Coed dorms, single-sex dorms, apartments, fraternity/sorority housing, substance-free housing available. $200 deposit. University scholars program honors facility available. **Activities:** Bands, choral groups, dance, drama, literary magazine, music ensembles, musical theater, opera, radio station, student government, student newspaper, symphony orchestra, College Republicans, Student Democrats, Pan-African Student Union, National Panhellenic Council, Hispanic-American organization, Student Athlete Advisory Council, Interfraternity Council, Golden Key, Omicron Delta Kappa, Gospel Choir, Panhellenic Council.

Athletics. NCAA. **Intercollegiate:** Baseball M, basketball, cross-country, football (tackle) M, golf, soccer W, softball W, swimming W, tennis, track and field, volleyball W. **Intramural:** Badminton, basketball, bowling, football (non-tackle), golf, handball, ice hockey, lacrosse, racquetball, soccer, softball, swimming, table tennis, tennis, volleyball, water polo. **Team name:** Penguins.

Student services. Adult student services, alcohol/substance abuse counseling, campus ministries, career counseling, student employment services, financial aid counseling, health services, minority student services, on-campus daycare, personal counseling, placement for graduates, veterans' counselor, women's services. **Physically disabled:** Services for visually, speech, hearing impaired.

Contact. E-mail: enroll@ysu.edu
Phone: (330) 941-2000 Toll-free number: (877) 468-6978
Fax: (330) 941-3674
Sue Davis, Director of Undergraduate Admissions, Youngstown State University, One University Plaza, Youngstown, OH 44555-0001

Oklahoma

Bacone College
Muskogee, Oklahoma
www.bacone.edu **CB code: 6030**

- Private 4-year liberal arts college affiliated with American Baptist Churches in the USA
- Commuter campus in large town
- 790 degree-seeking undergraduates: 22% part-time, 55% women, 23% African American, 4% Hispanic American, 36% Native American
- 50% of applicants admitted
- SAT or ACT required

General. Founded in 1880. Regionally accredited. Unique American Indian heritage and commitment to serving American Indians. Guided by Christian principles. **Degrees:** 49 bachelor's, 91 associate awarded. **Location:** 60 miles from Tulsa. **Calendar:** Semester, limited summer session. **Full-time faculty:** 26 total; 54% have terminal degrees, 35% minority, 73% women. **Part-time faculty:** 42 total; 17% have terminal degrees, 36% minority, 62% women. **Class size:** 70% < 20, 25% 20-39, 5% 40-49. **Special facilities:** Native American museum, Indian collection library.

Freshman class profile. 840 applied, 420 admitted, 220 enrolled.

Mid 50% test scores			
SAT verbal:	340-430	Rank in top quarter:	18%
SAT math:	350-460	Rank in top tenth:	6%
ACT:	15-20	End year in good standing:	56%
GPA 3.50 or higher:	18%	Return as sophomores:	57%
GPA 3.0-3.49:	24%	Out-of-state:	15%
GPA 2.0-2.99:	54%	Live on campus:	36%

Basis for selection. Student must meet high school GPA and ACT or SAT requirements. 2.0 High School GPA and 18 ACT required. Additional standards required for admission to nursing or radiography programs. ACT results used as basis for counseling. Interview recommended for nursing, radiologic technology programs. **Homeschooled:** Official transcript from an accredited home school organization or a General Education Diploma (GED). Home school and GED students must have ACT score of 18.

High school preparation. Recommended units include English 4, mathematics 3, history 2, science 2 (laboratory 2).

2005-2006 Annual costs. Tuition/fees: $9,220. Room/board: $5,700. Books/supplies: $1,000. Personal expenses: $500.

2005-2006 Financial aid. All financial aid based on need. Average need met was 89%. Average scholarship/grant was $5,300; average loan $2,625. 51% of total undergraduate aid awarded as scholarships/grants, 49% as loans/jobs.

Application procedures. Admission: No deadline. $25 fee, may be waived for applicants with need. Application may be submitted online. Admission notification on a rolling basis. **Financial aid:** Priority date 3/31; no closing date. FAFSA required. Applicants notified on a rolling basis starting 4/1; must reply within 2 week(s) of notification.

Academics. Special study options: Accelerated study, cross-registration, double major, dual enrollment of high school students, liberal arts/career combination. **Credit/placement by examination:** AP, CLEP, SAT, ACT, institutional tests. 15 credit hours maximum toward associate degree. **Support services:** Learning center, remedial instruction, tutoring.

Majors. Business: Business admin. **Education:** Early childhood, elementary, health, physical. **Health:** Nursing (RN). **Legal studies:** Prelaw.

Most popular majors. Business/marketing 57%, education 39%.

Computing on campus. 84 workstations in library, computer center. Commuter students can connect to campus network.

Student life. Freshman orientation: Mandatory. Preregistration for classes offered. **Policies:** Freshmen permitted cars on campus. **Housing:** Single-sex dorms available. $100 deposit. **Activities:** Choral groups, drama, student government, student newspaper, Christian Fellowship, Indian club, Black Student Union, cultural exchange student organization.

Athletics. NAIA. **Intercollegiate:** Baseball M, basketball, rodeo, soccer, softball W, wrestling. **Intramural:** Basketball, cross-country, football (tackle) M, golf, soccer, softball, table tennis, tennis, track and field, volleyball, wrestling. **Team name:** Warriors.

Student services. Career counseling, student employment services, health services, personal counseling, veterans' counselor. **Physically disabled:** Services for visually, speech, hearing impaired.

Contact. E-mail: admissionsoffice@bacone.edu
Phone: (918) 683-4581 ext. 7342 Toll-free number: (888) 682-5514 ext. 7342 Fax: (918) 781-7416
Rev. Leroy Thompson, Director of Admissions, Bacone College, 2299 Old Bacone Road, Muskogee, OK 74403

Cameron University
Lawton, Oklahoma **CB member**
www.cameron.edu **CB code: 6080**

- Public 4-year university and liberal arts college
- Commuter campus in small city
- 5,076 degree-seeking undergraduates: 38% part-time, 60% women, 19% African American, 3% Asian American, 9% Hispanic American, 8% Native American, 3% international
- 434 graduate students
- 30% graduate within 6 years

General. Founded in 1909. Regionally accredited. **Degrees:** 577 bachelor's, 150 associate awarded; master's offered. **ROTC:** Army. **Location:** 100 miles from Oklahoma City. **Calendar:** Semester, limited summer session. **Full-time faculty:** 180 total; 69% have terminal degrees, 14% minority, 36% women. **Part-time faculty:** 117 total; 14% have terminal degrees, 20% minority, 45% women. **Class size:** 43% < 20, 45% 20-39, 9% 40-49, 3% 50-99.

Freshman class profile. 2,826 applied, 2,819 admitted, 2,184 enrolled.

Mid 50% test scores			
ACT:	16-22	Out-of-state:	3%
Rank in top quarter:	31%	Live on campus:	7%
Rank in top tenth:	14%	Fraternities:	2%
Return as sophomores:	56%	Sororities:	2%

Basis for selection. Open admission, but selective for some programs. 2.7 GPA and rank in top half of class, or ACT composite score of 20 required for bachelor's degree programs. Open admissions for associate degree candidates only. Those who do not meet bachelor's criteria are admitted as associate degree candidates.

High school preparation. 15 units required. Required units include English 4, mathematics 3, history 2, science 2 (laboratory 2) and academic electives 3. One unit of citizenship elective in one of the following: government, geography, economics or non-Western culture.

2005-2006 Annual costs. Tuition/fees: $3,240; $7,830 out-of-state. Room/board: $3,292. Books/supplies: $1,050.

2004-2005 Financial aid. Need-based: 612 full-time freshmen applied for aid; 529 were judged to have need; 510 of these received aid. Average need met was 95%. Average scholarship/grant was $6,050; average loan $2,000. 49% of total undergraduate aid awarded as scholarships/grants, 51% as loans/jobs. **Non-need-based:** Awarded to 677 full-time undergraduates, including 364 freshmen. Scholarships awarded for academics, alumni affiliation, art, athletics, leadership, music/drama, ROTC.

Application procedures. Admission: Priority date 8/1; no deadline. $15 fee. Application may be submitted online. Admission notification on a rolling basis. **Financial aid:** Priority date 6/15; no closing date. FAFSA required. Applicants notified on a rolling basis starting 4/1; must reply within 2 week(s) of notification.

Academics. Special study options: Accelerated study, combined bachelor's/graduate degree, distance learning, double major, dual enrollment of high school students, honors, independent study, internships, liberal arts/career combination, teacher certification program. **Credit/placement by examination:** AP, CLEP, IB. 45 credit hours maximum toward associate degree, 64 toward bachelor's. **Support services:** Learning center, pre-admission summer program, reduced course load, remedial instruction, study skills assistance, tutoring, writing center.

Majors. **Agriculture:** General, agronomy, animal sciences, horticultural science. **Biology:** General. **Business:** Accounting, business admin. **Communications:** General, broadcast journalism, journalism, public relations. **Computer sciences:** General, computer science, web page design. **Education:** General, art, biology, chemistry, early childhood, elementary, English, history, mathematics, music, physical, science, secondary, social studies. **Engineering technology:** Electrical, mechanical drafting. **English:** English lit. **Family/consumer sciences:** General. **Foreign languages:** General, linguistics. **Health:** Clinical lab technology. **History:** General. **Interdisciplinary:** Biological/physical sciences, natural sciences. **Math:** General. **Parks/recreation:** Health/fitness. **Physical sciences:** Chemistry, physics. **Protective services:** Criminal justice. **Psychology:** General. **Social sciences:** Political science, sociology. **Visual/performing arts:** Art, dramatic, studio arts.

Most popular majors. Business/marketing 19%, computer/information sciences 13%, education 13%, interdisciplinary studies 10%, psychology 8%.

Computing on campus. 350 workstations in dormitories, library, computer center. Dormitories wired for high-speed internet access and linked to campus network. Commuter students can connect to campus network. Online library, helpline, student web hosting, wireless network available.

Student life. **Freshman orientation:** Mandatory. 7 sessions annually, June through August. **Policies:** Freshmen permitted cars on campus. **Housing:** Guaranteed on-campus for all undergraduates. Single-sex dorms, special housing for disabled, apartments, substance-free housing available. $200 fully refundable deposit, deadline 7/1. Quiet areas available. **Activities:** Bands, choral groups, drama, film society, literary magazine, music ensembles, musical theater, opera, radio station, student government, student newspaper, symphony orchestra, TV station, Ebony society, students of the Caribbean Alliance, American Indian student association, Latin alliance, international club, Asian/Pacific Islander student association, Cameron Campus Ministry, Baptist Collegiate Ministry, Chi Alpha, Young Republicans.

Athletics. NCAA. **Intercollegiate:** Baseball M, basketball, cross-country M, golf, softball W, tennis, volleyball W. **Intramural:** Badminton, basketball, bowling, football (non-tackle), golf, racquetball, softball, tennis, volleyball. **Team name:** Aggies.

Student services. Campus ministries, career counseling, services for economically disadvantaged, student employment services, financial aid counseling, minority student services, veterans' counselor. **Physically disabled:** Services for visually, speech, hearing impaired.

Contact. E-mail: zoed@cameron.edu
Phone: (580) 581-2230 Toll-free number: (888) 454-7600
Fax: (580) 581-5514
Zoe DuRant, Director of Admissions, Cameron University, 2800 West Gore Boulevard, Lawton, OK 73505-6377

East Central University

Ada, Oklahoma
www.ecok.edu **CB code: 6186**

- Public 4-year university
- Commuter campus in large town
- 4,065 degree-seeking undergraduates
- SAT or ACT required

General. Founded in 1909. Regionally accredited. **Degrees:** 620 bachelor's awarded; master's offered. **Location:** 86 miles from Oklahoma City. **Calendar:** Semester, extensive summer session. **Full-time faculty:** 160 total. **Part-time faculty:** 70 total.

Freshman class profile.

Out-of-state:	2%	**Fraternities:**	55%
Live on campus:	40%	**Sororities:**	45%

Basis for selection. Rank in top 50 percent of graduating class, 19 ACT score or SAT equivalent, 2.7 high school GPA and required course work.

High school preparation. 15 units required. Required and recommended units include English 4, mathematics 3, social studies 1, history 2, science 3 (laboratory 1), foreign language 1 and academic electives 4.

2005-2006 Annual costs. Tuition/fees: $3,256; $7,889 out-of-state. Room/board: $3,000. Books/supplies: $500.

2005-2006 Financial aid. **Non-need-based:** Scholarships awarded for academics, athletics.

Application procedures. **Admission:** No deadline. No application fee. Application may be submitted online. Admission notification on a rolling basis. **Financial aid:** Closing date 3/1. FAFSA, institutional form required. Applicants notified on a rolling basis starting 4/15; must reply within 2 week(s) of notification.

Academics. **Special study options:** Distance learning, double major, dual enrollment of high school students, exchange student, honors, independent study, internships, teacher certification program. **Credit/placement by examination:** AP, CLEP, IB, institutional tests. 94 credit hours maximum toward bachelor's degree. Students do not receive CLEP credit until 12 hours completed at ECU with GPA of 2.0 or higher. **Support services:** Learning center, pre-admission summer program, reduced course load, remedial instruction, tutoring, writing center.

Majors. **Biology:** General. **Business:** General, accounting, administrative services, business admin, finance, managerial economics, marketing, office management, operations, sales/distribution. **Communications:** General, broadcast journalism, journalism. **Computer sciences:** General. **Education:** Agricultural, business, drama/dance, early childhood, elementary, English, family/consumer sciences, history, mathematics, mentally handicapped, music, physical, physically handicapped, science, social studies, special, speech, technology/industrial arts, trade/industrial. **English:** Speech/rhetoric, technical writing. **Family/consumer sciences:** General, clothing/textiles. **Foreign languages:** Comparative lit. **Health:** Athletic training, environmental health, medical records technology, predentistry, premedicine, prepharmacy, preveterinary, vocational rehab counseling. **History:** General. **Legal studies:** Paralegal, prelaw. **Math:** General, applied. **Parks/recreation:** General, exercise sciences, health/fitness. **Physical sciences:** Chemistry, physics. **Protective services:** Criminal justice, police science. **Psychology:** General. **Public administration:** Community org/advocacy, human services, social work. **Social sciences:** General, cartography, criminology, political science, sociology. **Visual/performing arts:** Art, dramatic, piano/organ, studio arts, voice/opera.

Computing on campus. 485 workstations in library, computer center. Dormitories linked to campus network. Commuter students can connect to campus network. Helpline, repair service, wireless network available.

Student life. **Freshman orientation:** Mandatory. Preregistration for classes offered. **Policies:** Freshmen permitted cars on campus. **Housing:** Coed dorms, single-sex dorms, special housing for disabled, apartments, fraternity/sorority housing available. $50 deposit. **Activities:** Bands, choral groups, dance, drama, film society, literary magazine, music ensembles, musical theater, student government, student newspaper, Association of Black Students, Native American student association, Baptist Student Union, United Campus Ministry, Students with Disabilities, Church of Christ Bible Chair, Life House, Sigma Society, Panhellenic, Silent Friends Club.

Athletics. NCAA. **Intercollegiate:** Baseball M, basketball, cross-country, football (tackle) M, golf M, soccer W, softball W, tennis. **Intramural:** Basketball, soccer, softball, volleyball. **Team name:** Tigers.

Student services. Adult student services, career counseling, student employment services, financial aid counseling, health services, minority student services, on-campus daycare, personal counseling, placement for graduates, veterans' counselor. **Physically disabled:** Services for visually, speech, hearing impaired.

Contact. Phone: (580) 332-8000 Fax: (580) 310-5432
Pamla Armstrong, Registrar and Director of Admissions, East Central University, PMBJ8, 1100 East 14th Street, Ada, OK 74820

Family of Faith College

Shawnee, Oklahoma
www.familyoffaithcollege.com

- Private 4-year Bible and liberal arts college
- Residential campus

General. Accredited by ABHE. **Calendar:** Semester.

Annual costs/financial aid. Tuition/fees (2005-2006): $4,660. Room/board: $1,600.

Contact. Phone: (405) 275-5331
Vice President of Student Affairs, 30 Kinvill Road, Shawnee, OK 74802

Langston University

Langston, Oklahoma **CB member**
www.lunet.edu **CB code: 6361**

- Public 4-year liberal arts and teachers college
- Commuter campus in rural community

General. Founded in 1897. Regionally accredited. **Location:** 40 miles from Oklahoma City, 90 miles from Tulsa. **Calendar:** Semester.

Annual costs/financial aid. Tuition/fees (2005-2006): $3,241; $7,666 out-of-state. Room/board: $4,452. Books/supplies: $800. Personal expenses: $2,037. Need-based financial aid available to full-time and part-time students.

Contact. Phone: (405) 466-2231
Director of Enrollment Management, Box 728, Langston, OK 73050

Metropolitan College

Oklahoma City, Oklahoma
www.metropolitancollege.edu **CB code: 3066**

- Private 4-year business college
- Very large city
- 220 degree-seeking undergraduates

General. Accredited by ACCSCT. **Degrees:** 10 bachelor's, 43 associate awarded. **Calendar:** Trimester. **Full-time faculty:** 8 total. **Part-time faculty:** 25 total.

Basis for selection. Must pass 1-minute typing test. Applicants must submit SAT or ACT, or take Wonderlic exam (SLE) at Metropolitan.

2005-2006 Annual costs. Tuition varies by program and degree type. Certificate programs start at $7,410. Associate degrees start at $13,286. Bachelor's degrees range from $24,808 to $26,408. Costs are for the entire program and include books and fees.

Application procedures. Admission: No deadline. $50 fee.

Academics. Credit/placement by examination: CLEP.

Majors. Legal studies: Court reporting.

Contact. E-mail: metropolitan@mail.gorilla.net
Phone: (405) 843-1000 Fax: (405) 843-2325
Josita Baker, Director of Admissions, Metropolitan College, 1900 Northwest Expressway, Suite R302, Oklahoma City, OK 73118

Metropolitan College

Tulsa, Oklahoma
www.metropolitancollege.edu **CB code: 3072**

- Private 4-year college of legal studies
- Commuter campus in very large city
- 81 degree-seeking undergraduates
- Interview required

General. Accredited by ACCSCT. **Degrees:** 15 bachelor's, 32 associate awarded. **Calendar:** Continuous, extensive summer session. **Full-time faculty:** 4 total; 50% have terminal degrees, 25% minority, 75% women. **Part-time faculty:** 12 total; 33% have terminal degrees, 58% women.

Basis for selection. Open admission. Admission interview required, typing and problem-solving evaluation included.

Financial aid. All financial aid based on need.

Application procedures. Admission: No deadline. $50 fee. Admission notification on a rolling basis. **Financial aid:** No deadline. FAFSA required. Applicants notified on a rolling basis.

Academics. Credit/placement by examination: CLEP.

Majors. Legal studies: General, court reporting.

Student life. Freshman orientation: Mandatory.

Student services. Adult student services, financial aid counseling, placement for graduates.

Contact. E-mail: admissions@metropolitancollege.edu
Phone: (918) 627-9300 Fax: (918) 627-2122
Vicki Angelo, Admissions Director, Metropolitan College, 10820 E. 45th St. , Ste. #B-101, Tulsa, OK 74146

Mid-America Christian University

Oklahoma City, Oklahoma
www.macu.edu **CB code: 0918**

- Private 4-year university and liberal arts college affiliated with Church of God
- Residential campus in very large city
- 710 degree-seeking undergraduates: 10% African American, 4% Hispanic American, 9% Native American
- SAT or ACT required
- 38% graduate within 6 years

General. Founded in 1953. Regionally accredited; also accredited by ABHE. **Degrees:** 138 bachelor's, 2 associate awarded; master's offered. **Location:** 10 miles from downtown. **Calendar:** Semester, limited summer session. **Full-time faculty:** 20 total. **Part-time faculty:** 30 total. **Class size:** 100% 20-39.

Freshman class profile.

Out-of-state:	56%	**Live on campus:**	71%

Basis for selection. Applicants admitted who feel calling to full-time Christian vocations or seek God's will for their lives in spiritual environment. 2 references required. Interview, audition recommended. **Homeschooled:** Applicants without a GED must have a minimum ACT score of 15 in English and 14 in math.

High school preparation. 16 units recommended. Recommended units include English 4, mathematics 2, social studies 2, science 2 and foreign language 2.

2006-2007 Annual costs. Tuition/fees (projected): $11,100. Room/board: $4,550. Books/supplies: $800. Personal expenses: $660.

Financial aid. Non-need-based: Scholarships awarded for academics, leadership, minority status, music/drama.

Application procedures. Admission: Priority date 8/15; no deadline. $25 fee, may be waived for applicants with need. Admission notification on a rolling basis beginning on or about 2/1. **Financial aid:** Priority date 5/1; no closing date. FAFSA required. Applicants notified on a rolling basis starting 5/1.

Academics. Students must major in Bible/theology in addition to other majors offered. Degree-completion program available for enrollees 25 years of age and above with approximately 2 years of college experience. **Special study options:** Combined bachelor's/graduate degree, cooperative education, distance learning, double major, dual enrollment of high school students, external degree, independent study, internships, liberal arts/career combination, teacher certification program, weekend college. **Credit/placement by examination:** AP, CLEP, institutional tests. 30 credit hours maximum toward bachelor's degree. **Support services:** Remedial instruction, tutoring, writing center.

Majors. Business: Business admin, management information systems, management science. **Education:** Elementary, English, music, secondary, social science, social studies. **Interdisciplinary:** Behavioral sciences. **Philosophy/religion:** Religion. **Protective services:** Law enforcement admin. **Theology:** Bible, pastoral counseling, sacred music, theology. **Visual/performing arts:** Music performance.

Most popular majors. Business/marketing 35%, communications/journalism 10%, philosophy/religious studies 9%, psychology 17%, security/protective services 21%.

Computing on campus. 40 workstations in library, computer center. Dormitories wired for high-speed internet access and linked to campus network. Online library available.

Student life. Freshman orientation: Mandatory. Preregistration for classes offered. Held 1 day prior to start of classes. **Policies:** No smoking or drinking allowed on campus. Religious observance required. Freshmen permitted cars on campus. **Housing:** Guaranteed on-campus for freshmen. Single-sex dorms, substance-free housing available. $50 deposit. **Activities:** Concert band, choral groups, drama, music ensembles, musical theater, student government, Missions Club, Student Ministerial Fellowship, Ministry Refresher Institute.

Athletics. NCCAA. **Intercollegiate:** Baseball M, basketball, golf, soccer M, softball W, volleyball W. **Intramural:** Basketball, bowling, softball W, table tennis, volleyball. **Team name:** Evangels.

Student services. Campus ministries, career counseling, student employment services, financial aid counseling, health services, personal counseling, placement for graduates, veterans' counselor. **Physically disabled:** Services for speech impaired.

Contact. E-mail: info@macu.edu
Phone: (405) 692-3188 Toll-free number: (888) 436-3035
Fax: (405) 692-3165
Haley Hope, Director of Admissions, Mid-America Christian University, 3500 SW 119th Street, Oklahoma City, OK 73170

National Education Center: Spartan School of Aeronautics

Tulsa, Oklahoma
www.spartan.edu **CB code: 0336**

- For-profit 4-year technical college
- Commuter campus in large city
- 595 degree-seeking undergraduates
- Interview required

General. Founded in 1928. Accredited by ACCSCT. Multicampus institution. All campuses in Tulsa including one at Jones Airport. **Degrees:** 29 bachelor's, 192 associate awarded. **Location:** 100 miles from Oklahoma City. **Calendar:** Differs by program, extensive summer session. **Full-time faculty:** 101 total.

Freshman class profile.

Out-of-state:	90%	**Live on campus:**	24%

Basis for selection. ACT, SAT Subject Tests recommended.

2006-2007 Annual costs. Tech program tuition is $12,000 per academic year; flight program tuition is approximately $14,000 per academic year; bachelor' s program tuition is $8,910 per academic year. Books/Tools and supplies will vary by program. Books/supplies: $975. Personal expenses: $1,512.

Application procedures. Admission: No deadline. $100 fee. Admission notification on a rolling basis. **Financial aid:** No deadline. FAFSA, institutional form required. Applicants notified on a rolling basis starting 2/1; must reply within 2 week(s) of notification.

Academics. Special study options: Cross-registration. **Credit/placement by examination:** CLEP, institutional tests. No more than half of credits required for degree may be earned through examination. **Support services:** Remedial instruction, tutoring.

Majors. Transportation: Aviation management.

Computing on campus. Dormitories wired for high-speed internet access.

Student life. Freshman orientation: Mandatory. Usually held on Friday immediately preceding Monday start date of classes. Program introduces students to college's department heads and provides information on college procedures, policies and financial aid. **Policies:** Freshmen permitted cars on campus. **Housing:** Apartments available. **Activities:** Student government, student newspaper.

Athletics. Intramural: Baseball M, basketball M, bowling, soccer M, softball M, table tennis M, volleyball M.

Student services. Career counseling, student employment services, financial aid counseling, health services, personal counseling, placement for graduates, veterans' counselor.

Contact. E-mail: spartan@mail.spartan.edu
Phone: (918) 836-6886 Toll-free number: (800) 331-1204
Fax: (918) 831-5287
Mark Fowler, Vice President, Student Finance and Records, National Education Center: Spartan School of Aeronautics, Box 582833, Tulsa, OK 74158

Northeastern State University

Tahlequah, Oklahoma
www.nsuok.edu **CB code: 6485**

- Public 4-year university
- Commuter campus in large town
- 8,613 degree-seeking undergraduates: 24% part-time, 61% women, 6% African American, 1% Asian American, 2% Hispanic American, 29% Native American, 3% international
- 1,077 degree-seeking graduate students
- 76% of applicants admitted
- ACT (writing optional) required
- 32% graduate within 6 years; 8% enter graduate study

General. Founded in 1851. Regionally accredited. **Degrees:** 1,391 bachelor's awarded; master's, first professional offered. **ROTC:** Army. **Location:** 60 miles from Tulsa, 30 miles from Muskogee. **Calendar:** Semester, extensive summer session. **Full-time faculty:** 304 total; 72% have terminal degrees, 9% minority, 46% women. **Part-time faculty:** 156 total; 20% have terminal degrees, 13% minority, 60% women. **Class size:** 40% < 20, 47% 20-39, 6% 40-49, 6% 50-99, less than 1% >100. **Special facilities:** Center for the Study of Literacy, Center for Tribal Studies, Oklahoma Institute for Learning Styles.

Freshman class profile. 2,174 applied, 1,651 admitted, 1,169 enrolled.

Mid 50% test scores		**Out-of-state:**	9%
ACT:	18-23	**Live on campus:**	62%
Rank in top quarter:	47%	**International:**	3%
Rank in top tenth:	25%	**Fraternities:**	7%
Return as sophomores:	66%	**Sororities:**	1%

Basis for selection. Admissions based on secondary school record, class rank, and standardized test scores. Audition required, interview recommended for music program. Interview recommended for drama program; portfolio recommended for graphic art program.

High school preparation. College-preparatory program required. 15 units required. Required and recommended units include English 4, mathematics 3, social studies 2, history 2, science 2 (laboratory 2), foreign language 2 and academic electives 4.

2005-2006 Annual costs. Tuition/fees: $3,300; $8,100 out-of-state. Room/board: $3,100. Books/supplies: $900. Personal expenses: $1,080.

2005-2006 Financial aid. Need-based: Average need met was 63%. Average scholarship/grant was $1,845; average loan $1,107. 48% of total undergraduate aid awarded as scholarships/grants, 52% as loans/jobs. **Non-need-based:** Scholarships awarded for academics, alumni affiliation, art, athletics, leadership, minority status, music/drama, state residency. **Additional information:** Participates in off-campus job location & development program to assist students with off-campus employers to earn money for college expenses.

Application procedures. Admission: Closing date 8/1. No application fee. Application may be submitted online. Admission notification on a rolling basis. **Financial aid:** Priority date 4/15; no closing date. FAFSA, institutional form required. Applicants notified on a rolling basis starting 3/15; must reply within 3 week(s) of notification.

Academics. NSU College of Optometry on campus. **Special study options:** Combined bachelor's/graduate degree, cooperative education, distance learning, double major, dual enrollment of high school students, honors, independent study, internships, liberal arts/career combination, student-designed major, teacher certification program, weekend college. **Credit/placement by examination:** AP, CLEP, IB, ACT, institutional tests. 31 credit hours maximum toward bachelor's degree. **Support services:** Learning center, pre-admission summer program, reduced course load, remedial instruction, study skills assistance, tutoring, writing center.

Majors. Area/ethnic studies: Native American. **Biology:** General, cell/histology, marine. **Business:** Accounting, business admin, entrepreneurial studies, finance, human resources, international, management information systems, management science, marketing, tourism/travel. **Communications:** Journalism. **Computer sciences:** Computer science, networking. **Conservation:** Environmental science. **Education:** General, art, biology, chemistry, early childhood, elementary, English, family/consumer sciences, health, mathematics, music, physical, physics, science, secondary, social studies, Spanish, special, speech, technology/industrial arts. **Engineering:** Environmental, industrial, physics. **Engineering technology:** Industrial safety. **English:** Speech/rhetoric. **Family/consumer sciences:** General, food/nutrition. **Foreign languages:** Spanish. **Health:** Athletic training, audiology/speech pathology, clinical lab technology, health care admin, nursing (RN), prenursing. **History:** General. **Legal studies:** Paralegal. **Math:** General. **Parks/recreation:** Exercise sciences, health/fitness. **Physical sciences:** Chemistry. **Protective services:** Criminal justice. **Psychology:** General. **Public administration:** General, social work. **Social sciences:** Geography, political science, sociology. **Visual/performing arts:** Art, commercial/advertising art, dramatic, studio arts.

Most popular majors. Business/marketing 21%, education 29%, security/protective services 7%.

Computing on campus. 450 workstations in dormitories, library, computer center. Dormitories wired for high-speed internet access and linked to campus network. Commuter students can connect to campus network. Online library, helpline, repair service, student web hosting, wireless network available.

Student life. Freshman orientation: Mandatory. Preregistration for classes offered. **Policies:** Freshmen permitted cars on campus. **Housing:** Guaranteed on-campus for freshmen. Coed dorms, single-sex dorms, special housing for disabled, apartments, fraternity/sorority housing available. $50 deposit. **Activities:** Bands, choral groups, dance, drama, literary magazine, music ensembles, musical theater, student government, student newspaper, TV station, Native American Student Association, American Indian Science & Engineering Society, Black Student Society, Campus Christian Fellowship, Baptist Student Union, Methodist Wesley Foundation, Chi Alpha Christian Fellowship, Emerson, Catholic Student Organization, Native American Campus Ministries.

Athletics. NCAA. **Intercollegiate:** Baseball M, basketball, football (tackle) M, golf, soccer, softball W, tennis W. **Intramural:** Basketball, bowling, football (non-tackle), golf, racquetball, rugby M, soccer, softball, swimming, tennis, volleyball. **Team name:** Redmen.

Student services. Adult student services, alcohol/substance abuse counseling, campus ministries, career counseling, services for economically disadvantaged, student employment services, financial aid counseling, health services, personal counseling, placement for graduates, veterans' counselor. **Physically disabled:** Services for visually, speech, hearing impaired.

Contact. E-mail: nsuinfo@nsuok.edu
Phone: (918) 456-5511 ext. 2200 Toll-free number: (800) 722-9614
Fax: (918) 458-2342
Dawn Cain, Director of Admissions, Northeastern State University, 600 North Grand Avenue, Tahlequah, OK 74464

Northwestern Oklahoma State University

Alva, Oklahoma
www.nwalva.edu **CB code: 6493**

- Public 4-year university and teachers college
- Commuter campus in small town
- 1,775 degree-seeking undergraduates: 5% African American, 1% Asian American, 3% Hispanic American, 4% Native American, 3% international
- 240 graduate students
- 99% of applicants admitted
- ACT (writing optional) required
- 29% graduate within 6 years

General. Founded in 1897. Regionally accredited. **Degrees:** 385 bachelor's awarded; master's offered. **Location:** 160 miles from Oklahoma City, 70 miles from Enid. **Calendar:** Semester, limited summer session. **Full-time faculty:** 85 total. **Part-time faculty:** 70 total. **Class size:** 69% < 20, 28% 20-39, 2% 40-49, less than 1% 50-99. **Special facilities:** Museum, wellness center, farm.

Freshman class profile. 526 applied, 522 admitted, 497 enrolled.

Mid 50% test scores		Out-of-state:	15%
ACT:	18-23	Live on campus:	62%
Return as sophomores:	64%	International:	4%

Basis for selection. Applicants with 2.7 GPA and in top 50 percent of class or with ACT composite score of 19 admitted unconditionally. Others admitted provisionally. Audition recommended for music program.

High school preparation. 15 units required. Required and recommended units include English 4, mathematics 3, history 2, science 2 (laboratory 2), foreign language 2 and academic electives 3. One unit required from either government, economics, geography or non-Western culture.

2005-2006 Annual costs. Tuition/fees: $3,270; $8,100 out-of-state. Room/board: $2,980. Books/supplies: $800. Personal expenses: $1,100.

Financial aid. Non-need-based: Scholarships awarded for academics, alumni affiliation, art, athletics, leadership, music/drama.

Application procedures. Admission: No deadline. $15 fee, may be waived for applicants with need. Admission notification on a rolling basis. **Financial aid:** No deadline. FAFSA, institutional form required. Applicants notified on a rolling basis starting 5/1.

Academics. Special study options: Distance learning, double major, dual enrollment of high school students, independent study, internships, teacher certification program. 2-2 programs in many professional fields. **Credit/placement by examination:** AP, CLEP, institutional tests. **Support services:** Learning center, reduced course load, remedial instruction, tutoring, writing center.

Majors. Agriculture: General, business. **Biology:** General. **Business:** Accounting, business admin, e-commerce. **Communications:** Broadcast journalism, journalism, public relations. **Computer sciences:** General, information systems, programming. **Conservation:** Management/policy. **Education:** General, business, early childhood, elementary, English, health, learning disabled, mathematics, mentally handicapped, music, physical, science, social science, Spanish, special, technology/industrial arts. **English:** Speech/rhetoric. **Health:** Nursing (RN). **History:** General. **Legal studies:** Prelaw. **Math:** General. **Parks/recreation:** Health/fitness. **Physical sciences:** Chemistry. **Protective services:** Police science. **Psychology:** General. **Public administration:** Social work. **Social sciences:** General, political science, sociology. **Visual/performing arts:** Dramatic, music performance, piano/organ, voice/opera.

Computing on campus. 93 workstations in library, computer center.

Student life. Freshman orientation: Available. Preregistration for classes offered. **Policies:** Freshmen permitted cars on campus. **Housing:** Guaranteed on-campus for all undergraduates. Single-sex dorms, special housing for disabled available. $75 deposit. **Activities:** Bands, choral groups, dance, drama, music ensembles, musical theater, radio station, student government, student newspaper, TV station, Black student organization, International Student Association, Student Oklahoma Education Association, Fellowship of Christian Athletes, College Republicans, Student Government Association, nontraditional students organization, Los Listos, University Democrats.

Athletics. NAIA. **Intercollegiate:** Baseball M, basketball, cross-country W, football (tackle) M, golf, rodeo, soccer W, softball W, track and field. **Intramural:** Basketball, volleyball. **Team name:** Rangers.

Student services. Adult student services, career counseling, student employment services, financial aid counseling, health services, personal counseling, placement for graduates, veterans' counselor. **Physically disabled:** Services for visually, speech, hearing impaired.

Contact. E-mail: recruit@nwosu.edu
Phone: (580) 327-8546 Fax: (580) 327-8413
Jennifer Goucher, Director of Recruitment, Northwestern Oklahoma State University, 709 Oklahoma Boulevard, Alva, OK 73717-2799

Oklahoma Baptist University

Shawnee, Oklahoma **CB member**
www.okbu.edu **CB code: 6541**

- Private 4-year university and liberal arts college affiliated with Southern Baptist Convention
- Residential campus in large town
- 1,441 degree-seeking undergraduates: 3% part-time, 60% women, 3% African American, 1% Asian American, 2% Hispanic American, 4% Native American, 3% international
- 75% of applicants admitted
- SAT or ACT required
- 53% graduate within 6 years; 40% enter graduate study

General. Founded in 1910. Regionally accredited. Each summer approximately 250 students, faculty and staff serve in projects around the world. About 300 students participate in local service projects during the year. **Degrees:** 314 bachelor's, 5 associate awarded; master's offered. **ROTC:** Air Force. **Location:** 35 miles from Oklahoma City, 90 miles from Tulsa. **Calendar:** Semester, limited summer session. **Full-time faculty:** 105 total; 69% have terminal degrees, 2% minority, 37% women. **Part-time faculty:** 40 total; 38% have terminal degrees, 8% minority, 30% women. **Class size:** 62% < 20, 31% 20-39, 3% 40-49, 3% 50-99. **Special facilities:** Planetarium (operated by students), greenhouse, music technology laboratory, biblical research library.

Freshman class profile. 1,161 applied, 868 admitted, 371 enrolled.

Mid 50% test scores		Return as sophomores:	68%
SAT verbal:	520-610	Out-of-state:	38%
SAT math:	490-570	Live on campus:	94%
ACT:	16-21	International:	6%
End year in good standing:	86%		

Basis for selection. Minimum 20 ACT or 950 SAT (exclusive of writing), minimum 3.0 GPA or class rank in top half required. Interview recommended for borderline applicants; audition recommended for drama, music programs; portfolio recommended for art program.

High school preparation. 17 units recommended. Recommended units include English 4, mathematics 3, social studies 2, history 1, science 3 (laboratory 2), foreign language 2 and academic electives 2. Mathematics recommendation includes 2 algebra and 1 plane geometry.

2005-2006 Annual costs. Tuition/fees: $13,846. Room/board: $4,340. Books/supplies: $650. Personal expenses: $1,400.

2004-2005 Financial aid. Need-based: 353 full-time freshmen applied for aid; 238 were judged to have need; 238 of these received aid. Average need met was 65%. Average scholarship/grant was $3,446; average loan $3,151. 44% of total undergraduate aid awarded as scholarships/grants, 56% as loans/jobs. **Non-need-based:** Awarded to 1,433 full-time undergraduates, including 418 freshmen. Scholarships awarded for academics, athletics, ROTC.

Application procedures. Admission: Priority date 3/15; deadline 8/1 (postmark date). $25 fee, may be waived for applicants with need. Admission notification on a rolling basis. **Financial aid:** Priority date 3/1; no closing date. FAFSA required. Applicants notified on a rolling basis starting 4/1; must reply by 5/1 or within 2 week(s) of notification.

Academics. Opportunities for January-term travel to Europe, Russia, South America; also opportunity to teach English in China and Hungary. **Special study options:** Accelerated study, combined bachelor's/graduate degree, cooperative education, double major, ESL, exchange student, honors, independent study, internships, liberal arts/career combination, student-designed major, study abroad, teacher certification program. Exchange program with Seinan Gakuin University, Japan, and Hong Kong Baptist College; opportunities for January-term travel to Europe, Russia, South America. **Credit/placement by examination:** AP, CLEP, IB, ACT, institutional tests. 32 credit hours maximum toward bachelor's degree. Essay required for English, government, history exams; oral exam required for French, German and Spanish; lab exam required for information systems. **Support services:** Learning center, pre-admission summer program, reduced course load, remedial instruction, study skills assistance, tutoring.

Majors. Biology: General, biochemistry. **Business:** General, accounting, business admin, finance, international, international finance, management information systems, management science, marketing. **Communications:** General, broadcast journalism, journalism, public relations. **Computer sciences:** General, applications programming, computer science, information systems, systems analysis. **Education:** Art, biology, chemistry, early childhood, elementary, English, foreign languages, French, German, health, history, learning disabled, mathematics, mentally handicapped, music, physical, physics, science, secondary, social studies, Spanish, special, speech. **English:** Speech/rhetoric. **Foreign languages:** General, French, German, Spanish. **Health:** Athletic training, nursing (RN). **History:** General. **Interdisciplinary:** Math/computer science. **Liberal arts:** Arts/sciences. **Math:** General. **Parks/recreation:** Exercise sciences, facilities management, health/fitness, sports admin. **Philosophy/religion:** Philosophy, religion. **Physical sciences:** Chemistry, physics. **Psychology:** General. **Public administration:** Social work. **Social sciences:** General, anthropology, political science, sociology. **Theology:** Bible, missionary, religious ed, sacred music, theology. **Visual/performing arts:** Art, dramatic, music performance, music theory/composition, piano/organ, studio arts, voice/opera.

Most popular majors. Business/marketing 12%, education 16%, health sciences 12%, philosophy/religious studies 10%, psychology 7%, theological studies 12%, visual/performing arts 8%.

Computing on campus. 200 workstations in dormitories, library, computer center. Dormitories wired for high-speed internet access and linked to campus network. Online course registration, online library available.

Student life. Freshman orientation: Mandatory. Preregistration for classes offered. Held during the 3 days immediately prior to start of fall semester. **Policies:** Campus is alcohol/drug/smoke free. Freshmen permitted cars on campus. **Housing:** Guaranteed on-campus for all undergraduates. Single-sex dorms, apartments, substance-free housing available. **Activities:** Bands, choral groups, drama, literary magazine, music ensembles, musical theater, opera, student government, student newspaper, symphony orchestra, TV station, Campus Crusade, FCA, Baptist Collegiate Ministries, Collegiate Republicans, Young Democrats, Black Student Fellowship, International Student Union, Native American Heritage Association, residence hall association.

Athletics. NAIA. **Intercollegiate:** Baseball M, basketball, cross-country, golf, soccer, softball W, tennis, track and field. **Intramural:** Badminton, basketball, bowling, racquetball, soccer, softball, swimming, table tennis, tennis, volleyball. **Team name:** Bison.

Student services. Campus ministries, career counseling, student employment services, financial aid counseling, health services, personal counseling, placement for graduates, veterans' counselor. **Physically disabled:** Services for visually, hearing impaired.

Contact. E-mail: admissions@mail.okbu.edu
Phone: (405) 878-2033 Toll-free number: (800) 654-3285
Fax: (405) 878-2046
Trent Argo, Dean of Enrollment Management, Oklahoma Baptist University, 500 West University, Shawnee, OK 74804

Oklahoma Christian University

Oklahoma City, Oklahoma
www.oc.edu **CB code: 6086**

- Private 4-year liberal arts college affiliated with Church of Christ
- Residential campus in large city
- 1,835 degree-seeking undergraduates
- 220 graduate students
- 41% graduate within 6 years

General. Founded in 1950. Regionally accredited. **Degrees:** 266 bachelor's awarded; master's offered. **ROTC:** Army, Air Force. **Calendar:** Semester, extensive summer session. **Full-time faculty:** 85 total. **Part-time faculty:** 75 total. **Class size:** 53% < 20, 38% 20-39, 3% 40-49, 4% 50-99, less than 1% >100.

Freshman class profile. 1,421 applied, 1,421 admitted, 549 enrolled.

Mid 50% test scores			
SAT verbal:	580-610	GPA 2.0-2.99:	23%
SAT math:	420-620	Rank in top quarter:	49%
ACT:	20-27	Rank in top tenth:	22%
GPA 3.50 or higher:	41%	Return as sophomores:	71%
GPA 3.0-3.49:	33%	Out-of-state:	56%
		Live on campus:	96%

Basis for selection. Open admission.

High school preparation. 15 units recommended. Recommended units include English 4, mathematics 4, social studies 3 and science 4.

2005-2006 Annual costs. Tuition/fees: $13,932. Room/board: $5,060. Books/supplies: $800. Personal expenses: $1,360.

2005-2006 Financial aid. Need-based: 533 full-time freshmen applied for aid; 397 were judged to have need; 397 of these received aid. Average need met was 42%. Average scholarship/grant was $1,430; average loan $2,435. 23% of total undergraduate aid awarded as scholarships/grants, 77% as loans/jobs. **Non-need-based:** Scholarships awarded for academics, alumni affiliation, art, athletics, job skills, leadership, music/drama, religious affiliation, ROTC.

Application procedures. Admission: No deadline. $25 fee. Application may be submitted online. Admission notification on a rolling basis. **Financial aid:** Priority date 3/15, closing date 8/31. FAFSA, institutional form required. Applicants notified on a rolling basis starting 3/1; must reply within 4 week(s) of notification.

Academics. Special study options: Accelerated study, cross-registration, double major, dual enrollment of high school students, honors, independent study, internships, study abroad, teacher certification program. **Credit/placement by examination:** AP, CLEP, IB, institutional tests. 60 credit hours maximum toward bachelor's degree. **Support services:** Remedial instruction, tutoring.

Majors. Biology: General, biochemistry. **Business:** General, accounting, business admin, management science, market research. **Communications:** General, advertising, broadcast journalism, journalism, public relations. **Computer sciences:** General, computer science, information systems. **Education:** Art, early childhood, elementary, English, ESL, mathematics, middle, music, physical, science, secondary, social studies, speech. **Engineering:** Computer, electrical, mechanical, physics. **Engineering technology:** Mechanical. **English:** Creative writing, speech/rhetoric. **Family/consumer sciences:** Family studies, family/community services. **Foreign languages:** Spanish. **Health:** Clinical lab science, predentistry, premedicine, prenursing, prepharmacy, preveterinary. **History:** General. **Interdisciplinary:** Math/computer science. **Legal studies:** Prelaw. **Liberal arts:** Arts/sciences. **Math:** General. **Parks/recreation:** Health/fitness. **Philosophy/religion:** Religion. **Physical sciences:** Chemistry. **Psychology:** General. **Social sciences:** Political science. **Theology:** Bible, missionary, religious ed, theology, youth ministry. **Visual/performing arts:** Art, interior design, music performance, piano/organ, voice/opera.

Most popular majors. Business/marketing 18%, communications/journalism 8%, computer/information sciences 6%, education 16%, engineering/engineering technologies 11%, liberal arts 17%.

Computing on campus. PC or laptop required. 1,850 workstations in dormitories, library, computer center, student center. Dormitories wired for high-speed internet access and linked to campus network. Commuter students can connect to campus network. Online library, helpline, repair service, student web hosting, wireless network available.

Student life. **Freshman orientation:** Mandatory, $200 fee. Preregistration for classes offered. **Policies:** Religious observance required. Freshmen permitted cars on campus. **Housing:** Guaranteed on-campus for all undergraduates. Single-sex dorms, special housing for disabled, apartments available. $60 deposit. Single students must live on campus or with parents. Special arrangements considered. **Activities:** Bands, choral groups, drama, music ensembles, musical theater, opera, radio station, student government, student newspaper, TV station, Outreach, 13 social service clubs.

Athletics. NAIA. **Intercollegiate:** Basketball, cheerleading W, cross-country, golf M, soccer, softball W, tennis, track and field. **Intramural:** Basketball, bowling, cross-country, football (non-tackle), golf M, soccer, softball, swimming, table tennis, tennis, track and field, volleyball. **Team name:** Eagles.

Student services. Campus ministries, career counseling, student employment services, financial aid counseling, health services, personal counseling, placement for graduates, veterans' counselor. **Physically disabled:** Services for visually, speech, hearing impaired.

Contact. E-mail: info@oc.edu
Phone: (405) 425-5050 Toll-free number: (800) 877-5050
Fax: (405) 425-5069
Risa Forrester, Director of Admissions, Oklahoma Christian University, Box 11000, Oklahoma City, OK 73136-1100

Oklahoma City University

Oklahoma City, Oklahoma — **CB member**
www.okcu.edu — **CB code: 6543**

- Private 4-year university and liberal arts college affiliated with United Methodist Church
- Residential campus in very large city
- 1,911 degree-seeking undergraduates: 23% part-time, 63% women, 8% African American, 2% Asian American, 4% Hispanic American, 4% Native American, 20% international
- 1,777 degree-seeking graduate students
- 81% of applicants admitted
- SAT or ACT (ACT writing optional) required
- 50% graduate within 6 years

General. Founded in 1904. Regionally accredited. Institution embraces the United Methodist tradition of scholarship and service and welcomes all faiths. Service learning incorporated throughout the curriculum. **Degrees:** 415 bachelor's awarded; master's, first professional offered. **ROTC:** Army, Air Force. **Location:** 180 miles from Dallas, 350 miles from Kansas City. **Calendar:** Semester, limited summer session. **Full-time faculty:** 161 total; 86% have terminal degrees, 12% minority, 40% women. **Part-time faculty:** 121 total; 41% have terminal degrees, 11% minority, 44% women. **Class size:** 70% < 20, 29% 20-39, less than 1% 40-49, less than 1% 50-99. **Special facilities:** Art center, center for competitive enterprise, observatory.

Freshman class profile. 1,044 applied, 846 admitted, 370 enrolled.

Mid 50% test scores		**Rank in top tenth:**	30%
SAT verbal:	520-630	**Return as sophomores:**	72%
SAT math:	510-610	**Out-of-state:**	48%
ACT:	22-26	**Live on campus:**	82%
GPA 3.50 or higher:	69%	**International:**	5%
GPA 3.0-3.49:	24%	**Fraternities:**	16%
GPA 2.0-2.99:	7%	**Sororities:**	36%
Rank in top quarter:	65%		

Basis for selection. School achievement record, which includes class rank, and test scores most important. Admissions interview and counselor recommendations also considered. Essay, interview recommended for all; audition required for dance, music programs; portfolio required for art, graphic design programs. **Homeschooled:** Present official transcript, including course work and grades, from home schooling experience. Demonstrate that individual is graduating no earlier than their class in the public school system. Submit official copy of ACT or SAT test scores.

High school preparation. 15 units required. Required units include English 4, mathematics 3, social studies 3, science 3 (laboratory 1) and foreign language 2. Mathematics requirement includes 2 algebra and 1 geometry, trigonometry, math analysis, or calculus. Social studies requirement includes 1 world history, 1 state history or civics, and 1 United States history.

2005-2006 Annual costs. Tuition/fees: $17,535. Room/board: $6,250. Books/supplies: $900. Personal expenses: $1,000.

2004-2005 Financial aid. **Need-based:** 243 full-time freshmen applied for aid; 177 were judged to have need; 177 of these received aid. Average need met was 68%. Average scholarship/grant was $11,090; average loan $2,256. 78% of total undergraduate aid awarded as scholarships/grants, 22% as loans/jobs. **Non-need-based:** Awarded to 476 full-time undergraduates, including 129 freshmen. Scholarships awarded for academics, art, athletics, job skills, leadership, music/drama, religious affiliation.

Application procedures. **Admission:** Priority date 3/30; deadline 8/20 (postmark date). $30 fee, may be waived for applicants with need. Application may be submitted online. Admission notification on a rolling basis beginning on or about 10/15. Must reply by May 1 or within 2 week(s) if notified thereafter. **Financial aid:** Priority date 3/1, closing date 6/30. FAFSA, institutional form required. Applicants notified on a rolling basis starting 2/24; must reply within 2 week(s) of notification.

Academics. **Special study options:** Accelerated study, cooperative education, distance learning, double major, dual enrollment of high school students, ESL, exchange student, external degree, honors, independent study, internships, student-designed major, study abroad, teacher certification program, Washington semester. **Credit/placement by examination:** AP, CLEP, IB, SAT, ACT, institutional tests. 30 credit hours maximum toward bachelor's degree. **Support services:** Learning center, reduced course load, study skills assistance, tutoring, writing center.

Majors. **Area/ethnic studies:** American. **Biology:** General, biochemistry, biophysics. **Business:** General, accounting, business admin, finance, international, management information systems, management science, managerial economics, marketing. **Communications:** Advertising, broadcast journalism, journalism, media studies, public relations, radio/tv. **Computer sciences:** General, computer science. **Education:** General, art, business, elementary, English, foreign languages, French, German, health, history, mathematics, Montessori teacher, music, physical, science, secondary, social studies, Spanish, speech. **English:** English lit, speech/rhetoric. **Foreign languages:** French, German, Spanish. **Health:** Athletic training, nursing (RN), predentistry, premedicine, prepharmacy, preveterinary. **History:** General. **Interdisciplinary:** Biological/physical sciences. **Legal studies:** Prelaw. **Liberal arts:** Arts/sciences, humanities. **Math:** General. **Parks/recreation:** Health/fitness. **Philosophy/religion:** Philosophy, religion. **Physical sciences:** Chemistry, physics. **Protective services:** Corrections, law enforcement admin, police science. **Psychology:** General. **Public administration:** Social work. **Social sciences:** Economics, political science, sociology. **Theology:** Bible, religious ed, sacred music, youth ministry. **Visual/performing arts:** General, art, art history/conservation, arts management, cinematography, dance, dramatic, film/cinema, music management, music performance, music theory/composition, piano/organ, stringed instruments, studio arts, theater arts management, voice/opera.

Most popular majors. Business/marketing 13%, health sciences 10%, liberal arts 32%, visual/performing arts 19%.

Computing on campus. 218 workstations in dormitories, library, computer center, student center. Dormitories wired for high-speed internet access and linked to campus network. Commuter students can connect to campus network. Online course registration, online library, helpline, student web hosting, wireless network available.

Student life. **Freshman orientation:** Mandatory, $50 fee. Preregistration for classes offered. **Policies:** Freshmen permitted cars on campus. **Housing:** Guaranteed on-campus for all undergraduates. Single-sex dorms, apartments, fraternity/sorority housing, substance-free housing available. $100 partly refundable deposit. Learning communities available. **Activities:** Bands, choral groups, dance, drama, literary magazine, music ensembles, musical theater, opera, student government, student newspaper, symphony orchestra, TV station, Kappa Phi, Sigma Theta Epsilon, Association for People of Color, United Methodist Student Fellowship, Students of Arts Management, various international student organizations, Alpha Phi Sorority, Gamma Phi Beta Sorority, Lambda Chi Alpha Fraternity, Kappa Sigma Fraternity.

Athletics. NAIA. **Intercollegiate:** Baseball M, basketball, cheerleading, golf, rowing (crew), soccer, softball W. **Intramural:** Basketball, football (non-tackle) M, golf, softball, table tennis, volleyball. **Team name:** Stars.

Student services. Adult student services, campus ministries, career counseling, student employment services, financial aid counseling, health services, minority student services, personal counseling, placement for graduates, veterans' counselor. **Physically disabled:** Services for visually, hearing impaired.

Contact. E-mail: uadmissions@okcu.edu
Phone: (405) 208-5050 Toll-free number: (800) 633-7242
Fax: (405) 208-5916
Lloyd Musselman, Dean of Enrollment Services, Oklahoma City University, 2501 North Blackwelder Avenue, Oklahoma City, OK 73106

Four-Year Colleges

Oklahoma Panhandle State University
Goodwell, Oklahoma
www.opsu.edu **CB code: 6571**

- Public 4-year agricultural and liberal arts college
- Residential campus in rural community
- 1,046 degree-seeking undergraduates: 12% part-time, 54% women, 4% African American, 12% Hispanic American, 3% Native American, 3% international

General. Founded in 1909. Regionally accredited. **Degrees:** 180 bachelor's, 17 associate awarded. **Location:** 110 miles from Amarillo, Texas, 10 miles from Guymon. **Calendar:** Semester, limited summer session. **Full-time faculty:** 56 total; 36% have terminal degrees, 41% women. **Part-time faculty:** 33 total; 67% women. **Class size:** 78% < 20, 19% 20-39, less than 1% 40-49, less than 1% 50-99, less than 1% >100. **Special facilities:** Agronomy experiment station, historical museum, livestock facilities, farming area, rodeo arena, meat lab.

Freshman class profile. 257 applied, 257 admitted, 206 enrolled.

Out-of-state:	50%	**International:**	2%
Live on campus:	90%		

Basis for selection. Open admission. Incoming students with no ACT scores, or a score of 18 or below, must take ACCUPLACER test. **Homeschooled:** Transcript of courses and grades required.

High school preparation. 15 units recommended. Recommended units include English 4, mathematics 3, social studies 2, history 1, science 2 (laboratory 2) and academic electives 3.

2005-2006 Annual costs. Tuition/fees: $3,372; $5,618 out-of-state. Room/board: $4,270. Books/supplies: $180.

2004-2005 Financial aid. All financial aid based on need. 54% of total undergraduate aid awarded as scholarships/grants, 46% as loans/jobs.

Application procedures. Admission: No deadline. No application fee. Application must be submitted on paper. Admission notification on a rolling basis. **Financial aid:** Priority date 8/25; no closing date. FAFSA, institutional form required. Applicants notified on a rolling basis starting 6/15.

Academics. Special study options: Cooperative education, distance learning, double major, dual enrollment of high school students, ESL, independent study, internships, liberal arts/career combination, teacher certification program. **Credit/placement by examination:** AP, CLEP, institutional tests. 34 credit hours maximum toward associate degree, 60 toward bachelor's. **Support services:** Learning center, reduced course load, remedial instruction, study skills assistance, tutoring, writing center.

Majors. Agriculture: Agribusiness operations, agronomy, animal sciences, business, farm/ranch. **Biology:** General. **Business:** Accounting, business admin. **Computer sciences:** General, information systems. **Education:** Agricultural, business, elementary, music, technology/industrial arts. **Engineering technology:** Manufacturing. **English:** English lit, speech/rhetoric. **Foreign languages:** Spanish. **Health:** Clinical lab science, nursing (RN). **History:** General. **Interdisciplinary:** Biological/physical sciences, peace/conflict. **Liberal arts:** Humanities. **Math:** General. **Parks/recreation:** Health/fitness. **Physical sciences:** Chemistry. **Psychology:** General. **Social sciences:** General. **Visual/performing arts:** Art.

Most popular majors. Agriculture 21%, biology 11%, business/marketing 11%, education 17%, health sciences 6%, parks/recreation 7%, visual/performing arts 7%.

Computing on campus. 75 workstations in library, computer center, student center. Dormitories wired for high-speed internet access. Online library available.

Student life. Freshman orientation: Mandatory. Preregistration for classes offered. **Policies:** Freshmen permitted cars on campus. **Housing:** Guaranteed on-campus for all undergraduates. Single-sex dorms, special housing for disabled, apartments, substance-free housing available. Honors dormitory. **Activities:** Bands, choral groups, drama, literary magazine, music ensembles, musical theater, radio station, student government, student newspaper, Wesley Foundation, Baptist Student Union, Church of Christ Student Center, Circle-K, Newman Club, Methodist Student Center.

Athletics. NCAA. **Intercollegiate:** Baseball M, basketball, cheerleading, cross-country, equestrian, football (tackle) M, golf, rodeo, soccer M, softball, volleyball W. **Team name:** Aggies.

Student services. Adult student services, alcohol/substance abuse counseling, campus ministries, career counseling, student employment services, financial aid counseling, health services, minority student services, personal counseling, placement for graduates. **Physically disabled:** Services for visually, speech, hearing impaired.

Contact. E-mail: jolie@opsu.edu
Phone: (580) 349-1312 Toll-free number: (800) 664-6778
Fax: (580) 349-1371
Bobby Jenkins, Registrar and Director of Adminssion, Oklahoma Panhandle State University, OPSU Admissions, Goodwell, OK 73939-0430

Oklahoma State University
Stillwater, Oklahoma **CB member**
www.okstate.edu **CB code: 6546**

- Public 4-year university
- Residential campus in large town
- 18,773 degree-seeking undergraduates: 11% part-time, 48% women, 4% African American, 2% Asian American, 2% Hispanic American, 9% Native American, 4% international
- 4,099 degree-seeking graduate students
- 88% of applicants admitted
- SAT or ACT (ACT writing optional) required
- 59% graduate within 6 years

General. Founded in 1890. Regionally accredited. Campuses in Oklahoma City, Okmulgee, Tulsa; Center for Health Sciences (includes College of Osteopathic Medicine) at Tulsa. **Degrees:** 3,549 bachelor's awarded; master's, doctoral, first professional offered. **ROTC:** Army, Air Force. **Location:** 65 miles from Tulsa, 65 miles from Oklahoma City. **Calendar:** Semester, extensive summer session. **Full-time faculty:** 1,000 total; 90% have terminal degrees, 10% minority, 29% women. **Part-time faculty:** 237 total; 27% have terminal degrees, 8% minority, 55% women. **Class size:** 28% < 20, 44% 20-39, 11% 40-49, 12% 50-99, 5% >100. **Special facilities:** Laser research center with 8 laboratories and 30 laser systems, biotechnology and genetic engineering research center, telecommunication center.

Freshman class profile. 6,533 applied, 5,719 admitted, 3,315 enrolled.

Mid 50% test scores		**Rank in top tenth:**	27%
SAT verbal:	500-610	**Return as sophomores:**	79%
SAT math:	510-620	**Out-of-state:**	22%
ACT:	22-27	**Live on campus:**	85%
GPA 3.50 or higher:	58%	**International:**	2%
GPA 3.0-3.49:	33%	**Fraternities:**	18%
GPA 2.0-2.99:	9%	**Sororities:**	25%
Rank in top quarter:	55%		

Basis for selection. Applicants must earn a 3.0 high school GPA and rank in top 33% of their class, or have minimum 24 ACT or 1090 SAT (exclusive of Writing), or earn a 3.0 High School GPA in 15 required curricular units and have a 21 ACT or 980 SAT(exclusive of Writing). Early application encouraged. Test scores must be received no later than Friday before classes for fall-term admission. Interview recommended for academically borderline students. **Homeschooled:** Graduates of home school or unaccredited high schools must satisfy all the curricular requirements and meet the minimum ACT/SAT score requirements.

High school preparation. College-preparatory program required. 15 units required. Required and recommended units include English 4, mathematics 3, social studies 2, history 1, science 2 (laboratory 2), foreign language 2 and academic electives 3. One computer science recommended.

2005-2006 Annual costs. Tuition/fees: $4,365; $12,388 out-of-state. Room/board: $5,848. Books/supplies: $880. Personal expenses: $2,190.

2004-2005 Financial aid. Need-based: 2,074 full-time freshmen applied for aid; 1,449 were judged to have need; 1,418 of these received aid. Average need met was 75%. Average scholarship/grant was $3,869; average loan $2,722. 45% of total undergraduate aid awarded as scholarships/grants, 55% as loans/jobs. **Non-need-based:** Awarded to 7,295 full-time undergraduates, including 1,534 freshmen. Scholarships awarded for academics, alumni affiliation, art, athletics, job skills, leadership, music/drama, ROTC.

Application procedures. Admission: No deadline. $40 fee, may be waived for applicants with need. Application may be submitted online. Admission notification on a rolling basis beginning on or about 10/1. **Financial aid:** No deadline. FAFSA required. Applicants notified on a rolling basis starting 3/15; must reply within 2 week(s) of notification.

Academics. Special study options: Accelerated study, combined bachelor's/graduate degree, cooperative education, cross-registration, distance learning, double major, dual enrollment of high school students, ESL, exchange student, honors, independent study, internships, semester at sea, student-designed major, study abroad, teacher certification program, Washington semester. **Credit/placement by examination:** AP, CLEP, IB, SAT, ACT, institutional tests. Maximum number of credit hours towards degree is subject to university "residence credit" policy. **Support services:** Learning center, pre-admission summer program, reduced course load, remedial instruction, study skills assistance, tutoring, writing center.

Honors college/program. ACT of 27, SAT of 1210 (exclusive of Writing) and High School GPA of 3.75 required. Approximately 369 freshmen admitted.

Majors. Agriculture: Animal sciences, business, communications, economics, horticultural science, soil science. **Architecture:** Architecture, landscape. **Area/ethnic studies:** American. **Biology:** General, biochemistry, biomedical sciences, botany, ecology, entomology, microbiology, physiology, zoology. **Business:** Accounting, business admin, finance, hospitality admin, international, management information systems, management science, managerial economics, marketing. **Communications:** Journalism. **Computer sciences:** General, networking. **Conservation:** Environmental science, forestry. **Education:** General, agricultural, elementary, music, physical, secondary, voc/tech. **Engineering:** Aerospace, agricultural, architectural, chemical, civil, electrical, industrial, mechanical. **Engineering technology:** Construction, electrical, mechanical. **English:** English lit. **Family/consumer sciences:** Family studies, food/nutrition, housing. **Foreign languages:** French, German, Russian, Spanish. **Health:** Athletic training, clinical lab science, preveterinary, public health ed, speech pathology. **History:** General. **Liberal arts:** Arts/sciences. **Math:** General, statistics. **Parks/recreation:** General. **Philosophy/religion:** Philosophy. **Physical sciences:** Chemistry, geology, physics. **Protective services:** Fire safety technology. **Psychology:** General. **Social sciences:** Economics, geography, political science, sociology. **Transportation:** Aviation. **Visual/performing arts:** Art, dramatic.

Most popular majors. Agriculture 8%, business/marketing 29%, education 8%, engineering/engineering technologies 11%, family/consumer sciences 8%.

Computing on campus. 2,104 workstations in dormitories, library, computer center, student center. Dormitories wired for high-speed internet access and linked to campus network. Commuter students can connect to campus network. Online course registration, online library, helpline, repair service, wireless network available.

Student life. Freshman orientation: Mandatory. Preregistration for classes offered. One-day programs in June. Also ALPHA orientation program held the week before classes begin each fall semester. **Policies:** Freshmen permitted cars on campus. **Housing:** Guaranteed on-campus for freshmen. Coed dorms, single-sex dorms, special housing for disabled, apartments, fraternity/sorority housing, substance-free housing available. $150 fully refundable deposit. Honors housing, engineering floors, intensive study floors, graduate housing, disabled student rooms, foreign language floors. **Activities:** Bands, choral groups, dance, drama, literary magazine, music ensembles, musical theater, opera, radio station, student government, student newspaper, symphony orchestra, TV station, Campus Crusade for Christ, Flying Aggies, Rodeo Club, Young Democrats, Young Republicans, Fire Protection Society, Alpha Pi Omega, National Organization for Women, African American Student Association, Hispanic Student Association.

Athletics. NCAA. **Intercollegiate:** Baseball M, basketball, cross-country, equestrian W, football (tackle) M, golf, soccer W, softball W, tennis, track and field, wrestling M. **Intramural:** Archery, badminton, basketball, bowling, cross-country, football (tackle), golf, racquetball, soccer, softball, squash, swimming, table tennis, tennis, track and field, volleyball, water polo, weight lifting, wrestling M. **Team name:** Cowboys, Cowgirls.

Student services. Adult student services, alcohol/substance abuse counseling, career counseling, student employment services, financial aid counseling, health services, legal services, minority student services, personal counseling, placement for graduates, veterans' counselor, women's services. **Physically disabled:** Services for visually, speech, hearing impaired.

Contact. E-mail: admit@okstate.edu
Phone: (800) 233-5019 ext. 1 Toll-free number: (800) 852-1255
Fax: (405) 744-5285
Paul Carney, Director of Undergraduate Admissions, Oklahoma State University, 324 Student Union, Stillwater, OK 74078

Oklahoma Wesleyan University

Bartlesville, Oklahoma — **CB member**
www.okwu.edu — **CB code: 6135**

- Private 4-year liberal arts college affiliated with Wesleyan Church
- Residential campus in large town
- 966 degree-seeking undergraduates
- SAT or ACT (ACT writing optional) required

General. Founded in 1909. Regionally accredited. Dedicated to providing an education in a Christ-centered environment. **Degrees:** 215 bachelor's, 27 associate awarded. **ROTC:** Navy, Air Force. **Location:** 40 miles from Tulsa. **Calendar:** Semester, limited summer session. **Full-time faculty:** 30 total. **Part-time faculty:** 10 total. **Special facilities:** Nature preserve.

Freshman class profile.

Out-of-state:	80%	Live on campus:	90%

Basis for selection. In addition to required high school study, students must rank in top half of class and have 2.0 GPA or ACT score of 18. Interview recommended for academically weak, socially troubled applicants.

High school preparation. 15 units required. Required units include English 4, mathematics 2, social studies 2, science 1 (laboratory 1).

2006-2007 Annual costs. Tuition/fees: $14,550. Room/board: $5,350. Books/supplies: $650. Personal expenses: $1,000.

2005-2006 Financial aid. Need-based: 19% of total undergraduate aid awarded as scholarships/grants, 81% as loans/jobs.

Application procedures. Admission: No deadline. $25 fee, may be waived for applicants with need. Admission notification on a rolling basis beginning on or about 1/15. Application must be received prior to class start. **Financial aid:** Priority date 4/1; no closing date. FAFSA, institutional form required. Applicants notified on a rolling basis starting 4/1; must reply by 5/1 or within 2 week(s) of notification.

Academics. Special study options: Double major, dual enrollment of high school students, ESL, independent study, internships, student-designed major, study abroad, teacher certification program, Washington semester. **Credit/placement by examination:** AP, CLEP, institutional tests. 30 credit hours maximum toward associate degree, 36 toward bachelor's. **Support services:** Learning center, reduced course load, remedial instruction, tutoring.

Majors. Biology: General. **Business:** General, accounting, business admin. **Communications:** General. **Computer sciences:** General, computer science. **Education:** Business, elementary, English, mathematics, music, physical, science, social studies. **History:** General. **Interdisciplinary:** Behavioral sciences. **Math:** General. **Parks/recreation:** Exercise sciences. **Physical sciences:** Chemistry. **Social sciences:** General, political science. **Theology:** Bible, missionary, sacred music, theology.

Computing on campus. 30 workstations in library, computer center.

Student life. Freshman orientation: Available, $100 fee. **Policies:** Religious observance required. **Housing:** Guaranteed on-campus for freshmen. Single-sex dorms available. **Activities:** Marching band, choral groups, literary magazine, music ensembles, opera, symphony orchestra, TV station, Christian Services, Future Secretaries of America, Wesleyan Student Education Association, Campus Missionary Fellowship, Theology Fellowship, forensics, Fellowship of Christian Athletes.

Athletics. NAIA, NCCAA. **Intercollegiate:** Archery M, baseball M, basketball, golf M, soccer, volleyball W. **Intramural:** Archery, badminton, basketball, golf, handball, racquetball, soccer, softball, swimming, table tennis, tennis, track and field, volleyball.

Student services. Adult student services, career counseling, student employment services, health services, personal counseling, placement for graduates, veterans' counselor.

Contact. E-mail: admissions@okwu.edu
Phone: (918) 335-6219 Toll-free number: (800) 468-6292
Fax: (918) 335-6229
Jim Weidman, Vice President for Enrollment, Oklahoma Wesleyan University, 2201 Silver Lake Road, Bartlesville, OK 74006

Oral Roberts University

Tulsa, Oklahoma — **CB member**
www.oru.edu — **CB code: 6552**

- Private 4-year university and liberal arts college affiliated with nondenominational tradition
- Residential campus in large city
- 3,265 degree-seeking undergraduates
- 67% of applicants admitted
- SAT or ACT, application essay required

General. Founded in 1965. Regionally accredited. Integrated math and science academy sponsored by Oklahoma State Regents for Higher Education. **Degrees:** 547 bachelor's awarded; master's, doctoral, first professional offered. **ROTC:** Air Force. **Location:** 7 miles from downtown. **Calendar:** Semester, limited summer session. **Full-time faculty:** 198 total. **Part-time faculty:** 84 total. **Class size:** 58% < 20, 35% 20-39, 3% 40-49, 5% 50-99, less than 1% >100. **Special facilities:** Prayer tower.

Freshman class profile. 1,210 applied, 814 admitted, 453 enrolled.

Mid 50% test scores			
SAT verbal:	480-610	Rank in top quarter:	53%
SAT math:	480-600	Rank in top tenth:	27%
ACT:	20-26	Out-of-state:	71%
		Live on campus:	69%

Basis for selection. Academic record, test scores, personal essay, minister's recommendation, other recommendations, extracurricular activities considered. Students must provide immunization records. Interview recommended for all; audition required for music program; portfolio recommended for art program. **Homeschooled:** Under special circumstances, homeschooled applicants may be required to submit additional curricular information and/or proof of high school equivalency.

High school preparation. 16 units recommended. Recommended units include English 4, mathematics 2, social studies 2, science 1 (laboratory 1), foreign language 2 and academic electives 4. Students matriculating in a bachelor of science program may substitute additional mathematics for foreign language.

2005-2006 Annual costs. Tuition/fees: $15,880. Room/board: $6,530. Books/supplies: $1,000. Personal expenses: $1,500.

2005-2006 Financial aid. **Need-based:** Average need met was 86%. Average scholarship/grant was $8,414; average loan $6,716. 52% of total undergraduate aid awarded as scholarships/grants, 48% as loans/jobs. **Non-need-based:** Scholarships awarded for academics, art, athletics, job skills, leadership, music/drama.

Application procedures. **Admission:** No deadline. $35 fee, may be waived for applicants with need. Admission notification on a rolling basis. **Financial aid:** Priority date 3/15; no closing date. FAFSA required. Applicants notified on a rolling basis starting 2/15; must reply by 7/15.

Academics. **Special study options:** Distance learning, double major, dual enrollment of high school students, ESL, external degree, honors, independent study, internships, liberal arts/career combination, student-designed major, study abroad, teacher certification program, Washington semester, weekend college. **Credit/placement by examination:** AP, CLEP, institutional tests. 30 credit hours maximum toward bachelor's degree. **Support services:** Learning center, reduced course load, remedial instruction, study skills assistance, tutoring.

Majors. **Biology:** General, biochemistry. **Business:** Accounting, business admin, finance, international, international marketing, management information systems, management science, marketing, organizational behavior. **Communications:** General. **Computer sciences:** General, computer science. **Education:** Art, business, early childhood, elementary, English, foreign languages, health, mathematics, music, physical, science, social studies, Spanish, special. **Engineering:** General, biomedical, computer, electrical, mechanical, physics. **English:** Composition. **Foreign languages:** French, German, Spanish. **Health:** Clinical lab science, nursing (RN). **History:** General. **Liberal arts:** Arts/sciences. **Math:** General. **Parks/recreation:** Exercise sciences, facilities management, health/fitness. **Physical sciences:** Chemistry, physics. **Psychology:** General. **Public administration:** Social work. **Social sciences:** International relations, political science. **Theology:** Bible, missionary, pastoral counseling, religious ed, sacred music, theology. **Visual/performing arts:** Acting, art, commercial/advertising art, design, dramatic, music performance, music theory/composition, piano/organ, studio arts, theater design, voice/opera.

Computing on campus. 470 workstations in dormitories, library, computer center. Dormitories linked to campus network. Commuter students can connect to campus network.

Student life. **Freshman orientation:** Mandatory. **Policies:** Single students under 25 years of age must live in university housing or with parents. Religious observance required. **Housing:** Guaranteed on-campus for freshmen. Single-sex dorms, special housing for disabled available. $125 deposit. **Activities:** Bands, choral groups, dance, drama, film society, literary magazine, music ensembles, musical theater, opera, radio station, student government, student newspaper, symphony orchestra, TV station, community outreach, international students association, missions club, Young Republicans, Young Democrats, student activist society, Model United Nations.

Athletics. NCAA. **Intercollegiate:** Baseball M, basketball, cross-country, golf, soccer, tennis, track and field, volleyball W. **Intramural:** Badminton, basketball, bowling, cross-country, golf, racquetball, softball, swimming, table tennis, tennis, volleyball, wrestling M. **Team name:** Golden Eagles.

Student services. Campus ministries, career counseling, student employment services, financial aid counseling, health services, personal counseling, placement for graduates, veterans' counselor. **Physically disabled:** Services for visually, speech, hearing impaired.

Contact. E-mail: admissions@oru.edu
Phone: (918) 496-6518 Toll-free number: (800) 678-8876
Fax: (918) 495-6222
Chris Belcher, Director of Admissions, Oral Roberts University, 7777 South Lewis Avenue, Tulsa, OK 74171

Rogers State University

Claremore, Oklahoma
www.rsu.edu **CB code: 6545**

- Public 4-year university
- Commuter campus in large town
- 3,636 degree-seeking undergraduates: 50% part-time, 58% women, 3% African American, 1% Asian American, 3% Hispanic American, 27% Native American, 1% international
- SAT or ACT with writing required

General. Founded in 1909. Regionally accredited. **Degrees:** 124 bachelor's, 266 associate awarded. **ROTC:** Air Force. **Location:** 25 miles from Tulsa. **Calendar:** Semester, extensive summer session. **Full-time faculty:** 95 total. **Part-time faculty:** 109 total. **Class size:** 41% < 20, 54% 20-39, 4% 40-49, 1% 50-99. **Special facilities:** Conservation education reserve.

Freshman class profile. 1,355 applied, 1,164 admitted, 923 enrolled.

Mid 50% test scores			
ACT:	17-22	Rank in top quarter:	26%
GPA 3.50 or higher:	27%	Rank in top tenth:	8%
GPA 3.0-3.49:	26%	Out-of-state:	3%
GPA 2.0-2.99:	42%	Live on campus:	4%

Basis for selection. Open admission, but selective for some programs. Bachelor degree programs require minimum ACT score of 19 and no curricular deficiencies. Open admission for associate degree programs. TOEFL required of students who are not native speakers of English. Essay required for returning suspension students only.

High school preparation. 15 units required; 17 recommended. Required and recommended units include English 4, mathematics 3, social studies 2, history 3, science 2 (laboratory 2), foreign language 2 and academic electives 3. Mathematics units should include algebra I and II; 1 speech, 1 computer science also recommended; history units should include 1 unit of American history and 1 unit of citizenship (government, geography, etc.).

2005-2006 Annual costs. Tuition/fees: $3,300; $7,860 out-of-state. Books/supplies: $700. Personal expenses: $1,200.

2005-2006 Financial aid. **Need-based:** 653 full-time freshmen applied for aid; 561 were judged to have need; 544 of these received aid. Average need met was 14%. Average scholarship/grant was $1,850; average loan $1,200. 60% of total undergraduate aid awarded as scholarships/grants, 40% as loans/jobs. **Non-need-based:** Awarded to 535 full-time undergraduates, including 254 freshmen. Scholarships awarded for academics.

Application procedures. **Admission:** No deadline. No application fee. Application may be submitted online. Admission notification on a rolling basis. **Financial aid:** Priority date 3/1; no closing date. FAFSA, institutional form required. Applicants notified on a rolling basis starting 4/1; must reply within 3 week(s) of notification.

Academics. **Special study options:** Cooperative education, distance learning, double major, dual enrollment of high school students, honors, independent study, internships, liberal arts/career combination. **Credit/placement by examination:** AP, CLEP, ACT, institutional tests. 30 credit hours maximum toward associate degree, 45 toward bachelor's. **Support services:** Learning center, reduced course load, remedial instruction, study skills assistance, tutoring, writing center.

Majors. **Biology:** General. **Business:** Business admin. **Engineering technology:** Manufacturing. **Liberal arts:** Arts/sciences. **Protective services:** Law enforcement admin. **Social sciences:** General.

Most popular majors. Biology 10%, business/marketing 39%, engineering/engineering technologies 10%, liberal arts 8%, social sciences 33%.

Computing on campus. 300 workstations in dormitories, library, computer center. Dormitories wired for high-speed internet access. Commuter students can connect to campus network. Online library available.

Student life. Freshman orientation: Available. Preregistration for classes offered. **Policies:** Freshmen permitted cars on campus. **Housing:** Coed dorms, special housing for disabled, apartments available. **Activities:** Radio station, student government, TV station, Native American association, Baptist campus ministries, Defenders of Mother Earth, student art association, criminal justice association, student nursing association, Society for Computing and Business Machines, horse and agriculture club.

Athletics. Intramural: Basketball, bowling, football (non-tackle), soccer, softball, volleyball.

Student services. Adult student services, career counseling, services for economically disadvantaged, student employment services, financial aid counseling, on-campus daycare, personal counseling, placement for graduates, veterans' counselor. **Physically disabled:** Services for visually, hearing impaired.

Contact. Phone: (918) 343-7546 Toll-free number: (800) 256-7511
Fax: (918) 343-7595
Lindsay Fields, Director of Enrollment Management, Rogers State University, 1701 West Will Rogers Boulevard, Claremore, OK 74017

St. Gregory's University

Shawnee, Oklahoma
www.stgregorys.edu **CB code: 6621**

- Private 4-year university and liberal arts college affiliated with Roman Catholic Church
- Residential campus in large town
- 775 degree-seeking undergraduates: 38% part-time, 52% women, 6% African American, 1% Asian American, 7% Hispanic American, 8% Native American, 11% international
- 84% of applicants admitted
- SAT or ACT, application essay required
- 42% graduate within 6 years

General. Founded in 1875. Regionally accredited. A private institution in the Roman Catholic and Benedictine tradition. Special accelerated programs for non-traditional students in Shawnee and Tulsa, Oklahoma. **Degrees:** 92 bachelor's, 22 associate awarded; master's offered. **ROTC:** Army, Air Force. **Location:** 30 miles from Oklahoma City. **Calendar:** Semester, limited summer session. **Full-time faculty:** 30 total; 30% have terminal degrees, 7% minority, 57% women. **Part-time faculty:** 35 total; 26% have terminal degrees, 3% minority, 51% women. **Class size:** 89% < 20, 11% 20-39. **Special facilities:** Abbey, museum.

Freshman class profile. 339 applied, 286 admitted, 120 enrolled.

Mid 50% test scores		End year in good standing:	94%
SAT verbal:	460-600	Return as sophomores:	56%
SAT math:	450-580	Out-of-state:	17%
ACT:	19-25	Live on campus:	85%

Basis for selection. Core classes, GPA most important; test scores, class rank important. Interview required for students admitted on probation; audition required for dance, drama, and choral scholarships; portfolio required for art scholarships. **Homeschooled:** Interview required. **Learning Disabled:** Students with need beyond ADA standards may apply to Partners in Learning Program. Additional fee of approximately $7,000 required if admitted.

High school preparation. 17 units recommended. Recommended units include English 4, mathematics 3, social studies 2, history 2, science 2 (laboratory 2) and foreign language 2.

2005-2006 Annual costs. Tuition/fees: $12,636. Room/board: $5,320. Books/supplies: $800. Personal expenses: $1,746.

2004-2005 Financial aid. Need-based: 92 full-time freshmen applied for aid; 92 were judged to have need; 92 of these received aid. Average need met was 69%. Average scholarship/grant was $6,236; average loan $2,027. 46% of total undergraduate aid awarded as scholarships/grants, 54% as loans/jobs. **Non-need-based:** Awarded to 540 full-time undergraduates, including 130 freshmen. Scholarships awarded for academics, alumni affiliation, art, athletics, job skills, leadership, music/drama, religious affiliation.

Application procedures. Admission: Priority date 8/1; no deadline. $25 fee, may be waived for applicants with need. Application may be submitted online. Admission notification on a rolling basis. **Financial aid:** Priority date 4/1; no closing date. FAFSA, institutional form required. Applicants notified on a rolling basis starting 2/15; must reply within 2 week(s) of notification.

Academics. Special study options: Accelerated study, cooperative education, double major, ESL, honors, independent study, internships, student-designed major, study abroad, teacher certification program. **Credit/placement by examination:** AP, CLEP, IB, institutional tests. 12 credit hours maximum toward associate degree, 30 toward bachelor's. Course proficiency exams available in areas where no CLEP exams offered. **Support services:** Learning center, remedial instruction, study skills assistance, tutoring.

Majors. Biology: General. **Business:** General, accounting, business admin, hospitality/recreation. **Communications:** Journalism. **Computer sciences:** General. **Conservation:** General. **Education:** General, secondary. **History:** General. **Interdisciplinary:** Behavioral sciences, natural sciences. **Legal studies:** Prelaw. **Liberal arts:** Arts/sciences. **Math:** General. **Philosophy/religion:** Religion. **Psychology:** General. **Social sciences:** General, political science. **Visual/performing arts:** General, dramatic.

Most popular majors. Business/marketing 38%, parks/recreation 12%, physical sciences 7%, social sciences 23%.

Computing on campus. PC or laptop required. 60 workstations in dormitories, library, computer center, student center. Dormitories wired for high-speed internet access and linked to campus network. Commuter students can connect to campus network. Online library, helpline, repair service, student web hosting, wireless network available.

Student life. Freshman orientation: Mandatory. Preregistration for classes offered. Prior to start of fall term, 3 days plus evenings in first week of fall semester. **Policies:** Smoke-free; alcohol/drug-free; on-campus residency required under age 22. Freshmen permitted cars on campus. **Housing:** Guaranteed on-campus for freshmen. Single-sex dorms, substance-free housing available. $100 deposit. **Activities:** Jazz band, choral groups, dance, drama, student government, student newspaper, Knights of Columbus, academic honor society, Fellowship of Christian Athletes, buckley retreat team, history club, student alumni council.

Athletics. NAIA. **Intercollegiate:** Baseball M, basketball, cross-country, golf, soccer, softball W, volleyball W. **Intramural:** Basketball, football (non-tackle), racquetball, soccer, softball, table tennis, tennis, volleyball. **Team name:** Cavaliers.

Student services. Adult student services, alcohol/substance abuse counseling, campus ministries, career counseling, services for economically disadvantaged, student employment services, financial aid counseling, minority student services, personal counseling, placement for graduates, veterans' counselor. **Learning disabled:** Comprehensive services available.

Contact. E-mail: admissions@stgregorys.edu
Phone: (405) 878-5444 Toll-free number: (888) 784-7347
Fax: (405) 878-5198
Director of Admissions, St. Gregory's University, 1900 West MacArthur Drive, Shawnee, OK 74804

Southeastern Oklahoma State University

Durant, Oklahoma
www.sosu.edu **CB code: 6657**

- Public 4-year liberal arts and teachers college
- Commuter campus in large town
- 3,602 degree-seeking undergraduates: 17% part-time, 55% women
- 323 degree-seeking graduate students
- 71% of applicants admitted
- SAT or ACT with writing required
- 31% graduate within 6 years

General. Founded in 1909. Regionally accredited. Degree programs offered through Higher Education Centers at Ardmore, Idabel, McAlester, Tinker Air Force Base, Oklahoma City Community College, and Grayson County College. **Degrees:** 584 bachelor's awarded; master's offered. **Location:** 90 miles from Dallas, Texas. **Calendar:** Semester, extensive summer session. **Full-time faculty:** 141 total; 67% have terminal degrees, 21% minority, 36% women. **Part-time faculty:** 96 total; 20% have terminal degrees, 23% minority, 51% women. **Class size:** 44% < 20, 47% 20-39, 6% 40-49, 2% 50-99, less than 1% >100. **Special facilities:** Herbarium, equestrian facilities.

Freshman class profile. 1,101 applied, 782 admitted, 619 enrolled.

Mid 50% test scores			
ACT:	17-22	**Rank in top quarter:**	21%
GPA 3.50 or higher:	29%	**Rank in top tenth:**	14%
GPA 3.0-3.49:	38%	**Return as sophomores:**	58%
GPA 2.0-2.99:	30%	**Out-of-state:**	17%

Basis for selection. High school transcript and test scores important. Must have 2.7 GPA and rank in top half of class, 20 ACT or 940 SAT (exclusive of writing), score in top half on ACT scores, or attain 2.7 GPA in 15 core units. Audition required for drama, music programs. Interview required for alternative admissions. **Homeschooled:** ACT score of 20 required.

High school preparation. 15 units required. Required units include English 4, mathematics 3, history 2, science 2 (laboratory 2) and academic electives 3. One citizenship required.

2005-2006 Annual costs. Tuition/fees: $3,254; $8,075 out-of-state. Room/board: $3,250. Books/supplies: $600. Personal expenses: $1,312.

2004-2005 Financial aid. Need-based: 245 full-time freshmen applied for aid; 210 were judged to have need; 209 of these received aid. Average need met was 60%. Average scholarship/grant was $1,170; average loan $1,183. 48% of total undergraduate aid awarded as scholarships/grants, 52% as loans/jobs. **Non-need-based:** Awarded to 483 full-time undergraduates, including 135 freshmen. Scholarships awarded for academics, alumni affiliation, art, athletics, job skills, leadership, minority status, music/drama, religious affiliation, state residency.

Application procedures. Admission: No deadline. $20 fee. Application may be submitted online. Admission notification on a rolling basis. **Financial aid:** Priority date 3/1; no closing date. FAFSA, institutional form required. Applicants notified on a rolling basis starting 4/15; must reply within 2 week(s) of notification.

Academics. Programs in aviation, ecology, energy, health-related sciences, and criminology. **Special study options:** Distance learning, double major, honors, independent study, internships, teacher certification program. **Credit/placement by examination:** AP, CLEP, IB, institutional tests. 60 credit hours maximum toward bachelor's degree. **Support services:** Learning center, pre-admission summer program, reduced course load, remedial instruction, study skills assistance, tutoring, writing center.

Majors. Agriculture: Range science. **Area/ethnic studies:** Latin American. **Biology:** General, biophysics, biotechnology, zoology. **Business:** Accounting, business admin, finance, management science, marketing. **Communications:** General, advertising, broadcast journalism, journalism, public relations. **Computer sciences:** General, information systems. **Conservation:** General, environmental science. **Education:** General, art, early childhood, elementary, English, foreign languages, health, mathematics, multi-level teacher, music, science, secondary, social studies, Spanish, special, speech. **Engineering:** Aerospace. **Engineering technology:** General, electrical, occupational safety. **English:** English lit. **Foreign languages:** Spanish. **Health:** Clinical lab technology. **History:** General. **Math:** General. **Mechanic/repair:** Aircraft. **Parks/recreation:** General. **Physical sciences:** Chemistry. **Protective services:** Criminal justice. **Psychology:** General. **Social sciences:** Political science, sociology. **Transportation:** Airline/commercial pilot, aviation. **Visual/performing arts:** Art, music performance, theater design.

Most popular majors. Business/marketing 12%, communications/journalism 6%, education 23%, parks/recreation 6%, psychology 6%, trade and industry 7%.

Computing on campus. 398 workstations in dormitories, library, computer center. Dormitories wired for high-speed internet access. Online course registration, online library, wireless network available.

Student life. Freshman orientation: Available, $20 fee. Preregistration for classes offered. **Policies:** No alcohol at university events on/off campus. Freshmen permitted cars on campus. **Housing:** Coed dorms, single-sex dorms, special housing for disabled, apartments available. $50 deposit. **Activities:** Bands, choral groups, dance, drama, literary magazine, music ensembles, musical theater, opera, radio station, student government, student newspaper, international student club, Black American Society, Baptist Collegiate Ministries, Wesley Center, Student Bible Center, Chi Alpha, Young Democrats, College Republicans, Muslim Student Association.

Athletics. NCAA. **Intercollegiate:** Baseball M, basketball, cross-country W, football (tackle) M, golf M, rodeo, softball W, tennis, volleyball W. **Intramural:** Basketball, football (non-tackle), football (tackle) M, rodeo, soccer, softball, volleyball. **Team name:** Savage Storm.

Student services. Adult student services, alcohol/substance abuse counseling, campus ministries, career counseling, student employment services, financial aid counseling, health services, minority student services, personal counseling, placement for graduates, veterans' counselor. **Physically disabled:** Services for visually, speech, hearing impaired.

Contact. E-mail: admissions@sosu.edu
Phone: (580) 745-2060 Toll-free number: (800) 435-1327 ext. 2060
Fax: (580) 745-7502
Kyle Stafford, Director of Admission and Enrollment Services, Southeastern Oklahoma State University, 1405 North Fourth Avenue, PMB 4225, Durant, OK 74701-0607

Southern Nazarene University

Bethany, Oklahoma — **CB member**
www.snu.edu — **CB code: 6036**

- Private 4-year university and liberal arts college affiliated with Church of the Nazarene
- Residential campus in large town
- 1,762 degree-seeking undergraduates
- 437 graduate students

General. Founded in 1899. Regionally accredited. **Degrees:** 588 bachelor's, 2 associate awarded; master's offered. **ROTC:** Army, Air Force. **Location:** 10 miles from Oklahoma City. **Calendar:** Semester, limited summer session. **Full-time faculty:** 84 total. **Part-time faculty:** 60 total. **Special facilities:** Human cadaver laboratory, physics laser laboratory, laboratory school for children.

Basis for selection. Open admission. Students admitted on probation if high school GPA below 2.5, composite ACT below 17, combined SAT below 700 (exclusive of writing), or high school rank 40 percent or below. No test scores required for placement if student has 24 or more transfer credit hours or is over 25 years old. Interview recommended for all; audition recommended for music program. **Homeschooled:** Transcript of courses and grades required.

High school preparation. 13 units recommended. Recommended units include English 4, mathematics 3, social studies 2, science 2 and foreign language 2. One computer course recommended.

2005-2006 Annual costs. Tuition/fees: $13,160. Room/board: $5,466. Books/supplies: $600. Personal expenses: $1,200.

Financial aid. Non-need-based: Scholarships awarded for academics, athletics, ROTC, state residency.

Application procedures. Admission: Priority date 5/1; deadline 8/1. $25 fee, may be waived for applicants with need. Application may be submitted online. Admission notification on a rolling basis. **Financial aid:** Priority date 3/1; no closing date. FAFSA, institutional form required. Applicants notified on a rolling basis starting 5/1; must reply within 2 week(s) of notification.

Academics. Special study options: Combined bachelor's/graduate degree, double major, dual enrollment of high school students, external degree, independent study, internships, liberal arts/career combination, student-designed major, study abroad, teacher certification program, urban semester, Washington semester. **Credit/placement by examination:** AP, CLEP, IB, institutional tests. 30 credit hours maximum toward bachelor's degree. **Support services:** Remedial instruction, study skills assistance, tutoring, writing center.

Majors. Area/ethnic studies: American. **Biology:** General, biochemistry. **Business:** General, accounting, business admin, finance, marketing. **Communications:** General, journalism. **Communications technology:** General. **Computer sciences:** General, networking. **Conservation:** General. **Education:** General, biology, business, chemistry, early childhood, elementary, English, history, mathematics, music, physical, science, secondary, Spanish, speech. **English:** Speech/rhetoric. **Foreign languages:** Spanish. **Health:** Athletic training, clinical lab technology. **History:** General. **Interdisciplinary:** Behavioral sciences. **Legal studies:** Prelaw. **Liberal arts:** Arts/sciences. **Math:** General. **Parks/recreation:** Exercise sciences. **Philosophy/religion:** Philosophy, religion. **Physical sciences:** Chemistry, physics. **Protective services:** Criminal justice. **Psychology:** General. **Social sciences:** General, political science, sociology. **Theology:** Missionary, religious ed, sacred music, theology. **Transportation:** Aviation management. **Visual/performing arts:** General.

Computing on campus. 180 workstations in library, computer center. Dormitories wired for high-speed internet access and linked to campus network. Helpline, wireless network available.

Student life. Freshman orientation: Mandatory. Preregistration for classes offered. **Policies:** Religious observance required. Freshmen permitted cars on campus. **Housing:** Guaranteed on-campus for freshmen. Single-sex dorms, apartments available. $50 deposit, deadline 8/1. Single students under 23 required to live on campus or with relatives. **Activities:** Bands, choral groups, drama, film society, music ensembles, student government, student newspaper, symphony orchestra, Gospel Team, Mission Crusaders, Circle-K, Spanish Club, Mortar Board.

Athletics. NAIA. **Intercollegiate:** Baseball M, basketball, cross-country, equestrian, football (tackle) M, golf, soccer, softball W, tennis, track and field, volleyball W. **Intramural:** Basketball, football (tackle) M, golf M, softball, swimming, table tennis, tennis, track and field, volleyball. **Team name:** Crimson Storm.

Student services. Alcohol/substance abuse counseling, campus ministries, career counseling, services for economically disadvantaged, student employment services, financial aid counseling, health services, personal counseling, placement for graduates. **Physically disabled:** Services for visually, speech, hearing impaired.

Contact. E-mail: lhess@snu.edu
Phone: (405) 491-6324 Toll-free number: (800) 648-9899
Fax: (405) 491-6320
Larry Hess, Director of Admissions, Southern Nazarene University, 6729 NW 39th Expressway, Bethany, OK 73008

Southwestern Christian University

Bethany, Oklahoma
www.swcu.edu **CB code: 1433**

- Private 4-year Bible college affiliated with Pentecostal Holiness Church
- Residential campus in large town
- 188 degree-seeking undergraduates: 12% part-time, 50% women, 17% African American, 2% Asian American, 6% Hispanic American, 7% Native American, 2% international
- 74 degree-seeking graduate students
- 74% of applicants admitted
- Application essay, interview required

General. Founded in 1946. Regionally accredited. **Degrees:** 32 bachelor's, 9 associate awarded; master's offered. **Location:** 10 miles from Oklahoma City. **Calendar:** Semester, limited summer session. **Full-time faculty:** 8 total; 25% have terminal degrees, 38% women. **Part-time faculty:** 15 total; 53% have terminal degrees, 7% minority, 33% women. **Class size:** 77% < 20, 23% 20-39.

Freshman class profile. 84 applied, 62 admitted, 46 enrolled.

Mid 50% test scores			
SAT verbal:	390-530	GPA 2.0-2.99:	30%
SAT math:	460-610	Rank in top quarter:	27%
ACT:	16-20	Rank in top tenth:	5%
GPA 3.50 or higher:	22%	Out-of-state:	24%
GPA 3.0-3.49:	44%	Live on campus:	71%

Basis for selection. Must have either 2.5 GPA or ACT score of 19. Minister's recommendation important. SAT or ACT recommended. Essay is part of application.

High school preparation. Required units include English 4, mathematics 2, social studies 2, history 2, science 2 (laboratory 2).

2005-2006 Annual costs. Tuition/fees: $8,250. Adult Education Program is $295 per-credit-hour. Room/board: $4,400. Books/supplies: $750. Personal expenses: $1,100.

2005-2006 Financial aid. Need-based: 44 full-time freshmen applied for aid; 41 were judged to have need; 40 of these received aid. Average need met was 81%. Average scholarship/grant was $1,500; average loan $4,000. 40% of total undergraduate aid awarded as scholarships/grants, 60% as loans/jobs. **Non-need-based:** Awarded to 33 full-time undergraduates, including 11 freshmen. Scholarships awarded for academics, alumni affiliation, leadership, music/drama, religious affiliation.

Application procedures. Admission: Closing date 8/10 (postmark date). No application fee. Application may be submitted online. Admission notification on a rolling basis. **Financial aid:** Priority date 8/1; no closing date. FAFSA required. Applicants notified on a rolling basis starting 5/1; must reply within 2 week(s) of notification.

Academics. Applied Biblical Leadership Education (ABLE), an adult studies completion program. **Special study options:** Accelerated study, cross-registration, double major, dual enrollment of high school students, honors, independent study, internships, liberal arts/career combination. **Credit/placement by examination:** AP, CLEP, institutional tests. 30 credit hours maximum toward bachelor's degree. **Support services:** Learning center, reduced course load, remedial instruction, tutoring.

Majors. Business: Business admin. **Philosophy/religion:** Religion. **Theology:** Bible, missionary, pastoral counseling, religious ed, sacred music, theology, youth ministry. **Visual/performing arts:** Music performance.

Computing on campus. 9 workstations in library. Online library available.

Student life. Freshman orientation: Mandatory. Preregistration for classes offered. **Policies:** Extracurricular Christian programs and activities emphasized. Mandatory dress code. Students sign lifestyle covenant agreeing to certain behaviors. Religious observance required. Freshmen permitted cars on campus. **Housing:** Single-sex dorms available. $100 nonrefundable deposit, deadline 8/15. **Activities:** Choral groups, drama, music ensembles, musical theater, student government, student newspaper, Southwestern Ministerial Association, Robert Hough Missionary Society, Christian Education Association.

Athletics. NCCAA. **Intercollegiate:** Basketball M, cross-country, golf M, soccer M, softball, volleyball W. **Intramural:** Baseball M, basketball, cheerleading, football (non-tackle) M, softball, table tennis, volleyball. **Team name:** Eagles.

Student services. Adult student services, campus ministries, career counseling, student employment services, financial aid counseling, personal counseling, placement for graduates, veterans' counselor.

Contact. E-mail: megan@swcu.edu
Phone: (405) 789-7661 ext. 3439 Toll-free number: (888) 418-9272
Fax: (405) 495-0078
Megan Miles, Director of Admissions, Southwestern Christian University, Box 340, Bethany, OK 73008

Southwestern Oklahoma State University

Weatherford, Oklahoma **CB member**
www.swosu.edu **CB code: 6673**

- Public 4-year university
- Residential campus in large town
- 4,338 degree-seeking undergraduates
- 95% of applicants admitted
- SAT or ACT (ACT writing optional) required

General. Founded in 1901. Regionally accredited. Campus at Sayre offers lower division and remedial courses, as well as associate degrees. **Degrees:** 634 bachelor's, 103 associate awarded; master's, first professional offered. **Location:** 75 miles from Oklahoma City. **Calendar:** Semester, extensive summer session. **Full-time faculty:** 210 total. **Part-time faculty:** 40 total. **Class size:** 33% < 20, 47% 20-39, 12% 40-49, 7% 50-99, less than 1% >100.

Freshman class profile. 1,356 applied, 1,285 admitted, 906 enrolled.

Mid 50% test scores			
ACT:	18-24	Out-of-state:	7%
		Live on campus:	59%

Basis for selection. Bachelor degree programs require minimum ACT score of 19 and no curricular deficiencies. Open admission for certificate and associate degree programs. Last date to submit test scores is first day of classes. Essay required for returning suspension students only.

High school preparation. 15 units required; 17 recommended. Required and recommended units include English 4, mathematics 3, social studies 1, history 2, science 2 (laboratory 2) and academic electives 2. Social studies unit must be citizenship. Academic electives should be in fine arts. 3 units computer science or foreign language required.

2005-2006 Annual costs. Tuition/fees: $3,240; $7,740 out-of-state. Room/board: $3,339. Books/supplies: $756. Personal expenses: $996.

Financial aid. Non-need-based: Scholarships awarded for academics, alumni affiliation, art, athletics, music/drama, state residency.

Application procedures. Admission: No deadline. $15 fee. Admission notification on a rolling basis. **Financial aid:** Closing date 3/1. FAFSA, institutional form required. Applicants notified by 3/20; must reply by 4/6.

Academics. Special study options: Accelerated study, combined bachelor's/graduate degree, distance learning, double major, dual enrollment of high school students, independent study, internships, liberal arts/career combination, student-designed major, teacher certification program, weekend college. Weekend college for nursing only. **Credit/placement by examination:** AP, CLEP, IB, institutional tests. 62 credit hours maximum toward bachelor's degree. **Support services:** Pre-admission summer program, reduced course load, remedial instruction, study skills assistance, tutoring, writing center.

Majors. Biology: General, biophysics. **Business:** General, accounting, business admin, human resources, management information systems. **Communications:** General. **Computer sciences:** General, computer science, information systems. **Education:** Art, early childhood, elementary, English, health, history, learning disabled, mathematics, mentally handicapped, music, physical, science, social science, special, technology/industrial arts. **Engineering:** General, physics. **Engineering technology:** Manufacturing. **Health:** Athletic training, clinical lab technology, health care admin, medical records admin, music therapy, nursing (RN). **History:** General. **Math:** General. **Parks/ recreation:** General, facilities management. **Physical sciences:** Chemistry, physics. **Protective services:** Criminal justice. **Psychology:** General. **Public administration:** Social work. **Social sciences:** Political science, sociology. **Theology:** Sacred music. **Visual/performing arts:** Commercial/ advertising art, music management, music performance, music theory/ composition, piano/organ, voice/opera.

Most popular majors. Business/marketing 24%, education 23%, health sciences 12%, visual/performing arts 8%.

Computing on campus. 200 workstations in library, computer center. Dormitories wired for high-speed internet access. Commuter students can connect to campus network. Online library, wireless network available.

Student life. Freshman orientation: Mandatory, $60 fee. Preregistration for classes offered. Class meets 1 hour per week for the first 8 weeks of the fall semester. **Housing:** Guaranteed on-campus for all undergraduates. Single-sex dorms, apartments available. $60 deposit. Private rooms available on priority basis. Limited housing available for married students. **Activities:** Bands, choral groups, drama, music ensembles, musical theater, student government, student newspaper, symphony orchestra, 7 religious organizations, 4 political organizations, and approximately 75 social and professional clubs.

Athletics. NCAA. **Intercollegiate:** Baseball M, basketball, cheerleading, cross-country W, football (tackle) M, golf, rodeo, soccer, softball W. **Intramural:** Basketball, bowling, football (non-tackle), golf, racquetball, soccer, softball, swimming, tennis, volleyball. **Team name:** Bulldogs.

Student services. Adult student services, alcohol/substance abuse counseling, career counseling, student employment services, financial aid counseling, health services, personal counseling, placement for graduates, veterans' counselor. **Physically disabled:** Services for visually, hearing impaired.

Contact. Phone: (580) 774-3009 Fax: (580) 774-3795
Todd Boyd, Director of Admissions, Southwestern Oklahoma State University, 100 Campus Drive, Weatherford, OK 73096

University of Central Oklahoma

Edmond, Oklahoma
www.ucok.edu

CB member
CB code: 6091

- Public 4-year university
- Commuter campus in small city
- 14,625 degree-seeking undergraduates: 28% part-time, 59% women, 9% African American, 3% Asian American, 3% Hispanic American, 6% Native American, 7% international
- 1,261 degree-seeking graduate students
- SAT or ACT (ACT writing optional) required
- 34% graduate within 6 years

General. Founded in 1890. Regionally accredited. **Degrees:** 2,111 bachelor's awarded; master's offered. **ROTC:** Army. **Location:** 12 miles from Oklahoma City. **Calendar:** Semester, extensive summer session. **Full-time faculty:** 411 total; 73% have terminal degrees, 15% minority, 49% women. **Part-time faculty:** 401 total; 8% minority, 55% women. **Class size:** 26% < 20, 51% 20-39, 18% 40-49, 5% 50-99, less than 1% >100. **Special facilities:** Jazz lab, art museum, art gallery, library gallery.

Freshman class profile.

Mid 50% test scores		**Rank in top tenth:**	14%
ACT:	19-23	**Return as sophomores:**	71%
GPA 3.50 or higher:	40%	**Out-of-state:**	4%
GPA 3.0-3.49:	38%	**Live on campus:**	42%
GPA 2.0-2.99:	21%	**International:**	4%
Rank in top quarter:	36%		

Basis for selection. Must have 2.7 GPA, rank in top 50% of class, or minimum enhanced ACT composite score of 20. ACT recommended.

High school preparation. 15 units required; 16 recommended. Required and recommended units include English 4, mathematics 3-4, social studies 1, history 2, science 2-3 (laboratory 2-3), foreign language 2 and academic electives 3.

2005-2006 Annual costs. Tuition/fees: $3,292; $8,302 out-of-state. Room/ board: $4,476. Books/supplies: $1,000. Personal expenses: $2,000.

Financial aid. Non-need-based: Scholarships awarded for academics, alumni affiliation, art, athletics, leadership, minority status, music/drama, ROTC, state residency.

Application procedures. Admission: No deadline. $25 fee. Application may be submitted online. Admission notification on a rolling basis beginning on or about 4/1. **Financial aid:** Priority date 5/15; no closing date. FAFSA, institutional form required. Applicants notified on a rolling basis starting 4/15; must reply within 3 week(s) of notification.

Academics. Special study options: Accelerated study, distance learning, double major, dual enrollment of high school students, ESL, honors, independent study, internships, teacher certification program. **Credit/placement by examination:** AP, CLEP, ACT, institutional tests. 94 credit hours maximum toward bachelor's degree. **Support services:** Learning center, reduced course load, remedial instruction, tutoring, writing center.

Majors. Biology: General. **Business:** Accounting, actuarial science, apparel, business admin, finance, human resources, insurance, management information systems, managerial economics, marketing, nonprofit/public, operations. **Communications:** General, advertising, broadcast journalism, journalism, photojournalism, public relations. **Computer sciences:** General, information technology. **Education:** General, art, biology, business, chemistry, curriculum, drama/dance, early childhood, elementary, ESL, family/ consumer sciences, French, German, health occupations, history, instructional media, mathematics, music, physical, physics, reading, science, social studies, Spanish, special, technology/industrial arts. **Engineering:** Biomedical, physics. **Engineering technology:** General, industrial safety. **English:** Composition, English lit. **Family/consumer sciences:** General, aging, child development, family systems, food/nutrition. **Foreign languages:** French, German, Spanish. **Health:** Audiology/speech pathology, clinical lab science, nursing (RN), public health ed, speech pathology. **History:** General. **Liberal arts:** Arts/sciences. **Math:** General, applied, statistics. **Parks/ recreation:** General, exercise sciences. **Personal/culinary services:** Mortuary science. **Philosophy/religion:** Philosophy. **Physical sciences:** Chemistry, physics. **Protective services:** Corrections, criminal justice, forensics, juvenile corrections, police science. **Psychology:** General. **Social sciences:** Applied economics, economics, geography, political science, sociology, urban studies. **Visual/performing arts:** Art, art history/conservation, dance, dramatic, graphic design, interior design, music performance, piano/organ, stringed instruments, voice/opera.

Most popular majors. Business/marketing 28%, communications/ journalism 8%, education 11%, liberal arts 10%.

Computing on campus. 450 workstations in dormitories, library, computer center, student center. Dormitories wired for high-speed internet access. Commuter students can connect to campus network. Helpline available.

Student life. Freshman orientation: Mandatory, $35 fee. Preregistration for classes offered. 3-day orientation held the week before classes start in August. **Policies:** Freshmen permitted cars on campus. **Housing:** Coed dorms, single-sex dorms, apartments, fraternity/sorority housing, substance-free housing available. $150 fully refundable deposit. **Activities:** Bands, choral groups, dance, drama, music ensembles, musical theater, radio station, student government, student newspaper, symphony orchestra, TV station, Baptist Student Union, Fellowship of Christian Athletes, Young Democrats, Collegiate Republicans, Black student association, Malaysian student association, Association of Women Students, Webmasters.

Athletics. NCAA. **Intercollegiate:** Baseball M, basketball, cross-country, football (tackle) M, golf, soccer W, softball W, tennis, track and field, volleyball W, wrestling M. **Intramural:** Badminton, baseball M, basketball, bowling, football (non-tackle), golf, handball, soccer, softball, swimming, table tennis, tennis, track and field, volleyball, wrestling M. **Team name:** Bronchos.

Student services. Career counseling, student employment services, health services, personal counseling, placement for graduates, veterans' counselor. **Physically disabled:** Services for visually, speech, hearing impaired.

Contact. E-mail: admituco@ucok.edu
Phone: (405) 974-2338 Toll-free number: (800) 254-4215
Fax: (405) 341-4964
Linda Lofton, Director, Admissions & Records, University of Central Oklahoma, 100 North University Drive, Edmond, OK 73034-0151

University of Oklahoma

Norman, Oklahoma **CB member**
www.ou.edu **CB code: 6879**

- Public 4-year university
- Residential campus in small city
- 20,967 degree-seeking undergraduates: 13% part-time, 51% women, 5% African American, 5% Asian American, 4% Hispanic American, 7% Native American, 2% international
- 9,207 graduate students
- 86% of applicants admitted
- SAT or ACT (ACT writing optional) required
- 56% graduate within 6 years

General. Founded in 1890. Regionally accredited. Faculty-in-residence program has faculty live in student dorms and mix with students. **Degrees:** 3,995 bachelor's awarded; master's, doctoral, first professional offered. **ROTC:** Army, Navy, Air Force. **Location:** 20 miles from Oklahoma City, 200 miles from Dallas. **Calendar:** Semester, extensive summer session. **Full-time faculty:** 1,276 total; 84% have terminal degrees, 15% minority, 39% women. **Part-time faculty:** 377 total; 54% have terminal degrees, 10% minority, 46% women. **Class size:** 39% < 20, 43% 20-39, 6% 40-49, 8% 50-99, 4% >100. **Special facilities:** Museum of science and history, art museum, biological station, history of science collection, western history collection, national severe storms laboratory, energy center.

Freshman class profile. 7,388 applied, 6,331 admitted, 3,245 enrolled.

Mid 50% test scores		**Rank in top quarter:**	72%
ACT:	23-28	**Rank in top tenth:**	37%
GPA 3.50 or higher:	71%	**Return as sophomores:**	85%
GPA 3.0-3.49:	25%	**International:**	1%
GPA 2.0-2.99:	4%		

Basis for selection. Standardized test scores, class rank, and secondary school record very important. Applicants who do not meet requirements for guaranteed admission, but do meet certain performance minimums will be placed on wait list and admitted on space-available basis, with preference given to most academically qualified. High school GPA and class rank may be used in place of test scores for admission purposes. Audition required for dance, drama, music programs. **Homeschooled:** Must qualify for admission on ACT or SAT score. Need to submit a record or transcript of all courses completed at the high school level. **Learning Disabled:** Students with disabilities are held to same admission criteria as all applicants. These students must identify themselves after admission and provide documentation of disability in order to receive special services.

High school preparation. 15 units required. Required and recommended units include English 4, mathematics 3, social studies 2, history 1, science 2 (laboratory 2), foreign language 3 and academic electives 3. 1 computer science recommended. Must have 1 American history and 2 additional units from history, economics, geography, government, non-western culture.

2005-2006 Annual costs. Tuition/fees: $4,408; $12,301 out-of-state. Room/board: $6,361. Books/supplies: $1,067. Personal expenses: $3,176.

2004-2005 Financial aid. Need-based: 2,054 full-time freshmen applied for aid; 1,758 were judged to have need; 1,758 of these received aid. Average need met was 85%. Average scholarship/grant was $3,984; average loan $3,110. 33% of total undergraduate aid awarded as scholarships/grants, 67% as loans/jobs. **Non-need-based:** Awarded to 6,133 full-time undergraduates, including 1,475 freshmen. Scholarships awarded for academics, alumni affiliation, art, athletics, leadership, music/drama, religious affiliation, ROTC. **Additional information:** Institutional loans are available for early applicants who do not qualify for federal or state need-based aid.

Application procedures. Admission: Closing date 4/1 (receipt date). $40 fee, may be waived for applicants with need. Application may be submitted online. Admission notification on a rolling basis. April 1 application deadline for students applying for fall semesters, but freshman applicants encouraged to apply as soon as junior year in high school is completed or by scholarship deadline of February 1. Housing deposit is refundable if contract is voided before 6/15 for fall and 12/15 for spring. **Financial aid:** Priority date 3/1; no closing date. FAFSA required. Applicants notified on a rolling basis starting 3/15; must reply within 6 week(s) of notification.

Academics. OU College of Liberal Studies through distance learning provides non-traditional students with coherent interdisciplinary liberal arts programs. **Special study options:** Accelerated study, combined bachelor's/graduate degree, cooperative education, distance learning, double major, dual enrollment of high school students, ESL, external degree, honors, independent study, internships, liberal arts/career combination, student-designed major, study abroad, teacher certification program, Washington semester. **Credit/placement by examination:** AP, CLEP, IB, SAT, ACT, institutional tests. **Support services:** Learning center, pre-admission summer program, remedial instruction, study skills assistance, tutoring, writing center.

Honors college/program. Admission with 29 ACT or 1280 SAT score or higher (exclusive of Writing) and 3.75 high school GPA, or rank in top 10% of senior class. 400-500 word essay required. Approximately 400 freshmen admitted each year. Students must complete 15 hours of honors-designated courses, write honors thesis, and have a final GPA of 3.4 to graduate with an honors degree.

Majors. Architecture: Architecture, environmental design. **Area/ethnic studies:** African-American, Native American, women's. **Biology:** Biochemistry, botany, microbiology, zoology. **Business:** Accounting, business admin, construction management, finance, management information systems, management science, managerial economics, marketing. **Communications:** General, advertising, broadcast journalism, journalism. **Computer sciences:** Computer science, information systems. **Conservation:** Environmental science. **Education:** Early childhood, elementary, English, foreign languages, mathematics, music, science, social studies, special. **Engineering:** General, aerospace, architectural, chemical, civil, computer, electrical, environmental, industrial, mechanical, petroleum, physics. **English:** English lit. **Foreign languages:** Chinese, classics, French, Germanic, linguistics, Russian, Spanish. **Health:** Communication disorders, dental hygiene, medical radiologic technology/radiation therapy, nuclear medical technology, nursing (RN), sonography. **History:** General. **Interdisciplinary:** Global studies, nutrition sciences. **Liberal arts:** Arts/sciences, humanities. **Math:** General. **Parks/recreation:** Exercise sciences. **Philosophy/religion:** Philosophy, religion. **Physical sciences:** Astronomy, astrophysics, chemistry, geology, geophysics, meteorology, physics. **Psychology:** General. **Public administration:** General, social work. **Social sciences:** Anthropology, economics, geography, political science, sociology. **Transportation:** Aviation. **Visual/performing arts:** General, art history/conservation, dance, dramatic, film/cinema, interior design, music pedagogy, studio arts.

Most popular majors. Business/marketing 17%, communications/journalism 10%, engineering/engineering technologies 7%, health sciences 9%, liberal arts 8%, social sciences 11%.

Computing on campus. 3,385 workstations in dormitories, library, computer center, student center. Dormitories wired for high-speed internet access and linked to campus network. Commuter students can connect to campus network. Online course registration, online library, helpline, repair service, student web hosting, wireless network available.

Student life. Freshman orientation: Mandatory, $50 fee. Preregistration for classes offered. Summer enrollment program for entering freshmen consists of day-long series of activities. **Policies:** Freshmen permitted cars on campus. **Housing:** Guaranteed on-campus for freshmen. Coed dorms, single-sex dorms, special housing for disabled, apartments, fraternity/sorority housing, substance-free housing available. $175 fully refundable deposit. Honors, cultural, scholastic, National Merit housing available,. **Activities:** Bands, choral groups, dance, drama, film society, literary magazine, music ensembles, musical theater, opera, radio station, student government, student newspaper, symphony orchestra, TV station, American Indian, Black, Hispanic-American, Asian-American student associations, College Republicans, Young Democrats, Hillel Jewish student organization, Chi Alpha Christian Fellowship, Muslim student association, Alpha Phi Omega.

Athletics. NCAA. **Intercollegiate:** Baseball M, basketball, cheerleading, cross-country, football (tackle) M, golf, gymnastics, soccer W, softball W, tennis, track and field, volleyball W, wrestling M. **Intramural:** Badminton, basketball, bowling, cross-country, football (non-tackle), golf, handball, lacrosse M, racquetball, soccer, softball, squash, swimming, table tennis, tennis, track and field, volleyball, water polo. **Team name:** Sooners.

Student services. Adult student services, alcohol/substance abuse counseling, campus ministries, career counseling, services for economically disadvantaged, student employment services, financial aid counseling, health services, legal services, minority student services, on-campus daycare, personal counseling, placement for graduates, veterans' counselor, women's services. **Physically disabled:** Services for visually, speech, hearing impaired.

Contact. E-mail: admrec@ou.edu
Phone: (405) 325-2252 Toll-free number: (800) 234-6868
Fax: (405) 325-7124
Patricia Lynch, Director of Admissions and Records, University of Oklahoma, 1000 Asp Avenue, Norman, OK 73019-4076

University of Science and Arts of Oklahoma

Chickasha, Oklahoma
www.usao.edu **CB code: 6544**

- Public 4-year university and liberal arts college
- Commuter campus in large town
- 1,222 degree-seeking undergraduates: 13% part-time, 62% women, 6% African American, 1% Asian American, 3% Hispanic American, 13% Native American, 2% international
- 89% of applicants admitted
- SAT or ACT (ACT writing optional) required
- 32% graduate within 6 years; 29% enter graduate study

General. Founded in 1908. Regionally accredited. Founded in 1908, one of the oldest public liberal arts colleges in America. Only college or university offering trimester system classes, allowing for three-year graduation. **Degrees:** 182 bachelor's awarded. **Location:** 48 miles from Oklahoma City. **Calendar:** Trimester, extensive summer session. **Full-time faculty:** 48 total; 92% have terminal degrees, 15% minority, 48% women. **Part-time faculty:** 36 total; 25% have terminal degrees, 8% minority, 28% women. **Class size:** 56% < 20, 33% 20-39, 3% 40-49, 5% 50-99, 2% >100. **Special facilities:** Speech and hearing clinic, herbarium, child development center.

Freshman class profile. 448 applied, 397 admitted, 282 enrolled.

Mid 50% test scores			
ACT:	18-25	End year in good standing:	84%
GPA 3.50 or higher:	45%	Return as sophomores:	61%
GPA 3.0-3.49:	31%	Out-of-state:	6%
GPA 2.0-2.99:	24%	Live on campus:	61%
Rank in top quarter:	42%	International:	4%
Rank in top tenth:	13%	Fraternities:	4%
		Sororities:	8%

Basis for selection. One of the following is required for admission: minimum 21 ACT or 980 SAT (exclusive of writing), or minimum overall GPA of 2.85 and ranking in top 50% of high school graduating class, or GPA of 2.85 or higher in the 15-unit high school core curriculum and 18 ACT or 860 SAT. **Homeschooled:** Transcript of courses and grades required. 15 academic high school course units, minimum 21 composite ACT and 19 in each subtest (or 940 SAT) required.

High school preparation. College-preparatory program required. 15 units required; 21 recommended. Required and recommended units include English 4, mathematics 3-4, social studies 1, history 2, science 2-3 (laboratory 2-3), foreign language 2 and academic electives 3. 2 units each of fine arts and speech recommended.

2005-2006 Annual costs. Tuition/fees: $3,480; $8,220 out-of-state. Room/board: $4,170.

2005-2006 Financial aid. Need-based: 224 full-time freshmen applied for aid; 173 were judged to have need; 170 of these received aid. Average need met was 67%. Average scholarship/grant was $4,948; average loan $2,227. 58% of total undergraduate aid awarded as scholarships/grants, 42% as loans/jobs. **Non-need-based:** Awarded to 282 full-time undergraduates, including 90 freshmen. Scholarships awarded for academics, art, athletics, leadership, music/drama, state residency.

Application procedures. Admission: Closing date 9/6 (postmark date). $15 fee, may be waived for applicants with need. Application must be submitted on paper. Admission notification on a rolling basis beginning on or about 2/10. **Financial aid:** Priority date 3/15; no closing date. FAFSA, institutional form required. Applicants notified on a rolling basis starting 3/15; must reply within 4 week(s) of notification.

Academics. Special study options: Accelerated study, distance learning, double major, independent study, internships, liberal arts/career combination, student-designed major, study abroad, teacher certification program. **Credit/placement by examination:** AP, CLEP, ACT, institutional tests. 62 credit hours maximum toward bachelor's degree. **Support services:** Learning center, reduced course load, remedial instruction, study skills assistance, tutoring, writing center.

Majors. Area/ethnic studies: Native American. **Biology:** General. **Business:** Business admin. **Communications:** General. **Computer sciences:** Computer science. **Education:** Deaf/hearing impaired, early childhood, elementary. **English:** English lit. **Health:** Speech pathology. **History:** General. **Interdisciplinary:** Natural sciences. **Math:** General. **Parks/recreation:** Health/fitness. **Physical sciences:** Chemistry, physics. **Psychology:** General. **Social sciences:** Economics, political science, sociology. **Visual/performing arts:** Art, dramatic, studio arts.

Most popular majors. Business/marketing 21%, education 17%, parks/recreation 9%, psychology 9%, social sciences 9%, visual/performing arts 11%.

Computing on campus. 150 workstations in library, computer center. Dormitories wired for high-speed internet access and linked to campus network. Online library, helpline, student web hosting, wireless network available.

Student life. Freshman orientation: Mandatory. Preregistration for classes offered. **Policies:** Freshmen permitted cars on campus. **Housing:** Guaranteed on-campus for freshmen. Coed dorms, apartments available. $100 fully refundable deposit, deadline 4/1. **Activities:** Bands, choral groups, drama, film society, music ensembles, musical theater, student government, student newspaper, Ameslan culture club, Chi Alpha Christian Fellowship, College Democrats, College Republicans, African American student association, international student association, Inter-Tribal Heritage Club, student ambassadors, students with children club, feminist collective.

Athletics. NAIA. **Intercollegiate:** Baseball M, basketball, soccer, softball W. **Intramural:** Basketball, golf, volleyball. **Team name:** Drovers.

Student services. Alcohol/substance abuse counseling, career counseling, services for economically disadvantaged, student employment services, financial aid counseling, health services, minority student services, personal counseling, placement for graduates, veterans' counselor. **Physically disabled:** Services for visually, hearing impaired.

Contact. E-mail: usao-admissions@usao.edu
Phone: (405) 574-1204 Toll-free number: (800) 933-8726
Fax: (405) 574-1220
Joe Evans, Director of Admissions and Records, University of Science and Arts of Oklahoma, 1727 West Alabama, Chickasha, OK 73018-5322

University of Tulsa

Tulsa, Oklahoma **CB member**
www.utulsa.edu **CB code: 6883**

- Private 4-year university affiliated with Presbyterian Church (USA)
- Residential campus in large city
- 2,749 degree-seeking undergraduates: 5% part-time, 50% women, 7% African American, 2% Asian American, 4% Hispanic American, 5% Native American, 8% international
- 1,263 degree-seeking graduate students
- 75% of applicants admitted
- SAT or ACT (ACT writing optional) required
- 60% graduate within 6 years; 31% enter graduate study

General. Founded in 1894. Regionally accredited. **Degrees:** 536 bachelor's awarded; master's, doctoral, first professional offered. **ROTC:** Air Force. **Location:** 100 miles from Oklahoma City. **Calendar:** Semester, limited summer session. **Full-time faculty:** 306 total; 96% have terminal degrees, 13% minority, 34% women. **Part-time faculty:** 116 total; 96% have terminal degrees, 3% minority, 40% women. **Class size:** 60% < 20, 31% 20-39, 7% 40-49, 1% 50-99. **Special facilities:** Biotechnology institute, center for communicative disorders, communication lab, the Tall Grass Prairie Preserve.

Freshman class profile. 2,687 applied, 2,017 admitted, 631 enrolled.

Mid 50% test scores		Rank in top tenth:	63%
SAT verbal:	540-700	End year in good standing:	88%
SAT math:	550-710	Return as sophomores:	84%
ACT:	23-30	Out-of-state:	45%
GPA 3.50 or higher:	69%	Live on campus:	83%
GPA 3.0-3.49:	23%	International:	6%
GPA 2.0-2.99:	8%	Fraternities:	21%
Rank in top quarter:	81%	Sororities:	23%

Basis for selection. Primary requirements are school achievement records and test scores. High school guidance counselor recommendation required. Extracurricular activities, community involvement, and talents are taken into consideration. Essays and interviews are recommended for all; audition required for music, theater programs; portfolio required for art program. **Homeschooled:** Statement describing homeschool structure and mission, transcript of courses and grades, letter of recommendation (nonparent) required.

High school preparation. College-preparatory program recommended. 16 units recommended. Recommended units include English 4, mathematics 3, social studies 1, history 2, science 3 (laboratory 2), foreign language 2 and academic electives 1. 4 mathematics and 4 physical science recommended for engineering and natural science students.

2005-2006 Annual costs. Tuition/fees: $18,860. A one-time $375 fee is charged first-time students, for orientation, life-time transcripts, course drop/add transactions, and graduation/commencement. Room/board: $6,488. Books/supplies: $1,200. Personal expenses: $2,345.

2004-2005 Financial aid. Need-based: 631 full-time freshmen applied for aid; 358 were judged to have need; 358 of these received aid. Average need met was 83%. Average scholarship/grant was $4,736; average loan $4,457. 32% of total undergraduate aid awarded as scholarships/grants, 68% as loans/jobs. **Non-need-based:** Awarded to 2,138 full-time undergraduates, including 657 freshmen. Scholarships awarded for academics, alumni affiliation, art, athletics, leadership, minority status, music/drama, religious affiliation.

Application procedures. Admission: Priority date 2/1; no deadline. $35 fee, may be waived for applicants with need. Application may be submitted online. Admission notification on a rolling basis beginning on or about 10/1. Must reply by May 1 or within 2 week(s) if notified thereafter. **Financial aid:** Priority date 4/1; no closing date. FAFSA, institutional form required. Applicants notified on a rolling basis starting 3/1; must reply by 5/1 or within 2 week(s) of notification.

Academics. Special study options: Accelerated study, combined bachelor's/graduate degree, double major, ESL, honors, independent study, internships, liberal arts/career combination, student-designed major, study abroad, teacher certification program, Washington semester. **Credit/placement by examination:** AP, CLEP, IB, institutional tests. 36 credit hours maximum toward bachelor's degree. **Support services:** Learning center, reduced course load, study skills assistance, tutoring, writing center.

Majors. Biology: General, biochemistry. **Business:** Accounting, business admin, finance, international, management information systems, marketing. **Communications:** General. **Computer sciences:** General, computer science, information technology. **Conservation:** Environmental studies. **Education:** Chemistry, Deaf/hearing impaired, early childhood, elementary, mathematics, music. **Engineering:** Chemical, electrical, mechanical, petroleum, physics. **English:** English lit. **Foreign languages:** French, German, Spanish. **Health:** Athletic training, audiology/speech pathology, communication disorders, nursing (RN). **History:** General. **Interdisciplinary:** Global studies. **Legal studies:** General, prelaw. **Liberal arts:** Arts/sciences. **Math:** Applied. **Parks/recreation:** Exercise sciences. **Philosophy/religion:** Philosophy, religion. **Physical sciences:** Chemistry, geology, geophysics, physics. **Psychology:** General. **Social sciences:** Anthropology, economics, political science, sociology. **Visual/performing arts:** Art, art history/conservation, arts management, dramatic, film/cinema, music performance, music theory/composition, piano/organ, voice/opera.

Most popular majors. Biology 6%, business/marketing 24%, computer/information sciences 6%, engineering/engineering technologies 17%, visual/performing arts 9%.

Computing on campus. 900 workstations in dormitories, library, computer center, student center. Dormitories wired for high-speed internet access and linked to campus network. Commuter students can connect to campus network. Online course registration, online library, helpline, student web hosting, wireless network available.

Student life. Freshman orientation: Available, $275 fee. Preregistration for classes offered. Held the week prior to fall term, designed to help students form relationships with faculty, staff, and fellow students. **Policies:** Freshmen permitted cars on campus. **Housing:** Guaranteed on-campus for freshmen. Coed dorms, single-sex dorms, special housing for disabled, apartments, fraternity/sorority housing, substance-free housing available. $200 nonrefundable deposit. Honors house and Language house. **Activities:** Bands, choral groups, drama, literary magazine, music ensembles, musical theater, opera, radio station, student government, student newspaper, symphony orchestra, TV station, Baptist Student Union, Fellowship of Christian Athletes, Jewish student association, Young Democrats, Women's Law Caucus, Hispanic student association, College Republicans, International Fellowship House, Association of Black Collegians, volunteer income tax assistance project.

Athletics. NCAA. **Intercollegiate:** Basketball, cheerleading, cross-country, football (tackle) M, golf, rowing (crew) W, soccer, softball W, tennis, track and field, volleyball W. **Intramural:** Badminton, basketball, bowling, cross-country, diving, football (non-tackle), golf, racquetball, soccer, softball, squash, swimming, table tennis, tennis, track and field, volleyball, water polo, wrestling M. **Team name:** Golden Hurricane.

Student services. Adult student services, alcohol/substance abuse counseling, campus ministries, career counseling, student employment services, financial aid counseling, health services, legal services, minority student services, on-campus daycare, personal counseling, placement for graduates, veterans' counselor, women's services. **Physically disabled:** Services for visually, speech, hearing impaired.

Contact. E-mail: admission@utulsa.edu
Phone: (918) 631-2307 Toll-free number: (800) 331-3050
Fax: (918) 631-5003
John Corso, Associate Vice President and Dean of Admissions, University of Tulsa, 600 South College Avenue, Tulsa, OK 74104-3189

Oregon

Art Institute of Portland

Portland, Oregon
www.aipd.artinstitutes.edu
CB member
CB code: 4231

- For-profit 4-year visual arts and liberal arts college
- Commuter campus in large city
- 1,580 degree-seeking undergraduates: 32% part-time, 51% women, 2% African American, 6% Asian American, 5% Hispanic American, 2% Native American
- Application essay, interview required
- 37% graduate within 6 years

General. Founded in 1963. Regionally accredited. **Degrees:** 179 bachelor's, 27 associate awarded. **Calendar:** Quarter, extensive summer session. **Full-time faculty:** 35 total. **Part-time faculty:** 100 total. **Special facilities:** Specialized library, design laboratories, audio/visual laboratory.

Basis for selection. Proof of graduation from secondary school/GED required. Interview, essay, college transcripts, and/or English/math placement exam are considered. Portfolio recommended for Game Art and Design program.

2006-2007 Annual costs. Tuition/fees (projected): $17,460. Room/board: $5,625.

2004-2005 Financial aid. Need-based: 204 full-time freshmen applied for aid; 202 were judged to have need; 201 of these received aid. Average need met was 1%. Average scholarship/grant was $1,370; average loan $2,625. 30% of total undergraduate aid awarded as scholarships/grants, 70% as loans/jobs. **Non-need-based:** Awarded to 211 full-time undergraduates, including 101 freshmen. Scholarships awarded for art. **Additional information:** Applicants encouraged to apply early for financial aid. Scholarship deadlines range from January 1 to March 1.

Application procedures. Admission: No deadline. $50 fee. Application may be submitted online. Admission notification on a rolling basis. **Financial aid:** Priority date 3/1; no closing date. FAFSA required. Applicants notified on a rolling basis starting 1/1; must reply within 5 week(s) of notification.

Academics. Special study options: Accelerated study, distance learning, honors, independent study, internships, liberal arts/career combination, study abroad. **Credit/placement by examination:** AP, CLEP, IB, SAT, ACT, institutional tests. Credit by examination only offered for courses in writing, computing, graphics, drawing, and mathematics. **Support services:** Learning center, reduced course load, remedial instruction, study skills assistance, tutoring.

Majors. Communications technology: Animation/special effects. **Computer sciences:** Web page design. **Family/consumer sciences:** Clothing/textiles. **Visual/performing arts:** Arts management, commercial/advertising art, design, fashion design, graphic design, interior design, multimedia.

Computing on campus. 240 workstations in library, computer center. Dormitories wired for high-speed internet access. Commuter students can connect to campus network. Student web hosting available.

Student life. Freshman orientation: Mandatory. Preregistration for classes offered. Held before each quarter-registration, advising and student and community services available. **Policies:** Student code of conduct published in catalog. No alcohol or drugs on campus or in housing. Freshmen permitted cars on campus. **Housing:** Special housing for disabled, apartments, substance-free housing available. $250 partly refundable deposit. Apartments for 2 or 4 students. **Activities:** Drama, film society, student government, student newspaper.

Student services. Alcohol/substance abuse counseling, career counseling, student employment services, financial aid counseling, personal counseling, placement for graduates, veterans' counselor. **Physically disabled:** Services for visually, speech, hearing impaired.

Contact. E-mail: aipdadm@aii.edu
Phone: (503) 228-6528 Toll-free number: (888) 228-6528
Fax: (503) 227-1945
Lori Murray, Director of Admissions, Art Institute of Portland, 1122 Northwest Davis Street, Portland, OR 97209-2911

Concordia University

Portland, Oregon
www.cu-portland.edu
CB code: 4079

- Private 4-year university and liberal arts college affiliated with Lutheran Church - Missouri Synod
- Commuter campus in very large city
- 912 degree-seeking undergraduates: 13% part-time, 63% women
- 435 degree-seeking graduate students
- 66% of applicants admitted
- SAT or ACT (ACT writing optional) required
- 42% graduate within 6 years

General. Founded in 1905. Regionally accredited. About 5 percent of undergraduate students preparing for full-time service in Lutheran Church-Missouri Synod. **Degrees:** 196 bachelor's awarded; master's offered. **ROTC:** Air Force. **Location:** 5 miles from downtown. **Calendar:** Semester, limited summer session. **Full-time faculty:** 37 total; 54% have terminal degrees, 40% women. **Part-time faculty:** 89 total; 26% have terminal degrees, 2% minority, 54% women. **Class size:** 78% < 20, 21% 20-39, less than 1% 50-99. **Special facilities:** 2-way compressed video distance learning classroom.

Freshman class profile. 804 applied, 532 admitted, 171 enrolled.

Mid 50% test scores		**Rank in top quarter:**	49%
SAT verbal:	430-560	**Rank in top tenth:**	17%
SAT math:	460-570	**Return as sophomores:**	68%
ACT:	18-24	**Out-of-state:**	60%
GPA 3.50 or higher:	45%	**Live on campus:**	77%
GPA 3.0-3.49:	33%	**International:**	1%
GPA 2.0-2.99:	22%		

Basis for selection. 2.5 high school GPA, SAT verbal score greater than 480, or minimum ACT composite score of 18 required. **Homeschooled:** Statement describing homeschool structure and mission, state high school equivalency certificate, letter of recommendation (nonparent) required. Interview may be required.

High school preparation. College-preparatory program recommended. 19 units recommended. Recommended units include English 4, mathematics 3, social studies 3, science 3, foreign language 2 and academic electives 3. One computer/keyboarding recommended.

2006-2007 Annual costs. Tuition/fees: $19,090. Per-credit-hour charge for less than 6 credits in a given term: $314. Room/board: $3,305. Books/supplies: $500. Personal expenses: $1,000.

2004-2005 Financial aid. Need-based: 114 full-time freshmen applied for aid; 105 were judged to have need; 105 of these received aid. Average need met was 85%. Average scholarship/grant was $10,000; average loan $3,000. 65% of total undergraduate aid awarded as scholarships/grants, 35% as loans/jobs. **Non-need-based:** Awarded to 329 full-time undergraduates, including 118 freshmen. Scholarships awarded for academics, athletics, leadership, music/drama, religious affiliation.

Application procedures. Admission: Priority date 3/1; deadline 7/1 (postmark date). $20 fee, may be waived for applicants with need. Application may be submitted online. Admission notification on a rolling basis beginning on or about 1/1. Must reply by May 1 or within 2 week(s) if notified thereafter. **Financial aid:** No deadline. FAFSA required. Applicants notified on a rolling basis starting 3/15; must reply by 5/1 or within 3 week(s) of notification.

Academics. Special study options: Accelerated study, cross-registration, distance learning, double major, dual enrollment of high school students, ESL, exchange student, honors, independent study, internships, liberal arts/career combination, study abroad, teacher certification program. **Credit/placement by examination:** CLEP, institutional tests. **Support services:** Learning center, remedial instruction, tutoring, writing center.

Majors. Biology: General. **Business:** General, business admin, international. **Education:** General, biology, business, chemistry, early childhood, elementary, English, health, history, mathematics, middle, multi-level teacher, physical, science, secondary, social studies. **English:** English lit. **Health:** Athletic training, health care admin, nursing (RN), premedicine. **History:** General. **Liberal arts:** Arts/sciences. **Parks/recreation:** Health/fitness, sports admin. **Philosophy/religion:** Religion. **Physical sciences:** Chemistry. **Psychology:** General. **Public administration:** Social work. **Social sciences:** General. **Theology:** Religious ed, theology.

Most popular majors. Business/marketing 36%, education 28%, health sciences 10%.

Computing on campus. PC or laptop required. 60 workstations in dormitories, library, computer center. Dormitories wired for high-speed internet access and linked to campus network. Commuter students can connect to campus network. Online course registration, online library, helpline, wireless network available.

Student life. Freshman orientation: Mandatory. Preregistration for classes offered. Usually day before classes begin. **Policies:** Optional attendance for chapel services. Lutheran format, mixture of traditional and contemporary services offered. Freshmen permitted cars on campus. **Housing:** Coed dorms, single-sex dorms, special housing for disabled, apartments, substance-free housing available. $50 nonrefundable deposit, deadline 5/1. School rents nearby houses to students with families and maintains referral file. Homestay option for international students. **Activities:** Choral groups, drama, literary magazine, music ensembles, musical theater, radio station, student government, student newspaper, social service organization, Circle K, Spiritual Life, El Club Latino.

Athletics. NAIA. **Intercollegiate:** Baseball M, basketball, cross-country, golf, soccer, softball W, track and field, volleyball W. **Intramural:** Badminton, basketball, softball, tennis, volleyball. **Team name:** Cavaliers.

Student services. Adult student services, campus ministries, career counseling, financial aid counseling, health services, personal counseling, placement for graduates, veterans' counselor.

Contact. E-mail: admissions@cu-portland.edu
Phone: (503) 280-8501 Toll-free number: (800) 321-9371
Fax: (503) 280-8531
Bobi Swan, Dean of Admission, Concordia University, 2811 Northeast Holman Street, Portland, OR 97211

Corban College
Salem, Oregon
www.corban.edu **CB code: 4956**

- Private 4-year liberal arts college affiliated with Baptist faith
- Residential campus in small city
- 771 degree-seeking undergraduates: 15% part-time, 58% women, 1% African American, 2% Asian American, 2% Hispanic American, 1% Native American
- 47 degree-seeking graduate students
- 83% of applicants admitted
- SAT and SAT Subject Tests or ACT with writing, application essay required
- 59% graduate within 6 years

General. Founded in 1935. Regionally accredited. **Degrees:** 170 bachelor's, 5 associate awarded; master's offered. **ROTC:** Army, Air Force. **Location:** 45 miles from Portland. **Calendar:** Semester, limited summer session. **Full-time faculty:** 34 total. **Part-time faculty:** 34 total. **Class size:** 68% < 20, 25% 20-39, 4% 40-49, 2% 50-99. **Special facilities:** Archaeological museum, outdoor amphitheater.

Freshman class profile. 485 applied, 402 admitted, 205 enrolled.

Mid 50% test scores			
SAT verbal:	450-670	Rank in top quarter:	56%
SAT math:	420-650	Rank in top tenth:	29%
ACT:	20-31	Return as sophomores:	75%
GPA 3.50 or higher:	63%	Out-of-state:	31%
GPA 3.0-3.49:	22%	Live on campus:	86%
GPA 2.0-2.99:	15%	International:	1%

Basis for selection. Commitment to Christianity, high school GPA, test scores, recommendations, essays, school and community activities considered. Audition required for music program.

High school preparation. 13 units recommended. Recommended units include English 4, mathematics 3, social studies 3, science 2 and foreign language 1.

2006-2007 Annual costs. Tuition/fees (projected): $19,294. Room/board: $7,084. Books/supplies: $700. Personal expenses: $500.

2005-2006 Financial aid. Need-based: 155 full-time freshmen applied for aid; 142 were judged to have need; 141 of these received aid. Average need met was 71%. Average scholarship/grant was $8,981; average loan $5,659. 56% of total undergraduate aid awarded as scholarships/grants, 44% as loans/jobs. **Non-need-based:** Awarded to 131 full-time undergraduates, including 35 freshmen. Scholarships awarded for academics, alumni affiliation, athletics, leadership, music/drama.

Application procedures. Admission: Priority date 3/1; deadline 8/1 (receipt date). $35 fee, may be waived for applicants with need. Application may be submitted online. Admission notification on a rolling basis beginning on or about 10/1. Must reply by May 1 or within 2 week(s) if notified thereafter. **Financial aid:** Priority date 2/15; no closing date. FAFSA required. Applicants notified by 3/1; must reply within 4 week(s) of notification.

Academics. Special study options: Accelerated study, combined bachelor's/graduate degree, cross-registration, distance learning, double major, honors, independent study, internships, liberal arts/career combination, study abroad, teacher certification program, Washington semester, weekend college. **Credit/placement by examination:** AP, CLEP, institutional tests. 20 credit hours maximum toward associate degree, 32 toward bachelor's. **Support services:** Learning center, reduced course load, tutoring.

Majors. Business: General, accounting, accounting/business management, accounting/finance, business admin, communications, finance, management information systems. **Communications:** General, journalism. **Computer sciences:** Computer science. **Education:** General, biology, business, elementary, English, history, mathematics, middle, multi-level teacher, music, physical, science, secondary, social science, social studies. **Health:** Predentistry, premedicine, prenursing, prepharmacy, preveterinary. **History:** General. **Legal studies:** Prelaw. **Liberal arts:** Arts/sciences, humanities. **Math:** General. **Parks/recreation:** Health/fitness, sports admin. **Philosophy/religion:** Religion. **Psychology:** General. **Public administration:** Community org/advocacy. **Social sciences:** General. **Theology:** Bible, missionary, pastoral counseling, preministerial, religious ed, sacred music, theology, youth ministry. **Visual/performing arts:** Music performance, piano/organ, voice/opera.

Most popular majors. Business/marketing 27%, education 12%, interdisciplinary studies 11%, liberal arts 12%, psychology 23%.

Computing on campus. 34 workstations in dormitories, library, computer center, student center. Dormitories wired for high-speed internet access and linked to campus network. Commuter students can connect to campus network. Online library, helpline, repair service, wireless network available.

Student life. Freshman orientation: Mandatory. Preregistration for classes offered. Students assigned to core group of 12-18 students, with adviser to answer questions and schedule classes for fall semester. Core group advisers often visit students in their homes. **Policies:** Religious observance required. Freshmen permitted cars on campus. **Housing:** Guaranteed on-campus for freshmen. Single-sex dorms, substance-free housing available. $100 deposit, deadline 8/1. **Activities:** Bands, choral groups, drama, music ensembles, radio station, student government, student newspaper, symphony orchestra, Christian fellowships.

Athletics. NAIA, NCCAA. **Intercollegiate:** Baseball M, basketball, cross-country, golf M, soccer, softball W, volleyball W. **Intramural:** Basketball, football (non-tackle), soccer, softball, volleyball, weight lifting. **Team name:** Warriors.

Student services. Adult student services, campus ministries, career counseling, student employment services, financial aid counseling, health services, personal counseling, placement for graduates. **Physically disabled:** Services for visually, hearing impaired.

Contact. E-mail: admissions@corban.edu
Phone: (503) 375-7005 Toll-free number: (800) 845-3005
Fax: (503) 585-4316
Marty Ziesemer, Director of Admissions, Corban College, 5000 Deer Park Drive SE, Salem, OR 97301-9392

DeVry University: Portland
Portland, Oregon
www.devry.edu

- For-profit 4-year university
- Commuter campus in very large city
- 131 degree-seeking undergraduates: 38% part-time, 40% women, 6% African American, 18% Asian American, 34% Hispanic American, 1% Native American
- 35 graduate students

General. Degrees: 4 bachelor's awarded; master's offered. **Calendar:** Semester. **Part-time faculty:** 6 total; 50% minority, 50% women.

Freshman class profile. 42 enrolled.

Basis for selection. Applicants must have high school diploma or equivalent, or a degree from accredited postsecondary institution, demonstrate proficiency in basic college-level skills through SAT or ACT scores or institution-administered placement exams, and be at least 17 years of age on the first day of classes.

2005-2006 Annual costs. Tuition/fees: $11,900. Books/supplies: $1,250. Personal expenses: $1,950.

Financial aid. Non-need-based: Scholarships awarded for academics.

Application procedures. Admission: No deadline. $50 fee. Admission notification on a rolling basis. **Financial aid:** No deadline. FAFSA required. Applicants notified on a rolling basis.

Academics. Special study options: Accelerated study, cooperative education, distance learning. **Credit/placement by examination:** CLEP.

Majors. Business: Business admin. **Computer sciences:** General.

Student life. Housing: Private apartments, student-plan housing, private rooms.

Contact. Phone: (866) 543-3879
DeVry University: Portland, 9755 Southwest Barnes Road, Suite 150, Portland, OR 97225

Eastern Oregon University

LaGrande, Oregon
www.eou.edu **CB code: 4300**

- Public 4-year university and liberal arts college
- Residential campus in large town
- 2,956 degree-seeking undergraduates: 31% part-time, 60% women, 2% African American, 2% Asian American, 3% Hispanic American, 3% Native American, 3% international
- 191 degree-seeking graduate students
- 73% of applicants admitted
- SAT or ACT required
- 36% graduate within 6 years

General. Founded in 1929. Regionally accredited. **Degrees:** 489 bachelor's, 3 associate awarded; master's offered. **Location:** 260 miles from Portland; 180 miles from Boise, Idaho. **Calendar:** Quarter, limited summer session. **Full-time faculty:** 97 total; 60% have terminal degrees, 8% minority, 40% women. **Part-time faculty:** 31 total; 23% have terminal degrees, 10% minority, 52% women. **Class size:** 46% < 20, 44% 20-39, 4% 40-49, 5% 50-99, less than 1% >100. **Special facilities:** Wildlife habitat laboratory, agriculture experiment station.

Freshman class profile. 1,180 applied, 866 admitted, 383 enrolled.

Mid 50% test scores			
SAT verbal:	430-550	Rank in top quarter:	49%
SAT math:	430-550	Rank in top tenth:	21%
ACT:	18-24	Return as sophomores:	63%
GPA 3.0-3.49:	81%	Out-of-state:	33%
GPA 2.0-2.99:	18%	Live on campus:	69%
		International:	1%

Basis for selection. Secondary school record most important; high school GPA of 3.0 in 14 subject areas required. Students not meeting these requirements must submit portfolio including essay and 2 letters of recommendation. Limited number of students not meeting requirements may be admitted. **Homeschooled:** State high school equivalency certificate, letter of recommendation (nonparent) required. Applicants must present certificate of completion and portfolio including essay, letters of recommendation, standardized test scores.

High school preparation. 14 units required. Required units include English 4, mathematics 3, social studies 3, science 2 and foreign language 2. 1 lab science recommended.

2005-2006 Annual costs. Tuition/fees: $5,840; $5,840 out-of-state. Room/board: $7,300. Books/supplies: $1,068. Personal expenses: $1,146.

2005-2006 Financial aid. Need-based: 308 full-time freshmen applied for aid; 234 were judged to have need; 232 of these received aid. Average need met was 44%. Average scholarship/grant was $3,610; average loan $1,947. 39% of total undergraduate aid awarded as scholarships/grants, 61% as loans/jobs. **Non-need-based:** Awarded to 628 full-time undergraduates, including 169 freshmen. Scholarships awarded for academics, art, athletics, leadership, minority status, music/drama, state residency.

Application procedures. Admission: Priority date 8/1; deadline 9/1 (postmark date). $50 fee, may be waived for applicants with need. Application may be submitted online. Admission notification on a rolling basis beginning on or about 10/1. **Financial aid:** Priority date 3/1; no closing date. FAFSA required. Applicants notified on a rolling basis starting 4/1; must reply within 4 week(s) of notification.

Academics. Regional advisers for distance education students. **Special study options:** Combined bachelor's/graduate degree, cooperative education, cross-registration, distance learning, double major, dual enrollment of high school students, ESL, exchange student, external degree, honors, independent study, internships, liberal arts/career combination, semester at sea, student-designed major, study abroad, teacher certification program, weekend college. **Credit/placement by examination:** AP, CLEP, IB, SAT, ACT, institutional tests. 45 credit hours maximum toward bachelor's degree. **Support services:** Learning center, tutoring, writing center.

Majors. Agriculture: Agronomy, business, economics, range science, soil science. **Biology:** General. **Business:** General, accounting, business admin, managerial economics. **Computer sciences:** General, computer science, web page design. **Conservation:** General. **Education:** General, early childhood, elementary, ESL, German, middle, science, secondary, social science, social studies, Spanish. **Health:** Nursing (RN), ophthalmic lab technology, predentistry, premedicine, preop/surgical nursing, prepharmacy, preveterinary. **History:** General. **Legal studies:** Prelaw. **Liberal arts:** Arts/sciences. **Math:** General. **Parks/recreation:** Health/fitness. **Physical sciences:** Chemistry, physics. **Protective services:** Fire services admin. **Psychology:** General. **Social sciences:** Anthropology, political science, sociology. **Visual/performing arts:** Dramatic, studio arts.

Most popular majors. Business/marketing 24%, interdisciplinary studies 15%, liberal arts 30%, social sciences 8%.

Computing on campus. 150 workstations in dormitories, library, computer center, student center. Dormitories wired for high-speed internet access and linked to campus network. Commuter students can connect to campus network. Online course registration, online library, helpline, repair service, wireless network available.

Student life. Freshman orientation: Available. Preregistration for classes offered. **Policies:** Freshmen permitted cars on campus. **Housing:** Guaranteed on-campus for freshmen. Coed dorms, single-sex dorms, apartments available. $25 fully refundable deposit. Apartment-style suites for upper-division students. **Activities:** Bands, choral groups, dance, drama, literary magazine, music ensembles, musical theater, radio station, student government, student newspaper, symphony orchestra, international relations club, outdoor club, model United Nations, biology club, Fellowship of Christian Athletes, Latter-day Saint Student Association.

Athletics. NAIA. **Intercollegiate:** Baseball M, basketball, cheerleading, cross-country, football (tackle) M, rodeo, soccer W, softball W, track and field, volleyball W. **Intramural:** Badminton, baseball M, basketball, bowling, football (non-tackle), racquetball, softball, swimming, tennis, volleyball, water polo. **Team name:** Mountaineers.

Student services. Alcohol/substance abuse counseling, career counseling, student employment services, financial aid counseling, health services, minority student services, personal counseling, placement for graduates, veterans' counselor, women's services. **Physically disabled:** Services for visually, hearing impaired.

Contact. E-mail: admissions@eou.edu
Phone: (541) 962-3393 Toll-free number: (800) 452-8639
Fax: (541) 962-3418
Admissions Director, Eastern Oregon University, One University Boulevard, LaGrande, OR 97850

Eugene Bible College

Eugene, Oregon
www.ebc.edu **CB code: 4274**

- Private 4-year Bible college affiliated with Open Bible Standard Churches
- Residential campus in small city
- 180 degree-seeking undergraduates: 11% part-time, 44% women
- 47% of applicants admitted
- Application essay required
- 43% graduate within 6 years

General. Founded in 1925. Accredited by ABHE. **Degrees:** 24 bachelor's awarded. **Location:** 100 miles from Portland. **Calendar:** Quarter, extensive summer session. **Full-time faculty:** 10 total; 30% have terminal degrees, 20% minority, 40% women. **Part-time faculty:** 18 total; 28% have terminal degrees, 6% minority, 28% women. **Class size:** 54% < 20, 38% 20-39, 6% 40-49, 2% 50-99.

Freshman class profile. 217 applied, 102 admitted, 64 enrolled.

Mid 50% test scores		**Rank in top quarter:**	29%
SAT verbal:	450-580	**Rank in top tenth:**	8%
SAT math:	430-610	**End year in good standing:**	67%
ACT:	19-24	**Return as sophomores:**	68%
GPA 3.50 or higher:	27%	**Out-of-state:**	48%
GPA 3.0-3.49:	34%	**Live on campus:**	70%
GPA 2.0-2.99:	32%		

Basis for selection. School achievement and activities, test scores, recommendations, personal essay most important. Religious affiliation or commitment important factor. SAT or ACT recommended. TOEFL required of students who are non-native English speakers. **Homeschooled:** CAT test, SAT Subject Test, or ITBS recommended.

2005-2006 Annual costs. Tuition/fees: $8,301. Room/board: $4,575. Books/supplies: $800. Personal expenses: $450.

2005-2006 Financial aid. Need-based: Average need met was 55%. Average scholarship/grant was $2,000; average loan $2,625. 36% of total undergraduate aid awarded as scholarships/grants, 64% as loans/jobs. **Non-need-based:** Scholarships awarded for academics, athletics, leadership, music/drama. **Additional information:** Some early acceptance awards possible for those admitted by May 15. Distance awards to those coming from over 1000 miles away. Some awards for husbands and wives enrolled at same time.

Application procedures. Admission: Priority date 5/15; deadline 9/1 (receipt date). $30 fee. Application may be submitted online. Admission notification on a rolling basis. **Financial aid:** Priority date 5/1, closing date 9/1. FAFSA required. Applicants notified on a rolling basis starting 7/15; must reply within 4 week(s) of notification.

Academics. Transfer-track programs available in elementary education: first 2 years at college, final 2-3 years at other institutions. **Special study options:** Cooperative education, distance learning, double major, dual enrollment of high school students, independent study, internships, liberal arts/career combination. **Credit/placement by examination:** AP, CLEP, institutional tests. **Support services:** Reduced course load, remedial instruction, study skills assistance, tutoring.

Majors. Philosophy/religion: Christian, religion. **Theology:** Bible, missionary, pastoral counseling, religious ed, sacred music, theology, youth ministry.

Computing on campus. 18 workstations in dormitories, library, computer center, student center. Dormitories wired for high-speed internet access. Repair service available.

Student life. Freshman orientation: Mandatory. Preregistration for classes offered. Week-long program ends with camping retreat to mountains with fellow students and faculty. **Policies:** Students required to sign Code of Conduct agreement. Student ministry/community service required. Religious observance required. Freshmen permitted cars on campus. **Housing:** Guaranteed on-campus for freshmen. Single-sex dorms, apartments, substance-free housing available. $75 fully refundable deposit, deadline 9/1. **Activities:** Choral groups, drama, musical theater, student government, missions organizations, ministry outreach.

Athletics. Intramural: Basketball, soccer, volleyball. **Team name:** Deacons.

Student services. Campus ministries, student employment services, financial aid counseling, personal counseling, placement for graduates, veterans' counselor.

Contact. E-mail: admissions@ebc.edu
Phone: (541) 485-1780 Toll-free number: (800) 322-2638
Fax: (541) 343-5801
Trent Combs, Director of Admissions, Eugene Bible College, 2155 Bailey Hill Road, Eugene, OR 97405

George Fox University

Newberg, Oregon — **CB member**
www.georgefox.edu — **CB code: 4325**

- Private 4-year university and seminary college affiliated with Society of Friends (Quaker)
- Residential campus in large town
- 1,831 degree-seeking undergraduates: 16% part-time, 61% women, 1% African American, 5% Asian American, 2% Hispanic American, 1% Native American, 2% international
- 1,223 degree-seeking graduate students
- 83% of applicants admitted
- SAT or ACT (ACT writing optional), application essay required

General. Founded in 1891. Regionally accredited. **Degrees:** 457 bachelor's awarded; master's, doctoral, first professional offered. **ROTC:** Air Force. **Location:** 23 miles from Portland. **Calendar:** Semester, limited summer session. **Full-time faculty:** 144 total. **Part-time faculty:** 116 total. **Class size:** 62% < 20, 32% 20-39, 5% 40-49, 1% 50-99. **Special facilities:** Center for retreats and outdoor ministries, Quaker museum, Quaker library.

Freshman class profile. 1,503 applied, 1,251 admitted, 588 enrolled.

Mid 50% test scores		**Return as sophomores:**	82%
SAT verbal:	490-620	**Out-of-state:**	34%
SAT math:	500-620	**Live on campus:**	97%
ACT:	20-26	**International:**	1%

Basis for selection. 75% of decision based on grade transcript, test scores, recommendations from teacher and counselor; 25% based on church, school, and community activities. Interview recommended for all; audition recommended for drama, music programs.

High school preparation. 16 units recommended. Recommended units include English 4, mathematics 2, social studies 2, science 2, foreign language 2 and academic electives 3. One unit health or physical education.

2006-2007 Annual costs. Tuition/fees (projected): $22,570. Room/board: $7,210. Books/supplies: $700. Personal expenses: $1,380.

2005-2006 Financial aid. Need-based: 69% of total undergraduate aid awarded as scholarships/grants, 31% as loans/jobs. **Non-need-based:** Scholarships awarded for academics, alumni affiliation, art, minority status, music/drama, religious affiliation, state residency. **Additional information:** Audition required for music and drama scholarships.

Application procedures. Admission: Priority date 2/1; deadline 6/1 (postmark date). $40 fee, may be waived for applicants with need. Application may be submitted online. Admission notification on a rolling basis beginning on or about 9/1. Must reply by May 1 or within 2 week(s) if notified thereafter. **Financial aid:** Priority date 2/1; no closing date. FAFSA required. Applicants notified on a rolling basis starting 3/1; must reply within 6 week(s) of notification.

Academics. Special study options: Accelerated study, combined bachelor's/graduate degree, cooperative education, cross-registration, double major, dual enrollment of high school students, ESL, exchange student, external degree, honors, independent study, internships, liberal arts/career combination, student-designed major, study abroad, teacher certification program, Washington semester. **Credit/placement by examination:** AP, CLEP, IB, institutional tests. 32 credit hours maximum toward bachelor's degree. **Support services:** Learning center, reduced course load, remedial instruction, study skills assistance, tutoring, writing center.

Majors. Biology: General. **Business:** General, accounting, business admin, fashion, human resources, management information systems, managerial economics. **Communications:** General, public relations, radio/tv. **Computer sciences:** General, applications programming, computer science, information systems. **Education:** Elementary. **Engineering:** General, electrical, mechanical. **English:** English lit. **Family/consumer sciences:** General, family resources, food/nutrition. **Foreign languages:** Spanish. **Health:** Athletic training. **History:** General. **Math:** General. **Parks/recreation:** Sports admin. **Philosophy/religion:** Religion. **Physical sciences:** Chemistry. **Psychology:** General. **Public administration:** Social work. **Social sciences:** International relations, political science, sociology. **Theology:** Bible, missionary, religious ed. **Visual/performing arts:** Art, dramatic.

Most popular majors. Business/marketing 58%, education 6%, interdisciplinary studies 7%.

Computing on campus. 150 workstations in dormitories, library, computer center. Dormitories wired for high-speed internet access and linked to campus network. Commuter students can connect to campus network. Online library, helpline, repair service available.

Student life. Freshman orientation: Mandatory. Preregistration for classes offered. 5 one-day programs available during summer. New students attend 3-day program at start of semester. **Policies:** 3-year residency requirement for undergraduates. Required spiritual formation program and chapel program. Religious observance required. **Housing:** Guaranteed on-campus for all undergraduates. Single-sex dorms, special housing for disabled, apartments available. **Activities:** Bands, choral groups, dance, drama, literary magazine, music ensembles, musical theater, radio station, student government, student newspaper, symphony orchestra, TV station, Quaker Fellowship, Student Christian Union, Christian Service Committee, Multicultural Society, Fellowship of Christian Athletes.

Athletics. NCAA. **Intercollegiate:** Baseball M, basketball, cross-country, soccer, softball W, tennis, track and field, volleyball W. **Intramural:** Badminton, basketball, football (non-tackle), golf, racquetball, soccer, table tennis, tennis, volleyball, weight lifting. **Team name:** Bruins.

Student services. Alcohol/substance abuse counseling, campus ministries, career counseling, student employment services, financial aid counseling, health services, minority student services, personal counseling, placement for graduates, veterans' counselor. **Physically disabled:** Services for visually, speech, hearing impaired.

Contact. E-mail: admissions@georgefox.edu
Phone: (503) 554-2240 Toll-free number: (800) 765-4369
Fax: (503) 554-3110
Dale Seipp, Executive Director of Admissions, George Fox University, 414 North Meridian Street, Newberg, OR 97132-2697

ITT Technical Institute: Portland

Portland, Oregon
www.itt-tech.edu **CB code: 0947**

- For-profit 4-year technical college
- Commuter campus in large city

General. Founded in 1979. Accredited by ACICS. **Location:** 10 miles from downtown. **Calendar:** Quarter.

Annual costs/financial aid. Tuition varies by program, $260-$368 per credit hour.

Contact. Phone: (503) 255-6500
Director of Recruitment, 6035 Northeast 78th Court, Portland, OR 97218

Lewis & Clark College

Portland, Oregon **CB member**
www.lclark.edu **CB code: 4384**

- Private 4-year liberal arts college
- Residential campus in very large city
- 1,909 degree-seeking undergraduates: 1% part-time, 61% women, 1% African American, 6% Asian American, 4% Hispanic American, 1% Native American, 4% international
- 1,469 degree-seeking graduate students
- 59% of applicants admitted
- Application essay required
- 71% graduate within 6 years

General. Founded in 1867. Regionally accredited. **Degrees:** 377 bachelor's awarded; master's, doctoral, first professional offered. **Calendar:** Semester, limited summer session. **Full-time faculty:** 205 total; 2% have terminal degrees, 8% minority, 42% women. **Part-time faculty:** 118 total; 4% have terminal degrees, 9% minority, 59% women. **Class size:** 55% < 20, 41% 20-39, 2% 40-49, 2% 50-99. **Special facilities:** Scanning electron microscope, 3 diode array UV/visible spectrometers, gas chromatography/mass spectrometer, X-ray fluorescence spectrometer, atomic absorption spectrometer, solar telescope with spectrograph, imaging laboratory with high resolution optical microscope, observatory, holographic laboratory, electro-acoustic music studio, 85-rank Casavant organ, multi-media foreign language lab, greenhouse.

Freshman class profile. 4,196 applied, 2,495 admitted, 490 enrolled.

Mid 50% test scores			
SAT verbal:	610-700	Rank in top quarter:	78%
SAT math:	590-680	Rank in top tenth:	42%
ACT:	26-30	Return as sophomores:	86%
GPA 3.50 or higher:	76%	Out-of-state:	81%
GPA 3.0-3.49:	21%	Live on campus:	98%
GPA 2.0-2.99:	3%	International:	2%

Basis for selection. School curriculum and achievement most important. Standardized tests, recommendations, extracurricular involvement, essay and interview also considered. Portfolio Path option offered for admission, requiring academic portfolio (including 5 graded writing samples) and 2 additional teacher recommendations; standardized test scores optional. Interviews optional, audition recommended for music scholarships, portfolio required for Portfolio Path applicants. **Homeschooled:** School's Portfolio Path for admissions recommended. GED required, interview recommended.

High school preparation. Recommended units include English 4, mathematics 3, social studies 3, science 3 (laboratory 2) and foreign language 2. One unit fine arts recommended.

2005-2006 Annual costs. Tuition/fees: $27,710. Room/board: $7,648. Books/supplies: $1,800. Personal expenses: $900.

2005-2006 Financial aid. Need-based: 395 full-time freshmen applied for aid; 294 were judged to have need; 294 of these received aid. Average need met was 90%. Average scholarship/grant was $20,519; average loan $4,050. 76% of total undergraduate aid awarded as scholarships/grants, 24% as loans/jobs. **Non-need-based:** Awarded to 324 full-time undergraduates, including 98 freshmen. Scholarships awarded for academics, leadership, music/drama.

Application procedures. Admission: Closing date 2/1 (receipt date). $50 fee, may be waived for applicants with need. Application may be submitted online. Admission notification 4/1. Must reply by May 1 or within 2 week(s) if notified thereafter. **Financial aid:** Priority date 3/1; no closing date. FAFSA required. Applicants notified on a rolling basis starting 3/1; must reply by 5/1.

Academics. Special study options: Accelerated study, combined bachelor's/graduate degree, cross-registration, double major, dual enrollment of high school students, ESL, honors, independent study, internships, New York semester, student-designed major, study abroad, Washington semester. 3-2 engineering program with Columbia University, University of Southern California, Oregon Graduate Institute of Science and Engineering at OHSU, Washington University (St. Louis). **Credit/placement by examination:** AP, CLEP, IB, institutional tests. Up to 24 semester hours awarded for International Baccalaureate full diploma and a score of 36 or higher (16 hours for diploma with 32-35). Scores of 5 or higher on higher level exams get 4 credits. **Support services:** Learning center, reduced course load, study skills assistance, tutoring, writing center.

Majors. Area/ethnic studies: East Asian. **Biology:** General, biochemistry. **Communications:** General. **Computer sciences:** Computer science. **Conservation:** Environmental studies. **Foreign languages:** General, French, German, Spanish. **History:** General. **Interdisciplinary:** Math/computer science. **Liberal arts:** Arts/sciences. **Math:** General. **Philosophy/religion:** Philosophy, religion. **Physical sciences:** Chemistry, physics. **Psychology:** General. **Social sciences:** Anthropology, economics, international relations, political science, sociology. **Visual/performing arts:** Art, dramatic, music performance, studio arts.

Most popular majors. Biology 11%, communications/journalism 8%, English 6%, foreign language 11%, history 7%, psychology 11%, social sciences 19%, visual/performing arts 9%.

Computing on campus. 158 workstations in library, computer center, student center. Dormitories wired for high-speed internet access and linked to campus network. Commuter students can connect to campus network. Online library, helpline, repair service, student web hosting, wireless network available.

Student life. Freshman orientation: Mandatory. Preregistration for classes offered. 4 days preceding class in late August. **Housing:** Guaranteed on-campus for freshmen. Coed dorms, single-sex dorms, substance-free housing available. $100 deposit, deadline 5/1. Theme floors, apartment-style residence halls for upperclassmen. **Activities:** Bands, choral groups, dance, drama, literary magazine, music ensembles, musical theater, radio station, student government, student newspaper, symphony orchestra, TV station, Jewish Student Union, InterVarsity Christian Fellowship, Fellowship of Christian Athletes, Hawaii Club, Amnesty International, Black Student Union, Circle K, Forensics, Gringos y Latinos.

Athletics. NCAA. **Intercollegiate:** Baseball M, basketball, cross-country, football (tackle) M, golf, rowing (crew), soccer W, softball W, swimming, tennis, track and field, volleyball W. **Intramural:** Badminton, basketball, cross-country, softball, swimming, table tennis, tennis, volleyball, water polo. **Team name:** Pioneers, Pios.

Student services. Adult student services, alcohol/substance abuse counseling, campus ministries, career counseling, services for economically disadvantaged, student employment services, financial aid counseling, health services, legal services, minority student services, personal counseling, placement for graduates, veterans' counselor, women's services. **Physically disabled:** Services for visually, speech, hearing impaired.

Contact. E-mail: admissions@lclark.edu
Phone: (503) 768-7040 Toll-free number: (800) 444-4111
Fax: (503) 768-7055
Michael Sexton, Dean of Admissions, Lewis & Clark College, 0615 SW Palatine Hill Road, Portland, OR 97219-7899

Linfield College

McMinnville, Oregon — **CB member**
www.linfield.edu — **CB code: 4387**

- Private 4-year business and liberal arts college affiliated with American Baptist Churches in the USA
- Residential campus in large town
- 1,693 degree-seeking undergraduates: 1% part-time, 54% women, 1% African American, 6% Asian American, 2% Hispanic American, 1% Native American, 2% international
- 73% of applicants admitted
- SAT or ACT (ACT writing optional), application essay required
- 67% graduate within 6 years; 15% enter graduate study

General. Founded in 1849. Regionally accredited. Campus in Portland where students may transfer to major in nursing or health sciences. **Degrees:** 310 bachelor's awarded. **ROTC:** Air Force. **Location:** 38 miles from Portland. **Calendar:** 4-1-4, limited summer session. **Full-time faculty:** 107 total; 94% have terminal degrees, 8% minority, 40% women. **Part-time faculty:** 57 total; 39% have terminal degrees, 42% women. **Class size:** 60% < 20, 36% 20-39, 3% 40-49, 1% 50-99, less than 1% >100. **Special facilities:** Wilderness cabin, field station, anthropology museum, interactive writing laboratory.

Freshman class profile. 2,131 applied, 1,560 admitted, 488 enrolled.

Mid 50% test scores		**Rank in top tenth:**	38%
SAT verbal:	510-620	**End year in good standing:**	90%
SAT math:	520-640	**Return as sophomores:**	79%
ACT:	21-27	**Out-of-state:**	41%
GPA 3.50 or higher:	69%	**Live on campus:**	99%
GPA 3.0-3.49:	25%	**International:**	1%
GPA 2.0-2.99:	6%	**Fraternities:**	28%
Rank in top quarter:	68%	**Sororities:**	30%

Basis for selection. High school grades, official transcripts, counselor's recommendation and/or teacher recommendation, test scores, and essay important. Interview recommended.

High school preparation. 17 units recommended. Recommended units include English 4, mathematics 4, social studies 3, science 3 and foreign language 2.

2005-2006 Annual costs. Tuition/fees: $23,076. Room/board: $7,310. Books/supplies: $650. Personal expenses: $1,100.

2005-2006 Financial aid. Need-based: 317 full-time freshmen applied for aid; 317 were judged to have need; 317 of these received aid. Average need met was 85%. Average scholarship/grant was $7,730; average loan $3,304. 61% of total undergraduate aid awarded as scholarships/grants, 39% as loans/jobs. **Non-need-based:** Awarded to 1,073 full-time undergraduates, including 333 freshmen. Scholarships awarded for academics, music/drama.

Application procedures. Admission: $40 fee, may be waived for applicants with need. Application may be submitted online. Admission notification 4/1. Must reply by May 1 or within 2 week(s) if notified thereafter. **Financial aid:** Priority date 2/1; no closing date. FAFSA required. Applicants notified by 4/1; must reply by 5/1.

Academics. Special study options: Cross-registration, distance learning, double major, ESL, external degree, independent study, internships, liberal arts/career combination, semester at sea, student-designed major, study abroad, teacher certification program, Washington semester. Broad participation in semester abroad programs at Linfield centers in Austria, China, Costa Rica, Ecuador, England, France, Ireland, Japan, Korea, Mexico and Norway, as well as shorter term study abroad opportunities through January term. **Credit/placement by examination:** AP, CLEP, IB, institutional tests. 30 credit hours maximum toward bachelor's degree. **Support services:** Learning center, reduced course load, study skills assistance, tutoring, writing center.

Majors. Biology: General. **Business:** General, accounting, finance, international. **Communications:** General, media studies. **Computer sciences:** Computer science. **Conservation:** Environmental studies. **Education:** Elementary, music. **English:** Creative writing. **Foreign languages:** French, German, Japanese, Spanish. **Health:** Athletic training, nursing (RN). **History:** General. **Math:** General. **Parks/recreation:** Exercise sciences, health/fitness. **Philosophy/religion:** Philosophy, religion. **Physical sciences:** General, chemistry, physics. **Psychology:** General. **Social sciences:** Anthropology, economics, political science, sociology. **Visual/performing arts:** Art, dramatic, music performance, music theory/composition.

Most popular majors. Business/marketing 20%, education 11%, parks/recreation 8%, physical sciences 7%, psychology 6%, social sciences 10%.

Computing on campus. 266 workstations in dormitories, library, computer center, student center. Dormitories wired for high-speed internet access and linked to campus network. Commuter students can connect to campus network. Online course registration, online library, helpline, repair service, student web hosting, wireless network available.

Student life. Freshman orientation: Mandatory. Preregistration for classes offered. 4-day program held at beginning of fall semester includes one-on-one advising, peer mentoring. **Policies:** Freshmen permitted cars on campus. **Housing:** Guaranteed on-campus for freshmen. Coed dorms, single-sex dorms, special housing for disabled, apartments, fraternity/sorority housing, substance-free housing available. **Activities:** Bands, choral groups, dance, drama, literary magazine, music ensembles, musical theater, opera, radio station, student government, student newspaper, symphony orchestra, multicultural student club, Isis (Women's), Hawaiian club, Camas Literary Magazine, Fellowship of Christian Athletes, progressive student union, Circle-K, Habitat for Humanity, Gay/Straight Alliance, Linfield Republicans.

Athletics. NCAA. **Intercollegiate:** Baseball M, basketball, cross-country, football (tackle) M, golf, lacrosse W, soccer, softball, swimming, tennis, track and field, volleyball W. **Intramural:** Basketball, football (non-tackle), soccer, softball, volleyball. **Team name:** Wildcats.

Student services. Adult student services, alcohol/substance abuse counseling, campus ministries, career counseling, student employment services, financial aid counseling, health services, minority student services, personal counseling, placement for graduates, veterans' counselor, women's services. **Physically disabled:** Services for visually, speech, hearing impaired.

Contact. E-mail: admission@linfield.edu
Phone: (503) 883-2213 Toll-free number: (800) 640-2287
Fax: (503) 883-2472
Lisa Knodle-Bragiel, Director of Admission, Linfield College, 900 SE Baker Street, McMinnville, OR 97218-6894

Marylhurst University

Marylhurst, Oregon
www.marylhurst.edu — **CB code: 0440**

- Private 4-year university and liberal arts college affiliated with Roman Catholic Church
- Commuter campus in large town
- 730 degree-seeking undergraduates
- 388 graduate students

General. Founded in 1893. Regionally accredited. **Degrees:** 138 bachelor's awarded; master's offered. **Location:** 10 miles from Portland. **Calendar:** Quarter, extensive summer session. **Full-time faculty:** 37 total. **Part-time faculty:** 342 total. **Class size:** 98% < 20, 2% 20-39.

Freshman class profile. 34 applied, 15 admitted, 11 enrolled.

Basis for selection. Open admission, but selective for some programs. Admission to Music Therapy program based on GPA, SAT/ACT scores, essay, letters of recommendation, audition to demonstrate performance proficiency in an applied music area.

2005-2006 Annual costs. Tuition/fees: $14,220. Books/supplies: $600. Personal expenses: $1,800.

Financial aid. Non-need-based: Scholarships awarded for academics.

Application procedures. Admission: No deadline. $40 fee. Application may be submitted online. Admission notification on a rolling basis. **Financial aid:** Priority date 6/1; no closing date. FAFSA, institutional form required. Applicants notified on a rolling basis starting 5/1.

Academics. Special study options: Distance learning, double major, ESL, honors, independent study, internships, student-designed major, weekend college. **Credit/placement by examination:** AP, CLEP, IB, institutional tests. 45 credit hours maximum toward bachelor's degree. **Support services:** Learning center, study skills assistance, tutoring, writing center.

Majors. Business: General, business admin, communications, real estate. **Communications:** General. **Conservation:** General, environmental studies. **Interdisciplinary:** Natural sciences. **Liberal arts:** Arts/sciences. **Philosophy/religion:** Philosophy, religion. **Psychology:** General. **Social sciences:** General. **Visual/performing arts:** Art, interior design, studio arts.

Computing on campus. 41 workstations in library. Online course registration available.

Student life. Freshman orientation: Available. **Activities:** Jazz band, choral groups, music ensembles, musical theater, symphony orchestra.

Student services. Adult student services, career counseling, financial aid counseling, personal counseling, veterans' counselor. **Physically disabled:** Services for visually, hearing impaired.

Contact. E-mail: admissions@marylhurst.edu
Phone: (503) 699-6268 Toll-free number: (800) 634-9982 ext. 6268
Fax: (503) 635-6585
John French, Assistant Dean of Admissions and Enrollment Relations, Marylhurst University, PO Box 261, Marylhurst, OR 97036-0261

Mount Angel Seminary
St. Benedict, Oregon
www.mtangel.edu/Seminary/Seminary.htm CB code: 4491

- Private 4-year seminary college for men affiliated with Roman Catholic Church
- Residential campus in small town
- 175 undergraduates

General. Founded in 1887. Regionally accredited; also accredited by ATS. All undergraduates candidates for Roman Catholic priesthood. **Degrees:** 11 bachelor's awarded; master's, first professional offered. **Location:** 40 miles from Portland. **Calendar:** Semester. **Full-time faculty:** 26 total. **Part-time faculty:** 15 total.

Freshman class profile.

Out-of-state:	75%	Live on campus:	100%

Basis for selection. Primarily recommendations from sponsoring dioceses or clergymen, personal interview. Test scores considered. Adequate ESL scores for non-English speaking students. Interview recommended.

2005-2006 Annual costs. Tuition/fees: $11,300. Formation fee of $2,540 per year. Room/board: $7,660. Books/supplies: $800. Personal expenses: $1,000.

Application procedures. Admission: Closing date 6/15. $25 fee, may be waived for applicants with need. Admission notification on a rolling basis beginning on or about 9/1. **Financial aid:** No deadline. Institutional form required. Applicants notified on a rolling basis; must reply within 2 week(s) of notification.

Academics. Special study options: Cross-registration, double major, ESL. Interdivisional program, 3-week full-time pursuit of single approved course of study. **Credit/placement by examination:** CLEP, institutional tests.

Majors. Liberal arts: Arts/sciences. **Philosophy/religion:** Philosophy. **Theology:** Theology.

Most popular majors. Liberal arts 50%, philosophy/religious studies 50%.

Computing on campus. 10 workstations in dormitories, library, computer center.

Student life. Policies: Religious observance required. **Housing:** Guaranteed on-campus for all undergraduates. All full-time students working toward priesthood required to live on campus. **Activities:** Student government.

Athletics. Intramural: Basketball M, racquetball M, soccer M, swimming M, volleyball M.

Student services. Health services, personal counseling.

Contact. Phone: (503) 845-3951 Fax: (503) 845-3126
Sr. Virginia Schroeder, Admissions Director, Mount Angel Seminary, One Abbey Drive, St. Benedict, OR 97373

Multnomah Bible College
Portland, Oregon
www.multnomah.edu CB code: 4496

- Private 4-year Bible and seminary college affiliated with interdenominational tradition
- Residential campus in large city
- 590 degree-seeking undergraduates: 10% part-time, 47% women, 2% African American, 4% Asian American, 3% Hispanic American, 1% Native American
- 232 degree-seeking graduate students
- 84% of applicants admitted
- SAT or ACT (ACT writing recommended), application essay required
- 43% graduate within 6 years

General. Founded in 1936. Candidate for regional accreditation; also accredited by ABHE. Emphasis on preparation for Christian ministries. **Degrees:** 112 bachelor's awarded; master's, first professional offered. **Location:** 5 miles from downtown. **Calendar:** Semester, limited summer session. **Full-time faculty:** 24 total; 54% have terminal degrees, 12% minority, 21% women. **Part-time faculty:** 33 total; 15% have terminal degrees, 9% minority, 30% women. **Class size:** 54% < 20, 28% 20-39, 7% 40-49, 9% 50-99, 2% >100.

Freshman class profile. 185 applied, 155 admitted, 97 enrolled.

Mid 50% test scores		GPA 3.0-3.49:	35%
SAT verbal:	490-620	GPA 2.0-2.99:	27%
SAT math:	450-590	Rank in top quarter:	34%
ACT:	19-26	Rank in top tenth:	12%
GPA 3.50 or higher:	38%	Return as sophomores:	63%

Basis for selection. School achievement record, test scores, recommendations most important.

High school preparation. College-preparatory program recommended. Recommended units include English 4, mathematics 2, social studies 3, history 2, science 3 (laboratory 1) and foreign language 2.

2005-2006 Annual costs. Tuition/fees: $11,750. Room/board: $5,060. Books/supplies: $900. Personal expenses: $1,400.

2004-2005 Financial aid. Need-based: 75 full-time freshmen applied for aid; 60 were judged to have need; 60 of these received aid. Average need met was 50%. Average scholarship/grant was $4,089; average loan $2,420. 42% of total undergraduate aid awarded as scholarships/grants, 58% as loans/jobs. **Non-need-based:** Awarded to 77 full-time undergraduates, including 21 freshmen. Scholarships awarded for academics.

Application procedures. Admission: Priority date 3/1; deadline 7/15 (postmark date). $40 fee. Application must be submitted on paper. Admission notification on a rolling basis. Must reply by 8/15. **Financial aid:** Priority date 3/1, closing date 8/1. FAFSA, institutional form required. Applicants notified on a rolling basis starting 4/1; must reply within 3 week(s) of notification.

Academics. Special study options: Cooperative education, double major, internships, liberal arts/career combination. **Credit/placement by examination:** AP, CLEP, IB. 20 credit hours maximum toward bachelor's degree. **Support services:** Reduced course load, study skills assistance.

Majors. Communications: General, journalism. **Foreign languages:** Ancient Greek, Hebrew. **History:** General. **Theology:** Bible, missionary, pastoral counseling, religious ed, sacred music, theology, youth ministry.

Computing on campus. 42 workstations in dormitories, library, computer center. Dormitories wired for high-speed internet access and linked to campus network. Commuter students can connect to campus network. Online library, helpline, wireless network available.

Student life. Freshman orientation: Mandatory. **Policies:** No alcohol, smoking, gambling. Religious observance required. Freshmen permitted cars on campus. **Housing:** Guaranteed on-campus for freshmen. Single-sex dorms, apartments available. $125 partly refundable deposit, deadline 7/15. Houses for married students. **Activities:** Choral groups, drama, music ensembles, student government, student newspaper.

Athletics. NCCAA. **Intercollegiate:** Basketball M, volleyball W. **Intramural:** Basketball, football (non-tackle), soccer, volleyball. **Team name:** Ambassadors.

Student services. Campus ministries, career counseling, student employment services, financial aid counseling, health services, personal counseling, placement for graduates, veterans' counselor.

Contact. E-mail: admiss@multnomah.edu
Phone: (503) 255-0332 ext. 485 Toll-free number: (800) 275-4672
Fax: (503) 254-1268
Amy Stephens, Director of Admissions and Registrar, Multnomah Bible College, 8435 Northeast Glisan Street, Portland, OR 97220-5898

Northwest Christian College
Eugene, Oregon
www.nwcc.edu CB code: 4543

- Private 4-year liberal arts college affiliated with Christian Church (Disciples of Christ)
- Commuter campus in small city

- 391 degree-seeking undergraduates: 4% part-time, 59% women, 1% African American, 1% Asian American, 2% Hispanic American, 1% Native American
- 88 degree-seeking graduate students
- 64% of applicants admitted
- SAT or ACT (ACT writing recommended), application essay required
- 38% graduate within 6 years

General. Founded in 1895. Regionally accredited. **Degrees:** 103 bachelor's, 10 associate awarded; master's offered. **ROTC:** Army. **Location:** 110 miles from Portland. **Calendar:** Semester, limited summer session. **Full-time faculty:** 19 total; 47% have terminal degrees, 10% minority, 58% women. **Part-time faculty:** 42 total; 29% have terminal degrees, 2% minority, 38% women. **Class size:** 90% < 20, 7% 20-39, 1% 40-49, 1% 50-99.

Freshman class profile. 179 applied, 114 admitted, 50 enrolled.

Mid 50% test scores		**GPA 2.0-2.99:**	34%
SAT verbal:	430-590	**Rank in top quarter:**	36%
SAT math:	410-520	**Rank in top tenth:**	13%
ACT:	19-22	**Return as sophomores:**	62%
GPA 3.50 or higher:	32%	**Out-of-state:**	18%
GPA 3.0-3.49:	34%	**Live on campus:**	64%

Basis for selection. Admission based on evidence of ability to succeed academically and if applicant is appropriate match. Students failing to meet minimum admissions standards referred to admissions committee for final decision. Use ACT COMPASS if student does not submit ACT or SAT scores. Interview recommended, personal statement required. **Homeschooled:** Greater reliance on standardized test scores to demonstrate admissability. Flexible admission requirements enable student to demonstrate reasonable preparedness for college. **Learning Disabled:** Documented proof of disability.

High school preparation. 15 units recommended. Recommended units include English 4, mathematics 3, social studies 2, history 1, science 2 (laboratory 1) and foreign language 2. Computer literacy, humanities, and social science also recommended.

2005-2006 Annual costs. Tuition/fees: $18,380. Room/board: $5,918. Books/supplies: $825. Personal expenses: $900.

2005-2006 Financial aid. Need-based: 46 full-time freshmen applied for aid; 42 were judged to have need; 42 of these received aid. Average need met was 74%. Average scholarship/grant was $11,997; average loan $2,019. 55% of total undergraduate aid awarded as scholarships/grants, 45% as loans/jobs. **Non-need-based:** Scholarships awarded for academics, athletics, leadership, music/drama, religious affiliation.

Application procedures. Admission: No deadline. No application fee. Application may be submitted online. Admission notification on a rolling basis beginning on or about 10/15. **Financial aid:** Priority date 3/1; no closing date. FAFSA required. Applicants notified on a rolling basis starting 4/1.

Academics. Special study options: Accelerated study, distance learning, double major, ESL, independent study, internships, liberal arts/career combination, student-designed major, study abroad, teacher certification program. **Credit/placement by examination:** AP, CLEP, IB. 15 credit hours maximum toward associate degree, 30 toward bachelor's. **Support services:** Reduced course load, remedial instruction, tutoring, writing center.

Majors. Biology: Exercise physiology. **Business:** Accounting, business admin, management information systems. **Communications:** General. **Computer sciences:** General, programming. **Education:** Multi-level teacher. **Health:** Health services admin. **Psychology:** General. **Public administration:** Human services. **Theology:** Bible. **Visual/performing arts:** Music management.

Most popular majors. Business/marketing 51%, education 27%, psychology 6%.

Computing on campus. 46 workstations in dormitories, library, computer center. Dormitories wired for high-speed internet access and linked to campus network. Commuter students can connect to campus network. Online library, wireless network available.

Student life. Freshman orientation: Mandatory, $156 fee. Preregistration for classes offered. 4 day program held immediately before fall term. **Policies:** Attendance at chapel is required of all students. Religious observance required. Freshmen permitted cars on campus. **Housing:** Guaranteed on-campus for freshmen. Coed dorms, apartments available. $100 fully refundable deposit, deadline 6/1. **Activities:** Concert band, choral groups, drama, literary magazine, music ensembles, student government, student newspaper, education club, TESOL club, psychology club, ministry club, crochet club, dance club, gold club, running club, business club.

Athletics. USCAA. **Intercollegiate:** Basketball, softball W. **Intramural:** Basketball, volleyball W. **Team name:** Beacons.

Student services. Adult student services, alcohol/substance abuse counseling, campus ministries, career counseling, student employment services, financial aid counseling, health services, personal counseling, placement for graduates, veterans' counselor.

Contact. E-mail: admissions@nwcc.edu
Phone: (541) 684-7201 Toll-free number: (877) 463-6622
Fax: (541) 684-7317
Randy Jones, Dean of Admissions, Northwest Christian College, 828 East 11th Avenue, Eugene, OR 97401-3745

Oregon Health & Science University

Portland, Oregon — **CB member**
www.ohsu.edu — **CB code: 4900**

- Public upper-division university
- Commuter campus in large city
- 29% of applicants admitted
- Test scores, application essay required

General. Founded in 1887. Regionally accredited. **Degrees:** 246 bachelor's awarded; master's, doctoral, first professional offered. **Calendar:** Quarter. **Full-time faculty:** 900 total. **Part-time faculty:** 500 total.

Student profile. 649 degree-seeking undergraduates, 1,467 degree-seeking graduate students. 802 applied as first time-transfer students, 230 admitted, 195 enrolled.

Women:	88%	**Native American:**	1%
African American:	3%	**Part-time:**	27%
Asian American:	1%	**Live on campus:**	33%
Hispanic American:	3%		

Basis for selection. College transcript, application essay, standardized test scores required. Admission requirements vary with program. Transfer accepted as sophomores, juniors, seniors.

2005-2006 Annual costs. Tuition shown is for nursing program; costs for other programs vary. Room only: $3,560. Books/supplies: $461.

Application procedures. Admission: Deadline 1/15. $120 fee, may be waived for applicants with need. Application must be submitted online. Admission notification 3/25. Must reply by 4/15. **Financial aid:** FAFSA required.

Academics. Special study options: Combined bachelor's/graduate degree, exchange student. **Credit/placement by examination:** CLEP.

Majors. Health: Clinical lab technology, dental hygiene, medical radiologic technology/radiation therapy, nursing (RN).

Computing on campus. Commuter students can connect to campus network. Online library, helpline, wireless network available.

Student life. Activities: Student government.

Athletics. Intramural: Basketball, swimming, table tennis, tennis.

Student services. Career counseling, health services, on-campus daycare, personal counseling.

Contact. E-mail: proginfo@ohsu.edu
Phone: (503) 494-77725 Fax: (503) 494-4350
Jennifer Anderson, Director of Admission, Oregon Health & Science University, 3181 SW Sam Jackson Park Road, Portland, OR 97239

Oregon Institute of Technology

Klamath Falls, Oregon — **CB member**
www.oit.edu — **CB code: 4587**

- Public 4-year engineering and health science college
- Commuter campus in large town
- 2,578 degree-seeking undergraduates: 27% part-time, 45% women, 1% African American, 5% Asian American, 4% Hispanic American, 2% Native American, 1% international
- 17 degree-seeking graduate students
- 88% of applicants admitted
- SAT or ACT with writing required

General. Founded in 1947. Regionally accredited. Portland MetroCenter offers upper-division courses in electronics engineering technology, manufacturing engineering technology. Software engineering technology offered at Capital Center in Portland-Metro area. **Degrees:** 496 bachelor's, 74 associate awarded; master's offered. **ROTC:** Army. **Location:** 280 miles from Portland, 270 miles from Reno, Nevada. **Calendar:** Quarter, limited summer session. **Full-time faculty:** 119 total; 36% have terminal degrees, 6% minority, 35% women. **Part-time faculty:** 96 total; 17% have terminal degrees, 4% minority, 30% women. **Class size:** 56% < 20, 38% 20-39, 3% 40-49, 3% 50-99, less than 1% >100. **Special facilities:** Geo-heat center for research on geothermal energy, historical library, Oregon Renewable Energy Center.

Freshman class profile. 651 applied, 575 admitted, 265 enrolled.

Mid 50% test scores			
SAT verbal:	450-580	**Rank in top tenth:**	21%
SAT math:	480-610	**Return as sophomores:**	69%
ACT:	18-24	**Out-of-state:**	8%
Rank in top quarter:	54%	**Live on campus:**	54%

Basis for selection. Secondary school record and standardized test scores very important. Class rank, recommendations, essay, interview, character/personal qualities and work experience all considered. Applicants from non-standard or unaccredited high schools must take 3 SAT Subject Tests: 1 English, 1 math, 1 other of student's choice. Due to rolling admission process, the earlier test scores are received, the earlier an admission decision can be made. **Learning Disabled:** Tech opportunities available.

High school preparation. 14 units required. Required units include English 4, mathematics 3, social studies 3, science 2 (laboratory 1) and foreign language 2.

2005-2006 Annual costs. Tuition/fees: $5,457; $15,573 out-of-state. Room/board: $6,037. Books/supplies: $1,000. Personal expenses: $2,100.

2004-2005 Financial aid. Need-based: 37% of total undergraduate aid awarded as scholarships/grants, 63% as loans/jobs. **Non-need-based:** Scholarships awarded for academics, athletics, leadership, minority status.

Application procedures. Admission: $50 fee. Application may be submitted online. Admission notification on a rolling basis beginning on or about 8/1. Must reply by May 1 or within 4 week(s) if notified thereafter. **Financial aid:** Priority date 3/1; no closing date. FAFSA required. Applicants notified on a rolling basis starting 4/1; must reply within 3 week(s) of notification.

Academics. Special study options: Combined bachelor's/graduate degree, cooperative education, cross-registration, distance learning, double major, dual enrollment of high school students, external degree, internships, liberal arts/career combination, study abroad. **Credit/placement by examination:** AP, CLEP, SAT, ACT, institutional tests. No more than 25% of credits submitted for graduation may be credit by examination. **Support services:** Learning center, reduced course load, remedial instruction, study skills assistance, tutoring.

Majors. Business: Accounting, business admin, entrepreneurial studies, management information systems, marketing, operations, small business admin. **Communications:** General. **Computer sciences:** Information systems. **Conservation:** General. **Engineering technology:** Computer hardware, electrical, energy systems, manufacturing, mechanical, software, surveying. **Health:** Clinical lab science, dental hygiene, health services, medical radiologic technology/radiation therapy, radiologic technology/medical imaging, sonography. **Psychology:** General.

Computing on campus. 656 workstations in dormitories, library, computer center. Dormitories wired for high-speed internet access. Commuter students can connect to campus network. Online course registration, online library, helpline, repair service, student web hosting, wireless network available.

Student life. Freshman orientation: Mandatory. Preregistration for classes offered. **Policies:** Student clubs are very community oriented and compete for community service awards. Freshmen permitted cars on campus. **Housing:** Coed dorms available. $150 deposit, deadline 5/1. **Activities:** Choral groups, radio station, student government, student newspaper, symphony orchestra, TV station, Newman Club, Latter-day Saints, Christian Fellowship, Native American Club, international student club, Circle K, Latin American Club, residence hall association, Phi Delta Theta, College Republicans.

Athletics. NAIA. **Intercollegiate:** Baseball M, basketball, cross-country, soccer W, softball W, track and field, volleyball W. **Intramural:** Basketball, cheerleading, cross-country, football (tackle) M, lacrosse M, soccer, softball, track and field, volleyball. **Team name:** Owls.

Student services. Adult student services, alcohol/substance abuse counseling, career counseling, student employment services, financial aid counseling, health services, personal counseling, placement for graduates, veterans' counselor. **Physically disabled:** Services for visually, hearing impaired.

Contact. E-mail: oit@oit.edu
Phone: (541) 885-1150 Toll-free number: (800) 422-2017
Fax: (541) 885-1115
Palmer Muntz, Director of Admissions, Oregon Institute of Technology, 3201 Campus Drive, Klamath Falls, OR 97601

Oregon State University

Corvallis, Oregon — **CB member**
www.oregonstate.edu — **CB code: 4586**

- Public 4-year university
- Residential campus in small city
- 13,862 degree-seeking undergraduates
- 3,489 graduate students
- 90% of applicants admitted
- SAT or ACT with writing required

General. Founded in 1868. Regionally accredited. **Degrees:** 3,183 bachelor's awarded; master's, doctoral, first professional offered. **ROTC:** Army, Navy, Air Force. **Location:** 80 miles from Portland, 45 miles from Eugene. **Calendar:** Quarter, extensive summer session. **Full-time faculty:** 772 total; 80% have terminal degrees, 12% minority, 36% women. **Part-time faculty:** 459 total; 27% have terminal degrees, 10% minority, 63% women. **Class size:** 38% < 20, 33% 20-39, 11% 40-49, 10% 50-99, 7% >100. **Special facilities:** Arboretum, 13,429-acre forest, radiation center (with TRIGA Mark II Nuclear Reactor), wave research facility, marine science center museum and aquarium.

Freshman class profile. 6,917 applied, 6,225 admitted, 2,889 enrolled.

Mid 50% test scores			
SAT verbal:	470-590	**Return as sophomores:**	80%
SAT math:	490-610	**Out-of-state:**	10%
ACT:	20-26	**Live on campus:**	78%
Rank in top quarter:	48%	**Fraternities:**	16%
Rank in top tenth:	19%	**Sororities:**	17%

Basis for selection. 3.0 high school GPA, test scores most important. Students not meeting admission requirements may petition for exception. Students who do not meet subject requirements, who graduated from non-standard or unaccredited high schools, or who graduated prior to 1987 must submit SAT Subject Test scores in addition to SAT or ACT. Applicants with GED not required to submit test scores. **Homeschooled:** Must submit SAT or ACT, and SAT Subject Tests.

High school preparation. 14 units required. Required and recommended units include English 4, mathematics 3, social studies 3, science 2 (laboratory 1) and foreign language 2.

2005-2006 Annual costs. Tuition/fees: $5,442; $17,502 out-of-state. Room/board: $7,659. Books/supplies: $1,350. Personal expenses: $2,181.

2005-2006 Financial aid. Need-based: 2,124 full-time freshmen applied for aid; 1,508 were judged to have need; 1,458 of these received aid. Average need met was 69%. Average scholarship/grant was $2,344; average loan $2,153. 33% of total undergraduate aid awarded as scholarships/grants, 67% as loans/jobs. **Non-need-based:** Awarded to 670 full-time undergraduates, including 137 freshmen. Scholarships awarded for academics, athletics, job skills, leadership, minority status, ROTC, state residency.

Application procedures. Admission: Priority date 3/1; no deadline. $50 fee, may be waived for applicants with need. Application may be submitted online. Admission notification on a rolling basis beginning on or about 8/1. Must reply by May 1 or within 3 week(s) if notified thereafter. **Financial aid:** Priority date 2/1, closing date 5/1. FAFSA required. Applicants notified on a rolling basis starting 4/1; must reply within 4 week(s) of notification.

Academics. Special study options: Cooperative education, cross-registration, distance learning, double major, dual enrollment of high school students, ESL, exchange student, honors, independent study, internships, student-designed major, study abroad, teacher certification program, weekend college. **Credit/placement by examination:** AP, CLEP, IB, institutional tests. **Support services:** Learning center, remedial instruction, tutoring.

Majors. Agriculture: General, agronomy, animal sciences, business, economics, food science, horticultural science, plant sciences, range science.

Area/ethnic studies: American. **Biology:** General, bacteriology, biochemistry, biophysics, biotechnology, botany, entomology, zoology. **Business:** Business admin. **Computer sciences:** General. **Conservation:** General, environmental science, fisheries, forest management, forest resources, management/policy, wildlife. **Education:** Technology/industrial arts. **Engineering:** Biomedical, chemical, civil, computer, construction, electrical, environmental, forest, industrial, manufacturing, mechanical, mining, nuclear, physics. **English:** Speech/rhetoric. **Family/consumer sciences:** Clothing/textiles, family studies, food/nutrition, housing, merchandising. **Foreign languages:** French, German, Spanish. **Health:** Clinical lab technology, environmental health, health care admin, physics/radiologic health, public health ed. **History:** General. **Interdisciplinary:** Biological/physical sciences. **Liberal arts:** Arts/sciences. **Math:** General. **Parks/recreation:** General, health/fitness. **Philosophy/religion:** Philosophy. **Physical sciences:** Chemistry, geology, physics. **Psychology:** General. **Social sciences:** Anthropology, economics, geography, political science, sociology. **Visual/performing arts:** General, art, fashion design, interior design.

Computing on campus. 3,000 workstations in dormitories, library, computer center. Dormitories wired for high-speed internet access and linked to campus network. Commuter students can connect to campus network. Online course registration, helpline, repair service, student web hosting, wireless network available.

Student life. Freshman orientation: Available. Preregistration for classes offered. **Policies:** Freshmen permitted cars on campus. **Housing:** Coed dorms, single-sex dorms, special housing for disabled, apartments, cooperative housing, fraternity/sorority housing available. **Activities:** Bands, choral groups, dance, drama, film society, literary magazine, music ensembles, musical theater, opera, radio station, student government, student newspaper, symphony orchestra, TV station, 253 student organizations, 47 student honor and recognition societies.

Athletics. NCAA. **Intercollegiate:** Baseball M, basketball, cheerleading, cross-country W, football (tackle) M, golf, gymnastics W, rowing (crew), soccer, softball W, swimming W, volleyball W, wrestling M. **Intramural:** Badminton, basketball, bowling, cross-country, football (tackle) M, golf, racquetball, soccer, softball, swimming, tennis, track and field, volleyball, water polo, wrestling M. **Team name:** Beavers.

Student services. Adult student services, career counseling, student employment services, financial aid counseling, health services, legal services, minority student services, on-campus daycare, personal counseling, placement for graduates, veterans' counselor, women's services. **Physically disabled:** Services for visually, speech, hearing impaired.

Contact. E-mail: osuadmit@orst.edu
Phone: (541) 737-4411 Toll-free number: (800) 291-4192
Fax: (541) 737-2482
Michele Sandlin, Director of Admissions, Oregon State University, 104 Kerr Administration Building, Corvallis, OR 97331-2130

Pacific Northwest College of Art

Portland, Oregon
www.pnca.edu **CB code: 4504**

- Private 4-year visual arts college
- Commuter campus in large city
- 288 degree-seeking undergraduates: 12% part-time, 59% women, 1% African American, 3% Asian American, 3% Hispanic American, 1% Native American
- 72% of applicants admitted
- Application essay required
- 39% graduate within 6 years

General. Founded in 1909. Regionally accredited. **Degrees:** 71 bachelor's awarded. **Calendar:** Semester, limited summer session. **Full-time faculty:** 15 total. **Part-time faculty:** 40 total. **Class size:** 96% < 20, 4% 20-39. **Special facilities:** Student art galleries, printmaking center, individual studio spaces for seniors.

Freshman class profile. 120 applied, 87 admitted, 27 enrolled.

GPA 3.50 or higher:	30%	**Return as sophomores:**	66%
GPA 3.0-3.49:	24%	**Out-of-state:**	29%
GPA 2.0-2.99:	38%	**Live on campus:**	37%

Basis for selection. Portfolio, essays important. High school GPA average of at least 2.0 recommended for academic courses. Greater emphasis is on portfolio. Portfolio required; interview recommended. **Homeschooled:** Statement describing homeschool structure and mission, transcript of courses and grades, state high school equivalency certificate, letter of recommendation (nonparent) required. SAT/ACT exam recommended. Contact enrollment counselor for further details.

High school preparation. Recommended units include English 4, mathematics 3, social studies 3 and science 3. Visual arts classes recommended.

2005-2006 Annual costs. Tuition/fees: $17,296. Books/supplies: $985. Personal expenses: $615.

2005-2006 Financial aid. Need-based: 25 full-time freshmen applied for aid; 22 were judged to have need; 22 of these received aid. Average need met was 72%. Average scholarship/grant was $3,369; average loan $2,596. 56% of total undergraduate aid awarded as scholarships/grants, 44% as loans/jobs. **Non-need-based:** Scholarships awarded for academics, art.

Application procedures. Admission: Priority date 3/1; no deadline. $35 fee, may be waived for applicants with need. Application may be submitted online. Admission notification on a rolling basis. Must reply by May 1 or within 2 week(s) if notified thereafter. **Financial aid:** Priority date 3/1, closing date 8/1. FAFSA required. Applicants notified on a rolling basis starting 4/1; must reply by 5/1 or within 4 week(s) of notification.

Academics. Thesis required part of fourth-year curriculum. **Special study options:** Cooperative education, cross-registration, dual enrollment of high school students, exchange student, independent study, internships, New York semester, student-designed major, study abroad. 5-year BA/BFA program with Reed College. **Credit/placement by examination:** AP, CLEP. **Support services:** Study skills assistance, tutoring, writing center.

Majors. Visual/performing arts: Graphic design, illustration, multimedia, painting, photography, printmaking, sculpture, studio arts.

Computing on campus. 66 workstations in library, computer center, student center. Commuter students can connect to campus network. Online library, wireless network available.

Student life. Freshman orientation: Available. Preregistration for classes offered. 1-2 days prior to the start of each semester. **Policies:** Freshmen permitted cars on campus. **Housing:** Coed dorms available. $450 partly refundable deposit, deadline 6/15. Pets allowed in dorm rooms. Student housing available through partnership with College Housing Northwest. **Activities:** Student government.

Student services. Career counseling, financial aid counseling, personal counseling.

Contact. E-mail: admissions@pnca.edu
Phone: (503) 821-8972 Fax: (503) 821-8978
Rebecca Haas, Admissions, Pacific Northwest College of Art, 1241 NW Johnson Street, Portland, OR 97209

Pacific University

Forest Grove, Oregon
www.pacificu.edu **CB code: 4601**

- Private 4-year university affiliated with United Church of Christ
- Residential campus in large town
- 1,210 degree-seeking undergraduates: 3% part-time, 60% women, 1% African American, 20% Asian American, 3% Hispanic American, 1% Native American
- 1,304 degree-seeking graduate students
- 87% of applicants admitted
- SAT or ACT (ACT writing optional), application essay required
- 65% graduate within 6 years

General. Founded in 1849. Regionally accredited. Branch campuses in Portland and Eugene for selected professional programs. **Degrees:** 275 bachelor's awarded; master's, doctoral, first professional offered. **ROTC:** Army, Air Force. **Location:** 25 miles from Portland. **Calendar:** 4-1-4, limited summer session. **Full-time faculty:** 82 total; 88% have terminal degrees, 11% minority, 43% women. **Part-time faculty:** 46 total; 44% have terminal degrees, 4% minority, 44% women. **Class size:** 66% < 20, 30% 20-39, 1% 40-49, 2% 50-99. **Special facilities:** Wildlife refuge, museum, Holocaust Resource Center, performing arts center, arboretum, Center for Internet Studies, Institute for Ethics and Social Policy.

Freshman class profile. 1,324 applied, 1,147 admitted, 326 enrolled.

Mid 50% test scores		**Rank in top quarter:**	59%
SAT verbal:	500-620	**Rank in top tenth:**	28%
SAT math:	510-620	**Return as sophomores:**	80%
ACT:	23-28	**Out-of-state:**	55%
GPA 3.50 or higher:	57%	**Live on campus:**	92%
GPA 3.0-3.49:	30%	**Fraternities:**	4%
GPA 2.0-2.99:	13%	**Sororities:**	7%

Basis for selection. Strength of high school program, academic GPA, test scores, course selection, interview most important. Minimum combined SAT score of 1000 (exclusive of Writing) plus minimum 3.0 GPA recommended. Recommendation, essay, extracurricular activities, leadership involvement also important. Audition required for music program; portfolio recommended for art program. **Homeschooled:** Statement describing homeschool structure and mission, transcript of courses and grades, state high school equivalency certificate, interview, letter of recommendation (nonparent) required. Standardized test scores required. Applications considered on case-by-case basis.

High school preparation. 21 units recommended. Recommended units include English 4, mathematics 3, social studies 3, history 1, science 3 (laboratory 1), foreign language 2 and academic electives 4.

2005-2006 Annual costs. Tuition/fees: $21,468. Room/board: $6,052.

2005-2006 Financial aid. Need-based: 304 full-time freshmen applied for aid; 252 were judged to have need; 252 of these received aid. Average need met was 89%. Average scholarship/grant was $12,626; average loan $5,349. 63% of total undergraduate aid awarded as scholarships/grants, 37% as loans/jobs. **Non-need-based:** Awarded to 382 full-time undergraduates, including 91 freshmen. Scholarships awarded for academics, art, music/drama, religious affiliation.

Application procedures. Admission: Priority date 2/15; no deadline. $40 fee, may be waived for applicants with need. Application may be submitted online. Admission notification on a rolling basis beginning on or about 11/1. Must reply by May 1 or within 2 week(s) if notified thereafter. **Financial aid:** Priority date 2/15; no closing date. FAFSA required. Applicants notified on a rolling basis starting 3/1; must reply within 2 week(s) of notification.

Academics. Special study options: Combined bachelor's/graduate degree, cross-registration, double major, ESL, exchange student, independent study, internships, liberal arts/career combination, study abroad, teacher certification program, Washington semester. 3-2 engineering programs with Oregon Graduate Institute and Washington University, 3-2 applied physics program, 4-1 computer science, 4-1 environmental science programs with Oregon Graduate Institute, exchange programs with University of Vienna, Beijing Normal University, University of Edinburgh, other institutions in Europe and Asia; cooperative arrangement with Northwest Film Center. **Credit/placement by examination:** AP, CLEP, IB, institutional tests. **Support services:** Learning center, reduced course load, tutoring, writing center.

Majors. Biology: General. **Business:** Business admin. **Communications:** General, journalism. **Computer sciences:** General. **Education:** General. **English:** Creative writing. **Foreign languages:** General, Chinese, French, German, Japanese, Spanish. **History:** General. **Liberal arts:** Arts/sciences. **Math:** General. **Parks/recreation:** Exercise sciences. **Philosophy/religion:** Philosophy. **Physical sciences:** Chemistry, physics. **Psychology:** General. **Public administration:** Social work. **Social sciences:** Economics, international relations, political science, sociology. **Visual/performing arts:** General, art, dramatic, multimedia, music performance.

Most popular majors. Biology 14%, business/marketing 12%, education 11%, parks/recreation 11%, psychology 10%, social sciences 6%, visual/performing arts 7%.

Computing on campus. 200 workstations in dormitories, library, computer center, student center. Dormitories wired for high-speed internet access and linked to campus network. Commuter students can connect to campus network. Online library, helpline, repair service, student web hosting, wireless network available.

Student life. Freshman orientation: Mandatory. Preregistration for classes offered. **Policies:** Freshmen permitted cars on campus. **Housing:** Guaranteed on-campus for freshmen. Coed dorms, special housing for disabled, apartments, cooperative housing available. $200 fully refundable deposit, deadline 7/1. All unmarried freshman and sophomores under age 21 must live on campus unless living near campus with family. Limited number of houses available for married students. **Activities:** Bands, choral groups, dance, drama, film society, literary magazine, music ensembles, musical theater, radio station, student government, student newspaper, symphony orchestra, Hawaii Club, Christian Fellowship, Politics and Law Forum, international student club, Spurs, Circle K, Humanitarian Center, gay and lesbian support group, Bridges Ethnic Diversity Appreciation Club, United Church of Christ student organization.

Athletics. NCAA. **Intercollegiate:** Baseball M, basketball, cheerleading, cross-country, golf, lacrosse W, soccer, softball W, swimming, tennis, track and field, volleyball W, wrestling. **Intramural:** Basketball, football (tackle), golf, handball, racquetball, soccer, softball, tennis, volleyball. **Team name:** Boxers.

Student services. Career counseling, student employment services, financial aid counseling, health services, personal counseling, placement for graduates, veterans' counselor.

Contact. E-mail: admissions@pacificu.edu
Phone: (503) 352-2218 Toll-free number: (800) 677-6712
Fax: (503) 352-2975
Karen Dunston, Director of Undergraduate Admission, Pacific University, 2043 College Way, Forest Grove, OR 97116-1797

Pioneer Pacific College

Wilsonville, Oregon
www.pioneerpacific.edu **CB code: 0492**

- For-profit 4-year technical college
- Commuter campus in large town
- 370 degree-seeking undergraduates: 59% women
- Interview required

General. Accredited by ACICS. Four sites: Wilsonville - main campus, Wilsonville - health career institute, Clackamas - learning site, and Springfield - branch campus. **Degrees:** 242 associate awarded. **Location:** 20 miles from Portland. **Calendar:** Continuous, extensive summer session. **Full-time faculty:** 40 total. **Part-time faculty:** 90 total. **Class size:** 79% < 20, 21% 20-39.

Basis for selection. Open admission, but selective for some programs.

2006-2007 Annual costs. Tuition/fees (projected): $9,560. Costs vary by program from $9,358 to $22,053. Quoted annual tuition is for criminal justice. Certain programs have additional lab fees. Personal expenses: $1,169.

Financial aid. All financial aid based on need.

Application procedures. Admission: No deadline. $50 fee. Application must be submitted on paper. Admission notification on a rolling basis. **Financial aid:** No deadline. FAFSA required. Applicants notified on a rolling basis starting 3/15.

Academics. Special study options: Accelerated study, honors, liberal arts/career combination, weekend college. Externships. **Credit/placement by examination:** AP, CLEP, institutional tests. **Support services:** Study skills assistance, tutoring.

Majors. Business: Business admin. **Computer sciences:** Information technology. **Health:** Health care admin. **Protective services:** Criminal justice.

Computing on campus. 400 workstations in library, computer center. Online library, wireless network available.

Student life. Freshman orientation: Mandatory. **Policies:** Freshmen permitted cars on campus.

Student services. Career counseling, student employment services, financial aid counseling, placement for graduates.

Contact. E-mail: inquiries@pioneerpacific.edu
Phone: (503) 682-3903 Toll-free number: (866) 772-4636
Fax: (503) 682-1514
Sandey Church, Director of Admissions, Pioneer Pacific College, 27501 Southwest Parkway Avenue, Wilsonville, OR 97070

Portland State University

Portland, Oregon **CB member**
www.pdx.edu **CB code: 4610**

- Public 4-year university
- Commuter campus in very large city
- 15,797 degree-seeking undergraduates: 32% part-time, 54% women
- 5,028 degree-seeking graduate students
- 92% of applicants admitted
- SAT or ACT with writing required
- 33% graduate within 6 years

General. Founded in 1946. Regionally accredited. Courses offered at off-campus locations. **Degrees:** 2,931 bachelor's awarded; master's, doctoral offered. **ROTC:** Army, Air Force. **Calendar:** Quarter, extensive summer session. **Full-time faculty:** 737 total; 76% have terminal degrees, 14% minority, 42% women. **Part-time faculty:** 497 total; 25% have terminal degrees, 14% minority, 45% women. **Class size:** 25% < 20, 47% 20-39, 12% 40-49, 14% 50-99, 2% >100. **Special facilities:** Native American center.

Freshman class profile. 2,844 applied, 2,623 admitted, 1,427 enrolled.

Mid 50% test scores		Out-of-state:	17%
SAT verbal:	460-590	International:	4%
SAT math:	470-580	Fraternities:	4%
ACT:	20-25	Sororities:	4%
Return as sophomores:	68%		

Basis for selection. For automatic admission one needs a High school GPA of at least 3.0 or a combined test score of at least 1,000 (exclusive of Writing) on SAT or test score of at least 21 on ACT. There is also a combination of test scores and HS GPA that students may use to gain automatic admissions. (Contact admissions for table.) Those who do not qualify for automatic admission may qualify under special action by the admissions committee. Interview recommended for those who do not meet regular admission requirement.

High school preparation. College-preparatory program required. 14 units required. Required and recommended units include English 4, mathematics 3, social studies 2, history 1, science 2 (laboratory 1) and foreign language 2. One unit laboratory science recommended.

2005-2006 Annual costs. Tuition/fees: $5,202; $17,127 out-of-state. Room/board: $6,992. Books/supplies: $1,800. Personal expenses: $1,530.

2005-2006 Financial aid. Need-based: 804 full-time freshmen applied for aid; 577 were judged to have need; 561 of these received aid. Average need met was 46%. Average scholarship/grant was $3,983; average loan $2,748. 29% of total undergraduate aid awarded as scholarships/grants, 71% as loans/jobs. **Non-need-based:** Awarded to 906 full-time undergraduates, including 263 freshmen. Scholarships awarded for academics, art, athletics, music/drama, state residency.

Application procedures. Admission: Priority date 6/1; no deadline. $50 fee. Application must be submitted on paper. Admission notification on a rolling basis. **Financial aid:** No deadline. FAFSA required. Applicants notified on a rolling basis; must reply within 4 week(s) of notification.

Academics. Community based service and research projects offered in Portland area. All students required to complete 45 credit hour multidisciplinary core curriculum, including community service learning experience. Teaching certification only offered at graduate level. **Special study options:** Accelerated study, combined bachelor's/graduate degree, cooperative education, distance learning, double major, ESL, exchange student, honors, independent study, internships, liberal arts/career combination, study abroad, teacher certification program, Washington semester. Haystack Summer Program in the arts and sciences. **Credit/placement by examination:** AP, CLEP, institutional tests. 45 credit hours maximum toward bachelor's degree. **Support services:** Pre-admission summer program, reduced course load, tutoring, writing center.

Honors college/program. Students with combined 1200 SAT (exclusive of Writing) and high school 3.5 GPA or better eligible to apply. Limited to 200 participants.

Majors. Architecture: Architecture, urban/community planning. **Area/ethnic studies:** African, Central/Eastern European, East Asian, European, Latin American, Near/Middle Eastern, women's. **Biology:** General, biochemistry. **Business:** General, accounting, business admin, finance, human resources, logistics, management information systems, marketing. **Computer sciences:** Computer science. **Conservation:** General. **Education:** Health. **Engineering:** Civil, computer, electrical, mechanical. **English:** Speech/rhetoric. **Family/consumer sciences:** Family studies. **Foreign languages:** Chinese, French, German, Japanese, linguistics, Russian, Spanish. **Health:** Audiology/hearing, public health ed. **History:** General. **Interdisciplinary:** Biological/physical sciences. **Liberal arts:** Arts/sciences. **Math:** General. **Philosophy/religion:** Philosophy. **Physical sciences:** Chemistry, geology, physics. **Protective services:** Criminal justice, law enforcement admin. **Psychology:** General. **Social sciences:** General, anthropology, economics, geography, international relations, political science, sociology, urban studies. **Visual/performing arts:** Art, art history/conservation, commercial/advertising art, design, dramatic, drawing, music performance, painting, printmaking, sculpture, studio arts.

Most popular majors. Business/marketing 24%, liberal arts 7%, physical sciences 6%, psychology 7%, social sciences 19%.

Computing on campus. 725 workstations in dormitories, library, computer center, student center. Dormitories linked to campus network. Commuter students can connect to campus network. Online course registration, online library, helpline, repair service, student web hosting, wireless network available.

Student life. Freshman orientation: Available. **Policies:** Freshmen permitted cars on campus. **Housing:** Coed dorms, special housing for disabled, apartments, fraternity/sorority housing available. Pets allowed in dorm rooms.

Activities: Bands, choral groups, dance, drama, film society, literary magazine, music ensembles, musical theater, opera, radio station, student government, student newspaper, symphony orchestra, Campus Christian Ministry, student public interest research group, Black Cultural Affairs Board, United Indian Students in Higher Education, Women's Union, outdoor program, Disabled Student Union, Hispanic Student Union, Organization of International Students.

Athletics. NCAA. **Intercollegiate:** Baseball M, basketball, cross-country, football (tackle) M, golf, soccer W, softball W, tennis, track and field, volleyball W, wrestling M. **Intramural:** Archery, basketball, football (tackle) M, golf, racquetball, soccer W, softball, volleyball. **Team name:** Vikings.

Student services. Adult student services, alcohol/substance abuse counseling, campus ministries, career counseling, student employment services, financial aid counseling, health services, minority student services, on-campus daycare, personal counseling, placement for graduates, veterans' counselor, women's services. **Physically disabled:** Services for visually, speech, hearing impaired.

Contact. E-mail: admissions@pdx.edu
Phone: (503) 725-3511 Toll-free number: (800) 547-8887 ext. 3511
Fax: (503) 725-5525
Agnes Hoffman, Director of Admissions/Records, Portland State University, PO Box 751-ADM, Portland, OR 97207-0751

Reed College

Portland, Oregon — **CB member**
www.reed.edu — **CB code: 4654**

- Private 4-year liberal arts college
- Residential campus in very large city
- 1,283 degree-seeking undergraduates: 1% part-time, 55% women
- 31 degree-seeking graduate students
- 45% of applicants admitted
- SAT or ACT (ACT writing optional), application essay required
- 73% graduate within 6 years; 65% enter graduate study

General. Founded in 1909. Regionally accredited. All students take 1-year course in humanities. Seniors engage in 1-year research project in major field and prepare and defend thesis. **Degrees:** 299 bachelor's awarded; master's offered. **Location:** 5 miles from downtown. **Calendar:** Semester. **Full-time faculty:** 116 total; 90% have terminal degrees, 9% minority, 34% women. **Part-time faculty:** 15 total; 80% have terminal degrees, 33% women. **Class size:** 76% < 20, 20% 20-39, less than 1% 40-49, 1% 50-99, 2% >100. **Special facilities:** Nuclear research reactor, wildlife refuge, fish ladder.

Freshman class profile. 2,646 applied, 1,200 admitted, 354 enrolled.

Mid 50% test scores		Rank in top quarter:	86%
SAT verbal:	660-760	Rank in top tenth:	57%
SAT math:	620-710	Return as sophomores:	85%
ACT:	29-32	Out-of-state:	91%
GPA 3.50 or higher:	84%	Live on campus:	99%
GPA 3.0-3.49:	14%	International:	4%
GPA 2.0-2.99:	2%		

Basis for selection. Academic achievement, essay, recommendations, test scores most important. SAT Subject Tests recommended. Interview recommended. **Homeschooled:** Must document homeschool curriculum. High school diploma waived in some cases. Must be above age of compulsory education in home state. Require writing sample, essay, reference from evaluator or teacher not family member.

High school preparation. 23 units recommended. Recommended units include English 4, mathematics 4, social studies 1, history 3, science 4 (laboratory 3) and foreign language 4.

2005-2006 Annual costs. Tuition/fees: $32,590. Room/board: $8,516. Books/supplies: $950. Personal expenses: $900.

2005-2006 Financial aid. All financial aid based on need. 224 full-time freshmen applied for aid; 177 were judged to have need; 165 of these received aid. Average need met was 100%. Average scholarship/grant was $27,387; average loan $2,684. 83% of total undergraduate aid awarded as scholarships/grants, 17% as loans/jobs. **Additional information:** College meets demonstrated need of continuing students who have attended Reed minimum of 2 semesters, who file financial aid applications on time, and who maintain satisfactory academic progress. Institutional aid consideration is for a total of 8 semesters.

Application procedures. Admission: Closing date 1/15 (postmark date). $40 fee, may be waived for applicants with need. Application must be submitted on paper. Admission notification 4/1. Must reply by May 1 or within

2 week(s) if notified thereafter. **Financial aid:** Closing date 1/15. FAFSA, institutional form, CSS PROFILE required. Applicants notified by 4/1; must reply by 5/1 or within 2 week(s) of notification.

Academics. Special study options: Combined bachelor's/graduate degree, cooperative education, cross-registration, double major, dual enrollment of high school students, exchange student, independent study, internships, liberal arts/career combination, study abroad. Computer science program with University of Washington, computer science and engineering master of science program at Oregon Graduate Institute of Science and Engineering, engineering arrangement with California Institute of Technology, Columbia University School of Engineering and Applied Sciences and Rensselaer Polytechnic Institute, forestry-environmental sciences degree arrangement with Nicholas School of the Environment of Duke University, art program in conjunction with Pacific Northwest College of Art. **Credit/placement by examination:** AP, CLEP, IB, institutional tests. 30 credit hours maximum toward bachelor's degree. **Support services:** Learning center, study skills assistance, tutoring, writing center.

Majors. Area/ethnic studies: American. **Biology:** General, biochemistry, molecular. **English:** Creative writing. **Foreign languages:** Chinese, classics, comparative lit, French, German, linguistics, Russian, Spanish. **History:** General. **Interdisciplinary:** Biological/physical sciences. **Math:** General. **Philosophy/religion:** Philosophy, religion. **Physical sciences:** Chemistry, physics. **Psychology:** General. **Social sciences:** Anthropology, economics, political science, sociology. **Visual/performing arts:** Art history/conservation, dramatic, studio arts.

Most popular majors. Biology 14%, English 12%, foreign language 7%, history 6%, interdisciplinary studies 6%, philosophy/religious studies 10%, physical sciences 8%, psychology 8%, social sciences 20%, visual/performing arts 6%.

Computing on campus. 366 workstations in dormitories, library, computer center, student center. Dormitories wired for high-speed internet access and linked to campus network. Commuter students can connect to campus network. Online course registration, online library, helpline, repair service, student web hosting, wireless network available.

Student life. Freshman orientation: Mandatory. Preregistration for classes offered. Held 5 days before start of classes. **Policies:** Honor code. Freshmen permitted cars on campus. **Housing:** Guaranteed on-campus for freshmen. Coed dorms, single-sex dorms, special housing for disabled, apartments, cooperative housing, substance-free housing available. $100 deposit, deadline 6/15. Chinese, French, German, Russian, and Spanish language houses available for upper division students. First-year students required to live on campus. **Activities:** Choral groups, dance, drama, film society, literary magazine, music ensembles, radio station, student government, student newspaper, symphony orchestra, Christian Fellowship, Jewish Student Union, women's center, environmental coalition, politically active student groups, volunteer tutoring, language and outing clubs, poetry forum.

Athletics. Intramural: Archery, badminton, basketball M, diving, equestrian, fencing, golf, judo, rowing (crew), rugby, sailing, skiing, soccer, softball, squash, swimming, tennis, volleyball. **Team name:** Griffins.

Student services. Adult student services, alcohol/substance abuse counseling, career counseling, student employment services, financial aid counseling, health services, minority student services, personal counseling, placement for graduates. **Physically disabled:** Services for visually, speech, hearing impaired.

Contact. E-mail: admission@reed.edu
Phone: (503) 777-7511 Toll-free number: (800) 547-4750
Fax: (503) 777-7553
Paul Marthers, Dean of Admission, Reed College, 3203 Southeast Woodstock Boulevard, Portland, OR 97202-8199

Southern Oregon University

Ashland, Oregon **CB member**
www.sou.edu **CB code: 4702**

- Public 4-year university and liberal arts college
- Residential campus in large town
- 4,238 degree-seeking undergraduates: 18% part-time, 57% women, 1% African American, 3% Asian American, 4% Hispanic American, 2% Native American, 2% international
- 419 degree-seeking graduate students
- 80% of applicants admitted
- SAT or ACT (ACT writing optional) required

General. Founded in 1926. Regionally accredited. Designated by National Aeronautical and Space Administration to cooperate in NASA-directed joint space research by undergraduates. **Degrees:** 737 bachelor's awarded; master's offered. **Location:** 180 miles from Eugene, 285 miles from Portland. **Calendar:** Quarter, extensive summer session. **Full-time faculty:** 198 total. **Part-time faculty:** 114 total. **Class size:** 46% < 20, 42% 20-39, 6% 40-49, 5% 50-99, 1% >100. **Special facilities:** Herbarium, U.S. Fish and Wildlife forensics laboratory, public radio network studios, preschool and kindergarten, community television studio, center for visual arts, biotechnology center, institute for environmental economic and civic studies.

Freshman class profile. 2,157 applied, 1,726 admitted, 770 enrolled.

Mid 50% test scores			
SAT verbal:	450-580	Return as sophomores:	65%
SAT math:	460-570	Out-of-state:	19%
ACT:	20-25	Live on campus:	69%
		International:	1%

Basis for selection. 2.75 GPA from regionally accredited high school, 21 ACT composite score, 1010 SAT (exclusive of Writing), and 14 required high school academic units. Requests for special admission for undergraduates reviewed individually. TOEFL required of non-native English speakers. SAT Subject Tests required of students graduating from nonstandard or unaccredited high schools. **Homeschooled:** Submit SAT and SAT Subject Tests.

High school preparation. 14 units required. Required units include English 4, mathematics 3, social studies 3, science 2 and foreign language 2.

2005-2006 Annual costs. Tuition/fees: $5,085; $16,059 out-of-state. Room/board: $6,843. Books/supplies: $1,155. Personal expenses: $2,475.

2005-2006 Financial aid. Need-based: 54% of total undergraduate aid awarded as scholarships/grants, 46% as loans/jobs. **Non-need-based:** Scholarships awarded for academics, alumni affiliation, art, athletics, leadership, minority status, music/drama, religious affiliation, state residency.

Application procedures. Admission: No deadline. $50 fee, may be waived for applicants with need. Application may be submitted online. Admission notification on a rolling basis. **Financial aid:** No deadline. FAFSA required. Applicants notified on a rolling basis starting 3/1; must reply within 2 week(s) of notification.

Academics. Special study options: Accelerated study, combined bachelor's/graduate degree, cooperative education, cross-registration, distance learning, double major, dual enrollment of high school students, ESL, exchange student, honors, independent study, internships, liberal arts/career combination, student-designed major, study abroad, teacher certification program. **Credit/placement by examination:** AP, CLEP, IB, institutional tests. 24 credit hours maximum toward bachelor's degree. **Support services:** Learning center, reduced course load, remedial instruction, study skills assistance, tutoring, writing center.

Majors. Biology: General. **Business:** General, accounting, business admin, hospitality admin, marketing. **Communications:** General, journalism, public relations. **Computer sciences:** General, computer science, programming, security. **Conservation:** Environmental studies. **Education:** General. **English:** Speech/rhetoric. **Foreign languages:** General, Spanish. **Health:** Athletic training, nursing (RN), predentistry, premedicine, preop/surgical nursing, prepharmacy, preveterinary. **History:** General. **Interdisciplinary:** Biological/physical sciences, math/computer science. **Legal studies:** Prelaw. **Math:** General. **Parks/recreation:** Health/fitness, sports admin. **Physical sciences:** Chemistry, geology, physics. **Protective services:** Criminal justice, law enforcement admin, police science. **Psychology:** General. **Social sciences:** General, anthropology, criminology, economics, geography, political science, sociology. **Visual/performing arts:** Art, dramatic, music management.

Computing on campus. 750 workstations in dormitories, library, computer center, student center. Dormitories wired for high-speed internet access and linked to campus network. Commuter students can connect to campus network. Online course registration, online library, helpline, student web hosting, wireless network available.

Student life. Freshman orientation: Mandatory. Preregistration for classes offered. Early registration in July, orientation few days before start of classes. **Policies:** Freshmen permitted cars on campus. **Housing:** Guaranteed on-campus for freshmen. Coed dorms, special housing for disabled, apartments, substance-free housing available. $50 deposit. Special quiet, nonsmoking, older student or freshmen residence halls available. **Activities:** Bands, choral groups, dance, drama, literary magazine, music ensembles, musical theater, opera, radio station, student government, student newspaper, symphony orchestra, TV station, 100 clubs.

Athletics. NAIA. **Intercollegiate:** Basketball, cross-country, football (tackle) M, soccer W, softball W, tennis W, track and field, volleyball W, wrestling M. **Intramural:** Badminton, baseball M, basketball, bowling, golf, racquetball, rugby, sailing, skiing, soccer, softball, swimming, table tennis, tennis, track and field, volleyball, water polo. **Team name:** Raiders.

Student services. Adult student services, alcohol/substance abuse counseling, career counseling, services for economically disadvantaged, student employment services, financial aid counseling, health services, legal services, minority student services, on-campus daycare, personal counseling, placement for graduates, veterans' counselor, women's services. **Physically disabled:** Services for visually, speech, hearing impaired. **Learning disabled:** Comprehensive services available.

Contact. E-mail: admissions@sou.edu
Phone: (541) 552-6411 Toll-free number: (800) 482-7672
Fax: (541) 552-6614
Mara Affre, Assistant Vice President of Enrollment Services and Director of Admissions, Southern Oregon University, 1250 Siskiyou Boulevard, Ashland, OR 97520-5032

University of Oregon

Eugene, Oregon — **CB member**
www.uoregon.edu — **CB code: 4846**

- Public 4-year university
- Residential campus in small city
- 16,164 degree-seeking undergraduates: 8% part-time, 53% women, 2% African American, 6% Asian American, 3% Hispanic American, 1% Native American, 4% international
- 3,436 degree-seeking graduate students
- 90% of applicants admitted
- SAT or ACT with writing required
- 65% graduate within 6 years; 20% enter graduate study

General. Founded in 1876. Regionally accredited. **Degrees:** 3,960 bachelor's awarded; master's, doctoral, first professional offered. **ROTC:** Army. **Location:** 110 miles from Portland. **Calendar:** Quarter, extensive summer session. **Full-time faculty:** 785 total; 98% have terminal degrees, 19% minority, 39% women. **Part-time faculty:** 337 total; 91% have terminal degrees, 13% minority, 48% women. **Class size:** 39% < 20, 41% 20-39, 4% 40-49, 9% 50-99, 7% >100. **Special facilities:** Museum of natural and cultural history, Pine Mountain observatory, art museum, marine biology station on Oregon coast, sports marketing center.

Freshman class profile. 10,012 applied, 9,048 admitted, 3,207 enrolled.

Mid 50% test scores		**End year in good standing:**	89%
SAT verbal:	500-620	**Return as sophomores:**	84%
SAT math:	500-610	**Out-of-state:**	27%
GPA 3.50 or higher:	53%	**Live on campus:**	85%
GPA 3.0-3.49:	38%	**International:**	4%
GPA 2.0-2.99:	9%	**Fraternities:**	8%
Rank in top quarter:	58%	**Sororities:**	6%
Rank in top tenth:	25%		

Basis for selection. High school students with minimum 3.25 high school GPA and 16 college preparatory units guaranteed admission. For all others, secondary school record and test scores most important. Minimum 3.25 high school GPA in all academic subjects or predicted first-term GPA of 2.0 or better based on combination of high school GPA and SAT/ACT scores. Admissions essay required for all students with fewer than 16 college preparatory units or cumulative high school GPA below 3.25. Audition required for dance and music programs; portfolio required for arts, architecture, and interior architecture programs. **Learning Disabled:** If student does not meet admission requirements and has self-identified as having documented disability, secondary review will take place by disability review committee.

High school preparation. 14 units required. Required and recommended units include English 4, mathematics 3, social studies 3, science 2 (laboratory 1) and foreign language 2. One unit of laboratory science recommended. Additional 2 units in college preparatory areas required for guaranteed admission.

2005-2006 Annual costs. Tuition/fees: $5,613; $17,445 out-of-state. Room/board: $7,496. Books/supplies: $900. Personal expenses: $2,376.

2005-2006 Financial aid. Need-based: 2,008 full-time freshmen applied for aid; 1,174 were judged to have need; 1,106 of these received aid. Average need met was 55%. Average scholarship/grant was $4,005; average loan $3,669. 14% of total undergraduate aid awarded as scholarships/grants, 86% as loans/jobs. **Non-need-based:** Awarded to 2,860 full-time undergraduates, including 974 freshmen. Scholarships awarded for academics, athletics, leadership, minority status, music/drama, ROTC, state residency.

Application procedures. Admission: Priority date 11/1; deadline 1/15 (postmark date). $50 fee, may be waived for applicants with need. Application may be submitted online. Admission notification on a rolling basis. Must reply by May 1 or within 4 week(s) if notified thereafter. Additional applications required by major: architecture; art, 3/1; Clark Honors College, digital arts, 2/1; interior architecture; landscape architecture, 2/15; School of Music and Dance. **Financial aid:** Priority date 3/1, closing date 6/30. FAFSA required. Applicants notified on a rolling basis starting 4/15; must reply within 4 week(s) of notification.

Academics. Special study options: Distance learning, double major, dual enrollment of high school students, ESL, honors, independent study, internships, semester at sea, student-designed major, study abroad, teacher certification program. **Credit/placement by examination:** AP, CLEP, IB, SAT, ACT, institutional tests. **Support services:** Learning center, remedial instruction, study skills assistance, tutoring.

Honors college/program. Faculty Admission Committee considers several factors in making decision: SAT or ACT scores, unweighted grade point average, rigor and breadth of coursework, diversity, 2 teacher recommendations, and personal essay. Approximately 150 spaces available per year.

Majors. Architecture: Architecture, interior, landscape. **Area/ethnic studies:** Asian, Russian/Slavic, women's. **Biology:** General, biochemistry, marine, physiology. **Business:** General, accounting. **Communications:** General, advertising, digital media, journalism, media studies, public relations. **Computer sciences:** General. **Conservation:** Environmental science, environmental studies. **Education:** General, multi-level teacher, music. **English:** English lit. **Foreign languages:** Ancient Greek, Chinese, classics, comparative lit, French, German, Italian, Japanese, Latin, linguistics, Romance, Spanish. **Health:** Communication disorders. **History:** General. **Interdisciplinary:** Biological/physical sciences, global studies, math/computer science. **Liberal arts:** Humanities. **Math:** General. **Philosophy/religion:** Judaic, philosophy, religion. **Physical sciences:** Chemistry, geology, physics. **Psychology:** General. **Public administration:** General. **Social sciences:** General, anthropology, economics, geography, political science, sociology. **Visual/performing arts:** Art, art history/conservation, ceramics, dance, design, dramatic, fiber arts, jazz, metal/jewelry, multimedia, music performance, music theory/composition, painting, photography, printmaking, sculpture, studio arts.

Most popular majors. Business/marketing 12%, communications/journalism 9%, foreign language 7%, interdisciplinary studies 6%, psychology 7%, social sciences 21%, visual/performing arts 7%.

Computing on campus. 1,600 workstations in dormitories, library, computer center, student center. Dormitories wired for high-speed internet access and linked to campus network. Commuter students can connect to campus network. Online course registration, online library, helpline, repair service, student web hosting, wireless network available.

Student life. Freshman orientation: Mandatory. Preregistration for classes offered. IntroDUCKtion sessions offered throughout July. **Policies:** Freshmen permitted cars on campus. **Housing:** Coed dorms, special housing for disabled, apartments, fraternity/sorority housing, substance-free housing available. $250 fully refundable deposit, deadline 3/31. Residence halls have men's and women's floors. Special interest halls, graduate student housing available. **Activities:** Bands, choral groups, dance, drama, literary magazine, music ensembles, musical theater, opera, radio station, student government, student newspaper, symphony orchestra.

Athletics. NCAA. **Intercollegiate:** Basketball, cheerleading, cross-country, football (tackle) M, golf, lacrosse W, soccer W, softball W, tennis, track and field, volleyball W, wrestling M. **Intramural:** Basketball, cross-country, football (non-tackle), golf, racquetball, soccer, softball, swimming, tennis, track and field, volleyball, wrestling M. **Team name:** Ducks.

Student services. Adult student services, alcohol/substance abuse counseling, career counseling, student employment services, financial aid counseling, health services, legal services, minority student services, on-campus daycare, personal counseling, placement for graduates, veterans' counselor, women's services. **Physically disabled:** Services for visually, speech, hearing impaired. **Learning disabled:** Comprehensive services available.

Contact. E-mail: uoadmit@uoregon.edu
Phone: (541) 346-3201 Toll-free number: (800) 232-3825
Fax: (541) 346-5815
Martha Pitts, Assistant Vice President for Enrollment Services and Director of Admissions, University of Oregon, 1217 University of Oregon, Eugene, OR 97403-1217

University of Portland

Portland, Oregon — **CB member**
www.up.edu — **CB code: 4847**

- Private 4-year university affiliated with Roman Catholic Church
- Residential campus in large city

- 2,860 degree-seeking undergraduates: 1% part-time, 62% women, 2% African American, 9% Asian American, 4% Hispanic American, 1% Native American, 1% international
- 437 degree-seeking graduate students
- 81% of applicants admitted
- SAT or ACT (ACT writing optional), application essay required
- 68% graduate within 6 years; 25% enter graduate study

General. Founded in 1901. Regionally accredited. **Degrees:** 606 bachelor's awarded; master's offered. **ROTC:** Army, Air Force. **Location:** Located in North Portland. **Calendar:** Semester, limited summer session. **Full-time faculty:** 188 total; 86% have terminal degrees, 4% minority, 40% women. **Part-time faculty:** 91 total; 11% have terminal degrees, 2% minority, 45% women. **Class size:** 34% < 20, 54% 20-39, 8% 40-49, 3% 50-99, less than 1% >100. **Special facilities:** Rare book collection.

Freshman class profile. 3,026 applied, 2,445 admitted, 724 enrolled.

Mid 50% test scores		**Rank in top quarter:**	76%
SAT verbal:	540-640	**Rank in top tenth:**	44%
SAT math:	540-640	**Return as sophomores:**	86%
GPA 3.50 or higher:	71%	**Out-of-state:**	62%
GPA 3.0-3.49:	25%	**Live on campus:**	95%
GPA 2.0-2.99:	4%	**International:**	1%

Basis for selection. School achievement record, test scores, counselor recommendation, essay important. **Homeschooled:** Applicants need record of courses, SAT or ACT scores, letter of recommendation. Interview strongly encouraged.

High school preparation. Required and recommended units include English 3-4, mathematics 2-3, social studies 2, history 2, science 2, foreign language 3 and academic electives 7. Engineering, mathematics, and some science majors require additional mathematics and science courses.

2005-2006 Annual costs. Tuition/fees: $24,920. Room/board: $7,400. Books/supplies: $700. Personal expenses: $800.

2005-2006 Financial aid. Need-based: 632 full-time freshmen applied for aid; 482 were judged to have need; 480 of these received aid. Average need met was 86%. Average scholarship/grant was $13,807; average loan $2,944. 74% of total undergraduate aid awarded as scholarships/grants, 26% as loans/jobs. **Non-need-based:** Awarded to 1,619 full-time undergraduates, including 494 freshmen. Scholarships awarded for academics, athletics, music/drama, ROTC.

Application procedures. Admission: Priority date 2/1; deadline 6/1 (postmark date). $50 fee, may be waived for applicants with need. Application may be submitted online. Admission notification on a rolling basis beginning on or about 10/1. Must reply by May 1 or within 2 week(s) if notified thereafter. **Financial aid:** Priority date 3/1; no closing date. FAFSA, institutional form required. Applicants notified by 3/15; must reply within 3 week(s) of notification.

Academics. Special study options: Cross-registration, double major, honors, independent study, internships, liberal arts/career combination, student-designed major, study abroad, teacher certification program, Washington semester. **Credit/placement by examination:** AP, CLEP, IB, institutional tests. 45 credit hours maximum toward bachelor's degree. **Support services:** Learning center, study skills assistance, tutoring, writing center.

Majors. Biology: General. **Business:** Accounting, business admin, finance, international, marketing. **Communications:** Media studies, organizational. **Computer sciences:** Computer science. **Conservation:** Environmental science, environmental studies. **Education:** Elementary, music, secondary. **Engineering:** Civil, computer, electrical, environmental, mechanical. **English:** English lit. **Foreign languages:** Spanish. **Health:** Nursing (RN). **History:** General. **Math:** General. **Philosophy/religion:** Philosophy. **Physical sciences:** Chemistry, physics. **Psychology:** General. **Public administration:** Social work. **Social sciences:** Political science, sociology. **Theology:** Theology. **Visual/performing arts:** Dramatic, theater arts management.

Most popular majors. Biology 8%, business/marketing 17%, education 7%, engineering/engineering technologies 9%, health sciences 18%, social sciences 9%.

Computing on campus. 400 workstations in dormitories, library, computer center, student center. Dormitories wired for high-speed internet access and linked to campus network. Commuter students can connect to campus network. Online course registration, online library, helpline, student web hosting, wireless network available.

Student life. Freshman orientation: Available. Preregistration for classes offered. 5 days before classes begin. **Housing:** Guaranteed on-campus for freshmen. Coed dorms, single-sex dorms available. $100 nonrefundable deposit, deadline 6/1. Rental houses available. **Activities:** Bands, choral groups, dance, drama, literary magazine, music ensembles, musical theater, radio station, student government, student newspaper, symphony orchestra, Campus Ministry, volunteer services, Black Student Union, international club, Hawaiian Club, Society of Women Engineeers, feminist discussion group, Bible study group.

Athletics. NCAA. **Intercollegiate:** Baseball M, basketball, cross-country, golf, soccer, tennis, track and field, volleyball W. **Intramural:** Basketball, bowling, football (non-tackle), golf, skiing, soccer, softball, swimming, table tennis, tennis, volleyball, water polo, weight lifting. **Team name:** Pilots.

Student services. Adult student services, alcohol/substance abuse counseling, campus ministries, career counseling, student employment services, financial aid counseling, health services, personal counseling, placement for graduates, veterans' counselor. **Physically disabled:** Services for visually, speech, hearing impaired.

Contact. E-mail: admissio@up.edu
Phone: (503) 943-7147 Toll-free number: (888) 627-5601
Fax: (503) 943-7315
James Lyons, Dean of Admissions, University of Portland, 5000 North Willamette Boulevard, Portland, OR 97203-5798

Warner Pacific College
Portland, Oregon
www.warnerpacific.edu **CB code: 4595**

- Private 4-year liberal arts college affiliated with Church of God
- Residential campus in very large city
- 556 degree-seeking undergraduates: 2% part-time, 65% women, 4% African American, 2% Asian American, 3% Hispanic American, 1% Native American, 1% international
- 20 degree-seeking graduate students
- Application essay required
- 47% graduate within 6 years

General. Founded in 1937. Regionally accredited. **Degrees:** 138 bachelor's awarded; master's offered. **ROTC:** Army, Navy, Air Force. **Location:** 44 miles from Salem; 10 miles from Vancouver, Washington. **Calendar:** Semester, limited summer session. **Full-time faculty:** 30 total. **Part-time faculty:** 20 total.

Basis for selection. Open admission, but selective for some programs. High school GPA important; test scores, essay and signed lifestyle agreement required.

High school preparation. 11 units recommended. Recommended units include English 4, mathematics 2, social studies 3 and science 2.

2005-2006 Annual costs. Tuition/fees: $19,150. Per-credit-hour charges vary: part-time 1-5 credits $410; half-time 6-11 credits $800. Room/board: $5,360. Books/supplies: $600. Personal expenses: $2,350.

Financial aid. Non-need-based: Scholarships awarded for academics, athletics, leadership, minority status, music/drama, religious affiliation.

Application procedures. Admission: No deadline. $25 fee, may be waived for applicants with need. Application may be submitted online. Admission notification on a rolling basis. **Financial aid:** Priority date 6/1, closing date 8/15. FAFSA required. Applicants notified on a rolling basis starting 4/1; must reply within 4 week(s) of notification.

Academics. Special study options: Accelerated study, cooperative education, cross-registration, double major, independent study, internships, liberal arts/career combination, student-designed major, study abroad, teacher certification program, Washington semester. 2-2 nursing program with Walla Walla School of Nursing. **Credit/placement by examination:** CLEP, institutional tests. 30 credit hours maximum toward associate degree, 30 toward bachelor's. No more than 45 total alternative credits (maximum 30 of any one type). **Support services:** Learning center, reduced course load, remedial instruction, study skills assistance, tutoring.

Majors. Area/ethnic studies: American. **Biology:** General. **Business:** Business admin, international. **Education:** Music, physical. **Family/consumer sciences:** Family studies. **History:** General. **Liberal arts:** Arts/sciences. **Philosophy/religion:** Religion. **Physical sciences:** General. **Psychology:** General. **Public administration:** Social work. **Social sciences:** General. **Theology:** Preministerial.

Computing on campus. Dormitories wired for high-speed internet access and linked to campus network.

Student life. Freshman orientation: Available. Preregistration for classes offered. **Policies:** Religious observance required. Freshmen permitted cars on campus. **Housing:** Guaranteed on-campus for freshmen. Single-sex dorms, special housing for disabled, apartments available. $100 deposit. **Activities:** Bands, choral groups, drama, music ensembles, student government.

Athletics. NAIA, NCCAA. **Intercollegiate:** Basketball, cross-country, soccer, track and field, volleyball W. **Intramural:** Badminton, basketball, football (non-tackle), volleyball. **Team name:** Knights.

Student services. Adult student services, campus ministries, career counseling, student employment services, financial aid counseling, health services, minority student services, personal counseling, placement for graduates.

Contact. E-mail: admissions@warnerpacific.edu
Phone: (503) 517-1020 Toll-free number: (800) 804-1510
Fax: (503) 517-1352
Shannon Mackey, Executive Director of Enrollment Management, Warner Pacific College, 2219 SE 68th Avenue, Portland, OR 97215-4026

Western Oregon University

Monmouth, Oregon — **CB member**
www.wou.edu — **CB code: 4585**

- Public 4-year liberal arts and teachers college
- Residential campus in small town
- 4,136 degree-seeking undergraduates: 9% part-time, 58% women, 2% African American, 3% Asian American, 6% Hispanic American, 2% Native American, 1% international
- 225 degree-seeking graduate students
- 55% of applicants admitted
- SAT or ACT with writing required
- 44% graduate within 6 years

General. Founded in 1856. Regionally accredited. **Degrees:** 839 bachelor's, 3 associate awarded; master's offered. **ROTC:** Army, Navy, Air Force. **Location:** 15 miles from Salem, 60 miles from Portland. **Calendar:** Quarter, limited summer session. **Full-time faculty:** 179 total; 90% have terminal degrees, 7% minority, 46% women. **Part-time faculty:** 175 total; 38% have terminal degrees, 2% minority, 56% women. **Class size:** 79% < 20, 17% 20-39, 2% 40-49, 2% 50-99, less than 1% >100. **Special facilities:** Arctic museum, teaching research institute, early childhood and training development center.

Freshman class profile. 1,881 applied, 1,026 admitted, 834 enrolled.

Mid 50% test scores		Rank in top quarter:	27%
SAT verbal:	430-540	Rank in top tenth:	9%
SAT math:	430-550	End year in good standing:	90%
ACT:	17-23	Return as sophomores:	64%
GPA 3.50 or higher:	28%	Out-of-state:	10%
GPA 3.0-3.49:	38%	Live on campus:	80%
GPA 2.0-2.99:	33%		

Basis for selection. 2.75 high school GPA required. SAT combined score of 1000 (exclusive of Writing) strongly recommended, but only used in admissions decision if the applicant does not meet GPA or college preparation requirements. In the case that applicant does not meet academic requirements, other evidence of potential in the form of interviews, portfolios, auditions, essays, and the like considered. Applicant reviewed by admissions committee under special admissions criteria with weighting structure inclusive of other data indicators. **Homeschooled:** Minimum SAT score of 1000 (exclusive of writing) or ACT score of 21 required or minimum SAT Subject Tests combined score of 1410 in 3 subjects - must take 1 SAT Reasoning exam, 1 SAT subject exam in mathematics, and second exam in second language.

High school preparation. College-preparatory program required. 14 units required. Required and recommended units include English 4, mathematics 3, social studies 2, science 2 (laboratory 1) and foreign language 2. Algebra II or higher required.

2005-2006 Annual costs. Tuition/fees: $4,478; $13,709 out-of-state. Room/board: $6,654. Books/supplies: $1,125. Personal expenses: $2,475.

2004-2005 Financial aid. **Need-based:** 642 full-time freshmen applied for aid; 473 were judged to have need; 427 of these received aid. Average need met was 65%. Average scholarship/grant was $4,530; average loan $3,732. 37% of total undergraduate aid awarded as scholarships/grants, 63% as loans/jobs. **Non-need-based:** Awarded to 852 full-time undergraduates, including 223 freshmen. Scholarships awarded for academics, art, athletics, leadership, minority status, music/drama, ROTC, state residency.

Application procedures. **Admission:** No deadline. $50 fee. Application may be submitted online. Admission notification on a rolling basis. **Financial aid:** Priority date 3/1; no closing date. FAFSA required. Applicants notified on a rolling basis starting 4/1; must reply within 2 week(s) of notification.

Academics. **Special study options:** Distance learning, double major, dual enrollment of high school students, ESL, honors, independent study, internships, student-designed major, study abroad, teacher certification program. Preprofessional studies, interdisciplinary studies, nondegree licensure programs, service learning and career development. **Credit/placement by examination:** AP, CLEP, IB, SAT, ACT, institutional tests. 48 credit hours maximum toward bachelor's degree. **Support services:** Learning center, remedial instruction, study skills assistance, tutoring, writing center.

Majors. **Biology:** General. **Business:** General. **Communications:** General. **Computer sciences:** General. **Education:** General, elementary, health, instructional media, multi-level teacher, physical, secondary. **English:** Speech/rhetoric. **Foreign languages:** Sign language interpretation, Spanish. **History:** General. **Interdisciplinary:** Biological/physical sciences, math/computer science, natural sciences. **Liberal arts:** Arts/sciences. **Math:** General. **Philosophy/religion:** Philosophy. **Physical sciences:** Chemistry, geology, planetary. **Protective services:** Corrections, fire services admin, law enforcement admin. **Psychology:** General. **Public administration:** General. **Social sciences:** General, anthropology, economics, geography, political science, sociology. **Visual/performing arts:** General, art, dance, dramatic, studio arts, theater arts management.

Most popular majors. Business/marketing 11%, education 25%, interdisciplinary studies 9%, psychology 10%, security/protective services 7%, social sciences 12%, visual/performing arts 6%.

Computing on campus. 411 workstations in dormitories, library, computer center, student center. Dormitories wired for high-speed internet access and linked to campus network. Commuter students can connect to campus network. Online course registration, online library, helpline, repair service, wireless network available.

Student life. **Freshman orientation:** Available. Orientation held last weekend in June and the 2nd and 3rd weekends in July on Friday and/or Saturday. **Policies:** No alcohol permitted in residence halls even for those over 21 years of age. Freshmen permitted cars on campus. **Housing:** Guaranteed on-campus for freshmen. Coed dorms, special housing for disabled, apartments, substance-free housing available. $35 nonrefundable deposit, deadline 10/1. Family housing, housing by learning communities, community living options available. **Activities:** Bands, choral groups, dance, drama, literary magazine, music ensembles, musical theater, student government, student newspaper, symphony orchestra, TV station, Baptist Student Union, international students club, Big Brother/Big Sister, Multicultural Student Union, Campus Crusade for Christ, Circle-K, Environmental Action Committee, model United Nations.

Athletics. NCAA. **Intercollegiate:** Baseball M, basketball, cheerleading, cross-country, football (tackle) M, soccer W, softball W, track and field, volleyball W. **Intramural:** Basketball, bowling, cross-country, football (non-tackle), football (tackle) M, golf, racquetball, rifle, skiing, soccer, softball, swimming, table tennis, tennis, track and field, triathlon, volleyball, water polo, weight lifting, wrestling. **Team name:** Wolves.

Student services. Adult student services, alcohol/substance abuse counseling, campus ministries, career counseling, services for economically disadvantaged, student employment services, financial aid counseling, health services, minority student services, on-campus daycare, personal counseling, placement for graduates, veterans' counselor, women's services. **Physically disabled:** Services for visually, speech, hearing impaired.

Contact. E-mail: wolfgram@wou.edu
Phone: (503) 838-8211 Toll-free number: (877) 877-1593
Fax: (503) 838-8067
David McDonald, Dean of Admissions, Enrollment Management, and Retention, Western Oregon University, 345 North Monmouth Avenue, Monmouth, OR 97361

Willamette University

Salem, Oregon — **CB member**
www.willamette.edu — **CB code: 4954**

- Private 4-year university and liberal arts college affiliated with United Methodist Church
- Residential campus in small city
- 1,813 degree-seeking undergraduates: 1% part-time, 55% women, 2% African American, 7% Asian American, 4% Hispanic American, 1% Native American, 1% international
- 684 degree-seeking graduate students

- 74% of applicants admitted
- SAT or ACT with writing, application essay required
- 74% graduate within 6 years; 26% enter graduate study

General. Founded in 1842. Regionally accredited. Tokyo International University of America sister school located on campus. **Degrees:** 442 bachelor's awarded; master's, first professional offered. **ROTC:** Air Force. **Location:** 45 miles from Portland. **Calendar:** Semester. **Full-time faculty:** 184 total; 10% minority, 38% women. **Part-time faculty:** 117 total; 6% minority, 47% women. **Class size:** 68% < 20, 32% 20-39, less than 1% 40-49. **Special facilities:** Papers and memorabilia of Senator Mark O. Hatfield, botanical garden, Japanese garden, mountain retreat center, rural conference center, museum, science center, performing arts center.

Freshman class profile. 2,790 applied, 2,072 admitted, 444 enrolled.

Mid 50% test scores			
SAT verbal:	570-670	Rank in top quarter:	73%
SAT math:	570-650	Rank in top tenth:	40%
ACT:	25-29	Return as sophomores:	88%
GPA 3.50 or higher:	67%	Out-of-state:	67%
GPA 3.0-3.49:	26%	Live on campus:	95%
GPA 2.0-2.99:	7%	International:	1%

Basis for selection. School record most important, followed by test scores, essay, recommendations, school and community activities, interview. Audition recommended for music, theater programs; portfolio recommended for art program. **Homeschooled:** Recommend submission of accredited transcript from governing agency, if available.

High school preparation. Recommended units include English 4, mathematics 4, social studies 3, science 3 and foreign language 3.

2005-2006 Annual costs. Tuition/fees: $28,412. $440 optional health insurance. Room/board: $7,000. Books/supplies: $1,800.

2005-2006 Financial aid. **Need-based:** 353 full-time freshmen applied for aid; 297 were judged to have need; 297 of these received aid. Average need met was 92%. Average scholarship/grant was $18,666; average loan $3,797. 72% of total undergraduate aid awarded as scholarships/grants, 28% as loans/jobs. **Non-need-based:** Awarded to 715 full-time undergraduates, including 165 freshmen. Scholarships awarded for academics, leadership, minority status, music/drama.

Application procedures. **Admission:** Closing date 2/1 (postmark date). $50 fee, may be waived for applicants with need. Application may be submitted online. Admission notification 4/1. Must reply by May 1 or within 2 week(s) if notified thereafter. **Financial aid:** Closing date 2/1. FAFSA required. CSS PROFILE required of early action applicants. Applicants notified by 4/1; must reply by 5/1 or within 2 week(s) of notification.

Academics. **Special study options:** Accelerated study, combined bachelor's/graduate degree, cooperative education, cross-registration, double major, exchange student, independent study, internships, liberal arts/career combination, semester at sea, student-designed major, study abroad, teacher certification program, urban semester, Washington semester. Interdisciplinary freshman study program, undergraduate research grants, field studies program in ecology in Hawaii, Ecuador, American Southwest, Oregon; 3-2 program, master's degree in management; 3-2 program, bachelor's degree in computer science with Oregon Graduate Institute, University of Oregon; 3-2 program, master's degree in forestry with Duke University. **Credit/placement by examination:** AP, CLEP, IB, institutional tests. 28 credit hours maximum toward bachelor's degree. **Support services:** Reduced course load, study skills assistance, tutoring, writing center.

Majors. **Area/ethnic studies:** American, Japanese, Latin American. **Biology:** General. **Computer sciences:** General. **Conservation:** Environmental science. **English:** English lit, speech/rhetoric. **Foreign languages:** Classics, comparative lit, French, German, Spanish. **History:** General. **Interdisciplinary:** Global studies, science/society. **Liberal arts:** Humanities. **Math:** General. **Parks/recreation:** Exercise sciences. **Philosophy/religion:** Philosophy, religion. **Physical sciences:** Chemistry, physics. **Psychology:** General. **Social sciences:** Anthropology, economics, political science, sociology. **Visual/performing arts:** Art history/conservation, dramatic, music performance, music theory/composition, piano/organ, studio arts, voice/opera.

Most popular majors. Biology 8%, English 6%, foreign language 11%, physical sciences 6%, psychology 7%, social sciences 26%.

Computing on campus. 400 workstations in dormitories, library, computer center, student center. Dormitories wired for high-speed internet access and linked to campus network. Commuter students can connect to campus network. Online course registration, online library, helpline, repair service, student web hosting, wireless network available.

Student life. **Freshman orientation:** Mandatory. 5-day program before start of semester. **Policies:** Freshmen permitted cars on campus. **Housing:** Guaranteed on-campus for freshmen. Coed dorms, apartments, fraternity/sorority housing, substance-free housing available. International studies house, nonsmoking residence hall, quiet study residence hall, substance-free hall available. **Activities:** Bands, choral groups, dance, drama, literary magazine, music ensembles, musical theater, radio station, student government, student newspaper, symphony orchestra, Campus Ambassadors, College Democrats, College Republicans, Freaks And Geeks: WU Alternatives, Non-Traditional Student Association, SHE (strength-health-equality), Angles (Willamette's queer-straight alliance), Willamette International Student Association, Hawaii Club.

Athletics. NCAA. **Intercollegiate:** Baseball M, basketball, cross-country, football (tackle) M, golf, rowing (crew), soccer, softball W, swimming, tennis, track and field, volleyball W. **Intramural:** Badminton, basketball, bowling, cheerleading, fencing, football (non-tackle), lacrosse, racquetball, skiing, soccer, softball, table tennis, tennis, volleyball, water polo, weight lifting. **Team name:** Bearcats.

Student services. Adult student services, alcohol/substance abuse counseling, campus ministries, career counseling, student employment services, financial aid counseling, health services, minority student services, personal counseling, placement for graduates, veterans' counselor, women's services. **Physically disabled:** Services for visually, speech, hearing impaired.

Contact. E-mail: libarts@willamette.edu
Phone: (503) 370-6303 Toll-free number: (877) 542-2787
Fax: (503) 375-5363
Robin Brown, Vice President for Enrollment, Willamette University, 900 State Street, Salem, OR 97301-3922

Pennsylvania

Albright College

Reading, Pennsylvania **CB member**
www.albright.edu **CB code: 2004**

- Private 4-year liberal arts college affiliated with United Methodist Church
- Residential campus in small city
- 2,074 degree-seeking undergraduates: 58% women, 9% African American, 2% Asian American, 4% Hispanic American, 3% international
- 17 degree-seeking graduate students
- 69% of applicants admitted
- SAT or ACT, application essay required
- 57% graduate within 6 years

General. Founded in 1856. Regionally accredited. Flexible curriculum combines liberal arts education with hands-on experiences. Institution emphasizes faculty-student collaboration and has an active undergraduate research program, which also funds summer projects with faculty. **Degrees:** 441 bachelor's awarded; master's offered. **Location:** 50 miles from Philadelphia. **Calendar:** 4-1-4, limited summer session. **Full-time faculty:** 103 total; 82% have terminal degrees, 7% minority, 46% women. **Part-time faculty:** 52 total; 31% have terminal degrees, 2% minority, 54% women. **Class size:** 58% < 20, 37% 20-39, 3% 40-49, 1% 50-99, less than 1% >100. **Special facilities:** Satellite dish for foreign language program, transmission and scanning electron microscopes, Holocaust resource center, center for local government, wellness center, center for cultural ecology, center for Latin American studies.

Freshman class profile. 3,058 applied, 2,125 admitted, 451 enrolled.

Mid 50% test scores		**Return as sophomores:**	76%
SAT verbal:	470-580	**Out-of-state:**	37%
SAT math:	460-570	**Live on campus:**	89%
Rank in top quarter:	48%	**International:**	4%
Rank in top tenth:	23%	**Fraternities:**	3%
End year in good standing:	93%	**Sororities:**	4%

Basis for selection. High school performance (with emphasis on difficulty of curriculum pursued), personal statement, and recommendations most important. Community service, extracurricular activity and test scores considered. Interview recommended.

High school preparation. 16 units required; 20 recommended. Required and recommended units include English 4, mathematics 2-3, social studies 2, history 1-2, science 3-4 (laboratory 1-2), foreign language 2-3 and academic electives 2. Bachelor of science applicants should have 1 additional unit in science and 1 in mathematics. 2 units of laboratory science recommended.

2005-2006 Annual costs. Tuition/fees: $26,032. Room/board: $7,886. Books/supplies: $800. Personal expenses: $1,000.

2005-2006 Financial aid. Need-based: 406 full-time freshmen applied for aid; 365 were judged to have need; 364 of these received aid. Average need met was 78%. Average scholarship/grant was $16,255; average loan $3,948. 68% of total undergraduate aid awarded as scholarships/grants, 32% as loans/jobs. **Non-need-based:** Scholarships awarded for academics, alumni affiliation, art, leadership, minority status, music/drama, religious affiliation.

Application procedures. Admission: Priority date 3/1; no deadline. $25 fee, may be waived for applicants with need. Application may be submitted online. Admission notification on a rolling basis beginning on or about 10/1. Must reply by May 1 or within 2 week(s) if notified thereafter. **Financial aid:** Priority date 3/1; no closing date. FAFSA required. Applicants notified on a rolling basis starting 2/15; must reply by 5/1 or within 2 week(s) of notification.

Academics. Special study options: Accelerated study, combined bachelor's/graduate degree, cross-registration, double major, dual enrollment of high school students, ESL, exchange student, honors, independent study, internships, liberal arts/career combination, student-designed major, study abroad, teacher certification program, urban semester, Washington semester. Interdisciplinary studies, student research. **Credit/placement by examination:** AP, CLEP, IB. 28 credit hours maximum toward bachelor's degree. **Support services:** Learning center, pre-admission summer program, reduced course load, study skills assistance, tutoring, writing center.

Majors. Area/ethnic studies: American, Latin American, women's. **Biology:** General, biochemistry. **Business:** Accounting, business admin, finance, international, marketing. **Communications:** General. **Computer sciences:** General, information systems. **Conservation:** General, environmental science, environmental studies. **Education:** Art, early childhood, elementary, secondary, special. **English:** English lit. **Family/consumer sciences:** Clothing/textiles. **Foreign languages:** French, Spanish. **Health:** Predentistry, premedicine, preveterinary. **History:** General. **Math:** General. **Philosophy/religion:** Philosophy, religion. **Physical sciences:** Chemistry, optics, physics. **Psychology:** General. **Social sciences:** Anthropology, criminology, economics, political science, sociology. **Visual/performing arts:** Dramatic, studio arts.

Most popular majors. Business/marketing 28%, computer/information sciences 7%, psychology 14%, social sciences 15%, visual/performing arts 11%.

Computing on campus. 271 workstations in dormitories, library, computer center, student center. Dormitories wired for high-speed internet access and linked to campus network. Online library, helpline, wireless network available.

Student life. Freshman orientation: Mandatory. Preregistration for classes offered. Held the 4 days prior to start of fall classes. **Housing:** Guaranteed on-campus for all undergraduates. Coed dorms, apartments, substance-free housing available. $100 deposit, deadline 6/1. Honors housing, break housing suite, all freshmen housing, all female floors available. **Activities:** Bands, choral groups, dance, drama, literary magazine, music ensembles, musical theater, radio station, student government, student newspaper, TV station, Newman Association, Hillel, Christian Fellowship, African American society, Asian American society, international students organization, environmental action group, American Association of University Women, human services organization.

Athletics. NCAA. **Intercollegiate:** Badminton W, baseball M, basketball, cheerleading, cross-country, field hockey W, football (tackle) M, golf M, soccer, softball W, swimming, tennis, track and field, volleyball W, wrestling M. **Intramural:** Badminton W, basketball, bowling, football (non-tackle), softball, volleyball. **Team name:** Lions.

Student services. Adult student services, campus ministries, career counseling, student employment services, financial aid counseling, health services, minority student services, personal counseling, women's services. **Physically disabled:** Services for visually, hearing impaired.

Contact. E-mail: admission@albright.edu
Phone: (610) 921-7512 Toll-free number: (800) 252-1856
Fax: (610) 921-7294
Gregory Eichhorn, Vice-President for Enrollment Management and Dean of Admissions, Albright College, 13th & Bern Streets, Reading, PA 19612-5234

Allegheny College

Meadville, Pennsylvania **CB member**
www.allegheny.edu **CB code: 2006**

- Private 4-year liberal arts college affiliated with United Methodist Church
- Residential campus in large town
- 2,016 degree-seeking undergraduates: 53% women, 1% African American, 3% Asian American, 1% Hispanic American, 1% international
- 62% of applicants admitted
- SAT or ACT (ACT writing recommended), application essay required
- 73% graduate within 6 years; 52% enter graduate study

General. Founded in 1815. Regionally accredited. Operational decisions made according to Environmental Guiding Principles. **Degrees:** 381 bachelor's awarded. **Location:** 90 miles from Pittsburgh, 90 miles from Cleveland. **Calendar:** Semester, limited summer session. **Full-time faculty:** 135 total; 95% have terminal degrees, 8% minority, 36% women. **Part-time faculty:** 28 total; 18% have terminal degrees, 4% minority, 50% women. **Class size:** 58% < 20, 36% 20-39, 4% 40-49, 1% 50-99. **Special facilities:** Science complex, video conference facilities, planetarium, observatory, GIS lab, smart classrooms, art galleries, solid-volume glass sculpture grouping, environmental research reserve, 80-acre protected forest.

Freshman class profile. 3,540 applied, 2,206 admitted, 564 enrolled.

Mid 50% test scores			
SAT verbal:	570-660	Rank in top tenth:	45%
SAT math:	570-660	End year in good standing:	99%
ACT:	23-28	Return as sophomores:	90%
GPA 3.50 or higher:	79%	Out-of-state:	38%
GPA 3.0-3.49:	17%	Live on campus:	99%
GPA 2.0-2.99:	4%	International:	1%
Rank in top quarter:	77%	Fraternities:	19%
		Sororities:	27%

Basis for selection. Rigor of high school program most important, followed by high school achievement. Test scores important. Essay, minority status, alumni ties, geography considered. One recommendation from guidance counselor and 1 from teacher required. Interview recommended. **Homeschooled:** Applicants encouraged to schedule campus visit and individual interview with admissions counselor to discuss portfolios. **Learning Disabled:** Recommended interview with Director of Student Support Services.

High school preparation. College-preparatory program required. 16 units required. Required units include English 4, mathematics 3, social studies 3, science 3, foreign language 2 and academic electives 1.

2006-2007 Annual costs. Tuition/fees: $28,300. Room/board: $7,000. Books/supplies: $900. Personal expenses: $800.

2005-2006 Financial aid. Need-based: 478 full-time freshmen applied for aid; 395 were judged to have need; 395 of these received aid. Average need met was 94%. Average scholarship/grant was $15,625; average loan $4,360. 75% of total undergraduate aid awarded as scholarships/grants, 25% as loans/jobs. **Non-need-based:** Awarded to 836 full-time undergraduates, including 255 freshmen. Scholarships awarded for academics, leadership, minority status, state residency.

Application procedures. Admission: Closing date 2/15 (postmark date). $35 fee, may be waived for applicants with need. Application may be submitted online. Admission notification 4/1. Must reply by 5/1. **Financial aid:** Priority date 2/15; no closing date. FAFSA required. Applicants notified on a rolling basis starting 3/1; must reply by 5/1 or within 4 week(s) of notification.

Academics. Experiential learning term, partnerships with Columbia Teachers College, Xavier School of Education, Jefferson Medical College and Drexel College of Medicine. Combined bachelors degree for allied health; accelerated masters degree program with Carnegie Mellon University for public policy and management, arts management, health policy and management, information systems management, information technology. **Special study options:** Combined bachelor's/graduate degree, double major, dual enrollment of high school students, ESL, independent study, internships, student-designed major, study abroad, Washington semester. Preprofessional programs, cooperative program in teacher education, experiential learning terms, marine biology study program. **Credit/placement by examination:** AP, CLEP, IB, institutional tests. 20 credit hours maximum toward bachelor's degree. **Support services:** Learning center, reduced course load, study skills assistance, tutoring, writing center.

Majors. Area/ethnic studies: Women's. **Biology:** General, biochemistry. **Business:** Managerial economics. **Communications:** General, journalism, media studies. **Computer sciences:** Computer science. **Conservation:** Environmental science, environmental studies. **Education:** General. **Engineering:** Software. **English:** Creative writing, English lit, technical writing. **Foreign languages:** French, German, Spanish. **Health:** Predentistry, premedicine, prenursing, prepharmacy, preveterinary. **History:** General. **Interdisciplinary:** Global studies, neuroscience. **Legal studies:** Prelaw. **Math:** General. **Philosophy/religion:** Philosophy, religion. **Physical sciences:** Chemistry, geology, physics. **Psychology:** General. **Social sciences:** Applied economics, economics, international relations, political science. **Visual/performing arts:** Art, art history/conservation, dramatic, music performance, studio arts.

Most popular majors. Biology 13%, English 10%, history 7%, psychology 14%, social sciences 22%, visual/performing arts 6%.

Computing on campus. 311 workstations in dormitories, library, computer center, student center. Dormitories wired for high-speed internet access and linked to campus network. Commuter students can connect to campus network. Online library, helpline, repair service, student web hosting, wireless network available.

Student life. Freshman orientation: Mandatory. Held 4 days before classes begin. **Policies:** Honor code. Freshmen permitted cars on campus. **Housing:** Guaranteed on-campus for all undergraduates. Coed dorms, single-sex dorms, special housing for disabled, apartments, fraternity/sorority housing, substance-free housing available. Special interest housing, theme-based student apartments available. **Activities:** Bands, choral groups, dance, drama, literary magazine, music ensembles, musical theater, radio station, student government, student newspaper, symphony orchestra, TV station, Association for Asian and Asian-American Awareness, Advancement of Black Culture, Union Latina, Habitat for Humanity, Newman Association, Hillel, Christian Outreach, Students for Environmental Action, Alpha Phi Omega, Americorps Bonner Leaders.

Athletics. NCAA. **Intercollegiate:** Baseball M, basketball, cross-country, diving, football (tackle) M, golf, lacrosse W, soccer, softball W, swimming, tennis, track and field, volleyball W. **Intramural:** Basketball, bowling, football (non-tackle), golf, racquetball, soccer, softball, table tennis, tennis, volleyball. **Team name:** Gators.

Student services. Adult student services, alcohol/substance abuse counseling, campus ministries, career counseling, student employment services, financial aid counseling, health services, minority student services, personal counseling, placement for graduates. **Physically disabled:** Services for visually, speech, hearing impaired.

Contact. E-mail: admissions@allegheny.edu
Phone: (814) 332-4351 Toll-free number: (800) 521-5293
Fax: (814) 337-0431
Jennifer Winge, Director of Admissions, Allegheny College, 520 North Main Street, Meadville, PA 16335

Alvernia College

Reading, Pennsylvania — **CB member**
www.alvernia.edu — **CB code: 2431**

- Private 4-year liberal arts college affiliated with Roman Catholic Church
- Residential campus in small city
- 1,881 degree-seeking undergraduates: 20% part-time, 68% women
- 558 degree-seeking graduate students
- 76% of applicants admitted
- SAT or ACT (ACT writing optional) required
- 46% graduate within 6 years

General. Founded in 1958. Regionally accredited. Affiliated with Bernardine Sisters, Third Order of St. Francis. **Degrees:** 382 bachelor's, 9 associate awarded; master's offered. **ROTC:** Army. **Location:** 60 miles from Philadelphia. **Calendar:** Semester, limited summer session. **Full-time faculty:** 74 total; 68% have terminal degrees, 7% minority, 57% women. **Part-time faculty:** 161 total. **Class size:** 58% < 20, 41% 20-39, less than 1% 50-99.

Freshman class profile. 922 applied, 699 admitted, 284 enrolled.

Mid 50% test scores			
SAT verbal:	420-520	Rank in top quarter:	27%
SAT math:	420-530	Rank in top tenth:	8%
GPA 3.50 or higher:	23%	Return as sophomores:	77%
GPA 3.0-3.49:	26%	Out-of-state:	22%
GPA 2.0-2.99:	48%	Live on campus:	72%

Basis for selection. School achievement record, test scores important. Activities, counselor's recommendation, and interview considered. Essay, interview recommended for all. Interview required of nursing, occupational therapy and physical therapist assistant applicants.

2005-2006 Annual costs. Tuition/fees: $19,089. Room/board: $7,299. Books/supplies: $1,200.

2005-2006 Financial aid. Need-based: 269 full-time freshmen applied for aid; 240 were judged to have need; 240 of these received aid. Average need met was 84%. Average scholarship/grant was $6,784; average loan $3,496. **Non-need-based:** Scholarships awarded for academics, alumni affiliation.

Application procedures. Admission: No deadline. $25 fee, may be waived for applicants with need. Admission notification on a rolling basis. Must reply by May 1 or within 2 week(s) if notified thereafter. **Financial aid:** No deadline. FAFSA required. Applicants notified on a rolling basis starting 2/1; must reply within 2 week(s) of notification.

Academics. Special study options: Accelerated study, combined bachelor's/graduate degree, cross-registration, double major, dual enrollment of high school students, ESL, honors, independent study, internships, student-designed major, study abroad, teacher certification program, Washington semester. **Credit/placement by examination:** AP, CLEP, IB, SAT, institutional tests. 30 credit hours maximum toward associate degree, 30 toward bachelor's. Total of 30 credits allowed for all experiential credit, CLEP, life experience, challenge exam. **Support services:** Learning center, reduced course load, study skills assistance, tutoring, writing center.

Majors. **Biology:** General, biochemistry. **Business:** Accounting, business admin, human resources. **Communications:** General. **Computer sciences:** General. **Education:** General, biology, chemistry, early childhood, elementary, English, history, mathematics, physics, science, social studies, special. **Health:** Athletic training, clinical lab science, predentistry, premedicine, preop/surgical nursing, prepharmacy, preveterinary, substance abuse counseling. **History:** General. **Legal studies:** Prelaw. **Liberal arts:** Arts/sciences. **Math:** General. **Philosophy/religion:** Philosophy. **Physical sciences:** Chemistry. **Protective services:** Forensics, law enforcement admin. **Psychology:** General. **Public administration:** Social work. **Social sciences:** Political science.

Most popular majors. Business/marketing 23%, education 12%, health sciences 26%, security/protective services 14%.

Computing on campus. 113 workstations in dormitories, library, computer center. Dormitories wired for high-speed internet access and linked to campus network. Commuter students can connect to campus network. Online library, helpline available.

Student life. **Freshman orientation:** Mandatory. Preregistration for classes offered. Held weekend before classes start. **Policies:** Freshmen permitted cars on campus. **Housing:** Coed dorms, single-sex dorms, special housing for disabled available. Single-sex townhouses available. Single-sex floors in dorms. **Activities:** Choral groups, dance, drama, literary magazine, music ensembles, musical theater, student government, student newspaper.

Athletics. NCAA. **Intercollegiate:** Baseball M, basketball, cross-country, field hockey W, golf M, lacrosse, soccer, softball W, tennis, volleyball W. **Intramural:** Basketball, lacrosse M, skiing, volleyball M. **Team name:** Crusaders.

Student services. Adult student services, campus ministries, career counseling, services for economically disadvantaged, student employment services, financial aid counseling, health services, personal counseling, placement for graduates, veterans' counselor. **Physically disabled:** Services for visually impaired.

Contact. E-mail: admissions@alvernia.edu
Phone: (610) 796-8220 Toll-free number: (888) 258-3764
Fax: (610) 796-8336
Catherine Emery, Dean of Enrollment, Alvernia College, 400 St. Bernardine Street, Reading, PA 19607-1799

Arcadia University

Glenside, Pennsylvania — **CB member**
www.arcadia.edu — **CB code: 2039**

- Private 4-year university affiliated with Presbyterian Church (USA)
- Residential campus in large town
- 1,955 degree-seeking undergraduates: 11% part-time, 72% women
- 1,448 degree-seeking graduate students
- 76% of applicants admitted
- SAT or ACT with writing, application essay required
- 71% graduate within 6 years; 59% enter graduate study

General. Founded in 1853. Regionally accredited. **Degrees:** 381 bachelor's awarded; master's, doctoral offered. **ROTC:** Army. **Location:** 10 miles from Philadelphia. **Calendar:** Semester, limited summer session. **Full-time faculty:** 114 total. **Part-time faculty:** 215 total. **Class size:** 68% < 20, 30% 20-39, 1% 40-49, less than 1% 50-99, less than 1% >100. **Special facilities:** Observatory housing 14-inch Schmidt-Cassegrain telescope with extensive astrophotography capabilities, Grey Towers Castle (National Historic Landmark) used as residence hall.

Freshman class profile. 2,693 applied, 2,058 admitted, 441 enrolled.

Mid 50% test scores			
SAT verbal:	500-620	Rank in top tenth:	32%
SAT math:	490-600	Return as sophomores:	78%
ACT:	21-26	Out-of-state:	43%
Rank in top quarter:	65%	Live on campus:	72%
		International:	2%

Basis for selection. Emphasis placed on academic records, including type of program followed, courses taken, grades earned, class rank. Standardized test scores, counselor/ teacher recommendations, participation in school and community activities important. Character references also considered. Interview recommended for all. Portfolio review required for admission into fine arts department. Auditions required for BFA in acting. **Homeschooled:** Portfolio representing academic record/work and level of achievement for grades 9-12 required.

High school preparation. College-preparatory program required. Recommended units include English 4, mathematics 3, social studies 2, history 2, science 3 (laboratory 3) and foreign language 2. Additional units in foreign language, mathematics, and/or laboratory science are recommended. Math includes algebra II and geometry.

2005-2006 Annual costs. Tuition/fees: $24,270. Room/board: $9,300. Books/supplies: $800.

2005-2006 Financial aid. **Need-based:** Average need met was 82.49%. Average scholarship/grant was $15,216; average loan $4,840. 66% of total undergraduate aid awarded as scholarships/grants, 34% as loans/jobs. **Non-need-based:** Scholarships awarded for academics, alumni affiliation, art, leadership. **Additional information:** Early Financial Aid Estimate Service offered September through January. Students may use this service before applying for admission.

Application procedures. **Admission:** No deadline. $30 fee, may be waived for applicants with need. Application may be submitted online. Admission notification on a rolling basis. Supplementary materials demonstrating student's talents and potential recommended. Students who apply early but do not specify early decision will still receive priority consideration. **Financial aid:** Priority date 3/1; no closing date. FAFSA, institutional form required. Applicants notified on a rolling basis starting 2/15; must reply by 5/1.

Academics. **Special study options:** Combined bachelor's/graduate degree, cooperative education, cross-registration, double major, ESL, honors, independent study, internships, liberal arts/career combination, student-designed major, study abroad, teacher certification program, Washington semester, weekend college. 4-1 special education, 4-2 physician assistant studies, 4-3 physical therapy studies, 3-2 environmental studies, 4-2 international peace and conflict resolution with European Peace University, freshmen in good standing have opportunity to spend spring break in London or Scotland. **Credit/placement by examination:** AP, CLEP, IB, institutional tests. 64 credit hours maximum toward bachelor's degree. **Support services:** Learning center, pre-admission summer program, reduced course load, remedial instruction, study skills assistance, tutoring, writing center.

Majors. **Biology:** General. **Business:** General, accounting, business admin, finance, human resources, international, management information systems, marketing. **Communications:** General. **Computer sciences:** General, programming. **Conservation:** Environmental studies. **Education:** General, art, biology, chemistry, early childhood, elementary, English, mathematics, multi-level teacher, science, secondary, social science, social studies, special. **Engineering:** General. **Foreign languages:** Spanish. **Health:** Art therapy, health care admin, health services admin, medical illustrating. **History:** General. **Interdisciplinary:** Biological/physical sciences. **Legal studies:** General. **Liberal arts:** Arts/sciences. **Math:** General. **Philosophy/religion:** Philosophy. **Physical sciences:** Chemistry. **Psychology:** General. **Social sciences:** International relations, political science, sociology. **Visual/performing arts:** General, acting, art history/conservation, ceramics, commercial/advertising art, dramatic, graphic design, interior design, metal/jewelry, painting, photography, printmaking, studio arts, theater history.

Most popular majors. Biology 7%, business/marketing 15%, communications/journalism 7%, education 15%, psychology 10%, social sciences 9%, visual/performing arts 15%.

Computing on campus. 115 workstations in library, computer center. Dormitories wired for high-speed internet access and linked to campus network. Commuter students can connect to campus network. Online course registration, helpline, repair service, wireless network available.

Student life. **Freshman orientation:** Mandatory. Preregistration for classes offered. **Housing:** Guaranteed on-campus for all undergraduates. Coed dorms, single-sex dorms, special housing for disabled, apartments available. $200 deposit, deadline 5/1. Living and learning community available. **Activities:** Choral groups, dance, drama, literary magazine, music ensembles, musical theater, radio station, student government, student newspaper, TV station, approximately 35 different clubs and organizations.

Athletics. NCAA. **Intercollegiate:** Baseball M, basketball, cross-country, field hockey W, golf, lacrosse W, soccer, softball W, swimming, tennis, volleyball W. **Intramural:** Basketball, field hockey W, football (non-tackle), skiing, soccer, softball, swimming M, tennis, volleyball, weight lifting. **Team name:** Scarlet Knights.

Student services. Adult student services, alcohol/substance abuse counseling, career counseling, services for economically disadvantaged, student employment services, financial aid counseling, health services, minority student services, personal counseling, placement for graduates.

Contact. E-mail: admiss@arcadia.edu
Phone: (215) 572-2910 Toll-free number: (887) 272-2342
Fax: (215) 572-4049
Mark Lapreziosa, Assistant VP of Enrollment Management, Arcadia University, 450 South Easton Road, Glenside, PA 19038-3295

Art Institute of Philadelphia

Philadelphia, Pennsylvania
www.aiph.aii.edu **CB code: 2033**

- For-profit 4-year visual arts college
- Commuter campus in very large city
- 3,374 degree-seeking undergraduates: 28% part-time, 54% women
- Application essay, interview required

General. Founded in 1966. Accredited by ACICS. **Degrees:** 206 bachelor's, 347 associate awarded. **Calendar:** Quarter, extensive summer session. **Full-time faculty:** 99 total. **Part-time faculty:** 117 total. **Special facilities:** Recording studio utilizing Pro-tools software, digital photography laboratory, nonlinear digital editing suites using Avid and Media 100 technology, and full-service chef instructor/student-run restaurant.

Freshman class profile. 2,100 applied, 1,760 admitted, 947 enrolled.

Basis for selection. Open admission. Portfolio recommended.

High school preparation. Background or strong interest in chosen major preferred.

2006-2007 Annual costs. Tuition/fees (projected): $18,195. One-time activities fee of $50 for bachelor's, $35 for associate. Additionally, several programs have quarterly supplies fees that vary. Room only: $7,002.

2005-2006 Financial aid. Need-based: 12% of total undergraduate aid awarded as scholarships/grants, 88% as loans/jobs. **Additional information:** Institute-sponsored scholarships available.

Application procedures. Admission: No deadline. $50 fee. Application may be submitted online. Admission notification on a rolling basis. **Financial aid:** Closing date 5/1. FAFSA, institutional form required. Applicants notified on a rolling basis starting 3/1; must reply within 2 week(s) of notification.

Academics. Academic program designed to simulate working environment, focusing course work on job-related skills. **Special study options:** Independent study, internships. **Credit/placement by examination:** CLEP, IB, SAT, ACT. **Support services:** Learning center, reduced course load, remedial instruction, study skills assistance, tutoring.

Majors. Communications technology: Animation/special effects. **Computer sciences:** Web page design. **Visual/performing arts:** Cinematography, commercial/advertising art, design, industrial design, interior design.

Computing on campus. 507 workstations in dormitories, library, computer center. Dormitories wired for high-speed internet access. Online library, student web hosting available.

Student life. Freshman orientation: Available. **Housing:** Coed dorms, apartments available. **Activities:** Student government.

Student services. Career counseling, student employment services, financial aid counseling, personal counseling, placement for graduates.

Contact. E-mail: aiphadm@aii.edu
Phone: (215) 567-7080 Toll-free number: (800) 275-2474
Fax: (215) 405-6399
Larry McHugh, Director of Admissions, Art Institute of Philadelphia, 1622 Chestnut Street, Philadelphia, PA 19103-5198

Art Institute of Pittsburgh

Pittsburgh, Pennsylvania
www.aip.artinstitutes.edu **CB code: 2029**

- For-profit 4-year visual arts and technical college
- Commuter campus in large city
- 5,892 degree-seeking undergraduates: 49% part-time, 56% women
- Application essay, interview required

General. Founded in 1921. Accredited by ACICS. **Degrees:** 316 bachelor's, 183 associate awarded. **Calendar:** Continuous, extensive summer session. **Full-time faculty:** 122 total; 34% women. **Part-time faculty:** 445 total. **Special facilities:** Photography laboratory, art gallery for students and faculty, traveling exhibits, 24-track recording studio, restaurant.

Freshman class profile.

Out-of-state:	50%	**Live on campus:**	50%

Basis for selection. High school transcript most important. Essay required. Interview required. Limited portfolio required for some programs. **Homeschooled:** Statement describing homeschool structure and mission, transcript of courses and grades, state high school equivalency certificate, letter of recommendation (nonparent) required.

High school preparation. Prefer students with demonstrated interest in chosen major.

2005-2006 Annual costs. Tuition/fees: $17,837. Tuition and fees vary according to date of enrollment; tuition does not increase as long as student remains enrolled continuously. Room only: $5,175. Books/supplies: $1,000.

Application procedures. Admission: No deadline. $50 fee. Application may be submitted online. Admission notification on a rolling basis. **Financial aid:** No deadline. FAFSA, institutional form required. Applicants notified on a rolling basis starting 4/15.

Academics. Special study options: Cross-registration, distance learning, internships. **Credit/placement by examination:** AP, CLEP. **Support services:** Learning center, remedial instruction, tutoring.

Majors. Business: Fashion. **Communications technology:** Animation/special effects. **Computer sciences:** Web page design. **Personal/culinary services:** Chef training, restaurant/catering. **Visual/performing arts:** Cinematography, commercial/advertising art, design, industrial design, interior design, photography.

Computing on campus. 225 workstations in dormitories, library, computer center. Dormitories wired for high-speed internet access. Online course registration, online library, student web hosting, wireless network available.

Student life. Freshman orientation: Mandatory. One-day program held before start of classes. **Housing:** Coed dorms, apartments available. $100 deposit. **Activities:** Drama, film society, student government, student newspaper, Various community relations activities, international student organization, student success task force, student council.

Athletics. Intramural: Basketball M.

Student services. Career counseling, student employment services, financial aid counseling, personal counseling, placement for graduates, veterans' counselor. **Physically disabled:** Services for visually, speech, hearing impaired.

Contact. E-mail: aipadm@aii.edu
Phone: (412) 263-6600 Toll-free number: (800) 275-2470
Fax: (412) 263-6667
Jeffrey Bucklew, Director of Admissions, Art Institute of Pittsburgh, 420 Boulevard of the Allies, Pittsburgh, PA 15219

Art Institute Online

Pittsburgh, Pennsylvania
www.aionline.edu **CB code: 3835**

- For-profit 4-year virtual college
- Large city
- 5,900 undergraduates

General. Accredited by ACCSCT. A division of The Art Institute of Pittsburgh. **Degrees:** 316 bachelor's, 183 associate awarded. **Calendar:** Quarter. **Full-time faculty:** 285 total. **Part-time faculty:** 285 total.

Basis for selection. Must have high school GPA of 2.0 or bachelor's degree or higher. Applicants must submit completed enrollment agreement and $100 enrollment fee within 10 days of application. Applicants not accepted for admission will receive full refund of all fees paid.

Application procedures. Admission: $50 fee. Application may be submitted online.

Academics. Credit/placement by examination: CLEP.

Student life. Freshman orientation: Mandatory. Online student orientation teaches use of online software program and acquaints students with overall classroom environment. Conducted prior to beginning of classes.

Contact. E-mail: aioadm@aii.edu
Phone: (877) 872-8869 Toll-free number: (877) 872-8869
Fax: (412) 995-4320
Attn: Admissions, Art Institute Online, 1400 Penn Avenue, Pittsburgh, PA 15222

Baptist Bible College of Pennsylvania

Clarks Summit, Pennsylvania
www.bbc.edu **CB code: 2036**

- Private 4-year Bible and seminary college affiliated with Baptist faith
- Residential campus in small city
- 697 degree-seeking undergraduates: 4% part-time, 58% women, 1% African American, 1% Asian American, 2% Hispanic American, 2% international
- 185 degree-seeking graduate students
- 77% of applicants admitted
- SAT or ACT (ACT writing optional), application essay required
- 55% graduate within 6 years

General. Founded in 1932. Regionally accredited; also accredited by ABHE. Part of each student's curriculum includes ministry/service experiences in churches or social agencies. **Degrees:** 136 bachelor's, 16 associate awarded; master's, doctoral, first professional offered. **Location:** 7 miles from Scranton, 20 miles from Wilkes Barre. **Calendar:** Semester, limited summer session. **Full-time faculty:** 30 total. **Part-time faculty:** 2 total. **Class size:** 51% < 20, 29% 20-39, 7% 40-49, 11% 50-99, 1% >100.

Freshman class profile. 335 applied, 259 admitted, 200 enrolled.

Mid 50% test scores			
SAT verbal:	510-610	GPA 2.0-2.99:	22%
SAT math:	450-590	End year in good standing:	88%
ACT:	18-26	Return as sophomores:	76%
GPA 3.50 or higher:	48%	Out-of-state:	70%
GPA 3.0-3.49:	25%	Live on campus:	96%

Basis for selection. Academic record, test scores, references/recommendations most important. Audition required, interview recommended for all; portfolio required for music programs.

High school preparation. College-preparatory program recommended.

2006-2007 Annual costs. Tuition/fees: $13,980. Room/board: $5,600. Books/supplies: $600. Personal expenses: $1,144.

2005-2006 Financial aid. Non-need-based: Scholarships awarded for academics, leadership, music/drama, religious affiliation.

Application procedures. Admission: Priority date 5/1; deadline 8/15 (postmark date). $30 fee. Application may be submitted online. Admission notification on a rolling basis. Must reply by May 1 or within 4 week(s) if notified thereafter. **Financial aid:** Closing date 5/1. FAFSA, institutional form required. Applicants notified on a rolling basis starting 4/1.

Academics. Special study options: Combined bachelor's/graduate degree, distance learning, double major, dual enrollment of high school students, independent study, internships, study abroad, teacher certification program. **Credit/placement by examination:** AP, CLEP, IB, SAT, ACT, institutional tests. **Support services:** Reduced course load, remedial instruction, study skills assistance, tutoring, writing center.

Majors. Business: Administrative services. **Communications:** General. **Education:** Early childhood, elementary, multi-level teacher, music, physical, science, secondary, social studies. **Parks/recreation:** Health/fitness. **Theology:** Missionary, preministerial, sacred music, youth ministry.

Most popular majors. Education 26%, family/consumer sciences 6%, theological studies 64%.

Computing on campus. 30 workstations in library, computer center. Dormitories wired for high-speed internet access and linked to campus network. Online library available.

Student life. Freshman orientation: Mandatory. Preregistration for classes offered. Parent and student orientation weekend includes sessions on academics, student life, finances, and interaction with faculty. **Policies:** Religious observance required. **Housing:** Guaranteed on-campus for all undergraduates. Single-sex dorms, special housing for disabled, substance-free housing available. $250 nonrefundable deposit, deadline 5/1. **Activities:** Choral groups, drama, music ensembles, student government, student newspaper, several religious and service groups.

Athletics. NCAA, NCCAA. **Intercollegiate:** Baseball M, basketball, cheerleading W, cross-country, golf M, soccer, softball W, tennis W, track and field, volleyball, wrestling M. **Intramural:** Basketball, soccer, softball M, volleyball.

Student services. Adult student services, alcohol/substance abuse counseling, career counseling, student employment services, financial aid counseling, health services, personal counseling, placement for graduates.

Contact. E-mail: admissions@bbc.edu
Phone: (570) 586-2400 ext. 9271 Toll-free number: (800) 451-7664
Fax: (570) 585-9299
Glenn Amos, Vice President of Enrollment Management, Baptist Bible College of Pennsylvania, 538 Venard Road, Clarks Summit, PA 18411-1297

Bloomsburg University of Pennsylvania

Bloomsburg, Pennsylvania **CB member**
www.bloomu.edu **CB code: 2646**

- Public 4-year university and liberal arts college
- Residential campus in large town
- 7,575 degree-seeking undergraduates: 5% part-time, 60% women, 6% African American, 1% Asian American, 2% Hispanic American, 1% international
- 746 degree-seeking graduate students
- 68% of applicants admitted
- SAT or ACT (ACT writing optional) required
- 63% graduate within 6 years; 15% enter graduate study

General. Founded in 1839. Regionally accredited. **Degrees:** 1,403 bachelor's awarded; master's, doctoral offered. **ROTC:** Army, Air Force. **Location:** 40 miles from Wilkes-Barre, 80 miles from Harrisburg. **Calendar:** Semester, extensive summer session. **Full-time faculty:** 358 total; 80% have terminal degrees, 13% minority, 40% women. **Part-time faculty:** 42 total; 33% have terminal degrees, 50% women. **Class size:** 23% < 20, 65% 20-39, 5% 40-49, 4% 50-99, 3% >100.

Freshman class profile. 8,237 applied, 5,570 admitted, 1,697 enrolled.

Mid 50% test scores		Rank in top quarter:	35%
SAT verbal:	460-550	Rank in top tenth:	9%
SAT math:	470-560	Return as sophomores:	82%
GPA 3.50 or higher:	39%	Out-of-state:	13%
GPA 3.0-3.49:	34%	Live on campus:	89%
GPA 2.0-2.99:	26%		

Basis for selection. School achievement record and class rank most important. School's recommendation considered in borderline cases.

High school preparation. 16 units required; 20 recommended. Required and recommended units include English 4, mathematics 3-4, social studies 2, history 2, science 3-4 (laboratory 1-2), foreign language 2 and academic electives 2.

2005-2006 Annual costs. Tuition/fees: $6,226; $13,586 out-of-state. Room/board: $5,476. Books/supplies: $900. Personal expenses: $2,400.

2005-2006 Financial aid. Need-based: 1,490 full-time freshmen applied for aid; 1,416 were judged to have need; 1,373 of these received aid. Average need met was 65%. Average scholarship/grant was $4,491; average loan $2,479. 45% of total undergraduate aid awarded as scholarships/grants, 55% as loans/jobs. **Non-need-based:** Awarded to 1,414 full-time undergraduates, including 455 freshmen. Scholarships awarded for academics, art, athletics, job skills, leadership, minority status, music/drama, ROTC, state residency.

Application procedures. Admission: Priority date 12/1; no deadline. $30 fee, may be waived for applicants with need. Application may be submitted online. Admission notification on a rolling basis beginning on or about 10/1. Must reply by May 1 or within 2 week(s) if notified thereafter. **Financial aid:** Priority date 3/15; no closing date. FAFSA required. Applicants notified on a rolling basis starting 4/1.

Academics. Special study options: Combined bachelor's/graduate degree, cooperative education, distance learning, double major, honors, independent study, internships, liberal arts/career combination, study abroad, teacher certification program. **Credit/placement by examination:** AP, CLEP, institutional tests. 64 credit hours maximum toward bachelor's degree. **Support services:** Learning center, pre-admission summer program, reduced course load, remedial instruction, study skills assistance, tutoring, writing center.

Majors. Biology: General. **Business:** Accounting, business admin, managerial economics. **Communications:** General, media studies. **Computer sciences:** General, computer science. **Education:** Business, early childhood, elementary, science, social studies, special. **Engineering:** Electrical. **English:** English lit, speech/rhetoric. **Foreign languages:** French, German, Spanish. **Health:** Audiology/speech pathology, clinical lab science, clinical lab technology, medical radiologic technology/radiation therapy, nursing (RN), physics/radiologic health. **History:** General. **Math:** General. **Parks/recreation:** Exercise sciences. **Philosophy/religion:** Philosophy. **Physical sciences:** General, chemistry, geology, physics. **Protective services:** Criminal justice. **Psychology:** General. **Public administration:** Social work. **Social sciences:** Anthropology, economics, geography, political science, sociology. **Visual/performing arts:** Art history/conservation, dramatic, studio arts.

Most popular majors. Business/marketing 19%, education 18%, English 9%, health sciences 7%, social sciences 10%.

Computing on campus. 1,250 workstations in dormitories, library, computer center, student center. Dormitories wired for high-speed internet access and linked to campus network. Helpline, wireless network available.

Student life. **Freshman orientation:** Mandatory, $77 fee. 1-day program in July and 3-day program prior to start of classes. **Policies:** Freshmen permitted cars on campus. **Housing:** Guaranteed on-campus for freshmen. Coed dorms, apartments, substance-free housing available. $100 nonrefundable deposit, deadline 4/1. **Activities:** Bands, choral groups, dance, drama, literary magazine, music ensembles, radio station, student government, student newspaper, symphony orchestra, TV station, Bloomsburg Christian Fellowship, Catholic campus ministry, Hillel, Protestant campus ministry, University Democrats, College Republicans, community government association, Black Cultural Society, Student Organization of Latinos, Habitat for Humanity.

Athletics. NCAA. **Intercollegiate:** Baseball M, basketball, cross-country, field hockey W, football (tackle) M, lacrosse W, soccer, softball W, swimming, tennis, track and field, wrestling M. **Intramural:** Basketball, field hockey W, football (non-tackle) M, racquetball, soccer, softball, tennis, volleyball, wrestling M. **Team name:** Huskies.

Student services. Adult student services, alcohol/substance abuse counseling, campus ministries, career counseling, services for economically disadvantaged, student employment services, financial aid counseling, health services, legal services, minority student services, on-campus daycare, personal counseling, placement for graduates, veterans' counselor, women's services. **Physically disabled:** Services for visually, speech, hearing impaired.

Contact. E-mail: buadmiss@bloomu.edu
Phone: (570) 389-4316 Fax: (570) 389-4741
Christopher Keller, Director of Admissions and Records, Bloomsburg University of Pennsylvania, 104 Student Service Center, Bloomsburg, PA 17815

Bryn Athyn College of the New Church

Bryn Athyn, Pennsylvania
www.brynathyn.edu **CB code: 2002**

- Private 4-year liberal arts college affiliated with General Church of the New Jerusalem (Swedenborgian)
- Residential campus in small town
- 138 degree-seeking undergraduates: 4% part-time, 59% women, 1% Asian American, 1% Hispanic American, 17% international
- 18 degree-seeking graduate students
- 96% of applicants admitted
- SAT or ACT with writing, application essay required

General. Founded in 1876. Regionally accredited. **Degrees:** 20 bachelor's, 17 associate awarded; master's, first professional offered. **Location:** 15 miles from Philadelphia. **Calendar:** Trimester. **Full-time faculty:** 20 total; 70% have terminal degrees, 45% women. **Part-time faculty:** 29 total; 34% have terminal degrees, 38% women. **Class size:** 92% < 20, 8% 20-39. **Special facilities:** Performing arts center, museum, archives.

Freshman class profile. 52 applied, 50 admitted, 45 enrolled.

Mid 50% test scores		**GPA 2.0-2.99:**	34%
SAT verbal:	460-660	**End year in good standing:**	91%
SAT math:	470-610	**Return as sophomores:**	100%
ACT:	22-29	**Out-of-state:**	18%
GPA 3.50 or higher:	53%	**Live on campus:**	69%
GPA 3.0-3.49:	13%	**International:**	9%

Basis for selection. Applicants expected to have interest in the New Church. School achievement record important; test scores considered. TOEFL required of non-native English speakers. Interview recommended; may be required. **Homeschooled:** SAT Subject Tests in literature and mathematics recommended.

High school preparation. 15 units required. Required units include English 4, mathematics 3, science 3 and foreign language 2. 3 units social studies and/or history required.

2005-2006 Annual costs. Tuition/fees: $9,639. Room/board: $5,360. Books/supplies: $700. Personal expenses: $700.

2005-2006 Financial aid. **Need-based:** 30 full-time freshmen applied for aid; 24 were judged to have need; 24 of these received aid. Average need met was 74%. Average scholarship/grant was $6,162; average loan $877. 84% of total undergraduate aid awarded as scholarships/grants, 16% as loans/jobs. **Non-need-based:** Awarded to 22 full-time undergraduates, including 10 freshmen. Scholarships awarded for academics, leadership, religious affiliation.

Application procedures. **Admission:** Closing date 7/1 (receipt date). $30 fee, may be waived for applicants with need. Application may be submitted online. Admission notification on a rolling basis. Must reply by 8/1. **Financial aid:** Closing date 6/1. FAFSA, institutional form required. Applicants notified on a rolling basis starting 4/30; must reply by 9/30.

Academics. **Special study options:** Cooperative education, cross-registration, dual enrollment of high school students, ESL, independent study, internships, student-designed major, study abroad, teacher certification program. **Credit/placement by examination:** AP, CLEP, IB, institutional tests. **Support services:** Remedial instruction, study skills assistance, tutoring, writing center.

Majors. **Biology:** General. **Education:** General, biology, English, history. **English:** English lit. **History:** General. **Philosophy/religion:** Religion.

Most popular majors. Biology 9%, education 15%, English 6%, history 15%, interdisciplinary studies 50%, philosophy/religious studies 6%.

Computing on campus. 55 workstations in dormitories, library, computer center, student center. Dormitories wired for high-speed internet access and linked to campus network. Online library, helpline, repair service, wireless network available.

Student life. **Freshman orientation:** Mandatory. **Policies:** No alcohol on campus, restricted dorm visiting, required chapel attendance. Religious observance required. Freshmen permitted cars on campus. **Housing:** Guaranteed on-campus for all undergraduates. Single-sex dorms available. $150 deposit, deadline 7/15. Shared apartments. **Activities:** Choral groups, drama, student government, student newspaper, international club.

Athletics. **Intercollegiate:** Badminton, ice hockey M, lacrosse, soccer, volleyball W. **Team name:** Blaze.

Student services. Campus ministries, career counseling, student employment services, financial aid counseling, health services, personal counseling.

Contact. E-mail: sean.lawing@brynathyn.edu
Phone: (267) 502-2511 Fax: (267) 502-2658
Sean Lawing, Director of Admissions, Bryn Athyn College of the New Church, P.O. Box 717, Bryn Athyn, PA 19009-0717

Bryn Mawr College

Bryn Mawr, Pennsylvania **CB member**
www.brynmawr.edu **CB code: 2049**

- Private 4-year liberal arts college for women
- Residential campus in very large city
- 1,323 degree-seeking undergraduates: 1% part-time, 97% women, 5% African American, 12% Asian American, 3% Hispanic American, 7% international
- 441 degree-seeking graduate students
- 46% of applicants admitted
- SAT and SAT Subject Tests or ACT (ACT writing optional), application essay required
- 86% graduate within 6 years

General. Founded in 1885. Regionally accredited. Academic exchange with Haverford College, Swarthmore College, and University of Pennsylvania. Extracurricular and social coordination with Haverford. Most examinations self-scheduled. **Degrees:** 320 bachelor's awarded; master's, doctoral offered. **ROTC:** Air Force. **Location:** 11 miles from Philadelphia. **Calendar:** Semester, limited summer session. **Full-time faculty:** 150 total; 97% have terminal degrees, 20% minority, 51% women. **Part-time faculty:** 35 total; 51% have terminal degrees, 69% women. **Class size:** 71% < 20, 21% 20-39, 5% 40-49, 4% 50-99. **Special facilities:** Collections of minerals, archaeological and anthropological artifacts.

Freshman class profile. 1,938 applied, 899 admitted, 355 enrolled.

Mid 50% test scores		Rank in top tenth:	62%
SAT verbal:	620-720	Return as sophomores:	92%
SAT math:	590-680	Out-of-state:	87%
ACT:	27-30	Live on campus:	100%
Rank in top quarter:	87%	International:	6%

Basis for selection. School achievement record, recommendations, essay most important. Test scores, school and community activities, extracurricular achievements important. For those submitting SAT, 2 SAT Subject Tests required. Interview recommended. **Homeschooled:** Statement describing homeschool structure and mission, transcript of courses and grades, state high school equivalency certificate, interview, letter of recommendation (nonparent) required. Interview required, but may be completed with admissions officer or alumna.

High school preparation. 16 units recommended. Required and recommended units include English 4, mathematics 3, social studies 2, history 2, science 2 (laboratory 1), foreign language 3 and academic electives 2.

2006-2007 Annual costs. Tuition/fees (projected): $33,010. Room/board: $10,550. Books/supplies: $1,000. Personal expenses: $1,000.

2005-2006 Financial aid. All financial aid based on need. 252 full-time freshmen applied for aid; 202 were judged to have need; 202 of these received aid. Average need met was 98%. Average scholarship/grant was $24,396; average loan $3,525. 81% of total undergraduate aid awarded as scholarships/grants, 19% as loans/jobs.

Application procedures. Admission: Closing date 1/15 (postmark date). $50 fee, may be waived for applicants with need. Application may be submitted online. Admission notification 4/1. Must reply by 5/1. **Financial aid:** Closing date 2/4. FAFSA, CSS PROFILE required. Applicants notified by 3/23; must reply by 5/1.

Academics. Special study options: Accelerated study, combined bachelor's/graduate degree, cross-registration, double major, dual enrollment of high school students, exchange student, independent study, internships, liberal arts/career combination, student-designed major, study abroad, teacher certification program. 3-2 Program in City and Regional Planning with the University of Pennsylvania. A.B./B.S. 3-2 engineering programs with University of Pennsylvania. **Credit/placement by examination:** AP, CLEP, IB, institutional tests. 32 credit hours maximum toward bachelor's degree. **Support services:** Pre-admission summer program, reduced course load, study skills assistance, tutoring, writing center.

Majors. Architecture: Urban/community planning. **Area/ethnic studies:** African, East Asian. **Biology:** General. **Computer sciences:** Computer science. **Conservation:** General. **Foreign languages:** Ancient Greek, classics, comparative lit, French, German, Italian, Latin, Russian, Spanish. **History:** General. **Math:** General. **Philosophy/religion:** Philosophy, religion. **Physical sciences:** Astronomy, chemistry, geology, physics. **Psychology:** General. **Social sciences:** Anthropology, archaeology, economics, political science, sociology, urban studies. **Visual/performing arts:** Art history/conservation, studio arts.

Most popular majors. Biology 8%, English 12%, foreign language 12%, mathematics 8%, physical sciences 6%, psychology 7%, social sciences 29%, visual/performing arts 7%.

Computing on campus. 200 workstations in dormitories, library, computer center, student center. Dormitories linked to campus network. Commuter students can connect to campus network. Online course registration, online library, helpline, repair service, student web hosting, wireless network available.

Student life. Freshman orientation: Mandatory. Week-long program; students divided into groups of 10-20 students based on residence hall assignments. **Policies:** Self-governing student body, Honor Code: academic and social, Customs and Traditions programs. **Housing:** Guaranteed on-campus for all undergraduates. Coed dorms, apartments, cooperative housing, substance-free housing available. $200 fully refundable deposit, deadline 6/1. Students may live at Haverford. Foreign language houses available to students studying Chinese, French, German, Hebrew, Italian, Russsian or Spanish. Special housing available for non-traditional-aged students. **Activities:** Choral groups, dance, drama, film society, literary magazine, music ensembles, musical theater, radio station, student government, student newspaper, Asian students association, Mujeres, Rainbow Alliance, Muslim students association, Model U.N., Owl Investment Group, Catholic campus ministry, Jewish student union.

Athletics. NCAA. **Intercollegiate:** Badminton W, basketball W, cross-country W, field hockey W, lacrosse W, rowing (crew) W, soccer W, swimming W, tennis W, track and field W, volleyball W. **Intramural:** Tennis W, volleyball W. **Team name:** Owls.

Student services. Adult student services, alcohol/substance abuse counseling, campus ministries, career counseling, student employment services, financial aid counseling, health services, minority student services, personal counseling, placement for graduates, women's services. **Physically disabled:** Services for visually, speech, hearing impaired.

Contact. E-mail: admissions@brynmawr.edu
Phone: (610) 526-5152 Toll-free number: (800) 262-1885
Fax: (610) 526-7471
Jennifer Rickard, Dean of Admissions and Financial Aid, Bryn Mawr College, 101 North Merion Avenue, Bryn Mawr, PA 19010-2899

Bucknell University

Lewisburg, Pennsylvania — **CB member**
www.bucknell.edu — **CB code: 2050**

- Private 4-year university
- Residential campus in small town
- 3,460 degree-seeking undergraduates: 51% women, 3% African American, 7% Asian American, 2% Hispanic American, 3% international
- 88 degree-seeking graduate students
- 34% of applicants admitted
- SAT or ACT with writing, application essay required
- 90% graduate within 6 years; 24% enter graduate study

General. Founded in 1846. Regionally accredited. **Degrees:** 860 bachelor's awarded; master's offered. **ROTC:** Army. **Location:** 195 miles from Philadelphia, 140 miles from Baltimore. **Calendar:** Semester, limited summer session. **Full-time faculty:** 299 total; 97% have terminal degrees, 12% minority, 35% women. **Part-time faculty:** 29 total; 38% have terminal degrees, 55% women. **Class size:** 55% < 20, 40% 20-39, 2% 40-49, 1% 50-99, less than 1% >100. **Special facilities:** Observatory, 63-acre nature preserve, center for performing arts, poetry center, race/gender resource center, greenhouse, outdoor naturalistic primate facility, engineering structural test lab, gas chromatograph/mass spectrometer, nuclear magnetic resonance spectrometer, herbarium, 18-hole golf course, conference center, small business development center.

Freshman class profile. 8,306 applied, 2,820 admitted, 923 enrolled.

Mid 50% test scores		End year in good standing:	95%
SAT verbal:	600-680	Return as sophomores:	95%
SAT math:	630-710	Out-of-state:	76%
ACT:	27-30	Live on campus:	99%
Rank in top quarter:	93%	International:	3%
Rank in top tenth:	68%		

Basis for selection. Emphasis on school achievement. Test scores, recommendations, special talents and abilities, evidence of volunteer work, personal qualities important. If English is not student's first language and student submits SATs with Critical Reading score below 550, TOEFL required. SAT Subject Test in foreign language required for any student planning to enroll in foreign language study. Interview recommended for all; audition required for music program; portfolio recommended for art program. **Homeschooled:** Interview required. Interview, SAT, graded English paper, writing sample (not from English class), program description or certification from homeschooler's accrediting agency or school district, name/address/phone number of homeschool supervisor required.

High school preparation. 16 units required; 20 recommended. Required and recommended units include English 4, mathematics 3-4, social studies 2, history 2, science 2-3, foreign language 2-4 and academic electives 1.

2006-2007 Annual costs. Tuition/fees: $36,002. Room/board: $7,366. Personal expenses: $1,700.

2005-2006 Financial aid. Need-based: 541 full-time freshmen applied for aid; 418 were judged to have need; 418 of these received aid. Average need met was 100%. Average scholarship/grant was $18,400; average loan $4,000. 69% of total undergraduate aid awarded as scholarships/grants, 31% as loans/jobs. **Non-need-based:** Awarded to 74 full-time undergraduates, including 36 freshmen. Scholarships awarded for academics, art, athletics, leadership, music/drama, ROTC.

Application procedures. Admission: Closing date 1/1 (postmark date). $60 fee, may be waived for applicants with need. Application may be submitted online. Admission notification 4/1. Must reply by 5/1. **Financial aid:** Closing date 1/1. FAFSA, CSS PROFILE required. Applicants notified by 4/1; must reply by 5/1.

Academics. **Special study options:** Combined bachelor's/graduate degree, double major, dual enrollment of high school students, honors, independent study, internships, liberal arts/career combination, student-designed major, study abroad, teacher certification program, Washington semester. **Credit/placement by examination:** AP, CLEP, IB, institutional tests. No policy limit on number of credits. Only a few courses offer this option. **Support services:** Study skills assistance, tutoring, writing center.

Majors. **Area/ethnic studies:** East Asian, Latin American, women's. **Biology:** General, cellular/molecular. **Business:** Accounting, business admin. **Computer sciences:** General. **Conservation:** Environmental studies. **Education:** General, early childhood, elementary, evaluation, music, secondary. **Engineering:** Biomedical, chemical, civil, computer, electrical, mechanical. **English:** English lit. **Foreign languages:** Classics, French, German, Russian, Spanish. **History:** General. **Interdisciplinary:** Biopsychology. **Liberal arts:** Humanities. **Math:** General. **Philosophy/religion:** Philosophy, religion. **Physical sciences:** Chemistry, geology, physics. **Psychology:** General. **Social sciences:** Anthropology, economics, geography, international relations, political science, sociology. **Visual/performing arts:** Art, art history/conservation, dramatic, music history, music performance, music theory/composition, studio arts.

Most popular majors. Biology 9%, business/marketing 16%, engineering/engineering technologies 13%, English 6%, psychology 6%, social sciences 24%.

Computing on campus. 568 workstations in dormitories, library, computer center. Dormitories wired for high-speed internet access and linked to campus network. Commuter students can connect to campus network. Helpline, repair service, wireless network available.

Student life. **Freshman orientation:** Mandatory, $50 fee. Preregistration for classes offered. Held 5 days prior to start of classes. **Policies:** All first-year students must sign statement of student responsibility. **Housing:** Guaranteed on-campus for all undergraduates. Coed dorms, single-sex dorms, special housing for disabled, apartments, fraternity/sorority housing, substance-free housing available. Special interest houses, substance-free floors, quiet floors available. 6 residential colleges with themes: arts, humanities, global, environment, social justice, technology and society. **Activities:** Bands, choral groups, dance, drama, film society, literary magazine, music ensembles, opera, radio station, student government, student newspaper, symphony orchestra, Hillel, Fellowship of Christians, Students for Asian Awareness, BISON Volunteers, Chinese culture association, Brothers and Sisters empowered, Japan Society, Catholic campus ministry, Muslim student association, Cumbre.

Athletics. NCAA. **Intercollegiate:** Baseball M, basketball, cross-country, diving, field hockey W, football (tackle) M, golf, lacrosse, rowing (crew) W, soccer, softball W, swimming, tennis, track and field, volleyball W, water polo, wrestling M. **Intramural:** Basketball, bowling, cross-country, football (non-tackle), golf, racquetball, soccer, softball, squash, table tennis, tennis, volleyball, weight lifting M. **Team name:** Bison.

Student services. Alcohol/substance abuse counseling, campus ministries, career counseling, financial aid counseling, health services, minority student services, personal counseling, placement for graduates, women's services. **Physically disabled:** Services for visually, hearing impaired.

Contact. E-mail: admissions@bucknell.edu
Phone: (570) 577-1101 Fax: (570) 577-3538
Mark Davies, Dean of Admissions, Bucknell University, Freas Hall, Lewisburg, PA 17837-9988

Cabrini College

Radnor, Pennsylvania — **CB member**
www.cabrini.edu — **CB code: 2071**

- Private 4-year liberal arts college affiliated with Roman Catholic Church
- Residential campus in large town
- 1,715 degree-seeking undergraduates: 10% part-time, 68% women, 5% African American, 2% Asian American, 2% Hispanic American, 1% international
- 532 degree-seeking graduate students
- 65% of applicants admitted
- SAT or ACT (ACT writing optional) required
- 60% graduate within 6 years; 19% enter graduate study

General. Founded in 1957. Regionally accredited. College sponsored by Missionary Sisters of the Sacred Heart, international religious order serving 6 continents. **Degrees:** 339 bachelor's awarded; master's offered. **ROTC:** Army. **Location:** 18 miles from Philadelphia, 5 miles from King of Prussia. **Calendar:** Semester, extensive summer session. **Full-time faculty:** 65 total; 77% have terminal degrees, 5% minority, 54% women. **Part-time faculty:** 172 total; 23% have terminal degrees, 9% minority, 50% women. **Class size:** 55% < 20, 44% 20-39, 1% 40-49, less than 1% 50-99. **Special facilities:** College operated preschool (off-campus), human performance lab, video studio, graphic design lab and radio station.

Freshman class profile. 2,535 applied, 1,648 admitted, 539 enrolled.

Mid 50% test scores		**Rank in top quarter:**	27%
SAT verbal:	450-550	**Rank in top tenth:**	8%
SAT math:	440-540	**End year in good standing:**	89%
GPA 3.50 or higher:	40%	**Return as sophomores:**	72%
GPA 3.0-3.49:	25%	**Out-of-state:**	43%
GPA 2.0-2.99:	34%	**Live on campus:**	85%

Basis for selection. School achievement record, test scores, academic potential, and personal qualities most important. Special consideration for children of alumni and students with special backgrounds, skills or abilities. Community action required. Non-English-speaking international students may take TOEFL instead of SAT/ACT. Interview recommended for all; portfolio recommended for studio art program. **Homeschooled:** Provide as much external testing data as possible. Standardized test scores given more weight for homeschooled students.

High school preparation. 18 units required; 21 recommended. Required and recommended units include English 4, mathematics 3-4, social studies 3, history 3, science 3, foreign language 2 and academic electives 2. 2 arts and humanities also recommended. Additional mathematics and science units recommended for science students.

2005-2006 Annual costs. Tuition/fees: $24,000. Room/board: $9,340. Books/supplies: $900. Personal expenses: $1,000.

2005-2006 Financial aid. **Need-based:** 482 full-time freshmen applied for aid; 416 were judged to have need; 416 of these received aid. Average need met was 88%. Average scholarship/grant was $5,065; average loan $2,932. 57% of total undergraduate aid awarded as scholarships/grants, 43% as loans/jobs. **Non-need-based:** Awarded to 1,213 full-time undergraduates, including 465 freshmen. Scholarships awarded for academics, alumni affiliation.

Application procedures. **Admission:** Priority date 5/1; no deadline. $35 fee, may be waived for applicants with need. Application may be submitted online. Admission notification on a rolling basis beginning on or about 10/1. Recent documentation for students with learning disabilities required for support services. **Financial aid:** Closing date 4/1. FAFSA required. Applicants notified on a rolling basis starting 3/1.

Academics. Education fieldwork opportunities provided to education majors from sophomore to senior year. Students participate in community service. Internship or co-op programs offered in all majors. **Special study options:** Accelerated study, combined bachelor's/graduate degree, cooperative education, cross-registration, distance learning, double major, exchange student, honors, independent study, internships, liberal arts/career combination, student-designed major, study abroad, teacher certification program, Washington semester. Exchange programs with Eastern University, Rosemont College, Valley Forge Military College; cross-registration with Southeastern Pennsylvania Consortium for Higher Education (8-member consortium of private colleges/universities). **Credit/placement by examination:** AP, CLEP, IB, SAT, institutional tests. 30 credit hours maximum toward bachelor's degree. DANTES. **Support services:** Learning center, reduced course load, remedial instruction, study skills assistance, tutoring, writing center.

Majors. **Area/ethnic studies:** American. **Biology:** General, biotechnology. **Business:** Accounting, business admin, finance, human resources, management information systems, marketing, organizational behavior. **Communications:** General. **Computer sciences:** General, webmaster. **Education:** General, early childhood, elementary, special. **English:** English lit, technical writing. **Foreign languages:** French, Spanish. **Health:** Clinical lab science, premedicine. **History:** General. **Liberal arts:** Arts/sciences. **Math:** General. **Parks/recreation:** Exercise sciences. **Philosophy/religion:** Philosophy, religion. **Physical sciences:** Chemistry. **Psychology:** General. **Public administration:** Social work. **Social sciences:** Political science, sociology. **Visual/performing arts:** Graphic design, studio arts.

Most popular majors. Business/marketing 32%, communications/journalism 13%, education 20%, visual/performing arts 6%.

Computing on campus. 359 workstations in dormitories, library, computer center. Dormitories wired for high-speed internet access and linked to campus network. Online course registration, online library, helpline, student web hosting, wireless network available.

Student life. **Freshman orientation:** Mandatory, $210 fee. Preregistration for classes offered. 3-day program prior to the beginning of the fall semester. **Housing:** Coed dorms, single-sex dorms, special housing for disabled, apartments available. $350 fully refundable deposit, deadline 5/1. Special interest housing options designated for intensified study, honors, Hispanic culture and community service. **Activities:** Choral groups, dance, drama, literary magazine, music ensembles, musical theater, radio station, student government, student newspaper, TV station, Ethnic Student Alliance, campus ministry, Outreach to the Homeless, Respect Life, international club, Amnesty International, Latinos and Friends, Student Ambassadors, Cavalier Pride.

Athletics. NCAA. **Intercollegiate:** Basketball, cross-country, field hockey W, golf M, lacrosse, soccer, softball W, swimming W, tennis, track and field, volleyball W. **Intramural:** Badminton, basketball, football (non-tackle), football (tackle), lacrosse, racquetball, rugby, soccer, softball, squash, swimming, tennis, volleyball, water polo. **Team name:** Cavaliers.

Student services. Adult student services, alcohol/substance abuse counseling, campus ministries, career counseling, student employment services, financial aid counseling, health services, minority student services, personal counseling, placement for graduates. **Physically disabled:** Services for visually, hearing impaired.

Contact. E-mail: admit@cabrini.edu
Phone: (610) 902-8552 Toll-free number: (800) 848-1003
Fax: (610) 902-8508
Mark Osborn, Vice President for Enrollment Management, Cabrini College, 610 King of Prussia Road, Radnor, PA 19087-3698

California University of Pennsylvania

California, Pennsylvania **CB member**
www.cup.edu **CB code: 2647**

- Public 4-year university
- Commuter campus in small town
- 5,827 degree-seeking undergraduates: 10% part-time, 52% women
- 1,156 degree-seeking graduate students
- 78% of applicants admitted
- SAT required
- 50% graduate within 6 years; 14% enter graduate study

General. Founded in 1852. Regionally accredited. **Degrees:** 983 bachelor's, 47 associate awarded; master's offered. **ROTC:** Army. **Location:** 45 miles from Pittsburgh. **Calendar:** Semester, limited summer session. **Full-time faculty:** 289 total; 63% have terminal degrees, 12% minority, 42% women. **Part-time faculty:** 95 total; 6% minority, 42% women. **Class size:** 35% < 20, 46% 20-39, 9% 40-49, 11% 50-99. **Special facilities:** Fine arts museum.

Freshman class profile. 3,385 applied, 2,633 admitted, 1,259 enrolled.

Mid 50% test scores		**Rank in top quarter:**	23%
SAT verbal:	450-530	**Rank in top tenth:**	6%
SAT math:	440-530	**End year in good standing:**	75%
ACT:	17-21	**Return as sophomores:**	75%
GPA 3.50 or higher:	16%	**Out-of-state:**	4%
GPA 3.0-3.49:	31%	**Live on campus:**	62%
GPA 2.0-2.99:	52%	**International:**	1%

Basis for selection. School achievement record, test scores, activities, recommendations, interview considered. Essay recommended. **Homeschooled:** Transcript of courses and grades required.

High school preparation. 19 units required; 21 recommended. Required and recommended units include English 4, mathematics 3, social studies 2, history 2, science 1 (laboratory 1), foreign language 2 and academic electives 6.

2005-2006 Annual costs. Tuition/fees: $6,491; $8,945 out-of-state. Room/board: $7,908. Books/supplies: $650. Personal expenses: $1,242.

2004-2005 Financial aid. **Need-based:** 953 full-time freshmen applied for aid; 773 were judged to have need; 751 of these received aid. Average scholarship/grant was $3,794; average loan $2,602. 46% of total undergraduate aid awarded as scholarships/grants, 54% as loans/jobs. **Non-need-based:** Awarded to 819 full-time undergraduates, including 221 freshmen. Scholarships awarded for academics, athletics, minority status.

Application procedures. **Admission:** Priority date 5/1; no deadline. $25 fee, may be waived for applicants with need. Application may be submitted online. Admission notification on a rolling basis. **Financial aid:** Priority date 5/1; no closing date. FAFSA required. Applicants notified on a rolling basis starting 4/1; must reply within 3 week(s) of notification.

Academics. **Special study options:** Accelerated study, cooperative education, distance learning, double major, dual enrollment of high school students, exchange student, honors, independent study, internships, liberal arts/career combination, student-designed major, study abroad, teacher certification program, weekend college. **Credit/placement by examination:** AP, CLEP, SAT, institutional tests. **Support services:** Learning center, reduced course load, remedial instruction, study skills assistance, tutoring, writing center.

Honors college/program. Minimum 1100 SAT (exclusive of Writing), 3.0 GPA, letter of recommendation required. Admitted students work with adviser and dean to design course of study.

Majors. **Biology:** General. **Business:** Accounting, business admin. **Communications:** General. **Computer sciences:** General. **Conservation:** Environmental science. **Education:** General, elementary, kindergarten/preschool, special. **Engineering technology:** General, computer, electrical. **English:** English lit. **Foreign languages:** General, French, German, Russian, Spanish. **Health:** Athletic training, clinical lab technology, communication disorders, nursing (RN). **History:** General. **Interdisciplinary:** Gerontology. **Liberal arts:** Arts/sciences. **Math:** General. **Parks/recreation:** Facilities management, sports admin. **Philosophy/religion:** Philosophy. **Physical sciences:** General, chemistry, geology, physics. **Protective services:** Criminal justice. **Psychology:** General. **Public administration:** Social work. **Social sciences:** General, geography, political science. **Visual/performing arts:** Art, commercial/advertising art, dramatic, graphic design.

Most popular majors. Business/marketing 12%, education 20%, engineering/engineering technologies 7%, health sciences 7%, psychology 6%, security/protective services 8%.

Computing on campus. 1,220 workstations in dormitories, library, computer center, student center. Dormitories wired for high-speed internet access and linked to campus network. Commuter students can connect to campus network. Online course registration, online library, helpline available.

Student life. **Freshman orientation:** Available. Preregistration for classes offered. 1-day session during either July or August. **Policies:** Freshman students under 21 and not commuting from parental home required to live in dormitory. Freshmen permitted cars on campus. **Housing:** Coed dorms, single-sex dorms, apartments, fraternity/sorority housing, substance-free housing available. $235 partly refundable deposit. **Activities:** Bands, choral groups, drama, literary magazine, music ensembles, musical theater, radio station, student government, student newspaper, symphony orchestra, TV station.

Athletics. NCAA. **Intercollegiate:** Baseball M, basketball, cheerleading, cross-country, football (tackle) M, golf, rugby, soccer, softball, swimming W, tennis W, track and field, volleyball. **Intramural:** Baseball M, basketball, cheerleading, cross-country, football (tackle) M, golf, ice hockey, racquetball, soccer, softball W, swimming W, tennis W, track and field, volleyball. **Team name:** Vulcans.

Student services. Adult student services, alcohol/substance abuse counseling, campus ministries, career counseling, services for economically disadvantaged, student employment services, financial aid counseling, health services, legal services, minority student services, personal counseling, placement for graduates, veterans' counselor, women's services. **Physically disabled:** Services for visually, speech, hearing impaired.

Contact. E-mail: inquiry@cup.edu
Phone: (724) 938-4404 Fax: (724) 938-4564
William Edmonds, Dean of Admissions, California University of Pennsylvania, 250 University Avenue, California, PA 15419-1394

Carlow University

Pittsburgh, Pennsylvania
www.carlow.edu **CB code: 2421**

- Private 4-year liberal arts college for women affiliated with Roman Catholic Church
- Commuter campus in large city
- 1,602 degree-seeking undergraduates: 27% part-time, 94% women
- 488 degree-seeking graduate students
- 64% of applicants admitted
- SAT or ACT with writing required
- 34% graduate within 6 years; 16% enter graduate study

General. Founded in 1929. Regionally accredited. Sponsored by Sisters of Mercy. **Degrees:** 286 bachelor's awarded; master's offered. **ROTC:** Army, Navy, Air Force. **Location:** 3 miles from downtown. **Calendar:** Semester, limited summer session. **Full-time faculty:** 79 total; 75% have terminal degrees, 6% minority, 72% women. **Part-time faculty:** 154 total; 27% have terminal degrees, 7% minority, 67% women. **Class size:** 84% < 20, 16% 20-39, less than 1% 50-99. **Special facilities:** On-campus preschool and elementary laboratory school, hall of science and technology featuring research labs, greenhouse, darkroom and biochamber, children's science learning lab, theater, international poetry forum archives.

Freshman class profile. 1,076 applied, 684 admitted, 284 enrolled.

Mid 50% test scores			
SAT verbal:	470-570	Rank in top quarter:	43%
SAT math:	450-540	Rank in top tenth:	16%
ACT:	19-25	End year in good standing:	71%
GPA 3.50 or higher:	43%	Return as sophomores:	69%
GPA 3.0-3.49:	38%	Out-of-state:	4%
GPA 2.0-2.99:	19%	Live on campus:	64%

Basis for selection. Secondary school achievement record including quality of academic program and course grades of primary importance. Test scores important. 3.0 GPA and rank in upper two-fifths of class preferred. International students must take TOEFL and ACT or SAT exams. Essay, interview recommended for all, and in some cases, required. Portfolio recommended for all art programs. **Homeschooled:** Submit academic transcripts, evaluation from individual evaluator, personal statement, scores from SAT or ACT. Personal interview and portfolio from most recent year highly recommended. **Learning Disabled:** Contact Disabilities Services Coordinator separately from admissions process.

High school preparation. 18 units required. Required units include English 4, mathematics 3, science 3 and academic electives 4. 4 arts and humanities also required. Applicants to professional nursing programs must have completed 4 units of English, 3 units of social studies, 2 units of mathematics (1 must be algebra) and 2 units of laboratory science (1 must be chemistry).

2005-2006 Annual costs. Tuition/fees: $17,450. Room/board: $6,870. Books/supplies: $700. Personal expenses: $1,000.

2005-2006 Financial aid. Need-based: Average scholarship/grant was $7,430; average loan $3,113. 57% of total undergraduate aid awarded as scholarships/grants, 43% as loans/jobs. **Non-need-based:** Scholarships awarded for academics, athletics, leadership, religious affiliation.

Application procedures. Admission: Priority date 2/15; deadline 7/1. $20 fee, may be waived for applicants with need. Application may be submitted online. Admission notification on a rolling basis beginning on or about 7/1. Must reply by May 1 or within 2 week(s) if notified thereafter. **Financial aid:** Priority date 4/1; no closing date. FAFSA required. Applicants notified on a rolling basis starting 3/1; must reply within 2 week(s) of notification.

Academics. Special study options: Accelerated study, combined bachelor's/graduate degree, cooperative education, cross-registration, distance learning, double major, ESL, honors, independent study, internships, liberal arts/career combination, student-designed major, study abroad, teacher certification program, weekend college. 3-2 programs: chemistry/chemical engineering and mathematics/engineering with Carnegie Mellon, biology/environmental science and management with Duquesne (BA from Carlow, MS from Duquesne), biology/engineering with Carnegie Mellon University, programs with Duquesne University in athletic training (2-2), occupational therapy (2-3), physical therapy (3-3), and physician assistant (2-3), First Year Experience for freshmen, graduate certificates and minors in nursing, social sciences, education, accounting. **Credit/placement by examination:** AP, CLEP, IB, institutional tests. 30 credit hours maximum toward bachelor's degree. **Support services:** Learning center, reduced course load, remedial instruction, study skills assistance, tutoring.

Honors college/program. 3.5 high school GPA, 1100 SAT (exclusive of Writing), top 15% of high school class. 27 freshmen admitted, 15 enrolled.

Majors. Biology: General. **Business:** General, accounting, business admin, communications, human resources, international, management information systems, nonprofit/public. **Communications:** General. **Computer sciences:** Computer science, information systems. **Conservation:** Environmental science. **Education:** Art, early childhood, elementary, social studies, special. **English:** Creative writing, English lit, technical writing. **Foreign languages:** Spanish. **Health:** Athletic training, nursing (RN), physician assistant. **History:** General. **Liberal arts:** Arts/sciences. **Math:** General. **Philosophy/religion:** Philosophy. **Physical sciences:** Chemistry. **Psychology:** General. **Public administration:** Policy analysis, social work. **Social sciences:** General, political science, sociology. **Theology:** Theology. **Visual/performing arts:** Art, art history/conservation, commercial/advertising art, photography.

Most popular majors. Biology 6%, business/marketing 17%, education 21%, English 6%, health sciences 23%, liberal arts 6%, psychology 7%.

Computing on campus. 250 workstations in dormitories, library, computer center, student center. Dormitories wired for high-speed internet access and linked to campus network. Commuter students can connect to campus network. Online course registration, online library, helpline, student web hosting, wireless network available.

Student life. Freshman orientation: Mandatory. Preregistration for classes offered. 2 days prior to fall and spring semesters, providing new students with various seminars and team-building seminars, and social activities with other students and members of the faculty, staff and administration. **Housing:** $100 fully refundable deposit. **Activities:** Choral groups, drama, literary magazine, student government, student newspaper, community outreach office, Alpha Phi Omega, Carlow Against Drunk Driving, social work club, international students association, United Black Students, Alternative Spring Break, Mercy Neighborhood Ministry.

Athletics. NAIA. **Intercollegiate:** Basketball W, soccer W, softball W, tennis W, volleyball W. **Team name:** The Celtics.

Student services. Adult student services, alcohol/substance abuse counseling, campus ministries, career counseling, student employment services, financial aid counseling, health services, minority student services, on-campus daycare, personal counseling, placement for graduates, women's services. **Physically disabled:** Services for visually, speech, hearing impaired.

Contact. E-mail: admissions@carlow.edu
Phone: (412) 578-6059 Toll-free number: (800) 333-2275
Fax: (412) 578-6668
Christine Bell, Director of Admissions, Carlow University, 3333 Fifth Avenue, Pittsburgh, PA 15213-3165

Carnegie Mellon University

Pittsburgh, Pennsylvania **CB member**
www.cmu.edu **CB code: 2074**

- Private 4-year university
- Residential campus in large city
- 5,494 degree-seeking undergraduates: 2% part-time, 40% women, 5% African American, 24% Asian American, 5% Hispanic American, 12% international
- 4,394 degree-seeking graduate students
- 39% of applicants admitted
- SAT or ACT with writing, application essay required
- 86% graduate within 6 years; 41% enter graduate study

General. Founded in 1900. Regionally accredited. **Degrees:** 1,278 bachelor's awarded; master's, doctoral offered. **ROTC:** Army, Navy, Air Force. **Calendar:** Semester, limited summer session. **Full-time faculty:** 822 total; 98% have terminal degrees, 16% minority, 25% women. **Part-time faculty:** 173 total; 98% have terminal degrees, 8% minority, 43% women. **Class size:** 66% < 20, 21% 20-39, 3% 40-49, 6% 50-99, 3% >100. **Special facilities:** Botanical institute, art galleries, rare books collection, recording studios, design studios, photo shoot studio, music halls, theaters, radio station.

Freshman class profile. 15,777 applied, 6,135 admitted, 1,409 enrolled.

Mid 50% test scores			
SAT verbal:	610-710	Rank in top quarter:	94%
SAT math:	680-760	Rank in top tenth:	71%
ACT:	28-32	Return as sophomores:	94%
GPA 3.50 or higher:	67%	Out-of-state:	70%
GPA 3.0-3.49:	29%	Live on campus:	99%
GPA 2.0-2.99:	3%	International:	11%

Basis for selection. Academic and artistic potential; standardized tests; activities, jobs and other interests; interest in Carnegie Mellon; other personalized information. Deadline for fine arts applicants is December 1. SAT Subject Test requirements vary by college. SAT Subject Test scores not required for drama, design, art, or music school applicants. Interview recommended for all; audition required for drama, music programs; portfolio required for art, design programs. **Homeschooled:** Submit syllabus/course descriptions of work done; transcript of grades/evaluations; recommendation from counselor, representative of state board of education, homeschool association, or other person of authority.

High school preparation. Required and recommended units include English 4, mathematics 4, science 3 (laboratory 3), foreign language 2 and academic electives 3-4.

2006-2007 Annual costs. Tuition/fees (projected): $34,578. Room/board: $9,280.

2005-2006 Financial aid. Need-based: 969 full-time freshmen applied for aid; 755 were judged to have need; 752 of these received aid. Average need met was 80%. Average scholarship/grant was $17,288; average loan $3,470. 66% of total undergraduate aid awarded as scholarships/grants, 34%

as loans/jobs. **Non-need-based:** Awarded to 1,768 full-time undergraduates, including 436 freshmen. Scholarships awarded for academics, art, leadership, minority status, music/drama, state residency. **Additional information:** Early need analysis offered; merit awards available. Students notified within week to 10 days of receipt of financial aid application.

Application procedures. Admission: Closing date 1/1 (postmark date). $60 fee, may be waived for applicants with need. Application may be submitted online. Admission notification 4/15. Must reply by 5/1. Early decision deadline for fine arts applicants 11/1. Regular application deadline for fine arts 12/1. **Financial aid:** Priority date 2/15, closing date 5/1. FAFSA, institutional form required. Applicants notified by 3/15.

Academics. Special study options: Combined bachelor's/graduate degree, cooperative education, cross-registration, distance learning, double major, dual enrollment of high school students, exchange student, independent study, internships, liberal arts/career combination, student-designed major, study abroad, teacher certification program, Washington semester. **Credit/placement by examination:** AP, CLEP, IB, institutional tests. **Support services:** Learning center, pre-admission summer program, study skills assistance, tutoring, writing center.

Majors. Architecture: Architecture, history/criticism, technology. **Area/ethnic studies:** European, Latin American, Russian/Slavic. **Biology:** General, biophysics. **Business:** Business admin, managerial economics. **Computer sciences:** Computer science, information systems. **Conservation:** Management/policy. **Education:** ESL. **Engineering:** Biomedical, chemical, civil, materials science, mechanical, operations research. **English:** Creative writing, English lit, technical writing. **Foreign languages:** General, Chinese, French, German, Japanese, Spanish. **History:** European. **Interdisciplinary:** Behavioral sciences, biopsychology, cognitive science, science/society, systems science. **Liberal arts:** Arts/sciences. **Math:** Applied, computational, probability, statistics. **Philosophy/religion:** Ethics, logic, philosophy. **Physical sciences:** Astrophysics, chemical physics, chemistry, physics. **Psychology:** General. **Public administration:** Policy analysis. **Social sciences:** Economics, international relations, political science. **Visual/performing arts:** Art, dramatic, industrial design, music performance, music theory/composition, piano/organ, stringed instruments, voice/opera.

Most popular majors. Business/marketing 12%, computer/information sciences 11%, engineering/engineering technologies 26%, interdisciplinary studies 7%, visual/performing arts 11%.

Computing on campus. 388 workstations in dormitories, library. Dormitories wired for high-speed internet access and linked to campus network. Commuter students can connect to campus network. Online course registration, online library, helpline, repair service, student web hosting, wireless network available.

Student life. Freshman orientation: Mandatory, $190 fee. Week-long program held one week before start of classes. **Policies:** Freshmen required to live on campus. Freshmen permitted cars on campus. **Housing:** Guaranteed on-campus for freshmen. Coed dorms, single-sex dorms, special housing for disabled, apartments, fraternity/sorority housing available. $500 nonrefundable deposit, deadline 5/1. Special interest group housing available. **Activities:** Bands, choral groups, dance, drama, film society, literary magazine, music ensembles, musical theater, radio station, student government, student newspaper, symphony orchestra, TV station, Alpha Phi Omega, Hillel, Christian student organizations, minority women's club, service clubs, international student organizations, National Society of Black Engineers, Society of Women Engineers, Phi Beta Kappa, fraternities and sororities.

Athletics. NCAA. **Intercollegiate:** Basketball, cross-country, diving, football (tackle) M, golf M, soccer, swimming, tennis, track and field, volleyball W. **Intramural:** Badminton, basketball, bowling, cross-country, fencing, football (non-tackle), golf, racquetball, soccer, softball, squash, swimming, table tennis, tennis, track and field, volleyball, water polo. **Team name:** Tartans.

Student services. Alcohol/substance abuse counseling, campus ministries, career counseling, student employment services, financial aid counseling, health services, on-campus daycare, personal counseling, placement for graduates, women's services. **Physically disabled:** Services for visually, speech, hearing impaired. **Learning disabled:** Comprehensive services available.

Contact. E-mail: undergraduate-admissions@andrew.cmu.edu
Phone: (412) 268-2082 Fax: (412) 268-7838
Michael Steidel, Director of Admissions, Carnegie Mellon University, 5000 Forbes Avenue, Pittsburgh, PA 15213-3890

Cedar Crest College

Allentown, Pennsylvania — **CB member**
www.cedarcrest.edu — **CB code: 2079**

- Private 4-year liberal arts college for women
- Residential campus in small city
- 1,820 degree-seeking undergraduates: 48% part-time, 95% women, 6% African American, 3% Asian American, 6% Hispanic American
- 85 degree-seeking graduate students
- 66% of applicants admitted
- SAT or ACT (ACT writing optional) required

General. Founded in 1867. Regionally accredited. Men admitted to evening and weekend classes and daytime programs in nursing and nuclear medicine. **Degrees:** 326 bachelor's awarded; master's offered. **ROTC:** Army. **Location:** 55 miles from Philadelphia, 100 miles from New York City. **Calendar:** Semester, extensive summer session. **Full-time faculty:** 80 total; 70% have terminal degrees, 2% minority, 60% women. **Part-time faculty:** 77 total; 23% have terminal degrees, 5% minority, 75% women. **Class size:** 74% < 20, 21% 20-39, 2% 40-49, 3% 50-99, less than 1% >100. **Special facilities:** Wildlife sanctuary, outdoor Greek theater, arboretum, sculpture garden, aquatic center.

Freshman class profile. 1,444 applied, 955 admitted, 204 enrolled.

Mid 50% test scores		**GPA 2.0-2.99:**	36%
SAT verbal:	480-600	**Rank in top quarter:**	49%
SAT math:	460-570	**Rank in top tenth:**	21%
ACT:	22-27	**Return as sophomores:**	67%
GPA 3.50 or higher:	29%	**Out-of-state:**	42%
GPA 3.0-3.49:	34%	**Live on campus:**	77%

Basis for selection. Secondary school curriculum and grades most important. Test scores important. Special talents, potential for academic and personal growth considered. Interview and essay recommended for all.

High school preparation. 16 units required. Required and recommended units include English 4, mathematics 3, social studies 3, science 2 (laboratory 2), foreign language 2 and academic electives 3. Special natural science requirements for nuclear medicine and nursing.

2005-2006 Annual costs. Tuition/fees: $22,712. Fee of $300 required of resident students. Part-time evening/weekend per credit hour charge $339. Room/board: $7,903. Books/supplies: $1,000. Personal expenses: $300.

2005-2006 Financial aid. Need-based: 197 full-time freshmen applied for aid; 171 were judged to have need; 171 of these received aid. Average need met was 76%. Average scholarship/grant was $13,349; average loan $3,391. **Non-need-based:** Awarded to 180 full-time undergraduates, including 48 freshmen. Scholarships awarded for academics, alumni affiliation, art, leadership, music/drama.

Application procedures. Admission: No deadline. $30 fee, may be waived for applicants with need. Application may be submitted online. Admission notification on a rolling basis beginning on or about 8/2. Must reply by May 1 or within 2 week(s) if notified thereafter. **Financial aid:** No deadline. FAFSA, institutional form required. Applicants notified on a rolling basis starting 11/1; must reply by 5/1 or within 3 week(s) of notification.

Academics. Special study options: Accelerated study, combined bachelor's/graduate degree, cross-registration, distance learning, double major, dual enrollment of high school students, ESL, honors, independent study, internships, liberal arts/career combination, student-designed major, study abroad, teacher certification program, Washington semester, weekend college. **Credit/placement by examination:** AP, CLEP, IB, institutional tests. 18 credit hours maximum toward bachelor's degree. **Support services:** Reduced course load, remedial instruction, study skills assistance, tutoring, writing center.

Majors. Biology: General, biochemistry, conservation, genetics, human/medical genetics. **Business:** Accounting, business admin. **Communications:** General. **Computer sciences:** General, computer science, information systems. **Education:** Elementary, middle, science, secondary, special. **Engineering:** Biomedical. **Family/consumer sciences:** Food/nutrition. **Foreign languages:** Spanish. **Health:** Art therapy, dance therapy, nuclear medical technology. **History:** General. **Interdisciplinary:** Neuroscience. **Liberal arts:** Arts/sciences. **Math:** General. **Physical sciences:** Chemistry. **Psychology:** General. **Public administration:** Social work. **Social sciences:** Political science, sociology. **Visual/performing arts:** General, art, dance, dramatic, studio arts.

Most popular majors. Biology 14%, business/marketing 9%, education 6%, health sciences 22%, psychology 15%, visual/performing arts 6%.

Computing on campus. 257 workstations in dormitories, library, computer center, student center. Dormitories wired for high-speed internet access and linked to campus network. Commuter students can connect to campus network. Online library, helpline, repair service, student web hosting available.

Student life. Freshman orientation: Available. Preregistration for classes offered. 5-day academic and social program in August mandatory. 2-day academic testing and advising program in June suggested. **Policies:** Drinking under age 21 prohibited; honor philosophy exists. Freshmen permitted cars on campus. **Housing:** Special housing for disabled available. **Activities:** Choral groups, dance, drama, literary magazine, music ensembles, musical theater, radio station, student government, student newspaper, TV station, Sister Inc., Hillel, Crest Christian Fellowship, political society, SADD, Alpha Phi Omega, Islamic Awareness, International Student Organization, Amnesty International.

Athletics. NCAA. **Intercollegiate:** Basketball W, cross-country W, field hockey W, lacrosse W, soccer W, softball W, tennis W, volleyball W. **Intramural:** Badminton W, basketball W, soccer W, softball W, tennis W, volleyball W. **Team name:** Falcons.

Student services. Adult student services, alcohol/substance abuse counseling, campus ministries, career counseling, student employment services, financial aid counseling, health services, personal counseling, placement for graduates. **Physically disabled:** Services for visually, speech, hearing impaired.

Contact. E-mail: cccadmis@cedarcrest.edu
Phone: (610) 740-3780 Toll-free number: (800) 360-1222
Fax: (610) 606-4647
Judith Neyhart, Executive Vice President for Enrollment, Cedar Crest College, 100 College Drive, Allentown, PA 18104-6196

Central Pennsylvania College

Summerdale, Pennsylvania
www.centralpenn.edu **CB code: 1061**

- For-profit 4-year business and technical college
- Residential campus in rural community
- 981 degree-seeking undergraduates: 29% part-time, 65% women
- Interview required
- 63% graduate within 6 years

General. Founded in 1881. Regionally accredited. **Degrees:** 108 bachelor's, 109 associate awarded. **Location:** 5 miles from Harrisburg. **Calendar:** Trimester, extensive summer session. **Full-time faculty:** 29 total. **Part-time faculty:** 88 total. **Special facilities:** Student-run restaurant, travel agency and campus store; mock courtroom, optometric room, multimedia lab, medical office, child-care facility, advanced technology education center, conference facility.

Freshman class profile. 2,544 applied, 1,063 admitted, 225 enrolled.

Out-of-state:	21%	**Live on campus:**	49%

Basis for selection. Open admission, but selective for some programs. Admission to physical therapist assistant and paralegal programs based on high school achievement record; very important for these programs. Minimum SAT score of 900 (exclusive of Writing) required for admission into physical therapy assistant program. **Homeschooled:** Provide transcript of courses completed with grades and include parent/teacher/academy signatures. **Learning Disabled:** Students meet with academic dean to discuss provisions needed for individual learning experience.

2005-2006 Annual costs. Tuition/fees: $11,610. Room/board: $6,360. Books/supplies: $1,200. Personal expenses: $660.

Financial aid. Non-need-based: Scholarships awarded for academics, alumni affiliation, job skills, leadership, minority status, state residency.

Application procedures. Admission: Priority date 5/1; no deadline. No application fee. Application may be submitted online. Admission notification on a rolling basis. **Financial aid:** Priority date 3/15; no closing date. FAFSA, institutional form required. Applicants notified on a rolling basis starting 2/1; must reply within 2 week(s) of notification.

Academics. Special study options: Distance learning, double major, honors, internships, study abroad. **Credit/placement by examination:** AP, CLEP, institutional tests. 15 credit hours maximum toward associate degree, 15 toward bachelor's. **Support services:** Reduced course load, remedial instruction, study skills assistance, tutoring, writing center.

Majors. Business: Business admin. **Communications:** General. **Computer sciences:** Computer science, web page design. **Protective services:** Criminal justice.

Most popular majors. Business/marketing 45%, communications/journalism 6%, computer/information sciences 26%, security/protective services 23%.

Computing on campus. 150 workstations in library, computer center. Dormitories wired for high-speed internet access and linked to campus network. Commuter students can connect to campus network. Online course registration, online library, helpline, wireless network available.

Student life. Freshman orientation: Mandatory. Preregistration for classes offered. **Policies:** Dress code, attendance policy, no alcohol or drugs. Freshmen permitted cars on campus. **Housing:** Guaranteed on-campus for all undergraduates. Apartments available. $250 deposit. All resident housing is either single gender townhouses or apartments. **Activities:** Choral groups, literary magazine, student government, student newspaper, Debit Debit Credit, college council, Gamma Beta Phi, Delta Epsilon Chi, technology club, cheerleading, chorus, Club MED, Toastmasters.

Athletics. NJCAA. **Intercollegiate:** Basketball, bowling, golf, volleyball. **Intramural:** Basketball, football (non-tackle), softball, tennis, volleyball. **Team name:** Silver Knights.

Student services. Adult student services, career counseling, student employment services, financial aid counseling, on-campus daycare, personal counseling, placement for graduates.

Contact. E-mail: admissions@centralpenn.edu
Phone: (717) 728-2201 Toll-free number: (800) 759-2727
Fax: (717) 732-5254
Katie Bogovic, Director of Admissions, Central Pennsylvania College, College Hill & Valley Roads, Summerdale, PA 17093-0309

Chatham College

Pittsburgh, Pennsylvania **CB member**
www.chatham.edu **CB code: 2081**

- Private 4-year liberal arts college for women
- Residential campus in large city
- 470 degree-seeking undergraduates: 9% part-time, 100% women, 11% African American, 2% Asian American, 2% Hispanic American, 7% international
- 648 graduate students
- 61% of applicants admitted
- Application essay required
- 60% graduate within 6 years; 40% enter graduate study

General. Founded in 1869. Regionally accredited. **Degrees:** 103 bachelor's awarded; master's, doctoral offered. **ROTC:** Army, Navy, Air Force. **Location:** 6 miles from downtown. **Calendar:** 4-1-4, limited summer session. **Full-time faculty:** 70 total. **Part-time faculty:** 5 total. **Class size:** 80% < 20, 18% 20-39, less than 1% 40-49, less than 1% 50-99. **Special facilities:** Broadcast studio, science complex and green house, proscenium theatre, arboretum.

Freshman class profile. 457 applied, 280 admitted, 122 enrolled.

Mid 50% test scores		**Rank in top tenth:**	10%
SAT verbal:	480-600	**Return as sophomores:**	73%
SAT math:	440-580	**Out-of-state:**	25%
ACT:	19-25	**Live on campus:**	91%
Rank in top quarter:	35%	**International:**	6%

Basis for selection. School achievement record, essays, and test scores most important, though test scores not required. Students who do not submit SAT/ACT required to submit graded writing sample and resume/list of activities. Portfolios may also be submitted. Activities, talents, volunteer work, paid work, alumnae relationship, class rank, and recommendations considered. TOEFL or IELTS required for international students. SAT or ACT recommended. Campus visit or interviews recommended for all.

High school preparation. 11 units required; 15 recommended. Required and recommended units include English 4, mathematics 2-3, science 2-3 and foreign language 2. Require 3 units of social science.

2005-2006 Annual costs. Tuition/fees: $23,170. Room/board: $7,410. Books/supplies: $860. Personal expenses: $316.

2005-2006 Financial aid. Need-based: 112 full-time freshmen applied for aid; 88 were judged to have need; 88 of these received aid. Average need met was 70%. Average scholarship/grant was $9,339; average loan $4,625. 65% of total undergraduate aid awarded as scholarships/grants, 35% as loans/jobs. **Non-need-based:** Awarded to 47 full-time undergraduates, including 13 freshmen. Scholarships awarded for academics, alumni affiliation, leadership, music/drama.

Application procedures. Admission: Priority date 3/15; deadline 8/1. $35 fee, may be waived for applicants with need. Application may be submitted online. Admission notification on a rolling basis beginning on or about 10/15. Must reply by May 1 or within 2 week(s) if notified thereafter. **Financial aid:** Priority date 5/1; no closing date. FAFSA required. Applicants notified on a rolling basis starting 2/15; must reply by 5/1 or within 2 week(s) of notification.

Academics. All students eligible through PACE Center to receive free tutoring in every course offered. Specialized transitions courses also offered for students having academic difficulties, as well as career preparation courses to help students choose career path. **Special study options:** Accelerated study, combined bachelor's/graduate degree, cooperative education, cross-registration, distance learning, double major, ESL, exchange student, honors, independent study, internships, liberal arts/career combination, student-designed major, study abroad, teacher certification program, Washington semester. 5-year bachelor's/master's programs in 9 fields and 6-year bachelor's/doctorate in physical therapy; accelerated 5-year bachelor's/master's in 4 fields with Carnegie Mellon's Heinz School; 3-2 engineering with Carnegie Mellon and other institutions. **Credit/placement by examination:** AP, CLEP, IB. 12 credit hours maximum toward bachelor's degree. **Support services:** Learning center, reduced course load, remedial instruction, study skills assistance, tutoring, writing center.

Majors. Area/ethnic studies: Women's. **Biology:** General, biochemistry. **Business:** Accounting, business admin, international, managerial economics, marketing. **Communications:** General, broadcast journalism, public relations. **Conservation:** Environmental studies. **Education:** Early childhood, elementary. **Engineering:** General. **English:** English lit. **Foreign languages:** French, Spanish. **Health:** Nursing (RN), premedicine. **History:** General. **Interdisciplinary:** Intercultural. **Legal studies:** Prelaw. **Math:** General. **Parks/recreation:** Exercise sciences. **Physical sciences:** Chemistry, physics. **Protective services:** Forensics. **Psychology:** General. **Public administration:** Policy analysis, social work. **Social sciences:** Economics, international relations, political science. **Visual/performing arts:** Art history/conservation, arts management, dramatic, photography, studio arts.

Most popular majors. Biology 11%, business/marketing 11%, communications/journalism 8%, psychology 27%, public administration/social services 10%, social sciences 12%, visual/performing arts 14%.

Computing on campus. PC or laptop required. 300 workstations in dormitories, library, computer center. Dormitories wired for high-speed internet access and linked to campus network. Commuter students can connect to campus network. Online course registration, online library, helpline, repair service, student web hosting, wireless network available.

Student life. Freshman orientation: Mandatory. Preregistration for classes offered. Held immediately before classes begin in late August. Mini-orientations held during late spring and summer where students can register for courses. **Policies:** Honor code. **Housing:** Guaranteed on-campus for all undergraduates. Apartments, substance-free housing available. $100 nonrefundable deposit, deadline 5/1. Intercultural residence hall, community service floor and environmental floor within larger residence hall available. **Activities:** Choral groups, dance, drama, literary magazine, music ensembles, musical theater, student government, student newspaper, Black Student Union, Christian Fellowship, Jewish organization, feminist collective, Gateway Student Association, Green Horizons, International Student Association, Mortar Board, Students Against Sexual Oppression.

Athletics. NCAA. **Intercollegiate:** Basketball W, ice hockey W, soccer W, softball W, swimming W, tennis W, volleyball W. **Team name:** Cougars.

Student services. Adult student services, campus ministries, career counseling, services for economically disadvantaged, student employment services, financial aid counseling, health services, personal counseling, placement for graduates, women's services. **Physically disabled:** Services for visually, speech, hearing impaired.

Contact. E-mail: admissions@chatham.edu
Phone: (412) 365-1290 Toll-free number: (800) 837-1290
Fax: (412) 365-1609
Michael Poll, Vice President of Admissions, Chatham College, Woodland Road, Pittsburgh, PA 15232

Chestnut Hill College

Philadelphia, Pennsylvania — **CB member**
www.chc.edu — **CB code: 2082**

- Private 4-year liberal arts college affiliated with Roman Catholic Church
- Residential campus in very large city
- 1,000 degree-seeking undergraduates: 20% part-time, 73% women
- 555 degree-seeking graduate students
- 73% of applicants admitted
- SAT or ACT (ACT writing optional), application essay required
- 47% graduate within 6 years

General. Founded in 1924. Regionally accredited. **Degrees:** 182 bachelor's, 1 associate awarded; master's, doctoral offered. **Location:** 17 miles from center city. **Calendar:** Semester, limited summer session. **Full-time faculty:** 72 total; 83% have terminal degrees, 6% minority, 72% women. **Part-time faculty:** 184 total; 65% have terminal degrees, 8% minority, 55% women. **Class size:** 85% < 20, 15% 20-39. **Special facilities:** Observatory, planetarium, Irish literature collection, multimedia center, smart classrooms.

Freshman class profile. 1,255 applied, 921 admitted, 216 enrolled.

Mid 50% test scores		**Rank in top tenth:**	13%
SAT verbal:	450-550	**End year in good standing:**	66%
SAT math:	430-520	**Return as sophomores:**	74%
ACT:	18-24	**Out-of-state:**	20%
Rank in top quarter:	30%	**Live on campus:**	70%

Basis for selection. Secondary school record, essay very important. Standardized test scores, recommendations, character, interview, extracurricular activities important. Alumni connection, talent, volunteer activity, work experience considered. **Homeschooled:** Subscribe to a home-school agency.

High school preparation. 16 units recommended. Recommended units include English 4, mathematics 3, social studies 4, science 3 and foreign language 2.

2006-2007 Annual costs. Tuition/fees (projected): $22,750. Room/board: $7,950. Books/supplies: $1,160. Personal expenses: $180.

2004-2005 Financial aid. Need-based: 208 full-time freshmen applied for aid; 167 were judged to have need; 167 of these received aid. Average need met was 48%. Average scholarship/grant was $6,000; average loan $2,625. 56% of total undergraduate aid awarded as scholarships/grants, 44% as loans/jobs. **Non-need-based:** Awarded to 670 full-time undergraduates, including 163 freshmen. Scholarships awarded for academics, alumni affiliation, leadership, religious affiliation.

Application procedures. Admission: Priority date 1/20; no deadline. $35 fee, may be waived for applicants with need. Application may be submitted online. Admission notification on a rolling basis. Must reply by May 1 or within 3 week(s) if notified thereafter. **Financial aid:** Closing date 4/15. FAFSA required. Applicants notified on a rolling basis starting 1/31; must reply by 5/1 or within 3 week(s) of notification.

Academics. Montessori certification available with elementary and pre-elementary education. Secondary education certification available in major field of study. Interdisciplinary bachelor's degree in international business and culture. **Special study options:** Combined bachelor's/graduate degree, cooperative education, cross-registration, double major, dual enrollment of high school students, ESL, exchange student, honors, independent study, internships, student-designed major, study abroad, teacher certification program. 2-2 double bachelor's program in biology or chemistry and medical technology with Thomas Jefferson University School of Allied Health Sciences, 3-2 BA/MS psychology, 3-2 BS/MS applied technology, 5-year BS/MEd elementary education with emphasis in special education. **Credit/placement by examination:** AP, CLEP, IB, institutional tests. 12 credit hours maximum toward bachelor's degree. **Support services:** Learning center, pre-admission summer program, reduced course load, remedial instruction, study skills assistance, tutoring, writing center.

Majors. Biology: General, biochemistry, molecular. **Business:** Accounting, accounting/business management, business admin, communications, finance, human resources, international, marketing. **Computer sciences:** General, computer science. **Conservation:** Environmental science. **Education:** Early childhood, elementary, multi-level teacher. **English:** English lit. **Family/consumer sciences:** Aging, child care. **Foreign languages:** French, Spanish. **Health:** Health care admin. **History:** General. **Interdisciplinary:** Math/computer science. **Physical sciences:** Chemistry. **Protective services:** Law enforcement admin. **Psychology:** General. **Public administration:** Human services. **Social sciences:** Political science, sociology.

Most popular majors. Business/marketing 27%, education 10%, psychology 9%, public administration/social services 13%, security/protective services 9%.

Computing on campus. PC or laptop required. 65 workstations in library, computer center. Commuter students can connect to campus network. Helpline, repair service, wireless network available.

Student life. Freshman orientation: Available. Preregistration for classes offered. Held 2 days in summer. **Policies:** Freshmen permitted cars on campus. **Housing:** Single-sex dorms, special housing for disabled, substance-free housing available. $200 deposit, deadline 5/1. **Activities:** Choral groups, drama, literary magazine, music ensembles, musical theater, opera, radio station, student government, student newspaper, symphony orchestra, African-American Awareness Society, campus ministry, ecology club, Gay/Straight

Alliance, Griffin Hospitality Club, Hispanics in Action, Mosaic of Cultures Club, Students for Peace and Justice, student government association.

Athletics. NCAA. **Intercollegiate:** Basketball, cross-country, golf, lacrosse W, soccer, softball W, tennis, volleyball W. **Team name:** Griffins.

Student services. Adult student services, campus ministries, career counseling, services for economically disadvantaged, student employment services, financial aid counseling, health services, personal counseling, placement for graduates.

Contact. E-mail: apply@chc.edu
Phone: (215) 248-7001 Toll-free number: (800) 248-0052
Fax: (215) 248-7082
Jodie King, Director of Admissions, School of Undergraduate Studies, Chestnut Hill College, 9601 Germantown Avenue, Philadelphia, PA 19118-2693

Cheyney University of Pennsylvania

Cheyney, Pennsylvania — **CB member**
www.cheyney.edu — **CB code: 2648**

- Public 4-year university
- Residential campus in small town
- 1,351 degree-seeking undergraduates: 4% part-time, 54% women, 94% African American, 1% Hispanic American, 1% international
- 107 degree-seeking graduate students
- 56% of applicants admitted
- SAT or ACT, application essay required
- 32% graduate within 6 years

General. Founded in 1837. Regionally accredited. Courses offered at Philadelphia Urban Center. **Degrees:** 138 bachelor's awarded; master's offered. **ROTC:** Army. **Location:** 25 miles from Philadelphia. **Calendar:** Semester, limited summer session. **Full-time faculty:** 103 total; 63% have terminal degrees, 52% women. **Part-time faculty:** 24 total; 54% have terminal degrees, 58% women. **Class size:** 40% < 20, 58% 20-39, 2% 50-99. **Special facilities:** Planetarium, weather station, theater arts center.

Freshman class profile. 2,751 applied, 1,553 admitted, 675 enrolled.

Return as sophomores:	57%	**Live on campus:**	88%
Out-of-state:	17%		

Basis for selection. Test scores, class rank, high school GPA, counselor recommendation, extracurricular activities important. Minimum SAT combined score of 830 (exclusive of writing) or ACT composite score of 17 required. SAT Subject Tests recommended. Interview recommended.

High school preparation. 13 units required. Required units include English 4, mathematics 3, history 2, science 2 and foreign language 2.

2005-2006 Annual costs. Tuition/fees: $5,818; $13,178 out-of-state. Tuition for MD, NY, NJ and Delaware is $9,814. Required fees for all out of state students is $975. Room/board: $5,679. Books/supplies: $1,200.

Financial aid. Non-need-based: Scholarships awarded for academics, athletics.

Application procedures. Admission: Priority date 6/15; no deadline. $20 fee, may be waived for applicants with need. Application may be submitted online. Admission notification on a rolling basis. **Financial aid:** Priority date 5/1; no closing date. FAFSA required. Applicants notified on a rolling basis starting 4/1; must reply within 2 week(s) of notification.

Academics. Health and physical education courses required of most students. **Special study options:** Cooperative education, cross-registration, distance learning, double major, independent study, internships, teacher certification program. **Credit/placement by examination:** AP, CLEP, institutional tests. 23 credit hours maximum toward bachelor's degree. **Support services:** Learning center, pre-admission summer program, reduced course load, remedial instruction, tutoring.

Majors. Biology: General. **Business:** Accounting, business admin. **Communications:** General. **Communications technology:** General. **Computer sciences:** General. **Education:** Early childhood, elementary, special. **Family/consumer sciences:** Clothing/textiles. **Foreign languages:** French, Spanish. **Health:** Clinical lab science. **Interdisciplinary:** Biological/physical sciences. **Math:** General. **Parks/recreation:** Facilities management. **Physical sciences:** Chemistry. **Psychology:** General. **Social sciences:** General, economics, geography, political science, sociology. **Visual/performing arts:** Art, dramatic.

Most popular majors. Business/marketing 28%, communications/journalism 6%, parks/recreation 6%, psychology 12%, social sciences 35%.

Computing on campus. 296 workstations in dormitories, library, computer center, student center. Dormitories wired for high-speed internet access and linked to campus network. Online course registration, helpline, repair service available.

Student life. Freshman orientation: Mandatory. **Policies:** Ecumenical services held on campus. **Housing:** Guaranteed on-campus for freshmen. Coed dorms, single-sex dorms available. $100 deposit, deadline 5/11. Freshmen-only dormitory available. **Activities:** Bands, choral groups, dance, drama, film society, music ensembles, radio station, student government, student newspaper, TV station, Shades of Unity, Toastmasters, business club, education club, NAACP, Latino Students in Action, LaOriginale, Commuter Students Association.

Athletics. NCAA. **Intercollegiate:** Basketball, bowling W, cross-country, football (tackle) M, tennis W, track and field, volleyball W. **Intramural:** Basketball, football (tackle) M. **Team name:** Wolves.

Student services. Career counseling, student employment services, health services, personal counseling, placement for graduates, veterans' counselor.

Contact. E-mail: gstemley@cheyney.edu
Phone: (610) 399-2275 Toll-free number: (800) 243-9639
Fax: (610) 399-2099
Gemma Stemley, Director of Admissions, Cheyney University of Pennsylvania, 1837 University Circle/PO Box 200, Cheyney, PA 19319-0019

Clarion University of Pennsylvania

Clarion, Pennsylvania — **CB member**
www.clarion.edu — **CB code: 2649**

- Public 4-year university
- Commuter campus in small town
- 5,938 degree-seeking undergraduates: 11% part-time, 59% women, 5% African American, 1% Asian American, 1% Hispanic American, 1% international
- 594 graduate students
- 78% of applicants admitted
- SAT or ACT (ACT writing optional) required
- 51% graduate within 6 years

General. Founded in 1867. Regionally accredited. **Degrees:** 1,009 bachelor's, 119 associate awarded; master's offered. **ROTC:** Army. **Location:** 85 miles from Pittsburgh, 90 miles from Erie. **Calendar:** Semester, limited summer session. **Full-time faculty:** 254 total; 44% women. **Part-time faculty:** 50 total; 58% women. **Special facilities:** Planetarium, archaeology dig and display.

Freshman class profile. 3,346 applied, 2,609 admitted, 1,241 enrolled.

Rank in top quarter:	24%	**Out-of-state:**	4%

Basis for selection. School achievement record, class rank, GPA, test scores considered. Essay and interview required of nursing applicants, recommended for all others. Audition required for music, theater programs; portfolio required for art program.

High school preparation. College-preparatory program required. Required and recommended units include English 4, mathematics 2-4, social studies 4, science 3-4 and foreign language 2.

2005-2006 Annual costs. Tuition/fees: $6,437; $11,345 out-of-state. Room/board: $5,604. Books/supplies: $750. Personal expenses: $1,300.

2004-2005 Financial aid. Need-based: 1,121 full-time freshmen applied for aid; 905 were judged to have need; 866 of these received aid. Average need met was 76%. Average scholarship/grant was $5,592; average loan $2,452. 52% of total undergraduate aid awarded as scholarships/grants, 48% as loans/jobs. **Non-need-based:** Awarded to 1,461 full-time undergraduates, including 337 freshmen. Scholarships awarded for academics, alumni affiliation, art, athletics, leadership, minority status, music/drama, state residency. **Additional information:** Application closing date for academic scholarships March 15.

Application procedures. Admission: No deadline. $30 fee, may be waived for applicants with need. Application may be submitted online. Admission notification on a rolling basis beginning on or about 9/1. Must reply by May 1 or within 4 week(s) if notified thereafter. **Financial aid:** Priority date 5/1; no closing date. FAFSA required. Applicants notified on a rolling basis starting 5/15.

Academics. **Special study options:** Accelerated study, cooperative education, distance learning, double major, honors, independent study, internships, liberal arts/career combination, study abroad, teacher certification program. Co-op engineering program with 2 affiliate schools, nursing program at West Penn Hospital in Pittsburgh. Joint nursing programs with Slippery Rock University of Pennsylvania and Lock Haven University of Pennsylvania available. **Credit/placement by examination:** AP, CLEP, institutional tests. 38 credit hours maximum toward bachelor's degree. **Support services:** Learning center, pre-admission summer program, reduced course load, remedial instruction, study skills assistance, tutoring, writing center.

Majors. **Biology:** General, molecular. **Business:** Accounting, business admin, international, labor relations, managerial economics, marketing, real estate. **Communications:** General. **Computer sciences:** General, information systems. **Conservation:** General. **Education:** Early childhood, elementary, music, social studies, special. **English:** Speech/rhetoric. **Foreign languages:** French, Spanish. **Health:** Audiology/speech pathology, clinical lab technology, clinical/medical social work, medical radiologic technology/radiation therapy, nursing (RN). **History:** General. **Interdisciplinary:** Biological/physical sciences. **Liberal arts:** Arts/sciences, library science. **Math:** General. **Philosophy/religion:** Philosophy. **Physical sciences:** Chemistry, geology, physics, planetary. **Psychology:** General. **Social sciences:** General, anthropology, economics, geography, political science, sociology. **Visual/performing arts:** Art, dramatic, music management, music performance.

Most popular majors. Business/marketing 19%, communications/journalism 10%, education 27%, health sciences 7%.

Computing on campus. 400 workstations in dormitories, library, computer center, student center. Dormitories linked to campus network. Commuter students can connect to campus network. Online course registration, helpline, repair service available.

Student life. **Freshman orientation:** Available, $10 fee. Preregistration for classes offered. 2-day sessions held throughout the summer. **Policies:** Freshmen permitted cars on campus. **Housing:** Coed dorms, single-sex dorms, fraternity/sorority housing available. $75 deposit. **Activities:** Bands, choral groups, dance, drama, music ensembles, musical theater, radio station, student government, student newspaper, TV station, Christian and black student organizations, Young Democrats, Young Republicans, Circle K, service fraternities and sororities.

Athletics. NAIA, NCAA. **Intercollegiate:** Baseball M, basketball, cross-country, diving, football (tackle) M, golf M, soccer W, softball W, swimming, tennis W, track and field, volleyball W, wrestling M. **Intramural:** Badminton, basketball, bowling, boxing M, golf, handball, racquetball, soccer, softball, swimming, table tennis, tennis, volleyball, wrestling M. **Team name:** Eagles.

Student services. Adult student services, alcohol/substance abuse counseling, campus ministries, career counseling, student employment services, financial aid counseling, health services, minority student services, on-campus daycare, personal counseling, placement for graduates, veterans' counselor, women's services. **Physically disabled:** Services for visually, speech, hearing impaired.

Contact. E-mail: admissions@clarion.edu
Phone: (814) 393-2306 Toll-free number: (800) 672-7171
Fax: (814) 393-2030
William Bailey, Dean of Enrollment Management and Academic Records, Clarion University of Pennsylvania, Wood Street, Clarion, PA 16214

College Misericordia

Dallas, Pennsylvania — **CB member**
www.misericordia.edu — **CB code: 2087**

- Private 4-year liberal arts college affiliated with Roman Catholic Church
- Residential campus in small city
- 1,966 degree-seeking undergraduates: 27% part-time, 74% women, 2% African American, 1% Asian American, 2% Hispanic American
- 271 degree-seeking graduate students
- 81% of applicants admitted
- SAT or ACT (ACT writing optional) required
- 73% graduate within 6 years; 24% enter graduate study

General. Founded in 1924. Regionally accredited. Guaranteed Placement Program (within six months of graduation); Women with Children program for single women. **Degrees:** 397 bachelor's awarded; master's, doctoral offered. **ROTC:** Army, Air Force. **Location:** 9 miles from Wilkes-Barre, 20 miles from Scranton. **Calendar:** Semester, limited summer session. **Full-time faculty:** 90 total; 80% have terminal degrees, 2% minority, 51% women. **Part-time faculty:** 168 total; 15% have terminal degrees, 2% minority, 56% women. **Class size:** 61% < 20, 36% 20-39, 2% 40-49, less than 1% 50-99.

Freshman class profile. 1,071 applied, 865 admitted, 335 enrolled.

Mid 50% test scores		**Rank in top quarter:**	40%
SAT verbal:	450-540	**Rank in top tenth:**	11%
SAT math:	450-550	**End year in good standing:**	90%
ACT:	19-23	**Return as sophomores:**	79%
GPA 3.50 or higher:	23%	**Out-of-state:**	26%
GPA 3.0-3.49:	45%	**Live on campus:**	80%
GPA 2.0-2.99:	32%		

Basis for selection. In order of importance: high school achievement, test scores, character, recommendations from school teachers or counselors. Test scores weighed more heavily for health science programs. Essay, interview recommended. Essay required for occupational therapy applicants. **Homeschooled:** If applicant not affiliated with specific organization, college will accept transcript from home schooling parent which shows course work completed and grades achieved. GED not required. **Learning Disabled:** Essay, 3 letters of recommendation, documentation of disability, test results (i.e., WAIS) required. SAT/ACT not required.

High school preparation. 16 units required. Required units include English 4, mathematics 4, social studies 4 and science 4. 2 units science and algebra required for allied health applicants. Strong mathematics background required for computer science, physical therapy, chemistry and biology applicants.

2005-2006 Annual costs. Tuition/fees: $19,700. Room/board: $8,250. Books/supplies: $800. Personal expenses: $500.

2005-2006 Financial aid. **Need-based:** 302 full-time freshmen applied for aid; 260 were judged to have need; 260 of these received aid. Average need met was 72%. Average scholarship/grant was $9,934; average loan $5,176. 60% of total undergraduate aid awarded as scholarships/grants, 40% as loans/jobs. **Non-need-based:** Awarded to 377 full-time undergraduates, including 87 freshmen. Scholarships awarded for academics, alumni affiliation, leadership, minority status, state residency.

Application procedures. **Admission:** No deadline. $25 fee, may be waived for applicants with need. Application may be submitted online. Admission notification on a rolling basis beginning on or about 9/1. Must reply by May 1 or within 4 week(s) if notified thereafter. Essay required for applicants to 5-year occupational therapy bachelor's/master's program. Closing date for applications to 5-year physical therapy bachelor's/master's program is February 1. **Financial aid:** Priority date 3/1, closing date 5/1. FAFSA, institutional form required. Applicants notified on a rolling basis starting 3/15; must reply by 5/1.

Academics. **Special study options:** Accelerated study, combined bachelor's/graduate degree, cooperative education, cross-registration, distance learning, double major, dual enrollment of high school students, honors, independent study, internships, student-designed major, study abroad, teacher certification program, weekend college. **Credit/placement by examination:** AP, CLEP, IB, SAT, ACT, institutional tests. 40 credit hours maximum toward bachelor's degree. **Support services:** Learning center, pre-admission summer program, study skills assistance, tutoring, writing center.

Majors. **Biology:** General, biochemistry. **Business:** Accounting, business admin, management information systems, management science, marketing. **Communications:** General. **Computer sciences:** General, information technology. **Education:** Elementary, special. **English:** English lit. **Health:** Clinical lab science, medical radiologic technology/radiation therapy, nursing (RN). **History:** General. **Liberal arts:** Arts/sciences. **Math:** General. **Parks/recreation:** Sports admin. **Philosophy/religion:** Philosophy. **Physical sciences:** Chemistry. **Psychology:** General. **Public administration:** Social work.

Most popular majors. Business/marketing 24%, education 12%, health sciences 41%, psychology 6%.

Computing on campus. 100 workstations in dormitories, library, computer center, student center. Dormitories wired for high-speed internet access and linked to campus network. Commuter students can connect to campus network. Online course registration, online library, helpline, repair service, wireless network available.

Student life. **Freshman orientation:** Mandatory, $200 fee. Preregistration for classes offered. One-day testing for mathematics and English placement, adviser meetings, overall review of college. **Housing:** Guaranteed on-campus for all undergraduates. Coed dorms, substance-free housing available. $100 deposit, deadline 5/1. Leadership house, service house, apartment building for women with children located adjacent to campus. **Activities:** Jazz band, choral groups, dance, drama, literary magazine, music ensembles, radio station, student government, student newspaper, TV station, Young Republicans, Student Nurses Association, Student Council for

Exceptional Children, Circle-K, campus ministry, Peer Associates, international club, Diversity Institute.

Athletics. NCAA. **Intercollegiate:** Baseball M, basketball, cheerleading M, cross-country, field hockey W, golf M, lacrosse, soccer, softball W, swimming, tennis W, track and field, volleyball W. **Intramural:** Basketball, bowling, cross-country, football (non-tackle), golf, lacrosse, racquetball, soccer, softball, table tennis, tennis, volleyball. **Team name:** Cougars.

Student services. Adult student services, alcohol/substance abuse counseling, campus ministries, career counseling, services for economically disadvantaged, student employment services, financial aid counseling, health services, minority student services, personal counseling, placement for graduates, women's services. **Physically disabled:** Services for visually, speech, hearing impaired. **Learning disabled:** Comprehensive services available.

Contact. E-mail: admiss@misericordia.edu
Phone: (570) 674-6264 Toll-free number: (866) 262-6363
Fax: (570) 675-2441
Jane Dessoye, Executive Director of Admissions and Financial Aid, College Misericordia, 301 Lake Street, Dallas, PA 18612-1098

Curtis Institute of Music

Philadelphia, Pennsylvania
www.curtis.edu **CB code: 2100**

- Private 4-year music college
- Commuter campus in very large city
- 147 degree-seeking undergraduates: 48% women, 4% African American, 8% Asian American, 2% Hispanic American, 45% international
- 7 degree-seeking graduate students
- 5% of applicants admitted
- SAT required
- 100% graduate within 6 years

General. Founded in 1924. Regionally accredited. **Degrees:** 23 bachelor's awarded; master's offered. **Calendar:** Semester. **Part-time faculty:** 60 total; 7% have terminal degrees. **Special facilities:** 80,836 titles in audiovisual materials, sheet music, and books.

Freshman class profile. 304 applied, 16 admitted, 12 enrolled.

End year in good standing:	100%	**Out-of-state:**	94%
Return as sophomores:	93%	**International:**	17%

Basis for selection. Admission based on audition. Preference given to applicants demonstrating potential rather than proficiency. Test scores considered for applicants to bachelor's degree program.

High school preparation. Major emphasis on applied music activities.

2006-2007 Annual costs. All students given full-tuition scholarship. Required fees $1,910; for bachelor of music students $2,010; additional expenses per annum $15,000 (includes books, supplies, living expenses and miscellaneous).

2005-2006 Financial aid. All financial aid based on need. 10 full-time freshmen applied for aid; 10 were judged to have need; 10 of these received aid. Average need met was 79%. Average scholarship/grant was $5,745; average loan $2,756. 44% of total undergraduate aid awarded as scholarships/grants, 56% as loans/jobs. **Additional information:** All students accepted on full-tuition scholarship basis.

Application procedures. Admission: Closing date 12/15 (receipt date). $135 fee, may be waived for applicants with need. Application may be submitted online. Admission notification 4/1. Must reply by 5/1. **Financial aid:** Closing date 3/1. FAFSA, institutional form, CSS PROFILE required. Applicants notified by 4/1; must reply by 5/1.

Academics. Special study options: Double major, ESL. **Credit/placement by examination:** AP, CLEP, institutional tests. 47 credit hours maximum toward bachelor's degree. **Support services:** Remedial instruction, study skills assistance.

Majors. Visual/performing arts: Music performance, music theory/composition.

Computing on campus. 16 workstations in library, computer center, student center. Online library, repair service available.

Student life. Freshman orientation: Mandatory. Preregistration for classes offered. **Activities:** Music ensembles, opera, student government, symphony orchestra.

Student services. Alcohol/substance abuse counseling, career counseling, financial aid counseling, health services, personal counseling.

Contact. E-mail: admissions@curtis.edu
Phone: (215) 893-5262 Fax: (215) 893-7900
Christopher Hodges, Admissions Officer, Curtis Institute of Music, 1726 Locust Street, Philadelphia, PA 19103-6187

Delaware Valley College

Doylestown, Pennsylvania **CB member**
www.devalcol.edu **CB code: 2510**

- Private 4-year liberal arts college
- Residential campus in large town
- 1,843 degree-seeking undergraduates: 13% part-time, 55% women, 4% African American, 1% Asian American, 1% Hispanic American
- 49 degree-seeking graduate students
- 79% of applicants admitted
- SAT or ACT (ACT writing recommended), application essay required
- 57% graduate within 6 years

General. Founded in 1896. Regionally accredited. **Degrees:** 24 bachelor's, 281 associate awarded; master's offered. **Location:** 20 miles from Philadelphia, 70 miles from New York City. **Calendar:** Semester, extensive summer session. **Full-time faculty:** 78 total; 62% have terminal degrees, 6% minority, 35% women. **Part-time faculty:** 114 total; 22% have terminal degrees, 6% minority, 33% women. **Class size:** 57% < 20, 36% 20-39, 4% 40-49, 3% 50-99. **Special facilities:** Equine facility with indoor and outdoor arena, animal farms, dairy, arboretum greenhouses, tissue culture laboratories.

Freshman class profile. 1,476 applied, 1,164 admitted, 451 enrolled.

Mid 50% test scores		**Rank in top quarter:**	41%
SAT verbal:	460-570	**Rank in top tenth:**	15%
SAT math:	470-560	**Return as sophomores:**	75%
ACT:	20-25	**Out-of-state:**	44%
GPA 3.50 or higher:	54%	**Live on campus:**	88%
GPA 3.0-3.49:	29%	**Fraternities:**	4%
GPA 2.0-2.99:	17%	**Sororities:**	5%

Basis for selection. Academic achievement, class rank, test scores, letters of recommendation from mathematics or science teacher and guidance counselor, grades in mathematics and science considered. Interview, essay recommended.

High school preparation. College-preparatory program required. 15 units required. Required units include English 3, mathematics 2, social studies 2, science 2 (laboratory 1) and academic electives 6. For business administration 1 unit science only. Agriculture, biology, and chemistry majors need 6 additional units, business majors 7.

2005-2006 Annual costs. Tuition/fees: $21,794. $400 additional technology fee for resident students. Room/board: $8,130. Books/supplies: $750. Personal expenses: $200.

2005-2006 Financial aid. Need-based: 392 full-time freshmen applied for aid; 353 were judged to have need; 353 of these received aid. Average need met was 79%. Average scholarship/grant was $13,410; average loan $2,275. 75% of total undergraduate aid awarded as scholarships/grants, 25% as loans/jobs. **Non-need-based:** Awarded to 555 full-time undergraduates, including 146 freshmen. Scholarships awarded for academics, alumni affiliation, music/drama.

Application procedures. Admission: Priority date 5/1; no deadline. $35 fee, may be waived for applicants with need. Application may be submitted online. Admission notification on a rolling basis beginning on or about 10/31. Must reply by May 1 or within 4 week(s) if notified thereafter. **Financial aid:** Priority date 4/1; no closing date. FAFSA required. Applicants notified on a rolling basis starting 2/1; must reply by 5/1.

Academics. Students complete 24-week employment program related to major. **Special study options:** Combined bachelor's/graduate degree, cooperative education, cross-registration, distance learning, double major, honors, independent study, internships, liberal arts/career combination, study abroad, teacher certification program, weekend college. **Credit/placement by examination:** AP, CLEP, institutional tests. Credit for 5 courses may be granted through examination. **Support services:** Learning center, preadmission summer program, reduced course load, remedial instruction, tutoring.

Majors. Agriculture: Agribusiness operations, agronomy, animal sciences, crop production, dairy, equestrian studies, food science, horticultural science, horticulture, ornamental horticulture, turf management. **Biology:** General. **Business:** Accounting, business admin, management information systems, marketing. **Computer sciences:** General. **Conservation:** Wildlife. **Education:** Secondary. **English:** English lit. **Math:** General. **Physical sciences:** Chemistry. **Protective services:** Law enforcement admin.

Most popular majors. Agriculture 40%, biology 6%, business/marketing 30%, computer/information sciences 7%, security/protective services 9%.

Computing on campus. 150 workstations in dormitories, library, computer center, student center. Dormitories wired for high-speed internet access and linked to campus network. Online library, helpline, repair service, wireless network available.

Student life. Freshman orientation: Mandatory. **Housing:** Guaranteed on-campus for freshmen. Coed dorms, single-sex dorms available. $200 fully refundable deposit, deadline 5/1. **Activities:** Concert band, choral groups, drama, literary magazine, music ensembles, radio station, student government, student newspaper, Christian Fellowship, Hillel, Future Farmers of America, Minority Leadership Coalition, Environmental Awareness Club, Alpha Phi Omega, DVC Volunteer Corps, Newman Club, equine club, business club.

Athletics. NCAA. **Intercollegiate:** Baseball M, basketball, cheerleading M, cross-country, field hockey W, football (tackle) M, golf M, soccer, softball W, track and field, volleyball W, wrestling M. **Intramural:** Basketball, bowling, cross-country, equestrian, football (tackle) M, golf M, lacrosse M, soccer M, softball, tennis, volleyball. **Team name:** Aggies.

Student services. Adult student services, career counseling, student employment services, health services, personal counseling, placement for graduates. **Physically disabled:** Services for visually, speech, hearing impaired.

Contact. E-mail: admitme@devalcol.edu
Phone: (215) 489-2211 Toll-free number: (800) 233-5825
Fax: (215) 230-2968
Stephen Zenko, Director of Admissions, Delaware Valley College, 700 East Butler Avenue, Doylestown, PA 18901-2697

DeSales University

Center Valley, Pennsylvania — **CB member**
www.desales.edu — **CB code: 2021**

- Private 4-year university affiliated with Roman Catholic Church
- Residential campus in small town
- 2,489 degree-seeking undergraduates: 29% part-time, 58% women
- 793 degree-seeking graduate students
- 79% of applicants admitted
- SAT or ACT required
- 70% graduate within 6 years; 22% enter graduate study

General. Founded in 1964. Regionally accredited. **Degrees:** 443 bachelor's awarded; master's offered. **ROTC:** Army. **Location:** 7 miles from Allentown, 50 miles from Philadelphia. **Calendar:** Semester, limited summer session. **Full-time faculty:** 92 total; 72% have terminal degrees, 4% minority, 37% women. **Part-time faculty:** 71 total; 21% have terminal degrees, 1% minority, 56% women. **Class size:** 44% < 20, 52% 20-39, 1% 40-49, 3% 50-99.

Freshman class profile. 1,728 applied, 1,365 admitted, 434 enrolled.

Mid 50% test scores		**Rank in top tenth:**	20%
SAT verbal:	490-590	**End year in good standing:**	95%
SAT math:	490-590	**Return as sophomores:**	82%
ACT:	19-24	**Out-of-state:**	30%
Rank in top quarter:	48%	**Live on campus:**	88%

Basis for selection. High school achievement most important. Test scores and recommendations also considered. Essay, interview recommended for all; audition required for dance, theater programs. Interview required for physician assistant program.

High school preparation. 16 units required; 18 recommended. Required and recommended units include English 4, mathematics 3-4, social studies 3-4, science 2 (laboratory 2) and foreign language 2. Biology, chemistry, 3 math recommended for biology major. 3 math, including 2 algebra, recommended for business major. Chemistry, physics, 3 math recommended for chemistry major. Biology, chemistry, physics, 2 math recommended for nursing major. 2 biology, chemistry, or physics, and 3 math recommended for pre-med major. 4 math recommended for mathematics major.

2005-2006 Annual costs. Tuition/fees: $20,700. Room/board: $7,880. Books/supplies: $800. Personal expenses: $1,800.

2004-2005 Financial aid. Need-based: 56% of total undergraduate aid awarded as scholarships/grants, 44% as loans/jobs. **Non-need-based:** Scholarships awarded for academics, leadership, music/drama.

Application procedures. Admission: Priority date 3/1; deadline 8/1. $30 fee, may be waived for applicants with need. Application may be submitted online. Admission notification on a rolling basis. Must reply by May 1 or within 2 week(s) if notified thereafter. **Financial aid:** Priority date 2/1, closing date 5/1. FAFSA, institutional form required. Applicants notified on a rolling basis starting 2/15; must reply by 5/1 or within 2 week(s) of notification.

Academics. Special study options: Accelerated study, cross-registration, distance learning, double major, dual enrollment of high school students, ESL, honors, independent study, internships, liberal arts/career combination, study abroad, teacher certification program, weekend college. BS in medical studies, MS in physician assistant studies; cross-registration at consortium schools: Cedar Crest, Moravian, Muhlenberg, Lafayette, Lehigh. **Credit/placement by examination:** AP, CLEP, institutional tests. 24 credit hours maximum toward bachelor's degree. For AP credit for Physics B must complete lab component. Must submit research paper for CLEP English Composition with Essay to obtain 6 credits. **Support services:** Learning center, pre-admission summer program, reduced course load, study skills assistance, tutoring.

Majors. Biology: General. **Business:** General, accounting, business admin, e-commerce, finance, human resources, management information systems, management science, marketing. **Communications:** General. **Computer sciences:** General, computer science. **Conservation:** Environmental science. **Education:** Elementary. **Foreign languages:** Spanish. **Health:** Clinical lab science, nursing (RN), physician assistant. **History:** General. **Legal studies:** General. **Liberal arts:** Arts/sciences. **Math:** General. **Parks/recreation:** Exercise sciences, sports admin. **Philosophy/religion:** Philosophy. **Physical sciences:** Chemistry. **Protective services:** Criminal justice. **Psychology:** General. **Social sciences:** Political science. **Theology:** Theology. **Visual/performing arts:** Dance, dramatic, film/cinema.

Most popular majors. Business/marketing 30%, computer/information sciences 6%, education 12%, security/protective services 8%, visual/performing arts 16%.

Computing on campus. 150 workstations in library, computer center, student center. Dormitories wired for high-speed internet access and linked to campus network. Commuter students can connect to campus network. Online course registration, online library, helpline, student web hosting, wireless network available.

Student life. Freshman orientation: Mandatory, $100 fee. Preregistration for classes offered. One-day academic orientation in June; 3-day social and academic orientation in August. **Policies:** Students under 21 cannot possess or be in presence of alcohol. Access to dorm rooms of opposite sex restricted during certain hours. Freshmen permitted cars on campus. **Housing:** Guaranteed on-campus for all undergraduates. Coed dorms, single-sex dorms, substance-free housing available. Pets allowed in dorm rooms. Town houses for upperclassmen, common-interest housing available. **Activities:** Choral groups, dance, drama, film society, literary magazine, music ensembles, musical theater, radio station, student government, student newspaper, TV station, campus ministry, social outreach, Pro-Life club, SIFE, accounting and finance club, CEO dance club, rosary club, social work club, natural science club.

Athletics. NCAA. **Intercollegiate:** Baseball M, basketball, cross-country, field hockey W, golf M, lacrosse M, soccer, softball W, tennis, track and field, volleyball W. **Intramural:** Basketball, football (non-tackle), soccer, softball, volleyball. **Team name:** Bulldogs.

Student services. Adult student services, alcohol/substance abuse counseling, campus ministries, career counseling, services for economically disadvantaged, student employment services, financial aid counseling, health services, minority student services, personal counseling, placement for graduates, veterans' counselor.

Contact. E-mail: admiss@desales.edu
Phone: (610) 282-4443 Toll-free number: (877) 433-7253
Fax: (610) 282-0131
Peter Rautzhan, Dean of Enrollment Management, DeSales University, 2755 Station Avenue, Center Valley, PA 18034-9568

DeVry University: Ft. Washington

Fort Washington, Pennsylvania
www.devry.edu — **CB code: 3866**

- For-profit 4-year university
- Commuter campus in large town
- 710 degree-seeking undergraduates: 29% part-time, 43% women

- 92 graduate students
- Interview required

General. **Degrees:** 46 bachelor's, 18 associate awarded; master's offered. **Location:** 35 miles from Philadelphia. **Calendar:** Semester, extensive summer session. **Full-time faculty:** 44 total; 16% minority, 27% women. **Part-time faculty:** 40 total; 15% minority, 38% women.

Freshman class profile. 147 enrolled.

Basis for selection. Applicants must have high school diploma or equivalent, or a degree from accredited postsecondary institution, demonstrate proficiency in basic college-level skills through SAT or ACT scores or institution-administered placement exams, and be at least 17 years of age on the first day of classes. New students may enter at beginning of any semester. SAT or ACT recommended. CPT also accepted.

High school preparation. Required units include mathematics 1. Math unit must be algebra or higher.

2005-2006 Annual costs. Tuition/fees: $13,410. Books/supplies: $1,100. Personal expenses: $1,816.

Financial aid. All financial aid based on need.

Application procedures. **Admission:** No deadline. $50 fee. Application may be submitted online. Admission notification on a rolling basis. **Financial aid:** No deadline. FAFSA required. Applicants notified on a rolling basis.

Academics. **Special study options:** Accelerated study, cooperative education, distance learning. **Credit/placement by examination:** CLEP. **Support services:** Learning center, remedial instruction, tutoring.

Majors. **Business:** Small business admin. **Computer sciences:** LAN/WAN management, systems analysis. **Engineering technology:** Computer.

Most popular majors. Business/marketing 57%, computer/information sciences 24%, engineering/engineering technologies 19%.

Computing on campus. 407 workstations in library, computer center. Online course registration, online library, helpline available.

Student life. **Freshman orientation:** Mandatory. **Policies:** Freshmen permitted cars on campus. **Activities:** Campus Crusade for Christ, electronic gamers club, creative arts club.

Athletics. **Intramural:** Volleyball.

Student services. Career counseling, student employment services, financial aid counseling, placement for graduates, veterans' counselor. **Physically disabled:** Services for visually, hearing impaired.

Contact. E-mail: admissions@phi.devry.edu
Phone: (215) 591-5701 Toll-free number: (866) 303-3879
Fax: (215) 591-5745
Steve Cohen, Director of Admission, DeVry University: Ft. Washington, 1140 Virginia Drive, Fort Washington, PA 19034-3204

Dickinson College

Carlisle, Pennsylvania — **CB member**
www.dickinson.edu — **CB code: 2186**

- Private 4-year liberal arts college
- Residential campus in large town
- 2,301 degree-seeking undergraduates: 56% women, 4% African American, 4% Asian American, 4% Hispanic American, 5% international
- 49% of applicants admitted
- Application essay required
- 84% graduate within 6 years; 23% enter graduate study

General. Founded in 1783. Regionally accredited. **Degrees:** 536 bachelor's awarded. **ROTC:** Army. **Location:** 100 miles from Philadelphia, 90 miles from Washington, DC. **Calendar:** Semester, limited summer session. **Full-time faculty:** 175 total; 94% have terminal degrees, 10% minority, 42% women. **Part-time faculty:** 34 total; 41% have terminal degrees, 9% minority, 59% women. **Class size:** 68% < 20, 29% 20-39, 2% 40-49, less than 1% 50-99. **Special facilities:** Arts center, planetarium and multiple telescope observatory, intercontinental satellite communications for study-abroad programs, study of contemporary issues center.

Freshman class profile. 4,784 applied, 2,359 admitted, 648 enrolled.

Mid 50% test scores		**End year in good standing:**	97%
SAT verbal:	600-700	**Return as sophomores:**	89%
SAT math:	600-680	**Out-of-state:**	75%
ACT:	26-30	**Live on campus:**	100%
Rank in top quarter:	81%	**International:**	6%
Rank in top tenth:	52%		

Basis for selection. Academic potential as shown by school achievement record most important. Extracurricular activities very important. Counselor recommendation required. Motivation, personal character considered. Special consideration given to applicants of color. Preference given to academically qualified children of alumni if they satisfy above criteria. SAT or ACT recommended. Interview recommended.

High school preparation. 16 units required. Required and recommended units include English 4, mathematics 3, social studies 2, science 3 (laboratory 2), foreign language 2-3 and academic electives 2.

2006-2007 Annual costs. Tuition/fees: $33,829. Room/board: $8,480. Books/supplies: $1,000. Personal expenses: $1,190.

2005-2006 Financial aid. **Need-based:** 422 full-time freshmen applied for aid; 330 were judged to have need; 322 of these received aid. Average need met was 99%. Average scholarship/grant was $22,575; average loan $3,628. 76% of total undergraduate aid awarded as scholarships/grants, 24% as loans/jobs. **Non-need-based:** Awarded to 405 full-time undergraduates, including 108 freshmen. Scholarships awarded for academics, ROTC.

Application procedures. **Admission:** Closing date 2/1 (postmark date). $60 fee, may be waived for applicants with need. Application may be submitted online. Admission notification 3/31. Must reply by May 1 or within 2 week(s) if notified thereafter. **Financial aid:** Closing date 2/1. FAFSA, CSS PROFILE required. Applicants notified by 3/20; must reply by 5/1 or within 2 week(s) of notification.

Academics. Certificates in interdepartmental programs offered in Latin American studies in conjunction with bachelor's degree. Prebusiness, prelaw and premedical preparation available in conjunction with majors listed. **Special study options:** Accelerated study, combined bachelor's/graduate degree, cross-registration, double major, ESL, exchange student, independent study, internships, liberal arts/career combination, student-designed major, study abroad, teacher certification program, Washington semester. 3-2 engineering programs with University of Pennsylvania, Case Western Reserve University, Rensselaer Polytechnic Institute; 3-3 law degree with Dickinson School of Law of Penn State University. **Credit/placement by examination:** AP, CLEP, IB, institutional tests. **Support services:** Tutoring, writing center.

Majors. **Area/ethnic studies:** American, East Asian, Italian, Russian/Slavic, women's. **Biology:** General, biochemistry. **Business:** International. **Computer sciences:** General. **Conservation:** Environmental science, environmental studies. **Engineering:** General. **English:** English lit. **Foreign languages:** Classics, French, German, Italian, Russian, Spanish. **History:** General. **Interdisciplinary:** Medieval/Renaissance, neuroscience. **Legal studies:** General, prelaw. **Math:** General. **Philosophy/religion:** Judaic, philosophy, religion. **Physical sciences:** Chemistry, geology, physics. **Psychology:** General. **Public administration:** Policy analysis. **Social sciences:** Anthropology, archaeology, economics, international relations, political science, sociology. **Visual/performing arts:** Dramatic, studio arts.

Most popular majors. Biology 9%, business/marketing 7%, English 7%, foreign language 11%, history 7%, psychology 9%, social sciences 21%.

Computing on campus. 560 workstations in dormitories, library, computer center, student center. Dormitories wired for high-speed internet access and linked to campus network. Commuter students can connect to campus network. Online course registration, online library, helpline, repair service, wireless network available.

Student life. **Freshman orientation:** Mandatory. Preregistration for classes offered. **Housing:** Guaranteed on-campus for all undergraduates. Coed dorms, special housing for disabled, apartments, fraternity/sorority housing, substance-free housing available. Theme, foreign language, arts, environmental, multicultural housing available. **Activities:** Bands, choral groups, dance, drama, film society, literary magazine, music ensembles, musical theater, radio station, student government, student newspaper, symphony orchestra, public affairs, social service, religious, multicultural, foreign student organizations, College Democrats, Young Republicans, debate club.

Athletics. NCAA. **Intercollegiate:** Baseball M, basketball, cross-country, field hockey W, football (tackle) M, golf, lacrosse, soccer, softball W, swimming, tennis, track and field, volleyball W. **Intramural:** Badminton, basketball M, bowling M, field hockey W, football (non-tackle) M, golf, racquetball, soccer, softball, squash, table tennis, tennis, volleyball M. **Team name:** Red Devils.

Student services. Adult student services, alcohol/substance abuse counseling, career counseling, student employment services, financial aid counseling, health services, minority student services, on-campus daycare, personal counseling, placement for graduates. **Physically disabled:** Services for visually, speech, hearing impaired.

Contact. E-mail: admit@dickinson.edu
Phone: (717) 245-1231 Toll-free number: (800) 644-1773
Fax: (717) 245-1442
Christopher Allen, Dean of Admissions, Dickinson College, PO Box 1773, Carlisle, PA 17013-2896

Drexel University

Philadelphia, Pennsylvania — **CB member**
www.drexel.edu — **CB code: 2194**

- Private 5-year university
- Commuter campus in very large city
- 11,936 degree-seeking undergraduates: 15% part-time, 41% women, 9% African American, 12% Asian American, 3% Hispanic American, 6% international
- 5,881 degree-seeking graduate students
- 82% of applicants admitted
- SAT or ACT (ACT writing optional) required
- 60% graduate within 6 years

General. Founded in 1891. Regionally accredited. Most undergraduate programs require up to 18 months work experience within 5-year program of study. **Degrees:** 2,231 bachelor's, 7 associate awarded; master's, doctoral, first professional offered. **ROTC:** Army, Navy, Air Force. **Calendar:** Quarter, extensive summer session. **Full-time faculty:** 723 total; 14% minority, 38% women. **Part-time faculty:** 560 total. **Class size:** 55% < 20, 34% 20-39, 3% 40-49, 4% 50-99, 3% >100. **Special facilities:** Drexel University Collection (wide range of art objects), observatory, rifle range.

Freshman class profile. 12,093 applied, 9,946 admitted, 2,476 enrolled.

Mid 50% test scores		**Rank in top tenth:**	30%
SAT verbal:	530-630	**Return as sophomores:**	80%
SAT math:	550-660	**Out-of-state:**	51%
GPA 3.50 or higher:	51%	**Live on campus:**	83%
GPA 3.0-3.49:	30%	**International:**	6%
GPA 2.0-2.99:	18%	**Fraternities:**	5%
Rank in top quarter:	59%	**Sororities:**	5%

Basis for selection. Academic average, counselor's recommendation and test scores most important, followed by class rank, school, community and church activities. Employment also considered. Test scores used for placement in College of Engineering. Interview recommended for all; essay required and considered very important for architecture program only. **Homeschooled:** Applicants treated on case-by-case basis.

High school preparation. College-preparatory program required. Required and recommended units include mathematics 3, science 1 (laboratory 1) and foreign language 1. Engineering applicants required to have 4 units of math, including algebra I and II, geometry, trigonometry and precalculus; and 2 units of lab science, including chemistry and physics. Science applicants required to have 4 units of math, including algebra I and II, geometry and trigonometry; and 2 units of lab science including biology, chemistry or physics. Most other applicants must have algebra I and II and geometry as required math units.

2005-2006 Annual costs. Tuition/fees: $24,280. Tuition listed is for 5-year program. Room/board: $11,475. Books/supplies: $650. Personal expenses: $2,000.

2005-2006 Financial aid. Need-based: 2,257 full-time freshmen applied for aid; 1,679 were judged to have need; 1,671 of these received aid. Average need met was 64%. Average scholarship/grant was $4,388; average loan $3,002. 22% of total undergraduate aid awarded as scholarships/grants, 78% as loans/jobs. **Non-need-based:** Awarded to 7,916 full-time undergraduates, including 2,230 freshmen. Scholarships awarded for academics, alumni affiliation, art, athletics, leadership, music/drama, ROTC.

Application procedures. Admission: Closing date 3/1. $50 fee, may be waived for applicants with need. Application may be submitted online. Admission notification on a rolling basis. Must reply by May 1 or within 2 week(s) if notified thereafter. **Financial aid:** Closing date 3/1. FAFSA required. Applicants notified on a rolling basis starting 3/15.

Academics. Special study options: Accelerated study, combined bachelor's/graduate degree, cooperative education, distance learning, double major, ESL, honors, independent study, internships, semester at sea, study abroad, teacher certification program, weekend college. 3-3 programs in engineering with Lincoln University, Indiana University of Pennsylvania and Eastern Mennonite College. **Credit/placement by examination:** AP, CLEP, IB, institutional tests. 30 credit hours maximum toward bachelor's degree. **Support services:** Learning center, pre-admission summer program, reduced course load, remedial instruction, study skills assistance, tutoring, writing center.

Majors. Architecture: Architecture. **Biology:** General. **Business:** General, accounting, business admin, entrepreneurial studies, finance, human resources, international, management information systems, managerial economics, marketing, operations. **Communications:** General. **Computer sciences:** Computer science, information systems, systems analysis. **Conservation:** General. **Education:** Reading. **Engineering:** Architectural, chemical, civil, computer, electrical, environmental, materials, mechanical. **Engineering technology:** General. **English:** Technical writing. **Health:** Clinical lab science, EMT paramedic, health care admin, mental health services, nursing (RN), perfusion technology, physician assistant, substance abuse counseling. **History:** General. **Interdisciplinary:** Biological/physical sciences, nutrition sciences. **Liberal arts:** Arts/sciences. **Math:** General. **Parks/recreation:** Sports admin. **Personal/culinary services:** Culinary arts. **Physical sciences:** Atmospheric physics, chemistry, physics. **Psychology:** General. **Social sciences:** Anthropology, criminology, sociology, urban studies. **Visual/performing arts:** Cinematography, commercial/advertising art, design, fashion design, interior design, music management, photography, play/screenwriting.

Most popular majors. Business/marketing 28%, computer/information sciences 15%, engineering/engineering technologies 20%, health sciences 12%, visual/performing arts 8%.

Computing on campus. PC or laptop required. 610 workstations in dormitories, library, computer center, student center. Dormitories wired for high-speed internet access and linked to campus network. Commuter students can connect to campus network. Online course registration, online library, helpline, repair service, student web hosting, wireless network available.

Student life. Freshman orientation: Available. Preregistration for classes offered. Two-day overnight sessions held in July; 3-day program prior to start of classes. **Policies:** Freshmen permitted cars on campus. **Housing:** Guaranteed on-campus for freshmen. Coed dorms, special housing for disabled, apartments, fraternity/sorority housing available. $200 deposit, deadline 7/1. Freshmen required to live on campus unless living with parents. **Activities:** Bands, choral groups, dance, drama, film society, literary magazine, music ensembles, musical theater, radio station, student government, student newspaper, TV station, Protestant Ministry, Newman Center, Hillel, Alpha Phi Omega, NAACP, Eye Openers, Disciples in Deed, Drexel Christian Fellowship, Jewish Heritage Program.

Athletics. NCAA. **Intercollegiate:** Basketball, diving, field hockey W, golf M, lacrosse, rowing (crew), soccer, softball W, swimming, tennis, wrestling M. **Intramural:** Badminton, baseball M, basketball, fencing, football (tackle) M, ice hockey M, rifle, rugby, sailing, softball, squash, table tennis, tennis, volleyball, water polo. **Team name:** Dragons.

Student services. Adult student services, career counseling, student employment services, financial aid counseling, health services, minority student services, personal counseling, placement for graduates. **Physically disabled:** Services for visually, speech, hearing impaired.

Contact. E-mail: enroll@drexel.edu
Phone: (215) 895-2400 Toll-free number: (800) 237-3935
Fax: (215) 895-5939
Dana Davies, Director of Admissions, Drexel University, 3141 Chestnut Street, Philadelphia, PA 19104-2875

Duquesne University

Pittsburgh, Pennsylvania — **CB member**
www.duq.edu — **CB code: 2196**

- Private 4-year university affiliated with Roman Catholic Church
- Residential campus in large city
- 5,606 degree-seeking undergraduates: 5% part-time, 59% women, 4% African American, 2% Asian American, 1% Hispanic American, 2% international
- 4,239 degree-seeking graduate students
- 80% of applicants admitted
- SAT or ACT with writing, application essay required
- 69% graduate within 6 years; 33% enter graduate study

General. Founded in 1878. Regionally accredited. **Degrees:** 1,115 bachelor's awarded; master's, doctoral, first professional offered. **ROTC:** Army, Navy, Air Force. **Calendar:** Semester, extensive summer session. **Full-time**

faculty: 452 total; 87% have terminal degrees, 10% minority, 40% women. **Part-time faculty:** 479 total; 10% minority, 44% women. **Class size:** 47% < 20, 42% 20-39, 4% 40-49, 4% 50-99, 2% >100. **Special facilities:** Electronic studio, digital keyboards/computers and 24-track recording facility in school of music, family institute, pharmaceutical information center, center for pharmacy practice, center for pharmacy care, phenomenology center, center for pharmaceutical technology, pharmacy manufacturing lab, center for computational sciences, investment center.

Freshman class profile. 4,740 applied, 3,789 admitted, 1,328 enrolled.

Mid 50% test scores		Rank in top tenth:	28%
SAT verbal:	510-610	End year in good standing:	94%
SAT math:	510-620	Return as sophomores:	89%
ACT:	21-26	Out-of-state:	18%
GPA 3.50 or higher:	59%	Live on campus:	88%
GPA 3.0-3.49:	32%	International:	1%
GPA 2.0-2.99:	9%	Fraternities:	19%
Rank in top quarter:	58%	Sororities:	18%

Basis for selection. School achievement record, standardized test scores, recommendations, essay very important. Decisions based on overall GPA, standardized test scores, curriculum, volunteer activities, etc. Interview recommended for all; audition required for music program. **Learning Disabled:** Documentation of learning disabilities may be required.

High school preparation. 16 units required. Required units include English 4, mathematics 2, social studies 2, science 2, foreign language 2 and academic electives 4. 8 units in any combination from areas of social studies, language, mathematics, and science required.

2005-2006 Annual costs. Tuition/fees: $21,480. Room/board: $8,054. Books/supplies: $600. Personal expenses: $600.

2004-2005 Financial aid. **Need-based:** 1,037 full-time freshmen applied for aid; 864 were judged to have need; 861 of these received aid. Average need met was 82%. Average scholarship/grant was $11,689; average loan $3,571. 50% of total undergraduate aid awarded as scholarships/grants, 50% as loans/jobs. **Non-need-based:** Awarded to 3,926 full-time undergraduates, including 1,177 freshmen. Scholarships awarded for academics, athletics, music/drama, ROTC.

Application procedures. **Admission:** Priority date 11/1; deadline 7/1 (receipt date). $50 fee, may be waived for applicants with need. Application may be submitted online. Admission notification on a rolling basis beginning on or about 9/15. Must reply by May 1 or within 2 week(s) if notified thereafter. For international students applying to health sciences program, application closing date December 1 of year prior to year of entry. **Financial aid:** Closing date 5/1. FAFSA, institutional form required. Applicants notified on a rolling basis starting 3/1; must reply by 5/1 or within 3 week(s) of notification.

Academics. **Special study options:** Accelerated study, combined bachelor's/graduate degree, cross-registration, distance learning, double major, dual enrollment of high school students, ESL, exchange student, external degree, honors, independent study, internships, liberal arts/career combination, semester at sea, student-designed major, study abroad, teacher certification program, Washington semester, weekend college. **Credit/placement by examination:** AP, CLEP, IB, institutional tests. 90 credit hours maximum toward bachelor's degree. **Support services:** Learning center, pre-admission summer program, reduced course load, remedial instruction, study skills assistance, tutoring, writing center.

Majors. **Biology:** General, biochemistry. **Business:** General, accounting, communications, entrepreneurial studies, finance, international, investments/securities, logistics, management information systems, management science, managerial economics, marketing, nonprofit/public. **Communications:** General, journalism, public relations. **Computer sciences:** Computer science, web page design, webmaster. **Conservation:** Environmental science. **Education:** General, early childhood, elementary, English, Latin, mathematics, music, secondary, social studies, Spanish. **English:** English lit, speech/rhetoric. **Foreign languages:** General, ancient Greek, classics, Latin, Spanish. **Health:** Athletic training, health care admin, music therapy, nursing (RN), premedicine. **History:** General. **Math:** General. **Philosophy/religion:** Philosophy. **Physical sciences:** Chemistry, physics. **Psychology:** General. **Social sciences:** Economics, international relations, political science, sociology. **Theology:** Theology. **Visual/performing arts:** Art history/conservation, dramatic, music performance, studio arts.

Most popular majors. Biology 6%, business/marketing 26%, communications/journalism 7%, education 10%, health sciences 17%, liberal arts 6%, psychology 6%.

Computing on campus. 917 workstations in dormitories, library, computer center, student center. Dormitories wired for high-speed internet access and linked to campus network. Commuter students can connect to campus network. Online library, helpline, repair service, student web hosting, wireless network available.

Student life. **Freshman orientation:** Mandatory, $135 fee. Preregistration for classes offered. 5-day program in August; includes volunteer opportunities. **Policies:** All recognized student organizations must have faculty or staff adviser, have purpose consistent with university mission, and abide by Code of Rights, Responsibilities and Conduct. Freshmen permitted cars on campus. **Housing:** Guaranteed on-campus for all undergraduates. Coed dorms, special housing for disabled, apartments, fraternity/sorority housing, substance-free housing available. $300 nonrefundable deposit, deadline 5/1. Single-sex, sorority and fraternity, international, and club wings available. **Activities:** Bands, choral groups, dance, drama, film society, literary magazine, music ensembles, musical theater, opera, radio station, student government, student newspaper, symphony orchestra, TV station, United Nations Organization, Black Student Union, Duquesne University Volunteers, Commuter Council, Latin American student association, international student association, Evergreen, Indian student association, residence halls association.

Athletics. NCAA. **Intercollegiate:** Baseball M, basketball, cross-country, football (tackle) M, golf M, lacrosse W, rowing (crew) W, soccer, swimming, tennis, track and field, volleyball W, wrestling M. **Intramural:** Badminton, basketball, football (non-tackle), racquetball, skiing, soccer, softball, squash, swimming, table tennis, tennis, volleyball, water polo, weight lifting. **Team name:** Dukes.

Student services. Adult student services, alcohol/substance abuse counseling, campus ministries, career counseling, services for economically disadvantaged, student employment services, financial aid counseling, health services, minority student services, on-campus daycare, personal counseling, placement for graduates, women's services. **Physically disabled:** Services for visually, speech, hearing impaired.

Contact. E-mail: admissions@duq.edu
Phone: (412) 396-6222 Toll-free number: (800) 456-0590
Fax: (412) 396-5644
Paul Cukanna, Executive Director of Domestic Admissions, Duquesne University, 600 Forbes Avenue, Administration Building, Pittsburgh, PA 15282-0201

East Stroudsburg University of Pennsylvania

East Stroudsburg, Pennsylvania — **CB member**
www3.esu.edu — **CB code: 2650**

- Public 4-year university
- Residential campus in large town
- 5,441 degree-seeking undergraduates: 8% part-time, 58% women, 4% African American, 1% Asian American, 4% Hispanic American
- 836 degree-seeking graduate students
- 64% of applicants admitted
- SAT or ACT (ACT writing optional) required
- 43% graduate within 6 years

General. Founded in 1893. Regionally accredited. **Degrees:** 1,034 bachelor's awarded; master's offered. **ROTC:** Army, Air Force. **Location:** 40 miles from Allentown and Scranton. **Calendar:** Semester, extensive summer session. **Full-time faculty:** 259 total; 78% have terminal degrees, 11% minority, 43% women. **Part-time faculty:** 73 total; 30% have terminal degrees, 7% minority, 52% women. **Class size:** 26% < 20, 47% 20-39, 24% 40-49, 2% 50-99, 1% >100. **Special facilities:** 30-acre ecological studies area, business accelerator.

Freshman class profile. 5,063 applied, 3,264 admitted, 1,101 enrolled.

Mid 50% test scores		Rank in top tenth:	7%
SAT verbal:	450-530	Return as sophomores:	78%
SAT math:	450-550	Out-of-state:	28%
Rank in top quarter:	26%	Live on campus:	84%

Basis for selection. Academic achievement primary factor in selection process. Whole-person assessment also used, taking into account school and community activities, achievements and aspirations.

High school preparation. College-preparatory program recommended. 21 units recommended. Recommended units include English 4, mathematics 4, social studies 3, history 3, science 3 (laboratory 2) and foreign language 2.

2005-2006 Annual costs. Tuition/fees: $6,399; $13,719 out-of-state. Room/board: $4,794. Books/supplies: $1,000. Personal expenses: $2,012.

2004-2005 Financial aid. **Need-based:** 925 full-time freshmen applied for aid; 643 were judged to have need; 619 of these received aid. Average need met was 80%. Average scholarship/grant was $3,180; average loan $2,422. 40% of total undergraduate aid awarded as scholarships/grants, 60%

as loans/jobs. **Non-need-based:** Awarded to 1,185 full-time undergraduates, including 263 freshmen. Scholarships awarded for academics, alumni affiliation, art, athletics, leadership, minority status, music/drama, religious affiliation.

Application procedures. Admission: Closing date 4/1 (postmark date). $35 fee, may be waived for applicants with need. Application may be submitted online. Admission notification on a rolling basis beginning on or about 11/15. Must reply by May 1 or within 3 week(s) if notified thereafter. **Financial aid:** Closing date 3/1. FAFSA required. Applicants notified by 4/1; must reply by 5/1.

Academics. Special study options: Accelerated study, cross-registration, double major, dual enrollment of high school students, exchange student, honors, independent study, internships, student-designed major, study abroad, teacher certification program, urban semester. **Credit/placement by examination:** AP, CLEP, SAT, ACT, institutional tests. 24 credit hours maximum toward bachelor's degree. **Support services:** Learning center, pre-admission summer program, reduced course load, remedial instruction, study skills assistance, tutoring, writing center.

Majors. Biology: General, biochemistry, biotechnology, ecology, marine. **Business:** Business admin, hospitality admin. **Communications:** General. **Communications technology:** General. **Computer sciences:** General, security. **Education:** Early childhood, elementary, health, physical, special. **English:** English lit. **Foreign languages:** French, Spanish. **Health:** Athletic training, audiology/speech pathology, clinical lab science, health services admin, nursing (RN). **History:** General. **Interdisciplinary:** Biological/physical sciences. **Liberal arts:** Arts/sciences, humanities. **Math:** General. **Parks/recreation:** Exercise sciences, facilities management. **Philosophy/religion:** Philosophy. **Physical sciences:** General, chemistry, geology, physics. **Psychology:** General. **Social sciences:** General, economics, geography, political science, sociology. **Visual/performing arts:** General, dramatic, graphic design.

Most popular majors. Biology 6%, business/marketing 13%, education 24%, health sciences 8%, parks/recreation 9%, psychology 9%, social sciences 11%.

Computing on campus. 708 workstations in dormitories, library, computer center, student center. Dormitories linked to campus network. Online course registration, helpline, wireless network available.

Student life. Freshman orientation: Available. Preregistration for classes offered. 2-day event during summer with joint and separate sessions for parents. **Housing:** Guaranteed on-campus for freshmen. Coed dorms, single-sex dorms, special housing for disabled, apartments, substance-free housing available. $150 nonrefundable deposit. **Activities:** Bands, choral groups, dance, drama, literary magazine, music ensembles, musical theater, radio station, student government, student newspaper, symphony orchestra, Latin American Students Association, Campus Democrats, Young Republicans, African American Student Alliance, Fellowship of Christian Athletes, Newman Club, Women for Awareness.

Athletics. NCAA. **Intercollegiate:** Baseball M, basketball, cross-country, field hockey W, football (tackle) M, lacrosse W, soccer, softball W, swimming W, tennis, track and field, volleyball, wrestling M. **Intramural:** Badminton, basketball, football (non-tackle), racquetball, soccer, softball, tennis, volleyball, water polo. **Team name:** Warriors.

Student services. Adult student services, campus ministries, career counseling, student employment services, financial aid counseling, health services, minority student services, on-campus daycare, personal counseling, placement for graduates, veterans' counselor, women's services. **Physically disabled:** Services for visually, speech, hearing impaired.

Contact. E-mail: undergrads@po-box.esu.edu
Phone: (570) 422-3542 Toll-free number: (877) 230-5547
Fax: (570) 422-3933
Jennifer Serowick, Associate Director, East Stroudsburg University of Pennsylvania, 200 Prospect Street, East Stroudsburg, PA 18301-2999

Eastern University
St. Davids, Pennsylvania
www.eastern.edu **CB code: 2220**

- Private 4-year university affiliated with American Baptist Churches in the USA
- Residential campus in small town
- 2,216 degree-seeking undergraduates: 10% part-time, 65% women, 15% African American, 2% Asian American, 5% Hispanic American, 2% international
- 1,014 graduate students
- 77% of applicants admitted
- SAT or ACT (ACT writing optional), application essay required

General. Founded in 1952. Regionally accredited. **Degrees:** 548 bachelor's, 21 associate awarded; master's, doctoral, first professional offered. **ROTC:** Army, Air Force. **Location:** 10 miles from Philadelphia. **Calendar:** Semester, limited summer session. **Full-time faculty:** 80 total. **Part-time faculty:** 260 total. **Special facilities:** Planetarium, observatory.

Freshman class profile. 1,153 applied, 893 admitted, 404 enrolled.

Mid 50% test scores		Rank in top tenth:	17%
SAT verbal:	490-600	Return as sophomores:	80%
SAT math:	480-590	Out-of-state:	51%
ACT:	22-31	Live on campus:	94%
Rank in top quarter:	45%		

Basis for selection. SAT, high school GPA, and high school rank most important. Fit with school mission, slope of grades, attendance, interviews also evaluated. Interview recommended.

2005-2006 Annual costs. Tuition/fees: $18,875. Room/board: $7,840. Books/supplies: $800. Personal expenses: $1,604.

Application procedures. Admission: No deadline. $25 fee, may be waived for applicants with need. Application may be submitted online. Admission notification on a rolling basis. **Financial aid:** No deadline. FAFSA, institutional form required. Applicants notified on a rolling basis starting 4/1.

Academics. Special study options: Accelerated study, cross-registration, double major, honors, independent study, student-designed major, study abroad, teacher certification program, Washington semester. **Credit/placement by examination:** AP, CLEP, IB, SAT, ACT. 30 credit hours maximum toward associate degree, 60 toward bachelor's. **Support services:** Pre-admission summer program, remedial instruction, study skills assistance, tutoring, writing center.

Honors college/program. Students entering from high school must be in the top 9% of their graduating class and have SAT scores of 1300 (exclusive of Writing) or ACT scores of 30, or extraordinary leadership abilities with significant academic achievements. Transfer students must have a 3.4 grade-point average from prior institution and no more than 36 credits.

Majors. Biology: General, biochemistry. **Business:** Accounting, business admin, management information systems, nonprofit/public. **Communications:** General. **Conservation:** General. **Education:** Elementary, English, secondary. **English:** British lit, creative writing. **Foreign languages:** French, Spanish. **History:** General. **Math:** General. **Parks/recreation:** Health/fitness. **Philosophy/religion:** Philosophy. **Physical sciences:** Astronomy, chemistry. **Psychology:** General. **Public administration:** Social work. **Social sciences:** Economics, political science, sociology, urban studies. **Theology:** Bible, missionary, theology, youth ministry. **Visual/performing arts:** Art history/conservation, multimedia.

Most popular majors. Business/marketing 44%, education 8%, philosophy/religious studies 9%, psychology 6%, social sciences 6%.

Computing on campus. 131 workstations in dormitories, library, computer center, student center. Dormitories wired for high-speed internet access and linked to campus network. Commuter students can connect to campus network. Repair service available.

Student life. Freshman orientation: Mandatory. Preregistration for classes offered. Held 3 days before fall semester. **Policies:** Smoke-free campus. **Housing:** Coed dorms, apartments, substance-free housing available. $150 deposit, deadline 8/1. Students required to live on campus unless they receive permission from Dean of Students Office. **Activities:** Bands, choral groups, dance, drama, literary magazine, music ensembles, musical theater, student government, student newspaper, Black Student League, Penn State Education Association, yacht club, Gospel Outreach, Fellowship of Christian Athletes, Habitat for Humanity, Evangelicals for Social Action, Students Organized Against Racism, prison ministry, Latinos Unidos.

Athletics. NCAA. **Intercollegiate:** Baseball M, basketball, cross-country M, field hockey W, golf M, lacrosse, soccer, softball W, tennis, volleyball W. **Intramural:** Basketball, cheerleading, soccer, volleyball. **Team name:** Eagles.

Student services. Adult student services, alcohol/substance abuse counseling, campus ministries, career counseling, financial aid counseling, health services, legal services, minority student services, personal counseling, veterans' counselor, women's services. **Physically disabled:** Services for visually, speech, hearing impaired.

Contact. E-mail: ugadm@eastern.edu
Phone: (610) 341-5967 Toll-free number: (800) 452-0996
Fax: (610) 341-1723
David Urban, Executive Director for Enrollment, Eastern University, 1300 Eagle Road, St. Davids, PA 19087-3696

Edinboro University of Pennsylvania

Edinboro, Pennsylvania **CB member**
www.edinboro.edu **CB code: 2651**

- Public 4-year university
- Commuter campus in small town
- 6,312 degree-seeking undergraduates: 11% part-time, 57% women, 8% African American, 1% Asian American, 1% Hispanic American, 2% international
- 902 degree-seeking graduate students
- 82% of applicants admitted
- SAT or ACT with writing required
- 51% graduate within 6 years

General. Founded in 1857. Regionally accredited. Extensive programs and services for physically and learning disabled students available. Credit courses, continuing education, workshops, and seminars offered at Porreco Extension Center in Erie. **Degrees:** 1,174 bachelor's, 39 associate awarded; master's offered. **ROTC:** Army. **Location:** 18 miles from Erie. **Calendar:** Semester, extensive summer session. **Full-time faculty:** 363 total; 69% have terminal degrees, 9% minority, 44% women. **Part-time faculty:** 45 total; 4% minority, 53% women. **Class size:** 32% < 20, 51% 20-39, 12% 40-49, 5% 50-99. **Special facilities:** Observatory, planetarium, natural wildlife museum, robotics laboratory, center for performing arts, speech and hearing clinic, historical museum.

Freshman class profile. 3,541 applied, 2,903 admitted, 1,325 enrolled.

Mid 50% test scores		Rank in top tenth:	6%
SAT verbal:	420-540	Return as sophomores:	66%
SAT math:	420-530	Out-of-state:	10%
ACT:	16-21	Live on campus:	73%
Rank in top quarter:	21%	International:	1%

Basis for selection. High school curriculum, test scores, GPA, and class rank most important. Recommendations and activities record also reviewed. Interview and essay recommended for all; audition required for music program; portfolio recommended for art program. **Homeschooled:** Transcript of courses and grades, interview, letter of recommendation (nonparent) required.

High school preparation. College-preparatory program recommended. 15 units recommended. Recommended units include English 4, mathematics 3, social studies 3, science 3, foreign language 2 and academic electives 4. One unit of computer/word processing course recommended.

2005-2006 Annual costs. Tuition/fees: $6,289; $11,197 out-of-state. Room/board: $5,783. Books/supplies: $750. Personal expenses: $1,300.

2004-2005 Financial aid. **Need-based:** 1,195 full-time freshmen applied for aid; 1,027 were judged to have need; 999 of these received aid. Average need met was 78%. Average scholarship/grant was $2,832; average loan $2,107. 56% of total undergraduate aid awarded as scholarships/grants, 44% as loans/jobs. **Non-need-based:** Awarded to 1,764 full-time undergraduates, including 477 freshmen. Scholarships awarded for academics, alumni affiliation, art, athletics, job skills, leadership, minority status, music/drama, religious affiliation, ROTC, state residency.

Application procedures. **Admission:** Priority date 4/1; no deadline. $30 fee, may be waived for applicants with need. Application may be submitted online. Admission notification on a rolling basis. Must reply by May 1 or within 4 week(s) if notified thereafter. **Financial aid:** Priority date 3/15, closing date 5/1. FAFSA required. Applicants notified on a rolling basis starting 3/31; must reply within 2 week(s) of notification.

Academics. 60 credits of general education electives required for bachelor's degree. Associate degree counseling, peer tutoring, peer mentors, academic advising center, and trial admissions program offered. **Special study options:** Combined bachelor's/graduate degree, distance learning, double major, dual enrollment of high school students, honors, independent study, internships, liberal arts/career combination, student-designed major, study abroad, teacher certification program. **Credit/placement by examination:** AP, CLEP, SAT, ACT, institutional tests. 30 credit hours maximum toward associate degree, 30 toward bachelor's. **Support services:** Learning center, pre-admission summer program, reduced course load, remedial instruction, study skills assistance, tutoring, writing center.

Majors. **Area/ethnic studies:** German, Latin American, Spanish/Iberian. **Biology:** General. **Business:** Accounting, business admin, marketing, operations. **Communications:** General, broadcast journalism, journalism. **Computer sciences:** General, computer science. **Conservation:** General, environmental science, environmental studies. **Education:** Early childhood, elementary, reading, social studies, special. **English:** English lit. **Foreign languages:** German, Spanish. **Health:** Clinical lab technology, communication disorders, nursing (RN), predentistry, premedicine, preveterinary. **History:** General. **Interdisciplinary:** Biological/physical sciences. **Liberal arts:** Humanities. **Math:** General. **Parks/recreation:** Health/fitness, sports admin. **Philosophy/religion:** Philosophy. **Physical sciences:** Chemistry, geology, physics, planetary. **Protective services:** Criminal justice. **Psychology:** General. **Public administration:** Social work. **Social sciences:** General, anthropology, economics, geography, political science, sociology. **Visual/performing arts:** Art history/conservation, ceramics, dramatic, drawing, fiber arts, graphic design, painting, photography, printmaking, sculpture.

Most popular majors. Business/marketing 7%, communications/journalism 8%, education 14%, health sciences 8%, security/protective services 8%, visual/performing arts 15%.

Computing on campus. 717 workstations in dormitories, library, computer center, student center. Dormitories wired for high-speed internet access and linked to campus network. Commuter students can connect to campus network. Online course registration, online library, helpline, repair service available.

Student life. **Freshman orientation:** Available. Preregistration for classes offered. Summer program. **Policies:** Zero tolerance policy for alcohol and drugs on campus. Freshmen permitted cars on campus. **Housing:** Guaranteed on-campus for freshmen. Coed dorms, single-sex dorms, special housing for disabled, substance-free housing available. $75 partly refundable deposit, deadline 7/1. Living/learning by major and nonsmoking halls available. **Activities:** Bands, choral groups, dance, drama, film society, literary magazine, radio station, student government, student newspaper, TV station, 89 organizations on campus.

Athletics. NCAA. **Intercollegiate:** Basketball, cross-country, football (tackle) M, soccer W, softball W, swimming, track and field, volleyball W, wrestling M. **Intramural:** Basketball, football (non-tackle), racquetball, soccer, softball, volleyball, wrestling M. **Team name:** The Fighting Scots.

Student services. Adult student services, alcohol/substance abuse counseling, campus ministries, career counseling, student employment services, financial aid counseling, health services, minority student services, personal counseling, placement for graduates, veterans' counselor. **Physically disabled:** Services for visually, speech, hearing impaired. **Learning disabled:** Comprehensive services available.

Contact. E-mail: eup_admissions@edinboro.edu
Phone: (814) 732-2761 Toll-free number: (800) 626-2203
Fax: (814) 732-2420
Terrence Carlin, Assistant Vice President for Undergraduate Admissions, Edinboro University of Pennsylvania, 148 Meadville Street, Edinboro, PA 16444

Elizabethtown College

Elizabethtown, Pennsylvania **CB member**
www.etown.edu **CB code: 2225**

- Private 4-year liberal arts college affiliated with Church of the Brethren
- Residential campus in large town
- 2,082 degree-seeking undergraduates: 11% part-time, 66% women
- 38 degree-seeking graduate students
- 62% of applicants admitted
- SAT or ACT, application essay required
- 68% graduate within 6 years

General. Founded in 1899. Regionally accredited. **Degrees:** 442 bachelor's, 11 associate awarded; master's offered. **Location:** 20 miles from Harrisburg, 90 miles from Philadelphia. **Calendar:** Semester, limited summer session. **Full-time faculty:** 125 total; 80% have terminal degrees, 9% minority, 42% women. **Part-time faculty:** 82 total; 24% have terminal degrees, 7% minority, 58% women. **Class size:** 68% < 20, 31% 20-39, less than 1% 40-49, less than 1% 50-99, less than 1% >100. **Special facilities:** Center for study of Anabaptist and Pietist groups.

Freshman class profile. 2,708 applied, 1,692 admitted, 538 enrolled.

Mid 50% test scores		Rank in top tenth:	29%
SAT verbal:	510-610	Return as sophomores:	86%
SAT math:	500-620	Out-of-state:	32%
ACT:	21-26	Live on campus:	96%
Rank in top quarter:	63%		

Basis for selection. School achievement record most important. College preparatory program strongly recommended. Co-curricular activities also considered, particularly service-oriented activities. Applicants should be in top quarter of class. Interview required for occupational therapy and honors program. For international business applicants, essay must demonstrate interest in that subject area. Audition required for music, music education, music therapy programs; portfolio required for art program.

High school preparation. 15 units required; 20 recommended. Required and recommended units include English 4, mathematics 3-4, social studies 2, history 2, science 2-4 (laboratory 2-3), foreign language 2 and academic electives 2.

2005-2006 Annual costs. Tuition/fees: $25,200. Room/board: $6,900. Books/supplies: $700. Personal expenses: $600.

2005-2006 Financial aid. Need-based: 451 full-time freshmen applied for aid; 366 were judged to have need; 366 of these received aid. Average need met was 83%. Average scholarship/grant was $15,210; average loan $2,927. 75% of total undergraduate aid awarded as scholarships/grants, 25% as loans/jobs. **Non-need-based:** Awarded to 387 full-time undergraduates, including 150 freshmen. Scholarships awarded for academics, art, music/drama, religious affiliation.

Application procedures. Admission: Priority date 3/1; no deadline. $30 fee, may be waived for applicants with need. Application may be submitted online. Admission notification on a rolling basis beginning on or about 11/15. Must reply by May 1 or within 2 week(s) if notified thereafter. December 15 closing date for occupational therapy program. March 1 closing date for international business. January 15 closing date for honors program. **Financial aid:** Priority date 3/15; no closing date. FAFSA, institutional form required. Applicants notified on a rolling basis starting 3/1; must reply by 5/1 or within 2 week(s) of notification.

Academics. Special study options: Combined bachelor's/graduate degree, double major, dual enrollment of high school students, ESL, exchange student, external degree, honors, independent study, internships, liberal arts/career combination, study abroad, teacher certification program, Washington semester. 2-2 program with Thomas Jefferson University in nursing, laboratory sciences, diagnostic imaging; 3-3 program in physical therapy (DPT) with Thomas Jefferson University: 3-2 in engineering with Penn State; 3-2 with Duke University in forestry and environmental management; 3-3 in physical therapy with Widener University and University of Maryland, Baltimore; agreements for MBA programs at Lehigh University, Rutgers University, Loyola College (MD), Penn State University, Harrisburg. **Credit/placement by examination:** AP, CLEP, IB, institutional tests. Credit by examination unlimited provided student is able to fulfill residency requirement. Credit for International Baccalaureate awarded only for subject exams and only for earned scores from 4-7. **Support services:** Learning center, reduced course load, study skills assistance, tutoring, writing center.

Majors. Biology: General, biochemistry, biotechnology. **Business:** Accounting, actuarial science, business admin, international, management information systems, managerial economics. **Communications:** Advertising, media studies, public relations. **Computer sciences:** General, information systems. **Conservation:** Environmental science, forest management, forest sciences. **Education:** Biology, chemistry, early childhood, elementary, English, history, mathematics, multi-level teacher, music, science, social science, social studies. **Engineering:** General, computer, electrical, industrial, mechanics, physics. **English:** English lit, technical writing. **Foreign languages:** French, German, Japanese, Spanish. **Health:** Clinical lab science, music therapy, predentistry, premedicine, preveterinary. **History:** General. **Interdisciplinary:** Peace/conflict. **Math:** General, applied. **Philosophy/religion:** Christian, ethics, philosophy, religion. **Physical sciences:** Chemistry, physics. **Protective services:** Criminal justice. **Psychology:** General. **Public administration:** Social work. **Social sciences:** Anthropology, economics, political science, sociology. **Theology:** Theology. **Visual/performing arts:** Art, theater arts management.

Most popular majors. Business/marketing 25%, communications/journalism 8%, education 18%, health sciences 11%, social sciences 6%.

Computing on campus. 200 workstations in dormitories, library, computer center, student center. Dormitories wired for high-speed internet access and linked to campus network. Commuter students can connect to campus network. Online course registration, online library, helpline, student web hosting available.

Student life. Freshman orientation: Mandatory. One-day summer program in June and multi-day program at beginning of fall semester. **Policies:** Freshmen permitted cars on campus. **Housing:** Guaranteed on-campus for all undergraduates. Coed dorms, single-sex dorms, special housing for disabled, apartments, substance-free housing available. Special housing available for students involved in service learning and community service. All residence halls are smoke-free. **Activities:** Bands, choral groups, dance, drama, literary magazine, music ensembles, musical theater, radio station, student government, student newspaper, symphony orchestra, TV station, Newman Club, Intervarsity Christian Fellowship, international club, Hillel, Circle-K, Habitat for Humanity, Amnesty International, Colors United, College Democrats, Republican Club, many community service organizations.

Athletics. NCAA. **Intercollegiate:** Baseball M, basketball, cross-country, diving, field hockey W, golf M, lacrosse, soccer, softball W, swimming, tennis, track and field, volleyball W, wrestling M. **Intramural:** Basketball, racquetball, soccer, softball, tennis, volleyball. **Team name:** Blue Jays.

Student services. Adult student services, alcohol/substance abuse counseling, campus ministries, career counseling, student employment services, financial aid counseling, health services, minority student services, personal counseling, placement for graduates, veterans' counselor, women's services. **Physically disabled:** Services for visually, hearing impaired. **Learning disabled:** Comprehensive services available.

Contact. E-mail: admissions@etown.edu
Phone: (717) 361-1400 Fax: (717) 361-1365
Debra Murray, Director of Admissions, Elizabethtown College, One Alpha Drive, Elizabethtown, PA 17022-2298

Franklin & Marshall College

Lancaster, Pennsylvania — **CB member**
www.fandm.edu — **CB code: 2261**

- Private 4-year liberal arts college
- Residential campus in small city
- 1,981 degree-seeking undergraduates: 1% part-time, 47% women, 3% African American, 4% Asian American, 4% Hispanic American, 7% international
- 45% of applicants admitted
- SAT or ACT (ACT writing optional), application essay required
- 82% graduate within 6 years; 25% enter graduate study

General. Founded in 1787. Regionally accredited. **Degrees:** 449 bachelor's awarded. **Location:** 60 miles from Philadelphia, 120 miles from Washington, DC. **Calendar:** Semester, limited summer session. **Full-time faculty:** 175 total; 97% have terminal degrees, 9% minority, 38% women. **Part-time faculty:** 48 total; 58% have terminal degrees, 8% minority, 44% women. **Class size:** 50% < 20, 49% 20-39, 1% 40-49, less than 1% 50-99. **Special facilities:** Observatory, science library, retail sales complex, bronze casting foundry, field house, planetarium, natural history museum, concert hall, performing arts center.

Freshman class profile. 4,227 applied, 1,921 admitted, 582 enrolled.

Mid 50% test scores		Rank in top tenth:	54%
SAT verbal:	580-680	Return as sophomores:	92%
SAT math:	600-690	Out-of-state:	65%
ACT:	26-30	Live on campus:	99%
Rank in top quarter:	83%	International:	8%

Basis for selection. School achievement record, test scores, extracurricular activities, recommendations, essay considered. Students in top 10% of class or with cumulative GPA of 3.6 or higher (4.0 scale) not required to submit standardized test scores. 2 graded writing samples must then be submitted in lieu of standardized tests. Interview required for early decision applicants, strongly recommended for others. Auditions and portfolios recommended for all students who wish to demonstrate particular talent. **Homeschooled:** Interview required. Interview, accrediting and evaluative documenation from home state, and SAT or ACT required. 3 SAT Subject Tests highly recommended.

High school preparation. Required and recommended units include English 4, mathematics 3-4, social studies 1-3, history 2-3, science 2-3 (laboratory 2-3) and foreign language 2-4. One art, music or theater required.

2005-2006 Annual costs. Tuition/fees: $32,530. Room/board: $8,060. Books/supplies: $650. Personal expenses: $950.

2005-2006 Financial aid. Need-based: 475 full-time freshmen applied for aid; 367 were judged to have need; 365 of these received aid. Average need met was 100%. Average scholarship/grant was $20,967; average loan $3,507. 75% of total undergraduate aid awarded as scholarships/grants, 25% as loans/jobs. **Non-need-based:** Awarded to 903 full-time undergraduates,

including 274 freshmen. Scholarships awarded for academics, art, leadership, music/drama.

Application procedures. Admission: Closing date 2/1 (postmark date). $50 fee, may be waived for applicants with need. Application may be submitted online. Admission notification 4/1. Must reply by 5/1. Must reply by May 1 or within 2 week(s) if notified thereafter. **Financial aid:** Priority date 2/1, closing date 3/1. FAFSA, institutional form, CSS PROFILE required. Applicants notified by 3/15; must reply by 5/1.

Academics. Interdisciplinary minors offered. **Special study options:** Accelerated study, combined bachelor's/graduate degree, cross-registration, double major, dual enrollment of high school students, exchange student, honors, independent study, internships, liberal arts/career combination, New York semester, semester at sea, student-designed major, study abroad, teacher certification program, Washington semester. 3-2 programs in forestry, engineering, environmental studies; Columbia University's New York/Paris program. **Credit/placement by examination:** AP, CLEP, IB, institutional tests. 64 credit hours maximum toward bachelor's degree. **Support services:** Preadmission summer program, reduced course load, tutoring, writing center.

Majors. Area/ethnic studies: African, African-American, American. **Biology:** General, biochemistry. **Business:** Business admin. **Conservation:** Environmental science, environmental studies. **English:** Creative writing, English lit. **Foreign languages:** Ancient Greek, classics, French, German, Latin, Spanish. **History:** General. **Interdisciplinary:** Behavioral sciences, biopsychology, neuroscience. **Math:** General. **Philosophy/religion:** Philosophy, religion. **Physical sciences:** Astronomy, astrophysics, chemistry, geology, physics. **Psychology:** General. **Social sciences:** Anthropology, economics, political science, sociology. **Visual/performing arts:** Art history/conservation, dance, dramatic, studio arts.

Most popular majors. Biology 9%, business/marketing 13%, English 10%, foreign language 7%, interdisciplinary studies 8%, social sciences 29%.

Computing on campus. 125 workstations in library, computer center. Dormitories wired for high-speed internet access and linked to campus network. Commuter students can connect to campus network. Online course registration, online library, helpline, repair service, student web hosting, wireless network available.

Student life. Freshman orientation: Mandatory, $200 fee. Preregistration for classes offered. 4 days prior to start of classes, includes noncredit presemester academic experience. **Housing:** Guaranteed on-campus for freshmen. Coed dorms, special housing for disabled, apartments, substance-free housing available. Freshmen and sophomores required to live in college housing. French house, arts house, international house available to upperclassmen, community outreach house, men's and women's floors. **Activities:** Bands, choral groups, dance, drama, literary magazine, music ensembles, musical theater, opera, radio station, student government, student newspaper, symphony orchestra, TV station, East Asian Society, Catholic Campus Community, Hillel, Christian Fellowship, Habitat for Humanity, Voices for Women, Coalition for Choice, Environmental Action Alliance, Black Student Union, Mi Gente Latina.

Athletics. NCAA. **Intercollegiate:** Baseball M, basketball, cross-country, field hockey W, football (tackle) M, golf, lacrosse, soccer, softball W, squash, swimming, tennis, track and field, volleyball W, wrestling M. **Intramural:** Archery, badminton, basketball, bowling, cross-country, football (non-tackle) M, soccer, softball, squash, table tennis, tennis, volleyball. **Team name:** Diplomats.

Student services. Alcohol/substance abuse counseling, campus ministries, career counseling, student employment services, financial aid counseling, health services, minority student services, on-campus daycare, personal counseling, placement for graduates, women's services.

Contact. E-mail: admission@fandm.edu
Phone: (717) 291-3953 Fax: (717) 291-4389
Dennis Trotter, Vice President for Enrollment Management and Dean of Admission, Franklin & Marshall College, Box 3003, Lancaster, PA 17604-3003

Gannon University

Erie, Pennsylvania — **CB member**
www.gannon.edu — **CB code: 2270**

- Private 4-year university affiliated with Roman Catholic Church
- Residential campus in small city
- 2,394 degree-seeking undergraduates: 9% part-time, 60% women, 5% African American, 1% Asian American, 1% Hispanic American, 1% international
- 972 degree-seeking graduate students
- 86% of applicants admitted
- SAT or ACT (ACT writing optional) required
- 64% graduate within 6 years

General. Founded in 1925. Regionally accredited. **Degrees:** 423 bachelor's, 28 associate awarded; master's, doctoral offered. **ROTC:** Army. **Location:** 120 miles from Pittsburgh, 90 miles from Buffalo, New York. **Calendar:** Semester, extensive summer session. **Full-time faculty:** 180 total; 68% have terminal degrees, 11% minority, 43% women. **Part-time faculty:** 119 total; 24% have terminal degrees, 3% minority, 44% women. **Class size:** 57% < 20, 41% 20-39, 2% 40-49, less than 1% 50-99, less than 1% >100. **Special facilities:** Environmental studies center, computer integrated enterprise manufacturing center, floating laboratory providing hands-on environmental study on Lake Erie.

Freshman class profile. 2,443 applied, 2,111 admitted, 632 enrolled.

Mid 50% test scores			
SAT verbal:	470-570	Rank in top quarter:	48%
SAT math:	470-580	Rank in top tenth:	21%
ACT:	18-24	End year in good standing:	90%
GPA 3.50 or higher:	42%	Return as sophomores:	83%
GPA 3.0-3.49:	25%	Out-of-state:	28%
GPA 2.0-2.99:	31%	Live on campus:	76%
		International:	1%

Basis for selection. High school record important, including course selection, GPA, class rank, standardized test scores, recommendations, personal statement. Admission requirements vary by program. Limited number of students who do not meet all admissions requirements may be accepted into General Studies program. Essay recommended, interview recommended. **Homeschooled:** Interview required. **Learning Disabled:** Applicants screened through director must be interviewed.

High school preparation. 16 units required; 18 recommended. Required and recommended units include English 4, mathematics 4, social studies 1, history 1, science 2-4 (laboratory 1-2) and foreign language 2. 6 units of any combination of social sciences, foreign language, and academic electives. Requirements vary by program. Science students must have 4 units of science.

2005-2006 Annual costs. Tuition/fees: $18,690. Engineering and health sciences tuition $19,330. Room/board: $7,410. Books/supplies: $750. Personal expenses: $1,142.

2005-2006 Financial aid. Need-based: 597 full-time freshmen applied for aid; 537 were judged to have need; 537 of these received aid. Average need met was 75%. Average scholarship/grant was $12,687; average loan $2,182. 77% of total undergraduate aid awarded as scholarships/grants, 23% as loans/jobs. **Non-need-based:** Awarded to 477 full-time undergraduates, including 142 freshmen. Scholarships awarded for academics, athletics, leadership, music/drama, religious affiliation, ROTC.

Application procedures. Admission: No deadline. $25 fee, may be waived for applicants with need. Application may be submitted online. Admission notification on a rolling basis beginning on or about 9/1. Early application especially recommended for health science programs since space is limited. Closing date for occupational therapy, physican's assistant, radiological science programs January 15. Closing date for medical program December 15. **Financial aid:** Priority date 3/15; no closing date. FAFSA, institutional form required. Applicants notified on a rolling basis starting 11/15; must reply by 5/1 or within 4 week(s) of notification.

Academics. Preferred admission to doctorate physical therapy program granted to students with bachelor's degree from Gannon in physical therapy. Occupational therapy and physician assistant programs are 5-year master's degree programs. **Special study options:** Accelerated study, combined bachelor's/graduate degree, cooperative education, distance learning, double major, dual enrollment of high school students, ESL, external degree, honors, independent study, internships, liberal arts/career combination, study abroad, teacher certification program, Washington semester, weekend college. **Credit/placement by examination:** AP, CLEP, IB, institutional tests. 36 credit hours maximum toward bachelor's degree. **Support services:** Learning center, reduced course load, remedial instruction, study skills assistance, tutoring, writing center.

Honors college/program. Minimum 1150 SAT score (exclusive of Writing), minimum 3.0 high school GPA, rank in top tenth of high school class, college preparatory curriculum, extracurricular activities, community service. Recommendation, interview and essay also required. Approximately 50 freshmen admitted per year.

Majors. Biology: General, bioinformatics. **Business:** Accounting, business admin, finance, insurance, international, management information systems, marketing. **Communications:** Advertising. **Communications technology:** Radio/tv. **Computer sciences:** General, programming. **Conservation:** Environmental science. **Education:** Business, early childhood, elementary, multi-level teacher, secondary, social studies, special. **Engineering:** Chemical, electrical, environmental, industrial, mechanical. **English:** British lit. **Foreign languages:** General. **Health:** Athletic training, clinical lab science, dietetics, nursing (RN), physician assistant, predentistry, premedicine, prepharmacy, preveterinary, respiratory therapy technology. **History:** General. **Legal studies:** Paralegal, prelaw. **Liberal arts:** Arts/sciences. **Math:** General. **Personal/culinary services:** Mortuary science. **Philosophy/religion:** Philosophy. **Physical sciences:** Chemistry. **Protective services:** Criminal justice. **Psychology:** General. **Public administration:** Social work. **Science technology:** Biological. **Social sciences:** General, political science. **Theology:** Theology. **Visual/performing arts:** General, dramatic.

Most popular majors. Biology 6%, business/marketing 17%, education 12%, engineering/engineering technologies 8%, health sciences 20%, security/protective services 8%.

Computing on campus. 350 workstations in dormitories, library, computer center, student center. Dormitories wired for high-speed internet access and linked to campus network. Commuter students can connect to campus network. Online library, helpline, wireless network available.

Student life. **Freshman orientation:** Mandatory, $60 fee. Preregistration for classes offered. 4 separate sessions during summer. Open to parents and students. **Policies:** Freshmen permitted cars on campus. **Housing:** Guaranteed on-campus for freshmen. Coed dorms, special housing for disabled, apartments, substance-free housing available. $100 fully refundable deposit. **Activities:** Pep band, choral groups, dance, drama, literary magazine, music ensembles, musical theater, radio station, student government, student newspaper, campus ministry, Social Concerns, international student society, minority student union, College Democrats, College Republicans, activities programming board, debate, Vitality Through Exercise, residence union.

Athletics. NCAA. **Intercollegiate:** Baseball M, basketball, cheerleading, cross-country, diving, football (tackle) M, golf, lacrosse W, soccer, softball W, swimming, volleyball W, water polo, wrestling M. **Intramural:** Badminton, basketball, bowling, football (non-tackle), golf, handball, racquetball, soccer, softball, swimming, table tennis, volleyball, water polo, wrestling M. **Team name:** Golden Knights.

Student services. Adult student services, alcohol/substance abuse counseling, campus ministries, career counseling, services for economically disadvantaged, student employment services, financial aid counseling, health services, minority student services, personal counseling, placement for graduates, veterans' counselor. **Learning disabled:** Comprehensive services available.

Contact. E-mail: admissions@gannon.edu
Phone: (814) 871-7240 Toll-free number: (800) 426-6668
Fax: (814) 871-5803
Bill Eilola, Dean of Enrollment, Gannon University, 109 University Square, Erie, PA 16541-0001

Geneva College

Beaver Falls, Pennsylvania — **CB member**
www.geneva.edu — **CB code: 2273**

- Private 4-year liberal arts college affiliated with Reformed Presbyterian Church of North America
- Residential campus in large town
- 1,762 degree-seeking undergraduates: 9% African American, 1% Asian American, 1% international
- 354 graduate students
- 68% of applicants admitted
- SAT or ACT with writing, application essay required
- 55% graduate within 6 years

General. Founded in 1848. Regionally accredited. Christian college of arts, sciences, and Biblical studies, committed to diversity and development of servant leaders. **Degrees:** 430 bachelor's, 12 associate awarded; master's offered. **ROTC:** Army. **Location:** 35 miles from Pittsburgh. **Calendar:** Semester, extensive summer session. **Full-time faculty:** 80 total. **Part-time faculty:** 75 total. **Special facilities:** Collection of artifacts and records of Pittsburgh steel industry, center for technology development, observatory.

Freshman class profile. 1,328 applied, 905 admitted, 353 enrolled.

Mid 50% test scores		Return as sophomores:	75%
SAT verbal:	490-610	International:	1%
SAT math:	490-600		

Basis for selection. Academic performance and test scores most important. Recommendations important. Activities considered. Interview recommended for all; audition required for music program. **Homeschooled:** Help in preparing homeschooler's transcript available if necessary.

High school preparation. 16 units required. Required units include English 4, mathematics 2, social studies 3, science 1, foreign language 2 and academic electives 4. Engineering students should have 1 unit of chemistry and physics, 4 units of college-preparatory mathematics including trigonometry or precalculus.

2006-2007 Annual costs. Tuition/fees (projected): $18,460. Room/board: $6,960. Books/supplies: $800. Personal expenses: $1,150.

2005-2006 Financial aid. **Need-based:** Average need met was 75%. Average scholarship/grant was $9,987; average loan $3,187. 59% of total undergraduate aid awarded as scholarships/grants, 41% as loans/jobs. **Non-need-based:** Scholarships awarded for academics, athletics, music/drama, religious affiliation.

Application procedures. **Admission:** No deadline. $25 fee, may be waived for applicants with need. Application may be submitted online. Admission notification on a rolling basis beginning on or about 9/1. Must reply by May 1 or within 3 week(s) if notified thereafter. **Financial aid:** Priority date 3/15; no closing date. FAFSA required. Applicants notified on a rolling basis starting 3/1; must reply by 5/1 or within 4 week(s) of notification.

Academics. **Special study options:** Accelerated study, combined bachelor's/graduate degree, cooperative education, cross-registration, double major, dual enrollment of high school students, honors, independent study, internships, liberal arts/career combination, student-designed major, study abroad, teacher certification program, Washington semester. **Credit/placement by examination:** AP, CLEP, IB, SAT, ACT, institutional tests. 30 credit hours maximum toward bachelor's degree. **Support services:** Pre-admission summer program, reduced course load, remedial instruction, study skills assistance, tutoring, writing center.

Majors. **Biology:** General. **Business:** Accounting, business admin, human resources. **Communications:** General. **Computer sciences:** General. **Education:** General, biology, chemistry, elementary, English, history, mathematics, music, physics, social studies, special. **Engineering:** General, chemical. **English:** Composition, English lit, speech/rhetoric. **Foreign languages:** Spanish. **Health:** Speech pathology. **History:** General. **Liberal arts:** Arts/sciences. **Math:** Applied. **Philosophy/religion:** Philosophy. **Physical sciences:** Chemistry, physics. **Psychology:** General. **Public administration:** Social work. **Social sciences:** Political science, sociology. **Theology:** Bible, youth ministry. **Visual/performing arts:** Music management, music performance.

Most popular majors. Business/marketing 32%, education 21%, philosophy/religious studies 16%.

Computing on campus. 150 workstations in dormitories, library, computer center, student center. Dormitories wired for high-speed internet access and linked to campus network. Commuter students can connect to campus network. Online library, helpline, repair service, wireless network available.

Student life. **Freshman orientation:** Mandatory, $100 fee. **Policies:** Smoking, drinking, social or ballroom dancing not permitted on campus. Students must live on campus unless married, commuting, or over age 24. Religious observance required. Freshmen permitted cars on campus. **Housing:** Guaranteed on-campus for all undergraduates. Single-sex dorms, apartments, substance-free housing available. $150 deposit. Special interest, theme houses available. **Activities:** Bands, choral groups, dance, drama, literary magazine, music ensembles, radio station, student government, student newspaper, international student club, Christian ministry organizations, community service club, music ministry teams, Young Republicans, black student organization.

Athletics. NCAA, NCCAA. **Intercollegiate:** Baseball M, basketball, cheerleading, cross-country, football (tackle) M, soccer, softball W, tennis W, track and field, volleyball W. **Intramural:** Basketball, football (tackle) M, racquetball, soccer, softball, volleyball. **Team name:** Golden Tornadoes.

Student services. Campus ministries, career counseling, student employment services, financial aid counseling, health services, minority student services, personal counseling, placement for graduates. **Physically disabled:** Services for visually, hearing impaired.

Contact. E-mail: admissions@geneva.edu
Phone: (724) 847-6500 Toll-free number: (800) 847-8255
Fax: (724) 847-6776
David Layton, Dean of Enrollment, Geneva College, 3200 College Avenue, Beaver Falls, PA 15010

Gettysburg College

Gettysburg, Pennsylvania — **CB member**
www.gettysburg.edu — **CB code: 2275**

- Private 4-year liberal arts college
- Residential campus in large town

Four-Year Colleges

- 2,463 degree-seeking undergraduates: 52% women, 4% African American, 1% Asian American, 2% Hispanic American, 1% international
- 43% of applicants admitted
- SAT or ACT (ACT writing optional), application essay required
- 76% graduate within 6 years; 40% enter graduate study

General. Founded in 1832. Regionally accredited. **Degrees:** 588 bachelor's awarded. **ROTC:** Army. **Location:** 36 miles from Harrisburg, 80 miles from Washington, DC. **Calendar:** Semester. **Full-time faculty:** 187 total; 91% have terminal degrees, 18% minority, 44% women. **Part-time faculty:** 87 total; 3% minority, 47% women. **Class size:** 68% < 20, 30% 20-39, 2% 40-49, less than 1% 50-99. **Special facilities:** Observatory, planetarium, intercultural resource center, women's resource center, child study center, public service center, optics and plasma physics laboratories, infrared and NMR spectrometers, proton accelerator, science center, wireless computer labs, smart classrooms, college navigation portal, art gallery, special collections, outdoor climbing wall, language resource center for foreign language study, music conservatory.

Freshman class profile. 5,097 applied, 2,183 admitted, 697 enrolled.

Mid 50% test scores			
SAT verbal:	600-670	Return as sophomores:	92%
SAT math:	610-670	Out-of-state:	75%
Rank in top quarter:	89%	Live on campus:	100%
Rank in top tenth:	66%	International:	1%

Basis for selection. Academic record, test scores, recommendations, and activities most important. Audition required for music program; portfolio recommended for art program. Interview strongly recommended. **Homeschooled:** Statement describing homeschool structure and mission, transcript of courses and grades, interview, letter of recommendation (nonparent) required.

High school preparation. College-preparatory program required. Required and recommended units include English 4, mathematics 3-4, social studies 3-4, history 3-4, science 3-4 (laboratory 3-4) and foreign language 3-4.

2005-2006 Annual costs. Tuition/fees: $32,070. Room/board: $7,794. Books/supplies: $500.

2005-2006 Financial aid. **Need-based:** 479 full-time freshmen applied for aid; 384 were judged to have need; 384 of these received aid. Average need met was 100%. Average scholarship/grant was $20,095; average loan $3,466. 82% of total undergraduate aid awarded as scholarships/grants, 18% as loans/jobs. **Non-need-based:** Scholarships awarded for academics, music/drama.

Application procedures. **Admission:** Closing date 2/15 (postmark date). $45 fee, may be waived for applicants with need. Application may be submitted online. Admission notification 4/1. Must reply by May 1 or within 2 week(s) if notified thereafter. **Financial aid:** Closing date 2/15. FAFSA, CSS PROFILE required. Applicants notified by 3/27; must reply by 5/1.

Academics. **Special study options:** Combined bachelor's/graduate degree, double major, exchange student, independent study, internships, liberal arts/career combination, New York semester, semester at sea, student-designed major, study abroad, teacher certification program, United Nations semester, Washington semester. 3-2 programs in engineering with Columbia University, Rensselaer Polytechnic Institute, and Washington University in St. Louis; 3-2 program in nursing with Johns Hopkins University; 3-2 program in forestry with Duke University; pre-law and health professions advising available. **Credit/placement by examination:** AP, CLEP, IB, SAT, institutional tests. **Support services:** Study skills assistance, tutoring, writing center.

Majors. **Area/ethnic studies:** African-American, American, Asian, Asian-American, East Asian, Japanese, Latin American, women's. **Biology:** General, biochemistry, conservation, molecular. **Business:** Business admin, finance, international, management science, marketing, nonprofit/public. **Communications:** General, journalism. **Computer sciences:** General, computer science. **Conservation:** General, environmental science, environmental studies, forestry, management/policy, water/wetlands/marine. **Education:** Music. **Engineering:** General, aerospace, biomedical, chemical, civil, computer, electrical, environmental, mechanical, mechanics, nuclear, physics, science. **English:** American lit, British lit, creative writing. **Foreign languages:** Classics, comparative lit, French, German, Japanese, Latin, Spanish. **Health:** Health services, nursing (RN), predentistry, premedicine, prepharmacy, preveterinary. **History:** General, American, Asian, European. **Interdisciplinary:** Behavioral sciences, biological/physical sciences, global studies, math/computer science, medieval/Renaissance, natural sciences, neuroscience, peace/conflict. **Legal studies:** Prelaw. **Liberal arts:** Arts/sciences. **Math:** General. **Parks/recreation:** Exercise sciences, health/fitness, sports admin. **Philosophy/religion:** Philosophy, religion. **Physical sciences:** Astronomy, chemistry, physics. **Psychology:** General. **Social sciences:** Anthropology, economics, international relations, political science, sociology, U.S. government. **Theology:** Preministerial. **Visual/performing arts:** General, art, art history/conservation, dramatic, film/cinema, music performance, music theory/composition, piano/organ, studio arts, theater arts management, voice/opera.

Most popular majors. Biology 10%, business/marketing 22%, English 7%, history 7%, psychology 8%, social sciences 20%.

Computing on campus. 620 workstations in library, computer center, student center. Dormitories wired for high-speed internet access and linked to campus network. Commuter students can connect to campus network. Online course registration, online library, helpline, repair service, wireless network available.

Student life. **Freshman orientation:** Mandatory. Preregistration for classes offered. Begins 5 days prior to the start of fall semester classes. **Policies:** Freshmen permitted cars on campus. **Housing:** Guaranteed on-campus for all undergraduates. Coed dorms, single-sex dorms, apartments, fraternity/sorority housing, substance-free housing available. $500 nonrefundable deposit, deadline 5/1. Special interest and theme housing available. **Activities:** Bands, choral groups, dance, drama, film society, literary magazine, music ensembles, musical theater, radio station, student government, student newspaper, symphony orchestra, TV station, over 100 clubs available.

Athletics. NCAA. **Intercollegiate:** Baseball M, basketball, cheerleading, cross-country, field hockey W, football (tackle) M, golf, lacrosse, soccer, softball W, swimming, tennis, track and field, volleyball W, wrestling M. **Intramural:** Badminton, basketball, field hockey, football (non-tackle), golf, lacrosse W, skiing, soccer, softball, volleyball, weight lifting. **Team name:** Bullets.

Student services. Campus ministries, career counseling, student employment services, financial aid counseling, health services, minority student services, personal counseling, placement for graduates, women's services.

Contact. E-mail: admiss@gettysburg.edu
Phone: (717) 337-6100 Toll-free number: (800) 431-0803
Fax: (717) 337-6145
Gail Sweezey, Director of Admissions, Gettysburg College, 300 North Washington Street, Gettysburg, PA 17325-1484

Gratz College

Melrose Park, Pennsylvania
www.gratzcollege.edu **CB code: 2280**

- Private 4-year college of Jewish studies and Jewish education affiliated with Jewish faith
- Commuter campus in very large city
- 6 degree-seeking undergraduates: 67% part-time, 83% women
- 37 degree-seeking graduate students
- Application essay required

General. Founded in 1895. Regionally accredited. **Degrees:** 5 bachelor's awarded; master's offered. **Location:** 6 miles from Philadelphia. **Calendar:** Semester, limited summer session. **Full-time faculty:** 10 total. **Part-time faculty:** 125 total. **Special facilities:** Jewish music library and rare book collection, oral history Holocaust archives, Holocaust Awareness Museum.

Basis for selection. Application, personal statement, transcripts and commitment to Jewish Studies. Interview recommended.

2005-2006 Annual costs. Tuition/fees: $10,070. Books/supplies: $550. Personal expenses: $500.

Application procedures. **Admission:** No deadline. $50 fee. Admission notification on a rolling basis. **Financial aid:** Priority date 6/1; no closing date. FAFSA, institutional form required. Applicants notified on a rolling basis starting 11/1.

Academics. All education programs relate specifically to Jewish Studies. For bachelor's in Jewish Studies, 42 liberal arts credits from another accredited college or university required. **Special study options:** Cross-registration, distance learning, double major, independent study, internships, study abroad, teacher certification program. Double master's programs in Jewish education/Jewish music/Jewish studies. **Credit/placement by examination:** CLEP, institutional tests. **Support services:** Reduced course load, remedial instruction, tutoring.

Majors. **Philosophy/religion:** Judaic, religion.

Computing on campus. Wireless network available.

Student life. **Freshman orientation:** Available. **Policies:** Freshmen permitted cars on campus. **Activities:** Choral groups.

Student services. Adult student services, career counseling, financial aid counseling, personal counseling, placement for graduates.

Contact. E-mail: admissions@gratz.edu
Phone: (215) 635-7300 ext. 140 Toll-free number: (800) 475-4635 ext. 140
Fax: (215) 635-7399
Jill Sigman, Director of Admissions, Gratz College, 7605 Old York Road, Melrose Park, PA 19027

Grove City College

Grove City, Pennsylvania — **CB member**
www.gcc.edu — **CB code: 2277**

- Private 4-year liberal arts college affiliated with Presbyterian Church (USA)
- Residential campus in small town
- 2,310 degree-seeking undergraduates: 49% women, 2% Asian American, 1% international
- 45% of applicants admitted
- SAT or ACT with writing, application essay, interview required
- 81% graduate within 6 years; 20% enter graduate study

General. Founded in 1876. Regionally accredited. **Degrees:** 530 bachelor's awarded. **ROTC:** Army. **Location:** 60 miles from Pittsburgh. **Calendar:** Semester, extensive summer session. **Full-time faculty:** 125 total; 81% have terminal degrees, less than 1% minority, 22% women. **Part-time faculty:** 59 total; 22% have terminal degrees, 44% women. **Class size:** 36% < 20, 48% 20-39, 10% 40-49, 5% 50-99, 2% >100. **Special facilities:** Fine arts center.

Freshman class profile. 2,077 applied, 925 admitted, 582 enrolled.

Mid 50% test scores			
SAT verbal:	580-700	Rank in top tenth:	54%
SAT math:	580-700	End year in good standing:	91%
ACT:	25-30	Return as sophomores:	91%
GPA 3.50 or higher:	93%	Out-of-state:	51%
GPA 3.0-3.49:	7%	Live on campus:	90%
Rank in top quarter:	83%	Fraternities:	13%
		Sororities:	13%

Basis for selection. High school record, GPA or class rank, test scores, recommendations, interview, character, and extracurricular activities very important. Audition required for music program. **Homeschooled:** Transcript of courses and grades, interview, letter of recommendation (nonparent) required. Outside activities important.

High school preparation. 17 units recommended. Recommended units include English 4, mathematics 3, social studies 2, history 2, science 3 (laboratory 2) and foreign language 3. Engineering, science, and mathematics applicants must have 4 mathematics and 4 science.

2005-2006 Annual costs. Tuition/fees: $10,440. Tuition includes cost of tablet PC and printer. Room/board: $5,344. Books/supplies: $900. Personal expenses: $350.

2005-2006 Financial aid. **Need-based:** 352 full-time freshmen applied for aid; 241 were judged to have need; 241 of these received aid. Average need met was 56%. Average scholarship/grant was $5,104. 59% of total undergraduate aid awarded as scholarships/grants, 41% as loans/jobs. **Non-need-based:** Awarded to 857 full-time undergraduates, including 216 freshmen. Scholarships awarded for academics, leadership, minority status. **Additional information:** Institutional aid applications required for institutional scholarships, loans, and student employment.

Application procedures. **Admission:** Closing date 2/1 (postmark date). $50 fee, may be waived for applicants with need. Application may be submitted online. Admission notification on a rolling basis beginning on or about 3/15. Must reply by 5/1. **Financial aid:** Closing date 4/15. Institutional form required. Applicants notified on a rolling basis starting 3/15; must reply by 5/1.

Academics. All students required to complete 3-year interdisciplinary humanities sequence, which includes religion, philosophy, history, philosophy of science, literature, art, and music. **Special study options:** Accelerated study, double major, independent study, internships, study abroad, teacher certification program, Washington semester. **Credit/placement by examination:** AP, CLEP, IB. **Support services:** Reduced course load, tutoring.

Majors. **Biology:** General, biochemistry, molecular. **Business:** Accounting, business admin, communications, entrepreneurial studies, international, managerial economics, marketing. **Communications:** General. **Computer sciences:** General, applications programming, systems analysis. **Education:** Biology, chemistry, early childhood, elementary, English, French, history, mathematics, music, physics, science, secondary, social studies, Spanish. **Engineering:** Electrical, mechanical. **Engineering technology:** Industrial management. **Foreign languages:** French, Spanish. **Health:** Predentistry, premedicine, preveterinary. **History:** General. **Interdisciplinary:** Math/computer science. **Legal studies:** Prelaw. **Math:** General. **Philosophy/religion:** Philosophy, religion. **Physical sciences:** Chemistry, physics. **Psychology:** General. **Social sciences:** Economics, political science, sociology. **Visual/performing arts:** Music management, music performance.

Most popular majors. Biology 11%, business/marketing 21%, education 12%, engineering/engineering technologies 11%, English 7%, social sciences 6%.

Computing on campus. PC or laptop required. 50 workstations in library, computer center. Dormitories wired for high-speed internet access and linked to campus network. Commuter students can connect to campus network. Online course registration, online library, helpline, repair service, student web hosting, wireless network available.

Student life. **Freshman orientation:** Available. Preregistration for classes offered. One-day programs in June. **Policies:** Alcohol not permitted on campus. Chapel program consists of lectures, vespers, and seminars. Students must attend 16 chapels per semester. Religious observance required. **Housing:** Guaranteed on-campus for all undergraduates. Single-sex dorms, apartments, substance-free housing available. **Activities:** Bands, choral groups, dance, drama, literary magazine, music ensembles, musical theater, opera, radio station, student government, student newspaper, symphony orchestra, 22 Christian organizations, political, and many social service organizations.

Athletics. NCAA. **Intercollegiate:** Baseball M, basketball, cheerleading M, cross-country, diving, football (tackle) M, golf, soccer, softball W, swimming, tennis, track and field, volleyball W, water polo W. **Intramural:** Badminton, basketball, bowling, football (non-tackle), golf M, handball M, racquetball, soccer W, softball, swimming W, tennis, volleyball. **Team name:** Wolverines.

Student services. Campus ministries, career counseling, student employment services, financial aid counseling, health services, personal counseling, placement for graduates.

Contact. E-mail: admissions@gcc.edu
Phone: (724) 458-2100 Fax: (724) 458-3395
Jeffrey Mincey, Director of Admissions, Grove City College, 100 Campus Drive, Grove City, PA 16127-2104

Gwynedd-Mercy College

Gwynedd Valley, Pennsylvania — **CB member**
www.gmc.edu — **CB code: 2278**

- Private 4-year health science and liberal arts college affiliated with Roman Catholic Church
- Commuter campus in large town
- 2,031 degree-seeking undergraduates: 39% part-time, 75% women, 14% African American, 3% Asian American, 2% Hispanic American, 1% international
- 543 graduate students
- 65% of applicants admitted
- SAT or ACT (ACT writing optional) required
- 74% graduate within 6 years

General. Founded in 1948. Regionally accredited. Affiliated with the Religious Sisters of Mercy. 8-week evening sessions running 12 months for business and accounting majors. Accelerated degree program begins every 6 weeks. **Degrees:** 362 bachelor's, 192 associate awarded; master's offered. **Location:** 20 miles from Philadelphia. **Calendar:** Semester, limited summer session. **Full-time faculty:** 78 total; 54% have terminal degrees, 1% minority, 65% women. **Part-time faculty:** 196 total; 24% have terminal degrees, 6% minority, 52% women. **Class size:** 65% < 20, 32% 20-39, 3% 50-99, less than 1% >100. **Special facilities:** Lincoln-era collection, nursery laboratory school for early childhood education.

Freshman class profile. 1,622 applied, 1,052 admitted, 345 enrolled.

Mid 50% test scores			
SAT verbal:	440-530	Rank in top tenth:	4%
SAT math:	430-530	Return as sophomores:	72%
Rank in top quarter:	20%	Out-of-state:	11%
		Live on campus:	56%

Basis for selection. School achievement record most important, followed by test scores and recommendations. Extracurricular activities considered. Nursing program very competitive.

High school preparation. 16 units required. Required units include English 4, mathematics 3, history 1, science 3 and academic electives 3. Chemistry required for applicants to nursing, cardiovascular, biology, medical technology programs. Biology required for cardiovascular, health information technology programs. Physics required for radiation therapy, medical technology, biology programs. Chemistry or physics required for respiratory therapy.

2005-2006 Annual costs. Tuition/fees: $17,980. Tuition and fees for nursing and allied health programs $18,580; $430 per-credit-hour charge. Room/board: $8,290. Books/supplies: $450. Personal expenses: $1,000.

2004-2005 Financial aid. Need-based: 251 full-time freshmen applied for aid; 213 were judged to have need; 213 of these received aid. Average need met was 85%. Average scholarship/grant was $10,686; average loan $3,082. 69% of total undergraduate aid awarded as scholarships/grants, 31% as loans/jobs. **Non-need-based:** Awarded to 382 full-time undergraduates, including 119 freshmen. Scholarships awarded for academics, leadership.

Application procedures. Admission: Closing date 8/20 (receipt date). $25 fee, may be waived for applicants with need. Application may be submitted online. Admission notification on a rolling basis beginning on or about 9/20. Must reply by May 1 or within 3 week(s) if notified thereafter. Nursing program usually filled by May 1. **Financial aid:** Priority date 3/1, closing date 7/15. FAFSA, institutional form required. Applicants notified on a rolling basis starting 3/1; must reply by 5/1 or within 2 week(s) of notification.

Academics. Special study options: Accelerated study, combined bachelor's/graduate degree, cooperative education, cross-registration, double major, ESL, honors, independent study, internships, liberal arts/career combination, teacher certification program, weekend college. **Credit/placement by examination:** AP, CLEP, institutional tests. Credit by examination cannot be applied to open electives. **Support services:** Learning center, reduced course load, remedial instruction, study skills assistance, tutoring, writing center.

Majors. Biology: General. **Business:** Accounting, business admin. **Computer sciences:** General. **Education:** Business, elementary, special. **English:** English lit. **Family/consumer sciences:** Aging. **Health:** Cardiovascular technology, clinical lab science, medical radiologic technology/radiation therapy, medical records admin, nursing (RN), premedicine, preveterinary, respiratory therapy technology. **History:** General. **Math:** General. **Protective services:** Law enforcement admin. **Psychology:** General. **Social sciences:** Sociology.

Most popular majors. Business/marketing 39%, computer/information sciences 7%, education 20%, health sciences 18%, psychology 6%.

Computing on campus. 217 workstations in library, computer center. Dormitories wired for high-speed internet access and linked to campus network. Commuter students can connect to campus network. Online library available.

Student life. Freshman orientation: Available. Preregistration for classes offered. Multiple full-day sessions offered during the summer. **Policies:** Freshmen permitted cars on campus. **Housing:** Coed dorms, special housing for disabled available. $250 deposit, deadline 5/1. **Activities:** Choral groups, drama, literary magazine, student government, student newspaper, business society, honor societies, Mercy Corps, resident council, commuter club, education club, peer counseling, foreign student organization, psychology/sociology club, campus ministry.

Athletics. NCAA. **Intercollegiate:** Baseball M, basketball, cross-country, field hockey W, golf, lacrosse W, soccer, softball W, tennis, track and field, volleyball W. **Intramural:** Volleyball. **Team name:** Griffins.

Student services. Adult student services, campus ministries, career counseling, student employment services, financial aid counseling, health services, minority student services, on-campus daycare, personal counseling, placement for graduates.

Contact. E-mail: admissions@gmc.edu
Phone: (215) 646-7300 ext. 530 Toll-free number: (800) 342-5462
Fax: (215) 641-5556
James Abbuhl, Vice President for Enrollment Management,
Gwynedd-Mercy College, 1325 Sumneytown Pike, Gwynedd Valley, PA 19437-0901

Haverford College

Haverford, Pennsylvania **CB member**
www.haverford.edu **CB code: 2289**

- Private 4-year liberal arts college
- Residential campus in large town
- 1,155 degree-seeking undergraduates: 53% women, 7% African American, 13% Asian American, 8% Hispanic American, 1% Native American, 4% international
- 26% of applicants admitted
- SAT or ACT with writing, SAT Subject Tests, application essay required
- 88% graduate within 6 years; 17% enter graduate study

General. Founded in 1833. Regionally accredited. Founded by the Society of Friends (Quakers), but now independent. **Degrees:** 278 bachelor's awarded. **Location:** 10 miles from Philadelphia. **Calendar:** Semester. **Full-time faculty:** 111 total; 98% have terminal degrees, 22% minority, 46% women. **Part-time faculty:** 5 total; 80% have terminal degrees, 20% minority, 60% women. **Class size:** 72% < 20, 23% 20-39, 3% 40-49, 2% 50-99. **Special facilities:** Observatory, arboretum, fine arts foundry.

Freshman class profile. 3,112 applied, 816 admitted, 316 enrolled.

Mid 50% test scores		**Return as sophomores:**	97%
SAT verbal:	640-740	**Out-of-state:**	85%
SAT math:	650-730	**Live on campus:**	100%
Rank in top quarter:	96%	**International:**	4%
Rank in top tenth:	91%		

Basis for selection. School record, test scores, extracurricular achievements, and recommendations important. College seeks diversity of social, economic, and geographic backgrounds. Some preference given to children of alumni. First-year applicants must take SAT (all 3 tests, including Writing) or ACT plus 2 SAT Subject Tests before deadline for decision plan chosen. Interview required of applicants living within 150 miles of college, recommended for others.

High school preparation. 12 units required. Required and recommended units include English 4, mathematics 3-4, social studies 2, science 1-2 (laboratory 1) and foreign language 2-3.

2005-2006 Annual costs. Tuition/fees: $31,760. Freshmen subject to one-time fee of $160. Room/board: $9,840. Books/supplies: $890. Personal expenses: $1,270.

2005-2006 Financial aid. All financial aid based on need. 180 full-time freshmen applied for aid; 132 were judged to have need; 132 of these received aid. Average need met was 100%. Average scholarship/grant was $25,462; average loan $2,727. 87% of total undergraduate aid awarded as scholarships/grants, 13% as loans/jobs.

Application procedures. Admission: Closing date 1/15. $60 fee, may be waived for applicants with need. Application may be submitted online. Admission notification 4/15. Must reply by 5/1. Must reply by May 1 or within 2 week(s) if notified thereafter. **Financial aid:** Closing date 1/31. FAFSA required. Required for all students wishing to be considered for institutional funds. Applicants notified by 4/8; must reply by 5/1.

Academics. Academic Flexibility Program allows for advanced independent work and interdepartmental majors. Ample opportunity for student-faculty research. Senior seminars, comprehensive examination and/or senior thesis required for completion of all major programs. **Special study options:** Cross-registration, double major, exchange student, independent study, internships, liberal arts/career combination, student-designed major, study abroad, teacher certification program. Exchange programs with Spelman College (GA), Claremont McKenna College and Pitzer College (CA), Fisk University (TN); cross-registration with Bryn Mawr College, Swarthmore College, noncredit internships also available; 3-2 engineering program with California Institute of Technology. **Credit/placement by examination:** AP, CLEP, IB, SAT, ACT, institutional tests. **Support services:** Learning center, study skills assistance, tutoring, writing center.

Majors. Architecture: Urban/community planning. **Area/ethnic studies:** East Asian. **Biology:** General. **Computer sciences:** General. **English:** English lit. **Foreign languages:** Ancient Greek, classics, comparative lit, French, German, Italian, Latin, Russian, Spanish. **History:** General. **Liberal arts:** Arts/sciences. **Math:** General. **Philosophy/religion:** Philosophy, religion. **Physical sciences:** Astronomy, chemistry, geology, physics. **Psychology:** General. **Social sciences:** Anthropology, archaeology, economics, political science, sociology, urban studies. **Visual/performing arts:** Art history/conservation, studio arts.

Most popular majors. Biology 6%, social sciences 14%.

Computing on campus. 300 workstations in dormitories, library, computer center, student center. Dormitories wired for high-speed internet access and linked to campus network. Commuter students can connect to campus network. Online course registration, online library, helpline, student web hosting, wireless network available.

Student life. **Freshman orientation:** Mandatory, $170 fee. Preregistration for classes offered. **Policies:** Student conduct regulated by academic and social honor code, which allows for unsupervised examinations. Students serve on campus governance and policy-making committees. **Housing:** Guaranteed on-campus for all undergraduates. Coed dorms, single-sex dorms, apartments, substance-free housing available. Students may live at Bryn Mawr College through dormitory exchange program. Students at both colleges may eat meals on either campus. **Activities:** Choral groups, dance, drama, literary magazine, music ensembles, musical theater, radio station, student government, student newspaper, Quaker activities committee, Catholic Campus Ministry, Hillel, Christian Fellowship, environmental action committee, Black students league, Puerto Rican students at Haverford, Asian students association, Bisexual/Gay/Lesbian alliance, Eighth Dimension Volunteer Service Program.

Athletics. NCAA. **Intercollegiate:** Baseball M, basketball, cricket M, cross-country, fencing, field hockey W, lacrosse, soccer, softball W, squash, tennis, track and field, volleyball W. **Intramural:** Basketball, soccer, tennis.

Student services. Alcohol/substance abuse counseling, campus ministries, career counseling, student employment services, financial aid counseling, health services, minority student services, personal counseling, placement for graduates, women's services. **Physically disabled:** Services for visually, speech, hearing impaired.

Contact. E-mail: admitme@haverford.edu
Phone: (610) 896-1350 Fax: (610) 896-1338
Jess Lord, Director of Admissions, Haverford College, 370 West Lancaster Avenue, Haverford, PA 19041-1392

Holy Family University

Philadelphia, Pennsylvania — **CB member**
www.holyfamily.edu — **CB code: 2297**

- Private 4-year liberal arts college affiliated with Roman Catholic Church
- Commuter campus in very large city
- 2,335 degree-seeking undergraduates
- 69% of applicants admitted
- SAT or ACT (ACT writing optional) required

General. Founded in 1954. Regionally accredited. **Degrees:** 346 bachelor's, 23 associate awarded; master's offered. **Location:** 12 miles from downtown. **Calendar:** Semester, extensive summer session. **Full-time faculty:** 91 total. **Part-time faculty:** 255 total. **Class size:** 80% < 20, 20% 20-39. **Special facilities:** Early childhood center with nursery school and kindergarten.

Freshman class profile. 859 applied, 597 admitted, 327 enrolled.

Mid 50% test scores		SAT math:	430-510
SAT verbal:	440-520	Out-of-state:	6%

Basis for selection. High school record most important, followed by recommendations, interview and test scores. Motivation, schoolwork and community activities considered. Essay, interview recommended. **Homeschooled:** State-issued equivalency diploma required.

High school preparation. 14 units required; 16 recommended. Required and recommended units include English 4, mathematics 3, history 2, science 2, foreign language 2 and academic electives 3. All students must have algebra I and II and geometry. Mathematics majors need trigonometry. Nursing requires biology, chemistry, and science electives. Science requires biology, chemistry and trigonometry.

2005-2006 Annual costs. Tuition/fees: $17,740. Books/supplies: $640. Personal expenses: $3,110.

Financial aid. **Non-need-based:** Scholarships awarded for academics, alumni affiliation, athletics.

Application procedures. **Admission:** No deadline. $25 fee, may be waived for applicants with need. Application may be submitted online. Admission notification on a rolling basis. Must reply by May 1 or within 2 week(s) if notified thereafter. **Financial aid:** Priority date 3/1; no closing date. FAFSA, institutional form required. Applicants notified on a rolling basis starting 4/1; must reply within 2 week(s) of notification.

Academics. **Special study options:** Accelerated study, cooperative education, dual enrollment of high school students, independent study, internships, study abroad, teacher certification program. **Credit/placement by examination:** AP, CLEP, IB, institutional tests. 30 credit hours maximum toward bachelor's degree. **Support services:** Pre-admission summer program, remedial instruction, tutoring, writing center.

Majors. **Biology:** General, biochemistry. **Business:** Accounting, business admin, e-commerce, finance, hospitality/recreation, human resources, international, international marketing, marketing, operations, training/development. **Communications:** General. **Computer sciences:** General. **Education:** Biology, chemistry, early childhood, elementary, English, French, mathematics, science, secondary, social science, social studies, Spanish, special. **English:** American lit, British lit. **Foreign languages:** French, Spanish. **Health:** Clinical lab technology, medical radiologic technology/radiation therapy, predentistry, premedicine, preop/surgical nursing, prepharmacy, preveterinary. **History:** General. **Legal studies:** Prelaw. **Liberal arts:** Arts/sciences. **Math:** General. **Philosophy/religion:** Philosophy, religion. **Physical sciences:** Chemistry. **Psychology:** General. **Public administration:** Social work. **Social sciences:** Economics, sociology. **Theology:** Religious ed. **Visual/performing arts:** Art.

Most popular majors. Business/marketing 23%, education 36%, health sciences 13%, security/protective services 8%.

Computing on campus. 160 workstations in library, computer center. Helpline available.

Student life. **Freshman orientation:** Mandatory. **Policies:** Mature and intelligent student conduct expected in accordance with college's interests, standards, and ideals. Freshmen permitted cars on campus. **Housing:** On-campus housing available for some athletes. **Activities:** Drama, literary magazine, student government, student newspaper, community health and welfare organizations, social and departmental clubs, honor societies, campus ministry team.

Athletics. NCAA. **Intercollegiate:** Basketball, cross-country, golf M, soccer, softball W, tennis W, volleyball W. **Intramural:** Basketball, racquetball, volleyball. **Team name:** Tigers.

Student services. Adult student services, campus ministries, career counseling, student employment services, financial aid counseling, health services, personal counseling, placement for graduates. **Physically disabled:** Services for visually impaired.

Contact. E-mail: undergra@holyfamily.edu
Phone: (215) 637-3050 Toll-free number: (800) 637-1191
Fax: (215) 281-1022
Lauren McDermott, Director of Admissions, Holy Family University, 9801 Frankford Avenue, Philadelphia, PA 19114-2009

Immaculata University

Immaculata, Pennsylvania — **CB member**
www.immaculata.edu — **CB code: 2320**

- Private 4-year university and liberal arts college affiliated with Roman Catholic Church
- Residential campus in large town
- 691 degree-seeking undergraduates: 79% women
- 1,002 graduate students
- 80% of applicants admitted
- SAT or ACT required
- 60% graduate within 6 years

General. Founded in 1920. Regionally accredited. **Degrees:** 482 bachelor's, 35 associate awarded; master's, doctoral offered. **ROTC:** Army. **Location:** 20 miles from Philadelphia. **Calendar:** Semester, limited summer session. **Full-time faculty:** 87 total; 66% have terminal degrees, 5% minority, 71% women. **Part-time faculty:** 210 total; 30% have terminal degrees, 4% minority, 58% women. **Class size:** 74% < 20, 24% 20-39, 1% 40-49, less than 1% 50-99.

Freshman class profile. 1,394 applied, 1,119 admitted, 298 enrolled.

Mid 50% test scores		Out-of-state:	34%
SAT verbal:	420-520	Live on campus:	76%
SAT math:	450-550	Fraternities:	8%
Return as sophomores:	67%	Sororities:	5%

Basis for selection. Class rank, academic program, test scores, counselor recommendation important. Minimum 2.3 GPA preferred. Interviews, essay recommended. SAT Subject Tests recommended. Audition required for music program. **Homeschooled:** Transcript of courses and grades required. **Learning Disabled:** Proof of psychological or educational testing date must be supplied.

High school preparation. College-preparatory program recommended. 16 units required; 20 recommended. Required and recommended units include English 4, mathematics 2-3, social studies 2-3, science 2-4 (laboratory 1), foreign language 2-3 and academic electives 4. Music required for music majors.

2006-2007 Annual costs. Tuition/fees (projected): $20,575. Tuition and fees for entering freshmen guaranteed to not increase for the 4 years they are enrolled. Room/board: $9,335. Books/supplies: $1,100. Personal expenses: $1,575.

2004-2005 Financial aid. **Need-based:** 149 full-time freshmen applied for aid; 130 were judged to have need; 129 of these received aid. Average need met was 63%. Average scholarship/grant was $11,335; average loan $2,474. 50% of total undergraduate aid awarded as scholarships/grants, 50% as loans/jobs. **Non-need-based:** Awarded to 215 full-time undergraduates, including 39 freshmen. Scholarships awarded for academics, alumni affiliation, leadership, minority status, music/drama, religious affiliation, state residency.

Application procedures. **Admission:** Priority date 5/15; deadline 8/15 (postmark date). $35 fee, may be waived for applicants with need. Application may be submitted online. Admission notification on a rolling basis beginning on or about 9/15. Must reply by May 1 or within 2 week(s) if notified thereafter. **Financial aid:** Priority date 2/15, closing date 4/15. FAFSA required. Applicants notified on a rolling basis starting 1/1; must reply within 2 week(s) of notification.

Academics. **Special study options:** Accelerated study, combined bachelor's/graduate degree, cross-registration, double major, ESL, honors, independent study, internships, liberal arts/career combination, semester at sea, study abroad, teacher certification program, Washington semester. **Credit/placement by examination:** AP, CLEP, IB, institutional tests. 30 credit hours maximum toward associate degree, 63 toward bachelor's. **Support services:** Learning center, reduced course load, remedial instruction, study skills assistance, tutoring, writing center.

Majors. **Biology:** General. **Business:** Accounting, business admin, fashion, finance, human resources. **Computer sciences:** Information systems. **Conservation:** Environmental studies. **Education:** Business, elementary, family/consumer sciences, music. **English:** English lit. **Foreign languages:** French, Spanish. **Health:** Dietetics, health care admin, music therapy, nursing (RN), premedicine. **History:** General. **Interdisciplinary:** Biological/physical sciences, biopsychology, math/computer science. **Math:** General. **Parks/recreation:** Exercise sciences. **Physical sciences:** Chemistry. **Protective services:** Criminal justice. **Psychology:** General. **Public administration:** Policy analysis. **Social sciences:** Economics, international relations, political science, sociology. **Theology:** Theology. **Visual/performing arts:** Music performance.

Most popular majors. Business/marketing 34%, health sciences 37%, psychology 12%.

Computing on campus. 344 workstations in dormitories, library, computer center, student center. Dormitories wired for high-speed internet access and linked to campus network. Commuter students can connect to campus network. Online course registration, online library, helpline, wireless network available.

Student life. **Freshman orientation:** Mandatory, $300 fee. Preregistration for classes offered. 2-day session in summer. **Policies:** Freshmen permitted cars on campus. **Housing:** Coed dorms, single-sex dorms, special housing for disabled, apartments, substance-free housing available. $250 partly refundable deposit. **Activities:** Choral groups, dance, drama, literary magazine, music ensembles, musical theater, student government, student newspaper, symphony orchestra, campus ministry, international relations society, African American Cultural Society, American Music Therapy Association, Modern Foreign Language Association.

Athletics. NCAA. **Intercollegiate:** Basketball, cross-country W, field hockey W, golf, lacrosse W, soccer, softball W, tennis, volleyball W. **Intramural:** Basketball, cross-country W, field hockey W, lacrosse W, soccer W, softball W, swimming W, tennis W, volleyball W. **Team name:** Mighty Macs.

Student services. Adult student services, alcohol/substance abuse counseling, campus ministries, career counseling, student employment services, financial aid counseling, health services, minority student services, personal counseling, placement for graduates. **Physically disabled:** Services for visually, hearing impaired.

Contact. E-mail: admiss@immaculata.edu
Phone: (610) 647-4400 ext. 3060 Toll-free number: (877) 428-6329
Fax: (610) 640-0836
Rebecca Bowlby, Director of Admission, Immaculata University, PO Box 642, Immaculata, PA 19345-0642

Indiana University of Pennsylvania

Indiana, Pennsylvania — **CB member**
www.iup.edu — **CB code: 2652**

- Public 4-year university
- Residential campus in large town
- 11,788 degree-seeking undergraduates: 5% part-time, 55% women, 7% African American, 1% Asian American, 1% Hispanic American, 1% international
- 1,931 degree-seeking graduate students
- 55% of applicants admitted
- SAT or ACT (ACT writing optional) required
- 51% graduate within 6 years; 7% enter graduate study

General. Founded in 1875. Regionally accredited. Branch campuses located in Punxsutawney and Kittanning. **Degrees:** 1,972 bachelor's, 17 associate awarded; master's, doctoral offered. **ROTC:** Army. **Location:** 50 miles from Pittsburgh. **Calendar:** Semester, extensive summer session. **Full-time faculty:** 630 total. **Part-time faculty:** 60 total. **Class size:** 46% < 20, 36% 20-39, 9% 40-49, 6% 50-99, 2% >100. **Special facilities:** Museums, ski slopes, nature preserve, lodge, and sailing base.

Freshman class profile. 8,836 applied, 4,887 admitted, 2,654 enrolled.

Mid 50% test scores		Rank in top quarter:	35%
SAT verbal:	460-560	Rank in top tenth:	16%
SAT math:	460-550	Return as sophomores:	77%
GPA 3.50 or higher:	45%	Out-of-state:	3%
GPA 3.0-3.49:	51%	Live on campus:	79%
GPA 2.0-2.99:	4%	International:	1%

Basis for selection. School achievement record, recommendations and extracurricular activities considered, test scores, and high school rank important. Audition required for music program; portfolio required for art program. **Homeschooled:** Transcript of courses and grades required.

High school preparation. College-preparatory program recommended. 16 units recommended. Recommended units include English 4, mathematics 3, social studies 2, history 1, science 3, foreign language 2 and academic electives 1. Additional .5 unit computer science recommended.

2005-2006 Annual costs. Tuition/fees: $6,221; $13,581 out-of-state. Room/board: $4,988. Books/supplies: $900. Personal expenses: $2,749.

2005-2006 Financial aid. **Need-based:** Average need met was 79%. Average scholarship/grant was $4,052; average loan $3,036. 41% of total undergraduate aid awarded as scholarships/grants, 59% as loans/jobs. **Non-need-based:** Scholarships awarded for academics, alumni affiliation, art, athletics, job skills, leadership, music/drama, ROTC, state residency.

Application procedures. **Admission:** Priority date 12/31; no deadline. $35 fee, may be waived for applicants with need. Application may be submitted online. Admission notification on a rolling basis beginning on or about 9/1. Must reply by May 1 or within 2 week(s) if notified thereafter. **Financial aid:** Closing date 4/15. FAFSA required. Applicants notified on a rolling basis starting 3/15.

Academics. **Special study options:** Accelerated study, combined bachelor's/graduate degree, cooperative education, distance learning, double major, ESL, exchange student, honors, independent study, internships, study abroad, teacher certification program, urban semester, Washington semester, weekend college. **Credit/placement by examination:** AP, CLEP, IB, institutional tests. Unlimited number of hours of credit by examination may be counted toward degree. **Support services:** Learning center, pre-admission summer program, remedial instruction, study skills assistance, tutoring, writing center.

Honors college/program. 100 freshmen accepted each year through holistic admission process including review of essays, recommendations, and transcripts. Students participate in interdisciplinary, problem-solving course focusing on critical thinking, writing skills, and group dynamics.

Majors. **Architecture:** Interior, urban/community planning. **Biology:** General, biochemistry. **Business:** Accounting, business admin, finance, human resources, international, management information systems, office management. **Communications:** General, journalism. **Computer sciences:** General. **Education:** Art, business, Deaf/hearing impaired, early childhood, elementary, English, family/consumer sciences, mathematics, music, physical, physically handicapped, science, social studies, special, speech impaired, trade/industrial. **Engineering technology:** Occupational safety. **English:** English lit. **Family/consumer sciences:** General, consumer economics, family studies, food/nutrition. **Foreign languages:** French, German, Spanish. **Health:** Clinical lab science, nuclear medical technology, nursing (RN), respiratory therapy technology. **History:** General. **Interdisciplinary:** Biological/physical sciences. **Math:** General, applied. **Parks/recreation:** Health/fitness. **Philosophy/religion:** Philosophy, religion. **Physical sciences:** Chemistry, geology, physics. **Psychology:** General. **Social sciences:** Anthropology, criminology, economics, geography, international relations, political science, sociology. **Visual/performing arts:** Art, dramatic, multimedia, music performance.

Most popular majors. Business/marketing 23%, communications/journalism 7%, education 12%, social sciences 18%, visual/performing arts 7%.

Computing on campus. 3,500 workstations in dormitories, library, computer center. Dormitories wired for high-speed internet access and linked to campus network. Commuter students can connect to campus network. Online course registration, helpline, repair service, student web hosting, wireless network available.

Student life. Freshman orientation: Mandatory, $140 fee. Preregistration for classes offered. **Policies:** Freshmen permitted cars on campus. **Housing:** Guaranteed on-campus for freshmen. Coed dorms, single-sex dorms, special housing for disabled, apartments, substance-free housing available. $75 deposit, deadline 5/1. Honors college dormitory, substance-free housing, academic specialty floors available. **Activities:** Bands, choral groups, dance, drama, film society, literary magazine, music ensembles, musical theater, opera, radio station, student government, student newspaper, symphony orchestra, TV station, Alpha Phi Omega National Service Fraternity (coeducational), Gamma Sigma Sigma Service Sorority, African American Cultural Center, Campus Crusade for Christ, Coalition for Christian Outreach, Newman Center, Panhellenic Association, NAACP.

Athletics. NCAA. **Intercollegiate:** Baseball M, basketball, cross-country, diving, field hockey W, football (tackle) M, golf M, lacrosse W, soccer W, softball W, swimming, tennis W, track and field, volleyball W. **Intramural:** Archery, badminton, basketball, bowling, cross-country, fencing, football (non-tackle), golf, racquetball, soccer, softball, table tennis, tennis, track and field, volleyball, water polo, weight lifting, wrestling M. **Team name:** Indians.

Student services. Adult student services, alcohol/substance abuse counseling, campus ministries, career counseling, services for economically disadvantaged, student employment services, financial aid counseling, health services, legal services, minority student services, on-campus daycare, personal counseling, placement for graduates, veterans' counselor, women's services. **Physically disabled:** Services for visually, speech, hearing impaired.

Contact. E-mail: admissions_inquiry@iup.edu
Phone: (724) 357-2230 Toll-free number: (800) 442-6830
Fax: (724) 357-6281
Rhonda Luckey, Interim VP for Student Affairs, Indiana University of Pennsylvania, 117 John Sutton Hall, 1011 South Drive, Indiana, PA 15705-1088

Juniata College

Huntingdon, Pennsylvania — **CB member**
www.juniata.edu — **CB code: 2341**

- Private 4-year liberal arts college affiliated with Church of the Brethren
- Residential campus in small town
- 1,379 degree-seeking undergraduates: 1% part-time, 53% women, 2% African American, 2% Asian American, 1% Hispanic American, 3% international
- 68% of applicants admitted
- Application essay required
- 75% graduate within 6 years; 11% enter graduate study

General. Founded in 1876. Regionally accredited. **Degrees:** 296 bachelor's awarded. **Location:** 30 miles from Altoona and State College. **Calendar:** Semester, limited summer session. **Full-time faculty:** 94 total; 92% have terminal degrees, 4% minority, 36% women. **Part-time faculty:** 38 total; 45% have terminal degrees, 5% minority, 47% women. **Class size:** 66% < 20, 27% 20-39, 4% 40-49, 3% 50-99. **Special facilities:** Nature preserve, environmental studies field station, observatory, museum of art, early childhood education center.

Freshman class profile. 1,745 applied, 1,184 admitted, 388 enrolled.

Mid 50% test scores		**Rank in top quarter:**	79%
SAT verbal:	530-630	**Rank in top tenth:**	43%
SAT math:	550-640	**Return as sophomores:**	83%
GPA 3.50 or higher:	77%	**Out-of-state:**	27%
GPA 3.0-3.49:	17%	**Live on campus:**	98%
GPA 2.0-2.99:	6%	**International:**	1%

Basis for selection. School achievement record most important. Standardized test scores, school and community activities, recommendations and essay also important. SAT or ACT recommended. SAT required of foreign students whose entire secondary school experience was in American high school. Juniata requires 1 of the following as part of application requirements: If student chooses not to submit standardized test scores, then must submit 2 graded papers. Interview recommended.

High school preparation. 16 units required; 18 recommended. Required and recommended units include English 4, mathematics 3-4, social studies 1, history 3, science 3-4 (laboratory 2) and foreign language 2.

2006-2007 Annual costs. Tuition/fees (projected): $27,540. Room/board: $7,680. Books/supplies: $600. Personal expenses: $1,000.

2005-2006 Financial aid. Need-based: 347 full-time freshmen applied for aid; 310 were judged to have need; 310 of these received aid. Average need met was 78.6%. Average scholarship/grant was $15,668; average loan $3,448. 74% of total undergraduate aid awarded as scholarships/grants, 26% as loans/jobs. **Non-need-based:** Scholarships awarded for academics, art, leadership, minority status, music/drama, state residency.

Application procedures. Admission: Priority date 12/1; deadline 3/1 (postmark date). $30 fee, may be waived for applicants with need. Application may be submitted online. Admission notification on a rolling basis beginning on or about 2/28. Must reply by May 1 or within 2 week(s) if notified thereafter. **Financial aid:** Closing date 3/1. FAFSA required. Applicants notified on a rolling basis starting 3/1; must reply by 5/1 or within 2 week(s) of notification.

Academics. Majors replaced by Programs of Emphasis. Over 50% of students design individualized POE. **Special study options:** Accelerated study, combined bachelor's/graduate degree, distance learning, double major, dual enrollment of high school students, ESL, exchange student, honors, independent study, internships, student-designed major, study abroad, teacher certification program, urban semester, Washington semester. Marine biology with Duke University; 3-3 law with Duquesne University; 3-2 engineering with Columbia University, Pennsylvania State University, Clarkson University, Washington University, 3-4 dentistry with Temple University; 3-4 medicine with Tulane University School of Medicine, Lake Erie College of Osteopathic Medicine; 3-4 optometry with Pennsylvania College of Optometry; 3-4 podiatry with Temple University School of Podiatric Medicine and Ohio College of Podiatric Medicine; nursing with Thomas Jefferson University, Johns Hopkins University, Case Western University; biotechnology, cytogenetics/cytotechnology, diagnostic imaging/cardiovascular technology, occupational therapy with Thomas Jefferson University; physical therapy with Widener University, Drexel University; medical technology with Thomas Jefferson University, Altoona Regional Health Systems, Lancaster General College of Nursing & Health Sciences. **Credit/placement by examination:** AP, CLEP, IB, institutional tests. Unlimited number of hours of credit by examination may be counted toward degree. **Support services:** Reduced course load, study skills assistance, tutoring, writing center.

Majors. Biology: General, biochemistry, botany, cell/histology, ecology, marine, microbiology, molecular, zoology. **Business:** General, accounting, business admin, entrepreneurial studies, finance, human resources, information resources management, international, marketing. **Communications:** General, digital media, health. **Computer sciences:** General, information technology. **Conservation:** Environmental science, environmental studies. **Education:** General, biology, chemistry, early childhood, early childhood special, elementary, English, French, German, mathematics, multi-level teacher, physics, science, secondary, social studies, Spanish. **Engineering:** General, physics. **English:** English lit. **Foreign languages:** General, French, German, Russian, Spanish. **Health:** Predentistry, premedicine, prenursing, prepharmacy, preveterinary. **History:** General. **Interdisciplinary:** Global studies, museum, natural sciences, peace/conflict. **Legal studies:** Prelaw. **Liberal arts:** Arts/sciences, humanities. **Math:** General. **Philosophy/religion:** Philosophy, religion. **Physical sciences:** General, chemistry, geology, physics. **Psychology:** General. **Public administration:** General, social work. **Social sciences:** General, anthropology, criminology, economics, international relations, political science, sociology. **Theology:** Preministerial. **Visual/performing arts:** Art history/conservation, dramatic, studio arts.

Most popular majors. Biology 16%, business/marketing 14%, computer/information sciences 6%, education 15%, interdisciplinary studies 8%, physical sciences 6%, psychology 6%, social sciences 11%.

Computing on campus. 340 workstations in library, computer center, student center. Dormitories wired for high-speed internet access and linked to campus network. Commuter students can connect to campus network. Online course registration, online library, helpline, repair service, wireless network available.

Student life. Freshman orientation: Available. Preregistration for classes offered. 2 days in summer, parallel programs for new students and their parents. **Policies:** Freshmen permitted cars on campus. **Housing:** Guaranteed on-campus for all undergraduates. Coed dorms, single-sex dorms, apartments, substance-free housing available. $300 nonrefundable deposit, deadline 5/1. Special interest housing available. **Activities:** Bands, choral groups, dance, drama, literary magazine, music ensembles, musical theater, radio station, student government, student newspaper, symphony orchestra, Campus Ministry Board, Catholic Council, international club, Model United Nations club, United Cultures of Juniata College, Fellowship of Christian Athletes, emergency services club, Habitat for Humanity, JC Outreach, Juniata Coalition for Responsible Justice.

Athletics. NCAA. **Intercollegiate:** Baseball M, basketball, cheerleading M, cross-country, field hockey W, football (tackle) M, soccer, softball W, swimming W, tennis, track and field, volleyball. **Intramural:** Basketball, bowling, soccer, volleyball. **Team name:** Eagles.

Student services. Adult student services, alcohol/substance abuse counseling, campus ministries, career counseling, student employment services, financial aid counseling, health services, personal counseling, placement for graduates. **Physically disabled:** Services for visually, hearing impaired.

Contact. E-mail: admissions@juniata.edu
Phone: (814) 641-3420 Toll-free number: (877) 586-4282
Fax: (814) 641-3100
Michelle Bartol, Dean of Enrollment, Juniata College, 18th and Moore Streets, Huntingdon, PA 16652

Keystone College

La Plume, Pennsylvania — **CB member**
www.keystone.edu — **CB code: 2351**

- Private 4-year junior and liberal arts college
- Residential campus in small town
- 1,568 degree-seeking undergraduates: 22% part-time, 61% women, 3% African American, 1% Asian American, 1% Hispanic American, 1% international
- 91% of applicants admitted
- SAT or ACT (ACT writing optional) required

General. Founded in 1868. Regionally accredited. Students may enroll in up to 12 credits as nonmatriculating prior to making formal application to college. Trimester system for Adult Weekender Program. **Degrees:** 154 bachelor's, 137 associate awarded. **ROTC:** Army, Air Force. **Location:** 15 miles from Scranton. **Calendar:** Semester, limited summer session. **Full-time faculty:** 60 total. **Part-time faculty:** 145 total. **Class size:** 84% < 20, 16% 20-39, less than 1% 50-99. **Special facilities:** Observatory, children's center, Microsoft certified systems engineer training site, water discovery center, urban forestry center, restaurant (operated by culinary students), delayed harvest trout stream, Cisco training site, countryside conservancy.

Freshman class profile. 872 applied, 796 admitted, 384 enrolled.

Mid 50% test scores		**Rank in top tenth:**	3%
SAT verbal:	400-500	**Return as sophomores:**	66%
SAT math:	400-500	**Out-of-state:**	11%
ACT:	15-20	**Live on campus:**	30%
Rank in top quarter:	17%	**International:**	1%

Basis for selection. School achievement record, extracurricular activities, test scores, recommendations, class rank, preparation in proposed major area of study considered. Students whose primary language is not English should submit TOEFL or equivalent; may also take institutional TOEFL on campus. Students who have already graduated from high school do not need to submit SAT/ACT scores. Essay recommended for all. Portfolio and interviews required for all art and art education applications. **Homeschooled:** Interview required. Portfolio of high school level work also required. **Learning Disabled:** Current psychological report and Individualized Educational Program should be submitted at time of application. On campus interview generally required.

High school preparation. College-preparatory program recommended. 15 units required. Required and recommended units include English 4, mathematics 2-3, social studies 2, history 2, science 2 (laboratory 1), foreign language 2 and academic electives 3. Foreign language recommended for art, communications, and liberal arts curricula. 3 mathematics and 3 science (including 2 lab) recommended for allied health, environmental science, forestry and science curricula. Specific requirements vary between departments and majors.

2005-2006 Annual costs. Tuition/fees: $15,020. Room/board: $7,790. Books/supplies: $1,200. Personal expenses: $1,200.

2004-2005 Financial aid. Need-based: Average need met was 97%. Average scholarship/grant was $6,450; average loan $2,625. 51% of total undergraduate aid awarded as scholarships/grants, 49% as loans/jobs. **Non-need-based:** Awarded to 88 full-time undergraduates, including 42 freshmen. Scholarships awarded for academics, art, job skills, leadership, ROTC.

Application procedures. Admission: Priority date 5/1; deadline 7/1 (receipt date). $25 fee, may be waived for applicants with need. Application may be submitted online. Admission notification on a rolling basis. Must reply by May 1 or within 3 week(s) if notified thereafter. **Financial aid:** Priority date 5/1; no closing date. FAFSA required. Applicants notified on a rolling basis starting 11/1; must reply by 5/1 or within 3 week(s) of notification.

Academics. Students in good academic and financial standing who have not received at least 1 job offer or acceptance into transfer or graduate program within 6 months after graduating and fulfilling requirements of Career Development Center will be provided with additional courses and career counseling at no extra charge. **Special study options:** Accelerated study, combined bachelor's/graduate degree, cooperative education, cross-registration, double major, dual enrollment of high school students, honors, independent study, internships, student-designed major, study abroad, teacher certification program, weekend college. 2-2, 2-3, 3+3, 4-3 programs with various 4-year institutions for students studying allied health, health sciences, and environmental sciences. **Credit/placement by examination:** AP, CLEP, IB, SAT, ACT, institutional tests. 12 credit hours maximum toward associate degree, 18 toward bachelor's. A maximum of 32 credits for associate degree-seekers and 64 credits for bachelor's degree-seekers are awarded for prior work and/or life experience. **Support services:** Learning center, reduced course load, remedial instruction, study skills assistance, tutoring, writing center.

Honors college/program. Admissions requirements 1100 SAT (exclusive of Writing), 24 ACT, top 10% of class or high school GPA of 3.0. Students who do not meet criteria considered on case-by-case basis.

Majors. Biology: General, biochemistry, biomedical sciences, environmental. **Business:** General, accounting, accounting/business management, business admin, management information systems. **Communications:** General, journalism. **Computer sciences:** General, information systems, information technology, LAN/WAN management, networking, systems analysis. **Conservation:** General, management/policy, water/wetlands/marine. **Education:** General, art, early childhood, elementary, multi-level teacher. **Family/consumer sciences:** General, child care, child development, family systems. **Health:** Predentistry, premedicine, prepharmacy, preveterinary. **Interdisciplinary:** Biological/physical sciences, natural sciences. **Legal studies:** Prelaw. **Parks/recreation:** General, facilities management, sports admin. **Protective services:** Criminal justice, criminalistics, law enforcement admin. **Visual/performing arts:** Art, ceramics, drawing, illustration, painting, printmaking, sculpture, studio arts.

Most popular majors. Business/marketing 27%, communications/journalism 8%, computer/information sciences 14%, education 21%, parks/recreation 12%, security/protective services 14%.

Computing on campus. 120 workstations in dormitories, library, computer center, student center. Dormitories wired for high-speed internet access and linked to campus network. Commuter students can connect to campus network. Online course registration, helpline, wireless network available.

Student life. Freshman orientation: Mandatory, $100 fee. Preregistration for classes offered. One day program during summer for placement testing. Multi-day overnight program prior to start of classes; includes canoeing, hiking, camping, volunteer service, theatre, creative writing, and music. **Policies:** Freshmen permitted cars on campus. **Housing:** Guaranteed on-campus for all undergraduates. Coed dorms, single-sex dorms, special housing for disabled, substance-free housing available. $100 nonrefundable deposit, deadline 5/1. **Activities:** Choral groups, drama, literary magazine, musical theater, radio station, student government, student newspaper, art society, Phi Theta Kappa, ACT 101, Circle K, equestrian club, FADE (Facing Alcohol and Drugs through Education), service learning, MECA (Multi-Ethnic Cultural Association).

Athletics. NCAA. **Intercollegiate:** Baseball M, basketball, cross-country, golf M, soccer, softball W, tennis, track and field, volleyball W. **Intramural:** Basketball, football (non-tackle), lacrosse, soccer, softball, table tennis, tennis, volleyball, weight lifting. **Team name:** Giants.

Student services. Adult student services, alcohol/substance abuse counseling, campus ministries, career counseling, services for economically disadvantaged, student employment services, financial aid counseling, health services, minority student services, on-campus daycare, personal counseling, placement for graduates, veterans' counselor, women's services.

Contact. E-mail: admissions@keystone.edu
Phone: (570) 945-8111 Toll-free number: (877) 426-5534
Fax: (570) 945-7916
Sarah Keating, Director of Admissions, Keystone College, One College Green, La Plume, PA 18440-1099

King's College

Wilkes-Barre, Pennsylvania — **CB member**
www.kings.edu — **CB code: 2353**

- Private 4-year business and liberal arts college affiliated with Roman Catholic Church
- Residential campus in small city
- 1,955 degree-seeking undergraduates: 6% part-time, 46% women, 2% African American, 1% Asian American, 2% Hispanic American
- 145 degree-seeking graduate students

- 84% of applicants admitted
- SAT or ACT (ACT writing recommended) required
- 71% graduate within 6 years; 18% enter graduate study

General. Founded in 1946. Regionally accredited. Library offers computerized databases and access to research libraries nationwide. **Degrees:** 439 bachelor's, 6 associate awarded; master's offered. **ROTC:** Army, Air Force. **Location:** 110 miles from Philadelphia, 140 miles from New York City. **Calendar:** Semester, extensive summer session. **Full-time faculty:** 110 total; 83% have terminal degrees, 3% minority, 36% women. **Part-time faculty:** 91 total; 30% have terminal degrees, 1% minority, 47% women. **Class size:** 53% < 20, 47% 20-39, less than 1% 50-99. **Special facilities:** Rooftop greenhouse, molecular biology laboratory.

Freshman class profile. 1,654 applied, 1,388 admitted, 480 enrolled.

Mid 50% test scores		**Rank in top quarter:**	40%
SAT verbal:	470-560	**Rank in top tenth:**	16%
SAT math:	470-570	**Return as sophomores:**	80%
GPA 3.50 or higher:	40%	**Out-of-state:**	32%
GPA 3.0-3.49:	33%	**Live on campus:**	67%
GPA 2.0-2.99:	27%		

Basis for selection. Interview recommended. **Homeschooled:** Transcript of courses and grades required. **Learning Disabled:** Learning-disabled students applying for the first-year academic studies program must submit supplemental application with appropriate documentation. Contact Director of Academic Skills Center during admission process.

High school preparation. College-preparatory program required. 16 units required; 22 recommended. Required and recommended units include English 4, mathematics 3-4, social studies 3, history 1, science 3-4 (laboratory 2), foreign language 2-4 and academic electives 2.

2005-2006 Annual costs. Tuition/fees: $21,220. Room/board: $8,590. Books/supplies: $925. Personal expenses: $1,830.

2005-2006 Financial aid. **Need-based:** 449 full-time freshmen applied for aid; 399 were judged to have need; 399 of these received aid. Average need met was 76%. Average scholarship/grant was $5,699; average loan $3,674. 69% of total undergraduate aid awarded as scholarships/grants, 31% as loans/jobs. **Non-need-based:** Awarded to 1,427 full-time undergraduates, including 467 freshmen. Scholarships awarded for academics, leadership, ROTC. **Additional information:** Most minority students receive some aid in the form of a diversity scholarship.

Application procedures. **Admission:** No deadline. $30 fee, may be waived for applicants with need. Application may be submitted online. Admission notification on a rolling basis beginning on or about 10/1. Must reply by May 1 or within 2 week(s) if notified thereafter. **Financial aid:** Priority date 2/15; no closing date. FAFSA, institutional form required. Applicants notified on a rolling basis starting 3/1; must reply within 2 week(s) of notification.

Academics. **Special study options:** Accelerated study, cross-registration, distance learning, double major, dual enrollment of high school students, ESL, honors, independent study, internships, student-designed major, study abroad, teacher certification program, Washington semester, weekend college. Preprofessional programs in dentistry, medicine, pharmacy, veterinary science. **Credit/placement by examination:** AP, CLEP, IB, institutional tests. 15 credit hours maximum toward associate degree, 30 toward bachelor's. **Support services:** Learning center, pre-admission summer program, reduced course load, study skills assistance, tutoring, writing center.

Majors. **Biology:** General. **Business:** Accounting, business admin, finance, human resources, international, marketing. **Communications:** Media studies. **Computer sciences:** General, computer science. **Conservation:** Environmental science, environmental studies. **Education:** Early childhood, elementary, special. **English:** English lit. **Foreign languages:** French, Spanish. **Health:** Athletic training, clinical lab science, health services. **History:** General. **Interdisciplinary:** Biological/physical sciences, neuroscience. **Math:** General. **Philosophy/religion:** Philosophy. **Physical sciences:** Chemistry. **Protective services:** Criminal justice. **Psychology:** General. **Social sciences:** Economics, political science, sociology. **Theology:** Theology. **Visual/performing arts:** Dramatic.

Most popular majors. Business/marketing 26%, communications/journalism 6%, education 13%, health sciences 7%, psychology 9%, security/protective services 6%, social sciences 6%.

Computing on campus. 400 workstations in dormitories, library, computer center, student center. Dormitories wired for high-speed internet access and linked to campus network. Commuter students can connect to campus network. Online course registration, helpline, repair service, student web hosting, wireless network available.

Student life. **Freshman orientation:** Mandatory, $150 fee. Preregistration for classes offered. Held the 4 days prior to start of fall classes. **Policies:** Freshmen permitted cars on campus. **Housing:** Guaranteed on-campus for all undergraduates. Single-sex dorms, apartments available. $200 nonrefundable deposit, deadline 6/8. **Activities:** Choral groups, dance, drama, literary magazine, music ensembles, radio station, student government, student newspaper, association of campus events, organizations of various majors, Campion Society, Blood Council, Circle K, politics society, environmental awareness and outdoors club, residence hall council, service fraternity and sorority.

Athletics. NCAA. **Intercollegiate:** Baseball M, basketball, cheerleading, cross-country, field hockey W, football (tackle) M, golf M, lacrosse, soccer, softball W, swimming, tennis, volleyball W, wrestling M. **Intramural:** Basketball, soccer. **Team name:** Monarchs.

Student services. Adult student services, campus ministries, career counseling, student employment services, financial aid counseling, health services, personal counseling, placement for graduates.

Contact. E-mail: admissions@kings.edu
Phone: (570) 208-5858 Toll-free number: (888) 546-4772
Fax: (570) 208-5971
Michelle Lawrence-Schmude, Director of Admissions, King's College, 133 North River Street, Wilkes-Barre, PA 18711

Kutztown University of Pennsylvania

Kutztown, Pennsylvania — **CB member**
www.kutztown.edu — **CB code: 2653**

- Public 4-year university
- Residential campus in small town
- 8,267 degree-seeking undergraduates: 6% part-time, 58% women, 8% African American, 1% Asian American, 4% Hispanic American, 1% international
- 812 degree-seeking graduate students
- 79% of applicants admitted
- SAT or ACT (ACT writing optional) required
- 51% graduate within 6 years

General. Founded in 1866. Regionally accredited. **Degrees:** 1,388 bachelor's awarded; master's offered. **ROTC:** Army. **Location:** 20 miles from Allentown and Reading. **Calendar:** Semester, extensive summer session. **Full-time faculty:** 410 total; 60% have terminal degrees, 12% minority, 46% women. **Part-time faculty:** 42 total; 2% minority, 64% women. **Class size:** 26% < 20, 57% 20-39, 9% 40-49, 7% 50-99, 1% >100. **Special facilities:** Observatory, on-campus preschool, Pennsylvania German heritage cultural center, planetarium.

Freshman class profile. 10,423 applied, 8,253 admitted, 1,912 enrolled.

Mid 50% test scores		**Return as sophomores:**	76%
SAT verbal:	460-540	**Out-of-state:**	10.6%
SAT math:	450-540	**Live on campus:**	88%
Rank in top quarter:	20%	**Fraternities:**	4%
Rank in top tenth:	6%	**Sororities:**	4%
End year in good standing:	76%		

Basis for selection. School records and academic aptitude tests most important. Recommendations, essays, extracurricular activities considered. SAT Subject Tests (biology and chemistry) required for medical technology program. Audition required for music program; portfolio and/or art test required for art education, communication design, crafts, and fine arts programs. **Homeschooled:** Applicants must submit supporting data from Pennsylvania Home Schooling Association.

High school preparation. College-preparatory program recommended. 16 units recommended. Recommended units include English 4, mathematics 3, social studies 2, science 3 and foreign language 2. Course recommendations vary for specific programs.

2005-2006 Annual costs. Tuition/fees: $6,426; $13,786 out-of-state. Room/board: $5,508. Books/supplies: $1,100. Personal expenses: $2,600.

2004-2005 Financial aid. **Need-based:** 1,836 full-time freshmen applied for aid; 1,348 were judged to have need; 1,348 of these received aid. Average need met was 52%. Average scholarship/grant was $4,304; average loan $2,587. 42% of total undergraduate aid awarded as scholarships/grants, 58% as loans/jobs. **Non-need-based:** Awarded to 660 full-time undergraduates, including 137 freshmen. Scholarships awarded for academics, alumni affiliation, art, athletics, leadership, minority status, music/drama, state residency.

Application procedures. Admission: Priority date 1/1; no deadline. $30 fee, may be waived for applicants with need. Application may be submitted online. Admission notification on a rolling basis beginning on or about 8/1. Must reply by May 1 or within 4 week(s) if notified thereafter. **Financial aid:** Priority date 2/15; no closing date. FAFSA required. Applicants notified on a rolling basis starting 3/30.

Academics. Special study options: Combined bachelor's/graduate degree, cross-registration, distance learning, double major, dual enrollment of high school students, honors, independent study, internships, liberal arts/career combination, student-designed major, study abroad, teacher certification program. **Credit/placement by examination:** AP, CLEP, IB, institutional tests. **Support services:** Learning center, pre-admission summer program, remedial instruction, study skills assistance, tutoring, writing center.

Majors. Biology: General. **Business:** Accounting, business admin, finance, human resources, international, management science, marketing. **Communications:** General, digital media. **Computer sciences:** Information technology. **Conservation:** Environmental science. **Education:** General, early childhood, elementary, kindergarten/preschool, reading, secondary, special, speech impaired, visually handicapped. **English:** English lit, speech/rhetoric, technical writing. **Foreign languages:** French, German, Russian, Spanish. **Health:** Clinical lab science, nursing (RN). **History:** General. **Interdisciplinary:** Biological/physical sciences. **Liberal arts:** Arts/sciences, library science. **Math:** General. **Philosophy/religion:** Philosophy. **Physical sciences:** Chemistry, geology, oceanography, physics. **Protective services:** Criminal justice. **Psychology:** General. **Public administration:** General, social work. **Social sciences:** General, anthropology, geography, political science, sociology. **Visual/performing arts:** General, art, commercial/advertising art, crafts, dramatic, studio arts.

Most popular majors. Business/marketing 15%, education 20%, English 10%, psychology 8%, social sciences 6%, visual/performing arts 16%.

Computing on campus. 650 workstations in dormitories, library, computer center, student center. Dormitories wired for high-speed internet access and linked to campus network. Commuter students can connect to campus network. Online course registration, online library, helpline, student web hosting, wireless network available.

Student life. Freshman orientation: Mandatory, $80 fee. Preregistration for classes offered. 2-day, one overnight session in June, plus 2-day informational program preceding fall semester. **Policies:** No alcohol or drugs. Freshmen students may request permission to bring car on campus. Freshmen permitted cars on campus. **Housing:** Guaranteed on-campus for freshmen. Coed dorms, single-sex dorms, apartments, cooperative housing, substance-free housing available. $125 deposit, deadline 5/1. **Activities:** Bands, choral groups, dance, drama, literary magazine, music ensembles, musical theater, radio station, student government, student newspaper, TV station, Student Alliance for Learning, Success and Achievement, black student union, international students organization, Minority Achievement Coalition, Brothers and Sisters Seeking Excellence, Feminist Majority Leadership Alliance, Circle K, volunteer center, social work club.

Athletics. NCAA. **Intercollegiate:** Baseball M, basketball, cheerleading W, cross-country, field hockey W, football (tackle) M, golf W, soccer, softball W, swimming, tennis, track and field, volleyball W, wrestling M. **Intramural:** Badminton, basketball, cross-country, football (non-tackle), golf, soccer, softball, swimming, tennis, volleyball, weight lifting. **Team name:** Golden Bears.

Student services. Adult student services, alcohol/substance abuse counseling, career counseling, student employment services, financial aid counseling, health services, minority student services, on-campus daycare, personal counseling, veterans' counselor, women's services. **Physically disabled:** Services for visually, speech, hearing impaired.

Contact. E-mail: admission@kutztown.edu
Phone: (610) 683-4060 Toll-free number: (877) 628-1915
Fax: (610) 683-1375
William Stahler, Director of Admissions, Kutztown University of Pennsylvania, Admissions Center, Kutztown, PA 19530-0730

La Roche College

Pittsburgh, Pennsylvania **CB member**
www.laroche.edu **CB code: 2379**

- Private 4-year liberal arts college affiliated with Roman Catholic Church
- Commuter campus in large city
- 1,421 degree-seeking undergraduates: 15% part-time, 67% women, 4% African American, 1% Asian American, 1% Hispanic American, 1% Native American, 11% international
- 207 degree-seeking graduate students
- 65% of applicants admitted
- SAT or ACT required
- 62% graduate within 6 years

General. Founded in 1963. Regionally accredited. Founded and sponsored by Sisters of Divine Providence. **Degrees:** 323 bachelor's, 5 associate awarded; master's offered. **ROTC:** Army, Air Force. **Calendar:** Semester, limited summer session. **Full-time faculty:** 62 total; 86% have terminal degrees, 8% minority, 53% women. **Part-time faculty:** 163 total; 22% have terminal degrees, 3% minority, 55% women. **Class size:** 75% < 20, 25% 20-39, less than 1% 40-49.

Freshman class profile. 838 applied, 547 admitted, 305 enrolled.

Mid 50% test scores			
SAT verbal:	420-530	Rank in top quarter:	31%
SAT math:	430-530	Rank in top tenth:	11%
ACT:	17-22	End year in good standing:	80%
GPA 3.50 or higher:	31%	Return as sophomores:	67%
GPA 3.0-3.49:	33%	Out-of-state:	6%
GPA 2.0-2.99:	35%	Live on campus:	66%
		International:	17%

Basis for selection. Depth and rigor of curriculum considered. Standardized test scores considered in relation to other factors. Recommendation from guidance counselor important. Extracurricular involvement considered. Essay, interview recommended.

High school preparation. 15 units required; 22 recommended. Required and recommended units include English 3-4, mathematics 3-4, social studies 3-4, history 3-4, science 3-4 and foreign language 2.

2005-2006 Annual costs. Tuition/fees: $17,180. Room/board: $7,344. Books/supplies: $800. Personal expenses: $900.

2005-2006 Financial aid. Need-based: 218 full-time freshmen applied for aid; 185 were judged to have need; 185 of these received aid. Average need met was 89%. Average scholarship/grant was $3,030; average loan $2,783. 52% of total undergraduate aid awarded as scholarships/grants, 48% as loans/jobs. **Non-need-based:** Awarded to 1,024 full-time undergraduates, including 271 freshmen. Scholarships awarded for academics.

Application procedures. Admission: No deadline. $50 fee, may be waived for applicants with need. Application may be submitted online. Admission notification on a rolling basis. **Financial aid:** Priority date 4/15, closing date 5/1. FAFSA required. Applicants notified on a rolling basis starting 2/15; must reply within 2 week(s) of notification.

Academics. Special study options: Accelerated study, combined bachelor's/graduate degree, cross-registration, distance learning, double major, ESL, honors, independent study, internships, student-designed major, study abroad, teacher certification program, Washington semester. **Credit/placement by examination:** AP, CLEP. 60 credit hours maximum toward bachelor's degree. **Support services:** Learning center, reduced course load, remedial instruction, study skills assistance, tutoring, writing center.

Majors. Architecture: Interior. **Biology:** General. **Business:** Accounting, finance, international, management science, marketing, real estate. **Computer sciences:** General, computer science, information technology. **Education:** Biology, chemistry, elementary, English, mathematics, Spanish. **English:** Composition, English lit. **Health:** Medical radiologic technology/radiation therapy, nursing (RN), respiratory therapy technology. **History:** General. **Liberal arts:** Arts/sciences. **Math:** General. **Philosophy/religion:** Religion. **Physical sciences:** Chemistry. **Protective services:** Criminal justice. **Psychology:** General. **Public administration:** Human services. **Social sciences:** International relations, sociology. **Theology:** Religious ed. **Visual/performing arts:** Dance, design.

Most popular majors. Business/marketing 22%, computer/information sciences 13%, education 14%, health sciences 6%, psychology 7%, security/protective services 7%, visual/performing arts 9%.

Computing on campus. 200 workstations in dormitories, library, computer center. Dormitories wired for high-speed internet access and linked to campus network. Commuter students can connect to campus network. Online course registration, online library, helpline, wireless network available.

Student life. Freshman orientation: Mandatory. Preregistration for classes offered. **Policies:** Freshmen permitted cars on campus. **Housing:** Coed dorms available. $400 deposit. **Activities:** Choral groups, dance, drama, literary magazine, radio station, student government, student newspaper, campus ministry, professional organizations, multicultural student organization, Project Achievement, environment club, black student coalition, African Student Forum, GLOBE (international student), Rotaract Club, community service.

Athletics. NCAA. **Intercollegiate:** Baseball M, basketball, cross-country, golf M, soccer, softball W, volleyball W. **Intramural:** Basketball, racquetball, soccer, softball, table tennis, tennis, volleyball. **Team name:** Redhawks.

Student services. Adult student services, alcohol/substance abuse counseling, campus ministries, career counseling, services for economically disadvantaged, student employment services, financial aid counseling, health services, minority student services, personal counseling, placement for graduates, veterans' counselor. **Physically disabled:** Services for visually impaired. **Learning disabled:** Comprehensive services available.

Contact. E-mail: admissions@laroche.edu
Phone: (412) 536-1271 Toll-free number: (800) 838-4572
Fax: (412) 536-1048
Thomas Hassett, Director of Admissions, La Roche College, 9000 Babcock Boulevard, Pittsburgh, PA 15237

La Salle University

Philadelphia, Pennsylvania — **CB member**
www.lasalle.edu — **CB code: 2363**

- Private 4-year university and liberal arts college affiliated with Roman Catholic Church
- Residential campus in very large city
- 4,238 degree-seeking undergraduates: 21% part-time, 60% women, 16% African American, 3% Asian American, 8% Hispanic American, 1% international
- 1,776 degree-seeking graduate students
- 70% of applicants admitted
- SAT or ACT (ACT writing optional), application essay required
- 70% graduate within 6 years

General. Founded in 1863. Regionally accredited. Associate degree offered only through evening division. **Degrees:** 893 bachelor's, 30 associate awarded; master's, doctoral offered. **ROTC:** Army, Air Force. **Location:** 6 miles from Center City. **Calendar:** Semester, extensive summer session. **Full-time faculty:** 213 total; 82% have terminal degrees, 9% minority, 45% women. **Part-time faculty:** 265 total; 9% minority, 38% women. **Class size:** 47% < 20, 53% 20-39, less than 1% 40-49. **Special facilities:** Art museum, urban studies center, Japanese tea house, digital arts studio.

Freshman class profile. 4,674 applied, 3,284 admitted, 811 enrolled.

Mid 50% test scores		**Return as sophomores:**	83%
SAT verbal:	480-600	**Out-of-state:**	48%
SAT math:	480-600	**Live on campus:**	88%
Rank in top quarter:	45%	**Fraternities:**	7%
Rank in top tenth:	18%	**Sororities:**	18%

Basis for selection. High school GPA, class rank, test scores most important. Activities, recommendations considered. Admission through Academic Discovery Program (ADP) provides counseling and tutorial support for students who need academic assistance and meet certain criteria of financial need. Interview recommended.

High school preparation. College-preparatory program required. 16 units required. Required units include English 4, mathematics 3, history 1, science 1 (laboratory 1), foreign language 2 and academic electives 5.

2005-2006 Annual costs. Tuition/fees: $26,190. Room/board: $9,850. Books/supplies: $500. Personal expenses: $1,119.

2004-2005 Financial aid. Need-based: 716 full-time freshmen applied for aid; 641 were judged to have need; 641 of these received aid. Average need met was 74%. Average scholarship/grant was $13,822; average loan $3,059. 64% of total undergraduate aid awarded as scholarships/grants, 36% as loans/jobs. **Non-need-based:** Awarded to 1,004 full-time undergraduates, including 220 freshmen. Scholarships awarded for academics, athletics, ROTC.

Application procedures. Admission: No deadline. $35 fee, may be waived for applicants with need. Application may be submitted online. Admission notification on a rolling basis beginning on or about 11/15. Must reply by May 1 or within 2 week(s) if notified thereafter. **Financial aid:** Priority date 2/15; no closing date. FAFSA required. Applicants notified on a rolling basis starting 3/15; must reply by 5/1 or within 2 week(s) of notification.

Academics. Special study options: Accelerated study, combined bachelor's/graduate degree, cooperative education, double major, dual enrollment of high school students, ESL, honors, independent study, internships, study abroad, teacher certification program. 3-2 with Thomas Jefferson University. **Credit/placement by examination:** AP, CLEP, institutional tests. 70 credit hours maximum toward bachelor's degree. **Support services:** Learning center, pre-admission summer program, reduced course load, remedial instruction, tutoring, writing center.

Majors. Area/ethnic studies: Central/Eastern European, regional, Russian/Slavic. **Biology:** General, biochemistry. **Business:** General, accounting, banking/financial services, business admin, communications, finance, human resources, insurance, international, international marketing, labor relations, management science, managerial economics, market research, marketing, nonprofit/public, operations, organizational behavior, statistics. **Communications:** General, broadcast journalism, digital media, journalism, media studies, public relations, radio/tv. **Communications technology:** Desktop publishing, radio/tv. **Computer sciences:** General, applications programming, computer graphics, computer science, database management, information systems, information technology, programming, web page design. **Conservation:** General, environmental science. **Education:** General, bilingual, biology, chemistry, developmentally delayed, early childhood, early childhood special, elementary, emotionally handicapped, English, foreign languages, French, German, history, mathematics, mentally handicapped, middle, multi-level teacher, physically handicapped, science, secondary, social science, social studies, Spanish, special. **English:** American lit, British lit, composition, speech/rhetoric, technical writing. **Foreign languages:** General, Biblical, classics, comparative lit, French, German, Italian, Latin, Spanish. **Health:** Audiology/hearing, audiology/speech pathology, nursing (RN), predentistry, premedicine, preveterinary, speech pathology. **History:** General, American. **Interdisciplinary:** Biological/physical sciences, math/computer science, nutrition sciences, peace/conflict, systems science. **Legal studies:** Prelaw. **Liberal arts:** Arts/sciences. **Math:** General, applied, statistics. **Philosophy/religion:** Philosophy, religion. **Physical sciences:** Chemistry, geology, planetary. **Protective services:** Criminal justice. **Psychology:** General. **Public administration:** General, social work. **Social sciences:** General, criminology, economics, international economics, international relations, political science, sociology, U.S. government. **Theology:** Religious ed. **Visual/performing arts:** Art history/conservation, cinematography, film/cinema, music history, studio arts.

Most popular majors. Biology 6%, business/marketing 25%, communications/journalism 12%, education 6%, health sciences 11%, psychology 6%.

Computing on campus. 181 workstations in library, computer center. Dormitories wired for high-speed internet access and linked to campus network. Commuter students can connect to campus network. Online course registration, online library, helpline, student web hosting, wireless network available.

Student life. Freshman orientation: Mandatory, $100 fee. Preregistration for classes offered. **Policies:** Nonalcoholic nightclub and eatery available 7 days a week. Freshmen permitted cars on campus. **Housing:** Guaranteed on-campus for all undergraduates. Coed dorms, special housing for disabled, apartments, substance-free housing available. $200 nonrefundable deposit, deadline 5/1. Campus-owned and -operated townhouses available. **Activities:** Jazz band, choral groups, dance, drama, film society, literary magazine, musical theater, radio station, student government, student newspaper, TV station, Black Student Union, campus ministry, Hillel, women's center, international club, social work association, veterans club, Young Socialist Alliance, student council for exceptional children, urban center.

Athletics. NCAA. **Intercollegiate:** Baseball M, basketball, cheerleading, cross-country, diving, field hockey W, football (tackle) M, golf, lacrosse W, rowing (crew), soccer, softball W, swimming, tennis, track and field, volleyball W. **Intramural:** Basketball, football (non-tackle), rugby M, softball, volleyball. **Team name:** Explorers.

Student services. Adult student services, alcohol/substance abuse counseling, campus ministries, career counseling, services for economically disadvantaged, student employment services, health services, minority student services, on-campus daycare, personal counseling, placement for graduates, veterans' counselor.

Contact. E-mail: admiss@lasalle.edu
Phone: (215) 951-1500 Toll-free number: (800) 328-1910
Fax: (215) 951-1656
Robert Voss, Dean of Admissions and Financial Aid, La Salle University, 1900 West Olney Avenue, Philadelphia, PA 19141-1199

Lafayette College

Easton, Pennsylvania — **CB member**
www.lafayette.edu — **CB code: 2361**

- Private 4-year engineering and liberal arts college affiliated with Presbyterian Church (USA)
- Residential campus in large town
- 2,310 degree-seeking undergraduates: 2% part-time, 47% women, 5% African American, 2% Asian American, 4% Hispanic American, 6% international
- 37% of applicants admitted

- SAT or ACT with writing, application essay required
- 90% graduate within 6 years

General. Founded in 1826. Regionally accredited. **Degrees:** 532 bachelor's awarded. **ROTC:** Army. **Location:** 80 miles from New York City, 60 miles from Philadelphia. **Calendar:** Semester, limited summer session. **Full-time faculty:** 195 total; 100% have terminal degrees, 11% minority, 31% women. **Part-time faculty:** 41 total; 56% have terminal degrees, 7% minority, 49% women. **Class size:** 61% < 20, 35% 20-39, 2% 40-49, 2% 50-99, less than 1% >100. **Special facilities:** Advanced computer-aided design laboratory, satellite downlink capability.

Freshman class profile. 5,728 applied, 2,146 admitted, 603 enrolled.

Mid 50% test scores			
SAT verbal:	580-670	Rank in top quarter:	88%
SAT math:	600-700	Rank in top tenth:	62%
ACT:	25-30	Return as sophomores:	93%
GPA 3.50 or higher:	84%	Out-of-state:	73%
GPA 3.0-3.49:	16%	Live on campus:	99%
		International:	6%

Basis for selection. Academic performance, class rank, quality of courses taken, personal qualities, extracurricular record, recommendations, and standardized test results important. Special consideration to applicants who will contribute diversity to student body. SAT Subject Tests recommended. SAT Subject Tests, if submitted, are sometimes considered for placement in mathematics and foreign languages. Interview recommended for all; portfolio recommeded for art program.

High school preparation. 16 units recommended. Recommended units include English 4, mathematics 3, science 2 (laboratory 2), foreign language 2 and academic electives 5. 4 mathematics, chemistry, physics required of bachelor of science degree candidates.

2005-2006 Annual costs. Tuition/fees: $29,982. Room/board: $9,285. Books/supplies: $600. Personal expenses: $875.

2005-2006 Financial aid. Need-based: 397 full-time freshmen applied for aid; 322 were judged to have need; 322 of these received aid. Average need met was 100%. Average scholarship/grant was $24,266; average loan $3,250. 89% of total undergraduate aid awarded as scholarships/grants, 11% as loans/jobs. **Non-need-based:** Awarded to 317 full-time undergraduates, including 114 freshmen. Scholarships awarded for academics, leadership, ROTC. **Additional information:** Parent loans, of up to $7,500 annually, are available with college absorbing interest while student is enrolled. Family has 8 years after graduation to repay. Not limited to those demonstrating need.

Application procedures. Admission: Closing date 1/1. $60 fee, may be waived for applicants with need. Application may be submitted online. Admission notification 4/1. Must reply by 5/1. **Financial aid:** Closing date 2/15. FAFSA, CSS PROFILE required. Applicants notified on a rolling basis starting 3/15; must reply by 5/1.

Academics. Self-designed majors include psychobiology, pre-architecture, area studies. Interdisciplinary minors also offered. **Special study options:** Accelerated study, cross-registration, distance learning, double major, exchange student, honors, independent study, internships, liberal arts/career combination, New York semester, semester at sea, student-designed major, study abroad, urban semester, Washington semester. Interim sessions here and abroad. **Credit/placement by examination:** AP, CLEP, institutional tests. **Support services:** Reduced course load, tutoring.

Majors. Area/ethnic studies: American. **Biology:** General, biochemistry. **Computer sciences:** General. **Engineering:** General, chemical, civil, electrical, mechanical. **Foreign languages:** French, German, Russian, Spanish. **History:** General. **Math:** General. **Philosophy/religion:** Philosophy, religion. **Physical sciences:** Chemistry, geology, physics. **Psychology:** General. **Social sciences:** Anthropology, economics, international relations, political science, sociology. **Visual/performing arts:** Music history, studio arts.

Most popular majors. Biology 6%, engineering/engineering technologies 18%, English 7%, psychology 7%, social sciences 32%.

Computing on campus. 600 workstations in library, computer center. Dormitories wired for high-speed internet access and linked to campus network. Commuter students can connect to campus network. Online course registration, online library, helpline, repair service, student web hosting, wireless network available.

Student life. Freshman orientation: Mandatory. **Housing:** Guaranteed on-campus for freshmen. Coed dorms, single-sex dorms, special housing for disabled, apartments, fraternity/sorority housing available. $500 deposit, deadline 5/1. Scholars house, Black Cultural Center, Hillel House, arts house, special interest group floors in residence halls available. **Activities:** Bands, choral groups, dance, drama, film society, literary magazine, music ensembles, musical theater, radio station, student government, student newspaper, Hillel, Association for Black Collegians, international student association, association for Lafayette women, Muslim student association, apartheid awareness association, environmental awareness and protection group, community outreach center, Student Alliance of Latinos of South America.

Athletics. NCAA. **Intercollegiate:** Baseball M, basketball, cross-country, diving, fencing, field hockey W, football (tackle) M, golf, lacrosse, rowing (crew), rugby M, skiing, soccer, softball W, swimming, tennis, track and field, volleyball W, wrestling M. **Intramural:** Badminton, basketball, bowling, cross-country, equestrian, racquetball, skiing, soccer, softball, squash, swimming, table tennis, tennis, track and field, volleyball, water polo, wrestling M. **Team name:** Leopards.

Student services. Adult student services, career counseling, student employment services, health services, on-campus daycare, personal counseling, placement for graduates.

Contact. E-mail: admissions@lafayette.edu
Phone: (610) 330-5100 Fax: (610) 330-5355
Carol Rowlands, Director of Admissions, Lafayette College, 118 Markle Hall, Easton, PA 18042-1770

Lancaster Bible College

Lancaster, Pennsylvania

www.lbc.edu **CB code: 2388**

- Private 4-year Bible college affiliated with nondenominational tradition
- Residential campus in small city
- 679 degree-seeking undergraduates: 13% part-time, 51% women, 4% African American, 1% Asian American, 2% Hispanic American, 1% international
- 146 degree-seeking graduate students
- 57% of applicants admitted
- SAT or ACT (ACT writing recommended), application essay required
- 53% graduate within 6 years

General. Founded in 1933. Regionally accredited; also accredited by ABHE. **Degrees:** 124 bachelor's, 39 associate awarded; master's offered. **Location:** 64 miles from Philadelphia. **Calendar:** Semester, limited summer session. **Full-time faculty:** 30 total. **Part-time faculty:** 40 total. **Class size:** 57% < 20, 33% 20-39, 4% 40-49, 6% 50-99.

Freshman class profile. 223 applied, 127 admitted, 121 enrolled.

Mid 50% test scores			
SAT verbal:	480-580	Rank in top tenth:	16%
SAT math:	460-570	End year in good standing:	90%
ACT:	17-23	Return as sophomores:	73%
Rank in top quarter:	34%	Out-of-state:	30%
		Live on campus:	82%

Basis for selection. Application must include personal spiritual testimony, academic transcripts, SAT or ACT scores, and 3 references. Interview recommended for all; audition required for religious music program. **Homeschooled:** Yearly evaluations should be included with application.

2005-2006 Annual costs. Tuition/fees: $12,795. Room/board: $5,700. Books/supplies: $700. Personal expenses: $1,750.

2004-2005 Financial aid. Need-based: 68% of total undergraduate aid awarded as scholarships/grants, 32% as loans/jobs. **Non-need-based:** Scholarships awarded for academics, alumni affiliation, leadership, music/drama, state residency.

Application procedures. Admission: Priority date 8/1; no deadline. $25 fee, may be waived for applicants with need. Admission notification on a rolling basis. **Financial aid:** Priority date 5/1; no closing date. FAFSA required. Applicants notified on a rolling basis starting 3/15; must reply within 3 week(s) of notification.

Academics. Special study options: Accelerated study, double major, independent study, internships, study abroad, teacher certification program. **Credit/placement by examination:** AP, CLEP, SAT, ACT, institutional tests. 15 credit hours maximum toward associate degree, 30 toward bachelor's. **Support services:** Learning center, reduced course load, remedial instruction, study skills assistance, tutoring.

Majors. Education: Elementary, physical. **Theology:** Bible.

Computing on campus. 44 workstations in library, computer center. Dormitories wired for high-speed internet access and linked to campus network. Commuter students can connect to campus network. Online library, helpline available.

Student life. **Freshman orientation:** Mandatory, $40 fee. Preregistration for classes offered. 2 days prior to start of classes. **Policies:** Religious observance required. Freshmen permitted cars on campus. **Housing:** Guaranteed on-campus for freshmen. Single-sex dorms available. **Activities:** Concert band, choral groups, drama, music ensembles, student government, student newspaper, Christian Counseling Fellowship, international student fellowship, married couples fellowship, Helpers in Service teams, student missionary fellowship, resident affairs council, commuter affairs council.

Athletics. NCCAA. **Intercollegiate:** Baseball M, basketball, cheerleading, lacrosse W, soccer, volleyball. **Intramural:** Basketball, football (non-tackle) M, soccer, softball, table tennis, tennis, volleyball. **Team name:** Chargers.

Student services. Campus ministries, career counseling, student employment services, financial aid counseling, health services, personal counseling, placement for graduates. **Learning disabled:** Comprehensive services available.

Contact. E-mail: admissions@lbc.edu
Phone: (717) 560-8271 Toll-free number: (866) 522-4968
Fax: (717) 560-8213
Joanne Roper, Director of Admissions, Lancaster Bible College, 901 Eden Road, Lancaster, PA 17608-3403

Lebanon Valley College

Annville, Pennsylvania — **CB member**
www.lvc.edu — **CB code: 2364**

- Private 4-year liberal arts college affiliated with United Methodist Church
- Residential campus in small town
- 1,702 degree-seeking undergraduates: 6% part-time, 55% women, 2% African American, 2% Asian American, 2% Hispanic American
- 115 degree-seeking graduate students
- 77% of applicants admitted
- SAT or ACT (ACT writing optional) required
- 74% graduate within 6 years; 14% enter graduate study

General. Founded in 1866. Regionally accredited. **Degrees:** 374 bachelor's, 6 associate awarded; master's, first professional offered. **ROTC:** Army. **Location:** 7 miles from Hershey, 25 miles from Harrisburg. **Calendar:** Semester, limited summer session. **Full-time faculty:** 100 total; 84% have terminal degrees, 8% minority, 36% women. **Part-time faculty:** 99 total; 24% have terminal degrees, 2% minority, 46% women. **Class size:** 59% < 20, 39% 20-39, less than 1% 40-49, less than 1% 50-99. **Special facilities:** Electronic pianos, sound recording studio, transmission electron microscope, scanning electron microscope, Fourier transform infrared spectrometer, atomic absorption spectrometer, nuclear magnetic resonance spectrometer, molecular modeling lab, campus wetlands area for research, arboretum, art gallery.

Freshman class profile. 2,006 applied, 1,537 admitted, 454 enrolled.

Mid 50% test scores		**Return as sophomores:**	85%
SAT verbal:	500-610	**Out-of-state:**	23%
SAT math:	510-620	**Live on campus:**	87%
Rank in top quarter:	70%	**Fraternities:**	11%
Rank in top tenth:	36%	**Sororities:**	12%
End year in good standing:	92%		

Basis for selection. Record of high school achievement most important. Recommendations, test scores, school and community activities evaluated. Essay and interview recommended for all; interview required for physical therapy program; audition required for music program.

High school preparation. College-preparatory program required. 16 units required. Required and recommended units include English 4, mathematics 3, social studies 1, history 2, science 2-3 (laboratory 2) and foreign language 2-3.

2005-2006 Annual costs. Tuition/fees: $24,860. Room/board: $6,840. Books/supplies: $800. Personal expenses: $770.

2005-2006 Financial aid. **Need-based:** 426 full-time freshmen applied for aid; 366 were judged to have need; 365 of these received aid. Average need met was 88%. Average scholarship/grant was $15,235; average loan $3,622. 74% of total undergraduate aid awarded as scholarships/grants, 26% as loans/jobs. **Non-need-based:** Awarded to 452 full-time undergraduates, including 136 freshmen. Scholarships awarded for academics, alumni affiliation, music/drama, ROTC.

Application procedures. **Admission:** No deadline. $30 fee, may be waived for applicants with need. Application may be submitted online. Admission notification on a rolling basis beginning on or about 10/15. Must reply by May 1 or within 2 week(s) if notified thereafter. **Financial aid:** Priority date 3/1; no closing date. FAFSA, institutional form required. Applicants notified on a rolling basis starting 3/1; must reply by 5/1 or within 2 week(s) of notification.

Academics. **Special study options:** Combined bachelor's/graduate degree, double major, dual enrollment of high school students, independent study, internships, liberal arts/career combination, student-designed major, study abroad, teacher certification program, urban semester, Washington semester. **Credit/placement by examination:** AP, CLEP, IB, institutional tests. 15 credit hours maximum toward associate degree, 30 toward bachelor's. **Support services:** Reduced course load, study skills assistance, tutoring, writing center.

Majors. **Area/ethnic studies:** American. **Biology:** General, biochemistry, Biochemistry/biophysics and molecular biology. **Business:** Accounting, actuarial science, business admin. **Communications:** Digital media. **Communications technology:** Recording arts. **Computer sciences:** Computer science. **Education:** Elementary, music. **English:** English lit. **Foreign languages:** French, German, Spanish. **Health:** Health care admin. **History:** General. **Liberal arts:** Arts/sciences. **Math:** General. **Philosophy/religion:** Philosophy, religion. **Physical sciences:** Chemistry, physics. **Psychology:** General. **Social sciences:** Economics, political science, sociology. **Visual/performing arts:** Art history/conservation, music performance, studio arts.

Most popular majors. Biology 6%, business/marketing 18%, education 22%, health sciences 7%, psychology 11%, social sciences 6%, visual/performing arts 8%.

Computing on campus. 211 workstations in library, computer center, student center. Dormitories wired for high-speed internet access and linked to campus network. Commuter students can connect to campus network. Online course registration, online library, helpline, student web hosting, wireless network available.

Student life. **Freshman orientation:** Mandatory. Preregistration for classes offered. One-day programs in May and July; 3-day program in August. **Policies:** Freshmen permitted cars on campus. **Housing:** Guaranteed on-campus for all undergraduates. Coed dorms, single-sex dorms, special housing for disabled, apartments, substance-free housing available. Community service, suites, theme housing available. **Activities:** Bands, choral groups, drama, literary magazine, music ensembles, musical theater, radio station, student government, student newspaper, symphony orchestra, College Republicans, Circle K, College Democrats, Cornerstone, Down to Earth, council for international affairs, Best Buddies, Praise Him with Dance.

Athletics. NCAA. **Intercollegiate:** Baseball M, basketball, cross-country, field hockey W, football (tackle) M, golf M, ice hockey M, soccer, softball W, swimming, tennis, track and field, volleyball W. **Intramural:** Basketball, football (non-tackle), racquetball, softball. **Team name:** Flying Dutchmen.

Student services. Alcohol/substance abuse counseling, campus ministries, career counseling, student employment services, financial aid counseling, health services, minority student services, personal counseling, placement for graduates. **Physically disabled:** Services for visually, speech impaired. **Learning disabled:** Comprehensive services available.

Contact. E-mail: admission@lvc.edu
Phone: (717) 867-6181 Toll-free number: (866) 582-4236
Fax: (717) 867-6026
Susan Sarisky, Director of Admission, Lebanon Valley College, 101 North College Avenue, Annville, PA 17003

Lehigh University

Bethlehem, Pennsylvania — **CB member**
www.lehigh.edu — **CB code: 2365**

- Private 4-year university
- Residential campus in small city
- 4,656 degree-seeking undergraduates: 1% part-time, 41% women, 2% African American, 5% Asian American, 2% Hispanic American, 3% international
- 1,888 degree-seeking graduate students
- 41% of applicants admitted
- SAT or ACT with writing, application essay required
- 85% graduate within 6 years

General. Founded in 1865. Regionally accredited. **Degrees:** 1,113 bachelor's awarded; master's, doctoral offered. **ROTC:** Army. **Location:** 50 miles from Philadelphia, 75 miles from New York City. **Calendar:** Semester, limited summer session. **Full-time faculty:** 434 total; 99% have terminal degrees, 16% minority, 26% women. **Part-time faculty:** 187 total; 21% minority, 41% women. **Class size:** 67% < 20, 24% 20-39, 4% 40-49, 4% 50-99, 2% >100. **Special facilities:** Two aberration-corrected electron microscopes, financial service laboratory, broadband seismic station, multidirectional experimental laboratory, electron optical labs, particle accelerator, rock climbing wall.

Freshman class profile. 10,501 applied, 4,340 admitted, 1,223 enrolled.

Mid 50% test scores			
SAT verbal:	600-680	Out-of-state:	76%
SAT math:	640-720	Live on campus:	99%
Rank in top quarter:	95%	International:	2%
Rank in top tenth:	78%	Fraternities:	34%
Return as sophomores:	95%	Sororities:	41%

Basis for selection. Each application read individually by admissions staff. All submitted material considered. All decisions subsequently reviewed by committee of admissions staff. TOEFL recommended for international students. Campus visit recommended.

High school preparation. 16 units required. Required units include English 4, mathematics 3, social studies 2, (laboratory 2), foreign language 2 and academic electives 3. Chemistry required and physics recommended for engineering and science candidates. Waivers in mathematics granted by some departments to well qualified candidates.

2005-2006 Annual costs. Tuition/fees: $31,420. Room/board: $8,560. Books/supplies: $1,000. Personal expenses: $1,210.

2005-2006 Financial aid. Need-based: 754 full-time freshmen applied for aid; 573 were judged to have need; 568 of these received aid. Average need met was 97%. Average scholarship/grant was $19,990; average loan $3,215. 78% of total undergraduate aid awarded as scholarships/grants, 22% as loans/jobs. **Non-need-based:** Awarded to 579 full-time undergraduates, including 187 freshmen. Scholarships awarded for academics, art, athletics, leadership, music/drama, ROTC.

Application procedures. Admission: Closing date 1/1 (postmark date). $60 fee, may be waived for applicants with need. Application may be submitted online. Admission notification 4/1. Must reply by 5/1. **Financial aid:** Closing date 2/15. FAFSA, CSS PROFILE required. Applicants notified by 3/30; must reply by 5/1 or within 3 week(s) of notification.

Academics. Special study options: Accelerated study, combined bachelor's/graduate degree, cooperative education, cross-registration, double major, ESL, exchange student, external degree, honors, independent study, internships, liberal arts/career combination, study abroad, urban semester, Washington semester. **Credit/placement by examination:** AP, CLEP, IB, institutional tests. **Support services:** Learning center, study skills assistance, tutoring, writing center.

Majors. Architecture: Architecture. **Area/ethnic studies:** African-American, American, Asian, Russian/Slavic. **Biology:** General, biochemistry, ecology, molecular. **Business:** Accounting, finance, logistics, management science, managerial economics, marketing. **Communications:** Journalism. **Computer sciences:** Computer science, information systems. **Conservation:** Environmental science. **Engineering:** Biomedical, chemical, civil, computer, electrical, environmental, industrial, materials, mechanical, mechanics, physics, structural. **English:** English lit. **Foreign languages:** Classics, French, German, Spanish. **Health:** Predentistry, premedicine. **Interdisciplinary:** Biological/physical sciences, biopsychology, cognitive science, science/society. **Math:** General, statistics. **Philosophy/religion:** Philosophy, religion. **Physical sciences:** Astronomy, astrophysics, chemistry, geology, physics. **Psychology:** General. **Social sciences:** General, anthropology, international relations, political science, sociology, urban studies. **Visual/performing arts:** Art, art history/conservation, design, dramatic, music history.

Most popular majors. Business/marketing 27%, computer/information sciences 7%, engineering/engineering technologies 26%, psychology 7%, social sciences 9%.

Computing on campus. 580 workstations in library, computer center. Dormitories wired for high-speed internet access and linked to campus network. Commuter students can connect to campus network. Online course registration, online library, helpline, repair service, wireless network available.

Student life. Freshman orientation: Mandatory, $180 fee. Preregistration for classes offered. 4-day program held prior to the first day of classes. **Policies:** Project Impact program strives to alter drinking culture and bring about enduring changes in pattern of student life. **Housing:** Guaranteed on-campus for freshmen. Coed dorms, apartments, fraternity/sorority housing, substance-free housing available. $500 nonrefundable deposit, deadline 5/1. Special interest housing (theme housing); residential college (Taylor College) available. **Activities:** Bands, choral groups, dance, drama, film society, literary magazine, music ensembles, musical theater, radio station, student government, student newspaper, symphony orchestra, Global Union, Asian Cultural Society, Fellowship of Christian Athletes, Omicron Delta Kappa, Chinese culture club, Black Student Union, Muslim students association, Alpha Phi Omega Service Fraternity, Best Buddies (works with mentally retarded citizens).

Athletics. NCAA. **Intercollegiate:** Baseball M, basketball, cross-country, diving, field hockey W, football (tackle) M, golf, lacrosse, rowing (crew) W, soccer, softball W, swimming, tennis, track and field, volleyball W, wrestling M. **Intramural:** Basketball, football (non-tackle), soccer, softball, volleyball. **Team name:** Mountain Hawks.

Student services. Alcohol/substance abuse counseling, campus ministries, career counseling, student employment services, financial aid counseling, health services, minority student services, on-campus daycare, personal counseling, placement for graduates, veterans' counselor, women's services.

Contact. E-mail: admissions@lehigh.edu
Phone: (610) 758-3100 Fax: (610) 758-4361
Eric Kaplan, Dean of Admissions and Financial Aid, Lehigh University, 27 Memorial Drive West, Bethlehem, PA 18015-3094

Lincoln University

Lincoln University, Pennsylvania — **CB member**
www.lincoln.edu — **CB code: 2367**

- Public 4-year university and liberal arts college
- Residential campus in rural community
- 1,700 degree-seeking undergraduates: 3% part-time, 61% women, 93% African American, 6% international
- 497 degree-seeking graduate students
- 35% of applicants admitted
- SAT or ACT (ACT writing optional), application essay required

General. Founded in 1854. Regionally accredited. **Degrees:** 240 bachelor's awarded; master's offered. **ROTC:** Army. **Location:** 45 miles from Philadelphia. **Calendar:** Semester, limited summer session. **Full-time faculty:** 93 total; 76% have terminal degrees, 68% minority, 34% women. **Part-time faculty:** 90 total; 11% have terminal degrees, 80% minority, 50% women. **Class size:** 43% < 20, 53% 20-39, 3% 40-49, 1% 50-99. **Special facilities:** Special collections library.

Freshman class profile. 5,435 applied, 1,914 admitted, 636 enrolled.

Mid 50% test scores			
SAT verbal:	350-450	Rank in top quarter:	23%
SAT math:	350-440	Rank in top tenth:	7%
GPA 3.50 or higher:	10%	Return as sophomores:	68%
GPA 3.0-3.49:	34%	Out-of-state:	53%
GPA 2.0-2.99:	45%	Live on campus:	99%
		International:	2%

Basis for selection. Admissions based on secondary school record and class rank. Recommendations, standardized test scores, talent, and ability also important.

High school preparation. 21 units required. Required units include English 4, mathematics 3, social studies 3, science 3 and academic electives 5. 2 arts or humanities required.

2005-2006 Annual costs. Tuition/fees: $7,028; $10,704 out-of-state. Out of state students pay an additional $564 in fees. Room/board: $6,898.

2005-2006 Financial aid. Need-based: 599 full-time freshmen applied for aid; 553 were judged to have need; 547 of these received aid. Average need met was 45%. Average scholarship/grant was $5,142; average loan $2,673. 38% of total undergraduate aid awarded as scholarships/grants, 62% as loans/jobs. **Non-need-based:** Awarded to 607 full-time undergraduates, including 232 freshmen. Scholarships awarded for academics, alumni affiliation, leadership, music/drama.

Application procedures. Admission: Priority date 4/1; no deadline. $20 fee, may be waived for applicants with need. Application may be submitted online. Admission notification on a rolling basis beginning on or about 2/15. **Financial aid:** Closing date 5/1. FAFSA required. Applicants notified on a rolling basis starting 4/1; must reply within 3 week(s) of notification.

Academics. Special study options: Exchange student, honors, independent study, internships, study abroad, teacher certification program. 3-2 in advanced science/engineering with Drexel Univ; Penn State Univ; Howard Univ; Univ. of Delaware, Temple, Widener and New Jersey Institute of

Technology. **Credit/placement by examination:** AP, CLEP, IB, SAT, institutional tests. **Support services:** Learning center, reduced course load, remedial instruction, study skills assistance, tutoring, writing center.

Majors. **Area/ethnic studies:** African-American. **Biology:** General. **Business:** Accounting, actuarial science, business admin, finance, human resources. **Communications:** General, journalism. **Computer sciences:** General. **Conservation:** Environmental science. **Education:** Early childhood, elementary, English, mathematics, music, secondary, special. **Engineering:** General. **English:** English lit. **Foreign languages:** Chinese, French, Japanese, Spanish. **Health:** Recreational therapy. **History:** General. **Math:** General. **Parks/recreation:** Health/fitness. **Philosophy/religion:** Philosophy, religion. **Physical sciences:** General, chemistry, physics. **Protective services:** Criminal justice. **Psychology:** General. **Public administration:** General, human services. **Social sciences:** Economics, international relations, political science, sociology. **Visual/performing arts:** Studio arts.

Most popular majors. Business/marketing 18%, communications/journalism 10%, education 15%, parks/recreation 7%, public administration/social services 6%, security/protective services 10%, social sciences 8%.

Computing on campus. 299 workstations in dormitories, library, computer center. Dormitories wired for high-speed internet access and linked to campus network. Commuter students can connect to campus network. Online library, repair service, wireless network available.

Student life. **Freshman orientation:** Mandatory, $138 fee. Preregistration for classes offered. **Housing:** Guaranteed on-campus for freshmen. Coed dorms, single-sex dorms, apartments available. $275 nonrefundable deposit. **Activities:** Jazz band, choral groups, dance, drama, music ensembles, radio station, student government, student newspaper, TV station, Music Educator National Conference, Mu Phi Alpha, Tolson Society, Thurgood Marshall Law Society, Phi Kappa Epsilon Honor Society, fashion club, religious organizations and social clubs.

Athletics. NCAA. **Intercollegiate:** Baseball M, basketball, cross-country, soccer, tennis, track and field, volleyball W. **Intramural:** Baseball M, basketball, bowling, cheerleading W, cross-country, diving, football (tackle) M, softball, swimming, tennis, track and field, volleyball. **Team name:** Lions.

Student services. Alcohol/substance abuse counseling, campus ministries, career counseling, student employment services, financial aid counseling, health services, personal counseling, women's services.

Contact. E-mail: admiss@lincoln.edu
Phone: (610) 932-8300 ext. 3207 Toll-free number: (800) 790-0191
Fax: (610) 932-1209
Michael Taylor, Director of Admissions, Lincoln University, PO BOX 179, Lincoln University, PA 19352-0999

Lock Haven University of Pennsylvania

Lock Haven, Pennsylvania **CB member**
www.lhup.edu **CB code: 2654**

- Public 4-year university, liberal arts and teachers college
- Residential campus in small town
- 4,794 degree-seeking undergraduates: 6% part-time, 58% women, 5% African American, 1% Asian American, 2% Hispanic American, 1% international
- 232 degree-seeking graduate students
- 76% of applicants admitted
- SAT or ACT (ACT writing optional) required
- 52% graduate within 6 years

General. Founded in 1870. Regionally accredited. Branch campus in Clearfield. **Degrees:** 671 bachelor's, 113 associate awarded; master's offered. **ROTC:** Army. **Location:** 26 miles from Williamsport, 35 miles from State College. **Calendar:** Semester, limited summer session. **Full-time faculty:** 254 total; 77% have terminal degrees, 12% minority, 45% women. **Part-time faculty:** 19 total; 5% minority, 58% women. **Class size:** 30% < 20, 58% 20-39, 10% 40-49, 2% 50-99. **Special facilities:** Model United Nations, rural retreat conference center, cadaver dissection laboratory, electron microscope, primate laboratory.

Freshman class profile. 4,746 applied, 3,624 admitted, 1,247 enrolled.

Mid 50% test scores			
SAT verbal:	420-520	Rank in top quarter:	25%
SAT math:	430-530	Rank in top tenth:	7%
ACT:	16-21	Return as sophomores:	73%
GPA 3.50 or higher:	25%	Out-of-state:	10%
GPA 3.0-3.49:	35%	Live on campus:	80%
GPA 2.0-2.99:	38%	International:	1%

Basis for selection. Course selection, grades received, and test scores most important. Preferred test score report date February 1. Interview required for nursing program; audition required for music programs. **Homeschooled:** Provide as much documentation as possible. Interview required.

High school preparation. 16 units required; 21 recommended. Required and recommended units include English 4, mathematics 3-4, social studies 2, history 2, science 3-4 (laboratory 2-3) and foreign language 2. 4 units math required for mathematics, computer science, biology, physics, and chemistry majors. 1 unit each biology, chemistry, physics required for health science majors. 1 unit each biology, anatomy and physiology, chemistry recommended for health and physical education majors.

2005-2006 Annual costs. Tuition/fees: $6,258; $11,618 out-of-state. Room/board: $5,840. Books/supplies: $900. Personal expenses: $1,090.

2005-2006 Financial aid. **Need-based:** 1,104 full-time freshmen applied for aid; 861 were judged to have need; 861 of these received aid. Average need met was 73%. Average scholarship/grant was $4,283; average loan $2,500. 28% of total undergraduate aid awarded as scholarships/grants, 72% as loans/jobs. **Non-need-based:** Awarded to 706 full-time undergraduates, including 172 freshmen. Scholarships awarded for academics, art, athletics, leadership, minority status, music/drama, ROTC, state residency.

Application procedures. **Admission:** Priority date 3/1; no deadline. $35 fee, may be waived for applicants with need. Application may be submitted online. Admission notification on a rolling basis beginning on or about 10/1. Must reply by May 1 or within 2 week(s) if notified thereafter. **Financial aid:** Priority date 3/15; no closing date. FAFSA, institutional form required. Applicants notified on a rolling basis starting 3/1; must reply by 5/1 or within 2 week(s) of notification.

Academics. **Special study options:** Combined bachelor's/graduate degree, cross-registration, distance learning, double major, dual enrollment of high school students, honors, independent study, internships, student-designed major, study abroad, teacher certification program. Exchange program with institutions in Taiwan, Russia, Australia, France, England, Poland, Germany, Scotland, Costa Rica, China, Japan, Croatia, Italy, Kenya, Mexico. 2-2 program in music education with Clarion University of Pennsylvania and Millersville University of Pennsylvania. **Credit/placement by examination:** AP, CLEP, IB, SAT, institutional tests. 30 credit hours maximum toward bachelor's degree. **Support services:** Pre-admission summer program, reduced course load, remedial instruction, study skills assistance, tutoring, writing center.

Majors. **Area/ethnic studies:** Latin American. **Biology:** General. **Business:** Accounting, business admin. **Communications:** Journalism. **Computer sciences:** General, computer science. **Education:** Early childhood special, elementary, kindergarten/preschool, special. **English:** English lit, speech/rhetoric. **Foreign languages:** French, German, Spanish. **Health:** Nursing (RN). **History:** General. **Interdisciplinary:** Biological/physical sciences. **Legal studies:** Paralegal. **Liberal arts:** Arts/sciences, humanities, library science. **Math:** General. **Parks/recreation:** Facilities management, sports admin. **Philosophy/religion:** Philosophy. **Physical sciences:** Chemistry, geology, physics. **Protective services:** Law enforcement admin. **Psychology:** General. **Public administration:** Social work. **Social sciences:** General, economics, geography, international relations, political science, sociology. **Visual/performing arts:** Art, dramatic, studio arts.

Most popular majors. Business/marketing 9%, education 21%, health sciences 11%, parks/recreation 19%, security/protective services 8%.

Computing on campus. 290 workstations in dormitories, library, computer center, student center. Dormitories wired for high-speed internet access and linked to campus network. Online course registration, online library, helpline, repair service, student web hosting, wireless network available.

Student life. **Freshman orientation:** Available. Overnight new student and parent programs, run concurrently, held during June. **Policies:** Freshmen permitted cars on campus. **Housing:** Guaranteed on-campus for freshmen. Coed dorms, apartments, substance-free housing available. $100 nonrefundable deposit, deadline 5/1. **Activities:** Bands, choral groups, dance, drama, literary magazine, music ensembles, musical theater, radio station, student government, student newspaper, symphony orchestra, TV station, Newman Club, Black Cultural Society, Campus Crusade, Commonwealth Association of Students, Fellowship of Christian Athletes, social service society, Full Gospel Fellowship, New Life Student Fellowship.

Athletics. NCAA. **Intercollegiate:** Baseball M, basketball, boxing, cheerleading, cross-country, field hockey W, football (tackle) M, lacrosse W, soccer, softball W, swimming W, track and field, volleyball W, wrestling M. **Intramural:** Badminton, basketball, cross-country, field hockey W, golf, racquetball, skiing, soccer, softball, tennis, volleyball, water polo, wrestling M. **Team name:** Bald Eagles, Lady Eagles.

Student services. Adult student services, alcohol/substance abuse counseling, campus ministries, career counseling, student employment services, financial aid counseling, health services, minority student services, personal counseling, placement for graduates, veterans' counselor. **Physically disabled:** Services for visually, speech impaired.

Contact. E-mail: admissions@lhup.edu
Phone: (570) 893-2027 Toll-free number: (800) 233-8978
Fax: (570) 893-2201
Stephen Lee, Director of Admissions, Lock Haven University of Pennsylvania, Akeley Hall, Lock Haven, PA 17745

Lycoming College

Williamsport, Pennsylvania — **CB member**
www.lycoming.edu — **CB code: 2372**

- Private 4-year liberal arts college affiliated with United Methodist Church
- Residential campus in large town
- 1,450 degree-seeking undergraduates: 1% part-time, 57% women
- 77% of applicants admitted
- SAT or ACT (ACT writing optional), application essay required
- 64% graduate within 6 years; 20% enter graduate study

General. Founded in 1812. Regionally accredited. **Degrees:** 293 bachelor's awarded. **ROTC:** Army. **Location:** 90 miles from Harrisburg, 160 miles from Philadelphia. **Calendar:** Semester, limited summer session. **Full-time faculty:** 87 total; 92% have terminal degrees, 12% minority. **Part-time faculty:** 15 total; 27% have terminal degrees, 13% minority, 33% women. **Class size:** 60% < 20, 36% 20-39, 2% 40-49, less than 1% 50-99, less than 1% >100. **Special facilities:** Planetarium, electronic music studio.

Freshman class profile. 1,511 applied, 1,157 admitted, 358 enrolled.

Mid 50% test scores			
SAT verbal:	540-560	Rank in top tenth:	19%
SAT math:	520-560	End year in good standing:	94%
ACT:	21-24	Return as sophomores:	88%
		Out-of-state:	21%
Rank in top quarter:	45%	Live on campus:	90%

Basis for selection. Academic achievement as reflected in school record, class rank, and test scores most important. Curriculum, counselor and teacher recommendations also considered. Interview recommended for all; portfolio recommended for art program and creative writing program; audition recommended for music and theater programs.

High school preparation. 16 units required. Required and recommended units include English 4, mathematics 3-4, social studies 3-4, science 2-3 (laboratory 2-3), foreign language 2-3 and academic electives 2.

2005-2006 Annual costs. Tuition/fees: $24,330. Room/board: $6,540. Books/supplies: $800. Personal expenses: $800.

2005-2006 Financial aid. Need-based: 330 full-time freshmen applied for aid; 293 were judged to have need; 293 of these received aid. Average need met was 76%. Average scholarship/grant was $14,694; average loan $3,489. 70% of total undergraduate aid awarded as scholarships/grants, 30% as loans/jobs. **Non-need-based:** Awarded to 290 full-time undergraduates, including 82 freshmen. Scholarships awarded for academics, art, leadership, music/drama.

Application procedures. Admission: Priority date 4/1; deadline 7/1 (receipt date). $35 fee, may be waived for applicants with need. Application may be submitted online. Admission notification on a rolling basis beginning on or about 12/15. Must reply by May 1 or within 4 week(s) if notified thereafter. **Financial aid:** Priority date 3/1; no closing date. FAFSA, institutional form required. Applicants notified on a rolling basis starting 3/1; must reply by 5/1.

Academics. Teacher certification offered on elementary and secondary levels and special education certification as part of bachelor of arts program. **Special study options:** Accelerated study, combined bachelor's/graduate degree, cross-registration, double major, honors, independent study, internships, student-designed major, study abroad, teacher certification program, United Nations semester, Washington semester. **Credit/placement by examination:** AP, CLEP, IB, institutional tests. 64 credit hours maximum toward bachelor's degree. **Support services:** Learning center, study skills assistance, tutoring, writing center.

Majors. Area/ethnic studies: American. **Biology:** General. **Business:** Accounting, actuarial science, business admin. **Communications:** General. **Computer sciences:** General. **English:** English lit. **Foreign languages:** French, German, Spanish. **History:** General. **Math:** General. **Philosophy/religion:** Philosophy, religion. **Physical sciences:** Astronomy, chemistry, physics. **Protective services:** Criminal justice. **Psychology:** General. **Social sciences:** Anthropology, archaeology, economics, political science, sociology. **Visual/performing arts:** Art, art history/conservation, dramatic.

Most popular majors. Biology 11%, business/marketing 15%, communications/journalism 6%, psychology 17%, social sciences 16%, visual/performing arts 11%.

Computing on campus. 180 workstations in library, computer center, student center. Dormitories wired for high-speed internet access and linked to campus network. Commuter students can connect to campus network. Online course registration, online library, helpline, repair service, student web hosting, wireless network available.

Student life. Freshman orientation: Mandatory, $200 fee. Preregistration for classes offered. 2-day, 1-night event for students and parents. Choose 1 of 3 dates. **Policies:** Students must live in college-owned residence halls or apartments. Freshmen permitted cars on campus. **Housing:** Guaranteed on-campus for all undergraduates. Coed dorms, single-sex dorms, apartments, fraternity/sorority housing, substance-free housing available. $100 deposit, deadline 5/1. Substance-free housing, study-intensive housing, Creative Arts Society housing available. **Activities:** Bands, choral groups, dance, drama, film society, literary magazine, music ensembles, musical theater, opera, radio station, student government, student newspaper, symphony orchestra, TV station, Circle K, Habitat for Humanity, College Democrats, College Republicans, United Campus Ministry, environmental awareness foundation, Black Student Union.

Athletics. NCAA. **Intercollegiate:** Basketball, cross-country, football (tackle) M, golf M, lacrosse, soccer, softball W, swimming, tennis, volleyball W, wrestling M. **Intramural:** Basketball, football (non-tackle), soccer, softball, volleyball. **Team name:** Warriors.

Student services. Campus ministries, career counseling, student employment services, financial aid counseling, health services, personal counseling, placement for graduates, women's services.

Contact. E-mail: admissions@lycoming.edu
Phone: (570) 321-4026 Toll-free number: (800) 345-3920 ext. 4026
Fax: (570) 321-4317
James Spencer, Dean of Admissions and Financial Aid, Lycoming College, 700 College Place, Williamsport, PA 17701

Mansfield University of Pennsylvania

Mansfield, Pennsylvania
www.mnsfld.edu — **CB code: 2655**

- Public 4-year university and liberal arts college
- Residential campus in small town
- 2,886 degree-seeking undergraduates: 7% part-time, 62% women, 6% African American, 1% Asian American, 1% Hispanic American, 1% Native American, 1% international
- 357 degree-seeking graduate students
- 72% of applicants admitted
- SAT or ACT (ACT writing optional) required
- 52% graduate within 6 years

General. Founded in 1857. Regionally accredited. **Degrees:** 577 bachelor's, 30 associate awarded; master's offered. **Location:** 50 miles from Williamsport, 26 miles from Corning, New York. **Calendar:** Semester, limited summer session. **Full-time faculty:** 165 total; 93% have terminal degrees, 13% minority, 46% women. **Part-time faculty:** 58 total; 7% have terminal degrees, 2% minority, 64% women. **Class size:** 42% < 20, 45% 20-39, 6% 40-49, 7% 50-99, less than 1% >100. **Special facilities:** Planetarium, solar collector, science museum, animal collection.

Freshman class profile. 2,348 applied, 1,689 admitted, 680 enrolled.

Mid 50% test scores			
SAT verbal:	440-540	Rank in top tenth:	12%
SAT math:	430-540	Return as sophomores:	64%
GPA 3.50 or higher:	42%	Out-of-state:	15%
GPA 3.0-3.49:	27%	Live on campus:	80%
GPA 2.0-2.99:	29%	Fraternities:	3%
Rank in top quarter:	33%	Sororities:	4%

Basis for selection. Class rank, high school curriculum, test scores important; counselor's recommendation, extracurricular activities considered. Special consideration given to applicants eligible for Equal Education Opportunity Program. Entry competitive in X-ray technology, respiratory therapy, fisheries, music, art programs, premed, nursing, biology, chemistry. Essay recommended for all; interview required for radiology program; audition required for music program; portfolio required for art program.

High school preparation. College-preparatory program required. 21 units required; 25 recommended. Required and recommended units include English 4, mathematics 3-4, history 4, science 2-3 (laboratory 2-3), foreign language 2-4 and academic electives 6.

2005-2006 Annual costs. Tuition/fees: $6,408; $13,768 out-of-state. Room/board: $6,120. Books/supplies: $750. Personal expenses: $800.

2004-2005 Financial aid. **Need-based:** 656 full-time freshmen applied for aid; 528 were judged to have need; 528 of these received aid. Average need met was 52%. Average scholarship/grant was $4,051; average loan $2,600. 52% of total undergraduate aid awarded as scholarships/grants, 48% as loans/jobs. **Non-need-based:** Awarded to 611 full-time undergraduates, including 185 freshmen. Scholarships awarded for academics, art, athletics, leadership, music/drama, state residency.

Application procedures. **Admission:** No deadline. $25 fee, may be waived for applicants with need. Application may be submitted online. Admission notification on a rolling basis beginning on or about 7/1. Must reply by May 1 or within 2 week(s) if notified thereafter. Applicants to competitive programs should apply by January 15. **Financial aid:** Priority date 3/15; no closing date. FAFSA, institutional form required. Applicants notified on a rolling basis starting 3/15; must reply within 2 week(s) of notification.

Academics. **Special study options:** Cooperative education, cross-registration, distance learning, double major, dual enrollment of high school students, exchange student, honors, independent study, internships, liberal arts/career combination, student-designed major, study abroad, teacher certification program, Washington semester. **Credit/placement by examination:** CLEP, IB, institutional tests. **Support services:** Learning center, pre-admission summer program, reduced course load, remedial instruction, study skills assistance, tutoring, writing center.

Majors. **Architecture:** Urban/community planning. **Biology:** General, biochemistry, cell/histology, marine, molecular. **Business:** Accounting, actuarial science, business admin, human resources, international, marketing, tourism promotion, tourism/travel. **Communications:** General, broadcast journalism, journalism, public relations. **Computer sciences:** General, computer science, information systems. **Conservation:** General, environmental studies, fisheries. **Education:** Art, biology, chemistry, early childhood, elementary, English, foreign languages, French, German, history, mathematics, middle, multi-level teacher, music, physics, secondary, social studies, Spanish, special. **English:** Speech/rhetoric. **Foreign languages:** French, German, Spanish. **Health:** Clinical lab science, clinical lab technology, music therapy, predentistry, premedicine, preop/surgical nursing, prepharmacy, preveterinary. **History:** General. **Legal studies:** Prelaw. **Liberal arts:** Arts/sciences. **Math:** General. **Philosophy/religion:** Philosophy. **Physical sciences:** Chemistry, geology, physics. **Protective services:** Law enforcement admin. **Psychology:** General. **Public administration:** Social work. **Social sciences:** General, anthropology, economics, geography, political science, sociology. **Visual/performing arts:** Art, art history/conservation, dramatic, music management, music performance, piano/organ, studio arts, voice/opera.

Most popular majors. Business/marketing 12%, communications/journalism 10%, education 14%, English 7%, health sciences 8%, public administration/social services 6%, security/protective services 9%, visual/performing arts 9%.

Computing on campus. 715 workstations in dormitories, library, computer center. Dormitories linked to campus network. Commuter students can connect to campus network. Helpline available.

Student life. **Freshman orientation:** Mandatory, $65 fee. Preregistration for classes offered. 2-day program for students and parents. **Policies:** Freshmen permitted cars on campus. **Housing:** Guaranteed on-campus for all undergraduates. Coed dorms, fraternity/sorority housing available. **Activities:** Bands, choral groups, dance, drama, literary magazine, music ensembles, musical theater, radio station, student government, student newspaper, symphony orchestra, TV station, Black Awarenesss Association, Inter-Varsity Christian Fellowship, Commonwealth Association of Students.

Athletics. NCAA. **Intercollegiate:** Baseball M, basketball, cross-country, diving W, field hockey W, football (tackle) M, soccer W, softball W, swimming W, track and field, wrestling M. **Intramural:** Badminton, basketball, bowling, golf, handball, racquetball, skiing, soccer M, softball, tennis, volleyball, water polo. **Team name:** Mounties.

Student services. Adult student services, alcohol/substance abuse counseling, campus ministries, career counseling, services for economically disadvantaged, student employment services, financial aid counseling, health services, minority student services, on-campus daycare, personal counseling, placement for graduates, veterans' counselor, women's services. **Physically disabled:** Services for visually, speech, hearing impaired.

Contact. E-mail: admissns@mnsfld.edu
Phone: (570) 662-4243 Toll-free number: (800) 577-6826
Fax: (570) 662-4121
Brian Barden, Director of Admissions, Mansfield University of Pennsylvania, Alumni Hall, Mansfield, PA 16933

Marywood University

Scranton, Pennsylvania — **CB member**
www.marywood.edu — **CB code: 2407**

- Private 4-year university affiliated with Roman Catholic Church
- Residential campus in small city
- 1,807 degree-seeking undergraduates: 8% part-time, 73% women, 2% African American, 1% Asian American, 3% Hispanic American, 1% international
- 1,058 degree-seeking graduate students
- 77% of applicants admitted
- SAT or ACT (ACT writing optional) required
- 64% graduate within 6 years; 23% enter graduate study

General. Founded in 1915. Regionally accredited. Off-campus and distance education degree program available. **Degrees:** 349 bachelor's awarded; master's, doctoral offered. **ROTC:** Army, Air Force. **Location:** 110 miles from Philadelphia, 120 miles from New York City. **Calendar:** Semester, extensive summer session. **Full-time faculty:** 133 total; 81% have terminal degrees, 6% minority, 56% women. **Part-time faculty:** 175 total; 5% minority, 57% women. **Class size:** 61% < 20, 38% 20-39, less than 1% 40-49, less than 1% 50-99. **Special facilities:** Arboretum, art galleries, assistive technology lab, science multimedia laboratory, interactive voice laboratory, music computer laboratory, nursing laboratory, video conferencing facility, speech and hearing clinic, healthy families center, early childhood center.

Freshman class profile. 1,441 applied, 1,104 admitted, 308 enrolled.

Mid 50% test scores			
SAT verbal:	470-570	Rank in top quarter:	41%
SAT math:	470-510	Rank in top tenth:	16%
GPA 3.50 or higher:	47%	Return as sophomores:	73%
GPA 3.0-3.49:	30%	Out-of-state:	31%
GPA 2.0-2.99:	23%	Live on campus:	69%
		International:	1%

Basis for selection. Class rank and high school achievement weighed alongside performance on SAT/ACT. Course selection, achievement outside classroom, involvement in activities in and out of school, and letters or recommendations also considered. TOEFL used for admission of non-native English speakers. Essay recommended for all. Interview required for physician's assistant program; recommended for all others. Audition required for music program; portfolio recommended for art program. **Learning Disabled:** Students may request accommodation by submitting documentation to admissions office or coordinator of services for students with disabilities.

High school preparation. 16 units required. Required units include English 4, mathematics 2, social studies 3, science 1 (laboratory 1) and academic electives 6. Biological science must be laboratory science.

2005-2006 Annual costs. Tuition/fees: $21,580. Room/board: $9,100. Books/supplies: $700. Personal expenses: $700.

Financial aid. **Non-need-based:** Scholarships awarded for academics, alumni affiliation, art, leadership, minority status, music/drama, ROTC.

Application procedures. **Admission:** No deadline. $30 fee, may be waived for applicants with need. Application may be submitted online. Admission notification on a rolling basis beginning on or about 3/1. Must reply by May 1 or within 3 week(s) if notified thereafter. **Financial aid:** Priority date 2/15; no closing date. FAFSA, institutional form required. Applicants notified on a rolling basis starting 3/1; must reply by 5/1 or within 3 week(s) of notification.

Academics. Healthy Family Center provides opportunities for study and research in nutrition, dietetics, and athletic performance. **Special study options:** Accelerated study, combined bachelor's/graduate degree, cross-registration, distance learning, double major, dual enrollment of high school students, ESL, honors, independent study, internships, semester at sea, student-designed major, study abroad, teacher certification program. Study abroad programs in Italy, Thailand, Ireland. **Credit/placement by examination:** AP, CLEP, IB, institutional tests. 30 credit hours maximum toward associate degree, 66 toward bachelor's. **Support services:** Learning center, pre-admission summer program, reduced course load, remedial instruction, study skills assistance, tutoring, writing center.

Majors. Biology: General, biotechnology, ecology, systematic. **Business:** Accounting, business admin, financial planning, hospitality admin, international, management science, marketing. **Communications:** Advertising, broadcast journalism, digital media, public relations. **Communications technology:** Radio/tv. **Computer sciences:** General. **Conservation:** General, environmental science. **Education:** General, art, biology, Deaf/hearing impaired, drama/dance, early childhood, early childhood special, elementary, English, ESL, family/consumer sciences, foreign languages, French, health, mathematics, multi-level teacher, music, physical, science, secondary, Spanish, special, speech impaired. **English:** English lit. **Family/consumer sciences:** General, food/nutrition. **Foreign languages:** French, Spanish. **Health:** Art therapy, athletic training, clinical lab science, clinical nutrition, communication disorders, dietetics, facilities admin, health services, mental health counseling, music therapy, nursing (RN), prenursing, speech pathology, substance abuse counseling. **History:** General. **Legal studies:** Paralegal, prelaw. **Math:** General. **Parks/recreation:** General, exercise sciences, health/fitness. **Philosophy/religion:** Religion. **Protective services:** Law enforcement admin. **Psychology:** General. **Public administration:** General, community org/advocacy, social work. **Science technology:** Biological. **Social sciences:** General, criminology, sociology. **Theology:** Religious ed, sacred music. **Transportation:** Aviation management. **Visual/performing arts:** General, art history/conservation, arts management, ceramics, design, directing/producing, dramatic, graphic design, music performance, photography, studio arts, theater arts management.

Most popular majors. Education 21%, health sciences 23%, psychology 6%, visual/performing arts 15%.

Computing on campus. 382 workstations in dormitories, library, computer center, student center. Dormitories wired for high-speed internet access and linked to campus network. Commuter students can connect to campus network. Online course registration, online library, helpline, repair service, student web hosting available.

Student life. Freshman orientation: Mandatory, $175 fee. Preregistration for classes offered. Includes program for families, held in midsummer for 2 days. Additional 2-day program prior to start of classes. **Policies:** First- and second-year students under 21 not living at home with families in area required to live on campus. Freshmen permitted cars on campus. **Housing:** Guaranteed on-campus for freshmen. Coed dorms, single-sex dorms, special housing for disabled, apartments available. $300 fully refundable deposit, deadline 9/1. Volunteer services residential community and international students residential community available. **Activities:** Bands, choral groups, dance, drama, literary magazine, music ensembles, musical theater, radio station, student government, student newspaper, TV station, Amnesty International, Collegiate Volunteers, environmental club, Volunteers in Action, campus ministry, Psi Chi, Peer Mediators, international club, Gay-Straight Alliance, Americorps.

Athletics. NCAA. **Intercollegiate:** Baseball M, basketball, cross-country, field hockey W, soccer, softball W, tennis, volleyball W. **Intramural:** Badminton, baseball M, basketball, field hockey W, football (non-tackle), football (tackle) M, golf, ice hockey, racquetball, soccer, softball, swimming, table tennis, tennis, volleyball, water polo. **Team name:** Pacers.

Student services. Adult student services, alcohol/substance abuse counseling, campus ministries, career counseling, services for economically disadvantaged, student employment services, financial aid counseling, health services, minority student services, on-campus daycare, personal counseling, placement for graduates, women's services. **Physically disabled:** Services for visually, speech, hearing impaired. **Learning disabled:** Comprehensive services available.

Contact. E-mail: yourfuture@marywood.edu
Phone: (570) 348-6234 Toll-free number: (800) 346-5014
Fax: (570) 961-4763
Robert Reese, Director of Admissions, Marywood University, 2300 Adams Avenue, Scranton, PA 18509-1598

Mercyhurst College

Erie, Pennsylvania
www.mercyhurst.edu **CB code: 2410**

- Private 4-year liberal arts college affiliated with Roman Catholic Church
- Residential campus in small city
- 3,800 degree-seeking undergraduates: 11% part-time, 60% women, 4% African American, 2% Hispanic American, 4% international
- 274 degree-seeking graduate students
- 78% of applicants admitted
- SAT or ACT (ACT writing recommended) required
- 62% graduate within 6 years; 18% enter graduate study

General. Founded in 1926. Regionally accredited. **Degrees:** 558 bachelor's, 174 associate awarded; master's offered. **ROTC:** Army. **Location:** 100 miles from Pittsburgh, 90 miles from Buffalo, New York. **Calendar:** Trimester, limited summer session. **Full-time faculty:** 163 total; 54% have terminal degrees, 4% minority, 47% women. **Part-time faculty:** 85 total; 8% have terminal degrees, 4% minority, 45% women. **Class size:** 53% < 20, 46% 20-39, less than 1% 40-49, less than 1% 50-99. **Special facilities:** Observatory, archeological materials preservation laboratory.

Freshman class profile. 2,711 applied, 2,121 admitted, 698 enrolled.

Mid 50% test scores		**Rank in top quarter:**	43%
SAT verbal:	480-590	**Rank in top tenth:**	18%
SAT math:	490-590	**End year in good standing:**	91%
ACT:	19-25	**Return as sophomores:**	83%
GPA 3.50 or higher:	46%	**Out-of-state:**	57%
GPA 3.0-3.49:	32%	**Live on campus:**	92%
GPA 2.0-2.99:	22%	**International:**	6%

Basis for selection. Admissions based on secondary school record. Class rank, standardized test scores, talent, ability, character, and personal qualities also important. Essay, interview recommended for all; audition required for dance, music programs; portfolio required for art program. **Homeschooled:** SAT/ACT and transcript preferred.

High school preparation. College-preparatory program recommended. 16 units required. Required and recommended units include English 4, mathematics 3, social studies 4, history 1, science 2 (laboratory 1) and foreign language 2.

2005-2006 Annual costs. Tuition/fees: $19,113. Room/board: $7,074. Books/supplies: $1,000. Personal expenses: $2,000.

2005-2006 Financial aid. Need-based: 691 full-time freshmen applied for aid; 508 were judged to have need; 508 of these received aid. Average need met was 87%. Average scholarship/grant was $9,322; average loan $2,515. 57% of total undergraduate aid awarded as scholarships/grants, 43% as loans/jobs. **Non-need-based:** Awarded to 739 full-time undergraduates, including 384 freshmen. Scholarships awarded for academics, alumni affiliation, art, athletics, leadership, minority status, music/drama, religious affiliation, ROTC.

Application procedures. Admission: Priority date 3/15; no deadline. $30 fee, may be waived for applicants with need. Application may be submitted online. Admission notification on a rolling basis beginning on or about 11/15. Must reply by May 1 or within 2 week(s) if notified thereafter. **Financial aid:** Priority date 3/1; no closing date. FAFSA, institutional form required. Applicants notified on a rolling basis starting 2/15; must reply by 5/1 or within 2 week(s) of notification.

Academics. Education department offers graduate student-taught special education programs for learning disabled students. **Special study options:** Accelerated study, combined bachelor's/graduate degree, cooperative education, cross-registration, double major, dual enrollment of high school students, honors, independent study, internships, liberal arts/career combination, New York semester, semester at sea, student-designed major, study abroad, teacher certification program, Washington semester, weekend college. **Credit/placement by examination:** AP, CLEP, IB, SAT, ACT, institutional tests. 30 credit hours maximum toward bachelor's degree. **Support services:** Learning center, pre-admission summer program, reduced course load, remedial instruction, study skills assistance, tutoring, writing center.

Majors. Biology: General, biochemistry. **Business:** Accounting, business admin, finance, hospitality admin, international. **Communications:** General. **Computer sciences:** General. **Education:** Art, biology, business, chemistry, early childhood, elementary, English, family/consumer sciences, foreign languages, mathematics, music, science, secondary, social science, special.

English: English lit. **Family/consumer sciences:** General. **Foreign languages:** General. **Health:** Art therapy, health services, medical records technology. **History:** General. **Interdisciplinary:** Global studies. **Math:** General. **Philosophy/religion:** Philosophy, religion. **Physical sciences:** Chemistry, geology. **Protective services:** Criminal justice, forensics. **Psychology:** General. **Public administration:** Social work. **Social sciences:** Anthropology, political science, sociology. **Theology:** Religious ed. **Visual/performing arts:** Dance, music performance, studio arts.

Most popular majors. Business/marketing 24%, education 16%, family/consumer sciences 7%, health sciences 6%, interdisciplinary studies 6%, security/protective services 6%, visual/performing arts 7%.

Computing on campus. 330 workstations in dormitories, library, computer center, student center. Dormitories wired for high-speed internet access and linked to campus network. Commuter students can connect to campus network. Online course registration, online library, helpline, repair service, student web hosting, wireless network available.

Student life. **Freshman orientation:** Mandatory, $125 fee. Preregistration for classes offered. 3 sessions; July, August, September. **Housing:** Guaranteed on-campus for all undergraduates. Single-sex dorms, apartments available. $300 fully refundable deposit. **Activities:** Bands, choral groups, dance, drama, film society, literary magazine, music ensembles, musical theater, opera, radio station, student government, student newspaper, symphony orchestra, campus ministry, Association of Black Collegians, Habitat for Humanity, Amnesty International, ambassadors club.

Athletics. NCAA. **Intercollegiate:** Baseball M, basketball, cheerleading, cross-country, field hockey W, football (tackle) M, golf, ice hockey, lacrosse, rowing (crew), soccer, softball W, swimming M, tennis, volleyball, water polo, wrestling M. **Intramural:** Basketball, bowling, football (non-tackle) M, ice hockey, skiing, soccer, softball, table tennis. **Team name:** Lakers.

Student services. Adult student services, alcohol/substance abuse counseling, campus ministries, career counseling, services for economically disadvantaged, student employment services, financial aid counseling, health services, personal counseling, placement for graduates, veterans' counselor. **Physically disabled:** Services for hearing impaired. **Learning disabled:** Comprehensive services available.

Contact. E-mail: admissions@mercyhurst.edu
Phone: (814) 824-2202 Toll-free number: (800) 825-1926
Fax: (814) 824-2071
J.P. Cooney, Director of Admissions, Mercyhurst College, 501 East 38th Street, Erie, PA 16546-0001

Messiah College

Grantham, Pennsylvania — **CB member**
www.messiah.edu — **CB code: 2411**

- Private 4-year liberal arts college affiliated with interdenominational tradition
- Residential campus in small town
- 2,888 degree-seeking undergraduates: 1% part-time, 62% women, 2% African American, 2% Asian American, 2% Hispanic American, 3% international
- 75% of applicants admitted
- Application essay required
- 75% graduate within 6 years; 20% enter graduate study

General. Founded in 1909. Regionally accredited. **Degrees:** 633 bachelor's awarded. **Location:** 10 miles from Harrisburg, 20 miles from Gettysburg. **Calendar:** Semester, limited summer session. **Full-time faculty:** 170 total; 71% have terminal degrees, 6% minority, 35% women. **Part-time faculty:** 127 total; 6% minority, 49% women. **Class size:** 43% < 20, 53% 20-39, 2% 40-49, 2% 50-99, less than 1% >100. **Special facilities:** Brethren in Christ Historical Library and Archives, advanced studies center, natural history museum.

Freshman class profile. 2,730 applied, 2,036 admitted, 707 enrolled.

Mid 50% test scores			
SAT verbal:	550-660	Rank in top quarter:	71%
SAT math:	540-650	Rank in top tenth:	39%
ACT:	23-28	End year in good standing:	91%
GPA 3.50 or higher:	83%	Return as sophomores:	85%
GPA 3.0-3.49:	13%	Out-of-state:	51%
GPA 2.0-2.99:	4%	Live on campus:	98%
		International:	3%

Basis for selection. Students who enroll normally in top third of class and have B average or better. Statement of Christian commitment required. Tests required of standard choice applicants. Students in top 20% may apply without test scores but must submit graded writing sample and have on-campus interview. Interview recommended for all. **Homeschooled:** Comprehensive transcript of senior year academic program as well as courses and course evaluations of 9th through 11th grades required. If independent evaluation by qualified educator available, include with transcript. **Learning Disabled:** Autobiographical statement required. Psychoeducational report (done within last 4 years) and interview required only after admissions decision. High school IEP recommended.

High school preparation. 16 units required; 20 recommended. Required and recommended units include English 4, mathematics 2-3, social studies 2, history 2, science 2-3 (laboratory 2-3), foreign language 2 and academic electives 4.

2005-2006 Annual costs. Tuition/fees: $22,110. Room/board: $6,800. Books/supplies: $810. Personal expenses: $1,100.

2005-2006 Financial aid. **Need-based:** 605 full-time freshmen applied for aid; 484 were judged to have need; 484 of these received aid. Average need met was 63%. Average scholarship/grant was $4,742; average loan $2,069. 60% of total undergraduate aid awarded as scholarships/grants, 40% as loans/jobs. **Non-need-based:** Awarded to 2,258 full-time undergraduates, including 582 freshmen. Scholarships awarded for academics, alumni affiliation, art, leadership, music/drama, religious affiliation.

Application procedures. **Admission:** Priority date 5/1; no deadline. $30 fee, may be waived for applicants with need. Application may be submitted online. Admission notification on a rolling basis beginning on or about 7/1. Must reply by May 1 or within 4 week(s) if notified thereafter. **Financial aid:** Priority date 4/1; no closing date. FAFSA required. Applicants notified on a rolling basis starting 3/15; must reply by 5/1 or within 4 week(s) of notification.

Academics. **Special study options:** Accelerated study, double major, dual enrollment of high school students, ESL, exchange student, honors, independent study, internships, student-designed major, study abroad, teacher certification program, urban semester, Washington semester. Pass/Fail option. **Credit/placement by examination:** AP, CLEP, IB, institutional tests. 32 credit hours maximum toward bachelor's degree. **Support services:** Learning center, pre-admission summer program, reduced course load, remedial instruction, study skills assistance, tutoring, writing center.

Majors. **Biology:** General, biochemistry. **Business:** Accounting, business admin, e-commerce, entrepreneurial studies, human resources, international, managerial economics, marketing. **Communications:** General, journalism, radio/tv. **Computer sciences:** Computer science, information systems. **Conservation:** Environmental science, environmental studies. **Education:** Art, biology, chemistry, early childhood, elementary, English, family/consumer sciences, French, German, mathematics, music, physical, social studies, Spanish. **Engineering:** General. **English:** English lit. **Family/consumer sciences:** Family/community services. **Foreign languages:** French, German, Spanish. **Health:** Athletic training, clinical nutrition, nursing (RN), recreational therapy. **History:** General. **Interdisciplinary:** Biopsychology. **Liberal arts:** Humanities. **Math:** General. **Parks/recreation:** General, exercise sciences. **Philosophy/religion:** Philosophy, religion. **Physical sciences:** Chemistry, physics. **Protective services:** Criminal justice. **Psychology:** General. **Public administration:** Social work. **Social sciences:** Economics, political science, sociology. **Theology:** Bible, religious ed. **Visual/performing arts:** Art history/conservation, dramatic, studio arts.

Most popular majors. Biology 6%, business/marketing 10%, education 16%, health sciences 9%, psychology 7%, social sciences 7%.

Computing on campus. 527 workstations in dormitories, library, computer center, student center. Dormitories wired for high-speed internet access and linked to campus network. Commuter students can connect to campus network. Online course registration, helpline, student web hosting, wireless network available.

Student life. **Freshman orientation:** Mandatory. Preregistration for classes offered. 4-day orientation for students and parents during fall welcome weekend; includes placement exams and service day. **Policies:** Religious observance required. Freshmen permitted cars on campus. **Housing:** Guaranteed on-campus for all undergraduates. Coed dorms, single-sex dorms, special housing for disabled, apartments, substance-free housing available. $200 nonrefundable deposit, deadline 5/1. Students generally required to live on campus unless married or living with relatives. **Activities:** Bands, choral groups, dance, drama, film society, literary magazine, music ensembles, musical theater, radio station, student government, student newspaper, symphony orchestra, outreach teams, World Christian Fellowship, Nurses Christian Fellowship, Newman Club, Seek His Face Ministries, powerhouse band, acclamation dance, Alliance of Confessing Theologies, Orthodox Christian Fellowship, service trips.

Athletics. NCAA. **Intercollegiate:** Baseball M, basketball, cross-country, field hockey W, golf M, lacrosse, soccer, softball W, tennis, track and field, volleyball W, wrestling M. **Intramural:** Basketball, football (non-tackle), soccer, softball, volleyball. **Team name:** Falcons.

Student services. Campus ministries, career counseling, student employment services, financial aid counseling, health services, minority student services, personal counseling, placement for graduates. **Physically disabled:** Services for visually, speech, hearing impaired.

Contact. E-mail: admiss@messiah.edu
Phone: (717) 691-6000 Toll-free number: (800) 233-4220
Fax: (717) 796-5374
William Strausbaugh, Dean for Enrollment Management, Messiah College, PO Box 3005, Grantham, PA 17027-0800

Millersville University of Pennsylvania

Millersville, Pennsylvania — **CB member**
www.millersville.edu — **CB code: 2656**

- Public 4-year university and liberal arts college
- Residential campus in small town
- 6,847 degree-seeking undergraduates: 8% part-time, 57% women, 7% African American, 2% Asian American, 3% Hispanic American
- 525 degree-seeking graduate students
- 55% of applicants admitted
- SAT or ACT (ACT writing recommended) required
- 62% graduate within 6 years; 31% enter graduate study

General. Founded in 1855. Regionally accredited. **Degrees:** 1,391 bachelor's, 2 associate awarded; master's offered. **ROTC:** Army. **Location:** 3 miles from Lancaster, 35 miles from Harrisburg. **Calendar:** 4-1-4, limited summer session. **Full-time faculty:** 322 total; 16% minority, 46% women. **Part-time faculty:** 149 total; 3% minority, 49% women. **Class size:** 23% < 20, 66% 20-39, 6% 40-49, 4% 50-99, 1% >100. **Special facilities:** Early childhood center, teleconferencing center, weather station.

Freshman class profile. 6,413 applied, 3,555 admitted, 1,320 enrolled.

Mid 50% test scores			
SAT verbal:	480-570	Rank in top tenth:	15%
SAT math:	490-580	Return as sophomores:	80%
		Out-of-state:	4%
Rank in top quarter:	45%	Live on campus:	84%

Basis for selection. High school record most important, followed by class rank, followed by test scores and recommendations. Special consideration to students with special talents. Educationally and economically disadvantaged students may be admitted to Aim for Success enrichment program if they demonstrate potential for college success. Applicants without SAT scores may enroll as nondegree students and be admitted to degree-seeking status after completing 15 credits with 2.0 GPA. Interview required for applicants to disadvantaged program; recommended for all others. Audition required for music applicants; portfolio recommended for art applicants. RN required for nursing program.

High school preparation. 15 units required; 21 recommended. Required and recommended units include English 4, mathematics 3, social studies 3, history 2, science 3 (laboratory 1), foreign language 2 and academic electives 4.

2005-2006 Annual costs. Tuition/fees: $6,235; $13,595 out-of-state. Room/board: $5,878. Books/supplies: $850. Personal expenses: $1,756.

2004-2005 Financial aid. **Need-based:** 1,206 full-time freshmen applied for aid; 819 were judged to have need; 795 of these received aid. Average need met was 72%. Average scholarship/grant was $4,380; average loan $2,615. 52% of total undergraduate aid awarded as scholarships/grants, 48% as loans/jobs. **Non-need-based:** Awarded to 798 full-time undergraduates, including 239 freshmen. Scholarships awarded for academics, athletics, minority status.

Application procedures. **Admission:** Priority date 1/1; no deadline. $35 fee, may be waived for applicants with need. Application may be submitted online. Admission notification on a rolling basis beginning on or about 10/1. Must reply by 4/1. Extensions of reply date for accepted applicants granted upon request until May 1. **Financial aid:** Closing date 3/15. FAFSA required. Applicants notified on a rolling basis starting 3/19; must reply within 2 week(s) of notification.

Academics. All students must demonstrate competency in English composition, speech, mathematics, liberal arts and in an interdisciplinary perspectives course. **Special study options:** Accelerated study, combined bachelor's/graduate degree, cooperative education, cross-registration, distance learning, double major, dual enrollment of high school students, honors, independent study, internships, liberal arts/career combination, study abroad, teacher certification program. Adult and Continuing Education (ACE) program, off-campus study, learning disabilities services. **Credit/placement by examination:** AP, CLEP, institutional tests. **Support services:** Learning center, pre-admission summer program, reduced course load, remedial instruction, study skills assistance, tutoring, writing center.

Majors. **Biology:** General. **Business:** Business admin. **Communications:** General. **Computer sciences:** General. **Education:** Art, elementary, English, foreign languages, mathematics, music, science, secondary, social studies, special, technology/industrial arts. **Engineering technology:** Industrial, occupational safety. **English:** English lit. **Foreign languages:** French, German, Spanish. **Health:** Nursing (RN). **History:** General. **Math:** General. **Philosophy/religion:** Philosophy. **Physical sciences:** Atmospheric science, chemistry, geology, oceanography, physics. **Psychology:** General. **Public administration:** Social work. **Social sciences:** General, anthropology, economics, geography, international relations, political science, sociology. **Visual/performing arts:** Art.

Most popular majors. Business/marketing 12%, communications/journalism 8%, education 19%, engineering/engineering technologies 7%, psychology 7%, social sciences 11%, visual/performing arts 6%.

Computing on campus. 510 workstations in dormitories, library, computer center, student center. Dormitories wired for high-speed internet access and linked to campus network. Commuter students can connect to campus network. Online course registration, online library, helpline, repair service, wireless network available.

Student life. **Freshman orientation:** Mandatory, $120 fee. 2-day program in June and July includes parents. **Policies:** Freshmen permitted cars on campus. **Housing:** Guaranteed on-campus for freshmen. Coed dorms, apartments, substance-free housing available. $125 partly refundable deposit, deadline 4/1. Academic interest housing available for several subject areas. University-affiliated apartments and dormitory for single students adjacent to campus. **Activities:** Bands, choral groups, dance, drama, literary magazine, music ensembles, musical theater, radio station, student government, student newspaper, symphony orchestra, TV station, Black Campus Ministry, University Christian Fellowship, Black Student Union, College Republicans, Circle K, InterVarsity Christian Fellowship, United Campus Ministry, Hillel, Bible Campus Ministry, Habitat For Humanity.

Athletics. NCAA. **Intercollegiate:** Baseball M, basketball, cheerleading M, cross-country, field hockey W, football (tackle) M, golf M, lacrosse W, soccer, softball W, swimming W, tennis, track and field, volleyball W, wrestling M. **Intramural:** Badminton, basketball, golf, racquetball, soccer, softball, tennis, volleyball. **Team name:** Marauders.

Student services. Adult student services, alcohol/substance abuse counseling, campus ministries, career counseling, services for economically disadvantaged, student employment services, financial aid counseling, health services, minority student services, on-campus daycare, personal counseling, placement for graduates, veterans' counselor, women's services. **Physically disabled:** Services for visually, speech, hearing impaired.

Contact. E-mail: admissions@millersville.edu
Phone: (717) 872-3371 Toll-free number: (800) 682-3648
Fax: (717) 871-2147
Douglas Zander, Director of Admissions, Millersville University of Pennsylvania, PO Box 1002, Millersville, PA 17551-0302

Moore College of Art and Design

Philadelphia, Pennsylvania
www.moore.edu — **CB code: 2417**

- Private 4-year visual arts college for women
- Residential campus in very large city
- 493 degree-seeking undergraduates: 14% part-time, 99% women, 9% African American, 6% Asian American, 4% Hispanic American, 2% international
- 87% of applicants admitted
- SAT or ACT, interview required
- 86% graduate within 6 years

General. Founded in 1848. Regionally accredited. Only BFA-granting women's arts college in U.S. **Degrees:** 112 bachelor's awarded. **Location:** 90 miles from New York City. **Calendar:** Semester, limited summer session. **Full-time faculty:** 32 total; 69% have terminal degrees, 6% minority, 59% women. **Part-time faculty:** 74 total; 32% have terminal degrees, 14% minority, 69% women. **Class size:** 83% < 20, 17% 20-39. **Special facilities:** Professional galleries.

Freshman class profile. 223 applied, 195 admitted, 86 enrolled.

Mid 50% test scores			
SAT verbal:	450-560	GPA 2.0-2.99:	43%
SAT math:	420-540	Return as sophomores:	79%
ACT:	15-24	Out-of-state:	45%
GPA 3.50 or higher:	13%	Live on campus:	65%
GPA 3.0-3.49:	44%	International:	1%

Basis for selection. High school record, interview, portfolio, and test scores important. Minimum SAT combined score of 850 (exclusive of writing) or ACT composite score of 18, minimum high school GPA of 2.5 required. All students entering college must complete writing placement essay before they receive class schedule. Portfolio required; essay recommended for all. **Learning Disabled:** Students who request accommodations must provide qualifying documentation on professional letterhead and contain dates of assessment, signatures, titles, and license/certification numbers of diagnosing professionals. Documentation should be no more than 3 years old.

High school preparation. 14 units recommended. Recommended units include English 4, mathematics 2, social studies 4, science 2 and foreign language 2. 3 art recommended.

2005-2006 Annual costs. Tuition/fees: $22,846. Room/board: $8,654. Books/supplies: $2,000. Personal expenses: $2,000.

2005-2006 Financial aid. Need-based: 45% of total undergraduate aid awarded as scholarships/grants, 55% as loans/jobs. **Non-need-based:** Scholarships awarded for academics.

Application procedures. Admission: Priority date 3/1; deadline 9/15. $40 fee, may be waived for applicants with need. Application may be submitted online. Admission notification on a rolling basis. Must reply by May 1 or within 3 week(s) if notified thereafter. **Financial aid:** Priority date 3/1, closing date 5/1. FAFSA required. Applicants notified on a rolling basis starting 2/15; must reply within 2 week(s) of notification.

Academics. Special study options: Cooperative education, cross-registration, double major, exchange student, independent study, internships, study abroad, teacher certification program. **Credit/placement by examination:** CLEP, institutional tests. **Support services:** Learning center, pre-admission summer program, reduced course load, study skills assistance, tutoring.

Majors. Education: Art. **Interdisciplinary:** Museum. **Visual/performing arts:** Art history/conservation, fashion design, fiber arts, graphic design, illustration, interior design, photography, studio arts.

Most popular majors. Visual/performing arts 95%.

Computing on campus. 125 workstations in dormitories, library, computer center. Online course registration, wireless network available.

Student life. Freshman orientation: Mandatory, $55 fee. 4 days immediately prior to beginning of semester. **Policies:** Freshmen permitted cars on campus. **Housing:** Guaranteed on-campus for freshmen. Apartments, substance-free housing available. $250 deposit, deadline 7/15. **Activities:** Student government, student newspaper, Moore Environmental Committee, Emerging Leaders in the Arts, Judicial Board, Residence Life Mentors.

Student services. Adult student services, career counseling, student employment services, financial aid counseling, health services, personal counseling, placement for graduates.

Contact. E-mail: admiss@moore.edu
Phone: (215) 965-4014 Toll-free number: (800) 523-2025
Fax: (215) 568-3547
Heeseung Lee, Director of Admissions, Moore College of Art and Design, The Parkway at 20th Street, Philadelphia, PA 19103-1179

Moravian College

Bethlehem, Pennsylvania — **CB member**
www.moravian.edu — **CB code: 2418**

- Private 4-year liberal arts college affiliated with Moravian Church in America
- Residential campus in small city
- 1,636 degree-seeking undergraduates: 7% part-time, 59% women, 2% African American, 2% Asian American, 3% Hispanic American, 1% international
- 224 degree-seeking graduate students
- 65% of applicants admitted
- SAT or ACT with writing, application essay required
- 71% graduate within 6 years; 17% enter graduate study

General. Founded in 1742. Regionally accredited. Member of Lehigh Valley Association of Independent Colleges Consortium. Sixth oldest college in country. **Degrees:** 363 bachelor's awarded; master's, first professional offered. **ROTC:** Army. **Location:** 60 miles from Philadelphia, 90 miles from New York City. **Calendar:** Semester, extensive summer session. **Full-time faculty:** 115 total. **Part-time faculty:** 80 total. **Class size:** 66% < 20, 32% 20-39, 2% 40-49, less than 1% 50-99. **Special facilities:** Student art studios.

Freshman class profile. 1,890 applied, 1,231 admitted, 382 enrolled.

Mid 50% test scores			
SAT verbal:	520-620	Return as sophomores:	86%
SAT math:	520-630	Out-of-state:	43%
Rank in top quarter:	64%	Live on campus:	87%
Rank in top tenth:	31%	Fraternities:	14%
		Sororities:	19%

Basis for selection. High school performance, standardized test scores, recommendations, extracurricular activities, and potential for contributing to campus culture considered. TOEFL used for applicants who are not native speakers of English. Interviews strongly recommended; audition required for music applicants; portfolio recommended for art applicants. **Homeschooled:** Transcript of courses and grades, letter of recommendation (nonparent) required.

High school preparation. College-preparatory program required. 15 units required; 17 recommended. Required and recommended units include English 4, mathematics 3-4, social studies 4, science 2 (laboratory 2) and foreign language 2-3. 4 units mathematics recommended for business, science or math students.

2005-2006 Annual costs. Tuition/fees: $25,263. Room/board: $7,530. Books/supplies: $760. Personal expenses: $1,288.

2005-2006 Financial aid. Need-based: 343 full-time freshmen applied for aid; 277 were judged to have need; 277 of these received aid. Average need met was 76%. Average scholarship/grant was $12,492; average loan $3,307. 63% of total undergraduate aid awarded as scholarships/grants, 37% as loans/jobs. **Non-need-based:** Awarded to 447 full-time undergraduates, including 121 freshmen. Scholarships awarded for academics, alumni affiliation, leadership, music/drama, religious affiliation, ROTC.

Application procedures. Admission: Closing date 2/15 (postmark date). $40 fee, may be waived for applicants with need. Application may be submitted online. Admission notification 3/15. Must reply by May 1 or within 2 week(s) if notified thereafter. **Financial aid:** Priority date 2/14, closing date 3/15. FAFSA, CSS PROFILE required. Applicants notified on a rolling basis starting 4/1; must reply by 5/1 or within 2 week(s) of notification.

Academics. 4-year program of academic and career counseling. Learning Center offers partial program for learning disabled students. **Special study options:** Combined bachelor's/graduate degree, cross-registration, double major, honors, independent study, internships, semester at sea, student-designed major, study abroad, teacher certification program, Washington semester. Allied health program with Thomas Jefferson University, forestry program cooperative with Duke University, North Carolina, engineering programs cooperative with Lehigh University and Washington University (MO). **Credit/placement by examination:** AP, CLEP, IB, institutional tests. Some courses not included in credit-by-examination option. **Support services:** Learning center, reduced course load, study skills assistance, tutoring, writing center.

Majors. Area/ethnic studies: German. **Biology:** General, biochemistry. **Business:** Accounting, business admin, international. **Computer sciences:** Computer science. **Conservation:** Environmental science, environmental studies. **Education:** Music. **English:** Creative writing, English lit. **Foreign languages:** Classics, French, German, Spanish. **Health:** Nursing (RN). **History:** General. **Math:** General. **Philosophy/religion:** Philosophy, religion. **Physical sciences:** Chemistry, physics. **Protective services:** Criminal justice. **Psychology:** General. **Social sciences:** Economics, political science, sociology. **Theology:** Sacred music. **Visual/performing arts:** Art, art history/conservation, dramatic, graphic design, music performance, music theory/composition, studio arts.

Most popular majors. Biology 6%, business/marketing 14%, education 9%, English 9%, psychology 13%, social sciences 21%, visual/performing arts 7%.

Computing on campus. 236 workstations in library, computer center. Dormitories wired for high-speed internet access and linked to campus network. Commuter students can connect to campus network. Online library, helpline, repair service available.

Student life. **Freshman orientation:** Mandatory, $100 fee. Preregistration for classes offered. 3 days immediately before start of semester. **Housing:** Guaranteed on-campus for all undergraduates. Coed dorms, single-sex dorms, apartments, fraternity/sorority housing, substance-free housing available. $200 nonrefundable deposit, deadline 5/1. Special interest housing, townhouses and suites available. **Activities:** Bands, choral groups, dance, drama, literary magazine, music ensembles, radio station, student government, student newspaper, symphony orchestra, Hillel Society, Newman Association, international club, Moravian College Christian Fellowship, Spectrum, Catacombs, Campus Community Connection, The Forum, multicultural club, Moravians@Moravian.

Athletics. NCAA. **Intercollegiate:** Baseball M, basketball, cross-country, field hockey W, football (tackle) M, golf M, lacrosse, soccer, softball W, tennis, track and field, volleyball W. **Intramural:** Basketball, football (non-tackle), racquetball, soccer, softball, tennis, volleyball. **Team name:** Greyhounds.

Student services. Adult student services, alcohol/substance abuse counseling, campus ministries, career counseling, student employment services, financial aid counseling, health services, minority student services, personal counseling, placement for graduates, women's services. **Physically disabled:** Services for visually, speech, hearing impaired.

Contact. E-mail: admissions@moravian.edu
Phone: (610) 861-1320 Toll-free number: (800) 441-3191
Fax: (610) 625-7930
James Mackin, Director of Admission, Moravian College, 1200 Main Street, Bethlehem, PA 18018

Mount Aloysius College
Cresson, Pennsylvania
www.mtaloy.edu **CB code: 2420**

- Private 4-year liberal arts college affiliated with Roman Catholic Church
- Commuter campus in small town
- 1,424 degree-seeking undergraduates: 19% part-time, 72% women, 2% African American, 1% Hispanic American, 1% Native American, 2% international
- 57 degree-seeking graduate students
- 77% of applicants admitted
- SAT or ACT (ACT writing optional), application essay required
- 61% graduate within 6 years

General. Founded in 1939. Regionally accredited. Affiliated with Sisters of Mercy. **Degrees:** 157 bachelor's, 254 associate awarded; master's offered. **Location:** 12 miles from Altoona, 90 miles from Pittsburgh. **Calendar:** Semester, limited summer session. **Full-time faculty:** 62 total; 36% have terminal degrees, 2% minority, 66% women. **Part-time faculty:** 103 total; 7% have terminal degrees, 61% women. **Class size:** 67% < 20, 33% 20-39, less than 1% 40-49. **Special facilities:** Health and science center.

Freshman class profile. 949 applied, 728 admitted, 297 enrolled.

Mid 50% test scores			
SAT verbal:	410-520	Return as sophomores:	69%
SAT math:	420-510	Out-of-state:	3%
ACT:	16-20	Live on campus:	42%
		International:	1%

Basis for selection. School record, test scores, activities, talent, and character most important. TOEFL used for international students. Nursing entrance test not required for students with SAT of 900 (exclusive of Writing) or higher. Placement test waived if student scores 500 or higher in either section. Interview required for students with lower SAT scores and GPA. Interviews and essays required for physical therapist assistant majors. **Learning Disabled:** Admission interview required.

High school preparation. 16 units required. Required and recommended units include English 4, mathematics 3, social studies 3, history 3, science 3, foreign language 2 and academic electives 3. Algebra and 2 lab sciences required for nursing. Algebra, chemistry required for physical therapist assistant, radiography and medical imaging applicants. Biology required for occupational therapy assistant applicants.

2005-2006 Annual costs. Tuition/fees: $14,530. Room/board: $6,190. Books/supplies: $1,400. Personal expenses: $2,750.

2004-2005 Financial aid. **Need-based:** 277 full-time freshmen applied for aid; 238 were judged to have need; 238 of these received aid. Average need met was 23%. Average scholarship/grant was $2,800; average loan $2,600. 52% of total undergraduate aid awarded as scholarships/grants, 48% as loans/jobs. **Non-need-based:** Awarded to 153 full-time undergraduates, including 78 freshmen. Scholarships awarded for academics, art, leadership, music/drama, religious affiliation.

Application procedures. **Admission:** No deadline. $30 fee, may be waived for applicants with need. Application may be submitted online. Admission notification on a rolling basis beginning on or about 8/1. **Financial aid:** Priority date 2/15; no closing date. FAFSA required. Applicants notified on a rolling basis starting 3/15; must reply within 4 week(s) of notification.

Academics. **Special study options:** Accelerated study, combined bachelor's/graduate degree, distance learning, honors, independent study, internships, student-designed major, teacher certification program. **Credit/placement by examination:** AP, CLEP, institutional tests. 15 credit hours maximum toward associate degree, 30 toward bachelor's. **Support services:** Learning center, pre-admission summer program, reduced course load, remedial instruction, study skills assistance, tutoring, writing center.

Majors. **Business:** Accounting, accounting/business management, business admin. **Computer sciences:** General, information technology. **Education:** Early childhood, elementary. **Foreign languages:** Sign language interpretation. **Health:** Health services, nursing (RN), physician assistant, radiologic technology/medical imaging. **History:** General. **Interdisciplinary:** Behavioral sciences, math/computer science. **Legal studies:** Prelaw. **Liberal arts:** Arts/sciences, humanities. **Protective services:** Criminal justice. **Psychology:** General. **Social sciences:** General, criminology, political science.

Most popular majors. Business/marketing 15%, computer/information sciences 6%, education 8%, foreign language 6%, health sciences 29%, interdisciplinary studies 8%, legal studies 6%, security/protective services 10%.

Computing on campus. 175 workstations in dormitories, library, computer center, student center. Dormitories linked to campus network. Helpline, repair service available.

Student life. **Freshman orientation:** Mandatory. **Policies:** Freshmen permitted cars on campus. **Housing:** Guaranteed on-campus for all undergraduates. Coed dorms available. **Activities:** Choral groups, drama, student government, student newspaper, campus ministry, nursing, occupational therapy assistant, business, Phi Theta Kappa, student programming council.

Athletics. NCAA. **Intercollegiate:** Baseball M, basketball, cross-country, golf, soccer, softball W, volleyball W. **Intramural:** Baseball M, basketball, football (tackle), golf, skiing, soccer, softball W, table tennis, tennis, volleyball. **Team name:** Mounties.

Student services. Alcohol/substance abuse counseling, campus ministries, career counseling, student employment services, financial aid counseling, health services, on-campus daycare, personal counseling, placement for graduates, veterans' counselor. **Physically disabled:** Services for hearing impaired.

Contact. E-mail: admissions@mtaloy.edu
Phone: (814) 886-6383 Toll-free number: (888) 823-2220
Fax: (814) 886-6441
Frank Crouse, Dean of Enrollment Management, Mount Aloysius College, 7373 Admiral Peary Highway, Cresson, PA 16630

Muhlenberg College
Allentown, Pennsylvania **CB member**
www.muhlenberg.edu **CB code: 2424**

- Private 4-year liberal arts college affiliated with Evangelical Lutheran Church in America
- Residential campus in small city
- 2,396 degree-seeking undergraduates: 6% part-time, 58% women, 2% African American, 2% Asian American, 3% Hispanic American
- 43% of applicants admitted
- Application essay required
- 85% graduate within 6 years; 30% enter graduate study

General. Founded in 1848. Regionally accredited. **Degrees:** 589 bachelor's, 3 associate awarded. **ROTC:** Army. **Location:** 55 miles from Philadelphia, 90 miles from New York City. **Calendar:** Semester, limited summer session. **Full-time faculty:** 152 total; 86% have terminal degrees, 8% minority, 48% women. **Part-time faculty:** 104 total; 27% have terminal degrees, 7% minority, 44% women. **Class size:** 57% < 20, 41% 20-39, less than 1% 40-49, 1% 50-99, less than 1% >100. **Special facilities:** Theater complex, electronic music studio, natural history museum, 38-acre environmental field station, greenhouse, electron microscope, isolation laboratories, 20-foot boat for marine studies, 60-acre arboretum.

Freshman class profile. 4,217 applied, 1,809 admitted, 576 enrolled.

Mid 50% test scores		Rank in top quarter:	82%
SAT verbal:	560-660	Rank in top tenth:	42%
SAT math:	570-670	End year in good standing:	97%
ACT:	26-29	Return as sophomores:	93%
GPA 3.50 or higher:	56%	Out-of-state:	79%
GPA 3.0-3.49:	30%	Live on campus:	99%
GPA 2.0-2.99:	14%		

Basis for selection. High school courses, grades, class rank, test scores, personal qualities, essay, recommendations, special talents and activities important. Interview strongly recommended. In lieu of test scores, applicants may submit graded paper and interview with admissions staff. SAT or ACT required for 4-4 medical program, 3-4 dental program, 3-2 engineering program, and for consideration for merit scholarships. Audition recommended for dance, drama, music programs; portfolio recommended for art program. **Homeschooled:** Statement describing homeschool structure and mission, transcript of courses and grades, state high school equivalency certificate, letter of recommendation (nonparent) required. Interview strongly recommended.

High school preparation. 16 units required. Required and recommended units include English 4, mathematics 3-4, social studies 2, history 2, science 2-3 (laboratory 2), foreign language 2-4 and academic electives 1. Advanced placement and accelerated courses encouraged.

2006-2007 Annual costs. Tuition/fees: $30,715. Room/board: $7,525.

2005-2006 Financial aid. Need-based: 377 full-time freshmen applied for aid; 274 were judged to have need; 269 of these received aid. Average need met was 94%. Average scholarship/grant was $16,155; average loan $2,829. 83% of total undergraduate aid awarded as scholarships/grants, 17% as loans/jobs. **Non-need-based:** Awarded to 902 full-time undergraduates, including 267 freshmen. Scholarships awarded for academics, art, leadership, music/drama.

Application procedures. Admission: Closing date 2/15 (postmark date). $45 fee, may be waived for applicants with need. Application may be submitted online. Admission notification 3/15. Must reply by 5/1. **Financial aid:** Closing date 2/15. FAFSA, institutional form, CSS PROFILE required. Applicants notified by 4/1; must reply by 5/1.

Academics. Special study options: Accelerated study, combined bachelor's/graduate degree, cross-registration, double major, exchange student, honors, independent study, internships, student-designed major, study abroad, teacher certification program, Washington semester. Study abroad with Lehigh Valley Association of Independent Colleges, 3-2 engineering programs with Columbia University, Washington University, 3-2 forestry program with Duke University, over 60 agreements with foreign universities for study abroad. **Credit/placement by examination:** AP, CLEP, IB, SAT, ACT, institutional tests. 68 credit hours maximum toward bachelor's degree. 68 credit hours equivalent to 17 course units. **Support services:** Learning center, reduced course load, study skills assistance, tutoring, writing center.

Majors. Area/ethnic studies: American, German, Russian/Slavic. **Biology:** General, biochemistry. **Business:** Accounting, business admin, human resources, management information systems. **Communications:** General. **Computer sciences:** General. **Conservation:** Environmental science. **English:** English lit. **Foreign languages:** General, French, German, Spanish. **History:** General. **Interdisciplinary:** Natural sciences, neuroscience. **Legal studies:** Prelaw. **Math:** General. **Philosophy/religion:** Philosophy, religion. **Physical sciences:** General, chemistry, physics. **Psychology:** General. **Social sciences:** Anthropology, economics, international relations, political science, sociology. **Visual/performing arts:** Art, dance, dramatic.

Most popular majors. Business/marketing 27%, communications/journalism 8%, psychology 8%, social sciences 16%, visual/performing arts 11%.

Computing on campus. 486 workstations in dormitories, library, computer center. Dormitories wired for high-speed internet access and linked to campus network. Commuter students can connect to campus network. Helpline, repair service, wireless network available.

Student life. Freshman orientation: Mandatory, $120 fee. Preregistration for classes offered. 3-day program prior to start of classes. **Policies:** Students share responsibility for maintaining high standards and must pledge to abide by Academic Behavior Code. **Housing:** Guaranteed on-campus for all undergraduates. Coed dorms, single-sex dorms, special housing for disabled, apartments, fraternity/sorority housing, substance-free housing available. $400 deposit, deadline 5/1. College-owned houses in neighborhood surrounding campus. **Activities:** Bands, choral groups, dance, drama, literary magazine, music ensembles, musical theater, radio station, student government, student newspaper, TV station, over 100 clubs and organizations.

Athletics. NCAA. **Intercollegiate:** Baseball M, basketball, cheerleading, cross-country, field hockey W, football (tackle) M, golf, lacrosse, soccer, softball W, tennis, track and field, volleyball W, wrestling M. **Intramural:** Basketball, cross-country, football (non-tackle), racquetball, skiing, soccer, softball, squash, swimming, table tennis, tennis, volleyball. **Team name:** Mules.

Student services. Adult student services, alcohol/substance abuse counseling, campus ministries, career counseling, student employment services, financial aid counseling, health services, minority student services, personal counseling, placement for graduates, women's services. **Physically disabled:** Services for visually, speech, hearing impaired.

Contact. E-mail: admissions@muhlenberg.edu
Phone: (484) 664-3200 Fax: (484) 664-3234
Christopher Hooker-Haring, Dean of Admission and Financial Aid, Muhlenberg College, 2400 Chew Street, Allentown, PA 18104

Neumann College

Aston, Pennsylvania — **CB member**
www.neumann.edu — **CB code: 2628**

- Private 4-year liberal arts college affiliated with Roman Catholic Church
- Residential campus in large town
- 2,313 degree-seeking undergraduates: 21% part-time, 67% women, 13% African American, 1% Asian American, 2% Hispanic American, 2% international
- 497 degree-seeking graduate students
- 96% of applicants admitted
- SAT or ACT required
- 59% graduate within 6 years; 15% enter graduate study

General. Founded in 1965. Regionally accredited. Provides Catholic education in Franciscan tradition. **Degrees:** 395 bachelor's, 17 associate awarded; master's, doctoral offered. **ROTC:** Army. **Location:** 19 miles from Philadelphia. **Calendar:** Semester, limited summer session. **Full-time faculty:** 84 total; 56% have terminal degrees, 6% minority. **Part-time faculty:** 139 total; 17% have terminal degrees, 4% minority. **Class size:** 40% < 20, 59% 20-39, less than 1% 40-49, less than 1% 50-99. **Special facilities:** Institute for Franciscan studies, Betty Neumann archives.

Freshman class profile. 2,080 applied, 1,996 admitted, 522 enrolled.

Mid 50% test scores		Rank in top tenth:	10%
SAT verbal:	400-490	End year in good standing:	90%
SAT math:	380-490	Return as sophomores:	77%
GPA 3.50 or higher:	5%	Out-of-state:	32%
GPA 3.0-3.49:	45%	Live on campus:	72%
GPA 2.0-2.99:	50%	International:	4%
Rank in top quarter:	50%		

Basis for selection. Acceptance depends on major applied for, SAT scores and high school GPA. Interview recommended.

High school preparation. 16 units required; 17 recommended. Required and recommended units include English 4, mathematics 2, social studies 2, science 2-3, foreign language 2 and academic electives 4.

2005-2006 Annual costs. Tuition/fees: $17,920. Room/board: $8,076. Books/supplies: $1,500. Personal expenses: $1,000.

2005-2006 Financial aid. All financial aid based on need. 470 full-time freshmen applied for aid; 450 were judged to have need; 450 of these received aid. Average need met was 65%. Average scholarship/grant was $17,000; average loan $6,625. 59% of total undergraduate aid awarded as scholarships/grants, 41% as loans/jobs.

Application procedures. Admission: No deadline. $35 fee, may be waived for applicants with need. Admission notification on a rolling basis. Must reply by May 1 or within 2 week(s) if notified thereafter. **Financial aid:** No deadline. FAFSA required. Applicants notified on a rolling basis; must reply within 2 week(s) of notification.

Academics. Special study options: Accelerated study, combined bachelor's/graduate degree, cooperative education, distance learning, double major, honors, independent study, internships, liberal arts/career combination, student-designed major, study abroad, teacher certification program, weekend college. **Credit/placement by examination:** AP, CLEP, institutional tests. 15 credit hours maximum toward associate degree, 30 toward bachelor's. **Support services:** Learning center, reduced course load, remedial instruction, study skills assistance, tutoring, writing center.

Majors. **Biology:** General. **Business:** Accounting, business admin, international, marketing. **Communications:** General. **Computer sciences:** General. **Conservation:** Environmental studies. **Education:** Early childhood, elementary. **Health:** Clinical lab technology, nursing (RN). **Liberal arts:** Arts/sciences. **Parks/recreation:** Health/fitness, sports admin. **Philosophy/religion:** Religion. **Protective services:** Criminal justice. **Psychology:** General. **Social sciences:** Political science.

Most popular majors. Business/marketing 14%, education 15%, health sciences 14%, liberal arts 29%, parks/recreation 8%.

Computing on campus. 300 workstations in dormitories, library, computer center. Dormitories wired for high-speed internet access and linked to campus network. Commuter students can connect to campus network. Online library, helpline, wireless network available.

Student life. **Freshman orientation:** Mandatory. Preregistration for classes offered. Held the last weekend before classes begin, usually late August. **Policies:** Alcohol free campus. Freshmen permitted cars on campus. **Housing:** Guaranteed on-campus for all undergraduates. Coed dorms, apartments available. $200 nonrefundable deposit, deadline 8/1. **Activities:** Jazz band, choral groups, dance, drama, literary magazine, music ensembles, musical theater, student government, student newspaper, TV station, Black Student Union, environmental club, Neumann International Student Association, bio/sci club, Neumann Business Association, Professional Education Society, Student Nurses Association psychology club.

Athletics. NCAA. **Intercollegiate:** Baseball M, basketball, field hockey W, golf M, ice hockey, lacrosse, soccer, softball W, tennis, volleyball W. **Intramural:** Basketball, lacrosse M, softball W, table tennis, tennis, volleyball. **Team name:** Knights.

Student services. Adult student services, campus ministries, career counseling, services for economically disadvantaged, student employment services, financial aid counseling, health services, on-campus daycare, personal counseling, placement for graduates.

Contact. E-mail: neumann@neumann.edu
Phone: (610) 558-5616 Toll-free number: (800) 963-8626
Fax: (610) 558-5652
Dennis Murphy, Vice President for Enrollment Managament, Neumann College, One Neumann Drive, Aston, PA 19014-1298

Peirce College

Philadelphia, Pennsylvania — **CB member**
www.peirce.edu — **CB code: 2674**

- Private 4-year business and technical college
- Commuter campus in very large city
- 1,971 degree-seeking undergraduates: 58% part-time, 73% women, 50% African American, 1% Asian American, 5% Hispanic American, 3% international
- 55% graduate within 6 years; 14% enter graduate study

General. Founded in 1865. Regionally accredited. **Degrees:** 230 bachelor's, 144 associate awarded. **Calendar:** Continuous, limited summer session. **Full-time faculty:** 26 total; 46% have terminal degrees, 31% minority, 58% women. **Part-time faculty:** 115 total; 29% have terminal degrees, 29% minority, 33% women. **Class size:** 81% < 20, 19% 20-39.

Freshman class profile. 659 applied, 659 admitted, 294 enrolled.

End year in good standing:	78%	**Out-of-state:**	20%
Return as sophomores:	85%	**International:**	5%

Basis for selection. Open admission.

2005-2006 Annual costs. Tuition/fees: $12,760. Books/supplies: $1,000. Personal expenses: $2,000.

2004-2005 Financial aid. **Need-based:** 34 full-time freshmen applied for aid; 34 were judged to have need; 34 of these received aid. Average scholarship/grant was $1,500; average loan $4,000. 44% of total undergraduate aid awarded as scholarships/grants, 56% as loans/jobs. **Non-need-based:** Awarded to 124 full-time undergraduates, including 18 freshmen. Scholarships awarded for academics, leadership. **Additional information:** Tuition discounts available for U.S. students serving in U.S. military and in protect-and-serve fields.

Application procedures. **Admission:** No deadline. $50 fee, may be waived for applicants with need. Application may be submitted online. Admission notification on a rolling basis. Admission is continuous throughout the year, and is not specific to any term. **Financial aid:** Priority date 6/1; no closing date. FAFSA required. Applicants notified on a rolling basis; must reply within 3 week(s) of notification.

Academics. **Special study options:** Accelerated study, cooperative education, distance learning, double major, ESL, independent study, internships, weekend college. **Credit/placement by examination:** AP, CLEP, IB, institutional tests. 30 credit hours maximum toward associate degree, 90 toward bachelor's. **Support services:** Learning center, reduced course load, study skills assistance, tutoring, writing center.

Majors. **Business:** Business admin. **Computer sciences:** Information systems. **Legal studies:** Paralegal.

Most popular majors. Business/marketing 65%, computer/information sciences 23%, legal studies 12%.

Computing on campus. PC or laptop required. 39 workstations in library, computer center, student center. Online course registration, online library, helpline, wireless network available.

Student life. **Freshman orientation:** Mandatory, $450 fee. Preregistration for classes offered. **Activities:** Chi Alpha Epsilon Honor Society, Alpha Iota Chapter, Delta Mu Delta Honor Society, paralegal student association.

Student services. Adult student services, alcohol/substance abuse counseling, career counseling, services for economically disadvantaged, financial aid counseling, health services, placement for graduates, veterans' counselor. **Physically disabled:** Services for visually, hearing impaired.

Contact. E-mail: info@peirce.edu
Phone: (888) 467-3472 ext. 9214 Toll-free number: (888) 467-3472 ext. 9214 Fax: (215) 670-9366
Nadine Maher, Dean, Enrollment Management, Peirce College, 1420 Pine Street, Philadelphia, PA 19102-4699

Penn State Abington

Abington, Pennsylvania
www.abington.psu.edu — **CB code: 2660**

- Public 4-year branch campus college
- Commuter campus in small city
- 2,593 degree-seeking undergraduates: 12% part-time, 49% women, 12% African American, 14% Asian American, 5% Hispanic American, 1% international
- 78% of applicants admitted
- SAT or ACT (ACT writing optional) required
- 42% graduate within 6 years

General. Founded in 1950. Regionally accredited. **Degrees:** 359 bachelor's, 58 associate awarded. **ROTC:** Army, Air Force. **Location:** 15 miles from Philadelphia. **Calendar:** Semester, limited summer session. **Full-time faculty:** 109 total; 57% have terminal degrees, 9% minority, 40% women. **Part-time faculty:** 98 total; 31% have terminal degrees, 4% minority, 45% women. **Class size:** 42% < 20, 49% 20-39, 4% 40-49, 4% 50-99, less than 1% >100.

Freshman class profile. 2,694 applied, 2,099 admitted, 758 enrolled.

Mid 50% test scores		**Rank in top quarter:**	29%
SAT verbal:	400-520	**Rank in top tenth:**	10%
SAT math:	420-550	**Return as sophomores:**	76%
GPA 3.50 or higher:	18%	**Out-of-state:**	6%
GPA 3.0-3.49:	35%	**International:**	1%
GPA 2.0-2.99:	46%		

Basis for selection. Admission decisions based upon high school GPA, standardized test scores, class rank, personal statements, activities. Essay considered if submitted; portfolios required for select majors. **Homeschooled:** Provide complete documentation showing courses studied and all evaluations presented from homeschool evaluator or supervisor assigned to student in cooperation with local school district or evaluator approved through program.

High school preparation. Required units include English 4, mathematics 3, social studies 3, science 3 and foreign language 2.

2005-2006 Annual costs. Tuition/fees: $10,190; $15,322 out-of-state. Books/supplies: $1,040. Personal expenses: $1,854.

2004-2005 Financial aid. **Need-based:** 575 full-time freshmen applied for aid; 443 were judged to have need; 433 of these received aid. Average need met was 68%. Average scholarship/grant was $5,291; average loan $2,521. 58% of total undergraduate aid awarded as scholarships/grants, 42% as loans/jobs. **Non-need-based:** Awarded to 579 full-time undergraduates, including 312 freshmen. Scholarships awarded for academics, athletics, minority status, ROTC.

Application procedures. **Admission:** Priority date 11/30; no deadline. $50 fee, may be waived for applicants with need. Application may be submitted online. Admission notification on a rolling basis beginning on or about 11/1. Must reply by 5/1. All freshmen applications processed at University Park Campus. **Financial aid:** Priority date 2/15; no closing date. FAFSA required. Applicants notified on a rolling basis starting 2/15.

Academics. **Special study options:** Accelerated study, combined bachelor's/graduate degree, cooperative education, distance learning, double major, dual enrollment of high school students, ESL, exchange student, external degree, honors, independent study, internships, liberal arts/career combination, student-designed major, study abroad. **Credit/placement by examination:** AP, CLEP, IB, SAT. 60 credit hours maximum toward bachelor's degree. **Support services:** Learning center, pre-admission summer program, remedial instruction, study skills assistance, tutoring, writing center.

Majors. **Agriculture:** Agribusiness operations, agronomy, animal sciences, education services, equipment technology, food science, horticultural science, landscaping, soil science, turf management. **Area/ethnic studies:** African-American, American, East Asian, Latin American, women's. **Biology:** General, bacteriology, biochemistry. **Business:** General, accounting, actuarial science, business admin, finance, hospitality admin, insurance, international, labor relations, logistics, management information systems, management science, managerial economics, market research, real estate. **Communications:** Advertising, journalism, media studies. **Computer sciences:** Computer science, information systems. **Conservation:** Forest sciences, management/policy, wildlife, wood science. **Education:** Art, elementary, secondary, special. **Engineering:** Aerospace, agricultural, architectural, biomedical, chemical, civil, computer, electrical, environmental, industrial, materials, mechanical, nuclear, petroleum, science. **Engineering technology:** Telecommunications. **English:** Technical writing. **Family/consumer sciences:** Family studies, food/nutrition. **Foreign languages:** Classics, comparative lit, French, German, Italian, Japanese, Russian, Spanish. **Health:** Health services, nursing (RN), premedicine. **History:** General. **Interdisciplinary:** Biological/physical sciences, medieval/Renaissance. **Liberal arts:** Arts/sciences. **Math:** General, statistics. **Parks/recreation:** General, exercise sciences. **Philosophy/religion:** Judaic, religion. **Physical sciences:** Astronomy, atmospheric science, chemistry, geology, physics, planetary. **Protective services:** Criminal justice, law enforcement admin. **Psychology:** General. **Science technology:** Biological. **Social sciences:** Anthropology, economics, geography, international relations, political science, sociology. **Visual/performing arts:** General, acting, art, art history/conservation, cinematography, directing/producing, dramatic.

Most popular majors. Business/marketing 35%, computer/information sciences 11%, English 8%, liberal arts 7%, psychology 11%, security/protective services 18%.

Computing on campus. 376 workstations in library, computer center. Commuter students can connect to campus network. Online course registration, online library, helpline, repair service, student web hosting available.

Student life. **Freshman orientation:** Mandatory, $25 fee. Preregistration for classes offered. 3-part process before classes start: 1-day orientation, advising appointment, and new student day. **Policies:** Acts of intolerance and high-risk drinking discouraged at all locations. All facilities designated smoke-free. Students expected to abide by The Penn State Principles. Freshmen permitted cars on campus. **Activities:** Dance, drama, film society, literary magazine, music ensembles, student government, student newspaper, Christian Fellowship, Asian Club, Black Student Union, Hillel, Lesbian and Gay Alliance, Latino Student Association, Italian American Organization, Muslim Student Association, Praise and Worship Gospel Association.

Athletics. **Intercollegiate:** Baseball M, basketball, golf M, soccer, softball, tennis, volleyball W. **Intramural:** Basketball, cross-country, football (non-tackle) M, handball, soccer, softball, table tennis, tennis, volleyball. **Team name:** Nittany Lions.

Student services. Adult student services, alcohol/substance abuse counseling, career counseling, services for economically disadvantaged, student employment services, financial aid counseling, health services, minority student services, personal counseling, placement for graduates, veterans' counselor. **Physically disabled:** Services for visually, speech, hearing impaired.

Contact. E-mail: abingtonadmissions@psu.edu
Phone: (215) 881-7600 Fax: (215) 881-7655
Randall Deike, Asst. Vice Provost for Enrollment Management and Director of Admissions, Penn State Abington, 106 Sutherland Building, Abington, PA 19001

Penn State Altoona

Altoona, Pennsylvania
www.aa.psu.edu **CB code: 2660**

- Public 4-year branch campus college
- Residential campus in small city
- 3,499 degree-seeking undergraduates: 7% part-time, 50% women, 7% African American, 2% Asian American, 2% Hispanic American, 1% international
- 80% of applicants admitted
- SAT or ACT (ACT writing optional) required
- 64% graduate within 6 years

General. Founded in 1929. Regionally accredited. **Degrees:** 269 bachelor's, 125 associate awarded. **ROTC:** Army, Air Force. **Location:** 2 miles from downtown. **Calendar:** Semester, limited summer session. **Full-time faculty:** 155 total; 70% have terminal degrees, 10% minority, 43% women. **Part-time faculty:** 149 total; 23% have terminal degrees, 3% minority, 46% women. **Class size:** 41% < 20, 42% 20-39, 5% 40-49, 11% 50-99, less than 1% >100. **Special facilities:** MAC lab, CAD lab, robotics lab, manufacturing lab, automation lab, environmental studies lab, comprehensive art studio space.

Freshman class profile. 4,183 applied, 3,338 admitted, 1,216 enrolled.

Mid 50% test scores		**Rank in top quarter:**	27%
SAT verbal:	450-550	**Rank in top tenth:**	5%
SAT math:	460-570	**Return as sophomores:**	85%
GPA 3.50 or higher:	9%	**Out-of-state:**	21%
GPA 3.0-3.49:	41%	**Fraternities:**	7%
GPA 2.0-2.99:	49%	**Sororities:**	6%

Basis for selection. Admission decisions based upon high school GPA, test scores, class rank, personal statements, and activities. Essay considered if submitted; portfolios required for select majors. **Homeschooled:** Provide complete documentation showing courses studied and all evaluations presented from homeschool evaluator or supervisor assigned to student in cooperation with local school district or evaluator approved through program.

High school preparation. Required units include English 4, mathematics 3, social studies 3, science 3 and foreign language 2.

2005-2006 Annual costs. Tuition/fees: $10,626; $16,024 out-of-state. Room/board: $7,060. Books/supplies: $1,040. Personal expenses: $2,016.

2004-2005 Financial aid. **Need-based:** 1,041 full-time freshmen applied for aid; 830 were judged to have need; 812 of these received aid. Average need met was 63%. Average scholarship/grant was $4,250; average loan $2,694. 50% of total undergraduate aid awarded as scholarships/grants, 50% as loans/jobs. **Non-need-based:** Awarded to 880 full-time undergraduates, including 340 freshmen. Scholarships awarded for academics, athletics, minority status, ROTC.

Application procedures. **Admission:** Priority date 11/30; no deadline. $50 fee, may be waived for applicants with need. Application may be submitted online. Admission notification on a rolling basis beginning on or about 11/1. Must reply by 5/1. All freshmen applications processed at University Park Campus. **Financial aid:** Priority date 2/15; no closing date. FAFSA required. Applicants notified on a rolling basis starting 2/15.

Academics. **Special study options:** Cooperative education, cross-registration, distance learning, double major, dual enrollment of high school students, ESL, honors, independent study, internships, liberal arts/career combination, student-designed major, study abroad, teacher certification program. **Credit/placement by examination:** AP, CLEP, IB, SAT. 60 credit hours maximum toward bachelor's degree. **Support services:** Learning center, remedial instruction, study skills assistance, tutoring, writing center.

Majors. **Agriculture:** Agribusiness operations, agronomy, animal sciences, equipment technology, food science, horticultural science, landscaping, soil science, turf management. **Area/ethnic studies:** African-American, American, East Asian, Latin American, women's. **Biology:** General, bacteriology, biochemistry. **Business:** General, accounting, actuarial science, business admin, finance, hospitality admin, insurance, international, labor relations, logistics, management information systems, management science, managerial economics, market research, real estate. **Communications:** Advertising, journalism, media studies. **Computer sciences:** Computer science, information systems. **Conservation:** Environmental studies, forest sciences, management/policy, wildlife, wood science. **Education:** Art, elementary, secondary, special. **Engineering:** Aerospace, agricultural, architectural, biomedical, chemical, civil, computer, electrical, environmental, industrial, materials, mechanical, nuclear, petroleum, science. **English:** Speech/rhetoric. **Family/consumer sciences:** Family studies, food/nutrition. **Foreign languages:** Classics, comparative lit, French, German, Italian, Japanese, Russian, Spanish. **Health:** Nursing (RN), premedicine. **History:** General. **Interdisciplinary:** Biological/physical sciences, medieval/Renaissance. **Liberal arts:** Arts/sciences. **Math:** General, statistics. **Parks/recreation:** General, exercise sciences. **Philosophy/religion:** Judaic, philosophy, religion. **Physical sciences:** Astronomy, atmospheric science, chemistry, geology, physics, planetary. **Protective services:** Criminal justice. **Psychology:** General. **Science technology:** Biological. **Social sciences:** Anthropology, economics, geography, international relations, political science, sociology. **Visual/**

performing arts: General, acting, art, art history/conservation, cinematography, directing/producing, dramatic.

Most popular majors. Business/marketing 27%, education 12%, engineering/engineering technologies 9%, family/consumer sciences 7%, liberal arts 6%, security/protective services 17%.

Computing on campus. 464 workstations in dormitories, library, computer center. Dormitories wired for high-speed internet access and linked to campus network. Commuter students can connect to campus network. Online course registration, online library, helpline, student web hosting, wireless network available.

Student life. **Freshman orientation:** Mandatory. Preregistration for classes offered. Begins Saturday prior to start of classes and runs 2 weeks. **Policies:** Acts of intolerance and high-risk drinking discouraged at all locations. All facilities designated as smoke-free. Freshmen permitted cars on campus. **Housing:** Coed dorms, substance-free housing available. $100 partly refundable deposit, deadline 5/1. Suites, special interest housing available. **Activities:** Bands, choral groups, dance, drama, literary magazine, music ensembles, student government, student newspaper, Black Student Union, Circle K, Latin American student association, Catholic Campus Community, Students About Living Truth, Jewish student association, Asian student association, German club, Eco-Action, Being United for Social Transformation.

Athletics. NAIA. **Intercollegiate:** Baseball M, basketball, cross-country, diving, golf M, soccer, softball W, swimming, tennis, volleyball W. **Intramural:** Badminton, basketball, football (non-tackle), football (tackle), racquetball, soccer, softball, table tennis, track and field, triathlon, volleyball, weight lifting. **Team name:** Nittany Lions.

Student services. Adult student services, alcohol/substance abuse counseling, campus ministries, career counseling, services for economically disadvantaged, student employment services, financial aid counseling, health services, minority student services, personal counseling, placement for graduates, veterans' counselor, women's services. **Physically disabled:** Services for visually, speech, hearing impaired.

Contact. E-mail: aaadmit@psu.edu
Phone: (814) 949-5466 Toll-free number: (800) 848-9843
Fax: (814) 949-5564
Randall Deike, Asst. Vice Provost for Enrollment Management and Director of Admissions, Penn State Altoona, E108 E. Raymond Smith Building, Altoona, PA 16601-3760

Penn State Berks

Reading, Pennsylvania
www.bk.psu.edu **CB code: 2660**

- Public 4-year branch campus college
- Residential campus in small city
- 2,303 degree-seeking undergraduates: 8% part-time, 41% women, 7% African American, 4% Asian American, 4% Hispanic American, 1% international
- 44 graduate students
- 78% of applicants admitted
- SAT or ACT (ACT writing optional) required
- 58% graduate within 6 years

General. Founded in 1924. Regionally accredited. **Degrees:** 167 bachelor's, 71 associate awarded. **Location:** 5 miles from downtown. **Calendar:** Semester, limited summer session. **Full-time faculty:** 101 total; 69% have terminal degrees, 7% minority, 44% women. **Part-time faculty:** 81 total; 14% have terminal degrees, 4% minority, 38% women. **Class size:** 36% < 20, 46% 20-39, 7% 40-49, 11% 50-99, less than 1% >100.

Freshman class profile. 2,747 applied, 2,150 admitted, 856 enrolled.

Mid 50% test scores			
SAT verbal:	440-540	Rank in top quarter:	21%
SAT math:	440-570	Rank in top tenth:	5%
GPA 3.50 or higher:	7%	Return as sophomores:	84%
GPA 3.0-3.49:	30%	Out-of-state:	10%
GPA 2.0-2.99:	61%	International:	1%

Basis for selection. Admission decisions based upon high school GPA, test scores, class rank, personal statements, and activities. Essay considered if submitted; portfolios required for select majors. **Homeschooled:** Complete documentation showing courses studied and all evaluations presented from home school evaluator or supervisor assigned to student in cooperation with local school district or evaluator approved through program required.

High school preparation. Required units include English 4, mathematics 3, social studies 3, science 3 and foreign language 2.

2005-2006 Annual costs. Tuition/fees: $10,626; $16,024 out-of-state. Room/board: $7,670. Books/supplies: $1,040.

2004-2005 Financial aid. **Need-based:** 637 full-time freshmen applied for aid; 450 were judged to have need; 444 of these received aid. Average need met was 61%. Average scholarship/grant was $4,530; average loan $2,612. 51% of total undergraduate aid awarded as scholarships/grants, 49% as loans/jobs. **Non-need-based:** Awarded to 502 full-time undergraduates, including 201 freshmen. Scholarships awarded for academics, athletics, minority status, ROTC.

Application procedures. **Admission:** Priority date 11/30; no deadline. $50 fee, may be waived for applicants with need. Application may be submitted online. Admission notification on a rolling basis beginning on or about 11/1. Must reply by 5/1. All freshmen applications processed at University Park Campus. **Financial aid:** Priority date 2/15; no closing date. FAFSA required. Applicants notified on a rolling basis starting 2/15.

Academics. **Special study options:** Accelerated study, cooperative education, cross-registration, distance learning, dual enrollment of high school students, honors, independent study, internships, study abroad. **Credit/placement by examination:** AP, CLEP, IB, SAT. 60 credit hours maximum toward bachelor's degree. **Support services:** Learning center, preadmission summer program, remedial instruction, study skills assistance, tutoring, writing center.

Majors. **Agriculture:** Agribusiness operations, agronomy, animal sciences, education services, equipment technology, food science, horticultural science, landscaping, soil science, turf management. **Area/ethnic studies:** African-American, American, East Asian, Latin American, women's. **Biology:** General, bacteriology, biochemistry. **Business:** General, actuarial science, business admin, finance, hospitality admin, insurance, international, labor relations, logistics, management information systems, management science, managerial economics, market research, real estate. **Communications:** Advertising, journalism, media studies. **Computer sciences:** Computer science, information systems. **Conservation:** Forest sciences, management/policy, wildlife, wood science. **Education:** Art, elementary, secondary, special. **Engineering:** Aerospace, agricultural, architectural, biomedical, chemical, civil, computer, electrical, environmental, industrial, materials, mechanical, mining, nuclear, petroleum, science. **English:** Composition, speech/rhetoric. **Family/consumer sciences:** Family studies, food/nutrition. **Foreign languages:** Classics, comparative lit, French, German, Italian, Japanese, Russian, Spanish. **Health:** Health services, nursing (RN), premedicine. **History:** General. **Interdisciplinary:** Behavioral sciences, biological/physical sciences, medieval/Renaissance. **Liberal arts:** Arts/sciences. **Math:** General, statistics. **Parks/recreation:** General, exercise sciences. **Philosophy/religion:** Judaic, religion. **Physical sciences:** Astronomy, atmospheric science, chemistry, geology, physics, planetary. **Protective services:** Criminal justice. **Psychology:** General. **Science technology:** Biological. **Social sciences:** Anthropology, economics, geography, international relations, political science, sociology. **Visual/performing arts:** General, acting, art, art history/conservation, cinematography, directing/producing, dramatic.

Most popular majors. Business/marketing 48%, computer/information sciences 19%, engineering/engineering technologies 9%, interdisciplinary studies 6%, psychology 10%.

Computing on campus. 300 workstations in dormitories, library, computer center, student center. Dormitories wired for high-speed internet access and linked to campus network. Commuter students can connect to campus network. Online course registration, online library, helpline, repair service, student web hosting, wireless network available.

Student life. **Freshman orientation:** Mandatory. Preregistration for classes offered. Week prior to start of classes. Traditional orientation program 2 1/2 days long. Special pre-orientation programs that provide opportunities for community service, hiking and canoeing. Be a Part from the Start orientation program for new underrepresented students. **Policies:** All facilities smoke-free. Freshmen permitted cars on campus. **Housing:** Coed dorms, special housing for disabled, substance-free housing available. $100 partly refundable deposit, deadline 5/1. Honor students, suites, special interest houses available. **Activities:** Pep band, choral groups, dance, drama, radio station, student government, student newspaper, Christian Fellowship, Dimensions-the Ethnic Society, multicultural dance group, substance free, Rainbow Alliance, political science club, spiritual praise choir, international club, yoga and meditation Society.

Athletics. NCAA. **Intercollegiate:** Baseball M, basketball, cross-country, golf M, soccer, softball W, tennis, volleyball W. **Intramural:** Badminton, basketball, football (non-tackle), golf, soccer, volleyball. **Team name:** NIttany Lioms.

Student services. Adult student services, alcohol/substance abuse counseling, career counseling, services for economically disadvantaged, student employment services, financial aid counseling, health services, minority student services, personal counseling, placement for graduates, veterans' counselor. **Physically disabled:** Services for visually, speech, hearing impaired. **Learning disabled:** Comprehensive services available.

Contact. E-mail: admissionsbk@psu.edu
Phone: (610) 396-6060 Fax: (610) 396-6077
Randall Deike, Assistant Vice Provost for Enrollment Management and Director of Admissions, Penn State Berks, Tulpehocken Road, PO Box 7009, Reading, PA 19610-6009

Penn State Erie, The Behrend College

Erie, Pennsylvania
www.pennstatebehrend.psu.edu **CB code: 2660**

- Public 4-year branch campus college
- Residential campus in small city
- 3,231 degree-seeking undergraduates: 5% part-time, 34% women, 3% African American, 2% Asian American, 2% Hispanic American, 1% international
- 159 degree-seeking graduate students
- 80% of applicants admitted
- SAT or ACT (ACT writing optional) required
- 64% graduate within 6 years

General. Founded in 1926. Regionally accredited. **Degrees:** 656 bachelor's, 31 associate awarded; master's offered. **ROTC:** Army. **Calendar:** Semester, limited summer session. **Full-time faculty:** 200 total; 60% have terminal degrees, 12% minority, 28% women. **Part-time faculty:** 61 total; 15% have terminal degrees, 43% women. **Class size:** 39% < 20, 42% 20-39, 14% 40-49, 3% 50-99, 1% >100. **Special facilities:** Observatory, natural area for science field trips and experimentation, hiking trails, cross-country skiing.

Freshman class profile. 2,417 applied, 1,925 admitted, 838 enrolled.

Mid 50% test scores		**Rank in top tenth:**	12%
SAT verbal:	480-570	**Return as sophomores:**	83%
SAT math:	500-600	**Out-of-state:**	11%
GPA 3.50 or higher:	19%	**International:**	1%
GPA 3.0-3.49:	43%	**Fraternities:**	3%
GPA 2.0-2.99:	38%	**Sororities:**	3%
Rank in top quarter:	36%		

Basis for selection. Admission decisions based on high school GPA, standardized test scores, class rank, personal statements, and activities. Essay considered if submitted; portfolios required for select majors. **Homeschooled:** Complete documentation helpful, showing courses studied and all evaluations presented from a home school evaluator, supervisor assigned to student in cooperation with local school district, or evaluator approved through program.

High school preparation. College-preparatory program recommended. Required units include English 4, mathematics 3, social studies 3, science 3 and foreign language 2. Additional requirements for some programs. 3 additional units required in arts and humanities.

2005-2006 Annual costs. Tuition/fees: $10,626; $16,024 out-of-state. Room/board: $7,060. Books/supplies: $1,040. Personal expenses: $2,016.

2004-2005 Financial aid. Need-based: 750 full-time freshmen applied for aid; 602 were judged to have need; 592 of these received aid. Average need met was 68%. Average scholarship/grant was $4,511; average loan $2,848. 49% of total undergraduate aid awarded as scholarships/grants, 51% as loans/jobs. **Non-need-based:** Awarded to 996 full-time undergraduates, including 297 freshmen. Scholarships awarded for academics, athletics, minority status, ROTC.

Application procedures. Admission: Priority date 11/30; no deadline. $50 fee, may be waived for applicants with need. Application may be submitted online. Admission notification on a rolling basis beginning on or about 11/1. Must reply by 5/1. All freshmen applications processed at University Park Campus. **Financial aid:** Priority date 2/15; no closing date. FAFSA required. Applicants notified on a rolling basis starting 2/15.

Academics. Special study options: Accelerated study, combined bachelor's/graduate degree, cooperative education, distance learning, double major, dual enrollment of high school students, honors, independent study, internships, liberal arts/career combination, semester at sea, study abroad, teacher certification program. **Credit/placement by examination:** AP, CLEP, IB, SAT, institutional tests. 60 credit hours maximum toward bachelor's degree. **Support services:** Learning center, pre-admission summer program, remedial instruction, study skills assistance, tutoring, writing center.

Majors. Agriculture: Agribusiness operations, agronomy, animal sciences, education services, equipment technology, food science, horticultural science, landscaping, soil science, turf management. **Area/ethnic studies:** African-American, American, East Asian, Latin American, women's. **Biology:** General. **Business:** Accounting, business admin, finance, international, management information systems, managerial economics, marketing. **Communications:** General. **Conservation:** Forest sciences, management/policy, wildlife, wood science. **Engineering:** Computer, electrical, mechanical. **Engineering technology:** Electrical. **History:** General. **Liberal arts:** Arts/sciences. **Math:** General. **Physical sciences:** Chemistry, physics. **Psychology:** General. **Social sciences:** Economics, political science.

Most popular majors. Biology 6%, business/marketing 41%, engineering/engineering technologies 25%, psychology 7%.

Computing on campus. 642 workstations in dormitories, library, computer center, student center. Dormitories wired for high-speed internet access and linked to campus network. Commuter students can connect to campus network. Online course registration, online library, helpline, repair service, student web hosting available.

Student life. Freshman orientation: Mandatory. Preregistration for classes offered. Held during the 3 days before start of classes, orientation is a comprehensive introduction to college life in general and to life at Penn State Behrend. **Policies:** Acts of intolerance and high-risk drinking discouraged at all locations. All facilities designated as smoke-free. Freshmen permitted cars on campus. **Housing:** Coed dorms, single-sex dorms, special housing for disabled, apartments, substance-free housing available. $100 partly refundable deposit, deadline 5/1. Suites, special interest housing available. **Activities:** Bands, choral groups, dance, drama, film society, literary magazine, music ensembles, radio station, student government, student newspaper, Asian Student Organization, Association of Black Collegians, National Society of Black Engineers, Human Relations Programming Council, Multicultural Council, Irish American Society, Women Today, College Republicans, InterVarsity Christian Fellowship, gospel choir.

Athletics. NCAA. **Intercollegiate:** Baseball M, basketball, cheerleading, cross-country, diving, golf, soccer, softball W, swimming, tennis, track and field, volleyball W, water polo. **Intramural:** Badminton, basketball, bowling, cross-country, diving, football (non-tackle), golf, racquetball, skiing, soccer, softball, swimming, table tennis, tennis, track and field, triathlon, volleyball. **Team name:** Behrend Lions.

Student services. Adult student services, alcohol/substance abuse counseling, campus ministries, career counseling, services for economically disadvantaged, student employment services, financial aid counseling, health services, minority student services, on-campus daycare, personal counseling, placement for graduates, veterans' counselor, women's services. **Physically disabled:** Services for visually, speech, hearing impaired.

Contact. E-mail: behrendadmissions@psu.edu
Phone: (814) 898-6100 Toll-free number: (866) 374-3378
Fax: (814) 898-6044
Randall Deike, Assistant Vice Provost for Enrollment Management and Director of Admissions, Penn State Erie, The Behrend College, 5091 Station Road, Erie, PA 16563-0105

Penn State Harrisburg

Middletown, Pennsylvania
www.hbg.psu.edu **CB code: 2660**

- Public 4-year branch campus college
- Residential campus in small town
- 1,955 degree-seeking undergraduates: 20% part-time, 49% women, 8% African American, 7% Asian American, 3% Hispanic American, 1% international
- 1,525 degree-seeking graduate students
- 64% of applicants admitted
- SAT or ACT (ACT writing optional) required

General. Founded in 1966. Regionally accredited. **Degrees:** 600 bachelor's, 7 associate awarded; master's, doctoral offered. **ROTC:** Army. **Location:** 8 miles from Harrisburg. **Calendar:** Semester, limited summer session. **Full-time faculty:** 169 total; 83% have terminal degrees, 22% minority, 38% women. **Part-time faculty:** 104 total; 38% have terminal degrees, 10% minority, 39% women. **Class size:** 47% < 20, 50% 20-39, 2% 40-49, less than 1% 50-99. **Special facilities:** Outdoor sculpture garden, Black Cultural Arts Center lounge, humanities gallery, American studies archives.

Freshman class profile. 1,616 applied, 1,037 admitted, 219 enrolled.

Mid 50% test scores			
SAT verbal:	450-570	Rank in top quarter:	43%
SAT math:	470-600	Rank in top tenth:	10%
GPA 3.50 or higher:	15%	Return as sophomores:	85%
GPA 3.0-3.49:	46%	Out-of-state:	27%
GPA 2.0-2.99:	39%	International:	4%

Basis for selection. Admissions based on secondary school record and standardized test scores.

High school preparation. College-preparatory program recommended. Required units include English 4, mathematics 3, social studies 3, science 3 and foreign language 2.

2005-2006 Annual costs. Tuition/fees: $10,616; $16,014 out-of-state. Room/board: $8,560. Books/supplies: $1,040. Personal expenses: $2,016.

2004-2005 Financial aid. Need-based: 135 full-time freshmen applied for aid; 94 were judged to have need; 92 of these received aid. Average need met was 69%. Average scholarship/grant was $5,368; average loan $2,781. 47% of total undergraduate aid awarded as scholarships/grants, 53% as loans/jobs. **Non-need-based:** Awarded to 366 full-time undergraduates, including 61 freshmen. Scholarships awarded for academics, athletics, minority status, ROTC.

Application procedures. Admission: Priority date 11/30; no deadline. $50 fee, may be waived for applicants with need. Application may be submitted online. Admission notification on a rolling basis beginning on or about 11/1. Must reply by 5/1. All freshmen applications processed at University Park Campus. **Financial aid:** Priority date 2/15; no closing date. FAFSA required. Applicants notified on a rolling basis starting 2/15.

Academics. Special study options: Accelerated study, cooperative education, cross-registration, distance learning, double major, dual enrollment of high school students, honors, independent study, internships, student-designed major, study abroad, teacher certification program, weekend college. **Credit/placement by examination:** AP, CLEP, IB, SAT. 60 credit hours maximum toward bachelor's degree. **Support services:** Learning center, tutoring, writing center.

Majors. Area/ethnic studies: American. **Business:** Accounting, business admin, finance, management information systems, market research, organizational behavior. **Communications:** General. **Computer sciences:** Computer science, information systems. **Education:** Elementary, English, social studies. **Engineering:** Electrical, environmental, mechanical, structural. **Engineering technology:** Civil, electrical. **English:** American lit. **Health:** Health care admin, health services, nursing (RN). **Liberal arts:** Arts/sciences, humanities. **Math:** General, applied. **Protective services:** Criminal justice. **Psychology:** General. **Public administration:** Policy analysis. **Social sciences:** Sociology.

Most popular majors. Business/marketing 36%, communications/journalism 6%, computer/information sciences 8%, education 10%, engineering/engineering technologies 15%, psychology 8%, security/protective services 7%.

Computing on campus. 195 workstations in library, computer center. Dormitories wired for high-speed internet access and linked to campus network. Commuter students can connect to campus network. Online course registration, online library, helpline, repair service, student web hosting available.

Student life. Freshman orientation: Available. Preregistration for classes offered. Held 2 days prior to the start of classes. **Policies:** Acts of intolerance and high-risk drinking discouraged at all locations. All facilities designated smoke-free. Freshmen permitted cars on campus. **Housing:** Special housing for disabled, apartments, substance-free housing available. $100 partly refundable deposit, deadline 5/1. Special interest housing. **Activities:** Choral groups, drama, literary magazine, radio station, student government, student newspaper, Black Student Union, International Affairs Association, Christian Fellowship, Korean Student Association, Latino Student Union, Vietnamese Student Association, Chinese Student Association, Resident Community Council.

Athletics. Intercollegiate: Baseball M, cross-country M, soccer M, volleyball M. **Intramural:** Basketball, football (non-tackle) M, racquetball, softball, table tennis, volleyball. **Team name:** Nittany Lions.

Student services. Adult student services, alcohol/substance abuse counseling, career counseling, services for economically disadvantaged, student employment services, financial aid counseling, health services, minority student services, on-campus daycare, personal counseling, placement for graduates, veterans' counselor, women's services. **Physically disabled:** Services for visually, speech, hearing impaired.

Contact. E-mail: hbgadmit@psu.edu
Phone: (717) 948-6250 Toll-free number: (800) 222-2056
Fax: (717) 948-6325
Randall Deike, Asst. Vice Provost for Enrollment Management and Director of Admissions, Penn State Harrisburg, Swatapa Building, 777 West Harrisburg Pike, Middletown, PA 17057-4898

Penn State Lehigh Valley

Fogelsville, Pennsylvania
www.lv.psu.edu **CB code: 2660**

- Public 4-year branch campus college
- Commuter campus in rural community
- 592 degree-seeking undergraduates: 18% part-time, 36% women, 3% African American, 6% Asian American, 7% Hispanic American, 1% international
- 50 graduate students
- 75% of applicants admitted
- SAT or ACT (ACT writing optional) required
- 47% graduate within 6 years

General. Regionally accredited. **Degrees:** 62 bachelor's, 7 associate awarded. **ROTC:** Army. **Location:** 15 miles from Allentown, 30 miles from Easton. **Calendar:** Semester, limited summer session. **Full-time faculty:** 27 total; 63% have terminal degrees, 18% minority, 48% women. **Part-time faculty:** 39 total; 31% have terminal degrees, 33% women. **Class size:** 65% < 20, 30% 20-39, 4% 40-49, less than 1% 50-99.

Freshman class profile. 667 applied, 497 admitted, 153 enrolled.

Mid 50% test scores			
SAT verbal:	430-540	Rank in top quarter:	28%
SAT math:	450-570	Rank in top tenth:	4%
GPA 3.50 or higher:	13%	Return as sophomores:	75%
GPA 3.0-3.49:	29%	Out-of-state:	4%
GPA 2.0-2.99:	55%	International:	1%

Basis for selection. Admission decisions based on high school GPA, standardized test scores, class rank, personal statements, and activities. Essay considered if submitted; portfolios required for select majors. **Homeschooled:** Applicants should provide complete documentation showing courses studied and all evaluations presented from evaluator or supervisor assigned to student in cooperation with local school district or evaluator approved through program.

High school preparation. Required units include English 4, mathematics 3, social studies 3, science 3 and foreign language 2.

2005-2006 Annual costs. Tuition/fees: $10,200; $15,332 out-of-state. Books/supplies: $1,040. Personal expenses: $1,854.

2004-2005 Financial aid. Need-based: 134 full-time freshmen applied for aid; 96 were judged to have need; 93 of these received aid. Average need met was 68%. Average scholarship/grant was $4,533; average loan $2,712. 57% of total undergraduate aid awarded as scholarships/grants, 43% as loans/jobs. **Non-need-based:** Awarded to 136 full-time undergraduates, including 53 freshmen. Scholarships awarded for academics, athletics, minority status, ROTC.

Application procedures. Admission: Priority date 11/30; no deadline. $50 fee, may be waived for applicants with need. Application may be submitted online. Admission notification on a rolling basis beginning on or about 11/1. Must reply by 5/1. All freshmen applications processed at University Park Campus. **Financial aid:** Priority date 2/15; no closing date. FAFSA required. Applicants notified on a rolling basis starting 2/15.

Academics. Special study options: Accelerated study, cooperative education, cross-registration, distance learning, dual enrollment of high school students, honors, independent study, internships, study abroad. **Credit/placement by examination:** AP, CLEP, IB, SAT. 60 credit hours maximum toward bachelor's degree. **Support services:** Learning center, reduced course load, study skills assistance, tutoring, writing center.

Majors. Agriculture: Agribusiness operations, agronomy, animal sciences, education services, equipment technology, food science, horticultural science, landscaping, soil science, turf management. **Area/ethnic studies:** African-American, American, East Asian, Latin American, women's. **Biology:** General, biochemistry, microbiology. **Business:** General, accounting, actuarial science, business admin, finance, hospitality admin, insurance, international, labor relations, logistics, management information systems, management science, managerial economics, market research, real estate. **Communications:** Advertising, journalism, media studies. **Computer sciences:** Information systems. **Conservation:** Forest sciences, management/policy, wildlife, wood science. **Education:** Adult/continuing, art, elementary, secondary, special. **Engineering:** Aerospace, agricultural, architectural, biomedical, chemical, civil, computer, environmental, industrial, materials, mechanical, mining, nuclear, petroleum, science. **English:** Speech/rhetoric. **Family/consumer sciences:** Family studies, food/nutrition. **Foreign languages:** Classics, comparative lit, French, German, Italian, Japanese, Russian, Spanish. **Health:** Nursing (RN), premedicine. **History:** General. **Interdisciplinary:** Biological/physical sciences, medieval/Renaissance. **Liberal arts:** Arts/sciences. **Math:** General, statistics. **Parks/recreation:** General, exercise sciences. **Philosophy/religion:** Judaic, philosophy, religion. **Physical sciences:** Astronomy, atmospheric science, chemistry, geology, physics, planetary. **Protective services:** Criminal justice. **Psychology:** General. **Science technology:** Biological. **Social sciences:** Anthropology, economics, geography, international relations, political science, sociology. **Visual/performing arts:** General, acting, art, art history/conservation, cinematography, directing/producing, dramatic.

Most popular majors. Business/marketing 63%, computer/information sciences 21%, psychology 11%.

Computing on campus. 139 workstations in library, computer center. Commuter students can connect to campus network. Online course registration, online library, helpline, repair service, student web hosting, wireless network available.

Student life. Freshman orientation: Mandatory. Preregistration for classes offered. One day, prior to start of classes. **Policies:** Acts of intolerance and high risk drinking discouraged at all locations. All facilities designated as smoke-free. Students expected to abide by The Penn State Principles. Freshmen permitted cars on campus. **Activities:** Drama, student government, student newspaper, Asian Club, Christian Fellowship, Habitat for Humanity.

Athletics. Intramural: Basketball, football (non-tackle), skiing, soccer, volleyball. **Team name:** Nittany Lions.

Student services. Adult student services, alcohol/substance abuse counseling, career counseling, services for economically disadvantaged, student employment services, financial aid counseling, health services, minority student services, personal counseling, placement for graduates, veterans' counselor. **Physically disabled:** Services for visually, speech, hearing impaired. **Learning disabled:** Comprehensive services available.

Contact. E-mail: admission-lv@psu.edu
Phone: (610) 285-5035 Fax: (610) 285-5220
Randall Deike, Asst. Vice Provost for Enrollment Management and Director of Admissions, Penn State Lehigh Valley, 8380 Mohr Lane, Academic Building, Fogelsville, PA 18051-9999

Penn State Schuylkill - Capital College

Schuylkill Haven, Pennsylvania
www.sl.psu.edu **CB code: 2660**

- Public 4-year branch campus college
- Residential campus in small town
- 778 degree-seeking undergraduates: 12% part-time, 56% women, 21% African American, 2% Asian American, 3% Hispanic American
- 40 degree-seeking graduate students
- 81% of applicants admitted
- SAT or ACT (ACT writing optional) required
- 48% graduate within 6 years

General. Founded in 1934. Regionally accredited. **Degrees:** 53 bachelor's, 32 associate awarded. **Location:** 4 miles from Pottsville. **Calendar:** Semester, limited summer session. **Full-time faculty:** 45 total; 71% have terminal degrees, 4% minority, 42% women. **Part-time faculty:** 24 total; 29% have terminal degrees, 46% women. **Class size:** 50% < 20, 46% 20-39, 4% 40-49.

Freshman class profile. 686 applied, 559 admitted, 284 enrolled.

Mid 50% test scores		**GPA 2.0-2.99:**	63%
SAT verbal:	380-510	**Rank in top quarter:**	27%
SAT math:	390-520	**Rank in top tenth:**	6%
GPA 3.50 or higher:	6%	**Return as sophomores:**	75%
GPA 3.0-3.49:	29%	**Out-of-state:**	16%

Basis for selection. Admission decisions based upon high school GPA, standardized test scores, class rank, personal statements, and activities. Essay considered if submitted; portfolios required for select majors. **Homeschooled:** Applicants should provide complete documentation showing courses studied and all evaluations presented from evaluator or supervisor assigned to student in cooperation with local school district or evaluator approved through program.

High school preparation. Required units include English 4, mathematics 3, social studies 3, science 3 and foreign language 2.

2005-2006 Annual costs. Tuition/fees: $10,180; $15,312 out-of-state. Room only: $3,630. Books/supplies: $1,040. Personal expenses: $2,016.

2004-2005 Financial aid. Need-based: 246 full-time freshmen applied for aid; 217 were judged to have need; 215 of these received aid. Average need met was 61%. Average scholarship/grant was $5,009; average loan $2,621. 57% of total undergraduate aid awarded as scholarships/grants, 43% as loans/jobs. **Non-need-based:** Awarded to 252 full-time undergraduates, including 123 freshmen. Scholarships awarded for academics, athletics, minority status, ROTC.

Application procedures. Admission: Priority date 11/30; no deadline. $50 fee, may be waived for applicants with need. Application may be submitted online. Admission notification on a rolling basis beginning on or about 11/1. Must reply by 5/1. All freshmen applications processed at University Park Campus. **Financial aid:** Priority date 2/15; no closing date. FAFSA required. Applicants notified on a rolling basis starting 2/15.

Academics. Special study options: Accelerated study, cooperative education, distance learning, double major, dual enrollment of high school students, honors, independent study, internships, student-designed major, study abroad. **Credit/placement by examination:** CLEP, IB, SAT. 60 credit hours maximum toward bachelor's degree. **Support services:** Learning center, study skills assistance, tutoring, writing center.

Majors. Agriculture: Agribusiness operations, agronomy, animal sciences, education services, equipment technology, food science, horticultural science, landscaping, soil science, turf management. **Area/ethnic studies:** African-American, American, East Asian, Latin American, women's. **Biology:** General, bacteriology, biochemistry. **Business:** General, accounting, actuarial science, business admin, finance, hotel/motel admin, insurance, international, international marketing, labor relations, logistics, management information systems, management science, managerial economics, market research, marketing, real estate. **Communications:** Advertising, journalism, media studies. **Computer sciences:** General, information systems. **Conservation:** Forest sciences, management/policy, wildlife, wood science. **Education:** Art, elementary, secondary, special. **Engineering:** Aerospace, agricultural, architectural, biomedical, chemical, civil, computer, electrical, environmental, industrial, mechanical, metallurgical, mining, nuclear, petroleum, science. **Engineering technology:** Telecommunications. **English:** Speech/rhetoric. **Family/consumer sciences:** Family studies. **Foreign languages:** Classics, comparative lit, French, German, Italian, Japanese, Russian, Spanish. **Health:** Health services, nursing (RN), premedicine. **History:** General. **Interdisciplinary:** Biological/physical sciences, medieval/Renaissance. **Liberal arts:** Arts/sciences. **Math:** General, statistics. **Parks/recreation:** Exercise sciences, facilities management. **Philosophy/religion:** Judaic, religion. **Physical sciences:** Astronomy, astrophysics, chemistry, geology, meteorology, physics, planetary. **Protective services:** Criminal justice, law enforcement admin. **Psychology:** General. **Science technology:** Biological. **Social sciences:** Anthropology, applied economics, cartography, economics, international relations, political science, sociology. **Visual/performing arts:** General, art history/conservation, cinematography, dramatic, film/cinema.

Most popular majors. Business/marketing 28%, psychology 40%, security/protective services 30%.

Computing on campus. 157 workstations in computer center, student center. Dormitories wired for high-speed internet access and linked to campus network. Commuter students can connect to campus network. Online course registration, online library, helpline, repair service, student web hosting available.

Student life. Freshman orientation: Available. Preregistration for classes offered. 2 days, prior to the start of classes. **Policies:** Acts of intolerance and high-risk drinking discouraged at all locations. All facilities designated as smoke-free. Students expected to abide by The Penn State Principles. Freshmen permitted cars on campus. **Housing:** Special housing for disabled, apartments available. **Activities:** Choral groups, dance, drama, musical theater, student government, student newspaper, Campus Crusade for Christ, Criminal Justice, international club, Religious and Philosophical Forum, United Minority Leaders, Keystone Honor Society.

Athletics. Intercollegiate: Basketball, cheerleading, cross-country, golf M, soccer M, softball W, tennis, volleyball W. **Intramural:** Basketball, football (non-tackle) M, soccer, softball, table tennis M, volleyball. **Team name:** Nittany Lions.

Student services. Adult student services, career counseling, services for economically disadvantaged, student employment services, financial aid counseling, health services, minority student services, personal counseling, placement for graduates, veterans' counselor. **Physically disabled:** Services for visually, speech, hearing impaired.

Contact. E-mail: sl-admissions@psu.edu
Phone: (570) 385-6252 Fax: (570) 385-3672
Randall Deike, Asst. Vice Provost for Enrollment Management and Director of Admissions, Penn State Schuylkill - Capital College, 200 University Drive, A102 Administration Building, Schuylkill Haven, PA 17972-2208

Penn State University Park

University Park, Pennsylvania **CB member**
www.psu.edu **CB code: 2660**

- Public 4-year university
- Residential campus in large town
- 33,672 degree-seeking undergraduates: 3% part-time, 46% women, 4% African American, 6% Asian American, 3% Hispanic American, 2% international
- 5,795 degree-seeking graduate students
- 62% of applicants admitted
- SAT or ACT (ACT writing optional) required
- 84% graduate within 6 years; 24% enter graduate study

General. Founded in 1855. Regionally accredited. **Degrees:** 9,840 bachelor's, 90 associate awarded; master's, doctoral offered. **ROTC:** Army, Navy, Air Force. **Location:** 90 miles from Harrisburg. **Calendar:** Semester, extensive summer session. **Full-time faculty:** 2,233 total; 78% have terminal degrees, 18% minority, 34% women. **Part-time faculty:** 313 total; 32% have terminal degrees, 12% minority, 52% women. **Class size:** 30% < 20, 42% 20-39, 8% 40-49, 11% 50-99, 8% >100. **Special facilities:** Museums of art, entomology, anthropology, earth and mineral sciences, weather station, health and fitness center, environmental center, observatories.

Freshman class profile. 29,904 applied, 18,423 admitted, 6,496 enrolled.

Mid 50% test scores			
SAT verbal:	530-630	Rank in top quarter:	78%
SAT math:	570-670	Rank in top tenth:	40%
GPA 3.50 or higher:	58%	Return as sophomores:	93%
GPA 3.0-3.49:	38%	Out-of-state:	28%
GPA 2.0-2.99:	4%	International:	2%

Basis for selection. Admission decisions based upon high school GPA, standardized test scores, class rank, personal statements, and activities. Essay considered if submitted; portfolios required for select majors. **Homeschooled:** Applicants should provide complete documentation showing courses studied and all evaluations presented from evaluator or supervisor assigned to student in cooperation with local school district or evaluator approved through program.

High school preparation. Required units include English 4, mathematics 3, social studies 3, science 3 and foreign language 2. Additional requirements for some programs. 3 additional units required in arts and humanities.

2005-2006 Annual costs. Tuition/fees: $11,508; $21,744 out-of-state. Room/board: $7,060. Books/supplies: $1,040. Personal expenses: $2,016.

2004-2005 Financial aid. Need-based: 4,424 full-time freshmen applied for aid; 2,909 were judged to have need; 2,808 of these received aid. Average need met was 68%. Average scholarship/grant was $5,033; average loan $2,756. 50% of total undergraduate aid awarded as scholarships/grants, 50% as loans/jobs. **Non-need-based:** Awarded to 11,345 full-time undergraduates, including 2,454 freshmen. Scholarships awarded for academics, athletics, minority status, ROTC.

Application procedures. Admission: Priority date 11/30; no deadline. $50 fee, may be waived for applicants with need. Application may be submitted online. Admission notification on a rolling basis beginning on or about 11/1. Must reply by 5/1. All freshmen applications processed at University Park Campus. **Financial aid:** Priority date 2/15; no closing date. FAFSA required. Applicants notified on a rolling basis starting 2/15.

Academics. Special study options: Accelerated study, combined bachelor's/graduate degree, cooperative education, cross-registration, distance learning, double major, dual enrollment of high school students, ESL, exchange student, external degree, honors, independent study, internships, liberal arts/career combination, student-designed major, study abroad, teacher certification program. **Credit/placement by examination:** AP, CLEP, IB, SAT, institutional tests. 60 credit hours maximum toward bachelor's degree. **Support services:** Learning center, pre-admission summer program, study skills assistance, tutoring, writing center.

Honors college/program. 300 admitted university-wide each year. Generally, students with excellent high school records (near top of their class in grades and schedule strength) and SAT scores of at least 1350 (exclusive of Writing) are competitive applicants.

Majors. Agriculture: Agribusiness operations, agronomy, animal sciences, economics, education services, equipment technology, food science, horticultural science, landscaping, soil science, turf management. **Architecture:** Architecture, landscape. **Area/ethnic studies:** African-American, American, East Asian, Latin American, women's. **Biology:** General, bacteriology, biochemistry. **Business:** Accounting, actuarial science, business admin, finance, hospitality admin, insurance, international, international finance, international marketing, labor relations, logistics, management information systems, managerial economics, marketing, operations, real estate. **Communications:** General, advertising, journalism, media studies. **Computer sciences:** General, information systems, information technology. **Conservation:** General, economics, forest resources, forest sciences, management/policy, wildlife, wood science. **Education:** Agricultural, art, elementary, instructional media, music, secondary, special. **Engineering:** Aerospace, agricultural, architectural, biomedical, chemical, civil, computer, electrical, environmental, mechanical, metallurgical, mining, nuclear, petroleum, science. **Engineering technology:** Electrical, surveying, telecommunications. **English:** Speech/rhetoric. **Family/consumer sciences:** Family studies, food/nutrition. **Foreign languages:** Classics, comparative lit, French, German, Italian, Japanese, Russian, Spanish. **Health:** Audiology/speech pathology, health care admin, nursing (RN), premedicine. **History:** General. **Interdisciplinary:** Biological/physical sciences, medieval/Renaissance. **Liberal arts:** Arts/sciences. **Math:** General, statistics. **Parks/recreation:** Exercise sciences, facilities management. **Philosophy/religion:** Judaic, philosophy, religion. **Physical sciences:** Astronomy, astrophysics, atmospheric science, chemistry, geology, meteorology, physics, planetary. **Protective services:** Criminal justice, law enforcement admin. **Psychology:** General. **Public administration:** Policy analysis. **Science technology:** Biological. **Social sciences:** Anthropology, applied economics, economics, geography, international relations, political science, sociology. **Visual/performing arts:** General, art, art history/conservation, cinematography, commercial/advertising art, dramatic, film/cinema, music performance.

Most popular majors. Business/marketing 21%, communications/journalism 10%, education 6%, engineering/engineering technologies 13%.

Computing on campus. 4,768 workstations in dormitories, library, computer center, student center. Dormitories wired for high-speed internet access and linked to campus network. Commuter students can connect to campus network. Online course registration, online library, helpline, repair service, student web hosting available.

Student life. Freshman orientation: Mandatory. Preregistration for classes offered. Held during 2 days prior to start of classes. **Policies:** Acts of intolerance and high-risk drinking discouraged at all locations. All facilites designated as smoke-free. **Housing:** Coed dorms, single-sex dorms, special housing for disabled, apartments, fraternity/sorority housing, substance-free housing available. $100 partly refundable deposit, deadline 5/1. Suites, special interest housing, apartments available. **Activities:** Bands, choral groups, dance, drama, film society, literary magazine, music ensembles, musical theater, opera, radio station, student government, student newspaper, symphony orchestra, TV station, Adult Learners, Eco-action, Habitat for Humanity, Minorities in Agriculture and Natural Resources, National Society of Black Engineers, College Democrats, College Libertarians, Womyn's Concerns, Black Caucus, Alliance Christian Fellowship.

Athletics. NCAA. **Intercollegiate:** Baseball M, basketball, cheerleading, cross-country, diving, fencing, field hockey W, football (tackle) M, golf, gymnastics, lacrosse, soccer, softball W, swimming, tennis, track and field, volleyball, wrestling M. **Intramural:** Badminton, basketball, bowling, cross-country, diving, football (non-tackle), football (tackle), golf, gymnastics, racquetball, soccer, softball, squash, swimming, tennis, track and field, volleyball, wrestling. **Team name:** Nittany Lions.

Student services. Adult student services, alcohol/substance abuse counseling, campus ministries, career counseling, services for economically disadvantaged, student employment services, financial aid counseling, health services, legal services, minority student services, on-campus daycare, personal counseling, placement for graduates, veterans' counselor, women's services. **Physically disabled:** Services for visually, speech, hearing impaired.

Contact. E-mail: admissions@psu.edu
Phone: (814) 865-5471 Fax: (814) 863-7590
Randall Deike, Assistant Vice Provost for Enrollment Management and Director of Admissions, Penn State University Park, 201 Shields Building, University Park, PA 16804-3000

Penn State Wilkes-Barre

Lehman, Pennsylvania
www.wb.psu.edu **CB code: 2660**

- Public 4-year branch campus college
- Commuter campus in small city

- 565 degree-seeking undergraduates: 9% part-time, 33% women, 2% African American, 1% Asian American, 2% Hispanic American
- 33 graduate students
- 84% of applicants admitted
- SAT or ACT (ACT writing optional) required
- 49% graduate within 6 years

General. Founded in 1916. Regionally accredited. **Degrees:** 85 bachelor's, 38 associate awarded. **ROTC:** Army, Air Force. **Location:** 10 miles from Wilkes-Barre. **Calendar:** Semester, limited summer session. **Full-time faculty:** 36 total; 56% have terminal degrees, 19% minority, 17% women. **Part-time faculty:** 31 total; 19% have terminal degrees, 45% women. **Class size:** 61% < 20, 35% 20-39, 3% 40-49, 1% 50-99.

Freshman class profile. 427 applied, 360 admitted, 163 enrolled.

Mid 50% test scores		GPA 2.0-2.99:	53%
SAT verbal:	460-550	Rank in top quarter:	27%
SAT math:	450-560	Rank in top tenth:	8%
GPA 3.50 or higher:	16%	Return as sophomores:	71%
GPA 3.0-3.49:	31%	Out-of-state:	8%

Basis for selection. Admission decisions based upon high school GPA, standardized test scores, class rank, personal statements, and activities. Essay considered if submitted; portfolios required for select majors. **Homeschooled:** Applicants should provide complete documentation showing courses studied and all evaluations presented from evaluator or supervisor assigned to student in cooperation with local school district or evaluator approved through program. **Learning Disabled:** Prospective students with disabilities are encouraged to contact or visit the Office for Disability Services in their junior or senior years in high school in order to find out more about disability services at the college level.

High school preparation. Required units include English 4, mathematics 3, social studies 3, science 3 and foreign language 2.

2005-2006 Annual costs. Tuition/fees: $10,200; $15,332 out-of-state. Books/supplies: $1,040. Personal expenses: $1,854.

2004-2005 Financial aid. Need-based: 149 full-time freshmen applied for aid; 106 were judged to have need; 104 of these received aid. Average need met was 64%. Average scholarship/grant was $4,096; average loan $2,440. 57% of total undergraduate aid awarded as scholarships/grants, 43% as loans/jobs. **Non-need-based:** Awarded to 159 full-time undergraduates, including 50 freshmen. Scholarships awarded for academics, athletics, minority status, ROTC.

Application procedures. Admission: Priority date 11/30; no deadline. $50 fee, may be waived for applicants with need. Application may be submitted online. Admission notification on a rolling basis beginning on or about 11/1. Must reply by 5/1. All freshmen applications processed at University Park Campus. **Financial aid:** Priority date 2/15; no closing date. FAFSA required. Applicants notified on a rolling basis starting 2/15.

Academics. Special study options: Accelerated study, cross-registration, distance learning, double major, dual enrollment of high school students, honors, independent study, internships, student-designed major, study abroad. **Credit/placement by examination:** AP, CLEP, IB, SAT. 60 credit hours maximum toward bachelor's degree. **Support services:** Learning center, remedial instruction, study skills assistance, tutoring, writing center.

Majors. Agriculture: Agronomy, animal sciences, business, equipment technology, food science, horticultural science, landscaping, products processing, soil science, turf management. **Area/ethnic studies:** African-American, American, East Asian, Latin American, women's. **Biology:** General, bacteriology, biochemistry. **Business:** Accounting, actuarial science, business admin, finance, hotel/motel admin, insurance, international, labor relations, logistics, managerial economics, market research, real estate. **Communications:** Advertising, journalism, media studies. **Computer sciences:** Computer science, information systems, information technology. **Conservation:** Forest sciences, management/policy, wildlife. **Education:** Art, elementary, secondary, special. **Engineering:** Aerospace, architectural, biomedical, chemical, civil, computer, electrical, environmental, industrial, materials, mechanical, mining, nuclear, petroleum, science. **Engineering technology:** Surveying, telecommunications. **English:** Speech/rhetoric. **Family/consumer sciences:** Aging. **Foreign languages:** Classics, comparative lit, French, German, Italian, Japanese, Russian, Spanish. **Health:** Health services, nursing (RN), premedicine. **History:** General. **Interdisciplinary:** Biological/physical sciences, medieval/Renaissance. **Liberal arts:** Arts/sciences. **Math:** General, statistics. **Parks/recreation:** General, exercise sciences. **Philosophy/religion:** Religion. **Physical sciences:** Astronomy, chemistry, meteorology, physics, planetary. **Protective services:** Criminal justice. **Psychology:** General. **Science technology:** Biological. **Social sciences:** Anthropology, applied economics, economics, geography, international relations, political science, sociology. **Visual/performing arts:** General, art, art history/conservation, cinematography, dramatic.

Most popular majors. Business/marketing 42%, computer/information sciences 19%, engineering/engineering technologies 13%, security/protective services 24%.

Computing on campus. 157 workstations in library, computer center, student center. Commuter students can connect to campus network. Online course registration, online library, helpline, repair service, student web hosting available.

Student life. Freshman orientation: Available. Preregistration for classes offered. **Policies:** Acts of intolerance and high-risk drinking discouraged at all locations. All facilities designated smoke-free. Students expected to abide by The Penn State Principles. Freshmen permitted cars on campus. **Activities:** Radio station, student government, student newspaper, Model United Nations, Students for Justice club.

Athletics. Intercollegiate: Baseball M, basketball M, cross-country, golf, soccer, volleyball W. **Intramural:** Basketball, football (tackle), racquetball, softball, volleyball. **Team name:** Nittany Lions.

Student services. Adult student services, alcohol/substance abuse counseling, campus ministries, career counseling, services for economically disadvantaged, student employment services, financial aid counseling, health services, minority student services, personal counseling, placement for graduates. **Physically disabled:** Services for visually, hearing impaired.

Contact. E-mail: wbadmissions@psu.edu
Phone: (570) 675-9238 Toll-free number: (800) 966-6613
Fax: (570) 675-9113
Randall Deike, Assistant Vice Provost for Enrollment Management and Director of Admissions, Penn State Wilkes-Barre, Box PSU, Lehman, PA 18627-0217

Pennsylvania College of Art and Design

Lancaster, Pennsylvania
www.pcad.edu/

- Private 4-year art college
- Small city

General. Regionally accredited. **Calendar:** Semester.

Annual costs/financial aid. Tuition/fees (projected): $13,400.

Contact. Phone: (717) 396-7833
PO Box 59, Lancaster, PA 17608-0059

Pennsylvania College of Technology

Williamsport, Pennsylvania — **CB member**
www.pct.edu — **CB code: 2989**

- Public 4-year technical college
- Commuter campus in small city
- 6,440 degree-seeking undergraduates: 14% part-time, 35% women, 3% African American, 1% Asian American, 1% Hispanic American, 1% Native American
- 50% graduate within 6 years

General. Founded in 1965. Regionally accredited. **Degrees:** 393 bachelor's, 972 associate awarded. **ROTC:** Army. **Location:** 85 miles from Harrisburg, 70 miles from Wilkes-Barre. **Calendar:** Semester, limited summer session. **Full-time faculty:** 285 total. **Part-time faculty:** 185 total. **Class size:** 58% < 20, 42% 20-39. **Special facilities:** Automotic technology center, aviation center, plastics manufacturing center.

Freshman class profile. 2,793 applied, 2,712 admitted, 1,671 enrolled.

Return as sophomores:	66%	International:	1%
Out-of-state:	26%		

Basis for selection. Open admission, but selective for some programs. Competitive admissions to health science programs, using high school/college GPA, SAT scores, high school rank, selected course grades, completed developmental course work, college credits. Some programs have more specific requirements. SAT recommended for all bachelor's programs, dental hygiene, radiography, occupational therapy assistant, nursing applicants; college placement exams required for all applicants. Portfolio required for graphic design program. **Homeschooled:** Transcript of courses and grades, state high school equivalency certificate required.

2005-2006 Annual costs. Tuition/fees: $10,080; $12,660 out-of-state. Room/board: $6,900. Books/supplies: $1,000. Personal expenses: $2,450.

Financial aid. Non-need-based: Scholarships awarded for academics, alumni affiliation.

Application procedures. Admission: Closing date 7/1 (postmark date). $50 fee, may be waived for applicants with need. Application may be submitted online. Admission notification on a rolling basis. **Financial aid:** Priority date 4/1; no closing date. FAFSA, institutional form required. Applicants notified on a rolling basis starting 6/1; must reply by 7/1 or within 4 week(s) of notification.

Academics. Special study options: Accelerated study, cooperative education, cross-registration, distance learning, dual enrollment of high school students, exchange student, independent study, internships, student-designed major, study abroad, weekend college. **Credit/placement by examination:** AP, CLEP, institutional tests. 30 credit hours maximum toward associate degree, 30 toward bachelor's. **Support services:** Learning center, pre-admission summer program, remedial instruction, study skills assistance, tutoring.

Majors. Business: Accounting, business admin, management information systems. **Communications technology:** Graphic/printing. **Computer sciences:** Networking, security, systems analysis, web page design. **Construction:** Masonry. **Engineering technology:** Architectural, automotive, civil, construction, environmental, heat/ac/refrig, manufacturing, mechanical, plastics. **English:** Technical writing. **Health:** Cardiovascular technology, dental hygiene, surgical technology. **Mechanic/repair:** Avionics, electronics/electrical, heating/ac/refrig, industrial electronics. **Personal/culinary services:** Chef training. **Visual/performing arts:** Commercial/advertising art.

Most popular majors. Business/marketing 17%, computer/information sciences 19%, engineering/engineering technologies 38%, health sciences 14%, visual/performing arts 6%.

Computing on campus. 1,500 workstations in dormitories, library, computer center, student center. Dormitories wired for high-speed internet access and linked to campus network. Commuter students can connect to campus network. Online course registration, online library, helpline, wireless network available.

Student life. Freshman orientation: Available. **Policies:** Freshmen permitted cars on campus. **Housing:** Coed dorms, substance-free housing available. $300 partly refundable deposit. Coed apartments available. **Activities:** Dance, radio station, student government, Alpha Omega (Christian) Fellowship, human services club, multicultural society, American Institute of Architectural Students, American Society of Heating, Refrigeration and Engineering, avionics club.

Athletics. Intercollegiate: Archery, baseball M, basketball, bowling, cross-country, golf, soccer, softball W, tennis, volleyball. **Intramural:** Archery, badminton, basketball, bowling, football (non-tackle), golf, lacrosse, racquetball, soccer, softball, table tennis, tennis, volleyball, weight lifting, wrestling M. **Team name:** Wildcats.

Student services. Adult student services, alcohol/substance abuse counseling, career counseling, student employment services, financial aid counseling, health services, on-campus daycare, personal counseling, placement for graduates, veterans' counselor, women's services. **Physically disabled:** Services for visually, speech, hearing impaired.

Contact. Phone: (570) 327-4761 Toll-free number: (800) 367-9222
Fax: (570) 321-5536
Chester Schuman, Director of Admissions, Pennsylvania College of Technology, One College Avenue, Williamsport, PA 17701

Philadelphia Biblical University

Langhorne, Pennsylvania
www.pbu.edu **CB code: 2661**

- Private 4-year university and Bible college affiliated with Protestant Evangelical tradition
- Residential campus in small town
- 1,063 degree-seeking undergraduates: 8% part-time, 55% women, 11% African American, 3% Asian American, 3% Hispanic American, 2% international
- 300 degree-seeking graduate students
- 94% of applicants admitted
- SAT or ACT with writing, application essay required
- 52% graduate within 6 years; 38% enter graduate study

General. Founded in 1913. Regionally accredited; also accredited by ABHE. **Degrees:** 298 bachelor's awarded; master's, first professional offered. **ROTC:** Air Force. **Location:** 17 miles from Philadelphia, 5 miles from Trenton, New Jersey. **Calendar:** Semester, limited summer session. **Full-time faculty:** 64 total; 64% have terminal degrees, 11% minority, 31% women. **Part-time faculty:** 92 total; 27% have terminal degrees, 6% minority, 33% women. **Class size:** 52% < 20, 45% 20-39, 1% 40-49, 1% 50-99, 1% >100. **Special facilities:** Wooded walking trail.

Freshman class profile. 307 applied, 289 admitted, 233 enrolled.

Mid 50% test scores		**Rank in top quarter:**	45%
SAT verbal:	490-590	**Rank in top tenth:**	17%
SAT math:	460-580	**Return as sophomores:**	75%
ACT:	21-27	**Out-of-state:**	56%
GPA 3.50 or higher:	45%	**Live on campus:**	91%
GPA 3.0-3.49:	34%	**International:**	2%
GPA 2.0-2.99:	20%		

Basis for selection. High school GPA, pastor's references, autobiography, SAT or ACT scores required for some. Some applicants not meeting academic admissions requirements may be admitted and placed in remedial program. Interview recommended for all; audition required for music program.

High school preparation. 15 units recommended. Recommended units include English 4, mathematics 1, social studies 3, science 2 and foreign language 2.

2006-2007 Annual costs. Tuition/fees (projected): $15,875. Room/board: $6,550. Books/supplies: $800. Personal expenses: $100.

2005-2006 Financial aid. Need-based: 197 full-time freshmen applied for aid; 174 were judged to have need; 174 of these received aid. Average need met was 78.6%. Average scholarship/grant was $10,075; average loan $3,201. 67% of total undergraduate aid awarded as scholarships/grants, 33% as loans/jobs. **Non-need-based:** Awarded to 214 full-time undergraduates, including 67 freshmen. Scholarships awarded for academics, leadership, music/drama.

Application procedures. Admission: No deadline. $25 fee, may be waived for applicants with need. Admission notification on a rolling basis beginning on or about 9/1. Must reply by May 1 or within 4 week(s) if notified thereafter. **Financial aid:** Priority date 5/1; no closing date. FAFSA required. Applicants notified on a rolling basis starting 3/15.

Academics. Students may participate in semester studies in Israel. **Special study options:** Accelerated study, combined bachelor's/graduate degree, double major, dual enrollment of high school students, honors, internships, study abroad, teacher certification program. Cooperative agreement with Bucks County Community College. **Credit/placement by examination:** AP, CLEP, IB, SAT, ACT, institutional tests. 60 credit hours maximum toward bachelor's degree. **Support services:** Learning center, reduced course load, remedial instruction, study skills assistance, tutoring, writing center.

Majors. Business: Business admin. **Education:** Early childhood, elementary, English, mathematics, music, physical, social studies. **Parks/recreation:** Health/fitness. **Public administration:** Social work. **Theology:** Bible, missionary, pastoral counseling, religious ed, sacred music, theology. **Visual/performing arts:** Music performance, music theory/composition.

Computing on campus. 70 workstations in library, student center. Dormitories wired for high-speed internet access and linked to campus network. Commuter students can connect to campus network. Online library, helpline, wireless network available.

Student life. Freshman orientation: Mandatory. Preregistration for classes offered. **Policies:** Religious observance required. Freshmen permitted cars on campus. **Housing:** Guaranteed on-campus for freshmen. Single-sex dorms, special housing for disabled, apartments, substance-free housing available. $50 fully refundable deposit, deadline 7/15. **Activities:** Bands, choral groups, drama, music ensembles, musical theater, opera, student government, student newspaper, symphony orchestra, student missionary fellowship, commuter council, married student fellowship, resident council, student theological society, international student group, cultural awareness association, business club, university social committee.

Athletics. NCAA, NCCAA. **Intercollegiate:** Baseball M, basketball, cross-country, field hockey W, golf M, soccer, softball W, tennis, volleyball. **Intramural:** Basketball, football (non-tackle), lacrosse M, soccer, table tennis, tennis, volleyball. **Team name:** Eagles.

Student services. Adult student services, alcohol/substance abuse counseling, campus ministries, career counseling, student employment services, financial aid counseling, health services, minority student services, personal counseling, placement for graduates. **Physically disabled:** Services for visually, hearing impaired.

Contact. E-mail: admissions@pbu.edu
Phone: (215) 702-4235 Toll-free number: (800) 366-0049
Fax: (215) 702-4248
Lisa Yoder, Director of Admissions, Philadelphia Biblical University, 200 Manor Avenue, Langhorne, PA 19047-2990

Philadelphia University

Philadelphia, Pennsylvania — **CB member**
www.philau.edu — **CB code: 2666**

- Private 4-year university
- Residential campus in very large city
- 2,707 degree-seeking undergraduates: 10% part-time, 69% women, 9% African American, 4% Asian American, 3% Hispanic American, 3% international
- 486 degree-seeking graduate students
- 64% of applicants admitted
- SAT or ACT (ACT writing optional) required
- 54% graduate within 6 years

General. Founded in 1884. Regionally accredited. **Degrees:** 508 bachelor's, 4 associate awarded; master's, doctoral offered. **Location:** 9 miles from downtown. **Calendar:** Semester, limited summer session. **Full-time faculty:** 104 total; 76% have terminal degrees, 12% minority, 41% women. **Part-time faculty:** 314 total; 14% minority, 39% women. **Class size:** 64% < 20, 35% 20-39, less than 1% 40-49, less than 1% 50-99. **Special facilities:** Computer-aided design laboratories in architecture, grapic design and fashion design; CAD facilities, university design center, rapid prototyping.

Freshman class profile. 4,180 applied, 2,682 admitted, 692 enrolled.

Mid 50% test scores		**Rank in top tenth:**	12%
SAT verbal:	490-570	**Return as sophomores:**	74%
SAT math:	490-590	**Out-of-state:**	48%
GPA 3.50 or higher:	49%	**Live on campus:**	80%
GPA 3.0-3.49:	29%	**International:**	2%
GPA 2.0-2.99:	22%	**Fraternities:**	1%
Rank in top quarter:	38%	**Sororities:**	1%

Basis for selection. Academic record, high school GPA, and test scores most important. Extracurricular activities, counselor's recommendation and interview considered. Interview, essay recommended.

High school preparation. 15 units required; 19 recommended. Required and recommended units include English 4, mathematics 3-4, social studies 2-3, history 1-2, science 3-4 (laboratory 2), foreign language 2 and academic electives 2.

2005-2006 Annual costs. Tuition/fees: $22,140. Room/board: $7,936. Books/supplies: $1,000. Personal expenses: $1,789.

2005-2006 Financial aid. Need-based: 591 full-time freshmen applied for aid; 510 were judged to have need; 510 of these received aid. Average need met was 79%. Average scholarship/grant was $11,323; average loan $3,113. 56% of total undergraduate aid awarded as scholarships/grants, 44% as loans/jobs. **Non-need-based:** Awarded to 805 full-time undergraduates, including 221 freshmen. Scholarships awarded for academics, athletics, leadership.

Application procedures. Admission: No deadline. $35 fee, may be waived for applicants with need. Application must be submitted on paper. Admission notification on a rolling basis. Must reply by May 1 or within 3 week(s) if notified thereafter. **Financial aid:** Priority date 4/15; no closing date. FAFSA required. Applicants notified on a rolling basis starting 2/10; must reply by 5/1 or within 3 week(s) of notification.

Academics. Special study options: Combined bachelor's/graduate degree, cooperative education, distance learning, double major, honors, independent study, internships, study abroad. **Credit/placement by examination:** AP, CLEP, institutional tests. 60 credit hours maximum toward bachelor's degree. **Support services:** Learning center, reduced course load, remedial instruction, study skills assistance, tutoring, writing center.

Majors. Architecture: Architecture, interior, landscape. **Biology:** General, biochemistry, environmental. **Business:** Accounting, apparel, business admin, fashion, finance, international, management information systems, marketing. **Communications:** Digital media. **Communications technology:** Animation/special effects, graphics. **Engineering:** General, industrial, textile. **Family/consumer sciences:** Apparel marketing, clothing/textiles, textile science. **Health:** Health care admin, premedicine. **Interdisciplinary:** Biopsychology. **Physical sciences:** Chemistry. **Psychology:** General. **Visual/performing arts:** Fashion design, fiber arts, graphic design, industrial design, interior design.

Most popular majors. Architecture 20%, business/marketing 42%, visual/performing arts 20%.

Computing on campus. 400 workstations in library, computer center, student center. Dormitories wired for high-speed internet access and linked to campus network. Commuter students can connect to campus network. Online course registration, online library, helpline available.

Student life. Freshman orientation: Mandatory, $100 fee. Preregistration for classes offered. 3-day residental program in summer for orientation, advising and pre-registration. **Housing:** Guaranteed on-campus for freshmen. Coed dorms, single-sex dorms, apartments, substance-free housing available. $250 deposit, deadline 5/1. **Activities:** Choral groups, dance, drama, student government, student newspaper, 10 professional (major-related) organizations, international society, Black Awareness Society, Hillel, Christian Fellowship, community service corps, Minaret, Gemini Theatre, Phila Capella, Gay Lesbian Bisexual Allies Coalition.

Athletics. NCAA. **Intercollegiate:** Baseball M, basketball, cross-country, field hockey W, golf M, lacrosse W, rowing (crew), soccer, softball W, tennis, volleyball W. **Intramural:** Basketball, cross-country, football (tackle) M, skiing, soccer, softball, swimming, tennis, volleyball W. **Team name:** Rams.

Student services. Adult student services, alcohol/substance abuse counseling, career counseling, student employment services, financial aid counseling, health services, personal counseling, placement for graduates. **Physically disabled:** Services for visually, hearing impaired. **Learning disabled:** Comprehensive services available.

Contact. E-mail: admissions@philau.edu
Phone: (215) 951-2800 Toll-free number: (800) 951-7287
Fax: (215) 951-2907
Christine Greb, Director of Admissions, Philadelphia University, School House Lane and Henry Avenue, Philadelphia, PA 19144-5497

Point Park University

Pittsburgh, Pennsylvania — **CB member**
www.pointpark.edu — **CB code: 2676**

- Private 4-year university
- Commuter campus in large city
- 2,932 degree-seeking undergraduates: 23% part-time, 59% women, 18% African American, 1% Asian American, 2% Hispanic American, 1% international
- 439 degree-seeking graduate students
- 76% of applicants admitted
- SAT or ACT (ACT writing optional), application essay, interview required
- 43% graduate within 6 years

General. Founded in 1960. Regionally accredited. Numerous off-campus programs for college credits. Several accelerated programs available. Offers professionally oriented programs in arts, business, communications, and technology. **Degrees:** 610 bachelor's, 3 associate awarded; master's offered. **ROTC:** Army, Air Force. **Location:** Downtown. **Calendar:** Semester, extensive summer session. **Full-time faculty:** 87 total; 36% have terminal degrees, 6% minority, 39% women. **Part-time faculty:** 303 total. **Class size:** 75% < 20, 24% 20-39, less than 1% 40-49, less than 1% 50-99, less than 1% >100. **Special facilities:** Children's school.

Freshman class profile. 2,453 applied, 1,866 admitted, 472 enrolled.

Mid 50% test scores		**GPA 2.0-2.99:**	32%
SAT verbal:	470-580	**Rank in top quarter:**	38%
SAT math:	450-550	**Rank in top tenth:**	12%
ACT:	20-25	**Out-of-state:**	31%
GPA 3.50 or higher:	34%	**Live on campus:**	74%
GPA 3.0-3.49:	34%	**International:**	1%

Basis for selection. High school record, class rank, test scores most important. Recommendations, extracurricular activities, talent, character also important. Test scores must be submitted by class start. Audition required for some majors, portfolio recommended for multimedia, technical theater, stage management programs.

High school preparation. Recommended units include English 4, mathematics 3, social studies 3, history 3, science 3 and foreign language 2.

2005-2006 Annual costs. Tuition/fees: $16,740. Cost of tuition in bachelor of arts and bachelor of fine arts programs within conservatory of performing arts: $17540 or $498 per credit hour. Room/board: $7,420. Books/supplies: $1,000. Personal expenses: $1,141.

2005-2006 Financial aid. **Need-based:** Average need met was 70%. Average scholarship/grant was $7,716; average loan $4,530. 43% of total undergraduate aid awarded as scholarships/grants, 57% as loans/jobs. **Non-need-based:** Scholarships awarded for academics, alumni affiliation, art, athletics, job skills, leadership, music/drama.

Application procedures. **Admission:** No deadline. $40 fee, may be waived for applicants with need. Application may be submitted online. Admission notification on a rolling basis beginning on or about 10/1. Must reply by May 1 or within 4 week(s) if notified thereafter. **Financial aid:** Priority date 5/1; no closing date. FAFSA required. Applicants notified on a rolling basis starting 2/15; must reply within 3 week(s) of notification.

Academics. **Special study options:** Accelerated study, cooperative education, cross-registration, double major, ESL, honors, independent study, internships, student-designed major, study abroad, teacher certification program, weekend college. **Credit/placement by examination:** AP, CLEP, IB, SAT, institutional tests. 30 credit hours maximum toward associate degree, 60 toward bachelor's. **Support services:** Learning center, pre-admission summer program, reduced course load, remedial instruction, study skills assistance, tutoring.

Majors. **Biology:** General, biotechnology. **Business:** Accounting, business admin, human resources. **Communications:** Advertising, broadcast journalism, journalism, media studies, photojournalism. **Computer sciences:** Information technology. **Conservation:** Environmental science. **Education:** Biology, drama/dance, early childhood, elementary, English, mathematics. **Engineering technology:** Civil, mechanical. **English:** English lit. **History:** General. **Interdisciplinary:** Behavioral sciences. **Legal studies:** General. **Personal/culinary services:** Mortuary science. **Protective services:** Criminal justice, law enforcement admin. **Psychology:** General. **Public administration:** General. **Social sciences:** General, international relations, political science. **Visual/performing arts:** Cinematography, dance, dramatic, photography.

Most popular majors. Business/marketing 22%, communications/journalism 13%, computer/information sciences 6%, education 6%, security/protective services 15%, visual/performing arts 19%.

Computing on campus. 183 workstations in library, computer center, student center. Dormitories wired for high-speed internet access and linked to campus network. Commuter students can connect to campus network. Online library, helpline, student web hosting available.

Student life. **Freshman orientation:** Mandatory. Preregistration for classes offered. Students meet with faculty and register. **Policies:** Policies regarding student conduct, plagiarism and resident life. **Housing:** Guaranteed on-campus for all undergraduates. Coed dorms, single-sex dorms, special housing for disabled available. $100 deposit. Quiet floors, single gender floors available. **Activities:** Choral groups, dance, drama, film society, literary magazine, musical theater, radio station, student government, student newspaper, TV station, international club, black student union, Amnesty International.

Athletics. NAIA. **Intercollegiate:** Baseball M, basketball, cross-country, soccer M, softball W, volleyball W. **Intramural:** Basketball M, tennis, volleyball, weight lifting M. **Team name:** Pioneers.

Student services. Adult student services, alcohol/substance abuse counseling, career counseling, student employment services, financial aid counseling, health services, on-campus daycare, personal counseling, placement for graduates, veterans' counselor. **Physically disabled:** Services for visually, speech, hearing impaired.

Contact. E-mail: enroll@pointpark.edu
Phone: (412) 392-3430 Toll-free number: (800) 321-0129
Fax: (412) 391-1980
Joell Minford, Director of Admissions, Point Park University, 201 Wood Street, Pittsburgh, PA 15222-1984

Restaurant School

Philadelphia, Pennsylvania
www.walnuthillcollege.edu **CB code: 4883**

- For-profit 4-year culinary school and business college
- Commuter campus in very large city
- 615 undergraduates
- Application essay, interview required

General. Accredited by ACCSCT. Emphasis on fine dining and upscale hotels. **Degrees:** 17 bachelor's, 176 associate awarded. **Calendar:** Semester, extensive summer session. **Full-time faculty:** 15 total. **Special facilities:** Students interact with numerous food and beverage outlets open to public. 4 uniquely themed restaurants and pastry shop/cafe.

Freshman class profile.

Out-of-state:	51%	**Live on campus:**	30%

Basis for selection. Open admission, but selective for some programs. Students must submit two letters of reference and a 250-word essay and take a basic skills evaluation. SAT and SAT Subject Tests or ACT recommended. Students who score below 900 SAT (exclusive of Writing) total must take scholastic level exam at the Restaurant School. **Homeschooled:** Interview required.

2005-2006 Annual costs. Room only: $4,760.

Application procedures. **Admission:** No deadline. $200 fee. Application may be submitted online. Admission notification on a rolling basis.

Academics. **Special study options:** Independent study, internships. **Credit/placement by examination:** CLEP. **Support services:** Study skills assistance, tutoring.

Computing on campus. 24 workstations in dormitories, library, computer center. Dormitories linked to campus network. Online library available.

Student life. **Freshman orientation:** Mandatory. 3-day orientation held week prior to start of classes. **Policies:** Freshmen permitted cars on campus. **Housing:** Coed dorms available. $850 deposit. **Activities:** Literary magazine, student newspaper.

Student services. Career counseling, student employment services, financial aid counseling.

Contact. E-mail: info@walnuthillcollege.edu
Phone: (215) 222-4200 ext. 3011 Toll-free number: (877) 925-6884 ext. 3011 Fax: (215) 222-2811
Karl Becker, Director of Admissions, Restaurant School, 4207 Walnut Street, Philadelphia, PA 19104

Robert Morris University

Moon Township, Pennsylvania **CB member**
www.rmu.edu **CB code: 2769**

- Private 4-year university
- Commuter campus in large town
- 3,877 degree-seeking undergraduates: 20% part-time, 46% women, 8% African American, 1% Asian American, 1% Hispanic American, 2% international
- 984 degree-seeking graduate students
- 78% of applicants admitted
- SAT or ACT (ACT writing optional) required
- 55% graduate within 6 years; 3% enter graduate study

General. Founded in 1921. Regionally accredited. **Degrees:** 773 bachelor's, 2 associate awarded; master's, doctoral offered. **ROTC:** Army, Air Force. **Location:** 17 miles from Pittsburgh. **Calendar:** Semester, limited summer session. **Full-time faculty:** 157 total; 82% have terminal degrees, 12% minority, 34% women. **Part-time faculty:** 227 total; 25% have terminal degrees, 5% minority, 50% women. **Class size:** 50% < 20, 42% 20-39, 7% 40-49, less than 1% 50-99.

Freshman class profile. 2,584 applied, 2,024 admitted, 695 enrolled.

Mid 50% test scores		**Rank in top tenth:**	8%
SAT verbal:	450-540	**Return as sophomores:**	78%
SAT math:	460-570	**Out-of-state:**	19%
ACT:	19-23	**Live on campus:**	71%
GPA 3.50 or higher:	30%	**International:**	1%
GPA 3.0-3.49:	37%	**Fraternities:**	5%
GPA 2.0-2.99:	33%	**Sororities:**	4%
Rank in top quarter:	27%		

Basis for selection. Academic potential, high school GPA, class rank, test scores, and evidence of motivation important. Interview required of restricted-status applicants, recommended for all others.

High school preparation. College-preparatory program required. 16 units required; 18 recommended. Required and recommended units include English 4, mathematics 3, social studies 4, science 2, foreign language 2 and academic electives 3.

2005-2006 Annual costs. Tuition/fees: $15,152. Room/board: $7,670. Books/supplies: $1,000. Personal expenses: $1,606.

2005-2006 Financial aid. Need-based: 636 full-time freshmen applied for aid; 533 were judged to have need; 533 of these received aid. Average need met was 75%. Average scholarship/grant was $7,960; average loan $4,528. 39% of total undergraduate aid awarded as scholarships/grants, 61% as loans/jobs. **Non-need-based:** Awarded to 786 full-time undergraduates, including 211 freshmen. Scholarships awarded for academics, alumni affiliation, athletics, job skills, leadership, minority status, music/drama, religious affiliation, state residency.

Application procedures. Admission: Priority date 12/1; deadline 7/1 (postmark date). $30 fee, may be waived for applicants with need. Application may be submitted online. Admission notification on a rolling basis beginning on or about 8/1. Must reply by May 1 or within 3 week(s) if notified thereafter. **Financial aid:** No deadline. FAFSA required. Applicants notified on a rolling basis starting 3/15; must reply within 2 week(s) of notification.

Academics. Special study options: Combined bachelor's/graduate degree, cooperative education, cross-registration, distance learning, honors, independent study, internships, study abroad, teacher certification program, weekend college. **Credit/placement by examination:** AP, CLEP, SAT, ACT, institutional tests. 18 credit hours maximum toward associate degree, 30 toward bachelor's. **Support services:** Pre-admission summer program, reduced course load, remedial instruction, study skills assistance, tutoring.

Majors. Business: Accounting, actuarial science, business admin, entrepreneurial studies, finance, hospitality admin, human resources, logistics, management information systems, managerial economics, marketing, operations, organizational behavior. **Communications:** General. **Computer sciences:** Information systems. **Conservation:** Environmental science. **Education:** Business, elementary. **Engineering:** Manufacturing, software. **English:** English lit. **Health:** Health care admin, nursing (RN). **Math:** Applied. **Parks/recreation:** Sports admin. **Psychology:** General. **Social sciences:** General, economics. **Transportation:** Aviation management. **Visual/performing arts:** Design.

Most popular majors. Business/marketing 64%, communications/journalism 10%, computer/information sciences 9%.

Computing on campus. 300 workstations in dormitories, library, computer center, student center. Dormitories wired for high-speed internet access and linked to campus network. Commuter students can connect to campus network. Online course registration, online library, helpline, wireless network available.

Student life. Freshman orientation: Available. Preregistration for classes offered. 3-day program. **Policies:** Freshmen permitted cars on campus. **Housing:** Coed dorms, single-sex dorms, apartments available. $150 nonrefundable deposit, deadline 5/1. **Activities:** Bands, drama, musical theater, student government, student newspaper, TV station, minority student organization, international student organization, campus activities board, inter-residence hall council, interfraternity council/Panhellenic council, honor societies.

Athletics. NCAA. **Intercollegiate:** Basketball, cheerleading, cross-country, field hockey W, football (tackle) M, golf, ice hockey, lacrosse, rowing (crew) W, soccer, softball W, tennis, track and field, volleyball W. **Intramural:** Baseball M, basketball, boxing M, football (non-tackle) M, handball M, softball, volleyball W. **Team name:** Colonials.

Student services. Adult student services, alcohol/substance abuse counseling, campus ministries, career counseling, student employment services, financial aid counseling, health services, minority student services, personal counseling, placement for graduates, veterans' counselor. **Physically disabled:** Services for visually, speech, hearing impaired.

Contact. E-mail: enrollmentoffice@rmu.edu
Phone: (412) 262-8206 Toll-free number: (800) 762-0097
Fax: (412) 299-2425
Marianne Budziszewski, Associate VP, Academic & Enrollment Services, Robert Morris University, 6001 University Boulevard, Moon Township, PA 15108-1189

Rosemont College

Rosemont, Pennsylvania **CB member**
www.rosemont.edu **CB code: 2763**

- Private 4-year liberal arts college for women affiliated with Roman Catholic Church
- Residential campus in small town
- 644 degree-seeking undergraduates: 34% part-time, 87% women, 28% African American, 7% Asian American, 7% Hispanic American, 4% international
- 404 degree-seeking graduate students
- 66% of applicants admitted
- SAT or ACT, application essay required
- 62% graduate within 6 years; 35% enter graduate study

General. Founded in 1921. Regionally accredited. **Degrees:** 135 bachelor's awarded; master's offered. **ROTC:** Army, Air Force. **Location:** 11 miles from Philadelphia. **Calendar:** Semester, limited summer session. **Full-time faculty:** 32 total; 91% have terminal degrees, 3% minority, 59% women. **Part-time faculty:** 134 total; 81% have terminal degrees, 7% minority, 53% women. **Class size:** 92% < 20, 8% 20-39.

Freshman class profile. 434 applied, 285 admitted, 120 enrolled.

Mid 50% test scores		End year in good standing:	97%
SAT verbal:	480-620	Return as sophomores:	78%
SAT math:	460-600	Out-of-state:	30%
Rank in top quarter:	46%	Live on campus:	90%
Rank in top tenth:	24%	International:	3%

Basis for selection. School achievement record and curriculum, recommendations, test scores, extracurricular activities strongly considered. Interview recommended.

High school preparation. 18 units required. Required units include English 4, mathematics 2, social studies 2, history 2, science 2 (laboratory 2), foreign language 2 and academic electives 2.

2005-2006 Annual costs. Tuition/fees: $20,560. Room/board: $8,800. Books/supplies: $800. Personal expenses: $1,000.

2005-2006 Financial aid. Need-based: 106 full-time freshmen applied for aid; 98 were judged to have need; 98 of these received aid. Average need met was 77%. Average scholarship/grant was $16,507; average loan $3,108. 69% of total undergraduate aid awarded as scholarships/grants, 31% as loans/jobs. **Non-need-based:** Awarded to 90 full-time undergraduates, including 31 freshmen. Scholarships awarded for academics, alumni affiliation, art, job skills, religious affiliation.

Application procedures. Admission: No deadline. $35 fee, may be waived for applicants with need. Application may be submitted online. Admission notification on a rolling basis. Must reply by May 1 or within 2 week(s) if notified thereafter. $300 deposit required of all students intending to enroll. Refundable only if college notified by May 1 of decision not to attend. **Financial aid:** Priority date 2/15; no closing date. FAFSA required. Applicants notified on a rolling basis starting 2/15; must reply by 5/1 or within 4 week(s) of notification.

Academics. Special study options: Accelerated study, combined bachelor's/graduate degree, cross-registration, distance learning, double major, ESL, exchange student, honors, independent study, internships, liberal arts/career combination, student-designed major, study abroad, teacher certification program, Washington semester. **Credit/placement by examination:** AP, CLEP, IB, SAT, institutional tests. 30 credit hours maximum toward bachelor's degree. Students may be exempted if they demonstrate mastery of subject as determined by particular department. **Support services:** Learning center, reduced course load, remedial instruction, study skills assistance, tutoring, writing center.

Majors. Area/ethnic studies: Asian, women's. **Biology:** General, biochemistry. **Business:** General, accounting, business admin, communications, hospitality admin, human resources, management science, managerial economics, organizational behavior. **Communications:** General. **Conservation:** Environmental science. **Foreign languages:** General, French, German, Italian, Spanish. **History:** General. **Liberal arts:** Arts/sciences, humanities. **Math:** General. **Philosophy/religion:** Philosophy, religion. **Physical sciences:** Chemistry. **Psychology:** General. **Social sciences:** General, economics, political science, sociology. **Visual/performing arts:** Art history/conservation.

Most popular majors. Business/marketing 16%, English 14%, physical sciences 10%, psychology 13%, social sciences 15%, visual/performing arts 17%.

Computing on campus. 77 workstations in dormitories, library, computer center, student center. Dormitories wired for high-speed internet access and linked to campus network. Commuter students can connect to campus network. Online library, helpline, student web hosting available.

Student life. Freshman orientation: Mandatory, $245 fee. Preregistration for classes offered. **Policies:** Freshmen permitted cars on campus. **Housing:** Guaranteed on-campus for all undergraduates. **Activities:** Bands, choral groups, dance, drama, literary magazine, music ensembles, musical theater, opera, radio station, student government, student newspaper, campus ministry, premed club, politics club, Model UN, Rosemont Alcohol and Drug Awareness Resource, multicultural society, Organization of African American Students, Best Buddies, Triad, art society.

Athletics. NCAA. **Intercollegiate:** Basketball W, field hockey W, lacrosse W, softball W, tennis W, volleyball W. **Team name:** Ramblers.

Student services. Adult student services, alcohol/substance abuse counseling, campus ministries, career counseling, student employment services, financial aid counseling, health services, legal services, minority student services, on-campus daycare, personal counseling, placement for graduates, veterans' counselor, women's services. **Physically disabled:** Services for visually, speech, hearing impaired.

Contact. E-mail: admissions@rosemont.edu
Phone: (610) 526-2966 Toll-free number: (800) 331-0708
Fax: (610) 520-4399
Rennie Andrews, Vice President for Recruitment & Admissions, Rosemont College, 1400 Montgomery Avenue, Rosemont, PA 19010

St. Charles Borromeo Seminary - Overbrook

Wynnewood, Pennsylvania
www.scs.edu **CB code: 2794**

- Private 4-year seminary college for men affiliated with Roman Catholic Church
- Residential campus in large town
- 59 degree-seeking undergraduates: 2% Asian American, 2% Hispanic American, 3% international
- 133 degree-seeking graduate students
- 100% of applicants admitted
- Application essay, interview required
- 83% graduate within 6 years; 100% enter graduate study

General. Founded in 1832. Regionally accredited; also accredited by ATS. College and theology divisions enroll full-time seminary students. Religious studies division enrolls part-time undergraduate and graduate students who wish to pursue theological studies. Part-time programs open to men and women. **Degrees:** 12 bachelor's awarded; master's, first professional offered. **Location:** 4 miles from central Philadelphia. **Calendar:** Semester, limited summer session. **Full-time faculty:** 19 total; 68% have terminal degrees, 10% women. **Part-time faculty:** 12 total; 42% have terminal degrees, 8% minority, 25% women. **Class size:** 97% < 20, 3% 20-39. **Special facilities:** Rare book and special collections.

Freshman class profile. 9 applied, 9 admitted, 8 enrolled.

End year in good standing:	100%	**Out-of-state:**	50%
Return as sophomores:	82%	**Live on campus:**	100%

Basis for selection. Sponsorship by diocese or religious community required for admission to college and theology divisions. Seminary applicants holding bachelor's degree from accredited institution may enter special pretheology program. SAT or ACT recommended. **Homeschooled:** Transcript of courses and grades, letter of recommendation (nonparent) required.

High school preparation. 20 units recommended. Recommended units include English 4, mathematics 3, social studies 3, science 3 and foreign language 3. 3 to 4 units of religious education recommended. GED accepted on individual basis.

2005-2006 Annual costs. Tuition/fees: $11,175. Room/board: $7,500. Books/supplies: $800. Personal expenses: $500.

Application procedures. Admission: Priority date 3/1; deadline 7/15. No application fee. Admission notification on a rolling basis beginning on or about 4/1. Level of admission dependent on academic background in philosophy, theology, and classical languages.

Academics. Strong emphasis on philosophy, theology, classical languages, and liberal arts. **Special study options:** Accelerated study, ESL, independent study. **Credit/placement by examination:** AP, CLEP, institutional tests. 30 credit hours maximum toward bachelor's degree. **Support services:** Reduced course load, tutoring.

Majors. Philosophy/religion: Philosophy.

Computing on campus. 60 workstations in library, computer center. Online library available.

Student life. Freshman orientation: Mandatory. **Policies:** Religious observance required. Freshmen permitted cars on campus. **Housing:** Guaranteed on-campus for all undergraduates. Substance-free housing available. On-campus housing available for seminarians in college and theology divisions. On-campus housing available to students in religious studies division during summer session. **Activities:** Choral groups, drama, music ensembles, student government, student newspaper, Seminarians for Life.

Athletics. Intramural: Basketball M, football (tackle) M, soccer M, volleyball M.

Student services. Campus ministries, financial aid counseling, health services, personal counseling.

Contact. Phone: (610) 785-6271 Fax: (610) 617-9267
Msgr. Michael Fitzgerald, Vice Rector, St. Charles Borromeo Seminary - Overbrook, 100 East Wynnewood Road, Wynnewood, PA 19096

St. Francis University

Loretto, Pennsylvania **CB member**
www.francis.edu **CB code: 2797**

- Private 4-year university and liberal arts college affiliated with Roman Catholic Church
- Residential campus in rural community
- 1,360 degree-seeking undergraduates: 8% part-time, 61% women
- 513 degree-seeking graduate students
- 91% of applicants admitted
- SAT or ACT (ACT writing optional) required
- 60% graduate within 6 years

General. Founded in 1847. Regionally accredited. **Degrees:** 295 bachelor's, 4 associate awarded; master's, doctoral offered. **ROTC:** Army, Navy, Air Force. **Location:** 90 miles from Pittsburgh, 20 miles from Altoona. **Calendar:** Semester, limited summer session. **Full-time faculty:** 90 total. **Part-time faculty:** 75 total. **Class size:** 48% < 20, 46% 20-39, 6% 40-49, less than 1% 50-99. **Special facilities:** Nature trail, center for excellence in rural medically underserved areas, small business development center, center for social justice.

Freshman class profile. 1,246 applied, 1,132 admitted, 366 enrolled.

Mid 50% test scores		**Rank in top tenth:**	22%
SAT verbal:	470-570	**Return as sophomores:**	83%
SAT math:	480-580	**Out-of-state:**	27%
ACT:	19-26	**Live on campus:**	74%
Rank in top quarter:	28%		

Basis for selection. High school record most important, followed by counselor's recommendations, test scores, major area of interest, activities, honors. Relationship to alumni also considered. Campus visit highly recommended. Essay, interview recommended.

High school preparation. College-preparatory program recommended. Required and recommended units include English 4, mathematics 2-4, social studies 2, science 1, foreign language 2 and academic electives 7. One natural science for nonscience majors, 2 for science majors also required. One science unit must include laboratory. Remaining units in academic electives. 4 mathematics and 2 science required for physician assistant and occupational therapy. 4 mathematics and 4 science required for physical therapy.

2006-2007 Annual costs. Tuition/fees (projected): $22,428. Room/board: $7,946. Books/supplies: $800. Personal expenses: $1,250.

2005-2006 Financial aid. Need-based: 66% of total undergraduate aid awarded as scholarships/grants, 34% as loans/jobs. **Non-need-based:** Scholarships awarded for academics, alumni affiliation, athletics, music/drama, religious affiliation.

Application procedures. Admission: Priority date 7/6; no deadline. $30 fee, may be waived for applicants with need. Application may be submitted online. Admission notification on a rolling basis beginning on or about 10/6. Must reply by May 1 or within 2 week(s) if notified thereafter. Application closing date for physical therapy, occupational therapy and physican assistant January 15. Notification by February 1. **Financial aid:** Priority date 5/1; no closing date. FAFSA required. Applicants notified on a rolling basis starting 3/1.

Academics. Special study options: Combined bachelor's/graduate degree, cooperative education, distance learning, double major, honors, independent study, internships, liberal arts/career combination, semester at sea, student-designed major, study abroad, teacher certification program, Washington semester. **Credit/placement by examination:** AP, CLEP, IB, SAT, ACT, institutional tests. 15 credit hours maximum toward associate degree, 30 toward bachelor's. **Support services:** Learning center, pre-admission summer program, reduced course load, remedial instruction, study skills assistance, tutoring, writing center.

Honors college/program. 3.25 GPA, 1100 SAT (exclusive of Writing), and position in top 1/5 of high school class required. About 40 applicants admitted.

Majors. **Area/ethnic studies:** American, French. **Biology:** General, marine. **Business:** Accounting, business admin, finance, management information systems, marketing. **Communications:** General, public relations. **Computer sciences:** General, computer science, information systems, programming. **Conservation:** Environmental science, environmental studies, forest management, forestry. **Education:** General, biology, chemistry, elementary, English, foreign languages, French, history, mathematics, multi-level teacher, psychology, secondary, social science, social studies, Spanish, special, speech. **Engineering:** General. **English:** English lit. **Foreign languages:** General, French, Spanish. **Health:** Clinical lab technology, nursing (RN), physician assistant. **History:** General. **Interdisciplinary:** Math/computer science. **Math:** General. **Philosophy/religion:** Philosophy, religion. **Physical sciences:** Chemistry. **Psychology:** General. **Public administration:** General, social work. **Social sciences:** Economics, political science, sociology.

Most popular majors. Business/marketing 32%, education 7%, health sciences 24%.

Computing on campus. PC or laptop required. 60 workstations in dormitories, library, computer center, student center. Dormitories wired for high-speed internet access and linked to campus network. Commuter students can connect to campus network. Online library, helpline, wireless network available.

Student life. **Freshman orientation:** Mandatory. Preregistration for classes offered. Held at various times during spring and summer. **Policies:** Freshmen permitted cars on campus. **Housing:** Guaranteed on-campus for all undergraduates. Single-sex dorms, special housing for disabled, apartments, fraternity/sorority housing, substance-free housing available. $100 deposit. All students required to live on campus until 21st birthday unless commuter status or a senior by September 1 of academic year. **Activities:** Concert band, choral groups, drama, radio station, student government, student newspaper, TV station, Secular Franciscan Order, student activities organization, multicultural awareness club, Historians' Round Table, Knights of Columbus, Peace and Justice Center, current affairs club, pro-life club, prelaw club.

Athletics. NCAA. **Intercollegiate:** Basketball, cross-country, diving W, field hockey W, football (tackle) M, golf, lacrosse W, soccer, softball W, swimming W, tennis, track and field, volleyball. **Intramural:** Basketball, cross-country, football (non-tackle), golf, skiing, soccer, softball, swimming, table tennis, tennis, track and field, volleyball. **Team name:** Red Flash.

Student services. Adult student services, alcohol/substance abuse counseling, campus ministries, career counseling, student employment services, financial aid counseling, health services, minority student services, personal counseling, placement for graduates, veterans' counselor.

Contact. E-mail: admissions@francis.edu
Phone: (814) 472-3100 Toll-free number: (800) 342-5732
Fax: (814) 472-3335
Erin McCloskey, Dean for Enrollment Management, St. Francis University, Box 600, Loretto, PA 15940

St. Joseph's University

Philadelphia, Pennsylvania — **CB member**
www.sju.edu — **CB code: 2801**

- Private 4-year university affiliated with Roman Catholic Church
- Residential campus in very large city
- 4,979 degree-seeking undergraduates: 15% part-time, 53% women, 8% African American, 3% Asian American, 3% Hispanic American, 1% international
- 2,138 degree-seeking graduate students
- 47% of applicants admitted
- SAT or ACT (ACT writing optional), application essay required
- 76% graduate within 6 years; 20% enter graduate study

General. Founded in 1851. Regionally accredited. **Degrees:** 918 bachelor's, 12 associate awarded; master's, doctoral offered. **ROTC:** Army, Navy, Air Force. **Location:** 8 miles from downtown. **Calendar:** Semester, extensive summer session. **Full-time faculty:** 269 total; 88% have terminal degrees, 10% minority, 40% women. **Part-time faculty:** 329 total; 8% minority, 40% women. **Class size:** 37% < 20, 58% 20-39, 4% 40-49, 1% 50-99, less than 1% >100.

Freshman class profile. 9,021 applied, 4,282 admitted, 1,140 enrolled.

Mid 50% test scores			
SAT verbal:	520-620	Rank in top quarter:	78%
SAT math:	530-630	Rank in top tenth:	24%
ACT:	22-24	End year in good standing:	93%
GPA 3.50 or higher:	34%	Return as sophomores:	89%
GPA 3.0-3.49:	38%	Out-of-state:	56%
GPA 2.0-2.99:	28%	Live on campus:	93%
		International:	1%

Basis for selection. GED not accepted. Careful consideration is given to the applicant's high school curriculum, extra-curricular activities, recalculated academic grade point average, and standardized test scores. Preference is given to those applicants who have taken a more demanding curriculum, maintained a B grade point average, and rank in the upper 40% of their high school class.

High school preparation. 12 units required; 20 recommended. Required and recommended units include English 4, mathematics 3-4, history 1-4, science 2-4 (laboratory 1) and foreign language 2-4.

2005-2006 Annual costs. Tuition/fees: $27,455. Room/board: $9,940. Books/supplies: $1,500. Personal expenses: $2,500.

2005-2006 Financial aid. **Need-based:** 793 full-time freshmen applied for aid; 593 were judged to have need; 593 of these received aid. Average need met was 79%. Average scholarship/grant was $8,729; average loan $4,125. 50% of total undergraduate aid awarded as scholarships/grants, 50% as loans/jobs. **Non-need-based:** Awarded to 2,817 full-time undergraduates, including 707 freshmen. Scholarships awarded for academics, art, athletics, minority status, music/drama, ROTC.

Application procedures. **Admission:** Priority date 11/15; deadline 2/1 (postmark date). $55 fee, may be waived for applicants with need. Application may be submitted online. Admission notification 3/15. Must reply by 5/1. Housing deposit partially refundable only through May 1. **Financial aid:** Priority date 2/15, closing date 5/1. FAFSA required. Applicants notified on a rolling basis starting 2/15; must reply by 5/1.

Academics. **Special study options:** Accelerated study, combined bachelor's/graduate degree, cooperative education, distance learning, double major, dual enrollment of high school students, ESL, honors, independent study, internships, student-designed major, study abroad, teacher certification program, Washington semester, weekend college. Jesuit student exchange. **Credit/placement by examination:** AP, CLEP, IB, institutional tests. **Support services:** Learning center, pre-admission summer program, reduced course load, study skills assistance, tutoring, writing center.

Majors. **Area/ethnic studies:** European, French. **Biology:** General, biochemistry. **Business:** Accounting, actuarial science, business admin, finance, international, international marketing, management information systems, marketing, purchasing, special products marketing. **Communications:** General. **Computer sciences:** General, information systems. **Conservation:** Environmental studies. **Education:** Elementary, English, foreign languages, mathematics, science, secondary, social studies, special. **English:** English lit. **Foreign languages:** French, German, Italian, Latin, Spanish. **Health:** Facilities admin, health services. **History:** General. **Legal studies:** General. **Liberal arts:** Humanities. **Math:** General. **Philosophy/religion:** Philosophy, religion. **Physical sciences:** Chemistry, physics. **Psychology:** General. **Public administration:** General. **Social sciences:** General, criminology, economics, international relations, political science, sociology. **Visual/performing arts:** General.

Most popular majors. Business/marketing 45%, education 9%, English 7%, psychology 7%, social sciences 15%.

Computing on campus. 408 workstations in dormitories, library, computer center, student center. Dormitories wired for high-speed internet access and linked to campus network. Commuter students can connect to campus network. Online course registration, online library, helpline, repair service, student web hosting, wireless network available.

Student life. **Freshman orientation:** Available, $200 fee. **Housing:** Guaranteed on-campus for freshmen. Coed dorms, single-sex dorms, apartments, substance-free housing available. $400 partly refundable deposit, deadline 5/1. Special accommodations may be arranged for disabled students based upon need. **Activities:** Bands, choral groups, dance, drama, film society, literary magazine, musical theater, radio station, student government, student newspaper, black student union, international student association, Hand-in-Hand, College Democrats, College Republicans, Asian student association, Up-Til-Dawn, Project Mexico, Habitat for Humanity, Students for Life.

Athletics. NCAA. **Intercollegiate:** Baseball M, basketball, cheerleading, cross-country, field hockey W, golf M, lacrosse, rowing (crew), soccer, softball W, tennis, track and field. **Intramural:** Basketball, football (non-tackle), golf M, rugby, soccer, softball, tennis, volleyball. **Team name:** Hawks.

Student services. Adult student services, alcohol/substance abuse counseling, campus ministries, career counseling, services for economically disadvantaged, student employment services, financial aid counseling, health services, minority student services, personal counseling, women's services. **Physically disabled:** Services for visually, speech, hearing impaired. **Learning disabled:** Comprehensive services available.

Contact. E-mail: admit@sju.edu
Phone: (610) 660-1300 Toll-free number: (888) 232-4295
Fax: (610) 660-1314
Susan Kassab, Director of Admissions, St. Joseph's University, 5600 City Avenue, Philadelphia, PA 19131

St. Vincent College

Latrobe, Pennsylvania — **CB member**
www.stvincent.edu — **CB code: 2808**

- Private 4-year liberal arts college affiliated with Roman Catholic Church
- Residential campus in large town
- 1,483 degree-seeking undergraduates: 2% part-time, 52% women, 2% African American, 1% Asian American, 1% Hispanic American, 1% international
- 111 degree-seeking graduate students
- 73% of applicants admitted
- SAT or ACT (ACT writing optional), application essay required
- 69% graduate within 6 years; 35% enter graduate study

General. Founded in 1846. Regionally accredited. Affiliated with Order of Saint Benedict. **Degrees:** 262 bachelor's awarded; master's offered. **ROTC:** Air Force. **Location:** 35 miles from Pittsburgh. **Calendar:** Semester, extensive summer session. **Full-time faculty:** 95 total; 78% have terminal degrees, 2% minority, 21% women. **Part-time faculty:** 72 total; 26% have terminal degrees, 39% women. **Class size:** 44% < 20, 55% 20-39, 1% 40-49. **Special facilities:** Planetarium, observatory, radio telescope, wetlands program, rare book collection, spectrophotometer, spectrometer, physiograph workstations.

Freshman class profile. 1,488 applied, 1,088 admitted, 483 enrolled.

Mid 50% test scores			
SAT verbal:	480-590	**Rank in top quarter:**	53%
SAT math:	480-590	**Rank in top tenth:**	21%
ACT:	19-24	**End year in good standing:**	83%
GPA 3.50 or higher:	56%	**Return as sophomores:**	89%
GPA 3.0-3.49:	29%	**Out-of-state:**	10%
GPA 2.0-2.99:	14%	**Live on campus:**	91%
		International:	1%

Basis for selection. High school curriculum and grades most important; class rank, test scores, and essay important. Recommendations from school counselor considered. Interview recommended for all; audition required for music, theater programs; portfolio required for art, art therapy programs. **Learning Disabled:** All prior test results related to learning disability should be submitted.

High school preparation. 16 units required; 20 recommended. Required and recommended units include English 4, mathematics 3, social studies 3, science 1-3 (laboratory 1), foreign language 2 and academic electives 5. One plane geometry, 1 intermediate algebra, .5 trigonometry, and 1 physics required for 3-2 engineering program applicants.

2005-2006 Annual costs. Tuition/fees: $21,679. Room/board: $7,348. Books/supplies: $1,300.

2005-2006 Financial aid. Need-based: 480 full-time freshmen applied for aid; 392 were judged to have need; 392 of these received aid. Average need met was 93%. Average scholarship/grant was $12,849; average loan $1,905. 74% of total undergraduate aid awarded as scholarships/grants, 26% as loans/jobs. **Non-need-based:** Awarded to 1,567 full-time undergraduates, including 556 freshmen. Scholarships awarded for academics, leadership, minority status, music/drama.

Application procedures. Admission: Priority date 2/1; deadline 5/1 (postmark date). $25 fee, may be waived for applicants with need. Application may be submitted online. Admission notification on a rolling basis beginning on or about 10/1. Must reply by May 1 or within 3 week(s) if notified thereafter. **Financial aid:** Priority date 3/1, closing date 5/1. FAFSA required. Applicants notified on a rolling basis starting 3/1; must reply within 2 week(s) of notification.

Academics. College attempts to place career orientation in context of broader human and religious values with emphasis on liberal arts core curriculum. **Special study options:** Accelerated study, combined bachelor's/graduate degree, cooperative education, cross-registration, double major, dual enrollment of high school students, honors, independent study, internships, liberal arts/career combination, study abroad, teacher certification program. 3-2 engineering BA/BS program with University of Pittsburgh, Boston University, Catholic University of America, Pennsylvania State; 4-1 BS/MBA, 3-3 BA/JD, 3-2 occupational therapy, physical therapy, and physician's assistant, 2-4 pharmacy programs with Duquesne University; 3-4 podiatry with Ohio College of Pediatric Medicine and Pennsylvania College of Pediatric Medicine. **Credit/placement by examination:** AP, CLEP, IB, institutional tests. 62 credit hours maximum toward bachelor's degree. **Support services:** Learning center, pre-admission summer program, reduced course load, remedial instruction, study skills assistance, tutoring, writing center.

Majors. Biology: General, biochemistry, bioinformatics. **Business:** Accounting, business admin, finance, international, marketing. **Communications:** General. **Communications technology:** General. **Computer sciences:** General. **Conservation:** General, environmental science, environmental studies, management/policy. **Education:** Art, business, physics, psychology. **Engineering:** General. **English:** English lit. **Foreign languages:** French, Spanish. **Health:** Office assistant, predentistry, premedicine, prepharmacy, preveterinary. **History:** General. **Legal studies:** Prelaw. **Liberal arts:** Arts/sciences. **Math:** General. **Philosophy/religion:** Philosophy. **Physical sciences:** Chemistry, physics. **Psychology:** General. **Public administration:** Policy analysis. **Social sciences:** Anthropology, economics, political science, sociology. **Theology:** Religious ed, theology. **Visual/performing arts:** Art history/conservation, graphic design, music performance, studio arts.

Most popular majors. Biology 8%, business/marketing 21%, communications/journalism 12%, computer/information sciences 7%, history 8%, psychology 15%, social sciences 9%.

Computing on campus. 228 workstations in dormitories, library, computer center, student center. Dormitories wired for high-speed internet access and linked to campus network. Commuter students can connect to campus network. Online course registration, helpline, wireless network available.

Student life. Freshman orientation: Mandatory, $125 fee. Preregistration for classes offered. 6 weeks of activities to acclimate students to college on academic and social levels. **Policies:** Freshmen permitted cars on campus. **Housing:** Guaranteed on-campus for all undergraduates. Coed dorms available. $100 nonrefundable deposit, deadline 5/1. Single occupancy quiet study residence available. **Activities:** Pep band, choral groups, dance, drama, literary magazine, music ensembles, radio station, student government, student newspaper, TV station, campus ministry, pro-life club, Student Democrats, College Republicans, academic/social action/special interest groups, prelaw club, student educational association.

Athletics. NCAA. **Intercollegiate:** Baseball M, basketball, cross-country, field hockey W, golf, lacrosse, soccer, softball W, swimming, tennis, volleyball W. **Intramural:** Basketball, football (non-tackle), softball, table tennis, volleyball. **Team name:** Bearcats.

Student services. Adult student services, alcohol/substance abuse counseling, campus ministries, career counseling, student employment services, financial aid counseling, health services, on-campus daycare, personal counseling, placement for graduates. **Physically disabled:** Services for visually, speech, hearing impaired. **Learning disabled:** Comprehensive services available.

Contact. E-mail: admission@stvincent.edu
Phone: (724) 537-4540 Toll-free number: (800) 782-5549
Fax: (724) 532-5069
David Collins, Assistant Vice President of Admission and Financial Aid, St. Vincent College, 300 Fraser Purchase Road, Latrobe, PA 15650-2690

Seton Hill University

Greensburg, Pennsylvania — **CB member**
www.setonhill.edu — **CB code: 2812**

- Private 4-year university and liberal arts college affiliated with Roman Catholic Church
- Residential campus in large town
- 1,427 degree-seeking undergraduates: 14% part-time, 63% women, 8% African American, 1% Asian American, 1% Hispanic American, 2% international
- 312 degree-seeking graduate students
- 70% of applicants admitted
- Application essay required
- 54% graduate within 6 years; 29% enter graduate study

General. Founded in 1918. Regionally accredited. **Degrees:** 199 bachelor's awarded; master's offered. **ROTC:** Army. **Location:** 35 miles from

Pittsburgh. **Calendar:** Semester, extensive summer session. **Full-time faculty:** 68 total; 85% have terminal degrees, 7% minority, 54% women. **Part-time faculty:** 117 total; 20% have terminal degrees, 4% minority, 61% women. **Class size:** 60% < 20, 39% 20-39, 1% 40-49. **Special facilities:** Child development center, kindergarten, National Center for Women in Business, National Catholic Center for Holocaust Education.

Freshman class profile. 2,133 applied, 1,500 admitted, 336 enrolled.

Mid 50% test scores			
SAT verbal:	460-550	Rank in top quarter:	39%
SAT math:	460-560	Rank in top tenth:	14%
ACT:	17-22	End year in good standing:	85%
GPA 3.50 or higher:	24%	Return as sophomores:	78%
GPA 3.0-3.49:	26%	Out-of-state:	28%
GPA 2.0-2.99:	49%	Live on campus:	89%
		International:	1%

Basis for selection. School achievement record most important, followed by test scores and recommendations. Applicants from minorities or low-income families encouraged, accepted on basis of motivation and potential. SAT or ACT recommended. Students who have not taken SAT or ACT may submit 2 graded writing samples for consideration. Interview recommended for all; audition required for music, theater programs; portfolio required for art program. Additional application required for physician assistant program. **Homeschooled:** Must provide SAT/ACT scores and official transcript issued by a school district or agency approving the curriculum, or GED.

High school preparation. 15 units required. Required and recommended units include English 4, mathematics 2, social studies 2, science 1 (laboratory 1), foreign language 2 and academic electives 4. 4 mathematics recommended for science majors.

2005-2006 Annual costs. Tuition/fees: $23,180. Room/board: $7,450. Books/supplies: $1,000. Personal expenses: $2,400.

2005-2006 Financial aid. **Need-based:** 334 full-time freshmen applied for aid; 328 were judged to have need; 328 of these received aid. Average need met was 83%. Average scholarship/grant was $13,200; average loan $3,291. 74% of total undergraduate aid awarded as scholarships/grants, 26% as loans/jobs. **Non-need-based:** Awarded to 162 full-time undergraduates, including 45 freshmen. Scholarships awarded for academics, alumni affiliation, art, athletics, job skills, music/drama, religious affiliation. **Additional information:** Up to half tuition reduction for students in top 10% of high school class. Up to one-third tuition reduction for students in top 20% of high school class. Up to 25% tuition reduction for students in top 30% of class.

Application procedures. **Admission:** Priority date 5/1; deadline 8/15 (receipt date). $35 fee, may be waived for applicants with need. Application may be submitted online. Admission notification on a rolling basis beginning on or about 9/1. **Financial aid:** Priority date 6/1; no closing date. FAFSA, institutional form required. Applicants notified on a rolling basis starting 11/1; must reply within 2 week(s) of notification.

Academics. **Special study options:** Accelerated study, combined bachelor's/graduate degree, cross-registration, distance learning, double major, ESL, exchange student, honors, independent study, internships, liberal arts/career combination, New York semester, student-designed major, study abroad, teacher certification program, United Nations semester, Washington semester, weekend college. **Credit/placement by examination:** AP, CLEP, IB, SAT, ACT, institutional tests. 30 credit hours maximum toward bachelor's degree. **Support services:** Learning center, pre-admission summer program, reduced course load, remedial instruction, study skills assistance, tutoring, writing center.

Majors. **Biology:** General, biochemistry. **Business:** Accounting, business admin, entrepreneurial studies, finance, hospitality admin, human resources, international, management information systems, marketing, sales/distribution. **Communications:** General, journalism. **Computer sciences:** Computer science. **Education:** Art, biology, chemistry, English, family/consumer sciences, foreign languages, mathematics, music, Spanish. **Engineering:** General. **English:** Creative writing, English lit. **Family/consumer sciences:** General, child care, child development. **Foreign languages:** Spanish. **Health:** Art therapy, clinical lab science, dietetics, music therapy, nursing (RN), physician assistant. **History:** General. **Legal studies:** Prelaw. **Math:** General. **Philosophy/religion:** Religion. **Physical sciences:** Chemistry, physics. **Protective services:** Criminal justice, forensics. **Psychology:** General. **Public administration:** Human services, social work. **Social sciences:** Economics, international relations, political science, sociology. **Theology:** Sacred music. **Visual/performing arts:** Acting, art history/conservation, arts management, ceramics, commercial/advertising art, dramatic, drawing, metal/jewelry, music performance, painting, printmaking, sculpture, studio arts, theater arts management, theater design.

Most popular majors. Business/marketing 33%, psychology 7%, public administration/social services 10%, social sciences 7%, visual/performing arts 11%.

Computing on campus. 250 workstations in dormitories, library, computer center, student center. Dormitories wired for high-speed internet access and linked to campus network. Commuter students can connect to campus network. Online course registration, helpline, repair service available.

Student life. **Freshman orientation:** Mandatory, $25 fee. Preregistration for classes offered. One-day, on-campus family orientation in summer includes student testing, advising, and registration. 4-day orientation during weekend and weekdays prior to start of classes. **Policies:** Residence hall students involved in setting community standards. Freshmen permitted cars on campus. **Housing:** Guaranteed on-campus for all undergraduates. Coed dorms, single-sex dorms available. **Activities:** Bands, choral groups, dance, drama, literary magazine, music ensembles, musical theater, student government, student newspaper, symphony orchestra, social work club, campus ministry, liturgical groups, Respect Life, Operation Christmas Basket, Association of Black Collegians, National Coalition Building Institute, intercultural student organization, Helping Hands.

Athletics. NAIA. **Intercollegiate:** Baseball M, basketball, cross-country, equestrian, field hockey W, football (tackle) M, golf, lacrosse, soccer, softball W, tennis, volleyball W. **Intramural:** Basketball W, equestrian, soccer W, softball W, table tennis W, volleyball W. **Team name:** Griffins.

Student services. Adult student services, alcohol/substance abuse counseling, campus ministries, career counseling, services for economically disadvantaged, student employment services, financial aid counseling, health services, minority student services, on-campus daycare, personal counseling, placement for graduates, veterans' counselor. **Physically disabled:** Services for visually, hearing impaired.

Contact. E-mail: admit@setonhill.edu
Phone: (724) 838-4255 Toll-free number: (800) 826-6234
Fax: (724) 830-1294
Kim McCarty, Director of Admissions and Adult Student Services, Seton Hill University, Seton Hill Drive, Greensburg, PA 15601

Shippensburg University of Pennsylvania

Shippensburg, Pennsylvania — **CB member**
www.ship.edu — **CB code: 2657**

- Public 4-year university
- Residential campus in small town
- 6,395 degree-seeking undergraduates: 4% part-time, 52% women, 5% African American, 1% Asian American, 2% Hispanic American
- 884 degree-seeking graduate students
- 66% of applicants admitted
- SAT or ACT (ACT writing optional) required
- 63% graduate within 6 years

General. Founded in 1871. Regionally accredited. **Degrees:** 1,397 bachelor's awarded; master's offered. **ROTC:** Army. **Location:** 40 miles from Harrisburg. **Calendar:** Semester, extensive summer session. **Full-time faculty:** 305 total; 87% have terminal degrees, 12% minority, 40% women. **Part-time faculty:** 66 total; 30% have terminal degrees, 6% minority, 62% women. **Class size:** 25% < 20, 62% 20-39, 13% 40-49, less than 1% 50-99. **Special facilities:** On-campus elementary school for student teachers, planetarium, vertebrate museum, greenhouse, herbarium, electron microscope, NMR spectrometer, fashion archives, interfaith spiritual center.

Freshman class profile. 6,281 applied, 4,131 admitted, 1,503 enrolled.

Mid 50% test scores			
SAT verbal:	470-570	Rank in top quarter:	30%
SAT math:	470-570	Rank in top tenth:	10%
		End year in good standing:	79%
GPA 3.50 or higher:	32%	Return as sophomores:	76%
GPA 3.0-3.49:	33%	Out-of-state:	5%
GPA 2.0-2.99:	34%	Live on campus:	91%

Basis for selection. Secondary school record and test scores important. Summer Bridge Program provides access and academic support to students who do not meet regular admission criteria but have demonstrated potential, desire, and motivation to succeed in college. Rolling date for test scores, but application cannot be considered for admission until they are received. Interviews advisable in some situations. **Homeschooled:** Transcript of courses and grades, state high school equivalency certificate required. Those working with accredited agency must submit copy of both annual evaluation and homeschool diploma. All others encouraged to schedule interview and present portfolio, and must provide GED results. **Learning Disabled:** Students must register with Office of Social Equity and provide documentation from qualified professional that verifies disability. Documentation must be less than 3 years old. Reasonable support services provided to students who have documented disabilities.

High school preparation. 15 units recommended. Recommended units include English 4, mathematics 3, social studies 3, science 3 (laboratory 3) and foreign language 2.

2005-2006 Annual costs. Tuition/fees: $6,175; $13,598 out-of-state. Room/board: $5,710. Books/supplies: $1,000. Personal expenses: $1,729.

2005-2006 Financial aid. Need-based: 1,243 full-time freshmen applied for aid; 804 were judged to have need; 766 of these received aid. Average need met was 64%. Average scholarship/grant was $4,115; average loan $2,755. 43% of total undergraduate aid awarded as scholarships/grants, 57% as loans/jobs. **Non-need-based:** Awarded to 2,349 full-time undergraduates, including 261 freshmen. Scholarships awarded for academics, athletics.

Application procedures. Admission: No deadline. $30 fee, may be waived for applicants with need. Application may be submitted online. Admission notification on a rolling basis. Must reply by April 1 or request a May 1 extension in writing. **Financial aid:** Priority date 3/15; no closing date. FAFSA required. Applicants notified on a rolling basis; must reply within 2 week(s) of notification.

Academics. Web-based online courses and programs also available. **Special study options:** Accelerated study, cooperative education, distance learning, double major, dual enrollment of high school students, honors, independent study, internships, study abroad, teacher certification program, Washington semester. **Credit/placement by examination:** AP, CLEP, IB, SAT, ACT, institutional tests. 30 credit hours maximum toward bachelor's degree. **Support services:** Learning center, pre-admission summer program, reduced course load, remedial instruction, study skills assistance, tutoring, writing center.

Majors. Biology: General. **Business:** Accounting, business admin, finance, management science, marketing. **Communications:** Journalism. **Computer sciences:** General, systems analysis. **Conservation:** Environmental studies. **Education:** Elementary. **English:** English lit, speech/rhetoric. **Foreign languages:** French, Spanish. **Health:** Health care admin. **History:** General. **Math:** General. **Parks/recreation:** Exercise sciences. **Physical sciences:** Chemistry, geology, physics. **Protective services:** Criminal justice. **Psychology:** General. **Public administration:** General, social work. **Social sciences:** Economics, geography, political science, sociology. **Visual/performing arts:** Art.

Most popular majors. Business/marketing 22%, communications/journalism 7%, computer/information sciences 7%, education 17%, English 6%, psychology 6%, security/protective services 7%.

Computing on campus. 750 workstations in dormitories, library, computer center, student center. Dormitories wired for high-speed internet access and linked to campus network. Commuter students can connect to campus network. Online course registration, online library, helpline, wireless network available.

Student life. Freshman orientation: Mandatory, $50 fee. Orientation held in summer and prior to fall and spring semesters. **Policies:** University Student Code of Conduct. Freshmen permitted cars on campus. **Housing:** Guaranteed on-campus for freshmen. Coed dorms, single-sex dorms, special housing for disabled, apartments, substance-free housing available. $100 partly refundable deposit, deadline 4/1. **Activities:** Bands, choral groups, dance, drama, literary magazine, music ensembles, musical theater, radio station, student government, student newspaper, symphony orchestra, TV station, African American student organization, Fellowship of Christian Athletes, Christian Fellowship, Jewish student organization, Big Brother-Big Sister, United Campus Ministry, international student organization, nontraditional student organization, Latino student organization, Asian student organization.

Athletics. NCAA. **Intercollegiate:** Baseball M, basketball, cross-country, field hockey W, football (tackle) M, lacrosse W, soccer, softball W, swimming, tennis W, track and field, volleyball W, wrestling M. **Intramural:** Basketball, bowling, cross-country M, football (tackle) M, golf M, racquetball, softball, table tennis M, tennis W, volleyball, wrestling M. **Team name:** Raiders.

Student services. Adult student services, campus ministries, career counseling, student employment services, financial aid counseling, health services, minority student services, on-campus daycare, personal counseling, placement for graduates, veterans' counselor, women's services. **Physically disabled:** Services for visually, hearing impaired.

Contact. E-mail: admiss@ship.edu
Phone: (717) 477-1231 Toll-free number: (800) 822-8028
Fax: (717) 477-4016
Thomas Speakman, Dean of Enrollment Services, Shippensburg University of Pennsylvania, 1871 Old Main Drive, Shippensburg, PA 17257-2299

Slippery Rock University of Pennsylvania

Slippery Rock, Pennsylvania — **CB member**
www.sru.edu — **CB code: 2658**

- Public 4-year university
- Residential campus in rural community
- 7,336 degree-seeking undergraduates: 6% part-time, 55% women, 4% African American, 1% Asian American, 1% Hispanic American, 1% international
- 649 degree-seeking graduate students
- 41% of applicants admitted
- SAT or ACT (ACT writing optional) required
- 51% graduate within 6 years; 18% enter graduate study

General. Founded in 1889. Regionally accredited. **Degrees:** 1,559 bachelor's awarded; master's, doctoral offered. **ROTC:** Army. **Location:** 50 miles from Pittsburgh. **Calendar:** Semester, extensive summer session. **Full-time faculty:** 367 total; 80% have terminal degrees, 17% minority, 45% women. **Part-time faculty:** 34 total; 18% have terminal degrees, 9% minority, 59% women. **Class size:** 25% < 20, 53% 20-39, 16% 40-49, 5% 50-99, 3% >100. **Special facilities:** Environmental education centers.

Freshman class profile. 4,360 applied, 1,777 admitted, 1,455 enrolled.

Mid 50% test scores		**Rank in top tenth:**	8%
SAT verbal:	450-530	**End year in good standing:**	88%
SAT math:	450-550	**Return as sophomores:**	77%
ACT:	18-23	**Out-of-state:**	10%
GPA 3.50 or higher:	32%	**Live on campus:**	91%
GPA 3.0-3.49:	37%	**International:**	1%
GPA 2.0-2.99:	31%	**Fraternities:**	2%
Rank in top quarter:	28%	**Sororities:**	5%

Basis for selection. Recommended minimum 2.5 GPA, or 76 percent or higher average. Minimum score of 900 SAT or 20 ACT recommended. Interview recommended for all; audition required for dance, music, music education, and music therapy programs. **Homeschooled:** Documentation of homeschool diploma or certification information regarding how homeschool material covered required.

High school preparation. 16 units recommended. Recommended units include English 4, mathematics 3, social studies 3, history 3, science 3 (laboratory 1) and foreign language 2.

2005-2006 Annual costs. Tuition/fees: $6,211; $13,571 out-of-state. Room/board: $4,980. Books/supplies: $1,100. Personal expenses: $1,000.

2005-2006 Financial aid. Need-based: 1,355 full-time freshmen applied for aid; 928 were judged to have need; 915 of these received aid. Average need met was 77%. Average scholarship/grant was $3,300; average loan $2,352. 45% of total undergraduate aid awarded as scholarships/grants, 55% as loans/jobs. **Non-need-based:** Awarded to 2,602 full-time undergraduates, including 732 freshmen. Scholarships awarded for academics, alumni affiliation, art, athletics, job skills, leadership, minority status, music/drama, ROTC, state residency. **Additional information:** May 1 closing date for Pennsylvania state grants.

Application procedures. Admission: No deadline. $25 fee, may be waived for applicants with need. Application may be submitted online. Admission notification on a rolling basis beginning on or about 9/1. Must reply by May 1 or within 4 week(s) if notified thereafter. **Financial aid:** Priority date 5/1; no closing date. FAFSA required. Applicants notified on a rolling basis starting 3/15; must reply within 4 week(s) of notification.

Academics. Special study options: Combined bachelor's/graduate degree, distance learning, double major, exchange student, honors, independent study, internships, liberal arts/career combination, study abroad, teacher certification program. **Credit/placement by examination:** AP, CLEP, IB, SAT, ACT, institutional tests. 45 credit hours maximum toward bachelor's degree. **Support services:** Learning center, pre-admission summer program, reduced course load, remedial instruction, study skills assistance, tutoring, writing center.

Majors. Biology: General. **Business:** Business admin. **Communications:** General. **Computer sciences:** General, information technology. **Conservation:** General. **Education:** Elementary, special. **Engineering technology:** Occupational safety. **English:** English lit. **Foreign languages:** French, Spanish. **Health:** Athletic training, clinical lab technology, clinical/medical social work, cytotechnology, music therapy, nursing (RN). **History:** General. **Interdisciplinary:** Science/society. **Math:** General. **Parks/recreation:** Facilities management, health/fitness. **Philosophy/religion:** Philosophy. **Physical sciences:** Chemistry, geology, physics. **Psychology:** General. **Public administration:** Social work. **Social sciences:** Economics, geography, political science, sociology. **Visual/performing arts:** Art, dance, dramatic, music performance.

Most popular majors. Business/marketing 15%, communication technologies 7%, education 19%, health sciences 12%, parks/recreation 11%, social sciences 9%, visual/performing arts 6%.

Computing on campus. 1,050 workstations in dormitories, library, computer center, student center. Dormitories wired for high-speed internet access and linked to campus network. Commuter students can connect to campus network. Online course registration, online library, helpline, repair service available.

Student life. Freshman orientation: Mandatory, $80 fee. Preregistration for classes offered. Several sessions held during summer months. **Policies:** Freshmen permitted cars on campus. **Housing:** Guaranteed on-campus for freshmen. Coed dorms, single-sex dorms, special housing for disabled, apartments, fraternity/sorority housing, substance-free housing available. $150 partly refundable deposit. Special interest residence hall floors in education, humanities and fine arts, honors, wellness, technology, math/science, intensive study, ROTC, nontraditional/grad available. **Activities:** Bands, choral groups, dance, drama, literary magazine, music ensembles, musical theater, radio station, student government, student newspaper, symphony orchestra, TV station, Amnesty International, Black Action Society, Campus Crusade for Christ, Catholic campus ministry, environmental science society, international club, Latino student organization.

Athletics. NCAA. **Intercollegiate:** Baseball M, basketball, cheerleading, cross-country, diving, field hockey W, football (tackle) M, golf, soccer, softball W, swimming, tennis, track and field, volleyball W, water polo, wrestling M. **Intramural:** Badminton, basketball, cross-country, diving, football (non-tackle), golf, racquetball, soccer, softball, swimming, tennis, track and field, triathlon, volleyball, water polo, weight lifting, wrestling. **Team name:** Pride.

Student services. Adult student services, alcohol/substance abuse counseling, campus ministries, career counseling, services for economically disadvantaged, student employment services, financial aid counseling, health services, legal services, minority student services, on-campus daycare, personal counseling, placement for graduates, veterans' counselor, women's services. **Physically disabled:** Services for visually, speech, hearing impaired.

Contact. E-mail: asktherock@sru.edu
Phone: (724) 738-2015 Toll-free number: (800) 778-9111
Fax: (724) 738-2913
Mimi Conner, Associate Director of Admissions, Slippery Rock University of Pennsylvania, 1 Morrow Way, Slippery Rock, PA 16057-1383

Susquehanna University

Selinsgrove, Pennsylvania — **CB member**
www.susqu.edu — **CB code: 2820**

- Private 4-year university and liberal arts college affiliated with Evangelical Lutheran Church in America
- Residential campus in small town
- 1,898 degree-seeking undergraduates: 1% part-time, 55% women, 3% African American, 2% Asian American, 2% Hispanic American, 1% international
- 81% of applicants admitted
- Application essay required
- 80% graduate within 6 years; 21% enter graduate study

General. Founded in 1858. Regionally accredited. Associate degrees available in evening and only to residents of the greater Selinsgrove area. **Degrees:** 515 bachelor's awarded. **ROTC:** Army. **Location:** 50 miles from Harrisburg, 150 miles from Philadelphia. **Calendar:** Semester, limited summer session. **Full-time faculty:** 122 total; 90% have terminal degrees, 15% minority, 40% women. **Part-time faculty:** 63 total; 30% have terminal degrees, 6% minority, 51% women. **Class size:** 49% < 20, 50% 20-39, less than 1% 40-49. **Special facilities:** Ecology field station, film library, music library, rare book room, 24-hour study center, arboretum, observatory, 450-seat teaching theater, child development center, satellite dishes, distribution system for foreign language broadcasts, video conferencing facility, high technology center for business and communications.

Freshman class profile. 2,217 applied, 1,801 admitted, 512 enrolled.

Mid 50% test scores		**End year in good standing:**	91%
SAT verbal:	530-610	**Return as sophomores:**	85%
SAT math:	520-640	**Out-of-state:**	43%
Rank in top quarter:	63%	**Live on campus:**	97%
Rank in top tenth:	30%		

Basis for selection. School record and class rank most important, test scores secondary. Application essay, interview, teacher and counselor evaluations, activities, and interest in the university considered. Students have option of submitting 2 graded writing samples in place of SAT or ACT scores. Interview highly recommended for all; audition required for music majors; portfolio required for writing majors. **Homeschooled:** Student should have detailed description of course work taken.

High school preparation. 18 units required; 25 recommended. Required and recommended units include English 4, mathematics 3-4, social studies 1-3, history 1, science 3-4 (laboratory 2-3), foreign language 2-3 and academic electives 2-3.

2005-2006 Annual costs. Tuition/fees: $26,265. Room/board: $7,200. Books/supplies: $700. Personal expenses: $700.

2005-2006 Financial aid. Need-based: 418 full-time freshmen applied for aid; 338 were judged to have need; 336 of these received aid. Average need met was 79%. Average scholarship/grant was $14,709; average loan $3,238. 74% of total undergraduate aid awarded as scholarships/grants, 26% as loans/jobs. **Non-need-based:** Awarded to 653 full-time undergraduates, including 194 freshmen. Scholarships awarded for academics, alumni affiliation, leadership, minority status, music/drama, ROTC. **Additional information:** Graduated pay scale for federal work-study program.

Application procedures. Admission: Closing date 3/1 (postmark date). $35 fee, may be waived for applicants with need. Application may be submitted online. Admission notification on a rolling basis beginning on or about 1/15. Must reply by May 1 or within 2 week(s) if notified thereafter. **Financial aid:** Priority date 3/1, closing date 5/1. FAFSA, CSS PROFILE required. Applicants notified on a rolling basis starting 2/15; must reply by 5/1.

Academics. Special study options: Accelerated study, combined bachelor's/graduate degree, cross-registration, distance learning, double major, dual enrollment of high school students, exchange student, honors, independent study, internships, liberal arts/career combination, semester at sea, student-designed major, study abroad, teacher certification program, United Nations semester, urban semester, Washington semester. Internships abroad, 3-2 forestry or environmental management with Duke University, semester in London for junior business majors, 150-hour option in accounting to meet American Institute of CPA requirements, dentistry with Temple University, 2-2 allied health with Thomas Jefferson University. **Credit/placement by examination:** AP, CLEP, IB, SAT, institutional tests. 30 credit hours maximum toward associate degree, 65 toward bachelor's. **Support services:** Reduced course load, study skills assistance, tutoring, writing center.

Majors. Biology: General, biochemistry, ecology. **Business:** General, accounting, business admin, finance, human resources, marketing. **Communications:** General, broadcast journalism, journalism, media studies, public relations. **Computer sciences:** Computer science, information systems. **Conservation:** Environmental science. **Education:** Early childhood, elementary, music. **English:** Creative writing. **Foreign languages:** French, German, Spanish. **Health:** Predentistry, premedicine, preveterinary. **History:** General. **Interdisciplinary:** Global studies. **Legal studies:** Prelaw. **Math:** General. **Philosophy/religion:** Philosophy, religion. **Physical sciences:** Chemistry, physics. **Psychology:** General. **Social sciences:** Economics, political science, sociology. **Theology:** Preministerial, sacred music, theology. **Visual/performing arts:** Art, art history/conservation, graphic design, music performance, music theory/composition, piano/organ, stringed instruments, voice/opera.

Most popular majors. Business/marketing 31%, communications/journalism 11%, education 12%, psychology 7%, social sciences 8%.

Computing on campus. 305 workstations in dormitories, library, computer center, student center. Dormitories wired for high-speed internet access and linked to campus network. Commuter students can connect to campus network. Online course registration, online library, helpline, student web hosting available.

Student life. Freshman orientation: Mandatory. Preregistration for classes offered. Four-day program; includes community service projects. **Policies:** Freshmen permitted cars on campus. **Housing:** Guaranteed on-campus for all undergraduates. Coed dorms, single-sex dorms, apartments, fraternity/sorority housing, substance-free housing available. $400 nonrefundable deposit, deadline 5/1. Volunteer services living groups, scholars' house, international student house, townhouses and apartments available. **Activities:**

Bands, choral groups, dance, drama, film society, literary magazine, music ensembles, musical theater, opera, radio station, student government, student newspaper, symphony orchestra, volunteer services program, international club, Habitat for Humanity, Student Environmental Action Coalition, Hispanic and Latino, Black, and Asian student organizations, Amnesty International, astronomy club, investment club, Hillel, WomenSpeak.

Athletics. NCAA. **Intercollegiate:** Baseball M, basketball, cross-country, field hockey W, football (tackle) M, golf, lacrosse, rowing (crew), soccer, softball W, swimming, tennis, track and field, volleyball W. **Intramural:** Baseball M, basketball, football (non-tackle), ice hockey M, racquetball, soccer, softball, tennis, volleyball. **Team name:** Crusaders.

Student services. Adult student services, alcohol/substance abuse counseling, campus ministries, career counseling, student employment services, financial aid counseling, health services, minority student services, on-campus daycare, personal counseling, placement for graduates, veterans' counselor, women's services. **Physically disabled:** Services for visually impaired.

Contact. E-mail: suadmiss@susqu.edu
Phone: (570) 372-4260 Toll-free number: (800) 326-9672
Fax: (570) 372-2722
Chris Markle, Director of Admissions, Susquehanna University, 514 University Avenue, Selinsgrove, PA 17870-1040

Swarthmore College

Swarthmore, Pennsylvania — **CB member**
www.swarthmore.edu — **CB code: 2821**

- Private 4-year liberal arts college
- Residential campus in small town
- 1,461 degree-seeking undergraduates: 52% women, 7% African American, 15% Asian American, 10% Hispanic American, 1% Native American, 6% international
- 22% of applicants admitted
- SAT and SAT Subject Tests or ACT with writing, application essay required
- 92% graduate within 6 years; 27% enter graduate study

General. Founded in 1864. Regionally accredited. Quaker tradition. **Degrees:** 395 bachelor's awarded. **ROTC:** Army, Navy, Air Force. **Location:** 11 miles from Philadelphia. **Calendar:** Semester. **Full-time faculty:** 168 total; 100% have terminal degrees, 14% minority, 39% women. **Part-time faculty:** 27 total; 82% have terminal degrees, 7% minority, 63% women. **Class size:** 76% < 20, 20% 20-39, 1% 40-49, 2% 50-99, less than 1% >100. **Special facilities:** 330-acre arboretum, observatory, performing arts center with art gallery, solar energy laboratory, Friends Historical Library, Peace Collection in library.

Freshman class profile. 4,085 applied, 917 admitted, 389 enrolled.

Mid 50% test scores		**End year in good standing:**	96%
SAT verbal:	680-770	**Return as sophomores:**	96%
SAT math:	670-760	**Out-of-state:**	81%
Rank in top quarter:	95%	**Live on campus:**	100%
Rank in top tenth:	88%	**International:**	7%

Basis for selection. High school record, recommendations, class rank, test scores, essay, reading and experience in school and out, intellectual capacity and character important. Social responsibility considered. For students graduating from high school in 2006, Swarthmore will require: SAT with mandatory writing section and 2 SAT Subject Tests or old SAT with 3 SAT subject tests, 1 of which must be SAT II Writing test (last administered March 2005), or ACT with score from either ACT optional Writing test, new SAT Writing section, or SAT II Writing test (last administered March 2005). School will combine student's best test scores on SAT, even combining test scores from old and revised versions of SAT. Students interested in engineering strongly encouraged to take Math Level 2 SAT Subject Test/SAT II Math IIC. TOEFL or IELTS strongly encouraged for non-U.S. citizens whose first language is not English. Interview strongly recommended. Portfolios recommended if intended major is in the arts or music. **Homeschooled:** Include supplementary materials giving evidence of intellectual passion, personal commitments, special talents and interests. Additional essay on reasons for decision to home-school and its consequences would be helpful. **Learning Disabled:** Proper documentation required.

High school preparation. Recommended units include English 4, mathematics 3, social studies 3, history 3 and science 3. Study of 1 or 2 foreign languages and coursework in art and music recommended.

2005-2006 Annual costs. Tuition/fees: $31,516. Room/board: $9,764. Books/supplies: $982. Personal expenses: $962.

2005-2006 Financial aid. Need-based: 257 full-time freshmen applied for aid; 200 were judged to have need; 200 of these received aid. Average need met was 100%. Average scholarship/grant was $26,824; average loan $2,199. 86% of total undergraduate aid awarded as scholarships/grants, 14% as loans/jobs. **Non-need-based:** Awarded to 12 full-time undergraduates, including 3 freshmen. Scholarships awarded for academics, leadership, state residency. **Additional information:** Swarthmore meets 100% of demonstrated financial need for all admitted students.

Application procedures. Admission: Closing date 1/2 (postmark date). $60 fee, may be waived for applicants with need. Application may be submitted online. Admission notification 4/1. Must reply by 5/1. **Financial aid:** Closing date 2/15. FAFSA, institutional form, CSS PROFILE required. Applicants notified by 4/1; must reply by 5/1.

Academics. One course equals 1 credit. **Special study options:** Accelerated study, cross-registration, double major, exchange student, honors, independent study, internships, student-designed major, study abroad, teacher certification program. Cooperative exchange programs with Rice and Tufts universities and Harvey Mudd, Pomona, Mills, and Middlebury colleges. **Credit/placement by examination:** AP, CLEP, IB, institutional tests. AP credits listed are general guidelines; one course generally equals one credit. **Support services:** Study skills assistance, tutoring, writing center.

Majors. Area/ethnic studies: Asian, German. **Biology:** General, biochemistry. **Computer sciences:** General. **Education:** General. **Engineering:** General. **English:** English lit. **Foreign languages:** Ancient Greek, Chinese, classics, comparative lit, French, German, Latin, linguistics, Russian, Spanish. **History:** General. **Interdisciplinary:** Math/computer science, medieval/Renaissance. **Math:** General. **Philosophy/religion:** Philosophy, religion. **Physical sciences:** Astronomy, astrophysics, chemical physics, chemistry, physics. **Psychology:** General. **Social sciences:** Anthropology, economics, political science, sociology. **Visual/performing arts:** Art history/conservation, dance, dramatic, film/cinema, studio arts.

Most popular majors. Biology 13%, engineering/engineering technologies 6%, English 8%, foreign language 7%, philosophy/religious studies 7%, psychology 6%, social sciences 32%, visual/performing arts 6%.

Computing on campus. 177 workstations in dormitories, library, computer center, student center. Dormitories wired for high-speed internet access and linked to campus network. Commuter students can connect to campus network. Online course registration, online library, helpline, repair service, student web hosting, wireless network available.

Student life. Freshman orientation: Mandatory. General orientation lasts about 4 days; held before beginning of classes. Several-day optional Tri-College (with Haverford, Bryn Mawr) preorientation for new students of color. **Policies:** New students required to live on campus. **Housing:** Guaranteed on-campus for all undergraduates. Coed dorms, single-sex dorms, substance-free housing available. Overflow housing available in nearby condominium. **Activities:** Jazz band, choral groups, dance, drama, film society, literary magazine, music ensembles, opera, radio station, student government, student newspaper, symphony orchestra, religious organizations, women's resource center, international organizations, Amnesty International, Earthlust, Queer-Straight Alliance, College Republicans, College Democrats.

Athletics. NCAA. **Intercollegiate:** Badminton W, baseball M, basketball, cross-country, field hockey W, golf M, lacrosse, soccer, softball W, swimming, tennis, track and field, volleyball W. **Intramural:** Basketball, football (non-tackle), soccer, softball, table tennis, tennis, volleyball. **Team name:** Garnet Tide, Garnet.

Student services. Alcohol/substance abuse counseling, campus ministries, career counseling, services for economically disadvantaged, student employment services, financial aid counseling, health services, minority student services, personal counseling, placement for graduates, women's services. **Physically disabled:** Services for visually, hearing impaired.

Contact. E-mail: admissions@swarthmore.edu
Phone: (610) 328-8300 Toll-free number: (800) 667-3110
Fax: (610) 328-8580
James Bock, Dean of Admissions and Financial Aid, Swarthmore College, 500 College Avenue, Swarthmore, PA 19081

Talmudical Yeshiva of Philadelphia

Philadelphia, Pennsylvania
CB code: 1037

- Private 4-year rabbinical college for men affiliated with Jewish faith
- Residential campus in very large city
- 108 degree-seeking undergraduates
- Interview required

General. Founded in 1953. Accredited by AARTS. First Talmudic degree and ordination available. **Degrees:** 8 bachelor's awarded; first professional offered. **Calendar:** Trimester, extensive summer session. **Full-time faculty:** 5 total. **Part-time faculty:** 1 total.

Freshman class profile.

Out-of-state:	97%	**Live on campus:**	99%

Basis for selection. Institutional examinations required.

High school preparation. 20 units required. Required and recommended units include English 4, social studies 3, science 3 and foreign language 2.

2005-2006 Annual costs. Tuition/fees: $6,600. $75 fee for yeshiva linen. Room/board: $5,000. Books/supplies: $900.

Application procedures. Admission: Priority date 1/15; no deadline. No application fee. Admission notification on a rolling basis beginning on or about 7/15. **Financial aid:** Priority date 8/1, closing date 5/1. FAFSA required. Applicants notified on a rolling basis starting 3/15; must reply within 2 week(s) of notification.

Academics. Credit/placement by examination: CLEP, IB, institutional tests. **Support services:** Tutoring.

Majors. Theology: Talmudic.

Student life. Policies: Religious observance required. **Housing:** Guaranteed on-campus for all undergraduates.

Student services. Career counseling, health services, personal counseling, placement for graduates.

Contact. Phone: (215) 473-1212 Fax: (215) 477-5065
Rabbi Uri Mandelbaum, Admissions Director, Talmudical Yeshiva of Philadelphia, 6063 Drexel Road, Philadelphia, PA 19131

Temple University

Philadelphia, Pennsylvania — **CB member**
www.temple.edu — **CB code: 2906**

- Public 4-year university
- Commuter campus in very large city
- 23,450 degree-seeking undergraduates: 11% part-time, 57% women, 19% African American, 9% Asian American, 3% Hispanic American, 3% international
- 8,107 degree-seeking graduate students
- 63% of applicants admitted
- SAT or ACT (ACT writing optional) required
- 56% graduate within 6 years

General. Founded in 1884. Regionally accredited. Suburban campuses in Ambler and Fort Washington. Center City campus, Harrisburg campus, and foreign branches. **Degrees:** 4,263 bachelor's, 8 associate awarded; master's, doctoral, first professional offered. **ROTC:** Army, Navy, Air Force. **Location:** One mile from downtown. **Calendar:** Semester, extensive summer session. **Full-time faculty:** 1,206 total; 84% have terminal degrees, 18% minority, 36% women. **Part-time faculty:** 1,355 total; 21% minority, 43% women. **Class size:** 38% < 20, 46% 20-39, 8% 40-49, 5% 50-99, 3% >100. **Special facilities:** Observatory, theater, planetarium, arboretum.

Freshman class profile. 17,352 applied, 10,989 admitted, 3,871 enrolled.

Mid 50% test scores		**Rank in top quarter:**	51%
SAT verbal:	500-600	**Rank in top tenth:**	19%
SAT math:	500-600	**Return as sophomores:**	84%
ACT:	20-24	**Out-of-state:**	29%
GPA 3.50 or higher:	36%	**Live on campus:**	75%
GPA 3.0-3.49:	39%	**International:**	2%
GPA 2.0-2.99:	25%		

Basis for selection. Admissions process holistic; every aspect of student's academic history considered. Interview and essay required for health professions applicants. Audition required for dance, music programs; portfolio required for art.

High school preparation. 16 units required; 22 recommended. Required and recommended units include English 4, mathematics 3-4, social studies 2, history 1-2, science 2-3 (laboratory 1-2), foreign language 2 and academic electives 1-3. 3 of additional 6 recommended units should be in foreign language, math or social sciences.

2005-2006 Annual costs. Tuition/fees: $9,640; $17,236 out-of-state. Room/board: $8,188. Books/supplies: $800. Personal expenses: $3,966.

2004-2005 Financial aid. Need-based: 3,380 full-time freshmen applied for aid; 2,692 were judged to have need; 2,636 of these received aid. Average need met was 87%. Average scholarship/grant was $5,116; average loan $2,881. 50% of total undergraduate aid awarded as scholarships/grants, 50% as loans/jobs. **Non-need-based:** Awarded to 10,520 full-time undergraduates, including 2,515 freshmen. Scholarships awarded for academics, art, athletics, music/drama, ROTC.

Application procedures. Admission: Closing date 4/1 (postmark date). $35 fee, may be waived for applicants with need. Application may be submitted online. Admission notification on a rolling basis beginning on or about 12/1. Must reply by May 1 or within 2 week(s) if notified thereafter. College of Music freshman applicants must apply by 3/1 and transfer applicants by 5/1. Nursing transfer applications and health information management applications due by 4/1. **Financial aid:** Closing date 3/1. FAFSA required. Applicants notified on a rolling basis starting 2/15; must reply by 5/1 or within 3 week(s) of notification.

Academics. Special study options: Combined bachelor's/graduate degree, cooperative education, cross-registration, distance learning, double major, dual enrollment of high school students, ESL, exchange student, honors, independent study, internships, liberal arts/career combination, student-designed major, study abroad, teacher certification program. Present in a number of foreign countries: Japan, Italy, Costa Rica, France, Germany, Ghana, India, Spain, Turkey, United Kingdom and Brazil. **Credit/placement by examination:** AP, CLEP, IB, institutional tests. **Support services:** Learning center, pre-admission summer program, reduced course load, remedial instruction, study skills assistance, tutoring, writing center.

Majors. Agriculture: Horticultural science. **Architecture:** Architecture, landscape, urban/community planning. **Area/ethnic studies:** African-American, American, Asian, Latin American, women's. **Biology:** General, biochemistry, biophysics. **Business:** General, accounting, actuarial science, business admin, e-commerce, entrepreneurial studies, finance, hospitality admin, insurance, international, labor relations, management information systems, marketing, organizational behavior, real estate. **Communications:** Advertising, journalism, organizational, public relations. **Computer sciences:** General, information technology. **Conservation:** Environmental studies. **Education:** Art, business, elementary, English, foreign languages, health, mathematics, physical, sales/marketing, science, social studies, trade/industrial. **Engineering:** Civil, electrical, mechanical. **Engineering technology:** General, civil, environmental. **English:** English lit, speech/rhetoric. **Foreign languages:** Classics, French, German, Hebrew, Italian, linguistics, Russian, Spanish. **Health:** Audiology/speech pathology, medical records admin, music therapy, nursing (RN), public health ed, recreational therapy. **History:** General. **Liberal arts:** Arts/sciences. **Math:** General. **Philosophy/religion:** Judaic, philosophy, religion. **Physical sciences:** Chemistry, geology, physics. **Protective services:** Criminal justice. **Psychology:** General. **Public administration:** Social work. **Social sciences:** Anthropology, economics, geography, political science, sociology. **Visual/performing arts:** Acting, art, art history/conservation, ceramics, dance, dramatic, fiber arts, film/cinema, graphic design, jazz, metal/jewelry, music history, music pedagogy, music performance, music theory/composition, painting, photography, printmaking, sculpture, voice/opera.

Most popular majors. Business/marketing 21%, communications/journalism 10%, education 12%, psychology 6%, public administration/social services 6%, social sciences 6%, visual/performing arts 12%.

Computing on campus. 2,000 workstations in dormitories, library, computer center, student center. Dormitories wired for high-speed internet access and linked to campus network. Commuter students can connect to campus network. Online library, helpline, student web hosting, wireless network available.

Student life. Freshman orientation: Mandatory. Preregistration for classes offered. Includes placement testing. **Policies:** Freshmen permitted cars on campus. **Housing:** Guaranteed on-campus for freshmen. Coed dorms, special housing for disabled, apartments, fraternity/sorority housing, substance-free housing available. $250 fully refundable deposit, deadline 5/1. Living/Learning Centers. **Activities:** Bands, choral groups, dance, drama, film society, literary magazine, music ensembles, opera, radio station, student government, student newspaper, symphony orchestra, Newman Club, Hillel, Young Democrats, Young Republicans, international student association, professional organizations, public service, cultural, departmental, educational, honorary, sport, and special interest organizations.

Athletics. NCAA. **Intercollegiate:** Baseball M, basketball, cheerleading, cross-country, fencing W, field hockey W, football (tackle) M, golf M, gymnastics, lacrosse W, rowing (crew), soccer, softball W, tennis, track and field, volleyball W. **Intramural:** Basketball, football (non-tackle) M, racquetball, soccer M, softball, table tennis, tennis, volleyball, water polo. **Team name:** Owls.

Student services. Adult student services, alcohol/substance abuse counseling, campus ministries, career counseling, services for economically disadvantaged, student employment services, financial aid counseling, health services, legal services, personal counseling, placement for graduates, veterans' counselor. **Physically disabled:** Services for visually, speech, hearing impaired. **Learning disabled:** Comprehensive services available.

Contact. E-mail: tuadm@temple.edu
Phone: (215) 204-7200 Toll-free number: (888) 340-2222
Fax: (215) 204-5694
Timm Rinehart, Associate VP, Enrollment Management, Temple University, 1st Floor Conwell Hall, Philadelphia, PA 19122-6096

Thiel College

Greenville, Pennsylvania **CB member**
www.thiel.edu **CB code: 2910**

- Private 4-year liberal arts college affiliated with Evangelical Lutheran Church in America
- Residential campus in small town
- 1,295 degree-seeking undergraduates: 3% part-time, 45% women, 6% African American, 1% Asian American, 1% Hispanic American, 5% international
- 75% of applicants admitted
- SAT or ACT (ACT writing recommended), interview required
- 42% graduate within 6 years

General. Founded in 1866. Regionally accredited. **Degrees:** 213 bachelor's, 2 associate awarded. **Location:** 75 miles from Pittsburgh, 75 miles from Cleveland. **Calendar:** Semester, limited summer session. **Full-time faculty:** 61 total; 64% have terminal degrees, 5% minority, 38% women. **Part-time faculty:** 61 total; 21% have terminal degrees, 2% minority, 51% women. **Class size:** 48% < 20, 49% 20-39, 3% 40-49, less than 1% 50-99, less than 1% >100. **Special facilities:** Wildlife sanctuary, Greek Center for Excellence.

Freshman class profile. 2,397 applied, 1,803 admitted, 427 enrolled.

Mid 50% test scores			
SAT verbal:	420-530	**Rank in top quarter:**	24%
SAT math:	430-540	**Rank in top tenth:**	8%
ACT:	16-22	**Return as sophomores:**	69%
GPA 3.50 or higher:	20%	**Out-of-state:**	25%
GPA 3.0-3.49:	27%	**Live on campus:**	91%
GPA 2.0-2.99:	51%	**International:**	3%

Basis for selection. High school GPA, class rank, curriculum, and recommendation important. Essay recommended. **Learning Disabled:** Students with disabilities must submit evidence of disability to Office of Special Needs.

High school preparation. College-preparatory program recommended. 16 units recommended. Recommended units include English 4, mathematics 2, social studies 3, science 2 (laboratory 2), foreign language 2 and academic electives 1. Engineering, mathematics, and science majors should complete 3 years of college preparatory mathematics and science.

2005-2006 Annual costs. Tuition/fees: $17,590. Room/board: $6,990. Books/supplies: $600. Personal expenses: $1,600.

2005-2006 Financial aid. **Need-based:** 415 full-time freshmen applied for aid; 353 were judged to have need; 353 of these received aid. Average need met was 78%. Average scholarship/grant was $11,135; average loan $3,662. 70% of total undergraduate aid awarded as scholarships/grants, 30% as loans/jobs. **Non-need-based:** Awarded to 1,253 full-time undergraduates, including 427 freshmen. Scholarships awarded for academics, alumni affiliation, leadership, religious affiliation, state residency.

Application procedures. **Admission:** Priority date 4/1; deadline 6/30 (receipt date). $25 fee, may be waived for applicants with need. Application may be submitted online. Admission notification on a rolling basis beginning on or about 9/15. Must reply by May 1 or within 2 week(s) if notified thereafter. **Financial aid:** Priority date 3/15; no closing date. FAFSA required. Applicants notified on a rolling basis starting 2/15; must reply within 2 week(s) of notification.

Academics. **Special study options:** Combined bachelor's/graduate degree, cooperative education, double major, honors, independent study, internships, liberal arts/career combination, semester at sea, study abroad, teacher certification program, United Nations semester, Washington semester. 3-2 engineering with Case Western Reserve University and University of Pittsburgh, 3-2 engineering technologies with Point Park College, Pittsburgh, cooperative program with Art Institute of Pittsburgh, cooperative engineering with Youngstown State University, exchange with Duke University in forestry. **Credit/placement by examination:** AP, CLEP, SAT, ACT, institutional tests. 30 credit hours maximum toward bachelor's degree. **Support services:** Learning center, reduced course load, remedial instruction, study skills assistance, tutoring, writing center.

Majors. **Biology:** General. **Business:** Accounting, actuarial science, business admin, communications, international, management information systems. **Communications:** General. **Communications technology:** Radio/tv. **Computer sciences:** General, information systems. **Conservation:** General, environmental studies. **Education:** Biology, chemistry, elementary, English, history, mathematics, physics, science, social science, social studies, Spanish. **Engineering:** General. **Foreign languages:** Spanish. **Health:** Audiology/speech pathology, clinical lab technology, cytotechnology. **History:** General. **Math:** General. **Personal/culinary services:** General, mortuary science. **Philosophy/religion:** Philosophy, religion. **Physical sciences:** Chemistry, physics. **Protective services:** Criminal justice. **Psychology:** General. **Social sciences:** Political science, sociology. **Theology:** Religious ed. **Visual/performing arts:** Art.

Most popular majors. Biology 6%, business/marketing 34%, education 7%, psychology 11%, social sciences 11%.

Computing on campus. PC or laptop required. 300 workstations in dormitories, library, computer center, student center. Dormitories wired for high-speed internet access and linked to campus network. Commuter students can connect to campus network. Helpline, wireless network available.

Student life. **Freshman orientation:** Mandatory, $225 fee. Preregistration for classes offered. Weekend before classes start. **Policies:** Freshmen permitted cars on campus. **Housing:** Guaranteed on-campus for all undergraduates. Coed dorms, apartments, fraternity/sorority housing, substance-free housing available. $100 fully refundable deposit, deadline 6/30. Special interest housing, learning/living environment available. **Activities:** Bands, choral groups, dance, drama, literary magazine, music ensembles, musical theater, radio station, student government, student newspaper, symphony orchestra, Organization of Black Collegiates, Lutheran student movement, international students organization, Circle K, Christian Fellowship.

Athletics. NCAA. **Intercollegiate:** Baseball M, basketball, cheerleading, cross-country, football (tackle) M, golf, soccer, softball W, tennis, track and field, volleyball W, wrestling M. **Intramural:** Badminton, basketball, softball, table tennis, volleyball. **Team name:** Tomcats.

Student services. Alcohol/substance abuse counseling, campus ministries, career counseling, student employment services, financial aid counseling, health services, minority student services, personal counseling, placement for graduates. **Physically disabled:** Services for visually, hearing impaired.

Contact. E-mail: admission@thiel.edu
Phone: (724) 589-2345 Toll-free number: (800) 248-4435
Fax: (724) 589-2013
Gary Kelsey, Director of Admissions, Thiel College, 75 College Avenue, Greenville, PA 16125-2181

Thomas Jefferson University: College of Health Professions

Philadelphia, Pennsylvania **CB member**
www.jefferson.edu/jchp **CB code: 2903**

- Private upper-division health science and nursing college
- Residential campus in very large city
- 39% of applicants admitted
- Application essay required

General. Founded in 1824. Regionally accredited. Associate degree programs available in evening division. **Degrees:** 304 bachelor's, 4 associate awarded; master's, doctoral, first professional offered. **Articulation:** Agreements with Bloomsburg U of Pennsylvania, Bucks County CC, Cabrini College, CC of Philadelphia, Delaware County CC, Elizabethtown College, Juniata College, Keystone Junior College, La Salle U, Lebanon Valley College of Pennsylvania, Manor Junior College, Moravian College, Penn State - Delaware County Campus, St. Joseph's U, Shippensburg U of Pennsylvania, Susquehanna U, Villanova U, Gordon College, Burlington County College, Camden County College, Gloucester County College, Penn State-Abington Campus, Rider U, Muhlenberg College, Middlesex County College, Cumberland County College, Arcadia U. **ROTC:** Navy, Air Force. **Calendar:** Semester, limited summer session. **Full-time faculty:** 150 total. **Part-time faculty:** 55 total. **Class size:** 62% < 20, 17% 20-39, 12% 40-49, 7%

50-99, 1% >100. **Special facilities:** Rare book collection, simulation labs, human performance lab (for gait research).

Student profile. 802 degree-seeking undergraduates, 1,580 degree-seeking graduate students. 2,168 applied as first time-transfer students, 847 admitted, 620 enrolled. 80% entered as juniors, 20% entered as seniors. 55% transferred from two-year, 45% transferred from four-year institutions.

Women:	82%	**International:**	2%
African American:	14%	**Part-time:**	16%
Asian American:	8%	**Out-of-state:**	27%
Hispanic American:	2%	**Live on campus:**	30%
Native American:	1%		

Basis for selection. College transcript, application essay required. Decisions based on review of college transcripts, recommendations, written personal statement, and interview. Specific prerequisite credit requirements for each program. Volunteer experiences strongly recommended; 2 site visits required for OT applicants. Transfer accepted as sophomores, juniors, seniors.

2005-2006 Annual costs. Tuition/fees: $21,975. Books/supplies: $1,150. Personal expenses: $855.

Financial aid. Need-based: 479 applied for aid; 455 were judged to have need; 455 of these received aid. 46% of total undergraduate aid awarded as scholarships/grants, 54% as loans/jobs. **Non-need-based:** Scholarships awarded for academics, leadership, state residency.

Application procedures. Admission: Priority date 3/1. $50 fee, may be waived for applicants with need. Application may be submitted online. **Financial aid:** Applicants notified on a rolling basis starting 11/15; must reply within 2 weeks of notification. FAFSA, institutional form required.

Academics. PACE (Plan College Education Program) allows qualified high school seniors to reserve a place for future enrollment after completion of required college program. **Special study options:** Accelerated study, combined bachelor's/graduate degree, distance learning, independent study, internships, study abroad. **Credit/placement by examination:** AP, CLEP, institutional tests. 30 credit hours maximum toward bachelor's degree. **Support services:** Pre-admission summer program, study skills assistance, tutoring, writing center.

Majors. Biology: Biotechnology. **Health:** Cardiovascular technology, clinical lab science, cytotechnology, sonography. **Science technology:** Biological.

Computing on campus. 100 workstations in library, computer center, student center. Dormitories wired for high-speed internet access. Commuter students can connect to campus network. Online course registration, online library, helpline, wireless network available.

Student life. Housing: Guaranteed on-campus for all undergraduates. Coed dorms, special housing for disabled, apartments available. **Activities:** Choral groups, student government, student newspaper, Jefferson African American Student Society, TJU Chinese Students and Scholars Society, Hands of Hope, Jefferson Jewish Student Association, Medical Professionals for Choice, Asian Professional Society, Jefferson Latino Health Organization, Student Occupational Therapy Association, Student Physical Therapy Association, Student Nurses Association of Pennsylvania.

Athletics. Intramural: Basketball, golf, racquetball, rugby, softball, squash, swimming, table tennis, tennis, volleyball.

Student services. Adult student services, career counseling, student employment services, financial aid counseling, health services, minority student services, on-campus daycare, personal counseling, placement for graduates, veterans' counselor. **Physically disabled:** Services for visually, speech, hearing impaired.

Contact. E-mail: jchp@jefferson.edu
Phone: (215) 503-8890 Toll-free number: (877) 533-3247
Fax: (215) 503-7241
Karen Astle, Director of Admissions and Enrollment Management, Thomas Jefferson University: College of Health Professions, 130 South Ninth Street, Edison Building, Suite 100, Philadelphia, PA 19107

University of Pennsylvania

Philadelphia, Pennsylvania — **CB member**
www.upenn.edu — **CB code: 2926**

- Private 4-year university
- Residential campus in very large city
- 9,841 degree-seeking undergraduates: 3% part-time, 50% women, 7% African American, 18% Asian American, 6% Hispanic American, 9% international
- 8,973 degree-seeking graduate students
- 21% of applicants admitted
- SAT and SAT Subject Tests or ACT with writing, application essay required
- 94% graduate within 6 years; 22% enter graduate study

General. Founded in 1740. Regionally accredited. **Degrees:** 2,854 bachelor's, 2 associate awarded; master's, doctoral, first professional offered. **ROTC:** Army, Navy, Air Force. **Location:** One mile from downtown. **Calendar:** Semester, limited summer session. **Full-time faculty:** 1,388 total; 100% have terminal degrees, 17% minority, 31% women. **Part-time faculty:** 602 total; 100% have terminal degrees, 14% minority, 48% women. **Class size:** 73% < 20, 17% 20-39, 3% 40-49, 6% 50-99, 2% >100. **Special facilities:** Arthropology museum, contemporary art institute, arboretum, astronomical observatory, large animal research center, women's center, undergraduate research center, wind tunnel.

Freshman class profile. 18,824 applied, 3,913 admitted, 2,552 enrolled.

Mid 50% test scores		**Rank in top quarter:**	99%
SAT verbal:	660-750	**Rank in top tenth:**	94%
SAT math:	680-770	**End year in good standing:**	97%
ACT:	28-33	**Out-of-state:**	82%
GPA 3.50 or higher:	81%	**Live on campus:**	99%
GPA 3.0-3.49:	19%	**International:**	9%

Basis for selection. Transcript indicating rigor of course work and achievement/evaluation most important criteria. Co-curricular involvements and testing strongly considered, as are counselor and faculty recommendations. Personal commentary (essays) and interview considered as well. Interested in diverse geographic, economic, racial, ethnic student body. Portfolio suggested for Architecture and Fine Arts programs. **Homeschooled:** Statement describing homeschool structure and mission, transcript of courses and grades, letter of recommendation (nonparent) required. Commentary from primary instructor most important, and at least 1 other academic reference highly recommended. SAT Subject Tests in major academic areas highly recommended.

High school preparation. 20 units recommended. Recommended units include English 4, mathematics 4, social studies 1, history 3, science 4 and foreign language 4.

2005-2006 Annual costs. Tuition/fees: $32,364. Room/board: $9,402. Books/supplies: $830. Personal expenses: $1,674.

2004-2005 Financial aid. All financial aid based on need. 1,285 full-time freshmen applied for aid; 1,004 were judged to have need; 1,004 of these received aid. Average need met was 100%. Average scholarship/grant was $22,651; average loan $3,028. 68% of total undergraduate aid awarded as scholarships/grants, 32% as loans/jobs.

Application procedures. Admission: Closing date 1/1 (postmark date). $70 fee, may be waived for applicants with need. Application may be submitted online. Admission notification 4/1. Must reply by 5/1. Rolling admission notification for nursing school applicants; notification begins on or about February 15. **Financial aid:** Priority date 2/15; no closing date. FAFSA, institutional form, CSS PROFILE required. Applicants notified by 4/1; Applicants notified on a rolling basis starting 4/1; must reply by 5/1.

Academics. Special study options: Accelerated study, combined bachelor's/graduate degree, cross-registration, distance learning, double major, dual enrollment of high school students, ESL, exchange student, honors, independent study, internships, liberal arts/career combination, semester at sea, student-designed major, study abroad, teacher certification program, Washington semester. **Credit/placement by examination:** AP, CLEP, IB, institutional tests. No maximum number of semester hours of credit by examination counted toward degree. **Support services:** Learning center, pre-admission summer program, remedial instruction, study skills assistance, tutoring, writing center.

Majors. Architecture: Architecture, environmental design. **Area/ethnic studies:** African, African-American, American, East Asian, South Asian, women's. **Biology:** General, biochemistry, bioinformatics, biomedical sciences, biophysics. **Business:** Accounting, actuarial science, business admin, e-commerce, finance, human resources, insurance, international, management information systems, marketing, operations, real estate, sales/distribution, transportation. **Communications:** General. **Computer sciences:** General, computer graphics, networking. **Conservation:** Environmental studies. **Education:** General, elementary. **Engineering:** Biomedical, chemical, computer, electrical, environmental, materials, materials science, mechanical, systems. **English:** English lit. **Foreign languages:** Classics, comparative lit, East Asian, French, German, Italian, linguistics, Russian, Semitic,

Spanish. **Health:** Community health services, health care admin, nursing (RN). **History:** General, science/technology. **Interdisciplinary:** Cognitive science, global studies, neuroscience. **Legal studies:** General. **Liberal arts:** Arts/sciences, humanities. **Math:** General, statistics. **Philosophy/religion:** Judaic, logic, philosophy, religion. **Physical sciences:** Chemistry, geology, physics. **Psychology:** General. **Public administration:** Policy analysis. **Social sciences:** General, anthropology, economics, international relations, political science, sociology, urban studies. **Visual/performing arts:** General, art history/conservation, dramatic, film/cinema, studio arts.

Most popular majors. Biology 6%, business/marketing 20%, engineering/engineering technologies 10%, health sciences 6%, history 6%, social sciences 19%.

Computing on campus. 1,295 workstations in dormitories, library, computer center, student center. Dormitories wired for high-speed internet access and linked to campus network. Commuter students can connect to campus network. Online course registration, online library, helpline, repair service, student web hosting, wireless network available.

Student life. Freshman orientation: Mandatory. Preregistration for classes offered. **Policies:** Freshmen permitted cars on campus. **Housing:** Guaranteed on-campus for freshmen. Coed dorms, special housing for disabled, apartments, fraternity/sorority housing, substance-free housing available. **Activities:** Bands, choral groups, dance, drama, film society, literary magazine, music ensembles, musical theater, opera, radio station, student government, student newspaper, symphony orchestra, TV station, various religious, political, ethnic, social service, performing arts, cultural, and sports organizations.

Athletics. NCAA. **Intercollegiate:** Baseball M, basketball, cross-country, diving, fencing, field hockey W, football (tackle) M, golf, gymnastics W, lacrosse, rowing (crew), soccer, softball W, squash, swimming, tennis, track and field, volleyball W, wrestling M. **Intramural:** Basketball, cross-country, football (non-tackle), golf, soccer, softball, table tennis, tennis, track and field, volleyball. **Team name:** Quakers.

Student services. Adult student services, alcohol/substance abuse counseling, campus ministries, career counseling, services for economically disadvantaged, student employment services, financial aid counseling, health services, minority student services, on-campus daycare, personal counseling, placement for graduates, veterans' counselor, women's services. **Physically disabled:** Services for visually, speech, hearing impaired.

Contact. E-mail: info@admissions.uago.upenn.edu
Phone: (215) 898-7507 Fax: (215) 898-9670
Willis Stetson, Dean of Admissions, University of Pennsylvania, 1 College Hall, Philadelphia, PA 19104

University of Pittsburgh

Pittsburgh, Pennsylvania **CB member**
www.pitt.edu **CB code: 2927**

- Public 4-year university
- Residential campus in large city
- 16,585 degree-seeking undergraduates: 9% part-time, 52% women, 9% African American, 4% Asian American, 1% Hispanic American, 1% international
- 9,156 degree-seeking graduate students
- 53% of applicants admitted
- SAT or ACT with writing required

General. Founded in 1787. Regionally accredited. Regional campuses in Johnstown, Bradford, Titusville, and Greensburg. **Degrees:** 3,989 bachelor's awarded; master's, doctoral, first professional offered. **ROTC:** Army, Navy, Air Force. **Location:** 3 miles from downtown. **Calendar:** Semester, extensive summer session. **Full-time faculty:** 1,550 total. **Part-time faculty:** 535 total. **Class size:** 43% < 20, 34% 20-39, 7% 40-49, 10% 50-99, 6% >100. **Special facilities:** Observatory, nationality rooms, performance hall, museum, American music center, ecology laboratory.

Freshman class profile. 18,153 applied, 9,654 admitted, 3,249 enrolled.

Mid 50% test scores			
SAT verbal:	560-660	Rank in top tenth:	43%
SAT math:	570-670	Out-of-state:	21%
ACT:	24-29	Live on campus:	94%
Rank in top quarter:	80%	Fraternities:	6%
		Sororities:	7%

Basis for selection. GED not accepted. High school record, class rank, test scores, and activities considered. College of General Studies applicants must apply directly to that college, not through Admissions and Financial Aid. Students admitted as freshmen into School of Arts and Sciences, School of Engineering, School of Nursing, and College of Business Administration. Students may be conditionally accepted into the School of Pharmacy, PharmD program with the provision that they successfully complete 4 terms (2 years) of preprofessional study in School of Arts and Sciences. Interview and essay recommended for all; audition required for music program; portfolio recommended for studio art program; essay required for pharmacy applicants. **Homeschooled:** Statement describing homeschool structure and mission, transcript of courses and grades required. In some cases, committee will request end-of-year reviews by state approved educator, if transcript from an approved homeschooling association not provided, and/or course descriptions. In all cases, high school diploma or equivalent required showing date of graduation at end of senior year.

High school preparation. 15 units required. Required and recommended units include English 4, mathematics 3, social studies 1, science 3 (laboratory 3), foreign language 3 and academic electives 4. 4 electives required with 3 in single foreign language recommended. School of Engineering requires 4 English, 2 algebra, 1 geometry, 1 trigonometry/solid geometry, 1 chemistry, 1 physics and 5 1/2 academic electives. School of Nursing requires 4 English, 3 social studies, 5 academic electives with 2 foreign language recommended, 1 algebra I, 1 plane geometry or algebra II, 3 laboratory science (one must be in chemistry), 1 additional mathematics. School of Pharmacy requires 4 English, 4 math (algebra I, II, geometry, trig). 3 science and 5 academic electives and College of Business Administration requires 4 English, 4 math (algebra I, II, geometry, trig, pre-calculus, calculus), 2 lab science, 2 social science and history and 3 academic electives (3 units of same foreign language recommended).

2005-2006 Annual costs. Tuition/fees: $11,436; $20,784 out-of-state. Room/board: $8,830. Books/supplies: $700. Personal expenses: $1,500.

2005-2006 Financial aid. Need-based: 2,617 full-time freshmen applied for aid; 1,981 were judged to have need; 1,964 of these received aid. Average need met was 89%. Average scholarship/grant was $5,053; average loan $4,007. 34% of total undergraduate aid awarded as scholarships/grants, 66% as loans/jobs. **Non-need-based:** Awarded to 4,273 full-time undergraduates, including 1,140 freshmen. Scholarships awarded for academics, athletics.

Application procedures. Admission: Priority date 3/1; no deadline. $35 fee, may be waived for applicants with need. Application may be submitted online. Admission notification on a rolling basis beginning on or about 10/1. Must reply by May 1 or within 2 week(s) if notified thereafter. **Financial aid:** Priority date 3/1, closing date 6/1. FAFSA, institutional form required. Applicants notified on a rolling basis starting 3/1; must reply by 5/1 or within 2 week(s) of notification.

Academics. Accelerated high school program enables students to take courses in School of Arts and Sciences while in high school. **Special study options:** Accelerated study, combined bachelor's/graduate degree, cooperative education, cross-registration, distance learning, double major, dual enrollment of high school students, ESL, exchange student, external degree, honors, independent study, internships, liberal arts/career combination, student-designed major, study abroad, teacher certification program, Washington semester, weekend college. Freshman seminars, early admission to some graduate programs for exceptional students. **Credit/placement by examination:** AP, CLEP, IB, SAT, ACT, institutional tests. 30 credit hours maximum toward bachelor's degree. CLEP is awarded credit only with college of general studies. CLEP credits do not transfer to other University of Pittsburgh schools. **Support services:** Learning center, pre-admission summer program, reduced course load, remedial instruction, study skills assistance, tutoring, writing center.

Majors. Area/ethnic studies: African-American. **Biology:** General, ecology, microbiology, molecular. **Business:** Accounting, business admin, finance, marketing. **Communications:** Media studies. **Computer sciences:** Computer science, information systems. **Education:** Physical. **Engineering:** General, biomedical, chemical, civil, computer, electrical, industrial, materials, mechanical, physics. **English:** British lit, creative writing, speech/rhetoric. **Foreign languages:** Chinese, classics, French, German, Italian, Japanese, linguistics, Polish, Russian, Slavic, Spanish. **Health:** Audiology/speech pathology, dental hygiene, dietetics, medical records admin, nursing (RN). **History:** General, science/technology. **Interdisciplinary:** Neuroscience. **Liberal arts:** Arts/sciences, humanities. **Math:** General, applied, statistics. **Philosophy/religion:** Philosophy, religion. **Physical sciences:** General, chemistry, geology, physics. **Protective services:** Law enforcement admin. **Psychology:** General. **Public administration:** General, social work. **Social sciences:** General, anthropology, economics, political science, sociology, urban studies. **Visual/performing arts:** Art history/conservation, dramatic, film/cinema, studio arts.

Most popular majors. Business/marketing 14%, engineering/engineering technologies 9%, English 12%, health sciences 11%, psychology 10%, social sciences 11%.

Computing on campus. 600 workstations in dormitories, library, computer center, student center. Dormitories wired for high-speed internet access and linked to campus network. Commuter students can connect to campus network. Online library, helpline, repair service, wireless network available.

Student life. Freshman orientation: Available. Preregistration for classes offered. **Policies:** Freshmen permitted cars on campus. **Housing:** Guaranteed on-campus for freshmen. Coed dorms, single-sex dorms, apartments, fraternity/sorority housing, substance-free housing available. $325 deposit, deadline 5/1. Rooms can be adapted to meet disabled students' particular needs. **Activities:** Bands, choral groups, dance, drama, film society, literary magazine, music ensembles, radio station, student government, student newspaper, symphony orchestra, TV station, approximately 450 student organizations.

Athletics. NCAA. **Intercollegiate:** Baseball M, basketball, cross-country, diving, football (tackle) M, gymnastics W, soccer, softball W, swimming, tennis W, track and field, volleyball W, wrestling M. **Intramural:** Badminton, basketball, football (tackle) M, handball, racquetball, soccer, squash, swimming, volleyball, wrestling M. **Team name:** Panthers.

Student services. Adult student services, alcohol/substance abuse counseling, campus ministries, career counseling, student employment services, financial aid counseling, health services, personal counseling, placement for graduates, veterans' counselor. **Physically disabled:** Services for visually, speech, hearing impaired.

Contact. E-mail: oafa@pitt.edu
Phone: (412) 624-7488 Fax: (412) 648-8815
Betsy Porter, Director, Office of Admissions and Financial Aid, University of Pittsburgh, 4227 Fifth Avenue, 1st Floor, Alumni Hall, Pittsburgh, PA 15260

University of Pittsburgh at Bradford

Bradford, Pennsylvania — **CB member**
www.upb.pitt.edu — **CB code: 2935**

- Public 4-year university and liberal arts college
- Residential campus in large town
- 1,142 degree-seeking undergraduates: 18% part-time, 59% women, 4% African American, 1% Asian American, 1% Hispanic American, 1% Native American
- 76% of applicants admitted
- SAT or ACT (ACT writing optional) required
- 41% graduate within 6 years; 20% enter graduate study

General. Founded in 1963. Regionally accredited. **Degrees:** 151 bachelor's, 45 associate awarded. **ROTC:** Army. **Location:** 79 miles from Buffalo, New York, 160 miles from Pittsburgh. **Calendar:** Semester, extensive summer session. **Full-time faculty:** 65 total; 62% have terminal degrees, 12% minority, 34% women. **Part-time faculty:** 57 total; 18% have terminal degrees, 7% minority, 58% women. **Class size:** 69% < 20, 28% 20-39, 2% 40-49, 2% 50-99. **Special facilities:** Port-per-pillow resident Internet access. Located in the Allegheny National Forest.

Freshman class profile. 592 applied, 449 admitted, 239 enrolled.

Mid 50% test scores			
SAT verbal:	450-560	Rank in top quarter:	32%
SAT math:	460-550	Rank in top tenth:	11%
ACT:	19-23	End year in good standing:	59%
GPA 3.50 or higher:	41%	Return as sophomores:	65%
GPA 3.0-3.49:	33%	Out-of-state:	13%
GPA 2.0-2.99:	26%	Live on campus:	73%

Basis for selection. School achievement record, test scores, interview most important. Essay and recommendations considered. **Homeschooled:** Required: Complete listing of courses taken/completed/in progress, syllabus for each course, textbook used, 1 recommendation from educator, 1 outside recommendation, personal essay, personal interview, State requirement satisfaction.

High school preparation. College-preparatory program recommended. 15 units required; 16 recommended. Required and recommended units include English 4, mathematics 2, history 1, science 1-2 (laboratory 1-2), foreign language 2 and academic electives 5. Engineering and math students must have trigonometry and physics with a lab. Nursing majors must have 3 social science and 1 each of chemistry and biology with labs in both.

2005-2006 Annual costs. Tuition/fees: $10,538; $20,426 out-of-state. Room/board: $6,470. Books/supplies: $1,000. Personal expenses: $1,500.

2005-2006 Financial aid. Need-based: 46% of total undergraduate aid awarded as scholarships/grants, 54% as loans/jobs. **Non-need-based:** Scholarships awarded for academics, alumni affiliation, ROTC, state residency.

Application procedures. Admission: Priority date 5/1; no deadline. $35 fee, may be waived for applicants with need. Application may be submitted online. Admission notification on a rolling basis beginning on or about 11/15. Must reply by May 1 or within 2 week(s) if notified thereafter. **Financial aid:** Priority date 3/1; no closing date. FAFSA required. Applicants notified on a rolling basis starting 4/1; must reply within 2 week(s) of notification.

Academics. Special study options: Cross-registration, distance learning, double major, dual enrollment of high school students, external degree, independent study, internships, semester at sea, study abroad, teacher certification program. 3-4 preoptometry program with Pennsylvania College of Optometry, 1-4 pharmacy program with Oakland campus. **Credit/placement by examination:** AP, CLEP, IB, SAT, ACT, institutional tests. 30 credit hours maximum toward associate degree, 30 toward bachelor's. **Support services:** Learning center, reduced course load, remedial instruction, study skills assistance, tutoring.

Majors. Area/ethnic studies: American. **Biology:** General. **Business:** General, entrepreneurial studies. **Communications:** Media studies, public relations. **Computer sciences:** Computer science. **English:** Creative writing, English lit. **Health:** Athletic training, nursing (RN), radiologic technology/medical imaging. **Math:** Applied. **Parks/recreation:** Sports admin. **Physical sciences:** General, chemistry. **Protective services:** Corrections. **Psychology:** General. **Social sciences:** General, demography, economics, political science, sociology. **Visual/performing arts:** General.

Most popular majors. Business/marketing 19%, English 9%, health sciences 7%, security/protective services 15%, social sciences 17%.

Computing on campus. 123 workstations in library, computer center, student center. Dormitories wired for high-speed internet access and linked to campus network. Commuter students can connect to campus network. Helpline, student web hosting, wireless network available.

Student life. Freshman orientation: Mandatory, $90 fee. Preregistration for classes offered. 2-day program for students and parents in July; students register for classes. Additional 3-day program immediately prior to start of classes. **Policies:** Freshmen permitted cars on campus. **Housing:** Guaranteed on-campus for freshmen. Special housing for disabled, apartments, substance-free housing available. $125 nonrefundable deposit, deadline 6/1. Townhouse/apartment style housing available. **Activities:** Choral groups, dance, drama, literary magazine, radio station, student government, student newspaper, Black Action Committee, Christ in Action, Collegiate Liberals of America, Conservative Union, Habitat for Humanity, Ideology Expression Club.

Athletics. NCAA. **Intercollegiate:** Baseball M, basketball, cross-country, golf, soccer, softball W, volleyball W. **Intramural:** Basketball, football (non-tackle), golf, ice hockey, soccer, softball, table tennis, tennis, volleyball, water polo. **Team name:** Panthers.

Student services. Adult student services, alcohol/substance abuse counseling, campus ministries, career counseling, student employment services, financial aid counseling, health services, personal counseling, placement for graduates.

Contact. E-mail: admissions@www.upb.pitt.edu
Phone: (814) 362-7555 Toll-free number: (800) 872-1787
Fax: (814) 362-7578
Alexander Nazemetz, Director of Admissions, University of Pittsburgh at Bradford, 300 Campus Drive, Bradford, PA 16701

University of Pittsburgh at Greensburg

Greensburg, Pennsylvania
www.upg.pitt.edu — **CB code: 2936**

- Public 4-year branch campus and liberal arts college
- Commuter campus in large town
- 1,795 degree-seeking undergraduates: 9% part-time, 51% women, 3% African American, 2% Asian American, 1% Hispanic American
- SAT or ACT with writing required

General. Founded in 1963. Regionally accredited. **Degrees:** 297 bachelor's awarded. **ROTC:** Army, Air Force. **Location:** 35 miles from Pittsburgh. **Calendar:** Semester, limited summer session. **Full-time faculty:** 76 total; 82% have terminal degrees, 13% minority, 50% women. **Part-time faculty:** 62 total; 31% have terminal degrees, 6% minority, 45% women. **Class size:** 32% < 20, 52% 20-39, 7% 40-49, 9% 50-99. **Special facilities:** Wildlife sanctuary and nature trail, humanities village, behavioral science village, natural sciences and new technologies village, international village.

Freshman class profile.

Mid 50% test scores			
SAT verbal:	480-570	Rank in top quarter:	33%
SAT math:	490-580	Rank in top tenth:	10%
ACT:	20-23	Out-of-state:	1%
		Live on campus:	60%

Basis for selection. High school curriculum and grades most important, followed by class rank and SAT/ACT scores. Interviews, essays and letters of recommendation all optional. **Homeschooled:** Transcript of courses and grades required.

High school preparation. 15 units required; 20 recommended. Required and recommended units include English 4, mathematics 2-4, social studies 2, history 1, science 1-2 (laboratory 1-2), foreign language 3 and academic electives 4. For engineering applicants: 2 algebra, 1 geometry, 1 trigonometry, 1 physics required; calculus and computer science recommended.

2005-2006 Annual costs. Tuition/fees: $10,562; $20,450 out-of-state. Room/board: $6,960. Books/supplies: $1,000. Personal expenses: $1,500.

2004-2005 Financial aid. Need-based: 406 full-time freshmen applied for aid; 322 were judged to have need; 315 of these received aid. Average need met was 59%. Average scholarship/grant was $4,007; average loan $2,852. 43% of total undergraduate aid awarded as scholarships/grants, 57% as loans/jobs. **Non-need-based:** Awarded to 347 full-time undergraduates, including 135 freshmen. Scholarships awarded for academics, leadership, minority status.

Application procedures. Admission: Priority date 4/1; deadline 9/9 (receipt date). $35 fee, may be waived for applicants with need. Application may be submitted online. Admission notification on a rolling basis beginning on or about 10/1. Must reply by May 1 or within 3 week(s) if notified thereafter. **Financial aid:** Priority date 3/1, closing date 5/1. FAFSA, institutional form required. Applicants notified on a rolling basis starting 4/15; must reply within 3 week(s) of notification.

Academics. Special study options: Combined bachelor's/graduate degree, cross-registration, double major, dual enrollment of high school students, exchange student, independent study, internships, liberal arts/career combination, semester at sea, student-designed major, study abroad, Washington semester. **Credit/placement by examination:** AP, CLEP, institutional tests. 30 credit hours maximum toward bachelor's degree. **Support services:** Learning center, reduced course load, remedial instruction, study skills assistance, tutoring, writing center.

Majors. Area/ethnic studies: American. **Biology:** General. **Business:** Accounting, business admin, management information systems. **Communications:** General, journalism, public relations. **Computer sciences:** Information systems. **Conservation:** General. **Education:** General. **Engineering:** General. **English:** Composition. **Health:** Predentistry, premedicine, prepharmacy, preveterinary. **History:** General. **Liberal arts:** Arts/sciences. **Math:** Applied. **Protective services:** Law enforcement admin. **Psychology:** General. **Social sciences:** General, anthropology, criminology, political science.

Most popular majors. Business/marketing 25%, communications/journalism 6%, computer/information sciences 9%, English 8%, psychology 20%, social sciences 21%.

Computing on campus. 400 workstations in dormitories, library, computer center. Dormitories wired for high-speed internet access and linked to campus network. Commuter students can connect to campus network. Online library, helpline, repair service, student web hosting, wireless network available.

Student life. Freshman orientation: Mandatory, $55 fee. **Policies:** Freshmen permitted cars on campus. **Housing:** Coed dorms, special housing for disabled, apartments, substance-free housing available. $300 deposit, deadline 5/1. **Activities:** Concert band, choral groups, dance, drama, literary magazine, musical theater, student government, student newspaper, student activities board, honor societies, academic societies, Alpha Phi Omega, Circle K, Amnesty International, Christian fellowship club, College Republicans, intramurals, ski club.

Athletics. NCAA. **Intercollegiate:** Baseball M, basketball, cross-country, golf, soccer, softball W, tennis, volleyball W. **Intramural:** Baseball M, basketball, golf, racquetball, skiing, soccer, softball, table tennis, tennis, volleyball. **Team name:** Bobcats.

Student services. Adult student services, career counseling, student employment services, financial aid counseling, health services, personal counseling, placement for graduates. **Physically disabled:** Services for visually, hearing impaired.

Contact. E-mail: upgadmit@pitt.edu
Phone: (724) 836-9880 Fax: (724) 836-7160
Brandi Darr, Director of Admissions and Financial Aid, University of Pittsburgh at Greensburg, 1150 Mount Pleasant Road, Greensburg, PA 15601

University of Pittsburgh at Johnstown

Johnstown, Pennsylvania — **CB member**
www.upj.pitt.edu — **CB code: 2934**

- Public 4-year engineering and liberal arts college
- Residential campus in small city
- 3,113 degree-seeking undergraduates: 6% part-time, 48% women, 1% African American, 1% Asian American
- 85% of applicants admitted
- SAT or ACT (ACT writing recommended), application essay required
- 63% graduate within 6 years; 12% enter graduate study

General. Founded in 1927. Regionally accredited. **Degrees:** 501 bachelor's, 14 associate awarded. **Location:** 70 miles from Pittsburgh. **Calendar:** Semester, limited summer session. **Full-time faculty:** 140 total. **Part-time faculty:** 50 total. **Class size:** 28% < 20, 60% 20-39, 8% 40-49, 4% 50-99. **Special facilities:** 40-acre nature preserve maintained by biology department, performing arts center.

Freshman class profile. 2,589 applied, 2,189 admitted, 822 enrolled.

Mid 50% test scores		GPA 2.0-2.99:	28%
SAT verbal:	470-560	Rank in top quarter:	67%
SAT math:	470-570	Rank in top tenth:	22%
ACT:	18-23	Out-of-state:	1%
GPA 3.50 or higher:	34%	Live on campus:	82%
GPA 3.0-3.49:	38%		

Basis for selection. College preparatory curriculum, high school achievement, test scores, and class rank very important. Recommendations and essay considered. TOEFL required of non-native English speakers. Interview recommended.

High school preparation. College-preparatory program required. 15 units required. Required and recommended units include English 4, mathematics 2-3, social studies 4, science 2 (laboratory 1-2) and foreign language 2. One each of trigonometry, physics, and chemistry required for engineering technology program.

2005-2006 Annual costs. Tuition/fees: $10,540; $20,428 out-of-state. Room/board: $6,300. Books/supplies: $1,000. Personal expenses: $1,500.

2004-2005 Financial aid. Need-based: 775 full-time freshmen applied for aid; 667 were judged to have need; 621 of these received aid. Average need met was 44%. Average scholarship/grant was $4,061; average loan $2,355. 49% of total undergraduate aid awarded as scholarships/grants, 51% as loans/jobs. **Non-need-based:** Awarded to 805 full-time undergraduates, including 413 freshmen. Scholarships awarded for academics, athletics, leadership, minority status.

Application procedures. Admission: No deadline. $35 fee, may be waived for applicants with need. Application may be submitted online. Admission notification on a rolling basis beginning on or about 9/1. Must reply by May 1 or within 2 week(s) if notified thereafter. **Financial aid:** Priority date 4/1; no closing date. FAFSA required. Applicants notified on a rolling basis starting 3/15; must reply within 2 week(s) of notification.

Academics. Special study options: Accelerated study, combined bachelor's/graduate degree, cooperative education, cross-registration, distance learning, double major, dual enrollment of high school students, independent study, internships, liberal arts/career combination, student-designed major, study abroad, teacher certification program. **Credit/placement by examination:** AP, CLEP, IB, SAT, ACT, institutional tests. 90 credit hours maximum toward bachelor's degree. **Support services:** Learning center, reduced course load, study skills assistance, tutoring, writing center.

Majors. Area/ethnic studies: American. **Biology:** General. **Business:** General, accounting, finance, managerial economics. **Communications:** General, journalism. **Computer sciences:** General. **Conservation:** Environmental studies. **Education:** Biology, chemistry, elementary, English, mathematics, science, secondary, social science, social studies. **Engineering technology:** Civil, electrical, mechanical. **English:** American lit, British lit, creative writing. **Health:** Predentistry, premedicine, preveterinary. **History:** General. **Legal studies:** Prelaw. **Liberal arts:** Arts/sciences. **Math:** General. **Physical sciences:** Chemistry, geology. **Psychology:** General. **Social sciences:** General, economics, geography, political science, sociology. **Visual/performing arts:** Dramatic.

Most popular majors. Biology 6%, business/marketing 21%, communications/journalism 9%, computer/information sciences 7%, education 16%, engineering/engineering technologies 11%, psychology 7%, social sciences 14%.

Computing on campus. 150 workstations in library, computer center. Dormitories wired for high-speed internet access and linked to campus network. Commuter students can connect to campus network. Online library, helpline, student web hosting available.

Student life. Freshman orientation: Mandatory, $55 fee. Preregistration for classes offered. One-day program. **Policies:** To be eligible to hold office within group or organization, student must be full-time and have minimum GPA of 2.0. Freshmen permitted cars on campus. **Housing:** Guaranteed on-campus for all undergraduates. Coed dorms, apartments available. $300 fully refundable deposit, deadline 7/1. Townhouses, lodges, and single-sex residences available. **Activities:** Concert band, choral groups, dance, drama, literary magazine, music ensembles, musical theater, radio station, student government, student newspaper, TV station, Newman Students Association, Black Action Society, Student Outreach through Service, Time Out Christian Fellowship, Student Council on World Affairs, political science club, honor societies, academic clubs, Habitat for Humanity.

Athletics. NCAA. **Intercollegiate:** Baseball M, basketball, cross-country W, golf, soccer, track and field W, volleyball W, wrestling M. **Intramural:** Basketball, football (non-tackle), softball, volleyball. **Team name:** Mountain Cats.

Student services. Adult student services, alcohol/substance abuse counseling, campus ministries, career counseling, student employment services, financial aid counseling, health services, personal counseling, placement for graduates, veterans' counselor. **Physically disabled:** Services for visually, speech, hearing impaired.

Contact. E-mail: upjadmit@pitt.edu
Phone: (814) 269-7050 Toll-free number: (800) 765-4875
Fax: (814) 269-7044
James Gyure, Director of Admissions, University of Pittsburgh at Johnstown, 450 Schoolhouse Road, 157 Blackington Hall, Johnstown, PA 15904-1200

University of Scranton

Scranton, Pennsylvania — **CB member**
www.scranton.edu — **CB code: 2929**

- Private 4-year university and liberal arts college affiliated with Roman Catholic Church
- Residential campus in small city
- 4,014 degree-seeking undergraduates: 4% part-time, 58% women
- 1,022 degree-seeking graduate students
- 75% of applicants admitted
- SAT or ACT (ACT writing optional), application essay required
- 79% graduate within 6 years

General. Founded in 1888. Regionally accredited. **Degrees:** 868 bachelor's, 2 associate awarded; master's, doctoral offered. **ROTC:** Army, Air Force. **Location:** 125 miles from Philadelphia, 125 miles from New York City. **Calendar:** Semester, limited summer session. **Full-time faculty:** 251 total; 84% have terminal degrees, 8% minority, 34% women. **Part-time faculty:** 176 total; 15% have terminal degrees. **Class size:** 48% < 20, 50% 20-39, 1% 40-49, less than 1% 50-99. **Special facilities:** 2 cyber-cafes, conference and retreat center at Chapman Lake, performing arts center with seating for 700.

Freshman class profile. 6,343 applied, 4,777 admitted, 956 enrolled.

Mid 50% test scores		**Rank in top quarter:**	57%
SAT verbal:	520-600	**Rank in top tenth:**	26%
SAT math:	510-600	**Return as sophomores:**	88%
GPA 3.50 or higher:	37%	**Out-of-state:**	55%
GPA 3.0-3.49:	40%	**Live on campus:**	83%
GPA 2.0-2.99:	23%		

Basis for selection. Program taken, GPA, SAT scores, class rank most important. Essay, extracurricular/leadership activities, recommendations important. Interview recommended. **Homeschooled:** State high school equivalency certificate required.

High school preparation. College-preparatory program recommended. 16 units required. Required and recommended units include English 4, mathematics 3-4, social studies 2, science 1-2 and foreign language 2. Science and business students should have 4 mathematics; science students, 4 science.

2005-2006 Annual costs. Tuition/fees: $24,030. Room/board: $9,904. Books/supplies: $900. Personal expenses: $1,100.

2005-2006 Financial aid. All financial aid based on need. 799 full-time freshmen applied for aid; 632 were judged to have need; 629 of these received aid. Average need met was 73%. Average scholarship/grant was $11,571; average loan $3,422. 68% of total undergraduate aid awarded as scholarships/grants, 32% as loans/jobs.

Application procedures. Admission: Priority date 3/1; no deadline. $40 fee, may be waived for applicants with need. Application may be submitted online. Admission notification on a rolling basis beginning on or about 1/15. Must reply by May 1 or within 3 week(s) if notified thereafter. **Financial aid:** Priority date 2/15; no closing date. FAFSA required. Applicants notified on a rolling basis starting 3/1; must reply by 5/1 or within 2 week(s) of notification.

Academics. Special study options: Accelerated study, combined bachelor's/graduate degree, cross-registration, distance learning, double major, dual enrollment of high school students, exchange student, honors, independent study, internships, semester at sea, study abroad, teacher certification program, United Nations semester, Washington semester. Baccalaureate/master's degree programs available. **Credit/placement by examination:** AP, CLEP, IB, institutional tests. 30 credit hours maximum toward bachelor's degree. **Support services:** Learning center, pre-admission summer program, remedial instruction, study skills assistance, tutoring, writing center.

Majors. Biology: General, biochemistry, biophysics. **Business:** Accounting, business admin, finance, human resources, international, management science, marketing, operations. **Communications:** General. **Computer sciences:** General, information systems. **Conservation:** General. **Education:** Early childhood, elementary, secondary, special. **Engineering:** Electrical. **Foreign languages:** Ancient Greek, classics, French, German, Latin, Spanish. **Health:** Clinical lab science, health care admin. **History:** General. **Interdisciplinary:** Gerontology, neuroscience. **Math:** General. **Philosophy/religion:** Philosophy, religion. **Physical sciences:** Chemistry, physics. **Psychology:** General. **Public administration:** Human services. **Social sciences:** Economics, international relations, political science, sociology. **Visual/performing arts:** Dramatic.

Most popular majors. Biology 8%, business/marketing 20%, communications/journalism 10%, education 13%, health sciences 11%, psychology 6%, social sciences 9%.

Computing on campus. 906 workstations in dormitories, library, computer center, student center. Dormitories wired for high-speed internet access and linked to campus network. Commuter students can connect to campus network. Online course registration, online library, helpline, repair service, student web hosting, wireless network available.

Student life. Freshman orientation: Mandatory, $220 fee. Preregistration for classes offered. Overnight program (1.5 days) for students and parents, held between end of June and mid-July. **Housing:** Guaranteed on-campus for all undergraduates. Coed dorms, single-sex dorms, apartments available. $150 nonrefundable deposit, deadline 5/1. Theme houses (French, Spanish, international, service, education, arts) available. **Activities:** Bands, choral groups, dance, drama, literary magazine, music ensembles, radio station, student government, student newspaper, TV station, religious and social service organizations, veterans club, Young Democrats, Young Republicans, professional clubs, international students club, campus ministry, collegiate volunteers, multicultural club, debating club.

Athletics. NCAA. **Intercollegiate:** Baseball M, basketball, cross-country, field hockey W, golf M, ice hockey M, lacrosse, soccer, softball W, swimming, tennis, volleyball W, wrestling M. **Intramural:** Baseball M, basketball, bowling, cross-country, football (tackle) M, golf, handball, lacrosse, racquetball, rugby, skiing, soccer, softball, swimming, table tennis, tennis, track and field, volleyball, water polo M, wrestling M. **Team name:** Royals.

Student services. Adult student services, alcohol/substance abuse counseling, campus ministries, career counseling, student employment services, health services, personal counseling, placement for graduates, veterans' counselor. **Physically disabled:** Services for visually, hearing impaired.

Contact. E-mail: admissions@scranton.edu
Phone: (570) 941-7540 Toll-free number: (888) 727-2686
Fax: (570) 941-5928
Joseph Roback, Director of Admissions, University of Scranton, 800 Linden Street, Scranton, PA 18510-4699

University of the Arts

Philadelphia, Pennsylvania — **CB member**
www.uarts.edu — **CB code: 2664**

- Private 4-year visual arts and performing arts college
- Residential campus in very large city

- 2,057 degree-seeking undergraduates: 1% part-time, 55% women, 10% African American, 3% Asian American, 4% Hispanic American, 3% international
- 198 degree-seeking graduate students
- 49% of applicants admitted
- SAT or ACT (ACT writing optional) required
- 56% graduate within 6 years; 15% enter graduate study

General. Founded in 1870. Regionally accredited. **Degrees:** 406 bachelor's awarded; master's offered. **Calendar:** Semester, limited summer session. **Full-time faculty:** 118 total; 48% have terminal degrees, 8% minority, 38% women. **Part-time faculty:** 354 total; 4% minority, 45% women. **Class size:** 79% < 20, 21% 20-39, less than 1% 50-99. **Special facilities:** Digital multimedia laboratories, Oxberry animation stand, MIDI and recording studios, analog and digital electronic music studios, music calligraphy laboratory, center for publication arts, industrial design computer-aided product design center, genre-specific art galleries.

Freshman class profile. 2,283 applied, 1,114 admitted, 510 enrolled.

Mid 50% test scores			
SAT verbal:	480-600	Rank in top quarter:	32%
SAT math:	450-570	Rank in top tenth:	13%
ACT:	19-26	End year in good standing:	85%
GPA 3.50 or higher:	19%	Return as sophomores:	82%
GPA 3.0-3.49:	23%	Out-of-state:	64%
GPA 2.0-2.99:	55%	Live on campus:	85%
		International:	1%

Basis for selection. Academic records, art work portfolio, audition very important. SAT or ACT scores considered in relation to the former. Statement of purpose and letters of recommendation also important. Class placement in English composition through SAT/ACT scores. August 15 score deadline for placement, counseling and/or credit. Interview recommended for all; audition required for performing arts programs; portfolio required for multimedia, visual arts, writing programs; essay required for media arts, performing arts, and visual arts programs.

High school preparation. Required and recommended units include English 4, mathematics 3, social studies 2, history 2, science 2 and foreign language 2. Coursework in art, dance, music, creative writing, or theater as appropriate for specific programs recommended.

2005-2006 Annual costs. Tuition/fees: $24,330. Room only: $5,900. Books/supplies: $2,000. Personal expenses: $2,000.

Financial aid. Non-need-based: Scholarships awarded for academics, art, music/drama.

Application procedures. Admission: Priority date 3/1; no deadline. $60 fee, may be waived for applicants with need. Admission notification on a rolling basis beginning on or about 11/1. Must reply by May 1 or within 3 week(s) if notified thereafter. **Financial aid:** Priority date 2/15; no closing date. FAFSA required. Applicants notified on a rolling basis starting 3/15; must reply within 2 week(s) of notification.

Academics. Credit for course work may be given to entering freshmen by portfolio review (awarded after first year) or audition and placement testing. Art and design students declare major at end of first year, dance students at end of second year. **Special study options:** Accelerated study, cross-registration, double major, dual enrollment of high school students, ESL, exchange student, independent study, internships, teacher certification program. **Credit/placement by examination:** AP, CLEP, IB, SAT, ACT, institutional tests. Credit by examination counted toward bachelor's degree varies by program. **Support services:** Learning center, pre-admission summer program, reduced course load, remedial instruction, study skills assistance, tutoring, writing center.

Majors. Communications: General. **Visual/performing arts:** General, cinematography, commercial/advertising art, crafts, dance, dramatic, industrial design, jazz, music performance, music theory/composition, painting, photography, printmaking, sculpture, studio arts.

Most popular majors. Visual/performing arts 95%.

Computing on campus. 400 workstations in library, computer center, student center. Commuter students can connect to campus network. Online course registration, online library, helpline, wireless network available.

Student life. Freshman orientation: Available. Student leaders introduce first-time freshman and transfer students to the university and surrounding community, and conduct educational sessions on various social issues of university life. **Policies:** Campus code of conduct. **Housing:** Coed dorms, apartments available. $300 partly refundable deposit, deadline 6/1. All housing in apartment-style units. **Activities:** Jazz band, choral groups, dance, drama, film society, music ensembles, musical theater, student government, arts council, orientation committee, African American student union, Artists' Christian Fellowship, student government, Hispanic student union, Outreach Bible Study.

Athletics. Intramural: Volleyball.

Student services. Adult student services, alcohol/substance abuse counseling, career counseling, services for economically disadvantaged, student employment services, financial aid counseling, health services, personal counseling, placement for graduates, veterans' counselor. **Physically disabled:** Services for visually, speech, hearing impaired.

Contact. E-mail: admissions@uarts.edu
Phone: (215) 717-6049 Toll-free number: (800) 616-2787
Fax: (215) 717-6045
Susan Gandy, Director of Admission, University of the Arts, 320 South Broad Street, Philadelphia, PA 19102

University of the Sciences in Philadelphia

Philadelphia, Pennsylvania — **CB member**
www.usip.edu — **CB code: 2663**

- Private 4-year health science and pharmacy college
- Residential campus in very large city
- 1,962 degree-seeking undergraduates: 1% part-time, 61% women, 6% African American, 32% Asian American, 2% Hispanic American, 1% international
- 765 degree-seeking graduate students
- 65% of applicants admitted
- SAT or ACT with writing required
- 60% graduate within 6 years; 30% enter graduate study

General. Founded in 1821. Regionally accredited. Direct-entry admission for freshman pharmacy, DPT and MPT physical therapy program, occupational therapy and physician assistant programs. Students not required to reapply to professional phase of their majors. **Degrees:** 149 bachelor's awarded; master's, doctoral, first professional offered. **ROTC:** Army, Air Force. **Calendar:** Semester, limited summer session. **Full-time faculty:** 151 total; 80% have terminal degrees, 17% minority, 48% women. **Part-time faculty:** 98 total; 12% minority, 57% women. **Class size:** 35% < 20, 48% 20-39, 3% 40-49, 5% 50-99, 10% >100. **Special facilities:** History of pharmacy museum, center for advanced pharmacy study laboratory.

Freshman class profile. 2,897 applied, 1,891 admitted, 521 enrolled.

Mid 50% test scores			
SAT verbal:	530-610	Rank in top quarter:	74%
SAT math:	560-650	Rank in top tenth:	35%
ACT:	22-27	Return as sophomores:	83%
GPA 3.50 or higher:	62%	Out-of-state:	48%
GPA 3.0-3.49:	30%	Live on campus:	84%
GPA 2.0-2.99:	8%	International:	1%

Basis for selection. High school curriculum, GPA, class rank if provided by high school, and SAT or ACT test scores most important criteria. Essay and/or letters of recommendation not required, but reviewed if provided. **Learning Disabled:** If admitted under current admission process, students will be provided with necessary additional services to assist in academic success.

High school preparation. 19 units required. Required and recommended units include English 4, mathematics 3-4, social studies 1, history 1, science 3-4 (laboratory 3) and academic electives 4.

2005-2006 Annual costs. Tuition/fees: $23,982. Tiered cost structure applies to students enrolled in 5- and 6-year programs that lead to professional degrees. Room/board: $9,380. Books/supplies: $1,000. Personal expenses: $2,530.

Financial aid. Non-need-based: Scholarships awarded for academics, athletics.

Application procedures. Admission: No deadline. $45 fee, may be waived for applicants with need. Application may be submitted online. Admission notification on a rolling basis beginning on or about 10/1. Must reply by May 1 or within 2 week(s) if notified thereafter. **Financial aid:** Closing date 3/15. FAFSA required. Applicants notified on a rolling basis starting 1/15; must reply by 5/1 or within 2 week(s) of notification.

Academics. Special study options: Combined bachelor's/graduate degree, double major, ESL, honors, internships, liberal arts/career combination, teacher certification program. **Credit/placement by examination:** AP,

CLEP, IB, institutional tests. **Support services:** Learning center, pre-admission summer program, reduced course load, remedial instruction, study skills assistance, tutoring, writing center.

Majors. **Biology:** General, bacteriology, biochemistry, pharmacology, toxicology. **Business:** Marketing. **Computer sciences:** General. **Conservation:** Environmental science. **Health:** Clinical lab technology, physician assistant. **Physical sciences:** Chemistry. **Psychology:** General.

Most popular majors. Biology 40%, business/marketing 7%, health sciences 47%.

Computing on campus. 135 workstations in dormitories, library, computer center, student center. Dormitories wired for high-speed internet access and linked to campus network. Commuter students can connect to campus network. Online course registration, online library, helpline, repair service, wireless network available.

Student life. **Freshman orientation:** Mandatory. Programs for parents and students; placement testing. **Policies:** Campus alcohol free. **Housing:** Guaranteed on-campus for freshmen. Coed dorms, fraternity/sorority housing, substance-free housing available. $175 deposit, deadline 5/1. Honor halls. **Activities:** Concert band, choral groups, dance, drama, literary magazine, musical theater, student government, student newspaper, professional organizations, Greek letter organizations, religious groups, honor societies, student community involvement program, ethnic/diversity groups, student chapters of scientific organizations, and student publications.

Athletics. NAIA, NCAA. **Intercollegiate:** Baseball M, basketball, cross-country, golf, rifle, softball W, tennis, volleyball W. **Intramural:** Archery, badminton, basketball, bowling, rifle, table tennis, volleyball. **Team name:** Devils.

Student services. Adult student services, alcohol/substance abuse counseling, career counseling, student employment services, financial aid counseling, health services, personal counseling, placement for graduates, veterans' counselor. **Physically disabled:** Services for visually, speech, hearing impaired.

Contact. E-mail: admit@usip.edu
Phone: (215) 596-8810 Toll-free number: (888) 996-8747
Fax: (215) 596-8821
Louis Hegyes, Director of Admission, University of the Sciences in Philadelphia, 600 South 43rd Street, Philadelphia, PA 19104-4495

Ursinus College

Collegeville, Pennsylvania — **CB member**
www.ursinus.edu — **CB code: 2931**

- Private 4-year liberal arts college
- Residential campus in small town
- 1,555 degree-seeking undergraduates: 52% women, 7% African American, 4% Asian American, 3% Hispanic American, 1% international
- 75% of applicants admitted
- Application essay required
- 76% graduate within 6 years; 34% enter graduate study

General. Founded in 1869. Regionally accredited. All freshmen receive laptop computers (updated at beginning of junior year). **Degrees:** 295 bachelor's awarded. **Location:** 25 miles from Philadelphia. **Calendar:** Semester. **Full-time faculty:** 115 total; 93% have terminal degrees, 10% minority, 42% women. **Part-time faculty:** 50 total; 38% have terminal degrees, 68% women. **Class size:** 76% < 20, 23% 20-39, less than 1% 40-49, less than 1% 50-99. **Special facilities:** Performing arts center, art museum, smart classrooms.

Freshman class profile. 1,776 applied, 1,326 admitted, 426 enrolled.

Mid 50% test scores		**Return as sophomores:**	91%
SAT verbal:	550-660	**Out-of-state:**	40%
SAT math:	560-670	**Live on campus:**	98%
ACT:	22-28	**International:**	1%
Rank in top quarter:	65%	**Fraternities:**	12%
Rank in top tenth:	41%	**Sororities:**	33%
End year in good standing:	98%		

Basis for selection. Academic achievement most important, including courses taken, grades received. Test scores also important. Motivation and activities considered. Rank in top fifth of class preferred. Alumni children and minorities receive special consideration. SAT/ACT optional for students ranking in top 10% of class, or with minimum 3.5 GPA from non-ranking school. Interview recommended.

High school preparation. 16 units required; 20 recommended. Required and recommended units include English 4, mathematics 3-4, social studies 1-3, science 1-3 (laboratory 1), foreign language 2-4 and academic electives 5. Science majors should have minumum of 4 units each in mathematics and science.

2006-2007 Annual costs. Tuition/fees: $33,200. Room/board: $7,600. Books/supplies: $600. Personal expenses: $1,000.

2005-2006 Financial aid. **Need-based:** 411 full-time freshmen applied for aid; 326 were judged to have need; 326 of these received aid. Average need met was 85%. Average scholarship/grant was $20,243; average loan $3,649. 65% of total undergraduate aid awarded as scholarships/grants, 35% as loans/jobs. **Non-need-based:** Awarded to 348 full-time undergraduates, including 120 freshmen. Scholarships awarded for alumni affiliation.

Application procedures. **Admission:** Closing date 2/15 (receipt date). $50 fee, may be waived for applicants with need. Application may be submitted online. Admission notification 4/15. Must reply by 5/1. Rolling notification dates for both early decision and early action applicants, within 2 weeks of application receipt. **Financial aid:** Closing date 2/15. FAFSA, institutional form, CSS PROFILE required. Applicants notified by 4/1; must reply by 5/1.

Academics. Summer undergraduate research fellowships available. Independent Learning Experience required of all. Study abroad is encouraged. All first-year students complete two semesters of the Common Intellectual Experience, a wide-ranging, comprehensive overview of human thought, creativity, culture, history. **Special study options:** Accelerated study, combined bachelor's/graduate degree, double major, exchange student, honors, independent study, internships, semester at sea, student-designed major, study abroad, teacher certification program, United Nations semester, Washington semester. State capitol semester in Harrisburg (internship for state residents), Howard University semester. **Credit/placement by examination:** AP, CLEP, IB, institutional tests. **Support services:** Pre-admission summer program, tutoring, writing center.

Majors. **Area/ethnic studies:** American, East Asian. **Biology:** General. **Communications:** General. **Computer sciences:** Computer science. **Conservation:** Environmental studies. **English:** English lit. **Foreign languages:** Classics, French, German, Spanish. **History:** General. **Interdisciplinary:** Biological/physical sciences, neuroscience. **Math:** General. **Parks/recreation:** Health/fitness. **Philosophy/religion:** Philosophy. **Physical sciences:** Chemistry, physics. **Psychology:** General. **Social sciences:** Anthropology, economics, international relations, political science, sociology. **Visual/performing arts:** Art, art history/conservation, dance, dramatic.

Most popular majors. Biology 13%, communications/journalism 9%, English 8%, parks/recreation 6%, physical sciences 6%, psychology 12%, social sciences 23%.

Computing on campus. PC or laptop required. 1,625 workstations in dormitories, library, computer center, student center. Dormitories wired for high-speed internet access and linked to campus network. Commuter students can connect to campus network. Online course registration, online library, helpline, repair service, student web hosting, wireless network available.

Student life. **Freshman orientation:** Mandatory. Preregistration for classes offered. Choice of 1 of 2 weekends in June, plus 4 days in August before start of classes. **Housing:** Guaranteed on-campus for all undergraduates. Coed dorms, single-sex dorms, substance-free housing available. $500 nonrefundable deposit, deadline 5/1. Wellness house, quiet halls and houses, houses specializing in service, art, biology, honors, and literature available. **Activities:** Bands, choral groups, dance, drama, film society, literary magazine, music ensembles, musical theater, radio station, student government, student newspaper, TV station, Alternative Spring Break, Association of Latinos Motivated to Achieve, Best Buddies, College Democrats, College Republicans, Hillel, Inter-Faith Outreach, IMAAM, Sankofa Umoja Nia, student EMT crew.

Athletics. NCAA. **Intercollegiate:** Baseball M, basketball, cross-country, field hockey W, football (tackle) M, golf, gymnastics W, lacrosse, soccer, softball W, swimming, tennis, track and field, volleyball W, wrestling M. **Intramural:** Basketball, football (non-tackle) M, soccer, softball, squash, swimming, tennis, volleyball. **Team name:** Bears.

Student services. Adult student services, alcohol/substance abuse counseling, campus ministries, career counseling, student employment services, financial aid counseling, health services, minority student services, personal counseling, placement for graduates. **Physically disabled:** Services for visually, speech, hearing impaired.

Contact. E-mail: admissions@ursinus.edu
Phone: (610) 409-3200 Fax: (610) 489-3662
Director of Admissions, Ursinus College, P.O. Box 1000, Collegeville, PA 19426-1000

Valley Forge Christian College
Phoenixville, Pennsylvania
www.vfcc.edu **CB code: 2579**

- Private 4-year liberal arts college affiliated with Assemblies of God
- Residential campus in large town
- 878 degree-seeking undergraduates: 4% part-time, 53% women
- 75% of applicants admitted
- SAT or ACT with writing, application essay required
- 43% graduate within 6 years

General. Founded in 1938. Candidate for regional accreditation; also accredited by ABHE. **Degrees:** 119 bachelor's, 11 associate awarded. **Location:** 25 miles from Philadelphia. **Calendar:** Semester, limited summer session. **Full-time faculty:** 33 total; 46% have terminal degrees, 6% minority, 33% women. **Part-time faculty:** 35 total; 6% have terminal degrees, 3% minority, 34% women.

Freshman class profile. 398 applied, 297 admitted, 212 enrolled.

Basis for selection. School achievement record, pastor recommendation, written essay, test scores important. English, mathematics, Bible study skills tests required for all. Music, computer tests required for some. Interview recommended.

High school preparation. 16 units recommended. Recommended units include English 4, mathematics 2, social studies 4, science 4 and foreign language 2.

2006-2007 Annual costs. Tuition/fees: $11,755. Room/board: $5,850. Books/supplies: $748. Personal expenses: $1,660.

2005-2006 Financial aid. Need-based: Average need met was 47%. Average scholarship/grant was $4,812; average loan $2,568. 42% of total undergraduate aid awarded as scholarships/grants, 58% as loans/jobs. **Non-need-based:** Scholarships awarded for academics, leadership, music/drama, religious affiliation, state residency.

Application procedures. Admission: Priority date 5/1; deadline 8/1 (receipt date). $25 fee, may be waived for applicants with need. Application may be submitted online. Admission notification on a rolling basis beginning on or about 10/1. **Financial aid:** Priority date 5/1; no closing date. FAFSA required. Applicants notified on a rolling basis starting 3/15; must reply within 3 week(s) of notification.

Academics. Special study options: Accelerated study, combined bachelor's/graduate degree, distance learning, dual enrollment of high school students, ESL, independent study, internships, liberal arts/career combination, study abroad, teacher certification program, weekend college. **Credit/placement by examination:** AP, CLEP, institutional tests. 30 credit hours maximum toward bachelor's degree. **Support services:** Learning center, preadmission summer program, reduced course load, remedial instruction, study skills assistance, tutoring.

Majors. Business: Business admin. **Education:** Early childhood, elementary, music. **Theology:** Bible, missionary, pastoral counseling, religious ed, sacred music, theology. **Visual/performing arts:** Music performance.

Most popular majors. Education 13%, psychology 19%, theological studies 60%.

Computing on campus. 54 workstations in library, computer center. Dormitories wired for high-speed internet access and linked to campus network. Commuter students can connect to campus network. Online library, helpline available.

Student life. Freshman orientation: Mandatory, $55 fee. Preregistration for classes offered. Held weekend prior to classes beginning. **Policies:** Religious observance required. Freshmen permitted cars on campus. **Housing:** Guaranteed on-campus for freshmen. Single-sex dorms, special housing for disabled, apartments, substance-free housing available. $100 deposit. **Activities:** Bands, choral groups, drama, music ensembles, student government.

Athletics. NCCAA. **Intercollegiate:** Basketball, soccer, volleyball W. **Intramural:** Basketball, bowling, soccer, volleyball. **Team name:** Patriots.

Student services. Campus ministries, career counseling, student employment services, financial aid counseling, health services, personal counseling, placement for graduates, veterans' counselor.

Contact. E-mail: admission@vfcc.edu
Phone: (610) 935-0450 Toll-free number: (800) 432-8322
Fax: (610) 935-9353
William Chenco, Director of Admissions, Valley Forge Christian College, 1401 Charlestown Road, Phoenixville, PA 19460

Villanova University
Villanova, Pennsylvania **CB member**
www.villanova.edu **CB code: 2959**

- Private 4-year university affiliated with Roman Catholic Church
- Residential campus in small town
- 6,802 degree-seeking undergraduates: 5% part-time, 51% women, 4% African American, 6% Asian American, 5% Hispanic American, 2% international
- 3,042 degree-seeking graduate students
- 51% of applicants admitted
- SAT or ACT with writing, application essay required
- 85% graduate within 6 years; 25% enter graduate study

General. Founded in 1842. Regionally accredited. **Degrees:** 1,850 bachelor's, 4 associate awarded; master's, doctoral, first professional offered. **ROTC:** Army, Navy, Air Force. **Location:** 12 miles from Philadelphia. **Calendar:** Semester, extensive summer session. **Full-time faculty:** 545 total; 88% have terminal degrees, 11% minority, 31% women. **Part-time faculty:** 353 total; 42% have terminal degrees, 5% minority, 42% women. **Class size:** 42% < 20, 51% 20-39, 2% 40-49, 4% 50-99, less than 1% >100. **Special facilities:** Astronomy and astrophysics observatories, electron microscope, research with NASA, arboretum, structural engineering teaching and research laboratory.

Freshman class profile. 10,394 applied, 5,338 admitted, 1,629 enrolled.

Mid 50% test scores		**Rank in top quarter:**	83%
SAT verbal:	580-660	**Rank in top tenth:**	47%
SAT math:	600-690	**Return as sophomores:**	94%
ACT:	27-30	**Out-of-state:**	77%
GPA 3.50 or higher:	73%	**Live on campus:**	95%
GPA 3.0-3.49:	23%	**International:**	2%
GPA 2.0-2.99:	4%		

Basis for selection. High school record, class rank, standardized test scores, counselor recommendation, essay, extracurricular activities considered. Interview required for finalists of health affiliation programs and Presidential Scholarship consideration.

High school preparation. 22 units required; 25 recommended. Required and recommended units include English 4, mathematics 4, science 4 (laboratory 2-3), foreign language 2-4 and academic electives 2. 4 social studies and/or history required. Total units required varies by academic college.

2005-2006 Annual costs. Tuition/fees: $29,618. Tuition provided is average of costs for all 4 colleges within Villanova University. Room/board: $9,362. Books/supplies: $950. Personal expenses: $950.

2005-2006 Financial aid. Need-based: 1,054 full-time freshmen applied for aid; 741 were judged to have need; 733 of these received aid. Average need met was 85%. Average scholarship/grant was $18,878; average loan $3,110. 63% of total undergraduate aid awarded as scholarships/grants, 37% as loans/jobs. **Non-need-based:** Awarded to 1,364 full-time undergraduates, including 384 freshmen. Scholarships awarded for academics, alumni affiliation, athletics, leadership, minority status, religious affiliation, ROTC.

Application procedures. Admission: Closing date 1/7 (receipt date). $70 fee, may be waived for applicants with need. Application may be submitted online. Admission notification 4/1. Must reply by 5/1. November 1 is priority application date for scholarship consideration. Commuting students and nursing majors notified of decisions on a rolling basis beginning January 15. **Financial aid:** Closing date 2/7. FAFSA, institutional form required. Applicants notified by 3/24; must reply by 5/1.

Academics. Special study options: Accelerated study, combined bachelor's/graduate degree, cross-registration, distance learning, double major, dual enrollment of high school students, ESL, honors, independent study, internships, study abroad, teacher certification program, Washington semester. Cooperative certification programs in elementary education with Rosemont College. **Credit/placement by examination:** AP, CLEP, IB, institutional tests. 30 credit hours maximum toward bachelor's degree. Deans make decisions regarding prior work and life experiences on individual basis. **Support services:** Reduced course load, study skills assistance, tutoring, writing center.

Majors. Biology: General. **Business:** Accounting, business admin, finance, human resources, management information systems, managerial economics, marketing. **Communications:** General. **Computer sciences:** General, information systems. **Education:** Elementary, secondary. **Engineering:** Chemical, civil, computer, electrical, mechanical. **English:** English lit. **Foreign**

languages: Classics, French, German, Italian, Spanish. **Health:** Nursing (RN), predentistry, premedicine. **History:** General. **Interdisciplinary:** Biological/physical sciences. **Liberal arts:** Arts/sciences. **Math:** General. **Philosophy/religion:** Philosophy, religion. **Physical sciences:** Astronomy, astrophysics, chemistry, physics. **Psychology:** General. **Public administration:** Human services. **Social sciences:** Economics, geography, political science, sociology. **Visual/performing arts:** Art history/conservation.

Most popular majors. Business/marketing 35%, communications/journalism 9%, engineering/engineering technologies 11%, health sciences 7%, psychology 6%, social sciences 12%.

Computing on campus. PC or laptop required. 2,530 workstations in dormitories, library, computer center, student center. Dormitories wired for high-speed internet access and linked to campus network. Commuter students can connect to campus network. Online course registration, online library, helpline, repair service, student web hosting, wireless network available.

Student life. **Freshman orientation:** Mandatory, $125 fee. 4-day on-campus program prior to start of fall term. **Housing:** Guaranteed on-campus for freshmen. Coed dorms, single-sex dorms, apartments, substance-free housing available. $150 deposit, deadline 5/1. On-campus housing available for transfer students on space-available basis. **Activities:** Bands, choral groups, dance, drama, film society, literary magazine, music ensembles, musical theater, radio station, student government, student newspaper, TV station, Special Olympics, Amnesty International, Villanovans for Life, Black Cultural Society, Big Brother/Sister, Committee for the Homeless, Project Sunshine, Habitat for Humanity, Blue Key Society.

Athletics. NCAA. **Intercollegiate:** Baseball M, basketball, bowling W, cheerleading, cross-country, diving, field hockey W, football (tackle) M, golf M, lacrosse, rowing (crew) W, soccer, softball W, swimming, tennis, track and field, volleyball W, water polo W. **Intramural:** Basketball, cross-country, field hockey W, football (non-tackle), skiing, soccer, softball, tennis, volleyball. **Team name:** Wildcats.

Student services. Adult student services, alcohol/substance abuse counseling, campus ministries, career counseling, services for economically disadvantaged, student employment services, financial aid counseling, health services, minority student services, personal counseling, placement for graduates. **Physically disabled:** Services for visually, hearing impaired.

Contact. E-mail: gotovu@villanova.edu
Phone: (610) 519-4000 Fax: (610) 519-6450
Michael Gaynor, Director of University Admission, Villanova University, 800 Lancaster Avenue, Villanova, PA 19085-1672

Washington and Jefferson College

Washington, Pennsylvania — **CB member**
www.washjeff.edu — **CB code: 2967**

- Private 4-year liberal arts college
- Residential campus in large town
- 1,399 degree-seeking undergraduates: 48% women, 2% African American, 1% Asian American, 1% Hispanic American
- 39% of applicants admitted
- SAT or ACT (ACT writing recommended), application essay required
- 68% graduate within 6 years; 30% enter graduate study

General. Founded in 1781. Regionally accredited. **Degrees:** 258 bachelor's awarded. **ROTC:** Army, Air Force. **Location:** 27 miles from Pittsburgh. **Calendar:** 4-1-4, limited summer session. **Full-time faculty:** 97 total; 86% have terminal degrees, 9% minority, 34% women. **Part-time faculty:** 33 total; 27% have terminal degrees, 21% minority, 58% women. **Class size:** 65% < 20, 33% 20-39, 1% 40-49, less than 1% 50-99. **Special facilities:** Biological field station.

Freshman class profile. 4,477 applied, 1,737 admitted, 388 enrolled.

Mid 50% test scores		**Rank in top quarter:**	65%
SAT verbal:	520-610	**Rank in top tenth:**	31%
SAT math:	530-620	**End year in good standing:**	93%
ACT:	23-27	**Return as sophomores:**	86%
GPA 3.50 or higher:	41%	**Out-of-state:**	31%
GPA 3.0-3.49:	39%	**Live on campus:**	96%
GPA 2.0-2.99:	19%		

Basis for selection. High school record and class rank most important. Recommendations, test scores, essay, interview, extracurricular activities, character important.

High school preparation. College-preparatory program required. 15 units required. Required units include English 3, mathematics 3, science 1, foreign language 2 and academic electives 6.

2005-2006 Annual costs. Tuition/fees: $26,330. Room/board: $7,160. Books/supplies: $600. Personal expenses: $700.

2005-2006 Financial aid. **Need-based:** 353 full-time freshmen applied for aid; 301 were judged to have need; 301 of these received aid. Average need met was 80%. Average scholarship/grant was $14,800; average loan $2,696. 67% of total undergraduate aid awarded as scholarships/grants, 33% as loans/jobs. **Non-need-based:** Awarded to 365 full-time undergraduates, including 108 freshmen. Scholarships awarded for academics, alumni affiliation.

Application procedures. **Admission:** Priority date 1/15; deadline 3/1 (postmark date). $25 fee, may be waived for applicants with need. Application may be submitted online. Admission notification on a rolling basis beginning on or about 11/15. Must reply by 5/1. Must reply by May 1 or within 2 week(s) if notified thereafter. **Financial aid:** Priority date 2/15; no closing date. FAFSA required. Applicants notified on a rolling basis starting 3/1; must reply by 5/1.

Academics. **Special study options:** Accelerated study, combined bachelor's/graduate degree, double major, dual enrollment of high school students, honors, independent study, internships, student-designed major, study abroad, teacher certification program, Washington semester. **Credit/placement by examination:** AP, CLEP, IB, institutional tests. 68 credit hours maximum toward bachelor's degree. **Support services:** Learning center, reduced course load, study skills assistance, tutoring.

Majors. **Biology:** General, biochemistry. **Business:** General, accounting, international. **Computer sciences:** Information technology. **Education:** General, art. **English:** English lit. **Foreign languages:** French, German, Spanish. **History:** General. **Math:** General. **Philosophy/religion:** Philosophy. **Physical sciences:** Chemistry, physics. **Psychology:** General. **Social sciences:** Economics, political science, sociology. **Visual/performing arts:** Art, theater history.

Most popular majors. Biology 9%, business/marketing 32%, English 7%, history 9%, psychology 13%, social sciences 14%.

Computing on campus. 450 workstations in library, computer center. Dormitories wired for high-speed internet access and linked to campus network. Commuter students can connect to campus network. Online course registration, online library, helpline, repair service, student web hosting, wireless network available.

Student life. **Freshman orientation:** Mandatory. Preregistration for classes offered. Includes placement tests. **Policies:** All students required to live in campus housing unless granted written approval. Students not permitted to smoke in rooms, hallways, or lounges. Freshmen permitted cars on campus. **Housing:** Guaranteed on-campus for freshmen. Coed dorms, single-sex dorms, special housing for disabled, fraternity/sorority housing, substance-free housing available. On-campus suites available. **Activities:** Bands, choral groups, dance, drama, film society, literary magazine, music ensembles, musical theater, radio station, student government, student newspaper, Newman Club, Hillel Society, Young Republicans, College Democrats, liberal student union, Asian student association, Black Student Union, international club, Alpha Phi Omega, Get Involved in Volunteer Experiences.

Athletics. NCAA. **Intercollegiate:** Baseball M, basketball, cheerleading M, cross-country, diving, field hockey W, football (tackle) M, golf, lacrosse M, soccer, softball W, swimming, tennis, track and field, volleyball W, water polo, wrestling M. **Intramural:** Basketball, bowling, cross-country, football (non-tackle), racquetball, soccer, softball, table tennis, tennis, volleyball. **Team name:** Presidents.

Student services. Adult student services, alcohol/substance abuse counseling, career counseling, student employment services, financial aid counseling, health services, minority student services, personal counseling, placement for graduates.

Contact. E-mail: admission@washjeff.edu
Phone: (724) 223-6025 Toll-free number: (888) 926-3529
Fax: (724) 223-6534
Alton Newell, Vice President of Enrollment Management, Washington and Jefferson College, 60 South Lincoln Street, Washington, PA 15301

Waynesburg College

Waynesburg, Pennsylvania — **CB member**
www.waynesburg.edu — **CB code: 2969**

- Private 4-year liberal arts college affiliated with Presbyterian Church (USA)
- Residential campus in small town

- 1,440 degree-seeking undergraduates: 10% part-time, 60% women, 3% African American, 1% Hispanic American
- 520 graduate students
- 74% of applicants admitted
- SAT or ACT with writing required
- 52% graduate within 6 years

General. Founded in 1849. Regionally accredited. **Degrees:** 320 bachelor's, 22 associate awarded; master's offered. **ROTC:** Army. **Location:** 50 miles from Pittsburgh. **Calendar:** Semester, limited summer session. **Full-time faculty:** 62 total; 56% have terminal degrees, 3% minority, 45% women. **Part-time faculty:** 67 total; 30% have terminal degrees, 51% women. **Class size:** 67% < 20, 36% 20-39, 2% 40-49, less than 1% 50-99. **Special facilities:** Geological museum, historical museum.

Freshman class profile. 1,518 applied, 1,124 admitted, 341 enrolled.

Mid 50% test scores			
SAT verbal:	430-530	GPA 2.0-2.99:	23%
SAT math:	430-540	Rank in top quarter:	40%
ACT:	18-23	Rank in top tenth:	14%
GPA 3.50 or higher:	45%	Return as sophomores:	76%
GPA 3.0-3.49:	31%	Out-of-state:	15%
		Live on campus:	79%

Basis for selection. High school classes taken, grades, test scores, activities, community activities, interview, and recommendations considered. Note: one-half of $150 housing deposit is refundable if candidate does not enroll. Essay, interview recommended. **Homeschooled:** Statement describing homeschool structure and mission, transcript of courses and grades, state high school equivalency certificate required. College should be apprised if homeschooled applicant enrolled in program approved by state's department of education.

High school preparation. 16 units required. Required and recommended units include English 4, mathematics 3, social studies 2, science 2-3, foreign language 2 and academic electives 5.

2005-2006 Annual costs. Tuition/fees: $15,150. Room/board: $6,080. Books/supplies: $1,000. Personal expenses: $170.

2005-2006 Financial aid. Need-based: Average need met was 81%. Average scholarship/grant was $10,159; average loan $2,833. 65% of total undergraduate aid awarded as scholarships/grants, 35% as loans/jobs. **Non-need-based:** Scholarships awarded for academics, alumni affiliation, job skills, leadership, religious affiliation, state residency.

Application procedures. Admission: No deadline. $20 fee, may be waived for applicants with need. Application may be submitted online. Admission notification on a rolling basis. Rolling date as specified in deposit letter. **Financial aid:** Priority date 3/15; no closing date. FAFSA required. Applicants notified on a rolling basis starting 2/15; must reply within 2 week(s) of notification.

Academics. Nursing majors must complete 126 credit hours for bachelor of science degree. **Special study options:** Accelerated study, combined bachelor's/graduate degree, distance learning, double major, dual enrollment of high school students, honors, independent study, internships, liberal arts/career combination, study abroad, teacher certification program, Washington semester. 3-2 program in engineering with Case Western Reserve University (OH), Penn State University, Washington University (MO), 3-1 program in Marine Biology with Florida Institute of Technology, 3-3 law program with Duquesne University. **Credit/placement by examination:** AP, CLEP, IB, SAT, ACT, institutional tests. 15 credit hours maximum toward bachelor's degree. **Support services:** Learning center, reduced course load, study skills assistance, tutoring, writing center.

Majors. Biology: General, environmental, marine. **Business:** General, accounting, business admin, finance, international, international marketing. **Communications:** General, advertising, broadcast journalism, digital media, journalism, public relations. **Computer sciences:** General, computer science, information technology, networking. **Conservation:** General. **Education:** Biology, chemistry, elementary, English, history, mathematics, science, secondary, social studies, special. **English:** British lit, creative writing, English lit. **Family/consumer sciences:** Family studies. **Health:** Athletic training, nursing (RN), predentistry, premedicine, preveterinary. **History:** General. **Legal studies:** Prelaw. **Math:** General. **Parks/recreation:** Exercise sciences, sports admin. **Philosophy/religion:** Religion. **Physical sciences:** Chemistry. **Protective services:** Forensics, law enforcement admin. **Psychology:** General. **Public administration:** Human services. **Social sciences:** General, political science, sociology. **Theology:** Theology. **Visual/performing arts:** Art, arts management, commercial/advertising art, music management, theater arts management.

Most popular majors. Biology 7%, business/marketing 22%, communications/journalism 8%, education 12%, health sciences 22%, public administration/social services 10%.

Computing on campus. 160 workstations in library, computer center, student center. Dormitories wired for high-speed internet access and linked to campus network. Commuter students can connect to campus network. Online course registration, online library, helpline, wireless network available.

Student life. Freshman orientation: Mandatory. Preregistration for classes offered. 1-day summer program for parents and students; 2-day program prior to start of classes. **Policies:** No alcohol or drugs permitted on campus. **Housing:** Guaranteed on-campus for all undergraduates. Coed dorms, single-sex dorms available. $150 deposit. Upper class apartment style available. **Activities:** Bands, choral groups, dance, drama, literary magazine, music ensembles, musical theater, radio station, student government, student newspaper, TV station, Fellowship of Christian Athletes, Newman Club, international student organization, black student union, Waynesburg Christian Fellowship, Bonner Scholars (service group), Alpha Phi Omega, Habitat for Humanity, leadership program.

Athletics. NCAA. **Intercollegiate:** Baseball M, basketball, cross-country, football (tackle) M, golf, soccer, softball W, tennis, track and field, volleyball W, wrestling M. **Intramural:** Basketball, bowling, football (non-tackle), racquetball, softball, table tennis, volleyball W. **Team name:** Yellow Jackets.

Student services. Adult student services, campus ministries, career counseling, student employment services, financial aid counseling, health services, minority student services, personal counseling, placement for graduates.

Contact. E-mail: admissions@waynesburg.edu
Phone: (724) 852-3248 Toll-free number: (800) 225-7393
Fax: (724) 627-8124
Robin King, Director of Admissions, Waynesburg College, 51 West College Street, Waynesburg, PA 15370

West Chester University of Pennsylvania

West Chester, Pennsylvania **CB member**
www.wcupa.edu **CB code: 2659**

- Public 4-year university
- Commuter campus in large town
- 10,395 degree-seeking undergraduates: 7% part-time, 61% women
- 1,524 degree-seeking graduate students
- 49% of applicants admitted
- SAT or ACT with writing, application essay required
- 59% graduate within 6 years

General. Founded in 1871. Regionally accredited. **Degrees:** 2,020 bachelor's awarded; master's offered. **ROTC:** Army, Air Force. **Location:** 23 miles from Philadelphia. **Calendar:** Semester, extensive summer session. **Full-time faculty:** 567 total; 77% have terminal degrees, 15% minority, 47% women. **Part-time faculty:** 230 total; 30% have terminal degrees, 7% minority, 60% women. **Class size:** 27% < 20, 66% 20-39, 3% 40-49, 3% 50-99, 1% >100. **Special facilities:** Herbarium, natural area for environmental studies, planetarium.

Freshman class profile. 11,013 applied, 5,438 admitted, 1,901 enrolled.

Mid 50% test scores			
SAT verbal:	490-570	Rank in top quarter:	31%
SAT math:	490-580	Rank in top tenth:	9%
GPA 3.50 or higher:	40%	Return as sophomores:	84%
GPA 3.0-3.49:	40%	Out-of-state:	16%
GPA 2.0-2.99:	20%	Live on campus:	93%

Basis for selection. School achievement record, class rank, test scores important. Interview required for athletic training, music, and professional programs; audition required for music. **Homeschooled:** Students must have work certified by PA Homeschoolers' Association or their high school.

High school preparation. 16 units required; 21 recommended. Required and recommended units include English 4, mathematics 3-4, social studies 2, history 4, science 2-3 (laboratory 1-2), foreign language 2 and academic electives 1-2.

2005-2006 Annual costs. Tuition/fees: $6,147; $13,507 out-of-state. Room/board: $6,208. Books/supplies: $1,000. Personal expenses: $1,770.

Application procedures. Admission: Priority date 1/1; no deadline. $35 fee, may be waived for applicants with need. Application may be submitted online. Admission notification on a rolling basis beginning on or about 10/1. Must reply by May 1 or within 4 week(s) if notified thereafter. **Financial**

aid: Priority date 3/1; no closing date. FAFSA required. Applicants notified on a rolling basis starting 4/15; must reply within 3 week(s) of notification.

Academics. Special study options: Cooperative education, distance learning, double major, dual enrollment of high school students, ESL, exchange student, honors, independent study, internships, liberal arts/career combination, student-designed major, study abroad, teacher certification program. **Credit/placement by examination:** AP, CLEP, IB, SAT, institutional tests. 30 credit hours maximum toward bachelor's degree. **Support services:** Learning center, pre-admission summer program, reduced course load, remedial instruction, study skills assistance, tutoring, writing center.

Majors. Area/ethnic studies: American, women's. **Biology:** General, biochemistry, molecular. **Business:** General, accounting, business admin, entrepreneurial studies, finance, managerial economics, sales/distribution. **Communications:** General. **Computer sciences:** General. **Education:** Early childhood, elementary, mathematics, music, social science, special. **English:** American lit, speech/rhetoric. **Foreign languages:** Comparative lit, French, German, Latin, Russian, Spanish. **Health:** Athletic training, audiology/speech pathology, communication disorders, dietetics, health care admin, nursing (RN), premedicine. **History:** General. **Liberal arts:** Arts/sciences. **Math:** General. **Parks/recreation:** Exercise sciences, health/fitness. **Philosophy/religion:** Philosophy. **Physical sciences:** Analytical chemistry, chemistry, geology, physics. **Protective services:** Criminal justice. **Psychology:** General. **Public administration:** Social work. **Social sciences:** Anthropology, geography, international relations, political science, sociology. **Visual/performing arts:** Dramatic, music performance, music theory/composition, piano/organ, studio arts.

Most popular majors. Business/marketing 17%, education 18%, English 9%, health sciences 8%, liberal arts 9%, visual/performing arts 7%.

Computing on campus. 700 workstations in dormitories, library, computer center, student center. Dormitories wired for high-speed internet access and linked to campus network. Commuter students can connect to campus network. Helpline available.

Student life. Freshman orientation: Mandatory, $110 fee. Preregistration for classes offered. One-day program in late June/early July followed by 3-day program prior to start of classes. **Policies:** Code of conduct applicable on and off campus. **Housing:** Coed dorms, single-sex dorms, special housing for disabled, apartments, fraternity/sorority housing, substance-free housing available. $100 nonrefundable deposit, deadline 5/1. **Activities:** Bands, choral groups, dance, drama, literary magazine, music ensembles, musical theater, radio station, student government, student newspaper, Hillel, Newman Club, Crusade for Christ, international student association, Black Student Union, Latino American student organization, Asian American organization, Lesbian, Gay, Bisexual, and Transgender Association.

Athletics. NCAA. **Intercollegiate:** Baseball M, basketball, cross-country, diving, field hockey W, football (tackle) M, golf, gymnastics W, lacrosse W, rugby W, soccer, softball W, swimming, tennis, track and field, volleyball W. **Intramural:** Basketball, field hockey W, football (non-tackle), lacrosse, soccer, softball, tennis, volleyball. **Team name:** Rams.

Student services. Adult student services, alcohol/substance abuse counseling, campus ministries, career counseling, services for economically disadvantaged, student employment services, financial aid counseling, health services, legal services, minority student services, on-campus daycare, personal counseling, placement for graduates, women's services. **Physically disabled:** Services for visually, speech, hearing impaired. **Learning disabled:** Comprehensive services available.

Contact. E-mail: ugadmiss@wcupa.edu
Phone: (610) 436-3411 Toll-free number: (877) 315-2165
Fax: (610) 436-2907
Marsha Haug, Director of Admissions, West Chester University of Pennsylvania, Messikomer Hall, West Chester, PA 19383

Westminster College

New Wilmington, Pennsylvania — **CB member**
www.westminster.edu — **CB code: 2975**

- Private 4-year liberal arts college affiliated with Presbyterian Church (USA)
- Residential campus in small town
- 1,387 degree-seeking undergraduates: 1% part-time, 64% women
- 129 degree-seeking graduate students
- 77% of applicants admitted
- Application essay required
- 76% graduate within 6 years

General. Founded in 1852. Regionally accredited. General studies curriculum with a freshman common experience. **Degrees:** 239 bachelor's awarded; master's offered. **ROTC:** Army. **Location:** 60 miles from Pittsburgh, 17 miles from Youngstown, Ohio. **Calendar:** Semester, limited summer session. **Full-time faculty:** 103 total. **Part-time faculty:** 49 total. **Class size:** 63% < 20, 36% 20-39, less than 1% 40-49, less than 1% 50-99. **Special facilities:** Observatory, environmental outdoor laboratory, planetarium, electron microscopes, radar defractor.

Freshman class profile. 1,302 applied, 1,006 admitted, 359 enrolled.

Mid 50% test scores			
SAT verbal:	480-590	Rank in top quarter:	59%
SAT math:	480-590	Rank in top tenth:	26%
ACT:	20-25	Return as sophomores:	83%
GPA 3.50 or higher:	49%	Out-of-state:	19%
GPA 3.0-3.49:	32%	Live on campus:	97%
GPA 2.0-2.99:	19%	Fraternities:	33%
		Sororities:	35%

Basis for selection. Class rank most important. Test scores also important. SAT or ACT recommended. Interview recommended for all; audition recommended for music; portfolio recommended for art.

High school preparation. 16 units required. Required units include English 4, mathematics 3, social studies 2, history 1, science 2 (laboratory 2), foreign language 2 and academic electives 3.

2005-2006 Annual costs. Tuition/fees: $22,680. Room/board: $6,600. Books/supplies: $900. Personal expenses: $685.

2004-2005 Financial aid. Need-based: 70% of total undergraduate aid awarded as scholarships/grants, 30% as loans/jobs. **Non-need-based:** Scholarships awarded for academics, athletics.

Application procedures. Admission: Closing date 5/1. $35 fee, may be waived for applicants with need. Admission notification on a rolling basis beginning on or about 11/1. Must reply by May 1 or within 2 week(s) if notified thereafter. **Financial aid:** Closing date 5/1. FAFSA, institutional form, CSS PROFILE required. Applicants notified on a rolling basis starting 3/1.

Academics. Special study options: Double major, exchange student, honors, independent study, internships, liberal arts/career combination, semester at sea, student-designed major, study abroad, teacher certification program, Washington semester. 3-2 engineering programs with Case Western Reserve University (OH), Penn State, Washington University (MO), 3-2 law program with Duquesne University. **Credit/placement by examination:** AP, CLEP, institutional tests. **Support services:** Learning center, reduced course load, tutoring.

Majors. Biology: General, biochemistry, biophysics, ecology, molecular. **Business:** Accounting, business admin, finance, international, international finance, management science, managerial economics, organizational behavior. **Communications:** Broadcast journalism, public relations. **Computer sciences:** General, computer science, programming. **Education:** General, elementary, English, foreign languages, middle, multi-level teacher, secondary, social studies. **Engineering:** General. **English:** American lit, British lit, creative writing. **Foreign languages:** General, classics, French, German, Latin, Spanish. **Health:** Predentistry, premedicine, prepharmacy, preveterinary. **History:** General. **Interdisciplinary:** Biopsychology, math/computer science. **Legal studies:** Prelaw. **Math:** General. **Philosophy/religion:** Philosophy, religion. **Physical sciences:** Chemistry, physics. **Protective services:** Criminal justice. **Psychology:** General. **Public administration:** Social work. **Social sciences:** Economics, international relations, political science, sociology. **Theology:** Religious ed. **Visual/performing arts:** Art, dramatic, music performance, music theory/composition, piano/organ, studio arts, voice/opera.

Computing on campus. 160 workstations in library, computer center. Dormitories linked to campus network. Commuter students can connect to campus network. Helpline available.

Student life. Freshman orientation: Mandatory, $105 fee. 4-day general social and academic orientation. **Housing:** Guaranteed on-campus for freshmen. Coed dorms, single-sex dorms, special housing for disabled, fraternity/sorority housing available. **Activities:** Bands, choral groups, dance, drama, film society, literary magazine, music ensembles, musical theater, radio station, student government, student newspaper, symphony orchestra, TV station, Fellowship of Christian Athletes, mock convention, clown ministry, service organizations, social awareness and action groups, Students in Action Who Value the Environment, Habitat for Humanity, Alpha Phi Omega.

Athletics. NCAA. **Intercollegiate:** Baseball M, basketball, cross-country, football (tackle) M, golf, soccer, softball W, swimming, tennis, track and field, volleyball W. **Intramural:** Archery, badminton, basketball, equestrian, racquetball, rugby M, softball, track and field W, volleyball. **Team name:** Titans.

Student services. Adult student services, career counseling, student employment services, health services, personal counseling, placement for graduates.

Contact. E-mail: admis@westminster.edu
Phone: (724) 946-7100 Fax: (724) 946-7171
Douglas Swartz, Director of Admissions, Westminster College, Admissions, Westminster College, New Wilmington, PA 16172-0001

Widener University

Chester, Pennsylvania — **CB member**
www.widener.edu — **CB code: 2642**

- Private 4-year university
- Residential campus in large town
- 2,493 degree-seeking undergraduates: 5% part-time, 49% women, 13% African American, 2% Asian American, 2% Hispanic American, 2% international
- 3,059 degree-seeking graduate students
- 81% of applicants admitted
- SAT or ACT (ACT writing optional) required
- 68% graduate within 6 years

General. Founded in 1821. Regionally accredited. **Degrees:** 554 bachelor's, 25 associate awarded; master's, doctoral, first professional offered. **ROTC:** Army, Navy, Air Force. **Location:** 10 miles from Philadelphia, 10 miles from Wilmington, Delaware. **Calendar:** Semester, limited summer session. **Full-time faculty:** 220 total. **Part-time faculty:** 175 total. **Class size:** 47% < 20, 52% 20-39, less than 1% 40-49, less than 1% 50-99. **Special facilities:** Astronomical observatory, athletics complex, rock climbing wall, natural turf fields, restaurant lab, executive seminar facility, child development center, recording studio, education lab, commercial graphics lab, physical therapy lab, private art gallery.

Freshman class profile. 2,963 applied, 2,406 admitted, 650 enrolled.

Mid 50% test scores		**Rank in top tenth:**	11%
SAT verbal:	440-530	**Return as sophomores:**	66%
SAT math:	430-560	**Out-of-state:**	40%
GPA 3.50 or higher:	35%	**Live on campus:**	79%
GPA 3.0-3.49:	33%	**International:**	1%
GPA 2.0-2.99:	32%	**Fraternities:**	4%
Rank in top quarter:	32%	**Sororities:**	3%

Basis for selection. Strength of curriculum, GPA, standardized test scores, class rank most important; recommendations, strength of character important. Interview recommended. **Homeschooled:** Transcript of courses and grades required. Curriculum validation and interview with dean of admissions required.

High school preparation. 18 units required; 23 recommended. Required and recommended units include English 4, mathematics 3-4, social studies 3-4, science 3-4 (laboratory 2), foreign language 2 and academic electives 3.

2005-2006 Annual costs. Tuition/fees: $24,970. $800 additional fee for engineering students. Room/board: $8,500. Books/supplies: $840.

2005-2006 Financial aid. Need-based: 597 full-time freshmen applied for aid; 541 were judged to have need; 539 of these received aid. Average need met was 79%. Average scholarship/grant was $12,330; average loan $3,763. 55% of total undergraduate aid awarded as scholarships/grants, 45% as loans/jobs. **Non-need-based:** Awarded to 1,556 full-time undergraduates, including 446 freshmen. Scholarships awarded for academics, leadership, music/drama, ROTC.

Application procedures. Admission: Priority date 2/15; no deadline. $35 fee, may be waived for applicants with need. Application may be submitted online. Admission notification on a rolling basis beginning on or about 10/1. Must reply by May 1 or within 2 week(s) if notified thereafter. **Financial aid:** Priority date 2/15; no closing date. FAFSA required. Applicants notified on a rolling basis starting 3/15; must reply within 4 week(s) of notification.

Academics. Special study options: Accelerated study, combined bachelor's/graduate degree, cooperative education, distance learning, double major, honors, independent study, internships, student-designed major, study abroad, teacher certification program, weekend college. **Credit/placement by examination:** AP, CLEP, IB, institutional tests. Students can earn up to 2 years of credit in some fields via CLEP, challenge exams, and Advanced Placement exams. **Support services:** Learning center, pre-admission summer program, reduced course load, remedial instruction, study skills assistance, tutoring, writing center.

Majors. Area/ethnic studies: Women's. **Biology:** General, biochemistry. **Business:** Accounting, business admin, finance, financial planning, hospitality admin, human resources, international, management information systems, managerial economics, operations. **Communications:** General. **Computer sciences:** General, computer science, information systems. **Education:** Early childhood, elementary, science, special. **Engineering:** General, chemical, civil, electrical, mechanical. **English:** Creative writing, English lit. **Foreign languages:** French, Spanish. **Health:** Health services, nursing (RN), predentistry, premedicine, prenursing, preveterinary. **History:** General. **Legal studies:** Prelaw. **Liberal arts:** Arts/sciences. **Math:** General. **Physical sciences:** Chemistry, physics. **Protective services:** Law enforcement admin. **Psychology:** General. **Public administration:** Social work. **Social sciences:** Anthropology, economics, international relations, political science, sociology. **Visual/performing arts:** Studio arts.

Most popular majors. Business/marketing 34%, education 6%, engineering/engineering technologies 9%, health sciences 16%, psychology 8%, security/protective services 7%, social sciences 8%.

Computing on campus. 720 workstations in library, student center. Dormitories wired for high-speed internet access and linked to campus network. Commuter students can connect to campus network. Online course registration, online library, helpline, repair service, student web hosting, wireless network available.

Student life. Freshman orientation: Available. **Policies:** Freshmen permitted cars on campus. **Housing:** Guaranteed on-campus for all undergraduates. Coed dorms, single-sex dorms, apartments, cooperative housing, fraternity/sorority housing, substance-free housing available. $100 nonrefundable deposit. Special interest housing, academic clusters available. **Activities:** Bands, choral groups, dance, drama, film society, literary magazine, music ensembles, radio station, student government, student newspaper, TV station, Hillel, Black Student Union, political affairs club, Young Republicans, Young Democrats, environmental society, Widener Big Friends, Crusade for Christ, Alpha Phi Omega, Asian student association, presidential service corps.

Athletics. NCAA. **Intercollegiate:** Baseball M, basketball, cheerleading M, cross-country, field hockey W, football (tackle) M, golf M, lacrosse, soccer, softball W, swimming, track and field, volleyball W. **Intramural:** Basketball, cricket M, football (non-tackle), skiing, soccer, softball, volleyball, water polo M. **Team name:** Pioneers.

Student services. Adult student services, alcohol/substance abuse counseling, campus ministries, career counseling, services for economically disadvantaged, student employment services, financial aid counseling, health services, on-campus daycare, personal counseling, veterans' counselor, women's services. **Physically disabled:** Services for visually, speech, hearing impaired. **Learning disabled:** Comprehensive services available.

Contact. E-mail: admissions.office@widener.edu
Phone: (610) 499-4126 Toll-free number: (888) 943-3637
Fax: (610) 499-4676
Edwin Wright, Director of Admissions, Widener University, One University Place, Chester, PA 19013

Wilkes University

Wilkes-Barre, Pennsylvania — **CB member**
www.wilkes.edu — **CB code: 2977**

- Private 4-year university
- Residential campus in small city
- 2,147 degree-seeking undergraduates: 8% part-time, 53% women, 2% African American, 2% Asian American, 2% Hispanic American
- 2,292 degree-seeking graduate students
- 77% of applicants admitted
- SAT or ACT required
- 59% graduate within 6 years

General. Founded in 1933. Regionally accredited. **Degrees:** 405 bachelor's awarded; master's, first professional offered. **ROTC:** Army, Air Force. **Location:** 100 miles from Philadelphia, 140 miles from New York City. **Calendar:** Semester, extensive summer session. **Full-time faculty:** 131 total; 87% have terminal degrees, 8% minority, 38% women. **Part-time faculty:** 86 total; 5% minority, 57% women. **Class size:** 43% < 20, 49% 20-39, 3% 40-49, 5% 50-99, less than 1% >100. **Special facilities:** Performing arts center, field station, telecommunications center.

Freshman class profile. 2,702 applied, 2,084 admitted, 572 enrolled.

Mid 50% test scores		**Rank in top tenth:**	20%
SAT verbal:	480-580	**Return as sophomores:**	80%
SAT math:	480-600	**Out-of-state:**	23%
Rank in top quarter:	48%	**Live on campus:**	75%

Basis for selection. Combined SAT scores of 920 (exclusive of Writing) and/or rank in top 50% of high school class required for unconditional admission. Conditional admission may be offered to some applicants who do not meet these standards; must attend summer program prior to first semester. Interview recommended for all; audition required for music, theater arts programs.

High school preparation. College-preparatory program recommended. Recommended units include English 4, mathematics 3, social studies 3, science 3 (laboratory 2) and academic electives 1. Introduction to Computing recommended.

2005-2006 Annual costs. Tuition/fees: $21,646. Room/board: $8,670. Books/supplies: $1,050. Personal expenses: $1,000.

2004-2005 Financial aid. Need-based: 539 full-time freshmen applied for aid; 474 were judged to have need; 472 of these received aid. Average need met was 83%. Average scholarship/grant was $13,264; average loan $2,116. 61% of total undergraduate aid awarded as scholarships/grants, 39% as loans/jobs. **Non-need-based:** Awarded to 1,894 full-time undergraduates, including 547 freshmen. Scholarships awarded for academics, leadership, minority status, music/drama.

Application procedures. Admission: No deadline. $35 fee, may be waived for applicants with need. Application may be submitted online. Admission notification on a rolling basis. Must reply by May 1 or within 3 week(s) if notified thereafter. **Financial aid:** Priority date 3/1; no closing date. FAFSA, institutional form required. Applicants notified on a rolling basis starting 2/21.

Academics. Special study options: Combined bachelor's/graduate degree, cooperative education, cross-registration, distance learning, double major, dual enrollment of high school students, external degree, honors, independent study, internships, student-designed major, study abroad, teacher certification program, weekend college. **Credit/placement by examination:** AP, CLEP, institutional tests. Credit by examination may be given to within 30 credits of graduation. **Support services:** Learning center, preadmission summer program, reduced course load, remedial instruction, study skills assistance, tutoring, writing center.

Majors. Biology: General, biochemistry. **Business:** Accounting, business admin, entrepreneurial studies. **Communications:** General, digital media. **Computer sciences:** General, information systems. **Education:** Elementary, music, special. **Engineering:** Electrical, environmental, mechanical. **English:** English lit. **Foreign languages:** French, Spanish. **Health:** Clinical lab science, nursing (RN), premedicine. **History:** General. **Liberal arts:** Arts/sciences. **Math:** General. **Philosophy/religion:** Philosophy. **Physical sciences:** Chemistry, geology. **Protective services:** Criminal justice. **Psychology:** General. **Social sciences:** International relations, political science, sociology. **Visual/performing arts:** Dramatic, music performance.

Most popular majors. Biology 8%, business/marketing 16%, communications/journalism 7%, education 10%, engineering/engineering technologies 9%, liberal arts 14%, psychology 9%, social sciences 6%.

Computing on campus. 700 workstations in library, computer center, student center. Dormitories wired for high-speed internet access and linked to campus network. Commuter students can connect to campus network. Online course registration, online library, helpline, wireless network available.

Student life. Freshman orientation: Mandatory, $120 fee. Preregistration for classes offered. **Policies:** Freshmen permitted cars on campus. **Housing:** Guaranteed on-campus for all undergraduates. Coed dorms, single-sex dorms, apartments available. $100 fully refundable deposit. **Activities:** Bands, choral groups, dance, drama, literary magazine, music ensembles, musical theater, radio station, student government, student newspaper, TV station.

Athletics. NCAA. **Intercollegiate:** Baseball M, basketball, field hockey W, football (tackle) M, golf M, lacrosse W, soccer, softball W, tennis, volleyball W, wrestling M. **Intramural:** Basketball M, bowling, football (tackle) M, ice hockey M, racquetball, rowing (crew), rugby M, skiing, softball, table tennis, volleyball. **Team name:** Colonels.

Student services. Adult student services, career counseling, student employment services, financial aid counseling, health services, personal counseling, placement for graduates, veterans' counselor. **Physically disabled:** Services for visually, hearing impaired.

Contact. E-mail: admissions@wilkes.edu
Phone: (570) 408-4400 Toll-free number: (800) 945-5378
Fax: (570) 408-4904
Michael Frantz, Dean of Student Enrollment Services, Wilkes University, Chase Hall/184 South River Street, Wilkes-Barre, PA 18766

Williamson Free School of Mechanical Trades

Media, Pennsylvania
www.williamson.edu **CB code: 0765**

- Private 3-year technical college for men affiliated with nondenominational tradition
- Residential campus in large town
- 232 degree-seeking undergraduates
- Interview required

General. Founded in 1888. Accredited by ACCSCT. Discipline-oriented school that prepares students through academic instruction and hands-on training in a structured environment; scholarship-only students. **Degrees:** 57 associate awarded. **Location:** 14 miles from Philadelphia, 14 miles from Wilmington, Delaware. **Calendar:** Semester. **Full-time faculty:** 19 total. **Part-time faculty:** 13 total. **Special facilities:** Natural arboretum.

Freshman class profile.

Out-of-state:	15%	**Live on campus:**	100%

Basis for selection. Family economic need, high school performance, letters of character reference, interview important. First consideration given to applicants with 2.0 or better average in mathematics, science, and English. Applicant must have reached 16th birthday, but not have passed 20th birthday prior to June of year of admission. Armed Services Vocational Aptitude Battery (ASVAB) required by March 24th. Essay recommended.

High school preparation. 7 units required. Required units include English 3, mathematics 2 and science 2. Mathematics units must include algebra I and geometry. Science units should include chemistry and physics.

2006-2007 Annual costs. All students receive full scholarships covering tuition, room and board, and textbooks. Required fees, $985.

Application procedures. Admission: Closing date 3/15 (postmark date). Admission notification 4/15. Must reply by 5/24. Students who apply before November 30 will be brought in for January testing and interview session. **Financial aid:** No deadline.

Academics. Special study options: Cooperative education, internships. **Credit/placement by examination:** CLEP, institutional tests. **Support services:** Pre-admission summer program, tutoring.

Computing on campus. 35 workstations in library, computer center.

Student life. Freshman orientation: Mandatory. Takes place first 3 days of school and includes shop orientation, rules, classroom schedules and math testing. **Policies:** Student life carefully structured, including prescribed daily schedule, dress code, required chapel, and clearly defined privileges and responsibilities. Religious observance required. **Housing:** Guaranteed on-campus for all undergraduates. **Activities:** Jazz band, choral groups, student government, student newspaper, Campus Crusade for Christ, Bible study groups.

Athletics. NJCAA. **Intercollegiate:** Baseball M, basketball M, cross-country M, football (tackle) M, lacrosse M, soccer M, wrestling M. **Intramural:** Archery M, basketball M, table tennis M, volleyball M. **Team name:** Mechanics.

Student services. Alcohol/substance abuse counseling, career counseling, student employment services, health services, personal counseling, placement for graduates.

Contact. E-mail: ebailey@williamson.edu
Phone: (610) 566-1776 Fax: (610) 566-6502
Ed Bailey, Director of Admissions, Williamson Free School of Mechanical Trades, 106 South New Middletown Road, Media, PA 19063

Wilson College

Chambersburg, Pennsylvania **CB member**
www.wilson.edu **CB code: 2979**

- Private 4-year liberal arts college for women affiliated with Presbyterian Church (USA)
- Residential campus in large town
- 516 degree-seeking undergraduates: 37% part-time, 94% women, 5% African American, 1% Asian American, 3% Hispanic American, 5% international
- 57% of applicants admitted

- SAT or ACT (ACT writing optional), application essay required
- 62% graduate within 6 years; 30% enter graduate study

General. Founded in 1869. Regionally accredited. Men admitted to continuing studies division, adult learning program, associate degree programs, post baccalaureate teacher intern program. Residential program for single mothers with children. **Degrees:** 95 bachelor's, 16 associate awarded. **ROTC:** Army. **Location:** 90 miles from Washington, DC, 145 miles from Philadelphia. **Calendar:** 4-1-4, limited summer session. **Full-time faculty:** 40 total; 78% have terminal degrees, 5% minority, 52% women. **Part-time faculty:** 35 total; 43% have terminal degrees, 57% women. **Class size:** 85% < 20, 15% 20-39. **Special facilities:** Equestrian Center, Center for Sustainable Living, Veterinary Medical Center, Archival Center.

Freshman class profile. 441 applied, 250 admitted, 76 enrolled.

Mid 50% test scores		Rank in top quarter:	39%
SAT verbal:	460-580	Rank in top tenth:	9%
SAT math:	430-560	End year in good standing:	93%
ACT:	20-25	Return as sophomores:	63%
GPA 3.50 or higher:	39%	Out-of-state:	32%
GPA 3.0-3.49:	36%	Live on campus:	68%
GPA 2.0-2.99:	25%	International:	3%

Basis for selection. Admissions based on secondary school record. Class rank, recommendations, character, and personal qualities also important. Interview recommended. **Homeschooled:** Transcript of courses and grades, letter of recommendation (nonparent) required.

High school preparation. 15 units required. Required units include English 4, mathematics 3, social studies 4, science 2 (laboratory 2) and foreign language 2.

2005-2006 Annual costs. Tuition/fees: $20,050. Room/board: $7,610. Books/supplies: $800. Personal expenses: $800.

2005-2006 Financial aid. Need-based: 68 full-time freshmen applied for aid; 59 were judged to have need; 58 of these received aid. Average need met was 74%. Average scholarship/grant was $12,411; average loan $3,345. 92% of total undergraduate aid awarded as scholarships/grants, 8% as loans/jobs. **Non-need-based:** Awarded to 108 full-time undergraduates, including 24 freshmen. Scholarships awarded for academics, alumni affiliation, religious affiliation, state residency.

Application procedures. Admission: Priority date 4/30; no deadline. $35 fee, may be waived for applicants with need. Application may be submitted online. Admission notification on a rolling basis beginning on or about 6/30. Must reply by May 1 or within 3 week(s) if notified thereafter. **Financial aid:** Priority date 4/1; no closing date. FAFSA, institutional form required. Applicants notified on a rolling basis starting 2/15.

Academics. Special study options: Cooperative education, cross-registration, double major, ESL, honors, independent study, internships, liberal arts/career combination, student-designed major, study abroad, teacher certification program, Washington semester. Students with high academic achievement invited to pursue honors in major. **Credit/placement by examination:** AP, CLEP, IB. 4 credit hours maximum toward associate degree, 4 toward bachelor's. **Support services:** Learning center, reduced course load, remedial instruction, study skills assistance, tutoring, writing center.

Majors. Agriculture: Equestrian studies. **Biology:** General. **Business:** Accounting, business admin, international, management information systems, managerial economics. **Communications:** Media studies. **Conservation:** Environmental studies. **Education:** Elementary. **English:** English lit. **Foreign languages:** French, Spanish. **Health:** Premedicine, preveterinary, veterinary technology/assistant. **History:** General. **Interdisciplinary:** Behavioral sciences, biopsychology. **Math:** General. **Parks/recreation:** Exercise sciences. **Philosophy/religion:** Religion. **Physical sciences:** Chemistry. **Psychology:** General. **Social sciences:** General, international relations, political science, sociology. **Visual/performing arts:** Art.

Most popular majors. Agriculture 8%, biology 9%, business/marketing 13%, education 10%, health sciences 21%, social sciences 10%.

Computing on campus. 102 workstations in dormitories, library, computer center. Dormitories wired for high-speed internet access and linked to campus network. Online course registration, helpline, repair service, wireless network available.

Student life. Freshman orientation: Mandatory, $250 fee. Preregistration for classes offered. New student orientation is held in July, and in August for transfer and international students. **Policies:** Honor principle; shared governance. Freshmen permitted cars on campus. **Housing:** Guaranteed on-campus for all undergraduates. $200 deposit. Pets allowed in dorm rooms. Students of junior standing or above guaranteed single residence hall room, housing for single mothers with children available. **Activities:** Choral groups, dance, drama, literary magazine, music ensembles, radio station, student government, student newspaper, religious activities committee, language clubs, interfaith support group, Muhibbah Club (international), black student union, JOKO, Curran Scholars, Alternative Spring Break, Bible study.

Athletics. NCAA. **Intercollegiate:** Basketball W, equestrian W, field hockey W, gymnastics W, soccer W, softball W, tennis W, volleyball W. **Intramural:** Archery W, badminton W, basketball W, bowling W, cheerleading W, equestrian W, gymnastics W, tennis W, volleyball W. **Team name:** Phoenix.

Student services. Adult student services, alcohol/substance abuse counseling, campus ministries, career counseling, student employment services, financial aid counseling, health services, on-campus daycare, personal counseling, placement for graduates, women's services.

Contact. E-mail: admissions@wilson.edu
Phone: (717) 262-2002 Toll-free number: (800) 421-8402
Fax: (717) 262-2546
Mary Ann Naso, Director of Admissions, Wilson College, 1015 Philadelphia Avenue, Chambersburg, PA 17201-1285

Yeshivath Beth Moshe

Scranton, Pennsylvania

CB code: 1657

- Private 4-year rabbinical college for men affiliated with Jewish faith
- Small city
- 56 degree-seeking undergraduates

General. Founded in 1965. Accredited by AARTS. First and second Talmudic degrees offered. Ordination available. **Degrees:** 5 bachelor's awarded; master's offered. **Calendar:** Continuous. **Full-time faculty:** 6 total.

Basis for selection. Extensive oral examination given. Religious commitment important.

2005-2006 Annual costs. Tuition/fees: $8,100. Room/board: $3,600. Books/supplies: $150.

Application procedures. Admission: No deadline. No application fee. Admission notification on a rolling basis. **Financial aid:** No deadline. Applicants notified on a rolling basis.

Academics. Credit/placement by examination: CLEP.

Majors. Theology: Talmudic.

Student life. Activities: Choral groups, TV station.

Contact. Phone: (717) 346-1747 Fax: (717) 346-2251
Rabbi Chaim Bressler, Admissions Director, Yeshivath Beth Moshe, 930 Hickory Street, Scranton, PA 18505

York College of Pennsylvania

York, Pennsylvania **CB member**

www.ycp.edu **CB code: 2991**

- Private 4-year liberal arts college
- Residential campus in small city
- 5,170 degree-seeking undergraduates: 14% part-time, 59% women, 2% African American, 1% Asian American, 2% Hispanic American
- 297 degree-seeking graduate students
- 75% of applicants admitted
- SAT or ACT with writing required
- 63% graduate within 6 years

General. Founded in 1787. Regionally accredited. **Degrees:** 933 bachelor's, 32 associate awarded; master's offered. **ROTC:** Army. **Location:** 46 miles from Baltimore, 95 miles from Philadelphia. **Calendar:** Semester, extensive summer session. **Full-time faculty:** 134 total; 79% have terminal degrees, 4% minority, 37% women. **Part-time faculty:** 295 total; 20% have terminal degrees, 1% minority, 49% women. **Class size:** 34% < 20, 60% 20-39, 6% 40-49, less than 1% 50-99. **Special facilities:** Electronic classrooms, Abraham Lincoln artifacts collection, rare books collection, oral history room, video production studios, mechanical, electrical and computer engineering labs, nursing education center.

Freshman class profile. 4,152 applied, 3,101 admitted, 1,200 enrolled.

Mid 50% test scores		End year in good standing:	78%
SAT verbal:	500-600	Return as sophomores:	80%
SAT math:	500-590	Out-of-state:	50%
ACT:	18-24	Live on campus:	72%
Rank in top quarter:	65%	Fraternities:	5%
Rank in top tenth:	28%	Sororities:	5%

Basis for selection. High school record, standardized test results, and personal qualities most important. Interviews and essays recommended for academically borderline; audition required for music programs; portfolio recommended for art programs. **Homeschooled:** Diploma required from home school association or local school district.

High school preparation. 15 units required. Required and recommended units include English 4, mathematics 3-4, social studies 3, science 3 and foreign language 2. One biology, 2 chemistry, and 2 algebra required of nursing applicants.

2006-2007 Annual costs. Tuition/fees: $11,160. Room/board: $6,950. Books/supplies: $600. Personal expenses: $1,000.

2005-2006 Financial aid. Need-based: 933 full-time freshmen applied for aid; 558 were judged to have need; 550 of these received aid. Average need met was 71%. Average scholarship/grant was $4,225; average loan $2,512. 52% of total undergraduate aid awarded as scholarships/grants, 48% as loans/jobs. **Non-need-based:** Awarded to 891 full-time undergraduates, including 327 freshmen. Scholarships awarded for academics, art, music/drama.

Application procedures. Admission: No deadline. $30 fee, may be waived for applicants with need. Application may be submitted online. Admission notification on a rolling basis beginning on or about 10/1. **Financial aid:** Priority date 3/1; no closing date. FAFSA required. Applicants notified on a rolling basis starting 2/15; must reply within 4 week(s) of notification.

Academics. Special study options: Combined bachelor's/graduate degree, cooperative education, distance learning, double major, dual enrollment of high school students, honors, independent study, internships, student-designed major, study abroad, teacher certification program. **Credit/placement by examination:** AP, CLEP, IB, institutional tests. 30 credit hours maximum toward associate degree, 30 toward bachelor's. **Support services:** Learning center, reduced course load, remedial instruction, study skills assistance, tutoring, writing center.

Majors. Biology: General. **Business:** General, accounting, business admin, finance, knowledge management, managerial economics, marketing. **Communications:** General, digital media, media studies, public relations. **Computer sciences:** General, computer science, information systems. **Education:** General, biology, elementary, English, history, mathematics, music, science, secondary, special. **Engineering:** Computer, electrical, mechanical. **Engineering technology:** Industrial management. **English:** English lit, speech/rhetoric, technical writing. **Family/consumer sciences:** Aging. **Foreign languages:** Spanish. **Health:** Clinical lab technology, nuclear medical technology, nursing (RN), predentistry, premedicine, prepharmacy, preveterinary, recreational therapy, respiratory therapy technology. **History:** General. **Interdisciplinary:** Behavioral sciences. **Legal studies:** Prelaw. **Liberal arts:** Arts/sciences, humanities. **Math:** General. **Parks/recreation:** General, facilities management, sports admin. **Physical sciences:** Chemistry. **Protective services:** Corrections, forensics, law enforcement admin, police science, security services. **Psychology:** General. **Public administration:** General. **Social sciences:** General, economics, political science, sociology. **Visual/performing arts:** General, dramatic, graphic design, music performance, studio arts.

Most popular majors. Business/marketing 21%, communications/journalism 10%, education 12%, health sciences 10%, parks/recreation 6%, security/protective services 9%, social sciences 9%.

Computing on campus. 450 workstations in library, computer center. Dormitories wired for high-speed internet access and linked to campus network. Commuter students can connect to campus network. Online course registration, online library, helpline, wireless network available.

Student life. Freshman orientation: Mandatory. Preregistration for classes offered. 3-day program prior to fall semester. **Policies:** Freshmen permitted cars on campus. **Housing:** Guaranteed on-campus for freshmen. Coed dorms, single-sex dorms, special housing for disabled, apartments, substance-free housing available. $200 deposit. Minidorms featuring units of 10 students, suites, sponsored houses and apartments available. **Activities:** Bands, choral groups, drama, literary magazine, music ensembles, musical theater, radio station, student government, student newspaper, symphony orchestra, TV station, over 80 student organizations.

Athletics. NCAA. **Intercollegiate:** Baseball M, basketball, cheerleading, cross-country, field hockey W, golf M, lacrosse, soccer, softball W, swimming, tennis, track and field, volleyball W, wrestling M. **Intramural:** Badminton, basketball, football (non-tackle), lacrosse M, rugby M, skiing, soccer M, softball, swimming, tennis, track and field, volleyball, water polo M, wrestling M. **Team name:** Spartans.

Student services. Adult student services, alcohol/substance abuse counseling, campus ministries, career counseling, services for economically disadvantaged, student employment services, financial aid counseling, health services, minority student services, personal counseling, placement for graduates, veterans' counselor. **Physically disabled:** Services for visually, hearing impaired.

Contact. E-mail: admissions@ycp.edu
Phone: (717) 849-1600 Toll-free number: (800) 455-8018
Fax: (717) 849-1607
Nancy Spataro, Director of Admissions, York College of Pennsylvania, 441 Country Club Road, York, PA 17403-3651

Puerto Rico

American University of Puerto Rico

Bayamon, Puerto Rico **CB member**
www.aupr.edu **CB code: 0961**

- Private 4-year university and business college
- Commuter campus in large city
- 803 degree-seeking undergraduates
- 28 graduate students

General. Founded in 1963. Regionally accredited. Branch campus at Manati. **Degrees:** 275 bachelor's, 34 associate awarded. **ROTC:** Army. **Location:** 12 miles from San Juan. **Calendar:** Semester, limited summer session. **Full-time faculty:** 76 total. **Part-time faculty:** 168 total. **Special facilities:** Fully computerized classrooms.

Basis for selection. Open admission. SAT required for English-speaking applicants and NCAA student athletes. Interview recommended.

High school preparation. 18 units recommended. Recommended units include English 3, mathematics 2, social studies 2, history 1, science 2, foreign language 3 and academic electives 5.

2005-2006 Annual costs. Tuition/fees: $3,600. Books/supplies: $800.

Financial aid. All financial aid based on need.

Application procedures. Admission: No deadline. $15 fee, may be waived for applicants with need. Admission notification on a rolling basis. **Financial aid:** Priority date 4/30, closing date 5/31. FAFSA, institutional form required. Applicants notified by 6/1; must reply within 2 week(s) of notification.

Academics. Special study options: Cooperative education, honors, independent study, internships, liberal arts/career combination. **Credit/placement by examination:** CLEP, institutional tests. **Support services:** Learning center, reduced course load, tutoring.

Majors. Business: General, accounting, administrative services, business admin, office technology, office/clerical, purchasing. **Communications:** General. **Communications technology:** General. **Education:** General, business, elementary, ESL, mathematics, physical, secondary, Spanish, special. **Social sciences:** General.

Computing on campus. 75 workstations in computer center.

Student life. Freshman orientation: Mandatory. Preregistration for classes offered. **Activities:** Student government.

Athletics. NCAA. **Intercollegiate:** Basketball, cross-country, swimming, tennis, track and field, volleyball. **Intramural:** Basketball, cross-country, softball M, table tennis, track and field, volleyball. **Team name:** Pirates.

Student services. Career counseling, student employment services, health services, personal counseling, veterans' counselor. **Physically disabled:** Services for speech impaired.

Contact. E-mail: oficinaadmisiones@aupr.edu
Phone: (787) 620-2040 Fax: (787) 785-7377
Margarita Cruz, Director of Admissions, American University of Puerto Rico, Box 2037, Bayamon, PR 00960-2037

Atlantic College

Guaynabo, Puerto Rico
www.atlanticcollege-pr.com **CB code: 7137**

- Private 4-year visual arts and business college
- Commuter campus in small city
- 725 degree-seeking undergraduates: 14% part-time, 18% women, 100% Hispanic American
- 108 degree-seeking graduate students

General. Founded in 1983. Accredited by ACICS. **Degrees:** 98 bachelor's, 20 associate awarded; master's offered. **Location:** 20 miles from San Juan. **Calendar:** Quarter, extensive summer session. **Full-time faculty:** 13 total; 46% have terminal degrees, 54% minority, 38% women. **Part-time faculty:** 27 total; 15% have terminal degrees, 44% minority, 37% women. **Special facilities:** Graphic arts and computerized animation technology; motion caption laboratories, audio laboratories.

Basis for selection. Open admission.

High school preparation. 16 units recommended. Recommended units include English 3, mathematics 2, social studies 1, history 2, science 2, foreign language 3 and academic electives 3.

2005-2006 Annual costs. Tuition/fees: $4,230. Books/supplies: $500.

Financial aid. All financial aid based on need.

Application procedures. Admission: No deadline. $30 fee. Admission notification on a rolling basis. **Financial aid:** Closing date 6/30. FAFSA, institutional form required. Applicants notified on a rolling basis starting 4/1; must reply within 2 week(s) of notification.

Academics. Special study options: Combined bachelor's/graduate degree, honors, internships, liberal arts/career combination, student-designed major. **Credit/placement by examination:** CLEP. **Support services:** Learning center, pre-admission summer program, remedial instruction, tutoring.

Majors. Business: Accounting, administrative services, business admin. **Computer sciences:** Security. **Education:** Early childhood special. **Visual/performing arts:** Commercial/advertising art.

Most popular majors. Business/marketing 6%, computer/information sciences 12%, visual/performing arts 74%.

Computing on campus. 16 workstations in library, computer center. Online library, repair service, wireless network available.

Student life. Freshman orientation: Available. **Activities:** Dance, drama, student government, student newspaper.

Athletics. Intercollegiate: Basketball. **Intramural:** Basketball, volleyball.

Student services. Alcohol/substance abuse counseling, career counseling, financial aid counseling, health services, personal counseling, placement for graduates. **Physically disabled:** Services for hearing impaired.

Contact. E-mail: atlancol@coqui.net
Phone: (787) 720-1022 ext. 1104 Fax: (787) 720-1092
Heriberto Martinez, Dean of Technology and Marketing, Atlantic College, PO Box 3918, Guaynabo, PR 00970

Bayamon Central University

Bayamon, Puerto Rico **CB member**
www.ucb.edu.pr **CB code: 0840**

- Private 4-year university affiliated with Roman Catholic Church
- Commuter campus in large city
- 2,465 degree-seeking undergraduates: 19% part-time, 70% women, 100% Hispanic American
- 488 degree-seeking graduate students

General. Founded in 1970. Regionally accredited. Member of consortium of U.S. and South American universities. Virtually all students come from Spanish-speaking backgrounds. **Degrees:** 284 bachelor's, 16 associate awarded; master's offered. **ROTC:** Army, Air Force. **Location:** 9 miles from San Juan. **Calendar:** Semester, limited summer session. **Full-time faculty:** 60 total. **Part-time faculty:** 113 total. **Special facilities:** Library of Dominican Order.

Freshman class profile. 774 applied, 650 admitted, 262 enrolled.

GPA 3.50 or higher:	14%	**GPA 2.0-2.99:**	58%
GPA 3.0-3.49:	19%		

Basis for selection. Open admission, but selective for some programs and for out-of-state students. School achievement record and test scores most important. Minimum 2.0 high school GPA. Fluency in Spanish, basic knowledge of English necessary. Conditional admission to those identified as having underdeveloped academic potential. SAT or ACT accepted from English-speaking students. Score report must be received by 04/15. Essay recommended for all; interview recommended for academically weak.

High school preparation. Required units include English 3, mathematics 3, social studies 3 and science 1. 3 units of Spanish required.

2005-2006 Annual costs. Tuition/fees: $4,280. Books/supplies: $565. Personal expenses: $1,950.

Financial aid. All financial aid based on need.

Application procedures. **Admission:** Priority date 12/6; deadline 4/6 (postmark date). $15 fee, may be waived for applicants with need. Admission notification on a rolling basis beginning on or about 3/4. **Financial aid:** No deadline. FAFSA, institutional form required.

Academics. All classroom instruction conducted in Spanish. Core curriculum includes courses in Spanish. Course in methodology of learning must be satisfactorily completed. **Special study options:** Double major, independent study, teacher certification program. **Credit/placement by examination:** AP, CLEP. **Support services:** Learning center, reduced course load, tutoring.

Majors. **Biology:** General. **Business:** General, accounting, administrative services, business admin, finance, human resources, management information systems, management science, marketing. **Communications:** Journalism. **Conservation:** General. **Education:** Early childhood, elementary, English, instructional media, mathematics, physical, science, secondary, Spanish, special. **Foreign languages:** Spanish. **Health:** Occupational health. **Interdisciplinary:** Biological/physical sciences, natural sciences. **Philosophy/religion:** Philosophy, religion. **Physical sciences:** Chemistry. **Psychology:** General. **Public administration:** General, social work.

Computing on campus. 130 workstations in computer center. Online library available.

Student life. **Freshman orientation:** Mandatory. Preregistration for classes offered. **Policies:** Freshmen permitted cars on campus. **Activities:** Choral groups, drama, student government, student newspaper, various cultural, religious, and social activities.

Athletics. **Intercollegiate:** Basketball, cross-country, softball, swimming, table tennis, tennis, track and field, volleyball. **Intramural:** Basketball, track and field, volleyball. **Team name:** Halcones.

Student services. Career counseling, student employment services, financial aid counseling, health services, on-campus daycare, personal counseling, placement for graduates. **Physically disabled:** Services for visually, hearing impaired.

Contact. E-mail: chernandez@ucb.edu.pr
Phone: (787) 786-3030 ext. 2100 Fax: (787) 740-2200
Cristina Hernandez, Director of Admissions, Bayamon Central University, PO Box 1725, Bayamon, PR 00960-1725

Caribbean University

Bayamon, Puerto Rico — **CB member**
www.caribbean.edu — **CB code: 0779**

- Private 4-year business and liberal arts college
- Commuter campus in large city

General. Founded in 1969. Regionally accredited. **Location:** 12 miles from San Juan. **Calendar:** Semester.

Annual costs/financial aid. Books/supplies: $640. Personal expenses: $1,950.

Contact. Phone: (787) 780-0070 ext. 224
Admissions Director, PO Box 493, Bayamon, PR 00960-0493

Carlos Albizu University: San Juan

San Juan, Puerto Rico
www.albizu.edu

- Private upper-division university
- Large town

General. Regionally accredited. **Calendar:** Semester.

Contact. Phone: (787) 725-6500 ext. 21
151 Tanca Street, San Juan, PR 00901

Colegio Pentecostal Mizpa

San Juan, Puerto Rico

- Private 4-year Bible college
- Very large city

General. Accredited by ABHE. **Calendar:** Semester.

Annual costs/financial aid. Tuition/fees (projected): $1,720.

Contact. Phone: (787) 720-4476
PO Box 20966, San Juan, PR 00928-0966

Columbia College

Caguas, Puerto Rico
www.columbiaco.edu — **CB code: 2315**

- For-profit 4-year business and technical college
- Commuter campus in small city
- 810 degree-seeking undergraduates: 38% part-time, 69% women, 100% Hispanic American
- 49 degree-seeking graduate students
- Interview required

General. Founded in 1966. Accredited by ACICS. **Degrees:** 101 bachelor's, 107 associate awarded; master's offered. **Location:** 15 miles from San Juan. **Calendar:** Trimester, extensive summer session. **Full-time faculty:** 15 total; 13% have terminal degrees, 47% women. **Part-time faculty:** 50 total; 6% have terminal degrees, 50% women. **Class size:** 60% < 20, 40% 20-39.

Freshman class profile. 509 applied, 286 admitted, 259 enrolled.

Basis for selection. Open admission, but selective for some programs. Parent signature and vaccination certificate required for students under age 21. Portfolio required for adult education students.

High school preparation. 15 units required. Required units include English 3, mathematics 2, social studies 2, history 2, science 3 and academic electives 3.

2005-2006 Annual costs. Tuition/fees: $4,030. Books/supplies: $441. Personal expenses: $1,684.

2004-2005 Financial aid. All financial aid based on need. 212 full-time freshmen applied for aid; 212 were judged to have need; 212 of these received aid.

Application procedures. **Admission:** No deadline. $50 fee. Application must be submitted on paper. Admission notification on a rolling basis.

Academics. **Special study options:** Liberal arts/career combination. **Credit/placement by examination:** AP, CLEP. **Support services:** Tutoring.

Majors. **Business:** Business admin. **Health:** Nursing (RN).

Most popular majors. Business/marketing 67%, health sciences 34%.

Computing on campus. 27 workstations in library, computer center.

Student life. **Freshman orientation:** Mandatory. General orientation lasts about two hours. **Policies:** Freshmen permitted cars on campus.

Student services. Career counseling, student employment services, financial aid counseling, personal counseling, placement for graduates, veterans' counselor.

Contact. E-mail: info@columbiaco.edu
Phone: (787) 743-4041 ext. 240 Toll-free number: (800) 981-4877 ext. 240
Fax: (787) 744-7031
Ana Burgos, Marketing, Recruitment and Admissions Coordinator, Columbia College, PO Box 8517, Caguas, PR 00726

Conservatory of Music of Puerto Rico

San Juan, Puerto Rico
www.cmpr.edu — **CB code: 1115**

- Public 4-year music college
- Commuter campus in large city

- 304 degree-seeking undergraduates: 28% part-time, 27% women, 100% Hispanic American
- 52% of applicants admitted
- 27% graduate within 6 years

General. Founded in 1959. Regionally accredited. **Degrees:** 44 bachelor's awarded; master's offered. **Calendar:** Semester, limited summer session. **Full-time faculty:** 40 total. **Part-time faculty:** 27 total. **Class size:** 18% < 20, less than 1% 20-39, less than 1% 40-49, less than 1% 50-99. **Special facilities:** Library with 26,436 musical scores, technology lab (computers applied to music), piano lab, theater.

Freshman class profile. 111 applied, 58 admitted, 49 enrolled.

GPA 3.50 or higher:	53%	**End year in good standing:**	94%
GPA 3.0-3.49:	32%	**Return as sophomores:**	62%
GPA 2.0-2.99:	15%		

Basis for selection. Musical ability very important. School achievement record, test scores important. Recommendations considered. Must take entrance examination in both theory and instrument. SAT is accepted from applicants from US mainland. Audition required for music performance. Essays also required for Music Education. **Homeschooled:** State high school equivalency certificate required.

High school preparation. Required and recommended units include English 3, mathematics 3, history 3, science 3 and academic electives 3.

2005-2006 Annual costs. Books/supplies: $1,650. Personal expenses: $950.

2004-2005 Financial aid. All financial aid based on need. 39 full-time freshmen applied for aid; 39 were judged to have need; 39 of these received aid. Average need met was 40%. Average scholarship/grant was $927. 68% of total undergraduate aid awarded as scholarships/grants, 32% as loans/jobs.

Application procedures. **Admission:** Closing date 3/24 (receipt date). $35 fee. Admission notification 5/30. **Financial aid:** Priority date 6/30; no closing date. FAFSA, institutional form required. Applicants notified on a rolling basis starting 8/30.

Academics. **Special study options:** Cross-registration, dual enrollment of high school students, liberal arts/career combination, teacher certification program. **Credit/placement by examination:** AP, CLEP, institutional tests. 12 credit hours maximum toward bachelor's degree. **Support services:** Learning center, pre-admission summer program, reduced course load, remedial instruction, tutoring.

Majors. **Education:** Music. **Visual/performing arts:** Jazz, music performance, piano/organ, stringed instruments, voice/opera.

Computing on campus. 17 workstations in library, computer center.

Student life. **Freshman orientation:** Mandatory. Preregistration for classes offered. **Policies:** Freshmen permitted cars on campus. **Activities:** Bands, choral groups, music ensembles, opera, student government, symphony orchestra.

Student services. Career counseling, student employment services, financial aid counseling, personal counseling, placement for graduates.

Contact. E-mail: esantiag@cmpr.gobierno.pr
Phone: (787) 751-0160 ext. 275 Fax: (787) 758-8268
Eutimia Santiago, Director, Admissions Office and Institutional Research, Conservatory of Music of Puerto Rico, Rafael Lamar # 350 Esq. Roosevelt, San Juan, PR 00918-2199

Electronic Data Processing College of Puerto Rico

Hato Rey, Puerto Rico
www.edpcollege.edu **CB code: 2243**

- For-profit 4-year business and technical college
- Commuter campus in very large city

General. Founded in 1968. Candidate for regional accreditation. **Calendar:** Semester.

Annual costs/financial aid. Tuition/fees (2005-2006): $4,715. Books/supplies: $465. Personal expenses: $1,455.

Contact. Phone: (787) 765-3560
Admissions Director, PO Box 1923, Hato Rey, PR 00919-2303

Electronic Data Processing College: San Sebastian

San Sebastian, Puerto Rico
CB code: 3219

- For-profit 4-year business and health science college
- Commuter campus in small city
- 788 degree-seeking undergraduates: 37% part-time, 71% women
- Interview required

General. Accredited by ACICS. **Degrees:** 39 bachelor's, 67 associate awarded. **Location:** 28 miles from Mayaguez. **Calendar:** Semester, extensive summer session. **Full-time faculty:** 18 total; 11% have terminal degrees, 100% minority, 56% women. **Part-time faculty:** 38 total; 10% have terminal degrees, 100% minority, 47% women. **Class size:** 78% < 20, 22% 20-39.

Basis for selection. **Learning Disabled:** Interview with student doctor, vocational rehabilitation program, or other government agencies required.

High school preparation. 18 units required. Required units include English 3, mathematics 3, history 3, science 3, foreign language 3 and academic electives 3.

Application procedures. **Admission:** No deadline. $15 fee.

Academics. **Special study options:** Cooperative education, internships. **Credit/placement by examination:** CLEP. **Support services:** Learning center, reduced course load, remedial instruction, tutoring.

Computing on campus. 103 workstations in library, computer center.

Student life. **Freshman orientation:** Mandatory. **Policies:** Freshmen permitted cars on campus.

Athletics. **Intercollegiate:** Softball M, volleyball. **Team name:** Zoros.

Student services. Alcohol/substance abuse counseling, career counseling, services for economically disadvantaged, student employment services, financial aid counseling, personal counseling, placement for graduates.

Contact. Phone: (787) 896-2252 ext. 225 Toll-free number: (888) 915-3372 ext. 225 Fax: (787) 896-0066
Ingrid Gonzalez, Admissions Officer, Electronic Data Processing College: San Sebastian, PO Box 1674, San Sebastian, PR 00685

Escuela de Artes Plasticas de Puerto Rico

Old San Juan, Puerto Rico
www.eap.edu **CB code: 7036**

- Public 4-year art college
- Commuter campus in large city

General. Founded in 1965. Regionally accredited. **Location:** In Old San Juan. **Calendar:** Semester.

Annual costs/financial aid. Books/supplies: $2,250. Personal expenses: $1,750. Need-based financial aid available to full-time and part-time students.

Contact. Phone: (787) 725-8120 ext. 233
Registrar, PO Box 9021112, San Juan, PR 00902-1112

Inter American University of Puerto Rico: Aguadilla Campus

Aguadilla, Puerto Rico
www.aguadilla.inter.edu **CB code: 2042**

- Private 4-year university and liberal arts college
- Commuter campus in small city
- 4,059 degree-seeking undergraduates: 15% part-time, 58% women, 100% Hispanic American
- 70 degree-seeking graduate students

General. Founded in 1957. Regionally accredited. Adult higher education program, continuing education program. **Degrees:** 320 bachelor's, 45 associate awarded; master's offered. **ROTC:** Army. **Location:** 10 miles from Aguadilla City, 17 miles from Mayaguez. **Calendar:** Semester, extensive summer session. **Full-time faculty:** 75 total; 24% have terminal degrees,

57% women. **Part-time faculty:** 179 total; 5% have terminal degrees, 49% women. **Special facilities:** Manuel Mendez Bellester special collection.

Basis for selection. Regular program requires minimum 2.0 GPA from accredited secondary school and combined score of 800 on SAT (exclusive of Writing) or PAA. School achievement record, test scores very important. Pilot Program requires minimum 1.75 GPA from accredited secondary school and College Board examination test. SAT accepted for English-speaking applicants. Interview required for AVANCE, adult higher education, and Educational Services Programs.

High school preparation. 18 units required. Required units include English 3, mathematics 2, history 2, science 2, foreign language 3 and academic electives 6.

2005-2006 Annual costs. Tuition/fees: $4,564. Books/supplies: $640. Personal expenses: $880.

Financial aid. Non-need-based: Scholarships awarded for academics.

Application procedures. Admission: Priority date 5/1; deadline 5/15 (receipt date). No application fee. Application may be submitted online. Admission notification on a rolling basis. **Financial aid:** Closing date 4/30. FAFSA required. Applicants notified by 6/15; must reply by 8/8.

Academics. Special study options: Cross-registration, distance learning, dual enrollment of high school students, exchange student, honors, independent study, internships, teacher certification program, Washington semester, weekend college. **Credit/placement by examination:** AP, CLEP. **Support services:** Learning center, remedial instruction, study skills assistance, tutoring.

Majors. Biology: General, microbiology. **Business:** Accounting, administrative services, business admin, hotel/motel admin, management information systems, marketing. **Computer sciences:** Computer science. **Education:** Early childhood, elementary, secondary. **Engineering technology:** Electrical. **Health:** Nursing (RN). **Parks/recreation:** Facilities management. **Protective services:** Criminal justice.

Most popular majors. Business/marketing 33%, education 29%, public administration/social services 10%, security/protective services 12%.

Computing on campus. 485 workstations in library, computer center. Commuter students can connect to campus network. Online course registration, online library, wireless network available.

Student life. Freshman orientation: Mandatory. One-day program in August. **Policies:** Freshmen permitted cars on campus. **Activities:** Choral groups, dance, drama, radio station, student government, student newspaper, Juventud Universitaria Catolica, Asociacion Evangelica Universitaria, Future Teachers Association, Criminal Justice Association, Secretarial Sciences Association, Psychosocial Human Services Association, Hotel Management Association, Marketing Association, Honors Society.

Athletics. Intercollegiate: Baseball M, basketball, cheerleading, cross-country, judo, soccer M, softball, table tennis, tennis, track and field, volleyball, weight lifting. **Intramural:** Basketball, cross-country, softball, table tennis, tennis, track and field, volleyball, weight lifting. **Team name:** Tigers.

Student services. Adult student services, campus ministries, career counseling, student employment services, financial aid counseling, health services, personal counseling, placement for graduates, veterans' counselor.

Contact. Phone: (787) 891-0925 ext. 2100 Fax: (787) 882-3020
Doris Perez, Director of Admissions, Inter American University of Puerto Rico: Aguadilla Campus, Box 20000, Aguadilla, PR 00605

Inter American University of Puerto Rico: Arecibo Campus

Arecibo, Puerto Rico
www.arecibo.inter.edu **CB code: 1411**

- Private 4-year liberal arts college
- Commuter campus in small city
- 4,487 degree-seeking undergraduates

General. Founded in 1957. Regionally accredited. **Degrees:** 390 bachelor's, 42 associate awarded; master's offered. **Location:** 45 miles from San Juan. **Calendar:** Semester, limited summer session. **Full-time faculty:** 90 total. **Part-time faculty:** 183 total.

Basis for selection. Minimum 2.0 high school GPA. Test scores important; minimum admission index of 800 required. Special admissions policies apply to adults 21 years or older. SAT required of English-speaking applicants. Score reports by August 3. Interview recommended for academically weak.

High school preparation. 15 units required. Required units include English 3, mathematics 3, social studies 3, science 3 and foreign language 3.

2005-2006 Annual costs. Tuition/fees: $4,576. Books/supplies: $890. Personal expenses: $880.

Financial aid. Non-need-based: Scholarships awarded for athletics.

Application procedures. Admission: $19 fee. Admission notification on a rolling basis. **Financial aid:** Priority date 4/28; no closing date. FAFSA, institutional form required. Applicants notified on a rolling basis.

Academics. Special study options: Cooperative education, honors, independent study, internships, teacher certification program. **Credit/placement by examination:** CLEP, institutional tests. 15 credit hours maximum toward associate degree, 15 toward bachelor's. **Support services:** Preadmission summer program, remedial instruction, tutoring.

Majors. Biology: General, bacteriology. **Business:** Accounting, administrative services, business admin, management science. **Computer sciences:** General, computer science. **Education:** Biology, chemistry, early childhood, elementary, secondary, Spanish, special. **Health:** Nursing (RN). **Physical sciences:** Chemistry. **Protective services:** Criminal justice. **Public administration:** Social work.

Computing on campus. 322 workstations in library, computer center. Commuter students can connect to campus network. Helpline available.

Student life. Activities: Choral groups, drama, student government, student newspaper, Baptist Unity, Young Catholics Association, Criminal Justice Association, Haziel Evangelical Association, Future Social Workers Association, Bahai Association, Student Counseling Association, Society for Human Resources.

Athletics. Intercollegiate: Basketball, soccer, softball, table tennis, tennis, track and field, volleyball. **Intramural:** Basketball, soccer, softball, table tennis, tennis, track and field, volleyball. **Team name:** Tigers.

Student services. Adult student services, career counseling, student employment services, health services, personal counseling, veterans' counselor.

Contact. E-mail: pmontalvo@arecibo.inter.edu
Phone: (787) 878-5195 Fax: (787) 880-1624
Provi Montalvo, Director of Admissions, Inter American University of Puerto Rico: Arecibo Campus, Box 4050, Arecibo, PR 00614-4050

Inter American University of Puerto Rico: Barranquitas Campus

Barranquitas, Puerto Rico
www.br.inter.edu **CB code: 2067**

- Private 4-year university and branch campus college
- Commuter campus in large town
- 2,297 degree-seeking undergraduates: 18% part-time, 70% women, 100% Hispanic American
- 19 degree-seeking graduate students
- 50% of applicants admitted
- 31% graduate within 6 years

General. Founded in 1957. Regionally accredited. **Degrees:** 230 bachelor's, 18 associate awarded. **Location:** 35 miles from San Juan. **Calendar:** Semester, extensive summer session. **Full-time faculty:** 39 total; 13% have terminal degrees, 100% minority, 56% women. **Part-time faculty:** 105 total; 6% have terminal degrees, 100% minority, 48% women. **Special facilities:** Teleconference room, nature preserve, 35 e-classrooms.

Freshman class profile. 987 applied, 492 admitted, 417 enrolled.

Basis for selection. 2.0 high school GPA and minimum PAA or SAT score required. Interview, portfolio, essay recommended.

High school preparation. 15 units required. Required units include English 3, mathematics 2, social studies 2 and science 3. 3 units of Spanish required for Puerto Rican high school graduates, 2 units liberal arts recommended.

2005-2006 Annual costs. Tuition/fees: $4,564. Books/supplies: $900. Personal expenses: $2,731.

2005-2006 Financial aid. All financial aid based on need. Average need met was 1%. Average scholarship/grant was $87; average loan $172.

Application procedures. Admission: No deadline. No application fee. Application may be submitted online. Admission notification on a rolling basis. **Financial aid:** Closing date 4/30. FAFSA required. Applicants notified on a rolling basis; must reply within 2 week(s) of notification.

Academics. Special study options: Accelerated study, combined bachelor's/graduate degree, cross-registration, distance learning, ESL, honors, internships, liberal arts/career combination, teacher certification program, Washington semester, weekend college. **Credit/placement by examination:** CLEP. **Support services:** Learning center, pre-admission summer program, remedial instruction, study skills assistance, tutoring.

Majors. Biology: General. **Business:** General, accounting, administrative services, business admin. **Computer sciences:** General, computer science, information systems. **Education:** General, biology, early childhood, elementary, English, mathematics, secondary, social studies, Spanish, visually handicapped. **Health:** Audiology/speech pathology, nursing (RN).

Computing on campus. 43 workstations in library, computer center, student center. Commuter students can connect to campus network. Online course registration, online library, helpline, wireless network available.

Student life. Freshman orientation: Mandatory. **Activities:** Dance, literary magazine, musical theater, student government, student newspaper.

Athletics. NAIA. **Intercollegiate:** Baseball M, basketball M, cross-country, softball, tennis, volleyball. **Team name:** Tigers.

Student services. Adult student services, career counseling, personal counseling, veterans' counselor. **Physically disabled:** Services for visually, speech, hearing impaired.

Contact. Phone: (787) 857-3600 ext. 2011 Fax: (787) 857-2244
Maribel Diaz, Director of Admissions, Inter American University of Puerto Rico: Barranquitas Campus, PO Box 517, Barranquitas, PR 00794

Inter American University of Puerto Rico: Bayamon Campus

Bayamon, Puerto Rico
www.bc.inter.edu **CB code: 2043**

- Private 4-year university and engineering college
- Commuter campus in small city
- 5,184 degree-seeking undergraduates: 17% part-time, 43% women, 100% Hispanic American
- 53 degree-seeking graduate students
- 44% of applicants admitted

General. Founded in 1912. Regionally accredited. **Degrees:** 481 bachelor's, 32 associate awarded; master's offered. **ROTC:** Army, Navy, Air Force. **Location:** 15 miles from San Juan. **Calendar:** Semester, limited summer session. **Full-time faculty:** 99 total; 31% have terminal degrees, 48% women. **Part-time faculty:** 216 total; 12% have terminal degrees, 40% women. **Special facilities:** Wetland used as a natural laboratory, mata de platano field station.

Freshman class profile. 4,108 applied, 1,826 admitted, 1,189 enrolled.

Basis for selection. High school GPA and test scores most important. Minimum GPA of 2.0, minimum admission index (based on college formula) of 800. Achievment tests required for placement in math, English and Spanish. Interview recommended.

High school preparation. Required units include English 3, mathematics 3, social studies 1, history 2, science 3 and foreign language 3.

2005-2006 Annual costs. Tuition/fees: $4,612. Books/supplies: $890.

2004-2005 Financial aid. All financial aid based on need. 1,209 full-time freshmen applied for aid; 1,179 were judged to have need; 861 of these received aid. Average need met was 3%. Average scholarship/grant was $270; average loan $291. 35% of total undergraduate aid awarded as scholarships/grants, 65% as loans/jobs.

Application procedures. Admission: Closing date 5/1 (receipt date). No application fee. Application may be submitted online. Admission notification on a rolling basis. Must reply by 8/1. **Financial aid:** Priority date 6/30; no closing date. FAFSA required. Applicants notified on a rolling basis starting 5/10.

Academics. Special study options: Accelerated study, cooperative education, distance learning, honors, independent study, internships, study abroad. **Credit/placement by examination:** AP, CLEP. 225 credit hours maximum toward associate degree, 225 toward bachelor's. **Support services:** Learning center, pre-admission summer program, study skills assistance, tutoring.

Majors. Biology: General, bioinformatics, biomedical sciences, biotechnology, environmental, microbiology. **Business:** Accounting, administrative services, business admin, entrepreneurial studies, executive assistant, finance, human resources, management information systems, management science, managerial economics, marketing, office technology. **Communications technology:** General. **Computer sciences:** Computer science, information systems. **Conservation:** General, environmental science. **Engineering:** General, electrical, industrial, mechanical. **Engineering technology:** Electrical, industrial management. **Interdisciplinary:** Math/computer science. **Math:** General, applied. **Mechanic/repair:** Computer. **Physical sciences:** Chemistry. **Protective services:** Forensics. **Public administration:** General. **Science technology:** Chemical. **Transportation:** Air traffic control, airline/commercial pilot, aviation, aviation management, flight instructor.

Most popular majors. Biology 8%, business/marketing 48%, communication technologies 13%, engineering/engineering technologies 14%, trade and industry 11%.

Computing on campus. 757 workstations in library, computer center. Commuter students can connect to campus network. Online course registration, online library, repair service, wireless network available.

Student life. Freshman orientation: Mandatory. Preregistration for classes offered. **Policies:** Freshmen permitted cars on campus. **Housing:** Substance-free housing available. **Activities:** Concert band, choral groups, drama, student government, student newspaper, student council, business administration students association, Catholic students association, Christian university brotherhood association, society of joined students for science, photography club, ANCLA group, senior class association, engineering students association.

Athletics. Intercollegiate: Baseball M, basketball, cross-country, soccer M, softball, swimming, table tennis, tennis, track and field, volleyball, wrestling M. **Intramural:** Basketball, cross-country, softball, swimming, table tennis, tennis, track and field, volleyball, wrestling M. **Team name:** Tigers.

Student services. Adult student services, alcohol/substance abuse counseling, campus ministries, career counseling, student employment services, financial aid counseling, health services, on-campus daycare, personal counseling, placement for graduates, veterans' counselor. **Physically disabled:** Services for visually, speech, hearing impaired.

Contact. E-mail: calicea@bc.inter.edu
Phone: (787) 279-1912 ext. 2017 Fax: (787) 279-2205
Carlos Alicea, Director of Admissions, Inter American University of Puerto Rico: Bayamon Campus, 500 Dr. John Will Harris Road, Bayamon, PR 00957 .

Inter American University of Puerto Rico: Fajardo Campus

Fajardo, Puerto Rico
fajardo.inter.edu **CB code: 2065**

- Private 4-year university and branch campus college affiliated with nondenominational tradition
- Commuter campus in large town
- 2,206 undergraduates
- 50% of applicants admitted

General. Regionally accredited. **Degrees:** 252 bachelor's, 32 associate awarded. **ROTC:** Air Force. **Location:** 34 miles from San Juan. **Calendar:** Semester, limited summer session. **Full-time faculty:** 38 total; 26% have terminal degrees, 55% women. **Part-time faculty:** 113 total; 64% women. **Class size:** 70% < 20, 23% 20-39, 7% 40-49.

Freshman class profile. 1,394 applied, 696 admitted, 524 enrolled.

Basis for selection. High school students must have 2.0 GPA and average of 400 on first three parts of PAA. Special admissions policies apply to adults age 21 years or older. PAA test required for Spanish-speaking applicants; SAT or ACT required for English-speaking applicants. Interview required for adult education program.

High school preparation. 15 units required. Required units include English 3, mathematics 2, social studies 2 and science 3. 3 units Spanish required for Puerto Rican students.

2005-2006 Annual costs. Tuition/fees: $4,200. Books/supplies: $686.

2004-2005 Financial aid. Need-based: 467 full-time freshmen applied for aid; 460 were judged to have need; 406 of these received aid. Average need met was 2%. Average scholarship/grant was $129; average loan $278. 25% of total undergraduate aid awarded as scholarships/grants, 75% as loans/jobs. **Non-need-based:** Awarded to 4 full-time undergraduates, including 2 freshmen.

Application procedures. Admission: Closing date 5/15. No application fee. Application may be submitted online. Admission notification on a rolling basis. Early admissions applicants must have 3.0 GPA, 1175 admission index, interview and 2 recommendation letters. **Financial aid:** Closing date 4/30. FAFSA, institutional form required. Applicants notified on a rolling basis.

Academics. Special study options: Cross-registration, distance learning, double major, dual enrollment of high school students, ESL, honors, independent study, internships, Washington semester. Adult education program. **Credit/placement by examination:** CLEP, institutional tests. 15 credit hours maximum toward bachelor's degree. Maximum 24 credit hours counted for adult education students. **Support services:** Tutoring.

Majors. Business: General, accounting, administrative services, business admin. **Education:** General, biology, early childhood, elementary, ESL, secondary, social studies, Spanish. **Protective services:** Criminal justice.

Most popular majors. Business/marketing 70%, education 20%, social sciences 10%.

Computing on campus. 188 workstations in library, computer center. Commuter students can connect to campus network. Online library, wireless network available.

Student life. Freshman orientation: Mandatory. **Policies:** Freshmen permitted cars on campus. **Activities:** Dance, student government, student council, young Christian students fraternity, tourism student association, history club, human resources students association, future teachers association, criminal justice student association, multilingual student association, special education students association, computer science student association.

Athletics. Intramural: Basketball, softball, table tennis, tennis, track and field, volleyball.

Student services. Adult student services, campus ministries, career counseling, student employment services, financial aid counseling, health services, personal counseling, placement for graduates, veterans' counselor.

Contact. E-mail: adcaraba@inter.edu
Phone: (787) 860-3100 Fax: (787) 860-3470
Ada Caraballo, Admissions Director, Inter American University of Puerto Rico: Fajardo Campus, PO Box 70003, Fajardo, PR 00738-7003

Inter American University of Puerto Rico: Guayama Campus

Guayama, Puerto Rico
www.inter.edu **CB code: 2077**

- Private 4-year university
- Large town
- 2,155 degree-seeking undergraduates: 19% part-time, 70% women, 100% Hispanic American
- 43 degree-seeking graduate students
- 86% of applicants admitted
- Interview required
- 21% graduate within 6 years

General. Founded in 1957. Regionally accredited. **Degrees:** 255 bachelor's, 81 associate awarded; master's offered. **ROTC:** Army. **Location:** 18 miles from Ponce. **Calendar:** Semester, limited summer session. **Full-time faculty:** 46 total; 15% have terminal degrees, 54% women. **Part-time faculty:** 150 total; 2% have terminal degrees, 47% women. **Class size:** 60% < 20, 33% 20-39, 6% 40-49, 2% 50-99.

Freshman class profile. 698 applied, 601 admitted, 498 enrolled.

Basis for selection. High school graduates must have 2.0 GPA and 800 admission index.

2005-2006 Annual costs. Tuition/fees: $4,564. Books/supplies: $800. Personal expenses: $350.

2004-2005 Financial aid. All financial aid based on need. 437 full-time freshmen applied for aid; 427 were judged to have need; 298 of these received aid. Average need met was 3%. Average scholarship/grant was $128; average loan $298. 19% of total undergraduate aid awarded as scholarships/grants, 81% as loans/jobs.

Application procedures. Admission: Priority date 5/15; no deadline. No application fee. Application may be submitted online. Admission notification on a rolling basis beginning on or about 4/1. **Financial aid:** Closing date 4/29. FAFSA, institutional form required. Applicants notified by 6/15; must reply by 7/30.

Academics. Special study options: Accelerated study, cooperative education, dual enrollment of high school students, exchange student, external degree, honors, independent study, study abroad. **Credit/placement by examination:** CLEP. **Support services:** Learning center, remedial instruction, tutoring.

Majors. Biology: General. **Business:** Accounting, business admin, human resources, office management. **Education:** Early childhood special, elementary, ESL, kindergarten/preschool, physical. **Health:** Nursing (RN). **Mechanic/repair:** Computer. **Philosophy/religion:** Religion. **Protective services:** Law enforcement admin.

Computing on campus. 150 workstations in library, computer center, student center.

Student life. Freshman orientation: Mandatory. Detail to vocational, personal and academic orientation. **Activities:** Choral groups, dance, student government, religious circle.

Athletics. Intercollegiate: Baseball M, basketball, cross-country, soccer M. **Intramural:** Baseball M, basketball, cross-country M, softball, table tennis W, tennis W, track and field.

Student services. Adult student services, campus ministries, career counseling, student employment services, health services, on-campus daycare, personal counseling, placement for graduates, veterans' counselor.

Contact. E-mail: lferrer@inter.edu
Phone: (787) 864-7059 Fax: (787) 864-8232
Laura Ferrer Sanchez, Director of Admissions, Inter American University of Puerto Rico: Guayama Campus, PO Box 10004, Guayama, PR 00785

Inter American University of Puerto Rico: Metropolitan Campus

Rio Piedras, Puerto Rico **CB member**
www.metro.inter.edu **CB code: 0873**

- Private 4-year branch campus college
- Commuter campus in large city

General. Founded in 1962. Regionally accredited. **Location:** 9 miles from San Juan. **Calendar:** Semester.

Annual costs/financial aid. Tuition/fees (2005-2006): $4,616. Books/supplies: $831. Personal expenses: $2,731. Need-based financial aid available to full-time and part-time students.

Contact. Phone: (787) 250-1912
Admissions, Box 191293, San Juan, PR 00919-1293

Inter American University of Puerto Rico: Ponce Campus

Mercedita, Puerto Rico
ponce.inter.edu **CB code: 3531**

- Private 4-year university
- Large town
- 5,146 degree-seeking undergraduates: 17% part-time, 62% women, 100% Hispanic American
- 181 degree-seeking graduate students
- 63% of applicants admitted

General. Regionally accredited. **Degrees:** 453 bachelor's, 106 associate awarded; master's offered. **ROTC:** Navy. **Calendar:** Semester. **Full-time faculty:** 81 total; 28% have terminal degrees, 49% women. **Part-time faculty:** 176 total; 11% have terminal degrees, 57% women.

Freshman class profile. 2,123 applied, 1,347 admitted, 691 enrolled.

Basis for selection. 2.0 high school GPA and average of 400 on first three parts of PAA. Interview required for AVANCE program.

High school preparation. 18 units required. Required units include English 3, mathematics 3, social studies 1, history 3, science 3 (laboratory 1), foreign language 3 and academic electives 1.

2005-2006 Annual costs. Tuition/fees: $4,576. Books/supplies: $902. Personal expenses: $2,831.

2004-2005 Financial aid. All financial aid based on need. 894 full-time freshmen applied for aid; 846 were judged to have need; 600 of these received aid. Average need met was 2%. Average scholarship/grant was $127; average loan $270. 23% of total undergraduate aid awarded as scholarships/grants, 77% as loans/jobs.

Application procedures. Admission: Closing date 5/15 (receipt date). No application fee. Admission notification on a rolling basis. **Financial aid:** No deadline. FAFSA required.

Academics. Special study options: Cooperative education, distance learning, honors, independent study, internships, study abroad, teacher certification program, weekend college. Adult programs (AVANCE), development programs, PREAD program. **Credit/placement by examination:** CLEP. **Support services:** Learning center, remedial instruction, study skills assistance, tutoring.

Majors. Biology: General. **Business:** Accounting, administrative services, business admin, finance, hotel/motel admin, human resources, international, management information systems, management science, marketing, office technology, operations, training/development. **Communications:** Journalism, public relations. **Computer sciences:** Computer science, information systems. **Conservation:** General. **Education:** Biology, early childhood, elementary, ESL, secondary, special. **Health:** Nursing (RN). **Protective services:** Law enforcement admin.

Most popular majors. Biology 8%, business/marketing 43%, computer/information sciences 6%, education 16%, health sciences 7%, legal studies 17%.

Computing on campus. PC or laptop required. 268 workstations in library, computer center, student center. Commuter students can connect to campus network. Online course registration, online library, helpline available.

Student life. Freshman orientation: Available. Includes workshops, seminars, and social activities. **Policies:** Freshmen permitted cars on campus. **Activities:** Concert band, choral groups, dance, student government, student newspaper.

Athletics. Intercollegiate: Baseball M, basketball, judo, softball, swimming, table tennis, track and field, triathlon, volleyball, weight lifting, wrestling. **Intramural:** Baseball M, basketball M, softball, table tennis, track and field, volleyball, weight lifting. **Team name:** Tigers.

Student services. Adult student services, alcohol/substance abuse counseling, campus ministries, career counseling, student employment services, financial aid counseling, health services, on-campus daycare, personal counseling, placement for graduates, women's services. **Physically disabled:** Services for visually, speech, hearing impaired.

Contact. E-mail: fldiaz@poce.inter.edu
Phone: (787) 841-0110 Fax: (787) 841-0103
Franco Diaz Vega, Director of Admissions, Inter American University of Puerto Rico: Ponce Campus, 104 Turpo Industrial Park Road #1, Mercedita, PR 00715-1602

Inter American University of Puerto Rico: San German Campus

San German, Puerto Rico
www.sg.inter.edu **CB code: 0946**

- Private 4-year university
- Commuter campus in large town
- 4,872 degree-seeking undergraduates: 13% part-time, 53% women, 100% Hispanic American
- 907 degree-seeking graduate students
- 26% graduate within 6 years

General. Founded in 1912. Regionally accredited. **Degrees:** 551 bachelor's, 51 associate awarded; master's, doctoral offered. **ROTC:** Army, Air Force. **Location:** 14 miles from Mayaguez, 104 miles from San Juan. **Calendar:** Semester, extensive summer session. **Full-time faculty:** 137 total; 48% have terminal degrees, 54% women. **Part-time faculty:** 200 total; 11% have terminal degrees, 52% women. **Class size:** 42% < 20, 48% 20-39, 9% 40-49, 2% 50-99. **Special facilities:** Nature preserve, botanical garden, museum.

Freshman class profile.

Return as sophomores:	70%	**Live on campus:**	10%
Out-of-state:	2%		

Basis for selection. High school GPA and test scores important. SAT required of English-speaking applicants. Essay, interview recommended for all; audition recommended for music; portfolio recommended for art programs.

High school preparation. 18 units recommended. Recommended units include English 3, mathematics 3, history 3, science 3, foreign language 3 and academic electives 3. 3 units of Spanish required of Spanish-speaking students.

2005-2006 Annual costs. Tuition/fees: $4,616. Room/board: $2,400. Books/supplies: $890. Personal expenses: $880.

2004-2005 Financial aid. Need-based: 172 full-time freshmen applied for aid; 142 were judged to have need; 78 of these received aid. Average need met was 1%. Average scholarship/grant was $14; average loan $30. 23% of total undergraduate aid awarded as scholarships/grants, 77% as loans/jobs. **Non-need-based:** Awarded to 175 full-time undergraduates, including 7 freshmen. Scholarships awarded for academics, athletics.

Application procedures. Admission: Closing date 5/14 (receipt date). No application fee. Admission notification on a rolling basis beginning on or about 2/15. **Financial aid:** Closing date 5/14. FAFSA, institutional form required. Applicants notified on a rolling basis; must reply by 8/1.

Academics. Bilingual program enables students to learn English or Spanish while taking courses in their native language. **Special study options:** Accelerated study, cooperative education, cross-registration, distance learning, double major, dual enrollment of high school students, ESL, honors, independent study, internships, liberal arts/career combination, study abroad, teacher certification program. **Credit/placement by examination:** AP, CLEP, institutional tests. 12 credit hours maximum toward associate degree, 18 toward bachelor's. **Support services:** Learning center, reduced course load, remedial instruction, tutoring.

Majors. Architecture: Architecture. **Biology:** General. **Business:** Accounting, administrative services, business admin, finance, human resources, management information systems, management science, marketing. **Computer sciences:** General, computer science. **Education:** General, art, biology, chemistry, early childhood, elementary, English, ESL, history, mathematics, music, physical, secondary, Spanish, special, voc/tech. **Engineering technology:** Electrical. **Health:** Clinical lab science. **Math:** General. **Parks/recreation:** Health/fitness. **Physical sciences:** Chemistry. **Psychology:** General. **Public administration:** General. **Social sciences:** Political science, sociology. **Visual/performing arts:** General, ceramics, drawing, music performance, painting, photography, sculpture.

Most popular majors. Biology 12%, business/marketing 26%, computer/information sciences 7%, education 25%, psychology 8%, visual/performing arts 9%.

Computing on campus. 800 workstations in dormitories, library, computer center, student center. Dormitories wired for high-speed internet access and linked to campus network. Commuter students can connect to campus network. Online course registration, online library, wireless network available.

Student life. Freshman orientation: Mandatory. Preregistration for classes offered. General orientation program offered in spring, summer and fall. **Policies:** Freshmen permitted cars on campus. **Housing:** Single-sex dorms, apartments, substance-free housing available. $25 fully refundable deposit, deadline 6/30. **Activities:** Bands, choral groups, dance, drama, music ensembles, student government, student newspaper, Bahai association, student bible union, international students organization, counselors student association, Catholic student organization, bilingual English-Spanish organization.

Athletics. Intercollegiate: Baseball M, basketball, cross-country, soccer M, softball, swimming, table tennis, tennis, track and field, volleyball, weight lifting. **Intramural:** Basketball, cross-country, softball, table tennis, tennis, track and field, volleyball. **Team name:** Tigers.

Student services. Adult student services, alcohol/substance abuse counseling, campus ministries, career counseling, student employment services, financial aid counseling, health services, on-campus daycare, personal counseling, placement for graduates, veterans' counselor.

Contact. E-mail: milcama@sg.inter.edu
Phone: (787) 892-3090 Fax: (787) 892-6350
Mildred Camacho, Director of Admissions, Inter American University of Puerto Rico: San German Campus, Box 5100, San German, PR 00683-9801

Pontifical Catholic University of Puerto Rico

Ponce, Puerto Rico **CB member**
www.pucpr.edu **CB code: 0910**

- Private 4-year university affiliated with Roman Catholic Church
- Commuter campus in small city
- 7,273 degree-seeking undergraduates
- 68% of applicants admitted
- SAT or ACT (ACT writing optional) required

General. Founded in 1948. Regionally accredited. **Degrees:** 963 bachelor's, 17 associate awarded; master's, doctoral, first professional offered. **ROTC:** Army, Air Force. **Location:** 60 miles from San Juan. **Calendar:** Semester, limited summer session. **Full-time faculty:** 262 total. **Part-time faculty:** 238 total. **Class size:** 36% < 20, 57% 20-39, 5% 40-49, 1% 50-99, less than 1% >100.

Freshman class profile. 2,963 applied, 2,020 admitted, 1,497 enrolled.

Mid 50% test scores			
SAT verbal:	400-520	Live on campus:	4%
SAT math:	400-520	Fraternities:	1%
		Sororities:	1%

Basis for selection. School achievement record, test scores important. SAT required of English-speaking applicants. Interview required for special program.

High school preparation. 15 units required. Required units include English 4, mathematics 3, history 2, science 2 and foreign language 4. 3 units English, 3 units foreign language, 2 units mathematics, 1 unit science, 1 unit history required for 3-year high schools.

2005-2006 Annual costs. Books/supplies: $600. Personal expenses: $1,216.

2005-2006 Financial aid. Need-based: Average need met was 71%. Average scholarship/grant was $4,300; average loan $1,000. 47% of total undergraduate aid awarded as scholarships/grants, 53% as loans/jobs. **Non-need-based:** Scholarships awarded for academics, athletics.

Application procedures. Admission: Priority date 3/15; deadline 7/15 (receipt date). $15 fee, may be waived for applicants with need. Admission notification on a rolling basis beginning on or about 2/15. **Financial aid:** Priority date 5/1; no closing date. FAFSA, institutional form required. Applicants notified by 6/15; must reply within 4 week(s) of notification.

Academics. Special study options: Accelerated study, combined bachelor's/graduate degree, double major, dual enrollment of high school students, ESL, exchange student, honors, independent study, internships, liberal arts/career combination, study abroad. **Credit/placement by examination:** AP, CLEP, institutional tests. 30 credit hours maximum toward bachelor's degree. **Support services:** Learning center, pre-admission summer program, reduced course load, remedial instruction, tutoring.

Majors. Area/ethnic studies: Hispanic-American/Latino/Chicano. **Biology:** General. **Business:** General, accounting, administrative services, business admin, communications, finance, international, management information systems, managerial economics, marketing, tourism/travel. **Communications:** General. **Conservation:** General, environmental studies. **Education:** General, art, biology, business, chemistry, early childhood, elementary, English, ESL, family/consumer sciences, history, mathematics, music, physical, physically handicapped, physics, science, secondary, social studies, Spanish, special, speech impaired. **Family/consumer sciences:** General. **Foreign languages:** French, Latin, Spanish. **Health:** Clinical lab science. **History:** General. **Interdisciplinary:** Gerontology, natural sciences. **Legal studies:** General, prelaw. **Liberal arts:** Arts/sciences. **Math:** General. **Philosophy/religion:** Philosophy. **Physical sciences:** Chemistry, physics. **Psychology:** General. **Public administration:** General, social work. **Social sciences:** General, criminology, political science, sociology. **Visual/performing arts:** Studio arts.

Computing on campus. 419 workstations in library, computer center, student center. Commuter students can connect to campus network. Online library, wireless network available.

Student life. Freshman orientation: Mandatory. **Policies:** Freshmen permitted cars on campus. **Housing:** Single-sex dorms available. **Activities:** Choral groups, dance, drama, musical theater, radio station, student government, student newspaper, TV station, Pi Gamma Mu, Phi Alpha Theta, Beta Beta Beta, Alpha Beta Chi, Phi Delta Kappa, honor society for business students, Pioneer Students in Christ and Mary, Miles Jesu, Knights of Columbus, Phi Sigma Kappa.

Athletics. Intercollegiate: Baseball M, basketball M, cross-country, diving, soccer, softball, swimming, table tennis, tennis, track and field, volleyball, water polo M, wrestling M. **Intramural:** Archery, baseball M, basketball, cross-country, diving, softball, swimming, table tennis, tennis, track and field, volleyball, wrestling M. **Team name:** Pioneers.

Student services. Campus ministries, career counseling, student employment services, health services, on-campus daycare, personal counseling, placement for graduates, veterans' counselor. **Learning disabled:** Comprehensive services available.

Contact. E-mail: admisiones@pucpr.edu
Phone: (787) 841-2000 ext. 1000 Fax: (787) 840-4295
Ana Bonilla, Director of Admissions, Pontifical Catholic University of Puerto Rico, 2250 Las Americas Avenue, Suite 284, Ponce, PR 00717-9777

Turabo University

Gurabo, Puerto Rico
www.suagm.edu/ut **CB code: 0780**

- Private 4-year university
- Commuter campus in small city
- 11,921 degree-seeking undergraduates: 18% part-time, 60% women
- 2,848 degree-seeking graduate students
- 56% of applicants admitted
- 18% graduate within 6 years

General. Founded in 1972. Regionally accredited. 4 off-campus sites. **Degrees:** 740 bachelor's, 63 associate awarded; master's, doctoral offered. **ROTC:** Army. **Location:** 17 miles from San Juan. **Calendar:** Semester, limited summer session. **Full-time faculty:** 132 total; 50% have terminal degrees, 100% minority, 43% women. **Part-time faculty:** 685 total; 4% have terminal degrees, 100% minority, 52% women. **Class size:** 48% < 20, 47% 20-39, 4% 40-49, less than 1% 50-99. **Special facilities:** Museum.

Freshman class profile. 5,323 applied, 2,992 admitted, 2,407 enrolled.

GPA 3.50 or higher:	12%	GPA 2.0-2.99:	55%
GPA 3.0-3.49:	22%	Return as sophomores:	66%

Basis for selection. Minimum 2.0 high school GPA for secretarial applicants, 2.5 for science applicants. SAT required for admission to honors and science programs. Interview required for applicants with lower than 2.0 high school GPA.

High school preparation. 15 units required. Required units include English 3, mathematics 3, social studies 2, science 2 and foreign language 3.

2005-2006 Annual costs. Books/supplies: $600. Personal expenses: $2,620.

Financial aid. Non-need-based: Scholarships awarded for academics, athletics.

Application procedures. Admission: No deadline. $15 fee, may be waived for applicants with need. Admission notification on a rolling basis beginning on or about 3/1. **Financial aid:** Priority date 5/30; no closing date. FAFSA required. Applicants notified by 7/30.

Academics. Special study options: Accelerated study, combined bachelor's/graduate degree, distance learning, honors, independent study, internships, liberal arts/career combination, weekend college. Off-campus full-degree sites. **Credit/placement by examination:** CLEP, institutional tests. **Support services:** Reduced course load, remedial instruction, study skills assistance, tutoring.

Majors. Biology: General. **Business:** Accounting, administrative services, business admin, logistics, management information systems, marketing, office management. **Communications:** General. **Conservation:** Environmental science. **Education:** General, biology, chemistry, early childhood, elementary, English, history, mathematics, physical, science, social science, Spanish, special, trade/industrial. **Engineering:** Electrical, mechanical. **Engineering technology:** Architectural drafting, computer systems, electrical, industrial management, mechanical, quality control. **Health:** Nursing (RN), speech pathology. **Interdisciplinary:** Natural sciences. **Liberal arts:** Humanities. **Physical sciences:** Chemistry. **Psychology:** General. **Public administration:** General, social work. **Social sciences:** General, criminology. **Visual/performing arts:** Graphic design.

Most popular majors. Business/marketing 45%, education 19%, engineering/engineering technologies 6%, public administration/social services 6%, social sciences 11%.

Computing on campus. Commuter students can connect to campus network. Helpline available.

Student life. Freshman orientation: Available. Preregistration for classes offered. **Policies:** Freshmen permitted cars on campus. **Activities:** Choral groups, dance, drama, music ensembles, radio station, student government, student newspaper, TV station.

Athletics. NAIA. **Intercollegiate:** Baseball M, basketball, cross-country, judo, soccer M, softball, swimming, tennis, track and field, volleyball, weight lifting. **Intramural:** Basketball, softball, table tennis, tennis W, volleyball, weight lifting. **Team name:** Tainos.

Student services. Adult student services, alcohol/substance abuse counseling, career counseling, services for economically disadvantaged, student employment services, financial aid counseling, health services, personal counseling, placement for graduates, veterans' counselor. **Physically disabled:** Services for visually, hearing impaired.

Contact. Phone: (787) 746-3009 Toll-free number: (800) 747-8362
Virginia Gonzalez, Associate Director of Admissions and Financial Aid, Turabo University, PO Box 3030, Gurabo, PR 00778

Universidad Adventista de las Antillas

Mayaguez, Puerto Rico
www.uaa.edu **CB code: 1020**

- Private 4-year university and liberal arts college affiliated with Seventh-day Adventists
- Commuter campus in small city
- 760 degree-seeking undergraduates: 7% part-time, 60% women
- 71 degree-seeking graduate students

General. Founded in 1957. Regionally accredited. **Degrees:** 93 bachelor's, 35 associate awarded; master's offered. **Location:** 100 miles from San Juan. **Calendar:** Semester, limited summer session. **Full-time faculty:** 42 total; 26% have terminal degrees, 52% women. **Part-time faculty:** 21 total; 10% have terminal degrees, 43% women.

Freshman class profile. 446 applied, 401 admitted, 153 enrolled.

Out-of-state:	20%	**Live on campus:**	43%

Basis for selection. Open admission, but selective for some programs. SAT or ACT recommended for English-speaking applicants. Interview required for nursing program. **Homeschooled:** Unless home-schooling is accredited, applicant must take GED.

High school preparation. 18 units recommended. Recommended units include English 3, mathematics 3, social studies 3, science 3 and academic electives 3. 3 Spanish units recommended.

2006-2007 Annual costs. Tuition/fees (projected): $6,060. Tuition for nonresident aliens is the sum of private tuition ($3680) and the Form I-20 deposit ($4000); after the first year, these students receive credit refund at registration ($500 per semester). Room/board: $1,300. Books/supplies: $1,000. Personal expenses: $750.

Application procedures. Admission: No deadline. $20 fee, may be waived for applicants with need. Admission notification on a rolling basis. **Financial aid:** No deadline. FAFSA, institutional form required. Applicants notified on a rolling basis starting 8/15; must reply within 3 week(s) of notification.

Academics. Special study options: Cooperative education, double major, ESL, internships, liberal arts/career combination, teacher certification program. **Credit/placement by examination:** CLEP, institutional tests. 12 credit hours maximum toward associate degree, 12 toward bachelor's. **Support services:** Learning center, reduced course load, remedial instruction, tutoring.

Majors. Biology: General. **Business:** General, administrative services. **Computer sciences:** General, computer science, information systems. **Education:** Elementary, music, secondary. **Foreign languages:** Spanish. **Health:** Respiratory therapy technology. **History:** General. **Physical sciences:** Chemistry. **Theology:** Theology.

Most popular majors. Biology 8%, business/marketing 17%, education 13%, health sciences 31%, theological studies 13%.

Computing on campus. 62 workstations in library, computer center. Online library, repair service available.

Student life. Freshman orientation: Mandatory. Preregistration for classes offered. 2-day program at beginning of each semester. **Policies:** Religious environment designed for Seventh-day Adventist students. Freshmen permitted cars on campus. **Housing:** Guaranteed on-campus for freshmen. Single-sex dorms, apartments available. **Activities:** Concert band, choral groups, drama, music ensembles, student government, student newspaper, L.I.F.E., S.C.O.R., international club, ministerial club.

Athletics. Intramural: Basketball, bowling, gymnastics, soccer, softball M, swimming, table tennis, tennis, track and field, volleyball. **Team name:** Eagles Gym Team.

Student services. Alcohol/substance abuse counseling, campus ministries, career counseling, student employment services, financial aid counseling, health services, personal counseling, veterans' counselor.

Contact. E-mail: admissions@uaa.edu
Phone: (787) 834-9595 ext. 2208 Fax: (787) 834-9597
Evelyn del Valle, Director of Admissions/Continuing Education, Universidad Adventista de las Antillas, PO Box 118, Mayaguez, PR 00681-0118

Universidad Central del Caribe

Bayamon, Puerto Rico
www.uccaribe.edu/

- Private 4-year university
- Small city

General. Regionally accredited. **Calendar:** Differs by program.

Annual costs/financial aid. Tuition/fees (projected): $5,860.

Contact. Phone: (787) 740-1611
Decanato de Admisiones y Asuntos Estudiantiles, Bayamon, PR 00960-6032

Universidad del Este

Carolina, Puerto Rico **CB member**
www.suagm.edu **CB code: 0883**

- Private 4-year business and liberal arts college
- Commuter campus in small city
- 10,136 degree-seeking undergraduates: 27% part-time, 66% women, 100% Hispanic American
- 230 degree-seeking graduate students
- Interview required
- 12% graduate within 6 years

General. Founded in 1949. Regionally accredited. **Degrees:** 775 bachelor's, 89 associate awarded; master's offered. **ROTC:** Army. **Calendar:** Semester, limited summer session. **Full-time faculty:** 73 total; 41% have terminal degrees, 100% minority, 67% women. **Part-time faculty:** 675 total; 7% have terminal degrees, 100% minority, 59% women. **Class size:** 43% < 20, 52% 20-39, 4% 40-49.

Freshman class profile. 7,088 applied, 3,051 admitted, 2,067 enrolled.

GPA 3.50 or higher:	7%	**GPA 2.0-2.99:**	58%
GPA 3.0-3.49:	16%	**Return as sophomores:**	62%

Basis for selection. Open admission, but selective for some programs. Special requirements for health and science programs; interview recommended. SAT required of English-speaking freshman applicants.

2005-2006 Annual costs. Books/supplies: $700. Personal expenses: $2,620.

2004-2005 Financial aid. Need-based: 88% of total undergraduate aid awarded as scholarships/grants, 12% as loans/jobs. **Non-need-based:** Scholarships awarded for academics, athletics.

Application procedures. Admission: Priority date 3/30; no deadline. $15 fee, may be waived for applicants with need. Application may be submitted online. Admission notification on a rolling basis. **Financial aid:** Priority date 5/30; no closing date. FAFSA, institutional form required. Applicants notified by 7/30.

Academics. Special study options: Accelerated study, distance learning, honors, independent study, internships, liberal arts/career combination, teacher certification program, weekend college. **Credit/placement by examination:** CLEP. **Support services:** Reduced course load, remedial instruction, study skills assistance, tutoring.

Majors. Agriculture: Agribusiness operations. **Biology:** General, microbiology. **Business:** Accounting, administrative services, business admin, hotel/motel admin, insurance, management information systems, marketing, tourism/travel. **Computer sciences:** Applications programming, data processing. **Education:** Early childhood, health, physical, science. **Health:** Critical care nursing, health care admin, medical radiologic technology/radiation therapy, radiologic technology/medical imaging, sonography. **Legal studies:** Paralegal. **Personal/culinary services:** Restaurant/catering. **Protective services:** Law enforcement admin. **Psychology:** General. **Public administration:** Social work. **Social sciences:** Political science.

Most popular majors. Business/marketing 49%, education 16%, health sciences 6%, public administration/social services 14%, security/protective services 13%.

Computing on campus. Commuter students can connect to campus network. Online library, helpline, repair service available.

Student life. Freshman orientation: Available. **Policies:** Freshmen permitted cars on campus. **Activities:** Choral groups, dance, student government, student newspaper, Phi Theta Kappa, Future Secretaries of America, nursing club.

Athletics. Intercollegiate: Basketball, cross-country, softball W, table tennis, tennis, track and field, volleyball, weight lifting M. **Intramural:** Basketball, cross-country, softball, table tennis, tennis, volleyball. **Team name:** Pitirre.

Student services. Adult student services, alcohol/substance abuse counseling, career counseling, services for economically disadvantaged, student employment services, financial aid counseling, health services, personal counseling, placement for graduates, veterans' counselor.

Contact. Phone: (787) 257-7373 Toll-free number: (800) 981-6570
Fax: (787) 257-8744 ext. 3307
Magda Ostolaza, Director of Marketing and Recruitment, Universidad del Este, PO Box 2010, Carolina, PR 00981-2010

Universidad Metropolitana

Rio Piedras, Puerto Rico — **CB member**
www.suagm.edu/umet — **CB code: 1519**

- Private 4-year university and liberal arts college
- Commuter campus in large city
- 9,046 degree-seeking undergraduates: 21% part-time, 68% women
- 2,293 degree-seeking graduate students
- 14% graduate within 6 years

General. Founded in 1985. Regionally accredited. **Degrees:** 558 bachelor's, 74 associate awarded; master's, doctoral offered. **ROTC:** Army, Navy, Air Force. **Location:** 3 miles from San Juan. **Calendar:** Semester, limited summer session. **Full-time faculty:** 84 total; 38% have terminal degrees, 100% minority, 66% women. **Part-time faculty:** 663 total; 9% have terminal degrees, 100% minority, 51% women. **Class size:** 57% < 20, 41% 20-39, 2% 40-49.

Freshman class profile.

GPA 3.50 or higher:	8%	**GPA 2.0-2.99:**	58%
GPA 3.0-3.49:	20%		

Basis for selection. School achievement record and test scores considered. SAT required of English-speaking applicants. Interview required for academically weak.

2005-2006 Annual costs. Tuition/fees: $3,872. Books/supplies: $700. Personal expenses: $2,620.

2004-2005 Financial aid. All financial aid based on need.

Application procedures. Admission: Closing date 8/15 (receipt date). $15 fee, may be waived for applicants with need. Admission notification on a rolling basis. **Financial aid:** Priority date 5/30; no closing date. FAFSA required. Applicants notified by 7/30.

Academics. A flexible admissions policy allows Universidad Metropolitana to accept the challenge of providing all students with increased opportunities for success. **Special study options:** Accelerated study, combined bachelor's/graduate degree, distance learning, honors, independent study, internships, liberal arts/career combination, teacher certification program, Washington semester, weekend college. Off-campus full-degree sites. **Credit/placement by examination:** CLEP. **Support services:** Remedial instruction, tutoring.

Majors. Biology: General, cellular/anatomical. **Business:** Accounting, business admin, management information systems, managerial economics, marketing, office management. **Communications:** General, journalism. **Computer sciences:** Computer science. **Conservation:** Environmental studies. **Education:** Biology, elementary, English, history, physical, Spanish, special. **Health:** EMT paramedic, nursing (RN), respiratory therapy technology. **Physical sciences:** Chemistry. **Protective services:** Criminal justice. **Psychology:** General. **Public administration:** Social work. **Social sciences:** General.

Most popular majors. Business/marketing 44%, education 18%, health sciences 11%, public administration/social services 6%, security/protective services 8%.

Computing on campus. Commuter students can connect to campus network. Helpline, repair service available.

Student life. Freshman orientation: Mandatory. Preregistration for classes offered. Held 1 week before the beginning of the academic year. **Activities:** Choral groups, drama, student government, student newspaper, TV station, Business Students Association, Hermandad, Social Work, Students Association, Communication Students Association.

Athletics. Intercollegiate: Baseball, basketball, boxing, softball, table tennis, tennis, track and field, volleyball, weight lifting M. **Intramural:** Baseball, basketball, boxing, softball, table tennis, volleyball. **Team name:** Cocodrilo.

Student services. Adult student services, alcohol/substance abuse counseling, career counseling, services for economically disadvantaged, student employment services, financial aid counseling, health services, on-campus daycare, personal counseling, placement for graduates, veterans' counselor.

Contact. Phone: (787) 765-6262 Fax: (787) 759-7663
Julio Rodríguez, Director of Admission and Financial Aid, Universidad Metropolitana, Apartado 21150, Rio Piedras, PR 00928

Universidad Politecnica de Puerto Rico

Hato Rey, Puerto Rico — **CB member**
www.pupr.edu — **CB code: 0614**

- Private 5-year university and engineering college
- Commuter campus in large city
- 5,070 degree-seeking undergraduates: 50% part-time, 23% women
- 701 graduate students
- 93% of applicants admitted

General. Founded in 1966. Regionally accredited. **Degrees:** 477 bachelor's awarded; master's offered. **ROTC:** Army, Air Force. **Location:** 3 miles from San Juan. **Calendar:** Trimester, extensive summer session. **Full-time faculty:** 169 total; 22% have terminal degrees, 36% women. **Part-time faculty:** 131 total; 10% have terminal degrees, 30% women. **Special facilities:** TV studio.

Freshman class profile. 1,001 applied, 935 admitted, 740 enrolled.

Basis for selection. Minimum 2.5 high school GPA and PAA combined score of 1300 required. SAT in English or Spanish required.

High school preparation. 15 units required. Required units include English 3, mathematics 3, social studies 3, science 3, foreign language 3 and academic electives 3.

2005-2006 Annual costs. Tuition/fees: $5,922. Books/supplies: $1,070. Personal expenses: $1,978.

Financial aid. Non-need-based: Scholarships awarded for academics, music/drama.

Application procedures. Admission: Closing date 8/1. $30 fee. Application may be submitted online. Admission notification on a rolling basis. **Financial aid:** Closing date 6/30. FAFSA, institutional form required. Applicants notified by 7/15.

Academics. Special study options: Cooperative education, liberal arts/career combination. **Credit/placement by examination:** AP, CLEP. **Support services:** Pre-admission summer program, remedial instruction, study skills assistance, tutoring.

Majors. Architecture: Architecture. **Business:** General, business admin. **Engineering:** Civil, electrical, mechanical. **Engineering technology:** Surveying.

Computing on campus. 550 workstations in library, computer center. Online library available.

Student life. Freshman orientation: Available. Preregistration for classes offered. Week-long orientation offered every trimester. **Policies:** Freshmen permitted cars on campus. **Activities:** Choral groups, drama, student government, University Bible Association, Drugs and Alcohol Committee.

Athletics. Intercollegiate: Baseball M, basketball, cross-country, soccer M, table tennis, tennis, track and field, volleyball. **Intramural:** Basketball, cross-country W, table tennis, tennis, track and field, volleyball. **Team name:** Beavers.

Student services. Alcohol/substance abuse counseling, career counseling, services for economically disadvantaged, student employment services, financial aid counseling, health services, personal counseling, placement for graduates, veterans' counselor. **Physically disabled:** Services for hearing impaired.

Contact. Phone: (787) 754-8000 ext. 309 Fax: (787) 764-8712
Teresa Cardona, Director of Admissions, Universidad Politecnica de Puerto Rico, PO Box 192017, San Juan, PR 00918-2017

University of Puerto Rico: Aguadilla

Aguadilla, Puerto Rico
www.uprag.edu **CB code: 0983**

- Public 4-year liberal arts and technical college
- Commuter campus in small city
- 2,969 degree-seeking undergraduates: 12% part-time, 63% women, 100% Hispanic American
- 30% of applicants admitted
- 37% graduate within 6 years

General. Founded in 1972. Regionally accredited. **Degrees:** 371 bachelor's, 53 associate awarded. **ROTC:** Army. **Location:** 81 miles from San Juan. **Calendar:** Semester, limited summer session. **Full-time faculty:** 150 total; 15% have terminal degrees, 99% minority, 56% women. **Part-time faculty:** 16 total; 19% have terminal degrees, 100% minority, 38% women. **Class size:** 20% < 20, 80% 20-39.

Freshman class profile. 2,809 applied, 846 admitted, 761 enrolled.

GPA 3.50 or higher:	48%	**End year in good standing:**	74%
GPA 3.0-3.49:	35%	**Return as sophomores:**	78%
GPA 2.0-2.99:	17%		

Basis for selection. Admissions based on secondary school record and standardized test scores. Talent and ability considered. SAT and SAT Subject Tests in Spanish and math level I required of English-speaking applicants. **Homeschooled:** Copy of the curriculum of classes required.

High school preparation. Recommended units include English 3, mathematics 2 and social studies 2. 3 Spanish recommended.

2005-2006 Annual costs. Tuition/fees: $1,344; $3,192 out-of-state. Books/supplies: $1,320. Personal expenses: $1,000.

2004-2005 Financial aid. All financial aid based on need. 83% of total undergraduate aid awarded as scholarships/grants, 17% as loans/jobs.

Application procedures. Admission: Priority date 11/17; deadline 1/30 (receipt date). $20 fee, may be waived for applicants with need. Application must be submitted on paper. Admission notification 4/2. Admission notification on a rolling basis. Must reply by 4/30. **Financial aid:** Closing date 5/6. FAFSA, institutional form required. Applicants notified on a rolling basis starting 4/1; must reply within 1 week(s) of notification.

Academics. Special study options: Honors, liberal arts/career combination, teacher certification program. **Credit/placement by examination:** CLEP, institutional tests. **Support services:** Learning center, remedial instruction, tutoring.

Majors. Biology: General. **Business:** Accounting, finance, human resources, management information systems, marketing, office management. **Education:** Elementary, English. **Engineering technology:** Electrical.

Computing on campus. 220 workstations in library, computer center. Online library, student web hosting available.

Student life. Freshman orientation: Available. **Policies:** Freshmen permitted cars on campus. **Housing:** Family community housing and private guest house available. **Activities:** Concert band, choral groups, drama, student government, Organizacion Juventud en Cristo, Estudiantes Orientadores, Teatro Experimental 80, Bio-Study, Kayukembo Association, Companeros Alertas Ante Un Mundo Buscando Alternativas, alcohol and drug prevention organization.

Athletics. Intercollegiate: Baseball M, basketball, cross-country, softball W, table tennis, tennis, track and field, volleyball, weight lifting. **Intramural:** Baseball M, basketball, cross-country, softball W, table tennis, tennis, track and field, volleyball, weight lifting. **Team name:** Tiburones.

Student services. Career counseling, student employment services, health services, personal counseling, placement for graduates. **Physically disabled:** Services for visually impaired.

Contact. E-mail: melba_serrano@hotmail.com
Phone: (787) 890-2681 ext. 280
Melba Serrano, Admissions Officer, University of Puerto Rico: Aguadilla, Box 250160, Aguadilla, PR 00604

University of Puerto Rico: Arecibo

Arecibo, Puerto Rico
www.upra.edu **CB code: 0911**

- Public 4-year university
- Commuter campus in small city
- 3,931 degree-seeking undergraduates: 12% part-time, 67% women, 100% Hispanic American
- 31% of applicants admitted
- 36% graduate within 6 years

General. Founded in 1967. Regionally accredited. **Degrees:** 581 bachelor's, 85 associate awarded. **ROTC:** Army. **Location:** 48 miles from San Juan. **Calendar:** Semester, limited summer session. **Full-time faculty:** 193 total; 22% have terminal degrees, 54% women. **Part-time faculty:** 46 total; 6% have terminal degrees, 52% women. **Class size:** 28% < 20, 72% 20-39.

Freshman class profile. 3,715 applied, 1,152 admitted, 941 enrolled.

Basis for selection. Admissions based equally on College Board test scores and GPA. Each academic program has minimum requirements. SAT and SAT Subject Tests required of English-speaking applicants. The College Entrance Examination Board or CEEB (Spanish equivalent of the SAT) is a requirement for non-English speaking applicants. In 2006-07, CEEB subject scores will be used for placement in developmental courses in math, Spanish, and English. Interviews sometimes required.

2005-2006 Annual costs. Tuition/fees: $1,691; $3,539 out-of-state. Books/supplies: $1,320. Personal expenses: $1,000.

2004-2005 Financial aid. All financial aid based on need. 938 full-time freshmen applied for aid; 740 were judged to have need; 740 of these received aid. 89% of total undergraduate aid awarded as scholarships/grants, 11% as loans/jobs.

Application procedures. Admission: Closing date 11/30 (postmark date). $20 fee. Application may be submitted online. Admission notification 4/15. Must reply by 4/30. **Financial aid:** Closing date 4/27. FAFSA, institutional form required.

Academics. Special study options: Cooperative education, ESL, exchange student, honors, internships, liberal arts/career combination, study abroad, teacher certification program, Washington semester. Evening college, Continuing Education Program and Professional Improvement Program. **Credit/placement by examination:** AP, CLEP, IB. **Support services:** Learning center, pre-admission summer program, remedial instruction, study skills assistance, tutoring, writing center.

Majors. Biology: Bacteriology. **Business:** Accounting, administrative services, business admin, finance, market research. **Communications technology:** Radio/tv. **Computer sciences:** General. **Education:** Elementary.

Most popular majors. Biology 6%, business/marketing 23%, communication technologies 9%, computer/information sciences 6%, education 14%, psychology 7%.

Computing on campus. 240 workstations in library, computer center. Commuter students can connect to campus network. Online library, student web hosting, wireless network available.

Student life. Freshman orientation: Mandatory. Preregistration for classes offered. 4-day program held from 8 am to 12 pm in summer. 200 students attend every week until all students have attended. **Policies:** Freshmen permitted cars on campus. **Activities:** Concert band, choral groups, dance, drama, film society, music ensembles, student government, student newspaper, Teleradial Communications, ROTARAC, alcohol and drugs program, dance club, Juventud Universitaria Catolica (religious Catholic students), Federacion de Estudiantes Iberoamericanos, American marketing association.

Athletics. Intercollegiate: Baseball M, basketball, cross-country, judo, soccer M, softball W, track and field, volleyball, weight lifting, wrestling M. **Intramural:** Basketball, soccer M, softball W, volleyball. **Team name:** Los Lobos (Wolves).

Student services. Alcohol/substance abuse counseling, career counseling, services for economically disadvantaged, student employment services, financial aid counseling, health services, personal counseling, placement for graduates, women's services. **Physically disabled:** Services for visually impaired.

Contact. E-mail: dbarrios@upra.edu
Phone: (787) 815-0000 ext. 4110 Fax: (787) 817-3461
Delma Barrios, Admissions Officer, University of Puerto Rico: Arecibo, PO Box 4010, Arecibo, PR 00614-4010

University of Puerto Rico: Bayamon University College

Bayamon, Puerto Rico
www.uprb.edu **CB code: 0852**

- Public 4-year technical college
- Commuter campus in small city
- 4,638 degree-seeking undergraduates: 22% part-time, 56% women
- 1273% graduate within 6 years

General. Founded in 1971. Regionally accredited. **Degrees:** 546 bachelor's, 62 associate awarded. **ROTC:** Army. **Location:** 9 miles from San Juan. **Calendar:** Semester, limited summer session. **Full-time faculty:** 240 total; 25% have terminal degrees, 57% women. **Part-time faculty:** 48 total; 12% have terminal degrees, 56% women. **Special facilities:** Multimedia laboratory.

Basis for selection. High school GPA and test scores most important. Higher scores required of applicants to bachelor's programs. Special consideration given to applicants with special talents or handicaps. SAT and SAT Subject Tests recommended. SAT and 2 SAT Subject Tests (Spanish, mathematics) accepted for English speaking applicants from U.S. mainland. PAA required of Spanish-speaking applicants.

High school preparation. 12 units required. Required and recommended units include English 3, mathematics 3, social studies 1-3 and science 1. 3 units Spanish also required.

2005-2006 Annual costs. Tuition/fees: $1,344; $3,192 out-of-state. Books/supplies: $800. Personal expenses: $600.

Financial aid. All financial aid based on need.

Application procedures. Admission: Priority date 12/10; deadline 1/31. $15 fee. Application must be submitted on paper. Admission notification on a rolling basis beginning on or about 4/25. Must reply by 5/30. **Financial aid:** Closing date 6/15. Institutional form required. Applicants notified by 7/12; must reply within 4 week(s) of notification.

Academics. Special study options: Cooperative education, cross-registration, double major, ESL, exchange student, honors, internships. **Credit/placement by examination:** AP, CLEP. **Support services:** Pre-admission summer program, reduced course load, study skills assistance, tutoring.

Majors. Biology: General. **Business:** Accounting, administrative services, finance, management science, marketing. **Computer sciences:** Computer science. **Education:** Kindergarten/preschool, physically handicapped. **Engineering:** Materials.

Computing on campus. 370 workstations in computer center.

Student life. Freshman orientation: Available. **Activities:** Bands, choral groups, drama, student government, student newspaper, Confraternidad de Cristianos Unidos, Asociacion Juventud Catolica, Society for Human Resource Management, Asociacion de Estudiantes Orientadores, American Marketing Association, Asociacion de Estudiantes de Computadoras, Asociacion de Gerencia de Materiales.

Athletics. NCAA. **Intercollegiate:** Baseball M, basketball, cross-country, swimming, table tennis, tennis, track and field, volleyball, wrestling M. **Intramural:** Table tennis, tennis, volleyball. **Team name:** Vaqueros.

Student services. Adult student services, career counseling, student employment services, health services, personal counseling, placement for graduates.

Contact. E-mail: e_velez@cutb.upr.clu.edu
Phone: (787) 786-2885 Fax: (787) 798-1595
Vivian Rivera, Director of Admissions, University of Puerto Rico: Bayamon University College, 174 State Road #170 Parque Industrial Minillas, Bayamon, PR 00959

University of Puerto Rico: Carolina Regional College

Carolina, Puerto Rico
www.uprc.edu **CB code: 3891**

- Public 4-year university
- Commuter campus in small city
- 3,879 degree-seeking undergraduates: 30% part-time, 65% women

General. Founded in 1974. Regionally accredited. **Degrees:** 415 bachelor's, 186 associate awarded. **ROTC:** Army, Air Force. **Location:** 10 miles from San Juan. **Calendar:** Trimester, limited summer session. **Full-time faculty:** 117 total; 18% have terminal degrees, 43% women. **Part-time faculty:** 83 total; 17% have terminal degrees, 41% women.

Basis for selection. High school GPA and test scores important. SAT and SAT Subject Tests in Spanish, Math Level 1 required of English-speaking applicants. Interview recommended for those with exceptional ability; portfolio recommended for art.

High school preparation. 15 units required. Required units include English 3, mathematics 3, social studies 3, science 2 and foreign language 3.

2005-2006 Annual costs. Tuition/fees: $2,256; $3,192 out-of-state. Books/supplies: $1,980. Personal expenses: $1,000.

Financial aid. All financial aid based on need. 677 full-time freshmen applied for aid; 677 were judged to have need; 677 of these received aid. Average need met was 42%. Average scholarship/grant was $697.

Application procedures. Admission: Closing date 1/31 (postmark date). $20 fee. Application may be submitted online. Must reply by 6/12. **Financial aid:** Closing date 5/15. FAFSA, institutional form required. Applicants notified on a rolling basis starting 6/10.

Academics. Special study options: Cooperative education, ESL, independent study, internships, liberal arts/career combination. **Credit/placement by examination:** AP, CLEP. **Support services:** Learning center, pre-admission summer program, remedial instruction, tutoring.

Majors. Business: Administrative services, business admin, finance, hotel/motel admin, tourism promotion. **Communications:** Advertising. **Communications technology:** Graphic/printing. **Protective services:** Forensics, law enforcement admin.

Computing on campus. 451 workstations in library, computer center. Commuter students can connect to campus network. Online course registration, wireless network available.

Student life. Freshman orientation: Available. Preregistration for classes offered. **Activities:** Bands, choral groups, dance, drama, music ensembles, student government, religious, departmental, and athletic organizations.

Athletics. Intercollegiate: Baseball M, basketball, cross-country, softball W, table tennis, tennis, track and field, volleyball, weight lifting. **Intramural:** Basketball, cross-country, softball, table tennis, tennis, track and field, volleyball, weight lifting.

Student services. Alcohol/substance abuse counseling, career counseling, student employment services, financial aid counseling, health services, personal counseling, placement for graduates, veterans' counselor. **Physically disabled:** Services for visually, hearing impaired.

Contact. Phone: (787) 757-1485 Fax: (787) 750-7940
Celia Méndez, Admissions Officer, University of Puerto Rico: Carolina Regional College, PO Box 4800, Carolina, PR 00984-4800

University of Puerto Rico: Cayey University College

Cayey, Puerto Rico **CB member**
www.cayey.upr.edu **CB code: 0981**

- Public 4-year liberal arts college
- Commuter campus in large town

- 3,668 degree-seeking undergraduates: 13% part-time, 72% women, 100% Hispanic American
- 69% of applicants admitted
- SAT and SAT Subject Tests required
- 39% graduate within 6 years

General. Founded in 1967. Regionally accredited. **Degrees:** 509 bachelor's, 1 associate awarded. **ROTC:** Army. **Location:** 30 miles from San Juan. **Calendar:** Semester, limited summer session. **Full-time faculty:** 174 total; 57% have terminal degrees, 42% women. **Part-time faculty:** 38 total; 10% have terminal degrees, 58% women. **Special facilities:** Pio Lopez museum, Las Verdes Sombras Eco-Park.

Freshman class profile. 1,135 applied, 785 admitted, 734 enrolled.

Basis for selection. School achievement record, test scores most important. SAT required of English-speaking applicants. Audition, portfolio required of all; interview recommended for music, theater programs.

High school preparation. 18 units required. Required units include English 3, mathematics 3, social studies 3, history 3, science 2 and academic electives 3. 3 units Spanish required.

2005-2006 Annual costs. Tuition/fees: $1,344; $3,192 out-of-state.

2005-2006 Financial aid. All financial aid based on need. 568 full-time freshmen applied for aid; 505 were judged to have need; 505 of these received aid. 84% of total undergraduate aid awarded as scholarships/grants, 16% as loans/jobs.

Application procedures. Admission: Closing date 11/30 (postmark date). $20 fee. Application may be submitted online. Admission notification 4/4. Must reply by 5/4. **Financial aid:** Closing date 6/30. FAFSA required. Applicants notified by 7/30.

Academics. Special study options: Accelerated study, ESL, exchange student, honors, liberal arts/career combination, study abroad, teacher certification program. **Credit/placement by examination:** AP, CLEP. **Support services:** Pre-admission summer program, remedial instruction, tutoring.

Majors. Area/ethnic studies: Hispanic-American/Latino/Chicano. **Biology:** General. **Business:** General, accounting, administrative services, business admin, office management. **Education:** Early childhood special, elementary, ESL, history, mathematics, physical, science, secondary, social studies, Spanish, special. **English:** English lit. **Foreign languages:** Spanish. **History:** General. **Liberal arts:** Arts/sciences. **Math:** General. **Physical sciences:** Chemistry. **Psychology:** General. **Social sciences:** General, economics, sociology.

Most popular majors. Biology 13%, business/marketing 28%, education 27%, psychology 15%, social sciences 8%.

Computing on campus. 350 workstations in library, computer center. Online course registration available.

Student life. Freshman orientation: Mandatory. Preregistration for classes offered. **Policies:** Freshmen permitted cars on campus. **Activities:** Concert band, choral groups, drama, music ensembles, student government, student newspaper, Many religious, political, and social service organizations available.

Athletics. NCAA. **Intercollegiate:** Baseball M, basketball, cross-country, judo, soccer M, softball, swimming, table tennis, tennis, track and field, volleyball, weight lifting M, wrestling M. **Intramural:** Baseball M, basketball, football (tackle) M, soccer, softball M, swimming, table tennis, tennis, track and field, volleyball, weight lifting M, wrestling M. **Team name:** Bulls.

Student services. Career counseling, services for economically disadvantaged, student employment services, financial aid counseling, health services, on-campus daycare, personal counseling, placement for graduates, veterans' counselor. **Physically disabled:** Services for visually impaired.

Contact. E-mail: wilopez@cayey.upr.edu
Phone: (787) 738-2161 ext. 2208 Fax: (787) 738-5633
Wilfredo Lopez, Director of Admissions, University of Puerto Rico: Cayey University College, Oficina de Admisiones UPR- Cayey, Cayey, PR 00736

University of Puerto Rico: Humacao

Humacao, Puerto Rico
www.uprh.edu **CB code: 0874**

- Public 4-year university and liberal arts college
- Commuter campus in small city
- 3,976 degree-seeking undergraduates: 12% part-time, 70% women, 100% Hispanic American
- 47% of applicants admitted
- 46% graduate within 6 years

General. Founded in 1962. Regionally accredited. **Degrees:** 564 bachelor's, 91 associate awarded. **ROTC:** Army. **Location:** 30 miles from San Juan. **Calendar:** Semester, limited summer session. **Full-time faculty:** 253 total; 43% have terminal degrees, 57% women. **Part-time faculty:** 29 total; 7% have terminal degrees, 52% women. **Special facilities:** Observatory, census data center, museum, communication competencies center.

Freshman class profile. 2,178 applied, 1,015 admitted, 857 enrolled.

Mid 50% test scores		**GPA 3.0-3.49:**	28%
SAT verbal:	470-570	**GPA 2.0-2.99:**	10%
SAT math:	480-590	**Return as sophomores:**	85%
GPA 3.50 or higher:	62%		

Basis for selection. High school achievement record, test scores important. Non-native speakers of Spanish required to prove fluency through institutional examinations, interviews. Applicants for admission must take the Spanish version of Puerto Rico CEEB of the College Board: aptitude test (verbal and mathematics) and achievement test battery (Spanish, English and mathematics). In lieu of the above, applicants make take SAT and SAT Subject Tests (Spanish Composition and Spanish Reading). SAT and SAT Subject Tests (Spanish and Mathematics Level I) required of English-speaking applicants. **Homeschooled:** Sworn statement indicating that student received formal education at home. **Learning Disabled:** Director of Disabled Students Services Office (SERPI) evaluates learning disabled students to determine if they qualify for special admission.

High school preparation. 18 units recommended. Recommended units include English 3, mathematics 3, social studies 1, history 2, science 3, foreign language 3 and academic electives 3. Foreign language must be Spanish.

2005-2006 Annual costs. Tuition/fees: $1,344; $3,336 out-of-state. Books/supplies: $1,320. Personal expenses: $1,000.

2004-2005 Financial aid. Need-based: 90% of total undergraduate aid awarded as scholarships/grants, 10% as loans/jobs. **Non-need-based:** Scholarships awarded for academics, athletics, music/drama.

Application procedures. Admission: Priority date 11/15; deadline 11/30. $20 fee. Application must be submitted on paper. Admission notification 4/15. Must reply by 5/1. **Financial aid:** Closing date 7/31. FAFSA, institutional form required. Applicants notified by 9/30.

Academics. Course work conducted in Spanish. **Special study options:** Exchange student, honors, internships, teacher certification program. Students can travel to Europe during summer and earn 6 credits in elective courses. **Credit/placement by examination:** AP, CLEP, institutional tests. 40 credit hours maximum toward associate degree, 40 toward bachelor's. **Support services:** Learning center, pre-admission summer program, reduced course load, remedial instruction, study skills assistance, tutoring, writing center.

Majors. Biology: General, marine, microbiology. **Business:** General, accounting, administrative services, business admin, human resources, international. **Conservation:** Wildlife. **Education:** Elementary, ESL. **Health:** Nursing (RN). **Math:** Computational. **Physical sciences:** Physics. **Public administration:** Social work.

Most popular majors. Biology 11%, business/marketing 43%, education 20%, health sciences 7%, physical sciences 7%, public administration/social services 10%.

Computing on campus. 438 workstations in library, computer center. Commuter students can connect to campus network. Online course registration, wireless network available.

Student life. Freshman orientation: Available. One-day program. Students register for classes on this day. **Policies:** Freshmen permitted cars on campus. **Activities:** Choral groups, dance, drama, student government, various religious and social service organizations.

Athletics. Intercollegiate: Baseball M, basketball, cheerleading, cross-country, judo, softball W, swimming, tennis W, track and field, volleyball, weight lifting, wrestling M. **Intramural:** Basketball, softball W, volleyball, weight lifting. **Team name:** Buhos.

Student services. Alcohol/substance abuse counseling, career counseling, student employment services, health services, legal services, personal counseling, placement for graduates. **Physically disabled:** Services for visually, speech, hearing impaired.

Contact. E-mail: i_ferrer@webmail.uprh.edu
Phone: (787) 850-0000 ext. 9301 Fax: (787) 850-9428
Inara Ferrer, Admissions Officer, University of Puerto Rico: Humacao, 100 Road 908 CUH Station, Humacao, PR 00791

University of Puerto Rico: Mayaguez

Mayaguez, Puerto Rico **CB member**
www.uprm.edu **CB code: 0912**

- Public 4-year agricultural and engineering college
- Commuter campus in small city
- 10,981 degree-seeking undergraduates: 8% part-time, 49% women, 100% Hispanic American
- 1,059 degree-seeking graduate students
- 62% of applicants admitted
- 49% graduate within 6 years

General. Founded in 1911. Regionally accredited. Most courses conducted in Spanish. Students must have working knowledge of Spanish and English. **Degrees:** 1,575 bachelor's awarded; master's, doctoral offered. **ROTC:** Army, Air Force. **Location:** 100 miles from San Juan. **Calendar:** Semester, limited summer session. **Full-time faculty:** 619 total; 91% minority, 35% women. **Part-time faculty:** 21 total; 95% minority, 43% women. **Class size:** Less than 1% < 20, less than 1% 20-39, less than 1% 40-49, less than 1% 50-99, 98% >100. **Special facilities:** Planetarium, botanical garden, fine arts museum, agricultural extension service, agricultural experimental station, natural history collection, resource center for science and engineering.

Freshman class profile. 3,891 applied, 2,419 admitted, 2,158 enrolled.

Mid 50% test scores		**GPA 3.0-3.49:**	21%
SAT verbal:	490-620	**GPA 2.0-2.99:**	6%
SAT math:	510-670	**Out-of-state:**	1%
GPA 3.50 or higher:	73%		

Basis for selection. High school GPA and college entrance examination scores. SAT and SAT Subject Tests required for English-speaking applicants. Students from Puerto Rico are required to submit the score from the College Board Entrance Examination. The verbal and math aptitude is used for admission. The other component for admission is the high school GPA. The formula for admissions gives a weight of 50% to the GPA and 25% to each of the two aptitude test scores.

High school preparation. 18 units recommended. Recommended units include English 3, mathematics 2, social studies 2, history 2, science 2, foreign language 3 and academic electives 4.

2005-2006 Annual costs. Tuition/fees: $1,344; $3,336 out-of-state. Books/supplies: $1,320. Personal expenses: $800.

Financial aid. All financial aid based on need.

Application procedures. Admission: Closing date 1/31 (postmark date). $15 fee. Admission notification on a rolling basis beginning on or about 4/1. Must reply by 4/15. **Financial aid:** Closing date 6/30. FAFSA, institutional form required. Applicants notified by 9/30; must reply within 2 week(s) of notification.

Academics. Online support available. Spanish language skills (reading, writing) required to read most online course materials. **Special study options:** Cooperative education, distance learning, double major, ESL, exchange student, honors, internships, study abroad, teacher certification program. Four academic colleges: Arts and Sciences, Engineering, Agricultural Sciences and Business Administration; Public university; Master's university. **Credit/placement by examination:** AP, CLEP, institutional tests. 22 credit hours maximum toward bachelor's degree. **Support services:** Reduced course load, remedial instruction, tutoring.

Majors. Agriculture: Agribusiness operations, agronomy, animal sciences, business, economics, education services, horticultural science, plant protection, soil science. **Biology:** General, biotechnology, marine, microbiology. **Business:** Accounting, administrative services, business admin, finance, human resources, marketing, office management, organizational behavior, sales/distribution. **Computer sciences:** General, computer science, systems analysis. **Education:** Agricultural, mathematics, physical. **Engineering:** General, chemical, civil, computer, electrical, industrial, mechanical. **Engineering technology:** Surveying. **English:** English lit. **Foreign languages:** Comparative lit, French, Spanish. **Health:** Athletic training, nursing (RN), premedicine. **History:** General. **Interdisciplinary:** Math/computer science. **Math:** General. **Parks/recreation:** Facilities management, health/fitness. **Philosophy/religion:** Philosophy. **Physical sciences:** General, chemistry, geology, physics. **Psychology:** General. **Social sciences:** General, economics, political science, sociology. **Visual/performing arts:** Art history/conservation, studio arts.

Most popular majors. Agriculture 6%, biology 13%, business/marketing 12%, engineering/engineering technologies 42%.

Computing on campus. 1,000 workstations in library, computer center.

Student life. Freshman orientation: Mandatory. **Housing:** Housing available near campus. **Activities:** Bands, choral groups, dance, drama, literary magazine, radio station, student government, student newspaper, international associations, model of United Nations council.

Athletics. NCAA. **Intercollegiate:** Baseball M, basketball, cross-country, gymnastics, soccer M, softball W, swimming, table tennis, tennis, track and field, volleyball, water polo M, wrestling M. **Intramural:** Archery, baseball M, basketball, cross-country, racquetball, soccer M, softball, swimming, table tennis, tennis, volleyball, water polo M, wrestling M. **Team name:** Tarzanes "Bulldogs".

Student services. Career counseling, student employment services, health services, personal counseling, placement for graduates, veterans' counselor.

Contact. E-mail: admisiones@uprm.edu
Phone: (787) 265-3811 Fax: (787) 834-5265
Norma Torres, Director of Admissions, University of Puerto Rico: Mayaguez, Admsssions Office, Mayaguez, PR 00681-9021

University of Puerto Rico: Medical Sciences

San Juan, Puerto Rico
www.rcm.upr.edu **CB code: 0631**

- Public 4-year university
- Commuter campus in large city

General. Founded in 1950. Regionally accredited. **Calendar:** Differs by program. Semester or trimester.

Annual costs/financial aid. Tuition/fees (2005-2006): $1,344; $3,336 out-of-state. Books/supplies: $1,200. Personal expenses: $800. Need-based financial aid available to full-time and part-time students.

Contact. Phone: (787) 758-2525 ext. 5211
Director, Central Office of Admissions, P.O. Box 365067, San Juan, PR 00936-5067

University of Puerto Rico: Ponce

Ponce, Puerto Rico
upr-ponce.upr.edu **CB code: 0836**

- Public 4-year university and branch campus college
- Commuter campus in small city
- 3,158 degree-seeking undergraduates: 9% part-time, 65% women, 100% Hispanic American
- 28% of applicants admitted
- SAT and SAT Subject Tests required
- 30% graduate within 6 years

General. Founded in 1970. Regionally accredited. **Degrees:** 425 bachelor's, 94 associate awarded. **ROTC:** Army. **Location:** 68 miles from San Juan, 46 miles from Mayaguez. **Calendar:** Semester, limited summer session. **Full-time faculty:** 149 total; 20% have terminal degrees, 100% minority, 56% women. **Part-time faculty:** 45 total; 18% have terminal degrees, 100% minority, 47% women. **Class size:** 25% < 20, 75% 20-39.

Freshman class profile. 2,817 applied, 781 admitted, 750 enrolled.

Basis for selection. Admission based on general application index (GAI), combination of high school GPA and College Board test scores (50% each). Programs have their own GAI requirements. Interview required for academically weak and special ability.

High school preparation. College-preparatory program required. 18 units required. Required units include English 3, mathematics 3, social studies 3, science 3 and academic electives 2. 3 units Spanish, 1 unit fine arts.

2005-2006 Annual costs. Tuition/fees: $1,344; $3,336 out-of-state. Books/supplies: $1,320. Personal expenses: $800.

2005-2006 Financial aid. All financial aid based on need. 87% of total undergraduate aid awarded as scholarships/grants, 13% as loans/jobs.

Application procedures. Admission: Closing date 11/15. $15 fee. Admission notification on a rolling basis beginning on or about 4/15. Must reply by May 1 or within 3 week(s) if notified thereafter. **Financial aid:** Closing date 5/30. FAFSA, institutional form required. Applicants notified by 10/15.

Academics. Special study options: Dual enrollment of high school students, honors, internships. **Credit/placement by examination:** CLEP. **Support services:** Remedial instruction, tutoring.

Majors. Business: Accounting, administrative services, business admin, finance, marketing. **Computer sciences:** General. **Education:** Elementary. **Health:** Athletic training. **Math:** General. **Protective services:** Forensics. **Psychology:** General.

Most popular majors. Business/marketing 26%, education 26%, engineering/engineering technologies 12%, health sciences 18%, psychology 10%.

Computing on campus. 344 workstations in library, computer center.

Student life. Freshman orientation: Available. **Activities:** Bands, choral groups, dance, drama, student government, Catholic, Christian, and Baptist youth organizations.

Athletics. Intercollegiate: Basketball, cross-country, softball, table tennis, tennis, track and field, volleyball. **Intramural:** Basketball, cross-country, gymnastics, softball, table tennis, tennis, track and field, volleyball.

Student services. Career counseling, student employment services, health services, on-campus daycare, personal counseling, placement for graduates, veterans' counselor. **Physically disabled:** Services for visually impaired.

Contact. Phone: (787) 844-8181 ext. 2531 Fax: (787) 840-8108
William Rodriguez, Admissions Officer, University of Puerto Rico: Ponce, Box 7186, Ponce, PR 00732

University of Puerto Rico: Rio Piedras

San Juan, Puerto Rico — **CB member**
www.rrp.upr.edu — **CB code: 0979**

- Public 4-year university
- Commuter campus in large city
- 16,407 degree-seeking undergraduates: 18% part-time, 67% women
- 4,083 graduate students
- 22% of applicants admitted
- 48% graduate within 6 years

General. Founded in 1903. Regionally accredited. Most courses conducted in Spanish. Students must have working knowledge of Spanish and English. **Degrees:** 2,332 bachelor's awarded; master's, doctoral, first professional offered. **ROTC:** Army, Air Force. **Location:** 10 miles from Rio Piedras. **Calendar:** Semester, limited summer session. **Full-time faculty:** 1,087 total; 72% have terminal degrees, 50% women. **Part-time faculty:** 383 total; 27% have terminal degrees, 46% women. **Class size:** 30% < 20, 68% 20-39, 2% 40-49. **Special facilities:** Museums, theater, game room.

Freshman class profile. 13,494 applied, 2,966 admitted, 2,433 enrolled.

Mid 50% test scores		**GPA 3.0-3.49:**	25%
SAT verbal:	540-640	**GPA 2.0-2.99:**	9%
SAT math:	540-670	**Return as sophomores:**	88%
GPA 3.50 or higher:	66%	**Live on campus:**	10%

Basis for selection. Academic Aptitude Test and Achievement Test in Spanish, English and Mathematics offered by the College Board required. SAT accepted in English and Spanish from English-speaking and Spanish-speaking applicants. **Homeschooled:** State high school equivalency certificate required.

High school preparation. Required and recommended units include English 3, mathematics 2, social studies 1, history 1, science 2 and academic electives 6. 3 units Spanish required.

2005-2006 Annual costs. Tuition/fees: $1,344; $3,336 out-of-state. Tuition is based on per-credit-hour charge. For 2005-06 undergraduate credit cost is $40. First-time, first-year students take 12 to 15 credits per semester. Per-term required fees are: construction $47, technologies $25. Annual required fees ($216) represent 3 terms (first and second semester and one summer session). Room/board: $6,620. Books/supplies: $1,320. Personal expenses: $1,000.

2005-2006 Financial aid. All financial aid based on need. **Additional information:** Tuition waived for honor students, athletes, members of chorus, and others with special talents.

Application procedures. Admission: Closing date 2/15. $15 fee. Application may be submitted online. Admission notification 5/10. Must reply by 6/15. **Financial aid:** FAFSA required.

Academics. Special study options: Cooperative education, double major, ESL, exchange student, external degree, honors, internships, liberal arts/career combination, study abroad, Washington semester. Students can study abroad in the United States, Spain, France, Mexico, Costa Rica, Italy, Germany, Japan, China, Argentina, Nicaragua, as well as in other countries. **Credit/placement by examination:** AP, CLEP, institutional tests. 30 credit hours maximum toward bachelor's degree. **Support services:** Learning center, pre-admission summer program, remedial instruction, tutoring.

Majors. Architecture: Environmental design, urban/community planning. **Biology:** General. **Business:** General, accounting, administrative services, banking/financial services, business admin, entrepreneurial studies, finance, human resources, labor relations, management information systems, managerial economics, statistics. **Communications:** General. **Computer sciences:** General, computer science. **Conservation:** General. **Education:** Elementary, family/consumer sciences, secondary. **Family/consumer sciences:** General, child care, food/nutrition. **Foreign languages:** General, comparative lit, French, Spanish. **History:** General. **Interdisciplinary:** Natural sciences. **Legal studies:** Prelaw. **Liberal arts:** Arts/sciences. **Math:** General. **Philosophy/religion:** Philosophy. **Physical sciences:** Chemistry, physics. **Psychology:** General. **Public administration:** Social work. **Social sciences:** General, anthropology, economics, geography, political science, sociology. **Visual/performing arts:** General, art, art history/conservation, dramatic, drawing, multimedia, painting, sculpture, studio arts.

Most popular majors. Biology 12%, business/marketing 24%, communications/journalism 7%, education 18%, psychology 6%, social sciences 15%.

Computing on campus. 154 workstations in dormitories, library, computer center, student center. Dormitories linked to campus network. Commuter students can connect to campus network. Online library, wireless network available.

Student life. Freshman orientation: Available. Preregistration for classes offered. 3 days in summer. **Policies:** Students represented in university administration. **Housing:** Coed dorms, substance-free housing available. $35 deposit, deadline 10/29. **Activities:** Jazz band, choral groups, dance, drama, film society, literary magazine, musical theater, radio station, student government, student newspaper, TV station, Club Avanza, Confraternidad Universitaria de Avivamiento, Jovenes Cristianos Universitarios, Juventud Universitaria Popular, Club de la Cruz Roja Americana del Recinto de Rio Piedras.

Athletics. NAIA, NCAA. **Intercollegiate:** Basketball, cross-country, gymnastics, soccer M, softball, swimming, table tennis, tennis, track and field, volleyball, water polo M, wrestling M. **Intramural:** Basketball, cross-country, gymnastics, soccer M, softball, swimming, table tennis, tennis, track and field, volleyball, water polo, wrestling M. **Team name:** Gallitos/Gerezanas.

Student services. Adult student services, career counseling, student employment services, health services, on-campus daycare, personal counseling, placement for graduates, veterans' counselor. **Physically disabled:** Services for visually, speech, hearing impaired.

Contact. Phone: (787) 764-7290 Fax: (787) 763-4265
Cruz Valentin, Director of Admissions, University of Puerto Rico: Rio Piedras, Box 23344, San Juan, PR 00931-3344

University of Puerto Rico: Utuado

Utuado, Puerto Rico — **CB member**
http://upr-utuado.upr.clu.edu/ — **CB code: 3893**

- Public 4-year agricultural college
- Commuter campus in large town
- 1,395 degree-seeking undergraduates: 11% part-time, 60% women, 100% Hispanic American
- 32% of applicants admitted
- Interview required

General. Founded in 1979. Regionally accredited. **Degrees:** 96 bachelor's, 48 associate awarded. **ROTC:** Army. **Location:** 20 miles from Arecibo. **Calendar:** Semester, limited summer session. **Full-time faculty:** 67 total; 22% have terminal degrees, 100% minority, 45% women. **Part-time faculty:** 17 total; 100% minority, 53% women. **Special facilities:** 118-acre farm.

Freshman class profile. 1,626 applied, 523 admitted, 475 enrolled.

Basis for selection. GED not accepted. High school GPA, test scores important. SAT required of English-speaking students.

High school preparation. 10 units required. Required units include English 3, mathematics 2, history 3, science 2 and foreign language 3. 3 fine arts required.

2005-2006 Annual costs. Tuition/fees: $1,344; $3,336 out-of-state. Books/supplies: $1,320. Personal expenses: $1,000.

Financial aid. All financial aid based on need.

Application procedures. Admission: Priority date 11/15; no deadline. $20 fee, may be waived for applicants with need. Must reply by May 1 or within 2 week(s) if notified thereafter. **Financial aid:** Priority date 5/31; no closing date. FAFSA required. Applicants notified on a rolling basis starting 9/30; must reply within 4 week(s) of notification.

Academics. Special study options: Cooperative education, distance learning, dual enrollment of high school students, honors, internships, teacher certification program. **Credit/placement by examination:** AP, CLEP. **Support services:** Reduced course load, remedial instruction, tutoring.

Majors. Business: Accounting, office/clerical. **Education:** Elementary.

Most popular majors. Business/marketing 18%, education 67%.

Computing on campus. 90 workstations in library, computer center, student center. Online library available.

Student life. Freshman orientation: Mandatory. **Policies:** Freshmen permitted cars on campus. **Housing:** Substance-free housing available. **Activities:** Concert band, choral groups, dance, drama, student government.

Athletics. Intercollegiate: Baseball M, basketball, cross-country, softball W, tennis, track and field, volleyball, weight lifting. **Intramural:** Baseball M, basketball, cross-country, softball W, table tennis, tennis, track and field, volleyball, weight lifting. **Team name:** Guaraguao.

Student services. Alcohol/substance abuse counseling, career counseling, financial aid counseling, health services, personal counseling, placement for graduates, veterans' counselor.

Contact. Phone: (787) 894-2316 Fax: (787) 894-2891
Maria Robles, Admissions Officer, University of Puerto Rico: Utuado, PO Box 2500, Utuado, PR 00641

University of the Sacred Heart

Santurce, Puerto Rico — **CB member**
www.sagrado.edu — **CB code: 0913**

- Private 4-year university and liberal arts college affiliated with Roman Catholic Church
- Commuter campus in large city
- 4,324 degree-seeking undergraduates: 20% part-time, 65% women, 100% Hispanic American
- 854 degree-seeking graduate students

General. Founded in 1935. Regionally accredited. Campus is historical and educational landmark. **Degrees:** 521 bachelor's, 5 associate awarded; master's offered. **Calendar:** Semester, extensive summer session. **Full-time faculty:** 105 total; 35% have terminal degrees, 61% women. **Part-time faculty:** 215 total; 15% have terminal degrees, 46% women. **Class size:** 47% < 20, 53% 20-39. **Special facilities:** Jardin Escultorico, Museo de la Radio, Pabellon de las Artes, Patio de las Artes, Galeria Jose (Pepin) Mendez y Teatro Emilio S. Belaval.

Basis for selection. High school GPA and highest score CEEB important. SAT scores accepted in place of CEEB. Interview required for nursing program.

High school preparation. 15 units required. Required and recommended units include English 3, mathematics 3, social studies 2, science 3, foreign language 3 and academic electives 3.

2005-2006 Annual costs. Tuition/fees: $5,210. Room only: $1,900. Books/supplies: $1,398. Personal expenses: $2,246.

Financial aid. Non-need-based: Scholarships awarded for academics, athletics.

Application procedures. Admission: Priority date 12/15; deadline 6/30. $15 fee, may be waived for applicants with need. Application may be submitted online. Admission notification on a rolling basis. **Financial aid:** Closing date 5/30. FAFSA, institutional form required. Applicants notified on a rolling basis starting 6/15; must reply by 8/30.

Academics. Special study options: Combined bachelor's/graduate degree, cooperative education, cross-registration, double major, dual enrollment of high school students, exchange student, external degree, honors, independent study, internships, liberal arts/career combination, semester at sea, teacher certification program. International programs with universities in Mexico and Spain. **Credit/placement by examination:** AP, CLEP, institutional tests. **Support services:** Pre-admission summer program, reduced course load, remedial instruction, tutoring.

Majors. Biology: General. **Business:** Accounting, administrative services, business admin, tourism promotion. **Communications:** General, advertising, journalism. **Computer sciences:** Computer science, information systems. **Education:** General, bilingual, elementary, secondary. **Foreign languages:** French, Spanish. **Health:** Clinical lab technology, nursing (RN). **History:** General. **Interdisciplinary:** Natural sciences. **Math:** General. **Parks/recreation:** Health/fitness. **Physical sciences:** Chemistry. **Psychology:** General. **Public administration:** Social work. **Social sciences:** General. **Visual/performing arts:** General, dramatic.

Computing on campus. 500 workstations in dormitories, library, computer center, student center. Commuter students can connect to campus network. Repair service available.

Student life. Freshman orientation: Available. **Policies:** Freshmen permitted cars on campus. **Housing:** Single-sex dorms available. $125 deposit, deadline 6/15. **Activities:** Choral groups, drama, film society, literary magazine, radio station, student government, student newspaper, TV station, pastoral services organization, health and allied sciences organization, student council, senior class organization, judo club, soccer club, nursing club, Christian club, microbioloby club, psychology club, chemistry club, justice system, telecommunication club.

Athletics. Intercollegiate: Basketball M, cross-country, swimming, tennis M, track and field, volleyball, wrestling M. **Intramural:** Basketball M, softball M, swimming, table tennis, volleyball. **Team name:** Dolphins.

Student services. Alcohol/substance abuse counseling, career counseling, student employment services, financial aid counseling, health services, personal counseling, placement for graduates, veterans' counselor. **Physically disabled:** Services for visually, hearing impaired.

Contact. E-mail: admision@sagrado.edu
Phone: (787) 728-2070 Fax: (787) 728-2066
Luis Henriquez, Director of Admissions and Promotion, University of the Sacred Heart, Universidad del Sagrado Corazon Oficina de Nuevo Ingreso, San Juan, PR 00914-0383

Rhode Island

Brown University

Providence, Rhode Island **CB member**
www.brown.edu **CB code: 3094**

- Private 4-year university and liberal arts college
- Residential campus in small city
- 5,927 degree-seeking undergraduates: 1% part-time, 53% women, 7% African American, 14% Asian American, 7% Hispanic American, 1% Native American, 6% international
- 2,037 degree-seeking graduate students
- 15% of applicants admitted
- SAT and SAT Subject Tests or ACT with writing, application essay required
- 95% graduate within 6 years; 43% enter graduate study

General. Founded in 1764. Regionally accredited. **Degrees:** 1,499 bachelor's awarded; master's, doctoral, first professional offered. **ROTC:** Army. **Location:** 45 miles from Boston. **Calendar:** Semester, limited summer session. **Full-time faculty:** 630 total; 98% have terminal degrees, 16% minority, 30% women. **Part-time faculty:** 258 total; 98% have terminal degrees, 12% minority, 37% women. **Special facilities:** Museum of anthropology, observatory, center for the performing arts, center for information technology, institute for education, institute for international studies.

Freshman class profile. 16,911 applied, 2,587 admitted, 1,475 enrolled.

Mid 50% test scores			
SAT verbal:	660-760	Rank in top quarter:	98%
SAT math:	670-770	Rank in top tenth:	94%
ACT:	27-33	International:	7%

Basis for selection. GED not accepted. Strength of academic course load and student's achievement in courses most important. Extracurricular activities, recommendations, personal essay important; test scores strongly considered. Students submitting SAT should submit 2 SAT Subject Tests of their choice. ACT with Writing may take place of both SAT and SAT Subject Tests. Portfolio recommended for art, music programs. **Learning Disabled:** Untimed standardized tests accepted.

High school preparation. 16 units required; 19 recommended. Required and recommended units include English 4, mathematics 3-4, history 2, science 3-4 (laboratory 2-3), foreign language 3-4 and academic electives 1. At least 1 art unit (music or art) recommended. Familiarity with computers recommended. Physics, chemistry, and advanced mathematics recommended for prospective science or engineering majors.

2006-2007 Annual costs. Tuition/fees: $35,352. Room/board: $9,134. Books/supplies: $1,000. Personal expenses: $1,306.

Financial aid. All financial aid based on need.

Application procedures. **Admission:** Closing date 1/1 (postmark date). $70 fee, may be waived for applicants with need. Application may be submitted online. Admission notification 4/1. Must reply by 5/1. **Financial aid:** Closing date 2/1. FAFSA, CSS PROFILE required. Applicants notified by 4/1; must reply by 5/1.

Academics. Students must complete course requirements in major(s) of choice, but are free to choose courses without a core curriculum prior to designating a major. **Special study options:** Accelerated study, combined bachelor's/graduate degree, cross-registration, double major, exchange student, honors, independent study, internships, student-designed major, study abroad, teacher certification program. 8-year medical program, cross-registration with Rhode Island School of Design, early childhood certification (in teaching) program via Wheaton College courses. **Credit/placement by examination:** AP, CLEP, IB, institutional tests. **Support services:** Reduced course load, study skills assistance, tutoring, writing center.

Majors. **Architecture:** History/criticism. **Area/ethnic studies:** African, African-American, American, Asian, East Asian, European, French, German, Hispanic-American/Latino/Chicano, Italian, Latin American, Near/Middle Eastern, Slavic, South Asian, women's. **Biology:** General, aquatic, biochemistry, biophysics, cell/histology, molecular. **Computer sciences:** Computer science. **Conservation:** Environmental science, environmental studies. **Education:** General. **Engineering:** Biomedical, chemical, civil, computer, electrical, materials, mechanical, physics. **English:** American lit, British lit. **Foreign languages:** Ancient Greek, classics, comparative lit, French, German, Italian, Latin, linguistics, Portuguese, Slavic, Spanish. **Health:** Community health services. **History:** General. **Interdisciplinary:** Ancient studies, biological/physical sciences, cognitive science, math/computer science, medieval/Renaissance, neuroscience. **Math:** General, applied, statistics. **Philosophy/religion:** Judaic, philosophy, religion. **Physical sciences:** Chemical physics, chemistry, geochemistry, geology, geophysics, physics. **Psychology:** General. **Public administration:** Policy analysis. **Social sciences:** Anthropology, archaeology, economics, international economic development, international relations, political science, sociology, urban studies. **Visual/performing arts:** General, art history/conservation, dramatic, musicology, studio arts.

Most popular majors. Biology 17%, liberal arts 26%, physical sciences 12%, social sciences 44%.

Computing on campus. 400 workstations in dormitories, library, computer center. Dormitories linked to campus network. Commuter students can connect to campus network. Online course registration, helpline, repair service available.

Student life. **Freshman orientation:** Mandatory, $245 fee. Preregistration for classes offered. 6-day program, beginning Wednesday prior to Labor Day. **Policies:** Students must live in on-campus housing for first 3 years; those entering 7th semester may request off-campus residence. **Housing:** Guaranteed on-campus for all undergraduates. Coed dorms, single-sex dorms, cooperative housing, fraternity/sorority housing available. Language houses, social dormitories, cultural houses, special program housing (international students, technology students, environmental studies) available. **Activities:** Bands, choral groups, dance, drama, film society, literary magazine, music ensembles, musical theater, radio station, student government, student newspaper, symphony orchestra, TV station, African students association, ACLU, Amnesty International, Asian American students association, Big Brothers, Community Outreach, Catholic Pastoral Council, Latino American students association, International Organization, Canadian club.

Athletics. NCAA. **Intercollegiate:** Baseball M, basketball, cross-country, diving, equestrian W, fencing, field hockey W, football (tackle) M, golf, gymnastics W, ice hockey, lacrosse, rowing (crew), skiing W, soccer, softball W, squash, swimming, tennis, track and field, volleyball W, water polo, wrestling M. **Intramural:** Badminton, basketball, fencing, field hockey W, ice hockey, lacrosse, racquetball, rugby, soccer, softball, squash, swimming, tennis, volleyball, water polo. **Team name:** Bears.

Student services. Adult student services, alcohol/substance abuse counseling, campus ministries, career counseling, student employment services, financial aid counseling, health services, minority student services, personal counseling, placement for graduates, women's services. **Physically disabled:** Services for visually, hearing impaired.

Contact. E-mail: admission_undergraduate@brown.edu
Phone: (401) 863-2378 Fax: (401) 863-9300
James Miller, Director of Admission, Brown University, 45 Prospect Street, Providence, RI 02912

Bryant University

Smithfield, Rhode Island **CB member**
www.bryant.edu **CB code: 3095**

- Private 4-year business and liberal arts college
- Residential campus in large town
- 3,177 degree-seeking undergraduates: 5% part-time, 41% women, 3% African American, 2% Asian American, 4% Hispanic American, 2% international
- 430 degree-seeking graduate students
- 58% of applicants admitted
- SAT or ACT with writing, application essay required
- 69% graduate within 6 years; 4% enter graduate study

General. Founded in 1863. Regionally accredited. **Degrees:** 644 bachelor's awarded; master's offered. **ROTC:** Army. **Location:** 12 miles from Providence, 40 miles from Boston. **Calendar:** Semester, extensive summer session. **Full-time faculty:** 133 total; 86% have terminal degrees, 12% minority, 32% women. **Part-time faculty:** 129 total; 28% have terminal degrees, 51% women. **Class size:** 20% < 20, 78% 20-39, 2% 40-49. **Special facilities:** Wellness center, technology center, simulated financial trading floor, electronic classrooms, digital library, digital TV studio, high speed Unix lab with 20 Sun workstations.

Freshman class profile. 4,214 applied, 2,430 admitted, 822 enrolled.

Mid 50% test scores		Rank in top tenth:	18%
SAT verbal:	500-580	Return as sophomores:	88%
SAT math:	530-620	Out-of-state:	87%
ACT:	21-25	Live on campus:	94%
GPA 3.50 or higher:	33%	International:	1%
GPA 3.0-3.49:	45%	Fraternities:	1%
GPA 2.0-2.99:	22%	Sororities:	2%
Rank in top quarter:	56%		

Basis for selection. Secondary school curriculum, GPA, guidance counselor's recommendation, personal essay very important. Class rank and test scores important. Evidence of math ability is important for consideration to business programs. All files are carefully and thoroughly reviewed by professional admission staff. **Homeschooled:** Must be completing a state-accredited program. Course descriptions and progress reports required as part of application process. **Learning Disabled:** Foreign language requirement may be waived.

High school preparation. College-preparatory program required. 16 units required. Required and recommended units include English 4, mathematics 4, history 2-4, science 3 (laboratory 2) and foreign language 2. Mathematics must include a year beyond algebra II, with a preference for pre-calculus or calculus in senior year. History includes social sciences.

2005-2006 Annual costs. Tuition/fees: $24,762. $500 non-refundable enrollment commitment deposit is required of both residents and commuters. Room/board: $9,568.

2005-2006 Financial aid. Need-based: 531 full-time freshmen applied for aid; 460 were judged to have need; 460 of these received aid. Average need met was 77%. Average scholarship/grant was $10,040; average loan $4,390. 67% of total undergraduate aid awarded as scholarships/grants, 33% as loans/jobs. **Non-need-based:** Awarded to 1,549 full-time undergraduates, including 303 freshmen. Scholarships awarded for athletics, minority status, ROTC.

Application procedures. Admission: Closing date 2/15 (postmark date). $50 fee, may be waived for applicants with need. Application may be submitted online. Admission notification 3/15. Must reply by May 1 or within 2 week(s) if notified thereafter. **Financial aid:** Closing date 2/15. FAFSA required. Applicants notified by 3/24; must reply by 5/1.

Academics. Credit offered for military experience. **Special study options:** Double major, honors, independent study, internships, study abroad. **Credit/placement by examination:** AP, CLEP, IB, SAT, ACT, institutional tests. 30 credit hours maximum toward bachelor's degree. **Support services:** Learning center, study skills assistance, tutoring, writing center.

Majors. Business: Accounting, accounting technology, actuarial science, business admin, finance, financial planning, international, marketing. **Communications:** General. **Computer sciences:** General, information technology. **English:** English lit. **History:** General. **Psychology:** General. **Social sciences:** Economics, international relations.

Most popular majors. Business/marketing 86%, computer/information sciences 10%.

Computing on campus. PC or laptop required. 539 workstations in library, computer center. Dormitories wired for high-speed internet access and linked to campus network. Commuter students can connect to campus network. Online course registration, online library, helpline, repair service, student web hosting, wireless network available.

Student life. Freshman orientation: Mandatory, $75 fee. Preregistration for classes offered. 2-day program in June during which students and parents/guardians are housed in campus residence halls overnight. Students also take mathematics placement exam and register for elective courses. **Policies:** All residence halls are smoke free; all freshmen residence halls are alcohol free. Freshmen permitted cars on campus. **Housing:** Guaranteed on-campus for all undergraduates. Coed dorms, single-sex dorms, special housing for disabled, substance-free housing available. 24 hour quiet, honors, all women (upperclass), international business students. **Activities:** Bands, choral groups, dance, drama, literary magazine, radio station, student government, student newspaper, TV station, multicultural student union, international students organization, Hillel, Big Brothers/Big Sisters, Bryant Christian Fellowship, Amnesty International, student senate, greek leadership, alliance for women's awareness, Bryant Helps.

Athletics. NCAA. **Intercollegiate:** Baseball M, basketball, cross-country, field hockey W, football (tackle) M, golf M, lacrosse, soccer, softball W, swimming, tennis, track and field, volleyball W. **Intramural:** Basketball, field hockey W, football (non-tackle) M, lacrosse, soccer, softball, volleyball, water polo. **Team name:** Bulldogs.

Student services. Adult student services, alcohol/substance abuse counseling, campus ministries, career counseling, student employment services, financial aid counseling, health services, minority student services, personal counseling, placement for graduates, women's services. **Physically disabled:** Services for visually, hearing impaired.

Contact. E-mail: admission@bryant.edu
Phone: (401) 232-6100 Toll-free number: (800) 622-7001
Fax: (401) 232-6741
Director of Admission, Bryant University, 1150 Douglas Pike, Smithfield, RI 02917

Johnson & Wales University

Providence, Rhode Island — **CB member**
www.jwu.edu — **CB code: 3465**

- Private 4-year university
- Residential campus in small city
- 9,335 degree-seeking undergraduates: 10% part-time, 53% women, 8% African American, 2% Asian American, 5% Hispanic American, 4% international
- 259 degree-seeking graduate students
- 80% of applicants admitted

General. Founded in 1914. Regionally accredited. **Degrees:** 1,285 bachelor's, 1,643 associate awarded; master's, doctoral offered. **ROTC:** Army. **Location:** 200 miles from New York City, 50 miles from Boston. **Calendar:** Quarter, limited summer session. **Full-time faculty:** 278 total; 3% minority, 41% women. **Part-time faculty:** 120 total; 5% minority, 38% women. **Class size:** 29% < 20, 59% 20-39, 12% 40-49, less than 1% 50-99. **Special facilities:** 3 University-operated hotels and restaurants, banquet facilities, information kiosk, culinary archives and museum, equine center.

Freshman class profile. 15,258 applied, 12,235 admitted, 2,792 enrolled.

Mid 50% test scores		GPA 2.0-2.99:	58%
SAT verbal:	420-530	Rank in top quarter:	19%
SAT math:	410-540	Rank in top tenth:	4%
GPA 3.50 or higher:	15%	Out-of-state:	22%
GPA 3.0-3.49:	26%	Live on campus:	22%

Basis for selection. While academic record (secondary school curriculum, GPA, class rank, test scores) is important, student motivation and interest are given strong consideration. Interview and letter of recommendation generally required of students in bottom quarter of class, essay and interview recommended for all others.

High school preparation. 12 units recommended. Recommended units include English 4, mathematics 3, social studies 2 and science 3.

2006-2007 Annual costs. Tuition/fees (projected): $20,826. Room/board: $7,600. Books/supplies: $825. Personal expenses: $839.

2005-2006 Financial aid. Need-based: 2,069 full-time freshmen applied for aid; 1,793 were judged to have need; 1,784 of these received aid. Average need met was 63%. Average scholarship/grant was $5,175; average loan $6,203. 32% of total undergraduate aid awarded as scholarships/grants, 68% as loans/jobs. **Non-need-based:** Awarded to 4,584 full-time undergraduates, including 1,296 freshmen. Scholarships awarded for academics, leadership.

Application procedures. Admission: No deadline. No application fee. Admission notification on a rolling basis beginning on or about 10/1. **Financial aid:** No deadline. FAFSA required. Applicants notified on a rolling basis starting 3/1; must reply within 2 week(s) of notification.

Academics. Special study options: Accelerated study, cooperative education, dual enrollment of high school students, ESL, external degree, honors, independent study, internships, study abroad, weekend college. Externships, practicums (hands-on learning). **Credit/placement by examination:** CLEP, institutional tests. **Support services:** Learning center, pre-admission summer program, reduced course load, remedial instruction, study skills assistance, tutoring, writing center.

Majors. Agriculture: Equestrian studies, equine science. **Business:** Accounting, business admin, entrepreneurial studies, fashion, finance, hospitality admin, hospitality/recreation, international, investments/securities, marketing, public finance, tourism promotion, tourism/travel. **Computer sciences:** Information systems, webmaster. **Engineering:** Systems. **Engineering technology:** Drafting. **Interdisciplinary:** Nutrition sciences. **Legal studies:** Paralegal. **Parks/recreation:** Facilities management, sports admin. **Personal/culinary services:** Baking, chef training, culinary arts, food service, restaurant/catering. **Protective services:** Law enforcement admin.

Computing on campus. 400 workstations in library, computer center. Dormitories wired for high-speed internet access and linked to campus network. Commuter students can connect to campus network. Online library, helpline, wireless network available.

Student life. Freshman orientation: Mandatory, $250 fee. Preregistration for classes offered. **Policies:** Freshmen permitted cars on campus. **Housing:** Guaranteed on-campus for freshmen. Coed dorms, substance-free housing available. $300 deposit. Dormitory for National Student Organization scholarship winners, single rooms, women's floors available. **Activities:** Choral groups, drama, student government, student newspaper, Hillel, Christian student union, ACLU, Latin-American club, Asian club, T.R.U.E. (Together Realizing Unity Can Exist), College Republicans.

Athletics. NCAA. **Intercollegiate:** Baseball M, basketball, cross-country, equestrian, golf, ice hockey, soccer, softball W, tennis, volleyball, wrestling M. **Intramural:** Basketball, golf, soccer, softball, tennis. **Team name:** Wildcats.

Student services. Career counseling, student employment services, financial aid counseling, health services, personal counseling, placement for graduates, veterans' counselor, women's services. **Physically disabled:** Services for visually, speech, hearing impaired.

Contact. E-mail: admissions@jwu.edu
Phone: (401) 598-2310 Toll-free number: (800) 342-5598
Fax: (401) 598-2948
Maureen Dumas, Dean of Admissions, Johnson & Wales University, 8 Abbott Park Place, Providence, RI 02903-3703

New England Institute of Technology

Warwick, Rhode Island
www.neit.edu **CB code: 0339**

- Private 4-year technical college
- Commuter campus in small city
- 3,066 degree-seeking undergraduates: 5% African American, 3% Asian American, 6% Hispanic American, 6% international
- Interview required

General. Founded in 1940. Regionally accredited. **Degrees:** 195 bachelor's, 753 associate awarded. **Location:** 10 miles from Providence, 50 miles from Boston. **Calendar:** Quarter, extensive summer session. **Full-time faculty:** 100 total; 10% have terminal degrees. **Part-time faculty:** 135 total; 6% have terminal degrees.

Basis for selection. Open admission. Basic skills testing, Ronald P. Carver reading test used for placement. Portfolio recommended for drafting program.

2006-2007 Annual costs. Tuition/fees (projected): $15,765. Fees vary from $1,365 to $2,415 according to program. Books/supplies: $600. Personal expenses: $1,440.

Financial aid. Non-need-based: Scholarships awarded for academics. **Additional information:** Tuition at time of first enrollment guaranteed all students for 2 years.

Application procedures. Admission: No deadline. $25 fee. Application may be submitted online. Admission notification on a rolling basis. Must reply by May 1 or within 4 week(s) if notified thereafter. **Financial aid:** Priority date 6/1; no closing date. FAFSA, institutional form required. Applicants notified on a rolling basis starting 6/15.

Academics. Special study options: Accelerated study, cooperative education, double major, ESL, internships, student-designed major. **Credit/placement by examination:** AP, CLEP, institutional tests. 51 credit hours maximum toward associate degree. **Support services:** Learning center, preadmission summer program, reduced course load, remedial instruction, study skills assistance, tutoring, writing center.

Majors. Business: General. **Computer sciences:** General, computer science, information technology, systems analysis. **Engineering:** Architectural, manufacturing, mechanical. **Engineering technology:** Manufacturing. **Visual/performing arts:** Interior design.

Computing on campus. 50 workstations in library, computer center. Online course registration, online library, wireless network available.

Student life. Freshman orientation: Mandatory. Preregistration for classes offered. **Activities:** Radio station, student newspaper, TV station, international student club.

Student services. Career counseling, student employment services, financial aid counseling, personal counseling, placement for graduates, veterans' counselor.

Contact. E-mail: neit@neit.edu
Phone: (401) 467-7744 Toll-free number: (800) 736-7744 ext. 3357
Fax: (401) 738-5122
Michael Kwiatkowski, Director of Admissions, New England Institute of Technology, 2500 Post Road, Warwick, RI 02886-2286

Providence College

Providence, Rhode Island **CB member**
www.providence.edu **CB code: 3693**

- Private 4-year liberal arts college affiliated with Roman Catholic Church
- Residential campus in small city
- 3,889 degree-seeking undergraduates: 57% women, 1% African American, 2% Asian American, 2% Hispanic American, 1% international
- 486 degree-seeking graduate students
- 54% of applicants admitted
- SAT or ACT with writing, application essay required
- 83% graduate within 6 years

General. Founded in 1917. Regionally accredited. **Degrees:** 974 bachelor's, 6 associate awarded; master's offered. **ROTC:** Army. **Location:** 50 miles from Boston, 180 miles from New York City. **Calendar:** Semester, limited summer session. **Full-time faculty:** 287 total; 90% have terminal degrees, 8% minority, 32% women. **Part-time faculty:** 82 total; 6% minority, 52% women. **Class size:** 42% < 20, 54% 20-39, less than 1% 40-49, less than 1% 50-99, 3% >100.

Freshman class profile. 8,237 applied, 4,484 admitted, 1,069 enrolled.

Mid 50% test scores		**Rank in top quarter:**	79%
SAT verbal:	550-630	**Rank in top tenth:**	38%
SAT math:	560-650	**End year in good standing:**	93%
ACT:	23-27	**Return as sophomores:**	93%
GPA 3.50 or higher:	43%	**Out-of-state:**	90%
GPA 3.0-3.49:	45%	**Live on campus:**	98%
GPA 2.0-2.99:	12%	**International:**	1%

Basis for selection. GED not accepted. Emphasis placed on scholastic ability, motivation, character, and seriousness of purpose. School record and standardized ability and achievement tests important. Recommendations considered. SAT Subject Tests recommended. Audition recommended for music programs; portfolio recommended for art programs. **Homeschooled:** Transcript of courses and grades, state high school equivalency certificate, letter of recommendation (nonparent) required. **Learning Disabled:** Students must provide documentation of disability. Accomodations are then made as deemed appropriate.

High school preparation. College-preparatory program required. 16 units required; 18 recommended. Required and recommended units include English 4, mathematics 4, social studies 2, history 2, science 3-4 (laboratory 2) and foreign language 3.

2005-2006 Annual costs. Tuition/fees: $25,310. Room/board: $9,270. Books/supplies: $700. Personal expenses: $1,500.

2005-2006 Financial aid. Need-based: 785 full-time freshmen applied for aid; 579 were judged to have need; 579 of these received aid. Average need met was 88%. Average scholarship/grant was $12,796; average loan $3,625. 72% of total undergraduate aid awarded as scholarships/grants, 28% as loans/jobs. **Non-need-based:** Awarded to 980 full-time undergraduates, including 231 freshmen. Scholarships awarded for academics, athletics, minority status, ROTC.

Application procedures. Admission: Closing date 1/15 (postmark date). $55 fee, may be waived for applicants with need. Application may be submitted online. Admission notification 4/1. Must reply by 5/1. **Financial aid:** Closing date 2/1. FAFSA, CSS PROFILE required. Applicants notified by 4/1; must reply by 5/1.

Academics. Special study options: Combined bachelor's/graduate degree, cooperative education, cross-registration, double major, dual enrollment of high school students, honors, independent study, internships, student-designed major, study abroad, teacher certification program, Washington semester. **Credit/placement by examination:** AP, CLEP, IB, SAT, ACT, institutional tests. International Baccalaureate credit restricted to 5-7 higher level exams. **Support services:** Learning center, reduced course load, study skills assistance, tutoring, writing center.

Majors. **Area/ethnic studies:** American. **Biology:** General, biochemistry. **Business:** Accounting, business admin, finance, managerial economics, marketing, organizational behavior. **Computer sciences:** Computer science. **Education:** Music, secondary, special. **Engineering:** Physics. **English:** English lit. **Foreign languages:** French, Italian, Spanish. **Health:** Health care admin. **History:** General. **Interdisciplinary:** Global studies, systems science. **Liberal arts:** Arts/sciences, humanities. **Math:** General. **Philosophy/religion:** Philosophy. **Physical sciences:** Chemistry. **Psychology:** General. **Public administration:** Community org/advocacy, social work. **Social sciences:** General, econometrics, economics, political science, sociology. **Theology:** Theology. **Visual/performing arts:** General, art, art history/conservation.

Most popular majors. Biology 7%, business/marketing 29%, education 10%, English 8%, history 6%, psychology 6%, social sciences 14%.

Computing on campus. 150 workstations in library, computer center. Dormitories wired for high-speed internet access and linked to campus network. Commuter students can connect to campus network. Online course registration, online library, helpline, repair service, student web hosting, wireless network available.

Student life. **Freshman orientation:** Mandatory. Preregistration for classes offered. 2-day session held in the summer, involves both parents and students. **Housing:** Guaranteed on-campus for freshmen. Coed dorms, single-sex dorms, special housing for disabled, apartments, substance-free housing available. $700 nonrefundable deposit, deadline 5/1. **Activities:** Bands, choral groups, dance, drama, literary magazine, music ensembles, musical theater, radio station, student government, student newspaper, TV station, Afro-American society, Big Brothers and Sisters, pastoral service organization, campus ministry society, PC Pals, best buddies, College Democrats, College Republicans, Amigos Unidos, Asian American club.

Athletics. NCAA. **Intercollegiate:** Basketball, cross-country, diving, field hockey W, ice hockey, lacrosse M, soccer, softball W, swimming, tennis W, track and field, volleyball W. **Intramural:** Basketball, field hockey W, football (non-tackle), ice hockey, racquetball, soccer, softball, table tennis, tennis, volleyball. **Team name:** Friars.

Student services. Alcohol/substance abuse counseling, campus ministries, career counseling, student employment services, health services, minority student services, personal counseling, placement for graduates. **Physically disabled:** Services for visually, hearing impaired.

Contact. E-mail: pcadmiss@providence.edu
Phone: (401) 865-2535 Toll-free number: (800) 721-6444
Fax: (401) 865-2826
Christopher Lydon, Associate VP for Admissions and Enrollment Planning, Providence College, Harkins Hall 222, 549 River Avenue, Providence, RI 02918-0001

Rhode Island College

Providence, Rhode Island — **CB member**
www.ric.edu — **CB code: 3724**

- Public 4-year liberal arts college
- Commuter campus in small city
- 7,097 degree-seeking undergraduates: 27% part-time, 68% women, 5% African American, 2% Asian American, 5% Hispanic American
- 746 degree-seeking graduate students
- 75% of applicants admitted
- SAT or ACT with writing, application essay required
- 44% graduate within 6 years

General. Founded in 1854. Regionally accredited. **Degrees:** 1,142 bachelor's awarded; master's, doctoral offered. **ROTC:** Army. **Location:** 4 miles from downtown. **Calendar:** Semester, extensive summer session. **Full-time faculty:** 304 total; 85% have terminal degrees, 10% minority, 50% women. **Part-time faculty:** 340 total. **Class size:** 47% < 20, 51% 20-39, less than 1% 40-49, 1% 50-99, less than 1% >100.

Freshman class profile. 3,409 applied, 2,545 admitted, 1,098 enrolled.

Mid 50% test scores		**Rank in top tenth:**	7%
SAT verbal:	430-540	**Return as sophomores:**	78%
SAT math:	430-540	**Out-of-state:**	16%
Rank in top quarter:	33%		

Basis for selection. High school academic record and class rank most important, followed by test scores, essay, references. TOEFL required for applicants who are not native speakers of English. Interview available but not required; audition required for music performance; portfolio required for bachelor of fine arts.

High school preparation. 18 units required. Required units include English 4, mathematics 3, social studies 2, science 2 (laboratory 2), foreign language 2, academic electives 4.5. .5 unit in the arts (music, art, dance, theatre) is required. Biology and either chemistry or physics are required lab sciences. 2 years of the same foreign language is required. Algebra I, II and geometry required. All units must be college-preparatory.

2005-2006 Annual costs. Tuition/fees: $4,796; $12,108 out-of-state. Room/board: $6,750. Books/supplies: $750. Personal expenses: $1,000.

Financial aid. **Non-need-based:** Scholarships awarded for academics, alumni affiliation, art, music/drama.

Application procedures. **Admission:** Closing date 5/1 (postmark date). $50 fee, may be waived for applicants with need. Application may be submitted online. Admission notification on a rolling basis beginning on or about 12/15. Must reply by May 1 or within 2 week(s) if notified thereafter. $100 Enrollment Deposit. **Financial aid:** Priority date 3/1; no closing date. FAFSA, institutional form required. Applicants notified on a rolling basis starting 3/15; must reply within 3 week(s) of notification.

Academics. **Special study options:** Double major, exchange student, honors, independent study, internships, student-designed major, study abroad, teacher certification program. National Student Exchange Consortium. **Credit/placement by examination:** AP, CLEP, SAT, institutional tests. **Support services:** Learning center, pre-admission summer program, reduced course load, remedial instruction, study skills assistance, tutoring, writing center.

Majors. **Area/ethnic studies:** African-American, women's. **Biology:** General. **Business:** General, accounting, business admin, finance, human resources, international, labor relations, management information systems, managerial economics. **Communications:** General. **Computer sciences:** General, computer science. **Education:** Art, bilingual, biology, chemistry, early childhood, elementary, emotionally handicapped, English, foreign languages, French, health, history, mathematics, mentally handicapped, middle, multi-level teacher, multiple handicapped, music, physical, physically handicapped, physics, science, secondary, social studies, Spanish, special, technology/industrial arts, trade/industrial, voc/tech. **Foreign languages:** French, Spanish. **Health:** Clinical lab science, clinical lab technology, medical radiologic technology/radiation therapy, predentistry, premedicine, preveterinary. **History:** General. **Liberal arts:** Arts/sciences. **Math:** General. **Philosophy/religion:** Philosophy. **Physical sciences:** Chemistry, physics. **Protective services:** Criminal justice. **Psychology:** General. **Public administration:** General, social work. **Social sciences:** General, anthropology, economics, geography, political science, sociology. **Visual/performing arts:** Art history/conservation, ceramics, dramatic, drawing, fiber arts, film/cinema, metal/jewelry, music performance, painting, sculpture, studio arts, theater design.

Most popular majors. Business/marketing 16%, communications/journalism 6%, education 31%, health sciences 7%, psychology 12%, social sciences 9%, visual/performing arts 7%.

Computing on campus. 600 workstations in library, computer center, student center. Dormitories wired for high-speed internet access and linked to campus network. Commuter students can connect to campus network. Online course registration, online library, helpline, repair service, student web hosting available.

Student life. **Freshman orientation:** Available, $85 fee. Preregistration for classes offered. Held throughout the month of July in 2 day cycles. Some single days are available. **Policies:** Freshmen permitted cars on campus. **Housing:** Coed dorms, single-sex dorms, special housing for disabled available. $214 fully refundable deposit, deadline 5/1. **Activities:** Bands, choral groups, dance, drama, literary magazine, music ensembles, musical theater, radio station, student government, student newspaper, symphony orchestra, TV station, Catholic and Protestant religious organizations, Amnesty International, Cape Verdean student association, Habitat for Humanity, Intra-Varsity Student Fellowship, Latin American student association, Muslim students, RIC Angels RIC Republicans, Harambee, NAACP.

Athletics. NCAA. **Intercollegiate:** Baseball M, basketball, cross-country, golf M, gymnastics W, lacrosse W, soccer, softball W, tennis, track and field, volleyball W, wrestling M. **Intramural:** Basketball, bowling, gymnastics, softball, tennis, volleyball. **Team name:** Anchormen, Anchorwomen.

Student services. Adult student services, alcohol/substance abuse counseling, campus ministries, career counseling, student employment services, financial aid counseling, health services, on-campus daycare, personal counseling, placement for graduates, veterans' counselor. **Physically disabled:** Services for visually, speech, hearing impaired.

Contact. E-mail: admissions@ric.edu
Phone: (401) 456-8234 Toll-free number: (800) 669-5760
Fax: (401) 456-8817
Holly Shadoian, Director of Admissions, Rhode Island College, 600 Mount Pleasant Avenue, Providence, RI 02908

Rhode Island School of Design

Providence, Rhode Island
www.risd.edu
CB member
CB code: 3726

- Private 4-year visual arts college
- Residential campus in small city
- 1,878 degree-seeking undergraduates: 66% women
- 380 graduate students
- 35% of applicants admitted
- SAT or ACT with writing, application essay required

General. Founded in 1877. Regionally accredited. **Degrees:** 518 bachelor's awarded; master's offered. **Location:** 52 miles from Boston, 200 miles from New York City. **Calendar:** 4-1-4, limited summer session. **Full-time faculty:** 146 total; 12% minority, 45% women. **Part-time faculty:** 336 total. **Special facilities:** Fine art and design museum, extensive photograph and clipping collections, slide collection, recreational farm on Narragansett Bay, nature laboratory.

Freshman class profile. 2,512 applied, 870 admitted, 420 enrolled.

Mid 50% test scores			
SAT verbal:	530-650	Rank in top tenth:	40%
SAT math:	570-680	Out-of-state:	94%
Rank in top quarter:	72%	Live on campus:	96%

Basis for selection. Academic history, visual portfolio and 3 required drawings most important parts of application. Portfolio required for all applicants. **Homeschooled:** Proof of high school equivalent/GED required.

High school preparation. Architecture, interior architecture, landscape architecture, and industrial design applicants must have 2 algebra, .5 trigonometry, 1 science.

2005-2006 Annual costs. Tuition/fees: $29,775. Room/board: $8,355. Books/supplies: $2,000.

2004-2005 Financial aid. Need-based: 231 full-time freshmen applied for aid; 184 were judged to have need; 175 of these received aid. Average need met was 66%. Average scholarship/grant was $12,340; average loan $3,100. 57% of total undergraduate aid awarded as scholarships/grants, 43% as loans/jobs. **Non-need-based:** Awarded to 70 full-time undergraduates, including 4 freshmen.

Application procedures. Admission: Closing date 2/15 (postmark date). $50 fee, may be waived for applicants with need. Application may be submitted online. Admission notification 4/1. Must reply by 5/1. **Financial aid:** Closing date 2/15. FAFSA, CSS PROFILE required. Applicants notified by 4/1; must reply by 5/1.

Academics. Special study options: Cross-registration, exchange student, independent study, internships, study abroad, teacher certification program. **Credit/placement by examination:** AP, CLEP, IB. **Support services:** Remedial instruction, tutoring, writing center.

Majors. Architecture: Architecture, interior, landscape. **Visual/performing arts:** Ceramics, cinematography, fashion design, fiber arts, graphic design, illustration, industrial design, metal/jewelry, painting, photography, printmaking, sculpture, studio arts.

Most popular majors. Architecture 7%, visual/performing arts 93%.

Computing on campus. 425 workstations in dormitories, library, computer center, student center. Dormitories wired for high-speed internet access and linked to campus network. Commuter students can connect to campus network. Online course registration, helpline, wireless network available.

Student life. Freshman orientation: Mandatory. **Housing:** Guaranteed on-campus for freshmen. Coed dorms, apartments, substance-free housing available. $175 deposit, deadline 5/1. **Activities:** Dance, drama, film society, student government, student newspaper, all major religions represented on campus, professional societies, clubs.

Athletics. Intramural: Baseball M, basketball, ice hockey, soccer, softball.

Student services. Career counseling, student employment services, health services, legal services, minority student services, personal counseling, placement for graduates. **Physically disabled:** Services for hearing impaired.

Contact. E-mail: admissions@risd.edu
Phone: (401) 454-6300 Toll-free number: (800) 364-7473
Fax: (401) 454-6309
Edward Newhall, Director of Admissions, Rhode Island School of Design, Two College Street, Providence, RI 02903-2791

Roger Williams University

Bristol, Rhode Island
www.rwu.edu
CB member
CB code: 3729

- Private 4-year university and liberal arts college
- Residential campus in large town
- 4,358 degree-seeking undergraduates: 14% part-time, 49% women, 1% African American, 2% Asian American, 2% Hispanic American, 2% international
- 826 degree-seeking graduate students
- 78% of applicants admitted
- SAT or ACT (ACT writing recommended), application essay required
- 53% graduate within 6 years; 26% enter graduate study

General. Founded in 1956. Regionally accredited. Certificate and Associate programs offered only in continuing education. Continuing education in Providence and Bristol. **Degrees:** 829 bachelor's, 11 associate awarded; master's, first professional offered. **ROTC:** Army. **Location:** 18 miles from Providence, 10 miles from Newport. **Calendar:** Semester, limited summer session. **Full-time faculty:** 178 total; 80% have terminal degrees, 11% minority, 38% women. **Part-time faculty:** 220 total; 31% have terminal degrees, 3% minority, 42% women. **Class size:** 37% < 20, 62% 20-39, less than 1% 40-49, less than 1% 50-99. **Special facilities:** Marine and natural sciences building with marine biology wetlab.

Freshman class profile. 6,658 applied, 5,220 admitted, 1,189 enrolled.

Mid 50% test scores			
SAT verbal:	490-580	Rank in top quarter:	35%
SAT math:	500-600	Rank in top tenth:	11%
ACT:	21-25	Return as sophomores:	78%
GPA 3.50 or higher:	20%	Out-of-state:	91%
GPA 3.0-3.49:	37%	Live on campus:	97%
GPA 2.0-2.99:	42%	International:	1%

Basis for selection. High school record, standardized test scores, essay, extracurricular activities and achievements most important. Teacher or counselor recommendations considered. Interview recommended for all; audition required for dance; portfolio required for art, architecture programs. **Homeschooled:** State high school equivalency certificate required. Students must submit portfolio of their work.

High school preparation. 22 units required; 26 recommended. Required and recommended units include English 4, mathematics 3-4, social studies 2-3, history 2-3, science 2-3 (laboratory 2), foreign language 2 and academic electives 2-3. Specific subject requirements vary with intended major.

2006-2007 Annual costs. Tuition/fees (projected): $24,066. Tuition differential for architecture program. Room/board: $10,693. Books/supplies: $700. Personal expenses: $515.

2005-2006 Financial aid. Need-based: 935 full-time freshmen applied for aid; 746 were judged to have need; 734 of these received aid. Average need met was 78%. Average scholarship/grant was $8,734; average loan $3,091. 34% of total undergraduate aid awarded as scholarships/grants, 66% as loans/jobs. **Non-need-based:** Scholarships awarded for academics, ROTC.

Application procedures. Admission: Priority date 3/1; no deadline. $50 fee. Application may be submitted online. Admission notification on a rolling basis beginning on or about 1/2. Must reply by May 1 or within 2 week(s) if notified thereafter. Fall-term application deadline for architecture applicants February 1. Honors consideration deadline is also February 1. **Financial aid:** Closing date 2/1. FAFSA, CSS PROFILE required. Applicants notified on a rolling basis starting 3/20; must reply by 5/1 or within 2 week(s) of notification.

Academics. All students graduate with two areas of specialization: one in their major and a second in a liberal arts discipline; most students may complete two majors. **Special study options:** Combined bachelor's/graduate degree, cooperative education, distance learning, double major, dual enrollment of high school students, ESL, exchange student, external degree, honors, independent study, internships, liberal arts/career combination, semester at sea, student-designed major, study abroad, teacher certification program, Washington semester. **Credit/placement by examination:** AP, CLEP, IB, SAT, ACT, institutional tests. **Support services:** Learning center, reduced course load, study skills assistance, tutoring, writing center.

Honors college/program. Applicants must have minimum SAT score of 1250 (exclusive of Writing) and a 3.3 GPA. (1300/ 3.3 for Architecture and Marine Biology). Application deadline February 1.

Majors. Architecture: Architecture, history/criticism. **Area/ethnic studies:** American. **Biology:** General, marine. **Business:** Accounting, business admin, finance, international, management information systems, marketing. **Communications:** General, journalism, media studies. **Communications technology:** Graphics. **Computer sciences:** General, computer science. **Conservation:** General. **Construction:** Site management. **Education:** Elementary, health, secondary. **Engineering:** General, computer. **English:** British lit, creative writing. **Foreign languages:** General. **Health:** Health care admin, health services, premedicine. **History:** General. **Interdisciplinary:** Historic preservation. **Legal studies:** General, paralegal, prelaw. **Math:** General. **Philosophy/religion:** Philosophy. **Physical sciences:** Chemistry. **Protective services:** Criminal justice, law enforcement admin. **Psychology:** General. **Public administration:** General. **Social sciences:** Anthropology, political science, sociology. **Visual/performing arts:** Art history/conservation, dance, dramatic, graphic design, studio arts.

Most popular majors. Architecture 7%, biology 6%, business/marketing 23%, communications/journalism 6%, engineering/engineering technologies 7%, psychology 7%, security/protective services 15%, visual/performing arts 6%.

Computing on campus. 500 workstations in dormitories, library, computer center. Dormitories wired for high-speed internet access and linked to campus network. Commuter students can connect to campus network. Online course registration, helpline, repair service, wireless network available.

Student life. **Freshman orientation:** Mandatory. Preregistration for classes offered. Held during the summer months. 2-day program with overnight stay on campus. Separate orientations for transfer and international students. **Housing:** Guaranteed on-campus for all undergraduates. Coed dorms, special housing for disabled, apartments, substance-free housing available. $350 deposit, deadline 5/1. Special interest academic theme and honors housing available. **Activities:** Choral groups, dance, drama, literary magazine, musical theater, radio station, student government, student newspaper, Hillel, Inter-Varsity Christian Fellowship, multicultural student union, College Democrats, College Republicans, environmental and animal rights club, Model UN, Best Buddies of Rhode Island, Habitat for Humanity, student volunteer association.

Athletics. NCAA. **Intercollegiate:** Baseball M, basketball, cross-country, diving, equestrian, lacrosse, sailing, soccer, softball W, swimming, tennis, volleyball W, wrestling M. **Intramural:** Basketball, field hockey, football (non-tackle), golf, racquetball, skiing, soccer, softball, squash, tennis, volleyball, water polo. **Team name:** Hawks.

Student services. Campus ministries, career counseling, student employment services, financial aid counseling, health services, minority student services, personal counseling, women's services. **Physically disabled:** Services for visually, hearing impaired.

Contact. E-mail: admit@rwu.edu
Phone: (401) 254-3500 Toll-free number: (800) 458-7144 ext. 3500
Fax: (401) 254-3557
Michelle Beauregard, Director of Freshman Admissions, Roger Williams University, One Old Ferry Road, Bristol, RI 02809

Salve Regina University

Newport, Rhode Island — **CB member**
www.salve.edu — **CB code: 3759**

- Private 4-year university and liberal arts college affiliated with Roman Catholic Church
- Residential campus in small city
- 2,068 degree-seeking undergraduates: 4% part-time, 71% women, 1% African American, 1% Asian American, 2% Hispanic American, 1% international
- 309 degree-seeking graduate students
- 60% of applicants admitted
- SAT or ACT with writing, application essay required
- 60% graduate within 6 years

General. Founded in 1934. Regionally accredited. Affiliated with Religious Sisters of Mercy. **Degrees:** 427 bachelor's, 2 associate awarded; master's, doctoral offered. **ROTC:** Army. **Location:** 40 miles from Providence, 70 miles from Boston. **Calendar:** Semester, limited summer session. **Full-time faculty:** 122 total; 63% have terminal degrees, 8% minority, 56% women. **Part-time faculty:** 118 total; 55% women. **Class size:** 54% < 20, 46% 20-39, less than 1% 40-49, less than 1% 50-99. **Special facilities:** International relations and public policy center.

Freshman class profile. 4,555 applied, 2,727 admitted, 568 enrolled.

Mid 50% test scores			
SAT verbal:	500-580	Rank in top quarter:	54%
SAT math:	500-580	Rank in top tenth:	16%
ACT:	20-25	End year in good standing:	98%
GPA 3.50 or higher:	36%	Return as sophomores:	81%
GPA 3.0-3.49:	42%	Out-of-state:	91%
GPA 2.0-2.99:	22%	Live on campus:	96%
		International:	1%

Basis for selection. High school achievement most important, followed by rank in top half of high school class, test scores, recommendations, essay, activities, interview. Special consideration given to applicants from minority and low-income families. SAT or TOEFL required for international applicants. Audition and portfolio considered. **Homeschooled:** Statement describing homeschool structure and mission, transcript of courses and grades, letter of recommendation (nonparent) required. Require two recommendations, one of which must be academic. Course syllabus required for each course; results of SAT or ACT examinations; portfolio of academic accomplishments including a reading list, course descriptions and list of extracurricular/community involvement.

High school preparation. 16 units required. Required units include English 4, mathematics 3, social studies 1, science 2 (laboratory 2), foreign language 2 and academic electives 4. Additional course work may be required of students who have not completed recommended units. Social studies includes history.

2006-2007 Annual costs. Tuition/fees: $25,175. Room/board: $9,800. Books/supplies: $750. Personal expenses: $1,000.

2005-2006 Financial aid. **Need-based:** 474 full-time freshmen applied for aid; 381 were judged to have need; 375 of these received aid. Average need met was 72%. Average scholarship/grant was $13,425; average loan $2,710. 64% of total undergraduate aid awarded as scholarships/grants, 36% as loans/jobs. **Non-need-based:** Awarded to 352 full-time undergraduates, including 125 freshmen. Scholarships awarded for academics, music/drama, ROTC.

Application procedures. **Admission:** Priority date 3/1; no deadline. $40 fee, may be waived for applicants with need. Application may be submitted online. Admission notification on a rolling basis beginning on or about 12/15. Must reply by May 1 or within 2 week(s) if notified thereafter. **Financial aid:** Priority date 3/1; no closing date. FAFSA, CSS PROFILE required. Applicants notified on a rolling basis starting 3/1; must reply by 5/1 or within 2 week(s) of notification.

Academics. Credit may be awarded for learning associated with life experience. **Special study options:** Accelerated study, combined bachelor's/graduate degree, distance learning, double major, dual enrollment of high school students, ESL, exchange student, honors, independent study, internships, liberal arts/career combination, semester at sea, study abroad, teacher certification program, Washington semester. **Credit/placement by examination:** AP, CLEP, IB, SAT, ACT, institutional tests. **Support services:** Learning center, reduced course load, study skills assistance, tutoring, writing center.

Majors. **Area/ethnic studies:** American. **Biology:** General. **Business:** Accounting, business admin, finance, management science, market research. **Communications technology:** Animation/special effects. **Computer sciences:** Information systems. **Education:** Biology, drama/dance, early childhood, elementary, English, French, history, mathematics, music, secondary, Spanish, special. **English:** English lit. **Foreign languages:** French, Spanish. **Health:** Clinical lab science, nursing (RN). **History:** American, European. **Interdisciplinary:** Historic preservation. **Liberal arts:** Arts/sciences. **Math:** General. **Philosophy/religion:** Philosophy, religion. **Physical sciences:** Chemistry. **Protective services:** Law enforcement admin. **Psychology:** General. **Public administration:** Social work. **Social sciences:** Anthropology, economics, political science, sociology. **Visual/performing arts:** Art history/conservation, ceramics, dramatic, graphic design, painting, photography, studio arts.

Most popular majors. Biology 6%, business/marketing 17%, education 23%, English 6%, psychology 7%, security/protective services 9%.

Computing on campus. PC or laptop required. 120 workstations in dormitories, library, computer center, student center. Dormitories wired for high-speed internet access and linked to campus network. Commuter students can connect to campus network. Online course registration, online library, helpline, repair service, student web hosting, wireless network available.

Student life. **Freshman orientation:** Mandatory, $300 fee. Preregistration for classes offered. Two day Orientation Sessions are scheduled during June and July for full-time freshmen with separate sessions scheduled for international and transfer students. **Housing:** Guaranteed on-campus for freshmen. Coed dorms, single-sex dorms, special housing for disabled, apartments, substance-free housing available. $200 fully refundable deposit, deadline 5/1. Historic and conventional style housing options available on campus. Off-campus housing available to upperclassmen. **Activities:** Bands, choral groups, dance, drama, literary magazine, music ensembles, radio station, student government, student newspaper, The Artist's Guild, The Artist's Sanctuary, Circle K, environmental club, Student Outdoor Adventures, Volunteers Interested in Researching and Guiding, Women's Issues Now, Stagefright Theater Company.

Athletics. NCAA. **Intercollegiate:** Baseball M, basketball, cross-country, field hockey W, football (tackle) M, ice hockey, lacrosse, sailing, soccer, softball W, tennis, track and field W, volleyball W. **Intramural:** Basketball, field hockey W, football (non-tackle) W, football (tackle) M, racquetball, soccer, softball, tennis, track and field W, volleyball, weight lifting. **Team name:** Seahawks.

Student services. Campus ministries, career counseling, financial aid counseling, health services, minority student services, personal counseling, veterans' counselor. **Physically disabled:** Services for visually, hearing impaired.

Contact. E-mail: sruadmis@salve.edu
Phone: (401) 341-2908 Toll-free number: (888) 467-2583
Fax: (401) 848-2823
Colleen Emerson, Director of Admissions, Salve Regina University, 100 Ochre Point Avenue, Newport, RI 02840-4192

University of Rhode Island

Kingston, Rhode Island — **CB member**
www.uri.edu — **CB code: 3919**

- Public 4-year university
- Commuter campus in small town
- 11,162 degree-seeking undergraduates: 13% part-time, 57% women, 4% African American, 2% Asian American, 4% Hispanic American
- 2,512 degree-seeking graduate students
- 77% of applicants admitted
- SAT or ACT with writing required
- 56% graduate within 6 years

General. Founded in 1892. Regionally accredited. College of Continuing Education in Providence offers credit-bearing courses for degree and non-degree part-time students. **Degrees:** 1,899 bachelor's awarded; master's, doctoral, first professional offered. **ROTC:** Army. **Location:** 30 miles from Providence. **Calendar:** Semester, extensive summer session. **Full-time faculty:** 668 total; 90% have terminal degrees, 14% minority, 38% women. **Part-time faculty:** 23 total; 83% have terminal degrees, 13% minority, 39% women. **Class size:** 36% < 20, 50% 20-39, 6% 40-49, 5% 50-99, 3% >100. **Special facilities:** Center for robotics research, animal science farm, planetarium, Narragansett Bay Campus for Marine Sciences, American historic textiles museum, aquaculture center, fisheries and marine technology laboratory, biotechnology center, human performance laboratory.

Freshman class profile. 13,388 applied, 10,327 admitted, 2,461 enrolled.

Mid 50% test scores		Out-of-state:	47%
SAT verbal:	500-600	Live on campus:	90%
SAT math:	520-620	Fraternities:	11%
Rank in top tenth:	21%	Sororities:	10%
Return as sophomores:	80%		

Basis for selection. School record primary, test scores secondary. Extracurricular activities considered. Economically and socially disadvantaged students from Rhode Island admitted through special program for talent development.

High school preparation. College-preparatory program required. 18 units required; 20 recommended. Required and recommended units include English 4, mathematics 3-4, social studies 2-4, science 2-4 (laboratory 2), foreign language 2-4 and academic electives 5.

2005-2006 Annual costs. Tuition/fees: $7,284; $19,926 out-of-state. Room/board: $8,560.

2005-2006 Financial aid. **Need-based:** 2,134 full-time freshmen applied for aid; 1,656 were judged to have need; 1,333 of these received aid. Average need met was 67%. Average scholarship/grant was $6,353; average loan $6,184. 47% of total undergraduate aid awarded as scholarships/grants, 53% as loans/jobs. **Non-need-based:** Awarded to 943 full-time undergraduates, including 403 freshmen. Scholarships awarded for academics, alumni affiliation, art, athletics, leadership, minority status, music/drama, ROTC.

Application procedures. **Admission:** Priority date 12/15; no deadline. $50 fee ($50 out-of-state), may be waived for applicants with need. Application may be submitted online. Admission notification on a rolling basis beginning on or about 12/1. Must reply by May 1 or within 2 week(s) if notified thereafter. **Financial aid:** Priority date 3/1; no closing date. FAFSA required. Applicants notified on a rolling basis starting 3/21; must reply by 5/1 or within 2 week(s) of notification.

Academics. **Special study options:** Cooperative education, distance learning, double major, exchange student, external degree, honors, independent study, internships, liberal arts/career combination, study abroad, teacher certification program. **Credit/placement by examination:** AP, CLEP, institutional tests.

Majors. **Agriculture:** Animal sciences, soil science. **Architecture:** Landscape. **Area/ethnic studies:** African-American, Latin American, women's. **Biology:** General, marine, microbiology, zoology. **Business:** General, accounting, apparel, business admin, finance, financial planning, international, management information systems, marketing. **Communications:** General, journalism, public relations. **Computer sciences:** General. **Conservation:** Environmental studies, fisheries, management/policy, water/wetlands/marine, wildlife. **Education:** Elementary, music, secondary. **Engineering:** Biomedical, chemical, civil, computer, electrical, industrial, mechanical, ocean. **English:** English lit. **Family/consumer sciences:** Clothing/textiles, family studies, food/nutrition. **Foreign languages:** Classics, comparative lit, French, German, Italian, Spanish. **Health:** Clinical lab science, communication disorders, dental hygiene, dietetics, health care admin, nursing (RN). **History:** General. **Math:** General. **Philosophy/religion:** Philosophy. **Physical sciences:** Chemistry, geology, physics. **Psychology:** General. **Public administration:** Policy analysis. **Social sciences:** Anthropology, econometrics, economics, political science, sociology. **Visual/performing arts:** Art history/conservation, dramatic, music performance, music theory/composition, studio arts.

Most popular majors. Business/marketing 16%, communications/journalism 12%, education 7%, engineering/engineering technologies 10%, health sciences 6%, personal/culinary services 6%, psychology 6%, social sciences 6%.

Computing on campus. 800 workstations in dormitories, library, computer center, student center. Dormitories wired for high-speed internet access and linked to campus network. Commuter students can connect to campus network. Online course registration, online library, helpline, student web hosting, wireless network available.

Student life. **Freshman orientation:** Available, $150 fee. **Policies:** Freshmen permitted cars on campus. **Housing:** Guaranteed on-campus for freshmen. Coed dorms, special housing for disabled, apartments, fraternity/sorority housing available. $100 partly refundable deposit, deadline 5/1. **Activities:** Bands, choral groups, dance, drama, film society, literary magazine, music ensembles, musical theater, radio station, student government, student newspaper, TV station, African awareness association, Asian student association, business students of color, Cape Verdean student association, cultural Italian Amercian organization, French club, The Gay, Lesbian, Bisexual, Transgender Center, Habitat for Humanity, People Organized for Women's Equality and Resilience, students for social change.

Athletics. NCAA. **Intercollegiate:** Baseball M, basketball, cross-country, diving, field hockey W, football (tackle) M, golf M, gymnastics W, rowing (crew) W, skiing W, soccer, softball W, swimming, tennis, track and field, volleyball W. **Intramural:** Badminton, basketball, bowling, boxing, cross-country, football (tackle), golf, soccer, softball, swimming, tennis, volleyball, water polo. **Team name:** Rams.

Student services. Adult student services, alcohol/substance abuse counseling, campus ministries, career counseling, student employment services, health services, legal services, on-campus daycare, personal counseling, placement for graduates, veterans' counselor. **Physically disabled:** Services for visually, speech, hearing impaired.

Contact. E-mail: uriadmit@etal.uri.edu
Phone: (401) 874-7100 Fax: (401) 874-5523
Jame Lynch, Dean of Admissions, University of Rhode Island, 14 Upper College Road, Kingston, RI 02881-1391

Zion Bible Institute

Barrington, Rhode Island
www.zbc.edu — **CB code: 3942**

- Private 4-year Bible college affiliated with Assemblies of God
- Residential campus in large town

- 235 degree-seeking undergraduates: 9% part-time, 52% women, 11% African American, 1% Asian American, 9% Hispanic American, 4% international
- Application essay required

General. Accredited by ABHE. **Degrees:** 55 bachelor's awarded. **Location:** 10 miles from Providence. **Calendar:** Semester, limited summer session.

Freshman class profile.

Mid 50% test scores		ACT:	16-22
SAT verbal:	420-560	Out-of-state:	16%
SAT math:	390-520		

Basis for selection. Three references required for admission including a pastoral recommendation. High school transcript, immunizations, health certificate and test scores also required. **Homeschooled:** Applicants must produce diploma and transcript that verifies graduation by the state department of education, local school district or accrediting association. Students who cannot produce this must submit GED.

2005-2006 Annual costs. Tuition/fees: $6,405. Room/board: $4,800.

Application procedures. Admission: No deadline. $35 fee. Application may be submitted online. Admission notification on a rolling basis.

Academics. Special study options: Independent study, internships, weekend college. **Credit/placement by examination:** AP, CLEP. **Support services:** Learning center, reduced course load, study skills assistance.

Majors. Theology: Bible.

Computing on campus. 15 workstations in computer center. Online library available.

Student life. Freshman orientation: Mandatory. Preregistration for classes offered. **Policies:** Students have 10:30 pm curfew, except for Fridays when it is extended to 11:00 pm (midnight for seniors). Chapel attendance required Tuesday-Friday. No alcohol or drugs permitted on campus. Full-time students assigned to assist in area church. Religious observance required. Freshmen permitted cars on campus. **Housing:** Guaranteed on-campus for all undergraduates. Single-sex dorms, apartments available. $300 deposit. **Activities:** Choral groups, drama, student government, student newspaper.

Student services. Campus ministries, financial aid counseling.

Contact. E-mail: admissions@zbc.edu
Phone: (401) 246-0900 Toll-free number: (800) 356-4014
Fax: (401) 246-0906
David Hodge, Director, Admissions, Zion Bible Institute, 27 Middle Highway, Barrington, RI 02806

South Carolina

Allen University
Columbia, South Carolina
www.allenuniversity.edu **CB code: 5006**

- Private 4-year university and liberal arts college affiliated with African Methodist Episcopal Church
- Residential campus in large city
- 624 degree-seeking undergraduates: 4% part-time, 34% women

General. Founded in 1870. Regionally accredited. **Degrees:** 85 bachelor's awarded. **ROTC:** Army. **Location:** 112 miles from Charleston, 72 miles from Charlotte, North Carolina. **Calendar:** Semester, limited summer session. **Full-time faculty:** 25 total. **Part-time faculty:** 20 total. **Class size:** 65% < 20, 34% 20-39, 1% 40-49.

Freshman class profile.

Out-of-state:	30%	**Live on campus:**	85%

Basis for selection. Open admission. Interview, campus visit recommended. **Homeschooled:** Statement describing homeschool structure and mission, state high school equivalency certificate, interview, letter of recommendation (nonparent) required.

High school preparation. College-preparatory program recommended. Recommended units include English 4, mathematics 4, social studies 3, history 3, science 3 and foreign language 2.

2005-2006 Annual costs. Tuition/fees: $7,764. Room/board: $4,210. Books/supplies: $800.

Financial aid. Non-need-based: Scholarships awarded for academics, athletics, music/drama, ROTC.

Application procedures. Admission: Closing date 7/31 (postmark date). $20 fee, may be waived for applicants with need. Application may be submitted online. Admission notification on a rolling basis. **Financial aid:** Priority date 4/15, closing date 7/20. FAFSA required. Applicants notified on a rolling basis starting 4/1; must reply within 2 week(s) of notification.

Academics. Special study options: Cooperative education, honors, independent study, internships, teacher certification program, weekend college. Nontraditional program for returning students. **Credit/placement by examination:** CLEP, institutional tests. **Support services:** Learning center, remedial instruction, study skills assistance, tutoring, writing center.

Majors. Biology: General. **Business:** Business admin. **Math:** General. **Philosophy/religion:** Religion. **Physical sciences:** Chemistry. **Social sciences:** General.

Most popular majors. Business/marketing 23%, education 17%, philosophy/religious studies 39%, social sciences 15%.

Computing on campus. 55 workstations in library, computer center. Dormitories linked to campus network. Online course registration available.

Student life. Freshman orientation: Mandatory. Preregistration for classes offered. Week-long session. Students complete financial aid, register for class and receive dorm assignments. **Policies:** Freshmen permitted cars on campus. **Housing:** Guaranteed on-campus for freshmen. Single-sex dorms, apartments available. $50 nonrefundable deposit. **Activities:** Choral groups, student government, student newspaper, international students organization, social science club, NAACP, gospel choir.

Athletics. NAIA. **Intercollegiate:** Basketball, cross-country M, track and field M, volleyball W. **Team name:** Yellow Jackets.

Student services. Adult student services, career counseling, student employment services, financial aid counseling, health services, personal counseling, placement for graduates.

Contact. Phone: (803) 376-5735 Toll-free number: (877) 625-5368
Fax: (803) 758-2704
Aaron Bishop, Director of Admissions, Allen University, 1530 Harden Street, Columbia, SC 29204

Anderson University
Anderson, South Carolina **CB member**
www.ac.edu **CB code: 5008**

- Private 4-year liberal arts college affiliated with Southern Baptist Convention
- Residential campus in large town
- 1,418 degree-seeking undergraduates: 10% part-time, 63% women, 10% African American, 1% Asian American, 1% Hispanic American, 2% international
- 78% of applicants admitted
- SAT or ACT required
- 40% graduate within 6 years

General. Founded in 1911. Regionally accredited. **Degrees:** 254 bachelor's, 2 associate awarded; master's offered. **ROTC:** Army, Air Force. **Location:** 32 miles from Greenville, 100 miles from Atlanta. **Calendar:** Semester, limited summer session. **Full-time faculty:** 68 total; 60% have terminal degrees, 6% minority, 47% women. **Part-time faculty:** 82 total; 32% have terminal degrees, 6% minority, 40% women. **Class size:** 50% < 20, 50% 20-39. **Special facilities:** Fine arts center cultural program, on-campus audio recording studio, electronic classrooms.

Freshman class profile. 1,079 applied, 838 admitted, 371 enrolled.

Mid 50% test scores		**Rank in top quarter:**	44%
SAT verbal:	470-560	**Rank in top tenth:**	17%
SAT math:	470-580	**Return as sophomores:**	62%
ACT:	18-23	**Out-of-state:**	16%
GPA 3.50 or higher:	63%	**Live on campus:**	94%
GPA 3.0-3.49:	21%	**International:**	3%
GPA 2.0-2.99:	16%		

Basis for selection. High school achievement record, test scores important; recommendations considered. Minimum high school GPA of 2.5 and SAT (exclusive of writing) combined score of 1000 preferred. Each applicant considered individually. Applicants not meeting these guidelines may be admitted into developmental studies program. Recommendations, further grades or interview may be required for academically weak applicants. Interview recommended for some; audition required for art, music, theater programs. **Learning Disabled:** Applicants with diagnosed learning disabilities must meet regular requirements and supply summary of recent (within 1 year of enrollment) diagnostic testing.

High school preparation. 20 units required; 22 recommended. Required and recommended units include English 4, mathematics 3-4, social studies 2, history 2, science 3-4 (laboratory 2), foreign language 2 and academic electives 4.

2006-2007 Annual costs. Tuition/fees: $16,550. Room/board: $6,400. Books/supplies: $1,650. Personal expenses: $2,450.

2004-2005 Financial aid. Need-based: 362 full-time freshmen applied for aid; 323 were judged to have need; 323 of these received aid. Average need met was 64%. Average scholarship/grant was $8,098; average loan $3,608. 72% of total undergraduate aid awarded as scholarships/grants, 28% as loans/jobs. **Non-need-based:** Awarded to 981 full-time undergraduates, including 385 freshmen. Scholarships awarded for academics, alumni affiliation, art, athletics, leadership, minority status, music/drama, religious affiliation, state residency.

Application procedures. Admission: Closing date 7/1 (receipt date). $25 fee, may be waived for applicants with need. Application may be submitted online. Admission notification on a rolling basis beginning on or about 9/2. **Financial aid:** Priority date 3/1, closing date 7/30. FAFSA required. Applicants notified on a rolling basis starting 3/15; must reply within 2 week(s) of notification.

Academics. Special study options: Accelerated study, cooperative education, distance learning, double major, dual enrollment of high school students, honors, independent study, internships, liberal arts/career combination, study abroad, teacher certification program. **Credit/placement by examination:** AP, CLEP, IB, institutional tests. 24 credit hours maximum toward associate degree, 24 toward bachelor's. **Support services:** Learning center, reduced course load, remedial instruction, study skills assistance, tutoring, writing center.

Majors. Biology: General. **Business:** Accounting, business admin, finance, human resources, management information systems, marketing. **Communications:** General, journalism, media studies, public relations. **Computer sciences:** General. **Education:** Art, biology, early childhood, elementary, English, history, mathematics, multi-level teacher, music, physical, science, secondary, social studies, Spanish, special. **English:** Creative writing, English lit. **Foreign languages:** Spanish. **Health:** Athletic training, cytotechnology, health care admin. **History:** General. **Math:** General. **Parks/recreation:** Exercise sciences, health/fitness. **Philosophy/religion:** Religion. **Protective services:** Law enforcement admin. **Psychology:** General. **Public administration:** Human services. **Theology:** Sacred music, theology. **Visual/performing arts:** Art, ceramics, dramatic, drawing, graphic design, interior design, music performance, painting, studio arts, voice/opera.

Most popular majors. Business/marketing 33%, education 25%, parks/recreation 7%, psychology 8%, visual/performing arts 11%.

Computing on campus. 192 workstations in library, computer center, student center. Dormitories wired for high-speed internet access and linked to campus network. Commuter students can connect to campus network. Online course registration, online library, helpline, wireless network available.

Student life. **Freshman orientation:** Mandatory. Preregistration for classes offered. 2 orientation sessions held during summer. **Policies:** Freshmen permitted cars on campus. **Housing:** Coed dorms, single-sex dorms, apartments available. $100 deposit, deadline 7/1. **Activities:** Bands, choral groups, dance, drama, literary magazine, music ensembles, musical theater, student government, student newspaper, symphony orchestra, Baptist campus ministries, Gamma Beta Phi, campus activities board, Fellowship of Christian Athletes, Minorities for Change, student alumni council, Reformed University Fellowship, Young Life.

Athletics. NCAA. **Intercollegiate:** Baseball M, basketball, cheerleading M, cross-country, golf, soccer, softball W, tennis, track and field, volleyball W, wrestling M. **Intramural:** Basketball, football (non-tackle), racquetball, softball, tennis, volleyball, weight lifting M. **Team name:** Trojans.

Student services. Adult student services, campus ministries, career counseling, student employment services, financial aid counseling, health services, on-campus daycare, personal counseling, placement for graduates. **Physically disabled:** Services for visually impaired.

Contact. E-mail: admissions@ac.edu
Phone: (864) 231-2030 Toll-free number: (800) 542-3594
Fax: (864) 231-2033
Pam Bryant, Director of Admissions, Anderson University, 316 Boulevard, Anderson, SC 29621

Benedict College

Columbia, South Carolina — **CB member**
www.benedict.edu — **CB code: 5056**

- Private 4-year liberal arts college affiliated with American Baptist Churches in the USA
- Residential campus in very large city
- 2,552 degree-seeking undergraduates: 2% part-time, 51% women, 99% African American, 1% Hispanic American

General. Founded in 1870. Regionally accredited. **Degrees:** 312 bachelor's awarded. **ROTC:** Army, Air Force. **Location:** 110 miles from Greenville, 120 miles from Charleston. **Calendar:** Semester, limited summer session. **Full-time faculty:** 118 total; 59% have terminal degrees, 94% minority, 45% women. **Part-time faculty:** 35 total; 83% minority, 54% women. **Class size:** 43% < 20, 39% 20-39, 13% 40-49, 5% 50-99. **Special facilities:** Computer-assisted instruction facilities.

Freshman class profile.

Mid 50% test scores			
SAT verbal:	330-430	Rank in top quarter:	6%
SAT math:	330-430	Rank in top tenth:	1%
ACT:	13-16	End year in good standing:	83%
GPA 3.50 or higher:	4%	Return as sophomores:	56%
GPA 3.0-3.49:	14%	Out-of-state:	38%
GPA 2.0-2.99:	55%	Live on campus:	93%

Basis for selection. Open admission.

High school preparation. 20 units recommended. Recommended units include English 4, mathematics 3, social studies 3 and science 2.

2005-2006 Annual costs. Tuition/fees: $12,954. Room/board: $5,958. Books/supplies: $1,000. Personal expenses: $1,400.

Application procedures. **Admission:** No deadline. $25 fee. Admission notification on a rolling basis. **Financial aid:** Priority date 4/15; no closing date. FAFSA required. Applicants notified on a rolling basis starting 4/15.

Academics. **Special study options:** Accelerated study, double major, dual enrollment of high school students, external degree, honors, internships, teacher certification program, weekend college. **Credit/placement by examination:** AP, CLEP, institutional tests. 24 credit hours maximum toward bachelor's degree. **Support services:** Learning center, pre-admission summer program, reduced course load, remedial instruction, study skills assistance, tutoring, writing center.

Majors. **Biology:** General. **Business:** Accounting, business admin. **Computer sciences:** General, computer science. **Conservation:** Environmental science. **Education:** Early childhood, elementary. **Engineering technology:** Electrical. **Family/consumer sciences:** Family studies. **History:** General. **Math:** General. **Parks/recreation:** Health/fitness. **Physical sciences:** Chemistry, physics. **Public administration:** Social work. **Social sciences:** Economics, political science. **Visual/performing arts:** Art, multimedia.

Most popular majors. Biology 11%, business/marketing 24%, computer/information sciences 11%, education 9%, legal studies 12%, parks/recreation 8%.

Computing on campus. 385 workstations in dormitories, library, computer center, student center. Dormitories wired for high-speed internet access and linked to campus network. Commuter students can connect to campus network. Online library, helpline, repair service, wireless network available.

Student life. **Freshman orientation:** Mandatory. Preregistration for classes offered. **Policies:** Freshmen permitted cars on campus. **Housing:** Guaranteed on-campus for freshmen. Single-sex dorms available. **Activities:** Bands, choral groups, dance, drama, music ensembles, radio station, student government, student newspaper, Gordon-Jenkins Theological Association.

Athletics. NAIA. **Intercollegiate:** Baseball M, basketball, cross-country, football (tackle) M, golf, soccer M, softball, tennis, track and field, volleyball W, wrestling M. **Intramural:** Baseball M, basketball, softball W, volleyball W. **Team name:** Tigers.

Student services. Adult student services, campus ministries, career counseling, student employment services, financial aid counseling, health services, minority student services, on-campus daycare, personal counseling, placement for graduates, veterans' counselor.

Contact. E-mail: admissions@benedict.edu
Phone: (803) 253-5143 Toll-free number: (800) 868-6598
Fax: (803) 253-5167
Benedict College, 1600 Harden Street, Columbia, SC 29204

Charleston Southern University

Charleston, South Carolina — **CB member**
www.csuniv.edu — **CB code: 5079**

- Private 4-year university and liberal arts college affiliated with Southern Baptist Convention
- Commuter campus in large city
- 2,586 degree-seeking undergraduates: 15% part-time, 61% women, 28% African American, 2% Asian American, 1% Hispanic American, 1% Native American, 2% international
- 382 degree-seeking graduate students
- 71% of applicants admitted
- SAT or ACT with writing required

General. Founded in 1964. Regionally accredited. **Degrees:** 356 bachelor's awarded; master's offered. **ROTC:** Air Force. **Location:** 15 miles from downtown. **Calendar:** 4-1-4. 4-4-1. **Full-time faculty:** 107 total; 63% have terminal degrees, 2% minority, 45% women. **Part-time faculty:** 72 total; 26% have terminal degrees, 11% minority, 53% women. **Class size:** 53% < 20, 41% 20-39, 3% 40-49, 3% 50-99. **Special facilities:** Earthquake research center, center for economic forecasting.

Freshman class profile. 2,744 applied, 1,955 admitted, 632 enrolled.

Mid 50% test scores			
SAT verbal:	440-540	Rank in top tenth:	12%
SAT math:	460-540	Out-of-state:	24%
ACT:	18-22	Live on campus:	76%
Rank in top quarter:	34%	International:	1%

Basis for selection. School achievement record, academic course work, test scores, GPA, class rank most important. Interview and recommendations considered. Students may be required to take institutional math test for acceptance and/or placement. Essay, interview recommended for all; audition recommended for music programs. **Learning Disabled:** Special needs allowances require documentation and interview with Director of Special Needs.

High school preparation. College-preparatory program required. 23 units required. Required and recommended units include English 4, mathematics 3-4, social studies 2, history 2, science 3 (laboratory 2) and foreign language 2.

2006-2007 Annual costs. Tuition/fees (projected): $16,780. Room/board: $6,450.

2004-2005 Financial aid. Need-based: 472 full-time freshmen applied for aid; 432 were judged to have need; 432 of these received aid. Average need met was 73%. Average scholarship/grant was $10,161; average loan $3,432. 55% of total undergraduate aid awarded as scholarships/grants, 45% as loans/jobs. **Non-need-based:** Awarded to 608 full-time undergraduates, including 170 freshmen. Scholarships awarded for academics, athletics, religious affiliation, ROTC.

Application procedures. Admission: No deadline. $30 fee. Application may be submitted online. Admission notification on a rolling basis beginning on or about 9/1. **Financial aid:** Priority date 4/15; no closing date. FAFSA required. Applicants notified on a rolling basis starting 3/1; must reply within 2 week(s) of notification.

Academics. Special study options: Accelerated study, combined bachelor's/graduate degree, cooperative education, cross-registration, distance learning, double major, dual enrollment of high school students, honors, internships, study abroad, teacher certification program. **Credit/placement by examination:** AP, CLEP, IB, SAT, ACT, institutional tests. 30 credit hours maximum toward associate degree, 30 toward bachelor's. **Support services:** Learning center, remedial instruction, study skills assistance, tutoring, writing center.

Majors. Biology: General. **Business:** General, accounting, business admin, finance, management information systems, management science, marketing. **Computer sciences:** Information systems, programming. **Education:** General, elementary, foreign languages, mathematics, music, physical, science, secondary, social science, social studies, Spanish. **English:** English lit. **Foreign languages:** Spanish. **Health:** Music therapy, nursing (RN), predentistry, premedicine, prepharmacy. **History:** General. **Interdisciplinary:** Biological/physical sciences, math/computer science, natural sciences. **Liberal arts:** Arts/sciences, humanities. **Math:** General, applied. **Parks/recreation:** Health/fitness. **Philosophy/religion:** Religion. **Physical sciences:** Chemistry, geology, physics. **Protective services:** Criminal justice, law enforcement admin. **Psychology:** General. **Social sciences:** General, economics, political science, sociology. **Theology:** Bible, pastoral counseling, sacred music, theology, youth ministry. **Visual/performing arts:** General, dramatic, music performance, studio arts, voice/opera.

Most popular majors. Biology 8%, business/marketing 17%, education 14%, health sciences 10%, psychology 10%, security/protective services 8%, social sciences 13%.

Computing on campus. 150 workstations in dormitories, library, computer center, student center. Dormitories wired for high-speed internet access. Commuter students can connect to campus network. Online library, helpline, student web hosting, wireless network available.

Student life. Freshman orientation: Available. Preregistration for classes offered. **Policies:** Religious observance required. Freshmen permitted cars on campus. **Housing:** Guaranteed on-campus for freshmen. Single-sex dorms available. $200 fully refundable deposit. **Activities:** Bands, choral groups, dance, drama, literary magazine, music ensembles, musical theater, student government, student newspaper, College Republicans, Young Democrats, Afro-American Society, international club, Baptist Student Union, Fellowship of Christian Athletes, Campus Crusade, Future Teachers Society.

Athletics. NCAA. **Intercollegiate:** Baseball M, basketball, cross-country, football (tackle) M, golf, soccer, softball W, tennis, track and field, volleyball W. **Intramural:** Basketball, soccer, softball, volleyball. **Team name:** Buccaneer.

Student services. Adult student services, campus ministries, career counseling, student employment services, financial aid counseling, health services, personal counseling, placement for graduates, veterans' counselor. **Physically disabled:** Services for visually, speech, hearing impaired.

Contact. E-mail: enroll@csuniv.edu
Phone: (843) 863-7050 Toll-free number: (800) 947-7474
Fax: (843) 863-7070
Cheryl Burton, Director of Admissions, Charleston Southern University, 9200 University Boulevard, Charleston, SC 29423-8087

The Citadel

Charleston, South Carolina **CB member**
www.citadel.edu **CB code: 5108**

- Public 4-year military college
- Residential campus in large city
- 2,176 degree-seeking undergraduates: 3% part-time, 6% women, 7% African American, 2% Asian American, 4% Hispanic American, 2% international
- 806 degree-seeking graduate students
- 78% of applicants admitted
- SAT or ACT with writing required
- 66% graduate within 6 years

General. Founded in 1842. Regionally accredited. College of graduate and professional studies offers undergraduate and graduate evening programs. **Degrees:** 471 bachelor's awarded; master's offered. **ROTC:** Army, Navy, Air Force. **Location:** 110 miles from Columbia, 120 miles from Savannah, Georgia. **Calendar:** Semester, extensive summer session. **Full-time faculty:** 157 total; 94% have terminal degrees, 12% minority, 28% women. **Part-time faculty:** 75 total; 49% have terminal degrees, 8% minority, 36% women. **Class size:** 42% < 20, 49% 20-39, 4% 40-49, 4% 50-99. **Special facilities:** Archives museum, beach house, boating center.

Freshman class profile. 1,913 applied, 1,496 admitted, 585 enrolled.

Mid 50% test scores		**Rank in top quarter:**	31%
SAT verbal:	480-600	**Rank in top tenth:**	9%
SAT math:	500-600	**Return as sophomores:**	82%
ACT:	20-24	**Out-of-state:**	56%
GPA 3.50 or higher:	35%	**Live on campus:**	100%
GPA 3.0-3.49:	34%	**International:**	2%
GPA 2.0-2.99:	31%		

Basis for selection. Admissions based on class rank, test scores, GPA, alumni recommendations, extracurricular activities. Interview recommended.

High school preparation. 20 units required. Required units include English 4, mathematics 3, social studies 2, history 1, science 3 (laboratory 3), foreign language 2 and academic electives 4. One physical education or ROTC required.

2005-2006 Annual costs. Tuition/fees: $6,522; $15,918 out-of-state. Students in Corps of Cadets required to pay $998 in fees which include laundry and dry cleaning charges and infirmary fees. Freshmen also pay $5,200 deposit and upperclassmen pay $1,630 deposit for uniforms, books, and supplies. Room/board: $4,840.

2005-2006 Financial aid. Need-based: 456 full-time freshmen applied for aid; 319 were judged to have need; 305 of these received aid. Average need met was 56%. Average scholarship/grant was $9,231; average loan $3,154. 75% of total undergraduate aid awarded as scholarships/grants, 25% as loans/jobs. **Non-need-based:** Awarded to 1,102 full-time undergraduates, including 351 freshmen. Scholarships awarded for academics, athletics, leadership, music/drama, religious affiliation, ROTC, state residency.

Application procedures. Admission: No deadline. $40 fee, may be waived for applicants with need. Admission notification on a rolling basis beginning on or about 7/15. **Financial aid:** Closing date 3/1. FAFSA required. Applicants notified by 4/1; Applicants notified on a rolling basis starting 4/1; must reply within 2 week(s) of notification.

Academics. 4 years of ROTC required. **Special study options:** Combined bachelor's/graduate degree, cross-registration, double major, ESL, honors, independent study, internships, study abroad, teacher certification program. **Credit/placement by examination:** AP, CLEP, institutional tests. **Support services:** Learning center, study skills assistance, tutoring, writing center.

Majors. Biology: General. **Business:** Business admin. **Computer sciences:** General. **Education:** Physical, secondary. **Engineering:** Civil, electrical. **English:** English lit. **Foreign languages:** French, German, Spanish. **History:** General. **Math:** General. **Physical sciences:** Chemistry, physics. **Protective services:** Law enforcement admin. **Psychology:** General. **Social sciences:** Political science.

Most popular majors. Business/marketing 36%, education 9%, engineering/engineering technologies 9%, history 6%, security/protective services 12%, social sciences 10%.

Computing on campus. 350 workstations in dormitories, library, computer center. Dormitories linked to campus network. Commuter students can connect to campus network. Online course registration, online library, helpline, repair service available.

Student life. Freshman orientation: Mandatory. Preregistration for classes offered. **Housing:** Guaranteed on-campus for all undergraduates. Coed dorms available. $300 deposit, deadline 5/1. **Activities:** Bands, choral groups, drama, literary magazine, music ensembles, student government, student newspaper, African American Society, American Society of Civil Engineers, Association for Computing Machinery, Alpha Phi Omega, Summerall Guards,

African Methodist Episcopal, Baptist Student Union, Campus Crusade for Christ, Knights of Columbus, Army Aviator Association of America.

Athletics. NCAA. **Intercollegiate:** Baseball M, basketball M, cross-country, football (tackle) M, golf, soccer, tennis M, track and field, volleyball W, wrestling M. **Intramural:** Badminton, basketball, diving, football (non-tackle), handball, racquetball, softball, swimming, table tennis, tennis, track and field, triathlon, volleyball, water polo, weight lifting, wrestling. **Team name:** Bulldogs.

Student services. Alcohol/substance abuse counseling, campus ministries, career counseling, student employment services, financial aid counseling, health services, minority student services, personal counseling, placement for graduates, veterans' counselor.

Contact. E-mail: admissions@citadel.edu
Phone: (843) 953-5230 Toll-free number: (800) 868-1842
Fax: (843) 953-7036
John Powell, Director of Admissions, The Citadel, 171 Moultrie Street, Charleston, SC 29409

Claflin University

Orangeburg, South Carolina — **CB member**
www.claflin.edu — **CB code: 5109**

- Private 4-year liberal arts college affiliated with United Methodist Church
- Residential campus in large town
- 1,624 degree-seeking undergraduates: 2% part-time, 67% women
- 50 degree-seeking graduate students
- 40% of applicants admitted
- SAT or ACT (ACT writing optional) required
- 61% graduate within 6 years; 17% enter graduate study

General. Founded in 1869. Regionally accredited. **Degrees:** 284 bachelor's awarded; master's offered. **ROTC:** Army. **Location:** 40 miles from Columbia. **Calendar:** Semester, limited summer session. **Full-time faculty:** 92 total; 72% have terminal degrees, 60% minority, 40% women. **Part-time faculty:** 30 total. **Special facilities:** Center for excellence in science and math, center for excellence in mass communication, nuclear magnetic resonance, leadership development center, museum.

Freshman class profile. 2,744 applied, 1,103 admitted, 385 enrolled.

Mid 50% test scores			
SAT verbal:	430-580	Rank in top quarter:	46%
SAT math:	410-510	Rank in top tenth:	25%
GPA 3.50 or higher:	21%	Return as sophomores:	83%
GPA 3.0-3.49:	26%	Out-of-state:	4%
GPA 2.0-2.99:	51%	Live on campus:	90%
		International:	4%

Basis for selection. School achievement record, test scores, recommendation of high school officials, personal background, experience, character traits, educational objectives important. Audition required; essay, interview, portfolio recommended.

High school preparation. 20 units required. Required units include English 4, mathematics 3, social studies 2, history 1, (laboratory 2) and academic electives 7. Physical education.

2005-2006 Annual costs. Tuition/fees: $10,890. Room/board: $5,908. Books/supplies: $1,200. Personal expenses: $1,200.

2005-2006 Financial aid. Need-based: Average need met was 69%. Average scholarship/grant was $2,141; average loan $1,625. 48% of total undergraduate aid awarded as scholarships/grants, 52% as loans/jobs.

Application procedures. Admission: Closing date 7/15. $20 fee, may be waived for applicants with need. Application may be submitted online. Admission notification on a rolling basis beginning on or about 10/1. **Financial aid:** Priority date 4/15; no closing date. FAFSA, institutional form required. Applicants notified on a rolling basis starting 5/15; must reply within 2 week(s) of notification.

Academics. Special study options: Accelerated study, combined bachelor's/graduate degree, cooperative education, cross-registration, double major, dual enrollment of high school students, honors, independent study, internships, liberal arts/career combination, study abroad, teacher certification program, weekend college. **Credit/placement by examination:** AP, CLEP, institutional tests. 18 credit hours maximum toward bachelor's degree. **Support services:** Learning center, pre-admission summer program, reduced course load, remedial instruction, tutoring, writing center.

Honors college/program. 30 to 35 students admitted annually based on academic achievement, leadership, and SAT scores.

Majors. Area/ethnic studies: African-American, American. **Biology:** General, biochemistry, bioinformatics, biotechnology. **Business:** Business admin, management information systems, marketing, organizational behavior. **Communications:** Media studies. **Computer sciences:** Computer science. **Conservation:** Environmental science. **Education:** Art, early childhood, elementary, English, mathematics, music. **Engineering:** Software. **English:** English lit. **History:** General. **Math:** General. **Parks/recreation:** Health/fitness, sports admin. **Philosophy/religion:** Philosophy, religion. **Physical sciences:** Chemistry. **Protective services:** Law enforcement admin. **Social sciences:** Sociology. **Visual/performing arts:** Art.

Most popular majors. Biology 10%, business/marketing 20%, communications/journalism 6%, computer/information sciences 7%, education 10%, family/consumer sciences 11%, security/protective services 14%, social sciences 12%.

Computing on campus. 500 workstations in dormitories, library, computer center, student center. Dormitories wired for high-speed internet access and linked to campus network. Online course registration, online library, repair service, wireless network available.

Student life. Freshman orientation: Mandatory. Preregistration for classes offered. **Housing:** Guaranteed on-campus for freshmen. Single-sex dorms available. $50 deposit, deadline 4/15. **Activities:** Bands, drama, film society, literary magazine, music ensembles, radio station, student government, student newspaper, TV station, Alpha Kappa Mu (national honor society), Oxford Club, literature, art and film society, Phi Beta Lambda, Esquire XIII, Students in Free Enterprise, NAACP, religious leadership and volunteer organizations.

Athletics. NCAA. **Intercollegiate:** Baseball M, basketball, cross-country, softball W, tennis, track and field, volleyball W. **Intramural:** Baseball M, basketball. **Team name:** Panthers.

Student services. Adult student services, campus ministries, career counseling, student employment services, financial aid counseling, health services, minority student services, personal counseling, placement for graduates, veterans' counselor.

Contact. E-mail: mzeigler@claflin.edu
Phone: (803) 535-5340 Toll-free number: (800) 922-1276
Fax: (803) 535-5387
Michael Zeigler, Director of Admissions, Claflin University, 400 Magnolia Street, Orangeburg, SC 29115

Clemson University

Clemson, South Carolina — **CB member**
www.clemson.edu — **CB code: 5111**

- Public 4-year university
- Residential campus in small town
- 13,959 degree-seeking undergraduates: 5% part-time, 46% women, 7% African American, 2% Asian American, 1% Hispanic American
- 2,792 degree-seeking graduate students
- 57% of applicants admitted
- SAT or ACT with writing required
- 75% graduate within 6 years

General. Founded in 1889. Regionally accredited. **Degrees:** 3,005 bachelor's awarded; master's, doctoral offered. **ROTC:** Army, Air Force. **Location:** 32 miles from Greenville, 125 miles from Atlanta. **Calendar:** Semester, extensive summer session. **Full-time faculty:** 1,015 total; 86% have terminal degrees, 13% minority, 29% women. **Part-time faculty:** 163 total; 40% have terminal degrees, 7% minority, 42% women. **Class size:** 39% < 20, 43% 20-39, 7% 40-49, 7% 50-99, 3% >100. **Special facilities:** Planetarium, agricultural and forestry experimental facilities, geology museum, state botanical gardens, center for sustainable living, John C. Calhoun historical site and home, performing arts center.

Freshman class profile. 12,463 applied, 7,154 admitted, 2,904 enrolled.

Mid 50% test scores			
SAT verbal:	550-650	Return as sophomores:	87%
SAT math:	580-670	Out-of-state:	35%
ACT:	24-29	Live on campus:	98%
Rank in top quarter:	72%	Fraternities:	6%
Rank in top tenth:	42%	Sororities:	12%

Basis for selection. Admission is competitive and based largely on high school curriculum, performance in that curriculum, peer comparison, SAT or ACT scores, and choice of major. Campus visit recommended for all. Interview, portfolio recommended for architecture and art applicants. Audition required for performing arts program. **Homeschooled:** Include copies of all secondary school transcripts and course descriptions of any courses different from those traditionally offered in public school settings.

High school preparation. College-preparatory program required. 19 units required. Required and recommended units include English 4, mathematics 3-4, social studies 3, history 1, science 3 (laboratory 3-4), foreign language 3 and academic electives 2. Also require physical education or ROTC. 3 foreign language units must be in same language.

2005-2006 Annual costs. Tuition/fees: $9,016; $18,640 out-of-state. Laptop computer now required of all entering new students. This cost has been estimated at $1600. Room/board: $5,780. Books/supplies: $820. Personal expenses: $1,750.

2004-2005 Financial aid. **Need-based:** 37% of total undergraduate aid awarded as scholarships/grants, 63% as loans/jobs. **Non-need-based:** Scholarships awarded for academics, art, athletics, leadership, minority status, music/drama, ROTC, state residency.

Application procedures. **Admission:** Priority date 12/1; deadline 5/1 (postmark date). $50 fee, may be waived for applicants with need. Application may be submitted online. Admission notification on a rolling basis beginning on or about 2/15. Must reply by May 1 or within 4 week(s) if notified thereafter. Scholarship candidates notified on a rolling basis, beginning on or about October 1 for fall admission. **Financial aid:** Priority date 4/1; no closing date. FAFSA required. Applicants notified on a rolling basis starting 4/1; must reply within 3 week(s) of notification.

Academics. **Special study options:** Combined bachelor's/graduate degree, cooperative education, distance learning, double major, dual enrollment of high school students, exchange student, honors, independent study, internships, study abroad, teacher certification program, Washington semester. **Credit/placement by examination:** AP, CLEP, IB, institutional tests. Challenge examinations offered by each academic department. **Support services:** Learning center, pre-admission summer program, study skills assistance, tutoring, writing center.

Honors college/program. Less than 10 percent of freshman class invited to enroll in Honors College. Minimum peer comparison must show the student in top 3 percent of graduating secondary school class.

Majors. **Agriculture:** Agribusiness operations, animal sciences, dairy, economics, farm/ranch, food science, horticultural science, horticulture, plant sciences, poultry, soil science, turf management. **Architecture:** Architecture, landscape. **Biology:** General, bacteriology, biochemistry, genetics, plant pathology. **Business:** Accounting, business admin, international, operations, tourism/travel. **Communications:** General. **Computer sciences:** General, computer science, information systems. **Conservation:** Fisheries, forestry. **Education:** Agricultural, early childhood, elementary, mathematics, science, secondary, special, technology/industrial arts. **Engineering:** Agricultural, biomedical, ceramic, chemical, civil, computer, electrical, mechanical, textile. **English:** Speech/rhetoric. **Foreign languages:** General, French, German, Spanish. **Health:** Clinical lab science, premedicine, prepharmacy, preveterinary. **History:** General. **Interdisciplinary:** Nutrition sciences. **Legal studies:** Prelaw. **Math:** General. **Parks/recreation:** Facilities management. **Philosophy/religion:** Philosophy. **Physical sciences:** Chemistry, geology, physics. **Psychology:** General. **Social sciences:** Economics, political science, sociology. **Visual/performing arts:** Commercial/advertising art, design, industrial design, studio arts.

Most popular majors. Business/marketing 21%, education 10%, engineering/engineering technologies 15%, health sciences 7%, social sciences 6%.

Computing on campus. PC or laptop required. 875 workstations in library, computer center. Dormitories wired for high-speed internet access and linked to campus network. Commuter students can connect to campus network. Online course registration, online library, helpline, repair service, student web hosting, wireless network available.

Student life. **Freshman orientation:** Mandatory, $55 fee. Preregistration for classes offered. One and 1/2-day sessions held 8 times during June and July. Students must complete online mathematics placement exam prior to participating in orientation. **Policies:** Freshmen permitted cars on campus. **Housing:** Guaranteed on-campus for freshmen. Coed dorms, single-sex dorms, apartments, fraternity/sorority housing, substance-free housing available. $35 nonrefundable deposit. Housing guaranteed to freshmen and to students continuing in on-campus housing. **Activities:** Bands, choral groups, dance, drama, literary magazine, music ensembles, radio station, student government, student newspaper, symphony orchestra, TV station, religious organizations, Young Democrats, Young Republicans, minority awareness organizations, Blue Key, Alpha Phi Omega, Mortarboard, Hillel, Fellowship of Christian Athletes.

Athletics. NCAA. **Intercollegiate:** Baseball M, basketball, cross-country, diving, football (tackle) M, golf M, rowing (crew) W, soccer, swimming, tennis, track and field, volleyball W. **Intramural:** Basketball, diving, fencing, field hockey W, football (non-tackle), golf, racquetball, soccer, softball, table tennis, tennis, track and field, volleyball. **Team name:** Tigers.

Student services. Alcohol/substance abuse counseling, campus ministries, career counseling, student employment services, financial aid counseling, health services, minority student services, personal counseling, placement for graduates, veterans' counselor. **Physically disabled:** Services for visually, speech, hearing impaired.

Contact. E-mail: cuadmissions@clemson.edu
Phone: (864) 656-2287 Fax: (864) 656-2464
Robert Barkley, Director of Admissions, Clemson University, 105 Sikes Hall, Clemson, SC 29634-5124

Coastal Carolina University

Conway, South Carolina — **CB member**
www.coastal.edu — **CB code: 5837**

- Public 4-year university
- Commuter campus in small city
- 6,115 degree-seeking undergraduates: 6% part-time, 52% women, 12% African American, 1% Asian American, 2% Hispanic American, 1% Native American, 2% international
- 104 degree-seeking graduate students
- 74% of applicants admitted
- SAT or ACT (ACT writing optional) required
- 43% graduate within 6 years; 23% enter graduate study

General. Founded in 1954. Regionally accredited. **Degrees:** 887 bachelor's awarded; master's offered. **Location:** 9 miles from Myrtle Beach. **Calendar:** Semester, extensive summer session. **Full-time faculty:** 233 total; 78% have terminal degrees, 8% minority, 38% women. **Part-time faculty:** 181 total; 28% have terminal degrees, 7% minority, 50% women. **Class size:** 32% < 20, 48% 20-39, 14% 40-49, 6% 50-99, less than 1% >100. **Special facilities:** Barrier-reef island used for marine science field studies and research.

Freshman class profile. 5,427 applied, 4,015 admitted, 1,498 enrolled.

Mid 50% test scores			
SAT verbal:	470-550	Rank in top quarter:	43%
SAT math:	480-570	Rank in top tenth:	11%
ACT:	20-23	Return as sophomores:	64%
GPA 3.50 or higher:	40%	Out-of-state:	51%
GPA 3.0-3.49:	33%	Live on campus:	76%
GPA 2.0-2.99:	27%	Fraternities:	12%
		Sororities:	9%

Basis for selection. Secondary school record and test scores most important; class rank important. Applicants whose native language is not English must take TOEFL. Interview recommended for all. **Homeschooled:** Transcript of courses and grades required. Copy of declaration of intent to home school as filed with the local board of education. **Learning Disabled:** To become eligible for support services, students with disabilities must provide documentation of disability to Service for Students with Disabilities Office.

High school preparation. 20 units required. Required and recommended units include English 4, mathematics 3-4, social studies 2, history 1, science 3 (laboratory 3), foreign language 2 and academic electives 4. 1 unit of physical education or ROTC.

2005-2006 Annual costs. Tuition/fees: $6,940; $15,180 out-of-state. Room/board: $6,280. Books/supplies: $970. Personal expenses: $1,500.

2004-2005 Financial aid. **Need-based:** 1,021 full-time freshmen applied for aid; 839 were judged to have need; 838 of these received aid. Average need met was 58%. Average scholarship/grant was $3,347; average loan $6,088. 33% of total undergraduate aid awarded as scholarships/grants, 67% as loans/jobs. **Non-need-based:** Awarded to 2,408 full-time undergraduates, including 840 freshmen. Scholarships awarded for academics, art, athletics, leadership, music/drama, state residency.

Application procedures. **Admission:** Closing date 8/15. $45 fee, may be waived for applicants with need. Admission notification on a rolling basis beginning on or about 9/15. Must reply by May 1 or within 2 week(s) if notified thereafter. **Financial aid:** Priority date 3/1; no closing date. FAFSA required. Applicants notified on a rolling basis starting 3/1.

Academics. Professional golf management option in marketing program, accredited by PGA. Resort and international tourism management options in management program. CPA/CFA option in accounting. **Special study options:** Accelerated study, combined bachelor's/graduate degree, cooperative education, distance learning, double major, dual enrollment of high school students, honors, independent study, internships, liberal arts/career combination, student-designed major, study abroad, teacher certification program. 3-2 engineering program with Clemson University, nursing program with Francis Marion University and Medical University of South Carolina; master of educational administration with University of South Carolina. **Credit/placement by examination:** AP, CLEP, IB, SAT, institutional tests. 30 credit hours maximum toward bachelor's degree. **Support services:** Learning center, reduced course load, tutoring, writing center.

Majors. Biology: General, marine. **Business:** Accounting, business admin, finance, managerial economics, marketing, resort management. **Communications:** General. **Computer sciences:** General. **Education:** Early childhood, elementary, middle, physical, special. **English:** English lit. **Foreign languages:** Spanish. **Health:** Public health ed. **History:** General. **Liberal arts:** Arts/sciences. **Math:** Applied. **Parks/recreation:** Sports admin. **Philosophy/religion:** Philosophy. **Physical sciences:** Chemistry, physics. **Psychology:** General. **Social sciences:** Political science, sociology. **Visual/performing arts:** Dramatic, studio arts.

Most popular majors. Biology 14%, business/marketing 29%, education 14%, liberal arts 6%, psychology 7%, social sciences 7%.

Computing on campus. 600 workstations in dormitories, library, computer center, student center. Dormitories wired for high-speed internet access and linked to campus network. Commuter students can connect to campus network. Online library, wireless network available.

Student life. Freshman orientation: Mandatory, $85 fee. Preregistration for classes offered. 2-day programs. **Policies:** Freshmen permitted cars on campus. **Housing:** Coed dorms, special housing for disabled available. $150 partly refundable deposit, deadline 8/15. **Activities:** Bands, choral groups, dance, drama, literary magazine, music ensembles, musical theater, student government, student newspaper, Fellowship of Christian Athletes, African American Association, international club, gospel choir, Society for Advancement of Management, Students Taking Active Responsibility, fitness club, drama club.

Athletics. NCAA. **Intercollegiate:** Baseball M, basketball, cheerleading, cross-country, football (tackle) M, golf, soccer, softball W, tennis, track and field, volleyball W. **Intramural:** Badminton, basketball, bowling, football (tackle), golf, lacrosse, racquetball, rugby M, soccer, softball, swimming, table tennis, tennis, track and field, volleyball, water polo, weight lifting. **Team name:** Chanticleers.

Student services. Adult student services, alcohol/substance abuse counseling, career counseling, student employment services, financial aid counseling, health services, minority student services, personal counseling, placement for graduates, veterans' counselor, women's services. **Physically disabled:** Services for visually, speech, hearing impaired.

Contact. E-mail: admissions@coastal.edu
Phone: (843) 349-2026 Toll-free number: (800) 277-7000
Fax: (843) 349-2127
Judy Vogt, Vice President for Enrollment Services, Coastal Carolina University, PO Box 261954, Conway, SC 29528-6054

Coker College

Hartsville, South Carolina — **CB member**
www.coker.edu — **CB code: 5112**

- Private 4-year liberal arts college
- Residential campus in large town
- 548 degree-seeking undergraduates
- SAT or ACT required

General. Founded in 1908. Regionally accredited. **Degrees:** 79 bachelor's awarded. **Location:** 70 miles from Columbia, 80 miles from Charlotte, North Carolina. **Calendar:** Semester, limited summer session. **Full-time faculty:** 55 total. **Part-time faculty:** 15 total. **Class size:** 92% < 20, 8% 20-39. **Special facilities:** Botanical gardens.

Freshman class profile.

Mid 50% test scores			
SAT verbal:	440-570	ACT:	18-23
SAT math:	450-580	Out-of-state:	15%
		Live on campus:	82%

Basis for selection. Academic record and test scores, interview, school and community activities important. Recommendations also used to determine status. Applicants admitted on basis of test scores and GPA in academic core courses. Special talents and alumni relations important. Essay recommended for all; audition required for dance, music, theater programs; portfolio required for art programs.

High school preparation. 19 units required. Required and recommended units include English 4, mathematics 3, social studies 2, history 1, science 3 (laboratory 1), foreign language 3 and academic electives 3. Recommended science units includes 1 physical science, 1 biology.

2005-2006 Annual costs. Tuition/fees: $17,288. Room/board: $5,660. Books/supplies: $900. Personal expenses: $550.

2005-2006 Financial aid. Need-based: 50% of total undergraduate aid awarded as scholarships/grants, 50% as loans/jobs. **Non-need-based:** Scholarships awarded for academics, art, athletics, music/drama. **Additional information:** Endowed scholarship program for qualified applicants. June 1 deadline for filing South Carolina Tuition Grant forms.

Application procedures. Admission: No deadline. $15 fee, may be waived for applicants with need. Application may be submitted online. Admission notification on a rolling basis beginning on or about 6/1. Must reply by May 1 or within 3 week(s) if notified thereafter. Juniors allowed to apply and make admissions decision during summer prior to senior year. **Financial aid:** Priority date 4/1, closing date 6/1. FAFSA required. Applicants notified on a rolling basis starting 12/1; must reply by 5/1 or within 3 week(s) of notification.

Academics. Special study options: Cooperative education, double major, dual enrollment of high school students, ESL, honors, independent study, internships, liberal arts/career combination, student-designed major, study abroad, teacher certification program. 2-2 programs with two-year colleges, 3-1 program with regional medical facility. **Credit/placement by examination:** AP, CLEP, IB, institutional tests. Unlimited hours of credit by examination may be counted toward degree. **Support services:** Reduced course load, remedial instruction, study skills assistance, tutoring, writing center.

Majors. Biology: General. **Business:** Business admin. **Communications:** General. **Computer sciences:** Computer science. **Education:** General, art, biology, business, chemistry, early childhood, elementary, English, history, mathematics, music, physical. **English:** English lit, technical writing. **Foreign languages:** French, Spanish. **Health:** Clinical lab science, dance therapy, recreational therapy. **History:** General. **Math:** General. **Parks/recreation:** Exercise sciences, sports admin. **Physical sciences:** Chemistry. **Psychology:** General. **Public administration:** Social work. **Social sciences:** Criminology, political science, sociology. **Visual/performing arts:** Acting, art, commercial/advertising art, dance, dramatic, music performance, music theory/composition, photography, piano/organ, studio arts, theater design, voice/opera.

Most popular majors. Biology 7%, business/marketing 14%, education 11%, parks/recreation 17%, psychology 8%, social sciences 8%, visual/performing arts 9%.

Computing on campus. 49 workstations in dormitories, library, computer center, student center. Dormitories wired for high-speed internet access and linked to campus network. Online library, student web hosting available.

Student life. Freshman orientation: Mandatory. Preregistration for classes offered. 3-day session held immediately before fall classes begin. **Policies:** Freshmen permitted cars on campus. **Housing:** Guaranteed on-campus for freshmen. Coed dorms available. $75 deposit, deadline 5/1. **Activities:** Choral groups, dance, drama, literary magazine, musical theater, student government, student newspaper, Campus Crusade, Psi Chi, African American Sisterhood, Helping: Our Way of Life, Multicultural Affairs Committee.

Athletics. NCAA. **Intercollegiate:** Baseball M, basketball, cheerleading, cross-country, golf M, soccer, softball W, tennis, volleyball W. **Intramural:** Badminton, basketball, bowling, cross-country, football (non-tackle), handball, racquetball, rowing (crew) W, sailing, soccer, softball, swimming, table tennis, tennis, track and field, volleyball, water polo, weight lifting. **Team name:** Cobras.

Student services. Adult student services, campus ministries, career counseling, student employment services, financial aid counseling, health services, personal counseling, placement for graduates.

Contact. E-mail: admissions@coker.edu
Phone: (843) 383-8050 Toll-free number: (800) 950-1908
Fax: (843) 383-8056
Perry Wilson, Director of Admissions, Coker College, 300 East College Avenue, Hartsville, SC 29550

College of Charleston

Charleston, South Carolina **CB member**
www.cofc.edu **CB code: 5113**

- Public 4-year liberal arts college
- Residential campus in large city
- 9,501 degree-seeking undergraduates: 6% part-time, 64% women, 7% African American, 2% Asian American, 2% Hispanic American, 2% international
- 530 degree-seeking graduate students
- 66% of applicants admitted
- SAT or ACT (ACT writing optional), application essay required
- 59% graduate within 6 years

General. Founded in 1770. Regionally accredited. **Degrees:** 2,098 bachelor's awarded; master's offered. **ROTC:** Air Force. **Calendar:** Semester, limited summer session. **Full-time faculty:** 515 total; 85% have terminal degrees, 13% minority, 41% women. **Part-time faculty:** 343 total; 34% have terminal degrees, 11% minority, 60% women. **Class size:** 33% < 20, 57% 20-39, 7% 40-49, 3% 50-99, less than 1% >100. **Special facilities:** Communications museum, early childhood development center, observatory, marine science laboratory, sculpture studio, sailing center, African-American history and culture research center, bilingual legal interpreting center, media and technology studio, center for entrepreneurship.

Freshman class profile. 8,217 applied, 5,436 admitted, 1,993 enrolled.

Mid 50% test scores			
SAT verbal:	570-650	Rank in top quarter:	58%
SAT math:	570-640	Rank in top tenth:	25%
ACT:	22-25	Return as sophomores:	83%
GPA 3.50 or higher:	69%	Out-of-state:	42%
GPA 3.0-3.49:	27%	Live on campus:	86%
GPA 2.0-2.99:	4%	Fraternities:	13%
		Sororities:	14%

Basis for selection. School grades, class rank, curriculum most important, then test scores. Recommendations and activities helpful in borderline cases. Personal essay optional. Interview recommended for all. **Homeschooled:** Students should indicate which school district syllabus was followed during home schooling.

High school preparation. 20 units required. Required and recommended units include English 4, mathematics 3-4, social studies 3, history 2, science 3-4 (laboratory 3), foreign language 2-3 and academic electives 4. Mathematics requirement includes 2 algebra. Social science recommendation .5 economics and .5 government. 2 units of same foreign language, 1 additional unit of advanced mathematics, computer science, world history, world geography, or Western civilization required.

2005-2006 Annual costs. Tuition/fees: $6,668; $15,342 out-of-state. Room/board: $6,948. Books/supplies: $851. Personal expenses: $2,976.

Financial aid. Non-need-based: Scholarships awarded for academics, alumni affiliation, art, athletics, music/drama.

Application procedures. Admission: Priority date 11/1; deadline 4/1. $45 fee, may be waived for applicants with need. Application may be submitted online. Admission notification 4/1. Admission notification on a rolling basis. Must reply by May 1 or within 2 week(s) if notified thereafter. March 1 application date recommended for residence hall students. Admissions deposit refundable until May 1 for fall semester, December 1 for spring semester. Written notice required. **Financial aid:** Priority date 3/15; no closing date. FAFSA required. Applicants notified on a rolling basis starting 4/10; must reply within 8 week(s) of notification.

Academics. Special study options: Accelerated study, cooperative education, cross-registration, distance learning, double major, dual enrollment of high school students, ESL, exchange student, honors, independent study, internships, liberal arts/career combination, semester at sea, study abroad, teacher certification program, Washington semester. Internships and courses in conjunction with Spoleto US (international arts festival); 3-2 engineering program with Case Western Reserve University, Clemson University, University of South Carolina; marine engineering option with University of Michigan. **Credit/placement by examination:** AP, CLEP, IB, institutional tests. 30 credit hours maximum toward bachelor's degree. **Support services:** Learning center, pre-admission summer program, reduced course load, study skills assistance, tutoring, writing center.

Majors. Area/ethnic studies: Latin American. **Biology:** General, biochemistry, marine. **Business:** Accounting, business admin, hospitality admin, international. **Communications:** General. **Computer sciences:** General, computer science, information systems. **Education:** Elementary, physical, special. **English:** English lit. **Foreign languages:** Classics, French, German, Spanish. **Health:** Athletic training, predentistry, premedicine. **History:** General. **Interdisciplinary:** Historic preservation. **Math:** General. **Philosophy/religion:** Philosophy, religion. **Physical sciences:** Chemistry, geology, physics. **Psychology:** General. **Social sciences:** Anthropology, economics, political science, sociology, urban studies. **Visual/performing arts:** Art history/conservation, arts management, dramatic, studio arts.

Most popular majors. Biology 9%, business/marketing 20%, communications/journalism 15%, education 10%, psychology 9%, social sciences 11%, visual/performing arts 9%.

Computing on campus. PC or laptop required. 2,500 workstations in dormitories, library, computer center, student center. Dormitories wired for high-speed internet access and linked to campus network. Commuter students can connect to campus network. Online course registration, helpline, wireless network available.

Student life. Freshman orientation: Mandatory. Preregistration for classes offered. **Housing:** Coed dorms, single-sex dorms, special housing for disabled, fraternity/sorority housing available. $300 fully refundable deposit, deadline 4/1. Restored old Charleston houses used as residence halls, some with kitchen facilities in suite. **Activities:** Bands, choral groups, dance, drama, literary magazine, music ensembles, musical theater, opera, radio station, student government, student newspaper, symphony orchestra, over 100 organizations available.

Athletics. NCAA. **Intercollegiate:** Baseball M, basketball, cross-country, diving, equestrian W, golf, sailing, soccer, softball W, swimming, tennis, track and field W, volleyball W. **Intramural:** Badminton, basketball, equestrian W, fencing, football (tackle), racquetball, rowing (crew), rugby W, soccer, softball, tennis, volleyball, weight lifting. **Team name:** Cougars.

Student services. Adult student services, alcohol/substance abuse counseling, campus ministries, career counseling, student employment services, financial aid counseling, health services, legal services, minority student services, on-campus daycare, personal counseling, placement for graduates, veterans' counselor. **Physically disabled:** Services for visually, speech, hearing impaired.

Contact. E-mail: admissions@cofc.edu
Phone: (843) 953-5670 Fax: (843) 953-6322
Donald Burkard, Associate Vice President Admissions and Enrollment, College of Charleston, 66 George Street, Charleston, SC 29424-0001

Columbia College

Columbia, South Carolina **CB member**
www.columbiacollegesc.edu **CB code: 5117**

- Private 4-year liberal arts college for women affiliated with United Methodist Church
- Residential campus in large city
- 1,093 degree-seeking undergraduates: 21% part-time, 98% women, 43% African American, 1% Asian American, 2% Hispanic American, 2% international
- 379 degree-seeking graduate students
- 84% of applicants admitted
- SAT or ACT (ACT writing optional) required
- 50% graduate within 6 years

General. Founded in 1854. Regionally accredited. **Degrees:** 220 bachelor's awarded; master's offered. **ROTC:** Army. **Location:** 70 miles from Charlotte, North Carolina. **Calendar:** Semester, limited summer session. **Full-time faculty:** 82 total; 76% have terminal degrees, 11% minority, 68% women. **Part-time faculty:** 72 total; 39% have terminal degrees, 10% minority, 57% women. **Class size:** 74% < 20, 26% 20-39. **Special facilities:** Leadership center for women.

Freshman class profile. 767 applied, 642 admitted, 211 enrolled.

Mid 50% test scores			
SAT verbal:	460-600	Return as sophomores:	86%
SAT math:	450-580	Out-of-state:	8%
ACT:	18-23	Live on campus:	81%
End year in good standing:	86%	International:	1%

Basis for selection. School record, test scores, recommendations most important. Audition recommended for dance, music programs; portfolio recommended for art programs; essay, interview recommended for borderline applicants.

High school preparation. 16 units recommended. Recommended units include English 4, mathematics 3, social studies 2, history 1, (laboratory 2), foreign language 2 and academic electives 2. 2.5 units in music, dance, art also recommended.

2005-2006 Annual costs. Tuition/fees: $19,214. Room/board: $5,818. Books/supplies: $800. Personal expenses: $2,750.

2004-2005 Financial aid. Need-based: 240 full-time freshmen applied for aid; 199 were judged to have need; 199 of these received aid. Average need met was 82%. Average scholarship/grant was $8,309; average loan $3,444. 48% of total undergraduate aid awarded as scholarships/grants, 52% as loans/jobs. **Non-need-based:** Awarded to 424 full-time undergraduates, including 186 freshmen. Scholarships awarded for academics, alumni affiliation, art, athletics, leadership, music/drama.

Application procedures. Admission: No deadline. $25 fee, may be waived for applicants with need. Application may be submitted online. Admission notification on a rolling basis beginning on or about 10/1. Must reply by May 1 or within 4 week(s) if notified thereafter. **Financial aid:** Priority date 4/1; no closing date. FAFSA required. Applicants notified on a rolling basis starting 3/15; must reply within 2 week(s) of notification.

Academics. Special study options: Double major, dual enrollment of high school students, exchange student, honors, independent study, internships, student-designed major, study abroad, teacher certification program, Washington semester. **Credit/placement by examination:** AP, CLEP, IB, SAT, ACT, institutional tests. **Support services:** Learning center, reduced course load, remedial instruction, study skills assistance, tutoring, writing center.

Majors. Biology: General. **Business:** Accounting, business admin. **Communications:** General, journalism. **Computer sciences:** General. **Education:** Drama/dance, early childhood, elementary, music, special. **English:** English lit. **Family/consumer sciences:** Family studies. **Foreign languages:** French, Spanish. **Health:** Speech pathology. **History:** General. **Liberal arts:** Arts/sciences. **Math:** General. **Philosophy/religion:** Religion. **Physical sciences:** Chemistry. **Psychology:** General. **Public administration:** Social work. **Social sciences:** General, political science. **Theology:** Religious ed. **Visual/performing arts:** Art, dance, music performance, piano/organ, studio arts, voice/opera.

Most popular majors. Business/marketing 17%, education 15%, family/consumer sciences 6%, psychology 8%, public administration/social services 14%, social sciences 6%, visual/performing arts 10%.

Computing on campus. 165 workstations in dormitories, library, computer center, student center. Dormitories wired for high-speed internet access and linked to campus network. Online course registration, online library, helpline, repair service available.

Student life. Freshman orientation: Available, $150 fee. Preregistration for classes offered. 1 day program in June. 4 day program in August; where Students participate in community service project. **Policies:** All students are required to live on campus during thier first two years unless living with parent or guardian. All residence halls are non-smoking. Chapel requirements are in place for first year, sophomore, and junior level students. Religious observance required. Freshmen permitted cars on campus. **Housing:** Guaranteed on-campus for freshmen. Substance-free housing available. $100 fully refundable deposit, deadline 5/1. **Activities:** Concert band, choral groups, dance, drama, literary magazine, music ensembles, musical theater, student government, student newspaper, Young Republicans, Young Democrats, CC Serves, international student association, Sister to Sista, African-American Student Association, NAACP.

Athletics. NAIA. **Intercollegiate:** Basketball W, soccer W, tennis W, volleyball W. **Team name:** Koalas.

Student services. Adult student services, career counseling, student employment services, health services, personal counseling, placement for graduates.

Contact. E-mail: admissions@colacoll.edu
Phone: (803) 786-3871 Toll-free number: (800) 277-1301
Fax: (803) 786-3674
Ron White, Vice President of Enrollment Management, Columbia College, 1301 Columbia College Drive, Columbia, SC 29203

Columbia International University

Columbia, South Carolina
www.ciu.edu **CB code: 5116**

- Private 4-year university and Bible college affiliated with multidenominational/evangelical churches
- Residential campus in small city
- 540 degree-seeking undergraduates: 8% part-time, 58% women
- 452 degree-seeking graduate students
- 72% of applicants admitted
- SAT or ACT (ACT writing optional), application essay required
- 60% graduate within 6 years

General. Founded in 1923. Regionally accredited; also accredited by ABHE, ATS. **Degrees:** 119 bachelor's, 4 associate awarded; master's, doctoral, first professional offered. **Location:** 75 miles from Charlotte, North Carolina, 225 miles from Atlanta. **Calendar:** Semester, limited summer session. **Full-time faculty:** 20 total. **Part-time faculty:** 25 total. **Class size:** 61% < 20, 26% 20-39, 2% 40-49, 6% 50-99, 4% >100. **Special facilities:** Prayer towers.

Freshman class profile. 236 applied, 171 admitted, 93 enrolled.

Mid 50% test scores			
SAT verbal:	500-620	**Rank in top tenth:**	24%
SAT math:	470-600	**Return as sophomores:**	69%
ACT:	19-26	**Out-of-state:**	62%
Rank in top quarter:	48%	**Live on campus:**	91%
		International:	2%

Basis for selection. School achievement, recommendations, test scores, essay, school and community activities, religious commitment important. Audition required for church music program. **Homeschooled:** Transcripts should include GPA.

High school preparation. Recommended units include English 4, mathematics 2, social studies 2, science 1 and foreign language 2. Thorough background in English grammar and composition required.

2005-2006 Annual costs. Tuition/fees: $13,620. Room/board: $5,542. Books/supplies: $600. Personal expenses: $2,000.

Financial aid. Non-need-based: Scholarships awarded for academics, state residency. **Additional information:** Spouse scholarship program; special short quarter scholarships for missionaries on furlough.

Application procedures. Admission: Priority date 5/1; no deadline. $35 fee, may be waived for applicants with need. Application may be submitted online. Admission notification on a rolling basis. **Financial aid:** Closing date 3/15. FAFSA, institutional form required. Applicants notified on a rolling basis starting 4/1; must reply within 4 week(s) of notification.

Academics. Special study options: Combined bachelor's/graduate degree, cross-registration, distance learning, double major, independent study, internships, liberal arts/career combination, study abroad, teacher certification program. **Credit/placement by examination:** AP, CLEP. **Support services:** Learning center, reduced course load, remedial instruction, study skills assistance, tutoring.

Majors. Area/ethnic studies: Near/Middle Eastern. **Communications:** General. **Education:** Multi-level teacher. **Foreign languages:** Biblical. **Interdisciplinary:** Intercultural. **Liberal arts:** Humanities. **Psychology:** General. **Theology:** Bible, missionary, pastoral counseling, religious ed, sacred music, youth ministry. **Visual/performing arts:** Music performance.

Most popular majors. Communications/journalism 6%, liberal arts 7%, philosophy/religious studies 69%, psychology 7%.

Computing on campus. 46 workstations in library, computer center. Dormitories wired for high-speed internet access and linked to campus network. Online course registration, online library, helpline, repair service available.

Student life. Freshman orientation: Mandatory, $40 fee. Preregistration for classes offered. 3 sessions held prior to start of fall semester; 1 session held 3 days prior to start of spring semester. **Policies:** Mission of growing in Christlikeness, pursuing holiness and righteousness and striving to be biblical in all areas of our lives. Standards of Christian living are outlined in the Biblical Standards Handbook. Religious observance required. Freshmen permitted cars on campus. **Housing:** Guaranteed on-campus for all undergraduates. Single-sex dorms available. $75 deposit. Mobile home park available for married students. **Activities:** Concert band, choral groups, drama, music ensembles, radio station, student government, student newspaper, symphony orchestra, student missions connection, African-American Fellowship, student senate, student union, grad life council.

Athletics. Intramural: Basketball, football (non-tackle), soccer M, softball, table tennis, volleyball.

Student services. Campus ministries, career counseling, student employment services, financial aid counseling, health services, personal counseling, placement for graduates, veterans' counselor. **Physically disabled:** Services for visually, hearing impaired. **Learning disabled:** Comprehensive services available.

Contact. E-mail: yesciu@ciu.edu
Phone: (803) 754-4100 ext. 3024 Toll-free number: (800) 777-2227
Fax: (803) 333-0501
Michelle MacGregor, Associate Director of Admissions, Columbia International University, PO Box 3122, Columbia, SC 29230-3122

Converse College

Spartanburg, South Carolina — **CB member**
www.converse.edu — **CB code: 5121**

- Private 4-year music and liberal arts college for women
- Residential campus in small city
- 769 degree-seeking undergraduates: 16% part-time, 100% women, 14% African American, 1% Asian American, 3% Hispanic American, 4% international
- 481 degree-seeking graduate students
- 84% of applicants admitted
- SAT or ACT with writing, application essay required
- 51% graduate within 6 years; 15% enter graduate study

General. Founded in 1889. Regionally accredited. Men admitted to graduate programs in education and music. **Degrees:** 153 bachelor's awarded; master's offered. **ROTC:** Army. **Location:** 70 miles from Charlotte, North Carolina, 180 miles from Atlanta. **Calendar:** 4-1-4, limited summer session. **Full-time faculty:** 78 total; 88% have terminal degrees, 6% minority, 58% women. **Part-time faculty:** 90 total; 12% have terminal degrees, 6% minority, 64% women. **Class size:** 79% < 20, 21% 20-39. **Special facilities:** Music library.

Freshman class profile. 423 applied, 355 admitted, 185 enrolled.

Mid 50% test scores		**Rank in top tenth:**	28%
SAT verbal:	490-610	**Return as sophomores:**	76%
SAT math:	490-600	**Out-of-state:**	33%
ACT:	19-25	**Live on campus:**	90%
Rank in top quarter:	62%	**International:**	5%

Basis for selection. School record, class rank, test scores, extracurricular activities, school recommendation considered. Interview recommended for all; audition required for music programs.

High school preparation. 20 units required. Required units include English 4, mathematics 3, history 1, science 2 (laboratory 2), foreign language 2 and academic electives 6.

2006-2007 Annual costs. Tuition/fees: $22,234. Room/board: $6,848. Books/supplies: $750. Personal expenses: $1,500.

2005-2006 Financial aid. Need-based: 139 full-time freshmen applied for aid; 118 were judged to have need; 118 of these received aid. Average need met was 89%. Average scholarship/grant was $16,115; average loan $3,440. 73% of total undergraduate aid awarded as scholarships/grants, 27% as loans/jobs. **Non-need-based:** Scholarships awarded for academics, alumni affiliation, art, athletics, leadership, music/drama, ROTC, state residency.

Application procedures. Admission: Priority date 10/1; deadline 3/1 (receipt date). $40 fee, may be waived for applicants with need. Application must be submitted on paper. Admission notification on a rolling basis beginning on or about 10/1. Must reply by May 1 or within 2 week(s) if notified thereafter. **Financial aid:** Priority date 3/15; no closing date. FAFSA required. Applicants notified on a rolling basis starting 3/15; must reply by 5/1 or within 2 week(s) of notification.

Academics. Special study options: Cross-registration, double major, ESL, honors, independent study, internships, liberal arts/career combination, student-designed major, study abroad, teacher certification program. Women's leadership program. **Credit/placement by examination:** AP, CLEP, IB, SAT, ACT, institutional tests. 30 credit hours maximum toward bachelor's degree. **Support services:** Learning center, study skills assistance, tutoring, writing center.

Majors. Biology: General, biochemistry. **Business:** General, accounting, finance, international, organizational behavior. **Computer sciences:** General. **Education:** General, Deaf/hearing impaired, early childhood, elementary, special. **English:** English lit. **Foreign languages:** General, French, Spanish. **Health:** Art therapy. **History:** General. **Math:** General. **Philosophy/religion:** Religion. **Physical sciences:** Chemistry. **Psychology:** General. **Social sciences:** Economics, political science. **Visual/performing arts:** Art history/conservation, dramatic, interior design, music history, music pedagogy, music performance, music theory/composition, studio arts.

Computing on campus. 75 workstations in dormitories, library, computer center. Dormitories wired for high-speed internet access and linked to campus network. Commuter students can connect to campus network. Online library, helpline, repair service available.

Student life. Freshman orientation: Mandatory. Preregistration for classes offered. Orientation is a 3-day program. **Policies:** Strong honor tradition based on mutual trust and responsibility. Freshmen permitted cars on campus. **Housing:** Guaranteed on-campus for all undergraduates. $300 deposit, deadline 5/1. **Activities:** Concert band, choral groups, dance, drama, literary magazine, music ensembles, musical theater, opera, student government, student newspaper, symphony orchestra, Student Christian Association, student activities committee, Young Republicans, community service organizations, honor organizations, student volunteer services.

Athletics. NCAA. **Intercollegiate:** Basketball W, cross-country W, equestrian W, soccer W, tennis W, volleyball W. **Intramural:** Basketball W, soccer W, softball W, swimming W, synchronized swimming W, volleyball W. **Team name:** Allstars.

Student services. Adult student services, alcohol/substance abuse counseling, campus ministries, career counseling, student employment services, financial aid counseling, health services, personal counseling, placement for graduates. **Physically disabled:** Services for hearing impaired.

Contact. E-mail: admissions@converse.edu
Phone: (864) 596-9040 Toll-free number: (800) 766-1125
Fax: (864) 596-9225
Aaron Meis, Dean of Admissions, Converse College, 580 East Main Street, Spartanburg, SC 29302-0006

Erskine College

Due West, South Carolina — **CB member**
www.erskine.edu — **CB code: 5188**

- Private 4-year liberal arts and seminary college affiliated with Associate Reformed Presbyterian Church
- Residential campus in rural community
- 589 degree-seeking undergraduates: 1% part-time, 54% women, 6% African American, 1% Asian American, 1% Hispanic American, 2% international
- 283 degree-seeking graduate students
- 70% of applicants admitted
- SAT or ACT with writing required
- 65% graduate within 6 years

General. Founded in 1839. Regionally accredited. Affiliated with Erskine Theological Seminary. **Degrees:** 145 bachelor's awarded; master's, doctoral, first professional offered. **Location:** 18 miles from Anderson, 45 miles from Greenville. **Calendar:** 4-1-4, limited summer session. **Full-time faculty:** 37 total; 92% have terminal degrees, 8% minority, 43% women. **Part-time faculty:** 35 total. **Class size:** 72% < 20, 27% 20-39, 1% 40-49. **Special facilities:** Arts center.

Freshman class profile. 854 applied, 596 admitted, 181 enrolled.

Mid 50% test scores		**GPA 2.0-2.99:**	9%
SAT verbal:	480-620	**Rank in top quarter:**	58%
SAT math:	510-610	**Rank in top tenth:**	31%
ACT:	21-27	**Return as sophomores:**	77%
GPA 3.50 or higher:	70%	**Out-of-state:**	34%
GPA 3.0-3.49:	21%		

Basis for selection. School achievement record, with special emphasis on advanced placement and honor courses, most important. Consider high school courses twice as important as SAT scores. Test scores, counselor recommendations also important. Essay, interview, class rank, activities considered. Special consideration given to members of supporting church and alumni children. Essay recommended for all; interview required for academically weak; audition required for music. **Homeschooled:** High school diploma, GED, or college preparatory diploma certification required. Applicants must also submit portfolio of all high school work and 2 recommendations.

High school preparation. 14 units required. Required and recommended units include English 4, mathematics 2-4, social studies 2, science 3 (laboratory 2) and foreign language 2. Biology, chemistry, physics, history highly recommended. Preference given to students with more than minimum preparation.

2005-2006 Annual costs. Tuition/fees: $19,042. Room/board: $6,426. Books/supplies: $900.

2004-2005 Financial aid. Need-based: 170 full-time freshmen applied for aid; 143 were judged to have need; 143 of these received aid. Average need met was 84%. Average scholarship/grant was $8,501; average loan

$2,150. 69% of total undergraduate aid awarded as scholarships/grants, 31% as loans/jobs. **Non-need-based:** Awarded to 546 full-time undergraduates, including 211 freshmen. Scholarships awarded for academics, alumni affiliation, art, athletics, leadership, minority status, music/drama, religious affiliation, state residency. **Additional information:** Filing deadline 5/1 for institutional form, 6/30 for state form.

Application procedures. Admission: No deadline. $25 fee, may be waived for applicants with need. Application may be submitted online. Admission notification on a rolling basis. **Financial aid:** Priority date 4/1; no closing date. FAFSA, institutional form required. Applicants notified on a rolling basis starting 12/15; must reply within 2 week(s) of notification.

Academics. Special study options: Double major, independent study, internships, liberal arts/career combination, study abroad, teacher certification program. **Credit/placement by examination:** AP, CLEP, IB, institutional tests. 18 credit hours maximum toward bachelor's degree. **Support services:** Pre-admission summer program, tutoring.

Majors. Area/ethnic studies: American. **Biology:** General. **Business:** Business admin. **Education:** Early childhood, elementary, music, physical, secondary, social studies, special. **Foreign languages:** French, Spanish. **Health:** Athletic training, clinical lab technology. **History:** General. **Math:** General. **Parks/recreation:** General, health/fitness, sports admin. **Philosophy/religion:** Philosophy, religion. **Physical sciences:** Chemistry, physics. **Psychology:** General. **Theology:** Religious ed. **Visual/performing arts:** Art.

Most popular majors. Biology 10%, business/marketing 23%, education 14%, history 8%, philosophy/religious studies 6%, physical sciences 7%, psychology 9%.

Computing on campus. Dormitories wired for high-speed internet access and linked to campus network. Commuter students can connect to campus network. Helpline, repair service, student web hosting, wireless network available.

Student life. Freshman orientation: Mandatory. Preregistration for classes offered. Week-long orientation in August held 1 week prior to first day of classes. **Policies:** Religious observance required. Freshmen permitted cars on campus. **Housing:** Guaranteed on-campus for all undergraduates. Single-sex dorms, substance-free housing available. $300 deposit. **Activities:** Bands, choral groups, dance, drama, literary magazine, music ensembles, musical theater, radio station, student government, student newspaper, national honor societies for academics, drama, and leadership, association of minority students, denominational organizations, judicial council, Fellowship of Christian Athletes, Habitat for Humanity, council for exceptional children.

Athletics. NCAA. **Intercollegiate:** Baseball M, basketball, cross-country, soccer, softball W, tennis. **Intramural:** Basketball, football (non-tackle) W, football (tackle) M, racquetball, soccer, softball, tennis, volleyball. **Team name:** Flying Fleet.

Student services. Adult student services, campus ministries, career counseling, financial aid counseling, health services, personal counseling, placement for graduates.

Contact. E-mail: admissions@erskine.edu
Phone: (864) 379-8838 Toll-free number: (800) 241-8721
Fax: (864) 379-2167
Bart Walker, Director of Admissions, Erskine College, PO Box 338, Due West, SC 29639-0176

Francis Marion University

Florence, South Carolina — CB member
www.fmarion.edu — CB code: 5442

- Public 4-year university and liberal arts college
- Commuter campus in small city
- 3,182 degree-seeking undergraduates: 5% part-time, 64% women, 42% African American, 1% Asian American, 1% Hispanic American, 1% international
- 255 degree-seeking graduate students
- 71% of applicants admitted
- SAT or ACT (ACT writing optional) required
- 37% graduate within 6 years

General. Founded in 1970. Regionally accredited. **Degrees:** 493 bachelor's awarded; master's offered. **Location:** 7 miles from downtown, 80 miles from Columbia. **Calendar:** Semester, limited summer session. **Full-time faculty:** 176 total; 81% have terminal degrees, 6% minority, 36% women. **Part-time faculty:** 105 total; 25% have terminal degrees, 10% minority, 55% women. **Class size:** 40% < 20, 53% 20-39, 3% 40-49, 4% 50-99. **Special facilities:** Planetarium, observatory, arboretum, art museum.

Freshman class profile. 2,524 applied, 1,804 admitted, 803 enrolled.

Mid 50% test scores		**Rank in top tenth:**	14%
SAT verbal:	440-540	**End year in good standing:**	63%
SAT math:	440-530	**Return as sophomores:**	65%
ACT:	18-21	**Out-of-state:**	4%
GPA 3.50 or higher:	44%	**Live on campus:**	72%
GPA 3.0-3.49:	29%	**Fraternities:**	3%
GPA 2.0-2.99:	27%	**Sororities:**	3%
Rank in top quarter:	39%		

Basis for selection. Combination of standardized test scores and high school GPA important. Borderline cases may be admitted provisionally. Proficiency in math and English required. **Learning Disabled:** Accommodations provided with documentation.

High school preparation. College-preparatory program required. 20 units required. Required and recommended units include English 4, mathematics 3-4, social studies 3, history 1, science 3 (laboratory 3), foreign language 2 and academic electives 4. Social studies should include 1 history; 2 units of same foreign language required.

2005-2006 Annual costs. Tuition/fees: $5,984; $11,833 out-of-state. Room/board: $5,130.

2004-2005 Financial aid. Need-based: 611 full-time freshmen applied for aid; 519 were judged to have need; 458 of these received aid. 40% of total undergraduate aid awarded as scholarships/grants, 60% as loans/jobs. **Non-need-based:** Awarded to 703 full-time undergraduates, including 322 freshmen. Scholarships awarded for academics, music/drama.

Application procedures. Admission: No deadline. $30 fee, may be waived for applicants with need. Application must be submitted on paper. Admission notification on a rolling basis beginning on or about 9/1. April 1 reply date for dormitory students. **Financial aid:** Priority date 3/1; no closing date. FAFSA, institutional form required. Applicants notified on a rolling basis starting 4/15.

Academics. Special study options: Accelerated study, cross-registration, distance learning, double major, dual enrollment of high school students, honors, independent study, internships, study abroad, teacher certification program, Washington semester. **Credit/placement by examination:** AP, CLEP, institutional tests. **Support services:** Reduced course load, tutoring, writing center.

Majors. Biology: General. **Business:** Accounting, business admin, finance, management information systems, managerial economics, marketing. **Communications:** Media studies. **Computer sciences:** General. **Education:** Art, early childhood, elementary, English, history, mathematics, secondary, social studies. **English:** English lit. **Foreign languages:** French, German, Spanish. **Health:** Nursing (RN). **History:** General. **Liberal arts:** Arts/sciences. **Math:** General. **Physical sciences:** Chemistry, physics. **Psychology:** General. **Social sciences:** Economics, international relations, political science, sociology. **Visual/performing arts:** Art, dramatic.

Computing on campus. 551 workstations in dormitories, library, computer center. Dormitories wired for high-speed internet access. Online course registration, online library available.

Student life. Freshman orientation: Mandatory, $46 fee. Preregistration for classes offered. Held in summer for fall term. Session in January for spring. **Policies:** Freshmen permitted cars on campus. **Housing:** Single-sex dorms, special housing for disabled, apartments, substance-free housing available. $250 partly refundable deposit. **Activities:** Jazz band, choral groups, drama, literary magazine, music ensembles, student government, student newspaper, TV station, Baptist Collegiate Ministries, College Democrats, Young Republicans, NAACP, Rotoract, minority student association, psychology club, education club, Campus Crusade for Christ.

Athletics. NCAA. **Intercollegiate:** Baseball M, basketball, cross-country, golf M, soccer, softball W, tennis, track and field, volleyball W. **Intramural:** Basketball, bowling, football (non-tackle), golf, racquetball, soccer, softball, table tennis, tennis, track and field, volleyball. **Team name:** Patriots.

Student services. Adult student services, campus ministries, career counseling, student employment services, health services, minority student services, personal counseling, placement for graduates, veterans' counselor. **Physically disabled:** Services for visually, speech, hearing impaired.

Contact. E-mail: admission@fmarion.edu
Phone: (843) 661-1231 Toll-free number: (800) 368-7551
Fax: (843) 661-4635
Cynthia Harding, Director of Admissions, Francis Marion University, PO Box 100547, Florence, SC 29501-0547

Four-Year Colleges

Furman University

Greenville, South Carolina **CB member**
www.furman.edu **CB code: 5222**

- Private 4-year liberal arts college
- Residential campus in small city
- 2,774 degree-seeking undergraduates: 3% part-time, 56% women, 6% African American, 2% Asian American, 1% Hispanic American, 1% international
- 198 degree-seeking graduate students
- 53% of applicants admitted
- SAT or ACT with writing, application essay required
- 84% graduate within 6 years; 41% enter graduate study

General. Founded in 1826. Regionally accredited. Abundant internship and collaborative research opportunities. **Degrees:** 661 bachelor's awarded; master's offered. **ROTC:** Army. **Location:** 100 miles from Charlotte, North Carolina, 140 miles from Atlanta. **Calendar:** 3-2-3 (12 weeks-8 weeks-12 weeks). Extensive summer session. **Full-time faculty:** 220 total; 97% have terminal degrees, 7% minority, 30% women. **Part-time faculty:** 52 total; 36% have terminal degrees, 8% minority, 67% women. **Class size:** 53% < 20, 46% 20-39, less than 1% 40-49, less than 1% 50-99. **Special facilities:** Observatory, center for engaged learning, center for international education, center for collaborative learning and communication.

Freshman class profile. 4,007 applied, 2,119 admitted, 689 enrolled.

Mid 50% test scores		Rank in top tenth:	64%
SAT verbal:	600-700	End year in good standing:	99%
SAT math:	600-690	Return as sophomores:	93%
ACT:	25-30	Out-of-state:	72%
GPA 3.50 or higher:	73%	Live on campus:	98%
GPA 3.0-3.49:	21%	International:	2%
GPA 2.0-2.99:	6%	Fraternities:	35%
Rank in top quarter:	88%	Sororities:	40%

Basis for selection. High school record including courses taken and grades most important, then SAT scores (particularly verbal) or ACT scores. Special talents such as fine arts, athletic ability, writing ability considered. Special consideration given to children of alumni and minorities. Audition required for music scholarship applicants; portfolio required for art scholarship applicants. **Homeschooled:** SAT Subject Tests including math, subject of student's choice required. Interview strongly recommended.

High school preparation. 14 units required; 18 recommended. Required and recommended units include English 4, mathematics 3-4, social studies 3-4, science 2-3 (laboratory 2-3) and foreign language 2-3.

2006-2007 Annual costs. Tuition/fees: $28,840. Room/board: $7,552. Books/supplies: $750. Personal expenses: $712.

2005-2006 Financial aid. Need-based: 406 full-time freshmen applied for aid; 289 were judged to have need; 289 of these received aid. Average need met was 91%. Average scholarship/grant was $21,735; average loan $1,705. 69% of total undergraduate aid awarded as scholarships/grants, 31% as loans/jobs. **Non-need-based:** Awarded to 1,922 full-time undergraduates, including 515 freshmen. Scholarships awarded for academics, alumni affiliation, art, athletics, leadership, minority status, music/drama, religious affiliation, ROTC, state residency. **Additional information:** 5-point comprehensive education financing plan includes financial aid packaging, money management counseling, debt management counseling, outside scholarship coordination, and summer job-match program.

Application procedures. Admission: Closing date 1/15 (postmark date). $40 fee, may be waived for applicants with need. Application may be submitted online. Admission notification 3/15. Must reply by 5/1. **Financial aid:** Closing date 1/15. FAFSA, institutional form required. Applicants notified by 3/15; must reply by 5/1.

Academics. Strong emphasis on research, internships and other opportunities for engaged, hands-on learning. **Special study options:** Combined bachelor's/graduate degree, double major, independent study, internships, liberal arts/career combination, student-designed major, study abroad, teacher certification program, United Nations semester, Washington semester. Undergraduate research program, 3-2 engineering with Auburn University, Clemson University, Georgia Institute of Technology, North Carolina State, Washington University in St. Louis, 3-2 forestry program with Duke University, 3-1 dentistry and medicine programs with any accredited medical or dental school, 3-2 nursing, pharmacy, physical therapy, and physician assistant programs with any accredited medical school. **Credit/placement by examination:** AP, CLEP, IB, institutional tests. **Support services:** Learning center, reduced course load, study skills assistance, tutoring, writing center.

Majors. Area/ethnic studies: Asian. **Biology:** General. **Business:** Accounting, business admin, management information systems. **Communications:** General. **Computer sciences:** Computer science. **Conservation:** General, environmental studies. **Education:** General, music. **Foreign languages:** Ancient Greek, French, German, Latin, Spanish. **Health:** Predentistry, premedicine, prenursing, prepharmacy, preveterinary. **History:** General. **Interdisciplinary:** Math/computer science. **Legal studies:** Prelaw. **Math:** General. **Parks/recreation:** Health/fitness. **Philosophy/religion:** Philosophy, religion. **Physical sciences:** Chemistry, geology, physics. **Psychology:** General. **Social sciences:** Economics, political science, sociology, urban studies. **Visual/performing arts:** Art, art history/conservation, dramatic, music history, music performance, music theory/composition, piano/organ, studio arts, voice/opera.

Most popular majors. Biology 8%, business/marketing 10%, communications/journalism 7%, English 6%, foreign language 8%, history 9%, philosophy/religious studies 6%, social sciences 16%, visual/performing arts 10%.

Computing on campus. 340 workstations in library, computer center, student center. Dormitories wired for high-speed internet access and linked to campus network. Commuter students can connect to campus network. Online course registration, helpline, student web hosting, wireless network available.

Student life. Freshman orientation: Mandatory. 5-day orientation session, including academic placement testing, advisory services, entertainment, and recreation. **Policies:** Freshmen permitted cars on campus. **Housing:** Guaranteed on-campus for freshmen. Coed dorms, single-sex dorms, apartments available. $400 nonrefundable deposit, deadline 5/1. Language house for students focusing on specific language. Lakeside cottages and an environmentally equipped eco-cottage also available. **Activities:** Bands, choral groups, dance, drama, literary magazine, music ensembles, musical theater, opera, radio station, student government, student newspaper, symphony orchestra, TV station, Collegiate Educational Service Corps, Young Democrats, College Republicans, Student League for Black Culture, international students association, Fellowship of Christian Athletes, Council for Exceptional Children, Habitat for Humanity, arts students league, Amnesty International.

Athletics. NCAA. **Intercollegiate:** Baseball M, basketball, cheerleading, cross-country, football (tackle) M, golf, soccer, softball W, tennis, track and field, volleyball W. **Intramural:** Basketball, bowling, cross-country, football (non-tackle), golf, handball, racquetball, rowing (crew), soccer, softball, swimming, tennis, track and field, volleyball. **Team name:** Paladins.

Student services. Adult student services, alcohol/substance abuse counseling, campus ministries, career counseling, student employment services, financial aid counseling, health services, minority student services, personal counseling, placement for graduates, veterans' counselor. **Physically disabled:** Services for visually, hearing impaired.

Contact. E-mail: admissions@furman.edu
Phone: (864) 294-2034 Fax: (864) 294-2018
David O'Cain, Director of Admissions, Furman University, 3300 Poinsett Highway, Greenville, SC 29613

ITT Technical Institute: Greenville

Greenville, South Carolina
www.itt-tech.edu **CB code: 2708**

- For-profit 4-year technical college
- Commuter campus in large city

General. Accredited by ACICS. **Calendar:** Quarter.

Annual costs/financial aid. Tuition varies by program, $260-$368 per credit hour.

Contact. Phone: (864) 288-0777
Director of Recruitment, 6 Independence Pointe, Greenville, SC 29615

Lander University

Greenwood, South Carolina **CB member**
www.lander.edu **CB code: 5363**

- Public 4-year liberal arts and teachers college
- Residential campus in large town
- 2,552 degree-seeking undergraduates: 7% part-time, 66% women, 24% African American, 1% Hispanic American, 1% Native American, 2% international

- 35 degree-seeking graduate students
- 48% graduate within 6 years

General. Founded in 1872. Regionally accredited. **Degrees:** 466 bachelor's awarded; master's offered. **ROTC:** Army. **Location:** 55 miles from Greenville, 75 miles from Columbia. **Calendar:** Semester, limited summer session. **Full-time faculty:** 123 total; 68% have terminal degrees, 10% minority, 46% women. **Part-time faculty:** 70 total; 9% minority, 61% women. **Class size:** 37% < 20, 53% 20-39, 9% 40-49, 1% 50-99.

Freshman class profile. 1,851 applied, 1,345 admitted, 578 enrolled.

Mid 50% test scores			
SAT verbal:	420-530	Rank in top quarter:	33%
SAT math:	440-540	Rank in top tenth:	2%
ACT:	17-21	Return as sophomores:	63%
GPA 3.50 or higher:	44%	Out-of-state:	4%
GPA 3.0-3.49:	33%	Live on campus:	80%
GPA 2.0-2.99:	23%	International:	1%

Basis for selection. Open admission, but selective for some programs. Test scores, class rank, curriculum, and recommendations important. Out-of-state students must rank in top half of high school class. Selectivity of students may be based on transcripts and GED score. Audition required for music programs; interview recommended for art, music programs; portfolio recommended for art programs.

High school preparation. 20 units recommended. Recommended units include English 4, mathematics 3, social studies 2, history 1, science 3 (laboratory 3), foreign language 2 and academic electives 4. One unit physical education or ROTC also recommended.

2005-2006 Annual costs. Tuition/fees: $7,188; $13,528 out-of-state. Room/board: $5,332. Books/supplies: $840. Personal expenses: $2,520.

2004-2005 Financial aid. **Need-based:** 536 full-time freshmen applied for aid; 423 were judged to have need; 421 of these received aid. Average need met was 77%. Average scholarship/grant was $2,000; average loan $2,000. 66% of total undergraduate aid awarded as scholarships/grants, 34% as loans/jobs. **Non-need-based:** Awarded to 802 full-time undergraduates, including 357 freshmen. Scholarships awarded for academics, art, athletics, leadership, music/drama.

Application procedures. **Admission:** No deadline. $35 fee, may be waived for applicants with need. Application may be submitted online. Admission notification on a rolling basis. **Financial aid:** Priority date 4/15; no closing date. FAFSA required. Applicants notified on a rolling basis starting 4/15; must reply within 4 week(s) of notification.

Academics. **Special study options:** Cooperative education, distance learning, double major, dual enrollment of high school students, honors, independent study, internships, liberal arts/career combination, student-designed major, study abroad, teacher certification program. Dual degree in engineering with Clemson University; nursing (RN to BSN completion) offered online; MBA and M.Ed. in counseling/school administration from Clemson University offered on campus. **Credit/placement by examination:** AP, CLEP, IB, institutional tests. 30 credit hours maximum toward bachelor's degree. **Support services:** Learning center, pre-admission summer program, reduced course load, remedial instruction, study skills assistance, tutoring, writing center.

Majors. **Biology:** General. **Business:** Business admin. **Computer sciences:** General. **Conservation:** Environmental science. **Education:** Early childhood, elementary, music, physical, secondary, special. **English:** English lit. **Foreign languages:** Spanish. **Health:** Athletic training, nursing (RN). **History:** General. **Liberal arts:** Arts/sciences, humanities. **Math:** General. **Parks/recreation:** Exercise sciences. **Physical sciences:** Chemistry. **Psychology:** General. **Social sciences:** Political science, sociology. **Visual/performing arts:** Art.

Most popular majors. Business/marketing 24%, education 17%, health sciences 10%, psychology 7%, social sciences 12%, visual/performing arts 6%.

Computing on campus. PC or laptop required. 233 workstations in library, computer center. Dormitories linked to campus network. Commuter students can connect to campus network. Online course registration, online library, helpline, repair service, wireless network available.

Student life. **Freshman orientation:** Mandatory. Preregistration for classes offered. **Policies:** Freshmen permitted cars on campus. **Housing:** Coed dorms, single-sex dorms available. $75 deposit, deadline 4/15. **Activities:** Bands, choral groups, dance, drama, literary magazine, music ensembles, student government, student newspaper, Baptist Student Union, Bible study, Young Democrats, College Republicans, Minorities on the Move, Blue Key and Alpha Kappa Gamma (honor societies).

Athletics. NCAA. **Intercollegiate:** Baseball M, basketball, cross-country W, golf M, soccer, softball W, tennis, volleyball W. **Intramural:** Basketball, football (non-tackle), golf, soccer, softball, volleyball. **Team name:** Bearcats.

Student services. Adult student services, alcohol/substance abuse counseling, career counseling, student employment services, health services, minority student services, personal counseling, placement for graduates, veterans' counselor. **Physically disabled:** Services for visually, speech, hearing impaired.

Contact. E-mail: admissions@lander.edu
Phone: (864) 388-8307 Fax: (864) 388-8125
Jonathan Reece, Director of Admissions, Lander University, Stanley Avenue, Greenwood, SC 29649-2099

Limestone College

Gaffney, South Carolina
www.limestone.edu **CB code: 5366**

- Private 4-year liberal arts college
- Residential campus in large town
- 676 degree-seeking undergraduates: 2% part-time, 46% women, 18% African American, 2% Hispanic American, 1% Native American, 3% international
- 58% of applicants admitted
- SAT or ACT (ACT writing optional) required
- 43% graduate within 6 years

General. Founded in 1845. Regionally accredited. Evening classes at 10 off-campus sites throughout the state. **Degrees:** 108 bachelor's awarded. **ROTC:** Army. **Location:** 50 miles from Greenville, 50 miles from Charlotte, North Carolina. **Calendar:** Semester, limited summer session. **Full-time faculty:** 55 total; 62% have terminal degrees, 2% minority, 38% women. **Part-time faculty:** 32 total; 12% have terminal degrees, 25% women. **Class size:** 71% < 20, 27% 20-39, 1% 40-49. **Special facilities:** Computer graphics art lab.

Freshman class profile. 884 applied, 512 admitted, 172 enrolled.

Mid 50% test scores			
SAT verbal:	450-520	Rank in top tenth:	7%
SAT math:	460-540	End year in good standing:	84%
ACT:	17-21	Return as sophomores:	67%
GPA 3.50 or higher:	20%	Out-of-state:	19%
GPA 3.0-3.49:	36%	Live on campus:	79%
GPA 2.0-2.99:	42%	International:	8%
Rank in top quarter:	20%	Sororities:	1%

Basis for selection. SAT combined score of 880 (exclusive of Writing) and GPA of 2.0. Admissions committee must approve all applicants who do not meet these standards. SAT test requirement waived for freshmen who are 21 years of age or older or in military service. Interview required for lower-ranking applicants; recommended for all others. Audition required of first-time, first-year freshmen for music, music education, theatre programs; portfolio required for art education, studio art programs; essay required for honors program. **Learning Disabled:** Documentation required to be eligible for the Program for Alternative Learning Styles (PALS).

High school preparation. College-preparatory program recommended. 12 units required. Required units include English 4, mathematics 3, social studies 3, science 2 (laboratory 2).

2006-2007 Annual costs. Tuition/fees: $15,000. Room/board: $6,000. Books/supplies: $1,660. Personal expenses: $1,640.

2004-2005 Financial aid. **Need-based:** 180 full-time freshmen applied for aid; 151 were judged to have need; 151 of these received aid. Average need met was 66%. Average scholarship/grant was $7,644; average loan $2,372. 52% of total undergraduate aid awarded as scholarships/grants, 48% as loans/jobs. **Non-need-based:** Awarded to 289 full-time undergraduates, including 106 freshmen. Scholarships awarded for academics, alumni affiliation, art, athletics, job skills, leadership, music/drama, religious affiliation, ROTC, state residency.

Application procedures. **Admission:** Priority date 8/1; deadline 8/26 (receipt date). $25 fee, may be waived for applicants with need. Application may be submitted online. Admission notification on a rolling basis beginning on or about 6/1. **Financial aid:** Priority date 2/1; no closing date. FAFSA required. Applicants notified on a rolling basis starting 1/15; must reply within 3 week(s) of notification.

Academics. Special study options: Accelerated study, distance learning, double major, honors, independent study, internships, liberal arts/career combination, student-designed major, teacher certification program. **Credit/placement by examination:** AP, CLEP, institutional tests. 15 credit hours maximum toward associate degree, 30 toward bachelor's. **Support services:** Learning center, reduced course load, remedial instruction, study skills assistance, tutoring, writing center.

Majors. Biology: General. **Business:** Accounting, business admin, e-commerce, managerial economics, marketing, training/development. **Computer sciences:** Computer science, database management, programming, security, system admin, web page design, webmaster. **Education:** General, art, biology, elementary, English, mathematics, music, physical, secondary, social studies. **English:** English lit. **Health:** Athletic training, predentistry, premedicine, prenursing, prepharmacy, preveterinary. **History:** General. **Legal studies:** Prelaw. **Liberal arts:** Arts/sciences. **Math:** General. **Parks/recreation:** Exercise sciences, health/fitness, sports admin. **Physical sciences:** Chemistry. **Protective services:** Law enforcement admin. **Psychology:** General. **Public administration:** Social work. **Social sciences:** Economics. **Visual/performing arts:** Dramatic, graphic design, jazz, studio arts.

Most popular majors. Business/marketing 21%, education 38%, parks/recreation 6%, psychology 6%.

Computing on campus. 79 workstations in library, computer center, student center. Dormitories wired for high-speed internet access and linked to campus network. Commuter students can connect to campus network. Online library, helpline, repair service, wireless network available.

Student life. Freshman orientation: Mandatory. Preregistration for classes offered. Program held the 5 days prior to start of semester. **Policies:** Alcohol-free campus. Students must live on campus unless age 21, or have attained 90 credit hours, or live with immediate family within 50 miles of campus. Freshmen permitted cars on campus. **Housing:** Guaranteed on-campus for freshmen. Single-sex dorms, substance-free housing available. $50 fully refundable deposit. Off-campus apartments available. **Activities:** Bands, choral groups, drama, literary magazine, music ensembles, musical theater, student government, Fellowship of Christian Athletes, student alumni leadership council, student organization of social workers, students in free enterprise, Joyful Saints Gospel Choir, Christian Education and Leadership Program, Kappa Delta Kappa, student government association, Chi Alpha Sigma, outdoor recreation and education club.

Athletics. NCAA. **Intercollegiate:** Baseball M, basketball, cross-country, golf, lacrosse, soccer, softball W, swimming, tennis, volleyball W, wrestling M. **Intramural:** Basketball, bowling, softball, table tennis, tennis, volleyball. **Team name:** Saints.

Student services. Adult student services, alcohol/substance abuse counseling, campus ministries, career counseling, student employment services, financial aid counseling, health services, personal counseling, placement for graduates, veterans' counselor. **Physically disabled:** Services for visually, hearing impaired. **Learning disabled:** Comprehensive services available.

Contact. E-mail: cphenicie@limestone.edu
Phone: (864) 488-4554 Toll-free number: (800) 795-7151 ext. 4554
Fax: (864) 487-8706
Chris Phenicie, Vice President for Enrollment Services, Limestone College, 1115 College Drive, Gaffney, SC 29340-3799

Medical University of South Carolina

Charleston, South Carolina
www.musc.edu **CB code: 5407**

- Public upper-division health science and nursing college
- Commuter campus in large city
- 49% of applicants admitted
- Test scores, application essay required

General. Founded in 1824. Regionally accredited. Upper division/graduate academic health center consisting of six colleges: dental medicine, graduate studies, health professions, medicine, nursing, and pharmacy. College offers only 3 undergraduate degrees. **Degrees:** 188 bachelor's awarded; master's, doctoral, first professional offered. **Location:** 350 miles from Atlanta. **Calendar:** Semester, limited summer session. **Full-time faculty:** 338 total; 94% have terminal degrees, 10% minority, 39% women. **Part-time faculty:** 111 total; 58% have terminal degrees, 4% minority, 60% women. **Class size:** 86% < 20, 14% 20-39. **Special facilities:** Historical medical library, dental museum.

Student profile. 288 degree-seeking undergraduates, 2,183 graduate students. 523 applied as first time-transfer students, 256 admitted, 226 enrolled. 100% entered as juniors. 37% transferred from two-year, 63% transferred from four-year institutions.

Women:	85%	**International:**	1%
African American:	11%	**Part-time:**	29%
Asian American:	2%	**Out-of-state:**	22%
Hispanic American:	3%	**25 or older:**	60%

Basis for selection. College transcript, application essay, standardized test scores required. Admissions policies and dates are established by each of the six MUSC colleges due to varied nature of their academic programs. Transfer accepted as juniors.

2005-2006 Annual costs. Tuition/fees: $8,568; $23,344 out-of-state. Undergraduate costs vary by program, by year, and by college.

Financial aid. Need-based: Average need met was 51%. 15% of total undergraduate aid awarded as scholarships/grants, 85% as loans/jobs. **Non-need-based:** Scholarships awarded for academics, alumni affiliation, minority status, state residency.

Application procedures. Admission: $75 fee, may be waived for applicants with need. Application must be submitted online. **Financial aid:** FAFSA, institutional form required.

Academics. Offers a limited undergraduate degree program (3 majors). **Special study options:** Cross-registration, distance learning. **Credit/placement by examination:** AP, CLEP.

Majors. Health: Health care admin, nursing (RN), perfusion technology.

Computing on campus. 220 workstations in library. Commuter students can connect to campus network. Online library, helpline available.

Student life. Activities: Film society, literary magazine, student government, Christian Medical Society, campus crusade, student union, community help initiative, South Carolina health initiative, minority student union, Student National Medical Association.

Athletics. Intramural: Basketball, softball, volleyball.

Student services. Career counseling, financial aid counseling, health services, minority student services, personal counseling, veterans' counselor.

Contact. E-mail: oes-web@musc.edu
Phone: (843) 792-3281 Fax: (843) 792-6615
George Ohlandt, Director of Admissions, Medical University of South Carolina, 41 Bee Street, Charleston, SC 29425

Morris College

Sumter, South Carolina **CB member**
www.morris.edu **CB code: 5418**

- Private 4-year liberal arts college affiliated with Baptist faith
- Residential campus in large town
- 863 degree-seeking undergraduates: 2% part-time, 64% women, 100% African American
- 85% of applicants admitted
- SAT or ACT with writing required
- 40% graduate within 6 years; 14% enter graduate study

General. Founded in 1908. Regionally accredited. Affiliated with Baptist Educational and Missionary Convention of South Carolina. **Degrees:** 163 bachelor's awarded. **ROTC:** Army. **Location:** 45 miles from Columbia, 110 miles from Charlotte, North Carolina. **Calendar:** Semester, limited summer session. **Full-time faculty:** 47 total; 64% have terminal degrees, 55% minority, 53% women. **Part-time faculty:** 12 total; 33% have terminal degrees, 92% minority, 33% women. **Class size:** 60% < 20, 39% 20-39, 1% 40-49. **Special facilities:** Radio station/training lab, electronic learning lab, television production studio.

Freshman class profile. 896 applied, 760 admitted, 209 enrolled.

Mid 50% test scores		**GPA 2.0-2.99:**	61%
SAT verbal:	310-400	**Rank in top quarter:**	9%
SAT math:	310-410	**End year in good standing:**	64%
ACT:	13-16	**Return as sophomores:**	55%
GPA 3.50 or higher:	3%	**Out-of-state:**	20%
GPA 3.0-3.49:	18%	**Live on campus:**	92%

Basis for selection. High school record most important. Students with less than 2.0 high school GPA may be admitted on probation, limited to

13-credit-hour loads, and required to participate in tutorial and study sessions. Interview recommended.

High school preparation. 24 units required. Required and recommended units include English 4, mathematics 4, social studies 2, history 1, science 3, foreign language 1-2 and academic electives 7. 1 physical education or ROTC, 1 computer science.

2005-2006 Annual costs. Tuition/fees: $8,163. Room/board: $3,836. Books/supplies: $1,400. Personal expenses: $2,500.

2005-2006 Financial aid. All financial aid based on need. 209 full-time freshmen applied for aid; 203 were judged to have need; 203 of these received aid. Average need met was 86%. Average scholarship/grant was $8,150; average loan $2,625. 52% of total undergraduate aid awarded as scholarships/grants, 48% as loans/jobs. **Additional information:** Students are encouraged to complete FAFSA on the web.

Application procedures. Admission: Priority date 7/1; no deadline. $20 fee, may be waived for applicants with need. Application must be submitted on paper. Admission notification on a rolling basis beginning on or about 12/5. **Financial aid:** Priority date 3/30; no closing date. FAFSA, institutional form required. Applicants notified on a rolling basis starting 6/1; must reply within 2 week(s) of notification.

Academics. Special study options: Accelerated study, combined bachelor's/graduate degree, cooperative education, double major, honors, internships, liberal arts/career combination, teacher certification program. Adult Degree Program in Organizational Management offered through evening courses; students must be at least 25 years old and have earned 60 credit hours. **Credit/placement by examination:** AP, CLEP. 30 credit hours maximum toward bachelor's degree. **Support services:** Learning center, reduced course load, remedial instruction, study skills assistance, tutoring, writing center.

Majors. Biology: General. **Business:** Business admin, operations. **Communications:** Broadcast journalism, journalism. **Education:** Biology, early childhood, elementary, English, mathematics, social studies. **English:** English lit. **Health:** Community health services. **History:** General. **Liberal arts:** Arts/sciences. **Math:** General. **Parks/recreation:** Facilities management. **Protective services:** Law enforcement admin. **Social sciences:** Political science, sociology. **Theology:** Religious ed, theology.

Most popular majors. Business/marketing 26%, communications/journalism 7%, health sciences 18%, parks/recreation 9%, security/protective services 10%, social sciences 9%.

Computing on campus. 210 workstations in dormitories, library, computer center. Dormitories wired for high-speed internet access and linked to campus network.

Student life. Freshman orientation: Mandatory. Preregistration for classes offered. Held during first week of fall and spring semesters. **Policies:** College promotes drug-free, alcohol-free campus. Cigarette smoking prohibited in all buildings. **Housing:** Guaranteed on-campus for freshmen. Single-sex dorms, substance-free housing available. $100 nonrefundable deposit, deadline 8/1. **Activities:** Choral groups, dance, drama, literary magazine, radio station, student government, student newspaper, Baptist Student Union, NAACP, Alpha Phi Omega, social science club, Durham Ministerial Union.

Athletics. NAIA. **Intercollegiate:** Baseball M, basketball, cheerleading, cross-country, golf M, softball W, tennis, track and field, volleyball W. **Intramural:** Basketball, football (non-tackle), golf M, table tennis, tennis, volleyball. **Team name:** Hornets.

Student services. Adult student services, alcohol/substance abuse counseling, career counseling, student employment services, financial aid counseling, health services, personal counseling, placement for graduates, veterans' counselor.

Contact. E-mail: gscriven@morris.edu
Phone: (803) 934-3225 Toll-free number: (866) 853-1345
Fax: (803) 773-8241
Deborah Calhoun, Director of Admission and Records, Morris College, 100 West College Street, Sumter, SC 29150-3599

Newberry College

Newberry, South Carolina — **CB member**
www.newberry.edu — **CB code: 5493**

- Private 4-year liberal arts college affiliated with Evangelical Lutheran Church in America
- Residential campus in small city
- 841 degree-seeking undergraduates
- 59% of applicants admitted
- SAT or ACT required
- 51% graduate within 6 years

General. Founded in 1856. Regionally accredited. **Degrees:** 32 bachelor's awarded. **ROTC:** Army. **Location:** 40 miles from Columbia. **Calendar:** Semester, limited summer session. **Full-time faculty:** 51 total; 69% have terminal degrees, 8% minority, 43% women. **Part-time faculty:** 36 total; 28% have terminal degrees, 6% minority, 33% women. **Class size:** 60% < 20, 39% 20-39, 1% 40-49, less than 1% 50-99.

Freshman class profile. 1,102 applied, 654 admitted, 276 enrolled.

Mid 50% test scores			
SAT verbal:	430-530	ACT:	17-20
SAT math:	440-540	Rank in top quarter:	22%
		Rank in top tenth:	6%

Basis for selection. High school record and test scores important; recommendations and interview considered. Interview recommended for all; audition required for drama, music programs; portfolio required for art. **Homeschooled:** Submit transcripts from HS or home school association. If unavailable, submit major essays and course descriptions. References necessary from primary instructor and another source.

High school preparation. 15 units required. Required units include English 4, mathematics 3, social studies 2, history 1, science 2 (laboratory 2), foreign language 2 and academic electives 1.

2005-2006 Annual costs. Tuition/fees: $18,881. Room/board: $6,320. Books/supplies: $1,195. Personal expenses: $1,000.

2005-2006 Financial aid. Need-based: 264 full-time freshmen applied for aid; 194 were judged to have need; 194 of these received aid. Average need met was 70%. 97% of total undergraduate aid awarded as scholarships/grants, 3% as loans/jobs. **Non-need-based:** Scholarships awarded for academics, alumni affiliation, athletics, music/drama, religious affiliation, ROTC, state residency.

Application procedures. Admission: Priority date 1/30; no deadline. $30 fee, may be waived for applicants with need. Application may be submitted online. Admission notification on a rolling basis beginning on or about 9/15. Must reply by May 1 or within 3 week(s) if notified thereafter. **Financial aid:** Priority date 3/15; no closing date. FAFSA, institutional form required. Applicants notified on a rolling basis starting 3/1; must reply by 5/1 or within 2 week(s) of notification.

Academics. Special study options: Cooperative education, double major, dual enrollment of high school students, honors, independent study, internships, liberal arts/career combination, student-designed major, study abroad, teacher certification program. Dual degree programs in Engineering with Clemson University, Georgia Institute of Technology. Other dual degree programs with Duke and Medical University of South Carolina. **Credit/placement by examination:** AP, CLEP, IB, institutional tests. 30 credit hours maximum toward bachelor's degree. Sophomore standing available by earning 24 credit hours based on AP exam scores. **Support services:** Learning center, reduced course load, remedial instruction, tutoring, writing center.

Majors. Biology: General. **Business:** Business admin. **Communications:** General. **Education:** General, early childhood, elementary, music, physical. **Foreign languages:** General, French, German, Spanish. **Health:** Veterinary technology/assistant. **History:** General. **Interdisciplinary:** Global studies, math/computer science. **Math:** General. **Parks/recreation:** General, sports admin. **Physical sciences:** Chemistry. **Psychology:** General. **Social sciences:** International relations, political science, sociology. **Theology:** Sacred music. **Visual/performing arts:** Art, dramatic, music history, music performance, music theory/composition.

Most popular majors. Biology 6%, business/marketing 20%, communications/journalism 10%, education 17%, parks/recreation 9%, social sciences 11%, visual/performing arts 6%.

Computing on campus. 112 workstations in library, computer center. Dormitories wired for high-speed internet access and linked to campus network. Online library, helpline, student web hosting, wireless network available.

Student life. Freshman orientation: Mandatory, $100 fee. Preregistration for classes offered. 2-day event. Students stay overnight on campus. **Policies:** Freshmen permitted cars on campus. **Housing:** Guaranteed on-campus for freshmen. Coed dorms, single-sex dorms available. $100 deposit. **Activities:** Bands, choral groups, drama, literary magazine, music ensembles, musical theater, radio station, student government, student newspaper, TV station, Lutheran Student Movement, Baptist student union, Young Republicans, Intervarsity Fellowship of Christian Athletes, Students Organized for Community Service, South Carolina State Student Legislature.

Athletics. NCAA. **Intercollegiate:** Baseball M, basketball, cheerleading M, cross-country, football (tackle) M, golf, soccer, softball W, tennis, volleyball W, wrestling M. **Intramural:** Basketball, softball, volleyball W. **Team name:** Indians.

Student services. Alcohol/substance abuse counseling, campus ministries, career counseling, student employment services, financial aid counseling, health services, personal counseling, placement for graduates.

Contact. E-mail: admissions@newberry.edu
Phone: (803) 321-5127 Toll-free number: (800) 845-4955 ext. 5127
Fax: (803) 321-5138
Michael Robbins, Director of Admissions, Newberry College, 2100 College Street, Newberry, SC 29108

North Greenville College
Tigerville, South Carolina
www.ngc.edu **CB code: 5498**

- Private 4-year liberal arts college affiliated with Southern Baptist Convention
- Residential campus in rural community
- 1,724 degree-seeking undergraduates: 5% part-time, 49% women, 7% African American, 1% Hispanic American, 1% international
- 88% of applicants admitted
- SAT and SAT Subject Tests required
- 50% graduate within 6 years

General. Founded in 1891. Regionally accredited. Off-site receration and learning center for Ourdoor Leadership major. **Degrees:** 268 bachelor's, 26 associate awarded. **ROTC:** Army. **Location:** 18 miles from Greenville, 54 miles from Asheville, North Carolina. **Calendar:** Semester, limited summer session. **Full-time faculty:** 75 total; 1% minority, 39% women. **Part-time faculty:** 53 total; 2% minority, 53% women. **Class size:** 65% < 20, 35% 20-39, less than 1% 50-99. **Special facilities:** Bible museum.

Freshman class profile. 753 applied, 660 admitted, 439 enrolled.

Mid 50% test scores		**GPA 2.0-2.99:**	25%
SAT verbal:	440-580	**Rank in top quarter:**	38%
SAT math:	440-580	**Rank in top tenth:**	13%
ACT:	15-23	**Return as sophomores:**	69%
GPA 3.50 or higher:	41%	**Out-of-state:**	21%
GPA 3.0-3.49:	32%	**Live on campus:**	86%

Basis for selection. High school record, standardized test scores, class rank most important. Require 2 of the following: SAT 820 (exclusive of Writing); ACT 16; GPA 2.0; class rank top 60 percent. Computerized Placement Test required for those with SAT verbal and math scores below 500. Portfolio recommended for all; audition required for music, theater programs; essay required for English-deficient; interview recommended for music, theater programs. **Learning Disabled:** Meet with Director of Disability Services.

High school preparation. 12 units required; 16 recommended. Required and recommended units include English 4, mathematics 2, social studies 1-2, history 1-2, science 2, foreign language 2 and academic electives 2.

2006-2007 Annual costs. Tuition/fees (projected): $10,350. Room/board: $5,950. Books/supplies: $1,000. Personal expenses: $2,000.

2005-2006 Financial aid. All financial aid based on need. Average need met was 70%. Average scholarship/grant was $1,000; average loan $2,625. 78% of total undergraduate aid awarded as scholarships/grants, 22% as loans/jobs.

Application procedures. Admission: Priority date 6/1; deadline 8/26. $25 fee, may be waived for applicants with need. Admission notification on a rolling basis. **Financial aid:** Priority date 6/1, closing date 6/30. FAFSA required. Applicants notified on a rolling basis starting 8/1; must reply within 2 week(s) of notification.

Academics. Special study options: Cross-registration, double major, dual enrollment of high school students, ESL, honors, independent study, internships, student-designed major, teacher certification program. **Credit/placement by examination:** AP, CLEP, IB, institutional tests. 16 credit hours maximum toward associate degree, 30 toward bachelor's. CLEP and other exam credits cannot exceed 25 percent of hours needed for degree. **Support services:** Learning center, reduced course load, remedial instruction, study skills assistance, tutoring, writing center.

Majors. Business: General, accounting, business admin, international. **Communications:** Broadcast journalism, journalism. **Education:** Early childhood, elementary, music. **English:** English lit. **Health:** Predentistry, premedicine, prepharmacy. **Interdisciplinary:** Accounting/computer science. **Legal studies:** Prelaw. **Liberal arts:** Arts/sciences. **Parks/recreation:** Sports admin. **Philosophy/religion:** Christian. **Psychology:** General. **Theology:** Sacred music. **Visual/performing arts:** Music history, music performance, music theory/composition, piano/organ, theater arts management, voice/opera.

Most popular majors. Business/marketing 18%, communications/journalism 9%, education 16%, interdisciplinary studies 18%, philosophy/religious studies 30%.

Computing on campus. 75 workstations in library, computer center, student center. Dormitories wired for high-speed internet access. Helpline available.

Student life. Freshman orientation: Mandatory. Preregistration for classes offered. Held in August. **Policies:** Religious observance required. Freshmen permitted cars on campus. **Housing:** Guaranteed on-campus for all undergraduates. Single-sex dorms, special housing for disabled, apartments, substance-free housing available. $100 deposit, deadline 8/26. **Activities:** Bands, choral groups, drama, literary magazine, music ensembles, radio station, student government, student newspaper, symphony orchestra, Baptist student union, athletic ministries, Etude music society, Fellowship of Christians in Service, College Republicans.

Athletics. NCAA, NCCAA. **Intercollegiate:** Baseball M, basketball, cheerleading, cross-country, football (tackle) M, golf M, soccer, softball W, tennis, volleyball W. **Intramural:** Basketball, football (non-tackle) M, softball, table tennis, tennis, volleyball. **Team name:** Crusaders.

Student services. Campus ministries, career counseling, student employment services, financial aid counseling, health services, on-campus daycare, personal counseling, placement for graduates. **Physically disabled:** Services for visually impaired.

Contact. E-mail: admissions@ngc.edu
Phone: (864) 977-7001 Toll-free number: (800) 468-6642
Fax: (864) 977-7177
Charles Freeman, Executive Director of Admissions and Financial Aid, North Greenville College, PO Box 1892, Tigerville, SC 29688-1892

Presbyterian College
Clinton, South Carolina **CB member**
www.presby.edu **CB code: 5540**

- Private 4-year liberal arts college affiliated with Presbyterian Church (USA)
- Residential campus in small town
- 1,149 degree-seeking undergraduates: 1% part-time, 51% women, 5% African American, 1% Asian American, 1% Hispanic American
- 76% of applicants admitted
- SAT and SAT Subject Tests or ACT with writing, application essay required
- 73% graduate within 6 years; 25% enter graduate study

General. Founded in 1880. Regionally accredited. Academic student exchange with Finland, Japan, Korea, India, and Oxford University. Ecological research in Australia, Africa, Galapagos Islands, Alaska. Archaeological digs in western United States. Study abroad in England, Ireland, Scotland, Austria, France, Spain, Mexico, Greece, China. **Degrees:** 229 bachelor's awarded. **ROTC:** Army. **Location:** 40 miles from Greenville, 35 miles from Spartanburg. **Calendar:** Semester, limited summer session. **Full-time faculty:** 81 total; 96% have terminal degrees, 2% minority, 26% women. **Part-time faculty:** 29 total; 38% have terminal degrees, 14% minority, 45% women. **Class size:** 67% < 20, 33% 20-39, less than 1% 40-49, less than 1% 50-99. **Special facilities:** Scanning electron and transmission microscopes, ecological research center, Southeastern Center for Intercultural Studies.

Freshman class profile. 1,110 applied, 846 admitted, 313 enrolled.

Mid 50% test scores		**Rank in top tenth:**	31%
SAT verbal:	510-620	**End year in good standing:**	89%
SAT math:	520-620	**Return as sophomores:**	83%
ACT:	21-26	**Out-of-state:**	33%
GPA 3.50 or higher:	47%	**Live on campus:**	99%
GPA 3.0-3.49:	27%	**Fraternities:**	47%
GPA 2.0-2.99:	26%	**Sororities:**	35%
Rank in top quarter:	62%		

Basis for selection. Rigor of high school curriculum most important, followed by test scores, high school GPA, and high school recommendation. Extracurricular involvement and interview considered in some cases. Interview recommended.

High school preparation. 17 units required. Required units include English 4, mathematics 3, history 2, science 2 (laboratory 2), foreign language 2 and academic electives 2. 2 or more units of laboratory science for science majors recommended.

2006-2007 Annual costs. Tuition/fees: $24,626. Room/board: $7,756. Books/supplies: $1,072. Personal expenses: $2,680.

2005-2006 Financial aid. Need-based: 249 full-time freshmen applied for aid; 193 were judged to have need; 193 of these received aid. Average need met was 92%. Average scholarship/grant was $21,813; average loan $3,881. 77% of total undergraduate aid awarded as scholarships/grants, 23% as loans/jobs. **Non-need-based:** Awarded to 736 full-time undergraduates, including 211 freshmen. Scholarships awarded for academics, alumni affiliation, athletics, job skills, leadership, minority status, music/drama, religious affiliation, ROTC.

Application procedures. Admission: Priority date 5/1; no deadline. $30 fee, may be waived for applicants with need. Application may be submitted online. Admission notification on a rolling basis beginning on or about 10/1. Incoming students do not have a housing fee, but pay a $300 escrow deposit that is refundable until May 1st. **Financial aid:** Priority date 3/1; no closing date. FAFSA, institutional form required. Applicants notified on a rolling basis starting 4/1; must reply by 5/1.

Academics. Special study options: Accelerated study, combined bachelor's/graduate degree, double major, dual enrollment of high school students, exchange student, honors, independent study, internships, liberal arts/career combination, semester at sea, study abroad, teacher certification program, Washington semester. 3-2 environmental science program, 3-2 engineering program, religious educational program; dual degrees offered with Auburn University (AL), Clemson University, Vanderbilt University (TN), Mercer University (GA), Presbyterian School of Christian Education. **Credit/placement by examination:** AP, CLEP, IB, institutional tests. 40 credit hours maximum toward bachelor's degree. **Support services:** Preadmission summer program, reduced course load, study skills assistance, tutoring, writing center.

Majors. Biology: General. **Business:** Accounting, business admin. **Computer sciences:** Computer science. **Education:** Early childhood, middle, music, secondary, social studies. **English:** English lit. **Foreign languages:** French, German, Spanish. **History:** General. **Math:** General. **Philosophy/religion:** Religion. **Physical sciences:** Chemistry, physics. **Psychology:** General. **Social sciences:** Economics, political science, sociology. **Theology:** Religious ed. **Visual/performing arts:** Art, dramatic, music performance, studio arts.

Most popular majors. Biology 14%, business/marketing 22%, education 11%, philosophy/religious studies 7%, psychology 12%, social sciences 11%, visual/performing arts 7%.

Computing on campus. 120 workstations in dormitories, library, computer center, student center. Dormitories wired for high-speed internet access and linked to campus network. Commuter students can connect to campus network. Online course registration, helpline, student web hosting, wireless network available.

Student life. Freshman orientation: Mandatory. Preregistration for classes offered. Orientation includes registration, placement testing and organization fair. **Policies:** Honor code governs conduct inside and outside classroom. Cultural Enrichment Program requires students to attend 40 on-campus cultural events as part of graduation requirement. Freshmen permitted cars on campus. **Housing:** Guaranteed on-campus for all undergraduates. Coed dorms, single-sex dorms, apartments, fraternity/sorority housing, substance-free housing available. All full-time students, except those commuting daily from family's residence, required to live on campus. Sorority housing not available. **Activities:** Bands, choral groups, dance, drama, literary magazine, music ensembles, radio station, student government, student newspaper, volunteer organizations, multicultural student union, Young Democrats and Republicans, interdenominational organizations, Habitat for Humanity, Amnesty International, Fellowship of Christian Athletes.

Athletics. NCAA. **Intercollegiate:** Baseball M, basketball, cross-country, football (tackle) M, golf, lacrosse, soccer, softball W, tennis, volleyball W. **Intramural:** Basketball, football (tackle), golf, racquetball, soccer, softball, swimming, table tennis, tennis, volleyball. **Team name:** Blue Hose.

Student services. Campus ministries, career counseling, student employment services, financial aid counseling, health services, minority student services, personal counseling, placement for graduates.

Contact. E-mail: admissions@presby.edu
Phone: (864) 833-8230 Toll-free number: (800) 960-7583
Fax: (864) 833-8481
Leni Patterson, Vice President of Enrollment and Dean of Admissions, Presbyterian College, 503 South Broad Street, Clinton, SC 29325-9989

South Carolina State University

Orangeburg, South Carolina — **CB member**
www.scsu.edu — **CB code: 5618**

- Public 4-year university
- Residential campus in large town
- 3,839 degree-seeking undergraduates: 7% part-time, 58% women, 98% African American
- 462 degree-seeking graduate students
- 82% of applicants admitted
- SAT or ACT (ACT writing optional) required

General. Founded in 1896. Regionally accredited. **Degrees:** 499 bachelor's awarded; master's, doctoral offered. **ROTC:** Army, Air Force. **Location:** 40 miles from Columbia, 70 miles from Charleston. **Calendar:** Semester, limited summer session. **Full-time faculty:** 210 total. **Part-time faculty:** 55 total. **Special facilities:** Planetarium, museum.

Freshman class profile. 3,383 applied, 2,759 admitted, 1,013 enrolled.

Mid 50% test scores		**Rank in top tenth:**	12%
SAT verbal:	370-450	**Return as sophomores:**	22%
SAT math:	370-460	**Out-of-state:**	1%
ACT:	15-18	**Live on campus:**	96%
Rank in top quarter:	40%		

Basis for selection. Admission decisions based primarily on high school record, class rank, and standardized test scores. Audition required for music education program; portfolio required for art education program.

High school preparation. 20 units required. Required units include English 4, mathematics 3, social studies 3, science 3 (laboratory 3), foreign language 2 and academic electives 4. One unit of physical education or ROTC required.

2005-2006 Annual costs. Tuition/fees: $6,480; $13,288 out-of-state. Room/board: $4,920. Books/supplies: $1,000. Personal expenses: $700.

Financial aid. Non-need-based: Scholarships awarded for academics, athletics, ROTC.

Application procedures. Admission: Closing date 7/31 (postmark date). $25 fee, may be waived for applicants with need. Application may be submitted online. Admission notification on a rolling basis. **Financial aid:** Closing date 5/1. FAFSA required. Applicants notified on a rolling basis starting 6/15; must reply by 8/1 or within 4 week(s) of notification.

Academics. Special study options: Cooperative education, cross-registration, distance learning, double major, dual enrollment of high school students, exchange student, honors, internships, liberal arts/career combination, study abroad, teacher certification program. **Credit/placement by examination:** AP, CLEP, institutional tests. 30 credit hours maximum toward bachelor's degree. **Support services:** Learning center, remedial instruction, tutoring, writing center.

Majors. Agriculture: Agribusiness operations. **Biology:** General. **Business:** Accounting, business admin, fashion, managerial economics. **Computer sciences:** General. **Education:** Art, biology, business, chemistry, drama/dance, early childhood, elementary, emotionally handicapped, English, family/consumer sciences, French, health, history, learning disabled, mathematics, mentally handicapped, music, physical, social studies, Spanish, special, technology/industrial arts, trade/industrial. **Engineering:** Nuclear. **Engineering technology:** Civil, electrical. **Family/consumer sciences:** General, business, child care, food/nutrition. **Foreign languages:** French, Spanish. **Health:** Audiology/speech pathology, nursing (RN). **History:** General. **Math:** General. **Physical sciences:** Chemistry, physics. **Protective services:** Law enforcement admin. **Psychology:** General. **Public administration:** Social work. **Social sciences:** Political science, sociology. **Visual/performing arts:** Dramatic, music management, piano/organ, printmaking, voice/opera.

Computing on campus. 300 workstations in dormitories, library, computer center, student center. Dormitories wired for high-speed internet access and linked to campus network. Commuter students can connect to campus network. Online course registration, online library, helpline, repair service, wireless network available.

Student life. Freshman orientation: Available. Preregistration for classes offered. **Housing:** Guaranteed on-campus for freshmen. Single-sex dorms, apartments available. $25 deposit. **Activities:** Bands, choral groups, dance, drama, music ensembles, radio station, student government, student newspaper.

Athletics. NCAA. **Intercollegiate:** Basketball, bowling W, cross-country, football (tackle) M, golf, soccer W, softball W, tennis, track and field, volleyball W. **Intramural:** Basketball, softball. **Team name:** Bulldogs.

Student services. Adult student services, career counseling, health services, personal counseling, placement for graduates, veterans' counselor. **Physically disabled:** Services for speech, hearing impaired.

Contact. Phone: (803) 536-7185 Fax: (803) 536-8990
Dwight Bailey, Director, Admissions/Recruitment, South Carolina State University, 300 College Street NE, Orangeburg, SC 29117

South University

Columbia, South Carolina
www.southuniversity.com **CB code: 5097**

- For-profit 4-year university, business and health science college
- Commuter campus in small city
- 425 degree-seeking undergraduates: 32% part-time, 84% women, 90% African American, 1% Hispanic American, 1% Native American
- 65 degree-seeking graduate students

General. Founded in 1935. Regionally accredited. **Degrees:** 19 bachelor's, 53 associate awarded; master's offered. **Location:** 3 miles from downtown. **Calendar:** Quarter, extensive summer session. **Full-time faculty:** 10 total. **Part-time faculty:** 25 total.

Freshman class profile. 162 applied, 111 admitted, 111 enrolled.

Basis for selection. Open admission, but selective for some programs. Special requirements for pharmacy, nursing, physician assistant studies programs. SAT or ACT may be submitted in place of required institutional tests for placement. Score report due by September 15. **Homeschooled:** Transcript of courses and grades required.

Financial aid. All financial aid based on need.

Application procedures. Admission: No deadline. $25 fee, may be waived for applicants with need. Application may be submitted online. Admission notification on a rolling basis. **Financial aid:** Priority date 5/30; no closing date. FAFSA required. Applicants notified on a rolling basis starting 5/30.

Academics. Special study options: Cooperative education, distance learning, double major, internships, weekend college. **Credit/placement by examination:** AP, CLEP, institutional tests. **Support services:** Reduced course load, remedial instruction, study skills assistance, tutoring, writing center.

Majors. Computer sciences: Information technology. **Legal studies:** General. **Protective services:** Corrections, juvenile corrections, law enforcement admin, police science.

Computing on campus. 40 workstations in library, computer center. Helpline available.

Student life. Freshman orientation: Mandatory. Preregistration for classes offered. **Policies:** Freshmen permitted cars on campus.

Student services. Adult student services, career counseling, student employment services, financial aid counseling, personal counseling, placement for graduates, veterans' counselor. **Physically disabled:** Services for visually, speech, hearing impaired.

Contact. Phone: (803) 799-9082 Toll-free number: (866) 629-3031
Fax: (803) 799-9038
Trisha Sherwood, Director of Admissions, South University, 3810 Main Street, Columbia, SC 29203

Southern Wesleyan University

Central, South Carolina
www.swu.edu **CB code: 5896**

- Private 4-year university and liberal arts college affiliated with Wesleyan Church
- Commuter campus in small town
- 1,995 degree-seeking undergraduates: 4% part-time, 66% women, 36% African American, 1% Asian American, 2% Hispanic American, 1% Native American, 1% international
- 637 degree-seeking graduate students
- 66% of applicants admitted
- SAT or ACT (ACT writing recommended) required
- 55% graduate within 6 years

General. Founded in 1906. Regionally accredited. Christian world-view emphasized. **Degrees:** 381 bachelor's, 87 associate awarded; master's offered. **ROTC:** Army, Air Force. **Location:** 25 miles from Greenville. **Calendar:** Semester, limited summer session. **Full-time faculty:** 50 total; 76% have terminal degrees, 4% minority, 26% women. **Part-time faculty:** 178 total; 42% have terminal degrees, 19% minority, 39% women. **Class size:** 85% < 20, 14% 20-39, less than 1% 40-49, less than 1% 50-99. **Special facilities:** Electron microscope facility, Freedom's Hill historic site.

Freshman class profile. 401 applied, 264 admitted, 138 enrolled.

Mid 50% test scores		**GPA 2.0-2.99:**	21%
SAT verbal:	460-560	**Rank in top quarter:**	23%
SAT math:	460-570	**Rank in top tenth:**	13%
ACT:	17-23	**Return as sophomores:**	64%
GPA 3.50 or higher:	56%	**Out-of-state:**	38%
GPA 3.0-3.49:	22%	**Live on campus:**	64%

Basis for selection. GPA, class rank, test scores, and religious commitment important. Recommendations considered. Students admitted conditionally if combined SAT score is less than 800 (exclusive of Writing) or high school GPA is less than 2.3, and rank in bottom half of class. Students admitted conditionally take limited number of course hours and are on academic warning. Freshmen may be admitted provisionally and submit SAT scores by end of first semester. Audition required for music; interview recommended for applicants with special physical, emotional problems.

High school preparation. 10 units required. Required units include English 4, mathematics 2, social studies 2 and science 2.

2005-2006 Annual costs. Tuition/fees: $15,450. Room/board: $5,450. Books/supplies: $900. Personal expenses: $1,000.

2005-2006 Financial aid. Need-based: Average need met was 65%. Average scholarship/grant was $9,191; average loan $1,990. 51% of total undergraduate aid awarded as scholarships/grants, 49% as loans/jobs. **Non-need-based:** Scholarships awarded for academics, alumni affiliation, athletics, job skills, leadership, minority status, music/drama, religious affiliation, ROTC.

Application procedures. Admission: Closing date 8/1. $25 fee, may be waived for applicants with need. Admission notification on a rolling basis. **Financial aid:** Priority date 3/31, closing date 6/30. FAFSA, institutional form required. Applicants notified on a rolling basis starting 2/1; must reply within 3 week(s) of notification.

Academics. Special study options: Cooperative education, cross-registration, distance learning, double major, dual enrollment of high school students, external degree, honors, independent study, internships, liberal arts/career combination, student-designed major, study abroad, teacher certification program, Washington semester. **Credit/placement by examination:** AP, CLEP, IB. 48 credit hours maximum toward associate degree, 68 toward bachelor's. **Support services:** Learning center, reduced course load, remedial instruction, study skills assistance, tutoring, writing center.

Majors. Biology: General. **Business:** Accounting, business admin, e-commerce, human resources. **Communications:** General. **Computer sciences:** Computer science, information technology, security, webmaster. **Education:** Biology, early childhood, elementary, emotionally handicapped, English, learning disabled, mathematics, mentally handicapped, music, physical, special. **History:** General. **Math:** General. **Parks/recreation:** General, sports admin. **Philosophy/religion:** Religion. **Physical sciences:** Chemistry. **Protective services:** Forensics. **Psychology:** General. **Social sciences:** General.

Most popular majors. Business/marketing 73%, education 12%.

Computing on campus. 277 workstations in dormitories, library, computer center. Dormitories wired for high-speed internet access and linked to campus network. Commuter students can connect to campus network. Online library, helpline, repair service available.

Student life. Freshman orientation: Mandatory, $35 fee. Preregistration for classes offered. Held in June, July, and at beginning of fall and spring semesters. **Policies:** Students must agree to abide by lifestyle expectations of university. Religious observance required. Freshmen permitted cars on campus. **Housing:** Guaranteed on-campus for all undergraduates. Coed dorms, single-sex dorms, special housing for disabled, apartments, substance-free housing available. $200 deposit. **Activities:** Bands, choral groups, drama, literary magazine, music ensembles, musical theater, student government, Christian Service Organization, Student Missions Fellowship, Rotaract, gospel choir, Fellowship of Christian Athletes, Deeper, student activities board, intramural sports, Habitat for Humanity.

Athletics. NAIA, NCCAA. **Intercollegiate:** Baseball M, basketball, cheerleading, cross-country, golf M, soccer, softball W, volleyball W. **Intramural:** Basketball, soccer, softball, table tennis, tennis, volleyball. **Team name:** Warriors.

Student services. Adult student services, alcohol/substance abuse counseling, campus ministries, career counseling, financial aid counseling, health services, minority student services, personal counseling. **Physically disabled:** Services for visually, hearing impaired.

Contact. E-mail: admissions@swu.edu
Phone: (864) 644-5550 Toll-free number: (800) 282-8798
Fax: (864) 644-5972
Chad Peters, Director of Admissions, Southern Wesleyan University, PO Box 1020, Central, SC 29630-1020

University of South Carolina

Columbia, South Carolina — **CB member**
www.sc.edu — **CB code: 5818**

- Public 4-year university
- Residential campus in small city
- 17,781 degree-seeking undergraduates: 8% part-time, 54% women, 14% African American, 3% Asian American, 2% Hispanic American, 1% international
- 7,021 degree-seeking graduate students
- 68% of applicants admitted
- SAT or ACT with writing required
- 65% graduate within 6 years

General. Founded in 1801. Regionally accredited. **Degrees:** 3,286 bachelor's, 4 associate awarded; master's, doctoral, first professional offered. **ROTC:** Army, Navy, Air Force. **Location:** 200 miles from Atlanta, Georgia. **Calendar:** Semester, extensive summer session. **Full-time faculty:** 1,190 total; 86% have terminal degrees, 12% minority, 34% women. **Part-time faculty:** 377 total; 38% have terminal degrees, 7% minority, 41% women. **Class size:** 38% < 20, 44% 20-39, 7% 40-49, 8% 50-99, 3% >100. **Special facilities:** Museum, observatory, arboretum, green dorm with learning center focusing on sustainability.

Freshman class profile. 13,023 applied, 8,812 admitted, 3,734 enrolled.

Mid 50% test scores		**Return as sophomores:**	83%
SAT verbal:	520-630	**Out-of-state:**	15%
SAT math:	540-640	**Live on campus:**	90%
ACT:	22-27	**International:**	1%
Rank in top quarter:	60%	**Fraternities:**	4%
Rank in top tenth:	26%	**Sororities:**	6%
End year in good standing:	89%		

Basis for selection. Admission based on high school curriculum, grades in required high school courses, SAT and ACT scores. **Learning Disabled:** Diagnostic tests required for learning disabled students.

High school preparation. 19 units required. Required units include English 4, mathematics 3, social studies 2, history 1, science 3 (laboratory 3), foreign language 2 and academic electives 4. One unit of physical education or ROTC required.

2005-2006 Annual costs. Tuition/fees: $7,314; $18,956 out-of-state. Health professions (pharmacy, health, nursing), law and medical professions have higher undergraduate and graduate fees. Room/board: $6,083. Books/supplies: $782. Personal expenses: $2,420.

2004-2005 Financial aid. Need-based: 2,293 full-time freshmen applied for aid; 1,573 were judged to have need; 1,564 of these received aid. Average need met was 74%. Average scholarship/grant was $3,529; average loan $1,860. 50% of total undergraduate aid awarded as scholarships/grants, 50% as loans/jobs. **Non-need-based:** Awarded to 9,533 full-time undergraduates, including 2,969 freshmen. Scholarships awarded for academics, alumni affiliation, art, athletics, job skills, leadership, minority status, music/drama, religious affiliation, ROTC, state residency.

Application procedures. Admission: Closing date 12/1. $50 fee, may be waived for applicants with need. Application must be submitted on paper. Admission notification on a rolling basis beginning on or about 10/1. Must reply by May 1 or within 2 week(s) if notified thereafter. **Financial aid:** Priority date 4/1; no closing date. FAFSA required. Applicants notified on a rolling basis starting 4/1.

Academics. One-month May term which focuses on specialized topics. **Special study options:** Accelerated study, combined bachelor's/graduate degree, cooperative education, cross-registration, distance learning, double major, dual enrollment of high school students, ESL, exchange student, external degree, honors, independent study, internships, liberal arts/career combination, student-designed major, study abroad, teacher certification program, weekend college. International program. **Credit/placement by examination:** AP, CLEP, IB, institutional tests. Maximum number of semester hours of credit by examination allowed varies according to degree and program of study. **Support services:** Reduced course load.

Honors college/program. To be competitive for admission, students must have an SAT score of at least 1300 (exclusive of Writing) and a high school GPA of at least 3.5. 600 are admitted to yield a freshman class of 275. Academic program consists of 115-125 honors classes per semester across most disciplines and levels.

Majors. Area/ethnic studies: African-American, European, Latin American, women's. **Biology:** General, marine. **Business:** Accounting, business admin, finance, hospitality admin, insurance, management science, managerial economics, marketing, office management, real estate, retailing. **Communications:** Advertising, broadcast journalism, journalism, media studies, public relations. **Computer sciences:** General. **Education:** Art, early childhood, physical. **Engineering:** Chemical, civil, computer, electrical, mechanical. **Foreign languages:** Classics, French, German, Italian, Russian, Spanish. **Health:** Cardiovascular technology, nursing (RN). **History:** General. **Liberal arts:** Arts/sciences. **Math:** General, statistics. **Parks/recreation:** Exercise sciences, sports admin. **Philosophy/religion:** Philosophy, religion. **Physical sciences:** Chemistry, geology, geophysics, physics. **Protective services:** Law enforcement admin. **Social sciences:** Anthropology, economics, geography, international relations, political science, sociology. **Visual/performing arts:** Art history/conservation, dance, dramatic, film/cinema, studio arts.

Most popular majors. Business/marketing 26%, communications/journalism 9%, engineering/engineering technologies 6%, psychology 7%, social sciences 10%, visual/performing arts 7%.

Computing on campus. 2,800 workstations in dormitories, library, computer center, student center. Dormitories wired for high-speed internet access and linked to campus network. Commuter students can connect to campus network. Online course registration, online library, helpline, student web hosting, wireless network available.

Student life. Freshman orientation: Available, $60 fee. Preregistration for classes offered. Parents may also attend to view campus for $20 fee. **Policies:** Freshmen permitted cars on campus. **Housing:** Guaranteed on-campus for freshmen. Coed dorms, single-sex dorms, special housing for disabled, apartments, fraternity/sorority housing, substance-free housing available. $125 partly refundable deposit, deadline 12/1. Honors and wellness housing; residential college; communities for: pre-medical, engineering, athletic, teaching fellows. **Activities:** Bands, choral groups, dance, drama, literary magazine, music ensembles, musical theater, opera, radio station, student government, student newspaper, symphony orchestra, Campus Crusade for Christ, Baptist student union, Fellowship of Christian Athletes, Association of African American Students, Habitat for Humanity, dance marathon, alternative break corps.

Athletics. NCAA. **Intercollegiate:** Baseball M, basketball, cross-country W, diving, equestrian W, football (tackle) M, golf, soccer, softball W, swimming, tennis, track and field, volleyball W. **Intramural:** Badminton, basketball, bowling, football (tackle), golf, racquetball, soccer, softball, swimming, table tennis, tennis, track and field, volleyball, weight lifting. **Team name:** Fighting Gamecocks.

Student services. Adult student services, alcohol/substance abuse counseling, campus ministries, career counseling, services for economically disadvantaged, student employment services, financial aid counseling, health services, minority student services, on-campus daycare, personal counseling, placement for graduates, veterans' counselor. **Physically disabled:** Services for visually, speech, hearing impaired. **Learning disabled:** Comprehensive services available.

Contact. E-mail: admissions-ugrad@sc.edu
Phone: (803) 777-7700 Toll-free number: (800) 868-5872
Fax: (803) 777-0101
Scott Verzyl, Director of Undergraduate Admissions, University of South Carolina, Office of Undergraduate Admissions, Columbia, SC 29208

University of South Carolina at Aiken

Aiken, South Carolina — **CB member**
www.usca.edu — **CB code: 5840**

- Public 4-year university and liberal arts college
- Commuter campus in large town

- 2,851 degree-seeking undergraduates: 20% part-time, 67% women, 26% African American, 1% Asian American, 2% Hispanic American, 2% international
- 81 degree-seeking graduate students
- 48% of applicants admitted
- SAT or ACT (ACT writing recommended) required
- 43% graduate within 6 years

General. Founded in 1961. Regionally accredited. **Degrees:** 518 bachelor's, 49 associate awarded; master's offered. **Location:** 55 miles from Columbia, 15 miles from Augusta, Georgia. **Calendar:** Semester, limited summer session. **Full-time faculty:** 147 total; 76% have terminal degrees, 16% minority, 46% women. **Part-time faculty:** 99 total; 22% have terminal degrees, 11% minority, 59% women. **Class size:** 57% < 20, 42% 20-39, less than 1% 40-49, less than 1% 50-99. **Special facilities:** Fine arts center, science center, wellness center, natatorium, planetarium.

Freshman class profile. 2,064 applied, 982 admitted, 610 enrolled.

Mid 50% test scores			
SAT verbal:	440-540	Rank in top tenth:	15%
SAT math:	450-550	Return as sophomores:	60%
ACT:	18-21	Out-of-state:	9%
Rank in top quarter:	39%	International:	1%

Basis for selection. Test scores, high school core GPA important. Admission is based on course selection, standardized test scores and a Predicted College Grade Point Average (PCGPA). This average represents the academic average that a freshman applicant is predicted to earn at USC Aiken at the completion of his/her first year. The (PCGPA) is determined by a formula which uses two variables: the high school grade point average computed on college prep courses, and the SAT or ACT scores. Of these two variables, the high school grade point average is the more important and has more weight in the formula. Audition, essay, interview, portfolio recommended. **Learning Disabled:** Foreign language waivers accepted.

High school preparation. 21 units required. Required units include English 4, mathematics 4, social studies 2, history 1, science 3 (laboratory 3), foreign language 2 and academic electives 4. Elective college preparatory credits from 3 different fields. One unit computer science (not keyboarding) and 1 unit fine arts recommended.

2005-2006 Annual costs. Tuition/fees: $6,158; $12,300 out-of-state. Room/board: $5,560. Books/supplies: $800. Personal expenses: $1,500.

Application procedures. **Admission:** Priority date 7/1; deadline 8/1 (postmark date). $35 fee, may be waived for applicants with need. Application may be submitted online. Admission notification on a rolling basis. Must reply by May 1 or within 2 week(s) if notified thereafter. **Financial aid:** Priority date 3/15; no closing date. FAFSA required. Applicants notified on a rolling basis starting 5/20; must reply within 2 week(s) of notification.

Academics. **Special study options:** Cooperative education, distance learning, double major, dual enrollment of high school students, ESL, exchange student, honors, independent study, internships, liberal arts/career combination, student-designed major, study abroad, teacher certification program. **Credit/placement by examination:** AP, CLEP, institutional tests. 30 credit hours maximum toward bachelor's degree. **Support services:** Study skills assistance, tutoring, writing center.

Majors. **Biology:** General. **Business:** General, accounting, business admin, finance, managerial economics. **Communications:** General, journalism. **Education:** General, early childhood, elementary, English, mathematics, music, science, secondary, social science, social studies, special. **English:** English lit. **Health:** Nursing (RN). **History:** General. **Interdisciplinary:** Math/computer science. **Math:** Applied. **Parks/recreation:** Exercise sciences. **Physical sciences:** Chemistry. **Psychology:** General. **Social sciences:** Political science, sociology. **Visual/performing arts:** Studio arts.

Most popular majors. Biology 6%, business/marketing 28%, communications/journalism 7%, education 16%, health sciences 8%, parks/recreation 6%, social sciences 10%.

Computing on campus. 784 workstations in dormitories, library, computer center, student center. Dormitories wired for high-speed internet access and linked to campus network. Online course registration, helpline, wireless network available.

Student life. **Freshman orientation:** Mandatory, $75 fee. Preregistration for classes offered. Held in July and August. July orientation offers registration. **Policies:** Freshmen permitted cars on campus. **Housing:** Special housing for disabled, apartments available. $150 deposit. **Activities:** Bands, choral groups, dance, drama, literary magazine, music ensembles, student government, student newspaper, Campus Crusade for Christ, honor societies, Association for Women's Issues, Pacer Union Board, High Adventure Club, African American Students' Alliance, community action board, College Republicans, drama group.

Athletics. NCAA. **Intercollegiate:** Baseball M, basketball, cross-country W, golf M, soccer, softball W, tennis, volleyball W. **Intramural:** Badminton, baseball M, basketball, bowling, golf, soccer, softball, table tennis, tennis, volleyball. **Team name:** Pacers.

Student services. Adult student services, alcohol/substance abuse counseling, career counseling, student employment services, financial aid counseling, health services, minority student services, on-campus daycare, personal counseling, placement for graduates, veterans' counselor. **Physically disabled:** Services for visually, speech, hearing impaired.

Contact. E-mail: admit@sc.edu
Phone: (803) 641-3366 Toll-free number: (888) 969-8722
Fax: (803) 641-3727
Andrew Hendrix, Director of Admissions, University of South Carolina at Aiken, 471 University Parkway, Aiken, SC 29801

University of South Carolina at Beaufort

Beaufort, South Carolina — **CB member**
www.uscb.edu — **CB code: 5845**

- Public 4-year liberal arts college
- Commuter campus in large town
- 1,227 degree-seeking undergraduates: 45% part-time, 59% women, 16% African American, 1% Asian American, 4% Hispanic American, 1% Native American, 1% international
- SAT or ACT (ACT writing optional) required

General. Founded in 1959. Regionally accredited. **Degrees:** 107 bachelor's, 64 associate awarded. **Location:** 72 miles from Charleston, 42 miles from Savannah, Georgia. **Calendar:** Semester, limited summer session. **Full-time faculty:** 46 total; 78% have terminal degrees, 15% minority, 37% women. **Part-time faculty:** 57 total; 49% have terminal degrees, 7% minority, 42% women. **Class size:** 73% < 20, 25% 20-39, 2% 40-49, less than 1% 50-99. **Special facilities:** Pritchard's Island, a 1600-acre undeveloped island used for research, instruction, and as a center for the Loggerhead Sea Turtle Conservation Project.

Freshman class profile.

Mid 50% test scores			
SAT verbal:	430-540	Return as sophomores:	56%
SAT math:	420-540	Out-of-state:	11%
ACT:	17-21	Live on campus:	27%
		International:	1%

Basis for selection. Test scores, rank in class important. Minimum 2.0 GPA.

High school preparation. 20 units required. Required units include English 4, mathematics 3, social studies 2, history 1, science 3 (laboratory 3), foreign language 2 and academic electives 4. Computer course recommended.

2005-2006 Annual costs. Tuition/fees: $5,284; $12,200 out-of-state. Books/supplies: $744. Personal expenses: $1,307.

Financial aid. All financial aid based on need.

Application procedures. **Admission:** No deadline. $50 fee, may be waived for applicants with need. Admission notification on a rolling basis beginning on or about 2/1. Students may submit application through CollegeNET. **Financial aid:** Priority date 4/15; no closing date. FAFSA required. Applicants notified on a rolling basis starting 5/31; must reply within 2 week(s) of notification.

Academics. **Special study options:** Cooperative education, distance learning, dual enrollment of high school students, independent study, internships, student-designed major, study abroad, teacher certification program. **Credit/placement by examination:** CLEP, institutional tests. 15 credit hours maximum toward associate degree, 30 toward bachelor's. **Support services:** Learning center, reduced course load, study skills assistance, tutoring, writing center.

Majors. **Biology:** General. **Business:** Business admin, hospitality admin. **Education:** Early childhood. **English:** English lit. **Foreign languages:** General. **History:** General. **Liberal arts:** Arts/sciences. **Psychology:** General. **Social sciences:** General.

Computing on campus. 114 workstations in library, computer center. Dormitories wired for high-speed internet access. Online library available.

Student life. Freshman orientation: Mandatory. Preregistration for classes offered. **Policies:** Freshmen permitted cars on campus. **Housing:** Special housing for disabled, apartments, substance-free housing available. **Activities:** Drama, literary magazine, musical theater, student government, student newspaper, African American student association, Christian student fellowship, business club, veterans association, education club, Gamma Beta Phi honor society, psychology/sociology/anthropology club.

Athletics. Intramural: Football (non-tackle).

Student services. Career counseling, services for economically disadvantaged, student employment services, financial aid counseling, veterans' counselor.

Contact. E-mail: cacooney@gwm.sc.edu
Phone: (843) 208-8118 Fax: (843) 521-4194
Christine Cooney, Director of Admissions, University of South Carolina at Beaufort, 801 Carteret Street, Beaufort, SC 29902

University of South Carolina Upstate

Spartanburg, South Carolina
www.uscupstate.edu **CB code: 5850**

- Public 4-year university
- Commuter campus in small city
- 4,334 degree-seeking undergraduates: 1% part-time, 66% women
- 53 degree-seeking graduate students
- 64% of applicants admitted
- SAT or ACT (ACT writing optional) required
- 36% graduate within 6 years

General. Founded in 1967. Regionally accredited. **Degrees:** 839 bachelor's, 41 associate awarded; master's offered. **ROTC:** Army. **Location:** 70 miles from Charlotte, North Carolina, 30 miles from Greenville. **Calendar:** Semester, extensive summer session. **Full-time faculty:** 207 total; 65% have terminal degrees, 14% minority, 53% women. **Part-time faculty:** 149 total; 27% have terminal degrees, 15% minority, 50% women. **Class size:** 52% < 20, 45% 20-39, 3% 40-49, less than 1% 50-99. **Special facilities:** Arts studies film theater, recital hall, language laboratory, center for international studies and language services, audiovisual production center, digital lab.

Freshman class profile. 2,273 applied, 1,464 admitted, 736 enrolled.

Mid 50% test scores			
SAT verbal:	440-540	Rank in top tenth:	14%
SAT math:	450-550	Return as sophomores:	63%
ACT:	18-22	Out-of-state:	9%
Rank in top quarter:	38%	Live on campus:	17%

Basis for selection. Cumulative average of C or better in preparatory courses and minimum 850 SAT (exclusive of Writing), or 18 ACT required. Higher grades may offset lower SAT/ACT scores, and higher SAT/ACT scores may offset lower grades.

High school preparation. 20 units required; 22 recommended. Required and recommended units include English 4, mathematics 3-4, social studies 2, history 1, science 3 (laboratory 3), foreign language 2-3 and academic electives 4. One unit of physical education or ROTC required. 2 units of laboratory science and 1 elective required if student graduated from high school between 1988-2000.

2005-2006 Annual costs. Tuition/fees: $6,762; $13,600 out-of-state. Room/board: $5,860. Books/supplies: $1,000. Personal expenses: $200.

2004-2005 Financial aid. Need-based: 489 full-time freshmen applied for aid; 407 were judged to have need; 403 of these received aid. Average need met was 36%. Average scholarship/grant was $3,356; average loan $2,340. 40% of total undergraduate aid awarded as scholarships/grants, 60% as loans/jobs. **Non-need-based:** Awarded to 1,237 full-time undergraduates, including 440 freshmen. Scholarships awarded for academics, athletics, minority status, ROTC, state residency. **Additional information:** Out-of-state students who are recipients of financial aid may qualify for out-of-state fee waiver. Educational benefits available to veterans and children of deceased/disabled veterans.

Application procedures. Admission: Priority date 8/15; no deadline. $35 fee, may be waived for applicants with need. Admission notification on a rolling basis beginning on or about 9/15. **Financial aid:** Priority date 3/1, closing date 7/15. FAFSA, institutional form required. Applicants notified on a rolling basis starting 5/1; must reply within 2 week(s) of notification.

Academics. The Center for Student Success offers services such as free tutorials, advisement, study skills and time management assistance, study groups, supplementary instruction, consultation one-on-one, and referrals. **Special study options:** Accelerated study, cross-registration, distance learning, double major, exchange student, honors, independent study, internships, liberal arts/career combination, student-designed major, study abroad, teacher certification program, Washington semester. **Credit/placement by examination:** AP, CLEP, IB, institutional tests. 30 credit hours maximum toward bachelor's degree. **Support services:** Learning center, reduced course load, remedial instruction, study skills assistance, tutoring, writing center.

Majors. Biology: General. **Business:** Business admin. **Communications:** General. **Computer sciences:** General, information systems. **Education:** Early childhood, elementary, physical, secondary, special. **English:** English lit. **Foreign languages:** French, Spanish. **Health:** Nursing (RN). **History:** General. **Interdisciplinary:** Accounting/computer science. **Liberal arts:** Arts/sciences. **Math:** General, applied. **Physical sciences:** Chemistry. **Protective services:** Criminal justice. **Psychology:** General. **Social sciences:** Political science, sociology. **Visual/performing arts:** Commercial/advertising art, design.

Most popular majors. Business/marketing 15%, communications/journalism 6%, computer/information sciences 9%, education 18%, health sciences 19%, liberal arts 12%.

Computing on campus. 600 workstations in dormitories, library, computer center, student center. Dormitories wired for high-speed internet access and linked to campus network. Commuter students can connect to campus network. Online course registration, online library, helpline, repair service, student web hosting, wireless network available.

Student life. Freshman orientation: Available. Preregistration for classes offered. **Policies:** Freshmen permitted cars on campus. **Housing:** Coed dorms, apartments available. $135 deposit, deadline 6/1. **Activities:** Jazz band, choral groups, dance, drama, literary magazine, music ensembles, student government, student newspaper, African-American Association, Baptist student union, Campus Crusade for Christ, College Republicans, Young Democrats, student education association, campus activity board, Association for the Education of Young Children, environmental club, Amnesty International.

Athletics. NCAA. **Intercollegiate:** Baseball M, basketball, cheerleading, cross-country, golf, soccer, softball W, tennis, volleyball W. **Intramural:** Basketball, bowling, football (non-tackle), soccer, softball, table tennis, tennis, volleyball. **Team name:** Spartans.

Student services. Adult student services, alcohol/substance abuse counseling, campus ministries, career counseling, services for economically disadvantaged, student employment services, financial aid counseling, health services, minority student services, on-campus daycare, personal counseling, placement for graduates, veterans' counselor, women's services. **Physically disabled:** Services for visually, speech, hearing impaired. **Learning disabled:** Comprehensive services available.

Contact. E-mail: dstewart@uscupstate.edu
Phone: (864) 503-5246 Toll-free number: (800) 277-8727
Fax: (864) 503-5727
Donette Stewart, Assistant Vice Chancelor for Enrollment Services, University of South Carolina Upstate, 800 University Way, Spartanburg, SC 29303

Voorhees College

Denmark, South Carolina
www.voorhees.edu **CB code: 5863**

- Private 4-year liberal arts college affiliated with Episcopal Church
- Residential campus in small town
- 708 degree-seeking undergraduates
- 36% of applicants admitted

General. Founded in 1897. Regionally accredited. **Degrees:** 154 bachelor's awarded. **ROTC:** Army. **Location:** 50 miles from Columbia and Augusta, Georgia. **Calendar:** Semester, limited summer session. **Full-time faculty:** 40 total. **Part-time faculty:** 17 total.

Freshman class profile. 1,815 applied, 658 admitted, 134 enrolled.

Mid 50% test scores			
SAT verbal:	310-420	Rank in top quarter:	10%
SAT math:	310-440	Rank in top tenth:	2%
ACT:	13-16	Out-of-state:	10%
		Live on campus:	95%

Basis for selection. Secondary school record, GPA (2.0 or above), recommendations, and standardized test scores considered in admissions decisions. Interview required for Project Smart applicants.

High school preparation. 20 units recommended. Recommended units include English 4, mathematics 3, social studies 2, science 2, foreign language 2 and academic electives 7.

2005-2006 Annual costs. Tuition/fees: $7,726. Room/board: $4,572. Books/supplies: $600. Personal expenses: $1,365.

2005-2006 Financial aid. Need-based: 201 full-time freshmen applied for aid; 194 were judged to have need; 194 of these received aid. Average need met was 52%. Average scholarship/grant was $5,341; average loan $1,981. 52% of total undergraduate aid awarded as scholarships/grants, 48% as loans/jobs. **Non-need-based:** Awarded to 126 full-time undergraduates, including 59 freshmen.

Application procedures. Admission: Priority date 4/15; no deadline. $25 fee, may be waived for applicants with need. Application may be submitted online. Admission notification on a rolling basis beginning on or about 1/15. **Financial aid:** Priority date 4/15; no closing date. FAFSA, institutional form required. Applicants notified on a rolling basis starting 3/1; must reply within 2 week(s) of notification.

Academics. Special study options: Accelerated study, combined bachelor's/graduate degree, cooperative education, honors, independent study, internships, liberal arts/career combination, study abroad, weekend college. **Credit/placement by examination:** AP, CLEP, IB, institutional tests. 15 credit hours maximum toward bachelor's degree. **Support services:** Learning center, reduced course load, remedial instruction, study skills assistance, tutoring.

Honors college/program. Students are required to have SAT 1000 (exclusive of Writing) or higher and GPA 3.5 or higher.

Majors. Biology: General. **Business:** General, accounting, accounting/finance, business admin, management information systems, organizational behavior. **Communications:** Broadcast journalism, media studies. **Computer sciences:** General, computer science. **English:** English lit. **Health:** Predentistry, premedicine, prenursing. **Math:** General. **Parks/recreation:** Health/fitness. **Social sciences:** Sociology.

Computing on campus. 175 workstations in dormitories, library, computer center. Dormitories wired for high-speed internet access and linked to campus network. Commuter students can connect to campus network. Online library, helpline, wireless network available.

Student life. Freshman orientation: Mandatory. Preregistration for classes offered. One day orientation offered in June and July. One week orientation offered in August. **Policies:** Freshmen permitted cars on campus. **Housing:** Guaranteed on-campus for all undergraduates. Single-sex dorms available. $60 deposit, deadline 7/31. Accommodations for single mothers. **Activities:** Pep band, choral groups, dance, drama, radio station, student government, student newspaper.

Athletics. NAIA. **Intercollegiate:** Baseball M, basketball, cheerleading, cross-country, softball W, track and field, volleyball W. **Intramural:** Baseball M, basketball, softball W. **Team name:** Tigers.

Student services. Adult student services, campus ministries, career counseling, student employment services, financial aid counseling, health services, personal counseling, placement for graduates, veterans' counselor.

Contact. E-mail: bwatson@voorhees.edu
Phone: (803) 703-7112 Toll-free number: (800) 446-6250
Fax: (803) 793-1117
Benjamin Watson, Director of Admissions, Voorhees College, 213 Wiggins Road, Denmark, SC 29042

W.L. Bonner Bible College
Columbia, South Carolina

- Private 4-year Bible college

General. Accredited by ABHE.

Contact. Phone: (803) 754-3950
4430 Argent Court, Columbia, SC 29203

Winthrop University
Rock Hill, South Carolina — **CB member**
www.winthrop.edu — **CB code: 5910**

- Public 4-year university
- Residential campus in small city
- 5,000 degree-seeking undergraduates
- SAT or ACT with writing required

General. Founded in 1886. Regionally accredited. **Degrees:** 872 bachelor's awarded; master's offered. **Location:** 20 miles from Charlotte, North Carolina. **Calendar:** Semester, extensive summer session. **Full-time faculty:** 260 total. **Part-time faculty:** 230 total. **Class size:** 41% < 20, 47% 20-39, 8% 40-49, 4% 50-99. **Special facilities:** Nursery laboratory, music conservatory.

Freshman class profile.

Mid 50% test scores			
SAT verbal:	480-580	Rank in top tenth:	21%
SAT math:	480-580	Out-of-state:	12%
ACT:	19-24	Live on campus:	86%
Rank in top quarter:	56%	Sororities:	9%

Basis for selection. School achievement record, test scores, counselor recommendations important, school and community activities considered. Essay, interview recommended for all; audition recommended for dance, music, theater programs.

High school preparation. 20 units required; 21 recommended. Required and recommended units include English 4, mathematics 3-4, social studies 2, history 1, science 3 (laboratory 3), foreign language 2 and academic electives 4. Mathematics must include algebra I, II and geometry. Foreign language units must be in same language. Physical education or ROTC required.

2005-2006 Annual costs. Tuition/fees: $8,756; $16,150 out-of-state. Room/board: $5,352. Books/supplies: $750. Personal expenses: $1,236.

Financial aid. Non-need-based: Scholarships awarded for academics, art, athletics, music/drama, state residency. **Additional information:** Academic scholarships from $1,500 to full tuition and board awarded to approximately one-third of entering freshman class each year.

Application procedures. Admission: Priority date 6/1; no deadline. $40 fee, may be waived for applicants with need. Admission notification on a rolling basis beginning on or about 11/21. Must reply by May 1 or within 3 week(s) if notified thereafter. 8 monthly notification dates for fall between October and May on the 21st of the month. **Financial aid:** Priority date 3/1; no closing date. FAFSA required. Applicants notified on a rolling basis starting 4/1; must reply within 2 week(s) of notification.

Academics. Special study options: Cooperative education, cross-registration, distance learning, double major, exchange student, honors, independent study, internships, study abroad, teacher certification program, United Nations semester. **Credit/placement by examination:** AP, CLEP, IB, institutional tests. 30 credit hours maximum toward bachelor's degree. **Support services:** Pre-admission summer program, study skills assistance, tutoring, writing center.

Majors. Biology: General. **Business:** Business admin. **Communications:** Journalism, public relations. **Computer sciences:** General. **Education:** Early childhood, elementary, middle, music, physical, special. **English:** Technical writing. **Family/consumer sciences:** Food/nutrition. **Foreign languages:** General. **Health:** Clinical lab science, communication disorders. **History:** General. **Math:** General. **Parks/recreation:** Sports admin. **Philosophy/religion:** Philosophy, religion. **Physical sciences:** Chemistry. **Psychology:** General. **Public administration:** Social work. **Social sciences:** Political science, sociology. **Visual/performing arts:** Art, art history/conservation, dance, dramatic, studio arts.

Most popular majors. Business/marketing 22%, communications/journalism 7%, education 19%, psychology 7%, social sciences 10%, visual/performing arts 13%.

Computing on campus. 250 workstations in dormitories, library, computer center, student center. Dormitories linked to campus network. Online course registration, helpline, student web hosting, wireless network available.

Student life. Freshman orientation: Available. 3-day session in June. **Policies:** First and second year students are required to live on campus unless living with parents within 50 miles. Freshmen permitted cars on campus. **Housing:** Guaranteed on-campus for freshmen. Coed dorms, single-sex dorms, apartments, fraternity/sorority housing, substance-free housing available. $100 deposit. **Activities:** Bands, choral groups, dance, drama, literary magazine, music ensembles, musical theater, opera, radio station, student government, student newspaper, 115 clubs and organizations.

Athletics. NCAA. **Intercollegiate:** Baseball M, basketball, cross-country, golf, soccer, softball W, tennis, track and field, volleyball W. **Intramural:**

Badminton, basketball, cross-country, fencing, football (non-tackle), football (tackle) M, golf, handball, racquetball, soccer, softball, swimming, table tennis, tennis, volleyball. **Team name:** Eagles.

Student services. Adult student services, alcohol/substance abuse counseling, career counseling, student employment services, financial aid counseling, health services, minority student services, personal counseling, placement for graduates, veterans' counselor.

Contact. E-mail: admissions@winthrop.edu
Phone: (803) 323-2191 Toll-free number: (800) 763-0230
Fax: (803) 323-2137
Debi Barber, Director of Admissions, Winthrop University, 701 Oakland Avenue, Rock Hill, SC 29733

Wofford College

Spartanburg, South Carolina — **CB member**
www.wofford.edu — **CB code: 5912**

- Private 4-year liberal arts college affiliated with United Methodist Church
- Residential campus in small city
- 1,163 degree-seeking undergraduates: 1% part-time, 48% women, 6% African American, 2% Asian American, 1% Hispanic American, 1% international
- 66% of applicants admitted
- SAT or ACT with writing, application essay required
- 78% graduate within 6 years; 40% enter graduate study

General. Founded in 1854. Regionally accredited. **Degrees:** 256 bachelor's awarded. **ROTC:** Army. **Location:** 70 miles from Charlotte, North Carolina, 180 miles from Atlanta. **Calendar:** 4-1-4, limited summer session. **Full-time faculty:** 89 total; 92% have terminal degrees, 8% minority, 35% women. **Part-time faculty:** 33 total; 61% have terminal degrees, 3% minority, 33% women. **Class size:** 76% < 20, 23% 20-39, less than 1% 40-49, less than 1% 50-99. **Special facilities:** Arboretum.

Freshman class profile. 1,871 applied, 1,237 admitted, 321 enrolled.

Mid 50% test scores		**Return as sophomores:**	89%
SAT verbal:	570-660	**Out-of-state:**	53%
SAT math:	580-680	**Live on campus:**	99%
ACT:	22-27	**International:**	1%
Rank in top quarter:	83%	**Fraternities:**	45%
Rank in top tenth:	57%	**Sororities:**	60%
End year in good standing:	95%		

Basis for selection. High school record, including AP courses, most important. Test scores important. School recommendation, leadership, extracurricular activities considered. Minority applications encouraged. Interview recommended.

High school preparation. 20 units recommended. Recommended units include English 4, mathematics 4, social studies 2, history 1, (laboratory 3), foreign language 3 and academic electives 3.

2005-2006 Annual costs. Tuition/fees: $24,130. Room/board: $6,805. Books/supplies: $851. Personal expenses: $1,800.

2005-2006 Financial aid. Need-based: 224 full-time freshmen applied for aid; 162 were judged to have need; 162 of these received aid. Average need met was 85%. Average scholarship/grant was $16,532; average loan $2,942. 84% of total undergraduate aid awarded as scholarships/grants, 16% as loans/jobs. **Non-need-based:** Awarded to 716 full-time undergraduates, including 196 freshmen. Scholarships awarded for academics, athletics, leadership, music/drama, religious affiliation, ROTC, state residency.

Application procedures. Admission: Closing date 2/1 (postmark date). $40 fee, may be waived for applicants with need. Application must be submitted on paper. Admission notification 3/15. Must reply by 5/1. Must be admitted by December 15 to be eligible for Wofford Scholars (academic merit scholarship) program. **Financial aid:** Priority date 3/15; no closing date. FAFSA required. Applicants notified on a rolling basis starting 3/31; must reply by 5/1.

Academics. January interim program devoted to internships, foreign travel, independent study, and other nontraditional academic pursuits. **Special study options:** Accelerated study, cross-registration, double major, dual enrollment of high school students, independent study, internships, liberal arts/career combination, student-designed major, study abroad, teacher certification program, Washington semester. Presidential International Scholar program, summer intern programs at Milliken Research, Success Initiative and Bonner Scholars. **Credit/placement by examination:** AP, CLEP, IB. 30 credit hours maximum toward bachelor's degree. Chemistry majors must validate AP score of 4 in chemistry by successfully passing a departmental test. **Support services:** Tutoring, writing center.

Majors. Biology: General. **Business:** Accounting, finance, international, managerial economics. **Computer sciences:** General, computer science. **Foreign languages:** French, German, Spanish. **History:** General. **Liberal arts:** Arts/sciences. **Math:** General. **Philosophy/religion:** Philosophy, religion. **Physical sciences:** Chemistry, physics. **Psychology:** General. **Social sciences:** Economics, sociology, U.S. government. **Visual/performing arts:** Art history/conservation, theater design.

Most popular majors. Biology 16%, business/marketing 28%, English 7%, foreign language 9%, history 7%, psychology 6%, social sciences 13%.

Computing on campus. 35 workstations in library, computer center, student center. Dormitories linked to campus network. Commuter students can connect to campus network. Online course registration, online library, helpline, student web hosting available.

Student life. Freshman orientation: Mandatory. Preregistration for classes offered. Held 3 days before the semester begins. **Policies:** Honor code and honor council. Freshmen permitted cars on campus. **Housing:** Guaranteed on-campus for all undergraduates. Coed dorms, fraternity/sorority housing, substance-free housing available. $300 deposit, deadline 5/1. Students not living with immediate family member must secure permission to live off-campus. **Activities:** Bands, choral groups, drama, literary magazine, music ensembles, student government, student newspaper, Fellowship of Christian Athletes, Baptist student union, Association of African-American Students, student volunteer services, College Republicans, College Democrats, art and drama groups, service organizations, college bowl team, Lion's Club, and Rotaract Club.

Athletics. NCAA. **Intercollegiate:** Baseball M, basketball, cross-country, football (tackle) M, golf, rifle, soccer, tennis, track and field, volleyball W. **Intramural:** Basketball, racquetball, softball, tennis, volleyball. **Team name:** Terriers.

Student services. Alcohol/substance abuse counseling, campus ministries, career counseling, student employment services, financial aid counseling, health services, minority student services, personal counseling, placement for graduates. **Physically disabled:** Services for visually, speech, hearing impaired.

Contact. E-mail: admissions@wofford.edu
Phone: (864) 597-4130 Fax: (864) 597-4147
Brand Stille, Director of Admissions, Wofford College, 429 North Church Street, Spartanburg, SC 29303-3663

South Dakota

Augustana College

Sioux Falls, South Dakota **CB member**
www.augie.edu **CB code: 6015**

- Private 4-year liberal arts college affiliated with Evangelical Lutheran Church in America
- Residential campus in small city
- 1,621 degree-seeking undergraduates: 62% women
- 31 graduate students
- 80% of applicants admitted
- SAT or ACT (ACT writing optional) required
- 64% graduate within 6 years; 25% enter graduate study

General. Founded in 1860. Regionally accredited. **Degrees:** 360 bachelor's awarded; master's offered. **Location:** 160 miles from Omaha, Nebraska, 230 miles from Minneapolis-St. Paul. **Calendar:** 4-1-4, limited summer session. **Full-time faculty:** 108 total. **Part-time faculty:** 72 total. **Class size:** 44% < 20, 48% 20-39, 3% 40-49, 4% 50-99. **Special facilities:** Western studies museum and archives, archeology lab, liturgical art center, prairie garden.

Freshman class profile. 1,544 applied, 1,229 admitted, 405 enrolled.

Mid 50% test scores		**GPA 2.0-2.99:**	10%
SAT verbal:	530-650	**Rank in top quarter:**	62%
SAT math:	520-620	**Rank in top tenth:**	25%
ACT:	22-27	**Return as sophomores:**	79%
GPA 3.50 or higher:	64%	**Out-of-state:**	55%
GPA 3.0-3.49:	25%	**Live on campus:**	97%

Basis for selection. High school transcript, test scores, and 1 recommendation required. Minimum requirements: 20 ACT (or equivalent SAT), 2.5 GPA, class rank at 50% or higher. Interview recommended for all; supplementary essay questions/materials required for students who do not meet minimum admission requirements.

High school preparation. 16 units recommended. Recommended units include English 4, mathematics 4, social studies 3, science 4 (laboratory 3) and foreign language 2. 1 unit fine arts and 1/2 unit computer science also recommended.

2006-2007 Annual costs. Tuition/fees: $19,986. Room/board: $5,664. Books/supplies: $800. Personal expenses: $800.

2005-2006 Financial aid. Need-based: 62% of total undergraduate aid awarded as scholarships/grants, 38% as loans/jobs. **Non-need-based:** Scholarships awarded for academics, alumni affiliation, art, athletics, leadership, minority status, music/drama, religious affiliation.

Application procedures. Admission: Priority date 1/15; deadline 9/1. No application fee. Application may be submitted online. Admission notification on a rolling basis beginning on or about 10/1. Must reply by May 1 or within 2 week(s) if notified thereafter. **Financial aid:** Priority date 3/1; no closing date. FAFSA required. Applicants notified on a rolling basis starting 3/15; must reply by 5/1 or within 3 week(s) of notification.

Academics. Special study options: Accelerated study, combined bachelor's/graduate degree, cross-registration, double major, dual enrollment of high school students, independent study, internships, liberal arts/career combination, student-designed major, study abroad, teacher certification program, urban semester, Washington semester. **Credit/placement by examination:** AP, CLEP, IB, institutional tests. 32 credit hours maximum toward bachelor's degree. **Support services:** Learning center, pre-admission summer program, reduced course load, study skills assistance, tutoring, writing center.

Majors. Biology: General. **Business:** General, accounting, business admin, communications, management information systems. **Communications:** General, journalism. **Computer sciences:** Computer science. **Education:** Art, biology, Deaf/hearing impaired, elementary, emotionally handicapped, English, French, German, history, learning disabled, mathematics, mentally handicapped, multicultural, music, physical, physically handicapped, physics, psychology, secondary, social studies, Spanish, special, speech, speech impaired. **Engineering:** Physics. **English:** English lit. **Foreign languages:** General, French, German, Spanish. **Health:** Athletic training, audiology/speech pathology, clinical lab science, clinical lab technology, communication disorders, nursing (RN), predentistry, premedicine, prepharmacy, preveterinary. **History:** General. **Interdisciplinary:** Global studies. **Math:** General. **Parks/recreation:** Exercise sciences, health/fitness. **Philosophy/religion:** Philosophy, religion. **Physical sciences:** Chemistry, physics. **Protective services:** Forensics. **Psychology:** General. **Social sciences:** Economics, political science, sociology. **Visual/performing arts:** Art, dramatic.

Most popular majors. Biology 9%, business/marketing 15%, education 18%, health sciences 13%, philosophy/religious studies 6%, social sciences 11%.

Computing on campus. 375 workstations in dormitories, library, computer center, student center. Dormitories wired for high-speed internet access and linked to campus network. Commuter students can connect to campus network. Online course registration, online library, helpline, repair service, wireless network available.

Student life. Freshman orientation: Mandatory. Preregistration for classes offered. One day registration held during summer. 3 day orientation beginning on move-in day. **Policies:** Freshmen permitted cars on campus. **Housing:** Guaranteed on-campus for all undergraduates. Coed dorms, apartments, substance-free housing available. $100 deposit. Campus-owned theme houses available to upperclassmen. **Activities:** Bands, choral groups, dance, drama, film society, literary magazine, music ensembles, musical theater, opera, radio station, student government, student newspaper, symphony orchestra, Lutheran-ELCA congregation, Fellowship of Christian Athletes, Circle K, Augie Democrats, College Republicans, Augie Green, Catholics in Action, Augustana Coalition for Social Justice.

Athletics. NCAA. **Intercollegiate:** Baseball M, basketball, cross-country, football (tackle) M, golf, soccer W, softball W, tennis, track and field, volleyball W, wrestling M. **Intramural:** Basketball, football (non-tackle), golf, softball, triathlon, volleyball. **Team name:** Vikings.

Student services. Adult student services, alcohol/substance abuse counseling, campus ministries, career counseling, student employment services, financial aid counseling, health services, on-campus daycare, personal counseling, placement for graduates, veterans' counselor. **Physically disabled:** Services for visually, hearing impaired.

Contact. E-mail: admission@augie.edu
Phone: (605) 274-5516 Toll-free number: (800) 727-2844
Fax: (605) 274-5518
Nancy Davidson, Dean of Admission, Augustana College, 2001 South Summit Avenue, Sioux Falls, SD 57197-9990

Black Hills State University

Spearfish, South Dakota
www.bhsu.edu **CB code: 6042**

- Public 4-year liberal arts and teachers college
- Commuter campus in small town
- 3,166 degree-seeking undergraduates
- 94% of applicants admitted
- SAT or ACT (ACT writing optional) required

General. Founded in 1883. Regionally accredited. Evening degree program available at Ellsworth Air Force Base campus in Rapid City. **Degrees:** 38 bachelor's, 13 associate awarded; master's offered. **ROTC:** Army. **Location:** 45 miles from Rapid City. **Calendar:** Semester, extensive summer session. **Full-time faculty:** 111 total. **Part-time faculty:** 89 total. **Class size:** 21% < 20, 23% 20-39, 4% 40-49, less than 1% 50-99, 52% >100.

Freshman class profile. 1,432 applied, 1,349 admitted, 658 enrolled.

Mid 50% test scores		**Rank in top tenth:**	6%
ACT:	18-23	**Out-of-state:**	23%
Rank in top quarter:	23%		

Basis for selection. For bachelor's degree programs, minimum ACT composite score of 18 or class rank in top 60% (in-state applicants), top half (out-of-state applicants), or minimum GPA 2.6 in required courses. Portfolio recommended.

High school preparation. 14 units required. Required units include English 4, mathematics 3, social studies 3, science 3 (laboratory 3). One fine arts required.

2005-2006 Annual costs. Tuition/fees: $4,754; $9,741 out-of-state. Reciprocity agreements reduce tuition for some out-of-state students . Room/board: $3,960. Books/supplies: $600. Personal expenses: $1,252.

Financial aid. All financial aid based on need.

Application procedures. **Admission:** Closing date 7/15. $20 fee. Application may be submitted online. Admission notification on a rolling basis. **Financial aid:** Closing date 2/15. FAFSA required. Applicants notified on a rolling basis starting 5/15; must reply within 3 week(s) of notification.

Academics. **Special study options:** Cooperative education, distance learning, double major, dual enrollment of high school students, honors, independent study, internships, teacher certification program. **Credit/placement by examination:** AP, CLEP, institutional tests. 32 credit hours maximum toward bachelor's degree. **Support services:** Learning center, remedial instruction, study skills assistance, tutoring.

Majors. **Area/ethnic studies:** Native American. **Biology:** General. **Business:** Accounting, business admin, entrepreneurial studies, human resources, marketing, office management, tourism/travel. **Communications:** Media studies. **Education:** Art, biology, business, chemistry, elementary, English, foreign languages, history, kindergarten/preschool, mathematics, middle, music, physical, science, social science, special, speech, technology/industrial arts. **Engineering technology:** Industrial. **English:** English lit, speech/rhetoric. **Foreign languages:** Spanish. **Health:** Facilities admin. **History:** General. **Math:** General. **Parks/recreation:** General, exercise sciences, sports admin. **Physical sciences:** General, chemistry. **Psychology:** General. **Public administration:** Community org/advocacy. **Social sciences:** General, political science, sociology. **Visual/performing arts:** Art, commercial/advertising art.

Most popular majors. Business/marketing 24%, communications/journalism 6%, education 28%, psychology 7%, security/protective services 7%, social sciences 11%.

Computing on campus. 400 workstations in dormitories, library, student center. Dormitories wired for high-speed internet access and linked to campus network. Commuter students can connect to campus network. Online course registration, online library, helpline, wireless network available.

Student life. **Freshman orientation:** Available. Preregistration for classes offered. **Policies:** Freshmen permitted cars on campus. **Housing:** Guaranteed on-campus for freshmen. Coed dorms, single-sex dorms, apartments available. $100 deposit. Married student housing. **Activities:** Bands, choral groups, drama, music ensembles, radio station, student government, student newspaper, TV station, Native American Special Services, Inter-Greek Council, United Ministry, Veterans Club, Young Democrats, Young Republicans.

Athletics. NAIA. **Intercollegiate:** Basketball, cross-country, football (tackle) M, track and field, volleyball W. **Intramural:** Archery, badminton, basketball, bowling, golf, skiing, soccer, softball, swimming, table tennis, tennis, volleyball. **Team name:** Yellow Jackets.

Student services. Campus ministries, career counseling, student employment services, health services, on-campus daycare, personal counseling, placement for graduates, veterans' counselor. **Physically disabled:** Services for visually, speech, hearing impaired.

Contact. E-mail: admissions@bhsu.edu
Phone: (605) 642-6343 Toll-free number: (800) 255-2478
Fax: (605) 642-6022
Kristi Pearce, Dean of Enrollment, Black Hills State University, University Street Box 9502, Spearfish, SD 57799-9502

Dakota State University

Madison, South Dakota
www.dsu.edu **CB code: 6247**

- Public 4-year university
- Residential campus in small town
- 1,457 degree-seeking undergraduates: 20% part-time, 48% women, 1% African American, 1% Asian American, 1% Hispanic American, 1% Native American, 1% international
- 152 degree-seeking graduate students
- 97% of applicants admitted
- SAT or ACT (ACT writing optional) required
- 50% graduate within 6 years

General. Founded in 1881. Regionally accredited. Completely wireless environment. **Degrees:** 293 bachelor's, 47 associate awarded; master's offered. **ROTC:** Army, Air Force. **Location:** 45 miles from Sioux Falls. **Calendar:** Semester, limited summer session. **Full-time faculty:** 77 total; 34% have terminal degrees, 5% minority, 35% women. **Part-time faculty:** 31 total; 68% have terminal degrees, 3% minority, 52% women. **Class size:** 52% < 20, 44% 20-39, 1% 40-49, 2% 50-99, less than 1% >100. **Special facilities:** Museum.

Freshman class profile. 594 applied, 575 admitted, 314 enrolled.

Mid 50% test scores		**Out-of-state:**	18%
ACT:	19-24	**Live on campus:**	86%
Rank in top quarter:	20%	**International:**	1%
Rank in top tenth:	6%		

Basis for selection. All students must be either in top 60% of class or have minimum ACT composite scores of 18, or have high school minimum GPA of 2.6 in core courses. Underqualified applicants considered.

High school preparation. Recommended units include English 4, mathematics 3, social studies 3, science 3 (laboratory 3). One unit of fine arts required.

2005-2006 Annual costs. Tuition/fees: $4,832; $9,819 out-of-state. Reciprocity agreements reduce tuition for some out-of-state students . Room/board: $3,665. Books/supplies: $660.

2004-2005 Financial aid. **Need-based:** 276 full-time freshmen applied for aid; 220 were judged to have need; 216 of these received aid. Average need met was 78%. Average scholarship/grant was $2,764; average loan $2,953. 28% of total undergraduate aid awarded as scholarships/grants, 72% as loans/jobs. **Non-need-based:** Awarded to 628 full-time undergraduates, including 192 freshmen. Scholarships awarded for academics, alumni affiliation, art, athletics, leadership, minority status, music/drama, state residency. **Additional information:** Application deadline for grants and scholarships March 1. No deadline for loan and job applications.

Application procedures. **Admission:** No deadline. $20 fee. Application may be submitted online. Admission notification on a rolling basis. **Financial aid:** Priority date 3/1; no closing date. FAFSA required. Applicants notified on a rolling basis starting 4/15; must reply within 2 week(s) of notification.

Academics. Health information management degree and masters in information systems offered online. **Special study options:** Cooperative education, cross-registration, distance learning, double major, dual enrollment of high school students, ESL, honors, independent study, internships, teacher certification program. **Credit/placement by examination:** AP, CLEP, IB, institutional tests. 32 credit hours maximum toward bachelor's degree. **Support services:** Learning center, reduced course load, remedial instruction, study skills assistance, tutoring, writing center.

Majors. **Biology:** General. **Business:** General, business admin, e-commerce, management information systems, marketing. **Computer sciences:** General, computer graphics, computer science, information systems, web page design. **Education:** General, art, biology, business, chemistry, computer, elementary, English, health, history, mathematics, middle, multi-level teacher, music, physical, physics, sales/marketing, science, secondary, social studies, special. **Health:** Medical records admin, predentistry, premedicine, prepharmacy, preveterinary, respiratory therapy technology. **Legal studies:** Prelaw. **Math:** General, statistics. **Parks/recreation:** Health/fitness, sports admin. **Physical sciences:** Chemistry. **Visual/performing arts:** Studio arts.

Most popular majors. Business/marketing 28%, computer/information sciences 35%, education 20%.

Computing on campus. PC or laptop required. 417 workstations in dormitories, library, computer center, student center. Dormitories wired for high-speed internet access and linked to campus network. Commuter students can connect to campus network. Online course registration, online library, helpline, student web hosting, wireless network available.

Student life. **Freshman orientation:** Mandatory. Preregistration for classes offered. **Policies:** Freshmen permitted cars on campus. **Housing:** Guaranteed on-campus for freshmen. Coed dorms, single-sex dorms, apartments, substance-free housing available. $50 fully refundable deposit. Apartment style residence halls available. **Activities:** Bands, choral groups, dance, drama, literary magazine, music ensembles, musical theater, radio station, student government, student newspaper.

Athletics. NAIA. **Intercollegiate:** Baseball M, basketball, cross-country, football (tackle) M, soccer, softball W, tennis, volleyball W. **Intramural:** Basketball, racquetball, softball, table tennis, tennis, volleyball. **Team name:** Trojans.

Student services. Alcohol/substance abuse counseling, campus ministries, career counseling, student employment services, financial aid counseling, health services, minority student services, personal counseling, placement for graduates, veterans' counselor. **Physically disabled:** Services for visually, speech, hearing impaired.

Four-Year Colleges

Contact. E-mail: yourfuture@dsu.edu
Phone: (605) 256-5139 Toll-free number: (888) 378-9988
Fax: (605) 256-5020
Amy Crissinger, Director of Admission, Dakota State University, 820 North Washington Avenue, Madison, SD 57042

Dakota Wesleyan University
Mitchell, South Dakota
www.dwu.edu **CB code: 6155**

- Private 4-year university and liberal arts college affiliated with United Methodist Church
- Commuter campus in large town
- 755 degree-seeking undergraduates: 3% part-time, 59% women
- 783 graduate students
- SAT or ACT required

General. Founded in 1885. Regionally accredited. **Degrees:** 111 bachelor's, 30 associate awarded; master's offered. **Location:** 70 miles from Sioux Falls. **Calendar:** Semester, limited summer session. **Full-time faculty:** 45 total; 62% have terminal degrees, 2% minority, 47% women. **Part-time faculty:** 34 total; 29% have terminal degrees, 6% minority, 50% women. **Class size:** 74% < 20, 24% 20-39, 1% 40-49, 1% 50-99. **Special facilities:** Museum, observatory.

Freshman class profile.

Mid 50% test scores			
ACT:	18-23	Out-of-state:	37%
		Live on campus:	96%

Basis for selection. High school record, test scores, school activities, personal interview considered. Recommendations and personal interview used for marginal students. **Learning Disabled:** For special assistance, documentation of student's learning disability is required.

High school preparation. Recommended units include English 4, mathematics 4, social studies 4, history 3, science 3 (laboratory 1) and foreign language 2.

2005-2006 Annual costs. Tuition/fees: $15,700. Room/board: $4,800. Books/supplies: $800. Personal expenses: $1,200.

2005-2006 Financial aid. Need-based: 136 full-time freshmen applied for aid; 115 were judged to have need; 115 of these received aid. Average need met was 76%. Average scholarship/grant was $5,324; average loan $3,126. 59% of total undergraduate aid awarded as scholarships/grants, 41% as loans/jobs. **Non-need-based:** Scholarships awarded for academics, alumni affiliation, art, athletics, leadership, minority status, music/drama, religious affiliation.

Application procedures. Admission: Priority date 4/1; deadline 8/25 (receipt date). $25 fee, may be waived for applicants with need. Application may be submitted online. Admission notification on a rolling basis. **Financial aid:** Priority date 4/1; no closing date. FAFSA required. Applicants notified on a rolling basis starting 3/1; must reply within 2 week(s) of notification.

Academics. Special study options: Cross-registration, distance learning, double major, dual enrollment of high school students, exchange student, honors, independent study, internships, student-designed major, study abroad, teacher certification program, Washington semester. **Credit/placement by examination:** AP, CLEP, IB, institutional tests. 12 credit hours maximum toward associate degree, 63 toward bachelor's. **Support services:** Learning center, pre-admission summer program, reduced course load, remedial instruction, study skills assistance, tutoring, writing center.

Majors. Biology: General. **Business:** General, accounting. **Communications:** General, journalism. **Computer sciences:** Web page design. **Conservation:** Wildlife. **Education:** General, art, biology, business, elementary, English, mathematics, music, physical, science, social science, social studies, special. **Health:** Athletic training, predentistry, premedicine, prepharmacy, preveterinary. **History:** General. **Interdisciplinary:** Behavioral sciences. **Legal studies:** Prelaw. **Math:** General. **Parks/recreation:** Exercise sciences, sports admin. **Protective services:** Criminal justice. **Psychology:** General. **Social sciences:** General, sociology. **Theology:** Sacred music, youth ministry. **Visual/performing arts:** Art, dramatic.

Most popular majors. Business/marketing 25%, education 25%, parks/recreation 6%, security/protective services 18%.

Computing on campus. 85 workstations in dormitories, library, computer center, student center. Dormitories wired for high-speed internet access and linked to campus network. Commuter students can connect to campus network. Online library, helpline, repair service, student web hosting, wireless network available.

Student life. Freshman orientation: Mandatory. Preregistration for classes offered. In fall, held weekend before classes begin, 2 days. In spring, held first day of finalization. **Policies:** Freshmen permitted cars on campus. **Housing:** Guaranteed on-campus for freshmen. Coed dorms, single-sex dorms, apartments, substance-free housing available. Honor housing available for upperclassmen; ADA rooms and apartments available. **Activities:** Concert band, choral groups, drama, literary magazine, music ensembles, student government, student newspaper, Variety of religious, ethnic, minority, political, and service groups.

Athletics. NAIA. **Intercollegiate:** Baseball M, basketball, cheerleading, cross-country, football (tackle) M, golf, soccer, softball W, track and field, volleyball W, wrestling M. **Intramural:** Basketball, softball, volleyball, weight lifting. **Team name:** Tigers.

Student services. Adult student services, alcohol/substance abuse counseling, campus ministries, career counseling, services for economically disadvantaged, student employment services, financial aid counseling, health services, minority student services, on-campus daycare, personal counseling, placement for graduates. **Physically disabled:** Services for visually, hearing impaired.

Contact. E-mail: admissions@dwu.edu
Phone: (605) 995-2650 Toll-free number: (800) 333-8506
Fax: (605) 995-2699
Amy Novak, Admissions Operations and Outreach Programming, Dakota Wesleyan University, 1200 West University Avenue, Mitchell, SD 57301-4398

Mount Marty College
Yankton, South Dakota
www.mtmc.edu **CB code: 6416**

- Private 4-year liberal arts college affiliated with Roman Catholic Church
- Residential campus in large town
- 907 degree-seeking undergraduates: 22% part-time, 68% women, 2% African American, 2% Hispanic American, 3% Native American
- 100 degree-seeking graduate students
- 85% of applicants admitted
- SAT or ACT (ACT writing recommended) required
- 51% graduate within 6 years

General. Founded in 1936. Regionally accredited. **Degrees:** 166 bachelor's, 48 associate awarded; master's offered. **ROTC:** Army. **Location:** 75 miles from Sioux Falls, 60 miles from Sioux City, Iowa. **Calendar:** Semester, limited summer session. **Full-time faculty:** 48 total; 50% have terminal degrees, 8% minority, 46% women. **Part-time faculty:** 8 total; 50% women. **Class size:** 74% < 20, 22% 20-39, 3% 40-49, 1% 50-99, less than 1% >100.

Freshman class profile. 317 applied, 268 admitted, 148 enrolled.

Mid 50% test scores			
SAT verbal:	390-440	GPA 2.0-2.99:	22%
SAT math:	450-470	Rank in top quarter:	38%
ACT:	19-25	Rank in top tenth:	13%
GPA 3.50 or higher:	43%	Return as sophomores:	78%
GPA 3.0-3.49:	32%	Out-of-state:	45%
		Live on campus:	95%

Basis for selection. Academic record, test scores, GPA very important. Minimum 2.0 GPA and 18 ACT required for admission consideration. Interview recommended for all; audition required for scholarship recipients, music and theater programs. **Learning Disabled:** Students requesting disability services must submit a letter requesting services and documentation to support diagnosed disability.

2005-2006 Annual costs. Tuition/fees: $15,730. Room/board: $4,860. Books/supplies: $760. Personal expenses: $1,512.

2005-2006 Financial aid. Need-based: Average need met was 78%. Average scholarship/grant was $10,431; average loan $3,284. 12% of total undergraduate aid awarded as scholarships/grants, 88% as loans/jobs. **Non-need-based:** Scholarships awarded for academics, art, athletics, leadership, music/drama, religious affiliation. **Additional information:** Prestige scholarships application deadline 2/1.

Application procedures. Admission: Priority date 2/1; deadline 8/30 (receipt date). $35 fee, may be waived for applicants with need. Application may be submitted online. Admission notification on a rolling basis. **Financial aid:** Priority date 3/1; no closing date. FAFSA, institutional form required. Applicants notified on a rolling basis starting 3/15; must reply within 2 week(s) of notification.

Academics. **Special study options:** Accelerated study, cooperative education, double major, dual enrollment of high school students, honors, independent study, internships, liberal arts/career combination, student-designed major, teacher certification program, weekend college. **Credit/placement by examination:** AP, CLEP, IB, ACT, institutional tests. 88 credit hours maximum toward associate degree, 24 toward bachelor's. **Support services:** Learning center, reduced course load, remedial instruction, study skills assistance, tutoring, writing center.

Majors. **Biology:** General. **Business:** Accounting, business admin. **Computer sciences:** Computer science, information technology, programming. **Education:** Biology, chemistry, elementary, English, health, history, mathematics, middle, music, physical, science, secondary, social science. **English:** English lit. **Health:** Clinical lab science, medical radiologic technology/radiation therapy, nursing (RN). **History:** General. **Interdisciplinary:** Behavioral sciences. **Math:** General. **Parks/recreation:** Facilities management. **Philosophy/religion:** Religion. **Physical sciences:** Chemistry. **Protective services:** Criminal justice, forensics. **Psychology:** General. **Social sciences:** General. **Visual/performing arts:** Graphic design.

Most popular majors. Biology 6%, business/marketing 22%, education 23%, health sciences 20%, liberal arts 6%.

Computing on campus. PC or laptop required. 53 workstations in dormitories, library, computer center, student center. Dormitories wired for high-speed internet access and linked to campus network. Commuter students can connect to campus network. Online library, helpline, repair service, wireless network available.

Student life. **Freshman orientation:** Mandatory. Preregistration for classes offered. 3-day intensive orientation prior to beginning of fall semester. Orientation programs throughout academic year. **Policies:** Alcohol and drug free campus. Freshmen permitted cars on campus. **Housing:** Guaranteed on-campus for freshmen. Single-sex dorms, special housing for disabled available. $50 fully refundable deposit. All unmarried undergraduates under 21 required to live in college housing unless living with family. **Activities:** Bands, choral groups, drama, literary magazine, music ensembles, musical theater, student government, student newspaper, campus ministry, Yahoo outreach team, Habitat for Humanity, education club, nursing club, campus newspaper, English club.

Athletics. NAIA. **Intercollegiate:** Baseball M, basketball, cheerleading, cross-country, soccer, softball W, track and field, volleyball W. **Intramural:** Basketball. **Team name:** Lancers.

Student services. Adult student services, alcohol/substance abuse counseling, campus ministries, career counseling, student employment services, financial aid counseling, health services, on-campus daycare, personal counseling, placement for graduates, veterans' counselor. **Learning disabled:** Comprehensive services available.

Contact. E-mail: mmcadmit@mtmc.edu
Phone: (800) 658-4552 Toll-free number: (800) 658-4552
Fax: (605) 668-1607
Brandi Tschumper, Vice President of Enrollment Management, Mount Marty College, 1105 West Eighth Street, Yankton, SD 57078

National American University: Rapid City

Rapid City, South Dakota
www.national.edu/rc **CB code: 6464**

- For-profit 4-year business and technical college
- Residential campus in small city

General. Founded in 1941. Regionally accredited. **Location:** 400 miles from Denver. **Calendar:** Quarter.

Annual costs/financial aid. Tuition/fees (2005-2006): $10,665. Room/board: $4,230. Books/supplies: $1,125. Personal expenses: $1,053. Need-based financial aid available to full-time and part-time students.

Contact. Phone: (605) 394-48200
Director of Admissions, 321 Kansas City Street, Rapid City, SD 57701

Northern State University

Aberdeen, South Dakota
www.northern.edu **CB code: 6487**

- Public 4-year university and liberal arts college
- Residential campus in large town
- 1,872 degree-seeking undergraduates: 15% part-time, 57% women
- 150 degree-seeking graduate students
- 94% of applicants admitted
- ACT (writing optional) required
- 38% graduate within 6 years; 13% enter graduate study

General. Founded in 1901. Regionally accredited. Technology proficiency certification available for all degree programs. Emphasis on distance delivery technology in all degree programs especially in all levels of teacher preparation. **Degrees:** 293 bachelor's, 24 associate awarded; master's offered. **Location:** 285 miles from Minneapolis-St. Paul. **Calendar:** Semester, limited summer session. **Full-time faculty:** 94 total; 81% have terminal degrees, 11% minority, 30% women. **Class size:** 44% < 20, 47% 20-39, 4% 40-49, 5% 50-99. **Special facilities:** Art galleries, e-learning center, center of excellence for international business.

Freshman class profile. 783 applied, 737 admitted, 381 enrolled.

Mid 50% test scores		Return as sophomores:	69%
ACT:	18-24	Out-of-state:	18%

Basis for selection. Applicants to 4-year programs must meet the following: GPA in required courses or rank in top 60 of graduating class. Minimum ACT composite score of 18. Minimum GPA 2.6. Applicants lacking required high school units admitted provisionally. Equivalent work must be completed within 2 years. Interview recommended for borderline applicants; portfolio recommended for art program.

High school preparation. 13 units required. Required units include English 4, mathematics 3, social studies 3, science 3 (laboratory 3). Mathematics units must be algebra or above; .5 fine arts required.

2005-2006 Annual costs. Tuition/fees: $4,700; $9,687 out-of-state. Reciprocity agreements reduce tuition for some out-of-state students . Room/board: $3,821. Books/supplies: $650. Personal expenses: $2,350.

Financial aid. **Non-need-based:** Scholarships awarded for academics, athletics, state residency.

Application procedures. **Admission:** No deadline. $20 fee. Admission notification on a rolling basis. **Financial aid:** Priority date 3/1; no closing date. FAFSA required. Applicants notified on a rolling basis starting 5/1; must reply within 2 week(s) of notification.

Academics. **Special study options:** Distance learning, double major, dual enrollment of high school students, ESL, external degree, honors, independent study, internships, student-designed major, study abroad, teacher certification program, Washington semester, weekend college. **Credit/placement by examination:** AP, CLEP, institutional tests. 32 credit hours maximum toward bachelor's degree. **Support services:** Learning center, pre-admission summer program, reduced course load, remedial instruction, study skills assistance, tutoring, writing center.

Majors. **Biology:** General, ecology. **Business:** General, accounting, business admin, finance, international, management information systems, marketing, office/clerical. **Computer sciences:** General. **Education:** General, art, business, curriculum, early childhood, elementary, English, foreign languages, history, mathematics, multi-level teacher, music, physical, science, social science, special, speech. **Foreign languages:** French, German, Spanish. **Health:** Audiology/hearing, audiology/speech pathology, clinical lab science, speech pathology. **History:** General. **Math:** General. **Parks/recreation:** Health/fitness, sports admin. **Physical sciences:** Chemistry. **Psychology:** General. **Public administration:** Community org/advocacy, social work. **Social sciences:** Economics, political science, sociology. **Visual/performing arts:** Art.

Computing on campus. 900 workstations in dormitories, library, computer center. Dormitories wired for high-speed internet access and linked to campus network. Commuter students can connect to campus network. Online course registration, online library, helpline, repair service, student web hosting available.

Student life. **Freshman orientation:** Mandatory. **Housing:** Coed dorms, single-sex dorms available. $50 deposit. Married graduate student housing available for summer session only. **Activities:** Bands, choral groups, drama, literary magazine, music ensembles, musical theater, student government, student newspaper, symphony orchestra, Over 100 student organizations.

Athletics. NCAA. **Intercollegiate:** Baseball M, basketball, cross-country, football (tackle) M, golf, soccer W, softball W, tennis, track and field, volleyball W, wrestling M. **Intramural:** Badminton, baseball M, basketball, field hockey W, racquetball, softball, swimming, table tennis, tennis, volleyball. **Team name:** Wolves.

Student services. Adult student services, career counseling, student employment services, health services, on-campus daycare, personal counseling, placement for graduates, veterans' counselor. **Physically disabled:** Services for visually, speech, hearing impaired.

Contact. E-mail: admissions1@northern.edu
Phone: (605) 626-2544 Toll-free number: (800) 678-5330
Fax: (605) 626-2587
Allan Vogel, Director of Admissions, Northern State University, 1200 South Jay Street, Aberdeen, SD 57401-7198

Oglala Lakota College

Kyle, South Dakota
www.olc.edu **CB code: 1430**

- Public 4-year liberal arts college
- Rural community
- 1,500 degree-seeking undergraduates

General. Founded in 1971. Regionally accredited. Serves Oglala Lakota reservation. **Degrees:** 37 bachelor's, 71 associate awarded; master's offered. **Location:** 90 miles from Rapid City. **Calendar:** Semester, extensive summer session. **Full-time faculty:** 25 total. **Part-time faculty:** 30 total.

Basis for selection. Open admission.

2005-2006 Annual costs. Tuition/fees: $2,450; $2,900 out-of-state. Non-Native American students pay out-of-state tuition rate. Out-of-state Native Americans pay in-state tuition rate. Books/supplies: $260. Personal expenses: $450.

Financial aid. Additional information: Deadline for applications for Bureau of Indian Affairs Higher Education Grants, is March 15; applicants notified early summer.

Application procedures. Admission: No deadline. Admission notification on a rolling basis. **Financial aid:** No deadline. Applicants notified on a rolling basis.

Academics. College is one of 2 tribally chartered, fully accredited institutions in the United States. **Credit/placement by examination:** CLEP, institutional tests. 13 credit hours maximum toward bachelor's degree. **Support services:** Learning center, reduced course load, remedial instruction, tutoring.

Majors. Business: Business admin. **Education:** Business, elementary. **History:** General. **Protective services:** Firefighting. **Public administration:** Human services. **Social sciences:** Sociology.

Student life. Activities: Student government, student newspaper.

Athletics. NJCAA. **Intercollegiate:** Basketball, cross-country, volleyball.

Student services. Career counseling, personal counseling.

Contact. Phone: (605) 455-2321
Billi Hornbeck, Director of Admissions, Oglala Lakota College, Box 490, Kyle, SD 57752

Presentation College

Aberdeen, South Dakota
www.presentation.edu **CB code: 6582**

- Private 4-year business and health science college affiliated with Roman Catholic Church
- Commuter campus in large town
- 668 degree-seeking undergraduates
- 100% of applicants admitted

General. Founded in 1951. Regionally accredited. **Degrees:** 71 bachelor's, 18 associate awarded. **Location:** 200 miles from Sioux Falls, 280 miles from Minneapolis-St. Paul. **Calendar:** Semester, extensive summer session. **Full-time faculty:** 37 total. **Part-time faculty:** 50 total.

Freshman class profile. 315 applied, 314 admitted, 116 enrolled.

Mid 50% test scores		Out-of-state:	19%
ACT:	17-23	Live on campus:	90%

Basis for selection. Selective admissions to all programs. If not accepted to program of choice, student is still accepted to the college as a general student. ACT required for admission to radiologic technology program. ASSET assessment used for course placement. TOEFL required for ESL students. Interview recommended. **Homeschooled:** Official transcript from local schooling guild, detailed course descriptions, and textbooks used required. Letter of academic recommendation from primary educator also required.

High school preparation. 16 units recommended. Recommended units include English 4, mathematics 3, social studies 2 and science 2. CPR certificate required of nursing and allied health applicants.

2005-2006 Annual costs. Tuition/fees: $11,400. Room/board: $4,700. Books/supplies: $1,250. Personal expenses: $620.

Application procedures. Admission: Priority date 4/1; deadline 9/1 (receipt date). No application fee. Application may be submitted online. Admission notification on a rolling basis. **Financial aid:** Priority date 4/1; no closing date. FAFSA required. Applicants notified on a rolling basis starting 5/1; must reply within 2 week(s) of notification.

Academics. Special study options: Distance learning, double major, dual enrollment of high school students, external degree, internships, liberal arts/career combination. **Credit/placement by examination:** CLEP, institutional tests. 15 credit hours maximum toward associate degree, 30 toward bachelor's. **Support services:** Learning center, reduced course load, remedial instruction, study skills assistance, tutoring.

Majors. Business: Business admin. **Communications:** General. **Health:** Health care admin, medical radiologic technology/radiation therapy, nursing (RN). **Public administration:** Social work.

Computing on campus. 180 workstations in dormitories, library, computer center. Dormitories wired for high-speed internet access and linked to campus network.

Student life. Freshman orientation: Mandatory. Preregistration for classes offered. **Policies:** Freshmen permitted cars on campus. **Housing:** Coed dorms available. $100 deposit, deadline 7/15. **Activities:** Drama, student government, student newspaper, Native American club.

Athletics. NAIA. **Intercollegiate:** Baseball M, basketball, cross-country, golf, soccer, softball W, volleyball W. **Intramural:** Basketball, volleyball W. **Team name:** Saints.

Student services. Adult student services, career counseling, student employment services, health services, personal counseling, placement for graduates, veterans' counselor.

Contact. E-mail: admit@presentation.edu
Phone: (605) 229-8492 Toll-free number: (800) 437-6060
Fax: (605) 229-8425
Joddy Meidinger, Director of Admissions, Presentation College, 1500 North Main Street, Aberdeen, SD 57401

Si Tanka Huron University

Huron, South Dakota
www.sitanka.edu **CB code: 6279**

- Public 4-year business and teachers college
- Residential campus in large town

General. Founded in 1883. Regionally accredited. **Location:** 125 miles from Sioux Falls. **Calendar:** Semester.

Annual costs/financial aid. Books/supplies: $700. Personal expenses: $960. Need-based financial aid available to full-time and part-time students.

Contact. Phone: (605) 353-2401
Director of Admissions, 333 Ninth Street SW, Huron, SD 57350

Sinte Gleska University

Mission, South Dakota
www.sinte.edu **CB code: 7328**

- Public 4-year university and liberal arts college
- Commuter campus in rural community

General. Founded in 1970. Regionally accredited. **Location:** 90 miles from Pierre, 240 miles from Sioux Falls. **Calendar:** Semester.

Annual costs/financial aid. Tuition/fees (2005-2006): $2,520. Books/supplies: $500. Personal expenses: $500. Need-based financial aid available to full-time and part-time students.

Contact. Phone: (605) 747-2263
Registrar, Box 105, Mission, SD 57555

South Dakota School of Mines and Technology

Rapid City, South Dakota
www.sdsmt.edu **CB code: 6652**

- Public 4-year university and engineering college
- Commuter campus in small city
- 1,724 degree-seeking undergraduates: 11% part-time, 24% women, 1% African American, 1% Asian American, 1% Hispanic American, 3% Native American, 2% international
- 234 degree-seeking graduate students
- 94% of applicants admitted
- SAT or ACT (ACT writing recommended) required
- 40% graduate within 6 years

General. Founded in 1885. Regionally accredited. A leading institution in friction stir-welding technology. Competes in solar vehicle, chemical vehicle, and concrete canoe national competitions. **Degrees:** 249 bachelor's, 4 associate awarded; master's, doctoral offered. **ROTC:** Army. **Location:** 222 miles from Cheyenne, Wyoming. **Calendar:** Semester, limited summer session. **Full-time faculty:** 107 total; 85% have terminal degrees, 12% minority, 20% women. **Part-time faculty:** 33 total; 52% have terminal degrees, 6% minority, 21% women. **Class size:** 32% < 20, 48% 20-39, 11% 40-49, 8% 50-99, 1% >100. **Special facilities:** Geology/paleontology museum, engineering/mining experiment station, atmospheric science institute, camp-center for advanced manufacturing and production, advanced materials processing and joining lab, Analytical Characterization and Testing Laboratory, Additive Manufacturing Laboratory, Center for Accelerated Applications at the Nanoscale.

Freshman class profile. 727 applied, 682 admitted, 365 enrolled.

Mid 50% test scores			
SAT verbal:	480-570	Rank in top tenth:	21%
SAT math:	510-610	End year in good standing:	81%
ACT:	22-27	Return as sophomores:	73%
GPA 3.50 or higher:	55%	Out-of-state:	33%
GPA 3.0-3.49:	24%	Live on campus:	65%
GPA 2.0-2.99:	19%	International:	1%
Rank in top quarter:	50%	Fraternities:	11%
		Sororities:	13%

Basis for selection. Test scores and high school grades or class rank used in the selection process. **Homeschooled:** Must submit ACT or SAT scores, be 18 years of age, have graduated or completed GED with combined score of 225 and minimum of 40 on each test.

High school preparation. 20 units required. Required and recommended units include English 4, mathematics 3, social studies 3, science 3 (laboratory 3) and foreign language 2. 1 fine arts required.

2005-2006 Annual costs. Tuition/fees: $4,757; $9,744 out-of-state. Reciprocity agreements reduce tuition for some out-of-state students. Room/board: $3,904. Books/supplies: $900. Personal expenses: $1,550.

2004-2005 Financial aid. Need-based: 321 full-time freshmen applied for aid; 181 were judged to have need; 180 of these received aid. Average need met was 81%. Average scholarship/grant was $3,520; average loan $2,731. 30% of total undergraduate aid awarded as scholarships/grants, 70% as loans/jobs. **Non-need-based:** Awarded to 476 full-time undergraduates, including 165 freshmen. Scholarships awarded for academics, athletics, leadership, ROTC. **Additional information:** Closing date for scholarship applications February 1.

Application procedures. Admission: No deadline. $20 fee. Application may be submitted online. Admission notification on a rolling basis beginning on or about 11/1. **Financial aid:** Priority date 3/15; no closing date. FAFSA required. Applicants notified on a rolling basis starting 5/1; must reply within 3 week(s) of notification.

Academics. Special study options: Combined bachelor's/graduate degree, cooperative education, cross-registration, distance learning, double major, dual enrollment of high school students, ESL, independent study, internships, liberal arts/career combination, student-designed major, study abroad. ESL offered through National American University; web-based technical management MS program; student-designed BS interdisciplinary studies major. **Credit/placement by examination:** AP, CLEP, SAT, ACT, institutional tests. 36 credit hours maximum toward bachelor's degree. **Support services:** Learning center, reduced course load, remedial instruction, tutoring.

Majors. Computer sciences: Computer science. **Engineering:** Chemical, civil, computer, electrical, geological, industrial, mechanical, metallurgical. **Math:** General. **Physical sciences:** Chemistry, geology, physics.

Most popular majors. Computer/information sciences 10%, engineering/engineering technologies 68%, interdisciplinary studies 11%, physical sciences 8%.

Computing on campus. 210 workstations in dormitories, library, computer center, student center. Dormitories wired for high-speed internet access and linked to campus network. Commuter students can connect to campus network. Online course registration, online library, helpline, student web hosting, wireless network available.

Student life. Freshman orientation: Mandatory, $80 fee. Preregistration for classes offered. 2-day orientation program and placement testing in June, July and August and a 7-day welcome program. **Policies:** Freshmen permitted cars on campus. **Housing:** Guaranteed on-campus for freshmen. Coed dorms, special housing for disabled, fraternity/sorority housing, substance-free housing available. $100 deposit, deadline 8/15. **Activities:** Bands, choral groups, drama, music ensembles, radio station, student government, student newspaper, United Campus Ministries, Circle K, College Republicans, College Democrats, American Indian Science & Engineering Society, Habitat for Humanity, Muslim student association, Intervarsity Christian Fellowship.

Athletics. NAIA. **Intercollegiate:** Basketball, cross-country, football (tackle) M, track and field, volleyball W. **Intramural:** Basketball, bowling, golf, racquetball, skiing, softball, swimming, track and field, volleyball. **Team name:** Hardrockers.

Student services. Adult student services, alcohol/substance abuse counseling, campus ministries, career counseling, student employment services, financial aid counseling, health services, minority student services, on-campus daycare, personal counseling, placement for graduates, veterans' counselor, women's services. **Physically disabled:** Services for visually, speech, hearing impaired.

Contact. E-mail: admissions@sdsmt.edu
Phone: (605) 394-2400 Toll-free number: (800) 544-8162
Fax: (605) 394-1268
Barbara Dolan, Enrollment Manager, South Dakota School of Mines and Technology, 501 East St. Joseph Street, Rapid City, SD 57701

South Dakota State University

Brookings, South Dakota
www.sdstate.edu **CB code: 6653**

- Public 4-year university
- Commuter campus in large town
- 8,752 degree-seeking undergraduates: 12% part-time, 50% women, 1% African American, 1% Asian American, 1% Hispanic American, 1% Native American
- 1,216 degree-seeking graduate students
- 93% of applicants admitted
- SAT or ACT (ACT writing optional) required
- 55% graduate within 6 years

General. Founded in 1881. Regionally accredited. **Degrees:** 1,321 bachelor's, 20 associate awarded; master's, doctoral, first professional offered. **ROTC:** Army, Air Force. **Location:** 50 miles from Sioux Falls, 200 miles from Minneapolis-St. Paul. **Calendar:** Semester, limited summer session. **Full-time faculty:** 413 total; 78% have terminal degrees, 11% minority, 40% women. **Part-time faculty:** 171 total; 3% minority, 66% women. **Class size:** 38% < 20, 42% 20-39, 7% 40-49, 10% 50-99, 3% >100. **Special facilities:** Water resources research center, agricultural experiment station, cooperative extension service, biostress center, agricultural heritage museum, art museum, animal disease research and diagnostic laboratory, entrepreneur center, GIS Center of Excellence.

Freshman class profile. 3,641 applied, 3,376 admitted, 1,869 enrolled.

Mid 50% test scores			
ACT:	20-25	Rank in top quarter:	37%
GPA 3.50 or higher:	46%	Rank in top tenth:	15%
GPA 3.0-3.49:	30%	Return as sophomores:	74%
GPA 2.0-2.99:	23%	Out-of-state:	33%
		Live on campus:	97%

Basis for selection. School achievement record and test scores most important.

High school preparation. Required units include English 4, mathematics 3, social studies 3, science 3 (laboratory 3). One credit of fine arts and one-half unit computer science also required.

2005-2006 Annual costs. Tuition/fees: $4,732; $9,719 out-of-state. Reduced out-of-state tuition for Minnesota students. Room/board: $4,770. Books/supplies: $896. Personal expenses: $1,854.

2005-2006 Financial aid. Need-based: 1,559 full-time freshmen applied for aid; 1,418 were judged to have need; 1,414 of these received aid. Average need met was 86%. Average scholarship/grant was $3,148; average loan $1,804. 28% of total undergraduate aid awarded as scholarships/grants, 72% as loans/jobs. **Non-need-based:** Awarded to 4,658 full-time undergraduates, including 1,523 freshmen. Scholarships awarded for academics, art, athletics, leadership, minority status, music/drama, ROTC, state residency. **Additional information:** Financial aid awarded to approximately 87 percent of all undergraduates.

Application procedures. Admission: No deadline. $20 fee. Application may be submitted online. Admission notification on a rolling basis. **Financial aid:** Priority date 3/15; no closing date. FAFSA required. Applicants notified on a rolling basis starting 4/1; must reply within 3 week(s) of notification.

Academics. Evening, weekend and other condensed degree-awarding classes available at Sioux Falls Center for Public Higher Education. **Special study options:** Accelerated study, combined bachelor's/graduate degree, cooperative education, cross-registration, distance learning, double major, dual enrollment of high school students, exchange student, honors, independent study, internships, liberal arts/career combination, New York semester, study abroad, teacher certification program. **Credit/placement by examination:** AP, CLEP, IB, ACT, institutional tests. 32 credit hours maximum toward bachelor's degree. **Support services:** Pre-admission summer program, reduced course load, remedial instruction, study skills assistance, tutoring, writing center.

Majors. Agriculture: General, agribusiness operations, agronomy, animal sciences, dairy, economics, horticulture, landscaping, mechanization, range science. **Biology:** General, microbiology. **Business:** Hotel/motel admin. **Communications:** Journalism. **Computer sciences:** General. **Conservation:** Management/policy, wildlife. **Education:** Agricultural, early childhood, music, voc/tech. **Engineering:** Agricultural, civil, electrical, mechanical, physics, software. **Engineering technology:** Construction, electrical, industrial management, industrial safety, manufacturing. **English:** English lit, speech/rhetoric. **Family/consumer sciences:** Apparel marketing, consumer economics, family resources, family studies, food/nutrition. **Foreign languages:** French, German, Spanish. **Health:** Athletic training, clinical lab science, nursing (RN). **History:** General. **Interdisciplinary:** Global studies. **Liberal arts:** Arts/sciences. **Math:** General. **Parks/recreation:** General, facilities management, health/fitness. **Physical sciences:** Chemistry, physics. **Psychology:** General. **Social sciences:** Economics, geography, political science, sociology. **Visual/performing arts:** General, graphic design, interior design, music management.

Most popular majors. Agriculture 13%, education 6%, engineering/engineering technologies 9%, health sciences 22%, social sciences 9%.

Computing on campus. 1,022 workstations in dormitories, library, computer center, student center. Dormitories wired for high-speed internet access and linked to campus network. Commuter students can connect to campus network. Online course registration, online library, helpline, wireless network available.

Student life. Freshman orientation: Mandatory. Preregistration for classes offered. 2-day programs in June. **Policies:** Students out of high school for less than 2 years required to live in campus housing unless living with family. Freshmen permitted cars on campus. **Housing:** Guaranteed on-campus for freshmen. Coed dorms, special housing for disabled, apartments, fraternity/sorority housing, substance-free housing available. $50 deposit. Limited single rooms with optional meal plan available for upperclassmen. **Activities:** Bands, choral groups, dance, drama, literary magazine, music ensembles, musical theater, radio station, student government, student newspaper, symphony orchestra, Students' Association, University Program Council, Golden Key Honor Society, Campus Crusade for Christ, Fellowship of Christian Athletes, Native American Club, Circle K International, Black Student Alliance, Geography Club.

Athletics. NCAA. **Intercollegiate:** Baseball M, basketball, cross-country, equestrian W, football (tackle) M, golf, soccer W, softball W, swimming, tennis, track and field, volleyball W, wrestling M. **Intramural:** Badminton, basketball, football (non-tackle), golf, racquetball, soccer W, softball, swimming, table tennis, tennis, volleyball, wrestling M. **Team name:** Jackrabbits.

Student services. Adult student services, alcohol/substance abuse counseling, campus ministries, career counseling, services for economically disadvantaged, student employment services, financial aid counseling, health services, legal services, minority student services, personal counseling, placement for graduates, veterans' counselor. **Physically disabled:** Services for visually, speech, hearing impaired.

Contact. E-mail: SDSU.Admissions@sdstate.edu
Phone: (605) 688-4121 Toll-free number: (800) 952-3541
Fax: (605) 688-6891
Tracy Welsh, Director of Admissions and High School Relations, South Dakota State University, Box 2201 ADM 200, Brookings, SD 57007-0649

University of Sioux Falls

Sioux Falls, South Dakota
www.usiouxfalls.edu **CB code: 6651**

- Private 4-year liberal arts college affiliated with American Baptist Churches in the USA
- Residential campus in small city
- 1,262 degree-seeking undergraduates
- 344 graduate students
- 93% of applicants admitted
- SAT or ACT required

General. Founded in 1883. Regionally accredited. **Degrees:** 228 bachelor's, 2 associate awarded; master's offered. **Location:** 180 miles from Omaha, Nebraska. **Calendar:** 4-1-4, limited summer session. **Full-time faculty:** 65 total. **Part-time faculty:** 75 total. **Class size:** 58% < 20, 32% 20-39, 5% 40-49, 5% 50-99, less than 1% >100.

Freshman class profile. 750 applied, 695 admitted, 240 enrolled.

Mid 50% test scores			
SAT verbal:	390-480	ACT:	16-26
SAT math:	430-470	Out-of-state:	40%
		Live on campus:	83%

Basis for selection. Test scores, high school record, and rank in top half of graduating class important. Audition required for music, theater programs; portfolio recommended for art program.

High school preparation. Recommended units include English 4, mathematics 3, social studies 3, history 3 and science 2. One unit computer science recommended.

2005-2006 Annual costs. Tuition/fees: $16,100. Room/board: $4,900. Books/supplies: $640. Personal expenses: $2,000.

Financial aid. Non-need-based: Scholarships awarded for academics, alumni affiliation, art, athletics, job skills, leadership, minority status, music/drama, religious affiliation, state residency.

Application procedures. Admission: No deadline. $25 fee, may be waived for applicants with need. Admission notification on a rolling basis. **Financial aid:** Priority date 3/1; no closing date. FAFSA required. Applicants notified on a rolling basis starting 3/1; must reply within 2 week(s) of notification.

Academics. Degree completion program offered for adults 25 and older with 64 hours previous college education. **Special study options:** Accelerated study, cross-registration, distance learning, double major, dual enrollment of high school students, honors, independent study, internships, liberal arts/career combination, student-designed major, study abroad, teacher certification program, Washington semester. **Credit/placement by examination:** CLEP, institutional tests. 16 credit hours maximum toward bachelor's degree. **Support services:** Pre-admission summer program, reduced course load, remedial instruction, study skills assistance, tutoring, writing center.

Majors. Biology: General. **Business:** Accounting, business admin, hospitality admin, organizational behavior. **Communications:** Journalism. **Computer sciences:** General, computer science. **Education:** Art, elementary, health, multi-level teacher, music. **English:** Speech/rhetoric. **History:** General. **Liberal arts:** Arts/sciences. **Math:** General, applied. **Parks/recreation:** Exercise sciences. **Philosophy/religion:** Religion. **Physical sciences:** Chemistry. **Psychology:** General. **Public administration:** Social work. **Social sciences:** General, political science, sociology. **Theology:** Theology. **Visual/performing arts:** Art, dramatic.

Most popular majors. Biology 6%, business/marketing 49%, education 18%.

Computing on campus. 75 workstations in dormitories, library, computer center, student center. Dormitories wired for high-speed internet access and linked to campus network. Commuter students can connect to campus network. Student web hosting available.

Student life. Freshman orientation: Available. Preregistration for classes offered. Held 2 days immediately preceding fall semester. **Policies:** No alcohol at university-sponsored events. Freshmen permitted cars on campus. **Housing:** Coed dorms, single-sex dorms, apartments available. $100 deposit. Freshmen, sophomores required to live in college housing unless over 20 years of age or given permission by director of residence life. **Activities:** Bands, choral groups, dance, drama, music ensembles, musical theater, opera, radio station, student government, student newspaper, symphony orchestra, TV station, nontraditional student association, student volunteer groups, religious organizations, Fellowship of Christian Athletes.

Athletics. NAIA. **Intercollegiate:** Baseball M, basketball, cross-country, football (tackle) M, golf, soccer, softball W, tennis, track and field, volleyball W. **Intramural:** Basketball, golf, soccer, softball, table tennis, tennis, volleyball. **Team name:** Cougars.

Student services. Adult student services, alcohol/substance abuse counseling, campus ministries, career counseling, student employment services, financial aid counseling, health services, personal counseling, placement for graduates, veterans' counselor, women's services. **Physically disabled:** Services for hearing impaired.

Contact. E-mail: admissions@usiouxfalls.edu
Phone: (605) 331-6600 Toll-free number: (800) 888-1047
Fax: (605) 331-6615
Greg Fritz, Vice President of Admissions and Marketing, University of Sioux Falls, 1101 West 22nd Street, Sioux Falls, SD 57105-1699

University of South Dakota

Vermillion, South Dakota **CB member**
www.usd.edu **CB code: 6881**

- Public 4-year university
- Residential campus in small town
- 5,728 degree-seeking undergraduates: 26% part-time, 62% women, 1% African American, 1% Asian American, 1% Hispanic American, 2% Native American, 1% international
- 1,866 degree-seeking graduate students
- 86% of applicants admitted
- SAT and SAT Subject Tests or ACT (ACT writing optional), interview required
- 46% graduate within 6 years; 17% enter graduate study

General. Founded in 1862. Regionally accredited. **Degrees:** 757 bachelor's, 247 associate awarded; master's, doctoral, first professional offered. **ROTC:** Army. **Location:** 55 miles from Sioux Falls, 35 miles from Sioux City, Iowa. **Calendar:** Semester, extensive summer session. **Full-time faculty:** 389 total; 75% have terminal degrees, 10% minority, 45% women. **Part-time faculty:** 17 total; 65% have terminal degrees, 6% minority, 59% women. **Class size:** 54% < 20, 35% 20-39, 5% 40-49, 4% 50-99, 2% >100. **Special facilities:** Museums, center for instructional design and delivery, center for disabilities, governmental research bureau, state data center, federal technical procurement center, geological survey, archaeology lab, speech and hearing center, disaster mental health institute.

Freshman class profile. 2,829 applied, 2,439 admitted, 1,165 enrolled.

Mid 50% test scores		**Rank in top tenth:**	13%
SAT verbal:	440-610	**End year in good standing:**	78%
SAT math:	450-600	**Return as sophomores:**	69%
ACT:	19-25	**Out-of-state:**	27%
GPA 3.50 or higher:	37%	**Live on campus:**	82%
GPA 3.0-3.49:	30%	**Fraternities:**	8%
GPA 2.0-2.99:	32%	**Sororities:**	8%
Rank in top quarter:	35%		

Basis for selection. Admission in good standing granted with 2.0 GPA or higher in required courses, rank in top 60% of class, or ACT composite score of 18 or above or 2.6 high school GPA. Interview recommended for dental hygiene, nursing, physician assistant programs; audition recommended for music, theater programs; portfolio recommended for art progam.

High school preparation. 17 units required. Required units include English 4, mathematics 3, social studies 3, science 3 (laboratory 3). 1 fine arts required.

2005-2006 Annual costs. Tuition/fees: $4,829; $9,816 out-of-state. Reciprocity agreement in place for Minnesota residents. Reduced tuition for Iowa residents. Room/board: $4,240. Books/supplies: $750. Personal expenses: $2,000.

2004-2005 Financial aid. **Need-based:** 786 full-time freshmen applied for aid; 547 were judged to have need; 488 of these received aid. Average need met was 75%. Average scholarship/grant was $2,996; average loan $2,694. 30% of total undergraduate aid awarded as scholarships/grants, 70% as loans/jobs. **Non-need-based:** Awarded to 1,704 full-time undergraduates, including 597 freshmen. Scholarships awarded for academics, art, athletics, leadership, minority status, music/drama, ROTC.

Application procedures. **Admission:** No deadline. $20 fee. Application may be submitted online. Admission notification on a rolling basis beginning on or about 9/20. February 15 closing date for application to dental hygiene and nursing programs. **Financial aid:** Priority date 3/15; no closing date. FAFSA required. Applicants notified on a rolling basis starting 5/5.

Academics. **Special study options:** Accelerated study, combined bachelor's/graduate degree, cross-registration, distance learning, double major, dual enrollment of high school students, ESL, exchange student, external degree, honors, independent study, internships, liberal arts/career combination, student-designed major, study abroad, teacher certification program. **Credit/placement by examination:** AP, CLEP, institutional tests. 30 credit hours maximum toward bachelor's degree. **Support services:** Pre-admission summer program, reduced course load, remedial instruction, tutoring.

Honors college/program. University Honors Program open to students in all majors who displayed potential for honors work in high school through good grades, college preparatory curriculum, high ACT scores, and participation in school and community activities.

Majors. **Area/ethnic studies:** Native American. **Biology:** General. **Business:** Accounting, business admin, finance, managerial economics. **Communications:** General, journalism, media studies. **Computer sciences:** General. **Education:** Biology, chemistry, curriculum, drama/dance, early childhood, elementary, English, foreign languages, French, German, history, kindergarten/preschool, mathematics, music, physical, physics, science, social science, Spanish, special, speech. **English:** English lit, speech/rhetoric. **Foreign languages:** French, German, Spanish. **Health:** Communication disorders, dental hygiene, health services admin, substance abuse counseling. **History:** General. **Interdisciplinary:** Global studies. **Liberal arts:** Arts/sciences. **Math:** General. **Parks/recreation:** General. **Philosophy/religion:** Philosophy. **Physical sciences:** Chemistry, geology, physics. **Protective services:** Criminal justice. **Psychology:** General. **Public administration:** Social work. **Social sciences:** Anthropology, economics, political science, sociology. **Visual/performing arts:** Art, arts management, dramatic, music performance, studio arts.

Most popular majors. Biology 6%, business/marketing 21%, communications/journalism 8%, education 13%, health sciences 10%, psychology 10%, security/protective services 7%, social sciences 7%.

Computing on campus. 862 workstations in dormitories, library, computer center, student center. Dormitories wired for high-speed internet access and linked to campus network. Commuter students can connect to campus network. Online course registration, online library, helpline, student web hosting, wireless network available.

Student life. **Freshman orientation:** Mandatory. Preregistration for classes offered. **Policies:** Students required to live in residence halls for first 2 years unless living in fraternity or sorority housing, or commuting from home. Freshmen permitted cars on campus. **Housing:** Guaranteed on-campus for freshmen. Coed dorms, special housing for disabled, apartments, fraternity/sorority housing, substance-free housing available. $100 deposit, deadline 9/1. Apartments available for students with dependent children. **Activities:** Bands, choral groups, dance, drama, literary magazine, music ensembles, musical theater, opera, radio station, student government, student newspaper, symphony orchestra, TV station, Young Democrats, College Republicans, Campus Crusade for Christ, Chinese Student Friendship Association, Gay/Lesbian/Bisexual Alliance, Habitat for Humanity, international students club, nontraditional student association, political science league.

Athletics. NCAA. **Intercollegiate:** Baseball M, basketball, cross-country, diving, football (tackle) M, golf, soccer W, softball W, swimming, tennis W, track and field, volleyball W. **Intramural:** Badminton, basketball, bowling, cross-country, football (non-tackle), golf, racquetball, soccer, softball, swimming, table tennis, tennis, track and field, volleyball. **Team name:** Coyotes.

Student services. Adult student services, alcohol/substance abuse counseling, campus ministries, career counseling, services for economically disadvantaged, student employment services, financial aid counseling, health services, legal services, minority student services, on-campus daycare, personal counseling, placement for graduates, veterans' counselor. **Physically disabled:** Services for visually, speech, hearing impaired.

Contact. E-mail: admiss@usd.edu
Phone: (605) 677-5434 Toll-free number: (877) 269-6837
Fax: (605) 677-6753
Cecil Foster, Assistant Vice President of Enrollment, University of South Dakota, 414 East Clark Street, Vermillion, SD 57069-2390

Tennessee

American Baptist College of ABT Seminary
Nashville, Tennessee
www.abcnash.edu **CB code: 2401**

- Private 4-year Bible college affiliated with Baptist faith
- Commuter campus in very large city
- 105 degree-seeking undergraduates
- Application essay required

General. Founded in 1924. Accredited by ABHE. **Degrees:** 21 bachelor's, 3 associate awarded. **Calendar:** Semester. **Full-time faculty:** 7 total. **Part-time faculty:** 8 total.

Basis for selection. Recommendations, personal essay, religious commitment important. Admissions committee selects applicants best qualified to benefit from opportunities offered by college.

2005-2006 Annual costs. Tuition/fees: $5,160. Room only: $1,600. Books/supplies: $440.

Application procedures. Admission: Closing date 7/1. $20 fee. Admission notification on a rolling basis. **Financial aid:** No deadline. FAFSA required. Applicants notified on a rolling basis; must reply within 2 week(s) of notification.

Academics. All students major in Bible studies or theology. Additional major in business administration optional. **Special study options:** Double major. **Credit/placement by examination:** CLEP, institutional tests.

Majors. Area/ethnic studies: African-American. **Business:** Business admin. **Education:** General, history, social science. **Liberal arts:** Arts/sciences. **Social sciences:** General. **Theology:** Bible, pastoral counseling, religious ed, theology.

Student life. Housing: Single-sex dorms, apartments available. **Activities:** Student government.

Contact. Phone: (615) 256-1463 Fax: (615) 226-7855
Marcella Lockhart, Director of Enrollment Management, American Baptist College of ABT Seminary, 1800 Baptist World Center Drive, Nashville, TN 37207

Aquinas College
Nashville, Tennessee **CB member**
www.aquinas-tn.edu **CB code: 7318**

- Private 4-year nursing and liberal arts college affiliated with Roman Catholic Church
- Commuter campus in very large city
- 918 degree-seeking undergraduates: 64% part-time, 56% women, 16% African American, 3% Asian American, 3% Hispanic American

General. Founded in 1961. Regionally accredited. **Degrees:** 79 bachelor's, 91 associate awarded. **Location:** 1 mile from downtown Nashville, 195 miles from Knoxville. **Calendar:** Semester, limited summer session. **Full-time faculty:** 25 total; 52% have terminal degrees. **Part-time faculty:** 63 total; 35% have terminal degrees.

Freshman class profile. 58 enrolled.

Mid 50% test scores			
SAT verbal:	440-520	SAT math:	440-520
		ACT:	18-22

Basis for selection. School achievement record, test scores important. **Homeschooled:** Transcript of courses and grades required. Must provide copy of transcript from accredited home school agency along with official ACT Report.

High school preparation. 20 units recommended. Recommended units include English 4, mathematics 3, social studies 3, science 3, foreign language 2 and academic electives 5.

2006-2007 Annual costs. Tuition/fees (projected): $14,045. Additional $40 per-credit hour for nursing classes. Additional required fees for nursing and teacher education programs. Books/supplies: $1,000. Personal expenses: $1,500.

2005-2006 Financial aid. Need-based: 41% of total undergraduate aid awarded as scholarships/grants, 59% as loans/jobs. **Non-need-based:** Scholarships awarded for academics, alumni affiliation, leadership, religious affiliation.

Application procedures. Admission: Priority date 3/1; no deadline. $25 fee, may be waived for applicants with need. Application may be submitted online. Admission notification on a rolling basis. **Financial aid:** Priority date 3/1; no closing date. FAFSA required. Applicants notified on a rolling basis starting 3/1; must reply within 2 week(s) of notification.

Academics. Special study options: Accelerated study, independent study, liberal arts/career combination, teacher certification program. **Credit/placement by examination:** AP, CLEP, SAT, ACT, institutional tests. 30 credit hours maximum toward associate degree, 30 toward bachelor's. **Support services:** Learning center, reduced course load, remedial instruction, study skills assistance, tutoring, writing center.

Majors. Business: Business admin, management information systems. **Education:** Elementary. **Health:** Nursing (RN). **Liberal arts:** Arts/sciences.

Computing on campus. 50 workstations in library, computer center. Online library, helpline available.

Student life. Freshman orientation: Mandatory. **Policies:** Drug-free/alcohol-free campus. Freshmen permitted cars on campus. **Activities:** Choral groups, student government, Phi Beta Lambda, Delta Epsilon Sigma, Association of Student Nurses, Association for Supervision and Curriculum Development student chapter, Student Affairs Council, Frassati Society, Sigma Beta Delta,.

Athletics. Team name: Cavaliers.

Student services. Campus ministries, financial aid counseling.

Contact. E-mail: admissions@aquinas-tn.edu
Phone: (615) 297-7545 ext. 460 Toll-free number: (800) 649-9956
Fax: (615) 279-3893
Diane LeJeune, Director of Admissions, Aquinas College, 4210 Harding Road, Nashville, TN 37205-2086

Austin Peay State University
Clarksville, Tennessee **CB member**
www.apsu.edu **CB code: 1028**

- Public 4-year university and liberal arts college
- Commuter campus in small city
- 7,964 degree-seeking undergraduates: 27% part-time, 60% women, 19% African American, 2% Asian American, 5% Hispanic American, 1% Native American
- 514 degree-seeking graduate students
- 91% of applicants admitted
- 28% graduate within 6 years

General. Founded in 1927. Regionally accredited. **Degrees:** 914 bachelor's, 128 associate awarded; master's offered. **ROTC:** Army. **Location:** 45 miles from Nashville. **Calendar:** Semester, limited summer session. **Full-time faculty:** 262 total. **Part-time faculty:** 200 total. **Class size:** 43% < 20, 51% 20-39, 4% 40-49, 3% 50-99. **Special facilities:** Zoological museum.

Freshman class profile. 2,670 applied, 2,421 admitted, 1,278 enrolled.

Mid 50% test scores			
SAT verbal:	500-590	Return as sophomores:	61%
SAT math:	470-550	Out-of-state:	3%
ACT:	19-23	Live on campus:	35%

Basis for selection. SAT combined score of 720 to 740 (exclusive of Writing), ACT composite score of 19, or minimum high school GPA of 2.75 required. Additional testing required if criteria not met. **Learning Disabled:** Students with learning disabilities are admitted as regular students and make up approximately 5% of the freshman class.

High school preparation. 14 units required. Required units include English 4, mathematics 3, social studies 1, history 1, science 2 (laboratory 1) and foreign language 2. Mathematics units should be algebra I and II, 1 geometry or advanced mathematics. Social science units should be 1 social studies, 1 US history. Foreign language units must be in 1 language. 1 visual and/or performing arts also required.

2005-2006 Annual costs. Tuition/fees: $4,635; $13,947 out-of-state. Room/board: $4,800. Books/supplies: $1,350. Personal expenses: $3,000.

2004-2005 Financial aid. Need-based: 47% of total undergraduate aid awarded as scholarships/grants, 53% as loans/jobs. **Non-need-based:** Scholarships awarded for academics, art, athletics, leadership, minority status, music/drama, ROTC, state residency.

Application procedures. Admission: Closing date 8/29. $15 fee. Application may be submitted online. Admission notification on a rolling basis. **Financial aid:** Priority date 4/1; no closing date. FAFSA required. Applicants notified on a rolling basis starting 5/1; must reply within 2 week(s) of notification.

Academics. Special study options: Cooperative education, distance learning, double major, honors, independent study, internships, study abroad, teacher certification program. Service Members Opportunity College (associate and bachelor's degrees). **Credit/placement by examination:** AP, CLEP, institutional tests. 32 credit hours maximum toward associate degree, 64 toward bachelor's. **Support services:** Learning center, remedial instruction, study skills assistance, tutoring.

Majors. Biology: General. **Business:** General, nonprofit/public. **Communications:** Journalism. **Computer sciences:** General. **Education:** Health, special. **Engineering technology:** General. **Foreign languages:** General, Spanish. **Health:** Clinical lab science, medical radiologic technology/radiation therapy, nursing (RN). **History:** General. **Liberal arts:** Arts/sciences. **Math:** General. **Parks/recreation:** Health/fitness. **Philosophy/religion:** Philosophy. **Physical sciences:** Chemistry, geology, physics. **Psychology:** General. **Public administration:** General, social work. **Social sciences:** Political science, sociology. **Visual/performing arts:** Art.

Most popular majors. Business/marketing 15%, communications/journalism 7%, health sciences 9%, interdisciplinary studies 7%, liberal arts 6%, psychology 6%, public administration/social services 13%.

Computing on campus. 411 workstations in dormitories, library, computer center, student center. Commuter students can connect to campus network. Online library available.

Student life. Freshman orientation: Available. **Policies:** Alcohol not permitted on campus. **Housing:** Coed dorms, single-sex dorms, special housing for disabled, apartments, fraternity/sorority housing available. $100 deposit, deadline 8/15. Honors dorm available. **Activities:** Bands, choral groups, drama, literary magazine, music ensembles, musical theater, radio station, student government, student newspaper, TV station, Baptist Student Union, Wesley Foundation, Church of Christ Student Center, Catholic Community Organization.

Athletics. NCAA. **Intercollegiate:** Baseball M, basketball, cross-country, football (tackle) M, golf, rifle W, soccer W, softball W, tennis, track and field W, volleyball W. **Intramural:** Baseball M, basketball, racquetball, soccer M, softball, swimming, table tennis, track and field M, volleyball. **Team name:** Governors.

Student services. Adult student services, career counseling, student employment services, financial aid counseling, health services, minority student services, on-campus daycare, personal counseling, placement for graduates, veterans' counselor. **Physically disabled:** Services for visually, speech, hearing impaired.

Contact. E-mail: admissions@apsu.edu
Phone: (931) 221-7661 Toll-free number: (800) 844-2778
Fax: (931) 221-6168
Scott McDonald, Director of Admissions, Austin Peay State University, PO Box 4548, Clarksville, TN 37044

Baptist College of Health Sciences
Memphis, Tennessee
www.bchs.edu

- Private 4-year health science and nursing college
- Very large city

General. Regionally accredited. **Calendar:** Trimester.

Annual costs/financial aid. Tuition/fees (projected): $7,300.

Contact. Phone: (901) 575-2247
1003 Monroe Avenue, Memphis, TN 38104

Belmont University
Nashville, Tennessee
www.belmont.edu **CB code: 1058**

- Private 4-year university affiliated with Baptist faith
- Residential campus in very large city
- 3,570 degree-seeking undergraduates: 9% part-time, 61% women, 4% African American, 1% Asian American, 2% Hispanic American, 1% Native American, 1% international
- 657 degree-seeking graduate students
- 72% of applicants admitted
- SAT or ACT (ACT writing recommended), interview required
- 62% graduate within 6 years; 6% enter graduate study

General. Founded in 1951. Regionally accredited. **Degrees:** 649 bachelor's awarded; master's, doctoral offered. **ROTC:** Army, Navy. **Location:** 2 miles from downtown. **Calendar:** Semester, limited summer session. **Full-time faculty:** 214 total; 75% have terminal degrees, 2% minority, 48% women. **Part-time faculty:** 247 total; 5% minority, 52% women. **Class size:** 47% < 20, 52% 20-39, 1% 40-49. **Special facilities:** 22-track recording studio, Studio B on Music Row, 140-year-old antebellum mansion.

Freshman class profile. 2,184 applied, 1,579 admitted, 795 enrolled.

Mid 50% test scores		**Rank in top tenth:**	36%
SAT verbal:	530-630	**End year in good standing:**	78%
SAT math:	520-630	**Return as sophomores:**	79%
ACT:	22-28	**Out-of-state:**	64%
GPA 3.50 or higher:	55%	**Live on campus:**	98%
GPA 3.0-3.49:	35%	**International:**	1%
GPA 2.0-2.99:	10%	**Fraternities:**	1%
Rank in top quarter:	68%	**Sororities:**	2%

Basis for selection. Admissions based on test scores, course selection, GPA, class rank, recommendations, leadership activity. Interview required for music business; audition required for music programs.

High school preparation. 18 units required. Required and recommended units include English 4, mathematics 3-4, social studies 2, science 2-3 and foreign language 2.

2006-2007 Annual costs. Tuition/fees: $18,420. Room/board: $7,076. Books/supplies: $900. Personal expenses: $1,500.

2004-2005 Financial aid. Need-based: 657 full-time freshmen applied for aid; 384 were judged to have need; 368 of these received aid. Average need met was 45%. Average scholarship/grant was $4,797; average loan $2,586. 36% of total undergraduate aid awarded as scholarships/grants, 64% as loans/jobs. **Non-need-based:** Awarded to 1,314 full-time undergraduates, including 444 freshmen. Scholarships awarded for academics, art, athletics, leadership, music/drama, religious affiliation, state residency.

Application procedures. Admission: Priority date 3/15; deadline 5/1. $35 fee, may be waived for applicants with need. Application may be submitted online. Admission notification on a rolling basis beginning on or about 5/1. Must reply by May 1 or within 2 week(s) if notified thereafter. **Financial aid:** Priority date 3/1; no closing date. FAFSA required. Applicants notified on a rolling basis starting 3/15; must reply by 5/1 or within 2 week(s) of notification.

Academics. Special study options: Accelerated study, combined bachelor's/graduate degree, cooperative education, distance learning, double major, ESL, honors, independent study, internships, liberal arts/career combination, student-designed major, study abroad, teacher certification program, Washington semester. **Credit/placement by examination:** AP, CLEP, IB, institutional tests. 24 credit hours maximum toward bachelor's degree. **Support services:** Learning center, pre-admission summer program, reduced course load, remedial instruction, tutoring.

Majors. Biology: General, environmental, molecular, molecular biochemistry. **Business:** General, accounting, entrepreneurial studies, finance, hospitality admin, management information systems, management science, managerial economics, marketing. **Communications:** General, broadcast journalism, journalism, media studies, public relations. **Computer sciences:** Computer science, information systems. **Education:** General, art, biology, chemistry, early childhood, elementary, English, French, health, health occupations, history, mathematics, middle, music, physical, physics, science, secondary, social science, social studies, Spanish. **English:** Speech/rhetoric. **Family/consumer sciences:** Child care. **Foreign languages:** French, German, Spanish. **Health:** Nursing (RN). **History:** General. **Liberal arts:** Arts/sciences. **Math:** General. **Parks/recreation:** Exercise sciences, health/fitness. **Philosophy/religion:** Philosophy, religion. **Physical sciences:** Chemistry, physics. **Psychology:** General. **Public administration:** Social work. **Social sciences:** Economics, political science, sociology. **Theology:** Sacred music. **Visual/**

performing arts: Art, commercial/advertising art, dramatic, music management, music pedagogy, music performance, music theory/composition, piano/organ, voice/opera.

Most popular majors. Business/marketing 17%, communications/journalism 7%, health sciences 11%, liberal arts 6%, visual/performing arts 39%.

Computing on campus. 500 workstations in dormitories, library, computer center, student center. Dormitories wired for high-speed internet access and linked to campus network. Commuter students can connect to campus network. Online course registration, online library, helpline, wireless network available.

Student life. **Freshman orientation:** Mandatory, $60 fee. Preregistration for classes offered. 2-day program in summer or 4-day program in fall before classes start. **Policies:** Freshmen permitted cars on campus. **Housing:** Guaranteed on-campus for freshmen. Single-sex dorms, apartments, substance-free housing available. $100 deposit. **Activities:** Bands, choral groups, dance, drama, literary magazine, music ensembles, musical theater, opera, radio station, student government, student newspaper, symphony orchestra, TV station, Baptist student union, international student association, Christian music society, Campus Crusade for Christ, Fellowship of Christian Athletes, Black Student Alliance.

Athletics. NCAA. **Intercollegiate:** Baseball M, basketball, cross-country, golf, soccer, softball W, tennis, track and field, volleyball W. **Intramural:** Basketball, bowling, golf M, racquetball, softball, table tennis, tennis, volleyball. **Team name:** Bruins.

Student services. Adult student services, alcohol/substance abuse counseling, campus ministries, career counseling, student employment services, financial aid counseling, health services, minority student services, personal counseling, placement for graduates, veterans' counselor.

Contact. E-mail: buadmission@mail.belmont.edu
Phone: (615) 460-6785 Fax: (615) 460-5434
Kathy Baugher, Dean of Enrollment Services, Belmont University, 1900 Belmont Boulevard, Nashville, TN 37212-3757

Bethel College
McKenzie, Tennessee
www.bethel-college.edu **CB code: 1063**

- Private 4-year liberal arts college affiliated with Presbyterian Church (USA)
- Residential campus in small town
- 1,187 degree-seeking undergraduates: 19% part-time, 58% women
- 154 degree-seeking graduate students
- 60% of applicants admitted
- SAT or ACT (ACT writing optional) required

General. Founded in 1842. Regionally accredited. Students are provided with a laptop upon registration. **Degrees:** 301 bachelor's awarded; master's offered. **Location:** 115 miles from Nashville, 120 miles from Memphis. **Calendar:** Semester, limited summer session. **Full-time faculty:** 36 total. **Class size:** 72% < 20, 28% 20-39, less than 1% 40-49, less than 1% 50-99. **Special facilities:** Tennessee Wildlife Agency Research Laboratory.

Freshman class profile. 755 applied, 455 admitted, 252 enrolled.

Mid 50% test scores			
SAT verbal:	220-670	ACT:	9-28
SAT math:	250-740	Out-of-state:	7%
		Live on campus:	32%

Basis for selection. Counselor recommendation, interview considered for academically marginal applicants. High school GPA and academic units considered. **Homeschooled:** ACT of 19 or above and passing score on GED required.

High school preparation. Required units include English 4, mathematics 2, social studies 2 and science 2.

2005-2006 Annual costs. Tuition/fees: $10,016. Room/board: $5,760. Books/supplies: $1,000.

2005-2006 Financial aid. **Non-need-based:** Scholarships awarded for academics, athletics, music/drama, religious affiliation, state residency.

Application procedures. **Admission:** Priority date 2/3; no deadline. $30 fee. Admission notification on a rolling basis. **Financial aid:** Priority date 3/3, closing date 6/30. FAFSA, institutional form required. Applicants notified on a rolling basis starting 3/1.

Academics. Internship program including field experience offering up to 12 hours of credit. **Special study options:** Accelerated study, double major, internships, liberal arts/career combination, student-designed major, teacher certification program, weekend college. **Credit/placement by examination:** AP, CLEP, SAT, ACT, institutional tests. 30 credit hours maximum toward bachelor's degree. Accepts CLEP, DANTES, institutional exams for credit. **Support services:** Learning center, reduced course load, remedial instruction, study skills assistance, tutoring, writing center.

Majors. **Biology:** General, zoology. **Business:** Accounting, business admin. **Computer sciences:** General. **Education:** Art, elementary, English, health, history, physical, science, secondary, special. **History:** General. **Interdisciplinary:** Biological/physical sciences. **Liberal arts:** Arts/sciences. **Math:** General, applied. **Parks/recreation:** Exercise sciences. **Physical sciences:** Chemistry. **Psychology:** General. **Public administration:** Human services. **Social sciences:** General. **Visual/performing arts:** Dramatic, studio arts.

Most popular majors. Business/marketing 78%, education 7%.

Computing on campus. PC or laptop required. 650 workstations in dormitories, library, computer center, student center. Dormitories wired for high-speed internet access and linked to campus network. Commuter students can connect to campus network. Online library, helpline, repair service available.

Student life. **Freshman orientation:** Mandatory. Preregistration for classes offered. One-day orientations held in June, July, August on Saturday. **Policies:** Freshmen permitted cars on campus. **Housing:** Guaranteed on-campus for freshmen. Single-sex dorms available. $175 deposit. **Activities:** Bands, choral groups, drama, music ensembles, musical theater, student government, Fellowship of Christian Athletes, Christian Fellowship, Black Students United, honor societies, Christian Issues Organization, American Chemical Society, commuter club, business club, Student TN Education Association, wildlife club.

Athletics. NAIA. **Intercollegiate:** Baseball M, basketball, cross-country, football (tackle) M, golf, soccer, softball W, tennis, track and field, volleyball W. **Intramural:** Basketball, cheerleading, football (non-tackle), football (tackle), softball, swimming, table tennis, volleyball W. **Team name:** Wildcats.

Student services. Adult student services, alcohol/substance abuse counseling, campus ministries, career counseling, student employment services, financial aid counseling, personal counseling, placement for graduates, veterans' counselor. **Physically disabled:** Services for visually, speech, hearing impaired.

Contact. E-mail: admissions@bethel-college.edu
Phone: (731) 352-4030 Fax: (731) 352-4069
Tina Hodges, Director of Admission and Retention, Bethel College, 325 Cherry Avenue, McKenzie, TN 38201

Bryan College
Dayton, Tennessee
www.bryan.edu **CB code: 1908**

- Private 4-year liberal arts college affiliated with interdenominational tradition
- Residential campus in small town
- 765 degree-seeking undergraduates: 1% part-time, 57% women, 4% African American, 2% Hispanic American, 1% international
- SAT or ACT (ACT writing optional), application essay required
- 71% graduate within 6 years

General. Founded in 1930. Regionally accredited. All courses taught from Christian perspective. All faculty sign statement of faith annually. **Degrees:** 136 bachelor's awarded. **Location:** 40 miles from Chattanooga. **Calendar:** Semester, limited summer session. **Full-time faculty:** 33 total; 82% have terminal degrees, 18% women. **Part-time faculty:** 6 total; 17% women. **Special facilities:** Natural history museum.

Freshman class profile. 184 enrolled.

Mid 50% test scores			
SAT verbal:	500-660	Return as sophomores:	74%
SAT math:	450-610	Out-of-state:	60%
ACT:	21-27	Live on campus:	92%
		International:	1%

Basis for selection. High school record, Christian character supported by references, and SAT or ACT scores important. ACT composite score of 23 or SAT equivalent, or Pre-Professional Skills Test required of all teacher education applicants. Interview required for marginal applicants. **Home-schooled:** A detailed high school transcript of courses taken and grades received is required.

High school preparation. 20 units recommended. Recommended units include English 4, mathematics 3, social studies 3, science 3 and foreign language 2.

2006-2007 Annual costs. Tuition/fees (projected): $15,450. Room/board: $4,540. Books/supplies: $1,000. Personal expenses: $1,000.

2004-2005 Financial aid. Need-based: 42% of total undergraduate aid awarded as scholarships/grants, 58% as loans/jobs. **Non-need-based:** Scholarships awarded for academics, alumni affiliation, art, athletics, job skills, leadership, music/drama.

Application procedures. Admission: Priority date 5/1; deadline 7/31 (postmark date). $30 fee, may be waived for applicants with need. Application may be submitted online. Admission notification on a rolling basis. Must reply by May 1 or within 2 week(s) if notified thereafter. **Financial aid:** Priority date 3/1; no closing date. FAFSA, institutional form required. Applicants notified on a rolling basis starting 1/1; must reply within 2 week(s) of notification.

Academics. Special study options: Combined bachelor's/graduate degree, distance learning, double major, dual enrollment of high school students, honors, internships, study abroad, teacher certification program, Washington semester. Adult degree completion program. **Credit/placement by examination:** AP, CLEP, IB, SAT, ACT, institutional tests. 30 credit hours maximum toward associate degree, 31 toward bachelor's. **Support services:** Reduced course load, remedial instruction, study skills assistance, tutoring, writing center.

Majors. Biology: General. **Business:** General, business admin, management information systems. **Communications:** General, political. **Computer sciences:** Computer science. **Education:** General. **Foreign languages:** Spanish. **Health:** Athletic training. **History:** General. **Interdisciplinary:** Math/computer science. **Liberal arts:** Arts/sciences. **Math:** General. **Parks/recreation:** Exercise sciences. **Psychology:** General. **Theology:** Bible, religious ed. **Visual/performing arts:** Music management, music pedagogy, music performance, piano/organ, voice/opera.

Most popular majors. Biology 7%, business/marketing 22%, communications/journalism 15%, education 14%, English 6%, philosophy/religious studies 9%, visual/performing arts 7%.

Computing on campus. 100 workstations in dormitories, library, computer center, student center. Dormitories wired for high-speed internet access and linked to campus network. Commuter students can connect to campus network. Online library, helpline, student web hosting, wireless network available.

Student life. Freshman orientation: Mandatory. Preregistration for classes offered. **Policies:** No alcohol, tobacco, drugs. Curfew and dress code enforced. Religious observance required. Freshmen permitted cars on campus. **Housing:** Guaranteed on-campus for all undergraduates. Single-sex dorms, apartments available. $100 deposit, deadline 5/1. **Activities:** Choral groups, drama, music ensembles, musical theater, student government, student newspaper, Christian service organizations, community tutoring program, Practical Christian Ministry Involvement, Students for Life, international students organization, Fellowship of Christian Athletes.

Athletics. NAIA, NCCAA. **Intercollegiate:** Baseball M, basketball, cross-country, soccer, volleyball W. **Intramural:** Basketball, football (non-tackle) M, soccer, softball, table tennis, tennis, volleyball. **Team name:** Lions.

Student services. Adult student services, campus ministries, career counseling, student employment services, financial aid counseling, personal counseling, placement for graduates.

Contact. E-mail: admissions@bryan.edu
Phone: (423) 775-7204 Toll-free number: (800) 277-9522
Fax: (423) 775-7199
Michael Sapienza, Director of Admissions & Financial Aid, Bryan College, PO Box 7000, Dayton, TN 37321-7000

Carson-Newman College

Jefferson City, Tennessee — **CB member**
www.cn.edu — **CB code: 1102**

- Private 4-year liberal arts college affiliated with Southern Baptist Convention
- Residential campus in small town
- 1,834 degree-seeking undergraduates: 5% part-time, 54% women, 9% African American, 1% Hispanic American, 2% international
- 130 degree-seeking graduate students
- 78% of applicants admitted
- SAT or ACT required
- 56% graduate within 6 years

General. Founded in 1851. Regionally accredited. **Degrees:** 378 bachelor's awarded; master's offered. **ROTC:** Army, Air Force. **Location:** 30 miles from Knoxville. **Calendar:** Semester, extensive summer session. **Full-time faculty:** 128 total; 66% have terminal degrees. **Part-time faculty:** 67 total. **Class size:** 59% < 20, 38% 20-39, 2% 40-49, less than 1% 50-99. **Special facilities:** Appalachia Museum.

Freshman class profile. 1,066 applied, 828 admitted, 449 enrolled.

Mid 50% test scores		**Rank in top tenth:**	27%
ACT:	19-26	**Return as sophomores:**	69%
GPA 3.0-3.49:	68%	**Out-of-state:**	36%
GPA 2.0-2.99:	30%	**Live on campus:**	88%
Rank in top quarter:	47%	**International:**	1%

Basis for selection. Minimum 2.5 high school GPA, minimum ACT composite score of 19 or SAT combined score of 920 (exclusive of Writing), school and community activities, and recommendations important. Rank in top half of class considered. Essay required for marginal students; audition required for music; portfolio required for art; interview recommended for academically weak.

High school preparation. 20 units required. Required and recommended units include English 4, mathematics 2-3, social studies 3, history 2, science 2 (laboratory 1) and foreign language 2.

2006-2007 Annual costs. Tuition/fees (projected): $16,060. Room/board: $5,200. Books/supplies: $600. Personal expenses: $800.

2005-2006 Financial aid. Need-based: 445 full-time freshmen applied for aid; 363 were judged to have need; 363 of these received aid. Average need met was 87%. Average scholarship/grant was $10,199; average loan $3,101. 65% of total undergraduate aid awarded as scholarships/grants, 35% as loans/jobs. **Non-need-based:** Awarded to 1,368 full-time undergraduates, including 433 freshmen. Scholarships awarded for academics, art, athletics, leadership, minority status, music/drama, religious affiliation, ROTC.

Application procedures. Admission: Priority date 12/31; deadline 8/1. $25 fee, may be waived for applicants with need. Application may be submitted online. Admission notification on a rolling basis. Must reply by May 1 or within 4 week(s) if notified thereafter. **Financial aid:** Priority date 4/1; no closing date. FAFSA, institutional form required. Applicants notified on a rolling basis starting 2/1; must reply within 2 week(s) of notification.

Academics. 3-year pre-engineering programs available. **Special study options:** Accelerated study, double major, dual enrollment of high school students, ESL, exchange student, honors, independent study, internships, liberal arts/career combination, student-designed major, study abroad, teacher certification program, Washington semester, weekend college. **Credit/placement by examination:** AP, CLEP, institutional tests. 32 credit hours maximum toward associate degree, 32 toward bachelor's. **Support services:** Learning center, pre-admission summer program, reduced course load, remedial instruction, tutoring.

Majors. Biology: General. **Business:** General, accounting, business admin, managerial economics. **Communications:** General, journalism. **Computer sciences:** General, computer science. **Education:** General, early childhood, elementary, family/consumer sciences, music, physical, secondary, special. **English:** Speech/rhetoric. **Family/consumer sciences:** Clothing/textiles, family/community services, food/nutrition. **Foreign languages:** French, German, Spanish. **Health:** Athletic training, clinical lab science, health care admin, nursing (RN), predentistry, premedicine, prepharmacy. **History:** General. **Liberal arts:** Arts/sciences. **Math:** General. **Parks/recreation:** General, health/fitness. **Philosophy/religion:** Philosophy, religion. **Physical sciences:** Chemistry. **Psychology:** General. **Social sciences:** Economics, international economics, political science, sociology. **Theology:** Sacred music. **Visual/performing arts:** General, art, drawing, interior design, music performance, music theory/composition, painting, photography.

Most popular majors. Business/marketing 18%, communications/journalism 6%, education 19%, family/consumer sciences 6%, health sciences 7%, history 6%, psychology 7%.

Computing on campus. 100 workstations in dormitories, library, computer center.

Student life. Freshman orientation: Available. Preregistration for classes offered. **Policies:** Religious observance required. Freshmen permitted cars on campus. **Housing:** Guaranteed on-campus for freshmen. Single-sex dorms, apartments available. $50 deposit, deadline 8/1. Honors house available. **Activities:** Bands, choral groups, dance, drama, film society, literary magazine, music ensembles, musical theater, radio station, student government, student newspaper, TV station, Baptist Student Union, Fellowship of Christian Athletes, honor societies, Appalachian Outreach, Bonners Scholars Community Service.

Athletics. NCAA. **Intercollegiate:** Baseball M, basketball, cross-country, football (tackle) M, golf M, soccer, softball W, tennis, track and field, volleyball W, wrestling M. **Intramural:** Badminton, basketball, bowling, golf, racquetball, soccer, softball, swimming, table tennis, tennis, volleyball. **Team name:** Eagles.

Student services. Adult student services, career counseling, health services, personal counseling, placement for graduates, veterans' counselor. **Physically disabled:** Services for visually, hearing impaired.

Contact. E-mail: thuebner@cn.edu
Phone: (865) 471-3223 Fax: (865) 471-3502
Tom Huebner, Dean of Admissions, Carson-Newman College, 1646 Russell Avenue, Jefferson City, TN 37760

Christian Brothers University

Memphis, Tennessee — **CB member**
www.cbu.edu — **CB code: 1121**

- Private 4-year university affiliated with Roman Catholic Church
- Commuter campus in very large city
- 1,466 degree-seeking undergraduates: 22% part-time, 55% women, 36% African American, 5% Asian American, 2% Hispanic American, 2% international
- 281 degree-seeking graduate students
- 72% of applicants admitted
- SAT or ACT (ACT writing optional), application essay required
- 63% graduate within 6 years

General. Founded in 1871. Regionally accredited. **Degrees:** 313 bachelor's awarded; master's offered. **ROTC:** Army, Navy, Air Force. **Location:** 200 miles from Nashville; 150 miles from Little Rock, Arkansas. **Calendar:** Semester, limited summer session. **Full-time faculty:** 102 total; 89% have terminal degrees, 14% minority, 30% women. **Part-time faculty:** 52 total; 36% have terminal degrees, 17% minority, 48% women. **Class size:** 65% < 20, 35% 20-39, less than 1% 40-49.

Freshman class profile. 963 applied, 693 admitted, 261 enrolled.

Mid 50% test scores			
SAT verbal:	490-630	Rank in top quarter:	60%
SAT math:	480-620	Rank in top tenth:	35%
		Out-of-state:	22%
ACT:	21-27	Live on campus:	63%
GPA 3.50 or higher:	50%	International:	2%
GPA 3.0-3.49:	29%	Fraternities:	14%
GPA 2.0-2.99:	21%	Sororities:	14%

Basis for selection. Graduation from approved secondary school or GED equivalent, GPA of 2.0 and rank in upper 2/3 of graduating class, and satisfactory test scores required. SAT and ACT scores are used for math placement. Audition required for some programs; interview recommended for all. **Homeschooled:** Must have standardized test scores.

High school preparation. College-preparatory program recommended. Recommended units include English 4, mathematics 4 and science 4. College-preparatory program required of engineering applicants.

2005-2006 Annual costs. Tuition/fees: $19,150. Room/board: $5,500.

2004-2005 Financial aid. Need-based: 244 full-time freshmen applied for aid; 202 were judged to have need; 202 of these received aid. Average need met was 99%. Average scholarship/grant was $5,622; average loan $3,338. 47% of total undergraduate aid awarded as scholarships/grants, 53% as loans/jobs. **Non-need-based:** Awarded to 1,101 full-time undergraduates, including 272 freshmen. Scholarships awarded for academics, athletics, state residency. **Additional information:** ROTC scholarships available to qualified applicants.

Application procedures. Admission: Closing date 8/1 (postmark date). $25 fee, may be waived for applicants with need. Application may be submitted online. Admission notification on a rolling basis beginning on or about 12/1. Must reply by 5/1. **Financial aid:** Priority date 3/1; no closing date. FAFSA required. Applicants notified on a rolling basis starting 3/1; must reply within 2 week(s) of notification.

Academics. Special study options: Accelerated study, cross-registration, double major, dual enrollment of high school students, exchange student, honors, independent study, internships, liberal arts/career combination, study abroad, teacher certification program. **Credit/placement by examination:** AP, CLEP, SAT, ACT, institutional tests. 30 credit hours maximum toward bachelor's degree. **Support services:** Pre-admission summer program, reduced course load, tutoring, writing center.

Majors. Biology: General. **Business:** General, business admin. **Computer sciences:** Computer science. **Education:** Biology, chemistry, elementary, English, history, mathematics, physics, secondary. **Engineering:** Chemical, civil, computer, electrical, mechanical, physics. **English:** English lit. **History:** General. **Interdisciplinary:** Biological/physical sciences, math/computer science, natural sciences. **Liberal arts:** Arts/sciences. **Math:** General. **Philosophy/religion:** Philosophy, religion. **Physical sciences:** General, chemistry, physics. **Psychology:** General.

Most popular majors. Business/marketing 39%, education 6%, engineering/engineering technologies 15%, physical sciences 6%, psychology 22%.

Computing on campus. 300 workstations in dormitories, library, computer center, student center. Dormitories linked to campus network. Commuter students can connect to campus network. Online course registration, online library, helpline, wireless network available.

Student life. Freshman orientation: Mandatory. Preregistration for classes offered. Held Friday through Monday before classes begin in fall. Spring orientation held the Monday morning before classes begin on Tuesday. **Policies:** Freshmen permitted cars on campus. **Housing:** Guaranteed on-campus for freshmen. Single-sex dorms, apartments available. $450 fully refundable deposit, deadline 5/1. Juniors and seniors may live in on-campus apartments. Freshmen from outside Shelby County required to live on campus. Some houses are available. A private quiet study facility is available. **Activities:** Choral groups, drama, literary magazine, musical theater, student government, Black Student Association, The Chosen Generation, Intercultural Club, Lasallian Collegians, Student Peace Association, up 'til dawn.

Athletics. NCAA. **Intercollegiate:** Baseball M, basketball, cross-country, golf, soccer, softball W, tennis, volleyball W. **Intramural:** Basketball, football (non-tackle), soccer, softball, swimming, tennis, volleyball. **Team name:** Buccaneers.

Student services. Adult student services, alcohol/substance abuse counseling, campus ministries, career counseling, student employment services, financial aid counseling, health services, minority student services, personal counseling, placement for graduates.

Contact. E-mail: admissions@cbu.edu
Phone: (901) 321-3205 Toll-free number: (800) 288-7576
Fax: (901) 321-3202
Tracey Dysart, Dean of Admissions, Christian Brothers University, 650 East Parkway South, Memphis, TN 38104-5519

Crichton College

Memphis, Tennessee
www.crichton.edu — **CB code: 1782**

- Private 4-year liberal arts college affiliated with nondenominational tradition
- Commuter campus in very large city
- 972 degree-seeking undergraduates: 48% part-time, 65% women
- SAT or ACT (ACT writing optional), application essay required

General. Founded in 1941. Regionally accredited. Seeks to integrate Christian faith and learning throughout the disciplines. **Degrees:** 226 bachelor's awarded. **Location:** 7 miles from downtown. **Calendar:** Semester, limited summer session. **Full-time faculty:** 34 total; 59% have terminal degrees, 21% minority, 29% women. **Part-time faculty:** 73 total; 20% have terminal degrees, 11% minority, 41% women.

Freshman class profile. 80 enrolled.

Mid 50% test scores			
ACT:	20-26	Out-of-state:	36%
		Live on campus:	8%

Basis for selection. School achievement record, test scores, interview, references considered. Interview recommended. **Learning Disabled:** Psychoeducational assessments and/or medical documentation required.

High school preparation. 14 units required. Required units include English 3, mathematics 3, social studies 3, science 2 and foreign language 3.

2005-2006 Annual costs. Tuition/fees: $9,960. Room only: $3,600. Books/supplies: $500.

2005-2006 Financial aid. Need-based: Average need met was 57%. Average scholarship/grant was $4,943; average loan $2,938. 29% of total undergraduate aid awarded as scholarships/grants, 71% as loans/jobs. **Non-need-based:** Scholarships awarded for academics, alumni affiliation, athletics, leadership, music/drama, religious affiliation.

Application procedures. Admission: Priority date 1/1; no deadline. $25 fee, may be waived for applicants with need. Application may be submitted online. Admission notification on a rolling basis. **Financial aid:** Priority date 3/15; no closing date. FAFSA, institutional form required. Applicants notified on a rolling basis starting 3/1; must reply within 2 week(s) of notification.

Academics. Interdisciplinary team-taught core leading to work in the major field of study in business, education, Biblical studies, and the arts and sciences. Practicums (hands-on learning) and internships bridge classroom and workplace. Scheduling accommodates traditional and adult learners balancing family and professional obligations. Students over 25 who already have at least 60 credits may complete the major section of their degree in only 18 months by attending classes 1 night per week. **Special study options:** Accelerated study, cooperative education, distance learning, double major, dual enrollment of high school students, honors, independent study, internships, liberal arts/career combination, student-designed major, study abroad, teacher certification program, Washington semester, weekend college. Off-campus study options in Costa Rica, Los Angeles, London, and at the University of Oxford. **Credit/placement by examination:** AP, CLEP, IB, institutional tests. 30 credit hours maximum toward bachelor's degree. **Support services:** Learning center, reduced course load, remedial instruction, tutoring.

Majors. Biology: General. **Business:** Business admin, management information systems, nonprofit/public. **Education:** Biology, chemistry, elementary, English, secondary. **History:** General. **Legal studies:** Prelaw. **Liberal arts:** Arts/sciences. **Physical sciences:** Chemistry. **Psychology:** General. **Theology:** Bible, theology.

Most popular majors. Business/marketing 43%, education 33%, interdisciplinary studies 11%, theological studies 8%.

Computing on campus. 33 workstations in library, computer center. Dormitories wired for high-speed internet access. Online library, helpline, repair service, wireless network available.

Student life. Freshman orientation: Mandatory, $40 fee. Preregistration for classes offered. 2-day program teaches skills for success in college; helps establish relationships and a sense of community. **Policies:** Religious observance required. Freshmen permitted cars on campus. **Housing:** Special housing for disabled, apartments available. $150 deposit, deadline 8/15. **Activities:** Choral groups, dance, drama, film society, musical theater, student government, student newspaper, Operation Save, Praise and Worship Team, New Direction, Backyard Bible clubs, mission club, CRASH Ministries Leadership, chapel committee, Kingdom Kids puppet ministry, Alpha Chi Epsilon, Sigma Alpha Pi.

Athletics. NAIA, NCCAA. **Intercollegiate:** Baseball M, basketball M, cheerleading M, cross-country, soccer. **Intramural:** Football (non-tackle), softball, volleyball. **Team name:** Comets.

Student services. Adult student services, campus ministries, career counseling, student employment services, financial aid counseling, personal counseling, veterans' counselor.

Contact. E-mail: info@crichton.edu
Phone: (901) 320-9797 Toll-free number: (800) 960-9777
Fax: (901) 320-9791
Brian Duffy, Director of Admissions, Crichton College, 255 North Highland, Memphis, TN 38111

Cumberland University

Lebanon, Tennessee
www.cumberland.edu **CB code: 1146**

- Private 4-year university and liberal arts college
- Commuter campus in large town
- 1,031 degree-seeking undergraduates: 9% part-time, 57% women
- 425 degree-seeking graduate students
- 69% of applicants admitted
- ACT (writing optional) required
- 40% graduate within 6 years; 22% enter graduate study

General. Founded in 1842. Regionally accredited. **Degrees:** 170 bachelor's, 2 associate awarded; master's offered. **ROTC:** Army. **Location:** 30 miles from Nashville. **Calendar:** Semester, limited summer session. **Full-time faculty:** 60 total; 53% have terminal degrees, 8% minority, 38% women. **Part-time faculty:** 38 total; 13% have terminal degrees, 63% women. **Class size:** 56% < 20, 34% 20-39, 6% 40-49, 4% 50-99.

Freshman class profile. 1,038 applied, 717 admitted, 262 enrolled.

Mid 50% test scores		**Rank in top tenth:**	15%
SAT verbal:	410-530	**End year in good standing:**	70%
SAT math:	380-510	**Return as sophomores:**	60%
ACT:	17-22	**Out-of-state:**	12%
GPA 3.50 or higher:	12%	**Live on campus:**	60%
GPA 3.0-3.49:	60%	**Fraternities:**	19%
GPA 2.0-2.99:	25%	**Sororities:**	12%
Rank in top quarter:	38%		

Basis for selection. High school academic record and standardized test scores most important. Audition, portfolio required for some programs; interview recommended for academically weak. **Homeschooled:** Transcript of courses and grades required.

High school preparation. 16 units required; 19 recommended. Required and recommended units include English 4, mathematics 3-4, social studies 2, history 2, science 3 (laboratory 1-2) and foreign language 2.

2006-2007 Annual costs. Tuition/fees: $14,810. Room/board: $4,960. Books/supplies: $1,093. Personal expenses: $2,487.

2004-2005 Financial aid. Need-based: 186 full-time freshmen applied for aid; 163 were judged to have need; 163 of these received aid. Average need met was 59%. Average scholarship/grant was $4,959; average loan $2,185. 53% of total undergraduate aid awarded as scholarships/grants, 47% as loans/jobs. **Non-need-based:** Awarded to 1,010 full-time undergraduates, including 207 freshmen. Scholarships awarded for academics, art, athletics, music/drama.

Application procedures. Admission: Priority date 2/15; no deadline. $25 fee, may be waived for applicants with need. Application may be submitted online. Admission notification on a rolling basis beginning on or about 3/1. Permission of high school principal or guidance counselor required for early admission. Housing deposit refundable before August 1. **Financial aid:** Priority date 2/1; no closing date. FAFSA, institutional form required. Applicants notified on a rolling basis starting 5/1; must reply within 2 week(s) of notification.

Academics. Selection of major or minor not required. **Special study options:** Accelerated study, combined bachelor's/graduate degree, cooperative education, distance learning, double major, dual enrollment of high school students, honors, independent study, internships, liberal arts/career combination, teacher certification program. **Credit/placement by examination:** AP, CLEP, ACT. 30 credit hours maximum toward bachelor's degree. **Support services:** Learning center, pre-admission summer program, reduced course load, remedial instruction, study skills assistance, tutoring, writing center.

Honors college/program. Honors program requires minimum composite ACT score of 25 and consists of about 20 participating students per year.

Majors. Area/ethnic studies: American. **Biology:** General. **Business:** General, accounting, management science. **Education:** General, biology, early childhood, elementary, English, history, mathematics, middle, multi-level teacher, music, physical, secondary, social science, special. **English:** English lit. **Health:** Nursing (RN), predentistry, premedicine, prepharmacy, preveterinary. **History:** General. **Legal studies:** Prelaw. **Liberal arts:** Arts/sciences. **Math:** General. **Parks/recreation:** Health/fitness, sports admin. **Protective services:** Criminal justice. **Psychology:** General. **Public administration:** General. **Social sciences:** General, political science, sociology. **Visual/performing arts:** Studio arts.

Most popular majors. Business/marketing 18%, education 20%, health sciences 28%, liberal arts 9%, psychology 6%, security/protective services 7%.

Computing on campus. 60 workstations in library, computer center. Dormitories linked to campus network. Commuter students can connect to campus network. Online library, helpline, repair service, wireless network available.

Student life. Freshman orientation: Mandatory. Preregistration for classes offered. Freshman registration held June 25, July 8 and 21, August 5, 13, 16, and 23; 5 hours long. Freshman orientation held on August 27 and 28, 1 1/2 days long. **Policies:** Freshmen permitted cars on campus. **Housing:** Single-sex dorms, apartments, substance-free housing available. $200 fully refundable deposit, deadline 8/1. **Activities:** Bands, choral groups, dance, drama, music ensembles, musical theater, radio station, student government, student newspaper, Baptist Collegiate Ministries, Fellowship of Christian Athletes, African American Student Association, Campus Crusade for Christ, Champions for Christ.

Athletics. NAIA. **Intercollegiate:** Baseball M, basketball, cheerleading, cross-country, football (tackle) M, golf, soccer, softball W, tennis, volleyball W, wrestling M. **Intramural:** Basketball, bowling, football (non-tackle) M, softball, table tennis, volleyball. **Team name:** Bulldogs.

Student services. Adult student services, campus ministries, career counseling, student employment services, financial aid counseling, health services, personal counseling, placement for graduates. **Physically disabled:** Services for visually impaired.

Contact. E-mail: admissions@cumberland.edu
Phone: (615) 444-2562 ext. 1224 Toll-free number: (800) 467-0562
Fax: (615) 444-2569
Jason Brewer, Director of Admissions, Cumberland University, One Cumberland Square, Lebanon, TN 37087

East Tennessee State University

Johnson City, Tennessee — **CB member**
www.etsu.edu — **CB code: 1198**

- Public 4-year university
- Commuter campus in small city
- 9,486 degree-seeking undergraduates: 14% part-time, 58% women, 4% African American, 1% Asian American, 1% Hispanic American, 1% international
- 1,940 degree-seeking graduate students
- 81% of applicants admitted
- SAT or ACT (ACT writing optional) required
- 39% graduate within 6 years

General. Founded in 1911. Regionally accredited. Additional campuses in Kingsport, Bristol, and Greeneville. Paramedical center, medical college, many pre-professional programs. **Degrees:** 1,623 bachelor's, 4 associate awarded; master's, doctoral, first professional offered. **ROTC:** Army. **Location:** 90 miles from Knoxville, 60 miles from Asheville, North Carolina. **Calendar:** Semester, extensive summer session. **Full-time faculty:** 480 total; 70% have terminal degrees, 5% minority, 44% women. **Part-time faculty:** 309 total; 23% have terminal degrees, 3% minority, 55% women. **Class size:** 43% < 20, 43% 20-39, 6% 40-49, 6% 50-99, 2% >100. **Special facilities:** Museum, Appalachian archives, planetarium, observatory, arboretum.

Freshman class profile. 3,601 applied, 2,925 admitted, 1,595 enrolled.

Mid 50% test scores			
SAT verbal:	450-590	Rank in top tenth:	18%
SAT math:	450-570	Return as sophomores:	69%
ACT:	20-25	Out-of-state:	9%
GPA 3.50 or higher:	36%	Live on campus:	51%
GPA 3.0-3.49:	35%	International:	2%
GPA 2.0-2.99:	28%	Fraternities:	6%
Rank in top quarter:	38%	Sororities:	7%

Basis for selection. Completion of 14 specific high school units required by state. Minimum 2.3 GPA or ACT composite score of 19 or comparable SAT score required. Freshmen applicants age 21 or over not required to submit ACT or SAT scores but must complete assessment battery (ACT Compass) for placement purposes. Those with ACT composite scores below 19 or Math or English scores below 19 complete the appropriate assessment (Compass). Interview recommended for dental hygiene, health-related professions, nursing, physical therapy programs; audition required for music; portfolio recommended for art. **Homeschooled:** Transcript of courses and grades required.

High school preparation. 14 units required; 16 recommended. Required and recommended units include English 4, mathematics 3-4, social studies 1, history 1, science 2-3 (laboratory 1) and foreign language 2. One unit visual/performing arts also required.

2005-2006 Annual costs. Tuition/fees: $4,487; $13,799 out-of-state. Room/board: $5,428. Books/supplies: $942. Personal expenses: $4,795.

2005-2006 Financial aid. Need-based: 1,477 full-time freshmen applied for aid; 1,039 were judged to have need; 1,025 of these received aid. Average need met was 84%. Average scholarship/grant was $24,350; average loan $780. 4% of total undergraduate aid awarded as scholarships/grants, 96% as loans/jobs. **Non-need-based:** Awarded to 2,356 full-time undergraduates, including 529 freshmen. Scholarships awarded for academics, alumni affiliation, art, athletics, job skills, leadership, minority status, music/drama, religious affiliation, state residency. **Additional information:** Housing costs payable by installment.

Application procedures. Admission: Priority date 7/1; no deadline. $15 fee, may be waived for applicants with need. Application may be submitted online. Admission notification on a rolling basis. **Financial aid:** Priority date 3/1; no closing date. FAFSA required. Applicants notified on a rolling basis starting 5/15; must reply within 3 week(s) of notification.

Academics. Special study options: Accelerated study, combined bachelor's/graduate degree, cooperative education, distance learning, double major, dual enrollment of high school students, exchange student, honors, independent study, internships, study abroad, teacher certification program. **Credit/placement by examination:** AP, CLEP, IB, SAT, ACT, institutional tests. **Support services:** Learning center, reduced course load, study skills assistance, tutoring.

Honors college/program. Honors program selects 20 new freshmen each year for specifically designed courses. Requires minimum 29 ACT or comparable SAT, 3.5 high school GPA.

Majors. Biology: General. **Business:** Accounting, business admin, finance, managerial economics, marketing. **Communications:** Media studies. **Communications technology:** Animation/special effects. **Computer sciences:** General. **Education:** Special. **Engineering technology:** General, surveying. **English:** English lit, speech/rhetoric. **Family/consumer sciences:** General, child development, family studies. **Foreign languages:** General. **Health:** Dental hygiene, environmental health, health services, nursing (RN). **History:** General. **Liberal arts:** Arts/sciences. **Math:** General. **Parks/recreation:** Health/fitness, sports admin. **Philosophy/religion:** Philosophy. **Physical sciences:** Chemistry, physics. **Protective services:** Law enforcement admin. **Psychology:** General. **Public administration:** Social work. **Social sciences:** Economics, geography, political science, sociology. **Visual/performing arts:** Art.

Most popular majors. Business/marketing 16%, health sciences 17%, liberal arts 6%.

Computing on campus. 600 workstations in library, computer center, student center. Commuter students can connect to campus network. Online course registration, online library, helpline, repair service available.

Student life. Freshman orientation: Mandatory. Preregistration for classes offered. Five sessions during summer for 1 or 2 days in duration. **Policies:** Freshmen permitted cars on campus. **Housing:** Coed dorms, single-sex dorms, special housing for disabled, apartments, fraternity/sorority housing, substance-free housing available. $100 fully refundable deposit. **Activities:** Bands, choral groups, drama, literary magazine, music ensembles, radio station, student government, student newspaper, TV station, Baptist Student Union, Campus Crusade, Catholic Center, Christian Student Fellowship, Fellowship of Christian Athletes, Presbyterian ministry, Episcopal ministry, Real Life Fellowship, Wesley Foundation (Methodist), Black Affairs Association.

Athletics. NCAA. **Intercollegiate:** Baseball M, basketball, cross-country, golf, soccer W, softball W, tennis, track and field, volleyball W. **Intramural:** Basketball, cross-country, football (non-tackle), golf, handball, racquetball, softball, tennis, volleyball W, weight lifting M. **Team name:** Buccaneers.

Student services. Adult student services, alcohol/substance abuse counseling, campus ministries, career counseling, services for economically disadvantaged, student employment services, financial aid counseling, health services, legal services, minority student services, on-campus daycare, personal counseling, placement for graduates, veterans' counselor, women's services. **Physically disabled:** Services for visually, speech, hearing impaired.

Contact. E-mail: go2etsu@etsu.edu
Phone: (423) 439-4213 Toll-free number: (800) 462-3878
Fax: (423) 439-4630
T Pitts, Director of Admissions, East Tennessee State University, ETSU Box 70731, Johnson City, TN 37614-0731

Fisk University

Nashville, Tennessee — **CB member**
www.fisk.edu — **CB code: 1224**

- Private 4-year liberal arts college affiliated with United Church of Christ
- Residential campus in very large city
- 813 degree-seeking undergraduates: 5% part-time, 70% women
- 56 degree-seeking graduate students
- 80% of applicants admitted
- SAT or ACT (ACT writing optional), interview required
- 60% graduate within 6 years

General. Founded in 1866. Regionally accredited. **Degrees:** 140 bachelor's awarded; master's offered. **ROTC:** Army, Navy. **Location:** 216 miles from Memphis, 225 miles from Atlanta. **Calendar:** Semester. **Full-time faculty:** 52 total; 75% have terminal degrees, 71% minority, 42% women. **Part-time faculty:** 40 total; 12% have terminal degrees, 42% women. **Class size:** 62% < 20, 33% 20-39, 2% 40-49, 2% 50-99.

Freshman class profile. 1,643 applied, 1,310 admitted, 214 enrolled.

Mid 50% test scores		Rank in top quarter:	40%
SAT verbal:	430-560	Rank in top tenth:	17%
SAT math:	420-540	Return as sophomores:	86.5%
ACT:	18-22	Out-of-state:	70%
GPA 3.50 or higher:	28%	Live on campus:	92%
GPA 3.0-3.49:	28%	International:	2%
GPA 2.0-2.99:	44%		

Basis for selection. School achievement record, class rank, test scores, recommendations, activities important. Essay recommended for all; audition recommended for music. Interview required for scholarship nominees and must take place prior to 2/15.

High school preparation. 20 units recommended. Recommended units include English 4, mathematics 3, social studies 3, history 1, science 1, foreign language 1 and academic electives 6. 1 algebra and 1 geometry recommended.

2006-2007 Annual costs. Tuition/fees: $13,969. Room/board: $7,012. Books/supplies: $1,000. Personal expenses: $2,050.

2004-2005 Financial aid. All financial aid based on need. 158 full-time freshmen applied for aid; 151 were judged to have need; 149 of these received aid. Average need met was 51%. Average scholarship/grant was $4,974; average loan $3,483. 55% of total undergraduate aid awarded as scholarships/grants, 45% as loans/jobs.

Application procedures. Admission: Closing date 3/1 (receipt date). $50 fee, may be waived for applicants with need. Application must be submitted on paper. Admission notification on a rolling basis. Must reply by May 1 or within 2 week(s) if notified thereafter. **Financial aid:** Priority date 3/1, closing date 7/1. FAFSA required. Applicants notified on a rolling basis starting 4/1; must reply within 2 week(s) of notification.

Academics. Special study options: Combined bachelor's/graduate degree, cooperative education, cross-registration, double major, dual enrollment of high school students, exchange student, honors, independent study, internships, liberal arts/career combination, student-designed major, study abroad, teacher certification program. 2-2 program with Rush-Presbyterian-St. Luke's Medical Center in nursing, dual degree in science and engineering, dual degree in engineering and natural sciences in 5 years, 3-3 program with Howard University for Doctor of Pharmacy, 5-year MBA program with Vanderbilt University, 7-year MD, PhD, DDS programs with Meharry Medical College. **Credit/placement by examination:** AP, CLEP, IB, SAT, ACT, institutional tests. 30 credit hours maximum toward bachelor's degree. **Support services:** Learning center, pre-admission summer program, tutoring, writing center.

Majors. Biology: General. **Business:** Business admin. **Computer sciences:** Computer science. **Education:** Special. **English:** Speech/rhetoric. **Foreign languages:** Spanish. **Health:** Nursing (RN), premedicine. **History:** General. **Liberal arts:** Arts/sciences. **Math:** General. **Physical sciences:** Chemistry, physics. **Psychology:** General. **Social sciences:** Political science, sociology. **Visual/performing arts:** Art.

Most popular majors. Biology 12%, business/marketing 19%, English 6%, psychology 24%, social sciences 14%, visual/performing arts 6%.

Computing on campus. 100 workstations in dormitories, library, computer center. Dormitories wired for high-speed internet access and linked to campus network. Online course registration, helpline, student web hosting, wireless network available.

Student life. Freshman orientation: Available. Preregistration for classes offered. 3-5 day orientation held 1 week before classes. **Policies:** All students required to live on-campus, with few exceptions. All freshmen have curfew of 12:00 am. Freshmen permitted cars on campus. **Housing:** Guaranteed on-campus for all undergraduates. Single-sex dorms, special housing for disabled available. $100 nonrefundable deposit, deadline 7/15. **Activities:** Jazz band, choral groups, dance, drama, literary magazine, music ensembles, radio station, student government, student newspaper, TV station, Baptist student union, Muslim student association, Nation of Islam, Y.E.S. Ministries, Carribean student union, African student association, race relations students' organization.

Athletics. NCAA. **Intercollegiate:** Baseball M, basketball, cross-country, soccer, softball W, tennis, track and field, volleyball W. **Intramural:** Badminton, basketball, football (non-tackle) M, football (tackle) M, softball, volleyball. **Team name:** Bulldogs.

Student services. Career counseling, student employment services, financial aid counseling, health services, personal counseling, placement for graduates.

Contact. E-mail: admit@fisk.edu
Phone: (615) 329-8665 Toll-free number: (888) 702-0022
Fax: (615) 329-8774
Keith Chandler, Director of Admissions, Fisk University, 1000 17th Avenue North, Nashville, TN 37208-3051

Free Will Baptist Bible College

Nashville, Tennessee
www.fwbbc.edu **CB code: 1232**

- Private 4-year Bible college affiliated with Free Will Baptists
- Residential campus in very large city
- 357 degree-seeking undergraduates: 14% part-time, 47% women, 4% African American, 1% Hispanic American, 2% international
- Application essay required

General. Founded in 1942. Regionally accredited; also accredited by ABHE. **Degrees:** 48 bachelor's, 5 associate awarded. **ROTC:** Army, Air Force. **Calendar:** Semester, limited summer session. **Full-time faculty:** 23 total. **Part-time faculty:** 21 total. **Class size:** 81% < 20, 13% 20-39, 6% 50-99.

Freshman class profile. 69 enrolled.

Out-of-state:	67%	International:	1%
Live on campus:	93%		

Basis for selection. Open admission. References certifying evangelical Christian faith and character required. Applicants without high school diploma or GED must pass GED prior to receiving degree.

High school preparation. 22 units recommended. Recommended units include English 4, mathematics 4, social studies 3, history 2, science 4, foreign language 3 and academic electives 2.

2005-2006 Annual costs. Tuition/fees: $10,238. Room/board: $4,588. Books/supplies: $600. Personal expenses: $820.

Financial aid. Non-need-based: Scholarships awarded for academics, art, music/drama.

Application procedures. Admission: Priority date 4/15; no deadline. $35 fee. Application may be submitted online. Admission notification on a rolling basis. **Financial aid:** Priority date 4/15; no closing date. FAFSA, institutional form required. Applicants notified on a rolling basis starting 7/1; must reply within 2 week(s) of notification.

Academics. Special study options: Distance learning, double major, independent study, internships, teacher certification program. **Credit/placement by examination:** CLEP, IB, SAT, ACT, institutional tests. 16 credit hours maximum toward bachelor's degree. **Support services:** Reduced course load, remedial instruction, tutoring.

Majors. Business: Business admin. **Education:** Early childhood, elementary, music, physical, secondary. **Parks/recreation:** Exercise sciences. **Psychology:** General. **Theology:** Bible, missionary, religious ed, theology.

Most popular majors. Business/marketing 33%, education 19%, English 10%, parks/recreation 14%, psychology 19%.

Computing on campus. 38 workstations in library, computer center, student center. Online library, repair service, wireless network available.

Student life. Freshman orientation: Mandatory. **Policies:** Religious observance required. Freshmen permitted cars on campus. **Housing:** Single-sex dorms, apartments available. $100 fully refundable deposit, deadline 8/1. Single students required to live on campus unless living with parents or close relatives. **Activities:** Choral groups, drama, music ensembles, student government, ministerial and missionary organizations, Christian service assignments, organization for business students, literary societies.

Athletics. NCCAA. **Intercollegiate:** Baseball M, basketball, volleyball W. **Intramural:** Badminton W, basketball, soccer M, softball, swimming, table tennis M, tennis, volleyball. **Team name:** FLAMES.

Student services. Career counseling, student employment services, financial aid counseling, health services, personal counseling, placement for graduates.

Contact. E-mail: recruit@fwbbc.edu
Phone: (615) 383-1340 Toll-free number: (800) 763-9222
Fax: (615) 269-6028
Ryan Lewis, Director of Recruitment, Free Will Baptist Bible College, 3606 West End Avenue, Nashville, TN 37205-0117

Freed-Hardeman University
Henderson, Tennessee — **CB member**
www.fhu.edu — **CB code: 1230**

- Private 4-year university and liberal arts college affiliated with Church of Christ
- Residential campus in small town
- 1,459 degree-seeking undergraduates
- 530 graduate students
- 99% of applicants admitted
- SAT or ACT (ACT writing recommended) required

General. Founded in 1869. Regionally accredited. Henderson Church of Christ facilities adjacent to campus. Campus in Verviers, Belgium. **Degrees:** 256 bachelor's awarded; master's offered. **Location:** 15 miles from Jackson, 85 miles from Memphis. **Calendar:** Semester, limited summer session. **Full-time faculty:** 99 total; 75% have terminal degrees, 6% minority, 28% women. **Part-time faculty:** 36 total; 53% have terminal degrees, 3% minority, 33% women. **Class size:** 52% < 20, 40% 20-39, 4% 40-49, 3% 50-99. **Special facilities:** Cancer research institute.

Freshman class profile. 1,230 applied, 1,223 admitted, 374 enrolled.

Mid 50% test scores		**Rank in top tenth:**	30%
ACT:	20-26	**Out-of-state:**	49%
Rank in top quarter:	55%	**Live on campus:**	90%

Basis for selection. Admissions based on school achievement record, test scores, references. Applicants without minimum test score or high school GPA may be admitted with restrictions after further evaluation. **Homeschooled:** Applicants expected to take ACT or SAT.

High school preparation. 20 units recommended. Recommended units include English 4, mathematics 2, social studies 2, science 2 and academic electives 10. Additional science and mathematics courses recommended.

2005-2006 Annual costs. Tuition/fees: $12,440. Room/board: $6,200. Books/supplies: $1,500. Personal expenses: $1,660.

2005-2006 Financial aid. Need-based: 335 full-time freshmen applied for aid; 292 were judged to have need; 292 of these received aid. Average need met was 70%. Average scholarship/grant was $7,545; average loan $3,722. 47% of total undergraduate aid awarded as scholarships/grants, 53% as loans/jobs. **Non-need-based:** Scholarships awarded for academics, art, athletics, leadership, minority status, music/drama, state residency.

Application procedures. Admission: No deadline. No application fee. Application may be submitted online. Admission notification on a rolling basis. Housing deposit refundable up to 30 days prior to term. **Financial aid:** Priority date 3/1; no closing date. FAFSA required. Applicants notified on a rolling basis starting 3/1; must reply within 4 week(s) of notification.

Academics. Students enrolled for 12 or more undergraduate hours must register for Bible class. **Special study options:** Accelerated study, combined bachelor's/graduate degree, cooperative education, cross-registration, distance learning, double major, dual enrollment of high school students, honors, independent study, internships, liberal arts/career combination, student-designed major, study abroad, teacher certification program. 3-2 engineering, Honors College, study abroad program in Belgium. **Credit/placement by examination:** AP, CLEP, IB, institutional tests. 33 credit hours maximum toward bachelor's degree. **Support services:** Learning center, reduced course load, remedial instruction, study skills assistance, tutoring.

Honors college/program. Approximately 5% of freshmen class admitted to honors course work as result of competitive application process.

Majors. Biology: General, biochemistry. **Business:** Accounting, business admin, finance, human resources, management information systems, marketing. **Communications:** General, media studies, public relations. **Computer sciences:** General. **Education:** Art, biology, curriculum, early childhood, elementary, English, history, mathematics, middle, multi-level teacher, music, physical, science, secondary, special. **English:** English lit. **Family/consumer sciences:** Family studies. **Health:** Health care admin. **History:** General. **Liberal arts:** Arts/sciences. **Math:** General. **Parks/recreation:** Exercise sciences. **Philosophy/religion:** Philosophy. **Physical sciences:** General, chemistry. **Psychology:** General. **Public administration:** Social work. **Social sciences:** General. **Theology:** Bible, missionary, theology, youth ministry. **Visual/performing arts:** Acting, art, design, interior design, theater design.

Most popular majors. Biology 9%, business/marketing 13%, interdisciplinary studies 13%, psychology 7%, theological studies 15%.

Computing on campus. 238 workstations in dormitories, library, computer center. Dormitories wired for high-speed internet access and linked to campus network. Commuter students can connect to campus network. Online course registration, online library, helpline, wireless network available.

Student life. Freshman orientation: Mandatory. Preregistration for classes offered. Freshmen are put into groups of 15 along with upperclassmen. Held 4 days prior to start of classes in August. **Policies:** Daily chapel is mandatory. Nightly curfew. Religious observance required. Freshmen permitted cars on campus. **Housing:** Guaranteed on-campus for freshmen. Single-sex dorms, apartments, substance-free housing available. $50 deposit, deadline 4/1. Some student-teacher housing for education majors. **Activities:** Bands, choral groups, drama, music ensembles, musical theater, radio station, student government, student newspaper, TV station, evangelism forum, preachers club, student-alumni association, international club, university student ambassadors, university program council, youth workers club, Impact Team, Young Republicans, Young Democrats.

Athletics. NAIA. **Intercollegiate:** Baseball M, basketball, cheerleading W, soccer, softball W, tennis, volleyball W. **Intramural:** Badminton, basketball, cross-country, football (non-tackle), racquetball, soccer, softball, table tennis, tennis, volleyball. **Team name:** Lions.

Student services. Alcohol/substance abuse counseling, campus ministries, career counseling, student employment services, financial aid counseling, health services, on-campus daycare, personal counseling, placement for graduates, veterans' counselor. **Physically disabled:** Services for visually, hearing impaired.

Contact. E-mail: admissions@fhu.edu
Phone: (731) 989-6651 Toll-free number: (800) 630-3480
Fax: (731) 989-6045
Belinda Anderson, Director of Admissions, Freed-Hardeman University, 158 East Main Street, Henderson, TN 38340

International Academy of Design and Technology: Nashville
Nashville, Tennessee
www.iadtnashville.com

- For-profit 4-year branch campus and art college
- Very large city

General. Accredited by ACICS. **Calendar:** Quarter.

Annual costs/financial aid. Tuition/fees (projected): $15,875.

Contact. Phone: (866) 302-4238
1 Bridgestone Park, Nashville, TN 37214

ITT Technical Institute: Knoxville
Knoxville, Tennessee
www.itt-tech.edu — **CB code: 7139**

- For-profit 4-year technical college
- Commuter campus in small city

General. Accredited by ACICS. **Calendar:** Quarter.

Annual costs/financial aid. Tuition varies by program, $260-$368 per credit hour.

Contact. Phone: (865) 671-2800
Director of Recruitment, 10208 Technology Drive, Knoxville, TN 37932

ITT Technical Institute: Memphis
Cordova, Tennessee
www.itt-tech.edu — **CB code: 2731**

- For-profit 4-year technical college
- Commuter campus in very large city

General. Accredited by ACICS. **Calendar:** Quarter.

Annual costs/financial aid. Tuition varies by program, $260-$368 per credit hour.

Contact. Phone: (901) 762-0556
Director of Recruitment, 7260 Goodlett Farms Parkway, Cordova, TN 38016

ITT Technical Institute: Nashville

Nashville, Tennessee
www.itt-tech.edu **CB code: 7025**

- For-profit 4-year technical college
- Commuter campus in very large city

General. Accredited by ACICS. **Calendar:** Quarter.

Annual costs/financial aid. Tuition varies by program, $260-$368 per credit hour.

Contact. Phone: (615) 889-8700
Director of Recruitment, 2845 Elm Hill Pike, Nashville, TN 37214

Johnson Bible College

Knoxville, Tennessee
www.jbc.edu **CB code: 1345**

- Private 4-year Bible college affiliated with Christian Church
- Residential campus in small city
- 776 degree-seeking undergraduates: 1% part-time, 51% women, 2% African American, 1% Asian American, 1% Hispanic American, 2% international
- 130 degree-seeking graduate students
- 95% of applicants admitted
- SAT or ACT (ACT writing optional), application essay required
- 45% graduate within 6 years

General. Founded in 1893. Regionally accredited; also accredited by ABHE. **Degrees:** 127 bachelor's, 9 associate awarded; master's offered. **Location:** 7 miles from Knoxville. **Calendar:** Semester, limited summer session. **Full-time faculty:** 27 total; 63% have terminal degrees, 11% women. **Part-time faculty:** 36 total; 25% have terminal degrees, 39% women. **Class size:** 38% < 20, 31% 20-39, 13% 40-49, 19% 50-99.

Freshman class profile. 296 applied, 280 admitted, 184 enrolled.

Mid 50% test scores			
SAT verbal:	470-580	Rank in top quarter:	46%
SAT math:	470-560	Rank in top tenth:	20%
ACT:	20-24	Return as sophomores:	78%
GPA 3.50 or higher:	42%	Out-of-state:	83%
GPA 3.0-3.49:	30%	Live on campus:	96%
GPA 2.0-2.99:	28%	International:	1%

Basis for selection. High school transcript and 3 references, 1 from minister required. Combination of high school percentile rank and ACT score determines initial admission criteria. Interview recommended.

High school preparation. 16 units required. Required units include academic electives 4. 12 of the 16 units must be content courses such as English, history, mathematics, foreign language, and science.

2006-2007 Annual costs. Tuition/fees (projected): $6,930. Part-time students pay mandatory fee of $30.42 per credit hour. Room/board: $4,490. Books/supplies: $1,085. Personal expenses: $2,060.

2005-2006 Financial aid. Need-based: 183 full-time freshmen applied for aid; 154 were judged to have need; 154 of these received aid. Average need met was 42%. Average scholarship/grant was $1,620; average loan $1,150. 63% of total undergraduate aid awarded as scholarships/grants, 37% as loans/jobs. **Non-need-based:** Awarded to 315 full-time undergraduates, including 108 freshmen. Scholarships awarded for academics, leadership, minority status, music/drama, religious affiliation, state residency.

Application procedures. Admission: Closing date 7/1 (receipt date). $35 fee. Admission notification 9/1. Admission notification on a rolling basis. **Financial aid:** Priority date 5/1, closing date 8/1. FAFSA, institutional form required. Applicants notified by 4/30; must reply within 2 week(s) of notification.

Academics. All degree programs have major in Bible. Double majors in Bible and music, Bible and teacher education, Bible and counseling, Bible and preaching, Bible and youth ministry/preaching offered. **Special study options:** Accelerated study, combined bachelor's/graduate degree, cooperative education, distance learning, double major, ESL, honors, independent study, internships, teacher certification program. **Credit/placement by examination:** AP, CLEP, institutional tests. 32 credit hours maximum toward bachelor's degree. **Support services:** Learning center, remedial instruction, study skills assistance, tutoring.

Majors. Theology: Bible, sacred music.

Most popular majors. Education 13%, philosophy/religious studies 87%.

Computing on campus. 35 workstations in library, computer center. Dormitories linked to campus network. Helpline, student web hosting, wireless network available.

Student life. Freshman orientation: Mandatory. Preregistration for classes offered. Weekend preceeding first semester. **Policies:** Religious observance required. Freshmen permitted cars on campus. **Housing:** Single-sex dorms, apartments, substance-free housing available. $100 fully refundable deposit, deadline 8/1. Mobile homes, duplex houses, and apartments available for family housing. **Activities:** Choral groups, drama, music ensembles, musical theater, radio station, student government.

Athletics. NCCAA. **Intercollegiate:** Baseball M, basketball, soccer, volleyball W. **Intramural:** Basketball, softball, tennis, volleyball.

Student services. Alcohol/substance abuse counseling, campus ministries, career counseling, student employment services, financial aid counseling, health services, on-campus daycare, personal counseling, placement for graduates.

Contact. E-mail: twingfield@jbc.edu
Phone: (865) 251-2233 Toll-free number: (800) 827-2122
Fax: (865) 251-2336
Tim Wingfield, Director of Admissions, Johnson Bible College, 7900 Johnson Drive, Knoxville, TN 37998-0001

King College

Bristol, Tennessee **CB member**
www.king.edu **CB code: 1371**

- Private 4-year Bible and liberal arts college affiliated with Presbyterian Church (USA)
- Residential campus in large town
- 807 degree-seeking undergraduates: 2% part-time, 61% women, 3% African American, 2% Hispanic American, 3% international
- 97 degree-seeking graduate students
- 95% of applicants admitted
- SAT or ACT (ACT writing optional), application essay required
- 59% graduate within 6 years; 7% enter graduate study

General. Founded in 1867. Regionally accredited. Christian values emphasized. **Degrees:** 151 bachelor's awarded; master's offered. **Location:** 110 miles from Knoxville, 95 miles from Asheville, North Carolina. **Calendar:** Semester, limited summer session. **Full-time faculty:** 50 total; 76% have terminal degrees, 2% minority, 42% women. **Part-time faculty:** 44 total; 11% have terminal degrees, 7% minority, 54% women. **Class size:** 77% < 20, 22% 20-39, less than 1% 40-49, less than 1% 50-99. **Special facilities:** Observatory, nuclear physics laboratory.

Freshman class profile. 550 applied, 524 admitted, 109 enrolled.

Mid 50% test scores			
SAT verbal:	460-570	Rank in top quarter:	43%
SAT math:	490-570	Rank in top tenth:	19%
ACT:	20-24	Return as sophomores:	67%
GPA 3.50 or higher:	46%	Out-of-state:	45%
GPA 3.0-3.49:	29%	Live on campus:	94%
GPA 2.0-2.99:	25%	International:	1%

Basis for selection. Qualified applicants should have a minimum of a 2.4/4.0 GPA and a minimum ACT or SAT composite score of 19 or 890 (exclusive of Writing). Those who do not present this pattern may be conditionally accepted with permission from the Admissions Committee. Interview recommended.

High school preparation. 16 units required. Required units include English 4, mathematics 3, social studies 2, history 2, science 1, foreign language 2 and academic electives 4. 2 Algebra (Algebra I and II); one unit of Geometry; 1 Natural Science required.

2006-2007 Annual costs. Tuition/fees (projected): $18,345. Room/board: $6,200. Books/supplies: $850. Personal expenses: $2,000.

2005-2006 Financial aid. Need-based: 197 full-time freshmen applied for aid; 160 were judged to have need; 160 of these received aid. Average need met was 77%. Average scholarship/grant was $13,391; average loan $2,618. 69% of total undergraduate aid awarded as scholarships/grants, 31% as loans/jobs. **Non-need-based:** Awarded to 368 full-time undergraduates, including 122 freshmen. Scholarships awarded for academics, art, athletics, job skills, leadership, music/drama.

Application procedures. Admission: No deadline. $20 fee, may be waived for applicants with need. Application may be submitted online. Admission notification on a rolling basis. Refund available in full until May 1. **Financial aid:** Priority date 3/1; no closing date. FAFSA required. Applicants notified on a rolling basis starting 3/15; must reply within 2 week(s) of notification.

Academics. Special study options: Accelerated study, combined bachelor's/graduate degree, cross-registration, double major, dual enrollment of high school students, ESL, exchange student, honors, independent study, internships, student-designed major, study abroad, teacher certification program, Washington semester. **Credit/placement by examination:** AP, CLEP. 30 credit hours maximum toward bachelor's degree. **Support services:** Learning center, reduced course load, remedial instruction, study skills assistance, tutoring, writing center.

Honors college/program. Current students may be invited to join the Jack E. Snider Honors Center by invitation from a faculty member. Prospective students will meet entrance exam requirements.

Majors. Area/ethnic studies: American. **Biology:** General, biochemistry, biophysics. **Business:** Business admin. **Communications:** Digital media. **Computer sciences:** Computer science. **English:** English lit. **Foreign languages:** General, French, Spanish. **Health:** Clinical lab science, nursing (RN). **History:** General. **Interdisciplinary:** Behavioral sciences. **Math:** General. **Philosophy/religion:** Religion. **Physical sciences:** Chemistry, physics. **Psychology:** General. **Social sciences:** Political science. **Theology:** Bible, youth ministry. **Visual/performing arts:** General.

Most popular majors. Biology 7%, business/marketing 24%, English 9%, health sciences 22%, history 7%, psychology 7%, theological studies 7%.

Computing on campus. PC or laptop required. 88 workstations in library, computer center, student center. Dormitories wired for high-speed internet access and linked to campus network. Commuter students can connect to campus network. Online library, helpline, repair service, wireless network available.

Student life. Freshman orientation: Available. Preregistration for classes offered. **Policies:** Traditional undergraduate students participate in Chapel and Convocation series as a part of their service requirements necessary to fulfill degree requirements. Religious observance required. Freshmen permitted cars on campus. **Housing:** Guaranteed on-campus for all undergraduates. Single-sex dorms, special housing for disabled, apartments available. $50 fully refundable deposit. **Activities:** Bands, choral groups, dance, drama, literary magazine, music ensembles, musical theater, student government, student newspaper, Fellowship of Christian Athletes, Young Life Leadership, Student Life and Activities Committee at King, Students in Free Enterprise, King College Republicans, World Christian Fellowship, literary society.

Athletics. NAIA. **Intercollegiate:** Baseball M, basketball, bowling, cheerleading, cross-country M, golf, soccer, tennis, track and field, volleyball W, wrestling M. **Intramural:** Badminton, basketball, cross-country, football (non-tackle), golf, soccer, softball W, table tennis, track and field, volleyball. **Team name:** Tornado.

Student services. Campus ministries, career counseling, student employment services, financial aid counseling, health services, personal counseling, placement for graduates.

Contact. E-mail: admissions@king.edu
Phone: (423) 652-4861 Toll-free number: (800) 362-0014
Fax: (423) 652-4727
Melinda Clark, Associate Vice President of Enrollment Management, King College, 1350 King College Road, Bristol, TN 37620-2699

Lambuth University

Jackson, Tennessee
www.lambuth.edu **CB code: 1394**

- Private 4-year university and liberal arts college affiliated with United Methodist Church
- Residential campus in small city
- 786 degree-seeking undergraduates: 3% part-time, 54% women, 16% African American, 1% Asian American, 3% Hispanic American, 3% international
- 65% of applicants admitted
- SAT or ACT (ACT writing optional), application essay required
- 38% graduate within 6 years; 21% enter graduate study

General. Founded in 1843. Regionally accredited. Georgian revival buildings on 50 acre campus. **Degrees:** 154 bachelor's awarded. **Location:** 80 miles from Memphis, 120 miles from Nashville. **Calendar:** Semester, limited summer session. **Full-time faculty:** 52 total; 73% have terminal degrees, 6% minority, 35% women. **Part-time faculty:** 27 total; 22% have terminal degrees, 7% minority, 56% women. **Class size:** 72% < 20, 27% 20-39, less than 1% 50-99, less than 1% >100. **Special facilities:** Planetarium, art and interior design complex, biological field station, education curriculum lab, log house museum.

Freshman class profile. 1,333 applied, 861 admitted, 234 enrolled.

Mid 50% test scores			
SAT verbal:	480-600	Return as sophomores:	58%
SAT math:	500-590	Out-of-state:	28%
ACT:	21-26	Live on campus:	85%
Rank in top quarter:	52%	International:	5%
Rank in top tenth:	29%	Fraternities:	12%
		Sororities:	20%

Basis for selection. High school comprehensive record, test scores important. Applicants whose native language is not English need to provide evidence of English proficiency by results of TOEFL or results of ACT or SAT. Other approved English proficiency tests may be considered. Audition required for drama, music programs; portfolio recommended for art program; tryouts required for athletes. **Learning Disabled:** No special admissions requirements; appropriate documentation supporting request for accommodations must be provided to director of student disabilities. Accommodations determined on case-by-case basis.

High school preparation. College-preparatory program recommended. Recommended units include English 4, mathematics 4, social studies 2, history 2, science 3 (laboratory 1) and foreign language 2.

2006-2007 Annual costs. Tuition/fees (projected): $16,380. Room/board: $6,710. Books/supplies: $1,200. Personal expenses: $1,732.

2005-2006 Financial aid. Need-based: 217 full-time freshmen applied for aid; 180 were judged to have need; 180 of these received aid. Average need met was 83%. Average scholarship/grant was $12,871; average loan $1,346. 74% of total undergraduate aid awarded as scholarships/grants, 26% as loans/jobs. **Non-need-based:** Awarded to 337 full-time undergraduates, including 138 freshmen. Scholarships awarded for academics, alumni affiliation, art, athletics, job skills, leadership, minority status, music/drama, religious affiliation. **Additional information:** Part-time students eligible for federal and state aid, but not institutional aid.

Application procedures. Admission: No deadline. $25 fee, may be waived for applicants with need. Application may be submitted online. Admission notification on a rolling basis beginning on or about 10/1. Must reply by May 1 or within 2 week(s) if notified thereafter. **Financial aid:** Priority date 2/15; no closing date. FAFSA required. Applicants notified on a rolling basis starting 3/1; must reply by 5/1 or within 2 week(s) of notification.

Academics. Math and science study halls are held three nights during the week and are led by professors and peer tutors. **Special study options:** Accelerated study, combined bachelor's/graduate degree, cross-registration, double major, ESL, honors, independent study, internships, liberal arts/career combination, student-designed major, study abroad, teacher certification program, Washington semester. Legislative internships at state and national level. **Credit/placement by examination:** AP, CLEP, IB, SAT, ACT, institutional tests. 32 credit hours maximum toward bachelor's degree. **Support services:** Learning center, reduced course load, remedial instruction, study skills assistance, tutoring.

Majors. Biology: General. **Business:** General, accounting, accounting/business management, business admin, fashion, international, management information systems, managerial economics, marketing. **Communications:** General. **Computer sciences:** General. **Conservation:** Environmental science. **Education:** General, art, biology, business, chemistry, Deaf/hearing impaired, developmentally delayed, elementary, English, health, history, mathematics, mentally handicapped, middle, multiple handicapped, music, physical, secondary, special, speech impaired. **English:** English lit. **Family/consumer sciences:** General, clothing/textiles, food/nutrition. **Foreign languages:** General, French, Germanic, Spanish. **Health:** Athletic training, audiology/speech pathology, communication disorders, predentistry, premedicine, prenursing, prepharmacy, preveterinary. **History:** General. **Interdisciplinary:** Global studies. **Legal studies:** Prelaw. **Liberal arts:** Arts/sciences. **Math:** General. **Parks/recreation:** Facilities management, health/

fitness, sports admin. **Philosophy/religion:** Religion. **Physical sciences:** Chemistry. **Protective services:** Law enforcement admin. **Psychology:** General. **Social sciences:** International relations, political science, sociology. **Theology:** Preministerial, sacred music. **Visual/performing arts:** General, art, art history/conservation, design, dramatic, interior design, music performance, piano/organ, studio arts, voice/opera.

Most popular majors. Business/marketing 30%, communications/journalism 6%, education 11%, parks/recreation 9%, social sciences 10%, visual/performing arts 10%.

Computing on campus. 100 workstations in dormitories, library, computer center, student center. Dormitories wired for high-speed internet access and linked to campus network. Commuter students can connect to campus network. Online course registration, online library, helpline, repair service, wireless network available.

Student life. Freshman orientation: Mandatory, $55 fee. Preregistration for classes offered. Week before fall semester begins, includes testing, advising, registration, social activities, community service. **Policies:** No alcohol containers, full or empty regardless of age; no drug paraphernalia, hazing, fireworks, or firearms. Freshmen permitted cars on campus. **Housing:** Guaranteed on-campus for freshmen. Coed dorms, single-sex dorms, special housing for disabled, apartments, fraternity/sorority housing, substance-free housing available. $100 nonrefundable deposit, deadline 5/1. **Activities:** Bands, choral groups, dance, drama, film society, literary magazine, music ensembles, musical theater, radio station, student government, student newspaper, Black Student Union, international students association, Alpha Omega, Gamma Beta Phi, Fellowship of Christian Athletes, Best Buddies, Phi Sigma Eta, Religious Life Council, Companions in Christ, Discipleship/Accountability groups.

Athletics. NAIA. **Intercollegiate:** Baseball M, basketball, cheerleading, cross-country, football (tackle) M, golf, soccer, softball W, swimming, tennis, volleyball W. **Intramural:** Basketball, football (non-tackle), softball, swimming, table tennis, volleyball. **Team name:** Eagles.

Student services. Campus ministries, career counseling, student employment services, financial aid counseling, health services, personal counseling, placement for graduates. **Physically disabled:** Services for visually, speech, hearing impaired.

Contact. E-mail: admit@lambuth.edu
Phone: (731) 425-3223 Toll-free number: (800) 526-2884
Fax: (731) 425-3496
Rueben Burnley, Director of Admission, Lambuth University, 705 Lambuth Boulevard, Jackson, TN 38301-5296

Lane College

Jackson, Tennessee
www.lanecollege.edu **CB code: 1395**

- Private 4-year liberal arts college affiliated with Christian Methodist Episcopal Church
- Residential campus in small city

General. Founded in 1882. Regionally accredited. **Location:** 80 miles from Memphis, 126 miles from Nashville. **Calendar:** Semester.

Annual costs/financial aid. Tuition/fees (2005-2006): $7,176. Room/board: $4,534. Books/supplies: $550. Personal expenses: $675. Need-based financial aid available to full-time and part-time students.

Contact. Phone: (731) 426-7532
Director of Admissions, 545 Lane Avenue, Jackson, TN 38301-4598

Lee University

Cleveland, Tennessee
www.leeuniversity.edu **CB code: 1401**

- Private 4-year university and liberal arts college affiliated with Church of God
- Residential campus in large town
- 3,573 degree-seeking undergraduates: 7% part-time, 58% women, 4% African American, 1% Asian American, 3% Hispanic American, 1% Native American, 5% international
- 258 degree-seeking graduate students
- SAT or ACT (ACT writing optional) required
- 47% graduate within 6 years

General. Founded in 1918. Regionally accredited. **Degrees:** 631 bachelor's awarded; master's offered. **Location:** 30 miles from Chattanooga, 75 miles from Knoxville. **Calendar:** Semester, limited summer session. **Full-time faculty:** 148 total; 75% have terminal degrees, 10% minority, 27% women. **Part-time faculty:** 164 total; 29% have terminal degrees, 7% minority, 44% women. **Class size:** 52% < 20, 34% 20-39, 8% 40-49, 5% 50-99, 1% >100.

Freshman class profile. 1,465 applied, 895 admitted, 761 enrolled.

Mid 50% test scores			
SAT verbal:	480-610	Rank in top quarter:	43%
SAT math:	450-600	Rank in top tenth:	19%
ACT:	19-26	Return as sophomores:	73%
GPA 3.50 or higher:	47%	Out-of-state:	67%
GPA 3.0-3.49:	26%	Live on campus:	89%
GPA 2.0-2.99:	26%	International:	5%

Basis for selection. Open admission, but selective for some programs. School achievement record and test scores considered. SAT Subject Tests recommended. SAT or ACT required for placement only, except for applicants with 16 college semester hours (24 college semester hours for TN residents). Interview recommended for all; audition required for music program. **Homeschooled:** Must have high school transcript with date of graduation and 17 on ACT or 860 on SAT (exclusive of Writing).

High school preparation. College-preparatory program recommended. 13 units required; 14 recommended. Required and recommended units include English 4, mathematics 3, social studies 2, history 1, science 2 and foreign language 1. 1 unit computer skills recommended.

2005-2006 Annual costs. Tuition/fees: $9,610. Room/board: $4,830. Books/supplies: $700. Personal expenses: $1,510.

2005-2006 Financial aid. Need-based: Average need met was 62%. Average scholarship/grant was $7,000; average loan $2,819. 45% of total undergraduate aid awarded as scholarships/grants, 55% as loans/jobs. **Non-need-based:** Scholarships awarded for academics, alumni affiliation, athletics, leadership, minority status, music/drama, religious affiliation, state residency.

Application procedures. Admission: Closing date 9/1. $25 fee. Application may be submitted online. Admission notification on a rolling basis beginning on or about 9/1. **Financial aid:** Priority date 3/15; no closing date. FAFSA required. Applicants notified on a rolling basis starting 2/1; must reply within 3 week(s) of notification.

Academics. Special study options: Distance learning, double major, dual enrollment of high school students, ESL, exchange student, external degree, honors, independent study, internships, liberal arts/career combination, study abroad, teacher certification program, Washington semester. **Credit/placement by examination:** AP, CLEP, SAT, ACT. 32 credit hours maximum toward bachelor's degree. **Support services:** Learning center, pre-admission summer program, reduced course load, remedial instruction, tutoring, writing center.

Majors. Biology: Biochemistry. **Business:** General, accounting, business admin, office management. **Communications:** General, journalism, public relations. **Computer sciences:** Information systems. **Education:** General, business, early childhood, elementary, English, foreign languages, history, mathematics, music, physical, science, secondary, Spanish, special. **Family/consumer sciences:** Family studies. **Foreign languages:** General, French, Spanish. **History:** General. **Liberal arts:** Arts/sciences. **Math:** General. **Parks/recreation:** Health/fitness. **Physical sciences:** Chemistry. **Psychology:** General. **Social sciences:** General, political science, sociology. **Theology:** Bible, missionary, religious ed, sacred music. **Visual/performing arts:** Music performance.

Most popular majors. Business/marketing 10%, communications/journalism 13%, education 21%, health sciences 6%, philosophy/religious studies 16%, psychology 11%, social sciences 9%.

Computing on campus. 232 workstations in dormitories, library, computer center, student center. Dormitories wired for high-speed internet access and linked to campus network. Helpline, wireless network available.

Student life. Freshman orientation: Mandatory. Preregistration for classes offered. **Policies:** Religious observance required. Freshmen permitted cars on campus. **Housing:** Guaranteed on-campus for freshmen. Single-sex dorms, apartments, substance-free housing available. $200 fully refundable deposit, deadline 9/1. Lee University leases apartments and houses for students. **Activities:** Bands, choral groups, drama, literary magazine, music ensembles, musical theater, opera, student government, student newspaper, symphony orchestra, 10 Greek councils, Student Leadership Council, international club, Collegiate Sertoma, Married Students Fellowship, Pioneers for Christ, Fellowship of Christian Athletes, Missions Alive, Deaf Ministry Association.

Athletics. NAIA, NCCAA. **Intercollegiate:** Baseball M, basketball, cross-country, golf M, soccer, softball W, tennis, volleyball W. **Intramural:** Basketball, bowling, racquetball, soccer, softball, table tennis, tennis, volleyball. **Team name:** Flames.

Student services. Campus ministries, career counseling, student employment services, financial aid counseling, health services, personal counseling, placement for graduates, veterans' counselor.

Contact. E-mail: admissions@leeuniversity.edu
Phone: (423) 614-8500 Toll-free number: (800) 533-9930
Fax: (423) 614-8533
Phil Cook, Director of Admissions, Lee University, 1120 North Ocoee Street, Cleveland, TN 37320-3450

LeMoyne-Owen College

Memphis, Tennessee — **CB member**
www.loc.edu — **CB code: 1403**

- Private 4-year liberal arts college affiliated with United Church of Christ and Tennessee Baptist Convention
- Commuter campus in very large city
- 809 degree-seeking undergraduates: 15% part-time, 68% women, 97% African American, 2% international
- SAT or ACT required

General. Founded in 1862. Regionally accredited. **Degrees:** 104 bachelor's awarded. **ROTC:** Army, Air Force. **Location:** 200 miles from Nashville. **Calendar:** Semester, extensive summer session. **Full-time faculty:** 62 total; 48% have terminal degrees, 81% minority, 48% women. **Part-time faculty:** 56 total.

Freshman class profile. 111 enrolled.

Return as sophomores:	47%	**Live on campus:**	10%
Out-of-state:	5%		

Basis for selection. High school transcript, test scores, letter of recommendation, and interview important. Special consideration given to children of alumni. Essay, interview recommended.

High school preparation. 15 units required. Required units include English 4, mathematics 3, history 2, science 3, foreign language 2 and academic electives 1.

2005-2006 Annual costs. Tuition/fees: $9,618. Room/board: $4,620. Books/supplies: $750. Personal expenses: $1,800.

Application procedures. Admission: Closing date 4/15. $25 fee, may be waived for applicants with need. Application may be submitted online. Admission notification on a rolling basis. Must reply by May 1 or within 2 week(s) if notified thereafter. **Financial aid:** Priority date 4/15; no closing date. FAFSA required. Applicants notified on a rolling basis starting 4/1.

Academics. Special study options: Accelerated study, cooperative education, cross-registration, distance learning, double major, dual enrollment of high school students, exchange student, honors, internships, liberal arts/career combination, student-designed major, study abroad, teacher certification program, weekend college. **Credit/placement by examination:** AP, CLEP, IB, institutional tests. 24 credit hours maximum toward bachelor's degree. **Support services:** Learning center, pre-admission summer program, reduced course load, remedial instruction, tutoring.

Majors. Biology: General. **Business:** Business admin. **Computer sciences:** Computer science. **Education:** Early childhood, special. **English:** English lit. **History:** General. **Interdisciplinary:** Behavioral sciences. **Liberal arts:** Humanities. **Math:** General. **Physical sciences:** Chemistry. **Public administration:** Social work. **Social sciences:** General, political science, sociology. **Visual/performing arts:** Art, music performance.

Most popular majors. Biology 7%, business/marketing 41%, liberal arts 7%, social sciences 27%.

Computing on campus. 223 workstations in library, computer center. Helpline, repair service available.

Student life. Freshman orientation: Mandatory. The freshman seminar is designed to prepare entering students for college life. **Policies:** Freshmen permitted cars on campus. **Housing:** Single-sex dorms, substance-free housing available. $100 deposit. **Activities:** Jazz band, choral groups, dance, drama, music ensembles, student government, student newspaper, NAACP, Social Work Club, Students for Free Enterprise, Pre-Alumni Council, National Student Business Organization.

Athletics. NCAA. **Intercollegiate:** Baseball M, basketball, cross-country, golf, soccer, softball W, tennis, volleyball W. **Intramural:** Basketball. **Team name:** Magicians.

Student services. Adult student services, career counseling, student employment services, health services, personal counseling, placement for graduates, veterans' counselor.

Contact. E-mail: admission@loc.edu
Phone: (901) 435-1500 Fax: (901) 435-1524
Mark Green, Director of Admissions/Recruitment, LeMoyne-Owen College, 807 Walker Avenue, Memphis, TN 38126

Lincoln Memorial University

Harrogate, Tennessee — **CB member**
www.lmunet.edu — **CB code: 1408**

- Private 4-year university and liberal arts college
- Commuter campus in small town
- 1,225 degree-seeking undergraduates: 17% part-time, 74% women
- 1,486 graduate students
- 37% of applicants admitted
- 37% graduate within 6 years

General. Founded in 1897. Regionally accredited. **Degrees:** 146 bachelor's, 153 associate awarded; master's offered. **Location:** 50 miles from Knoxville. **Calendar:** Semester, limited summer session. **Full-time faculty:** 91 total; 55% women. **Part-time faculty:** 57 total; 63% women. **Class size:** 75% < 20, 23% 20-39, 2% 40-49, less than 1% 50-99. **Special facilities:** Abraham Lincoln Library and Museum, Cumberland Mountain Research Center.

Freshman class profile. 1,350 applied, 494 admitted, 184 enrolled.

Mid 50% test scores		**Out-of-state:**	52%
SAT verbal:	460-550	**Live on campus:**	32%
SAT math:	430-580	**Fraternities:**	5%
ACT:	18-23	**Sororities:**	10%

Basis for selection. Academic record, ACT or SAT, recommendations, interviews for some programs. Specialized programs often have admission requirements in addition to those of the general university. In some programs, specialized admission tests also required. Interviews and essays help candidates seeking academic or talent related scholarships. **Homeschooled:** Must submit SAT or ACT scores.

High school preparation. 10 units required; 22 recommended. Required and recommended units include English 4, mathematics 2-3, social studies 1-2, history 1, science 2, foreign language 2 and academic electives 7.

2005-2006 Annual costs. Tuition/fees: $13,104. Room/board: $5,040.

Financial aid. Non-need-based: Scholarships awarded for academics, athletics, music/drama, state residency.

Application procedures. Admission: Priority date 3/1; no deadline. $25 fee, may be waived for applicants with need. Admission notification on a rolling basis beginning on or about 9/1. **Financial aid:** Priority date 4/1; no closing date. FAFSA required. Applicants notified on a rolling basis starting 4/15; must reply within 3 week(s) of notification.

Academics. Special study options: Double major, ESL, independent study, internships, liberal arts/career combination, teacher certification program. **Credit/placement by examination:** AP, CLEP, IB, institutional tests. 16 credit hours maximum toward associate degree, 32 toward bachelor's. **Support services:** Learning center, reduced course load, remedial instruction, study skills assistance, tutoring.

Majors. Area/ethnic studies: American. **Biology:** General. **Business:** General, accounting, business admin, management science, managerial economics, office/clerical. **Communications:** General, broadcast journalism. **Computer sciences:** General. **Conservation:** General, fisheries, wildlife. **Education:** General, art, biology, business, chemistry, early childhood, elementary, English, health, history, mathematics, middle, physical, science, secondary, social science, social studies. **Health:** Athletic training, clinical lab science, clinical lab technology, nursing (RN), predentistry, premedicine, prepharmacy, preveterinary, veterinary technology/assistant. **History:** General. **Legal studies:** Prelaw. **Liberal arts:** Arts/sciences. **Math:** General. **Parks/recreation:** Health/fitness. **Physical sciences:** Chemistry. **Psychology:** General. **Public administration:** Social work. **Social sciences:** General. **Visual/performing arts:** General, art.

Computing on campus. 150 workstations in library, computer center. Dormitories wired for high-speed internet access and linked to campus network. Commuter students can connect to campus network. Online library available.

Student life. Freshman orientation: Mandatory. Preregistration for classes offered. Four times during the summer months proceeding fall semester. **Policies:** Freshmen permitted cars on campus. **Housing:** Guaranteed on-campus for all undergraduates. Coed dorms, single-sex dorms, apartments available. $100 deposit, deadline 8/1. **Activities:** Choral groups, drama, literary magazine, radio station, student government, student newspaper, TV station, Baptist Student Union, Wesley Foundation.

Athletics. NCAA. **Intercollegiate:** Baseball M, basketball, cheerleading, cross-country, golf, soccer, softball W, tennis, volleyball W. **Intramural:** Basketball, soccer M, softball, table tennis, volleyball. **Team name:** Railsplitters.

Student services. Alcohol/substance abuse counseling, career counseling, financial aid counseling, on-campus daycare, personal counseling, placement for graduates, veterans' counselor.

Contact. E-mail: admissions@lmunet.edu
Phone: (423) 869-3611 ext. 6280 Toll-free
number: (800) 325-0900 ext. 6280 Fax: (423) 869-6250
Conrad Daniels, Dean of Admissions, Lincoln Memorial University, 6965 Cumberland Gap Parkway, Harrogate, TN 37752

Lipscomb University
Nashville, Tennessee
www.lipscomb.edu **CB code: 1161**

- Private 4-year Bible and liberal arts college affiliated with Church of Christ
- Residential campus in very large city
- 2,278 degree-seeking undergraduates: 9% part-time, 57% women, 5% African American, 1% Asian American, 2% Hispanic American, 1% international
- 206 degree-seeking graduate students
- 76% of applicants admitted
- SAT or ACT (ACT writing optional) required
- 54% graduate within 6 years

General. Founded in 1891. Regionally accredited. **Degrees:** 530 bachelor's awarded; master's, first professional offered. **ROTC:** Army, Air Force. **Location:** 4 miles from downtown. **Calendar:** Semester, extensive summer session. **Full-time faculty:** 115 total; 77% have terminal degrees. **Part-time faculty:** 105 total; 42% have terminal degrees. **Class size:** 73% < 20, 58% 20-39, 10% 40-49, 5% 50-99.

Freshman class profile. 1,599 applied, 1,210 admitted, 535 enrolled.

Mid 50% test scores		Rank in top quarter:	51%
SAT verbal:	460-680	Rank in top tenth:	25%
SAT math:	450-670	Return as sophomores:	71%
ACT:	19-29	Out-of-state:	37%
GPA 3.50 or higher:	59%	Live on campus:	92%
GPA 3.0-3.49:	25%	International:	1%
GPA 2.0-2.99:	16%		

Basis for selection. School achievement record, test scores, educational and personal references required. Strong moral character desired. Essay recommended for all; audition required for music; portfolio required for art; interview recommended for art, honors, music programs.

High school preparation. 14 units required. Required units include English 4, mathematics 2, social studies 2, science 2, foreign language 2 and academic electives 2. Math units preferably Algebra I, II. Foreign language units in the same language. 2 academic electives should be selected from natural sciences, mathematics, foreign languages, or social sciences.

2005-2006 Annual costs. Tuition/fees: $14,567. Room/board: $6,706.

2004-2005 Financial aid. Need-based: 430 full-time freshmen applied for aid; 309 were judged to have need; 288 of these received aid. Average need met was 84%. Average scholarship/grant was $2,789; average loan $2,479. 40% of total undergraduate aid awarded as scholarships/grants, 60% as loans/jobs. **Non-need-based:** Awarded to 2,242 full-time undergraduates, including 432 freshmen. Scholarships awarded for academics, alumni affiliation, art, athletics, music/drama, religious affiliation, ROTC.

Application procedures. Admission: No deadline. $50 fee, may be waived for applicants with need. Admission notification on a rolling basis beginning on or about 12/15. **Financial aid:** Priority date 3/1; no closing date. FAFSA required. Applicants notified on a rolling basis starting 3/15.

Academics. Special study options: Accelerated study, double major, dual enrollment of high school students, honors, independent study, internships, liberal arts/career combination, study abroad, teacher certification program. **Credit/placement by examination:** AP, CLEP, IB, SAT, ACT, institutional tests. 30 credit hours maximum toward bachelor's degree. **Support services:** Learning center, reduced course load, remedial instruction, study skills assistance, tutoring, writing center.

Majors. Area/ethnic studies: American. **Biology:** General, biochemistry. **Business:** Accounting, business admin, fashion, human resources, managerial economics, marketing. **Communications:** Journalism, media studies, organizational, public relations. **Computer sciences:** Computer science, information technology. **Conservation:** Environmental science. **Education:** Art, biology, chemistry, drama/dance, elementary, English, French, German, history, mathematics, music, physical, physics, Spanish. **Engineering:** Mechanics, science. **English:** English lit, speech/rhetoric. **Family/consumer sciences:** General, clothing/textiles, family systems, institutional food production. **Foreign languages:** French, German, Spanish. **Health:** Athletic training, dietetics, nursing (RN), predentistry, premedicine, prenursing, prepharmacy, preveterinary. **History:** General. **Math:** General. **Parks/recreation:** Exercise sciences. **Philosophy/religion:** Philosophy. **Physical sciences:** Chemistry, physics. **Psychology:** General. **Public administration:** General, social work. **Social sciences:** Political science, urban studies. **Theology:** Bible, missionary, youth ministry. **Visual/performing arts:** Commercial/advertising art, dramatic, music performance, music theory/composition, piano/organ, studio arts, voice/opera.

Most popular majors. Biology 8%, business/marketing 34%, communications/journalism 7%, education 10%, psychology 6%.

Computing on campus. 245 workstations in dormitories, library, computer center. Dormitories wired for high-speed internet access and linked to campus network. Commuter students can connect to campus network. Online course registration, helpline, wireless network available.

Student life. Freshman orientation: Mandatory. Preregistration for classes offered. **Policies:** Daily chapel service and Bible studies required. Religious observance required. Freshmen permitted cars on campus. **Housing:** Single-sex dorms available. $100 deposit, deadline 7/15. Out-of-town undergraduates required to live on campus, except for seniors and students over age of 21 and married students. **Activities:** Bands, choral groups, drama, music ensembles, musical theater, radio station, student government, student newspaper, social service organizations, College Republicans, Young Democrats, honorary societies, social clubs.

Athletics. NCAA. **Intercollegiate:** Baseball M, basketball, cross-country, golf, soccer, softball W, tennis, track and field, volleyball W. **Intramural:** Basketball, football (non-tackle) M, softball, volleyball. **Team name:** Bisons.

Student services. Adult student services, career counseling, student employment services, health services, minority student services, personal counseling, placement for graduates. **Physically disabled:** Services for visually, speech, hearing impaired.

Contact. E-mail: admissions@lipscomb.edu
Phone: (615) 269-1776 Toll-free number: (877) 582-4766
Fax: (615) 269-1804
Ricky Holaway, Director of Admissions, Lipscomb University, 3901 Granny White Pike, Nashville, TN 37204-3951

Martin Methodist College
Pulaski, Tennessee
www.martinmethodist.edu **CB code: 1449**

- Private 4-year liberal arts college affiliated with United Methodist Church
- Residential campus in small town
- 728 degree-seeking undergraduates: 20% part-time, 59% women, 14% African American, 2% Hispanic American, 10% international
- SAT or ACT (ACT writing optional) required

General. Founded in 1870. Regionally accredited. **Degrees:** 124 bachelor's, 31 associate awarded. **Location:** 70 miles from Nashville, 40 miles from Huntsville, Alabama. **Calendar:** Semester, limited summer session. **Full-time faculty:** 37 total. **Part-time faculty:** 13 total. **Class size:** 78% < 20, 21% 20-39, less than 1% 40-49.

Freshman class profile. 595 applied, 578 admitted, 221 enrolled.

Mid 50% test scores		Out-of-state:	16%
ACT:	17-23	Live on campus:	46%
Return as sophomores:	17%	International:	9%

Basis for selection. Open admission, but selective for some programs. High school record, interview, test scores important. Minimum 2.0 high school GPA, ACT composite score of 18, or rank in upper 50% of class. Must meet 2 of these 3 criteria for admission or apply for "special circumstances" admission status. Students whose academic record or test scores do not qualify them for admission can be conditionally admitted and offered full enrollment if they complete a semester with a 2.0 GPA. Audition recommended for music; portfolio recommended for art.

High school preparation. 12 units required. Required and recommended units include English 4, mathematics 2, social studies 1, science 1 and foreign language 2.

2006-2007 Annual costs. Tuition/fees (projected): $15,391. Room/board: $5,600. Books/supplies: $750. Personal expenses: $1,200.

2004-2005 Financial aid. Need-based: 74% of total undergraduate aid awarded as scholarships/grants, 26% as loans/jobs. **Non-need-based:** Scholarships awarded for academics, art, athletics, leadership, music/drama, religious affiliation, state residency.

Application procedures. Admission: Priority date 5/1; deadline 8/1 (postmark date). $30 fee. Admission notification on a rolling basis. **Financial aid:** No deadline. FAFSA, institutional form required. Applicants notified on a rolling basis starting 3/1; must reply within 2 week(s) of notification.

Academics. Special study options: Dual enrollment of high school students, ESL, honors, independent study, study abroad. **Credit/placement by examination:** CLEP, SAT, ACT. 30 credit hours maximum toward associate degree. **Support services:** Learning center, pre-admission summer program, reduced course load, study skills assistance, tutoring.

Majors. Biology: General. **Business:** General, accounting. **Education:** Elementary, middle, secondary. **Health:** Health care admin. **Parks/recreation:** Sports admin. **Philosophy/religion:** Religion. **Psychology:** General. **Public administration:** Human services.

Most popular majors. Business/marketing 40%, education 19%, psychology 32%.

Computing on campus. 50 workstations in library, computer center. Dormitories wired for high-speed internet access. Wireless network available.

Student life. Freshman orientation: Mandatory. Preregistration for classes offered. 3 days prior to other students coming on campus. **Policies:** Freshmen permitted cars on campus. **Housing:** Guaranteed on-campus for all undergraduates. Single-sex dorms available. $100 deposit, deadline 6/1. **Activities:** Choral groups, drama, music ensembles, student government, student newspaper, Student Christian Association, Black Student Union, Fellowship of Christian Athletes.

Athletics. NAIA, NJCAA. **Intercollegiate:** Baseball M, basketball, cross-country, golf M, soccer, softball W, tennis, volleyball W. **Intramural:** Basketball, racquetball, softball, swimming, table tennis, volleyball. **Team name:** RedHawks.

Student services. Adult student services, campus ministries, career counseling, student employment services, financial aid counseling, personal counseling, placement for graduates, veterans' counselor.

Contact. E-mail: mkelley@martinmethodist.edu
Phone: (931) 363-9804 Toll-free number: (800) 467-1273
Fax: (931) 363-9818
Michael Kelley, Director of Admissions, Martin Methodist College, 433 West Madison, Pulaski, TN 38478-2799

Maryville College

Maryville, Tennessee — **CB member**
www.maryvillecollege.edu — **CB code: 1454**

- Private 4-year liberal arts college affiliated with Presbyterian Church (USA)
- Residential campus in small city
- 1,120 degree-seeking undergraduates: 2% part-time, 54% women, 6% African American, 1% Asian American, 1% Hispanic American, 4% international
- 79% of applicants admitted
- Application essay required
- 55% graduate within 6 years; 29% enter graduate study

General. Founded in 1819. Regionally accredited. **Degrees:** 172 bachelor's awarded. **Location:** 15 miles from Knoxville. **Calendar:** 4-1-4, limited summer session. **Full-time faculty:** 73 total; 93% have terminal degrees, 3% minority, 55% women. **Part-time faculty:** 37 total; 24% have terminal degrees, 14% minority, 40% women. **Class size:** 62% < 20, 38% 20-39, less than 1% 40-49. **Special facilities:** Science center, fine arts center, Mountain Challenge outdoor program, college woods with ropes courses, equestrian center.

Freshman class profile. 1,496 applied, 1,183 admitted, 333 enrolled.

Mid 50% test scores		Rank in top quarter:	57%
SAT verbal:	490-620	Rank in top tenth:	27%
SAT math:	460-600	End year in good standing:	74.7%
ACT:	21-28	Return as sophomores:	72%
GPA 3.50 or higher:	55%	Out-of-state:	30%
GPA 3.0-3.49:	32%	Live on campus:	86%
GPA 2.0-2.99:	13%	International:	1%

Basis for selection. Students are admitted based on academic criteria, extracurricular involvement, and personal achievement, without regard to financial need. Successful students typically follow strong college preparatory curriculums in high school and rank in the top 25% of their classes. International students who score at least 525 on TOEFL or 80 on Michigan Test eligible to enroll full time. Others may enroll in limited number of college level courses until they complete international students' orientation. SAT or ACT recommended. Writing component not required for Fall 2007, although writing samples are encouraged for assistance in admissions decisions. Essay, interview recommended for all; audition required for music; portfolio recommended for art. **Homeschooled:** Pursue rigorous curriculum that includes strong emphasis on writing and reasoning.

High school preparation. 15 units required. Required and recommended units include English 4, mathematics 3, social studies 2, history 1, science 2 (laboratory 1), foreign language 2 and academic electives 1.

2005-2006 Annual costs. Tuition/fees: $22,224. Room/board: $7,000. Books/supplies: $630. Personal expenses: $1,350.

2005-2006 Financial aid. Need-based: 333 full-time freshmen applied for aid; 270 were judged to have need; 270 of these received aid. Average need met was 91%. Average scholarship/grant was $13,991; average loan $1,575. 95% of total undergraduate aid awarded as scholarships/grants, 5% as loans/jobs. **Non-need-based:** Awarded to 837 full-time undergraduates, including 329 freshmen. Scholarships awarded for academics, art, leadership, minority status, music/drama, religious affiliation, state residency.

Application procedures. Admission: Priority date 1/15; deadline 3/1 (postmark date). , may be waived for applicants with need. No application fee. Application may be submitted online. Admission notification on a rolling basis beginning on or about 12/1. Must reply by May 1 or within 2 week(s) if notified thereafter. Required enrollment deposit of $200 includes housing deposit, refundable before May 1. **Financial aid:** Priority date 3/1; no closing date. FAFSA required. Applicants notified on a rolling basis starting 3/15; must reply within 4 week(s) of notification.

Academics. All students complete 6 credit-hour research project and comprehensive examination in their major area of study. **Special study options:** Combined bachelor's/graduate degree, double major, ESL, honors, independent study, internships, liberal arts/career combination, student-designed major, study abroad, teacher certification program, Washington semester. **Credit/placement by examination:** AP, CLEP, IB, institutional tests. 32 credit hours maximum toward bachelor's degree. Students may petition individual departments for credit by examination. **Support services:** Learning center, reduced course load, remedial instruction, study skills assistance, tutoring, writing center.

Majors. Biology: General, biochemistry. **Business:** Business admin, international. **Computer sciences:** General. **Conservation:** Environmental studies. **Education:** General, biology, chemistry, English, ESL, health, history, mathematics, music, physical, social science, social studies, Spanish. **Engineering:** General. **English:** English lit, technical writing. **Foreign languages:** American Sign Language, sign language interpretation, Spanish. **Health:** Nursing (RN), predentistry, premedicine, prenursing, prepharmacy, preveterinary. **History:** General. **Interdisciplinary:** Math/computer science. **Math:** General. **Parks/recreation:** General, health/fitness. **Philosophy/religion:** Religion. **Physical sciences:** Chemical physics, chemistry. **Psychology:** General. **Social sciences:** Economics, international relations, political science, sociology. **Visual/performing arts:** Art, dramatic, music performance, studio arts.

Most popular majors. Biology 8%, business/marketing 20%, education 15%, psychology 15%, social sciences 10%, visual/performing arts 10%.

Computing on campus. 265 workstations in library, computer center. Dormitories wired for high-speed internet access and linked to campus network. Commuter students can connect to campus network. Online course registration, online library, helpline, repair service, wireless network available.

Student life. Freshman orientation: Mandatory, $25 fee. Preregistration for classes offered. Includes Mountain Challenge component. Begins several days before registration. Optional 3-day wilderness experience. **Policies:** Freshmen permitted cars on campus. **Housing:** Guaranteed on-campus for all undergraduates. Coed dorms, single-sex dorms, special housing for disabled, apartments, substance-free housing available. $200 deposit, deadline 5/1. **Activities:** Bands, choral groups, dance, drama, literary magazine, music ensembles, radio station, student government, student newspaper, symphony orchestra, Habitat for Humanity, Literary Corps, Fellowship of Christian Athletes, MC Wellness Council, Student Programming Board, Black student association.

Athletics. NCAA. **Intercollegiate:** Baseball M, basketball, cross-country, equestrian, football (tackle) M, soccer, softball W, tennis, volleyball W. **Intramural:** Archery, badminton, baseball M, basketball, bowling, football (non-tackle), golf, racquetball, rugby, skiing, soccer, softball, swimming, table tennis, tennis, track and field, volleyball, water polo. **Team name:** Scots.

Student services. Adult student services, alcohol/substance abuse counseling, campus ministries, career counseling, student employment services, financial aid counseling, health services, minority student services, personal counseling, placement for graduates. **Physically disabled:** Services for visually, speech, hearing impaired.

Contact. E-mail: admissions@maryvillecollege.edu
Phone: (865) 981-8092 Toll-free number: (800) 597-2687
Fax: (865) 981-8005
Ned Willard, Assistant Vice President for Admissions, Maryville College, 502 East Lamar Alexander Parkway, Maryville, TN 37804-5907

Memphis College of Art
Memphis, Tennessee
www.mca.edu **CB code: 1511**

- Private 4-year visual arts college
- Residential campus in very large city
- 314 degree-seeking undergraduates: 14% part-time, 50% women, 15% African American, 2% Asian American, 4% Hispanic American, 1% Native American, 1% international
- 12 degree-seeking graduate students
- 45% of applicants admitted
- SAT or ACT (ACT writing optional) required
- 42% graduate within 6 years

General. Founded in 1936. Regionally accredited. Situated in 324-acre city park with bicycle trails and golf course. Students have access to Memphis Brooks Museum of Art and Overton Park Zoo. Consortium with four other colleges provides greater selection of liberal studies classes. Mobility program with 30+ other independent colleges of art around the country and in Canada available. **Degrees:** 47 bachelor's awarded; master's offered. **Location:** 500 miles from New Orleans, Louisiana, 700 miles from Dallas, Texas. **Calendar:** Semester, limited summer session. **Full-time faculty:** 22 total; 86% have terminal degrees, 9% minority, 41% women. **Part-time faculty:** 23 total. **Special facilities:** 5 on-campus galleries for faculty, student and visiting artist exhibitions.

Freshman class profile. 505 applied, 226 admitted, 64 enrolled.

Mid 50% test scores			
ACT:	17-28	Return as sophomores:	79%
GPA 3.50 or higher:	25%	Out-of-state:	65%
GPA 3.0-3.49:	27%	Live on campus:	72%
GPA 2.0-2.99:	35%	International:	2%

Basis for selection. Art portfolio, high school transcript, test scores required; letter of recommendation from art teacher and essay considered, but not required. Portfolio required; essay, interview recommended for all.

High school preparation. Portfolio should include 10 to 20 pieces of work, originals or slides, with focus on direct observational drawing.

2005-2006 Annual costs. Tuition/fees: $17,460. Room/board: $7,400. Books/supplies: $1,300. Personal expenses: $1,000.

2005-2006 Financial aid. Need-based: 55 full-time freshmen applied for aid; 49 were judged to have need; 49 of these received aid. Average need met was 90%. Average scholarship/grant was $3,000; average loan $3,500. 45% of total undergraduate aid awarded as scholarships/grants, 55% as loans/jobs. **Non-need-based:** Awarded to 270 full-time undergraduates, including 50 freshmen. Scholarships awarded for academics, art. **Additional information:** Students considered for institutional resources through admissions application process.

Application procedures. Admission: Priority date 3/31; no deadline. $25 fee, may be waived for applicants with need. Application may be submitted online. Admission notification on a rolling basis beginning on or about 11/15. Must reply by May 1 or within 3 week(s) if notified thereafter. **Financial aid:** Priority date 3/1; no closing date. FAFSA required. Applicants notified on a rolling basis; must reply within 3 week(s) of notification.

Academics. Foundation courses incorporate computer use in writing and design. **Special study options:** Combined bachelor's/graduate degree, cross-registration, double major, exchange student, independent study, internships, New York semester, study abroad. New York Studio Exchange Program. Mobility semester exchange at 30+ independent art colleges across the country (AICAD consortium). **Credit/placement by examination:** AP, CLEP, IB, SAT, ACT, institutional tests. 15 credit hours maximum toward bachelor's degree. **Support services:** Reduced course load, remedial instruction, study skills assistance, tutoring, writing center.

Majors. Computer sciences: Computer graphics. **Visual/performing arts:** Art, ceramics, commercial photography, commercial/advertising art, crafts, design, fiber arts, graphic design, illustration, metal/jewelry, multimedia, painting, photography, printmaking, sculpture, studio arts.

Computing on campus. 200 workstations in dormitories, library, computer center. Dormitories wired for high-speed internet access.

Student life. Freshman orientation: Mandatory. Preregistration for classes offered. 4-day session and parent sessions. **Policies:** Freshmen permitted cars on campus. **Housing:** Guaranteed on-campus for freshmen. Coed dorms, apartments, substance-free housing available. $300 nonrefundable deposit. Considerable assistance available in matching roommates and helping students find affordable housing within walking distance. **Activities:** Student government, student newspaper, international student club, photography club, student alliance, multicultural student association.

Student services. Adult student services, career counseling, student employment services, financial aid counseling, personal counseling, placement for graduates, veterans' counselor.

Contact. E-mail: info@mca.edu
Phone: (901) 272-5151 Toll-free number: (800) 727-1088
Fax: (901) 272-5158
Annette Moore, Director of Admissions, Memphis College of Art, Overton Park, 1930 Poplar Avenue, Memphis, TN 38104-2764

Middle Tennessee State University
Murfreesboro, Tennessee **CB member**
www.mtsu.edu **CB code: 1466**

- Public 4-year university
- Commuter campus in small city
- 20,279 degree-seeking undergraduates: 15% part-time, 53% women, 12% African American, 3% Asian American, 2% Hispanic American
- 1,953 degree-seeking graduate students
- 85% of applicants admitted
- SAT or ACT (ACT writing optional) required

General. Founded in 1911. Regionally accredited. Centers for Historic Preservation and Popular Music, largest recording industry program in the nation. **Degrees:** 3,475 bachelor's, 2 associate awarded; master's, doctoral offered. **ROTC:** Army. **Location:** 32 miles from Nashville. **Calendar:** Semester, extensive summer session. **Full-time faculty:** 881 total; 68% have terminal degrees, 16% minority, 44% women. **Part-time faculty:** 286 total; 55% women. **Class size:** 36% < 20, 54% 20-39, 5% 40-49, 4% 50-99, less than 1% >100. **Special facilities:** 3 recording studios, observatory, flight simulators, weather center, electronic music laboratory, digital audio edit laboratory, satellite mapping equipment, seismograph, 3 television studios, electronic newsroom, radio and television stations.

Freshman class profile. 6,394 applied, 5,430 admitted, 3,208 enrolled.

Mid 50% test scores			
SAT verbal:	480-590	Rank in top tenth:	13%
SAT math:	500-590	Out-of-state:	7%
ACT:	20-24	Live on campus:	10%
Rank in top quarter:	33%	Fraternities:	3%
		Sororities:	4%

Basis for selection. Must meet high school curriculum requirements and have 3.0 high school GPA or ACT composite score of 22 or a combination of a 19 ACT and a 2.7 GPA. Personal statement required of students who do not meet standard requirements.

High school preparation. 14 units required. Required units include English 4, mathematics 3, social studies 1, history 1, science 2 (laboratory 1) and foreign language 2. Foreign language units must be in single language. Mathematics units must include algebra I and II, geometry or other advanced mathematics. 1 visual or performing arts, 1 US history, 1 global studies also required.

2005-2006 Annual costs. Tuition/fees: $4,600; $13,912 out-of-state. Room/board: $5,626. Books/supplies: $1,000. Personal expenses: $1,400.

2004-2005 Financial aid. Need-based: Average need met was 84%. Average scholarship/grant was $2,295; average loan $1,553. 26% of total undergraduate aid awarded as scholarships/grants, 74% as loans/jobs. **Non-need-based:** Scholarships awarded for academics, alumni affiliation, art, athletics, job skills, leadership, minority status, music/drama, religious affiliation, ROTC, state residency. **Additional information:** Application filing deadline for scholarships February 15.

Application procedures. Admission: Closing date 7/1 (postmark date). $25 fee. Application may be submitted online. Admission notification on a rolling basis. **Financial aid:** Priority date 5/1; no closing date. FAFSA required. Applicants notified on a rolling basis starting 4/15; must reply within 2 week(s) of notification.

Academics. Special study options: Cooperative education, distance learning, double major, dual enrollment of high school students, honors, independent study, internships, study abroad, teacher certification program. Academic basic skills. **Credit/placement by examination:** AP, CLEP, IB, SAT, ACT, institutional tests. 66 credit hours maximum toward bachelor's degree. Up to 66 semester hours from correspondence study, credit-by-examination, credit for service-related experience, and flight training may be counted toward degree. **Support services:** Learning center, pre-admission summer program, reduced course load, remedial instruction, study skills assistance, tutoring, writing center.

Honors college/program. Must have minimum ACT composite score of 26 (1170 SAT, exclusive of Writing) and 3.0 GPA or 3.5 GPA and ACT of 22 (950 SAT); returning or transfer students must have overall college GPA of 3.0 or higher.

Majors. Agriculture: Agribusiness operations, animal sciences, plant sciences, soil science. **Biology:** General. **Business:** Accounting, business admin, finance, management information systems, managerial economics, marketing, office management, purchasing, sales/distribution. **Communications:** Media studies. **Computer sciences:** General, computer science. **Education:** Art, business, early childhood, health, kindergarten/preschool, sales/marketing, special, technology/industrial arts. **Engineering technology:** General, architectural, environmental, industrial, industrial management. **English:** English lit. **Family/consumer sciences:** Clothing/textiles, family resources, food/nutrition. **Foreign languages:** General. **Health:** Athletic training, nursing (RN). **History:** General. **Interdisciplinary:** Biological/physical sciences. **Liberal arts:** Arts/sciences. **Math:** General. **Parks/recreation:** Facilities management, health/fitness. **Philosophy/religion:** Philosophy. **Physical sciences:** Chemistry, geology, physics. **Protective services:** Law enforcement admin. **Psychology:** General. **Public administration:** Social work. **Social sciences:** Anthropology, economics, international relations, political science, sociology. **Transportation:** Aviation. **Visual/performing arts:** Art, art history/conservation, dramatic, interior design, music management.

Most popular majors. Business/marketing 21%, communications/journalism 11%, interdisciplinary studies 9%, visual/performing arts 13%.

Computing on campus. 2,300 workstations in dormitories, library, computer center, student center. Dormitories wired for high-speed internet access and linked to campus network. Commuter students can connect to campus network. Online course registration, online library, helpline, wireless network available.

Student life. Freshman orientation: Mandatory, $45 fee. Preregistration for classes offered. Held from mid-June to mid-July. **Policies:** Parents notified when student under age of 21 found responsible for use and/or possession of drugs or alcohol. Freshmen permitted cars on campus. **Housing:** Coed dorms, single-sex dorms, apartments, fraternity/sorority housing, substance-free housing available. $200 partly refundable deposit. Honors living, learning hall, freshman year experience hall available. **Activities:** Bands, choral groups, dance, drama, literary magazine, music ensembles, musical theater, radio station, student government, student newspaper, TV station, Golden Key National Honor Society, African American student association, Fellowship of Christian Athletes, Collegiate Women International, Citizens for Action, Baptist Student Union, Aerospace Maintenance Club, agricultural council, Student Tennessee Education Association.

Athletics. NCAA. **Intercollegiate:** Baseball M, basketball, cross-country, football (tackle) M, golf, soccer W, softball W, tennis, track and field, volleyball W. **Intramural:** Basketball M, boxing M, equestrian, football (tackle) M, racquetball, rugby M, soccer, softball, swimming, tennis, volleyball. **Team name:** Blue Raiders.

Student services. Adult student services, campus ministries, career counseling, student employment services, financial aid counseling, health services, minority student services, on-campus daycare, personal counseling, placement for graduates, veterans' counselor, women's services. **Physically disabled:** Services for visually, speech, hearing impaired.

Contact. E-mail: admissions@mtsu.edu
Phone: (615) 898-2111 Fax: (615) 898-5478
Lynn Palmer, Director of Admissions, Middle Tennessee State University, 1301 East Main Street, Murfreesboro, TN 37132

Milligan College

Milligan College, Tennessee
www.milligan.edu **CB code: 1469**

- Private 4-year liberal arts college affiliated with independent Christian churches
- Residential campus in small city
- 744 degree-seeking undergraduates: 2% part-time, 61% women, 1% African American, 1% Asian American, 1% Hispanic American, 1% Native American, 2% international
- 192 degree-seeking graduate students
- 78% of applicants admitted
- SAT or ACT (ACT writing optional), application essay required
- 59% graduate within 6 years

General. Founded in 1866. Regionally accredited. Weekly chapels, convocation programs, vespers. **Degrees:** 177 bachelor's awarded; master's offered. **ROTC:** Army. **Location:** 3 miles from Johnson City. **Calendar:** Semester, limited summer session. **Full-time faculty:** 69 total; 71% have terminal degrees, 1% minority, 51% women. **Part-time faculty:** 39 total; 15% have terminal degrees, 46% women. **Class size:** 69% < 20, 28% 20-39, less than 1% 40-49, less than 1% 50-99, 1% >100.

Freshman class profile. 686 applied, 536 admitted, 168 enrolled.

Mid 50% test scores		**GPA 2.0-2.99:**	13%
SAT verbal:	500-600	**Return as sophomores:**	73%
SAT math:	480-590	**Out-of-state:**	62%
ACT:	21-26	**Live on campus:**	88%
GPA 3.50 or higher:	61%	**International:**	2%
GPA 3.0-3.49:	26%		

Basis for selection. Academic work, test scores, and references from minister or church leader and high school principal or counselor required for admission. Portfolio required; audition required for music; interview recommended in some instances.

High school preparation. College-preparatory program recommended. 17 units recommended. Recommended units include English 4, mathematics 3, social studies 2, history 3, science 3 and foreign language 2.

2005-2006 Annual costs. Tuition/fees: $17,240. Room/board: $5,150. Books/supplies: $750. Personal expenses: $1,100.

2004-2005 Financial aid. Need-based: 174 full-time freshmen applied for aid; 143 were judged to have need; 143 of these received aid. Average need met was 66%. Average scholarship/grant was $4,738; average loan $2,611. 47% of total undergraduate aid awarded as scholarships/grants, 53% as loans/jobs. **Non-need-based:** Awarded to 801 full-time undergraduates, including 232 freshmen. Scholarships awarded for academics, alumni affiliation, art, athletics, job skills, minority status, music/drama, religious affiliation, state residency.

Application procedures. Admission: Priority date 4/1; deadline 8/1 (postmark date). $30 fee, may be waived for applicants with need. Application may be submitted online. Admission notification on a rolling basis beginning on or about 10/1. Must reply by May 1 or within 2 week(s) if notified thereafter. Enrollment deposits are not refunded after May 1. **Financial aid:** Priority date 3/1; no closing date. FAFSA required. Applicants notified on a rolling basis starting 3/15; must reply within 2 week(s) of notification.

Academics. Special study options: Cross-registration, double major, independent study, internships, study abroad, teacher certification program, Washington semester. Students may apply for participation in the following programs through the Council for Christian Colleges and Universities: American Studies Program in Washington, D.C.; Australia Studies Center; China

Studies Program; Contemporary Music Center in Martha's Vineyard; Latin American Studies Program in Costa Rica; Los Angeles Film Studies Center; Middle East Studies Program in Egypt; Russian Studies Program; Scholars' Semester in Oxford; Uganda Studies Program; Summer Institute of Journalism in Washington, D.C.; Oxford Summer Programme. **Credit/placement by examination:** AP, CLEP, IB, SAT, ACT, institutional tests. 32 credit hours maximum toward bachelor's degree. DANTES credit may be earned for scores at or above B level. Students may not receive credit by examination upon achieving a total of 64 credit hours. **Support services:** Reduced course load, remedial instruction, study skills assistance, tutoring, writing center.

Majors. Biology: General. **Business:** Accounting, business admin. **Communications:** General. **Computer sciences:** General. **Education:** General, early childhood, music. **English:** English lit. **Health:** Nursing (RN). **History:** General. **Liberal arts:** Humanities. **Math:** General. **Parks/recreation:** Health/fitness. **Physical sciences:** Chemistry. **Psychology:** General. **Public administration:** Human services. **Social sciences:** Sociology. **Theology:** Bible. **Visual/performing arts:** General.

Most popular majors. Biology 7%, business/marketing 25%, communications/journalism 10%, education 7%, English 7%, philosophy/religious studies 7%, psychology 8%, visual/performing arts 7%.

Computing on campus. 102 workstations in dormitories, library, computer center. Dormitories wired for high-speed internet access and linked to campus network. Commuter students can connect to campus network. Online library, helpline, repair service, student web hosting, wireless network available.

Student life. Freshman orientation: Available, $10 fee. Preregistration for classes offered. Weekend sessions available in April or June for students and parents. Students may register for classes and meet with an adviser during orientation. An abbreviated version is offered the weekend prior to the first day of fall classes. **Policies:** Smoking, alcoholic beverages, and dancing are not permitted on campus. Religious observance required. Freshmen permitted cars on campus. **Housing:** Guaranteed on-campus for all undergraduates. Single-sex dorms, apartments, substance-free housing available. $200 deposit, deadline 8/15. Students must live in college housing unless married or living with members of immediate family. **Activities:** Bands, choral groups, drama, literary magazine, music ensembles, musical theater, radio station, student government, student newspaper, symphony orchestra, Fellowship of Christian Athletes, missions club, service seekers, student government association, Beacon (missions organization), campus ministry team, College Republicans, Habitat for Humanity, political awareness group, Roteract.

Athletics. NAIA. **Intercollegiate:** Baseball M, basketball, cross-country, golf M, soccer, softball W, tennis, track and field, volleyball W. **Intramural:** Basketball, football (non-tackle), softball, volleyball. **Team name:** Buffaloes.

Student services. Adult student services, campus ministries, career counseling, student employment services, financial aid counseling, health services, personal counseling, placement for graduates.

Contact. E-mail: admissions@milligan.edu
Phone: (423) 461-8730 Toll-free number: (800) 262-8337
Fax: (423) 461-8982
Tracy Brinn, Director of Enrollment Management, Milligan College, Box 210, Milligan College, TN 37682

O'More College of Design

Franklin, Tennessee
www.omorecollege.edu **CB code: 1545**

- Private 4-year visual arts college
- Commuter campus in large town
- 70 degree-seeking undergraduates
- 39% of applicants admitted
- SAT or ACT (ACT writing optional) required

General. Founded in 1970. Accredited by ACCSCT. Housed in two historic mansions. Accredited by Foundation for Interior Design Education Research. **Degrees:** 30 bachelor's awarded. **Location:** 15 miles from Nashville. **Calendar:** Semester, limited summer session. **Full-time faculty:** 10 total. **Part-time faculty:** 40 total.

Freshman class profile. 115 applied, 45 admitted, 31 enrolled.

Mid 50% test scores			
SAT verbal:	480-540	GPA 3.50 or higher:	40%
SAT math:	460-510	GPA 3.0-3.49:	30%
ACT:	20-26	GPA 2.0-2.99:	30%

Basis for selection. High school record most important. Test scores, grades given equal weight. Portfolio or departmental home exam may be required. Portfolio recommended for most. If student does not have portfolio and does not meet admittance criteria on basis of their grades alone, student will need to contact chair of department to which he or she seeks admittance for instructions on completing department's home exam.

High school preparation. 18 units recommended. Recommended units include English 4, mathematics 3, social studies 1, history 2, science 3, foreign language 2 and academic electives 3. Art, mechanical drawing, and design courses are recommended.

2005-2006 Annual costs. Tuition/fees: $12,880. Books/supplies: $750.

2005-2006 Financial aid. All financial aid based on need. Average need met was 20%. Average scholarship/grant was $2,000; average loan $1,500. 23% of total undergraduate aid awarded as scholarships/grants, 77% as loans/jobs.

Application procedures. Admission: Closing date 8/1 (postmark date). $40 fee, may be waived for applicants with need. Application may be submitted online. Admission notification on a rolling basis. **Financial aid:** Priority date 4/1, closing date 7/30. FAFSA required. Applicants notified on a rolling basis starting 8/1; must reply by 7/30.

Academics. Students may attend Belmont University (Nashville) and get a minor there. Belmont students may receive a minor at O'More as well. **Special study options:** Dual enrollment of high school students, internships, semester at sea. **Credit/placement by examination:** CLEP, institutional tests. 9 credit hours maximum toward bachelor's degree.

Majors. Business: Fashion. **Visual/performing arts:** Commercial/advertising art, interior design.

Computing on campus. 25 workstations in library, computer center.

Student life. Freshman orientation: Mandatory. Preregistration for classes offered. **Policies:** Freshmen permitted cars on campus. **Activities:** Student government, student chapter of American Society of Interior Designers, O'More Fashion Merchandisers Association, Student Government Association, American Institute of Graphic Arts, International Interior Design Association.

Student services. Career counseling.

Contact. E-mail: admissions@omorecollege.edu
Phone: (615) 794-4254 Fax: (615) 790-1662
Christopher Lee, Director of Enrollment Management, O'More College of Design, 423 South Margin Street, Franklin, TN 37064-0908

Rhodes College

Memphis, Tennessee **CB member**
www.rhodes.edu **CB code: 1730**

- Private 4-year liberal arts college affiliated with Presbyterian Church (USA)
- Residential campus in very large city
- 1,655 degree-seeking undergraduates: 5% part-time, 58% women, 5% African American, 4% Asian American, 1% Hispanic American
- 13 degree-seeking graduate students
- 49% of applicants admitted
- SAT or ACT (ACT writing optional), application essay required
- 79% graduate within 6 years

General. Founded in 1848. Regionally accredited. **Degrees:** 317 bachelor's awarded; master's offered. **ROTC:** Army, Air Force. **Location:** 4 miles from downtown. **Calendar:** Semester. **Full-time faculty:** 141 total; 95% have terminal degrees, 10% minority, 40% women. **Part-time faculty:** 43 total; 67% have terminal degrees, 19% minority, 42% women. **Class size:** 74% < 20, 25% 20-39, less than 1% 40-49, less than 1% 50-99. **Special facilities:** Arboretum, scanning electron microscope, rooftop observatory, cell culture facility, nuclear magnetic resonance instrument.

Freshman class profile. 3,695 applied, 1,823 admitted, 446 enrolled.

Mid 50% test scores			
SAT verbal:	580-680	Rank in top tenth:	50%
SAT math:	580-670	Return as sophomores:	88%
ACT:	25-30	Out-of-state:	77%
GPA 3.50 or higher:	69%	Live on campus:	100%
GPA 3.0-3.49:	23%	International:	1%
GPA 2.0-2.99:	8%	Fraternities:	47%
Rank in top quarter:	79%	Sororities:	53%

Basis for selection. Academic record, standardized test scores, class rank, recommendations, essay, school and community activities important. Applications sought from international students, minorities, and children of alumni. Interview recommended. **Homeschooled:** Applicants must submit two SAT Subject Tests other than mathematics or literature in addition to usual requirements.

High school preparation. 16 units required. Required and recommended units include English 4, mathematics 3-4, social studies 2, science 2 (laboratory 2), foreign language 2 and academic electives 3. 4 mathematics recommended for applicants in mathematics, natural science, computer science, and economics.

2006-2007 Annual costs. Tuition/fees: $29,112. Room/board: $7,180. Books/supplies: $870. Personal expenses: $1,240.

2005-2006 Financial aid. Need-based: 267 full-time freshmen applied for aid; 152 were judged to have need; 151 of these received aid. Average need met was 94%. Average scholarship/grant was $15,983; average loan $4,076. 76% of total undergraduate aid awarded as scholarships/grants, 24% as loans/jobs. **Non-need-based:** Awarded to 816 full-time undergraduates, including 260 freshmen. Scholarships awarded for academics, art, minority status, music/drama, religious affiliation. **Additional information:** Auditions required for theater and music achievement awards and art achievement awards. Interviews recommended for merit scholarships.

Application procedures. Admission: Priority date 1/15; no deadline. $45 fee, may be waived for applicants with need. Application may be submitted online. Admission notification 4/1. Must reply by 5/1. Notification of admissions decision for Bellingrath Scholarship applicants by 03/15; must reply by 05/01. **Financial aid:** Closing date 1/15. FAFSA, CSS PROFILE required. Applicants notified by 4/1; must reply by 5/1.

Academics. Expense-paid summer internships in businesses abroad. Model United Nations program, opportunities for participation in computer-simulated international negotiating, mock trial program. **Special study options:** Combined bachelor's/graduate degree, cooperative education, cross-registration, double major, dual enrollment of high school students, exchange student, honors, independent study, internships, liberal arts/career combination, student-designed major, study abroad, Washington semester. **Credit/placement by examination:** AP, CLEP, IB, institutional tests. 28 credit hours maximum toward bachelor's degree. **Support services:** Tutoring, writing center.

Majors. Area/ethnic studies: Latin American, Russian/Slavic. **Biology:** General, Biochemistry/biophysics and molecular biology. **Business:** Business admin, managerial economics. **Computer sciences:** Computer science. **English:** English lit. **Foreign languages:** Classics, French, German, modern Greek, Russian, Spanish. **History:** General. **Math:** General. **Philosophy/religion:** Philosophy, religion. **Physical sciences:** Chemistry, physics. **Psychology:** General. **Social sciences:** Anthropology, economics, international relations, political science, sociology, urban studies. **Visual/performing arts:** Art, dramatic.

Most popular majors. Biology 12%, business/marketing 12%, English 13%, foreign language 6%, history 7%, philosophy/religious studies 6%, psychology 9%, social sciences 25%.

Computing on campus. 220 workstations in library, computer center, student center. Dormitories wired for high-speed internet access and linked to campus network. Commuter students can connect to campus network. Online course registration, online library, helpline, wireless network available.

Student life. Freshman orientation: Mandatory. Preregistration for classes offered. 5-day orientation acquaints students with academic expectations and regulations and gives opportunity to plan program of study with help from advisor. **Policies:** Student-run honor system central to campus life. Freshmen permitted cars on campus. **Housing:** Guaranteed on-campus for freshmen. Coed dorms, single-sex dorms, apartments, substance-free housing available. Special interest townhouses. **Activities:** Pep band, choral groups, dance, drama, literary magazine, music ensembles, musical theater, student government, student newspaper, symphony orchestra, Black Student Association, Kinney (social service), Inter-Varsity Christian Fellowship, international house, Habitat for Humanity, Interfaith Circle, Diversity Group, College Democrats, College Republicans.

Athletics. NCAA. **Intercollegiate:** Baseball M, basketball, cross-country, field hockey W, football (tackle) M, golf, soccer, softball W, swimming, tennis, track and field, volleyball W. **Intramural:** Basketball, football (non-tackle), football (tackle), racquetball, soccer, squash M, table tennis, tennis, volleyball. **Team name:** Lynx.

Student services. Campus ministries, career counseling, student employment services, financial aid counseling, health services, minority student services, personal counseling, placement for graduates. **Physically disabled:** Services for visually, speech, hearing impaired.

Contact. E-mail: adminfo@rhodes.edu
Phone: (901) 843-3700 Toll-free number: (800) 844-5969
Fax: (901) 843-3631
David Wottle, Dean of Admissions and Financial Aid, Rhodes College, 2000 North Parkway, Memphis, TN 38112

South College
Knoxville, Tennessee
www.southcollegetn.edu **CB code: 0711**

- For-profit 4-year liberal arts college
- Commuter campus in small city
- 502 degree-seeking undergraduates: 26% part-time, 84% women, 12% African American, 1% Asian American, 1% international
- 52 graduate students
- SAT or ACT with writing, interview required

General. Founded in 1882. Regionally accredited; also accredited by ACICS. **Degrees:** 10 bachelor's, 104 associate awarded. **Location:** Downtown. **Calendar:** Quarter, extensive summer session. **Full-time faculty:** 60 total. **Part-time faculty:** 25 total.

Basis for selection. CPTS examination required. SAT/ACT or CPAT required for admission.

2005-2006 Annual costs. Tuition $17,200 for physical therapy assistance, radiography, health science, post-baccalaureate education certificate, and nursing pre-professional programs. Books/supplies: $1,300. Personal expenses: $1,200.

Financial aid. All financial aid based on need.

Application procedures. Admission: No deadline. $40 fee. Admission notification on a rolling basis. **Financial aid:** No deadline. FAFSA, institutional form required. Applicants notified on a rolling basis.

Academics. Special study options: Accelerated study, double major, dual enrollment of high school students, internships, teacher certification program. **Credit/placement by examination:** CLEP, institutional tests. **Support services:** Learning center, reduced course load, study skills assistance, tutoring, writing center.

Majors. Business: Business admin. **Legal studies:** General.

Computing on campus. 85 workstations in library, computer center. Online library, wireless network available.

Student life. Freshman orientation: Mandatory. Preregistration for classes offered. **Policies:** Freshmen permitted cars on campus. **Activities:** Literary magazine, student government, student newspaper, Collegiate Secretaries International, paralegal association, student affairs advisory council, Empowerment Club (business), students of medical assisting, movie club, community service club.

Student services. Career counseling, student employment services, financial aid counseling, placement for graduates, veterans' counselor.

Contact. E-mail: admissions@southcollegetn.edu
Phone: (865) 251-1800 Fax: (865) 470-8737
Walter Hosea, Admissions Director, South College, 200 Hayfield Road, Knoxville, TN 37922

Southern Adventist University
Collegedale, Tennessee
www.southern.edu **CB code: 1727**

- Private 4-year university and liberal arts college affiliated with Seventh-day Adventists
- Residential campus in small town
- 2,390 degree-seeking undergraduates
- 132 graduate students

- 69% of applicants admitted
- SAT and SAT Subject Tests or ACT (ACT writing optional) required
- 55% graduate within 6 years; 16% enter graduate study

General. Founded in 1892. Regionally accredited. **Degrees:** 381 bachelor's, 117 associate awarded; master's offered. **Location:** 18 miles from Chattanooga. **Calendar:** Semester, limited summer session. **Full-time faculty:** 131 total; 66% have terminal degrees, 12% minority, 35% women. **Part-time faculty:** 86 total; 37% have terminal degrees, 15% minority, 55% women. **Class size:** 50% < 20, 34% 20-39, 6% 40-49, 10% 50-99, less than 1% >100. **Special facilities:** Civil War collection, Lincoln collection, Anton Memorial Organ.

Freshman class profile. 1,471 applied, 1,022 admitted, 605 enrolled.

Mid 50% test scores			
SAT verbal:	210-540	GPA 3.0-3.49:	29%
SAT math:	220-500	GPA 2.0-2.99:	24%
ACT:	19-24	Return as sophomores:	72%
GPA 3.50 or higher:	47%	Out-of-state:	79%
		Live on campus:	89%

Basis for selection. School achievement record and test scores important. Interview recommended for all; audition required for music, gymnastics programs. **Homeschooled:** Home-school organization must be academically accredited or student must take GED. GED recommended in all home-schooled situations.

High school preparation. College-preparatory program recommended. 18 units required; 24 recommended. Required and recommended units include English 3-4, mathematics 2-3, social studies 1, history 1-2, science 2-3, foreign language 2 and academic electives 9. One unit chemistry (2.0 GPA or better) required for nursing majors. 2 units foreign language required for BA program applicants. Computer competency strongly recommended.

2006-2007 Annual costs. Tuition/fees (projected): $14,784. Room/board: $4,604. Books/supplies: $900. Personal expenses: $2,000.

2005-2006 Financial aid. Need-based: Average need met was 60%. Average scholarship/grant was $4,500; average loan $3,700. 48% of total undergraduate aid awarded as scholarships/grants, 52% as loans/jobs. **Non-need-based:** Scholarships awarded for academics, alumni affiliation, art, leadership, music/drama.

Application procedures. Admission: Closing date 9/8 (receipt date). $25 fee, may be waived for applicants with need. Application may be submitted online. Admission notification on a rolling basis. Must reply by 9/8. **Financial aid:** Priority date 3/1; no closing date. FAFSA required. Applicants notified on a rolling basis starting 2/15; must reply within 2 week(s) of notification.

Academics. Special study options: Combined bachelor's/graduate degree, double major, dual enrollment of high school students, ESL, honors, independent study, internships, study abroad, teacher certification program. **Credit/placement by examination:** AP, CLEP, institutional tests. 12 credit hours maximum toward bachelor's degree. **Support services:** Learning center, reduced course load, remedial instruction, study skills assistance, tutoring, writing center.

Majors. Biology: General, biochemistry, biophysics. **Business:** Accounting, actuarial science, business admin, international, management information systems, management science, marketing, nonprofit/public. **Communications:** Advertising, broadcast journalism, journalism, media studies, public relations. **Communications technology:** General. **Computer sciences:** Computer science, programming, system admin. **Education:** Art, biology, chemistry, elementary, English, French, history, mathematics, music, physical, physics, Spanish. **English:** English lit. **Family/consumer sciences:** Family studies. **Foreign languages:** General, French, Spanish. **Health:** Art therapy, clinical lab science, health care admin, nursing (RN). **History:** General. **Math:** General. **Parks/recreation:** Exercise sciences, sports admin. **Philosophy/religion:** Religion. **Physical sciences:** Chemistry, physics. **Psychology:** General. **Public administration:** Social work. **Social sciences:** Archaeology. **Theology:** Pastoral counseling, religious ed, theology. **Visual/performing arts:** Art, cinematography, commercial/advertising art, music performance, music theory/composition, photography.

Most popular majors. Biology 6%, business/marketing 15%, communications/journalism 7%, education 8%, health sciences 15%, psychology 6%, theological studies 9%, visual/performing arts 12%.

Computing on campus. 200 workstations in dormitories, library, computer center. Dormitories wired for high-speed internet access and linked to campus network. Commuter students can connect to campus network. Online course registration, online library, wireless network available.

Student life. Freshman orientation: Mandatory. Preregistration for classes offered. Orientation prior to registration for fall term. Includes exams and instruction in course planning as well as social occasions for students to meet faculty and fellow students. **Policies:** Alcohol and drug free. Religious observance required. Freshmen permitted cars on campus. **Housing:** Guaranteed on-campus for all undergraduates. Single-sex dorms, apartments available. $250 fully refundable deposit, deadline 7/15. **Activities:** Bands, choral groups, drama, film society, music ensembles, radio station, student government, student newspaper, symphony orchestra, TV station, African club, campus ministries, Black Christian Union, Partners at Wellness, Association of South East Asian Nation Students.

Athletics. Intramural: Badminton, basketball, racquetball, soccer, softball, table tennis, tennis, volleyball.

Student services. Campus ministries, career counseling, student employment services, financial aid counseling, health services, personal counseling, placement for graduates, veterans' counselor.

Contact. E-mail: admissions@southern.edu
Phone: (423) 236-2844 Toll-free number: (800) 768-8437
Fax: (423) 236-1844
Marc Grundy, Director of Admissions, Southern Adventist University, Box 370, Collegedale, TN 37315-0370

Tennessee State University

Nashville, Tennessee — **CB member**
www.tnstate.edu — **CB code: 1803**

- Public 4-year university
- Residential campus in large city
- 6,423 degree-seeking undergraduates: 16% part-time, 66% women
- 1,521 degree-seeking graduate students
- 43% of applicants admitted
- SAT or ACT required

General. Founded in 1912. Regionally accredited. **Degrees:** 982 bachelor's, 132 associate awarded; master's, doctoral offered. **ROTC:** Air Force. **Location:** 130 miles from Chattanooga, 210 miles from Memphis. **Calendar:** Semester, limited summer session. **Full-time faculty:** 430 total; 79% have terminal degrees, 60% minority, 42% women. **Part-time faculty:** 151 total; 26% have terminal degrees, 54% minority, 54% women. **Class size:** 40% < 20, 50% 20-39, 7% 40-49, less than 1% 50-99, 3% >100.

Freshman class profile. 6,950 applied, 2,962 admitted, 1,205 enrolled.

Mid 50% test scores			
SAT verbal:	400-500	ACT:	16-20
SAT math:	410-500	Out-of-state:	42%
		Live on campus:	75%

Basis for selection. School achievement record, test scores important. Interview required for allied health, nursing, physical therapy programs.

High school preparation. 14 units required. Required units include English 4, mathematics 3, social studies 2, science 2 (laboratory 1) and foreign language 2. One unit visual and/or performing arts recommended.

2005-2006 Annual costs. Tuition/fees: $4,334; $13,646 out-of-state. Room/board: $4,620. Books/supplies: $875. Personal expenses: $2,800.

2005-2006 Financial aid. Need-based: 36% of total undergraduate aid awarded as scholarships/grants, 64% as loans/jobs. **Non-need-based:** Scholarships awarded for academics.

Application procedures. Admission: Closing date 8/1. $15 fee. Admission notification on a rolling basis. **Financial aid:** Priority date 4/1; no closing date. FAFSA required. Applicants notified on a rolling basis starting 7/10; must reply within 2 week(s) of notification.

Academics. Special study options: Cooperative education, cross-registration, distance learning, double major, ESL, exchange student, honors, independent study, study abroad, teacher certification program, weekend college. **Credit/placement by examination:** AP, CLEP, institutional tests. 33 credit hours maximum toward bachelor's degree. **Support services:** Learning center, remedial instruction, study skills assistance, tutoring, writing center.

Majors. Agriculture: Animal sciences. **Architecture:** Architecture. **Biology:** General, biochemistry. **Business:** Accounting, administrative services, business admin, managerial economics. **Communications:** General, journalism. **Computer sciences:** General, programming. **Education:** General, early childhood, physical, secondary, special. **Engineering:** General, architectural, civil, electrical. **Family/consumer sciences:** General, clothing/textiles, family studies, food/nutrition. **Foreign languages:** French, Spanish. **Health:** Audiology/speech pathology, dental hygiene, health care admin, medical records admin. **History:** General. **Interdisciplinary:** Biological/

physical sciences. **Liberal arts:** Arts/sciences. **Math:** General. **Physical sciences:** Chemistry, physics. **Protective services:** Criminal justice. **Psychology:** General. **Public administration:** Social work. **Social sciences:** General, political science, sociology. **Visual/performing arts:** Art history/ conservation, dramatic.

Computing on campus. 450 workstations in library, computer center, student center. Dormitories linked to campus network. Commuter students can connect to campus network. Online course registration, online library, helpline available.

Student life. Freshman orientation: Mandatory. Preregistration for classes offered. **Policies:** Freshmen permitted cars on campus. **Housing:** Coed dorms, single-sex dorms, apartments available. $50 deposit, deadline 4/1. **Activities:** Bands, choral groups, dance, drama, film society, music ensembles, musical theater, radio station, student government, student newspaper, religious organizations, foreign student organization, honor organization, literary organization.

Athletics. NCAA. **Intercollegiate:** Baseball M, basketball, cross-country, football (tackle) M, golf, softball W, tennis, track and field, volleyball W. **Intramural:** Basketball, racquetball, tennis, track and field, volleyball. **Team name:** Tigers.

Student services. Career counseling, student employment services, financial aid counseling, health services, minority student services, on-campus daycare, personal counseling, placement for graduates, veterans' counselor. **Physically disabled:** Services for visually, speech, hearing impaired.

Contact. E-mail: jcade@tnstate.edu
Phone: (615) 963-5101 Fax: (615) 963-5108
John Cade, Dean of Admissions, Tennessee State University, 3500 John A. Merritt Boulevard, Nashville, TN 37209-1561

Tennessee Technological University

Cookeville, Tennessee **CB member**
www.tntech.edu **CB code: 1804**

- Public 4-year university
- Residential campus in large town
- 7,167 degree-seeking undergraduates: 10% part-time, 46% women, 4% African American, 1% Asian American, 1% Hispanic American, 1% international
- 1,436 degree-seeking graduate students
- 75% of applicants admitted
- 44% graduate within 6 years

General. Founded in 1915. Regionally accredited. **Degrees:** 1,270 bachelor's awarded; master's, doctoral offered. **ROTC:** Army, Air Force. **Location:** 80 miles from Nashville, 100 miles from Knoxville. **Calendar:** Semester, extensive summer session. **Full-time faculty:** 380 total; 83% have terminal degrees, 14% minority, 34% women. **Part-time faculty:** 180 total; 29% have terminal degrees, 3% minority, 53% women. **Class size:** 51% < 20, 36% 20-39, 7% 40-49, 4% 50-99, 2% >100. **Special facilities:** Center for crafts,cooperative fishery research unit, agricultural pavilion, center for energy systems research, center for manufacturing research, center for the management, utilization and protection of water resources, childcare resource center.

Freshman class profile. 3,292 applied, 2,475 admitted, 1,423 enrolled.

Mid 50% test scores			
SAT verbal:	490-600	Rank in top quarter:	53%
SAT math:	500-630	Rank in top tenth:	24%
ACT:	20-26	Return as sophomores:	73%
GPA 3.50 or higher:	38%	Out-of-state:	4%
GPA 3.0-3.49:	33%	Live on campus:	52%
GPA 2.0-2.99:	29%	Fraternities:	18%
		Sororities:	12%

Basis for selection. All students must complete 14 specific high school courses. In addition to these required courses, applicants must fall into one of the following two categories to be admitted: 1) have a 19 ACT composite (900 SAT) and a 2.00 high school GPA; 2) have a 17 ACT composite (810 SAT) and a 2.5 high school GPA. Engineering applicants need ACT mathematics score of 20, composite score of 20 and GPA of 2.35. Computer science and mathematics applicants need ACT mathematics score of 21. (SAT scores are exclusive of Writing). Interview recommended for all; audition recommended for music; portfolio recommended for arts, crafts. **Homeschooled:** Must have same core units as high school curriculum, 2.50 GPA and 19 ACT; GED required otherwise.

High school preparation. 14 units required. Required units include English 4, mathematics 3, social studies 1, history 1, science 2 (laboratory 1) and foreign language 2. Mathematics units must include algebra I and II and geometry or advanced mathematics course. Science units must be biology, chemistry, or physics with laboratories (can include physical sciences). Foreign language units must be in single language. 1 US history, 1 unit visual and/or performing arts also required. Social studies must be either world, ancient, modern, or European history, or world geography.

2005-2006 Annual costs. Tuition/fees: $4,424; $13,736 out-of-state. Room/ board: $5,820. Books/supplies: $633. Personal expenses: $840.

2004-2005 Financial aid. Need-based: 1,381 full-time freshmen applied for aid; 819 were judged to have need; 804 of these received aid. Average need met was 84%. Average scholarship/grant was $3,476; average loan $1,477. 39% of total undergraduate aid awarded as scholarships/grants, 61% as loans/jobs. **Non-need-based:** Awarded to 3,431 full-time undergraduates, including 1,149 freshmen. Scholarships awarded for academics, alumni affiliation, art, athletics, leadership, minority status, music/drama, ROTC, state residency. **Additional information:** Tuition and/or fee waivers available for children of Tennessee public school teachers.

Application procedures. Admission: Priority date 5/1; deadline 8/1 (postmark date). $15 fee, may be waived for applicants with need. Application may be submitted online. Admission notification on a rolling basis. **Financial aid:** Priority date 3/15; no closing date. FAFSA required. Applicants notified on a rolling basis starting 3/15; must reply within 2 week(s) of notification.

Academics. Special study options: Accelerated study, cooperative education, distance learning, double major, dual enrollment of high school students, ESL, honors, independent study, internships, liberal arts/career combination, study abroad, teacher certification program. **Credit/placement by examination:** AP, CLEP, IB, institutional tests. 33 credit hours maximum toward bachelor's degree. **Support services:** Learning center, preadmission summer program, reduced course load, remedial instruction, study skills assistance, tutoring, writing center.

Majors. Agriculture: Agribusiness operations, agronomy, animal sciences, horticultural science, horticulture, landscaping, nursery operations, soil science. **Biology:** General, biochemistry. **Business:** General, accounting, finance, labor relations, management science, managerial economics, operations. **Communications:** General, journalism. **Communications technology:** General. **Computer sciences:** General, computer science, web page design. **Conservation:** General, fisheries, wildlife. **Education:** General, agricultural, early childhood, English, health, music, physical, secondary, special. **Engineering:** Chemical, civil, computer, electrical, mechanical. **Engineering technology:** Manufacturing. **English:** Technical writing. **Family/ consumer sciences:** General, clothing/textiles, family/community services, food/nutrition, housing. **Foreign languages:** French, German, Spanish. **Health:** Nursing (RN), predentistry, premedicine, prepharmacy, preveterinary. **History:** General. **Math:** General. **Physical sciences:** Chemistry, geology, physics. **Psychology:** General. **Social sciences:** Economics, political science, sociology. **Visual/performing arts:** Ceramics, drawing, fiber arts, music performance, painting, sculpture, studio arts.

Most popular majors. Business/marketing 21%, engineering/ engineering technologies 20%, interdisciplinary studies 13%, social sciences 6%.

Computing on campus. 600 workstations in dormitories, library, computer center. Dormitories wired for high-speed internet access and linked to campus network. Commuter students can connect to campus network. Online course registration, online library, helpline, wireless network available.

Student life. Freshman orientation: Mandatory, $45 fee. Preregistration for classes offered. **Policies:** Freshmen permitted cars on campus. **Housing:** Guaranteed on-campus for freshmen. Coed dorms, single-sex dorms, special housing for disabled, apartments, fraternity/sorority housing available. $50 fully refundable deposit. **Activities:** Bands, choral groups, dance, drama, literary magazine, music ensembles, musical theater, opera, radio station, student government, student newspaper, symphony orchestra, TV station, more than 190 student organizations.

Athletics. NCAA. **Intercollegiate:** Baseball M, basketball, cheerleading, cross-country, football (tackle) M, golf, rifle, soccer W, softball W, tennis, track and field W, volleyball W. **Intramural:** Basketball, bowling, golf M, handball, racquetball, rugby M, soccer, softball, tennis, volleyball, wrestling M. **Team name:** Golden Eagles.

Student services. Alcohol/substance abuse counseling, career counseling, student employment services, financial aid counseling, health services, minority student services, on-campus daycare, personal counseling, placement for graduates, veterans' counselor, women's services. **Physically disabled:** Services for visually, speech, hearing impaired. **Learning disabled:** Comprehensive services available.

Contact. E-mail: admissions@tntech.edu
Phone: (931) 372-3888 Toll-free number: (800) 255-8881
Fax: (931) 372-6250
Rebecca Tolbert, Associate Vice President for Academic Affairs and Enrollment Management, Tennessee Technological University, Office of Admissions, Cookeville, TN 38505-0001

Tennessee Temple University

Chattanooga, Tennessee
www.tntemple.edu **CB code: 1818**

- Private 4-year university and Bible college affiliated with Baptist faith
- Residential campus in small city
- 423 degree-seeking undergraduates
- SAT or ACT with writing, application essay required

General. Founded in 1946. Accredited by ABHE. **Degrees:** 95 bachelor's, 9 associate awarded; master's offered. **Location:** 120 miles from Atlanta, Georgia. **Calendar:** Semester, limited summer session. **Full-time faculty:** 24 total; 54% have terminal degrees, 33% women. **Part-time faculty:** 23 total; 30% women. **Class size:** 77% < 20, 17% 20-39, 4% 40-49, less than 1% 50-99, less than 1% >100.

Freshman class profile. 110 enrolled.

Mid 50% test scores			
ACT:	14-25	Out-of-state:	26%
		Live on campus:	72%

Basis for selection. Test scores, one personal reference, one pastoral reference and a written personal testimony about applicant's faith are required. **Homeschooled:** Relevant experiences that may indicate and support ability to succeed in college work may be substituted for high school diploma or GED. Students should submit a transcript and other supporting information, such as course or curriculum descriptions, grades, graduation date, and the signatures of the instructor. Students should submit official transcripts from other secondary or post secondary institutions attended. Students must submit official scores from the ACT Enhanced Test or SAT Test.

High school preparation. 10 units required; 15 recommended. Required and recommended units include English 4, mathematics 2-3, social studies 2-3, science 2-3 and foreign language 2. Computer fundamentals recommended.

2005-2006 Annual costs. Tuition/fees: $8,000. Room/board: $5,750. Books/supplies: $700. Personal expenses: $850.

2005-2006 Financial aid. Need-based: 46% of total undergraduate aid awarded as scholarships/grants, 54% as loans/jobs. **Non-need-based:** Scholarships awarded for academics, alumni affiliation, athletics, leadership, music/drama, state residency.

Application procedures. Admission: Priority date 3/31; deadline 8/1 (receipt date). $30 fee, may be waived for applicants with need. Application may be submitted online. Admission notification on a rolling basis. **Financial aid:** Priority date 3/31; no closing date. FAFSA required. Applicants notified on a rolling basis starting 2/15; must reply within 2 week(s) of notification.

Academics. Special study options: Distance learning, double major, dual enrollment of high school students, external degree, independent study, internships, liberal arts/career combination, teacher certification program, Washington semester. **Credit/placement by examination:** AP, CLEP, IB, institutional tests. 16 credit hours maximum toward associate degree, 32 toward bachelor's. **Support services:** Reduced course load, remedial instruction, study skills assistance, tutoring, writing center.

Majors. Biology: General. **Business:** General, administrative services, business admin, office management. **Computer sciences:** Computer science. **Education:** Biology, Deaf/hearing impaired, elementary, English, history, mathematics, music, science, secondary, speech. **English:** English lit, speech/rhetoric. **Health:** Premedicine. **History:** General. **Legal studies:** Prelaw. **Liberal arts:** Arts/sciences. **Math:** General. **Physical sciences:** General. **Psychology:** General. **Social sciences:** Political science. **Theology:** Bible, missionary, religious ed, sacred music, theology.

Computing on campus. 105 workstations in dormitories, library, computer center. Dormitories wired for high-speed internet access and linked to campus network. Commuter students can connect to campus network. Wireless network available.

Student life. Freshman orientation: Mandatory, $25 fee. Held 2-3 days prior to beginning of classes. **Policies:** Religious observance required. Freshmen permitted cars on campus. **Housing:** Guaranteed on-campus for all undergraduates. Single-sex dorms, apartments available. $100 deposit, deadline 5/31. **Activities:** Choral groups, drama, music ensembles, radio station, student government, student newspaper, Student Missions Fellowship, Student Preachers Fellowship.

Athletics. NCCAA. **Intercollegiate:** Baseball M, basketball, soccer M, volleyball W. **Intramural:** Basketball, football (tackle) M, soccer, softball, table tennis, tennis, volleyball, wrestling M. **Team name:** Crusaders.

Student services. Campus ministries, student employment services, financial aid counseling, personal counseling, placement for graduates, veterans' counselor. **Physically disabled:** Services for visually, hearing impaired.

Contact. E-mail: ttuinfo@tntemple.edu
Phone: (423) 493-4371 Toll-free number: (800) 553-4050
Fax: (423) 493-4497
Chris Dooley, Director of Enrollment Services, Tennessee Temple University, 1815 Union Avenue, Chattanooga, TN 37404

Tennessee Wesleyan College

Athens, Tennessee
www.twcnet.edu **CB code: 1805**

- Private 4-year nursing, liberal arts and teachers college affiliated with United Methodist Church
- Commuter campus in large town
- 847 degree-seeking undergraduates: 14% part-time, 68% women, 3% African American, 1% Asian American, 2% Hispanic American, 3% international
- 77% of applicants admitted
- SAT or ACT (ACT writing recommended) required
- 32% graduate within 6 years; 39% enter graduate study

General. Founded in 1857. Regionally accredited. Baccalaureate programs in nursing and business through Knoxville campus. **Degrees:** 195 bachelor's awarded. **Location:** 50 miles from Chattanooga and Knoxville. **Calendar:** Semester, extensive summer session. **Full-time faculty:** 46 total; 59% have terminal degrees, 2% minority, 50% women. **Part-time faculty:** 40 total; 32% have terminal degrees, 2% minority, 45% women. **Class size:** 65% < 20, 27% 20-39, 8% 40-49, less than 1% 50-99.

Freshman class profile. 515 applied, 399 admitted, 169 enrolled.

Mid 50% test scores			
SAT verbal:	400-500	Rank in top quarter:	25%
SAT math:	460-550	End year in good standing:	77%
ACT:	18-23	Return as sophomores:	65%
GPA 3.50 or higher:	37%	Out-of-state:	6%
GPA 3.0-3.49:	32%	Live on campus:	57%
GPA 2.0-2.99:	30%	International:	3%
		Sororities:	4%

Basis for selection. Test scores, school records, recommendations and GPA very important. Michigan test used for placement. Essay recommended for all; interview recommended for academically weak; audition required for music and theater. **Homeschooled:** Must take the ACT or SAT before being considered for admission.

High school preparation. 10 units recommended. Recommended units include English 4, mathematics 2, social studies 1, history 1 and science 2.

2005-2006 Annual costs. Tuition/fees: $13,550. Room/board: $5,100. Books/supplies: $1,000. Personal expenses: $1,000.

2005-2006 Financial aid. Need-based: Average need met was 73%. Average scholarship/grant was $8,552; average loan $1,881. 60% of total undergraduate aid awarded as scholarships/grants, 40% as loans/jobs. **Non-need-based:** Scholarships awarded for academics, alumni affiliation, athletics, job skills, minority status, music/drama, religious affiliation.

Application procedures. Admission: No deadline. $25 fee, may be waived for applicants with need. Application may be submitted online. Admission notification on a rolling basis. **Financial aid:** No deadline. FAFSA, institutional form required. Applicants notified on a rolling basis starting 2/15; must reply within 2 week(s) of notification.

Academics. Service and leadership are components of Tennessee Wesleyan College's mission. Several academic programs on campus require students to demonstrate servant leadership as well as to provide documentation of service to the campus, community or other worthwhile organizations. Study abroad opportunities are also available for students wishing to extend their learning globally. **Special study options:** Accelerated study, combined bachelor's/graduate degree, cooperative education, double major, dual enrollment of high school students, exchange student, honors, independent study, internships, liberal arts/career combination, student-designed major, study abroad, teacher certification program. Member of the Private College Consortium for International Studies (semester in London program). **Credit/placement by examination:** AP, CLEP, IB, institutional tests. 12 credit hours maximum toward bachelor's degree. **Support services:** Learning center, reduced course load, remedial instruction, study skills assistance, tutoring.

Honors college/program. Open to second semester freshmen, sophomores, juniors, and seniors based on standardized test scores and/or past classroom performance. The Honors Program explores the general theme of Culture, Ideas, and Values from an interdisciplinary perspective. The courses are designed to open the barriers that separate disciplines, teaching the student to appreciate the interrelationships among history, literature, mathematics, philosophy, religion and science.

Majors. **Area/ethnic studies:** American. **Biology:** General. **Business:** Accounting, business admin, finance, human resources. **Computer sciences:** General. **Conservation:** Environmental studies. **Education:** Biology, chemistry, English, history, music, physical, science. **English:** English lit. **Health:** Nursing (RN), predentistry, premedicine, prenursing, prepharmacy, preveterinary. **History:** General. **Interdisciplinary:** Behavioral sciences, global studies, intercultural. **Legal studies:** Prelaw. **Math:** General. **Parks/recreation:** Health/fitness, sports admin. **Philosophy/religion:** Religion. **Physical sciences:** Chemistry. **Psychology:** General. **Public administration:** Human services. **Theology:** Preministerial.

Most popular majors. Business/marketing 30%, computer/information sciences 6%, education 11%, health sciences 16%, parks/recreation 11%, public administration/social services 11%.

Computing on campus. 95 workstations in library, computer center. Dormitories wired for high-speed internet access. Online library available.

Student life. **Freshman orientation:** Mandatory. Preregistration for classes offered. Held in August. Participation in orientation earns students one credit hour. **Policies:** Religious observance required. Freshmen permitted cars on campus. **Housing:** Guaranteed on-campus for freshmen. Single-sex dorms, apartments, substance-free housing available. $100 deposit. **Activities:** Choral groups, drama, literary magazine, musical theater, student government, student newspaper, Business Club, Circle K, Hackberry and Oak Society, The International Club, The National Student Nurses Association, The Psychology Club, Student Activities Board, Student Government Association and Student Ambassadors.

Athletics. NAIA. **Intercollegiate:** Baseball M, basketball, cross-country, golf, soccer, softball W, tennis, volleyball W. **Intramural:** Badminton, basketball, table tennis, volleyball. **Team name:** Bulldogs.

Student services. Adult student services, campus ministries, career counseling, student employment services, financial aid counseling, health services, personal counseling, placement for graduates, veterans' counselor. **Physically disabled:** Services for visually, hearing impaired. **Learning disabled:** Comprehensive services available.

Contact. E-mail: cawoodr@twcnet.edu
Phone: (423) 745-7504 Toll-free number: (800) 742-5892
Fax: (423) 745-9335
Ruthie Cawood, Director of Admissions, Tennessee Wesleyan College, 204 East College Street, Athens, TN 37371-0040

Trevecca Nazarene University

Nashville, Tennessee
www.trevecca.edu **CB code: 1809**

- Private 4-year university and liberal arts college affiliated with Church of the Nazarene
- Residential campus in very large city
- 1,172 degree-seeking undergraduates: 20% part-time, 54% women, 8% African American, 1% Asian American, 2% Hispanic American, 2% international
- 924 degree-seeking graduate students
- 69% of applicants admitted
- SAT or ACT (ACT writing optional) required
- 40% graduate within 6 years

General. Founded in 1901. Regionally accredited. **Degrees:** 459 bachelor's awarded; master's, doctoral offered. **ROTC:** Army. **Location:** 200 miles from Memphis, 175 miles from Knoxville. **Calendar:** Semester, limited summer session. **Full-time faculty:** 73 total; 74% have terminal degrees, 32% women. **Part-time faculty:** 144 total; 49% have terminal degrees, 42% women. **Class size:** 62% < 20, 29% 20-39, 6% 40-49, 2% 50-99.

Freshman class profile. 762 applied, 522 admitted, 250 enrolled.

Mid 50% test scores			
SAT verbal:	470-580	Rank in top quarter:	48%
SAT math:	450-590	Rank in top tenth:	20%
ACT:	19-25	Return as sophomores:	68%
GPA 3.50 or higher:	39%	Out-of-state:	59%
GPA 3.0-3.49:	26%	Live on campus:	84%
GPA 2.0-2.99:	31%	International:	2%

Basis for selection. Freshmen required to meet one of two conditions: a minimum 18 ACT composite (860 SAT composite, exclusive of Writing) or 2.5 high school GPA based on 4.0 scale. Latest date SAT or ACT scores must be received for fall admission is day of registration. The specific procedures for the following programs are described in the music, natrual and applied sciences, and teacher education department sections of the University Catalog: Church Music, Medical Technology, Music, Music Business, Music Education, Nursing, Teacher Education. **Homeschooled:** Transcript with all subjects and grades should be provided by the correspondence-school based organization or the parent depending on the method of homeschooling. **Learning Disabled:** Contact the coordinator of disability services in the Academic Support Center for information concerning the documentation of a disability and the services available.

High school preparation. College-preparatory program recommended. 15 units recommended. Recommended units include English 4, mathematics 2, social studies 1, history 1, science 1, foreign language 2 and academic electives 4.

2006-2007 Annual costs. Tuition/fees (projected): $14,774. Room/board: $6,470. Books/supplies: $888. Personal expenses: $1,338.

2004-2005 Financial aid. **Need-based:** 180 full-time freshmen applied for aid; 154 were judged to have need; 101 of these received aid. Average need met was 47%. Average scholarship/grant was $8,176; average loan $3,820. 29% of total undergraduate aid awarded as scholarships/grants, 71% as loans/jobs. **Non-need-based:** Awarded to 369 full-time undergraduates, including 150 freshmen. Scholarships awarded for academics, alumni affiliation, athletics, leadership, music/drama, religious affiliation.

Application procedures. **Admission:** Priority date 7/1; no deadline. $25 fee. Application may be submitted online. Admission notification on a rolling basis. **Financial aid:** Priority date 3/1; no closing date. FAFSA required. Applicants notified on a rolling basis starting 3/15.

Academics. **Special study options:** Double major, internships, study abroad, teacher certification program. Adult degree completion program. **Credit/placement by examination:** AP, CLEP, IB, SAT, ACT. 22 credit hours maximum toward associate degree, 45 toward bachelor's. Credit awarded after one semester and tuition paid. **Support services:** Learning center, remedial instruction, study skills assistance, tutoring.

Majors. **Biology:** General. **Business:** Accounting, business admin, e-commerce, management information systems, marketing. **Communications:** General, media studies, organizational. **Computer sciences:** Information technology, web page design. **Education:** Biology, chemistry, drama/dance, elementary, English, history, mathematics, music, physical, secondary, speech. **English:** English lit. **Health:** Clinical lab science, health services, nursing (RN). **History:** General. **Interdisciplinary:** Behavioral sciences. **Math:** General. **Parks/recreation:** Health/fitness. **Philosophy/religion:** Religion. **Physical sciences:** Chemistry, physics. **Psychology:** General. **Public administration:** Social work. **Social sciences:** General. **Theology:** Sacred music. **Visual/performing arts:** Dramatic, music management.

Most popular majors. Business/marketing 68%.

Computing on campus. 200 workstations in dormitories, library, computer center, student center. Dormitories linked to campus network. Commuter students can connect to campus network.

Student life. **Freshman orientation:** Mandatory. Preregistration for classes offered. **Policies:** Chapel attendance required for traditional undergraduate students. Freshmen permitted cars on campus. **Housing:** Single-sex dorms, apartments available. $25 fully refundable deposit, deadline 5/1. **Activities:** Bands, choral groups, drama, literary magazine, music ensembles, musical theater, radio station, student government, student newspaper, symphony orchestra, Mission Club, Trevecca Ministerial Association, Phi Beta Lambda.

Athletics. NAIA. **Intercollegiate:** Baseball M, basketball, golf, soccer, softball W, volleyball W. **Intramural:** Badminton, basketball, football (tackle)

M, golf, racquetball, softball, table tennis, track and field, volleyball. **Team name:** Trojans.

Student services. Campus ministries, career counseling, student employment services, financial aid counseling, health services, personal counseling, placement for graduates.

Contact. E-mail: admissions_und@trevecca.edu
Phone: (615) 248-1320 Toll-free number: (888) 210-4868
Fax: (615) 248-7406
Patty Cook, Director of Admissions, Trevecca Nazarene University, 333 Murfreesboro Road, Nashville, TN 37210

Tusculum College

Greeneville, Tennessee **CB member**
www.tusculum.edu **CB code: 1812**

- Private 4-year liberal arts college affiliated with Presbyterian Church (USA)
- Residential campus in large town
- 2,289 degree-seeking undergraduates: 2% part-time, 56% women, 12% African American, 1% Asian American, 1% Hispanic American, 3% international
- 367 degree-seeking graduate students
- 67% of applicants admitted
- SAT or ACT (ACT writing optional), application essay required
- 41% graduate within 6 years; 12% enter graduate study

General. Founded in 1794. Regionally accredited. Strong civic arts focus and service-learning curriculum. Focused calendar: students take one class at a time. **Degrees:** 386 bachelor's awarded; master's offered. **Location:** 70 miles from Knoxville, 30 miles from Johnson City. **Calendar:** Differs by program, limited summer session. **Full-time faculty:** 75 total. **Part-time faculty:** 70 total. **Class size:** 83% < 20, 17% 20-39. **Special facilities:** Museum.

Freshman class profile. 1,969 applied, 1,320 admitted, 259 enrolled.

Mid 50% test scores			
SAT verbal:	410-540	Return as sophomores:	61%
SAT math:	410-540	Out-of-state:	48%
ACT:	18-23	Live on campus:	81%
		International:	5%

Basis for selection. Admissions based on secondary school record and standardized test scores. Essay also important. Math and English placement tests may be required based on ACT or SAT scores. Interview recommended.

High school preparation. 12 units required. Required units include English 4, mathematics 3, social studies 3 and science 2.

2005-2006 Annual costs. Tuition/fees: $15,415. Room/board: $6,230. Books/supplies: $500.

Financial aid. Non-need-based: Scholarships awarded for academics, athletics, leadership, religious affiliation, state residency.

Application procedures. Admission: No deadline. No application fee. Application may be submitted online. Admission notification on a rolling basis. **Financial aid:** Closing date 2/15. FAFSA required. Applicants notified on a rolling basis starting 3/1; must reply within 3 week(s) of notification.

Academics. Semesters are comprised of 4 blocks, each 3 1/2 weeks long. Students take one course per block. Students and faculty can concentrate on one course at a time. Intensive 16-month professional studies program designed for non-traditional students also offered. **Special study options:** Accelerated study, double major, honors, independent study, internships, student-designed major, study abroad, teacher certification program. **Credit/placement by examination:** AP, CLEP, institutional tests. 30 credit hours maximum toward bachelor's degree. **Support services:** Learning center, pre-admission summer program, study skills assistance, tutoring, writing center.

Majors. Biology: General. **Business:** Accounting, business admin, entrepreneurial studies. **Communications:** Journalism. **Conservation:** General, environmental studies. **Education:** Art, early childhood, elementary, English, history, mathematics, middle, physical, science, secondary, special. **Health:** Athletic training, clinical lab science, premedicine, prepharmacy. **History:** General. **Interdisciplinary:** Museum. **Legal studies:** Prelaw. **Math:** General. **Parks/recreation:** Health/fitness, sports admin. **Psychology:** General. **Social sciences:** Political science. **Visual/performing arts:** General.

Most popular majors. Business/marketing 71%, education 22%.

Computing on campus. 160 workstations in library, computer center, student center. Dormitories wired for high-speed internet access and linked to campus network. Commuter students can connect to campus network. Online library, helpline, repair service available.

Student life. Freshman orientation: Mandatory. Preregistration for classes offered. **Policies:** Freshmen permitted cars on campus. **Housing:** Guaranteed on-campus for freshmen. Single-sex dorms available. $200 nonrefundable deposit, deadline 6/1. **Activities:** Choral groups, drama, literary magazine, radio station, student government, student newspaper, Bonwandi, Campus Activities Board, Fellowship of Christian Athletes, "Tusculana" yearbook.

Athletics. NAIA, NCAA. **Intercollegiate:** Baseball M, basketball, cheerleading M, cross-country, football (tackle) M, golf, soccer, softball W, tennis, volleyball W. **Intramural:** Basketball, football (tackle) M, soccer, softball, table tennis, tennis, volleyball. **Team name:** Pioneers.

Student services. Adult student services, campus ministries, career counseling, student employment services, health services, personal counseling, placement for graduates, veterans' counselor.

Contact. E-mail: gwolf@tusculum.edu
Phone: (423) 636-7300 Toll-free number: (800) 729-0256
Fax: (423) 638-7166
Tony England, Director of Admissions, Tusculum College, 60 Shiloh Road, Greeneville, TN 37743

Union University

Jackson, Tennessee
www.uu.edu **CB code: 1826**

- Private 4-year university and liberal arts college affiliated with Southern Baptist Convention
- Residential campus in small city
- 2,038 degree-seeking undergraduates: 21% part-time, 61% women, 8% African American, 1% Asian American, 1% Hispanic American, 2% international
- 776 degree-seeking graduate students
- 86% of applicants admitted
- SAT or ACT (ACT writing optional) required
- 59% graduate within 6 years

General. Founded in 1823. Regionally accredited. **Degrees:** 428 bachelor's, 2 associate awarded; master's, doctoral offered. **Location:** 80 miles from Memphis, 120 miles from Nashville. **Calendar:** Semester, extensive summer session. **Full-time faculty:** 152 total; 82% have terminal degrees, 7% minority, 42% women. **Part-time faculty:** 126 total; 36% have terminal degrees, 14% minority, 60% women. **Class size:** 73% < 20, 23% 20-39, 3% 40-49, 1% 50-99. **Special facilities:** Aquatic center, creative communications center, health and wellness center.

Freshman class profile. 1,090 applied, 936 admitted, 408 enrolled.

Mid 50% test scores		Rank in top quarter:	66%
SAT verbal:	530-650	Rank in top tenth:	37%
SAT math:	510-620	Out-of-state:	39%
ACT:	22-27	Live on campus:	89%
GPA 3.50 or higher:	65%	International:	2%
GPA 3.0-3.49:	23%	Fraternities:	12%
GPA 2.0-2.99:	11%	Sororities:	19%

Basis for selection. School achievement, recommendations, special talents, test scores important. Minimum 22 ACT or 1030 SAT (exclusive of Writing), top 50% of high school class, and 2.5 GPA required. SAT and SAT Subject Tests or ACT recommended. Interview recommended for all; audition required for music; portfolio recommended for art, communications. Essay required for academic and leadership scholarships.

High school preparation. 15 units required; 22 recommended. Required and recommended units include English 4, mathematics 3-4, social studies 2, history 1-2, science 3-4 (laboratory 2), foreign language 1-2 and academic electives 1-4.

2005-2006 Annual costs. Tuition/fees: $16,450. Room/board: $5,790. Books/supplies: $600.

2005-2006 Financial aid. Need-based: 352 full-time freshmen applied for aid; 287 were judged to have need; 287 of these received aid. Average scholarship/grant was $8,010; average loan $3,316. 43% of total undergraduate aid awarded as scholarships/grants, 57% as loans/jobs. **Non-need-based:** Awarded to 694 full-time undergraduates, including 182 freshmen. Scholarships awarded for academics, alumni affiliation, art, athletics, leadership, minority status, music/drama, religious affiliation.

Application procedures. Admission: Priority date 12/1; deadline 8/1 (postmark date). $25 fee, may be waived for applicants with need. Application may be submitted online. Admission notification on a rolling basis beginning on or about 11/1. Must reply by May 1 or within 2 week(s) if notified thereafter. **Financial aid:** Priority date 2/1, closing date 3/1. FAFSA, institutional form required. Applicants notified on a rolling basis starting 2/15; must reply by 5/1 or within 2 week(s) of notification.

Academics. Special study options: Accelerated study, combined bachelor's/graduate degree, cooperative education, cross-registration, distance learning, double major, dual enrollment of high school students, ESL, exchange student, honors, independent study, internships, study abroad, teacher certification program, Washington semester. **Credit/placement by examination:** CLEP, IB, institutional tests. 32 credit hours maximum toward bachelor's degree. **Support services:** Learning center, pre-admission summer program, reduced course load, remedial instruction, study skills assistance, tutoring.

Majors. Biology: General. **Business:** Accounting, business admin, finance, international, management science, managerial economics, marketing. **Communications:** General, advertising, broadcast journalism, digital media, journalism, public relations. **Computer sciences:** General. **Education:** General, art, biology, business, chemistry, early childhood, early childhood special, elementary, English, ESL, foreign languages, French, history, mathematics, middle, music, physical, science, secondary, Spanish, special. **Engineering:** Electrical, mechanical. **English:** Composition, speech/rhetoric. **Family/consumer sciences:** Family systems. **Foreign languages:** French, Spanish. **Health:** Athletic training, clinical lab technology, nursing (RN), predentistry, premedicine, preop/surgical nursing, prepharmacy, preveterinary. **History:** General. **Interdisciplinary:** Intercultural. **Legal studies:** Prelaw. **Math:** General. **Parks/recreation:** Exercise sciences, sports admin. **Philosophy/religion:** Ethics, philosophy. **Physical sciences:** General, chemical physics, chemistry, physics. **Psychology:** General. **Public administration:** Social work. **Social sciences:** Economics, political science, sociology. **Theology:** Bible, sacred music, theology, youth ministry. **Visual/performing arts:** Art, dramatic, music performance, music theory/composition, piano/organ, sculpture, voice/opera.

Most popular majors. Business/marketing 21%, education 9%, health sciences 27%, philosophy/religious studies 7%.

Computing on campus. 215 workstations in dormitories, library, computer center, student center. Dormitories wired for high-speed internet access and linked to campus network. Commuter students can connect to campus network. Online course registration, online library, helpline, repair service, wireless network available.

Student life. Freshman orientation: Available, $70 fee. Preregistration for classes offered. Held 4 days before classes begin for freshmen and transfer students. **Policies:** Full-time resident students required to attend 14 chapel services per semester. Smoke and alcohol-free campus. Religious observance required. Freshmen permitted cars on campus. **Housing:** Guaranteed on-campus for all undergraduates. Single-sex dorms, special housing for disabled, apartments available. $100 nonrefundable deposit, deadline 5/1. **Activities:** Bands, choral groups, drama, film society, literary magazine, music ensembles, musical theater, opera, student government, student newspaper, symphony orchestra, TV station, Fellowship of Christian Athletes, Ministerial Association, student activity council, Mu Kappa, honors student association, Tennessee Intercollegiate State Legislature, international student organization, LIFE Groups, Klemata, weekend ministry teams.

Athletics. NAIA. **Intercollegiate:** Baseball M, basketball, cheerleading M, cross-country, golf M, soccer, softball W, tennis, volleyball W. **Intramural:** Basketball, cheerleading W, cross-country, football (non-tackle), golf, racquetball, softball, swimming, table tennis, tennis, volleyball, weight lifting. **Team name:** Bulldogs.

Student services. Adult student services, alcohol/substance abuse counseling, campus ministries, career counseling, student employment services, financial aid counseling, health services, personal counseling, placement for graduates, veterans' counselor. **Physically disabled:** Services for visually, speech, hearing impaired.

Contact. E-mail: info@uu.edu
Phone: (731) 661-5000 Toll-free number: (800) 338-6466
Fax: (731) 661-5017
Rich Grimm, Vice President for Enrollment Services, Union University, 1050 Union University Drive, Jackson, TN 38305-3697

University of Memphis

Memphis, Tennessee
www.memphis.edu **CB code: 1459**

- Public 4-year university
- Commuter campus in very large city
- 15,228 degree-seeking undergraduates: 25% part-time, 61% women, 38% African American, 2% Asian American, 1% Hispanic American, 2% international
- 3,612 degree-seeking graduate students
- 71% of applicants admitted
- SAT or ACT (ACT writing optional) required
- 35% graduate within 6 years

General. Founded in 1912. Regionally accredited. **Degrees:** 2,328 bachelor's awarded; master's, doctoral, first professional offered. **ROTC:** Army, Navy, Air Force. **Location:** 10 miles from downtown. **Calendar:** Semester, extensive summer session. **Full-time faculty:** 743 total; 78% have terminal degrees, 20% minority, 36% women. **Part-time faculty:** 542 total; 32% have terminal degrees, 18% minority, 55% women. **Class size:** 39% < 20, 47% 20-39, 5% 40-49, 8% 50-99, 2% >100. **Special facilities:** Technology institute, Chucalissa Indian Village and Museum, speech and hearing center, Institute of Egyptian Art and Archaeology, center for earthquake research.

Freshman class profile. 5,131 applied, 3,665 admitted, 2,073 enrolled.

Mid 50% test scores		Rank in top quarter:	45%
SAT verbal:	460-600	Rank in top tenth:	18%
SAT math:	480-600	Return as sophomores:	72%
ACT:	18-24	Out-of-state:	7%
GPA 3.50 or higher:	27%	Live on campus:	27%
GPA 3.0-3.49:	34%	International:	2%
GPA 2.0-2.99:	38%		

Basis for selection. High school GPA and test scores are important. Applicants whose Admisssion Index (3.0 GPA+ACT) is 95 or greater, will be guaranteed admission. Applicants who do not meet the Admission Index requirement but provide an ACT composite score of 26 or greater or a cumulative GPA of 3.0 or greater will also be admitted. Interview required for university college; audition required for music; portfolio required for fine arts. **Homeschooled:** Transcript of courses and grades required. Applicants must comply with state law by submitting proof of registration with the local education agency.

High school preparation. Required units include English 4, mathematics 3, social studies 2, history 1, science 2 (laboratory 1) and foreign language 2. 1 visual and/or performing arts also required.

2005-2006 Annual costs. Tuition/fees: $5,084; $14,898 out-of-state. Room/board: $6,069. Books/supplies: $900.

2004-2005 Financial aid. All financial aid based on need. 1,412 full-time freshmen applied for aid; 1,063 were judged to have need; 1,043 of these received aid. Average need met was 82%. Average scholarship/grant was $3,299; average loan $1,665. 50% of total undergraduate aid awarded as scholarships/grants, 50% as loans/jobs.

Application procedures. Admission: Closing date 7/1 (postmark date). $25 fee. Application may be submitted online. Admission notification on a rolling basis. Must reply by registration deadline. **Financial aid:** Priority date 3/1, closing date 6/30. FAFSA required. Applicants notified on a rolling basis starting 3/1; must reply within 2 week(s) of notification.

Academics. University enables students to create non-traditional degrees. **Special study options:** Accelerated study, combined bachelor's/graduate degree, cooperative education, cross-registration, distance learning, double major, dual enrollment of high school students, ESL, exchange student, external degree, honors, independent study, internships, liberal arts/career combination, student-designed major, study abroad, teacher certification program. **Credit/placement by examination:** AP, CLEP, IB, SAT, ACT, institutional tests. Number of credits awarded decided by individual departments. **Support services:** Learning center, pre-admission summer program, reduced course load, remedial instruction, study skills assistance, tutoring, writing center.

Honors college/program. ACT of 27 or high or a combined SAT score of 1200 or more (exclusive of Writing); 3.5 cumulative high school GPA.

Majors. Architecture: Architecture. **Area/ethnic studies:** African-American. **Biology:** General. **Business:** Accounting, business admin, finance, hospitality admin, international, logistics, management information systems, managerial economics, marketing, resort management, sales/distribution. **Communications:** Journalism, media studies. **Computer sciences:** Computer science. **Education:** Elementary, multi-level teacher, physical, special. **Engineering:** Biomedical, civil, computer, electrical, mechanical. **Engineering technology:** Computer, electrical, manufacturing. **English:** English lit. **Foreign languages:** General. **Health:** Nursing (RN). **History:** General. **Liberal arts:** Arts/sciences. **Math:** General. **Parks/recreation:** Exercise sciences, sports admin. **Philosophy/religion:** Philosophy. **Physical sciences:** Chemistry, geology, physics. **Protective services:** Law enforcement admin.

Psychology: General. **Public administration:** Social work. **Social sciences:** Anthropology, economics, geography, international relations, political science, sociology. **Visual/performing arts:** Art, art history/conservation, dramatic, music management.

Most popular majors. Business/marketing 20%, communications/journalism 8%, education 8%, interdisciplinary studies 10%, psychology 6%, social sciences 7%, visual/performing arts 6%.

Computing on campus. 2,000 workstations in dormitories, library, computer center, student center. Dormitories linked to campus network. Commuter students can connect to campus network. Online course registration, online library, helpline, repair service, wireless network available.

Student life. Freshman orientation: Mandatory. Preregistration for classes offered. One- or 2-day sessions, evening program for adult students. Fees vary by program. **Policies:** Freshmen permitted cars on campus. **Housing:** Coed dorms, single-sex dorms, special housing for disabled, apartments, fraternity/sorority housing available. **Activities:** Bands, choral groups, dance, drama, literary magazine, music ensembles, musical theater, opera, radio station, student government, student newspaper, symphony orchestra.

Athletics. NCAA. **Intercollegiate:** Baseball M, basketball, cross-country, football (tackle) M, golf, rifle, soccer, softball W, tennis, track and field, volleyball W. **Intramural:** Basketball, bowling, cross-country, football (non-tackle), golf, racquetball, soccer, softball, table tennis, tennis, volleyball. **Team name:** Tigers.

Student services. Adult student services, career counseling, student employment services, health services, minority student services, on-campus daycare, personal counseling, placement for graduates, veterans' counselor, women's services. **Physically disabled:** Services for visually, speech, hearing impaired.

Contact. E-mail: recruitment@memphis.edu
Phone: (901) 678-2111 Toll-free number: (800) 669-2678
Fax: (901) 678-3053
David Wallace, Director of Admissions, University of Memphis, 101 Wilder Tower, Memphis, TN 38152

University of Tennessee Health Science Center

Memphis, Tennessee
www.utmem.edu **CB code: 1850**

- Public upper-division university and health science college
- Commuter campus in very large city

General. Founded in 1911. Regionally accredited. **Location:** 220 miles from Nashville, 299 miles from St. Louis, Missouri. **Calendar:** Semester.

Annual costs/financial aid. Tuition/fees (2005-2006): $4,149; $9,593 out-of-state. Above cost are for bachelor's program in nursing. Other programs vary by cost. Need-based financial aid available to full-time and part-time students.

Contact. Phone: (901) 448-5560
Registrar, 800 Madison Avenue, Memphis, TN 38163

University of Tennessee: Chattanooga

Chattanooga, Tennessee
www.utc.edu **CB code: 1831**

- Public 4-year university
- Commuter campus in large city
- 7,115 degree-seeking undergraduates: 13% part-time, 57% women, 23% African American, 3% Asian American, 1% Hispanic American, 1% Native American, 1% international
- 1,318 degree-seeking graduate students
- 84% of applicants admitted
- SAT or ACT (ACT writing optional) required
- 45% graduate within 6 years

General. Founded in 1886. Regionally accredited. **Degrees:** 1,290 bachelor's awarded; master's, doctoral, first professional offered. **Location:** 130 miles from Nashville, 118 miles from Atlanta. **Calendar:** Semester, extensive summer session. **Full-time faculty:** 372 total; 76% have terminal degrees, 11% minority, 44% women. **Part-time faculty:** 249 total; 18% have terminal degrees, 9% minority, 51% women. **Class size:** 38% < 20, 50% 20-39, 9% 40-49, 3% 50-99, less than 1% >100. **Special facilities:** 2 art galleries, theater, observatory.

Freshman class profile. 3,580 applied, 3,021 admitted, 1,454 enrolled.

Mid 50% test scores		**GPA 2.0-2.99:**	31%
ACT:	17-23	**Return as sophomores:**	64%
GPA 3.50 or higher:	20%	**Out-of-state:**	6%
GPA 3.0-3.49:	24%	**Live on campus:**	70%

Basis for selection. High school curriculum and GPA (minimum 2.75), test scores, special talents, recommendations, essay or personal statement considered. Conditional admission for GPA between 2.0 and 2.74 and SAT combined score between 640 and 900 (exclusive of Writing) or ACT composite score between 12 and 19. Essay recommended.

High school preparation. 14 units required; 15 recommended. Required and recommended units include English 4, mathematics 3, social studies 2, history 1, science 2-4 (laboratory 2) and foreign language 2. Foreign language units must be in same language. Social science units should be US history and world/European history or world geography, one fine arts unit.

2005-2006 Annual costs. Tuition/fees: $4,500; $14,424 out-of-state. Room/board: $6,474. Books/supplies: $900. Personal expenses: $1,272.

2005-2006 Financial aid. Need-based: 1,296 full-time freshmen applied for aid; 787 were judged to have need; 729 of these received aid. Average need met was 83%. Average scholarship/grant was $3,865; average loan $2,560. 41% of total undergraduate aid awarded as scholarships/grants, 59% as loans/jobs. **Non-need-based:** Awarded to 3,362 full-time undergraduates, including 995 freshmen. Scholarships awarded for academics, alumni affiliation, art, athletics, job skills, leadership, minority status, music/drama, religious affiliation, state residency.

Application procedures. Admission: Priority date 8/1; no deadline. $25 fee, may be waived for applicants with need. Application may be submitted online. Admission notification on a rolling basis. **Financial aid:** Priority date 4/1; no closing date. FAFSA, institutional form required. Applicants notified on a rolling basis starting 3/15.

Academics. Special study options: Combined bachelor's/graduate degree, cooperative education, cross-registration, distance learning, double major, dual enrollment of high school students, ESL, honors, independent study, internships, study abroad, teacher certification program. Cooperative program in criminal justice with Cleveland State Community College. **Credit/placement by examination:** AP, CLEP, institutional tests. 24 credit hours maximum toward bachelor's degree. May only be used for elective credit hours. **Support services:** Learning center, pre-admission summer program, reduced course load, remedial instruction, study skills assistance, tutoring, writing center.

Majors. Biology: General. **Business:** Business admin. **Communications:** General. **Computer sciences:** General. **Conservation:** General. **Education:** Art, English, foreign languages, mathematics, middle, music, science, secondary, social studies, special. **Engineering:** General. **Engineering technology:** Industrial management. **English:** English lit. **Family/consumer sciences:** General. **Foreign languages:** Classics, French, Latin, Spanish. **Health:** Nursing (RN). **History:** General. **Legal studies:** Paralegal. **Liberal arts:** Arts/sciences, humanities. **Math:** General, applied. **Parks/recreation:** Exercise sciences. **Physical sciences:** Chemistry, geology, physics. **Protective services:** Law enforcement admin. **Psychology:** General. **Public administration:** Community org/advocacy, social work. **Social sciences:** General, economics, political science, sociology. **Visual/performing arts:** Art, dramatic.

Most popular majors. Business/marketing 26%, education 8%, family/consumer sciences 8%, health sciences 7%, psychology 6%.

Computing on campus. 1,200 workstations in library, computer center, student center. Dormitories wired for high-speed internet access and linked to campus network. Commuter students can connect to campus network. Online course registration, online library, helpline, wireless network available.

Student life. Freshman orientation: Mandatory, $50 fee. Preregistration for classes offered. Held in summer, 2 days, at 5 different times. **Policies:** Freshmen permitted cars on campus. **Housing:** Coed dorms, apartments, fraternity/sorority housing available. $75 partly refundable deposit. **Activities:** Bands, choral groups, dance, drama, film society, music ensembles, radio station, student government, student newspaper, symphony orchestra, several religious, political, ethnic, and social service organizations.

Athletics. NCAA. **Intercollegiate:** Basketball, cross-country, football (tackle) M, golf, rowing (crew), soccer W, softball W, tennis, track and field, volleyball W, wrestling M. **Intramural:** Archery, badminton, basketball, bowling, fencing, football (non-tackle), golf, racquetball, soccer, softball W, swimming, table tennis, tennis, track and field, volleyball, weight lifting, wrestling M. **Team name:** Moccasins.

Student services. Adult student services, campus ministries, career counseling, student employment services, financial aid counseling, health services, minority student services, on-campus daycare, personal counseling, placement for graduates, veterans' counselor. **Physically disabled:** Services for visually, hearing impaired.

Contact. E-mail: yancy-freeman@utc.edu
Phone: (423) 425-4662 Toll-free number: (800) 882-6627
Fax: (423) 425-4157
Yancy Freeman, Director of Student Recruitment and Admissions, University of Tennessee: Chattanooga, 615 McCallie Avenue, Chattanooga, TN 37403

University of Tennessee: Knoxville

Knoxville, Tennessee **CB member**
www.tennessee.edu **CB code: 1843**

- Public 4-year university
- Residential campus in large city
- 19,878 degree-seeking undergraduates: 6% part-time, 51% women, 9% African American, 3% Asian American, 1% Hispanic American, 1% international
- 10,419 degree-seeking graduate students
- 74% of applicants admitted
- SAT or ACT, application essay required
- 57% graduate within 6 years

General. Founded in 1794. Regionally accredited. **Degrees:** 3,762 bachelor's awarded; master's, doctoral, first professional offered. **ROTC:** Army, Air Force. **Location:** 224 miles from Atlanta, 178 miles from Nashville. **Calendar:** Semester, extensive summer session. **Full-time faculty:** 1,476 total; 82% have terminal degrees, 14% minority, 35% women. **Part-time faculty:** 81 total; 78% have terminal degrees, 9% minority, 32% women. **Class size:** 37% < 20, 50% 20-39, 6% 40-49, 5% 50-99, 2% >100. **Special facilities:** Museum, 2 theaters, science/engineering research facility, international house, Olympic track, baseball stadium.

Freshman class profile. 12,251 applied, 9,060 admitted, 4,265 enrolled.

Mid 50% test scores		**Rank in top tenth:**	34%
SAT verbal:	520-630	**Return as sophomores:**	80%
SAT math:	530-640	**Out-of-state:**	17%
ACT:	23-28	**Live on campus:**	91%
GPA 3.50 or higher:	59%	**International:**	1%
GPA 3.0-3.49:	27%	**Fraternities:**	25%
GPA 2.0-2.99:	13%	**Sororities:**	23%
Rank in top quarter:	63%		

Basis for selection. Admission based on high school grades in core academic subjects and standardized test scores. Other factors that indicate future academic success considered, as are special talents, student statement, extracurricular leadership, community involvement, class rank, and background. Essay required, portfolio recommended for architecture; audition required for music; interview recommended for marginally prepared, reentry.

High school preparation. 14 units required. Required units include English 4, mathematics 3, social studies 1, history 1, science 2 (laboratory 1), foreign language 2 and academic electives 1. Social science units must be 1 US history and either world history, European history, or world geography. Mathematics units must include algebra I, algebra II, and 1 unit of either geometry, trigonometry, advanced mathematics, or calculus. One unit of fine or performing arts required. One unit of visual or performing arts required.

2005-2006 Annual costs. Tuition/fees: $5,290; $16,060 out-of-state. Out-of-state students pay additional required fees. Room/board: $5,210. Books/supplies: $998. Personal expenses: $2,002.

2004-2005 Financial aid. All financial aid based on need. 2,161 full-time freshmen applied for aid; 1,403 were judged to have need; 1,314 of these received aid. Average need met was 66%. Average scholarship/grant was $6,225; average loan $2,582. 40% of total undergraduate aid awarded as scholarships/grants, 60% as loans/jobs. **Additional information:** Application priority date for scholarships 2/1.

Application procedures. Admission: Priority date 11/1; deadline 2/1 (postmark date). $25 fee, may be waived for applicants with need. Application may be submitted online. Admission notification on a rolling basis beginning on or about 2/1. Must reply by 5/1. **Financial aid:** Priority date 3/1; no closing date. FAFSA required. Applicants notified on a rolling basis starting 3/15; must reply within 3 week(s) of notification.

Academics. Special study options: Combined bachelor's/graduate degree, cooperative education, distance learning, double major, dual enrollment of high school students, ESL, exchange student, honors, independent study, internships, liberal arts/career combination, student-designed major, study abroad, teacher certification program. **Credit/placement by examination:** AP, CLEP, IB, institutional tests. Departmental proficiency available. Up to 50 hours of credit awarded for International Baccalaureate. **Support services:** Study skills assistance, tutoring, writing center.

Majors. Agriculture: Animal sciences, food science, ornamental horticulture, plant sciences, soil science. **Architecture:** Architecture. **Area/ethnic studies:** African-American, American, Asian, Latin American, Russian/Slavic, women's. **Biology:** General, bacteriology, biochemistry, botany, zoology. **Business:** General, accounting, business admin, finance, logistics, statistics. **Communications:** Advertising, broadcast journalism, journalism. **Computer sciences:** General, computer science. **Conservation:** Forestry. **Education:** General, agricultural, art, business, Deaf/hearing impaired, early childhood, family/consumer sciences, music, sales/marketing, trade/industrial. **Engineering:** Aerospace, agricultural, chemical, civil, electrical, materials science, mechanical, nuclear, physics, science. **English:** Composition. **Family/consumer sciences:** General, clothing/textiles, family/community services, food/nutrition. **Foreign languages:** Ancient Greek, classics, comparative lit, French, Italian, Latin, linguistics, Portuguese, Russian, Spanish. **Health:** Audiology/hearing, clinical lab science, dental hygiene, medical radiologic technology/radiation therapy, nursing (RN), occupational health nursing, office admin, optician, predentistry, premedicine, preop/surgical nursing, prepharmacy, preveterinary, speech pathology. **History:** General. **Interdisciplinary:** Medieval/Renaissance. **Legal studies:** Prelaw. **Math:** General. **Parks/recreation:** General, exercise sciences, health/fitness, sports admin. **Philosophy/religion:** Philosophy, religion. **Physical sciences:** Chemistry, geology, physics. **Protective services:** Criminal justice. **Psychology:** General. **Public administration:** General, social work. **Social sciences:** Anthropology, economics, geography, political science, sociology, urban studies. **Visual/performing arts:** Art, art history/conservation, commercial/advertising art, dramatic, film/cinema, interior design, music theory/composition, piano/organ, studio arts, voice/opera.

Most popular majors. Business/marketing 16%, communications/journalism 8%, engineering/engineering technologies 8%, health sciences 6%, psychology 10%, social sciences 13%.

Computing on campus. 1,000 workstations in dormitories, library, computer center, student center. Dormitories linked to campus network. Commuter students can connect to campus network. Online course registration, helpline, repair service, student web hosting available.

Student life. Freshman orientation: Mandatory, $85 fee. Preregistration for classes offered. Orientation charge includes all expenses for 2 days for students. Parents may also attend orientation for $20 per parent. Fee does not include housing. **Policies:** Freshmen permitted cars on campus. **Housing:** Guaranteed on-campus for freshmen. Coed dorms, single-sex dorms, apartments, fraternity/sorority housing available. $15 deposit, deadline 2/1. Foreign language housing available. Freshmen must live on campus unless residing with parent or legal guardian. **Activities:** Bands, choral groups, dance, drama, film society, literary magazine, music ensembles, musical theater, opera, radio station, student government, student newspaper, symphony orchestra, Black cultural center, variety of student political, ethnic, social, and service organizations, women's center.

Athletics. NCAA. **Intercollegiate:** Baseball M, basketball, cricket, cross-country, diving, football (tackle) M, golf, rowing (crew) W, soccer W, softball W, swimming, tennis, track and field, volleyball W. **Intramural:** Badminton, basketball, bowling, cross-country, field hockey, golf, racquetball, skin diving, soccer, softball, swimming, table tennis, tennis, track and field, volleyball. **Team name:** Volunteers.

Student services. Adult student services, alcohol/substance abuse counseling, campus ministries, career counseling, student employment services, financial aid counseling, health services, minority student services, on-campus daycare, personal counseling, placement for graduates, veterans' counselor, women's services. **Physically disabled:** Services for visually, speech, hearing impaired.

Contact. E-mail: admissions@utk.edu
Phone: (865) 974-2184 Toll-free number: (800) 221-8657
Fax: (865) 974-6341
Nancy McGlasson, Director of Admissions, University of Tennessee: Knoxville, 320 Student Services Building, Knoxville, TN 37996-0230

University of Tennessee: Martin

Martin, Tennessee
www.utm.edu **CB code: 1844**

- Public 4-year university
- Commuter campus in small town

- 5,489 degree-seeking undergraduates: 9% part-time, 57% women, 15% African American, 1% Hispanic American, 2% international
- 483 degree-seeking graduate students
- 78% of applicants admitted
- SAT or ACT (ACT writing optional) required
- 40% graduate within 6 years; 20% enter graduate study

General. Founded in 1927. Regionally accredited. Sponsors only collegiate rodeo team in Tennessee. **Degrees:** 835 bachelor's awarded; master's offered. **ROTC:** Army. **Location:** 125 miles from Memphis, 150 miles from Nashville. **Calendar:** Semester, extensive summer session. **Full-time faculty:** 245 total; 69% have terminal degrees, 11% minority, 43% women. **Part-time faculty:** 171 total; 21% have terminal degrees, 8% minority, 48% women. **Class size:** 49% < 20, 38% 20-39, 5% 40-49, 8% 50-99, less than 1% >100. **Special facilities:** Museum/archives, nature preserve, research farm, center for environmental and conservation education.

Freshman class profile. 2,803 applied, 2,184 admitted, 1,250 enrolled.

Mid 50% test scores			
ACT:	19-24	**End year in good standing:**	74%
GPA 3.50 or higher:	39%	**Return as sophomores:**	71%
GPA 3.0-3.49:	35%	**Out-of-state:**	5%
GPA 2.0-2.99:	26%	**Live on campus:**	65%
Rank in top quarter:	50%	**International:**	1%
Rank in top tenth:	20%	**Fraternities:**	22%
		Sororities:	15%

Basis for selection. School achievement record and test scores very important. High school GPA of 2.75 and minimum ACT composite score of 17, or GPA of 2.40 and minimum ACT score of 20 required. Students not meeting regular admission requirements may be considered for conditional admission. **Homeschooled:** 19 ACT and 2.6 GPA.

High school preparation. College-preparatory program required. 14 units required. Required units include English 4, mathematics 3, history 2, science 2 (laboratory 1) and foreign language 2. Requirements include algebra I and II plus additional unit in geometry or advanced mathematics, 1 laboratory course in biology, chemistry, or physics, 1 US history and additional unit in European history, world history, or geography, 2 units in natural sciences, and 1 unit in fine or performing arts.

2005-2006 Annual costs. Tuition/fees: $4,493; $13,547 out-of-state. Room/board: $4,220. Books/supplies: $1,200. Personal expenses: $2,200.

2005-2006 Financial aid. All financial aid based on need. Average need met was 75%. Average scholarship/grant was $4,493; average loan $2,680. 51% of total undergraduate aid awarded as scholarships/grants, 49% as loans/jobs.

Application procedures. Admission: Priority date 2/1; deadline 8/1. $25 fee. Application may be submitted online. Admission notification on a rolling basis beginning on or about 9/1. **Financial aid:** Priority date 3/1; no closing date. FAFSA required. Applicants notified by 4/1; Applicants notified on a rolling basis starting 4/1.

Academics. Special study options: Accelerated study, cooperative education, distance learning, double major, dual enrollment of high school students, ESL, honors, independent study, internships, student-designed major, study abroad. 3-1 pharmacy program, 3-1 veterinary medicine program, 3-1 dentistry program, 3-1 medicine program, 3-1 optometry program, 3-1 podiatry program, 3-1 chiropractory program. **Credit/placement by examination:** AP, CLEP, ACT, institutional tests. 30 credit hours maximum toward bachelor's degree. **Support services:** Learning center, remedial instruction, study skills assistance, tutoring, writing center.

Honors college/program. University Scholars: approximately 15 freshmen admitted, requires 28 ACT or 1240 SAT (exclusive of Writing), 3.50 high school GPA and complete application. Honors seminar: approximately 70 admitted, requires 28 ACT or 1240 SAT (exclusive of Writing), 3.50 high school GPA and complete application.

Majors. Agriculture: General. **Biology:** General. **Business:** Accounting, business admin, management information systems, managerial economics, marketing. **Communications:** General. **Computer sciences:** Computer science. **Conservation:** Management/policy. **Education:** Biology, business, chemistry, English, French, geography, German, history, mathematics, Spanish, special. **Engineering:** General. **English:** English lit. **Family/consumer sciences:** General. **Foreign languages:** French, Spanish. **Health:** Nursing (RN). **History:** General. **Math:** General. **Parks/recreation:** Health/fitness. **Philosophy/religion:** Philosophy. **Physical sciences:** Chemistry, geology. **Protective services:** Law enforcement admin. **Psychology:** General. **Public administration:** General, social work. **Social sciences:** Economics, international relations, political science, sociology. **Visual/performing arts:** General.

Most popular majors. Agriculture 6%, business/marketing 22%, interdisciplinary studies 20%.

Computing on campus. 836 workstations in dormitories, library, computer center, student center. Dormitories wired for high-speed internet access and linked to campus network. Commuter students can connect to campus network. Online course registration, online library, helpline, repair service, student web hosting, wireless network available.

Student life. Freshman orientation: Available, $165 fee. Preregistration for classes offered. August 26-28, meet with advisor and discuss career choices. **Policies:** Freshmen and sophomores must live on campus. Freshmen permitted cars on campus. **Housing:** Coed dorms, single-sex dorms, special housing for disabled, apartments, fraternity/sorority housing, substance-free housing available. $100 fully refundable deposit, deadline 8/1. Honors floors available. Year-round accommodations available. **Activities:** Bands, choral groups, dance, drama, literary magazine, music ensembles, musical theater, opera, radio station, student government, student newspaper, TV station, student government association, Panhellenic Council, Baptist Collegiate Ministry, Reformed University Fellowship, students for the American Red Cross, Alpha Phi Omega, Black student association, College Republicans, College Democrats, Taiwanese student association.

Athletics. NCAA. **Intercollegiate:** Baseball M, basketball, cheerleading, cross-country, football (tackle) M, golf M, rifle, rodeo, soccer W, softball W, tennis, volleyball W. **Intramural:** Basketball, cross-country, football (non-tackle), golf, soccer, softball, tennis, volleyball. **Team name:** Skyhawks.

Student services. Adult student services, alcohol/substance abuse counseling, campus ministries, career counseling, services for economically disadvantaged, student employment services, financial aid counseling, health services, minority student services, on-campus daycare, personal counseling, placement for graduates, veterans' counselor, women's services. **Physically disabled:** Services for visually, speech, hearing impaired. **Learning disabled:** Comprehensive services available.

Contact. E-mail: jrayburn@utm.edu
Phone: (731) 881-7020 Toll-free number: (800) 829-8861
Fax: (731) 881-7029
Judy Rayburn, Director of Admissions, University of Tennessee: Martin, 200 Hall Moody Administration Building, Martin, TN 38238

University of the South

Sewanee, Tennessee — **CB member**
www.sewanee.edu — **CB code: 1842**

- Private 4-year university affiliated with Episcopal Church
- Residential campus in small town
- 1,402 degree-seeking undergraduates: 54% women, 4% African American, 2% Asian American, 2% Hispanic American, 2% international
- 91 degree-seeking graduate students
- 67% of applicants admitted
- SAT or ACT with writing, application essay required
- 82% graduate within 6 years

General. Founded in 1857. Regionally accredited; also accredited by ATS. **Degrees:** 292 bachelor's awarded; master's, doctoral, first professional offered. **Location:** 45 miles from Chattanooga, 90 miles from Nashville. **Calendar:** Semester, limited summer session. **Full-time faculty:** 130 total; 95% have terminal degrees, 9% minority, 35% women. **Part-time faculty:** 44 total; 68% have terminal degrees, 9% minority, 46% women. **Class size:** 72% < 20, 28% 20-39, less than 1% 40-49. **Special facilities:** Observatory, 10,000-acre wooded campus, hiking and horseback riding trail, materials analysis laboratory with electron microscopy.

Freshman class profile. 2,027 applied, 1,358 admitted, 421 enrolled.

Mid 50% test scores			
SAT verbal:	590-670	**Rank in top tenth:**	42%
SAT math:	570-660	**Return as sophomores:**	88%
ACT:	25-29	**Out-of-state:**	80%
GPA 3.50 or higher:	62%	**Live on campus:**	100%
GPA 3.0-3.49:	29%	**International:**	1%
GPA 2.0-2.99:	9%	**Fraternities:**	64%
Rank in top quarter:	78%	**Sororities:**	57%

Basis for selection. GED not accepted. School achievement record, recommendations, extracurricular activities, test scores, essay important. Children of alumni and minority applicants given special consideration. Interview recommended.

High school preparation. 13 units required; 20 recommended. Required and recommended units include English 4, mathematics 3-4, social studies 1-2, history 1-2, science 2-4 (laboratory 2-3) and foreign language 2-4.

2005-2006 Annual costs. Tuition/fees: $27,095. Room/board: $7,550. Books/supplies: $550. Personal expenses: $810.

2005-2006 Financial aid. Need-based: 248 full-time freshmen applied for aid; 168 were judged to have need; 168 of these received aid. Average need met was 94%. Average scholarship/grant was $17,663; average loan $3,182. 83% of total undergraduate aid awarded as scholarships/grants, 17% as loans/jobs. **Non-need-based:** Awarded to 275 full-time undergraduates, including 76 freshmen. Scholarships awarded for academics, minority status, religious affiliation.

Application procedures. Admission: Closing date 2/1 (postmark date). $45 fee, may be waived for applicants with need. Admission notification 4/1. Must reply by May 1 or within 2 week(s) if notified thereafter. **Financial aid:** Priority date 3/1; no closing date. FAFSA, institutional form required. Applicants notified by 4/1; must reply within 4 week(s) of notification.

Academics. Special study options: Double major, independent study, internships, semester at sea, student-designed major, study abroad, teacher certification program, Washington semester. Oak Ridge semester in experimental science, summer science program on St. Catherines Island, Georgia. **Credit/placement by examination:** AP, CLEP, SAT, ACT, institutional tests. 60 credit hours maximum toward bachelor's degree. **Support services:** Tutoring.

Majors. Area/ethnic studies: American, Asian, French, German, Russian/Slavic. **Biology:** General. **Computer sciences:** General, computer science. **Conservation:** Environmental studies, forestry, management/policy. **Foreign languages:** Ancient Greek, comparative lit, French, German, Latin, modern Greek, Russian, Spanish. **History:** General. **Interdisciplinary:** Math/computer science, medieval/Renaissance. **Math:** General. **Philosophy/religion:** Philosophy, religion. **Physical sciences:** Chemistry, geology, physics. **Psychology:** General. **Social sciences:** Anthropology, economics, political science. **Visual/performing arts:** General, art history/conservation, studio arts.

Most popular majors. Biology 6%, English 18%, foreign language 6%, history 15%, natural resources/environmental science 7%, philosophy/religious studies 7%, psychology 7%, social sciences 15%, visual/performing arts 9%.

Computing on campus. 200 workstations in dormitories, library, computer center. Dormitories wired for high-speed internet access and linked to campus network. Commuter students can connect to campus network. Online course registration, helpline, repair service, student web hosting, wireless network available.

Student life. Freshman orientation: Mandatory. Several days before the college opens in the fall. Students dine with the faculty advisor, sign the Honor Code, and participate in discussions of the summer reading. **Policies:** Student-administered honor code strictly observed. Freshmen permitted cars on campus. **Housing:** Guaranteed on-campus for freshmen. Coed dorms, single-sex dorms, special housing for disabled, apartments, fraternity/sorority housing, substance-free housing available. $300 nonrefundable deposit, deadline 5/1. German, French, Spanish, Russian language houses available. **Activities:** Jazz band, choral groups, dance, drama, film society, literary magazine, music ensembles, musical theater, radio station, student government, student newspaper, symphony orchestra, tutoring center for disadvantaged youth, religious organizations, Big Brother-Big Sister program.

Athletics. NCAA. **Intercollegiate:** Baseball M, basketball, cross-country, diving, equestrian, fencing, field hockey W, football (tackle) M, golf, lacrosse M, rowing (crew), rugby M, skiing, soccer, softball W, swimming, tennis, track and field, volleyball W. **Intramural:** Basketball, cross-country, diving, golf, handball, racquetball, skin diving, soccer, softball, swimming, table tennis, tennis, track and field, volleyball, wrestling M. **Team name:** Tigers.

Student services. Campus ministries, career counseling, student employment services, health services, minority student services, on-campus daycare, personal counseling, placement for graduates. **Physically disabled:** Services for visually, hearing impaired.

Contact. E-mail: collegeadmission@sewanee.edu
Phone: (931) 598-1238 Toll-free number: (800) 522-2234
Fax: (931) 538-3248
David Lesesne, Dean of Admission, University of the South, 735 University Avenue, Sewanee, TN 37383

Vanderbilt University

Nashville, Tennessee — **CB member**
www.vanderbilt.edu — **CB code: 1871**

- Private 4-year university
- Residential campus in very large city
- 6,286 degree-seeking undergraduates: 1% part-time, 52% women, 8% African American, 6% Asian American, 5% Hispanic American, 2% international
- 4,965 degree-seeking graduate students
- 35% of applicants admitted
- SAT or ACT with writing, application essay required
- 88% graduate within 6 years

General. Founded in 1873. Regionally accredited. University's internal divisions include Blair School of Music, Peabody College (education and human development). **Degrees:** 1,519 bachelor's awarded; master's, doctoral, first professional offered. **ROTC:** Army, Navy, Air Force. **Location:** 240 miles from Atlanta, 300 miles from St. Louis. **Calendar:** Semester, limited summer session. **Full-time faculty:** 785 total; 15% minority, 32% women. **Class size:** 66% < 20, 25% 20-39, 3% 40-49, 5% 50-99, 2% >100. **Special facilities:** Observatory, free electron laser, electron microscopes, television news archive, national arboretum, video productions, Black cultural center, women's center, cinema and art museum.

Freshman class profile. 11,663 applied, 4,115 admitted, 1,622 enrolled.

Mid 50% test scores			
SAT verbal:	630-720	Return as sophomores:	95%
SAT math:	650-740	Out-of-state:	84%
ACT:	28-33	Live on campus:	100%
Rank in top quarter:	93%	International:	2%
Rank in top tenth:	77%	Fraternities:	34%
		Sororities:	50%

Basis for selection. Academic achievement, recommendation, essay, test scores, activities important. SAT Subject Tests recommended. Audition required for music program.

High school preparation. 13 units required; 20 recommended. Required and recommended units include English 4, mathematics 3-4, social studies 2-4, science 2-4 (laboratory 2-4) and foreign language 2-4. Additional unit in mathematics and 2 in science recommended for engineering applicants. Blair does not require 2 units of science. Engineering recommends 2 years of language. Peabody does not require language. Peabody, Blair, and Engineering require 1 year of history.

2005-2006 Annual costs. Tuition/fees: $31,730. Room/board: $10,286. Books/supplies: $1,072. Personal expenses: $1,902.

2005-2006 Financial aid. Need-based: 864 full-time freshmen applied for aid; 753 were judged to have need; 751 of these received aid. Average need met was 100%. Average scholarship/grant was $25,749; average loan $3,096. 86% of total undergraduate aid awarded as scholarships/grants, 14% as loans/jobs. **Non-need-based:** Awarded to 2,288 full-time undergraduates, including 734 freshmen. Scholarships awarded for academics, minority status, music/drama, state residency. **Additional information:** Various payment plans available.

Application procedures. Admission: Closing date 1/3. $50 fee, may be waived for applicants with need. Application may be submitted online. Admission notification 4/1. Must reply by 5/1. **Financial aid:** Priority date 2/1; no closing date. FAFSA, CSS PROFILE required. Applicants notified on a rolling basis starting 4/1; must reply by 5/1.

Academics. All undergraduates take portion of coursework in College of Arts and Science. **Special study options:** Accelerated study, combined bachelor's/graduate degree, cooperative education, cross-registration, distance learning, double major, dual enrollment of high school students, ESL, honors, independent study, internships, student-designed major, study abroad, teacher certification program, Washington semester. **Credit/placement by examination:** CLEP, IB, institutional tests. 30 credit hours maximum toward bachelor's degree. **Support services:** Learning center, tutoring.

Majors. Area/ethnic studies: African, African-American, American, East Asian, European, Latin American. **Biology:** Molecular. **Business:** Human resources. **Communications:** General. **Computer sciences:** General. **Education:** General, early childhood, elementary, secondary, social studies, special. **Engineering:** Biomedical, chemical, civil, computer, electrical, mechanical, science. **Family/consumer sciences:** Family studies. **Foreign languages:** General, classics, French, German, Russian, Spanish. **History:** General. **Math:** General. **Philosophy/religion:** Philosophy, religion. **Physical sciences:** Chemistry, geology, physics. **Psychology:** General. **Social sciences:** Anthropology, economics, political science, sociology, urban studies. **Visual/performing arts:** Dramatic, music performance, music theory/composition, studio arts.

Most popular majors. Engineering/engineering technologies 14%, English 6%, foreign language 6%, psychology 7%, social sciences 27%.

Computing on campus. 400 workstations in library, computer center, student center. Dormitories wired for high-speed internet access and linked

to campus network. Commuter students can connect to campus network. Online course registration, online library, helpline, repair service, student web hosting, wireless network available.

Student life. Freshman orientation: Mandatory. Preregistration for classes offered. Series of programs to introduce students to faculty, staff, facilities, campus organizations. Academic and social programs also included. **Housing:** Guaranteed on-campus for freshmen. Coed dorms, single-sex dorms, special housing for disabled, apartments available. Housing for students with interest in foreign languages or philosophy available. **Activities:** Bands, choral groups, dance, drama, film society, literary magazine, music ensembles, musical theater, opera, radio station, student government, student newspaper, symphony orchestra, over 200 clubs and organizations.

Athletics. NCAA. **Intercollegiate:** Baseball M, basketball, bowling W, cross-country, football (tackle) M, golf, lacrosse W, soccer, tennis, track and field W. **Intramural:** Badminton, basketball, bowling, football (non-tackle), golf, racquetball, soccer, softball, squash, swimming, table tennis, tennis, track and field, volleyball, water polo, wrestling.

Student services. Alcohol/substance abuse counseling, campus ministries, career counseling, student employment services, financial aid counseling, health services, minority student services, on-campus daycare, personal counseling, placement for graduates, women's services. **Physically disabled:** Services for visually, speech, hearing impaired.

Contact. E-mail: admissions@vanderbilt.edu
Phone: (615) 322-2561 Toll-free number: (800) 288-0432
Fax: (615) 343-7765
William Shain, Dean of Undergraduate Admissions, Vanderbilt University, 2305 West End Avenue, Nashville, TN 37203-1727

Williamson Christian College
Franklin, Tennessee
www.williamsoncc.edu

- Private 4-year liberal arts college affiliated with interdenominational tradition
- Commuter campus in small city
- 58 degree-seeking undergraduates

General. Accredited by ABHE. Accelerated degree completion programs available for working adults. **Degrees:** 12 bachelor's awarded. **Location:** 15 miles from downtown. **Calendar:** Semester, limited summer session. **Full-time faculty:** 4 total. **Part-time faculty:** 25 total. **Class size:** 100% < 20.

Basis for selection. Open admission, but selective for some programs.

2005-2006 Annual costs. Tuition/fees: $6,780. Books/supplies: $800. Personal expenses: $3,800.

Application procedures. Admission: No deadline. $25 fee. Application must be submitted on paper. Admission notification on a rolling basis. **Financial aid:** No deadline.

Academics. Special study options: Accelerated study, distance learning, liberal arts/career combination, weekend college. **Credit/placement by examination:** CLEP. 15 credit hours maximum toward associate degree, 32 toward bachelor's.

Majors. Business: Nonprofit/public. **Philosophy/religion:** Religion.

Most popular majors. Business/marketing 50%, philosophy/religious studies 50%.

Computing on campus. 3 workstations in computer center.

Student life. Policies: Freshmen permitted cars on campus. **Activities:** Student government.

Student services. Adult student services, campus ministries, financial aid counseling, personal counseling.

Contact. E-mail: lucy@williamsoncc.edu
Phone: (615) 771-7821 Fax: (615) 771-7810
Lucy Sircy, Director of Admissions, Williamson Christian College, 200 Seaboard Lane, Franklin, TN 37067

Texas

Abilene Christian University

Abilene, Texas
www.acu.edu
CB member
CB code: 6001

- Private 4-year university affiliated with Church of Christ
- Residential campus in small city
- 4,079 degree-seeking undergraduates: 4% part-time, 55% women, 7% African American, 1% Asian American, 7% Hispanic American, 1% Native American, 4% international
- 544 degree-seeking graduate students
- 54% of applicants admitted
- SAT or ACT (ACT writing optional) required
- 56% graduate within 6 years

General. Founded in 1906. Regionally accredited. **Degrees:** 812 bachelor's awarded; master's, doctoral, first professional offered. **Location:** 180 miles from Dallas. **Calendar:** Semester, limited summer session. **Full-time faculty:** 218 total; 78% have terminal degrees, 8% minority, 33% women. **Part-time faculty:** 141 total; 24% have terminal degrees, 6% minority, 46% women. **Class size:** 45% < 20, 41% 20-39, 6% 40-49, 7% 50-99, less than 1% >100. **Special facilities:** Observatory, 3 college farms (for agriculture majors), center for Biblical studies, voice institute.

Freshman class profile. 3,695 applied, 1,990 admitted, 1,020 enrolled.

Mid 50% test scores			
SAT verbal:	490-630	Rank in top tenth:	22%
SAT math:	490-620	Return as sophomores:	73%
ACT:	20-26	Out-of-state:	18%
Rank in top quarter:	50%	Live on campus:	95%
		International:	2%

Basis for selection. Rank in top half of class and/or 960 SAT (exclusive of Writing) or 20 ACT required. Interview, portfolio recommended for all; audition required for debate, forensics, music, theater programs. **Homeschooled:** Transcript of courses and grades required.

High school preparation. 12 units recommended. Recommended units include English 4, mathematics 3, science 3 (laboratory 2) and foreign language 2.

2005-2006 Annual costs. Tuition/fees: $15,160. Room/board: $5,670. Books/supplies: $800. Personal expenses: $1,578.

2004-2005 Financial aid. Need-based: 941 full-time freshmen applied for aid; 572 were judged to have need; 570 of these received aid. Average need met was 73%. Average scholarship/grant was $8,057; average loan $2,830. 45% of total undergraduate aid awarded as scholarships/grants, 55% as loans/jobs. **Non-need-based:** Awarded to 3,009 full-time undergraduates, including 865 freshmen. Scholarships awarded for academics, art, athletics, leadership, minority status, music/drama, religious affiliation, state residency. **Additional information:** Early estimate service available.

Application procedures. Admission: Priority date 2/1; deadline 8/1 (postmark date). $25 fee. Application may be submitted online. Admission notification on a rolling basis beginning on or about 8/1. **Financial aid:** Priority date 3/1; no closing date. FAFSA, institutional form required. Applicants notified on a rolling basis starting 4/1.

Academics. Special study options: Cross-registration, distance learning, double major, dual enrollment of high school students, ESL, honors, independent study, internships, student-designed major, study abroad, teacher certification program. Campus abroad programs in England, Mexico, Uruguay; pass/fail grading option. **Credit/placement by examination:** AP, CLEP, IB, institutional tests. 15 credit hours maximum toward associate degree, 30 toward bachelor's. **Support services:** Pre-admission summer program, reduced course load, remedial instruction, study skills assistance, tutoring.

Majors. Agriculture: Agribusiness operations, animal sciences. **Biology:** General, biochemistry. **Business:** Accounting, business admin, finance, marketing. **Communications:** Digital media, journalism. **Computer sciences:** Computer science. **Conservation:** Environmental science. **Education:** Art, biology, elementary, English, history, mathematics, middle, music, physical, reading, science, secondary, social studies, Spanish, special. **Engineering:** General, computer hardware, physics, science. **English:** English lit, speech/rhetoric. **Family/consumer sciences:** Family studies. **Foreign languages:** Spanish. **Health:** Clinical lab science, dietetics, nursing (RN), ophthalmic lab technology, predentistry, premedicine, prepharmacy, preveterinary, speech pathology. **History:** General. **Interdisciplinary:** Global studies. **Legal studies:** Prelaw. **Liberal arts:** Arts/sciences. **Math:** General. **Parks/recreation:** Health/fitness, sports admin. **Physical sciences:** Chemistry, physics. **Psychology:** General. **Public administration:** Social work. **Social sciences:** Criminology, political science, sociology. **Theology:** Bible, missionary, pastoral counseling, youth ministry. **Visual/performing arts:** Art, commercial/advertising art, dramatic, interior design, piano/organ, studio arts, voice/opera.

Computing on campus. 650 workstations in dormitories, library, computer center, student center. Dormitories wired for high-speed internet access and linked to campus network. Commuter students can connect to campus network. Online course registration, online library, helpline, student web hosting available.

Student life. Freshman orientation: Mandatory, $115 fee. Preregistration for classes offered. Overnight program, held twice in summer; includes assessment testing and registration. **Policies:** Religious observance required. Freshmen permitted cars on campus. **Housing:** Guaranteed on-campus for freshmen. Single-sex dorms, special housing for disabled, apartments available. $100 deposit. **Activities:** Bands, choral groups, drama, literary magazine, music ensembles, musical theater, opera, radio station, student government, student newspaper, symphony orchestra, TV station, student association, Seekers of the Word, international student association, campus activities team, Hispanos Unidos, College Democrats, African Missions Fellowship, Essence of Ebony, mission student committee, College Republicans.

Athletics. NCAA. **Intercollegiate:** Baseball M, basketball, cross-country, football (tackle) M, golf M, softball W, tennis, track and field, volleyball W. **Intramural:** Badminton, basketball, bowling, cross-country, racquetball, soccer, softball, table tennis, tennis, track and field, volleyball, water polo M. **Team name:** Wildcats.

Student services. Adult student services, career counseling, student employment services, health services, minority student services, personal counseling, placement for graduates, veterans' counselor. **Physically disabled:** Services for visually, speech, hearing impaired.

Contact. E-mail: info@admissions.acu.edu
Phone: (325) 674-2650 Toll-free number: (800) 460-6228 ext. 2650
Fax: (325) 674-2130
Robert Heil, Director of Admissions & Enrollment Mgmt., Abilene Christian University, ACU Box 29000, Abilene, TX 79699

Amberton University

Garland, Texas
www.amberu.edu
CB code: 6140

- Private upper-division university affiliated with nondenominational tradition
- Commuter campus in small city

General. Founded in 1971. Regionally accredited. Upper level and graduate institution designed for adult students. Must have previous college and be over 21 years old to attend. **Degrees:** 150 bachelor's awarded; master's offered. **Articulation:** Agreements with Dallas County Community College District, East Texas State University, Collin County Community College, Tarrant County Junior College. **Location:** 12 miles from downtown Dallas. **Calendar:** Four 10-week sessions. Extensive summer session. **Full-time faculty:** 15 total; 93% have terminal degrees. **Part-time faculty:** 60 total; 92% have terminal degrees.

Student profile. 465 degree-seeking undergraduates, 1,072 degree-seeking graduate students. 50% entered as juniors, 50% entered as seniors. 50% transferred from two-year, 50% transferred from four-year institutions.

Women:	58%	Native American:	1%
African American:	29%	Part-time:	43%
Asian American:	2%	Out-of-state:	2%
Hispanic American:	5%	25 or older:	94%

Basis for selection. Open admission. College transcript required. Transfer candidates must have completed 30 hours of course work with at least 2.0 GPA at regionally accredited institution. Must be at least 21. Interview required for international applicants. Must have completed some college. Transfer accepted as juniors, seniors.

2005-2006 Annual costs. Tuition/fees: $6,000. Books/supplies: $500.

Application procedures. Admission: Rolling admission. No application fee. Application must be submitted on paper.

Academics. **Special study options:** Distance learning, independent study, weekend college. **Credit/placement by examination:** CLEP. 30 credit hours maximum toward bachelor's degree.

Majors. **Business:** General, accounting, business admin. **Liberal arts:** Arts/sciences.

Most popular majors. Business/marketing 90%, liberal arts 10%.

Computing on campus. 25 workstations in library, computer center.

Student services. Adult student services, career counseling, personal counseling, placement for graduates, veterans' counselor.

Contact. E-mail: advisor@amberton.edu
Phone: (972) 279-6511 Fax: (972) 279-9773
Algia Allen, Vice President for Academic Services, Amberton University, 1700 Eastgate Drive, Garland, TX 75041-5595

Angelo State University

San Angelo, Texas — **CB member**
www.angelo.edu — **CB code: 6644**

- Public 4-year university
- Residential campus in small city
- 5,658 degree-seeking undergraduates: 15% part-time, 54% women, 6% African American, 1% Asian American, 23% Hispanic American, 1% international
- 395 degree-seeking graduate students
- 100% of applicants admitted
- SAT or ACT (ACT writing optional) required
- 34% graduate within 6 years

General. Founded in 1928. Regionally accredited. **Degrees:** 856 bachelor's, 71 associate awarded; master's offered. **ROTC:** Air Force. **Location:** 215 miles from San Antonio, 200 miles from Austin. **Calendar:** Semester, extensive summer session. **Full-time faculty:** 233 total; 74% have terminal degrees, 12% minority, 42% women. **Part-time faculty:** 117 total; 20% have terminal degrees, 8% minority, 50% women. **Class size:** 25% < 20, 52% 20-39, 11% 40-49, 11% 50-99, less than 1% >100. **Special facilities:** Planetarium; management, instruction, and research center; food safety and product development laboratory; West Texas collection.

Freshman class profile. 2,224 applied, 2,216 admitted, 1,304 enrolled.

Mid 50% test scores		**Return as sophomores:**	61%
SAT verbal:	420-540	**Out-of-state:**	2%
SAT math:	430-550	**Live on campus:**	54%
ACT:	17-23	**Fraternities:**	3%
Rank in top quarter:	40%	**Sororities:**	4%
Rank in top tenth:	12%		

Basis for selection. Applicants must graduate from an accredited high school and satisfactorily complete recommended high school program or an advanced college-prep curriculum, or rank in top half of high school class. If ranked in third quarter, applicant must have ACT of 23 or SAT of 1030 (exclusive of Writing). If ranked in fourth quarter, applicant must have ACT 30 or SAT of 1270.

High school preparation. College-preparatory program recommended. 23 units recommended. Recommended units include English 4, mathematics 3, social studies 3, science 3 and foreign language 2. One computer science recommended.

2005-2006 Annual costs. Tuition/fees: $4,290; $12,570 out-of-state. Room/board: $5,314. Books/supplies: $1,000.

2004-2005 Financial aid. **Need-based:** 917 full-time freshmen applied for aid; 569 were judged to have need; 569 of these received aid. Average need met was 75%. Average scholarship/grant was $2,495; average loan $1,960. 45% of total undergraduate aid awarded as scholarships/grants, 55% as loans/jobs. **Non-need-based:** Awarded to 2,140 full-time undergraduates, including 593 freshmen. Scholarships awarded for academics, athletics, leadership, music/drama, ROTC.

Application procedures. **Admission:** Closing date 8/15 (postmark date). $20 fee. Application may be submitted online. Admission notification on a rolling basis. Notification within 5 working days of receipt of completed application. **Financial aid:** Priority date 5/1; no closing date. FAFSA, institutional form required. Applicants notified on a rolling basis starting 4/1.

Academics. **Special study options:** Combined bachelor's/graduate degree, distance learning, double major, dual enrollment of high school students, honors, independent study, internships, study abroad, teacher certification program. 3-2 engineering-physics and 3-2 agriculture-education programs with Texas A&M and University of Texas El Paso. **Credit/placement by examination:** AP, CLEP. Unlimited credits by examination provided student meets hours required in residence. **Support services:** Learning center, reduced course load, remedial instruction, tutoring, writing center.

Majors. **Agriculture:** Animal husbandry, animal sciences. **Biology:** General, biochemistry. **Business:** Accounting, business admin, finance, international, marketing, real estate. **Communications:** General, journalism. **Computer sciences:** General. **Conservation:** Management/policy. **English:** English lit. **Foreign languages:** French, German, Spanish. **Health:** Athletic training, clinical lab science, nursing (RN). **History:** General. **Math:** General. **Parks/recreation:** Health/fitness. **Physical sciences:** Chemistry, physics. **Protective services:** Criminal justice. **Psychology:** General. **Social sciences:** Political science, sociology. **Visual/performing arts:** Art, dramatic, studio arts.

Most popular majors. Business/marketing 23%, communications/journalism 6%, health sciences 11%, interdisciplinary studies 14%, parks/recreation 10%, psychology 10%.

Computing on campus. 700 workstations in dormitories, library, computer center, student center. Dormitories wired for high-speed internet access and linked to campus network. Commuter students can connect to campus network. Online course registration, online library, helpline, student web hosting, wireless network available.

Student life. **Freshman orientation:** Available, $25 fee. Preregistration for classes offered. Sessions offered several times during the summer. **Policies:** Single undergraduates with less than 60 semester credit hours of college level work who carry 12 or more semester credit hours total and who do not live at full-time, established residence of their parent(s) required to reside in University-owned housing. Freshmen permitted cars on campus. **Housing:** Coed dorms, single-sex dorms, special housing for disabled, apartments, substance-free housing available. $100 fully refundable deposit. **Activities:** Bands, choral groups, dance, drama, film society, literary magazine, music ensembles, musical theater, radio station, student government, student newspaper, TV station, College Republicans, Young Democrats, Baptist student union, international students organization, residence hall association, Block and Bridle, Newman Center, nontraditional sudent organization.

Athletics. NCAA. **Intercollegiate:** Baseball M, basketball, cross-country, football (tackle) M, soccer W, softball W, track and field, volleyball W. **Intramural:** Badminton, basketball, football (non-tackle), golf, racquetball, soccer, softball, swimming, table tennis, tennis, volleyball, weight lifting. **Team name:** Rams.

Student services. Adult student services, alcohol/substance abuse counseling, campus ministries, career counseling, services for economically disadvantaged, student employment services, financial aid counseling, health services, minority student services, personal counseling, placement for graduates, veterans' counselor. **Physically disabled:** Services for visually, hearing impaired.

Contact. E-mail: admissions@angelo.edu
Phone: (325) 942-2185 Toll-free number: (800) 946-8627
Fax: (325) 942-2078
Frederic Dietz, Director of Admissions, Angelo State University, ASU Station #11014, San Angelo, TX 76909-1014

Arlington Baptist College

Arlington, Texas
www.abconline.edu — **CB code: 6039**

- Private 4-year Bible college affiliated with Baptist faith
- Residential campus in very large city
- 181 degree-seeking undergraduates: 21% part-time, 49% women
- Application essay required

General. Founded in 1939. Accredited by ABHE. **Degrees:** 25 bachelor's awarded. **Location:** 10 miles from Fort Worth, 25 miles from Dallas. **Calendar:** Semester, limited summer session. **Full-time faculty:** 7 total; 14% minority, 29% women. **Part-time faculty:** 13 total; 15% have terminal degrees, 31% women. **Class size:** 73% < 20, 18% 20-39, 8% 40-49.

Freshman class profile. 72 applied, 72 admitted, 35 enrolled.

GPA 3.50 or higher:	27%	Return as sophomores:	46%
GPA 3.0-3.49:	25%	Out-of-state:	17%
GPA 2.0-2.99:	46%	Live on campus:	82%
Rank in top quarter:	24%	International:	3%
End year in good standing:	50%		

Basis for selection. Open admission. Interview recommended for all; audition required for music. **Homeschooled:** Advised to obtain GED.

High school preparation. 16 units recommended. Recommended units include English 3, mathematics 2, social studies 3, history 3 and science 1.

2005-2006 Annual costs. Tuition/fees: $5,490. Room/board: $3,800. Books/supplies: $750. Personal expenses: $720.

2005-2006 Financial aid. All financial aid based on need. 32 full-time freshmen applied for aid; 30 were judged to have need; 30 of these received aid. 40% of total undergraduate aid awarded as scholarships/grants, 60% as loans/jobs.

Application procedures. Admission: Priority date 8/1; no deadline. $15 fee, may be waived for applicants with need. Application must be submitted on paper. Admission notification on a rolling basis. **Financial aid:** Priority date 8/15; no closing date. FAFSA required. Applicants notified on a rolling basis.

Academics. Special study options: Distance learning, double major, dual enrollment of high school students, teacher certification program. **Credit/placement by examination:** AP, CLEP, institutional tests. 30 credit hours maximum toward bachelor's degree. **Support services:** Reduced course load, remedial instruction.

Majors. Education: General, elementary, music. **Philosophy/religion:** Religion. **Theology:** Bible, missionary, pastoral counseling, religious ed, sacred music, youth ministry.

Most popular majors. Education 15%, philosophy/religious studies 45%.

Computing on campus. 17 workstations in library, computer center.

Student life. Freshman orientation: Mandatory. Preregistration for classes offered. Orientation includes placement testing. **Policies:** Religious observance required. Freshmen permitted cars on campus. **Housing:** Guaranteed on-campus for freshmen. Single-sex dorms, substance-free housing available. $25 fully refundable deposit. **Activities:** Choral groups, music ensembles, student government, student newspaper, student missionary association, Student Preachers' Fellowship, International Students Fellowship, 4:12 Group (Youth Majors).

Athletics. NCCAA. **Intercollegiate:** Baseball M, basketball, volleyball W. **Team name:** Patriots.

Student services. Career counseling, student employment services, financial aid counseling, personal counseling, placement for graduates, veterans' counselor.

Contact. E-mail: jhall@abconline.org
Phone: (817) 461-8741 Fax: (817) 274-1138
Janie Taylor, Registrar, Arlington Baptist College, 3001 West Division, Arlington, TX 76012

Art Institute of Dallas

Dallas, Texas
www.aid.edu — **CB code: 2680**

- For-profit 4-year visual arts college
- Very large city
- 1,010 full-time, degree-seeking undergraduates

General. Regionally accredited. **Degrees:** 42 bachelor's, 282 associate awarded. **Calendar:** Continuous. **Full-time faculty:** 100 total. **Part-time faculty:** 40 total.

Basis for selection. Open admission, but selective for some programs. Some animation, art and design associate degree programs may require portfolio evaluation.

2005-2006 Annual costs. Tuition for full bachelor's degree programs (180 credits): $64,800.00; for full associate degree programs (105 credits) $37,800. Per credit hour cost $360. Personal expenses: $2,880.

Application procedures. Admission: No deadline. $50 fee. Admission notification on a rolling basis. **Financial aid:** FAFSA required. Applicants notified on a rolling basis.

Academics. Credit/placement by examination: CLEP.

Majors. Visual/performing arts: Studio arts.

Contact. E-mail: crispm@aii.edu
Phone: (214) 692-8080 Toll-free number: (800) 275-4243
Art Institute of Dallas, Two North Park, 8080 Park Lane, Dallas, TX 75231

Art Institute of Houston

Houston, Texas
www.aih.artinstitutes.edu — **CB code: 8271**

- For-profit 4-year visual arts college
- Very large city
- 1,130 full-time, degree-seeking undergraduates
- 32% of applicants admitted

General. Regionally accredited. **Degrees:** 31 bachelor's, 379 associate awarded. **Calendar:** Quarter. **Full-time faculty:** 47 total. **Part-time faculty:** 32 total.

Freshman class profile. 845 applied, 271 admitted, 253 enrolled.

Basis for selection. Based on high school record or GED and personal interview with admissions representative; test scores optional but may be considered if submitted. Observes TASP guidelines. ASSET or COMPASS testing may be required. Remediation may be required if test scores fall below required ranges; some remediation available on campus.

Application procedures. Admission: No deadline. No application fee. Admission notification on a rolling basis. **Financial aid:** FAFSA, institutional form required.

Academics. Credit/placement by examination: CLEP.

Majors. Visual/performing arts: Graphic design, interior design.

Contact. E-mail: aihadm@aii.edu
Phone: (713) 623-2040 Toll-free number: (800) 275-4244
Brian Shumaker, Director of Admission, Art Institute of Houston, 1900 Yorktown, Houston, TX 77056-4115

Austin College

Sherman, Texas — **CB member**
www.austincollege.edu — **CB code: 6016**

- Private 4-year liberal arts and teachers college affiliated with Presbyterian Church (USA)
- Residential campus in small city
- 1,291 degree-seeking undergraduates: 55% women, 4% African American, 12% Asian American, 9% Hispanic American, 1% Native American, 1% international
- 28 degree-seeking graduate students
- 67% of applicants admitted
- SAT or ACT with writing, application essay required
- 74% graduate within 6 years; 47% enter graduate study

General. Founded in 1849. Regionally accredited. **Degrees:** 290 bachelor's awarded; master's offered. **Location:** 60 miles from Dallas. **Calendar:** 4-1-4, limited summer session. **Full-time faculty:** 91 total; 98% have terminal degrees, 7% minority, 32% women. **Part-time faculty:** 40 total; 48% have terminal degrees, 15% minority, 52% women. **Class size:** 60% < 20, 35% 20-39, 3% 40-49, 2% 50-99. **Special facilities:** Environmental research areas totaling 174 acres, lake recreation area, tissue culture facility for study of cellular molecular interactions of eukaryotic cells, high performance numeric and graphics computing facility for advanced scientific computing and 3-D graphics.

Freshman class profile. 1,530 applied, 1,029 admitted, 348 enrolled.

Mid 50% test scores		**Return as sophomores:**	88%
SAT verbal:	580-680	**Out-of-state:**	8%
SAT math:	580-670	**Live on campus:**	97%
ACT:	23-28	**International:**	1%
Rank in top quarter:	75%	**Fraternities:**	20%
Rank in top tenth:	44%	**Sororities:**	23%
End year in good standing:	95%		

Basis for selection. Academic transcript record, test scores, recommendations, extracurricular involvement, essay important. Interview considered. Interview recommended for all; audition recommended for music, theater (required for scholarship consideration); portfolio recommended for art (required for scholarship consideration).

High school preparation. Required and recommended units include English 4, mathematics 3-4, social studies 2-3, science 3-4 (laboratory 2-3), foreign language 2-3 and academic electives 1. One fine arts required, 2 fine arts recommended.

2006-2007 Annual costs. Tuition/fees: $23,355. Room/board: $7,741. Books/supplies: $800. Personal expenses: $950.

2005-2006 Financial aid. Need-based: 273 full-time freshmen applied for aid; 194 were judged to have need; 194 of these received aid. Average need met was 100%. Average scholarship/grant was $14,574; average loan $5,724. 69% of total undergraduate aid awarded as scholarships/grants, 31% as loans/jobs. **Non-need-based:** Awarded to 718 full-time undergraduates, including 208 freshmen. Scholarships awarded for academics, alumni affiliation, art, leadership, music/drama, religious affiliation, state residency.

Application procedures. Admission: Priority date 1/15; deadline 5/1 (postmark date). $35 fee, may be waived for applicants with need. Application may be submitted online. By April 1 and on space available basis thereafter. Must reply by May 1 or within 2 week(s) if notified thereafter. **Financial aid:** Priority date 4/1; no closing date. FAFSA, institutional form required. Applicants notified on a rolling basis starting 3/1; must reply by 5/1.

Academics. Special study options: Double major, exchange student, honors, independent study, internships, liberal arts/career combination, student-designed major, study abroad, teacher certification program, Washington semester. 3-2 dual degree engineering program with University of Texas Dallas, Washington University in St. Louis, Columbia University, Texas A&M University. **Credit/placement by examination:** AP, CLEP, IB, institutional tests. **Support services:** Learning center, study skills assistance, tutoring.

Majors. Area/ethnic studies: American, Latin American. **Biology:** General, biochemistry. **Business:** General. **Communications:** General. **Computer sciences:** Computer science. **Conservation:** Environmental studies. **English:** English lit. **Foreign languages:** Classics, French, German, Latin, Spanish. **History:** General. **Math:** General. **Philosophy/religion:** Philosophy, religion. **Physical sciences:** Chemistry, physics. **Psychology:** General. **Social sciences:** Economics, international economics, international relations, political science, sociology. **Visual/performing arts:** Art.

Most popular majors. Biology 8%, business/marketing 13%, English 8%, foreign language 9%, history 7%, philosophy/religious studies 6%, psychology 14%, social sciences 17%.

Computing on campus. 160 workstations in dormitories, library, computer center, student center. Dormitories wired for high-speed internet access and linked to campus network. Commuter students can connect to campus network. Online library, helpline, student web hosting, wireless network available.

Student life. Freshman orientation: Mandatory. Preregistration for classes offered. Held the weekend prior to the first day of classes. **Policies:** Freshmen permitted cars on campus. **Housing:** Guaranteed on-campus for all undergraduates. Coed dorms, single-sex dorms, special housing for disabled, apartments available. Language emphasis residence; suite-style housing for upper-level students with private bedroom, common area, and kitchenette. **Activities:** Jazz band, choral groups, dance, drama, literary magazine, music ensembles, musical theater, student government, student newspaper, symphony orchestra, Alpha Phi Omega, Intervarsity Christian Fellowship, student international organization, Black Expressions, Young Democrats, Service Station, Los Amigos, Habitat for Humanity, Activators, Amnesty International.

Athletics. NCAA. **Intercollegiate:** Baseball M, basketball, diving, football (tackle) M, golf M, soccer, swimming, tennis, volleyball W. **Intramural:** Basketball, football (non-tackle), soccer, softball. **Team name:** Roos.

Student services. Campus ministries, career counseling, student employment services, financial aid counseling, health services, personal counseling.

Contact. E-mail: admission@austincollege.edu
Phone: (903) 813-3000 Toll-free number: (800) 442-5363
Fax: (903) 813-3198
Nan Davis, Vice President for Institutional Enrollment, Austin College, 900 North Grand, Suite 6N, Sherman, TX 75090-4400

Austin Graduate School of Theology

Austin, Texas
www.austingrad.edu **CB code: 4969**

- Private upper-division Bible and seminary college affiliated with Church of Christ
- Commuter campus in large city
- 91% of applicants admitted
- Application essay required

General. Founded in 1917. Regionally accredited. **Degrees:** 5 bachelor's awarded; master's offered. **Location:** 80 miles from San Antonio, 150 miles from Houston. **Calendar:** Semester, limited summer session. **Full-time faculty:** 4 total; 100% have terminal degrees. **Part-time faculty:** 5 total; 60% have terminal degrees, 20% women. **Class size:** 90% < 20, 10% 20-39.

Student profile. 27 degree-seeking undergraduates, 34 degree-seeking graduate students. 22 applied as first time-transfer students, 20 admitted, 19 enrolled.

Women:	41%	**Hispanic American:**	11%
African American:	30%	**Part-time:**	89%

Basis for selection. Open admission. College transcript, application essay required. Transcript, GPA, recommendations required. High school transcript, test scores required for applicants with fewer than 35 hours. Transfer accepted as sophomores, juniors, seniors.

2005-2006 Annual costs. Tuition/fees: $5,700. Books/supplies: $400. Personal expenses: $1,728.

Financial aid. Need-based: 54% of total undergraduate aid awarded as scholarships/grants, 46% as loans/jobs. **Non-need-based:** Scholarships awarded for academics, leadership. **Additional information:** Generous scholarships for students taking at least 12 hours. Federal work study program available. Institutional work study program (need-based) available.

Application procedures. Admission: Priority date 6/1. No application fee. Application must be submitted on paper. **Financial aid:** No deadline. FAFSA, institutional form required.

Academics. Special study options: Dual enrollment of high school students, liberal arts/career combination. Liberal arts/career combination program in religion; combined bachelor's/graduate program in ministry. **Credit/placement by examination:** AP, CLEP. 18 credit hours maximum toward bachelor's degree.

Majors. Theology: Bible, theology.

Computing on campus. 8 workstations in library, computer center, student center. Online library available.

Student life. Policies: Religious observance required. **Activities:** Student government.

Student services. Financial aid counseling, personal counseling.

Contact. E-mail: admissions@austingrad.edu
Phone: (512) 476-2772 Toll-free number: (866) 287-4723
Fax: (512) 476-3919
Kirk Eason, Director of Admissions, Austin Graduate School of Theology, 1909 University Avenue, Austin, TX 78705

Baptist Missionary Association Theological Seminary

Jacksonville, Texas
www.bmats.edu **CB code: 7042**

- Private 4-year Bible and seminary college affiliated with Baptist faith
- Commuter campus in large town
- 55 degree-seeking undergraduates: 60% part-time, 11% women
- 67 degree-seeking graduate students

General. Founded in 1955. Regionally accredited. **Degrees:** 3 bachelor's awarded; master's, first professional offered. **Location:** 120 miles from Dallas. **Calendar:** Semester, limited summer session. **Full-time faculty:** 5 total; 100% have terminal degrees. **Part-time faculty:** 4 total; 100% have terminal degrees.

Basis for selection. Open admission, but selective for some programs. Essay or personal statement very important. Religious commitment, interview, recommendations, school and community activities important.

2005-2006 Annual costs. Tuition/fees: $2,800. Room/board: $2,400.

Application procedures. Admission: No deadline. $35 fee.

Academics. Special study options: Internships. **Credit/placement by examination:** CLEP.

Majors. Philosophy/religion: Religion. **Theology:** Theology.

Computing on campus. 2 workstations in library.

Student life. Activities: Student government.

Student services. Career counseling, personal counseling.

Contact. E-mail: bmatsem@bmats.edu
Phone: (903) 586-2501 Fax: (903) 586-0378
Philip Attebery, Dean/Registrar, Baptist Missionary Association Theological Seminary, 1530 East Pine Street, Jacksonville, TX 75766

Baptist University of the Americas
San Antonio, Texas

- Private 4-year Bible college
- Commuter campus
- 180 degree-seeking undergraduates

General. Accredited by ABHE. **Degrees:** 25 bachelor's awarded. **Calendar:** Semester. **Full-time faculty:** 7 total. **Part-time faculty:** 9 total.

Basis for selection. Open admission. Observes THEA requirements.

2005-2006 Annual costs. Tuition/fees: $3,250.

Application procedures. Admission: Closing date 2/15. $25 fee. **Financial aid:** No deadline.

Academics. Credit/placement by examination: CLEP.

Majors. Theology: Bible, theology.

Student life. Freshman orientation: Available. **Housing:** $200 deposit.

Contact. Phone: (210) 924-4338
Mary Ranjel, Director of Admissions, Baptist University of the Americas, 8019 South Pan Am Expressway, San Antonio, TX 78224

Baylor University
Waco, Texas — **CB member**
www.baylor.edu — **CB code: 6032**

- Private 4-year university affiliated with Baptist faith
- Residential campus in small city
- 11,751 degree-seeking undergraduates: 3% part-time, 58% women, 8% African American, 7% Asian American, 10% Hispanic American, 1% Native American, 1% international
- 2,150 degree-seeking graduate students
- 66% of applicants admitted
- SAT or ACT with writing, application essay required
- 72% graduate within 6 years

General. Founded in 1845. Regionally accredited. **Degrees:** 2,533 bachelor's awarded; master's, doctoral, first professional offered. **ROTC:** Air Force. **Location:** 100 miles from Dallas-Fort Worth, 100 miles from Austin. **Calendar:** Semester, extensive summer session. **Full-time faculty:** 755 total; 77% have terminal degrees, 8% minority, 35% women. **Part-time faculty:** 155 total; 5% minority, 50% women. **Class size:** 36% < 20, 46% 20-39, 8% 40-49, 7% 50-99, 3% >100. **Special facilities:** Museum of natural science, Texas collection library.

Freshman class profile. 15,443 applied, 10,157 admitted, 3,168 enrolled.

Mid 50% test scores			
SAT verbal:	540-650	End year in good standing:	87%
SAT math:	550-660	Return as sophomores:	83%
ACT:	22-27	Out-of-state:	18%
Rank in top quarter:	68%	Live on campus:	98%
Rank in top tenth:	38%	International:	1%

Basis for selection. Competitive high school performance and competitive scores on ACT or SAT most important; above-average achievement and potential expected. Audition required for music and theater programs; interview recommended for marginal achievers; portfolio recommended for art. **Homeschooled:** Transcript of courses and grades required. If applicant graduated from home school not officially recognized by state in which school located, applicant must be 17 before first day of class unless GED certificate submitted prior to registration.

High school preparation. Required units include English 4, mathematics 3, social studies 1, history 1, science 2 (laboratory 2) and foreign language 2.

2006-2007 Annual costs. Tuition/fees: $22,814. Room/board: $7,125. Books/supplies: $1,502. Personal expenses: $2,108.

2005-2006 Financial aid. Need-based: 2,282 full-time freshmen applied for aid; 1,739 were judged to have need; 1,739 of these received aid. Average need met was 70%. Average scholarship/grant was $12,114; average loan $2,015. 55% of total undergraduate aid awarded as scholarships/grants, 45% as loans/jobs. **Non-need-based:** Awarded to 8,198 full-time undergraduates, including 2,874 freshmen. Scholarships awarded for academics, art, athletics, job skills, leadership, music/drama, ROTC.

Application procedures. Admission: Priority date 3/1; no deadline. $50 fee, may be waived for applicants with need. Application must be submitted online. Must reply by May 1 or within 2 week(s) if notified thereafter. **Financial aid:** Priority date 3/1; no closing date. FAFSA required. Applicants notified on a rolling basis starting 3/10; must reply by 5/1 or within 2 week(s) of notification.

Academics. Special study options: Accelerated study, combined bachelor's/graduate degree, double major, honors, internships, student-designed major, study abroad, teacher certification program. Architecture program with Washington University, forestry with Duke University. **Credit/placement by examination:** AP, CLEP, IB, institutional tests. 60 credit hours maximum toward bachelor's degree. **Support services:** Learning center, reduced course load, study skills assistance, tutoring, writing center.

Honors college/program. Require SAT 1270 (exclusive of Writing) or ACT 30 and maintenance of 3.5 GPA.

Majors. Architecture: Architecture. **Area/ethnic studies:** American, Asian, Latin American, Slavic. **Biology:** General, biochemistry, bioinformatics, exercise physiology. **Business:** General, accounting, business admin, entrepreneurial studies, fashion, finance, financial planning, human resources, insurance, international, management information systems, managerial economics, marketing, operations, real estate, sales/distribution. **Communications:** General, journalism, radio/tv. **Computer sciences:** Computer science. **Conservation:** Environmental science, environmental studies, forestry. **Education:** General, art, computer, early childhood, elementary, English, health occupations, mathematics, music, physical, science, social studies, special. **Engineering:** General, electrical, mechanical. **English:** Composition, English lit. **Family/consumer sciences:** General, family studies, human nutrition. **Foreign languages:** Ancient Greek, Biblical, classics, French, German, Latin, linguistics, Russian, Spanish. **Health:** Athletic training, clinical lab science, communication disorders, health services, nursing (RN), predentistry, premedicine, prenursing. **History:** General. **Interdisciplinary:** Museum, neuroscience. **Liberal arts:** Humanities. **Math:** General, applied, statistics. **Parks/recreation:** Health/fitness. **Philosophy/religion:** Philosophy, religion. **Physical sciences:** Chemistry, geology, geophysics, physics. **Protective services:** Forensics. **Psychology:** General. **Public administration:** General, social work. **Social sciences:** Anthropology, archaeology, geography, international relations, political science, sociology. **Theology:** Sacred music. **Transportation:** Airline/commercial pilot. **Visual/performing arts:** Acting, art history/conservation, dramatic, fashion design, interior design, music history, music pedagogy, music performance, music theory/composition, studio arts, theater design.

Most popular majors. Biology 7%, business/marketing 27%, communications/journalism 10%, education 8%, health sciences 7%, psychology 6%, social sciences 6%, visual/performing arts 6%.

Computing on campus. 1,688 workstations in dormitories, library, computer center, student center. Dormitories wired for high-speed internet access and linked to campus network. Commuter students can connect to campus network. Online course registration, online library, helpline, repair service, student web hosting, wireless network available.

Student life. **Freshman orientation:** Mandatory. Preregistration for classes offered. 10 2-day sessions primarily in June. **Policies:** All students required to participate in chapel for 2 semesters. Freshmen permitted cars on campus. **Housing:** Guaranteed on-campus for freshmen. Single-sex dorms, special housing for disabled, apartments, substance-free housing available. $200 deposit, deadline 5/1. Engineering & computer science living-learning center, honors college living-learning center, leadership living-learning center. **Activities:** Bands, choral groups, dance, drama, film society, literary magazine, music ensembles, musical theater, opera, radio station, student government, student newspaper, symphony orchestra, TV station, Baptist Student Ministries, Campus Crusade for Christ, College Republicans, Young Democrats, association of black students, Hispanic student association, Asian student association, Habitat for Humanity, Alpha Phi Omega, Baylor Chamber of Commerce.

Athletics. NCAA. **Intercollegiate:** Baseball M, basketball, cross-country, equestrian W, football (tackle) M, golf, soccer W, softball W, tennis, track and field, volleyball W. **Intramural:** Basketball, bowling, cross-country, equestrian, football (non-tackle), golf, lacrosse, racquetball, soccer, softball, swimming, table tennis, tennis, track and field, volleyball, weight lifting. **Team name:** Bears.

Student services. Campus ministries, career counseling, student employment services, financial aid counseling, health services, legal services, personal counseling, placement for graduates. **Physically disabled:** Services for visually, speech, hearing impaired.

Contact. E-mail: admissions@baylor.edu
Phone: (254) 710-3435 Toll-free number: (800) 229-5678
Fax: (254) 710-3436
Stephanie Willis, Director of Admissions Counseling, Baylor University, One Bear Place #97056, Waco, TX 76798-7056

College of Biblical Studies-Houston

Houston, Texas
www.cbshouston.edu **CB code: 3946**

- Private 4-year Bible college
- Commuter campus in very large city
- 635 degree-seeking undergraduates

General. Accredited by ABHE. Multidenominational Christian Bible college. **Degrees:** 106 bachelor's, 10 associate awarded. **Calendar:** Trimester, extensive summer session. **Full-time faculty:** 8 total; 25% have terminal degrees, 25% minority. **Part-time faculty:** 54 total; 24% have terminal degrees, 52% minority, 9% women.

Freshman class profile. 206 applied, 206 admitted, 206 enrolled.

Basis for selection. Open admission, but selective for some programs. ASSET testing may be required for associate or baccalaureate level programs. **Homeschooled:** State high school equivalency certificate required.

2005-2006 Annual costs. Tuition/fees: $2,920.

Application procedures. **Admission:** No deadline. $20 fee. Application must be submitted on paper. Admission notification on a rolling basis.

Academics. **Special study options:** Accelerated study, dual enrollment of high school students, ESL, independent study. **Credit/placement by examination:** CLEP. **Support services:** Learning center, remedial instruction.

Majors. **Theology:** Bible, preministerial.

Computing on campus. 14 workstations in library. Online course registration available.

Student life. **Freshman orientation:** Available. Preregistration for classes offered. 2 sessions lasting 2 hours held week before classes begin; new students requested to attend 1 session. **Policies:** Religious observance required. Freshmen permitted cars on campus. **Activities:** Student government.

Student services. Adult student services, campus ministries, financial aid counseling.

Contact. E-mail: cbs@cbshouston.edu
Phone: (713) 785-5995 Fax: (713) 785-5998
Daniel Lopez, Director of Enrollment Management/Registrar, College of Biblical Studies-Houston, 7000 Regency Square Boulevard, #110, Houston, TX 77036-3211

College of Saint Thomas More

Fort Worth, Texas
www.cstm.edu **CB code: 0169**

- Private 4-year liberal arts college affiliated with Roman Catholic Church
- Commuter campus in very large city
- 37 degree-seeking undergraduates: 43% part-time, 43% women
- SAT, interview required

General. Regionally accredited. All students take three trips: to Rome, Greece, and Oxford, England. **Degrees:** 5 bachelor's awarded. **Calendar:** Semester, limited summer session. **Full-time faculty:** 3 total; 100% have terminal degrees, 33% women. **Part-time faculty:** 5 total; 20% have terminal degrees, 40% women.

Basis for selection. Secondary school record, essay, interview, test scores important; 2 letters of recommendation required.

2005-2006 Annual costs. Tuition/fees: $12,000. Books/supplies: $500.

Application procedures. **Admission:** No deadline. $35 fee. Admission notification on a rolling basis.

Academics. **Special study options:** Dual enrollment of high school students, study abroad. **Credit/placement by examination:** CLEP. **Support services:** Remedial instruction, study skills assistance, tutoring, writing center.

Majors. **Liberal arts:** Arts/sciences.

Computing on campus. 10 workstations in library, student center.

Student life. **Freshman orientation:** Mandatory. Preregistration for classes offered. **Policies:** Freshmen permitted cars on campus. **Housing:** Apartments available. **Activities:** Student government.

Student services. Alcohol/substance abuse counseling, campus ministries, career counseling, financial aid counseling, personal counseling.

Contact. E-mail: jpatrick@cstm.edu
Phone: (817) 923-8459 Toll-free number: (800) 583-6489
Fax: (817) 924-3206
James Patrick, Chancellor, College of Saint Thomas More, 3020 Lubbock Avenue, Fort Worth, TX 76109

Concordia University at Austin

Austin, Texas
www.concordia.edu **CB code: 6127**

- Private 4-year university and liberal arts college affiliated with Lutheran Church - Missouri Synod
- Commuter campus in very large city
- 1,021 degree-seeking undergraduates: 26% part-time, 58% women, 9% African American, 1% Asian American, 16% Hispanic American
- 90 degree-seeking graduate students
- 73% of applicants admitted
- SAT or ACT (ACT writing optional) required
- 35% graduate within 6 years

General. Founded in 1926. Regionally accredited. Offers new cutting-edge emphases in leadership training, wellness, student service, experiential learning and honors program. **Degrees:** 151 bachelor's, 16 associate awarded; master's offered. **ROTC:** Army, Air Force. **Calendar:** Semester, extensive summer session. **Full-time faculty:** 35 total; 74% have terminal degrees, 3% minority, 31% women. **Part-time faculty:** 100 total; 31% have terminal degrees, 10% minority, 41% women. **Class size:** 81% < 20, 18% 20-39, less than 1% 40-49, less than 1% >100.

Freshman class profile. 728 applied, 532 admitted, 195 enrolled.

Mid 50% test scores		**GPA 2.0-2.99:**	23%
SAT verbal:	450-560	**Rank in top quarter:**	36%
SAT math:	460-560	**Rank in top tenth:**	10%
ACT:	18-23	**Return as sophomores:**	60%
GPA 3.50 or higher:	30%	**Out-of-state:**	12%
GPA 3.0-3.49:	46%		

Basis for selection. School achievement record, test scores, and 2.5 GPA important. Interview recommended for academically weak.

High school preparation. Do not recommend specific number of units, just basic college preparatory program.

2005-2006 Annual costs. Tuition/fees: $16,850. Room/board: $6,900. Books/supplies: $600. Personal expenses: $1,050.

Financial aid. Non-need-based: Scholarships awarded for academics, leadership, music/drama, religious affiliation.

Application procedures. Admission: Priority date 4/1; deadline 8/15. $25 fee, may be waived for applicants with need. Application may be submitted online. Admission notification on a rolling basis. Reply by August 15 if dormitory applicant. **Financial aid:** Priority date 4/15, closing date 7/1. FAFSA, institutional form required. Applicants notified on a rolling basis starting 3/1; must reply within 2 week(s) of notification.

Academics. Special study options: Accelerated study, combined bachelor's/graduate degree, double major, dual enrollment of high school students, independent study, internships, study abroad, teacher certification program. Simultaneous enrollment with other institutions of Concordia University System for two semesters. **Credit/placement by examination:** AP, CLEP, IB, SAT, ACT, institutional tests. 15 credit hours maximum toward associate degree, 30 toward bachelor's. **Support services:** Reduced course load, remedial instruction, tutoring.

Majors. Biology: General. **Business:** General, business admin, training/development. **Communications:** General. **Computer sciences:** Computer science. **Conservation:** Environmental studies. **Education:** Elementary, secondary. **Health:** Health care admin. **History:** General. **Legal studies:** Prelaw. **Liberal arts:** Arts/sciences. **Math:** General. **Parks/recreation:** Exercise sciences. **Philosophy/religion:** Religion. **Protective services:** Law enforcement admin. **Social sciences:** General. **Theology:** Religious ed, sacred music. **Visual/performing arts:** Conducting, piano/organ.

Most popular majors. Business/marketing 44%, education 12%, social sciences 9%, theological studies 6%.

Computing on campus. 45 workstations in library, computer center. Dormitories wired for high-speed internet access and linked to campus network. Commuter students can connect to campus network. Helpline, student web hosting available.

Student life. Freshman orientation: Mandatory. **Policies:** Freshmen permitted cars on campus. **Housing:** Guaranteed on-campus for freshmen. Coed dorms, single-sex dorms available. $250 nonrefundable deposit, deadline 7/1. **Activities:** Jazz band, choral groups, drama, music ensembles, student government, Sisters in Christ, Lutheran Student Fellowship, Lutheran Women's Missionary League, Pro Life, College Republicans, Pre-Sem Club (preseminary students), Fellowship of Christian Athletes, students active for the environment, writer's guild.

Athletics. NCAA. **Intercollegiate:** Baseball M, basketball, cross-country, golf, soccer, softball W, tennis, volleyball W. **Intramural:** Badminton, basketball, bowling, handball, racquetball, softball, table tennis, tennis, volleyball. **Team name:** Tornadoes.

Student services. Adult student services, alcohol/substance abuse counseling, campus ministries, career counseling, student employment services, financial aid counseling, personal counseling, placement for graduates, veterans' counselor.

Contact. E-mail: admissions@concordia.edu
Phone: (512) 486-2000 Toll-free number: (800) 865-4282
Fax: (512) 459-8517
Kristi Kirk, Associate Director of Admissions, Concordia University at Austin, 3400 Interstate 35 North, Austin, TX 78705-2799

Criswell College

Dallas, Texas
www.criswell.edu **CB code: 0794**

- Private 4-year Bible and seminary college affiliated with Southern Baptist Convention
- Commuter campus in very large city
- 125 full-time, degree-seeking undergraduates
- SAT or ACT (ACT writing optional), application essay required

General. Founded in 1970. Regionally accredited. **Degrees:** 25 bachelor's, 1 associate awarded; master's offered. **Calendar:** Semester, limited summer session. **Full-time faculty:** 15 total. **Part-time faculty:** 20 total.

Basis for selection. Test scores and 2 letters of recommendation required. School achievement, essay, religious affiliation very important. Interview recommended.

High school preparation. Recommended units include English 4, mathematics 2, social studies 2, science 3 and foreign language 2.

2005-2006 Annual costs. Tuition/fees: $6,370. Books/supplies: $500.

Application procedures. Admission: Priority date 5/1; no deadline. $30 fee, may be waived for applicants with need. Admission notification on a rolling basis. Must reply by May 1 or within 2 week(s) if notified thereafter. **Financial aid:** Priority date 6/1; no closing date. CSS PROFILE required. Applicants notified on a rolling basis.

Academics. Special study options: Double major, dual enrollment of high school students, independent study, internships. **Credit/placement by examination:** CLEP. **Support services:** Reduced course load, study skills assistance, tutoring.

Majors. Philosophy/religion: Philosophy, religion. **Theology:** Bible, missionary, pastoral counseling, theology.

Computing on campus. 25 workstations in computer center. Online course registration available.

Student life. Policies: Religious observance required. **Activities:** Student government, student newspaper, missionary fellowship, international fellowship, student council.

Athletics. Intramural: Basketball, soccer, softball, table tennis, volleyball.

Student services. Career counseling, student employment services, personal counseling, veterans' counselor.

Contact. E-mail: tccsa@criswell.edu
Phone: (214) 818-1305 Toll-free number: (800) 899-0012
Fax: (214) 818-1310
Danny Blair, Academic and Enrollment Services, Criswell College, 4010 Gaston Avenue, Dallas, TX 75246-1537

Dallas Baptist University

Dallas, Texas **CB member**
www.dbu.edu **CB code: 6159**

- Private 4-year university affiliated with Baptist faith
- Commuter campus in very large city
- 3,567 degree-seeking undergraduates: 41% part-time, 60% women, 17% African American, 1% Asian American, 10% Hispanic American, 1% Native American, 7% international
- 1,421 degree-seeking graduate students
- 64% of applicants admitted
- SAT or ACT with writing, application essay required
- 48% graduate within 6 years

General. Founded in 1898. Regionally accredited. **Degrees:** 803 bachelor's, 1 associate awarded; master's, doctoral offered. **ROTC:** Army, Air Force. **Location:** 13 miles from downtown, 29 miles from Fort Worth. **Calendar:** 4-1-4, extensive summer session. **Full-time faculty:** 100 total; 81% have terminal degrees, 12% minority, 41% women. **Part-time faculty:** 356 total; 33% have terminal degrees, 8% minority, 43% women. **Class size:** 60% < 20, 35% 20-39, 1% 40-49, 3% 50-99, less than 1% >100. **Special facilities:** Corrie ten Boom collection.

Freshman class profile. 937 applied, 599 admitted, 362 enrolled.

Mid 50% test scores		**GPA 2.0-2.99:**	13%
SAT verbal:	480-580	**Rank in top quarter:**	43%
SAT math:	480-580	**Rank in top tenth:**	18%
ACT:	19-24	**Return as sophomores:**	68%
GPA 3.50 or higher:	58%	**Out-of-state:**	8%
GPA 3.0-3.49:	28%	**Live on campus:**	92%

Basis for selection. All factors considered for admission, including test scores, class rank, essay and GPA. Interview recommended. **Homeschooled:** Transcript of courses and grades required. If student is not in accredited home school program, GED required.

High school preparation. 16 units recommended. Recommended units include English 4, mathematics 3, social studies 3, history 2, science 2 and foreign language 2.

2005-2006 Annual costs. Tuition/fees: $12,270. Room/board: $4,770. Books/supplies: $930. Personal expenses: $1,422.

2005-2006 Financial aid. Need-based: 330 full-time freshmen applied for aid; 202 were judged to have need; 197 of these received aid. Average

need met was 70%. Average scholarship/grant was $2,742; average loan $2,438. 43% of total undergraduate aid awarded as scholarships/grants, 57% as loans/jobs. **Non-need-based:** Awarded to 1,421 full-time undergraduates, including 260 freshmen. Scholarships awarded for academics, alumni affiliation, athletics, job skills, leadership, music/drama, religious affiliation.

Application procedures. Admission: Priority date 1/15; no deadline. $25 fee. Application may be submitted online. Admission notification on a rolling basis. **Financial aid:** Priority date 3/15, closing date 5/1. FAFSA, institutional form required. Applicants notified on a rolling basis.

Academics. Special study options: Accelerated study, combined bachelor's/graduate degree, distance learning, double major, dual enrollment of high school students, ESL, honors, independent study, internships, study abroad, teacher certification program, Washington semester, weekend college. **Credit/placement by examination:** AP, CLEP, institutional tests. Credit by examination not counted toward residency hours. Credits recorded on permanent record after student has completed minimum of 12 hours in residence. **Support services:** Learning center, pre-admission summer program, remedial instruction, study skills assistance, tutoring, writing center.

Majors. Biology: General. **Business:** General, accounting, business admin, finance, management information systems, managerial economics, marketing. **Communications:** General. **Computer sciences:** General, computer science. **Education:** General, early childhood, elementary, music, physical, science, secondary. **English:** English lit. **Health:** Health care admin. **History:** General. **Liberal arts:** Arts/sciences. **Math:** General. **Philosophy/religion:** Philosophy. **Protective services:** Criminal justice. **Psychology:** General. **Social sciences:** Political science, sociology. **Theology:** Bible, pastoral counseling, religious ed, sacred music. **Visual/performing arts:** Art, music theory/composition, piano/organ, voice/opera.

Computing on campus. 220 workstations in dormitories, library, computer center, student center. Dormitories wired for high-speed internet access and linked to campus network. Commuter students can connect to campus network. Online library, helpline, wireless network available.

Student life. Freshman orientation: Available. Preregistration for classes offered. **Policies:** Religious observance required. Freshmen permitted cars on campus. **Housing:** Single-sex dorms, special housing for disabled, apartments, substance-free housing available. $100 fully refundable deposit. **Activities:** Choral groups, drama, music ensembles, musical theater, opera, student government, College Republicans, Spanish-speaking students association, Baptist student ministry, Chinese student association, Ministerial Alliance, Japanese student association, Korean student association.

Athletics. NCAA, NCCAA. **Intercollegiate:** Baseball M, cross-country, golf, soccer, tennis, track and field, volleyball W. **Intramural:** Badminton, basketball, football (non-tackle), golf M, softball, table tennis, tennis, volleyball. **Team name:** Patriots.

Student services. Adult student services, alcohol/substance abuse counseling, campus ministries, career counseling, student employment services, financial aid counseling, health services, personal counseling, placement for graduates, veterans' counselor. **Physically disabled:** Services for visually, speech, hearing impaired.

Contact. E-mail: admiss@dbu.edu
Phone: (214) 333-5360 Toll-free number: (800) 460-1328
Fax: (214) 333-5447
Erin Spivey, Director of Undergraduate Admissions, Dallas Baptist University, 3000 Mountain Creek Parkway, Dallas, TX 75211-9299

Dallas Christian College
Dallas, Texas
www.dallas.edu **CB code: 0792**

- Private 4-year Bible college affiliated with nondenominational tradition
- Commuter campus in very large city
- 260 full-time, degree-seeking undergraduates
- 48% of applicants admitted
- SAT or ACT required

General. Founded in 1950. Accredited by ABHE. Special program for adult, nontraditional students. **Degrees:** 66 bachelor's awarded. **Location:** 10 miles from downtown. **Calendar:** 4-1-4, limited summer session. **Full-time faculty:** 8 total; 50% have terminal degrees, 12% minority, 25% women. **Part-time faculty:** 48 total; 23% have terminal degrees, 8% minority, 17% women.

Freshman class profile. 336 applied, 161 admitted, 40 enrolled.

Mid 50% test scores			
SAT verbal:	430-560	Rank in top quarter:	14%
SAT math:	400-560	Rank in top tenth:	2%
ACT:	18-23	Out-of-state:	8%
		Live on campus:	85%

Basis for selection. School record and recommendation, followed by test scores. Class rank also important. Interview recommended, essays required for some.

2005-2006 Annual costs. Tuition/fees: $8,185. Room/board: $5,000. Books/supplies: $600.

Application procedures. Admission: Priority date 7/1; deadline 8/15 (postmark date). $40 fee, may be waived for applicants with need. Application may be submitted online. Admission notification on a rolling basis. Must reply by 8/15. **Financial aid:** Closing date 4/15. FAFSA, institutional form required. Applicants notified on a rolling basis; must reply within 2 week(s) of notification.

Academics. Special study options: Distance learning, double major, dual enrollment of high school students, independent study, internships, liberal arts/career combination, teacher certification program. Evening degree-seeking program for adults. **Credit/placement by examination:** AP, CLEP, institutional tests. 30 credit hours maximum toward bachelor's degree. **Support services:** Reduced course load, remedial instruction, study skills assistance.

Majors. Business: Business admin. **Liberal arts:** Arts/sciences. **Psychology:** General. **Theology:** Bible, religious ed, sacred music, theology.

Most popular majors. Business/marketing 20%, philosophy/religious studies 80%.

Computing on campus. 16 workstations in library, computer center. Dormitories wired for high-speed internet access. Online library, wireless network available.

Student life. Freshman orientation: Mandatory, $100 fee. Preregistration for classes offered. Held 2 days prior to registration. **Policies:** All resident students as well as those taking 8 hours or more required to attend campus chapel services 2 times a week. Freshmen permitted cars on campus. **Housing:** Guaranteed on-campus for all undergraduates. Single-sex dorms available. $50 deposit, deadline 8/10. **Activities:** Pep band, choral groups, drama, music ensembles, student government, urban ministries program.

Athletics. NCCAA. **Intercollegiate:** Basketball, soccer M, volleyball W. **Team name:** Crusaders.

Student services. Adult student services, campus ministries, student employment services, financial aid counseling, personal counseling, placement for graduates.

Contact. E-mail: dcc@dallas.edu
Phone: (972) 241-3371 ext. 153 Toll-free number: (800) 688-1029
Fax: (972) 241-8021
Marty McKee, Director of Admissions, Dallas Christian College, 2700 Christian Parkway, Dallas, TX 75234-7299

DeVry University: Houston
Houston, Texas
www.devry.edu

- For-profit 4-year university
- Commuter campus
- 611 degree-seeking undergraduates: 38% part-time, 38% women
- 83 graduate students

General. Degrees: 20 bachelor's, 1 associate awarded; master's offered. **Calendar:** Semester. **Full-time faculty:** 1 total; 100% women. **Part-time faculty:** 96 total; 29% minority, 32% women.

Freshman class profile. 158 enrolled.

Return as sophomores:	41%	International:	1%

Basis for selection. Interview, high school GPA, and test scores most important. DeVry-administered admissions tests may be submitted in place of SAT/ACT.

2005-2006 Annual costs. Tuition/fees: $12,140.

Financial aid. Non-need-based: Scholarships awarded for academics.

Application procedures. **Admission:** No deadline. $50 fee. Admission notification on a rolling basis. **Financial aid:** No deadline. FAFSA required. Applicants notified on a rolling basis.

Academics. **Special study options:** Accelerated study, cooperative education, distance learning. **Credit/placement by examination:** CLEP.

Most popular majors. Business/marketing 95%.

Contact. Phone: (713) 973-3000 Fax: (713) 896-7650
DeVry University: Houston, 11125 Equity Drive, Houston, TX 77041

DeVry University: Irving

Dallas, Texas — **CB member**
www.devry.edu — **CB code: 6180**

- For-profit 4-year university
- Commuter campus in small city
- 1,596 degree-seeking undergraduates: 31% part-time, 60% women
- 218 graduate students
- Interview required

General. Founded in 1969. Regionally accredited. **Degrees:** 413 bachelor's, 61 associate awarded; master's offered. **Location:** 12 miles from Dallas. **Calendar:** Semester, extensive summer session. **Full-time faculty:** 59 total; 22% minority, 36% women. **Part-time faculty:** 68 total; 28% minority, 40% women.

Freshman class profile. 248 enrolled.

Return as sophomores:	41%	**Out-of-state:**	6%

Basis for selection. Applicants must have a high school diploma or equivalent or a degree from an accredited postsecondary institution, demonstrating proficiency in basic college-level skills through SAT or ACT scores or institution-administered placement examinations, and be at least 17 years of age on the first day of classes. New students may enter at beginning of any semester. SAT or ACT recommended. CPT also accepted.

High school preparation. College-preparatory program recommended. Required units include mathematics 1. Math unit must be algebra or higher.

2005-2006 Annual costs. Tuition/fees: $12,140. Books/supplies: $1,100. Personal expenses: $1,750.

2004-2005 Financial aid. All financial aid based on need. 192 full-time freshmen applied for aid; 180 were judged to have need; 177 of these received aid. Average need met was 42%. Average scholarship/grant was $4,383; average loan $5,422. 18% of total undergraduate aid awarded as scholarships/grants, 82% as loans/jobs.

Application procedures. **Admission:** No deadline. $50 fee. Application may be submitted online. Admission notification on a rolling basis. **Financial aid:** No deadline. FAFSA required. Applicants notified on a rolling basis starting 7/1.

Academics. **Special study options:** Accelerated study, cooperative education, distance learning. **Credit/placement by examination:** CLEP, institutional tests. No more than 35% of credit toward graduation requirement accepted. **Support services:** Learning center, remedial instruction, tutoring.

Majors. **Biology:** Bioinformatics. **Business:** General. **Computer sciences:** Information technology, networking, systems analysis. **Engineering technology:** Biomedical, computer, electrical. **Health:** Medical records technology.

Most popular majors. Business/marketing 49%, computer/information sciences 39%, engineering/engineering technologies 12%.

Computing on campus. 450 workstations in library, computer center. Online course registration, online library, helpline available.

Student life. **Freshman orientation:** Mandatory. **Policies:** Freshmen permitted cars on campus. **Activities:** Student newspaper, Association of Information Technology Professionals, campus Bible study, Christian Students Fellowship, Habitat for Humanity, Institute of Electrical and Electronics Engineers, Institute of Management Accountants, minority student union, National Society of Black Engineers, Society of Women Engineers, Telecommunications Management and Associations, Society of Hispanic Professionals Engineers, gamers.

Athletics. **Intramural:** Basketball, football (tackle) M, volleyball.

Student services. Career counseling, student employment services, financial aid counseling, placement for graduates, veterans' counselor. **Physically disabled:** Services for visually, hearing impaired.

Contact. E-mail: cwilliams@mail.dal.devry.edu
Phone: (972) 929-5777 Toll-free number: (800) 633-3879
Fax: (972) 929-2860
Chad Williams, Director of Admissions, DeVry University: Irving, 4800 Regent Boulevard, Dallas, TX 75063-2439

East Texas Baptist University

Marshall, Texas
www.etbu.edu — **CB code: 6187**

- Private 4-year university and liberal arts college affiliated with Baptist faith
- Residential campus in large town
- 1,241 degree-seeking undergraduates: 5% part-time, 55% women, 15% African American, 4% Hispanic American, 1% Native American, 1% international
- 79% of applicants admitted
- SAT or ACT (ACT writing optional) required
- 48% graduate within 6 years

General. Founded in 1912. Regionally accredited. **Degrees:** 265 bachelor's awarded. **Location:** 35 miles from Shreveport, Louisiana, 20 miles from Longview. **Calendar:** Semester. 4-4-1. Extensive summer session. **Full-time faculty:** 66 total; 85% have terminal degrees, 4% minority, 33% women. **Part-time faculty:** 41 total; 15% have terminal degrees, 20% minority, 54% women. **Class size:** 43% < 20, 45% 20-39, 9% 40-49, 3% 50-99. **Special facilities:** Caddo Lake international wetlands.

Freshman class profile. 851 applied, 670 admitted, 303 enrolled.

Mid 50% test scores		**Rank in top tenth:**	16%
SAT verbal:	440-530	**End year in good standing:**	81%
SAT math:	440-540	**Return as sophomores:**	53%
ACT:	18-24	**Out-of-state:**	1%
Rank in top quarter:	44%	**Live on campus:**	95%

Basis for selection. School achievement record and test scores most important. Evidence of good character also important. Applicants should be in top 40% of class. Interview recommended for academically deficient; audition recommended for music, speech, theater arts programs. **Learning Disabled:** Student should provide documentation of learning disability to Office of Student Services, which verifies documentation and assists in acquiring reasonable accommodations.

High school preparation. 22 units recommended. Recommended units include English 4, mathematics 3, social studies 2.5, science 2 and academic electives 1. 0.5 economics, 1.5 physical education, 0.5 health education, 1 technology applications.

2006-2007 Annual costs. Tuition/fees: $13,700. Room/board: $4,190. Books/supplies: $800. Personal expenses: $1,281.

2005-2006 Financial aid. **Need-based:** 294 full-time freshmen applied for aid; 242 were judged to have need; 242 of these received aid. Average need met was 89%. Average scholarship/grant was $5,284; average loan $2,605. 57% of total undergraduate aid awarded as scholarships/grants, 43% as loans/jobs. **Non-need-based:** Scholarships awarded for academics, alumni affiliation, leadership, music/drama, religious affiliation.

Application procedures. **Admission:** Closing date 8/17 (receipt date). $25 fee, may be waived for applicants with need. Application may be submitted online. Admission notification on a rolling basis beginning on or about 9/1. **Financial aid:** Closing date 6/1. FAFSA, institutional form required. Applicants notified on a rolling basis starting 1/15; must reply within 3 week(s) of notification.

Academics. **Special study options:** Accelerated study, double major, dual enrollment of high school students, exchange student, honors, independent study, internships, liberal arts/career combination, study abroad, teacher certification program, Washington semester. **Credit/placement by examination:** AP, CLEP, IB, institutional tests. 15 credit hours maximum toward associate degree, 30 toward bachelor's. ACT required for placement. Departmental examinations administered on request upon approval of department chair. **Support services:** Learning center, reduced course load, study skills assistance, tutoring, writing center.

Majors. **Biology:** General. **Business:** General, accounting, management information systems. **Communications:** Media studies. **Computer sciences:** General. **Education:** General, biology, chemistry, drama/dance, elementary, English, history, mathematics, music, physical, social studies, Spanish, speech. **English:** English lit, speech/rhetoric. **Foreign languages:** Spanish.

Health: Athletic training, clinical lab science, nursing (RN). **History:** General. **Liberal arts:** Arts/sciences. **Math:** General. **Parks/recreation:** Health/fitness. **Philosophy/religion:** Religion. **Physical sciences:** Chemistry. **Psychology:** General. **Social sciences:** General, sociology. **Theology:** Bible, missionary, pastoral counseling, religious ed, sacred music, youth ministry. **Visual/performing arts:** Dramatic, piano/organ, voice/opera.

Most popular majors. Biology 6%, business/marketing 16%, education 22%, English 6%, health sciences 7%, psychology 9%, theological studies 14%.

Computing on campus. 206 workstations in dormitories, library, computer center, student center. Dormitories wired for high-speed internet access and linked to campus network. Commuter students can connect to campus network. Online course registration, online library, helpline, repair service, student web hosting, wireless network available.

Student life. Freshman orientation: Mandatory, $50 fee. Preregistration for classes offered. Full week prior to start of fall classes. **Policies:** Graded curfew, weekly clean room check. Religious observance required. Freshmen permitted cars on campus. **Housing:** Guaranteed on-campus for all undergraduates. Single-sex dorms, apartments, substance-free housing available. $100 deposit, deadline 8/15. **Activities:** Bands, choral groups, drama, literary magazine, music ensembles, student government, student newspaper, symphony orchestra, Baptist student ministries, Fellowship of Christian Athletes, political awareness society, United Voices of Praise, Delta Cho Rho, Delta Pi Theta, Pi Sigma, Sigma Sigma Epsilon.

Athletics. NCAA. **Intercollegiate:** Baseball M, basketball, cross-country, football (tackle) M, soccer, softball W, volleyball W. **Intramural:** Basketball, football (non-tackle) M, softball, volleyball. **Team name:** Tigers.

Student services. Adult student services, campus ministries, career counseling, student employment services, financial aid counseling, health services, personal counseling, placement for graduates, veterans' counselor. **Physically disabled:** Services for hearing impaired.

Contact. E-mail: admissions@etbu.edu
Phone: (903) 923-2000 Toll-free number: (800) 804-3828
Fax: (903) 923-2001
Vince Blankenship, Dean of Admissions and Marketing, East Texas Baptist University, 1209 North Grove, Marshall, TX 75670-1498

Hardin-Simmons University

Abilene, Texas — **CB member**
www.hsutx.edu — **CB code: 6268**

- Private 4-year university affiliated with Baptist faith
- Residential campus in small city
- 1,987 degree-seeking undergraduates: 10% part-time, 55% women, 5% African American, 1% Asian American, 10% Hispanic American, 1% Native American
- 395 degree-seeking graduate students
- 66% of applicants admitted
- SAT or ACT with writing required
- 51% graduate within 6 years; 41% enter graduate study

General. Founded in 1891. Regionally accredited. Part of 3-member consortium (with Abilene Christian University and McMurry University) comprising Abilene Intercollegiate School of Nursing. **Degrees:** 308 bachelor's awarded; master's, doctoral, first professional offered. **Location:** 150 miles from Fort Worth. **Calendar:** Semester, extensive summer session. **Full-time faculty:** 131 total; 74% have terminal degrees, 2% minority, 34% women. **Part-time faculty:** 48 total; 31% have terminal degrees, 4% minority, 44% women. **Class size:** 54% < 20, 42% 20-39, 3% 40-49, 1% 50-99. **Special facilities:** Rare and fine book room, observatory.

Freshman class profile. 1,179 applied, 782 admitted, 436 enrolled.

Mid 50% test scores			
SAT verbal:	460-580	Rank in top quarter:	45%
SAT math:	470-570	Rank in top tenth:	21%
ACT:	19-24	End year in good standing:	82%
GPA 3.50 or higher:	68%	Return as sophomores:	69%
GPA 3.0-3.49:	19%	Out-of-state:	3%
GPA 2.0-2.99:	13%	Live on campus:	92%

Basis for selection. Applicants admitted on basis of acceptable combination of test scores and prior academic record. Special cases considered individually. Non-native speakers of English require score of 550 on TOEFL, unless transferring 24 or more credits. Audition required for music program; interview recommended for special cases. Written essay, interview, and separate application required for honors program. **Homeschooled:** GED scores required only if applicant plans to apply for federal need-based financial aid.

High school preparation. 16 units required. Required units include English 3, mathematics 2, social studies 2, science 2 and academic electives 7. Mathematics must include algebra I and above. English must be English I, II and III.

2006-2007 Annual costs. Tuition/fees: $15,626. Room/board: $4,580. Books/supplies: $750. Personal expenses: $1,482.

2005-2006 Financial aid. Need-based: 434 full-time freshmen applied for aid; 306 were judged to have need; 306 of these received aid. Average need met was 67%. Average scholarship/grant was $4,431; average loan $2,394. 65% of total undergraduate aid awarded as scholarships/grants, 35% as loans/jobs. **Non-need-based:** Awarded to 1,255 full-time undergraduates, including 366 freshmen. Scholarships awarded for academics, art, job skills, leadership, music/drama, religious affiliation.

Application procedures. Admission: No deadline. $50 fee. Application may be submitted online. Admission notification on a rolling basis beginning on or about 9/1. **Financial aid:** Priority date 3/15; no closing date. FAFSA required. Applicants notified on a rolling basis starting 1/1.

Academics. Special study options: Accelerated study, cross-registration, distance learning, double major, dual enrollment of high school students, honors, independent study, internships, New York semester, study abroad, teacher certification program, United Nations semester, Washington semester. **Credit/placement by examination:** AP, CLEP, SAT, ACT, institutional tests. 32 credit hours maximum toward bachelor's degree. Maximum 14 hours in any one discipline. **Support services:** Pre-admission summer program, reduced course load, remedial instruction, tutoring, writing center.

Majors. Agriculture: Agronomy, animal sciences, business. **Biology:** General, Biochemistry/biophysics and molecular biology. **Business:** Accounting, business admin, finance, management science, marketing. **Communications:** General, broadcast journalism, media studies, public relations, radio/tv. **Computer sciences:** Programming. **Conservation:** Environmental science. **Education:** Art, business, computer, drama/dance, early childhood, English, history, mathematics, music, physical, reading, science, social studies, Spanish, speech. **English:** English lit, speech/rhetoric. **Foreign languages:** Spanish. **Health:** Athletic training, audiology/speech pathology, nursing (RN), predentistry, premedicine. **History:** General. **Legal studies:** Prelaw. **Math:** General. **Parks/recreation:** Exercise sciences, health/fitness. **Philosophy/religion:** Philosophy. **Physical sciences:** Chemistry, geology, physics. **Protective services:** Corrections, police science. **Psychology:** General. **Public administration:** Social work. **Social sciences:** Economics, political science, sociology. **Theology:** Bible, missionary, preministerial, sacred music, theology, youth ministry. **Visual/performing arts:** Dramatic, graphic design, music history, music management, music performance, music theory/composition, piano/organ, stringed instruments, studio arts, voice/opera.

Most popular majors. Biology 8%, business/marketing 13%, communications/journalism 6%, education 18%, health sciences 9%, parks/recreation 8%, psychology 7%, visual/performing arts 8%.

Computing on campus. 200 workstations in dormitories, library, computer center, student center. Dormitories wired for high-speed internet access and linked to campus network. Online library, helpline, wireless network available.

Student life. Freshman orientation: Available, $75 fee. Preregistration for classes offered. Held Tuesday through Sunday the week before classes begin. **Policies:** Single, undergraduate students under 21 who have not completed 60 credit hours and are not living at home required to live in residence halls. Religious observance required. Freshmen permitted cars on campus. **Housing:** Guaranteed on-campus for freshmen. Single-sex dorms, special housing for disabled, apartments, substance-free housing available. $100 fully refundable deposit. Single and duplex housing available with priority given to families. **Activities:** Bands, choral groups, drama, literary magazine, music ensembles, musical theater, opera, student government, student newspaper, symphony orchestra, unity group, Baptist student ministry, student foundation, black student fellowship, moot court team, Latin American club, United Mexican American Students, social work club, criminal justice club, Students in Free Enterprise, Collegiates for Racial Harmony.

Athletics. NCAA. **Intercollegiate:** Baseball M, basketball, cheerleading, football (tackle) M, golf, soccer, softball W, tennis, volleyball W. **Intramural:** Badminton, basketball, bowling, football (non-tackle), football (tackle), golf, handball, racquetball, soccer, softball, tennis, volleyball. **Team name:** Cowboys/Cowgirls.

Student services. Campus ministries, career counseling, student employment services, financial aid counseling, health services, personal counseling, placement for graduates, veterans' counselor. **Physically disabled:** Services for visually, speech, hearing impaired.

Contact. E-mail: enroll@hsutx.edu
Phone: (325) 670-1206 Toll-free number: (877) 464-7889
Fax: (325) 671-2115
Shane Davidson, Associate Vice President of Enrollment Services,
Hardin-Simmons University, PO Box 16050, Abilene, TX 79698-0001

Houston Baptist University

Houston, Texas — **CB member**
www.hbu.edu — **CB code: 6282**

- Private 4-year university and liberal arts college affiliated with Baptist General Convention of Texas
- Commuter campus in very large city
- 1,873 degree-seeking undergraduates: 14% part-time, 67% women, 19% African American, 13% Asian American, 15% Hispanic American, 6% international
- 362 degree-seeking graduate students
- 65% of applicants admitted
- SAT or ACT with writing, application essay required
- 59% graduate within 6 years

General. Founded in 1960. Regionally accredited. Quarter calendar used, but semester credit hours granted. **Degrees:** 349 bachelor's, 6 associate awarded; master's offered. **ROTC:** Army, Navy. **Location:** 180 miles from San Antonio. **Calendar:** Quarter, extensive summer session. **Full-time faculty:** 103 total; 81% have terminal degrees, 10% minority, 48% women. **Part-time faculty:** 66 total; 33% have terminal degrees, 14% minority, 46% women. **Class size:** 49% < 20, 48% 20-39, 2% 40-49, less than 1% >100. **Special facilities:** Decorative arts museum, Bible in America museum, wellness center.

Freshman class profile. 867 applied, 567 admitted, 313 enrolled.

Mid 50% test scores			
SAT verbal:	480-600	**Rank in top tenth:**	24%
SAT math:	480-600	**End year in good standing:**	90%
ACT:	19-25	**Return as sophomores:**	74%
Rank in top quarter:	44%	**Out-of-state:**	2%
		International:	5%

Basis for selection. School achievement record, test scores, recommendations, class rank, special talents, and skills most important. Audition required for music majors; portfolio required for art majors; interview recommended for academically weak students.

High school preparation. 18 units recommended. Recommended units include English 4, mathematics 3, social studies 2, history 2, science 3 (laboratory 1), foreign language 2 and academic electives 2.

2005-2006 Annual costs. Tuition/fees: $13,950. Room/board: $4,710.

2005-2006 Financial aid. Need-based: Average need met was 59%. Average scholarship/grant was $7,021; average loan $2,162. 47% of total undergraduate aid awarded as scholarships/grants, 53% as loans/jobs. **Non-need-based:** Scholarships awarded for academics, alumni affiliation, art, athletics, leadership, music/drama, religious affiliation.

Application procedures. Admission: No deadline. $25 fee, may be waived for applicants with need. Application may be submitted online. Admission notification on a rolling basis. **Financial aid:** Priority date 3/1, closing date 4/15. FAFSA required. Applicants notified on a rolling basis starting 3/10.

Academics. Special study options: Accelerated study, combined bachelor's/graduate degree, double major, dual enrollment of high school students, ESL, honors, independent study, internships, liberal arts/career combination, teacher certification program. **Credit/placement by examination:** AP, CLEP, IB, institutional tests. CLEP credit limited to students with 63 or fewer credit hours. **Support services:** Reduced course load, remedial instruction, tutoring, writing center.

Majors. Biology: General, molecular. **Business:** General, accounting, business admin, entrepreneurial studies, finance, information resources management, management information systems, managerial economics, marketing. **Communications:** General, media studies. **Education:** Art, early childhood, English, mathematics, middle, music, physical, science, secondary, social studies. **English:** Creative writing, English lit. **Family/consumer sciences:** Child development. **Foreign languages:** French, Spanish. **Health:** Nursing (RN). **History:** General. **Interdisciplinary:** Accounting/computer science. **Math:** General. **Parks/recreation:** Exercise sciences, health/fitness. **Philosophy/religion:** Christian. **Physical sciences:** Chemistry, physics. **Psychology:** General. **Social sciences:** Economics, political science, sociology. **Theology:** Pastoral counseling, sacred music. **Visual/performing arts:** Music performance, music theory/composition, studio arts.

Most popular majors. Biology 12%, business/marketing 32%, communications/journalism 6%, education 11%, philosophy/religious studies 6%, psychology 11%.

Computing on campus. 95 workstations in dormitories, library, computer center. Dormitories wired for high-speed internet access and linked to campus network. Commuter students can connect to campus network. Online course registration, online library, helpline, repair service, wireless network available.

Student life. Freshman orientation: Available. Preregistration for classes offered. 2-and-a-half-day camp held off campus. **Policies:** Spiritual Life Program graduation requirement for all undergraduate students. Freshmen permitted cars on campus. **Housing:** Guaranteed on-campus for freshmen. Single-sex dorms, apartments, substance-free housing available. $200 partly refundable deposit. **Activities:** Bands, choral groups, drama, literary magazine, music ensembles, musical theater, opera, student government, student newspaper, symphony orchestra, TV station, Christian Life on Campus, Psi Chi, Nursing Association, international club, Black Student Fellowship, Toastmasters, Digital Eon, Vietnamese Student Association, Indian Student Association, Sisters for the Lord, Brothers Under Christ.

Athletics. NAIA. **Intercollegiate:** Baseball M, basketball, cheerleading, softball W, volleyball W. **Intramural:** Badminton, basketball, bowling, football (non-tackle), golf, soccer, softball, table tennis, tennis, volleyball. **Team name:** Huskies.

Student services. Adult student services, alcohol/substance abuse counseling, campus ministries, career counseling, student employment services, financial aid counseling, health services, personal counseling, placement for graduates, women's services. **Physically disabled:** Services for visually, speech, hearing impaired.

Contact. E-mail: unadm@hbu.edu
Phone: (281) 649-3211 Toll-free number: (800) 969-3210
Fax: (281) 649-3217
David Melton, Associate Vice President of Admissions and Marketing,
Houston Baptist University, 7502 Fondren Road, Houston, TX 77074-3298

Howard Payne University

Brownwood, Texas
www.hputx.edu — **CB code: 6278**

- Private 4-year liberal arts and teachers college affiliated with Baptist faith
- Residential campus in large town
- 1,364 degree-seeking undergraduates: 6% African American, 1% Asian American, 14% Hispanic American, 1% Native American
- 1,364 graduate students
- 71% of applicants admitted
- SAT or ACT with writing required
- 37% graduate within 6 years

General. Founded in 1889. Regionally accredited. **Degrees:** 173 bachelor's, 2 associate awarded. **Location:** 150 miles from Dallas, 77 miles from Abilene. **Calendar:** Semester, limited summer session. **Full-time faculty:** 75 total; 59% have terminal degrees, 5% minority, 36% women. **Part-time faculty:** 65 total; 28% have terminal degrees, 8% minority, 28% women. **Class size:** 78% < 20, 20% 20-39, 2% 40-49, less than 1% 50-99.

Freshman class profile. 1,076 applied, 763 admitted, 297 enrolled.

Mid 50% test scores		**Rank in top quarter:**	42%
SAT verbal:	440-570	**Rank in top tenth:**	20%
SAT math:	440-550	**Return as sophomores:**	57%
ACT:	17-23	**Out-of-state:**	2%
GPA 3.50 or higher:	50%	**Live on campus:**	91%
GPA 3.0-3.49:	41%	**Fraternities:**	15%
GPA 2.0-2.99:	9%	**Sororities:**	15%

Basis for selection. Applicants must meet at least one of the following criteria: ACT score of at least 19 or SAT score of at least 910 (exclusive of Writing), B average throughout high school, or rank in top half of class. Those not meeting requirements may be eligible for provisional or conditional admission. ACT/SAT scores used to exempt students from placement tests in English, math, or reading. Interview required for academic program applicants, recommended for all others. Interview may be required by admissions committee. Audition required for music program. **Homeschooled:** Admissions committee assesses on individual basis.

High school preparation. 15 units required; 22 recommended. Required and recommended units include English 4, mathematics 3, social studies 2.5, science 2, academic electives 10.5. Remaining credits must be among those listed in approved courses provided by Texas Education Agency.

2005-2006 Annual costs. Tuition/fees: $12,500. Room/board: $4,615. Books/supplies: $1,000. Personal expenses: $1,500.

Financial aid. Non-need-based: Scholarships awarded for academics, alumni affiliation, art, job skills, music/drama.

Application procedures. Admission: Priority date 8/15; no deadline. $25 fee. Admission notification on a rolling basis. **Financial aid:** Priority date 3/1; no closing date. FAFSA, institutional form required. Applicants notified on a rolling basis starting 3/30; must reply within 3 week(s) of notification.

Academics. Special study options: Accelerated study, cooperative education, distance learning, double major, dual enrollment of high school students, ESL, honors, independent study, internships, liberal arts/career combination, study abroad, teacher certification program. Extension classes in El Paso, Corpus Christi, Harlingen, Ft. Worth. **Credit/placement by examination:** AP, CLEP, institutional tests. 30 credit hours maximum toward bachelor's degree. **Support services:** Reduced course load, remedial instruction, study skills assistance, tutoring, writing center.

Majors. Biology: General. **Business:** General, accounting, business admin, finance, marketing. **Communications:** General, public relations. **Computer sciences:** Information systems. **Education:** General, art, biology, business, chemistry, drama/dance, elementary, English, history, mathematics, multi-level teacher, music, physical, science, secondary, social science, Spanish, speech. **English:** Speech/rhetoric. **Foreign languages:** Biblical, Spanish. **Health:** Athletic training, premedicine. **History:** General. **Liberal arts:** Arts/sciences. **Math:** General. **Parks/recreation:** General, exercise sciences, health/fitness, sports admin. **Philosophy/religion:** Philosophy, religion. **Physical sciences:** Chemistry. **Psychology:** General. **Public administration:** Social work. **Social sciences:** General, political science, sociology. **Theology:** Bible, religious ed, sacred music, theology, youth ministry. **Visual/performing arts:** Art, dramatic, music performance, piano/organ, stringed instruments, studio arts, voice/opera.

Computing on campus. 260 workstations in dormitories, library, computer center, student center. Dormitories wired for high-speed internet access and linked to campus network. Online library, helpline, wireless network available.

Student life. Freshman orientation: Available, $50 fee. Preregistration for classes offered. Held the weekend before fall semester classes begin. **Policies:** Religious observance required. Freshmen permitted cars on campus. **Housing:** Guaranteed on-campus for freshmen. Single-sex dorms, apartments, substance-free housing available. $100 deposit, deadline 8/15. **Activities:** Bands, choral groups, dance, drama, literary magazine, music ensembles, musical theater, opera, radio station, student government, student newspaper, Baptist Student Ministry, Student Foundation, Ministerial Alliance, Fellowship of Christian Athletes.

Athletics. NCAA. **Intercollegiate:** Baseball M, basketball, cheerleading, football (tackle) M, softball W, tennis, track and field, volleyball W. **Intramural:** Basketball, football (non-tackle), softball, table tennis, tennis, volleyball. **Team name:** Yellow Jackets.

Student services. Adult student services, campus ministries, career counseling, student employment services, financial aid counseling, health services, personal counseling, placement for graduates.

Contact. E-mail: enroll@hputx.edu
Phone: (325) 649-8027 Toll-free number: (800) 880-4478
Fax: (325) 649-8901
Brad Johnson, Vice President for Enrollment Services, Howard Payne University, 1000 Fisk Avenue, Brownwood, TX 76801

Huston-Tillotson College

Austin, Texas — **CB member**
www.htu.edu — **CB code: 6280**

- Private 4-year liberal arts college affiliated with United Church of Christ and United Methodist Church
- Residential campus in very large city
- 630 degree-seeking undergraduates: 7% part-time, 55% women
- SAT or ACT, application essay required

General. Founded in 1876. Regionally accredited. **Degrees:** 58 bachelor's awarded. **ROTC:** Army, Navy, Air Force. **Location:** Downtown. **Calendar:** Semester, extensive summer session. **Full-time faculty:** 37 total; 70% have terminal degrees, 62% minority, 54% women. **Part-time faculty:** 25 total; 32% have terminal degrees, 36% minority, 52% women. **Class size:** 76% < 20, 22% 20-39, 1% 40-49, less than 1% 50-99, less than 1% >100.

Freshman class profile.

Mid 50% test scores			
SAT verbal:	340-460	Rank in top tenth:	7%
SAT math:	340-460	Return as sophomores:	58%
ACT:	14-18	Out-of-state:	14%
Rank in top quarter:	23%	Live on campus:	81%

Basis for selection. School achievement record important. Test scores and interview considered.

High school preparation. 22 units required. Required and recommended units include English 4, mathematics 3, social studies 2.5, science 2, foreign language 2 and academic electives 1.

2005-2006 Annual costs. Tuition/fees: $8,780. Room/board: $5,610. Books/supplies: $635. Personal expenses: $1,306.

2004-2005 Financial aid. Need-based: 161 full-time freshmen applied for aid; 161 were judged to have need; 149 of these received aid. Average need met was 77%. Average scholarship/grant was $1,263; average loan $2,325. 53% of total undergraduate aid awarded as scholarships/grants, 47% as loans/jobs. **Non-need-based:** Awarded to 357 full-time undergraduates, including 134 freshmen. Scholarships awarded for academics, alumni affiliation, art, athletics, job skills, leadership, minority status, music/drama, religious affiliation, ROTC, state residency.

Application procedures. Admission: Priority date 3/1; deadline 8/1. $25 fee, may be waived for applicants with need. Admission notification on a rolling basis beginning on or about 1/1. **Financial aid:** Priority date 3/15, closing date 4/1. FAFSA, institutional form required. Applicants notified on a rolling basis starting 4/1; must reply within 4 week(s) of notification.

Academics. Special study options: Cross-registration, distance learning, double major, dual enrollment of high school students, external degree, honors, independent study, internships, liberal arts/career combination, study abroad, teacher certification program. 3-2 engineering program with Prairie View A&M University. **Credit/placement by examination:** AP, CLEP, institutional tests. 15 credit hours maximum toward bachelor's degree. **Support services:** Learning center, remedial instruction, tutoring.

Majors. Biology: General. **Business:** Accounting, business admin, marketing. **Computer sciences:** General, computer science. **Education:** General, physical. **English:** Composition. **Liberal arts:** Arts/sciences. **Math:** General. **Physical sciences:** Chemistry. **Social sciences:** General, political science, sociology.

Computing on campus. 400 workstations in dormitories, library, computer center, student center. Dormitories wired for high-speed internet access and linked to campus network. Commuter students can connect to campus network. Online library, helpline, wireless network available.

Student life. Freshman orientation: Mandatory. Preregistration for classes offered. **Policies:** Freshmen permitted cars on campus. **Housing:** Guaranteed on-campus for all undergraduates. Single-sex dorms, substance-free housing available. **Activities:** Choral groups, literary magazine, music ensembles, student government, student newspaper, Brothers and Sisters in Christ.

Athletics. NAIA. **Intercollegiate:** Baseball M, basketball, soccer M, track and field W, volleyball W. **Intramural:** Basketball, soccer M, softball, table tennis, volleyball. **Team name:** Rams.

Student services. Adult student services, career counseling, student employment services, financial aid counseling, health services, personal counseling, placement for graduates, veterans' counselor.

Contact. Phone: (512) 505-3028 Fax: (512) 505-3190
Nadine Jenkins, Dean of Enrollment Management, Huston-Tillotson College, 900 Chicon Street, Austin, TX 78702-2795

Jarvis Christian College

Hawkins, Texas
www.jarvis.edu — **CB code: 6319**

- Private 4-year liberal arts and teachers college affiliated with Christian Church (Disciples of Christ)
- Residential campus in rural community
- 561 degree-seeking undergraduates: 54% women, 98% African American, 1% Hispanic American
- 59% of applicants admitted

General. Founded in 1912. Regionally accredited. **Degrees:** 57 bachelor's awarded. **Location:** 100 miles from Dallas; 100 miles from Shreveport,

Louisiana. **Calendar:** Semester, extensive summer session. **Full-time faculty:** 36 total; 44% have terminal degrees, 61% minority, 33% women. **Part-time faculty:** 19 total; 26% have terminal degrees, 63% minority, 58% women. **Class size:** 58% < 20, 37% 20-39, 2% 40-49, 2% 50-99, less than 1% >100. **Special facilities:** Observatory, natatorium, archives of black Christian church (Disciples of Christ).

Freshman class profile. 398 applied, 236 admitted, 161 enrolled.

GPA 3.50 or higher:	5%	**End year in good standing:**	100%
GPA 3.0-3.49:	28%	**Return as sophomores:**	65%
GPA 2.0-2.99:	54%	**Out-of-state:**	8%
Rank in top quarter:	10%	**Live on campus:**	96%
Rank in top tenth:	3%		

Basis for selection. Admission granted to applicants who present evidence of adequate college preparation and show promise of profiting from experiences provided by the College. **Homeschooled:** State high school equivalency certificate required.

High school preparation. College-preparatory program recommended. 16 units recommended. Recommended units include English 3, mathematics 2, social studies 3, science 1 and academic electives 7.

2006-2007 Annual costs. Tuition/fees (projected): $6,980. Room/board: $4,156. Books/supplies: $800. Personal expenses: $950.

2004-2005 Financial aid. Need-based: 98 full-time freshmen applied for aid; 81 were judged to have need; 81 of these received aid. Average need met was 79%. Average scholarship/grant was $3,400; average loan $1,313. 63% of total undergraduate aid awarded as scholarships/grants, 37% as loans/jobs. **Non-need-based:** Awarded to 86 full-time undergraduates, including 71 freshmen. Scholarships awarded for academics, athletics, religious affiliation. **Additional information:** High school transcript required for scholarship consideration.

Application procedures. Admission: No deadline. $25 fee, may be waived for applicants with need. Application may be submitted online. Admission notification on a rolling basis beginning on or about 4/1. **Financial aid:** Priority date 6/30; no closing date. FAFSA required. Applicants notified on a rolling basis starting 5/1; must reply within 2 week(s) of notification.

Academics. Special study options: Accelerated study, combined bachelor's/graduate degree, cooperative education, cross-registration, distance learning, double major, dual enrollment of high school students, honors, internships, liberal arts/career combination, student-designed major, teacher certification program, Washington semester. **Credit/placement by examination:** AP, CLEP, IB, institutional tests. 18 credit hours maximum toward bachelor's degree. **Support services:** Learning center, reduced course load, remedial instruction, study skills assistance, tutoring, writing center.

Majors. Biology: General. **Business:** Business admin. **Communications:** Journalism. **Computer sciences:** General. **Education:** General, biology, business, early childhood, elementary, English, history, mathematics, middle, physical, reading, secondary, special. **Health:** Premedicine. **History:** General. **Math:** General. **Philosophy/religion:** Religion. **Physical sciences:** Chemistry. **Protective services:** Criminal justice. **Social sciences:** Sociology.

Most popular majors. Business/marketing 37%, computer/information sciences 14%, education 9%, health sciences 14%, history 9%, social sciences 11%.

Computing on campus. 359 workstations in dormitories, library, computer center. Dormitories wired for high-speed internet access and linked to campus network. Online library, repair service, wireless network available.

Student life. Freshman orientation: Mandatory. Preregistration for classes offered. **Policies:** Religious services available, regardless of denomination. Religious observance required. Freshmen permitted cars on campus. **Housing:** Guaranteed on-campus for all undergraduates. Single-sex dorms, special housing for disabled, apartments available. $100 nonrefundable deposit, deadline 8/1. Single parents housing available on limited basis. **Activities:** Bands, choral groups, music ensembles, student government, student ministers' association, United Campus Christian Fellowship, pre-law club, National Society of Black Accountants, Student National Educational Association, Students in Free Enterprise, Phi Beta Lambda English Club, college church.

Athletics. NAIA. **Intercollegiate:** Baseball M, basketball, cheerleading, volleyball W. **Intramural:** Baseball M, basketball, football (non-tackle), football (tackle) M, golf, soccer, softball, swimming, table tennis, tennis, volleyball, weight lifting, wrestling M. **Team name:** Bulldogs.

Student services. Campus ministries, career counseling, services for economically disadvantaged, student employment services, financial aid counseling, health services, personal counseling, placement for graduates, veterans' counselor. **Physically disabled:** Services for visually, speech, hearing impaired.

Contact. E-mail: felecia_tyiska@jarvis.edu
Phone: (903) 769-5734 Fax: (903) 769-1282
Felecia Tyiska, Director of Admissions, Jarvis Christian College, PO Box 1470, Hawkins, TX 75765-1470

Lamar University

Beaumont, Texas **CB member**
www.lamar.edu **CB code: 6360**

- Public 4-year university
- Commuter campus in small city
- 9,682 degree-seeking undergraduates: 31% part-time, 60% women, 26% African American, 3% Asian American, 6% Hispanic American, 1% Native American, 1% international
- 911 degree-seeking graduate students
- 68% of applicants admitted
- SAT or ACT required

General. Founded in 1923. Regionally accredited. **Degrees:** 1,202 bachelor's, 29 associate awarded; master's, doctoral offered. **Location:** 75 miles from Houston. **Calendar:** Semester, limited summer session. **Full-time faculty:** 372 total; 62% have terminal degrees, 19% minority, 44% women. **Part-time faculty:** 170 total; 17% have terminal degrees, 15% minority, 51% women. **Class size:** 27% < 20, 48% 20-39, 13% 40-49, 10% 50-99, 2% >100. **Special facilities:** Coastal and marine studies center, space exploration center, environmental chemistry laboratory, criminal justice studies center, hazardous substance research center, Spindletop/Gladys City museum.

Freshman class profile. 5,213 applied, 3,523 admitted, 1,683 enrolled.

Mid 50% test scores		**End year in good standing:**	71%
SAT verbal:	410-520	**Return as sophomores:**	61%
SAT math:	400-520	**Out-of-state:**	1%
ACT:	16-20	**Live on campus:**	43%
Rank in top quarter:	34%	**Fraternities:**	1%
Rank in top tenth:	12%	**Sororities:**	1%

Basis for selection. Admission decision based on high school class rank, SAT scores, and completion of 14 high school units of college preparatory courses. SAT Subject Tests recommended for students with strong academic backgrounds. Interview required of students accepted with GED tests and required for early entry. **Homeschooled:** Transcript of courses and grades required. Must submit SAT and meet state TASP testing requirements.

High school preparation. 15 units required. Required and recommended units include English 4, mathematics 3, social studies 3, science 2, foreign language 2 and academic electives 3.

2005-2006 Annual costs. Tuition/fees: $4,650; $12,930 out-of-state. Room/board: $5,254. Books/supplies: $692. Personal expenses: $1,892.

2005-2006 Financial aid. Need-based: 1,109 full-time freshmen applied for aid; 713 were judged to have need; 600 of these received aid. Average need met was 65%. 54% of total undergraduate aid awarded as scholarships/grants, 46% as loans/jobs. **Non-need-based:** Awarded to 2,030 full-time undergraduates, including 1,075 freshmen.

Application procedures. Admission: Closing date 8/1. No application fee. Admission notification on a rolling basis. **Financial aid:** Priority date 4/1; no closing date. FAFSA, institutional form required. Applicants notified on a rolling basis starting 4/1; must reply within 2 week(s) of notification.

Academics. Special study options: Accelerated study, cooperative education, distance learning, double major, dual enrollment of high school students, ESL, honors, independent study, internships, study abroad, teacher certification program. **Credit/placement by examination:** AP, CLEP, institutional tests. 15 credit hours maximum toward associate degree, 30 toward bachelor's. **Support services:** Learning center, pre-admission summer program, reduced course load, remedial instruction, study skills assistance, tutoring, writing center.

Majors. Architecture: Interior. **Biology:** General, marine. **Business:** General, accounting, business admin, finance, human resources, management information systems, managerial economics, marketing, office management, sales/distribution. **Communications:** General, advertising. **Computer sciences:** General. **Conservation:** General, environmental studies. **Education:** Art, Deaf/hearing impaired, early childhood, elementary, family/consumer sciences, health, mathematics, music, physical, school counseling, science, secondary, social studies, special. **Engineering:** General, chemical, civil, electrical, environmental, industrial, mechanical. **Engineering technology:** Industrial, industrial management. **English:** Speech/rhetoric. **Family/consumer sciences:** General, clothing/textiles, family/community services, food/nutrition. **Foreign languages:** French, Spanish. **Health:** Audiology/speech pathology, clinical lab science, nursing (RN). **History:** General. **Liberal arts:** Arts/sciences. **Math:** General, applied. **Parks/recreation:** Health/fitness. **Physical sciences:** Chemistry, geology, physics, planetary. **Protective services:** Criminal justice. **Psychology:** General. **Public administration:** Social work. **Social sciences:** Economics, political science, sociology. **Visual/performing arts:** Art, commercial/advertising art, dance, dramatic, voice/opera.

Most popular majors. Business/marketing 23%, engineering/engineering technologies 9%, health sciences 10%, interdisciplinary studies 15%, liberal arts 10%.

Computing on campus. 644 workstations in dormitories, library, computer center, student center. Dormitories wired for high-speed internet access and linked to campus network. Commuter students can connect to campus network. Online course registration, online library, helpline, repair service, student web hosting available.

Student life. **Freshman orientation:** Available, $10 fee. Preregistration for classes offered. One-day program available June-August. **Policies:** Freshmen permitted cars on campus. **Housing:** Guaranteed on-campus for freshmen. Coed dorms, single-sex dorms, special housing for disabled, substance-free housing available. $100 deposit, deadline 8/1. Coed halls with single rooms. **Activities:** Bands, choral groups, dance, drama, film society, literary magazine, music ensembles, musical theater, opera, radio station, student government, student newspaper, symphony orchestra, TV station, Catholic student union, Church of Latter-day Saints, Episcopal Center, Church of Christ Student Center, Wesley Foundation, Vietnamese student organization.

Athletics. NCAA. **Intercollegiate:** Baseball M, basketball, cross-country, golf, tennis, track and field, volleyball W. **Intramural:** Badminton, basketball, cross-country, racquetball, soccer, softball, swimming, table tennis, tennis, track and field, volleyball, weight lifting. **Team name:** Cardinals.

Student services. Adult student services, career counseling, student employment services, health services, on-campus daycare, personal counseling, placement for graduates, veterans' counselor. **Physically disabled:** Services for visually, speech, hearing impaired.

Contact. E-mail: admissions@hal.lamar.edu
Phone: (409) 880-8888 Fax: (409) 880-8463
James Rush, Director of Academic Services, Lamar University, Box 10009, Beaumont, TX 77705

LeTourneau University

Longview, Texas
www.letu.edu **CB code: 6365**

- Private 4-year university affiliated with nondenominational tradition
- Residential campus in small city
- 3,565 degree-seeking undergraduates: 61% part-time, 56% women, 22% African American, 1% Asian American, 8% Hispanic American, 1% international
- 374 degree-seeking graduate students
- 76% of applicants admitted
- SAT or ACT with writing, application essay required
- 52% graduate within 6 years

General. Founded in 1946. Regionally accredited. Centers in Tyler, Dallas, Houston and Bedford. **Degrees:** 523 bachelor's, 1 associate awarded; master's offered. **Location:** 120 miles from Dallas; 60 miles from Shreveport, Louisiana. **Calendar:** Semester, limited summer session. **Full-time faculty:** 72 total; 72% have terminal degrees, 10% minority, 17% women. **Part-time faculty:** 243 total; 42% have terminal degrees, 12% minority, 49% women. **Class size:** 80% < 20, 18% 20-39, 2% 40-49, less than 1% 50-99. **Special facilities:** Microprocessor and robotics laboratory, CAD laboratory, scanning electronic microscope, dynamic simulation laboratory, fleet of nine up-to-date airplanes, museum, biomedical engineering laboratory with motion analysis system.

Freshman class profile. 920 applied, 703 admitted, 352 enrolled.

Mid 50% test scores			
SAT verbal:	500-650	Rank in top quarter:	60%
SAT math:	520-650	Rank in top tenth:	32%
ACT:	21-28	Return as sophomores:	72%
GPA 3.50 or higher:	66%	Out-of-state:	55%
GPA 3.0-3.49:	24%	Live on campus:	90%
GPA 2.0-2.99:	10%	International:	2%

Basis for selection. Applicants should rank in top half of high school graduating class, have minimum ACT of 20 or minimum SAT of 950 (exclusive of Writing), and GPA of 2.5. Interview recommended. **Homeschooled:** Require SAT or ACT, transcript; recommend GED and detailed summary of curriculum used.

High school preparation. 16 units required. Required and recommended units include English 4, mathematics 3, social studies 2, history 1, science 3 (laboratory 3), foreign language 1 and academic electives 2. 4 math (including trigonometry) recommended for engineering applicants.

2005-2006 Annual costs. Tuition/fees: $15,890. Tuition for 1-6 hours is $286 per credit, for 7-11 hours is $628 per credit. Room/board: $6,286. Books/supplies: $1,095. Personal expenses: $1,000.

2004-2005 Financial aid. **Need-based:** 302 full-time freshmen applied for aid; 252 were judged to have need; 252 of these received aid. Average need met was 79%. Average scholarship/grant was $8,864; average loan $3,276. 42% of total undergraduate aid awarded as scholarships/grants, 58% as loans/jobs. **Non-need-based:** Awarded to 665 full-time undergraduates, including 246 freshmen. Scholarships awarded for academics, leadership.

Application procedures. **Admission:** Priority date 12/31; deadline 8/1. $25 fee, may be waived for applicants with need. Application may be submitted online. Admission notification on a rolling basis beginning on or about 8/1. Must reply by 5/1. **Financial aid:** Priority date 2/15; no closing date. FAFSA required. Applicants notified on a rolling basis starting 3/1; must reply within 3 week(s) of notification.

Academics. Peer advisers, student resource center, CARE committee, freshman year experience course available. **Special study options:** Accelerated study, cooperative education, distance learning, double major, dual enrollment of high school students, honors, independent study, internships, study abroad, teacher certification program, weekend college. **Credit/placement by examination:** AP, CLEP, IB, SAT, ACT, institutional tests. Credit must be established by end of student's first year at school. **Support services:** Reduced course load, remedial instruction, tutoring.

Majors. **Biology:** General. **Business:** General, accounting, business admin, finance, human resources, international, management information systems, marketing, operations. **Computer sciences:** General, computer science, information systems. **Education:** Business, computer, elementary, English, history, mathematics, middle, multi-level teacher, physical, science, secondary, social studies. **Engineering:** General, biomedical, computer, electrical, mechanical. **Engineering technology:** Aerospace, computer, electrical, mechanical. **English:** English lit. **Health:** Clinical lab science, predentistry, premedicine, prepharmacy, preveterinary. **History:** General. **Interdisciplinary:** Math/computer science. **Legal studies:** Prelaw. **Math:** General. **Mechanic/repair:** Aircraft, aircraft powerplant. **Parks/recreation:** Exercise sciences, sports admin. **Physical sciences:** Chemistry, physical chemistry. **Psychology:** General. **Social sciences:** Political science. **Theology:** Bible. **Transportation:** Airline/commercial pilot, aviation.

Most popular majors. Business/marketing 23%, education 11%, engineering/engineering technologies 33%, trade and industry 13%.

Computing on campus. 200 workstations in library, computer center. Dormitories wired for high-speed internet access and linked to campus network. Commuter students can connect to campus network. Online library, helpline, wireless network available.

Student life. **Freshman orientation:** Mandatory, $65 fee. Preregistration for classes offered. 3-day event for students and parents held before classes start. **Policies:** Religious observance required. Freshmen permitted cars on campus. **Housing:** Guaranteed on-campus for all undergraduates. Single-sex dorms, special housing for disabled, apartments available. $100 deposit, deadline 5/1. Residential societies available. **Activities:** Jazz band, choral groups, drama, music ensembles, student government, student newspaper, international student organization, Fellowship of Christian Athletes, Student Foundation, Habitat for Humanity, summer missions, married student fellowship, student ministries, 2 CARE Council.

Athletics. NCAA, NCCAA. **Intercollegiate:** Baseball M, basketball, cross-country, golf, soccer, softball W, tennis, volleyball W. **Intramural:** Badminton, basketball, cross-country, football (non-tackle), golf, racquetball, soccer, softball, swimming, table tennis, tennis, volleyball. **Team name:** Yellowjackets.

Student services. Campus ministries, career counseling, student employment services, financial aid counseling, health services, personal counseling, placement for graduates, veterans' counselor. **Physically disabled:** Services for visually, speech, hearing impaired.

Contact. E-mail: admissions@letu.edu
Phone: (903) 233-3400 Toll-free number: (800) 759-8811
Fax: (903) 233-3411
James Townsend, Director of Admissions, LeTourneau University, PO Box 7001, Longview, TX 75607

Lubbock Christian University
Lubbock, Texas
www.lcu.edu **CB code: 6378**

- Private 4-year university and liberal arts college affiliated with Church of Christ
- Commuter campus in small city
- 1,764 degree-seeking undergraduates: 22% part-time, 57% women, 7% African American, 1% Asian American, 15% Hispanic American, 1% international
- 244 degree-seeking graduate students
- 74% of applicants admitted
- SAT or ACT (ACT writing recommended) required
- 41% graduate within 6 years; 59% enter graduate study

General. Founded in 1957. Regionally accredited. **Degrees:** 387 bachelor's, 1 associate awarded; master's, first professional offered. **Location:** 300 miles from Dallas, 325 miles from Albuquerque, New Mexico. **Calendar:** Semester, limited summer session. **Full-time faculty:** 81 total; 59% have terminal degrees, 2% minority, 40% women. **Part-time faculty:** 73 total; 29% have terminal degrees, 3% minority, 42% women. **Class size:** 57% < 20, 36% 20-39, 4% 40-49, 2% 50-99. **Special facilities:** 2 farms totaling 450 acres.

Freshman class profile. 912 applied, 671 admitted, 320 enrolled.

Mid 50% test scores			
SAT verbal:	430-570	Rank in top tenth:	14%
SAT math:	430-560	End year in good standing:	69%
ACT:	17-24	Return as sophomores:	69%
GPA 3.50 or higher:	51%	Out-of-state:	13%
GPA 3.0-3.49:	33%	Live on campus:	69%
GPA 2.0-2.99:	15%	International:	1%
Rank in top quarter:	41%	Fraternities:	32%
		Sororities:	36%

Basis for selection. Standardized test scores and secondary academic record considered. **Homeschooled:** Transcript of courses and grades required. **Learning Disabled:** Applicants accepted for admission who claim disabilities must provide evidence of disabilities to Disability Coordinator.

High school preparation. 22 units recommended. Recommended units include English 4, mathematics 3, social studies 2, history 2, science 3 (laboratory 2), foreign language 2 and academic electives 4.

2006-2007 Annual costs. Tuition/fees: $13,644. Room/board: $4,600.

2005-2006 Financial aid. Need-based: 240 full-time freshmen applied for aid; 201 were judged to have need; 199 of these received aid. Average need met was 70%. Average scholarship/grant was $6,796; average loan $3,254. 39% of total undergraduate aid awarded as scholarships/grants, 61% as loans/jobs. **Non-need-based:** Awarded to 318 full-time undergraduates, including 102 freshmen. Scholarships awarded for academics, art, athletics, leadership, music/drama.

Application procedures. Admission: Closing date 8/1 (receipt date). $20 fee, may be waived for applicants with need. Application may be submitted online. Admission notification on a rolling basis. **Financial aid:** Priority date 6/1, closing date 8/1. FAFSA, institutional form required. Applicants notified on a rolling basis starting 3/1; must reply within 2 week(s) of notification.

Academics. Computer use integrated into the curriculum. **Special study options:** Distance learning, double major, dual enrollment of high school students, honors, internships, liberal arts/career combination, student-designed major, study abroad, teacher certification program, weekend college. **Credit/placement by examination:** AP, CLEP, IB, SAT, ACT, institutional tests. 45 credit hours maximum toward bachelor's degree. **Support services:** Learning center, pre-admission summer program, reduced course load, remedial instruction, study skills assistance, tutoring.

Majors. Agriculture: General, animal sciences, business, plant sciences. **Biology:** General. **Business:** Accounting, business admin, finance, management information systems, marketing. **Communications:** General, organizational. **Education:** Agricultural, art, biology, business, chemistry, computer, early childhood, elementary, English, history, mathematics, multi-level teacher, music, physical, science, secondary, social studies, Spanish, special, speech. **Engineering:** General. **Family/consumer sciences:** Work/family studies. **Health:** Athletic training, nursing (RN), predentistry, premedicine, prenursing, prepharmacy, preveterinary. **Legal studies:** Prelaw. **Liberal arts:** Humanities. **Math:** General. **Parks/recreation:** Exercise sciences, health/fitness, sports admin. **Physical sciences:** Chemistry. **Protective services:** Law enforcement admin. **Psychology:** General. **Public administration:** Social work. **Theology:** Bible, missionary, sacred music, youth ministry. **Visual/performing arts:** Design.

Most popular majors. Business/marketing 29%, education 23%, health sciences 6%, liberal arts 6%, public administration/social services 7%.

Computing on campus. 235 workstations in dormitories, library, computer center, student center. Dormitories wired for high-speed internet access and linked to campus network. Commuter students can connect to campus network. Online course registration, online library, helpline, repair service, wireless network available.

Student life. Freshman orientation: Available, $145 fee. Preregistration for classes offered. Week-long orientation held the week before fall semester begins. **Policies:** Chapel attendance required for full-time students age 24 or under. Religious observance required. Freshmen permitted cars on campus. **Housing:** Guaranteed on-campus for freshmen. Single-sex dorms, special housing for disabled, apartments, substance-free housing available. $90 deposit, deadline 8/15. **Activities:** Jazz band, choral groups, drama, music ensembles, student government, student newspaper, Best Friends, Missions Club, Fellowship of Christian Athletes, Students in Free Enterprise, Social Work Outreach Association, social clubs, Organization of Latin American Students.

Athletics. NAIA. **Intercollegiate:** Baseball M, basketball, golf, volleyball W. **Intramural:** Badminton, basketball, bowling, football (non-tackle), soccer, softball, table tennis, tennis, volleyball. **Team name:** Chaparrals.

Student services. Adult student services, alcohol/substance abuse counseling, campus ministries, career counseling, student employment services, financial aid counseling, health services, personal counseling, placement for graduates, veterans' counselor.

Contact. E-mail: admissions@lcu.edu
Phone: (806) 720-7151 Toll-free number: (800) 933-7601 ext. 7151
Fax: (806) 720-7162
Brad Rogers, Director of Admissions, Lubbock Christian University, 5601 19th Street, Lubbock, TX 79407

McMurry University
Abilene, Texas **CB member**
www.mcm.edu **CB code: 6402**

- Private 4-year university and liberal arts college affiliated with United Methodist Church
- Residential campus in small city
- 1,396 degree-seeking undergraduates: 15% part-time, 50% women, 11% African American, 1% Asian American, 14% Hispanic American, 1% Native American, 1% international
- 86% of applicants admitted
- SAT or ACT (ACT writing recommended) required
- 41% graduate within 6 years; 17% enter graduate study

General. Founded in 1923. Regionally accredited. 3-week May term available; additional off-campus extension at Dyess Air Force Base; part of 3-member consortium providing collegiate nursing education in Texas. **Degrees:** 248 bachelor's awarded. **ROTC:** Air Force. **Location:** 155 miles from Fort Worth, 220 miles from Austin. **Calendar:** Semester, extensive summer session. **Full-time faculty:** 77 total; 78% have terminal degrees, 5% minority, 31% women. **Part-time faculty:** 51 total; 14% have terminal degrees, 10% minority, 55% women. **Class size:** 64% < 20, 34% 20-39, less than 1% 40-49, 1% 50-99. **Special facilities:** Buffalo Gap historical village.

Freshman class profile. 917 applied, 785 admitted, 292 enrolled.

Mid 50% test scores			
SAT verbal:	420-540	Rank in top quarter:	41%
SAT math:	440-570	Rank in top tenth:	17%
ACT:	18-23	End year in good standing:	80%
GPA 3.50 or higher:	52%	Return as sophomores:	65%
GPA 3.0-3.49:	24%	Out-of-state:	6%
GPA 2.0-2.99:	23%	Live on campus:	80%

Basis for selection. Applicants evaluated on basis of ACT or SAT scores, high school rank and GPA, academic preparation, and extracurricular activities; character considered. Interview recommended for all; essay required for borderline applicants; audition required for music, theater programs; portfolio required for art; interview required for admission to Honors Program. **Learning Disabled:** Appropriate documentation required for students seeking special accommodations.

High school preparation. 12 units required; 16 recommended. Required and recommended units include English 4, mathematics 3, social studies 3-4, science 2-3 and foreign language 2. 2 units of foreign language strongly recommended; those who enroll with fewer than 2 units required to take 8 hours of foreign language.

2006-2007 Annual costs. Tuition/fees (projected): $15,150. Room/board: $5,852. Books/supplies: $1,000. Personal expenses: $1,800.

2005-2006 Financial aid. **Need-based:** 276 full-time freshmen applied for aid; 240 were judged to have need; 240 of these received aid. Average need met was 88%. Average scholarship/grant was $9,181; average loan $2,764. 69% of total undergraduate aid awarded as scholarships/grants, 31% as loans/jobs. **Non-need-based:** Awarded to 536 full-time undergraduates, including 156 freshmen. Scholarships awarded for academics, art, music/drama, religious affiliation, ROTC.

Application procedures. **Admission:** Priority date 3/15; deadline 8/15 (receipt date). $20 fee, may be waived for applicants with need. Application may be submitted online. Admission notification on a rolling basis beginning on or about 9/1. Must reply by May 1 or within 2 week(s) if notified thereafter. **Financial aid:** Priority date 3/15; no closing date. FAFSA required. Applicants notified on a rolling basis starting 2/1; must reply within 3 week(s) of notification.

Academics. Students receive credit for both nontraditional and traditional courses on and off campus during 3-week May term. Opportunities for bachelor's degree after early admission to dental, medical, or veterinary school. **Special study options:** Accelerated study, combined bachelor's/graduate degree, cross-registration, double major, dual enrollment of high school students, honors, independent study, internships, liberal arts/career combination, study abroad, teacher certification program. Engineering with Texas Tech University and Texas A&M. **Credit/placement by examination:** AP, CLEP, SAT, ACT, institutional tests. 45 credit hours maximum toward bachelor's degree. Special examinations may be given, upon approval of neccesary department, for credit in areas not covered by AP or CLEP. **Support services:** Learning center, reduced course load, remedial instruction, study skills assistance, tutoring, writing center.

Majors. **Biology:** General, biochemistry. **Business:** General, accounting, business admin, finance, management information systems, marketing. **Communications:** General. **Computer sciences:** General, information systems, web page design. **Conservation:** General, environmental science. **Education:** Art, early childhood, elementary, middle, music, physical, secondary. **English:** Creative writing, English lit, speech/rhetoric. **Foreign languages:** French, German, Spanish. **Health:** Nursing (RN). **History:** General. **Interdisciplinary:** Biological/physical sciences, math/computer science, natural sciences. **Math:** General. **Philosophy/religion:** Philosophy, religion. **Physical sciences:** Chemistry, physics. **Psychology:** General. **Social sciences:** Political science, sociology. **Theology:** Sacred music. **Visual/performing arts:** Art, ceramics, dramatic, graphic design, painting, piano/organ, studio arts, voice/opera.

Most popular majors. Biology 6%, business/marketing 14%, communications/journalism 7%, education 27%, health sciences 11%, social sciences 9%.

Computing on campus. 236 workstations in library, computer center, student center. Dormitories wired for high-speed internet access and linked to campus network. Commuter students can connect to campus network. Online library, helpline, student web hosting, wireless network available.

Student life. **Freshman orientation:** Available, $150 fee. Preregistration for classes offered. Summer weekend orientation plus 4-day orientation before first week of classes. **Policies:** Freshmen permitted cars on campus. **Housing:** Guaranteed on-campus for all undergraduates. Single-sex dorms, special housing for disabled, apartments, substance-free housing available. $150 partly refundable deposit, deadline 5/1. **Activities:** Bands, choral groups, drama, literary magazine, music ensembles, musical theater, student government, student newspaper, Alpha Phi Omega, Fellowship of Christian Athletes, Religious Life, Servant Leadership, Students in Free Enterprise, West Texas Model United Nations, Kappa Delta Sigma, Association of Information Technology Professionals.

Athletics. NCAA. **Intercollegiate:** Baseball M, basketball, cheerleading, cross-country, diving, football (tackle) M, golf, soccer, swimming, tennis, track and field, volleyball W. **Intramural:** Basketball, football (non-tackle), golf, racquetball, soccer, softball, tennis, volleyball. **Team name:** Indians.

Student services. Alcohol/substance abuse counseling, campus ministries, career counseling, student employment services, financial aid counseling, health services, personal counseling, placement for graduates, veterans' counselor.

Contact. E-mail: admissions@mcm.edu
Phone: (325) 793-4700 Toll-free number: (800) 460-2392
Fax: (325) 793-4718
Scott Smiley, Director of Admission, McMurry University, South 14th and Sayles Boulevard, Abilene, TX 79697-0001

Midwestern State University

Wichita Falls, Texas — **CB member**
www.mwsu.edu — **CB code: 6408**

- Public 4-year university and liberal arts college
- Commuter campus in small city
- 5,537 degree-seeking undergraduates: 28% part-time, 57% women, 13% African American, 3% Asian American, 9% Hispanic American, 1% Native American, 5% international
- 579 degree-seeking graduate students
- 83% of applicants admitted
- SAT or ACT with writing required

General. Founded in 1922. Regionally accredited. **Degrees:** 934 bachelor's, 42 associate awarded; master's offered. **ROTC:** Air Force. **Location:** 130 miles from Dallas-Fort Worth. **Calendar:** Semester, extensive summer session. **Full-time faculty:** 208 total; 70% have terminal degrees, 10% minority, 44% women. **Part-time faculty:** 112 total; 18% have terminal degrees, 5% minority, 52% women. **Class size:** 35% < 20, 49% 20-39, 5% 40-49, 10% 50-99, less than 1% >100. **Special facilities:** Kurzweil reading machine for the blind, planetarium, greenhouse, college operated museum, 2 biologic study properties.

Freshman class profile. 1,561 applied, 1,291 admitted, 876 enrolled.

Mid 50% test scores		Rank in top tenth:	12%
SAT verbal:	430-540	End year in good standing:	65%
SAT math:	440-540	Return as sophomores:	60%
ACT:	18-23	Out-of-state:	4%
GPA 3.50 or higher:	38%	Live on campus:	55%
GPA 3.0-3.49:	30%	International:	1%
GPA 2.0-2.99:	31%	Fraternities:	13%
Rank in top quarter:	33%	Sororities:	11%

Basis for selection. For unconditional admission, students must graduate from accredited high school, meet requirements, submit official transcripts and ACT/SAT scores. Entrance exams determined by class rank. Texas public universities require THEA test score on file prior to enrollment unless student exempt. Audition required for applied music program.

High school preparation. 15 units required. Required units include English 4, mathematics 3, science 2 and academic electives 6.

2006-2007 Annual costs. Tuition/fees: $4,566; $12,816 out-of-state. Room/board: $5,220. Books/supplies: $1,050. Personal expenses: $1,275.

2005-2006 Financial aid. **Need-based:** Average need met was 71%. Average scholarship/grant was $4,414; average loan $2,526. 45% of total undergraduate aid awarded as scholarships/grants, 55% as loans/jobs. **Non-need-based:** Awarded to 858 full-time undergraduates, including 212 freshmen. Scholarships awarded for academics, alumni affiliation, art, athletics, leadership, minority status, music/drama. **Additional information:** Employees offered educational incentive plan in which tuition reimbursed provided employee meets stated criteria. Additionally, dependents and children of faculty and staff may receive scholarship to defer local tuition and fees.

Application procedures. **Admission:** Priority date 7/1; deadline 8/7 (receipt date). $25 fee. Application may be submitted online. Admission notification on a rolling basis beginning on or about 9/1. **Financial aid:** Priority date 5/1; no closing date. FAFSA, institutional form required. Applicants notified on a rolling basis starting 3/15; must reply within 2 week(s) of notification.

Academics. **Special study options:** Combined bachelor's/graduate degree, distance learning, double major, dual enrollment of high school students, ESL, honors, independent study, internships, liberal arts/career combination, study abroad, teacher certification program. Study abroad in England and France. **Credit/placement by examination:** AP, CLEP, IB, SAT, ACT, institutional tests. 15 credit hours maximum toward associate degree, 30 toward bachelor's. Advanced Placement up to 60 hours. **Support services:** Learning center, reduced course load, remedial instruction, study skills assistance, tutoring, writing center.

Majors. **Biology:** General. **Business:** General, accounting, business admin, finance, international, management information systems, marketing. **Communications:** Media studies. **Computer sciences:** General. **Conservation:** Environmental science. **Education:** Bilingual, early childhood, English. **Engineering:** General, mechanical. **Engineering technology:** Manufacturing. **English:** English lit. **Foreign languages:** Spanish. **Health:** Athletic training, clinical lab science, dental hygiene, nursing (RN), predentistry, premedicine, prepharmacy, preveterinary, radiologic technology/medical imaging, respiratory therapy technology. **History:** General. **Interdisciplinary:** Global studies. **Legal studies:** Prelaw. **Liberal arts:** Humanities. **Math:** General. **Parks/recreation:** Exercise sciences, facilities management, health/

fitness. **Physical sciences:** General, chemistry, geology, physics. **Protective services:** Criminal justice. **Psychology:** General. **Public administration:** Social work. **Social sciences:** Economics, political science, sociology. **Visual/performing arts:** Art, dramatic, studio arts.

Most popular majors. Business/marketing 22%, education 9%, health sciences 13%, interdisciplinary studies 20%, security/protective services 7%.

Computing on campus. 454 workstations in dormitories, library, computer center, student center. Dormitories wired for high-speed internet access and linked to campus network. Commuter students can connect to campus network. Online course registration, online library available.

Student life. **Freshman orientation:** Available. Preregistration for classes offered. **Policies:** Freshmen permitted cars on campus. **Housing:** Guaranteed on-campus for freshmen. Coed dorms, single-sex dorms, special housing for disabled, apartments, substance-free housing available. $100 fully refundable deposit, deadline 4/9. Cooperative housing units for honors students and biology students. **Activities:** Bands, choral groups, dance, drama, film society, literary magazine, music ensembles, student government, student newspaper, TV station, Methodist student foundation, Baptist student center, Catholic campus ministries, Student Ambassadors, black student union, organization of Hispanic students, international students association, University Democrats, College Republicans, Amnesty International, academic and special interest honor societies.

Athletics. NCAA. **Intercollegiate:** Basketball, cross-country W, football (tackle) M, soccer, softball W, tennis, volleyball W. **Intramural:** Archery, badminton, basketball, bowling, football (non-tackle), football (tackle) M, golf, soccer M, softball, table tennis, tennis, track and field, volleyball. **Team name:** Mustangs.

Student services. Alcohol/substance abuse counseling, career counseling, student employment services, financial aid counseling, health services, personal counseling, placement for graduates, veterans' counselor. **Physically disabled:** Services for visually, speech, hearing impaired.

Contact. E-mail: admissions@mwsu.edu
Phone: (940) 397-4334 Toll-free number: (800) 842-1922
Fax: (940) 397-4672
Barbara Merkle, Director of Admissions, Midwestern State University, 3410 Taft Boulevard, Wichita Falls, TX 76308-2099

Northwood University: Texas Campus

Cedar Hill, Texas
www.northwood.edu **CB code: 6499**

- Private 4-year university and business college
- Residential campus in large town
- 578 degree-seeking undergraduates: 3% part-time, 48% women, 18% African American, 3% Asian American, 26% Hispanic American, 4% international
- 54% of applicants admitted
- SAT or ACT (ACT writing optional), application essay required

General. Founded in 1966. Regionally accredited. Specialty university offering only business degrees in management; 3 residential campuses in Texas, Florida, and Michigan; 44 program centers; Library Center in Maine. **Degrees:** 92 bachelor's, 71 associate awarded. **Location:** 18 miles from Dallas, 28 miles from Fort Worth. **Calendar:** Quarter, limited summer session. **Full-time faculty:** 23 total; 22% have terminal degrees, 17% minority, 35% women. **Part-time faculty:** 7 total; 14% have terminal degrees, 14% minority, 29% women. **Class size:** 57% < 20, 43% 20-39.

Freshman class profile. 635 applied, 344 admitted, 137 enrolled.

Mid 50% test scores			
SAT verbal:	430-510	Rank in top quarter:	23%
SAT math:	420-530	Rank in top tenth:	9%
ACT:	18-21	End year in good standing:	72%
GPA 3.50 or higher:	18%	Return as sophomores:	60%
GPA 3.0-3.49:	75%	Out-of-state:	8%
GPA 2.0-2.99:	7%	Live on campus:	46%
		International:	2%

Basis for selection. Miminum GPA of 2.0 and strong interest in business or related field. Test scores considered. Students with lower GPA possibly admitted on probation. Interview recommended. **Homeschooled:** Transcript of courses and grades required.

High school preparation. 16 units recommended. Recommended units include English 4, mathematics 3, social studies 3, science 2 (laboratory 1) and foreign language 3.

2005-2006 Annual costs. Tuition/fees: $15,183. Room/board: $6,849. Books/supplies: $1,305. Personal expenses: $1,509.

2005-2006 Financial aid. **Need-based:** 117 full-time freshmen applied for aid; 101 were judged to have need; 101 of these received aid. Average need met was 61%. Average scholarship/grant was $5,709; average loan $2,441. 53% of total undergraduate aid awarded as scholarships/grants, 47% as loans/jobs. **Non-need-based:** Awarded to 275 full-time undergraduates, including 56 freshmen. Scholarships awarded for academics, alumni affiliation, athletics, leadership, minority status, state residency.

Application procedures. **Admission:** No deadline. $25 fee, may be waived for applicants with need. Application may be submitted online. Admission notification on a rolling basis. **Financial aid:** No deadline. FAFSA required. Applicants notified on a rolling basis starting 3/1.

Academics. **Special study options:** Accelerated study, distance learning, double major, dual enrollment of high school students, external degree, honors, independent study, internships, liberal arts/career combination, study abroad, weekend college. **Credit/placement by examination:** AP, CLEP, IB, SAT, ACT, institutional tests. 12 credit hours maximum toward associate degree, 12 toward bachelor's. **Support services:** Learning center, reduced course load, remedial instruction, study skills assistance, tutoring, writing center.

Majors. **Business:** Accounting, banking/financial services, business admin, entrepreneurial studies, fashion, hotel/motel admin, international, management information systems, marketing, vehicle parts marketing. **Communications:** Advertising. **Computer sciences:** General. **Legal studies:** Court reporting. **Parks/recreation:** Sports admin.

Most popular majors. Business/marketing 89%, parks/recreation 7%.

Computing on campus. 50 workstations in library, computer center. Dormitories wired for high-speed internet access and linked to campus network. Commuter students can connect to campus network. Online course registration, online library, helpline, student web hosting, wireless network available.

Student life. **Freshman orientation:** Mandatory, $125 fee. Preregistration for classes offered. 5 days in early September. **Policies:** Freshmen permitted cars on campus. **Housing:** Guaranteed on-campus for freshmen. Single-sex dorms, apartments, substance-free housing available. $100 partly refundable deposit. **Activities:** Choral groups, dance, drama, literary magazine, student government, student newspaper, Christian Fellowship.

Athletics. NAIA. **Intercollegiate:** Baseball M, cross-country, golf, soccer, softball W, track and field. **Intramural:** Basketball, volleyball. **Team name:** Knights.

Student services. Adult student services, career counseling, student employment services, financial aid counseling, health services, personal counseling, placement for graduates.

Contact. E-mail: txadmit@northwood.edu
Phone: (972) 293-5400 Toll-free number: (800) 927-9663
Fax: (972) 291-3824
Sylvia Correa, Director of Admissions, Northwood University: Texas Campus, 1114 West FM 1382, Cedar Hill, TX 75104

Our Lady of the Lake University of San Antonio

San Antonio, Texas **CB member**
www.ollusa.edu **CB code: 6550**

- Private 4-year university affiliated with Roman Catholic Church
- Commuter campus in very large city
- 1,792 degree-seeking undergraduates: 31% part-time, 76% women, 8% African American, 1% Asian American, 71% Hispanic American, 1% international
- 1,080 degree-seeking graduate students
- 53% of applicants admitted
- SAT or ACT (ACT writing optional) required

General. Founded in 1895. Regionally accredited. **Degrees:** 341 bachelor's awarded; master's, doctoral offered. **ROTC:** Army, Air Force. **Location:** 4 miles from downtown, 90 miles from Austin. **Calendar:** Semester, limited summer session. **Full-time faculty:** 118 total; 36% minority, 52% women. **Part-time faculty:** 107 total; 34% minority, 48% women. **Class size:** 72% < 20, 27% 20-39, less than 1% 40-49, less than 1% 50-99. **Special facilities:** International center, international folk culture center, speech and hearing clinic, community counseling center, elementary school, child development center, center for social work research, center for women in church and society.

Freshman class profile. 2,214 applied, 1,173 admitted, 271 enrolled.

Mid 50% test scores			
SAT verbal:	430-520	Rank in top quarter:	47%
SAT math:	420-520	Rank in top tenth:	22%
ACT:	16-21	End year in good standing:	80%
GPA 3.50 or higher:	33%	Return as sophomores:	62%
GPA 3.0-3.49:	45%	Out-of-state:	2%
GPA 2.0-2.99:	21%	International:	1%

Basis for selection. High school academic record and test scores important. **Homeschooled:** Transcript of courses and grades required.

High school preparation. College-preparatory program recommended. 16 units required. Required and recommended units include English 4, mathematics 2-3, social studies 3, science 2 (laboratory 2), foreign language 3 and academic electives 3.

2005-2006 Annual costs. Tuition/fees: $17,048. Room/board: $5,384. Books/supplies: $1,000. Personal expenses: $1,850.

2004-2005 Financial aid. Need-based: 42% of total undergraduate aid awarded as scholarships/grants, 58% as loans/jobs. **Non-need-based:** Scholarships awarded for academics, alumni affiliation, art, music/drama.

Application procedures. Admission: Priority date 5/1; deadline 7/15 (receipt date). $25 fee, may be waived for applicants with need. Application may be submitted online. Admission notification on a rolling basis. **Financial aid:** Priority date 4/1; no closing date. FAFSA required. Applicants notified on a rolling basis starting 4/1; must reply within 2 week(s) of notification.

Academics. Special study options: Combined bachelor's/graduate degree, cooperative education, cross-registration, distance learning, double major, dual enrollment of high school students, ESL, independent study, internships, liberal arts/career combination, study abroad, teacher certification program, weekend college. Service learning. **Credit/placement by examination:** AP, CLEP, IB, institutional tests. No limit to number of credit hours that may be awarded through CLEP or that may be counted towards bachelor's degree. **Support services:** Learning center, pre-admission summer program, reduced course load, remedial instruction, study skills assistance, tutoring.

Majors. Biology: General. **Business:** Accounting, business admin, human resources, management information systems, marketing. **Communications:** General, broadcast journalism, journalism, public relations. **Computer sciences:** General. **Education:** Special, speech impaired. **English:** English lit. **Family/consumer sciences:** Family/community services. **Foreign languages:** Spanish. **History:** General. **Interdisciplinary:** Natural sciences. **Liberal arts:** Arts/sciences. **Math:** General. **Philosophy/religion:** Philosophy, religion. **Physical sciences:** Chemistry. **Psychology:** General. **Public administration:** Social work. **Social sciences:** General, political science, sociology. **Visual/performing arts:** Art, dramatic.

Most popular majors. Business/marketing 22%, computer/information sciences 7%, education 8%, liberal arts 8%, psychology 16%, public administration/social services 8%, social sciences 7%.

Computing on campus. Dormitories wired for high-speed internet access and linked to campus network. Commuter students can connect to campus network. Online course registration, helpline, repair service, wireless network available.

Student life. Freshman orientation: Mandatory, $50 fee. Preregistration for classes offered. Overnight program, 3 times during the summer. Familiarity with faculty, staff, campus, and assessment testing. Parent participation encouraged. **Policies:** Freshmen permitted cars on campus. **Housing:** Guaranteed on-campus for freshmen. Coed dorms, single-sex dorms, special housing for disabled, substance-free housing available. $100 nonrefundable deposit, deadline 8/1. **Activities:** Jazz band, choral groups, dance, drama, music ensembles, musical theater, student government, student newspaper, symphony orchestra, TV station, religious organizations, black and Hispanic clubs, service clubs.

Athletics. Intramural: Basketball, football (non-tackle), golf, racquetball, soccer, softball, swimming, tennis, volleyball. **Team name:** Armadillos.

Student services. Adult student services, alcohol/substance abuse counseling, campus ministries, career counseling, student employment services, financial aid counseling, health services, personal counseling, placement for graduates, veterans' counselor, women's services. **Physically disabled:** Services for visually, speech, hearing impaired.

Contact. E-mail: admission@lake.ollusa.edu
Phone: (210) 434-6711 ext. 2314 Toll-free number: (800) 436-6558
Fax: (210) 431-4036
Mary Cooper, Dean of Enrollment Management, Our Lady of the Lake University of San Antonio, 411 Southwest 24th Street, San Antonio, TX 78207-4689

Paul Quinn College

Dallas, Texas
www.pqc.edu **CB code: 6577**

- Private 4-year liberal arts college affiliated with African Methodist Episcopal Church
- Residential campus in very large city
- 850 full-time, degree-seeking undergraduates
- 7% of applicants admitted
- SAT or ACT (ACT writing optional) required

General. Founded in 1872. Regionally accredited. Oldest historically black institution west of the Mississippi River. **Degrees:** 146 bachelor's awarded. **Location:** 12 miles from Dallas. **Calendar:** Semester, limited summer session. **Full-time faculty:** 35 total. **Part-time faculty:** 15 total.

Freshman class profile. 1,713 applied, 128 admitted, 96 enrolled.

Mid 50% test scores		ACT:	8-17
SAT verbal:	210-420	Out-of-state:	10%
SAT math:	220-440	Live on campus:	80%

Basis for selection. 2.0 GPA and test scores most important.

High school preparation. Required and recommended units include English 4, mathematics 3, social studies 2, science 3 and foreign language 2.

2005-2006 Annual costs. Tuition/fees: $6,410. Room/board: $4,600. Books/supplies: $1,000. Personal expenses: $500.

Financial aid. All financial aid based on need.

Application procedures. Admission: Priority date 7/1; no deadline. $35 fee, may be waived for applicants with need. Admission notification on a rolling basis. **Financial aid:** No deadline. FAFSA, institutional form required. Applicants notified on a rolling basis starting 7/15; must reply within 2 week(s) of notification.

Academics. Special study options: Combined bachelor's/graduate degree, cooperative education, distance learning, honors, internships, liberal arts/career combination, teacher certification program. Program with Texas State Technical Institute leading to bachelor of applied science in 24 fields. **Credit/placement by examination:** CLEP. 12 credit hours maximum toward bachelor's degree. **Support services:** Reduced course load, remedial instruction, study skills assistance, tutoring.

Majors. Biology: General. **Computer sciences:** General. **Education:** Elementary, secondary. **Philosophy/religion:** Religion. **Protective services:** Criminal justice.

Computing on campus. 30 workstations in computer center.

Student life. Freshman orientation: Mandatory. **Policies:** Religious observance required. Freshmen permitted cars on campus. **Housing:** Guaranteed on-campus for all undergraduates. Single-sex dorms available. $75 deposit. **Activities:** Jazz band, choral groups, drama, student government, student newspaper, student ministerial council, Christian student organization.

Athletics. NAIA. **Intercollegiate:** Baseball M, basketball, cross-country, football (tackle) M, softball W, track and field, volleyball. **Intramural:** Basketball, softball, table tennis, volleyball. **Team name:** Tigers.

Student services. Career counseling, student employment services, health services, on-campus daycare, personal counseling, placement for graduates, veterans' counselor.

Contact. Phone: (214) 302-3575 Toll-free number: (800) 237-2648
Fax: (214) 302-3613
Nina Taylor Richey, Director of Recruitment, Paul Quinn College, 3837 Simpson Stuart Road, Dallas, TX 75241

Prairie View A&M University

Prairie View, Texas **CB member**
www.pvamu.edu **CB code: 6580**

- Public 4-year university
- Commuter campus in small town

- 5,402 degree-seeking undergraduates: 10% part-time, 55% women
- 2,210 degree-seeking graduate students
- 60% of applicants admitted
- SAT or ACT required
- 35% graduate within 6 years

General. Founded in 1876. Regionally accredited. Historically black college. **Degrees:** 792 bachelor's awarded; master's, doctoral offered. **ROTC:** Army, Navy. **Location:** 45 miles from Houston. **Calendar:** Semester, extensive summer session. **Full-time faculty:** 394 total; 64% have terminal degrees, 39% women. **Part-time faculty:** 118 total; 39% have terminal degrees, 54% women. **Special facilities:** Nuclear magnetic resonance spectrometric differentiator, scanning calorimeter, high pressure liquid chromatograph, solid state engineering laboratory, computer-aided design and drafting laboratory, center for learning and teaching effectiveness, international dairy goat research center, cooperative agricultural research center, solar observatory.

Freshman class profile. 4,323 applied, 2,581 admitted, 1,101 enrolled.

Mid 50% test scores			
SAT verbal:	390-470	GPA 3.0-3.49:	31%
SAT math:	390-470	GPA 2.0-2.99:	61%
ACT:	16-19	Rank in top quarter:	17%
GPA 3.50 or higher:	8%	Rank in top tenth:	4%
		Live on campus:	75%

Basis for selection. Score on institution's entrance examination, personal qualities, high school GPA important. Students may be admitted conditionally if grades or test scores are below minimum requirement.

High school preparation. 16 units required; 18 recommended. Required and recommended units include English 4, mathematics 3-4, social studies 2, science 3, foreign language 2 and academic electives 4. Recommend 1 computer science.

2005-2006 Annual costs. Tuition/fees: $4,906; $13,186 out-of-state. Room/board: $6,204. Books/supplies: $794. Personal expenses: $1,961.

2005-2006 Financial aid. **Need-based:** Average need met was 76%. Average scholarship/grant was $2,765; average loan $3,875. 44% of total undergraduate aid awarded as scholarships/grants, 56% as loans/jobs. **Non-need-based:** Scholarships awarded for academics, athletics, ROTC.

Application procedures. **Admission:** Closing date 6/1 (postmark date). $25 fee, may be waived for applicants with need. Application may be submitted online. Admission notification on a rolling basis. **Financial aid:** Closing date 3/1. FAFSA, institutional form required. Applicants notified by 6/1; must reply by 8/1.

Academics. **Special study options:** Accelerated study, combined bachelor's/graduate degree, cooperative education, cross-registration, distance learning, double major, dual enrollment of high school students, exchange student, external degree, honors, independent study, internships, liberal arts/career combination, study abroad, teacher certification program, weekend college. **Credit/placement by examination:** AP, CLEP. 30 credit hours maximum toward bachelor's degree. **Support services:** Learning center, preadmission summer program, reduced course load, remedial instruction, tutoring.

Majors. **Agriculture:** General. **Architecture:** Architecture. **Biology:** General. **Business:** Accounting, business admin, finance, management information systems. **Communications:** General. **Computer sciences:** General. **Engineering:** Chemical, civil, computer, electrical, mechanical. **Engineering technology:** Computer, construction, drafting, electrical, industrial. **English:** English lit. **Family/consumer sciences:** Food/nutrition. **Foreign languages:** Spanish. **Health:** Clinical lab science, health services, nursing (RN). **History:** General. **Math:** General. **Parks/recreation:** Health/fitness. **Physical sciences:** Chemistry, physics. **Protective services:** Criminal justice. **Psychology:** General. **Public administration:** Social work. **Social sciences:** Political science, sociology. **Visual/performing arts:** Dramatic, music performance, piano/organ, voice/opera.

Most popular majors. Biology 6%, business/marketing 19%, engineering/engineering technologies 17%, health sciences 12%, interdisciplinary studies 7%, security/protective services 8%.

Computing on campus. 500 workstations in library, computer center, student center. Dormitories linked to campus network. Commuter students can connect to campus network. Online library, helpline available.

Student life. **Freshman orientation:** Mandatory, $60 fee. Preregistration for classes offered. 2 overnights in summer. **Policies:** Freshmen permitted cars on campus. **Housing:** Guaranteed on-campus for freshmen. Coed dorms, special housing for disabled, apartments, substance-free housing available. $150 deposit. **Activities:** Bands, choral groups, dance, drama, film society, literary magazine, music ensembles, musical theater, radio station, student government, student newspaper, symphony orchestra, College Republicans, Spanish-speaking students association, Baptist student ministry, Chinese student association, ministerial alliance, Japanese student association, Korean student association.

Athletics. NAIA, NCAA. **Intercollegiate:** Baseball M, basketball, bowling W, cross-country, football (tackle) M, golf, soccer W, softball W, tennis, track and field, volleyball W. **Intramural:** Basketball, bowling W, golf, soccer W, softball, tennis, track and field, volleyball W. **Team name:** Panthers.

Student services. Adult student services, career counseling, student employment services, financial aid counseling, health services, personal counseling, placement for graduates, veterans' counselor. **Physically disabled:** Services for hearing impaired.

Contact. E-mail: mary_gooch@pvamu.edu
Phone: (936) 857-2626 Fax: (936) 857-2699
Mary Gooch, Director Admissions, Prairie View A&M University, PO Box 3089, Prairie View, TX 77446

Rice University

Houston, Texas — **CB member**
www.rice.edu — **CB code: 6609**

- Private 4-year university
- Residential campus in very large city
- 2,988 degree-seeking undergraduates: 1% part-time, 48% women, 7% African American, 16% Asian American, 12% Hispanic American, 1% Native American, 3% international
- 1,983 degree-seeking graduate students
- 25% of applicants admitted
- SAT or ACT with writing, SAT Subject Tests, application essay required
- 90% graduate within 6 years; 40% enter graduate study

General. Founded in 1891. Regionally accredited. Every student member of one of 9 residential colleges. **Degrees:** 970 bachelor's awarded; master's, doctoral offered. **ROTC:** Army, Navy, Air Force. **Location:** 3 miles from downtown. **Calendar:** Semester, limited summer session. **Full-time faculty:** 567 total; 95% have terminal degrees, 16% minority, 27% women. **Part-time faculty:** 143 total; 61% have terminal degrees, 6% minority, 35% women. **Class size:** 61% < 20, 25% 20-39, 4% 40-49, 8% 50-99, 2% >100. **Special facilities:** Art museum, wetland center for biochemical research, nanotechnology lab, center for study of languages and culture, civil engineering lab, concert hall with grand organ, institutes for public policy.

Freshman class profile. 7,890 applied, 1,970 admitted, 722 enrolled.

Mid 50% test scores			
SAT verbal:	660-760	Rank in top tenth:	88%
SAT math:	670-780	Return as sophomores:	96%
ACT:	30-34	Out-of-state:	54%
Rank in top quarter:	96%	Live on campus:	98%
		International:	3%

Basis for selection. High school course selection and performance, test scores, teacher and counselor recommendations, extracurricular activity, and application answers/essay most important. 2 SAT Subject Tests required. Audition required for music; portfolio required for architecture. Interview recommended for all.

High school preparation. 16 units required; 20 recommended. Required and recommended units include English 4, mathematics 3-4, social studies 2, science 2-4 (laboratory 2-3), foreign language 2-4 and academic electives 3. Trigonometry (pre-calculus), physics, and chemistry required of engineering and natural science majors, although 2nd year chemistry or biology may replace physics requirement.

2005-2006 Annual costs. Tuition/fees: $23,746. Room/board: $9,122. Books/supplies: $800. Personal expenses: $1,550.

2005-2006 Financial aid. **Need-based:** 533 full-time freshmen applied for aid; 287 were judged to have need; 287 of these received aid. Average need met was 100%. Average scholarship/grant was $21,157; average loan $1,276. 84% of total undergraduate aid awarded as scholarships/grants, 16% as loans/jobs. **Non-need-based:** Awarded to 1,008 full-time undergraduates, including 237 freshmen. Scholarships awarded for academics, alumni affiliation, art, athletics, leadership, minority status, music/drama, ROTC, state residency.

Application procedures. **Admission:** Closing date 1/10 (postmark date). $50 fee, may be waived for applicants with need. Application may be submitted online. Admission notification 4/1. Must reply by May 1 or within 2 week(s) if notified thereafter. **Financial aid:** Priority date 3/1; no closing date. FAFSA, CSS PROFILE required. Applicants notified by 4/15; must reply by 5/1.

Academics. Academic honor code. **Special study options:** Combined bachelor's/graduate degree, cross-registration, double major, dual enrollment of high school students, honors, independent study, internships, liberal arts/career combination, student-designed major, study abroad, teacher certification program. 8-year guaranteed medical school program with Baylor College of Medicine. **Credit/placement by examination:** AP, CLEP, IB, institutional tests. **Support services:** Tutoring.

Majors. Architecture: Architecture. **Area/ethnic studies:** Asian, German, Hispanic-American/Latino/Chicano, Latin American, Slavic, women's. **Biology:** General, biochemistry, ecology, evolutionary. **Business:** Business admin. **Computer sciences:** Computer science. **Engineering:** Biomedical, chemical, civil, computer, electrical, environmental, materials, mechanical. **Foreign languages:** Ancient Greek, classics, French, German, Latin, linguistics, Slavic, Spanish. **History:** General. **Interdisciplinary:** Classical/archaeology, cognitive science, medieval/Renaissance. **Math:** General, applied, statistics. **Parks/recreation:** Exercise sciences. **Philosophy/religion:** Philosophy, religion. **Physical sciences:** Astronomy, astrophysics, chemical physics, chemistry, geology, geophysics, physical chemistry, physics. **Psychology:** General. **Public administration:** Policy analysis. **Social sciences:** General, anthropology, economics, political science, sociology. **Visual/performing arts:** General, art, art history/conservation, music history, music performance, music theory/composition, studio arts.

Most popular majors. Biology 8%, engineering/engineering technologies 13%, English 6%, psychology 6%, social sciences 20%, visual/performing arts 6%.

Computing on campus. 523 workstations in dormitories, library, computer center, student center. Dormitories wired for high-speed internet access and linked to campus network. Commuter students can connect to campus network. Online course registration, online library, helpline, student web hosting, wireless network available.

Student life. Freshman orientation: Mandatory, $225 fee. Held the week before start of classes. **Policies:** Freshmen permitted cars on campus. **Housing:** Guaranteed on-campus for freshmen. Coed dorms, special housing for disabled available. $50 nonrefundable deposit, deadline 5/1. **Activities:** Bands, choral groups, dance, drama, film society, literary magazine, music ensembles, musical theater, opera, radio station, student government, student newspaper, symphony orchestra, TV station, Hispanic student association, Hillel, black student association, Young Democrats, Young Republicans, Chinese student association, Baptist Student Union, Catholic student center, international student association, student volunteer program.

Athletics. NCAA. **Intercollegiate:** Baseball M, basketball, cross-country, football (tackle) M, golf M, soccer W, swimming W, tennis, track and field, volleyball W. **Intramural:** Badminton, basketball, football (non-tackle), racquetball, softball, swimming, table tennis, tennis, track and field, volleyball. **Team name:** Owls.

Student services. Alcohol/substance abuse counseling, campus ministries, career counseling, student employment services, financial aid counseling, health services, minority student services, personal counseling, placement for graduates, women's services. **Physically disabled:** Services for visually, speech, hearing impaired.

Contact. Phone: (713) 348-7423 Toll-free number: (800) 527-6957
Fax: (713) 348-5952
Julie Browning, Dean for Undergraduate Enrollment, Rice University, 6100 Main Street, MS17, Houston, TX 77251-1892

St. Edward's University

Austin, Texas — **CB member**
www.stedwards.edu — **CB code: 6619**

- Private 4-year university and liberal arts college affiliated with Roman Catholic Church
- Commuter campus in very large city
- 3,930 degree-seeking undergraduates: 24% part-time, 58% women, 5% African American, 2% Asian American, 30% Hispanic American, 1% Native American, 2% international
- 946 degree-seeking graduate students
- 69% of applicants admitted
- SAT or ACT with writing, application essay required
- 53% graduate within 6 years

General. Founded in 1885. Regionally accredited. **Degrees:** 758 bachelor's awarded; master's offered. **ROTC:** Army, Air Force. **Location:** 80 miles from San Antonio, 180 miles from Dallas. **Calendar:** Semester, limited summer session. **Full-time faculty:** 155 total; 83% have terminal degrees, 11% minority, 45% women. **Part-time faculty:** 285 total; 35% have terminal degrees, 15% minority, 45% women. **Class size:** 49% < 20, 49% 20-39, 1% 40-49, less than 1% 50-99. **Special facilities:** Fine arts facility with photography laboratory; natural sciences center including laboratories, classrooms and seminar rooms.

Freshman class profile. 2,217 applied, 1,530 admitted, 650 enrolled.

Mid 50% test scores		**End year in good standing:**	93%
SAT verbal:	510-620	**Return as sophomores:**	84%
SAT math:	500-590	**Out-of-state:**	8%
ACT:	21-26	**Live on campus:**	89%
Rank in top quarter:	45%	**International:**	1%
Rank in top tenth:	15%		

Basis for selection. High school grades and curriculum, rank in top half of class, composite test scores in top 50th percentile nationally, leadership experience, extracurricular involvement, and quality of admission essay. ELPT will be considered if submitted by non-native English speakers. **Homeschooled:** Assessment done on individual basis. **Learning Disabled:** Students may submit learning disability documentation with admission application.

High school preparation. College-preparatory program recommended. 14 units required; 19 recommended. Required and recommended units include English 4, mathematics 3-4, social studies 1, history 2-3, science 2-3 (laboratory 2-3), foreign language 2-3 and academic electives 1.

2006-2007 Annual costs. Tuition/fees: $18,800. Room/board: $6,900. Books/supplies: $1,000. Personal expenses: $2,730.

2005-2006 Financial aid. Need-based: 530 full-time freshmen applied for aid; 402 were judged to have need; 401 of these received aid. Average need met was 80%. Average scholarship/grant was $12,129; average loan $3,563. 70% of total undergraduate aid awarded as scholarships/grants, 30% as loans/jobs. **Non-need-based:** Awarded to 1,149 full-time undergraduates, including 330 freshmen. Scholarships awarded for academics, art, athletics, leadership, music/drama, ROTC.

Application procedures. Admission: Priority date 2/1; deadline 5/1 (postmark date). $45 fee, may be waived for applicants with need. Application may be submitted online. Admission notification on a rolling basis beginning on or about 11/1. Must reply by May 1 or within 2 week(s) if notified thereafter. Applicants seeking scholarship consideration must apply by February 1. **Financial aid:** Priority date 3/1; no closing date. FAFSA required. Applicants notified on a rolling basis starting 2/15; must reply by 5/1 or within 2 week(s) of notification.

Academics. Special study options: Double major, honors, internships, liberal arts/career combination, semester at sea, study abroad, teacher certification program. **Credit/placement by examination:** AP, CLEP, IB, SAT, ACT, institutional tests. 90 credit hours maximum toward bachelor's degree. **Support services:** Learning center, reduced course load, remedial instruction, study skills assistance, tutoring, writing center.

Majors. Area/ethnic studies: Latin American. **Biology:** General, biochemistry, bioinformatics. **Business:** Accounting, accounting technology, business admin, entrepreneurial studies, finance, international, marketing. **Communications:** Media studies. **Computer sciences:** General, computer science. **Conservation:** Environmental studies. **Education:** Art, biology, drama/dance, history, mathematics, physical, social studies, Spanish. **English:** Composition, English lit. **Foreign languages:** Spanish. **History:** General. **Liberal arts:** Arts/sciences. **Math:** General. **Parks/recreation:** Exercise sciences. **Philosophy/religion:** Philosophy. **Physical sciences:** Chemistry. **Protective services:** Criminal justice, forensics. **Psychology:** General. **Public administration:** Social work. **Social sciences:** Criminology, economics, international relations, political science, sociology. **Theology:** Religious ed. **Visual/performing arts:** Art, dramatic, graphic design, photography.

Most popular majors. Business/marketing 36%, communications/journalism 10%, psychology 7%, social sciences 7%.

Computing on campus. 501 workstations in dormitories, library, computer center, student center. Dormitories wired for high-speed internet access and linked to campus network. Commuter students can connect to campus network. Online course registration, online library, helpline, student web hosting, wireless network available.

Student life. Freshman orientation: Mandatory, $150 fee. Preregistration for classes offered. 2-day sessions held 5 times during summer. **Policies:** Student organizations must receive annual university recognition through office of student life. Freshmen permitted cars on campus. **Housing:** Guaranteed on-campus for freshmen. Coed dorms, single-sex dorms, special housing for disabled, apartments available. $150 nonrefundable deposit, deadline 5/1. Community-style living in casitas available. **Activities:** Choral groups, dance, drama, literary magazine, music ensembles, musical theater, student government, student newspaper, 60 registered student organizations.

Athletics. NCAA. **Intercollegiate:** Baseball M, basketball, cross-country, golf, soccer, softball W, tennis, volleyball W. **Intramural:** Basketball, racquetball, soccer, softball, tennis, volleyball. **Team name:** Hilltoppers.

Student services. Adult student services, alcohol/substance abuse counseling, campus ministries, career counseling, student employment services, financial aid counseling, health services, personal counseling, placement for graduates, veterans' counselor. **Physically disabled:** Services for visually, speech, hearing impaired.

Contact. E-mail: seu.admit@admin.stedwards.edu
Phone: (512) 448-8500 Toll-free number: (800) 555-0164
Fax: (512) 464-8877
Tracy Manier, Dean of Undergraduate Admission, St. Edward's University, 3001 South Congress Avenue, Austin, TX 78704

St. Mary's University

San Antonio, Texas — **CB member**
www.stmarytx.edu — **CB code: 6637**

- Private 4-year university affiliated with Roman Catholic Church
- Residential campus in very large city
- 2,374 degree-seeking undergraduates: 8% part-time, 60% women, 4% African American, 3% Asian American, 70% Hispanic American, 4% international
- 1,540 degree-seeking graduate students
- 72% of applicants admitted
- SAT or ACT with writing, application essay required
- 61% graduate within 6 years; 44% enter graduate study

General. Founded in 1852. Regionally accredited. Writing across the curriculum program requires students in all undergraduate programs to take writing-intensive courses. **Degrees:** 509 bachelor's awarded; master's, doctoral, first professional offered. **ROTC:** Army, Air Force. **Location:** 5 miles from downtown. **Calendar:** Semester, limited summer session. **Full-time faculty:** 184 total; 92% have terminal degrees, 22% minority, 34% women. **Part-time faculty:** 149 total; 50% have terminal degrees, 22% minority, 37% women. **Class size:** 39% < 20, 59% 20-39, 1% 40-49, less than 1% 50-99.

Freshman class profile. 1,942 applied, 1,400 admitted, 494 enrolled.

Mid 50% test scores			
SAT verbal:	470-570	**Rank in top quarter:**	63%
SAT math:	480-580	**Rank in top tenth:**	32%
ACT:	20-24	**End year in good standing:**	90%
GPA 3.50 or higher:	47%	**Return as sophomores:**	78%
GPA 3.0-3.49:	38%	**Out-of-state:**	3%
GPA 2.0-2.99:	14%	**Live on campus:**	66%
		International:	2%

Basis for selection. Recommendations, talent/ability, character/personal qualities very important. Secondary school record, class rank, standardized test scores, essay and volunteer work important. Interviews, extracurricular activities, alumni/ae relation, religious affiliation or commitment, and work experience considered.

High school preparation. 17 units required; 21 recommended. Required and recommended units include English 4, mathematics 3-4, social studies 3-4, science 3-4 (laboratory 1), foreign language 2-3 and academic electives 1.

2005-2006 Annual costs. Tuition/fees: $19,474. Room/board: $6,688. Books/supplies: $1,500. Personal expenses: $1,177.

2004-2005 Financial aid. Need-based: 395 full-time freshmen applied for aid; 363 were judged to have need; 363 of these received aid. Average need met was 74%. Average scholarship/grant was $12,236; average loan $4,224. 61% of total undergraduate aid awarded as scholarships/grants, 39% as loans/jobs. **Non-need-based:** Awarded to 1,521 full-time undergraduates, including 352 freshmen. Scholarships awarded for academics, alumni affiliation, athletics, leadership, music/drama, ROTC.

Application procedures. Admission: Priority date 1/15; no deadline. $30 fee, may be waived for applicants with need. Application may be submitted online. Admission notification on a rolling basis beginning on or about 10/1. Must reply by May 1 or within 2 week(s) if notified thereafter. **Financial aid:** Priority date 2/15; no closing date. FAFSA required. Applicants notified on a rolling basis starting 5/1; must reply within 2 week(s) of notification.

Academics. Special study options: Cooperative education, cross-registration, distance learning, double major, dual enrollment of high school students, exchange student, honors, independent study, internships, liberal arts/career combination, study abroad, teacher certification program, Washington semester. Evening studies program. **Credit/placement by examination:** AP, CLEP, institutional tests. 30 credit hours maximum toward bachelor's degree. **Support services:** Learning center, pre-admission summer program, reduced course load, remedial instruction, study skills assistance, tutoring, writing center.

Majors. Area/ethnic studies: Latin American. **Biology:** General, biochemistry, biophysics. **Business:** General, accounting, entrepreneurial studies, human resources, international, marketing. **Communications:** General. **Computer sciences:** General, computer science. **Engineering:** Computer, electrical, science. **English:** English lit. **Foreign languages:** French, German, Spanish. **Health:** Clinical lab science. **History:** General. **Liberal arts:** Arts/sciences. **Math:** General. **Parks/recreation:** Exercise sciences. **Philosophy/religion:** Philosophy. **Physical sciences:** Chemistry, geology, physics. **Protective services:** Criminal justice. **Social sciences:** International relations, political science, sociology. **Theology:** Theology.

Most popular majors. Biology 9%, business/marketing 27%, communications/journalism 6%, physical sciences 6%, public administration/social services 6%, social sciences 19%.

Computing on campus. PC or laptop required. 100 workstations in dormitories, library, computer center, student center. Dormitories wired for high-speed internet access and linked to campus network. Commuter students can connect to campus network. Online library, helpline, repair service, wireless network available.

Student life. Freshman orientation: Available. Preregistration for classes offered. June orientation weekend with residence accommodations for students and parents. **Policies:** Freshmen permitted cars on campus. **Housing:** Guaranteed on-campus for freshmen. Coed dorms, single-sex dorms, special housing for disabled available. $100 deposit, deadline 5/1. Nontraditional residence halls for students 22 years old or above available. Freshmen must live on campus or with parents or relative. **Activities:** Bands, choral groups, dance, drama, literary magazine, music ensembles, musical theater, student government, student newspaper, university ministry, We the People, Circle K, Amnesty International, black student union, College Democrats, emerging leaders, environmental rescue, Habitat for Humanity, League of United Latin American Citizens.

Athletics. NAIA, NCAA. **Intercollegiate:** Baseball M, basketball, cross-country W, golf, soccer, softball W, tennis, volleyball W. **Intramural:** Badminton, basketball, bowling, cross-country, soccer, softball, swimming, table tennis, tennis, volleyball. **Team name:** Rattlers.

Student services. Adult student services, campus ministries, career counseling, student employment services, financial aid counseling, health services, personal counseling, placement for graduates, veterans' counselor. **Physically disabled:** Services for visually, speech, hearing impaired.

Contact. E-mail: uadm@stmarytx.edu
Phone: (210) 436-3126 Toll-free number: (800) 367-7868
Fax: (210) 431-6742
Maria Ramos-Smalling, Director of Admissions, St. Mary's University, One Camino Santa Maria, San Antonio, TX 78228

Sam Houston State University

Huntsville, Texas — **CB member**
www.shsu.edu — **CB code: 6643**

- Public 4-year university
- Residential campus in large town
- 13,200 degree-seeking undergraduates: 15% part-time, 58% women, 15% African American, 1% Asian American, 11% Hispanic American, 1% Native American, 1% international
- 2,164 degree-seeking graduate students
- 75% of applicants admitted
- SAT or ACT (ACT writing optional) required
- 41% graduate within 6 years

General. Founded in 1879. Regionally accredited. **Degrees:** 2,256 bachelor's awarded; master's, doctoral offered. **ROTC:** Army. **Location:** 69 miles from Houston, 170 miles from Dallas. **Calendar:** Semester, extensive summer session. **Full-time faculty:** 417 total; 98% have terminal degrees, 13% minority, 41% women. **Part-time faculty:** 167 total; 8% minority, 50% women. **Class size:** 19% < 20, 54% 20-39, 9% 40-49, 17% 50-99, 2% >100. **Special facilities:** Sam Houston Memorial Museum, Huntsville State Park.

Freshman class profile. 6,307 applied, 4,718 admitted, 2,216 enrolled.

Mid 50% test scores			
SAT verbal:	450-550	Rank in top tenth:	13%
SAT math:	460-560	Return as sophomores:	70%
ACT:	19-23	Out-of-state:	2%
Rank in top quarter:	43%	Live on campus:	83%

Basis for selection. Test scores, school achievement records very important. Students graduating in top quarter of accredited high school exempt from test requirements. **Homeschooled:** Must have minimum requirements in ACT or SAT.

High school preparation. Required and recommended units include English 4, mathematics 3, social studies 3-4, science 2-3, foreign language 2 and academic electives 1-4.

2006-2007 Annual costs. Tuition/fees (projected): $4,560; $12,240 out-of-state. Room/board: $4,400. Books/supplies: $708. Personal expenses: $1,506.

2005-2006 Financial aid. Need-based: 1,531 full-time freshmen applied for aid; 1,062 were judged to have need; 1,062 of these received aid. Average scholarship/grant was $4,285; average loan $2,407. 47% of total undergraduate aid awarded as scholarships/grants, 53% as loans/jobs. **Non-need-based:** Awarded to 2,087 full-time undergraduates, including 744 freshmen. Scholarships awarded for academics, athletics, ROTC.

Application procedures. Admission: Closing date 8/1 (postmark date). $35 fee, may be waived for applicants with need. Application may be submitted online. Admission notification on a rolling basis beginning on or about 9/1. **Financial aid:** Priority date 3/31, closing date 5/31. FAFSA, institutional form required. Applicants notified on a rolling basis starting 5/1; must reply within 4 week(s) of notification.

Academics. Special study options: Combined bachelor's/graduate degree, distance learning, double major, dual enrollment of high school students, ESL, honors, independent study, internships, liberal arts/career combination, study abroad, teacher certification program, weekend college. **Credit/placement by examination:** AP, CLEP, IB, institutional tests. 30 credit hours maximum toward bachelor's degree. **Support services:** Learning center, pre-admission summer program, reduced course load, remedial instruction, study skills assistance, tutoring, writing center.

Majors. Agriculture: General, agribusiness operations, animal sciences, horticultural science, mechanization. **Architecture:** Interior. **Biology:** General. **Business:** General, accounting, banking/financial services, business admin, fashion, finance, human resources, international, management information systems, managerial economics, marketing, operations. **Communications:** Advertising, journalism, public relations, radio/tv. **Computer sciences:** General. **Conservation:** Environmental science. **Engineering technology:** Construction, drafting, electrical, industrial, manufacturing. **English:** English lit, speech/rhetoric. **Family/consumer sciences:** General, food/nutrition. **Foreign languages:** French, Spanish. **Health:** Clinical lab science, health services, music therapy. **History:** General. **Math:** General. **Parks/recreation:** Health/fitness. **Personal/culinary services:** Institutional food service. **Philosophy/religion:** Philosophy. **Physical sciences:** Chemistry, geology, physics. **Protective services:** Criminal justice. **Psychology:** General. **Social sciences:** General, geography, political science, sociology. **Visual/performing arts:** Art, commercial/advertising art, dance, dramatic, music history, music performance, music theory/composition, photography, studio arts.

Most popular majors. Business/marketing 30%, interdisciplinary studies 10%, psychology 6%, security/protective services 17%.

Computing on campus. 552 workstations in library, computer center, student center. Dormitories wired for high-speed internet access and linked to campus network. Commuter students can connect to campus network. Online course registration, online library, helpline, repair service, student web hosting, wireless network available.

Student life. Freshman orientation: Available, $125 fee. Preregistration for classes offered. Overnight program throughout summer and before classes commence. Parent participation. **Policies:** Freshmen permitted cars on campus. **Housing:** Guaranteed on-campus for freshmen. Coed dorms, single-sex dorms, apartments, fraternity/sorority housing, substance-free housing available. $200 partly refundable deposit. **Activities:** Bands, choral groups, dance, drama, music ensembles, musical theater, radio station, student government, student newspaper, symphony orchestra, TV station, Democratic and Republican student associations, Baptist student ministry, Church of Christ student center, Lutheran student center, Hillel, Muslim students association, student Pagan association, ROTARACT, Habitat for Humanity.

Athletics. NCAA. **Intercollegiate:** Baseball M, basketball, cross-country, equestrian, football (tackle) M, golf, rifle, rodeo, soccer, softball W, tennis, track and field, volleyball W. **Intramural:** Basketball, bowling, diving, football (tackle) M, golf, gymnastics W, handball, lacrosse M, racquetball, rugby M, soccer, softball, swimming, tennis, volleyball, water polo. **Team name:** Bearkats.

Student services. Alcohol/substance abuse counseling, career counseling, student employment services, financial aid counseling, health services, legal services, minority student services, on-campus daycare, personal counseling, placement for graduates, veterans' counselor. **Physically disabled:** Services for visually impaired.

Contact. E-mail: admissions@shsu.edu
Phone: (936) 294-1828 Toll-free number: (866) 232-7528
Fax: (936) 294-3758
Trevor Thorn, Director of Admissions, Sam Houston State University, Box 2418, Huntsville, TX 77341-2418

Schreiner University

Kerrville, Texas — **CB member**
www.schreiner.edu — **CB code: 6647**

- Private 4-year liberal arts college affiliated with Presbyterian Church (USA)
- Residential campus in large town
- 765 degree-seeking undergraduates: 10% part-time, 60% women, 4% African American, 1% Asian American, 20% Hispanic American, 1% Native American, 1% international
- 52 degree-seeking graduate students
- 68% of applicants admitted
- SAT or ACT with writing required
- 36% graduate within 6 years

General. Founded in 1923. Regionally accredited. **Degrees:** 120 bachelor's awarded; master's offered. **Location:** 60 miles from San Antonio, 80 miles from Austin. **Calendar:** Semester, limited summer session. **Full-time faculty:** 49 total; 69% have terminal degrees, 4% minority, 41% women. **Part-time faculty:** 33 total; 12% have terminal degrees, 3% minority, 46% women. **Class size:** 66% < 20, 34% 20-39, less than 1% 40-49.

Freshman class profile. 565 applied, 387 admitted, 173 enrolled.

Mid 50% test scores		Rank in top quarter:	18%
SAT verbal:	420-520	Rank in top tenth:	10%
SAT math:	430-540	Return as sophomores:	59%
ACT:	17-21	Live on campus:	79%
GPA 3.50 or higher:	51%	Fraternities:	9%
GPA 3.0-3.49:	36%	Sororities:	27%
GPA 2.0-2.99:	13%		

Basis for selection. High school courses taken, grades, class rank, extracurricular activities, test scores, recommendations, interviews considered. Students admitted to Learning Support Services program not required to take SAT or ACT. Interview recommended for all; essay required for applicants not meeting certain admissions standards; portfolio recommended for fine arts.

High school preparation. College-preparatory program recommended. Recommended units include English 4, mathematics 3, social studies 2, science 2 (laboratory 2).

2005-2006 Annual costs. Tuition/fees: $15,142. Room/board: $6,812. Books/supplies: $1,000. Personal expenses: $1,000.

2004-2005 Financial aid. Need-based: 184 full-time freshmen applied for aid; 162 were judged to have need; 161 of these received aid. Average need met was 65%. Average scholarship/grant was $8,566; average loan $2,084. 63% of total undergraduate aid awarded as scholarships/grants, 37% as loans/jobs. **Non-need-based:** Awarded to 178 full-time undergraduates, including 61 freshmen. Scholarships awarded for academics, alumni affiliation, art, job skills, leadership, music/drama, religious affiliation.

Application procedures. Admission: Priority date 5/1; deadline 8/1. $25 fee, may be waived for applicants with need. Application may be submitted online. Admission notification on a rolling basis beginning on or about 12/1. Must reply by 5/1. **Financial aid:** Priority date 4/1, closing date 8/1. Institutional form required. Applicants notified on a rolling basis starting 2/21; must reply within 2 week(s) of notification.

Academics. Special study options: Accelerated study, double major, dual enrollment of high school students, honors, independent study, internships, liberal arts/career combination, student-designed major, study abroad, teacher certification program, weekend college. **Credit/placement by examination:** AP, CLEP, IB, SAT, ACT, institutional tests. **Support services:** Learning center, reduced course load, remedial instruction, study skills assistance, tutoring, writing center.

Majors. **Biology:** General, biochemistry. **Business:** General, accounting, management information systems. **Education:** General, biology, early childhood, elementary, English, history, mathematics, middle, music, physical, secondary. **Engineering:** General. **English:** English lit. **Health:** Predentistry. **History:** General. **Interdisciplinary:** Accounting/computer science. **Legal studies:** Prelaw. **Liberal arts:** Arts/sciences, humanities. **Math:** General. **Parks/recreation:** Exercise sciences. **Philosophy/religion:** Religion. **Physical sciences:** Chemistry. **Psychology:** General. **Social sciences:** Political science. **Visual/performing arts:** Dramatic, graphic design.

Most popular majors. Biology 10%, business/marketing 28%, education 14%, English 7%, parks/recreation 11%, psychology 12%.

Computing on campus. 103 workstations in dormitories, library, computer center, student center. Dormitories wired for high-speed internet access and linked to campus network. Commuter students can connect to campus network. Online library, repair service, student web hosting, wireless network available.

Student life. **Freshman orientation:** Mandatory. Preregistration for classes offered. Overnight program before classes begin. **Policies:** Freshmen permitted cars on campus. **Housing:** Guaranteed on-campus for all undergraduates. Coed dorms, special housing for disabled, apartments, substance-free housing available. $100 nonrefundable deposit, deadline 5/1. **Activities:** Pep band, choral groups, drama, literary magazine, music ensembles, musical theater, student government, student newspaper, symphony orchestra, community outreach program, Best Buddies, BACCHUS (Boosting Alcohol Consciousness Concerning the Health of University Students), Baptist student ministries, Celtic Cross, Episcopal-Lutheran Association, Fellowship of Christian Athletes, Methodist student ministries, Young Catholic Adults, Young Republicans.

Athletics. NCAA. **Intercollegiate:** Baseball M, basketball, cheerleading M, golf, soccer, softball W, tennis, volleyball W. **Intramural:** Basketball, football (non-tackle), football (tackle), golf, racquetball, soccer, swimming, table tennis, tennis, volleyball. **Team name:** Mountaineers.

Student services. Adult student services, campus ministries, career counseling, student employment services, health services, personal counseling, placement for graduates. **Physically disabled:** Services for visually, speech, hearing impaired. **Learning disabled:** Comprehensive services available.

Contact. E-mail: admissions@schreiner.edu
Phone: (830) 792-7217 Toll-free number: (800) 343-4919
Fax: (830) 792-7226
Sandra Speed, Director of Admissions, Schreiner University, 2100 Memorial Boulevard, Kerrville, TX 78028-5697

Southern Methodist University

Dallas, Texas — **CB member**
www.smu.edu — **CB code: 6660**

- Private 4-year university affiliated with United Methodist Church
- Residential campus in large town
- 6,196 degree-seeking undergraduates: 4% part-time, 54% women, 5% African American, 6% Asian American, 8% Hispanic American, 1% Native American, 5% international
- 4,209 degree-seeking graduate students
- 58% of applicants admitted
- SAT or ACT (ACT writing optional), application essay required
- 71% graduate within 6 years

General. Founded in 1911. Regionally accredited. Campus in Taos, New Mexico. Courses offered in Carrollton, Houston/Galveston, Plano, and Richardson. **Degrees:** 1,492 bachelor's awarded; master's, doctoral, first professional offered. **ROTC:** Army, Air Force. **Location:** 5 miles from downtown. **Calendar:** Semester, limited summer session. **Full-time faculty:** 604 total; 84% have terminal degrees, 14% minority, 33% women. **Part-time faculty:** 329 total; 36% women. **Class size:** 50% < 20, 30% 20-39, 9% 40-49, 9% 50-99, 2% >100. **Special facilities:** Sculpture garden, film/video archives, New Mexico archeological dig of 13th century Indian pueblo, theater, institute for the study of Earth and man, seismological observatory, electron microscopy laboratory, paleontology museum, business information center.

Freshman class profile. 6,981 applied, 4,076 admitted, 1,402 enrolled.

Mid 50% test scores			
SAT verbal:	560-660	Rank in top tenth:	35%
SAT math:	570-670	Return as sophomores:	87%
ACT:	24-28	Out-of-state:	45%
Rank in top quarter:	64%	Live on campus:	95%
		International:	4%

Basis for selection. GED not accepted. Students evaluated comprehensively. High school curriculum, GPA, test scores, school/community activities, recommendations, and essay important. Special talents considered. Interview recommended for all; audition required for performing arts; portfolio recommended for studio art. **Homeschooled:** SAT Subject Tests required.

High school preparation. 15 units required. Required and recommended units include English 4, mathematics 3-4, social studies 1-2, history 2-3, science 3-4 (laboratory 2-3) and foreign language 2-3.

2006-2007 Annual costs. Tuition/fees: $28,630. Room/board: $10,115. Books/supplies: $600. Personal expenses: $1,100.

2005-2006 Financial aid. **Need-based:** 644 full-time freshmen applied for aid; 471 were judged to have need; 468 of these received aid. Average need met was 91%. Average scholarship/grant was $11,918; average loan $2,555. 75% of total undergraduate aid awarded as scholarships/grants, 25% as loans/jobs. **Non-need-based:** Awarded to 3,394 full-time undergraduates, including 1,044 freshmen. Scholarships awarded for academics, art, athletics, leadership, music/drama, religious affiliation, ROTC, state residency.

Application procedures. **Admission:** Priority date 1/15; deadline 3/15 (postmark date). $50 fee, may be waived for applicants with need. Application may be submitted online. Admission notification on a rolling basis beginning on or about 12/31. Must reply by 5/1. **Financial aid:** Priority date 2/15; no closing date. FAFSA, CSS PROFILE required. Applicants notified on a rolling basis starting 3/15.

Academics. **Special study options:** Accelerated study, cooperative education, distance learning, double major, ESL, exchange student, honors, independent study, internships, student-designed major, study abroad, teacher certification program, Washington semester. **Credit/placement by examination:** AP, CLEP, IB, institutional tests. No limit on number of AP credits that may be counted toward bachelor's degree. Maximum of 8 hours of International Baccalaureate credits may be counted toward bachelor's degree. **Support services:** Learning center, pre-admission summer program, remedial instruction, study skills assistance, tutoring, writing center.

Majors. **Area/ethnic studies:** African-American, German, Hispanic-American/Latino/Chicano, Italian, Latin American, regional, Russian/Slavic. **Biology:** General, biochemistry. **Business:** Accounting, business admin, finance, financial planning, management information systems, management science, marketing, organizational behavior, real estate. **Communications:** Advertising, journalism, media studies, public relations, radio/tv. **Computer sciences:** Computer science. **Conservation:** Environmental science. **Education:** Music. **Engineering:** Civil, computer, electrical, environmental, mechanical. **Engineering technology:** Industrial management. **English:** Creative writing, English lit. **Foreign languages:** General, French, German, Russian, Spanish. **Health:** Music therapy. **History:** General. **Interdisciplinary:** Medieval/Renaissance. **Liberal arts:** Humanities. **Math:** General, statistics. **Philosophy/religion:** Philosophy, religion. **Physical sciences:** Chemistry, geology, geophysics, physics. **Psychology:** General. **Public administration:** Policy analysis. **Social sciences:** General, anthropology, applied economics, econometrics, economics, international relations, political science, sociology. **Visual/performing arts:** Art, art history/conservation, dance, dramatic, film/cinema, music performance, music theory/composition, piano/organ, studio arts, voice/opera.

Most popular majors. Business/marketing 26%, communications/journalism 12%, psychology 9%, social sciences 15%, visual/performing arts 8%.

Computing on campus. 758 workstations in dormitories, library, computer center, student center. Dormitories wired for high-speed internet access and linked to campus network. Commuter students can connect to campus network. Online course registration, online library, helpline, repair service, student web hosting, wireless network available.

Student life. **Freshman orientation:** Mandatory. **Policies:** Freshmen permitted cars on campus. **Housing:** Guaranteed on-campus for freshmen. Coed dorms, apartments, fraternity/sorority housing, substance-free housing available. $100 nonrefundable deposit, deadline 5/1. Theme residence halls available. **Activities:** Bands, choral groups, dance, drama, film society, literary magazine, music ensembles, musical theater, opera, radio station, student government, student newspaper, symphony orchestra, over 130 groups available.

Athletics. NCAA. **Intercollegiate:** Basketball, cross-country W, diving, equestrian W, football (tackle) M, golf, rowing (crew) W, soccer, swimming, tennis, track and field W, volleyball W. **Intramural:** Basketball, bowling, diving, football (tackle), golf, racquetball, soccer, softball, swimming, tennis, volleyball, water polo, weight lifting. **Team name:** Mustangs.

Student services. Adult student services, alcohol/substance abuse counseling, campus ministries, career counseling, student employment services,

financial aid counseling, health services, on-campus daycare, personal counseling, placement for graduates, women's services. **Physically disabled:** Services for visually, speech, hearing impaired.

Contact. E-mail: enrol_serv@smu.edu
Phone: (214) 768-3417 Toll-free number: (800) 323-0672
Fax: (214) 768-0202
Ron Moss, Executive Director of Enrollment Services, Southern Methodist University, PO Box 750181, Dallas, TX 75275-0181

Southwestern Adventist University

Keene, Texas
www.swau.edu CB code: 6671

- Private 4-year university and liberal arts college affiliated with Seventh-day Adventists
- Residential campus in small town
- 870 degree-seeking undergraduates
- 20 graduate students

General. Founded in 1893. Regionally accredited. **Degrees:** 150 bachelor's, 38 associate awarded; master's offered. **Location:** 55 miles from Dallas, 25 miles from Fort Worth. **Calendar:** Semester, limited summer session. **Full-time faculty:** 55 total. **Part-time faculty:** 18 total. **Class size:** 65% < 20, 24% 20-39, 9% 40-49, 2% 50-99, less than 1% >100. **Special facilities:** Observatory, museum of student life.

Freshman class profile.

Mid 50% test scores			
SAT verbal:	440-570	ACT:	19-24
SAT math:	420-540	Out-of-state:	44%
		Live on campus:	35%

Basis for selection. Secondary school record, test scores important. Additional requirements for nursing, education, social work programs. SAT or ACT recommended. SAT preferred for placement.

High school preparation. Recommended units include English 4, mathematics 2, social studies 2.5, science 2 and foreign language 2.

2005-2006 Annual costs. Tuition/fees: $12,484. Room/board: $5,806. Books/supplies: $700. Personal expenses: $1,040.

Financial aid. Non-need-based: Scholarships awarded for academics, athletics, leadership, music/drama.

Application procedures. Admission: Closing date 8/31. No application fee. Application may be submitted online. Admission notification on a rolling basis. **Financial aid:** Priority date 3/15; no closing date. FAFSA, institutional form required. Applicants notified on a rolling basis starting 4/15.

Academics. Special study options: Accelerated study, combined bachelor's/graduate degree, cooperative education, cross-registration, distance learning, double major, ESL, external degree, honors, independent study, internships, liberal arts/career combination, student-designed major, study abroad, teacher certification program. **Credit/placement by examination:** AP, CLEP, IB, institutional tests. **Support services:** Reduced course load, remedial instruction, tutoring, writing center.

Majors. Biology: General, biostatistics. **Business:** Accounting, administrative services, business admin, communications, international, management information systems, management science, office management. **Communications:** General, broadcast journalism, journalism. **Computer sciences:** General, computer science, information systems. **Education:** Business, elementary. **Health:** Clinical lab technology, health care admin, medical secretary, nursing (RN). **History:** General. **Math:** General, applied. **Parks/recreation:** Health/fitness. **Philosophy/religion:** Religion. **Physical sciences:** Chemistry, physics, theoretical physics. **Protective services:** Criminal justice. **Psychology:** General. **Public administration:** Social work. **Social sciences:** General, international relations. **Theology:** Theology.

Computing on campus. 150 workstations in library, computer center. Dormitories wired for high-speed internet access and linked to campus network. Commuter students can connect to campus network. Helpline, repair service, student web hosting, wireless network available.

Student life. Freshman orientation: Mandatory. Preregistration for classes offered. Held the week prior to fall registration. **Policies:** Freshmen permitted cars on campus. **Housing:** Guaranteed on-campus for all undergraduates. Single-sex dorms, apartments available. $50 deposit, deadline 8/31. **Activities:** Concert band, choral groups, drama, music ensembles, musical theater, radio station, student government, student newspaper, symphony orchestra, TV station, campus ministries, multicultural student organization.

Athletics. Intramural: Baseball M, basketball, gymnastics, soccer M, volleyball W.

Student services. Adult student services, career counseling, student employment services, financial aid counseling, health services, personal counseling, placement for graduates, veterans' counselor.

Contact. E-mail: admissions@swau.edu
Phone: (817) 202-6252 Toll-free number: (800) 433-2240
Fax: (817) 556-4744
Fred Harder, Enrollment and Marketing Vice President, Southwestern Adventist University, Box 567, Keene, TX 76059

Southwestern Assemblies of God University

Waxahachie, Texas
www.sagu.edu CB code: 6669

- Private 4-year university and Bible college affiliated with Assemblies of God
- Residential campus in large town
- 1,300 full-time, degree-seeking undergraduates
- 200 graduate students
- 52% of applicants admitted
- SAT or ACT (ACT writing optional), application essay required

General. Founded in 1927. Regionally accredited; also accredited by ABHE. **Degrees:** 292 bachelor's, 66 associate awarded; master's offered. **ROTC:** Army. **Location:** 20 miles from Dallas. **Calendar:** Semester, limited summer session. **Full-time faculty:** 40 total. **Part-time faculty:** 25 total.

Freshman class profile. 489 applied, 252 admitted, 252 enrolled.

Mid 50% test scores			
SAT verbal:	420-520	ACT:	16-23
SAT math:	410-510	Out-of-state:	45%
		Live on campus:	80%

Basis for selection. Minister's reference and 1 personal reference required. Interview recommended. **Learning Disabled:** Enrollment with the Achievement Center indicated.

2005-2006 Annual costs. Tuition/fees: $10,110. Room/board: $4,715. Books/supplies: $612. Personal expenses: $1,479.

Application procedures. Admission: Priority date 7/1; no deadline. $35 fee. Admission notification on a rolling basis beginning on or about 3/1. **Financial aid:** Priority date 3/1, closing date 6/1. FAFSA required. Applicants notified on a rolling basis starting 6/1; must reply within 2 week(s) of notification.

Academics. Special study options: Distance learning, double major, dual enrollment of high school students, external degree, independent study, internships, teacher certification program. **Credit/placement by examination:** CLEP, institutional tests. 15 credit hours maximum toward associate degree, 30 toward bachelor's. **Support services:** Learning center, reduced course load, remedial instruction, tutoring.

Majors. Business: General, accounting, business admin, marketing. **Education:** Early childhood, elementary, English, music, reading, secondary, social studies. **Health:** Clinical pastoral counseling. **History:** General. **Philosophy/religion:** Christian. **Theology:** Bible, missionary, pastoral counseling, religious ed, sacred music, youth ministry. **Visual/performing arts:** Music performance, piano/organ, voice/opera.

Computing on campus. 45 workstations in library, computer center. Dormitories wired for high-speed internet access and linked to campus network. Online library, repair service available.

Student life. Freshman orientation: Mandatory. Preregistration for classes offered. **Policies:** Dress code observed. Religious observance required. Freshmen permitted cars on campus. **Housing:** Guaranteed on-campus for freshmen. Coed dorms, single-sex dorms, apartments available. Unmarried students 23 and under required to live in college housing unless alternative arrangements agreed to upon enrollment. **Activities:** Bands, choral groups, drama, music ensembles, musical theater, student government, student newspaper, prayer groups, ministry labs.

Athletics. NAIA, NCCAA. **Intercollegiate:** Baseball M, basketball, cheerleading, football (tackle) M, soccer M, volleyball W. **Intramural:** Basketball, football (non-tackle) W, racquetball, softball, table tennis, volleyball. **Team name:** Lions.

Student services. Adult student services, campus ministries, career counseling, student employment services, financial aid counseling, health services, personal counseling, placement for graduates, veterans' counselor.

Contact. E-mail: admissions@sagu.edu
Phone: (972) 937-4010 ext. 1125 Toll-free number: (888) 937-7248 ext. 1125 Fax: (972) 923-0006
Pat Thompson, Admissions Counselor, Southwestern Assemblies of God University, 1200 Sycamore Street, Waxahachie, TX 75165

Southwestern Christian College

Terrell, Texas
www.swcc.edu **CB code: 6705**

- Private 4-year Bible and liberal arts college affiliated with Church of Christ
- Residential campus in large town
- 253 degree-seeking undergraduates

General. Founded in 1949. Regionally accredited. **Degrees:** 8 bachelor's, 37 associate awarded. **Location:** 30 miles from Dallas. **Calendar:** Semester. **Full-time faculty:** 12 total. **Part-time faculty:** 11 total.

Freshman class profile.

Out-of-state:	85%	**Live on campus:**	94%

Basis for selection. Open admission. Interview recommended.

2005-2006 Annual costs. Tuition/fees: $5,314. Room/board: $3,742. Books/supplies: $460. Personal expenses: $400.

Application procedures. Admission: Closing date 7/31. $20 fee. Admission notification on a rolling basis. **Financial aid:** Closing date 7/15. Applicants notified on a rolling basis starting 7/15.

Academics. Special study options: Independent study, internships. **Credit/placement by examination:** CLEP, institutional tests. 8 credit hours maximum toward associate degree, 16 toward bachelor's. **Support services:** Learning center, reduced course load, remedial instruction.

Majors. Theology: Bible.

Student life. Freshman orientation: Mandatory. **Policies:** High moral standards required. Profanity, vulgarity, gambling, drinking alcoholic beverages, attending dances or places of questionable amusement are against college's ideals and rules. **Housing:** Single-sex dorms available. **Activities:** Jazz band, choral groups, drama, music ensembles, student government, student newspaper.

Athletics. NJCAA. **Intercollegiate:** Basketball, track and field.

Student services. Career counseling, personal counseling.

Contact. Phone: (972) 524-3341 Fax: (972) 563-7133
John Edmerson, Director of Admissions, Southwestern Christian College, Box 10, Terrell, TX 75160

Southwestern University

Georgetown, Texas **CB member**
www.southwestern.edu **CB code: 6674**

- Private 4-year liberal arts college affiliated with United Methodist Church
- Residential campus in large town
- 1,296 degree-seeking undergraduates: 1% part-time, 59% women, 3% African American, 5% Asian American, 14% Hispanic American, 1% Native American
- 67% of applicants admitted
- SAT or ACT (ACT writing optional), application essay required
- 78% graduate within 6 years; 84% enter graduate study

General. Founded in 1840. Regionally accredited. **Degrees:** 311 bachelor's awarded. **Location:** 28 miles from Austin. **Calendar:** Semester, limited summer session. **Full-time faculty:** 118 total; 99% have terminal degrees, 13% minority, 48% women. **Part-time faculty:** 49 total; 53% have terminal degrees, 12% minority, 55% women. **Class size:** 76% < 20, 24% 20-39, less than 1% 40-49, less than 1% 50-99. **Special facilities:** Electronic classrooms, language learning center.

Freshman class profile. 1,760 applied, 1,178 admitted, 329 enrolled.

Mid 50% test scores		**Return as sophomores:**	89%
SAT verbal:	580-690	**Out-of-state:**	7%
SAT math:	570-670	**Live on campus:**	100%
ACT:	24-29	**Fraternities:**	29%
Rank in top quarter:	83%	**Sororities:**	31%
Rank in top tenth:	47%		

Basis for selection. School record, class rank, recommendations, test scores, and essay most important. Audition required for music, theater programs; portfolio required for art program.

High school preparation. Required units include English 4, mathematics 4, social studies 3, history 3, science 3 (laboratory 2) and foreign language 2.

2006-2007 Annual costs. Tuition/fees: $23,650. Room/board: $7,590.

2005-2006 Financial aid. Need-based: 231 full-time freshmen applied for aid; 175 were judged to have need; 175 of these received aid. Average need met was 98%. Average scholarship/grant was $16,275; average loan $2,760. 67% of total undergraduate aid awarded as scholarships/grants, 33% as loans/jobs. **Non-need-based:** Awarded to 678 full-time undergraduates, including 196 freshmen. Scholarships awarded for academics, art, music/drama. **Additional information:** Family loan program (PATH): borrow up to $22,500 annually with a fixed, monthly payment plan; students who ranked in top 10% of high school class or received an academic merit scholarship may be subsidized.

Application procedures. Admission: Closing date 2/15 (postmark date). $40 fee, may be waived for applicants with need. Application may be submitted online. Admission notification 4/1. Must reply by 5/1. Applicants accepted after 2/15 if space allows. **Financial aid:** Closing date 3/1. FAFSA required. Applicants notified on a rolling basis starting 3/21; must reply by 5/1 or within 2 week(s) of notification.

Academics. Students must demonstrate computer skills and grasp of major through capstone project, course, or examination prior to graduation. **Special study options:** Combined bachelor's/graduate degree, double major, exchange student, honors, independent study, internships, liberal arts/career combination, New York semester, student-designed major, study abroad, teacher certification program, Washington semester. **Credit/placement by examination:** AP, CLEP, IB, institutional tests. **Support services:** Reduced course load, study skills assistance, tutoring, writing center.

Majors. Area/ethnic studies: American, women's. **Biology:** General. **Business:** General, accounting. **Communications:** General. **Computer sciences:** General. **Education:** General, elementary, music, physical. **English:** English lit. **Foreign languages:** Classics, French, German, Latin, Spanish. **Health:** Athletic training. **History:** General. **Math:** General. **Philosophy/religion:** Philosophy, religion. **Physical sciences:** Chemistry, physics. **Psychology:** General. **Social sciences:** General, anthropology, economics, international relations, political science, sociology. **Theology:** Sacred music. **Visual/performing arts:** Art, art history/conservation, dramatic, music history, music performance, studio arts.

Most popular majors. Biology 6%, business/marketing 12%, communications/journalism 15%, English 7%, psychology 6%, social sciences 17%, visual/performing arts 6%.

Computing on campus. 233 workstations in dormitories, library, computer center, student center. Dormitories wired for high-speed internet access and linked to campus network. Helpline, repair service, student web hosting, wireless network available.

Student life. Freshman orientation: Mandatory. 5 or 6-day orientation for all new students prior to opening of classes in fall. **Policies:** Freshmen permitted cars on campus. **Housing:** Guaranteed on-campus for freshmen. Coed dorms, single-sex dorms, special housing for disabled, apartments, fraternity/sorority housing available. $250 deposit, deadline 5/1. **Activities:** Bands, choral groups, drama, film society, literary magazine, music ensembles, musical theater, opera, student government, student newspaper, symphony orchestra, TV station, Alpha Phi Omega, Ebony, Mexican American student association, political science society, international club, Equal Voice For Women's Perspective.

Athletics. NCAA. **Intercollegiate:** Baseball M, basketball, cross-country, diving, golf, soccer, swimming, tennis, track and field, volleyball W. **Intramural:** Archery, basketball, bowling, cross-country, diving M, fencing, golf, racquetball M, soccer M, softball, swimming, table tennis, tennis, track and field. **Team name:** Bucs/Pirates.

Student services. Alcohol/substance abuse counseling, campus ministries, career counseling, student employment services, financial aid counseling, health services, minority student services, personal counseling, placement for graduates. **Physically disabled:** Services for hearing impaired.

Contact. E-mail: admission@southwestern.edu
Phone: (512) 863-1200 Toll-free number: (800) 252-3166
Fax: (512) 863-9601
Tom Oliver, Vice President Enrollment Services, Southwestern University, 1001 East University Avenue, Georgetown, TX 78626

Stephen F. Austin State University

Nacogdoches, Texas — **CB member**
www.sfasu.edu — **CB code: 6682**

- Public 4-year university
- Residential campus in large town
- 9,806 degree-seeking undergraduates: 13% part-time, 60% women, 17% African American, 1% Asian American, 8% Hispanic American, 1% Native American, 1% international
- 1,111 degree-seeking graduate students
- 74% of applicants admitted
- SAT or ACT with writing required

General. Founded in 1923. Regionally accredited. **Degrees:** 1,785 bachelor's awarded; master's, doctoral offered. **ROTC:** Army. **Location:** 140 miles from Houston, 70 miles from Longview. **Calendar:** Semester, extensive summer session. **Full-time faculty:** 434 total; 76% have terminal degrees, 7% minority, 41% women. **Part-time faculty:** 148 total; 40% have terminal degrees, 8% minority, 47% women. **Class size:** 29% < 20, 52% 20-39, 10% 40-49, 8% 50-99, 2% >100. **Special facilities:** Computerized observatory; experimental forest; on-campus arboretum; beef, poultry and swine research facilities; biotechnology/environmental science research center; Stone Fort museum; agricultural pond; forest resources institute; geographic information systems lab.

Freshman class profile. 6,506 applied, 4,823 admitted, 1,921 enrolled.

Mid 50% test scores		Rank in top tenth:	14%
SAT verbal:	430-560	Out-of-state:	2%
SAT math:	450-560	Live on campus:	86%
ACT:	17-23	Fraternities:	4%
Rank in top quarter:	42%	Sororities:	3%

Basis for selection. Applicants must complete prescribed high school preparation and submit official high school transcript and SAT or ACT scores. No minimum score required for those ranking in top quartile; those in second quartile must have composite score (exclusive of Writing) of 850 SAT, 18 ACT; third quartile 1050 SAT, 23 ACT; fourth quartile 1250 SAT, 28 ACT. Applicants not meeting rank-in-class and test requirements reviewed on individual basis. SAT or ACT scores must be received by last day of registration for fall term admission. **Homeschooled:** Applicants assessed on individual basis; those whose academic background indicates probability of success may be admitted.

High school preparation. 12 units required; 18 recommended. Required and recommended units include English 4, mathematics 3, social studies 3, science 3 and foreign language 2. 1 fine arts, 1 computer science, and 1 government/economics recommended.

2005-2006 Annual costs. Tuition/fees: $4,718; $12,998 out-of-state. Room/board: $5,459. Books/supplies: $905. Personal expenses: $1,412.

2004-2005 Financial aid. Need-based: 1,199 full-time freshmen applied for aid; 784 were judged to have need; 774 of these received aid. Average need met was 65%. Average scholarship/grant was $1,340; average loan $1,238. 45% of total undergraduate aid awarded as scholarships/grants, 55% as loans/jobs. **Non-need-based:** Awarded to 2,335 full-time undergraduates, including 642 freshmen. Scholarships awarded for academics, alumni affiliation, art, athletics, leadership, music/drama, ROTC, state residency.

Application procedures. Admission: No deadline. $25 fee, may be waived for applicants with need. Application may be submitted online. Admission notification on a rolling basis beginning on or about 9/1. **Financial aid:** Priority date 4/1, closing date 4/15. FAFSA required. Applicants notified on a rolling basis starting 5/1; must reply within 3 week(s) of notification.

Academics. Special study options: Accelerated study, combined bachelor's/graduate degree, distance learning, double major, dual enrollment of high school students, honors, independent study, internships, liberal arts/career combination, student-designed major, study abroad, teacher certification program. **Credit/placement by examination:** AP, CLEP, IB, institutional tests. 32 credit hours maximum toward bachelor's degree. **Support services:** Learning center, pre-admission summer program, reduced course load, remedial instruction, study skills assistance, tutoring, writing center.

Majors. Agriculture: General, agribusiness operations, agronomy, animal sciences, horticultural science, horticulture, mechanization, poultry, production. **Architecture:** Interior. **Biology:** General. **Business:** General, accounting, business admin, fashion, finance, hospitality admin, international, managerial economics, marketing, office management. **Communications:** General, journalism, radio/tv. **Computer sciences:** General, data processing. **Conservation:** Environmental science, forest management, forestry, wildlife. **English:** English lit, speech/rhetoric. **Family/consumer sciences:** General, family studies, food/nutrition. **Foreign languages:** French, Spanish. **Health:** Audiology/hearing, audiology/speech pathology, clinical lab science, health services, nursing (RN). **History:** General. **Interdisciplinary:** Gerontology. **Legal studies:** Paralegal. **Liberal arts:** Arts/sciences, humanities. **Math:** General. **Parks/recreation:** Facilities management, health/fitness. **Physical sciences:** Chemistry, geology, physics. **Protective services:** Corrections, criminal justice, police science. **Psychology:** General. **Public administration:** General, social work. **Social sciences:** General, economics, geography, political science, sociology. **Visual/performing arts:** Art, art history/conservation, dance, dramatic, music performance.

Computing on campus. 1,000 workstations in dormitories, library, computer center, student center. Dormitories wired for high-speed internet access and linked to campus network. Commuter students can connect to campus network. Online course registration, online library, helpline, student web hosting available.

Student life. Freshman orientation: Available, $120 fee. Preregistration for classes offered. **Policies:** Freshmen permitted cars on campus. **Housing:** Guaranteed on-campus for freshmen. Coed dorms, single-sex dorms, special housing for disabled, apartments, fraternity/sorority housing, substance-free housing available. $100 deposit. Students must live in college housing until 60 semester hours completed. **Activities:** Bands, choral groups, dance, drama, film society, literary magazine, music ensembles, musical theater, opera, radio station, student government, student newspaper, symphony orchestra, TV station, African American student association, Baptist student ministries, Campus Christian organization, Canterbury Episcopal student association, Campus Crusade for Christ, Jewish Student Fellowship, Habitat for Humanity, SFA Democrats, Young Republicans, social services.

Athletics. NCAA. **Intercollegiate:** Baseball M, basketball, cross-country, equestrian W, football (tackle) M, golf M, soccer W, softball W, tennis W, track and field, volleyball W. **Intramural:** Badminton, baseball M, basketball, cross-country, gymnastics, lacrosse M, racquetball, rodeo, rugby, soccer M, softball, table tennis, tennis, volleyball, water polo, wrestling M. **Team name:** Lumberjacks/Ladyjacks.

Student services. Adult student services, alcohol/substance abuse counseling, career counseling, student employment services, financial aid counseling, health services, on-campus daycare, personal counseling, placement for graduates, veterans' counselor. **Physically disabled:** Services for visually, speech, hearing impaired.

Contact. E-mail: admissions@sfasu.edu
Phone: (936) 468-2504 Toll-free number: (800) 731-2902
Fax: (936) 468-3849
Monique Cossich, Executive Director of Enrollment Management, Stephen F. Austin State University, Box 13051, SFA Station, Nacogdoches, TX 75962-3051

Sul Ross State University

Alpine, Texas — **CB member**
www.sulross.edu — **CB code: 6685**

- Public 4-year university
- Residential campus in small town
- 1,500 full-time, degree-seeking undergraduates
- 900 graduate students
- SAT or ACT (ACT writing optional) required

General. Founded in 1917. Regionally accredited. Off-campus upper-level and graduate programs available in Del Rio, Eagle Pass, and Uvalde. **Degrees:** 396 bachelor's, 11 associate awarded; master's offered. **Location:** 140 miles from Odessa, 220 miles from El Paso. **Calendar:** Semester, limited summer session. **Full-time faculty:** 90 total. **Part-time faculty:** 45 total. **Class size:** 61% < 20, 33% 20-39, 4% 40-49, 3% 50-99. **Special facilities:** Center for Big Bend studies, museum, materials characterization laboratory.

Freshman class profile.

Out-of-state:	3%	Live on campus:	74%

Basis for selection. Students must meet one of following criteria: ACT score of 20, SAT score of 800 (exclusive of Writing), or rank in top half of graduating class. Probational admission for all other applicants.

High school preparation. 16 units required; 25.5 recommended. Required and recommended units include English 4, mathematics 3-4, social studies 2, history 1-2, science 2-4 (laboratory 2), foreign language 3, academic electives 2.5. 1 fine art, 1 computer science required.

2005-2006 Annual costs. Tuition/fees: $4,118; $12,398 out-of-state. Room/board: $4,110. Books/supplies: $678. Personal expenses: $1,576.

Financial aid. Non-need-based: Scholarships awarded for academics, alumni affiliation, leadership.

Application procedures. Admission: No deadline. $25 fee, may be waived for applicants with need. Application may be submitted online. Admission notification on a rolling basis. **Financial aid:** Priority date 5/1; no closing date. FAFSA, institutional form required. Applicants notified on a rolling basis starting 5/1; must reply within 2 week(s) of notification.

Academics. Special study options: Distance learning, honors, internships, teacher certification program. **Credit/placement by examination:** AP, CLEP, institutional tests. 30 credit hours maximum toward bachelor's degree. **Support services:** Learning center, pre-admission summer program, reduced course load, remedial instruction, study skills assistance, tutoring, writing center.

Majors. Agriculture: Agribusiness operations, animal health, animal sciences, equestrian studies, food science, range science. **Biology:** General. **Business:** General, accounting, administrative services, business admin, finance, marketing, office management. **Communications:** General. **Computer sciences:** General. **Conservation:** General, management/policy, wildlife. **Education:** Elementary. **English:** Speech/rhetoric. **Foreign languages:** Spanish. **History:** General. **Math:** General. **Parks/recreation:** Health/fitness. **Physical sciences:** Chemistry, geology. **Protective services:** Criminal justice. **Psychology:** General. **Social sciences:** General, political science. **Visual/performing arts:** Art, dramatic.

Computing on campus. 200 workstations in library, computer center. Dormitories wired for high-speed internet access and linked to campus network. Commuter students can connect to campus network. Online library, helpline, repair service, wireless network available.

Student life. Freshman orientation: Available. Preregistration for classes offered. **Policies:** Freshmen permitted cars on campus. **Housing:** Guaranteed on-campus for freshmen. Coed dorms, single-sex dorms, special housing for disabled, apartments available. $100 deposit, deadline 8/1. Students not living with their parents must live on campus until they reach 20 years of age and complete 45 semester credit hours. **Activities:** Bands, choral groups, dance, drama, literary magazine, music ensembles, musical theater, radio station, student government, student newspaper, Wesley Foundation, Newman Club, Baptist Student Union, Fellowship of Christian Athletes, Spanish club, rodeo club, black student association, international student association, nontraditional student association.

Athletics. NCAA. **Intercollegiate:** Baseball M, basketball, cross-country, football (tackle) M, softball W, tennis, track and field, volleyball W. **Intramural:** Basketball, football (non-tackle), racquetball, soccer, softball, tennis, volleyball, water polo, weight lifting. **Team name:** Lobos.

Student services. Alcohol/substance abuse counseling, campus ministries, career counseling, student employment services, financial aid counseling, health services, on-campus daycare, personal counseling, placement for graduates, veterans' counselor. **Physically disabled:** Services for visually, hearing impaired.

Contact. E-mail: admissions@sulross.edu
Phone: (432) 837-8050 Toll-free number: (888) 722-7778
Fax: (432) 837-8431
Greg Schwab, Director of Recruiting and Admission, Sul Ross State University, Box C-2, Alpine, TX 79832

Tarleton State University

Stephenville, Texas — **CB member**
www.tarleton.edu — **CB code: 6817**

- Public 4-year university
- Residential campus in large town
- 7,595 degree-seeking undergraduates: 20% part-time, 57% women, 8% African American, 1% Asian American, 8% Hispanic American, 1% Native American, 1% international
- 1,447 degree-seeking graduate students
- 84% of applicants admitted
- SAT or ACT (ACT writing recommended) required
- 48% graduate within 6 years

General. Founded in 1899. Regionally accredited. Graduate courses available at several off-campus locations within 150-mile radius. Upper level/graduate program offered at Tarleton University System Center in Killeen. Educational progam for prison inmates offered in Gatesville on Fort Hood Military Post. **Degrees:** 1,165 bachelor's awarded; master's, doctoral offered. **ROTC:** Army. **Location:** 65 miles from Fort Worth. **Calendar:** Semester, extensive summer session. **Full-time faculty:** 292 total; 70% have terminal degrees, 11% minority, 42% women. **Part-time faculty:** 242 total; 10% minority, 46% women. **Class size:** 37% < 20, 48% 20-39, 6% 40-49, 7% 50-99, 1% >100. **Special facilities:** University farm and equine center, planetarium.

Freshman class profile. 2,247 applied, 1,893 admitted, 1,247 enrolled.

Mid 50% test scores			
SAT verbal:	430-530	Rank in top quarter:	33%
SAT math:	450-550	Rank in top tenth:	10%
ACT:	18-22	Return as sophomores:	65%
		Out-of-state:	1%

Basis for selection. Unconditional admission requires 930 SAT (exclusive of Writing) or 20 ACT. Rank in top quarter of class ensures unconditional admission if student has taken 4 years English and 3 years mathematics. **Homeschooled:** Must provide proof of curriculum completed from an agency or teacher. **Learning Disabled:** Contact Director of Disability Services for appropriate accommodation.

High school preparation. 19 units required. Required and recommended units include English 4, mathematics 3, social studies 2, history 1, science 2-3 (laboratory 2), foreign language 2 and academic electives 2-4.

2005-2006 Annual costs. Tuition/fees: $4,171; $12,451 out-of-state. Distance learning fee additional $40 per credit hour. Room/board: $5,514. Books/supplies: $800. Personal expenses: $2,156.

2004-2005 Financial aid. Need-based: 967 full-time freshmen applied for aid; 900 were judged to have need; 817 of these received aid. Average need met was 71%. Average scholarship/grant was $4,100; average loan $2,116. 49% of total undergraduate aid awarded as scholarships/grants, 51% as loans/jobs. **Non-need-based:** Awarded to 2,106 full-time undergraduates, including 512 freshmen. Scholarships awarded for academics, alumni affiliation, art, athletics, leadership, ROTC.

Application procedures. Admission: Priority date 7/1; deadline 8/1 (receipt date). $25 fee. Application may be submitted online. Admission notification on a rolling basis beginning on or about 2/1. Early acceptance available to applicants who rank in top 10% of class; notification on rolling basis beginning January 1. **Financial aid:** Priority date 4/1, closing date 10/15. FAFSA required. Applicants notified on a rolling basis starting 2/1; must reply within 2 week(s) of notification.

Academics. Special study options: Accelerated study, distance learning, double major, dual enrollment of high school students, honors, internships, study abroad, teacher certification program. Specialized bachelor of applied arts and science degree for students with practical work experience in field of study; cooperative doctoral program in educational administration offered in partnership with Texas A&M University-Commerce; 2-2 engineering with Texas A&M University and University of Texas Arlington. **Credit/placement by examination:** AP, CLEP, SAT, ACT, institutional tests. Students can earn the majority of credits toward their degree by examination. **Support services:** Learning center, pre-admission summer program, reduced course load, remedial instruction, study skills assistance, tutoring, writing center.

Majors. Agriculture: General, agribusiness operations, agronomy, animal husbandry, animal sciences, business, economics, livestock, mechanization, ornamental horticulture, supplies. **Biology:** General, zoology. **Business:** General, accounting, business admin, finance, human resources, management information systems, marketing, office management. **Communications:** General. **Computer sciences:** General. **Conservation:** Wildlife. **Education:** Computer, science. **Engineering:** Environmental, physics. **Engineering technology:** General, industrial, manufacturing. **English:** English lit. **Family/consumer sciences:** General. **Foreign languages:** Spanish. **Health:** Clinical lab science, nursing (RN). **History:** General. **Liberal arts:** Arts/sciences. **Math:** General. **Parks/recreation:** Health/fitness. **Physical sciences:** Chemistry, geology, hydrology, physics. **Protective services:** Criminal justice. **Psychology:** General. **Public administration:** Social work. **Social sciences:** Economics, political science, sociology. **Transportation:** Airline/commercial pilot, aviation management. **Visual/performing arts:** Dramatic, studio arts.

Most popular majors. Agriculture 13%, business/marketing 23%, interdisciplinary studies 10%, parks/recreation 8%.

Computing on campus. 1,600 workstations in dormitories, library, computer center, student center. Dormitories wired for high-speed internet access and linked to campus network. Commuter students can connect to campus network. Online course registration, online library, helpline, repair service, student web hosting, wireless network available.

Student life. **Freshman orientation:** Available, $125 fee. Preregistration for classes offered. Held first week of August and 1 week prior to start of classes. **Policies:** Freshmen permitted cars on campus. **Housing:** Guaranteed on-campus for freshmen. Coed dorms, single-sex dorms, apartments, fraternity/sorority housing, substance-free housing available. $100 fully refundable deposit, deadline 3/1. **Activities:** Bands, choral groups, dance, drama, literary magazine, music ensembles, musical theater, radio station, student government, student newspaper, symphony orchestra, Los Tejanos, Chinese student association, progressive united black student organization, student social work association, Alpha Phi Omega, Circle K, Fellowship of Christian Athletes, Fellowship of Christian Cowboys, College Republicans, Young Democrats.

Athletics. NCAA. **Intercollegiate:** Baseball M, basketball, cheerleading, cross-country, football (tackle) M, golf W, rodeo, softball W, tennis W, track and field, volleyball W. **Intramural:** Archery, basketball, football (non-tackle) M, football (tackle), golf, racquetball, rodeo, soccer, softball, table tennis, tennis, volleyball. **Team name:** Texans.

Student services. Adult student services, alcohol/substance abuse counseling, campus ministries, career counseling, student employment services, financial aid counseling, health services, legal services, minority student services, on-campus daycare, personal counseling, placement for graduates, veterans' counselor. **Physically disabled:** Services for visually, speech, hearing impaired.

Contact. E-mail: uadm@tarleton.edu
Phone: (254) 968-9125 Toll-free number: (800) 687-8236
Fax: (254) 968-9951
Cindy Hess, Director of Admissions, Tarleton State University, Box T-0030, Stephenville, TX 76402

Texas A&M International University

Laredo, Texas — **CB member**
www.tamiu.edu — **CB code: 0359**

- Public 4-year university
- Commuter campus in small city

General. Founded in 1969. Regionally accredited. **Location:** 150 miles from San Antonio and Corpus Christi. **Calendar:** Semester.

Annual costs/financial aid. Tuition/fees (2005-2006): $4,218; $12,498 out-of-state. Room/board: $6,390. Books/supplies: $1,000. Personal expenses: $2,027. Need-based financial aid available to full-time and part-time students.

Contact. Phone: (956) 326-2200
Director of Admissions, 5201 University Boulevard, Laredo, TX 78041-1900

Texas A&M University

College Station, Texas — **CB member**
www.tamu.edu — **CB code: 6003**

- Public 4-year university
- Residential campus in small city
- 36,227 degree-seeking undergraduates: 9% part-time, 49% women, 3% African American, 4% Asian American, 11% Hispanic American, 1% international
- 8,223 degree-seeking graduate students
- 70% of applicants admitted
- SAT or ACT with writing, application essay required

General. Founded in 1876. Regionally accredited. **Degrees:** 7,711 bachelor's awarded; master's, doctoral, first professional offered. **ROTC:** Army, Navy, Air Force. **Location:** 90 miles from Houston, 100 miles from Austin. **Calendar:** Semester, extensive summer session. **Full-time faculty:** 1,922 total; 90% have terminal degrees, 20% minority, 25% women. **Part-time faculty:** 830 total; 69% have terminal degrees, 17% minority, 33% women. **Class size:** 20% < 20, 47% 20-39, 9% 40-49, 13% 50-99, 12% >100. **Special facilities:** Reactor, cyclotron, observatory, agriculture research property, 18-hole golf course, supercomputer center, oceanographic research vessel, Italian study center, George H. W. Bush Presidential Library and Museum.

Freshman class profile. 17,871 applied, 12,503 admitted, 7,104 enrolled.

Mid 50% test scores			
SAT verbal:	530-640	Out-of-state:	4%
SAT math:	560-670	Live on campus:	71%
ACT:	23-28	International:	1%
Rank in top quarter:	79%	Fraternities:	6%
Rank in top tenth:	50%	Sororities:	15%

Basis for selection. Automatic admission to applicants in top 10% of Texas high school class (with completed application), as specified by state law. Strong senior year course schedule recommended. Test scores required of all applicants but not used for admission of applicants from top 10% of any Texas high school class. **Learning Disabled:** Must provide documentation of disability from qualified professional licensed or certified to diagnose disability.

High school preparation. 17.5 units required; 18.5 recommended. Required and recommended units include English 4, mathematics 3.5, social studies 2, history 1, science 3 (laboratory 2) and foreign language 2. 1 unit computer usage required.

2005-2006 Annual costs. Tuition/fees: $6,399; $14,679 out-of-state. Room/board: $6,952. Books/supplies: $1,180. Personal expenses: $1,476.

2005-2006 Financial aid. **Need-based:** Average need met was 71%. Average scholarship/grant was $7,103; average loan $3,153. 22% of total undergraduate aid awarded as scholarships/grants, 78% as loans/jobs. **Non-need-based:** Scholarships awarded for academics, alumni affiliation, art, athletics, job skills, leadership, music/drama, ROTC, state residency. **Additional information:** Short-term loans available. Out-of-state students awarded academic scholarships of $1,000 or more are eligible for waiver of out-of-state tuition.

Application procedures. **Admission:** Closing date 2/1 (receipt date). $50 fee, may be waived for applicants with need. Application may be submitted online. Admission notification on a rolling basis beginning on or about 9/1. Must reply by 5/1. **Financial aid:** No deadline. FAFSA, institutional form required. Applicants notified on a rolling basis starting 4/1; must reply within 4 week(s) of notification.

Academics. Core curriculum requirements in foreign language and computer science may be satisfied by selected high school courses. **Special study options:** Accelerated study, combined bachelor's/graduate degree, cooperative education, distance learning, double major, dual enrollment of high school students, ESL, honors, independent study, internships, liberal arts/career combination, study abroad, teacher certification program. Exchange programs in architecture with Instituto Tecnologico y de Estudios Superiores de Monterrey, King's College London (England), University of Lancaster (England), Denmark's international study program, Ruhr University Bochum (Germany), University of Lausanne (Switzerland). **Credit/placement by examination:** AP, CLEP, IB, institutional tests. **Support services:** Learning center, pre-admission summer program, remedial instruction, tutoring, writing center.

Majors. **Agriculture:** Agribusiness operations, agronomy, animal husbandry, animal sciences, aquaculture, business, dairy, economics, farm/ranch, food science, horticultural science, horticulture, ornamental horticulture, plant breeding, plant protection, plant sciences, poultry, production, range science, soil science, turf management. **Architecture:** Environmental design, landscape. **Area/ethnic studies:** American. **Biology:** General, bacteriology, biochemistry, biomedical sciences, botany, cell/histology, cellular/molecular, entomology, genetics, marine, molecular, zoology. **Business:** Accounting, finance, marketing, tourism promotion, tourism/travel. **Communications:** Journalism. **Computer sciences:** General, computer science. **Conservation:** General, environmental science, fisheries, forest management, forestry, management/policy, wildlife. **Education:** Adult/continuing. **Engineering:** Aerospace, agricultural, biomedical, chemical, civil, computer, electrical, industrial, mechanical, nuclear, ocean, petroleum, systems. **Engineering technology:** General, construction, electrical, manufacturing, telecommunications. **English:** English lit, speech/rhetoric. **Family/consumer sciences:** Food/nutrition. **Foreign languages:** French, German, Russian, Spanish. **Health:** Physics/radiologic health, predentistry, premedicine, preveterinary. **History:** General. **Interdisciplinary:** Biological/physical sciences, museum, nutrition sciences. **Liberal arts:** Arts/sciences. **Math:** General, applied. **Parks/recreation:** General, facilities management, health/fitness. **Philosophy/religion:** Philosophy. **Physical sciences:** Atmospheric science, chemistry, geology, geophysics, physics, planetary. **Psychology:** General. **Public administration:** Community org/advocacy. **Social sciences:** Anthropology, cartography, economics, geography, political science, sociology. **Visual/performing arts:** Dramatic.

Most popular majors. Agriculture 12%, biology 9%, business/marketing 17%, engineering/engineering technologies 16%, English 6%, interdisciplinary studies 8%, social sciences 9%.

Computing on campus. 1,300 workstations in dormitories, library, computer center, student center. Dormitories wired for high-speed internet access and linked to campus network. Commuter students can connect to campus network. Online course registration, online library, helpline, repair service, student web hosting, wireless network available.

Student life. **Freshman orientation:** Mandatory, $35 fee. Preregistration for classes offered. 2 1/2 day program throughout the summer. **Policies:** Freshmen permitted cars on campus. **Housing:** Coed dorms, single-sex dorms, special housing for disabled, apartments, fraternity/sorority housing, substance-free housing available. $300 deposit. Campus housing guaranteed to members of Corps of Cadets and recipients of major 4-year endowed academic scholarships. Freshman honors dorm available. **Activities:** Bands, choral groups, dance, drama, film society, literary magazine, music ensembles, musical theater, radio station, student government, student newspaper, symphony orchestra, TV station, black awareness committee, committee for the awareness of Mexican American culture, student Y association, student conference on national affairs, social service organizations, College Republicans, Aggie Democrats, political forum, united campus ministries, Aggies for Christ.

Athletics. NCAA. **Intercollegiate:** Archery W, baseball M, basketball, cross-country, diving, equestrian W, football (tackle) M, golf, soccer W, softball W, swimming, tennis, track and field, volleyball W. **Intramural:** Archery, badminton, basketball, bowling, diving, golf, lacrosse, racquetball, rodeo, soccer, softball, squash, swimming, table tennis, track and field, volleyball. **Team name:** Aggies.

Student services. Alcohol/substance abuse counseling, career counseling, student employment services, financial aid counseling, health services, legal services, minority student services, on-campus daycare, personal counseling, placement for graduates, veterans' counselor, women's services. **Physically disabled:** Services for visually, speech, hearing impaired.

Contact. E-mail: admissions@tamu.edu
Phone: (979) 845-3741 Fax: (979) 458-1808
Monique Snowden, Director of Admissions, Texas A&M University, PO Box 30014, College Station, TX 77842-3014

Texas A&M University-Baylor College of Dentistry

Dallas, Texas
www.bcd.tamhsc.edu **CB code: 6059**

- Public upper-division health science college
- Commuter campus in very large city
- 31% of applicants admitted
- Application essay, interview required

General. Founded in 1905. Regionally accredited. **Degrees:** 27 bachelor's awarded; master's, doctoral, first professional offered. **Articulation:** Agreement with Collin Community College District. **Calendar:** Semester. **Full-time faculty:** 106 total; 100% have terminal degrees, 24% minority, 33% women. **Part-time faculty:** 122 total; 100% have terminal degrees, 45% minority, 30% women.

Student profile. 59 degree-seeking undergraduates, 382 degree-seeking graduate students. 114 applied as first time-transfer students, 35 admitted, 30 enrolled. 60% transferred from two-year, 40% transferred from four-year institutions.

Women:	100%	**Part-time:**	2%
African American:	2%	**Out-of-state:**	3%
Asian American:	14%	**25 or older:**	25%
Hispanic American:	7%		

Basis for selection. High school transcript, college transcript, application essay, interview required. School achievement most important. Essay, interview, and recommendations highly considered. Transfer accepted as juniors.

2005-2006 Annual costs. Tuition/fees: $4,117; $12,397 out-of-state. Personal expenses: $2,700.

Financial aid. **Need-based:** 26% of total undergraduate aid awarded as scholarships/grants, 74% as loans/jobs. **Non-need-based:** Scholarships awarded for academics.

Application procedures. **Admission:** Priority date 12/31. $35 fee. **Financial aid:** FAFSA, institutional form required.

Academics. Participation in research activities under faculty sponsorship and annual research fellowships awarded by college offered. **Special study options:** Combined bachelor's/graduate degree, internships. **Credit/placement by examination:** CLEP. **Support services:** Pre-admission summer program, reduced course load, remedial instruction, tutoring.

Majors. **Health:** Dental hygiene.

Computing on campus. 25 workstations in library, computer center. Commuter students can connect to campus network. Online library, helpline, wireless network available.

Student life. **Housing:** Baylor Medical Center nursing dormitory housing available. **Activities:** Student government.

Student services. Student employment services, financial aid counseling, health services, personal counseling.

Contact. Phone: (214) 828-8230 Fax: (214) 828-8346
Barbara Miller, Director, Texas A&M University-Baylor College of Dentistry, PO Box 660677, Dallas, TX 75266-0677

Texas A&M University-Commerce

Commerce, Texas **CB member**
www.tamu-commerce.edu **CB code: 6188**

- Public 4-year university
- Residential campus in small town
- 6,234 degree-seeking undergraduates
- 2,447 graduate students
- 57% of applicants admitted
- SAT or ACT required

General. Founded in 1889. Regionally accredited. **Degrees:** 1,080 bachelor's awarded; master's, doctoral offered. **Location:** 60 miles from Dallas. **Calendar:** Semester, extensive summer session. **Full-time faculty:** 281 total; 6% minority, 37% women. **Part-time faculty:** 238 total. **Class size:** 48% < 20, 39% 20-39, 8% 40-49, 5% 50-99, less than 1% >100. **Special facilities:** Instructional university farm, science building with planetarium.

Freshman class profile. 2,017 applied, 1,156 admitted, 620 enrolled.

Mid 50% test scores			
SAT verbal:	440-550	**Rank in top quarter:**	42%
SAT math:	430-550	**Rank in top tenth:**	16%
ACT:	18-23	**End year in good standing:**	92%

Basis for selection. ACT or SAT scores most important, followed by high school grades and class rank. Students admitted with 20 ACT or 920 SAT (exclusive of Writing). TASP scores may exempt student from SAT or ACT tests. If student is TASP remedial, must take TASP within first semester of enrolling. Portfolio required for advertising art program; audition recommended for music program. **Homeschooled:** Must earn GED and be at least 18 years of age.

High school preparation. 12 units required. Required and recommended units include English 4, mathematics 3, science 2 and foreign language 2. 2.5 hours history/social studies required.

2005-2006 Annual costs. Tuition/fees: $4,136; $12,416 out-of-state. Room/board: $6,060. Books/supplies: $900. Personal expenses: $1,470.

2005-2006 Financial aid. **Need-based:** Average need met was 80%. Average scholarship/grant was $5,875; average loan $1,545. 44% of total undergraduate aid awarded as scholarships/grants, 56% as loans/jobs. **Additional information:** Work-study also available for full-time students.

Application procedures. **Admission:** Closing date 8/1 (postmark date). $25 fee ($50 out-of-state). Application may be submitted online. Admission notification on a rolling basis beginning on or about 10/1. High school seniors may enroll part-time before graduation with consent of high school principal if they meet requirements. **Financial aid:** Priority date 4/1; no closing date. FAFSA, institutional form required. Applicants notified on a rolling basis starting 4/1; must reply within 2 week(s) of notification.

Academics. **Special study options:** Combined bachelor's/graduate degree, cooperative education, distance learning, double major, dual enrollment of high school students, external degree, honors, independent study, internships, liberal arts/career combination, study abroad, teacher certification program, weekend college. **Credit/placement by examination:** AP, CLEP, IB, institutional tests. 6 credit hours maximum toward bachelor's degree. **Support services:** Learning center, pre-admission summer program, remedial instruction, study skills assistance, tutoring, writing center.

Majors. **Agriculture:** Animal sciences, communications, economics, food science, plant sciences, soil science. **Biology:** General, cell/histology. **Business:** General, accounting, business admin, human resources, management information systems, managerial economics, marketing, office management, office/clerical, operations, public finance. **Communications:** General, advertising, broadcast journalism, digital media, journalism, photojournalism, public relations. **Communications technology:** Graphic/printing. **Computer sciences:** General, computer science, information systems. **Conservation:** General, environmental studies, wildlife. **Construction:** Maintenance. **Education:** Bilingual, biology, chemistry, driver/safety, early childhood, elementary, middle, multi-level teacher, physical, special. **Engineering:** Operations research. **Engineering technology:** Construction, manufacturing. **English:** American lit, British lit, composition, speech/rhetoric. **Foreign languages:** German, Spanish. **Health:** Athletic training, health care admin, medical records admin, predentistry, premedicine, prepharmacy, preveterinary. **History:** General. **Interdisciplinary:** Biological/physical sciences. **Legal studies:** Legal secretary, paralegal, prelaw. **Liberal arts:** Arts/sciences, library science. **Math:** General. **Parks/recreation:** Health/fitness. **Physical sciences:** Chemistry, geology, organic chemistry, physics, planetary. **Protective services:** Criminal justice, law enforcement admin. **Psychology:** General. **Public administration:** Social work. **Social sciences:** General, anthropology, criminology, economics, geography, political science, sociology. **Theology:** Preministerial. **Visual/performing arts:** General, art, arts management, ceramics, commercial photography, commercial/advertising art, design, dramatic, industrial design, metal/jewelry, music history, music pedagogy, music performance, music theory/composition, musicology, painting, photography, piano/organ, printmaking, sculpture, voice/opera.

Computing on campus. 1,500 workstations in dormitories, library, computer center. Dormitories linked to campus network. Commuter students can connect to campus network. Online course registration, online library, helpline, repair service, wireless network available.

Student life. Freshman orientation: Mandatory, $70 fee. Preregistration for classes offered. Held throughout summer; includes advising, assessment testing, and parental involvement. **Policies:** Freshmen permitted cars on campus. **Housing:** Coed dorms, single-sex dorms, special housing for disabled, apartments, fraternity/sorority housing, substance-free housing available. $100 deposit. Shared freshman experience housing available. **Activities:** Bands, choral groups, dance, drama, film society, literary magazine, music ensembles, musical theater, opera, radio station, student government, student newspaper, symphony orchestra, TV station, Baptist student union, Church of Christ Bible chair, Newman Club, university Christian center, Young Democrats, association cultural de Hispanos-Americanos, Chinese student association, Muslim society, NAACP, Thai students association, Alpha Phi Omega.

Athletics. NCAA. **Intercollegiate:** Basketball, cross-country, football (tackle) M, golf, soccer W, track and field, volleyball W. **Intramural:** Archery, badminton, baseball M, basketball, bowling, cross-country, golf, racquetball, softball, swimming, table tennis, tennis, track and field, volleyball. **Team name:** Lions.

Student services. Alcohol/substance abuse counseling, campus ministries, career counseling, student employment services, financial aid counseling, health services, legal services, on-campus daycare, personal counseling, placement for graduates, veterans' counselor. **Physically disabled:** Services for visually, speech, hearing impaired.

Contact. E-mail: randy_mcdonald@tamu-commerce.edu
Phone: (903) 886-5081 Toll-free number: (888) 886-2682
Fax: (903) 468-6080
Randy McDonald, Director of Admissions, Texas A&M University-Commerce, Box 3011, Commerce, TX 75429-3011

Texas A&M University-Corpus Christi

Corpus Christi, Texas — **CB member**
www.tamucc.edu — **CB code: 0366**

- Public 4-year university
- Commuter campus in large city

General. Founded in 1947. Regionally accredited. **Location:** 150 miles from San Antonio, 200 miles from Houston. **Calendar:** Semester.

Annual costs/financial aid. Tuition/fees (2005-2006): $4,516; $12,796 out-of-state. Room/board: $7,800. Books/supplies: $840. Personal expenses: $1,245. Need-based financial aid available to full-time and part-time students.

Contact. Phone: (361) 825-2624
Director of Admissions, 6300 Ocean Drive, Corpus Christi, TX 78412

Texas A&M University-Galveston

Galveston, Texas — **CB member**
www.tamug.edu — **CB code: 6835**

- Public 4-year university and branch campus college
- Residential campus in small city
- 1,636 degree-seeking undergraduates: 9% part-time, 42% women
- 41 degree-seeking graduate students
- 96% of applicants admitted
- SAT or ACT (ACT writing optional), application essay required
- 48% graduate within 6 years; 35% enter graduate study

General. Founded in 1962. Regionally accredited. Institution houses Texas Maritime Academy, 1 of 5 seacoast maritime academies in the US preparing graduates for licensing as officers in the Merchant Marine. All academic programs are ocean-related. **Degrees:** 248 bachelor's awarded; master's offered. **ROTC:** Navy. **Location:** 50 miles from Houston. **Calendar:** Semester, limited summer session. **Full-time faculty:** 92 total; 65% have terminal degrees, 13% minority, 20% women. **Part-time faculty:** 78 total; 22% have terminal degrees, 14% minority, 42% women. **Class size:** 67% < 20, 23% 20-39, 4% 40-49, 4% 50-99, 2% >100. **Special facilities:** Fleet of research and training boats, 300-acre wetlands on west Galveston Bay, wetlands research center, ship bridge simulator.

Freshman class profile. 1,171 applied, 1,119 admitted, 466 enrolled.

Rank in top quarter:	40%	**Out-of-state:**	14%
Rank in top tenth:	11%	**Live on campus:**	75%
Return as sophomores:	72%	**International:**	1%

Basis for selection. School achievement record and test scores most important. Adverse circumstances, leadership, exceptional talents, course selections, and references reviewed on individual basis.

High school preparation. 13 units required; 19 recommended. Required and recommended units include English 4, mathematics 3-4, social studies 3, science 3-4 (laboratory 2) and foreign language 3. 1 unit computer literacy required. Science courses must be selected from biology, chemistry or physics.

2005-2006 Annual costs. Tuition/fees: $5,118; $13,398 out-of-state. Room/board: $4,870. Books/supplies: $1,180. Personal expenses: $1,960.

2004-2005 Financial aid. Need-based: Average need met was 13%. Average scholarship/grant was $3,987; average loan $1,912. 28% of total undergraduate aid awarded as scholarships/grants, 72% as loans/jobs. **Non-need-based:** Scholarships awarded for academics, state residency.

Application procedures. Admission: No deadline. $35 fee, may be waived for applicants with need. Application may be submitted online. Admission notification on a rolling basis. **Financial aid:** Priority date 4/1; no closing date. FAFSA required. Applicants notified on a rolling basis starting 3/15; must reply within 3 week(s) of notification.

Academics. USCG ship officer's license may be earned through license option program. **Special study options:** Accelerated study, cooperative education, double major, dual enrollment of high school students, independent study, internships, liberal arts/career combination, semester at sea, study abroad, teacher certification program. Merchant marine licensing program available with marine biology, marine science, marine transportation, and marine engineering technology degrees. **Credit/placement by examination:** AP, CLEP, IB, institutional tests. **Support services:** Learning center, pre-admission summer program, remedial instruction, study skills assistance, tutoring.

Majors. Agriculture: Aquaculture. **Biology:** General, aquatic, biomedical sciences, botany, marine, zoology. **Business:** Business admin, international, international finance, tourism/travel, transportation. **Conservation:** General, fisheries. **Education:** Biology, science. **Engineering:** Marine, ocean, systems. **Engineering technology:** Mechanical. **Interdisciplinary:** Biological/physical sciences. **Liberal arts:** Arts/sciences. **Parks/recreation:** General. **Physical sciences:** General, geology, hydrology, oceanography. **Transportation:** General, commercial fishing, marine science/Merchant Marine.

Computing on campus. 130 workstations in dormitories, library, computer center. Dormitories wired for high-speed internet access and linked to campus network. Commuter students can connect to campus network. Helpline, repair service available.

Student life. Freshman orientation: Mandatory, $50 fee. Preregistration for classes offered. 4 days in June and August. **Policies:** Freshmen permitted cars on campus. **Housing:** Coed dorms, single-sex dorms, special housing for disabled, apartments, substance-free housing available. $250 fully refundable deposit. **Activities:** Choral groups, dance, drama, literary magazine, student government, student newspaper, Circle K, Campus Crusade for Christ, emergency care team, outdoor and environmental conservation, Catholic student association, SEED (Students Encouraging Ethnic Diversity), Wesley Foundation.

Athletics. Intercollegiate: Rowing (crew), sailing. **Intramural:** Basketball, football (non-tackle), racquetball, soccer, softball, tennis, volleyball, water polo. **Team name:** Aggies.

Student services. Alcohol/substance abuse counseling, campus ministries, career counseling, student employment services, financial aid counseling, health services, minority student services, personal counseling, placement for graduates, veterans' counselor. **Physically disabled:** Services for hearing impaired.

Contact. E-mail: seaaggie@tamug.edu
Phone: (409) 740-4414 Toll-free number: (877) 322-4443
Fax: (409) 740-4731
Cheryl Moon, Director of Admissions and Records, Texas A&M University-Galveston, PO Box 1675, Galveston, TX 77553-1675

Texas A&M University-Kingsville

Kingsville, Texas **CB member**
www.tamuk.edu **CB code: 6822**

- Public 4-year university
- Commuter campus in large town
- 4,665 full-time, degree-seeking undergraduates
- 97% of applicants admitted

General. Founded in 1925. Regionally accredited. **Degrees:** 1,005 bachelor's awarded; master's, doctoral offered. **ROTC:** Army. **Location:** 40 miles from Corpus Christi, 250 miles from Houston. **Calendar:** Semester, extensive summer session. **Full-time faculty:** 346 total. **Part-time faculty:** 120 total. **Class size:** 41% < 20, 51% 20-39, 5% 40-49, 2% 50-99, less than 1% >100. **Special facilities:** Equine facilities, observatory, college-operated farms, research center for citrus.

Freshman class profile. 1,800 applied, 1,753 admitted, 659 enrolled.

Mid 50% test scores		Out-of-state:	1%
SAT verbal:	410-520	Live on campus:	60%
SAT math:	410-540	Fraternities:	2%
ACT:	16-21	Sororities:	2%

Basis for selection. High school GPA, class rank, test scores important. Audition required, portfolio recommended for music program.

High school preparation. 24 units recommended. Recommended units include English 4, mathematics 3, social studies 4, history 3, science 3, foreign language 3 and academic electives 3. One fine arts, 1 computer indicated.

2005-2006 Annual costs. Tuition/fees: $4,326; $12,606 out-of-state. Room/board: $4,654. Books/supplies: $614. Personal expenses: $2,108.

Financial aid. Non-need-based: Scholarships awarded for academics, leadership.

Application procedures. Admission: No deadline. $15 fee, may be waived for applicants with need. Admission notification on a rolling basis. **Financial aid:** FAFSA required. Applicants notified on a rolling basis.

Academics. Special study options: Cooperative education, distance learning, double major, ESL, honors, internships, study abroad, teacher certification program. **Credit/placement by examination:** AP, CLEP.

Majors. Agriculture: Agribusiness operations, animal sciences, business, food science, plant sciences, range science. **Architecture:** Interior. **Biology:** General. **Business:** General, accounting, finance, international, management information systems, management science, managerial economics. **Communications:** General. **Conservation:** Wildlife. **Education:** General, agricultural, art, bilingual, elementary, family/consumer sciences, health, music, physical, secondary. **Engineering:** Chemical, civil, computer, electrical, mechanical, petroleum. **Engineering technology:** Industrial management. **Family/consumer sciences:** General, clothing/textiles, family studies, food/nutrition. **Foreign languages:** Spanish. **Health:** Speech pathology. **History:** General. **Math:** General. **Physical sciences:** Chemistry, geology, physics. **Psychology:** General. **Social sciences:** Anthropology, political science, sociology. **Visual/performing arts:** Dramatic, interior design, studio arts.

Student life. Freshman orientation: Mandatory. **Housing:** Guaranteed on-campus for freshmen. Coed dorms, single-sex dorms, apartments available. **Activities:** Bands, choral groups, dance, drama, music ensembles, musical theater, radio station, student government, student newspaper, TV station, Muslim student association, Baptist Student Associates, Black Student Union, La Barraca Tejana, American Society of Women Engineers, Society of Hispanic Professional Engineers, Pre-Law Society.

Athletics. NCAA. **Intercollegiate:** Baseball M, basketball, cross-country, football (tackle) M, softball W, tennis, track and field, volleyball W. **Intramural:** Archery, bowling, equestrian, golf, racquetball, softball, volleyball.

Student services. Adult student services, career counseling, student employment services, health services, on-campus daycare, personal counseling, placement for graduates, veterans' counselor. **Physically disabled:** Services for visually, speech, hearing impaired.

Contact. E-mail: ksossrx@tamuk.edu
Phone: (361) 593-2315 Toll-free number: (800) 687-6000
Fax: (361) 593-2195
Maggie Williams, Director of Admissions and Registrar, Texas A&M University-Kingsville, MSC 105, Kingsville, TX 78363-8201

Texas A&M University-Texarkana

Texarkana, Texas
www.tamut.edu **CB code: 6206**

- Public upper-division university
- Commuter campus in small city
- 66% of applicants admitted
- Test scores required

General. Founded in 1971. Regionally accredited. **Degrees:** 286 bachelor's awarded; master's offered. **Articulation:** Agreements with Texarkana College, Northeast Texas Community College, Panola College, Paris Junior College, Cossatot College, Rich Mountain College, University of Arkansas Community College at Hope. **Location:** 180 miles from Dallas, 145 miles from Little Rock, Arkansas. **Calendar:** Semester, limited summer session. **Full-time faculty:** 55 total; 93% have terminal degrees, 11% minority, 49% women. **Part-time faculty:** 45 total; 20% have terminal degrees, 4% minority, 69% women.

Student profile. 1,000 degree-seeking undergraduates, 519 degree-seeking graduate students. 472 applied as first time-transfer students, 312 admitted, 256 enrolled.

Women:	75%	Out-of-state:	24%
Part-time:	62%		

Basis for selection. Open admission. College transcript, standardized test scores required. Minimum 2.0 GPA for 75 hours or more; 1.75 GPA for less than 75 hours; must satisfy Texas Success Initiative. Transfer accepted as sophomores, juniors, seniors.

2005-2006 Annual costs. Tuition/fees: $3,185; $11,465 out-of-state. Books/supplies: $896. Personal expenses: $1,512.

Financial aid. All financial aid based on need. 52% of total undergraduate aid awarded as scholarships/grants, 48% as loans/jobs.

Application procedures. Admission: Rolling admission. No application fee. Application may be submitted online. **Financial aid:** No deadline. Must have completed minimum of 54 semester hours of transferable college credit to apply for financial aid. Notified applicants must reply within 45 days from date of award letter. Exceptions made on individual basis. March 1 financial aid deadline for scholarships. FAFSA, institutional form required.

Academics. Special study options: Combined bachelor's/graduate degree, cross-registration, distance learning, independent study, internships, liberal arts/career combination, student-designed major, teacher certification program. **Credit/placement by examination:** AP, CLEP, IB, institutional tests. BAAS degree limits credit by exam to 18 semester credit hours. **Support services:** Tutoring, writing center.

Majors. Biology: General. **Business:** General, accounting, business admin, finance, human resources, international, management information systems, marketing. **Communications:** Media studies. **Computer sciences:** General. **English:** English lit. **Health:** Nursing (RN). **History:** General. **Math:** General. **Protective services:** Criminal justice. **Psychology:** General.

Most popular majors. Business/marketing 19%, history 10%, interdisciplinary studies 33%, liberal arts 10%, psychology 11%.

Computing on campus. 104 workstations in library, computer center. Commuter students can connect to campus network. Online library, wireless network available.

Student life. Activities: Student government, student newspaper, multicultural association.

Student services. Career counseling, student employment services, financial aid counseling, personal counseling, placement for graduates, veterans' counselor. **Physically disabled:** Services for visually, hearing impaired.

Contact. E-mail: admissions@tamut.edu
Phone: (903) 223-3069 Fax: (903) 233-3140
Pat Black, Director of Admissions and Registrar, Texas A&M University-Texarkana, 2600 North Robinson Road, Texarkana, TX 75505

Texas Christian University

Fort Worth, Texas — **CB member**
www.tcu.edu — **CB code: 6820**

- Private 4-year university affiliated with Christian Church (Disciples of Christ)
- Residential campus in large city
- 7,056 degree-seeking undergraduates: 5% part-time, 61% women, 5% African American, 2% Asian American, 6% Hispanic American, 1% Native American, 4% international
- 1,561 degree-seeking graduate students
- 67% of applicants admitted
- SAT or ACT (ACT writing recommended), application essay required
- 69% graduate within 6 years

General. Founded in 1873. Regionally accredited. 2 comprehensive leadership programs offered. Leadership center, information and resources related to leadership development and training. **Degrees:** 1,537 bachelor's awarded; master's, doctoral, first professional offered. **ROTC:** Army, Air Force. **Location:** 3 miles from downtown, 29 miles from Dallas. **Calendar:** Semester, limited summer session. **Full-time faculty:** 465 total; 90% have terminal degrees, 13% minority, 40% women. **Part-time faculty:** 345 total; 32% have terminal degrees, 6% minority, 48% women. **Class size:** 50% < 20, 33% 20-39, 10% 40-49, 5% 50-99, 2% >100. **Special facilities:** Geological center for remote sensing, nuclear magnetic resonance facility, observatory, film library, performance complex, behavioral research institute, meteorite collection, lab school, speech and hearing clinic.

Freshman class profile. 8,155 applied, 5,471 admitted, 1,610 enrolled.

Mid 50% test scores		**Return as sophomores:**	84%
SAT verbal:	520-630	**Out-of-state:**	24%
SAT math:	540-640	**Live on campus:**	95%
ACT:	23-28	**International:**	3%
Rank in top quarter:	61%	**Fraternities:**	45%
Rank in top tenth:	28%	**Sororities:**	50%

Basis for selection. GED not accepted. Academic credentials most important; talents, leadership potential, and applicant's determination to make difference considered. Audition, portfolio required for fine arts students; interview recommended for all. **Homeschooled:** Interview with admissions officer recommended, additional weight may be placed on SAT/ACT scores in admissions process.

High school preparation. 17 units required; 24 recommended. Required and recommended units include English 4, mathematics 3-4, social studies 3-4, science 3-4, foreign language 2-4 and academic electives 2-4.

2006-2007 Annual costs. Tuition/fees: $23,028. Room/board: $7,520. Books/supplies: $720. Personal expenses: $1,920.

2005-2006 Financial aid. Need-based: 875 full-time freshmen applied for aid; 613 were judged to have need; 610 of these received aid. Average need met was 71%. Average scholarship/grant was $10,246; average loan $4,809. 50% of total undergraduate aid awarded as scholarships/grants, 50% as loans/jobs. **Non-need-based:** Awarded to 2,874 full-time undergraduates, including 765 freshmen. Scholarships awarded for academics, alumni affiliation, art, athletics, leadership, minority status, music/drama, religious affiliation, ROTC, state residency.

Application procedures. Admission: Priority date 11/15; deadline 2/15. $40 fee, may be waived for applicants with need. Application must be submitted on paper. Admission notification 4/1. Admission notification on a rolling basis. Must reply by 5/1. **Financial aid:** Closing date 5/1. FAFSA, institutional form required. Applicants notified on a rolling basis starting 3/1; must reply by 5/1 or within 2 week(s) of notification.

Academics. Premajor option and accompanying special academic advising for entering students unsure of major; can be used for up to 4 semesters. **Special study options:** Accelerated study, combined bachelor's/graduate degree, cross-registration, distance learning, double major, ESL, honors, independent study, internships, liberal arts/career combination, semester at sea, study abroad, teacher certification program, Washington semester. **Credit/placement by examination:** AP, CLEP, IB, institutional tests. **Support services:** Study skills assistance, tutoring, writing center.

Majors. Area/ethnic studies: Latin American. **Biology:** General, biochemistry. **Business:** Accounting, e-commerce, fashion, finance, international, international finance, international marketing, management science, marketing, real estate. **Communications:** General, advertising, broadcast journalism, journalism, radio/tv. **Computer sciences:** General. **Conservation:** Environmental science. **Education:** Art, bilingual, Deaf/hearing impaired, early childhood, elementary, English, gifted/talented, mathematics, music, physical, science, secondary, social studies, voc/tech. **Engineering:** General. **English:** English lit. **Foreign languages:** French, Spanish. **Health:** Dietetics, movement therapy, nursing (RN), speech pathology. **History:** General. **Interdisciplinary:** Neuroscience. **Liberal arts:** Arts/sciences. **Math:** General. **Parks/recreation:** Health/fitness. **Philosophy/religion:** Philosophy, religion. **Physical sciences:** Chemistry, geology, physics. **Protective services:** Criminal justice. **Psychology:** General. **Public administration:** Social work. **Social sciences:** Anthropology, economics, international economics, international relations, political science, sociology. **Visual/performing arts:** Art history/conservation, ballet, directing/producing, dramatic, graphic design, interior design, music performance, music theory/composition, painting, photography, piano/organ, printmaking, sculpture, studio arts, theater history.

Most popular majors. Business/marketing 27%, communications/journalism 16%, education 8%, health sciences 8%, social sciences 6%, visual/performing arts 7%.

Computing on campus. 645 workstations in dormitories, library, computer center, student center. Dormitories wired for high-speed internet access and linked to campus network. Commuter students can connect to campus network. Online course registration, helpline, repair service available.

Student life. Freshman orientation: Mandatory, $115 fee. Preregistration for classes offered. 2 to 3-day program for students and parents. **Policies:** Freshmen permitted cars on campus. **Housing:** Guaranteed on-campus for freshmen. Coed dorms, single-sex dorms, apartments, fraternity/sorority housing available. $250 partly refundable deposit, deadline 5/1. Designated rooms available for ADA needs. **Activities:** Bands, choral groups, dance, drama, literary magazine, music ensembles, musical theater, opera, radio station, student government, student newspaper, TV station, over 190 social, religious, service, academic, and preprofessional organizations.

Athletics. NCAA. **Intercollegiate:** Baseball M, basketball, cross-country, diving, football (tackle) M, golf, rifle W, soccer W, swimming, tennis, track and field, volleyball W. **Team name:** Horned Frogs.

Student services. Adult student services, alcohol/substance abuse counseling, campus ministries, career counseling, student employment services, financial aid counseling, health services, minority student services, personal counseling, placement for graduates, veterans' counselor, women's services. **Physically disabled:** Services for visually, speech, hearing impaired.

Contact. E-mail: frogmail@tcu.edu
Phone: (817) 257-7490 Toll-free number: (800) 828-3764
Fax: (817) 257-7268
Ray Brown, Dean of Admissions, Texas Christian University, TCU Box 297013, Fort Worth, TX 76129

Texas College

Tyler, Texas
www.texascollege.edu — **CB code: 6821**

- Private 4-year liberal arts college affiliated with Christian Methodist Episcopal Church
- Residential campus in small city
- 794 degree-seeking undergraduates

General. Founded in 1894. Regionally accredited. **Degrees:** 1 bachelor's awarded. **Location:** 90 miles from Dallas, 100 miles from Shreveport, Louisiana. **Calendar:** Semester, limited summer session. **Full-time faculty:** 30 total. **Part-time faculty:** 20 total. **Class size:** 61% < 20, 24% 20-39, 13% 40-49, 3% 50-99. **Special facilities:** Black studies collection, Texas college historical collection.

Freshman class profile.

Rank in top quarter:	10%	**Live on campus:**	85%
Rank in top tenth:	3%	**Fraternities:**	10%
Out-of-state:	15%	**Sororities:**	15%

Basis for selection. Open admission. Students admitted based on completion of minimum of 16 high school units and submission of official high school transcript or GED test scores. SAT/ACT recommended for scholarships and placement.

High school preparation. 16 units required. Required units include English 4, mathematics 2, social studies 2, science 2 and academic electives 6.

2006-2007 Annual costs. Tuition/fees (projected): $7,910. Room/board: $5,600. Books/supplies: $800. Personal expenses: $1,740.

2004-2005 Financial aid. All financial aid based on need. 68% of total undergraduate aid awarded as scholarships/grants, 32% as loans/jobs.

Application procedures. Admission: No deadline. $20 fee, may be waived for applicants with need. Application must be submitted on paper. Admission notification on a rolling basis. **Financial aid:** Priority date 6/1; no closing date. FAFSA, institutional form required. Applicants notified on a rolling basis starting 4/15; must reply within 2 week(s) of notification.

Academics. Special study options: Accelerated study, cooperative education, distance learning, double major, dual enrollment of high school students, independent study, internships, liberal arts/career combination, teacher certification program. **Credit/placement by examination:** AP, CLEP, institutional tests. 32 credit hours maximum toward bachelor's degree. **Support services:** Reduced course load, remedial instruction, study skills assistance, tutoring.

Majors. Biology: General. **Business:** Business admin. **Computer sciences:** General. **Education:** Art, biology, elementary, history, mathematics, middle, music, physical. **English:** English lit. **History:** General. **Liberal arts:** Arts/sciences. **Math:** General. **Public administration:** Social work. **Social sciences:** Political science, sociology. **Visual/performing arts:** Studio arts.

Computing on campus. 105 workstations in dormitories, library, computer center. Dormitories linked to campus network. Online library, helpline, repair service, wireless network available.

Student life. Freshman orientation: Mandatory. Preregistration for classes offered. Held first week of school. **Policies:** Students required to attend weekly religious-natured assembly program twice a month. Religious observance required. Freshmen permitted cars on campus. **Housing:** Guaranteed on-campus for freshmen. Single-sex dorms, substance-free housing available. $75 deposit, deadline 8/15. **Activities:** Bands, choral groups, dance, music ensembles, student government, student newspaper, Young Adults for Christ, NAACP, Fellowship of Christian Athletes, criminal justice association, Students in Free Enterprise, student ministerial alliance, pre-alumni council, Young Republicans.

Athletics. NAIA. **Intercollegiate:** Baseball M, basketball, football (tackle) M, soccer, softball W, track and field, volleyball W. **Intramural:** Basketball, football (non-tackle) M, softball W, volleyball W. **Team name:** Steers.

Student services. Adult student services, campus ministries, career counseling, services for economically disadvantaged, student employment services, financial aid counseling, health services, on-campus daycare, personal counseling, veterans' counselor.

Contact. E-mail: afrancis@texascollege.edu
Phone: (903) 593-8311 ext. 2297 Toll-free number: (800) 306-6299
Fax: (903) 596-0001
Anetha Francis, Director of Enrollment Services, Texas College, 2404 North Grand Avenue, Tyler, TX 75712-4500

Texas Lutheran University

Seguin, Texas — **CB member**
www.tlu.edu — **CB code: 6823**

- Private 4-year university and liberal arts college affiliated with Evangelical Lutheran Church in America
- Residential campus in large town
- 1,360 degree-seeking undergraduates: 3% part-time, 53% women
- 73% of applicants admitted
- SAT or ACT (ACT writing optional), application essay required
- 75% graduate within 6 years

General. Founded in 1891. Regionally accredited. **Degrees:** 263 bachelor's awarded. **ROTC:** Army, Air Force. **Location:** 30 miles from San Antonio, 55 miles from Austin. **Calendar:** Semester, limited summer session. **Full-time faculty:** 66 total; 79% have terminal degrees, 11% minority, 44% women. **Part-time faculty:** 49 total; 37% have terminal degrees, 10% minority, 47% women. **Class size:** 68% < 20, 52% 20-39, 2% 40-49. **Special facilities:** Biology field station, Mexican-American study center, life enrichment center, geological museum.

Freshman class profile. 1,147 applied, 832 admitted, 380 enrolled.

Mid 50% test scores		**GPA 2.0-2.99:**	15%
SAT verbal:	440-560	**Rank in top quarter:**	57%
SAT math:	450-580	**Rank in top tenth:**	24%
ACT:	18-24	**Return as sophomores:**	67%
GPA 3.50 or higher:	57%	**Out-of-state:**	1%
GPA 3.0-3.49:	28%	**Live on campus:**	88%

Basis for selection. Quality of academic curriculum pursued and class rank most important. Academic record and test scores also important. Interview recommended. **Homeschooled:** Transcript of courses and grades, letter of recommendation (nonparent) required. Greater emphasis placed on homeschooled applicants' SAT or ACT scores.

High school preparation. 23 units recommended. Recommended units include English 4, mathematics 3, social studies 3, history 2, science 3 (laboratory 2), foreign language 2 and academic electives 4.

2005-2006 Annual costs. Tuition/fees: $17,720. Room/board: $5,810. Books/supplies: $740. Personal expenses: $1,100.

2004-2005 Financial aid. Need-based: 356 full-time freshmen applied for aid; 284 were judged to have need; 284 of these received aid. Average need met was 72%. Average scholarship/grant was $5,700; average loan $3,148. 61% of total undergraduate aid awarded as scholarships/grants, 39% as loans/jobs. **Non-need-based:** Awarded to 1,245 full-time undergraduates, including 381 freshmen. Scholarships awarded for academics, alumni affiliation, art, job skills, leadership, music/drama, religious affiliation.

Application procedures. Admission: Priority date 5/6; deadline 8/6 (postmark date). $25 fee, may be waived for applicants with need. Application may be submitted online. Admission notification on a rolling basis beginning on or about 10/1. **Financial aid:** Priority date 4/1; no closing date. FAFSA required. Applicants notified on a rolling basis starting 3/1; must reply within 2 week(s) of notification.

Academics. Special study options: Combined bachelor's/graduate degree, double major, dual enrollment of high school students, honors, independent study, internships, liberal arts/career combination, study abroad, teacher certification program, Washington semester. International studies curriculum, dual BS program in applied science and engineering in conjunction with Texas state institutions. **Credit/placement by examination:** AP, CLEP, IB, institutional tests. 30 credit hours maximum toward bachelor's degree. **Support services:** Study skills assistance, tutoring, writing center.

Majors. Biology: General, molecular. **Business:** General, accounting, business admin. **Communications:** General. **Computer sciences:** General, computer science, information systems. **Education:** Elementary, English, history, mathematics, middle, multi-level teacher, music, physical, reading, social studies. **English:** English lit. **Foreign languages:** Spanish. **Health:** Athletic training. **History:** General, public archives. **Math:** General. **Parks/recreation:** Exercise sciences, health/fitness, sports admin. **Philosophy/religion:** Philosophy. **Physical sciences:** Chemistry, physics. **Psychology:** General. **Social sciences:** Economics, political science, sociology. **Theology:** Preministerial, youth ministry. **Visual/performing arts:** General, art, dramatic, music history, music performance.

Computing on campus. 48 workstations in dormitories, library, computer center, student center. Dormitories wired for high-speed internet access and linked to campus network. Commuter students can connect to campus network. Online library, helpline, wireless network available.

Student life. Freshman orientation: Mandatory. Preregistration for classes offered. Held 2 days prior to start of fall semester. **Policies:** Freshmen permitted cars on campus. **Housing:** Guaranteed on-campus for freshmen. Coed dorms, single-sex dorms, apartments available. $200 deposit, deadline 8/6. **Activities:** Bands, choral groups, dance, drama, literary magazine, music ensembles, musical theater, student government, student newspaper, symphony orchestra, black student union, Mexican American student association, Young Democrats, College Republicans, Fellowship of Christian Athletes, Students Make a Difference, Lutheran student movement, Canterbury, Catholic student organization, international student association.

Athletics. NCAA. **Intercollegiate:** Baseball M, basketball, cross-country W, football (tackle) M, golf, soccer, softball W, tennis, track and field W, volleyball W. **Intramural:** Basketball, bowling, football (non-tackle), handball, racquetball, softball, swimming, tennis, volleyball. **Team name:** Bulldogs.

Student services. Alcohol/substance abuse counseling, campus ministries, career counseling, student employment services, financial aid counseling, health services, personal counseling, placement for graduates, veterans' counselor.

Contact. E-mail: admissions@tlu.edu
Phone: (830) 372-8050 Toll-free number: (800) 771-8521
Fax: (830) 372-8096
Jamie Kocian, Associate Director of Admissions, Texas Lutheran University, 1000 West Court Street, Seguin, TX 78155-5999

Texas Southern University

Houston, Texas — **CB member**
www.tsu.edu — **CB code: 6824**

- Public 4-year university
- Commuter campus in very large city
- 9,760 degree-seeking undergraduates: 21% part-time, 58% women, 90% African American, 2% Asian American, 3% Hispanic American, 3% international
- 2,143 degree-seeking graduate students

General. Founded in 1947. Regionally accredited. **Degrees:** 538 bachelor's awarded; master's, doctoral, first professional offered. **ROTC:** Army. **Location:** 2 miles from downtown. **Calendar:** Semester, extensive summer session. **Full-time faculty:** 330 total. **Part-time faculty:** 205 total. **Class size:** 64% < 20, 27% 20-39, 5% 40-49, 4% 50-99. **Special facilities:** Museum.

Freshman class profile.

Out-of-state:	16%	**Fraternities:**	3%
Live on campus:	45%	**Sororities:**	1%
International:	2%		

Basis for selection. Open admission, but selective for some programs. Special requirements for pharmacy, law, accounting, marketing, and computer science programs. For selective programs high school achievement, interview, essay important; test scores, individual abilities, high school activities considered.

High school preparation. Recommended units include English 4, mathematics 3, social studies 4, science 2, foreign language 2 and academic electives 6.

2005-2006 Annual costs. Tuition/fees: $4,468; $12,748 out-of-state. Room/board: $6,296. Books/supplies: $819. Personal expenses: $1,700.

Financial aid. All financial aid based on need.

Application procedures. Admission: Priority date 7/31; deadline 8/15 (postmark date). $42 fee, may be waived for applicants with need. Application may be submitted online. Admission notification on a rolling basis. Must reply by 7/31. **Financial aid:** Priority date 5/1; no closing date. FAFSA required. Applicants notified on a rolling basis starting 6/1.

Academics. Special study options: Cooperative education, distance learning, double major, ESL, honors, internships, teacher certification program, weekend college. **Credit/placement by examination:** CLEP, institutional tests. **Support services:** Learning center, pre-admission summer program, remedial instruction, study skills assistance, tutoring.

Majors. Architecture: Urban/community planning. **Area/ethnic studies:** African-American. **Biology:** General. **Business:** General, accounting, banking/financial services, marketing, office/clerical. **Communications:** General, broadcast journalism, journalism. **Computer sciences:** General, computer science. **Conservation:** Environmental studies. **Education:** Curriculum. **Engineering technology:** Biomedical, civil, drafting, electrical. **Family/consumer sciences:** Food/nutrition. **Foreign languages:** French, Spanish. **Health:** Clinical lab science, health care admin, medical records admin, prepharmacy, respiratory therapy technology. **History:** General. **Math:** General. **Mechanic/repair:** General. **Parks/recreation:** Health/fitness. **Physical sciences:** Chemistry. **Protective services:** Law enforcement admin. **Psychology:** General. **Public administration:** General, human services, social work. **Social sciences:** Economics, political science, sociology. **Transportation:** Aviation, aviation management. **Visual/performing arts:** Art, dramatic, studio arts.

Most popular majors. Biology 11%, business/marketing 24%, communications/journalism 6%, engineering/engineering technologies 8%, health sciences 9%, psychology 6%, public administration/social services 8%, security/protective services 6%.

Computing on campus. 500 workstations in library, computer center, student center. Online course registration available.

Student life. Freshman orientation: Mandatory. Preregistration for classes offered. **Policies:** Freshmen permitted cars on campus. **Housing:** Guaranteed on-campus for freshmen. Single-sex dorms, apartments available. $300 deposit, deadline 6/2. **Activities:** Bands, choral groups, drama, film society, music ensembles, musical theater, opera, radio station, student government, student newspaper, symphony orchestra, TV station, Alpha Phi Omega, Baptist student ministry, Campus Crusade for Christ, health information management association, Impact campus ministry, Integrity Plus campus ministry, sociology club, political science club, student psychological club, NAACP.

Athletics. NAIA, NCAA. **Intercollegiate:** Baseball M, basketball, bowling W, cross-country, football (tackle) M, golf, soccer W, softball W, tennis, track and field, volleyball W. **Intramural:** Basketball, bowling, softball, swimming, table tennis, tennis, track and field, volleyball. **Team name:** Tigers.

Student services. Campus ministries, career counseling, student employment services, financial aid counseling, health services, on-campus daycare, personal counseling, placement for graduates, veterans' counselor. **Physically disabled:** Services for speech impaired.

Contact. Phone: (713) 313-7472 Fax: (713) 313-4317
Joyce Waddell, Director of Admissions, Recruitment, and Academic Advisement, Texas Southern University, 3100 Cleburne Street, Houston, TX 77004

Texas State University: San Marcos

San Marcos, Texas — **CB member**
www.txstate.edu — **CB code: 6667**

- Public 4-year university
- Commuter campus in large town
- 22,986 degree-seeking undergraduates: 20% part-time, 55% women, 5% African American, 2% Asian American, 20% Hispanic American, 1% Native American, 1% international
- 3,355 degree-seeking graduate students
- 76% of applicants admitted
- SAT or ACT with writing, application essay required
- 52% graduate within 6 years; 20% enter graduate study

General. Founded in 1899. Regionally accredited. **Degrees:** 4,314 bachelor's awarded; master's, doctoral offered. **ROTC:** Army, Air Force. **Location:** 30 miles from Austin, 49 miles from San Antonio. **Calendar:** Semester, extensive summer session. **Full-time faculty:** 775 total; 76% have terminal degrees, 17% minority, 42% women. **Part-time faculty:** 522 total; 26% have terminal degrees, 13% minority, 52% women. **Class size:** 15% < 20, 57% 20-39, 8% 40-49, 14% 50-99, 7% >100. **Special facilities:** Ranch, natural spring with unique aquatic plants and animals, Southwestern writers collection (original manuscripts), observatory with 17-inch telescope, archeological forensic laboratory.

Freshman class profile. 9,284 applied, 7,095 admitted, 3,073 enrolled.

Mid 50% test scores		**End year in good standing:**	84%
SAT verbal:	490-580	**Return as sophomores:**	74%
SAT math:	500-590	**Out-of-state:**	2%
ACT:	21-25	**Live on campus:**	91%
Rank in top quarter:	50%	**International:**	1%
Rank in top tenth:	13%		

Basis for selection. Applicants who rank in top 10% of high school class have no minimum test score requirements. Otherwise score requirements are as follows: rank in next 15%, 920 SAT or 20 ACT; rank in second quarter, 1010 SAT, 22 ACT; rank in third quarter, 1180 SAT, 26 ACT; rank in bottom quarter, 1270 SAT, 29 ACT (SAT scores exclusive of Writing). SAT Subject Tests required for placement in certain higher level courses. Writing sections of ACT or SAT used as supplemental information and not in admissions decisions. Audition required for music program. **Homeschooled:** Transcript of courses and grades required. Minimum 26 ACT or 1180 SAT (exclusive of Writing) and admissions essay.

High school preparation. 24 units required. Required and recommended units include English 4, mathematics 3, social studies 3.5-4.5, science 3 (laboratory 2), foreign language 2-3, academic electives 3.5. 1 computer literacy, 1 fine arts, 0.5 economics, 0.5 speech required.

2005-2006 Annual costs. Tuition/fees: $5,252; $13,532 out-of-state. Room/board: $5,610. Books/supplies: $950. Personal expenses: $2,370.

2005-2006 Financial aid. Need-based: 1,996 full-time freshmen applied for aid; 1,389 were judged to have need; 1,292 of these received aid. Average need met was 73%. Average scholarship/grant was $4,550; average loan $2,395. 43% of total undergraduate aid awarded as scholarships/grants, 57% as loans/jobs. **Non-need-based:** Awarded to 3,435 full-time undergraduates, including 956 freshmen. Scholarships awarded for academics, art, athletics, leadership, music/drama, ROTC, state residency.

Application procedures. Admission: Closing date 5/1 (receipt date). $40 fee, may be waived for applicants with need. Application may be submitted online. Admission notification on a rolling basis beginning on or about 10/1. Housing deposit refundable if student does not enroll but refund request must be made prior to August 1. **Financial aid:** Priority date 4/1; no closing date. FAFSA required. Applicants notified on a rolling basis starting 5/1; must reply within 3 week(s) of notification.

Academics. Special study options: Accelerated study, combined bachelor's/graduate degree, distance learning, double major, dual enrollment of high school students, ESL, exchange student, honors, independent study, internships, study abroad, teacher certification program, Washington semester, weekend college. **Credit/placement by examination:** AP, CLEP, IB, institutional tests. 30 credit hours maximum toward bachelor's degree. SAT Subject Test scores used to award credit only. Credit hours earned by exam do not count as credit earned in residence. **Support services:** Learning center, remedial instruction, study skills assistance, tutoring, writing center.

Majors. Agriculture: General, agribusiness operations, animal sciences. **Architecture:** Urban/community planning. **Area/ethnic studies:** American, Asian, European, Near/Middle Eastern, Russian/Slavic. **Biology:** General, animal physiology, aquatic, biochemistry, botany, marine, microbiology, wildlife, zoology. **Business:** Accounting, business admin, fashion, finance, management information systems, managerial economics, marketing. **Communications:** Advertising, journalism, media studies, public relations, radio/tv. **Communications technology:** Desktop publishing, recording arts. **Computer sciences:** General, data processing. **Conservation:** Environmental science, water/wetlands/marine. **Engineering:** Industrial, manufacturing. **Engineering technology:** General, construction, industrial, manufacturing. **English:** English lit, speech/rhetoric. **Family/consumer sciences:** General, family studies, food/nutrition. **Foreign languages:** French, German, Spanish. **Health:** Athletic training, audiology/speech pathology, clinical lab science, facilities admin, health care admin, health services, medical radiologic technology/radiation therapy, medical records admin, respiratory therapy technology. **History:** General. **Interdisciplinary:** Global studies. **Math:** General, applied. **Parks/recreation:** Facilities management, health/fitness, sports admin. **Philosophy/religion:** Philosophy. **Physical sciences:** Chemistry, physics. **Protective services:** Corrections, criminal justice, police science. **Psychology:** General. **Public administration:** General, social work. **Social sciences:** Anthropology, cartography, economics, geography, international relations, political science, sociology. **Visual/performing arts:** Art, dance, dramatic, graphic design, interior design, jazz, music performance, studio arts.

Most popular majors. Business/marketing 22%, communications/journalism 6%, English 6%, interdisciplinary studies 13%, parks/recreation 6%, social sciences 8%, visual/performing arts 9%.

Computing on campus. 1,480 workstations in dormitories, library, computer center, student center. Dormitories wired for high-speed internet access and linked to campus network. Commuter students can connect to campus network. Online course registration, helpline, repair service, student web hosting, wireless network available.

Student life. Freshman orientation: Mandatory, $25 fee. Preregistration for classes offered. 2-day program of advising, campus tour and partial payment of tuition and fees combined with welcome week prior to start of semester. **Policies:** Freshmen permitted cars on campus. **Housing:** Guaranteed on-campus for freshmen. Coed dorms, single-sex dorms, apartments, fraternity/sorority housing, substance-free housing available. $100 deposit. **Activities:** Bands, choral groups, dance, drama, film society, literary magazine, music ensembles, musical theater, opera, radio station, student government, student newspaper, symphony orchestra, over 250 social, service, religious, political, and professional organizations.

Athletics. NCAA. **Intercollegiate:** Baseball M, basketball, cheerleading, cross-country, football (tackle) M, golf, soccer W, softball W, tennis W, track and field, volleyball W. **Intramural:** Basketball, bowling, football (non-tackle), golf, racquetball, soccer, softball, tennis, volleyball. **Team name:** Bobcats.

Student services. Adult student services, alcohol/substance abuse counseling, campus ministries, career counseling, student employment services, financial aid counseling, health services, legal services, minority student services, personal counseling, placement for graduates, veterans' counselor. **Physically disabled:** Services for visually, speech, hearing impaired.

Contact. E-mail: admissions@txstate.edu
Phone: (512) 245-2364 Fax: (512) 245-8044
Christie Kangas, Director of Admissions, Texas State University: San Marcos, 429 North Guadalupe Street, San Marcos, TX 78666-5709

Texas Tech University

Lubbock, Texas — **CB member**
www.ttu.edu — **CB code: 6827**

- Public 4-year university
- Commuter campus in small city
- 22,967 degree-seeking undergraduates: 9% part-time, 45% women, 3% African American, 2% Asian American, 11% Hispanic American, 1% Native American, 1% international
- 4,714 degree-seeking graduate students
- 71% of applicants admitted
- SAT or ACT with writing required
- 55% graduate within 6 years

General. Founded in 1923. Regionally accredited. **Degrees:** 4,264 bachelor's awarded; master's, doctoral, first professional offered. **ROTC:** Army, Air Force. **Location:** 320 miles from Dallas, 320 miles from Albuquerque, New Mexico. **Calendar:** Semester, extensive summer session. **Full-time faculty:** 1,046 total; 88% have terminal degrees, 15% minority, 33% women. **Part-time faculty:** 77 total; 43% have terminal degrees, 10% minority, 61% women. **Class size:** 23% < 20, 44% 20-39, 13% 40-49, 12% 50-99, 8% >100. **Special facilities:** Museum, national ranching heritage center, archaeological dig/state park, international cultural center, international textile research center, science research laboratory, arid and semi-arid land studies center, seismological observatory, child development research center, institutes for environmental and human health, Vietnam center.

Freshman class profile. 12,583 applied, 8,927 admitted, 3,779 enrolled.

Mid 50% test scores			
SAT verbal:	510-600	End year in good standing:	87%
SAT math:	530-620	Return as sophomores:	84%
ACT:	22-26	Out-of-state:	5%
Rank in top quarter:	55%	Live on campus:	89%
Rank in top tenth:	22%	International:	1%

Basis for selection. Class rank and test scores considered first, and students meeting the following score requirements (exclusive of Writing) eligible for unconditional admission: class rank in top 10%, no minimum test scores; rank in next 15%, with 1140 SAT or 25 ACT; rank in second quarter, with 1230 SAT or 28 ACT; rank in lower half, with 1270 SAT or 29 ACT. Applicants who do not meet assured admission criteria will have records reviewed in holistic manner. Response to Topic C on State of Texas Common Application may be helpful in review process as well as following additional information: high school course work; honors or advanced placement; extracurricular activities; leadership experiences; proposed field of study; civic or other service activities; socioeconomic background; family educational background; bilingual proficiency; family affiliation with Texas Tech; special talents or awards. Auditions and portfolios required for admission to some programs.

High school preparation. 11 units required. Required units include English 4, mathematics 3, science 2 (laboratory 2) and foreign language 2. Algebra I, geometry, and algebra II recommended for required math units. Biology I, chemistry I or physics I recommended for science units. If 2 years of foreign language not completed in high school, at least 2 semesters of single foreign language will be required at college level.

2005-2006 Annual costs. Tuition/fees: $6,152; $14,432 out-of-state. Students from adjacent counties in New Mexico and Oklahoma pay in-state tuition rates; students from all other counties in New Mexico and Oklahoma pay reduced out-of-state tuition rates. Room/board: $6,506. Books/supplies: $900. Personal expenses: $1,850.

2004-2005 Financial aid. Need-based: 3,048 full-time freshmen applied for aid; 1,739 were judged to have need; 1,669 of these received aid. Average scholarship/grant was $4,485; average loan $2,310. 46% of total undergraduate aid awarded as scholarships/grants, 54% as loans/jobs. **Non-need-based:** Awarded to 8,614 full-time undergraduates, including 2,654 freshmen. Scholarships awarded for academics, art, athletics, job skills, leadership, music/drama, ROTC.

Application procedures. Admission: Closing date 5/1 (receipt date). $50 fee, may be waived for applicants with need. Application may be submitted online. Admission notification on a rolling basis. **Financial aid:** Priority date 5/1; no closing date. FAFSA required. Applicants notified on a rolling basis; must reply within 2 week(s) of notification.

Academics. Special study options: Accelerated study, combined bachelor's/graduate degree, cooperative education, cross-registration, distance learning, double major, dual enrollment of high school students, ESL, exchange student, external degree, honors, independent study, internships, liberal arts/career combination, semester at sea, student-designed major, study abroad, teacher certification program. **Credit/placement by examination:** AP, CLEP, IB, SAT, ACT, institutional tests. **Support services:** Learning center, preadmission summer program, remedial instruction, study skills assistance, tutoring, writing center.

Honors college/program. Requires separate application, minimum 1200 SAT (exclusive of Writing) or 26 ACT, or top 10% class rank, essays, 2 teacher recommendations. 260 freshmen admitted. Average SAT score: 1322; total enrollment 895. 2 tracks offered to students: nondegree program working with all colleges and majors to provide honors academic, cocurricular and social program; and interdisciplinary degree program for bachelor of arts degree in natural history and humanities or Honors Arts and Letters.

Majors. Agriculture: General, agronomy, animal sciences, business, communications, economics, food science, horticulture, plant protection, range science. **Architecture:** Architecture, interior, landscape. **Area/ethnic studies:** Latin American, Russian/Slavic. **Biology:** General, biochemistry, cellular/molecular, microbiology, zoology. **Business:** General, accounting, business admin, fashion, finance, hotel/motel admin, international, management information systems, marketing. **Communications:** Advertising, journalism, photojournalism, public relations, radio/tv. **Computer sciences:** General. **Conservation:** General, fisheries, wildlife. **Engineering:** General, chemical, civil, computer, electrical, environmental, industrial, mechanical, petroleum, physics. **Engineering technology:** General, architectural, electrical, mechanical. **English:** English lit, speech/rhetoric. **Family/consumer sciences:** General, child development, clothing/textiles, family studies, family systems, food/nutrition, work/family studies. **Foreign languages:** Classics, French, German, Spanish. **Health:** Dietetics, health services. **History:** General. **Interdisciplinary:** Biological/physical sciences. **Liberal arts:** Arts/sciences. **Math:** General. **Parks/recreation:** Health/fitness. **Philosophy/religion:** Philosophy. **Physical sciences:** Chemistry, geology, geophysics, physics. **Psychology:** General. **Public administration:** Social work. **Social sciences:** Anthropology, economics, geography, political science, sociology. **Visual/performing arts:** Acting, art, art history/conservation, dance, dramatic, fashion design, graphic design, music performance, music theory/composition, studio arts, theater design.

Most popular majors. Business/marketing 28%, communications/journalism 6%, engineering/engineering technologies 8%, family/consumer sciences 14%.

Computing on campus. 3,000 workstations in dormitories, library, computer center, student center. Dormitories wired for high-speed internet access and linked to campus network. Commuter students can connect to campus network. Online course registration, online library, helpline, repair service, student web hosting, wireless network available.

Student life. Freshman orientation: Mandatory, $55 fee. Preregistration for classes offered. **Policies:** Freshmen required to live on campus. Freshmen permitted cars on campus. **Housing:** Guaranteed on-campus for freshmen. Coed dorms, single-sex dorms, special housing for disabled, apartments, substance-free housing available. $450 partly refundable deposit, deadline 5/1. **Activities:** Bands, choral groups, dance, drama, film society, literary magazine, music ensembles, musical theater, opera, radio station, student government, student newspaper, symphony orchestra, TV station, College Republicans, Wesley Foundation, Baptist student ministries, black student association, Hispanic student society, Alpha Phi Omega, Christ in action student ministries, women's service organization, University Democrats, Campus Crusade for Christ.

Athletics. NCAA. **Intercollegiate:** Baseball M, basketball, cross-country, football (tackle) M, golf, soccer W, softball W, tennis, track and field, volleyball W. **Intramural:** Badminton, baseball, basketball, bowling, football (non-tackle), golf, racquetball, soccer, softball, swimming, table tennis, tennis, volleyball, water polo, weight lifting. **Team name:** Red Raiders/ Lady Raiders.

Student services. Adult student services, alcohol/substance abuse counseling, career counseling, student employment services, financial aid counseling, health services, legal services, personal counseling, placement for graduates, veterans' counselor. **Physically disabled:** Services for visually, speech, hearing impaired. **Learning disabled:** Comprehensive services available.

Contact. E-mail: admissions@ttu.edu
Phone: (806) 742-1480 Fax: (806) 742-0062
Djuana Young, Director of Admissions, Texas Tech University, Box 45005, Lubbock, TX 79409-5005

Texas Tech University Health Sciences Center

Lubbock, Texas
www.ttuhsc.edu **CB code: 3423**

- Public 4-year university
- Commuter campus in small city
- 633 degree-seeking undergraduates: 15% part-time, 85% women, 8% African American, 3% Asian American, 13% Hispanic American
- 1,758 degree-seeking graduate students

General. Founded in 1969. Regionally accredited. **Degrees:** 364 bachelor's awarded; master's, doctoral, first professional offered. **Calendar:** Semester. **Full-time faculty:** 674 total; 67% have terminal degrees, 18% minority, 37% women. **Part-time faculty:** 97 total; 65% have terminal degrees, 14% minority, 40% women.

Basis for selection. Admission requirements vary by program.

2005-2006 Annual costs. Tuition and fees vary by school and program: $106 per-credit-hour in-state for School of Allied Health Sciences or $382 out-of-state; $126 per-credit-hour in-state for School of Nursing and School of Pharmacy or $402 out-of-state.

Application procedures. Admission: $40 fee.

Academics. Special study options: Combined bachelor's/graduate degree, distance learning. **Credit/placement by examination:** CLEP.

Majors. Health: Clinical lab science, communication disorders, health care admin, health services, nursing (RN).

Student services. Physically disabled: Services for visually, speech, hearing impaired.

Contact. Phone: (806) 743-2300
Texas Tech University Health Sciences Center, 3601 Fourth Street, Lubbock, TX 79430

Texas Wesleyan University

Fort Worth, Texas
www.txwesleyan.edu **CB code: 6828**

- Private 4-year university affiliated with United Methodist Church
- Commuter campus in large city
- 1,335 degree-seeking undergraduates: 27% part-time, 66% women, 17% African American, 2% Asian American, 22% Hispanic American, 1% Native American
- 1,298 degree-seeking graduate students
- 46% of applicants admitted
- SAT or ACT, application essay required

General. Founded in 1890. Regionally accredited. **Degrees:** 272 bachelor's awarded; master's, first professional offered. **ROTC:** Army, Air Force. **Location:** 1 mile from downtown. **Calendar:** Semester, limited summer session. **Full-time faculty:** 150 total; 71% have terminal degrees, 12% minority, 45% women. **Part-time faculty:** 94 total; 6% minority, 48% women. **Class size:** 62% < 20, 36% 20-39, 1% 40-49, less than 1% 50-99.

Freshman class profile. 590 applied, 273 admitted, 180 enrolled.

Mid 50% test scores			
		ACT:	17-23
SAT verbal:	450-550	**Out-of-state:**	3%
SAT math:	430-550	**Live on campus:**	10%

Basis for selection. High school record and standardized test scores most important. Class rank and interview also important. Interview required for applicants in bottom half of high school class; recommended for all others. Essay recommended for all; audition required for music, theater programs; portfolio required for art program.

High school preparation. 20 units recommended. Recommended units include English 4, mathematics 4, social studies 2, history 1, science 2 and academic electives 7.

2005-2006 Annual costs. Tuition/fees: $14,000. Room/board: $4,760. Books/supplies: $675. Personal expenses: $1,590.

Financial aid. All financial aid based on need.

Application procedures. Admission: No deadline. $25 fee, may be waived for applicants with need. Application may be submitted online. Admission notification on a rolling basis. **Financial aid:** Priority date 4/15; no closing date. FAFSA, institutional form required. Applicants notified on a rolling basis starting 4/15; must reply within 2 week(s) of notification.

Academics. Special study options: Accelerated study, combined bachelor's/graduate degree, distance learning, double major, dual enrollment of high school students, ESL, exchange student, independent study, internships, liberal arts/career combination, study abroad, teacher certification program, weekend college. 3-2 engineering programs with Case Western Reserve University and Southern Methodist University. **Credit/placement by examination:** AP, CLEP, institutional tests. 30 credit hours maximum toward bachelor's degree. **Support services:** Learning center, pre-admission summer program, reduced course load, remedial instruction, tutoring, writing center.

Majors. Biology: General, biochemistry. **Business:** Accounting, business admin, finance, international marketing, management science, office technology. **Communications:** General, journalism, public relations, radio/tv. **Computer sciences:** General, computer science, information systems. **Education:** General, bilingual, biology, business, chemistry, early childhood, elementary, English, history, mathematics, multi-level teacher, music, physical, reading, secondary, social science, social studies, Spanish. **Foreign languages:** Spanish. **Health:** Athletic training, predentistry, premedicine. **History:** General. **Legal studies:** Paralegal, prelaw. **Math:** General. **Parks/recreation:** Facilities management, health/fitness. **Physical sciences:** Chemistry. **Psychology:** General. **Social sciences:** General, political science. **Theology:** Religious ed. **Visual/performing arts:** General, art, dramatic.

Most popular majors. Business/marketing 18%, communications/journalism 7%, education 23%, interdisciplinary studies 8%, psychology 9%, social sciences 8%.

Computing on campus. 300 workstations in library, computer center. Dormitories wired for high-speed internet access. Online library available.

Student life. Freshman orientation: Mandatory. Preregistration for classes offered. **Policies:** Resident chaplain on staff. Freshmen permitted cars on campus. **Housing:** Coed dorms, single-sex dorms, apartments available. $100 deposit. **Activities:** Bands, choral groups, drama, literary magazine, music ensembles, musical theater, opera, student government, student newspaper, Methodist and Baptist student unions, Student Foundation, Alpha Phi Omega, Fellowship of Christian Athletes.

Athletics. NAIA. **Intercollegiate:** Baseball M, basketball, golf M, soccer, softball W, table tennis M, volleyball W. **Intramural:** Badminton, basketball, bowling, diving, golf M, soccer, softball, swimming, table tennis, tennis W, volleyball. **Team name:** Rams.

Student services. Adult student services, alcohol/substance abuse counseling, campus ministries, career counseling, student employment services, financial aid counseling, health services, personal counseling, placement for graduates, veterans' counselor.

Contact. E-mail: freshman@txwesleyan.edu
Phone: (817) 531-4422 Toll-free number: (800) 580-8980
Fax: (817) 531-4231
Andera Canales, Director of Freshman Admission, Texas Wesleyan University, 1201 Wesleyan Street, Fort Worth, TX 76105-1536

Texas Woman's University

Denton, Texas — **CB member**
www.twu.edu — **CB code: 6826**

- Public 4-year university
- Commuter campus in small city
- 6,226 degree-seeking undergraduates: 27% part-time, 93% women, 21% African American, 6% Asian American, 14% Hispanic American, 1% Native American, 3% international
- 4,527 degree-seeking graduate students
- 64% of applicants admitted
- SAT or ACT (ACT writing optional) required
- 37% graduate within 6 years

General. Founded in 1901. Regionally accredited. Primarily women's university. **Degrees:** 1,130 bachelor's awarded; master's, doctoral offered. **ROTC:** Army, Air Force. **Location:** 35 miles from Dallas and Fort Worth. **Calendar:** Semester, extensive summer session. **Full-time faculty:** 426 total; 76% women. **Part-time faculty:** 266 total; 75% women. **Class size:** 75% < 20, 24% 20-39, 1% 40-49, less than 1% 50-99. **Special facilities:** History of Texas women collection, DAR museum, historical collection.

Freshman class profile. 2,796 applied, 1,794 admitted, 744 enrolled.

Mid 50% test scores			
SAT verbal:	430-540	**Rank in top quarter:**	30%
SAT math:	420-540	**Rank in top tenth:**	17%
ACT:	17-24	**Return as sophomores:**	75%
GPA 3.50 or higher:	35%	**Out-of-state:**	1%
GPA 3.0-3.49:	44%	**Live on campus:**	70%
GPA 2.0-2.99:	21%	**International:**	1%
		Sororities:	1%

Basis for selection. School achievement record and test scores most important: Texas Academic Skills Program, SAT of 950 (exclusive of Writing) or ACT of 20. Interview and audition required for drama and music programs; interview required and portfolio recommended for art program.

High school preparation. 22 units required. Required units include English 4, mathematics 3, social studies 2, science 2 and academic electives 11.

2006-2007 Annual costs. Tuition/fees: $5,010; $13,290 out-of-state. Room/board: $5,598. Books/supplies: $930. Personal expenses: $1,818.

2005-2006 Financial aid. Need-based: 538 full-time freshmen applied for aid; 402 were judged to have need; 394 of these received aid. Average need met was 98%. Average scholarship/grant was $4,206; average loan $2,230. 52% of total undergraduate aid awarded as scholarships/grants, 48% as loans/jobs. **Non-need-based:** Awarded to 1,121 full-time undergraduates, including 265 freshmen.

Application procedures. Admission: Priority date 2/1; deadline 7/15 (receipt date). $30 fee, may be waived for applicants with need. Application may be submitted online. Admission notification on a rolling basis beginning on or about 3/1. **Financial aid:** Priority date 4/1; no closing date. FAFSA, institutional form required. Applicants notified on a rolling basis starting 3/1; must reply within 2 week(s) of notification.

Academics. Special study options: Accelerated study, combined bachelor's/graduate degree, cooperative education, cross-registration, distance learning, double major, dual enrollment of high school students, honors, independent study, internships, liberal arts/career combination, study abroad, teacher certification program, weekend college. **Credit/placement by examination:** AP, CLEP, SAT, ACT, institutional tests. 30 credit hours maximum toward bachelor's degree. **Support services:** Learning center, preadmission summer program, reduced course load, remedial instruction, study skills assistance, tutoring, writing center.

Majors. Biology: General, zoology. **Business:** Accounting, administrative services, business admin, fashion, marketing. **Communications:** Journalism, media studies. **Computer sciences:** General. **Family/consumer sciences:** General, child development, family studies, food/nutrition. **Health:** Audiology/speech pathology, clinical lab science, community health services, dental hygiene, dietetics, health services, music therapy, nursing (RN). **History:** General. **Interdisciplinary:** Nutrition sciences. **Legal studies:** Paralegal. **Math:** General. **Parks/recreation:** Health/fitness. **Physical sciences:** Chemistry. **Protective services:** Criminal justice. **Psychology:** General. **Public administration:** Social work. **Social sciences:** Political science, sociology. **Visual/performing arts:** Art, dance, dramatic, fashion design.

Most popular majors. Business/marketing 7%, health sciences 44%, interdisciplinary studies 13%.

Computing on campus. 1,000 workstations in dormitories, library, computer center, student center. Dormitories linked to campus network. Commuter students can connect to campus network. Online course registration, helpline available.

Student life. Freshman orientation: Mandatory, $25 fee. Preregistration for classes offered. During a one day event, orientation includes a tour of the campus, meetings with academic advisors and faculty and class registration. **Policies:** Freshmen permitted cars on campus. **Housing:** Guaranteed on-campus for all undergraduates. Coed dorms, single-sex dorms, special housing for disabled, apartments, cooperative housing, fraternity/sorority housing, substance-free housing available. $100 fully refundable deposit. Family housing, honors students housing, theme floors available. **Activities:** Jazz band, choral groups, dance, drama, music ensembles, musical theater, opera, student government, student newspaper, Alpha Theta Omega, Hispanic organization for leadership and advancement, international student association, multicultural African organization, NAACP, Alpha Kappa Alpha Sorority, Delta Sigma Theta Sorority, Zeta Phi Beta Sorority, United Campus Ministries of Denton, Golden Key international honor society.

Athletics. NCAA. **Intercollegiate:** Basketball W, gymnastics W, soccer W, softball W, volleyball W. **Intramural:** Badminton, basketball, bowling, golf, soccer, softball, table tennis M, volleyball. **Team name:** Pioneers.

Student services. Adult student services, alcohol/substance abuse counseling, career counseling, student employment services, financial aid counseling, health services, minority student services, on-campus daycare, personal counseling, placement for graduates, veterans' counselor, women's services. **Physically disabled:** Services for visually, speech, hearing impaired.

Contact. E-mail: admissions@twu.edu
Phone: (940) 898-3188 Toll-free number: (888) 948-9984
Fax: (940) 898-3081
Erma Nieto, Director of Admissions, Texas Woman's University, Box 425589, Denton, TX 76204-5589

Trinity University

San Antonio, Texas — **CB member**
www.trinity.edu — **CB code: 6831**

- Private 4-year liberal arts college affiliated with Presbyterian Church (USA)
- Residential campus in very large city

- 2,523 degree-seeking undergraduates: 2% part-time, 54% women, 3% African American, 6% Asian American, 11% Hispanic American, 1% Native American, 3% international
- 232 degree-seeking graduate students
- 63% of applicants admitted
- SAT and SAT Subject Tests or ACT (ACT writing optional), application essay required
- 74% graduate within 6 years

General. Founded in 1869. Regionally accredited. **Degrees:** 528 bachelor's awarded; master's offered. **ROTC:** Air Force. **Location:** 3 miles from downtown. **Calendar:** Semester, limited summer session. **Full-time faculty:** 225 total; 99% have terminal degrees, 12% minority, 32% women. **Part-time faculty:** 67 total; 9% minority, 49% women. **Class size:** 51% < 20, 46% 20-39, 2% 40-49, 1% 50-99, less than 1% >100.

Freshman class profile. 3,864 applied, 2,442 admitted, 651 enrolled.

Mid 50% test scores		**Rank in top quarter:**	81%
SAT verbal:	600-690	**Rank in top tenth:**	47%
SAT math:	610-690	**Return as sophomores:**	89%
ACT:	27-30	**Out-of-state:**	27%
GPA 3.50 or higher:	54%	**Live on campus:**	100%
GPA 3.0-3.49:	39%	**International:**	4%
GPA 2.0-2.99:	7%		

Basis for selection. GPA, high school rank, test scores, essay, interview, recommendations, extracurricular involvement, and achievement important. **Homeschooled:** At least 3 SAT Subject Tests recommended, including natural science and foreign language.

High school preparation. 18.5 units required; 20 recommended. Required and recommended units include English 4, mathematics 3.5-4, social studies 3, science 3-4 (laboratory 2-3), foreign language 2-3 and academic electives 1.

2005-2006 Annual costs. Tuition/fees: $21,582. Room/board: $7,880. Books/supplies: $640. Personal expenses: $950.

Financial aid. Non-need-based: Scholarships awarded for academics, leadership, music/drama.

Application procedures. Admission: Closing date 2/1 (postmark date). $50 fee, may be waived for applicants with need. Application may be submitted online. Admission notification 4/1. Must reply by 5/1. **Financial aid:** Priority date 2/1, closing date 4/1. FAFSA required. Applicants notified by 4/1; must reply by 5/1 or within 4 week(s) of notification.

Academics. Special study options: Accelerated study, combined bachelor's/graduate degree, dual enrollment of high school students, honors, independent study, internships, liberal arts/career combination, New York semester, semester at sea, student-designed major, study abroad, teacher certification program, United Nations semester, urban semester, Washington semester. **Credit/placement by examination:** AP, CLEP, IB, institutional tests. 36 credit hours maximum toward bachelor's degree. **Support services:** Writing center.

Majors. Area/ethnic studies: Asian, European, Latin American. **Biology:** General, biochemistry. **Business:** Accounting, business admin, finance, international, management science, marketing. **Communications:** General. **Computer sciences:** General. **Education:** Elementary. **Engineering:** Science. **English:** Speech/rhetoric. **Foreign languages:** Chinese, classics, French, German, Russian, Spanish. **History:** General. **Math:** General. **Philosophy/religion:** Philosophy, religion. **Physical sciences:** Chemistry, geology, physics. **Psychology:** General. **Social sciences:** Anthropology, economics, political science, sociology, urban studies. **Visual/performing arts:** Art, art history/conservation, dramatic, music performance, music theory/composition, theater design, voice/opera.

Most popular majors. Business/marketing 21%, English 6%, foreign language 11%, social sciences 20%.

Computing on campus. 400 workstations in library, computer center, student center. Dormitories wired for high-speed internet access and linked to campus network. Online course registration, online library, helpline, student web hosting, wireless network available.

Student life. Freshman orientation: Available. **Policies:** Freshmen permitted cars on campus. **Housing:** Coed dorms available. $500 nonrefundable deposit, deadline 5/1. **Activities:** Bands, choral groups, dance, drama, film society, literary magazine, music ensembles, musical theater, opera, radio station, student government, student newspaper, symphony orchestra, TV station, Phi Beta Kappa, 20+ academic honor societies, activities council, Young Democrats, Young Republicans, association of student representatives, Alpha Phi Omega, various religious organizations, Hispanic, black and Asian student organizations.

Athletics. NCAA. **Intercollegiate:** Baseball M, basketball, cross-country, diving, football (tackle) M, golf, soccer, softball W, swimming, tennis, track and field, volleyball W. **Intramural:** Basketball, cross-country, football (non-tackle), golf, racquetball, soccer, softball, swimming, table tennis, tennis, track and field, volleyball, wrestling M. **Team name:** Tigers.

Student services. Campus ministries, career counseling, student employment services, financial aid counseling, health services, personal counseling, placement for graduates, veterans' counselor. **Physically disabled:** Services for visually, hearing impaired.

Contact. E-mail: admissions@trinity.edu
Phone: (210) 999-7207 Toll-free number: (800) 874-6489
Fax: (210) 999-8164
Christopher Ellertson, Dean of Admissions and Financial Aid, Trinity University, One Trinity Place, San Antonio, TX 78212

University of Dallas

Irving, Texas — **CB member**
www.udallas.edu — **CB code: 6868**

- Private 4-year university and liberal arts college affiliated with Roman Catholic Church
- Residential campus in small city
- 1,058 degree-seeking undergraduates: 1% part-time, 58% women, 2% African American, 5% Asian American, 15% Hispanic American, 1% international
- 1,709 degree-seeking graduate students
- 81% of applicants admitted
- SAT or ACT with writing, application essay required

General. Founded in 1956. Regionally accredited. Campus in Rome, Italy. **Degrees:** 244 bachelor's awarded; master's, doctoral offered. **ROTC:** Army, Air Force. **Location:** 5 miles from Dallas. **Calendar:** Semester, limited summer session. **Full-time faculty:** 116 total; 91% have terminal degrees, 5% minority, 26% women. **Part-time faculty:** 105 total; 24% have terminal degrees, 12% minority, 22% women. **Class size:** 49% < 20, 46% 20-39, 3% 40-49, 1% 50-99. **Special facilities:** Observatory with several telescopes, art galleries.

Freshman class profile. 817 applied, 662 admitted, 256 enrolled.

Mid 50% test scores		**GPA 2.0-2.99:**	7%
SAT verbal:	580-700	**Rank in top quarter:**	55%
SAT math:	540-650	**Rank in top tenth:**	31%
ACT:	23-29	**Out-of-state:**	49%
GPA 3.50 or higher:	72%	**Live on campus:**	95%
GPA 3.0-3.49:	21%	**International:**	1%

Basis for selection. Sufficient academic preparation and ability to do the work required along with evidence of good character. Critical writing and composition skills important. Interview recommended for academically marginal; audition recommended for theater program; portfolio recommended for art program.

High school preparation. Required and recommended units include English 4, mathematics 3-4, social studies 3-4, history 3-4, science 3-4, foreign language 2-3 and academic electives 4.

2005-2006 Annual costs. Tuition/fees: $20,411. Room/board: $7,026. Books/supplies: $1,000. Personal expenses: $1,100.

2004-2005 Financial aid. Need-based: 203 full-time freshmen applied for aid; 161 were judged to have need; 161 of these received aid. Average need met was 78%. Average scholarship/grant was $11,388; average loan $2,638. 67% of total undergraduate aid awarded as scholarships/grants, 33% as loans/jobs. **Non-need-based:** Awarded to 423 full-time undergraduates, including 104 freshmen. Scholarships awarded for academics, art, leadership, music/drama.

Application procedures. Admission: Priority date 1/15; deadline 8/1 (postmark date). $40 fee, may be waived for applicants with need. Application may be submitted online. Admission notification on a rolling basis beginning on or about 2/1. Must reply by May 1 or within 4 week(s) if notified thereafter. **Financial aid:** Priority date 3/1, closing date 7/1. FAFSA required. Applicants notified on a rolling basis starting 3/1; must reply by 5/1 or within 2 week(s) of notification.

Academics. 80% of undergraduates spend semester of sophomore year at university's campus in Rome, Italy. Optional credit-bearing intersession available. **Special study options:** Accelerated study, combined bachelor's/graduate degree, double major, dual enrollment of high school students, independent study, internships, liberal arts/career combination, student-designed major, study abroad, teacher certification program. Intensive honors chemistry summer program for entering freshmen. **Credit/placement by examination:** AP, CLEP, IB, institutional tests. 32 credit hours maximum toward bachelor's degree. **Support services:** Learning center, pre-admission summer program, reduced course load, tutoring, writing center.

Majors. Biology: General, biochemistry. **Business:** Business admin. **Education:** General, elementary. **English:** English lit. **Foreign languages:** Ancient Greek, French, German, Latin, Spanish. **History:** General. **Math:** General. **Philosophy/religion:** Philosophy. **Physical sciences:** Chemistry, physics. **Psychology:** General. **Social sciences:** Economics, political science. **Theology:** Preministerial, theology. **Visual/performing arts:** Art history/conservation, ceramics, dramatic, painting, printmaking, sculpture.

Most popular majors. Biology 10%, business/marketing 6%, English 14%, foreign language 9%, history 8%, philosophy/religious studies 7%, social sciences 16%, theological studies 8%, visual/performing arts 8%.

Computing on campus. 125 workstations in library, computer center, student center. Dormitories wired for high-speed internet access and linked to campus network. Commuter students can connect to campus network. Online library, wireless network available.

Student life. Freshman orientation: Mandatory. One-day program prior to fall semester. **Policies:** Freshmen permitted cars on campus. **Housing:** Guaranteed on-campus for freshmen. Coed dorms, single-sex dorms, apartments available. $100 nonrefundable deposit, deadline 8/1. **Activities:** Choral groups, dance, drama, film society, literary magazine, music ensembles, musical theater, radio station, student government, student newspaper, Best Buddies, Society of St. Vincent de Paul, Alpha Phi Omega, Crusaders for Life, Asian student organization.

Athletics. NCAA. **Intercollegiate:** Baseball M, basketball, cross-country, golf M, lacrosse W, soccer, softball W, tennis, track and field, volleyball W. **Intramural:** Basketball M, football (non-tackle), soccer, softball, volleyball. **Team name:** Crusaders.

Student services. Campus ministries, career counseling, student employment services, financial aid counseling, health services, personal counseling, placement for graduates. **Physically disabled:** Services for visually impaired.

Contact. E-mail: ugadmis@udallas.edu
Phone: (972) 721-5266 Toll-free number: (800) 628-6999
Fax: (972) 721-5017
Curt Eley, Dean of Enrollment Management, University of Dallas, 1845 East Northgate Drive, Irving, TX 75062-4736

University of Houston

Houston, Texas **CB member**
www.uh.edu **CB code: 6870**

- Public 4-year university
- Commuter campus in very large city
- 26,959 degree-seeking undergraduates: 27% part-time, 52% women, 16% African American, 21% Asian American, 21% Hispanic American, 5% international
- 7,158 degree-seeking graduate students
- 80% of applicants admitted
- SAT or ACT (ACT writing optional) required
- 40% graduate within 6 years

General. Founded in 1927. Regionally accredited. Institution has large number of nontraditional students (older adults working full-time). **Degrees:** 4,562 bachelor's awarded; master's, doctoral, first professional offered. **ROTC:** Army, Navy, Air Force. **Calendar:** Semester, extensive summer session. **Full-time faculty:** 1,190 total. **Part-time faculty:** 435 total. **Special facilities:** Theater complex, observatory, opera house, coastal center, underground satellite center.

Freshman class profile. 8,875 applied, 7,130 admitted, 3,445 enrolled.

Mid 50% test scores		**Rank in top tenth:**	21%
SAT verbal:	460-580	**Return as sophomores:**	78%
SAT math:	490-610	**Out-of-state:**	2%
ACT:	19-24	**Live on campus:**	25%
GPA 3.50 or higher:	26%	**International:**	4%
GPA 3.0-3.49:	40%	**Fraternities:**	2%
GPA 2.0-2.99:	34%	**Sororities:**	3%
Rank in top quarter:	50%		

Basis for selection. Class rank, completion of high school academic core curriculum with GPA of 2.5 or higher, and test scores from ACT or SAT important. Applicants who do not qualify under standard admission policy may request application review through individual admission process. Review based on overall assessment of applicant's circumstances in respect to academic success and/or personal statement, recommendations from high school or college personnel. SAT Subject Tests recommended. SAT Writing component required but not used in admissions decision. Audition required for music program; essay recommended for honors college. **Homeschooled:** Must submit minimum SAT score of 1180 (exclusive of Writing) and transcript (can be created by parent). In order to qualify for financial aid, must pass GED exam. SAT not recognized by financial aid department. **Learning Disabled:** Intake appointment with counselor scheduled upon receipt of required documentation indicating that disability substantially limits some major life activity.

High school preparation. Required and recommended units include English 4, mathematics 3, social studies 2, history 2, science 2 (laboratory 2) and foreign language 2. 1 chemistry, 1 physics, 1 mechanical drawing recommended for engineering and science applicants.

2005-2006 Annual costs. Tuition/fees: $5,163; $13,443 out-of-state. Room/board: $6,030. Books/supplies: $1,050. Personal expenses: $2,900.

2005-2006 Financial aid. All financial aid based on need. 1,393 full-time freshmen applied for aid; 1,245 were judged to have need; 1,153 of these received aid. Average need met was 53%. Average scholarship/grant was $5,847; average loan $2,736. 45% of total undergraduate aid awarded as scholarships/grants, 55% as loans/jobs. **Additional information:** 45-day and 90-day institutional loans available.

Application procedures. Admission: Closing date 4/1. $50 fee ($75 out-of-state), may be waived for applicants with need. Application may be submitted online. Admission notification on a rolling basis beginning on or about 9/1. **Financial aid:** No deadline. FAFSA required. Applicants notified on a rolling basis starting 5/1; must reply within 4 week(s) of notification.

Academics. Many academic support and other support programs available. **Special study options:** Accelerated study, cooperative education, cross-registration, distance learning, double major, dual enrollment of high school students, ESL, exchange student, honors, independent study, internships, semester at sea, study abroad, teacher certification program, Washington semester, weekend college. Continuing education programs, academic enrichment programs, certification programs and affiliated studies. **Credit/placement by examination:** AP, CLEP, IB, institutional tests. **Support services:** Learning center, reduced course load, remedial instruction, study skills assistance, tutoring, writing center.

Majors. Architecture: Architecture, environmental design, interior. **Area/ethnic studies:** German, Russian/Slavic. **Biology:** General, biochemistry, biophysics. **Business:** Accounting, communications, entrepreneurial studies, finance, human resources, management information systems, managerial economics, marketing, merchandising, operations, organizational behavior, personal/financial services, sales/distribution, statistics. **Communications:** General, journalism, public relations, radio/tv. **Computer sciences:** General, information systems, systems analysis. **Education:** Health, physical, trade/industrial. **Engineering:** Chemical, civil, computer, electrical, mechanical. **Engineering technology:** Architectural, civil, construction, electrical, industrial, industrial management, manufacturing. **English:** Speech/rhetoric. **Family/consumer sciences:** General, business, family studies, food/nutrition. **Foreign languages:** Classics, French, German, Italian, Latin, Spanish. **Health:** Audiology/speech pathology, clinical lab science, communication disorders, kinesiotherapy, nuclear medical technology, optician, prepharmacy. **History:** General. **Math:** General, applied. **Parks/recreation:** Exercise sciences, health/fitness, sports admin. **Philosophy/religion:** Philosophy. **Physical sciences:** Chemistry, geology, geophysics, physics, planetary. **Psychology:** General. **Social sciences:** Anthropology, economics, political science, sociology, urban studies. **Visual/performing arts:** Art, art history/conservation, ceramics, commercial/advertising art, dance, dramatic, graphic design, industrial design, interior design, metal/jewelry, music performance, music theory/composition, painting, photography, printmaking, sculpture, studio arts.

Most popular majors. Business/marketing 34%, communications/journalism 6%, communication technologies 6%, engineering/engineering technologies 12%, psychology 9%, social sciences 7%.

Computing on campus. 850 workstations in dormitories, library, computer center, student center. Dormitories wired for high-speed internet access and linked to campus network. Commuter students can connect to campus network. Helpline, repair service available.

Student life. Freshman orientation: Mandatory, $90 fee. Preregistration for classes offered. 2-day conferences include advising, phone registration, placement testing, textbook orders. **Policies:** Freshmen permitted cars on campus. **Housing:** Coed dorms, special housing for disabled, apartments, fraternity/sorority housing available. $100 fully refundable deposit, deadline 4/1. **Activities:** Bands, choral groups, dance, drama, film society, literary magazine, music ensembles, musical theater, opera, radio station, student government, student newspaper, symphony orchestra, TV station, Asian student association, Hispanic student association, Habitat for Humanity, Hillel, College Republicans/Democrats, NAACP, Green Party, Indian student association, Muslim students association, Bahai student association.

Athletics. NCAA. **Intercollegiate:** Baseball M, basketball, cross-country, diving W, football (tackle) M, golf M, soccer W, softball W, swimming W, tennis W, track and field, volleyball W. **Intramural:** Badminton, basketball, bowling, cross-country, diving, football (tackle) M, golf, racquetball, soccer, softball, swimming, table tennis, tennis, track and field, volleyball, water polo. **Team name:** Cougars.

Student services. Adult student services, campus ministries, career counseling, student employment services, financial aid counseling, health services, on-campus daycare, personal counseling, placement for graduates, veterans' counselor, women's services. **Physically disabled:** Services for visually, speech, hearing impaired.

Contact. E-mail: admissions@uh.edu
Phone: (713) 743-1010 Fax: (713) 743-9633
Susanna Finnell, Director of Admission, University of Houston, 122 East Cullen Building, Houston, TX 77204-2023

University of Houston: Clear Lake

Houston, Texas — **CB member**
www.uhcl.edu — **CB code: 6916**

- Public upper-division university
- Commuter campus in very large city
- 64% of applicants admitted

General. Founded in 1971. Regionally accredited. **Degrees:** 1,057 bachelor's awarded; master's offered. **Articulation:** Agreements with all community colleges in Houston metropolitan area, Houston CC, North Harris CC, San Jacinto College, Brazosport College, Galveston College, Alvin CC, Lee College, College of the Mainland, Kingwood College, Montgomery College, Tomball College, Wharton County JC. **Location:** 21 miles from Houston. **Calendar:** Semester, limited summer session. **Full-time faculty:** 230 total; 90% have terminal degrees, 14% minority, 38% women. **Part-time faculty:** 294 total; 42% have terminal degrees, 18% minority, 55% women. **Class size:** 45% < 20, 44% 20-39, 8% 40-49, 2% 50-99, less than 1% >100.

Student profile. 3,913 degree-seeking undergraduates, 3,527 degree-seeking graduate students. 1,957 applied as first time-transfer students, 1,250 admitted, 983 enrolled. 82% entered as juniors, 18% entered as seniors.

Women:	69%	**Part-time:**	47%
African American:	7%	**Out-of-state:**	1%
Asian American:	6%	**Live on campus:**	3%
Hispanic American:	17%	**25 or older:**	55%
International:	1%		

Basis for selection. College transcript required. Students with 54 hours of credit with grades 2.0 or better (exclusive of remedial or development or repeated courses) from regionally accredited institution will be admitted. Students must also have completed college algebra or higher mathematics course and have passing scores on THEA. Students must be eligible to return to last institution attended. Transfer accepted as juniors, seniors.

2006-2007 Annual costs. Tuition/fees (projected): $4,653; $13,595 out-of-state. Room only: $6,456. Books/supplies: $918.

Financial aid. Need-based: 903 applied for aid; 802 were judged to have need; 799 of these received aid. Average need met was 54%. 24% of total undergraduate aid awarded as scholarships/grants, 76% as loans/jobs. **Non-need-based:** Awarded to 86 undergraduates. Scholarships awarded for academics, state residency.

Application procedures. Admission: Priority date 6/2. $35 fee. Application may be submitted online. **Financial aid:** Priority date 4/1, no deadline. Applicants notified by 5/15; must reply within 4 weeks of notification. FAFSA, institutional form required.

Academics. Special study options: Combined bachelor's/graduate degree, cooperative education, distance learning, double major, dual enrollment of high school students, independent study, internships, student-designed major, study abroad, teacher certification program, weekend college. **Credit/placement by examination:** AP, CLEP. 18 credit hours maximum toward bachelor's degree.

Majors. Biology: General. **Business:** General, accounting, business admin, finance, management information systems, marketing. **Communications:** General. **Computer sciences:** General, computer science. **Conservation:** General, environmental science, environmental studies. **Education:** General. **Engineering:** Computer. **English:** English lit. **Health:** Health care admin. **History:** General. **Interdisciplinary:** Behavioral sciences, math/computer science. **Legal studies:** Prelaw. **Liberal arts:** Arts/sciences, humanities. **Math:** General. **Parks/recreation:** Health/fitness. **Physical sciences:** Chemistry. **Psychology:** General. **Public administration:** Policy analysis, social work. **Social sciences:** Anthropology, criminology, geography, political science, sociology. **Visual/performing arts:** Art.

Most popular majors. Business/marketing 32%, interdisciplinary studies 19%, psychology 8%.

Computing on campus. 715 workstations in library, computer center. Commuter students can connect to campus network. Online course registration, online library, helpline, wireless network available.

Student life. Housing: Limited apartments on campus. **Activities:** Film society, literary magazine, student government, student newspaper, Catholic campus ministries, international student organization, black student association, Chinese Christian student fellowship, Hispanic advancement in culture and education, student organization for Native American studies, student council for exceptional children, unity club, clinical psychology club, Muslim student association.

Student services. Alcohol/substance abuse counseling, career counseling, student employment services, financial aid counseling, health services, minority student services, personal counseling, placement for graduates, veterans' counselor, women's services. **Physically disabled:** Services for visually, speech, hearing impaired.

Contact. E-mail: admissions@uhcl.edu
Phone: (281) 283-2521 Fax: (281) 283-2530
Rauchelle Jones, Interim Director of Admissions, University of Houston: Clear Lake, 2700 Bay Area Boulevard, Houston, TX 77058-1098

University of Houston: Downtown

Houston, Texas — **CB member**
www.uhd.edu — **CB code: 6922**

- Public 4-year university
- Commuter campus in very large city
- 11,359 degree-seeking undergraduates: 48% part-time, 59% women, 26% African American, 10% Asian American, 37% Hispanic American, 4% international
- 125 degree-seeking graduate students

General. Founded in 1974. Regionally accredited. Locations in Sugar Land, Cinco Ranch, The Woodlands, and East Harris County. **Degrees:** 1,619 bachelor's awarded; master's offered. **ROTC:** Army. **Location:** 240 miles from Dallas, 200 miles from San Antonio. **Calendar:** Semester, limited summer session. **Full-time faculty:** 277 total; 80% have terminal degrees, 29% minority, 45% women. **Part-time faculty:** 296 total; 25% have terminal degrees, 36% minority, 50% women. **Class size:** 26% < 20, 65% 20-39, 6% 40-49, 3% 50-99. **Special facilities:** Live theater.

Freshman class profile. 1,726 applied, 1,726 admitted, 1,029 enrolled.

Return as sophomores:	61%	**International:**	5%
Out-of-state:	2%		

Basis for selection. Open admission.

High school preparation. 25 units recommended. Recommended units include English 4, mathematics 3, social studies 3.5, science 3, foreign language 3 and academic electives 1. Fine arts, speech, technology, health education, economics, and physical education recommended 7.5 units.

2005-2006 Annual costs. Tuition/fees: $4,069; $12,349 out-of-state. Books/supplies: $1,020.

2004-2005 Financial aid. Need-based: 693 full-time freshmen applied for aid; 656 were judged to have need; 569 of these received aid. Average need met was 28%. Average scholarship/grant was $3,591; average loan $2,155. 51% of total undergraduate aid awarded as scholarships/grants, 49% as loans/jobs. **Non-need-based:** Awarded to 393 full-time undergraduates, including 213 freshmen. Scholarships awarded for academics, leadership.

Application procedures. Admission: Closing date 7/1 (postmark date). $25 fee, may be waived for applicants with need. Application may be submitted online. Admission notification on a rolling basis. **Financial aid:** Closing date 4/1. FAFSA, institutional form required. Applicants notified on a rolling basis starting 6/1; must reply within 4 week(s) of notification.

Academics. Special study options: Cooperative education, distance learning, double major, dual enrollment of high school students, ESL, honors, independent study, internships, study abroad, teacher certification program, weekend college. **Credit/placement by examination:** AP, CLEP, IB. 24 credit hours maximum toward bachelor's degree. **Support services:** Learning center, reduced course load, remedial instruction, study skills assistance, tutoring, writing center.

Majors. Biology: General, microbiology. **Business:** General, accounting, business admin, finance, international, management information systems, marketing, office management, purchasing. **Computer sciences:** General. **Engineering technology:** Civil, computer, mechanical, occupational safety. **English:** English lit, speech/rhetoric, technical writing. **Foreign languages:** Spanish. **History:** General. **Interdisciplinary:** Biological/physical sciences. **Liberal arts:** Arts/sciences, humanities. **Math:** Applied. **Philosophy/religion:** Philosophy. **Physical sciences:** Chemistry. **Protective services:** Criminal justice. **Psychology:** General. **Social sciences:** General, political science, sociology.

Most popular majors. Business/marketing 43%, interdisciplinary studies 7%, liberal arts 22%, psychology 7%, security/protective services 7%.

Computing on campus. 1,003 workstations in library, computer center, student center. Commuter students can connect to campus network. Online library, helpline, student web hosting, wireless network available.

Student life. Freshman orientation: Available, $20 fee. Preregistration for classes offered. One-day program. **Activities:** Jazz band, drama, literary magazine, student government, student newspaper, Chinese student association, friends of Central America student association, Kingdom Connections, Latin American student services organization, Vietnamese student association, black student alliance, Alpha Kappa Alpha Sorority, Sigma Lambda Beta Fraternity, international student organization, Mexican student organization.

Athletics. Intramural: Badminton, basketball, bowling, football (non-tackle) M, softball, table tennis, volleyball, weight lifting. **Team name:** Gator.

Student services. Alcohol/substance abuse counseling, career counseling, student employment services, financial aid counseling, health services, personal counseling, placement for graduates, veterans' counselor. **Physically disabled:** Services for visually, hearing impaired.

Contact. E-mail: uhdadmit@dt.uh.edu
Phone: (713) 221-8522 Fax: (713) 221-8157
Carmen Holland, Director of Admissions, University of Houston: Downtown, One Main Street, 350-South, Houston, TX 77002

University of Houston: Victoria

Victoria, Texas
www.uhv.edu **CB code: 6917**

- Public upper-division university
- Commuter campus in small city
- 83% of applicants admitted
- Test scores required

General. Founded in 1973. Regionally accredited. **Degrees:** 330 bachelor's awarded; master's offered. **Articulation:** Agreements with Bee County College, Victoria College, Wharton County Junior College, Blinn College. **Location:** 120 miles from Houston and Austin. **Calendar:** Semester, limited summer session. **Full-time faculty:** 74 total; 100% have terminal degrees, 43% minority, 32% women. **Part-time faculty:** 56 total; 45% have terminal degrees, 11% minority, 68% women.

Student profile. 1,188 degree-seeking undergraduates, 1,262 graduate students. 517 applied as first time-transfer students, 431 admitted, 316 enrolled. 90% entered as juniors, 10% entered as seniors. 80% transferred from two-year, 20% transferred from four-year institutions.

Women:	75%	**Native American:**	1%
African American:	7%	**Part-time:**	62%
Asian American:	3%	**25 or older:**	70%
Hispanic American:	23%		

Basis for selection. College transcript, standardized test scores required. Minimum of 54 semester hours of transferable credit with minimum 2.0 GPA required. Transfer accepted as juniors, seniors.

2005-2006 Annual costs. Tuition/fees: $4,350; $12,630 out-of-state.

Financial aid. Need-based: 313 applied for aid; 262 were judged to have need; 241 of these received aid. Average need met was 53%. 43% of total undergraduate aid awarded as scholarships/grants, 57% as loans/jobs. **Non-need-based:** Awarded to 36 undergraduates. Scholarships awarded for academics, leadership, state residency. **Additional information:** Short-term loans available at registration.

Application procedures. Admission: Rolling admission. No application fee. **Financial aid:** FAFSA, institutional form required.

Academics. Degree program in liberal arts for graduates of 2-year vocational programs. **Special study options:** Distance learning, double major, independent study, internships, study abroad, teacher certification program. **Credit/placement by examination:** CLEP.

Majors. Biology: General. **Business:** Accounting, business admin, marketing. **Communications:** General. **Computer sciences:** General, information systems. **Education:** General. **English:** Speech/rhetoric. **History:** General. **Math:** General. **Psychology:** General.

Most popular majors. Business/marketing 17%, communications/journalism 7%, computer/information sciences 9%, education 31%, psychology 9%.

Computing on campus. 150 workstations in library, computer center. Commuter students can connect to campus network. Online library, helpline, repair service available.

Student life. Activities: Student government, student newspaper.

Student services. Career counseling, student employment services, financial aid counseling, placement for graduates, veterans' counselor. **Physically disabled:** Services for visually, hearing impaired.

Contact. E-mail: admission@uhv.edu
Phone: (361) 570-4110 Toll-free number: (877) 970-4848 ext. 110
Fax: (361) 570-4114
Richard Phillips, Director of Enrollment Management, University of Houston: Victoria, 3007 North Ben Wilson, Victoria, TX 77901-4450

University of Mary Hardin-Baylor

Belton, Texas **CB member**
www.umhb.edu **CB code: 6396**

- Private 4-year university affiliated with Baptist faith
- Residential campus in large town
- 2,532 degree-seeking undergraduates: 11% part-time, 63% women, 11% African American, 1% Asian American, 11% Hispanic American, 1% international
- 124 degree-seeking graduate students
- 75% of applicants admitted
- SAT or ACT with writing required
- 42% graduate within 6 years

General. Founded in 1845. Regionally accredited. Information, counseling, and administrative services, as well as limited number of undergraduate and graduate level evening courses, offered at Fort Hood. Affiliated with Baptist General Convention of Texas. **Degrees:** 489 bachelor's awarded; master's offered. **ROTC:** Air Force. **Location:** 60 miles from Austin. **Calendar:** Semester, limited summer session. **Full-time faculty:** 133 total; 69% have terminal degrees, 8% minority, 56% women. **Part-time faculty:** 94 total; 21% have terminal degrees, 1% minority, 50% women. **Class size:** 50% < 20, 45% 20-39, 4% 40-49, 1% 50-99.

Freshman class profile. 1,261 applied, 942 admitted, 501 enrolled.

Mid 50% test scores		**Rank in top tenth:**	19%
SAT verbal:	480-570	**End year in good standing:**	80%
SAT math:	480-570	**Return as sophomores:**	71%
ACT:	20-25	**Out-of-state:**	1%
Rank in top quarter:	46%	**Live on campus:**	90%

Basis for selection. School achievement record and test scores important. First-time freshmen must rank in top 10 percent of accredited high school graduating class, or score minimum of 910 on SAT (exclusive of Writing), or minimum of 19 on ACT. Academically deficient students may be accepted on individual basis by approval of admissions committee. Interview recommended for academically marginal; audition recommended for music. **Homeschooled:** Must submit list of classes, grades, and graduation date. Since there is no ranking, admission made on ACT or SAT test scores.

High school preparation. 22 units required. Required units include English 4, mathematics 3, social studies 2.5.

2006-2007 Annual costs. Tuition/fees (projected): $15,710. Room/board: $4,200. Books/supplies: $900. Personal expenses: $1,869.

2005-2006 Financial aid. **Need-based:** 472 full-time freshmen applied for aid; 360 were judged to have need; 353 of these received aid. Average need met was 64%. Average scholarship/grant was $5,334; average loan $2,514. 51% of total undergraduate aid awarded as scholarships/grants, 49% as loans/jobs. **Non-need-based:** Awarded to 1,755 full-time undergraduates, including 412 freshmen. Scholarships awarded for academics, art, leadership, music/drama, religious affiliation.

Application procedures. **Admission:** Priority date 7/1; no deadline. $35 fee. Application may be submitted online. Admission notification on a rolling basis. **Financial aid:** Priority date 3/1; no closing date. FAFSA, institutional form required. Applicants notified on a rolling basis starting 2/1; must reply within 2 week(s) of notification.

Academics. **Special study options:** Accelerated study, combined bachelor's/graduate degree, double major, dual enrollment of high school students, ESL, honors, independent study, internships, study abroad, teacher certification program. Servicemember Opportunity Colleges (SOC) programs, military degree completion programs, tuition exchange program with other participating universities. **Credit/placement by examination:** AP, CLEP, institutional tests. 31 credit hours maximum toward bachelor's degree. No more than one-fourth of total credit hours required for degree may be earned through credit by examination. **Support services:** Learning center, preadmission summer program, reduced course load, remedial instruction, study skills assistance, tutoring.

Majors. **Biology:** Biomedical sciences. **Business:** General, accounting, business admin, finance, management information systems, marketing. **Communications:** General. **Computer sciences:** General, computer graphics, computer science, information systems. **Education:** Chemistry, elementary, English, mathematics, music, physical, science, social studies, special. **English:** English lit. **Foreign languages:** Spanish. **Health:** Athletic training, clinical lab science, nursing (RN). **History:** General. **Math:** General. **Parks/recreation:** General, sports admin. **Philosophy/religion:** Christian, religion. **Physical sciences:** Chemistry. **Protective services:** Law enforcement admin. **Psychology:** General. **Public administration:** Social work. **Social sciences:** Political science, sociology. **Theology:** Bible, pastoral counseling, sacred music, theology. **Visual/performing arts:** Dramatic, music performance, music theory/composition, studio arts.

Most popular majors. Biology 6%, business/marketing 12%, computer/information sciences 9%, education 16%, health sciences 14%, liberal arts 8%, psychology 7%.

Computing on campus. 275 workstations in dormitories, library, computer center, student center. Dormitories wired for high-speed internet access and linked to campus network. Online library available.

Student life. **Freshman orientation:** Available, $40 fee. Preregistration for classes offered. One-day orientation in summer for students and parents. Full-week orientation for students only before start of classes. **Policies:** Religious observance required. Freshmen permitted cars on campus. **Housing:** Guaranteed on-campus for freshmen. Single-sex dorms, special housing for disabled, apartments, substance-free housing available. $150 deposit. **Activities:** Bands, choral groups, drama, literary magazine, music ensembles, musical theater, opera, student government, student newspaper, symphony orchestra, Baptist student ministry, Catholic student organization, College Democrats, College Republicans, Crusaders for Christ, Fellowship of Christian Athletes, Focus (community-wide worship), Habitat for Humanity, international student union.

Athletics. NCAA. **Intercollegiate:** Baseball M, basketball, football (tackle) M, golf, soccer, softball W, tennis, volleyball W. **Intramural:** Basketball, football (non-tackle), golf, soccer, softball, table tennis, tennis, volleyball, water polo. **Team name:** Crusaders.

Student services. Alcohol/substance abuse counseling, campus ministries, career counseling, student employment services, financial aid counseling, health services, personal counseling, placement for graduates, veterans' counselor. **Physically disabled:** Services for visually, speech, hearing impaired.

Contact. E-mail: admissions@umhb.edu
Phone: (254) 295-4520 Toll-free number: (800) 727-8642 ext. 4520
Fax: (254) 295-5049
Robbin Steen, Director of Admissions and Recruiting, University of Mary Hardin-Baylor, 900 College Street, Belton, TX 76513

University of North Texas

Denton, Texas — **CB member**
www.unt.edu — **CB code: 6481**

- Public 4-year university and liberal arts college
- Commuter campus in small city
- 25,308 degree-seeking undergraduates: 22% part-time, 56% women, 12% African American, 5% Asian American, 11% Hispanic American, 1% Native American, 3% international
- 6,739 degree-seeking graduate students
- 69% of applicants admitted
- SAT or ACT (ACT writing optional) required
- 43% graduate within 6 years

General. Founded in 1890. Regionally accredited. **Degrees:** 4,391 bachelor's awarded; master's, doctoral offered. **ROTC:** Army, Air Force. **Location:** 35 miles from Dallas-Fort Worth. **Calendar:** Semester, extensive summer session. **Full-time faculty:** 936 total; 17% minority, 35% women. **Part-time faculty:** 610 total; 50% women. **Class size:** 38% < 20, 40% 20-39, 10% 40-49, 8% 50-99, 4% >100. **Special facilities:** Laser, observatory, accelerators, recreational facility.

Freshman class profile. 11,282 applied, 7,834 admitted, 3,635 enrolled.

Mid 50% test scores		**Return as sophomores:**	75%
SAT verbal:	500-600	**Out-of-state:**	3%
SAT math:	500-610	**Live on campus:**	80%
ACT:	20-24	**International:**	1%
Rank in top quarter:	48%	**Fraternities:**	14%
Rank in top tenth:	19%	**Sororities:**	10%

Basis for selection. School achievement record most important. Test score minimums vary with class rank: top 10% no minimum. Students seeking early admission before high school graduation must be in top quarter of class with strong B average, complete 3 units of English and 2 each of mathematics, social science, natural science; present minimum SAT score of 1180 (exclusive of Writing) or ACT 27. Audition required for music program.

High school preparation. College-preparatory program recommended. 19 units required; 26 recommended. Required and recommended units include English 4, mathematics 3-4, social studies 2-3, history 2, science 3, foreign language 2-3 and academic electives 3. Units in health and physical education, computer sciences, fine arts recommended.

2005-2006 Annual costs. Tuition/fees: $6,110; $14,390 out-of-state. Room/board: $5,350. Books/supplies: $1,030. Personal expenses: $1,110.

2005-2006 Financial aid. **Need-based:** 2,442 full-time freshmen applied for aid; 1,567 were judged to have need; 1,541 of these received aid. Average need met was 73%. Average scholarship/grant was $4,034; average loan $2,534. 39% of total undergraduate aid awarded as scholarships/grants, 61% as loans/jobs. **Non-need-based:** Awarded to 3,270 full-time undergraduates, including 926 freshmen. Scholarships awarded for academics.

Application procedures. **Admission:** Closing date 6/15 (postmark date). $40 fee, may be waived for applicants with need. Application may be submitted online. Admission notification on a rolling basis. **Financial aid:** Priority date 6/1; no closing date. FAFSA required. Applicants notified on a rolling basis starting 4/1.

Academics. **Special study options:** Accelerated study, combined bachelor's/graduate degree, cooperative education, cross-registration, distance learning, double major, dual enrollment of high school students, ESL, exchange student, external degree, honors, independent study, internships, study abroad, teacher certification program, weekend college. **Credit/placement by examination:** AP, CLEP, IB, institutional tests. 24 credit hours maximum toward bachelor's degree. **Support services:** Learning center, study skills assistance, tutoring, writing center.

Majors. **Architecture:** Interior, urban/community planning. **Biology:** General, biochemistry. **Business:** General, accounting, banking/financial services, business admin, fashion, finance, hospitality admin, human resources, insurance, labor relations, management information systems, managerial economics, marketing, office management, operations, organizational behavior, public finance, real estate. **Communications:** General, advertising, broadcast journalism, journalism, public relations. **Computer sciences:** General. **Education:** Art, early childhood, elementary. **Engineering technology:** Construction, electrical. **English:** Composition, speech/rhetoric. **Family/consumer sciences:** Business, child care, clothing/textiles, family studies, housing. **Foreign languages:** Comparative lit, French, German, Latin, Spanish. **Health:** Audiology/speech pathology, clinical lab science, cytotechnology, EMT paramedic. **History:** General. **Interdisciplinary:** Gerontology. **Liberal arts:** Arts/sciences, library science. **Math:** General. **Parks/recreation:** General, facilities management, health/fitness. **Philosophy/religion:** Philosophy. **Physical sciences:** Chemistry, physics. **Protective services:** Criminal justice. **Psychology:** General. **Public administration:** General, social work. **Social sciences:** General, anthropology, economics, geography, political science, sociology. **Visual/performing arts:** Art history/conservation, ceramics, commercial/advertising art, crafts, dance, dramatic, drawing, fashion design, fiber arts, interior design, jazz, metal/jewelry, music history, music performance, music theory/composition, painting, photography, printmaking, sculpture, studio arts.

Most popular majors. Business/marketing 26%, communications/journalism 7%, education 9%, social sciences 8%, visual/performing arts 9%.

Computing on campus. 575 workstations in dormitories, library, computer center.

Student life. Freshman orientation: Mandatory, $164 fee. Preregistration for classes offered. 8 sessions during June and July; each 2 nights and 3 days. **Policies:** Freshmen permitted cars on campus. **Housing:** Guaranteed on-campus for freshmen. Coed dorms, single-sex dorms, special housing for disabled, apartments, fraternity/sorority housing available. $400 partly refundable deposit. **Activities:** Bands, choral groups, dance, drama, film society, literary magazine, music ensembles, musical theater, opera, radio station, student government, student newspaper, symphony orchestra, TV station, honorary societies, religious, ethnic, and social service organizations.

Athletics. NCAA. **Intercollegiate:** Basketball, cross-country, football (tackle) M, golf, soccer W, softball, swimming W, tennis W, track and field, volleyball W. **Intramural:** Badminton, basketball, bowling, football (non-tackle), golf, racquetball, soccer, softball, tennis, track and field, volleyball W, water polo. **Team name:** Eagles.

Student services. Adult student services, alcohol/substance abuse counseling, career counseling, student employment services, financial aid counseling, health services, legal services, minority student services, on-campus daycare, personal counseling, placement for graduates, veterans' counselor, women's services. **Physically disabled:** Services for visually, speech, hearing impaired.

Contact. E-mail: undergrad@unt.edu
Phone: (940) 565-2681 Toll-free number: (800) 868-8211
Fax: (940) 565-2408
Marcilla Collinsworth, Director of Admissions and School Relations, University of North Texas, 1401 West Prairie, Suite 309, Denton, TX 76203

University of St. Thomas

Houston, Texas **CB member**
www.stthom.edu **CB code: 6880**

- Private 4-year university and liberal arts college affiliated with Roman Catholic Church
- Commuter campus in very large city
- 1,776 degree-seeking undergraduates: 24% part-time, 61% women, 6% African American, 12% Asian American, 30% Hispanic American, 1% Native American, 3% international
- 1,132 degree-seeking graduate students
- 92% of applicants admitted
- SAT or ACT with writing required
- 53% graduate within 6 years

General. Founded in 1947. Regionally accredited. **Degrees:** 334 bachelor's awarded; master's, doctoral, first professional offered. **ROTC:** Army. **Location:** 3 miles from downtown. **Calendar:** Semester, limited summer session. **Full-time faculty:** 121 total; 88% have terminal degrees, 7% minority, 35% women. **Part-time faculty:** 151 total; 64% have terminal degrees, 9% minority, 51% women. **Class size:** 52% < 20, 48% 20-39, less than 1% 40-49. **Special facilities:** Chapel of St. Basil, archaeology gallery.

Freshman class profile. 807 applied, 744 admitted, 295 enrolled.

Mid 50% test scores		**Rank in top quarter:**	58%
SAT verbal:	530-640	**Rank in top tenth:**	29%
SAT math:	520-640	**End year in good standing:**	79%
ACT:	22-28	**Return as sophomores:**	71%
GPA 3.50 or higher:	49%	**Out-of-state:**	4%
GPA 3.0-3.49:	28%	**Live on campus:**	42%
GPA 2.0-2.99:	23%		

Basis for selection. School achievement record, test scores, and graded essay most important. Cumulative high school GPA of 2.5 or higher in a minimum of 18 college preparatory units required, as well as minimum 1020 SAT (exclusive of Writing) or 22 ACT. High school class rank in the upper 50% required, if high school attended ranks graduates. Audition required for applied music, drama, voice programs; portfolio required for art program.

High school preparation. 18 units required. Required units include English 4, mathematics 3, social studies 2, history 1, science 3 (laboratory 2), foreign language 2 and academic electives 3.

2005-2006 Annual costs. Tuition/fees: $17,110. Room/board: $7,300.

2005-2006 Financial aid. Need-based: 203 full-time freshmen applied for aid; 173 were judged to have need; 171 of these received aid. Average need met was 68%. Average scholarship/grant was $9,958; average loan $2,815. 67% of total undergraduate aid awarded as scholarships/grants, 33% as loans/jobs. **Non-need-based:** Awarded to 375 full-time undergraduates, including 62 freshmen. Scholarships awarded for academics, leadership, music/drama, religious affiliation, state residency.

Application procedures. Admission: Priority date 2/1; no deadline. $35 fee, may be waived for applicants with need. Application may be submitted online. Admission notification on a rolling basis beginning on or about 10/1. Must reply by May 1 or within 2 week(s) if notified thereafter. **Financial aid:** Priority date 3/1; no closing date. FAFSA required. Applicants notified on a rolling basis starting 3/1; must reply within 4 week(s) of notification.

Academics. Special study options: Combined bachelor's/graduate degree, cross-registration, distance learning, double major, honors, independent study, internships, study abroad, teacher certification program. First-year experiences, learning communities, service learning, senior capstone or culminating academic experiences, undergraduate research/creative projects. **Credit/placement by examination:** AP, CLEP, IB, SAT, ACT, institutional tests. 30 credit hours maximum toward bachelor's degree. Validation of credit by examination contingent upon completion of at least 24 semester hours in residence at institution. **Support services:** Learning center, reduced course load, remedial instruction, study skills assistance, tutoring, writing center.

Majors. Biology: General, bioinformatics. **Business:** Accounting, business admin, finance, management information systems, marketing. **Communications:** General. **Conservation:** Environmental studies. **Education:** General, elementary, music, secondary. **English:** English lit. **Foreign languages:** French, Spanish. **History:** General. **Liberal arts:** Arts/sciences. **Math:** General. **Philosophy/religion:** Philosophy. **Physical sciences:** Chemistry. **Psychology:** General. **Social sciences:** Economics, international relations, political science. **Theology:** Pastoral counseling, theology. **Visual/performing arts:** Dramatic, studio arts.

Most popular majors. Biology 6%, business/marketing 27%, education 6%, liberal arts 16%, psychology 7%, social sciences 12%.

Computing on campus. 156 workstations in dormitories, library, computer center, student center. Dormitories wired for high-speed internet access. Online library, helpline, wireless network available.

Student life. Freshman orientation: Available. Preregistration for classes offered. Held in August and January. **Policies:** Freshmen permitted cars on campus. **Housing:** Coed dorms, apartments available. $300 deposit. Pets allowed in dorm rooms. Houses and living-learning center available. **Activities:** Bands, choral groups, drama, literary magazine, music ensembles, musical theater, student government, student newspaper, Best Buddies, black student union, campus ministry, Muslim student association, Society of St. Vincent de Paul, student organization of Latinos, Vietnamese student association, Filipino student association, international students association.

Athletics. Intercollegiate: Basketball M. **Intramural:** Basketball, golf, racquetball, table tennis, tennis, volleyball.

Student services. Adult student services, campus ministries, career counseling, student employment services, financial aid counseling, health services, personal counseling, placement for graduates.

Contact. E-mail: admissions@stthom.edu
Phone: (713) 525-3500 Toll-free number: (800) 856-8565
Fax: (713) 525-3558
Eduardo Prieto, Dean of Admissions, University of St. Thomas, 3800 Montrose Boulevard, Houston, TX 77006-4696

University of Texas at Arlington

Arlington, Texas **CB member**
www.uta.edu **CB code: 6013**

- Public 4-year university
- Large city
- 19,222 degree-seeking undergraduates: 29% part-time, 53% women, 14% African American, 11% Asian American, 15% Hispanic American, 1% Native American, 5% international
- 5,783 degree-seeking graduate students
- 74% of applicants admitted

- SAT or ACT with writing required
- 40% graduate within 6 years

General. Founded in 1895. Regionally accredited. **Degrees:** 3,378 bachelor's awarded; master's, doctoral offered. **ROTC:** Army, Air Force. **Location:** 15 miles from Dallas and Fort Worth. **Calendar:** 4-1-4-1 (January and May terms). Extensive summer session. **Full-time faculty:** 781 total; 20% minority, 36% women. **Part-time faculty:** 332 total; 14% minority, 47% women. **Class size:** 27% < 20, 40% 20-39, 8% 40-49, 18% 50-99, 7% >100. **Special facilities:** Library special collections, robotics center, observatory, planetarium, maps collection, minority cultures collection, cartographic history library, library of Texana and Mexican War material.

Freshman class profile. 5,465 applied, 4,050 admitted, 2,130 enrolled.

Mid 50% test scores		**Return as sophomores:**	69%
SAT verbal:	460-570	**Out-of-state:**	2%
SAT math:	480-590	**Live on campus:**	43%
ACT:	19-24	**International:**	2%
Rank in top quarter:	60%	**Fraternities:**	5%
Rank in top tenth:	20%	**Sororities:**	4%
End year in good standing:	73%		

Basis for selection. GED not accepted. Admission based on test scores and high school rank. Fourth quarter of high school class must be approved by director of admissions or associate director. Interview recommended for academically weak; audition recommended for music; portfolio recommended for art, architecture programs. **Homeschooled:** Transcript of courses and grades, letter of recommendation (nonparent) required.

High school preparation. 20 units required. Required and recommended units include English 4, mathematics 3-4, social studies 3-4, science 3, foreign language 2-3 and academic electives 5. 1 computing profiency, 1 fine arts, 1 music, theatre art recommended.

2005-2006 Annual costs. Tuition/fees: $5,561; $13,843 out-of-state. Room/board: $6,628. Books/supplies: $800. Personal expenses: $1,350.

2005-2006 Financial aid. **Need-based:** 1,180 full-time freshmen applied for aid; 1,035 were judged to have need; 1,035 of these received aid. Average need met was 71%. Average scholarship/grant was $3,998; average loan $4,096. 39% of total undergraduate aid awarded as scholarships/grants, 61% as loans/jobs. **Non-need-based:** Awarded to 4,722 full-time undergraduates, including 1,051 freshmen. Scholarships awarded for academics, art, athletics, leadership, music/drama, ROTC.

Application procedures. **Admission:** Priority date 6/1; no deadline. $35 fee ($50 out-of-state), may be waived for applicants with need. Application may be submitted online. Admission notification on a rolling basis. **Financial aid:** Priority date 5/15; no closing date. FAFSA required. Applicants notified on a rolling basis starting 4/1; must reply within 3 week(s) of notification.

Academics. **Special study options:** Combined bachelor's/graduate degree, cooperative education, cross-registration, distance learning, double major, dual enrollment of high school students, ESL, honors, independent study, internships, student-designed major, study abroad, teacher certification program. **Credit/placement by examination:** AP, CLEP, IB, institutional tests. Credit by exam does not count as credit earned in residence. **Support services:** Learning center, reduced course load, remedial instruction, study skills assistance, tutoring, writing center.

Majors. **Architecture:** Architecture, interior. **Biology:** General, biochemistry, microbiology. **Business:** Accounting, banking/financial services, business admin, international, management information systems, managerial economics, marketing, real estate. **Communications:** Advertising, digital media, journalism, public relations, radio/tv. **Computer sciences:** Computer science. **Engineering:** Aerospace, civil, computer, electrical, industrial, mechanical, software. **English:** English lit, speech/rhetoric. **Family/consumer sciences:** Child development. **Foreign languages:** General, classics, French, German, Russian, Spanish. **Health:** Athletic training, clinical lab science, nursing (RN). **History:** General. **Math:** General. **Parks/recreation:** Health/fitness. **Philosophy/religion:** Philosophy. **Physical sciences:** Chemistry, geology, physics. **Protective services:** Criminal justice. **Psychology:** General. **Public administration:** Social work. **Social sciences:** Anthropology, economics, political science, sociology. **Visual/performing arts:** Art, art history/conservation, dramatic, studio arts.

Most popular majors. Biology 7%, business/marketing 28%, communications/journalism 6%, engineering/engineering technologies 9%, health sciences 9%, interdisciplinary studies 9%.

Computing on campus. 1,000 workstations in dormitories, library, computer center. Dormitories wired for high-speed internet access and linked to campus network. Commuter students can connect to campus network. Online course registration, online library, helpline, student web hosting, wireless network available.

Student life. **Freshman orientation:** Mandatory. Preregistration for classes offered. One-and-a-half-day sessions held in June, July, August. Students stay in residence halls. **Policies:** Freshmen permitted cars on campus. **Housing:** Coed dorms, single-sex dorms, apartments, fraternity/sorority housing available. $350 deposit. Priority given to students with dependent children. **Activities:** Bands, choral groups, dance, drama, film society, literary magazine, music ensembles, opera, radio station, student government, student newspaper, symphony orchestra, University Democrats, Circle K, Baptist student ministry, international students organization, association of Mexican American students, Vietnamese student association, Wesley Foundation.

Athletics. NCAA. **Intercollegiate:** Baseball M, basketball, cross-country, golf M, softball W, tennis, track and field, volleyball W. **Intramural:** Badminton, basketball, bowling, football (non-tackle), golf, racquetball, soccer, softball, squash, swimming, table tennis, tennis, track and field, volleyball, weight lifting. **Team name:** Mavericks.

Student services. Alcohol/substance abuse counseling, campus ministries, career counseling, services for economically disadvantaged, student employment services, financial aid counseling, health services, legal services, minority student services, on-campus daycare, personal counseling, placement for graduates, veterans' counselor. **Physically disabled:** Services for visually, hearing impaired.

Contact. E-mail: admissions@uta.edu
Phone: (817) 272-6287 Fax: (817) 272-3435
Hans Gatterdam, Director of Admissions & Records, University of Texas at Arlington, Box 19111, Arlington, TX 76019

University of Texas at Austin

Austin, Texas — **CB member**
www.utexas.edu — **CB code: 6882**

- Public 4-year university
- Commuter campus in very large city
- 35,734 degree-seeking undergraduates: 7% part-time, 52% women, 4% African American, 17% Asian American, 16% Hispanic American, 3% international
- 12,672 degree-seeking graduate students
- 51% of applicants admitted
- SAT or ACT with writing, application essay required
- 75% graduate within 6 years

General. Founded in 1883. Regionally accredited. **Degrees:** 8,836 bachelor's awarded; master's, doctoral, first professional offered. **ROTC:** Army, Navy, Air Force. **Location:** 70 miles from San Antonio, 163 miles from Houston. **Calendar:** Semester, extensive summer session. **Full-time faculty:** 2,482 total; 17% minority. **Part-time faculty:** 252 total; 13% minority. **Class size:** 33% < 20, 38% 20-39, 6% 40-49, 13% 50-99, 10% >100. **Special facilities:** Humanities and scientific research centers, observatory, marine science institute, fusion reactor, presidential library and museum, art galleries, performing arts center.

Freshman class profile. 23,925 applied, 12,207 admitted, 6,836 enrolled.

Mid 50% test scores		**Return as sophomores:**	93%
SAT verbal:	540-670	**Out-of-state:**	5%
SAT math:	570-690	**Live on campus:**	54%
ACT:	23-29	**International:**	3%
Rank in top quarter:	92%	**Fraternities:**	12%
Rank in top tenth:	68%	**Sororities:**	16%
End year in good standing:	93%		

Basis for selection. Applicants from top 10% of class from accredited Texas high school automatically admitted with completed application. Off-campus coordinated admission program available for Texans who complete all required high school units and apply immediately upon high school graduation, but are not otherwise eligible for regular admission. Audition required, interview recommended for music program; interview recommended for art, liberal arts honors program.

High school preparation. College-preparatory program recommended. 15.5 units required. Required and recommended units include English 4, mathematics 3-4, social studies 3, science 2-3, foreign language 2-3, academic electives 1.5. Foreign language must be same language; .5 fine arts elective strongly recommended.

2005-2006 Annual costs. Tuition/fees: $6,972; $16,310 out-of-state. Room/board: $6,360. Books/supplies: $800. Personal expenses: $2,150.

2005-2006 Financial aid. Need-based: 4,550 full-time freshmen applied for aid; 4,000 were judged to have need; 3,950 of these received aid. Average need met was 90%. Average scholarship/grant was $6,750; average loan $3,650. 53% of total undergraduate aid awarded as scholarships/grants, 47% as loans/jobs. **Non-need-based:** Awarded to 9,750 full-time undergraduates, including 1,140 freshmen. Scholarships awarded for academics, art, athletics, leadership, music/drama, ROTC, state residency.

Application procedures. Admission: Closing date 2/1 (receipt date). $60 fee, may be waived for applicants with need. Application may be submitted online. Admission notification on a rolling basis beginning on or about 11/15. Must reply by May 1 or within 2 week(s) if notified thereafter. **Financial aid:** Priority date 4/1; no closing date. FAFSA required. Applicants notified on a rolling basis starting 3/15; must reply within 4 week(s) of notification.

Academics. Special study options: Accelerated study, combined bachelor's/graduate degree, cooperative education, distance learning, double major, dual enrollment of high school students, ESL, honors, independent study, internships, liberal arts/career combination, student-designed major, study abroad, teacher certification program, Washington semester. **Credit/placement by examination:** CLEP, IB, institutional tests. **Support services:** Learning center, reduced course load, remedial instruction, study skills assistance, tutoring, writing center.

Majors. Architecture: Architecture. **Area/ethnic studies:** American, Asian, Latin American, Near/Middle Eastern, Russian/Slavic. **Biology:** General, biochemistry, botany, ecology, microbiology, zoology. **Business:** General, accounting, business admin, finance, management information systems, marketing. **Communications:** General, advertising, journalism, public relations, radio/tv. **Computer sciences:** General. **Engineering:** Aerospace, architectural, biomedical, chemical, civil, electrical, mechanical, petroleum. **English:** English lit. **Family/consumer sciences:** General, clothing/textiles, family studies, food/nutrition. **Foreign languages:** General, ancient Greek, Arabic, classics, Czech, East Asian, French, German, Hebrew, Italian, Latin, linguistics, Persian, Portuguese, Russian, Scandinavian, Semitic, Spanish, Turkish. **Health:** Athletic training, clinical lab science, communication disorders, health services, nursing (RN). **History:** General. **Interdisciplinary:** Ancient studies. **Liberal arts:** Arts/sciences, humanities. **Math:** General. **Parks/recreation:** Health/fitness, sports admin. **Philosophy/religion:** Islamic, Judaic, philosophy, religion. **Physical sciences:** Astronomy, chemistry, geology, geophysics, hydrology, physics. **Psychology:** General. **Public administration:** Social work. **Social sciences:** Anthropology, archaeology, economics, geography, political science, sociology, urban studies. **Visual/performing arts:** General, art, art history/conservation, dance, design, dramatic, interior design, music history, music performance, music theory/composition, studio arts.

Most popular majors. Biology 8%, business/marketing 13%, communications/journalism 13%, engineering/engineering technologies 10%, social sciences 16%.

Computing on campus. Dormitories wired for high-speed internet access and linked to campus network. Commuter students can connect to campus network. Online course registration, online library, helpline, repair service, student web hosting, wireless network available.

Student life. Freshman orientation: Available, $105 fee. Held during summer. **Policies:** Freshmen permitted cars on campus. **Housing:** Coed dorms, single-sex dorms, apartments available. $300 nonrefundable deposit. Honors residence and living learning centers available for first-time freshmen. **Activities:** Bands, choral groups, dance, drama, film society, literary magazine, music ensembles, musical theater, opera, radio station, student government, student newspaper, symphony orchestra, TV station, wide variety of religious, political, ethnic, and social service organizations.

Athletics. NCAA. **Intercollegiate:** Baseball M, basketball, cross-country, diving, football (tackle) M, golf, rowing (crew) W, soccer W, softball W, swimming, tennis, track and field, volleyball W. **Intramural:** Badminton, basketball, bowling, football (non-tackle), golf, handball, racquetball, soccer, softball, squash, swimming, table tennis, tennis, track and field, volleyball, weight lifting. **Team name:** Longhorns.

Student services. Adult student services, alcohol/substance abuse counseling, campus ministries, career counseling, services for economically disadvantaged, student employment services, financial aid counseling, health services, legal services, minority student services, on-campus daycare, personal counseling, placement for graduates, veterans' counselor, women's services. **Physically disabled:** Services for visually, speech, hearing impaired. **Learning disabled:** Comprehensive services available.

Contact. Phone: (512) 475-7399
Bruce Walker, Vice Provost and Director of Admissions, University of Texas at Austin, PO Box 8058, Austin, TX 78713-8058

University of Texas at Brownsville

Brownsville, Texas — **CB member**
www.utb.edu — **CB code: 2054**

- Public 4-year university and community college
- Commuter campus in small city
- 10,690 degree-seeking undergraduates
- 880 graduate students

General. Founded in 1977. Regionally accredited. Campus has both lower and upper division students. Close association with Texas Southmost College, which shares campus. **Degrees:** 697 bachelor's awarded; master's offered. **Calendar:** Semester, extensive summer session. **Full-time faculty:** 334 total; 52% have terminal degrees, 48% minority, 42% women. **Part-time faculty:** 297 total; 9% have terminal degrees, 62% minority, 45% women. **Class size:** 59% < 20, 32% 20-39, 3% 40-49, 5% 50-99, less than 1% >100.

Freshman class profile.

Rank in top quarter:	29%	**Out-of-state:**	1%
Rank in top tenth:	16%	**Live on campus:**	1%

Basis for selection. Open admission, but selective for some programs. Special requirements for nursing and allied health programs.

2005-2006 Annual costs. Tuition/fees: $3,895; $12,175 out-of-state. Books/supplies: $534. Personal expenses: $2,188.

Application procedures. Admission: Priority date 3/1; deadline 7/1 (receipt date). No application fee. Application may be submitted online. Admission notification on a rolling basis. **Financial aid:** Priority date 4/1, closing date 8/15. FAFSA required. Applicants notified on a rolling basis; must reply within 4 week(s) of notification.

Academics. Special study options: Combined bachelor's/graduate degree, cooperative education, cross-registration, distance learning, double major, dual enrollment of high school students, ESL, independent study, internships, liberal arts/career combination, teacher certification program. **Credit/placement by examination:** AP, CLEP, IB, institutional tests. **Support services:** Learning center, pre-admission summer program, reduced course load, remedial instruction, study skills assistance, tutoring.

Majors. Biology: General. **Business:** General, accounting, business admin, finance, marketing. **Communications:** General. **Computer sciences:** General, information systems. **Engineering:** Physics. **Engineering technology:** Electrical, industrial, manufacturing, mechanical. **English:** English lit. **Foreign languages:** Spanish. **Health:** Health services, nursing (RN). **History:** General. **Liberal arts:** Arts/sciences. **Math:** General. **Parks/recreation:** Health/fitness. **Physical sciences:** Chemistry, physics. **Protective services:** Corrections, law enforcement admin. **Psychology:** General. **Social sciences:** Political science, sociology. **Visual/performing arts:** Art.

Computing on campus. 650 workstations in dormitories, library, computer center. Dormitories wired for high-speed internet access and linked to campus network. Commuter students can connect to campus network. Online course registration, online library, helpline, repair service, student web hosting, wireless network available.

Student life. Freshman orientation: Available. **Policies:** Freshmen permitted cars on campus. **Housing:** Coed dorms, substance-free housing available. **Activities:** Jazz band, choral groups, dance, music ensembles, student government, student newspaper.

Athletics. NJCAA. **Intercollegiate:** Baseball M, golf, volleyball W. **Team name:** Scorpions.

Student services. Career counseling, services for economically disadvantaged, student employment services, financial aid counseling, health services, minority student services, on-campus daycare, personal counseling, placement for graduates, veterans' counselor. **Physically disabled:** Services for visually, hearing impaired.

Contact. E-mail: admissions@utb.edu
Phone: (956) 882-8295 Toll-free number: (800) 850-0160
Fax: (956) 882-7810
Rene Villarreal, Director of Admissions, University of Texas at Brownsville, 80 Fort Brown, Brownsville, TX 78520

University of Texas at Dallas

Richardson, Texas — **CB member**
www.utdallas.edu — **CB code: 6897**

- Public 4-year university
- Commuter campus in very large city

- 9,243 degree-seeking undergraduates: 29% part-time, 46% women, 7% African American, 20% Asian American, 10% Hispanic American, 1% Native American, 5% international
- 4,331 degree-seeking graduate students
- 51% of applicants admitted
- SAT or ACT with writing required
- 56% graduate within 6 years

General. Founded in 1969. Regionally accredited. Established internships in industrial practice positions with over 200 advanced technology firms located near the university. **Degrees:** 2,020 bachelor's awarded; master's, doctoral offered. **ROTC:** Army, Air Force. **Location:** 18 miles from downtown Dallas. **Calendar:** Semester, extensive summer session. **Full-time faculty:** 457 total; 92% have terminal degrees, 26% minority, 25% women. **Part-time faculty:** 239 total; 61% have terminal degrees, 20% minority, 48% women. **Class size:** 28% < 20, 33% 20-39, 8% 40-49, 25% 50-99, 6% >100. **Special facilities:** Geological information library, history of aviation library, rare book library, philatelic research library, collection of petroleum well logs and associated geological data, center for communications disorders, Holocaust collection, translation library.

Freshman class profile. 5,584 applied, 2,850 admitted, 1,060 enrolled.

Mid 50% test scores		**Rank in top tenth:**	42%
SAT verbal:	540-670	**End year in good standing:**	86%
SAT math:	580-700	**Return as sophomores:**	82%
ACT:	24-29	**Out-of-state:**	4%
GPA 3.50 or higher:	67%	**Live on campus:**	74%
GPA 3.0-3.49:	25%	**International:**	3%
GPA 2.0-2.99:	8%	**Fraternities:**	7%
Rank in top quarter:	75%	**Sororities:**	8%

Basis for selection. 1140 SAT (exclusive of Writing) or 25 ACT, rank in top 25% of class, completion of required high school course work required for automatic admission. 1270 SAT (exclusive of Writing) or 29 ACT required of nonresident applicants. All others reviewed for admission. In-state high school students finishing in top 10% of class automatically admitted to state public universities. Texas Higher Education Assessment test required for some based on high school performance.

High school preparation. 18 units required; 24 recommended. Required and recommended units include English 4, mathematics 3.5-4, social studies 3-4, science 3 (laboratory 3), foreign language 2-3, academic electives 1.5-2.5. 0.5 unit of fine art, 1 unit computer science, 1 unit fine art required.

2005-2006 Annual costs. Tuition/fees: $6,831; $15,111 out-of-state. Room/board: $6,244. Books/supplies: $1,200. Personal expenses: $1,812.

2004-2005 Financial aid. Need-based: 651 full-time freshmen applied for aid; 446 were judged to have need; 446 of these received aid. Average need met was 64%. Average scholarship/grant was $3,996; average loan $4,506. 39% of total undergraduate aid awarded as scholarships/grants, 61% as loans/jobs. **Non-need-based:** Awarded to 1,283 full-time undergraduates, including 252 freshmen. Scholarships awarded for academics.

Application procedures. Admission: Closing date 7/1 (postmark date). $50 fee. Application may be submitted online. Admission notification on a rolling basis. **Financial aid:** Priority date 3/1, closing date 4/12. FAFSA required. Applicants notified by 4/15; must reply within 3 week(s) of notification.

Academics. Special study options: Accelerated study, combined bachelor's/graduate degree, cooperative education, cross-registration, distance learning, double major, dual enrollment of high school students, honors, independent study, internships, student-designed major, study abroad, teacher certification program, Washington semester, weekend college. 3-2 engineering and 2-2 transfer programs. **Credit/placement by examination:** AP, CLEP, IB, institutional tests. 30 credit hours maximum toward bachelor's degree. No limit on lower-level courses, 6 hours limit on upper-level courses. SAT Subject Tests in Math Level I and II and are accepted for advanced placement. **Support services:** Learning center, pre-admission summer program, reduced course load, remedial instruction, study skills assistance, tutoring, writing center.

Majors. Area/ethnic studies: American, women's. **Biology:** General, biochemistry, molecular. **Business:** General, accounting. **Computer sciences:** General. **Engineering:** Electrical, software. **Foreign languages:** Comparative lit. **Health:** Audiology/speech pathology. **History:** General. **Interdisciplinary:** Cognitive science, neuroscience. **Liberal arts:** Arts/sciences. **Math:** General, applied, statistics. **Physical sciences:** Chemistry, geology, physics. **Psychology:** General. **Public administration:** General. **Social sciences:** Criminology, economics, geography, political science, sociology. **Visual/performing arts:** General, studio arts.

Most popular majors. Business/marketing 31%, computer/information sciences 11%, engineering/engineering technologies 9%, interdisciplinary studies 15%, psychology 7%, social sciences 7%.

Computing on campus. 630 workstations in library, computer center. Dormitories linked to campus network. Commuter students can connect to campus network. Online course registration, online library, helpline, wireless network available.

Student life. Freshman orientation: Available, $50 fee. Preregistration for classes offered. New student 1-day sessions held in May. Family 1-day sessions and freshman 2-day sessions held in July and August. **Policies:** Freshmen permitted cars on campus. **Housing:** Apartments available. $100 fully refundable deposit, deadline 6/30. Pets allowed in dorm rooms. 900-unit complex of 1-, 2- and 4-bedroom apartments located on campus; scholarship and graduate students given priority consideration for occupancy. **Activities:** Dance, drama, radio station, student government, student newspaper, College Republicans, campus Hispanic association, African American student alliance, Friendship Association of Chinese Students and Visiting Scholars, Indian students association, multicultural association, Campus Crusade for Christ, Muslim students association, Pacific Asian student association.

Athletics. NCAA. **Intercollegiate:** Baseball M, basketball, cross-country, golf, soccer, softball W, tennis, volleyball W. **Intramural:** Basketball, cheerleading, golf, racquetball, soccer, softball, table tennis, tennis, volleyball. **Team name:** Comets.

Student services. Alcohol/substance abuse counseling, career counseling, student employment services, financial aid counseling, health services, legal services, minority student services, on-campus daycare, personal counseling, placement for graduates, veterans' counselor, women's services. **Physically disabled:** Services for visually, speech, hearing impaired.

Contact. E-mail: admissions-status@utdallas.edu
Phone: (972) 883-2342 Toll-free number: (800) 889-2443
Fax: (972) 883-2599
Bryan Bradford, Director of Admissions, University of Texas at Dallas, Office of Admissions, Richardson, TX 75083-0688

University of Texas at El Paso

El Paso, Texas — CB member
www.utep.edu — CB code: 6829

- Public 4-year university
- Commuter campus in very large city
- 15,806 degree-seeking undergraduates: 31% part-time, 55% women, 2% African American, 1% Asian American, 76% Hispanic American, 10% international
- 2,600 degree-seeking graduate students
- 99% of applicants admitted

General. Founded in 1913. Regionally accredited. Bilingual community, programs, and student body. Located within 100 yards of Mexico. **Degrees:** 1,646 bachelor's awarded; master's, doctoral offered. **ROTC:** Army, Air Force. **Calendar:** Semester, extensive summer session. **Full-time faculty:** 680 total; 32% minority, 38% women. **Part-time faculty:** 379 total; 45% minority, 46% women. **Class size:** 31% < 20, 49% 20-39, 7% 40-49, 10% 50-99, 3% >100. **Special facilities:** Museum, solar energy facility.

Freshman class profile. 4,012 applied, 3,984 admitted, 2,289 enrolled.

Mid 50% test scores		**Rank in top tenth:**	17%
SAT verbal:	400-520	**Return as sophomores:**	69%
SAT math:	400-510	**Out-of-state:**	3%
ACT:	15-20	**Live on campus:**	9%
GPA 3.50 or higher:	100%	**International:**	8%
Rank in top quarter:	41%		

Basis for selection. Minimum GED score of 45, or top half of high school class with 20 ACT or 920 SAT (exclusive of Writing). Provisional admission for in-state residents not meeting these criteria. For students in top quarter of high school class, any score acceptable. SAT or ACT, when required, may be used for counseling. Credit may be given for selected SAT Subject Tests.

High school preparation. 21 units recommended. Recommended units include English 4, mathematics 3, social studies 2, history 2, science 3 and foreign language 2. One computer science, 1 fine arts, 1 additional math for science and engineering majors.

2005-2006 Annual costs. Tuition/fees: $4,888; $13,218 out-of-state. Mexican citizens who show need may qualify for in-state tuition. Books/supplies: $890. Personal expenses: $1,376.

2004-2005 Financial aid. **Need-based:** 1,950 full-time freshmen applied for aid; 1,536 were judged to have need; 1,519 of these received aid. Average need met was 71%. Average scholarship/grant was $5,068; average loan $2,773. 43% of total undergraduate aid awarded as scholarships/grants, 57% as loans/jobs. **Non-need-based:** Awarded to 1,413 full-time undergraduates, including 432 freshmen. Scholarships awarded for academics, alumni affiliation, art, athletics, job skills, leadership, minority status, music/drama, religious affiliation, ROTC, state residency. **Additional information:** Emergency loans available.

Application procedures. **Admission:** Priority date 5/1; deadline 7/31 (postmark date). No application fee. Application may be submitted online. Admission notification on a rolling basis. Notification of early action applicants when admission file is complete. **Financial aid:** Closing date 3/15. FAFSA, institutional form required. Applicants notified by 6/30; must reply within 2 week(s) of notification.

Academics. **Special study options:** Accelerated study, combined bachelor's/graduate degree, cooperative education, cross-registration, distance learning, double major, dual enrollment of high school students, ESL, exchange student, honors, independent study, internships, study abroad, teacher certification program, weekend college. **Credit/placement by examination:** AP, CLEP, IB, institutional tests. **Support services:** Learning center, preadmission summer program, reduced course load, remedial instruction, study skills assistance, tutoring, writing center.

Majors. **Area/ethnic studies:** Hispanic-American/Latino/Chicano, Latin American. **Biology:** General, microbiology. **Business:** General, accounting, business admin, finance, management information systems, managerial economics, marketing, operations. **Communications:** General, advertising, journalism, media studies, public relations. **Computer sciences:** General. **Conservation:** Environmental science. **Education:** General, elementary, middle, special. **Engineering:** General, civil, electrical, industrial, mechanical, metallurgical. **English:** Creative writing. **Foreign languages:** Comparative lit, French, German, linguistics, Spanish. **Health:** Audiology/speech pathology, clinical lab science, community health services, health services, nursing (RN). **History:** General. **Interdisciplinary:** Biological/physical sciences. **Liberal arts:** Arts/sciences. **Math:** General, applied, statistics. **Parks/recreation:** Health/fitness. **Philosophy/religion:** Philosophy. **Physical sciences:** General, chemistry, geology, geophysics, physics. **Protective services:** Criminal justice. **Psychology:** General. **Public administration:** Social work. **Social sciences:** Anthropology, political science, sociology. **Visual/performing arts:** Art, ceramics, dance, dramatic, drawing, graphic design, metal/jewelry, music performance, music theory/composition, painting, piano/organ, printmaking, sculpture, studio arts, voice/opera.

Most popular majors. Biology 6%, business/marketing 21%, communications/journalism 6%, engineering/engineering technologies 10%, health sciences 10%, interdisciplinary studies 16%, security/protective services 6%.

Computing on campus. 2,500 workstations in library, computer center, student center. Dormitories wired for high-speed internet access. Commuter students can connect to campus network. Online course registration, online library, helpline, student web hosting, wireless network available.

Student life. **Freshman orientation:** Available. Preregistration for classes offered. 3-5 day program. **Policies:** Freshmen permitted cars on campus. **Housing:** Special housing for disabled, apartments available. $200 deposit. **Activities:** Bands, choral groups, dance, drama, film society, literary magazine, music ensembles, musical theater, opera, radio station, student government, student newspaper, symphony orchestra, Black Student Coalition, Mexican student organizations, Society of Hispanic Professional Engineers.

Athletics. NCAA. **Intercollegiate:** Basketball, cross-country, football (tackle) M, golf, rifle, soccer W, softball W, tennis, track and field, volleyball W. **Intramural:** Badminton, baseball M, basketball, bowling, fencing, football (tackle) M, golf, gymnastics, handball, racquetball, skiing, soccer, softball, squash, swimming, table tennis, tennis, track and field, volleyball, water polo, wrestling M. **Team name:** Miners.

Student services. Alcohol/substance abuse counseling, campus ministries, career counseling, student employment services, financial aid counseling, health services, on-campus daycare, personal counseling, placement for graduates, veterans' counselor, women's services. **Physically disabled:** Services for visually, speech, hearing impaired.

Contact. E-mail: futureminer@utep.edu
Phone: (915) 747-5890 Toll-free number: (877) 746-4636
Fax: (915) 747-8893
Tammie Aragon-Campos, Director of Admissions, University of Texas at El Paso, 500 West University Avenue, El Paso, TX 79968-0510

University of Texas at San Antonio

San Antonio, Texas **CB member**
www.utsa.edu **CB code: 6919**

- Public 4-year university
- Commuter campus in very large city
- 23,282 degree-seeking undergraduates: 25% part-time, 53% women, 7% African American, 5% Asian American, 46% Hispanic American, 1% Native American, 2% international
- 3,609 degree-seeking graduate students
- 99% of applicants admitted
- SAT or ACT with writing required

General. Founded in 1969. Regionally accredited. Second campus in downtown area. **Degrees:** 3,258 bachelor's awarded; master's, doctoral offered. **ROTC:** Army, Air Force. **Location:** 15 miles from downtown. **Calendar:** Semester, limited summer session. **Full-time faculty:** 860 total; 26% minority, 42% women. **Part-time faculty:** 223 total; 26% minority, 44% women. **Class size:** 25% < 20, 44% 20-39, 8% 40-49, 14% 50-99, 9% >100. **Special facilities:** Institute of Texan cultures, center for archaelogical research, neuroscience research center, center for water research, center for lasers and materials science, center for economic development, culture and policy institute, institute for music research, center for professional excellence.

Freshman class profile. 9,144 applied, 9,087 admitted, 4,452 enrolled.

Mid 50% test scores			
SAT verbal:	450-560	Return as sophomores:	58%
SAT math:	460-570	Out-of-state:	3%
ACT:	18-23	Live on campus:	6%
Rank in top quarter:	35%	International:	2%
Rank in top tenth:	9%	Fraternities:	2%
End year in good standing:	56%	Sororities:	2%

Basis for selection. Texas residents who graduate in top 10% of high school graduating class admitted, regardless of ACT or SAT scores. Those not in top 10% must meet appropriate ACT or SAT scores based on class rank. If test score/rank criteria not met, additional factors may be taken into consideration. Out-of-state applicants must graduate in top half of graduating class in addition to meeting corresponding ACT or SAT score requirements. **Homeschooled:** Conditional admissions decision based on SAT score over 970 (exclusive of Writing) plus high school educational record (courses taken and grades earned) signed and dated by person responsible for conducting educational program. Upon high school graduation, final high school record indicating graduation date signed and dated by responsible educator must be submitted.

High school preparation. 16.5 units recommended. Recommended units include English 4, mathematics 3, social studies 3.5, science 3, foreign language 2 and academic electives 1. One fine arts recommended.

2005-2006 Annual costs. Tuition/fees: $5,544; $13,824 out-of-state. Room/board: $6,965. Books/supplies: $1,000. Personal expenses: $2,162.

2004-2005 Financial aid. **Need-based:** 3,518 full-time freshmen applied for aid; 2,619 were judged to have need; 2,490 of these received aid. Average need met was 56%. Average scholarship/grant was $4,195; average loan $2,356. 36% of total undergraduate aid awarded as scholarships/grants, 64% as loans/jobs. **Non-need-based:** Awarded to 2,713 full-time undergraduates, including 986 freshmen. Scholarships awarded for academics, alumni affiliation, art, athletics, job skills, leadership, music/drama, ROTC, state residency.

Application procedures. **Admission:** Priority date 4/1; deadline 7/1 (receipt date). $30 fee, may be waived for applicants with need. Application may be submitted online. Admission notification on a rolling basis beginning on or about 9/1. **Financial aid:** Priority date 3/31; no closing date. FAFSA, institutional form required. Applicants notified on a rolling basis starting 4/1; must reply within 4 week(s) of notification.

Academics. Freshman Initiative includes learning communities and freshman seminar program, enhancing academic services for new students in order to increase retention and success in college. **Special study options:** Distance learning, double major, dual enrollment of high school students, ESL, exchange student, honors, independent study, internships, liberal arts/career combination, study abroad, teacher certification program. 2-2 programs with Alamo Community College District, Southwest Texas Junior College, Laredo Junior College, Victoria College, Del Mar College, Coastal Bend Community College, Austin Community College; telecampus agreement with UT System. **Credit/placement by examination:** AP, CLEP, institutional tests. Some departments have limits on number of credits earned by examination. **Support services:** Learning center, pre-admission summer program, remedial instruction, study skills assistance, tutoring, writing center.

Majors. **Architecture:** Architecture, interior. **Area/ethnic studies:** American, Hispanic-American/Latino/Chicano. **Biology:** General. **Business:** General, accounting, actuarial science, business admin, finance, human resources, international, management information systems, management science, managerial economics, marketing, operations, sales/distribution, tourism/travel. **Communications:** General, media studies, public relations. **Computer sciences:** General, security. **Conservation:** Environmental science.

Engineering: Civil, computer, electrical, mechanical. **English:** English lit, speech/rhetoric, technical writing. **Foreign languages:** Classics, French, German, Spanish. **Health:** Clinical lab science, health services. **History:** General. **Interdisciplinary:** Biological/physical sciences. **Liberal arts:** Humanities. **Math:** General, statistics. **Parks/recreation:** Health/fitness. **Philosophy/religion:** Philosophy. **Physical sciences:** Chemistry, geology, physics. **Protective services:** Criminal justice. **Psychology:** General. **Social sciences:** Anthropology, geography, political science, sociology. **Visual/performing arts:** Art, art history/conservation, music management, music performance, music theory/composition, studio arts.

Most popular majors. Biology 9%, business/marketing 30%, interdisciplinary studies 12%, psychology 8%, security/protective services 6%, social sciences 6%.

Computing on campus. 550 workstations in dormitories, library, computer center, student center. Dormitories wired for high-speed internet access and linked to campus network. Commuter students can connect to campus network. Online course registration, online library, helpline, repair service, student web hosting, wireless network available.

Student life. **Freshman orientation:** Mandatory, $55 fee. Preregistration for classes offered. One-day sessions held throughout the year; optional 2-day camp held in August. **Policies:** Freshmen permitted cars on campus. **Housing:** Coed dorms, apartments available. $200 partly refundable deposit. **Activities:** Bands, choral groups, drama, literary magazine, music ensembles, musical theater, opera, student government, student newspaper, symphony orchestra, IDS student association, pre-med society, Golden Key national honor society, Intervarsity Christian Fellowship, S/B Alph Chi national honor society, Catholic student association, Mortar Board national college senior honor society, Texas Association of Chicanos in Higher Education.

Athletics. NCAA. **Intercollegiate:** Baseball M, basketball, cross-country, golf, soccer W, softball W, tennis, track and field, volleyball W. **Intramural:** Badminton, basketball, bowling, football (non-tackle), golf, racquetball, soccer, softball, table tennis, tennis, volleyball, weight lifting. **Team name:** Roadrunners.

Student services. Career counseling, student employment services, financial aid counseling, health services, personal counseling, placement for graduates, veterans' counselor. **Physically disabled:** Services for visually, speech, hearing impaired.

Contact. E-mail: prospects@utsa.edu
Phone: (210) 458-8000 Toll-free number: (800) 669-0919
Fax: (210) 458-2001
George Norton, Director of Admissions, University of Texas at San Antonio, 6900 North Loop 1604 West, San Antonio, TX 78249-0617

University of Texas at Tyler

Tyler, Texas — **CB member**
www.uttyler.edu — **CB code: 0389**

- Public 4-year university
- Commuter campus in small city
- 4,618 degree-seeking undergraduates: 23% part-time, 59% women, 10% African American, 2% Asian American, 6% Hispanic American, 1% Native American, 1% international
- 984 degree-seeking graduate students
- 75% of applicants admitted
- SAT or ACT (ACT writing optional) required
- 52% graduate within 6 years

General. Founded in 1971. Regionally accredited. Off-campus sites at Palestine, Mexia. Internet courses and telecampus available. **Degrees:** 711 bachelor's awarded; master's offered. **Location:** 80 miles from Dallas. **Calendar:** Semester, limited summer session. **Full-time faculty:** 218 total; 72% have terminal degrees, 10% minority, 46% women. **Part-time faculty:** 142 total; 31% have terminal degrees, 4% minority, 53% women. **Class size:** 42% < 20, 38% 20-39, 7% 40-49, 13% 50-99, less than 1% >100. **Special facilities:** Desktop manufacturing lab to demonstrate key manufacturing technologies, computer-based virtual lab instruments to provide specialized measurement capabilities.

Freshman class profile. 1,497 applied, 1,127 admitted, 549 enrolled.

Mid 50% test scores			
SAT verbal:	480-580	Return as sophomores:	60%
SAT math:	490-600	Out-of-state:	3%
ACT:	20-25	Live on campus:	46%

Basis for selection. Top 10% accepted automatically, others admitted based on ACT/SAT scores and high school preparation.

High school preparation. Required and recommended units include English 4, mathematics 3-4, social studies 3, science 3 and foreign language 2. Math requirement must be algebra I and higher. 4 mathematics recommended for science, engineering, and other technical fields.

2005-2006 Annual costs. Tuition/fees: $4,244; $12,524 out-of-state.

Financial aid. **Non-need-based:** Scholarships awarded for academics, art, leadership, music/drama. **Additional information:** Apply early for all programs.

Application procedures. **Admission:** No deadline. No application fee. Application may be submitted online. Admission notification on a rolling basis. Must reply by May 1 or within 4 week(s) if notified thereafter. **Financial aid:** Priority date 4/1; no closing date. FAFSA required. Applicants notified on a rolling basis starting 4/15; must reply within 3 week(s) of notification.

Academics. **Special study options:** Cooperative education, distance learning, double major, ESL, exchange student, independent study, internships, student-designed major, study abroad, teacher certification program, weekend college. **Credit/placement by examination:** AP, CLEP, IB. AP, CLEP and International Baccalaureate awarded transfer credit with no maximum limit. **Support services:** Learning center, study skills assistance, tutoring, writing center.

Majors. **Biology:** General. **Business:** Accounting, business admin, finance, managerial economics, marketing, sales/distribution. **Communications:** Journalism. **Computer sciences:** General. **Engineering:** Civil, electrical, mechanical. **Engineering technology:** General, industrial, occupational safety. **English:** English lit, speech/rhetoric. **Foreign languages:** General, Spanish. **Health:** Clinical lab science, community health services, nursing (RN). **History:** General. **Math:** General. **Parks/recreation:** Health/fitness. **Physical sciences:** Chemistry. **Protective services:** Criminal justice. **Psychology:** General. **Social sciences:** Political science, sociology. **Visual/performing arts:** Art.

Most popular majors. Business/marketing 20%, health sciences 18%, interdisciplinary studies 18%.

Computing on campus. 175 workstations in library, computer center, student center. Dormitories wired for high-speed internet access and linked to campus network. Online course registration, online library, wireless network available.

Student life. **Freshman orientation:** Mandatory, $35 fee. Preregistration for classes offered. One-day orientation in summer for students and parents. **Policies:** Freshmen permitted cars on campus. **Housing:** Coed dorms, apartments available. **Activities:** Bands, choral groups, drama, film society, literary magazine, music ensembles, musical theater, opera, student government, student newspaper, campus Bible study fellowship, Baptist student ministry, University Democrats, University Republicans, criminal justice club, Nurses Christian Fellowship, foreign language club, Webb Historical Society, press club.

Athletics. NCAA. **Intercollegiate:** Baseball M, basketball, cheerleading, cross-country, golf, soccer, softball W, tennis, volleyball W. **Intramural:** Baseball M, basketball, bowling, football (non-tackle), football (tackle), golf, racquetball, soccer, softball, swimming, table tennis, tennis, volleyball W. **Team name:** Patriots.

Student services. Adult student services, alcohol/substance abuse counseling, career counseling, student employment services, financial aid counseling, health services, personal counseling, veterans' counselor. **Physically disabled:** Services for visually, speech, hearing impaired.

Contact. E-mail: admissions@mail.uttyl.edu
Phone: (903) 566-7202 Toll-free number: (800) 888-9537
Fax: (903) 566-7068
Jim Hutto, Dean of Enrollment Management, University of Texas at Tyler, 3900 University Boulevard, Tyler, TX 75799

University of Texas Health Science Center at Houston

Houston, Texas
www.uth.tmc.edu — **CB code: 6888**

- Public upper-division university and health science college
- Commuter campus in very large city
- Interview required

General. Founded in 1972. Regionally accredited. Located in the Texas Medical Center. **Degrees:** 177 bachelor's awarded; master's, doctoral, first professional offered. **Location:** 5 miles from downtown. **Calendar:** Semester, limited summer session. **Full-time faculty:** 925 total. **Part-time faculty:** 275 total.

Student profile. 380 degree-seeking undergraduates, 3,000 graduate students. 70% entered as juniors.

Basis for selection. College transcript, interview required. Applicants must submit official transcript from all previous institutions. Application closing dates/admissions policies vary by program. Dental hygiene application closing date: December 31. Minimum number of credits: 28. Nursing application closing date: January 1. Minimum number of credits: 60. Transfer accepted as sophomores, juniors.

2005-2006 Annual costs. Tuition/fees: $5,602; $17,268 out-of-state. Nursing program students must attend for full calendar year (fall, spring, summer semesters). Room/board: $6,060. Books/supplies: $1,050. Personal expenses: $2,964.

Financial aid. All financial aid based on need.

Application procedures. Admission: Deadline 12/31. $30 fee. Application may be submitted online. **Financial aid:** FAFSA, institutional form required.

Academics. Upper division bachelor's program for nursing, with accelerated RN-master's program. **Special study options:** Accelerated study, combined bachelor's/graduate degree, distance learning. **Credit/placement by examination:** AP, CLEP. All CLEP must appear on college transcript with credit hours and grade.

Majors. Health: Dental hygiene, nursing (RN).

Computing on campus. PC or laptop required. Helpline available.

Student life. Housing: Apartments available. University operates apartment complex as only student housing available. Complex located approximately 1 mile from campus. **Activities:** Student government.

Student services. Adult student services, alcohol/substance abuse counseling, financial aid counseling, health services, on-campus daycare, personal counseling. **Physically disabled:** Services for visually, hearing impaired.

Contact. E-mail: admissions@uth.tmc.edu
Phone: (713) 500-3361 Fax: (713) 500-3356
Carrie Streeter, Associate Registrar, University of Texas Health Science Center at Houston, Box 20036, Houston, TX 77225

University of Texas Health Science Center at San Antonio

San Antonio, Texas — CB member
www.uthscsa.edu — CB code: 6908

- Public upper-division university and health science college
- Commuter campus in very large city

General. Founded in 1969. Regionally accredited. Located in South Texas Medical Center. **Degrees:** 351 bachelor's awarded; master's, doctoral, first professional offered. **Location:** 10 miles from downtown. **Calendar:** Semester, limited summer session. **Full-time faculty:** 1,154 total. **Part-time faculty:** 355 total.

Student profile. 676 degree-seeking undergraduates. 99% entered as juniors, 1% entered as seniors.

Basis for selection. High school transcript, college transcript required. Admission varies with each program. In many cases, academic records and interview required. Application closing and priority dates vary with each program. Transfer accepted as juniors.

2005-2006 Annual costs. Tuition/fees: $3,260; $11,540 out-of-state. Tuition and fees vary by program. Books/supplies: $850. Personal expenses: $1,100.

Financial aid. Need-based: 19% of total undergraduate aid awarded as scholarships/grants, 81% as loans/jobs. **Additional information:** Students strongly advised to provide parental information on need analysis form regardless of dependency status.

Application procedures. Admission: Application fees vary from $10 to $55 depending on program. **Financial aid:** FAFSA, institutional form required.

Academics. Special study options: Combined bachelor's/graduate degree, cross-registration, internships. Pharmacy program with University of Texas-Austin; joint degree program with University of Texas-San Antonio allied health sciences; joint PhD nursing program with Texas Tech University. **Credit/placement by examination:** CLEP, institutional tests.

Majors. Health: Clinical lab science, dental hygiene, dental lab technology, nursing (RN), physician assistant, respiratory therapy technology.

Computing on campus. 50 workstations in library. Commuter students can connect to campus network. Helpline, wireless network available.

Student life. Activities: Student government, student newspaper, Texas Association of Mexican-American Medical Students, Latin-American Nursing Student Association, Diversified Dental Students.

Athletics. Intramural: Baseball M, basketball, softball, tennis, volleyball.

Student services. Financial aid counseling, health services, personal counseling.

Contact. E-mail: registrars@uthscsa.edu
Phone: (210) 567-2621 Fax: (210) 567-2685
Debra Goode, Registrar, University of Texas Health Science Center at San Antonio, 7703 Floyd Curl Drive, San Antonio, TX 78229

University of Texas Medical Branch at Galveston

Galveston, Texas
www.utmb.edu — CB code: 6887

- Public upper-division health science and nursing college
- Commuter campus in small city

General. Founded in 1881. Regionally accredited. **Degrees:** 223 bachelor's awarded; master's, doctoral, first professional offered. **Location:** 50 miles from Houston. **Calendar:** Semester, limited summer session. **Full-time faculty:** 95 total. **Part-time faculty:** 10 total.

Student profile. 500 degree-seeking undergraduates, 1,673 degree-seeking graduate students.

Women:	78%	**Out-of-state:**	1%
Part-time:	46%	**25 or older:**	61%

Basis for selection. College transcript required. Students with 60 hours from accredited college or university considered. Nonresident enrollment limited by legislature to not more than 10% of any class. Transfer decisions based on competitive comparison of transcripts, allied health experience, departmental testing, and personal interviews. Specific prerequisites and application closing dates vary by program. Transfer accepted as juniors.

2005-2006 Annual costs. Tuition/fees: $3,401; $11,681 out-of-state. Required fees and tuition vary by program.

Financial aid. Need-based: 7% of total undergraduate aid awarded as scholarships/grants, 93% as loans/jobs. **Non-need-based:** Scholarships awarded for academics, minority status, state residency.

Application procedures. Admission: Rolling admission. $30 fee. Application may be submitted online. Application closing dates vary with school and program. **Financial aid:** FAFSA required.

Academics. Institution located in a medical complex. Curriculum provides clinical experience in 6 hospitals, 85 clinics, Shriners Burn Institute, and school for children with cerebral palsy. **Special study options:** Distance learning, independent study, internships. **Credit/placement by examination:** AP, CLEP, IB. 30 credit hours maximum toward bachelor's degree. **Support services:** Learning center, pre-admission summer program, reduced course load, remedial instruction, study skills assistance, tutoring.

Majors. Health: Clinical lab science, nursing (RN), respiratory therapy technology.

Computing on campus. Dormitories wired for high-speed internet access and linked to campus network. Commuter students can connect to campus network. Online course registration, online library, helpline, repair service, wireless network available.

Student life. Housing: Coed dorms, apartments, fraternity/sorority housing available. **Activities:** Student government, student newspaper, Baptist Student Ministry, Wesley Foundation, Newman Center, sports clubs, Christian Medical and Dental Society, Jewish Student and Faculty Organization, multicultural awareness council, student national medical association, Texas Association of Latin American Medical Students.

Athletics. **Intramural:** Basketball, football (non-tackle), soccer, softball, volleyball.

Student services. Alcohol/substance abuse counseling, campus ministries, career counseling, student employment services, financial aid counseling, health services, legal services, on-campus daycare, personal counseling, veterans' counselor, women's services. **Physically disabled:** Services for visually, speech, hearing impaired.

Contact. E-mail: enrollment.services@utmb.edu
Phone: (409) 772-1215 Fax: (409) 772-4466
Vicki Brewer, Registrar, University of Texas Medical Branch at Galveston, 301 University Boulevard, Galveston, TX 77555-1305

University of Texas of the Permian Basin

Odessa, Texas — **CB member**
www.utpb.edu — **CB code: 0448**

- Public 4-year university
- Commuter campus in small city
- 2,621 degree-seeking undergraduates
- 785 graduate students
- 95% of applicants admitted
- SAT or ACT (ACT writing optional) required

General. Founded in 1969. Regionally accredited. **Degrees:** 452 bachelor's awarded; master's offered. **Location:** 150 miles from Lubbock, 350 miles from Dallas. **Calendar:** Semester, extensive summer session. **Full-time faculty:** 105 total. **Part-time faculty:** 55 total. **Class size:** 43% < 20, 42% 20-39, 7% 40-49, 8% 50-99, less than 1% >100.

Freshman class profile. 547 applied, 520 admitted, 264 enrolled.

Mid 50% test scores		**ACT:**	19-24
SAT verbal:	430-560	**Out-of-state:**	1%
SAT math:	430-560	**Live on campus:**	38%

Basis for selection. Secondary school record, class rank, test scores important. Foreign students whose native language is not English must take TOEFL. Requirement may be waived for non-English speakers transferring from a US college or high school.

High school preparation. 20 units required. Required and recommended units include English 4, mathematics 3, social studies 2, history 1, science 2, foreign language 2 and academic electives 6. 1 English unit in developmental writing recommended.

2005-2006 Annual costs. Tuition/fees: $4,147; $12,427 out-of-state. New Mexico residents pay $4,170 for full-year tuition or $139 per-credit-hour. Room/board: $4,058. Books/supplies: $555. Personal expenses: $1,375.

Financial aid. **Non-need-based:** Scholarships awarded for academics.

Application procedures. **Admission:** Closing date 7/15. No application fee. Admission notification on a rolling basis. **Financial aid:** Priority date 5/1; no closing date. FAFSA, institutional form required. Applicants notified on a rolling basis starting 6/1; must reply within 2 week(s) of notification.

Academics. **Special study options:** Distance learning, double major, independent study, internships, teacher certification program. **Credit/placement by examination:** CLEP, institutional tests. 28 credit hours maximum toward bachelor's degree. Credit/placement awarded on AP or CLEP exams, special exams administered by School of Business. **Support services:** Learning center, reduced course load, remedial instruction, study skills assistance, writing center.

Majors. **Biology:** General. **Business:** Accounting, business admin, finance, managerial economics. **Communications:** General. **Computer sciences:** General, information systems. **Conservation:** Environmental studies. **English:** English lit. **Family/consumer sciences:** Family studies. **Foreign languages:** Spanish. **History:** General. **Liberal arts:** Arts/sciences. **Math:** General. **Parks/recreation:** Health/fitness. **Physical sciences:** Chemistry, geology, planetary. **Psychology:** General. **Social sciences:** Criminology, political science, sociology. **Visual/performing arts:** Art.

Computing on campus. 50 workstations in dormitories, library, computer center, student center. Dormitories linked to campus network. Commuter students can connect to campus network. Online course registration, student web hosting, wireless network available.

Student life. **Freshman orientation:** Available. Preregistration for classes offered. 3 separate sessions in June, July and August, lasting at least 2 days with some meals, refreshments provided. Limited lodging for out-of-town students. **Policies:** Freshmen permitted cars on campus. **Housing:** Special housing for disabled, apartments available. $100 deposit. **Activities:** Dance, literary magazine, student government, student newspaper, Baptist student ministries, Genesis Bible study, political science club, black student organization, students in philanthropy, Catholic student organization.

Athletics. NAIA. **Intercollegiate:** Basketball, cheerleading W, soccer, softball W, swimming, volleyball W. **Intramural:** Badminton, baseball M, basketball, bowling, golf, handball, racquetball, rugby M, soccer, softball, swimming, table tennis, tennis, volleyball, weight lifting. **Team name:** Falcons.

Student services. Campus ministries, career counseling, student employment services, financial aid counseling, personal counseling, placement for graduates, veterans' counselor. **Physically disabled:** Services for visually, speech, hearing impaired.

Contact. E-mail: admissions@utpb.edu
Phone: (432) 552-2605 Toll-free number: (866) 552-8872
Fax: (432) 552-3605
Vickie Gomez, Director of Admissions, University of Texas of the Permian Basin, 4901 East University Boulevard, Odessa, TX 79762

University of Texas Southwestern Medical Center at Dallas

Dallas, Texas
www.utsouthwestern.edu — **CB code: 0273**

- Public upper-division university and health science college
- Commuter campus in very large city
- 52% of applicants admitted
- Application essay required

General. Founded in 1943. Regionally accredited. Four teaching hospitals adjoin campus. **Degrees:** 49 bachelor's awarded; master's, doctoral, first professional offered. **Articulation:** Agreements with Dallas County Community College District, Collin County Community College, Tarrant County College District. **Location:** 3 miles from downtown. **Calendar:** Semester, limited summer session. **Full-time faculty:** 60 total. **Part-time faculty:** 45 total. **Class size:** 88% < 20, 12% 20-39.

Student profile. 116 degree-seeking undergraduates, 2,257 degree-seeking graduate students. 73 applied as first time-transfer students, 38 admitted, 37 enrolled. 92% entered as juniors, 8% entered as seniors.

Women:	66%	**International:**	11%
African American:	10%	**Part-time:**	16%
Asian American:	15%	**Out-of-state:**	7%
Hispanic American:	15%	**25 or older:**	63%

Basis for selection. College transcript, application essay required. Application closing dates vary by program. No limit on transferable credits. Students must complete prescribed professional curriculum and be Texas Core Curriculum complete. Transfer accepted as juniors, seniors.

2006-2007 Annual costs. Tuition/fees (projected): $3,810; $12,150 out-of-state. Books/supplies: $750.

Financial aid. **Need-based:** Average need met was 86%. 17% of total undergraduate aid awarded as scholarships/grants, 83% as loans/jobs.

Application procedures. **Admission:** Rolling admission. $10 fee. Application may be submitted online.

Academics. Offers 2-year upper division baccalaureate and master's programs in allied health professions. **Special study options:** Cross-registration, distance learning, independent study, internships. **Credit/placement by examination:** CLEP, institutional tests. Credit granted in English, government and history via advanced standing exams. Cannot exceed 3 semester hours in each subject.

Majors. **Health:** Clinical lab science, dietetics, health care admin, orthotics/prosthetics, vocational rehab counseling.

Computing on campus. 150 workstations in library, computer center. Commuter students can connect to campus network. Online library, helpline available.

Student life. **Activities:** Student Dietetic Association, student membership in American Physical Therapy Association, American Academy of Physician Assistants, American Dietetic Association, American Society for Medical Technology, National Rehabilitation Association, American Society of Allied Health Professions.

Athletics. **Intramural:** Basketball, golf, softball, table tennis, tennis, volleyball.

Student services. Career counseling, financial aid counseling, health services, personal counseling, placement for graduates, veterans' counselor.

Contact. E-mail: admissions@utsouthwestern.edu
Phone: (214) 648-5617 Fax: (214) 648-3289
J. Scott Wright, Director of Admissions, University of Texas Southwestern Medical Center at Dallas, 5323 Harry Hines Boulevard, Dallas, TX 75390-9162

University of Texas: Pan American

Edinburg, Texas **CB member**
www.utpa.edu **CB code: 6570**

- Public 4-year university
- Commuter campus in small city
- 14,129 degree-seeking undergraduates: 25% part-time, 58% women, 1% Asian American, 88% Hispanic American, 4% international
- 2,106 degree-seeking graduate students
- SAT or ACT (ACT writing optional) required

General. Founded in 1927. Regionally accredited. Hispanic Serving Institution. **Degrees:** 1,987 bachelor's awarded; master's, doctoral offered. **ROTC:** Army, Air Force. **Location:** 250 miles from San Antonio, 300 miles from Austin. **Calendar:** Semester, extensive summer session. **Full-time faculty:** 587 total; 46% minority, 39% women. **Part-time faculty:** 119 total; 67% minority, 49% women. **Class size:** 19% < 20, 58% 20-39, 9% 40-49, 14% 50-99, less than 1% >100. **Special facilities:** Coastal studies laboratory on South Padre Island.

Freshman class profile. 2,434 enrolled.

Mid 50% test scores			
SAT verbal:	410-520	Rank in top tenth:	21%
SAT math:	420-530	End year in good standing:	59%
ACT:	16-21	Return as sophomores:	68%
Rank in top quarter:	48%	Out-of-state:	1%
		International:	5%

Basis for selection. For regular admission, rank in top quartile of class or acceptable ACT/SAT scores required. Students who do not meet criteria for regular or clear admission placed in PEP (Provisional Enrollment Program).

High school preparation. 24 units required. Required units include English 4, mathematics 3, social studies 4, science 3, foreign language 2 and academic electives 4. Economics .5, health education .5, fine arts 1, speech .5, technology 1.

2006-2007 Annual costs. Tuition/fees (projected): $4,160; $12,410 out-of-state. Mexican citizens may be eligible for in-state tuition rates. Room/board: $5,095. Books/supplies: $600. Personal expenses: $3,000.

2004-2005 Financial aid. **Need-based:** 1,463 full-time freshmen applied for aid; 1,390 were judged to have need; 1,377 of these received aid. Average need met was 73%. Average scholarship/grant was $6,958; average loan $1,449. 67% of total undergraduate aid awarded as scholarships/grants, 33% as loans/jobs. **Non-need-based:** Awarded to 612 full-time undergraduates, including 126 freshmen. Scholarships awarded for academics, alumni affiliation, art, athletics, leadership, music/drama, ROTC, state residency.

Application procedures. **Admission:** Priority date 2/1; deadline 8/11 (receipt date). No application fee. Application may be submitted online. Admission notification on a rolling basis. **Financial aid:** Closing date 3/1. FAFSA required. Applicants notified on a rolling basis starting 3/15; must reply within 2 week(s) of notification.

Academics. **Special study options:** Combined bachelor's/graduate degree, cooperative education, distance learning, double major, dual enrollment of high school students, ESL, exchange student, honors, independent study, internships, study abroad, teacher certification program, weekend college. Concurrent enrollment (high school students taking limited number of college classes either on campus or through distance learning). **Credit/placement by examination:** AP, CLEP, IB, institutional tests. 45 credit hours maximum toward bachelor's degree. **Support services:** Learning center, pre-admission summer program, remedial instruction, study skills assistance, tutoring, writing center.

Majors. **Area/ethnic studies:** American, Hispanic-American/Latino/Chicano. **Biology:** General. **Business:** Accounting, business admin, finance, international, management information systems, marketing. **Communications:** General, journalism. **Computer sciences:** General, computer science. **Engineering:** Electrical, manufacturing, mechanical. **English:** English lit. **Foreign languages:** Spanish. **Health:** Audiology/speech pathology, clinical lab science, dietetics, health services, nursing (RN), physician assistant, substance abuse counseling, vocational rehab counseling. **History:** General. **Interdisciplinary:** Biological/physical sciences. **Math:** General. **Parks/recreation:** Health/fitness. **Philosophy/religion:** Philosophy. **Physical sciences:** Chemistry, physics. **Protective services:** Law enforcement admin. **Psychology:** General. **Public administration:** Social work. **Social sciences:** General, anthropology, economics, political science, sociology. **Visual/performing arts:** Dance, dramatic, illustration, studio arts.

Most popular majors. Biology 7%, business/marketing 18%, health sciences 11%, interdisciplinary studies 20%, security/protective services 7%, social sciences 7%.

Computing on campus. 900 workstations in dormitories, library, computer center. Dormitories wired for high-speed internet access and linked to campus network. Commuter students can connect to campus network. Online course registration, helpline, wireless network available.

Student life. **Freshman orientation:** Mandatory, $15 fee. Preregistration for classes offered. Several 1-day sessions held prior to beginning of each semester. **Policies:** Freshmen permitted cars on campus. **Housing:** Coed dorms, single-sex dorms, apartments available. $75 fully refundable deposit. **Activities:** Bands, choral groups, dance, drama, music ensembles, musical theater, student government, student newspaper, symphony orchestra, United Methodist campus ministries, Episcopal Canterbury Association, Latter-day Saints student association, Baha'i association, Baptist student union, Campus Crusade for Christ, Fellowship of Christian Athletes, international student organization, Asian American students association, Society of Hispanic Professional Engineers.

Athletics. NCAA. **Intercollegiate:** Baseball M, basketball, cross-country, golf, tennis, track and field, volleyball W. **Intramural:** Badminton, basketball, bowling, cheerleading, football (non-tackle), golf, racquetball, soccer, softball, tennis, volleyball. **Team name:** Broncs/Lady Broncs.

Student services. Alcohol/substance abuse counseling, career counseling, services for economically disadvantaged, student employment services, financial aid counseling, health services, on-campus daycare, personal counseling, placement for graduates, veterans' counselor, women's services. **Physically disabled:** Services for visually, speech, hearing impaired.

Contact. E-mail: admissions@panam.edu
Phone: (956) 381-2201 Fax: (956) 381-2212
Magdalena Williams, Dean of Admissions & Enrollment Services, University of Texas: Pan American, 1201 West University Drive, Edinburg, TX 78541-2999

University of the Incarnate Word

San Antonio, Texas **CB member**
www.uiw.edu **CB code: 6303**

- Private 4-year university and liberal arts college affiliated with Roman Catholic Church
- Commuter campus in very large city
- 4,278 degree-seeking undergraduates: 40% part-time, 67% women, 7% African American, 2% Asian American, 56% Hispanic American, 1% Native American, 3% international
- 841 degree-seeking graduate students
- 75% of applicants admitted
- SAT or ACT (ACT writing optional) required
- 43% graduate within 6 years

General. Founded in 1881. Regionally accredited. Off-campus courses available at US Automobile Association, Randolph Air Force Base, City Public Service Board, Santa Rosa Hospital, Northeast Campus, Delmar Campus. **Degrees:** 645 bachelor's, 2 associate awarded; master's, doctoral, first professional offered. **ROTC:** Army, Air Force. **Location:** 5 miles from downtown. **Calendar:** Semester, limited summer session. **Full-time faculty:** 160 total; 69% have terminal degrees, 29% minority, 58% women. **Part-time faculty:** 284 total; 31% minority, 45% women. **Class size:** 46% < 20, 51% 20-39, 2% 40-49, less than 1% 50-99. **Special facilities:** Teaching theater.

Freshman class profile. 2,070 applied, 1,560 admitted, 578 enrolled.

Mid 50% test scores			
SAT verbal:	430-540	Rank in top quarter:	42%
SAT math:	430-540	Rank in top tenth:	17%
ACT:	17-22	Return as sophomores:	70%
GPA 3.50 or higher:	39%	Out-of-state:	2%
GPA 3.0-3.49:	51%	Live on campus:	46%
GPA 2.0-2.99:	10%	International:	1%

Basis for selection. Test scores and school achievement record most important. Interview helpful. Interview recommended for academically weak.

High school preparation. 16 units required; 18 recommended. Required and recommended units include English 4, mathematics 3-4, social studies 3-4, science 3 and foreign language 2. One fine arts unit required.

2006-2007 Annual costs. Tuition/fees: $18,272. Pharmacy annual tuition $25,500 and fees $500. Room/board: $6,475. Books/supplies: $1,000. Personal expenses: $1,500.

2005-2006 Financial aid. **Need-based:** 542 full-time freshmen applied for aid; 425 were judged to have need; 425 of these received aid. Average need met was 68%. Average scholarship/grant was $8,274; average loan $2,838. 54% of total undergraduate aid awarded as scholarships/grants, 46% as loans/jobs. **Non-need-based:** Awarded to 1,906 full-time undergraduates, including 253 freshmen. Scholarships awarded for academics, alumni affiliation, art, athletics, leadership, music/drama, religious affiliation, ROTC. **Additional information:** Students encouraged to pursue outside scholarship programs.

Application procedures. **Admission:** Priority date 3/1; no deadline. $20 fee, may be waived for applicants with need. Application may be submitted online. Admission notification on a rolling basis beginning on or about 11/1. Response by May 1 encouraged. **Financial aid:** Priority date 1/1; no closing date. FAFSA required. Applicants notified on a rolling basis starting 2/15; must reply within 2 week(s) of notification.

Academics. **Special study options:** Accelerated study, cooperative education, cross-registration, distance learning, double major, dual enrollment of high school students, ESL, exchange student, independent study, internships, liberal arts/career combination, study abroad, teacher certification program. Adult Degree Completion Program: accelerated 8-week term program. **Credit/placement by examination:** AP, CLEP, institutional tests. 30 credit hours maximum toward bachelor's degree. **Support services:** Learning center, reduced course load, remedial instruction, study skills assistance, tutoring, writing center.

Majors. **Area/ethnic studies:** Native American. **Biology:** General. **Business:** Business admin, fashion, human resources, organizational behavior. **Communications:** Media studies. **Computer sciences:** Computer graphics, information technology. **Conservation:** Environmental science. **Education:** General, elementary, secondary. **Engineering:** General. **English:** English lit. **Family/consumer sciences:** Child care. **Foreign languages:** Spanish. **Health:** Athletic training, music therapy, nuclear medical technology, nursing (RN). **History:** General. **Interdisciplinary:** Intercultural, nutrition sciences. **Math:** General. **Parks/recreation:** Health/fitness. **Philosophy/religion:** Philosophy, religion. **Physical sciences:** Chemistry. **Psychology:** General. **Social sciences:** Political science, sociology. **Visual/performing arts:** Art, dramatic, fashion design, interior design, music management, music performance.

Most popular majors. Business/marketing 46%, communications/journalism 6%, health sciences 9%, liberal arts 8%, visual/performing arts 7%.

Computing on campus. PC or laptop required. 161 workstations in library, computer center. Dormitories wired for high-speed internet access and linked to campus network. Commuter students can connect to campus network. Online course registration, online library, helpline, repair service, wireless network available.

Student life. **Freshman orientation:** Mandatory, $40 fee. Preregistration for classes offered. Overnight program for out-of-towners and 1-day session for local students. Parents encouraged to participate. **Policies:** Freshmen permitted cars on campus. **Housing:** Guaranteed on-campus for freshmen. Coed dorms, single-sex dorms, apartments, substance-free housing available. $200 partly refundable deposit. **Activities:** Bands, choral groups, dance, drama, literary magazine, music ensembles, musical theater, radio station, student government, student newspaper, Hispanic student association, black student association, international student association, student ambassadors, Crusaders for Christ.

Athletics. NCAA. **Intercollegiate:** Baseball M, basketball, cross-country, golf, soccer, softball W, swimming W, synchronized swimming W, tennis, track and field, volleyball W. **Intramural:** Archery, badminton, basketball, bowling, cross-country, golf, racquetball, soccer, softball, swimming, table tennis, tennis, track and field, volleyball. **Team name:** Cardinals.

Student services. Campus ministries, career counseling, student employment services, financial aid counseling, health services, personal counseling, placement for graduates.

Contact. E-mail: admis@uiwtx.edu
Phone: (210) 829-6005 Toll-free number: (800) 749-9673
Fax: (210) 829-3921
Andrea Cyterski-Acosta, Director of Admissions, University of the Incarnate Word, 4301 Broadway, San Antonio, TX 78209-6397

Wayland Baptist University

Plainview, Texas — **CB member**
www.wbu.edu — **CB code: 6930**

- Private 4-year university and liberal arts college affiliated with Southern Baptist Convention
- Residential campus in large town
- 937 degree-seeking undergraduates: 10% part-time, 57% women, 4% African American, 1% Asian American, 24% Hispanic American, 1% Native American, 2% international
- 74 degree-seeking graduate students
- 65% of applicants admitted
- SAT or ACT (ACT writing optional) required

General. Founded in 1908. Regionally accredited. Off-campus sites in Amarillo, Lubbock, San Antonio, Wichita Falls, Alaska, Arizona, Hawaii, Oklahoma, New Mexico. **Degrees:** 144 bachelor's awarded; master's offered. **ROTC:** Army, Air Force. **Location:** 50 miles from Lubbock, 70 miles from Amarillo. **Calendar:** Semester, limited summer session. **Full-time faculty:** 67 total; 70% have terminal degrees, 4% minority, 31% women. **Part-time faculty:** 35 total; 26% have terminal degrees, 3% minority, 37% women. **Class size:** 72% < 20, 28% 20-39, less than 1% 50-99. **Special facilities:** Museum of the Llano Estacado.

Freshman class profile. 511 applied, 333 admitted, 226 enrolled.

Mid 50% test scores		Rank in top tenth:	23%
SAT verbal:	430-580	Return as sophomores:	69%
SAT math:	450-570	Out-of-state:	16%
ACT:	17-25	Live on campus:	72%
GPA 3.50 or higher:	47%	International:	2%
GPA 3.0-3.49:	35%	Fraternities:	3%
GPA 2.0-2.99:	17%	Sororities:	4%
Rank in top quarter:	53%		

Basis for selection. Regular freshman admission is based on a combination of class rank and the score on either the ACT composite or SAT. Interview, audition recommended.

High school preparation. 9 units required. Required and recommended units include English 3, mathematics 2-3, social studies 2 and science 2-3.

2005-2006 Annual costs. Tuition/fees: $9,900. Room/board: $3,506. Books/supplies: $586. Personal expenses: $1,228.

2005-2006 Financial aid. **Need-based:** 175 full-time freshmen applied for aid; 146 were judged to have need; 146 of these received aid. Average need met was 77%. Average scholarship/grant was $7,632; average loan $2,037. 59% of total undergraduate aid awarded as scholarships/grants, 41% as loans/jobs. **Non-need-based:** Awarded to 292 full-time undergraduates, including 74 freshmen. Scholarships awarded for academics, alumni affiliation, art, athletics, job skills, leadership, minority status, music/drama, religious affiliation, state residency.

Application procedures. **Admission:** Priority date 8/1; no deadline. $35 fee. Application may be submitted online. Admission notification on a rolling basis beginning on or about 3/1. **Financial aid:** Priority date 5/1; no closing date. FAFSA, institutional form required. Applicants notified on a rolling basis starting 2/15; must reply within 4 week(s) of notification.

Academics. **Special study options:** Accelerated study, distance learning, double major, dual enrollment of high school students, external degree, honors, internships, teacher certification program. **Credit/placement by examination:** AP, CLEP, IB, SAT, ACT, institutional tests. 30 credit hours maximum toward bachelor's degree. **Support services:** Learning center, reduced course load, remedial instruction, study skills assistance, tutoring.

Majors. **Biology:** General. **Business:** Business admin. **Communications:** Media studies. **Education:** Elementary, music, physical, technology/industrial arts, trade/industrial. **English:** English lit. **Foreign languages:** Spanish. **History:** General. **Math:** General. **Philosophy/religion:** Christian. **Physical sciences:** General, chemistry. **Protective services:** Criminal justice. **Psychology:** General. **Public administration:** Human services. **Social sciences:** Political science, sociology. **Theology:** Religious ed, sacred music. **Visual/performing arts:** Art, dramatic.

Most popular majors. Business/marketing 21%, education 24%, philosophy/religious studies 10%, security/protective services 7%, theological studies 7%.

Computing on campus. 123 workstations in library, computer center. Dormitories linked to campus network. Commuter students can connect to campus network.

Student life. **Freshman orientation:** Mandatory, $15 fee. Preregistration for classes offered. Entry seminar course designed to help students succeed academically, socially, and spiritually. Taken during initial term of enrollment. **Policies:** Religious observance required. Freshmen permitted cars on campus. **Housing:** Guaranteed on-campus for freshmen. Single-sex dorms, apartments, substance-free housing available. $100 fully refundable deposit. **Activities:** Bands, choral groups, drama, music ensembles, musical theater, radio station, student government, student newspaper, TV station, Over 20 religious, service, and special interest organizations available.

Athletics. NAIA. **Intercollegiate:** Baseball M, basketball, cross-country, golf M, track and field, volleyball W. **Intramural:** Basketball, football (non-tackle), golf, softball, volleyball. **Team name:** Pioneers, Flying Queens.

Student services. Campus ministries, career counseling, student employment services, financial aid counseling, health services, personal counseling, placement for graduates.

Contact. E-mail: admityou@wbu.edu
Phone: (806) 291-3500 Toll-free number: (800) 588-1928
Fax: (806) 291-1960
Director of Admissions, Wayland Baptist University, 1900 West Seventh Street, CMB #712, Plainview, TX 79072

West Texas A&M University

Canyon, Texas — **CB member**
www.wtamu.edu — **CB code: 6938**

- Public 4-year university
- Commuter campus in large town
- 5,730 degree-seeking undergraduates: 22% part-time, 58% women, 4% African American, 1% Asian American, 16% Hispanic American, 1% Native American, 1% international
- 1,494 degree-seeking graduate students
- 73% of applicants admitted
- SAT or ACT (ACT writing optional) required

General. Founded in 1909. Regionally accredited. **Degrees:** 980 bachelor's awarded; master's, doctoral offered. **Location:** 17 miles from Amarillo. **Calendar:** Semester, limited summer session. **Full-time faculty:** 246 total; 70% have terminal degrees, 7% minority, 41% women. **Part-time faculty:** 75 total; 20% have terminal degrees, 7% minority, 57% women. **Class size:** 44% < 20, 40% 20-39, 9% 40-49, 8% 50-99, less than 1% >100. **Special facilities:** 24,000-acre farm and ranch, alternative energy institute, historical museum, event center.

Freshman class profile. 1,903 applied, 1,392 admitted, 797 enrolled.

Mid 50% test scores		**Return as sophomores:**	66%
SAT verbal:	400-630	**Out-of-state:**	12%
SAT math:	400-620	**Live on campus:**	84%
ACT:	17-26	**International:**	1%
Rank in top quarter:	43%	**Fraternities:**	4%
Rank in top tenth:	14%	**Sororities:**	4%
End year in good standing:	68%		

Basis for selection. Freshman applicants must be in top half of graduating class, have minimum 950 SAT (exclusive of writing) or 20 ACT, or attend a summer provisional term. Texas Success Initiative Testing required of all incoming students before entrance. Audition required for music program; portfolio recommended for art, theater programs.

High school preparation. 24 units recommended. Recommended units include English 4, mathematics 4, social studies 3.5, history 2, science 3, foreign language 2, academic electives 7.5.

2005-2006 Annual costs. Tuition/fees: $3,756; $12,036 out-of-state. Out-of-district students from border counties pay in-state tuition. Tuition reduction plan available to students from border states. Books/supplies: $800. Personal expenses: $1,574.

2004-2005 Financial aid. **Need-based:** 621 full-time freshmen applied for aid; 458 were judged to have need; 447 of these received aid. Average need met was 77%. Average scholarship/grant was $4,562; average loan $2,123. 50% of total undergraduate aid awarded as scholarships/grants, 50% as loans/jobs. **Non-need-based:** Awarded to 1,555 full-time undergraduates, including 603 freshmen. Scholarships awarded for academics, art, athletics, leadership, music/drama, state residency. **Additional information:** Scholarship deadline February 1.

Application procedures. **Admission:** No deadline. $25 fee, may be waived for applicants with need. Application may be submitted online. Admission notification on a rolling basis. **Financial aid:** Priority date 4/15; no closing date. FAFSA required. Applicants notified on a rolling basis starting 3/1; must reply within 2 week(s) of notification.

Academics. **Special study options:** Accelerated study, combined bachelor's/graduate degree, cooperative education, distance learning, double major, ESL, honors, independent study, internships, student-designed major, study abroad, teacher certification program, Washington semester. **Credit/placement by examination:** AP, CLEP, IB, institutional tests. Only 6 of a student's last 30 hours can come from CLEP. **Support services:** Learning center, remedial instruction, study skills assistance, tutoring, writing center.

Majors. **Agriculture:** General, agribusiness operations, animal sciences, business, equestrian studies, plant protection, plant sciences. **Biology:** General, biotechnology. **Business:** General, accounting, business admin, finance, management information systems, managerial economics, marketing. **Communications:** Advertising, broadcast journalism, journalism. **Computer sciences:** General. **Conservation:** Environmental science, wildlife. **Engineering:** Mechanical. **Engineering technology:** Industrial. **English:** English lit, speech/rhetoric. **Foreign languages:** Spanish. **Health:** Athletic training, clinical lab science, communication disorders, music therapy, nursing (RN). **History:** General. **Legal studies:** Prelaw. **Math:** General. **Parks/recreation:** Health/fitness. **Physical sciences:** Chemistry, geology, physics. **Protective services:** Law enforcement admin. **Psychology:** General. **Public administration:** General, social work. **Social sciences:** General, economics, geography, political science, sociology. **Visual/performing arts:** Art, dance, dramatic, graphic design, music performance, music theory/composition, studio arts.

Most popular majors. Biology 6%, business/marketing 20%, health sciences 7%, interdisciplinary studies 14%, liberal arts 14%, visual/performing arts 6%.

Computing on campus. 1,800 workstations in dormitories, library, computer center, student center. Dormitories wired for high-speed internet access and linked to campus network. Commuter students can connect to campus network. Online course registration, online library, helpline, student web hosting, wireless network available.

Student life. **Freshman orientation:** Available, $50 fee. Preregistration for classes offered. 2-day summer orientation and preregistration and 3-day orientation before school starts. **Policies:** Students with fewer than 60 semester hours accumulated, enrolled in 9 or more semester hours, and under 21 on first day of class each semester required to live in university residence halls. Freshmen permitted cars on campus. **Housing:** Guaranteed on-campus for all undergraduates. Coed dorms, single-sex dorms available. $100 fully refundable deposit. Honors hall for students in honors program available. **Activities:** Bands, choral groups, dance, drama, literary magazine, music ensembles, musical theater, radio station, student government, student newspaper, Chinese student association, Hispanic association, agriculture organizations, Students in Free Enterprise, preprofessional organizations, Baptist student ministries, United Campus Ministries, Black students association, College Republicans, Catholic student association.

Athletics. NCAA. **Intercollegiate:** Baseball M, basketball, cross-country, equestrian W, football (tackle) M, golf, soccer, softball W, volleyball W. **Intramural:** Archery, badminton, basketball, bowling, football (non-tackle), golf, racquetball, rodeo, soccer, softball, swimming, table tennis, tennis, volleyball. **Team name:** Buffaloes.

Student services. Alcohol/substance abuse counseling, career counseling, services for economically disadvantaged, student employment services, financial aid counseling, health services, on-campus daycare, personal counseling, placement for graduates, veterans' counselor. **Physically disabled:** Services for visually, speech, hearing impaired.

Contact. E-mail: admissions@mail.wtamu.edu
Phone: (806) 651-2020 Toll-free number: (800) 999-8268
Fax: (806) 651-5268
Lila Vars, Director of Admissions, West Texas A&M University, 2501 Fourth Avenue, WTAMU Box 60907, Canyon, TX 79016-0001

Wiley College

Marshall, Texas — **CB member**
www.wileyc.edu — **CB code: 6940**

- Private 4-year liberal arts college affiliated with United Methodist Church
- Residential campus in large town
- 792 degree-seeking undergraduates: 9% part-time, 61% women

General. Founded in 1873. Regionally accredited. **Degrees:** 125 bachelor's awarded. **Location:** 40 miles from Shreveport, Louisiana, 150 miles from Dallas. **Calendar:** Semester, extensive summer session. **Full-time faculty:** 47 total; 68% have terminal degrees, 85% minority, 30% women.

Part-time faculty: 11 total; 9% have terminal degrees, 91% minority, 46% women. **Class size:** 60% < 20, 35% 20-39, 3% 40-49, 2% 50-99. **Special facilities:** Nature trail.

Freshman class profile.

Mid 50% test scores			
SAT verbal:	320-430	Rank in top quarter:	15%
SAT math:	320-430	Rank in top tenth:	3%
ACT:	13-17	Out-of-state:	38%
		Live on campus:	90%

Basis for selection. Open admission, but selective for some programs.

High school preparation. 16 units recommended. Recommended units include English 4, mathematics 2, social studies 2, science 2 and academic electives 6.

2005-2006 Annual costs. Tuition/fees: $7,334. Room/board: $4,510. Books/supplies: $1,320. Personal expenses: $1,002.

2004-2005 Financial aid. All financial aid based on need. 119 full-time freshmen applied for aid; 117 were judged to have need; 117 of these received aid. Average need met was 45%. Average scholarship/grant was $4,652; average loan $1,986. 59% of total undergraduate aid awarded as scholarships/grants, 41% as loans/jobs.

Application procedures. Admission: Priority date 8/15; no deadline. $25 fee. Admission notification on a rolling basis. **Financial aid:** No deadline. FAFSA, institutional form required. Applicants notified on a rolling basis.

Academics. Special study options: Accelerated study, cross-registration, distance learning, double major, dual enrollment of high school students, honors, independent study, internships, liberal arts/career combination, study abroad, teacher certification program, weekend college. **Credit/placement by examination:** AP, CLEP, institutional tests. **Support services:** Learning center, reduced course load, remedial instruction, study skills assistance, tutoring.

Majors. Biology: General. **Business:** Accounting, business admin, operations. **Communications:** Journalism. **Computer sciences:** Computer science. **Education:** Elementary, physical, secondary. **History:** General. **Math:** General. **Physical sciences:** Chemistry. **Social sciences:** Sociology.

Most popular majors. Business/marketing 66%, education 6%.

Computing on campus. 177 workstations in dormitories, library, computer center. Dormitories wired for high-speed internet access and linked to campus network. Commuter students can connect to campus network. Online course registration, online library, helpline, wireless network available.

Student life. Freshman orientation: Mandatory. Preregistration for classes offered. **Policies:** Religious observance required. Freshmen permitted cars on campus. **Housing:** Single-sex dorms, substance-free housing available. $50 deposit. **Activities:** Choral groups, drama, music ensembles, radio station, student government, student newspaper, national service fraternity, interdenominational student movement, religion majors club.

Athletics. NAIA. **Intercollegiate:** Baseball M, basketball, cross-country, softball W, track and field, volleyball W. **Intramural:** Baseball M, basketball, cheerleading, softball, table tennis, tennis, track and field, volleyball, weight lifting M. **Team name:** Wildcats.

Student services. Adult student services, campus ministries, career counseling, services for economically disadvantaged, student employment services, financial aid counseling, health services, personal counseling, placement for graduates, veterans' counselor.

Contact. E-mail: admissions@wileyc.edu
Phone: (903) 927-3311 Toll-free number: (800) 658-6889
Fax: (903) 927-3366
Lalita Estes, Director of Enrollment Management Services, Wiley College, 711 Wiley Avenue, Marshall, TX 75670

Utah

Brigham Young University

Provo, Utah
www.byu.edu

CB member
CB code: 4019

- Private 4-year university affiliated with Church of Jesus Christ of Latter-day Saints
- Residential campus in small city
- 30,798 degree-seeking undergraduates: 11% part-time, 49% women
- 3,269 graduate students
- 78% of applicants admitted
- SAT or ACT (ACT writing optional), application essay, interview required
- 70% graduate within 6 years

General. Founded in 1875. Regionally accredited. Additional educational center in Salt Lake City. **Degrees:** 6,951 bachelor's awarded; master's, doctoral, first professional offered. **ROTC:** Army, Air Force. **Location:** 45 miles from Salt Lake City. **Calendar:** Semester, limited summer session. **Full-time faculty:** 1,321 total; 4% minority, 20% women. **Part-time faculty:** 441 total; 7% minority, 59% women. **Class size:** 44% < 20, 38% 20-39, 7% 40-49, 8% 50-99, 3% >100. **Special facilities:** Aquatic ecology laboratory, science and anthropological museums, veterinary pathology laboratory, fine arts museum, reading and writing laboratories, mathematics and language computer laboratories, supercomputer.

Freshman class profile. 8,696 applied, 6,794 admitted, 5,335 enrolled.

Mid 50% test scores			
SAT verbal:	550-660	GPA 2.0-2.99:	2%
SAT math:	570-670	Rank in top quarter:	84%
ACT:	25-29	Rank in top tenth:	49%
GPA 3.50 or higher:	86%	Return as sophomores:	95%
GPA 3.0-3.49:	12%	Out-of-state:	72%
		Live on campus:	80%

Basis for selection. School achievement record, test scores, endorsements and recommendations important. Students must maintain ideals and standards in harmony with The Church of Jesus Christ of Latter-day Saints. ACT recommended. Interview is ecclesiastical. **Homeschooled:** Portfolio not considered in placement. **Learning Disabled:** Untimed ACT accepted.

High school preparation. Required and recommended units include English 4, mathematics 3-4, history 2, science 2-3 (laboratory 2-3) and foreign language 2-4. 2 units of literature/writing required.

2005-2006 Annual costs. Tuition/fees: $3,410. Undergraduate 2-semester tuition $5,116 for nonmembers of The Church of Jesus Christ of Latter-day Saints. Undergraduate per-credit-hour charge $262 for nonmembers. Room/board: $5,790. Books/supplies: $1,240. Personal expenses: $3,150.

2004-2005 Financial aid. Need-based: 5,793 full-time freshmen applied for aid; 1,353 were judged to have need; 1,178 of these received aid. Average need met was 30%. Average scholarship/grant was $1,756; average loan $837. 60% of total undergraduate aid awarded as scholarships/grants, 40% as loans/jobs. **Non-need-based:** Awarded to 15,038 full-time undergraduates, including 2,781 freshmen. Scholarships awarded for academics, art, athletics, leadership, minority status, music/drama, religious affiliation, ROTC, state residency.

Application procedures. Admission: Closing date 2/15 (receipt date). $30 fee, may be waived for applicants with need. Application may be submitted online. Admission notification on a rolling basis. **Financial aid:** Closing date 6/30. FAFSA required. Applicants notified on a rolling basis starting 4/1.

Academics. Special study options: Accelerated study, combined bachelor's/graduate degree, cooperative education, cross-registration, distance learning, double major, ESL, external degree, honors, independent study, internships, liberal arts/career combination, study abroad, teacher certification program, Washington semester. **Credit/placement by examination:** AP, CLEP, IB, ACT, institutional tests. **Support services:** Learning center, pre-admission summer program, reduced course load, remedial instruction, study skills assistance, tutoring, writing center.

Majors. Agriculture: Crop production, food processing, food science, landscaping, soil science. **Area/ethnic studies:** American, Asian, Latin American. **Biology:** General, biochemistry, bioinformatics, biophysics, biostatistics, biotechnology, botany, microbiology, molecular, physiology. **Business:** General, accounting, actuarial science, business admin, construction management, entrepreneurial studies, finance, financial planning, information resources management, logistics, management information systems, marketing, statistics. **Communications:** Journalism. **Communications technology:** Animation/special effects. **Computer sciences:** Computer science, information technology. **Conservation:** Wildlife. **Education:** Chemistry, drama/dance, early childhood, elementary, English, family/consumer sciences, French, German, health, history, Latin, mathematics, music, physical, physics, science, social science, special, speech, technology/industrial arts. **Engineering:** Chemical, civil, computer, electrical, manufacturing, mechanical. **English:** English lit, speech/rhetoric. **Family/consumer sciences:** General, family resources, family studies. **Foreign languages:** General, ancient Greek, Biblical, Chinese, classics, comparative lit, French, German, Italian, Japanese, Korean, Latin, linguistics, Portuguese, Russian, Spanish, translation. **Health:** Athletic training, audiology/speech pathology, clinical lab science, dietetics, nursing (RN), recreational therapy. **History:** General. **Interdisciplinary:** Biological/physical sciences, neuroscience, nutrition sciences. **Liberal arts:** Arts/sciences, humanities. **Math:** General, statistics. **Parks/recreation:** General, health/fitness. **Philosophy/religion:** Philosophy. **Physical sciences:** Astronomy, chemistry, geology, hydrology, physics. **Psychology:** General. **Public administration:** Social work. **Social sciences:** Anthropology, archaeology, cartography, economics, geography, international relations, political science, sociology. **Visual/performing arts:** Acting, art, art history/conservation, ballet, dance, design, dramatic, film/cinema, graphic design, illustration, industrial design, jazz, music history, music performance, music theory/composition, photography, piano/organ, stringed instruments, studio arts, voice/opera.

Most popular majors. Business/marketing 16%, education 12%, engineering/engineering technologies 6%, family/consumer sciences 6%, visual/performing arts 7%.

Computing on campus. 2,000 workstations in dormitories, library, computer center, student center. Dormitories wired for high-speed internet access and linked to campus network. Commuter students can connect to campus network. Online course registration, online library, helpline, repair service, student web hosting, wireless network available.

Student life. Freshman orientation: Available. Preregistration for classes offered. **Policies:** Honor code enforced. Religious observance required. Freshmen permitted cars on campus. **Housing:** Single-sex dorms, special housing for disabled, apartments, substance-free housing available. $150 deposit. Language houses (for students studying one of 9 selected languages) available. **Activities:** Bands, choral groups, dance, drama, film society, literary magazine, music ensembles, musical theater, opera, radio station, student government, student newspaper, symphony orchestra, TV station, College Republicans, College Democrats, African American club, Black Student Union, Latin American student association, international student association, Intercollegiate Knights, Circle-K International, Southeast Asian club, Baptist Student Union.

Athletics. NCAA. **Intercollegiate:** Baseball M, basketball, cheerleading, cross-country, diving, football (tackle) M, golf, gymnastics W, soccer W, softball W, swimming, tennis, track and field, volleyball. **Intramural:** Badminton, basketball, football (non-tackle), football (tackle), golf, racquetball, soccer, softball, tennis, volleyball, water polo, wrestling M. **Team name:** Cougars.

Student services. Campus ministries, career counseling, services for economically disadvantaged, student employment services, financial aid counseling, health services, minority student services, personal counseling, placement for graduates, veterans' counselor, women's services. **Physically disabled:** Services for visually, speech, hearing impaired.

Contact. E-mail: admissions@byu.edu
Phone: (801) 422-2507 Fax: (801) 422-0005
Tom Gourley, Director of Admissions, Brigham Young University, A-153 ASB, BYU, Provo, UT 84602

ITT Technical Institute: Murray

Murray, Utah
www.itt-tech.edu

CB code: 3601

- For-profit 4-year technical college
- Commuter campus in small city

General. Founded in 1984. Accredited by ACICS. **Location:** 10 miles from Salt Lake City. **Calendar:** Quarter.

Annual costs/financial aid. Tuition varies by program, $260-$368 per credit hour.

Contact. Phone: (801) 263-3313
Director of Recruitment, 920 West LeVoy Drive, Murray, UT 84123

Neumont University
South Jordan, Utah
www.neumont.edu

- For-profit 4-year engineering and technical college
- Residential campus in very large city
- 270 degree-seeking undergraduates: 7% women
- SAT or ACT (ACT writing optional), application essay, interview required

General. Accredited by ACICS. **Location:** 20 miles from Salt Lake City. **Calendar:** Quarter, extensive summer session. **Full-time faculty:** 18 total; 22% have terminal degrees. **Part-time faculty:** 5 total.

Freshman class profile. 255 applied, 240 admitted, 100 enrolled.

Out-of-state:	50%	Live on campus:	50%

Basis for selection. Open admission, but selective for some programs. Academic potential, computer experience, and interest and motivation for the program all considered. **Homeschooled:** State high school equivalency certificate required.

2006-2007 Annual costs. Tuition/fees (projected): $21,325.

Application procedures. Admission: No deadline. $35 fee. Application may be submitted online. Admission notification on a rolling basis. **Financial aid:** No deadline.

Academics. Special study options: Accelerated study, internships. **Credit/placement by examination:** AP, CLEP. **Support services:** Remedial instruction, study skills assistance, tutoring.

Majors. Computer sciences: Computer science.

Computing on campus. PC or laptop required. Commuter students can connect to campus network. Online library, helpline, repair service, student web hosting, wireless network available.

Student life. Freshman orientation: Mandatory. Preregistration for classes offered. **Policies:** Freshmen permitted cars on campus. **Housing:** Apartments available. $275 partly refundable deposit.

Student services. Career counseling, financial aid counseling, placement for graduates.

Contact. E-mail: info@neumont.edu
Phone: (801) 302-2800 Toll-free number: (866) 622-3448
Fax: (801) 302-2880
Scott Sainsbury, Director of Admissions, Neumont University, 10701 South River Front Parkway, Suite 300, South Jordan, UT 84095

Southern Utah University
Cedar City, Utah
www.suu.edu **CB code: 4092**

- Public 4-year university
- Residential campus in large town
- 4,999 degree-seeking undergraduates: 1% African American, 2% Asian American, 2% Hispanic American, 2% Native American, 1% international
- 394 graduate students
- 80% of applicants admitted
- SAT or ACT (ACT writing optional) required
- 34% graduate within 6 years

General. Founded in 1897. Regionally accredited. **Degrees:** 971 bachelor's, 34 associate awarded; master's offered. **ROTC:** Army. **Location:** 265 miles from Salt Lake City, 160 miles from Las Vegas. **Calendar:** Semester, extensive summer session. **Full-time faculty:** 211 total; 73% have terminal degrees, 5% minority, 30% women. **Part-time faculty:** 63 total; 3% have terminal degrees, 5% minority, 48% women. **Class size:** 46% < 20, 41% 20-39, 7% 40-49, 5% 50-99, less than 1% >100. **Special facilities:** Natural life museum, observatory, Shakespearean theater.

Freshman class profile. 2,492 applied, 2,001 admitted, 1,075 enrolled.

Mid 50% test scores		Rank in top tenth:	28%
SAT verbal:	440-560	Return as sophomores:	59%
SAT math:	430-560	Out-of-state:	19%
ACT:	18-24	Live on campus:	41%
GPA 3.50 or higher:	51%	International:	1%
GPA 3.0-3.49:	29%	Fraternities:	4%
GPA 2.0-2.99:	18%	Sororities:	4%
Rank in top quarter:	51%		

Basis for selection. ACT/SAT scores and high school academic record used to calculate admissions index, which in turn determines admission.

High school preparation. College-preparatory program recommended. Recommended units include English 4, mathematics 3, social studies 3, science 3 (laboratory 1) and foreign language 2.

2005-2006 Annual costs. Tuition/fees: $3,358; $9,878 out-of-state. Room/board: $4,154.

2004-2005 Financial aid. Need-based: Average need met was 70%. Average scholarship/grant was $2,530; average loan $2,966. 56% of total undergraduate aid awarded as scholarships/grants, 44% as loans/jobs. **Non-need-based:** Awarded to 841 full-time undergraduates, including 287 freshmen. Scholarships awarded for academics, art, athletics, job skills, leadership, music/drama, state residency.

Application procedures. Admission: Closing date 8/1. $35 fee. Decision sent immediately. **Financial aid:** No deadline. FAFSA, institutional form required. Applicants notified on a rolling basis starting 2/1.

Academics. Special study options: Combined bachelor's/graduate degree, cooperative education, distance learning, double major, ESL, honors, independent study, internships, liberal arts/career combination, teacher certification program, weekend college. **Credit/placement by examination:** AP, CLEP, ACT. 25 credit hours maximum toward associate degree, 25 toward bachelor's. **Support services:** Learning center, pre-admission summer program, reduced course load, remedial instruction, study skills assistance, tutoring, writing center.

Majors. Agriculture: Business. **Biology:** General, botany, zoology. **Business:** Accounting, business admin, finance, management information systems, managerial economics, marketing. **Communications:** General, advertising, journalism, public relations. **Computer sciences:** Computer science, information systems. **Construction:** Maintenance. **Education:** General, art, biology, business, chemistry, drama/dance, elementary, English, family/consumer sciences, foreign languages, French, German, history, learning disabled, mathematics, music, science, secondary, social science, Spanish, special, speech, technology/industrial arts, trade/industrial. **Engineering:** General. **English:** British lit, speech/rhetoric. **Family/consumer sciences:** General. **Foreign languages:** General, French, German, Spanish. **Health:** Nursing (RN), predentistry, premedicine, prepharmacy, preveterinary. **History:** General. **Interdisciplinary:** Behavioral sciences. **Legal studies:** Prelaw. **Math:** General, statistics. **Philosophy/religion:** Philosophy. **Physical sciences:** Chemistry, geology, planetary. **Protective services:** Criminal justice. **Psychology:** General. **Social sciences:** General, economics, political science, sociology. **Visual/performing arts:** Art, commercial/advertising art, dance, dramatic.

Most popular majors. Business/marketing 13%, communications/journalism 9%, education 28%, psychology 6%, social sciences 8%, visual/performing arts 6%.

Computing on campus. 300 workstations in dormitories, library, computer center. Dormitories wired for high-speed internet access and linked to campus network. Commuter students can connect to campus network. Online library, helpline, wireless network available.

Student life. Freshman orientation: Mandatory. Preregistration for classes offered. One-day program held throughout the summer. Parents are welcome and encouraged to attend. **Policies:** Freshmen permitted cars on campus. **Housing:** Coed dorms, single-sex dorms, special housing for disabled, apartments, fraternity/sorority housing available. $200 fully refundable deposit. **Activities:** Bands, choral groups, dance, drama, literary magazine, music ensembles, musical theater, opera, radio station, student government, student newspaper, symphony orchestra, TV station, intercultural club, LDSSA, Newman Club, Campus Christian Fellowship, College Republicans, College Democrats.

Athletics. NAIA, NCAA. **Intercollegiate:** Badminton, baseball M, basketball, cross-country, football (tackle) M, golf M, gymnastics W, rodeo, soccer W, softball W, tennis W, track and field. **Intramural:** Badminton, basketball, golf, soccer, tennis, volleyball. **Team name:** Thunderbirds.

Student services. Career counseling, student employment services, health services, minority student services, personal counseling, placement for graduates, veterans' counselor. **Physically disabled:** Services for speech impaired.

Contact. E-mail: adminfo@suu.edu
Phone: (435) 586-7740 Fax: (435) 865-8223
Stephen Allen, Director of Admissions, Southern Utah University, 351 West Center Street, Cedar City, UT 84720

Stevens-Henager College
Ogden, Utah
www.stevenshenager.edu **CB code: 4751**

- For-profit 4-year liberal arts college
- Commuter campus in small city
- 470 full-time, degree-seeking undergraduates
- 470 graduate students
- Interview required

General. Accredited by ACCSCT. **Degrees:** 38 bachelor's, 79 associate awarded. **Location:** 35 miles from Salt Lake City. **Calendar:** Continuous. **Full-time faculty:** 15 total. **Part-time faculty:** 15 total.

Basis for selection. Open admission, but selective for some programs. Special requirements for Surgical Technology program.

High school preparation. Required units include history 4.

Application procedures. Admission: No deadline. No application fee. Application must be submitted on paper. Admission notification on a rolling basis.

Academics. Special study options: Accelerated study, cooperative education, distance learning, liberal arts/career combination. **Credit/placement by examination:** AP, CLEP. **Support services:** Tutoring.

Majors. Business: Accounting, business admin. **Computer sciences:** General. **Health:** Health care admin.

Computing on campus. 15 workstations in library, computer center. Commuter students can connect to campus network. Online library available.

Student life. Freshman orientation: Mandatory. **Policies:** Freshmen permitted cars on campus. **Housing:** Single-sex dorms available. $100 deposit.

Student services. Financial aid counseling, placement for graduates.

Contact. Phone: (801) 394-7791 Fax: (801) 621-0853
Cynthia Williams, Director of Admissions, Stevens-Henager College, 1890 South 1350 West, Ogden, UT 84401

Stevens-Henager College of Business
Orem, Utah
www.stevenshenager.edu **CB code: 4751**

- For-profit 3-year business and technical college
- Small city
- 327 degree-seeking undergraduates

General. Founded in 1891. Accredited by ACICS. **Degrees:** 85 bachelor's, 150 associate awarded; master's offered. **Calendar:** Continuous, extensive summer session. **Full-time faculty:** 8 total; 12% have terminal degrees, 38% women.

Freshman class profile.

Out-of-state:	10%	**Live on campus:**	16%

Basis for selection. Open admission.

2005-2006 Annual costs. Associate program ranges from $29,950 to $36,650. Tuition for bachelor's programs starts at $54,600. Tuition and fees vary by program. Personal expenses: $2,123.

Application procedures. Admission: No deadline. No application fee. Admission notification on a rolling basis. **Financial aid:** No deadline. Applicants notified on a rolling basis; must reply within 3 week(s) of notification.

Academics. Special study options: Accelerated study, dual enrollment of high school students, ESL, independent study, internships. **Credit/placement by examination:** AP, CLEP, institutional tests. **Support services:** Reduced course load, tutoring.

Majors. Business: Accounting, business admin.

Computing on campus. 26 workstations in library, computer center.

Student life. Freshman orientation: Mandatory. **Housing:** Single-sex dorms available. **Activities:** Student government, Future Business Leaders Association, Latter-day Saints student association.

Student services. Career counseling, student employment services, personal counseling, placement for graduates.

Contact. Phone: (801) 375-5455
Daniel Write, Director of Admissions, Stevens-Henager College of Business, 1476 South Sand Hill Road, Orem, UT 84058

University of Utah
Salt Lake City, Utah **CB member**
www.utah.edu **CB code: 4853**

- Public 4-year university
- Commuter campus in large city
- 21,695 degree-seeking undergraduates: 29% part-time, 44% women, 1% African American, 4% Asian American, 4% Hispanic American, 1% Native American, 2% international
- 6,351 degree-seeking graduate students
- 85% of applicants admitted
- SAT or ACT (ACT writing optional) required
- 55% graduate within 6 years

General. Founded in 1850. Regionally accredited. **Degrees:** 5,198 bachelor's awarded; master's, doctoral, first professional offered. **ROTC:** Army, Navy, Air Force. **Location:** 2 miles from downtown. **Calendar:** Semester, limited summer session. **Full-time faculty:** 1,175 total; 86% have terminal degrees, 11% minority, 37% women. **Part-time faculty:** 512 total; 38% have terminal degrees, 6% minority, 44% women. **Class size:** 35% < 20, 39% 20-39, 7% 40-49, 13% 50-99, 5% >100. **Special facilities:** Arboretum, fine arts museum, natural history museum, architecture exhibition hall, Olympic Cauldron Park.

Freshman class profile. 6,687 applied, 5,684 admitted, 2,821 enrolled.

Mid 50% test scores		**Rank in top tenth:**	27%
SAT verbal:	500-630	**End year in good standing:**	85%
SAT math:	500-630	**Return as sophomores:**	83%
ACT:	21-26	**Out-of-state:**	17%
GPA 3.50 or higher:	58%	**Live on campus:**	30%
GPA 3.0-3.49:	30%	**International:**	2%
GPA 2.0-2.99:	12%	**Fraternities:**	2%
Rank in top quarter:	51%	**Sororities:**	4%

Basis for selection. High school course requirements, admissions index using high school GPA and test scores important. Recommendation, extracurricular activities considered. Audition required for dance, drama, music programs; portfolio required for art program. **Homeschooled:** ACT score of 23 or SAT score of 1060 (exclusive of Writing), official high school transcript, GED composite scores of at least 550.

High school preparation. 16 units required. Required units include English 4, mathematics 2, history 1, science 3 (laboratory 1), foreign language 2 and academic electives 4. 3 science units required include 1 science lab unit. Also 4 units from at least 2 of the following: history, English, mathematics beyond algebra, laboratory science, foreign language, social science, fine arts.

2005-2006 Annual costs. Tuition/fees: $4,299; $13,372 out-of-state. Room/board: $5,678. Books/supplies: $1,086. Personal expenses: $2,412.

2005-2006 Financial aid. Need-based: 1,301 full-time freshmen applied for aid; 715 were judged to have need; 705 of these received aid. Average need met was 47%. Average scholarship/grant was $4,414; average loan $2,903. 39% of total undergraduate aid awarded as scholarships/grants, 61% as loans/jobs. **Non-need-based:** Awarded to 646 full-time undergraduates, including 280 freshmen. Scholarships awarded for academics, art, athletics, leadership, minority status, music/drama, ROTC, state residency.

Application procedures. Admission: Priority date 2/1; deadline 4/1 (postmark date). $35 fee. Application may be submitted online. Admission notification on a rolling basis. **Financial aid:** Priority date 3/15; no closing date. FAFSA, institutional form required. Applicants notified on a rolling basis starting 4/15; must reply within 6 week(s) of notification.

Academics. **Special study options:** Accelerated study, combined bachelor's/graduate degree, cooperative education, distance learning, double major, ESL, exchange student, honors, independent study, internships, liberal arts/career combination, New York semester, semester at sea, student-designed major, study abroad, teacher certification program, Washington semester. **Credit/placement by examination:** AP, CLEP, IB, SAT, ACT, institutional tests. 32 credit hours maximum toward bachelor's degree. **Support services:** Learning center, pre-admission summer program, reduced course load, remedial instruction, study skills assistance, tutoring, writing center.

Majors. **Architecture:** Architecture. **Area/ethnic studies:** Asian, Near/Middle Eastern, women's. **Biology:** General, biochemistry, cell/histology, cellular/molecular, human/medical genetics, neurobiology/physiology, oncology, pathology, physiology. **Business:** General, accounting, business admin, finance, management information systems, marketing. **Communications:** General, media studies. **Computer sciences:** Computer science. **Conservation:** Environmental science. **Education:** Art, biology, chemistry, drama/dance, elementary, English, foreign languages, French, geography, German, health, history, mathematics, multi-level teacher, music, psychology, science, social science, social studies, Spanish, special, speech. **Engineering:** General, biomedical, chemical, civil, computer, electrical, environmental, geological, materials, mechanical, metallurgical, mining, nuclear, petroleum. **English:** English lit. **Family/consumer sciences:** Consumer economics, family resources, family studies. **Foreign languages:** General, Chinese, classics, French, German, Japanese, linguistics, Russian, Spanish. **Health:** Audiology/hearing, audiology/speech pathology, clinical lab science, medical records technology, nursing (RN), predentistry, premedicine, prepharmacy, public health ed. **History:** General. **Interdisciplinary:** Global studies, math/computer science. **Legal studies:** Prelaw. **Liberal arts:** Humanities. **Math:** General. **Parks/recreation:** General, health/fitness. **Philosophy/religion:** Philosophy. **Physical sciences:** Chemistry, geology, geophysics, meteorology, molecular physics, physics. **Psychology:** General. **Public administration:** Social work. **Social sciences:** General, anthropology, economics, geography, political science, sociology, urban studies. **Visual/performing arts:** General, art, art history/conservation, ballet, dance, dramatic, film/cinema.

Most popular majors. Business/marketing 13%, communications/journalism 9%, engineering/engineering technologies 6%, health sciences 6%, social sciences 20%, visual/performing arts 7%.

Computing on campus. 8,800 workstations in dormitories, library, computer center, student center. Dormitories wired for high-speed internet access and linked to campus network. Commuter students can connect to campus network. Online course registration, online library, helpline, repair service, student web hosting, wireless network available.

Student life. **Freshman orientation:** Mandatory. Preregistration for classes offered. One-day, 2-day, and 4-day programs offered before fall semester. Late orientations offered in August and mini-orientations held the first day of class. **Policies:** Freshmen permitted cars on campus. **Housing:** Single-sex dorms, apartments, fraternity/sorority housing, substance-free housing available. $75 fully refundable deposit, deadline 3/28. Theme housing. **Activities:** Bands, choral groups, dance, drama, film society, literary magazine, music ensembles, musical theater, opera, radio station, student government, student newspaper, symphony orchestra, TV station, political and religious groups, ethnic clubs, outdoor clubs, community service organization.

Athletics. NCAA. **Intercollegiate:** Baseball M, basketball, cheerleading, cross-country W, diving, football (tackle) M, golf M, gymnastics W, skiing, soccer W, softball W, swimming, tennis, track and field, volleyball W. **Intramural:** Fencing, lacrosse, racquetball, rugby M, soccer M, volleyball M, water polo M. **Team name:** Utes.

Student services. Adult student services, alcohol/substance abuse counseling, campus ministries, career counseling, student employment services, financial aid counseling, health services, minority student services, on-campus daycare, personal counseling, placement for graduates, veterans' counselor, women's services. **Physically disabled:** Services for visually, speech, hearing impaired.

Contact. E-mail: admissions@sa.utah.edu
Phone: (801) 581-7281 Toll-free number: (800) 685-8856
Fax: (801) 581-7864
John Boswell, Director of Admissions, University of Utah, 201 South 1460 East Room 250S, Salt Lake City, UT 84112-9057

Utah State University

Logan, Utah
www.usu.edu **CB code: 4857**

- Public 4-year university
- Residential campus in small city
- 12,530 degree-seeking undergraduates: 16% part-time, 49% women, 1% African American, 1% Asian American, 2% Hispanic American, 3% international
- 1,632 degree-seeking graduate students
- SAT or ACT (ACT writing optional) required
- 46% graduate within 6 years; 23% enter graduate study

General. Founded in 1888. Regionally accredited. **Degrees:** 2,609 bachelor's, 35 associate awarded; master's, doctoral offered. **ROTC:** Army, Air Force. **Location:** 80 miles from Salt Lake City. **Calendar:** Semester, extensive summer session. **Full-time faculty:** 727 total; 86% have terminal degrees, 6% minority, 31% women. **Part-time faculty:** 37 total; 51% have terminal degrees, 5% minority, 65% women. **Class size:** 41% < 20, 37% 20-39, 9% 40-49, 10% 50-99, 3% >100. **Special facilities:** Agricultural experiment stations, water research laboratory, space shuttle experiments, forestry research facility, botanical gardens, teaching greenhouse, research park, laboratory school, art museum, off-campus theater performance lab, anthropology museum.

Freshman class profile. 2,054 enrolled.

Mid 50% test scores		**Rank in top quarter:**	51%
SAT verbal:	470-620	**Rank in top tenth:**	25%
SAT math:	490-620	**Out-of-state:**	21%
ACT:	21-27	**International:**	4%
GPA 3.50 or higher:	62%	**Fraternities:**	2%
GPA 3.0-3.49:	25%	**Sororities:**	2%
GPA 2.0-2.99:	12%		

Basis for selection. High school record, test scores most important. Audition required for music; portfolio required for art. **Homeschooled:** Early entry policy applies: junior equivalent, ACT, letters of approval.

High school preparation. Required and recommended units include English 4, mathematics 3, history 1, science 3 (laboratory 1), foreign language 2 and academic electives 4. Some social studies required as part of electives.

2005-2006 Annual costs. Tuition/fees: $3,672; $10,616 out-of-state. Room/board: $4,330.

Financial aid. All financial aid based on need.

Application procedures. **Admission:** No deadline. $40 fee. Application may be submitted online. Admission notification on a rolling basis. **Financial aid:** No deadline. FAFSA, institutional form required. Applicants notified on a rolling basis starting 4/1; must reply within 4 week(s) of notification.

Academics. **Special study options:** Accelerated study, cooperative education, cross-registration, distance learning, double major, dual enrollment of high school students, ESL, exchange student, honors, independent study, internships, liberal arts/career combination, student-designed major, study abroad, teacher certification program, weekend college. **Credit/placement by examination:** AP, CLEP, IB, SAT, ACT, institutional tests. 16 credits of lower division course work per language. **Support services:** Learning center, pre-admission summer program, reduced course load, remedial instruction, study skills assistance, tutoring, writing center.

Majors. **Agriculture:** Agronomy, animal sciences, business, dairy, economics, equipment technology, food science, horticultural science, ornamental horticulture, range science, soil science. **Architecture:** Landscape. **Area/ethnic studies:** American, Asian. **Biology:** General, botany, ecology, entomology, zoology. **Business:** General, accounting, administrative services, business admin, fashion, finance, human resources, marketing, operations. **Communications:** Journalism. **Computer sciences:** General, information systems. **Conservation:** Forestry, wildlife. **Education:** Agricultural, biology, business, chemistry, curriculum, early childhood, elementary, family/consumer sciences, health, mathematics, multi-level teacher, music, physical, physics, sales/marketing, science, secondary, social studies, special, technology/industrial arts, voc/tech. **Engineering:** General, aerospace, agricultural, civil, computer, electrical, environmental, mechanical. **Engineering technology:** Electrical. **English:** Speech/rhetoric. **Family/consumer sciences:** Clothing/textiles, family studies, food/nutrition, housing. **Foreign languages:** French, German, Spanish. **Health:** Audiology/speech pathology, clinical lab science, music therapy, predentistry, premedicine, preveterinary. **History:** General. **Legal studies:** Prelaw. **Liberal arts:** Arts/sciences. **Math:** General, statistics. **Mechanic/repair:** Aircraft. **Parks/recreation:** General, facilities management. **Philosophy/religion:** Philosophy. **Physical sciences:** Chemistry, geology, hydrology, physics. **Psychology:** General. **Public administration:** Social work. **Social sciences:** Anthropology, economics, geography, political science, sociology. **Visual/performing arts:** Art, dance, dramatic, interior design.

Most popular majors. Business/marketing 16%, education 13%, engineering/engineering technologies 9%, family/consumer sciences 8%, social sciences 7%, visual/performing arts 6%.

Computing on campus. 910 workstations in dormitories, library, computer center, student center. Dormitories wired for high-speed internet access and linked to campus network. Commuter students can connect to campus network. Online course registration, helpline, repair service, student web hosting available.

Student life. Freshman orientation: Mandatory, $25 fee. Preregistration for classes offered. Half-day, 1, 2 and 4-day orientation sessions available in June and July for fall semester, half-day session in November for spring semester, and half-day session in March for summer semester. **Policies:** Freshmen permitted cars on campus. **Housing:** Coed dorms, single-sex dorms, special housing for disabled, apartments, fraternity/sorority housing, substance-free housing available. $150 partly refundable deposit, deadline 7/1. Mobile home park available. **Activities:** Bands, choral groups, drama, music ensembles, musical theater, opera, student government, student newspaper, symphony orchestra, Latter-day Saints, Catholic, Lutheran, Baptist student organizations, Crusade for Christ, Christian Fellowship, black student union, Hispanic student union, Native American student union, Polynesian student union, Asian American student union.

Athletics. NCAA. **Intercollegiate:** Basketball, cross-country, football (tackle) M, golf M, gymnastics W, soccer W, softball W, tennis, track and field, volleyball W. **Intramural:** Badminton, basketball, cross-country, football (non-tackle), golf, racquetball, soccer, softball, table tennis, tennis, triathlon, volleyball. **Team name:** Aggies.

Student services. Adult student services, alcohol/substance abuse counseling, career counseling, student employment services, financial aid counseling, health services, minority student services, on-campus daycare, personal counseling, placement for graduates, veterans' counselor, women's services. **Physically disabled:** Services for visually, speech, hearing impaired.

Contact. E-mail: admit@cc.usu.edu
Phone: (435) 797-1079 Toll-free number: (800) 488-8108
Fax: (435) 797-3708
Jimmy Moore, Director of Admissions, Utah State University, 0160 Old Main Hill, Logan, UT 84322-0160

Utah Valley State College

Orem, Utah
www.uvsc.edu **CB code: 4870**

- Public 4-year university and technical college
- Commuter campus in small city
- 19,331 degree-seeking undergraduates: 43% part-time, 43% women, 1% African American, 2% Asian American, 4% Hispanic American, 1% Native American, 1% international
- 45% graduate within 6 years

General. Founded in 1941. Regionally accredited. Access to libraries at Brigham Young University. Over 30 four-year bachelor degree programs available. **Degrees:** 1,189 bachelor's, 2,072 associate awarded. **ROTC:** Army, Air Force. **Location:** 45 miles from Salt Lake City. **Calendar:** Semester, limited summer session. **Full-time faculty:** 407 total; 46% have terminal degrees, 12% minority, 34% women. **Part-time faculty:** 924 total; 9% minority, 32% women. **Class size:** 44% < 20, 48% 20-39, 4% 40-49, 4% 50-99, less than 1% >100. **Special facilities:** Airport.

Freshman class profile. 4,473 applied, 4,473 admitted, 3,713 enrolled.

Mid 50% test scores		**Rank in top quarter:**	19%
SAT verbal:	440-540	**Rank in top tenth:**	6%
SAT math:	430-530	**End year in good standing:**	68%
ACT:	18-23	**Return as sophomores:**	43%
GPA 3.50 or higher:	27%	**Out-of-state:**	79%
GPA 3.0-3.49:	31%	**International:**	1%
GPA 2.0-2.99:	38%		

Basis for selection. Open admission. Students will be admitted without ACT/SAT scores, but all full/part-time students under 21 must complete ACT/SAT prior to registration. Students who do not have minimum ACT/SAT score competencies will be required to also take New Student Assessment prior to being cleared for registrations. Minimum scores are ACT English and Math 19, SAT Verbal and Math 500. SAT or ACT scores used for placement and counseling, particularly for math and English courses.

High school preparation. 11 units recommended. Recommended units include English 4, mathematics 3, science 2 and foreign language 2.

2005-2006 Annual costs. Tuition/fees: $3,022; $9,472 out-of-state. Books/supplies: $1,487. Personal expenses: $1,552.

2005-2006 Financial aid. Need-based: Average need met was 54%. Average scholarship/grant was $2,889; average loan $2,123. 39% of total undergraduate aid awarded as scholarships/grants, 61% as loans/jobs. **Non-need-based:** Scholarships awarded for academics, alumni affiliation, art, athletics, leadership, minority status, music/drama.

Application procedures. Admission: Closing date 8/15. $30 fee, may be waived for applicants with need. Application may be submitted online. Admission notification on a rolling basis. **Financial aid:** Priority date 5/1; no closing date. FAFSA, institutional form required. Applicants notified on a rolling basis starting 1/1; must reply within 2 week(s) of notification.

Academics. Special study options: Accelerated study, cooperative education, cross-registration, distance learning, dual enrollment of high school students, ESL, honors, independent study, internships, liberal arts/career combination, student-designed major, study abroad, teacher certification program, weekend college. Evening school. **Credit/placement by examination:** AP, CLEP, IB, SAT, ACT, institutional tests. 16 credit hours maximum toward associate degree, 16 toward bachelor's. No more than 25% of credits applied toward associate degree, diploma, or certificate may be awarded through challenge credit. Regardless of certificate, diploma, or degree (to include a BS degree), maximum 16 credit hours of challenge credit. **Support services:** Learning center, reduced course load, remedial instruction, study skills assistance, tutoring, writing center.

Majors. Biology: General. **Business:** Accounting, business admin, hospitality admin, operations. **Communications:** Digital media. **Computer sciences:** Computer science, data processing. **Education:** Biology, business, chemistry, drama/dance, early childhood, elementary, English, health, history, kindergarten/preschool, mathematics, physical, science, Spanish. **English:** English lit. **Foreign languages:** Spanish. **Health:** Community health, nursing (RN). **History:** General. **Legal studies:** Paralegal. **Math:** General. **Parks/recreation:** Health/fitness. **Philosophy/religion:** Philosophy. **Physical sciences:** Chemistry, geology, physics. **Protective services:** Fire services admin, law enforcement admin. **Psychology:** General. **Social sciences:** Political science. **Transportation:** Airline/commercial pilot. **Visual/performing arts:** Dance, design.

Most popular majors. Business/marketing 34%, computer/information sciences 8%, education 14%, interdisciplinary studies 7%, psychology 14%, trade and industry 6%.

Computing on campus. 1,000 workstations in library, computer center, student center. Commuter students can connect to campus network. Online course registration, online library, helpline, repair service, wireless network available.

Student life. Freshman orientation: Mandatory. Preregistration for classes offered. 3-day adventure session (mountain setting with river rafting, rock climbing). On-campus session also available. **Policies:** Freshmen permitted cars on campus. **Activities:** Bands, choral groups, dance, drama, literary magazine, music ensembles, musical theater, student government, student newspaper, symphony orchestra, TV station, Baptist Student Union, Black Student Union, German Club, International Student Council, Japan Club, Latin American Club, Latter-day Saint Student Association, Multi-Cultural Voices, Native Sun, Russian Club.

Athletics. NCAA. **Intercollegiate:** Baseball M, basketball, cross-country, golf, soccer W, softball W, track and field, volleyball W, wrestling M. **Intramural:** Football (tackle), table tennis. **Team name:** Wolverines.

Student services. Adult student services, alcohol/substance abuse counseling, career counseling, services for economically disadvantaged, student employment services, financial aid counseling, health services, legal services, minority student services, on-campus daycare, personal counseling, placement for graduates, veterans' counselor, women's services. **Physically disabled:** Services for visually, speech, hearing impaired.

Contact. E-mail: info@uvsc.edu
Phone: (801) 863-8466 Fax: (801) 225-4677
Liz Childs, Director of Admissions, Utah Valley State College, 800 West University Parkway, Orem, UT 84058-5999

Weber State University

Ogden, Utah
www.weber.edu **CB code: 4941**

- Public 4-year university
- Commuter campus in small city
- 17,688 degree-seeking undergraduates: 42% part-time, 50% women, 1% African American, 2% Asian American, 4% Hispanic American, 1% Native American, 1% international

- 404 degree-seeking graduate students
- 44% graduate within 6 years; 22% enter graduate study

General. Founded in 1889. Regionally accredited. **Degrees:** 2,069 bachelor's, 1,531 associate awarded; master's offered. **ROTC:** Army, Navy, Air Force. **Location:** 35 miles from Salt Lake City. **Calendar:** Semester, extensive summer session. **Full-time faculty:** 465 total; 85% have terminal degrees, 8% minority, 40% women. **Part-time faculty:** 480 total. **Class size:** 40% < 20, 47% 20-39, 6% 40-49, 6% 50-99, less than 1% >100. **Special facilities:** Museum of natural history, planetarium, aerospace technology center.

Freshman class profile. 5,196 applied, 5,196 admitted, 2,759 enrolled.

Mid 50% test scores		End year in good standing:	79%
SAT verbal:	440-570	Return as sophomores:	71%
SAT math:	430-570	Out-of-state:	7%
ACT:	18-24	Live on campus:	3%
GPA 3.50 or higher:	43%	International:	1%
GPA 3.0-3.49:	27%	Fraternities:	1%
GPA 2.0-2.99:	26%	Sororities:	1%
Rank in top quarter:	68%		

Basis for selection. Open admission, but selective for some programs. Selective admission to nursing, dental health, health professions. Based on test scores, freshmen placed on college or university tier; students with higher scores have fewer restrictions on courses. General Aptitude Test battery required for nursing, dental health, and health professions programs. If student has not taken SAT or ACT, ACT will be administered upon enrollment.

High school preparation. 15 units recommended. Recommended units include English 4, mathematics 2, history 1, science 2, foreign language 2 and academic electives 4. 4 additional courses, at least 2 of which should be from the following: history, English, mathematics beyond algebra, laboratory science, fine arts and computer science.

2005-2006 Annual costs. Tuition/fees: $3,138; $9,599 out-of-state. Room/board: $6,400. Books/supplies: $900. Personal expenses: $1,275.

2004-2005 Financial aid. All financial aid based on need. 1,041 full-time freshmen applied for aid; 863 were judged to have need; 477 of these received aid. Average need met was 54%. Average scholarship/grant was $2,865; average loan $1,841. 51% of total undergraduate aid awarded as scholarships/grants, 49% as loans/jobs.

Application procedures. Admission: Closing date 8/22. $30 fee. Application may be submitted online. Admission notification on a rolling basis. **Financial aid:** Priority date 3/1; no closing date. FAFSA, institutional form required. Applicants notified on a rolling basis starting 3/15; must reply within 2 week(s) of notification.

Academics. Students apply for upper-division courses in junior year. **Special study options:** Accelerated study, cooperative education, distance learning, double major, dual enrollment of high school students, ESL, exchange student, external degree, honors, independent study, internships, New York semester, semester at sea, student-designed major, study abroad, teacher certification program, United Nations semester, Washington semester. First-year experience. **Credit/placement by examination:** AP, CLEP, IB, institutional tests. 30 credit hours maximum toward bachelor's degree. **Support services:** Learning center, pre-admission summer program, reduced course load, remedial instruction, study skills assistance, tutoring, writing center.

Majors. Area/ethnic studies: African-American, Hispanic-American/Latino/Chicano, Native American. **Biology:** Bacteriology, botany, zoology. **Business:** Accounting, administrative services, business admin, finance, human resources, logistics, management information systems, managerial economics, marketing, office management. **Communications:** Broadcast journalism, journalism, public relations. **Computer sciences:** General, computer science, information systems, networking. **Construction:** Maintenance. **Education:** Art, bilingual, biology, business, chemistry, drama/dance, early childhood, elementary, English, French, German, history, mathematics, music, physical, physics, science, secondary, social science, social studies, Spanish. **Engineering:** Physics. **Engineering technology:** Electrical. **English:** Technical writing. **Family/consumer sciences:** Family studies. **Foreign languages:** French, German, Spanish. **Health:** Athletic training, clinical lab science, dental hygiene, health care admin, medical radiologic technology/radiation therapy, nuclear medical technology, nursing (RN), respiratory therapy technology, sonography. **History:** General. **Interdisciplinary:** Gerontology. **Liberal arts:** Arts/sciences. **Math:** General, applied. **Military:** General. **Parks/recreation:** Exercise sciences, health/fitness. **Physical sciences:** Chemistry, geology, physics. **Protective services:** Corrections, criminal justice, police science. **Psychology:** General. **Public administration:** Social work. **Social sciences:** Economics, geography, political science, sociology. **Visual/performing arts:** General, art, commercial/advertising art, dance, design, dramatic, music performance, photography, piano/organ, studio arts, voice/opera.

Most popular majors. Business/marketing 22%, computer/information sciences 7%, education 10%, health sciences 13%, security/protective services 7%.

Computing on campus. 558 workstations in dormitories, library, computer center, student center. Dormitories wired for high-speed internet access and linked to campus network. Commuter students can connect to campus network. Online course registration, online library, helpline, repair service, student web hosting, wireless network available.

Student life. Freshman orientation: Available. Preregistration for classes offered. April 19 through 25, 4 hours in length. **Policies:** Freshmen permitted cars on campus. **Housing:** Single-sex dorms, special housing for disabled, apartments, substance-free housing available. $175 partly refundable deposit, deadline 8/1. **Activities:** Bands, choral groups, dance, drama, film society, literary magazine, music ensembles, musical theater, opera, radio station, student government, student newspaper, symphony orchestra, TV station, Latter-day Saint Student Association, Newman Center, Black Scholars United, international student association, physically challenged student association.

Athletics. NCAA. **Intercollegiate:** Basketball, cross-country, football (tackle) M, golf, soccer W, tennis, track and field, volleyball W. **Intramural:** Baseball M, basketball, bowling, racquetball, soccer, softball, tennis, track and field, volleyball. **Team name:** Wildcats.

Student services. Adult student services, alcohol/substance abuse counseling, campus ministries, career counseling, services for economically disadvantaged, student employment services, financial aid counseling, health services, legal services, minority student services, on-campus daycare, personal counseling, placement for graduates, veterans' counselor, women's services. **Physically disabled:** Services for visually, speech, hearing impaired.

Contact. E-mail: admissions@weber.edu
Phone: (801) 626-6744 Toll-free number: (800) 848-7770
Fax: (801) 626-6747
Christopher Rivera, Director of Admissions, Weber State University, 1137 University Circle, Ogden, UT 84408-1137

Western Governors University

Salt Lake City, Utah
www.wgu.edu **CB code: 3349**

- Private 4-year virtual college
- Very large city
- 4,000 undergraduates
- 1,000 graduate students

General. Candidate for regional accreditation; also accredited by DETC. **Degrees:** 130 bachelor's, 12 associate awarded; master's offered. **Calendar:** Continuous. **Full-time faculty:** 50 total. **Part-time faculty:** 10 total.

Basis for selection. Open admission. ACT or SAT not required for admission but will be accepted if submitted.

2005-2006 Annual costs. Tuition/fees: $5,670. Tuition is based on 6 month terms.

Academics. Credit/placement by examination: CLEP.

Majors. Business: Human resources. **Computer sciences:** General.

Contact. E-mail: info@wgu.edu
Phone: (801) 274-3280 Toll-free number: (877) 435-7948
Fax: (801) 274-3305
Chris Mallett, Director of Enrollment, Western Governors University, 4001 South 700 East, Suite 700, Salt Lake City, UT 84107

Westminster College

Salt Lake City, Utah
www.westminstercollege.edu **CB code: 4948**

- Private 4-year liberal arts college
- Residential campus in large city
- 1,842 degree-seeking undergraduates: 11% part-time, 58% women, 1% African American, 3% Asian American, 6% Hispanic American, 2% international
- 571 degree-seeking graduate students
- 89% of applicants admitted

- SAT or ACT (ACT writing recommended) required
- 57% graduate within 6 years; 27% enter graduate study

General. Founded in 1875. Regionally accredited. Curriculum combines professional and liberal arts study. **Degrees:** 470 bachelor's awarded; master's offered. **ROTC:** Army, Navy, Air Force. **Location:** 6 miles from downtown. **Calendar:** 4-1-4, limited summer session. **Full-time faculty:** 121 total; 91% have terminal degrees, 3% minority, 51% women. **Part-time faculty:** 138 total; 55% have terminal degrees, less than 1% minority, 56% women. **Class size:** 69% < 20, 28% 20-39, 2% 40-49. **Special facilities:** Meade Lx200 telescope.

Freshman class profile. 897 applied, 801 admitted, 350 enrolled.

Mid 50% test scores			
SAT verbal:	490-630	**Rank in top quarter:**	57%
SAT math:	470-610	**Rank in top tenth:**	30%
ACT:	21-26	**End year in good standing:**	92%
GPA 3.50 or higher:	62%	**Return as sophomores:**	74%
GPA 3.0-3.49:	25%	**Out-of-state:**	20%
GPA 2.0-2.99:	13%	**Live on campus:**	55%

Basis for selection. Academic performance in high school and GPA are important. Essay, interview recommended.

High school preparation. Required and recommended units include English 4-6, mathematics 2-3, social studies 2, history 1, science 3, foreign language 2-3 and academic electives 2-3.

2005-2006 Annual costs. Tuition/fees: $19,724. Room/board: $5,932. Books/supplies: $1,000. Personal expenses: $1,225.

2005-2006 Financial aid. Need-based: 271 full-time freshmen applied for aid; 221 were judged to have need; 221 of these received aid. Average need met was 91%. Average scholarship/grant was $11,241; average loan $3,397. 57% of total undergraduate aid awarded as scholarships/grants, 43% as loans/jobs. **Non-need-based:** Awarded to 554 full-time undergraduates, including 154 freshmen. Scholarships awarded for academics, alumni affiliation, art, athletics, leadership, minority status, music/drama, religious affiliation.

Application procedures. Admission: $40 fee, may be waived for applicants with need. Application may be submitted online. Admission notification on a rolling basis beginning on or about 10/1. Must reply by May 1 or within 3 week(s) if notified thereafter. **Financial aid:** Priority date 4/15; no closing date. FAFSA required. Applicants notified on a rolling basis starting 3/15; must reply within 3 week(s) of notification.

Academics. Special study options: Accelerated study, combined bachelor's/graduate degree, cooperative education, double major, dual enrollment of high school students, honors, independent study, internships, liberal arts/career combination, semester at sea, student-designed major, study abroad, teacher certification program, weekend college. **Credit/placement by examination:** AP, CLEP, IB, SAT, ACT, institutional tests. 40 credit hours maximum toward bachelor's degree. **Support services:** Remedial instruction, study skills assistance, tutoring, writing center.

Honors college/program. 35 freshman per year, admission by invitation.

Majors. Biology: General. **Business:** General, accounting, business admin, international. **Communications:** General. **Computer sciences:** Computer science. **Education:** General, early childhood, elementary, secondary, special. **English:** English lit. **History:** General. **Math:** General. **Philosophy/religion:** Philosophy. **Physical sciences:** Chemistry, physics. **Psychology:** General. **Social sciences:** General, political science, sociology. **Transportation:** Aviation, aviation management. **Visual/performing arts:** Art.

Most popular majors. Business/marketing 36%, communications/journalism 6%, education 7%, health sciences 11%, psychology 8%.

Computing on campus. 412 workstations in dormitories, library, computer center, student center. Dormitories wired for high-speed internet access and linked to campus network. Commuter students can connect to campus network. Online course registration, online library, helpline, student web hosting, wireless network available.

Student life. Freshman orientation: Mandatory. Preregistration for classes offered. **Policies:** Freshmen permitted cars on campus. **Housing:** Guaranteed on-campus for freshmen. Coed dorms, single-sex dorms, apartments available. $200 nonrefundable deposit, deadline 6/1. **Activities:** Jazz band, choral groups, dance, drama, film society, literary magazine, music ensembles, musical theater, student government, student newspaper, symphony orchestra, Campus Ministry, College Democrats, College Republicans, Habitat for Humanity, Earth Effort, Latter-day Saint Student Association, Native American Club, Volunteer Club, Pride Club.

Athletics. NAIA. **Intercollegiate:** Basketball, cross-country, golf, soccer M, volleyball W. **Intramural:** Basketball, bowling, cross-country, football (non-tackle), skiing, soccer, table tennis, tennis, volleyball, weight lifting. **Team name:** Griffins.

Student services. Alcohol/substance abuse counseling, campus ministries, career counseling, student employment services, financial aid counseling, health services, minority student services, personal counseling, placement for graduates, veterans' counselor. **Physically disabled:** Services for visually, hearing impaired.

Contact. E-mail: admission@westminstercollege.edu
Phone: (801) 832-2200 Toll-free number: (800) 748-4753
Fax: (801) 832-3101
Bonnie Sofarelli, Director of Admissions, Westminster College, 1840 South 1300 East, Salt Lake City, UT 84105

Vermont

Bennington College

Bennington, Vermont — **CB member**
www.bennington.edu — **CB code: 3080**

- Private 4-year liberal arts college
- Residential campus in large town
- 571 degree-seeking undergraduates: 1% part-time, 66% women, 2% African American, 2% Asian American, 3% Hispanic American, 3% international
- 141 degree-seeking graduate students
- 62% of applicants admitted
- Application essay required
- 60% graduate within 6 years; 11% enter graduate study

General. Founded in 1932. Regionally accredited. **Degrees:** 138 bachelor's awarded; master's offered. **Location:** 45 miles from Albany, New York, 150 miles from Boston and New York City. **Calendar:** 15-week fall and spring terms; 7-week winter work term (January/February). **Full-time faculty:** 66 total; 74% have terminal degrees, 14% minority, 41% women. **Part-time faculty:** 24 total; 25% have terminal degrees, 17% minority, 29% women. **Class size:** 90% < 20, 10% 20-39, less than 1% 50-99. **Special facilities:** Center for Languages and Cultures, Center for Creative Teaching, science center, early childhood center; computer center and media labs, digital arts lab, art gallery; architecture, drawing, painting, printmaking, and sculpture studios, ceramics studio and kilns, color and black-and-white photography darkrooms, film and video editing studio, several fully equipped professional theatres, scripts library, dance studios and archives, electronic music and sound recording studios, music practice rooms and music library, radio station, student run cafe, fitness center, observatory; greenhouse, and 550 acres of forest, ponds, wetlands, fields for biological study.

Freshman class profile. 723 applied, 445 admitted, 137 enrolled.

GPA 3.50 or higher:	41%	**End year in good standing:**	95%
GPA 3.0-3.49:	37%	**Return as sophomores:**	87%
GPA 2.0-2.99:	22%	**Out-of-state:**	98%
Rank in top quarter:	74%	**Live on campus:**	99%
Rank in top tenth:	30%	**International:**	2%

Basis for selection. Admissions decisions are based upon the strength of an applicants academic record and extracurricular activities, the quality of the ideas expressed in the application, and the support of teachers and guidance counselor in discussing the student's performance in school. Phone and in-person interviews with large portion of applicant pool for more in-depth discussions. Portfolio reviews not offered or required. **Homeschooled:** Statement describing homeschool structure and mission, transcript of courses and grades, state high school equivalency certificate, letter of recommendation (nonparent) required. Documentation of academic work (course descriptions and a reading list) required. Strongly encourage standardized test, SAT or ACT.

High school preparation. 18 units recommended. Recommended units include English 4, mathematics 3, social studies 2, history 3, science 3 and foreign language 3. Students are expected to take a full academic course load each term.

2005-2006 Annual costs. Tuition/fees: $33,570. Room/board: $8,320. Books/supplies: $800. Personal expenses: $1,684.

2005-2006 Financial aid. Need-based: 98 full-time freshmen applied for aid; 91 were judged to have need; 91 of these received aid. Average need met was 75%. Average scholarship/grant was $21,211; average loan $2,281. 77% of total undergraduate aid awarded as scholarships/grants, 23% as loans/jobs. **Non-need-based:** Awarded to 36 full-time undergraduates, including 6 freshmen. Scholarships awarded for academics. **Additional information:** All applicants for undergraduate admission will be considered for scholarships based on the quality of their overall application.

Application procedures. Admission: Closing date 1/3 (postmark date). $60 fee, may be waived for applicants with need. Application may be submitted online. Admission notification 4/1. Must reply by May 1 or within 2 week(s) if notified thereafter. **Financial aid:** Priority date 3/1; no closing date. FAFSA, institutional form required. CSS profile required of early decision applicants only. Applicants notified by 3/30; must reply by 5/1 or within 2 week(s) of notification.

Academics. Internships and field work offered. **Special study options:** Accelerated study, combined bachelor's/graduate degree, cooperative education, cross-registration, double major, ESL, independent study, internships, student-designed major, study abroad, teacher certification program. Post-baccalaureate plan of study for those preparing for medical or allied health grad programs. **Credit/placement by examination:** AP, CLEP. **Support services:** Reduced course load, study skills assistance, tutoring, writing center.

Majors. Architecture: Architecture. **Area/ethnic studies:** American, Asian, European, gay/lesbian, women's. **Biology:** General, botany, cellular/molecular, ecology, environmental, evolutionary, zoology. **Communications:** Journalism. **Communications technology:** Animation/special effects. **Computer sciences:** Computer science. **Conservation:** Environmental science, environmental studies. **Education:** General, early childhood, elementary, middle, secondary. **English:** American lit, British lit, composition, creative writing, English lit. **Foreign languages:** General, Chinese, French, Italian, Japanese, Spanish. **Health:** Premedicine. **History:** General, American, European. **Interdisciplinary:** Global studies, math/computer science, peace/conflict. **Legal studies:** Prelaw. **Liberal arts:** Arts/sciences, humanities. **Math:** General. **Philosophy/religion:** Philosophy. **Physical sciences:** General, astronomy, chemistry, physics. **Psychology:** General. **Social sciences:** General, anthropology, international relations, political science, sociology, U.S. government. **Visual/performing arts:** General, acting, ceramics, cinematography, dance, design, directing/producing, dramatic, drawing, film/cinema, jazz, multimedia, music history, music performance, music theory/composition, musicology, painting, photography, piano/organ, play/screenwriting, printmaking, sculpture, stringed instruments, studio arts, theater design, theater history, voice/opera.

Most popular majors. English 15%, social sciences 12%, visual/performing arts 53%.

Computing on campus. 75 workstations in library, computer center, student center. Dormitories wired for high-speed internet access and linked to campus network. Commuter students can connect to campus network. Helpline, wireless network available.

Student life. Freshman orientation: Available. Preregistration for classes offered. 6-day orientation program prior to the start of fall classes. International students have 1 extra day. Students may also participate in pre-orientation camping trips run by the outing club. **Policies:** Freshmen permitted cars on campus. **Housing:** Guaranteed on-campus for all undergraduates. Coed dorms, special housing for disabled, cooperative housing, substance-free housing available. **Activities:** Bands, choral groups, dance, drama, film society, literary magazine, music ensembles, radio station, student government, student newspaper, symphony orchestra, Amnesty International, Legal Aliens, Student Endowment for the Arts, Literature Gathering, Open Critique Night, Outing Club, Student Action Network, Queer Student Union, Community Garden, Social Science Colloquium.

Athletics. Intramural: Soccer.

Student services. Career counseling, student employment services, financial aid counseling, health services, on-campus daycare, personal counseling, placement for graduates. **Physically disabled:** Services for hearing impaired.

Contact. E-mail: admissions@bennington.edu
Phone: (802) 440-4312 Toll-free number: (800) 833-6845
Fax: (802) 440-4320
Ken Himmelman, Dean of Admissions and Financial Aid, Bennington College, One College Drive, Bennington, VT 05201-6003

Burlington College

Burlington, Vermont
www.burlingtoncollege.edu — **CB code: 1119**

- Private 4-year liberal arts college
- Commuter campus in small city
- 188 degree-seeking undergraduates
- Application essay, interview required

General. Founded in 1972. Regionally accredited. Flexible liberal arts education offered for adult learners. **Degrees:** 38 bachelor's awarded. **Location:** 100 miles from Montreal, Canada, 200 miles from Boston. **Calendar:** Semester, limited summer session. **Full-time faculty:** 5 total. **Part-time faculty:** 80 total. **Class size:** 99% < 20, 1% 20-39. **Special facilities:** Film production facilities, special cinema studies collection.

Freshman class profile.

Out-of-state:	50%	**Live on campus:**	96%

Basis for selection. Applicants must demonstrate ability to write at beginning college level or higher. Writing samples needed for external degree program. Two letters of recommendation. SAT or ACT scores not required, but students must take assessments for math, writing, and computer literacy. **Homeschooled:** Portfolio-style transcripts accepted.

High school preparation. Recommended units include English 4, mathematics 3, social studies 4, history 3, science 3 (laboratory 1), foreign language 2 and academic electives 4.

2005-2006 Annual costs. Tuition/fees: $14,670. Books/supplies: $600. Personal expenses: $900.

Financial aid. All financial aid based on need.

Application procedures. Admission: Closing date 7/30 (postmark date). $35 fee. Admission notification on a rolling basis. Application fee may be deferred until enrollment for qualified financial aid applicants. **Financial aid:** Priority date 6/1, closing date 8/1. FAFSA required. Applicants notified on a rolling basis starting 4/1; must reply by 8/1.

Academics. Special study options: Combined bachelor's/graduate degree, cross-registration, distance learning, double major, dual enrollment of high school students, external degree, independent study, internships, liberal arts/career combination, student-designed major, study abroad, weekend college. **Credit/placement by examination:** CLEP, IB, institutional tests. 42 credit hours maximum toward associate degree, 90 toward bachelor's. **Support services:** Learning center, reduced course load, remedial instruction, study skills assistance, tutoring, writing center.

Majors. Area/ethnic studies: Latin American, women's. **Communications technology:** Animation/special effects, photo/film/video. **English:** Composition, creative writing. **Foreign languages:** Comparative lit. **Health:** Art therapy. **History:** General. **Legal studies:** General. **Liberal arts:** Arts/sciences, humanities. **Philosophy/religion:** Philosophy, religion. **Psychology:** General. **Public administration:** Human services. **Social sciences:** General. **Visual/performing arts:** General, cinematography, drawing, film/cinema, painting, photography, studio arts, theater history.

Most popular majors. English 17%, psychology 54%, visual/performing arts 20%.

Computing on campus. 21 workstations in library, computer center, student center. Commuter students can connect to campus network. Online library available.

Student life. Freshman orientation: Mandatory, $150 fee. Preregistration for classes offered. **Policies:** Freshmen permitted cars on campus. **Housing:** Apartments available. $575 deposit. **Activities:** Drama, film society, literary magazine, student government, student newspaper, with 5 other colleges in the area, students are offered many social, cultural, and outdoor recreational opportunities year-round.

Student services. Adult student services, career counseling, student employment services, financial aid counseling, personal counseling.

Contact. E-mail: admissions@burlcol.edu
Phone: (802) 862-9616 Toll-free number: (800) 862-9616
Fax: (802) 660-4331
Cathleen Sullivan, Director of Admissions, Burlington College, 95 North Avenue, Burlington, VT 05401

Castleton State College

Castleton, Vermont — **CB member**
www.castleton.edu — **CB code: 3765**

- Public 4-year liberal arts college
- Residential campus in small town
- 1,840 degree-seeking undergraduates: 9% part-time, 58% women, 1% African American, 1% Asian American, 1% Hispanic American, 1% Native American
- 53 degree-seeking graduate students
- 79% of applicants admitted
- SAT or ACT with writing, application essay required
- 40% graduate within 6 years

General. Founded in 1787. Regionally accredited. **Degrees:** 239 bachelor's, 73 associate awarded; master's offered. **ROTC:** Army. **Location:** 12 miles from Rutland. **Calendar:** Semester, limited summer session. **Full-time faculty:** 89 total; 93% have terminal degrees, 7% minority, 48% women. **Part-time faculty:** 112 total; 29% have terminal degrees, 46% women. **Class size:** 73% < 20, 26% 20-39, less than 1% 40-49, 1% 50-99, less than 1% >100. **Special facilities:** Medical society museum, outdoor classroom.

Freshman class profile. 1,715 applied, 1,348 admitted, 467 enrolled.

Mid 50% test scores			
SAT verbal:	430-550	Rank in top quarter:	20%
SAT math:	460-540	Rank in top tenth:	5%
ACT:	17-21	Return as sophomores:	66%
GPA 3.50 or higher:	13%	Out-of-state:	43%
GPA 3.0-3.49:	28%	Live on campus:	80%
GPA 2.0-2.99:	59%	International:	1%

Basis for selection. School achievement record, test scores, recommendations important. Class rank, if available, considered. Interview recommended for all; audition recommended for music.

High school preparation. College-preparatory program required. 14 units required; 16 recommended. Required and recommended units include English 4, mathematics 3, social studies 3-4, science 3-4 (laboratory 2) and foreign language 2.

2005-2006 Annual costs. Tuition/fees: $6,484; $13,804 out-of-state. New England Board of Higher Education rate for students from other New England states: 150% of Vermont resident tuition. Room/board: $6,674. Books/supplies: $800. Personal expenses: $600.

Financial aid. Non-need-based: Scholarships awarded for academics, alumni affiliation, art, leadership, music/drama, state residency.

Application procedures. Admission: No deadline. $35 fee, may be waived for applicants with need. Admission notification on a rolling basis beginning on or about 10/1. **Financial aid:** Priority date 2/15; no closing date. FAFSA required. Applicants notified on a rolling basis starting 1/1; must reply by 5/1 or within 2 week(s) of notification.

Academics. Special study options: Combined bachelor's/graduate degree, cooperative education, cross-registration, double major, dual enrollment of high school students, honors, independent study, internships, liberal arts/career combination, student-designed major, study abroad, teacher certification program. 5-year MBA with Clarkson University; 7-year physical therapy with Sage Graduate School; 6-year occupational therapy with Sage Graduate School. **Credit/placement by examination:** AP, CLEP, SAT, ACT, institutional tests. 30 credit hours maximum toward associate degree, 60 toward bachelor's. **Support services:** Learning center, reduced course load, remedial instruction, study skills assistance, tutoring, writing center.

Majors. Biology: General. **Business:** General, accounting, business admin, management science, marketing. **Communications:** Digital media, journalism, media studies. **Computer sciences:** General, webmaster. **Conservation:** Environmental science. **Education:** Art, biology, chemistry, drama/dance, elementary, English, foreign languages, history, mathematics, middle, music, physical, physics, science, secondary, social science, social studies, Spanish. **English:** American lit. **Foreign languages:** Spanish. **Health:** Athletic training. **History:** General. **Interdisciplinary:** Biological/physical sciences, math/computer science, natural sciences. **Math:** General, statistics. **Parks/recreation:** Exercise sciences, health/fitness, sports admin. **Physical sciences:** Geology. **Protective services:** Criminal justice. **Psychology:** General. **Public administration:** Social work. **Social sciences:** General, criminology, sociology. **Visual/performing arts:** General, art, dramatic.

Most popular majors. Business/marketing 18%, communications/journalism 8%, interdisciplinary studies 8%, parks/recreation 10%, psychology 7%, social sciences 7%, visual/performing arts 14%.

Computing on campus. 200 workstations in dormitories, library, computer center. Dormitories wired for high-speed internet access and linked to campus network. Commuter students can connect to campus network. Repair service available.

Student life. Freshman orientation: Mandatory. Preregistration for classes offered. 2 and a half day program. **Policies:** Freshmen permitted cars on campus. **Housing:** Guaranteed on-campus for freshmen. Coed dorms, substance-free housing available. $200 nonrefundable deposit, deadline 5/1. **Activities:** Jazz band, choral groups, dance, drama, literary magazine, music ensembles, musical theater, radio station, student government, student newspaper, TV station, Christian fellowships, political discussion group, Spanish club, social issues club, community service club, women's issues group.

Athletics. NCAA. **Intercollegiate:** Baseball M, basketball, cross-country, field hockey W, golf M, ice hockey, lacrosse, skiing, soccer, softball W, tennis, volleyball W. **Intramural:** Basketball, football (non-tackle), racquetball, soccer, softball, swimming, table tennis, tennis, volleyball. **Team name:** Spartans.

Student services. Adult student services, alcohol/substance abuse counseling, career counseling, services for economically disadvantaged, student employment services, financial aid counseling, health services, personal counseling, placement for graduates.

Contact. E-mail: info@castleton.edu
Phone: (802) 468-1213 Toll-free number: (800) 639-8521
Fax: (802) 468-1476
Maurice Ouimet, Director of Admissions, Castleton State College, Seminary Street, Castleton, VT 05735

Champlain College

Burlington, Vermont — **CB member**
www.champlain.edu — **CB code: 3291**

- Private 4-year business and liberal arts college
- Residential campus in small city
- 2,296 degree-seeking undergraduates: 23% part-time, 48% women, 1% African American, 1% Asian American, 1% Hispanic American
- 55 degree-seeking graduate students
- 67% of applicants admitted
- SAT or ACT (ACT writing optional), application essay required

General. Founded in 1878. Regionally accredited. **Degrees:** 161 bachelor's, 361 associate awarded; master's offered. **ROTC:** Army. **Location:** 200 miles from Boston, 90 miles from Montreal. **Calendar:** Semester, limited summer session. **Full-time faculty:** 65 total; 37% have terminal degrees, 2% minority, 38% women. **Part-time faculty:** 191 total; 26% have terminal degrees, 1% minority, 44% women. **Class size:** 37% < 20, 63% 20-39, less than 1% 40-49.

Freshman class profile. 1,850 applied, 1,244 admitted, 461 enrolled.

Mid 50% test scores			
SAT verbal:	490-590	Rank in top tenth:	10%
SAT math:	480-590	Return as sophomores:	82%
ACT:	18-20	Out-of-state:	70%
Rank in top quarter:	15%	Live on campus:	90%

Basis for selection. GPA, level of difficulty of high school curriculum, essay, interview, counselor recommendations most important. Waiting list for Radiography and Electronic Gaming and Interactive Design programs only. Interview strongly recommended. **Homeschooled:** GED or two SAT Subject Tests required.

High school preparation. 20 units required. Required and recommended units include English 4, mathematics 3-4, social studies 2, history 2-4, science 3-4 (laboratory 2-3), foreign language 2 and academic electives 2.

2006-2007 Annual costs. Tuition/fees: $16,250. Room/board: $10,125. Books/supplies: $600. Personal expenses: $600.

2004-2005 Financial aid. Need-based: 361 full-time freshmen applied for aid; 268 were judged to have need; 257 of these received aid. Average need met was 58%. Average scholarship/grant was $4,869; average loan $4,886. 37% of total undergraduate aid awarded as scholarships/grants, 63% as loans/jobs. **Non-need-based:** Awarded to 286 full-time undergraduates, including 95 freshmen. Scholarships awarded for academics, leadership.

Application procedures. Admission: Closing date 8/30. $40 fee, may be waived for applicants with need. Application may be submitted online. Admission notification on a rolling basis beginning on or about 9/15. Must reply by May 1 or within 2 week(s) if notified thereafter. Housing deposit refundable prior to 5/1 only. **Financial aid:** Closing date 5/1. FAFSA, institutional form required. Applicants notified on a rolling basis starting 3/1; must reply within 2 week(s) of notification.

Academics. 96% of majors include required internship. **Special study options:** Accelerated study, combined bachelor's/graduate degree, cooperative education, cross-registration, distance learning, double major, honors, independent study, internships, liberal arts/career combination, study abroad, teacher certification program. Clinical internships at Flether Allen Medical Center, "Plus Two" format for all majors. **Credit/placement by examination:** AP, CLEP, IB, institutional tests. 30 credit hours maximum toward associate degree, 75 toward bachelor's. **Support services:** Reduced course load, study skills assistance, tutoring, writing center.

Majors. Business: General, accounting, accounting/business management, accounting/finance, business admin, communications, e-commerce, hospitality admin, hospitality/recreation, hotel/motel admin, human resources, international, marketing, organizational behavior, restaurant/food services, small business admin, tourism promotion, tourism/travel, travel services. **Communications:** Digital media, journalism, media studies, organizational, public relations. **Communications technology:** Animation/special effects, graphics. **Computer sciences:** General, computer graphics, computer science, information systems, LAN/WAN management, networking, security, system admin, systems analysis, web page design, webmaster. **Education:** General, early childhood, elementary, kindergarten/preschool, middle, secondary. **Engineering:** Software. **English:** Composition, creative writing, technical writing. **Family/consumer sciences:** Family/community services. **Legal studies:** Paralegal, prelaw. **Liberal arts:** Arts/sciences. **Personal/culinary services:** Restaurant/catering. **Protective services:** Criminal justice, forensics, law enforcement admin, security management, security services. **Psychology:** General. **Public administration:** Human services, social work. **Visual/performing arts:** Cinematography, design, graphic design, multimedia.

Most popular majors. Business/marketing 43%, computer/information sciences 9%, education 10%, liberal arts 30%, visual/performing arts 7%.

Computing on campus. 260 workstations in library, computer center, student center. Dormitories wired for high-speed internet access and linked to campus network. Commuter students can connect to campus network. Online course registration, online library, helpline, wireless network available.

Student life. Freshman orientation: Available, $60 fee. Preregistration for classes offered. 4-day/3-night program focusing on introductions to campus, academics and Burlington. **Policies:** No alcohol permitted on campus. **Housing:** Guaranteed on-campus for freshmen. Coed dorms, single-sex dorms, substance-free housing available. $150 deposit, deadline 5/1. Wellness, music-focus, and community service theme dorms available. **Activities:** Choral groups, dance, drama, literary magazine, musical theater, radio station, student government, student newspaper, cultural diversity committee, GET REAL community service, international club, outing club, Champlain Heritage Society, Reader's Exchange, flash animation club, Intercollegiate Writers Exchange.

Athletics. Intramural: Basketball, bowling, golf, ice hockey, skiing, soccer, volleyball.

Student services. Adult student services, alcohol/substance abuse counseling, career counseling, student employment services, financial aid counseling, health services, personal counseling, placement for graduates. **Physically disabled:** Services for visually, hearing impaired.

Contact. E-mail: admission@champlain.edu
Phone: (802) 860-2727 Toll-free number: (800) 570-5858
Fax: (802) 860-2767
Josephine Churchill, Director of Admissions, Champlain College, 163 South Willard Street, Burlington, VT 05402-0670

College of St. Joseph in Vermont

Rutland, Vermont — **CB member**
www.csj.edu — **CB code: 3297**

- Private 4-year liberal arts and teachers college affiliated with Roman Catholic Church
- Residential campus in large town
- 236 degree-seeking undergraduates: 26% part-time, 61% women, 4% African American, 1% Asian American, 2% Hispanic American
- 162 degree-seeking graduate students
- 68% of applicants admitted
- SAT or ACT (ACT writing optional), application essay required

General. Founded in 1950. Regionally accredited. **Degrees:** 61 bachelor's, 10 associate awarded; master's offered. **Location:** 70 miles from Burlington, 100 miles from Albany, New York. **Calendar:** Semester, extensive summer session. **Full-time faculty:** 11 total; 73% have terminal degrees, 9% minority, 27% women. **Part-time faculty:** 59 total; 29% have terminal degrees, 2% minority, 52% women. **Class size:** 91% < 20, 9% 20-39. **Special facilities:** Photography and ceramics studios.

Freshman class profile. 157 applied, 107 admitted, 45 enrolled.

Mid 50% test scores			
SAT verbal:	400-520	End year in good standing:	92%
SAT math:	370-500	Return as sophomores:	81%
Rank in top quarter:	5%	Out-of-state:	53%
Rank in top tenth:	1%	Live on campus:	55%
		International:	2%

Basis for selection. Criteria include high school record, 2.0 high school GPA in college preparatory course work, essay, test scores; 2 recommendations and extracurricular activities considered. Interview recommended. **Homeschooled:** Interview required. Personal evaluation required.

High school preparation. 16 units required. Required and recommended units include English 4, mathematics 3, social studies 2, science 2, foreign language 2 and academic electives 5.

2005-2006 Annual costs. Tuition/fees: $14,050. Room/board: $6,850. Books/supplies: $650. Personal expenses: $900.

2005-2006 Financial aid. **Need-based:** 42 full-time freshmen applied for aid; 36 were judged to have need; 36 of these received aid. Average need met was 84%. Average scholarship/grant was $10,748; average loan $3,920. 53% of total undergraduate aid awarded as scholarships/grants, 47% as loans/jobs. **Non-need-based:** Awarded to 19 full-time undergraduates, including 5 freshmen. Scholarships awarded for academics, athletics. **Additional information:** Instructors at local Catholic schools are granted a tuition reduction.

Application procedures. **Admission:** Priority date 3/1; no deadline. $25 fee, may be waived for applicants with need. Application may be submitted online. Admission notification on a rolling basis. Must reply by May 1 or within 2 week(s) if notified thereafter. **Financial aid:** Priority date 3/1; no closing date. FAFSA, institutional form required. Applicants notified on a rolling basis starting 3/15.

Academics. Experiential educational options including internships available. **Special study options:** Accelerated study, combined bachelor's/graduate degree, double major, dual enrollment of high school students, ESL, independent study, internships, liberal arts/career combination, teacher certification program. **Credit/placement by examination:** AP, CLEP, IB, institutional tests. 12 credit hours maximum toward associate degree, 12 toward bachelor's. **Support services:** Learning center, reduced course load, study skills assistance, tutoring, writing center.

Majors. **Business:** General, accounting, business admin, management science, operations, resort management. **Education:** Early childhood, elementary, English, history, middle, multi-level teacher, secondary, social studies, special. **History:** General. **Liberal arts:** Arts/sciences. **Parks/recreation:** Sports admin. **Psychology:** General. **Public administration:** Human services.

Most popular majors. Business/marketing 36%, education 28%, liberal arts 20%, psychology 11%.

Computing on campus. 35 workstations in library, computer center. Dormitories wired for high-speed internet access and linked to campus network. Online library available.

Student life. **Freshman orientation:** Mandatory, $100 fee. Preregistration for classes offered. 3-day weekend before freshmen move into dorms. **Policies:** Freshmen permitted cars on campus. **Housing:** Guaranteed on-campus for all undergraduates. Single-sex dorms available. $200 deposit, deadline 5/1. Some single rooms available. **Activities:** Choral groups, drama, literary magazine, student government, student newspaper, campus ministry, Student Ambassadors, human services club, education club; honor societies.

Athletics. NAIA. **Intercollegiate:** Baseball M, basketball, cross-country, soccer, softball W, volleyball W. **Intramural:** Basketball, bowling, golf, racquetball, skiing, soccer, softball, tennis, volleyball, weight lifting. **Team name:** Fighting Saints.

Student services. Adult student services, alcohol/substance abuse counseling, campus ministries, career counseling, student employment services, financial aid counseling, personal counseling, placement for graduates, veterans' counselor. **Physically disabled:** Services for visually, speech, hearing impaired.

Contact. E-mail: admissions@csj.edu
Phone: (802) 773-5900 ext. 3206 Toll-free number: (877) 270-9998
Fax: (802) 776-5258
Patricia Ryan, Director of Admissions and Marketing, College of St. Joseph in Vermont, 71 Clement Road, Rutland, VT 05701-3899

Goddard College

Plainfield, Vermont
www.goddard.edu **CB code: 3416**

- Private 4-year liberal arts college
- Rural community
- 159 degree-seeking undergraduates: 61% women, 3% African American, 1% Asian American, 3% Hispanic American, 2% Native American
- 395 degree-seeking graduate students
- Application essay, interview required

General. Founded in 1938. Regionally accredited. Non-traditional institution; independent study programs designed for working adults. **Degrees:** 80 bachelor's awarded; master's offered. **Location:** 10 miles from Montpelier. **Calendar:** Semester. **Full-time faculty:** 2 total; 100% have terminal degrees, 50% women. **Part-time faculty:** 72 total; 94% have terminal degrees, 74% women. **Special facilities:** Community radio station.

Freshman class profile. 13 applied, 13 admitted, 12 enrolled.

Basis for selection. Open admission, but selective for some programs. Academic potential, maturity, ability to work independently, personal statement, and interview important. SAT/ACT scores optional. Students are encouraged to include a portfolio with their application. **Homeschooled:** GED recommended.

2005-2006 Annual costs. Books/supplies: $765. Personal expenses: $1,127.

2005-2006 Financial aid. **Need-based:** Average need met was 37%. Average scholarship/grant was $5,400; average loan $2,177. 27% of total undergraduate aid awarded as scholarships/grants, 73% as loans/jobs. **Non-need-based:** Scholarships awarded for academics, art, job skills, leadership, music/drama, state residency.

Application procedures. **Admission:** No deadline. $40 fee, may be waived for applicants with need. Application may be submitted online. Admission notification on a rolling basis. Must reply by May 1 or within 4 week(s) if notified thereafter. **Financial aid:** FAFSA required. Applicants notified on a rolling basis starting 4/15; must reply within 4 week(s) of notification.

Academics. Written evaluations replace grades. Individually designed majors at bachelor's and master's levels. Students design programs of study in collaboration with faculty mentor. Students on campus for 8 days at the beginning of each semester and then work from home following a study plan that is designed by students in collaboration with their advisor. **Special study options:** Distance learning, external degree, independent study, internships, liberal arts/career combination, student-designed major, study abroad, teacher certification program. **Credit/placement by examination:** AP, CLEP, IB. 30 credit hours maximum toward bachelor's degree.

Majors. **Area/ethnic studies:** African-American, American, European, Latin American, Native American, Near/Middle Eastern, women's. **Biology:** General, ecology. **Business:** Business admin. **Conservation:** Environmental studies. **Education:** General, art, early childhood, elementary, English, middle, secondary, social studies. **English:** Creative writing. **History:** General. **Interdisciplinary:** Peace/conflict. **Liberal arts:** Arts/sciences. **Philosophy/religion:** Judaic, philosophy, religion. **Psychology:** General. **Public administration:** Community org/advocacy, social work. **Social sciences:** General. **Visual/performing arts:** General, crafts, studio arts.

Computing on campus. PC or laptop required. 100 workstations in dormitories, library, computer center, student center. Dormitories wired for high-speed internet access and linked to campus network. Commuter students can connect to campus network. Online library, helpline, wireless network available.

Student life. **Freshman orientation:** Mandatory, $105 fee. Held day before registration. **Policies:** Freshmen permitted cars on campus. **Housing:** Guaranteed on-campus for all undergraduates. Substance-free housing available. Housing available 8 days per semester. **Activities:** Radio station.

Contact. E-mail: admissions@goddard.edu
Phone: (802) 454-8311 ext. 241 Toll-free number: (800) 906-8312 ext. 241
Fax: (802) 454-1029
Brenda Hawkins, Director of Admissions, Goddard College, 123 Pitkin Road, Plainfield, VT 05667

Green Mountain College

Poultney, Vermont **CB member**
www.greenmtn.edu **CB code: 3418**

- Private 4-year liberal arts college affiliated with United Methodist Church
- Residential campus in small town
- 684 degree-seeking undergraduates: 4% part-time, 48% women, 3% African American, 1% Asian American, 2% Hispanic American, 1% Native American, 1% international
- 91% of applicants admitted
- SAT or ACT (ACT writing optional), application essay required
- 39% graduate within 6 years; 17% enter graduate study

General. Founded in 1834. Regionally accredited. Liberal arts college with environmental core curriculum. **Degrees:** 107 bachelor's awarded; master's offered. **Location:** 20 miles from Rutland, 35 miles from Killington. **Calendar:** Differs by program. **Full-time faculty:** 41 total; 90% have terminal degrees, 29% women. **Part-time faculty:** 24 total; 21% have terminal degrees, 46% women. **Class size:** 54% < 20, 46% 20-39. **Special facilities:** Collection of Welsh artifacts and literature, collection of early American decoration, art collection, student-operated organically managed farm, ropes course, nature preserve.

Freshman class profile. 927 applied, 840 admitted, 253 enrolled.

Mid 50% test scores		**Rank in top tenth:**	9%
SAT verbal:	470-600	**End year in good standing:**	89%
SAT math:	430-560	**Return as sophomores:**	72%
ACT:	18-23	**Out-of-state:**	86%
Rank in top quarter:	24%	**Live on campus:**	99%

Basis for selection. Academic achievement, recommendations, interview, test scores, personal statement, school and community activities considered. Interview recommended; audition recommended for choral, theater; portfolio recommended for art. **Homeschooled:** Statement describing homeschool structure and mission, transcript of courses and grades, state high school equivalency certificate, letter of recommendation (nonparent) required. Applicants advised to develop thorough portfolio of all work completed. Students are highly encouraged to interview on campus.

High school preparation. College-preparatory program required. 21 units required. Required and recommended units include English 4, mathematics 3-4, social studies 3, history 1-2, science 3-4 (laboratory 2), foreign language 2-3 and academic electives 5.

2006-2007 Annual costs. Tuition/fees (projected): $23,404. Room/board: $8,760. Books/supplies: $800. Personal expenses: $850.

2005-2006 Financial aid. **Need-based:** Average need met was 80%. Average scholarship/grant was $14,444; average loan $4,492. 62% of total undergraduate aid awarded as scholarships/grants, 38% as loans/jobs. **Non-need-based:** Scholarships awarded for academics, art, leadership, music/drama, religious affiliation. **Additional information:** Service/recognition awards available to all students.

Application procedures. **Admission:** Priority date 3/1; no deadline. $30 fee, may be waived for applicants with need. Application may be submitted online. Admission notification on a rolling basis beginning on or about 9/1. Must reply by May 1 or within 2 week(s) if notified thereafter. **Financial aid:** Priority date 3/1; no closing date. FAFSA required. CSS Profile is recommended and is optional to receive an earlier financial aid package. Applicants notified on a rolling basis starting 1/1; must reply by 5/1 or within 4 week(s) of notification.

Academics. **Special study options:** Accelerated study, double major, ESL, exchange student, honors, independent study, internships, liberal arts/career combination, student-designed major, study abroad, teacher certification program. Exchange programs at Aberystwyth University (Wales) and Hannam University (Korea), credit granted for programs of National Outdoor Leadership School. Member of Eco-League Consortium - students can spend up to two semesters at one of five other schools - Alaska Pacific University, Antioch University, College of the Atlantic, Northand College, Prescott College. **Credit/placement by examination:** AP, CLEP, IB, SAT, ACT, institutional tests. **Support services:** Learning center, pre-admission summer program, reduced course load, remedial instruction, study skills assistance, tutoring, writing center.

Majors. **Biology:** General. **Business:** Business admin, hospitality admin, hospitality/recreation, resort management. **Communications:** General, journalism. **Conservation:** General, environmental studies, management/policy. **Education:** Art, elementary, English, middle, secondary, social studies, special. **English:** Creative writing, English lit. **Health:** Predentistry, premedicine, preveterinary. **History:** General. **Legal studies:** Prelaw. **Liberal arts:** Arts/sciences. **Parks/recreation:** General, facilities management. **Philosophy/religion:** Philosophy. **Psychology:** General. **Social sciences:** Anthropology, sociology. **Visual/performing arts:** General, art, arts management, studio arts.

Computing on campus. 60 workstations in dormitories, library, computer center, student center. Dormitories wired for high-speed internet access and linked to campus network. Online library, helpline available.

Student life. **Freshman orientation:** Mandatory, $400 fee. Preregistration for classes offered. Orientation is held the week before classes begin in August (Fall term) and January (Spring Term). Students have the option of participating in a Wilderness Challenge for an additional fee. **Policies:** Freshmen permitted cars on campus. **Housing:** Guaranteed on-campus for all undergraduates. Coed dorms, substance-free housing available. The college offers theme floors including substance free, sustainable living, adventure recreation, creative arts, quiet floor, honors floor. **Activities:** Bands, choral groups, drama, film society, literary magazine, music ensembles, student government, student newspaper, Olympics/Senior Games, outdoor adventure programs, Poultney Partners Mentoring Program, environmental volunteer and research groups, African American Culture Club.

Athletics. NCAA. **Intercollegiate:** Basketball, cross-country, golf M, lacrosse M, skiing, soccer, softball W, tennis, volleyball W. **Intramural:** Basketball, skiing, soccer, softball, table tennis, tennis, volleyball. **Team name:** Eagles.

Student services. Alcohol/substance abuse counseling, campus ministries, career counseling, student employment services, financial aid counseling, health services, personal counseling, placement for graduates.

Contact. E-mail: admiss@greenmtn.edu
Phone: (802) 287-8207 Toll-free number: (800) 776-6675
Fax: (802) 287-8099
Jessica Day, Director of Admissions, Green Mountain College, One College Circle, Poultney, VT 05764

Johnson State College

Johnson, Vermont — **CB member**
www.jsc.vsc.edu — **CB code: 3766**

- Public 4-year liberal arts college
- Residential campus in small town
- 1,452 degree-seeking undergraduates: 30% part-time, 61% women, 1% African American, 1% Asian American, 1% Hispanic American, 1% Native American
- 184 degree-seeking graduate students
- 95% of applicants admitted
- SAT or ACT (ACT writing optional), application essay required

General. Founded in 1828. Regionally accredited. Special tuition rate for New England residents who apply to selected fields of study. **Degrees:** 296 bachelor's, 22 associate awarded; master's offered. **ROTC:** Army. **Location:** 50 miles from Burlington, 90 miles from Montreal. **Calendar:** Semester, limited summer session. **Full-time faculty:** 49 total; 76% have terminal degrees, 4% minority, 29% women. **Part-time faculty:** 89 total; 15% have terminal degrees, 2% minority, 62% women. **Special facilities:** 1,000-acre nature preserve, visual arts center, human performance laboratory, interactive multimedia math and science laboratory, community service learning center, Vermont Interactive Television site.

Freshman class profile. 770 applied, 728 admitted, 251 enrolled.

Return as sophomores:	63%	**Live on campus:**	74%
Out-of-state:	37%		

Basis for selection. High school transcript, GPA, SAT or ACT scores, class rank, recommendations, and essay important. Tests not required for any student who graduated high school at least one year ago, nor for students taking the GED. Interview recommended. **Homeschooled:** SAT required. Applicants encouraged to complete the GED or other state certified achievement test to demonstrate aptitude.

High school preparation. 9 units required; 15 recommended. Required and recommended units include English 4, mathematics 3-4, social studies 2, history 2, science 2-3 (laboratory 1-2) and foreign language 2. Mathematics units to include algebra II.

2005-2006 Annual costs. Tuition/fees: $6,484; $13,804 out-of-state. New England Board of Higher Education rate for students from other New England states: 150% of Vermont resident tuition. Available to degree candidates in academic areas not offered by educational institutions in their home states. Room/board: $6,674. Books/supplies: $800. Personal expenses: $650.

2004-2005 Financial aid. **Need-based:** 10% of total undergraduate aid awarded as scholarships/grants, 90% as loans/jobs. **Non-need-based:** Scholarships awarded for academics.

Application procedures. **Admission:** Priority date 3/1; no deadline. $30 fee, may be waived for applicants with need. Application may be submitted online. Admission notification on a rolling basis beginning on or about 12/1. Must reply by May 1 or within 2 week(s) if notified thereafter. Although students are admitted and notified on a rolling basis, we strongly recommend students apply for admission before March 1 in order to insure optimal financial aid consideration. **Financial aid:** Priority date 3/1; no closing date. FAFSA required. Applicants notified on a rolling basis starting 4/1; must reply within 3 week(s) of notification.

Academics. **Special study options:** Accelerated study, cross-registration, distance learning, double major, dual enrollment of high school students, ESL, exchange student, external degree, independent study, internships, study abroad, teacher certification program. **Credit/placement by examination:** AP, CLEP. **Support services:** Learning center, pre-admission summer program, reduced course load, remedial instruction, study skills assistance, tutoring, writing center.

Majors. **Biology:** General, cell/histology, molecular. **Business:** General, business admin, hospitality admin, tourism/travel. **Communications:** Journalism. **Conservation:** General, environmental studies, management/policy.

Education: General, art, biology, drama/dance, elementary, English, history, mathematics, middle, multi-level teacher, music, physical, science, secondary, social science, social studies. **Foreign languages:** Comparative lit. **Health:** Athletic training, premedicine. **History:** General. **Liberal arts:** Arts/sciences. **Math:** General. **Parks/recreation:** General, exercise sciences, health/fitness, sports admin. **Psychology:** General. **Social sciences:** General, anthropology, political science, sociology. **Visual/performing arts:** General, art, dance, dramatic, jazz, music history, music management, music performance, music theory/composition, piano/organ, studio arts, theater design, voice/opera.

Most popular majors. Business/marketing 13%, education 15%, history 6%, liberal arts 21%, psychology 17%, visual/performing arts 11%.

Computing on campus. 131 workstations in library, computer center. Dormitories wired for high-speed internet access and linked to campus network. Commuter students can connect to campus network. Online course registration, helpline, wireless network available.

Student life. **Freshman orientation:** Mandatory, $150 fee. Preregistration for classes offered. 3-day program. **Policies:** Freshmen permitted cars on campus. **Housing:** Guaranteed on-campus for all undergraduates. Coed dorms, apartments, substance-free housing available. $200 deposit, deadline 5/1. Alcohol and Drug Free Dorm. **Activities:** Jazz band, choral groups, dance, drama, film society, literary magazine, music ensembles, musical theater, radio station, student government, student newspaper, behavioral science club, Christian Fellowship Club, diversity committee, political awareness club, international club, Little Brother/Little Sister, Habitat for Humanity, Native American Club, Students Enriching and Responding Through Volunteer Efforts (SERVE), earth awareness club.

Athletics. NAIA, NCAA. **Intercollegiate:** Basketball, cross-country, lacrosse M, rugby, soccer, softball W, tennis. **Intramural:** Badminton, basketball, bowling, cross-country, football (non-tackle), golf, lacrosse, racquetball, rugby, soccer, softball, swimming, table tennis, tennis, volleyball, water polo, weight lifting. **Team name:** Badgers.

Student services. Adult student services, alcohol/substance abuse counseling, career counseling, services for economically disadvantaged, student employment services, financial aid counseling, health services, on-campus daycare, personal counseling, placement for graduates. **Physically disabled:** Services for visually, hearing impaired.

Contact. E-mail: jscapply@badger.jsc.vsc.edu
Phone: (802) 635-1219 Toll-free number: (800) 635-2356
Fax: (802) 635-1230
Penny Howrigan, Associate Dean of Enrollment Services, Johnson State College, 337 College Hill, Johnson, VT 05656

Lyndon State College

Lyndonville, Vermont — **CB member**
www.lyndonstate.edu — **CB code: 3767**

- Public 4-year liberal arts and teachers college
- Residential campus in small town
- 1,273 degree-seeking undergraduates: 10% part-time, 49% women
- 46 degree-seeking graduate students
- 94% of applicants admitted
- SAT or ACT with writing, application essay required

General. Founded in 1911. Regionally accredited. **Degrees:** 191 bachelor's, 33 associate awarded; master's offered. **ROTC:** Air Force. **Location:** 10 miles from St. Johnsbury, 85 miles from Burlington. **Calendar:** Semester, limited summer session. **Full-time faculty:** 55 total. **Part-time faculty:** 85 total. **Class size:** 75% < 20, 25% 20-39, less than 1% 40-49. **Special facilities:** Museum, meteorology laboratory, ropes course.

Freshman class profile. 994 applied, 938 admitted, 333 enrolled.

Mid 50% test scores		Out-of-state:	58%
SAT verbal:	420-520	Live on campus:	65%
SAT math:	410-530		

Basis for selection. High school courses and grades most important, then class rank (top half preferred), recommendations, and test scores. Interview recommended.

High school preparation. Required and recommended units include English 4, mathematics 3-4, social studies 2, history 1, science 2-4 (laboratory 2) and foreign language 2. Physics and advanced mathematics for meteorology and computer science recommended.

2005-2006 Annual costs. Tuition/fees: $6,484; $13,804 out-of-state. New England Board of Higher Education rate for students from other New England states: 150% of Vermont resident tuition. Available to degree candidates in academic areas not offered by educational institutions in their home states. Room/board: $6,674. Books/supplies: $600. Personal expenses: $900.

Financial aid. **Non-need-based:** Scholarships awarded for academics, leadership.

Application procedures. **Admission:** Priority date 5/1; no deadline. $35 fee, may be waived for applicants with need. Application may be submitted online. Admission notification on a rolling basis beginning on or about 11/1. **Financial aid:** Priority date 2/1; no closing date. FAFSA required. Applicants notified on a rolling basis starting 4/1; must reply within 2 week(s) of notification.

Academics. **Special study options:** Accelerated study, combined bachelor's/graduate degree, cooperative education, double major, dual enrollment of high school students, honors, internships, liberal arts/career combination, student-designed major, study abroad, teacher certification program. **Credit/placement by examination:** AP, CLEP, IB. 60 credit hours maximum toward bachelor's degree. **Support services:** Learning center, reduced course load, remedial instruction, study skills assistance, tutoring, writing center.

Majors. **Business:** Accounting, business admin, entrepreneurial studies. **Communications:** General, journalism, radio/tv. **Communications technology:** General. **Computer sciences:** General. **Education:** General, early childhood, elementary, English, physical, science, social science, special. **Health:** Athletic training. **Interdisciplinary:** Biological/physical sciences. **Liberal arts:** Arts/sciences. **Math:** General. **Parks/recreation:** Facilities management. **Physical sciences:** Atmospheric science. **Psychology:** General. **Public administration:** Human services. **Social sciences:** General. **Visual/performing arts:** Graphic design.

Most popular majors. Business/marketing 13%, communications/journalism 10%, education 12%, liberal arts 13%, parks/recreation 10%, physical sciences 6%, social sciences 11%, visual/performing arts 10%.

Computing on campus. 50 workstations in library, computer center. Dormitories wired for high-speed internet access and linked to campus network. Commuter students can connect to campus network. Online library, helpline available.

Student life. **Freshman orientation:** Mandatory. Preregistration for classes offered. Held weekend before classes start. **Policies:** Freshmen permitted cars on campus. **Housing:** Guaranteed on-campus for freshmen. Coed dorms, single-sex dorms, special housing for disabled, substance-free housing available. $100 deposit, deadline 5/1. All students under 23 years of age must live on campus for four full semesters unless residing with parents or must live within 45-mile commuting distance. **Activities:** Choral groups, dance, drama, radio station, student government, student newspaper, symphony orchestra, TV station, American Meteorological Society (student chapter), community service learning group.

Athletics. NAIA. **Intercollegiate:** Baseball M, basketball, cross-country, ice hockey, soccer, softball W, tennis. **Intramural:** Basketball, cross-country, handball, ice hockey, lacrosse, racquetball, rugby, soccer, softball, squash, swimming, table tennis, tennis, track and field, volleyball, water polo M, weight lifting. **Team name:** Hornets.

Student services. Alcohol/substance abuse counseling, career counseling, student employment services, financial aid counseling, health services, personal counseling, placement for graduates, veterans' counselor. **Physically disabled:** Services for visually, hearing impaired.

Contact. E-mail: admissions@lyndonstate.edu
Phone: (802) 626-6413 Toll-free number: (800) 225-1998
Fax: (802) 626-6335
Michelle McCaffrey, Assistant Dean of Admissions, Lyndon State College, 1001 College Road, Lyndonville, VT 05851

Marlboro College

Marlboro, Vermont — **CB member**
www.marlboro.edu — **CB code: 3509**

- Private 4-year liberal arts college
- Residential campus in rural community
- 340 degree-seeking undergraduates: 4% part-time, 61% women, 1% African American, 1% Asian American, 2% Hispanic American, 1% Native American, 1% international
- 58% of applicants admitted
- SAT or ACT (ACT writing optional), application essay required
- 53% graduate within 6 years; 68% enter graduate study

General. Founded in 1946. Regionally accredited. **Degrees:** 68 bachelor's awarded; master's offered. **Location:** 12 miles from Brattleboro, 70 miles from Albany, NY. **Calendar:** Semester. **Full-time faculty:** 36 total; 81% have terminal degrees, 42% women. **Part-time faculty:** 14 total; 50% have terminal degrees, 7% minority, 36% women. **Class size:** 88% < 20, 12% 20-39. **Special facilities:** Aviary, observatory, darkroom, theater 3/4 round, robotics lab, DNA lab.

Freshman class profile. 497 applied, 289 admitted, 102 enrolled.

Mid 50% test scores			
SAT verbal:	590-690	Return as sophomores:	83%
SAT math:	510-650	Out-of-state:	90%
ACT:	24-32	Live on campus:	98%
End year in good standing:	98%	International:	1%

Basis for selection. Academic ability, intellectual potential, writing skills, demonstrated leadership qualities and compatibility with college community most important. Each candidate for admission is evaluated and considered as a unique individual possessing qualities which are not necessarily quantifiable. Selected applicants may be required to interview at the discretion of the admission committee. **Homeschooled:** Statement describing homeschool structure and mission required. Provide documentation of homeschool curriculum and projects. List of textbooks is preferred. Writing sample is required. **Learning Disabled:** Additional documentation may be required.

High school preparation. Recommended units include English 4, mathematics 3, social studies 2, history 2, science 3 (laboratory 3), foreign language 3 and academic electives 5. Advanced electives in area of interest and in performing and/or visual arts also recommended.

2006-2007 Annual costs. Tuition/fees: $29,240. Room/board: $8,600. Books/supplies: $600.

2005-2006 Financial aid. Need-based: 63 full-time freshmen applied for aid; 50 were judged to have need; 50 of these received aid. Average need met was 80%. Average scholarship/grant was $9,940; average loan $3,542. 68% of total undergraduate aid awarded as scholarships/grants, 32% as loans/jobs. **Non-need-based:** Awarded to 235 full-time undergraduates, including 22 freshmen. Scholarships awarded for academics, art, leadership, music/drama.

Application procedures. Admission: Priority date 1/15; deadline 2/15 (postmark date). $50 fee, may be waived for applicants with need. Application may be submitted online. Admission notification 4/15. Admission notification on a rolling basis beginning on or about 2/1. Must reply by May 1 or within 2 week(s) if notified thereafter. **Financial aid:** Priority date 3/1; no closing date. FAFSA required. Applicants notified on a rolling basis starting 2/15; must reply by 5/1 or within 2 week(s) of notification.

Academics. Students self-design a field of study, which is often interdisciplinary in nature. They work very closely with faculty to determine a "Plan of Concentration", which results in a formal review in the senior year by both internal and external faculty. **Special study options:** Double major, dual enrollment of high school students, independent study, internships, student-designed major, study abroad. World Studies Program - opportunity to integrate a study abroad experience and/or internship to the undergraduate course of study or plan of concentration. **Credit/placement by examination:** AP, CLEP, IB, institutional tests. **Support services:** Learning center, reduced course load, study skills assistance, tutoring, writing center.

Majors. Area/ethnic studies: American, Asian, Central/Eastern European, East Asian, European, Latin American, Near/Middle Eastern, Russian/Slavic, South Asian, Southeast Asian, Western European. **Biology:** General, biochemistry, botany, cell/histology, ecology, genetics, molecular, plant physiology. **Computer sciences:** General, computer science. **Conservation:** General, environmental studies. **English:** American lit, British lit, composition, creative writing. **Foreign languages:** General, comparative lit, French, linguistics, Spanish, translation. **History:** General. **Interdisciplinary:** Biological/physical sciences, global studies, math/computer science, peace/conflict. **Legal studies:** Prelaw. **Liberal arts:** Arts/sciences. **Math:** General. **Philosophy/religion:** Philosophy, religion. **Physical sciences:** Astronomy, chemistry, organic chemistry, physics, theoretical physics. **Psychology:** General. **Social sciences:** General, anthropology, economics, political science, sociology. **Visual/performing arts:** General, art, art history/conservation, ceramics, cinematography, dance, dramatic, drawing, film/cinema, music history, painting, photography, play/screenwriting, sculpture, studio arts, theater design, theater history.

Computing on campus. 45 workstations in dormitories, library, computer center. Dormitories wired for high-speed internet access and linked to campus network. Commuter students can connect to campus network. Online library, helpline, wireless network available.

Student life. Freshman orientation: Mandatory, $100 fee. 5-day program in late August, option to go on pre-orientation outdoor trips for the week prior to on-campus orientation. **Policies:** Self-governing community based on the old-fashioned, historical New England-style town meeting. Students, faculty, and staff have equal vote. Elected community court enforces bylaws. Freshmen permitted cars on campus. **Housing:** Guaranteed on-campus for freshmen. Coed dorms, single-sex dorms, apartments, substance-free housing available. $300 deposit, deadline 5/1. **Activities:** Choral groups, dance, drama, film society, literary magazine, music ensembles, musical theater, student government, student newspaper, Amnesty International, animal rights, gay/lesbian and bisexual group, Committee on Environmental Quality, fire and safety commission.

Athletics. Intercollegiate: Soccer. **Intramural:** Basketball, cross-country, fencing, soccer, softball, swimming, table tennis, volleyball, weight lifting. **Team name:** Fighting Dead Trees.

Student services. Alcohol/substance abuse counseling, career counseling, financial aid counseling, health services, personal counseling. **Physically disabled:** Services for visually impaired.

Contact. E-mail: admissions@marlboro.edu
Phone: (802) 258-9236 Toll-free number: (800) 343-0049
Fax: (802) 451-7555
Alan Young, Dean of Enrollment and Financial Aid, Marlboro College, PO Box A, Marlboro, VT 05344-0300

Middlebury College

Middlebury, Vermont — **CB member**
www.middlebury.edu — **CB code: 3526**

- Private 4-year liberal arts college
- Residential campus in small town
- 2,415 degree-seeking undergraduates: 1% part-time, 51% women, 3% African American, 7% Asian American, 5% Hispanic American, 1% Native American, 9% international
- 24% of applicants admitted
- SAT and SAT Subject Tests or ACT (ACT writing optional), application essay required

General. Founded in 1800. Regionally accredited. Affiliated with Monterey Institute of International Studies. **Degrees:** 613 bachelor's awarded; master's, doctoral offered. **ROTC:** Army. **Location:** 200 miles from Boston, 250 miles from New York City. **Calendar:** 4-1-4, limited summer session. **Full-time faculty:** 254 total; 94% have terminal degrees, 14% minority, 40% women. **Part-time faculty:** 46 total; 83% have terminal degrees, 35% women. **Class size:** 68% < 20, 20% 20-39, 6% 40-49, 7% 50-99. **Special facilities:** Art museum, observatory, fine arts center, ski area, interactive language laboratories, 18-hole golf course.

Freshman class profile. 5,254 applied, 1,241 admitted, 555 enrolled.

Mid 50% test scores			
SAT verbal:	630-750	Rank in top tenth:	84%
SAT math:	650-730	Out-of-state:	92%
ACT:	27-32	Live on campus:	100%
Rank in top quarter:	96%	International:	13%

Basis for selection. School record most important (including course selection and course load), followed by class rank, extracurricular activities, letters of recommendation and test scores. Candidates must submit standardized tests in at least 3 areas of study. Requirement may be met by submitting ACT, old SAT and SAT Subject Tests, new SAT, or 3 exams in different areas of study which may be selected from SAT Subject Tests, AP tests or International Baccalaureate exams.

High school preparation. Recommended units include English 4, mathematics 4, social studies 3, science 3 (laboratory 3) and foreign language 4. Music, art, or drama recommended.

2005-2006 Annual costs. Comprehensive fee: $42,340. Books/supplies: $750. Personal expenses: $1,000.

2004-2005 Financial aid. All financial aid based on need. 318 full-time freshmen applied for aid; 257 were judged to have need; 257 of these received aid. Average need met was 100%. Average scholarship/grant was $24,002; average loan $3,411. 85% of total undergraduate aid awarded as scholarships/grants, 15% as loans/jobs. **Additional information:** College maintains need-blind admissions policy and meets full demonstrated financial need of students who qualify for admission, to degree resources permit.

Application procedures. Admission: Closing date 1/1 (postmark date). $55 fee, may be waived for applicants with need. Application may be submitted online. Admission notification 4/1. Must reply by 5/1. **Financial aid:**

Priority date 11/15, closing date 1/1. FAFSA, institutional form, CSS PROFILE required. Applicants notified by 4/1; must reply by 5/1.

Academics. **Special study options:** Accelerated study, double major, exchange student, honors, independent study, internships, semester at sea, student-designed major, study abroad, teacher certification program, Washington semester. Williams College-Mystic Seaport Program in American Maritime Studies, Oxford University summer program, independent scholar program, exchange programs with Berea College and Swarthmore College, 3-year international major. **Credit/placement by examination:** AP, CLEP, IB, institutional tests. **Support services:** Learning center, pre-admission summer program, reduced course load, study skills assistance, tutoring, writing center.

Majors. **Area/ethnic studies:** American, Central/Eastern European, East Asian, Russian/Slavic, women's. **Biology:** General, biochemistry, molecular. **Computer sciences:** Computer science. **Conservation:** Environmental studies. **English:** American lit, English lit. **Foreign languages:** Chinese, classics, French, German, Italian, Japanese, Russian, Spanish. **History:** General. **Interdisciplinary:** Neuroscience. **Liberal arts:** Arts/sciences. **Math:** General. **Philosophy/religion:** Philosophy, religion. **Physical sciences:** Chemistry, geology, physics. **Psychology:** General. **Social sciences:** Economics, geography, international relations, political science, sociology. **Visual/performing arts:** Art history/conservation, cinematography, dance, dramatic, studio arts.

Computing on campus. 494 workstations in dormitories, library, computer center, student center. Dormitories wired for high-speed internet access and linked to campus network. Commuter students can connect to campus network. Online course registration, online library, helpline, repair service, student web hosting, wireless network available.

Student life. **Freshman orientation:** Mandatory. Elective portion of orientation carries cost of $150. **Policies:** Freshmen permitted cars on campus. **Housing:** Guaranteed on-campus for all undergraduates. Coed dorms, special housing for disabled, apartments, substance-free housing available. $200 nonrefundable deposit, deadline 5/1. Multicultural, environmental, foreign language, and 5 social houses available. Commons System organizes residence halls into 5 groups, each with own budget, government, faculty, and staff associates. **Activities:** Jazz band, choral groups, dance, drama, film society, literary magazine, music ensembles, musical theater, radio station, student government, student newspaper, symphony orchestra, African-American alliance, Alianza Latinoamerica y Caribena, Asian students organization, environmental quality, international students organization, Hillel, Gay Lesbian Bisexual Alliance, mountain club, volunteer service program, women's organization.

Athletics. NCAA. **Intercollegiate:** Baseball M, basketball, cross-country, diving, field hockey W, football (tackle) M, golf, ice hockey, lacrosse, skiing, soccer, softball W, squash W, swimming, tennis, track and field, volleyball W. **Intramural:** Badminton, basketball, cross-country, diving, football (non-tackle), golf, ice hockey, lacrosse, skiing, soccer, softball, squash W, swimming, table tennis, tennis, triathlon, volleyball. **Team name:** Panthers.

Student services. Alcohol/substance abuse counseling, campus ministries, career counseling, student employment services, financial aid counseling, health services, minority student services, personal counseling, placement for graduates, women's services. **Physically disabled:** Services for visually, speech, hearing impaired.

Contact. E-mail: admissions@middlebury.edu
Phone: (802) 443-3000 Fax: (802) 443-0258
Robert Clagett, Dean of Admissions, Middlebury College, The Emma Willard House, Middlebury, VT 05753-6002

Norwich University

Northfield, Vermont — **CB member**
www.norwich.edu — **CB code: 3669**

- Private 4-year university and military college
- Residential campus in small town
- 1,900 degree-seeking undergraduates
- 74% of applicants admitted
- SAT or ACT (ACT writing optional) required
- 37% graduate within 6 years

General. Founded in 1819. Regionally accredited. Oldest private military college in U.S. Adult programs, baccalaureate and masters, are self-designed, individually mentored programs. Both military and civilian students. **Degrees:** 269 bachelor's awarded; master's offered. **ROTC:** Army, Navy, Air Force. **Location:** 50 miles from Burlington, 180 miles from Boston. **Calendar:** Semester, limited summer session. **Full-time faculty:** 125 total. **Part-time faculty:** 137 total.

Freshman class profile. 1,981 applied, 1,470 admitted, 578 enrolled.

Mid 50% test scores		**Return as sophomores:**	53%
SAT verbal:	470-600	**Out-of-state:**	80%
SAT math:	480-600	**Live on campus:**	98%
ACT:	19-24		

Basis for selection. High school record, recommendations, activities, honors, awards, test scores important. Class rank considered in admissions decisions and will be criterion for financial aid awarding.

High school preparation. 18 units recommended. Recommended units include English 4, mathematics 3, social studies 2, science 1 and foreign language 2.

2005-2006 Annual costs. Tuition/fees: $21,138. Military students pay an additional $1,320 per year for cadet uniform for first and second years. Room/board: $7,374. Books/supplies: $500. Personal expenses: $400.

Financial aid. **Non-need-based:** Scholarships awarded for academics, leadership, music/drama, ROTC. **Additional information:** Winners of ROTC scholarships receive full room and board; must maintain 2.75 GPA. Renewable up to 4 years.

Application procedures. **Admission:** Priority date 5/1; no deadline. $35 fee, may be waived for applicants with need. Application may be submitted online. Admission notification on a rolling basis beginning on or about 11/30. Must reply by May 1 or within 3 week(s) if notified thereafter. **Financial aid:** Priority date 3/1; no closing date. FAFSA, institutional form, CSS PROFILE required. Applicants notified on a rolling basis starting 12/15.

Academics. **Special study options:** Accelerated study, combined bachelor's/graduate degree, distance learning, double major, external degree, honors, independent study, internships, liberal arts/career combination, student-designed major, study abroad, teacher certification program. **Credit/placement by examination:** AP, CLEP, institutional tests. **Support services:** Learning center, pre-admission summer program, reduced course load, remedial instruction, tutoring.

Majors. **Biology:** General, biochemistry, biomedical sciences. **Business:** Accounting, business admin. **Communications:** General. **Computer sciences:** General, computer science. **Conservation:** General. **Education:** Physical. **Engineering:** Civil, electrical, mechanical. **Health:** Athletic training. **History:** General. **Interdisciplinary:** Peace/conflict. **Legal studies:** Prelaw. **Liberal arts:** Arts/sciences. **Math:** General. **Physical sciences:** Chemistry, geology, physics. **Protective services:** Criminal justice. **Psychology:** General. **Social sciences:** Economics, international relations, political science.

Computing on campus. 150 workstations in library, computer center. Dormitories linked to campus network. Commuter students can connect to campus network. Helpline available.

Student life. **Freshman orientation:** Available, $10 fee. Preregistration for classes offered. Wednesday through Sunday, including one-day program on a cruise, dinner included. **Housing:** Guaranteed on-campus for all undergraduates. Coed dorms available. $250 deposit, deadline 5/1. ROTC participants must live in dormitories. **Activities:** Bands, choral groups, drama, literary magazine, music ensembles, musical theater, radio station, student government, student newspaper, symphony orchestra, Arnold Air Society, international student organization, special operations company association of the United States Army, Norwich University Volunteer Organization, Norwich Christian Fellowship, ambulance rescue squad, Young Republicans, Square and Compass.

Athletics. NCAA. **Intercollegiate:** Baseball M, basketball, cross-country, diving, football (tackle) M, golf, ice hockey M, lacrosse, rifle, rugby W, soccer, softball W, swimming, tennis, track and field, wrestling M. **Intramural:** Basketball, cross-country, fencing, football (tackle) M, ice hockey M, lacrosse M, racquetball, skiing, soccer, softball, tennis, track and field, volleyball. **Team name:** Cadets.

Student services. Adult student services, career counseling, student employment services, health services, personal counseling, placement for graduates, veterans' counselor.

Contact. E-mail: nuadm@norwich.edu
Phone: (802) 485-2002 Toll-free number: (800) 468-6679
Fax: (802) 485-2002
Karen McGrath, Dean of Enrollment, Norwich University, 158 Harmon Drive, Northfield, VT 05663

St. Michael's College

Colchester, Vermont — **CB member**
www.smcvt.edu — **CB code: 3757**

- Private 4-year liberal arts college affiliated with Roman Catholic Church
- Residential campus in large town

- 1,950 degree-seeking undergraduates: 1% part-time, 54% women, 1% African American, 1% Asian American, 1% Hispanic American, 2% international
- 294 degree-seeking graduate students
- 72% of applicants admitted
- SAT or ACT with writing, application essay required
- 76% graduate within 6 years; 16% enter graduate study

General. Founded in 1904. Regionally accredited. **Degrees:** 494 bachelor's awarded; master's offered. **ROTC:** Army, Air Force. **Location:** 3 miles from Burlington, 100 miles from Montreal, Canada. **Calendar:** Semester, limited summer session. **Full-time faculty:** 150 total; 85% have terminal degrees, 6% minority, 43% women. **Part-time faculty:** 67 total; 51% have terminal degrees, 2% minority, 61% women. **Class size:** 60% < 20, 38% 20-39, 1% 40-49, less than 1% 50-99, less than 1% >100. **Special facilities:** Observatory.

Freshman class profile. 2,924 applied, 2,119 admitted, 597 enrolled.

Mid 50% test scores			
SAT verbal:	520-620	Rank in top quarter:	58%
SAT math:	520-610	Rank in top tenth:	26%
ACT:	21-26	End year in good standing:	93%
GPA 3.50 or higher:	48%	Return as sophomores:	88%
GPA 3.0-3.49:	30%	Out-of-state:	79%
GPA 2.0-2.99:	22%	Live on campus:	99%

Basis for selection. Admitted students are typically in the top 25% of their class, have taken a strong college prep curriculum and have a middle 50% SAT range of 1060 - 1260 (exclusive of Writing). Students applying for fall 2006 will have taken the SAT Reasoning Test with different scoring . While we have not yet collected data on the test, we do anticipate that average total scores will range soemwhere between 1590 and 1860. Essay, recommendations, and activities are also important considerations. All students required to achieve intermediate level of second-language proficiency to graduate. AP exams or SAT Subject Tests can be used to determine placement in foreign language or fulfill foreign language requirement. The College administers language placement tests during Academic Orientation prior to the beginning of each semester. Interviews recommended. **Homeschooled:** Statement describing homeschool structure and mission, state high school equivalency certificate required.

High school preparation. College-preparatory program required. 16 units required; 20 recommended. Required and recommended units include English 4, mathematics 3-4, social studies 3-4, science 3-4 (laboratory 2-3) and foreign language 3-4. Physics, mathematics, chemistry, biology emphasized for science applicants. History courses fulfill the social studies requirement.

2005-2006 Annual costs. Tuition/fees: $26,770. Room/board: $6,560. Books/supplies: $1,200. Personal expenses: $310.

2005-2006 Financial aid. Need-based: 494 full-time freshmen applied for aid; 411 were judged to have need; 411 of these received aid. Average need met was 88%. Average scholarship/grant was $14,611; average loan $3,809. 73% of total undergraduate aid awarded as scholarships/grants, 27% as loans/jobs. **Non-need-based:** Awarded to 495 full-time undergraduates, including 141 freshmen. Scholarships awarded for academics, athletics, ROTC.

Application procedures. Admission: Priority date 11/1; deadline 2/1 (postmark date). $45 fee, may be waived for applicants with need. Application may be submitted online. Admission notification 4/1. Must reply by May 1 or within 2 week(s) if notified thereafter. Institution has two Early Action deadlines: November 1, and December 1. The corresponding Early Action notification of admission decision dates are January 1, and February 1. The regular application deadline in February 1, with notification of admission decision sent by April 1. **Financial aid:** Closing date 3/15. FAFSA required. CSS Profile should be submitted by students who apply for early action and wish early estimate on aid. Applicants notified on a rolling basis starting 4/1; must reply by 5/1 or within 2 week(s) of notification.

Academics. Special study options: Combined bachelor's/graduate degree, double major, ESL, honors, independent study, internships, liberal arts/career combination, semester at sea, student-designed major, study abroad, teacher certification program, Washington semester. 3-2 engineering with University of Vermont and Clarkson University, 4-1 MBA with Clarkson University, international exchange student program. **Credit/placement by examination:** AP, CLEP, IB, institutional tests. 30 credit hours maximum toward bachelor's degree. **Support services:** Learning center, reduced course load, study skills assistance, tutoring, writing center.

Majors. Area/ethnic studies: American. **Biology:** General, biochemistry. **Business:** Accounting, business admin. **Communications:** Journalism. **Computer sciences:** Computer science, information systems. **Conservation:** Environmental science. **Education:** Art, elementary. **Engineering:** General. **Foreign languages:** General, classics, French, Latin, Spanish. **History:** General. **Math:** General. **Philosophy/religion:** Philosophy, religion. **Physical sciences:** General, chemistry, physics. **Psychology:** General. **Social sciences:** Anthropology, economics, political science, sociology. **Visual/performing arts:** Art, dramatic, studio arts.

Most popular majors. Biology 8%, business/marketing 20%, communications/journalism 6%, education 7%, English 10%, psychology 15%, social sciences 12%.

Computing on campus. 233 workstations in dormitories, library, computer center, student center. Dormitories wired for high-speed internet access and linked to campus network. Commuter students can connect to campus network. Online course registration, online library, helpline, student web hosting, wireless network available.

Student life. Freshman orientation: Mandatory. Preregistration for classes offered. 1 day Academic orientation held in July. 4 day New Student Orientation held in August prior to the first day of classes. An off-campus weekend experience during the summer is offered to all new students. **Policies:** A limited number of permits are available for first-time, first-year students to have cars on campus during the Spring semester. **Housing:** Guaranteed on-campus for all undergraduates. Coed dorms, single-sex dorms, special housing for disabled, apartments, substance-free housing available. $500 deposit, deadline 5/1. Theme housing. **Activities:** Bands, choral groups, dance, drama, literary magazine, music ensembles, musical theater, radio station, student government, student newspaper, Fire and Rescue Squad, Mobilization of Volunteer Efforts, Martin Luther King Society, Diversity Coalition, campus ministry, LEAP Retreat, political science club, Alianza Society, Peace and Justice, Student Global AIDS Campaign.

Athletics. NCAA. **Intercollegiate:** Baseball M, basketball, cross-country, diving, field hockey W, golf M, ice hockey, lacrosse, skiing, soccer, softball W, swimming, tennis, volleyball W. **Intramural:** Badminton, basketball, bowling, football (non-tackle), ice hockey, racquetball, soccer, softball, squash, table tennis, volleyball. **Team name:** Purple Knights.

Student services. Alcohol/substance abuse counseling, campus ministries, career counseling, student employment services, financial aid counseling, health services, minority student services, on-campus daycare, personal counseling, placement for graduates, women's services. **Physically disabled:** Services for visually, speech, hearing impaired.

Contact. E-mail: admission@smcvt.edu
Phone: (802) 654-3000 Toll-free number: (800) 762-8000
Fax: (802) 654-2906
Jacqueline Murphy, Director of Admissions, St. Michael's College, One Winooski Park, Colchester, VT 05439

Southern Vermont College

Bennington, Vermont
www.svc.edu **CB code: 3796**

- Private 4-year liberal arts college
- Residential campus in large town
- 387 degree-seeking undergraduates: 17% part-time, 72% women, 4% African American, 1% Asian American, 2% Hispanic American, 1% international
- 66% of applicants admitted
- SAT or ACT with writing, application essay required

General. Founded in 1926. Regionally accredited. **Degrees:** 76 bachelor's, 26 associate awarded. **Location:** 40 miles from Albany, New York, 90 miles from Springfield, Massachusetts. **Calendar:** Semester, limited summer session. **Full-time faculty:** 19 total. **Part-time faculty:** 20 total. **Class size:** 65% < 20, 35% 20-39. **Special facilities:** 25 miles of trails, 2 natural ponds, 27-room Edwardian mansion.

Freshman class profile. 359 applied, 237 admitted, 74 enrolled.

Mid 50% test scores			
SAT verbal:	400-520	GPA 2.0-2.99:	67%
SAT math:	390-510	Rank in top quarter:	4%
ACT:	14-18	Return as sophomores:	66%
GPA 3.50 or higher:	2%	Out-of-state:	71%
GPA 3.0-3.49:	30%	Live on campus:	86%

Basis for selection. Potential for academic achievement most important. Test scores, interview, personal references important. None of the admissions criteria are intended as absolute cut-offs, but students failing to meet these standards must demonstrate their potential for academic success in other ways. May submit Southern Vermont College Placement tests in lieu of SAT/ACT. Interview strongly recommended.

High school preparation. Required and recommended units include English 4, mathematics 3, social studies 4, history 4, science 4, foreign language 2 and academic electives 4.

2005-2006 Annual costs. Tuition/fees: $14,374. Health insurance, if applicable, $450/semester. Room/board: $6,948. Books/supplies: $750. Personal expenses: $690.

2004-2005 Financial aid. **Need-based:** 31% of total undergraduate aid awarded as scholarships/grants, 69% as loans/jobs. **Non-need-based:** Scholarships awarded for academics, leadership. **Additional information:** Financial aid provided through Vermont Student Assistance Corporation (VSAC).

Application procedures. **Admission:** Priority date 3/1; no deadline. $30 fee, may be waived for applicants with need. Application may be submitted online. Admission notification on a rolling basis beginning on or about 1/1. Must reply by May 1 or within 2 week(s) if notified thereafter. Students accepted in the junior year must deposit by June 30 of junior year to secure placement. Tuition is locked at current cost for 3 years (senior year in high school and first and second year at the college). **Financial aid:** Priority date 5/1; no closing date. FAFSA, institutional form required. Applicants notified on a rolling basis starting 3/1; must reply by 5/1 or within 2 week(s) of notification.

Academics. Students can receive free walk-in tutoring, individualized tutoring, study group sessions, workshops for skill review, proofreading, and note-taking. Disabilities Support Program. **Special study options:** Accelerated study, cooperative education, cross-registration, double major, dual enrollment of high school students, honors, independent study, internships, liberal arts/career combination, semester at sea, student-designed major, study abroad. **Credit/placement by examination:** CLEP, institutional tests. 45 credit hours maximum toward associate degree, 90 toward bachelor's. **Support services:** Learning center, reduced course load, remedial instruction, study skills assistance, tutoring, writing center.

Majors. **Business:** Business admin. **Communications:** General. **Conservation:** Environmental studies. **English:** Creative writing. **Family/consumer sciences:** Family studies. **Health:** Nursing (RN). **Legal studies:** Prelaw. **Liberal arts:** Arts/sciences. **Psychology:** General. **Public administration:** Social work.

Most popular majors. Business/marketing 17%, communications/journalism 10%, health sciences 10%, liberal arts 17%, natural resources/environmental science 11%, psychology 13%, security/protective services 13%.

Computing on campus. 35 workstations in library, computer center. Dormitories wired for high-speed internet access and linked to campus network. Commuter students can connect to campus network. Online library, student web hosting available.

Student life. **Freshman orientation:** Mandatory. 4-day experience held with 3-part theme: academics, student life, outdoor recreation. Outdoor component parallels what students encounter during first semester: learning to adapt to unfamiliar environment. **Policies:** Freshmen permitted cars on campus. **Housing:** Guaranteed on-campus for freshmen. Coed dorms, substance-free housing available. $200 deposit, deadline 5/1. Quiet, substance-free, non-smoking, and freshman residence halls available. **Activities:** Drama, literary magazine, radio station, student government, student newspaper, criminal justice club, Everyone's Earth, multicultural international student association, community action program.

Athletics. NCAA. **Intercollegiate:** Baseball M, basketball, cross-country, soccer, softball W, volleyball. **Intramural:** Basketball, ice hockey, skiing, soccer, softball, table tennis, tennis, volleyball. **Team name:** Mountaineers.

Student services. Adult student services, alcohol/substance abuse counseling, career counseling, student employment services, financial aid counseling, health services, personal counseling, placement for graduates. **Physically disabled:** Services for visually, hearing impaired.

Contact. E-mail: admis@svc.edu
Phone: (802) 447-6304 Toll-free number: (800) 378-2782
Fax: (802) 447-4695
Kathleen James, Director of Admissions, Southern Vermont College, 982 Mansion Drive, Bennington, VT 05201

Sterling College

Craftsbury Common, Vermont — **CB member**
www.sterlingcollege.edu — **CB code: 3752**

- Private 4-year agricultural and liberal arts college
- Residential campus in rural community
- 97 degree-seeking undergraduates: 7% part-time, 33% women, 2% Asian American, 1% Hispanic American, 1% Native American
- 65% of applicants admitted
- Application essay required

General. Founded in 1958. Regionally accredited. We offer international field programs in Nepal, Lapland, Labrador, Scotland, Newfoundland, Iceland, Canada, Japan, India, Belize, Mexico, and Scandinavian countries. Member of National Work Colleges Consortium. **Degrees:** 7 bachelor's, 15 associate awarded. **Location:** 40 miles from Montpelier, 70 miles from Burlington. **Calendar:** Semester, limited summer session. **Full-time faculty:** 15 total; 33% have terminal degrees, 7% minority, 53% women. **Part-time faculty:** 30 total; 10% have terminal degrees, 3% minority, 43% women. **Class size:** 94% < 20, 6% 20-39. **Special facilities:** Managed woodlots, livestock farm, extensive cross-country ski trails, back-country recreation, solar and wind powered barns, organic gardens, greenhouse, 32-foot climbing tower, challenge course, sugar house, 350 acre educational Bear Swamp (boreal forest and muskeg).

Freshman class profile. 55 applied, 36 admitted, 17 enrolled.

Mid 50% test scores			
SAT verbal:	550-660	Return as sophomores:	83%
SAT math:	480-610	Out-of-state:	82%
		Live on campus:	100%

Basis for selection. Demonstrated interest in programs, motivation, interview, academic record, recommendations important. Test scores considered. **Homeschooled:** A portfolio of educational and life experience may be submitted in lieu of a diploma or equivalency.

High school preparation. Required and recommended units include English 4, mathematics 3-4, social studies 2, history 2, science 2-3 (laboratory 1-2) and foreign language 2.

2005-2006 Annual costs. Tuition/fees: $16,950. Students receive $1,400 tuition and book credit in exchange for work done on campus. Room/board: $6,335. Books/supplies: $750. Personal expenses: $600.

2004-2005 Financial aid. **Need-based:** 17 full-time freshmen applied for aid; 14 were judged to have need; 14 of these received aid. Average need met was 77%. Average scholarship/grant was $9,255; average loan $2,625. 56% of total undergraduate aid awarded as scholarships/grants, 44% as loans/jobs. **Non-need-based:** Awarded to 5 full-time undergraduates, including 2 freshmen. Scholarships awarded for academics, leadership, state residency.

Application procedures. **Admission:** Priority date 3/1; no deadline. $35 fee, may be waived for applicants with need. Application may be submitted online. Admission notification on a rolling basis beginning on or about 1/15. Must reply by May 1 or within 2 week(s) if notified thereafter. **Financial aid:** Priority date 3/15; no closing date. FAFSA, institutional form required. Applicants notified on a rolling basis starting 2/1; must reply by 5/1 or within 2 week(s) of notification.

Academics. **Special study options:** Combined bachelor's/graduate degree, exchange student, independent study, internships, liberal arts/career combination, New York semester, semester at sea, student-designed major, study abroad, United Nations semester, urban semester, Washington semester. **Credit/placement by examination:** AP, CLEP. **Support services:** Learning center, reduced course load, remedial instruction, study skills assistance, tutoring, writing center.

Majors. **Agriculture:** General, agronomy, animal breeding, animal health, animal husbandry, animal nutrition, animal sciences, business, communications, crop production, dairy, dairy husbandry, equestrian studies, equine science, farm/ranch, greenhouse operations, horticultural science, horticulture, international, livestock, plant breeding, plant protection, plant sciences, poultry, products processing, range science, soil science. **Architecture:** Environmental design. **Area/ethnic studies:** Canadian, Scandinavian. **Biology:** Conservation, ecology, environmental, systematic, wildlife. **Conservation:** General, environmental studies, fisheries, forest management, forest resources, forest sciences, forestry, land use planning, management/policy, water/wetlands/marine, wildlife, wood science. **Education:** Agricultural, comparative, curriculum, foundations, science, Waldorf/Steiner teacher. **Engineering technology:** Energy systems, environmental, solar energy. **History:** Canadian history. **Interdisciplinary:** Biological/physical sciences, cultural resource management, global studies, intercultural, natural sciences, systems science. **Liberal arts:** Arts/sciences. **Parks/recreation:** General, facilities management. **Social sciences:** Canadian government.

Most popular majors. Agriculture 14%, natural resources/environmental science 72%, parks/recreation 14%.

Computing on campus. 15 workstations in library, computer center. Dormitories wired for high-speed internet access. Online library, repair service, wireless network available.

Student life. **Freshman orientation:** Mandatory. All entering freshman participate in a series of adventure challenge and academic activities to acquaint students with college life, faculty, and the local and college community. **Policies:** Freshmen permitted cars on campus. **Housing:** Guaranteed on-campus for all undergraduates. Coed dorms, apartments available. $150 fully refundable deposit. Pets allowed in dorm rooms. **Activities:** Choral groups, dance, music ensembles, student government.

Athletics. Intramural: Archery, baseball, basketball, bowling, boxing, cross-country, equestrian, ice hockey, rifle, skiing, soccer, softball, swimming, table tennis, volleyball, weight lifting.

Student services. Adult student services, alcohol/substance abuse counseling, career counseling, student employment services, financial aid counseling, health services, on-campus daycare, personal counseling, placement for graduates, women's services.

Contact. E-mail: admissions@sterlingcollege.edu
Phone: (802) 586-7711 ext. 100 Toll-free number: (800) 648-3591
Fax: (802) 586-2596
Gwyn Harris, Director of Admissions, Sterling College, PO Box 72, Craftsbury Common, VT 05827-0072

University of Vermont

Burlington, Vermont — **CB member**
www.uvm.edu — **CB code: 3920**

- Public 4-year university
- Residential campus in large town
- 8,784 degree-seeking undergraduates: 4% part-time, 55% women, 1% African American, 2% Asian American, 2% Hispanic American, 1% international
- 1,706 degree-seeking graduate students
- 80% of applicants admitted
- SAT or ACT with writing, application essay required
- 65% graduate within 6 years

General. Founded in 1791. Regionally accredited. **Degrees:** 1,795 bachelor's awarded; master's, doctoral, first professional offered. **ROTC:** Army. **Location:** 225 miles from Boston, 100 miles from Montreal. **Calendar:** Semester, extensive summer session. **Full-time faculty:** 560 total; 87% have terminal degrees, 12% minority, 39% women. **Part-time faculty:** 163 total; 45% have terminal degrees, 5% minority, 56% women. **Class size:** 47% < 20, 37% 20-39, 5% 40-49, 6% 50-99, 4% >100. **Special facilities:** Art museum, horse farm, dairy farm, geology museum, art galleries, natural areas, science center, research vessel on Lake Champlain, ecosystem science laboratory on Lake Champlain.

Freshman class profile. 13,015 applied, 10,439 admitted, 2,394 enrolled.

Mid 50% test scores		**Rank in top tenth:**	21%
SAT verbal:	530-620	**Return as sophomores:**	88%
SAT math:	540-630	**Out-of-state:**	72%
ACT:	22-27	**Live on campus:**	94%
Rank in top quarter:	55%	**International:**	1%

Basis for selection. School achievement record of primary importance; test scores also important. Essay, extracurricular activities considered. Letter of recommendation required. Special consideration to Vermont residents, children of alumni, minority students, and foreign students. Audition required for music performance. Informational interview recommended. **Homeschooled:** Applicants must provide proof of completion of minimum entrance requirements and completion of GED.

High school preparation. 16 units required. Required units include English 4, mathematics 3, social studies 3, science 2 (laboratory 1) and foreign language 2. Additional mathematics and/or science units required in engineering, business, and health science programs.

2005-2006 Annual costs. Tuition/fees: $10,748; $24,934 out-of-state. Additional $24 fee for on-campus students. Room/board: $7,321. Books/supplies: $832. Personal expenses: $975.

2004-2005 Financial aid. Need-based: 1,395 full-time freshmen applied for aid; 1,102 were judged to have need; 1,094 of these received aid. Average need met was 87%. Average scholarship/grant was $12,913; average loan $5,455. 62% of total undergraduate aid awarded as scholarships/grants, 38% as loans/jobs. **Non-need-based:** Awarded to 1,206 full-time undergraduates, including 384 freshmen. Scholarships awarded for academics, art, athletics, ROTC.

Application procedures. Admission: Closing date 1/15 (postmark date). $45 fee, may be waived for applicants with need. Application may be submitted online. Admission notification 3/31. Must reply by May 1 or within 3 week(s) if notified thereafter. Early action candidates may have a final decision deferred until completion of fall semester review. **Financial aid:** Priority date 2/10; no closing date. FAFSA required. Applicants notified on a rolling basis starting 3/15; must reply within 4 week(s) of notification.

Academics. Students in School of Business Administration must have microcomputers. **Special study options:** Combined bachelor's/graduate degree, cooperative education, distance learning, double major, dual enrollment of high school students, exchange student, honors, independent study, internships, liberal arts/career combination, student-designed major, study abroad, teacher certification program, Washington semester. Evening university option in approximately six major programs, limited English as a second language. **Credit/placement by examination:** AP, CLEP, IB, institutional tests. Half of major and half of minor requirements must be completed in residence. **Support services:** Learning center, pre-admission summer program, reduced course load, study skills assistance, tutoring, writing center.

Majors. Agriculture: General, animal sciences, economics, horticulture, plant sciences, soil science. **Area/ethnic studies:** Asian, Canadian, Central/Eastern European, European, Latin American, Russian/Slavic, women's. **Biology:** General, bacteriology, biochemistry, botany, molecular, zoology. **Business:** Business admin. **Computer sciences:** General, computer science, information systems. **Conservation:** General, environmental science, environmental studies, forestry, management/policy, wildlife. **Education:** General, art, early childhood, elementary, English, foreign languages, kindergarten/preschool, mathematics, middle, music, physical, science, secondary, social science. **Engineering:** General, civil, electrical, environmental, mechanical. **Engineering technology:** Industrial management. **Family/consumer sciences:** General, family studies, family/community services, food/nutrition. **Foreign languages:** General, ancient Greek, classics, French, German, Latin, Russian, Spanish. **Health:** Clinical lab science, communication disorders, medical radiologic technology/radiation therapy, nuclear medical technology, nursing (RN), speech pathology. **History:** General. **Interdisciplinary:** Nutrition sciences. **Liberal arts:** Arts/sciences. **Math:** General, statistics. **Philosophy/religion:** Philosophy, religion. **Physical sciences:** Chemistry, geology, physics. **Psychology:** General. **Public administration:** Social work. **Social sciences:** General, anthropology, economics, geography, political science, sociology. **Visual/performing arts:** General, art history/conservation, dramatic, music performance, studio arts.

Most popular majors. Biology 6%, business/marketing 10%, education 8%, English 7%, health sciences 7%, natural resources/environmental science 6%, psychology 9%, social sciences 21%.

Computing on campus. 685 workstations in dormitories, library, computer center, student center. Dormitories wired for high-speed internet access and linked to campus network. Commuter students can connect to campus network. Online course registration, online library, helpline, repair service, wireless network available.

Student life. Freshman orientation: Mandatory. Preregistration for classes offered. 2-day session in June (dates vary) plus session prior to start of fall classes. **Housing:** Guaranteed on-campus for freshmen. Coed dorms, apartments, fraternity/sorority housing, substance-free housing available. **Activities:** Bands, choral groups, dance, drama, film society, literary magazine, music ensembles, musical theater, radio station, student government, student newspaper, TV station, Hillel, black student union, Asian American student union, gay/lesbian/bisexual/transgender alliance, Alianza Latina, Catholic center, Volunteers in Action, Vermont student environmental program.

Athletics. NCAA. **Intercollegiate:** Baseball M, basketball, cross-country, diving W, field hockey W, ice hockey, lacrosse, skiing, soccer, softball W, swimming W, track and field. **Intramural:** Basketball, bowling, cricket, football (non-tackle), ice hockey, racquetball, soccer, softball, tennis, volleyball. **Team name:** Catamounts.

Student services. Alcohol/substance abuse counseling, campus ministries, career counseling, services for economically disadvantaged, student employment services, financial aid counseling, health services, minority student services, on-campus daycare, personal counseling, veterans' counselor, women's services. **Physically disabled:** Services for visually, speech, hearing impaired. **Learning disabled:** Comprehensive services available.

Contact. E-mail: admissions@uvm.edu
Phone: (802) 656-3370 Fax: (802) 656-8611
Donald Honeman, Dean of Admission and Enrollment Planning, University of Vermont, 194 South Prospect Street, Burlington, VT 05401-3596

Vermont Technical College

Randolph Center, Vermont — **CB member**
www.vtc.edu — **CB code: 3941**

- Public 4-year agricultural and engineering college
- Residential campus in small town

- 1,216 degree-seeking undergraduates: 15% part-time, 39% women, 1% African American, 2% Asian American, 1% Hispanic American, 1% Native American
- 70% of applicants admitted
- 67% graduate within 6 years

General. Founded in 1866. Regionally accredited. Some classes offered on Vermont Interactive Television and broadcasted to 12 locations in Vermont. Vermont Academy of Science and Technology enrolls high school seniors who excel in math/science to complete their last year of high school and first year of college simultaneously. **Degrees:** 64 bachelor's, 300 associate awarded. **ROTC:** Army. **Location:** 20 miles from Montpelier, 50 miles from Burlington. **Calendar:** Semester, limited summer session. **Full-time faculty:** 78 total; 53% have terminal degrees, 44% women. **Part-time faculty:** 61 total; 41% have terminal degrees, 44% women. **Special facilities:** Biotechnology laboratories, 500-acre farmstead and orchard, lighted ski hill, nursing laboratory.

Freshman class profile. 742 applied, 516 admitted, 258 enrolled.

Mid 50% test scores			
SAT verbal:	440-540	Rank in top quarter:	25%
SAT math:	450-560	Rank in top tenth:	10%
GPA 3.50 or higher:	6%	End year in good standing:	61%
GPA 3.0-3.49:	32%	Return as sophomores:	63%
GPA 2.0-2.99:	56%	Out-of-state:	25%
		Live on campus:	80%

Basis for selection. School achievement record most important, followed by test scores, recommendations, interview. Interview and essay required for veterinary applicants. Entrance exam required for nursing applicants. Veterinary technology and nursing programs highly selective. SAT or ACT not required of nursing applicants or non-traditional students. Essay recommended for all. Interviews recommended for all and required for Veterinary Technology program. **Homeschooled:** Statement describing homeschool structure and mission required. May choose affiliated Vermont Academy of Science and Technology to get high school diploma and first year of college simultaneously.

High school preparation. College-preparatory program recommended. 16 units required. Required and recommended units include English 4, mathematics 3-4, social studies 2, history 2, science 2-3 (laboratory 1-2), foreign language 2 and academic electives 2.

2005-2006 Annual costs. Tuition/fees: $7,852; $14,812 out-of-state. New England Board of Higher Education rate for students from other New England states: 150% of Vermont resident tuition. Available to degree candidates in academic areas not offered by educational institutions in their home states. Dental Hygiene program: $9624/$24,096 in-state/out-of-state per year. LPN program: $10,560/$20,130 in-state/out-of-state per year. Room/board: $6,674. Books/supplies: $750. Personal expenses: $650.

2004-2005 Financial aid. Need-based: 212 full-time freshmen applied for aid; 180 were judged to have need; 179 of these received aid. Average need met was 68%. Average scholarship/grant was $4,104; average loan $2,856. 38% of total undergraduate aid awarded as scholarships/grants, 62% as loans/jobs. **Non-need-based:** Awarded to 71 full-time undergraduates, including 14 freshmen. Scholarships awarded for academics.

Application procedures. Admission: Priority date 3/1; no deadline. $35 fee, may be waived for applicants with need. Application may be submitted online. Admission notification on a rolling basis beginning on or about 12/15. Must reply by May 1 or within 4 week(s) if notified thereafter. **Financial aid:** Priority date 3/1; no closing date. FAFSA required. Applicants notified on a rolling basis starting 3/15; must reply within 2 week(s) of notification.

Academics. 3-year preparatory program options for students planning engineering programs. **Special study options:** Accelerated study, distance learning, double major, dual enrollment of high school students, ESL, honors, independent study, internships. Vermont Academy of Science and Technology program combines senior year of high school and first year of college. **Credit/placement by examination:** CLEP, institutional tests. 36 credit hours maximum toward associate degree, 36 toward bachelor's. **Support services:** Learning center, pre-admission summer program, reduced course load, remedial instruction, study skills assistance, tutoring, writing center.

Majors. Computer sciences: General, information technology, LAN/WAN management, networking, programming, security, system admin. **Engineering:** Computer, software. **Engineering technology:** Architectural.

Most popular majors. Architecture 37%, engineering/engineering technologies 63%.

Computing on campus. 225 workstations in dormitories, library, computer center. Dormitories linked to campus network. Commuter students can connect to campus network. Online library, helpline available.

Student life. Freshman orientation: Mandatory, $60 fee. Preregistration for classes offered. 2 days prior to start of classes. **Policies:** Freshmen permitted cars on campus. **Housing:** Coed dorms, special housing for disabled available. $100 deposit, deadline 6/1. Theme housing, substance-free housing. **Activities:** Drama, radio station, student government, student newspaper, TV station, international club, national student chapters of: American Institute of Architects (AIA), American Society of Civil Engineers (ASCE), Institute of Electrical and Electronic Engineers (IEEE), Society of Manufacturing Engineers (SME), Society of Women Engineers, National Association of Veterinary Technicians, Women Issues Christian Fellowship, Phi Theta Kappa, Tau Alpha Pi.

Athletics. Intercollegiate: Baseball M, basketball, cross-country, soccer, softball W, volleyball. **Intramural:** Basketball, football (non-tackle), golf, ice hockey, racquetball, skiing, soccer, softball, swimming, table tennis, tennis, volleyball, water polo. **Team name:** Knights.

Student services. Alcohol/substance abuse counseling, career counseling, services for economically disadvantaged, student employment services, financial aid counseling, health services, minority student services, personal counseling, placement for graduates, veterans' counselor, women's services. **Physically disabled:** Services for visually, hearing impaired.

Contact. E-mail: admissions@vtc.edu
Phone: (802) 728-1242 Toll-free number: (800) 442-8821
Fax: (802) 728-1390
Dwight Cross, Assistant Dean of Enrollment, Vermont Technical College, PO Box 500, Randolph Center, VT 05061-0500

Woodbury College

Montpelier, Vermont
www.woodbury-college.edu **CB code: 2600**

- Private 4-year technical college
- Commuter campus in small town
- 131 degree-seeking undergraduates: 29% part-time, 85% women, 1% African American
- 10 degree-seeking graduate students
- Application essay, interview required
- 58% graduate within 6 years

General. Regionally accredited. Woodbury's Dispute Resolution Center provides mediation and facilitation services to the community, and serves as a learning laboratory for mediation and conflict management students. **Degrees:** 23 bachelor's, 8 associate awarded; master's offered. **Location:** 38 miles from Burlington. **Calendar:** Trimester. **Full-time faculty:** 15 total. **Part-time faculty:** 50 total.

Freshman class profile. 68 applied, 40 admitted, 8 enrolled.

Basis for selection. Open admission, but selective for some programs. All certificate programs require an associate degree as minimum qualification. Mediation and conflict management certificate program more selective. **Homeschooled:** Transcript of courses and grades required.

2005-2006 Annual costs. Tuition/fees: $15,150. Books/supplies: $600. Personal expenses: $2,400.

Application procedures. Admission: No deadline. $30 fee, may be waived for applicants with need. Application must be submitted on paper. Admission notification on a rolling basis. **Financial aid:** FAFSA required.

Academics. Special study options: Cooperative education, distance learning, double major, independent study, internships, liberal arts/career combination, student-designed major, weekend college. **Credit/placement by examination:** CLEP, institutional tests. 30 credit hours maximum toward associate degree, 90 toward bachelor's. Credit by examination treated like transfer credits. **Support services:** Reduced course load, remedial instruction, study skills assistance, tutoring.

Majors. Legal studies: General, paralegal, prelaw. **Public administration:** Community org/advocacy, human services.

Most popular majors. Interdisciplinary studies 32%, legal studies 59%, security/protective services 9%.

Computing on campus. 18 workstations in library, computer center. Commuter students can connect to campus network. Online library, wireless network available.

Student life. Freshman orientation: Mandatory. Preregistration for classes offered. **Policies:** Freshmen permitted cars on campus.

Student services. Adult student services, career counseling, financial aid counseling, personal counseling.

Contact. E-mail: admiss@woodbury-college.edu
Phone: (802) 229-0516 ext. 275 Toll-free number: (800) 639-6039 ext. 275
Fax: (802) 229-2141
Kathleen Moore, Director of Admissions, Woodbury College, 660 Elm Street, Montpelier, VT 05602

Virginia

Art Institute of Washington
Arlington, Virginia
www.aiw.artinstitutes.edu **CB code: 3836**

- For-profit 4-year culinary school and visual arts college
- Commuter campus in small city
- 1,100 degree-seeking undergraduates
- 53% of applicants admitted
- Application essay, interview required

General. Regionally accredited. **Degrees:** 88 bachelor's, 54 associate awarded. **Location:** 1 mile from Washington, DC. **Calendar:** Quarter, extensive summer session. **Full-time faculty:** 25 total. **Part-time faculty:** 60 total.

Freshman class profile. 623 applied, 329 admitted, 329 enrolled.

Basis for selection. Secondary school record, essay, interview most important; portfolio also considered.

2005-2006 Annual costs. Tuition/fees: $17,472. Room only: $6,120.

Application procedures. Admission: No deadline. $50 fee. Admission notification on a rolling basis. **Financial aid:** FAFSA, institutional form required.

Academics. Credit/placement by examination: AP, CLEP.

Majors. Communications: Advertising, digital media. **Communications technology:** Animation/special effects. **Computer sciences:** Web page design. **Visual/performing arts:** Graphic design, interior design.

Student life. Freshman orientation: Available.

Contact. E-mail: aiwadm@aii.edu
Phone: (703) 358-9550 Fax: (703) 358-9759
Sara Cruley, Director of Admissions, Art Institute of Washington, 1820 North Fort Myer Drive, Arlington, VA 22209-1802

Averett University
Danville, Virginia **CB member**
www.averett.edu **CB code: 5017**

- Private 4-year university and liberal arts college
- Residential campus in small city
- 824 degree-seeking undergraduates: 4% part-time, 48% women, 23% African American, 1% Asian American, 2% Hispanic American, 2% international
- 65 degree-seeking graduate students
- 84% of applicants admitted
- SAT or ACT (ACT writing optional) required
- 49% graduate within 6 years

General. Founded in 1859. Regionally accredited. **Degrees:** 473 bachelor's, 36 associate awarded; master's offered. **Location:** 45 miles from Greensboro; North Carolina, 150 miles from Richmond. **Calendar:** Semester, limited summer session. **Full-time faculty:** 66 total; 77% have terminal degrees, 6% minority, 33% women. **Part-time faculty:** 173 total; 32% have terminal degrees, 20% minority, 37% women. **Class size:** 84% < 20, 16% 20-39, less than 1% 50-99. **Special facilities:** 100-acre equestrian center, flight center.

Freshman class profile. 1,202 applied, 1,006 admitted, 258 enrolled.

Mid 50% test scores			
SAT verbal:	440-530	Rank in top tenth:	9%
SAT math:	450-540	End year in good standing:	95%
ACT:	17-22	Return as sophomores:	48%
GPA 3.50 or higher:	26%	Out-of-state:	49%
GPA 3.0-3.49:	33%	Live on campus:	85%
GPA 2.0-2.99:	40%	International:	2%
Rank in top quarter:	34%	Fraternities:	3%
		Sororities:	7%

Basis for selection. Rigor of secondary school record and GPA very important; standardized test scores important. Recommendations, essay, interview, extracurricular activities, talent/ability/ alumni/ae relation, volunteer work, work experience and level of interest all considered. Auditions required for Music program; Portfolios for Art recommended. Essay recommended.

High school preparation. 21 units required; 23 recommended. Required and recommended units include English 4, mathematics 2-3, social studies 3, history 3, science 3 (laboratory 3), foreign language 2 and academic electives 3-5.

2005-2006 Annual costs. Tuition/fees: $19,040. Room/board: $5,880. Books/supplies: $900. Personal expenses: $1,400.

2005-2006 Financial aid. Need-based: 220 full-time freshmen applied for aid; 186 were judged to have need; 186 of these received aid. Average need met was 73%. Average scholarship/grant was $11,097; average loan $3,968. 63% of total undergraduate aid awarded as scholarships/grants, 37% as loans/jobs. **Non-need-based:** Scholarships awarded for academics, alumni affiliation, art, leadership, minority status, music/drama, religious affiliation, state residency.

Application procedures. Admission: Closing date 7/1 (receipt date). No application fee. Application may be submitted online. Admission notification on a rolling basis. Must reply by May 1 or within 2 week(s) if notified thereafter. Housing deposits are taken until July 1, but are only refundable if paid before May 1. **Financial aid:** Priority date 4/1; no closing date. FAFSA required. Applicants notified on a rolling basis starting 2/15; must reply within 2 week(s) of notification.

Academics. Special study options: Accelerated study, combined bachelor's/ graduate degree, cross-registration, double major, dual enrollment of high school students, exchange student, honors, independent study, internships, student-designed major, study abroad, teacher certification program, Washington semester. Undergraduates may take graduate level classes. **Credit/ placement by examination:** AP, CLEP, IB, SAT, ACT, institutional tests. 27 credit hours maximum toward associate degree, 90 toward bachelor's. **Support services:** Learning center, reduced course load, remedial instruction, study skills assistance, tutoring, writing center.

Majors. Agriculture: Equestrian studies. **Biology:** General, ecology. **Business:** General, accounting, business admin, finance, management science, marketing. **Communications:** Journalism. **Computer sciences:** Information systems. **Conservation:** Environmental science. **Education:** Art, biology, chemistry, drama/dance, English, health, mathematics, multi-level teacher, social studies. **English:** English lit. **Health:** Athletic training, clinical lab science, medical radiologic technology/radiation therapy, premedicine. **History:** General. **Interdisciplinary:** Biological/physical sciences, math/ computer science. **Liberal arts:** Arts/sciences. **Math:** General. **Parks/ recreation:** Health/fitness, sports admin. **Philosophy/religion:** Religion. **Physical sciences:** Chemistry. **Protective services:** Law enforcement admin. **Social sciences:** Political science, sociology. **Transportation:** Airline/ commercial pilot, aviation management. **Visual/performing arts:** Art, dramatic, theater history.

Most popular majors. Business/marketing 70%.

Computing on campus. 135 workstations in library, computer center. Dormitories wired for high-speed internet access. Online course registration, online library, helpline, student web hosting available.

Student life. Freshman orientation: Mandatory, $50 fee. Preregistration for classes offered. 11 day orientation; begins on Saturday and lasts until classes start. **Policies:** No alcohol on campus. Freshmen permitted cars on campus. **Housing:** Guaranteed on-campus for all undergraduates. Coed dorms, apartments available. $400 fully refundable deposit, deadline 5/1. Coed housing by floor or suite. **Activities:** Choral groups, drama, literary magazine, music ensembles, musical theater, student government, student newspaper, AU College Republicans, AU Gospel Choir, Baptist Student Union, Brothers and Sisters in Christ, Habitat for Humanity, Catholic Campus Ministries, Environmental Club, Multicultural Student Association, International Student Association, Gay-Straight Alliance.

Athletics. NCAA. **Intercollegiate:** Baseball M, basketball, cross-country, football (tackle) M, golf M, lacrosse W, soccer, softball W, tennis, volleyball W. **Intramural:** Basketball M, cheerleading, football (non-tackle) M, softball. **Team name:** Cougars.

Student services. Alcohol/substance abuse counseling, career counseling, student employment services, financial aid counseling, personal counseling. **Physically disabled:** Services for visually, speech, hearing impaired.

Contact. E-mail: admit@averett.edu
Phone: (434) 791-4996 Toll-free number: (800) 283-7388
Fax: (434) 797-2784
Kathie Tune, Dean of Admissions, Averett University, 420 West Main Street, Danville, VA 24541

Bluefield College

Bluefield, Virginia
www.bluefield.edu **CB code: 5063**

- Private 4-year liberal arts college affiliated with Southern Baptist Convention
- Commuter campus in large town
- 776 degree-seeking undergraduates: 11% part-time, 60% women, 18% African American, 1% Asian American, 1% Hispanic American
- 776 graduate students
- SAT or ACT (ACT writing optional) required
- 42% graduate within 6 years

General. Founded in 1920. Regionally accredited. **Degrees:** 220 bachelor's awarded. **Location:** 90 miles from Roanoke, 80 miles from Charleston, West Virginia. **Calendar:** Semester, limited summer session. **Full-time faculty:** 33 total; 64% have terminal degrees, 30% women. **Part-time faculty:** 77 total; 40% have terminal degrees, 9% minority, 32% women. **Class size:** 86% < 20, 14% 20-39.

Freshman class profile.

Mid 50% test scores			
SAT verbal:	430-520	**Live on campus:**	71%
SAT math:	420-510	**International:**	1%
ACT:	16-21	**Fraternities:**	5%
Out-of-state:	6%	**Sororities:**	7%

Basis for selection. Students must have minimum 2.0 GPA, 18 ACT or SAT equivalent, and rank in upper 50% of graduating class. Interview, portfolio recommended; audition required for music program. **Homeschooled:** Must supply written description and transcript of home-school curriculum. **Learning Disabled:** Must provide documentation of learning disability.

High school preparation. 22 units required. Required units include English 4, mathematics 3, social studies 3, science 3 (laboratory 1) and academic electives 6. 2 units of health and physical education; 1 unit of fine arts.

2005-2006 Annual costs. Tuition/fees: $11,430. Room/board: $5,705. Books/supplies: $1,100. Personal expenses: $1,210.

Financial aid. Non-need-based: Scholarships awarded for academics, art, athletics, leadership, music/drama, religious affiliation.

Application procedures. Admission: Closing date 8/1. $30 fee, may be waived for applicants with need. Application may be submitted online. Admission notification on a rolling basis beginning on or about 9/1. Must reply by May 1 or within 3 week(s) if notified thereafter. **Financial aid:** Priority date 3/1; no closing date. FAFSA, institutional form required. Applicants notified on a rolling basis; must reply within 3 week(s) of notification.

Academics. Special study options: Accelerated study, double major, dual enrollment of high school students, honors, internships, student-designed major, study abroad, teacher certification program, weekend college. **Credit/placement by examination:** AP, CLEP, institutional tests. 30 credit hours maximum toward associate degree, 30 toward bachelor's. Hours of credit by examination that may be counted toward degree varies. **Support services:** Learning center, reduced course load, remedial instruction, study skills assistance, tutoring, writing center.

Majors. Biology: General. **Business:** General, accounting, business admin, human resources. **Communications:** Journalism. **Computer sciences:** General. **Education:** General, business, early childhood, elementary, middle, music, physical, science, secondary. **Health:** Athletic training. **History:** General. **Liberal arts:** Arts/sciences. **Math:** General. **Parks/recreation:** Exercise sciences. **Philosophy/religion:** Christian, philosophy. **Physical sciences:** Chemistry. **Protective services:** Correctional facilities, law enforcement admin, police science. **Psychology:** General. **Social sciences:** General. **Theology:** Bible, preministerial, sacred music. **Visual/performing arts:** Art, dramatic, music performance.

Computing on campus. 100 workstations in dormitories, library, computer center. Dormitories wired for high-speed internet access and linked to campus network. Commuter students can connect to campus network. Online library available.

Student life. Freshman orientation: Mandatory, $55 fee. Preregistration for classes offered. Held in June or July. **Policies:** Religious observance required. Freshmen permitted cars on campus. **Housing:** Guaranteed on-campus for freshmen. Coed dorms, single-sex dorms, substance-free housing available. $100 deposit. **Activities:** Choral groups, drama, literary magazine, music ensembles, musical theater, radio station, student government, student newspaper, Baptist Student Union, Fellowship of Christian Athletes, ministerial association, Alpha Delta, Phi Mu Delta, Kappa Psi Omicron, Sigma Alpha Alpha.

Athletics. NAIA. **Intercollegiate:** Baseball M, basketball, golf M, soccer, softball W, tennis, volleyball W. **Intramural:** Badminton, basketball, football (non-tackle), softball, table tennis, tennis, volleyball. **Team name:** Rams.

Student services. Adult student services, campus ministries, career counseling, financial aid counseling, health services, personal counseling, placement for graduates, veterans' counselor.

Contact. E-mail: admissions@mail.bluefield.edu
Phone: (276) 326-4214 Toll-free number: (800) 872-0175
Fax: (276) 326-4288
Timothy Havens, Director of Admissions, Bluefield College, 3000 College Drive, Bluefield, VA 24605

Bridgewater College

Bridgewater, Virginia **CB member**
www.bridgewater.edu **CB code: 5069**

- Private 4-year liberal arts college affiliated with Church of the Brethren
- Residential campus in small town
- 1,493 degree-seeking undergraduates: 57% women, 8% African American, 1% Asian American, 1% Hispanic American, 1% international
- 86% of applicants admitted
- SAT or ACT (ACT writing optional) required
- 68% graduate within 6 years

General. Founded in 1880. Regionally accredited. **Degrees:** 277 bachelor's awarded. **Location:** 8 miles from Harrisonburg, 130 miles from Washington, DC. **Calendar:** 4-1-4, limited summer session. **Full-time faculty:** 96 total; 79% have terminal degrees, 1% minority, 38% women. **Part-time faculty:** 30 total; 30% have terminal degrees, 7% minority, 63% women. **Class size:** 56% < 20, 41% 20-39, 1% 40-49, 2% 50-99. **Special facilities:** Historical museum.

Freshman class profile. 1,502 applied, 1,292 admitted, 394 enrolled.

Mid 50% test scores		**GPA 2.0-2.99:**	15%
SAT verbal:	480-570	**Rank in top quarter:**	44%
SAT math:	480-580	**Rank in top tenth:**	17%
ACT:	19-24	**Return as sophomores:**	77%
GPA 3.50 or higher:	48%	**Out-of-state:**	24%
GPA 3.0-3.49:	37%	**Live on campus:**	88%

Basis for selection. High school GPA most important, followed by test scores and letters of recommendation. Prefer applicants in top half of high school class. Consider those in bottom half with strong compensating qualities. Interview required for some, recommended for all.

High school preparation. 15 units required; 22 recommended. Required and recommended units include English 4, mathematics 3-4, science 2-4 (laboratory 2), foreign language 3 and academic electives 4. Social studies and history: 2 required, 3 recommended.

2006-2007 Annual costs. Tuition/fees: $20,190. Room/board: $9,060. Books/supplies: $960. Personal expenses: $990.

2005-2006 Financial aid. Need-based: 348 full-time freshmen applied for aid; 275 were judged to have need; 275 of these received aid. Average need met was 85%. Average scholarship/grant was $14,547; average loan $2,570. 69% of total undergraduate aid awarded as scholarships/grants, 31% as loans/jobs. **Non-need-based:** Awarded to 1,451 full-time undergraduates, including 387 freshmen. Scholarships awarded for academics, minority status, music/drama, religious affiliation, state residency. **Additional information:** GED required of home-schooled students applying for Title IV federal aid.

Application procedures. Admission: No deadline. $30 fee, may be waived for applicants with need. Application may be submitted online. Admission notification on a rolling basis beginning on or about 9/1. Must reply by May 1 or within 2 week(s) if notified thereafter. **Financial aid:** Priority date 3/1; no closing date. FAFSA required. Applicants notified on a rolling basis starting 3/15; must reply within 2 week(s) of notification.

Academics. **Special study options:** Combined bachelor's/graduate degree, double major, honors, independent study, internships, liberal arts/career combination, study abroad, teacher certification program, Washington semester. 3-2 engineering with George Washington University, 3-2 engineering with Virginia Tech, 3-2 forestry with Duke University (BA/MS), 3-2 nursing with Vanderbilt University (BA/MN), 3-2 physical therapy with George Washington University (BA/MPT), 3-4 physical therapy with Shenandoah University (BA/DPT), 3-4 veterinary medicine with Virginia Tech (BA/DVM). **Credit/placement by examination:** AP, CLEP, IB, SAT, ACT, institutional tests. **Support services:** Reduced course load, study skills assistance, tutoring, writing center.

Majors. **Biology:** General. **Business:** Business admin, management information systems. **Communications:** Media studies. **Computer sciences:** Computer science. **Conservation:** Environmental science. **Education:** Family/consumer sciences, physical. **English:** English lit. **Family/consumer sciences:** General, food/nutrition. **Foreign languages:** French, Spanish. **Health:** Athletic training, clinical lab science. **History:** General. **Liberal arts:** Arts/sciences. **Math:** General. **Parks/recreation:** Exercise sciences, health/fitness. **Philosophy/religion:** Philosophy, religion. **Physical sciences:** Chemistry, physics. **Psychology:** General. **Social sciences:** Economics, international relations, political science, sociology. **Visual/performing arts:** Music history, studio arts.

Most popular majors. Biology 13%, business/marketing 20%, communications/journalism 8%, education 14%, parks/recreation 8%, psychology 6%, social sciences 10%.

Computing on campus. 176 workstations in library. Dormitories wired for high-speed internet access and linked to campus network. Commuter students can connect to campus network. Online library, helpline, repair service, student web hosting, wireless network available.

Student life. **Freshman orientation:** Mandatory. Preregistration for classes offered. Students choose one of 3 one-day orientation sessions held during summer. Further orientation during 2 days prior to beginning of classes. Parents included in summer sessions. **Policies:** Alcoholic beverages not permitted on campus. Co-ed visitation hours. Smoking and other tobacco products are permitted only in designated areas a minimum of 20' from the residence hall. Freshmen permitted cars on campus. **Housing:** Guaranteed on-campus for all undergraduates. Single-sex dorms, special housing for disabled, apartments, substance-free housing available. Honor housing available. Unmarried students under age 23 must live on campus unless living with parents. **Activities:** Bands, choral groups, dance, drama, literary magazine, music ensembles, musical theater, radio station, student government, student newspaper, Brethren Student Fellowship, Baptist Student Union, Catholic Campus Ministry, College Republicans, Young Democrats, Black Student Association, Fellowship of Christian Athletes, International Club, Amnesty International, Habitat for Humanity.

Athletics. NCAA. **Intercollegiate:** Baseball M, basketball, cross-country, equestrian, field hockey W, football (tackle) M, golf M, lacrosse W, soccer, softball W, tennis, track and field, volleyball W. **Intramural:** Badminton, basketball, bowling, football (non-tackle), golf, racquetball, soccer, softball, table tennis, tennis, volleyball. **Team name:** Eagles.

Student services. Campus ministries, career counseling, student employment services, financial aid counseling, health services, personal counseling, placement for graduates. **Physically disabled:** Services for visually impaired.

Contact. E-mail: admissions@bridgewater.edu
Phone: (540) 828-5375 Toll-free number: (800) 759-8328
Fax: (540) 828-5481
Linda Stout, Director of Enrollment Operations, Bridgewater College, 402 East College Street, Bridgewater, VA 22812-1599

Catholic Distance University
Hamilton, Virginia
www.cdu.edu

- Private upper-division virtual university
- Rural community

General. Accredited by DETC. **Location:** We are a Distance Learning University with no requirement for on-site classes We are close to Leesburg, Virginia and just outside Washington, DC. **Calendar:** Differs by program.

Contact. Phone: (540) 338-2700
120 East Colonial Highway, Hamilton, VA 20158-9012

Christendom College
Front Royal, Virginia
www.christendom.edu **CB code: 5691**

- Private 4-year liberal arts college affiliated with Roman Catholic Church
- Residential campus in large town
- 379 degree-seeking undergraduates: 2% part-time, 57% women, 1% African American, 2% Asian American, 3% Hispanic American, 2% international
- 56 degree-seeking graduate students
- 76% of applicants admitted
- SAT or ACT with writing, application essay required
- 70% graduate within 6 years

General. Founded in 1977. Regionally accredited. Junior semester in Rome. **Degrees:** 87 bachelor's, 1 associate awarded; master's offered. **Location:** 70 miles from Washington, DC. **Calendar:** Semester, limited summer session. **Full-time faculty:** 23 total; 78% have terminal degrees, 9% women. **Part-time faculty:** 16 total; 44% have terminal degrees, 25% women. **Class size:** 59% < 20, 37% 20-39, 2% 40-49, 2% 50-99.

Freshman class profile. 249 applied, 190 admitted, 105 enrolled.

Mid 50% test scores		**Rank in top tenth:**	15%
SAT verbal:	600-700	**End year in good standing:**	96%
SAT math:	530-630	**Return as sophomores:**	88%
GPA 3.50 or higher:	64%	**Out-of-state:**	73%
GPA 3.0-3.49:	29%	**Live on campus:**	98%
GPA 2.0-2.99:	7%	**International:**	2%
Rank in top quarter:	75%		

Basis for selection. Secondary school record, essay, test scores, recommendations important. Applicants can present additional material and explain scores, evaluations, etc. which they believe do not adequately reflect their abilities. Interview recommended. **Homeschooled:** Home school transcript forms required (available from college).

High school preparation. 14 units recommended. Recommended units include English 4, mathematics 2, social studies 1, history 2, science 2, foreign language 2 and academic electives 1.

2006-2007 Annual costs. Tuition/fees: $16,740. Room/board: $6,066. Books/supplies: $500. Personal expenses: $300.

2005-2006 Financial aid. **Need-based:** Average need met was 90%. Average scholarship/grant was $8,500; average loan $4,705. 48% of total undergraduate aid awarded as scholarships/grants, 52% as loans/jobs. **Non-need-based:** Scholarships awarded for academics, alumni affiliation. **Additional information:** Christendom accepts no direct federal aid, nor does it participate in indirect programs of federal aid.

Application procedures. **Admission:** Priority date 3/1; no deadline. $25 fee. Application may be submitted online. Admission notification on a rolling basis. **Financial aid:** Priority date 4/1, closing date 6/1. Institutional form required. Applicants notified on a rolling basis starting 2/1; must reply within 4 week(s) of notification.

Academics. **Special study options:** Double major, honors, independent study, internships, study abroad. **Credit/placement by examination:** AP, CLEP, institutional tests. **Support services:** Pre-admission summer program, writing center.

Majors. **Foreign languages:** Classics. **History:** General. **Philosophy/religion:** Philosophy. **Social sciences:** Political science.

Most popular majors. English 10%, history 25%, philosophy/religious studies 30%, social sciences 16%, theological studies 17%.

Computing on campus. 70 workstations in library.

Student life. **Freshman orientation:** Mandatory. Preregistration for classes offered. Orientation held weekend before school starts. **Policies:** Although no student is required to participate, the college encourages religious activities. Freshmen permitted cars on campus. **Housing:** Guaranteed on-campus for all undergraduates. Single-sex dorms, substance-free housing available. $500 fully refundable deposit, deadline 3/15. **Activities:** Choral groups, drama, film society, literary magazine, musical theater, student government, student newspaper, Legion of Mary, Shield of Roses, St. Genesius Society, Holy Rood Guild, College Republicans, works of mercy group.

Athletics. USCAA. **Intercollegiate:** Baseball M, basketball, soccer, softball W, volleyball W. **Intramural:** Basketball, cross-country, football (non-tackle), handball, racquetball, rugby M, soccer, softball, table tennis, tennis, volleyball. **Team name:** Crusaders.

Student services. Campus ministries, career counseling, health services, personal counseling, placement for graduates.

Contact. E-mail: admissions@christendom.edu
Phone: (540) 636-2900 Toll-free number: (800) 877-5456
Fax: (540) 636-1655
Tom McFadden, Director of Admissions, Christendom College, 134 Christendom Drive, Front Royal, VA 22630

Christopher Newport University

Newport News, Virginia — **CB member**
www.cnu.edu — **CB code: 5128**

- Public 4-year university and liberal arts college
- Residential campus in small city
- 4,496 degree-seeking undergraduates: 7% part-time, 54% women, 8% African American, 2% Asian American, 2% Hispanic American, 1% Native American
- 123 degree-seeking graduate students
- SAT or ACT (ACT writing optional) required
- 45% graduate within 6 years

General. Founded in 1960. Regionally accredited. **Degrees:** 834 bachelor's awarded; master's offered. **ROTC:** Army. **Location:** 20 miles from Norfolk, 70 miles from Richmond. **Calendar:** Semester, extensive summer session. **Full-time faculty:** 195 total. **Part-time faculty:** 125 total. **Class size:** 30% < 20, 53% 20-39, 12% 40-49, 5% 50-99, less than 1% >100.

Freshman class profile.

Mid 50% test scores		Rank in top quarter:	49%
SAT verbal:	530-620	Rank in top tenth:	16%
SAT math:	530-610	End year in good standing:	80%
ACT:	21-25	Return as sophomores:	75%
GPA 3.50 or higher:	44%	Out-of-state:	4%
GPA 3.0-3.49:	44%	Live on campus:	92%
GPA 2.0-2.99:	12%		

Basis for selection. Minimum 3.0 GPA, rank in top half of class. Type of diploma and difficulty of classes taken considered. Test scores required for all freshman applicants who graduated from high school within past 2 years. Audition required for music; interview recommended for marginal; portfolio recommended for art. **Homeschooled:** Applicants should submit a copy of their high school transcript and descriptions, along with an ACT or SAT score.

High school preparation. 23 units required. Required and recommended units include English 4, mathematics 4, history 3, science 3 and foreign language 3.

2005-2006 Annual costs. Tuition/fees: $5,826; $12,898 out-of-state. Room/board: $7,500. Books/supplies: $704. Personal expenses: $1,557.

2005-2006 Financial aid. Need-based: 916 full-time freshmen applied for aid; 517 were judged to have need; 512 of these received aid. Average need met was 72%. Average scholarship/grant was $3,461; average loan $1,983. 48% of total undergraduate aid awarded as scholarships/grants, 52% as loans/jobs. **Non-need-based:** Awarded to 596 full-time undergraduates, including 245 freshmen. Scholarships awarded for academics, leadership, music/drama, ROTC, state residency.

Application procedures. Admission: Priority date 12/1; deadline 3/1 (receipt date). $35 fee, may be waived for applicants with need. Application may be submitted online. Admission notification on a rolling basis beginning on or about 12/1. Must reply by May 1 or within 2 week(s) if notified thereafter. **Financial aid:** Priority date 3/1; no closing date. FAFSA required. Applicants notified on a rolling basis starting 2/21; must reply within 2 week(s) of notification.

Academics. Special study options: Cross-registration, double major, dual enrollment of high school students, exchange student, honors, independent study, internships, student-designed major, study abroad, teacher certification program. Member of the Virginia Tidewater Consortium. **Credit/placement by examination:** AP, CLEP, IB, institutional tests. **Support services:** Pre-admission summer program, reduced course load, study skills assistance, tutoring, writing center.

Majors. Agriculture: Ornamental horticulture. **Biology:** General. **Business:** Accounting, business admin, finance, managerial economics, marketing. **Communications:** General. **Computer sciences:** General, computer science. **Conservation:** Environmental science. **Engineering:** Computer. **English:** English lit. **Foreign languages:** French, German, Spanish. **History:** General. **Math:** General. **Philosophy/religion:** Philosophy. **Physical sciences:** Chemistry, physics. **Psychology:** General. **Public administration:** Social work. **Social sciences:** Political science, sociology. **Visual/performing arts:** Dramatic, studio arts.

Most popular majors. Biology 8%, business/marketing 19%, communications/journalism 7%, computer/information sciences 7%, English 6%, psychology 13%, social sciences 17%.

Computing on campus. 302 workstations in dormitories, library, computer center. Dormitories wired for high-speed internet access and linked to campus network. Commuter students can connect to campus network. Online course registration, online library, helpline, student web hosting, wireless network available.

Student life. Freshman orientation: Mandatory, $175 fee. Preregistration for classes offered. 2 programs: 1.5-day mandatory program (Setting Sail) with overnight stay in the residence halls, offered June-July, and a "Welcome Week" program prior to the start of classes in fall. **Policies:** Alcohol not permitted on campus; 1st and 2nd year students will be required to live on campus unless they reside with their parents or legal guardians in Gloucester, Hampton, Isle of Wight, James City County, Matthews County, Newport News, Poquoson, Williamsburg or York County (of Virginia). Freshmen permitted cars on campus. **Housing:** Guaranteed on-campus for freshmen. Coed dorms, apartments, substance-free housing available. $100 nonrefundable deposit, deadline 5/1. Learning communities. **Activities:** Bands, choral groups, dance, drama, literary magazine, music ensembles, musical theater, opera, radio station, student government, student newspaper, symphony orchestra, Baptist Student Union, Catholic Campus Ministries, Intervarsity Christian Fellowship, Lions Club, Lutheran student association, Model United Nations, multicultural student association, student government association, various honor societies.

Athletics. NCAA. **Intercollegiate:** Baseball M, basketball, cheerleading, cross-country, equestrian, field hockey W, football (tackle) M, golf M, lacrosse, sailing, soccer, softball W, tennis, track and field, volleyball W. **Intramural:** Basketball, football (non-tackle) M, soccer, softball, tennis, volleyball. **Team name:** Captains.

Student services. Campus ministries, career counseling, student employment services, financial aid counseling, health services, minority student services, personal counseling, placement for graduates, veterans' counselor. **Physically disabled:** Services for visually, speech, hearing impaired.

Contact. E-mail: admit@cnu.edu
Phone: (757) 594-7015 Toll-free number: (800) 333-4268
Fax: (757) 594-7333
Patricia Cavender, Dean of Admissions, Christopher Newport University, 1 University Place, Newport News, VA 23606

College of William and Mary

Williamsburg, Virginia — **CB member**
www.wm.edu — **CB code: 5115**

- Public 4-year university
- Residential campus in large town
- 5,540 degree-seeking undergraduates: 1% part-time, 54% women, 6% African American, 7% Asian American, 5% Hispanic American, 1% Native American, 1% international
- 1,859 degree-seeking graduate students
- 31% of applicants admitted
- SAT or ACT (ACT writing optional), application essay required
- 91% graduate within 6 years

General. Founded in 1693. Regionally accredited. **Degrees:** 1,472 bachelor's awarded; master's, doctoral, first professional offered. **ROTC:** Army. **Location:** 50 miles from Richmond, 50 miles from Norfolk. **Calendar:** Semester, extensive summer session. **Full-time faculty:** 596 total; 89% have terminal degrees, 10% minority, 34% women. **Part-time faculty:** 167 total; 50% have terminal degrees, 6% minority, 49% women. **Special facilities:** Observatory, continuous beam accelerator, 3 interdisciplinary centers in humanities, international studies, writing resources, marine science institute, materials processes research center, public policy research center.

Freshman class profile. 10,610 applied, 3,292 admitted, 1,344 enrolled.

Mid 50% test scores		Rank in top quarter:	97%
SAT verbal:	630-730	Rank in top tenth:	79%
SAT math:	630-710	Return as sophomores:	95%
ACT:	28-31	Out-of-state:	33%
GPA 3.50 or higher:	92%	Live on campus:	100%
GPA 3.0-3.49:	8%	International:	2%

Basis for selection. Academic preparation most important, with particular emphasis on course selection and grades, test scores, special talents and abilities. Special consideration given to children of alumni. Preference given to Virginia residents. Diverse backgrounds, special abilities, unique interests and experiences preferred. Applications evaluated on own merits without specific course requirements. Most candidates present as strong a college preparatory program as possible. Advanced placement, honors, accelerated courses strongly weighed in evaluation process.

High school preparation. 20 units recommended. Recommended units include English 4, mathematics 4, social studies 4, science 4 (laboratory 3) and foreign language 4. Recommend most demanding high school course available.

2005-2006 Annual costs. Tuition/fees: $7,723; $22,993 out-of-state. Room/board: $6,916. Books/supplies: $800. Personal expenses: $970.

2004-2005 Financial aid. **Need-based:** 62% of total undergraduate aid awarded as scholarships/grants, 38% as loans/jobs. **Non-need-based:** Scholarships awarded for academics, athletics, leadership.

Application procedures. **Admission:** Closing date 1/1 (postmark date). $60 fee, may be waived for applicants with need. Application may be submitted online. Admission notification 4/1. Must reply by 5/1. **Financial aid:** Priority date 2/15, closing date 3/15. FAFSA required. CSS PROFILE required of early decision applicants only. Applicants notified on a rolling basis starting 3/10; must reply by 5/1.

Academics. **Special study options:** Accelerated study, combined bachelor's/graduate degree, double major, dual enrollment of high school students, exchange student, honors, independent study, internships, semester at sea, student-designed major, study abroad, teacher certification program, Washington semester. Early assurance program with Eastern Virginia Medical School. **Credit/placement by examination:** AP, CLEP, IB, institutional tests. **Support services:** Pre-admission summer program, reduced course load, study skills assistance, tutoring, writing center.

Majors. **Area/ethnic studies:** African, African-American, American, East Asian, European, Latin American, Near/Middle Eastern, Russian/Slavic, women's. **Biology:** General. **Business:** Business admin. **Computer sciences:** General. **Conservation:** Environmental studies. **Foreign languages:** Ancient Greek, classics, French, German, Latin, linguistics, Spanish. **History:** General. **Interdisciplinary:** Biopsychology, medieval/Renaissance, neuroscience. **Math:** General. **Parks/recreation:** Health/fitness. **Philosophy/religion:** Philosophy, religion. **Physical sciences:** Chemistry, geology, physics. **Psychology:** General. **Public administration:** Policy analysis. **Social sciences:** Anthropology, economics, international relations, political science, sociology. **Visual/performing arts:** Art, art history/conservation, dramatic, studio arts.

Most popular majors. Biology 8%, business/marketing 12%, English 9%, interdisciplinary studies 7%, physical sciences 6%, psychology 10%, social sciences 24%.

Computing on campus. PC or laptop required. 350 workstations in dormitories, library, computer center, student center. Dormitories wired for high-speed internet access and linked to campus network. Commuter students can connect to campus network. Online course registration, online library, helpline, repair service, student web hosting, wireless network available.

Student life. **Freshman orientation:** Mandatory, $83 fee. 5-day program. **Policies:** Honor system in effect. Freshmen permitted cars on campus. **Housing:** Guaranteed on-campus for freshmen. Coed dorms, single-sex dorms, fraternity/sorority housing available. $200 deposit, deadline 2/17. Special interest housing (Italian, French, German, Asian, Russian, Spanish, Project Plus, international studies, ecology) available. **Activities:** Bands, choral groups, dance, drama, film society, literary magazine, music ensembles, musical theater, opera, radio station, student government, student newspaper, symphony orchestra, TV station, black student organization, College Republicans, Young Democrats, women's issues group, College Partnerships for Kids, Student Environmental Action Coalition, ecumenical council, Asian student union, club international, Hispanic cultural organization.

Athletics. NCAA. **Intercollegiate:** Baseball M, basketball, cross-country, diving, field hockey W, football (tackle) M, golf, gymnastics, lacrosse W, soccer, swimming, tennis, track and field, volleyball W. **Intramural:** Badminton, baseball M, basketball, bowling, cross-country, golf, racquetball, soccer, softball, table tennis, tennis, track and field, weight lifting, wrestling M. **Team name:** Tribe.

Student services. Alcohol/substance abuse counseling, campus ministries, career counseling, student employment services, financial aid counseling, health services, legal services, minority student services, on-campus daycare, personal counseling, placement for graduates. **Physically disabled:** Services for visually, hearing impaired.

Contact. E-mail: admiss@wm.edu
Phone: (757) 221-4223 Fax: (757) 221-1242
Henry Broaddus, Dean of Admissions, College of William and Mary, PO Box 8795, Williamsburg, VA 23187-8795

DeVry University: Arlington

Arlington, Virginia
www.crys.devry.edu **CB code: 3813**

- For-profit 4-year university
- Commuter campus in very large city
- 459 degree-seeking undergraduates: 33% part-time, 47% women
- 122 graduate students
- Interview required

General. **Degrees:** 103 bachelor's, 30 associate awarded; master's offered. **Calendar:** Semester, extensive summer session. **Full-time faculty:** 20 total; 30% minority, 30% women. **Part-time faculty:** 42 total; 36% minority, 14% women.

Basis for selection. Applicant must have high school diploma or equivalent, degree from an accredited postsecondary institution, or submit acceptable test scores and be at least 17 years of age. CPT also accepted.

High school preparation. Required units include mathematics 1. Math unit must be algebra or higher.

2005-2006 Annual costs. Tuition/fees: $13,410. Books/supplies: $1,100. Personal expenses: $1,550.

2004-2005 Financial aid. All financial aid based on need. 97 full-time freshmen applied for aid; 92 were judged to have need; 92 of these received aid. Average need met was 35%. Average scholarship/grant was $3,770; average loan $5,877. 17% of total undergraduate aid awarded as scholarships/grants, 83% as loans/jobs.

Application procedures. **Admission:** No deadline. $50 fee. Application may be submitted online. Admission notification on a rolling basis. **Financial aid:** No deadline. FAFSA required. Applicants notified on a rolling basis starting 7/1.

Academics. **Special study options:** Accelerated study, cooperative education, distance learning. **Credit/placement by examination:** CLEP. **Support services:** Learning center, remedial instruction, tutoring.

Majors. **Business:** Business admin. **Computer sciences:** Information systems, networking. **Engineering technology:** Electrical.

Most popular majors. Business/marketing 31%, computer/information sciences 48%, engineering/engineering technologies 21%.

Computing on campus. Online course registration, online library, helpline available.

Student life. **Freshman orientation:** Mandatory. **Policies:** Freshmen permitted cars on campus. **Activities:** Linux user's group.

Athletics. **Intramural:** Basketball, volleyball.

Student services. Career counseling, student employment services, financial aid counseling, placement for graduates, veterans' counselor. **Physically disabled:** Services for visually, hearing impaired.

Contact. E-mail: admissions@crys.devry.edu
Phone: (703) 414-4100 Toll-free number: (866) 338-7932
Fax: (703) 414-4040
Bob Pavlovics, Director of Admissions, DeVry University: Arlington, 2450 Crystal Drive, Arlington, VA 22202

Eastern Mennonite University

Harrisonburg, Virginia — **CB member**
www.emu.edu — **CB code: 5181**

- Private 4-year university and liberal arts college affiliated with Mennonite Church
- Residential campus in large town
- 998 degree-seeking undergraduates: 3% part-time, 63% women, 7% African American, 2% Asian American, 3% Hispanic American, 5% international
- 270 degree-seeking graduate students
- 77% of applicants admitted
- SAT or ACT with writing required
- 60% graduate within 6 years; 5% enter graduate study

General. Founded in 1917. Regionally accredited. **Degrees:** 315 bachelor's, 1 associate awarded; master's, first professional offered. **Location:** 110 miles from Richmond, 110 miles from Washington, DC. **Calendar:** Semester, limited summer session. **Full-time faculty:** 116 total; 71% have terminal degrees, 7% minority, 40% women. **Part-time faculty:** 47 total; 36% have terminal degrees, 19% minority, 45% women. **Class size:** 62% < 20, 34% 20-39, 1% 40-49, 2% 50-99, less than 1% >100. **Special facilities:** Historical library, museum of natural history, planetarium, arboretum.

Freshman class profile. 636 applied, 490 admitted, 202 enrolled.

Mid 50% test scores			
SAT verbal:	480-630	Rank in top quarter:	44%
SAT math:	480-630	Rank in top tenth:	21%
ACT:	22-28	End year in good standing:	87%
GPA 3.50 or higher:	57%	Return as sophomores:	74%
GPA 3.0-3.49:	20%	Out-of-state:	57%
GPA 2.0-2.99:	23%	Live on campus:	92%
		International:	2%

Basis for selection. 2.2 high school GPA and SAT score of 920 (exclusive of Writing) required. ACT minimum composite score of 20 required. Conditional admission possible for motivated applicants who fail to reach minimum admissions requirements. **Homeschooled:** Detailed record of coursework completed for grades 9-12, SAT or ACT required. **Learning Disabled:** Interview recommended for learning disabled.

High school preparation. College-preparatory program recommended. 21 units recommended. Recommended units include English 4, mathematics 3, social studies 3, science 3 (laboratory 3), foreign language 2 and academic electives 6.

2006-2007 Annual costs. Tuition/fees (projected): $20,670. Room/board: $6,550. Books/supplies: $900. Personal expenses: $700.

2005-2006 Financial aid. Need-based: 184 full-time freshmen applied for aid; 169 were judged to have need; 169 of these received aid. Average need met was 88%. Average scholarship/grant was $7,010; average loan $4,600. 66% of total undergraduate aid awarded as scholarships/grants, 34% as loans/jobs. **Non-need-based:** Awarded to 688 full-time undergraduates, including 178 freshmen. Scholarships awarded for academics, alumni affiliation, music/drama, religious affiliation, state residency.

Application procedures. Admission: No deadline. $25 fee, may be waived for applicants with need. Application may be submitted online. Admission notification on a rolling basis. **Financial aid:** Priority date 4/15; no closing date. FAFSA required. Applicants notified on a rolling basis starting 2/1; must reply within 4 week(s) of notification.

Academics. Missions programs available. Cross-cultural education component required in 3-week or 3-month assignments to locations around the world. **Special study options:** Double major, dual enrollment of high school students, ESL, honors, independent study, internships, liberal arts/career combination, study abroad, teacher certification program, Washington semester. **Credit/placement by examination:** AP, CLEP, IB, SAT, ACT, institutional tests. **Support services:** Learning center, reduced course load, remedial instruction, study skills assistance, tutoring, writing center.

Majors. Agriculture: International. **Biology:** General, biochemistry. **Business:** Accounting, business admin, international, organizational behavior. **Communications:** General. **Computer sciences:** Computer science, systems analysis. **Conservation:** Environmental science. **Education:** Physical, teacher assistance. **English:** English lit. **Foreign languages:** French, German, Spanish. **Health:** Clinical lab science, nursing (RN), predentistry, premedicine, preveterinary. **History:** General. **Interdisciplinary:** Peace/conflict. **Liberal arts:** Arts/sciences. **Math:** General. **Parks/recreation:** Sports admin. **Physical sciences:** Chemistry. **Psychology:** General. **Public administration:** Social work. **Social sciences:** General, economics, international economic development, sociology. **Theology:** Bible, preministerial, theology. **Visual/performing arts:** Art, dramatic.

Most popular majors. Business/marketing 26%, education 10%, health sciences 14%, liberal arts 17%.

Computing on campus. 100 workstations in dormitories, library, computer center, student center. Dormitories wired for high-speed internet access and linked to campus network. Online library, helpline, student web hosting, wireless network available.

Student life. Freshman orientation: Mandatory. Preregistration for classes offered. Mandatory 1-week orientation begins 5 days before fall semester. **Policies:** Alcohol and drug use by students prohibited. Chapel attendance expected. Students must sign and adhere to the Community Lifestyle Commitment. Freshmen permitted cars on campus. **Housing:** Guaranteed on-campus for freshmen. Coed dorms, single-sex dorms, special housing for disabled, apartments, substance-free housing available. $200 fully refundable deposit, deadline 3/24. Intentional communities. **Activities:** Bands, choral groups, dance, drama, literary magazine, music ensembles, musical theater, radio station, student government, student newspaper, symphony orchestra, young people's Christian association, peace fellowship, Black Student Union, international student organization, Latino Student alliance, Earth Keepers, campus activities council, student Virginia education association, social work is people, Substance education committee.

Athletics. NCAA. **Intercollegiate:** Baseball M, basketball, cross-country, field hockey W, soccer, softball W, tennis, track and field, volleyball. **Intramural:** Basketball, football (tackle) M, golf, soccer, table tennis, tennis, volleyball. **Team name:** Royals.

Student services. Adult student services, alcohol/substance abuse counseling, campus ministries, career counseling, student employment services, financial aid counseling, health services, minority student services, personal counseling, placement for graduates. **Physically disabled:** Services for visually, speech, hearing impaired.

Contact. E-mail: admiss@emu.edu
Phone: (540) 432-4118 Toll-free number: (800) 368-2665
Fax: (540) 432-4444
Stephanie Shafer, Director of Admissions, Eastern Mennonite University, 1200 Park Road, Harrisonburg, VA 22802-2462

ECPI College of Technology

Virginia Beach, Virginia
www.ecpi.edu — **CB code: 7140**

- For-profit 4-year health science and technical college
- Commuter campus in large city
- 4,853 degree-seeking undergraduates: 4% part-time, 52% women, 48% African American, 1% Asian American, 1% Hispanic American
- Interview required
- 56% graduate within 6 years

General. Founded in 1966. Regionally accredited. **Degrees:** 755 associate awarded. **Calendar:** Continuous, extensive summer session. **Class size:** 80% < 20, 20% 20-39.

Basis for selection. Requirements include interview and program specific admissions test. No special considerations given.

High school preparation. Recommended units include English 4, mathematics 2, social studies 2, history 2 and science 2.

2005-2006 Annual costs. Required fee is for books. Personal expenses: $1,710.

Financial aid. Non-need-based: Scholarships awarded for academics.

Application procedures. Admission: No deadline. $50 fee. Application may be submitted online. Admission notification on a rolling basis. **Financial aid:** No deadline. Institutional form required. Applicants notified on a rolling basis.

Academics. Special study options: Accelerated study, cooperative education, distance learning, double major, dual enrollment of high school students, independent study, internships. **Credit/placement by examination:** AP, CLEP, institutional tests. 18 credit hours maximum toward associate degree, 33 toward bachelor's. **Support services:** Learning center, remedial instruction, study skills assistance, tutoring, writing center.

Majors. Computer sciences: General.

Computing on campus. 2,700 workstations in library, computer center, student center. Commuter students can connect to campus network. Online library available.

Student life. Freshman orientation: Mandatory. Half-day orientation held the day prior to each term start. **Policies:** Freshmen permitted cars on campus. **Activities:** Student Electronic Technicians Association, Information Technology Exchange, accounting society, International Association of Administrative Professionals, Phi Theta Kappa.

Student services. Student employment services, financial aid counseling, placement for graduates, veterans' counselor.

Contact. Phone: (757) 671-7171 Toll-free number: (800) 986-1200
Fax: (757) 671-8661
Frances Hinton, Director of Admissions, ECPI College of Technology, 5555 Greenwich Road, Suite 300, Virginia Beach, VA 23462-6542

ECPI Technical College: Glen Allen

Glen Allen, Virginia
www.ecpitech.edu

- For-profit 4-year technical college
- Commuter campus in large town
- 443 degree-seeking undergraduates: 29% women, 37% African American, 3% Asian American, 4% Hispanic American
- Interview required

General. Accredited by ACCSCT. **Degrees:** 152 associate awarded. **Calendar:** Semester, extensive summer session.

Basis for selection. Program specific admission test required. Admissions test required.

Application procedures. Admission: No deadline. $50 fee. Admission notification on a rolling basis.

Academics. Special study options: Distance learning, internships, study abroad. **Credit/placement by examination:** AP, CLEP, institutional tests. **Support services:** Remedial instruction, tutoring.

Majors. Computer sciences: General.

Computing on campus. 300 workstations in library, computer center. Online library available.

Student life. Freshman orientation: Mandatory. Preregistration for classes offered. **Policies:** Freshmen permitted cars on campus.

Student services. Adult student services, career counseling, student employment services, financial aid counseling, placement for graduates, veterans' counselor.

Contact. Phone: (804) 934-0100
Sharon Fitzgerald, Admissions, ECPI Technical College: Glen Allen, 4305 Cox Road, Glen Allen, VA 23060

Emory & Henry College

Emory, Virginia — **CB member**
www.ehc.edu — **CB code: 5185**

- Private 4-year liberal arts college affiliated with United Methodist Church
- Residential campus in rural community
- 1,027 degree-seeking undergraduates: 3% part-time, 49% women
- 25 degree-seeking graduate students
- 76% of applicants admitted
- SAT or ACT (ACT writing optional), application essay required
- 52% graduate within 6 years

General. Founded in 1836. Regionally accredited. **Degrees:** 196 bachelor's awarded; master's offered. **Location:** 25 miles from Bristol. **Calendar:** Semester, limited summer session. **Full-time faculty:** 68 total; 88% have terminal degrees, 7% minority, 28% women. **Part-time faculty:** 27 total; 26% have terminal degrees, 4% minority, 52% women. **Class size:** 72% < 20, 28% 20-39. **Special facilities:** Observatory.

Freshman class profile. 1,329 applied, 1,009 admitted, 338 enrolled.

Mid 50% test scores			
SAT verbal:	480-590	Rank in top tenth:	21%
SAT math:	460-560	Return as sophomores:	72%
ACT:	20-26	Out-of-state:	30%
Rank in top quarter:	51%	Live on campus:	90%

Basis for selection. School achievement record, test scores, volunteer work very important; class rank, recommendations also important. Audition recommended for drama, music programs; portfolio recommended for art programs.

High school preparation. 14 units required. Required units include English 4, mathematics 3, social studies 2, science 3 (laboratory 3) and foreign language 2.

2005-2006 Annual costs. Tuition/fees: $19,530. Room/board: $7,040. Books/supplies: $700. Personal expenses: $1,000.

2005-2006 Financial aid. All financial aid based on need. 317 full-time freshmen applied for aid; 276 were judged to have need; 276 of these received aid. Average need met was 74%. Average scholarship/grant was $11,711; average loan $2,543. 78% of total undergraduate aid awarded as scholarships/grants, 22% as loans/jobs. **Additional information:** Virginia residents eligible for additional in-state tuition grants.

Application procedures. Admission: No deadline. $30 fee, may be waived for applicants with need. Application may be submitted online. Admission notification on a rolling basis beginning on or about 8/1. Must reply by May 1 or within 2 week(s) if notified thereafter. **Financial aid:** Priority date 4/1, closing date 8/1. FAFSA required. Applicants notified on a rolling basis starting 2/1; must reply within 4 week(s) of notification.

Academics. Special study options: Combined bachelor's/graduate degree, cooperative education, double major, dual enrollment of high school students, honors, independent study, internships, liberal arts/career combination, student-designed major, study abroad, teacher certification program. **Credit/placement by examination:** AP, CLEP, IB, institutional tests. **Support services:** Learning center, pre-admission summer program, reduced course load, study skills assistance, tutoring, writing center.

Majors. Area/ethnic studies: East Asian, European, Near/Middle Eastern. **Biology:** General. **Business:** Business admin. **Communications:** General. **Computer sciences:** General, computer science. **Conservation:** Environmental studies. **Foreign languages:** French, Spanish. **Health:** Athletic training, clinical lab technology. **History:** General. **Math:** General. **Parks/recreation:** Health/fitness. **Philosophy/religion:** Philosophy, religion. **Physical sciences:** Chemistry, physics. **Psychology:** General. **Public administration:** Community org/advocacy. **Social sciences:** Anthropology, economics, geography, political science, sociology. **Visual/performing arts:** Art, dramatic.

Most popular majors. Business/marketing 13%, education 13%, physical sciences 6%, psychology 6%, social sciences 16%.

Computing on campus. 128 workstations in dormitories, library, computer center, student center. Dormitories wired for high-speed internet access and linked to campus network. Commuter students can connect to campus network. Online library, helpline available.

Student life. Freshman orientation: Mandatory. Preregistration for classes offered. Orientation occurs before registration. Students participate in a community service activity and attend a fine arts event the following weekend as a part of extended orientation. **Policies:** Freshmen permitted cars on campus. **Housing:** Guaranteed on-campus for all undergraduates. Single-sex dorms, substance-free housing available. $200 deposit. Religious life and honor houses available. **Activities:** Pep band, choral groups, drama, literary magazine, music ensembles, musical theater, opera, radio station, student government, student newspaper, TV station, Young Democrats, Young Republicans, Alpha Phi Omega, Fellowship of Christian Athletes, Bible study groups, Habitat for Humanity, Campus Christian Fellowship, Multi-Cultural Student Association.

Athletics. NCAA. **Intercollegiate:** Baseball M, basketball, cheerleading M, cross-country, football (tackle) M, golf M, soccer, softball W, swimming W, tennis, volleyball W. **Intramural:** Badminton, basketball, football (non-tackle), golf, racquetball, skiing, soccer, softball, swimming, table tennis, tennis, volleyball, water polo, weight lifting. **Team name:** Wasps.

Student services. Alcohol/substance abuse counseling, campus ministries, career counseling, student employment services, financial aid counseling, health services, personal counseling, placement for graduates, veterans' counselor. **Physically disabled:** Services for visually impaired.

Contact. E-mail: ehadmiss@ehc.edu
Phone: (276) 944-6133 Toll-free number: (800) 848-5493
Fax: (276) 944-6935
Liz Daniels, Director of Admissions and Financial Aid, Emory & Henry College, Box 10, Emory, VA 24327

Ferrum College

Ferrum, Virginia — **CB member**
www.ferrum.edu — **CB code: 5213**

- Private 4-year liberal arts college affiliated with United Methodist Church
- Residential campus in rural community
- 991 degree-seeking undergraduates: 3% part-time, 42% women, 20% African American, 1% Asian American, 2% Hispanic American, 1% Native American, 1% international
- 72% of applicants admitted
- SAT or ACT (ACT writing recommended) required
- 33% graduate within 6 years

General. Founded in 1913. Regionally accredited. **Degrees:** 140 bachelor's awarded. **Location:** 35 miles from Roanoke, 65 miles from Greensboro, North Carolina. **Calendar:** Semester, limited summer session. **Full-time faculty:** 62 total; 77% have terminal degrees, 5% minority, 39% women. **Part-time faculty:** 33 total; 9% have terminal degrees, 36% women. **Class size:** 71% < 20, 29% 20-39. **Special facilities:** Blue Ridge Institute and Farm Museum; State Center for Blue Ridge Folklore; forest and agricultural acreage used as outdoor labs in science, high and low ropes courses.

Freshman class profile. 1,248 applied, 896 admitted, 347 enrolled.

Mid 50% test scores			
SAT verbal:	410-490	Rank in top quarter:	13%
SAT math:	400-490	Rank in top tenth:	1%
ACT:	15-19	End year in good standing:	77%
GPA 3.50 or higher:	13%	Return as sophomores:	55%
GPA 3.0-3.49:	16%	Out-of-state:	16%
GPA 2.0-2.99:	65%	Live on campus:	89%
		International:	1%

Basis for selection. High school record is most important, followed by test scores, counselor recommendations, areas of intended college study, and extracurricular activities. Essay and interview are recommended. **Homeschooled:** Transcript of courses and grades required.

High school preparation. Recommended units include English 4, mathematics 3, social studies 3, science 2 (laboratory 1), foreign language 2 and academic electives 2.

2006-2007 Annual costs. Tuition/fees: $19,520. Room/board: $6,300. Books/supplies: $800. Personal expenses: $1,300.

Financial aid. Non-need-based: Scholarships awarded for academics, job skills, leadership, religious affiliation, state residency.

Application procedures. Admission: Priority date 3/1; deadline 8/15 (postmark date). $25 fee, may be waived for applicants with need. Application may be submitted online. Admission notification on a rolling basis. Must reply no later than 30 days after receiving official acceptance letter. **Financial aid:** Priority date 4/1; no closing date. FAFSA required. Applicants notified on a rolling basis starting 3/1.

Academics. Field experiences and internships are emphasized. **Special study options:** Cooperative education, double major, dual enrollment of high school students, honors, independent study, internships, liberal arts/career combination, student-designed major, study abroad, teacher certification program. **Credit/placement by examination:** AP, CLEP, institutional tests. 12 credit hours maximum toward bachelor's degree. **Support services:** Learning center, pre-admission summer program, reduced course load, remedial instruction, study skills assistance, tutoring, writing center.

Majors. Agriculture: Business, horticultural science. **Biology:** General. **Business:** Accounting, business admin. **Computer sciences:** Computer science, information systems. **Conservation:** Environmental science. **Education:** General. **English:** English lit. **Foreign languages:** Russian, Spanish. **Health:** Clinical lab science, health services. **History:** General. **Interdisciplinary:** Global studies. **Liberal arts:** Arts/sciences. **Math:** General. **Parks/recreation:** General, health/fitness, sports admin. **Philosophy/religion:** Philosophy, religion. **Physical sciences:** Chemistry. **Protective services:** Criminal justice. **Psychology:** General. **Public administration:** Social work. **Social sciences:** General, international relations, political science. **Visual/performing arts:** General, art, dramatic.

Most popular majors. Business/marketing 23%, computer/information sciences 7%, education 9%, history 8%, parks/recreation 14%, psychology 10%, public administration/social services 7%.

Computing on campus. 500 workstations in dormitories, library, computer center, student center. Dormitories wired for high-speed internet access and linked to campus network. Commuter students can connect to campus network. Online course registration, online library, helpline, repair service, student web hosting, wireless network available.

Student life. Freshman orientation: Mandatory. Preregistration for classes offered. A two-day student orientation is held immediately prior to fall semester. **Policies:** Freshmen permitted cars on campus. **Housing:** Guaranteed on-campus for all undergraduates. Coed dorms, single-sex dorms, apartments, substance-free housing available. $200 fully refundable deposit. Housing substance-free; no alcohol or tobacco products allowed. **Activities:** Jazz band, choral groups, dance, drama, literary magazine, music ensembles, musical theater, radio station, student government, student newspaper, Organization for World Understanding, African American Student Association, Students Achieving Volunteer Service, Bonner Scholars, Student Christian Fellowship, Catholic Campus Ministry, Kappa Delta Chi, Habitat for Humanity, Canterbury Club.

Athletics. NCAA. **Intercollegiate:** Baseball M, basketball, cheerleading, cross-country, football (tackle) M, golf M, lacrosse W, soccer, softball W, tennis, volleyball W. **Intramural:** Basketball, bowling, football (non-tackle) M, racquetball, softball, swimming, table tennis, tennis, volleyball. **Team name:** Panthers.

Student services. Adult student services, alcohol/substance abuse counseling, campus ministries, career counseling, student employment services, financial aid counseling, health services, minority student services, personal counseling, placement for graduates, veterans' counselor.

Contact. E-mail: admissions@ferrum.edu
Phone: (540) 365-4290 Toll-free number: (800) 868-9797
Fax: (540) 365-4266
Gilda Woods, Director of Admissions, Ferrum College, Spilman-Daniel House, Ferrum, VA 24088

George Mason University

Fairfax, Virginia — **CB member**
www.gmu.edu — **CB code: 5827**

- Public 4-year university
- Commuter campus in large town
- 17,529 degree-seeking undergraduates: 23% part-time, 54% women, 8% African American, 17% Asian American, 8% Hispanic American, 4% international
- 9,248 degree-seeking graduate students
- 69% of applicants admitted
- SAT or ACT (ACT writing optional) required
- 52% graduate within 6 years

General. Founded in 1972. Regionally accredited. **Degrees:** 3,415 bachelor's awarded; master's, doctoral, first professional offered. **ROTC:** Army, Air Force. **Location:** 15 miles from Washington, DC. **Calendar:** Semester, extensive summer session. **Full-time faculty:** 997 total; 90% have terminal degrees, 15% minority, 39% women. **Part-time faculty:** 958 total; 43% have terminal degrees, 14% minority, 54% women. **Class size:** 32% < 20, 45% 20-39, 9% 40-49, 10% 50-99, 3% >100. **Special facilities:** Library of Congress Federal Theater Project collection, arts center.

Freshman class profile. 10,344 applied, 7,109 admitted, 2,529 enrolled.

Mid 50% test scores			
SAT verbal:	490-600	Rank in top quarter:	44%
SAT math:	510-610	Rank in top tenth:	14%
ACT:	20-24	Return as sophomores:	84%
GPA 3.50 or higher:	33%	Out-of-state:	17%
GPA 3.0-3.49:	52%	Live on campus:	63%
GPA 2.0-2.99:	15%	International:	2%

Basis for selection. Test scores, class rank, academic record with emphasis on courses taken, and GPA most important. Special talents and abilities and counselor recommendations also important. SAT Subject Tests recommended. Essay recommended for all; audition required for dance, music programs.

High school preparation. College-preparatory program required. 18 units required; 24 recommended. Required and recommended units include English 4, mathematics 3-4, social studies 3-4, science 3-4 (laboratory 3-4), foreign language 2-3 and academic electives 3-5. Additional mathematics and science units required for engineering, mathematics, and computer science applicants.

2005-2006 Annual costs. Tuition/fees: $5,922; $17,202 out-of-state. Room/board: $6,480. Books/supplies: $810. Personal expenses: $1,336.

2004-2005 Financial aid. Need-based: 1,380 full-time freshmen applied for aid; 918 were judged to have need; 866 of these received aid. Average need met was 64%. Average scholarship/grant was $4,708; average loan $2,787. 42% of total undergraduate aid awarded as scholarships/grants, 58% as loans/jobs. **Non-need-based:** Awarded to 1,526 full-time undergraduates, including 512 freshmen. Scholarships awarded for academics, athletics, minority status, music/drama, ROTC, state residency.

Application procedures. Admission: Priority date 12/1; deadline 1/15 (postmark date). $60 fee, may be waived for applicants with need. Application may be submitted online. Admission notification 4/1. Admission notification on a rolling basis. Must reply by May 1 or within 3 week(s) if notified thereafter. **Financial aid:** Priority date 3/1; no closing date. FAFSA required. Applicants notified by 4/1; Applicants notified on a rolling basis starting 4/1; must reply within 3 week(s) of notification.

Academics. Special study options: Accelerated study, combined bachelor's/graduate degree, cooperative education, cross-registration, distance learning, double major, dual enrollment of high school students, ESL, exchange student, external degree, honors, independent study, internships, liberal arts/career combination, student-designed major, study abroad, teacher certification program. Alternative interdisciplinary core curriculum program. **Credit/placement by examination:** AP, CLEP, IB, institutional tests. 30 credit hours maximum toward bachelor's degree. **Support services:** Learning center, pre-admission summer program, study skills assistance, tutoring, writing center.

Majors. Area/ethnic studies: Russian/Slavic. **Biology:** General. **Business:** General, accounting, business admin, finance, marketing. **Computer sciences:** General. **Education:** Health, physical. **Engineering:** Civil, electrical, systems. **English:** Speech/rhetoric. **Foreign languages:** General. **Health:** Clinical lab science, nursing (RN). **History:** General. **Liberal arts:** Arts/sciences. **Math:** General. **Parks/recreation:** General, health/fitness. **Philosophy/religion:** Philosophy. **Physical sciences:** Chemistry, geology, physics, planetary. **Protective services:** Police science. **Psychology:** General. **Public administration:** General, social work. **Social sciences:** Anthropology, economics, geography, international relations, political science, sociology. **Visual/performing arts:** Art, art history/conservation, dance, dramatic, music performance, studio arts.

Most popular majors. Business/marketing 21%, communications/journalism 9%, computer/information sciences 7%, health sciences 10%, interdisciplinary studies 7%, psychology 8%, social sciences 10%, visual/performing arts 7%.

Computing on campus. 1,500 workstations in dormitories, library, computer center, student center. Dormitories wired for high-speed internet access and linked to campus network. Commuter students can connect to campus network. Online course registration, online library, helpline, repair service, student web hosting, wireless network available.

Student life. Freshman orientation: Available. Preregistration for classes offered. **Policies:** Freshmen permitted cars on campus. **Housing:** Guaranteed on-campus for freshmen. Coed dorms, single-sex dorms, special housing for disabled, apartments available. $300 nonrefundable deposit, deadline 5/1. **Activities:** Bands, choral groups, dance, drama, film society, literary magazine, music ensembles, musical theater, opera, radio station, student government, student newspaper, symphony orchestra, TV station.

Athletics. NCAA. **Intercollegiate:** Baseball M, basketball, cross-country, diving, golf M, lacrosse W, rifle, rowing (crew) W, soccer, softball W, swimming, tennis, track and field, volleyball, wrestling M. **Intramural:** Basketball, lacrosse M, racquetball, soccer, softball, table tennis, volleyball. **Team name:** Patriots.

Student services. Alcohol/substance abuse counseling, campus ministries, career counseling, student employment services, financial aid counseling, health services, minority student services, on-campus daycare, personal counseling, placement for graduates, veterans' counselor, women's services. **Physically disabled:** Services for visually, hearing impaired.

Contact. E-mail: admissions@gmu.edu
Phone: (703) 993-2400 Fax: (703) 993-2392
Andrew Flagel, Dean of Admissions, George Mason University, 4400 University Drive, MSN 3A4, Fairfax, VA 22030

Gibbs College

Vienna, Virginia
www.gibbsva.edu **CB code: 5655**

- For-profit 4-year business and technical college
- Large city

General. Accredited by ACICS. **Calendar:** Quarter.

Contact. Phone: (703) 556-8888
1980 Gallows Road, Vienna, VA 22182

Hampden-Sydney College

Hampden-Sydney, Virginia **CB member**
www.hsc.edu **CB code: 5291**

- Private 4-year liberal arts college for men affiliated with Presbyterian Church (USA)
- Residential campus in rural community
- 1,060 degree-seeking undergraduates
- 67% of applicants admitted
- SAT or ACT with writing required
- 61% graduate within 6 years

General. Founded in 1776. Regionally accredited. **Degrees:** 214 bachelor's awarded. **ROTC:** Army. **Location:** 60 miles from Richmond, 69 miles from Charlottesville. **Calendar:** Semester, limited summer session. **Full-time faculty:** 91 total; 88% have terminal degrees, 4% minority, 26% women. **Part-time faculty:** 17 total; 82% have terminal degrees, 6% minority, 18% women. **Class size:** 67% < 20, 33% 20-39. **Special facilities:** International communications center, observatory, museum.

Freshman class profile. 1,376 applied, 922 admitted, 322 enrolled.

Mid 50% test scores		**Rank in top quarter:**	25%
SAT verbal:	520-630	**Rank in top tenth:**	12%
SAT math:	530-640	**Return as sophomores:**	83%
ACT:	21-27	**Out-of-state:**	35%
GPA 3.50 or higher:	41%	**Live on campus:**	100%
GPA 3.0-3.49:	32%	**International:**	2%
GPA 2.0-2.99:	27%	**Fraternities:**	34%

Basis for selection. High school academic record most important. Recommendations, test scores, extracurricular activities, essay also important. SAT Subject Tests recommended. SAT Subject Test in Math Level 1 recommended. Interview recommended.

High school preparation. 16 units required. Required and recommended units include English 4, mathematics 3-4, social studies 1, science 2-3 (laboratory 1), foreign language 2-3 and academic electives 3.

2006-2007 Annual costs. Tuition/fees (projected): $26,344. Room/board: $8,125. Books/supplies: $1,000. Personal expenses: $1,000.

2005-2006 Financial aid. Need-based: 240 full-time freshmen applied for aid; 159 were judged to have need; 159 of these received aid. Average need met was 88.5%. Average scholarship/grant was $15,444; average loan $2,974. 76% of total undergraduate aid awarded as scholarships/grants, 24% as loans/jobs. **Non-need-based:** Awarded to 645 full-time undergraduates, including 206 freshmen. Scholarships awarded for academics, leadership, religious affiliation, ROTC, state residency.

Application procedures. Admission: Closing date 3/1 (postmark date). $30 fee, may be waived for applicants with need. Application must be submitted on paper. Admission notification 4/15. Must reply by 5/1. **Financial aid:** Priority date 3/1; no closing date. FAFSA, CSS PROFILE required. Applicants notified on a rolling basis starting 3/1; must reply by 5/1 or within 2 week(s) of notification.

Academics. Public service concentration for men interested in government involves classwork and internship followed by paper presented and defended publicly. **Special study options:** Cross-registration, double major, exchange student, honors, independent study, internships, semester at sea, study abroad, Washington semester. Appalachian semester, junior year exchange program with members of Virginia consortium. **Credit/placement by examination:** AP, CLEP, IB, SAT, ACT, institutional tests. **Support services:** Reduced course load, study skills assistance, tutoring, writing center.

Majors. Biology: General, biochemistry, biophysics. **Business:** Managerial economics. **Computer sciences:** Computer science. **English:** English lit. **Foreign languages:** Ancient Greek, classics, French, German, Latin,

Spanish. **History:** General. **Interdisciplinary:** Math/computer science. **Liberal arts:** Humanities. **Math:** General, applied. **Philosophy/religion:** Philosophy, religion. **Physical sciences:** Chemistry, physics. **Psychology:** General. **Social sciences:** Econometrics, economics, international relations, political science. **Visual/performing arts:** Studio arts.

Most popular majors. Biology 9%, business/marketing 10%, history 13%, philosophy/religious studies 9%, physical sciences 8%, psychology 7%, social sciences 29%.

Computing on campus. 98 workstations in dormitories, library, computer center. Dormitories wired for high-speed internet access and linked to campus network. Commuter students can connect to campus network. Online course registration, helpline, repair service, wireless network available.

Student life. **Freshman orientation:** Mandatory, $150 fee. Preregistration for classes offered. 4-day program before start of classes. **Policies:** Freshmen permitted cars on campus. **Housing:** Guaranteed on-campus for all undergraduates. Apartments, fraternity/sorority housing available. $300 deposit, deadline 5/1. **Activities:** Pep band, choral groups, drama, literary magazine, music ensembles, radio station, student government, student newspaper, Inter-Varsity Christian Fellowship, Republican Society, volunteer fire department, Good Men and Good Citizens (community service), Student Environmental Action Coalition, museum board, Fellowship of Christian Athletes, Minority Student Union, Young Democrats.

Athletics. NCAA. **Intercollegiate:** Baseball M, basketball M, cross-country M, football (tackle) M, golf M, lacrosse M, soccer M, tennis M. **Intramural:** Basketball M, racquetball M, rugby M, soccer M, softball M, volleyball M. **Team name:** Tigers.

Student services. Alcohol/substance abuse counseling, campus ministries, career counseling, student employment services, financial aid counseling, health services, minority student services, personal counseling, placement for graduates.

Contact. E-mail: hsapp@hsc.edu
Phone: (434) 223-6120 Toll-free number: (800) 755-0733
Fax: (434) 223-6346
Anita Garland, Dean of Admissions, Hampden-Sydney College, Box 667, Hampden-Sydney, VA 23943

Hampton University

Hampton, Virginia **CB member**
www.hamptonu.edu **CB code: 5292**

- Private 4-year university
- Residential campus in small city
- 5,225 degree-seeking undergraduates: 6% part-time, 65% women, 94% African American, 1% Asian American, 1% Hispanic American
- 566 degree-seeking graduate students
- 54% of applicants admitted
- SAT or ACT, application essay required

General. Founded in 1868. Regionally accredited. **Degrees:** 817 bachelor's, 5 associate awarded; master's, doctoral, first professional offered. **ROTC:** Army, Navy. **Location:** 10 miles from Norfolk. **Calendar:** Semester, extensive summer session. **Full-time faculty:** 325 total. **Part-time faculty:** 125 total. **Class size:** 51% < 20, 38% 20-39, 7% 40-49, 4% 50-99, less than 1% >100. **Special facilities:** African American literature and history collection; university archives; North American Indian, African, Oceanic and Black American art collections; 5 national historic landmarks.

Freshman class profile. 7,598 applied, 4,128 admitted, 1,201 enrolled.

Mid 50% test scores			
SAT verbal:	470-560	Out-of-state:	68%
SAT math:	460-550	Live on campus:	71%
ACT:	17-21	Fraternities:	5%
		Sororities:	4%

Basis for selection. Academic record, rank in top half of graduating class, personal references, intended major, test scores and personal statement important. Extracurricular activities, essay, school recommendation considered. Audition required for music. **Homeschooled:** Transcript of courses and grades required. Must present secondary school record if it exists, GED test scores, verification by state/regional official, SAT or ACT results.

High school preparation. 17 units required. Required and recommended units include English 4, mathematics 3, social studies 2, science 2 (laboratory 2), foreign language 2 and academic electives 6. One chemistry, biology with lab, algebra I and II, geometry required.

2005-2006 Annual costs. Tuition/fees: $14,182. Room/board: $6,746. Books/supplies: $750. Personal expenses: $1,103.

2005-2006 Financial aid. **Need-based:** 36% of total undergraduate aid awarded as scholarships/grants, 64% as loans/jobs. **Non-need-based:** Scholarships awarded for academics, athletics, leadership, music/drama, ROTC.

Application procedures. **Admission:** Priority date 12/1; deadline 3/1 (postmark date). $25 fee. Application may be submitted online. Admission notification on a rolling basis beginning on or about 12/15. Must reply by 5/1. **Financial aid:** Priority date 3/1; no closing date. FAFSA required. Applicants notified on a rolling basis starting 4/15; must reply within 2 week(s) of notification.

Academics. Students who have completed one semester with minimum 3.2 GPA may apply to honors college. Academic skills workshops held throughout year available for all students. Students may take courses at other Tidewater consortium schools. **Special study options:** Accelerated study, combined bachelor's/graduate degree, cooperative education, cross-registration, distance learning, double major, dual enrollment of high school students, honors, independent study, internships, study abroad, teacher certification program. Grad level programs for undergraduates, coop programs in arts, business, education, engineering, social/behavioral science. **Credit/placement by examination:** AP, CLEP, IB, institutional tests. 30 credit hours maximum toward bachelor's degree. **Support services:** Learning center, pre-admission summer program, reduced course load, remedial instruction, tutoring, writing center.

Majors. **Architecture:** Architecture. **Biology:** General, marine, molecular. **Business:** Accounting, banking/financial services, business admin, finance, management information systems, managerial economics, marketing. **Communications:** Advertising, broadcast journalism, journalism, media studies, public relations. **Computer sciences:** General, computer science, networking. **Conservation:** Environmental science. **Education:** General, health, physical, special. **Engineering:** General, chemical, computer, electrical. **English:** English lit, speech/rhetoric. **Foreign languages:** Spanish. **Health:** Audiology/speech pathology, communication disorders, nursing (RN). **History:** General. **Legal studies:** Paralegal, prelaw. **Liberal arts:** Arts/sciences. **Math:** General. **Parks/recreation:** General, facilities management, sports admin. **Physical sciences:** Chemistry, physics. **Protective services:** Fire services admin, law enforcement admin. **Psychology:** General. **Social sciences:** Political science, sociology. **Theology:** Theology. **Transportation:** Aviation management. **Visual/performing arts:** Art, commercial/advertising art, dramatic, music performance.

Most popular majors. Biology 11%, business/marketing 25%, communications/journalism 8%, health sciences 8%, psychology 11%, social sciences 10%.

Computing on campus. 1,500 workstations in dormitories, library, computer center, student center. Dormitories wired for high-speed internet access and linked to campus network. Commuter students can connect to campus network. Online course registration, online library, helpline, repair service, student web hosting, wireless network available.

Student life. **Freshman orientation:** Mandatory. Preregistration for classes offered. One-week orientation held in August. **Housing:** Guaranteed on-campus for freshmen. Coed dorms, single-sex dorms, substance-free housing available. $500 deposit, deadline 5/1. **Activities:** Bands, choral groups, dance, drama, music ensembles, musical theater, opera, radio station, student government, student newspaper, symphony orchestra, TV station, Student Christian Association, Big Brothers/Big Sisters, political science/prelaw club, Women in Communications, Muslim Student Fellowship, international student association, service learning and leadership organizations, National Leadership of Black Journalists.

Athletics. NCAA. **Intercollegiate:** Basketball, bowling W, cheerleading M, cross-country, football (tackle) M, golf, sailing, softball W, tennis, track and field, volleyball W. **Intramural:** Basketball, bowling W, softball W, swimming. **Team name:** Pirates.

Student services. Campus ministries, career counseling, services for economically disadvantaged, student employment services, financial aid counseling, health services, on-campus daycare, personal counseling, placement for graduates, veterans' counselor. **Physically disabled:** Services for visually, speech, hearing impaired.

Contact. E-mail: admit@hamptonu.edu
Phone: (757) 727-5328 Toll-free number: (800) 624-3328
Fax: (757) 727-5095
Angela Boyd, Director of Admissions, Hampton University, Office of Admissions, Hampton, VA 23668

Hollins University

Roanoke, Virginia **CB member**
www.hollins.edu **CB code: 5294**

- Private 4-year university and liberal arts college for women
- Residential campus in small city

- 818 degree-seeking undergraduates: 6% part-time, 100% women, 8% African American, 1% Asian American, 2% Hispanic American, 1% Native American, 2% international
- 250 degree-seeking graduate students
- 86% of applicants admitted
- SAT or ACT (ACT writing optional), application essay required
- 62% graduate within 6 years; 32% enter graduate study

General. Founded in 1842. Regionally accredited. **Degrees:** 178 bachelor's awarded; master's offered. **Location:** 175 miles from Richmond, 250 miles from Washington, DC. **Calendar:** 4-1-4, limited summer session. **Full-time faculty:** 68 total; 98% have terminal degrees, 9% minority, 53% women. **Part-time faculty:** 41 total; 42% have terminal degrees, 5% minority, 49% women. **Class size:** 79% < 20, 19% 20-39, 2% 40-49. **Special facilities:** Electron microscope facilities, EEG and biofeedback equipment, research facilities for chromatography, spectrophotometry, electrochemistry, gas kinetics, centrifugation, visual arts center museum.

Freshman class profile. 686 applied, 589 admitted, 184 enrolled.

Mid 50% test scores			
SAT verbal:	530-640	Rank in top quarter:	55%
SAT math:	490-590	Rank in top tenth:	19%
ACT:	22-27	Return as sophomores:	79%
GPA 3.50 or higher:	50%	Out-of-state:	58%
GPA 3.0-3.49:	34%	Live on campus:	98%
GPA 2.0-2.99:	15%	International:	1%

Basis for selection. School achievement record, school recommendation, and test scores very important. Essay, talent/ability important. Interview, class rank, character, alumni relation, extracurricular activities, volunteer work, work experience considered. Interview recommended. **Homeschooled:** Applicants encouraged to take 3 SAT Subject Tests.

High school preparation. 16 units required. Required units include English 4, mathematics 3, social studies 3, science 3 and foreign language 3.

2006-2007 Annual costs. Tuition/fees: $24,325. Room/board: $8,650. Books/supplies: $800. Personal expenses: $850.

2005-2006 Financial aid. Need-based: 165 full-time freshmen applied for aid; 130 were judged to have need; 130 of these received aid. Average need met was 81%. Average scholarship/grant was $13,042; average loan $3,287. 73% of total undergraduate aid awarded as scholarships/grants, 27% as loans/jobs. **Non-need-based:** Awarded to 467 full-time undergraduates, including 115 freshmen. Scholarships awarded for academics, alumni affiliation, art, leadership, minority status, music/drama, state residency.

Application procedures. Admission: Priority date 2/1; no deadline. $35 fee, may be waived for applicants with need. Application may be submitted online. Admission notification on a rolling basis beginning on or about 12/15. Must reply by May 1 or within 2 week(s) if notified thereafter. **Financial aid:** Priority date 2/15; no closing date. FAFSA required. Applicants notified on a rolling basis starting 3/15; must reply by 5/1.

Academics. Special study options: Accelerated study, combined bachelor's/graduate degree, cooperative education, cross-registration, double major, dual enrollment of high school students, exchange student, independent study, internships, liberal arts/career combination, student-designed major, study abroad, teacher certification program, Washington semester. Numerous college exchange programs; 5- and 6-year dual degree programs in engineering with Washington University in St. Louis and Virginia Tech; Louis D. Rubin, Jr., Semester in Creative Writing. **Credit/placement by examination:** AP, CLEP, IB, institutional tests. **Support services:** Tutoring, writing center.

Majors. Area/ethnic studies: Women's. **Biology:** General, environmental. **Business:** General. **Communications:** General. **Conservation:** Environmental studies. **English:** Creative writing. **Foreign languages:** Classics, French, German, Spanish. **History:** General. **Math:** General. **Philosophy/religion:** Philosophy, religion. **Physical sciences:** Chemistry, physics. **Psychology:** General. **Social sciences:** Economics, political science, sociology. **Visual/performing arts:** Art history/conservation, dance, dramatic, studio arts.

Most popular majors. Biology 7%, business/marketing 6%, communications/journalism 8%, English 16%, foreign language 7%, interdisciplinary studies 6%, psychology 9%, social sciences 15%, visual/performing arts 16%.

Computing on campus. 100 workstations in dormitories, library, computer center. Dormitories wired for high-speed internet access and linked to campus network. Online library, helpline, wireless network available.

Student life. Freshman orientation: Mandatory. 5-day program includes group meetings, mini-classes, individual student-faculty advisor meetings, social events, community service. **Policies:** Freshmen permitted cars on campus. **Housing:** Guaranteed on-campus for all undergraduates. Special housing for disabled, apartments, substance-free housing available. Special interest housing. **Activities:** Choral groups, dance, drama, film society, literary magazine, music ensembles, musical theater, student government, student newspaper, TV station, Religious Life Association, Black Student Alliance, College Democrats, College Republicans, Colleges Against Cancer, Student Health Advisory Board, Students Helping Achieve Rewarding Experiences, Model United Nations, Mujeres Unidas, Circle K.

Athletics. NCAA. **Intercollegiate:** Basketball W, equestrian W, field hockey W, golf W, lacrosse W, soccer W, swimming W, tennis W, volleyball W.

Student services. Adult student services, alcohol/substance abuse counseling, campus ministries, career counseling, student employment services, financial aid counseling, health services, minority student services, personal counseling, placement for graduates, women's services. **Physically disabled:** Services for visually, hearing impaired.

Contact. E-mail: huadm@hollins.edu
Phone: (540) 362-6401 Toll-free number: (800) 456-9595
Fax: (540) 362-6218
Rebecca Eckstein, Dean of Admissions, Hollins University, P.O. Box 9707, Roanoke, VA 24020-1707

ITT Technical Institute: Chantilly

Chantilly, Virginia

CB code: 4086

- For-profit 4-year technical college
- Commuter campus

General. Accredited by ACICS. **Calendar:** Quarter.

Annual costs/financial aid. Tuition varies by program, $260-$368 per credit hour.

Contact. Phone: (703) 263-2541
Director of Recruitment, 14420 Albemarle Point Place, Chantilly, VA 20151

ITT Technical Institute: Norfolk

Norfolk, Virginia
www.itt-tech.edu

CB code: 2737

- For-profit 4-year technical college
- Commuter campus in large city

General. Accredited by ACICS. **Location:** 81 miles from Richmond, 145 miles from Washington, DC. **Calendar:** Quarter.

Annual costs/financial aid. Tuition varies by program, $260-$368 per credit hour.

Contact. Phone: (757) 466-1260
Director of Recruitment, 863 Glenrock Road, Norfolk, VA 23502

ITT Technical Institute: Richmond

Richmond, Virginia
www.itt-tech.edu

CB code: 2748

- For-profit 4-year technical college
- Commuter campus in small city

General. Accredited by ACICS. **Location:** 98 miles from Washington, DC. **Calendar:** Quarter.

Annual costs/financial aid. Tuition varies by program, $260-$368 per credit hour. Books/supplies: $3,100.

Contact. Phone: (804) 330-4992
Director of Recruitment, 300 Gateway Centre Parkway, Richmond, VA 23235

ITT Technical Institute: Springfield

Springfield, Virginia

- For-profit 4-year technical college
- Commuter campus

General. Accredited by ACICS. **Calendar:** Quarter.

Annual costs/financial aid. Tuition varies by program, $260-$368 per credit hour.

Contact. Phone: (703) 440-9535
Director of Recruitment, 7300 Boston Boulevard, Springfield, VA 22153

James Madison University

Harrisonburg, Virginia — **CB member**
www.jmu.edu — **CB code: 5392**

- Public 4-year university
- Residential campus in large town
- 15,287 degree-seeking undergraduates: 3% part-time, 61% women, 3% African American, 5% Asian American, 2% Hispanic American, 1% international
- 1,067 degree-seeking graduate students
- 68% of applicants admitted
- SAT or ACT (ACT writing optional) required
- 80% graduate within 6 years; 27% enter graduate study

General. Founded in 1908. Regionally accredited. **Degrees:** 3,329 bachelor's awarded; master's, doctoral offered. **ROTC:** Army, Air Force. **Location:** 123 miles from Washington, DC. **Calendar:** Semester, extensive summer session. **Full-time faculty:** 795 total; 80% have terminal degrees, 7% minority, 42% women. **Part-time faculty:** 369 total; 26% have terminal degrees, 4% minority, 50% women. **Class size:** 29% < 20, 49% 20-39, 8% 40-49, 10% 50-99, 4% >100. **Special facilities:** Planetarium, arboretum.

Freshman class profile. 16,388 applied, 11,094 admitted, 3,798 enrolled.

Mid 50% test scores		**GPA 2.0-2.99:**	2%
SAT verbal:	530-620	**Rank in top quarter:**	74%
SAT math:	540-630	**Rank in top tenth:**	28%
ACT:	21-26	**Return as sophomores:**	91%
GPA 3.50 or higher:	68%	**Out-of-state:**	37%
GPA 3.0-3.49:	30%	**Live on campus:**	99%

Basis for selection. Rigor of high school curriculum, as shown by the quantity and quality of courses, most important. Class rank or GPA, test scores, extracurricular activities, special skills or talents important. Counselor recommendation considered. Applicants with solid achievement in 5 or more academic courses each of the 4 years of high school have decided advantage in admissions process. Audition required for dance, music, theatre programs; portfolio and interview required for art. Nursing students must apply to the Nursing Department in addition to applying for undergraduate admission.

High school preparation. Required and recommended units include English 4, mathematics 4, social studies 1-2, history 2, science 3 (laboratory 3) and foreign language 3-4. 3 units of of same language required, or 2 of one language and 2 of another.

2005-2006 Annual costs. Tuition/fees: $5,886; $15,322 out-of-state. Room/board: $6,124.

2005-2006 Financial aid. Need-based: 2,769 full-time freshmen applied for aid; 1,403 were judged to have need; 1,205 of these received aid. Average need met was 62%. Average scholarship/grant was $5,827; average loan $2,904. 36% of total undergraduate aid awarded as scholarships/grants, 64% as loans/jobs. **Non-need-based:** Awarded to 1,463 full-time undergraduates, including 653 freshmen. Scholarships awarded for academics, alumni affiliation, art, athletics, leadership, minority status, music/drama, state residency.

Application procedures. Admission: Priority date 11/1; deadline 1/15 (postmark date). $40 fee, may be waived for applicants with need. Application may be submitted online. Admission notification 4/1. Must reply by 5/1. **Financial aid:** Priority date 3/1; no closing date. FAFSA required. Applicants notified on a rolling basis starting 4/1; must reply within 4 week(s) of notification.

Academics. Special study options: Accelerated study, combined bachelor's/graduate degree, distance learning, double major, honors, independent study, internships, study abroad, teacher certification program, Washington semester. **Credit/placement by examination:** AP, CLEP, IB, institutional tests. 30 credit hours maximum toward bachelor's degree. CLEP credit awarded only to students seeking bachelor's in Individualized Study. **Support services:** Learning center, study skills assistance, tutoring.

Majors. Biology: General, biotechnology. **Business:** Accounting, business admin, finance, hospitality admin, international, managerial economics, marketing. **Communications:** General. **Computer sciences:** General, information systems. **Education:** Business. **English:** English lit, technical writing. **Family/consumer sciences:** Food/nutrition. **Foreign languages:** General. **Health:** Athletic training, community health services, health care admin, nursing (RN), speech pathology. **History:** General. **Interdisciplinary:** Science/society. **Liberal arts:** Arts/sciences. **Math:** General. **Parks/recreation:** Health/fitness. **Physical sciences:** Chemistry, geology, physics. **Psychology:** General. **Public administration:** General, social work. **Social sciences:** General, anthropology, economics, geography, international relations, political science, sociology. **Visual/performing arts:** Art, art history/conservation, dramatic, music performance.

Most popular majors. Business/marketing 21%, communications/journalism 8%, health sciences 9%, liberal arts 6%, psychology 7%, social sciences 12%, visual/performing arts 7%.

Computing on campus. 1,583 workstations in dormitories, library, computer center. Dormitories wired for high-speed internet access and linked to campus network. Commuter students can connect to campus network. Online course registration, helpline, student web hosting, wireless network available.

Student life. Freshman orientation: Mandatory, $125 fee. Preregistration for classes offered. One-day orientation in June or July, plus 5-day program in August prior to the beginning of classes. **Housing:** Guaranteed on-campus for freshmen. Coed dorms, apartments, fraternity/sorority housing, substance-free housing available. $250 nonrefundable deposit, deadline 5/1. **Activities:** Bands, choral groups, dance, drama, literary magazine, music ensembles, musical theater, opera, radio station, student government, student newspaper, symphony orchestra, 287 student organizations and clubs.

Athletics. NCAA. **Intercollegiate:** Archery, baseball M, basketball, cross-country, diving, fencing W, field hockey W, football (tackle) M, golf, gymnastics, lacrosse W, soccer, softball W, swimming, tennis, track and field, volleyball W, wrestling M. **Intramural:** Badminton, basketball, bowling, football (tackle), golf, racquetball, soccer, softball, table tennis, tennis, volleyball. **Team name:** Dukes.

Student services. Adult student services, alcohol/substance abuse counseling, career counseling, student employment services, health services, personal counseling, placement for graduates. **Physically disabled:** Services for visually, speech, hearing impaired.

Contact. E-mail: admissions@jmu.edu
Phone: (540) 568-5681 Fax: (540) 568-3332
Michael Walsh, Director of Admissions, James Madison University, Sonner Hall MSC 0101, Harrisonburg, VA 22807

Jefferson College of Health Sciences

Roanoke, Virginia
www.jchs.edu — **CB code: 5099**

- Private 4-year health science and nursing college
- Commuter campus in small city
- 873 degree-seeking undergraduates
- 21 degree-seeking graduate students
- SAT or ACT (ACT writing recommended) required

General. Founded in 1982. Regionally accredited. Access to educational seminars broadcast live by American Hospital Association, Hospital Satellite network, and other networks. One of 50 demonstration centers nationwide for interactive video in nursing education. **Degrees:** 50 bachelor's, 150 associate awarded; master's offered. **Calendar:** Semester, limited summer session. **Full-time faculty:** 35 total. **Part-time faculty:** 20 total.

Freshman class profile.

End year in good standing:	90%	**Live on campus:**	50%
Return as sophomores:	80%		

Basis for selection. Certification required for some programs. Emergency health sciences program requires emergency medical technician ambulance certification prior to entering program.

High school preparation. 16 units required. Required units include English 4, mathematics 2 and science 2.

2005-2006 Annual costs. Tuition/fees: $12,960. Tuition for physician assistant program: $44,750 for full 2-year program. Books/supplies: $800. Personal expenses: $2,100.

Financial aid. Non-need-based: Scholarships awarded for academics.

Application procedures. **Admission:** No deadline. $35 fee. Application may be submitted online. Admission notification on a rolling basis. Must reply by May 1 or within 2 week(s) if notified thereafter. **Financial aid:** No deadline. FAFSA, institutional form required. Applicants notified on a rolling basis; must reply within 2 week(s) of notification.

Academics. LPN mobility program provides opportunities for LPNs to become eligible for registered nurse licensure. Students uncertain about health care profession and those who have limited or unsatisfactory academic background can enter associate degree in science program. **Special study options:** Accelerated study, cross-registration, distance learning, independent study, internships, liberal arts/career combination. **Credit/placement by examination:** CLEP, institutional tests. Maximum of 18 credit hours may be satisfied by AP examinations. **Support services:** Learning center, preadmission summer program, tutoring.

Majors. **Biology:** Biomedical sciences. **Health:** Nursing (RN), physician assistant, premedicine, prenursing, prepharmacy. **Interdisciplinary:** Biological/physical sciences.

Computing on campus. 56 workstations in library, computer center. Dormitories wired for high-speed internet access. Online library, repair service available.

Student life. **Freshman orientation:** Mandatory. Preregistration for classes offered. One-day orientation held multiple times during summer. **Policies:** Freshmen permitted cars on campus. **Housing:** Coed dorms available. $200 deposit. **Activities:** Student government, student newspaper, Student nurse association, student occupational therapy association, student physical therapy assistant assembly, Good Samaritan Club, Crossroads.

Student services. Adult student services, career counseling, student employment services, financial aid counseling, health services, personal counseling, placement for graduates.

Contact. E-mail: jmckeon@jchs.edu
Phone: (540) 985-8483 Fax: (540) 985-9773
Judith McKeon, Director of Admissions, Jefferson College of Health Sciences, Box 13186, Roanoke, VA 24031-3186

Liberty University

Lynchburg, Virginia **CB member**
www.liberty.edu **CB code: 5385**

- Private 4-year university and seminary college affiliated with Baptist faith
- Residential campus in small city
- 9,879 degree-seeking undergraduates: 15% part-time, 52% women, 10% African American, 2% Asian American, 3% Hispanic American, 1% Native American, 4% international
- 2,422 degree-seeking graduate students
- 67% of applicants admitted
- SAT or ACT (ACT writing optional), application essay required
- 33% graduate within 6 years

General. Founded in 1971. Regionally accredited. **Degrees:** 1,292 bachelor's, 65 associate awarded; master's, doctoral, first professional offered. **ROTC:** Army, Air Force. **Location:** 120 miles from Richmond, 150 miles from Raleigh, North Carolina. **Calendar:** Semester, limited summer session. **Full-time faculty:** 336 total; 64% have terminal degrees, 6% minority, 32% women. **Part-time faculty:** 165 total; 14% have terminal degrees, 5% minority, 43% women. **Class size:** 26% < 20, 58% 20-39, 2% 40-49, 8% 50-99, 6% >100. **Special facilities:** Ice rink.

Freshman class profile. 6,504 applied, 4,376 admitted, 1,985 enrolled.

Mid 50% test scores			
SAT verbal:	440-570	Rank in top quarter:	14%
SAT math:	430-550	Rank in top tenth:	4%
ACT:	18-24	Return as sophomores:	73%
GPA 3.50 or higher:	33%	Out-of-state:	67%
GPA 3.0-3.49:	29%	Live on campus:	88%
GPA 2.0-2.99:	35%	International:	5%

Basis for selection. Secondary school record, standardized test scores, and essay most important. TOEFL required for international students. **Homeschooled:** Submit ACT or SAT scores. **Learning Disabled:** Applicants who fail to meet the minimum required GPA may be admitted on academic warning status and will be limited to 13 semester hours of coursework, including CLST 100/Foundations for Academic success or CLST 101/College Learning Strategies.

High school preparation. College-preparatory program required. 17 units recommended. Recommended units include English 4, mathematics 3, social studies 2, science 2 (laboratory 2), foreign language 2 and academic electives 2.

2006-2007 Annual costs. Tuition/fees: $15,350. Room/board: $5,400. Books/supplies: $1,000. Personal expenses: $1,000.

2005-2006 Financial aid. **Need-based:** 1,800 full-time freshmen applied for aid; 1,458 were judged to have need; 1,451 of these received aid. Average need met was 57%. Average scholarship/grant was $2,895; average loan $2,445. 32% of total undergraduate aid awarded as scholarships/grants, 68% as loans/jobs. **Non-need-based:** Awarded to 7,857 full-time undergraduates, including 1,923 freshmen. Scholarships awarded for academics, alumni affiliation, athletics, leadership, music/drama, religious affiliation, ROTC, state residency.

Application procedures. **Admission:** Priority date 6/30; no deadline. $35 fee, may be waived for applicants with need. Application may be submitted online. Admission notification on a rolling basis. Must reply by May 1 or within 2 week(s) if notified thereafter. **Financial aid:** Closing date 3/1. FAFSA required. Applicants notified on a rolling basis starting 3/15; must reply within 3 week(s) of notification.

Academics. **Special study options:** Accelerated study, cooperative education, distance learning, double major, dual enrollment of high school students, ESL, external degree, honors, independent study, internships, liberal arts/career combination, student-designed major, teacher certification program, weekend college. Associate school of the Institute of Holy Land Studies in Jerusalem. **Credit/placement by examination:** AP, CLEP, IB, SAT, ACT, institutional tests. 30 credit hours maximum toward bachelor's degree. **Support services:** Learning center, reduced course load, remedial instruction, study skills assistance, tutoring.

Majors. **Biology:** General, biochemistry. **Business:** General, accounting, business admin, fashion, finance, management information systems, marketing. **Communications:** General, advertising, broadcast journalism, journalism, public relations. **Communications technology:** Radio/tv. **Computer sciences:** General. **Education:** Biology, business, computer, English, ESL, family/consumer sciences, health, history, mathematics, multi-level teacher, music, social science, Spanish, special. **English:** English lit. **Family/consumer sciences:** General, aging. **Foreign languages:** Spanish. **Health:** Athletic training, community health, health services, nursing (RN). **History:** General. **Math:** General. **Parks/recreation:** Exercise sciences, health/fitness, sports admin. **Philosophy/religion:** Philosophy, religion. **Protective services:** Criminal justice, law enforcement admin. **Psychology:** General. **Social sciences:** General, economics, political science. **Theology:** Bible, missionary, pastoral counseling, sacred music, youth ministry. **Transportation:** Aviation. **Visual/performing arts:** Dramatic, graphic design.

Most popular majors. Business/marketing 15%, communications/journalism 7%, education 7%, health sciences 8%, interdisciplinary studies 11%, philosophy/religious studies 15%, psychology 16%.

Computing on campus. 406 workstations in library, computer center, student center. Dormitories wired for high-speed internet access and linked to campus network. Commuter students can connect to campus network. Online course registration, online library, helpline, repair service, wireless network available.

Student life. **Freshman orientation:** Mandatory, $480 fee. Preregistration for classes offered. Freshmen orientation is a one semester hour class held the first week before regular classes begin for first-time freshmen. **Policies:** All students involved in Christian or community service. Freshmen permitted cars on campus. **Housing:** Guaranteed on-campus for all undergraduates. Single-sex dorms, special housing for disabled, apartments, substance-free housing available. $250 nonrefundable deposit. Students required to live on campus unless living with parents, over age 21, or married. **Activities:** Bands, choral groups, drama, music ensembles, musical theater, opera, radio station, student government, student newspaper, TV station, Circle K, Youthquest, Light Ministries, Fellowship of Christian Athletes, Students Teaching Elementary School, College Republicans, Campus SERVE.

Athletics. NCAA. **Intercollegiate:** Baseball M, basketball, cheerleading, cross-country, football (tackle) M, golf M, soccer, softball W, tennis, track and field, volleyball W. **Intramural:** Basketball, football (non-tackle), soccer, softball, tennis, volleyball. **Team name:** Flames.

Student services. Campus ministries, career counseling, student employment services, financial aid counseling, health services, minority student services, personal counseling, placement for graduates, veterans' counselor, women's services. **Physically disabled:** Services for hearing impaired.

Contact. E-mail: admissions@liberty.edu
Phone: (434) 582-5985 Toll-free number: (800) 543-5317
Fax: (800) 542-2311
Chris Johnson, Executive Director, Resident Recruitment, Liberty University, 1971 University Boulevard, Lynchburg, VA 24502

Longwood University

Farmville, Virginia **CB member**
www.whylongwood.com **CB code: 5368**

- Public 4-year university
- Residential campus in small town
- 3,674 degree-seeking undergraduates: 2% part-time, 66% women, 6% African American, 2% Asian American, 2% Hispanic American, 1% international
- 334 degree-seeking graduate students
- 76% of applicants admitted
- SAT or ACT (ACT writing optional), application essay required
- 64% graduate within 6 years; 22% enter graduate study

General. Founded in 1839. Regionally accredited. **Degrees:** 802 bachelor's awarded; master's offered. **ROTC:** Army. **Location:** 65 miles from Richmond, 60 miles from Charlottesville. **Calendar:** Semester, limited summer session. **Full-time faculty:** 201 total; 84% have terminal degrees, 8% minority, 42% women. **Part-time faculty:** 35 total. **Class size:** 38% < 20, 52% 20-39, 7% 40-49, 3% 50-99, less than 1% >100. **Special facilities:** Telecommunications network, golf course, flora collection, visual arts center, greenhouse.

Freshman class profile. 3,369 applied, 2,574 admitted, 958 enrolled.

Mid 50% test scores		**Rank in top tenth:**	10%
SAT verbal:	500-580	**Return as sophomores:**	76%
SAT math:	450-570	**Out-of-state:**	10%
GPA 3.50 or higher:	26%	**Live on campus:**	97%
GPA 3.0-3.49:	46%	**International:**	1%
GPA 2.0-2.99:	28%	**Fraternities:**	2%
Rank in top quarter:	39%	**Sororities:**	2%

Basis for selection. Rank in top half of class, combined SAT score (exclusive of Writing) of 1000 minimum and minimum cumulative GPA of 2.7 in college preparatory courses required. Extracurricular activities and recommendations also considered. Modern language majors required to take SAT subject test in intended language of study for placement. An audition is required for music. **Homeschooled:** Applications reviewed on case by case basis.

High school preparation. 18 units required; 23 recommended. Required and recommended units include English 4, mathematics 3-4, social studies 1, history 3, science 3-4 (laboratory 2), foreign language 2-3 and academic electives 3-4. 1 unit fine or practical arts required.

2005-2006 Annual costs. Tuition/fees: $7,020; $13,704 out-of-state. Required laptop computer for first year students $2,000. Room/board: $5,586. Books/supplies: $700. Personal expenses: $1,330.

2004-2005 Financial aid. Need-based: 648 full-time freshmen applied for aid; 411 were judged to have need; 411 of these received aid. Average need met was 76%. Average scholarship/grant was $4,673; average loan $3,230. 51% of total undergraduate aid awarded as scholarships/grants, 49% as loans/jobs. **Non-need-based:** Awarded to 1,305 full-time undergraduates, including 328 freshmen. Scholarships awarded for academics, alumni affiliation, art, athletics, leadership, music/drama, ROTC, state residency.

Application procedures. Admission: Priority date 3/1; no deadline. $40 fee, may be waived for applicants with need. Application may be submitted online. Admission notification on a rolling basis beginning on or about 1/15. Must reply by May 1 or within 2 week(s) if notified thereafter. For Early Action consideration, applicants must have a 3.0 High School Grade Point Average and 1000 on the SAT (exclusive of Writing). **Financial aid:** Priority date 3/1; no closing date. FAFSA required. Applicants notified on a rolling basis starting 4/1; must reply within 2 week(s) of notification.

Academics. Strong liberal arts program focus. General Education requirements for all majors. **Special study options:** Accelerated study, combined bachelor's/graduate degree, cross-registration, distance learning, double major, dual enrollment of high school students, ESL, exchange student, honors, independent study, internships, liberal arts/career combination, study abroad, teacher certification program. Summer field programs in archaeology and botany. **Credit/placement by examination:** AP, CLEP, IB, institutional tests. **Support services:** Learning center, reduced course load, study skills assistance, tutoring, writing center.

Majors. Biology: General. **Business:** General, accounting, business admin, finance, management information systems, management science, marketing. **Communications:** General. **Computer sciences:** General, computer science. **Education:** General, art, biology, business, chemistry, early childhood, elementary, English, French, German, health, history, mathematics, middle, multi-level teacher, music, physical, physics, science, social studies, Spanish, special, speech impaired. **Foreign languages:** French, German, Spanish. **Health:** Athletic training, predentistry, premedicine, prepharmacy, preveterinary, recreational therapy. **History:** General, public archives. **Legal studies:** Prelaw. **Liberal arts:** Arts/sciences. **Math:** General. **Parks/recreation:** Exercise sciences, health/fitness. **Physical sciences:** Chemistry, physics. **Protective services:** Criminal justice. **Psychology:** General. **Public administration:** Social work. **Social sciences:** Anthropology, criminology, economics, political science, sociology. **Visual/performing arts:** General, art, art history/conservation, commercial/advertising art, dramatic, music performance, studio arts.

Most popular majors. Business/marketing 23%, liberal arts 22%, psychology 6%, social sciences 9%, visual/performing arts 7%.

Computing on campus. PC or laptop required. 270 workstations in dormitories, library, computer center, student center. Dormitories wired for high-speed internet access and linked to campus network. Commuter students can connect to campus network. Online course registration, online library, helpline, repair service, student web hosting, wireless network available.

Student life. Freshman orientation: Mandatory, $75 fee. Preregistration for classes offered. 1-day orientation held during spring and summer. **Housing:** Guaranteed on-campus for freshmen. Coed dorms, single-sex dorms, special housing for disabled, apartments, fraternity/sorority housing, substance-free housing available. $400 nonrefundable deposit, deadline 5/1. Honor student housing. **Activities:** Bands, choral groups, dance, drama, literary magazine, music ensembles, musical theater, opera, radio station, student government, student newspaper, College Democrats, unity alliance, inter-fraternity council, Fellowship of Christian Athletes, Alpha Phi Omega, students educating for active leadership, College Republicans, peer helpers, Big Sibling Program, Catholic Campus Ministries.

Athletics. NCAA. **Intercollegiate:** Baseball M, basketball, cheerleading, cross-country, field hockey W, golf, lacrosse W, soccer, softball W, tennis. **Intramural:** Basketball, bowling, football (non-tackle), golf, soccer, softball, swimming, table tennis, tennis, volleyball. **Team name:** Lancers.

Student services. Adult student services, alcohol/substance abuse counseling, campus ministries, career counseling, student employment services, financial aid counseling, health services, minority student services, personal counseling, placement for graduates, women's services. **Physically disabled:** Services for visually, speech, hearing impaired.

Contact. E-mail: admissions@longwood.edu
Phone: (434) 395-2060 Toll-free number: (800) 281-4677 ext. 2
Fax: (434) 395-2332
Robert Chonko, Dean of Enrollment Management, Longwood University, 201 High Street, Farmville, VA 23909-1898

Lynchburg College

Lynchburg, Virginia **CB member**
www.lynchburg.edu **CB code: 5372**

- Private 4-year liberal arts college affiliated with Christian Church (Disciples of Christ)
- Residential campus in small city
- 1,998 degree-seeking undergraduates: 4% part-time, 59% women, 8% African American, 2% Asian American, 3% Hispanic American, 1% Native American
- 287 degree-seeking graduate students
- 72% of applicants admitted
- SAT or ACT (ACT writing optional) required
- 56% graduate within 6 years; 10% enter graduate study

General. Founded in 1903. Regionally accredited. **Degrees:** 349 bachelor's awarded; master's offered. **Location:** 180 miles from Washington, DC, 60 miles from Roanoke. **Calendar:** Semester, extensive summer session. **Full-time faculty:** 135 total; 74% have terminal degrees. **Part-time faculty:** 75 total; 33% have terminal degrees. **Class size:** 53% < 20, 47% 20-39, less than 1% 40-49, less than 1% 50-99. **Special facilities:** Nature study center, center for media development, art gallery, cadaver lab, geographic information system lab.

Freshman class profile. 4,009 applied, 2,883 admitted, 554 enrolled.

Mid 50% test scores			
SAT verbal:	470-560	Rank in top quarter:	26%
SAT math:	460-560	Rank in top tenth:	13%
ACT:	18-22	End year in good standing:	78%
GPA 3.50 or higher:	23%	Return as sophomores:	74%
GPA 3.0-3.49:	31%	Out-of-state:	45%
GPA 2.0-2.99:	46%	Live on campus:	94%

Basis for selection. School record, test scores, school and community involvement, recommendation, academic quality of secondary school attended, essay, interview important. Audition recommended for music, theater arts programs; portfolio recommended for studio art. Essay or personal statement is strongly encouraged, but not formally required. **Learning Disabled:** Documentation must be received no later than 45 days prior to the first day of class.

High school preparation. 16 units required; 20 recommended. Required and recommended units include English 4, mathematics 3-4, social studies 2, history 2, science 3-4 (laboratory 2), foreign language 2-3 and academic electives 1.

2006-2007 Annual costs. Tuition/fees: $25,565. Room/board: $6,800. Books/supplies: $600. Personal expenses: $500.

2005-2006 Financial aid. Need-based: 457 full-time freshmen applied for aid; 352 were judged to have need; 352 of these received aid. Average need met was 95%. Average scholarship/grant was $15,060; average loan $3,076. 73% of total undergraduate aid awarded as scholarships/grants, 27% as loans/jobs. **Non-need-based:** Awarded to 1,480 full-time undergraduates, including 398 freshmen. Scholarships awarded for academics, art, leadership, music/drama, state residency.

Application procedures. Admission: No deadline. $30 fee, may be waived for applicants with need. Application may be submitted online. Admission notification on a rolling basis beginning on or about 9/1. Must reply by May 1 or within 2 week(s) if notified thereafter. **Financial aid:** Priority date 3/1; no closing date. FAFSA required. Applicants notified on a rolling basis starting 3/5; must reply by 5/1 or within 2 week(s) of notification.

Academics. Special study options: Accelerated study, cross-registration, double major, dual enrollment of high school students, honors, independent study, internships, study abroad, teacher certification program. **Credit/placement by examination:** AP, CLEP, IB, institutional tests. **Support services:** Study skills assistance, tutoring, writing center.

Majors. Biology: General, ecology, exercise physiology. **Business:** Accounting, business admin, international, marketing. **Communications:** General. **Computer sciences:** General. **Conservation:** Environmental science. **Education:** Elementary, health, physical. **English:** English lit. **Family/consumer sciences:** Family studies. **Foreign languages:** Comparative lit, French, Spanish. **Health:** Athletic training, nursing (RN). **History:** General. **Math:** General. **Parks/recreation:** Health/fitness, sports admin. **Philosophy/religion:** Philosophy, religion. **Physical sciences:** Chemistry, physics. **Psychology:** General. **Social sciences:** Economics, international relations, political science, sociology. **Visual/performing arts:** Art, dramatic.

Most popular majors. Biology 6%, business/marketing 14%, communications/journalism 13%, education 12%, English 6%, health sciences 8%, psychology 7%, social sciences 10%.

Computing on campus. 217 workstations in dormitories, library, computer center, student center. Dormitories wired for high-speed internet access and linked to campus network. Online library, repair service, wireless network available.

Student life. Freshman orientation: Mandatory. **Policies:** Honor system promoted and adhered to. **Housing:** Guaranteed on-campus for all undergraduates. Coed dorms, single-sex dorms, special housing for disabled, fraternity/sorority housing, substance-free housing available. $200 nonrefundable deposit, deadline 5/1. **Activities:** Bands, choral groups, dance, drama, literary magazine, music ensembles, student government, student newspaper, TV station, Over 50 clubs and organizations.

Athletics. NCAA. **Intercollegiate:** Baseball M, basketball, cross-country, equestrian, field hockey W, golf M, lacrosse, soccer, softball W, tennis, track and field, volleyball W. **Intramural:** Basketball, bowling, field hockey W, football (non-tackle) M, lacrosse M, skiing, soccer, softball, volleyball. **Team name:** Hornets.

Student services. Adult student services, campus ministries, career counseling, student employment services, health services, personal counseling.

Contact. E-mail: admissions@lynchburg.edu
Phone: (434) 544-8300 Toll-free number: (800) 426-8101 ext. 8300
Fax: (434) 544-8653
Sharon Walters-Bower, Director of Recruitment, Lynchburg College, 1501 Lakeside Drive, Lynchburg, VA 24501

Mary Baldwin College

Staunton, Virginia — **CB member**
www.mbc.edu — **CB code: 5397**

- Private 4-year liberal arts college for women affiliated with Presbyterian Church (USA)
- Residential campus in large town
- 1,339 degree-seeking undergraduates: 29% part-time, 94% women, 20% African American, 3% Asian American, 3% Hispanic American, 1% Native American, 2% international
- 205 degree-seeking graduate students
- 77% of applicants admitted
- SAT or ACT (ACT writing optional), interview required
- 43% graduate within 6 years; 23% enter graduate study

General. Founded in 1842. Regionally accredited. Bachelor's degree available for younger women (13-15) in program for exceptionally gifted. Adult degree program available on main campus and at several satellite campuses throughout Virginia. Men admitted to adult program. **Degrees:** 293 bachelor's awarded; master's offered. **ROTC:** Army, Navy, Air Force. **Location:** 100 miles from Richmond, 150 miles from Washington, DC. **Calendar:** 4-4-1 semester system for traditional students. **Full-time faculty:** 76 total; 93% have terminal degrees, 7% minority, 54% women. **Part-time faculty:** 58 total; 10% minority, 62% women. **Class size:** 67% < 20, 33% 20-39, less than 1% 50-99. **Special facilities:** Electron microscope, gas chromatoscope.

Freshman class profile. 1,273 applied, 985 admitted, 335 enrolled.

Mid 50% test scores			
SAT verbal:	470-630	Rank in top quarter:	29%
SAT math:	450-560	Rank in top tenth:	14%
ACT:	18-26	Return as sophomores:	228%
GPA 3.50 or higher:	37%	Out-of-state:	42%
GPA 3.0-3.49:	26%	Live on campus:	92%
GPA 2.0-2.99:	36%	International:	1%

Basis for selection. School achievement record most important; test scores, involvement in school or civic groups also important; recommendations considered. 3.0 GPA recommended. Portfolio recommended for art majors.

High school preparation. Required and recommended units include English 4, mathematics 3, social studies 3, science 2 (laboratory 1), foreign language 2-3 and academic electives 2. Higher requirements for Virginia Women's Institute for Leadership (VWIL).

2005-2006 Annual costs. Tuition/fees: $20,605. Room/board: $5,860. Books/supplies: $700. Personal expenses: $1,615.

2004-2005 Financial aid. Need-based: 244 full-time freshmen applied for aid; 217 were judged to have need; 215 of these received aid. Average need met was 88%. Average scholarship/grant was $12,133; average loan $1,852. 59% of total undergraduate aid awarded as scholarships/grants, 41% as loans/jobs. **Non-need-based:** Awarded to 1,051 full-time undergraduates, including 255 freshmen. Scholarships awarded for academics, leadership, state residency.

Application procedures. Admission: No deadline. $35 fee, may be waived for applicants with need. Application may be submitted online. Admission notification on a rolling basis beginning on or about 9/1. Regular admission notification within 48 hours of receipt of all necessary materials. **Financial aid:** Priority date 5/15; no closing date. FAFSA required. Applicants notified on a rolling basis starting 2/1.

Academics. Students complete requirements in experiential education, international education, women's studies. May term offers opportunity for individualized programming, externships, study abroad. Institute combines academics, physical training and leadership development in rigorous 4-year bachelor's program. **Special study options:** Accelerated study, combined bachelor's/graduate degree, cooperative education, cross-registration, distance learning, double major, dual enrollment of high school students, ESL, exchange student, external degree, honors, independent study, internships, liberal arts/career combination, semester at sea, student-designed major, study abroad, teacher certification program. Summer exchange program with Doshisha Women's College in Kyoto, Japan. **Credit/placement by examination:** AP, CLEP, IB, institutional tests. 25% of required credits may be counted toward bachelor's degree. **Support services:** Learning center, reduced course load, study skills assistance, tutoring, writing center.

Honors college/program. Minimum SAT score of 1150 (exclusive of Writing) or ACT score of 25, minimum 3.5 high school GPA, essay, interview required for admission. About 36 freshmen admitted.

Majors. Area/ethnic studies: Asian. **Biology:** General, biochemistry. **Business:** Business admin. **Communications:** General. **Computer sciences:** General, computer science, information systems. **English:** English lit. **Foreign languages:** French, German, Spanish. **Health:** Clinical lab science, health care admin. **History:** General. **Math:** General, applied. **Philosophy/religion:** Philosophy. **Physical sciences:** Chemistry, physics. **Psychology:** General. **Public administration:** Social work. **Social sciences:** Economics, international relations, political science, sociology. **Visual/performing arts:** Art, arts management, dramatic.

Most popular majors. Biology 6%, business/marketing 13%, communications/journalism 7%, English 7%, history 7%, psychology 16%, social sciences 18%, visual/performing arts 12%.

Computing on campus. 227 workstations in dormitories, library, computer center. Dormitories wired for high-speed internet access and linked to campus network. Commuter students can connect to campus network. Online course registration, online library, helpline, repair service, wireless network available.

Student life. Freshman orientation: Mandatory. Preregistration for classes offered. Full-year program. **Policies:** College prohibits drinking under age 21. Honor code observed. Freshmen permitted cars on campus. **Housing:** Guaranteed on-campus for all undergraduates. Apartments available. $300 deposit. Special interest houses focusing on Japan, honors, leadership, and community service available. **Activities:** Marching band, choral groups, dance, drama, film society, literary magazine, music ensembles, musical theater, radio station, student government, student newspaper, TV station, Circle K, Habitat for Humanity, College Republicans, College Democrats, Black Student Alliance, Latinas Unidas, Christian Student Union, Campus Crusade for Christ, Anointed Voices of Praise Gospel Choir.

Athletics. NCAA. **Intercollegiate:** Basketball W, cross-country W, field hockey W, soccer W, softball W, swimming W, tennis W, volleyball W. **Team name:** Squirrels.

Student services. Adult student services, campus ministries, career counseling, student employment services, health services, minority student services, personal counseling, placement for graduates, women's services. **Physically disabled:** Services for visually, hearing impaired.

Contact. E-mail: admit@mbc.edu
Phone: (540) 887-7019 Toll-free number: (800) 468-2262
Fax: (540) 887-7279
Lisa Branson, Dean of Admissions and Financial Aid, Mary Baldwin College, Office of Admissions, Staunton, VA 24401

Marymount University

Arlington, Virginia — **CB member**
www.marymount.edu — **CB code: 5405**

- Private 4-year university affiliated with Roman Catholic Church
- Residential campus in small city
- 2,268 degree-seeking undergraduates: 18% part-time, 75% women, 14% African American, 9% Asian American, 11% Hispanic American, 7% international
- 1,263 degree-seeking graduate students
- 83% of applicants admitted
- SAT or ACT (ACT writing optional) required
- 53% graduate within 6 years; 32% enter graduate study

General. Founded in 1950. Regionally accredited. Classes available in Loudoun County and government sites including Office of Naval Research and Navy Federal Credit Union. Extensive utilization of local resources in Washington, DC area, including placement in senior internships. **Degrees:** 349 bachelor's, 118 associate awarded; master's, doctoral offered. **ROTC:** Army. **Location:** 7 miles from Washington, DC. **Calendar:** Semester, extensive summer session. **Full-time faculty:** 134 total; 85% have terminal degrees, 6% minority, 69% women. **Part-time faculty:** 218 total; 43% have terminal degrees, 6% minority, 60% women.

Freshman class profile. 1,802 applied, 1,491 admitted, 426 enrolled.

Mid 50% test scores			
SAT verbal:	450-560	Rank in top quarter:	30%
SAT math:	440-550	Rank in top tenth:	12%
ACT:	17-23	End year in good standing:	87%
GPA 3.50 or higher:	18%	Return as sophomores:	73%
GPA 3.0-3.49:	34%	Out-of-state:	54%
GPA 2.0-2.99:	48%	Live on campus:	66%
		International:	5%

Basis for selection. GPA in academic courses and test scores are most important. Class rank, recommendations from guidance counselors and teachers are also important. Essay, interview recommended.

High school preparation. 15 units required. Required and recommended units include English 4, mathematics 3, social studies 3, science 2 and foreign language 3.

2005-2006 Annual costs. Tuition/fees: $18,114. Room/board: $7,820. Books/supplies: $800. Personal expenses: $900.

2005-2006 Financial aid. Need-based: 325 full-time freshmen applied for aid; 246 were judged to have need; 241 of these received aid. Average need met was 78%. Average scholarship/grant was $7,253; average loan $2,629. 57% of total undergraduate aid awarded as scholarships/grants, 43% as loans/jobs. **Non-need-based:** Awarded to 1,027 full-time undergraduates, including 276 freshmen. Scholarships awarded for academics, alumni affiliation, leadership, state residency.

Application procedures. Admission: Priority date 5/1; no deadline. $35 fee, may be waived for applicants with need. Application may be submitted online. Admission notification on a rolling basis. Must reply by May 1 or within 3 week(s) if notified thereafter. **Financial aid:** Priority date 6/1; no closing date. FAFSA required. Applicants notified on a rolling basis; must reply within 2 week(s) of notification.

Academics. All undergraduates complete an internship before graduation. **Special study options:** Accelerated study, combined bachelor's/graduate degree, cross-registration, double major, honors, independent study, internships, student-designed major, study abroad, teacher certification program. Member of the Consortium of Universities in Washington, DC. **Credit/placement by examination:** AP, CLEP, IB, institutional tests. 30 credit hours maximum toward associate degree, 30 toward bachelor's. Credit for prior work/life experience through Marymount's Porftolio Assessment and Credit by Examination (PACE) program. **Support services:** Learning center, reduced course load, tutoring.

Honors college/program. Admission is competitive and limited to 20 students each year. Minimum high school or college GPA of 3.5, minimum composite SAT score of 1200 (exclusive of writing) or ACT of 26, minimum TOEFL score of 617 (paper) or 260 (computer) for international students, composition proficiency as demonstrated by credit for English 101 (AP or transfer), satisfactory score on the MU writing test recommended.

Majors. Biology: General, cellular/molecular. **Business:** Accounting, business admin, fashion, finance, human resources, international, marketing. **Communications:** General. **Computer sciences:** General, computer science, information systems. **Conservation:** Environmental science. **English:** English lit. **Health:** Nursing (RN). **History:** General. **Legal studies:** Paralegal. **Liberal arts:** Arts/sciences. **Math:** General. **Parks/recreation:** Exercise sciences. **Philosophy/religion:** Philosophy, religion. **Protective services:** Criminal justice. **Psychology:** General. **Social sciences:** Criminology, economics, political science, sociology. **Visual/performing arts:** Fashion design, graphic design, interior design, studio arts.

Most popular majors. Business/marketing 21%, computer/information sciences 10%, health sciences 7%, liberal arts 7%, psychology 22%, social sciences 8%, visual/performing arts 21%.

Computing on campus. 270 workstations in dormitories, library, computer center. Dormitories wired for high-speed internet access and linked to campus network. Commuter students can connect to campus network. Online course registration, helpline, wireless network available.

Student life. Freshman orientation: Mandatory, $125 fee. Preregistration for classes offered. 3 weekend orientation sessions in the summer. **Housing:** Guaranteed on-campus for freshmen. Coed dorms, single-sex dorms available. $300 nonrefundable deposit, deadline 5/1. **Activities:** Choral groups, dance, drama, literary magazine, student government, student newspaper, Campus Ministry, Black Student Alliance, International Club, Students in Free Enterprise, College Democrats/College Republicans, Best Buddies.

Athletics. NCAA. **Intercollegiate:** Basketball, cross-country, golf M, lacrosse, soccer, swimming, volleyball W. **Intramural:** Basketball, football (non-tackle), golf M, soccer, softball, swimming, volleyball, water polo, weight lifting. **Team name:** Saints.

Student services. Campus ministries, career counseling, student employment services, financial aid counseling, health services, personal counseling. **Physically disabled:** Services for visually, speech, hearing impaired.

Contact. E-mail: admissions@marymount.edu
Phone: (703) 284-1500 Toll-free number: (800) 548-7638
Fax: (703) 522-0349
Chris Domes, Vice President for Enrollment and Student Services, Marymount University, 2807 North Glebe Road, Arlington, VA 22207-4299

National College of Business & Technology: Salem

Roanoke, Virginia
www.ncbt.edu — **CB code: 5502**

- For-profit 4-year business college
- Commuter campus in large city
- 639 degree-seeking undergraduates
- Interview required

General. Founded in 1886. Accredited by ACICS. **Degrees:** 38 bachelor's, 102 associate awarded; master's offered. **Calendar:** Quarter, extensive summer session, limited summer session. **Full-time faculty:** 14 total. **Part-time faculty:** 71 total.

Basis for selection. Open admission.

2006-2007 Annual costs. Tuition/fees: $8,976.

Financial aid. All financial aid based on need.

Application procedures. Admission: Closing date 9/1 (receipt date). $30 fee, may be waived for applicants with need. Application may be submitted online. Admission notification on a rolling basis. **Financial aid:** No deadline. FAFSA required. Applicants notified on a rolling basis.

Academics. Special study options: Double major, internships. **Credit/placement by examination:** CLEP, institutional tests. **Support services:** Tutoring.

Majors. Business: Accounting, business admin.

Computing on campus. 35 workstations in library, computer center.

Student life. Freshman orientation: Mandatory. Preregistration for classes offered. **Policies:** Freshmen permitted cars on campus. **Housing:** Coed dorms available. Hotel accommodations available. **Activities:** Student government.

Student services. Career counseling, financial aid counseling, placement for graduates.

Contact. Phone: (540) 986-1800 Fax: (540) 444-4198
Larry Steele, Vice President of Admissions, National College of Business & Technology: Salem, PO Box 6400, Roanoke, VA 24017-0400

Norfolk State University

Norfolk, Virginia — **CB member**
www.nsu.edu — **CB code: 5864**

- Public 4-year university
- Commuter campus in small city
- 5,246 degree-seeking undergraduates: 16% part-time, 62% women, 89% African American, 1% Asian American, 2% Hispanic American, 1% international
- 591 degree-seeking graduate students
- 71% of applicants admitted
- SAT or ACT (ACT writing optional) required

General. Founded in 1935. Regionally accredited. **Degrees:** 722 bachelor's, 62 associate awarded; master's, doctoral offered. **ROTC:** Army, Navy. **Location:** 5 miles from downtown. **Calendar:** Semester, extensive summer session. **Full-time faculty:** 285 total. **Part-time faculty:** 135 total. **Class size:** 62% < 20, 32% 20-39, 4% 40-49, 2% 50-99. **Special facilities:** Planetarium, crystal laboratory, laser laboratory, nuclear magnetic resonance laboratory, institute for service learning, literacy center for entrepreneurial studies, center for materials research, institute for minorities in applied sciences, assistive technology laboratory.

Freshman class profile. 4,696 applied, 3,315 admitted, 996 enrolled.

Mid 50% test scores			
SAT verbal:	410-490	Rank in top tenth:	4%
SAT math:	400-490	End year in good standing:	73%
ACT:	17-20	Out-of-state:	34%
GPA 3.50 or higher:	7%	Live on campus:	71%
GPA 3.0-3.49:	20%	International:	1%
GPA 2.0-2.99:	71%	Fraternities:	10%
Rank in top quarter:	21%	Sororities:	10%

Basis for selection. NSU seeks to admit applicants whose combination of academic preparation, aptitude, achievements, and motivation predict a reasonable probability of success. Interview recommended for electronics, engineering, nursing programs; audition recommended for music; portfolio recommended for art. **Homeschooled:** Transcript of courses and grades required. Transcript required.

High school preparation. College-preparatory program recommended. 22 units required. Required units include English 4, mathematics 3, history 3, science 3 and academic electives 9. 2 science required for nursing applicants: 1 chemistry, 1 biology. 2 units high school math (1 unit of algebra), 2 units science required for business applicants. 1 unit geometry, 2 algebra units recommended for mathematics applicants. 2 mathematics units must include algebra for computer science applicants.

2006-2007 Annual costs. Tuition/fees (projected): $4,670; $14,480 out-of-state. Room/board: $6,474. Books/supplies: $1,000. Personal expenses: $1,700.

2004-2005 Financial aid. Need-based: 897 full-time freshmen applied for aid; 782 were judged to have need; 772 of these received aid. Average need met was 83%. Average scholarship/grant was $5,521; average loan $2,918. 37% of total undergraduate aid awarded as scholarships/grants, 63% as loans/jobs. **Non-need-based:** Awarded to 1,372 full-time undergraduates, including 381 freshmen. Scholarships awarded for academics, alumni affiliation, athletics, leadership, music/drama, ROTC, state residency.

Application procedures. Admission: Closing date 5/31 (postmark date). $25 fee, may be waived for applicants with need. Application may be submitted online. Admission notification on a rolling basis. Must reply by May 1 or within 2 week(s) if notified thereafter. **Financial aid:** Priority date 5/31; no closing date. FAFSA required. Applicants notified on a rolling basis starting 4/1; must reply within 2 week(s) of notification.

Academics. Special study options: Combined bachelor's/graduate degree, cooperative education, cross-registration, distance learning, double major, dual enrollment of high school students, ESL, honors, independent study, internships, liberal arts/career combination, teacher certification program. **Credit/placement by examination:** AP, CLEP, SAT, ACT, institutional tests. There is no limit on number of credits the university will accept, as long as the student passes the exam and has departmental approval. **Support services:** Learning center, reduced course load, study skills assistance, tutoring, writing center.

Majors. Biology: General. **Business:** General, accounting, hospitality admin. **Communications:** Journalism, media studies. **Computer sciences:** General. **Education:** Business, early childhood, special, trade/industrial. **Engineering:** Electrical. **Engineering technology:** CAD/CADD, computer, construction, electrical. **Health:** Clinical lab science, health care admin, medical records admin, nursing (RN). **History:** General. **Math:** General. **Parks/recreation:** Exercise sciences. **Physical sciences:** Chemistry, optics, physics. **Psychology:** General. **Public administration:** Social work. **Social sciences:** Political science, sociology. **Visual/performing arts:** Art.

Most popular majors. Business/marketing 15%, communications/journalism 8%, health sciences 7%, interdisciplinary studies 17%, psychology 9%, public administration/social services 6%, social sciences 13%.

Computing on campus. 978 workstations in dormitories, library, computer center. Dormitories linked to campus network. Online library, helpline available.

Student life. Freshman orientation: Mandatory. Preregistration for classes offered. Held during June, July and August. **Housing:** Single-sex dorms, special housing for disabled, substance-free housing available. $300 nonrefundable deposit, deadline 5/1. **Activities:** Bands, choral groups, dance, drama, music ensembles, radio station, student government, student newspaper, symphony orchestra, TV station, Beta Psi Club, Omega Psi Phi, Alpha Kappa Alpha, Delta Sigma Theta, Alpha Delta Mu, Young Democrats, Young Republicans, Alpha Phi Alpha, Kappa Alpha Psi.

Athletics. NCAA. **Intercollegiate:** Baseball M, basketball, bowling W, cross-country, football (tackle) M, softball W, tennis, track and field, volleyball W. **Intramural:** Basketball, bowling, cheerleading, football (non-tackle) M, soccer M, softball, swimming, table tennis, tennis, volleyball. **Team name:** Spartans.

Student services. Adult student services, alcohol/substance abuse counseling, campus ministries, career counseling, student employment services, financial aid counseling, health services, on-campus daycare, personal counseling, placement for graduates, veterans' counselor, women's services. **Physically disabled:** Services for visually, speech, hearing impaired.

Contact. E-mail: admissions@nsu.edu
Phone: (757) 823-8396 Fax: (757) 823-2078
Michelle Marable, Director of Admissions, Norfolk State University, 700 Park Avenue, Norfolk, VA 23504

Old Dominion University

Norfolk, Virginia — **CB member**
www.odu.edu — **CB code: 5126**

- Public 4-year university
- Commuter campus in small city
- 14,605 degree-seeking undergraduates: 27% part-time, 59% women, 23% African American, 6% Asian American, 3% Hispanic American, 1% Native American, 2% international
- 3,743 degree-seeking graduate students
- 69% of applicants admitted
- SAT or ACT with writing, application essay required
- 48% graduate within 6 years; 48% enter graduate study

General. Founded in 1930. Regionally accredited. Classes are offered on the main campus in Norfolk, Virginia, at four regional Centers of Higher Education, and through the distance learning network TELETECHNET, which includes more than 40 sites across Virginia, Georgia, Illinois, Arizona, Washington, the Bahamas and the District of Columbia, along with U.S. Navy ships at sea. **Degrees:** 2,411 bachelor's awarded; master's, doctoral offered. **ROTC:** Army, Navy. **Location:** 2 miles from downtown, 200 miles from Washington, DC. **Calendar:** Semester, extensive summer session. **Full-time faculty:** 617 total; 81% have terminal degrees, 21% minority, 37% women. **Part-time faculty:** 283 total; 13% minority, 55% women. **Class size:** 30% < 20, 47% 20-39, 13% 40-49, 6% 50-99, 4% >100. **Special facilities:** Student art gallery, centers for urban research/service, economic education and child study centers, laser optics lab, planetarium, robotics lab, sub-/super-sonic wind tunnels, marine science research vessel, random wave pool.

Freshman class profile. 7,067 applied, 4,904 admitted, 2,094 enrolled.

Mid 50% test scores		**Rank in top tenth:**	15%
SAT verbal:	480-580	**End year in good standing:**	77%
SAT math:	480-580	**Return as sophomores:**	77%
ACT:	19-23	**Out-of-state:**	9%
GPA 3.50 or higher:	28%	**Live on campus:**	61%
GPA 3.0-3.49:	44%	**International:**	1%
GPA 2.0-2.99:	28%	**Fraternities:**	7%
Rank in top quarter:	44%	**Sororities:**	4%

Basis for selection. Students who submit acceptable GPA and SAT/ACT scores are admitted. Those who do not meet the acceptable GPA or SAT scores are reviewed by an Admissions Committee. The committee looks at grades in core curriculum courses, student essay, student activity, resume/letters of recommendation, high school attended, IB and AP courses taken, etc. Audition required for music; portfolio required for art. **Homeschooled:** Scores from SAT or ACT must be submitted. The GED is not required. Students who are not attending a program that requires regular curriculum review and submission of test scores to a local school board must submit Stanford 9 results. **Learning Disabled:** Documentation of disabilities must be submitted before receiving services from Office of Disability Services.

High school preparation. College-preparatory program recommended. 17 units required. Required and recommended units include English 4, mathematics 3, social studies 3, history 3, science 3 (laboratory 2), foreign language 3 and academic electives 1. 3 years of one foreign language or 2 years each of 2 different foreign languages. 3 units of mathematics required for engineering technology applicants, 4 units for engineering applicants.

2006-2007 Annual costs. Tuition/fees (projected): $5,614; $15,394 out-of-state. Room/board: $6,292. Books/supplies: $900. Personal expenses: $1,875.

2005-2006 Financial aid. **Need-based:** 1,550 full-time freshmen applied for aid; 1,421 were judged to have need; 1,224 of these received aid. Average need met was 68%. Average scholarship/grant was $3,954; average loan $2,678. 45% of total undergraduate aid awarded as scholarships/grants, 55% as loans/jobs. **Non-need-based:** Awarded to 2,060 full-time undergraduates, including 682 freshmen. Scholarships awarded for academics, alumni affiliation, art, athletics, leadership, music/drama, ROTC, state residency.

Application procedures. **Admission:** Priority date 12/15; deadline 3/15 (receipt date). $40 fee, may be waived for applicants with need. Application may be submitted online. Admission notification on a rolling basis beginning on or about 1/15. Students are required to submit the following: $40 application fee, high school transcripts, application, SAT or ACT scores, 1-3 letters of recommendation, one essay, one student activity resume. **Financial aid:** Priority date 2/15, closing date 3/15. FAFSA required. Applicants notified on a rolling basis starting 2/1; must reply within 2 week(s) of notification.

Academics. Guaranteed work or internship experience for credit in all fields of study. **Special study options:** Accelerated study, combined bachelor's/graduate degree, cooperative education, cross-registration, distance learning, double major, dual enrollment of high school students, ESL, exchange student, honors, independent study, internships, liberal arts/career combination, student-designed major, study abroad, teacher certification program, weekend college. Experiential learning. **Credit/placement by examination:** AP, CLEP, IB, institutional tests. 60 credit hours maximum toward bachelor's degree. Work life credits awarded through certification or department evaluations. Essay required to receive CLEP credit in American History I and II, Analysis and Interpretation of Literature, and Western Civilization I and II. **Support services:** Learning center, pre-admission summer program, reduced course load, study skills assistance, tutoring, writing center.

Majors. **Area/ethnic studies:** Asian, women's. **Biology:** General, biochemistry, marine. **Business:** Accounting, business admin, finance, international, management information systems, managerial economics, marketing. **Communications:** General. **Computer sciences:** General. **Education:** Art, biology, chemistry, drama/dance, English, foreign languages, French, geography, German, history, mathematics, music, physical, physics, sales/marketing, Spanish, technology/industrial arts. **Engineering:** Civil, computer, electrical, environmental, mechanical. **Engineering technology:** General, civil, computer, electrical, mechanical, nuclear. **English:** English lit, speech/rhetoric. **Foreign languages:** General, French, German, Spanish. **Health:** Audiology/speech pathology, clinical lab science, community health services, cytotechnology, dental hygiene, environmental health, health services, nuclear medical technology, nursing (RN), ophthalmic technology. **History:** General. **Math:** General. **Parks/recreation:** Exercise sciences, facilities management, sports admin. **Philosophy/religion:** Philosophy. **Physical sciences:** Chemistry, geology, oceanography, physics. **Psychology:** General. **Social sciences:** Anthropology, criminology, economics, geography, international relations, political science, sociology. **Visual/performing arts:** Acting, art, art history/conservation, dance, dramatic, graphic design, music performance, studio arts.

Most popular majors. Business/marketing 21%, engineering/engineering technologies 11%, English 10%, health sciences 18%, interdisciplinary studies 6%, psychology 6%, social sciences 9%.

Computing on campus. 500 workstations in library, computer center, student center. Dormitories wired for high-speed internet access and linked to campus network. Commuter students can connect to campus network. Online course registration, online library, helpline, repair service, wireless network available.

Student life. **Freshman orientation:** Mandatory, $100 fee. Preregistration for classes offered. Consists of campus tours, available Monday through Friday at 10am, Monday and Friday at 2pm, and Saturday at 11am. Special tours can be arranged within the Office of Admissions. Summer orientation programs include advising. **Policies:** Freshmen permitted cars on campus. **Housing:** Coed dorms, special housing for disabled, apartments, substance-free housing available. $150 fully refundable deposit, deadline 5/1. **Activities:** Bands, choral groups, dance, drama, literary magazine, music ensembles, musical theater, radio station, student government, student newspaper, TV station, approximately 220 student clubs and organizations available.

Athletics. NCAA. **Intercollegiate:** Baseball M, basketball, diving, field hockey W, golf, lacrosse W, sailing, soccer, swimming, tennis, wrestling M. **Intramural:** Badminton, basketball, bowling, cross-country, football (non-tackle), golf, sailing M, soccer, softball, swimming, table tennis, tennis, volleyball, water polo, weight lifting, wrestling. **Team name:** Monarchs.

Student services. Adult student services, alcohol/substance abuse counseling, campus ministries, career counseling, services for economically disadvantaged, student employment services, financial aid counseling, health services, minority student services, on-campus daycare, personal counseling, placement for graduates, veterans' counselor, women's services. **Physically disabled:** Services for visually, speech, hearing impaired.

Contact. E-mail: admit@odu.edu
Phone: (757) 683-3685 Toll-free number: (800) 348-7926
Fax: (757) 683-3255
Alice McAdory, Director of Admissions, Old Dominion University, 108 Rollins Hall, 5115 Hampton Boulevard, Norfolk, VA 23529

Potomac College
Herndon, Virginia
www.potomac.edu

- For-profit 4-year business college
- Residential campus in large town
- 140 degree-seeking undergraduates

General. Accredited by ACICS. **Degrees:** 11 bachelor's awarded. **Location:** 30 miles from Washington, DC. **Calendar:** Continuous, extensive summer session. **Full-time faculty:** 1 total. **Part-time faculty:** 4 total.

2005-2006 Annual costs. Tuition/fees: $17,920.

Application procedures. Admission: No deadline. $15 fee, may be waived for applicants with need. Admission notification on a rolling basis.

Academics. Special study options: Accelerated study, independent study. **Credit/placement by examination:** CLEP, institutional tests.

Majors. Business: Business admin. **Computer sciences:** General, information technology.

Computing on campus. 16 workstations in library, computer center. Wireless network available.

Student life. Freshman orientation: Mandatory. Preregistration for classes offered.

Contact. Phone: (703) 709-5875 Fax: (703) 709-8972
Ron Parker, Director of Admissions, Potomac College, 1029 Herndon Parkway, Herndon, VA 20170

Radford University
Radford, Virginia **CB member**
www.radford.edu **CB code: 5565**

- Public 4-year university
- Residential campus in large town
- 8,419 degree-seeking undergraduates: 5% part-time, 58% women, 6% African American, 2% Asian American, 3% Hispanic American, 1% international
- 866 degree-seeking graduate students
- 81% of applicants admitted
- SAT or ACT (ACT writing optional) required
- 51% graduate within 6 years

General. Founded in 1910. Regionally accredited. **Degrees:** 1,795 bachelor's awarded; master's offered. **ROTC:** Army. **Location:** 36 miles from Roanoke. **Calendar:** Semester, limited summer session. **Full-time faculty:** 377 total; 83% have terminal degrees, 9% minority, 45% women. **Part-time faculty:** 193 total; 26% have terminal degrees, 5% minority, 62% women. **Class size:** 30% < 20, 53% 20-39, 11% 40-49, 5% 50-99, less than 1% >100. **Special facilities:** Planetarium, greenhouse, nature and recreational conservatory, art museum, speech and hearing clinic, center for advancement of teaching and learning, family clinics, gender studies center, experiential learning and career development center, Center for Music Technology, Center for Health Resources.

Freshman class profile. 5,792 applied, 4,719 admitted, 1,896 enrolled.

Mid 50% test scores			
SAT verbal:	460-550	Rank in top quarter:	22%
SAT math:	450-550	Rank in top tenth:	4%
ACT:	18-22	Return as sophomores:	79%
GPA 3.50 or higher:	15%	Out-of-state:	9%
GPA 3.0-3.49:	38%	Live on campus:	97%
GPA 2.0-2.99:	47%	International:	1%

Basis for selection. Students are selected on the basis of their high school records; SAT, ACT, or TOEFL exam results; optional student essay; and evidence of interest and motivation as indicated in the supplied materials. Audition required for music, theater, dance programs; portfolio required for art. **Homeschooled:** Must take either the ACT or SAT and SAT Subject tests.

High school preparation. 24 units recommended. Recommended units include English 4, mathematics 4, social studies 2, history 2, science 4 (laboratory 3), foreign language 3 and academic electives 5. Pre-nursing students should complete units in both biology and chemistry.

2005-2006 Annual costs. Tuition/fees: $5,130; $12,368 out-of-state. Room/board: $6,120. Books/supplies: $800. Personal expenses: $1,600.

2004-2005 Financial aid. Need-based: 1,148 full-time freshmen applied for aid; 731 were judged to have need; 701 of these received aid. Average need met was 70%. Average scholarship/grant was $5,241; average loan $2,492. 41% of total undergraduate aid awarded as scholarships/grants, 59% as loans/jobs. **Non-need-based:** Awarded to 1,260 full-time undergraduates, including 418 freshmen. Scholarships awarded for academics, athletics, ROTC. **Additional information:** Student's need and grades considered. Top consideration given to those with greatest need and who apply by deadline.

Application procedures. Admission: Closing date 2/1 (postmark date). $35 fee, may be waived for applicants with need. Application may be submitted online. Admission notification 3/20. Admission notification on a rolling basis beginning on or about 1/9. Must reply by 5/1. Must reply by May 1 or within 2 week(s) if notified thereafter. **Financial aid:** Priority date 3/1; no closing date. FAFSA required. Applicants notified on a rolling basis starting 4/15.

Academics. Special study options: Accelerated study, combined bachelor's/graduate degree, cross-registration, distance learning, double major, ESL, honors, independent study, internships, student-designed major, study abroad, teacher certification program. **Credit/placement by examination:** AP, CLEP, IB. **Support services:** Learning center, study skills assistance, tutoring, writing center.

Majors. Biology: General. **Business:** Accounting, business admin, finance, management information systems, marketing. **Communications:** Journalism. **Computer sciences:** Computer science, information systems. **Education:** Health, physical. **English:** English lit. **Family/consumer sciences:** Family studies, food/nutrition. **Foreign languages:** General. **Health:** Clinical lab science, communication disorders, music therapy, nursing (RN). **History:** General. **Liberal arts:** Arts/sciences. **Math:** General. **Parks/recreation:** General. **Philosophy/religion:** Philosophy, religion. **Physical sciences:** General, chemistry, geology. **Protective services:** Criminal justice. **Psychology:** General. **Public administration:** Social work. **Social sciences:** General, anthropology, economics, geography, political science, sociology. **Visual/performing arts:** Art, dance, design, dramatic, studio arts.

Most popular majors. Business/marketing 19%, communications/journalism 9%, health sciences 6%, interdisciplinary studies 12%, security/protective services 10%, social sciences 9%, visual/performing arts 9%.

Computing on campus. 566 workstations in dormitories, library, computer center, student center. Dormitories wired for high-speed internet access and linked to campus network. Commuter students can connect to campus network. Online course registration, online library, helpline, repair service, student web hosting, wireless network available.

Student life. Freshman orientation: Available, $200 fee. Preregistration for classes offered. 5 two day sessions in June or August. **Policies:** Freshmen permitted cars on campus. **Housing:** Guaranteed on-campus for freshmen. Coed dorms, special housing for disabled, apartments, substance-free housing available. $200 nonrefundable deposit, deadline 5/1. **Activities:** Jazz band, choral groups, dance, drama, literary magazine, music ensembles, musical theater, radio station, student government, student newspaper, TV station, Campus Crusade for Christ, Hillel B'nai Brith, Deliverance Gospel Choir, Alpha Phi Omega, American Red Cross, Habitat for Humanity, Educated Women of Color, NAACP, Hispanic and Asian American Student Association, Legislative Action Committee.

Athletics. NCAA. **Intercollegiate:** Baseball M, basketball, cross-country, field hockey W, golf, soccer, softball W, swimming W, tennis, track and field, volleyball W. **Intramural:** Basketball, bowling, football (tackle), racquetball, rugby M, soccer, softball, tennis, volleyball, weight lifting. **Team name:** Highlanders.

Student services. Adult student services, alcohol/substance abuse counseling, campus ministries, career counseling, services for economically disadvantaged, student employment services, financial aid counseling, health services, minority student services, personal counseling, placement for graduates, veterans' counselor, women's services. **Physically disabled:** Services for visually, speech, hearing impaired.

Contact. E-mail: ruadmiss@radford.edu
Phone: (540) 831-5371 Toll-free number: (800) 890-4265
Fax: (540) 831-5038
David Kraus, Director of Admissions, Radford University, Radford University Admissions, 209 Martin Hall, Radford, VA 24142

Randolph-Macon College
Ashland, Virginia **CB member**
www.rmc.edu **CB code: 5566**

- Private 4-year liberal arts college affiliated with United Methodist Church
- Residential campus in small town

- 1,097 degree-seeking undergraduates: 1% part-time, 51% women, 7% African American, 1% Asian American, 1% Hispanic American, 1% international
- 79% of applicants admitted
- SAT or ACT (ACT writing recommended), application essay required
- 74% graduate within 6 years; 27% enter graduate study

General. Founded in 1830. Regionally accredited. **Degrees:** 196 bachelor's awarded. **ROTC:** Army. **Location:** 15 miles from Richmond, 90 miles from Washington, DC. **Calendar:** 4-1-4, limited summer session. **Full-time faculty:** 90 total; 96% have terminal degrees, 7% minority, 39% women. **Part-time faculty:** 53 total; 43% have terminal degrees, 8% minority, 60% women. **Class size:** 74% < 20, 26% 20-39. **Special facilities:** Observatory with 12-inch reflecting telescope and 3-meter radio telescope, 6 historic buildings, greenhouse.

Freshman class profile. 1,727 applied, 1,357 admitted, 305 enrolled.

Mid 50% test scores		**Rank in top tenth:**	20%
SAT verbal:	510-600	**End year in good standing:**	86%
SAT math:	500-580	**Return as sophomores:**	76%
GPA 3.50 or higher:	35%	**Out-of-state:**	30%
GPA 3.0-3.49:	33%	**Live on campus:**	95%
GPA 2.0-2.99:	32%	**International:**	1%
Rank in top quarter:	43%		

Basis for selection. School achievement record, class rank, and test scores most important. Personal recommendations, leadership skills and participation considered. Interview recommended. **Homeschooled:** Statement describing homeschool structure and mission, transcript of courses and grades, letter of recommendation (nonparent) required. **Learning Disabled:** Students with learning disabilities are encouraged to meet with the director of disability support services.

High school preparation. 16 units required; 22 recommended. Required and recommended units include English 4, mathematics 3-4, social studies 1-2, history 2, science 3-4 (laboratory 2-4), foreign language 2-4 and academic electives 1-2.

2006-2007 Annual costs. Tuition/fees: $25,345. Room/board: $7,695. Books/supplies: $1,000. Personal expenses: $720.

2005-2006 Financial aid. Need-based: 239 full-time freshmen applied for aid; 189 were judged to have need; 189 of these received aid. Average need met was 86%. Average scholarship/grant was $14,629; average loan $4,645. 70% of total undergraduate aid awarded as scholarships/grants, 30% as loans/jobs. **Non-need-based:** Awarded to 497 full-time undergraduates, including 144 freshmen. Scholarships awarded for academics, alumni affiliation, minority status, religious affiliation, state residency.

Application procedures. Admission: Priority date 2/1; deadline 3/1 (postmark date). $30 fee, may be waived for applicants with need. Application may be submitted online. Admission notification 4/1. Must reply by 5/1. Must reply by May 1 or within 2 week(s) if notified thereafter. Applications accepted after March 1 on space-available basis. **Financial aid:** Priority date 2/1, closing date 3/1. FAFSA required. Applicants notified by 3/15; must reply by 5/1 or within 2 week(s) of notification.

Academics. Comprehensive liberal arts core curriculum. All students must complete an Internship, study abroad, or original research project for graduation. Interdisciplinary First-Year Experience program for all freshmen students. **Special study options:** Accelerated study, combined bachelor's/graduate degree, cross-registration, double major, dual enrollment of high school students, exchange student, honors, independent study, internships, liberal arts/career combination, study abroad, teacher certification program, United Nations semester, Washington semester. Member of Seven College consortium; 3-2 program in engineering with Columbia University and University of Virginia; 3-2 in forestry with Duke University; 4-1 in accounting with Virginia Commonwealth University. **Credit/placement by examination:** AP, CLEP, IB, institutional tests. 75 credit hours maximum toward bachelor's degree. At least one-half major course of study must be completed at Randolph-Macon College. **Support services:** Learning center, reduced course load, study skills assistance, tutoring, writing center.

Majors. Area/ethnic studies: Women's. **Biology:** General. **Business:** Accounting, managerial economics. **Computer sciences:** General. **Conservation:** Environmental studies. **English:** English lit. **Foreign languages:** Ancient Greek, classics, French, German, Latin, Spanish. **History:** General. **Interdisciplinary:** Global studies. **Math:** General. **Philosophy/religion:** Philosophy, religion. **Physical sciences:** Chemistry, physics. **Psychology:** General. **Social sciences:** Economics, political science, sociology. **Visual/performing arts:** Art history/conservation, arts management, dramatic, studio arts.

Most popular majors. Business/marketing 18%, English 7%, foreign language 6%, history 6%, psychology 10%, social sciences 26%, visual/performing arts 7%.

Computing on campus. 350 workstations in library, computer center, student center. Dormitories wired for high-speed internet access and linked to campus network. Commuter students can connect to campus network. Online course registration, online library, helpline, repair service, student web hosting, wireless network available.

Student life. Freshman orientation: Mandatory, $100 fee. Preregistration for classes offered. 4-day program held for students and parents prior to start of fall classes. **Policies:** Freshmen permitted cars on campus. **Housing:** Guaranteed on-campus for all undergraduates. Coed dorms, single-sex dorms, special housing for disabled, apartments, fraternity/sorority housing, substance-free housing available. $300 fully refundable deposit, deadline 5/1. Honors house, special interest housing available. **Activities:** Bands, choral groups, dance, drama, film society, literary magazine, musical theater, radio station, student government, student newspaper, TV station, Over 100 clubs and organizations.

Athletics. NCAA. **Intercollegiate:** Baseball M, basketball, field hockey W, football (tackle) M, golf M, lacrosse, soccer, softball W, swimming W, tennis, volleyball W. **Intramural:** Basketball, football (non-tackle), lacrosse, racquetball, soccer, softball, table tennis, tennis, volleyball. **Team name:** Yellow Jackets.

Student services. Alcohol/substance abuse counseling, campus ministries, career counseling, student employment services, financial aid counseling, health services, minority student services, personal counseling, placement for graduates, women's services. **Physically disabled:** Services for visually, speech, hearing impaired.

Contact. E-mail: admissions@rmc.edu
Phone: (804) 752-7305 Toll-free number: (800) 888-1762
Fax: (804) 752-4707
John Conkright, Dean of Admissions and Financial Aid, Randolph-Macon College, PO Box 5005, Ashland, VA 23005-5505

Randolph-Macon Woman's College

Lynchburg, Virginia — **CB member**
www.rmwc.edu — **CB code: 5567**

- Private 4-year liberal arts college for women affiliated with United Methodist Church
- Residential campus in small city
- 681 degree-seeking undergraduates: 2% part-time, 100% women, 9% African American, 3% Asian American, 4% Hispanic American, 1% Native American, 10% international
- 87% of applicants admitted
- SAT or ACT (ACT writing optional), application essay required
- 63% graduate within 6 years

General. Founded in 1891. Regionally accredited. **Degrees:** 155 bachelor's awarded; master's offered. **Location:** 60 miles from Roanoke and Charlottesville. **Calendar:** Semester, limited summer session. **Full-time faculty:** 72 total; 94% have terminal degrees, 11% minority, 57% women. **Part-time faculty:** 18 total; 33% have terminal degrees, 6% minority, 78% women. **Class size:** 82% < 20, 18% 20-39. **Special facilities:** Observatory, 3 nature preserves, botanical garden, 100-acre equestrian center, museum of American art, science and mathematics resource center, learning resources center, writing lab.

Freshman class profile. 774 applied, 675 admitted, 184 enrolled.

Mid 50% test scores		**Rank in top quarter:**	70%
SAT verbal:	540-670	**Rank in top tenth:**	36%
SAT math:	510-630	**Return as sophomores:**	71%
ACT:	21-29	**Out-of-state:**	65%
GPA 3.50 or higher:	42%	**Live on campus:**	98%
GPA 3.0-3.49:	45%	**International:**	11%
GPA 2.0-2.99:	13%		

Basis for selection. Rigor of high school curriculum and achievement most important, followed by teacher and counselor recommendations, test scores, activities, personal achievement. International students may submit SAT in lieu of TOEFL. Interview recommended. Essay submission may be an essay written on a topic of the applicant's choice or a copy of a graded essay written by the applicant in the 11th or 12th grade. **Learning Disabled:** Any student with a diagnosed disability should submit documentation to the Director of the Learning Resources Center, who will work in consultation with the Office of the Dean of the College and faculty to determine reasonable and appropriate accommodations.

High school preparation. College-preparatory program required. 16 units required. Required and recommended units include English 4, mathematics 3, history 2, science 2 (laboratory 2), foreign language 3-4 and academic electives 1-2. Recommended academic units represent a minimum expected program. Three years of one foreign language are recommended, but applicants may offer 2 units of each of 2 languages instead. A student must have successfully completed or be enrolled in algebra II senior year in order for the application to be considered.

2005-2006 Annual costs. Tuition/fees: $23,030. Room and board charges include free use of laundry facilities. Room/board: $8,610. Books/supplies: $800. Personal expenses: $1,000.

2005-2006 Financial aid. Need-based: 138 full-time freshmen applied for aid; 112 were judged to have need; 112 of these received aid. Average need met was 92%. Average scholarship/grant was $17,465; average loan $2,526. 70% of total undergraduate aid awarded as scholarships/grants, 30% as loans/jobs. **Non-need-based:** Awarded to 290 full-time undergraduates, including 95 freshmen. Scholarships awarded for academics, alumni affiliation, art, leadership, minority status, music/drama, religious affiliation, state residency. **Additional information:** College offers approximately $2 million annually to incoming first-year students. Grants range up to full tuition. Student must reapply each year.

Application procedures. Admission: Priority date 3/1; no deadline. $35 fee, may be waived for applicants with need. Application may be submitted online. Admission notification on a rolling basis beginning on or about 11/1. Must reply by May 1 or within 2 week(s) if notified thereafter. **Financial aid:** Priority date 3/1; no closing date. FAFSA required. Applicants notified on a rolling basis starting 3/1; must reply by 5/1 or within 2 week(s) of notification.

Academics. Honor system includes self-scheduled examinations. **Special study options:** Accelerated study, cross-registration, double major, dual enrollment of high school students, exchange student, honors, independent study, internships, liberal arts/career combination, student-designed major, study abroad, teacher certification program, Washington semester. 7-college exchange with Washington and Lee University, Hollins University, Hampden-Sydney College, Mary Baldwin College, Sweet Briar College, Randolph-Macon College; junior year abroad program with University of Reading, England; affiliate abroad programs in Greece, France, Denmark, Japan, Italy, Ireland, Mexico, Germany, Czech Republic, Spain; assistance with non-affiliated abroad programs; Marine Biological Laboratory Semester in Environmental Science; American Culture program (1-semester program including study on-site at key locations in and near Virginia), Tri-College Consortium with Lynchburg College and Sweet Briar College. **Credit/placement by examination:** AP, CLEP, IB, SAT, ACT, institutional tests. Applicants with scores at or above 50th percentile awarded credit for CLEP subject examinations in subject areas offered by college. However, subject tests in foreign languages granted credit only if they represent acheivement beyond that of previous high school or college preparation. **Support services:** Learning center, reduced course load, study skills assistance, tutoring, writing center.

Majors. Area/ethnic studies: American, German, Russian/Slavic. **Biology:** General. **Communications:** General. **Conservation:** Environmental studies. **Engineering:** Physics. **English:** British lit, creative writing. **Foreign languages:** Ancient Greek, classics, French, Latin, Spanish. **History:** General. **Interdisciplinary:** Museum. **Math:** General. **Philosophy/religion:** Philosophy, religion. **Physical sciences:** Chemistry, physics. **Psychology:** General. **Social sciences:** Economics, political science, sociology. **Visual/performing arts:** Art history/conservation, dance, dramatic, music history, music performance, music theory/composition, studio arts.

Most popular majors. Biology 12%, communications/journalism 8%, English 7%, history 8%, psychology 9%, social sciences 27%, visual/performing arts 10%.

Computing on campus. 154 workstations in dormitories, library, computer center, student center. Dormitories wired for high-speed internet access and linked to campus network. Commuter students can connect to campus network. Helpline, student web hosting, wireless network available.

Student life. Freshman orientation: Mandatory. Preregistration for classes offered. Program held 5 days before start of classes. **Policies:** Freshmen permitted cars on campus. **Housing:** Guaranteed on-campus for all undergraduates. $300 deposit, deadline 5/1. All students under 24 years of age required to live in college housing unless living with family. **Activities:** Choral groups, dance, drama, film society, literary magazine, music ensembles, radio station, student government, student newspaper, international relations and current affairs clubs, Young Democrats, College Republicans, Black Women's Alliance, women's organizations, Christian Fellowship, language clubs, volunteer service organizations.

Athletics. NCAA. **Intercollegiate:** Basketball W, equestrian W, field hockey W, soccer W, softball W, swimming W, tennis W, volleyball W. **Intramural:** Basketball W, softball W, table tennis W. **Team name:** Wildcats.

Student services. Adult student services, alcohol/substance abuse counseling, campus ministries, career counseling, student employment services, financial aid counseling, health services, minority student services, personal counseling, placement for graduates, women's services. **Physically disabled:** Services for visually, hearing impaired.

Contact. E-mail: admissions@rmwc.edu
Phone: (434) 947-8100 Toll-free number: (800) 745-7692
Fax: (434) 947-8996
Patricia LeDonne, Director of Admissions, Randolph-Macon Woman's College, 2500 Rivermont Avenue, Lynchburg, VA 24503-1526

Regent University

Virginia Beach, Virginia
www.regent.edu **CB code: 4452**

- Private 4-year university affiliated with interdenominational tradition
- Commuter campus in large city
- 982 degree-seeking undergraduates: 49% part-time, 68% women
- 3,081 degree-seeking graduate students
- SAT or ACT (ACT writing optional), application essay required

General. Founded in 1977. Regionally accredited. **Degrees:** 121 bachelor's awarded; master's, doctoral, first professional offered. **Calendar:** Semester, limited summer session. **Full-time faculty:** 150 total. **Part-time faculty:** 300 total.

Freshman class profile. 165 enrolled.

GPA 3.50 or higher:	30%	**GPA 2.0-2.99:**	36%
GPA 3.0-3.49:	23%	**End year in good standing:**	100%

Basis for selection. Homeschooled: Transcript of courses and grades required.

Application procedures. Admission: Closing date 8/14 (receipt date). $40 fee. Application may be submitted online. Admission notification on a rolling basis.

Academics. Special study options: Combined bachelor's/graduate degree, distance learning, double major, dual enrollment of high school students, study abroad, teacher certification program. **Credit/placement by examination:** CLEP. **Support services:** Remedial instruction, study skills assistance, tutoring, writing center.

Majors. Business: Business admin, international, organizational behavior. **Communications:** General. **Education:** General. **Philosophy/religion:** Religion. **Psychology:** General. **Social sciences:** Political science. **Theology:** Youth ministry.

Computing on campus. Online course registration, online library, helpline available.

Student life. Freshman orientation: Mandatory. **Policies:** Freshmen permitted cars on campus. **Activities:** Student government.

Athletics. Intramural: Football (non-tackle), soccer, volleyball.

Student services. Campus ministries, financial aid counseling.

Contact. E-mail: admissions@regent.edu
Phone: (757) 226-4127 Toll-free number: (800) 373-5504
Kristen Prescott, Director of Enrollment Management, Regent University, 1000 Regent University Drive, Virginia Beach, VA 23464-9800

Roanoke College

Salem, Virginia **CB member**
www.roanoke.edu **CB code: 5571**

- Private 4-year liberal arts college affiliated with Evangelical Lutheran Church in America
- Residential campus in large town
- 1,877 degree-seeking undergraduates: 3% part-time, 56% women, 4% African American, 2% Asian American, 2% Hispanic American, 1% Native American, 1% international
- 74% of applicants admitted
- SAT or ACT (ACT writing optional) required
- 65% graduate within 6 years; 20% enter graduate study

General. Founded in 1842. Regionally accredited. **Degrees:** 402 bachelor's awarded. **Location:** 7 miles from Roanoke. **Calendar:** Semester, extensive summer session. **Full-time faculty:** 133 total; 87% have terminal degrees, 8% minority, 47% women. **Part-time faculty:** 41 total; 32% have terminal degrees, 12% minority, 46% women. **Class size:** 57% < 20, 42% 20-39, 1% 40-49. **Special facilities:** Fine arts center with 3 galleries, multimedia classrooms, greenhouse, nuclear magnetic resonance equipment, center for community research, center for church and society, center for teaching and learning.

Freshman class profile. 3,016 applied, 2,220 admitted, 534 enrolled.

Mid 50% test scores			
SAT verbal:	520-610	Rank in top tenth:	23%
SAT math:	510-600	Return as sophomores:	85%
GPA 3.50 or higher:	34%	Out-of-state:	46%
GPA 3.0-3.49:	31%	Live on campus:	90%
GPA 2.0-2.99:	35%	International:	1%
Rank in top quarter:	50%	Fraternities:	15%
		Sororities:	19%

Basis for selection. School achievement record and class rank most important. Essay, interview recommended for all; audition recommended for music; portfolio recommended for graphic arts. **Learning Disabled:** Documentation of learning disability is needed for special services after enrollment.

High school preparation. 18 units required. Required and recommended units include English 4, mathematics 3, social studies 2, science 2 (laboratory 2), foreign language 4 and academic electives 5. Mathematics must include algebra II.

2005-2006 Annual costs. Tuition/fees: $23,453. Room/board: $7,295. Books/supplies: $850. Personal expenses: $750.

2005-2006 Financial aid. Need-based: 398 full-time freshmen applied for aid; 396 were judged to have need; 396 of these received aid. Average need met was 93%. Average scholarship/grant was $16,416; average loan $3,230. 69% of total undergraduate aid awarded as scholarships/grants, 31% as loans/jobs. **Non-need-based:** Awarded to 1,298 full-time undergraduates, including 468 freshmen. Scholarships awarded for academics, minority status, music/drama, religious affiliation.

Application procedures. Admission: Priority date 12/15; deadline 3/15 (postmark date). $30 fee, may be waived for applicants with need. Application may be submitted online. Admission notification 4/1. Must reply by May 1 or within 2 week(s) if notified thereafter. **Financial aid:** Priority date 3/1; no closing date. FAFSA required. Applicants notified on a rolling basis starting 11/1; must reply within 2 week(s) of notification.

Academics. Special study options: Accelerated study, combined bachelor's/graduate degree, cross-registration, double major, dual enrollment of high school students, ESL, honors, independent study, internships, liberal arts/career combination, study abroad, teacher certification program, Washington semester. **Credit/placement by examination:** AP, CLEP, IB, institutional tests. 27 credit hours maximum toward bachelor's degree. **Support services:** Learning center, reduced course load, study skills assistance, tutoring.

Majors. Biology: General, biochemistry. **Business:** Business admin. **Computer sciences:** General, computer science, information systems. **Conservation:** Environmental science, management/policy. **Education:** Physical. **Foreign languages:** French, Spanish. **Health:** Athletic training, clinical lab science. **History:** General. **Math:** General. **Parks/recreation:** Health/fitness. **Philosophy/religion:** Philosophy, religion. **Physical sciences:** Chemistry, physics. **Protective services:** Criminal justice. **Psychology:** General. **Social sciences:** Economics, international relations, political science, sociology. **Theology:** Theology. **Visual/performing arts:** Art, art history/conservation, dramatic.

Most popular majors. Business/marketing 22%, English 12%, history 11%, psychology 8%, social sciences 16%.

Computing on campus. 175 workstations in library, computer center, student center. Dormitories wired for high-speed internet access and linked to campus network. Commuter students can connect to campus network. Online course registration, online library, helpline, repair service, student web hosting, wireless network available.

Student life. Freshman orientation: Mandatory, $125 fee. Preregistration for classes offered. **Policies:** Freshmen permitted cars on campus. **Housing:** Guaranteed on-campus for freshmen. Coed dorms, single-sex dorms, apartments, fraternity/sorority housing, substance-free housing available. $250 nonrefundable deposit, deadline 5/1. Theme houses for a variety of student interests available. **Activities:** Bands, choral groups, dance, drama, film society, literary magazine, music ensembles, musical theater, radio station, student government, student newspaper, Alpha Phi Omega, Earthbound, Fellowship of Christian Athletes, Habitat for Humanity, Lutheran Student Movement, Model United Nations, Baptist Student Union, Shades of Maroon.

Athletics. NCAA. **Intercollegiate:** Baseball M, basketball, cross-country, field hockey W, golf M, lacrosse, soccer, softball W, tennis, track and field, volleyball W. **Intramural:** Badminton, baseball M, basketball, field hockey W, football (non-tackle), golf W, racquetball, soccer, softball, table tennis, tennis, volleyball. **Team name:** Maroons.

Student services. Adult student services, alcohol/substance abuse counseling, campus ministries, career counseling, student employment services, financial aid counseling, health services, minority student services, personal counseling, placement for graduates.

Contact. E-mail: admissions@roanoke.edu
Phone: (540) 375-2270 Toll-free number: (800) 388-2276
Fax: (540) 375-2267
Michael Maxey, Vice President of Admissions Services, Roanoke College, 221 College Lane, Salem, VA 24153-3794

St. Paul's College

Lawrenceville, Virginia — **CB member**
www.saintpauls.edu — **CB code: 5604**

- Private 4-year liberal arts college affiliated with Episcopal Church
- Residential campus in small town
- 690 full-time, degree-seeking undergraduates
- 72% of applicants admitted
- SAT or ACT (ACT writing optional) required

General. Founded in 1888. Regionally accredited. **Degrees:** 102 bachelor's awarded. **ROTC:** Army. **Location:** 80 miles from Richmond. **Calendar:** Semester, limited summer session. **Full-time faculty:** 26 total. **Part-time faculty:** 6 total. **Class size:** 73% < 20, 13% 20-39, 2% 40-49, 7% 50-99, 5% >100.

Freshman class profile. 534 applied, 383 admitted, 224 enrolled.

Mid 50% test scores			
SAT verbal:	300-410	Rank in top quarter:	1%
SAT math:	290-400	Rank in top tenth:	1%
ACT:	14-18	Out-of-state:	32%
		Live on campus:	89%

Basis for selection. School achievement record most important. School recommendations considered. Rank in top half of class important. 3.0 GPA recommended. Essay, interview recommended.

High school preparation. 10 units required. Required units include English 4, mathematics 2, social studies 2 and science 2.

2005-2006 Annual costs. Tuition/fees: $10,640. Room/board: $5,530. Books/supplies: $500. Personal expenses: $700.

2004-2005 Financial aid. Need-based: 51% of total undergraduate aid awarded as scholarships/grants, 49% as loans/jobs. **Non-need-based:** Scholarships awarded for academics, athletics, leadership.

Application procedures. Admission: No deadline. $20 fee, may be waived for applicants with need. Application may be submitted online. Admission notification on a rolling basis. Must reply by May 1 or within 2 week(s) if notified thereafter. **Financial aid:** No deadline. FAFSA required. Applicants notified on a rolling basis starting 1/15; must reply by 7/1 or within 4 week(s) of notification.

Academics. Special study options: Accelerated study, cooperative education, cross-registration, double major, exchange student, honors, independent study, internships, student-designed major, teacher certification program. Organizational Management Program for adults 25 and older. **Credit/placement by examination:** AP, CLEP, institutional tests. 24 credit hours maximum toward bachelor's degree. **Support services:** Learning center, pre-admission summer program, reduced course load, remedial instruction, tutoring.

Majors. Biology: General, marine. **Business:** Accounting, administrative services, business admin, management information systems, operations. **Computer sciences:** General. **Conservation:** General. **Education:** Business. **English:** English lit. **Math:** General. **Philosophy/religion:** Philosophy, religion. **Protective services:** Criminal justice. **Social sciences:** General, political science, sociology.

Most popular majors. Business/marketing 64%, liberal arts 8%, security/protective services 6%, social sciences 10%.

Computing on campus. 100 workstations in library, computer center, student center. Dormitories wired for high-speed internet access and linked to campus network. Commuter students can connect to campus network. Helpline, repair service, wireless network available.

Student life. Freshman orientation: Mandatory. Preregistration for classes offered. **Policies:** Freshmen permitted cars on campus. **Housing:** Single-sex dorms available. $50 deposit. **Activities:** Choral groups, dance, student government, Altar Guild, veterans club, Canterbury club, NAACP, single parent support system.

Athletics. NCAA. **Intercollegiate:** Baseball M, basketball, bowling, cross-country, football (tackle) M, golf, softball W, tennis, track and field, volleyball W. **Intramural:** Basketball, softball, volleyball. **Team name:** Tigers.

Student services. Adult student services, career counseling, student employment services, financial aid counseling, health services, on-campus daycare, personal counseling, placement for graduates, veterans' counselor.

Contact. E-mail: admissions@saintpauls.edu
Phone: (434) 848-3111 Toll-free number: (800) 678-7071
Fax: (434) 848-1846
Rosemary Lewis, Director of Admissions, St. Paul's College, 115 College Drive, Lawrenceville, VA 23868

Shenandoah University

Winchester, Virginia — **CB member**
www.su.edu — **CB code: 5613**

- Private 4-year university affiliated with United Methodist Church
- Commuter campus in small city
- 1,562 degree-seeking undergraduates: 3% part-time, 60% women, 2% African American, 1% Asian American, 4% international
- 1,227 degree-seeking graduate students
- 70% of applicants admitted
- SAT or ACT (ACT writing optional) required
- 46% graduate within 6 years; 42% enter graduate study

General. Founded in 1875. Regionally accredited. **Degrees:** 268 bachelor's, 2 associate awarded; master's, doctoral, first professional offered. **Location:** 100 miles from Baltimore, 75 miles from Washington, DC. **Calendar:** Differs by program, limited summer session. **Full-time faculty:** 181 total; 80% have terminal degrees, 7% minority, 46% women. **Part-time faculty:** 170 total; 29% have terminal degrees, 5% minority, 65% women. **Class size:** 69% < 20, 28% 20-39, 2% 40-49, less than 1% 50-99. **Special facilities:** Arts and media centers, conservatory, recording studio.

Freshman class profile. 1,479 applied, 1,036 admitted, 370 enrolled.

Mid 50% test scores		**Rank in top quarter:**	37%
SAT verbal:	400-640	**Rank in top tenth:**	15%
SAT math:	430-580	**End year in good standing:**	89%
ACT:	20-26	**Return as sophomores:**	70%
GPA 3.50 or higher:	33%	**Out-of-state:**	45%
GPA 3.0-3.49:	28%	**Live on campus:**	81%
GPA 2.0-2.99:	39%	**International:**	4%

Basis for selection. Applicants are evaluated on the basis of GPA and standardized test scores along with 1 recommendation. Conservatory students must pass an audition. In-house English proficiency tests administered. Interview recommended for all; audition required for dance, music, and theatre programs. **Homeschooled:** May request a GED score.

High school preparation. 15 units required. Required and recommended units include English 4, mathematics 3-4, social studies 2-4, history 2-4, science 2-4 (laboratory 1), foreign language 2-3 and academic electives 2-4. 2 history or social studies required, 4 recommended.

2005-2006 Annual costs. Tuition/fees: $20,050. Room/board: $7,550. Books/supplies: $1,000. Personal expenses: $1,500.

2004-2005 Financial aid. Need-based: 245 full-time freshmen applied for aid; 245 were judged to have need; 245 of these received aid. Average need met was 84%. Average scholarship/grant was $4,897; average loan $3,677. 36% of total undergraduate aid awarded as scholarships/grants, 64% as loans/jobs. **Non-need-based:** Awarded to 639 full-time undergraduates, including 151 freshmen. Scholarships awarded for academics, job skills, music/drama, religious affiliation, state residency.

Application procedures. Admission: Priority date 3/1; deadline 8/29 (postmark date). $30 fee, may be waived for applicants with need. Application may be submitted online. Admission notification on a rolling basis beginning on or about 10/1. Must reply by May 1 or within 2 week(s) if notified thereafter. **Financial aid:** Priority date 2/15; no closing date. FAFSA required. Applicants notified on a rolling basis starting 3/15; must reply within 2 week(s) of notification.

Academics. Special study options: Accelerated study, combined bachelor's/graduate degree, cooperative education, distance learning, double major, ESL, independent study, internships, liberal arts/career combination, student-designed major, study abroad, teacher certification program, weekend college. **Credit/placement by examination:** AP, CLEP, IB, SAT, ACT, institutional tests. 15 credit hours maximum toward associate degree, 15 toward bachelor's. AP placement grade may be higher for exams taken in student's major. CEEB, CLEP, academic department exams used. **Support services:** Learning center, reduced course load, remedial instruction, study skills assistance, tutoring, writing center.

Majors. Area/ethnic studies: American. **Biology:** General. **Business:** Business admin. **Communications:** General. **Conservation:** General. **Education:** Drama/dance, ESL, music, physical. **English:** English lit. **Foreign languages:** Spanish. **Health:** Music therapy, nursing (RN), respiratory therapy technology. **History:** General. **Liberal arts:** Arts/sciences. **Math:** General. **Philosophy/religion:** Religion. **Physical sciences:** Chemistry. **Protective services:** Law enforcement admin. **Psychology:** General. **Public administration:** General. **Social sciences:** Sociology. **Visual/performing arts:** General, acting, arts management, dance, dramatic, music performance, music theory/composition, piano/organ, theater design.

Most popular majors. Biology 6%, business/marketing 17%, education 15%, health sciences 13%, visual/performing arts 29%.

Computing on campus. 175 workstations in dormitories, library, computer center, student center. Dormitories wired for high-speed internet access and linked to campus network. Commuter students can connect to campus network. Online course registration, online library, helpline, repair service, wireless network available.

Student life. Freshman orientation: Mandatory. Preregistration for classes offered. **Policies:** Freshmen permitted cars on campus. **Housing:** Guaranteed on-campus for freshmen. Coed dorms, special housing for disabled, substance-free housing available. $100 partly refundable deposit, deadline 7/1. **Activities:** Bands, choral groups, dance, drama, literary magazine, music ensembles, musical theater, opera, radio station, student government, student newspaper, symphony orchestra, TV station, Circle K, Alpha Chi Honor Society, Alpha Lambda Delta, freshman honor society, nursing honor society, Christian Pharmacists Fellowship International, Omicron Delta Kappa, College Democrats, College Republicans.

Athletics. NCAA. **Intercollegiate:** Baseball M, basketball, cross-country, field hockey W, football (tackle) M, golf M, lacrosse, soccer, softball W, tennis, volleyball W. **Intramural:** Basketball, football (non-tackle), soccer, table tennis, tennis, volleyball. **Team name:** Hornets.

Student services. Adult student services, alcohol/substance abuse counseling, campus ministries, career counseling, student employment services, financial aid counseling, health services, minority student services, personal counseling, placement for graduates, veterans' counselor. **Physically disabled:** Services for visually, speech, hearing impaired.

Contact. E-mail: admit@su.edu
Phone: (540) 665-4581 Toll-free number: (800) 432-2266
Fax: (540) 665-4627
David Anthony, Dean of Admissions, Shenandoah University, 1460 University Drive, Winchester, VA 22601-5195

Southern Virginia University

Buena Vista, Virginia
www.southernvirginia.edu — **CB member**

- Private 4-year liberal arts college
- Small town

General. Calendar: Semester.

Annual costs/financial aid. Tuition/fees (projected): $15,350.

Contact. Phone: (540) 261-2756
One University Hill Drive, Buena Vista, VA 24416

Stratford University: Falls Church

Falls Church, Virginia
www.stratford.edu — **CB code: 3778**

- For-profit 4-year university

General. Accredited by ACICS. **Calendar:** Quarter.

Contact. Phone: (703) 821-8570
Director of Admissions, 7777 Leesburg Pike, Falls Church, VA 22043

Stratford University: Woodbridge

Woodbridge, Virginia
www.stratford.edu

- For-profit 4-year university

General. Accredited by ACICS. **Calendar:** Quarter.

Contact. Phone: (703) 897-1982
Director of Admissions, 13576 Minnieville Road, Woodbridge, VA 22192

Sweet Briar College

Sweet Briar, Virginia **CB member**
www.sbc.edu **CB code: 5634**

- Private 4-year liberal arts college for women
- Residential campus in rural community
- 556 degree-seeking undergraduates: 2% part-time, 100% women, 3% African American, 2% Asian American, 2% Hispanic American, 1% Native American, 2% international
- 13 degree-seeking graduate students
- 79% of applicants admitted
- SAT or ACT with writing, application essay required
- 67% graduate within 6 years

General. Founded in 1901. Regionally accredited. Studio art building houses 4 large studios for painting, drawing and printmaking, a photo studio and darkroom, and faculty offices. **Degrees:** 126 bachelor's awarded; master's offered. **Location:** 12 miles from Lynchburg, 167 miles from Washington, DC. **Calendar:** Semester, limited summer session. **Full-time faculty:** 64 total; 100% have terminal degrees, 2% minority, 48% women. **Part-time faculty:** 35 total; 43% have terminal degrees, 3% minority, 60% women. **Class size:** 91% < 20, 9% 20-39. **Special facilities:** Fine arts center, museum, indoor and outdoor riding facilities, 3 nature sanctuaries, college-run nursery school and kindergarten for student teaching, observatory, Environmental Education and Nature Center.

Freshman class profile. 623 applied, 495 admitted, 182 enrolled.

Mid 50% test scores		**Rank in top quarter:**	64%
SAT verbal:	530-640	**Rank in top tenth:**	25%
SAT math:	500-590	**End year in good standing:**	80%
ACT:	22-27	**Return as sophomores:**	75%
GPA 3.50 or higher:	54%	**Out-of-state:**	53%
GPA 3.0-3.49:	27%	**Live on campus:**	95%
GPA 2.0-2.99:	19%	**International:**	1%

Basis for selection. High school curriculum and grades are of primary importance, followed by school and teacher recommendations, test scores, and writing ability as demonstrated by essay or personal statement. Interview, extracurricular activities, and personal characteristics are also considered. **Learning Disabled:** If an applicant believes that an accommodated admission review is warranted, the applicant must initiate the process. The applicant must submit a written request for an accommodated admissions review to the Office of Admissions and enclose with that request the appropriate documentation.

High school preparation. College-preparatory program required. 16 units required; 20 recommended. Required and recommended units include English 4, mathematics 3-4, social studies 3-4, science 3-4 (laboratory 2-3) and foreign language 2-4. Mathematics preparation must be at least through Algebra II. Foreign language must include 2 consecutive years of same language.

2006-2007 Annual costs. Tuition/fees: $23,540. Room/board: $9,480. Books/supplies: $600. Personal expenses: $750.

2005-2006 Financial aid. **Need-based:** 123 full-time freshmen applied for aid; 123 were judged to have need; 122 of these received aid. Average need met was 36%. Average scholarship/grant was $14,320; average loan $3,848. 87% of total undergraduate aid awarded as scholarships/grants, 13% as loans/jobs. **Non-need-based:** Awarded to 492 full-time undergraduates, including 170 freshmen. Scholarships awarded for academics, art, leadership, music/drama, state residency.

Application procedures. **Admission:** Priority date 2/1; deadline 2/1 (postmark date). $40 fee, may be waived for applicants with need. Application may be submitted online. Admission notification 3/15. Must reply by 5/1. **Financial aid:** Priority date 3/1; no closing date. FAFSA required. Applicants notified on a rolling basis starting 3/1; must reply by 5/1 or within 2 week(s) of notification.

Academics. General Education Program: students complete requirements that involve communication and quantitative reasoning skills; rationale for broad liberal arts background; emphasis on internships; regular progress self-assessments. Summer research program provides opportunities for high-level work with faculty. **Special study options:** Accelerated study, combined bachelor's/graduate degree, cross-registration, double major, dual enrollment of high school students, exchange student, honors, independent study, internships, liberal arts/career combination, student-designed major, study abroad, teacher certification program, Washington semester. **Credit/placement by examination:** AP, CLEP, IB, institutional tests. Exemption from one or more of the degree requirements and/or admission to advanced courses may be granted on the basis of Advanced Placement Tests, the International Baccalaureate (IB) Program, transfer credit, or, in some cases, placement tests taken at Sweet Briar. Any student who has not participated in the Advanced Placement or International Baccalaureate programs, but believes she is capable of doing the work of an advance course or should be exempted from a degree requirement, may so indicate to the Dean. Placement tests and conferences with department chairs will be arranged to meet the needs of such students. **Support services:** Learning center, study skills assistance, tutoring, writing center.

Majors. **Area/ethnic studies:** German, Italian. **Biology:** General, biochemistry, molecular. **Business:** General. **Computer sciences:** Computer science. **Conservation:** Environmental science, environmental studies. **Engineering:** Science. **Engineering technology:** Industrial management. **English:** Creative writing, English lit. **Foreign languages:** General, classics, French, German, Spanish. **History:** General. **Liberal arts:** Arts/sciences. **Math:** General. **Philosophy/religion:** Philosophy, religion. **Physical sciences:** Chemistry, physics, theoretical physics. **Psychology:** General. **Social sciences:** Anthropology, economics, international relations, political science, sociology. **Visual/performing arts:** Art history/conservation, dance, dramatic, studio arts.

Most popular majors. Biology 6%, English 9%, foreign language 7%, psychology 11%, social sciences 25%, visual/performing arts 10%.

Computing on campus. 117 workstations in library, computer center. Dormitories wired for high-speed internet access and linked to campus network. Commuter students can connect to campus network. Online course registration, online library, helpline, repair service, student web hosting, wireless network available.

Student life. **Freshman orientation:** Mandatory. Preregistration for classes offered. SBC's formal Orientation period, begins on a Saturday in August through the following Thursday; which is the official beginning of classes. Students register for classes, tour the library, become familiar with academic standards and pledge the Honor Code. First Year Advisors (FYAs) meet new students at check-in and act as guides for Orientation. **Policies:** Self-governing student body; honor system observed. Freshmen permitted cars on campus. **Housing:** Guaranteed on-campus for all undergraduates. Substance-free housing available. **Activities:** Choral groups, dance, drama, film society, literary magazine, music ensembles, musical theater, radio station, student government, student newspaper, symphony orchestra, TV station, Campus Christian Fellowship, Campus Spirituality Coalition, College Republicans, College Democrats, Circle K, Habitat for Humanity, Student Environmental Organization, Vixen PAWS, Newman Club.

Athletics. NCAA. **Intercollegiate:** Field hockey W, lacrosse W, soccer W, softball W, swimming W, tennis W, volleyball W. **Team name:** Vixens.

Student services. Alcohol/substance abuse counseling, campus ministries, career counseling, student employment services, financial aid counseling, health services, personal counseling, placement for graduates, women's services. **Physically disabled:** Services for hearing impaired.

Contact. E-mail: admissions@sbc.edu
Phone: (434) 381-6142 Toll-free number: (800) 381-6142
Fax: (434) 381-6152
Ken Huus, Dean of Admissions, Sweet Briar College, PO Box B, Sweet Briar, VA 24595

University of Management and Technology

Arlington, Virginia
www.umtweb.edu

- For-profit 4-year business and engineering college
- Very large city

General. Accredited by DETC. **Calendar:** Continuous.

Annual costs/financial aid. Tuition/fees (projected): $11,940.

Contact. Phone: (703) 516-0035
1901 N Fort Myer Drive/Suite 700, Arlington, VA 22209

University of Mary Washington

Fredericksburg, Virginia **CB member**
www.umw.edu **CB code: 5398**

- Public 4-year liberal arts college
- Residential campus in small city
- 3,951 degree-seeking undergraduates: 11% part-time, 66% women, 4% African American, 5% Asian American, 3% Hispanic American
- 555 degree-seeking graduate students
- 64% of applicants admitted
- SAT or ACT (ACT writing optional), application essay required
- 75% graduate within 6 years; 26% enter graduate study

General. Founded in 1908. Regionally accredited. **Degrees:** 878 bachelor's awarded; master's offered. **Location:** 50 miles from Richmond, 50 miles from Washington, DC. **Calendar:** Semester, limited summer session. **Full-time faculty:** 231 total; 78% have terminal degrees, 10% minority, 41% women. **Part-time faculty:** 107 total; 10% minority, 51% women. **Class size:** 44% < 20, 52% 20-39, 3% 40-49, less than 1% 50-99. **Special facilities:** Center for Historic Preservation, computer access center for visually impaired, campus-wide fiber-optic network, wireless in all academic and administrative buildings, James Monroe Museum, Center for Asian Studies.

Freshman class profile. 4,635 applied, 2,979 admitted, 914 enrolled.

Mid 50% test scores			
SAT verbal:	580-670	Rank in top quarter:	83%
SAT math:	560-640	Rank in top tenth:	38%
ACT:	25-29	End year in good standing:	87%
GPA 3.50 or higher:	69%	Return as sophomores:	86%
GPA 3.0-3.49:	27%	Out-of-state:	36%
GPA 2.0-2.99:	4%	Live on campus:	97%

Basis for selection. Rigor of high school program most important, followed by GPA, standardized test scores, activities, essays, recommendations. SAT Subject Tests recommended. SAT Subject Tests recommended including mathematics. **Homeschooled:** Students are strongly advised to take 3 SAT Subject Tests: math and two other subject areas of their choice.

High school preparation. Required and recommended units include English 4, mathematics 3-4, social studies 2, history 1-2, science 3-4 (laboratory 3-4) and foreign language 2-4.

2005-2006 Annual costs. Tuition/fees: $5,634; $14,776 out-of-state. Room/board: $7,134. Books/supplies: $900. Personal expenses: $1,678.

2005-2006 Financial aid. Need-based: 610 full-time freshmen applied for aid; 392 were judged to have need; 392 of these received aid. Average need met was 60%. Average scholarship/grant was $2,825; average loan $2,515. 46% of total undergraduate aid awarded as scholarships/grants, 54% as loans/jobs. **Non-need-based:** Awarded to 680 full-time undergraduates, including 275 freshmen. Scholarships awarded for academics, art, leadership, minority status, music/drama, state residency.

Application procedures. Admission: Priority date 1/15; deadline 2/1 (postmark date). $45 fee, may be waived for applicants with need. Application may be submitted online. Admission notification 4/1. Must reply by 5/1. Applicants for regular admission who complete application by January 15 eligible for honor admission (early notification). **Financial aid:** Priority date 3/1; no closing date. FAFSA required. Applicants notified by 4/15; must reply by 5/1 or within 2 week(s) of notification.

Academics. College provides grants for undergraduate research program enabling students to work individually with faculty members. **Special study options:** Combined bachelor's/graduate degree, double major, independent study, internships, semester at sea, student-designed major, study abroad, teacher certification program, Washington semester. **Credit/placement by examination:** AP, CLEP, IB, institutional tests. Credit from CLEP scores applicable to adult degree program only. **Support services:** Pre-admission summer program, study skills assistance, tutoring, writing center.

Majors. Area/ethnic studies: American. **Biology:** General. **Business:** Business admin. **Computer sciences:** Computer science. **Conservation:** General. **Foreign languages:** Classics, French, German, Latin, Spanish. **History:** General. **Interdisciplinary:** Historic preservation. **Math:** General. **Philosophy/religion:** Philosophy, religion. **Physical sciences:** Chemistry, geology, physics. **Psychology:** General. **Social sciences:** Anthropology, economics, geography, international relations, political science, sociology. **Visual/performing arts:** Art history/conservation, dramatic, music history, music performance, studio arts.

Most popular majors. Biology 8%, business/marketing 14%, English 10%, interdisciplinary studies 6%, liberal arts 9%, psychology 9%, social sciences 18%.

Computing on campus. 236 workstations in library, computer center, student center. Dormitories wired for high-speed internet access and linked to campus network. Commuter students can connect to campus network. Online course registration, online library, helpline, repair service, wireless network available.

Student life. Freshman orientation: Mandatory. Preregistration for classes offered. 1-day preview held in July for freshmen and transfer students. 5-day freshmen/transfer orientation held in August prior to start of classes. **Policies:** Honor system. **Housing:** Guaranteed on-campus for freshmen. Coed dorms, single-sex dorms, special housing for disabled, apartments, substance-free housing available. $250 deposit, deadline 5/1. Special interest housing options include foreign language and leadership/service living areas. Guaranteed on-campus housing for freshmen and sophomores. **Activities:** Bands, choral groups, dance, drama, film society, literary magazine, music ensembles, musical theater, radio station, student government, student newspaper, symphony orchestra, Amnesty International, Baptist Student Union, Catholic Student Union, Hillel, Hispanic student association, model UN, Asian student association, Young Democrats, Campus Christian Community, College Republicans.

Athletics. NCAA. **Intercollegiate:** Baseball M, basketball, cross-country, equestrian, field hockey W, lacrosse, rowing (crew), soccer, softball W, swimming, tennis, track and field, volleyball W. **Intramural:** Basketball, football (non-tackle) M, golf, ice hockey, racquetball, soccer, softball, volleyball, water polo. **Team name:** Eagles.

Student services. Adult student services, campus ministries, career counseling, student employment services, financial aid counseling, health services, minority student services, personal counseling, placement for graduates, veterans' counselor, women's services. **Physically disabled:** Services for visually, speech, hearing impaired.

Contact. E-mail: admit@umw.edu
Phone: (540) 654-2000 Toll-free number: (800) 468-5614
Fax: (540) 654-1857
Martin Wilder, Vice-President for Enrollment, University of Mary Washington, 1301 College Avenue, Fredericksburg, VA 22401-5358

University of Northern Virginia

Manassas, Virginia
www.unva.edu

- For-profit 4-year university
- Large town
- 45 degree-seeking undergraduates
- 250 graduate students

General. Accredited by ACICS. Branch campuses in London, Hong Kong, Prague and Cyprus. **Location:** 25 miles from Washington, DC. **Calendar:** Quadmester. Extensive summer session. **Full-time faculty:** 7 total; 43% have terminal degrees, 57% minority. **Part-time faculty:** 30 total; 30% have terminal degrees, 83% minority, 3% women. **Class size:** 100% < 20.

2005-2006 Annual costs. Books/supplies: $920.

Academics. Special study options: Accelerated study, combined bachelor's/graduate degree, cooperative education, cross-registration, distance learning, double major, ESL, exchange student, independent study, internships, study abroad, teacher certification program. **Credit/placement by examination:** AP, CLEP. **Support services:** Learning center, reduced course load, tutoring, writing center.

Majors. Business: Business admin, international, marketing. **Computer sciences:** General, information technology.

Computing on campus. PC or laptop required. Commuter students can connect to campus network. Online library, helpline, repair service, student web hosting, wireless network available.

Contact. Phone: (703) 392-0771 ext. 2033 Fax: (703) 392-0756
Robert Frantz, Director of Admissions, University of Northern Virginia, 10021 Balls Ford Road, Manassas, VA 20109

University of Richmond

University of Richmond, Virginia **CB member**
www.richmond.edu **CB code: 5569**

- Private 4-year university and liberal arts college
- Residential campus in very large city

- 2,853 degree-seeking undergraduates: 1% part-time, 51% women, 4% African American, 3% Asian American, 2% Hispanic American, 4% international
- 763 degree-seeking graduate students
- 47% of applicants admitted
- SAT or ACT (ACT writing optional), application essay required
- 84% graduate within 6 years

General. Founded in 1830. Regionally accredited. **Degrees:** 729 bachelor's awarded; master's, first professional offered. **ROTC:** Army. **Location:** 6 miles from Richmond, 100 miles from Washington, DC. **Calendar:** Semester, limited summer session. **Full-time faculty:** 262 total; 90% have terminal degrees, 11% minority, 38% women. **Part-time faculty:** 58 total; 76% have terminal degrees, 9% minority, 50% women. **Class size:** 64% < 20, 35% 20-39, less than 1% 40-49, less than 1% 50-99, less than 1% >100. **Special facilities:** Greenhouse, electron microscope, radionuclide complex, museum-quality art gallery, gem, rock, and mineral gallery, neuroscience research laboratory, music technology laboratory.

Freshman class profile. 5,778 applied, 2,743 admitted, 772 enrolled.

Mid 50% test scores			
SAT verbal:	610-690	Rank in top quarter:	88%
SAT math:	630-700	Rank in top tenth:	58%
ACT:	26-30	Return as sophomores:	93%
GPA 3.50 or higher:	39%	Out-of-state:	87%
GPA 3.0-3.49:	48%	Live on campus:	99%
GPA 2.0-2.99:	13%	International:	4%

Basis for selection. Students are evaluated on high school transcript, test scores, essay, personal qualities and letter of reference. Campus visits recommended; interviews not offered. SAT Subject Tests in foreign languages may be used for placement, but are not required. The January SAT and SAT Subject Test date and the February ACT test date are the last acceptable testing dates for fall admission. Character statement required. **Homeschooled:** Interview conducted by admissions officer. Applicant must submit narrative description of home-schooling environment. Two SAT Subject Tests in history and natural science strongly recommended. SAT and SAT Subject Tests or ACT required of all applicants.

High school preparation. College-preparatory program recommended. 16 units required; 20 recommended. Required and recommended units include English 4, mathematics 3-4, history 2-4, science 2-4 (laboratory 2-4) and foreign language 2-4.

2006-2007 Annual costs. Tuition/fees: $36,550. Room/board: $6,060. Books/supplies: $1,050.

2005-2006 Financial aid. Need-based: Average need met was 100%. Average scholarship/grant was $23,594; average loan $2,829. 89% of total undergraduate aid awarded as scholarships/grants, 11% as loans/jobs. **Non-need-based:** Scholarships awarded for academics, art, athletics, leadership, minority status, music/drama, ROTC, state residency. **Additional information:** Interview required for University, Oldham, Ethyl, and CIGNA. Undergraduate research grants available.

Application procedures. Admission: Closing date 1/15 (postmark date). $50 fee, may be waived for applicants with need. Application may be submitted online. Admission notification 4/1. Must reply by 5/1. Must reply by May 1 or within 2 week(s) if notified thereafter. **Financial aid:** Closing date 2/25. FAFSA, institutional form required. Applicants notified by 4/1; must reply by 5/1 or within 4 week(s) of notification.

Academics. New minors: Chinese, Italian studies, Japanese, Jewish studies; new concentration: fine arts management. **Special study options:** Accelerated study, cross-registration, distance learning, double major, ESL, exchange student, honors, independent study, internships, student-designed major, study abroad, teacher certification program, Washington semester. 86 different programs to over 30 different countries; English as a Second Language (ESL) English Language Institute held during the summer for enrolling International students only. **Credit/placement by examination:** AP, CLEP, IB, institutional tests. 30 credit hours maximum toward bachelor's degree. School of Continuing Studies follows different guidelines and credit granting procedures. **Support services:** Learning center, study skills assistance, tutoring, writing center.

Majors. Area/ethnic studies: American, women's. **Biology:** General, biochemistry, molecular. **Business:** Accounting, business admin. **Communications:** Journalism. **Computer sciences:** Computer science. **Education:** Early childhood, middle, secondary. **English:** Speech/rhetoric. **Foreign languages:** Ancient Greek, classics, French, German, Latin, Spanish. **History:** General. **Interdisciplinary:** Math/computer science. **Math:** General. **Philosophy/religion:** Philosophy, religion. **Physical sciences:** Chemistry, physics. **Protective services:** Criminal justice. **Psychology:** General. **Social sciences:** Economics, political science, sociology, urban studies. **Visual/performing arts:** Art history/conservation, dramatic, music history, music performance, music theory/composition, studio arts.

Most popular majors. Biology 7%, business/marketing 24%, English 8%, foreign language 6%, history 7%, psychology 6%, social sciences 19%.

Computing on campus. 600 workstations in dormitories, library, computer center. Dormitories wired for high-speed internet access and linked to campus network. Commuter students can connect to campus network. Online course registration, helpline, repair service, student web hosting, wireless network available.

Student life. Freshman orientation: Mandatory. 3 days before upperclassmen arrive in the fall. **Policies:** Undergraduate students become members of residential colleges: Richmond College (men) and Westhampton College (women). Classes and extracurricular activities co-educational. Separate student government, honor/judicial councils and deans. Freshmen permitted cars on campus. **Housing:** Single-sex dorms, special housing for disabled, apartments, substance-free housing available. $250 nonrefundable deposit, deadline 5/1. Limited university apartments available for foreign language students. 2 houses available for students interested in an international community. Substance-free housing available. **Activities:** Bands, choral groups, dance, drama, literary magazine, music ensembles, musical theater, radio station, student government, student newspaper, symphony orchestra, over 200 organizations.

Athletics. NCAA. **Intercollegiate:** Baseball M, basketball, cross-country, diving W, field hockey W, football (tackle) M, golf, lacrosse W, soccer, swimming W, tennis, track and field. **Intramural:** Badminton, basketball, golf, handball, racquetball, soccer, softball, squash, swimming, synchronized swimming W, table tennis, tennis, volleyball, water polo M, wrestling M. **Team name:** Spiders.

Student services. Alcohol/substance abuse counseling, campus ministries, career counseling, student employment services, financial aid counseling, health services, minority student services, personal counseling, placement for graduates, veterans' counselor. **Physically disabled:** Services for visually, speech, hearing impaired.

Contact. E-mail: admissions@richmond.edu
Phone: (804) 289-8640 Toll-free number: (800) 700-1662
Fax: (804) 289-6003
Pamela Spence, Dean of Admissions, University of Richmond, 28 Westhampton Way, University of Richmond, VA 23173

University of Virginia

Charlottesville, Virginia — **CB member**
www.virginia.edu — **CB code: 5820**

- Public 4-year university
- Residential campus in small city
- 13,387 degree-seeking undergraduates: 2% part-time, 54% women, 9% African American, 11% Asian American, 4% Hispanic American, 4% international
- 6,322 degree-seeking graduate students
- 38% of applicants admitted
- SAT or ACT with writing, application essay required
- 93% graduate within 6 years

General. Founded in 1819. Regionally accredited. **Degrees:** 3,353 bachelor's awarded; master's, doctoral, first professional offered. **ROTC:** Army, Navy, Air Force. **Location:** 70 miles of Richmond, 120 miles of Washington, DC. **Calendar:** Semester, extensive summer session. **Full-time faculty:** 1,193 total; 90% have terminal degrees, 10% minority, 32% women. **Part-time faculty:** 137 total; 50% have terminal degrees, 6% minority, 47% women. **Class size:** 47% < 20, 32% 20-39, 5% 40-49, 9% 50-99, 7% >100. **Special facilities:** Art museum, observatory, center for biological timing.

Freshman class profile. 15,657 applied, 5,898 admitted, 3,112 enrolled.

Mid 50% test scores			
SAT verbal:	600-710	Rank in top quarter:	97%
SAT math:	620-720	Rank in top tenth:	86%
ACT:	25-30	End year in good standing:	99%
GPA 3.50 or higher:	94%	Return as sophomores:	97%
GPA 3.0-3.49:	5%	Out-of-state:	29%
GPA 2.0-2.99:	1%	Live on campus:	100%
		International:	5%

Basis for selection. School achievement record, class rank, test scores most important. Extracurricular activities and interests, quality of writing, recommendation also important. Special consideration for minorities and children of alumni. School diploma may be waived for especially qualified applicants. Following international tests accepted: International Baccalaureate, German Abitur, British AICE, French Baccalaureate, Swiss Federal Maturity Certificate. SAT Subject Tests recommended. **Homeschooled:** Academic writing samples, community involvement, interview, recommendations, at least 3 SAT Subject Tests required.

High school preparation. 16 units required. Required and recommended units include English 4, mathematics 4-5, social studies 1-4, science 2-4 and foreign language 2-5. 3 science (1 chemistry, 1 physics) required for engineering and applied science programs.

2005-2006 Annual costs. Tuition/fees: $7,133; $23,877 out-of-state. Room/board: $6,389.

2005-2006 Financial aid. Need-based: 1,652 full-time freshmen applied for aid; 737 were judged to have need; 737 of these received aid. Average need met was 100%. Average scholarship/grant was $11,886; average loan $3,828. 71% of total undergraduate aid awarded as scholarships/grants, 29% as loans/jobs. **Non-need-based:** Awarded to 2,506 full-time undergraduates, including 662 freshmen. Scholarships awarded for academics, athletics, leadership, minority status, state residency.

Application procedures. Admission: Closing date 1/2 (postmark date). $60 fee, may be waived for applicants with need. Application may be submitted online. Admission notification 4/1. Must reply by May 1 or within 2 week(s) if notified thereafter. **Financial aid:** Priority date 3/1; no closing date. FAFSA, institutional form required. Applicants notified by 4/5; must reply by 5/1.

Academics. Special study options: Accelerated study, combined bachelor's/graduate degree, cooperative education, double major, ESL, honors, independent study, internships, liberal arts/career combination, student-designed major, study abroad, teacher certification program. Echols and Rodman Scholar programs for highest-achieving high school students. **Credit/placement by examination:** AP, CLEP, IB, institutional tests. **Support services:** Learning center, pre-admission summer program, reduced course load, study skills assistance, tutoring, writing center.

Majors. Architecture: Architecture, history/criticism, urban/community planning. **Area/ethnic studies:** African-American, Latin American. **Biology:** General. **Business:** General. **Computer sciences:** General. **Conservation:** Environmental science. **Education:** Physical. **Engineering:** General, aerospace, chemical, civil, computer, electrical, mechanical, systems. **English:** English lit. **Foreign languages:** Classics, comparative lit, French, German, Italian, Slavic, Spanish. **Health:** Audiology/speech pathology, nursing (RN). **History:** General. **Liberal arts:** Arts/sciences. **Math:** General, applied. **Philosophy/religion:** Philosophy, religion. **Physical sciences:** Astronomy, chemistry, physics. **Psychology:** General. **Social sciences:** Anthropology, economics, international relations, political science, sociology. **Visual/performing arts:** Art, dramatic.

Most popular majors. Business/marketing 8%, engineering/engineering technologies 9%, English 7%, history 6%, liberal arts 6%, psychology 8%, social sciences 25%.

Computing on campus. 2,050 workstations in dormitories, library, computer center. Dormitories wired for high-speed internet access and linked to campus network. Commuter students can connect to campus network. Online course registration, online library, helpline, repair service, student web hosting, wireless network available.

Student life. Freshman orientation: Mandatory, $185 fee. Preregistration for classes offered. 2-day program held in July; August session held for international students. **Housing:** Guaranteed on-campus for freshmen. Coed dorms, apartments, fraternity/sorority housing available. French, German, Russian and Spanish language houses, 3 residential colleges available. **Activities:** Bands, choral groups, dance, drama, film society, literary magazine, music ensembles, musical theater, opera, radio station, student government, student newspaper, symphony orchestra, TV station, community service group, Black Student Alliance, general clubs and religious organizations, political organizations, service fraternities and sororities, debating union.

Athletics. NCAA. **Intercollegiate:** Baseball M, basketball, cross-country, diving, field hockey W, football (tackle) M, golf, lacrosse, rowing (crew) W, soccer, softball W, swimming, tennis, track and field, volleyball W, wrestling M. **Intramural:** Basketball, field hockey W, football (non-tackle), golf, racquetball, rowing (crew), soccer, softball, tennis, volleyball, water polo. **Team name:** Cavaliers.

Student services. Alcohol/substance abuse counseling, career counseling, student employment services, financial aid counseling, health services, legal services, minority student services, on-campus daycare, personal counseling, placement for graduates, veterans' counselor, women's services. **Physically disabled:** Services for visually, speech, hearing impaired.

Contact. E-mail: undergradadmission@virginia.edu
Phone: (434) 982-3200 Fax: (434) 924-3587
John Blackburn, Dean of Admission, University of Virginia, Office of Admission, Charlottesville, VA 22904-4160

University of Virginia's College at Wise

Wise, Virginia — **CB member**
www.uvawise.edu — **CB code: 5124**

- Public 4-year liberal arts college
- Commuter campus in small town
- 1,623 degree-seeking undergraduates: 11% part-time, 52% women, 6% African American, 1% Asian American, 2% Hispanic American, 1% international
- 76% of applicants admitted
- SAT or ACT (ACT writing recommended) required
- 40% graduate within 6 years

General. Founded in 1954. Regionally accredited. **Degrees:** 287 bachelor's awarded. **Location:** 60 miles from Bristol. **Calendar:** Semester, limited summer session. **Full-time faculty:** 89 total; 62% have terminal degrees, 9% minority, 40% women. **Part-time faculty:** 51 total; 29% have terminal degrees, 4% minority, 53% women. **Class size:** 63% < 20, 34% 20-39, 3% 40-49, less than 1% 50-99. **Special facilities:** Observatory, scanning electron microscope, oral communication center, nursing assessment stations.

Freshman class profile. 1,085 applied, 824 admitted, 366 enrolled.

Mid 50% test scores		**Rank in top quarter:**	49%
SAT verbal:	440-550	**Rank in top tenth:**	25%
SAT math:	430-540	**End year in good standing:**	79%
ACT:	18-22	**Return as sophomores:**	73%
GPA 3.50 or higher:	39%	**Out-of-state:**	6%
GPA 3.0-3.49:	27%	**Live on campus:**	63%
GPA 2.0-2.99:	34%		

Basis for selection. Applications reviewed on rolling basis. Emphasis given to academic courses and grades earned in those courses. Interview required for marginal applicants.

High school preparation. 18 units required. Required units include English 4, mathematics 3, social studies 1, history 1, science 2 (laboratory 2), foreign language 2 and academic electives 5. 1 American history, 1 world history required.

2005-2006 Annual costs. Tuition/fees: $5,081; $15,159 out-of-state. Capital fee of $50 for out of state students. Room/board: $5,995. Books/supplies: $700. Personal expenses: $890.

2004-2005 Financial aid. Need-based: 340 full-time freshmen applied for aid; 262 were judged to have need; 262 of these received aid. Average need met was 95%. Average scholarship/grant was $4,163; average loan $2,125. 62% of total undergraduate aid awarded as scholarships/grants, 38% as loans/jobs. **Non-need-based:** Awarded to 866 full-time undergraduates, including 217 freshmen. Scholarships awarded for academics, alumni affiliation, art, athletics, job skills, leadership, music/drama, religious affiliation, state residency.

Application procedures. Admission: Priority date 12/1; deadline 8/15 (postmark date). $25 fee, may be waived for applicants with need. Application may be submitted online. Admission notification 8/20. Admission notification on a rolling basis beginning on or about 8/15. Must reply by May 1 or within 2 week(s) if notified thereafter. Early action notification on a rolling basis. **Financial aid:** Priority date 4/1; no closing date. FAFSA required. Applicants notified on a rolling basis starting 2/15; must reply within 4 week(s) of notification.

Academics. Special study options: Cooperative education, double major, dual enrollment of high school students, honors, independent study, internships, liberal arts/career combination, student-designed major, study abroad, teacher certification program. **Credit/placement by examination:** AP, CLEP, IB, institutional tests. **Support services:** Learning center, reduced course load, remedial instruction, study skills assistance, tutoring, writing center.

Majors. Biology: General. **Business:** Accounting, business admin, management information systems. **Communications:** General. **Computer sciences:** Computer science. **Conservation:** Environmental studies. **English:** English lit. **Foreign languages:** General, French, Spanish. **Health:** Clinical lab science, nursing (RN). **History:** General. **Liberal arts:** Arts/sciences. **Math:** General. **Physical sciences:** Chemistry. **Protective services:** Criminal justice. **Psychology:** General. **Public administration:** General. **Social**

sciences: Economics, political science, sociology. **Visual/performing arts:** Art, dramatic.

Most popular majors. Biology 7%, business/marketing 25%, history 12%, liberal arts 12%, psychology 9%, social sciences 16%.

Computing on campus. 300 workstations in dormitories, library, computer center. Dormitories wired for high-speed internet access and linked to campus network. Commuter students can connect to campus network. Helpline, repair service, student web hosting available.

Student life. Freshman orientation: Mandatory, $30 fee. Preregistration for classes offered. 2-day program held for students and parents. Dormitory space available (free for students, $35 per night for parents). **Policies:** Freshmen permitted cars on campus. **Housing:** Coed dorms, single-sex dorms, special housing for disabled, apartments available. $150 deposit, deadline 5/1. **Activities:** Concert band, choral groups, dance, drama, literary magazine, music ensembles, musical theater, radio station, student government, student newspaper, TV station, Young Republicans, Young Democrats, international students organization, multicultural alliance, honors societies, professional organizations, student activities board, Baptist Student Union, Wesley Foundation.

Athletics. NAIA. **Intercollegiate:** Baseball M, basketball, cross-country, football (tackle) M, golf M, softball W, tennis, track and field, volleyball W. **Intramural:** Badminton, basketball, football (non-tackle), racquetball, soccer, softball, table tennis, tennis, volleyball, water polo. **Team name:** Cavaliers.

Student services. Alcohol/substance abuse counseling, campus ministries, career counseling, services for economically disadvantaged, student employment services, financial aid counseling, health services, minority student services, personal counseling, placement for graduates. **Physically disabled:** Services for visually, speech, hearing impaired.

Contact. E-mail: admissions@uvawise.edu
Phone: (276) 328-0102 Toll-free number: (888) 282-9324
Fax: (276) 328-0251
Russell Necessary, Vice Chancellor of Enrollment Management, University of Virginia's College at Wise, One College Avenue, Wise, VA 24293-4412

Virginia Commonwealth University

Richmond, Virginia — **CB member**
www.vcu.edu — **CB code: 5570**

- Public 4-year university
- Commuter campus in small city
- 18,691 degree-seeking undergraduates: 14% part-time, 60% women, 20% African American, 9% Asian American, 3% Hispanic American, 1% Native American, 2% international
- 6,379 degree-seeking graduate students
- 68% of applicants admitted
- SAT or ACT (ACT writing optional), application essay required
- 41% graduate within 6 years

General. Founded in 1838. Regionally accredited. **Degrees:** 2,684 bachelor's awarded; master's, doctoral, first professional offered. **Location:** 100 miles from Washington, DC. **Calendar:** Semester, extensive summer session. **Full-time faculty:** 1,744 total; 80% have terminal degrees, 18% minority, 41% women. **Part-time faculty:** 1,069 total; 14% minority, 51% women. **Class size:** 43% < 20, 40% 20-39, 6% 40-49, 6% 50-99, 6% >100. **Special facilities:** Center for environmental life sciences.

Freshman class profile. 11,764 applied, 8,020 admitted, 3,540 enrolled.

Mid 50% test scores			
SAT verbal:	480-600	Rank in top quarter:	44%
SAT math:	480-590	Rank in top tenth:	16%
ACT:	18-23	End year in good standing:	74%
GPA 3.50 or higher:	29%	Return as sophomores:	80%
GPA 3.0-3.49:	37%	Out-of-state:	8%
GPA 2.0-2.99:	34%	Live on campus:	72%
		International:	3%

Basis for selection. High school record, GPA, and standardized test scores important. **Homeschooled:** Transcript of courses and grades required.

High school preparation. 20 units required; 24 recommended. Required and recommended units include English 4, mathematics 3-4, social studies 1, history 2-3, science 3-4 (laboratory 1), foreign language 3 and academic electives 3-4.

2005-2006 Annual costs. Tuition/fees: $5,445; $17,380 out-of-state. Capital Outlay Fee of $60 additional for out-of-state students. Room/board: $7,315.

2004-2005 Financial aid. Need-based: 2,445 full-time freshmen applied for aid; 1,766 were judged to have need; 1,699 of these received aid. Average need met was 42%. Average scholarship/grant was $3,959; average loan $2,857. 43% of total undergraduate aid awarded as scholarships/grants, 57% as loans/jobs. **Non-need-based:** Awarded to 2,472 full-time undergraduates, including 791 freshmen. Scholarships awarded for academics, art, athletics, leadership, music/drama.

Application procedures. Admission: Closing date 2/1 (postmark date). $30 fee, may be waived for applicants with need. Application may be submitted online. Admission notification on a rolling basis beginning on or about 11/15. Must reply by May 1 or within 3 week(s) if notified thereafter. **Financial aid:** Priority date 3/1; no closing date. FAFSA required. Applicants notified by 3/15; must reply by 5/1 or within 2 week(s) of notification.

Academics. Special study options: Accelerated study, combined bachelor's/graduate degree, cooperative education, cross-registration, distance learning, double major, dual enrollment of high school students, ESL, exchange student, honors, independent study, internships, liberal arts/career combination, student-designed major, study abroad, teacher certification program, urban semester, Washington semester. **Credit/placement by examination:** AP, CLEP, IB, SAT, ACT, institutional tests. **Support services:** Learning center, reduced course load, study skills assistance, tutoring, writing center.

Majors. Area/ethnic studies: African-American. **Biology:** General, bioinformatics. **Business:** Accounting, business admin, managerial economics, marketing. **Communications:** Media studies. **Computer sciences:** General, information systems. **Conservation:** Environmental studies. **Education:** Art, health. **Engineering:** Biomedical, chemical, computer, electrical, mechanical. **English:** English lit. **Foreign languages:** General. **Health:** Clinical lab science, dental hygiene, nursing (RN), radiologic technology/medical imaging. **History:** General. **Interdisciplinary:** Biological/physical sciences, global studies. **Math:** General. **Parks/recreation:** General. **Philosophy/religion:** Philosophy, religion. **Physical sciences:** Chemistry, physics. **Protective services:** Forensics, law enforcement admin. **Psychology:** General. **Public administration:** Social work. **Social sciences:** Anthropology, political science, sociology, urban studies. **Visual/performing arts:** Art history/conservation, crafts, dance, design, dramatic, fashion design, interior design, music performance, painting, photography, sculpture.

Computing on campus. PC or laptop required. Dormitories wired for high-speed internet access and linked to campus network. Commuter students can connect to campus network. Online course registration, online library, helpline, repair service, student web hosting, wireless network available.

Student life. Freshman orientation: Available. Preregistration for classes offered. **Policies:** Most events open to VCU students with I.D. Events are sponsored by activity fees. Freshmen permitted cars on campus. **Housing:** Guaranteed on-campus for freshmen. Coed dorms, single-sex dorms, special housing for disabled available. $250 fully refundable deposit, deadline 6/15. Special housing for honors program and engineering. Suites for upperclassmen. Guaranteed on-campus housing for freshmen. **Activities:** Bands, choral groups, dance, drama, literary magazine, music ensembles, opera, radio station, student government, student newspaper, symphony orchestra, Baptist Student Union, Catholic campus ministry, College Republicans, Young Democrats, NAACP, Black Student Alliance, International Student Union, activities programming board, Sexual Minority Student Alliance, Chinese students, scholars association.

Athletics. NAIA, NCAA. **Intercollegiate:** Baseball M, basketball, cheerleading, cross-country, field hockey W, golf M, soccer, tennis, track and field, volleyball W. **Intramural:** Badminton, basketball, football (non-tackle), soccer, softball, tennis, volleyball, water polo. **Team name:** Rams.

Student services. Adult student services, career counseling, student employment services, financial aid counseling, health services, on-campus daycare, personal counseling, placement for graduates, veterans' counselor. **Physically disabled:** Services for visually, speech, hearing impaired.

Contact. E-mail: ugrad@vcu.edu
Phone: (804) 828-1222 Toll-free number: (800) 841-3638
Fax: (804) 828-1899
Delores Taylor, Director of Admissions, Virginia Commonwealth University, Box 842526, Richmond, VA 23284-2526

Virginia Intermont College

Bristol, Virginia
www.vic.edu — **CB code: 5857**

- Private 4-year liberal arts college affiliated with Baptist faith
- Residential campus in large town

- 1,126 degree-seeking undergraduates: 13% part-time, 70% women, 7% African American, 1% Asian American, 2% Hispanic American, 1% Native American, 1% international
- 63% of applicants admitted
- SAT or ACT with writing required
- 30% graduate within 6 years

General. Founded in 1884. Regionally accredited. Adult Degree Studies program available for working adults 23 years of age or older. Limited majors available. **Degrees:** 224 bachelor's, 7 associate awarded. **Location:** 144 miles from Roanoke, 114 miles from Knoxville, Tennessee. **Calendar:** Semester, limited summer session. **Full-time faculty:** 45 total; 67% have terminal degrees, 7% minority, 42% women. **Part-time faculty:** 44 total; 36% have terminal degrees, 2% minority, 43% women. **Class size:** 85% < 20, 15% 20-39, less than 1% 40-49. **Special facilities:** 120-acre riding center with 2 indoor riding arenas, two culinary training facilities.

Freshman class profile. 802 applied, 505 admitted, 182 enrolled.

Mid 50% test scores			
SAT verbal:	430-550	Rank in top quarter:	24%
SAT math:	410-510	Rank in top tenth:	11%
ACT:	18-22	End year in good standing:	93%
GPA 3.50 or higher:	26%	Return as sophomores:	72%
GPA 3.0-3.49:	34%	Out-of-state:	53%
GPA 2.0-2.99:	38%	Live on campus:	72%
		International:	1%

Basis for selection. School achievement record, SAT or ACT scores, school and community activities important. Essay, interview recommended for all; audition recommended for dance, equine studies, performing arts; portfolio recommended for art, photography. **Homeschooled:** SAT or ACT scores, record of academic achievement must be submitted. **Learning Disabled:** Students admitted conditionally, restricted to 12 credit hours in first semester.

High school preparation. 15 units required. Required units include English 4, mathematics 2, social studies 2, (laboratory 1) and academic electives 6.

2005-2006 Annual costs. Tuition/fees: $16,450. Room/board: $5,750. Books/supplies: $820. Personal expenses: $2,190.

2004-2005 Financial aid. Need-based: 133 full-time freshmen applied for aid; 111 were judged to have need; 111 of these received aid. Average need met was 58%. Average scholarship/grant was $10,186; average loan $2,516. 48% of total undergraduate aid awarded as scholarships/grants, 52% as loans/jobs. **Non-need-based:** Awarded to 271 full-time undergraduates, including 67 freshmen. Scholarships awarded for academics, alumni affiliation, art, athletics, minority status, music/drama, religious affiliation, state residency.

Application procedures. Admission: No deadline. $15 fee, may be waived for applicants with need. Application may be submitted online. Admission notification on a rolling basis. **Financial aid:** Closing date 3/1. FAFSA required. Applicants notified on a rolling basis starting 2/15; must reply within 3 week(s) of notification.

Academics. Special study options: Accelerated study, cross-registration, distance learning, double major, honors, independent study, internships, teacher certification program. **Credit/placement by examination:** AP, CLEP, IB, institutional tests. **Support services:** Learning center, reduced course load, study skills assistance, tutoring, writing center.

Majors. Agriculture: Equestrian studies. **Biology:** General. **Business:** Business admin, international, marketing. **Computer sciences:** General. **Conservation:** Environmental studies. **Education:** General, art, biology, elementary, English, physical, secondary, social studies, special. **Health:** Premedicine, preveterinary. **History:** General. **Legal studies:** General, paralegal, prelaw. **Liberal arts:** Arts/sciences. **Parks/recreation:** Health/fitness, sports admin. **Personal/culinary services:** Baking, chef training, restaurant/catering. **Philosophy/religion:** Religion. **Protective services:** Law enforcement admin. **Psychology:** General. **Public administration:** General, social work. **Social sciences:** Political science. **Visual/performing arts:** Art, dance, dramatic, photography.

Most popular majors. Business/marketing 23%, computer/information sciences 9%, education 32%, social sciences 6%, visual/performing arts 13%.

Computing on campus. 100 workstations in dormitories, library, computer center. Dormitories wired for high-speed internet access and linked to campus network. Commuter students can connect to campus network. Online library, wireless network available.

Student life. Freshman orientation: Mandatory. Preregistration for classes offered. Students assigned orientation mentors; diagnostic testing done. **Policies:** Alcohol and tobacco use is prohibited on campus. Freshmen permitted cars on campus. **Housing:** Guaranteed on-campus for freshmen. Coed dorms, single-sex dorms, apartments, substance-free housing available. $200 deposit. Juniors and seniors may live off campus, but all other students under 21 years of age not living with parents must live on campus. Special accommodations for learning disabled. **Activities:** Choral groups, dance, drama, music ensembles, musical theater, student government, Christian Student Union, Cardinal Key, social work action group, Fellowship of Christian Athletes, international student club, Alpha Phi Omega, Black Student Alliance, multicultural affairs program.

Athletics. NAIA. **Intercollegiate:** Baseball M, basketball, cheerleading M, cross-country, equestrian, golf M, soccer, softball W, tennis, track and field, volleyball W. **Intramural:** Basketball, bowling, football (non-tackle), football (tackle) M, golf, skiing, softball, swimming, table tennis, tennis, volleyball, weight lifting. **Team name:** Cobras.

Student services. Adult student services, alcohol/substance abuse counseling, campus ministries, career counseling, student employment services, financial aid counseling, health services, minority student services, personal counseling, placement for graduates. **Physically disabled:** Services for visually, hearing impaired.

Contact. E-mail: viadmit@vic.edu
Phone: (276) 466-7856 Toll-free number: (800) 451-1842
Fax: (276) 466-7855
Roger Lowe, Director of Admissions, Virginia Intermont College, 1013 Moore Street, Bristol, VA 24201

Virginia Military Institute

Lexington, Virginia — **CB member**
www.vmi.edu — **CB code: 5858**

- Public 4-year liberal arts and military college
- Residential campus in small town
- 1,369 degree-seeking undergraduates: 8% women, 5% African American, 3% Asian American, 3% Hispanic American, 2% international
- 50% of applicants admitted
- SAT or ACT (ACT writing optional) required
- 62% graduate within 6 years

General. Founded in 1839. Regionally accredited. Mandatory ROTC classes and optional commissioning in the Army, Air Force, Navy, or Marines. **Degrees:** 299 bachelor's awarded. **ROTC:** Army, Navy, Air Force. **Location:** 55 miles from Roanoke, 140 miles from Richmond. **Calendar:** Semester, limited summer session. **Full-time faculty:** 110 total. **Part-time faculty:** 40 total. **Class size:** 67% < 20, 33% 20-39. **Special facilities:** Historical museums, research library, observatory, particle accelerator.

Freshman class profile. 1,811 applied, 913 admitted, 391 enrolled.

Mid 50% test scores			
SAT verbal:	520-630	Rank in top quarter:	44%
SAT math:	530-620	Rank in top tenth:	12%
ACT:	22-26	Return as sophomores:	84%
GPA 3.50 or higher:	35%	Out-of-state:	44%
GPA 3.0-3.49:	44%	Live on campus:	100%
GPA 2.0-2.99:	21%	International:	1%

Basis for selection. GED not accepted. Admissions based on secondary school record, class rank, standardized test scores, character, and personal qualities. Interview, extracurricular activities, state residency, minority status, and volunteer work also important. **Homeschooled:** Require transcript with list of texts used or group affiliation.

High school preparation. College-preparatory program required. Required and recommended units include English 4, mathematics 3-4, science 3 (laboratory 3) and foreign language 3-4.

2005-2006 Annual costs. Tuition/fees: $8,666; $22,826 out-of-state. Room/board: $5,666. Books/supplies: $650. Personal expenses: $1,000.

2004-2005 Financial aid. Need-based: 243 full-time freshmen applied for aid; 194 were judged to have need; 193 of these received aid. Average need met was 93%. Average scholarship/grant was $7,459; average loan $3,400. 74% of total undergraduate aid awarded as scholarships/grants, 26% as loans/jobs. **Non-need-based:** Awarded to 440 full-time undergraduates, including 123 freshmen. Scholarships awarded for academics, alumni affiliation, athletics, leadership, music/drama, ROTC, state residency.

Application procedures. Admission: Closing date 2/15 (postmark date). $35 fee, may be waived for applicants with need. Application may be submitted online. Admission notification on a rolling basis beginning on or

about 1/1. Must reply by 5/1. Must reply by May 1 or within 2 week(s) if notified thereafter. **Financial aid:** Closing date 3/1. FAFSA, institutional form required. Applicants notified on a rolling basis starting 3/1.

Academics. 12 hours minimum course load each semester. All full-time faculty teach and serve as student advisers. All courses taught by full or part-time faculty, not graduate assistants. **Special study options:** Accelerated study, double major, exchange student, honors, independent study, internships, study abroad, teacher certification program. **Credit/placement by examination:** AP, CLEP, IB, institutional tests. No policy, but it is unlikely any student would receive more than 36 hours credit. **Support services:** Learning center, pre-admission summer program, study skills assistance, tutoring, writing center.

Majors. Biology: General. **Computer sciences:** Computer science. **Engineering:** Civil, electrical, mechanical. **Foreign languages:** General. **History:** General. **Interdisciplinary:** Global studies. **Math:** General. **Physical sciences:** Chemistry, physics. **Psychology:** General. **Social sciences:** Economics.

Most popular majors. Biology 7%, engineering/engineering technologies 20%, history 19%, psychology 8%, social sciences 29%.

Computing on campus. PC or laptop required. 200 workstations in library, computer center. Dormitories wired for high-speed internet access and linked to campus network. Online library, helpline, repair service, wireless network available.

Student life. Freshman orientation: Mandatory. Held in August, 8 days before beginning of class. **Policies:** Student-run honor system integral part of institution. **Housing:** Guaranteed on-campus for all undergraduates. Barracks house 3-5 students per room. **Activities:** Bands, choral groups, drama, literary magazine, music ensembles, musical theater, student government, student newspaper, More than 50 clubs and student organizations available.

Athletics. NCAA. **Intercollegiate:** Baseball M, basketball M, cross-country, diving M, football (tackle) M, golf M, lacrosse M, rifle M, soccer, swimming, tennis M, track and field, wrestling M. **Intramural:** Basketball, football (non-tackle), soccer, softball. **Team name:** Keydets.

Student services. Alcohol/substance abuse counseling, campus ministries, career counseling, student employment services, financial aid counseling, health services, personal counseling, placement for graduates.

Contact. E-mail: admissions@vmi.edu
Phone: (540) 464-7211 Toll-free number: (800) 767-4207
Fax: (540) 464-7746
Col. Vernon Beitzel, Director of Admissions, Virginia Military Institute, Office of Admissions, Lexington, VA 24450-9967

Virginia Polytechnic Institute and State University

Blacksburg, Virginia — **CB member**
www.vt.edu — **CB code: 5859**

- Public 4-year university
- Residential campus in large town
- 21,534 degree-seeking undergraduates: 2% part-time, 41% women, 5% African American, 7% Asian American, 2% Hispanic American, 2% international
- 6,349 degree-seeking graduate students
- 72% of applicants admitted
- SAT or ACT (ACT writing recommended) required
- 76% graduate within 6 years

General. Founded in 1872. Regionally accredited. Option of enrolling as member of cadet corps. **Degrees:** 4,835 bachelor's, 51 associate awarded; master's, doctoral, first professional offered. **ROTC:** Army, Navy, Air Force. **Location:** 38 miles from Roanoke. **Calendar:** Semester, extensive summer session. **Full-time faculty:** 1,304 total; 89% have terminal degrees, 13% minority, 29% women. **Part-time faculty:** 228 total; 8% minority, 42% women. **Class size:** 24% < 20, 44% 20-39, 12% 40-49, 13% 50-99, 8% >100. **Special facilities:** Natural history, geology and art museums, observatory, wind tunnel, black cultural center, digital music center, robotics laboratory, multimedia laboratory, media center, women's center, math emporium, advanced communications/information technology center.

Freshman class profile. 17,681 applied, 12,714 admitted, 5,049 enrolled.

Mid 50% test scores			
SAT verbal:	540-630	Rank in top quarter:	78%
SAT math:	570-660	Rank in top tenth:	37%
GPA 3.50 or higher:	74%	Return as sophomores:	88%
GPA 3.0-3.49:	23%	Out-of-state:	29%
GPA 2.0-2.99:	2%	Live on campus:	98%
		International:	2%

Basis for selection. High school course work, grades, test scores most important. Prospective students encouraged to pursue rigorous preparatory course of study through senior year. SAT subject test scores in math (level Ic or IIc) and a second area of study to be chosen by the applicant recommended. Audition required for music. **Homeschooled:** Transcript of courses and grades required. Must submit standardized test scores; statement describing homeschool structure and mission recommended but not required.

High school preparation. 18 units required. Required and recommended units include English 4, mathematics 3-4, social studies 1, history 1, science 2-3 (laboratory 2), foreign language 3 and academic electives 4. Preference given to applicants with mathematics beyond Algebra II. 4 mathematics required for general engineering, biochemistry, chemistry, computer science, math, physics and statistics. 3 science including physics required for engineering and recommended for all science-related majors.

2005-2006 Annual costs. Tuition/fees: $6,378; $17,717 out-of-state. Room/board: $4,760. Books/supplies: $1,030. Personal expenses: $1,409.

2004-2005 Financial aid. Need-based: 3,426 full-time freshmen applied for aid; 2,292 were judged to have need; 1,832 of these received aid. Average need met was 71%. Average scholarship/grant was $5,199; average loan $3,240. 48% of total undergraduate aid awarded as scholarships/grants, 52% as loans/jobs. **Non-need-based:** Awarded to 2,490 full-time undergraduates, including 885 freshmen. Scholarships awarded for art, athletics, ROTC.

Application procedures. Admission: Closing date 1/15 (postmark date). $40 fee, may be waived for applicants with need. Application may be submitted online. Admission notification 4/1. Must reply by 5/1. $400 matriculation deposit required. **Financial aid:** Priority date 3/11; no closing date. FAFSA required. Applicants notified on a rolling basis starting 3/30; must reply by 5/1 or within 4 week(s) of notification.

Academics. Special study options: Accelerated study, combined bachelor's/graduate degree, cooperative education, cross-registration, distance learning, double major, dual enrollment of high school students, ESL, exchange student, honors, independent study, internships, liberal arts/career combination, student-designed major, study abroad, teacher certification program, Washington semester. Cadet corps, 3 year combined bachelors/masters degree program offered to qualifying honors program students. **Credit/placement by examination:** AP, CLEP, IB, institutional tests. 12 credit hours maximum toward associate degree, 12 toward bachelor's. **Support services:** Learning center, study skills assistance, tutoring, writing center.

Majors. Agriculture: General, agronomy, animal sciences, dairy, economics, food science, horticultural science. **Architecture:** Architecture, landscape. **Biology:** General, biochemistry. **Business:** Accounting, business admin, construction management, finance, hotel/motel admin, management science, managerial economics, marketing. **Communications:** General. **Computer sciences:** General. **Conservation:** Environmental science, environmental studies, forestry. **Education:** Secondary. **Engineering:** Aerospace, agricultural, chemical, civil, computer, electrical, industrial, materials, mechanical, mechanics, mining. **English:** English lit. **Family/consumer sciences:** Business, family studies, food/nutrition. **Foreign languages:** General. **History:** General. **Liberal arts:** Arts/sciences. **Math:** General, statistics. **Philosophy/religion:** Philosophy. **Physical sciences:** Chemistry, geology, physics. **Psychology:** General. **Public administration:** Policy analysis. **Social sciences:** Economics, geography, international relations, political science, sociology. **Visual/performing arts:** Art, dramatic, industrial design, interior design.

Most popular majors. Biology 7%, business/marketing 22%, engineering/engineering technologies 18%, family/consumer sciences 8%, social sciences 7%.

Computing on campus. PC or laptop required. 912 workstations in dormitories, library, computer center, student center. Dormitories wired for high-speed internet access and linked to campus network. Commuter students can connect to campus network. Online course registration, online library, helpline, repair service, student web hosting, wireless network available.

Student life. Freshman orientation: Available, $100 fee. Preregistration for classes offered. Day and a half long program held in July. **Policies:** Freshmen required to live on campus, unless living with parents or close relatives, married, veteran, or at least 21 years old. Honor system in force. Freshmen permitted cars on campus. **Housing:** Guaranteed on-campus for freshmen. Coed dorms, single-sex dorms, special housing for disabled, fraternity/sorority housing, substance-free housing available. Cadets live in cadet residence halls. Foreign language hall and academic success hall available. **Activities:** Bands, choral groups, dance, drama, literary magazine, music ensembles, musical theater, radio station, student government, student newspaper, 400 clubs and organizations available.

Athletics. NCAA. **Intercollegiate:** Baseball M, basketball, cheerleading, cross-country, diving, football (tackle) M, golf M, lacrosse W, soccer, softball W, swimming, tennis, track and field, volleyball W, wrestling M. **Intramural:** Basketball, bowling, football (non-tackle), golf, handball, racquetball, soccer, softball, squash, swimming, table tennis, tennis, volleyball, water polo. **Team name:** Hokies.

Student services. Alcohol/substance abuse counseling, campus ministries, career counseling, student employment services, financial aid counseling, health services, legal services, minority student services, personal counseling, placement for graduates, veterans' counselor, women's services. **Physically disabled:** Services for visually, hearing impaired.

Contact. E-mail: vtadmiss@vt.edu
Phone: (540) 231-6267 Fax: (540) 231-3242
Norrine Spencer, Associate Provost and Director of Undergraduate Admissions, Virginia Polytechnic Institute and State University, 201 Burruss Hall, Blacksburg, VA 24061-0202

Virginia State University

Petersburg, Virginia **CB member**
www.vsu.edu **CB code: 5860**

- Public 4-year university
- Residential campus in large town
- 4,278 degree-seeking undergraduates: 5% part-time, 61% women, 96% African American, 1% Hispanic American
- 444 degree-seeking graduate students
- 79% of applicants admitted
- SAT or ACT (ACT writing optional) required
- 44% graduate within 6 years

General. Founded in 1882. Regionally accredited. **Degrees:** 727 bachelor's awarded; master's, doctoral offered. **ROTC:** Army. **Location:** 25 miles from Richmond. **Calendar:** Semester, limited summer session. **Full-time faculty:** 226 total; 80% have terminal degrees, 69% minority, 38% women. **Part-time faculty:** 101 total; 32% have terminal degrees, 72% minority, 50% women. **Class size:** 41% < 20, 47% 20-39, 7% 40-49, 5% 50-99, less than 1% >100.

Freshman class profile. 4,000 applied, 3,143 admitted, 1,107 enrolled.

Mid 50% test scores		**Rank in top quarter:**	19%
SAT verbal:	380-460	**Rank in top tenth:**	4%
SAT math:	370-460	**Out-of-state:**	40%
ACT:	16-19	**Live on campus:**	93%

Basis for selection. School achievement record most important; recommendation required. Essay recommended for all; audition required for music; portfolio recommended for art.

High school preparation. 11 units required. Required and recommended units include English 4, mathematics 3, social studies 2, science 2 (laboratory 1) and foreign language 2. Mathematics requirement must include algebra I.

2005-2006 Annual costs. Tuition/fees: $4,834; $9,852 out-of-state. Out-of-state residents pay an addition $58 state capital outlay fee. Room/board: $6,484. Books/supplies: $790. Personal expenses: $532.

2004-2005 Financial aid. Need-based: 37% of total undergraduate aid awarded as scholarships/grants, 63% as loans/jobs. **Non-need-based:** Scholarships awarded for academics, alumni affiliation, art, athletics, job skills, leadership, music/drama, religious affiliation, ROTC. **Additional information:** Strongly recommend that students apply for scholarship assistance through federal, state, local and private agencies.

Application procedures. Admission: Priority date 3/31; deadline 5/1 (postmark date). $25 fee, may be waived for applicants with need. Application may be submitted online. Admission notification on a rolling basis. Must reply by May 1 or within 2 week(s) if notified thereafter. **Financial aid:** Priority date 3/31, closing date 5/1. FAFSA, institutional form required. Applicants notified on a rolling basis starting 5/1; must reply within 2 week(s) of notification.

Academics. Special study options: Cooperative education, double major, dual enrollment of high school students, exchange student, honors, independent study, internships, teacher certification program. **Credit/placement by examination:** AP, CLEP, institutional tests. 12 credit hours maximum toward bachelor's degree. **Support services:** Study skills assistance, tutoring, writing center.

Majors. Agriculture: General. **Biology:** General. **Business:** Accounting, business admin, hospitality admin, managerial economics, marketing. **Communications:** Media studies. **Computer sciences:** Computer science, information technology. **Education:** Business, physical, trade/industrial. **Engineering:** Computer, manufacturing. **Engineering technology:** General, electrical, mechanical. **English:** English lit. **Family/consumer sciences:** Communication. **History:** General. **Liberal arts:** Arts/sciences. **Math:** General. **Physical sciences:** Chemistry, physics. **Protective services:** Criminal justice. **Psychology:** General. **Public administration:** General, social work. **Social sciences:** Political science, sociology. **Visual/performing arts:** General, music performance.

Most popular majors. Business/marketing 15%, computer/information sciences 6%, education 11%, interdisciplinary studies 8%, liberal arts 10%, psychology 6%, security/protective services 7%, social sciences 7%.

Computing on campus. 750 workstations in dormitories, library, student center. Dormitories wired for high-speed internet access and linked to campus network. Commuter students can connect to campus network. Online course registration, online library, helpline, repair service available.

Student life. Freshman orientation: Mandatory, $75 fee. Preregistration for classes offered. Two-day orientation held at various times in the summer. **Housing:** Guaranteed on-campus for freshmen. Coed dorms, single-sex dorms, apartments, substance-free housing available. $150 deposit. **Activities:** Bands, choral groups, dance, drama, literary magazine, music ensembles, radio station, student government, student newspaper, TV station, NAACP, Black Students Against Drugs, Muslim Student Organization, Peer Mediators, Betterment of Brothers and Sisters, New Generation Campus Ministries, Caribbean Students Association, Institute for Leadership Development.

Athletics. NCAA. **Intercollegiate:** Baseball M, basketball, bowling W, cheerleading, cross-country, football (tackle) M, golf, softball W, tennis, track and field, volleyball W. **Intramural:** Basketball, football (tackle) M, swimming, table tennis, tennis, track and field, volleyball W. **Team name:** Trojans.

Student services. Alcohol/substance abuse counseling, campus ministries, career counseling, services for economically disadvantaged, student employment services, financial aid counseling, health services, personal counseling, placement for graduates, veterans' counselor. **Physically disabled:** Services for visually, hearing impaired.

Contact. E-mail: admiss@vsu.edu
Phone: (804) 524-5902 Toll-free number: (800) 871-7611
Fax: (804) 524-5055
Irene Logan, Director of Admissions, Virginia State University, One Hayden Street, Petersburg, VA 23806

Virginia Union University

Richmond, Virginia **CB member**
www.vuu.edu **CB code: 5862**

- Private 4-year university and liberal arts college affiliated with Baptist faith
- Residential campus in small city
- 1,344 degree-seeking undergraduates: 3% part-time, 58% women, 96% African American, 1% Hispanic American
- 356 degree-seeking graduate students
- 58% of applicants admitted
- SAT or ACT (ACT writing recommended) required

General. Founded in 1865. Regionally accredited. **Degrees:** 151 bachelor's awarded; master's, doctoral, first professional offered. **ROTC:** Army. **Location:** 90 miles from Norfolk, 100 miles from Washington, DC. **Calendar:** Semester, limited summer session. **Full-time faculty:** 85 total. **Special facilities:** Police academy, learning resource center.

Freshman class profile. 3,933 applied, 2,264 admitted, 341 enrolled.

Mid 50% test scores			
SAT verbal:	350-430	Rank in top quarter:	8%
SAT math:	330-410	Rank in top tenth:	4%
ACT:	13-16	End year in good standing:	75%
GPA 3.50 or higher:	2%	Return as sophomores:	59%
GPA 3.0-3.49:	8%	Out-of-state:	54%
GPA 2.0-2.99:	69%	Live on campus:	80%

Basis for selection. Secondary school record, test scores, extracurricular activities most important. Essay, interview, and talent or ability also important. Essay recommended for all. Interview recommended for academically weak. Audition required for band, choir, music, university players.

High school preparation. College-preparatory program required. 16 units required. Required units include English 4, mathematics 3, social studies 2, science 2, foreign language 2 and academic electives 3.

2005-2006 Annual costs. Tuition/fees: $12,770. Room/board: $5,662. Books/supplies: $500. Personal expenses: $1,000.

2005-2006 Financial aid. Need-based: 329 full-time freshmen applied for aid; 299 were judged to have need; 297 of these received aid. Average need met was 81%. Average scholarship/grant was $3,959; average loan $3,642. 41% of total undergraduate aid awarded as scholarships/grants, 59% as loans/jobs. **Non-need-based:** Awarded to 778 full-time undergraduates, including 317 freshmen. Scholarships awarded for academics, athletics, ROTC, state residency.

Application procedures. Admission: Priority date 6/30; no deadline. $25 fee, may be waived for applicants with need. Application may be submitted online. Admission notification on a rolling basis. **Financial aid:** Priority date 4/27; no closing date. FAFSA required. Applicants notified on a rolling basis starting 5/1; must reply within 2 week(s) of notification.

Academics. Special study options: Combined bachelor's/graduate degree, cooperative education, honors, independent study, internships, liberal arts/career combination, teacher certification program. **Credit/placement by examination:** AP, CLEP, IB, institutional tests. 18 credit hours maximum toward bachelor's degree. **Support services:** Learning center, reduced course load, remedial instruction, tutoring, writing center.

Majors. Biology: General. **Business:** Accounting, business admin, finance, management information systems, sales/distribution. **Communications:** Journalism. **Computer sciences:** General. **Education:** Multi-level teacher. **History:** General. **Interdisciplinary:** Natural sciences. **Math:** General. **Philosophy/religion:** Religion. **Physical sciences:** Chemistry. **Psychology:** General. **Public administration:** Social work. **Social sciences:** Political science, sociology. **Visual/performing arts:** Art, dramatic, music theory/composition, piano/organ, voice/opera.

Most popular majors. Biology 8%, business/marketing 21%, communications/journalism 6%, legal studies 23%, psychology 7%, social sciences 11%.

Computing on campus. PC or laptop required. 148 workstations in library, computer center. Dormitories linked to campus network. Online course registration, wireless network available.

Student life. Freshman orientation: Mandatory. **Policies:** Freshmen permitted cars on campus. **Housing:** Coed dorms, single-sex dorms available. $250 partly refundable deposit, deadline 7/1. **Activities:** Bands, choral groups, dance, drama, music ensembles, musical theater, opera, student government, student newspaper, social work club, sociology club, student education association, Ministers Alliance.

Athletics. NCAA. **Intercollegiate:** Basketball, bowling W, cross-country, football (tackle) M, golf, softball W, tennis, track and field, volleyball W. **Intramural:** Basketball, football (non-tackle) M, softball, table tennis. **Team name:** Panthers.

Student services. Career counseling, student employment services, health services, personal counseling, placement for graduates.

Contact. E-mail: admissions@vuu.edu
Phone: (804) 329-8440 Toll-free number: (800) 368-3227
Fax: (804) 329-8477
Gil Powell, Director of Admissions, Virginia Union University, 1500 North Lombardy Street, Richmond, VA 23220

Virginia Wesleyan College

Norfolk, Virginia — **CB member**
www.vwc.edu — **CB code: 5867**

- Private 4-year liberal arts college affiliated with United Methodist Church
- Residential campus in large city
- 1,313 degree-seeking undergraduates: 15% part-time, 63% women, 15% African American, 2% Asian American, 3% Hispanic American, 1% international
- 78% of applicants admitted
- SAT or ACT (ACT writing optional), application essay required
- 37% graduate within 6 years

General. Founded in 1961. Regionally accredited. Special 3-week winter session offered, adult studies program, alternative certification for teaching (ACT). **Degrees:** 287 bachelor's awarded. **ROTC:** Army. **Location:** 10 miles from downtown Norfolk and Virginia Beach. **Calendar:** 4-1-4, limited summer session. **Full-time faculty:** 80 total; 76% have terminal degrees, 8% minority, 45% women. **Part-time faculty:** 58 total; 21% have terminal degrees, 14% minority, 60% women. **Class size:** 79% < 20, 21% 20-39. **Special facilities:** Greenhouse, Center for Study of Religious Freedom, 142-acre woodlands, rock climbing wall.

Freshman class profile. 1,357 applied, 1,065 admitted, 323 enrolled.

Mid 50% test scores			
SAT verbal:	450-560	GPA 2.0-2.99:	44%
SAT math:	440-570	Rank in top quarter:	31%
ACT:	17-22	Rank in top tenth:	13%
GPA 3.50 or higher:	25%	Return as sophomores:	66%
GPA 3.0-3.49:	31%	Out-of-state:	33%
		Live on campus:	78%

Basis for selection. Above average grades in solid college-preparatory curriculum, SAT scores, campus interview, personal statement, extracurricular activities important.

High school preparation. 12 units required; 19 recommended. Required and recommended units include English 4, mathematics 3, social studies 2, history 1, science 2-3 (laboratory 2-3) and foreign language 3.

2006-2007 Annual costs. Tuition/fees (projected): $23,136. Damage deposit of $75 for residents. Room/board: $6,850. Books/supplies: $800. Personal expenses: $1,800.

2004-2005 Financial aid. Need-based: 344 full-time freshmen applied for aid; 305 were judged to have need; 271 of these received aid. Average need met was 71%. Average scholarship/grant was $4,061; average loan $3,214. 26% of total undergraduate aid awarded as scholarships/grants, 74% as loans/jobs. **Non-need-based:** Awarded to 1,082 full-time undergraduates, including 336 freshmen. Scholarships awarded for academics, art, leadership, music/drama, religious affiliation, state residency.

Application procedures. Admission: Priority date 3/1; no deadline. $40 fee, may be waived for applicants with need. Application may be submitted online. Admission notification on a rolling basis beginning on or about 11/1. Must reply by May 1 or within 3 week(s) if notified thereafter. **Financial aid:** Priority date 3/1; no closing date. FAFSA required. Applicants notified on a rolling basis starting 2/15; must reply by 5/1 or within 2 week(s) of notification.

Academics. Writing proficiency examination and one writing course per semester required. **Special study options:** Cross-registration, distance learning, double major, honors, independent study, internships, liberal arts/career combination, student-designed major, study abroad, teacher certification program. Externships; 4-year competitive honors program integrates liberal arts and experiential learning. **Credit/placement by examination:** AP, CLEP, IB, institutional tests. 30 credit hours maximum toward bachelor's degree. **Support services:** Learning center, reduced course load, remedial instruction, study skills assistance, tutoring, writing center.

Majors. Area/ethnic studies: American. **Biology:** General. **Business:** Business admin. **Communications:** General. **Computer sciences:** Computer science. **Conservation:** Environmental studies. **Education:** Art. **English:** Creative writing, English lit. **Foreign languages:** General, French, German, Spanish. **Health:** Predentistry, premedicine, prepharmacy, preveterinary. **History:** General. **Interdisciplinary:** Global studies, math/computer science, natural sciences. **Legal studies:** Prelaw. **Liberal arts:** Arts/sciences, humanities. **Math:** General. **Parks/recreation:** General, facilities management. **Philosophy/religion:** Philosophy, religion. **Physical sciences:** Chemistry, geology. **Protective services:** Criminal justice, law enforcement admin. **Psychology:** General. **Public administration:** Human services. **Social sciences:** General, criminology, economics, international relations, political science, sociology. **Visual/performing arts:** Art, dramatic, studio arts, theater history.

Most popular majors. Business/marketing 20%, communications/journalism 11%, interdisciplinary studies 10%, legal studies 9%, parks/recreation 7%, social sciences 14%.

Computing on campus. 96 workstations in library, computer center, student center. Dormitories wired for high-speed internet access and linked to campus network. Online library, helpline, repair service, student web hosting, wireless network available.

Student life. **Freshman orientation:** Mandatory, $100 fee. Preregistration for classes offered. 2-day event scheduled twice in july; all-day retreat in August. Just prior to the beginning of classes also available. **Policies:** Freshmen permitted cars on campus. **Housing:** Guaranteed on-campus for freshmen. Coed dorms, single-sex dorms, special housing for disabled, apartments, fraternity/sorority housing available. $500 nonrefundable deposit, deadline 5/1. Coed dorms house men and women on alternating floors. Honors and Scholars hall provided. **Activities:** Bands, choral groups, dance, drama, literary magazine, music ensembles, musical theater, radio station, student government, student newspaper, international student organization, political science association, Model United Nations, Habitat for Humanity, black student union, Shalom, Honors & Scholars, Campus Kaleidoscope, SALSA, Wesleyan activities council.

Athletics. NCAA. **Intercollegiate:** Baseball M, basketball, cheerleading M, cross-country, field hockey W, golf M, lacrosse, soccer, softball W, tennis, track and field, volleyball W. **Intramural:** Basketball, field hockey W, football (tackle), soccer, softball, table tennis, volleyball. **Team name:** Marlins.

Student services. Adult student services, alcohol/substance abuse counseling, campus ministries, career counseling, student employment services, financial aid counseling, health services, minority student services, personal counseling, veterans' counselor, women's services. **Physically disabled:** Services for visually, hearing impaired.

Contact. E-mail: admissions@vwc.edu
Phone: (757) 455-3208 Toll-free number: (800) 737-8684
Fax: (757) 461-5238
Richard Hinshaw, Vice President for Enrollment Management and Dean of Admissions, Virginia Wesleyan College, 1584 Wesleyan Drive, Norfolk, VA 23502-5599

Washington and Lee University

Lexington, Virginia — **CB member**
www.wlu.edu — **CB code: 5887**

- Private 4-year university and liberal arts college
- Residential campus in small town
- 1,745 degree-seeking undergraduates: 50% women, 4% African American, 3% Asian American, 1% Hispanic American, 3% international
- 407 graduate students
- 29% of applicants admitted
- SAT or ACT with writing, SAT Subject Tests, application essay required
- 87% graduate within 6 years; 23% enter graduate study

General. Founded in 1749. Regionally accredited. Front campus and Lee Chapel are designated as a National Historic Landmark. **Degrees:** 463 bachelor's awarded; master's, first professional offered. **ROTC:** Army. **Location:** 50 miles from Roanoke, 60 miles from Charlottesville. **Calendar:** 4-4-2. **Full-time faculty:** 215 total; 94% have terminal degrees, 6% minority, 30% women. **Part-time faculty:** 2 total; 50% women. **Class size:** 66% < 20, 33% 20-39, less than 1% 50-99. **Special facilities:** Asian export pottery center, Asian art pavilion, chapel and history museum, performing arts center, university special collections, multimedia center, archaeology museum.

Freshman class profile. 3,950 applied, 1,141 admitted, 464 enrolled.

Mid 50% test scores			
SAT verbal:	660-730	**End year in good standing:**	98%
SAT math:	660-720	**Return as sophomores:**	95%
ACT:	28-31	**Out-of-state:**	87%
Rank in top quarter:	96%	**Live on campus:**	100%
Rank in top tenth:	76%	**International:**	3%

Basis for selection. School achievement record most important, followed closely by test scores, school and community activities, recommendations and personal qualities. Special consideration given to children of alumni and applicants from minorities and low-income families. Two unrelated SAT Subject Tests required. Interview recommended. **Homeschooled:** Recommend taking 5 SAT Subject Tests in unrelated fields.

High school preparation. College-preparatory program recommended. 16 units required. Required and recommended units include English 4, mathematics 3-4, social studies 1, history 1-2, science 1-3 (laboratory 1), foreign language 2-3 and academic electives 4.

2006-2007 Annual costs. Tuition/fees: $31,850. Room/board: $7,942. Books/supplies: $1,500. Personal expenses: $1,630.

2004-2005 Financial aid. **Need-based:** 232 full-time freshmen applied for aid; 172 were judged to have need; 167 of these received aid. Average need met was 99%. Average scholarship/grant was $19,728; average loan $3,273. 78% of total undergraduate aid awarded as scholarships/grants, 22% as loans/jobs. **Non-need-based:** Awarded to 399 full-time undergraduates, including 86 freshmen. Scholarships awarded for academics. **Additional information:** Various memorial and endowed scholarships are available. Interested students should refer to the W&L Financial Assistance brochure available from Financial Aid.

Application procedures. **Admission:** Closing date 1/15 (postmark date). $50 fee, may be waived for applicants with need. Application may be submitted online. Admission notification 4/1. Admission notification on a rolling basis. Must reply by 5/1. **Financial aid:** Priority date 2/1; no closing date. FAFSA, CSS PROFILE required. Applicants notified by 4/3; must reply by 5/1.

Academics. **Special study options:** Combined bachelor's/graduate degree, double major, exchange student, honors, independent study, internships, liberal arts/career combination, student-designed major, study abroad, teacher certification program, Washington semester. Member Seven College Consortium, professional ethics seminars in business, law, medicine, journalism. **Credit/placement by examination:** AP, CLEP, IB, institutional tests. **Support services:** Study skills assistance, tutoring, writing center.

Majors. **Area/ethnic studies:** East Asian, Russian/Slavic. **Biology:** General. **Business:** Accounting, business admin. **Communications:** Journalism. **Computer sciences:** General. **Engineering:** Chemical, physics. **English:** English lit. **Foreign languages:** General, classics, French, German, Spanish. **History:** General. **Interdisciplinary:** Medieval/Renaissance, neuroscience. **Math:** General. **Philosophy/religion:** Philosophy, religion. **Physical sciences:** Chemistry, geology, physics. **Psychology:** General. **Public administration:** Policy analysis. **Social sciences:** Anthropology, archaeology, economics, political science, sociology. **Visual/performing arts:** Art history/conservation, dramatic, studio arts.

Most popular majors. Biology 6%, business/marketing 18%, communications/journalism 8%, social sciences 32%.

Computing on campus. 320 workstations in dormitories, library, computer center, student center. Dormitories wired for high-speed internet access and linked to campus network. Commuter students can connect to campus network. Online course registration, online library, helpline, repair service, wireless network available.

Student life. **Freshman orientation:** Mandatory. Preregistration for classes offered. 4 days prior to beginning of fall term. **Policies:** Student-run honor system, observed with single sanction. Freshmen permitted cars on campus. **Housing:** Guaranteed on-campus for freshmen. Coed dorms, apartments, fraternity/sorority housing, substance-free housing available. $150 nonrefundable deposit, deadline 5/1. Outing Club House, Spanish House, Chavis House. **Activities:** Bands, choral groups, dance, drama, film society, literary magazine, music ensembles, radio station, student government, student newspaper, symphony orchestra, TV station, Alpha Phi Omega, General's Christian Fellowship, Nabors Service League, Hillel, Habitat for Humanity, Minority Student Association, Outing Club, Student Association for International Learning.

Athletics. NCAA. **Intercollegiate:** Baseball M, basketball, cross-country, equestrian W, field hockey W, football (tackle) M, golf M, lacrosse, soccer, swimming, tennis, track and field, volleyball W, wrestling M. **Intramural:** Badminton, basketball, football (non-tackle), soccer, softball, swimming, table tennis, tennis, volleyball, water polo, wrestling M. **Team name:** Generals.

Student services. Alcohol/substance abuse counseling, career counseling, student employment services, health services, personal counseling, placement for graduates. **Physically disabled:** Services for visually, hearing impaired.

Contact. E-mail: admissions@wlu.edu
Phone: (540) 458-8710 Fax: (540) 458-8062
William Hartog, Dean of Admissions and Financial Aid, Washington and Lee University, 204 West Washington Street, Lexington, VA 24450-2116

World College

Virginia Beach, Virginia
www.cie-wc.edu — **CB code: 3970**

- For-profit 4-year technical college
- Large city
- 283 degree-seeking undergraduates

General. Accredited by DETC. Affiliated with Cleveland Institute of Electronics. **Degrees:** 8 bachelor's awarded. **Calendar:** Continuous. **Full-time faculty:** 3 total. **Part-time faculty:** 3 total.

2006-2007 Annual costs. Tuition/fees (projected): $3,540.

Application procedures. Admission: No deadline. No application fee. Admission notification on a rolling basis.

Academics. Credit/placement by examination: CLEP.

Majors. Engineering technology: Electrical.

Computing on campus. PC or laptop required.

Contact. E-mail: info@cie-wc.edu
Phone: (800) 696-7532 Toll-free number: (800) 696-7532
World College, Lake Shore Plaza, 5193 Shore Drive, Suite 105, Virginia Beach, VA 23455-2500

Four-Year Colleges

Washington

Antioch University Seattle
Seattle, Washington
www.antiochsea.edu **CB code: 3070**

- Private upper-division university and liberal arts college
- Commuter campus in very large city
- Application essay, interview required

General. Founded in 1976. Regionally accredited. Individualized degree programs offered on both graduate and undergraduate levels. **Degrees:** 83 bachelor's awarded; master's offered. **Calendar:** Quarter, extensive summer session. **Full-time faculty:** 10 total. **Part-time faculty:** 10 total.

Student profile. 260 degree-seeking undergraduates, 700 graduate students.

Basis for selection. High school transcript, college transcript, application essay, interview required. Transfer accepted as juniors, seniors.

2005-2006 Annual costs. Tuition/fees: $18,135. Books/supplies: $918. Personal expenses: $555.

Financial aid. Need-based: Average need met was 70%. 44% of total undergraduate aid awarded as scholarships/grants, 56% as loans/jobs.

Application procedures. Admission: Rolling admission. $50 fee. **Financial aid:** FAFSA, institutional form required.

Academics. Bachelor's program is a completion program only. Students generally transfer in with at least 90 credits. **Special study options:** Cross-registration, independent study, student-designed major, teacher certification program. **Credit/placement by examination:** CLEP. **Support services:** Tutoring.

Majors. Liberal arts: Arts/sciences.

Computing on campus. 16 workstations in library, computer center. Commuter students can connect to campus network.

Student life. Activities: Student government, student newspaper.

Student services. Career counseling, financial aid counseling, personal counseling, veterans' counselor. **Physically disabled:** Services for visually impaired.

Contact. E-mail: admissions@antiochsea.edu
Phone: (206) 441-5352 ext. 5201 Toll-free number: (888) 268-4477
Fax: (206) 441-3307
Pam Smith-Mentz, Director of Admissions, Antioch University Seattle, 2326 Sixth Avenue, Seattle, WA 98121-1814

Art Institute of Seattle
Seattle, Washington
www.ais.edu **CB code: 4805**

- For-profit 4-year visual arts and technical college
- Commuter campus in very large city
- 3,020 degree-seeking undergraduates
- Application essay, interview required

General. Founded in 1982. Regionally accredited; also accredited by ACCSCT. **Degrees:** 1 bachelor's, 655 associate awarded. **Location:** Downtown. **Calendar:** Quarter, extensive summer session. **Full-time faculty:** 82 total; 16% have terminal degrees, 4% minority, 37% women. **Part-time faculty:** 90 total; 9% have terminal degrees, 6% minority, 41% women. **Class size:** 49% < 20, 49% 20-39, less than 1% 40-49, 1% 50-99. **Special facilities:** Gallery with rotating art/design shows.

Freshman class profile.

Out-of-state:	40%	**Live on campus:**	20%

Basis for selection. Secondary school record, essay, interview most important; class rank, recommendations, academic records, test scores considered. SAT or ACT recommended. **Learning Disabled:** Admissions notifies counselors of student who discloses learning disability and special needs students. Referral sent to counselor who determines eligibility.

2005-2006 Annual costs. Tuition/fees: $17,100. Room/board: $9,045. Books/supplies: $975. Personal expenses: $2,265.

Financial aid. Non-need-based: Scholarships awarded for academics, art.

Application procedures. Admission: No deadline. $50 fee. Application may be submitted online. Admission notification on a rolling basis. **Financial aid:** Priority date 4/15; no closing date. FAFSA required. Applicants notified on a rolling basis; must reply within 4 week(s) of notification.

Academics. Special study options: Cooperative education, ESL, internships. **Credit/placement by examination:** AP, CLEP, IB, institutional tests. 12 credit hours maximum toward associate degree, 12 toward bachelor's. Course waived by proficiency exam; credit does not count toward degree. **Support services:** Learning center, reduced course load, remedial instruction, study skills assistance, tutoring.

Majors. Visual/performing arts: General, graphic design, interior design.

Computing on campus. 494 workstations in library, computer center. Dormitories wired for high-speed internet access. Online course registration, online library, student web hosting available.

Student life. Freshman orientation: Available. Preregistration for classes offered. 1 to 4-day program held 3 weeks before start of the quarter. **Policies:** Freshmen permitted cars on campus. **Housing:** Guaranteed on-campus for all undergraduates. Coed dorms available. $200 deposit. AIS housing located 1 mile from campus. Students share 1 bedroom and studio apartments in secured apartment complexes. **Activities:** Student government, student newspaper.

Athletics. Intramural: Soccer, softball.

Student services. Adult student services, career counseling, student employment services, financial aid counseling, personal counseling, placement for graduates, veterans' counselor. **Physically disabled:** Services for visually, speech, hearing impaired.

Contact. E-mail: aisadm@aii.edu
Phone: (206) 448-6600 Toll-free number: (800) 275-2471
Fax: (206) 269-0275
Karen Shea, Director of Admissions, Art Institute of Seattle, 2323 Elliott Avenue, Seattle, WA 98121

Bastyr University
Kenmore, Washington
www.bastyr.edu **CB code: 0181**

- Private upper-division university and health science college
- Commuter campus in small city
- 80% of applicants admitted
- Application essay required

General. Founded in 1978. Regionally accredited. **Degrees:** 65 bachelor's awarded; master's, doctoral, first professional offered. **Location:** 16 miles from Seattle. **Calendar:** Quarter, limited summer session. **Full-time faculty:** 41 total; 98% have terminal degrees, 20% minority, 51% women. **Part-time faculty:** 107 total; 75% have terminal degrees, 15% minority, 57% women.

Student profile. 239 degree-seeking undergraduates, 814 degree-seeking graduate students. 235 applied as first time-transfer students, 187 admitted, 124 enrolled. 100% entered as juniors. 80% transferred from two-year, 20% transferred from four-year institutions.

Women:	84%	**Live on campus:**	5%
Part-time:	11%	**25 or older:**	56%
Out-of-state:	50%		

Basis for selection. College transcript, application essay required. Transfer accepted as juniors, seniors.

2005-2006 Annual costs. Tuition/fees: $15,381. Books/supplies: $900.

Financial aid. All financial aid based on need.

Application procedures. Admission: Priority date 3/15. $60 fee. **Financial aid:** FAFSA, institutional form required.

Academics. **Special study options:** Double major, internships. Selected tracks within major. **Credit/placement by examination:** AP, CLEP.

Majors. **Health:** Acupuncture, Chinese medicine/herbology, herbalism. **Interdisciplinary:** Nutrition sciences. **Psychology:** General.

Most popular majors. Health sciences 33%, interdisciplinary studies 41%, psychology 26%.

Computing on campus. 44 workstations in library, computer center. Dormitories wired for high-speed internet access and linked to campus network. Online library, helpline, wireless network available.

Student life. **Housing:** Coed dorms available. **Activities:** Student government, student newspaper, Student Physicians for Social Responsibility.

Athletics. **Intramural:** Basketball, soccer.

Student services. Career counseling, financial aid counseling, health services, on-campus daycare, personal counseling, placement for graduates. **Physically disabled:** Services for visually impaired.

Contact. E-mail: admiss@bastyr.edu
Phone: (425) 602-3330 Fax: (425) 602-3090
Richard Dent, Dean of Enrollment, Bastyr University, 14500 Juanita Drive NE, Kenmore, WA 98028

Central Washington University

Ellensburg, Washington — **CB member**
www.cwu.edu — **CB code: 4044**

- Public 4-year university
- Residential campus in large town
- 9,148 degree-seeking undergraduates
- 76% of applicants admitted
- SAT or ACT (ACT writing optional) required

General. Founded in 1890. Regionally accredited. **Degrees:** 2,126 bachelor's awarded; master's offered. **ROTC:** Army, Air Force. **Location:** 105 miles from Seattle. **Calendar:** Quarter, limited summer session. **Full-time faculty:** 369 total. **Part-time faculty:** 201 total. **Class size:** 36% < 20, 50% 20-39, 9% 40-49, 5% 50-99, less than 1% >100. **Special facilities:** Chimpanzee and Human Communication Institute, geodesy lab, data analysis center, education technology center, Museum of Northwest Native American and Circum-Pacific Artifacts.

Freshman class profile. 4,656 applied, 3,554 admitted, 1,435 enrolled.

Mid 50% test scores			
SAT verbal:	440-570	Rank in top quarter:	30%
SAT math:	460-570	Rank in top tenth:	9%
ACT:	18-24	Out-of-state:	3%
		Live on campus:	97%

Basis for selection. Admission generally based on weighted combination of test scores and GPA. Interview, essay, and recommendations required for students whose grades or test scores do not reflect their potential for success. Additional academic support provided within alternate admission program. ACT COMPASS may be substituted for SAT or ACT. SAT/ACT scores also used for placement into appropriate levels of math and English classes. **Homeschooled:** Must submit transcripts for any periods enrolled in secondary school, submit ACT or SAT scores, write substantial essay about applicant's preparation for college and how schooling meets or parallels core requirements.

High school preparation. 15 units required; 17 recommended. Required and recommended units include English 4, mathematics 3, social studies 3, science 2-3 (laboratory 1) and foreign language 2-3. 1 year of performing or fine arts or additional year of study in any main subject area also required. Course work in U.S. history and government recommended and will count toward social studies requirements.

2005-2006 Annual costs. Tuition/fees: $4,766; $13,100 out-of-state. Room/board: $6,924. Books/supplies: $810. Personal expenses: $2,094.

2004-2005 Financial aid. **Need-based:** 43% of total undergraduate aid awarded as scholarships/grants, 57% as loans/jobs. **Non-need-based:** Scholarships awarded for academics, alumni affiliation, art, athletics, job skills, leadership, minority status, music/drama, religious affiliation, ROTC, state residency.

Application procedures. **Admission:** Closing date 4/1 (receipt date). $50 fee, may be waived for applicants with need. Application may be submitted online. Admission notification on a rolling basis beginning on or about 12/1. **Financial aid:** Priority date 3/1; no closing date. FAFSA required. Applicants notified on a rolling basis starting 4/15; must reply within 4 week(s) of notification.

Academics. Extended degree programs at locations in Yakima, Wenatchee, and greater Seattle area. **Special study options:** Cooperative education, distance learning, double major, dual enrollment of high school students, ESL, exchange student, honors, independent study, internships, student-designed major, study abroad, teacher certification program, weekend college. **Credit/placement by examination:** AP, CLEP, IB, institutional tests. 45 credit hours maximum toward bachelor's degree. **Support services:** Learning center, reduced course load, remedial instruction, study skills assistance, tutoring, writing center.

Honors college/program. General education program emphasizes history, philosophy, literature. Applicants should score in upper 10 percent on SAT and ACT Verbal Composite and Quantitative Composite. 3.0 GPA required. 25 freshmen generally admitted.

Majors. **Area/ethnic studies:** Asian. **Biology:** General. **Business:** Accounting, business admin, construction management, fashion, office management. **Communications:** General, journalism, public relations. **Computer sciences:** General. **Education:** Art, biology, business, chemistry, drama/dance, early childhood, elementary, English, family/consumer sciences, foreign languages, French, German, health, history, mathematics, music, physical, science, social science, Spanish, special, technology/industrial arts, trade/industrial. **Engineering technology:** Construction, electrical, industrial, mechanical. **Family/consumer sciences:** General, food/nutrition. **Foreign languages:** Chinese, French, German, Japanese, Russian, Spanish. **Health:** Occupational health. **History:** General. **Interdisciplinary:** Gerontology. **Math:** General. **Parks/recreation:** General, sports admin. **Philosophy/religion:** Philosophy, religion. **Physical sciences:** Chemistry, geology, physics, planetary. **Protective services:** Criminal justice. **Psychology:** General. **Public administration:** Human services, policy analysis. **Social sciences:** General, anthropology, economics, geography, political science, sociology. **Transportation:** Aviation. **Visual/performing arts:** Art, commercial/advertising art, dramatic, music management, music performance, music theory/composition, piano/organ, stringed instruments, studio arts, voice/opera.

Computing on campus. 700 workstations in dormitories, library, computer center, student center. Dormitories linked to campus network. Commuter students can connect to campus network. Helpline, student web hosting, wireless network available.

Student life. **Freshman orientation:** Mandatory. Preregistration for classes offered. 2-day introduction to campus held for students and parents. **Policies:** Freshmen permitted cars on campus. **Housing:** Guaranteed on-campus for freshmen. Coed dorms, single-sex dorms, special housing for disabled, apartments, substance-free housing available. $200 deposit. Academic interests, upperclasmen, and 21 years old and older. **Activities:** Bands, choral groups, dance, drama, film society, literary magazine, music ensembles, musical theater, opera, radio station, student government, student newspaper, symphony orchestra, religious, political, ethnic, minority student organizations, professional societies, major field clubs available.

Athletics. NAIA, NCAA. **Intercollegiate:** Baseball M, basketball, cheerleading, cross-country, football (tackle) M, soccer W, softball W, track and field, volleyball W. **Intramural:** Badminton, basketball, football (non-tackle), golf, racquetball, rugby, soccer, softball, tennis, volleyball. **Team name:** Wildcats.

Student services. Adult student services, alcohol/substance abuse counseling, campus ministries, career counseling, services for economically disadvantaged, student employment services, financial aid counseling, health services, on-campus daycare, personal counseling, placement for graduates, veterans' counselor, women's services. **Physically disabled:** Services for visually, speech, hearing impaired.

Contact. E-mail: cwuadmis@cwu.edu
Phone: (509) 963-1211 Toll-free number: (866) 298-4968
Fax: (509) 963-3022
Lisa Garcia-Hanson, Director of Admissions, Central Washington University, 400 East University Way, Ellensburg, WA 98926-7463

City University

Bellevue, Washington — **CB member**
www.cityu.edu — **CB code: 4042**

- Private 4-year university
- Commuter campus in very large city
- 1,131 full-time, degree-seeking undergraduates

General. Founded in 1973. Regionally accredited. University maintains satellite sites in Renton, Everett, North Seattle, Spokane, Tacoma, Vancouver, Tri-Cities Yakima, Kitsap, San Jose (CA), Los Angeles (CA), Canada,

Germany, Switzerland, Slovakia, Denmark. **Degrees:** 600 bachelor's, 21 associate awarded; master's offered. **Location:** 12 miles from Seattle. **Calendar:** Quarter, extensive summer session. **Full-time faculty:** 30 total. **Part-time faculty:** 1,189 total. **Class size:** 52% < 20, 43% 20-39, 1% 40-49, 3% 50-99, less than 1% >100.

Freshman class profile. 15 applied, 15 admitted, 15 enrolled.

Basis for selection. Open admission.

2006-2007 Annual costs. Tuition/fees (projected): $12,435. Books/supplies: $860.

Financial aid. Non-need-based: Scholarships awarded for academics. **Additional information:** All degree programs approved for veteran's administration educational benefits.

Application procedures. Admission: No deadline. $80 fee. Admission notification on a rolling basis. **Financial aid:** No deadline. FAFSA, institutional form required. Applicants notified on a rolling basis.

Academics. Special study options: Accelerated study, distance learning, double major, dual enrollment of high school students, ESL, external degree, internships, student-designed major, teacher certification program, weekend college. **Credit/placement by examination:** CLEP, IB, institutional tests. 45 credit hours maximum toward associate degree, 90 toward bachelor's.

Majors. Business: Accounting, business admin, marketing. **Communications:** Journalism. **Computer sciences:** Programming. **Liberal arts:** Arts/sciences. **Philosophy/religion:** Philosophy. **Protective services:** Law enforcement admin. **Psychology:** General. **Social sciences:** International relations, political science, sociology.

Most popular majors. Business/marketing 45%, computer/information sciences 21%, education 22%, liberal arts 7%.

Computing on campus. 80 workstations in computer center. Commuter students can connect to campus network. Helpline, repair service available.

Student services. Adult student services, career counseling, financial aid counseling, veterans' counselor. **Physically disabled:** Services for visually, hearing impaired.

Contact. E-mail: info@cityu.edu
Phone: (425) 637-1010 Toll-free number: (800) 426-5596
Fax: (425) 277-2437
Melissa Mecham, Vice President Admissions/Student Affairs, City University, 11900 NE 1st Street, Bellevue, WA 98005

Cornish College of the Arts
Seattle, Washington
www.cornish.edu **CB code: 0058**

- Private 4-year visual arts and music college
- Commuter campus in very large city
- 663 degree-seeking undergraduates: 3% African American, 4% Asian American, 4% Hispanic American, 1% Native American, 3% international
- 51% of applicants admitted
- Application essay required

General. Founded in 1914. Regionally accredited. **Degrees:** 126 bachelor's awarded. **Calendar:** Semester, limited summer session. **Full-time faculty:** 54 total. **Part-time faculty:** 92 total. **Class size:** 87% < 20, 13% 20-39. **Special facilities:** Electronic music laboratory, experimental books laboratory, music listening center, costumemaking facilities, video editing facilities.

Freshman class profile. 1,081 applied, 546 admitted, 270 enrolled.

End year in good standing:	99%	**Out-of-state:**	40%
Return as sophomores:	90%	**International:**	2%

Basis for selection. Portfolio (for visual artists) or audition (for performing artists), academic achievement history, creative ability, and artistic goals considered. SAT or ACT recommended. Interview recommended for all; audition required for dance, music, theater; portfolio required for art, design, performance production. Alternative audition and portfolio arrangements for long-distance applicants. **Homeschooled:** Transcript of courses and grades, state high school equivalency certificate required.

High school preparation. Required and recommended units include English 4, mathematics 2-4, social studies 3, science 2-4 (laboratory 1) and foreign language 2.

2006-2007 Annual costs. Tuition/fees (projected): $22,400. Design Major required to have a laptop computer and Adobe software, estimated cost = $3000.00. Books/supplies: $1,800. Personal expenses: $2,000.

Financial aid. Non-need-based: Scholarships awarded for academics.

Application procedures. Admission: Priority date 2/1; deadline 8/15 (receipt date). $35 fee, may be waived for applicants with need. Application may be submitted online. Admission notification on a rolling basis beginning on or about 1/1. Must reply by May 1 or within 2 week(s) if notified thereafter. **Financial aid:** Priority date 2/15; no closing date. FAFSA, institutional form required. Applicants notified on a rolling basis starting 4/15; must reply by 5/1 or within 2 week(s) of notification.

Academics. Special study options: Cooperative education, independent study, internships, study abroad. **Credit/placement by examination:** AP, CLEP, institutional tests. 30 credit hours maximum toward bachelor's degree. A total of 30 credits through a combination of prior work experience and credit by exam allowed. **Support services:** Remedial instruction, study skills assistance, tutoring, writing center.

Majors. Visual/performing arts: General, acting, art, cinematography, commercial/advertising art, dance, design, directing/producing, dramatic, drawing, graphic design, illustration, interior design, jazz, music performance, music theory/composition, painting, photography, piano/organ, play/screenwriting, printmaking, sculpture, stringed instruments, studio arts, theater design, voice/opera.

Computing on campus. 91 workstations in library, computer center, student center. Online library, helpline, wireless network available.

Student life. Freshman orientation: Mandatory. Preregistration for classes offered. Begins one week before class starts each fall. Students will meet the Chair of their department and register for classes. **Policies:** Freshmen permitted cars on campus. **Activities:** Bands, choral groups, dance, drama, film society, literary magazine, music ensembles, musical theater, opera, student government, student newspaper, art history club, Birds and Whistles, Black student alliance, bowling club, digital illustration club, Inform the Misinformed Campaign/Corporate Watchdogs, movie club, Salt and Light (Bible study), sports/intramural club.

Student services. Adult student services, alcohol/substance abuse counseling, career counseling, student employment services, financial aid counseling, personal counseling, placement for graduates. **Physically disabled:** Services for visually impaired.

Contact. E-mail: admissions@cornish.edu
Phone: (206) 726-5016 Toll-free number: (800) 726-2787
Fax: (206) 720-1011
Eric Pedersen, Director of Admissions, Cornish College of the Arts, 1000 Lenora Street, Seattle, WA 98121

Crown College
Tacoma, Washington
www.crowncollege.edu **CB code: 3129**

- For-profit 4-year business college
- Commuter campus in large city
- 293 undergraduates
- Interview required

General. Accredited by ACCSCT. **Degrees:** 75 bachelor's, 80 associate awarded. **Location:** 30 miles from Seattle. **Calendar:** Continuous, extensive summer session. **Full-time faculty:** 7 total; 100% have terminal degrees, 14% minority, 29% women. **Part-time faculty:** 17 total; 100% have terminal degrees, 24% minority, 41% women.

Basis for selection. Open admission, but selective for some programs. Criminal justice applicants must not have felony or domestic violence convictions. Transfer into Bachelor completion requires 2.5 GPA from Associate program. **Homeschooled:** Statement describing homeschool structure and mission, transcript of courses and grades, state high school equivalency certificate required.

2006-2007 Annual costs. Tuition/fees (projected): $7,500.

Financial aid. All financial aid based on need.

Application procedures. Admission: No deadline. $135 fee. Application may be submitted online. Admission notification on a rolling basis. **Financial aid:** FAFSA required.

Academics. **Special study options:** Accelerated study, distance learning, internships, liberal arts/career combination. **Credit/placement by examination:** CLEP, institutional tests. **Support services:** Learning center, study skills assistance, tutoring.

Majors. **Business:** Business admin. **Computer sciences:** Information technology.

Computing on campus. 90 workstations in library, computer center, student center. Commuter students can connect to campus network. Online course registration, online library, helpline available.

Student life. **Freshman orientation:** Mandatory. Preregistration for classes offered. 4 hours at start of new freshman class. **Policies:** Freshmen permitted cars on campus.

Athletics. **Team name:** Golden Eagles.

Student services. Career counseling, student employment services, financial aid counseling, placement for graduates. **Physically disabled:** Services for visually, speech, hearing impaired.

Contact. E-mail: admissions@crowncollege.edu
Phone: (253) 531-3123 Toll-free number: (888) 689-3688
Fax: (253) 531-3521
Jesica McMulline, Director of Admissions, Crown College, 8739 South Hosmer Street, Tacoma, WA 98444-1836

DeVry University: Federal Way

Federal Way, Washington
www.sea.devry.edu **CB code: 3696**

- For-profit 4-year university
- Commuter campus in large city
- 773 degree-seeking undergraduates: 29% part-time, 29% women
- 103 graduate students
- Interview required

General. **Degrees:** 201 bachelor's, 20 associate awarded; master's offered. **Calendar:** Semester, extensive summer session. **Full-time faculty:** 32 total; 22% minority, 19% women. **Part-time faculty:** 18 total; 6% minority, 22% women.

Freshman class profile. 96 enrolled.

Basis for selection. Applicants must have high school diploma or equivalent, or a degree from an accredited postsecondary institution. Must demonstrate proficiency in basic college level skills through test scores and/or institutionally-administered placement exams, and be at least 17 years of age on the first day of classes. New students may enter at the beginning of any semester. CPT also accepted.

High school preparation. Required units include mathematics 1. Math unit must be algebra or higher.

2005-2006 Annual costs. Tuition/fees: $13,410. Books/supplies: $1,250. Personal expenses: $1,950.

Financial aid. All financial aid based on need.

Application procedures. **Admission:** No deadline. $50 fee. Application may be submitted online. Admission notification on a rolling basis. **Financial aid:** No deadline. FAFSA required. Applicants notified on a rolling basis.

Academics. **Special study options:** Accelerated study, cooperative education, distance learning. **Credit/placement by examination:** CLEP. **Support services:** Learning center, remedial instruction, tutoring.

Majors. **Business:** General. **Computer sciences:** Information technology, systems analysis. **Engineering technology:** Computer, electrical.

Most popular majors. Business/marketing 35%, computer/information sciences 40%, engineering/engineering technologies 25%.

Computing on campus. 335 workstations in library, computer center. Online course registration, online library, helpline available.

Student life. **Freshman orientation:** Mandatory. **Policies:** Freshmen permitted cars on campus. **Activities:** Student government, student newspaper, alternative sports, business & technology club, gaming, robotics, Institution of Electrical and Electronic Engineers, network gaming.

Student services. Career counseling, student employment services, financial aid counseling, placement for graduates, veterans' counselor. **Physically disabled:** Services for visually, hearing impaired.

Contact. E-mail: admissions@sea.devry.edu
Phone: (253) 943-2810 Toll-free number: (877) 923-3879
Fax: (253) 943-3291
Fred Pressel, Director of Admissions, DeVry University: Federal Way, 3600 South 344th Way, Federal Way, WA 98001-9558

DigiPen Institute of Technology

Redmond, Washington
www.digipen.edu **CB code: 4138**

- For-profit 4-year visual arts and engineering college
- Commuter campus in large town
- 618 degree-seeking undergraduates: 5% women
- 20 degree-seeking graduate students
- 47% of applicants admitted
- SAT or ACT (ACT writing optional), application essay required

General. Accredited by ACCSCT. **Degrees:** 42 bachelor's, 26 associate awarded; master's offered. **Location:** 20 miles from downtown Seattle. **Calendar:** Semester, limited summer session. **Full-time faculty:** 60 total. **Part-time faculty:** 20 total.

Freshman class profile. 563 applied, 263 admitted, 179 enrolled.

Mid 50% test scores		ACT:	25-29
SAT verbal:	540-650	End year in good standing:	89%
SAT math:	580-670	Return as sophomores:	80%

Basis for selection. Applicants must submit official transcripts, test scores, and recommendation letters, a personal statement. Non-native English speakers must provide a minimum TOEFL iBT score of 80. Portfolios of 10-20 pieces of work required for art school applicants. **Homeschooled:** Home schooled applicants who have completed an accredited high school curriculum may submit official transcripts as proof of their high school equivalency. Applicants who did not complete an accredited program must show proof of their high school equivalency through an official high school equivalency test, such as the GED, and submit those scores. **Learning Disabled:** Contact Student Services Director (ADA Coordinator) to arrange accommodations.

Financial aid. All financial aid based on need.

Application procedures. **Admission:** Priority date 2/1; no deadline. $75 fee, may be waived for applicants with need. Application may be submitted online. Admission notification on a rolling basis. Applicants must respond by the date listed on their individual acceptance letters. **Financial aid:** No deadline. FAFSA, institutional form required. Applicants notified on a rolling basis starting 1/1; must reply within 4 week(s) of notification.

Academics. **Special study options:** Independent study, internships. **Credit/placement by examination:** AP, CLEP, IB, institutional tests. **Support services:** Tutoring.

Majors. **Computer sciences:** Computer science.

Computing on campus. Online course registration available.

Student life. **Freshman orientation:** Mandatory. A 3-4 day orientation is held the week before classes begin. **Policies:** Freshmen permitted cars on campus. **Activities:** Student government.

Student services. Financial aid counseling. **Physically disabled:** Services for hearing impaired.

Contact. E-mail: admissions@digipen.edu
Phone: (425) 558-0299 Fax: (425) 558-0378
Angela Kugler, Admissions and Outreach Manager, DigiPen Institute of Technology, 5001-150th Avenue NE., Redmond, WA 98052

Eastern Washington University

Cheney, Washington **CB member**
www.ewu.edu **CB code: 4301**

- Public 4-year university
- Commuter campus in large town
- 9,356 degree-seeking undergraduates: 14% part-time, 58% women
- 1,244 degree-seeking graduate students

- 83% of applicants admitted
- SAT or ACT with writing required

General. Founded in 1882. Regionally accredited. **Degrees:** 1,859 bachelor's awarded; master's, doctoral offered. **ROTC:** Army. **Location:** 17 miles from Spokane, 200 miles from Seattle. **Calendar:** Quarter, extensive summer session. **Full-time faculty:** 396 total; 96% have terminal degrees, 8% minority, 43% women. **Part-time faculty:** 165 total; 100% have terminal degrees, 4% minority, 57% women. **Class size:** 24% < 20, 52% 20-39, 10% 40-49, 12% 50-99, 1% >100. **Special facilities:** Planetarium, 17,000-acre national wildlife refuge, on-campus elementary school, anthropology museum, laboratory for ecological studies, photography and print gallery, children's center, English language institute, state crime lab.

Freshman class profile. 4,365 applied, 3,602 admitted, 1,637 enrolled.

Mid 50% test scores		**GPA 2.0-2.99:**	24%
SAT verbal:	440-550	**Rank in top quarter:**	44%
SAT math:	450-560	**Rank in top tenth:**	19%
ACT:	18-24	**Out-of-state:**	9%
GPA 3.50 or higher:	34%	**Live on campus:**	70%
GPA 3.0-3.49:	42%		

Basis for selection. Admission based on index combining GPA, test scores and requisite high school core curriculum. Essay and special review considered for applicants who do not meet these standards. Limited number enrolled below index and core requirements. Letters of recommendation from teachers and/or counselors encouraged. Interview or essay required for returning adult applicants and high school students below admission index. **Homeschooled:** Must show evidence of completing required core courses.

High school preparation. 15 units required. Required and recommended units include English 4, mathematics 3-4, social studies 3, science 2 (laboratory 1), foreign language 2 and academic electives 1. Math requirement includes algebra, geometry, and trigonometry or advanced algebra. One year fine arts or core elective required. Foreign language requirement includes 2 years in 1 foreign language (American Sign Language accepted).

2005-2006 Annual costs. Tuition/fees: $4,301; $13,574 out-of-state. Room/board: $5,933. Books/supplies: $690. Personal expenses: $1,908.

2004-2005 Financial aid. Need-based: 1,374 full-time freshmen applied for aid; 1,032 were judged to have need; 999 of these received aid. Average need met was 43%. Average scholarship/grant was $4,468; average loan $2,335. 34% of total undergraduate aid awarded as scholarships/grants, 66% as loans/jobs. **Non-need-based:** Awarded to 872 full-time undergraduates, including 365 freshmen. Scholarships awarded for academics, alumni affiliation, athletics, ROTC. **Additional information:** Prepaid tuition plan available to Washington state residents.

Application procedures. Admission: $35 fee. Application may be submitted online. Admission notification on a rolling basis beginning on or about 12/1. Must reply by May 1 or within 4 week(s) if notified thereafter. Application deadline is 10 days prior to start of quarter. **Financial aid:** Priority date 4/1; no closing date. FAFSA required. Applicants notified on a rolling basis starting 4/1; must reply within 4 week(s) of notification.

Academics. Extensive internship opportunities available. **Special study options:** Cooperative education, distance learning, double major, ESL, honors, independent study, internships, student-designed major, study abroad, teacher certification program, weekend college. Nursing consortium with Washington State University, Whitworth College, Gonzaga University. Dual degree program: Master's of Social Work (EWU) and Law (Gonzaga). **Credit/placement by examination:** AP, CLEP, IB, institutional tests. 45 credit hours maximum toward bachelor's degree. **Support services:** Learning center, pre-admission summer program, remedial instruction, study skills assistance, tutoring, writing center.

Majors. Architecture: Urban/community planning. **Biology:** General, anatomy, bacteriology, biochemistry, botany, environmental toxicology, zoology. **Business:** Accounting, business admin, human resources, management information systems, management science, marketing, operations, public finance. **Communications:** General, broadcast journalism, journalism, public relations. **Communications technology:** General. **Computer sciences:** Computer science, information systems. **Education:** General, art, business, elementary, health, music, physical, reading, sales/marketing, social science, technology/industrial arts. **Engineering:** Computer. **Engineering technology:** Construction, electrical, manufacturing. **English:** Technical writing. **Family/consumer sciences:** Child development. **Foreign languages:** Comparative lit, French, German, Spanish. **Health:** Athletic training, audiology/speech pathology, communication disorders, dental hygiene, health care admin, predentistry, premedicine, prepharmacy, preveterinary, public health ed, recreational therapy. **History:** General. **Legal studies:** Prelaw. **Liberal arts:** Arts/sciences. **Math:** General. **Parks/recreation:** General, exercise sciences, facilities management, health/fitness. **Physical sciences:** Chemistry, geology, physics, planetary. **Psychology:** General. **Public administration:** Social work. **Social sciences:** Anthropology, economics, geography, international relations, political science, sociology. **Visual/performing arts:** General, art, art history/conservation, commercial/advertising art, dramatic, music performance, music theory/composition, piano/organ, studio arts, voice/opera.

Computing on campus. 226 workstations in dormitories, library, computer center, student center. Dormitories wired for high-speed internet access and linked to campus network. Commuter students can connect to campus network. Online course registration, online library, helpline, wireless network available.

Student life. Freshman orientation: Mandatory. Preregistration for classes offered. One-day sessions from late June through summer. 3-day program prior to start of classes with advising, student activities, enrollment services. **Policies:** Student conduct code, academic integrity policy, alcohol/substance use and abuse policy. Freshmen permitted cars on campus. **Housing:** Coed dorms, single-sex dorms, special housing for disabled, apartments, fraternity/sorority housing, substance-free housing available. $200 deposit, deadline 5/1. Apartments for students with children. **Activities:** Bands, choral groups, dance, drama, literary magazine, music ensembles, musical theater, opera, radio station, student government, student newspaper, symphony orchestra, TV station, Circle K, Native American Student Association, MECHA, Catholic Newman Center, Black Student Union, Model United Nations, United Ministries, international affairs club, environmental club, debate club.

Athletics. NCAA. **Intercollegiate:** Basketball, cross-country, football (tackle) M, golf W, soccer W, tennis, track and field, volleyball W. **Intramural:** Badminton, basketball, bowling, cross-country, football (tackle), golf, racquetball, soccer, softball, tennis, triathlon, volleyball. **Team name:** Eagles.

Student services. Alcohol/substance abuse counseling, career counseling, student employment services, financial aid counseling, health services, minority student services, on-campus daycare, personal counseling, placement for graduates, veterans' counselor, women's services. **Physically disabled:** Services for visually, speech, hearing impaired.

Contact. E-mail: admissions@mail.ewu.edu
Phone: (509) 359-2397 Fax: (509) 359-6692
Shannon Carr, Director of Admissions, Eastern Washington University, 101 Sutton Hall, Cheney, WA 99004-2447

Evergreen State College

Olympia, Washington — **CB member**
www.evergreen.edu — **CB code: 4292**

- Public 4-year liberal arts college
- Commuter campus in small city
- 3,962 degree-seeking undergraduates: 8% part-time, 55% women, 5% African American, 5% Asian American, 4% Hispanic American, 4% Native American
- 290 degree-seeking graduate students
- 97% of applicants admitted
- SAT or ACT (ACT writing optional) required
- 56% graduate within 6 years; 28% enter graduate study

General. Founded in 1967. Regionally accredited. **Degrees:** 1,169 bachelor's awarded; master's offered. **Location:** 6 miles from downtown Olympia, 60 miles from Seattle. **Calendar:** Quarter, limited summer session. **Full-time faculty:** 158 total; 86% have terminal degrees, 25% minority, 50% women. **Part-time faculty:** 63 total; 44% have terminal degrees, 16% minority, 52% women. **Class size:** 43% < 20, 35% 20-39, 11% 40-49, 11% 50-99. **Special facilities:** Organic farm; 3,000 feet of waterfront property on Puget Sound, 1,000 acres of forest.

Freshman class profile. 1,657 applied, 1,611 admitted, 605 enrolled.

Mid 50% test scores		**Rank in top quarter:**	24%
SAT verbal:	530-650	**Rank in top tenth:**	8%
SAT math:	480-600	**End year in good standing:**	69%
ACT:	21-27	**Return as sophomores:**	70%
GPA 3.50 or higher:	18%	**Out-of-state:**	40%
GPA 3.0-3.49:	38%	**Live on campus:**	81%
GPA 2.0-2.99:	43%		

Basis for selection. School achievement record, test scores, diversity factors, understanding of interdisciplinary study important. Official TOEFL test scores are required for most students whose native language is not English. Applicants 25 years old and older may submit a personal resume and personal statement (PDF) in lieu of SAT or ACT scores. Essay recommended. Interviews optional (by appointment for non-residents.). **Homeschooled:** Transcript of courses and grades required.

High school preparation. College-preparatory program required. 15 units required. Required units include English 4, mathematics 3, social studies 3, science 2 (laboratory 1), foreign language 2 and academic electives 1. One fine, visual, or performing arts elective or other college prep elective from the areas above required.

2005-2006 Annual costs. Tuition/fees: $4,337; $14,747 out-of-state. Room/board: $6,924. Books/supplies: $894. Personal expenses: $1,566.

2004-2005 Financial aid. Need-based: 415 full-time freshmen applied for aid; 229 were judged to have need; 218 of these received aid. Average need met was 77%. Average scholarship/grant was $4,815; average loan $2,862. 52% of total undergraduate aid awarded as scholarships/grants, 48% as loans/jobs. **Non-need-based:** Awarded to 356 full-time undergraduates, including 146 freshmen. Scholarships awarded for academics, athletics, state residency. **Additional information:** Application deadline for merit and cultural diversity scholarships February 1. Minority students may apply for tuition and fee waiver scholarships; amount of award equal to in-state tuition and fees. Discount waiver for employees. To meet priority deadline for required financial aid forms, official results of FAFSA must be received by March 15.

Application procedures. Admission: Priority date 3/1; no deadline. $50 fee, may be waived for applicants with need. Application may be submitted online. Admission notification on a rolling basis beginning on or about 12/1. Must reply by May 1 or within 4 week(s) if notified thereafter. **Financial aid:** Priority date 3/15; no closing date. FAFSA, institutional form required. Applicants notified on a rolling basis starting 4/15; must reply within 4 week(s) of notification.

Academics. Special study options: Accelerated study, double major, exchange student, independent study, internships, student-designed major, study abroad, teacher certification program. **Credit/placement by examination:** AP, CLEP, IB. 135 credit hours maximum toward bachelor's degree. **Support services:** Learning center, reduced course load, study skills assistance, tutoring, writing center.

Majors. Area/ethnic studies: Native American. **Biology:** General. **Business:** Business admin. **Computer sciences:** General. **Conservation:** Environmental studies. **Education:** General. **Foreign languages:** Classics. **Interdisciplinary:** Biological/physical sciences, global studies, intercultural, natural sciences. **Liberal arts:** Arts/sciences, humanities. **Physical sciences:** General. **Social sciences:** General, political science. **Visual/performing arts:** General, art, cinematography, dramatic, multimedia, studio arts.

Computing on campus. 300 workstations in dormitories, library, computer center. Dormitories wired for high-speed internet access and linked to campus network. Commuter students can connect to campus network. Online course registration, online library, helpline, student web hosting, wireless network available.

Student life. Freshman orientation: Available. Preregistration for classes offered. Week-long orientation offers academic and social events to familiarize students with teaching, learning, and resources at campus. **Policies:** Freshmen permitted cars on campus. **Housing:** Guaranteed on-campus for freshmen. Coed dorms, special housing for disabled, apartments, substance-free housing available. $250 fully refundable deposit, deadline 7/15. First-year experience residence halls, quiet housing, alcohol/drug-free housing, smoke-free housing, Community Action House, Sustainability House. **Activities:** Choral groups, dance, drama, film society, literary magazine, music ensembles, radio station, student newspaper, TV station, Native Student Alliance, Evergreen Queer Alliance, Women of Color Coalition, Students for Christ, Radical Catholics for Justice and Peace, MECHA, Women's Resource Center, Evergreen Political Information Center, Students for Ecological Design, Asian Solidarity in Action.

Athletics. NAIA. **Intercollegiate:** Basketball, cross-country, soccer, track and field, volleyball W. **Intramural:** Badminton, basketball, fencing, racquetball, soccer, softball, tennis, volleyball, water polo. **Team name:** Geoducks.

Student services. Adult student services, alcohol/substance abuse counseling, career counseling, services for economically disadvantaged, student employment services, financial aid counseling, health services, minority student services, on-campus daycare, personal counseling, placement for graduates, veterans' counselor, women's services. **Physically disabled:** Services for visually, speech, hearing impaired.

Contact. E-mail: admissions@evergreen.edu
Phone: (360) 867-6170 Fax: (360) 867-6576
Doug Scrima, Director of Admissions, Evergreen State College, 2700 Evergreen Parkway NW, Olympia, WA 98505

Gonzaga University

Spokane, Washington **CB member**
www.gonzaga.edu **CB code: 4330**

- Private 4-year university and liberal arts college affiliated with Roman Catholic Church
- Residential campus in large city
- 4,060 degree-seeking undergraduates: 3% part-time, 54% women, 1% African American, 6% Asian American, 4% Hispanic American, 1% Native American, 1% international
- 2,028 degree-seeking graduate students
- 73% of applicants admitted
- SAT or ACT (ACT writing optional), application essay required
- 74% graduate within 6 years

General. Founded in 1887. Regionally accredited. **Degrees:** 932 bachelor's awarded; master's, doctoral, first professional offered. **ROTC:** Army. **Location:** 300 miles from Seattle. **Calendar:** Semester, extensive summer session. **Full-time faculty:** 325 total; 86% have terminal degrees, 10% minority. **Part-time faculty:** 300 total; 1% have terminal degrees, less than 1% minority, 45% women. **Class size:** 51% < 20, 45% 20-39, 2% 40-49, 2% 50-99. **Special facilities:** 2 electron microscopes.

Freshman class profile. 4,328 applied, 3,173 admitted, 986 enrolled.

Mid 50% test scores		**Rank in top quarter:**	71%
SAT verbal:	540-640	**Rank in top tenth:**	40%
SAT math:	550-650	**End year in good standing:**	98%
ACT:	24-29	**Return as sophomores:**	90%
GPA 3.50 or higher:	71%	**Out-of-state:**	45%
GPA 3.0-3.49:	25%	**Live on campus:**	96%
GPA 2.0-2.99:	4%	**International:**	1%

Basis for selection. GED not accepted. Academic achievement, scholastic aptitude, personal characteristics important. GPA below 3.0 reevaluated to include only grades in academic subjects. Course content and test scores important. Interview recommended for all; audition recommended for music. **Homeschooled:** Test scores, interview by admissions representative required.

High school preparation. Required and recommended units include English 4, mathematics 3-4, social studies 2-3, history 2-3, science 3-4 (laboratory 3-4), foreign language 3-4 and academic electives 3. Algebra, geometry, trigonometry required of engineering applicants. Of 6 additional electives 4 must be from subjects mentioned and the arts.

2005-2006 Annual costs. Tuition/fees: $23,680. Room/board: $6,700. Books/supplies: $750. Personal expenses: $1,700.

2004-2005 Financial aid. Need-based: 824 full-time freshmen applied for aid; 610 were judged to have need; 608 of these received aid. Average need met was 83%. Average scholarship/grant was $12,554; average loan $4,097. 63% of total undergraduate aid awarded as scholarships/grants, 37% as loans/jobs. **Non-need-based:** Awarded to 2,346 full-time undergraduates, including 591 freshmen. Scholarships awarded for academics, alumni affiliation, athletics, leadership, minority status, music/drama, ROTC.

Application procedures. Admission: Closing date 2/1 (postmark date). $45 fee, may be waived for applicants with need. Application may be submitted online. Admission notification 3/15. Must reply by 5/1. **Financial aid:** Priority date 2/1, closing date 6/30. FAFSA required. Applicants notified on a rolling basis starting 3/1; must reply by 5/1 or within 3 week(s) of notification.

Academics. Special study options: Accelerated study, combined bachelor's/graduate degree, double major, ESL, exchange student, honors, internships, semester at sea, study abroad, teacher certification program, Washington semester, weekend college. **Credit/placement by examination:** AP, CLEP, IB, SAT, ACT. 32 credit hours maximum toward bachelor's degree. **Support services:** Pre-admission summer program, study skills assistance, writing center.

Majors. Area/ethnic studies: Asian, European, Latin American, women's. **Biology:** General, biochemistry. **Business:** Accounting, banking/financial services, business admin, international, management information systems, managerial economics. **Communications:** Broadcast journalism, journalism, public relations. **Computer sciences:** Computer science. **Education:** Music, physical, special. **Engineering:** General, civil, computer, electrical, mechanical. **English:** Speech/rhetoric. **Foreign languages:** Comparative lit, French, Italian, Spanish. **Health:** Preop/surgical nursing. **History:** General. **Liberal arts:** Arts/sciences. **Math:** General. **Philosophy/religion:** Philosophy, religion. **Physical sciences:** Chemistry, physics. **Protective services:**

Criminal justice. **Psychology:** General. **Social sciences:** Economics, international relations, political science, sociology. **Visual/performing arts:** Dramatic, music performance, studio arts.

Most popular majors. Biology 6%, business/marketing 23%, communications/journalism 8%, engineering/engineering technologies 9%, social sciences 12%.

Computing on campus. 560 workstations in library, computer center. Dormitories wired for high-speed internet access and linked to campus network. Commuter students can connect to campus network. Online course registration, online library, helpline, repair service, student web hosting available.

Student life. **Freshman orientation:** Mandatory, $60 fee. Preregistration for classes offered. **Policies:** Freshmen permitted cars on campus. **Housing:** Guaranteed on-campus for freshmen. Coed dorms, single-sex dorms, special housing for disabled, apartments, substance-free housing available. $200 fully refundable deposit, deadline 5/1. International students, freshmen and sophomores under 21 must live on campus, unless living at home. **Activities:** Bands, choral groups, dance, drama, literary magazine, music ensembles, radio station, student government, student newspaper, symphony orchestra, TV station, 102 student clubs and service organizations.

Athletics. NCAA. **Intercollegiate:** Baseball M, basketball, cross-country, golf, rowing (crew), soccer, tennis, track and field, volleyball W. **Intramural:** Badminton, basketball, racquetball, soccer, softball, tennis, volleyball, weight lifting, wrestling M. **Team name:** Bulldogs.

Student services. Adult student services, alcohol/substance abuse counseling, campus ministries, career counseling, student employment services, financial aid counseling, health services, minority student services, personal counseling, veterans' counselor. **Physically disabled:** Services for visually, speech, hearing impaired.

Contact. E-mail: mcculloh@gu.gonzaga.edu
Phone: (509) 323-6572 Toll-free number: (800) 322-2584
Fax: (509) 323-5780
Julie McCulloh, Dean of Admissions, Gonzaga University, 502 East Boone Avenue, Spokane, WA 99258-0001

Henry Cogswell College

Everett, Washington
www.henrycogswell.edu **CB code: 0584**

- Private 4-year engineering and liberal arts college
- Commuter campus in small city
- 200 degree-seeking undergraduates: 41% part-time, 26% women, 2% African American, 8% Asian American, 7% Hispanic American, 1% Native American
- 77% of applicants admitted
- Application essay required
- 42% graduate within 6 years

General. Founded in 1979. Regionally accredited. **Degrees:** 63 bachelor's awarded. **Location:** 30 miles from Seattle. **Calendar:** Trimester, extensive summer session. **Full-time faculty:** 14 total; 43% have terminal degrees, 29% women. **Part-time faculty:** 18 total; 28% have terminal degrees, 22% women. **Class size:** 88% < 20, 12% 20-39.

Freshman class profile. 86 applied, 66 admitted, 56 enrolled.

Mid 50% test scores		**ACT:**	12-20
SAT verbal:	510-560	**Return as sophomores:**	64%
SAT math:	560-610		

Basis for selection. Standardized test scores and secondary school record are most important. Institutional tests in mathematics and English may be required for placement. Interview recommended for all; portfolio required of art students. **Learning Disabled:** Campus interview recommended.

High school preparation. 13 units required; 16 recommended. Required and recommended units include English 4, mathematics 2-3, social studies 3, history 1, science 2-3 (laboratory 2-3), foreign language 1 and academic electives 2. 2 art required for digital arts majors.

2005-2006 Annual costs. Tuition/fees: $16,680. Personal expenses: $1,720.

2005-2006 Financial aid. All financial aid based on need. 31 full-time freshmen applied for aid; 28 were judged to have need; 28 of these received aid. Average need met was 29%. Average scholarship/grant was $1,606; average loan $1,666. 29% of total undergraduate aid awarded as scholarships/grants, 71% as loans/jobs. **Additional information:** Many students qualify for tuition reimbursement from industry employers.

Application procedures. **Admission:** No deadline. $50 fee, may be waived for applicants with need. Application may be submitted online. Admission notification on a rolling basis beginning on or about 9/1. Must reply by May 1 or within 4 week(s) if notified thereafter. **Financial aid:** Priority date 3/1; no closing date. FAFSA, institutional form required. Applicants notified by 4/1; must reply within 4 week(s) of notification.

Academics. **Special study options:** Accelerated study, cooperative education, double major, independent study, internships, liberal arts/career combination. **Credit/placement by examination:** AP, CLEP, IB, institutional tests. 30 credit hours maximum toward bachelor's degree. **Support services:** Remedial instruction, study skills assistance, tutoring.

Majors. **Business:** General, business admin. **Communications technology:** Desktop publishing. **Computer sciences:** Computer science. **Engineering:** Electrical, mechanical. **Visual/performing arts:** Commercial/advertising art.

Most popular majors. Business/marketing 16%, computer/information sciences 12%, engineering/engineering technologies 24%, visual/performing arts 48%.

Computing on campus. 150 workstations in library, computer center. Online library available.

Student life. **Freshman orientation:** Mandatory. 2-day event the week before the start of fall term, culminates in registration, lunch provided. **Policies:** Freshmen permitted cars on campus. **Activities:** Student government, student newspaper, Institute of Electrical and Electronic Engineers, American Society for Mechanical Engineering, Association for Computing Machinery, Sigma Iota Epsilon.

Student services. Adult student services, career counseling, student employment services, financial aid counseling, personal counseling, veterans' counselor.

Contact. E-mail: admissions@henrycogswell.edu
Phone: (425) 258-3351 Toll-free number: (866) 411-4224
Fax: (425) 257-0405
Jane Buckman, Dean of Enrollment, Henry Cogswell College, 3002 Colby Avenue, Everett, WA 98201

Heritage University

Toppenish, Washington
www.heritage.edu **CB code: 4344**

- Private 4-year liberal arts and teachers college affiliated with interdenominational tradition
- Commuter campus in small town
- 756 degree-seeking undergraduates: 28% part-time, 73% women, 1% African American, 1% Asian American, 54% Hispanic American, 10% Native American
- 504 degree-seeking graduate students
- 60% of applicants admitted

General. Founded in 1982. Regionally accredited. **Degrees:** 77 bachelor's, 11 associate awarded; master's offered. **Location:** 165 miles from Seattle, 20 miles from Yakima. **Calendar:** Semester, limited summer session. **Full-time faculty:** 47 total; 38% have terminal degrees, 23% minority, 49% women. **Part-time faculty:** 140 total; 17% have terminal degrees, 19% minority, 39% women. **Class size:** 76% < 20, 24% 20-39. **Special facilities:** Solar telescope, portable planetarium, greenhouse.

Freshman class profile. 475 applied, 285 admitted, 89 enrolled.

Basis for selection. Heritage University considers each applicant on an individual basis. Acceptance results from an overall assessment of background, rather than arbitrary standards for grades, test scores, courses taken, or achievements. All students take institutional placement test.

High school preparation. Recommended units include English 3, mathematics 2, history 3, science 1 (laboratory 1) and academic electives 4.

2006-2007 Annual costs. Tuition/fees (projected): $9,645. Books/supplies: $750. Personal expenses: $1,968.

2004-2005 Financial aid. **Need-based:** 94 full-time freshmen applied for aid; 91 were judged to have need; 82 of these received aid. Average need met was 57%. Average scholarship/grant was $7,033; average loan $1,960. 57% of total undergraduate aid awarded as scholarships/grants, 43% as loans/jobs. **Non-need-based:** Awarded to 12 full-time undergraduates, including 2 freshmen. Scholarships awarded for academics, leadership, minority status.

Application procedures. Admission: Priority date 3/15; no deadline. No application fee. Application must be submitted on paper. Admission notification on a rolling basis. **Financial aid:** Priority date 2/10; no closing date. FAFSA, institutional form required. Applicants notified on a rolling basis; must reply within 2 week(s) of notification.

Academics. Special study options: Cooperative education, distance learning, double major, dual enrollment of high school students, ESL, honors, independent study, internships, liberal arts/career combination, student-designed major, teacher certification program. **Credit/placement by examination:** AP, CLEP, institutional tests. 14 credit hours maximum toward associate degree, 30 toward bachelor's. **Support services:** Learning center, reduced course load, remedial instruction, study skills assistance, tutoring, writing center.

Majors. Agriculture: Horticulture. **Area/ethnic studies:** American. **Biology:** General. **Business:** General, accounting, business admin, entrepreneurial studies, human resources, marketing. **Computer sciences:** General. **Conservation:** General, environmental science. **Education:** General, bilingual, biology, chemistry, computer, early childhood, elementary, English, ESL, history, mathematics, middle, reading, science, secondary, Spanish, special. **English:** English lit. **Health:** Health care admin. **Interdisciplinary:** Math/computer science, natural sciences. **Math:** General. **Physical sciences:** General, chemistry. **Psychology:** General. **Public administration:** Social work.

Computing on campus. 160 workstations in library, computer center. Commuter students can connect to campus network. Online library, wireless network available.

Student life. Freshman orientation: Available. Preregistration for classes offered. Typically held one day during the week before classes start for the fall and spring semesters. **Policies:** Freshmen permitted cars on campus. **Activities:** Dance, drama, literary magazine, music ensembles, student government, student newspaper, Native American, Heritage Community Volunteers in Action, Heritage Educators Association, social work club, Nursing students club.

Student services. Adult student services, career counseling, services for economically disadvantaged, student employment services, financial aid counseling, on-campus daycare, personal counseling, placement for graduates, veterans' counselor.

Contact. E-mail: 3w_Admissions@heritage.edu
Phone: (509) 865-8508 Toll-free number: (888) 272-6190
Fax: (509) 865-8659
Lettie Garcia, Director of Admissions, Heritage University, 3240 Fort Road, Toppenish, WA 98948-9599

ITT Technical Institute: Everett

Everett, Washington
www.itt-tech.edu **CB code: 2697**

- For-profit 4-year technical college
- Commuter campus in large town

General. Accredited by ACICS. **Calendar:** Quarter.

Annual costs/financial aid. Tuition varies by program, $260-$368 per credit hour.

Contact. Phone: (425) 485-0303
Director of Recruitment, 1615 75th Street, S.W., Everett, WA 98203

ITT Technical Institute: Seattle

Seattle, Washington
www.itt-tech.edu **CB code: 3599**

- For-profit 4-year technical college
- Commuter campus in very large city

General. Founded in 1932. Accredited by ACICS. **Location:** 12 miles from downtown. **Calendar:** Quarter.

Annual costs/financial aid. Tuition varies by program, $260-$368 per credit hour.

Contact. Phone: (206) 244-3300
Director of Recruitment, 12720 Gateway Drive, Suite 100, Seattle, WA 98168

ITT Technical Institute: Spokane

Spokane Valley, Washington
www.itt-tech.edu **CB code: 7027**

- For-profit 4-year technical college
- Commuter campus in small city

General. Accredited by ACICS. **Location:** 5 miles from downtown. **Calendar:** Quarter.

Annual costs/financial aid. Tuition varies by program, $260-$368 per credit hour.

Contact. Phone: (509) 926-2900
Director of Recruitment, 13518 East Indiana Avenue, Spokane Valley, WA 99216

Northwest College of Art

Poulsbo, Washington
www.nca.edu **CB code: 2432**

- For-profit 4-year visual arts college
- Commuter campus in small town
- 140 undergraduates
- Application essay, interview required

General. Founded in 1982. Accredited by ACCSCT. **Location:** 30 miles from Seattle, 60 miles from Tacoma. **Calendar:** Semester, extensive summer session.

Basis for selection. Requirements include minimum 2.5 GPA, 2 interviews, 3 letters of recommendation, 2-3 page typed essay, portfolio. TOEFL test required for international students from non-english speaking countries. SAT required for students with a GED. Portfolio required. **Homeschooled:** GED required except when home-school programs show proof of school or program accreditation.

2006-2007 Annual costs. Tuition/fees: $14,400.

Financial aid. Non-need-based: Scholarships awarded for academics, art.

Application procedures. Admission: Priority date 3/1; deadline 6/1 (postmark date). $50 fee. Application must be submitted on paper. Admission notification on a rolling basis. **Financial aid:** Priority date 3/1, closing date 6/1. FAFSA required. Applicants notified on a rolling basis.

Academics. Special study options: Double major, internships. **Credit/placement by examination:** AP, CLEP.

Majors. Visual/performing arts: Design, studio arts.

Student life. Freshman orientation: Mandatory, $15 fee. Preregistration for classes offered. **Policies:** Freshmen permitted cars on campus.

Student services. Adult student services, career counseling, student employment services, financial aid counseling, personal counseling, placement for graduates, veterans' counselor.

Contact. E-mail: kperigard@nca.edu
Phone: (360) 779-9993 Toll-free number: (800) 769-2787
Fax: (360) 779-9933
Mark Stoddard, Northwest College of Art, Northwest College of Art, 16301 Creative Drive NE, Poulsbo, WA 98370

Northwest University

Kirkland, Washington
www.northwestu.edu **CB code: 4541**

- Private 4-year university and liberal arts college affiliated with Assemblies of God
- Residential campus in small city
- 1,089 degree-seeking undergraduates: 5% part-time, 63% women
- 107 degree-seeking graduate students
- 83% of applicants admitted
- SAT or ACT (ACT writing optional), application essay required
- 42% graduate within 6 years

General. Founded in 1934. Regionally accredited. **Degrees:** 239 bachelor's, 2 associate awarded; master's offered. **ROTC:** Army. **Location:** 10

miles from Seattle. **Calendar:** Semester, limited summer session. **Full-time faculty:** 55 total. **Part-time faculty:** 35 total. **Class size:** 48% < 20, 44% 20-39, 4% 40-49, 5% 50-99.

Freshman class profile. 427 applied, 356 admitted, 132 enrolled.

GPA 3.50 or higher:	41%	**Return as sophomores:**	74%
GPA 3.0-3.49:	32%	**Out-of-state:**	18%
GPA 2.0-2.99:	27%	**International:**	2%

Basis for selection. Entire application reviewed: includes essay, references, transcript, SAT or ACT. GPA of 2.3 required: those with GPA below 2.3 but greater than 2.0 admitted on academic probation if space available. TOEFL (minimum score 500) required for non-native speakers of English. Audition recommended for music and drama scholarships. **Learning Disabled:** Interview with Director of Student Success.

High school preparation. 16 units recommended. Recommended units include English 4, mathematics 3, social studies 2, history 2, science 2, foreign language 2 and academic electives 3.

2006-2007 Annual costs. Tuition/fees: $18,144. Room/board: $6,450. Books/supplies: $900. Personal expenses: $1,600.

2005-2006 Financial aid. Need-based: 163 full-time freshmen applied for aid; 138 were judged to have need; 135 of these received aid. Average need met was 70%. Average scholarship/grant was $8,644; average loan $2,931. 50% of total undergraduate aid awarded as scholarships/grants, 50% as loans/jobs. **Non-need-based:** Awarded to 275 full-time undergraduates, including 64 freshmen. Scholarships awarded for academics, art, athletics, leadership, music/drama, religious affiliation.

Application procedures. Admission: Priority date 3/1; deadline 8/1 (postmark date). $30 fee, may be waived for applicants with need. Application may be submitted online. Admission notification on a rolling basis beginning on or about 10/1. **Financial aid:** Priority date 3/1; no closing date. FAFSA, institutional form required. Applicants notified by 3/31; Applicants notified on a rolling basis starting 3/3; must reply within 4 week(s) of notification.

Academics. Special study options: Accelerated study, double major, dual enrollment of high school students, ESL, independent study, internships, student-designed major, study abroad, teacher certification program, Washington semester. **Credit/placement by examination:** AP, CLEP, IB, SAT, ACT, institutional tests. 30 credit hours maximum toward associate degree, 30 toward bachelor's. **Support services:** Learning center, reduced course load, remedial instruction, study skills assistance, tutoring, writing center.

Majors. Business: Business admin. **Communications:** General, organizational. **Conservation:** Environmental science. **Education:** Elementary, middle, secondary. **English:** English lit. **Health:** Nursing (RN). **History:** General. **Liberal arts:** Arts/sciences. **Philosophy/religion:** Philosophy. **Psychology:** General. **Social sciences:** Political science. **Theology:** Bible, missionary, pastoral counseling, religious ed, sacred music, theology, youth ministry.

Most popular majors. Business/marketing 26%, communications/journalism 6%, education 13%, health sciences 10%, psychology 15%, theological studies 18%.

Computing on campus. 100 workstations in dormitories, library, computer center, student center. Dormitories wired for high-speed internet access and linked to campus network. Commuter students can connect to campus network. Online course registration, online library, helpline, repair service, student web hosting, wireless network available.

Student life. Freshman orientation: Mandatory. Held end of August, one week before start of classes. **Policies:** Religious observance required. Freshmen permitted cars on campus. **Housing:** Guaranteed on-campus for all undergraduates. Single-sex dorms, apartments available. $200 fully refundable deposit, deadline 5/1. **Activities:** Bands, choral groups, drama, music ensembles, musical theater, radio station, student government, student newspaper, community outreach groups, Psi Chi Honor Society (psychology), Association of International Students, Environmental Stewardship Club, Students in Free Enterprise.

Athletics. NAIA, NCCAA. **Intercollegiate:** Basketball, cross-country, soccer, track and field, volleyball W. **Intramural:** Basketball, football (non-tackle), soccer W. **Team name:** Eagles.

Student services. Adult student services, alcohol/substance abuse counseling, campus ministries, career counseling, student employment services, financial aid counseling, health services, personal counseling, veterans' counselor. **Physically disabled:** Services for visually impaired.

Contact. E-mail: admissions@northwestu.edu
Phone: (425) 889-5231 Toll-free number: (800) 669-3781
Fax: (425) 889-5224
Myles Corrigan, Associate Vice President, Enrollment, Northwest University, 5520 108th Avenue NE, Kirkland, WA 98083-0579

Pacific Lutheran University

Tacoma, Washington — **CB member**
www.plu.edu — **CB code: 4597**

- Private 4-year university affiliated with Evangelical Lutheran Church in America
- Residential campus in large city
- 3,331 degree-seeking undergraduates: 5% part-time, 64% women, 2% African American, 6% Asian American, 2% Hispanic American, 1% Native American, 6% international
- 302 degree-seeking graduate students
- 76% of applicants admitted
- SAT or ACT (ACT writing recommended), application essay required
- 66% graduate within 6 years

General. Founded in 1890. Regionally accredited. **Degrees:** 691 bachelor's awarded; master's offered. **ROTC:** Army. **Location:** 7 miles from Tacoma, 30 miles from Seattle. **Calendar:** 4-1-4, extensive summer session. **Full-time faculty:** 236 total; 86% have terminal degrees, 12% minority, 45% women. **Part-time faculty:** 24 total; 50% have terminal degrees, 8% minority, 71% women. **Class size:** 44% < 20, 48% 20-39, 4% 40-49, 3% 50-99, less than 1% >100. **Special facilities:** Herbarium, invertebrate and vertebrate museums, greenhouse, field station and boat equipped for studies of Puget Sound, Scandinavian cultural center, observatory, performing arts center, language and culture residence hall.

Freshman class profile. 2,112 applied, 1,614 admitted, 690 enrolled.

Mid 50% test scores		**GPA 2.0-2.99:**	8%
SAT verbal:	500-620	**Rank in top quarter:**	65%
SAT math:	500-620	**Rank in top tenth:**	33%
ACT:	21-27	**Out-of-state:**	24%
GPA 3.50 or higher:	65%	**Live on campus:**	88%
GPA 3.0-3.49:	27%	**International:**	3%

Basis for selection. Grades, test scores, essay, recommendations, service, leadership. Admission on rolling basis until class is full. Interview recommended for borderline, exceptional; audition required for music, forensics, theater; portfolio recommended for art. **Homeschooled:** Must provide proof of high-school equivalency.

High school preparation. 17 units required. Required and recommended units include English 4, mathematics 2-3, science 2 (laboratory 2), foreign language 2-3 and academic electives 3. Computer science, speech, debate, music also recommended. 2 years visual or performing arts recommended.

2005-2006 Annual costs. Tuition/fees: $22,040. Room/board: $6,765. Books/supplies: $750. Personal expenses: $2,094.

2004-2005 Financial aid. Need-based: 640 full-time freshmen applied for aid; 508 were judged to have need; 506 of these received aid. Average need met was 93%. Average scholarship/grant was $8,538; average loan $4,329. 56% of total undergraduate aid awarded as scholarships/grants, 44% as loans/jobs. **Non-need-based:** Awarded to 1,592 full-time undergraduates, including 383 freshmen. Scholarships awarded for academics, alumni affiliation, art, leadership, music/drama, ROTC.

Application procedures. Admission: Priority date 2/15; no deadline. $40 fee, may be waived for applicants with need. Application may be submitted online. Admission notification on a rolling basis beginning on or about 10/1. Must reply by May 1 or within 2 week(s) if notified thereafter. Housing deposit is refundable only through May 1. **Financial aid:** Priority date 1/31; no closing date. FAFSA required. Applicants notified on a rolling basis starting 3/1; must reply by 5/1 or within 4 week(s) of notification.

Academics. Freshman year program includes topic-oriented writing and critical conversation classes. **Special study options:** Cooperative education, double major, ESL, exchange student, independent study, internships, liberal arts/career combination, student-designed major, study abroad, teacher certification program. **Credit/placement by examination:** AP, CLEP, IB, institutional tests. 30 credit hours maximum toward bachelor's degree. **Support services:** Pre-admission summer program, reduced course load, study skills assistance, tutoring, writing center.

Majors. Area/ethnic studies: Scandinavian, women's. **Biology:** General. **Business:** Business admin. **Communications:** General. **Computer sciences:** Computer science. **Conservation:** Environmental science. **Education:** Elementary, secondary. **Engineering:** Computer, science. **English:** English lit. **Foreign languages:** Chinese, classics, French, German, Norwegian, Spanish. **Health:** Nursing (RN). **History:** General. **Interdisciplinary:** Global studies. **Math:** General. **Parks/recreation:** General, health/fitness. **Philosophy/religion:** Philosophy, religion. **Physical sciences:** Chemistry, geology, physics. **Psychology:** General. **Public administration:** Social work. **Social sciences:** Anthropology, economics, political science, sociology. **Visual/performing arts:** Art, studio arts, theater arts management.

Most popular majors. Business/marketing 14%, communications/journalism 6%, education 16%, health sciences 8%, psychology 7%, social sciences 13%, visual/performing arts 6%.

Computing on campus. 250 workstations in library, student center. Dormitories wired for high-speed internet access and linked to campus network. Commuter students can connect to campus network. Helpline, student web hosting available.

Student life. Freshman orientation: Available. Preregistration for classes offered. **Policies:** Freshmen permitted cars on campus. **Housing:** Guaranteed on-campus for all undergraduates. Coed dorms, single-sex dorms, apartments, substance-free housing available. $200 deposit, deadline 5/1. All single, full-time students must live in university housing, unless student lives at home with parent or legal guardian, is 20 years of age or older on or before a specific college-designated date, or has achieved junior status. **Activities:** Bands, choral groups, dance, drama, film society, literary magazine, music ensembles, musical theater, opera, radio station, student government, student newspaper, symphony orchestra, TV station, Intervarsity Christian Fellowship, Advocates for Social Justice, Asian & Pacific Islanders club, B.L.A.C.K. at PLU, environmental action, Puentes, social work organization, Amnesty International, Habitat for Humanity, Young Life.

Athletics. NCAA. **Intercollegiate:** Baseball M, basketball, cheerleading, cross-country, football (tackle) M, golf, rowing (crew), soccer, softball W, swimming, tennis, track and field, volleyball W. **Intramural:** Badminton, basketball, bowling, cross-country, football (non-tackle), golf, handball, racquetball, soccer, softball, squash, table tennis, tennis, track and field, volleyball. **Team name:** Lutes.

Student services. Adult student services, campus ministries, career counseling, student employment services, financial aid counseling, health services, minority student services, personal counseling, placement for graduates, veterans' counselor, women's services. **Physically disabled:** Services for visually, speech, hearing impaired.

Contact. E-mail: admissions@plu.edu
Phone: (253) 535-7151 Toll-free number: (800) 274-6758
Fax: (253) 536-5136
Karl Stumo, Dean of Admission and Financial Aid, Pacific Lutheran University, Office of Admissions, Tacoma, WA 98447-0003

Puget Sound Christian College

Everett, Washington
www.pscc.edu **CB code: 4618**

- Private 4-year Bible college affiliated with nondenominational tradition
- Commuter campus in large town
- 140 degree-seeking undergraduates
- SAT or ACT (ACT writing optional) required

General. Founded in 1950. Accredited by ABHE. **Degrees:** 27 bachelor's, 3 associate awarded. **Location:** 15 miles from Seattle. **Calendar:** Semester, limited summer session. **Full-time faculty:** 8 total. **Part-time faculty:** 30 total. **Class size:** 81% < 20, 17% 20-39, 2% 40-49.

Freshman class profile.

Mid 50% test scores			
SAT verbal:	430-590	Out-of-state:	60%
SAT math:	410-600	Live on campus:	85%

Basis for selection. 3 recommendations, 2.0 high school GPA, and test scores considered. Applicants who do not meet these standards will be evaluated individually. College will award placement and credit for SAT Subject Test scores. **Homeschooled:** Must be monitored by local high school to confirm graduation requirements or submit GED. **Learning Disabled:** Must submit documentation of need.

High school preparation. 15 units recommended. Recommended units include English 3, mathematics 3, social studies 1, history 3, science 3 and foreign language 2. One speech recommended.

2005-2006 Annual costs. Tuition/fees: $10,120. Room/board: $5,770. Books/supplies: $900. Personal expenses: $2,800.

Financial aid. Non-need-based: Scholarships awarded for academics, alumni affiliation, music/drama, religious affiliation.

Application procedures. Admission: Priority date 5/1; deadline 8/15 (receipt date). $25 fee, may be waived for applicants with need. Admission notification on a rolling basis. **Financial aid:** Priority date 5/1, closing date 8/15. FAFSA, institutional form required. Applicants notified on a rolling basis starting 4/15; must reply within 3 week(s) of notification.

Academics. All students' first major is Bible; second major relates to professional choice (most are related to church ministry careers). 32 to 40 credit hours of Bible, depending on second major, required for bachelor's degree. 24 Bible credit hours for associate's degree. **Special study options:** Combined bachelor's/graduate degree, double major, dual enrollment of high school students, internships, liberal arts/career combination. Degree-completion program. **Credit/placement by examination:** AP, CLEP. 16 credit hours maximum toward associate degree, 32 toward bachelor's. **Support services:** Reduced course load, remedial instruction, study skills assistance, tutoring.

Majors. Social sciences: General. **Theology:** Bible, missionary, religious ed, sacred music, theology.

Computing on campus. 12 workstations in computer center. Repair service available.

Student life. Freshman orientation: Mandatory, $120 fee. Preregistration for classes offered. Held for 1 week prior to start of classes. **Policies:** No smoking, no alcohol, no drugs allowed on campus. Religious observance required. Freshmen permitted cars on campus. **Housing:** Guaranteed on-campus for freshmen. Single-sex dorms, apartments available. $50 deposit, deadline 8/1. **Activities:** Choral groups, drama, music ensembles, student government, student newspaper, outreach ministries, mission trips, community service.

Athletics. NCCAA. **Intercollegiate:** Basketball, volleyball W. **Intramural:** Baseball M, basketball, skiing, table tennis, tennis, volleyball. **Team name:** Anchormen.

Student services. Adult student services, career counseling, student employment services, financial aid counseling, personal counseling, veterans' counselor.

Contact. E-mail: admissions@pscc.edu
Phone: (425) 257-3090 ext. 554 Toll-free number: (888) 775-8699
Fax: (425) 258-1488
Mark Krause, Dean, Puget Sound Christian College, 2610 Wetmore Avenue, Everett, WA 98206

Saint Martin's University

Lacey, Washington **CB member**
www.stmartin.edu **CB code: 4674**

- Private 4-year liberal arts college affiliated with Roman Catholic Church
- Commuter campus in large town
- 936 full-time, degree-seeking undergraduates
- 73% of applicants admitted
- SAT or ACT with writing, application essay required

General. Founded in 1895. Regionally accredited. Campus is home to Benedictine Monastery where 40 monks live and work. **Degrees:** 435 bachelor's awarded; master's offered. **ROTC:** Army. **Location:** 3 miles from Olympia, 60 miles from Seattle. **Calendar:** Semester, limited summer session. **Full-time faculty:** 67 total. **Part-time faculty:** 7 total. **Class size:** 77% < 20, 22% 20-39, less than 1% 40-49.

Freshman class profile. 522 applied, 382 admitted, 173 enrolled.

Mid 50% test scores			
SAT verbal:	450-590	Rank in top quarter:	48%
SAT math:	450-570	Rank in top tenth:	22%
ACT:	19-23	Out-of-state:	18%
		Live on campus:	82%

Basis for selection. School achievement record most important. Test scores important. 3.0 GPA required for regular admittance. TOEFL required for international applicants. Interview recommended. **Learning Disabled:** Recommend students self-identify to Director of Access Services for information on support services.

High school preparation. 14 units recommended. Recommended units include English 4, mathematics 3, social studies 2, science 2 (laboratory 1), foreign language 2 and academic electives 3.

2006-2007 Annual costs. Tuition/fees (projected): $21,155. Room/board: $6,400. Books/supplies: $894. Personal expenses: $1,560.

2005-2006 Financial aid. **Need-based:** 56% of total undergraduate aid awarded as scholarships/grants, 44% as loans/jobs. **Non-need-based:** Scholarships awarded for academics, alumni affiliation, athletics, music/drama, state residency.

Application procedures. **Admission:** Priority date 3/1; no deadline. $35 fee, may be waived for applicants with need. Application must be submitted on paper. Admission notification on a rolling basis beginning on or about 11/1. Must reply by May 1 or within 3 week(s) if notified thereafter. **Financial aid:** Priority date 3/1; no closing date. FAFSA required. Applicants notified on a rolling basis starting 3/15; must reply within 3 week(s) of notification.

Academics. **Special study options:** Accelerated study, combined bachelor's/graduate degree, double major, ESL, exchange student, independent study, internships, liberal arts/career combination, study abroad, teacher certification program, Washington semester. **Credit/placement by examination:** AP, CLEP, IB, institutional tests. 30 credit hours maximum toward associate degree, 60 toward bachelor's. **Support services:** Learning center, reduced course load, remedial instruction, study skills assistance, tutoring, writing center.

Majors. **Biology:** General. **Business:** Accounting, business admin. **Computer sciences:** General, computer science. **Education:** Elementary, secondary, special. **Engineering:** Civil, mechanical. **Health:** Predentistry, premedicine, prepharmacy, preveterinary. **History:** General. **Liberal arts:** Humanities. **Math:** General. **Philosophy/religion:** Religion. **Physical sciences:** Chemistry. **Protective services:** Criminal justice. **Psychology:** General. **Social sciences:** Political science, sociology. **Visual/performing arts:** Dramatic.

Computing on campus. 140 workstations in library, computer center. Dormitories linked to campus network. Commuter students can connect to campus network. Online library, helpline available.

Student life. **Freshman orientation:** Mandatory, $150 fee. Preregistration for classes offered. Occurs the 5 days prior to fall classes. **Policies:** Dry campus. Freshmen permitted cars on campus. **Housing:** Guaranteed on-campus for freshmen. Coed dorms, apartments available. $200 deposit, deadline 7/1. **Activities:** Concert band, choral groups, drama, music ensembles, student government, student newspaper, international student club, Circle K, Hawaiian club, nontraditional student group, social action club, Young Republicans, women's club, gay/straight alliance, Democratic club, HANDS (campus ministry club).

Athletics. NCAA. **Intercollegiate:** Baseball M, basketball, cross-country, golf, softball W, track and field, volleyball W. **Intramural:** Basketball, bowling, soccer, softball, tennis, volleyball. **Team name:** Saints.

Student services. Adult student services, alcohol/substance abuse counseling, campus ministries, career counseling, student employment services, financial aid counseling, personal counseling, placement for graduates, veterans' counselor. **Physically disabled:** Services for visually, hearing impaired.

Contact. E-mail: admissions@stmartin.edu
Phone: (360) 438-4311 Toll-free number: (800) 368-8803
Fax: (360) 412-6189
Todd Abbott, Director of Admissions, Saint Martin's University, 5300 Pacific Avenue Southeast, Lacey, WA 98503

Seattle Pacific University

Seattle, Washington — **CB member**
www.spu.edu — **CB code: 4694**

- Private 4-year university affiliated with Free Methodist Church of North America
- Residential campus in very large city
- 2,978 degree-seeking undergraduates: 4% part-time, 67% women, 2% African American, 6% Asian American, 3% Hispanic American, 1% Native American, 1% international
- 744 degree-seeking graduate students
- 85% of applicants admitted
- SAT or ACT with writing, application essay required
- 67% graduate within 6 years

General. Founded in 1891. Regionally accredited. **Degrees:** 673 bachelor's awarded; master's, doctoral offered. **ROTC:** Army, Navy, Air Force. **Location:** 3 miles from downtown. **Calendar:** Quarter, limited summer session. **Full-time faculty:** 185 total; 84% have terminal degrees, 8% minority, 37% women. **Part-time faculty:** 150 total; 9% have terminal degrees, 6% minority, 61% women. **Class size:** 46% < 20, 42% 20-39, 8% 40-49, 3% 50-99, less than 1% >100. **Special facilities:** 2 island campuses used for biological studies.

Freshman class profile. 1,858 applied, 1,576 admitted, 710 enrolled.

Mid 50% test scores			
SAT verbal:	530-650	GPA 2.0-2.99:	4%
SAT math:	520-630	Rank in top quarter:	67%
ACT:	22-28	Rank in top tenth:	39%
GPA 3.50 or higher:	71%	Return as sophomores:	85%
GPA 3.0-3.49:	25%	Out-of-state:	58%
		Live on campus:	98%

Basis for selection. Audition required for music, performing art workshop; portfolio required for fine art scholarship.

High school preparation. Recommended units include English 4, mathematics 3, social studies 1, history 2, science 3 and foreign language 3.

2006-2007 Annual costs. Tuition/fees: $23,391. Room/board: $7,818. Books/supplies: $813. Personal expenses: $1,635.

2005-2006 Financial aid. **Need-based:** 578 full-time freshmen applied for aid; 467 were judged to have need; 467 of these received aid. Average need met was 81%. Average scholarship/grant was $15,431; average loan $4,778. 59% of total undergraduate aid awarded as scholarships/grants, 41% as loans/jobs. **Non-need-based:** Awarded to 847 full-time undergraduates, including 203 freshmen. Scholarships awarded for academics, alumni affiliation, art, athletics, leadership, minority status, music/drama, religious affiliation, ROTC.

Application procedures. **Admission:** Priority date 3/1; deadline 6/1. $45 fee. Admission notification 6/1. Must reply by May 1 or within 3 week(s) if notified thereafter. **Financial aid:** Priority date 1/31; no closing date. FAFSA required. Applicants notified on a rolling basis starting 3/15; must reply by 5/1 or within 4 week(s) of notification.

Academics. **Special study options:** Cooperative education, cross-registration, distance learning, double major, ESL, exchange student, external degree, honors, independent study, internships, liberal arts/career combination, student-designed major, study abroad, teacher certification program, Washington semester, weekend college. **Credit/placement by examination:** AP, CLEP, IB, SAT, ACT, institutional tests. 45 credit hours maximum toward bachelor's degree. **Support services:** Learning center, reduced course load, remedial instruction, tutoring, writing center.

Majors. **Area/ethnic studies:** European, Latin American. **Biology:** General, biochemistry. **Business:** Accounting, business admin, managerial economics, organizational behavior. **Communications:** General. **Computer sciences:** General, networking. **Education:** Art, biology, English, family/consumer sciences, mathematics, music, physical, science, social science, special. **Engineering:** Computer, electrical, science. **Family/consumer sciences:** Clothing/textiles, communication, food/nutrition. **Foreign languages:** Classics, French, German, Latin, Russian, Spanish. **Health:** Nursing (RN), predentistry, premedicine. **History:** General. **Legal studies:** Prelaw. **Math:** General, computational. **Parks/recreation:** Exercise sciences. **Philosophy/religion:** Philosophy. **Physical sciences:** Chemistry, physics. **Psychology:** General. **Social sciences:** Economics, political science, sociology. **Theology:** Religious ed. **Visual/performing arts:** General, art, dramatic.

Most popular majors. Business/marketing 16%, communications/journalism 8%, English 7%, family/consumer sciences 9%, health sciences 11%, psychology 6%, social sciences 9%, visual/performing arts 7%.

Computing on campus. 150 workstations in dormitories, library, computer center, student center. Dormitories wired for high-speed internet access and linked to campus network. Commuter students can connect to campus network. Online course registration, online library, helpline, repair service, wireless network available.

Student life. **Freshman orientation:** Mandatory. Preregistration for classes offered. **Policies:** Religious observance required. Freshmen permitted cars on campus. **Housing:** Coed dorms, apartments, substance-free housing available. $300 deposit. **Activities:** Jazz band, choral groups, drama, literary magazine, music ensembles, radio station, student government, student newspaper, symphony orchestra, more than 25 clubs and organizations.

Athletics. NCAA. **Intercollegiate:** Basketball, cross-country, gymnastics W, rowing (crew), soccer, track and field, volleyball W. **Intramural:** Badminton, basketball, bowling, cross-country, football (tackle) M, golf, skiing, soccer, softball, swimming, table tennis, tennis, track and field, volleyball, wrestling M. **Team name:** Falcons.

Student services. Adult student services, campus ministries, career counseling, student employment services, health services, personal counseling, placement for graduates, veterans' counselor. **Physically disabled:** Services for visually, hearing impaired.

Contact. E-mail: admissions@spu.edu
Phone: (206) 281-2021 Toll-free number: (800) 366-3344
Fax: (206) 281-2554
Jennifer Kenney, Director of Undergraduate Admissions, Seattle Pacific University, 3307 Third Avenue West, Seattle, WA 98119-1997

Seattle University

Seattle, Washington **CB member**
www.seattleu.edu **CB code: 4695**

- Private 4-year university affiliated with Roman Catholic Church
- Residential campus in very large city
- 4,110 degree-seeking undergraduates: 7% part-time, 61% women, 5% African American, 20% Asian American, 7% Hispanic American, 1% Native American, 7% international
- 2,899 degree-seeking graduate students
- 68% of applicants admitted
- SAT or ACT with writing, application essay required
- 63% graduate within 6 years

General. Founded in 1891. Regionally accredited. Courses also offered at Bellevue Campus. **Degrees:** 986 bachelor's awarded; master's, doctoral, first professional offered. **ROTC:** Army, Navy, Air Force. **Location:** One mile from downtown. **Calendar:** Quarter, extensive summer session. **Full-time faculty:** 387 total; 85% have terminal degrees, 18% minority, 49% women. **Part-time faculty:** 195 total; 63% have terminal degrees, 6% minority, 45% women. **Class size:** 49% < 20, 48% 20-39, 2% 40-49, less than 1% 50-99. **Special facilities:** Design center (where engineering students work with major companies in the area), observatory.

Freshman class profile. 4,339 applied, 2,935 admitted, 763 enrolled.

Mid 50% test scores			
SAT verbal:	520-630	Rank in top quarter:	60%
SAT math:	530-620	Rank in top tenth:	32%
ACT:	22-28	Return as sophomores:	87%
GPA 3.50 or higher:	59%	Out-of-state:	50%
GPA 3.0-3.49:	36%	Live on campus:	88%
GPA 2.0-2.99:	5%	International:	1%

Basis for selection. 2.75 GPA minimum, higher for some programs. Secondary school record, recommendations, test scores most important. Essay, school, community activities also important. Applicants must submit one test with a writing component. The ACT writing component is required if the applicant does not submit the SAT Reasoning scores. Interview recommended for marginal students.

High school preparation. Required and recommended units include English 4, mathematics 3-4, social studies 3-4, science 2-3 (laboratory 2-3), foreign language 2 and academic electives 2. History included in social studies.

2005-2006 Annual costs. Tuition/fees: $22,905. $200 admission fee, $90 matriculation fee required. $90 per-credit-hour charge for credit by examination. $90 per-credit-hour charge for validation of field experience. $65 removal fee for incompletes. Room/board: $8,403. Books/supplies: $945. Personal expenses: $162.

2005-2006 Financial aid. Need-based: 674 full-time freshmen applied for aid; 514 were judged to have need; 509 of these received aid. Average need met was 86%. Average scholarship/grant was $19,528; average loan $3,464. 61% of total undergraduate aid awarded as scholarships/grants, 39% as loans/jobs. **Non-need-based:** Awarded to 1,122 full-time undergraduates, including 244 freshmen. Scholarships awarded for academics, alumni affiliation, athletics, leadership, minority status, music/drama, ROTC, state residency.

Application procedures. Admission: Priority date 2/1; no deadline. $45 fee. Application may be submitted online. Admission notification on a rolling basis beginning on or about 1/31. Must reply by May 1 or within 2 week(s) if notified thereafter. **Financial aid:** Priority date 2/1; no closing date. FAFSA required. Applicants notified by 3/21; Applicants notified on a rolling basis starting 3/21; must reply by 5/1 or within 2 week(s) of notification.

Academics. Special study options: Combined bachelor's/graduate degree, cooperative education, cross-registration, double major, honors, independent study, internships, liberal arts/career combination, student-designed major, study abroad, teacher certification program. **Credit/placement by examination:** AP, CLEP, IB, SAT, ACT, institutional tests. 45 credit hours maximum toward bachelor's degree. Special arrangements for nursing majors who take NLN exams. 50 credits maximum. **Support services:** Learning center, reduced course load, study skills assistance, tutoring, writing center.

Majors. Biology: General, biochemistry. **Business:** General, accounting, business admin, e-commerce, finance, international, managerial economics, marketing. **Communications:** Journalism, media studies, public relations. **Computer sciences:** Computer science. **Conservation:** General. **Engineering:** Civil, electrical, mechanical. **English:** Creative writing, English lit. **Foreign languages:** French, Spanish. **Health:** Clinical lab science, medical records admin, nurse practitioner, nursing (RN), public health nursing, sonography. **History:** General. **Interdisciplinary:** Global studies. **Liberal arts:** Arts/sciences, humanities. **Math:** General. **Philosophy/religion:** Philosophy, religion. **Physical sciences:** General, chemistry, physics. **Protective services:** Criminal justice, criminalistics. **Psychology:** General. **Public administration:** General, social work. **Social sciences:** Economics, political science, sociology. **Visual/performing arts:** General, art history/conservation, dramatic.

Most popular majors. Business/marketing 27%, health sciences 11%, psychology 7%.

Computing on campus. 401 workstations in dormitories, library, computer center, student center. Dormitories wired for high-speed internet access and linked to campus network. Commuter students can connect to campus network. Helpline, student web hosting available.

Student life. Freshman orientation: Mandatory. Preregistration for classes offered. 3 days prior to start of classes. **Policies:** Freshmen permitted cars on campus. **Housing:** Guaranteed on-campus for freshmen. Coed dorms, special housing for disabled, apartments available. $300 nonrefundable deposit, deadline 5/1. Single-gender floors available. **Activities:** Jazz band, choral groups, drama, literary magazine, music ensembles, musical theater, radio station, student government, student newspaper, 65 clubs available.

Athletics. NCAA. **Intercollegiate:** Basketball, cross-country, soccer, softball W, swimming, tennis W, track and field, volleyball W. **Intramural:** Basketball, football (non-tackle), soccer, softball, tennis, volleyball. **Team name:** Redhawks.

Student services. Adult student services, alcohol/substance abuse counseling, campus ministries, career counseling, student employment services, financial aid counseling, health services, minority student services, personal counseling, placement for graduates, veterans' counselor, women's services. **Physically disabled:** Services for visually, speech, hearing impaired.

Contact. E-mail: admissions@seattleu.edu
Phone: (206) 296-2000 Toll-free number: (800) 426-7123
Fax: (206) 296-5656
Michael McKeon, Dean of Admissions, Seattle University, 901 12th Avenue, Seattle, WA 98122-4340

Trinity Lutheran College

Issaquah, Washington
www.tlc.edu **CB code: 4408**

- Private 4-year Bible and liberal arts college affiliated with Lutheran Church
- Residential campus in large town
- 107 degree-seeking undergraduates: 15% part-time, 46% women
- 62% of applicants admitted
- SAT or ACT (ACT writing optional) required

General. Founded in 1944. Regionally accredited. All students participate in off-campus service learning practicums. **Degrees:** 27 bachelor's, 6 associate awarded. **Location:** 18 miles from Seattle. **Calendar:** Quarter. **Full-time faculty:** 10 total. **Part-time faculty:** 18 total. **Special facilities:** Children, Youth & Family Resource Center; preschool and Christian school.

Freshman class profile. 105 applied, 65 admitted, 38 enrolled.

Basis for selection. High school GPA, test scores, 2 recommendations. Interview considered.

High school preparation. Recommended units include English 3, mathematics 2, history 2, science 2 and foreign language 1.

2005-2006 Annual costs. Tuition/fees: $12,000. Room/board: $5,900. Books/supplies: $642. Personal expenses: $1,818.

Financial aid. **Non-need-based:** Scholarships awarded for academics, alumni affiliation, art, leadership, music/drama.

Application procedures. **Admission:** Priority date 3/1; deadline 9/15 (receipt date). $30 fee, may be waived for applicants with need. Application may be submitted online. Admission notification on a rolling basis beginning on or about 10/1. Must reply by May 1 or within 2 week(s) if notified thereafter. **Financial aid:** Priority date 3/1; no closing date. FAFSA, institutional form required. Applicants notified on a rolling basis starting 3/15; must reply within 2 week(s) of notification.

Academics. **Special study options:** Combined bachelor's/graduate degree, cooperative education, dual enrollment of high school students, independent study, internships, liberal arts/career combination, student-designed major, study abroad, urban semester. Study trips to Holy Lands, Italy, Greece. **Credit/placement by examination:** AP, CLEP, institutional tests. 15 credit hours maximum toward associate degree, 15 toward bachelor's. **Support services:** Reduced course load, remedial instruction, study skills assistance, tutoring, writing center.

Majors. **Communications:** Media studies. **Education:** Early childhood, early childhood special. **Philosophy/religion:** Christian. **Psychology:** General. **Public administration:** Social work. **Theology:** Bible, missionary, religious ed, sacred music, theology, youth ministry.

Computing on campus. 15 workstations in dormitories, library, computer center, student center. Dormitories wired for high-speed internet access and linked to campus network. Commuter students can connect to campus network. Online library, helpline, wireless network available.

Student life. **Freshman orientation:** Mandatory. Preregistration for classes offered. **Policies:** Freshmen permitted cars on campus. **Housing:** Guaranteed on-campus for all undergraduates. Single-sex dorms, special housing for disabled, apartments available. $75 deposit, deadline 5/1. **Activities:** Choral groups, drama, music ensembles, musical theater, student government, student newspaper, Social Service teams, Global Concerns Mission, Worship Commission, Environmental Commission.

Athletics. **Intercollegiate:** Basketball M. **Intramural:** Basketball, football (non-tackle), soccer, softball, table tennis, tennis, volleyball. **Team name:** Eagles.

Student services. Adult student services, campus ministries, career counseling, student employment services, financial aid counseling, health services, personal counseling, placement for graduates.

Contact. E-mail: admission@tlc.edu
Phone: (425) 961-5510 Toll-free number: (800) 843-5659
Fax: (425) 392-0404
Jon Olson, Director of College Advancement, Trinity Lutheran College, 4221 228th Avenue Southeast, Issaquah, WA 98029

University of Puget Sound

Tacoma, Washington — **CB member**
www.ups.edu — **CB code: 4067**

- Private 4-year university and liberal arts college
- Residential campus in small city
- 2,589 degree-seeking undergraduates: 1% part-time, 58% women, 2% African American, 9% Asian American, 4% Hispanic American, 1% Native American
- 263 degree-seeking graduate students
- 71% of applicants admitted
- SAT or ACT (ACT writing recommended), application essay required
- 73% graduate within 6 years; 35% enter graduate study

General. Founded in 1888. Regionally accredited. Institution also offers community service opportunities, forensics & debate, diversity & leadership training, multiple speaker/lecturer programs. School of Music performances are abundant. **Degrees:** 619 bachelor's awarded; master's, first professional offered. **ROTC:** Army. **Location:** 35 miles from Seattle, 28 miles from Olympia. **Calendar:** Semester, limited summer session. **Full-time faculty:** 224 total; 88% have terminal degrees, 8% minority, 44% women. **Part-time faculty:** 59 total; 37% have terminal degrees, 3% minority, 54% women. **Class size:** 51% < 20, 46% 20-39, 2% 40-49, less than 1% 50-99. **Special facilities:** Natural history museum, arboretum, x-ray laboratory, electron microscope lab, observatory, concert hall, sculpture building, greenhouse, sedimentology lab, rock and mineral collection, exercise science lab, physiology labs, end stage.

Freshman class profile. 4,711 applied, 3,343 admitted, 670 enrolled.

Mid 50% test scores			
SAT verbal:	580-690	Rank in top quarter:	68%
SAT math:	560-660	Rank in top tenth:	37%
ACT:	24-29	End year in good standing:	93%
GPA 3.50 or higher:	55%	Return as sophomores:	87%
GPA 3.0-3.49:	35%	Out-of-state:	73%
GPA 2.0-2.99:	10%	Live on campus:	98%
		International:	1%

Basis for selection. High school record most important followed by test scores. Writing ability as demonstrated through the essay and short answer questions. Recommendations and activities important. If applicants have taken both SAT and ACT, they should submit both. Interview recommended for all; audition required for music; portfolio recommended for art; audition recommended for theatre. **Homeschooled:** Applicants should show work in writing, critical reading, mathematics, history; and social, physical, and natural sciences. Foreign language recommended.

High school preparation. 19 units recommended. Recommended units include English 4, mathematics 4, social studies 3, history 3, science 4 (laboratory 4), foreign language 3 and academic electives 1. One fine, visual or performing art recommended.

2005-2006 Annual costs. Tuition/fees: $28,460. Room/board: $7,450.

2005-2006 Financial aid. **Need-based:** 491 full-time freshmen applied for aid; 393 were judged to have need; 393 of these received aid. Average need met was 82%. Average scholarship/grant was $16,270; average loan $3,699. 64% of total undergraduate aid awarded as scholarships/grants, 36% as loans/jobs. **Non-need-based:** Awarded to 1,418 full-time undergraduates, including 335 freshmen. Scholarships awarded for academics, alumni affiliation, art, leadership, music/drama, religious affiliation. **Additional information:** Cooperative education allows qualified upperclassmen to alternate semesters of full-time study and full-time work.

Application procedures. **Admission:** Priority date 2/1; deadline 2/1 (postmark date). $40 fee, may be waived for applicants with need. Application may be submitted online. Admission notification 4/1. Must reply by May 1 or within 2 week(s) if notified thereafter. **Financial aid:** Priority date 2/1; no closing date. FAFSA required. Applicants notified on a rolling basis starting 3/15; must reply by 5/1 or within 2 week(s) of notification.

Academics. All students complete core curriculum, including courses in writing and rhetoric, scholarly and creative inquiry, fine arts, humanistic, mathematical, natural scientific and social scientific approaches, and a connections course intended to develop an understanding of the interrelationship of fields of knowledge. **Special study options:** Combined bachelor's/graduate degree, cooperative education, double major, honors, independent study, internships, student-designed major, study abroad, teacher certification program. One-year of study in Asia, 3-2 engineering program, business leadership program. **Credit/placement by examination:** AP, CLEP, IB, institutional tests. **Support services:** Learning center, reduced course load, study skills assistance, tutoring, writing center.

Majors. **Area/ethnic studies:** Asian. **Biology:** General. **Business:** Business admin. **Communications:** General. **Computer sciences:** General, computer science. **Education:** Music. **English:** English lit. **Foreign languages:** Classics, French, German, Spanish. **History:** General. **Interdisciplinary:** Natural sciences, science/society. **Math:** General. **Parks/recreation:** Exercise sciences. **Philosophy/religion:** Philosophy, religion. **Physical sciences:** Chemistry, geology, physics. **Psychology:** General. **Social sciences:** Economics, international economics, political science, sociology. **Visual/performing arts:** Art, dramatic, music management, music performance.

Most popular majors. Biology 7%, business/marketing 14%, English 8%, foreign language 6%, psychology 7%, social sciences 23%, visual/performing arts 9%.

Computing on campus. 324 workstations in dormitories, library, computer center, student center. Dormitories wired for high-speed internet access and linked to campus network. Commuter students can connect to campus network. Online course registration, online library, helpline, repair service, student web hosting, wireless network available.

Student life. **Freshman orientation:** Available. Offers 9-day introduction to academic life and campus community. **Policies:** Freshmen permitted cars on campus. **Housing:** Guaranteed on-campus for freshmen. Coed dorms, single-sex dorms, special housing for disabled, fraternity/sorority housing, substance-free housing available. $200 fully refundable deposit, deadline 5/1. 56 university-owned homes on campus. Variety of theme houses and residence hall theme floors (i.e. languages, music, adventure education hall, healthy options, substance free). **Activities:** Bands, choral groups, dance, drama, film society, literary magazine, music ensembles, musical theater, opera, radio station, student government, student newspaper, symphony orchestra, Black Student Union (BSU); Hui-o-Hawaii; Circle K; Jewish student organization; Bisexuals, Gays, Lesbians, and Allies for Diversity (B-GLAD); Pacific American student union; Students for Peace and Justice; First Nations; Habitat for Humanity; film and theatre society.

Athletics. NCAA. **Intercollegiate:** Baseball M, basketball, cheerleading, cross-country, football (tackle) M, golf, lacrosse W, rowing (crew), soccer, softball W, swimming, tennis, track and field, volleyball W. **Intramural:** Badminton, basketball, football (non-tackle), racquetball, soccer, softball, tennis, volleyball. **Team name:** Loggers.

Student services. Alcohol/substance abuse counseling, campus ministries, career counseling, student employment services, financial aid counseling, health services, legal services, minority student services, personal counseling, placement for graduates. **Physically disabled:** Services for visually, speech, hearing impaired.

Contact. E-mail: admission@ups.edu
Phone: (253) 879-3211 Toll-free number: (800) 396-7191
Fax: (253) 879-3993
George Mills, Vice President for Enrollment, University of Puget Sound, 1500 North Warner Street, Tacoma, WA 98416-1062

University of Washington

Seattle, Washington **CB member**
www.washington.edu **CB code: 4854**

- Public 4-year university
- Commuter campus in very large city
- 25,469 degree-seeking undergraduates: 9% part-time, 51% women
- 11,763 degree-seeking graduate students
- 67% of applicants admitted
- SAT or ACT with writing, application essay required
- 74% graduate within 6 years

General. Founded in 1861. Regionally accredited. **Degrees:** 7,300 bachelor's awarded; master's, doctoral, first professional offered. **ROTC:** Army, Navy, Air Force. **Location:** 5 miles from downtown. **Calendar:** Quarter, extensive summer session. **Full-time faculty:** 2,847 total; 93% have terminal degrees, 17% minority. **Part-time faculty:** 622 total; 91% have terminal degrees, 11% minority. **Class size:** 31% < 20, 50% 20-39, 6% 40-49, 8% 50-99, 4% >100. **Special facilities:** Arboretum, observatory, anthropological museum, applied physics laboratory, planetarium.

Freshman class profile. 15,923 applied, 10,681 admitted, 5,124 enrolled.

Mid 50% test scores		**Rank in top tenth:**	82%
SAT verbal:	530-650	**Return as sophomores:**	93%
SAT math:	580-670	**Out-of-state:**	77%
ACT:	23-28	**Live on campus:**	55%
GPA 3.50 or higher:	80%	**International:**	3%
GPA 3.0-3.49:	18%	**Fraternities:**	23%
GPA 2.0-2.99:	2%	**Sororities:**	17%
Rank in top quarter:	96%		

Basis for selection. Applicants evaluated and ranked on completion of core subject requirements, grades and test scores and supplemental factors including personal statement, completion of substantial number of courses beyond minimum, grades in college-preparatory courses, enrollment in AP or honors courses, cultural diversity and documented evidence of exceptional artistic talent. Audition required for performing arts. **Homeschooled:** Must fulfill core subject requirements and provide transcript documenting course titles or subjects studied.

High school preparation. 15 units required. Required and recommended units include English 4, mathematics 3-4, social studies 3-4, science 2-3 (laboratory 1-2) and foreign language 2-3. One semester (.5) elective from required subjects list and .5 fine arts course.

2005-2006 Annual costs. Tuition/fees: $5,620; $19,917 out-of-state. Room/board: $7,164. Books/supplies: $798. Personal expenses: $2,187.

2005-2006 Financial aid. Need-based: Average need met was 87%. Average scholarship/grant was $5,000; average loan $4,200. 58% of total undergraduate aid awarded as scholarships/grants, 42% as loans/jobs. **Non-need-based:** Scholarships awarded for academics, alumni affiliation, art, athletics, leadership, music/drama, ROTC. **Additional information:** Tuition not due until third week of term.

Application procedures. Admission: Priority date 12/1; deadline 1/15 (postmark date). $38 fee, may be waived for applicants with need. Application may be submitted online. Admission notification on a rolling basis beginning on or about 12/1. Must reply by May 1 or within 2 week(s) if notified thereafter. Applications accepted after closing date on space-available basis. **Financial aid:** Priority date 2/28; no closing date. FAFSA required. Applicants notified on a rolling basis starting 4/1; must reply within 3 week(s) of notification.

Academics. Special study options: Combined bachelor's/graduate degree, cooperative education, distance learning, double major, ESL, exchange student, honors, independent study, internships, liberal arts/career combination, student-designed major, study abroad, teacher certification program, Washington semester. Quarter at Friday Harbor Laboratories, San Juan Islands. **Credit/placement by examination:** AP, CLEP, IB, institutional tests. 90 credit hours maximum toward bachelor's degree. **Support services:** Learning center, pre-admission summer program, reduced course load, remedial instruction, study skills assistance, tutoring, writing center.

Majors. Architecture: Architecture, landscape, urban/community planning. **Area/ethnic studies:** African, African-American, Asian, Asian-American, Canadian, Central/Eastern European, Chinese, European, French, German, Hispanic-American/Latino/Chicano, Italian, Japanese, Korean, Latin American, Native American, Near/Middle Eastern, Russian/Slavic, Scandinavian, Slavic, South Asian, Southeast Asian, women's. **Biology:** General, bacteriology, biochemistry, botany, ecology, marine, microbiology, zoology. **Business:** Accounting, business admin, construction management, finance, human resources, international, management information systems, organizational behavior. **Communications:** General. **Computer sciences:** General, computer science, information systems, information technology. **Conservation:** General, fisheries, forest resources, forestry, wildlife. **Education:** Music. **Engineering:** General, aerospace, biomedical, ceramic, chemical, civil, computer, electrical, environmental, forest, industrial, materials, materials science, mechanical, metallurgical. **English:** English lit, speech/rhetoric, technical writing. **Foreign languages:** Ancient Greek, Arabic, Chinese, classics, comparative lit, Danish, East Asian, French, German, Germanic, Hebrew, Italian, Japanese, Korean, Latin, linguistics, Norwegian, Russian, Scandinavian, South Asian, Southeast Asian, Spanish, Swedish, Turkish, Ukrainian. **Health:** Audiology/speech pathology, clinical lab science, dental hygiene, environmental health, nursing (RN), orthotics/prosthetics, physician assistant. **History:** General. **Interdisciplinary:** Peace/conflict. **Liberal arts:** Arts/sciences. **Math:** General, applied. **Philosophy/religion:** Judaic, philosophy, religion. **Physical sciences:** Astronomy, astrophysics, atmospheric science, chemistry, geology, oceanography, physics, planetary. **Psychology:** General. **Public administration:** Social work. **Social sciences:** General, anthropology, economics, geography, international relations, political science, sociology. **Visual/performing arts:** Art, art history/conservation, ceramics, commercial/advertising art, dance, dramatic, fiber arts, industrial design, metal/jewelry, music history, music performance, music theory/composition, musicology, painting, photography, piano/organ, printmaking, sculpture, stringed instruments, voice/opera.

Most popular majors. Biology 7%, business/marketing 13%, engineering/engineering technologies 7%, interdisciplinary studies 6%, social sciences 17%.

Computing on campus. 1,500 workstations in dormitories, library, computer center, student center. Dormitories wired for high-speed internet access and linked to campus network. Commuter students can connect to campus network. Online course registration, online library, helpline, repair service, student web hosting, wireless network available.

Student life. Freshman orientation: Available, $250 fee. Preregistration for classes offered. Advising and registration happens throughout the summer. **Policies:** Freshmen permitted cars on campus. **Housing:** Guaranteed on-campus for freshmen. Coed dorms, special housing for disabled, apartments, fraternity/sorority housing, substance-free housing available. $300 deposit. Special interest houses available. **Activities:** Bands, choral groups, dance, drama, literary magazine, music ensembles, musical theater, opera, radio station, student government, student newspaper, symphony orchestra, TV station, over 500 organizations.

Athletics. NCAA. **Intercollegiate:** Baseball M, basketball, cheerleading, cross-country, diving, fencing W, football (tackle) M, golf, gymnastics W, ice hockey M, rowing (crew), soccer, softball W, swimming, tennis, track and field, volleyball W. **Intramural:** Basketball, bowling, fencing, handball, racquetball, soccer, softball, squash, tennis, volleyball. **Team name:** Huskies.

Student services. Alcohol/substance abuse counseling, career counseling, services for economically disadvantaged, student employment services, financial aid counseling, health services, legal services, minority student services, on-campus daycare, personal counseling, placement for graduates, veterans' counselor, women's services. **Physically disabled:** Services for visually, speech, hearing impaired.

Contact. Phone: (206) 543-9686 Fax: (206) 685-3655
Philip Ballinger, Director of Admissions, University of Washington, 1410 Northeast Campus Parkway, Box 355852, Seattle, WA 98195-5852

Walla Walla College

College Place, Washington
www.wwc.edu **CB code: 4940**

- Private 4-year university and liberal arts college affiliated with Seventh-day Adventists
- Residential campus in large town

- 1,596 degree-seeking undergraduates: 5% part-time, 48% women, 3% African American, 5% Asian American, 7% Hispanic American, 1% Native American, 1% international
- 271 degree-seeking graduate students
- 78% of applicants admitted
- SAT or ACT required
- 44% graduate within 6 years

General. Founded in 1892. Regionally accredited. Branch campus in Portland, Oregon, for final two years of nursing program. Summer biology courses offered at marine research facility near Anacortes. Graduate social work program in Billings and Missoula, Montana. **Degrees:** 295 bachelor's, 7 associate awarded; master's offered. **Location:** 270 miles from Seattle, 250 miles from Portland, Oregon. **Calendar:** Quarter, extensive summer session. **Full-time faculty:** 122 total; 4% have terminal degrees, 7% minority, 38% women. **Part-time faculty:** 72 total; 1% have terminal degrees, 3% minority, 61% women. **Class size:** 60% < 20, 32% 20-39, 6% 40-49, 2% 50-99, less than 1% >100. **Special facilities:** Biological research facility, observatory.

Freshman class profile. 452 applied, 351 admitted, 292 enrolled.

GPA 3.50 or higher:	44%	**Return as sophomores:**	72%
GPA 3.0-3.49:	25%	**Out-of-state:**	69%
GPA 2.0-2.99:	31%	**Live on campus:**	80%

Basis for selection. Must have a combined high 2.0 high school GPA. If entering with GED must have an average score of 500 or higher and each test must be 450 or higher. Official TOEFL scores required for prospective students whose first language is not English. Audition recommended. **Homeschooled:** May be admitted by acceptable score on ACT test, GED test, or transcript from accredited home school organization.

High school preparation. 10 units required. Required and recommended units include English 4, mathematics 3, social studies 1, history 2, science 1 (laboratory 1) and foreign language 2. Mathematics units must be algebra and geometry. 2 laboratory units recommended.

2006-2007 Annual costs. Tuition/fees (projected): $19,917. Room/board: $4,572. Books/supplies: $924. Personal expenses: $1,608.

2004-2005 Financial aid. Need-based: 336 full-time freshmen applied for aid; 230 were judged to have need; 229 of these received aid. Average need met was 88%. Average scholarship/grant was $5,632; average loan $5,219. 51% of total undergraduate aid awarded as scholarships/grants, 49% as loans/jobs. **Non-need-based:** Awarded to 1,051 full-time undergraduates, including 307 freshmen. Scholarships awarded for academics, leadership, music/drama.

Application procedures. Admission: Priority date 9/1; no deadline. $40 fee, may be waived for applicants with need. Application may be submitted online. Admission notification on a rolling basis beginning on or about 9/5. **Financial aid:** No deadline. FAFSA, institutional form required. Applicants notified on a rolling basis starting 3/15.

Academics. Special study options: Combined bachelor's/graduate degree, cooperative education, distance learning, double major, honors, internships, study abroad, teacher certification program. **Credit/placement by examination:** AP, CLEP, IB, institutional tests. 12 credit hours maximum toward associate degree, 24 toward bachelor's. **Support services:** Learning center, pre-admission summer program, reduced course load, remedial instruction, study skills assistance, tutoring, writing center.

Majors. Biology: General, biochemistry, biophysics. **Business:** Accounting, business admin, finance, human resources, international, management science. **Communications:** General, journalism, media studies. **Communications technology:** Graphic/printing. **Computer sciences:** General, computer graphics, computer science, data processing, information systems. **Education:** General, business, elementary, music, physical, special, voc/tech. **Engineering:** General, biomedical, civil, computer, electrical, mechanical. **Foreign languages:** French, German, Spanish. **Health:** Nursing (RN). **History:** General. **Liberal arts:** Arts/sciences. **Math:** General. **Mechanic/repair:** Automotive. **Philosophy/religion:** Religion. **Physical sciences:** Chemistry, physics. **Psychology:** General. **Public administration:** Social work. **Social sciences:** Sociology. **Theology:** Theology. **Visual/performing arts:** Art, music performance.

Most popular majors. Business/marketing 16%, education 12%, engineering/engineering technologies 15%, health sciences 19%, visual/performing arts 6%.

Computing on campus. 105 workstations in dormitories, library, computer center. Dormitories wired for high-speed internet access and linked to campus network. Commuter students can connect to campus network. Online course registration, online library, helpline, repair service, student web hosting, wireless network available.

Student life. Freshman orientation: Mandatory. Preregistration for classes offered. Held during week before classes begin. **Policies:** Chapel requirement once a week; worship policy for resident students. Religious observance required. Freshmen permitted cars on campus. **Housing:** Guaranteed on-campus for all undergraduates. Single-sex dorms, special housing for disabled, apartments available. $150 fully refundable deposit, deadline 8/1. **Activities:** Concert band, choral groups, drama, music ensembles, radio station, student government, student newspaper, symphony orchestra, TV station, Student entrepeneur group, student missionary groups, drama, foreign student organizations, academic department clubs, service clubs, music groups.

Athletics. NCCAA. **Intercollegiate:** Basketball, golf, ice hockey M, soccer M, softball W, volleyball. **Intramural:** Badminton, basketball, football (non-tackle), racquetball, soccer, softball, table tennis, tennis, volleyball. **Team name:** Wolves.

Student services. Campus ministries, career counseling, student employment services, financial aid counseling, health services, minority student services, personal counseling, placement for graduates, veterans' counselor. **Physically disabled:** Services for visually, speech, hearing impaired.

Contact. E-mail: info@wwc.edu
Phone: (509) 527-2327 Toll-free number: (800) 541-8900
Fax: (509) 527-2397
Victor Brown, Vice President for Admissions and Marketing, Walla Walla College, 204 South College Avenue, College Place, WA 99324-3000

Washington State University

Pullman, Washington — **CB member**
www.wsu.edu — **CB code: 4705**

- Public 4-year university
- Residential campus in large town
- 19,077 degree-seeking undergraduates: 13% part-time, 52% women, 3% African American, 6% Asian American, 4% Hispanic American, 1% Native American, 3% international
- 3,959 degree-seeking graduate students
- 74% of applicants admitted
- SAT or ACT with writing, application essay required
- 63% graduate within 6 years

General. Founded in 1890. Regionally accredited. Institute for Technology Entrepreneurship with Pacific Northwest National Laboratory. **Degrees:** 4,133 bachelor's awarded; master's, doctoral, first professional offered. **ROTC:** Army, Navy, Air Force. **Location:** 80 miles from Spokane. **Calendar:** Semester, extensive summer session. **Full-time faculty:** 1,057 total; 89% have terminal degrees, 11% minority, 37% women. **Part-time faculty:** 392 total; 44% have terminal degrees, 5% minority, 49% women. **Class size:** 36% < 20, 38% 20-39, 7% 40-49, 13% 50-99, 6% >100. **Special facilities:** Anthropology museum, art museum, geological collections, historic textiles and costume collection, entomological collection, observatory, mycological herbarium, soil monolith collection, veterinary anatomy teaching museum, laboratory for atmospheric research, laboratory for biotechnology and bioanalysis, electron microscopy center, envirnomental research center, geoanalytical laboratory, nuclear radiation center, social and economic sciences research center, State of Washington Water research center, Center for Spectroscopy, recording studio.

Freshman class profile. 9,193 applied, 6,793 admitted, 2,878 enrolled.

Mid 50% test scores		**End year in good standing:**	88%
SAT verbal:	490-600	**Return as sophomores:**	84%
SAT math:	510-610	**Out-of-state:**	7%
GPA 3.50 or higher:	47%	**Live on campus:**	91%
GPA 3.0-3.49:	42%	**International:**	1%
GPA 2.0-2.99:	11%	**Fraternities:**	24%
Rank in top quarter:	57%	**Sororities:**	25%
Rank in top tenth:	37%		

Basis for selection. Admission based on combination of high school GPA and SAT or ACT scores, completion of course work, and personal statement. Special circumstances, community activities and recommendations considered in some cases. Various exemptions to English proficiency testing available to those who can otherwise demonstrate successful experience in use of the English language in secondary or post-secondary studies. Essay, interview recommended for students not meeting minimum admission index requirement; audition required for music; portfolio required for art, architecture, landscape architecture. **Homeschooled:** Required is one of the following: Official transcripts from GED exam or an academic resume that provides documentation of all subjects studied. Details of how the home-based instruction fulfills our core requirements must be provided. **Learning Disabled:** At the time of offer, a card is mailed to student that they can opt to return to Disability Services if they wish to have assistance with their disability.

High school preparation. 15 units required; 17 recommended. Required and recommended units include English 4, mathematics 3-4, social studies 2, history 1, science 2 (laboratory 1), foreign language 2 and academic electives 1. Mathematics units must include one year each, algebra, geometry, and advanced algebra. Foreign language must be 2 years of single language (Native American or American Sign Language are accepted). One unit fine/performing arts or additional academic elective.

2005-2006 Annual costs. Tuition/fees: $6,010; $15,018 out-of-state. Room/board: $6,746.

2004-2005 Financial aid. **Need-based:** 2,191 full-time freshmen applied for aid; 1,395 were judged to have need; 1,389 of these received aid. Average need met was 95%. Average scholarship/grant was $4,771; average loan $3,042. 48% of total undergraduate aid awarded as scholarships/grants, 52% as loans/jobs. **Non-need-based:** Awarded to 4,146 full-time undergraduates, including 1,356 freshmen. Scholarships awarded for academics, alumni affiliation, art, athletics, job skills, leadership, minority status, music/drama, religious affiliation, ROTC, state residency.

Application procedures. **Admission:** Priority date 1/31; no deadline. $50 fee, may be waived for applicants with need. Application may be submitted online. Admission notification on a rolling basis beginning on or about 12/1. Must reply by May 1 or within 2 week(s) if notified thereafter. Applications accepted after May 1 and later if space is still available. **Financial aid:** Priority date 3/1; no closing date. FAFSA required. Applicants notified on a rolling basis starting 4/15.

Academics. **Special study options:** Combined bachelor's/graduate degree, cooperative education, cross-registration, distance learning, double major, dual enrollment of high school students, ESL, exchange student, honors, independent study, internships, liberal arts/career combination, student-designed major, study abroad, teacher certification program. **Credit/placement by examination:** AP, CLEP, IB, institutional tests. 60 credit hours maximum toward bachelor's degree. **Support services:** Learning center, study skills assistance, tutoring, writing center.

Honors college/program. Acceptance into the Honors College is competitive, and spaces are limited. Selection Committee considers: GPA and SAT/ACT scores, essay responses, strength of high school curriculum, Running Start credits, AP/IP programs, honors courses, foreign language skills at the intermediate level, letters of recommendation from 2 teachers who know you well, and overall motivation, organizational skills, and desire to challenge yourself.

Majors. **Agriculture:** General, agronomy, animal sciences, business, communications, crop production, economics, education services, horticultural science, mechanization, plant protection, soil science. **Architecture:** Architecture, interior, landscape. **Area/ethnic studies:** American, Asian, women's. **Biology:** General, animal genetics, bacteriology, biochemistry, biotechnology, entomology, microbiology, molecular genetics, plant genetics, zoology. **Business:** General, accounting, accounting technology, business admin, e-commerce, entrepreneurial studies, finance, hospitality admin, hotel/motel admin, human resources, insurance, international, management information systems, management science, managerial economics, marketing, operations, real estate. **Communications:** General, digital media, media studies. **Computer sciences:** General, computer science. **Conservation:** General, environmental science, forestry, wildlife. **Education:** General, agricultural, bilingual, biology, chemistry, early childhood, elementary, English, ESL, family/consumer sciences, foreign languages, French, German, health, history, kindergarten/preschool, mathematics, multi-level teacher, music, physical, physics, reading, science, secondary, social studies, Spanish, special. **Engineering:** Agricultural, chemical, civil, computer, electrical, manufacturing, materials, mechanical. **Engineering technology:** Construction. **English:** English lit. **Family/consumer sciences:** Clothing/textiles, family studies, food/nutrition. **Foreign languages:** General, French, German, linguistics, Russian, Spanish. **Health:** Athletic training, audiology/speech pathology, nursing (RN), premedicine. **History:** General. **Interdisciplinary:** Biological/physical sciences, neuroscience. **Legal studies:** Prelaw. **Liberal arts:** Arts/sciences, humanities. **Math:** General, applied. **Parks/recreation:** Exercise sciences, facilities management, health/fitness, sports admin. **Philosophy/religion:** Philosophy, religion. **Physical sciences:** General, chemistry, geology, physics. **Protective services:** Law enforcement admin. **Psychology:** General. **Public administration:** General, policy analysis. **Social sciences:** General, anthropology, economics, political science, sociology. **Visual/performing arts:** Art, dramatic, music performance.

Most popular majors. Business/marketing 19%, communications/journalism 8%, engineering/engineering technologies 6%, health sciences 7%, social sciences 13%.

Computing on campus. 8,500 workstations in dormitories, library, computer center, student center. Dormitories wired for high-speed internet access and linked to campus network. Commuter students can connect to campus network. Online course registration, online library, helpline, repair service, student web hosting, wireless network available.

Student life. **Freshman orientation:** Available, $150 fee. Two and a half day programs for students and families. **Policies:** Freshmen permitted cars on campus. **Housing:** Guaranteed on-campus for freshmen. Coed dorms, single-sex dorms, apartments, fraternity/sorority housing, substance-free housing available. $400 fully refundable deposit, deadline 6/1. Single undergraduate freshmen under 20 required to live on campus. **Activities:** Bands, choral groups, dance, drama, film society, literary magazine, music ensembles, opera, radio station, student government, student newspaper, symphony orchestra, TV station, Over 200 clubs and special interest groups.

Athletics. NCAA. **Intercollegiate:** Baseball M, basketball, cross-country, football (tackle) M, golf, rowing (crew) W, soccer W, swimming W, tennis W, track and field, volleyball W. **Intramural:** Badminton, basketball, bowling, football (non-tackle), football (tackle), golf, racquetball, soccer, softball, table tennis, tennis W, volleyball, wrestling M. **Team name:** Cougars.

Student services. Alcohol/substance abuse counseling, campus ministries, career counseling, student employment services, financial aid counseling, health services, legal services, minority student services, on-campus daycare, personal counseling, placement for graduates, veterans' counselor, women's services. **Physically disabled:** Services for visually, speech, hearing impaired.

Contact. E-mail: admiss2@wsu.edu
Phone: (509) 335-5586 Toll-free number: (888) 468-6978
Fax: (509) 335-4902
Wendy Peterson, Director of Admissions, Washington State University, 370 Lighty Student Services Bldg, Pullman, WA 99164-1067

Western Washington University

Bellingham, Washington — **CB member**
www.wwu.edu — **CB code: 4947**

- Public 4-year university
- Residential campus in small city
- 12,816 degree-seeking undergraduates: 7% part-time, 56% women, 2% African American, 8% Asian American, 3% Hispanic American, 2% Native American
- 1,245 degree-seeking graduate students
- 67% of applicants admitted
- SAT or ACT (ACT writing optional), application essay required

General. Founded in 1893. Regionally accredited. **Degrees:** 2,888 bachelor's awarded; master's offered. **Location:** 90 miles from Seattle, 60 miles from Vancouver, Canada. **Calendar:** Quarter, extensive summer session. **Full-time faculty:** 472 total; 84% have terminal degrees, 12% minority, 38% women. **Part-time faculty:** 156 total; 40% have terminal degrees, 11% minority, 49% women. **Class size:** 52% < 20, 33% 20-39, 4% 40-49, 8% 50-99, 3% >100. **Special facilities:** Wind tunnel, electron microscope, neutron generator laboratory, planetarium, air pollution laboratory, motor vehicle research laboratory, electronic music studio, 11-acre recreational park on lake, marine laboratory.

Freshman class profile. 8,645 applied, 5,778 admitted, 2,381 enrolled.

Mid 50% test scores			
SAT verbal:	510-620	GPA 2.0-2.99:	3%
SAT math:	520-620	Rank in top quarter:	64%
ACT:	20-26	Rank in top tenth:	31%
GPA 3.50 or higher:	62%	Out-of-state:	9%
GPA 3.0-3.49:	35%	Live on campus:	93%

Basis for selection. Academic achievement most significant factor. Curriculum rigor (level and difficulty of courses), grade trends, school, community activities, special talent, multicultural experience, personal circumstances considered. All students encouraged to take courses beyond minimums. Consideration given to motivation, achievements outside of classroom, multicultural experience, and attributes that will enhance institution's learning community. Audition recommended for music; portfolio required for art.

High school preparation. 15 units required. Required units include English 4, mathematics 3, social studies 3, science 2 (laboratory 1), foreign language 2 and academic electives 1. Mathematics requirement includes 2 algebra. Sciences include 1 algebra-based chemistry or physics. Foreign language should be in 1 language. .5 fine arts and .5 academic elective required.

2005-2006 Annual costs. Tuition/fees: $4,737; $14,688 out-of-state. Room/board: $6,524. Books/supplies: $906. Personal expenses: $1,830.

2005-2006 Financial aid. **Need-based:** 1,651 full-time freshmen applied for aid; 844 were judged to have need; 819 of these received aid. Average need met was 87%. Average scholarship/grant was $5,608; average loan $2,895. 50% of total undergraduate aid awarded as scholarships/grants, 50% as loans/jobs. **Non-need-based:** Awarded to 491 full-time undergraduates, including 106 freshmen. Scholarships awarded for academics, alumni affiliation, art, athletics, leadership, minority status, music/drama, state residency. **Additional information:** Short-term student loans ranging from $100 to $1,000 available on a quarterly basis.

Application procedures. Admission: Closing date 3/1 (postmark date). $50 fee, may be waived for applicants with need. Application may be submitted online. Admission notification on a rolling basis beginning on or about 12/1. Must reply by May 1 or within 2 week(s) if notified thereafter. **Financial aid:** Priority date 2/15; no closing date. FAFSA required. Applicants notified on a rolling basis starting 3/20; must reply within 3 week(s) of notification.

Academics. Special study options: Double major, ESL, exchange student, honors, independent study, internships, liberal arts/career combination, student-designed major, study abroad, teacher certification program. **Credit/placement by examination:** AP, CLEP, IB, institutional tests. 135 credit hours maximum toward bachelor's degree. **Support services:** Learning center, study skills assistance, tutoring, writing center.

Majors. Area/ethnic studies: American, Canadian, East Asian. **Biology:** General, biochemistry, botany, cell/histology, cellular/molecular, ecology, evolutionary, marine, zoology. **Business:** Accounting, business admin, finance, human resources, international, management information systems, marketing, operations. **Communications:** General, journalism. **Computer sciences:** General. **Conservation:** Environmental science, environmental studies. **Education:** Art, biology, chemistry, drama/dance, elementary, English, German, history, mathematics, music, physical, science, social science, social studies, Spanish, special, speech, technology/industrial arts. **Engineering technology:** Electrical, industrial, manufacturing, plastics. **English:** Creative writing, English lit. **Family/consumer sciences:** Child development. **Foreign languages:** General, French, German, linguistics, Spanish. **Health:** Audiology/speech pathology, community health services. **History:** General. **Interdisciplinary:** Accounting/computer science, biological/physical sciences. **Liberal arts:** Humanities. **Math:** General, applied. **Parks/recreation:** General, health/fitness. **Philosophy/religion:** Philosophy. **Physical sciences:** Chemistry, geology, geophysics, physics. **Psychology:** General. **Public administration:** Human services. **Social sciences:** Anthropology, archaeology, economics, geography, political science, sociology. **Visual/performing arts:** General, art, art history/conservation, ceramics, commercial/advertising art, dance, design, dramatic, drawing, fiber arts, graphic design, industrial design, multimedia, music history, music performance, music theory/composition, painting, photography, printmaking, sculpture.

Most popular majors. Business/marketing 14%, English 7%, psychology 7%, social sciences 13%, visual/performing arts 6%.

Computing on campus. 745 workstations in dormitories, library, computer center, student center. Dormitories wired for high-speed internet access and linked to campus network. Commuter students can connect to campus network. Online course registration, online library, helpline, repair service, student web hosting, wireless network available.

Student life. Freshman orientation: Available. Preregistration for classes offered. 6 programs offered for students and family members, early-mid August. Program 1-2 days, based on housing needs. **Policies:** Freshmen permitted cars on campus. **Housing:** Coed dorms, special housing for disabled, apartments, substance-free housing available. $200 partly refundable deposit, deadline 6/15. Wellness floors, multicultural floors available. **Activities:** Bands, choral groups, dance, drama, literary magazine, music ensembles, musical theater, opera, radio station, student government, student newspaper, symphony orchestra, TV station, Lesbian/Gay/Bisexual Alliance, veteran's outreach center, volunteer services and resources, international student club, The Inn (nondenominational), Campus Christian Fellowship, ethnic student center, Mecha, Circle K, American Red Cross chapter.

Athletics. NCAA. **Intercollegiate:** Basketball, cross-country, football (tackle) M, golf, rowing (crew), soccer, softball W, track and field, volleyball W. **Intramural:** Badminton, basketball, football (non-tackle), golf, racquetball, soccer, softball, table tennis, tennis, volleyball. **Team name:** Vikings.

Student services. Adult student services, alcohol/substance abuse counseling, campus ministries, career counseling, student employment services, financial aid counseling, health services, minority student services, on-campus daycare, personal counseling, placement for graduates, veterans' counselor. **Physically disabled:** Services for visually, speech, hearing impaired.

Contact. E-mail: admit@wwu.edu
Phone: (360) 650-3440 Fax: (360) 650-7369
Karen Copetas, Director of Admissions and Enrollment Planning, Western Washington University, 516 High Street, Bellingham, WA 98225-9009

Whitman College

Walla Walla, Washington — **CB member**
www.whitman.edu — **CB code: 4951**

- Private 4-year liberal arts college
- Residential campus in large town
- 1,488 degree-seeking undergraduates: 1% part-time, 54% women, 2% African American, 9% Asian American, 4% Hispanic American, 1% Native American, 3% international
- 49% of applicants admitted
- SAT or ACT with writing, application essay required
- 86% graduate within 6 years

General. Founded in 1883. Regionally accredited. **Degrees:** 359 bachelor's awarded. **Location:** 150 miles from Spokane, 235 miles from Portland, Oregon. **Calendar:** Semester. **Full-time faculty:** 115 total; 97% have terminal degrees, 11% minority, 37% women. **Part-time faculty:** 76 total; 60% have terminal degrees, 5% minority, 46% women. **Class size:** 70% < 20, 28% 20-39, 2% 40-49, less than 1% 50-99. **Special facilities:** Asian art collection, natural history museum, planetarium, 2 electron microscopes, outdoor observatory, indoor and outdoor rock-climbing walls, outdoor sculpture walk, organic garden.

Freshman class profile. 2,544 applied, 1,251 admitted, 361 enrolled.

Mid 50% test scores		**Rank in top tenth:**	60%
SAT verbal:	620-750	**Return as sophomores:**	95%
SAT math:	620-700	**Out-of-state:**	60%
ACT:	27-31	**Live on campus:**	100%
GPA 3.50 or higher:	83%	**International:**	3%
GPA 3.0-3.49:	15%	**Fraternities:**	19%
GPA 2.0-2.99:	2%	**Sororities:**	17%
Rank in top quarter:	91%		

Basis for selection. Scholastic record, test scores, quality of written expression, and level of motivation are very important. Evidence of talent, imagination, creativity, leadership, responsibility, and maturity are also considered. Writing for all students. TOEFL, ELPT, or APIEL accepted as language proficiency exams. Interview recommended.

High school preparation. 16 units recommended. Recommended units include English 4, mathematics 4, social studies 2, history 2, science 3 (laboratory 2) and foreign language 2. Arts (1 unit).

2006-2007 Annual costs. Tuition/fees: $30,806. Room/board: $7,840. Books/supplies: $1,250.

2005-2006 Financial aid. Need-based: Average need met was 98%. Average scholarship/grant was $17,400; average loan $3,450. 76% of total undergraduate aid awarded as scholarships/grants, 24% as loans/jobs. **Non-need-based:** Scholarships awarded for academics, art, minority status, music/drama.

Application procedures. Admission: Priority date 11/15; deadline 1/15 (postmark date). $45 fee, may be waived for applicants with need. Application may be submitted online. Admission notification 4/1. Must reply by 5/1. Must reply by May 1 or within 2 week(s) if notified thereafter. **Financial aid:** Priority date 1/15, closing date 2/1. FAFSA, CSS PROFILE required. Applicants notified on a rolling basis starting 12/20; must reply within 2 week(s) of notification.

Academics. Library open 24 hours, seven days a week during academic year. **Special study options:** Accelerated study, combined bachelor's/graduate degree, cooperative education, cross-registration, double major, dual enrollment of high school students, exchange student, honors, independent study, liberal arts/career combination, student-designed major, study abroad, urban semester, Washington semester. Study abroad opportunities in over 20 countries; Whitman-In-China allows recent graduates to spend a year teaching English in one of 3 Chinese universities; 3-2 engineering and computer science programs with California Institute of Technology, Columbia University (NY), Duke University (NC), Washington University (MO) and University of Washington; 3-2 oceanography and biology or geology program with University of Washington; 3-3 law program with Columbia University; 3-2 program with Monterey Institute of International Studies; 4-1 program with Bank Street College of Education; undergraduate research conference; Semester in the West field study. **Credit/placement by examination:** AP, CLEP, IB, institutional tests. 30 credit hours maximum toward bachelor's degree. **Support services:** Learning center, reduced course load, study skills assistance, tutoring, writing center.

Majors. Area/ethnic studies: Asian. **Biology:** General, Biochemistry/biophysics and molecular biology. **Conservation:** Environmental studies. **English:** English lit. **Foreign languages:** Classics, French, German, Spanish. **History:** General. **Math:** General. **Philosophy/religion:** Philosophy, religion. **Physical sciences:** Astronomy, chemistry, geology, physics. **Psychology:** General. **Social sciences:** Anthropology, economics, political science, sociology. **Visual/performing arts:** Art history/conservation, dramatic, film/cinema, studio arts.

Most popular majors. Biology 13%, English 8%, history 7%, physical sciences 8%, psychology 10%, social sciences 23%, visual/performing arts 13%.

Computing on campus. 410 workstations in dormitories, library, computer center, student center. Dormitories wired for high-speed internet access and linked to campus network. Commuter students can connect to campus network. Online library, helpline, student web hosting available.

Student life. Freshman orientation: Available. **Policies:** Freshmen permitted cars on campus. **Housing:** Guaranteed on-campus for freshmen. Coed dorms, single-sex dorms, apartments, fraternity/sorority housing available. $300 nonrefundable deposit, deadline 5/1. German, French, Spanish, Japanese language houses. Asian Studies, multiethnic, environmental, fine arts, community service, writing, global awareness houses available, college-owned rentals. **Activities:** Bands, choral groups, dance, drama, film society, literary magazine, music ensembles, musical theater, opera, radio station, student government, student newspaper, symphony orchestra, multiethnic cultural association, community service, political organizations, environmental groups, sexual-assault prevention educators.

Athletics. NCAA. **Intercollegiate:** Baseball M, basketball, cross-country, golf, skiing, soccer, swimming, tennis, volleyball W. **Intramural:** Bowling, football (non-tackle), tennis, volleyball. **Team name:** Missionaries.

Student services. Adult student services, alcohol/substance abuse counseling, career counseling, student employment services, financial aid counseling, health services, minority student services, on-campus daycare, personal counseling, placement for graduates, veterans' counselor, women's services. **Physically disabled:** Services for visually, speech, hearing impaired.

Contact. E-mail: admission@whitman.edu
Phone: (509) 527-5176 Toll-free number: (877) 462-9448
Fax: (509) 527-4967
Tony Cabasco, Dean of Admission and Financial Aid, Whitman College, 345 Boyer Avenue, Walla Walla, WA 99362-2046

Whitworth College

Spokane, Washington — **CB member**
www.whitworth.edu — **CB code: 4953**

- Private 4-year liberal arts college affiliated with Presbyterian Church (USA)
- Residential campus in large city
- 2,156 degree-seeking undergraduates: 5% part-time, 60% women, 2% African American, 4% Asian American, 2% Hispanic American, 1% Native American, 1% international
- 180 degree-seeking graduate students
- 67% of applicants admitted
- SAT or ACT (ACT writing optional), application essay required
- 76% graduate within 6 years

General. Founded in 1890. Regionally accredited. **Degrees:** 467 bachelor's awarded; master's offered. **ROTC:** Army. **Location:** 6 miles from downtown Spokane, 280 miles from Seattle. **Calendar:** 4-1-4, limited summer session. **Full-time faculty:** 119 total; 71% have terminal degrees, 5% minority, 37% women. **Part-time faculty:** 162 total; 3% minority, 45% women. **Class size:** 59% < 20, 34% 20-39, 4% 40-49, 2% 50-99, less than 1% >100.

Freshman class profile. 2,062 applied, 1,372 admitted, 451 enrolled.

Mid 50% test scores			
SAT verbal:	540-650	Rank in top quarter:	70%
SAT math:	540-650	Rank in top tenth:	40%
ACT:	24-29	End year in good standing:	98%
GPA 3.50 or higher:	73%	Return as sophomores:	87%
GPA 3.0-3.49:	21%	Out-of-state:	33%
GPA 2.0-2.99:	6%	Live on campus:	96%
		International:	1%

Basis for selection. School achievement, extracurricular activities, recommendations most important. Interview recommended.

High school preparation. College-preparatory program recommended. 18 units recommended. Recommended units include English 4, mathematics 3, social studies 3, history 3, science 3 (laboratory 2) and foreign language 2.

2005-2006 Annual costs. Tuition/fees: $22,678. Room/board: $6,760. Books/supplies: $888. Personal expenses: $1,710.

2005-2006 Financial aid. Need-based: 399 full-time freshmen applied for aid; 317 were judged to have need; 316 of these received aid. Average need met was 83%. Average scholarship/grant was $12,851; average loan $3,757. 66% of total undergraduate aid awarded as scholarships/grants, 34% as loans/jobs. **Non-need-based:** Scholarships awarded for academics, alumni affiliation, art, music/drama, religious affiliation, ROTC.

Application procedures. Admission: Closing date 3/1 (postmark date). No application fee. Application may be submitted online. Admission notification on a rolling basis beginning on or about 12/20. Must reply by 5/1. **Financial aid:** Priority date 3/1; no closing date. FAFSA required. Applicants notified on a rolling basis starting 3/1; must reply by 5/1 or within 4 week(s) of notification.

Academics. Special study options: Accelerated study, cooperative education, cross-registration, distance learning, double major, dual enrollment of high school students, ESL, honors, independent study, internships, student-designed major, study abroad, teacher certification program, Washington semester. 3-2 engineering programs. **Credit/placement by examination:** AP, CLEP, IB, SAT, ACT, institutional tests. 32 credit hours maximum toward bachelor's degree. **Support services:** Learning center, reduced course load, study skills assistance, tutoring, writing center.

Majors. Area/ethnic studies: American. **Biology:** General. **Business:** Accounting, business admin, international, marketing. **Communications:** General, journalism. **Computer sciences:** General, computer science. **Education:** General, art, biology, chemistry, computer, drama/dance, elementary, English, ESL, foreign languages, French, health, history, mathematics, middle, multi-level teacher, music, physical, physics, reading, school counseling, science, secondary, social science, social studies, Spanish, special, speech. **Engineering:** General. **Foreign languages:** French, Spanish. **Health:** Athletic training. **History:** General. **Interdisciplinary:** Peace/conflict. **Liberal arts:** Arts/sciences. **Math:** General, applied. **Parks/recreation:** Health/fitness. **Philosophy/religion:** Philosophy, religion. **Physical sciences:** Chemistry, physics. **Psychology:** General. **Social sciences:** General, economics, international relations, political science, sociology. **Theology:** Theology. **Visual/performing arts:** General, art, jazz, music performance, piano/organ, theater history, voice/opera.

Most popular majors. Business/marketing 21%, education 13%, English 7%, philosophy/religious studies 6%, psychology 7%, social sciences 7%, visual/performing arts 8%.

Computing on campus. 150 workstations in library, computer center, student center. Dormitories wired for high-speed internet access and linked to campus network. Commuter students can connect to campus network. Online course registration, helpline, repair service available.

Student life. Freshman orientation: Mandatory. Preregistration for classes offered. **Housing:** Guaranteed on-campus for freshmen. Coed dorms, single-sex dorms, special housing for disabled, apartments available. $70 partly refundable deposit, deadline 5/1. Pets allowed in dorm rooms. Theme houses. **Activities:** Bands, choral groups, dance, drama, literary magazine, music ensembles, musical theater, radio station, student government, student newspaper, symphony orchestra, Black Student Union, Fellowship of Christian Athletes, international club, Hawaiian club, political activist club, Native American club, Amnesty International, Habitat for Humanity, Asian American club, Circle-K International.

Athletics. NCAA. **Intercollegiate:** Baseball M, basketball, cross-country, football (tackle) M, golf, soccer, softball W, swimming, tennis, track and field, volleyball W. **Intramural:** Basketball, soccer, softball, table tennis, tennis, volleyball. **Team name:** Pirates.

Student services. Adult student services, campus ministries, career counseling, student employment services, financial aid counseling, health services, minority student services, personal counseling, placement for graduates, veterans' counselor. **Physically disabled:** Services for visually, speech, hearing impaired.

Contact. E-mail: admissions@whitworth.edu
Phone: (509) 777-3212 Fax: (509) 777-3773
Fred Pfursich, Dean of Enrollment Services, Whitworth College, 300 West Hawthorne Road, Spokane, WA 99251-0002

West Virginia

Alderson-Broaddus College
Philippi, West Virginia
www.ab.edu **CB code: 5005**

- Private 4-year liberal arts college affiliated with American Baptist Churches in the USA
- Commuter campus in small town
- 623 degree-seeking undergraduates: 8% part-time, 68% women, 2% African American, 1% Asian American, 1% Hispanic American, 2% international
- 131 degree-seeking graduate students
- 75% of applicants admitted
- SAT and SAT Subject Tests or ACT (ACT writing optional) required
- 71% graduate within 6 years; 15% enter graduate study

General. Founded in 1871. Regionally accredited. **Degrees:** 132 bachelor's, 13 associate awarded; master's offered. **Location:** 100 miles from Charleston, 125 miles from Pittsburgh. **Calendar:** Semester, limited summer session. **Full-time faculty:** 58 total; 24% have terminal degrees, 12% minority, 53% women. **Part-time faculty:** 29 total; 31% have terminal degrees, 59% women. **Special facilities:** Gross anatomy laboratory.

Freshman class profile. 480 applied, 362 admitted, 125 enrolled.

Mid 50% test scores			
SAT verbal:	520-580	Rank in top tenth:	17%
SAT math:	430-540	Out-of-state:	25%
ACT:	20-23	Live on campus:	42%
Rank in top quarter:	49%	International:	1%

Basis for selection. High school record, rank in top half of class, test scores, interview very important. Physician's assistant and nursing applicants should have strong background in science. Interview required for physician's assistant applicants, recommended for all others. Audition required for music. **Homeschooled:** ACT/SAT and results from Iowa Tests required.

High school preparation. College-preparatory program recommended. 15 units recommended. Recommended units include English 4, mathematics 3, social studies 2, history 2, science 3 and foreign language 1.

2005-2006 Annual costs. Tuition/fees: $18,136. Room/board: $5,870. Books/supplies: $800. Personal expenses: $1,500.

2004-2005 Financial aid. Need-based: 150 full-time freshmen applied for aid; 145 were judged to have need; 145 of these received aid. Average need met was 91%. Average scholarship/grant was $9,735; average loan $3,594. 67% of total undergraduate aid awarded as scholarships/grants, 33% as loans/jobs. **Non-need-based:** Awarded to 123 full-time undergraduates, including 21 freshmen. Scholarships awarded for academics, athletics, music/drama.

Application procedures. Admission: No deadline. $10 fee, may be waived for applicants with need. Application may be submitted online. Admission notification on a rolling basis. **Financial aid:** Priority date 3/1; no closing date. FAFSA required. Applicants notified on a rolling basis starting 2/15; must reply within 2 week(s) of notification.

Academics. Special study options: Accelerated study, cross-registration, double major, dual enrollment of high school students, exchange student, external degree, honors, independent study, internships, study abroad, teacher certification program. Business department offers an on-line certificate program. **Credit/placement by examination:** AP, CLEP, institutional tests. 40 credit hours maximum toward associate degree, 60 toward bachelor's. **Support services:** Learning center, reduced course load, remedial instruction, study skills assistance, tutoring.

Majors. Biology: General. **Business:** Accounting, business admin, management information systems. **Computer sciences:** Computer science. **Conservation:** General. **Education:** General, elementary, middle, multi-level teacher, music, secondary, special. **Family/consumer sciences:** Family/community services. **Health:** Athletic training, medical radiologic technology/radiation therapy, nursing (RN), physician assistant, recreational therapy. **History:** General. **Interdisciplinary:** Natural sciences. **Liberal arts:** Arts/sciences. **Math:** Applied. **Parks/recreation:** General. **Philosophy/religion:** Religion. **Physical sciences:** Chemistry. **Psychology:** General. **Theology:** Theology. **Visual/performing arts:** Music performance, painting.

Most popular majors. Business/marketing 8%, education 15%, health sciences 39%, philosophy/religious studies 9%, visual/performing arts 7%.

Computing on campus. 75 workstations in library, student center. Dormitories wired for high-speed internet access and linked to campus network. Commuter students can connect to campus network. Online library, helpline, student web hosting available.

Student life. Freshman orientation: Available. Preregistration for classes offered. On Saturday prior to start of fall classes. **Policies:** Participation in campus activities stressed. Voluntary weekly chapel service offered. Freshmen permitted cars on campus. **Housing:** Guaranteed on-campus for all undergraduates. Coed dorms, single-sex dorms, special housing for disabled, apartments, substance-free housing available. $100 deposit. **Activities:** Bands, choral groups, dance, drama, literary magazine, music ensembles, musical theater, opera, radio station, student government, student newspaper, TV station, A-B Collegiate 4-H, association of women's studies, Baptist campus ministries, College Players, Fellowship of Christian Athletes, Students in Free Enterprise, Students Learning in Community Education, A-B mission team.

Athletics. NCAA. **Intercollegiate:** Baseball M, basketball, cross-country, golf, soccer M, softball W, track and field, volleyball W. **Intramural:** Badminton, basketball, bowling, football (non-tackle), golf, gymnastics, handball, racquetball, skiing, soccer, softball W, swimming, table tennis, tennis, volleyball, water polo, weight lifting. **Team name:** Battlers.

Student services. Adult student services, alcohol/substance abuse counseling, campus ministries, career counseling, financial aid counseling, health services, personal counseling, placement for graduates, veterans' counselor. **Physically disabled:** Services for visually, hearing impaired.

Contact. E-mail: admissions@ab.edu
Phone: (304) 457-6256 Toll-free number: (800) 263-1549
Fax: (304) 457-6239
Kimberly Klaus, Director of Admissions, Alderson-Broaddus College, College Hill, Philippi, WV 26416

American Military University
Charles Town, West Virginia
www.apus.edu/amu **CB code: 3955**

- Private 4-year university and military college
- Large town

General. Accredited by DETC. **Calendar:** Semester.

Contact. Phone: (703) 396-6860
10648 Wakeman Court, Manassas, VA 20110

American Public University
Charles Town, West Virginia
www.apu.apus.edu/index.htm

- For-profit 4-year university and liberal arts college
- Small town

General. Accredited by DETC. **Calendar:** Continuous.

Annual costs/financial aid. Distance learning only.

Contact. Phone: (877) 468-6268
Director of Admissions, 111 West Congress Street, Charles Town, WV 25414

Appalachian Bible College
Bradley, West Virginia
www.abc.edu **CB code: 7305**

- Private 4-year Bible college affiliated with nondenominational tradition
- Residential campus in rural community
- 230 degree-seeking undergraduates: 7% part-time, 48% women, 2% African American, 1% Asian American, 2% international
- 69% of applicants admitted
- SAT or ACT (ACT writing optional), application essay required

General. Founded in 1950. Regionally accredited; also accredited by ABHE. **Degrees:** 41 bachelor's, 8 associate awarded; master's offered. **Location:** 5 miles from Beckley. **Calendar:** Semester, limited summer session. **Full-time faculty:** 10 total. **Part-time faculty:** 5 total.

Freshman class profile. 101 applied, 70 admitted, 48 enrolled.

Mid 50% test scores			
SAT verbal:	470-680	Return as sophomores:	73%
SAT math:	460-590	Out-of-state:	64%
ACT:	18-23	Live on campus:	89%

Basis for selection. Profession of Jesus Christ as Saviour, essential agreement with doctrinal statement of college, approved character very important. Minimum 2.0 GPA, test scores, achievement and potential in English also considered. If no scores are submitted, student must test on first available test date after enrollment and must take developmental English. Interview recommended. **Homeschooled:** Must provide accurate record of curriculum used, subjects studied, grades earned for grade levels 9-12.

High school preparation. Recommended units include English 4, mathematics 3, social studies 3, history 3, science 3, foreign language 1 and academic electives 4.

2006-2007 Annual costs. Tuition/fees: $8,820. Room/board: $4,680. Books/supplies: $1,000. Personal expenses: $1,080.

2004-2005 Financial aid. **Need-based:** 64% of total undergraduate aid awarded as scholarships/grants, 36% as loans/jobs.

Application procedures. **Admission:** No deadline. $10 fee, may be waived for applicants with need. Application may be submitted online. Admission notification on a rolling basis. **Financial aid:** Closing date 6/15. FAFSA, institutional form required. Applicants notified on a rolling basis starting 6/15; must reply by 8/1 or within 4 week(s) of notification.

Academics. **Special study options:** Cooperative education, dual enrollment of high school students, independent study, internships, teacher certification program. **Credit/placement by examination:** AP, CLEP, SAT, ACT, institutional tests. 29 credit hours maximum toward bachelor's degree. **Support services:** Reduced course load, remedial instruction, study skills assistance, tutoring.

Majors. **Theology:** Bible.

Computing on campus. 10 workstations in library. Dormitories wired for high-speed internet access and linked to campus network. Online library, repair service available.

Student life. **Freshman orientation:** Mandatory. Preregistration for classes offered. Held for 3 days immediately prior to beginning of semester. **Policies:** Chapel held three times a week. Annual Spiritual Life Conference, Distinguished Christian Lecture Series, Bible and missions conferences. Religious observance required. Freshmen permitted cars on campus. **Housing:** Single-sex dorms, apartments available. **Activities:** Choral groups, drama, music ensembles, student government.

Athletics. NCCAA. **Intercollegiate:** Basketball, soccer M, volleyball W. **Intramural:** Basketball, soccer M, table tennis, tennis, volleyball. **Team name:** Warriors.

Student services. Career counseling, financial aid counseling, health services, personal counseling, placement for graduates, veterans' counselor.

Contact. E-mail: admissions@abc.edu
Phone: (304) 877-6428 ext. 3213 Toll-free number: (800) 678-9222
Fax: (304) 877-5082
Angela Harding, Director of Admissions, Appalachian Bible College, PO Box ABC, Bradley, WV 25818-1353

Bethany College

Bethany, West Virginia — **CB member**
www.bethanywv.edu — **CB code: 5060**

- Private 4-year liberal arts college affiliated with Christian Church (Disciples of Christ)
- Residential campus in rural community
- 888 degree-seeking undergraduates: 54% women, 4% African American, 1% Hispanic American, 4% international
- 75% of applicants admitted
- SAT or ACT (ACT writing recommended), application essay required
- 69% graduate within 6 years; 24% enter graduate study

General. Founded in 1840. Regionally accredited. **Degrees:** 153 bachelor's awarded. **Location:** 14 miles from Wheeling, 40 miles from Pittsburgh. **Calendar:** Semester. **Full-time faculty:** 63 total; 54% have terminal degrees, 6% minority, 33% women. **Part-time faculty:** 23 total; 13% have terminal degrees, 52% women. **Class size:** 71% < 20, 21% 20-39, 5% 40-49, 3% 50-99, less than 1% >100. **Special facilities:** 1300 acres of nature preserves, 5 national historic sites, Peace Point Equestrian Center adjacent to campus.

Freshman class profile. 859 applied, 645 admitted, 219 enrolled.

Mid 50% test scores			
SAT verbal:	430-550	Rank in top quarter:	30%
SAT math:	440-540	Rank in top tenth:	11%
ACT:	19-24	End year in good standing:	94%
GPA 3.50 or higher:	27%	Return as sophomores:	75%
GPA 3.0-3.49:	33%	Out-of-state:	71%
GPA 2.0-2.99:	39%	Live on campus:	98%
		International:	3%

Basis for selection. Rank in top half of graduating class, test scores, interview, activities, and recommendations important. Interviews are strongly reccomended, but not required. **Homeschooled:** Statement describing home-school structure and mission required. **Learning Disabled:** Submit official diagnosis of learning disability after acceptance.

High school preparation. 15 units required. Required and recommended units include English 4, mathematics 3, social studies 3, science 3 (laboratory 1), foreign language 2 and academic electives 2.

2006-2007 Annual costs. Tuition/fees (projected): $15,940. Room/board: $7,625. Books/supplies: $600. Personal expenses: $900.

2005-2006 Financial aid. **Need-based:** 233 full-time freshmen applied for aid; 233 were judged to have need; 233 of these received aid. Average loan was $5,568. 57% of total undergraduate aid awarded as scholarships/grants, 43% as loans/jobs. **Non-need-based:** Scholarships awarded for academics, alumni affiliation, art, leadership, music/drama, religious affiliation. **Additional information:** Scholarships available for travel program.

Application procedures. **Admission:** Priority date 4/1; no deadline. $25 fee, may be waived for applicants with need. Application may be submitted online. Admission notification on a rolling basis beginning on or about 10/1. Must reply by May 1 or within 3 week(s) if notified thereafter. **Financial aid:** Priority date 3/1, closing date 5/1. FAFSA required. Applicants notified on a rolling basis starting 2/1; must reply within 3 week(s) of notification.

Academics. Students with learning disabilities must apply by Febuary 15 for priority consideration in limited-enrollment learning disabled program. **Special study options:** Accelerated study, double major, dual enrollment of high school students, ESL, independent study, internships, liberal arts/career combination, student-designed major, study abroad, teacher certification program, United Nations semester, Washington semester. **Credit/placement by examination:** AP, CLEP, IB, institutional tests. 80 credit hours maximum toward bachelor's degree. **Support services:** Learning center, remedial instruction, study skills assistance, tutoring.

Majors. **Biology:** General, biochemistry. **Business:** General, accounting, finance, international, international finance. **Communications:** General, advertising, broadcast journalism, journalism, public relations, radio/tv. **Communications technology:** Graphics. **Computer sciences:** General, computer science. **Conservation:** Environmental studies. **Education:** General, art, biology, chemistry, elementary, English, foreign languages, French, German, history, learning disabled, mathematics, multi-level teacher, multiple handicapped, physical, secondary, social studies, Spanish, special. **Foreign languages:** French, German, Spanish. **History:** General. **Interdisciplinary:** Global studies, math/computer science. **Math:** General. **Parks/recreation:** Health/fitness, sports admin. **Philosophy/religion:** Philosophy, religion. **Physical sciences:** Chemistry, physics. **Psychology:** General. **Public administration:** Social work. **Social sciences:** Economics, international relations, political science. **Visual/performing arts:** General, art, design, dramatic, studio arts.

Computing on campus. 145 workstations in dormitories, library, computer center, student center. Dormitories wired for high-speed internet access and linked to campus network. Commuter students can connect to campus network. Online library, helpline, repair service, student web hosting, wireless network available.

Student life. **Freshman orientation:** Mandatory, $100 fee. Preregistration for classes offered. Summer registration and orientation to campus and facilities and/or pre-college orientation in late August for students who cannot participate in summer programs. **Policies:** Freshmen permitted cars on campus. **Housing:** Guaranteed on-campus for all undergraduates. Coed dorms, single-sex dorms, special housing for disabled, apartments, fraternity/sorority housing available. Off-campus housing available in the village of Bethany for students who meet requirements. **Activities:** Bands, choral groups, drama, film society, literary magazine, music ensembles, musical theater, radio station, student government, student newspaper, TV station, community service organization, ecumenical religious organization, Model UN, multicultural students club, advertising club, international students association, social work club, Amnesty International, Coalition for Christian Outreach, Circle K, Equestrian Club.

Athletics. NCAA. **Intercollegiate:** Baseball M, basketball, cheerleading, cross-country, diving, football (tackle) M, golf M, soccer, softball W, swimming, tennis, track and field, volleyball W. **Intramural:** Basketball, football (non-tackle) M, handball, racquetball, soccer, softball, swimming, tennis, volleyball. **Team name:** Bison.

Student services. Alcohol/substance abuse counseling, campus ministries, career counseling, student employment services, financial aid counseling, health services, minority student services, personal counseling, placement for graduates, women's services. **Physically disabled:** Services for visually, speech, hearing impaired. **Learning disabled:** Comprehensive services available.

Contact. E-mail: wblair@bethanywv.edu
Phone: (304) 829-7611 Toll-free number: (800) 922-7611
Fax: (304) 829-7142
Wray Blair, Director of Admission, Bethany College, Office of Admission, Bethany, WV 26032-0428

Bluefield State College

Bluefield, West Virginia
www.bluefieldstate.edu **CB code: 5064**

- Public 4-year community and technical college
- Commuter campus in large town
- 1,790 degree-seeking undergraduates
- SAT or ACT with writing required

General. Founded in 1895. Regionally accredited. Off-campus locations at Lewisburg, Welch, Beckley, and Summersville. **Degrees:** 185 bachelor's, 182 associate awarded. **Location:** 100 miles from Charleston, 100 miles from Roanoke, Virginia. **Calendar:** Semester, limited summer session. **Full-time faculty:** 92 total; 40% have terminal degrees, 10% minority, 55% women. **Part-time faculty:** 174 total; 9% have terminal degrees, 9% minority, 49% women. **Class size:** 63% < 20, 35% 20-39, 3% 40-49. **Special facilities:** Instructional technology center.

Freshman class profile.

Mid 50% test scores			
SAT verbal:	430-560	Out-of-state:	3%
SAT math:	400-520	Fraternities:	1%
ACT:	16-21	Sororities:	1%

Basis for selection. 2.5 minimum GPA, college preparatory program, test scores required for applicants to health, teacher education, humanities, social science and business administration programs. High school requirements not necessary for associate's program.

High school preparation. 17 units required. Required and recommended units include English 4, mathematics 3, social studies 3, history 1, science 3 (laboratory 2), foreign language 2 and academic electives 1.

2005-2006 Annual costs. Tuition/fees: $3,410; $7,014 out-of-state. Books/supplies: $800. Personal expenses: $840.

2004-2005 Financial aid. Need-based: 450 full-time freshmen applied for aid; 375 were judged to have need; 375 of these received aid. Average need met was 70%. Average scholarship/grant was $3,010; average loan $3,000. 66% of total undergraduate aid awarded as scholarships/grants, 34% as loans/jobs. **Non-need-based:** Awarded to 585 full-time undergraduates, including 165 freshmen. Scholarships awarded for academics, alumni affiliation, athletics, leadership, minority status, state residency.

Application procedures. Admission: No deadline. No application fee. Application may be submitted online. Admission notification on a rolling basis. **Financial aid:** Closing date 3/1. FAFSA, institutional form required. Applicants notified on a rolling basis starting 6/1.

Academics. Special study options: Distance learning, honors, internships, liberal arts/career combination, student-designed major, teacher certification program. **Credit/placement by examination:** AP, CLEP, IB, institutional tests. **Support services:** Learning center, pre-admission summer program, reduced course load, remedial instruction, study skills assistance, tutoring, writing center.

Majors. Business: Accounting, business admin. **Computer sciences:** General. **Education:** Elementary, middle. **Engineering technology:** Architectural, civil, electrical. **Interdisciplinary:** Biological/physical sciences. **Liberal arts:** Arts/sciences. **Protective services:** Criminal justice. **Social sciences:** General.

Most popular majors. Business/marketing 15%, computer/information sciences 10%, education 18%, health sciences 14%, liberal arts 10%.

Computing on campus. 358 workstations in library, computer center. Online library, helpline, student web hosting, wireless network available.

Student life. Freshman orientation: Available. Preregistration for classes offered. One day in July or August. **Policies:** Freshmen permitted cars on campus. **Housing:** Off-campus housing services provided. **Activities:** Choral groups, radio station, student government, student newspaper, Baptist Student Union, Christian fellowship organization, international student organization, Minorities on the Move, Model UN, student nurses association.

Athletics. NCAA. **Intercollegiate:** Baseball M, basketball, cheerleading, cross-country, golf M, softball W, tennis, volleyball W. **Intramural:** Badminton, basketball, bowling, football (non-tackle) M, handball, skiing, softball, swimming, table tennis, tennis, volleyball, water polo. **Team name:** Big Blues.

Student services. Career counseling, student employment services, financial aid counseling, health services, minority student services, personal counseling, placement for graduates, veterans' counselor. **Physically disabled:** Services for visually, speech, hearing impaired.

Contact. E-mail: bscadmit@bluefieldstate.edu
Phone: (304) 327-4065 Toll-free number: (800) 654-7798
Fax: (304) 325-7747
John Cardwell, Director of Enrollment Management, Bluefield State College, 219 Rock Street, Bluefield, WV 24701

Concord University

Athens, West Virginia **CB member**
www.concord.edu **CB code: 5120**

- Public 4-year university
- Residential campus in small town
- 3,015 degree-seeking undergraduates
- SAT or ACT with writing required

General. Founded in 1872. Regionally accredited. **Degrees:** 448 bachelor's awarded; master's offered. **Location:** 5 miles from Princeton, 80 miles from Charleston. **Calendar:** Semester, limited summer session. **Full-time faculty:** 80 total. **Part-time faculty:** 95 total. **Class size:** 64% < 20, 30% 20-39, 4% 40-49, 3% 50-99, less than 1% >100.

Freshman class profile.

Mid 50% test scores	ACT:	17-36

Basis for selection. 2.0 high school GPA and 810 SAT (exclusive of Writing) required.

High school preparation. Required and recommended units include English 4, mathematics 3, social studies 2, history 1, science 1 (laboratory 2), foreign language 2 and academic electives 6. Mathematics courses must include algebra I and another higher level course. Social science requirement includes 1 US history.

2005-2006 Annual costs. Tuition/fees: $3,912; $8,686 out-of-state. Room/board: $5,796. Books/supplies: $1,000.

Financial aid. Non-need-based: Scholarships awarded for academics, alumni affiliation, art, athletics, job skills, leadership, minority status, music/drama, state residency. **Additional information:** Room and board may be paid in 2 installments each semester: 60% at registration, 40% six weeks later. March 1 is priority deadline for state forms. April 15 is priority deadline for FAFSA.

Application procedures. Admission: No deadline. No application fee. Admission notification on a rolling basis beginning on or about 9/1. **Financial aid:** FAFSA, institutional form required. Applicants notified on a rolling basis starting 3/1; must reply within 2 week(s) of notification.

Academics. Special study options: Cooperative education, distance learning, double major, dual enrollment of high school students, ESL, honors, internships, liberal arts/career combination, student-designed major, study abroad, teacher certification program. English as a second language program for foreign students, mentoring programs for pre-law and pre-med students. **Credit/placement by examination:** AP, CLEP, institutional tests.

Support services: Learning center, reduced course load, remedial instruction, study skills assistance, tutoring, writing center.

Majors. Biology: General, genetics. **Business:** General, accounting, business admin, finance, hospitality admin, hospitality/recreation, hotel/motel admin, human resources, managerial economics, marketing, resort management, restaurant/food services, tourism promotion, tourism/travel. **Communications:** General, advertising, broadcast journalism, journalism, public relations. **Computer sciences:** General, computer science. **Education:** General, art, biology, business, chemistry, early childhood, elementary, English, health, learning disabled, mathematics, mentally handicapped, music, physical, science, social studies, speech. **English:** British lit, composition, English lit. **Health:** Athletic training, clinical lab science, predentistry, premedicine, prepharmacy, preveterinary. **History:** General. **Interdisciplinary:** Global studies. **Legal studies:** Prelaw. **Liberal arts:** Arts/sciences, library science. **Math:** General. **Parks/recreation:** General, facilities management, health/fitness, sports admin. **Personal/culinary services:** Restaurant/catering. **Physical sciences:** Chemistry, geology. **Psychology:** General. **Public administration:** General, social work. **Social sciences:** Geography, political science, sociology. **Visual/performing arts:** Art, commercial/advertising art, dramatic, graphic design, studio arts.

Computing on campus. 250 workstations in dormitories, library, computer center, student center. Online library, helpline, repair service, wireless network available.

Student life. Freshman orientation: Mandatory, $40 fee. Preregistration for classes offered. **Policies:** Freshmen permitted cars on campus. **Housing:** Guaranteed on-campus for all undergraduates. Coed dorms, single-sex dorms, special housing for disabled, apartments, fraternity/sorority housing, substance-free housing available. $50 deposit. **Activities:** Bands, choral groups, dance, drama, film society, literary magazine, music ensembles, radio station, student government, student newspaper, TV station, Black Student Union, social service club, student activities committee, Bonner Scholars SNEA chapter, student social work organization.

Athletics. NCAA. **Intercollegiate:** Baseball M, basketball, cross-country, football (tackle) M, golf M, soccer W, softball W, tennis, track and field, volleyball W. **Intramural:** Archery, badminton, basketball, bowling, football (tackle) M, golf, handball, racquetball, soccer W, softball, swimming, tennis, track and field, volleyball, water polo. **Team name:** Mountain Lions.

Student services. Career counseling, student employment services, financial aid counseling, health services, on-campus daycare, personal counseling, placement for graduates, veterans' counselor. **Learning disabled:** Comprehensive services available.

Contact. E-mail: admissions@concord.edu
Phone: (304) 384-5248 Toll-free number: (888) 384-5249
Fax: (304) 384-3218
Michael Curry, Vice President of Admissions and Financial Aid, Concord University, PO Box 1000, Athens, WV 24712-1000

Davis and Elkins College

Elkins, West Virginia — **CB member**
www.davisandelkins.edu — **CB code: 5151**

- Private 4-year liberal arts college affiliated with Presbyterian Church (USA)
- Residential campus in small town
- 543 degree-seeking undergraduates: 10% part-time, 60% women
- 46% of applicants admitted
- SAT or ACT with writing required
- 65% graduate within 6 years; 13% enter graduate study

General. Founded in 1904. Regionally accredited. **Degrees:** 82 bachelor's, 50 associate awarded. **Location:** 130 miles from Pittsburgh, 200 miles from Washington, DC. **Calendar:** 4-1-4, extensive summer session. **Full-time faculty:** 44 total; 84% have terminal degrees, 11% minority, 50% women. **Part-time faculty:** 40 total; 18% have terminal degrees, 48% women. **Class size:** 80% < 20, 16% 20-39, 2% 40-49, 2% 50-99. **Special facilities:** Pearl S. Buck collection, observatory, greenhouse, planetarium, 8 buildings on the national historic registry.

Freshman class profile. 654 applied, 300 admitted, 110 enrolled.

Mid 50% test scores		**End year in good standing:**	82%
SAT verbal:	440-550	**Return as sophomores:**	64%
SAT math:	430-550	**Out-of-state:**	41%
ACT:	18-23	**Live on campus:**	82%
Rank in top quarter:	33%	**Fraternities:**	25%
Rank in top tenth:	12%	**Sororities:**	17%

Basis for selection. Admission is based on school achievement record (must have minimum cumulative GPA of 2.0), test scores, and extracurricular activities. Recommended interview also important. Tests are required for admission and must be submitted before application can be evaluated. Essay, academic/personal recommendations recommended for all applicants; audition required for musicians and theatre students; portfolio required for art students. **Learning Disabled:** Must complete Supported Learning Program application at same time general application is completed.

High school preparation. 14 units required. Required and recommended units include English 4, mathematics 3-4, social studies 3-4, science 3-4 (laboratory 1-2), foreign language 1-2 and academic electives 4. Mathematics units must include Algebra I or Algebra II, and Geometry.

2005-2006 Annual costs. Tuition/fees: $16,832. Room/board: $6,104. Books/supplies: $800.

2004-2005 Financial aid. All financial aid based on need. 124 full-time freshmen applied for aid; 89 were judged to have need; 89 of these received aid. Average need met was 86%. Average scholarship/grant was $2,115; average loan $2,219. 78% of total undergraduate aid awarded as scholarships/grants, 22% as loans/jobs.

Application procedures. Admission: Priority date 5/1; no deadline. $35 fee, may be waived for applicants with need. Application may be submitted online. Admission notification on a rolling basis beginning on or about 9/30. Must reply by May 1 or within 2 week(s) if notified thereafter. **Financial aid:** Priority date 3/1; no closing date. FAFSA required. Applicants notified on a rolling basis starting 5/1; must reply within 2 week(s) of notification.

Academics. Special study options: Combined bachelor's/graduate degree, cooperative education, cross-registration, double major, dual enrollment of high school students, external degree, honors, independent study, internships, liberal arts/career combination, student-designed major, study abroad, teacher certification program, Washington semester. **Credit/placement by examination:** AP, CLEP, IB, institutional tests. Hours of credit by examination is limited only by the circumstances of the individual student. **Support services:** Learning center, reduced course load, remedial instruction, study skills assistance, tutoring, writing center.

Majors. Biology: General. **Business:** General, accounting, business admin, hospitality admin, international, marketing, office management, tourism/travel. **Communications:** General. **Computer sciences:** Applications programming, computer science. **Conservation:** General, environmental studies. **Education:** General, elementary, secondary. **English:** English lit. **Foreign languages:** General, French, Spanish. **Health:** Health care admin, predentistry, premedicine, prepharmacy, preveterinary. **History:** General. **Math:** General. **Parks/recreation:** Exercise sciences, sports admin. **Philosophy/religion:** Philosophy, religion. **Physical sciences:** Chemistry. **Psychology:** General. **Social sciences:** Political science, sociology. **Visual/performing arts:** Art, dramatic, music management, voice/opera.

Most popular majors. Business/marketing 34%, education 14%, psychology 6%, social sciences 8%.

Computing on campus. 106 workstations in library, computer center. Dormitories wired for high-speed internet access and linked to campus network. Commuter students can connect to campus network. Helpline, repair service, wireless network available.

Student life. Freshman orientation: Mandatory. Preregistration for classes offered. **Policies:** Freshmen permitted cars on campus. **Housing:** Guaranteed on-campus for all undergraduates. Coed dorms, single-sex dorms, fraternity/sorority housing, substance-free housing available. $200 nonrefundable deposit, deadline 5/1. **Activities:** Bands, choral groups, drama, literary magazine, music ensembles, musical theater, radio station, student government, student newspaper, International Student Organization, Black Student Assembly, Common Ground, Food For Thought.

Athletics. NCAA. **Intercollegiate:** Baseball M, basketball, cross-country, golf M, skiing, soccer, softball W, volleyball W. **Intramural:** Basketball, soccer, tennis, volleyball. **Team name:** Senators.

Student services. Alcohol/substance abuse counseling, campus ministries, career counseling, student employment services, financial aid counseling, health services, personal counseling, placement for graduates, veterans' counselor. **Learning disabled:** Comprehensive services available.

Contact. E-mail: admiss@davisandelkins.edu
Phone: (304) 637-1230 Toll-free number: (800) 624-3157 ext. 1230
Fax: (304) 637-1800
Renee Heckel, Director of Enrollment Management, Davis and Elkins College, 100 Campus Drive, Elkins, WV 26241

Fairmont State University
Fairmont, West Virginia
www.fairmontstate.edu **CB code: 5211**

- Public 4-year liberal arts and teachers college
- Commuter campus in large town

General. Founded in 1865. Regionally accredited. **Location:** 90 miles from Pittsburgh. **Calendar:** Semester.

Annual costs/financial aid. Tuition/fees (2005-2006): $4,030; $8,620 out-of-state. Associate degree program: $3,090 annually or $132 per credit hour for residents; $7,110 annually or $300 per credit hour for nonresidents. Room/board: $6,252. Books/supplies: $1,200. Personal expenses: $1,200. Need-based financial aid available to full-time and part-time students.

Contact. Phone: (304) 367-4892
Executive Director of Enrollment Services, 1201 Locust Avenue, Fairmont, WV 26554-2470

Glenville State College
Glenville, West Virginia **CB member**
www.glenville.edu **CB code: 5254**

- Public 4-year liberal arts and teachers college
- Residential campus in rural community
- 1,305 degree-seeking undergraduates: 9% part-time, 50% women, 6% African American, 1% Asian American, 1% Hispanic American
- 100% of applicants admitted
- SAT or ACT required
- 34% graduate within 6 years

General. Founded in 1872. Regionally accredited. **Degrees:** 182 bachelor's, 50 associate awarded. **Location:** 100 miles from Charleston, 100 miles from Morgantown. **Calendar:** Semester, limited summer session. **Full-time faculty:** 51 total; 51% have terminal degrees, 2% minority, 37% women. **Part-time faculty:** 29 total; 14% have terminal degrees, 3% minority, 52% women. **Class size:** 39% < 20, 52% 20-39, 5% 40-49, 3% 50-99, less than 1% >100. **Special facilities:** Law enforcement teaching and training center.

Freshman class profile. 857 applied, 857 admitted, 304 enrolled.

Mid 50% test scores			
SAT verbal:	380-460	**GPA 2.0-2.99:**	41%
SAT math:	370-500	**Rank in top quarter:**	27%
ACT:	16-22	**Rank in top tenth:**	10%
GPA 3.50 or higher:	23%	**End year in good standing:**	80%
GPA 3.0-3.49:	31%	**Return as sophomores:**	60%
		Live on campus:	67%

Basis for selection. Students must have graduated from an accredited high school with at least a 2.0 average or an ACT composite score of at least 17 or an SAT of 820 (exclusive of Writing). Associate degree programs open to all students who have graduated from any high school or hold a GED. Students who want to pursue a bachelor's degree program, but who do not meet the admissions requirements outlined above, may enter a two-year program and later transfer into a bachelor's degree program. Audition required for music education. **Homeschooled:** GED is required.

High school preparation. 28 units required. Required and recommended units include English 4, mathematics 3, social studies 3, science 3 (laboratory 2), foreign language 2 and academic electives 15. Mathematics should be algebra and higher. The laboratory science units should be from coordinated and thematic science, biology, chemistry, physics and other courses with a strong laboratory orientation. Social studies should include U.S. history. English should include courses in grammar, composition and literature.

2005-2006 Annual costs. Tuition/fees: $3,628; $8,640 out-of-state. Room/board: $5,300. Books/supplies: $900. Personal expenses: $1,906.

2004-2005 Financial aid. Need-based: 282 full-time freshmen applied for aid; 243 were judged to have need; 231 of these received aid. Average need met was 79%. Average scholarship/grant was $4,484; average loan $3,029. 55% of total undergraduate aid awarded as scholarships/grants, 45% as loans/jobs. **Non-need-based:** Awarded to 520 full-time undergraduates, including 156 freshmen. Scholarships awarded for academics, art, athletics, music/drama.

Application procedures. Admission: No deadline. No application fee. Application may be submitted online. Admission notification on a rolling basis. **Financial aid:** Priority date 3/1; no closing date. FAFSA required. Applicants notified on a rolling basis starting 4/1; must reply within 2 week(s) of notification.

Academics. Credit for employment, military, and life experience awarded only in nontraditional Regents Bachelor of Arts degree program (designed for adult students). **Special study options:** Accelerated study, cooperative education, distance learning, double major, ESL, honors, internships, student-designed major, teacher certification program. **Credit/placement by examination:** AP, CLEP, institutional tests. Unlimited number of hours of credit may be counted for degree. **Support services:** Remedial instruction, study skills assistance, tutoring, writing center.

Majors. Biology: General. **Business:** Business admin. **Conservation:** Management/policy. **Education:** Elementary, kindergarten/preschool, secondary, special. **English:** English lit. **Health:** Nursing (RN). **History:** General. **Physical sciences:** Chemistry.

Most popular majors. Business/marketing 20%, education 29%, liberal arts 10%, social sciences 18%.

Computing on campus. 171 workstations in library, computer center, student center. Dormitories wired for high-speed internet access and linked to campus network. Commuter students can connect to campus network. Online library, helpline, wireless network available.

Student life. Freshman orientation: Mandatory, $80 fee. Preregistration for classes offered. Held immediately preceding the start of classes each semester, assists students in becoming acclimated to campus. Addresses transitional issues critical to first year success. **Policies:** All unmarried students who have earned less than 58 credit hours are required to reside on campus so long as space is available. Alcoholic beverages, tobacco and controlled substances are not permitted on campus. All students are required to adhere to the Student Code of Conduct. Community service required of student organizations. Freshmen permitted cars on campus. **Housing:** Guaranteed on-campus for freshmen. Single-sex dorms, special housing for disabled, apartments, substance-free housing available. $75 nonrefundable deposit. **Activities:** Bands, choral groups, drama, literary magazine, music ensembles, student government, student newspaper, Baptist Campus Ministry, fellowship of Christian athletes, environmental organization, students in free enterprise, Student National Education Association, student athlete advisory committee, student awareness organization.

Athletics. NCAA. **Intercollegiate:** Basketball, cross-country, football (tackle) M, golf, softball W, track and field, volleyball W. **Intramural:** Badminton, basketball, bowling, fencing, field hockey, football (non-tackle), soccer, softball, swimming, table tennis, tennis, track and field, volleyball, water polo, weight lifting, wrestling. **Team name:** Pioneers.

Student services. Adult student services, alcohol/substance abuse counseling, career counseling, services for economically disadvantaged, student employment services, financial aid counseling, health services, personal counseling, placement for graduates, veterans' counselor. **Physically disabled:** Services for visually, speech, hearing impaired.

Contact. E-mail: admissions@glenville.edu
Phone: (304) 462-4128 Toll-free number: (800) 924-2010
Fax: (304) 462-8619
Michelle Wicks, Director of Admissions, Glenville State College, 200 High Street, Glenville, WV 26351-1292

Marshall University
Huntington, West Virginia **CB member**
www.marshall.edu **CB code: 5396**

- Public 4-year university
- Commuter campus in small city
- 9,161 degree-seeking undergraduates: 11% part-time, 56% women, 5% African American, 1% Asian American, 1% Hispanic American, 1% international
- 3,542 degree-seeking graduate students
- SAT or ACT with writing required
- 39% graduate within 6 years

General. Founded in 1837. Regionally accredited. **Degrees:** 1,487 bachelor's, 90 associate awarded; master's, doctoral, first professional offered. **ROTC:** Army. **Location:** 126 miles from Lexington, Kentucky, 160 miles from Columbus, Ohio. **Calendar:** Semester, limited summer session. **Full-time faculty:** 469 total; 80% have terminal degrees, 12% minority, 40% women. **Part-time faculty:** 253 total; 10% have terminal degrees, 7% minority, 51% women. **Class size:** 36% < 20, 50% 20-39, 10% 40-49, 4% 50-99, less than 1% >100. **Special facilities:** Confederate history collection, superconducting nuclear magnetic resonance spectrometer.

Freshman class profile.

Mid 50% test scores		GPA 3.0-3.49:	28%
SAT verbal:	460-570	GPA 2.0-2.99:	24%
SAT math:	450-570	Return as sophomores:	72%
ACT:	20-25	Out-of-state:	21%
GPA 3.50 or higher:	46%	International:	1%

Basis for selection. Open admission, but selective for some programs and for out-of-state students. Full admission requires a 2.0 GPA and ACT 19 or SAT 910 (exclusive of Writing). Conditional admission is granted below a 2.0 GPA or the above scores, on a limited, first-come, first-served basis. Programs and colleges may have different requirements for admissions. Audition required for music majors; interview recommended for academically weak, learning disabled; portfolio recommended. **Homeschooled:** Applicants should apply early and have home schooling well documented.

High school preparation. 15 units required. Required and recommended units include English 4, mathematics 3, social studies 3, science 3 (laboratory 2) and foreign language 2.

2005-2006 Annual costs. Tuition/fees: $3,932; $10,634 out-of-state. Room/board: $6,262. Books/supplies: $800. Personal expenses: $2,453.

2005-2006 Financial aid. Need-based: 1,060 full-time freshmen applied for aid; 733 were judged to have need; 724 of these received aid. Average need met was 52%. Average scholarship/grant was $4,015; average loan $3,578. 35% of total undergraduate aid awarded as scholarships/grants, 65% as loans/jobs. **Non-need-based:** Awarded to 3,606 full-time undergraduates, including 822 freshmen. Scholarships awarded for academics, art, athletics, minority status, music/drama, ROTC, state residency.

Application procedures. Admission: No deadline. $25 fee ($35 out-of-state), may be waived for applicants with need. Application may be submitted online. Admission notification on a rolling basis beginning on or about 9/1. **Financial aid:** Priority date 3/1; no closing date. FAFSA required. Applicants notified on a rolling basis starting 5/1; must reply within 2 week(s) of notification.

Academics. Special study options: Accelerated study, combined bachelor's/graduate degree, cooperative education, cross-registration, distance learning, double major, ESL, exchange student, honors, independent study, internships, study abroad, teacher certification program, Washington semester. 2-2 preengineering program, 3-2 program in forestry with Duke University. **Credit/placement by examination:** AP, CLEP, IB, SAT, ACT, institutional tests. **Support services:** Learning center, pre-admission summer program, reduced course load, remedial instruction, study skills assistance, tutoring, writing center.

Majors. Biology: General. **Business:** Accounting, business admin, finance, managerial economics, marketing. **Communications:** Journalism. **Computer sciences:** General. **Conservation:** Environmental science. **Education:** Elementary, physical, school counseling, secondary. **Engineering technology:** Computer, occupational safety. **English:** English lit, speech/rhetoric. **Family/consumer sciences:** General. **Foreign languages:** General. **Health:** Clinical lab science, communication disorders, cytotechnology, dietetics, nursing (RN), speech pathology. **History:** General. **Interdisciplinary:** Systems science. **Liberal arts:** Humanities. **Math:** General. **Parks/recreation:** Facilities management. **Physical sciences:** Chemistry, geology, physics. **Protective services:** Criminal justice. **Psychology:** General. **Public administration:** Social work. **Social sciences:** General, economics, geography, international relations, political science, sociology. **Visual/performing arts:** Art.

Most popular majors. Business/marketing 23%, education 21%, health sciences 6%, liberal arts 14%, psychology 6%.

Computing on campus. 1,854 workstations in dormitories, library, computer center, student center. Dormitories wired for high-speed internet access and linked to campus network. Commuter students can connect to campus network. Online course registration, online library, helpline, student web hosting available.

Student life. Freshman orientation: Available. Preregistration for classes offered. One-day programs in June, July, August. **Policies:** Freshmen permitted cars on campus. **Housing:** Guaranteed on-campus for freshmen. Coed dorms, single-sex dorms, special housing for disabled, apartments, fraternity/sorority housing, substance-free housing available. $150 fully refundable deposit. **Activities:** Bands, choral groups, drama, literary magazine, music ensembles, musical theater, opera, radio station, student government, student newspaper, symphony orchestra, TV station, Black United Students, Baptist Campus Ministry, College Republicans, Lambda Society, Habitat for Humanity, Presbyterian Campus Ministry, Student Organization for Alumni Relations.

Athletics. NCAA. **Intercollegiate:** Baseball M, basketball, cross-country, football (tackle) M, golf, soccer, softball W, swimming W, tennis W, track and field, volleyball W. **Intramural:** Basketball, bowling, football (tackle), golf, racquetball, soccer, softball, swimming, tennis, track and field, volleyball. **Team name:** Thundering Herd.

Student services. Adult student services, alcohol/substance abuse counseling, campus ministries, career counseling, student employment services, health services, minority student services, on-campus daycare, personal counseling, placement for graduates, veterans' counselor, women's services. **Physically disabled:** Services for visually, speech, hearing impaired.

Contact. E-mail: admissions@marshall.edu
Phone: (304) 696-3160 Toll-free number: (800) 642-3499
Fax: (304) 696-3135
Craig Grooms, Director of Admissions, Marshall University, One John Marshall Drive, Huntington, WV 25755

Mountain State University

Beckley, West Virginia — **CB member**
www.mountainstate.edu — **CB code: 5054**

- Private 4-year university and health science college
- Commuter campus in large town
- 3,837 degree-seeking undergraduates: 10% African American, 1% Asian American, 2% Hispanic American, 1% Native American, 2% international
- 426 graduate students
- 27% graduate within 6 years; 20% enter graduate study

General. Founded in 1933. Regionally accredited. **Degrees:** 410 bachelor's, 169 associate awarded; master's offered. **Location:** 55 miles from Charleston. **Calendar:** Semester, limited summer session. **Full-time faculty:** 79 total; 34% have terminal degrees, 9% minority, 65% women. **Part-time faculty:** 237 total; 22% have terminal degrees, 4% minority, 53% women. **Class size:** 65% < 20, 34% 20-39, less than 1% 40-49. **Special facilities:** YMCA, medicinal botanical garden and greenhouse, family practice medical clinic.

Freshman class profile. 1,224 applied, 1,224 admitted, 365 enrolled.

Mid 50% test scores		Rank in top quarter:	13%
SAT verbal:	450-520	Rank in top tenth:	2%
SAT math:	420-640	End year in good standing:	38%
ACT:	16-21	Return as sophomores:	52%
GPA 3.50 or higher:	7%	Out-of-state:	16%
GPA 3.0-3.49:	24%	Live on campus:	14%
GPA 2.0-2.99:	58%	International:	2%

Basis for selection. Open admission, but selective for some programs. Special requirements for health science programs. ACT or SAT scores required for nursing and physician's assistant programs. **Homeschooled:** Provide official home-schooled academic records.

High school preparation. 13 units required; 15 recommended. Required and recommended units include English 4, mathematics 2, social studies 3, history 2, science 2 (laboratory 2).

2005-2006 Annual costs. Tuition/fees: $7,350. Room/board: $5,526. Books/supplies: $1,300.

2004-2005 Financial aid. Need-based: 288 full-time freshmen applied for aid; 221 were judged to have need; 221 of these received aid. Average need met was 37%. Average scholarship/grant was $3,319; average loan $2,533. 43% of total undergraduate aid awarded as scholarships/grants, 57% as loans/jobs. **Non-need-based:** Awarded to 124 full-time undergraduates, including 22 freshmen. Scholarships awarded for academics, alumni affiliation, athletics, leadership, minority status.

Application procedures. Admission: No deadline. $25 fee, may be waived for applicants with need. Application may be submitted online. Admission notification on a rolling basis. **Financial aid:** No deadline. FAFSA required. Applicants notified on a rolling basis starting 4/1.

Academics. Special study options: Accelerated study, combined bachelor's/graduate degree, cooperative education, cross-registration, distance learning, double major, dual enrollment of high school students, ESL, independent study, internships, liberal arts/career combination, student-designed major, weekend college. Degree completion program, credit for prior learning (challenge exam and portfolio assessment). **Credit/placement by examination:** AP, CLEP, IB, institutional tests. 32 credit hours maximum toward associate degree, 64 toward bachelor's. CLEP, DANTES and Challenge exams available. **Support services:** Learning center, reduced course load, remedial instruction, study skills assistance, tutoring, writing center.

Majors. Business: General, accounting, business admin, e-commerce, entrepreneurial studies, financial planning, hospitality admin, hospitality/

recreation, human resources, international, logistics, management science, marketing, nonprofit/public, office management, organizational behavior, tourism/travel. **Communications:** Media studies. **Computer sciences:** Computer science, information systems, networking, webmaster. **Conservation:** General, environmental studies. **English:** English lit. **Health:** EMT ambulance attendant, health care admin, health services, nursing (RN), occupational health, premedicine, public health ed, respiratory therapy assistant, respiratory therapy technology, sonography. **Interdisciplinary:** Accounting/computer science, behavioral sciences, biological/physical sciences, math/computer science. **Legal studies:** General. **Liberal arts:** Arts/sciences, humanities, library science. **Personal/culinary services:** Chef training. **Physical sciences:** General. **Protective services:** Criminal justice, forensics, law enforcement admin. **Psychology:** General. **Public administration:** Social work. **Transportation:** Aviation management.

Most popular majors. Biology 7%, business/marketing 43%, health sciences 18%, interdisciplinary studies 9%, security/protective services 18%.

Computing on campus. 90 workstations in library, computer center. Dormitories wired for high-speed internet access and linked to campus network. Commuter students can connect to campus network. Online course registration, online library, helpline, repair service, student web hosting, wireless network available.

Student life. Freshman orientation: Available. Preregistration for classes offered. One-day orientation during summer. Special sessions for parents. **Policies:** Freshmen permitted cars on campus. **Housing:** Guaranteed on-campus for freshmen. Coed dorms available. $150 nonrefundable deposit. Handicapped-accessible dorms, off-campus housing for athletes. **Activities:** Pep band, choral groups, drama, student government, student newspaper, Christian student organization, international student organization, American Association of Medical Assistants, criminal justice association, forensic club, legal club, student association for respiratory care, student nursing association, Students in Free Enterprise, student social work organization.

Athletics. NAIA. **Intercollegiate:** Basketball M, cheerleading, softball W, volleyball W. **Intramural:** Basketball, soccer, softball, table tennis, volleyball. **Team name:** Cougars.

Student services. Adult student services, alcohol/substance abuse counseling, career counseling, student employment services, financial aid counseling, health services, on-campus daycare, personal counseling, placement for graduates, veterans' counselor.

Contact. E-mail: gomsu@mountainstate.edu
Phone: (304) 929-1433 Toll-free number: (800) 766-6067
Fax: (304) 253-3463
Tammy Toney, Director of the Admissions Process, Mountain State University, 609 South Kanawha Street, Beckley, WV 25802-9003

Ohio Valley University

Vienna, West Virginia
www.ovc.edu **CB code: 5519**

- Private 4-year university and liberal arts college affiliated with Church of Christ
- Residential campus in small city
- 516 degree-seeking undergraduates: 3% part-time, 52% women, 4% African American, 1% Hispanic American, 1% Native American, 6% international
- SAT or ACT (ACT writing optional) required
- 35% graduate within 6 years

General. Founded in 1960. Regionally accredited. **Degrees:** 101 bachelor's, 26 associate awarded. **Location:** 95 miles from Columbus, 120 miles from Pittsburgh. **Calendar:** Semester, limited summer session. **Full-time faculty:** 25 total; 36% have terminal degrees, 32% women. **Part-time faculty:** 35 total; 17% have terminal degrees, 37% women. **Class size:** 78% < 20, 22% 20-39.

Freshman class profile.

Mid 50% test scores		**Rank in top quarter:**	32%
SAT verbal:	510-600	**Rank in top tenth:**	10%
SAT math:	460-540	**Return as sophomores:**	74%
ACT:	17-23	**Out-of-state:**	26%
GPA 3.50 or higher:	19%	**Live on campus:**	90%
GPA 3.0-3.49:	34%	**International:**	8%
GPA 2.0-2.99:	44%		

Basis for selection. School achievement record, test scores considered, reference. Essay, interview recommended. **Homeschooled:** Transcript of courses and grades required.

High school preparation. 12 units recommended. Recommended units include English 3, mathematics 3, social studies 2, history 1, science 3 (laboratory 1).

2005-2006 Annual costs. Tuition/fees: $13,092. Room/board: $5,660. Books/supplies: $1,000. Personal expenses: $750.

2005-2006 Financial aid. Need-based: 86 full-time freshmen applied for aid; 65 were judged to have need; 65 of these received aid. Average need met was 63%. Average scholarship/grant was $7,219; average loan $2,971. 48% of total undergraduate aid awarded as scholarships/grants, 52% as loans/jobs. **Non-need-based:** Scholarships awarded for academics, athletics, job skills, leadership, music/drama.

Application procedures. Admission: $20 fee, may be waived for applicants with need. Application may be submitted online. Admission notification on a rolling basis. **Financial aid:** Priority date 2/15; no closing date. FAFSA required. Applicants notified on a rolling basis starting 3/15; must reply within 4 week(s) of notification.

Academics. Full-time students required to take a Bible course each semester. **Special study options:** Cooperative education, double major, dual enrollment of high school students, ESL, honors, independent study, internships, student-designed major, teacher certification program, weekend college. Degree completion programs and special certifications. **Credit/placement by examination:** AP, CLEP, IB, SAT, ACT, institutional tests. 30 credit hours maximum toward associate degree, 30 toward bachelor's. Challenge course testing. **Support services:** Learning center, pre-admission summer program, reduced course load, remedial instruction, study skills assistance, tutoring.

Majors. Business: Accounting, business admin, human resources, nonprofit/public. **Computer sciences:** Information technology. **Education:** General, elementary, English, mathematics, multi-level teacher, physical, science, secondary, social studies. **Liberal arts:** Arts/sciences. **Philosophy/religion:** Religion. **Psychology:** General. **Theology:** Bible.

Most popular majors. Business/marketing 20%, education 11%, liberal arts 33%, philosophy/religious studies 29%, psychology 7%.

Computing on campus. 34 workstations in dormitories, library, computer center. Dormitories wired for high-speed internet access and linked to campus network. Commuter students can connect to campus network. Online library, repair service, wireless network available.

Student life. Freshman orientation: Mandatory. Preregistration for classes offered. Orientation programs held in the summer and fall are designed to integrate incoming students into the campus community. **Policies:** Chapel/Assembly attendance required. Freshmen permitted cars on campus. **Housing:** Guaranteed on-campus for all undergraduates. Single-sex dorms, apartments, substance-free housing available. $100 fully refundable deposit, deadline 8/20. **Activities:** Bands, choral groups, drama, literary magazine, music ensembles, musical theater, student government, student newspaper, symphony orchestra, prospective ministers and prospective missionaries clubs, women's club, diversity of the university, student government association.

Athletics. NCAA. **Intercollegiate:** Baseball M, basketball, cross-country, golf, soccer, softball W, volleyball W. **Intramural:** Basketball, bowling, cross-country, football (non-tackle), soccer, softball, table tennis, track and field, volleyball. **Team name:** Fighting Scots.

Student services. Adult student services, alcohol/substance abuse counseling, campus ministries, career counseling, student employment services, financial aid counseling, health services, minority student services, personal counseling.

Contact. E-mail: admissions@ovc.edu
Phone: (304) 865-6200 Toll-free number: (877) 446-8668
Fax: (304) 865-6001
Rob Dudley, Director of Admissions, Ohio Valley University, One Campus View Drive, Vienna, WV 26105

Salem International University

Salem, West Virginia
www.salemiu.edu **CB code: 5608**

- For-profit 4-year university and liberal arts college
- Residential campus in small town
- 489 degree-seeking undergraduates: 18% part-time, 39% women
- 339 degree-seeking graduate students
- SAT or ACT with writing required

General. Founded in 1888. Regionally accredited. **Degrees:** 76 bachelor's awarded; master's offered. **Location:** 12 miles from Clarksburg, 125 miles from Pittsburgh. **Calendar:** Modular, 6 modules of 8 weeks each divided into 3 terms. Limited summer session. **Full-time faculty:** 22 total. **Part-time faculty:** 15 total. **Class size:** 73% < 20, 27% 20-39.

Freshman class profile.

Mid 50% test scores		Out-of-state:	55%
SAT verbal:	390-560	Live on campus:	90%
SAT math:	410-550	Fraternities:	5%
ACT:	18-23	Sororities:	8%

Basis for selection. School achievement record, test scores, counselor recommendations most important. Applicants not meeting admissions standards referred to committee which may or may not recommend their acceptance. Essay, interview recommended. **Homeschooled:** State high school equivalency certificate required.

High school preparation. 16 units recommended. Recommended units include English 4, mathematics 2, social studies 3, science 2 and foreign language 2. 16 required units should be in academic areas.

2005-2006 Annual costs. Tuition/fees: $11,040. First year students tuition is $10,100. All returning students tuition is $15,295. Room/board: $4,790. Books/supplies: $660. Personal expenses: $320.

Financial aid. Non-need-based: Scholarships awarded for academics.

Application procedures. Admission: No deadline. $25 fee, may be waived for applicants with need. Application may be submitted online. Admission notification on a rolling basis. **Financial aid:** Priority date 4/15; no closing date. FAFSA required. Applicants notified on a rolling basis starting 2/15; must reply within 4 week(s) of notification.

Academics. In keeping with college's mission to foster global awareness, all students required to complete international core curriculum. **Special study options:** Accelerated study, cooperative education, distance learning, double major, dual enrollment of high school students, ESL, independent study, internships, liberal arts/career combination, student-designed major, study abroad, teacher certification program, Washington semester. **Credit/placement by examination:** AP, CLEP, IB, SAT, ACT, institutional tests. 32 credit hours maximum toward bachelor's degree. **Support services:** Learning center, reduced course load, remedial instruction, study skills assistance, tutoring, writing center.

Majors. Biology: General. **Business:** Business admin. **Computer sciences:** General, computer science. **Education:** Multi-level teacher, secondary. **Liberal arts:** Arts/sciences. **Protective services:** Criminal justice.

Most popular majors. Agriculture 14%, area/ethnic studies 6%, biology 12%, business/marketing 17%, education 11%, English 15%, health sciences 6%, liberal arts 8%.

Computing on campus. 50 workstations in dormitories, library, computer center. Dormitories wired for high-speed internet access and linked to campus network. Commuter students can connect to campus network. Wireless network available.

Student life. Freshman orientation: Available, $30 fee. Preregistration for classes offered. Program includes introduction to international aspects of college. Special orientation for international students with U.S. life-skills training. **Policies:** Freshmen permitted cars on campus. **Housing:** Guaranteed on-campus for all undergraduates. Coed dorms, single-sex dorms, substance-free housing available. $200 deposit. Unless local resident, freshmen and sophomores required to live on-campus. Private rooms subject to availability. **Activities:** Music ensembles, student government, student newspaper, Gamma Beta Phi Honor Society, Alpha Phi Omega fraternity service organization, TriBeta biology society, international friends, Campus Crusade for Christ, Rainbow Alliance, International Woman's Alliance, Christian Student Fellowship, Indian student association, Chinese student association.

Athletics. NCAA. **Intercollegiate:** Baseball M, basketball, cross-country M, golf, soccer, softball W, tennis, volleyball W, water polo M. **Intramural:** Basketball, cricket, football (non-tackle), racquetball, soccer, swimming, table tennis, tennis, volleyball. **Team name:** Tigers.

Student services. Career counseling, services for economically disadvantaged, financial aid counseling, health services, personal counseling.

Contact. E-mail: admissions@salemiu.edu
Phone: (304) 326-1336 Toll-free number: (800) 283-4562
Fax: (304) 326-1592
Kimberly Neucall, Director of Admissions Operations, Salem International University, 223 West Main Street, Salem, WV 26426

Shepherd University
Shepherdstown, West Virginia — **CB member**
www.shepherd.edu — **CB code: 5615**

- Public 4-year university
- Commuter campus in small town
- 3,436 degree-seeking undergraduates: 15% part-time, 57% women
- 92 degree-seeking graduate students
- 93% of applicants admitted
- SAT or ACT with writing required
- 40% graduate within 6 years; 19% enter graduate study

General. Founded in 1871. Regionally accredited. **Degrees:** 537 bachelor's, 139 associate awarded; master's offered. **ROTC:** Air Force. **Location:** 8 miles from Martinsburg, 70 miles from Washington, DC. **Calendar:** Semester, extensive summer session. **Full-time faculty:** 109 total; 83% have terminal degrees, 12% minority, 38% women. **Part-time faculty:** 144 total; 26% have terminal degrees, 4% minority, 46% women. **Class size:** 37% < 20, 60% 20-39, 2% 40-49, 1% 50-99. **Special facilities:** Creative arts center with computer-controlled theater, recital hall with concert grand piano, recording studio, nursery school, 3 theaters, Civil War center, observatory; Robert C. Byrd Center for Legislative Studies.

Freshman class profile. 1,593 applied, 1,485 admitted, 675 enrolled.

Mid 50% test scores		Return as sophomores:	69%
SAT verbal:	470-560	Out-of-state:	39%
SAT math:	460-550	Live on campus:	46%
ACT:	19-24	International:	1%
GPA 3.50 or higher:	31%	Fraternities:	1%
GPA 3.0-3.49:	31%	Sororities:	1%
GPA 2.0-2.99:	36%		

Basis for selection. Minimum 2.0 academic GPA and 19 ACT or 910 SAT (exclusive of Writing) required. Essays and recommendations are optional but important. Interview required for honors program and nursing applicants; recommended for others. Audition required for music; portfolio required for transfer students in art, photography, graphic design. **Homeschooled:** ACT and/or SAT test scores, portfolio of work completed.

High school preparation. 21 units required. Required and recommended units include English 4, mathematics 3, social studies 3, history 1, science 3 (laboratory 2), foreign language 2 and academic electives 6. History unit must include US history; science unit must include biology.

2005-2006 Annual costs. Tuition/fees: $4,046; $10,618 out-of-state. Room/board: $6,020. Books/supplies: $850. Personal expenses: $2,000.

2005-2006 Financial aid. Need-based: 571 full-time freshmen applied for aid; 333 were judged to have need; 319 of these received aid. Average need met was 70%. Average scholarship/grant was $3,627; average loan $2,368. 38% of total undergraduate aid awarded as scholarships/grants, 62% as loans/jobs. **Non-need-based:** Awarded to 1,055 full-time undergraduates, including 295 freshmen. Scholarships awarded for academics, art, athletics, job skills, leadership, minority status, music/drama, state residency.

Application procedures. Admission: Priority date 2/1; no deadline. $35 fee, may be waived for applicants with need. Application may be submitted online. Admission notification on a rolling basis beginning on or about 9/1. Must reply by May 1 or within 3 week(s) if notified thereafter. **Financial aid:** Priority date 3/1; no closing date. FAFSA required. Applicants notified on a rolling basis starting 3/15; must reply within 3 week(s) of notification.

Academics. Special study options: Cooperative education, double major, honors, independent study, internships, liberal arts/career combination, teacher certification program, Washington semester. **Credit/placement by examination:** AP, CLEP, IB, SAT, ACT, institutional tests. 32 credit hours maximum toward bachelor's degree. No limit for students pursuing Regents' Bachelor of Arts degree. **Support services:** Learning center, preadmission summer program, reduced course load, remedial instruction, study skills assistance, tutoring, writing center.

Majors. Biology: General. **Business:** Accounting, business admin. **Communications:** General. **Computer sciences:** General, applications programming. **Conservation:** General, environmental studies. **Education:** Elementary, secondary. **Family/consumer sciences:** General. **Health:** Nursing (RN). **History:** General. **Math:** General. **Parks/recreation:** General. **Physical sciences:** Chemistry. **Psychology:** General. **Public administration:** Social work. **Social sciences:** Economics, political science, sociology. **Visual/performing arts:** Art.

Most popular majors. Business/marketing 13%, education 15%, liberal arts 16%, parks/recreation 8%, social sciences 7%, visual/performing arts 6%.

Computing on campus. 350 workstations in dormitories, library, computer center, student center. Dormitories wired for high-speed internet access and linked to campus network. Commuter students can connect to campus network. Online course registration, helpline, student web hosting available.

Student life. Freshman orientation: Mandatory, $75 fee. Preregistration for classes offered. 2-day advising and registration sessions held in June and July for students and parents. August orientation program for all new students held on the Thursday, Friday, and Saturday prior to the first day of classes. **Policies:** Freshmen permitted cars on campus. **Housing:** Guaranteed on-campus for all undergraduates. Coed dorms, apartments, substance-free housing available. $200 deposit, deadline 6/1. Living/learning center, honors housing, freshmen housing. Housing guaranteed if deadlines met. **Activities:** Bands, choral groups, dance, drama, literary magazine, music ensembles, musical theater, radio station, student government, student newspaper, symphony orchestra, College Republicans, College Democrats, Christians in Action, NAACP, United Brothers, international student union, Shepherd Greens, Allies, Sistaz, student community services.

Athletics. NCAA. **Intercollegiate:** Baseball M, basketball, football (tackle) M, golf M, soccer, softball W, tennis, volleyball W. **Intramural:** Basketball, bowling, football (non-tackle), racquetball, soccer, softball, swimming, table tennis, tennis, volleyball, weight lifting, wrestling. **Team name:** Rams.

Student services. Adult student services, alcohol/substance abuse counseling, campus ministries, career counseling, student employment services, financial aid counseling, health services, minority student services, personal counseling, placement for graduates, veterans' counselor. **Physically disabled:** Services for visually, hearing impaired.

Contact. E-mail: admissions@shepherd.edu
Phone: (304) 876-5212 Toll-free number: (800) 344-5231
Fax: (304) 876-5165
Kimberly Scranage, Director of Admissions, Shepherd University, PO Box 3210, Shepherdstown, WV 25443-3210

University of Charleston

Charleston, West Virginia — **CB member**
www.ucwv.edu — **CB code: 5419**

- Private 4-year university and liberal arts college
- Commuter campus in small city
- 900 degree-seeking undergraduates: 5% part-time, 60% women, 11% African American, 1% Asian American, 1% Hispanic American, 1% international
- 19 degree-seeking graduate students
- 96% of applicants admitted
- SAT or ACT (ACT writing optional) required
- 41% graduate within 6 years

General. Founded in 1888. Regionally accredited. **Degrees:** 123 bachelor's, 34 associate awarded; master's offered. **ROTC:** Army. **Location:** 200 miles from Pittsburgh, 200 miles from Charlotte, North Carolina. **Calendar:** Semester, limited summer session. **Full-time faculty:** 59 total; 46% have terminal degrees, 7% minority, 56% women. **Part-time faculty:** 31 total; 10% have terminal degrees, 6% minority, 52% women. **Class size:** 62% < 20, 34% 20-39, 2% 40-49, 2% 50-99. **Special facilities:** Sports medicine clinic, clinics at nearby hospital.

Freshman class profile. 1,124 applied, 1,074 admitted, 278 enrolled.

Mid 50% test scores			
SAT verbal:	430-530	**Rank in top quarter:**	48%
SAT math:	420-540	**Rank in top tenth:**	21%
ACT:	19-25	**End year in good standing:**	87%
GPA 3.50 or higher:	44%	**Return as sophomores:**	66%
GPA 3.0-3.49:	25%	**Out-of-state:**	50%
GPA 2.0-2.99:	31%	**Live on campus:**	83%

Basis for selection. School achievement record and courses taken most important. Test scores, school recommendation, school and community activities, class rank, and interview also considered. High school GPA recomputed to reflect performance in academic subjects only. UC accepts the TOEFL score from students who are not native speakers of English. SAT Subject Tests recommended. Essay, interview, portfolio recommended for all; audition required for music. **Homeschooled:** If part of diploma-granting organization, list of coursework completed and level of performance required. Otherwise, detailed portfolio required (e.g. research project, resume, reading list, community service, athletic and/or artistic endeavors, and study abroad). Essay, 3 letters of reference, on-campus interview recommended. **Learning Disabled:** Documentation from a professional within last 2 years required.

High school preparation. 16 units recommended. Recommended units include English 4, mathematics 3, social studies 3, history 2, science 3 and foreign language 1. Chemistry, algebra required for 4-year nursing program.

2006-2007 Annual costs. Tuition/fees: $21,000. Tuition for pharmacy students: $23,200. Room/board: $7,600. Books/supplies: $800. Personal expenses: $500.

2005-2006 Financial aid. Need-based: Average need met was 88%. Average scholarship/grant was $5,800; average loan $6,500. 58% of total undergraduate aid awarded as scholarships/grants, 42% as loans/jobs. **Non-need-based:** Scholarships awarded for academics, alumni affiliation, art, athletics, leadership, music/drama, ROTC.

Application procedures. Admission: Priority date 5/2; no deadline. $25 fee, may be waived for applicants with need. Application must be submitted on paper. Admission notification on a rolling basis. Must reply by May 1 or within 2 week(s) if notified thereafter. For most health science programs, application deadline is January 15, early decision recommended. **Financial aid:** Closing date 3/1. FAFSA required. Applicants notified on a rolling basis starting 4/1; must reply by 5/1 or within 4 week(s) of notification.

Academics. Students can fulfill course requirements at their own pace. **Special study options:** Accelerated study, combined bachelor's/graduate degree, cooperative education, distance learning, double major, dual enrollment of high school students, independent study, internships, liberal arts/career combination, student-designed major, study abroad, teacher certification program, Washington semester. **Credit/placement by examination:** AP, CLEP, IB, institutional tests. 30 credit hours maximum toward associate degree, 60 toward bachelor's. **Support services:** Learning center, reduced course load, remedial instruction, study skills assistance, tutoring, writing center.

Majors. Biology: General, environmental. **Business:** Accounting, business admin, finance, financial planning, marketing. **Communications:** Journalism, media studies. **Computer sciences:** General, information technology. **Conservation:** Environmental science. **Education:** General, biology, elementary, health, music, science, secondary, social studies. **English:** Creative writing, English lit. **Health:** Athletic training, nursing (RN), radiologic technology/medical imaging. **History:** General. **Parks/recreation:** Sports admin. **Physical sciences:** Chemistry. **Psychology:** General. **Social sciences:** Political science. **Visual/performing arts:** Art, interior design, music management.

Most popular majors. Business/marketing 18%, communications/journalism 7%, education 11%, health sciences 26%, liberal arts 6%, visual/performing arts 9%.

Computing on campus. 65 workstations in library, student center. Dormitories wired for high-speed internet access and linked to campus network. Helpline, student web hosting, wireless network available.

Student life. Freshman orientation: Mandatory. Preregistration for classes offered. **Policies:** Freshmen permitted cars on campus. **Housing:** Guaranteed on-campus for freshmen. Coed dorms, special housing for disabled available. $100 deposit. On-campus housing required for dependent freshmen and sophomores not living with parents or legal guardian in local area. Single rooms and suites available. **Activities:** Choral groups, drama, music ensembles, musical theater, student government, student newspaper, honorary fraternities, international student association, Fellowship Christian Athletes, Young Republicans, College Democrats, Baptist Campus Ministries.

Athletics. NCAA. **Intercollegiate:** Baseball M, basketball, cheerleading, cross-country, football (tackle) M, golf M, rowing (crew), soccer, softball W, swimming, tennis, track and field, volleyball W. **Intramural:** Basketball, bowling, tennis, volleyball, water polo. **Team name:** Golden Eagles.

Student services. Career counseling, student employment services, financial aid counseling, personal counseling, placement for graduates.

Contact. E-mail: admissions@ucwv.edu
Phone: (304) 357-4750 Toll-free number: (800) 995-4682
Fax: (304) 357-4781
Bradley Parrish, Associate Vice President for Enrollment, University of Charleston, 2300 MacCorkle Avenue, SE, Charleston, WV 25304

West Liberty State College

West Liberty, West Virginia
www.wlsc.edu — **CB code: 5901**

- Public 4-year liberal arts college
- Residential campus in rural community
- 2,160 degree-seeking undergraduates: 9% part-time, 57% women, 3% African American, 1% Hispanic American

- 5 graduate students
- 81% of applicants admitted
- SAT or ACT with writing required

General. Founded in 1837. Regionally accredited. **Degrees:** 436 bachelor's, 38 associate awarded. **Location:** 10 miles from Wheeling, 50 miles from Pittsburgh. **Calendar:** Semester, limited summer session. **Full-time faculty:** 98 total; 45% have terminal degrees, 40% women. **Part-time faculty:** 58 total; 2% have terminal degrees, 5% minority, 60% women. **Class size:** 54% < 20, 38% 20-39, 6% 40-49, 3% 50-99. **Special facilities:** Rare book room, rare sheet music collection.

Freshman class profile. 1,379 applied, 1,113 admitted, 421 enrolled.

Out-of-state:	33%	**International:**	1%
Live on campus:	80%		

Basis for selection. Minimum 2.0 high school GPA required or 17 on enhanced ACT or 810 (exclusive of writing) on SAT. Audition required for music education; portfolio recommended for art.

High school preparation. 11 units required; 13 recommended. Required and recommended units include English 4, mathematics 2, social studies 2, history 1, science 2 (laboratory 2) and foreign language 2. Mathematics must be algebra I and higher. Social science must include American History.

2005-2006 Annual costs. Tuition/fees: $3,686; $9,054 out-of-state. Room/board: $5,456. Books/supplies: $800. Personal expenses: $1,000.

2005-2006 Financial aid. Need-based: 430 full-time freshmen applied for aid; 261 were judged to have need; 249 of these received aid. Average need met was 76%. Average scholarship/grant was $3,807; average loan $2,582. 42% of total undergraduate aid awarded as scholarships/grants, 58% as loans/jobs. **Non-need-based:** Awarded to 662 full-time undergraduates, including 229 freshmen. Scholarships awarded for academics, alumni affiliation, art, athletics, leadership, music/drama. **Additional information:** Non-need based student employment available at food service, college union, bookstore, and tutoring office. Resident assistant and campus security jobs also available.

Application procedures. Admission: No deadline. No application fee. Application may be submitted online. Admission notification on a rolling basis beginning on or about 9/1. **Financial aid:** Priority date 3/1; no closing date. FAFSA required. Applicants notified on a rolling basis starting 2/15; must reply within 2 week(s) of notification.

Academics. Freshman experience course available. **Special study options:** Accelerated study, double major, external degree, honors, independent study, internships, student-designed major, teacher certification program, Washington semester. **Credit/placement by examination:** AP, CLEP, institutional tests. **Support services:** Reduced course load, remedial instruction, tutoring.

Majors. Biology: General, bacteriology, biotechnology. **Business:** General, accounting, banking/financial services, business admin, managerial economics, tourism promotion, tourism/travel. **Communications:** General. **Computer sciences:** Information systems. **Education:** Art, biology, chemistry, early childhood, elementary, English, health, mathematics, mentally handicapped, music, physical, science, secondary, social science, special. **Health:** Clinical lab science, dental hygiene. **History:** General. **Liberal arts:** Arts/sciences. **Math:** General. **Parks/recreation:** Exercise sciences. **Physical sciences:** Chemistry. **Protective services:** Criminal justice. **Psychology:** General. **Social sciences:** General, political science, sociology. **Visual/performing arts:** Commercial/advertising art.

Computing on campus. 300 workstations in dormitories, library, computer center, student center. Dormitories wired for high-speed internet access and linked to campus network. Commuter students can connect to campus network. Online course registration, helpline, repair service available.

Student life. Freshman orientation: Mandatory, $30 fee. Preregistration for classes offered. Held friday through Sunday before first day of classes. **Policies:** Freshmen permitted cars on campus. **Housing:** Guaranteed on-campus for all undergraduates. Coed dorms, single-sex dorms, special housing for disabled, apartments available. $100 deposit, deadline 6/1. Honors residence for students who meet criteria specifications. **Activities:** Bands, choral groups, drama, literary magazine, music ensembles, musical theater, radio station, student government, student newspaper, TV station, Amnesty International, WLSC Students for Life, B-Pride, Electric Square, international students organization, non-traditional student support group, Students in Free Enterprise, pep club, Students for Unity and Understanding.

Athletics. NCAA. **Intercollegiate:** Baseball M, basketball, cross-country, football (tackle) M, golf, softball W, tennis, track and field, volleyball W, wrestling M. **Intramural:** Basketball, golf, handball M, racquetball, softball, table tennis, tennis, volleyball. **Team name:** Hilltoppers.

Student services. Campus ministries, career counseling, student employment services, financial aid counseling, health services, personal counseling, placement for graduates, veterans' counselor. **Physically disabled:** Services for visually, hearing impaired.

Contact. E-mail: wladmsn1@wlsc.edu
Phone: (304) 336-8076 Toll-free number: (800) 732-6204
Fax: (304) 336-8403
Brenda King, Director of Admissions, West Liberty State College, Box 295, West Liberty, WV 26074-0295

West Virginia State University

Institute, West Virginia — **CB member**
www.wvstateu.edu — **CB code: 5903**

- Public 4-year liberal arts and teachers college
- Commuter campus in small town
- 3,455 degree-seeking undergraduates: 31% part-time, 59% women, 15% African American, 1% Asian American, 1% Hispanic American
- 36 graduate students
- 50% of applicants admitted
- SAT or ACT with writing required
- 30% graduate within 6 years

General. Founded in 1891. Regionally accredited. **Degrees:** 438 bachelor's awarded; master's offered. **ROTC:** Army. **Location:** 8 miles from Charleston. **Calendar:** Semester, limited summer session. **Full-time faculty:** 120 total; 64% have terminal degrees, 25% minority, 42% women. **Part-time faculty:** 74 total; 12% have terminal degrees, 12% minority, 57% women.

Freshman class profile. 862 applied, 428 admitted, 381 enrolled.

Basis for selection. School achievement record and test scores considered for 4-year programs. Open admission for community college component. Interview recommended for academically weak applicants to regents bachelor of arts programs. **Homeschooled:** Must provide detailed description of home school curriculum.

High school preparation. 14 units required. Required units include English 4, mathematics 2, social studies 3, science 3 (laboratory 2) and foreign language 2.

2005-2006 Annual costs. Tuition/fees: $3,548; $8,124 out-of-state. Room/board: $4,850. Books/supplies: $948. Personal expenses: $1,288.

Financial aid. Non-need-based: Scholarships awarded for academics, athletics, ROTC, state residency.

Application procedures. Admission: No deadline. No application fee. Admission notification on a rolling basis. **Financial aid:** Priority date 3/1, closing date 6/15. FAFSA required. Applicants notified on a rolling basis starting 2/15; must reply within 2 week(s) of notification.

Academics. Special study options: Cooperative education, cross-registration, distance learning, double major, dual enrollment of high school students, external degree, honors, internships, teacher certification program, weekend college. Nontraditional life experience degree program. **Credit/placement by examination:** AP, CLEP, IB, institutional tests. **Support services:** Learning center, reduced course load, remedial instruction, study skills assistance, tutoring.

Majors. Biology: General. **Business:** General, accounting, banking/financial services, business admin. **Communications:** General. **Computer sciences:** Computer science. **Education:** General, art, early childhood, elementary, English, gifted/talented, health, mathematics, mentally handicapped, middle, music, physical, science, secondary, social studies, special. **English:** Technical writing. **Health:** Recreational therapy. **History:** General. **Liberal arts:** Arts/sciences. **Math:** General, applied. **Parks/recreation:** Facilities management. **Physical sciences:** Chemistry, physics. **Protective services:** Criminal justice, police science. **Psychology:** General. **Public administration:** Social work. **Social sciences:** Economics, political science, sociology. **Visual/performing arts:** Ceramics, commercial/advertising art, drawing, fiber arts, painting, photography, printmaking, sculpture, studio arts.

Computing on campus. 200 workstations in dormitories, library, computer center, student center. Dormitories linked to campus network. Commuter students can connect to campus network. Helpline available.

Student life. Freshman orientation: Mandatory. Preregistration for classes offered. **Policies:** Freshmen permitted cars on campus. **Housing:** Guaranteed on-campus for freshmen. Single-sex dorms, apartments available. **Activities:** Bands, choral groups, drama, film society, literary magazine, music ensembles, radio station, student government, student newspaper, TV station, DNA science club, Pre-Alumni Club, College Students for Christ, NAACP, Access Awareness Council, Fellowship for Christian Athletes, poetry workshop.

Athletics. NCAA. **Intercollegiate:** Baseball M, basketball, football (tackle) M, golf, softball W, tennis, track and field, volleyball W. **Intramural:** Basketball, bowling, football (tackle) M, softball, swimming, tennis, volleyball. **Team name:** Yellow Jackets.

Student services. Career counseling, student employment services, health services, on-campus daycare, personal counseling, placement for graduates, veterans' counselor. **Physically disabled:** Services for visually, speech, hearing impaired.

Contact. E-mail: admission@wvstateu.edu
Phone: (304) 766-3221 Toll-free number: (800) 987-2112
Fax: (304) 766-4104
Tryreno Sowell, Director, West Virginia State University, Campus Box 197, Institute, WV 25112-1000

West Virginia University

Morgantown, West Virginia — **CB member**
www.wvu.edu — **CB code: 5904**

- Public 4-year university
- Residential campus in small city
- 19,510 degree-seeking undergraduates: 5% part-time, 46% women, 4% African American, 2% Asian American, 2% Hispanic American, 2% international
- 6,541 degree-seeking graduate students
- 92% of applicants admitted
- SAT or ACT with writing required
- 55% graduate within 6 years

General. Founded in 1867. Regionally accredited. Regional centers at Charleston, Clarksburg, Parkersburg, Potomac State College in Keyser, Shepherdstown, WVU Institute of Technology, and West Liberty. Health Sciences Center operates division in Charleston. **Degrees:** 3,157 bachelor's awarded; master's, doctoral, first professional offered. **ROTC:** Army, Air Force. **Location:** 70 miles from Pittsburgh, 200 miles from Baltimore. **Calendar:** Semester, extensive summer session. **Full-time faculty:** 785 total; 75% have terminal degrees, 11% minority, 34% women. **Part-time faculty:** 337 total. **Class size:** 34% < 20, 38% 20-39, 10% 40-49, 10% 50-99, 9% >100. **Special facilities:** Personal rapid transit system (PRT), arboretum, planetarium, herbarium, pharmacy museum, 2 art galleries, 8 experimental farms, 4 forests, software development center, mineral and energy resources museum, center for Black culture and research, student recreation center.

Freshman class profile. 10,957 applied, 10,110 admitted, 4,574 enrolled.

Mid 50% test scores		**Rank in top tenth:**	18%
SAT verbal:	470-560	**Return as sophomores:**	81%
SAT math:	480-580	**Out-of-state:**	49%
ACT:	20-26	**Live on campus:**	83%
GPA 3.50 or higher:	40%	**International:**	1%
GPA 3.0-3.49:	30%	**Fraternities:**	9%
GPA 2.0-2.99:	30%	**Sororities:**	10%
Rank in top quarter:	43%		

Basis for selection. High school GPA and SAT or ACT scores most important. Minimum 2.0 GPA and SAT of 910 (exclusive of Writing) or ACT of 19 required of state residents. Minimum 2.25 GPA and SAT of 950 or ACT of 20 required of nonresidents. Applicants with high GPA, high test scores, or special talents (athletics or the arts) who do not meet all admissions criteria may be considered on individual basis. Up to 5% of each incoming class may be admitted under this special policy. Internal placement test for math, chemistry, & foreign languages. Interview required for dental hygiene; audition required for drama, music; portfolio required for art. Essay required for some programs. **Homeschooled:** Students should submit ACT or SAT scores, transcript or descriptions of class background and/or experience.

High school preparation. 13 units required. Required and recommended units include English 4, mathematics 3, social studies 3, science 3 (laboratory 2) and foreign language 2. Math units should include 2 algebra and 1 geometry. 3 units combined from social studies and history required. Recommended electives include computer science, fine arts, humanities.

2005-2006 Annual costs. Tuition/fees: $4,164; $12,874 out-of-state. Room/board: $6,342. Books/supplies: $825. Personal expenses: $1,315.

2005-2006 Financial aid. Need-based: 2,525 full-time freshmen applied for aid; 2,014 were judged to have need; 1,917 of these received aid. Average need met was 87%. Average scholarship/grant was $3,149; average loan $3,493. 40% of total undergraduate aid awarded as scholarships/grants, 60% as loans/jobs. **Non-need-based:** Awarded to 11,915 full-time undergraduates, including 2,386 freshmen. Scholarships awarded for academics, alumni affiliation, art, athletics, job skills, leadership, minority status, music/drama, state residency. **Additional information:** February 1 closing date for freshman scholarships.

Application procedures. Admission: Priority date 3/1; deadline 8/1. $25 fee ($40 out-of-state), may be waived for applicants with need. Application may be submitted online. Admission notification on a rolling basis beginning on or about 9/15. **Financial aid:** Closing date 3/1. FAFSA required. Applicants notified on a rolling basis starting 3/15; must reply within 4 week(s) of notification.

Academics. Special study options: Accelerated study, combined bachelor's/graduate degree, cooperative education, distance learning, double major, ESL, exchange student, external degree, honors, independent study, internships, semester at sea, student-designed major, study abroad, teacher certification program, Washington semester. **Credit/placement by examination:** AP, CLEP, IB, SAT, ACT, institutional tests. 38 credit hours maximum toward bachelor's degree. **Support services:** Learning center, pre-admission summer program, reduced course load, remedial instruction, study skills assistance, tutoring, writing center.

Majors. Agriculture: Agronomy, animal sciences, business, economics, horticultural science, plant sciences, soil science. **Architecture:** Landscape. **Biology:** General, biochemistry, exercise physiology. **Business:** Accounting, business admin, finance, management information systems, managerial economics, marketing. **Communications:** Advertising, broadcast journalism, journalism, public relations. **Computer sciences:** Computer science. **Conservation:** Forest management, wildlife, wood science. **Education:** Agricultural, physical. **Engineering:** Aerospace, chemical, civil, computer, electrical, industrial, mechanical, mining, petroleum. **English:** English lit. **Family/consumer sciences:** General, clothing/textiles, family/community services, food/nutrition. **Foreign languages:** General. **Health:** Athletic training, audiology/speech pathology, clinical lab science, dental hygiene, nursing (RN), prenursing, prepharmacy. **History:** General. **Liberal arts:** Arts/sciences. **Math:** General. **Parks/recreation:** Exercise sciences, facilities management, health/fitness, sports admin. **Philosophy/religion:** Philosophy. **Physical sciences:** Chemistry, geology, physics. **Protective services:** Criminalistics, forensics. **Psychology:** General. **Public administration:** Social work. **Social sciences:** Economics, geography, political science, sociology. **Visual/performing arts:** General, art, dramatic.

Most popular majors. Business/marketing 12%, communications/journalism 10%, engineering/engineering technologies 9%, health sciences 6%, liberal arts 11%, social sciences 8%.

Computing on campus. 2,500 workstations in dormitories, library, computer center, student center. Dormitories wired for high-speed internet access and linked to campus network. Commuter students can connect to campus network. Online course registration, online library, helpline, repair service, student web hosting available.

Student life. Freshman orientation: Available. Preregistration for classes offered. Held during summer; several options ranging in length and fees. **Policies:** Anti-hazing, affirmative action and nondiscrimination policies. Mandatory freshmen housing program places faculty residence hall leaders adjacent to residence halls. Freshmen permitted cars on campus. **Housing:** Guaranteed on-campus for freshmen. Coed dorms, single-sex dorms, special housing for disabled, apartments, fraternity/sorority housing, substance-free housing available. $150 partly refundable deposit, deadline 5/1. Special interest floors available. **Activities:** Bands, choral groups, dance, drama, literary magazine, music ensembles, musical theater, opera, radio station, student government, student newspaper, symphony orchestra, TV station, Sierra student coalition, Hillel House, Gamma Beta Phi, Collegiate 4-H, Circle K, Campus Crusade for Christ, College Republicans, Muslim student association.

Athletics. NCAA. **Intercollegiate:** Baseball M, basketball, cross-country W, diving, football (tackle) M, gymnastics W, rifle, rowing (crew) W, soccer, swimming, tennis W, track and field W, volleyball W, wrestling M. **Intramural:** Badminton, basketball, bowling M, football (non-tackle), golf, racquetball, rifle, soccer, swimming, tennis W, track and field W, volleyball, wrestling M. **Team name:** Mountaineers.

Student services. Adult student services, alcohol/substance abuse counseling, campus ministries, career counseling, services for economically disadvantaged, student employment services, financial aid counseling, health

services, legal services, minority student services, personal counseling, placement for graduates, veterans' counselor, women's services. **Physically disabled:** Services for visually, speech, hearing impaired.

Contact. E-mail: wvuadmissions@arc.wvu.edu
Phone: (304) 293-2121 Toll-free number: (800) 344-9881
Fax: (304) 293-3080
Cheng Khoo, Director of Admissions and Records, West Virginia University, Admissions and Records Office, Morgantown, WV 26506-6009

West Virginia University at Parkersburg

Parkersburg, West Virginia
www.wvup.edu **CB code: 5932**

- Public 4-year community college
- Commuter campus in large town
- 3,114 degree-seeking undergraduates: 30% part-time, 65% women, 1% African American, 1% Asian American, 1% Hispanic American

General. Founded in 1971. Regionally accredited. Regional campus of West Virginia University. **Degrees:** 82 bachelor's, 312 associate awarded. **Location:** 80 miles from Charleston, 110 miles from Columbus, Ohio. **Calendar:** Semester, limited summer session. **Full-time faculty:** 86 total; 15% have terminal degrees, 4% minority, 49% women. **Part-time faculty:** 160 total; 3% have terminal degrees, 2% minority, 53% women. **Class size:** 57% < 20, 40% 20-39, 2% 40-49, 2% 50-99.

Freshman class profile. 700 applied, 700 admitted, 659 enrolled.

GPA 3.50 or higher:	20%	**End year in good standing:**	70%
GPA 3.0-3.49:	28%	**Return as sophomores:**	33%
GPA 2.0-2.99:	44%	**Out-of-state:**	1%

Basis for selection. Open admission, but selective for some programs. Special requirements for nursing, surgical technology, and bachelor's degree programs. SAT or ACT scores required but not used in admission decisions; ACT preferred. Interview required for nursing program.

High school preparation. 16 units recommended. Recommended units include English 4, mathematics 3, social studies 4, science 3 (laboratory 2). Social studies requirements may be fulfilled with history units.

2005-2006 Annual costs. Tuition/fees: $1,668; $5,892 out-of-state. Bachelor degree program: $2,280 annually or $95 per credit hour for residents; $6,024 annually or $251 per credit hour for nonresidents. Books/supplies: $800. Personal expenses: $1,400.

2005-2006 Financial aid. Need-based: Average need met was 78%. Average scholarship/grant was $5,200; average loan $2,800. 97% of total undergraduate aid awarded as scholarships/grants, 3% as loans/jobs. **Non-need-based:** Scholarships awarded for academics, state residency.

Application procedures. Admission: No deadline. No application fee. Application may be submitted online. Admission notification on a rolling basis. **Financial aid:** Priority date 3/1; no closing date. FAFSA required. Applicants notified on a rolling basis; must reply within 2 week(s) of notification.

Academics. Special study options: Cooperative education, distance learning, double major, dual enrollment of high school students, independent study, internships, teacher certification program. **Credit/placement by examination:** AP, CLEP, institutional tests. **Support services:** Learning center, reduced course load, remedial instruction, study skills assistance, tutoring.

Majors. Business: Business admin. **Education:** Elementary. **Engineering technology:** Industrial management.

Most popular majors. Business/marketing 56%, education 24%, engineering/engineering technologies 20%.

Computing on campus. 250 workstations in library, computer center.

Student life. Freshman orientation: Available. Preregistration for classes offered. Held several weeks prior to the start of classes. **Policies:** Freshmen permitted cars on campus. **Activities:** Choral groups, drama, student government, student newspaper, Campus Christian Fellowship, criminal justice organization, social service organization.

Athletics. Intramural: Basketball, bowling, softball, table tennis, volleyball.

Student services. Adult student services, career counseling, services for economically disadvantaged, financial aid counseling, health services, on-campus daycare, placement for graduates, veterans' counselor. **Physically disabled:** Services for visually, speech, hearing impaired.

Contact. E-mail: info@mail.wvup.edu
Phone: (304) 424-8220 Fax: (304) 424-8332
Cecelia Malhotra, Registrar, West Virginia University at Parkersburg, 300 Campus Drive, Parkersburg, WV 26104-8647

West Virginia University Institute of Technology

Montgomery, West Virginia
www.wvutech.edu **CB code: 5902**

- Public 4-year engineering and technical college
- Commuter campus in small town
- 1,959 degree-seeking undergraduates
- 69% of applicants admitted
- SAT or ACT with writing required

General. Founded in 1895. Regionally accredited. **Degrees:** 210 bachelor's awarded; master's offered. **ROTC:** Army. **Location:** 30 miles from Charleston. **Calendar:** Semester, limited summer session. **Full-time faculty:** 119 total. **Part-time faculty:** 57 total. **Class size:** 64% < 20, 31% 20-39, 3% 40-49, 2% 50-99, less than 1% >100. **Special facilities:** Hiking trail.

Freshman class profile. 1,139 applied, 785 admitted, 350 enrolled.

Basis for selection. School achievement record and test scores important. Out-of-state applicants must rank in top three-quarters of class or have SAT combined score of 820 (exclusive of Writing) or ACT composite score of 17. Higher requirements for both in-state and out-of-state engineering applicants. Selective admission to dental hygiene, respiratory therapy and surgical technology. For associate degree programs, SAT/ACT required for placement but not admission. Interview recommended for engineering. **Homeschooled:** Students may be required to take GED exam.

High school preparation. 17 units required. Required and recommended units include English 4, mathematics 2, social studies 3, history 3, science 2 (laboratory 2). 2 algebra, 1 plane geometry, 1 advanced mathematics required of engineering majors. 1 algebra, 1 chemistry, 1 biology required of dental hygiene majors. 2 laboratory sciences, including chemistry, 2 higher mathematics required for nursing program.

2005-2006 Annual costs. Tuition/fees: $4,078; $10,416 out-of-state. Room/board: $4,810. Books/supplies: $800. Personal expenses: $1,600.

Financial aid. Additional information: Room and board may be deferred for up to 60 days. First 50% due in 30 days.

Application procedures. Admission: Closing date 8/15. No application fee. Application may be submitted online. Admission notification on a rolling basis. Must reply by May 1 or within 2 week(s) if notified thereafter. **Financial aid:** Priority date 2/1, closing date 4/1. FAFSA, institutional form required. Applicants notified on a rolling basis; must reply within 3 week(s) of notification.

Academics. Special study options: Combined bachelor's/graduate degree, cooperative education, distance learning, double major, dual enrollment of high school students, external degree, internships, liberal arts/career combination, student-designed major. Cooperative programs in engineering and business. **Credit/placement by examination:** AP, CLEP, institutional tests. 90 credit hours maximum toward bachelor's degree. **Support services:** Learning center, pre-admission summer program, reduced course load, remedial instruction, tutoring.

Majors. Biology: General. **Business:** General, business admin. **Computer sciences:** General, computer science, programming. **Education:** Physical. **Engineering:** Chemical, civil, electrical, mechanical. **Engineering technology:** Electrical. **History:** General. **Math:** General. **Physical sciences:** Chemistry.

Most popular majors. Business/marketing 21%, engineering/engineering technologies 42%, health sciences 10%, liberal arts 11%.

Computing on campus. 500 workstations in dormitories, library, computer center, student center. Dormitories wired for high-speed internet access and linked to campus network. Online library, helpline, wireless network available.

Student life. Freshman orientation: Available, $25 fee. Preregistration for classes offered. **Policies:** Freshmen permitted cars on campus. **Housing:** Guaranteed on-campus for all undergraduates. Coed dorms, single-sex dorms, fraternity/sorority housing available. $100 deposit. **Activities:** Bands, choral groups, drama, music ensembles, student government, student newspaper, Christian Student Union, Alpha Phi Omega service fraternity.

Athletics. NCAA. **Intercollegiate:** Baseball M, basketball, football (tackle) M, golf M, soccer W, softball W, tennis, volleyball W. **Intramural:** Badminton, basketball, handball, racquetball, rowing (crew), softball, swimming, table tennis, tennis, volleyball, water polo, wrestling M. **Team name:** Golden Bears.

Student services. Adult student services, career counseling, student employment services, financial aid counseling, health services, on-campus daycare, personal counseling, placement for graduates, veterans' counselor. **Physically disabled:** Services for speech impaired.

Contact. E-mail: admissions@wvutech.edu
Phone: (304) 442-3167 Toll-free number: (888) 554-8324
Fax: (304) 442-3097
Donna Varney, Director of Admissions, West Virginia University Institute of Technology, 405 Fayette Pike, Montgomery, WV 25136-2436

West Virginia Wesleyan College

Buckhannon, West Virginia — **CB member**
www.wvwc.edu — **CB code: 5905**

- Private 4-year liberal arts college affiliated with United Methodist Church
- Residential campus in small town
- 1,366 degree-seeking undergraduates: 2% part-time, 54% women
- 42 degree-seeking graduate students
- 77% of applicants admitted
- SAT or ACT with writing required
- 54% graduate within 6 years; 36% enter graduate study

General. Founded in 1890. Regionally accredited. **Degrees:** 297 bachelor's awarded; master's offered. **Location:** 115 miles from Charleston, 135 miles from Pittsburgh. **Calendar:** Semester, limited summer session. **Full-time faculty:** 87 total; 77% have terminal degrees, 2% minority, 41% women. **Part-time faculty:** 80 total. **Special facilities:** Planetarium, botany museum, herbarium, greenhouse.

Freshman class profile. 1,268 applied, 982 admitted, 348 enrolled.

Mid 50% test scores			
SAT verbal:	460-580	Rank in top tenth:	25%
SAT math:	460-570	End year in good standing:	84%
ACT:	20-25	Return as sophomores:	72%
Rank in top quarter:	53%	Out-of-state:	47%
		Live on campus:	95%

Basis for selection. School achievement record and test scores required. Essay, interview recommended for all; audition recommended for drama, music; portfolio recommended for art.

High school preparation. 24 units required. Required and recommended units include English 4, mathematics 3, social studies 2, history 2, science 3 (laboratory 2), foreign language 2-3 and academic electives 3.

2006-2007 Annual costs. Tuition/fees (projected): $21,250. Room/board: $5,550. Books/supplies: $1,000. Personal expenses: $2,500.

2005-2006 Financial aid. Need-based: 314 full-time freshmen applied for aid; 278 were judged to have need; 278 of these received aid. Average need met was 89%. Average scholarship/grant was $16,861; average loan $3,098. 72% of total undergraduate aid awarded as scholarships/grants, 28% as loans/jobs. **Non-need-based:** Awarded to 830 full-time undergraduates, including 214 freshmen. Scholarships awarded for academics, alumni affiliation, art, athletics, leadership, music/drama, religious affiliation.

Application procedures. Admission: Priority date 1/1; deadline 7/1 (postmark date). $35 fee, may be waived for applicants with need. Application may be submitted online. Admission notification on a rolling basis beginning on or about 12/1. Must reply by May 1 or within 4 week(s) if notified thereafter. **Financial aid:** Priority date 2/15; no closing date. FAFSA required. Applicants notified on a rolling basis starting 3/15; must reply within 4 week(s) of notification.

Academics. Special study options: Combined bachelor's/graduate degree, double major, ESL, exchange student, honors, independent study, internships, student-designed major, study abroad, teacher certification program, Washington semester. Wesleyan Scholars program, Bonner Scholars program, May term travel. **Credit/placement by examination:** AP, CLEP, IB, institutional tests. 60 credit hours maximum toward bachelor's degree. **Support services:** Learning center, reduced course load, remedial instruction, study skills assistance, tutoring, writing center.

Majors. Biology: General. **Business:** Accounting, business admin, finance, international, managerial economics, marketing. **Communications:** General, public relations. **Computer sciences:** General, computer science, information systems. **Conservation:** Environmental science. **Education:** General, art, biology, chemistry, elementary, English, health, history, kindergarten/preschool, learning disabled, mathematics, music, physical, science, secondary, social studies, special. **English:** Creative writing, English lit. **Health:** Athletic training, predentistry, premedicine, prepharmacy, preveterinary. **History:** General. **Legal studies:** Prelaw. **Math:** General. **Parks/recreation:** Health/fitness, sports admin. **Philosophy/religion:** Philosophy, religion. **Physical sciences:** Chemistry, physics. **Protective services:** Law enforcement admin. **Psychology:** General. **Social sciences:** Economics, international relations, political science, sociology. **Theology:** Religious ed. **Visual/performing arts:** Art, arts management, ceramics, dramatic, drawing, graphic design, painting, studio arts, theater arts management.

Computing on campus. PC or laptop required. Dormitories wired for high-speed internet access and linked to campus network. Commuter students can connect to campus network. Online library, helpline, repair service, wireless network available.

Student life. Freshman orientation: Mandatory, $200 fee. Preregistration for classes offered. One-credit semester long course. **Policies:** Freshmen permitted cars on campus. **Housing:** Guaranteed on-campus for all undergraduates. Coed dorms, single-sex dorms, special housing for disabled, apartments, fraternity/sorority housing, substance-free housing available. Full-time students required to live on campus unless married, living with parents, or have received written permission from the Housing Committee to live off campus. **Activities:** Bands, choral groups, dance, drama, literary magazine, music ensembles, musical theater, radio station, student government, student newspaper, TV station, Christian Life Council, Fellowship of Christian Athletes, Alpha Phi Omega service fraternity, Black Student Union, international student organization, College Republicans, Young Democrats, Green Club, Wesleyan service corps.

Athletics. NCAA. **Intercollegiate:** Baseball M, basketball, cross-country, football (tackle) M, golf M, soccer, softball W, swimming, tennis, track and field, volleyball W. **Intramural:** Basketball M, football (non-tackle), racquetball, softball, table tennis, volleyball, water polo M. **Team name:** Bobcats.

Student services. Alcohol/substance abuse counseling, campus ministries, career counseling, financial aid counseling, health services, minority student services, personal counseling, placement for graduates. **Physically disabled:** Services for visually, speech, hearing impaired.

Contact. E-mail: admission@wvwc.edu
Phone: (304) 473-8510 Toll-free number: (800) 722-9933
Fax: (304) 473-8108
West Virginia Wesleyan College, 59 College Avenue, Buckhannon, WV 26201-2998

Wheeling Jesuit University

Wheeling, West Virginia — **CB member**
www.wju.edu — **CB code: 5906**

- Private 4-year university and liberal arts college affiliated with Roman Catholic Church
- Residential campus in small city
- 1,188 degree-seeking undergraduates: 12% part-time, 59% women
- 212 degree-seeking graduate students
- 75% of applicants admitted
- SAT or ACT (ACT writing optional), application essay required
- 60% graduate within 6 years

General. Founded in 1954. Regionally accredited. **Degrees:** 273 bachelor's awarded; master's, doctoral offered. **Location:** 55 miles from Pittsburgh, 125 miles from Columbus, Ohio. **Calendar:** Semester, limited summer session. **Full-time faculty:** 75 total; 72% have terminal degrees, 4% minority, 45% women. **Part-time faculty:** 40 total; 30% have terminal degrees, 5% minority, 45% women. **Class size:** 57% < 20, 42% 20-39, less than 1% 40-49, less than 1% 50-99. **Special facilities:** NASA Classroom of the Future.

Freshman class profile. 1,132 applied, 853 admitted, 285 enrolled.

Mid 50% test scores		Rank in top quarter:	41%
SAT verbal:	460-580	Rank in top tenth:	20%
SAT math:	450-570	End year in good standing:	72%
ACT:	19-24	Return as sophomores:	72%
GPA 3.50 or higher:	43%	Out-of-state:	65%
GPA 3.0-3.49:	37%	Live on campus:	85%
GPA 2.0-2.99:	20%	International:	3%

Basis for selection. High school GPA, quality of courses taken, and test scores most important. Some exception made to minimum when warranted by high school record. Personal recommendations and extracurricular activities important. In-state and out-of-state applicants treated equally. Interview recommended. **Learning Disabled:** Students need to submit written documentation of disability.

High school preparation. 15 units required. Required and recommended units include English 4, mathematics 2, social studies 2, history 2, science 1 (laboratory 1), foreign language 2 and academic electives 6. Applicants for programs in the natural sciences should have 1 unit of biology and 1 of chemistry. Applicants preparing for future study in the physical therapy doctorate program should have a minimum of 3 years of college preparatory math and 3 years of lab science, including physics.

2006-2007 Annual costs. Tuition/fees (projected): $22,186. Room/board: $6,808. Books/supplies: $800. Personal expenses: $600.

2005-2006 Financial aid. Need-based: 267 full-time freshmen applied for aid; 237 were judged to have need; 237 of these received aid. Average need met was 95%. Average scholarship/grant was $7,200; average loan $2,380. 55% of total undergraduate aid awarded as scholarships/grants, 45% as loans/jobs. **Non-need-based:** Awarded to 847 full-time undergraduates, including 264 freshmen. Scholarships awarded for academics, alumni affiliation, athletics, leadership, music/drama.

Application procedures. Admission: No deadline. $25 fee, may be waived for applicants with need. Application may be submitted online. Admission notification on a rolling basis beginning on or about 9/1. Must reply by May 1 or within 2 week(s) if notified thereafter. **Financial aid:** Priority date 2/15; no closing date. FAFSA required. Applicants notified on a rolling basis starting 3/15; must reply within 2 week(s) of notification.

Academics. All students required to participate in 2 offerings for each of 8 dimensions of university's wellness program. **Special study options:** Combined bachelor's/graduate degree, distance learning, double major, ESL, honors, independent study, internships, liberal arts/career combination, semester at sea, student-designed major, study abroad, teacher certification program, United Nations semester, Washington semester. **Credit/placement by examination:** AP, CLEP, SAT, ACT. 30 credit hours maximum toward bachelor's degree. **Support services:** Learning center, remedial instruction, study skills assistance, tutoring, writing center.

Majors. Biology: General. **Business:** Accounting, business admin, international. **Computer sciences:** Computer science. **Education:** Science. **English:** Creative writing, English lit. **Foreign languages:** French, Spanish. **Health:** Health care admin, nuclear medical technology, respiratory therapy technology. **History:** General. **Liberal arts:** Arts/sciences. **Math:** General. **Philosophy/religion:** Philosophy. **Physical sciences:** Chemistry, physics. **Protective services:** Criminal justice. **Psychology:** General. **Social sciences:** International relations, political science. **Theology:** Theology.

Most popular majors. Business/marketing 32%, English 8%, health sciences 18%, liberal arts 7%, psychology 7%, security/protective services 6%.

Computing on campus. 243 workstations in dormitories, library, computer center. Dormitories wired for high-speed internet access and linked to campus network. Commuter students can connect to campus network. Online library, helpline, student web hosting available.

Student life. Freshman orientation: Available. Preregistration for classes offered. **Policies:** Freshmen permitted cars on campus. **Housing:** Guaranteed on-campus for all undergraduates. Coed dorms, single-sex dorms, apartments available. $100 fully refundable deposit. **Activities:** Pep band, choral groups, dance, drama, literary magazine, student government, student newspaper, TV station, social service outreach organization, international student club, academic clubs, campus ministry leadership/faith sharing groups, leadership development group.

Athletics. NCAA. **Intercollegiate:** Baseball M, basketball, cheerleading, cross-country, golf, lacrosse M, soccer, softball W, swimming, track and field, volleyball W. **Intramural:** Basketball, soccer, softball, tennis, volleyball. **Team name:** Cardinals.

Student services. Adult student services, alcohol/substance abuse counseling, campus ministries, career counseling, student employment services, financial aid counseling, health services, minority student services, personal counseling, placement for graduates, veterans' counselor.

Contact. E-mail: admiss@wju.edu
Phone: (304) 243-2359 Toll-free number: (800) 624-6992
Fax: (304) 243-2397
Carol Descak, Dean of Admissions, Wheeling Jesuit University, 316 Washington Avenue, Wheeling, WV 26003-6295

Wisconsin

Alverno College
Milwaukee, Wisconsin
www.alverno.edu **CB code: 1012**

- Private 4-year liberal arts college for women affiliated with Roman Catholic Church
- Commuter campus in very large city
- 2,047 degree-seeking undergraduates: 26% part-time, 100% women, 20% African American, 5% Asian American, 11% Hispanic American, 1% Native American, 1% international
- 175 degree-seeking graduate students
- 56% of applicants admitted
- SAT or ACT (ACT writing optional), application essay required
- 47% graduate within 6 years; 17% enter graduate study

General. Founded in 1887. Regionally accredited. Students in every major area spend from 8 to 12 hours per week for one semester in field internship. **Degrees:** 234 bachelor's, 15 associate awarded; master's offered. **ROTC:** Army, Air Force. **Location:** 5 miles from downtown. **Calendar:** Semester, limited summer session. **Full-time faculty:** 104 total; 88% have terminal degrees, 8% minority, 75% women. **Part-time faculty:** 121 total; 56% have terminal degrees, 7% minority, 79% women. **Class size:** 62% < 20, 38% 20-39. **Special facilities:** Multimedia productions facility, independent science research areas, native prairie, clinical nursing resource center.

Freshman class profile. 789 applied, 438 admitted, 280 enrolled.

Mid 50% test scores		**Return as sophomores:**	76%
ACT:	17-22	**Out-of-state:**	3%
GPA 3.50 or higher:	19%	**Live on campus:**	32%
GPA 3.0-3.49:	35%	**International:**	1%
GPA 2.0-2.99:	42%	**Sororities:**	2%

Basis for selection. Review of high school transcripts, including GPA, academic units completed, standardized test scores, essay, Communication Placement Assessment results. Audition required for music therapy; portfolio required for studio art. **Homeschooled:** Portfolio of work required.

High school preparation. College-preparatory program required. 17 units recommended. Recommended units include English 4, mathematics 3, social studies 3, science 3 and foreign language 2. Science, social studies, and math course requirements vary according to intended program of study.

2005-2006 Annual costs. Tuition/fees: $16,062. Slightly higher per credit charge for nursing majors. Room/board: $5,660. Books/supplies: $1,050. Personal expenses: $1,730.

2004-2005 Financial aid. Need-based: 61% of total undergraduate aid awarded as scholarships/grants, 39% as loans/jobs. **Non-need-based:** Scholarships awarded for academics, alumni affiliation, leadership, minority status, music/drama.

Application procedures. Admission: Closing date 8/1. $20 fee, may be waived for applicants with need. Application may be submitted online. Admission notification on a rolling basis beginning on or about 9/1. Must reply by May 1 or within 2 week(s) if notified thereafter. **Financial aid:** Priority date 4/15; no closing date. FAFSA, institutional form required. Applicants notified on a rolling basis starting 4/15; must reply within 2 week(s) of notification.

Academics. Required internships in all majors provide research opportunities through federal government, local organizations and businesses. Degrees with honor awarded based on outstanding achievement and application of learning in service to others. **Special study options:** Double major, independent study, internships, semester at sea, student-designed major, study abroad, teacher certification program, weekend college. **Credit/placement by examination:** AP, CLEP, IB, institutional tests. **Support services:** Learning center, pre-admission summer program, reduced course load, remedial instruction, study skills assistance, tutoring, writing center.

Majors. Biology: General, molecular. **Business:** Accounting/finance, business admin, international. **Communications:** General. **Computer sciences:** General. **Conservation:** Environmental science. **Education:** General, art, elementary, English, middle, music. **English:** English lit. **Health:** Art therapy, music therapy, nursing (RN). **History:** General. **Liberal arts:** Arts/sciences. **Math:** General. **Philosophy/religion:** Philosophy, religion. **Physical sciences:** Chemistry. **Psychology:** General. **Public administration:** Community org/advocacy. **Social sciences:** General, international relations, political science, sociology. **Visual/performing arts:** Art.

Most popular majors. Business/marketing 23%, communications/journalism 12%, education 11%, English 6%, health sciences 20%, psychology 7%, public administration/social services 6%.

Computing on campus. 450 workstations in dormitories, library, computer center. Dormitories linked to campus network. Commuter students can connect to campus network. Online library, wireless network available.

Student life. Freshman orientation: Mandatory. Includes evening event before school begins plus 2 days at start of school year. **Policies:** Freshmen permitted cars on campus. **Housing:** Guaranteed on-campus for all undergraduates. $100 partly refundable deposit. Smoke-free areas available, semi-apartment living within residence halls available to older students. **Activities:** Choral groups, dance, drama, literary magazine, music ensembles, student newspaper, Alliance of the Sciences, Alverno College Entrepreneurs, Alverno Student Education Organization, Artourage, Circle K, Hispanic Women of Alverno, Student Nurses Association, Students in Free Enterprise, Women in Communications, Inc., Women of Asian Ethnicity.

Athletics. NCAA. **Intercollegiate:** Basketball W, cross-country W, soccer W, softball W, volleyball W. **Intramural:** Basketball W, volleyball W. **Team name:** Alverno Inferno.

Student services. Adult student services, campus ministries, career counseling, financial aid counseling, health services, on-campus daycare, personal counseling. **Physically disabled:** Services for visually, speech, hearing impaired.

Contact. E-mail: admissions@alverno.edu
Phone: (414) 382-6100 Toll-free number: (800) 933-3401
Fax: (414) 382-6354
Mary Kay Farrell, Director Admissions, Alverno College, 3400 South 43rd Street, Milwaukee, WI 53234-3922

Bellin College of Nursing
Green Bay, Wisconsin
www.bcon.edu **CB code: 1046**

- Private 4-year nursing college
- Commuter campus in small city
- 247 degree-seeking undergraduates: 14% part-time, 93% women, 2% Asian American, 1% Hispanic American, 1% Native American
- 36 degree-seeking graduate students
- 45% of applicants admitted
- ACT (writing optional), interview required
- 91% graduate within 6 years

General. Founded in 1909. Regionally accredited. **Degrees:** 39 bachelor's awarded; master's offered. **ROTC:** Army. **Location:** 120 miles from Milwaukee. **Calendar:** Semester, limited summer session. **Full-time faculty:** 17 total; 18% have terminal degrees, 100% women. **Part-time faculty:** 2 total; 100% women. **Class size:** 12% < 20, 60% 20-39, 4% 40-49, 24% 50-99.

Freshman class profile. 75 applied, 34 admitted, 23 enrolled.

Mid 50% test scores		**GPA 3.0-3.49:**	30%
ACT:	22-25	**End year in good standing:**	82%
GPA 3.50 or higher:	70%	**Return as sophomores:**	82%

Basis for selection. ACT composite of 23 and a 3.25 high school GPA required. Personal interview very important. Three references required, including 1 academic and 1 from employer if working.

High school preparation. 13 units required. Required units include English 4, mathematics 3, social studies 3 and science 3. Math must include 1 algebra and 2 advanced mathematics. Sciences must include 1 chemistry, 1 biology, and 1 advanced science.

2005-2006 Annual costs. Tuition/fees: $14,791. Books/supplies: $560. Personal expenses: $665.

2004-2005 Financial aid. Need-based: 42% of total undergraduate aid awarded as scholarships/grants, 58% as loans/jobs. **Non-need-based:** Scholarships awarded for academics. **Additional information:** Freshmen and sophomores receive aid through University of Wisconsin-Green Bay. Juniors and seniors receive aid through Bellin College of Nursing.

Application procedures. **Admission:** No deadline. $30 fee, may be waived for applicants with need. Admission notification on a rolling basis beginning on or about 9/1. Must reply by May 1 or within 3 week(s) if notified thereafter. Limited freshman applications accepted. Application closing date only if targeted number reached. **Financial aid:** Priority date 3/1; no closing date. FAFSA required. Applicants notified on a rolling basis starting 4/1; must reply within 2 week(s) of notification.

Academics. Students fulfill general education requirements at University of Wisconsin-Green Bay or another accredited college or university of their choice. **Special study options:** Accelerated study, independent study, semester at sea. **Credit/placement by examination:** AP, CLEP. **Support services:** Study skills assistance, tutoring.

Majors. **Health:** Nursing (RN).

Computing on campus. 18 workstations in computer center. Commuter students can connect to campus network.

Student life. **Freshman orientation:** Mandatory. Preregistration for classes offered. One day in early summer and 1 day within a week prior to fall semester. **Housing:** Students can live in dorms on University of Wisconsin-Green Bay campus. **Activities:** Student government, student nurses association, ambassadors club.

Student services. Financial aid counseling, health services, personal counseling.

Contact. E-mail: admisso@bcon.edu
Phone: (920) 433-5803 Toll-free number: (800) 236-8707
Fax: (920) 433-7416
Penny Croghan, Director of Admissions, Bellin College of Nursing, PO Box 23400, Green Bay, WI 54305-3400

Beloit College

Beloit, Wisconsin — **CB member**
www.beloit.edu — **CB code: 1059**

- Private 4-year liberal arts college
- Residential campus in large town
- 1,328 degree-seeking undergraduates: 1% part-time, 59% women, 3% African American, 4% Asian American, 2% Hispanic American, 1% Native American, 5% international
- 64% of applicants admitted
- SAT or ACT (ACT writing optional), application essay required
- 72% graduate within 6 years; 37% enter graduate study

General. Founded in 1846. Regionally accredited. Emphasis on international education, interdisciplinary study, and experiential learning. **Degrees:** 291 bachelor's awarded. **Location:** 70 miles from Milwaukee, 90 miles from Chicago. **Calendar:** Semester, limited summer session. **Full-time faculty:** 103 total; 95% have terminal degrees, 12% minority, 43% women. **Part-time faculty:** 24 total; 62% have terminal degrees, 21% minority, 54% women. **Class size:** 70% < 20, 29% 20-39, less than 1% 40-49. **Special facilities:** Art museum, anthropology museum, observatory, 2 nature preserves, social science research laboratory, limnology laboratory, 2 electron microscopes, superconducting NMR, ICAP spectrometer, marketing research center, center for entrepreneurship.

Freshman class profile. 2,054 applied, 1,324 admitted, 326 enrolled.

Mid 50% test scores		**Rank in top quarter:**	64%
SAT verbal:	590-700	**Rank in top tenth:**	37%
SAT math:	560-660	**End year in good standing:**	98%
ACT:	24-31	**Return as sophomores:**	89%
GPA 3.50 or higher:	58%	**Out-of-state:**	83%
GPA 3.0-3.49:	33%	**Live on campus:**	100%
GPA 2.0-2.99:	9%	**International:**	3%

Basis for selection. Rigor of high school curriculum and high school record most important. Test scores, recommendations, essay, interview, and extracurricular activities important. Writing section of the SAT or ACT not considered for purposes of admission. Interview recommended. **Home-schooled:** Letter of recommendation (nonparent) required.

High school preparation. Recommended units include English 4, mathematics 4, social studies 4, history 4, science 3 and foreign language 2.

2006-2007 Annual costs. Tuition/fees: $28,350. Room/board: $6,162. Books/supplies: $500. Personal expenses: $1,000.

2005-2006 Financial aid. **Need-based:** 309 full-time freshmen applied for aid; 262 were judged to have need; 262 of these received aid. Average need met was 100%. Average scholarship/grant was $15,676; average loan $4,420. 69% of total undergraduate aid awarded as scholarships/grants, 31% as loans/jobs. **Non-need-based:** Awarded to 726 full-time undergraduates, including 209 freshmen. Scholarships awarded for academics, leadership, minority status, music/drama.

Application procedures. **Admission:** Closing date 1/15 (postmark date). $35 fee, may be waived for applicants with need. Application may be submitted online. Admission notification 3/15. Admission notification on a rolling basis. Must reply by May 1 or within 2 week(s) if notified thereafter. First early action deadline November 15; notification December 15. **Financial aid:** Priority date 1/15, closing date 3/1. FAFSA, institutional form required. Applicants notified on a rolling basis starting 3/15; must reply by 5/1 or within 2 week(s) of notification.

Academics. Students participate in field terms, internships, work-study experiences. First-Year Initiative combines orientation program with advising, academic course work, and volunteer service. **Special study options:** Combined bachelor's/graduate degree, double major, ESL, exchange student, independent study, internships, liberal arts/career combination, student-designed major, study abroad, teacher certification program, urban semester, Washington semester. Field schools in archeology and geology, Center for Language Studies, intensive summer foreign language program, reserved admission to Medical College of Wisconsin. 3-2 programs in engineering, nursing, med tech and forestry. **Credit/placement by examination:** AP, CLEP, IB. 32 credit hours maximum toward bachelor's degree. **Support services:** Learning center, tutoring, writing center.

Majors. **Area/ethnic studies:** Women's. **Biology:** General, biochemistry, cell/histology, cellular/molecular, environmental, molecular. **Business:** Business admin, managerial economics. **Computer sciences:** Computer science. **Conservation:** Forestry. **Education:** General, art, science. **Engineering:** General. **English:** Creative writing, speech/rhetoric. **Foreign languages:** General, classics, comparative lit, French, German, Russian, Spanish. **Health:** Nursing (RN). **History:** General. **Interdisciplinary:** Behavioral sciences. **Liberal arts:** Arts/sciences. **Math:** General. **Physical sciences:** Chemistry, geology, physics. **Psychology:** General. **Public administration:** Social work. **Social sciences:** Anthropology, economics, international relations, political science, sociology. **Visual/performing arts:** Art history/conservation, dramatic.

Most popular majors. Biology 6%, business/marketing 6%, English 11%, foreign language 8%, history 8%, psychology 11%, social sciences 20%, visual/performing arts 12%.

Computing on campus. 132 workstations in dormitories, library, computer center, student center. Dormitories wired for high-speed internet access and linked to campus network. Commuter students can connect to campus network. Helpline, student web hosting, wireless network available.

Student life. **Freshman orientation:** Mandatory. Preregistration for classes offered. **Policies:** Residence hall system is student managed. Freshmen permitted cars on campus. **Housing:** Guaranteed on-campus for all undergraduates. Coed dorms, single-sex dorms, apartments, cooperative housing, fraternity/sorority housing, substance-free housing available. French house, Spanish house, German house, Russian house, arts co-op, women's center available. **Activities:** Jazz band, choral groups, dance, drama, film society, literary magazine, music ensembles, musical theater, radio station, student government, student newspaper, symphony orchestra, TV station, volunteer community tutoring service, women's center program, International Club, various religious interest clubs, Students for Social Responsibility, Gay Alliance, Young Republicans, Young Democrats, Science Fiction and Fantasy Association, outing-environmental Club, multicultural center.

Athletics. NCAA. **Intercollegiate:** Baseball M, basketball, cross-country, diving, football (tackle) M, golf, soccer, softball W, swimming, tennis, track and field, volleyball W. **Intramural:** Basketball, fencing, handball, ice hockey M, racquetball, rugby M, sailing, soccer, softball, swimming, tennis, volleyball, water polo. **Team name:** Bucs.

Student services. Career counseling, services for economically disadvantaged, student employment services, financial aid counseling, health services, minority student services, on-campus daycare, personal counseling, placement for graduates, women's services. **Physically disabled:** Services for visually, hearing impaired.

Contact. E-mail: admiss@beloit.edu
Phone: (608) 363-2500 Toll-free number: (800) 923-5648
Fax: (608) 363-2075
Nancy Monnich, Vice President of Enrollment Services, Beloit College, 700 College Street, Beloit, WI 53511-5595

Cardinal Stritch University

Milwaukee, Wisconsin
www.stritch.edu — **CB code: 1100**

- Private 4-year liberal arts college affiliated with Roman Catholic Church
- Commuter campus in very large city

- 3,100 degree-seeking undergraduates
- 92% of applicants admitted
- SAT or ACT (ACT writing optional), application essay required

General. Founded in 1937. Regionally accredited. **Degrees:** 595 bachelor's, 245 associate awarded; master's, doctoral offered. **Location:** 7 miles from downtown, 85 miles from Chicago. **Calendar:** Semester, limited summer session. **Full-time faculty:** 50 total. **Part-time faculty:** 242 total. **Class size:** 89% < 20, 11% 20-39.

Freshman class profile. 701 applied, 646 admitted, 176 enrolled.

Mid 50% test scores			
SAT verbal:	470-510	ACT:	19-24
SAT math:	480-520	Out-of-state:	19%
		Live on campus:	19%

Basis for selection. High school GPA of 2.0, rank in top half of class, minimum ACT test score of 20 or SAT combined score of 840 (exclusive of Writing). Interview, activities, recommendations considered. Conditional admission available to applicants not meeting all admissions criteria. Institutional tests used for admission of academically weak students. Interview recommended for all; portfolio recommended for art.

High school preparation. 16 units required; 18 recommended. Required and recommended units include English 4, mathematics 2-3, social studies 1, history 1, science 2-3, foreign language 2 and academic electives 4.

2006-2007 Annual costs. Tuition/fees (projected): $16,830. Additional $55 per credit for the nursing program. Room/board: $5,430. Books/supplies: $500. Personal expenses: $1,200.

Financial aid. Non-need-based: Scholarships awarded for academics, art, athletics, music/drama.

Application procedures. Admission: Priority date 4/1; no deadline. $25 fee, may be waived for applicants with need. Application may be submitted online. Notification sent within 2 weeks after date of application. **Financial aid:** Priority date 4/15; no closing date. FAFSA, institutional form required. Applicants notified on a rolling basis starting 3/1; must reply within 3 week(s) of notification.

Academics. Special study options: Accelerated study, cooperative education, distance learning, double major, dual enrollment of high school students, ESL, external degree, honors, independent study, internships, student-designed major, teacher certification program. **Credit/placement by examination:** AP, CLEP, IB, institutional tests. 30 credit hours maximum toward associate degree, 60 toward bachelor's. **Support services:** Learning center, reduced course load, remedial instruction, study skills assistance, tutoring, writing center.

Majors. Biology: General. **Business:** General, accounting, business admin, international, management information systems. **Communications:** General, public relations. **Education:** General. **English:** Creative writing. **Foreign languages:** French, Spanish. **Health:** Nursing (RN). **History:** General. **Interdisciplinary:** Math/computer science. **Math:** General. **Philosophy/religion:** Religion. **Physical sciences:** Chemistry. **Psychology:** General. **Social sciences:** General, political science, sociology. **Visual/performing arts:** Art, commercial/advertising art, dramatic, music performance, photography, studio arts.

Most popular majors. Business/marketing 80%, education 6%.

Computing on campus. 236 workstations in dormitories, library, computer center. Dormitories linked to campus network. Commuter students can connect to campus network. Helpline available.

Student life. Freshman orientation: Mandatory. Preregistration for classes offered. One week long program prior to first week of classes. **Policies:** Freshmen permitted cars on campus. **Housing:** Coed dorms available. $50 deposit. **Activities:** Bands, choral groups, dance, drama, literary magazine, music ensembles, musical theater, radio station, student government, student newspaper, Students for Political Awareness, model United Nations, multicultural committee, Asian club, Black student union, United Latino Organization, Fellowship of Christian Students, service corps, peer helpers, student campus ministry.

Athletics. NAIA. **Intercollegiate:** Baseball M, basketball, cross-country, soccer, softball W, volleyball. **Intramural:** Basketball, volleyball. **Team name:** Wolves.

Student services. Adult student services, alcohol/substance abuse counseling, campus ministries, career counseling, student employment services, financial aid counseling, health services, personal counseling, placement for graduates, veterans' counselor. **Physically disabled:** Services for hearing impaired.

Contact. E-mail: admityou@stritch.edu
Phone: (414) 410-4040 Toll-free number: (800) 347-8822 ext. 4040
Fax: (414) 410-4058
Kristy Bueno, Director of Admission, Cardinal Stritch University, 6801 North Yates Road, Box 516, Milwaukee, WI 53217-7516

Carroll College
Waukesha, Wisconsin
www.cc.edu **CB code: 1101**

- Private 4-year liberal arts college affiliated with Presbyterian Church (USA)
- Residential campus in small city
- 2,663 degree-seeking undergraduates: 15% part-time, 66% women, 2% African American, 1% Asian American, 3% Hispanic American, 2% international
- 239 graduate students
- 77% of applicants admitted
- SAT and SAT Subject Tests or ACT (ACT writing recommended) required
- 62% graduate within 6 years

General. Founded in 1846. Regionally accredited. **Degrees:** 414 bachelor's awarded; master's offered. **ROTC:** Army, Air Force. **Location:** 15 miles from Milwaukee. **Calendar:** Semester, extensive summer session. **Full-time faculty:** 99 total; 70% have terminal degrees, 3% minority, 56% women. **Part-time faculty:** 147 total; 55% women. **Class size:** 59% < 20, 36% 20-39, 1% 40-49, 4% 50-99. **Special facilities:** Scientific study and conservancy area, research station in 20-acre laboratory and watershed.

Freshman class profile. 2,517 applied, 1,944 admitted, 610 enrolled.

Mid 50% test scores		Out-of-state:	26%
ACT:	21-24	Live on campus:	85%
Rank in top quarter:	51%	International:	1%
Rank in top tenth:	15%	Fraternities:	4%
Return as sophomores:	77%	Sororities:	9%

Basis for selection. School achievement record most important, followed by test scores. Recommendations, essay, interview considered. Essay, interview recommended for all; audition recommended for music, theater; portfolio recommended for art.

High school preparation. Recommended units include English 4, mathematics 4, social studies 3, history 3, science 3 (laboratory 1) and foreign language 2.

2006-2007 Annual costs. Tuition/fees (projected): $19,900. Room/board: $6,070. Books/supplies: $872. Personal expenses: $1,460.

2005-2006 Financial aid. Need-based: 557 full-time freshmen applied for aid; 451 were judged to have need; 451 of these received aid. Average need met was 94%. Average scholarship/grant was $10,512; average loan $2,531. 73% of total undergraduate aid awarded as scholarships/grants, 27% as loans/jobs. **Non-need-based:** Awarded to 2,000 full-time undergraduates, including 516 freshmen. Scholarships awarded for academics, alumni affiliation, art, leadership, minority status, music/drama, religious affiliation, ROTC, state residency.

Application procedures. Admission: Priority date 4/15; no deadline. No application fee. Application may be submitted online. Admission notification on a rolling basis. **Financial aid:** Priority date 4/15; no closing date. FAFSA required. Applicants notified on a rolling basis starting 2/15; must reply by 5/1 or within 2 week(s) of notification.

Academics. Education majors must maintain 2.75 GPA in major. Nursing students must maintain 2.5 GPA. 4 majors available for pre-physical therapy programs. **Special study options:** Distance learning, double major, exchange student, honors, independent study, internships, student-designed major, study abroad, teacher certification program, United Nations semester, Washington semester. **Credit/placement by examination:** AP, CLEP, IB, institutional tests. 48 credit hours maximum toward bachelor's degree. **Support services:** Learning center, reduced course load, study skills assistance, tutoring, writing center.

Majors. Biology: General, animal behavior, biochemistry. **Business:** Accounting, actuarial science, business admin, finance, human resources, management information systems, marketing, organizational behavior. **Communications:** General, journalism, organizational, public relations. **Communications technology:** Graphics, printing management. **Computer sciences:** General, information systems. **Conservation:** General. **Education:** General, art, biology, chemistry, early childhood, elementary, English, foreign languages, geography, health, history, mathematics, middle, music, physical, psychology, science, social science, social studies, Spanish. **Engineering:** Software. **English:** Creative writing. **Foreign languages:** Spanish. **Health:** Athletic training, clinical lab science, nursing (RN), predentistry, premedicine, prepharmacy, preveterinary. **History:** General. **Math:** General, applied. **Parks/recreation:** Exercise sciences, facilities management, health/fitness. **Philosophy/religion:** Religion. **Physical sciences:** Chemistry. **Protective services:** Criminal justice, forensics. **Psychology:** General. **Social sciences:** International relations, political science, sociology. **Visual/performing arts:** Art, commercial/advertising art, dramatic, photography, studio arts.

Most popular majors. Business/marketing 17%, communications/journalism 8%, computer/information sciences 6%, education 11%, health sciences 15%, psychology 8%, social sciences 7%, visual/performing arts 6%.

Computing on campus. 250 workstations in dormitories, library, computer center, student center. Dormitories wired for high-speed internet access and linked to campus network. Online library, helpline, student web hosting, wireless network available.

Student life. **Freshman orientation:** Mandatory. Preregistration for classes offered. **Policies:** Freshmen permitted cars on campus. **Housing:** Guaranteed on-campus for freshmen. Coed dorms, single-sex dorms, apartments available. $200 nonrefundable deposit. **Activities:** Bands, choral groups, dance, drama, literary magazine, music ensembles, radio station, student government, student newspaper, symphony orchestra, College Democrats, Bible Study Group, Environmental Conservation Organization, Intervarsity Christian Fellowship, Outright.

Athletics. NCAA. **Intercollegiate:** Baseball M, basketball, cross-country, football (tackle) M, golf, soccer, softball W, swimming, tennis, track and field, volleyball W. **Intramural:** Basketball, football (non-tackle), soccer, softball, table tennis, volleyball, water polo. **Team name:** Pioneers.

Student services. Adult student services, campus ministries, career counseling, student employment services, financial aid counseling, health services, minority student services, personal counseling, veterans' counselor. **Physically disabled:** Services for visually, hearing impaired.

Contact. E-mail: info@cc.edu
Phone: (262) 524-7220 Toll-free number: (800) 227-7655
Fax: (262) 951-3037
Jim Wiseman, Vice President for Enrollment, Carroll College, 100 North East Avenue, Waukesha, WI 53186-9988

Carthage College

Kenosha, Wisconsin — **CB member**
www.carthage.edu — **CB code: 1103**

- Private 4-year liberal arts college affiliated with Evangelical Lutheran Church in America
- Residential campus in small city
- 2,432 degree-seeking undergraduates: 12% part-time, 58% women, 5% African American, 1% Asian American, 4% Hispanic American, 1% international
- 105 degree-seeking graduate students
- 76% of applicants admitted
- SAT or ACT (ACT writing optional) required
- 53% graduate within 6 years

General. Founded in 1847. Regionally accredited. **Degrees:** 396 bachelor's awarded; master's offered. **ROTC:** Army, Air Force. **Location:** 60 miles from Chicago, 30 miles from Milwaukee. **Calendar:** 4-1-4, extensive summer session. **Full-time faculty:** 125 total; 78% have terminal degrees, 5% minority, 30% women. **Part-time faculty:** 85 total; 12% have terminal degrees, 5% minority, 48% women. **Class size:** 47% < 20, 52% 20-39, 2% 40-49, less than 1% 50-99. **Special facilities:** Planetarium, Civil War museum, undergraduate science research laboratory, computer/mathematics research laboratory, greenhouse, arboretum, Audubon Sanctuary, geographic information systems (GIS) lab, 24-hour cyber-cafe.

Freshman class profile. 4,000 applied, 3,036 admitted, 598 enrolled.

Mid 50% test scores		**Rank in top tenth:**	18%
SAT verbal:	500-630	**End year in good standing:**	85%
SAT math:	500-620	**Return as sophomores:**	75%
ACT:	21-27	**Out-of-state:**	71%
GPA 3.50 or higher:	36%	**Live on campus:**	85%
GPA 3.0-3.49:	33%	**Fraternities:**	19%
GPA 2.0-2.99:	30%	**Sororities:**	27%
Rank in top quarter:	43%		

Basis for selection. High school GPA (calculated based on academic courses) and test scores most important. Interview recommended; audition recommended for music and theater. **Homeschooled:** Transcript of courses and grades required.

High school preparation. College-preparatory program recommended. 18 units recommended. Recommended units include English 4, mathematics 3, social studies 3, science 3 (laboratory 2), foreign language 2 and academic electives 3.

2006-2007 Annual costs. Tuition/fees (projected): $23,650. Room/board: $6,800. Books/supplies: $1,200. Personal expenses: $1,500.

2005-2006 Financial aid. **Need-based:** 519 full-time freshmen applied for aid; 428 were judged to have need; 427 of these received aid. Average need met was 69%. Average scholarship/grant was $10,520; average loan $4,554. 64% of total undergraduate aid awarded as scholarships/grants, 36% as loans/jobs. **Non-need-based:** Awarded to 748 full-time undergraduates, including 204 freshmen. Scholarships awarded for academics, alumni affiliation, art, leadership, minority status, music/drama, religious affiliation.

Application procedures. **Admission:** No deadline. $25 fee, may be waived for applicants with need. Application may be submitted online. Admission notification on a rolling basis. Must reply by May 1 or within 2 week(s) if notified thereafter. **Financial aid:** Priority date 2/15; no closing date. FAFSA required. Applicants notified on a rolling basis starting 3/1.

Academics. All students take the Heritage Seminar Series, a 2-course combination of oral and written communication skills and cross-cultural studies. Students must also complete a Carthage symposium and a senior thesis in their major. **Special study options:** Accelerated study, combined bachelor's/graduate degree, cooperative education, cross-registration, double major, dual enrollment of high school students, honors, independent study, internships, liberal arts/career combination, student-designed major, study abroad, teacher certification program, Washington semester, weekend college. **Credit/placement by examination:** AP, CLEP, IB, institutional tests. 32 credit hours maximum toward bachelor's degree. **Support services:** Preadmission summer program, reduced course load, study skills assistance, tutoring, writing center.

Majors. **Area/ethnic studies:** Women's. **Biology:** General. **Business:** Accounting, business admin, marketing. **Communications:** General. **Computer sciences:** Computer science, information technology. **Conservation:** Environmental science. **Education:** General, elementary, learning disabled, mentally handicapped, music, physical, special. **English:** English lit. **Foreign languages:** French, German, Spanish. **Health:** Athletic training. **History:** General. **Interdisciplinary:** Classical/archaeology, neuroscience. **Math:** General. **Parks/recreation:** Exercise sciences. **Philosophy/religion:** Philosophy, religion. **Physical sciences:** Chemistry, physics. **Protective services:** Criminal justice. **Psychology:** General. **Public administration:** Social work. **Social sciences:** General, economics, geography, international economics, political science, sociology. **Visual/performing arts:** Art, commercial/advertising art, dramatic, music performance, piano/organ, studio arts, voice/opera.

Most popular majors. Business/marketing 27%, education 9%, psychology 6%, visual/performing arts 6%.

Computing on campus. 150 workstations in dormitories, library, computer center, student center. Dormitories wired for high-speed internet access and linked to campus network. Commuter students can connect to campus network. Online library, helpline, repair service, student web hosting, wireless network available.

Student life. **Freshman orientation:** Mandatory. Preregistration for classes offered. **Policies:** Worship opportunities available on Sunday evening, chapel services offered Monday, Wednesday and Friday. Freshmen permitted cars on campus. **Housing:** Guaranteed on-campus for freshmen. Coed dorms, single-sex dorms, fraternity/sorority housing available. $300 fully refundable deposit, deadline 5/1. **Activities:** Bands, choral groups, dance, drama, film society, literary magazine, music ensembles, musical theater, opera, radio station, student government, student newspaper, symphony orchestra, Fellowship of Christian Athletes, black student union, international students association, United Women of Color, Carthage Christian Fellowship, Circle K International, College Republicans, Young Democrats.

Athletics. NCAA. **Intercollegiate:** Baseball M, basketball, cross-country, football (tackle) M, golf, soccer, softball W, swimming, tennis, track and field, volleyball, water polo. **Intramural:** Basketball, football (non-tackle), racquetball, soccer, softball, tennis, volleyball. **Team name:** Red Men, Lady Reds.

Student services. Adult student services, alcohol/substance abuse counseling, campus ministries, career counseling, student employment services, financial aid counseling, health services, personal counseling, placement for graduates.

Contact. E-mail: admissions@carthage.edu
Phone: (262) 551-6000 Toll-free number: (800) 351-4058
Fax: (262) 551-5762
Brenda Poggendorf, Vice President for Enrollment, Carthage College, 2001 Alford Park Drive, Kenosha, WI 53140-1994

Columbia College of Nursing
Milwaukee, Wisconsin
www.ccon.edu **CB code: 3409**

- Private 4-year nursing college
- Commuter campus in very large city
- 259 degree-seeking undergraduates
- SAT or ACT (ACT writing optional) required

General. Founded in 1901. Regionally accredited. Joint bachelor's degree in nursing awarded with Mount Mary College. **Degrees:** 85 bachelor's awarded. **Location:** 90 miles from Chicago. **Calendar:** Semester, limited summer session. **Full-time faculty:** 14 total. **Part-time faculty:** 5 total. **Class size:** 23% < 20, 15% 20-39, 38% 40-49, 23% 50-99.

Basis for selection. Class rank, high school GPA, test scores important. **Learning Disabled:** All students must meet Technical Standards for Admission to and Progression in the Nursing Porgram.

High school preparation. 3 units required. Required and recommended units include English 4, mathematics 1-2, science 2-3 and foreign language 2. Algebra required. Chemistry, biology required as science units.

2006-2007 Annual costs. Tuition/fees (projected): $18,600. Room/board: $5,000. Books/supplies: $734. Personal expenses: $1,234.

2005-2006 Financial aid. Non-need-based: Scholarships awarded for academics, minority status. **Additional information:** Students must apply to and meet financial aid requirements of Carroll College.

Application procedures. Admission: No deadline. $25 fee, may be waived for applicants with need. Application may be submitted online. Admission notification on a rolling basis beginning on or about 10/1. Students submit application to Mt. Mary College and must fulfill its requirements for admission. **Financial aid:** No deadline. FAFSA required. Applicants notified on a rolling basis starting 2/15; must reply by 5/1 or within 2 week(s) of notification.

Academics. Students generally complete first 2 years on Mt. Mary campus and last 2 years on Columbia campus. **Special study options:** Accelerated study, combined bachelor's/graduate degree, cooperative education, double major, ESL, honors, independent study, study abroad. Cultural immersion options. **Credit/placement by examination:** AP, CLEP, SAT, ACT, institutional tests. **Support services:** Learning center, pre-admission summer program, reduced course load, remedial instruction, study skills assistance, tutoring, writing center.

Majors. Health: Nursing (RN).

Computing on campus. 18 workstations in library, computer center. Commuter students can connect to campus network.

Student life. Freshman orientation: Mandatory. Preregistration for classes offered. **Policies:** Freshmen permitted cars on campus. **Housing:** Single-sex dorms available. Freshmen and sophomores guaranteed housing on Mt. Mary or Carroll College campuses. Juniors and seniors have the option to live in Columbia College housing. Apartments for married students and fraternity housing for undergraduates available on the Carroll Campus. **Activities:** Bands, choral groups, dance, drama, literary magazine, music ensembles, musical theater, radio station, student government, student newspaper, student nursing organization, black student organization, campus ministry, Amnesty International, international student groups.

Athletics. NCAA. **Intercollegiate:** Basketball W, cross-country W, diving W, golf W, soccer W, softball W, swimming W, tennis W, track and field W, volleyball W. **Intramural:** Badminton W, basketball W, bowling W, golf W, soccer W, softball W, swimming W, table tennis W, tennis W, volleyball W.

Student services. Alcohol/substance abuse counseling, campus ministries, career counseling, financial aid counseling, health services, minority student services, personal counseling, placement for graduates.

Contact. E-mail: admiss@mtmary.edu
Phone: (414) 256-1219 Toll-free number: (800) 321-6265
Fax: (414) 256-0180
Ronda Bond, Admissions Counselor, Mount Mary College, Columbia College of Nursing, Mount Mary College Enrollment Office; 2900 North Menominee River Parkway, Milwaukee, WI 53222-4597

Concordia University Wisconsin
Mequon, Wisconsin
www.cuw.edu **CB code: 1139**

- Private 4-year university and liberal arts college affiliated with Lutheran Church - Missouri Synod
- Residential campus in large town
- 3,650 degree-seeking undergraduates: 46% part-time, 64% women, 13% African American, 1% Asian American, 3% Hispanic American, 1% Native American, 1% international
- 1,436 graduate students
- 84% of applicants admitted
- ACT (writing optional) required
- 61% graduate within 6 years; 19% enter graduate study

General. Founded in 1881. Regionally accredited. **Degrees:** 483 bachelor's, 23 associate awarded; master's, doctoral offered. **Location:** 15 miles from Milwaukee. **Calendar:** 4-1-4, limited summer session. **Full-time faculty:** 89 total; 70% have terminal degrees, 6% minority, 40% women. **Part-time faculty:** 110 total; 60% have terminal degrees, 62% women. **Class size:** 65% < 20, 31% 20-39, 4% 40-49, less than 1% 50-99. **Special facilities:** Access to Lake Michigan.

Freshman class profile. 1,274 applied, 1,076 admitted, 386 enrolled.

Mid 50% test scores		**Rank in top tenth:**	19%
ACT:	19-26	**Return as sophomores:**	80%
GPA 3.50 or higher:	41%	**Out-of-state:**	33%
GPA 3.0-3.49:	28%	**Live on campus:**	90%
GPA 2.0-2.99:	29%	**International:**	1%
Rank in top quarter:	38%		

Basis for selection. School achievement record and test scores important. Essay, interview recommended; audition recommended for music.

High school preparation. 16 units required. Required and recommended units include English 3-4, mathematics 2-3, social studies 2, science 2, foreign language 2 and academic electives 5. Two liberal arts required.

2005-2006 Annual costs. Tuition/fees: $17,280. Room/board: $6,540. Books/supplies: $750. Personal expenses: $1,700.

2005-2006 Financial aid. Need-based: 373 full-time freshmen applied for aid; 300 were judged to have need; 300 of these received aid. Average need met was 78%. Average scholarship/grant was $10,099; average loan $4,860. 62% of total undergraduate aid awarded as scholarships/grants, 38% as loans/jobs. **Non-need-based:** Scholarships awarded for academics, alumni affiliation, music/drama, religious affiliation.

Application procedures. Admission: Priority date 5/1; deadline 8/15. $35 fee, may be waived for applicants with need. Application may be submitted online. Admission notification on a rolling basis beginning on or about 10/15. **Financial aid:** Priority date 5/1; no closing date. FAFSA, institutional form required. Applicants notified on a rolling basis starting 1/15; must reply within 3 week(s) of notification.

Academics. Special study options: Accelerated study, combined bachelor's/graduate degree, cross-registration, distance learning, double major, dual enrollment of high school students, ESL, exchange student, independent study, internships, liberal arts/career combination, student-designed major, study abroad, teacher certification program, weekend college. Cooperative programs with Cardinal Stritch University, Marquette University, and Milwaukee Institute of Art and Design. **Credit/placement by examination:** AP, CLEP, IB, institutional tests. 15 credit hours maximum toward associate degree, 30 toward bachelor's. **Support services:** Learning center, reduced course load, remedial instruction, tutoring, writing center.

Majors. Biology: General. **Business:** General, accounting, business admin, finance, international finance, marketing. **Communications:** General, broadcast journalism, digital media, media studies. **Computer sciences:** General.

Education: General, art, biology, business, early childhood, elementary, English, health, history, kindergarten/preschool, mathematics, middle, multi-level teacher, music, physical, science, secondary, social science, social studies, Spanish. **English:** English lit. **Foreign languages:** German, Spanish. **Health:** Athletic training, clinical/medical social work, health services, medical radiologic technology/radiation therapy, nursing (RN). **History:** General. **Legal studies:** Prelaw. **Liberal arts:** Arts/sciences, humanities. **Math:** General. **Philosophy/religion:** Religion. **Protective services:** Criminal justice. **Psychology:** General. **Public administration:** Social work. **Social sciences:** Economics. **Theology:** Bible, missionary, pastoral counseling, preministerial, religious ed, sacred music, theology, youth ministry. **Visual/performing arts:** Art, commercial/advertising art, graphic design, illustration, interior design, music performance, photography, piano/organ.

Most popular majors. Business/marketing 38%, education 16%, health sciences 15%, legal studies 11%.

Computing on campus. 200 workstations in dormitories, library, computer center, student center. Dormitories wired for high-speed internet access and linked to campus network. Commuter students can connect to campus network. Online library, helpline, repair service available.

Student life. Freshman orientation: Available. Preregistration for classes offered. Held before start of fall semester, includes sessions for parents. **Policies:** Lutheran church services available every Sunday. Chapel services held daily. Freshmen permitted cars on campus. **Housing:** Single-sex dorms, substance-free housing available. $160 deposit, deadline 4/15. **Activities:** Bands, choral groups, dance, drama, music ensembles, musical theater, radio station, student government, student newspaper, International student services and center, Jeremiah Project, Servant Events, Campus Ministry.

Athletics. NCAA. **Intercollegiate:** Baseball M, basketball, cross-country, football (tackle) M, golf, soccer, softball W, tennis, track and field, volleyball, wrestling M. **Intramural:** Basketball, soccer, softball, table tennis, tennis, volleyball. **Team name:** Falcons.

Student services. Adult student services, alcohol/substance abuse counseling, campus ministries, career counseling, student employment services, financial aid counseling, health services, minority student services, personal counseling, placement for graduates, veterans' counselor. **Physically disabled:** Services for hearing impaired.

Contact. E-mail: admission@cuw.edu
Phone: (262) 243-5700 Fax: (262) 243-4545
Kenneth Gaschk, Vice President of Enrollment Services, Concordia University Wisconsin, 12800 North Lake Shore Drive, Mequon, WI 53097

DeVry University: Milwaukee
Milwaukee, Wisconsin

- For-profit 4-year university
- Commuter campus
- 73 degree-seeking undergraduates: 62% part-time, 67% women, 55% African American, 1% Asian American, 7% Hispanic American, 1% Native American
- 142 graduate students

General. Calendar: Semester. **Full-time faculty:** 1 total; 100% women. **Part-time faculty:** 16 total; 6% minority, 19% women.

Basis for selection. Interview important.

2005-2006 Annual costs. Tuition/fees: $12,000. Books/supplies: $1,250. Personal expenses: $1,740.

Application procedures. Admission: No deadline. $50 fee. Admission notification on a rolling basis. **Financial aid:** Applicants notified on a rolling basis.

Academics. Special study options: Accelerated study, cooperative education, distance learning. **Credit/placement by examination:** CLEP.

Majors. Business: Business admin. **Computer sciences:** General.

Contact. Phone: (414) 278-7677
DeVry University: Milwaukee, 100 East Wisconsin Avenue, Suite 2550, Milwaukee, WI 53202

Edgewood College
Madison, Wisconsin — **CB member**
www.edgewood.edu — **CB code: 1202**

- Private 4-year liberal arts college affiliated with Roman Catholic Church
- Commuter campus in small city
- 1,826 degree-seeking undergraduates: 21% part-time, 73% women, 2% African American, 2% Asian American, 2% Hispanic American, 1% international
- 487 degree-seeking graduate students
- 81% of applicants admitted
- SAT or ACT required
- 49% graduate within 6 years

General. Founded in 1927. Regionally accredited. **Degrees:** 343 bachelor's awarded; master's, doctoral offered. **Location:** 82 miles from Milwaukee, 140 miles from Chicago, Illinois. **Calendar:** 4-1-4, limited summer session. **Full-time faculty:** 100 total; 81% have terminal degrees, 7% minority, 44% women. **Part-time faculty:** 159 total; 31% have terminal degrees, 6% minority, 54% women. **Class size:** 69% < 20, 30% 20-39, less than 1% 40-49, less than 1% 50-99. **Special facilities:** Science center, biological research station, nursery school.

Freshman class profile. 1,035 applied, 835 admitted, 353 enrolled.

Mid 50% test scores		**Rank in top tenth:**	11%
ACT:	20-24	**Return as sophomores:**	74%
GPA 3.50 or higher:	39%	**Out-of-state:**	8%
GPA 3.0-3.49:	34%	**Live on campus:**	71%
GPA 2.0-2.99:	27%	**International:**	2%
Rank in top quarter:	34%		

Basis for selection. High school transcript and test scores most important.

High school preparation. College-preparatory program recommended. 16 units recommended. Recommended units include English 4, mathematics 2, social studies 2, history 1, science 2 (laboratory 1) and foreign language 2.

2005-2006 Annual costs. Tuition/fees: $17,000. Room/board: $5,862. Books/supplies: $750. Personal expenses: $1,968.

2004-2005 Financial aid. Need-based: 47% of total undergraduate aid awarded as scholarships/grants, 53% as loans/jobs. **Non-need-based:** Scholarships awarded for academics, alumni affiliation, art, leadership, minority status, music/drama, religious affiliation. **Additional information:** Auditions required for music scholarships, portfolios required for fine arts scholarships, essays required for a number of institutional scholarships, including AHANA Student Advancement Award, Alumni Association Scholarship, O'Connor Memorial Scholarship.

Application procedures. Admission: Closing date 8/26 (receipt date). $25 fee, may be waived for applicants with need. Application may be submitted online. Admission notification on a rolling basis beginning on or about 9/1. **Financial aid:** Priority date 3/15; no closing date. FAFSA, institutional form required. Applicants notified on a rolling basis starting 3/30; must reply within 2 week(s) of notification.

Academics. Special study options: Accelerated study, cross-registration, distance learning, double major, dual enrollment of high school students, honors, independent study, internships, liberal arts/career combination, student-designed major, study abroad, teacher certification program, weekend college. **Credit/placement by examination:** AP, CLEP, IB, institutional tests. 30 credit hours maximum toward associate degree, 60 toward bachelor's. **Support services:** Learning center, reduced course load, remedial instruction, study skills assistance, tutoring, writing center.

Majors. Area/ethnic studies: American. **Biology:** General. **Business:** General, accounting, business admin, finance, management information systems, market research. **Communications:** Media studies. **Communications technology:** Graphics. **Computer sciences:** General, information systems. **Education:** General, art, biology, business, chemistry, early childhood, elementary, English, foreign languages, French, history, kindergarten/preschool, mathematics, middle, music, science, secondary, social science, Spanish, special. **English:** English lit. **Foreign languages:** French, Spanish. **Health:** Art therapy, cytotechnology, nursing (RN). **History:** General. **Interdisciplinary:** Natural sciences. **Liberal arts:** Arts/sciences. **Math:** General. **Philosophy/religion:** Religion. **Physical sciences:** Chemistry. **Protective services:** Criminal justice. **Psychology:** General. **Social sciences:** General, economics, international relations, political science, sociology. **Theology:** Religious ed. **Visual/performing arts:** General, art, commercial/advertising art.

Most popular majors. Business/marketing 18%, education 25%, health sciences 13%, psychology 11%, visual/performing arts 9%.

Computing on campus. 100 workstations in dormitories, library, computer center, student center. Dormitories wired for high-speed internet access and linked to campus network. Commuter students can connect to campus network. Online course registration, online library, helpline available.

Student life. **Freshman orientation:** Available. Preregistration for classes offered. 3-day program in the fall. **Housing:** Coed dorms, single-sex dorms, special housing for disabled, apartments available. $150 fully refundable deposit. Student leadership house. **Activities:** Bands, choral groups, drama, literary magazine, music ensembles, musical theater, student government, student newspaper, symphony orchestra, international student organization, Student Business Association, Student Nurse Association, Amnesty International, Habitat for Humanity, Student Association of Various Ethnicities; on-campus coffee house provides alternative environment.

Athletics. NCAA. **Intercollegiate:** Baseball M, basketball, cross-country, golf, soccer, softball W, tennis, volleyball W. **Intramural:** Basketball, bowling, diving, skiing, softball, swimming, table tennis, volleyball, weight lifting. **Team name:** Eagles.

Student services. Campus ministries, career counseling, student employment services, financial aid counseling, health services, minority student services, personal counseling, placement for graduates, veterans' counselor.

Contact. E-mail: admissions@edgewood.edu
Phone: (608) 663-2294 Toll-free number: (800) 444-4861 ext. 2294
Fax: (608) 663-3291
Christine Benedict, Director of Undergraduate Admissions, Edgewood College, 1000 Edgewood College Drive, Madison, WI 53711-1997

Herzing College

Madison, Wisconsin
www.herzing.edu **CB code: 0388**

- For-profit 3-year business and technical college
- Commuter campus in small city
- 652 degree-seeking undergraduates
- Interview required

General. Founded in 1948. Accredited by ACCSCT. **Degrees:** 109 bachelor's, 181 associate awarded. **Location:** 90 miles from Milwaukee, 150 miles from Chicago. **Calendar:** Semester, extensive summer session. **Full-time faculty:** 15 total. **Part-time faculty:** 31 total.

Freshman class profile. 514 enrolled.

Basis for selection. Open admission. Interview and placement test required prior to acceptance. **Homeschooled:** State high school equivalency certificate required. High school diploma or GED required before enrolling. **Learning Disabled:** Must provide documentation to counselor, prior to starting classes.

2006-2007 Annual costs. For associate degrees: $11,475 for computer, electronics and telecommunications program, $11,385 for CAD drafting program, $12,445 for computer information systems program, $12,530 for computer network technology program. For bachelor's degrees: $10,875 for technology management program, $12,445 for computer information systems program.

Application procedures. **Admission:** No deadline. No application fee. Admission notification on a rolling basis. **Financial aid:** No deadline. FAFSA, institutional form required. Applicants notified on a rolling basis.

Academics. Bachelors degree may be acquired in 3 years, associate degree in 1 year, 8 months. **Special study options:** Accelerated study, cooperative education, distance learning, honors, internships. **Credit/placement by examination:** AP, CLEP. **Support services:** Learning center, preadmission summer program, reduced course load, remedial instruction, study skills assistance, tutoring, writing center.

Majors. **Business:** Business admin. **Communications technology:** Animation/special effects. **Computer sciences:** Computer graphics, information technology, networking, programming. **Engineering technology:** Drafting, electrical. **Mechanic/repair:** Electronics/electrical.

Computing on campus. 300 workstations in library, computer center, student center. Online library, helpline, repair service, wireless network available.

Student life. **Freshman orientation:** Mandatory. **Policies:** Freshmen permitted cars on campus. **Activities:** Student government, student newspaper.

Student services. Adult student services, career counseling, student employment services, financial aid counseling, placement for graduates.

Contact. E-mail: info@msn.herzing.edu
Phone: (608) 249-6611 Toll-free number: (800) 582-1227
Fax: (608) 249-8593
Rebecca Abrams, Director of Admissions, Herzing College, 5218 East Terrace Drive, Madison, WI 53718

ITT Technical Institute: Green Bay

Green Bay, Wisconsin
www.itt-tech.edu

- For-profit 4-year technical college
- Small city

General. Accredited by ACICS. **Calendar:** Trimester.

Annual costs/financial aid. Tuition varies by program, $260-$368 per credit hour.

Contact. Phone: (920) 662-9000
Director of Recruitment, 470 Security Boulevard, Green Bay, WI 54313

ITT Technical Institute: Greenfield

Greenfield, Wisconsin
www.itt-tech.edu **CB code: 2706**

- For-profit 4-year technical college
- Commuter campus in large town

General. Accredited by ACICS. **Calendar:** Quarter.

Annual costs/financial aid. Tuition varies by program, $260-$368 per credit hour.

Contact. Phone: (414) 282-9494
Director of Recruitment, 6300 West Layton Avenue, Greenfield, WI 53220-4612

Lakeland College

Sheboygan, Wisconsin
www.lakeland.edu **CB code: 1393**

- Private 4-year liberal arts college affiliated with United Church of Christ
- Residential campus in small city
- 3,373 degree-seeking undergraduates
- 71% of applicants admitted
- SAT or ACT (ACT writing recommended) required

General. Founded in 1862. Regionally accredited. Evening, online, and graduate classes offered for nontraditional students at 7 in-state sites. Associate program available at Tokyo, Japan campus. **Degrees:** 712 bachelor's, 30 associate awarded; master's offered. **Location:** 60 miles from Milwaukee, 60 miles from Green Bay. **Calendar:** 4-4-1. Limited summer session. **Full-time faculty:** 55 total. **Part-time faculty:** 260 total. **Class size:** 69% < 20, 30% 20-39, 1% 40-49. **Special facilities:** Museum.

Freshman class profile. 872 applied, 617 admitted, 210 enrolled.

Mid 50% test scores		**Rank in top tenth:**	7%
SAT verbal:	390-500	**Out-of-state:**	15%
SAT math:	430-520	**Live on campus:**	90%
ACT:	18-23	**Fraternities:**	3%
Rank in top quarter:	23%	**Sororities:**	3%

Basis for selection. High school graduates who have an ACT composite score of 19, rank in the top half of class, and have a minimum high school GPA of 2.0. Essays are recommended.

High school preparation. Recommended units include English 4, mathematics 2, social studies 2, history 2, science 2, foreign language 2 and academic electives 2.

2006-2007 Annual costs. Tuition/fees (projected): $16,796. Room/board: $5,920. Books/supplies: $600. Personal expenses: $750.

2005-2006 Financial aid. **Need-based:** 46% of total undergraduate aid awarded as scholarships/grants, 54% as loans/jobs. **Non-need-based:** Scholarships awarded for academics.

Application procedures. **Admission:** No deadline. $20 fee, may be waived for applicants with need. Application may be submitted online. Admission notification on a rolling basis. **Financial aid:** Priority date 5/1, closing date 7/1. FAFSA, institutional form required. Applicants notified on a rolling basis starting 2/1; must reply within 2 week(s) of notification.

Academics. Applicants whose test scores reflect weakness in basic skills must take basic skills courses in freshman year. **Special study options:**

Combined bachelor's/graduate degree, cooperative education, distance learning, double major, dual enrollment of high school students, ESL, honors, independent study, internships, liberal arts/career combination, study abroad, teacher certification program. Engineering program with University of Wisconsin-Madison, nursing program with Bellin College of Nursing. **Credit/placement by examination:** AP, CLEP, IB, institutional tests. 32 credit hours maximum toward bachelor's degree. **Support services:** Learning center, reduced course load, remedial instruction, study skills assistance, tutoring, writing center.

Majors. **Biology:** General, biochemistry. **Business:** Accounting, business admin, international, marketing, nonprofit/public, resort management. **Computer sciences:** Computer science. **Education:** Elementary, kindergarten/preschool, middle, secondary. **English:** Composition. **Foreign languages:** German, Spanish. **History:** General. **Math:** General. **Philosophy/religion:** Religion. **Physical sciences:** Chemistry. **Protective services:** Law enforcement admin. **Psychology:** General. **Social sciences:** Sociology. **Visual/performing arts:** Art.

Most popular majors. Business/marketing 68%, computer/information sciences 19%, education 11%.

Computing on campus. 218 workstations in dormitories, library, computer center, student center. Dormitories wired for high-speed internet access and linked to campus network. Commuter students can connect to campus network. Online course registration, online library, helpline available.

Student life. **Freshman orientation:** Mandatory. Preregistration for classes offered. **Policies:** Freshmen permitted cars on campus. **Housing:** Guaranteed on-campus for freshmen. Coed dorms, single-sex dorms, special housing for disabled, apartments available. $50 deposit. Honor apartments and apartments for students with senior standing available. **Activities:** Concert band, choral groups, drama, music ensembles, student government, student newspaper, campus activities board, student association, Black student union, Mortar Board, Global Students Association, business fraternity, Inter-Greek Council.

Athletics. NCAA. **Intercollegiate:** Baseball M, basketball, cross-country, football (tackle) M, golf, soccer, softball W, tennis, track and field, volleyball W, wrestling M. **Team name:** Muskies.

Student services. Alcohol/substance abuse counseling, campus ministries, career counseling, services for economically disadvantaged, student employment services, financial aid counseling, health services, on-campus daycare, personal counseling, placement for graduates, veterans' counselor. **Physically disabled:** Services for visually impaired.

Contact. E-mail: admissions@lakeland.edu
Phone: (920) 565-1217 Toll-free number: (800) 242-3347
Fax: (920) 565-1206
Nathan Dehne, Director of Admissions, Lakeland College, Box 359, Sheboygan, WI 53082-0359

Lawrence University

Appleton, Wisconsin — **CB member**
www.lawrence.edu — **CB code: 1398**

- Private 4-year music and liberal arts college
- Residential campus in small city
- 1,405 degree-seeking undergraduates: 3% part-time, 54% women, 2% African American, 3% Asian American, 3% Hispanic American, 7% international
- 68% of applicants admitted
- Application essay required
- 75% graduate within 6 years; 23% enter graduate study

General. Founded in 1847. Regionally accredited. **Degrees:** 294 bachelor's awarded. **Location:** 100 miles from Milwaukee, 30 miles from Green Bay. **Calendar:** Trimester. **Full-time faculty:** 144 total; 99% have terminal degrees, 8% minority, 33% women. **Part-time faculty:** 32 total; 31% have terminal degrees, 6% minority, 47% women. **Class size:** 71% < 20, 25% 20-39, 2% 40-49, 2% 50-99. **Special facilities:** Laser physics laboratory, 250 MHz nuclear magnetic resonance spectrometer, physics/computational graphics laboratory, art galleries.

Freshman class profile. 2,060 applied, 1,407 admitted, 401 enrolled.

Mid 50% test scores		**Rank in top tenth:**	41%
SAT verbal:	590-700	**Return as sophomores:**	87%
SAT math:	600-690	**Out-of-state:**	59%
ACT:	25-30	**Live on campus:**	99%
GPA 3.50 or higher:	52%	**International:**	4%
GPA 3.0-3.49:	32%	**Fraternities:**	23%
GPA 2.0-2.99:	16%	**Sororities:**	10%
Rank in top quarter:	72%		

Basis for selection. GED not accepted. Strength of curriculum, school achievement record most important. Recommendations, out-of-class activities, test scores considered. Music applicants judged on musicianship, teacher's recommendations, and academic ability. Interview recommended; portfolio recommended for studio art. Audition required for conservatory of music study. **Homeschooled:** Require some standardized test results, evidence of coursework completed and level of performance, letters of recommendation, and GED if applicable.

High school preparation. 16 units required. Required and recommended units include English 4, mathematics 3, social studies 2, history 2, science 3 and foreign language 2. Strong musical preparation required of music applicants.

2006-2007 Annual costs. Tuition/fees: $29,598. Room/board: $6,382. Books/supplies: $600. Personal expenses: $1,005.

2005-2006 Financial aid. **Need-based:** 318 full-time freshmen applied for aid; 250 were judged to have need; 250 of these received aid. Average need met was 100%. Average scholarship/grant was $17,080; average loan $4,510. 72% of total undergraduate aid awarded as scholarships/grants, 28% as loans/jobs. **Non-need-based:** Awarded to 436 full-time undergraduates, including 125 freshmen. Scholarships awarded for academics, alumni affiliation, minority status, music/drama, state residency. **Additional information:** The first $1,000 (aggregate) of independently-sponsored scholarships received by a needy student will reduce student's loan or work-study commitment. Half of scholarships in excess of $1,000 will offset loan or work-study and the other half will reduce institutional grant funding.

Application procedures. **Admission:** Closing date 1/15 (postmark date). $40 fee, may be waived for applicants with need. Application may be submitted online. Admission notification 4/1. Must reply by 5/1. **Financial aid:** Priority date 3/15; no closing date. FAFSA, institutional form required. Applicants notified on a rolling basis starting 3/15; must reply by 5/1 or within 2 week(s) of notification.

Academics. As an adjunct to a major, students may pursue 1 interdisciplinary area of study: biomedical ethics, international studies, neuroscience, or cognitive science. **Special study options:** Combined bachelor's/graduate degree, double major, ESL, independent study, internships, liberal arts/career combination, student-designed major, study abroad, teacher certification program, urban semester, Washington semester. Study abroad programs in 12 countries; marine biology term, marine geology term, Oak Ridge science semester; urban semester in Chicago; Newberry Library Program in humanities; environmental studies and forestry programs with Duke University; occupational therapy program with Washington University, St. Louis. **Credit/placement by examination:** AP, CLEP, IB, institutional tests. 30 credit hours maximum toward bachelor's degree. Course credit awarded for scores of at least 5 on International Baccalaureate examinations. Sophomore status granted for completion of full IB diploma. **Support services:** Learning center, reduced course load, study skills assistance, tutoring, writing center.

Majors. **Area/ethnic studies:** Asian, Chinese, East Asian, Japanese, Russian/Slavic, women's. **Biology:** General, animal behavior, aquatic, biochemistry, Biochemistry/biophysics and molecular biology, botany, cellular/anatomical, ecology, embryology, environmental, evolutionary, genetics, marine, microbiology, molecular biochemistry, zoology. **Business:** International finance, management information systems. **Computer sciences:** General. **Conservation:** Environmental studies. **Education:** Music. **English:** American lit, British lit, English lit. **Foreign languages:** Ancient Greek, Biblical, Chinese, classics, East Asian, French, German, Japanese, Latin, linguistics, Russian, Spanish. **Health:** Predentistry, premedicine, prepharmacy, preveterinary. **History:** General. **Interdisciplinary:** Biological/physical sciences, cognitive science, global studies, intercultural, math/computer science, natural sciences, neuroscience. **Legal studies:** Prelaw. **Liberal arts:** Arts/sciences. **Math:** General. **Philosophy/religion:** Philosophy, religion. **Physical sciences:** Chemistry, geology, geophysics, physics, theoretical physics. **Psychology:** General. **Social sciences:** Anthropology, economics, political science. **Visual/performing arts:** Art, art history/conservation, dramatic, jazz, music history, music performance, music theory/composition, piano/organ, studio arts, voice/opera.

Most popular majors. Biology 7%, English 8%, foreign language 9%, history 7%, interdisciplinary studies 8%, psychology 8%, social sciences 13%, visual/performing arts 23%.

Computing on campus. 175 workstations in dormitories, library, computer center. Dormitories wired for high-speed internet access and linked to campus network. Commuter students can connect to campus network. Online course registration, online library, helpline, repair service, wireless network available.

Student life. Freshman orientation: Mandatory. Preregistration for classes offered. New student orientation held 5 days prior to start of fall classes. **Policies:** Honor code in effect. All single students are required to live in university residence halls for 4 years. Freshmen permitted cars on campus. **Housing:** Guaranteed on-campus for all undergraduates. Coed dorms, single-sex dorms, apartments, substance-free housing available. 14 theme/group houses available. **Activities:** Bands, choral groups, dance, drama, film society, literary magazine, music ensembles, musical theater, opera, radio station, student government, student newspaper, symphony orchestra, Lawrence Christian Fellowship, Lawrence International, Chavurah, Black Organization of Students, Latin American student organization, social service groups, international, political and academic clubs, professional sororities and fraternities.

Athletics. NCAA. **Intercollegiate:** Baseball M, basketball, cross-country, diving, fencing, football (tackle) M, golf M, ice hockey M, lacrosse, soccer, softball W, swimming, tennis, track and field, volleyball W, wrestling M. **Intramural:** Badminton, basketball, bowling, cross-country, diving, fencing, football (non-tackle), golf, handball, lacrosse, racquetball, rowing (crew), skiing, soccer, softball, squash, swimming, table tennis, tennis, track and field, volleyball, water polo. **Team name:** Vikings.

Student services. Alcohol/substance abuse counseling, career counseling, student employment services, financial aid counseling, health services, minority student services, personal counseling, placement for graduates. **Physically disabled:** Services for visually, speech, hearing impaired.

Contact. E-mail: excel@lawrence.edu
Phone: (920) 832-6500 Toll-free number: (800) 227-0982
Fax: (920) 832-6782
Steven Syverson, Dean of Admissions and Financial Aid, Lawrence University, Box 599, Appleton, WI 54912-0599

Maranatha Baptist Bible College

Watertown, Wisconsin
www.mbbc.edu **CB code: 2732**

- Private 4-year Bible college affiliated with Baptist faith
- Residential campus in large town
- 786 degree-seeking undergraduates: 5% part-time, 54% women, 2% African American, 1% Asian American, 1% Hispanic American
- 47 degree-seeking graduate students
- 66% of applicants admitted
- ACT (writing optional), application essay required
- 50% graduate within 6 years; 10% enter graduate study

General. Founded in 1968. Regionally accredited. **Degrees:** 143 bachelor's, 18 associate awarded; master's offered. **ROTC:** Air Force. **Location:** 45 miles from Milwaukee, 38 miles from Madison. **Calendar:** Semester, limited summer session. **Full-time faculty:** 44 total; 27% have terminal degrees, 4% minority, 27% women. **Part-time faculty:** 28 total; 11% have terminal degrees, 43% women. **Class size:** 61% < 20, 27% 20-39, 4% 40-49, 6% 50-99, 2% >100.

Freshman class profile. 390 applied, 258 admitted, 223 enrolled.

Mid 50% test scores		**Return as sophomores:**	78%
ACT:	18-24	**Out-of-state:**	71%
End year in good standing:	86%	**Live on campus:**	75%

Basis for selection. Recommendations, religious commitment most important. Secondary school record, test scores, character also important. Class rank, essay considered. At-risk students placed on admissions probation. Audition required for fine arts.

High school preparation. College-preparatory program recommended. 18 units recommended. Recommended units include English 4, mathematics 3, social studies 3, history 3, science 3 and foreign language 2. One unit of keyboarding (typing or computer science) recommended.

2006-2007 Annual costs. Tuition/fees (projected): $9,110. Room/board: $5,200. Books/supplies: $600. Personal expenses: $1,700.

Financial aid. Non-need-based: Scholarships awarded for academics.

Application procedures. Admission: No deadline. $50 fee. Admission notification on a rolling basis. **Financial aid:** Priority date 3/1; no closing date. FAFSA required. Applicants notified on a rolling basis starting 2/1; must reply within 2 week(s) of notification.

Academics. Hands-on ministerial work available. **Special study options:** Distance learning, double major, dual enrollment of high school students, independent study, internships, liberal arts/career combination, study abroad, teacher certification program. **Credit/placement by examination:** AP, CLEP, institutional tests. 12 credit hours maximum toward associate degree, 12 toward bachelor's. Only 6 credits may be counted in any one field of study. **Support services:** Reduced course load, remedial instruction, study skills assistance, tutoring.

Majors. Biology: General. **Business:** Accounting/business management, business admin, management information systems, marketing, office management. **Education:** General, business, early childhood, elementary, English, history, mathematics, music, physical, science, secondary, social studies, speech. **Health:** Nursing (RN). **Liberal arts:** Humanities. **Theology:** Bible, missionary, pastoral counseling, sacred music, youth ministry. **Visual/performing arts:** Music pedagogy, music performance, piano/organ.

Most popular majors. Business/marketing 12%, education 39%, liberal arts 8%, philosophy/religious studies 38%.

Computing on campus. 120 workstations in dormitories, library, computer center. Dormitories wired for high-speed internet access and linked to campus network. Online library, repair service, student web hosting, wireless network available.

Student life. Freshman orientation: Mandatory. Preregistration for classes offered. Held Saturday through Tuesday before classes begin. **Policies:** Church attendance required. Religious observance required. Freshmen permitted cars on campus. **Housing:** Guaranteed on-campus for all undergraduates. Single-sex dorms available. $175 nonrefundable deposit. **Activities:** Concert band, choral groups, drama, music ensembles, musical theater, student government, symphony orchestra, annual missionary conferences, evangelistic meetings, bible conferences, artist series, public speaking, societies for ministry outreach.

Athletics. NCAA, NCCAA. **Intercollegiate:** Baseball M, basketball, cross-country, football (tackle) M, soccer, softball W, volleyball W, wrestling M. **Intramural:** Basketball, soccer W, volleyball. **Team name:** Crusaders.

Student services. Career counseling, health services, on-campus day-care, personal counseling, placement for graduates, veterans' counselor.

Contact. E-mail: admissions@mbbc.edu
Phone: (920) 261-9300 Toll-free number: (800) 611-1947
Fax: (920) 261-9109
James Harrison, Director of Admissions, Maranatha Baptist Bible College, 745 West Main Street, Watertown, WI 53094

Marian College of Fond du Lac

Fond du Lac, Wisconsin **CB member**
www.mariancollege.edu **CB code: 1443**

- Private 4-year liberal arts college affiliated with Roman Catholic Church
- Residential campus in large town
- 1,872 degree-seeking undergraduates: 29% part-time, 73% women, 4% African American, 1% Asian American, 1% Hispanic American, 1% Native American, 1% international
- 613 degree-seeking graduate students
- 86% of applicants admitted
- SAT or ACT (ACT writing optional) required

General. Founded in 1936. Regionally accredited. **Degrees:** 335 bachelor's awarded; master's, doctoral offered. **ROTC:** Army. **Location:** 60 miles from Milwaukee, 65 miles from Green Bay. **Calendar:** Semester, extensive summer session. **Full-time faculty:** 78 total; 60% have terminal degrees, 9% minority, 42% women. **Part-time faculty:** 207 total; 12% have terminal degrees, 4% minority, 52% women. **Class size:** 71% < 20, 27% 20-39, 2% 40-49, less than 1% 50-99.

Freshman class profile. 766 applied, 661 admitted, 262 enrolled.

Mid 50% test scores		**Return as sophomores:**	72%
ACT:	18-22	**Out-of-state:**	10%
GPA 3.50 or higher:	26%	**Live on campus:**	74%
GPA 3.0-3.49:	29%	**International:**	2%
GPA 2.0-2.99:	41%	**Fraternities:**	9%
Rank in top quarter:	31%	**Sororities:**	6%
Rank in top tenth:	11%		

Basis for selection. School achievement record most important, followed by test scores. Applicants must meet 2 of following 3 criteria: minimum 2.0 high school GPA, top half of class, minimum ACT composite score of 18. Special admissions procedures required for nursing and education divisions. If admission criteria not met, students may be admitted on provisional basis. Interview, audition recommended.

High school preparation. College-preparatory program required. Required and recommended units include English 4, mathematics 2-3, history 1, science 1-2 (laboratory 1) and foreign language 2. Biology and chemistry prerequisite for nursing program.

2005-2006 Annual costs. Tuition/fees: $16,705. Room/board: $5,300. Books/supplies: $700. Personal expenses: $1,530.

2005-2006 Financial aid. **Need-based:** 261 full-time freshmen applied for aid; 221 were judged to have need; 221 of these received aid. Average need met was 90%. Average scholarship/grant was $9,521; average loan $3,488. 53% of total undergraduate aid awarded as scholarships/grants, 47% as loans/jobs. **Non-need-based:** Awarded to 1,059 full-time undergraduates, including 241 freshmen. Scholarships awarded for academics, ROTC, state residency.

Application procedures. **Admission:** Priority date 4/1; no deadline. $20 fee, may be waived for applicants with need. Application may be submitted online. Admission notification on a rolling basis. Must reply by May 1 or within 4 week(s) if notified thereafter. **Financial aid:** Priority date 3/1; no closing date. FAFSA, institutional form required. Applicants notified on a rolling basis starting 3/1; must reply within 4 week(s) of notification.

Academics. **Special study options:** Accelerated study, cooperative education, distance learning, double major, dual enrollment of high school students, honors, independent study, internships, liberal arts/career combination, student-designed major, study abroad, teacher certification program. Accelerated programs for adults in business, nursing, operation management, radiologic technology, administration of justice. **Credit/placement by examination:** AP, CLEP, IB, institutional tests. 30 credit hours maximum toward bachelor's degree. Writing sample required for placement and counseling. **Support services:** Learning center, pre-admission summer program, reduced course load, remedial instruction, study skills assistance, tutoring, writing center.

Majors. **Biology:** General. **Business:** General, accounting, business admin, human resources, managerial economics, marketing, operations. **Communications:** General, organizational. **Computer sciences:** Information technology. **Education:** General, art, biology, chemistry, early childhood, elementary, English, history, mathematics, music, science, secondary, social studies, Spanish. **English:** British lit, composition, English lit. **Foreign languages:** General, Spanish. **Health:** Art therapy, cytotechnology, nursing (RN), radiologic technology/medical imaging. **History:** General. **Liberal arts:** Arts/sciences. **Math:** General. **Parks/recreation:** Sports admin. **Physical sciences:** Chemistry. **Protective services:** Law enforcement admin. **Psychology:** General. **Public administration:** Social work. **Social sciences:** Political science, sociology. **Visual/performing arts:** Graphic design, studio arts.

Most popular majors. Business/marketing 36%, education 14%, health sciences 16%, security/protective services 10%.

Computing on campus. 275 workstations in dormitories, library, computer center, student center. Dormitories wired for high-speed internet access and linked to campus network. Commuter students can connect to campus network. Online course registration, online library, helpline available.

Student life. **Freshman orientation:** Mandatory. Preregistration for classes offered. **Policies:** Emphasis on community volunteer activity. Service transcript available for graduates. Freshmen permitted cars on campus. **Housing:** Guaranteed on-campus for all undergraduates. Coed dorms, special housing for disabled, apartments, fraternity/sorority housing, substance-free housing available. $100 deposit. Townhouses, penthouses and residential suites available. **Activities:** Bands, choral groups, drama, literary magazine, music ensembles, student government, student newspaper, symphony orchestra, Campus Ministry, Circle K, Eco club, Minority Students Association, Social Justice Committee, Multicultural Association.

Athletics. NCAA. **Intercollegiate:** Baseball M, basketball, golf, ice hockey M, soccer, softball W, tennis, volleyball W. **Intramural:** Badminton, basketball, bowling, football (non-tackle) M, skiing, softball M, tennis, volleyball. **Team name:** Sabre Cats.

Student services. Adult student services, alcohol/substance abuse counseling, campus ministries, career counseling, services for economically disadvantaged, student employment services, financial aid counseling, health services, minority student services, on-campus daycare, personal counseling, placement for graduates, women's services. **Physically disabled:** Services for visually, speech, hearing impaired.

Contact. E-mail: admissions@mariancollege.edu
Phone: (920) 923-7650 Toll-free number: (800) 262-7426
Fax: (920) 923-8755
Eric Peterson, Dean of Admission, Marian College of Fond du Lac, 45 South National Avenue, Fond du Lac, WI 54935-4699

Marquette University

Milwaukee, Wisconsin **CB member**
www.marquette.edu **CB code: 1448**

- Private 4-year university affiliated with Roman Catholic Church
- Residential campus in very large city
- 7,718 degree-seeking undergraduates: 4% part-time, 55% women, 5% African American, 4% Asian American, 4% Hispanic American, 2% international
- 3,467 degree-seeking graduate students
- 70% of applicants admitted
- SAT or ACT with writing, application essay required
- 80% graduate within 6 years; 29% enter graduate study

General. Founded in 1881. Regionally accredited. College in the Jesuit tradition. **Degrees:** 1,562 bachelor's awarded; master's, doctoral, first professional offered. **ROTC:** Army, Navy, Air Force. **Location:** Downtown. **Calendar:** Semester, extensive summer session. **Full-time faculty:** 592 total; 88% have terminal degrees, 11% minority, 36% women. **Part-time faculty:** 454 total; 47% have terminal degrees, 10% minority, 40% women. **Class size:** 44% < 20, 37% 20-39, 9% 40-49, 8% 50-99, 3% >100. **Special facilities:** St. Joan of Arc chapel.

Freshman class profile. 10,348 applied, 7,257 admitted, 1,784 enrolled.

Mid 50% test scores			
SAT verbal:	540-650	Rank in top tenth:	34%
SAT math:	540-660	Return as sophomores:	90%
ACT:	24-29	Out-of-state:	59%
Rank in top quarter:	65%	Live on campus:	93%
		International:	1%

Basis for selection. High school course selection, trend of performance, test scores and class rank most important. Essay, leadership, community service and extracurricular activities considered. Interview recommended. **Homeschooled:** Provide detailed list of curriculum and bibliography. Personal interview may be required.

High school preparation. 16 units required; 22 recommended. Required and recommended units include English 4, mathematics 2-4, social studies 2-3, science 2-3 (laboratory 2-3), foreign language 2 and academic electives 2-5. Algebra, geometry, and intermediate algebra required for arts & sciences, business administration and health sciences. Algebra and geometry required for nursing. 3 years of science recommended for premedical, predental and science majors. Students interested in international business strongly urged to complete 4 units of single foreign language.

2005-2006 Annual costs. Tuition/fees: $23,346. Room/board: $7,720. Books/supplies: $900. Personal expenses: $1,350.

2005-2006 Financial aid. **Need-based:** 1,421 full-time freshmen applied for aid; 1,093 were judged to have need; 1,091 of these received aid. Average need met was 78%. Average scholarship/grant was $14,044; average loan $3,696. 59% of total undergraduate aid awarded as scholarships/grants, 41% as loans/jobs. **Non-need-based:** Awarded to 1,046 full-time undergraduates, including 353 freshmen. Scholarships awarded for academics, athletics, leadership, music/drama, ROTC.

Application procedures. **Admission:** Closing date 12/1 (postmark date). $30 fee, may be waived for applicants with need. Application may be submitted online. Admission notification 1/31. Admission notification on a rolling basis. Must reply by May 1 or within 2 week(s) if notified thereafter. Application closing date for physical therapy and athletic training programs is 12/1 for direct admits. **Financial aid:** Priority date 2/1; no closing date. FAFSA required. Applicants notified on a rolling basis starting 4/1; must reply by 5/1 or within 3 week(s) of notification.

Academics. **Special study options:** Accelerated study, combined bachelor's/graduate degree, cooperative education, cross-registration, double major, dual enrollment of high school students, ESL, honors, internships, study abroad, teacher certification program, Washington semester, weekend college. **Credit/placement by examination:** AP, CLEP, IB, institutional tests. 30 credit hours maximum toward bachelor's degree. **Support services:** Learning center, pre-admission summer program, reduced course load, study skills assistance, tutoring, writing center.

Majors. **Area/ethnic studies:** African-American, women's. **Biology:** General, biochemistry, molecular. **Business:** Accounting, accounting technology, business admin, e-commerce, finance, human resources, international, management information systems, managerial economics, marketing. **Communications:** General, advertising, broadcast journalism, journalism, media studies, public relations. **Computer sciences:** Computer science, information systems. **Education:** Elementary, English, foreign languages, mathematics, middle, science, secondary, social science, social studies. **Engineering:** General, biomedical, civil, computer, electrical, environmental, manufacturing, mechanical. **Engineering technology:** Industrial management. **English:** Creative writing, English lit, speech/rhetoric. **Foreign languages:** Classics, French, German, Spanish. **Health:** Athletic training, audiology/speech pathology, clinical lab technology, nursing (RN), predentistry, premedicine. **History:** General. **Interdisciplinary:** Global studies, intercultural, math/computer science. **Legal studies:** Prelaw. **Math:** General, computational, statistics. **Parks/recreation:** Exercise sciences. **Philosophy/religion:** Philosophy, religion. **Physical sciences:** Chemistry, physics. **Psychology:** General. **Social sciences:** General, anthropology, criminology, economics, international relations, political science, sociology. **Visual/performing arts:** Dramatic.

Most popular majors. Biology 7%, business/marketing 22%, communications/journalism 14%, education 6%, engineering/engineering technologies 10%, health sciences 8%, social sciences 10%.

Computing on campus. 1,200 workstations in dormitories, library, computer center, student center. Dormitories wired for high-speed internet access and linked to campus network. Commuter students can connect to campus network. Online course registration, online library, helpline, student web hosting, wireless network available.

Student life. **Freshman orientation:** Available. Preregistration for classes offered. 4-day session held week before classes begin in fall. Summer preview program in June also available. **Policies:** Written policies concerning racial and sexual harassment, alcohol, drugs and safety. Students provided materials detailing policies and programs. Freshmen permitted cars on campus. **Housing:** Guaranteed on-campus for freshmen. Coed dorms, single-sex dorms, special housing for disabled, apartments, fraternity/sorority housing available. $200 nonrefundable deposit, deadline 5/1. Special housing for engineering, nursing, and honor students. **Activities:** Bands, choral groups, dance, drama, literary magazine, music ensembles, musical theater, radio station, student government, student newspaper, symphony orchestra, TV station, JUSTICE, College Republicans, College Democrats, Campus Crusade for Christ, Intervarsity, Latin American student organization.

Athletics. NCAA. **Intercollegiate:** Basketball, cheerleading, cross-country, golf M, soccer, tennis, track and field, volleyball W. **Intramural:** Badminton, basketball, football (tackle), golf, racquetball, soccer, softball, squash, tennis, track and field, volleyball, water polo, weight lifting. **Team name:** Golden Eagles.

Student services. Adult student services, alcohol/substance abuse counseling, campus ministries, career counseling, services for economically disadvantaged, student employment services, financial aid counseling, health services, minority student services, on-campus daycare, personal counseling, placement for graduates. **Physically disabled:** Services for visually, speech, hearing impaired.

Contact. E-mail: admissions@marquette.edu
Phone: (414) 288-7302 Toll-free number: (800) 222-6544
Fax: (414) 288-3764
Robert Blust, Dean of Undergraduate Admissions, Marquette University, PO Box 1881, Milwaukee, WI 53201-1881

Milwaukee Institute of Art & Design

Milwaukee, Wisconsin
www.miad.edu **CB code: 1506**

- Private 4-year art college
- Commuter campus in very large city

General. Founded in 1974. Regionally accredited. **Location:** Located in Milwaukee, Wisconsin. Located 90 miles from Chicago. **Calendar:** Semester.

Annual costs/financial aid. Tuition/fees (2005-2006): $22,350. Room/board: $6,750. Books/supplies: $1,650. Personal expenses: $1,624. Need-based financial aid available to full-time and part-time students.

Contact. Phone: (414) 291-8070
Director of Admissions, 273 East Erie Street, Milwaukee, WI 53202

Milwaukee School of Engineering

Milwaukee, Wisconsin **CB member**
www.msoe.edu **CB code: 1476**

- Private 4-year university
- Residential campus in very large city
- 2,092 degree-seeking undergraduates: 13% part-time, 17% women, 4% African American, 3% Asian American, 3% Hispanic American, 1% Native American, 2% international
- 223 degree-seeking graduate students
- 69% of applicants admitted
- SAT or ACT (ACT writing optional) required
- 55% graduate within 6 years; 42% enter graduate study

General. Founded in 1903. Regionally accredited. **Degrees:** 361 bachelor's, 3 associate awarded; master's offered. **ROTC:** Army, Navy, Air Force. **Location:** 72 miles from Chicago. **Calendar:** Quarter, limited summer session. **Full-time faculty:** 120 total; 65% have terminal degrees, 8% minority, 22% women. **Part-time faculty:** 94 total; 31% have terminal degrees, 12% minority, 30% women. **Class size:** 47% < 20, 53% 20-39. **Special facilities:** Laboratories for fluid power motion control, construction engineering, energy systems and rapid prototyping, software development.

Freshman class profile. 1,742 applied, 1,203 admitted, 456 enrolled.

Mid 50% test scores		**End year in good standing:**	79%
SAT verbal:	530-650	**Return as sophomores:**	81%
SAT math:	570-660	**Out-of-state:**	34%
ACT:	23-28	**Live on campus:**	83%
GPA 3.50 or higher:	47%	**International:**	1%
GPA 3.0-3.49:	38%	**Fraternities:**	4%
GPA 2.0-2.99:	15%	**Sororities:**	20%

Basis for selection. Admissions based on secondary school record and standardized test scores. **Homeschooled:** Transcript of courses and grades required. ACT or SAT scores required. **Learning Disabled:** Untimed standardized tests required.

High school preparation. College-preparatory program recommended. 10 units required. Required and recommended units include English 4, mathematics 4, science 2 (laboratory 2). For business and technical communication, mathematics units should include 1 algebra. For biomedical engineering, science units should include 1 biological science.

2006-2007 Annual costs. Tuition/fees (projected): $24,960. $1,140 technology package required for all first-year students. Room/board: $6,189. Books/supplies: $1,500. Personal expenses: $2,940.

2004-2005 Financial aid. **Need-based:** 412 full-time freshmen applied for aid; 369 were judged to have need; 368 of these received aid. Average need met was 72%. Average scholarship/grant was $13,919; average loan $2,702. 64% of total undergraduate aid awarded as scholarships/grants, 36% as loans/jobs. **Non-need-based:** Awarded to 399 full-time undergraduates, including 115 freshmen. Scholarships awarded for academics, ROTC. **Additional information:** More than 90 percent of full-time students receive financial assistance. More than 60 percent receive academic scholarships.

Application procedures. **Admission:** Priority date 2/1; no deadline. $25 fee, may be waived for applicants with need. Application may be submitted online. Admission notification on a rolling basis beginning on or about 10/1. **Financial aid:** Priority date 3/15; no closing date. FAFSA required. Applicants notified on a rolling basis starting 3/1; must reply within 2 week(s) of notification.

Academics. Average of 600 hours of laboratory experience for each program. **Special study options:** Combined bachelor's/graduate degree, distance learning, double major, dual enrollment of high school students, ESL, internships, study abroad. Bachelor of Science in business, mechanical engineering, and in electrical engineering with Lubeck University of Applied Sciences, Germany; exchange program with Czech Technical University, bachelor's or master's option in an engineering discipline and master's in environmental engineering. **Credit/placement by examination:** AP, CLEP, IB, SAT, ACT. **Support services:** Learning center, pre-admission summer program, reduced course load, study skills assistance, tutoring, writing center.

Majors. **Business:** General, business admin, construction management, international, management information systems. **Communications:** General. **Engineering:** Architectural, biomedical, computer, electrical, industrial, mechanical, software. **Engineering technology:** Electrical, mechanical. **English:** Technical writing. **Health:** Nursing (RN).

Most popular majors. Business/marketing 20%, engineering/engineering technologies 77%.

Computing on campus. PC or laptop required. 150 workstations in dormitories, library, computer center, student center. Dormitories wired for high-speed internet access and linked to campus network. Commuter students can connect to campus network. Online course registration, online library, helpline, repair service, student web hosting, wireless network available.

Student life. Freshman orientation: Available. Preregistration for classes offered. 3- to 4-day program. **Policies:** Freshmen permitted cars on campus. **Housing:** Guaranteed on-campus for freshmen. Coed dorms, apartments, fraternity/sorority housing, substance-free housing available. $75 fully refundable deposit, deadline 6/1. **Activities:** Pep band, choral groups, drama, literary magazine, radio station, student government, student newspaper, symphony orchestra, Inter-Varsity Christian Fellowship, residence hall association, Circle-K, Society of International Students, Asian Student Organization, Society of Hispanic Professional Engineers, National Society of Black Engineers, National Student Nurses Association, Campus Crusade for Christ.

Athletics. NCAA. **Intercollegiate:** Baseball M, basketball, cheerleading, cross-country, golf, ice hockey M, soccer, softball W, tennis, track and field, volleyball, wrestling M. **Intramural:** Basketball, football (non-tackle), soccer, softball, volleyball. **Team name:** Raiders.

Student services. Adult student services, alcohol/substance abuse counseling, campus ministries, career counseling, services for economically disadvantaged, student employment services, financial aid counseling, health services, minority student services, personal counseling, placement for graduates, veterans' counselor, women's services. **Physically disabled:** Services for visually, speech, hearing impaired. **Learning disabled:** Comprehensive services available.

Contact. E-mail: explore@msoe.edu
Phone: (414) 277-6763 Toll-free number: (800) 332-6763
Fax: (414) 277-7475
Paul Borens, Dean of Enrollment Management, Milwaukee School of Engineering, 1025 North Broadway, Milwaukee, WI 53202-3109

Mount Mary College

Milwaukee, Wisconsin
www.mtmary.edu **CB code: 1490**

- Private 4-year liberal arts college for women affiliated with Roman Catholic Church
- Commuter campus in very large city
- 1,346 degree-seeking undergraduates: 32% part-time, 98% women, 18% African American, 5% Asian American, 5% Hispanic American, 1% Native American, 1% international
- 234 degree-seeking graduate students
- 66% of applicants admitted
- SAT or ACT (ACT writing optional) required
- 47% graduate within 6 years; 10% enter graduate study

General. Founded in 1913. Regionally accredited. Open to all faiths. Small number of men admitted as part-time non-degree-seeking students and for joint nursing students with Columbia College of Nursing. **Degrees:** 164 bachelor's awarded; master's offered. **Location:** 7 miles from downtown. **Calendar:** Semester, limited summer session. **Full-time faculty:** 64 total; 64% have terminal degrees, 3% minority, 78% women. **Part-time faculty:** 134 total; 19% have terminal degrees, 5% minority, 78% women. **Class size:** 92% < 20, 13% 20-39, 1% 40-49, less than 1% 50-99. **Special facilities:** Historic costume collection, labyrinth.

Freshman class profile. 438 applied, 288 admitted, 160 enrolled.

Mid 50% test scores			
SAT verbal:	510-650	Rank in top quarter:	50%
SAT math:	400-600	Rank in top tenth:	22%
ACT:	16-22	End year in good standing:	73%
GPA 3.50 or higher:	30%	Return as sophomores:	65%
GPA 3.0-3.49:	32%	Out-of-state:	8%
GPA 2.0-2.99:	36%	Live on campus:	37%
		International:	2%

Basis for selection. Academic record, test scores and supplemental information are reviewed. Class rank, core curriculum, test scores and GPA important. Interview recommended and essay required for students who do not meet direct admission requirements. **Homeschooled:** Transcript of courses and grades required. **Learning Disabled:** Students encouraged to talk with Disabilities Coordinator, at least one semester prior to enrollment, to determine if reasonable accommodations can be made.

High school preparation. 16 units required. Required and recommended units include English 4, mathematics 2-3, social studies 2, history 2, science 2 (laboratory 2), foreign language 2 and academic electives 4.

2006-2007 Annual costs. Tuition/fees: $18,128. Room/board: $5,990. Books/supplies: $950. Personal expenses: $1,398.

2005-2006 Financial aid. Need-based: 125 full-time freshmen applied for aid; 115 were judged to have need; 115 of these received aid. Average need met was 72%. Average scholarship/grant was $9,679; average loan $3,113. 51% of total undergraduate aid awarded as scholarships/grants, 49% as loans/jobs. **Non-need-based:** Awarded to 188 full-time undergraduates, including 47 freshmen. Scholarships awarded for academics, alumni affiliation, art, leadership, music/drama.

Application procedures. Admission: No deadline. $25 fee, may be waived for applicants with need. Application may be submitted online. Admission notification on a rolling basis beginning on or about 9/1. Must reply by May 1 or within 2 week(s) if notified thereafter. **Financial aid:** Priority date 3/1; no closing date. FAFSA required. Applicants notified on a rolling basis starting 1/1; must reply within 2 week(s) of notification.

Academics. Special study options: Accelerated study, combined bachelor's/graduate degree, distance learning, double major, dual enrollment of high school students, honors, independent study, internships, liberal arts/career combination, student-designed major, study abroad, teacher certification program. **Credit/placement by examination:** AP, CLEP, IB, ACT, institutional tests. Maximum of 24 credits earned through a combination of credit exams, credit from life experience, directed and independent study. **Support services:** Learning center, reduced course load, remedial instruction, study skills assistance, tutoring.

Majors. Biology: General. **Business:** Accounting, business admin, fashion, marketing. **Communications:** General, public relations. **Computer sciences:** Computer graphics, computer science. **Education:** General, art, bilingual, biology, business, chemistry, early childhood, elementary, English, foreign languages, French, history, mathematics, music, science, secondary, social studies, Spanish. **English:** English lit, technical writing. **Foreign languages:** French, Spanish. **Health:** Art therapy, dietetics, nursing (RN), predentistry, premedicine, preveterinary. **History:** General. **Interdisciplinary:** Behavioral sciences, biological/physical sciences. **Legal studies:** Prelaw. **Math:** General. **Philosophy/religion:** Philosophy, religion. **Physical sciences:** Chemistry. **Protective services:** Criminal justice. **Psychology:** General. **Public administration:** Social work. **Social sciences:** General, international relations. **Theology:** Religious ed. **Visual/performing arts:** Art, commercial/advertising art, fashion design, interior design.

Most popular majors. Business/marketing 10%, health sciences 15%, social sciences 38%, visual/performing arts 15%.

Computing on campus. Dormitories wired for high-speed internet access and linked to campus network. Commuter students can connect to campus network. Helpline available.

Student life. Freshman orientation: Mandatory. Preregistration for classes offered. **Policies:** No overnight male visitation. Freshmen permitted cars on campus. **Housing:** Guaranteed on-campus for freshmen. $100 fully refundable deposit, deadline 5/1. **Activities:** Choral groups, dance, drama, literary magazine, music ensembles, student government, student newspaper, campus ministry, international club, commuter council, hall council, gospel choir, programming and activities council, student athletes, department-affiliated clubs.

Athletics. NCAA. **Intercollegiate:** Basketball W, soccer W, softball W, tennis W, volleyball W. **Intramural:** Basketball W, bowling W, golf W, skiing W, soccer W, swimming W, tennis W, track and field W, volleyball W. **Team name:** Blue Angels.

Student services. Campus ministries, career counseling, student employment services, financial aid counseling, health services, minority student services, on-campus daycare, personal counseling. **Physically disabled:** Services for visually impaired.

Contact. E-mail: admiss@mtmary.edu
Phone: (414) 256-1219 Toll-free number: (800) 321-6265
Fax: (414) 256-0180
Brooke Konopacki, Dean of Enrollment, Mount Mary College, 2900 North Menomonee River Parkway, Milwaukee, WI 53222

Northland College

Ashland, Wisconsin **CB member**
www.northland.edu **CB code: 1561**

- Private 4-year liberal arts college affiliated with United Church of Christ
- Residential campus in small town
- 691 degree-seeking undergraduates: 7% part-time, 57% women, 2% African American, 1% Asian American, 2% Hispanic American, 3% Native American, 1% international

- 75% of applicants admitted
- SAT or ACT (ACT writing optional), application essay required

General. Founded in 1892. Regionally accredited. **Degrees:** 191 bachelor's awarded. **Location:** 220 miles from Minneapolis-St. Paul, 65 miles from Duluth, Minnesota. **Calendar:** 4-4-1 semester system. Limited summer session. **Full-time faculty:** 41 total; 85% have terminal degrees, 7% minority, 22% women. **Part-time faculty:** 57 total; 39% have terminal degrees, 2% minority, 46% women. **Class size:** 77% < 20, 22% 20-39, 2% 40-49. **Special facilities:** Field stations for natural science courses, atmospheric environmental satellite links.

Freshman class profile. 804 applied, 605 admitted, 180 enrolled.

Mid 50% test scores		**GPA 2.0-2.99:**	21%
SAT verbal:	510-590	**Rank in top quarter:**	50%
SAT math:	490-570	**Rank in top tenth:**	28%
ACT:	22-26	**Out-of-state:**	67%
GPA 3.50 or higher:	44%	**Live on campus:**	95%
GPA 3.0-3.49:	34%		

Basis for selection. High school curriculum evaluation, class rank, guidance counselor recommendation, grade point average, and standardized test scores considered. Audition, portfolio recommended; interview required for borderline applicants.

High school preparation. Required and recommended units include English 3-4, mathematics 3, social studies 3, history 1, science 3 (laboratory 2), foreign language 2 and academic electives 3.

2006-2007 Annual costs. Tuition/fees: $20,789. Room/board: $5,891. Books/supplies: $700. Personal expenses: $1,200.

2004-2005 Financial aid. Need-based: 122 full-time freshmen applied for aid; 108 were judged to have need; 108 of these received aid. Average need met was 83%. Average scholarship/grant was $11,340; average loan $3,464. 67% of total undergraduate aid awarded as scholarships/grants, 33% as loans/jobs. **Non-need-based:** Awarded to 55 full-time undergraduates, including 5 freshmen. Scholarships awarded for academics, alumni affiliation, leadership, minority status, music/drama.

Application procedures. Admission: Priority date 12/1; no deadline. $25 fee, may be waived for applicants with need. Admission notification on a rolling basis beginning on or about 11/1. Must reply by May 1 or within 3 week(s) if notified thereafter. **Financial aid:** Priority date 4/15; no closing date. FAFSA required. Applicants notified on a rolling basis starting 3/1; must reply by 5/1 or within 4 week(s) of notification.

Academics. Accelerated evening degree completion business program offered; classes meet one night a week over 16-month period. Accelerated Bachelor of Nursing for students who have an earned RN. **Special study options:** Combined bachelor's/graduate degree, cooperative education, distance learning, double major, exchange student, independent study, internships, liberal arts/career combination, student-designed major, study abroad, teacher certification program. 3-2 cooperative degree programs in environmental engineering and forestry with Michigan Technological University. Ecoleague exchange with Antioch, Alaska Pacific, Green Mountain, Prescott, College of the Atlantic. **Credit/placement by examination:** AP, CLEP, IB, institutional tests. 28 credit hours maximum toward bachelor's degree. **Support services:** Learning center, reduced course load, study skills assistance, tutoring, writing center.

Majors. Architecture: Urban/community planning. **Area/ethnic studies:** Native American. **Biology:** General, ecology. **Business:** General, business admin, management science. **Computer sciences:** General, computer science, information systems. **Conservation:** General, environmental studies, fisheries, forestry, management/policy, wildlife. **Education:** Elementary. **English:** Creative writing. **Health:** Predentistry, premedicine, prepharmacy, preveterinary, recreational therapy. **History:** General. **Interdisciplinary:** Biological/physical sciences, global studies, natural sciences, peace/conflict. **Legal studies:** Prelaw. **Liberal arts:** Arts/sciences. **Math:** General. **Parks/recreation:** General. **Philosophy/religion:** Religion. **Physical sciences:** Atmospheric science, chemistry, geology, planetary. **Psychology:** General. **Public administration:** Policy analysis. **Social sciences:** General, economics, sociology. **Visual/performing arts:** Art, music performance, studio arts, voice/opera.

Most popular majors. Biology 10%, business/marketing 12%, education 22%, natural resources/environmental science 21%, physical sciences 8%, psychology 7%.

Computing on campus. 125 workstations in dormitories, library, computer center, student center. Dormitories wired for high-speed internet access and linked to campus network. Commuter students can connect to campus network. Online course registration, online library, helpline, repair service, wireless network available.

Student life. Freshman orientation: Mandatory. Preregistration for classes offered. Outdoor orientation or North County orientation. **Policies:** Freshmen permitted cars on campus. **Housing:** Guaranteed on-campus for freshmen. Coed dorms, single-sex dorms, special housing for disabled, apartments, cooperative housing available. $100 nonrefundable deposit. Environmental living and learning residential hall available. **Activities:** Bands, choral groups, dance, drama, film society, literary magazine, music ensembles, radio station, student government, student newspaper, symphony orchestra, Native American Council, veterans organization, environmental group, international students association, ecology club.

Athletics. NAIA, NCAA. **Intercollegiate:** Baseball M, basketball, cross-country, ice hockey M, soccer, softball W, volleyball W. **Intramural:** Archery, badminton, basketball, football (non-tackle), ice hockey, racquetball, rugby, skiing, soccer, softball, table tennis, tennis, volleyball, water polo. **Team name:** Lumberjacks, Lumberjills.

Student services. Adult student services, alcohol/substance abuse counseling, campus ministries, career counseling, services for economically disadvantaged, student employment services, financial aid counseling, health services, minority student services, personal counseling, placement for graduates, women's services. **Physically disabled:** Services for visually, hearing impaired.

Contact. E-mail: admit@northland.edu
Phone: (715) 682-1224 Toll-free number: (800) 753-1840
Fax: (715) 682-1258
Jason Turley, Director of Admission, Northland College, 1411 Ellis Avenue, Ashland, WI 54806

Ripon College

Ripon, Wisconsin — **CB member**
www.ripon.edu — **CB code: 1664**

- Private 4-year liberal arts college affiliated with United Church of Christ
- Residential campus in small town
- 945 degree-seeking undergraduates: 1% part-time, 50% women
- 81% of applicants admitted
- SAT or ACT (ACT writing optional), application essay required
- 70% graduate within 6 years; 9% enter graduate study

General. Founded in 1851. Regionally accredited. **Degrees:** 178 bachelor's awarded. **ROTC:** Army. **Location:** 80 miles from Milwaukee, 80 miles from Madison. **Calendar:** Semester. **Full-time faculty:** 49 total; 94% have terminal degrees, 6% minority, 41% women. **Part-time faculty:** 38 total; 42% have terminal degrees, 5% minority, 42% women. **Class size:** 58% < 20, 37% 20-39, 3% 40-49, 2% 50-99, less than 1% >100. **Special facilities:** Woodland preservation area with outdoor classroom.

Freshman class profile. 976 applied, 791 admitted, 262 enrolled.

Mid 50% test scores		**Rank in top tenth:**	23%
SAT verbal:	480-650	**End year in good standing:**	94%
SAT math:	500-620	**Return as sophomores:**	84%
ACT:	21-27	**Out-of-state:**	29%
GPA 3.50 or higher:	47%	**Live on campus:**	95%
GPA 3.0-3.49:	31%	**International:**	1%
GPA 2.0-2.99:	22%	**Fraternities:**	34%
Rank in top quarter:	50%	**Sororities:**	24%

Basis for selection. School achievement record, interview, class rank, test scores, recommendations, extracurricular or community activities important.

High school preparation. 17 units required. Required and recommended units include English 4, mathematics 2-4, social studies 2-4, science 2-4 and foreign language 2. Math must include 1 algebra and geometry. 7 units chosen from additional units in math, science, social science, foreign language.

2006-2007 Annual costs. Tuition/fees: $22,437. Room/board: $6,060. Books/supplies: $750. Personal expenses: $700.

2004-2005 Financial aid. Need-based: 253 full-time freshmen applied for aid; 204 were judged to have need; 204 of these received aid. Average need met was 95%. Average scholarship/grant was $14,360; average loan $4,156. 74% of total undergraduate aid awarded as scholarships/grants, 26% as loans/jobs. **Non-need-based:** Awarded to 314 full-time undergraduates, including 100 freshmen. Scholarships awarded for academics, alumni affiliation, art, leadership, minority status, music/drama, religious affiliation, ROTC, state residency. **Additional information:** Institution strives to meet 100 percent of students' demonstrated financial need for all four years.

Application procedures. **Admission:** Priority date 3/15; no deadline. $30 fee, may be waived for applicants with need. Application may be submitted online. Admission notification on a rolling basis beginning on or about 9/1. Must reply by May 1 or within 2 week(s) if notified thereafter. **Financial aid:** Priority date 3/1; no closing date. FAFSA required. Applicants notified on a rolling basis starting 3/1; must reply within 2 week(s) of notification.

Academics. **Special study options:** Accelerated study, combined bachelor's/graduate degree, double major, exchange student, internships, liberal arts/career combination, student-designed major, study abroad, teacher certification program, urban semester, Washington semester. Domestic and international off-campus study programs. **Credit/placement by examination:** AP, CLEP, IB, institutional tests. Amount of credit and placement for AP exams subject to departmental approval. **Support services:** Learning center, reduced course load, tutoring.

Majors. **Area/ethnic studies:** Latin American, women's. **Biology:** General, biochemistry. **Business:** Business admin. **Communications:** General. **Computer sciences:** Computer science. **Conservation:** Environmental studies. **Education:** General. **Foreign languages:** General, classics, French, German, Spanish. **Health:** Predentistry, premedicine, prenursing, prepharmacy, preveterinary. **History:** General. **Interdisciplinary:** Biopsychology, global studies. **Legal studies:** Prelaw. **Math:** General. **Parks/recreation:** Exercise sciences. **Philosophy/religion:** Philosophy, religion. **Physical sciences:** General, chemistry, physics. **Psychology:** General. **Social sciences:** Anthropology, economics, political science, sociology. **Visual/performing arts:** Art, art history/conservation, dramatic.

Most popular majors. Biology 10%, business/marketing 8%, education 15%, English 7%, foreign language 7%, history 8%, psychology 8%, social sciences 15%, visual/performing arts 7%.

Computing on campus. 150 workstations in dormitories, library, computer center. Dormitories linked to campus network. Commuter students can connect to campus network. Helpline, student web hosting available.

Student life. **Freshman orientation:** Mandatory, $45 fee. Preregistration for classes offered. 2-day orientation held in late June. **Policies:** Freshmen permitted cars on campus. **Housing:** Guaranteed on-campus for all undergraduates. Coed dorms, single-sex dorms, fraternity/sorority housing, substance-free housing available. $200 deposit, deadline 8/15. **Activities:** Bands, choral groups, dance, drama, film society, literary magazine, music ensembles, musical theater, radio station, student government, student newspaper, symphony orchestra, international club, Christian Fellowship, Big Brother/Big Sister, multicultural club, romance language club, environmental group, Feminists for Equality, College Democrats, College Republicans.

Athletics. NCAA. **Intercollegiate:** Baseball M, basketball, cross-country, diving, football (tackle) M, golf, soccer, softball W, swimming, tennis, track and field, volleyball W. **Intramural:** Basketball, bowling, fencing, football (tackle), golf, handball, racquetball, soccer, softball, table tennis, tennis, volleyball. **Team name:** Red Hawks.

Student services. Career counseling, student employment services, financial aid counseling, health services, personal counseling, placement for graduates.

Contact. E-mail: adminfo@ripon.edu
Phone: (920) 748-8114 Toll-free number: (800) 947-4766
Fax: (920) 748-8335
Leigh Mlodzik, Director of Admission, Ripon College, 300 Seward Street, Ripon, WI 54971-0248

St. Norbert College

De Pere, Wisconsin **CB member**
www.snc.edu **CB code: 1706**

- Private 4-year liberal arts college affiliated with Roman Catholic Church
- Residential campus in large town
- 1,942 degree-seeking undergraduates: 1% part-time, 57% women, 1% African American, 1% Asian American, 2% Hispanic American, 1% Native American, 2% international
- 58 degree-seeking graduate students
- 86% of applicants admitted
- SAT or ACT (ACT writing optional) required
- 71% graduate within 6 years; 16% enter graduate study

General. Founded in 1898. Regionally accredited. Study abroad is strongly supported, and students are allowed to apply all of their financial aid to their study abroad program costs; student/faculty collaborative research. **Degrees:** 462 bachelor's awarded; master's offered. **ROTC:** Army. **Location:** 5 miles from Green Bay. **Calendar:** Semester, limited summer session. **Full-time faculty:** 109 total; 92% have terminal degrees, 6% minority, 34% women. **Part-time faculty:** 52 total; 31% have terminal degrees, 2% minority, 44% women. **Class size:** 52% < 20, 47% 20-39, less than 1% 40-49, less than 1% 50-99. **Special facilities:** Center for leadership and service, art galleries, scanning electron microscope, center for adaptive education and assistive technology, visual and performing arts center, center for international education, riverfront campus center with marina, peace and justice center, career services, children's center in cooperation with early childhood education, center of economic education, survey center, chapels in residence halls, women's center, men's center.

Freshman class profile. 1,683 applied, 1,453 admitted, 511 enrolled.

Mid 50% test scores		**Rank in top tenth:**	24%
ACT:	21-27	**End year in good standing:**	86%
GPA 3.50 or higher:	38%	**Return as sophomores:**	88%
GPA 3.0-3.49:	30%	**Live on campus:**	95%
GPA 2.0-2.99:	32%	**International:**	1%
Rank in top quarter:	50%		

Basis for selection. Rigor of high school classes selected, GPA, ACT/SAT scores, co-curricular activities, letters of recommendation and personal statement. Essay, interview recommended for all; audition recommended for music. **Learning Disabled:** Students with learning disabilities should submit documentation of specific disability to receive proper level of support from institution.

High school preparation. 16 units recommended. Recommended units include English 4, mathematics 3, social studies 2, history 2, science 3 (laboratory 3) and foreign language 2. As many college-prep elective units as possible.

2005-2006 Annual costs. Tuition/fees: $22,509. Room/board: $6,068. Books/supplies: $500. Personal expenses: $750.

2004-2005 Financial aid. **Need-based:** 416 full-time freshmen applied for aid; 344 were judged to have need; 344 of these received aid. Average need met was 88%. Average scholarship/grant was $12,740; average loan $3,881. 60% of total undergraduate aid awarded as scholarships/grants, 40% as loans/jobs. **Non-need-based:** Awarded to 731 full-time undergraduates, including 200 freshmen. Scholarships awarded for academics, art, leadership, minority status, music/drama, ROTC, state residency.

Application procedures. **Admission:** Priority date 4/1; no deadline. $25 fee, may be waived for applicants with need. Application may be submitted online. Admission notification on a rolling basis beginning on or about 10/1. Must reply by May 1 or within 3 week(s) if notified thereafter. **Financial aid:** Priority date 3/1; no closing date. FAFSA required. Applicants notified on a rolling basis starting 3/15; must reply within 2 week(s) of notification.

Academics. **Special study options:** Distance learning, double major, ESL, honors, independent study, internships, student-designed major, study abroad, teacher certification program, Washington semester. Foundation for International Education (London) Internship. **Credit/placement by examination:** AP, CLEP, IB, institutional tests. **Support services:** Learning center, reduced course load, remedial instruction, study skills assistance, tutoring, writing center.

Majors. **Biology:** General. **Business:** General, accounting, international. **Communications:** General. **Computer sciences:** General. **Conservation:** Environmental science, environmental studies. **Education:** Elementary, music. **English:** English lit. **Foreign languages:** French, German, Spanish. **History:** General. **Interdisciplinary:** Biological/physical sciences. **Liberal arts:** Humanities. **Math:** General. **Philosophy/religion:** Philosophy, religion. **Physical sciences:** Chemistry, geology, physics. **Psychology:** General. **Social sciences:** Economics, international relations, political science, sociology. **Visual/performing arts:** Art, commercial/advertising art.

Most popular majors. Business/marketing 26%, communications/journalism 11%, education 12%, history 6%, social sciences 11%.

Computing on campus. 219 workstations in dormitories, library, computer center, student center. Dormitories wired for high-speed internet access and linked to campus network. Commuter students can connect to campus network. Online course registration, online library, helpline, repair service, wireless network available.

Student life. **Freshman orientation:** Mandatory. Preregistration for classes offered. 2-day summer program for students and parents. **Policies:** Freshmen permitted cars on campus. **Housing:** Guaranteed on-campus for all undergraduates. Coed dorms, single-sex dorms, special housing for disabled, apartments available. $350 nonrefundable deposit, deadline 5/1. Living/learning residence hall experience for freshman seminar students, townhouses, college-owned houses near campus also available. **Activities:** Bands, choral groups, drama, film society, literary magazine, music ensembles, musical theater, radio station, student government, student newspaper, TV station, campus ministries, InterVarsity Christian Fellowship, Amnesty International, Unity Among Friends, Japan club, Discoveries International, Circle K, Athletes for Life.

Athletics. NCAA. **Intercollegiate:** Baseball M, basketball, cross-country, diving W, football (tackle) M, golf, ice hockey M, soccer, softball W, swimming W, tennis, track and field, volleyball W. **Intramural:** Basketball, football (non-tackle), softball, volleyball. **Team name:** Green Knights.

Student services. Alcohol/substance abuse counseling, campus ministries, career counseling, student employment services, financial aid counseling, health services, minority student services, on-campus daycare, personal counseling, placement for graduates, women's services. **Physically disabled:** Services for visually, speech, hearing impaired.

Contact. E-mail: admit@snc.edu
Phone: (920) 403-3005 Toll-free number: (800) 236-4878
Fax: (920) 403-4072
Bridget O'Connor, Associate Vice President for Enrollment Management, St. Norbert College, 100 Grant Street, De Pere, WI 54115-2099

Silver Lake College
Manitowoc, Wisconsin
www.sl.edu **CB code: 1300**

- Private 4-year liberal arts college affiliated with Roman Catholic Church
- Commuter campus in large town
- 413 degree-seeking undergraduates: 53% part-time, 77% women, 1% Hispanic American, 4% Native American
- 176 degree-seeking graduate students
- 83% of applicants admitted
- SAT or ACT (ACT writing optional) required
- 58% graduate within 6 years

General. Founded in 1935. Regionally accredited. **Degrees:** 128 bachelor's awarded; master's offered. **Location:** 80 miles from Milwaukee, 30 miles from Green Bay. **Calendar:** Trimester, extensive summer session. **Full-time faculty:** 44 total; 48% have terminal degrees, 7% minority, 73% women. **Part-time faculty:** 119 total; 18% have terminal degrees, 2% minority, 59% women. **Class size:** 97% < 20, 3% 20-39. **Special facilities:** Nature preserve.

Freshman class profile. 102 applied, 85 admitted, 33 enrolled.

Mid 50% test scores			
ACT:	17-22	Rank in top quarter:	35%
GPA 3.50 or higher:	19%	Rank in top tenth:	5%
GPA 3.0-3.49:	28%	End year in good standing:	71%
GPA 2.0-2.99:	53%	Return as sophomores:	64%
		Live on campus:	70%

Basis for selection. High school GPA, test scores very important. Audition required, interview recommended for music; portfolio, interview recommended for art. **Homeschooled:** State high school equivalency certificate required.

High school preparation. College-preparatory program recommended. 16 units required. Required and recommended units include English 3, mathematics 2, social studies 1, history 1, science 1 (laboratory 1) and academic electives 7.

2006-2007 Annual costs. Tuition/fees: $17,108. Room only: $4,400. Books/supplies: $800. Personal expenses: $1,200.

2005-2006 Financial aid. Need-based: 31 full-time freshmen applied for aid; 27 were judged to have need; 27 of these received aid. Average need met was 84%. Average scholarship/grant was $12,279; average loan $2,572. 47% of total undergraduate aid awarded as scholarships/grants, 53% as loans/jobs. **Non-need-based:** Awarded to 24 full-time undergraduates, including 7 freshmen. Scholarships awarded for academics, art, athletics, leadership, music/drama, religious affiliation, state residency.

Application procedures. Admission: Priority date 8/1; no deadline. $35 fee, may be waived for applicants with need. Application may be submitted online. Admission notification on a rolling basis beginning on or about 9/1. **Financial aid:** Priority date 3/15; no closing date. FAFSA required. Applicants notified on a rolling basis starting 3/15; must reply within 2 week(s) of notification.

Academics. Special study options: Accelerated study, combined bachelor's/graduate degree, double major, dual enrollment of high school students, independent study, internships, liberal arts/career combination, student-designed major, teacher certification program. **Credit/placement by examination:** AP, CLEP, IB, SAT, ACT, institutional tests. 30 credit hours maximum toward associate degree, 60 toward bachelor's. **Support services:** Learning center, reduced course load, remedial instruction, study skills assistance, tutoring.

Majors. Biology: General. **Business:** Accounting, business admin, human resources. **Computer sciences:** Computer science, information systems. **Education:** General, art, early childhood, elementary, emotionally handicapped, learning disabled, mentally handicapped, music. **History:** General. **Math:** General. **Philosophy/religion:** Religion. **Psychology:** General. **Public administration:** General. **Social sciences:** General. **Theology:** Theology. **Visual/performing arts:** Art.

Most popular majors. Business/marketing 51%, education 22%, engineering/engineering technologies 6%, psychology 10%.

Computing on campus. 40 workstations in library, computer center, student center. Commuter students can connect to campus network. Online course registration, online library, wireless network available.

Student life. Freshman orientation: Mandatory. Preregistration for classes offered. **Policies:** Freshmen permitted cars on campus. **Housing:** Apartments, substance-free housing available. $100 nonrefundable deposit. Men's and women's housing available, located off campus. **Activities:** Jazz band, choral groups, dance, literary magazine, music ensembles, student government, student newspaper, campus ministry, student forum, student Wisconsin Education Association, student Wisconsin Early Childhood Association, student council for exceptional children, music educators national conference for students.

Athletics. USCAA. **Intercollegiate:** Basketball W, cross-country. **Intramural:** Table tennis, volleyball. **Team name:** Lakers.

Student services. Campus ministries, career counseling, student employment services, financial aid counseling, health services, personal counseling, placement for graduates.

Contact. E-mail: admslc@silver.sl.edu
Phone: (920) 686-6175 Toll-free number: (800) 236-4752 ext. 175
Fax: (920) 684-7082
Jan Algozine, Dean of Student Development, Silver Lake College, 2406 South Alverno Road, Manitowoc, WI 54220

University of Wisconsin-Eau Claire
Eau Claire, Wisconsin
www.uwec.edu **CB code: 1913**

- Public 4-year university
- Residential campus in small city
- 9,929 degree-seeking undergraduates: 6% part-time, 59% women, 3% Asian American, 1% Hispanic American, 1% Native American, 1% international
- 408 degree-seeking graduate students
- 70% of applicants admitted
- SAT or ACT (ACT writing optional) required
- 59% graduate within 6 years; 11% enter graduate study

General. Founded in 1916. Regionally accredited. **Degrees:** 1,849 bachelor's, 7 associate awarded; master's offered. **Location:** 90 miles from Minneapolis-St. Paul. **Calendar:** Semester, extensive summer session. **Full-time faculty:** 401 total; 86% have terminal degrees, 9% minority, 43% women. **Part-time faculty:** 107 total; 36% have terminal degrees, 2% minority, 62% women. **Class size:** 28% < 20, 48% 20-39, 11% 40-49, 10% 50-99, 3% >100. **Special facilities:** Observatories, planetarium, bird museum, 200-acre reserve for study of flora and fauna, collections of Native American materials.

Freshman class profile. 7,134 applied, 5,007 admitted, 2,068 enrolled.

Mid 50% test scores			
SAT verbal:	520-630	End year in good standing:	91%
SAT math:	540-640	Return as sophomores:	83%
ACT:	22-26	Out-of-state:	24%
Rank in top quarter:	60%	Live on campus:	91%
Rank in top tenth:	23%	International:	1%
		Fraternities:	1%

Basis for selection. Applicants must present required combination of rank and test scores. Special consideration to disadvantaged, veterans, and minority applicants. Applicants with rank in top 50% and/or ACT score of 23 or better given first priority. Some applicants not admitted to the fall semester may be considered for admission to the following spring semester.

Wisconsin residents required to take ACT; non-residents may submit SAT. Audition required for music programs.

High school preparation. College-preparatory program required. 17 units required. Required units include English 4, mathematics 3, social studies 3, science 3, foreign language 2 and academic electives 2. 3 units English must be composition and/or literature. One of the 3 social studies units must be world or American history.

2005-2006 Annual costs. Tuition/fees: $5,179; $15,225 out-of-state. Room/board: $4,737. Books/supplies: $400. Personal expenses: $2,030.

2004-2005 Financial aid. **Need-based:** 1,524 full-time freshmen applied for aid; 844 were judged to have need; 836 of these received aid. Average need met was 95%. Average scholarship/grant was $3,643; average loan $3,516. 33% of total undergraduate aid awarded as scholarships/grants, 67% as loans/jobs. **Non-need-based:** Awarded to 852 full-time undergraduates, including 329 freshmen. Scholarships awarded for academics, art, leadership, minority status, music/drama, state residency.

Application procedures. **Admission:** Priority date 12/1; no deadline. $35 fee, may be waived for applicants with need. Application may be submitted online. Admission notification on a rolling basis beginning on or about 9/15. Must reply by May 1 or within 2 week(s) if notified thereafter. Closing and priority dates vary. **Financial aid:** Priority date 4/15; no closing date. FAFSA required. Applicants notified on a rolling basis starting 4/15.

Academics. Baccalaureate degree includes service-learning requirement, freshman seminars, capstone courses, internships in most majors, and opportunities for students to collaborate with faculty on research and scholarly projects. **Special study options:** Accelerated study, cooperative education, distance learning, double major, dual enrollment of high school students, ESL, exchange student, honors, independent study, internships, study abroad, teacher certification program. Program with University of Wisconsin: Stout in early childhood education. **Credit/placement by examination:** AP, CLEP, IB, institutional tests. 15 credit hours maximum toward associate degree, 30 toward bachelor's. **Support services:** Learning center, pre-admission summer program, reduced course load, remedial instruction, study skills assistance, tutoring, writing center.

Majors. **Area/ethnic studies:** Latin American, Native American. **Biology:** Biomedical sciences, molecular. **Business:** Accounting, business admin, finance, information resources management, marketing. **Communications:** General, journalism, media studies. **Computer sciences:** General. **Education:** Elementary, science, social studies, special. **English:** English lit. **Foreign languages:** French, Germanic, Spanish. **Health:** Athletic training, communication disorders, environmental health, health care admin, music therapy, nursing (RN). **History:** General. **Math:** General. **Parks/recreation:** Exercise sciences. **Philosophy/religion:** Philosophy, religion. **Physical sciences:** Chemistry, geology, physics. **Protective services:** Criminal justice. **Psychology:** General. **Public administration:** Social work. **Social sciences:** Economics, geography, political science, sociology. **Visual/performing arts:** Art, dramatic.

Most popular majors. Biology 6%, business/marketing 25%, communications/journalism 8%, education 11%, health sciences 9%, social sciences 6%, visual/performing arts 6%.

Computing on campus. 1,150 workstations in dormitories, library, computer center, student center. Dormitories wired for high-speed internet access and linked to campus network. Commuter students can connect to campus network. Online course registration, online library, helpline, wireless network available.

Student life. **Freshman orientation:** Mandatory, $40 fee. Preregistration for classes offered. **Policies:** Freshmen permitted cars on campus. **Housing:** Guaranteed on-campus for freshmen. Coed dorms, single-sex dorms, apartments, substance-free housing available. $75 fully refundable deposit. **Activities:** Bands, choral groups, dance, drama, film society, literary magazine, music ensembles, musical theater, opera, radio station, student government, student newspaper, symphony orchestra, TV station, College Republicans, College Democrats, Newman Student Association, ecumenical religious center student association, Alpha Phi Omega service fraternity, Mortar Board, Black student organization, Native American student organization, Hmong student association.

Athletics. NCAA. **Intercollegiate:** Basketball, cross-country, diving, football (tackle) M, golf, gymnastics W, ice hockey, soccer W, softball W, swimming, tennis, track and field, volleyball W, wrestling M. **Intramural:** Badminton, baseball M, basketball, bowling, diving, football (tackle), golf, ice hockey, racquetball, rugby, skiing, soccer, softball, swimming, table tennis, tennis, volleyball, water polo M, weight lifting. **Team name:** Blugolds.

Student services. Adult student services, alcohol/substance abuse counseling, career counseling, student employment services, financial aid counseling, health services, legal services, minority student services, on-campus daycare, personal counseling, placement for graduates, veterans' counselor. **Physically disabled:** Services for visually, speech, hearing impaired.

Contact. E-mail: admissions@uwec.edu
Phone: (715) 836-5415 Fax: (715) 836-2409
Kristina Anderson, Director of Admissions, University of Wisconsin-Eau Claire, 112 Schofield Hall, Eau Claire, WI 54701

University of Wisconsin-Green Bay

Green Bay, Wisconsin — **CB member**
www.uwgb.edu — **CB code: 1859**

- Public 4-year university and liberal arts college
- Residential campus in small city
- 5,321 degree-seeking undergraduates: 16% part-time, 66% women, 1% African American, 3% Asian American, 1% Hispanic American, 1% Native American, 1% international
- 132 degree-seeking graduate students
- 66% of applicants admitted
- SAT or ACT (ACT writing optional) required
- 47% graduate within 6 years; 20% enter graduate study

General. Founded in 1965. Regionally accredited. **Degrees:** 928 bachelor's, 5 associate awarded; master's offered. **ROTC:** Army. **Location:** 80 miles from Milwaukee. **Calendar:** Semester, limited summer session. **Full-time faculty:** 179 total; 88% have terminal degrees, 12% minority, 40% women. **Part-time faculty:** 100 total; 16% have terminal degrees, 6% minority, 59% women. **Class size:** 27% < 20, 46% 20-39, 12% 40-49, 11% 50-99, 4% >100. **Special facilities:** Natural history museum, herbarium, 290-acre arboretum, performing arts center.

Freshman class profile. 3,350 applied, 2,222 admitted, 910 enrolled.

Mid 50% test scores			
SAT verbal:	480-560	End year in good standing:	86%
SAT math:	520-610	Return as sophomores:	76%
ACT:	21-25	Out-of-state:	4%
GPA 3.50 or higher:	37%	Live on campus:	77%
GPA 3.0-3.49:	44%	International:	1%
GPA 2.0-2.99:	19%	Fraternities:	1%
		Sororities:	1%

Basis for selection. ACT score, high school GPA and extracurricular or community involvement very important. Priority given to students with ACT of 23 or higher or high school GPA of 3.25 or higher. Students not meeting standard admission requirements (17 ACT and 2.25 GPA) may be considered on an individual basis. ACT requirement may be waived for international students. ACT reports should be supplied prior to receiving admission. Interview may be requested of borderline applicants; audition required for music.

High school preparation. College-preparatory program required. 17 units required; 19 recommended. Required and recommended units include English 4, mathematics 3, social studies 3, science 3 (laboratory 1), foreign language 2 and academic electives 4. Mathematics must include algebra or more advanced course. 2 of the 4 required academic electives must be from English, mathematics, science, social studies, or foreign language.

2005-2006 Annual costs. Tuition/fees: $5,425; $15,471 out-of-state. Room/board: $4,775. Books/supplies: $700. Personal expenses: $1,836.

2005-2006 Financial aid. **Need-based:** 773 full-time freshmen applied for aid; 498 were judged to have need; 463 of these received aid. Average need met was 74%. Average scholarship/grant was $4,125; average loan $3,030. 43% of total undergraduate aid awarded as scholarships/grants, 57% as loans/jobs. **Non-need-based:** Awarded to 931 full-time undergraduates, including 205 freshmen. Scholarships awarded for academics, art, athletics, leadership, minority status, music/drama. **Additional information:** Auditions required for music and theater scholarships.

Application procedures. **Admission:** Priority date 1/1; no deadline. $35 fee, may be waived for applicants with need. Application may be submitted online. Admission notification on a rolling basis beginning on or about 10/15. **Financial aid:** Priority date 4/15; no closing date. FAFSA required. Applicants notified on a rolling basis starting 11/1; must reply within 3 week(s) of notification.

Academics. Minimum credit hours required in major for bachelor's degree varies depending on field. Teacher certification available in conjunction with bachelor's degree. **Special study options:** Combined bachelor's/graduate degree, distance learning, double major, dual enrollment of high school students, exchange student, external degree, independent study, internships, liberal arts/career combination, student-designed major, study abroad, teacher certification program. **Credit/placement by examination:** AP, CLEP,

IB, ACT, institutional tests. 47 credit hours maximum toward associate degree, 93 toward bachelor's. **Support services:** Pre-admission summer program, reduced course load, remedial instruction, study skills assistance, tutoring, writing center.

Majors. **Area/ethnic studies:** Native American, women's. **Biology:** General. **Business:** Accounting, business admin. **Communications:** General. **Computer sciences:** Computer science, information systems. **Conservation:** Environmental science, environmental studies. **Education:** Elementary. **Foreign languages:** French, German, Spanish. **Health:** Nursing (RN). **History:** General. **Interdisciplinary:** Biological/physical sciences. **Liberal arts:** Arts/sciences, humanities. **Math:** General. **Philosophy/religion:** Philosophy. **Physical sciences:** Chemistry, physics. **Psychology:** General. **Public administration:** General, social work. **Social sciences:** Economics, political science, sociology, urban studies. **Visual/performing arts:** General, art, dramatic.

Most popular majors. Biology 10%, business/marketing 20%, communications/journalism 9%, psychology 18%.

Computing on campus. 550 workstations in dormitories, library, computer center, student center. Dormitories wired for high-speed internet access and linked to campus network. Commuter students can connect to campus network. Online course registration, online library, helpline, repair service, wireless network available.

Student life. **Freshman orientation:** Available, $200 fee. Preregistration for classes offered. Freshmen register in June; they can move into campus housing the week before fall term for an intensive academic and social program, which continues in a less intensive manner throughout the year. **Policies:** Freshmen permitted cars on campus. **Housing:** Coed dorms, apartments, substance-free housing available. $225 fully refundable deposit. Suite-style apartments with private bathrooms. **Activities:** Bands, choral groups, dance, drama, literary magazine, music ensembles, radio station, student government, student newspaper, TV station, College Republicans, College Democrats, Habitat for Humanity, Circle K, Ten Percent Society, Athletes in Action, American Marketing Association, psychology and human development club, student government association, Wisconsin Education Assocation Council.

Athletics. NCAA. **Intercollegiate:** Basketball, cheerleading, cross-country, diving, golf M, skiing, soccer, softball W, swimming, tennis, volleyball W. **Intramural:** Basketball, football (non-tackle), golf, racquetball, soccer, softball, tennis, volleyball. **Team name:** Phoenix.

Student services. Alcohol/substance abuse counseling, career counseling, student employment services, financial aid counseling, health services, minority student services, personal counseling, placement for graduates, veterans' counselor. **Physically disabled:** Services for visually, hearing impaired.

Contact. E-mail: admissions@uwgb.edu
Phone: (920) 465-2111 Toll-free number: (888) 674-8942
Fax: (920) 465-5754
Pam Harvey-Jacobs, Director of Admissions, University of Wisconsin-Green Bay, 2420 Nicolet Drive, Green Bay, WI 54311-7001

University of Wisconsin-La Crosse

La Crosse, Wisconsin
www.uwlax.edu **CB code: 1914**

- Public 4-year university
- Residential campus in small city
- 7,908 degree-seeking undergraduates: 4% part-time, 59% women, 1% African American, 3% Asian American, 1% Hispanic American, 1% Native American, 1% international
- 1,124 degree-seeking graduate students
- 67% of applicants admitted
- SAT or ACT (ACT writing recommended) required
- 64% graduate within 6 years; 24% enter graduate study

General. Founded in 1909. Regionally accredited. **Degrees:** 1,524 bachelor's awarded; master's offered. **ROTC:** Army. **Location:** 140 miles from Madison, 160 miles from Minneapolis-St. Paul. **Calendar:** Semester, limited summer session. **Full-time faculty:** 339 total; 79% have terminal degrees, 14% minority, 39% women. **Part-time faculty:** 109 total; 25% have terminal degrees, 10% minority, 51% women. **Class size:** 39% < 20, 45% 20-39, 9% 40-49, 6% 50-99, 2% >100. **Special facilities:** Museum, art galleries, greenhouse, planetarium, nuclear radiation laboratory, river studies center, archaeology center.

Freshman class profile. 6,347 applied, 4,237 admitted, 1,764 enrolled.

Mid 50% test scores		End year in good standing:	93%
SAT verbal:	500-610	Return as sophomores:	90%
SAT math:	520-660	Out-of-state:	16%
ACT:	23-27	Live on campus:	90%
Rank in top quarter:	80%	Fraternities:	1%
Rank in top tenth:	30%	Sororities:	1%

Basis for selection. Applicants should rank in top 25% of class, minimum ACT composite score of 23 (or rank in upper 30% of class with score of 26), and complete a rigorous college prep curriculum. Interviews not required, but may be considered in admission decision. Auditions may be required for some scholarships. Portfolios and essays may be included with application and will be considered in admission decision. **Homeschooled:** Interview may be required. **Learning Disabled:** Information regarding a learning disability may be considered in admission decision.

High school preparation. 17 units required; 21 recommended. Required and recommended units include English 4, mathematics 3-4, social studies 3-4, science 3-4 (laboratory 2), foreign language 3 and academic electives 4.

2005-2006 Annual costs. Tuition/fees: $5,074; $15,120 out-of-state. Minnesota Reciprocity Tuition: $4,780; $199 per credit hour. Room/board: $4,820. Books/supplies: $300. Personal expenses: $2,000.

2004-2005 Financial aid. **Need-based:** 1,122 full-time freshmen applied for aid; 886 were judged to have need; 851 of these received aid. Average need met was 80%. Average scholarship/grant was $1,609; average loan $3,265. 33% of total undergraduate aid awarded as scholarships/grants, 67% as loans/jobs. **Non-need-based:** Awarded to 885 full-time undergraduates, including 139 freshmen. Scholarships awarded for academics, alumni affiliation, art, leadership, minority status, music/drama, ROTC. **Additional information:** "Return to Wisconsin" program provides 25 percent waiver of nonresident portion of tuition to children and grandchildren of alumni who are residents of states other than Wisconsin and Minnesota.

Application procedures. **Admission:** Priority date 2/1; no deadline. $35 fee, may be waived for applicants with need. Application may be submitted online. Admission notification on a rolling basis beginning on or about 9/15. **Financial aid:** Priority date 3/15; no closing date. FAFSA, institutional form required. Applicants notified on a rolling basis starting 3/10; must reply by 5/10 or within 3 week(s) of notification.

Academics. **Special study options:** Cooperative education, cross-registration, distance learning, double major, dual enrollment of high school students, ESL, honors, independent study, internships, study abroad, teacher certification program. **Credit/placement by examination:** AP, CLEP, IB, SAT, ACT, institutional tests. 16 credit hours maximum toward associate degree, 32 toward bachelor's. **Support services:** Learning center, pre-admission summer program, reduced course load, remedial instruction, study skills assistance, tutoring, writing center.

Majors. **Biology:** General, biochemistry, microbiology. **Business:** Accounting, business admin, finance, international, management information systems, marketing. **Communications:** General. **Computer sciences:** General. **Education:** Elementary, health, science, social studies. **English:** English lit. **Foreign languages:** French, German, Spanish. **Health:** Athletic training, clinical lab science, community health, nuclear medical technology, physician assistant, recreational therapy. **History:** General. **Math:** General. **Parks/recreation:** Exercise sciences, facilities management. **Philosophy/religion:** Philosophy. **Physical sciences:** Chemistry, physics. **Psychology:** General. **Social sciences:** Archaeology, economics, geography, political science, sociology. **Visual/performing arts:** Art, dramatic.

Most popular majors. Biology 10%, business/marketing 21%, communications/journalism 6%, education 9%, health sciences 9%, parks/recreation 13%, psychology 7%, social sciences 10%.

Computing on campus. 600 workstations in dormitories, library, computer center, student center. Dormitories wired for high-speed internet access and linked to campus network. Commuter students can connect to campus network. Online course registration, online library, helpline, wireless network available.

Student life. **Freshman orientation:** Available. Preregistration for classes offered. Held week prior to classes. **Policies:** Freshmen permitted cars on campus. **Housing:** Coed dorms, single-sex dorms, special housing for disabled, fraternity/sorority housing, substance-free housing available. $75 deposit, deadline 5/1. **Activities:** Bands, choral groups, dance, drama, literary magazine, music ensembles, musical theater, radio station, student government, student newspaper, symphony orchestra, TV station, Black Students Unity, Native American Council, Hispanic student organization, Asian association, Amnesty International, United Campus Ministry, Newman Club, hall councils, Intervarsity Christian Fellowship, Campus Crusade.

Athletics. NAIA, NCAA. **Intercollegiate:** Baseball M, basketball, cross-country, diving, football (tackle) M, gymnastics W, soccer W, softball W, swimming, tennis, track and field, volleyball W, wrestling M. **Intramural:** Badminton, basketball, football (non-tackle), golf M, racquetball, soccer, softball, tennis, volleyball. **Team name:** Eagles.

Student services. Adult student services, alcohol/substance abuse counseling, campus ministries, career counseling, services for economically disadvantaged, student employment services, financial aid counseling, health services, legal services, minority student services, on-campus daycare, personal counseling, placement for graduates, veterans' counselor, women's services. **Physically disabled:** Services for visually, speech, hearing impaired.

Contact. E-mail: admissions@uwlax.edu
Phone: (608) 785-8939 Fax: (608) 785-8940
Kathryn Kiefer, Associate Director of Admissions, University of Wisconsin-La Crosse, 1725 State Street, Room 115 Main Hall, La Crosse, WI 54601

University of Wisconsin-Madison

Madison, Wisconsin — **CB member**
www.wisc.edu — **CB code: 1846**

- Public 4-year university
- Residential campus in small city
- 28,458 degree-seeking undergraduates: 5% part-time, 54% women, 3% African American, 5% Asian American, 3% Hispanic American, 1% Native American, 3% international
- 11,374 degree-seeking graduate students
- 68% of applicants admitted
- SAT or ACT with writing, application essay required
- 78% graduate within 6 years

General. Founded in 1849. Regionally accredited. **Degrees:** 6,303 bachelor's awarded; master's, doctoral, first professional offered. **ROTC:** Army, Navy, Air Force. **Location:** 90 miles from Milwaukee, 150 miles from Chicago. **Calendar:** Semester, extensive summer session. **Full-time faculty:** 2,371 total; 92% have terminal degrees, 14% minority, 32% women. **Part-time faculty:** 602 total; 65% have terminal degrees, 10% minority, 51% women. **Class size:** 43% < 20, 34% 20-39, 5% 40-49, 9% 50-99, 10% >100. **Special facilities:** Art museum, teaching nuclear reactor, biotron for simulating environments, nature preserve, observatory.

Freshman class profile. 21,682 applied, 14,718 admitted, 6,141 enrolled.

Mid 50% test scores		**Rank in top tenth:**	56%
SAT verbal:	560-670	**Return as sophomores:**	94%
SAT math:	600-700	**Out-of-state:**	39%
ACT:	26-30	**Live on campus:**	79%
GPA 3.50 or higher:	74%	**International:**	3%
GPA 3.0-3.49:	20%	**Fraternities:**	9%
GPA 2.0-2.99:	6%	**Sororities:**	8%
Rank in top quarter:	91%		

Basis for selection. Secondary school record, including grades and/or rank, test scores most important. Candidate statement, recommendations, extracurricular activities and community service also important. Audition required for music; portfolio recommended for fine arts.

High school preparation. 17 units required; 20 recommended. Required and recommended units include English 4, mathematics 3-4, social studies 3-4, science 3-4, foreign language 2-4 and academic electives 2. Math units must include 1 each algebra and geometry, plus 1 year advanced math. Computer science or statistics will not fulfill math requirement. Applicants strongly advised to present academic credentials well in excess of minimum units.

2005-2006 Annual costs. Tuition/fees: $6,280; $20,280 out-of-state. Minnesota Reciprocity Tuition: $7,806. Room/board: $6,500. Books/supplies: $860. Personal expenses: $1,920.

2004-2005 Financial aid. **Need-based:** 3,777 full-time freshmen applied for aid; 1,885 were judged to have need; 1,753 of these received aid. Average scholarship/grant was $5,919; average loan $3,775. 31% of total undergraduate aid awarded as scholarships/grants, 69% as loans/jobs. **Non-need-based:** Awarded to 7,196 full-time undergraduates, including 2,300 freshmen. Scholarships awarded for academics, alumni affiliation, athletics, minority status, music/drama, ROTC.

Application procedures. **Admission:** Closing date 2/1 (postmark date). $35 fee, may be waived for applicants with need. Application may be submitted online. Admission notification on a rolling basis beginning on or about 10/1. Must reply by May 1 or within 3 week(s) if notified thereafter. **Financial aid:** No deadline. FAFSA, institutional form required. Applicants notified on a rolling basis starting 4/1; must reply within 3 week(s) of notification.

Academics. **Special study options:** Accelerated study, combined bachelor's/graduate degree, cooperative education, distance learning, double major, dual enrollment of high school students, ESL, honors, independent study, internships, liberal arts/career combination, student-designed major, study abroad, teacher certification program. **Credit/placement by examination:** AP, CLEP, IB, institutional tests. **Support services:** Learning center, pre-admission summer program, reduced course load, remedial instruction, study skills assistance, tutoring, writing center.

Majors. **Agriculture:** Agronomy, animal sciences, business, communications, dairy, economics, food science, horticultural science, poultry, soil science. **Area/ethnic studies:** African-American, Asian, Latin American, Scandinavian, South Asian, women's. **Biology:** General, bacteriology, biochemistry, botany, conservation, entomology, genetics, microbiology, molecular, pharmacology/toxicology, plant pathology, zoology. **Business:** General, accounting, actuarial science, business admin, finance, insurance, international, management information systems, marketing, operations, real estate. **Communications:** General, journalism. **Computer sciences:** General. **Conservation:** Forest sciences, wildlife. **Education:** Agricultural, art, elementary, family/consumer sciences, music, social studies, special. **Engineering:** Agricultural, biomedical, chemical, civil, computer, electrical, geological, industrial, marine, materials, mechanical, mechanics, nuclear, physics. **English:** English lit. **Family/consumer sciences:** General, clothing/textiles, communication, consumer economics, family studies, merchandising. **Foreign languages:** Ancient Greek, Chinese, classics, comparative lit, French, Germanic, Hebrew, Italian, Japanese, Latin, linguistics, Polish, Portuguese, Romance, Russian, Spanish. **Health:** Audiology/speech pathology, clinical lab science, communication disorders, nursing (RN), physician assistant, vocational rehab counseling. **History:** General, science/technology. **Interdisciplinary:** Behavioral sciences, global studies. **Legal studies:** General. **Math:** General, applied, statistics. **Parks/recreation:** Exercise sciences, facilities management. **Philosophy/religion:** Philosophy, religion. **Physical sciences:** Astronomy, astrophysics, atmospheric science, chemistry, geology, geophysics, physics, planetary. **Protective services:** Criminal justice. **Psychology:** General. **Public administration:** Social work. **Social sciences:** Anthropology, cartography, economics, geography, political science, sociology. **Visual/performing arts:** Art, art history/conservation, ceramics, cinematography, commercial/advertising art, conducting, dance, design, dramatic, fashion design, fiber arts, film/cinema, interior design, jazz, metal/jewelry, music history, music performance, music theory/composition, painting, piano/organ, printmaking, sculpture, theater design, voice/opera.

Most popular majors. Biology 10%, business/marketing 9%, communications/journalism 7%, engineering/engineering technologies 10%, social sciences 14%.

Computing on campus. 3,350 workstations in dormitories, library, computer center, student center. Dormitories wired for high-speed internet access and linked to campus network. Commuter students can connect to campus network. Online course registration, online library, helpline, repair service, student web hosting, wireless network available.

Student life. **Freshman orientation:** Mandatory. Preregistration for classes offered. **Housing:** Coed dorms, single-sex dorms, apartments, cooperative housing, fraternity/sorority housing, substance-free housing available. $50 nonrefundable deposit. Residential learning communities available. **Activities:** Bands, choral groups, dance, drama, film society, literary magazine, music ensembles, musical theater, opera, radio station, student government, student newspaper, symphony orchestra, TV station.

Athletics. NCAA. **Intercollegiate:** Basketball, cheerleading, cross-country, football (tackle) M, golf, ice hockey, rowing (crew), soccer, softball W, swimming, tennis, track and field, volleyball W, wrestling M. **Team name:** Badgers.

Student services. Adult student services, alcohol/substance abuse counseling, career counseling, services for economically disadvantaged, student employment services, financial aid counseling, health services, minority student services, personal counseling, placement for graduates, veterans' counselor, women's services. **Physically disabled:** Services for visually, speech, hearing impaired.

Contact. E-mail: onwisconsin@admissions.wisc.edu
Phone: (608) 262-3961 Fax: (608) 262-7706
Robert Seltzer, Director of Admissions, University of Wisconsin-Madison, Armory & Gymnasium, Madison, WI 53706-1481

University of Wisconsin-Milwaukee

Milwaukee, Wisconsin **CB member**
www.uwm.edu **CB code: 1473**

- Public 4-year university
- Commuter campus in very large city
- 21,662 degree-seeking undergraduates: 14% part-time, 53% women, 7% African American, 4% Asian American, 4% Hispanic American, 1% Native American, 1% international
- 4,066 degree-seeking graduate students
- 81% of applicants admitted
- SAT or ACT (ACT writing recommended) required
- 42% graduate within 6 years

General. Founded in 1956. Regionally accredited. **Degrees:** 3,181 bachelor's awarded; master's, doctoral offered. **ROTC:** Army, Air Force. **Location:** 90 miles from Chicago. **Calendar:** Semester, extensive summer session. **Class size:** 36% < 20, 44% 20-39, 6% 40-49, 7% 50-99, 8% >100. **Special facilities:** Planetarium, geological museum, art galleries, American Geological Society Collection.

Freshman class profile. 11,238 applied, 9,070 admitted, 4,300 enrolled.

Mid 50% test scores			
SAT verbal:	480-620	Rank in top tenth:	8%
SAT math:	490-610	Return as sophomores:	71%
ACT:	20-25	Out-of-state:	3%
Rank in top quarter:	28%	Live on campus:	35%

Basis for selection. High school academic record and class rank (top half) important. If applicant ranks in lower half of class, minimum enhanced ACT score of 21 required. ACT (or equivalent SAT score) for out-of-state residents required. Additional requirements for architecture. Students who do not meet standard admission requirements may apply through Academic Opportunity Program Office. SAT and ACT may be accepted for foreign students in lieu of other criteria. Audition required for dance, music, theater.

High school preparation. 17 units required; 19 recommended. Required and recommended units include English 4, mathematics 3, social studies 3, science 3 (laboratory 1), foreign language 2 and academic electives 4. Mathematics includes algebra, geometry, and beyond.

2005-2006 Annual costs. Tuition/fees: $6,220; $18,972 out-of-state. Room/board: $6,078. Books/supplies: $700. Personal expenses: $1,388.

2004-2005 Financial aid. Need-based: 2,714 full-time freshmen applied for aid; 1,930 were judged to have need; 1,803 of these received aid. Average need met was 58%. Average scholarship/grant was $4,243; average loan $2,755. 27% of total undergraduate aid awarded as scholarships/grants, 73% as loans/jobs. **Non-need-based:** Awarded to 1,409 full-time undergraduates, including 514 freshmen.

Application procedures. Admission: Priority date 6/30; deadline 8/1. $35 fee, may be waived for applicants with need. Admission notification on a rolling basis beginning on or about 9/15. **Financial aid:** Priority date 3/1; no closing date. FAFSA required. Applicants notified on a rolling basis starting 3/1.

Academics. Special study options: Accelerated study, cooperative education, cross-registration, distance learning, ESL, honors, independent study, internships, student-designed major, study abroad, teacher certification program, United Nations semester, Washington semester. **Credit/placement by examination:** AP, CLEP, institutional tests. **Support services:** Learning center, pre-admission summer program, reduced course load, remedial instruction, tutoring.

Majors. Architecture: Architecture. **Area/ethnic studies:** African. **Biology:** General, conservation. **Business:** Accounting, finance, human resources, management information systems, marketing, operations, real estate. **Communications:** General, journalism. **Computer sciences:** Computer science. **Education:** General, art, music. **Engineering:** Civil, electrical, materials, mechanical. **Foreign languages:** Classics, comparative lit, French, German, Hebrew, Italian, linguistics, Russian, Spanish. **Health:** Clinical lab science, communication disorders, medical records admin, nursing (RN), predentistry, premedicine, prepharmacy, preveterinary. **History:** General. **Legal studies:** Prelaw. **Liberal arts:** Arts/sciences. **Math:** General, applied. **Parks/recreation:** General, exercise sciences. **Philosophy/religion:** Philosophy, religion. **Physical sciences:** Chemistry, geology, physics. **Protective services:** Criminal justice. **Psychology:** General. **Public administration:** Social work. **Social sciences:** General, anthropology, economics, geography, political science, sociology, urban studies. **Visual/performing arts:** Art, art history/conservation, dance, dramatic, film/cinema, multimedia.

Most popular majors. Business/marketing 19%, communication technologies 9%, education 11%, health sciences 11%, social sciences 9%, visual/performing arts 7%.

Computing on campus. 400 workstations in dormitories, library, computer center, student center.

Student life. Housing: Coed dorms, special housing for disabled, apartments available. **Activities:** Bands, choral groups, dance, drama, film society, literary magazine, music ensembles, musical theater, radio station, student government, student newspaper, symphony orchestra.

Athletics. NCAA. **Intercollegiate:** Baseball M, basketball, cross-country, diving, soccer, swimming, tennis, track and field, volleyball. **Intramural:** Badminton, baseball M, basketball, bowling, diving, fencing, football (tackle) M, golf, handball, racquetball, rugby, sailing, skiing, soccer, softball, swimming, tennis, volleyball, water polo, wrestling M.

Student services. Adult student services, career counseling, student employment services, health services, on-campus daycare, personal counseling, placement for graduates, veterans' counselor. **Physically disabled:** Services for visually, speech, hearing impaired.

Contact. E-mail: uwmlook@uwm.edu
Phone: (414) 229-2222 Fax: (414) 229-6940
Beth Weckmueller, Executive Director of Enrollment Services and Registrar, University of Wisconsin-Milwaukee, Box 749, Milwaukee, WI 53201

University of Wisconsin-Oshkosh

Oshkosh, Wisconsin **CB member**
www.uwosh.edu **CB code: 1916**

- Public 4-year university
- Residential campus in small city
- 9,592 degree-seeking undergraduates: 11% part-time, 60% women, 1% African American, 3% Asian American, 1% Hispanic American, 1% Native American, 1% international
- 1,043 degree-seeking graduate students
- 79% of applicants admitted
- ACT (writing optional) required
- 46% graduate within 6 years

General. Founded in 1871. Regionally accredited. **Degrees:** 1,553 bachelor's, 2 associate awarded; master's offered. **ROTC:** Army. **Location:** 90 miles from Milwaukee. **Calendar:** Semester, limited summer session. **Full-time faculty:** 381 total; 85% have terminal degrees, 13% minority, 40% women. **Part-time faculty:** 185 total; 27% have terminal degrees, 6% minority, 63% women. **Class size:** 27% < 20, 54% 20-39, 6% 40-49, 9% 50-99, 4% >100. **Special facilities:** Planetarium.

Freshman class profile. 4,777 applied, 3,796 admitted, 1,634 enrolled.

Mid 50% test scores			
ACT:	20-24	Rank in top quarter:	38%
GPA 3.50 or higher:	32%	Rank in top tenth:	11%
GPA 3.0-3.49:	47%	Return as sophomores:	76%
GPA 2.0-2.99:	21%	Out-of-state:	2%
		Live on campus:	69%

Basis for selection. Students must rank in top half of high school class or have ACT composite score of 22 if rank is in third quartile. Out-of-state applicants may submit SAT scores. Interview recommended for all; audition required for music.

High school preparation. 17 units required. Required and recommended units include English 4, mathematics 3-4, social studies 3, history 1, science 3-4, foreign language 2 and academic electives 4. Social studies must include 1 history.

2005-2006 Annual costs. Tuition/fees: $4,977; $15,023 out-of-state. Room/board: $4,784. Books/supplies: $750. Personal expenses: $2,000.

2004-2005 Financial aid. Need-based: 1,305 full-time freshmen applied for aid; 914 were judged to have need; 914 of these received aid. Average need met was 50%. Average scholarship/grant was $1,800; average loan $2,500. 26% of total undergraduate aid awarded as scholarships/grants, 74% as loans/jobs. **Non-need-based:** Awarded to 4,178 full-time undergraduates, including 936 freshmen. Scholarships awarded for academics, alumni affiliation, art, leadership, minority status, music/drama, state residency.

Application procedures. Admission: No deadline. $35 fee, may be waived for applicants with need. Application may be submitted online. Admission notification on a rolling basis. **Financial aid:** Priority date 3/15; no

closing date. FAFSA required. Applicants notified on a rolling basis starting 5/1; must reply within 2 week(s) of notification.

Academics. **Special study options:** Accelerated study, cooperative education, distance learning, double major, dual enrollment of high school students, ESL, exchange student, honors, independent study, internships, student-designed major, study abroad, teacher certification program, weekend college. **Credit/placement by examination:** AP, CLEP, IB, institutional tests. 32 credit hours maximum toward bachelor's degree. **Support services:** Learning center, pre-admission summer program, reduced course load, study skills assistance, tutoring, writing center.

Majors. **Biology:** General, bacteriology. **Business:** Accounting, finance, human resources, management information systems, operations. **Communications:** General, broadcast journalism, journalism. **Computer sciences:** Computer science. **Education:** Elementary, emotionally handicapped, learning disabled, mentally handicapped, music, physical, science, secondary, social science, special. **Foreign languages:** French, German, Spanish. **Health:** Clinical lab technology, nursing (RN), predentistry, premedicine, prepharmacy, preveterinary. **History:** General. **Legal studies:** Prelaw. **Liberal arts:** Arts/sciences. **Math:** General. **Philosophy/religion:** Philosophy, religion. **Physical sciences:** Chemistry, geology, physics. **Psychology:** General. **Public administration:** Human services, social work. **Social sciences:** Anthropology, economics, geography, political science, sociology, urban studies. **Visual/performing arts:** Art, cinematography, dramatic, studio arts.

Most popular majors. Business/marketing 20%, communications/journalism 8%, education 16%, health sciences 11%, public administration/social services 6%, social sciences 7%.

Computing on campus. 475 workstations in dormitories, library, computer center, student center. Dormitories wired for high-speed internet access and linked to campus network. Commuter students can connect to campus network. Online course registration, helpline available.

Student life. **Freshman orientation:** Available. **Policies:** Select group of freshmen take part in residential college experience for more individualized instruction. Freshmen permitted cars on campus. **Housing:** Guaranteed on-campus for freshmen. Coed dorms, single-sex dorms available. $125 deposit, deadline 6/15. **Activities:** Bands, choral groups, dance, drama, film society, literary magazine, music ensembles, musical theater, opera, radio station, student government, student newspaper, symphony orchestra, TV station, Black Student Union, Asian student association, American Indian student association, Hispanic Cultures United, InterVarsity Christian Fellowship, Athletes in Action, Crusade for Christ, United Ministries student group, community involvement program, Habitat for Humanity.

Athletics. NCAA. **Intercollegiate:** Baseball M, basketball, cross-country, diving, football (tackle) M, golf W, gymnastics W, rifle, soccer, softball W, swimming, tennis, track and field, volleyball W, wrestling M. **Intramural:** Basketball, racquetball, skiing, soccer, softball, volleyball. **Team name:** Titans.

Student services. Adult student services, alcohol/substance abuse counseling, career counseling, services for economically disadvantaged, student employment services, financial aid counseling, health services, minority student services, on-campus daycare, personal counseling, placement for graduates, veterans' counselor, women's services. **Physically disabled:** Services for visually, speech, hearing impaired.

Contact. E-mail: oshadmuw@uwosh.edu
Phone: (920) 424-0202 Fax: (920) 424-1098
Jill Endries, Director of Admissions, University of Wisconsin-Oshkosh, 800 Algoma Boulevard, Oshkosh, WI 54901-8602

University of Wisconsin-Parkside

Kenosha, Wisconsin — **CB member**
www.uwp.edu — **CB code: 1860**

- Public 4-year university
- Commuter campus in small city
- 4,590 degree-seeking undergraduates: 23% part-time, 57% women
- 86 degree-seeking graduate students
- 92% of applicants admitted

General. Founded in 1968. Regionally accredited. **Degrees:** 589 bachelor's awarded; master's offered. **ROTC:** Army. **Location:** 30 miles from Milwaukee, 60 miles from Chicago. **Calendar:** Semester, extensive summer session. **Full-time faculty:** 181 total; 74% have terminal degrees, 22% minority, 45% women. **Part-time faculty:** 132 total; 22% have terminal degrees, 15% minority, 42% women. **Class size:** 46% < 20, 37% 20-39, 8% 40-49, 9% 50-99, less than 1% >100. **Special facilities:** Communication arts building.

Freshman class profile. 1,868 applied, 1,726 admitted, 877 enrolled.

Mid 50% test scores		**Out-of-state:**	5%
ACT:	18-22	**Live on campus:**	50%
Rank in top quarter:	23%	**International:**	1%
Rank in top tenth:	5%	**Fraternities:**	1%
Return as sophomores:	65%	**Sororities:**	1%

Basis for selection. Rank in top half of graduating class with specified distribution of high school units for standard admission. Students can be admitted on conditional status if in top 65 percent of class or with ACT composite of 18 or higher. Audition required for theater, recommended for music; portfolio recommended for art. **Homeschooled:** Applicants reviewed on an individual basis.

High school preparation. College-preparatory program required. 17 units required; 22 recommended. Required and recommended units include English 4, mathematics 3-4, social studies 3, history 1, science 3-4 (laboratory 2), foreign language 2 and academic electives 4.

2005-2006 Annual costs. Tuition/fees: $5,001; $15,767 out-of-state. Room/board: $5,550. Books/supplies: $784. Personal expenses: $1,328.

2004-2005 Financial aid. **Need-based:** 621 full-time freshmen applied for aid; 586 were judged to have need; 503 of these received aid. Average need met was 87%. Average scholarship/grant was $3,108; average loan $2,666. 53% of total undergraduate aid awarded as scholarships/grants, 47% as loans/jobs. **Non-need-based:** Awarded to 318 full-time undergraduates, including 168 freshmen. Scholarships awarded for academics, art, athletics, minority status, music/drama, state residency.

Application procedures. **Admission:** Priority date 3/1; deadline 8/1 (postmark date). $35 fee, may be waived for applicants with need. Application may be submitted online. Admission notification on a rolling basis beginning on or about 9/15. **Financial aid:** Priority date 3/15; no closing date. FAFSA required. Applicants notified on a rolling basis starting 4/1; must reply within 2 week(s) of notification.

Academics. **Special study options:** Accelerated study, double major, dual enrollment of high school students, exchange student, honors, independent study, internships, liberal arts/career combination, study abroad, teacher certification program, weekend college. Cooperative nursing program with University of Wisconsin: Milwaukee. **Credit/placement by examination:** AP, CLEP, IB, institutional tests. 30 credit hours maximum toward bachelor's degree. Retroactive credit policy for foreign language study. **Support services:** Learning center, reduced course load, remedial instruction, study skills assistance, tutoring, writing center.

Majors. **Area/ethnic studies:** French, German. **Biology:** General, molecular. **Business:** General, accounting, business admin, finance, human resources, management information systems. **Communications:** General. **Computer sciences:** Computer science. **Foreign languages:** French, German, Spanish. **Health:** Predentistry, premedicine, preveterinary. **History:** General. **Interdisciplinary:** Math/computer science. **Legal studies:** Prelaw. **Liberal arts:** Arts/sciences. **Math:** General. **Parks/recreation:** Sports admin. **Philosophy/religion:** Philosophy. **Physical sciences:** Chemistry, geology, physics. **Protective services:** Criminal justice. **Psychology:** General. **Social sciences:** Economics, geography, political science, sociology. **Visual/performing arts:** Art, dramatic.

Most popular majors. Biology 7%, business/marketing 21%, communications/journalism 8%, English 6%, psychology 8%, security/protective services 11%, social sciences 14%, visual/performing arts 8%.

Computing on campus. 225 workstations in dormitories, library, computer center, student center. Dormitories wired for high-speed internet access and linked to campus network. Commuter students can connect to campus network. Online course registration, online library, helpline, student web hosting, wireless network available.

Student life. **Freshman orientation:** Mandatory, $52 fee. Preregistration for classes offered. Day-long session offered several times throughout summer before fall semester. **Policies:** Freshmen permitted cars on campus. **Housing:** Coed dorms, special housing for disabled, apartments available. $50 deposit. **Activities:** Bands, choral groups, dance, drama, literary magazine, music ensembles, musical theater, radio station, student government, student newspaper, symphony orchestra, College Democrats, Campus Crusade for Christ, optimist club, black student union, Latinos Unidos, community outreach club, Habitat for Humanity, adult student alliance, rugby club, activities board.

Athletics. NCAA. **Intercollegiate:** Baseball M, basketball, cross-country, golf M, soccer, softball W, track and field, volleyball W, wrestling M. **Intramural:** Basketball, racquetball, soccer, softball, table tennis, tennis, volleyball. **Team name:** Rangers.

Student services. Adult student services, alcohol/substance abuse counseling, career counseling, services for economically disadvantaged, student employment services, financial aid counseling, health services, minority student services, on-campus daycare, personal counseling, placement for graduates, veterans' counselor, women's services. **Physically disabled:** Services for visually, speech, hearing impaired.

Contact. E-mail: matthew.jensen@uwp.edu
Phone: (262) 595-2355 Fax: (262) 595-2008
Matthew Jensen, Director of Admissions, University of Wisconsin-Parkside, PO Box 2000, Kenosha, WI 53141-2000

University of Wisconsin-Platteville

Platteville, Wisconsin — **CB member**
www.uwplatt.edu — **CB code: 1917**

- Public 4-year university
- Residential campus in large town
- 5,631 degree-seeking undergraduates: 8% part-time, 38% women, 1% African American, 1% Asian American, 1% Hispanic American
- 535 degree-seeking graduate students
- 85% of applicants admitted
- ACT (writing recommended) required
- 51% graduate within 6 years

General. Founded in 1866. Regionally accredited. **Degrees:** 883 bachelor's awarded; master's offered. **Location:** 25 miles from Dubuque, Iowa, 75 miles from Madison. **Calendar:** Semester, limited summer session. **Full-time faculty:** 249 total; 83% have terminal degrees, 16% minority, 31% women. **Part-time faculty:** 99 total; 17% have terminal degrees, 3% minority, 37% women. **Class size:** 51% < 20, 39% 20-39, 5% 40-49, 4% 50-99, less than 1% >100.

Freshman class profile. 3,075 applied, 2,620 admitted, 1,218 enrolled.

Mid 50% test scores		**Out-of-state:**	15%
ACT:	20-25	**Live on campus:**	90%
Rank in top quarter:	35%	**Fraternities:**	7%
Rank in top tenth:	12%	**Sororities:**	7%
Return as sophomores:	76%		

Basis for selection. Rank in top 40% of graduating class or ACT composite score of 22 for standard admission. Applicants in top 65% of class or with ACT composite score of 20 may be put on waiting list. Competency Based Admission requirements. Audition required for music scholarships. **Homeschooled:** Submit ACT scores.

High school preparation. 7 units required. Required and recommended units include English 4, mathematics 3, social studies 3, science 3, foreign language 2 and academic electives 4. 3 units natural science (2 from biology, chemistry, or physics), 3 units algebra I, geometry, algebra II, or higher.

2005-2006 Annual costs. Tuition/fees: $4,981; $15,027 out-of-state. Minnesota reciprocity tuition: $4,780 full-time, $199 per credit hour. Room/board: $4,658. Books/supplies: $300. Personal expenses: $1,170.

Financial aid. All financial aid based on need.

Application procedures. Admission: Priority date 1/1; no deadline. $35 fee. Application may be submitted online. Admission notification on a rolling basis beginning on or about 9/15. **Financial aid:** Priority date 3/15; no closing date. FAFSA required. Applicants notified on a rolling basis starting 6/1; must reply within 2 week(s) of notification.

Academics. Special study options: Combined bachelor's/graduate degree, distance learning, double major, exchange student, external degree, honors, independent study, internships, student-designed major, study abroad, teacher certification program. **Credit/placement by examination:** AP, CLEP, institutional tests. 30 credit hours maximum toward bachelor's degree. **Support services:** Learning center, study skills assistance, tutoring, writing center.

Majors. Agriculture: Agribusiness operations, agronomy, animal sciences, economics. **Biology:** General. **Business:** General, accounting, business admin, entrepreneurial studies, finance, human resources, investments/securities, organizational behavior. **Communications:** General. **Computer sciences:** Computer science. **Conservation:** General. **Construction:** Maintenance. **Education:** Agricultural, art, biology, chemistry, early childhood, elementary, English, German, history, mathematics, science, social science, social studies, Spanish, speech, technology/industrial arts, voc/tech. **Engineering:** Civil, electrical, mechanical, physics. **Foreign languages:** German, Spanish. **History:** General. **Math:** General. **Parks/recreation:** Health/fitness. **Philosophy/religion:** Philosophy. **Physical sciences:** Chemistry. **Protective services:** Law enforcement admin. **Psychology:** General. **Social sciences:** General, economics, geography, political science, sociology. **Visual/performing arts:** Art, commercial/advertising art, dramatic.

Most popular majors. Agriculture 8%, business/marketing 13%, education 12%, engineering/engineering technologies 32%, security/protective services 9%.

Computing on campus. 483 workstations in dormitories, library, computer center. Dormitories wired for high-speed internet access and linked to campus network. Commuter students can connect to campus network. Online course registration, online library, helpline, repair service, student web hosting available.

Student life. Freshman orientation: Available. **Policies:** Freshmen permitted cars on campus. **Housing:** Guaranteed on-campus for freshmen. Coed dorms, single-sex dorms, fraternity/sorority housing available. $100 nonrefundable deposit. All residence halls have connections to campus computer network in every room. **Activities:** Bands, choral groups, dance, drama, literary magazine, music ensembles, musical theater, opera, radio station, student government, student newspaper, symphony orchestra, TV station, Black student union, A.S.I.A. student group, Hmong club, inter-tribal council, Young Democrats, College Republicans, Circle K.

Athletics. NCAA. **Intercollegiate:** Baseball M, basketball, cross-country, football (tackle) M, golf W, soccer, softball W, track and field, volleyball W, wrestling M. **Intramural:** Basketball, bowling, racquetball, soccer, softball, tennis, volleyball, water polo M.

Student services. Adult student services, alcohol/substance abuse counseling, campus ministries, career counseling, student employment services, financial aid counseling, health services, minority student services, on-campus daycare, personal counseling, placement for graduates, veterans' counselor, women's services. **Physically disabled:** Services for visually, speech, hearing impaired.

Contact. E-mail: admit@uwplatt.edu
Phone: (608) 342-1125 Toll-free number: (800) 362-5515
Fax: (608) 342-1122
Angela Udelhofen, Dean of Admissions and Enrollment Management, University of Wisconsin-Platteville, One University Plaza, Platteville, WI 53818

University of Wisconsin-River Falls

River Falls, Wisconsin
www.uwrf.edu — **CB code: 1918**

- Public 4-year university
- Residential campus in large town
- 5,504 degree-seeking undergraduates: 5% part-time, 61% women, 1% African American, 3% Asian American, 1% Hispanic American, 1% international
- 370 degree-seeking graduate students
- 80% of applicants admitted
- ACT (writing optional) required
- 56% graduate within 6 years; 15% enter graduate study

General. Founded in 1874. Regionally accredited. **Degrees:** 990 bachelor's awarded; master's offered. **ROTC:** Army. **Location:** 30 miles from Minneapolis-St. Paul. **Calendar:** Semester, limited summer session. **Full-time faculty:** 223 total. **Part-time faculty:** 101 total. **Class size:** 27% < 20, 51% 20-39, 13% 40-49, 8% 50-99, 1% >100. **Special facilities:** 2 laboratory farms, 20-inch reflecting telescope, USDA-approved food science laboratory, computerized greenhouse, 42-foot rapelling and climbing wall, indoor track and field house, on campus ice arena, electron microscope, observatory, education regional archive collection.

Freshman class profile. 3,223 applied, 2,580 admitted, 1,209 enrolled.

Mid 50% test scores		**Return as sophomores:**	76%
ACT:	20-25	**Out-of-state:**	46%
Rank in top quarter:	37%	**Live on campus:**	90%
Rank in top tenth:	14%	**Fraternities:**	5%
End year in good standing:	90%	**Sororities:**	5%

Basis for selection. High school rank in top 40 percent of class with minimum ACT composite score of 18, or if high school rank in top 60 percent with minimum ACT composite score of 22. Minority student applications given special consideration. Elementary education applicants must rank in the top 40 percent of high school class and earn 24 or higher on ACT.

High school preparation. College-preparatory program required. 17 units required. Required and recommended units include English 4, mathematics

3-4, social studies 3-4, science 3-4, foreign language 1 and academic electives 4. Vocational agriculture units also recommended for applicants to College of Agriculture. Wisconsin residents who receive GED must also complete Wisconsin high school equivalency diploma.

2005-2006 Annual costs. Tuition/fees: $4,962; $15,008 out-of-state. Minnesota reciprocity tuition: $4,780 full-time, $199 per-credit-hour. Room/board: $4,400. Books/supplies: $200. Personal expenses: $1,106.

2004-2005 Financial aid. All financial aid based on need. 34% of total undergraduate aid awarded as scholarships/grants, 66% as loans/jobs.

Application procedures. **Admission:** Priority date 2/1; no deadline. $35 fee, may be waived for applicants with need. Application may be submitted online. Admission notification on a rolling basis beginning on or about 9/15. Late applicants considered on individual basis through appeal procedure. **Financial aid:** Priority date 3/15; no closing date. FAFSA required. Applicants notified on a rolling basis starting 4/1; must reply within 3 week(s) of notification.

Academics. **Special study options:** Accelerated study, combined bachelor's/graduate degree, cooperative education, cross-registration, distance learning, double major, dual enrollment of high school students, exchange student, honors, independent study, internships, liberal arts/career combination, student-designed major, study abroad, teacher certification program. **Credit/placement by examination:** AP, CLEP, IB, ACT, institutional tests. 27 credit hours maximum toward bachelor's degree. Placement in English, foreign languages, and math based on university system placement exams. **Support services:** Learning center, reduced course load, remedial instruction, study skills assistance, tutoring, writing center.

Majors. **Agriculture:** General, agronomy, animal sciences, business, dairy, equipment technology, food science, horticultural science, soil science. **Biology:** General, biotechnology. **Business:** Accounting, business admin. **Communications:** Journalism. **Computer sciences:** General. **Conservation:** General, management/policy. **Education:** Agricultural, art, elementary, ESL, music, physical, speech impaired. **English:** Speech/rhetoric. **Foreign languages:** French, German, Spanish. **Health:** Communication disorders. **History:** General. **Interdisciplinary:** Biological/physical sciences, global studies. **Math:** General. **Physical sciences:** Chemistry, geology, organic chemistry, physics, planetary, polymer chemistry. **Psychology:** General. **Public administration:** Social work. **Social sciences:** General, economics, geography, political science, sociology. **Visual/performing arts:** Art, studio arts.

Most popular majors. Agriculture 14%, biology 6%, business/marketing 17%, communications/journalism 9%, education 16%, social sciences 6%.

Computing on campus. 700 workstations in dormitories, library, computer center, student center. Dormitories wired for high-speed internet access and linked to campus network. Commuter students can connect to campus network. Online course registration, online library, helpline, repair service, student web hosting, wireless network available.

Student life. **Freshman orientation:** Mandatory. Preregistration for classes offered. Orientation is held over Labor Day weekend prior to classes starting. **Policies:** Freshmen and sophomores must live in residence halls unless they reside with parents. Freshmen permitted cars on campus. **Housing:** Guaranteed on-campus for freshmen. Coed dorms, single-sex dorms, apartments, fraternity/sorority housing, substance-free housing available. $125 partly refundable deposit. **Activities:** Bands, choral groups, dance, drama, literary magazine, music ensembles, musical theater, radio station, student government, student newspaper, symphony orchestra, TV station, African American Alliance, Hispanic Student Coalition, Native American Council, Hmong student association, Habitat for Humanity, Fellowship of Christian Athletes, Young Democrats, Young Republicans, Young Life, Intervarsity Christian Fellowship.

Athletics. NCAA. **Intercollegiate:** Basketball, cross-country, diving, football (tackle) M, golf W, ice hockey, soccer W, softball W, swimming, tennis W, track and field, volleyball W. **Intramural:** Badminton, basketball, bowling, cheerleading, football (non-tackle), golf, ice hockey, racquetball, softball, swimming, tennis, volleyball, water polo. **Team name:** Falcons.

Student services. Adult student services, alcohol/substance abuse counseling, campus ministries, career counseling, services for economically disadvantaged, student employment services, financial aid counseling, health services, minority student services, on-campus daycare, personal counseling, placement for graduates, veterans' counselor. **Physically disabled:** Services for visually, speech, hearing impaired.

Contact. E-mail: admit@uwrf.edu
Phone: (715) 425-3500 Fax: (715) 425-0676
Alan Tuchtenhagen, Director of Admissions, University of Wisconsin-River Falls, 410 South Third Street, River Falls, WI 54022-5001

University of Wisconsin-Stevens Point

Stevens Point, Wisconsin — **CB member**
www.uwsp.edu — **CB code: 1919**

- Public 4-year university
- Residential campus in large town
- 8,328 degree-seeking undergraduates: 7% part-time, 54% women, 1% African American, 2% Asian American, 1% Hispanic American, 1% Native American, 1% international
- 202 degree-seeking graduate students
- 80% of applicants admitted
- SAT or ACT (ACT writing optional) required
- 58% graduate within 6 years; 16% enter graduate study

General. Founded in 1894. Regionally accredited. **Degrees:** 1,536 bachelor's, 13 associate awarded; master's offered. **ROTC:** Army. **Location:** 110 miles from Madison, 240 miles from Chicago. **Calendar:** Semester, extensive summer session. **Full-time faculty:** 357 total; 87% have terminal degrees, 7% minority, 38% women. **Part-time faculty:** 80 total; 40% have terminal degrees, 4% minority, 49% women. **Class size:** 30% < 20, 46% 20-39, 8% 40-49, 12% 50-99, 4% >100. **Special facilities:** Natural history museum, planetarium and observatory, nature preserve, Foucault pendulum, electron microscope, 1,000-acre natural resources summer camp, fire science center, multicultural center.

Freshman class profile. 4,583 applied, 3,681 admitted, 1,523 enrolled.

Mid 50% test scores		**Rank in top tenth:**	14%
SAT verbal:	470-580	**Return as sophomores:**	76%
SAT math:	440-610	**Out-of-state:**	6%
ACT:	20-25	**Live on campus:**	89%
GPA 3.50 or higher:	39%	**International:**	2%
GPA 3.0-3.49:	43%	**Fraternities:**	1%
GPA 2.0-2.99:	18%	**Sororities:**	1%
Rank in top quarter:	42%		

Basis for selection. Rank in the top 25 percent of high school class; or have a minimum cumulative GPA of 3.25 (on a 4.0 scale) with a minimum ACT score of 21 or SAT 990 (exclusive of Writing); or rank in the top 50 percent of class with a minimum ACT score of 21 (SAT 990). The SAT is accepted in lieu of TOEFL. Standardized test scores required of all applicants under 21 years of age. Campus visit recommended.

High school preparation. 17 units required. Required units include English 4, mathematics 3, social studies 3 and science 3. Additional 2 units from English, mathematics, social sciences, sciences, or foreign language and 2 units from above areas or fine arts, computer science, or other academic areas.

2005-2006 Annual costs. Tuition/fees: $4,928; $14,974 out-of-state. Minnesota Reciprocity tuition $4,780 full-year or $199 per-credit-hour. Room/board: $4,322. Books/supplies: $450. Personal expenses: $1,730.

2004-2005 Financial aid. **Need-based:** 1,284 full-time freshmen applied for aid; 752 were judged to have need; 714 of these received aid. Average need met was 93%. Average scholarship/grant was $4,078; average loan $3,206. 36% of total undergraduate aid awarded as scholarships/grants, 64% as loans/jobs. **Non-need-based:** Awarded to 846 full-time undergraduates, including 151 freshmen. Scholarships awarded for academics, ROTC.

Application procedures. **Admission:** No deadline. $35 fee, may be waived for applicants with need. Application may be submitted online. Admission notification on a rolling basis beginning on or about 9/15. **Financial aid:** Priority date 3/15, closing date 6/15. FAFSA required. Applicants notified on a rolling basis starting 5/1; must reply within 4 week(s) of notification.

Academics. **Special study options:** Accelerated study, cooperative education, distance learning, double major, dual enrollment of high school students, ESL, independent study, internships, student-designed major, study abroad, teacher certification program. Cooperative program with University of Wisconsin: Eau Claire and St. Joseph's Hospital; collaborative degree program with University of Wisconsin-Marshfield, University of Wisconsin-Marathon and University of Wisconsin-Marinette. **Credit/placement by examination:** AP, CLEP, IB, institutional tests. 16 credit hours maximum toward associate degree, 32 toward bachelor's. **Support services:** Learning center, pre-admission summer program, reduced course load, remedial instruction, study skills assistance, tutoring, writing center.

Majors. **Agriculture:** Soil science. **Biology:** General. **Business:** Accounting, business admin. **Communications:** General. **Computer sciences:** General, web page design. **Conservation:** General, forestry, water/wetlands/marine, wildlife, wood science. **Education:** Early childhood, elementary, family/consumer sciences, music, physical, secondary. **Foreign languages:** French, German, Spanish. **Health:** Athletic training, audiology/speech pathology, clinical lab science. **History:** General. **Interdisciplinary:** Biological/physical sciences. **Liberal arts:** Arts/sciences. **Math:** General. **Parks/recreation:** Health/fitness. **Philosophy/religion:** Philosophy. **Physical sciences:** Chemistry, physics. **Psychology:** General. **Public administration:** General. **Social sciences:** General, economics, geography, political science, sociology. **Visual/performing arts:** General, art, arts management, dance, dramatic, interior design, music history, music performance.

Most popular majors. Biology 9%, business/marketing 10%, communications/journalism 7%, education 7%, natural resources/environmental science 13%, social sciences 10%, visual/performing arts 8%.

Computing on campus. 879 workstations in dormitories, library, computer center, student center. Dormitories linked to campus network. Commuter students can connect to campus network. Online course registration, helpline, student web hosting, wireless network available.

Student life. **Freshman orientation:** Mandatory, $35 fee. **Policies:** Nonsmoking policy for all campus buildings. Freshmen permitted cars on campus. **Housing:** Coed dorms, single-sex dorms, substance-free housing available. $125 deposit. Intercultural program hall; language hall; quiet wings/floors; upper class/nontraditional hall; eco hall. **Activities:** Bands, choral groups, dance, drama, film society, literary magazine, music ensembles, musical theater, radio station, student government, student newspaper, symphony orchestra, TV station, American Indians Reaching for Opportunities, Black Student Union, College Republicans, College Democrats, Lutheran Collegians, Association for Community Tasks, Newman Catholic Student Association, Habitat for Humanity, United Nations Student Organization, Gay-Straight Alliance.

Athletics. NCAA. **Intercollegiate:** Baseball M, basketball, cross-country, diving, football (tackle) M, golf W, ice hockey, soccer W, softball W, swimming, tennis W, track and field, volleyball W, wrestling M. **Intramural:** Badminton, basketball, football (non-tackle), football (tackle) M, golf, ice hockey, racquetball, soccer, softball, tennis, volleyball. **Team name:** Pointers.

Student services. Adult student services, alcohol/substance abuse counseling, career counseling, services for economically disadvantaged, student employment services, financial aid counseling, health services, minority student services, on-campus daycare, personal counseling, placement for graduates, veterans' counselor, women's services. **Physically disabled:** Services for visually, speech, hearing impaired.

Contact. E-mail: admiss@uwsp.edu
Phone: (715) 346-2441 Fax: (715) 346-3296
Catherine Glennon, Director of Admissions, University of Wisconsin-Stevens Point, Student Services Center, Stevens Point, WI 54481

University of Wisconsin-Stout
Menomonie, Wisconsin
www.uwstout.edu **CB code: 1740**

- Public 4-year university
- Residential campus in large town
- 7,248 degree-seeking undergraduates: 9% part-time, 49% women, 1% African American, 2% Asian American, 1% Hispanic American, 1% Native American, 1% international
- 527 degree-seeking graduate students
- SAT or ACT (ACT writing optional) required
- 48% graduate within 6 years

General. Founded in 1891. Regionally accredited. **Degrees:** 1,239 bachelor's awarded; master's offered. **Location:** 60 miles from Minneapolis-St. Paul. **Calendar:** 4-1-4, limited summer session. **Full-time faculty:** 289 total; 78% have terminal degrees, 10% minority, 40% women. **Part-time faculty:** 105 total; 26% have terminal degrees, 3% minority, 46% women. **Class size:** 30% < 20, 60% 20-39, 4% 40-49, 4% 50-99, 1% >100. **Special facilities:** Teleproduction center, technology transfer institute, vocational rehabilitation institute.

Freshman class profile. 1,694 enrolled.

Mid 50% test scores		**Return as sophomores:**	73%
ACT:	19-23	**Out-of-state:**	35%
GPA 3.50 or higher:	25%	**Live on campus:**	96%
GPA 3.0-3.49:	42%	**International:**	1%
GPA 2.0-2.99:	32%	**Fraternities:**	5%
Rank in top quarter:	28%	**Sororities:**	12%
Rank in top tenth:	6%		

Basis for selection. Rank in top half of high school class or ACT score of 22 or better required. Rolling admissions with limited enrollment in all programs. Art-graphic design deadline of November 1 with selective admission from qualified applications; not all qualified applicants will be admitted. Applied science and manufacturing engineering require upper 40% of class or ACT score of 22 or higher, along with an ACT-Math score of at least 22. If student is in top half of high school class, ACT scores need not be submitted until first day of classes. **Homeschooled:** Transcripts of completed coursework and ACT/SAT test results required. **Learning Disabled:** Current IEP may be submitted with application.

High school preparation. College-preparatory program required. Required and recommended units include English 4, mathematics 3, social studies 3, science 3, foreign language 2 and academic electives 4. Electives in English, math, social sciences, and sciences, technology business, fine art, family & consumer education, sciences.

2005-2006 Annual costs. Tuition/fees: $6,452; $16,785 out-of-state. Room/board: $4,572. Books/supplies: $306. Personal expenses: $1,620.

2005-2006 Financial aid. **Need-based:** 1,305 full-time freshmen applied for aid; 816 were judged to have need; 816 of these received aid. Average need met was 83%. Average scholarship/grant was $3,811; average loan $3,170. 33% of total undergraduate aid awarded as scholarships/grants, 67% as loans/jobs. **Non-need-based:** Awarded to 1,197 full-time undergraduates, including 613 freshmen. Scholarships awarded for academics.

Application procedures. **Admission:** Priority date 1/1; no deadline. $35 fee, may be waived for applicants with need. Application may be submitted online. Admission notification on a rolling basis beginning on or about 9/15. Enrollment limited. Early application recommended. **Financial aid:** Priority date 3/15; no closing date. FAFSA required. Applicants notified on a rolling basis starting 4/1; must reply within 4 week(s) of notification.

Academics. **Special study options:** Accelerated study, cooperative education, cross-registration, distance learning, double major, dual enrollment of high school students, exchange student, external degree, honors, independent study, internships, study abroad, teacher certification program. **Credit/placement by examination:** AP, CLEP, IB, institutional tests. **Support services:** Learning center, pre-admission summer program, reduced course load, remedial instruction, study skills assistance, tutoring, writing center.

Majors. **Business:** Business admin, customer service, hospitality admin, operations, sales/distribution. **Communications technology:** Printing management. **Computer sciences:** Networking. **Education:** Art, early childhood, family/consumer sciences, mentally handicapped, sales/marketing, technology/industrial arts, voc/tech. **Engineering:** Manufacturing. **Engineering technology:** General, construction. **English:** Technical writing. **Family/consumer sciences:** Clothing/textiles, family studies, institutional food production. **Health:** Dietetics, vocational rehab counseling. **Math:** Applied. **Psychology:** General. **Visual/performing arts:** Commercial/advertising art, studio arts.

Most popular majors. Business/marketing 38%, education 17%, engineering/engineering technologies 7%, family/consumer sciences 8%, health sciences 6%, psychology 6%, visual/performing arts 9%.

Computing on campus. PC or laptop required. 590 workstations in dormitories, library, computer center, student center. Dormitories wired for high-speed internet access and linked to campus network. Commuter students can connect to campus network. Online course registration, helpline, repair service, student web hosting, wireless network available.

Student life. **Freshman orientation:** Available. One-day program with additional activities week immediately before classes begin. **Policies:** Freshmen permitted cars on campus. **Housing:** Guaranteed on-campus for freshmen. Coed dorms, special housing for disabled, substance-free housing available. $125 partly refundable deposit. Freshman housing, smoke-free housing, upperclass/graduate housing, alcohol-free housing. **Activities:** Bands, choral groups, drama, film society, literary magazine, music ensembles, radio station, student government, student newspaper, black student union, Hmong Stout student organization, Lutheran student fellowship, College Democrats, College Republicans, Chi Alpha Christians in Action, single parent association, Club Los Hispanos.

Athletics. NCAA. **Intercollegiate:** Baseball M, basketball, cross-country, football (tackle) M, gymnastics W, ice hockey M, soccer W, softball W, tennis W, track and field, volleyball W. **Intramural:** Baseball M, basketball, golf, ice hockey, racquetball, soccer, softball, volleyball. **Team name:** Blue Devils.

Student services. Campus ministries, career counseling, student employment services, health services, on-campus daycare, personal counseling, placement for graduates, veterans' counselor. **Physically disabled:** Services for visually, speech, hearing impaired.

Contact. E-mail: admissions@uwstout.edu
Phone: (715) 232-1411 Toll-free number: (800) 447-8688
Fax: (715) 232-1667
Cindy Gilberts, Executive Director of Enrollment Services, University of Wisconsin-Stout, Menomonie, WI 54751

University of Wisconsin-Superior

Superior, Wisconsin
www.uwsuper.edu **CB code: 1920**

- Public 4-year university and liberal arts college
- Commuter campus in large town
- 2,507 degree-seeking undergraduates: 15% part-time, 60% women, 1% African American, 1% Asian American, 1% Hispanic American, 3% Native American, 5% international
- 237 degree-seeking graduate students
- 74% of applicants admitted
- SAT or ACT (ACT writing optional) required
- 41% graduate within 6 years

General. Founded in 1893. Regionally accredited. **Degrees:** 446 bachelor's, 9 associate awarded; master's offered. **ROTC:** Air Force. **Location:** 2 miles from Duluth, Minnesota, 150 miles from Minneapolis-St. Paul. **Calendar:** Semester, limited summer session. **Full-time faculty:** 117 total; 73% have terminal degrees, 11% minority, 39% women. **Part-time faculty:** 52 total; 23% have terminal degrees, 6% minority, 46% women. **Class size:** 48% < 20, 44% 20-39, 4% 40-49, 4% 50-99, less than 1% >100. **Special facilities:** Observatory, wetlands.

Freshman class profile. 918 applied, 679 admitted, 346 enrolled.

Mid 50% test scores			
SAT verbal:	490-610	Rank in top tenth:	14%
SAT math:	500-630	Return as sophomores:	71%
ACT:	20-24	Out-of-state:	41%
Rank in top quarter:	44%	Live on campus:	60%
		International:	6%

Basis for selection. Admissions based on secondary school record and class rank. Standardized test scores also important. Essay, audition, portfolio, interview recommended. **Homeschooled:** Statement describing homeschool structure and mission, transcript of courses and grades required.

High school preparation. 17 units required. Required units include English 4, mathematics 3, social studies 3, science 3 and academic electives 4. Math must include algebra, geometry and higher.

2005-2006 Annual costs. Tuition/fees: $5,182; $15,228 out-of-state. Minnesota reciprocity tuition: $4,780 full-time, $199 per-credit-hour. Room/board: $4,422. Books/supplies: $860. Personal expenses: $1,690.

2005-2006 Financial aid. Need-based: Average scholarship/grant was $4,173; average loan $2,657. 41% of total undergraduate aid awarded as scholarships/grants, 59% as loans/jobs. **Non-need-based:** Scholarships awarded for academics, art, leadership, minority status, music/drama. **Additional information:** Tuition Assistance Program (TAP) available to non-resident students on limited basis.

Application procedures. Admission: Priority date 4/1; no deadline. $35 fee, may be waived for applicants with need. Application may be submitted online. Admission notification on a rolling basis beginning on or about 10/1. Must reply by May 1 or within 4 week(s) if notified thereafter. **Financial aid:** Priority date 4/15; no closing date. FAFSA required. Applicants notified on a rolling basis starting 3/15.

Academics. Post-bachelor's certificates offered in early childhood education, counseling, and secondary education. Post-master's certificate offered in library science. **Special study options:** Combined bachelor's/graduate degree, cooperative education, cross-registration, distance learning, double major, dual enrollment of high school students, ESL, exchange student, external degree, honors, independent study, internships, liberal arts/career combination, student-designed major, study abroad, teacher certification program. Engineering with University of Wisconsin-Madison. **Credit/placement by examination:** AP, CLEP, IB, ACT, institutional tests. 32 credit hours maximum toward associate degree, 32 toward bachelor's. **Support services:** Learning center, pre-admission summer program, reduced course load, remedial instruction, study skills assistance, tutoring, writing center.

Majors. Biology: General, aquatic, botany, cell/histology, ecology, environmental, molecular. **Business:** General, accounting, business admin, finance, international, management information systems, marketing. **Communications:** General, broadcast journalism, journalism, media studies. **Computer sciences:** Computer science. **Education:** Art, biology, chemistry, English, history, mathematics, multi-level teacher, music, physical, science, social science. **English:** Speech/rhetoric. **Health:** Art therapy. **History:** General. **Interdisciplinary:** Biological/physical sciences. **Legal studies:** General, prelaw. **Liberal arts:** Arts/sciences. **Math:** General. **Physical sciences:** Chemistry. **Protective services:** Criminal justice. **Psychology:** General. **Public administration:** General, policy analysis, social work. **Social sciences:** General, economics, political science, sociology. **Transportation:** General. **Visual/performing arts:** General, art, art history/conservation, dramatic, music performance, studio arts.

Most popular majors. Biology 6%, business/marketing 21%, communications/journalism 8%, education 19%, psychology 7%, public administration/social services 7%, social sciences 8%.

Computing on campus. 340 workstations in dormitories, library, computer center, student center. Dormitories wired for high-speed internet access and linked to campus network. Commuter students can connect to campus network. Online course registration, online library, helpline, student web hosting, wireless network available.

Student life. Freshman orientation: Mandatory, $70 fee. Preregistration for classes offered. Held in the spring and summer and a 2 1/2 day program just prior to classes beginning. **Policies:** Freshmen permitted cars on campus. **Housing:** Guaranteed on-campus for freshmen. Coed dorms, single-sex dorms, special housing for disabled, substance-free housing available. $125 partly refundable deposit, deadline 7/1. Suites available in nontraditional residence halls for married students. Single parents have access to student residences. **Activities:** Bands, choral groups, dance, drama, music ensembles, radio station, student government, student newspaper, symphony orchestra, TV station, Asian Pacific/Islander student association, criminal justice association, American Indian student organization, black student union, College Democrats, world student association, social work student association, College Republicans, intervarsity Christian fellowship, student government association.

Athletics. NCAA. **Intercollegiate:** Baseball M, basketball, cross-country, golf W, ice hockey, soccer, softball W, track and field, volleyball W. **Intramural:** Badminton, basketball, bowling, cheerleading, cross-country, golf, ice hockey, racquetball, rifle, skiing, soccer, softball, swimming, tennis, volleyball. **Team name:** Yellowjackets.

Student services. Adult student services, alcohol/substance abuse counseling, campus ministries, career counseling, student employment services, financial aid counseling, health services, minority student services, on-campus daycare, personal counseling, veterans' counselor, women's services. **Physically disabled:** Services for visually, hearing impaired.

Contact. E-mail: admissions@uwsuper.edu
Phone: (715) 394-8230 Fax: (715) 394-8407
Jim Miller, Director of Admissions, University of Wisconsin-Superior, Belknap and Catlin, PO Box 2000, Superior, WI 54880

University of Wisconsin-Whitewater

Whitewater, Wisconsin
www.uww.edu **CB code: 1921**

- Public 4-year university
- Residential campus in large town
- 9,123 degree-seeking undergraduates: 7% part-time, 51% women, 4% African American, 2% Asian American, 2% Hispanic American, 1% Native American, 1% international
- 1,363 graduate students
- 55% of applicants admitted
- 50% graduate within 6 years

General. Founded in 1868. Regionally accredited. **Degrees:** 1,797 bachelor's, 6 associate awarded; master's offered. **ROTC:** Army, Air Force. **Location:** 40 miles from Madison, 50 miles from Milwaukee. **Calendar:** Semester, extensive summer session. **Full-time faculty:** 399 total; 84% have terminal degrees, 17% minority, 45% women. **Part-time faculty:** 98 total; 34% have terminal degrees, 5% minority, 53% women. **Class size:** 35% < 20, 50% 20-39, 10% 40-49, 4% 50-99, less than 1% >100. **Special facilities:** Observatory, nature preserve and recreation area, weather station.

Freshman class profile. 5,403 applied, 2,981 admitted, 1,708 enrolled.

Mid 50% test scores		**End year in good standing:**	92%
ACT:	20-24	**Return as sophomores:**	76%
GPA 3.50 or higher:	29%	**Out-of-state:**	5%
GPA 3.0-3.49:	42%	**Live on campus:**	90%
GPA 2.0-2.99:	29%	**International:**	1%
Rank in top quarter:	32%	**Fraternities:**	7%
Rank in top tenth:	8%	**Sororities:**	6%

Basis for selection. Rank in top 40% of high school class very important. Others may qualify on basis of combined class rank and ACT/SAT percentile. Special consideration given to minority, disabled and adult applicants. SAT or ACT recommended. ACT required of Wisconsin applicants. Test scores required for admission if student ranks in lower half of class or is unranked. All new freshmen under age 25 must provide test scores prior to registration. Audition required for music; portfolio recommended for art. **Homeschooled:** Transcript of courses and grades required.

High school preparation. College-preparatory program required. 17 units required; 20 recommended. Required and recommended units include English 4, mathematics 3-4, social studies 3-4, science 3-4 (laboratory 1), foreign language 2 and academic electives 4.

2005-2006 Annual costs. Tuition/fees: $5,305; $15,703 out-of-state. Minnesota reciprocity tuition: $4,780 full-time, $199 per-credit-hour. Room/board: $4,070. Books/supplies: $120. Personal expenses: $1,600.

2005-2006 Financial aid. Need-based: 1,427 full-time freshmen applied for aid; 949 were judged to have need; 887 of these received aid. Average need met was 70%. Average scholarship/grant was $4,860; average loan $3,014. 35% of total undergraduate aid awarded as scholarships/grants, 65% as loans/jobs. **Non-need-based:** Awarded to 1,068 full-time undergraduates, including 417 freshmen. Scholarships awarded for academics, alumni affiliation, art, leadership, minority status, music/drama, ROTC, state residency.

Application procedures. Admission: Priority date 1/1; no deadline. $35 fee, may be waived for applicants with need. Application may be submitted online. Admission notification on a rolling basis beginning on or about 9/15. **Financial aid:** Priority date 3/15; no closing date. FAFSA required. Applicants notified on a rolling basis starting 4/1; must reply within 2 week(s) of notification.

Academics. Special study options: Accelerated study, combined bachelor's/graduate degree, cooperative education, cross-registration, distance learning, double major, dual enrollment of high school students, ESL, exchange student, external degree, honors, independent study, internships, liberal arts/career combination, student-designed major, study abroad, teacher certification program, weekend college. **Credit/placement by examination:** AP, CLEP, IB, SAT, ACT, institutional tests. 60 credit hours maximum toward bachelor's degree. **Support services:** Learning center, pre-admission summer program, reduced course load, remedial instruction, study skills assistance, tutoring, writing center.

Majors. Area/ethnic studies: Women's. **Biology:** General. **Business:** General, accounting, business admin, finance, human resources, managerial economics, marketing, office/clerical, operations. **Communications:** General, broadcast journalism, journalism, public relations. **Computer sciences:** General, information technology, systems analysis. **Education:** General, art, biology, business, computer, drama/dance, early childhood, elementary, English, French, German, history, learning disabled, mathematics, music, physical, sales/marketing, science, secondary, social science, Spanish, special, speech. **Engineering technology:** Occupational safety. **English:** Creative writing, speech/rhetoric. **Foreign languages:** French, German, Spanish. **Health:** Speech pathology. **History:** General. **Interdisciplinary:** Global studies. **Legal studies:** Prelaw. **Liberal arts:** Arts/sciences. **Math:** General. **Physical sciences:** Chemistry, physics. **Psychology:** General. **Public administration:** General, policy analysis, social work. **Social sciences:** General, economics, geography, political science, sociology. **Visual/performing arts:** Art, art history/conservation, dance, dramatic, music theory/composition, theater arts management, theater history.

Most popular majors. Business/marketing 32%, communications/journalism 9%, education 14%, public administration/social services 6%, social sciences 7%.

Computing on campus. 1,373 workstations in dormitories, library, computer center, student center. Dormitories wired for high-speed internet access and linked to campus network. Commuter students can connect to campus network. Online course registration, online library, helpline, repair service, student web hosting, wireless network available.

Student life. Freshman orientation: Mandatory, $55 fee. Preregistration for classes offered. Full-day program held in summer. **Policies:** Freshmen permitted cars on campus. **Housing:** Guaranteed on-campus for freshmen. Coed dorms, single-sex dorms, special housing for disabled, fraternity/sorority housing, substance-free housing available. $125 deposit. **Activities:** Bands, choral groups, dance, drama, literary magazine, music ensembles, musical theater, opera, radio station, student government, student newspaper, symphony orchestra, TV station.

Athletics. NCAA. **Intercollegiate:** Baseball M, basketball, bowling W, cross-country, diving, football (tackle) M, golf W, gymnastics W, soccer, softball W, swimming, tennis, track and field, volleyball W, wrestling M. **Intramural:** Badminton, basketball, bowling, football (non-tackle), golf, racquetball, soccer, softball, table tennis, tennis, volleyball, water polo. **Team name:** Warhawks.

Student services. Adult student services, alcohol/substance abuse counseling, campus ministries, career counseling, services for economically disadvantaged, student employment services, financial aid counseling, health services, legal services, minority student services, on-campus daycare, personal counseling, placement for graduates, veterans' counselor, women's services. **Physically disabled:** Services for visually, speech, hearing impaired. **Learning disabled:** Comprehensive services available.

Contact. E-mail: uwwadmit@uww.edu
Phone: (262) 472-1440 Fax: (262) 472-1515
Stephen McKellips, Director of Admissions, University of Wisconsin-Whitewater, 800 West Main Street, Whitewater, WI 53190-1790

Viterbo University

La Crosse, Wisconsin — **CB member**
www.viterbo.edu — **CB code: 1878**

- Private 4-year university and liberal arts college affiliated with Roman Catholic Church
- Residential campus in small city
- 1,778 degree-seeking undergraduates
- 86% of applicants admitted
- ACT (writing optional) required

General. Founded in 1890. Regionally accredited. **Degrees:** 384 bachelor's awarded; master's offered. **ROTC:** Army. **Location:** 150 miles from Minneapolis-St. Paul, 150 miles from Madison. **Calendar:** Semester, limited summer session. **Full-time faculty:** 119 total. **Part-time faculty:** 105 total. **Class size:** 68% < 20, 30% 20-39, less than 1% 40-49, 2% 50-99. **Special facilities:** Center for ethics, science and technology; fine arts center; center for recreation and education.

Freshman class profile. 1,098 applied, 939 admitted, 284 enrolled.

Mid 50% test scores		**Rank in top tenth:**	11%
ACT:	19-24	**Out-of-state:**	22%
Rank in top quarter:	32%	**Live on campus:**	79%

Basis for selection. High school cumulative GPA and ACT score most important; testing and interview required for some students. Auditions and portfolio reviews required for students applying to School of Fine Arts (music, theater, art, dance). Interview required for students not meeting admission requirements. **Homeschooled:** Submission of academic transcript and ACT scores requested. **Learning Disabled:** All students encouraged to file ADA petition for reasonable accommodations, preferably 8 weeks prior to start of classes.

High school preparation. 16 units required; 19 recommended. Required and recommended units include English 3-4, mathematics 2, social studies 2, history 2, science 2 (laboratory 2), foreign language 2 and academic electives 5. Chemistry required for nursing, dietetics, natural sciences, allied health preprofessional students. Portfolios or auditions required for fine arts students.

2006-2007 Annual costs. Tuition/fees: $17,640. Additional fees for some art, dietetics, science courses, and nursing clinicals. Room/board: $5,640. Books/supplies: $650. Personal expenses: $1,800.

Financial aid. Non-need-based: Scholarships awarded for academics, alumni affiliation, art, athletics, leadership, minority status, music/drama, ROTC. **Additional information:** Approximately 97 percent of traditional undergraduate students receive financial aid. Average financial aid package $15,270.

Application procedures. Admission: Priority date 8/1; no deadline. $25 fee, may be waived for applicants with need. Application may be submitted online. Admission notification on a rolling basis. Must reply by May 1 or within 2 week(s) if notified thereafter. **Financial aid:** Priority date 3/15; no closing date. FAFSA, institutional form required. Applicants notified on a rolling basis starting 4/1; must reply within 3 week(s) of notification.

Academics. Learning Center offers individual and small group tutoring in all subject areas daily. Library services available weekends and evenings.

Computer help desk services available weekdays. **Special study options:** Accelerated study, cross-registration, distance learning, double major, dual enrollment of high school students, exchange student, independent study, internships, liberal arts/career combination, student-designed major, study abroad, teacher certification program, urban semester, Washington semester, weekend college. **Credit/placement by examination:** AP, CLEP, IB, institutional tests. 30 credit hours maximum toward bachelor's degree. 16 hours awarded for military services. **Support services:** Learning center, reduced course load, remedial instruction, study skills assistance, tutoring, writing center.

Majors. **Biology:** General, biochemistry. **Business:** Accounting, business admin, management information systems, marketing, nonprofit/public, restaurant/food services. **Computer sciences:** General. **Education:** Art, biology, business, chemistry, drama/dance, elementary, English, mathematics, middle, music, secondary, social studies, Spanish, technology/industrial arts. **English:** English lit. **Foreign languages:** Spanish. **Health:** Dietetics, nursing (RN). **Liberal arts:** Arts/sciences. **Math:** General. **Philosophy/religion:** Religion. **Physical sciences:** Chemistry. **Protective services:** Criminal justice. **Psychology:** General. **Public administration:** Social work. **Social sciences:** General, sociology. **Theology:** Preministerial, religious ed. **Visual/performing arts:** General, art, arts management, design, dramatic, graphic design, music pedagogy, music performance, studio arts.

Most popular majors. Business/marketing 20%, education 9%, health sciences 30%, interdisciplinary studies 7%, visual/performing arts 9%.

Computing on campus. 278 workstations in library, computer center. Dormitories wired for high-speed internet access and linked to campus network. Commuter students can connect to campus network. Online library, helpline, wireless network available.

Student life. **Freshman orientation:** Mandatory. Preregistration for classes offered. One-day program offered four times in the summer for incoming freshmen and parents. **Policies:** Standards of conduct, sexual harassment code, anti-hazing initiation policy, academic honesty policy, academic due process, campus security policy, residence hall terms and conditions, alcohol and drug policy, student event policies. **Housing:** Guaranteed on-campus for freshmen. Coed dorms, apartments, substance-free housing available. $100 deposit, deadline 8/1. University-owned theme houses, theme floors. **Activities:** Pep band, choral groups, dance, drama, literary magazine, music ensembles, musical theater, opera, student government, student newspaper, campus ministry, Connect, Students in Free Enterprise, Circle K, student nurses association, education club, Sigma Pi Delta, CREW, Global Rhythms, psychology club.

Athletics. NAIA. **Intercollegiate:** Baseball M, basketball, soccer, softball W, volleyball W. **Intramural:** Badminton, basketball, bowling, cross-country, golf, handball, racquetball, skiing, soccer, softball, table tennis, tennis, volleyball. **Team name:** V-Hawks.

Student services. Adult student services, alcohol/substance abuse counseling, campus ministries, career counseling, services for economically disadvantaged, student employment services, financial aid counseling, health services, personal counseling, placement for graduates, women's services. **Physically disabled:** Services for visually, hearing impaired.

Contact. E-mail: admission@viterbo.edu
Phone: (608) 796-3012 Toll-free number: (800) 848-3726
Fax: (608) 796-3020
Roland Nelson, Vice President for Enrollment, Viterbo University, 900 Viterbo Drive, La Crosse, WI 54601-8804

Wisconsin Lutheran College

Milwaukee, Wisconsin
www.wlc.edu **CB code: 1513**

- Private 4-year liberal arts college affiliated with Wisconsin Evangelical Lutheran Synod
- Residential campus in very large city
- 691 degree-seeking undergraduates
- SAT or ACT (ACT writing optional) required

General. Founded in 1973. Regionally accredited. Challenging academic program in a conservative Christian environment. **Degrees:** 139 bachelor's awarded. **ROTC:** Army, Navy, Air Force. **Calendar:** Semester, limited summer session. **Full-time faculty:** 48 total. **Part-time faculty:** 45 total. **Class size:** 62% < 20, 38% 20-39.

Freshman class profile.

Mid 50% test scores			
SAT verbal:	500-630	Rank in top quarter:	53%
SAT math:	540-620	Rank in top tenth:	23%
ACT:	22-27	Out-of-state:	19%
		Live on campus:	86%

Basis for selection. Test scores, class rank, GPA most important. Interview recommended for some; audition required for music scholarships.

High school preparation. 16 units required; 20 recommended. Required and recommended units include English 4, mathematics 3-4, history 2, science 2-3 (laboratory 1-2), foreign language 2-4 and academic electives 3. Mathematics or science majors should complete 4 units of mathematics and 3-4 units of appropriate science courses.

2005-2006 Annual costs. Tuition/fees: $17,470. Room/board: $6,080. Books/supplies: $700. Personal expenses: $1,470.

Financial aid. **Non-need-based:** Scholarships awarded for academics, art, leadership, minority status, music/drama, state residency.

Application procedures. **Admission:** Priority date 3/1; no deadline. $20 fee, may be waived for applicants with need. Application may be submitted online. Admission notification on a rolling basis beginning on or about 9/1. Must reply by May 1 or within 2 week(s) if notified thereafter. **Financial aid:** Priority date 3/1; no closing date. FAFSA, institutional form required. Applicants notified on a rolling basis starting 3/15; must reply within 2 week(s) of notification.

Academics. Special graduation requirements include freshman seminar. **Special study options:** Double major, dual enrollment of high school students, independent study, internships, student-designed major, study abroad, teacher certification program. **Credit/placement by examination:** AP, CLEP, institutional tests. **Support services:** Learning center, reduced course load, study skills assistance, tutoring, writing center.

Majors. **Biology:** General, biochemistry. **Business:** Managerial economics. **Communications:** General. **Education:** Elementary. **Foreign languages:** Spanish. **History:** General. **Math:** General. **Physical sciences:** Chemistry. **Psychology:** General. **Social sciences:** General, political science. **Theology:** Theology. **Visual/performing arts:** Art, dramatic.

Most popular majors. Biology 12%, business/marketing 11%, communications/journalism 20%, education 11%, English 8%, psychology 11%, visual/performing arts 12%.

Computing on campus. 200 workstations in dormitories, library, computer center, student center. Dormitories wired for high-speed internet access and linked to campus network. Commuter students can connect to campus network. Online library, helpline, repair service, wireless network available.

Student life. **Freshman orientation:** Mandatory. Preregistration for classes offered. Intensive 2-day program held week before start of fall semester; includes social activities, introduction to student support services. **Policies:** Drug free campus program. No alcohol on campus. Smoking permitted outside only. Freshmen permitted cars on campus. **Housing:** Guaranteed on-campus for all undergraduates. Single-sex dorms, apartments available. $100 deposit, deadline 5/1. All traditional age, unmarried students less than 5 years out of high school must live in college housing. Upperclassmen eligible for college apartments. **Activities:** Bands, choral groups, dance, drama, music ensembles, student government, student newspaper.

Athletics. NCAA. **Intercollegiate:** Baseball M, basketball, cross-country, football (tackle) M, golf, soccer, softball W, tennis W, track and field, volleyball W. **Intramural:** Basketball, football (tackle), softball, volleyball. **Team name:** Warriors.

Student services. Adult student services, campus ministries, career counseling, student employment services, financial aid counseling, health services, personal counseling, placement for graduates. **Physically disabled:** Services for visually, hearing impaired.

Contact. E-mail: admissions@wlc.edu
Phone: (414) 443-8811 Toll-free number: (888) 947-5884
Fax: (414) 443-8514
Craig Swiontek, Director of Admissions, Wisconsin Lutheran College, 8800 West Bluemound Road, Milwaukee, WI 53226-4699

Wyoming

University of Wyoming

Laramie, Wyoming **CB member**
www.uwyo.edu/ **CB code: 4855**

- Public 4-year university
- Residential campus in large town
- 8,984 degree-seeking undergraduates: 15% part-time, 52% women, 1% African American, 1% Asian American, 4% Hispanic American, 1% Native American, 1% international
- 2,171 degree-seeking graduate students
- 95% of applicants admitted
- 56% graduate within 6 years

General. Founded in 1886. Regionally accredited. Undergraduate and graduate degree programs offered in Casper. Extension classes available in off-campus locations throughout the state. Online classes offered nationally. **Degrees:** 1,695 bachelor's awarded; master's, doctoral, first professional offered. **ROTC:** Army, Air Force. **Location:** 45 miles from Cheyenne, 130 miles from Denver. **Calendar:** Semester, extensive summer session. **Full-time faculty:** 643 total; 84% have terminal degrees, 8% minority, 32% women. **Part-time faculty:** 49 total; 49% have terminal degrees, 2% minority, 45% women. **Class size:** 40% < 20, 44% 20-39, 6% 40-49, 7% 50-99, 4% >100. **Special facilities:** Geology museum, American Heritage Center, national park research center in Grand Teton National Park, planetarium, state veterinary laboratory, environmental biology laboratory, anthropology museum, on-site elementary school, infrared telescope observatory, lysimeter lab, insect museum, gallery room.

Freshman class profile. 3,155 applied, 3,008 admitted, 1,421 enrolled.

Mid 50% test scores			
SAT verbal:	480-610	Rank in top quarter:	48%
SAT math:	500-610	Rank in top tenth:	20%
ACT:	20-26	End year in good standing:	77%
GPA 3.50 or higher:	50%	Return as sophomores:	74%
GPA 3.0-3.49:	32%	Out-of-state:	44%
GPA 2.0-2.99:	18%	Live on campus:	71%
		International:	1%

Basis for selection. High school or college GPA, ACT or SAT scores and completion of 13 units in the stated pre-college curriculum. **Home-schooled:** Transcript of courses and grades required. **Learning Disabled:** Must present documentation of disability in order to receive assistance from University Disability Support Services.

High school preparation. 13 units required; 19 recommended. Required and recommended units include English 4, mathematics 3, science 3 (laboratory 3). 3 cultural context electives required. 3 behavioral or social sciences, 3 visual or performing arts, and 3 humanities or earth/space sciences recommended.

2005-2006 Annual costs. Tuition/fees: $3,429; $9,819 out-of-state. International students must pay an additional $35 fee per semester. Room/board: $6,240. Books/supplies: $1,000. Personal expenses: $2,000.

2004-2005 Financial aid. Need-based: 1,257 full-time freshmen applied for aid; 843 were judged to have need; 826 of these received aid. Average need met was 75%. Average scholarship/grant was $1,849; average loan $2,010. 41% of total undergraduate aid awarded as scholarships/grants, 59% as loans/jobs. **Non-need-based:** Awarded to 4,096 full-time undergraduates, including 753 freshmen. Scholarships awarded for academics, alumni affiliation, art, athletics, leadership, minority status, music/drama, religious affiliation, ROTC, state residency.

Application procedures. Admission: Priority date 3/1; deadline 8/10 (postmark date). $30 fee, may be waived for applicants with need. Application may be submitted online. Admission notification on a rolling basis. Early application recommended for students seeking financial aid and university housing preferences. **Financial aid:** Priority date 2/1; no closing date. FAFSA required. Applicants notified on a rolling basis starting 3/1; must reply within 3 week(s) of notification.

Academics. Remedial instruction offered on campus through Laramie County Community College. **Special study options:** Accelerated study, combined bachelor's/graduate degree, distance learning, double major, dual enrollment of high school students, ESL, exchange student, external degree, honors, independent study, internships, student-designed major, study abroad, teacher certification program, Washington semester. **Credit/placement by examination:** AP, CLEP, IB, SAT, ACT, institutional tests. Individual departments may also allow additional tests on case-by-case basis. **Support services:** Learning center, pre-admission summer program, reduced course load, study skills assistance, tutoring, writing center.

Majors. Agriculture: Agribusiness operations, communications, range science. **Area/ethnic studies:** American, women's. **Biology:** General, botany, microbiology, molecular, zoology. **Business:** Accounting, business admin, finance, management information systems, management science, managerial economics, marketing. **Communications:** General, journalism. **Computer sciences:** Computer science. **Conservation:** General, environmental studies. **Education:** Agricultural, elementary, music, physical, secondary, special, technology/industrial arts, trade/industrial. **Engineering:** Architectural, chemical, civil, computer, electrical, mechanical. **English:** English lit. **Family/consumer sciences:** General. **Foreign languages:** French, German, Russian, Spanish. **Health:** Audiology/speech pathology, dental hygiene, health services, nursing (RN). **History:** General. **Liberal arts:** Humanities. **Math:** General, statistics. **Parks/recreation:** Exercise sciences, facilities management. **Philosophy/religion:** Philosophy. **Physical sciences:** Chemistry, geology, physics. **Protective services:** Criminal justice. **Psychology:** General. **Public administration:** Social work. **Social sciences:** General, anthropology, geography, international relations, political science, sociology. **Visual/performing arts:** Art, dramatic, music performance, music theory/composition.

Most popular majors. Agriculture 6%, business/marketing 17%, education 17%, engineering/engineering technologies 10%, health sciences 7%, social sciences 6%.

Computing on campus. 1,300 workstations in dormitories, library, computer center, student center. Dormitories wired for high-speed internet access and linked to campus network. Commuter students can connect to campus network. Online course registration, online library, helpline, student web hosting, wireless network available.

Student life. Freshman orientation: Available, $35 fee. Preregistration for classes offered. Eight 2-day sessions held in June. **Policies:** New freshmen subject to live-in policy. Freshmen permitted cars on campus. **Housing:** Guaranteed on-campus for all undergraduates. Coed dorms, special housing for disabled, apartments, fraternity/sorority housing, substance-free housing available. $100 deposit. Floor-specific living plans in residence halls, health sciences living house available. **Activities:** Bands, choral groups, dance, drama, literary magazine, music ensembles, musical theater, opera, radio station, student government, student newspaper, symphony orchestra, TV station, Association of Black Student Leaders, Keepers of the Fire, local church organizations, College Republicans, Rocky Mountain Democrats, Fellowship of Christian Athletes, Amnesty International, Spectrum (lesbian/gay/bisexual/transgendered association), Movimiento Estudiantil Chicanos de Atzlan, Rocky Mountain Activist Network.

Athletics. NCAA. **Intercollegiate:** Basketball, cheerleading, cross-country, diving, football (tackle) M, golf, soccer W, swimming, tennis W, track and field, volleyball W, wrestling M. **Intramural:** Archery, badminton, baseball, basketball, bowling, cricket, fencing, football (non-tackle), football (tackle), golf, racquetball, skiing, soccer, softball, swimming, table tennis, tennis, track and field, triathlon, volleyball, water polo, weight lifting, wrestling. **Team name:** Cowboys, Cowgirls.

Student services. Adult student services, alcohol/substance abuse counseling, campus ministries, career counseling, services for economically disadvantaged, student employment services, financial aid counseling, health services, legal services, minority student services, on-campus daycare, personal counseling, placement for graduates, veterans' counselor, women's services. **Physically disabled:** Services for visually, speech, hearing impaired. **Learning disabled:** Comprehensive services available.

Contact. E-mail: why-wyo@uwyo.edu
Phone: (307) 766-5160 Toll-free number: (800) 342-5996
Fax: (307) 766-4042
Sara Axelson, Associate Vice President for Enrollment Management and Director of Admissions, University of Wyoming, Department 3314/1000 East University Avenue, Laramie, WY 82071

Guam

University of Guam

Mangilao, Guam
www.uog.edu CB code: 0959

- Public 4-year university
- Small town
- 2,713 degree-seeking undergraduates: 27% part-time, 60% women
- 214 degree-seeking graduate students

General. Founded in 1952. Regionally accredited. **Degrees:** 290 bachelor's awarded; master's offered. **ROTC:** Army. **Calendar:** Semester, limited summer session. **Full-time faculty:** 190 total. **Part-time faculty:** 50 total. **Special facilities:** University-operated athletic center, planetarium, marine lab, Pacific and Micronesian library resources.

Freshman class profile. 775 applied, 553 admitted, 553 enrolled.

Out-of-state:	35%	**Live on campus:**	20%

Basis for selection. Open admission, but selective for some programs.

2005-2006 Annual costs. Tuition/fees: $4,350; $12,030 out-of-state. Room only: $1,940. Books/supplies: $705. Personal expenses: $1,830.

Application procedures. Admission: Closing date 6/6. $49 fee. Admission notification on a rolling basis. **Financial aid:** Priority date 4/15; no closing date. FAFSA required. Applicants notified on a rolling basis starting 6/1; must reply within 2 week(s) of notification.

Academics. Special study options: Double major, internships. **Credit/placement by examination:** CLEP, institutional tests. **Support services:** Reduced course load, remedial instruction, tutoring.

Majors. Biology: General. **Business:** Accounting, business admin, finance, international. **Communications:** General. **Computer sciences:** General. **Education:** Bilingual, early childhood, elementary, physical, secondary, special. **Family/consumer sciences:** General. **Health:** Nursing (RN). **History:** General. **Math:** General. **Physical sciences:** Chemistry. **Protective services:** Criminal justice. **Psychology:** General. **Public administration:** General, social work. **Social sciences:** Anthropology, economics, political science, sociology. **Visual/performing arts:** Art.

Student life. Housing: Single-sex dorms available. **Activities:** Choral groups, dance, drama, student government, student newspaper.

Athletics. Intercollegiate: Archery, badminton, baseball M, basketball, bowling, boxing M, cross-country, diving, equestrian, fencing, field hockey W, football (tackle) M, golf, gymnastics, handball, ice hockey, lacrosse, racquetball, rifle, rowing (crew), rugby, sailing, skiing, soccer, softball, squash, swimming, table tennis, tennis, track and field, volleyball, water polo, wrestling M. **Intramural:** Archery, badminton, baseball M, basketball, bowling, boxing M, cross-country, diving, equestrian, fencing, field hockey W, football (tackle) M, golf, gymnastics, handball, ice hockey, lacrosse, racquetball, rifle, rowing (crew), rugby, sailing, skiing, skin diving, soccer, softball, squash, swimming, table tennis, tennis, track and field, volleyball, water polo, wrestling M. **Team name:** Tritons.

Student services. Student employment services, health services, on-campus daycare, personal counseling, placement for graduates.

Contact. E-mail: admitme@uog.edu
Phone: (671) 735-2201
Deborah Leon Guerrero, Registrar, University of Guam, UOG Station, Mangilao, GU 96923

Virgin Islands, U.S.

University of the Virgin Islands

St. Thomas, Virgin Islands, U.S. CB member
www.uvi.edu CB code: 0879

- Public 4-year university
- Commuter campus in small city
- 1,987 degree-seeking undergraduates: 39% part-time, 77% women
- 183 degree-seeking graduate students
- 72% of applicants admitted
- SAT or ACT (ACT writing optional) required
- 26% graduate within 6 years

General. Founded in 1962. Regionally accredited. Additional campus on St. Croix. Housing available on St. Thomas and St. Croix. **Degrees:** 172 bachelor's, 92 associate awarded; master's offered. **ROTC:** Army. **Location:** 45 miles from San Juan, Puerto Rico. **Calendar:** Semester, limited summer session. **Full-time faculty:** 107 total; 69% have terminal degrees, 48% minority, 47% women. **Part-time faculty:** 148 total; 16% have terminal degrees, 78% minority, 49% women. **Class size:** 74% < 20, 26% 20-39, less than 1% 40-49. **Special facilities:** Outdoor amphitheater, Caribbean collection, African art collection.

Freshman class profile. 802 applied, 581 admitted, 361 enrolled.

Mid 50% test scores		**GPA 2.0-2.99:**	62%
SAT verbal:	370-470	**End year in good standing:**	84%
SAT math:	340-450	**Return as sophomores:**	72%
GPA 3.50 or higher:	9%	**Out-of-state:**	6%
GPA 3.0-3.49:	26%		

Basis for selection. Secondary school record very important. Must have at least a 2.0 GPA. Nursing Aptitude Test required of nursing applicants.

High school preparation. College-preparatory program recommended. 11 units required. Required units include English 4, mathematics 2, social studies 2, science 2 and foreign language 1.

2005-2006 Annual costs. Tuition/fees: $3,726; $10,326 out-of-state. Room/board: $7,550. Books/supplies: $500. Personal expenses: $411.

2004-2005 Financial aid. Need-based: 274 full-time freshmen applied for aid; 243 were judged to have need; 219 of these received aid. Average need met was 60%. Average scholarship/grant was $3,800; average loan $2,000. 74% of total undergraduate aid awarded as scholarships/grants, 26% as loans/jobs. **Non-need-based:** Awarded to 88 full-time undergraduates, including 33 freshmen. Scholarships awarded for academics, athletics.

Application procedures. Admission: Priority date 2/1; deadline 4/30 (postmark date). $25 fee. Admission notification on a rolling basis. Must reply by 6/30. **Financial aid:** Closing date 3/1. FAFSA required. Applicants notified on a rolling basis starting 4/1; must reply within 2 week(s) of notification.

Academics. Special study options: Combined bachelor's/graduate degree, distance learning, exchange student, external degree, independent study, internships. **Credit/placement by examination:** AP, CLEP, institutional tests. **Support services:** Learning center, pre-admission summer program, reduced course load, remedial instruction, study skills assistance, tutoring.

Majors. Biology: General, marine. **Business:** Accounting, business admin. **Computer sciences:** Computer science. **Education:** Elementary, music, trade/industrial. **Liberal arts:** Arts/sciences. **Math:** General. **Physical sciences:** Chemistry. **Psychology:** General. **Social sciences:** General.

Computing on campus. 50 workstations in library, computer center. Dormitories linked to campus network. Helpline, wireless network available.

Student life. Freshman orientation: Mandatory, $50 fee. **Policies:** Freshmen permitted cars on campus. **Housing:** Single-sex dorms available. $100 nonrefundable deposit, deadline 6/1. **Activities:** Jazz band, choral groups, drama, music ensembles, student government, political clubs, president's club, Future Business Leaders of America, explorer's club, Virgin Islands student association, British Virgin Islands student association, Baptist Student Union, environment association, peer health educators.

Athletics. NCAA. **Intercollegiate:** Basketball, cross-country, tennis, volleyball. **Intramural:** Archery, badminton, basketball, fencing, golf, gymnastics, racquetball, softball, swimming, table tennis, tennis, track and field, volleyball. **Team name:** Bucs.

Student services. Career counseling, student employment services, health services, personal counseling, placement for graduates. **Physically disabled:** Services for visually, speech, hearing impaired.

Contact. E-mail: admissions@uvi.edu
Phone: (340) 693-1150 Fax: (340) 693-1155
Carolyn Cook-Roberts, Director of Admissions and New Student Services, University of the Virgin Islands, No. 2 John Brewers Bay, St. Thomas, VI 00802-9990

Arab Republic of Egypt

American University in Cairo

Cairo, Arab Republic of Egypt **CB member**
www.aucegypt.edu **CB code: 0903**

- Private 4-year university
- Commuter campus in very large city
- 3,890 degree-seeking undergraduates: 9% part-time, 51% women
- 1,013 degree-seeking graduate students
- 60% of applicants admitted
- 85% graduate within 6 years

General. Founded in 1919. Regionally accredited. Language of instruction is English; 75 percent of degree-seeking students must be of Egyptian nationality. **Degrees:** 889 bachelor's awarded; master's offered. **Location:** Center of Cairo. **Calendar:** Semester, extensive summer session. **Full-time faculty:** 310 total; 67% have terminal degrees, 47% women. **Part-time faculty:** 256 total; 59% have terminal degrees, 59% women. **Class size:** 55% < 20, 38% 20-39, 7% 40-49, less than 1% 50-99. **Special facilities:** Located near Cairo Museum with world's largest collection of Egyptian antiquities. Many historical sites representing Pharonic, Greco-Roman, Coptic (early Christian) and early Moslem periods in the area.

Freshman class profile. 1,973 applied, 1,186 admitted, 876 enrolled.

Mid 50% test scores		**GPA 3.0-3.49:**	29%
SAT verbal:	410-500	**GPA 2.0-2.99:**	20%
SAT math:	510-610	**Return as sophomores:**	92%
GPA 3.50 or higher:	51%		

Basis for selection. GED not accepted. Undergraduate degree applicants from the United States expected to have completed college preparatory (academic) high school program and to have taken SAT; minimum combined score of 1000 (exclusive of Writing) required. Arab students must take Thanawiya 'Amma; minimum score of 65% required. CE/GCSE/IGCSE certificates will also be considered for admission. SAT Subject Tests required for applicants who have graduated from American-style high schools with less than 3 semesters in residence.

High school preparation. Recommended units include English 3, mathematics 3, social studies 3, science 2 and foreign language 2. One unit fine arts recommended.

2005-2006 Annual costs. Tuition/fees: $13,829. Room only: $3,375. Books/supplies: $700. Personal expenses: $2,200.

2005-2006 Financial aid. Need-based: 461 full-time freshmen applied for aid; 423 were judged to have need; 356 of these received aid. **Non-need-based:** Scholarships awarded for academics, art, athletics, leadership, music/drama, state residency. **Additional information:** Up to 15 fellowships awarded annually in teaching English as a foreign language. To facilitate attendance of year-abroad U.S. students from state universities, tuition equivalent to difference between university's tuition and out-of-state tuition offered. Up to 20 graduate fellowships for qualified applicants from African countries. On-campus jobs paid at local (Egyptian) wage scale. Non-Egyptian nationals placing in top quarter of applicant pool for the year may receive $4,000 per year Academic Achievement Scholarship; those in the second or third quartile may receive $2,000 per year.

Application procedures. Admission: Closing date 6/15. $50 fee. Application may be submitted online. Admission notification on a rolling basis. **Financial aid:** Closing date 5/15. Institutional form required. Applicants notified by 10/15.

Academics. Special study options: Double major, ESL, independent study, liberal arts/career combination, study abroad. **Credit/placement by examination:** CLEP, IB, SAT, institutional tests. 30 credit hours maximum toward bachelor's degree. **Support services:** Learning center, reduced course load, remedial instruction, study skills assistance, writing center.

Majors. Area/ethnic studies: Near/Middle Eastern. **Biology:** General. **Business:** Accounting, actuarial science, business admin. **Communications:** Journalism. **Computer sciences:** General. **Engineering:** Construction, electrical, mechanical. **English:** English lit. **Foreign languages:** Arabic, comparative lit. **History:** General, Asian. **Math:** General. **Philosophy/religion:** Philosophy. **Physical sciences:** Chemistry, physics. **Psychology:** General. **Social sciences:** Anthropology, archaeology, economics, political science, sociology. **Visual/performing arts:** Art, dramatic.

Most popular majors. Business/marketing 22%, communications/journalism 16%, computer/information sciences 12%, engineering/engineering technologies 17%, social sciences 23%.

Computing on campus. 840 workstations in dormitories, library, computer center. Dormitories linked to campus network. Commuter students can connect to campus network. Online course registration, online library, helpline, repair service available.

Student life. Freshman orientation: Available. **Policies:** Non-smoking campus. **Housing:** Single-sex dorms available. $300 fully refundable deposit, deadline 6/30. 435 spaces available for international students; preference given to female students. **Activities:** Choral groups, dance, drama, film society, literary magazine, music ensembles, radio station, student government, student newspaper, African students association, community service society, Model United Nations, Model Arab League.

Athletics. Intercollegiate: Basketball, diving W, fencing, gymnastics, rowing (crew), soccer M, squash, swimming, table tennis, tennis, track and field, volleyball, water polo M, wrestling M. **Intramural:** Basketball, soccer, table tennis, tennis, volleyball.

Student services. Adult student services, career counseling, health services, personal counseling, placement for graduates.

Contact. E-mail: mdavidson@aucnyo.edu
Phone: (212) 730-8800 ext. 223 Fax: (212) 730-1600
Mary Davidson, Senior Student Affairs Officer, American University in Cairo, 420 Fifth Avenue, Third Floor, New York, NY 10018-2729

Bolivia

Universidad Privada Boliviana

Cochabamba, Bolivia **CB member**
www.upb.edu **CB code: 0856**

- Private 4-year university
- Very large city

General. Founded in 1992. **Location:** 391 kilometers from Santa Cruz, 497 kilometers from La Paz. **Calendar:** Semester.

Annual costs/financial aid. Books/supplies: $400.

Contact. Phone: (4) 268-287
Km 6.5 Camimo Antiguo a Quillacollo, Casilla 3967, Cochabamba, BO

Canada

Acadia University

Wolfville, Canada
www.acadiau.ca
CB member
CB code: 0901

- Public 4-year university
- Residential campus in small town
- 3,540 degree-seeking undergraduates
- 142 graduate students
- SAT required

General. Regionally accredited. Acadia Advantage program provides each student with notebook computer. **Degrees:** 757 bachelor's awarded; master's, first professional offered. **Location:** 60 miles from Halifax. **Calendar:** Semester, limited summer session. **Full-time faculty:** 220 total. **Part-time faculty:** 60 total. **Special facilities:** Environmental science center and botanical gardens.

Basis for selection. GED not accepted. Academic record and recommendations most important. Class rank and standardized test scores also important.

High school preparation. Required and recommended units include English 3, mathematics 2, history 2 and science 2.

2006-2007 Annual costs. Costs reported in Canadian dollars: $13,810 annually for tuition/fees for international students and $7760 annually for Canadian students, $6,999 for room & board. $503 health insurance fee for non-Canadian international students, $177 for Canadian students.

Financial aid. Non-need-based: Scholarships awarded for academics, athletics.

Application procedures. Admission: Priority date 3/1; no deadline. $25 fee, may be waived for applicants with need. Application may be submitted online. Admission notification on a rolling basis beginning on or about 10/1.

Academics. Special study options: Combined bachelor's/graduate degree, cooperative education, distance learning, double major, ESL, exchange student, honors, independent study, internships, liberal arts/career combination, study abroad, teacher certification program. **Credit/placement by examination:** CLEP. **Support services:** Remedial instruction, study skills assistance, tutoring, writing center.

Majors. Area/ethnic studies: Canadian. **Biology:** General. **Business:** General. **Computer sciences:** General. **Education:** General. **Family/consumer sciences:** Food/nutrition. **Foreign languages:** General. **Math:** General. **Parks/recreation:** General, exercise sciences. **Physical sciences:** Chemistry, geology. **Psychology:** General. **Social sciences:** Economics, political science, sociology. **Visual/performing arts:** Art, dramatic.

Computing on campus. PC or laptop required. Dormitories wired for high-speed internet access and linked to campus network. Commuter students can connect to campus network. Online course registration, online library, helpline, repair service, student web hosting, wireless network available.

Student life. Freshman orientation: Available. Preregistration for classes offered. **Policies:** Freshmen permitted cars on campus. **Housing:** Guaranteed on-campus for all undergraduates. Coed dorms, single-sex dorms, special housing for disabled, substance-free housing available. $100 deposit. **Activities:** Bands, choral groups, dance, drama, literary magazine, music ensembles, musical theater, opera, radio station, student government, student newspaper, symphony orchestra.

Athletics. Intercollegiate: Basketball, cross-country W, football (tackle) M, ice hockey M, rugby W, soccer W, volleyball W. **Intramural:** Badminton, baseball, basketball, cheerleading, football (non-tackle) M, football (tackle) M, ice hockey, rugby, soccer, softball, track and field, volleyball. **Team name:** Axemen/Axewomen.

Student services. Campus ministries, career counseling, student employment services, financial aid counseling, health services, legal services, minority student services, personal counseling, women's services. **Physically disabled:** Services for visually, hearing impaired.

Contact. E-mail: admissions@acadiau.ca
Phone: (902) 585-1016 Fax: (902) 585-1081
Anne Scott, Manager of Admissions, Acadia University, PO Box 40, Wolfville, CN B4P-2R6

McGill University

Montreal, Canada
www.mcgill.ca
CB member
CB code: 0935

- Public 4-year university
- Commuter campus in very large city
- 19,805 degree-seeking undergraduates: 12% part-time, 61% women, 17% international
- 8,622 degree-seeking graduate students
- 56% of applicants admitted
- 83% graduate within 6 years

General. Founded in 1821. **Degrees:** 4,277 bachelor's awarded; master's, doctoral, first professional offered. **Location:** City center. **Calendar:** Semester, limited summer session. **Full-time faculty:** 1,597 total; 95% have terminal degrees, 28% women. **Part-time faculty:** 805 total; 46% have terminal degrees, 43% women. **Class size:** 33% < 20, 29% 20-39, 7% 40-49, 21% 50-99, 11% >100. **Special facilities:** Museum of Canadian history, museum of natural history, entomological museum and research laboratory, ecomuseum, collection of Canadiana, Canadian architecture collection, arboretum, nature reserve, herbarium, Canadian history archives, research institute, arctic research station, subarctic research station, sound recording studio.

Freshman class profile. 18,963 applied, 10,689 admitted, 4,834 enrolled.

Mid 50% test scores			
SAT verbal:	620-720	GPA 3.0-3.49:	42%
SAT math:	650-720	Return as sophomores:	92%
ACT:	27-30	Out-of-state:	33%
GPA 3.50 or higher:	58%	Live on campus:	46%
		International:	17%

Basis for selection. GED not accepted. School achievement record, grades in prerequisite courses, test scores most important. Advanced Placement (AP) results, class rank, recommendations also considered. Generally minimum of 3.3 high school GPA required. For demonstration of English proficiency, TOEFL (600 paper, 250 computer for management students only) Michigan, IELTS or APIEL is acceptable. SAT and SAT Subject Tests or ACT required for U.S. students, optional for Canadian. Audition required of music majors. Portfolio required of architecture majors. Language tests required for ESL/FSL education programs. **Homeschooled:** Statement describing homeschool structure and mission, transcript of courses and grades, letter of recommendation (nonparent) required. Description should include a comprehensive list of all texts (and editions) studied; a personal statement from the applicant and a separate statement from the home educator explaining the basis of the university application and estimation of readiness to handle university-level study. In some cases, further information and/or interview(s) with an admissions officer, associate dean, or program director may be required. **Learning Disabled:** McGill does not have any special admission requirements for students with learning disabilities, and it does not make specific allowances for admission of students with learning disabilities. Students are not asked questions about disabilities in the admissions application. Students are free to add extenuating circumstances information with the application.

High school preparation. 15 units recommended. Recommended units include English 4, mathematics 4, social studies 1, history 1, science 3 (laboratory 3) and foreign language 3. 15-20 total recommended academic units; three or more combined recommended units for social studies and history.

2005-2006 Annual costs. Costs reported in Canadian dollars. Full-time tuition for Quebec residents $1,668, for other Canadian students $4,651, for international students $11,970 to $15,000 depending on program. Required fees range from $1,118 to $1,562 depending on program. Room and board $7,964 to $10,760. Per-credit hour charges for Quebec residents $55.61, for other Canadian students $155.03, for international students $399-$500 depending on program. Estimated cost of books and supplies $1,000; compulsory health insurance for international students is $663. Books/supplies: $1,000. Personal expenses: $2,000.

2004-2005 Financial aid. All financial aid based on need. 23% of total undergraduate aid awarded as scholarships/grants, 77% as loans/jobs. **Additional information:** McGill offers awards ranging in value from $3,000 renewable to $10,000 renewable and based on outstanding academic achievement or a combination of outstanding academic achievement and leadership qualities. Finalists for the scholarships valued at over $5,000 may be interviewed. Students who meet the following eligibility conditions may apply for entrance awards: must be entering a university for the first time to undertake a full-time undergraduate degree program (transfer students are not eligible); must be in the top 5% of their class based on the last two years of full-time studies.

Application procedures. **Admission:** Closing date 1/15 (postmark date). $60 fee. Application may be submitted online. Admission notification on a rolling basis beginning on or about 1/16. Must reply by May 1 or within 3 week(s) if notified thereafter. **Financial aid:** Priority date 6/1; no closing date. FAFSA, institutional form required. Applicants notified by 3/15; Applicants notified on a rolling basis starting 3/15; must reply within 4 week(s) of notification.

Academics. Students are permitted to submit papers and exams in French. **Special study options:** Accelerated study, combined bachelor's/graduate degree, cooperative education, cross-registration, distance learning, double major, ESL, exchange student, honors, independent study, internships, study abroad, teacher certification program, Washington semester. **Credit/placement by examination:** AP, CLEP, IB, institutional tests. 30 credit hours maximum toward bachelor's degree. Maximum 30 AP credits on 120-credit program. **Support services:** Learning center, pre-admission summer program, reduced course load, remedial instruction, study skills assistance, tutoring, writing center.

Majors. **Agriculture:** Agronomy, animal sciences, business, economics, food science, horticultural science, horticulture, plant sciences, soil science. **Architecture:** Architecture. **Area/ethnic studies:** African, Canadian, Caribbean, East Asian, German, Hispanic-American/Latino/Chicano, Italian, Latin American, Near/Middle Eastern, regional, Russian/Slavic, Spanish/Iberian, women's. **Biology:** General, anatomy, animal behavior, aquatic, bacteriology, biochemistry, botany, cell/histology, cellular/anatomical, ecology, environmental, genetics, marine, microbiology, molecular, neuroanatomy, wildlife, zoology. **Business:** General, accounting, accounting/finance, entrepreneurial studies, finance, human resources, international, international finance, labor relations, management science, managerial economics, marketing, operations, organizational behavior. **Computer sciences:** General, computer science. **Conservation:** General, economics, environmental science, environmental studies, management/policy, wildlife. **Education:** General, bilingual, biology, chemistry, early childhood, elementary, English, ESL, French, geography, health, history, mathematics, music, physical, physics, science, secondary, social science, social studies. **Engineering:** Agricultural, biomedical, chemical, civil, computer, electrical, materials, mechanical, metallurgical, mining, software. **English:** English lit. **Family/consumer sciences:** Food/nutrition, human nutrition. **Foreign languages:** Classics, East Asian, French, German, Italian, linguistics, Russian, Spanish, translation. **Health:** Nursing (RN). **History:** General, Asian, Canadian history, European. **Interdisciplinary:** Biological/physical sciences, cognitive science, math/computer science, natural sciences, nutrition sciences. **Legal studies:** General. **Liberal arts:** Humanities. **Math:** General, applied, probability, statistics. **Parks/recreation:** Exercise sciences, health/fitness. **Philosophy/religion:** Judaic, philosophy, religion. **Physical sciences:** Analytical chemistry, atmospheric physics, atmospheric science, chemistry, geophysics, hydrology, inorganic chemistry, organic chemistry, physics, planetary. **Psychology:** General. **Public administration:** Social work. **Social sciences:** Anthropology, economics, geography, political science, sociology, urban studies. **Theology:** Religious ed, sacred music, theology. **Visual/performing arts:** Art history/conservation, dramatic, jazz, music history, music pedagogy, music performance, music theory/composition, piano/organ, stringed instruments, voice/opera.

Most popular majors. Biology 11%, business/marketing 11%, education 7%, engineering/engineering technologies 8%, health sciences 6%, psychology 7%, social sciences 18%.

Computing on campus. 3,491 workstations in dormitories, library, computer center, student center. Dormitories wired for high-speed internet access and linked to campus network. Commuter students can connect to campus network. Online course registration, online library, helpline, repair service, wireless network available.

Student life. **Freshman orientation:** Available. New undergraduate students may sign up for a one-day campus-wide orientation session held at the end of August. Students learn about Student Services and the Students' Society of McGill University, and they receive information about their individual Faculty/School programs. On this day, students meet administrators and senior students from their programs. **Policies:** Freshmen permitted cars on campus. **Housing:** Coed dorms, single-sex dorms, apartments, substance-free housing available. $1,000 partly refundable deposit, deadline 6/15. Shared facilities houses. **Activities:** Bands, choral groups, dance, drama, literary magazine, music ensembles, musical theater, opera, radio station, student government, student newspaper, symphony orchestra, over 100 clubs, service groups, and independent student organizations with interests that include sports, social activities, religion and politics.

Athletics. **Intercollegiate:** Badminton, baseball M, basketball, cheerleading, cross-country, fencing, field hockey W, football (tackle) M, golf, ice hockey, lacrosse, rowing (crew), rugby, sailing, skiing, soccer, squash, swimming, synchronized swimming W, tennis, track and field, volleyball, wrestling. **Intramural:** Badminton, basketball, cricket M, football (non-tackle), football (tackle) M, ice hockey, soccer, squash, table tennis, tennis, volleyball. **Team name:** Redmen, Martlets.

Student services. Adult student services, alcohol/substance abuse counseling, campus ministries, career counseling, services for economically disadvantaged, student employment services, financial aid counseling, health services, legal services, minority student services, on-campus daycare, personal counseling, placement for graduates, women's services. **Physically disabled:** Services for visually, speech, hearing impaired.

Contact. E-mail: admissions@mcgill.ca
Phone: (514) 398-3910 Fax: (514) 398-4193
Kim Bartlett, Director of Admissions, McGill University, 845 Sherbrooke Street West, Montreal, CN H3A-2T5

Memorial University of Newfoundland

St. John's, Newfoundland, Canada — **CB member**
www.mun.ca — **CB code: 0885**

- Public 4-year university
- Commuter campus in small city

General. Founded in 1925. **Calendar:** Trimester.

Annual costs/financial aid. Costs reported in Canadian dollars. Annual tuition for Canadians $2,550; for non-Canadians $8,800. Required fees $185. Room and board $4,826. Books/supplies: $700. Need-based financial aid available for full-time students.

Contact. Phone: (709) 737-4431
Registrar, Memorial University of Newfoundland, Admissions Office-Arts and Admin. Bldg, St. John's, Newfoundland, Canada, 99 A1C-S7

Simon Fraser University

Burnaby, Canada — **CB member**
www.sfu.ca — **CB code: 0999**

- Public 4-year university
- Commuter campus in very large city
- 19,937 degree-seeking undergraduates: 49% part-time, 56% women
- 3,666 degree-seeking graduate students
- 72% of applicants admitted
- SAT or ACT required

General. Founded in 1965. Regionally accredited. Harbour Centre in downtown Vancouver; Surrey campus in Surrey, British Columbia. **Degrees:** 3,856 bachelor's awarded; master's, doctoral offered. **Location:** 9 miles from Vancouver. **Calendar:** Semester, extensive summer session. **Full-time faculty:** 823 total; 87% have terminal degrees, 32% women. **Class size:** 28% < 20, 36% 20-39, 6% 40-49, 17% 50-99, 13% >100. **Special facilities:** Climbing wall, child care facility, hyperbaric chamber, underwater laboratory, combative room, apiary, archaeology museum, theater.

Freshman class profile. 9,418 applied, 6,794 admitted, 2,697 enrolled.

Basis for selection. GED not accepted. Secondary school graduation with a GPA of 3.2 or higher based on a combination of grade 11 and 12 academic courses, test scores (typically SAT verbal and math combined scores greater than 1200 or ACT greater than 26). Other factors will be considered, such as honors, rank in class, and advanced academic courses (e.g. international baccalaureate, advanced placement program). The required score for the new SAT test has not yet been determined. Academic background, especially GPA, rank in class, and test scores most important. Canadian residents not required to submit SAT or ACT. Audition/interview may be required for school of contemporary arts. Applicants may submit personal information profile and at least 1 letter of reference. Campus visit recommended. Those who meet our minimum admission standards and have demonstrated commitment or excellence in other endeavours, or who have succeeded in their studies in spite of difficult circumstances, may also gain admission via the Diverse Qualifications process. Note: applicants who have been required to withdraw from a recognized university are not eligible to apply. **Homeschooled:** Applicants must meet state high school graduation requirements.

High school preparation. 13 units required. Required units include English 4, mathematics 3, social studies 1, history 1, science 2 and foreign language 2.

2005-2006 Annual costs. Costs reported in Canadian dollars. Tuition per year for Canadian students $4,356; for non-Canadian students $14,358. Required fees $503. Per-credit-hour charges for Canadian students $145; for non-Canadian students $479. Full-time students may opt to attend 2 or 3 semesters in academic year. Room only is $3,134 - $4,232 depending on accommodation.

2004-2005 Financial aid. **Need-based:** 19% of total undergraduate aid awarded as scholarships/grants, 81% as loans/jobs. **Non-need-based:** Scholarships awarded for academics, art, athletics, leadership, minority status, music/drama, state residency.

Application procedures. **Admission:** Priority date 2/28; deadline 4/30 (receipt date). $45 fee. Application may be submitted online. Admission notification 6/30. Admission notification on a rolling basis beginning on or about 1/15. Must reply by May 1 or within 3 week(s) if notified thereafter. Document evaluation fee of $55 (Canadian) if academic records originate outside of Canada. **Financial aid:** Priority date 7/1, closing date 11/15. Institutional form required.

Academics. **Special study options:** Cooperative education, distance learning, double major, exchange student, honors, independent study, study abroad, teacher certification program. **Credit/placement by examination:** CLEP, IB. 60 credit hours maximum toward bachelor's degree. **Support services:** Reduced course load, study skills assistance.

Majors. **Area/ethnic studies:** Canadian, women's. **Biology:** General, biochemistry, molecular. **Business:** Business admin, management information systems. **Communications:** General. **Computer sciences:** General, information systems, programming. **Conservation:** General, environmental science, environmental studies. **Education:** General. **Engineering:** Science. **Foreign languages:** French, linguistics. **History:** General. **Interdisciplinary:** Cognitive science, math/computer science, systems science. **Liberal arts:** Arts/sciences. **Math:** General, applied, statistics. **Parks/recreation:** Exercise sciences. **Philosophy/religion:** Philosophy. **Physical sciences:** Chemistry, physics, planetary. **Psychology:** General. **Social sciences:** Anthropology, archaeology, criminology, economics, geography, political science, sociology. **Visual/performing arts:** General, cinematography, dance, design, dramatic.

Most popular majors. Biology 6%, business/marketing 14%, communications/journalism 8%, computer/information sciences 7%, English 7%, liberal arts 6%, psychology 6%, social sciences 30%.

Computing on campus. 900 workstations in library, computer center, student center. Commuter students can connect to campus network. Online course registration, helpline, repair service available.

Student life. **Freshman orientation:** Available. One-day or one-evening session. **Policies:** Freshmen permitted cars on campus. **Housing:** Coed dorms, single-sex dorms, special housing for disabled, apartments available. Nonrefundable housing deposit $450 (Canadian) due 1 month prior to lease commencement. Guaranteed on-campus housing for academic scholars, athletic scholars, university exchange students, First Nations students, graduate scholars, and students registered with the Centre for Students with Disabilities. **Activities:** Dance, drama, film society, radio station, student government, student newspaper, Native student center, center for students with disabilities, crisis line, Simon Fraser Public Interest Research Group, women's center, interfaith center, harassment resolution office, Canadian Federation of Students, Simon Fraser Student Society.

Athletics. NAIA. **Intercollegiate:** Basketball, cross-country, diving, field hockey W, football (tackle) M, golf M, soccer, softball W, swimming, track and field, volleyball W, wrestling. **Intramural:** Badminton, basketball, football (non-tackle), soccer, softball, tennis, volleyball. **Team name:** The Clan.

Student services. Alcohol/substance abuse counseling, campus ministries, career counseling, financial aid counseling, health services, legal services, minority student services, on-campus daycare, personal counseling, women's services. **Physically disabled:** Services for visually, speech, hearing impaired.

Contact. E-mail: undergraduate-admissions@sfu.ca
Phone: (604) 291-3224 Fax: (604) 291-4969
Nick Heath, Director, Admissions, Simon Fraser University, 8888 University Drive, Burnaby, CN V5A 1-6

University of Alberta

Edmonton, Canada — **CB member**
www.ualberta.ca — **CB code: 0963**

- Public 4-year university
- Commuter campus in very large city
- 28,737 degree-seeking undergraduates
- 5,880 graduate students

General. Founded in 1906. Regionally accredited. **Degrees:** 6,300 bachelor's awarded; master's, doctoral, first professional offered. **Location:** 180 miles from Calgary. **Calendar:** Semester, extensive summer session. **Full-time faculty:** 1,513 total. **Special facilities:** Fine arts center, botanical gardens, research farm (including several agricultural research stations), field mission scanning electron microscope, professional development center, National Institute for Nanotechnology.

Basis for selection. GED not accepted. Admission is based on completion of five appropriate Grade 12 subjects (faculty/program specific), including English. Applicant must present a competitive average for admission, with a minimum grade of 50% in each subject. Competitive averages range from 70-85%. SAT Subject Tests recommended. Auditions, portfolios, letters of intent/essays or interviews are required for several programs; however, admission to most programs is based solely on academic merit.

High school preparation. 3 units required. Required and recommended units include English 3, mathematics 3, social studies 3, history 3, science 3 (laboratory 3), foreign language 3 and academic electives 3. Specific course requirements vary depending on program.

2005-2006 Annual costs. Tuition amounts vary by year, program and citizenship status. Books/supplies: $1,000. Personal expenses: $1,000.

Financial aid. **Additional information:** American students may use U.S. federal aid and student loans towards university tuition, but must apply for that aid in United States prior to attending university.

Application procedures. **Admission:** Closing date 5/1 (postmark date). $100 fee. Application may be submitted online. Admission notification on a rolling basis beginning on or about 7/1. Must reply by 8/15. Conditional admission to qualified applicants begins in late November or in December. If applicants maintain the necessary GPA and meet all deadlines, they will be admitted for the fall. **Financial aid:** Closing date 5/1. Applicants notified on a rolling basis; must reply by 8/15.

Academics. **Special study options:** Combined bachelor's/graduate degree, cooperative education, distance learning, double major, ESL, exchange student, honors, internships, student-designed major, study abroad, teacher certification program. **Credit/placement by examination:** AP, CLEP, IB. **Support services:** Learning center, pre-admission summer program, reduced course load, remedial instruction, study skills assistance, tutoring, writing center.

Majors. **Agriculture:** General, animal sciences, business, crop production, economics, food science, horticultural science. **Area/ethnic studies:** African, Central/Eastern European, East Asian, Latin American, Near/Middle Eastern, Scandinavian, Southeast Asian, women's. **Biology:** General, animal physiology, biochemistry, bioinformatics, botany, cell/histology, environmental, microbiology, molecular genetics, neurobiology/physiology, pharmacology, physiology, plant molecular, zoology. **Business:** General, accounting, actuarial science, business admin, communications, entrepreneurial studies, finance, human resources, international, international finance, management information systems, marketing, operations, organizational behavior, retailing, sales/distribution. **Computer sciences:** Computer science, programming. **Conservation:** General, forestry, wildlife. **Education:** Agricultural, art, biology, comparative, computer, drama/dance, early childhood, English, ESL, foreign languages, French, mathematics, middle, music, physical, physics, science, social studies, special, trade/industrial. **Engineering:** General, chemical, civil, computer, electrical, materials, mechanical, mechanics, mining, petroleum, physics, software. **Family/consumer sciences:** Clothing/textiles, family/community services, food/nutrition. **Foreign languages:** General, Chinese, classics, French, German, Italian, Japanese, Latin, linguistics, modern Greek, Romance, Scandinavian, Spanish. **Health:** Athletic training, clinical lab technology, dental hygiene, hematology, nursing (RN), occupational therapy assistant, predentistry, premedicine, preop/surgical nursing, prepharmacy, preveterinary. **History:** General. **Legal studies:** General. **Math:** General, computational, statistics. **Parks/recreation:** General, exercise sciences, sports admin. **Philosophy/religion:** Philosophy, religion. **Physical sciences:** Atmospheric science, chemistry, physics. **Protective services:** Criminal justice. **Psychology:** General. **Social sciences:** Anthropology, criminology, economics, geography, international relations, political science, sociology. **Visual/performing arts:** Dramatic, film/cinema, metal/jewelry, music history, music theory/composition, printmaking, studio arts, theater design.

Most popular majors. Business/marketing 9%, education 21%, health sciences 12%, liberal arts 18%.

Computing on campus. 1,200 workstations in dormitories, library, computer center, student center. Dormitories wired for high-speed internet access and linked to campus network. Commuter students can connect to campus network. Online course registration, online library, helpline, wireless network available.

Student life. **Freshman orientation:** Available. Preregistration for classes offered. **Policies:** Freshmen permitted cars on campus. **Housing:** Coed dorms, single-sex dorms, special housing for disabled, apartments, fraternity/sorority housing available. $175 partly refundable deposit. **Activities:** Bands, choral groups, dance, drama, film society, literary magazine, music ensembles, musical theater, opera, radio station, student government, student newspaper, symphony orchestra, more than 300 clubs available.

Athletics. Intercollegiate: Basketball, cross-country, field hockey W, football (tackle) M, gymnastics, ice hockey, soccer, swimming, tennis, track and field, volleyball, wrestling. **Intramural:** Badminton, baseball, basketball, cross-country, diving, football (tackle) M, gymnastics, ice hockey, judo, racquetball, rugby, skiing, soccer, squash, swimming, tennis, track and field, volleyball, water polo, wrestling. **Team name:** Golden Bears, Pandas.

Student services. Adult student services, alcohol/substance abuse counseling, campus ministries, career counseling, services for economically disadvantaged, student employment services, financial aid counseling, health services, legal services, minority student services, on-campus daycare, personal counseling, placement for graduates, women's services. **Physically disabled:** Services for visually, speech, hearing impaired. **Learning disabled:** Comprehensive services available.

Contact. Phone: (780) 492-3113 Fax: (780) 492-7172
Gerry Kendal, Associate Registrar and Director of Enrolment Management, University of Alberta, Administration Building, Room 201, Edmonton, CN T6G 2-M7

University of British Columbia

Vancouver, Canada — **CB member**
www.ubc.ca — **CB code: 0965**

- Public 4-year university
- Commuter campus in very large city
- 27,186 degree-seeking undergraduates: 28% part-time, 55% women
- 12,516 graduate students
- 57% of applicants admitted
- 75% graduate within 6 years; 50% enter graduate study

General. Founded in 1915. Campuses in Vancouver on Canada's Pacific coast and in Okanagan (Kelowna) in the interior of British Columbia. Undergraduate students may study abroad at any one of 130 partner institutions in 30 different countries. **Degrees:** 5,125 bachelor's awarded; master's, doctoral, first professional offered. **Location:** 6 miles from downtown. **Calendar:** Semester, limited summer session. **Full-time faculty:** 2,048 total; 13% minority, 30% women. **Class size:** 30% < 20, 31% 20-39, 10% 40-49, 17% 50-99, 12% >100. **Special facilities:** Museum of Anthropology (Canada's largest teaching museum), Museum of Geological Sciences, botany collection and herbarium, fine arts gallery, Botanical Garden Nitobe Japanese Garden, astronomical observatory, First Nations House of Learning, performing arts center, theater, study of global issues center, TRIUMF Cyclatron (world's largest), campus-wide wireless network.

Freshman class profile. 17,001 applied, 9,724 admitted, 4,795 enrolled.

Rank in top quarter:	79%	**Return as sophomores:**	91%
Rank in top tenth:	13%		

Basis for selection. GED not accepted. Admission is competitive, with academic averages most important. Minimum requirement is a strong B + average; for science and engineering-based programs, a strong A average is likely to be required. Evaluation of those from the American curriculum will be made on the best 8 academic courses from junior and senior years. In addition, applicants schooled out of Canada are encouraged to submit a Broader Based Admission package (including a personal statement, references, and special academic & extracurricular achievements). UBC encourages applications from students who are completing enriched secondary school programs, such as the International Baccalaureate (IB), Advanced Placement (AP), and the General Certificate of Education (GCE). Generous first-year credit is offered to students with high academic achievement in these programs. In general, results of standardized achievement tests (SAT, Sat Subject Tests, or ACT) are not required. Results may be submitted, however; combined score of 1300 on the SAT, or a 27 on the ACT or higher would strengthen an application. Interviews are generally not required. Exceptions at UBC Vancouver are applications to School of Music (interview, audition, and/or portfolio required) and to the Sauder School of Business (supplemental application demonstrating documented leadership and accomplishment required). At UBC Okanagan application to the Fine Arts program requires a portfolio and letter of intent.

High school preparation. 8 units required. Required units include English 4, mathematics 3 and academic electives 1.

2005-2006 Annual costs. Canadian residents pay $136 per-credit-hour, non-residents pay $554; figures are in Canadian dollars. Books/supplies: $1,200.

2004-2005 Financial aid. Non-need-based: Scholarships awarded for academics, athletics. **Additional information:** Need-based financial aid from public funds available only to domestic students (Canadian citizens or permanent residents of Canada). UBC is committed to providing domestic students access to undergraduate programs, regardless of financial need. Need-based financial aid to international students is limited; applicants must generally be able to meet their tuition and living costs for the full length of their studies. A major scholarship open to outstanding international students is the International Leader of Tomorrow award; other scholarships for academic excellence, athletics, and on other criteria are available, some in specific programs.

Application procedures. Admission: Closing date 2/28 (postmark date). $100 fee ($100 out-of-state). Application may be submitted online. Admission notification on a rolling basis beginning on or about 1/30. No set date for accepting an offer of admission, except for students applying for on-campus student housing, who must accept their offer of admission by May 31 in order to retain an offer of housing placement. Students not required to accept admission offers by May 1. However, applicants will receive an admissions decision by the May 1 deadline, provided they submit all required supporting documents by March 31. **Financial aid:** Closing date 2/28. Applicants notified by 4/14.

Academics. Special study options: Combined bachelor's/graduate degree, cooperative education, cross-registration, distance learning, double major, dual enrollment of high school students, ESL, exchange student, honors, internships, liberal arts/career combination, student-designed major, study abroad, teacher certification program. **Credit/placement by examination:** AP, CLEP, IB. **Support services:** Learning center, reduced course load, study skills assistance, tutoring, writing center.

Majors. Agriculture: General, agronomy, animal sciences, aquaculture, economics, food processing, food science, horticultural science, plant sciences, soil science. **Architecture:** Environmental design. **Area/ethnic studies:** Asian, Canadian, Central/Eastern European, East Asian, European, German, Hispanic-American/Latino/Chicano, Italian, Latin American, Russian/Slavic, Scandinavian, Slavic, South Asian, Southeast Asian, Western European, women's. **Biology:** General, anatomy, animal physiology, bacteriology, biochemistry, biophysics, biotechnology, cell/histology, conservation, ecology, environmental, epidemiology, genetics, molecular, molecular biochemistry, pathology, pharmacology/toxicology, physiology, reproductive. **Business:** General, accounting, business admin, finance, human resources, international, international finance, international marketing, investments/securities, labor relations, management information systems, management science, managerial economics, marketing, operations, real estate, transportation. **Computer sciences:** General, a.i./robotics, computer science. **Conservation:** General, economics, environmental science, environmental studies, forest management, forest resources, forest sciences, forestry, management/policy, wood science. **Education:** General, elementary, middle, multi-level teacher, Native American, physical, secondary. **Engineering:** General, biomedical, chemical, civil, computer, electrical, environmental, forest, geological, materials, materials science, mechanical, mechanics, metallurgical, mining, operations research, physics, software. **English:** British lit, Canadian lit, creative writing. **Family/consumer sciences:** General, family/community services, food/nutrition, human nutrition. **Foreign languages:** Chinese, classics, French, German, Germanic, Italian, Japanese, Korean, Latin, linguistics, Native American, Portuguese, Romance, Slavic, South Asian, Spanish, Urdu. **Health:** Athletic training, clinical lab assistant, community health, dental hygiene, nurse midwife, nursing (RN), occupational health, preveterinary. **History:** General. **Interdisciplinary:** Ancient studies, biological/physical sciences, classical/archaeology, cognitive science, medieval/Renaissance, neuroscience, nutrition sciences. **Legal studies:** General. **Math:** General, applied, statistics. **Parks/recreation:** Exercise sciences, facilities management, health/fitness, sports admin. **Philosophy/religion:** Philosophy, religion. **Physical sciences:** Astronomy, atmospheric science, chemistry, geology, geophysics, oceanography, physics, planetary, theoretical physics. **Psychology:** General. **Public administration:** Social work. **Science technology:** Biological. **Social sciences:** Anthropology, archaeology, Canadian government, economics, geography, international relations, political science, sociology. **Transportation:** General. **Visual/performing arts:** General, art, art history/conservation, cinematography, conducting, dramatic, film/cinema, music history, music performance, music theory/composition, musicology, piano/organ, stringed instruments, theater arts management, theater design, voice/opera.

Computing on campus. 1,100 workstations in library, computer center, student center. Dormitories wired for high-speed internet access and linked to campus network. Commuter students can connect to campus network. Online course registration, online library, helpline, repair service, wireless network available.

Student life. Freshman orientation: Available. Preregistration for classes offered. Three different orientation programs: GALA, the largest international student orientation in North America, is a three-day event held in the week before the start of Winter term; parents orientation takes place on the Sunday before the start of term; IMAGINE UBC is the official welcome and orientation experience for all first-year students and takes place on the first day of Winter term. **Policies:** Freshmen permitted cars on campus.

Housing: Guaranteed on-campus for freshmen. Coed dorms, single-sex dorms, apartments, fraternity/sorority housing available. $50 nonrefundable deposit, deadline 5/1. Cultural theme houses in partnership with universities in Japan, Korea, and Mexico. **Activities:** Bands, choral groups, dance, drama, film society, literary magazine, music ensembles, musical theater, opera, radio station, student government, student newspaper, symphony orchestra, TV station, over 250 clubs, societies, and other groups.

Athletics. NAIA. **Intercollegiate:** Baseball M, basketball, cross-country, field hockey W, football (tackle) M, golf, ice hockey, rowing (crew), rugby, skiing, soccer, swimming, track and field, volleyball. **Intramural:** Badminton, basketball, cheerleading, cross-country, football (non-tackle), ice hockey, racquetball, soccer, softball, squash, swimming, table tennis, tennis, triathlon, volleyball, water polo, wrestling M. **Team name:** Thunderbirds.

Student services. Alcohol/substance abuse counseling, campus ministries, career counseling, student employment services, financial aid counseling, health services, minority student services, on-campus daycare, personal counseling, placement for graduates, women's services. **Physically disabled:** Services for visually, speech, hearing impaired.

Contact. E-mail: international.reception@ubc.ca
Phone: (604) 822-8999 Toll-free number: (877) 272-1422
Fax: (604) 822-9858
Rosalie Vlaar, Associate Director, Undergraduate Admissions, University of British Columbia, 2016 - 1874 East Mall, Vancouver, CN V6T 1-1

University of Manitoba

Winnipeg, Canada — **CB member**
www.umanitoba.ca — **CB code: 0973**

- Public 4-year university
- Commuter campus in very large city
- 24,267 undergraduates
- 3,332 graduate students

General. Founded in 1877. **Location:** 10 miles from downtown Winnipeg. **Calendar:** Semester, limited summer session. **Full-time faculty:** 2,274 total. **Part-time faculty:** 724 total. **Special facilities:** Planetarium.

Basis for selection. Open admission, but selective for some programs.

High school preparation. 28 units required.

Application procedures. Admission: $90 fee. Application may be submitted online.

Academics. Special study options: Combined bachelor's/graduate degree, cooperative education, distance learning, double major, ESL, honors, independent study, internships, liberal arts/career combination, study abroad, teacher certification program, weekend college. **Credit/placement by examination:** CLEP, IB. 30 credit hours maximum toward bachelor's degree. **Support services:** Learning center, reduced course load, study skills assistance.

Majors. Agriculture: General, agribusiness operations, agronomy, animal health, animal nutrition, animal sciences, business, dairy, economics, farm/ranch, food science, horticultural science, ornamental horticulture, plant breeding, plant protection, plant sciences, poultry, soil science. **Architecture:** Environmental design. **Area/ethnic studies:** Asian, Canadian, Central/Eastern European, Latin American, Near/Middle Eastern, Russian/Slavic, women's. **Biology:** Bacteriology, biochemistry, botany, cell/histology, ecology, entomology, genetics, molecular, pathology, pharmacology, plant pathology, plant physiology, zoology. **Business:** Accounting, actuarial science, business admin, finance, international, labor relations, market research. **Computer sciences:** General, computer science, data processing, information systems, programming, systems analysis. **Conservation:** General, environmental studies. **Education:** General, adult ed admin, business, curriculum, early childhood, elementary, ESL, family/consumer sciences, foundations, instructional media, leadership, middle, multi-level teacher, music, physical, secondary, special, technology/industrial arts. **Engineering:** General, agricultural, civil, computer, electrical, materials science, mechanical. **English:** American lit, British lit, composition, creative writing. **Family/consumer sciences:** General, clothing/textiles, family/community services, food/nutrition. **Foreign languages:** Biblical, classics, comparative lit, French, German, Hebrew, Italian, linguistics, modern Greek, Russian, Spanish. **Health:** Athletic training, dental hygiene, nursing (RN), occupational therapy, physical therapy. **History:** General. **Interdisciplinary:** Behavioral sciences, gerontology, global studies, math/computer science, medieval/Renaissance, nutrition sciences. **Legal studies:** General. **Math:** General, applied, statistics. **Parks/recreation:** General, exercise sciences, health/fitness, sports admin. **Philosophy/religion:** Judaic, philosophy, religion. **Physical sciences:** Astronomy, chemistry, geology, physics. **Psychology:** General, clinical, counseling, educational. **Public administration:** General, social work. **Social sciences:** Anthropology, criminology, economics, geography, political science, sociology. **Visual/performing arts:** Art, art history/conservation, commercial/advertising art, dramatic, film/cinema, interior design, music history, music performance, music theory/composition, piano/organ, studio arts, theater history, voice/opera.

Computing on campus. 392 workstations in library, computer center. Commuter students can connect to campus network. Online course registration, online library, helpline, repair service, student web hosting available.

Student life. Freshman orientation: Mandatory. **Activities:** Bands, choral groups, dance, drama, music ensembles, radio station, student government, student newspaper, symphony orchestra.

Athletics. Intercollegiate: Basketball, cross-country, diving, field hockey W, football (tackle) M, gymnastics, ice hockey, skiing, swimming, synchronized swimming W, tennis, track and field, volleyball, weight lifting M, wrestling. **Intramural:** Archery, basketball, cross-country, diving, field hockey W, football (non-tackle) M, handball, ice hockey, judo M, racquetball, soccer, squash, swimming, tennis, volleyball. **Team name:** Bisons.

Student services. Adult student services, alcohol/substance abuse counseling, campus ministries, career counseling, student employment services, financial aid counseling, health services, legal services, on-campus daycare, personal counseling, placement for graduates. **Physically disabled:** Services for visually, speech, hearing impaired.

Contact. E-mail: admissions@umanitoba.ca
Phone: (204) 474-8808 Fax: (204) 474-7554
Peter Dueck, Executive Director of Enrollment Services, University of Manitoba, 424 University Centre, Winnipeg, CN R3T 2-N2

France

American University of Paris

Paris, France — **CB member**
www.aup.edu — **CB code: 0866**

- Private 4-year university and liberal arts college
- Commuter campus in very large city
- 209 degree-seeking undergraduates: 23% part-time, 63% women
- 33 degree-seeking graduate students
- 71% of applicants admitted
- Application essay required

General. Founded in 1962. Regionally accredited. **Degrees:** 175 bachelor's awarded; master's offered. **Calendar:** Semester, extensive summer session. **Full-time faculty:** 59 total. **Part-time faculty:** 70 total.

Freshman class profile. 541 applied, 382 admitted, 156 enrolled.

Mid 50% test scores			
		SAT math:	520-640
SAT verbal:	550-660	**Return as sophomores:**	64%

Basis for selection. Non-English speakers are required to take TOEFL or TOEIC or IELTS. **Homeschooled:** Statement describing homeschool structure and mission required.

High school preparation. 18 units recommended. Recommended units include English 4, mathematics 3, social studies 3, history 2, science 2 (laboratory 1) and foreign language 3.

2005-2006 Annual costs. Books/supplies: $1,200.

2005-2006 Financial aid. Need-based: 86% of total undergraduate aid awarded as scholarships/grants, 14% as loans/jobs. **Non-need-based:** Scholarships awarded for academics, alumni affiliation.

Application procedures. Admission: Closing date 3/15 (postmark date). $50 fee. Application may be submitted online. Admission notification on a rolling basis. **Financial aid:** No deadline. FAFSA, institutional form required.

Academics. **Special study options:** Cooperative education, cross-registration, double major, exchange student, independent study, internships, study abroad. **Credit/placement by examination:** AP, CLEP, IB, institutional tests. 30 credit hours maximum toward bachelor's degree. **Support services:** Reduced course load, study skills assistance, tutoring, writing center.

Majors. **Area/ethnic studies:** European, French. **Business:** Finance, international. **Communications:** General. **Computer sciences:** General, computer science. **Foreign languages:** General, comparative lit, French. **History:** General. **Psychology:** General. **Social sciences:** Economics, international relations. **Visual/performing arts:** Art history/conservation, film/cinema.

Most popular majors. Business/marketing 36%, communications/journalism 24%.

Computing on campus. 120 workstations in library, computer center, student center. Commuter students can connect to campus network. Online library, wireless network available.

Student life. **Freshman orientation:** Mandatory, $420 fee. Held the week before the first week of classes. Students are assisted in the housing process, receive academic advising, attend workshops on living in Paris. **Policies:** Freshmen permitted cars on campus. **Activities:** Dance, drama, literary magazine, music ensembles, musical theater, student government, student newspaper.

Student services. Career counseling, student employment services, financial aid counseling, personal counseling.

Contact. E-mail: usoffice@aup.edu
Phone: (303) 757-6333 Fax: (303) 757-6444
Marc Montheard, Vice President and Dean of Student Services, American University of Paris, 950 South Cherry Street, Suite 210, Denver, CO 80246

Germany

University of Karlsruhe

Karlsruhe, Germany — **CB member**
www.uni-karlsruhe.de — **CB code: 3592**

- Public 4-year university
- Small city

General. **Calendar:** Continuous.

Contact. Phone: (721) 608-6378
Kaiserstr. 12, Karlsruhe, GE 76128

Guatemala

Universidad del Valle de Guatemala

Guatemala City, Guatemala — **CB member**
www.uvg.edu.gt — **CB code: 3875**

- Private 5-year university and engineering college
- Commuter campus in very large city
- 1,453 degree-seeking undergraduates
- Application essay required

General. **Degrees:** 167 bachelor's awarded; master's offered. **Calendar:** Semester. **Full-time faculty:** 54 total. **Part-time faculty:** 426 total.

Basis for selection. Open admission, but selective for some programs and for out-of-state students. **Homeschooled:** Transcript of courses and grades, letter of recommendation (nonparent) required.

Application procedures. **Admission:** $55 fee, may be waived for applicants with need. Application must be submitted on paper.

Academics. **Special study options:** Combined bachelor's/graduate degree, exchange student, weekend college. **Credit/placement by examination:** CLEP.

Majors. **Agriculture:** General, food processing. **Computer sciences:** General. **Education:** General. **Engineering:** Agricultural, chemical, civil, computer, electrical, forest, industrial, mechanical, mechanics. **History:** General. **Math:** General. **Psychology:** General. **Social sciences:** Anthropology, archaeology, sociology.

Computing on campus. Commuter students can connect to campus network. Student web hosting, wireless network available.

Student life. **Freshman orientation:** Mandatory. **Activities:** Concert band, choral groups, drama, music ensembles, student government.

Student services. Career counseling, financial aid counseling.

Contact. E-mail: info@uvg.edu.gt
Phone: (502) 364-0336 ext. 453
Eugenia Rosales, Secretaria General, Universidad del Valle de Guatemala, 18 Avenida 11-95 zona 15, Vista Hermosa III, Guatemala City, GT 01015

Lebanon

American University of Beirut

Beirut, Lebanon — **CB member**
www.aub.edu.lb — **CB code: 0902**

- Private 4-year university
- Commuter campus in very large city
- 5,674 degree-seeking undergraduates: 3% part-time, 47% women
- 1,448 degree-seeking graduate students
- 68% of applicants admitted
- SAT required
- 82% graduate within 6 years; 17% enter graduate study

General. Regionally accredited. **Degrees:** 1,272 bachelor's awarded; master's, first professional offered. **Location:** In Beirut City. **Calendar:** Semester, extensive summer session. **Full-time faculty:** 402 total; 88% have terminal degrees, 38% women. **Part-time faculty:** 244 total; 37% have terminal degrees, 40% women. **Class size:** 33% < 20, 51% 20-39, 5% 40-49, 7% 50-99, 3% >100. **Special facilities:** Archaeological museum, geological museum, rare biological collection.

Freshman class profile. 3,296 applied, 2,257 admitted, 1,387 enrolled.

Mid 50% test scores		**Rank in top tenth:**	29%
SAT verbal:	440-530	**End year in good standing:**	93%
SAT math:	570-680	**Return as sophomores:**	94%
Rank in top quarter:	56%	**Live on campus:**	16%

Basis for selection. Admission based on composite scores: 50% SAT (25% verbal, 25% math) and 50% standardized school grades. Holders of Lebanese, French and International Baccalaureate, among other regional governmental secondary diplomas, will be admittted directly into the sophomore class. SAT must be taken before January of the year preceding admissions. **Homeschooled:** Most applicants must take 3 SAT Subject Tests.

2006-2007 Annual costs. Tuition/fees (projected): $10,407. Room only: $2,574. Books/supplies: $300. Personal expenses: $100.

2005-2006 Financial aid. **Need-based:** 60 full-time freshmen applied for aid; 57 were judged to have need; 57 of these received aid. Average scholarship/grant was $3,198. 86% of total undergraduate aid awarded as scholarships/grants, 14% as loans/jobs. **Non-need-based:** Awarded to 78 full-time undergraduates, including 8 freshmen. Scholarships awarded for academics.

Application procedures. **Admission:** Priority date 11/30; deadline 1/15 (receipt date). $50 fee. Application may be submitted online. Admission notification on a rolling basis beginning on or about 4/15. Must reply by 6/30. Early action applicants must have a minimum SAT and must have been in top 40th percentile of their class for the past two years. **Financial aid:** Priority date 10/3, closing date 2/2. Institutional form required. Applicants notified by 5/30.

Academics. **Special study options:** Cross-registration, ESL, honors, independent study, internships, liberal arts/career combination, study abroad, teacher certification program. **Credit/placement by examination:** AP, CLEP, IB. **Support services:** Learning center, remedial instruction, study skills assistance, writing center.

Majors. **Agriculture:** General, food science, landscaping. **Architecture:** Architecture. **Biology:** General. **Business:** Business admin. **Computer sciences:** Computer science. **Education:** Elementary. **Engineering:** Civil, computer, electrical, mechanical. **Engineering technology:** Petroleum. **English:** British lit. **Foreign languages:** Arabic. **Health:** Clinical lab technology, dietetics, environmental health, nursing (RN). **History:** General. **Math:** General, statistics. **Philosophy/religion:** Philosophy. **Physical sciences:** Chemistry, geology, physics. **Psychology:** General. **Public administration:** General. **Social sciences:** Archaeology, economics, political science. **Visual/performing arts:** Graphic design.

Most popular majors. Biology 11%, business/marketing 29%, computer/information sciences 9%, engineering/engineering technologies 16%, health sciences 6%, social sciences 6%.

Computing on campus. 906 workstations in dormitories, library, computer center, student center. Dormitories wired for high-speed internet access and linked to campus network. Commuter students can connect to campus network. Online course registration, online library, helpline, repair service, student web hosting, wireless network available.

Student life. **Freshman orientation:** Mandatory. Preregistration for classes offered. 3-day program held during first days of registration period. **Housing:** Guaranteed on-campus for all undergraduates. Single-sex dorms available. $67 nonrefundable deposit, deadline 8/31. **Activities:** Choral groups, dance, drama, music ensembles, student government, student newspaper, Arab Heritage Club, Gulf Club, Palestinian Cultural Club, Syrian Cultural Club, Jordanian Cultural Club, Lebanese Armenian Heritage Club, Lebanese Red Cross Club, Human Rights & Peace Club, Special Support Club for Special People, Women's Rights Club.

Athletics. **Intercollegiate:** Badminton, basketball, boxing, cross-country, gymnastics, handball, rugby M, skiing, soccer, swimming, table tennis, tennis, track and field, volleyball. **Intramural:** Badminton, basketball, boxing, cheerleading W, cross-country, handball, soccer, swimming, table tennis, tennis, volleyball, weight lifting.

Student services. Career counseling, student employment services, financial aid counseling, health services, personal counseling, placement for graduates. **Physically disabled:** Services for visually, hearing impaired.

Contact. E-mail: admissions@aub.edu.lb
Phone: (961) 137-4374 ext. 2590 Fax: (961) 175-0775
Salim Kanaan, Director of Admissions, American University of Beirut, PO Box 11-0236, Beirut, LB

Mexico

Instituto Tecnologico Autonomo de Mexico

Colonia Tizapan, San Angel, Mexico — **CB member**
www.itam.mx — **CB code: 7144**

- Public 4-year university and business college
- Commuter campus in very large city
- 4,500 degree-seeking undergraduates

General. **Degrees:** 550 bachelor's awarded; master's, doctoral, first professional offered. **Location:** Southern part of Mexico City. **Calendar:** Semester, limited summer session. **Full-time faculty:** 479 total. **Part-time faculty:** 409 total.

Basis for selection. Open admission. High school records and admission test mandatory. English language tests for continuation required. **Homeschooled:** Complete high school diploma, minimum GPA, and admission test.

Application procedures. **Admission:** No deadline. $50 fee, may be waived for applicants with need. Application must be submitted on paper. Admission notification on a rolling basis.

Academics. **Special study options:** Combined bachelor's/graduate degree, double major, exchange student, liberal arts/career combination, study abroad. **Credit/placement by examination:** CLEP.

Majors. **Business:** Accounting, accounting/business management, actuarial science, business admin. **Communications:** Digital media. **Communications technology:** Computer typography. **Computer sciences:** General. **Engineering:** Computer. **Engineering technology:** General. **Interdisciplinary:** Science/society. **Legal studies:** General, prelaw. **Math:** Applied. **Social sciences:** Economics, international relations, political science.

Computing on campus. 140 workstations in computer center. Online library available.

Student life. **Activities:** Dance, drama, literary magazine, radio station, student newspaper.

Student services. Student employment services.

Contact. E-mail: admisiones@itam.mx
Phone: (5) 628-4156 Fax: (5) 490-4655
Marisol Villanueva, Jefe de Admisiones, Instituto Tecnologico Autonomo de Mexico, Rio Hondo 1, Colonia Tizapan, San Angel, MX 1000

Instituto Tecnologico y de Estudios Superiores de Occidente

Tlaquepaque, Jalisco, Mexico — **CB member**
www.iteso.mx — **CB code: 7145**

- Private 4-year university, business and engineering college affiliated with Roman Catholic Church
- Commuter campus in very large city

General. **Location:** In metropolitan Guadalajara. **Calendar:** Semester.

Annual costs/financial aid. Tuition ranges from 392 to 409 Mexican pesos per-credit-hour.

Contact. Phone: (52) 333-6693535
Chief of the Admission Office, AP 31-175, Zapopan Jalisco, MX 45090

Universidad Anahuac

México City, Mexico — **CB member**
www.anahuac.mx — **CB code: 7146**

- Private 6-year university affiliated with Roman Catholic Church
- Commuter campus in small city
- 5,235 degree-seeking undergraduates: 48% women
- 1,230 degree-seeking graduate students
- 87% of applicants admitted
- Interview required

General. Founded in 1964. **Degrees:** 698 bachelor's awarded; master's, doctoral offered. **Location:** 10 miles from Mexico City. **Calendar:** Semester, limited summer session. **Full-time faculty:** 191 total; 84% have terminal degrees, 47% women. **Part-time faculty:** 770 total; 23% women.

Freshman class profile. 1,908 applied, 1,652 admitted, 1,532 enrolled.

Basis for selection. GED not accepted. Admission decisions are based on careful consideration of all factors in a process of personal attention to each applicant and not on numerical factors alone. SAT or ACT recommended. Recommend that U.S. mainland applicants take the PAA; SAT or ACT accepted in lieu of the PAA.

High school preparation. 13 units required. Required units include English 2, mathematics 2, social studies 1, history 2, science 2, foreign language 3 and academic electives 1.

2005-2006 Annual costs. Books/supplies: $200. Personal expenses: $550.

Financial aid. All financial aid based on need.

Application procedures. Admission: Priority date 5/1; deadline 7/7. $92 fee, may be waived for applicants with need. Admission notification on a rolling basis beginning on or about 6/16. Must reply by 7/25. **Financial aid:** Priority date 7/20; no closing date. Institutional form required. Applicants notified on a rolling basis starting 8/13; must reply within 2 week(s) of notification.

Academics. Special study options: Cooperative education, distance learning, double major, ESL, exchange student, internships, liberal arts/career combination, study abroad, teacher certification program. **Credit/placement by examination:** CLEP, SAT. **Support services:** Learning center, pre-admission summer program, reduced course load, remedial instruction, study skills assistance, tutoring, writing center.

Majors. Architecture: Architecture. **Business:** Accounting, actuarial science, business admin, international, international marketing, tourism/travel. **Communications:** General. **Computer sciences:** Information systems. **Engineering:** Civil, electrical, mechanics, systems. **Engineering technology:** Industrial management. **Family/consumer sciences:** General. **Legal studies:** General. **Psychology:** General. **Social sciences:** Economics. **Visual/performing arts:** Commercial/advertising art, drawing, industrial design.

Computing on campus. Online course registration, online library, helpline available.

Student life. Freshman orientation: Available. **Housing:** Host families provide housing for international and out-of-state students. **Activities:** Choral groups, drama, film society, music ensembles, musical theater, student government, student newspaper, Anahuac Challenge, Anahuac for Mexico, Anahuac Social Action, Anahuac Social Foundation, Campus Ministry, Center for Integral Community Development, Perpetual Adoration Society, Red Cross, Youth Weekend Mission Program, Youth for the Third Millennium.

Athletics. Intercollegiate: Basketball, ice hockey M, racquetball, soccer, swimming, tennis, track and field, volleyball. **Intramural:** Basketball, ice hockey M, racquetball, soccer, swimming, tennis, track and field, volleyball. **Team name:** Halcones.

Student services. Career counseling, student employment services, health services, personal counseling, placement for graduates.

Contact. E-mail: pbertha@anahuac.mx
Phone: (5) 627-0210 Toll-free number: (800) 508-9800 Fax: (5) 596-1938
Bertha Perez Vera, Director of Admissions, Universidad Anahuac, Av. Lomas Anahuac s/n, Mexico City, MX

Universidad Autonoma de Aguascalientes

Aguascalientes, Mexico — **CB member**
www.uaa.mx — **CB code: 7147**

- Public 4-year university
- Residential campus in very large city

General. Founded in 1974. Regionally accredited. **Location:** 319 miles from Mexico City. **Calendar:** Semester.

Annual costs/financial aid. Tuition/fees (2005-2006): $676. Tuition and fee costs: $676 pesos for non-U.S. students, $17,424 pesos for U.S. students. Need-based financial aid available for full-time students.

Contact. Phone: (449) 910-7422
Jefe de Departamento de Control Escolar, Av. Universidad No. 940, Aguascalientes, MX 20100

Universidad Autonoma de Coahuila

Saltillo, Mexico — **CB member**
www.uadec.mx — **CB code: 7148**

- Public 4-year university
- Very large city

General. Calendar: Semester.

Annual costs/financial aid. Tuition for residents, $780. Tuition for nonresident aliens, $1,710.

Contact. Phone: (844) 4-3-81729
Rector, Boulevard V. Carranza y Gonzalez, 25280 Saltillo, Coahuila, Mexico, MX

Universidad de Monterrey

San Pedro Garza Garcia, NL, Mexico
www.udem.edu.mx — **CB member**

- Private 4-year university affiliated with Roman Catholic Church
- Residential campus in very large city

General. Calendar: Semester.

Annual costs/financial aid. Tuition for full semester, 37,620 Mexican pesos, plus required fees of 2,540 pesos for insurance. Non-Mexican applicants are subject to an additional fee of 5,643 pesos.

Contact. Phone: (81) 812-41010
Dean of Admissions, Avenida Ignacio Morones Prieto, 4500 Pte., San Pedro Garza Garcia, NL, MX 66238

Monaco

International University of Monaco

Monaco, Monaco
www.monaco.edu — **CB member**

- For-profit 3-year business college
- Large town
- 182 degree-seeking undergraduates: 48% women
- 70 degree-seeking graduate students
- Application essay required

General. Unique international atmosphere both in the classrooms and in the Principality itself. **Degrees:** 21 bachelor's awarded; master's offered. **Calendar:** Trimester. **Full-time faculty:** 40 total; 65% have terminal degrees, 48% women. **Part-time faculty:** 19 total; 5% have terminal degrees, 21% women. **Class size:** 74% < 20, 26% 20-39. **Special facilities:** Principality of Monaco features high-quality sports facilities, museums and other leisure activities.

Basis for selection. Open admission.

2005-2006 Annual costs. Monegasque nationals and residents, as well as French nationals, pay 6,750 (euros) for academic year. All others pay 11,250 (euros). One-time enrollment fee of 1,500 (euros) for freshmen. Housing costs range from 450 to 950 (euros) per month. If students live and pay rent in France, it is possible to receive housing subsidy from French government.

Application procedures. Admission: Closing date 6/15. $160 fee. Application must be submitted on paper. Admission notification on a rolling basis.

Academics. Special study options: Combined bachelor's/graduate degree, ESL, study abroad. **Credit/placement by examination:** CLEP.

Majors. Business: Business admin, finance, international finance, marketing.

Computing on campus. 100 workstations in library, computer center. Online library, helpline, repair service available.

Student life. Freshman orientation: Mandatory. Preregistration for classes offered. **Policies:** Freshmen permitted cars on campus. **Housing:** Apartments available.

Athletics. Intramural: Golf, soccer, tennis.

Student services. Career counseling, student employment services, placement for graduates.

Contact. E-mail: info@monaco.edu
Phone: (377) 979-86994 Fax: (377) 920-52830
Gisele Dudognon, Director of Admissions, International University of Monaco, 2 Avenue Prince Hereditaire Albert, Monaco, MC 98000

Singapore

Singapore Management University

Singapore **CB member**
www.smu.edu.sg **CB code: 3873**

- Private 4-year university
- Very large city

General. **Calendar:** Semester.

Contact. Phone: (656) 822-0200
469 Bukit Timah Road, SG 25975

Switzerland

Franklin College: Switzerland

Lugano, Switzerland **CB member**
www.fc.edu **CB code: 0922**

- Private 4-year liberal arts college
- Residential campus in small city
- 321 degree-seeking undergraduates: 3% part-time, 59% women
- 70% of applicants admitted
- SAT or ACT with writing, application essay required
- 40% graduate within 6 years

General. Founded in 1969. Regionally accredited. Undergraduate degree programs are accredited in United States and in Switzerland. Instruction in English. Students from 50 nations. **Degrees:** 52 bachelor's, 3 associate awarded. **Location:** 60 miles from Milan, Italy, 80 miles from Lucerne. **Calendar:** Semester, extensive summer session. **Full-time faculty:** 20 total; 80% have terminal degrees, 25% women. **Part-time faculty:** 25 total; 32% have terminal degrees, 56% women. **Class size:** 75% < 20, 25% 20-39.

Freshman class profile. 413 applied, 290 admitted, 101 enrolled.

Mid 50% test scores			
SAT verbal:	550-660	GPA 3.0-3.49:	36%
SAT math:	540-650	GPA 2.0-2.99:	31%
ACT:	24-27	End year in good standing:	89%
GPA 3.50 or higher:	33%	Return as sophomores:	66%
		Live on campus:	99%

Basis for selection. High school academic record, recommendations, extracurricular participation most important. Essay, test scores, interview also important. TOEFL required for students whose first language is not English. SAT Subject Tests recommended. Essay and personal statement required. Interview recommended for all.

High school preparation. College-preparatory program required. 19 units recommended. Recommended units include English 4, mathematics 3, social studies 1, history 3, science 3, foreign language 3 and academic electives 2. Electives include computer science, art, music.

2006-2007 Annual costs. Tuition/fees: $29,030. Tuition includes required 2-week, credit-bearing academic travel program each semester. All costs reported in U.S. dollars. Room/board: $10,500. Books/supplies: $1,000. Personal expenses: $2,000.

2004-2005 Financial aid. All financial aid based on need. 59 full-time freshmen applied for aid; 48 were judged to have need; 48 of these received aid. Average need met was 60%. Average scholarship/grant was $5,104; average loan $2,740. 56% of total undergraduate aid awarded as scholarships/grants, 44% as loans/jobs.

Application procedures. Admission: $65 fee. Application may be submitted online. Admission notification on a rolling basis beginning on or about 12/15. Must reply by 1/5. Must reply by May 1 or within 2 week(s) if notified thereafter. **Financial aid:** Priority date 2/15, closing date 3/30. FAFSA, institutional form required. CSS PROFILE preferred. Applicants notified on a rolling basis starting 2/15; must reply by 5/1 or within 3 week(s) of notification.

Academics. 2-week credit-bearing academic travel program required each semester. **Special study options:** Double major, ESL, exchange student, honors, independent study, internships, study abroad. Sophomore and junior year abroad programs with cooperating colleges/universities. **Credit/placement by examination:** AP, CLEP, IB, institutional tests. 15 credit hours maximum toward associate degree, 30 toward bachelor's. **Support services:** Reduced course load, study skills assistance, tutoring, writing center.

Majors. Area/ethnic studies: European. **Business:** Banking/financial services, international, international finance, international marketing. **Communications:** General. **English:** English lit. **Foreign languages:** General, French, Italian. **History:** General. **Liberal arts:** Arts/sciences. **Social sciences:** Economics, international economics, international relations. **Visual/performing arts:** General, art history/conservation, design.

Most popular majors. Business/marketing 38%, communications/journalism 13%, interdisciplinary studies 6%, social sciences 29%, visual/performing arts 8%.

Computing on campus. 75 workstations in library, computer center, student center. Dormitories wired for high-speed internet access and linked to campus network. Online library, repair service, student web hosting, wireless network available.

Student life. Freshman orientation: Mandatory, $250 fee. **Policies:** All students live within the Lugano community; 55% from United States. Freshmen permitted cars on campus. **Housing:** Guaranteed on-campus for freshmen. Coed dorms, single-sex dorms, apartments, substance-free housing available. $300 nonrefundable deposit, deadline 6/20. College-owned and leased apartments on and adjacent to campus and in Lugano; freshmen and sophomores must live in college housing. **Activities:** Dance, drama, literary magazine, music ensembles, radio station, student government, student newspaper, international business club, language clubs, numerous sports clubs, international relations club, cultural clubs, booster club, improv club, film society, Amnesty International, Far Lawn Club.

Athletics. Intramural: Basketball, soccer, tennis, volleyball. **Team name:** Falcons.

Student services. Alcohol/substance abuse counseling, career counseling, student employment services, financial aid counseling, health services, personal counseling, placement for graduates, women's services.

Contact. E-mail: info@fc.edu
Phone: (718) 335-6800 Fax: (718) 335-6733
Karen Ballard, Director of Admissions, Franklin College: Switzerland, 91-31 Queens Boulevard, Suite 411, Elmhurst, NY 11373

United Arab Emirates

American University in Dubai - United Arab Emirates

Dubai, United Arab Emirates **CB member**
www.aud.edu **CB code: 2688**

- Private 4-year university and branch campus college
- Residential campus in very large city
- 1,403 degree-seeking undergraduates: 21% part-time, 47% women
- 98 degree-seeking graduate students
- Application essay required
- 42% graduate within 6 years

General. Regionally accredited. Branch campus of American InterContinental University, Atlanta, Georgia. **Degrees:** 234 bachelor's awarded; master's offered. **Calendar:** Semester, extensive summer session. **Full-time faculty:** 40 total. **Part-time faculty:** 62 total. **Class size:** 24% < 20, 76% 20-39.

Freshman class profile.

End year in good standing:	74%	Return as sophomores:	87%

Basis for selection. GED not accepted. Applications reviewed on a rolling basis. Students will be notified of their admissions status within two weeks after applying. Students can sit for the Math placement test at AUD or submit an acceptable SAT score. All Engineering applicants must take SAT. Combined score of 1090 (exclusive of Writing) is required for admissions to the program. **Learning Disabled:** Student should declare disability upon applying. Student services provides support on a case by case basis.

2005-2006 Annual costs. Tuition/fees: $12,891. Room only: $3,870. Books/supplies: $600.

Application procedures. Admission: Closing date 8/20. $50 fee. Application must be submitted on paper. Admission notification on a rolling basis.

Academics. Special study options: Combined bachelor's/graduate degree, ESL, internships, study abroad. **Credit/placement by examination:** AP, CLEP, IB, SAT, institutional tests. **Support services:** Pre-admission summer program, reduced course load, tutoring.

Majors. Business: General, accounting, banking/financial services, e-commerce, management science, marketing. **Communications technology:** Graphics. **Computer sciences:** Information technology. **Engineering:** Civil, computer, electrical. **Visual/performing arts:** Commercial/advertising art, graphic design, illustration, interior design, photography.

Computing on campus. 65 workstations in library, computer center. Dormitories wired for high-speed internet access. Online library, helpline, wireless network available.

Student life. Freshman orientation: Mandatory. **Policies:** Dress code; no alcohol on campus. Freshmen permitted cars on campus. **Housing:** Single-sex dorms, special housing for disabled available. $680 deposit, deadline 6/5. **Activities:** Dance, drama, student government, student newspaper, African, Egyptian, Indian cultural clubs, Khaleej, Lebanese, Palestinian, and Pakistani student associations, Syrian & Islamic Awareness club.

Athletics. Intercollegiate: Basketball, soccer, swimming, tennis, track and field, volleyball. **Intramural:** Soccer, table tennis, volleyball, water polo.

Student services. Alcohol/substance abuse counseling, career counseling, student employment services, health services, personal counseling, placement for graduates. **Physically disabled:** Services for visually, speech, hearing impaired.

Contact. E-mail: admissions@aud.edu
Phone: (009) 714-3999000 Fax: (009) 714-3998899
Carol Maalouf, Associate Director of Admissions, American University in Dubai - United Arab Emirates, PO Box 28282, Dubai, AE

United Kingdom

Richmond, The American International University in London

Richmond-upon-Thames, United Kingdom — **CB member**
www.richmond.ac.uk — **CB code: 0823**

- Private 4-year university and liberal arts college
- Residential campus in very large city
- 698 degree-seeking undergraduates
- 75% of applicants admitted
- Application essay required

General. Founded in 1972. Regionally accredited. International student body with over 100 countries represented. Students spend their first two years on the Richmond Hill campus and the second two on the Kensington campus in London. Study centers in Florence and Rome, Italy. Degrees accredited in the both the US and the UK. **Degrees:** 166 bachelor's awarded; master's offered. **Location:** Located in London, England. **Calendar:** Semester, extensive summer session. **Full-time faculty:** 73 total; 41% have terminal degrees, 32% women. **Part-time faculty:** 75 total; 19% have terminal degrees, 45% women. **Class size:** 69% < 20, 31% 20-39.

Freshman class profile. 1,237 applied, 930 admitted, 259 enrolled.

Mid 50% test scores			
SAT verbal:	490-620	Rank in top quarter:	38%
SAT math:	460-600	Rank in top tenth:	30%
ACT:	24-28	Live on campus:	90%

Basis for selection. School achievement record most important. Letters of recommendations and personal statement considered. SAT/ACT scores also considered. Admission criteria geared to educational requirements not normally recognized in United States. Only 8% of student body holds U.S. citizenship. SAT or ACT recommended.

High school preparation. Required units include English 4, mathematics 3, science 3 and foreign language 2.

2005-2006 Annual costs. Tuition/fees: $21,020. Room/board: $10,970. Books/supplies: $600. Personal expenses: $4,500.

2004-2005 Financial aid. Need-based: Average need met was 9%. Average loan was $2,785. **Non-need-based:** Scholarships awarded for academics. **Additional information:** U.S. government loan programs available for eligible U.S. citizens/students.

Application procedures. Admission: Priority date 3/1; no deadline. $50 fee, may be waived for applicants with need. Application may be submitted online. Admission notification on a rolling basis beginning on or about 11/1. Must reply by May 1 or within 4 week(s) if notified thereafter. **Financial aid:** Priority date 3/15, closing date 8/1. FAFSA required. Applicants notified on a rolling basis starting 3/1; must reply by 5/1 or within 4 week(s) of notification.

Academics. English language development programs for non-native English speakers. **Special study options:** Combined bachelor's/graduate degree, cross-registration, double major, ESL, honors, independent study, internships, liberal arts/career combination, study abroad. Joint engineering program with George Washington University. **Credit/placement by examination:** AP, CLEP, IB, institutional tests. 30 credit hours maximum toward associate degree, 60 toward bachelor's. **Support services:** Reduced course load, remedial instruction, tutoring, writing center.

Majors. Business: General, business admin, communications, finance, international, international finance, international marketing, managerial economics, marketing. **Communications:** General, advertising, digital media, journalism, media studies, photojournalism, public relations. **Communications technology:** Graphics, photo/film/video. **Computer sciences:** General, applications programming, computer graphics, computer science, information systems, programming. **Engineering:** General, computer. **History:** General. **Liberal arts:** Arts/sciences. **Psychology:** General. **Social sciences:** General, economics, international economics, international relations, political science, sociology. **Visual/performing arts:** Cinematography, commercial photography, commercial/advertising art, design, graphic design, photography, studio arts.

Computing on campus. 250 workstations in library, computer center, student center. Online library, helpline, repair service, wireless network available.

Student life. Freshman orientation: Mandatory. **Housing:** Guaranteed on-campus for all undergraduates. Coed dorms, single-sex dorms, apartments, substance-free housing available. $550 deposit, deadline 5/1. **Activities:** Choral groups, dance, drama, literary magazine, music ensembles, student government, student newspaper, Community Outreach Club, Amnesty International, Pan-African Club, Middle Eastern Society, Literary Society, International Night, Student Ambassadors, Kuwaiti United, History/Politics Society, Royal United Services Institute for Defense and Security Studies (RUSI for Richmond University).

Student services. Alcohol/substance abuse counseling, career counseling, financial aid counseling, health services, minority student services, personal counseling, placement for graduates.

Contact. E-mail: enroll@richmond.ac.uk
Phone: (617) 450-5617 Fax: (617) 450-5601
Brian Davis, Director, US Office of Admissions, Richmond, The American International University in London, 343 Congress Street, Suite 3100, Boston, MA 02210-1214

Two-year colleges

Alabama

Alabama Southern Community College
Monroeville, Alabama
www.ascc.edu **CB code: 1644**

- Public 2-year community and junior college
- Commuter campus in small town

General. Founded in 1965. Regionally accredited. Institution has 3 campuses and 3 centers. **Enrollment:** 1,300 degree-seeking undergraduates. **Degrees:** 209 associate awarded. **Location:** 85 miles from Mobile. **Calendar:** Quarter, extensive summer session. **Full-time faculty:** 41 total. **Part-time faculty:** 66 total. **Special facilities:** Nature trail.

Basis for selection. Open admission.

2005-2006 Annual costs. Tuition/fees: $2,700; $4,830 out-of-state. Per-credit charge: $71 in-state; $142 out-of-state. Books/supplies: $750.

Application procedures. Admission: No deadline. No application fee. Admission notification on a rolling basis. **Financial aid:** Priority date 7/15; no closing date. FAFSA required. Applicants notified on a rolling basis; must reply within 4 week(s) of notification.

Academics. Special study options: Accelerated study, dual enrollment of high school students, honors, independent study. Degrees in allied health available through University of Alabama at Birmingham, registered nurse program through Jefferson Davis State Junior College. **Credit/placement by examination:** CLEP, institutional tests. 30 credit hours maximum toward associate degree. **Support services:** Learning center, pre-admission summer program, reduced course load, remedial instruction, tutoring.

Majors. Business: General, accounting, administrative services, banking/financial services, operations. **Computer sciences:** General. **Conservation:** Forest resources, forestry. **Construction:** Carpentry, power transmission. **Engineering:** Civil, electrical, mechanics. **Engineering technology:** Electrical. **Health:** EMT paramedic, licensed practical nurse, nursing (RN), nursing assistant, predentistry, premedicine, prepharmacy, preveterinary. **Legal studies:** Prelaw. **Liberal arts:** Arts/sciences. **Mechanic/repair:** Auto body, diesel, electronics/electrical, industrial. **Personal/culinary services:** General, cosmetic. **Protective services:** Firefighting.

Student life. Activities: Bands, choral groups, dance, drama, student government, Baptist student union, Circle K, ethnic student society, Phi Theta Kappa, Phi Beta Lambda, Baptist campus ministry, Students in Free Enterprise.

Athletics. NJCAA. **Intercollegiate:** Baseball M, basketball M. **Intramural:** Basketball M, softball, table tennis, tennis, volleyball.

Student services. Adult student services, career counseling, personal counseling, placement for graduates, veterans' counselor.

Contact. Phone: (251) 575-3156 Fax: (251) 575-5238
Ann Clanton, Dean of Students, Alabama Southern Community College, Box 2000, Monroeville, AL 36461

Bevill State Community College
Sumiton, Alabama
www.bscc.edu **CB code: 0723**

- Public 2-year community college
- Commuter campus in small town

General. Founded in 1969. Regionally accredited. Walker (main), Brewer, and Hamilton campuses. Learning sites in Jasper, Solligent, Carrollton. **Enrollment:** 3,707 degree-seeking undergraduates. **Degrees:** 499 associate awarded. **Location:** 25 miles from Birmingham. **Calendar:** Semester, limited summer session. **Full-time faculty:** 119 total. **Part-time faculty:** 216 total. **Special facilities:** Observatory, simulated underground mine.

Basis for selection. Open admission, but selective for some programs. Admission to nursing programs competitive and limited. High school diploma not required in some technical programs. ASSET required for placement.

2005-2006 Annual costs. Tuition/fees: $2,700; $4,830 out-of-state. Per-credit charge: $71 in-state; $142 out-of-state. Room-only rates for Bevill campuses: Fayette, $1,350; Hamilton, $900; Jasper, $990; Sumiton, $1,100. Books/supplies: $900. Personal expenses: $2,125.

Application procedures. Admission: No deadline. No application fee. Admission notification on a rolling basis beginning on or about 7/1. **Financial aid:** Priority date 5/1, closing date 8/25. FAFSA required. Applicants notified on a rolling basis starting 7/1.

Academics. Special study options: Accelerated study, cooperative education, distance learning, dual enrollment of high school students, honors, weekend college. **Credit/placement by examination:** CLEP, institutional tests. **Support services:** Learning center, reduced course load, remedial instruction, tutoring.

Majors. Business: Business admin. **Computer sciences:** General, computer science. **Construction:** Power transmission. **Engineering technology:** Drafting. **Health:** Medical transcription, nursing (RN). **Liberal arts:** Arts/sciences. **Mechanic/repair:** Auto body, electronics/electrical, heating/ac/refrig.

Computing on campus. 105 workstations in library, computer center.

Student life. Freshman orientation: Available, $30 fee. **Housing:** Apartments available. Housing for student athletes. **Activities:** Bands, choral groups, dance, drama, music ensembles, student government, Inter-Varsity Christian Fellowship, Black Student Union, Circle-K.

Athletics. NJCAA. **Intercollegiate:** Baseball M, basketball, cross-country M, golf M, softball W, volleyball W. **Intramural:** Basketball, softball, table tennis, volleyball.

Student services. Adult student services, career counseling, student employment services, health services, personal counseling, placement for graduates, veterans' counselor. **Physically disabled:** Services for visually, speech, hearing impaired. **Transfer:** Special adviser, orientation for new students. Transfer adviser for students transferring to 4-year colleges.

Contact. Phone: (205) 648-3271 ext. 5432 Fax: (205) 648-3311
Melissa Stowe, Director of Enrollment Services, Bevill State Community College, Box 800, Sumiton, AL 35148

Bishop State Community College
Mobile, Alabama
www.bishop.edu **CB code: 1517**

- Public 2-year community college
- Commuter campus in small city

General. Founded in 1963. Regionally accredited. 4 off-campus sites for technical and health-related programs. **Enrollment:** 4,887 degree-seeking undergraduates. **Degrees:** 350 associate awarded. **ROTC:** Army, Air Force. **Calendar:** Semester, limited summer session. **Full-time faculty:** 118 total. **Part-time faculty:** 75 total. **Partnerships:** Training for business and industry, JTPA Assessment Center, formal partnership with Mobile County public school system.

Basis for selection. Open admission, but selective for some programs.

2005-2006 Annual costs. Tuition/fees: $2,700; $4,800 out-of-state. Per-credit charge: $72 in-state; $144 out-of-state. Books/supplies: $700. Personal expenses: $1,033.

2004-2005 Financial aid. **Need-based:** 90% of total undergraduate aid awarded as scholarships/grants, 10% as loans/jobs. **Non-need-based:** Scholarships awarded for academics, athletics.

Application procedures. **Admission:** No deadline. No application fee. Admission notification on a rolling basis. **Financial aid:** Priority date 4/1; no closing date. FAFSA, institutional form required. Applicants notified on a rolling basis; must reply within 2 week(s) of notification.

Academics. Students must complete 112 credit hours for graduation from technical programs. **Special study options:** Accelerated study, cooperative education, cross-registration, dual enrollment of high school students, honors, internships, weekend college. Degree programs available in allied health through University of Alabama at Birmingham. License preparation in nursing. **Credit/placement by examination:** CLEP. **Support services:** Learning center, pre-admission summer program, reduced course load, remedial instruction, tutoring.

Majors. **Business:** Accounting, administrative services, business admin. **Computer sciences:** General. **Education:** General. **Engineering technology:** Civil, drafting. **Health:** Medical records technology, nursing (RN), physical therapy assistant. **Liberal arts:** Arts/sciences. **Mechanic/repair:** Electronics/electrical. **Personal/culinary services:** Culinary arts, mortuary science. **Protective services:** Fire services admin, law enforcement admin.

Computing on campus. 71 workstations in library, computer center.

Student life. **Freshman orientation:** Available. **Activities:** Bands, choral groups, dance, drama, music ensembles, radio station, student government, student newspaper, social service organization, Baptist Student Union, Young Democrats.

Athletics. NJCAA. **Intercollegiate:** Baseball M, basketball, softball W.

Student services. Adult student services, career counseling, student employment services, health services, on-campus daycare, personal counseling, placement for graduates, veterans' counselor. **Physically disabled:** Services for visually, speech, hearing impaired. **Transfer:** Special adviser, orientation for new students. Transfer adviser for students transferring to 4-year colleges.

Contact. Phone: (251) 690-6801 Fax: (251) 438-5403
Wanda Daniels, Director of Admissions, Bishop State Community College, 351 North Broad Street, Mobile, AL 36603-5898

Calhoun Community College

Decatur, Alabama — **CB member**
www.calhoun.edu — **CB code: 1356**

- Public 2-year community and liberal arts college
- Commuter campus in small city

General. Founded in 1963. Regionally accredited. Two off-campus sites in Huntsville offer evening and weekend classes. Numerous courses available online and by videocassette. **Enrollment:** 8,249 degree-seeking undergraduates. **Degrees:** 732 associate awarded. **Location:** 75 miles from Birmingham, 30 miles from Huntsville. **Calendar:** Semester, limited summer session. **Full-time faculty:** 120 total. **Part-time faculty:** 300 total. **Partnerships:** Formal partnership with Boeing.

Student profile. Among degree-seeking undergraduates, 30% enrolled in a transfer program, 68% enrolled in a vocational program, 3,794 transferred in from other institutions.

Part-time:	61%	**Asian American:**	1%
Out-of-state:	1%	**Hispanic American:**	2%
Women:	56%	**Native American:**	2%
African American:	19%		

Transfer out. **Colleges most students transferred to 2005:** Athens University, University of North Alabama, University of Alabama-Huntsville, Wallace State, Auburn University.

Basis for selection. Open admission, but selective for some programs. SAT/ACT scores used for placement. Students from unaccredited high schools are required to have a minimum ACT score of 16 or SAT score of 790 (exclusive of Writing). Portfolio recommended for art majors. **Homeschooled:** Must have ACT score of at least 16, SAT score of 790 (exclusive of Writing), successfully complete GED or high school graduation examination.

High school preparation. 26 units recommended. Recommended units include English 4, mathematics 4, social studies 4, science 4, foreign language 2 and academic electives 10. In-state high school graduates must pass state high school competency examination.

2005-2006 Annual costs. Tuition/fees: $2,700; $4,830 out-of-state. Per-credit charge: $71 in-state; $142 out-of-state. Books/supplies: $1,500. Personal expenses: $1,000.

Financial aid. **Need-based:** Work study available for part-time students. **Non-need-based:** Scholarships awarded for academics.

Application procedures. **Admission:** No deadline. No application fee. Application must be submitted on paper. Admission notification on a rolling basis. **Financial aid:** Priority date 5/1; no closing date. FAFSA, institutional form required. Applicants notified on a rolling basis starting 7/1; must reply within 2 week(s) of notification.

Academics. **Special study options:** Accelerated study, distance learning, dual enrollment of high school students, liberal arts/career combination, weekend college. License preparation in dental hygiene, nursing, paramedic, real estate. **Credit/placement by examination:** AP, CLEP, institutional tests. 30 credit hours maximum toward associate degree. AP Exam credit limited to 18 semester hours. **Support services:** GED preparation and test center, reduced course load, remedial instruction, tutoring, writing center.

Majors. **Business:** Accounting, business admin. **Communications technology:** General, photo/film/video. **Computer sciences:** General, applications programming, programming. **Construction:** Electrician. **Education:** General, early childhood, elementary, secondary. **Engineering technology:** Aerospace, drafting, heat/ac/refrig. **Family/consumer sciences:** Child care, child development. **Health:** Cytogenetics, dental assistant, EMT paramedic, nursing (RN), predentistry, premedicine, prenursing, prepharmacy, preveterinary. **Liberal arts:** Arts/sciences. **Math:** General. **Mechanic/repair:** Heating/ac/refrig. **Production:** Machine tool, tool and die. **Visual/performing arts:** Commercial/advertising art.

Most popular majors. Business/marketing 22%, computer/information sciences 6%, education 10%, health sciences 25%, liberal arts 22%, military 14%.

Computing on campus. 166 workstations in library, student center. Online course registration available.

Student life. **Freshman orientation:** Mandatory, $95 fee. Preregistration for classes offered. Class held the first semester of attendance. **Policies:** Freshmen permitted cars on campus. **Activities:** Jazz band, choral groups, drama, music ensembles, student government, student newspaper, TV station, BACCHUS/SADD, campus ministries, Black Students Alliance Club, drama club, criminal justice club, Native American club, Phi Theta Kappa, Allied Health Students Association, The Centurians.

Student services. Career counseling, financial aid counseling, minority student services, on-campus daycare, veterans' counselor. **Transfer:** Special adviser, orientation for new students. Transfer adviser, college fairs on campus for students transferring to 4-year colleges.

Contact. E-mail: pml@calhoun.edu
Phone: (256) 306-2593 Toll-free number: (800) 626-3628
Fax: (256) 306-2941
M. Tosh, Director of Admissions and Registrar, Calhoun Community College, Box 2216, Decatur, AL 35609-2216

Central Alabama Community College

Childersburg, Alabama
www.cacc.cc.al.us — **CB code: 0715**

- Public 2-year community college
- Commuter campus in large town

General. Founded in 1965. Regionally accredited. 2 campuses: Childersburg, predominantly for technical courses, and Alexander City, predominantly for transfer courses. **Enrollment:** 2,000 degree-seeking undergraduates. **Degrees:** 260 associate awarded. **Location:** 50 miles from Montgomery, 35 miles from Birmingham. **Calendar:** Semester, extensive summer session. **Full-time faculty:** 50 total. **Part-time faculty:** 60 total. **Special facilities:** Wildlife museum, wellness center, pioneer village.

Student profile.

Out-of-state:	1%	**25 or older:**	48%

Basis for selection. Open admission, but selective for some programs. Graduates of non-accredited high schools and certain nursing applicants may be required to take SAT or ACT.

2005-2006 Annual costs. Tuition/fees: $2,700; $4,830 out-of-state. Per-credit charge: $71 in-state; $142 out-of-state. Books/supplies: $300. Personal expenses: $500.

Financial aid. Non-need-based: Scholarships awarded for academics, athletics, state residency.

Application procedures. Admission: Closing date 8/5. No application fee. Admission notification on a rolling basis. **Financial aid:** Priority date 7/15; no closing date. FAFSA, institutional form required. Applicants notified on a rolling basis.

Academics. Special study options: Cooperative education, dual enrollment of high school students, independent study. **Credit/placement by examination:** CLEP, institutional tests. 48 credit hours maximum toward associate degree. **Support services:** GED preparation and test center, learning center, remedial instruction, study skills assistance, tutoring.

Majors. Agriculture: Business. **Business:** General, administrative services, business admin, management information systems. **Computer sciences:** General. **Education:** General. **Engineering:** General. **Engineering technology:** Drafting, electrical. **Health:** Clinical lab science, EMT paramedic, health services, medical assistant, medical radiologic technology/radiation therapy, medical records technology, occupational therapy assistant, physical therapy assistant, respiratory therapy technology. **Liberal arts:** Arts/sciences. **Protective services:** Criminal justice, firefighting, police science.

Computing on campus. 45 workstations in library, computer center, student center.

Student life. Freshman orientation: Mandatory. **Policies:** Freshmen permitted cars on campus. **Activities:** Jazz band, choral groups, dance, drama, radio station, student government.

Athletics. NJCAA. **Intercollegiate:** Baseball M, golf M, softball W, tennis, volleyball W. **Team name:** Trojans.

Student services. Career counseling, personal counseling, veterans' counselor. **Transfer:** Special adviser, pre-admission transcript evaluation for new students. Transfer adviser, college fairs on campus for students transferring to 4-year colleges.

Contact. Phone: (256) 215-4255 Toll-free number: (800) 643-2657
Betty Graham, Director of Admissions, Central Alabama Community College, 34091 US Highway 280 South, Childersburg, AL 35044

Chattahoochee Valley Community College

Phenix City, Alabama
www.cv.edu **CB code: 1187**

- Public 2-year community and junior college
- Commuter campus in large town

General. Founded in 1974. Regionally accredited. **Enrollment:** 2,031 degree-seeking undergraduates. **Degrees:** 162 associate awarded. **ROTC:** Army. **Location:** 2 miles from Columbus, Georgia. **Calendar:** Semester, extensive summer session. **Full-time faculty:** 30 total. **Part-time faculty:** 76 total.

Student profile. Among degree-seeking undergraduates, 80% enrolled in a transfer program, 20% enrolled in a vocational program. Of all enrolled students, 5% already have a bachelor's degree or higher.

Transfer out. Colleges most students transferred to 2005: Columbus State University, Auburn University, Columbus Technical College, Southern Union State Community College, Troy State University.

Basis for selection. Open admission, but selective for some programs. Additional requirements for health occupation programs. SAT and ACT considered if submitted. ASSET waived for students submitting appropriate ACT/SAT scores.

2005-2006 Annual costs. Tuition/fees: $2,700; $4,830 out-of-state. Per-credit charge: $71 in-state; $142 out-of-state. Books/supplies: $800. Personal expenses: $750.

2004-2005 Financial aid. Need-based: 98% of total undergraduate aid awarded as scholarships/grants, 2% as loans/jobs. Need-based aid available for part-time students. Work study available nights, weekends and for part-time students. **Non-need-based:** Scholarships awarded for academics, art, athletics, leadership, music/drama.

Application procedures. Admission: Priority date 7/15; no deadline. No application fee. Admission notification on a rolling basis. **Financial aid:** Priority date 7/1; no closing date. FAFSA required. Applicants notified on a rolling basis; must reply within 1 week(s) of notification.

Academics. Special study options: Accelerated study, distance learning, dual enrollment of high school students, honors, independent study, liberal arts/career combination. License preparation in nursing. **Credit/placement by examination:** CLEP, institutional tests. 18 credit hours maximum toward associate degree. **Support services:** GED test center, learning center, reduced course load, remedial instruction.

Majors. Biology: General. **Business:** Accounting, administrative services, business admin. **Computer sciences:** General, data processing. **Conservation:** Forestry. **Education:** Business, elementary, physical, secondary. **Engineering:** General. **Health:** Medical records technology, nursing (RN). **Liberal arts:** Arts/sciences. **Math:** General. **Parks/recreation:** Health/fitness. **Physical sciences:** Chemistry, physics. **Protective services:** Criminal justice, firefighting. **Visual/performing arts:** Art history/conservation, dramatic.

Computing on campus. 150 workstations in library, computer center. Online library available.

Student life. Freshman orientation: Available. Preregistration for classes offered. **Policies:** Freshmen permitted cars on campus. **Activities:** Choral groups, drama, music ensembles, musical theater, student government, student newspaper.

Athletics. NJCAA. **Intercollegiate:** Baseball M, softball W. **Team name:** Pirates.

Student services. Adult student services, career counseling, personal counseling, placement for graduates, veterans' counselor. **Physically disabled:** Services for visually, hearing impaired. **Transfer:** Special adviser for new students.

Contact. Phone: (334) 291-4995 Fax: (334) 291-4994
David Hodge, Dean of Student and Administrative Services, Chattahoochee Valley Community College, 2602 College Drive, Phenix City, AL 36869

Community College of the Air Force

Maxwell Air Force Base, Alabama **CB member**
www.au.af.mil/au/ccaf **CB code: 1175**

- Public 2-year community and technical college
- Commuter campus in small city
- Interview required

General. Founded in 1972. Regionally accredited. Multicampus, worldwide, for United States Air Force enlisted personnel. Administrative offices at Maxwell Air Force Base. Primary campuses are technical training centers located at 5 Air Force bases in 3 states. Other campuses include USAF PME Centers, USAF Command Sponsored Schools, and Field Training Detachments. **Enrollment:** 354,000 degree-seeking undergraduates. **Degrees:** 16,521 associate awarded. **Location:** 160 miles from Atlanta, 90 miles from Birmingham. **Calendar:** Continuous, extensive summer session. **Full-time faculty:** 6,735 total.

Basis for selection. Open admission. For Air Force enlisted personnel, enlisted members of Selected Reserve in Air National Guard, Air Force Reserve Units, or mobilization augmentees who have completed basic training. All USAF enlisted personnel automatically registered upon completion of basic military training and assignment to an Air Force career field. All applicants must take the Armed Services Vocational Aptitude Battery. **Adult students:** Entrance exam policies same as for first-time freshmen.

High school preparation. 16 units recommended. Recommended units include English 4, mathematics 3, social studies 3, science 2 and foreign language 2.

2006-2007 Annual costs. Students pay no tuition or fees.

Financial aid. Additional information: Air Force Tuition Assistance program available for general and technical education courses taken at civilian colleges and universities. Pays 75% of tuition costs.

Application procedures. Admission: No deadline. No application fee. Admission notification on a rolling basis. **Financial aid:** No deadline.

Academics. Special study options: Accelerated study, distance learning, independent study, internships, liberal arts/career combination. License preparation in aviation, physical therapy, radiology. **Credit/placement by examination:** AP, CLEP, institutional tests. 30 credit hours maximum toward associate degree. **Support services:** Reduced course load, remedial instruction, tutoring.

Majors. Business: Human resources, management information systems, office management, operations, purchasing. **Communications:** Public relations. **Communications technology:** General. **Computer sciences:** General, networking. **Construction:** General. **Education:** Technology/industrial arts. **Engineering technology:** Construction, electrical. **Health:** Cardiovascular technology, dental assistant, dental lab technology, health care admin, health services, histologic assistant, medical assistant, nuclear medical technology, ophthalmic lab technology, pharmacy assistant, physical therapy assistant, radiologic technology/medical imaging, sonography, surgical technology. **History:** General, public archives. **Interdisciplinary:** Nutrition sciences. **Legal studies:** Paralegal. **Mechanic/repair:** Aircraft, electronics/electrical, heating/ac/refrig, industrial. **Military:** General. **Parks/recreation:** General. **Physical sciences:** Atmospheric science. **Protective services:** Criminal justice, fire safety technology. **Public administration:** Social work. **Transportation:** General, air traffic control, aviation, aviation management.

Student life. Policies: Air Force bases provide housing, student services, activities, and athletics. Freshmen permitted cars on campus. **Housing:** Coed dorms, single-sex dorms, apartments available.

Athletics. Intramural: Badminton, baseball M, basketball, bowling, boxing M, cross-country, golf, handball, racquetball, rifle, soccer M, softball, squash, swimming, table tennis, tennis, track and field, volleyball, weight lifting.

Student services. Adult student services, alcohol/substance abuse counseling, career counseling, financial aid counseling, health services, legal services, on-campus daycare, personal counseling, veterans' counselor. **Transfer:** Special adviser for new students. Transfer center, transfer adviser, college fairs on campus for students transferring to 4-year colleges.

Contact. E-mail: registrar.ccat@maxwell.af.mil
Phone: (334) 953-2794 Fax: (334) 953-5231
CMSgt. Bobby McAlexander, Director of Enrollment Management and Registrar Division, Community College of the Air Force, 130 West Maxwell Boulevard, Maxwell Air Force Base, AL 36112-6613

Enterprise-Ozark Community College

Enterprise, Alabama
www.eocc.edu **CB code: 1213**

- Public 2-year junior college
- Commuter campus in large town

General. Founded in 1963. Regionally accredited. Courses offered at Enterprise, Ozark, Fort Rucker, and Mobile. **Enrollment:** 1,810 degree-seeking undergraduates. **Degrees:** 270 associate awarded. **ROTC:** Air Force. **Location:** 85 miles from Montgomery, 30 miles from Dothan. **Calendar:** Semester, limited summer session. **Full-time faculty:** 61 total. **Part-time faculty:** 150 total.

Transfer out. Colleges most students transferred to 2005: Troy State University, Troy State University at Dothan, Auburn University.

Basis for selection. Open admission.

High school preparation. 28 units recommended. Recommended units include English 4, mathematics 4, social studies 4 and science 4.

2005-2006 Annual costs. Tuition/fees: $2,700; $4,830 out-of-state. Per-credit charge: $71 in-state; $142 out-of-state. Books/supplies: $500. Personal expenses: $500.

Financial aid. Need-based: Work study available for part-time students. **Non-need-based:** Scholarships awarded for academics, art, athletics, leadership, music/drama, state residency.

Application procedures. Admission: No deadline. No application fee. Admission notification on a rolling basis. **Financial aid:** No deadline. FAFSA, institutional form required. Applicants notified on a rolling basis starting 7/1; must reply within 2 week(s) of notification.

Academics. Special study options: Distance learning, dual enrollment of high school students, ESL, honors, internships, weekend college. License preparation in paramedic, real estate. **Credit/placement by examination:** CLEP, institutional tests. 30 credit hours maximum toward associate degree. **Support services:** GED preparation and test center, learning center, pre-admission summer program, remedial instruction, tutoring.

Majors. Agriculture: Business. **Business:** General, administrative services, business admin, management information systems, office management, real estate. **Communications:** General. **Computer sciences:** General, applications programming. **Construction:** Power transmission. **Engineering technology:** Automotive. **Family/consumer sciences:** Institutional food production. **Health:** Clinical lab science, EMT paramedic, medical assistant, medical records technology, nuclear medical technology, occupational therapy assistant, physical therapy assistant, respiratory therapy technology. **Legal studies:** Paralegal, prelaw. **Liberal arts:** Arts/sciences. **Mechanic/repair:** General, aircraft, avionics. **Parks/recreation:** Facilities management. **Protective services:** Police science.

Computing on campus. 125 workstations in library, computer center, student center. Online library available.

Student life. Freshman orientation: Mandatory, $10 fee. Preregistration for classes offered. **Activities:** Concert band, choral groups, dance, literary magazine, music ensembles, student government, student newspaper, scholastic honorary fraternity, African American organizations.

Athletics. NJCAA. **Intercollegiate:** Baseball M, basketball, softball W. **Team name:** Boll Weevils.

Student services. Adult student services, career counseling, student employment services, on-campus daycare, personal counseling, placement for graduates, veterans' counselor, women's services. **Physically disabled:** Services for visually, speech, hearing impaired. **Transfer:** Special adviser, orientation for new students. Transfer adviser, college fairs on campus for students transferring to 4-year colleges.

Contact. E-mail: rwyatt@eocc.edu
Phone: (334) 347-2623 ext. 234 Fax: (334) 393-6223
Gary Deas, Registrar, Enterprise-Ozark Community College, Box 1300, Enterprise, AL 36331

Gadsden State Community College

Gadsden, Alabama
www.gadsdenstate.edu **CB code: 1262**

- Public 2-year community college
- Commuter campus in large town

General. Founded in 1985. Regionally accredited. Off-campus sites include Ayers Campus, McClellan Campus and Cherokee County Center. **Enrollment:** 5,426 degree-seeking undergraduates. **Degrees:** 492 associate awarded. **ROTC:** Army. **Location:** 60 miles from Birmingham. **Calendar:** Semester, limited summer session. **Full-time faculty:** 141 total. **Part-time faculty:** 157 total. **Special facilities:** Advanced technology center, language institute, aquaculture education and development center.

Student profile. Among degree-seeking undergraduates, 1,658 enrolled as first-time, first-year students.

Part-time:	45%	**Asian American:**	2%
Out-of-state:	4%	**Hispanic American:**	2%
Women:	62%	**25 or older:**	46%
African American:	20%	**Live on campus:**	4%

Transfer out. Colleges most students transferred to 2005: Jacksonville State University, Auburn University, University of Alabama, University of Alabama at Birmingham, University of Alabama at Huntsville.

Basis for selection. Open admission, but selective for some programs. Special requirements for health-related programs. Career Program Assessment Test required for some programs. Interview recommended for computer technology, court reporting, and most health science majors. **Adult students:** Entrance exam policies same as for first-time freshmen. **Home-schooled:** Transcript of courses and grades required. An ACT score of 16 or a SAT score 790.

High school preparation. 27 units recommended. Recommended units include English 4, mathematics 4, social studies 4, science 4 (laboratory 2), academic electives 8.5. Electives must include .5 unit computer, .5 unit of fine arts.

2005-2006 Annual costs. Tuition/fees: $2,700; $4,830 out-of-state. Per-credit charge: $71 in-state; $142 out-of-state. Room only: $2,800. Books/supplies: $800. Personal expenses: $825.

2005-2006 Financial aid. Need-based: Need-based aid available for part-time students. Work study available for part-time students. **Non-need-based:** Scholarships awarded for academics, athletics, state residency.

Application procedures. Admission: No deadline. No application fee. Admission notification on a rolling basis. **Financial aid:** Priority date 4/15; no closing date. FAFSA, institutional form required. Applicants notified on a rolling basis starting 6/10; must reply within 2 week(s) of notification.

Academics. Special study options: Accelerated study, cooperative education, cross-registration, distance learning, dual enrollment of high school students, ESL, independent study, internships, weekend college. License preparation in nursing, paramedic. **Credit/placement by examination:** CLEP, institutional tests. 20 credit hours maximum toward associate degree. **Support services:** GED preparation and test center, remedial instruction, study skills assistance, tutoring, writing center.

Majors. Agriculture: General. **Area/ethnic studies:** American. **Biology:** General. **Business:** Accounting technology, administrative services, business admin, sales/distribution. **Communications:** General. **Communications technology:** General, graphics. **Computer sciences:** General, computer science, information systems, information technology, LAN/WAN management, networking, programming. **Conservation:** Forestry. **Education:** General, early childhood, elementary, kindergarten/preschool, mathematics. **Engineering:** General. **Engineering technology:** Civil, civil drafting, computer systems, electrical, heat/ac/refrig, industrial, mechanical, mechanical drafting, telecommunications. **Family/consumer sciences:** Child development. **Health:** Clinical lab assistant, clinical lab technology, EMT paramedic, medical radiologic technology/radiation therapy, medical records technology, nursing (RN), predentistry, premedicine, prenursing, prepharmacy, preveterinary, substance abuse counseling. **History:** General. **Legal studies:** Court reporting, paralegal, prelaw. **Liberal arts:** Arts/sciences. **Math:** General. **Mechanic/repair:** Electronics/electrical, heating/ac/refrig, industrial. **Parks/recreation:** Health/fitness. **Philosophy/religion:** Religion. **Physical sciences:** Chemistry. **Protective services:** Law enforcement admin. **Psychology:** General. **Social sciences:** Sociology. **Visual/performing arts:** Art.

Computing on campus. 250 workstations in library, computer center, student center. Online course registration, online library available.

Student life. Freshman orientation: Available, $90 fee. Preregistration for classes offered. **Policies:** Freshmen permitted cars on campus. **Housing:** Coed dorms, substance-free housing available. **Activities:** Bands, choral groups, dance, drama, student government, Circle-K, International Club, Baptist Student Union, Phi Beta Lambda (business service organization).

Athletics. NJCAA. **Intercollegiate:** Baseball M, basketball, cross-country W, golf M, softball W, volleyball W. **Team name:** Cardinals.

Student services. Adult student services, career counseling, services for economically disadvantaged, student employment services, personal counseling, placement for graduates, veterans' counselor. **Physically disabled:** Services for visually, speech, hearing impaired. **Transfer:** Special adviser, orientation, pre-admission transcript evaluation for new students. Transfer adviser, college fairs on campus for students transferring to 4-year colleges.

Contact. E-mail: info@gadsdenstate.edu
Phone: (256) 549-8210 ext. 8210 Toll-free number: (800) 226-5563
Fax: (256) 549-8205
Teresa Rhea, Registrar & Associate Dean, Gadsden State Community College, 1001 George Wallace Drive, Gadsden, AL 35902-0227

George C. Wallace Community College at Dothan

Dothan, Alabama
www.wallace.edu **CB code: 1264**

- Public 2-year community college
- Commuter campus in small city

General. Founded in 1949. Regionally accredited. Additional campuses in Eufula and Ft. Rucker. **Enrollment:** 3,601 degree-seeking undergraduates. **Degrees:** 353 associate awarded. **Location:** 6 miles from downtown. **Calendar:** Semester, extensive summer session. **Full-time faculty:** 127 total. **Part-time faculty:** 110 total.

Student profile. Among degree-seeking undergraduates, 29% enrolled in a transfer program, 28% enrolled in a vocational program, 866 enrolled as first-time, first-year students.

Part-time:	45%	**Women:**	64%
Out-of-state:	4%	**25 or older:**	42%

Transfer out. Colleges most students transferred to 2005: University of Alabama, Auburn University, and University of Alabama at Birmingham.

Basis for selection. Open admission, but selective for some programs. Additional requirements for allied health and nursing programs. National League for Nursing examination required for nursing applicants. Interview required of nursing majors.

2005-2006 Annual costs. Tuition/fees: $2,700; $4,890 out-of-state. Per-credit charge: $71 in-state; $142 out-of-state. Books/supplies: $900. Personal expenses: $500.

Financial aid. Need-based: Work study available for part-time students. **Non-need-based:** Scholarships awarded for academics, athletics, leadership.

Application procedures. Admission: No deadline. No application fee. Admission notification on a rolling basis. **Financial aid:** No deadline. FAFSA required. Applicants notified on a rolling basis.

Academics. Special study options: Accelerated study, combined bachelor's/graduate degree, cooperative education, cross-registration, distance learning, dual enrollment of high school students, ESL, honors, weekend college. License preparation in nursing, paramedic, physical therapy, radiology. **Credit/placement by examination:** AP, CLEP, institutional tests. 48 credit hours maximum toward associate degree. **Support services:** GED preparation and test center, learning center, pre-admission summer program, remedial instruction, study skills assistance, tutoring.

Majors. Business: Administrative services. **Computer sciences:** General. **Construction:** Electrician. **Engineering technology:** Drafting. **Health:** EMT paramedic, medical assistant, medical radiologic technology/radiation therapy, respiratory therapy technology. **Legal studies:** Legal secretary. **Liberal arts:** Arts/sciences. **Mechanic/repair:** Electronics/electrical.

Student life. Freshman orientation: Mandatory. Preregistration for classes offered. **Policies:** Freshmen permitted cars on campus. **Activities:** Jazz band, choral groups, drama, music ensembles, student government, student newspaper, Association of Student Practical Nursing, Wallace Chorus, Diplomats, Elite Club, Jazz Band, National Vocational-Technical Honor Society, Phi Theta Kappa, Phi Beta Lambda, Refuge, Respiratory Therapy Association for Better Breathing.

Athletics. NJCAA. **Intercollegiate:** Baseball M, softball W. **Team name:** Govs, Lady Govs.

Student services. Adult student services, career counseling, services for economically disadvantaged, student employment services, financial aid counseling, personal counseling, placement for graduates, veterans' counselor. **Learning disabled:** Comprehensive services available. **Transfer:** Special adviser, orientation for new students. Transfer adviser, college fairs on campus for students transferring to 4-year colleges.

Contact. E-mail: bbarnes@wallace.edu
Phone: (334) 983-3521 Toll-free number: (800) 543-2426
Fax: (334) 983-6066
Brenda Barnes, Assistant Dean of Student Affairs, George C. Wallace Community College at Dothan, 1141 Wallace Drive, Dothan, AL 36303-0943

George C. Wallace State Community College at Selma

Selma, Alabama
wccs.edu **CB code: 3146**

- Public 2-year community and technical college
- Commuter campus in large town

General. Founded in 1963. Regionally accredited. **Enrollment:** 2,100 degree-seeking undergraduates. **Degrees:** 180 associate awarded. **Location:** 50 miles from Montgomery, 90 miles from Birmingham. **Calendar:** Semester, extensive summer session. **Full-time faculty:** 50 total. **Part-time faculty:** 50 total.

Basis for selection. Open admission, but selective for some programs. Generic/mobility (RN) nursing candidates need minimum ACT composite score of 20. Practical (LPN) nursing candidates need minimum ACT composite score of 18, or score 41 composite on the Nursing Entrance Test.

2005-2006 Annual costs. Tuition/fees: $2,700; $4,860 out-of-state. Per-credit charge: $72 in-state; $144 out-of-state. Books/supplies: $690. Personal expenses: $976.

Financial aid. Non-need-based: Scholarships awarded for academics, athletics.

Application procedures. Admission: No deadline. No application fee. Admission notification on a rolling basis. **Financial aid:** Priority date 6/1; no closing date. FAFSA required. Applicants notified on a rolling basis starting 6/15.

Academics. Special study options: Accelerated study, double major, dual enrollment of high school students. **Credit/placement by examination:** CLEP, institutional tests. 30 credit hours maximum toward associate degree. **Support services:** GED preparation and test center, learning center, reduced course load, remedial instruction, study skills assistance, tutoring.

Majors. Business: Administrative services, business admin. **Computer sciences:** General. **Engineering technology:** Drafting. **Health:** Nursing (RN). **Liberal arts:** Arts/sciences. **Mechanic/repair:** General.

Student life. Freshman orientation: Available. Preregistration for classes offered. **Activities:** Student government, Baptist Student Union, Phi Theta Kappa, Fellowship of Christian Athletes (FCA).

Athletics. NJCAA. **Intercollegiate:** Baseball M, basketball, softball W. **Intramural:** Baseball M, basketball, softball. **Team name:** Patriots.

Student services. Career counseling, student employment services, personal counseling, placement for graduates, veterans' counselor. **Physically disabled:** Services for visually, speech, hearing impaired. **Transfer:** Special adviser, orientation for new students. Transfer adviser, college fairs on campus for students transferring to 4-year colleges.

Contact. Phone: (334) 876-9295 Fax: (334) 876-9300
Gail May, Dean of Students, George C. Wallace State Community College at Selma, PO Box 2530, Selma, AL 36702-2530

J. F. Drake State Technical College

Huntsville, Alabama
www.drakestate.edu **CB code: 2108**

- Public 2-year technical college
- Commuter campus in small city

General. Founded in 1961. Regionally accredited. **Enrollment:** 759 degree-seeking undergraduates. **Degrees:** 58 associate awarded. **Location:** 100 miles from Birmingham, 200 miles from Atlanta. **Calendar:** Semester. **Full-time faculty:** 23 total. **Part-time faculty:** 51 total. **Class size:** 65% < 20, 29% 20-39, 4% 40-49, 2% 50-99.

Student profile.

Part-time:	40%	**Women:**	50%
Out-of-state:	2%	**25 or older:**	53%

Basis for selection. Open admission, but selective for some programs. Nursing applicants must pass pre-entrance examination. COMPASS required for all students for placement only.

2005-2006 Annual costs. Tuition/fees: $2,700; $4,830 out-of-state. Per-credit charge: $72 in-state; $144 out-of-state.

2005-2006 Financial aid. Need-based: Need-based aid available for part-time students. Work study available for part-time students. **Non-need-based:** Scholarships awarded for academics, state residency.

Application procedures. Admission: Priority date 7/1; no deadline. No application fee. Admission notification on a rolling basis. **Financial aid:** Priority date 7/1; no closing date. FAFSA required. Applicants notified on a rolling basis.

Academics. Special study options: Cooperative education, dual enrollment of high school students, internships. License preparation in nursing. **Credit/placement by examination:** CLEP, institutional tests. **Support services:** GED preparation, learning center, reduced course load, remedial instruction, tutoring.

Majors. Business: Accounting, administrative services. **Communications technology:** Graphic/printing. **Computer sciences:** Data processing, programming. **Engineering technology:** Drafting. **Mechanic/repair:** Electronics/electrical. **Production:** Machine tool.

Computing on campus. 130 workstations in library, computer center, student center. Online library, repair service available.

Student life. Freshman orientation: Available. Preregistration for classes offered. One-day program includes a study skills seminar. **Activities:** Student government, student newspaper, Phi Beta Lambda, VICA, National Vocational Technical Honor Society.

Student services. Career counseling, services for economically disadvantaged, student employment services, financial aid counseling, personal counseling, placement for graduates, veterans' counselor. **Physically disabled:** Services for hearing impaired. **Transfer:** Special adviser, orientation, pre-admission transcript evaluation for new students. Transfer adviser for students transferring to 4-year colleges.

Contact. E-mail: clemons@drakestate.edu
Phone: (256) 551-3109 Toll-free number: (888) 413-7253
Fax: (256) 539-6439
Shirley Clemons, Director of Admissions, J. F. Drake State Technical College, 3421 Meridian Street North, Huntsville, AL 35811

James H. Faulkner State Community College

Bay Minette, Alabama
www.faulknerstate.edu **CB code: 1939**

- Public 2-year community college
- Commuter campus in large town

General. Founded in 1965. Regionally accredited. Two off-campus sites in Fairhope and Gulf Shores. **Enrollment:** 2,200 degree-seeking undergraduates. **Degrees:** 375 associate awarded. **Location:** 35 miles from Mobile. **Calendar:** Semester, extensive summer session. **Full-time faculty:** 60 total. **Part-time faculty:** 100 total.

Transfer out. Colleges most students transferred to 2005: University of Alabama, Auburn University, University of South Alabama.

Basis for selection. Open admission, but selective for some programs. Students applying for dental assisting program must take and pass Health Occupations Aptitude exam. Audition recommended for music majors, portfolio for art majors. **Homeschooled:** If school is non-accredited, ACT composite of 16 or better or GED is required.

2005-2006 Annual costs. Tuition/fees: $2,790; $4,920 out-of-state. Per-credit charge: $71 in-state; $142 out-of-state. Room/board: $2,930. Books/supplies: $450. Personal expenses: $800.

Application procedures. Admission: No deadline. No application fee. Admission notification on a rolling basis. **Financial aid:** Priority date 7/1, closing date 8/1. FAFSA, institutional form required. Applicants notified on a rolling basis starting 8/1.

Academics. Special study options: Accelerated study, cooperative education, distance learning, double major, dual enrollment of high school students, honors, independent study, internships. **Credit/placement by examination:** CLEP. 20 credit hours maximum toward associate degree. **Support services:** GED preparation and test center, learning center, remedial instruction, tutoring.

Majors. Agriculture: General, business, landscaping. **Biology:** General. **Business:** Administrative services, business admin, finance, hospitality admin, office technology. **Communications:** Journalism. **Computer sciences:** General, computer graphics, systems analysis. **Conservation:** Forestry. **Education:** Business, early childhood, elementary, physical. **Engineering technology:** Hazardous materials. **Family/consumer sciences:** General. **Health:** Clinical lab science, clinical lab technology, dental assistant, EMT paramedic, medical secretary, predentistry, premedicine, prenursing, prepharmacy, preveterinary. **Legal studies:** Court reporting, legal secretary, paralegal. **Liberal arts:** Arts/sciences. **Math:** General. **Parks/recreation:** Facilities management. **Personal/culinary services:** Culinary arts. **Physical sciences:** Chemistry. **Social sciences:** General. **Visual/performing arts:** General, art, commercial/advertising art, studio arts.

Computing on campus. 16 workstations in library, computer center.

Student life. Freshman orientation: Available. **Policies:** Freshmen permitted cars on campus. **Housing:** Single-sex dorms available. $35 deposit. **Activities:** Jazz band, choral groups, drama, music ensembles, student government, student newspaper, Pow-wow leadership, Phi Beta Lambda, Baptist Campus Ministries, Phi Theta Kappa, Psi Beta, association of computational machinery.

Athletics. NJCAA. **Intercollegiate:** Baseball M, basketball, cheerleading, golf, softball W, tennis, volleyball. **Intramural:** Basketball M, bowling, racquetball, softball, volleyball W. **Team name:** Sun Chiefs.

Student services. Career counseling, student employment services, health services, personal counseling, placement for graduates, veterans' counselor. **Physically disabled:** Services for visually impaired. **Transfer:** Special adviser, orientation for new students. Transfer adviser for students transferring to 4-year colleges.

Contact. E-mail: pduck@faulknerstate.edu
Phone: (251) 580-2111 Toll-free number: (800) 231-3752
Fax: (251) 580-2285
Betty Shefield, Director of Admissions, James H. Faulkner State Community College, 1900 Highway 31 South, Bay Minette, AL 36507

Jefferson Davis Community College

Brewton, Alabama
www.jdcc.edu **CB code: 1355**

- Public 2-year nursing and community college
- Commuter campus in small town

General. Founded in 1965. Regionally accredited. **Enrollment:** 860 full-time, degree-seeking students. **Degrees:** 180 associate awarded. **Location:** 60 miles from Pensacola, Florida. **Calendar:** Semester, limited summer session. **Full-time faculty:** 45 total. **Part-time faculty:** 55 total. **Special facilities:** Museum, golf course, telecommunications center.

Basis for selection. Open admission, but selective for some programs. Special requirements for nursing programs. **Homeschooled:** ACT score of 16 or higher required.

High school preparation. 24 units recommended. Recommended units include English 4, mathematics 4, social studies 4, science 4 and academic electives 8.

2005-2006 Annual costs. Tuition/fees: $2,708; $4,838 out-of-state. Per-credit charge: $72 in-state; $143 out-of-state. Room only: $2,800. Books/supplies: $800. Personal expenses: $400.

Financial aid. Non-need-based: Scholarships awarded for academics, athletics.

Application procedures. Admission: No deadline. No application fee. Application may be submitted online. Admission notification on a rolling basis. **Financial aid:** No deadline. FAFSA required. Applicants notified on a rolling basis.

Academics. Special study options: Cooperative education, distance learning, dual enrollment of high school students, ESL, honors, independent study, weekend college. License preparation in nursing. **Credit/placement by examination:** AP, CLEP. **Support services:** GED preparation and test center, learning center, remedial instruction, study skills assistance, tutoring.

Majors. Health: Nursing (RN). **Liberal arts:** Arts/sciences. **Protective services:** Law enforcement admin.

Student life. Policies: Freshmen permitted cars on campus. **Housing:** Coed dorms available. $150 deposit. **Activities:** Student government, Baptist student union, Phi Theta Kappa, Phi Beta Lambda, Psi Beta.

Athletics. NJCAA. **Intercollegiate:** Baseball M, basketball M, softball W. **Team name:** Warhawks.

Student services. Adult student services, career counseling, veterans' counselor. **Transfer:** Special adviser, pre-admission transcript evaluation for new students.

Contact. Phone: (251) 809-1594 Fax: (251) 809-1593
Robin Sessions, Coordinator of Admissions and Records, Jefferson Davis Community College, PO Box 958, Brewton, AL 36427

Jefferson State Community College

Birmingham, Alabama
www.jeffstateonline.com **CB code: 1352**

- Public 2-year community college
- Commuter campus in large city

General. Founded in 1963. Regionally accredited. **Enrollment:** 5,660 degree-seeking undergraduates; 1,347 non-degree-seeking students. **Degrees:** 574 associate awarded. **ROTC:** Army, Air Force. **Location:** 12 miles from downtown. **Calendar:** Semester, extensive summer session. **Full-time faculty:** 110 total; 21% have terminal degrees, 16% minority, 66% women. **Part-time faculty:** 272 total; 12% have terminal degrees, 18% minority, 53% women. **Class size:** 49% < 20, 44% 20-39, 4% 40-49. **Special facilities:** Museum of natural history, learning success center, nature trail.

Student profile. Among degree-seeking undergraduates, 56% enrolled in a transfer program, 44% enrolled in a vocational program, 1,170 enrolled as first-time, first-year students, 578 transferred in from other institutions.

Part-time:	54%	**Asian American:**	1%
Out-of-state:	1%	**Hispanic American:**	1%
Women:	62%	**International:**	2%
African American:	20%	**25 or older:**	36%

Basis for selection. Open admission, but selective for some programs. Special requirements for allied health programs. Applicants from non-accredited high schools admitted with high school diploma and minimum ACT score of 16 or equivalent SAT score. Students registering for five (plus) hours of credit must take ACT ASSET or ACT COMPASS prior to registration. Placement test exemptions are given for students who have completed college level math or English courses, or students who have equivalent ACT scores. **Homeschooled:** Must have minimum ACT score of 16 or pass Alabama Public High School Graduation Exam.

High school preparation. Recommended units include English 4, mathematics 4, social studies 2, science 3 and foreign language 2.

2005-2006 Annual costs. Tuition/fees: $3,060; $5,190 out-of-state. Per-credit charge: $71 in-state; $142 out-of-state. Books/supplies: $1,120. Personal expenses: $2,896.

Financial aid. Need-based: Need-based aid available for part-time students. Work study available nights and for part-time students. **Non-need-based:** Scholarships awarded for academics, art, athletics, leadership, music/drama. **Additional information:** Any Alabama resident over age 60 may attend classes tuition free.

Application procedures. Admission: No deadline. No application fee. Application may be submitted online. Admission notification on a rolling basis. **Financial aid:** Priority date 5/1; no closing date. FAFSA, institutional form required. Applicants notified on a rolling basis starting 6/1.

Academics. Special study options: Accelerated study, distance learning, honors, independent study, internships. Bachelor's degree programs available on campus. **Credit/placement by examination:** AP, CLEP, IB, institutional tests. 20 credit hours maximum toward associate degree. **Support services:** GED preparation and test center, learning center, reduced course load, remedial instruction, study skills assistance, tutoring.

Majors. Agriculture: Business. **Business:** General, accounting technology, administrative services, banking/financial services, hospitality admin. **Communications technology:** Radio/tv. **Computer sciences:** General. **Engineering technology:** General, biomedical, construction. **Family/consumer sciences:** Child care, home furnishings. **Health:** Clinical lab technology, medical radiologic technology/radiation therapy, nursing (RN), physical therapy assistant, veterinary technology/assistant. **Liberal arts:** Arts/sciences. **Personal/culinary services:** Mortuary science. **Protective services:** Fire services admin, police science.

Most popular majors. Business/marketing 19%, health sciences 25%, liberal arts 35%.

Computing on campus. Commuter students can connect to campus network. Online course registration, online library, helpline available.

Student life. Freshman orientation: Available. Preregistration for classes offered. **Policies:** Freshmen permitted cars on campus. **Activities:** Choral groups, drama, literary magazine, music ensembles, musical theater, radio station, student government, student newspaper, Baptist campus ministries, senior adult student club, African American Society, BACCHUS, students in free enterprise, Ambassadors.

Athletics. NJCAA. **Intercollegiate:** Baseball M, softball W. **Intramural:** Badminton, basketball, bowling, soccer, softball, tennis, volleyball. **Team name:** Pioneers.

Student services. Adult student services, career counseling, student employment services, placement for graduates, veterans' counselor, women's services. **Physically disabled:** Services for visually, hearing impaired. **Transfer:** Special adviser, orientation for new students. Transfer adviser, college fairs on campus for students transferring to 4-year colleges.

Contact. E-mail: hlawley@jeffstateonline.com
Phone: (205) 853-1200 ext. 7704 Toll-free number: (800) 239-5900
Fax: (205) 856-6070
Lillian Owens, Director, Admissions, Jefferson State Community College, 2601 Carson Road, Birmingham, AL 35215-3098

Lawson State Community College

Birmingham, Alabama **CB member**
www.lawsonstate.edu **CB code: 1933**

- Public 2-year community college
- Commuter campus in small city

General. Founded in 1949. Regionally accredited. **Enrollment:** 3,370 degree-seeking undergraduates. **Degrees:** 127 associate awarded. **Calendar:** Semester, limited summer session. **Full-time faculty:** 104 total. **Part-time faculty:** 127 total. **Class size:** 100% >100.

Student profile. Among degree-seeking undergraduates, 60% enrolled in a transfer program, 40% enrolled in a vocational program, 864 enrolled as first-time, first-year students, 422 transferred in from other institutions.

Part-time:	48%	**Women:**	65%
Out-of-state:	1%		

Transfer out. 40% of students enrolled in the transfer program go on to 4-year colleges. **Colleges most students transferred to 2005:** Miles College, University of Alabama at Birmingham, Alabama A&M University, Alabama State University, Jefferson State Community College.

Basis for selection. Open admission, but selective for some programs. Advanced placement option for licensed practical nurses (LPN) and nursing education. Nursing students must pass nursing entrance exam or have composite ACT of 20 or comparable SAT. **Adult students:** Entrance exam policies same as for first-time freshmen.

2005-2006 Annual costs. Tuition/fees: $2,700; $4,830 out-of-state. Per-credit charge: $72 in-state; $144 out-of-state. Books/supplies: $1,390. Personal expenses: $920.

2005-2006 Financial aid. All financial aid based on need. Average need met was 40%. Average scholarship/grant was $465. 98% of total undergraduate aid awarded as scholarships/grants, 2% as loans/jobs. Need-based aid available for part-time students. Work study available nights and for part-time students.

Application procedures. Admission: No deadline. No application fee. Admission notification on a rolling basis. **Financial aid:** Priority date 6/1; no closing date. FAFSA required. Applicants notified on a rolling basis starting 8/1; must reply within 2 week(s) of notification.

Academics. Special study options: Accelerated study, double major, dual enrollment of high school students, internships, liberal arts/career combination, student-designed major. License preparation in dental hygiene, nursing, real estate. **Credit/placement by examination:** AP, CLEP, institutional tests. **Support services:** GED preparation and test center, learning center, reduced course load, remedial instruction, tutoring.

Majors. Biology: General. **Business:** Accounting, administrative services, business admin, office management, office technology, operations. **Computer sciences:** Computer science. **Construction:** General. **Education:** General, early childhood, health, health occupations, multi-level teacher, physical, social studies. **Engineering:** General, electrical. **Engineering technology:** Architectural, automotive, construction, drafting, electrical, mechanical drafting. **English:** English lit. **Health:** Medical secretary, nursing (RN). **History:** General. **Legal studies:** Legal secretary, prelaw. **Liberal arts:** Arts/sciences. **Math:** General. **Mechanic/repair:** Auto body. **Parks/recreation:** Health/fitness. **Protective services:** Criminal justice. **Psychology:** General. **Public administration:** Social work. **Social sciences:** Economics, political science, sociology.

Most popular majors. Biological/life sciences 7%, business/marketing 17%, computer/information sciences 11%, education 12%, health sciences 19%, security/protective services 7%, social sciences 9%.

Computing on campus. 421 workstations in library, computer center, student center. Online course registration, online library available.

Student life. Freshman orientation: Mandatory. Preregistration for classes offered. **Policies:** Freshmen permitted cars on campus. **Activities:** Jazz band, choral groups, dance, drama, music ensembles, radio station, student government, student newspaper, TV station, Scholars Bowl Team, Sophist Club.

Athletics. NJCAA. **Intercollegiate:** Baseball M, basketball, track and field M, volleyball W. **Intramural:** Baseball M, basketball. **Team name:** Cougars.

Student services. Adult student services, career counseling, services for economically disadvantaged, student employment services, financial aid counseling, health services, on-campus daycare, personal counseling, placement for graduates, veterans' counselor. **Physically disabled:** Services for hearing impaired. **Transfer:** Special adviser, orientation for new students. College fairs on campus for students transferring to 4-year colleges.

Contact. E-mail: dallen@lawsonstate.edu
Phone: (205) 929-6309 Fax: (205) 923-7106
Darren Allen, Director of Admissions and Records, Lawson State Community College, 3060 Wilson Road SW, Birmingham, AL 35221-1717

Lurleen B. Wallace Community College

Andalusia, Alabama
www.lbw.edu **CB code: 1429**

- Public 2-year junior college
- Commuter campus in small town

General. Founded in 1969. Regionally accredited. MacArthur campus in Opp and Greenville campus in Greenville. **Enrollment:** 1,500 degree-seeking undergraduates. **Degrees:** 200 associate awarded. **Location:** 90 miles from Montgomery. **Calendar:** Semester, limited summer session. **Full-time faculty:** 48 total. **Part-time faculty:** 60 total. **Special facilities:** Nature trail.

Transfer out. Colleges most students transferred to 2005: Troy State University, Auburn University, Auburn University in Montgomery.

Basis for selection. Open admission. COMPASS required for placement unless student scores 20 or higher in math and English on ACT. **Adult students:** Entrance exam policies same as for first-time freshmen.

2005-2006 Annual costs. Tuition/fees: $2,700; $4,830 out-of-state. Per-credit charge: $71 in-state; $142 out-of-state. Books/supplies: $450. Personal expenses: $600.

Financial aid. Non-need-based: Scholarships awarded for academics, art, athletics, leadership, music/drama, state residency.

Application procedures. Admission: No deadline. No application fee. Admission notification on a rolling basis. **Financial aid:** Priority date 5/1; no closing date. Applicants notified on a rolling basis starting 7/1; must reply within 2 week(s) of notification.

Academics. Special study options: Accelerated study, cooperative education, dual enrollment of high school students, honors. License preparation in paramedic. **Credit/placement by examination:** CLEP, institutional tests. 30 credit hours maximum toward associate degree. **Support services:** GED preparation and test center, learning center, reduced course load, remedial instruction, tutoring.

Majors. Conservation: Forest resources. **Health:** EMT paramedic. **Liberal arts:** Arts/sciences.

Most popular majors. Liberal arts 87%.

Computing on campus. 50 workstations in computer center.

Student life. Freshman orientation: Available. **Activities:** Jazz band, choral groups, drama, music ensembles, musical theater, student government, student newspaper, Collegiate Civitan Club, Circle-K, Christian Student Union, adult re-entry club.

Athletics. NJCAA. **Intercollegiate:** Baseball M, basketball, cross-country, softball W. **Team name:** Saints.

Student services. Career counseling, student employment services, personal counseling, placement for graduates, veterans' counselor. **Transfer:** Special adviser for new students. Transfer adviser, college fairs on campus for students transferring to 4-year colleges.

Contact. Phone: (334) 222-6591 ext. 271 Fax: (334) 222-0136
Mackie Stephens, Director of Admissions, Lurleen B. Wallace Community College, Box 1418, Andalusia, AL 36420-1418

Marion Military Institute

Marion, Alabama
www.marionmilitary.edu **CB code: 1447**

- Private 2-year junior and military college
- Residential campus in small town
- SAT or ACT required

General. Founded in 1842. Regionally accredited. The oldest military junior college in the nation. **Enrollment:** 175 degree-seeking undergraduates. **Degrees:** 46 associate awarded. **ROTC:** Army, Air Force. **Location:** 70 miles from Birmingham, 52 miles from Tuscaloosa. **Calendar:** Semester. **Full-time faculty:** 12 total. **Part-time faculty:** 5 total. **Class size:** 75% < 20, 20% 20-39, 3% 40-49, 3% >100. **Special facilities:** Alabama Military Hall of Honor, golf course, bird sanctuary.

Student profile.

Out-of-state:	85%	**Live on campus:**	100%

Transfer out. Colleges most students transferred to 2005: University of Alabama, Auburn University, Florida State University.

Basis for selection. Academic record, recommendations, test scores, character and personal qualities important. Extracurricular activities and alumni relation also important. Interview recommended. **Homeschooled:** Applicants must have been enrolled in approved programs.

High school preparation. 25 units required. Required and recommended units include English 4, mathematics 4, social studies 1, history 3, science 4, foreign language 1-2 and academic electives 8.

2006-2007 Annual costs. Tuition/fees (projected): $775; $13,955 out-of-state. Additional $1600 for uniforms. Room/board: $3,180. Books/supplies: $900. Personal expenses: $3,400.

2004-2005 Financial aid. Need-based: 52% of total undergraduate aid awarded as scholarships/grants, 48% as loans/jobs. Need-based aid available for part-time students. **Non-need-based:** Scholarships awarded for academics, alumni affiliation, athletics, leadership, music/drama, ROTC.

Application procedures. Admission: Closing date 8/15 (receipt date). $100 fee, may be waived for applicants with need. Admission notification on a rolling basis. **Financial aid:** No deadline. FAFSA required. Applicants notified on a rolling basis starting 6/15; must reply within 6 week(s) of notification.

Academics. Special preparation for national service academies offered. **Special study options:** Cross-registration, dual enrollment of high school students, ESL. **Credit/placement by examination:** CLEP, institutional tests. **Support services:** Reduced course load, remedial instruction, tutoring.

Majors. Liberal arts: Arts/sciences.

Computing on campus. 420 workstations in dormitories, library, computer center. Dormitories wired for high-speed internet access and linked to campus network. Online library available.

Student life. Freshman orientation: Mandatory. Preregistration for classes offered. **Policies:** Structured military school environment. **Housing:** Guaranteed on-campus for all undergraduates. Single-sex dorms available. $100 deposit. Students must live on campus. **Activities:** Bands, choral groups, drama, music ensembles, musical theater, student government, Jefferson Society, student campus service organizations, Dolphins environmental society, Normandy Society, history society. Students have option to participate in precision drill team, orienteering team, and United States Army Ranger-type training.

Athletics. NJCAA. **Intercollegiate:** Basketball M. **Intramural:** Basketball, cross-country, diving, golf, handball, rifle, soccer M, softball, swimming, tennis, track and field, volleyball, water polo M, weight lifting. **Team name:** Tigers.

Student services. Adult student services, campus ministries, career counseling, student employment services, financial aid counseling, health services, personal counseling, veterans' counselor. **Transfer:** Special adviser, orientation for new students. Transfer adviser for students transferring to 4-year colleges.

Contact. E-mail: admissions@marionmilitary.edu
Phone: (334) 683-2305 Toll-free number: (800) 664-1842
Fax: (334) 683-2383
Robert Sumlin, Vice President for Enrollment, Marion Military Institute, 1101 Washington Street, Marion, AL 36756-0420

Northeast Alabama Community College

Rainsville, Alabama
www.nacc.edu **CB code: 1576**

- Public 2-year community college
- Commuter campus in rural community

General. Founded in 1963. Regionally accredited. **Enrollment:** 1,710 degree-seeking undergraduates. **Degrees:** 220 associate awarded. **Location:** 55 miles from Huntsville, 110 miles from Birmingham. **Calendar:** Semester, extensive summer session. **Full-time faculty:** 34 total. **Class size:** 63% < 20, 30% 20-39, 6% 40-49, less than 1% 50-99. **Special facilities:** Community theater, lakeside walking trail.

Student profile. Among degree-seeking undergraduates, 90% enrolled in a transfer program, 10% enrolled in a vocational program.

Out-of-state:	1%	**25 or older:**	37%

Transfer out. Colleges most students transferred to 2005: Jacksonville State University, University of Alabama: Huntsville, Athens State University.

Basis for selection. Open admission, but selective for some programs. **Adult students:** Entrance exam policies same as for first-time freshmen. **Homeschooled:** Must provide official transcript and have ACT score of 16. **Learning Disabled:** Students who may require accommodations are encouraged to communicate with Disability Services.

High school preparation. College-preparatory program recommended. 24 units recommended. Recommended units include English 4, mathematics 4, social studies 2, history 2, science 4 (laboratory 2), foreign language 2 and academic electives 4.

2005-2006 Annual costs. Tuition/fees: $2,700; $4,830 out-of-state. Per-credit charge: $71 in-state; $142 out-of-state. In-state costs apply to on-campus or distance-learning courses. Out-of-state distance-learning students pay $5,400 for academic year (or $180 per-credit-hour). Personal expenses: $1,500.

2004-2005 Financial aid. Need-based: 78% of total undergraduate aid awarded as scholarships/grants, 22% as loans/jobs. Need-based aid available for part-time students. Work study available for part-time students. **Non-need-based:** Scholarships awarded for academics, art, leadership, minority status, music/drama.

Application procedures. Admission: No deadline. No application fee. Application may be submitted online. Admission notification on a rolling basis. **Financial aid:** No deadline. FAFSA required. Applicants notified on a rolling basis.

Academics. Special study options: Accelerated study, double major, dual enrollment of high school students, honors, independent study, study abroad. 2-year degree programs in allied health available requiring 1 year study at Wallace State Community College at Hanceville. Bachelor's degree programs available on campus. License preparation in nursing, paramedic. **Credit/placement by examination:** AP, CLEP, institutional tests. **Support services:** GED preparation and test center, learning center, remedial instruction, study skills assistance, tutoring, writing center.

Majors. Agriculture: Animal sciences, business. **Biology:** General. **Business:** General, accounting, administrative services, banking/financial services, business admin, office management. **Computer sciences:** General, computer science. **Conservation:** Forestry. **Education:** Elementary, family/consumer sciences, secondary, voc/tech. **Engineering:** General, chemical. **Engineering technology:** CAD/CADD, electrical. **English:** English lit. **Family/consumer sciences:** General. **Health:** EMT paramedic, nursing (RN), predentistry, premedicine, prenursing, prepharmacy, preveterinary. **History:** General. **Legal studies:** Paralegal. **Liberal arts:** Arts/sciences. **Math:** General. **Parks/recreation:** Health/fitness. **Physical sciences:** Chemistry, physics. **Psychology:** General. **Visual/performing arts:** Art, dramatic.

Computing on campus. 212 workstations in library, computer center. Commuter students can connect to campus network. Online course registration, online library, helpline, wireless network available.

Student life. Freshman orientation: Mandatory. Preregistration for classes offered. Groups of 100 meet for an afternoon. **Policies:** Freshmen permitted cars on campus. **Activities:** Bands, choral groups, drama, literary magazine, music ensembles, musical theater, student government, Baptist campus ministries.

Athletics. Intramural: Basketball. **Team name:** Mustangs.

Student services. Career counseling, student employment services, financial aid counseling, personal counseling, placement for graduates, veterans' counselor. **Physically disabled:** Services for visually, speech, hearing impaired. **Transfer:** Special adviser, orientation, pre-admission transcript evaluation for new students. Transfer adviser, college fairs on campus for students transferring to 4-year colleges.

Contact. E-mail: yatesw@nacc.edu
Phone: (256) 228-6001 ext. 222 Fax: (256) 638-6043
Joe Burke, Director of Admissions and Student Services, Northeast Alabama Community College, Admissions Office, NACC, Rainsville, AL 35986-0159

Northwest-Shoals Community College

Muscle Shoals, Alabama
www.nwscc.edu **CB code: 0188**

- Public 2-year community and technical college
- Commuter campus in large town

General. Founded in 1966. Regionally accredited. Two campuses: Phil Campbell and Muscle Shoals. **Enrollment:** 3,380 degree-seeking undergraduates. **Degrees:** 412 associate awarded. **ROTC:** Army. **Location:** 120 miles from Birmingham, 134 miles from Memphis, Tennessee. **Calendar:** Semester, extensive summer session. **Full-time faculty:** 75 total. **Part-time faculty:** 171 total. **Partnerships:** Formal agreement with high schools for Tech prep articulation programs.

Two-Year Colleges

Student profile. Among degree-seeking undergraduates, 580 enrolled as first-time, first-year students, 2 transferred in from other institutions.

Part-time:	37%	**Hispanic American:**	1%
Out-of-state:	1%	**Native American:**	2%
Women:	61%	**25 or older:**	34%
African American:	12%	**Live on campus:**	2%

Transfer out. Colleges most students transferred to 2005: University of North Alabama, University of Alabama, Athens State University, University of Alabama at Huntsville.

Basis for selection. Open admission, but selective for some programs. Additional requirements for health occupation programs. **Homeschooled:** Equivalent number of required units for graduation and ACT score of 16 or SAT score of 790 (exclusive of Writing) required.

High school preparation. 22 units recommended. Recommended units include English 4, mathematics 2, social studies 3 and science 4.

2005-2006 Annual costs. Tuition/fees: $2,700; $4,830 out-of-state. Per-credit charge: $71 in-state; $142 out-of-state. Room only: $1,600. Books/supplies: $1,000.

2005-2006 Financial aid. Need-based: 53% of total undergraduate aid awarded as scholarships/grants, 47% as loans/jobs. Need-based aid available for part-time students. Work study available nights, weekends and for part-time students. **Non-need-based:** Scholarships awarded for academics, art, athletics, leadership, minority status, music/drama.

Application procedures. Admission: No deadline. No application fee. Admission notification on a rolling basis. **Financial aid:** Priority date 4/1; no closing date. FAFSA, institutional form required. Applicants notified on a rolling basis; must reply within 2 week(s) of notification.

Academics. Special study options: Accelerated study, cooperative education, cross-registration, distance learning, dual enrollment of high school students, independent study, internships, liberal arts/career combination, weekend college. License preparation in nursing, paramedic. **Credit/placement by examination:** AP, CLEP, institutional tests. 30 credit hours maximum toward associate degree. **Support services:** GED preparation and test center, learning center, pre-admission summer program, remedial instruction, tutoring.

Majors. Business: Accounting technology, administrative services. **Computer sciences:** General, applications programming, data processing, information systems, information technology, programming. **Conservation:** Environmental studies. **Engineering technology:** CAD/CADD, drafting, electrical, environmental. **Family/consumer sciences:** Child care. **Health:** EMT paramedic, nursing (RN). **Liberal arts:** Arts/sciences. **Mechanic/repair:** Industrial. **Protective services:** Police science.

Most popular majors. Business/marketing 14%, health sciences 21%, liberal arts 43%.

Computing on campus. 650 workstations in library, computer center, student center. Online course registration, online library, helpline, repair service, wireless network available.

Student life. Freshman orientation: Available, $10 fee. Program includes components for developing research skills and good study habits. Occupational students also receive orientation to work ethics and workplace readiness. **Policies:** Freshmen permitted cars on campus. **Housing:** Coed dorms, substance-free housing available. $75 fully refundable deposit. **Activities:** Bands, choral groups, music ensembles, student government, Phi Theta Kappa, Ambassadors, Baptist Campus Ministry, Fellowship of Christian Athletes, Music Educators National Conference, VICA, Student Government Association, College Bowl Team, Science Club, American Society of Heating, Refrigerating and Air Conditioning Engineers.

Athletics. NJCAA. **Intercollegiate:** Baseball M, basketball, cheerleading, cross-country M, golf M, softball W, tennis W, volleyball W. **Intramural:** Basketball, softball, table tennis, tennis. **Team name:** Patriots.

Student services. Career counseling, student employment services, on-campus daycare, personal counseling, placement for graduates, veterans' counselor. **Physically disabled:** Services for hearing impaired. **Transfer:** Special adviser, orientation, pre-admission transcript evaluation for new students. Transfer adviser, college fairs on campus for students transferring to 4-year colleges.

Contact. Phone: (256) 331-5363 Fax: (256) 331-5366
Karen Berryhill, Vice President for Student Development Services, Northwest-Shoals Community College, PO Box 2545, Muscle Shoals, AL 35662

Prince Institute of Professional Studies

Montgomery, Alabama
www.princeinstitute.edu **CB code: 3450**

- For-profit 2-year technical college
- Commuter campus in large city

General. Accredited by ACICS. **Enrollment:** 38 degree-seeking undergraduates. **Degrees:** 9 associate awarded. **Calendar:** Quarter, extensive summer session. **Full-time faculty:** 10 total. **Part-time faculty:** 5 total.

Student profile. Among degree-seeking undergraduates, 100% enrolled in a vocational program, 5 enrolled as first-time, first-year students.

Part-time:	39%	**Women:**	95%

Basis for selection. Open admission. High school diploma or GED required.

2005-2006 Annual costs. Tuition/fees: $6,131. Additional required fees vary per program. Books/supplies: $272. Personal expenses: $1,674.

Financial aid. All financial aid based on need. Need-based aid available for part-time students.

Application procedures. Admission: No deadline. No application fee. Applications must be received before class start. **Financial aid:** No deadline. FAFSA required.

Academics. Special study options: Distance learning. **Credit/placement by examination:** CLEP.

Majors. Computer sciences: Information systems. **Health:** Medical transcription. **Legal studies:** Court reporting.

Student life. Freshman orientation: Available. Preregistration for classes offered.

Contact. E-mail: admissions@princeinstitute.edu
Phone: (334) 271-1670 Toll-free number: (877) 853-5569
Fax: (334) 271-1671
Sherry Hill, Admissions Director, Prince Institute of Professional Studies, 7735 Atlanta Highway, Montgomery, AL 36117-4231

Remington College: Mobile

Mobile, Alabama
www.educationamerica.com **CB code: 3157**

- Private 2-year technical college
- Commuter campus in large city

General. Accredited by ACCSCT. **Enrollment:** 300 undergraduates. **Degrees:** 30 bachelor's, 89 associate awarded. **Calendar:** Quarter, extensive summer session. **Full-time faculty:** 30 total. **Part-time faculty:** 15 total.

Basis for selection. Open admission. **Adult students:** Entrance exam policies same as for first-time freshmen. **Homeschooled:** Must take CDAT Test.

2005-2006 Annual costs. Bachelor programs $28,890. Associate programs $31,490. Diploma programs (allied health) $11,730. Cost includes tuition, fees and books.

Financial aid. All financial aid based on need. Work study available nights.

Application procedures. Admission: No deadline. $50 fee. **Financial aid:** FAFSA required.

Academics. Special study options: Cooperative education, honors, liberal arts/career combination. Bachelor's degree programs available on campus. **Credit/placement by examination:** CLEP. **Support services:** Tutoring.

Majors. Business: Business admin. **Computer sciences:** General. **Engineering:** Electrical. **Engineering technology:** Drafting.

Computing on campus. PC or laptop required. Helpline, repair service available.

Student life. Freshman orientation: Available. Preregistration for classes offered. Held the week before class for 2 1/2 hours. **Policies:** Freshmen permitted cars on campus.

Student services. Career counseling, financial aid counseling, placement for graduates. **Transfer:** Special adviser, orientation, pre-admission transcript evaluation for new students.

Contact. Phone: (251) 343-8200 Toll-free number: (800) 866-0850
Fax: (251) 343-8200
Stephanie Darst, Director of Admissions, Remington College: Mobile, 828 Downtowner Loop West, Mobile, AL 36609-5404

Shelton State Community College

Tuscaloosa, Alabama
www.sheltonstate.edu **CB code: 3338**

- Public 2-year community and technical college
- Commuter campus in small city

General. Founded in 1963. Regionally accredited. Designated as Alabama's Community College of the Fine Arts; includes C.A. Fredd campus, an Historically Black College. **Enrollment:** 4,622 degree-seeking undergraduates; 579 non-degree-seeking students. **Degrees:** 241 associate awarded. **ROTC:** Army, Air Force. **Location:** 60 miles from Birmingham. **Calendar:** Semester, extensive summer session. **Full-time faculty:** 82 total; 11% have terminal degrees, 17% minority, 54% women. **Part-time faculty:** 162 total; 4% have terminal degrees, 25% minority, 58% women. **Class size:** 42% < 20, 48% 20-39, 10% 40-49, less than 1% 50-99. **Special facilities:** Observatories, wellness center.

Student profile. Among degree-seeking undergraduates, 54% enrolled in a transfer program, 46% enrolled in a vocational program, 1% already have a bachelor's degree or higher, 1,523 enrolled as first-time, first-year students, 27 transferred in from other institutions.

Part-time:	35%	**Asian American:**	1%
Out-of-state:	5%	**Hispanic American:**	1%
Women:	59%	**25 or older:**	32%
African American:	33%		

Transfer out. Colleges most students transferred to 2005: University of Alabama, Auburn University, Stillman College, University of Alabama at Birmingham.

Basis for selection. Open admission. COMPASS test required of all first-time freshmen for placement unless students have taken ACT. **Adult students:** Entrance exam policies same as for first-time freshmen.

2005-2006 Annual costs. Tuition/fees: $2,730; $4,890 out-of-state. Per-credit charge: $72 in-state; $144 out-of-state. Books/supplies: $750. Personal expenses: $200.

Financial aid. All financial aid based on need. Need-based aid available for part-time students. Work study available nights.

Application procedures. Admission: No deadline. No application fee. Application may be submitted online. Admission notification on a rolling basis. **Financial aid:** Priority date 6/30; no closing date. FAFSA required. Applicants notified on a rolling basis starting 7/30.

Academics. Special study options: Accelerated study, distance learning, double major, dual enrollment of high school students, honors, liberal arts/career combination. License preparation in nursing, real estate. **Credit/placement by examination:** AP, CLEP, IB, institutional tests. 20 credit hours maximum toward associate degree. **Support services:** GED preparation and test center, learning center, reduced course load, remedial instruction, study skills assistance, tutoring.

Majors. Business: Administrative services. **Construction:** Electrician. **Education:** General, music, secondary. **Engineering:** General. **Engineering technology:** Drafting, heat/ac/refrig. **Health:** Nursing (RN), respiratory therapy technology. **Liberal arts:** Arts/sciences. **Math:** General. **Mechanic/repair:** Industrial electronics. **Production:** General, tool and die. **Public administration:** Social work.

Most popular majors. Business/marketing 20%, health sciences 25%, liberal arts 38%, trade and industry 12%.

Computing on campus. 200 workstations in library, computer center. Commuter students can connect to campus network. Online course registration, wireless network available.

Student life. Freshman orientation: Mandatory. Preregistration for classes offered. **Policies:** Freshmen permitted cars on campus. **Activities:** Jazz band, choral groups, dance, drama, music ensembles, musical theater, student government, student newspaper, Phi Theta Kappa, Circle K.

Athletics. NJCAA. **Intercollegiate:** Baseball M, basketball, cheerleading, soccer W, softball W. **Team name:** Buccaneers.

Student services. Career counseling, student employment services, financial aid counseling, personal counseling, placement for graduates, veterans' counselor. **Transfer:** Special adviser, orientation for new students. College fairs on campus for students transferring to 4-year colleges.

Contact. Phone: (205) 391-2214 Fax: (205) 391-3910
Tommy Taylor, Dean of Student Services, Shelton State Community College, 9500 Old Greensboro Road, Tuscaloosa, AL 35405-8522

Snead State Community College

Boaz, Alabama
www.snead.edu **CB code: 1721**

- Public 2-year community college
- Commuter campus in small town
- Interview required

General. Founded in 1898. Regionally accredited. Upper-level courses offered on campus through Athens College and distance learning. **Enrollment:** 1,695 degree-seeking undergraduates. **Degrees:** 160 associate awarded. **Location:** 65 miles from Birmingham, 60 miles from Huntsville. **Calendar:** Semester, limited summer session. **Special facilities:** Museum, state diagnostic lab. **Partnerships:** Marshall County Tech Prep Consortium (grant writer and fiscal agent for eight secondary schools).

Student profile.

Out-of-state:	2%	**Live on campus:**	2%

Transfer out. Colleges most students transferred to 2005: Jacksonville State University, Auburn University, University of Alabama, University of Alabama at Birmingham, University of Alabama in Huntsville.

Basis for selection. Open admission, but selective for some programs. Veterinary technician applicants must pass personal interview for admission. **Adult students:** Entrance exam policies same as for first-time freshmen. **Homeschooled:** Minimum ACT score of 16 or equivalent score on SAT required for high school graduates from non-accredited schools and for those receiving occupational diplomas.

High school preparation. 24 units recommended. Recommended units include English 4, mathematics 4, social studies 4, science 4, foreign language 2 and academic electives 8. Half unit fine arts, 1/2 computer applications, 5 1/2 electives recommended.

2005-2006 Annual costs. Tuition/fees: $2,820; $4,950 out-of-state. Per-credit charge: $71 in-state; $142 out-of-state. Room/board: $2,474. Books/supplies: $1,050. Personal expenses: $1,200.

Financial aid. Need-based: Need-based aid available for part-time students. Work study available nights and for part-time students. **Non-need-based:** Scholarships awarded for academics, alumni affiliation, art, athletics, leadership, music/drama.

Application procedures. Admission: Closing date 8/14 (postmark date). No application fee. Application must be submitted on paper. Admission notification on a rolling basis. **Financial aid:** Priority date 4/15; no closing date. FAFSA required. Applicants notified on a rolling basis starting 4/15.

Academics. Special study options: Accelerated study, distance learning, dual enrollment of high school students, independent study, internships, student-designed major. **Credit/placement by examination:** AP, CLEP, institutional tests. 20 credit hours maximum toward associate degree. **Support services:** GED preparation and test center, learning center, remedial instruction, study skills assistance, tutoring, writing center.

Majors. Business: Administrative services, business admin. **Computer sciences:** General. **Engineering:** General. **Engineering technology:** General. **Family/consumer sciences:** Child care. **Liberal arts:** Arts/sciences.

Most popular majors. Computer/information sciences 6%, engineering/engineering technologies 6%, family/consumer sciences 7%, health sciences 8%, interdisciplinary studies 8%, liberal arts 59%.

Computing on campus. 350 workstations in library, computer center, student center. Online course registration, online library available.

Student life. Freshman orientation: Available, $94 fee. Preregistration for classes offered. Orientation offered as one credit-hour course on 2 consecutive Fridays or Saturdays. **Policies:** Freshmen permitted cars on campus. **Housing:** Coed dorms available. $25 deposit. **Activities:** Jazz band, choral groups, music ensembles, student government, student newspaper,

Baptist Campus Ministry, Ambassadors, Snead Agricultural Organization, Phi Beta Lambda, Phi Theta Kappa, student government association, College Republicans, Civitans.

Athletics. NJCAA. **Intercollegiate:** Baseball M, basketball, softball W, tennis W. **Intramural:** Basketball, softball, table tennis, volleyball. **Team name:** Parsons.

Student services. Campus ministries, career counseling, services for economically disadvantaged, student employment services, financial aid counseling, personal counseling, placement for graduates, veterans' counselor. **Physically disabled:** Services for visually, speech, hearing impaired. **Transfer:** Special adviser, orientation, pre-admission transcript evaluation for new students. Transfer center, transfer adviser, college fairs on campus for students transferring to 4-year colleges.

Contact. E-mail: mbuchanan@snead.edu
Phone: (256) 593-5120 ext. 207 Fax: (256) 593-7180
Martha Buchanan, Admissions and Records Director, Snead State Community College, PO Box 734, Boaz, AL 35957-0734

Southern Union State Community College

Wadley, Alabama
suscc.edu **CB code: 1728**

- Public 2-year community and technical college
- Commuter campus in small city

General. Founded in 1963. Regionally accredited. 3 campuses located in Wadley, Opelika Valley. **Enrollment:** 4,560 undergraduates. **Degrees:** 438 associate awarded. **Location:** 90 miles from Atlanta, 90 miles from Birmingham. **Calendar:** Semester, extensive summer session. **Full-time faculty:** 81 total; 6% have terminal degrees, 9% minority, 60% women. **Part-time faculty:** 144 total.

Student profile. 75% enrolled in a transfer program, 25% enrolled in a vocational program.

Out-of-state:	20%	**Live on campus:**	4%
25 or older:	25%		

Basis for selection. Open admission, but selective for some programs. Criteria for some health sciences programs include test scores.

2005-2006 Annual costs. Tuition/fees: $2,700; $4,830 out-of-state. Per-credit charge: $71 in-state; $142 out-of-state. Room/board: $2,400. Books/supplies: $400. Personal expenses: $1,100.

Financial aid. Need-based: Need-based aid available for part-time students.

Application procedures. Admission: No deadline. No application fee. Admission notification on a rolling basis. **Financial aid:** No deadline. FAFSA required. Applicants notified on a rolling basis.

Academics. Special study options: Accelerated study, distance learning, dual enrollment of high school students. License preparation in nursing, paramedic, radiology. **Credit/placement by examination:** CLEP. **Support services:** GED preparation and test center, remedial instruction, tutoring.

Majors. Biology: General. **Business:** Accounting, office management. **Communications:** General. **Computer sciences:** General. **Construction:** Carpentry. **Education:** Physical. **Engineering technology:** Drafting. **Health:** EMT paramedic, insurance coding, nursing (RN), radiologic technology/medical imaging. **Mechanic/repair:** Heating/ac/refrig. **Physical sciences:** Chemistry, theoretical physics. **Social sciences:** General.

Student life. Freshman orientation: Available. Preregistration for classes offered. Held during June and July. **Policies:** Freshmen permitted cars on campus. **Housing:** Single-sex dorms, substance-free housing available. **Activities:** Choral groups, dance, drama, musical theater, student government, student newspaper, Student Government Association, Association of Radiologic Students, Baptist Campus Ministries, Global Environmental Organization of Students, Music Club, Letterman's Club, National Student Nurses' Association, Phi Beta Lambda, Phi Theta Kappa, Southern Union Players.

Athletics. NJCAA. **Intercollegiate:** Baseball M, basketball, cheerleading, cross-country, softball W, volleyball W. **Team name:** Bison's.

Student services. Adult student services, career counseling, financial aid counseling. **Transfer:** Special adviser, orientation for new students.

Contact. Phone: (256) 395-2211 Fax: (256) 395-2215
Cathryn Stringfellow, Registrar, Southern Union State Community College, 750 Roberts Street, Wadley, AL 36276

Trenholm State Technical College

Montgomery, Alabama
www.trenholmtech.cc.al.us **CB code: 0207**

- Public 2-year technical college
- Commuter campus in large city

General. Founded in 1966. Regionally accredited. Two campuses: Patterson and Trenholm. **Enrollment:** 1,379 degree-seeking undergraduates; 36 non-degree-seeking students. **Degrees:** 49 associate awarded. **Location:** 100 miles from Birmingham, 170 miles from Atlanta, Georgia. **Calendar:** Semester, limited summer session. **Full-time faculty:** 72 total; 14% have terminal degrees, 54% minority, 54% women. **Part-time faculty:** 62 total; 19% have terminal degrees, 56% minority, 58% women. **Class size:** 79% < 20, 19% 20-39, less than 1% 40-49, 1% 50-99. **Special facilities:** Archives.

Student profile. Among degree-seeking undergraduates, 100% enrolled in a vocational program, 378 enrolled as first-time, first-year students.

Part-time:	48%	**25 or older:**	48%
Women:	52%		

Transfer out. Colleges most students transferred to 2005: Alabama State University, Alabama A&M University, Troy State University.

Basis for selection. Open admission, but selective for some programs. Additional requirements for Licensed Practical Nursing. COMPASS required of all students for placement and counseling; ACT or SAT accepted instead. COMPASS required for admission for applicants to Health Services Technology Division; ACT of 16 or better may be submitted in lieu of failed COMPASS. Minimum score of 16 in mathematics and 20 in reading required. Interview recommended for dental assistant applicants, and required for practical nursing applicants. **Adult students:** Entrance exam policies same as for first-time freshmen.

High school preparation. Required units include English 4, mathematics 4, history 4 and science 4.

2005-2006 Annual costs. Tuition/fees: $2,700; $4,860 out-of-state. Per-credit charge: $71 in-state; $142 out-of-state. Books/supplies: $1,500. Personal expenses: $2,050.

2004-2005 Financial aid. Need-based: 432 full-time freshmen applied for aid; 194 were judged to have need; 194 of these received aid. Average need met was .81%. Average scholarship/grant was $1,816. 95% of total undergraduate aid awarded as scholarships/grants, 5% as loans/jobs. Need-based aid available for part-time students. Work study available for part-time students. **Non-need-based:** Awarded to 96 full-time undergraduates, including 26 freshmen. Scholarships awarded for academics, leadership, state residency.

Application procedures. Admission: No deadline. No application fee. Admission notification on a rolling basis beginning on or about 7/31. **Financial aid:** No deadline. FAFSA required. Applicants notified on a rolling basis.

Academics. Special study options: Cooperative education, distance learning, dual enrollment of high school students, independent study, internships. **Credit/placement by examination:** AP, CLEP, institutional tests. 15 credit hours maximum toward associate degree. **Support services:** GED preparation and test center, learning center, reduced course load, remedial instruction, study skills assistance, tutoring.

Majors. Agriculture: Ornamental horticulture. **Business:** Accounting technology, administrative services. **Communications technology:** Graphics. **Computer sciences:** General. **Construction:** Building inspection, electrician. **Engineering technology:** Automotive, drafting, heat/ac/refrig. **Family/consumer sciences:** Child care. **Health:** Dental assistant, dental lab technology, EMT paramedic, licensed practical nurse, medical assistant. **Mechanic/repair:** Industrial, industrial electronics. **Personal/culinary services:** Chef training. **Production:** Tool and die.

Most popular majors. Business/marketing 10%, health sciences 9%, trade and industry 13%.

Computing on campus. 650 workstations in library, computer center. Online course registration, online library, wireless network available.

Student life. Freshman orientation: Mandatory. Preregistration for classes offered. **Policies:** Freshmen permitted cars on campus. **Activities:** Choral groups, student government, Vocational and Industrial Clubs of America, Phi Beta Lambda, Ambassadors club.

Student services. Adult student services, career counseling, services for economically disadvantaged, student employment services, financial aid counseling, on-campus daycare, personal counseling, placement for graduates, veterans' counselor. **Physically disabled:** Services for visually, speech, hearing impaired. **Transfer:** Special adviser, orientation, re-entry adviser, pre-admission transcript evaluation for new students. Transfer adviser, college fairs on campus for students transferring to 4-year colleges.

Contact. Phone: (334) 420-4300 Fax: (334) 420-4344
Tennie McBryde, Coordinator of Admissions, Trenholm State Technical College, 1225 Air Base Boulevard, Montgomery, AL 36108

Virginia College at Mobile
Mobile, Alabama
www.vc.edu/mobile

- For-profit 2-year technical college
- Commuter campus

General. Accredited by ACICS.

Contact. Phone: (251) 343-7227
Director of Admissions, 2970 Cottage Hill Road, Mobile, AL 36606

Virginia College Technical
Pelham, Alabama
www.vctechnical.com

- For-profit 2-year technical college
- Commuter campus

General. Accredited by ACICS. **Enrollment:** 204 undergraduates. **Degrees:** 29 associate awarded. **Calendar:** Quarter. **Full-time faculty:** 18 total.

Basis for selection. Open admission.

Application procedures. **Admission:** No deadline. $100 fee.

Academics. **Credit/placement by examination:** CLEP.

Majors. **Mechanic/repair:** Auto body, automotive. **Production:** Welding.

Contact. E-mail: vctech@vc.edu
Phone: (205) 943-2100 Toll-free number: (877) 582-8324
Lynn Berg-Daigle, Director, Virginia College Technical, 2790 Pelham Parkway, Pelham, AL 35124-1734

Wallace State Community College at Hanceville
Hanceville, Alabama
www.wallacestate.edu **CB code: 0528**

- Public 2-year health science and community college
- Commuter campus in rural community

General. Founded in 1966. Regionally accredited. **Enrollment:** 4,871 degree-seeking undergraduates. **Degrees:** 742 associate awarded. **Location:** 35 miles from Birmingham, 50 miles from Huntsville. **Calendar:** Semester, limited summer session. **Full-time faculty:** 122 total. **Part-time faculty:** 130 total. **Special facilities:** Extensive genealogy collection, recording studio, nature trail.

Transfer out. **Colleges most students transferred to 2005:** Athens State College, University of Alabama, University of Alabama in Huntsville, University of Alabama at Birmingham, Auburn University.

Basis for selection. Open admission, but selective for some programs. Additional requirements for nursing and allied health programs. ACT required of applicants to certain allied health programs. National League for Nursing, Pre-Nursing and Guidance Examination required for nursing applicants. Interview recommended for health program applicants; auditions recommended for music education majors. **Adult students:** Entrance exam policies same as for first-time freshmen.

2005-2006 Annual costs. Tuition/fees: $2,700; $4,830 out-of-state. Per-credit charge: $71 in-state; $142 out-of-state. Room only: $1,450. Books/supplies: $700. Personal expenses: $2,650.

2004-2005 Financial aid. All financial aid based on need. Need-based aid available for part-time students. Work study available nights.

Application procedures. **Admission:** No deadline. No application fee. Application may be submitted online. Admission notification on a rolling basis beginning on or about 7/15. **Financial aid:** Priority date 5/1; no closing date. FAFSA required. Applicants notified on a rolling basis starting 7/15; must reply within 2 week(s) of notification.

Academics. **Special study options:** Accelerated study, cooperative education, distance learning, double major, dual enrollment of high school students, internships, weekend college. License preparation in aviation, dental hygiene, nursing, occupational therapy, paramedic, physical therapy, radiology, real estate. **Credit/placement by examination:** AP, CLEP, institutional tests. 26 credit hours maximum toward associate degree. **Support services:** GED preparation and test center, learning center, reduced course load, remedial instruction, study skills assistance, tutoring.

Majors. **Agriculture:** Agribusiness operations. **Business:** General, accounting, banking/financial services, fashion, insurance, labor relations, office management, office/clerical, sales/distribution. **Computer sciences:** Data processing, programming. **Education:** General. **Engineering:** General, electrical. **Engineering technology:** Drafting. **Family/consumer sciences:** Child care, food/nutrition, institutional food production. **Health:** Athletic training, clinical lab technology, dental assistant, dental hygiene, EMT paramedic, health services, medical assistant, medical radiologic technology/radiation therapy, medical records technology, nursing (RN), occupational therapy assistant, physical therapy assistant, respiratory therapy technology, sonography, substance abuse counseling. **Legal studies:** Legal secretary, paralegal, prelaw. **Liberal arts:** Arts/sciences. **Mechanic/repair:** Auto body, automotive, diesel, electronics/electrical, heating/ac/refrig. **Parks/recreation:** Facilities management. **Production:** Woodworking. **Protective services:** Police science. **Visual/performing arts:** Art, fashion design, interior design.

Most popular majors. Business/marketing 6%, health sciences 61%, liberal arts 17%.

Computing on campus. 65 workstations in library, computer center. Commuter students can connect to campus network. Online course registration, online library, helpline, wireless network available.

Student life. **Freshman orientation:** Available. Preregistration for classes offered. **Policies:** Freshmen permitted cars on campus. **Housing:** Single-sex dorms, substance-free housing available. $200 fully refundable deposit. **Activities:** Bands, choral groups, drama, music ensembles, student government, student newspaper, Baptist Campus Ministry.

Athletics. NJCAA. **Intercollegiate:** Baseball M, basketball, cross-country, golf M, soccer M, softball W, track and field M, volleyball. **Intramural:** Badminton, basketball, softball, tennis, track and field, volleyball. **Team name:** Lions.

Student services. Campus ministries, career counseling, student employment services, financial aid counseling, placement for graduates, veterans' counselor. **Physically disabled:** Services for visually, speech, hearing impaired. **Transfer:** Special adviser, orientation for new students. Transfer adviser, college fairs on campus for students transferring to 4-year colleges.

Contact. Phone: (256) 352-8236 Toll-free number: (866) 350-9722
Fax: (256) 352-8129
Linda Sperling, Director of Admissions/Registrar, Wallace State Community College at Hanceville, P. O. Box 2000, Hanceville, AL 35077-2000

Alaska

Ilisagvik College
Barrow, Alaska
www.ilisagvik.cc **CB code: 0469**

- Public 2-year community college
- Rural community

General. Many Inupiat Eskimo traditional courses offered. **Enrollment:** 425 degree-seeking undergraduates. **Degrees:** 6 associate awarded. **Location:** 500 miles from Fairbanks. **Calendar:** Semester, limited summer session. **Full-time faculty:** 12 total. **Part-time faculty:** 10 total.

Basis for selection. Open admission.

2005-2006 Annual costs. $9868 per year includes tuition, fees, room and board.

Application procedures. Admission: No deadline. No application fee.

Academics. Credit/placement by examination: CLEP.

Student life. Freshman orientation: Available.

Contact. E-mail: diana.perkett@ilisagvik.cc
Phone: (907) 852-1763 Toll-free number: (907) 478-7337 ext. 1784
Diana Perkett, Registrar, Ilisagvik College, 100 Stevenson Road, Barrow, AK 99723

Prince William Sound Community College
Valdez, Alaska
www.pwscc.edu **CB code: 4636**

- Public 2-year community college
- Commuter campus in small town

General. Founded in 1978. Regionally accredited. Service area of 44,000 square miles. Full schedule of courses plus videotapes and audio conferencing for students in remote areas. Home of nationally recognized "Last Frontier Theatre Conference" featuring Edward Albee's plays. Off-campus centers at Cordova and Glennallen offer credit-bearing courses. **Enrollment:** 105 degree-seeking undergraduates; 1,033 non-degree-seeking students. **Degrees:** 27 associate awarded. **Location:** 300 miles from Anchorage. **Calendar:** Semester, limited summer session. **Full-time faculty:** 6 total; 17% have terminal degrees, 83% women. **Part-time faculty:** 55 total; 71% women. **Class size:** 94% < 20, 5% 20-39, less than 1% 40-49, less than 1% 50-99, less than 1% >100. **Special facilities:** Largest Alaska native museum.

Student profile. Among degree-seeking undergraduates, 5% already have a bachelor's degree or higher, 85 enrolled as first-time, first-year students, 18 transferred in from other institutions.

Part-time:	28%	**Women:**	74%

Transfer out. Colleges most students transferred to 2005: University of Alaska - Anchorage.

Basis for selection. Open admission. **Homeschooled:** Statement describing homeschool structure and mission required.

2005-2006 Annual costs. Tuition/fees: $3,060. Per-credit charge: $94. Room only: $3,634. Books/supplies: $600.

Financial aid. Need-based: Need-based aid available for part-time students. **Non-need-based:** Scholarships awarded for state residency.

Application procedures. Admission: No deadline. $10 fee. Application must be submitted on paper. Admission notification on a rolling basis. **Financial aid:** Priority date 6/30; no closing date. FAFSA required. Applicants notified on a rolling basis.

Academics. Special study options: Distance learning, double major, dual enrollment of high school students, ESL, external degree, honors, independent study, internships. Bachelor's degree programs available on campus. **Credit/placement by examination:** AP, CLEP, IB, institutional tests. **Support services:** GED preparation and test center, learning center, reduced course load, remedial instruction, study skills assistance, tutoring.

Majors. Business: Office management. **Engineering technology:** Electrical. **Liberal arts:** Arts/sciences.

Computing on campus. 50 workstations in dormitories, library, computer center. Online library, helpline available.

Student life. Freshman orientation: Available. Preregistration for classes offered. **Policies:** Freshmen permitted cars on campus. **Housing:** Coed dorms, apartments, substance-free housing available. $200 fully refundable deposit. **Activities:** Drama, film society, student government.

Student services. Adult student services, career counseling, financial aid counseling, veterans' counselor. **Transfer:** Special adviser, orientation for new students. Transfer adviser, college fairs on campus for students transferring to 4-year colleges.

Contact. E-mail: vnsmf@uaa.alaska.edu
Phone: (907) 834-1632 Toll-free number: (800) 478-8800
Fax: (907) 834-1635
Shannon Foster, Registrar, Prince William Sound Community College, Box 97, Valdez, AK 99686

Arizona

Arizona Automotive Institute

Glendale, Arizona
www.azautoinst.com **CB code: 2127**

- For-profit 2-year technical college
- Commuter campus in small city

General. Founded in 1967. Accredited by ACCSCT. **Location:** 3 miles from Phoenix. **Calendar:** Quarter.

Annual costs/financial aid. Total cost of associate degree program ranges from $17,644 to $21,901 including tuition, books, supplies, tools. Other non-degree programs available at a range of $11,796 to $14,534.

Contact. Phone: (623) 934-7273
Director of Admissions, 6829 North 46th Avenue, Glendale, AZ 85301

Arizona Western College

Yuma, Arizona **CB member**
www.azwestern.edu **CB code: 4013**

- Public 2-year community college
- Commuter campus in small city

General. Founded in 1963. Regionally accredited. Satellite sites in Parker, San Luis-Somerton, Wellton. Campus shared with Northern Arizona University, which offers completion of bachelor's, master's and doctoral programs. **Enrollment:** 5,602 degree-seeking undergraduates; 1,129 non-degree-seeking students. **Degrees:** 495 associate awarded. **Location:** 7 miles from downtown. **Calendar:** Semester, limited summer session. **Full-time faculty:** 109 total; 16% have terminal degrees, 16% minority, 46% women. **Part-time faculty:** 235 total; 5% have terminal degrees, 22% minority, 44% women. **Partnerships:** Formal partnerships with Yuma Educational Consortium and Yuma Regional Medical Center.

Student profile. Among degree-seeking undergraduates, 60% enrolled in a transfer program, 23% enrolled in a vocational program, 1,456 enrolled as first-time, first-year students, 3,836 transferred in from other institutions.

Part-time:	69%	**Hispanic American:**	56%
Women:	60%	**Native American:**	2%
African American:	3%	**International:**	11%
Asian American:	1%	**25 or older:**	40%

Transfer out. Colleges most students transferred to 2005: Northern Arizona University at Yuma, Arizona State University, University of Arizona.

Basis for selection. Open admission, but selective for some programs. Out-of-state applicants screened for social or disciplinary problems. Selective admission for nursing program. Mandatory testing for placement.

2006-2007 Annual costs. Tuition/fees: $1,200; $5,760 out-of-state. Per-credit charge: $40 in-state; $46 out-of-state. Room/board: $4,468.

Financial aid. Need-based: Need-based aid available for part-time students. Work study available nights, weekends and for part-time students. **Non-need-based:** Scholarships awarded for academics, athletics.

Application procedures. Admission: No deadline. No application fee. Admission notification on a rolling basis. **Financial aid:** Priority date 4/1; no closing date. FAFSA, institutional form required. Applicants notified on a rolling basis starting 5/1.

Academics. Special study options: Accelerated study, combined bachelor's/graduate degree, cooperative education, distance learning, dual enrollment of high school students, ESL, honors, independent study, internships, study abroad, teacher certification program, weekend college. Bachelor's degree programs available on campus. License preparation in nursing, paramedic. **Credit/placement by examination:** AP, CLEP, institutional tests. 45 credit hours maximum toward associate degree. **Support services:** GED preparation, learning center, reduced course load, remedial instruction, study skills assistance, tutoring.

Majors. Agriculture: General, business, plant sciences, production. **Biology:** General. **Business:** General, administrative services, business admin, hospitality admin, management information systems, tourism/travel. **Communications:** Broadcast journalism. **Computer sciences:** General, computer graphics. **Conservation:** Environmental science. **Education:** Early childhood, elementary, secondary, technology/industrial arts. **Engineering:** General. **Engineering technology:** Drafting. **Family/consumer sciences:** Child care, communication. **Foreign languages:** Spanish. **Health:** EMT paramedic, medical radiologic technology/radiation therapy, nursing (RN). **History:** General. **Math:** General. **Mechanic/repair:** Automotive, heating/ac/refrig. **Parks/recreation:** Exercise sciences. **Philosophy/religion:** Philosophy. **Physical sciences:** Chemistry, geology, physics. **Production:** Welding. **Protective services:** Criminal justice, firefighting. **Psychology:** General. **Social sciences:** Political science, sociology. **Visual/performing arts:** Dramatic, multimedia, studio arts.

Most popular majors. Business/marketing 9%, education 9%, health sciences 6%, liberal arts 37%.

Computing on campus. 200 workstations in dormitories, library, computer center, student center. Dormitories linked to campus network. Commuter students can connect to campus network. Online course registration, online library, helpline, repair service available.

Student life. Freshman orientation: Mandatory. Preregistration for classes offered. **Policies:** Freshmen permitted cars on campus. **Housing:** Guaranteed on-campus for all undergraduates. Coed dorms, single-sex dorms, special housing for disabled, substance-free housing available. $100 deposit. **Activities:** Bands, choral groups, dance, drama, literary magazine, music ensembles, radio station, student government, student newspaper, TV station, Phi Theta Kappa, Native American club, Hispanic students club, international club.

Athletics. NJCAA. **Intercollegiate:** Baseball M, basketball, football (tackle) M, soccer M, softball W, volleyball W. **Intramural:** Basketball, football (tackle) M, softball, volleyball. **Team name:** Matadors.

Student services. Adult student services, career counseling, services for economically disadvantaged, student employment services, financial aid counseling, health services, minority student services, on-campus daycare, personal counseling, placement for graduates, veterans' counselor, women's services. **Physically disabled:** Services for visually, hearing impaired. **Transfer:** Special adviser for new students. Transfer adviser, college fairs on campus for students transferring to 4-year colleges.

Contact. E-mail: admissions@azwestern.edu
Phone: (928) 317-6000 Toll-free number: (888) 293-0392
Fax: (928) 344-7543
Bryan Doak, Associate Dean of Enrollment Services, Arizona Western College, P.O. Box 929, Yuma, AZ 85366-0929

Bryman School

Phoenix, Arizona
www.hightechschools.com **CB code: 3040**

- For-profit 2-year health science college
- Very large city

General. Accredited by ACCSCT. **Enrollment:** 1,100 full-time, degree-seeking students. **Degrees:** 540 associate awarded. **Calendar:** Continuous. **Full-time faculty:** 60 total.

Basis for selection. Open admission. Wonderlich exam required.

2005-2006 Annual costs. Diploma programs range in price from $8,000 to $12,000. Associate degree programs range from $20,000 to $24,000. Registration fee of $50. Books/supplies: $424. Personal expenses: $3,360.

Application procedures. Admission: No deadline. No application fee. Admission notification on a rolling basis.

Academics. Credit/placement by examination: CLEP.

Majors. Health: Insurance coding, insurance specialist.

Student life. Freshman orientation: Mandatory.

Contact. Phone: (602) 274-4300 Toll-free number: (800) 987-0110
Teri Garver, Director of Admissions, Bryman School, 2250 West Peoria Ave, Phoenix, AZ 85029-4919

Central Arizona College

Coolidge, Arizona
www.centralaz.edu **CB code: 4122**

- Public 2-year community college
- Commuter campus in rural community

General. Founded in 1962. Regionally accredited. **Enrollment:** 4,155 degree-seeking undergraduates; 2,233 non-degree-seeking students. **Degrees:** 249 associate awarded. **ROTC:** Army. **Location:** 45 miles from Phoenix. **Calendar:** Semester, limited summer session. **Full-time faculty:** 95 total. **Part-time faculty:** 270 total. **Special facilities:** Observatory, visual and performing art center. **Partnerships:** Formal partnership with CAVIT.

Student profile. Among degree-seeking undergraduates, 1,118 enrolled as first-time, first-year students.

Part-time:	58%	**Women:**	61%
Out-of-state:	3%	**Live on campus:**	4%

Basis for selection. Open admission, but selective for some programs. Special requirements for nursing programs. Placement tests required of all degree-seeking students. **Learning Disabled:** Contact special needs coordinator.

2006-2007 Annual costs. Tuition/fees (projected): $1,348; $6,388 out-of-state. Per-credit charge: $47 in-state; $94 out-of-state. Room/board: $4,200. Books/supplies: $400. Personal expenses: $1,500.

Financial aid. Need-based: Need-based aid available for part-time students. Work study available nights, weekends and for part-time students.

Application procedures. Admission: No deadline. No application fee. Application may be submitted online. Admission notification on a rolling basis. **Financial aid:** Priority date 5/1, closing date 7/15. FAFSA required. Applicants notified by 5/30; must reply within 3 week(s) of notification.

Academics. Special study options: Distance learning, dual enrollment of high school students, ESL, honors, independent study, internships, liberal arts/career combination, student-designed major. Bachelor's degree programs available on campus. License preparation in nursing, real estate. **Credit/placement by examination:** AP, CLEP, institutional tests. 30 credit hours maximum toward associate degree. **Support services:** GED preparation and test center, learning center, pre-admission summer program, reduced course load, remedial instruction, study skills assistance, tutoring, writing center.

Majors. Agriculture: Business. **Biology:** General. **Business:** General, accounting, administrative services, business admin, hospitality/recreation, management information systems, office management, office technology. **Computer sciences:** General, applications programming, data processing, programming. **Education:** General, early childhood, elementary, multi-level teacher, special. **Engineering:** General, civil, mechanical, mechanics. **Engineering technology:** Electrical, industrial management, manufacturing. **Family/consumer sciences:** Family studies. **Health:** EMT paramedic, medical assistant, medical secretary, medical transcription, nursing (RN), pharmacy assistant, preveterinary. **Interdisciplinary:** Biological/physical sciences. **Legal studies:** Legal secretary. **Liberal arts:** Arts/sciences, humanities. **Math:** General. **Mechanic/repair:** Automotive, diesel, industrial. **Parks/recreation:** Exercise sciences. **Personal/culinary services:** Culinary arts. **Physical sciences:** Chemistry. **Protective services:** Corrections, criminal justice, firefighting. **Psychology:** General. **Social sciences:** General, criminology. **Visual/performing arts:** General, art, dramatic.

Computing on campus. 500 workstations in dormitories, library, computer center, student center. Dormitories wired for high-speed internet access. Commuter students can connect to campus network. Online course registration, helpline, wireless network available.

Student life. Freshman orientation: Available. Preregistration for classes offered. **Policies:** Declaration of Civility, Student Code of Conduct. Freshmen permitted cars on campus. **Housing:** Coed dorms, special housing for disabled, substance-free housing available. $100 deposit. **Activities:** Bands, choral groups, drama, music ensembles, musical theater, student government, student newspaper, TV station, Native American club, Movimiento Estudiante Chicano de Aztlan, religious groups, Phi Theta Kappa.

Athletics. NJCAA. **Intercollegiate:** Baseball M, basketball, cross-country, rodeo, softball W, track and field. **Intramural:** Swimming, tennis. **Team name:** Vaqueros.

Student services. Adult student services, alcohol/substance abuse counseling, career counseling, student employment services, financial aid counseling, on-campus daycare, personal counseling, placement for graduates. **Physically disabled:** Services for visually, hearing impaired. **Transfer:** Special adviser, orientation, re-entry adviser for new students. Transfer center, transfer adviser for students transferring to 4-year colleges.

Contact. E-mail: wanna_kim@centralaz.edu
Phone: (520) 426-4260 Fax: (520) 876-1983
Leonor Machado, Director of Student Records, Central Arizona College, 8470 North Overfield Road, Coolidge, AZ 85228-9778

Chandler-Gilbert Community College: Pecos

Chandler, Arizona
www.cgc.maricopa.edu **CB code: 0535**

- Public 2-year community college
- Commuter campus in small town

General. Regionally accredited. **Enrollment:** 987 full-time, degree-seeking students. **Degrees:** 286 associate awarded. **Calendar:** Semester. **Full-time faculty:** 104 total. **Part-time faculty:** 400 total.

Basis for selection. Open admission.

2005-2006 Annual costs. Tuition/fees: $1,810; $7,750 out-of-state. Per-credit charge: $60 in-state; $258 out-of-state.

2005-2006 Financial aid. Need-based: 52% of total undergraduate aid awarded as scholarships/grants, 48% as loans/jobs.

Application procedures. Admission: No deadline. No application fee.

Academics. Special study options: Distance learning, dual enrollment of high school students, ESL, honors, independent study, weekend college. License preparation in aviation. **Credit/placement by examination:** CLEP, IB, institutional tests. 30 credit hours maximum toward associate degree. **Support services:** Learning center, reduced course load, remedial instruction, study skills assistance, tutoring, writing center.

Majors. Business: General, accounting, office technology. **Computer sciences:** Vendor certification. **Mechanic/repair:** Aircraft, avionics. **Transportation:** Aviation.

Computing on campus. 75 workstations in library, computer center. Online course registration, wireless network available.

Student life. Freshman orientation: Available. **Policies:** Freshmen permitted cars on campus. **Housing:** Coed dorms available. **Activities:** Bands, choral groups, dance, drama, music ensembles, musical theater, student government.

Athletics. NJCAA. **Intercollegiate:** Baseball M, basketball, soccer, softball W, volleyball W.

Student services. Adult student services, alcohol/substance abuse counseling, career counseling, services for economically disadvantaged, student employment services, financial aid counseling, personal counseling, placement for graduates, veterans' counselor. **Physically disabled:** Services for visually, speech, hearing impaired.

Contact. Phone: (480) 732-7320
Irene Pearl, Supervisor of Admission Records and Registration, Chandler-Gilbert Community College: Pecos, 2626 East Pecos Road, Chandler, AZ 85225

Chandler-Gilbert Community College: Sun Lakes Education Center

Sun Lakes, Arizona
www.cgc.maricopa.edu **CB code: 3826**

- Public 2-year community college
- Small town

General. Regionally accredited. **Calendar:** Semester.

Annual costs/financial aid. Tuition/fees (2005-2006): $1,810; $7,750 out-of-state.

Contact. Phone: (480) 857-5500
Supervisor of Admissions Records and Registration, 25105 South Alma School Road, Sun Lakes, AZ 85248-7158

Chandler-Gilbert Community College: Williams Campus

Chandler, Arizona
www.cgc.maricopa.edu **CB code: 3827**

- Public 2-year community college
- Commuter campus in very large city

General. Regionally accredited. **Enrollment:** 987 degree-seeking undergraduates; 7,676 non-degree-seeking students. **Degrees:** 384 associate awarded. **ROTC:** Army, Air Force. **Calendar:** Semester, extensive summer session. **Full-time faculty:** 15 total. **Part-time faculty:** 90 total.

Student profile. Among degree-seeking undergraduates, 70% enrolled in a transfer program, 30% enrolled in a vocational program, 5% already have a bachelor's degree or higher, 260 enrolled as first-time, first-year students.

Part-time:	52%	**Hispanic American:**	16%
Out-of-state:	6%	**Native American:**	3%
Women:	51%	**International:**	1%
African American:	4%	**25 or older:**	31%
Asian American:	3%		

Transfer out. Colleges most students transferred to 2005: Arizona State University, Northern Arizona University, University of Arizona.

Basis for selection. Open admission, but selective for some programs. Special requirements for nursing and aviation.

2005-2006 Annual costs. Tuition/fees: $1,840; $7,780 out-of-state. Per-credit charge: $60 in-state; $258 out-of-state.

Application procedures. Admission: No deadline. No application fee. Application may be submitted online.

Academics. Special study options: Distance learning, double major, dual enrollment of high school students, ESL, honors, internships, teacher certification program. License preparation in aviation, nursing. **Credit/placement by examination:** CLEP. **Support services:** Learning center, remedial instruction, study skills assistance, tutoring, writing center.

Majors. Computer sciences: General, applications programming, networking. **Education:** General. **Liberal arts:** Arts/sciences. **Physical sciences:** General. **Psychology:** General.

Computing on campus. Commuter students can connect to campus network. Online course registration, helpline, wireless network available.

Student life. Freshman orientation: Available. Preregistration for classes offered. **Policies:** Freshmen permitted cars on campus. **Activities:** Bands, choral groups, dance, drama, music ensembles, musical theater, student government.

Athletics. NJCAA. **Team name:** Coyotes.

Student services. Adult student services, career counseling, student employment services, financial aid counseling, personal counseling, placement for graduates. **Physically disabled:** Services for visually, speech, hearing impaired. **Transfer:** Special adviser, orientation, re-entry adviser for new students. Transfer center, transfer adviser, college fairs on campus for students transferring to 4-year colleges.

Contact. E-mail: irene.pearl@cgcmail.maricopa.edu
Phone: (480) 732-7320 Fax: (480) 732-7099
Irene Pearl, Supervisor of Admissions, Records and Registration, Chandler-Gilbert Community College: Williams Campus, 2626 East Pecos Road, Chandler, AZ 85225-2499

Cochise College

Douglas, Arizona **CB member**
www.cochise.edu **CB code: 4097**

- Public 2-year community college
- Commuter campus in large town

General. Founded in 1962. Regionally accredited. Courses offered at 12 locations throughout county. **Enrollment:** 3,289 degree-seeking undergraduates. **Degrees:** 667 associate awarded. **Location:** 120 miles from Tucson. **Calendar:** Semester, limited summer session. **Full-time faculty:** 90 total. **Part-time faculty:** 285 total. **Special facilities:** Asian art collection, college airport.

Student profile.

Out-of-state:	3%	**Live on campus:**	3%
25 or older:	38%		

Transfer out. Colleges most students transferred to 2005: University of Arizona, Arizona State University, Northern Arizona University, Western New Mexico University.

Basis for selection. Open admission, but selective for some programs. Special requirements for air transportation (professional pilot, aviation maintenance) and nursing programs; interview required. Walk-in admission available.

2006-2007 Annual costs. Tuition/fees (projected): $1,440. Room/board: $3,671. Books/supplies: $600. Personal expenses: $1,125.

2004-2005 Financial aid. Need-based: 97% of total undergraduate aid awarded as scholarships/grants, 3% as loans/jobs. Need-based aid available for part-time students.

Application procedures. Admission: No deadline. No application fee in-state; $10 out-of-state. Admission notification on a rolling basis. **Financial aid:** Closing date 4/15. FAFSA required. Applicants notified on a rolling basis starting 6/15; must reply within 2 week(s) of notification.

Academics. Special study options: Cooperative education, cross-registration, distance learning, double major, dual enrollment of high school students, ESL, honors, independent study, internships, teacher certification program, weekend college. License preparation in aviation, nursing. **Credit/placement by examination:** CLEP, institutional tests. 30 credit hours maximum toward associate degree. **Support services:** GED preparation, learning center, reduced course load, remedial instruction, tutoring.

Majors. Biology: General. **Business:** Administrative services, business admin, international, management information systems, office management, office/clerical. **Communications:** General, journalism. **Computer sciences:** General, computer science, information systems. **Education:** General. **Engineering technology:** Drafting, electrical. **Foreign languages:** General, Spanish. **Health:** EMT paramedic, medical secretary, nursing (RN). **History:** General. **Legal studies:** Legal secretary. **Liberal arts:** Arts/sciences. **Mechanic/repair:** Aircraft, avionics. **Physical sciences:** Chemistry. **Protective services:** Fire safety technology, police science. **Psychology:** General. **Public administration:** Social work. **Social sciences:** Anthropology, political science. **Transportation:** Airline/commercial pilot, aviation. **Visual/performing arts:** Studio arts.

Most popular majors. Business/marketing 11%, computer/information sciences 6%, engineering/engineering technologies 6%, health sciences 12%, liberal arts 56%.

Computing on campus. 150 workstations in dormitories, library, computer center. Online course registration available.

Student life. Freshman orientation: Available. Preregistration for classes offered. **Policies:** Freshmen permitted cars on campus. **Housing:** Single-sex dorms, apartments available. $150 deposit. **Activities:** Concert band, choral groups, drama, literary magazine, music ensembles, student government, student newspaper, Alpha Delta Omega, Alpha Eta Rho, Armed Forces Communication and Electronics Association (AFCEA), Aviation Maintenance Specialist Club (AMS), Campus Activities Board, ECO Club (Hispanic American), Vocational Industrial Clubs of America, Future Teacher's Club, Phi Beta Lambda, Phi Theta Kappa, Students of Diversity.

Athletics. NJCAA. **Intercollegiate:** Baseball M, basketball, rodeo, soccer W. **Intramural:** Basketball, football (non-tackle), volleyball. **Team name:** Apaches.

Student services. Career counseling, student employment services, health services, personal counseling, placement for graduates, veterans' counselor. **Physically disabled:** Services for visually, hearing impaired. **Transfer:** Special adviser for new students. Transfer adviser, college fairs on campus for students transferring to 4-year colleges.

Contact. E-mail: admissions@cochise.edu
Phone: (520) 417-4046 Toll-free number: (800) 966-7943
Fax: (520) 417-4761
Debbie Quick, Director of Admissions, Cochise College, 4190 West Highway 80, Douglas, AZ 85607-6190

Coconino County Community College

Flagstaff, Arizona
www.coconino.edu **CB code: 1712**

- Public 2-year community college
- Commuter campus in small city

General. Regionally accredited. **Enrollment:** 1,574 degree-seeking undergraduates. **Degrees:** 117 associate awarded. **ROTC:** Army, Air Force. **Location:** 140 miles from Phoenix. **Calendar:** Semester, limited summer session. **Full-time faculty:** 34 total. **Part-time faculty:** 245 total.

Basis for selection. Open admission, but selective for some programs. Special requirements for nursing program. High school students must complete additional paperwork. **Adult students:** Entrance exam policies same as for first-time freshmen.

2005-2006 Annual costs. Tuition/fees: $1,344; $5,376 out-of-state. Per-credit charge: $56 in-state; $224 out-of-state.

2004-2005 Financial aid. Need-based: 95% of total undergraduate aid awarded as scholarships/grants, 5% as loans/jobs.

Application procedures. Admission: No deadline. No application fee. Application must be submitted on paper. Admission notification on a rolling basis. **Financial aid:** Priority date 4/15, closing date 6/30.

Academics. Special study options: Distance learning, dual enrollment of high school students, honors, internships. License preparation in nursing, paramedic, real estate. **Credit/placement by examination:** CLEP. **Support services:** GED test center, learning center, remedial instruction, study skills assistance, tutoring, writing center.

Majors. Business: Hospitality admin. **Construction:** Carpentry. **Education:** Early childhood. **Engineering technology:** CAD/CADD, construction, software, solar energy. **Health:** Medical secretary. **Legal studies:** Paralegal. **Protective services:** Firefighting.

Computing on campus. 100 workstations in computer center, student center. Online course registration, online library available.

Student life. Freshman orientation: Available. Preregistration for classes offered. **Policies:** Freshmen permitted cars on campus. **Housing:** Some dorm opportunities may be available through Northern Arizona University. **Activities:** Jazz band, dance, symphony orchestra.

Student services. Adult student services, career counseling, financial aid counseling, on-campus daycare, veterans' counselor. **Physically disabled:** Services for visually, speech, hearing impaired. **Transfer:** Special adviser, orientation, pre-admission transcript evaluation for new students. College fairs on campus for students transferring to 4-year colleges.

Contact. E-mail: marrianna.dougherty@coconino.edu
Phone: (928) 527-1222 ext. 4299 Toll-free
number: (800) 350-7122 ext. 4299 Fax: (928) 226-4110
Steve Miller, Registrar/Director for Admissions, Coconino County Community College, 2800 S Lone Tree Road, Flagstaff, AZ 86001

Dine College
Tsaile, Arizona
www.dinecollege.edu **CB member** **CB code: 4550**

- Public 2-year community college
- Residential campus in rural community

General. Founded in 1968. Regionally accredited. The first tribally controlled community college in the United States; chartered by the Navajo Nation. **Enrollment:** 1,753 degree-seeking undergraduates; 3 non-degree-seeking students. **Degrees:** 224 associate awarded. **Location:** 55 miles from Window Rock. **Calendar:** Semester, limited summer session. **Full-time faculty:** 60 total. **Part-time faculty:** 100 total. **Special facilities:** Museum.

Student profile. Among degree-seeking undergraduates, 388 enrolled as first-time, first-year students.

Part-time:	52%	**Native American:**	99%
Out-of-state:	15%	**25 or older:**	49%
Women:	76%	**Live on campus:**	20%

Transfer out. Colleges most students transferred to 2005: Northern Arizona University, Arizona State University, Fort Lewis College, University of Arizona, University of New Mexico.

Basis for selection. Open admission. **Adult students:** Entrance exam policies same as for first-time freshmen.

2005-2006 Annual costs. Tuition/fees: $800. Per-credit charge: $30. Room/board: $3,764.

2004-2005 Financial aid. Need-based: 46 full-time freshmen applied for aid; 43 were judged to have need; 43 of these received aid. Average need met was 4%. Average scholarship/grant was $4,025. 97% of total undergraduate aid awarded as scholarships/grants, 3% as loans/jobs. Need-based aid available for part-time students. **Non-need-based:** Awarded to 59 full-time undergraduates, including 6 freshmen.

Application procedures. Admission: No deadline. $20 fee. Application must be submitted on paper. Admission notification on a rolling basis. **Financial aid:** Priority date 4/15; no closing date. FAFSA, institutional form required. Applicants notified on a rolling basis starting 5/1; must reply within 4 week(s) of notification.

Academics. Special study options: Cooperative education, distance learning, double major, independent study. **Credit/placement by examination:** CLEP, institutional tests. 12 credit hours maximum toward associate degree. **Support services:** Learning center, pre-admission summer program, remedial instruction, tutoring.

Majors. Area/ethnic studies: Native American. **Biology:** General. **Business:** Administrative services, business admin, office/clerical. **Computer sciences:** General, computer science. **Conservation:** Environmental science. **Education:** General. **Foreign languages:** Native American. **Health:** Public health ed. **Liberal arts:** Arts/sciences. **Psychology:** General. **Social sciences:** General. **Visual/performing arts:** Studio arts.

Computing on campus. 104 workstations in dormitories, library, computer center, student center. Dormitories wired for high-speed internet access and linked to campus network. Repair service, wireless network available.

Student life. Freshman orientation: Available. Preregistration for classes offered. **Housing:** Coed dorms, single-sex dorms available. **Activities:** Student government, Red Dawn Indian club.

Athletics. NJCAA. **Intercollegiate:** Archery, cross-country, rodeo. **Intramural:** Archery, cross-country, rodeo. **Team name:** Warrior.

Student services. Career counseling, personal counseling, veterans' counselor. **Transfer:** Special adviser, orientation for new students. Transfer adviser, college fairs on campus for students transferring to 4-year colleges.

Contact. Phone: (928) 724-6630 Fax: (928) 724-3349
Louise Litzin, Registrar, Dine College, Box 67, Tsaile, AZ 86556

Eastern Arizona College
Thatcher, Arizona
www.eac.edu **CB code: 4297**

- Public 2-year community college
- Commuter campus in large town

General. Founded in 1888. Regionally accredited. Near archaeological sites. Several continuing education centers within 165 miles of campus. **Enrollment:** 2,758 degree-seeking undergraduates; 2,481 non-degree-seeking students. **Degrees:** 276 associate awarded. **Location:** 160 miles from Phoenix, 130 miles from Tucson. **Calendar:** Semester, limited summer session. **Full-time faculty:** 88 total; 12% have terminal degrees, 7% minority, 34% women. **Part-time faculty:** 210 total; 1% have terminal degrees, 10% minority, 58% women. **Class size:** 76% < 20, 21% 20-39, 2% 40-49, 2% 50-99, less than 1% >100. **Special facilities:** Observatory, golf course, wilderness area. **Partnerships:** Formal partnerships with local high schools allow high school students to obtain degrees in areas such as office technology and drafting.

Student profile. Among degree-seeking undergraduates, 54% enrolled in a transfer program, 46% enrolled in a vocational program, 1,197 enrolled as first-time, first-year students.

Part-time:	53%	**Hispanic American:**	17%
Out-of-state:	5%	**Native American:**	10%
Women:	59%	**International:**	1%
African American:	3%	**25 or older:**	46%
Asian American:	1%	**Live on campus:**	6%

Basis for selection. Open admission, but selective for some programs. Special requirements for nursing and several paramedical programs. **Adult students:** Entrance exam policies same as for first-time freshmen.

High school preparation. 15 units recommended. Recommended units include English 4, mathematics 4, social studies 1, history 1, science 3 (laboratory 3) and foreign language 2.

2006-2007 Annual costs. Tuition/fees (projected): $1,220; $6,460 out-of-state. Per-credit charge: $50 in-state; $100 out-of-state. Room/board: $4,320. Books/supplies: $800. Personal expenses: $1,750.

2005-2006 Financial aid. **Need-based:** 387 full-time freshmen applied for aid; 298 were judged to have need; 250 of these received aid. Average need met was 45%. Average scholarship/grant was $3,978. 94% of total undergraduate aid awarded as scholarships/grants, 6% as loans/jobs. Need-based aid available for part-time students. Work study available nights, weekends and for part-time students. **Non-need-based:** Scholarships awarded for academics, art, athletics, leadership, music/drama, state residency. **Additional information:** Limited number of tuition waivers for New Mexico residents. Unlimited number of waivers for those meeting WUE requirements.

Application procedures. **Admission:** No deadline. No application fee. Application may be submitted online. Admission notification on a rolling basis. **Financial aid:** Priority date 3/1; no closing date. FAFSA, institutional form required. Applicants notified on a rolling basis starting 3/15.

Academics. **Special study options:** Cooperative education, distance learning, double major, dual enrollment of high school students, independent study. Bachelor's degree programs available on campus. License preparation in nursing, paramedic. **Credit/placement by examination:** AP, CLEP, IB, institutional tests. 48 credit hours maximum toward associate degree. All students intending to enroll in mathematics or English composition courses must take appropriate placement tests. Tests waived for students who score 21 on both English and math ACT, or 530 on English, 520 on math SAT. **Support services:** GED preparation and test center, learning center, reduced course load, remedial instruction, study skills assistance, tutoring, writing center.

Majors. **Agriculture:** Agribusiness operations. **Biology:** General, wildlife. **Business:** Administrative services, business admin, entrepreneurial studies, office technology. **Computer sciences:** Information systems, system admin. **Conservation:** Forestry. **Education:** Art, business, elementary, secondary, technology/industrial arts. **Engineering technology:** Civil, drafting, mining. **English:** English lit. **Foreign languages:** General. **Health:** EMT paramedic, nursing (RN), pharmacy assistant, premedicine, prepharmacy. **History:** General. **Legal studies:** Prelaw. **Liberal arts:** Arts/sciences. **Math:** General. **Mechanic/repair:** Automotive. **Parks/recreation:** Health/fitness. **Personal/culinary services:** Cosmetic. **Physical sciences:** Chemistry, geology, physics. **Protective services:** Law enforcement admin, police science. **Psychology:** General. **Social sciences:** Anthropology, political science, sociology. **Visual/performing arts:** Art, commercial/advertising art, dramatic, studio arts.

Most popular majors. Business/marketing 11%, education 11%, health sciences 17%, liberal arts 41%, social sciences 6%.

Computing on campus. 543 workstations in library, computer center. Dormitories wired for high-speed internet access and linked to campus network. Online course registration, online library available.

Student life. **Freshman orientation:** Available. Preregistration for classes offered. Half-day session given the week prior to beginning of classes each semester and weekly during summer months. **Policies:** Freshmen permitted cars on campus. **Housing:** Single-sex dorms, substance-free housing available. $150 deposit. **Activities:** Bands, choral groups, dance, drama, literary magazine, music ensembles, musical theater, student government, symphony orchestra, Latter-Day-Saints Student Association, Newman Club, Drama Club, Hispanic Leaders, Intertribal Club, Phi Theta Kappa, Spanish Club, Choir Club, Gila Force, Rowdy Reptiles, International Club.

Athletics. NJCAA. **Intercollegiate:** Baseball M, basketball, football (tackle) M, golf M, softball W, tennis W, volleyball W. **Intramural:** Basketball, soccer, swimming, tennis, volleyball. **Team name:** Gila Monsters.

Student services. Adult student services, alcohol/substance abuse counseling, career counseling, services for economically disadvantaged, student employment services, financial aid counseling, minority student services, personal counseling, placement for graduates, veterans' counselor, women's services. **Physically disabled:** Services for visually, speech, hearing impaired. **Transfer:** Special adviser, orientation, re-entry adviser, pre-admission transcript evaluation for new students. Transfer adviser, college fairs on campus for students transferring to 4-year colleges.

Contact. E-mail: admissions@eac.edu
Phone: (928) 428-8272 Toll-free number: (800) 678-3808
Fax: (928) 428-8462
Jeff Savage, Coordinator Office of Admissions, Eastern Arizona College, 615 North Stadium Avenue, Thatcher, AZ 85552-0769

Estrella Mountain Community College

Avondale, Arizona
www.emc.maricopa.edu **CB code: 3810**

- Public 2-year community college
- Commuter campus in small city

General. Regionally accredited. **Enrollment:** 1,870 degree-seeking undergraduates. **Degrees:** 280 associate awarded. **ROTC:** Air Force. **Location:** 15 miles from Phoenix. **Calendar:** Semester, limited summer session. **Full-time faculty:** 61 total. **Part-time faculty:** 175 total.

Student profile.

Out-of-state:	1%	**25 or older:**	46%

Transfer out. **Colleges most students transferred to 2005:** Arizona State University.

Basis for selection. Open admission. **Adult students:** Entrance exam policies same as for first-time freshmen.

2005-2006 Annual costs. Tuition/fees: $1,810; $7,750 out-of-state. Per-credit charge: $60 in-state; $258 out-of-state. Books/supplies: $848.

2004-2005 Financial aid. **Need-based:** 67% of total undergraduate aid awarded as scholarships/grants, 33% as loans/jobs. Need-based aid available for part-time students. Work study available nights and for part-time students. **Non-need-based:** Scholarships awarded for leadership.

Application procedures. **Admission:** Closing date 3/1. $5 fee. Application may be submitted online. **Financial aid:** Priority date 4/1; no closing date. Applicants notified on a rolling basis starting 4/15.

Academics. **Special study options:** Accelerated study, dual enrollment of high school students, ESL, honors, independent study, weekend college. **Credit/placement by examination:** CLEP, IB. 30 credit hours maximum toward associate degree. **Support services:** GED test center, learning center, pre-admission summer program, reduced course load, remedial instruction, study skills assistance, tutoring, writing center.

Majors. **Business:** Business admin, hotel/motel admin, organizational behavior. **Computer sciences:** Applications programming, data entry, LAN/WAN management, vendor certification. **Education:** General, elementary, secondary, teacher assistance. **Liberal arts:** Arts/sciences. **Personal/culinary services:** Chef training, culinary arts. **Protective services:** Criminal justice. **Psychology:** General. **Public administration:** Social work.

Computing on campus. 185 workstations in library, computer center. Online course registration, online library, helpline, wireless network available.

Student life. **Freshman orientation:** Available. Preregistration for classes offered. **Policies:** Freshmen permitted cars on campus. **Activities:** Literary magazine, student government.

Student services. Adult student services, alcohol/substance abuse counseling, career counseling, financial aid counseling, personal counseling, veterans' counselor. **Physically disabled:** Services for visually, speech, hearing impaired. **Transfer:** Special adviser, pre-admission transcript evaluation for new students. College fairs on campus for students transferring to 4-year colleges.

Contact. Phone: (623) 935-8000
Barbara Boros, Director of Admission and Records, Estrella Mountain Community College, 3000 North Dysart Road, Avondale, AZ 85323

Everest College

Phoenix, Arizona
www.everest-college.com **CB code: 2172**

- For-profit 2-year business and technical college
- Commuter campus in very large city
- Interview required

General. Founded in 1982. Regionally accredited. **Enrollment:** 650 degree-seeking undergraduates. **Degrees:** 130 associate awarded. **Location:** 10 miles from downtown Phoenix. **Calendar:** Differs by program, extensive summer session. **Full-time faculty:** 11 total. **Part-time faculty:** 50 total.

Student profile.

Out-of-state:	5%	**25 or older:**	65%

Transfer out. **Colleges most students transferred to 2005:** Arizona State University, Northern Arizona University, University of Phoenix.

Basis for selection. Open admission. Interview very important. Essay required of legal assistant majors.

2005-2006 Annual costs. Tuition/fees: $6,051. Per-credit charge: $249. Tuition varies by program.

Application procedures. **Admission:** No deadline. No application fee. Admission notification on a rolling basis. **Financial aid:** No deadline. FAFSA required. Applicants notified on a rolling basis.

Academics. **Special study options:** Cooperative education, distance learning, independent study, internships. Bachelor's degree programs available on campus. **Credit/placement by examination:** CLEP. **Support services:** Reduced course load, remedial instruction, tutoring.

Majors. **Business:** Accounting, administrative services, business admin, office management, office technology, office/clerical. **Computer sciences:** General, information systems. **Education:** Business. **Engineering:** Software. **Legal studies:** Legal secretary.

Most popular majors. Business/marketing 30%, computer/information sciences 30%, legal studies 40%.

Computing on campus. 120 workstations in library, computer center. Helpline available.

Student life. **Freshman orientation:** Mandatory. **Activities:** Collegiate Secretaries International.

Student services. Career counseling, student employment services, personal counseling, placement for graduates. **Transfer:** Special adviser, orientation, pre-admission transcript evaluation for new students. Transfer adviser for students transferring to 4-year colleges.

Contact. E-mail: magee@cci.edu
Phone: (602) 942-4141 Toll-free number: (888) 741-4271
Fax: (602) 943-0960
Melissa Agee, Director of Admissions, Everest College, 10400 North 25th Avenue Suite 190, Phoenix, AZ 85021

Gateway Community College

Phoenix, Arizona
www.gwc.maricopa.edu **CB code: 0455**

- Public 2-year community and technical college
- Commuter campus in very large city

General. Founded in 1968. Regionally accredited. **Enrollment:** 8,500 degree-seeking undergraduates. **Degrees:** 340 associate awarded. **ROTC:** Army, Navy, Air Force. **Calendar:** Semester, extensive summer session. **Full-time faculty:** 86 total; 19% minority, 63% women. **Part-time faculty:** 245 total. **Partnerships:** Formal partnerships with Intel, Johnson Control, Toyota, Motorola.

Student profile.

Out-of-state:	5%	**25 or older:**	80%

Transfer out. **Colleges most students transferred to 2005:** Arizona State Unversity, Northern Arizona University, University of Arizona.

Basis for selection. Open admission, but selective for some programs. Special requirements for nursing and some allied health programs. General Aptitude Test Battery required of health science applicants.

2005-2006 Annual costs. Tuition/fees: $1,810; $7,750 out-of-state. Per-credit charge: $60 in-state; $258 out-of-state.

Financial aid. **Need-based:** Need-based aid available for part-time students. Work study available nights, weekends and for part-time students. **Non-need-based:** Scholarships awarded for athletics.

Application procedures. **Admission:** No deadline. No application fee. Application may be submitted online. Admission notification on a rolling basis. **Financial aid:** Priority date 4/15; no closing date. FAFSA, institutional form required. Applicants notified on a rolling basis starting 7/1; must reply within 4 week(s) of notification.

Academics. **Special study options:** Accelerated study, combined bachelor's/graduate degree, cooperative education, cross-registration, distance learning, double major, dual enrollment of high school students, ESL, honors, independent study, internships, liberal arts/career combination, study abroad, teacher certification program. License preparation in nursing, physical therapy, radiology. **Credit/placement by examination:** CLEP, IB, institutional tests. 30 credit hours maximum toward associate degree. **Support services:** GED test center, learning center, reduced course load, remedial instruction, study skills assistance, tutoring, writing center.

Majors. **Business:** General, accounting, administrative services, banking/financial services, international, office management. **Computer sciences:** General, information systems, LAN/WAN management, networking, system admin, systems analysis. **Construction:** Carpentry, electrician, maintenance, masonry, pipefitting, power transmission. **Education:** General, elementary. **Engineering:** General, aerospace, water resource. **Engineering technology:** Aerospace, hazardous materials, manufacturing, occupational safety, water quality. **Health:** Health care admin, medical radiologic technology/radiation therapy, medical transcription, nuclear medical technology, nursing (RN), physical therapy assistant, respiratory therapy technology, sonography, surgical technology. **Legal studies:** Court reporting. **Liberal arts:** Arts/sciences. **Mechanic/repair:** Automotive, electronics/electrical, heating/ac/refrig. **Social sciences:** Sociology.

Most popular majors. Health sciences 67%, liberal arts 23%.

Computing on campus. 100 workstations in library, computer center, student center. Commuter students can connect to campus network. Online course registration, online library, helpline available.

Student life. **Freshman orientation:** Available. Preregistration for classes offered. **Activities:** Film society, student government, student newspaper, Newman Club, MEHCA, Indian Tribal Club, Single Parents Association, VA Club, internatilonal student club, women's club, health sciences club, business club.

Athletics. NJCAA. **Intercollegiate:** Cross-country, golf, tennis. **Team name:** Geckos.

Student services. Adult student services, alcohol/substance abuse counseling, career counseling, services for economically disadvantaged, student employment services, financial aid counseling, minority student services, on-campus daycare, personal counseling, placement for graduates, veterans' counselor, women's services. **Physically disabled:** Services for visually, speech, hearing impaired. **Learning disabled:** Comprehensive services available. **Transfer:** Special adviser, orientation, re-entry adviser, pre-admission transcript evaluation for new students. Transfer center, transfer adviser, college fairs on campus for students transferring to 4-year colleges.

Contact. E-mail: cathy.gibson@gwmail.maricopa.edu
Phone: (602) 286-8200 Fax: (602) 286-8072
Cathy Gibson, Director Admissions and Records, Gateway Community College, 108 North 40th Street, Phoenix, AZ 85034

Glendale Community College

Glendale, Arizona
www.gc.maricopa.edu **CB code: 4338**

- Public 2-year community college
- Commuter campus in small city

General. Founded in 1965. Regionally accredited. Extension site at Glendale Community College North in Peoria. **Enrollment:** 4,431 degree-seeking undergraduates; 16,218 non-degree-seeking students. **Degrees:** 854 associate awarded. **Location:** 17 miles from Phoenix. **Calendar:** Semester, extensive summer session. **Full-time faculty:** 240 total. **Part-time faculty:** 600 total. **Class size:** 50% < 20, 47% 20-39, 2% 40-49, less than 1% 50-99. **Special facilities:** Performing arts center, high-technology centers, international student center. **Partnerships:** Formal partnerships with General Motors, Ford, Chrysler, Best Western, and John Deere.

Student profile.

Part-time:	60%	**Hispanic American:**	22%
Out-of-state:	4%	**Native American:**	3%
Women:	57%	**International:**	1%
African American:	7%	**25 or older:**	44%
Asian American:	4%		

Transfer out. **Colleges most students transferred to 2005:** Arizona State University, Arizona State University West, University of Arizona, Grand Canyon University.

Basis for selection. Open admission, but selective for some programs. Special requirements for nursing, basic emergency medical technology, General Motors and Ford automotive programs, international students. **Adult students:** Entrance exam policies same as for first-time freshmen. **Home-schooled:** If under 18, special admissions required.

2005-2006 Annual costs. Tuition/fees: $1,810; $7,750 out-of-state. Per-credit charge: $60 in-state; $258 out-of-state. Books/supplies: $1,000. Personal expenses: $2,400.

Financial aid. **Need-based:** Need-based aid available for part-time students. Work study available nights, weekends and for part-time students.

Application procedures. **Admission:** No deadline. No application fee. Application may be submitted online. Admission notification on a rolling basis. **Financial aid:** Priority date 4/30, closing date 8/1. FAFSA required. Applicants notified on a rolling basis starting 6/1.

Academics. **Special study options:** Cooperative education, distance learning, dual enrollment of high school students, ESL, honors, independent study, internships, weekend college. ACE Plus (Achieving College Education), a high school bridge program, intensive English program. License preparation in nursing, paramedic. **Credit/placement by examination:** AP, CLEP, institutional tests. 30 credit hours maximum toward associate degree. **Support services:** GED preparation and test center, learning center, remedial instruction, study skills assistance, tutoring, writing center.

Majors. **Agriculture:** Horticulture, supplies. **Business:** General, accounting technology, administrative services, business admin, management information systems, operations. **Communications:** Public relations. **Communications technology:** Radio/tv. **Computer sciences:** Applications programming, LAN/WAN management, networking. **Education:** Elementary. **Engineering technology:** Architectural drafting, computer, electrical, nuclear. **Family/consumer sciences:** Child care, food/nutrition. **Health:** EMT paramedic, nursing (RN). **Liberal arts:** Arts/sciences. **Mechanic/repair:** Automotive. **Physical sciences:** General. **Protective services:** Firefighting, police science. **Psychology:** General. **Public administration:** Social work. **Visual/performing arts:** Commercial/advertising art.

Most popular majors. Business/marketing 22%, education 6%, health sciences 10%, liberal arts 42%, trade and industry 6%.

Computing on campus. 1,500 workstations in library, computer center. Commuter students can connect to campus network. Online course registration, online library, student web hosting, wireless network available.

Student life. **Freshman orientation:** Available. Preregistration for classes offered. **Policies:** Freshmen permitted cars on campus. **Activities:** Bands, choral groups, dance, drama, literary magazine, music ensembles, musical theater, opera, student government, student newspaper.

Athletics. NJCAA. **Intercollegiate:** Baseball M, basketball, cheerleading, cross-country, football (tackle) M, golf M, soccer, softball W, tennis, track and field, volleyball W. **Team name:** Gauchos.

Student services. Adult student services, campus ministries, career counseling, student employment services, financial aid counseling, minority student services, on-campus daycare, veterans' counselor. **Physically disabled:** Services for visually, speech, hearing impaired. **Transfer:** Special adviser, orientation for new students. Transfer adviser, college fairs on campus for students transferring to 4-year colleges.

Contact. E-mail: info@gc.maricopa.edu
Phone: (623) 845-3300 Fax: (623) 845-3303
Mary Massal, Associate Dean of Enrollment Services, Glendale Community College, 6000 West Olive Avenue, Glendale, AZ 85302

Golf Academy of Arizona

Scottsdale, Arizona
www.sdgagolf.com/golfacademyarizona.html
CB code: 3460

- For-profit 2-year college of golf course management
- Small city

General. Accredited by ACICS. **Calendar:** Semester.

Annual costs/financial aid. Books/supplies: $650. Personal expenses: $2,862.

Contact. Phone: (480) 905-9288
7373 North Scottsdale Road, Suite B-100, Scottsdale, AZ 85253

High-Tech Institute

Phoenix, Arizona
www.hightechinstitute.edu
CB code: 3170

- For-profit 2-year technical college
- Commuter campus in very large city
- Interview required

General. Accredited by ACCSCT. **Enrollment:** 2,044 degree-seeking undergraduates. **Degrees:** 727 associate awarded. **Calendar:** Continuous, extensive summer session. **Full-time faculty:** 55 total.

Student profile. Among degree-seeking undergraduates, 100% enrolled in a vocational program, 576 enrolled as first-time, first-year students, 37 transferred in from other institutions.

Out-of-state:	70%	**Hispanic American:**	25%
African American:	20%	**Native American:**	7%
Asian American:	3%		

Basis for selection. Open admission. **Homeschooled:** Transcript of courses and grades, state high school equivalency certificate, interview required.

2005-2006 Annual costs. Total costs of associate degrees vary by program and range from $18,450 to $25,850. Total costs of diplomas vary by program and range from $8,850 to $16,250. Personal expenses: $205.

Financial aid. All financial aid based on need.

Application procedures. **Admission:** No deadline. $50 fee. Application must be submitted on paper. Admission notification on a rolling basis. **Financial aid:** No deadline.

Academics. **Special study options:** Distance learning. **Credit/placement by examination:** CLEP, institutional tests. **Support services:** GED preparation, study skills assistance, tutoring.

Majors. **Computer sciences:** Security, web page design. **Engineering:** General, electrical. **Engineering technology:** Drafting. **Health:** Insurance specialist, office computer specialist. **Protective services:** Law enforcement admin.

Most popular majors. Computer/information sciences 73%, health sciences 27%.

Computing on campus. 2 workstations in library, computer center. Commuter students can connect to campus network. Online course registration, online library, helpline available.

Student life. **Freshman orientation:** Mandatory.

Student services. Financial aid counseling, placement for graduates. **Transfer:** Pre-admission transcript evaluation for new students.

Contact. Phone: (602) 279-9700 Toll-free number: (800) 832-4011
Fax: (602) 279-2999
Rhonda Rains, Director of Admissions, High-Tech Institute, 1515 East Indian School Road, Phoenix, AZ 85014-4901

International Institute of the Americas: Phoenix

Phoenix, Arizona
www.iia.edu
CB code: 2188

- Private 2-year business and health science college
- Commuter campus in very large city
- Interview required

General. Accredited by ACICS. Institution comprised of 5 campuses located in West Phoenix, Phoenix, Mesa, Tucson, and Albuquerque, New Mexico. **Enrollment:** 450 degree-seeking undergraduates. **Degrees:** 1 bachelor's, 2 associate awarded. **Calendar:** Continuous. **Full-time faculty:** 55 total; 36% have terminal degrees, 46% women. **Part-time faculty:** 40 total; 10% have terminal degrees, 40% women. **Special facilities:** Child activity centers for children of students.

Student profile. Among degree-seeking undergraduates, 228 enrolled as first-time, first-year students.

African American:	15%	**Native American:**	3%
Hispanic American:	32%		

Basis for selection. Open admission.

2006-2007 Annual costs. Tuition/fees (projected): $10,050. Tuition and fees may vary by program.

Financial aid. All financial aid based on need.

Application procedures. **Admission:** No deadline. No application fee. Application must be submitted on paper. Admission notification on a rolling basis. **Financial aid:** No deadline. FAFSA, institutional form required.

Academics. **Special study options:** Distance learning. Bachelor's degree programs available on campus. License preparation in nursing. **Credit/**

placement by examination: CLEP. **Support services:** GED preparation and test center, learning center.

Majors. Business: Accounting, business admin. **Health:** Health care admin, nursing (RN). **Legal studies:** Paralegal.

Computing on campus. 240 workstations in library, computer center. Commuter students can connect to campus network. Online library available.

Student life. Freshman orientation: Mandatory. **Policies:** Freshmen permitted cars on campus.

Student services. Career counseling, services for economically disadvantaged, student employment services, financial aid counseling, on-campus daycare, personal counseling, placement for graduates. **Transfer:** Special adviser, orientation, pre-admission transcript evaluation for new students.

Contact. E-mail: jpechota@iia.edu
Phone: (602) 242-6265 Toll-free number: (800) 793-2428
Fax: (602) 589-1348
John Pechota, Director of Admission, International Institute of the Americas: Phoenix, 6049 North 43rd Avenue, Phoenix, AZ 85019

Lamson College

Tempe, Arizona
www.lamsoncollege.com **CB code: 1899**

- For-profit 2-year junior and technical college
- Commuter campus in very large city
- Interview required

General. Founded in 1889. Accredited by ACICS. **Enrollment:** 300 degree-seeking undergraduates. **Degrees:** 55 associate awarded. **Calendar:** Quarter, extensive summer session.

Student profile. Among degree-seeking undergraduates, 100% enrolled in a vocational program.

Basis for selection. Open admission. **Adult students:** Entrance exam policies same as for first-time freshmen.

Financial aid. Need-based: Need-based aid available for part-time students.

Application procedures. Admission: No deadline. $25 fee. Application must be submitted on paper. Admission notification on a rolling basis. **Financial aid:** No deadline. FAFSA required. Applicants notified on a rolling basis.

Academics. Special study options: Independent study, internships. **Credit/placement by examination:** CLEP. **Support services:** Learning center, tutoring.

Majors. Business: Accounting, business admin. **Health:** Medical assistant. **Legal studies:** Paralegal.

Computing on campus. 73 workstations in library, computer center.

Student life. Freshman orientation: Mandatory.

Student services. Career counseling, student employment services, financial aid counseling, placement for graduates, veterans' counselor. **Transfer:** Special adviser, orientation, pre-admission transcript evaluation for new students.

Contact. E-mail: Lamsonadmissions@gryphoncolleges.edu
Phone: (480) 898-7000 Toll-free number: (800) 898-7017
Fax: (480) 967-6645
Al Frazier, Director of Admission, Lamson College, 1126 North Scottsdale Road, Suite 17, Tempe, AZ 85281-1700

Long Technical College

Phoenix, Arizona
www.longtechnicalcollege.com **CB code: 3052**

- For-profit 2-year technical college
- Very large city
- Interview required

General. Accredited by ACICS, ACCSCT. **Enrollment:** 400 degree-seeking undergraduates. **Degrees:** 111 associate awarded. **Calendar:** Continuous. **Full-time faculty:** 40 total.

Basis for selection. Open admission, but selective for some programs. Entrance exam (Wonderlic or CPAT) required.

2005-2006 Annual costs. Tuition and fees vary by degree program. Prices range from $9,515- $28,760.

Application procedures. Admission: No deadline. $25 fee.

Academics. Credit/placement by examination: CLEP. **Support services:** Learning center, tutoring.

Majors. Health: Respiratory therapy technology.

Student life. Freshman orientation: Available.

Contact. E-mail: mcrone@longtechnicalcollege.com
Phone: (602) 548-1955 ext. 1366 Toll-free number: (877) 548-1955 ext. 1366 Fax: (602) 548-1956
Glenn Sheppard, Director of Admissions, Long Technical College, 13450 North Black Canyon Highway, Suite 104, Phoenix, AZ 85029

Mesa Community College

Mesa, Arizona
www.mc.maricopa.edu **CB code: 4513**

- Public 2-year community college
- Commuter campus in very large city

General. Founded in 1965. Regionally accredited. Motorola University business and industry training for Motorola Corporation employees. **Enrollment:** 2,781 degree-seeking undergraduates. **Degrees:** 1,479 associate awarded. **ROTC:** Army, Navy, Air Force. **Location:** 5 miles from Phoenix. **Calendar:** Semester, extensive summer session. **Full-time faculty:** 318 total. **Part-time faculty:** 879 total. **Special facilities:** High technology laboratory/information commons.

Basis for selection. Open admission, but selective for some programs. General education requirements and minimum 2.5 GPA required for nursing, mortuary science, and fire academy.

2005-2006 Annual costs. Tuition/fees: $1,810; $7,750 out-of-state. Per-credit charge: $60 in-state; $258 out-of-state. Books/supplies: $500.

Financial aid. Non-need-based: Scholarships awarded for academics, athletics. **Additional information:** Awards available for Maricopa County residents.

Application procedures. Admission: No deadline. No application fee. Admission notification on a rolling basis. Diploma or GED required for applicants under 18. **Financial aid:** Priority date 5/1; no closing date. Institutional form required. Applicants notified on a rolling basis starting 7/1.

Academics. Associate of General Studies degree allows students to take half of credits in required courses, and dictate own program of electives. **Special study options:** Cooperative education, cross-registration, distance learning, dual enrollment of high school students, ESL, honors, independent study, internships, study abroad, weekend college. **Credit/placement by examination:** CLEP, IB, institutional tests. 30 credit hours maximum toward associate degree. **Support services:** Learning center, remedial instruction, tutoring.

Honors college/program. Honors courses open to all students with minimum 3.5 GPA.

Majors. Agriculture: Agribusiness operations, horticulture, landscaping. **Business:** Accounting, business admin, fashion, marketing, office management, office/clerical. **Communications:** Journalism. **Computer sciences:** General, applications programming, computer science, networking. **Education:** Teacher assistance. **Engineering:** General. **Engineering technology:** Architectural. **Family/consumer sciences:** Clothing/textiles, food/nutrition. **Health:** Nursing (RN). **Liberal arts:** Library assistant. **Visual/performing arts:** Interior design.

Computing on campus. 1,000 workstations in library, computer center, student center. Commuter students can connect to campus network. Online course registration, helpline available.

Student life. Freshman orientation: Available. **Housing:** Coed dorms, apartments available. Housing available at Williams campus. **Activities:** Jazz band, choral groups, dance, drama, music ensembles, musical theater, student government, student newspaper.

Athletics. NJCAA. **Intercollegiate:** Baseball M, basketball, cross-country, football (tackle) M, golf, gymnastics W, soccer, softball W, swimming M, track and field, volleyball W, wrestling M. **Intramural:** Basketball, bowling, cross-country, football (tackle) M, softball, track and field, volleyball, wrestling M. **Team name:** Thunderbirds.

Student services. Adult student services, career counseling, student employment services, on-campus daycare, personal counseling, placement for graduates, veterans' counselor. **Physically disabled:** Services for visually, speech, hearing impaired. **Transfer:** Special adviser for new students. Transfer adviser for students transferring to 4-year colleges.

Contact. E-mail: admissions@mc.maricipa.edu
Phone: (480) 461-7000 Fax: (480) 461-7805
Carol Petersen, Director of Admissions and Records, Mesa Community College, 1833 West Southern Avenue, Mesa, AZ 85202

Mohave Community College
Kingman, Arizona
www.mohave.edu **CB code: 0443**

- Public 2-year community college
- Commuter campus in large town

General. Founded in 1971. Regionally accredited. **Enrollment:** 2,690 degree-seeking undergraduates; 3,357 non-degree-seeking students. **Degrees:** 228 associate awarded. **Location:** 200 miles from Phoenix, 100 miles from Las Vegas. **Calendar:** Semester, limited summer session.

Student profile. Among degree-seeking undergraduates, 30% enrolled in a transfer program, 70% enrolled in a vocational program, 7% already have a bachelor's degree or higher, 501 enrolled as first-time, first-year students.

Part-time:	54%	**Asian American:**	2%
Women:	75%	**Hispanic American:**	9%
African American:	1%	**Native American:**	2%

Basis for selection. Open admission, but selective for some programs. Special requirements for nursing, dental hygiene and EMT/paramedic programs.

2006-2007 Annual costs. Tuition/fees (projected): $1,500; $4,500 out-of-state. Per-credit charge: $50 in-state; $150 out-of-state.

Financial aid. Need-based: Need-based aid available for part-time students. Work study available nights and for part-time students.

Application procedures. Admission: No deadline. No application fee. Application may be submitted online. **Financial aid:** Priority date 4/15; no closing date. FAFSA, institutional form required. Applicants notified on a rolling basis starting 5/1; must reply within 2 week(s) of notification.

Academics. Special study options: Distance learning, dual enrollment of high school students, ESL, independent study, internships, liberal arts/career combination, student-designed major. License preparation in dental hygiene, nursing, paramedic, real estate. **Credit/placement by examination:** CLEP, IB, institutional tests. 20 credit hours maximum toward associate degree. **Support services:** GED preparation and test center, learning center, reduced course load, remedial instruction, study skills assistance, tutoring.

Majors. Business: Administrative services, business admin. **Computer sciences:** General. **Education:** General. **Family/consumer sciences:** Child care. **Health:** Dental hygiene, nursing (RN). **Liberal arts:** Arts/sciences. **Mechanic/repair:** Automotive, heating/ac/refrig. **Protective services:** Firefighting, police science. **Visual/performing arts:** Metal/jewelry.

Computing on campus. 300 workstations in library, computer center. Online course registration, online library, helpline, wireless network available.

Student life. Freshman orientation: Available. Preregistration for classes offered. **Policies:** Freshmen permitted cars on campus. **Activities:** Bands, choral groups, dance, drama, music ensembles, musical theater, student government, symphony orchestra.

Student services. Adult student services, career counseling, student employment services, financial aid counseling, veterans' counselor. **Physically disabled:** Services for visually, speech, hearing impaired. **Transfer:** Special adviser, orientation for new students. Transfer adviser for students transferring to 4-year colleges.

Contact. E-mail: johwil@mohave.edu
Phone: (928) 757-0847 Toll-free number: (866) 664-2832
Fax: (928) 757-0808
John Wilson, Director of Admissions, Mohave Community College, 1971 Jagerson Avenue, Kingman, AZ 86409

Northland Pioneer College
Holbrook, Arizona
www.npc.edu **CB code: 0325**

- Public 2-year community college
- Commuter campus in small town

General. Founded in 1973. Regionally accredited. 10 locations in Navajo and Apache Counties. **Enrollment:** 1,500 degree-seeking undergraduates. **Degrees:** 151 associate awarded. **Location:** 200 miles from Phoenix, 90 miles from Flagstaff. **Calendar:** Semester, limited summer session. **Full-time faculty:** 58 total. **Part-time faculty:** 260 total.

Student profile.

Out-of-state:	2%	**Live on campus:**	1%

Transfer out. Colleges most students transferred to 2005: Northern Arizona University, University of Arizona, Arizona State University, Western New Mexico University, Brigham Young University.

Basis for selection. Open admission, but selective for some programs. Limited admission for nursing, criminal justice, and cosmetology.

2005-2006 Annual costs. Tuition/fees: $1,008; $6,600 out-of-state. Per-credit charge: $42 in-state; $72 out-of-state. Room only: $2,000. Books/supplies: $580. Personal expenses: $1,150.

Financial aid. Need-based: Need-based aid available for part-time students. Work study available nights, weekends and for part-time students. **Non-need-based:** Scholarships awarded for academics, art, job skills, leadership, minority status, music/drama, state residency.

Application procedures. Admission: No deadline. No application fee. Admission notification on a rolling basis. **Financial aid:** Priority date 6/1; no closing date. FAFSA, institutional form required. Applicants notified on a rolling basis starting 5/15; must reply within 2 week(s) of notification.

Academics. Special study options: Cooperative education, dual enrollment of high school students, honors, independent study. License preparation in nursing, paramedic, real estate. **Credit/placement by examination:** CLEP, IB, institutional tests. 52 credit hours maximum toward associate degree. **Support services:** Learning center, remedial instruction, tutoring.

Majors. Agriculture: Turf management. **Business:** General, accounting, administrative services, business admin. **Communications technology:** General. **Computer sciences:** General, computer graphics, data processing. **Construction:** Carpentry. **Engineering technology:** Electrical. **Family/consumer sciences:** Child care. **Health:** EMT paramedic, medical assistant, medical transcription, nursing (RN). **Interdisciplinary:** Biological/physical sciences. **Legal studies:** Court reporting, legal secretary, paralegal. **Liberal arts:** Arts/sciences, library assistant. **Personal/culinary services:** Cosmetic. **Protective services:** Corrections, criminal justice, firefighting, police science.

Computing on campus. 36 workstations in library, computer center.

Student life. Freshman orientation: Available. Preregistration for classes offered. **Housing:** Coed dorms available. $100 deposit, deadline 8/1. **Activities:** Jazz band, choral groups, drama, musical theater, student government, symphony orchestra, National Honor Society, Phi Theta Kappa.

Athletics. NJCAA. **Intercollegiate:** Basketball, golf, rodeo. **Team name:** Golden Eagles.

Student services. Career counseling, services for economically disadvantaged, student employment services, financial aid counseling, placement for graduates, veterans' counselor. **Physically disabled:** Services for visually impaired. **Transfer:** Special adviser for new students. Transfer adviser, college fairs on campus for students transferring to 4-year colleges.

Contact. E-mail: dsimper@npc.edu
Phone: (928) 536-6257 Toll-free number: (800) 266-7845
Fax: (928) 524-7612
David Simper, Director of Admissions, Northland Pioneer College, PO Box 610, Holbrook, AZ 86025-0610

Paradise Valley Community College

Phoenix, Arizona — **CB member**
www.pvc.maricopa.edu — **CB code: 2179**

- Public 2-year community college
- Commuter campus in very large city

General. Founded in 1985. Regionally accredited. **Enrollment:** 2,862 degree-seeking undergraduates; 5,535 non-degree-seeking students. **Degrees:** 340 associate awarded. **ROTC:** Army. **Calendar:** Semester, limited summer session. **Full-time faculty:** 92 total; 18% minority, 52% women. **Part-time faculty:** 275 total. **Special facilities:** Studio theater, performing arts center.

Student profile. Among degree-seeking undergraduates, 85% enrolled in a transfer program, 15% enrolled in a vocational program, 10% already have a bachelor's degree or higher, 296 transferred in from other institutions.

Part-time:	61%	**Asian American:**	3%
Out-of-state:	3%	**Hispanic American:**	10%
Women:	59%	**Native American:**	2%
African American:	3%	**25 or older:**	50%

Transfer out. Colleges most students transferred to 2005: Arizona State University, Arizona State University West, Northern Arizona University, University of Arizona.

Basis for selection. Open admission.

2005-2006 Annual costs. Tuition/fees: $1,810; $7,750 out-of-state. Per-credit charge: $60 in-state; $258 out-of-state. Books/supplies: $700. Personal expenses: $1,185.

Financial aid. Need-based: Need-based aid available for part-time students.

Application procedures. Admission: No deadline. No application fee. Admission notification on a rolling basis. **Financial aid:** No deadline. FAFSA required. Applicants notified on a rolling basis starting 6/1.

Academics. Special study options: Accelerated study, cooperative education, cross-registration, distance learning, ESL, honors, independent study, internships, teacher certification program, weekend college. License preparation in nursing, paramedic. **Credit/placement by examination:** AP, CLEP, institutional tests. 30 credit hours maximum toward associate degree. **Support services:** Learning center, remedial instruction, study skills assistance, tutoring, writing center.

Majors. Business: General, accounting, administrative services, international, office technology, office/clerical, organizational behavior. **Computer sciences:** General, word processing. **Engineering technology:** Hazardous materials. **Liberal arts:** Arts/sciences. **Visual/performing arts:** Music.

Computing on campus. 600 workstations in library, computer center, student center. Commuter students can connect to campus network. Online course registration, helpline available.

Student life. Freshman orientation: Available. **Activities:** Jazz band, choral groups, dance, drama, literary magazine, music ensembles, musical theater, opera, student government, student newspaper, Phi Theta Kappa, Student Christian Association, human service club, Returning Adults to Education, ECO Watch (environmental club), Latter Day Saints Student Association, international student club, recreational outdoor club.

Athletics. NJCAA. **Intercollegiate:** Cross-country, golf, soccer, tennis, track and field. **Team name:** Pumas.

Student services. Adult student services, career counseling, student employment services, financial aid counseling, minority student services, on-campus daycare, personal counseling, placement for graduates, veterans' counselor. **Physically disabled:** Services for visually, speech, hearing impaired. **Transfer:** Special adviser, orientation for new students. Transfer adviser, college fairs on campus for students transferring to 4-year colleges.

Contact. Phone: (602) 787-7020 Fax: (602) 787-6625
Shirley Green, Associate Dean Student Services, Paradise Valley Community College, 18401 North 32nd Street, Phoenix, AZ 85032

Paralegal Institute

Phoenix, Arizona
www.theparalegalinstitute.com — **CB code: 3888**

- For-profit 2-year community college
- Very large city

General. Accredited by DETC. **Enrollment:** 500 undergraduates. **Calendar:** Continuous.

Basis for selection. Open admission.

2006-2007 Annual costs. Tuition for certificate and diploma programs range from $2,175-$2,250 associate degree programs are $3600.

Application procedures. Admission: No deadline. No application fee. Application must be submitted on paper.

Academics. Credit/placement by examination: CLEP.

Majors. Legal studies: Paralegal.

Contact. E-mail: paralegalinst@mindspring.com
Phone: (602) 212-0501 Toll-free number: (800) 354-1254
Fax: (602) 212-0502
Paralegal Institute, 2933 West Indian School Road, Drawer 11408, Phoenix, AZ 85061-1408

Phoenix College

Phoenix, Arizona
www.pc.maricopa.edu — **CB code: 4606**

- Public 2-year community college
- Commuter campus in very large city

General. Founded in 1920. Regionally accredited. **Enrollment:** 12,200 undergraduates. **Degrees:** 822 associate awarded. **ROTC:** Army, Air Force. **Calendar:** Semester, limited summer session. **Full-time faculty:** 146 total. **Part-time faculty:** 450 total.

Student profile.

Out-of-state:	2%	**25 or older:**	53%

Basis for selection. Open admission, but selective for some programs. ASSET, COMPASS and Celsa test scores used for placement.

2005-2006 Annual costs. Tuition/fees: $1,810; $7,750 out-of-state. Per-credit charge: $60 in-state; $258 out-of-state. Books/supplies: $700. Personal expenses: $3,654.

Financial aid. Need-based: Work study available weekends.

Application procedures. Admission: No deadline. No application fee. Application may be submitted online. Admission notification on a rolling basis. **Financial aid:** Priority date 6/30; no closing date. FAFSA required. Applicants notified on a rolling basis starting 5/1.

Academics. Special study options: Cooperative education, cross-registration, distance learning, dual enrollment of high school students, ESL, honors, independent study, internships, liberal arts/career combination, study abroad. License preparation in nursing. **Credit/placement by examination:** CLEP, institutional tests. 30 credit hours maximum toward associate degree. **Support services:** GED test center, learning center, reduced course load, remedial instruction, tutoring.

Honors college/program. Requires 3.0 GPA.

Majors. Architecture: Interior. **Business:** General, accounting, banking/financial services, business admin, management information systems, management science, marketing, tourism promotion, tourism/travel. **Communications:** General. **Computer sciences:** General, computer graphics, information systems. **Education:** General, family/consumer sciences. **Engineering:** General, software. **Engineering technology:** Civil. **Family/consumer sciences:** General, child care, institutional food production. **Foreign languages:** Sign language interpretation. **Health:** Clinical lab science, dental assistant, dental hygiene, EMT paramedic, medical records technology, medical transcription, nursing (RN), premedicine. **Legal studies:** Legal secretary, paralegal. **Liberal arts:** Arts/sciences. **Physical sciences:** Chemistry. **Protective services:** Firefighting, police science. **Visual/performing arts:** Art, commercial/advertising art, interior design.

Student life. Freshman orientation: Available. Preregistration for classes offered. **Activities:** Bands, choral groups, dance, drama, music ensembles, musical theater, opera, student newspaper, symphony orchestra, TV station.

Athletics. NJCAA. **Intercollegiate:** Baseball M, basketball, cross-country, football (tackle) M, golf M, soccer M, softball W, tennis, track and field, volleyball W. **Team name:** PC Bears.

Student services. Adult student services, career counseling, services for economically disadvantaged, student employment services, legal services, on-campus daycare, personal counseling, placement for graduates, veterans' counselor. **Physically disabled:** Services for visually, speech, hearing impaired. **Transfer:** Special adviser, orientation, re-entry adviser, pre-admission transcript evaluation for new students. Transfer adviser, college fairs on campus for students transferring to 4-year colleges.

Contact. Phone: (602) 285-7502 Fax: (602) 285-7813
Mary Blackwell, Director of Admissions, Phoenix College, 1202 West Thomas Road, Phoenix, AZ 85013

Pima Community College

Tucson, Arizona — **CB member**
www.pima.edu — **CB code: 4623**

- Public 2-year community and technical college
- Commuter campus in very large city

General. Founded in 1966. Regionally accredited. 6 campuses, 3 centers and Public Safety Institute serve Tucson metropolitan area. **Enrollment:** 25,145 degree-seeking undergraduates; 5,739 non-degree-seeking students. **Degrees:** 1,835 associate awarded. **ROTC:** Army, Navy, Air Force. **Calendar:** Semester, limited summer session. **Full-time faculty:** 300 total; 25% minority, 55% women. **Part-time faculty:** 1,067 total. **Special facilities:** Arts center.

Student profile. Among degree-seeking undergraduates, 47% enrolled in a transfer program, 23% enrolled in a vocational program, 4% already have a bachelor's degree or higher, 5,456 enrolled as first-time, first-year students.

Part-time:	67%	**Hispanic American:**	31%
Out-of-state:	5%	**Native American:**	3%
Women:	58%	**International:**	1%
African American:	4%	**25 or older:**	41%
Asian American:	3%		

Transfer out. Colleges most students transferred to 2005: University of Arizona, Arizona State University, Northern Arizona University, University of Phoenix.

Basis for selection. Open admission, but selective for some programs. Special requirements for nursing, dental hygiene, and pharmacy technology.

2005-2006 Annual costs. Tuition/fees: $1,405; $6,565 out-of-state. Per-credit charge: $44 in-state; $74 out-of-state. Books/supplies: $720. Personal expenses: $2,734.

Financial aid. Need-based: Need-based aid available for part-time students. **Non-need-based:** Scholarships awarded for academics, alumni affiliation, art, athletics, minority status, music/drama.

Application procedures. Admission: No deadline. No application fee. Application may be submitted online. Admission notification on a rolling basis. **Financial aid:** Priority date 3/15; no closing date. FAFSA required. Applicants notified on a rolling basis starting 7/1; must reply within 2 week(s) of notification.

Academics. Special study options: Accelerated study, cooperative education, distance learning, double major, dual enrollment of high school students, ESL, honors, independent study, internships, student-designed major, teacher certification program, weekend college. License preparation in dental hygiene, nursing, radiology. **Credit/placement by examination:** AP, CLEP, institutional tests. 30 credit hours maximum toward associate degree. **Support services:** GED preparation and test center, learning center, remedial instruction, study skills assistance, tutoring.

Majors. Area/ethnic studies: Native American. **Business:** Accounting, administrative services, banking/financial services, business admin, hospitality admin, international, management information systems, real estate, tourism/travel. **Computer sciences:** General, networking, systems analysis. **Construction:** Maintenance. **Education:** Early childhood. **Engineering technology:** Drafting, electrical. **Foreign languages:** Sign language interpretation. **Health:** Dental hygiene, dental lab technology, EMT paramedic, medical radiologic technology/radiation therapy, medical records technology, nursing (RN), pharmacy assistant, respiratory therapy technology, substance abuse counseling, veterinary technology/assistant. **Legal studies:** Paralegal. **Liberal arts:** Arts/sciences. **Mechanic/repair:** Aircraft, automotive, electronics/electrical. **Personal/culinary services:** Culinary arts. **Protective services:** Criminal justice, firefighting, police science. **Social sciences:** Anthropology, political science, sociology. **Visual/performing arts:** Art, design, dramatic.

Most popular majors. Business/marketing 12%, health sciences 16%, liberal arts 54%.

Computing on campus. 1,500 workstations in library, computer center. Commuter students can connect to campus network.

Student life. Freshman orientation: Mandatory. Orientation programs based on majors. **Policies:** Freshmen permitted cars on campus. **Activities:** Bands, choral groups, dance, drama, literary magazine, music ensembles, student government, student newspaper, TV station, forensics activities, speech communication program, clubs for different groups such as Native American or Hispanic student clubs.

Athletics. NJCAA. **Intercollegiate:** Baseball M, basketball, cross-country, football (tackle) M, golf, soccer, softball W, tennis, track and field, volleyball W. **Intramural:** Badminton, baseball M, basketball, cross-country, football (non-tackle) M, golf, racquetball, tennis, track and field, volleyball. **Team name:** Aztecs.

Student services. Career counseling, student employment services, health services, minority student services, on-campus daycare, personal counseling, placement for graduates, veterans' counselor. **Physically disabled:** Services for visually, speech, hearing impaired. **Transfer:** Special adviser, orientation for new students. Transfer adviser, college fairs on campus for students transferring to 4-year colleges.

Contact. E-mail: coadmit@pima.edu
Phone: (520) 206-4640 Fax: (520) 206-4790
Wendy Kilgore, Enrollment Services/Registrar, Pima Community College, 4905B East Broadway, Tucson, AZ 85709-1120

Refrigeration School

Phoenix, Arizona
www.refrigerationschool.com — **CB code: 2888**

- For-profit 1-year technical college
- Very large city

General. Accredited by ACCSCT. **Enrollment:** 40 degree-seeking undergraduates. **Degrees:** 40 associate awarded. **Calendar:** 3, 6 or 8 month programs. **Full-time faculty:** 12 total. **Part-time faculty:** 14 total.

Basis for selection. Open admission.

2005-2006 Annual costs. Tuition varies by program and ranges from $6,500 to $16,500.

Application procedures. Admission: No deadline. No application fee.

Academics. Credit/placement by examination: CLEP.

Majors. Engineering technology: Energy systems.

Contact. Phone: (602) 275-7133 Fax: (602) 267-4805
Mary Simmons, Admissions Director, Refrigeration School, 4210 East Washington Street, Phoenix, AZ 85034-1816

Remington College: Tempe

Tempe, Arizona
CB code: 3459

- Private 2-year technical college
- Large city

General. Accredited by ACICS. **Calendar:** Quarter.

Annual costs/financial aid. $31,490 total costs for each associate degree program offered. $11,730 for the diploma programs.

Contact. Phone: (480) 834-1000
Director of Recruitment, 875 West Elliot Road, Suite 126, Tempe, AZ 85284

Rio Salado College

Tempe, Arizona — **CB member**
www.riosalado.edu — **CB code: 0997**

- Public 2-year virtual community college
- Commuter campus in very large city

General. Founded in 1978. Regionally accredited. Access to libraries at Arizona State University and 10 Maricopa County community colleges. Agreement with Army allows military personnel to take Internet courses. Online

Nursing and Clinical Dental Assisting programs. **Enrollment:** 16,604 undergraduates. **Degrees:** 260 associate awarded. **Location:** 120 miles from Tucson, 10 miles from Phoenix. **Calendar:** Semester, extensive summer session. **Full-time faculty:** 29 total. **Part-time faculty:** 1,053 total. **Special facilities:** Public radio stations.

Student profile.

Out-of-state:	3.5%	**25 or older:**	46%

Transfer out. Colleges most students transferred to 2005: Arizona State University, University of Arizona, Northern Arizona University.

Basis for selection. Open admission, but selective for some programs. GPA requirements for dental hygiene program.

2006-2007 Annual costs. Tuition/fees (projected): $1,810; $7,750 out-of-state. Per-credit charge: $60 in-state; $258 out-of-state. Books/supplies: $1,024. Personal expenses: $2,454.

2004-2005 Financial aid. All financial aid based on need. 32% of total undergraduate aid awarded as scholarships/grants, 68% as loans/jobs. Need-based aid available for part-time students.

Application procedures. Admission: No deadline. No application fee. Application may be submitted online. Admission notification on a rolling basis. **Financial aid:** Priority date 6/30; no closing date. FAFSA, institutional form required. Applicants notified on a rolling basis starting 6/30.

Academics. Special study options: Accelerated study, combined bachelor's/graduate degree, cooperative education, cross-registration, distance learning, double major, dual enrollment of high school students, ESL, honors, independent study, internships, liberal arts/career combination, weekend college. License preparation in dental hygiene. **Credit/placement by examination:** AP, CLEP, institutional tests. 30 credit hours maximum toward associate degree. Placement testing required for students taking English, reading, and mathematics courses. **Support services:** GED preparation, learning center, remedial instruction, study skills assistance, tutoring, writing center.

Majors. Business: General, accounting, banking/financial services, business admin, international, office management. **Computer sciences:** General. **Engineering technology:** Water quality. **Health:** Dental hygiene, nursing assistant, substance abuse counseling. **Protective services:** Law enforcement admin. **Public administration:** General.

Computing on campus. 750 workstations in computer center. Commuter students can connect to campus network. Online course registration, online library, helpline, wireless network available.

Student life. Policies: Freshmen permitted cars on campus. **Activities:** Radio station, Phi Theta Kappa.

Student services. Adult student services, career counseling, student employment services, financial aid counseling, personal counseling, veterans' counselor. **Physically disabled:** Services for visually, speech, hearing impaired. **Transfer:** Special adviser, re-entry adviser, pre-admission transcript evaluation for new students. Transfer adviser for students transferring to 4-year colleges.

Contact. E-mail: admissions@email.rio.maricopa.edu
Phone: (480) 517-8150 Toll-free number: (800) 729-1197
Fax: (480) 517-8199
Ruby Miller, Director of Registration and Records, Rio Salado College, 2323 West 14th Street, Tempe, AZ 85281

Scottsdale Community College

Scottsdale, Arizona
www.sc.maricopa.edu **CB code: 4755**

- Public 2-year community college
- Commuter campus in small city

General. Founded in 1969. Regionally accredited. **Enrollment:** 3,168 degree-seeking undergraduates. **Degrees:** 784 associate awarded. **Location:** 10 miles from Tempe. **Calendar:** Semester, limited summer session. **Full-time faculty:** 167 total; 23% have terminal degrees, 13% minority, 46% women. **Part-time faculty:** 477 total; 6% have terminal degrees, 10% minority, 51% women. **Class size:** 57% < 20, 41% 20-39, 1% 40-49, 1% 50-99, less than 1% >100. **Special facilities:** Student-operated restaurant associated with school of culinary arts.

Student profile. Among degree-seeking undergraduates, 28% enrolled in a transfer program, 46% enrolled in a vocational program, 7% already have a bachelor's degree or higher.

Out-of-state:	5%	**25 or older:**	46%

Basis for selection. Open admission.

High school preparation. 16 units recommended. Recommended units include English 4, mathematics 4, social studies 2, history 1, science 3 and foreign language 2.

2005-2006 Annual costs. Tuition/fees: $1,810; $7,750 out-of-state. Per-credit charge: $60 in-state; $258 out-of-state. Books/supplies: $848. Personal expenses: $4,194.

2004-2005 Financial aid. Need-based: 35% of total undergraduate aid awarded as scholarships/grants, 65% as loans/jobs. **Non-need-based:** Scholarships awarded for academics, athletics. **Additional information:** Athletic scholarships offered in rodeo. All athletic scholarships limited to county residents.

Application procedures. Admission: No deadline. No application fee. Application may be submitted online. Admission notification on a rolling basis. **Financial aid:** Priority date 6/30; no closing date. FAFSA, institutional form required. Applicants notified on a rolling basis starting 4/1; must reply by 7/15 or within 3 week(s) of notification.

Academics. Special study options: Cooperative education, cross-registration, distance learning, dual enrollment of high school students, ESL, honors, internships, study abroad. **Credit/placement by examination:** AP, CLEP, institutional tests. 52 credit hours maximum toward associate degree. **Support services:** Learning center, remedial instruction, tutoring, writing center.

Majors. Agriculture: Equestrian studies. **Architecture:** Environmental design. **Area/ethnic studies:** Native American. **Business:** General, accounting, administrative services, fashion, hospitality admin, international, management information systems, retailing. **Communications:** Public relations. **Computer sciences:** General, information systems. **Education:** Early childhood. **Family/consumer sciences:** Child care. **Health:** EMT paramedic, medical radiologic technology/radiation therapy, nursing (RN). **Personal/culinary services:** Culinary arts. **Protective services:** Criminal justice, firefighting, law enforcement admin. **Visual/performing arts:** Cinematography, interior design.

Most popular majors. Business/marketing 6%, communication technologies 6%, health sciences 20%, liberal arts 42%, visual/performing arts 6%.

Computing on campus. 600 workstations in library, computer center, student center. Commuter students can connect to campus network. Online course registration, online library, helpline available.

Student life. Freshman orientation: Available. Preregistration for classes offered. **Activities:** Bands, choral groups, dance, drama, music ensembles, student government, student newspaper, symphony orchestra, TV station.

Athletics. NAIA, NJCAA. **Intercollegiate:** Baseball M, basketball, cross-country, football (tackle) M, golf M, soccer M, softball W, tennis, track and field, volleyball W. **Intramural:** Baseball M. **Team name:** Artichokes.

Student services. Adult student services, alcohol/substance abuse counseling, career counseling, student employment services, financial aid counseling, on-campus daycare, personal counseling, placement for graduates, veterans' counselor. **Physically disabled:** Services for visually, speech, hearing impaired. **Transfer:** Special adviser, orientation for new students. Transfer adviser, college fairs on campus for students transferring to 4-year colleges.

Contact. E-mail: admissions@sccmail.maricopa.edu
Phone: (480) 423-6100 Fax: (480) 423-6200
Fran Watkins, Director of Admissions and Records, Scottsdale Community College, 9000 East Chaparral Road, Scottsdale, AZ 85256-2626

Scottsdale Culinary Institute

Scottsdale, Arizona
www.scichefs.com **CB code: 3028**

- Private 2-year art and technical college
- Commuter campus in large city

General. Accredited by ACCSCT. **Location:** 2 miles from downtown. **Calendar:** Continuous.

Annual costs/financial aid. Tuition and fees vary by degree and by program. Total costs of program (including fees): certificate programs start at $20,295; Associate degree programs start at $30,695; Bachelor's degree programs start at $59,095. Books/supplies: $910. Personal expenses: $2,275.

Contact. Phone: (480) 990-3773
Director of Admissions, 8100 East Camelback Road, Suite 1001, Scottsdale, AZ 85251

South Mountain Community College

Phoenix, Arizona
www.smc.maricopa.edu **CB code: 4734**

- Public 2-year community college
- Commuter campus in very large city

General. Founded in 1979. Regionally accredited. Learning Center in Guadalupe, Arizona. Arizona Agribusiness Equine Charter. **Enrollment:** 4,295 undergraduates. **Degrees:** 259 associate awarded. **Location:** 8 miles from downtown Phoenix. **Calendar:** Semester, limited summer session. **Full-time faculty:** 52 total. **Part-time faculty:** 125 total. **Partnerships:** Agribusiness charter school on campus.

Student profile.

Out-of-state:	2%	**25 or older:**	45%

Basis for selection. Open admission.

2005-2006 Annual costs. Tuition/fees: $1,810; $7,750 out-of-state. Per-credit charge: $60 in-state; $258 out-of-state. Books/supplies: $760. Personal expenses: $1,250.

Financial aid. Need-based: Need-based aid available for part-time students. Work study available nights, weekends and for part-time students. **Non-need-based:** Scholarships awarded for academics, athletics, minority status, music/drama.

Application procedures. Admission: No deadline. No application fee. Application may be submitted online. Admission notification on a rolling basis. **Financial aid:** Priority date 5/1; no closing date. FAFSA required. Applicants notified on a rolling basis starting 5/15; must reply within 3 week(s) of notification.

Academics. Special study options: Cooperative education, cross-registration, dual enrollment of high school students, ESL, honors, independent study. **Credit/placement by examination:** CLEP, IB, institutional tests. 30 credit hours maximum toward associate degree. ASSET used for placement in math, reading, and English. **Support services:** GED preparation and test center, learning center, remedial instruction, tutoring.

Majors. Biology: General. **Business:** Administrative services, business admin, international, logistics, office technology. **Computer sciences:** General, information systems, security, system admin, systems analysis. **Education:** General, early childhood, music, physical. **Engineering technology:** Software. **Family/consumer sciences:** General. **History:** General. **Liberal arts:** Arts/sciences. **Math:** General. **Physical sciences:** General, chemistry, physics. **Psychology:** General. **Social sciences:** Political science, sociology. **Visual/performing arts:** Art, music.

Most popular majors. Computer/information sciences 6%, liberal arts 83%.

Computing on campus. 125 workstations in library, computer center.

Student life. Freshman orientation: Available. **Activities:** Concert band, choral groups, dance, drama, music ensembles, student government, student newspaper, African-American Unity Coalition, Society of Hispanic Engineers and Scientists, Christian Student Club, Star Native American Club, forensic club, music club, volunteers program, Phi Theta Kappa.

Athletics. NJCAA. **Intercollegiate:** Baseball M, basketball, golf, soccer M, softball W, tennis, volleyball W. **Team name:** Cougars.

Student services. Career counseling, student employment services, on-campus daycare, personal counseling, veterans' counselor. **Transfer:** Special adviser, orientation, re-entry adviser, pre-admission transcript evaluation for new students. Transfer adviser, college fairs on campus for students transferring to 4-year colleges.

Contact. Phone: (602) 243-8123 Fax: (602) 243-8199
Tony Bracamonte, Associate Dean of Student Services, South Mountain Community College, 7050 South 24th Street, Phoenix, AZ 85042

Tohono O'odham Community College

Sells, Arizona
www.tocc.cc.az.us

- Public 2-year community college
- Commuter campus in rural community

General. Enrollment: 52 degree-seeking undergraduates. **Degrees:** 12 associate awarded. **Location:** 60 miles from Tucson. **Calendar:** Semester, limited summer session. **Full-time faculty:** 15 total; 13% have terminal degrees. **Part-time faculty:** 15 total.

Student profile. Among degree-seeking undergraduates, 14% enrolled in a transfer program, 22% enrolled in a vocational program, 112 enrolled as first-time, first-year students, 46 transferred in from other institutions.

Basis for selection. Open admission. **Homeschooled:** Transcript of courses and grades, state high school equivalency certificate required.

2005-2006 Annual costs. Tuition/fees: $1,270; $6,340 out-of-state. Per-credit charge: $42 in-state; $72 out-of-state.

2004-2005 Financial aid. All financial aid based on need. 11 full-time freshmen applied for aid; 11 were judged to have need; 11 of these received aid. Average scholarship/grant was $4,050. 97% of total undergraduate aid awarded as scholarships/grants, 3% as loans/jobs. Need-based aid available for part-time students. Work study available for part-time students.

Application procedures. Admission: $15 fee. **Financial aid:** No deadline. FAFSA, institutional form required. Applicants notified on a rolling basis.

Academics. Special study options: Distance learning, independent study. **Credit/placement by examination:** CLEP. **Support services:** GED preparation, learning center, remedial instruction, study skills assistance, tutoring, writing center.

Majors. Business: Business admin. **Computer sciences:** System admin. **Construction:** Carpentry, electrician, painting, plumbing. **Education:** Early childhood special. **Liberal arts:** Arts/sciences. **Social sciences:** General.

Student life. Freshman orientation: Mandatory. Preregistration for classes offered. Orientation class offers information on student services and academic support services. **Policies:** Freshmen permitted cars on campus. **Activities:** Student government.

Student services. Adult student services, career counseling, student employment services, financial aid counseling, personal counseling, placement for graduates. **Transfer:** Special adviser, orientation, re-entry adviser, pre-admission transcript evaluation for new students. College fairs on campus for students transferring to 4-year colleges.

Contact. E-mail: lluna@tocc.cc.az.us
Phone: (520) 383-8401 ext. 35 Fax: (520) 383-0029
Leslie Luna, Registar, Tohono O'odham Community College, P.O. Box 3129, Sells, AZ 85634-3129

Universal Technical Institute

Avondale, Arizona
www.uticorp.com **CB code: 2504**

- For-profit 2-year technical college
- Commuter campus in large town

General. Founded in 1965. Accredited by ACCSCT. **Enrollment:** 2,840 degree-seeking undergraduates. **Degrees:** 1,485 associate awarded. **Location:** 17 miles from Phoenix, 11 miles from Glendale. **Calendar:** Continuous, extensive summer session.

Student profile. Among degree-seeking undergraduates, 100% enrolled in a vocational program.

Basis for selection. Open admission. **Homeschooled:** Must pass the Wonderlic Scholastic Level Exam.

2005-2006 Annual costs. Tuition varies by program and by campus and ranges from $20,000 -$32,900.

Application procedures. Admission: No deadline. No application fee. Admission notification on a rolling basis. **Financial aid:** No deadline. FAFSA required.

Academics. Special study options: Distance learning. **Credit/placement by examination:** AP, CLEP. **Support services:** Tutoring.

Majors. Mechanic/repair: Automotive, diesel.

Student life. Freshman orientation: Mandatory.

Student services. Career counseling, services for economically disadvantaged, student employment services, financial aid counseling, veterans' counselor.

Contact. E-mail: info@uticorp.com
Phone: (623) 245-4600 Toll-free number: (800) 859-1202
Fax: (602) 245-4601
Melissa Maclee, Campus Admissions Director, Universal Technical Institute, 10695 West Pierce Street, Avondale, AZ 85323

Yavapai College

Prescott, Arizona
www.yc.edu **CB code: 4996**

- Public 2-year community college
- Commuter campus in large town

General. Founded in 1966. Regionally accredited. Classes offered at branch campus in Clarkdale and several locations in Yavapai County. **Enrollment:** 4,035 degree-seeking undergraduates; 3,387 non-degree-seeking students. **Degrees:** 304 associate awarded. **ROTC:** Army, Air Force. **Location:** 100 miles from Phoenix. **Calendar:** Semester, limited summer session. **Full-time faculty:** 102 total; 4% minority, 49% women. **Part-time faculty:** 393 total; 5% minority, 47% women. **Class size:** 78% < 20, 21% 20-39, less than 1% 40-49. **Special facilities:** Solar laboratory, solar greenhouse, performance hall.

Student profile. Among degree-seeking undergraduates, 672 enrolled as first-time, first-year students.

Part-time:	69%	**Hispanic American:**	7%
Out-of-state:	6%	**Native American:**	4%
Women:	61%	**25 or older:**	24%
African American:	1%	**Live on campus:**	10%
Asian American:	1%		

Transfer out. 80% of students enrolled in the transfer program go on to 4-year colleges. **Colleges most students transferred to 2005:** Arizona State University, Northern Arizona University, University of Arizona, Old Dominion University.

Basis for selection. Open admission, but selective for some programs. Limited admission for registered nursing, gunsmithing, and independent filmmaking. Interview required of nursing majors. Essay for independent filmmaking.

2005-2006 Annual costs. Tuition/fees: $1,320; $7,120 out-of-state. Per-credit charge: $44 in-state; $237 out-of-state. Room/board: $4,940. Books/supplies: $800. Personal expenses: $1,500.

Financial aid. Need-based: Need-based aid available for part-time students. **Non-need-based:** Scholarships awarded for academics, athletics.

Application procedures. Admission: No deadline. No application fee. Application may be submitted online. Admission notification on a rolling basis. **Financial aid:** Priority date 4/15; no closing date. FAFSA required. Applicants notified on a rolling basis.

Academics. Special study options: Accelerated study, distance learning, dual enrollment of high school students, ESL, honors, independent study, internships, liberal arts/career combination, teacher certification program, weekend college. 2-2 program with Northern Arizona University for bachelor degree in education and business, program with Old Dominion University offering bachelor degree completion. Bachelor's degree programs available on campus. License preparation in nursing, paramedic, real estate. **Credit/placement by examination:** AP, CLEP, IB, institutional tests. 30 credit hours maximum toward associate degree. **Support services:** GED preparation and test center, learning center, pre-admission summer program, reduced course load, remedial instruction, study skills assistance, tutoring, writing center.

Majors. Agriculture: Business. **Architecture:** Environmental design. **Business:** Accounting, administrative services, business admin, office management, office technology. **Computer sciences:** General. **Construction:** Maintenance. **Education:** Early childhood. **Engineering technology:** Manufacturing. **Health:** Medical secretary, nursing (RN). **Legal studies:** Legal secretary, paralegal. **Liberal arts:** Arts/sciences. **Mechanic/repair:** Automotive, gunsmithing. **Protective services:** Firefighting, law enforcement admin. **Visual/performing arts:** Commercial/advertising art, industrial design.

Computing on campus. 677 workstations in dormitories, library, computer center. Dormitories wired for high-speed internet access and linked to campus network. Online course registration, online library available.

Student life. Freshman orientation: Available. Preregistration for classes offered. **Policies:** Freshmen permitted cars on campus. **Housing:** Coed dorms, special housing for disabled, substance-free housing available. $150 deposit. **Activities:** Bands, choral groups, dance, drama, literary magazine, music ensembles, musical theater, student government, student newspaper, nursing association, Native American club, international student club, Hispanic Club, Campus Crusade for Christ, Bahai Club, PTK, Veterans' Club.

Athletics. NJCAA. **Intercollegiate:** Baseball M, basketball, cross-country W, soccer M, volleyball W. **Team name:** Roughriders.

Student services. Adult student services, career counseling, student employment services, financial aid counseling, health services, personal counseling, placement for graduates, veterans' counselor. **Physically disabled:** Services for visually, hearing impaired. **Transfer:** Special adviser, orientation for new students. College fairs on campus for students transferring to 4-year colleges.

Contact. E-mail: registration@yc.edu
Phone: (928) 445-7300 ext. 2148 Toll-free number: (800) 922-6787
Fax: (928) 776-2151
David Van Ness, Registrar, Yavapai College, 1100 East Sheldon Street, Prescott, AZ 86301

Arkansas

Arkansas Northeastern College

Blytheville, Arkansas
www.anc.edu **CB code: 1267**

- Public 2-year community college
- Commuter campus in large town

General. Founded in 1974. Regionally accredited. **Enrollment:** 1,559 degree-seeking undergraduates; 271 non-degree-seeking students. **Degrees:** 253 associate awarded. **Location:** 65 miles from Memphis, Tennessee. **Calendar:** Semester, limited summer session. **Full-time faculty:** 73 total; 6% have terminal degrees, 7% minority, 71% women. **Part-time faculty:** 100 total; 3% have terminal degrees, 16% minority, 66% women. **Class size:** 66% < 20, 32% 20-39, less than 1% 40-49, 1% 50-99. **Partnerships:** Formal partnership with Tech Prep for business and technical courses.

Student profile. Among degree-seeking undergraduates, 40% enrolled in a transfer program, 45% enrolled in a vocational program, 1% already have a bachelor's degree or higher, 370 enrolled as first-time, first-year students, 110 transferred in from other institutions.

Part-time:	41%	**Asian American:**	1%
Out-of-state:	18%	**Hispanic American:**	1%
Women:	70%	**25 or older:**	50%
African American:	30%		

Transfer out. 20% of students enrolled in the transfer program go on to 4-year colleges. **Colleges most students transferred to 2005:** Arkansas State University, Southeast Missouri State University.

Basis for selection. Open admission, but selective for some programs. Entrance exam required for nursing program. **Adult students:** Entrance exam policies same as for first-time freshmen.

High school preparation. Recommended units include English 4, mathematics 4, social studies 1, history 2, science 3 (laboratory 3).

2005-2006 Annual costs. Tuition/fees: $1,610; $1,910 out-of-district; $3,410 out-of-state. Per-credit charge: $47 in-district; $57 out-of-district; $107 out-of-state. Books/supplies: $595. Personal expenses: $3,747.

2005-2006 Financial aid. Need-based: 290 full-time freshmen applied for aid; 267 were judged to have need; 253 of these received aid. Average need met was 40%. Average scholarship/grant was $1,889; average loan $1,589. 85% of total undergraduate aid awarded as scholarships/grants, 15% as loans/jobs. Need-based aid available for part-time students. Work study available nights and for part-time students. **Non-need-based:** Awarded to 31 full-time undergraduates, including 18 freshmen. Scholarships awarded for academics, minority status, music/drama, state residency.

Application procedures. Admission: No deadline. No application fee. Admission notification on a rolling basis. **Financial aid:** Priority date 4/15; no closing date. FAFSA, institutional form required. Applicants notified on a rolling basis starting 5/1; must reply within 2 week(s) of notification.

Academics. Special study options: Distance learning, double major, dual enrollment of high school students, weekend college. Bachelor's degree programs available on campus. License preparation in nursing, paramedic. **Credit/placement by examination:** CLEP, institutional tests. 15 credit hours maximum toward associate degree. Placement tests required for algebra, English composition. **Support services:** GED preparation and test center, learning center, reduced course load, remedial instruction, study skills assistance, tutoring, writing center.

Majors. Agriculture: Food science, horticulture. **Business:** General, administrative services, management information systems. **Education:** Middle. **Engineering technology:** Metallurgical. **Health:** Nursing (RN). **Liberal arts:** Arts/sciences. **Mechanic/repair:** Industrial. **Protective services:** Police science.

Most popular majors. Business/marketing 12%, education 8%, health sciences 12%, liberal arts 58%.

Computing on campus. 400 workstations in library, computer center. Commuter students can connect to campus network. Online library available.

Student life. Freshman orientation: Available. Preregistration for classes offered. **Policies:** Freshmen permitted cars on campus. **Activities:** Choral groups, music ensembles, student newspaper, Cultural Diversity Association, Baptist College Ministry, Adult Student Association.

Student services. Adult student services, career counseling, services for economically disadvantaged, student employment services, financial aid counseling, on-campus daycare, personal counseling, placement for graduates, veterans' counselor. **Physically disabled:** Services for visually, speech, hearing impaired. **Transfer:** Special adviser, orientation, pre-admission transcript evaluation for new students. Transfer adviser, college fairs on campus for students transferring to 4-year colleges.

Contact. E-mail: jwalters@anc.edu
Phone: (870) 762-1020 ext. 1114 Fax: (870) 763-1654
June Walters, Vice President for Student Services and Registrar, Arkansas Northeastern College, Box 1109, Blytheville, AR 72316-1109

Arkansas State University: Beebe

Beebe, Arkansas
www.asub.edu **CB code: 0782**

- Public 2-year branch campus and community college
- Commuter campus in small town

General. Founded in 1927. Regionally accredited. Approved as Serviceman's Opportunity College. **Enrollment:** 3,200 degree-seeking undergraduates. **Degrees:** 469 associate awarded. **Location:** 35 miles from Little Rock. **Calendar:** Semester, extensive summer session. **Full-time faculty:** 100 total. **Part-time faculty:** 85 total.

Student profile.

Out-of-state:	1%	**Live on campus:**	4%

Basis for selection. Open admission.

High school preparation. 15 units recommended. Recommended units include English 3, mathematics 1, social studies 2 and science 2.

2005-2006 Annual costs. Tuition/fees: $2,280; $3,750 out-of-state. Per-credit charge: $68 in-state; $117 out-of-state. Room/board: $2,480. Books/supplies: $800. Personal expenses: $1,900.

Financial aid. Need-based: Need-based aid available for part-time students. Work study available nights, weekends and for part-time students. **Non-need-based:** Scholarships awarded for academics, leadership, minority status, music/drama.

Application procedures. Admission: No deadline. No application fee. Admission notification on a rolling basis beginning on or about 8/1. **Financial aid:** Priority date 7/1; no closing date. FAFSA, institutional form required. Applicants notified on a rolling basis starting 6/1; must reply within 2 week(s) of notification.

Academics. Special study options: Accelerated study, double major, dual enrollment of high school students, honors, independent study. **Credit/placement by examination:** CLEP. 30 credit hours maximum toward associate degree. **Support services:** Learning center, reduced course load, remedial instruction, tutoring.

Majors. Agriculture: Business. **Biology:** General, botany, zoology. **Business:** General, administrative services, business admin, office management, office technology. **Computer sciences:** General. **Education:** General, music. **Engineering technology:** Drafting, electrical. **English:** Speech/rhetoric. **History:** General. **Liberal arts:** Arts/sciences. **Math:** General. **Social sciences:** General, sociology.

Student life. Freshman orientation: Available. Preregistration for classes offered. **Housing:** Single-sex dorms available. **Activities:** Choral groups, drama, student government, student newspaper, Gamma Beta Phi.

Athletics. NJCAA. **Intramural:** Archery, badminton, basketball, bowling, softball, table tennis, tennis, track and field, volleyball.

Student services. Career counseling, personal counseling, veterans' counselor. **Transfer:** Transfer adviser, college fairs on campus for students transferring to 4-year colleges.

Contact. E-mail: rahayes@asub.edu
Phone: (501) 882-8260 Toll-free number: (800) 632-9985
Fax: (501) 882-8370
Robin Hayes, Registrar and Director of Admissions, Arkansas State University: Beebe, PO Box 1000, Beebe, AR 72012-1000

Two-Year Colleges

Arkansas State University: Mountain Home

Mountain Home, Arkansas
www.asumh.edu **CB code: 6057**

- Public 2-year community and technical college
- Commuter campus in large town

General. Enrollment: 1,031 degree-seeking undergraduates; 188 non-degree-seeking students. **Degrees:** 180 associate awarded. **Location:** 130 miles from Little Rock. **Calendar:** Semester, limited summer session. **Full-time faculty:** 40 total; 25% have terminal degrees, 55% women. **Part-time faculty:** 17 total; 6% have terminal degrees, 47% women. **Class size:** 68% < 20, 32% 20-39.

Student profile. Among degree-seeking undergraduates, 25% enrolled in a transfer program, 37% enrolled in a vocational program, 305 enrolled as first-time, first-year students, 97 transferred in from other institutions.

Part-time:	39%	**Women:**	67%
Out-of-state:	3%	**25 or older:**	46%

Transfer out. Colleges most students transferred to 2005: Arkansas State University-Jonesboro, University of Central Arkansas-Conway, University of Arkansas-Fayetteville.

Basis for selection. Open admission, but selective for some programs. Additional requirements for practical nursing program, respiratory care program, and phlebotomy program. **Adult students:** Entrance exam policies same as for first-time freshmen. **Homeschooled:** Statement describing homeschool structure and mission, transcript of courses and grades required. **Learning Disabled:** Students with learning disabilities must document them with disability coordinator.

High school preparation. Recommended units include English 4, mathematics 4, social studies 3 and science 4.

2005-2006 Annual costs. Tuition/fees: $2,280; $3,750 out-of-state. Per-credit charge: $68 in-state; $117 out-of-state. Books/supplies: $800.

Financial aid. Need-based: Need-based aid available for part-time students. **Non-need-based:** Scholarships awarded for academics, state residency.

Application procedures. Admission: Closing date 8/22 (receipt date). No application fee. Application must be submitted on paper. Admission notification on a rolling basis. **Financial aid:** Priority date 7/1; no closing date. FAFSA, institutional form required. Applicants notified on a rolling basis starting 5/1; must reply within 2 week(s) of notification.

Academics. Special study options: Cooperative education, distance learning, dual enrollment of high school students, independent study, liberal arts/career combination. License preparation in funeral sciences; AAS in Hearing Healthcare or Opticianry is online. Bachelor's degree programs available on campus. License preparation in nursing, paramedic, radiology. **Credit/placement by examination:** AP, CLEP. 15 credit hours maximum toward associate degree, 15 toward bachelor's. **Support services:** GED preparation and test center, learning center, remedial instruction, study skills assistance, tutoring, writing center.

Majors. Business: Administrative services. **Computer sciences:** Information systems. **Education:** Middle. **Health:** EMT paramedic, nursing (RN), optician. **Liberal arts:** Arts/sciences. **Mechanic/repair:** Industrial. **Personal/culinary services:** Mortuary science. **Protective services:** Law enforcement admin.

Most popular majors. Business/marketing 8%, computer/information sciences 8%, liberal arts 59%, personal/culinary services 12%, security/protective services 6%.

Computing on campus. 40 workstations in library, computer center. Commuter students can connect to campus network. Online course registration, online library, wireless network available.

Student life. Freshman orientation: Available. **Policies:** Freshmen permitted cars on campus. **Housing:** This campus does not offer housing. Apartment complexes and condominiums are available. **Activities:** Choral groups, dance, drama, literary magazine, student government, Baptist Collegiate Ministries, Circle K, criminal justice club, mortuary science club, student ambassadors, student practical nurses association, Phi Beta Lambda, Phi Delta Kappa, Phi Theta Kappa, Rotaract.

Student services. Adult student services, campus ministries, career counseling, financial aid counseling, veterans' counselor. **Physically disabled:** Services for visually, hearing impaired. **Transfer:** Special adviser, orientation for new students. College fairs on campus for students transferring to 4-year colleges.

Contact. E-mail: rblagg@asumh.edu
Phone: (870) 508-6104 Fax: (870) 508-6287
Rosalyn Blagg, Registrar/Director of Admissions, Arkansas State University: Mountain Home, 1600 South College Street, Mountain Home, AR 72653

Arkansas State University: Newport

Newport, Arkansas
www.asun.edu

- Public 2-year community and liberal arts college
- Small town

General. Enrollment: 1,217 degree-seeking undergraduates. **Degrees:** 73 associate awarded. **Location:** 100 miles from Little Rock. **Calendar:** Semester, limited summer session. **Full-time faculty:** 37 total. **Part-time faculty:** 44 total.

Basis for selection. Open admission.

2005-2006 Annual costs. Tuition/fees: $2,190; $3,660 out-of-state. Per-credit charge: $68 in-state; $117 out-of-state.

2004-2005 Financial aid. Need-based: 70% of total undergraduate aid awarded as scholarships/grants, 30% as loans/jobs.

Academics. Special study options: Cooperative education, distance learning, dual enrollment of high school students, independent study, internships, liberal arts/career combination. License preparation in aviation, nursing, paramedic. **Credit/placement by examination:** CLEP. **Support services:** GED preparation and test center.

Majors. Business: General, management information systems. **Education:** Middle. **Engineering technology:** Computer. **Health:** EMT paramedic. **Liberal arts:** Arts/sciences.

Contact. Phone: (870) 512-7800 Toll-free number: (800) 976-1676
Tara Byrd, Registrar/Director of Admissions, Arkansas State University: Newport, 7648 Victory Boulevard, Newport, AR 72112

Black River Technical College

Pocahontas, Arkansas
www.blackrivertech.org **CB code: 3879**

- Public 2-year technical college
- Large town

General. Regionally accredited. **Enrollment:** 1,710 degree-seeking undergraduates. **Degrees:** 185 associate awarded. **Calendar:** Semester. **Full-time faculty:** 50 total. **Part-time faculty:** 50 total.

Basis for selection. High school transcript and standardized test scores most important.

2005-2006 Annual costs. Tuition/fees: $1,650; $2,070 out-of-district; $5,430 out-of-state. Per-credit charge: $52 in-district; $66 out-of-district; $178 out-of-state.

Application procedures. Admission: No deadline. No application fee.

Academics. Credit/placement by examination: CLEP.

Majors. Business: Accounting, business admin, management information systems. **Education:** Early childhood, elementary. **Foreign languages:** German. **Math:** General. **Protective services:** Criminal justice. **Social sciences:** Economics. **Visual/performing arts:** Art.

Contact. E-mail: elisec@blackrivertech.org
Phone: (870) 248-4000
Jim Ulmer, Director of Admissions, Black River Technical College, Highway 304 East, Pocahontas, AR 72455

Cossatot Community College of the University of Arkansas

De Queen, Arkansas
http://cccua.edu **CB code: 3613**

- Public 2-year community college
- Commuter campus in small town

General. Regionally accredited. Off-campus sites located in Nashville and Ashdown. **Enrollment:** 633 degree-seeking undergraduates; 372 non-degree-seeking students. **Degrees:** 74 associate awarded. **Location:** 60 miles from Texarkana. **Calendar:** Semester, limited summer session. **Full-time faculty:** 26 total; 8% minority, 62% women. **Part-time faculty:** 29 total; 72% women. **Class size:** 69% < 20, 31% 20-39. **Partnerships:** Secondary Vocational Center for local high schools.

Student profile. Among degree-seeking undergraduates, 40% enrolled in a transfer program, 24% enrolled in a vocational program, 129 enrolled as first-time, first-year students, 93 transferred in from other institutions.

Part-time:	46%	**Women:**	79%
Out-of-state:	2%	**25 or older:**	39%

Transfer out. **Colleges most students transferred to 2005:** Henderson State University, Texas A&M - Texarkana, Arkansas Tech University, University of Central Arkansas, Southern Arkansas University.

Basis for selection. Open admission, but selective for some programs. Admission to Nursing programs are based upon test scores and previous course grades. **Adult students:** Entrance exam policies same as for first-time freshmen.

High school preparation. College-preparatory program required. 22 units required. Required units include English 4, mathematics 4, social studies 2, history 1, science 3 (laboratory 2), foreign language 1 and academic electives 5.

2005-2006 Annual costs. Tuition/fees: $1,546; $1,846 out-of-district; $5,146 out-of-state. Per-credit charge: $45 in-district; $55 out-of-district; $165 out-of-state. Residents of bordering out-of-state counties may qualify for in-state tuition. Books/supplies: $1,100. Personal expenses: $1,564.

2004-2005 Financial aid. **Need-based:** 61 full-time freshmen applied for aid; 60 were judged to have need; 60 of these received aid. Average scholarship/grant was $1,762. 96% of total undergraduate aid awarded as scholarships/grants, 4% as loans/jobs. Need-based aid available for part-time students. Work study available nights and for part-time students. **Non-need-based:** Awarded to 66 full-time undergraduates, including 28 freshmen. **Additional information:** Active or honorably discharged military and their dependents receive tuition discounts.

Application procedures. **Admission:** No deadline. No application fee. Application may be submitted online. Admission notification on a rolling basis. **Financial aid:** Priority date 5/1; no closing date. FAFSA, institutional form required. Applicants notified on a rolling basis starting 3/1.

Academics. **Special study options:** Combined bachelor's/graduate degree, cooperative education, distance learning, double major, dual enrollment of high school students, ESL, exchange student, independent study, internships, liberal arts/career combination, student-designed major. Bachelor's degree programs available on campus. License preparation in nursing. **Credit/placement by examination:** AP, CLEP, institutional tests. 15 credit hours maximum toward associate degree. **Support services:** GED preparation and test center, learning center, remedial instruction, study skills assistance, tutoring.

Majors. **Business:** General, management information systems. **Construction:** Carpentry. **Education:** Elementary, middle. **Engineering technology:** Environmental. **Family/consumer sciences:** Child care. **Health:** Medical assistant, nursing (RN). **Liberal arts:** Arts/sciences. **Mechanic/repair:** Automotive. **Protective services:** Forensics, law enforcement admin.

Most popular majors. Business/marketing 23%, liberal arts 68%.

Computing on campus. 95 workstations in library, computer center. Commuter students can connect to campus network. Online course registration, online library, helpline, wireless network available.

Student life. **Freshman orientation:** Available. Preregistration for classes offered. Course offered each semester. **Policies:** Freshmen permitted cars on campus. **Activities:** Student government, student newspaper, Baptist Collegiate Ministry, Phi Theta Kappa, Journalism Club, Arkansas Licensed Practical Nursing Association, Amnesty International, SkillsUSA.

Student services. Adult student services, alcohol/substance abuse counseling, career counseling, services for economically disadvantaged, student employment services, financial aid counseling, minority student services, on-campus daycare, personal counseling, placement for graduates, veterans' counselor. **Physically disabled:** Services for visually, speech, hearing impaired. **Transfer:** Special adviser, orientation, pre-admission transcript evaluation for new students. Transfer adviser, college fairs on campus for students transferring to 4-year colleges.

Contact. E-mail: ncowling@cccua.edu
Phone: (870) 584-4471 ext. 344 Toll-free number: (800) 844-4471
Fax: (870) 642-8766
Kay Cobb, Dean of Student Services, Cossatot Community College of the University of Arkansas, 183 Highway 399, De Queen, AR 71832

Crowley's Ridge College

Paragould, Arkansas
www.crowleysridgecollege.edu **CB code: 6131**

- Private 2-year junior college affiliated with Church of Christ
- Commuter campus in large town

General. Regionally accredited. **Enrollment:** 165 degree-seeking undergraduates. **Degrees:** 25 associate awarded. **Location:** 23 miles from Jonesboro. **Calendar:** Semester, limited summer session. **Full-time faculty:** 10 total. **Part-time faculty:** 15 total.

Transfer out. **Colleges most students transferred to 2005:** Arkansas State University, Williams Baptist College, Harding University, Freed-Hardeman University.

Basis for selection. Open admission. Placement in freshman composition and algebra determined by ACT and ASSET scores. Development courses required for students with ACT score under 19. **Adult students:** Entrance exam policies same as for first-time freshmen.

2006-2007 Annual costs. Tuition/fees: $7,700. Per-credit charge: $240. Technology fee for non-resident students is $75 per semester. Room/board: $4,700.

Financial aid. **Need-based:** Work study available nights and weekends. **Non-need-based:** Scholarships awarded for academics, leadership, music/drama.

Application procedures. **Admission:** No deadline. $15 fee. Admission notification on a rolling basis. **Financial aid:** FAFSA required.

Academics. **Special study options:** Dual enrollment of high school students, independent study. **Credit/placement by examination:** CLEP. 34 credit hours maximum toward associate degree. **Support services:** Remedial instruction, study skills assistance, tutoring.

Majors. **Liberal arts:** Arts/sciences. **Philosophy/religion:** Religion.

Computing on campus. 15 workstations in dormitories, library, computer center. Dormitories linked to campus network.

Student life. **Freshman orientation:** Available. Preregistration for classes offered. Takes place first week of August. **Policies:** Chapel attendance required. Freshmen permitted cars on campus. **Housing:** Guaranteed on-campus for all undergraduates. Single-sex dorms available. $100 deposit. **Activities:** Choral groups, music ensembles, student government.

Athletics. **Intercollegiate:** Baseball M, basketball, volleyball W. **Intramural:** Basketball, softball, tennis, volleyball. **Team name:** Pioneers.

Student services. Campus ministries, financial aid counseling. **Transfer:** Special adviser, orientation, pre-admission transcript evaluation for new students. College fairs on campus for students transferring to 4-year colleges.

Contact. E-mail: njoneshill@crowleysridgecollege.edu
Phone: (870) 236-6901 ext. 14 Toll-free number: (800) 264-1096
Fax: (870) 236-7748
Nancy Joneshill, Admissions Director, Crowley's Ridge College, 100 College Drive, Paragould, AR 72450

East Arkansas Community College

Forrest City, Arkansas
www.eacc.edu **CB code: 0847**

- Public 2-year community college
- Commuter campus in large town

General. Founded in 1973. Regionally accredited. **Enrollment:** 1,267 degree-seeking undergraduates; 210 non-degree-seeking students. **Degrees:** 146 associate awarded. **Location:** 40 miles from Memphis, Tennessee. **Calendar:** Semester, limited summer session. **Full-time faculty:** 35 total; 9% minority, 63% women. **Part-time faculty:** 58 total; 22% minority, 59% women.

Two-Year Colleges

Student profile. Among degree-seeking undergraduates, 275 enrolled as first-time, first-year students.

Part-time:	41%	**Women:**	69%
Out-of-state:	1%	**25 or older:**	47%

Transfer out. Colleges most students transferred to 2005: Arkansas State University.

Basis for selection. Open admission. ASSET may be substituted for ACT or SAT for placement. Interview required of nursing, emergency medical technology majors.

2005-2006 Annual costs. Tuition/fees: $1,620; $1,860 out-of-district; $2,220 out-of-state. Per-credit charge: $49 in-district; $57 out-of-district; $69 out-of-state. Books/supplies: $700. Personal expenses: $1,000.

Financial aid. All financial aid based on need. Need-based aid available for part-time students.

Application procedures. Admission: No deadline. No application fee. Application must be submitted on paper. Admission notification on a rolling basis. **Financial aid:** Priority date 3/1, closing date 7/1. FAFSA required. Applicants notified on a rolling basis starting 5/15; must reply within 2 week(s) of notification.

Academics. Special study options: Distance learning, dual enrollment of high school students, honors, internships, liberal arts/career combination. License preparation in nursing, paramedic, radiology. **Credit/placement by examination:** AP, CLEP, institutional tests. 12 credit hours maximum toward associate degree. **Support services:** Learning center, remedial instruction, tutoring.

Majors. Agriculture: General. **Business:** Administrative services, business admin, finance, management information systems. **Computer sciences:** Web page design. **Education:** Middle. **Engineering technology:** Environmental, mechanical drafting. **Family/consumer sciences:** Child care. **Health:** EMT paramedic, medical radiologic technology/radiation therapy, nursing (RN). **Mechanic/repair:** Industrial. **Protective services:** Police science.

Most popular majors. Business/marketing 13%, health sciences 15%, liberal arts 60%, security/protective services 11%.

Computing on campus. 35 workstations in library, computer center.

Student life. Activities: Choral groups, student government, student newspaper.

Athletics. Intramural: Basketball, softball, tennis, volleyball.

Student services. Career counseling, student employment services, health services, personal counseling, placement for graduates, veterans' counselor. **Physically disabled:** Services for visually, hearing impaired. **Transfer:** Special adviser, orientation for new students. Transfer adviser, college fairs on campus for students transferring to 4-year colleges.

Contact. E-mail: dadams@eacc.edu
Phone: (870) 633-4480 ext. 335 Toll-free number: (877) 797-3222
Fax: (870) 633-3840
DeAnna Adams, Director of Enrollment Management/Institutional Research, East Arkansas Community College, 1700 Newcastle Road, Forrest City, AR 72335-9598

Mid-South Community College

West Memphis, Arkansas
www.midsouthcc.edu **CB code: 3880**

- Public 2-year community and junior college
- Commuter campus in large town

General. Regionally accredited. **Enrollment:** 965 degree-seeking undergraduates; 502 non-degree-seeking students. **Degrees:** 84 associate awarded. **Location:** 8 miles from Memphis, Tennessee. **Calendar:** Semester, limited summer session. **Full-time faculty:** 36 total; 3% have terminal degrees, 28% minority, 53% women. **Part-time faculty:** 74 total; 10% have terminal degrees, 24% minority, 54% women. **Class size:** 76% < 20, 24% 20-39.

Student profile. Among degree-seeking undergraduates, 36% enrolled in a transfer program, 29% enrolled in a vocational program, 1% already have a bachelor's degree or higher, 210 enrolled as first-time, first-year students, 58 transferred in from other institutions.

Part-time:	55%	**Asian American:**	1%
Out-of-state:	65%	**Hispanic American:**	1%
Women:	71%	**25 or older:**	30%
African American:	49%		

Transfer out. Colleges most students transferred to 2005: Arkansas State University, University of Memphis.

Basis for selection. Open admission. **Adult students:** Entrance exam policies same as for first-time freshmen. **Homeschooled:** Transcript of courses and grades required.

2006-2007 Annual costs. Tuition/fees: $1,620; $1,950 out-of-district; $3,360 out-of-state. Per-credit charge: $47 in-district; $58 out-of-district; $105 out-of-state. Books/supplies: $900. Personal expenses: $2,000.

Financial aid. Need-based: Need-based aid available for part-time students. Work study available nights and for part-time students. **Non-need-based:** Scholarships awarded for academics, state residency.

Application procedures. Admission: No deadline. No application fee. Application may be submitted online. Admission notification on a rolling basis. **Financial aid:** No deadline. FAFSA, institutional form required. Applicants notified on a rolling basis starting 6/1; must reply within 2 week(s) of notification.

Academics. Special study options: Cooperative education, distance learning, dual enrollment of high school students, liberal arts/career combination. **Credit/placement by examination:** AP, CLEP, institutional tests. 18 credit hours maximum toward associate degree. **Support services:** GED preparation and test center, learning center, reduced course load, remedial instruction, study skills assistance, tutoring, writing center.

Majors. Business: Business admin. **Computer sciences:** General. **Education:** Middle. **Liberal arts:** Arts/sciences.

Most popular majors. Business/marketing 8%, computer/information sciences 10%, liberal arts 82%.

Computing on campus. 250 workstations in library, computer center, student center. Commuter students can connect to campus network. Online course registration, online library, helpline available.

Student life. Freshman orientation: Available. Preregistration for classes offered. **Policies:** Freshmen permitted cars on campus. **Activities:** Choral groups, TV station.

Student services. Adult student services, career counseling, services for economically disadvantaged, student employment services, financial aid counseling, minority student services, veterans' counselor. **Physically disabled:** Services for visually, speech, hearing impaired. **Transfer:** Special adviser, orientation for new students. Transfer adviser, college fairs on campus for students transferring to 4-year colleges.

Contact. E-mail: admission@midsouthcc.edu
Phone: (870) 733-6728 Fax: (870) 733-6719
Leslie Anderson, Director of Admissions/ Registrar, Mid-South Community College, 2000 West Broadway, West Memphis, AR 72301

National Park Community College

Hot Springs, Arkansas
www.npcc.edu **CB code: 6243**

- Public 2-year community college
- Commuter campus in large town

General. Founded in 1973. Regionally accredited. **Enrollment:** 2,200 degree-seeking undergraduates. **Degrees:** 270 associate awarded. **Location:** 53 miles from Little Rock. **Calendar:** Semester, extensive summer session. **Full-time faculty:** 70 total. **Part-time faculty:** 100 total. **Class size:** 63% < 20, 37% 20-39, less than 1% 40-49, less than 1% 50-99.

Student profile.

Out-of-state:	1%	**25 or older:**	56%

Transfer out. Colleges most students transferred to 2005: Henderson State University, Arkadelphia-University of Arkansas, University of Arkansas-Little Rock, University of Arkansas-Fayetteville.

Basis for selection. Open admission, but selective for some programs. Limited admission to allied health programs and nursing. Interview required for some health-related majors. **Adult students:** Entrance exam policies same as for first-time freshmen.

High school preparation. 18 units recommended. Recommended units include English 4, mathematics 4, social studies 3, history 2, science 3 (laboratory 3) and foreign language 2.

2005-2006 Annual costs. Tuition/fees: $1,230; $1,470 out-of-district; $3,030 out-of-state. Per-credit charge: $50 in-district; $60 out-of-district; $125 out-of-state. Books/supplies: $700. Personal expenses: $1,420.

Financial aid. Need-based: Need-based aid available for part-time students. Work study available nights, weekends and for part-time students. **Non-need-based:** Scholarships awarded for academics, minority status, music/drama, state residency.

Application procedures. Admission: No deadline. No application fee. Application may be submitted online. Admission notification on a rolling basis beginning on or about 3/1. **Financial aid:** Priority date 7/1; no closing date. FAFSA, institutional form required. Applicants notified on a rolling basis starting 3/1.

Academics. Special study options: Cooperative education, cross-registration, distance learning, double major, dual enrollment of high school students, honors, independent study, internships, liberal arts/career combination, student-designed major. License preparation in aviation, nursing, paramedic, radiology, real estate. **Credit/placement by examination:** AP, CLEP, institutional tests. 18 credit hours maximum toward associate degree. **Support services:** Learning center, reduced course load, remedial instruction, study skills assistance, tutoring, writing center.

Majors. Business: Accounting, hospitality admin, hospitality/recreation, office management, office technology. **Computer sciences:** General, applications programming, computer graphics. **Engineering technology:** Electrical. **Health:** Clinical lab technology, EMT paramedic, medical assistant, medical radiologic technology/radiation therapy, medical records technology, medical secretary, nursing (RN). **Liberal arts:** Arts/sciences. **Parks/recreation:** General. **Visual/performing arts:** Commercial/advertising art.

Computing on campus. 470 workstations in library, computer center, student center. Online library available.

Student life. Freshman orientation: Mandatory. Preregistration for classes offered. 2-day orientation, held one week prior to beginning of classes. **Activities:** Choral groups, dance, literary magazine, music ensembles, student government, student newspaper, Baptist Student Union, Black Awareness, Association for Barrier Awareness.

Athletics. Intramural: Baseball, basketball, bowling, skin diving, softball, table tennis, tennis, volleyball.

Student services. Adult student services, career counseling, services for economically disadvantaged, student employment services, financial aid counseling, health services, personal counseling, placement for graduates, veterans' counselor. **Physically disabled:** Services for visually, speech, hearing impaired. **Learning disabled:** Comprehensive services available. **Transfer:** Special adviser, orientation, pre-admission transcript evaluation for new students. Transfer adviser, college fairs on campus for students transferring to 4-year colleges.

Contact. E-mail: admissions@npcc.edu
Phone: (501) 767-4222 Toll-free number: (800) 761-1825
Fax: (501) 760-4100
Brad Moody, Director of Admissions, National Park Community College, 101 College Drive, Hot Springs, AR 71913

North Arkansas College

Harrison, Arkansas
www.northark.edu **CB code: 1423**

- Public 2-year community and technical college
- Commuter campus in large town

General. Founded in 1974. Regionally accredited. **Enrollment:** 1,715 degree-seeking undergraduates; 472 non-degree-seeking students. **Degrees:** 200 associate awarded. **Location:** 75 miles from Fayetteville. **Calendar:** Semester, limited summer session. **Full-time faculty:** 66 total; 12% have terminal degrees, 53% women. **Part-time faculty:** 90 total; 53% women. **Class size:** 69% < 20, 29% 20-39, less than 1% 40-49, less than 1% 50-99, less than 1% >100.

Student profile. Among degree-seeking undergraduates, 42% enrolled in a transfer program, 58% enrolled in a vocational program, 2% already have a bachelor's degree or higher, 474 enrolled as first-time, first-year students, 177 transferred in from other institutions.

Part-time:	35%	**Asian American:**	1%
Out-of-state:	2%	**Hispanic American:**	2%
Women:	64%	**Native American:**	1%
African American:	1%	**25 or older:**	41%

Transfer out. 57% of students enrolled in the transfer program go on to 4-year colleges. **Colleges most students transferred to 2005:** Arkansas Tech University, College of the Ozarks, University of Arkansas, University of Central Arkansas, Southwest Missouri State University.

Basis for selection. Open admission, but selective for some programs. Allied health programs require separate application. Regarding CLEP examinations, to receive college credit, a student must score at the 50th percentile or higher, based on national norms, and may not have earned college credit nor have ever been enrolled in the course for which he/she is writing the test. **Adult students:** Entrance exam policies same as for first-time freshmen.

High school preparation. 17 units recommended. Recommended units include English 4, mathematics 4, social studies 2, history 1, science 3 (laboratory 3).

2005-2006 Annual costs. Tuition/fees: $1,590; $2,130 out-of-district; $4,110 out-of-state. Per-credit charge: $53 in-district; $71 out-of-district; $137 out-of-state. Books/supplies: $820. Personal expenses: $1,764.

2005-2006 Financial aid. Need-based: 297 full-time freshmen applied for aid; 277 were judged to have need; 263 of these received aid. Average need met was 49%. Average scholarship/grant was $3,958; average loan $2,517. 63% of total undergraduate aid awarded as scholarships/grants, 37% as loans/jobs. Need-based aid available for part-time students. Work study available nights and for part-time students. **Non-need-based:** Awarded to 48 full-time undergraduates, including 35 freshmen. Scholarships awarded for academics, athletics, state residency.

Application procedures. Admission: No deadline. No application fee. Application must be submitted on paper. Admission notification on a rolling basis. **Financial aid:** Priority date 5/1; no closing date. FAFSA, institutional form required. Applicants notified on a rolling basis starting 5/1.

Academics. Special study options: Distance learning, dual enrollment of high school students, ESL, honors, independent study, internships, student-designed major. Bachelor's degree programs available on campus. License preparation in nursing, paramedic, radiology, real estate. **Credit/placement by examination:** AP, CLEP, institutional tests. 20 credit hours maximum toward associate degree. Only one-third of the credit hours for a degree can be from Advanced Placement, CLEP, the College Now Program, Challenge Test, various other examinations, or independent studies. Credit for Advanced Placement, CLEP, or Professional Certification Examinations will not be posted to an academic record until the student has successfully completed at least 12 semester credit hours of work. **Support services:** GED preparation and test center, learning center, remedial instruction, study skills assistance, tutoring, writing center.

Majors. Agriculture: General, business. **Biology:** Biomedical sciences. **Business:** General, administrative services, hotel/motel admin, management information systems. **Computer sciences:** General. **Education:** Middle. **Engineering technology:** Biomedical, drafting, electrical, electromechanical. **Health:** Clinical lab technology, EMT paramedic, medical radiologic technology/radiation therapy, nursing (RN), surgical technology. **Liberal arts:** Arts/sciences. **Mechanic/repair:** Automotive, communications systems, industrial electronics. **Personal/culinary services:** Institutional food service. **Production:** Machine tool, welding. **Protective services:** Forensics, law enforcement admin, police science.

Most popular majors. Business/marketing 10%, health sciences 31%, liberal arts 49%.

Computing on campus. 250 workstations in library, computer center. Online course registration, online library, repair service, wireless network available.

Student life. Activities: Choral groups, drama, student government, Baptist Student Union, Future Farmers of America, Health Occupations Students of America, Phi Beta Lambda, Phi Theta Kappa, Pioneer Hands Club, Rad Tech Club, Skills USA, student government, student nurses association.

Athletics. NJCAA. **Intercollegiate:** Baseball M, basketball, softball W. **Intramural:** Archery, badminton, basketball, football (non-tackle) M, golf, racquetball, softball, table tennis, volleyball. **Team name:** Pioneers.

Student services. Adult student services, alcohol/substance abuse counseling, career counseling, student employment services, financial aid counseling, placement for graduates, veterans' counselor. **Physically disabled:**

Services for visually, speech, hearing impaired. **Transfer:** Special adviser, pre-admission transcript evaluation for new students. Transfer adviser, college fairs on campus for students transferring to 4-year colleges.

Contact. E-mail: charlam@northark.edu
Phone: (870) 391-3505 Toll-free number: (800) 679-6622
Fax: (870) 391-3339
Charla Jennings, Director of Admissions, North Arkansas College, 1515 Pioneer Drive, Harrison, AR 72601

Northwest Arkansas Community College

Bentonville, Arkansas
www.nwacc.edu **CB code: 7101**

- Public 2-year community college
- Commuter campus in large town

General. Regionally accredited. **Enrollment:** 4,753 degree-seeking undergraduates; 714 non-degree-seeking students. **Degrees:** 114 associate awarded. **ROTC:** Army, Air Force. **Location:** 30 miles from Fayetteville. **Calendar:** Semester, extensive summer session. **Full-time faculty:** 92 total. **Part-time faculty:** 215 total.

Student profile. Among degree-seeking undergraduates, 55% enrolled in a transfer program, 45% enrolled in a vocational program, 905 enrolled as first-time, first-year students, 805 transferred in from other institutions.

Part-time:	61%	**Women:**	60%
Out-of-state:	1%	**25 or older:**	20%

Transfer out. Colleges most students transferred to 2005: University of Arkansas.

Basis for selection. Open admission, but selective for some programs. Additional requirements for nursing, physical therapy, respiratory therapy, emergency medical technician/paramedic programs. **Adult students:** Entrance exam policies same as for first-time freshmen.

High school preparation. 21 units recommended. Recommended units include English 4, mathematics 3, social studies 1, history 1, science 2, foreign language 1 and academic electives 10.

2005-2006 Annual costs. Tuition/fees: $1,878; $2,868 out-of-district; $3,918 out-of-state. Per-credit charge: $55 in-district; $88 out-of-district; $123 out-of-state. Books/supplies: $936.

Financial aid. Need-based: Need-based aid available for part-time students. Work study available nights, weekends and for part-time students. **Non-need-based:** Scholarships awarded for academics, leadership, music/drama, state residency.

Application procedures. Admission: No deadline. $10 fee. Application must be submitted on paper. Admission notification on a rolling basis. **Financial aid:** Priority date 4/1; no closing date. FAFSA, institutional form required. Applicants notified on a rolling basis starting 4/1; must reply within 2 week(s) of notification.

Academics. Special study options: Distance learning, dual enrollment of high school students, ESL, honors, independent study, internships, liberal arts/career combination, weekend college. Bachelor's degree programs available on campus. License preparation in aviation, nursing, paramedic, physical therapy. **Credit/placement by examination:** AP, CLEP. 15 credit hours maximum toward associate degree. **Support services:** GED preparation and test center, learning center, remedial instruction, study skills assistance, tutoring, writing center.

Majors. Business: Accounting, administrative services, banking/financial services, business admin. **Computer sciences:** General, LAN/WAN management, programming, webmaster. **Engineering:** Environmental. **Engineering technology:** Drafting, electrical. **Family/consumer sciences:** Child care. **Health:** EMT paramedic, nursing (RN), physical therapy assistant, respiratory therapy technology. **Legal studies:** Paralegal. **Liberal arts:** Arts/sciences. **Mechanic/repair:** Aircraft. **Protective services:** Firefighting, law enforcement admin. **Transportation:** Aviation. **Visual/performing arts:** Commercial/advertising art.

Most popular majors. Business/marketing 8%, health sciences 24%, liberal arts 50%.

Computing on campus. 75 workstations in library, computer center. Commuter students can connect to campus network. Online course registration, online library available.

Student life. Freshman orientation: Available. Preregistration for classes offered. **Activities:** Choral groups, drama, literary magazine, music ensembles, musical theater, student government, student newspaper, symphony orchestra.

Athletics. Intramural: Archery, basketball, bowling, golf, soccer, softball, table tennis, volleyball.

Student services. Adult student services, alcohol/substance abuse counseling, career counseling, financial aid counseling, personal counseling, placement for graduates, veterans' counselor. **Transfer:** Special adviser, orientation for new students. College fairs on campus for students transferring to 4-year colleges.

Contact. E-mail: askregistration@nwacc.edu
Phone: (479) 619-4398 Toll-free number: (800) 995-6922
Fax: (479) 619-2229
John Honey, Admissions Officer, Northwest Arkansas Community College, One College Drive, Bentonville, AR 72712

Ouachita Technical College

Malvern, Arkansas
www.otcweb.edu **CB code: 3619**

- Public 2-year community and technical college
- Commuter campus in large town

General. Regionally accredited. **Enrollment:** 1,591 undergraduates. **Degrees:** 85 associate awarded. **ROTC:** Army. **Location:** 45 miles from Little Rock. **Calendar:** Semester, limited summer session. **Full-time faculty:** 26 total; 8% have terminal degrees, 58% women. **Part-time faculty:** 59 total; 14% have terminal degrees, 5% minority, 56% women.

Transfer out. Colleges most students transferred to 2005: Henderson State University, University of Central Arkansas.

Basis for selection. Open admission, but selective for some programs. Practical nursing and cosmetology program applicants admitted based on ASSET score. **Adult students:** Entrance exam policies same as for first-time freshmen.

2005-2006 Annual costs. Tuition/fees: $1,920; $4,980 out-of-state. Per-credit charge: $51 in-state; $153 out-of-state. Books/supplies: $700. Personal expenses: $1,148.

Financial aid. Need-based: Need-based aid available for part-time students. Work study available nights.

Application procedures. Admission: No deadline. No application fee. Application may be submitted online. **Financial aid:** Closing date 6/30. FAFSA required. Applicants notified on a rolling basis starting 7/1; must reply within 6 week(s) of notification.

Academics. Associate of Arts in General Education and Associate of Applied Science in Criminal Justice offered online. **Special study options:** Distance learning, dual enrollment of high school students, independent study, internships, liberal arts/career combination. License preparation in nursing. **Credit/placement by examination:** AP, CLEP, institutional tests. **Support services:** GED preparation and test center, learning center, remedial instruction, study skills assistance, tutoring.

Majors. Business: General, business admin. **Computer sciences:** General. **Education:** Early childhood. **Family/consumer sciences:** Child care. **Liberal arts:** Arts/sciences. **Production:** General. **Protective services:** Criminal justice, forensics.

Most popular majors. Business/marketing 20%, computer/information sciences 20%, education 6%, liberal arts 46%.

Computing on campus. 100 workstations in library, computer center. Online library, wireless network available.

Student life. Freshman orientation: Mandatory. Preregistration for classes offered. Mandatory orientation can be completed online. Optional orientation offered on-campus. **Activities:** Student government.

Student services. Adult student services, alcohol/substance abuse counseling, campus ministries, career counseling, services for economically disadvantaged, student employment services, financial aid counseling, personal counseling, placement for graduates, veterans' counselor. **Physically disabled:** Services for visually, speech, hearing impaired. **Transfer:** Special adviser, orientation, pre-admission transcript evaluation for new students. College fairs on campus for students transferring to 4-year colleges.

Contact. E-mail: lindaj@octweb.edu
Phone: (501) 337-5000 ext. 1118 Fax: (501) 337-9382
Linda Johnson, Vice President for Student Affairs, Ouachita Technical College, One College Circle, Malvern, AR 72104

Ozarka College
Melbourne, Arkansas
www.ozarka.edu **CB code: 3621**

- Public 2-year community and technical college
- Commuter campus in rural community

General. Regionally accredited. **Enrollment:** 765 degree-seeking undergraduates. **Degrees:** 109 associate awarded. **Location:** 125 miles from Little Rock, 160 miles from Memphis, Tennessee. **Calendar:** Semester, limited summer session. **Full-time faculty:** 25 total. **Part-time faculty:** 45 total.

Student profile. Among degree-seeking undergraduates, 60% enrolled in a transfer program, 40% enrolled in a vocational program, 1% already have a bachelor's degree or higher, 200 transferred in from other institutions.

Transfer out. Colleges most students transferred to 2005: Arkansas State University, Lyon College, University of Arkansas, University of Central Arkansas, Williams Baptist College.

Basis for selection. Open admission, but selective for some programs. Admission to licensed practical nursing, Registered Nursing, and culinary arts programs based on test scores, and/or essay, interview. **Adult students:** Entrance exam policies same as for first-time freshmen. ACT/ASSET/COMPASS/SAT are accepted test scores used for placement in math and English. **Homeschooled:** Transcript of courses and grades required.

2005-2006 Annual costs. Tuition/fees: $2,015; $5,255 out-of-state. Per-credit charge: $60 in-state; $168 out-of-state. Books/supplies: $800. Personal expenses: $4,900.

Financial aid. Need-based: Need-based aid available for part-time students.

Application procedures. Admission: No deadline. No application fee. Application may be submitted online. Admission notification on a rolling basis. **Financial aid:** No deadline. FAFSA required. Applicants notified on a rolling basis; must reply within 2 week(s) of notification.

Academics. Special study options: Combined bachelor's/graduate degree, cooperative education, distance learning, dual enrollment of high school students, liberal arts/career combination. Bachelor's degree programs available on campus. License preparation in nursing. **Credit/placement by examination:** AP, CLEP, institutional tests. 36 credit hours maximum toward associate degree. **Support services:** GED preparation and test center, learning center, remedial instruction, study skills assistance, tutoring.

Majors. Business: Business admin, information resources management. **Computer sciences:** Information systems. **Education:** General, elementary, middle. **Engineering technology:** General. **Health:** Licensed practical nurse, medical transcription. **Liberal arts:** Arts/sciences. **Mechanic/repair:** Automotive. **Personal/culinary services:** Culinary arts. **Protective services:** Law enforcement admin.

Computing on campus. 175 workstations in library, computer center. Commuter students can connect to campus network. Online course registration, helpline, wireless network available.

Student life. Freshman orientation: Mandatory. **Activities:** Student government.

Athletics. Team name: Eagles.

Student services. Campus ministries, career counseling, services for economically disadvantaged, financial aid counseling, on-campus daycare, veterans' counselor, women's services. **Transfer:** Special adviser, orientation, pre-admission transcript evaluation for new students. College fairs on campus for students transferring to 4-year colleges.

Contact. E-mail: rscaggs@ozarka.edu
Phone: (870) 368-2028 Toll-free number: (800) 821-4335 ext. 2028
Fax: (870) 368-2091
Randy Scaggs, Director of Admissions, Ozarka College, 218 College Drive, Melbourne, AR 72556-0010

Phillips Community College of the University of Arkansas
Helena, Arkansas
www.pccua.edu **CB code: 6583**

- Public 2-year community college
- Commuter campus in large town

General. Founded in 1965. Regionally accredited. Campuses in Helena, Phillips County and Stuttgart and DeWitt in Arkansas county. **Enrollment:** 1,600 degree-seeking undergraduates. **Degrees:** 195 associate awarded. **Location:** 117 miles from Little Rock, 70 miles from Memphis, Tennessee. **Calendar:** Semester, limited summer session. **Full-time faculty:** 73 total; 4% have terminal degrees, 14% minority, 73% women. **Part-time faculty:** 47 total; 6% have terminal degrees, 19% minority, 62% women. **Class size:** 78% < 20, 22% 20-39, less than 1% 50-99. **Special facilities:** Performing arts center.

Student profile. Among degree-seeking undergraduates, 268 enrolled as first-time, first-year students.

Basis for selection. Open admission, but selective for some programs. Additional requirements for nursing program. Interview required of applicants with no high school transcript or test scores.

2005-2006 Annual costs. Tuition/fees: $1,760; $2,030 out-of-district; $3,170 out-of-state. Per-credit charge: $50 in-district; $59 out-of-district; $97 out-of-state. Books/supplies: $1,000. Personal expenses: $3,660.

Financial aid. All financial aid based on need. Need-based aid available for part-time students. Work study available nights and for part-time students.

Application procedures. Admission: No deadline. No application fee. Admission notification on a rolling basis. **Financial aid:** Priority date 4/1, closing date 5/1. FAFSA required. Applicants notified on a rolling basis starting 4/1; must reply within 2 week(s) of notification.

Academics. Special study options: Distance learning, dual enrollment of high school students, honors, independent study, internships, weekend college. Bachelor's degree programs available on campus. License preparation in nursing. **Credit/placement by examination:** CLEP, institutional tests. 30 credit hours maximum toward associate degree. **Support services:** GED preparation and test center, learning center, remedial instruction, study skills assistance, tutoring.

Majors. Biology: General. **Business:** General, business admin, office technology. **Communications technology:** Graphic/printing. **Computer sciences:** Computer science, information technology, LAN/WAN management. **Education:** General, early childhood, elementary. **Engineering:** General. **Engineering technology:** Biomedical, drafting, manufacturing. **English:** Speech/rhetoric. **Health:** Nursing (RN), phlebotomy. **Legal studies:** Prelaw. **Liberal arts:** Arts/sciences. **Math:** General. **Mechanic/repair:** Industrial. **Physical sciences:** Chemistry, physics. **Psychology:** General. **Social sciences:** General. **Visual/performing arts:** Printmaking.

Most popular majors. Business/marketing 17%, computer/information sciences 35%, education 19%, health sciences 10%, legal studies 6%, liberal arts 8%.

Computing on campus. 200 workstations in library, computer center.

Student life. Freshman orientation: Available. Preregistration for classes offered. **Activities:** Choral groups, dance, drama, musical theater, Baptist Collegiate Ministries.

Athletics. Intramural: Archery, badminton, basketball, football (non-tackle) M, golf, softball, table tennis, tennis, volleyball.

Student services. Adult student services, career counseling, services for economically disadvantaged, student employment services, financial aid counseling, personal counseling, placement for graduates, veterans' counselor. **Physically disabled:** Services for visually, hearing impaired. **Transfer:** Special adviser, orientation for new students. Transfer adviser, college fairs on campus for students transferring to 4-year colleges.

Contact. E-mail: lboone@pccua.edu
Phone: (870) 338-6474 ext. 1336 Fax: (870) 338-7542
Lynn Boone, Vice Chancellor for Student Services/Registrar, Phillips Community College of the University of Arkansas, 1000 Campus Drive, Helena, AR 72342

Two-Year Colleges

Pulaski Technical College
North Little Rock, Arkansas
www.pulaskitech.edu **CB code: 3622**

- Public 2-year community and technical college
- Commuter campus in small city

General. Regionally accredited. **Enrollment:** 6,740 degree-seeking undergraduates. **Degrees:** 378 associate awarded. **Location:** 5 miles from Little Rock. **Calendar:** Semester, extensive summer session. **Full-time faculty:** 80 total. **Part-time faculty:** 150 total.

Student profile. Among degree-seeking undergraduates, 1,117 transferred in from other institutions.

Transfer out. Colleges most students transferred to 2005: University of Arkansas at Little Rock, University of Central Arkansas.

Basis for selection. Open admission, but selective for some programs. Additional requirements for dental assisting, practical nursing, respiratory therapy programs. **Adult students:** Entrance exam policies same as for first-time freshmen.

2005-2006 Annual costs. Tuition/fees: $2,340; $3,660 out-of-state. Per-credit charge: $68 in-state; $112 out-of-state. Books/supplies: $800.

2005-2006 Financial aid. Need-based: 35% of total undergraduate aid awarded as scholarships/grants, 65% as loans/jobs. Need-based aid available for part-time students.

Application procedures. Admission: No deadline. No application fee. Admission notification on a rolling basis. **Financial aid:** Priority date 5/15; no closing date. FAFSA, institutional form required. Applicants notified on a rolling basis starting 5/1; must reply within 2 week(s) of notification.

Academics. Special study options: Cooperative education, distance learning, dual enrollment of high school students, external degree, internships, liberal arts/career combination, weekend college. License preparation in aviation, dental hygiene, nursing. **Credit/placement by examination:** AP, CLEP, institutional tests. **Support services:** Learning center, remedial instruction, study skills assistance, tutoring.

Majors. Business: General, management information systems. **Computer sciences:** General, computer science, LAN/WAN management, programming, web page design, webmaster. **Construction:** General. **Education:** Early childhood. **Engineering technology:** Drafting. **Family/consumer sciences:** Child care. **Health:** Respiratory therapy technology. **Legal studies:** Paralegal. **Liberal arts:** Arts/sciences. **Mechanic/repair:** Aircraft, electronics/electrical, heating/ac/refrig.

Most popular majors. Business/marketing 10%, computer/information sciences 20%, health sciences 7%, liberal arts 50%.

Computing on campus. 60 workstations in library, computer center, student center. Commuter students can connect to campus network. Online course registration, online library, helpline, repair service, wireless network available.

Student life. Freshman orientation: Available. Preregistration for classes offered. Online Orientation. **Policies:** Freshmen permitted cars on campus. **Activities:** Literary magazine, student government, Metro Student Ministries, culture shock, philoshophy club, student ambassadors, Phi Theta Kappa.

Student services. Adult student services, career counseling, student employment services, financial aid counseling, personal counseling, veterans' counselor. **Physically disabled:** Services for visually, hearing impaired. **Learning disabled:** Comprehensive services available. **Transfer:** Special adviser, orientation for new students. Transfer adviser, college fairs on campus for students transferring to 4-year colleges.

Contact. E-mail: jhurd@pulaskitech.edu
Phone: (501) 812-2231 Fax: (501) 812-2316
Clark Atkins, Director of Admissions, Pulaski Technical College, 3000 West Scenic Drive, North Little Rock, AR 72118

Remington College: Little Rock
Little Rock, Arkansas
www.remingtoncollege.edu

- For-profit 2-year technical college
- Commuter campus in very large city

General. Accredited by ACCSCT. **Enrollment:** 350 degree-seeking undergraduates. **Degrees:** 30 associate awarded. **Calendar:** Quarter. **Full-time faculty:** 25 total. **Part-time faculty:** 3 total.

Basis for selection. Wonderlic Exam required for admission. Can be retaken.

2005-2006 Annual costs. Tuition/fees: $10,980. Per-credit charge: $256. Cost of 2-year IT programs is $29,330. 8-month medical and other programs cost $10,650. Cost includes tuition, fees and books.

Application procedures. Admission: No deadline. $50 fee. Admission notification on a rolling basis. **Financial aid:** No deadline. FAFSA required.

Academics. Credit/placement by examination: AP, CLEP.

Majors. Computer sciences: Networking. **Protective services:** Law enforcement admin.

Student life. Activities: American Association of Medical Assistants, National Technical Honor Society, Professional Business Leaders of America.

Student services. Career counseling, financial aid counseling.

Contact. Phone: (501) 312-0007 Fax: (501) 225-3819
Carla Larson, Director of Admissions, Remington College: Little Rock, 19 Remington Drive, Little Rock, AR 72204

Rich Mountain Community College
Mena, Arkansas
www.rmcc.edu **CB code: 0226**

- Public 2-year community college
- Commuter campus in small town

General. Founded in 1983. Regionally accredited. **Enrollment:** 550 degree-seeking undergraduates. **Degrees:** 57 associate awarded. **Location:** 85 miles from Fort Smith, 80 miles from Hot Springs. **Calendar:** Semester, limited summer session. **Full-time faculty:** 22 total. **Part-time faculty:** 43 total.

Student profile.

Out-of-state:	25%	25 or older:	51%

Transfer out. Colleges most students transferred to 2005: Henderson State University, Arkansas Tech University, Westark College, Cossatot Community College.

Basis for selection. Open admission, but selective for some programs. Limited admission to licensed practical nurse program.

High school preparation. 18 units recommended. Recommended units include English 4, mathematics 3, social studies 2 and science 4.

2005-2006 Annual costs. Tuition/fees: $1,290; $1,890 out-of-district; $4,590 out-of-state. Per-credit charge: $40 in-district; $50 out-of-district; $150 out-of-state. Books/supplies: $800. Personal expenses: $3,000.

2005-2006 Financial aid. Need-based: Need-based aid available for part-time students. Work study available for part-time students. **Non-need-based:** Scholarships awarded for academics.

Application procedures. Admission: No deadline. No application fee. Admission notification on a rolling basis. **Financial aid:** Priority date 7/1; no closing date. FAFSA, institutional form required. Applicants notified on a rolling basis starting 6/1; must reply within 2 week(s) of notification.

Academics. MBA, masters in education leadership offered on campus by Henderson State University. **Special study options:** Cooperative education, distance learning, dual enrollment of high school students, external degree, internships, student-designed major. License preparation in nursing. **Credit/placement by examination:** AP, CLEP, institutional tests. 30 credit hours maximum toward associate degree. **Support services:** GED preparation and test center, pre-admission summer program, remedial instruction, study skills assistance, tutoring.

Majors. Agriculture: General. **Business:** Administrative services, business admin, management information systems. **Computer sciences:** General, information systems, LAN/WAN management, programming, systems analysis. **Education:** General. **Engineering technology:** Computer hardware. **Liberal arts:** Arts/sciences. **Production:** Machine tool.

Most popular majors. Business/marketing 17%, liberal arts 78%.

Computing on campus. 73 workstations in library, computer center. Commuter students can connect to campus network.

Student life. Freshman orientation: Available. Preregistration for classes offered. **Policies:** Freshmen permitted cars on campus. **Activities:** Radio station, student government, TV station, Baptist student union, student government association.

Student services. Adult student services, career counseling, services for economically disadvantaged, financial aid counseling, personal counseling, veterans' counselor. **Physically disabled:** Services for visually, hearing impaired. **Transfer:** Special adviser, orientation, pre-admission transcript evaluation for new students. Transfer adviser, college fairs on campus for students transferring to 4-year colleges.

Contact. Phone: (501) 394-7622 ext. 1410 Fax: (501) 394-2760
Tammy Young, Dean of Students, Rich Mountain Community College, 1100 College Drive, Mena, AR 71953

South Arkansas Community College

El Dorado, Arkansas
www.southark.edu **CB code: 1550**

- Public 2-year community and junior college
- Commuter campus in large town

General. Founded in 1975. Regionally accredited. **Enrollment:** 1,400 degree-seeking undergraduates. **Degrees:** 82 associate awarded. **Location:** 115 miles from Little Rock. **Calendar:** Semester, limited summer session. **Full-time faculty:** 55 total. **Part-time faculty:** 40 total.

Transfer out. Colleges most students transferred to 2005: Southern Arkansas University, Louisiana Tech.

Basis for selection. Open admission. ACT, ASSET or COMPASS required for placement. **Adult students:** Entrance exam policies same as for first-time freshmen.

2005-2006 Annual costs. Tuition/fees: $1,900; $2,140 out-of-district; $3,790 out-of-state. Per-credit charge: $57 in-district; $65 out-of-district; $120 out-of-state. $25 lab fee for most courses. Books/supplies: $600. Personal expenses: $550.

Financial aid. Need-based: Need-based aid available for part-time students.

Application procedures. Admission: No deadline. No application fee. Admission notification on a rolling basis. **Financial aid:** Priority date 7/1; no closing date. FAFSA, institutional form required. Applicants notified on a rolling basis starting 7/1; must reply within 2 week(s) of notification.

Academics. Special study options: Dual enrollment of high school students, liberal arts/career combination. License preparation in nursing, occupational therapy, paramedic, physical therapy, radiology, real estate. **Credit/placement by examination:** AP, CLEP, IB, institutional tests. 30 credit hours maximum toward associate degree. **Support services:** GED preparation and test center, learning center, reduced course load, remedial instruction, tutoring.

Majors. Business: General, administrative services, business admin. **Communications:** Digital media. **Communications technology:** Desktop publishing. **Computer sciences:** General, applications programming, computer graphics, computer science, information technology, programming. **Conservation:** General. **Education:** General, early childhood, elementary, kindergarten/preschool, middle, multi-level teacher, secondary. **Family/consumer sciences:** Child care. **Health:** Clinical lab technology, EMT paramedic, medical radiologic technology/radiation therapy, nursing (RN), occupational therapy assistant, physical therapy assistant, radiologic technology/medical imaging. **Liberal arts:** Arts/sciences. **Mechanic/repair:** Automotive, industrial. **Protective services:** Police science. **Visual/performing arts:** Commercial/advertising art.

Computing on campus. 250 workstations in library, computer center. Student web hosting available.

Student life. Freshman orientation: Available. Preregistration for classes offered. **Policies:** Freshmen permitted cars on campus. **Activities:** Choral groups, literary magazine, Phi Beta Lambda, Phi Theta Kappa, student leadership group.

Athletics. Intramural: Basketball, tennis, volleyball.

Student services. Adult student services, career counseling, services for economically disadvantaged, student employment services, financial aid counseling, personal counseling, placement for graduates, veterans' counselor. **Physically disabled:** Services for visually, hearing impaired. **Transfer:** Special adviser for new students. Transfer adviser, college fairs on campus for students transferring to 4-year colleges.

Contact. E-mail: registrar@southark.edu
Phone: (870) 862-8131 Toll-free number: (800) 955-2289
Fax: (870) 864-7137
Dean Inman, Director of Enrollment Services, South Arkansas Community College, Box 7010, El Dorado, AR 71731-7010

Southeast Arkansas College

Pine Bluff, Arkansas
www.seark.edu **CB code: 3624**

- Public 2-year community and technical college
- Commuter campus in small city

General. Regionally accredited. **Enrollment:** 1,560 degree-seeking undergraduates. **Degrees:** 186 associate awarded. **Location:** 42 miles from Little Rock. **Calendar:** Semester, limited summer session. **Full-time faculty:** 50 total. **Part-time faculty:** 75 total. **Class size:** 64% < 20, 36% 20-39, less than 1% 40-49.

Transfer out. Colleges most students transferred to 2005: University of Arkansas at Pine Bluff, University of Arkansas at Monticello, University of Arkansas at Little Rock.

Basis for selection. Open admission, but selective for some programs. Additional requirements for some health programs. ACT, ASSET or COMPASS required for placement. **Adult students:** Entrance exam policies same as for first-time freshmen.

High school preparation. Recommended units include English 4, mathematics 2, social studies 2, history 2, science 2 and foreign language 1.

2005-2006 Annual costs. Tuition/fees: $1,660; $3,160 out-of-state. Per-credit charge: $50 in-state; $100 out-of-state. $5 per credit hour technology fee. $5 assessment fee. Books/supplies: $700. Personal expenses: $2,450.

Financial aid. Need-based: Need-based aid available for part-time students. Work study available nights, weekends and for part-time students. **Non-need-based:** Scholarships awarded for academics, leadership, state residency.

Application procedures. Admission: No deadline. No application fee. **Financial aid:** Priority date 6/1; no closing date. FAFSA required. Applicants notified on a rolling basis starting 5/1; must reply within 2 week(s) of notification.

Academics. Special study options: Cooperative education, distance learning, independent study, internships. License preparation in nursing, paramedic, real estate. **Credit/placement by examination:** AP, CLEP. 15 credit hours maximum toward associate degree. Credit awarded through challenge exams. **Support services:** GED preparation and test center, learning center, remedial instruction, tutoring.

Majors. Biology: Biotechnology. **Business:** General. **Computer sciences:** General, networking, web page design, webmaster. **Engineering technology:** Drafting. **Family/consumer sciences:** Child care. **Health:** EMT paramedic, medical assistant, medical radiologic technology/radiation therapy, nursing (RN), surgical technology. **Legal studies:** Paralegal. **Liberal arts:** Arts/sciences. **Mechanic/repair:** Electronics/electrical, industrial. **Protective services:** Criminal justice, firefighting.

Most popular majors. Business/marketing 14%, computer/information sciences 19%, health sciences 16%, liberal arts 32%.

Computing on campus. PC or laptop required. 500 workstations in library, computer center.

Student life. Freshman orientation: Available. Preregistration for classes offered. 1-hour program held Sunday afternoon before start of classes. **Policies:** Freshmen permitted cars on campus. **Activities:** Student government.

Student services. Adult student services, alcohol/substance abuse counseling, career counseling, services for economically disadvantaged, student employment services, financial aid counseling, personal counseling, placement for graduates, veterans' counselor. **Physically disabled:** Services for visually, speech, hearing impaired. **Learning disabled:** Comprehensive services available. **Transfer:** Special adviser, pre-admission transcript evaluation for new students. College fairs on campus for students transferring to 4-year colleges.

Contact. E-mail: hpost@seark.edu
Phone: (870) 543-5903 Fax: (870) 543-5956
Barbara Dunn, Admissions and Enrollment Management Coordinator, Southeast Arkansas College, 1900 Hazel Street, Pine Bluff, AR 71603

Southern Arkansas University Tech
Camden, Arkansas
www.sautech.edu **CB code: 6704**

- Public 2-year junior and technical college
- Commuter campus in large town

General. Founded in 1967. Regionally accredited. **Enrollment:** 757 degree-seeking undergraduates; 1,011 non-degree-seeking students. **Degrees:** 88 associate awarded. **Location:** 90 miles from Little Rock. **Calendar:** Semester, limited summer session. **Full-time faculty:** 41 total; 7% have terminal degrees, 15% minority, 49% women. **Part-time faculty:** 59 total; 7% have terminal degrees, 10% minority, 54% women. **Class size:** 66% < 20, 28% 20-39, 1% 40-49, 5% 50-99. **Special facilities:** Fire training academy, environmental science academy, law enforcement academy, career academy, business and industry center. **Partnerships:** Formal partnerships with area businesses/industries and high schools.

Student profile. Among degree-seeking undergraduates, 15% enrolled in a transfer program, 53% enrolled in a vocational program, 1% already have a bachelor's degree or higher, 165 enrolled as first-time, first-year students, 131 transferred in from other institutions.

Part-time:	36%	**Hispanic American:**	1%
Out-of-state:	2%	**Native American:**	1%
Women:	44%	**25 or older:**	45%
African American:	25%		

Transfer out. Colleges most students transferred to 2005: Southern Arkansas University, Henderson State University, University of Arkansas at Monticello, University of Central Arkansas, South Arkansas Community College.

Basis for selection. Open admission, but selective for some programs. Additional requirements for nursing program. **Adult students:** Entrance exam policies same as for first-time freshmen. **Homeschooled:** State high school equivalency certificate required. Applicants must take the GED test.

High school preparation. 23 units recommended. Recommended units include English 4, mathematics 4, social studies 2, history 2, science 3, foreign language 2 and academic electives 6.

2006-2007 Annual costs. Tuition/fees (projected): $2,106; $2,626 out-of-state. Per-credit charge: $60 in-state; $80 out-of-state. Books/supplies: $700. Personal expenses: $3,500.

Financial aid. Need-based: Need-based aid available for part-time students. Work study available for part-time students. **Non-need-based:** Scholarships awarded for academics, state residency.

Application procedures. Admission: Priority date 7/15; deadline 6/1 (postmark date). No application fee. Application may be submitted online. Admission notification on a rolling basis. **Financial aid:** Priority date 6/1; no closing date. FAFSA required. Applicants notified on a rolling basis starting 5/1.

Academics. Special study options: Distance learning, double major, dual enrollment of high school students, honors, independent study, internships. Articulation agreements for Nursing Assistant and Practical Nursing programs. License preparation in aviation, nursing. **Credit/placement by examination:** AP, CLEP, institutional tests. 15 credit hours maximum toward associate degree. **Support services:** GED preparation and test center, learning center, pre-admission summer program, remedial instruction, tutoring, writing center.

Majors. Business: Office management. **Computer sciences:** Computer science, networking, programming. **Education:** Instructional media, middle. **Engineering technology:** Environmental. **Mechanic/repair:** Aircraft powerplant, industrial. **Protective services:** Firefighting. **Visual/performing arts:** Commercial/advertising art.

Most popular majors. Business/marketing 10%, computer/information sciences 28%, education 9%, liberal arts 27%, trade and industry 11%, visual/performing arts 7%.

Computing on campus. 155 workstations in library, computer center. Dormitories wired for high-speed internet access and linked to campus network. Commuter students can connect to campus network. Online course registration, online library, helpline, repair service, wireless network available.

Student life. Freshman orientation: Mandatory. Preregistration for classes offered. One-day program in late July or early August. **Policies:** Freshmen permitted cars on campus. **Housing:** $100 deposit. Off-campus housing is available. **Activities:** Radio station, student government, TV station, Multi-Cultural Club, Aviation Club, IMEDIO (multimedia graphics, audio/video) CCUB, Computer Club, Electronics Club, Phi Beta Lambda, Phi Theta Kappa, SAU Tech Ambassadors, Allied Health Student Club, Student Advisers.

Athletics. Intramural: Basketball, football (non-tackle), soccer, softball, tennis, volleyball, weight lifting. **Team name:** Varmits.

Student services. Adult student services, campus ministries, career counseling, student employment services, financial aid counseling, on-campus daycare, personal counseling, placement for graduates, veterans' counselor. **Physically disabled:** Services for visually, speech, hearing impaired. **Transfer:** Special adviser, orientation, re-entry adviser, pre-admission transcript evaluation for new students. Transfer center, transfer adviser, college fairs on campus for students transferring to 4-year colleges.

Contact. E-mail: bclark@sautech.edu
Phone: (870) 574-4558 Fax: (870) 574-4478
Patricia Sindle, Director, Enrollment Services, Southern Arkansas University Tech, P.O. Box 3499, East Camden, AR 71711-1599

University of Arkansas Community College at Morrilton
Morrilton, Arkansas
www.uaccm.edu **CB code: 3881**

- Public 2-year community college
- Commuter campus in small town

General. Regionally accredited. **Enrollment:** 1,653 degree-seeking undergraduates; 86 non-degree-seeking students. **Degrees:** 120 associate awarded. **Location:** 26 miles from Russellville. **Calendar:** Semester, limited summer session. **Full-time faculty:** 45 total. **Part-time faculty:** 50 total.

Student profile. Among degree-seeking undergraduates, 503 enrolled as first-time, first-year students.

Part-time:	26%	**Hispanic American:**	2%
Women:	61%	**Native American:**	1%
African American:	6%	**25 or older:**	42%
Asian American:	1%		

Transfer out. Colleges most students transferred to 2005: University of Central Arkansas, Arkansas Tech University, University of Arkansas at Fayetteville.

Basis for selection. Open admission. ASSET or COMPASS test scores required for placement. **Adult students:** Entrance exam policies same as for first-time freshmen.

2005-2006 Annual costs. Tuition/fees: $2,260; $2,440 out-of-district; $3,400 out-of-state. Per-credit charge: $64 in-district; $70 out-of-district; $102 out-of-state.

Application procedures. Admission: No deadline. No application fee. Application must be submitted on paper.

Academics. Special study options: Distance learning, internships, liberal arts/career combination. License preparation in nursing. **Credit/placement by examination:** AP, CLEP, institutional tests. 53 credit hours maximum toward associate degree. **Support services:** GED preparation and test center, learning center, remedial instruction, study skills assistance, tutoring, writing center.

Majors. Business: General. **Engineering technology:** General. **Liberal arts:** Arts/sciences.

Student life. Freshman orientation: Available. Preregistration for classes offered. **Policies:** Freshmen permitted cars on campus. **Activities:** Choral groups, drama, student government.

Athletics. NJCAA. **Intercollegiate:** Golf M. **Intramural:** Table tennis, volleyball. **Team name:** Timberwolves.

Student services. Career counseling, financial aid counseling, on-campus daycare, placement for graduates. **Physically disabled:** Services for visually, speech, hearing impaired. **Transfer:** College fairs on campus for students transferring to 4-year colleges.

Contact. E-mail: adm@uaccm.edu
Phone: (501) 977-2053 Toll-free number: (800) 264-1094
Fax: (501) 977-2123
Susan Dewey, Director of Admissions, University of Arkansas Community College at Morrilton, 1537 University Boulevard, Morrilton, AR 72110

University of Arkansas: Community College at Batesville

Batesville, Arkansas
www.uaccb.edu **CB code: 3628**

- Public 2-year community college
- Commuter campus in small town

General. Regionally accredited. **Enrollment:** 1,007 degree-seeking undergraduates. **Degrees:** 120 associate awarded. **Location:** 90 miles from Little Rock. **Calendar:** Semester, limited summer session. **Full-time faculty:** 41 total. **Part-time faculty:** 75 total.

Transfer out. Colleges most students transferred to 2005: Lyon College, Arkansas State University, University of Arkansas, University of Central Arkansas, Arkansas Tech University.

Basis for selection. Open admission, but selective for some programs. Admission to nursing program based on GPA in prerequisite courses. **Adult students:** Entrance exam policies same as for first-time freshmen. **Home-schooled:** Transcript of courses and grades required.

2005-2006 Annual costs. Tuition/fees: $1,860; $2,220 out-of-district; $3,930 out-of-state. Per-credit charge: $48 in-district; $60 out-of-district; $117 out-of-state. Books/supplies: $700. Personal expenses: $2,100.

Financial aid. All financial aid based on need. Work study available nights, weekends and for part-time students.

Application procedures. Admission: No deadline. No application fee. Admission notification on a rolling basis. **Financial aid:** No deadline. FAFSA required. Applicants notified on a rolling basis starting 3/1; must reply within 2 week(s) of notification.

Academics. Special study options: Cooperative education, distance learning, dual enrollment of high school students, ESL, independent study, internships, liberal arts/career combination, weekend college. Bachelor's degree programs available on campus. License preparation in paramedic. **Credit/placement by examination:** CLEP. **Support services:** GED preparation and test center, remedial instruction, study skills assistance, tutoring.

Majors. Business: General, accounting, administrative services, business admin. **Computer sciences:** General. **Education:** Early childhood. **Health:** EMT paramedic, nursing (RN). **Liberal arts:** Arts/sciences. **Mechanic/repair:** General, electronics/electrical, industrial. **Protective services:** Criminal justice.

Computing on campus. 25 workstations in computer center.

Student life. Freshman orientation: Available. Preregistration for classes offered. **Policies:** Freshmen permitted cars on campus. **Activities:** Student government, Baptist Collegiate Ministry, Young Democrats, College Republicans.

Student services. Adult student services, career counseling, services for economically disadvantaged, student employment services, financial aid counseling, personal counseling, veterans' counselor. **Physically disabled:** Services for visually, speech, hearing impaired. **Transfer:** Special adviser, orientation, pre-admission transcript evaluation for new students. College fairs on campus for students transferring to 4-year colleges.

Contact. E-mail: elacy@uaccb.edu
Phone: (870) 612-2010 Toll-free number: (800) 508-7878
Fax: (870) 612-2129
Shelly Moser, Director of Student Records and Information, University of Arkansas: Community College at Batesville, Box 3350, Batesville, AR 72503

University of Arkansas: Community College at Hope

Hope, Arkansas
www.uacch.edu **CB code: 3629**

- Public 2-year community and technical college
- Commuter campus in small town

General. Regionally accredited. **Enrollment:** 923 degree-seeking undergraduates; 241 non-degree-seeking students. **Degrees:** 132 associate awarded. **Location:** 30 miles from Texarkana. **Calendar:** Semester, limited summer session. **Full-time faculty:** 38 total; 5% have terminal degrees, 8% minority, 45% women. **Part-time faculty:** 23 total; 48% women.

Student profile. Among degree-seeking undergraduates, 36% enrolled in a transfer program, 64% enrolled in a vocational program, 1% already have a bachelor's degree or higher, 226 enrolled as first-time, first-year students, 75 transferred in from other institutions.

Part-time:	39%	**Hispanic American:**	2%
Women:	71%	**Native American:**	1%
African American:	36%	**25 or older:**	40%
Asian American:	1%		

Basis for selection. Open admission, but selective for some programs. Additional requirements for nursing, funeral services, respiratory therapy programs. **Adult students:** Entrance exam policies same as for first-time freshmen.

High school preparation. 15 units recommended. Recommended units include English 4, mathematics 3, social studies 1, history 2, science 3 and academic electives 2.

2005-2006 Annual costs. Tuition/fees: $1,690; $1,840 out-of-district; $3,460 out-of-state. Per-credit charge: $52 in-district; $57 out-of-district; $111 out-of-state. Books/supplies: $900. Personal expenses: $500.

2004-2005 Financial aid. Need-based: 89% of total undergraduate aid awarded as scholarships/grants, 11% as loans/jobs. Need-based aid available for part-time students. Work study available nights and for part-time students. **Non-need-based:** Scholarships awarded for academics.

Application procedures. Admission: No deadline. No application fee. Application may be submitted online. Admission notification on a rolling basis. **Financial aid:** Priority date 7/6; no closing date. FAFSA, institutional form required. Applicants notified on a rolling basis starting 1/1; must reply within 4 week(s) of notification.

Academics. Special study options: Distance learning, double major, dual enrollment of high school students, ESL, independent study, liberal arts/career combination. Bachelor's degree programs available on campus. License preparation in nursing, paramedic. **Credit/placement by examination:** AP, CLEP, institutional tests. **Support services:** GED test center, remedial instruction, study skills assistance, tutoring.

Majors. Agriculture: General. **Business:** General. **Education:** Middle. **Family/consumer sciences:** Child care. **Health:** Respiratory therapy technology. **Legal studies:** Paralegal. **Liberal arts:** Arts/sciences. **Personal/culinary services:** Mortuary science. **Protective services:** Forensics, law enforcement admin, police science.

Most popular majors. Business/marketing 7%, health sciences 9%, legal studies 6%, liberal arts 62%, personal/culinary services 7%.

Computing on campus. 20 workstations in library. Commuter students can connect to campus network. Online course registration, online library, helpline, wireless network available.

Student life. Freshman orientation: Available. **Policies:** Freshmen permitted cars on campus. **Activities:** Jazz band, choral groups, drama, music ensembles, student government, student newspaper.

Student services. Adult student services, alcohol/substance abuse counseling, campus ministries, career counseling, services for economically disadvantaged, student employment services, financial aid counseling, personal counseling, placement for graduates, veterans' counselor. **Physically disabled:** Services for visually, speech, hearing impaired. **Transfer:** Special adviser, orientation, pre-admission transcript evaluation for new students. College fairs on campus for students transferring to 4-year colleges.

Contact. E-mail: dormand@uacch.edu
Phone: (870) 777-5722 Fax: (870) 722-6630
Danita Ormand, Director for Enrollment Services, University of Arkansas: Community College at Hope, 2500 South Main, Hope, AR 71802-0140

California

Allan Hancock College
Santa Maria, California
www.hancockcollege.edu **CB code: 4002**

- Public 2-year community college
- Commuter campus in small city

General. Founded in 1920. Regionally accredited. **Enrollment:** 6,446 degree-seeking undergraduates. **Degrees:** 1,121 associate awarded. **Location:** 70 miles from Santa Barbara, 175 miles from Los Angeles. **Calendar:** Semester, extensive summer session. **Full-time faculty:** 152 total; 50% women. **Part-time faculty:** 442 total; 39% women.

Transfer out. Colleges most students transferred to 2005: California Polytechnic State University-San Luis Obispo, California State University-Fresno, University of California-Santa Barbara, California State University-San Diego.

Basis for selection. Open admission, but selective for some programs. Special requirements for allied health and drama programs. Students required to make separate application for admission to nursing, drama, police academy programs. Interviews required for allied health applicants. Auditions required for drama applicants.

2005-2006 Annual costs. Tuition/fees: $818; $5,348 out-of-state. Per-credit charge: $26 in-state; $177 out-of-state. Books/supplies: $1,200. Personal expenses: $1,620.

Financial aid. All financial aid based on need. Need-based aid available for part-time students. Work study available for part-time students.

Application procedures. Admission: No deadline. No application fee. Admission notification on a rolling basis. **Financial aid:** Priority date 5/1; no closing date. FAFSA required. Applicants notified on a rolling basis starting 6/1.

Academics. Special study options: Accelerated study, cooperative education, distance learning, double major, dual enrollment of high school students, ESL, independent study, internships, study abroad. Bachelor's degree programs available on campus. License preparation in paramedic, real estate. **Credit/placement by examination:** AP, CLEP, institutional tests. 30 credit hours maximum toward associate degree. **Support services:** GED test center, learning center, reduced course load, remedial instruction, tutoring, writing center.

Majors. Agriculture: Agribusiness operations. **Biology:** General. **Business:** General, accounting, administrative services, business admin, international marketing, management information systems, management science, office technology, office/clerical. **Communications technology:** Graphic/printing. **Computer sciences:** General, information systems. **Education:** General, early childhood, elementary, physical. **Engineering:** General, aerospace. **Engineering technology:** Architectural, civil, electrical. **Family/consumer sciences:** General. **Foreign languages:** Spanish. **Health:** Dental assistant, health services, licensed practical nurse, medical assistant, medical records admin, medical records technology, nursing (RN), physical therapy assistant. **Legal studies:** Legal secretary. **Liberal arts:** Arts/sciences. **Mechanic/repair:** General, auto body, automotive, diesel, electronics/electrical. **Parks/recreation:** General. **Personal/culinary services:** Cosmetic. **Physical sciences:** Chemistry, physics. **Protective services:** Fire safety technology. **Public administration:** Human services. **Social sciences:** General, international relations. **Visual/performing arts:** Art, commercial photography, commercial/advertising art, dance, design, fashion design, film/cinema, interior design, photography.

Most popular majors. Liberal arts 69%.

Computing on campus. 180 workstations in library, computer center. Online library available.

Student life. Freshman orientation: Available. **Policies:** Freshmen permitted cars on campus. **Activities:** Bands, choral groups, dance, drama, film society, literary magazine, music ensembles, musical theater, student government, student newspaper.

Athletics. Intercollegiate: Baseball M, basketball, cross-country, football (tackle) M, golf, soccer, tennis, track and field, volleyball W. **Team name:** Bulldogs.

Student services. Adult student services, career counseling, services for economically disadvantaged, student employment services, health services, on-campus daycare, personal counseling, placement for graduates, veterans' counselor. **Physically disabled:** Services for visually, hearing impaired. **Transfer:** Special adviser, pre-admission transcript evaluation for new students. Transfer center, transfer adviser, college fairs on campus for students transferring to 4-year colleges.

Contact. Phone: (805) 922-6966 ext. 3248 Fax: (805) 922-3477
Marian Quaid-Maltagliati, Interim Director, Admissions and Records, Allan Hancock College, 800 South College Drive, Santa Maria, CA 93454-6399

American Academy of Dramatic Arts: West
Los Angeles, California
www.aada.org **CB code: 7024**

- Private 2-year performing arts college
- Commuter campus in very large city
- Application essay, interview required

General. Founded in 1974. Regionally accredited. **Enrollment:** 258 degree-seeking undergraduates. **Degrees:** 13 associate awarded. **Calendar:** Semester. **Full-time faculty:** 1 total; 100% women. **Part-time faculty:** 27 total; 11% minority, 63% women. **Class size:** 93% < 20, 7% 20-39. **Special facilities:** Performance theater.

Student profile. Among degree-seeking undergraduates, 119 enrolled as first-time, first-year students. Of all enrolled students, 2% already have a bachelor's degree or higher.

Out-of-state:	84%	**25 or older:**	20%
Women:	54%		

Basis for selection. Student attitude, seriousness of intent, and potential as professional actor as indicated by written recommendations, interview, and audition. All applicants must have full command of English language. Auditions required.

2006-2007 Annual costs. Tuition/fees: $17,450. Books/supplies: $600. Personal expenses: $1,232.

2004-2005 Financial aid. Need-based: 48% of total undergraduate aid awarded as scholarships/grants, 52% as loans/jobs. **Non-need-based:** Scholarships awarded for academics, music/drama.

Application procedures. Admission: No deadline. $50 fee. Application may be submitted online. Admission notification on a rolling basis. SAT or ACT recommended for applicants attending directly from high school. **Financial aid:** Priority date 7/1; no closing date. Institutional form required. Applicants notified on a rolling basis starting 6/1; must reply within 3 week(s) of notification.

Academics. Select group of students invited to return for additional year of study and performance after graduation in repertory situation. **Special study options:** Cross-registration, exchange student. Students may study 1 year in each of 2 campuses (NY and CA). **Credit/placement by examination:** AP, CLEP. **Support services:** Pre-admission summer program, tutoring, writing center.

Majors. Visual/performing arts: Acting.

Computing on campus. 10 workstations in computer center.

Student life. Freshman orientation: Mandatory. **Policies:** Freshmen permitted cars on campus. **Activities:** Student government.

Student services. Alcohol/substance abuse counseling, career counseling, financial aid counseling, personal counseling, veterans' counselor.

Contact. Phone: (323) 464-2777 ext. 109 Toll-free number: (800) 222-2867 Fax: (818) 464-1250
Dan Justin, Director of Admissions, American Academy of Dramatic Arts: West, 1336 N. La Brea Avenue, Los Angeles, CA 90028

American River College
Sacramento, California
www.arc.losrios.edu **CB code: 4004**

- Public 2-year community college
- Commuter campus in large city

General. Founded in 1955. Regionally accredited. **Enrollment:** 32,241 undergraduates. **Degrees:** 1,274 associate awarded. **Location:** 10 miles from downtown. **Calendar:** Semester, limited summer session. **Full-time faculty:** 650 total. **Part-time faculty:** 220 total.

Basis for selection. Open admission, but selective for some programs. Limited admission to nursing program. **Homeschooled:** Transcript of courses and grades, interview, letter of recommendation (nonparent) required.

2005-2006 Annual costs. Tuition/fees: $812; $5,342 out-of-state. Per-credit charge: $26 in-state; $177 out-of-state. International students pay additional $50 application fee. Books/supplies: $500. Personal expenses: $756.

Financial aid. All financial aid based on need. Need-based aid available for part-time students.

Application procedures. Admission: No deadline. No application fee in-state; $177 out-of-state. Application must be submitted online. Admission notification on a rolling basis beginning on or about 7/1. **Financial aid:** Priority date 3/2; no closing date. FAFSA required. Applicants notified on a rolling basis starting 7/1; must reply within 2 week(s) of notification.

Academics. Special study options: Accelerated study, cooperative education, cross-registration, independent study. **Credit/placement by examination:** CLEP, IB. 15 credit hours maximum toward associate degree. **Support services:** Learning center, pre-admission summer program, reduced course load, remedial instruction, study skills assistance, tutoring, writing center.

Majors. Architecture: Landscape. **Business:** Accounting, administrative services, fashion, hospitality/recreation, management information systems, office/clerical, real estate. **Communications technology:** Graphic/printing. **Education:** Teacher assistance. **Engineering technology:** Drafting. **Family/consumer sciences:** General, child care, institutional food production. **Health:** Health services, nursing (RN), respiratory therapy technology. **Interdisciplinary:** Biological/physical sciences, gerontology. **Legal studies:** Paralegal. **Liberal arts:** Arts/sciences. **Mechanic/repair:** Automotive. **Parks/recreation:** General. **Protective services:** Fire safety technology, police science. **Visual/performing arts:** Dramatic, interior design.

Student life. Activities: Bands, choral groups, dance, drama, literary magazine, music ensembles, musical theater, student government, student newspaper, symphony orchestra.

Athletics. Intercollegiate: Baseball M, basketball, cross-country, football (tackle) M, soccer M, softball W, swimming, tennis, track and field, volleyball W. **Team name:** Beavers.

Student services. Adult student services, career counseling, services for economically disadvantaged, student employment services, financial aid counseling, health services, minority student services, on-campus daycare, personal counseling, placement for graduates, veterans' counselor. **Physically disabled:** Services for visually, speech, hearing impaired. **Learning disabled:** Comprehensive services available.

Contact. Phone: (916) 484-8261 Fax: (916) 484-8864
Robin Neal, Dean of Enrollment Services, American River College, 4700 College Oak Drive, Sacramento, CA 95841

Antelope Valley College

Lancaster, California
www.avc.edu **CB code: 4005**

- Public 2-year community college
- Commuter campus in large city

General. Founded in 1929. Regionally accredited. Shares campus with Cal State Bakersfield. **Enrollment:** 7,450 degree-seeking undergraduates. **Degrees:** 862 associate awarded. **ROTC:** Air Force. **Location:** 50 miles from Los Angeles. **Calendar:** Semester, limited summer session. **Full-time faculty:** 181 total. **Part-time faculty:** 495 total. **Class size:** 27% < 20, 63% 20-39, 6% 40-49, 3% 50-99, less than 1% >100. **Partnerships:** Formal partnerships with local high schools to provide paraprofessional teacher training; Department of Labor grant provides aerospace worker training for Lockheed Martin and Boeing.

Transfer out. Colleges most students transferred to 2005: CSU Northridge, CSU Bakersfield, UC Los Angeles.

Basis for selection. Open admission, but selective for some programs. High school graduate, GED or 18 years of age. **Adult students:** Entrance exam policies same as for first-time freshmen.

2005-2006 Annual costs. Tuition/fees: $782; $5,312 out-of-state. Per-credit charge: $26 in-state; $177 out-of-state. Personal expenses: $2,250.

Financial aid. Need-based: Need-based aid available for part-time students. Work study available for part-time students.

Application procedures. Admission: No deadline. No application fee in-state; $175 out-of-state. Application may be submitted online. Admission notification on a rolling basis. **Financial aid:** Priority date 3/2; no closing date. FAFSA, institutional form required. Applicants notified on a rolling basis starting 7/15; must reply within 2 week(s) of notification.

Academics. Special study options: Accelerated study, cooperative education, distance learning, double major, dual enrollment of high school students, ESL, honors, independent study, internships, study abroad, teacher certification program, weekend college. Bachelor's degree programs available on campus. License preparation in aviation, nursing, real estate. **Credit/placement by examination:** AP, CLEP, institutional tests. Maximum of 4 courses allowed. **Support services:** GED preparation, learning center, reduced course load, remedial instruction, study skills assistance, tutoring, writing center.

Majors. Agriculture: Landscaping, ornamental horticulture. **Biology:** General. **Business:** General, administrative services, business admin, real estate. **Communications technology:** Graphic/printing. **Computer sciences:** General, computer graphics, computer science, data processing, information systems, programming. **Education:** Teacher assistance. **Engineering:** General. **Engineering technology:** Aerospace, construction, drafting. **Family/consumer sciences:** General, child care, child development, clothing/textiles, communication, family resources, food/nutrition, home furnishings. **Foreign languages:** American Sign Language. **Health:** Medical assistant, medical secretary, nursing (RN), office assistant. **Liberal arts:** Arts/sciences. **Math:** General. **Mechanic/repair:** Aircraft, auto body, automotive, electronics/electrical. **Parks/recreation:** Health/fitness. **Production:** Welding. **Protective services:** Fire safety technology. **Visual/performing arts:** General, cinematography, interior design, multimedia, photography.

Computing on campus. 300 workstations in library, computer center, student center. Online course registration, online library available.

Student life. Freshman orientation: Available. Preregistration for classes offered. Online orientation available. **Policies:** Freshmen permitted cars on campus. **Activities:** Bands, choral groups, dance, drama, music ensembles, musical theater, student government, student newspaper, symphony orchestra.

Athletics. NCAA. **Intercollegiate:** Baseball M, basketball, cheerleading, cross-country, football (tackle) M, golf, soccer W, softball W, track and field, volleyball W. **Intramural:** Basketball, tennis, volleyball W. **Team name:** Marauders.

Student services. Adult student services, career counseling, services for economically disadvantaged, student employment services, financial aid counseling, health services, minority student services, on-campus daycare, personal counseling, veterans' counselor. **Physically disabled:** Services for visually, speech, hearing impaired. **Learning disabled:** Comprehensive services available. **Transfer:** Special adviser, orientation, re-entry adviser for new students. Transfer center, transfer adviser, college fairs on campus for students transferring to 4-year colleges.

Contact. Phone: (661) 722-6332 Fax: (661) 722-6531
Michelle St. John, Dean of Counseling and Admissions and Records, Antelope Valley College, 3041 West Avenue K, Lancaster, CA 93536-5426

Art Institute of California: Los Angeles

Santa Monica, California
www.aila.artinstitutes.edu **CB code: 2490**

- For-profit 2-year visual arts college
- Commuter campus in small city
- Application essay, interview required

General. Accredited by ACICS. **Enrollment:** 2,102 degree-seeking undergraduates. **Degrees:** 175 bachelor's, 182 associate awarded. **Calendar:** Continuous. **Full-time faculty:** 75 total. **Part-time faculty:** 53 total. **Class size:** 57% < 20, 43% 20-39.

Basis for selection. High school record and general appropriateness of educational background to specific program applied for most important. Portfolio, interview, standardized test scores also important.

2006-2007 Annual costs. Tuition/fees (projected): $19,874. Room only: $9,594. Books/supplies: $1,733. Personal expenses: $1,500.

2005-2006 Financial aid. Need-based: 52% of total undergraduate aid awarded as scholarships/grants, 48% as loans/jobs. Need-based aid available for part-time students. Work study available nights, weekends and for part-time students. **Non-need-based:** Scholarships awarded for academics.

Application procedures. **Admission:** No deadline. $50 fee. Application may be submitted online. **Financial aid:** No deadline. FAFSA required. Applicants notified on a rolling basis.

Academics. **Special study options:** Internships. Bachelor's degree programs available on campus. **Credit/placement by examination:** CLEP. **Support services:** Reduced course load, tutoring, writing center.

Majors. **Computer sciences:** Computer graphics, web page design. **Personal/culinary services:** Culinary arts. **Visual/performing arts:** Cinematography, commercial/advertising art, design.

Computing on campus. 250 workstations in library, computer center. Student web hosting available.

Student life. **Freshman orientation:** Mandatory. Preregistration for classes offered. One day program before start of quarter. **Policies:** Freshmen permitted cars on campus. **Housing:** Guaranteed on-campus for all undergraduates. Apartments available. $250 deposit. **Activities:** Literary magazine, Gay, Lesbian, Straight Alliance.

Athletics. **Intramural:** Basketball, softball, volleyball.

Student services. Alcohol/substance abuse counseling, career counseling, student employment services, financial aid counseling, personal counseling, placement for graduates.

Contact. E-mail: ailaadm@aii.edu
Phone: (310) 752-4700 Toll-free number: (888) 646-4610
Andrea Sylvester, Director of Admissions, Art Institute of California: Los Angeles, 2900 31st Street, Santa Monica, CA 90405-3035

Bakersfield College

Bakersfield, California
www.bakersfieldcollege.edu **CB code: 4015**

- Public 2-year community college
- Small city

General. Founded in 1913. Regionally accredited. **Enrollment:** 9,864 degree-seeking undergraduates. **Degrees:** 904 associate awarded. **Location:** 114 miles from Los Angeles. **Calendar:** Semester, limited summer session. **Full-time faculty:** 252 total. **Part-time faculty:** 247 total.

Basis for selection. Open admission, but selective for some programs. Nursing and other allied health programs have selective admission requirements including required coursework.

2005-2006 Annual costs. Tuition/fees: $818; $5,768 out-of-state. Per-credit charge: $26 in-state; $191 out-of-state. Books/supplies: $650. Personal expenses: $1,420.

Application procedures. **Admission:** No deadline. No application fee. Admission notification on a rolling basis. **Financial aid:** Priority date 3/2; no closing date. FAFSA required. Applicants notified on a rolling basis starting 6/1; must reply within 2 week(s) of notification.

Academics. **Special study options:** Double major, dual enrollment of high school students. **Credit/placement by examination:** CLEP, institutional tests. 12 credit hours maximum toward associate degree. **Support services:** Learning center, pre-admission summer program, reduced course load, remedial instruction, tutoring.

Majors. **Agriculture:** Agribusiness operations, animal sciences, horticulture, ornamental horticulture. **Biology:** General, bacteriology. **Business:** Accounting, administrative services, business admin, management information systems, office technology, office/clerical, real estate. **Communications:** Broadcast journalism, journalism. **Communications technology:** General, graphic/printing. **Computer sciences:** Applications programming, data processing. **Conservation:** Forestry. **Construction:** Carpentry, masonry, pipefitting, power transmission. **Engineering technology:** Aerospace, drafting. **Family/consumer sciences:** General, food/nutrition, institutional food production. **Foreign languages:** German, Spanish. **Health:** Dental assistant, EMT paramedic, licensed practical nurse, medical radiologic technology/radiation therapy, nursing (RN), predentistry, premedicine, prepharmacy, preveterinary. **History:** General. **Legal studies:** Prelaw. **Liberal arts:** Arts/sciences. **Math:** General. **Mechanic/repair:** Automotive. **Parks/recreation:** General. **Personal/culinary services:** Culinary arts. **Philosophy/religion:** Philosophy. **Physical sciences:** Chemistry, geology, physics. **Production:** Woodworking. **Protective services:** Fire safety technology, police science. **Psychology:** General. **Social sciences:** Anthropology, criminology, economics, geography, political science, sociology. **Visual/performing arts:** Interior design, photography.

Student life. **Housing:** Single-sex dorms available. **Activities:** Bands, choral groups, drama, literary magazine, radio station, student government, student newspaper.

Athletics. **Intercollegiate:** Baseball M, basketball, cross-country, diving, football (tackle) M, golf M, softball W, swimming, tennis, track and field, volleyball W, wrestling M. **Team name:** Renegades.

Student services. Career counseling, student employment services, health services, on-campus daycare.

Contact. Phone: (661) 395-4301
Sue Vaughn, Director of Enrollment Services, Bakersfield College, 1801 Panorama Drive, Bakersfield, CA 93305

Barstow College

Barstow, California
www.barstow.edu **CB code: 4020**

- Public 2-year community college
- Large town

General. Founded in 1959. Regionally accredited. **Enrollment:** 2,175 degree-seeking undergraduates. **Degrees:** 447 associate awarded. **Location:** 70 miles from San Bernardino. **Calendar:** Semester, limited summer session. **Full-time faculty:** 36 total. **Part-time faculty:** 69 total.

Basis for selection. Open admission. Interviews required of full-time applicants.

2005-2006 Annual costs. Tuition/fees: $780; $5,190 out-of-state. Per-credit charge: $26 in-state; $173 out-of-state. Books/supplies: $685. Personal expenses: $1,500.

Financial aid. All financial aid based on need. Need-based aid available for part-time students.

Application procedures. **Admission:** Priority date 8/22; no deadline. No application fee. Admission notification on a rolling basis. **Financial aid:** Closing date 5/22. FAFSA required. Applicants notified on a rolling basis starting 7/1.

Academics. **Special study options:** Accelerated study, cooperative education, distance learning, dual enrollment of high school students, honors, independent study, internships, weekend college. **Credit/placement by examination:** CLEP, institutional tests. 30 credit hours maximum toward associate degree. **Support services:** Learning center, pre-admission summer program, reduced course load, remedial instruction, tutoring.

Majors. **Biology:** General. **Business:** General, accounting, administrative services, business admin, management information systems, managerial economics, office management, office technology, office/clerical, real estate. **Communications:** General. **Computer sciences:** General, applications programming, programming. **Education:** General, elementary, teacher assistance. **Family/consumer sciences:** Child care. **Liberal arts:** Arts/sciences. **Math:** General. **Production:** Welding. **Protective services:** Fire safety technology, police science. **Psychology:** General. **Social sciences:** General. **Visual/performing arts:** Dramatic, studio arts.

Computing on campus. 40 workstations in library, computer center.

Student life. **Activities:** Bands, choral groups, dance, drama, music ensembles, musical theater, student government, student newspaper, Circle-K, Christian club, Alpha Gamma Sigma.

Athletics. NJCAA. **Intercollegiate:** Baseball M, basketball M, cross-country, golf, soccer, tennis, volleyball W. **Intramural:** Badminton, baseball M, basketball, bowling, soccer, softball, swimming, tennis, volleyball.

Student services. Adult student services, career counseling, student employment services, personal counseling, placement for graduates, veterans' counselor. **Physically disabled:** Services for visually, speech, hearing impaired. **Transfer:** Special adviser, orientation for new students. Transfer adviser for students transferring to 4-year colleges.

Contact. Phone: (760) 252-2411 Fax: (760) 252-1875
Heather Porter, Director of Admissions, Barstow College, 2700 Barstow Road, Barstow, CA 92311-9984

Brooks College

Long Beach, California
www.brookscollege.edu **CB code: 1263**

- For-profit 2-year technical college
- Residential campus in very large city
- Interview required

General. Founded in 1971. Regionally accredited. Campuses in Long Beach, Sunnyvale. **Enrollment:** 700 degree-seeking undergraduates. **Degrees:** 612 associate awarded. **Location:** 15 miles from Los Angeles. **Calendar:** Quarter, extensive summer session. **Full-time faculty:** 16 total. **Part-time faculty:** 70 total. **Special facilities:** Antique clothing collection.

Student profile.

Out-of-state:	35%	**Live on campus:**	40%
25 or older:	14%		

Basis for selection. Open admission.

2005-2006 Annual costs. Quoted tuition for animation, graphic design, and multimedia programs. Tuition $11,000 for fashion design, fashion merchandising, and interior design programs. Books/supplies: $1,500. Personal expenses: $1,100.

Financial aid. Non-need-based: Scholarships awarded for academics.

Application procedures. Admission: No deadline. $50 fee, may be waived for applicants with need. Admission notification on a rolling basis. **Financial aid:** No deadline. FAFSA required. Applicants notified on a rolling basis starting 5/1; must reply within 2 week(s) of notification.

Academics. Curriculum is designed to prepare students for profession in fashion merchandising, fashion design, interior design, multimedia, and graphic design. **Special study options:** Cooperative education, ESL, internships. **Credit/placement by examination:** CLEP, IB. **Support services:** Learning center, remedial instruction, tutoring.

Majors. Business: Fashion. **Visual/performing arts:** Commercial/advertising art, fashion design, interior design.

Computing on campus. 30 workstations in library, computer center.

Student life. Freshman orientation: Mandatory. Held within 3 days of beginning of classes. **Policies:** Student activities council offers on-campus entertainment and intramural sports programs,trips to Europe, trips to off-campus sporting and cultural events, and participation in community programs. **Housing:** Single-sex dorms available. **Activities:** Drama, student government, student newspaper, international club.

Athletics. Intramural: Baseball M, basketball, softball, volleyball.

Student services. Adult student services, alcohol/substance abuse counseling, career counseling, services for economically disadvantaged, student employment services, financial aid counseling, placement for graduates, veterans' counselor.

Contact. Phone: (562) 498-2441 Fax: (562) 597-7412
Christine Varon, Dean of Admissions, Brooks College, 4825 East Pacific Coast Highway, Long Beach, CA 90804

Brooks College: Sunnyvale
Sunnyvale, California

- For-profit 2-year technical college
- Residential campus

General. Accredited by ACICS.

Contact. Phone: (408) 328-5700
1120 Kiefer Road, Sunnyvale, CA 94086

Butte College
Oroville, California
www.butte.edu **CB code: 4226**

- Public 2-year community college
- Commuter campus in small city

General. Founded in 1966. Regionally accredited. **Enrollment:** 8,356 degree-seeking undergraduates. **Degrees:** 982 associate awarded. **Location:** 100 miles from Sacramento. **Calendar:** Semester, extensive summer session. **Full-time faculty:** 130 total. **Part-time faculty:** 470 total. **Special facilities:** 900-acre wild game refuge, nature trails.

Basis for selection. Open admission, but selective for some programs. Nursing, allied health programs have selective admission. Interviews required for allied health applicants.

2005-2006 Annual costs. Tuition/fees: $946; $6,196 out-of-state. Per-credit charge: $26 in-state; $201 out-of-state. Books/supplies: $500. Personal expenses: $1,430.

Application procedures. Admission: No deadline. No application fee. Admission notification on a rolling basis. **Financial aid:** Priority date 5/1; no closing date. FAFSA required. Applicants notified on a rolling basis starting 8/1.

Academics. Special study options: Cooperative education, cross-registration, distance learning, double major, dual enrollment of high school students, ESL, honors, independent study, study abroad. **Credit/placement by examination:** CLEP, institutional tests. 9 credit hours maximum toward associate degree. **Support services:** Learning center, remedial instruction, tutoring.

Majors. Agriculture: Agronomy, animal sciences, business, horticulture, ornamental horticulture. **Business:** General, accounting, administrative services, business admin, fashion, management information systems, marketing, office technology, real estate, tourism promotion. **Communications:** Broadcast journalism, journalism. **Communications technology:** General, graphic/printing. **Computer sciences:** General, applications programming, networking. **Construction:** Maintenance. **Education:** General, bilingual, early childhood, physical. **Engineering technology:** Civil, construction, drafting, electrical. **Family/consumer sciences:** General, child care. **Health:** Cardiovascular technology, EMT paramedic, licensed practical nurse, medical assistant, medical secretary, nursing (RN), respiratory therapy technology, substance abuse counseling. **Legal studies:** Court reporting, legal secretary, paralegal, prelaw. **Liberal arts:** Arts/sciences. **Math:** General. **Mechanic/repair:** Automotive. **Parks/recreation:** Facilities management. **Personal/culinary services:** Cosmetic. **Production:** Welding. **Protective services:** Fire safety technology, police science. **Social sciences:** General. **Visual/performing arts:** Ceramics, commercial photography, commercial/advertising art, fashion design, photography, studio arts.

Computing on campus. 200 workstations in library, computer center.

Student life. Activities: Bands, drama, film society, music ensembles, radio station, student government, symphony orchestra, TV station.

Athletics. NJCAA. **Intercollegiate:** Baseball M, basketball, cross-country, field hockey W, football (tackle) M, golf, soccer, softball W, tennis, track and field, volleyball W.

Student services. Adult student services, career counseling, student employment services, health services, on-campus daycare, personal counseling, placement for graduates, veterans' counselor. **Physically disabled:** Services for visually, speech, hearing impaired. **Transfer:** Orientation, re-entry adviser for new students. Transfer center, transfer adviser for students transferring to 4-year colleges.

Contact. E-mail: admissions@butte.edu
Phone: (530) 895-2361 Fax: (530) 895-2411
Don Gray, Director of Admissions and Records, Butte College, 3536 Butte Campus Drive, Oroville, CA 95965

Cabrillo College
Aptos, California
www.cabrillo.edu **CB code: 4084**

- Public 2-year community college
- Commuter campus in large town

General. Founded in 1959. Regionally accredited. **Enrollment:** 7,264 degree-seeking undergraduates. **Degrees:** 798 associate awarded. **Location:** 25 miles from San Jose. **Calendar:** Semester, extensive summer session. **Full-time faculty:** 210 total. **Part-time faculty:** 360 total. **Special facilities:** Observatory, planetarium, horticulture garden.

Student profile. Among degree-seeking undergraduates, 52% enrolled in a transfer program.

Out-of-state:	2%	**25 or older:**	50%

Basis for selection. Open admission, but selective for some programs. Special prerequisite requirements for nursing, dental hygiene, and radiologic technology. International applicants have special admission requirements.

2005-2006 Annual costs. Tuition/fees: $818; $5,738 out-of-state. Per-credit charge: $26 in-state; $190 out-of-state. Books/supplies: $846. Personal expenses: $1,595.

Application procedures. Admission: No deadline. No application fee. Application may be submitted online. Admission notification on a rolling

basis beginning on or about 6/1. **Financial aid:** No deadline. FAFSA, institutional form required. Applicants notified on a rolling basis starting 7/31; must reply within 3 week(s) of notification.

Academics. **Special study options:** Dual enrollment of high school students, honors, independent study, internships, liberal arts/career combination, study abroad. License preparation in dental hygiene, nursing, radiology. **Credit/placement by examination:** AP, CLEP, institutional tests. **Support services:** Learning center, pre-admission summer program, reduced course load, remedial instruction, tutoring.

Majors. **Agriculture:** Ornamental horticulture. **Area/ethnic studies:** Asian. **Biology:** General. **Business:** General, accounting, banking/financial services, business admin, construction management, entrepreneurial studies, office technology, real estate. **Communications:** Journalism. **Computer sciences:** General, data processing. **Engineering technology:** Hazardous materials, solar energy. **English:** Speech/rhetoric. **Family/consumer sciences:** General, child care. **Foreign languages:** General, Chinese, French, German, Italian, Japanese, Russian, Spanish. **Health:** Dental hygiene, licensed practical nurse, medical assistant, medical radiologic technology/radiation therapy, nursing (RN). **History:** General. **Liberal arts:** Arts/sciences, library science. **Math:** General. **Mechanic/repair:** Industrial. **Physical sciences:** Chemistry, physics. **Protective services:** Firefighting, police science. **Psychology:** General. **Social sciences:** General, anthropology, economics, geography, political science, sociology. **Visual/performing arts:** General, art, dance, studio arts.

Computing on campus. 350 workstations in library, computer center.

Student life. **Freshman orientation:** Available. Preregistration for classes offered. **Activities:** Bands, choral groups, dance, drama, music ensembles, musical theater, student government, student newspaper, various clubs, literacy, recreational, cultural and/or ethnic organizations.

Athletics. **Intercollegiate:** Baseball M, basketball, cross-country, diving, football (tackle) M, golf M, soccer M, softball W, swimming, tennis, track and field, volleyball W, water polo M. **Team name:** Seahawks.

Student services. Adult student services, career counseling, student employment services, health services, personal counseling, placement for graduates, veterans' counselor. **Physically disabled:** Services for visually, speech, hearing impaired. **Transfer:** Special adviser, orientation for new students. Transfer adviser for students transferring to 4-year colleges.

Contact. Phone: (831) 479-6201 Fax: (831) 479-5782
Gloria Garing, Registrar, Cabrillo College, 6500 Soquel Drive, Aptos, CA 95003

California Culinary Academy

San Francisco, California
www.caculinary.edu **CB code: 2209**

- For-profit 2-year culinary school
- Commuter campus in very large city
- Interview required

General. Founded in 1977. Accredited by ACCSCT. Housed in historic landmark building in San Francisco. Most culinary programs offered sanctioned by Le Cordon Bleu. **Enrollment:** 1,030 degree-seeking undergraduates. **Degrees:** 1,682 associate awarded. **Location:** Downtown. **Calendar:** Continuous. **Full-time faculty:** 80 total. **Part-time faculty:** 2 total. **Class size:** 100% 20-39. **Special facilities:** 2 student-staffed public restaurants, retail store, mixology lab, gaming room, professional production kitchens, demonstration kitchens, pastry kitchens, confisseries, lecture classrooms with wireless network access, library.

Student profile.

Out-of-state:	10%	**Live on campus:**	32%
25 or older:	25%		

Basis for selection. Interview important, character and personal qualities and work experience considered. Wonderlic required for baking and pastry certificate program. **Adult students:** Entrance exam policies same as for first-time freshmen.

2005-2006 Annual costs. Books/supplies: $2,664.

Financial aid. **Additional information:** Financial aid forms due 60 days prior to first day of classes.

Application procedures. **Admission:** No deadline. $65 fee, may be waived for applicants with need. Application may be submitted online. Admission notification on a rolling basis. **Financial aid:** No deadline. FAFSA required. Applicants notified on a rolling basis; must reply within 1 week(s) of notification.

Academics. Hands-on associate degree programs in Le Cordon Bleu Culinary Arts and Hospitality & Restaurant Management, and certificate program in Baking & Pastry Arts offered. **Special study options:** Honors, internships. **Credit/placement by examination:** CLEP. **Support services:** Study skills assistance.

Majors. **Personal/culinary services:** Culinary arts, restaurant/catering.

Computing on campus. 35 workstations in library, computer center. Wireless network available.

Student life. **Freshman orientation:** Mandatory. **Housing:** Coed dorms available. $600 deposit. **Activities:** Brewing arts association, Cuisine Des Femmes, Asian food club, baking and pastry arts club, dinner club, wine club.

Student services. Career counseling, student employment services, financial aid counseling, placement for graduates. **Transfer:** Special adviser, orientation, re-entry adviser, pre-admission transcript evaluation for new students.

Contact. E-mail: admissions@caculinary.edu
Phone: (415) 771-3500 Toll-free number: (800) 229-2433
Fax: (415) 771-2194
Heatlher McBreen, Senior Director of Admissions, California Culinary Academy, 625 Polk Street, San Francisco, CA 94102

California Design College

Los Angeles, California
www.cdc.edu **CB code: 3463**

- For-profit 2-year visual arts and technical college
- Very large city
- Application essay, interview required

General. Accredited by ACICS. **Enrollment:** 360 degree-seeking undergraduates. **Degrees:** 97 associate awarded. **Calendar:** Quarter. **Full-time faculty:** 5 total. **Part-time faculty:** 50 total.

Basis for selection. Interview, academic transcripts, essay important.

2005-2006 Annual costs. Cost for 7-quarter continuous enrollment associate degree program $42,560; cost for 12-quarter continuous enrollment bachelor's degree program $72,960. Fees vary by program. Books/supplies: $630. Personal expenses: $1,694.

Application procedures. **Admission:** No application fee.

Academics. **Credit/placement by examination:** CLEP.

Majors. **Visual/performing arts:** Fashion design.

Contact. E-mail: aicdcadm@aii.edu
Phone: (213) 251-3636 ext. 220
Jesus Moreno, Director of Admissions, California Design College, 3440 Wilshire Boulevard, 10th Floor, Los Angeles, CA 90010

California School of Culinary Arts

Pasadena, California
www.csca.edu

- For-profit 2-year culinary school
- Commuter campus in very large city
- Interview required

General. Accredited by ACICS. **Enrollment:** 1,686 degree-seeking undergraduates. **Degrees:** 687 associate awarded. **Location:** 15 miles from downtown Los Angeles. **Calendar:** Continuous. **Full-time faculty:** 80 total; 1% have terminal degrees, 30% minority, 38% women. **Part-time faculty:** 11 total; 36% minority, 54% women. **Class size:** 100% 20-39. **Special facilities:** School cafe and fine-dining restaurant where students gain practical work experience.

Student profile. Among degree-seeking undergraduates, 100% enrolled in a vocational program, 3% already have a bachelor's degree or higher, 896 enrolled as first-time, first-year students, 4 transferred in from other institutions.

Transfer out. Colleges most students transferred to 2005: California Culinary Academy, Scottsdale Culinary Institute.

Basis for selection. Open admission. Students whose first language is not English are required to submit evidence of English Proficiency. This may be done by submitting a TOEFL test score of 500 or higher (for the CPT version, a score of 150 or higher). Entrance Test is required by state agency (BPPVE) for diploma programs. CSCA utilizes the Wonderlic SLE Exam to comply with these regulations. **Learning Disabled:** Students requesting special needs and services are required to submit an Application for Auxiliary Aid request. The application must include supporting documentation as evidence of the disability.

2005-2006 Annual costs. Books/supplies: $1,500. Personal expenses: $1,347.

2004-2005 Financial aid. Need-based: 26% of total undergraduate aid awarded as scholarships/grants, 74% as loans/jobs. Need-based aid available for part-time students. Work study available nights and weekends.

Application procedures. Admission: No deadline. $100 fee. Application may be submitted online. Admission notification on a rolling basis. **Financial aid:** No deadline. FAFSA required. Applicants notified on a rolling basis.

Academics. Special study options: Honors. **Credit/placement by examination:** AP, CLEP. **Support services:** Learning center, reduced course load, study skills assistance, tutoring.

Majors. Personal/culinary services: Chef training.

Computing on campus. 35 workstations in library. Online library available.

Student life. Freshman orientation: Mandatory. **Policies:** Freshmen permitted cars on campus. **Housing:** Outside agency handles all housing issues for participating students. **Activities:** Student newspaper.

Student services. Adult student services, career counseling, financial aid counseling, placement for graduates. **Transfer:** Re-entry adviser, preadmission transcript evaluation for new students.

Contact. E-mail: ecolon@scsca.com
Phone: (626) 229-1300 Toll-free number: (888) 900-2433
Fax: (626) 403-4835
Ed Colon, Vice President of Admissions, California School of Culinary Arts, 521 East Green Street, Pasadena, CA 91101

Canada College

Redwood City, California
canadacollege.edu **CB code: 4109**

- Public 2-year community college
- Commuter campus in small city

General. Founded in 1968. Regionally accredited. **Enrollment:** 2,931 degree-seeking undergraduates. **Degrees:** 174 associate awarded. **Location:** 20 miles from San Francisco. **Calendar:** Semester, limited summer session. **Full-time faculty:** 80 total. **Part-time faculty:** 120 total.

Student profile. Among degree-seeking undergraduates, 80% enrolled in a transfer program, 20% enrolled in a vocational program, 19% already have a bachelor's degree or higher.

Basis for selection. Open admission, but selective for some programs. Special admission to radiologic technology programs.

2005-2006 Annual costs. Tuition/fees: $806; $5,876 out-of-state. Per-credit charge: $26 in-state; $195 out-of-state. Books/supplies: $630. Personal expenses: $1,450.

Application procedures. Admission: No deadline. No application fee. Admission notification on a rolling basis. **Financial aid:** Priority date 5/8; no closing date. FAFSA required. Applicants notified on a rolling basis starting 7/15; must reply within 2 week(s) of notification.

Academics. Special study options: Cooperative education, cross-registration, distance learning, double major, dual enrollment of high school students, ESL, independent study, internships, study abroad. **Credit/placement by examination:** AP, CLEP, IB, institutional tests. 12 credit hours maximum toward associate degree. **Support services:** Learning center, reduced course load, remedial instruction, study skills assistance, tutoring, writing center.

Majors. Biology: General. **Business:** General, accounting, administrative services, banking/financial services, business admin, fashion, management information systems, management science, office technology, office/clerical, tourism/travel. **Communications:** Journalism. **Computer sciences:** General, applications programming, programming. **Education:** Early childhood. **Engineering technology:** Computer hardware. **Family/consumer sciences:** General, child care. **Foreign languages:** French, Spanish. **Health:** Medical radiologic technology/radiation therapy, ophthalmic lab technology. **History:** General. **Legal studies:** Paralegal. **Liberal arts:** Arts/sciences. **Math:** General. **Philosophy/religion:** Philosophy. **Physical sciences:** Chemistry, physics. **Psychology:** General. **Public administration:** Human services. **Social sciences:** General, anthropology, geography, political science. **Visual/performing arts:** Art, dramatic, interior design, multimedia.

Computing on campus. 300 workstations in library, computer center. Online course registration available.

Student life. Freshman orientation: Available. Preregistration for classes offered. **Activities:** Concert band, choral groups, dance, drama, music ensembles, student government, symphony orchestra, Latin American club, Rotarians, international student club, black student union.

Athletics. NJCAA. **Intercollegiate:** Baseball M, basketball M, golf M, soccer W, tennis M. **Team name:** Colts.

Student services. Adult student services, career counseling, health services, personal counseling, veterans' counselor. **Physically disabled:** Services for visually, hearing impaired. **Transfer:** Special adviser, orientation for new students. Transfer adviser, college fairs on campus for students transferring to 4-year colleges.

Contact. Phone: (650) 306-3226 Fax: (650) 306-3113
Ruth Miller, Assistant Registrar, Canada College, 4200 Farm Hill Boulevard, Redwood City, CA 94061

Cerritos Community College

Norwalk, California **CB member**
www.cerritos.edu **CB code: 4083**

- Public 2-year community college
- Commuter campus in small city

General. Founded in 1955. Regionally accredited. **Enrollment:** 21,000 undergraduates. **Degrees:** 1,232 associate awarded. **Location:** 15 miles from Los Angeles. **Calendar:** Semester, limited summer session. **Full-time faculty:** 285 total. **Part-time faculty:** 585 total.

Basis for selection. Open admission, but selective for some programs. Limited admissions to nursing program.

2005-2006 Annual costs. Tuition/fees: $808; $5,338 out-of-state. Per-credit charge: $26 in-state; $177 out-of-state. Books/supplies: $648. Personal expenses: $1,710.

Application procedures. Admission: No deadline. No application fee. Admission notification on a rolling basis. **Financial aid:** Priority date 5/8; no closing date. FAFSA required. Applicants notified on a rolling basis; must reply within 2 week(s) of notification.

Academics. Special study options: Cooperative education, distance learning, dual enrollment of high school students, honors. License preparation in dental hygiene, nursing, physical therapy. **Credit/placement by examination:** CLEP, institutional tests. 12 credit hours maximum toward associate degree. **Support services:** Learning center, remedial instruction, tutoring.

Majors. Agriculture: Ornamental horticulture. **Area/ethnic studies:** Hispanic-American/Latino/Chicano. **Biology:** General, bacteriology, biomedical sciences, botany, zoology. **Business:** General, accounting, administrative services, banking/financial services, business admin, human resources, logistics, office management, office/clerical, real estate. **Communications:** Journalism. **Computer sciences:** General, applications programming, data processing, programming, systems analysis. **Conservation:** Wildlife. **Education:** Bilingual, early childhood, special, teacher assistance. **Engineering technology:** Drafting, electrical, manufacturing, plastics, robotics. **English:** Speech/rhetoric. **Family/consumer sciences:** General, clothing/textiles, institutional food production. **Foreign languages:** French, German, Spanish. **Health:** Dental assistant, dental hygiene, licensed practical nurse, medical assistant, medical records technology, nursing (RN), physical therapy assistant. **History:** General. **Legal studies:** Court reporting, paralegal. **Liberal arts:** Arts/sciences. **Math:** General. **Mechanic/repair:** General, auto body, electronics/electrical. **Parks/recreation:** General. **Philosophy/religion:** Philosophy. **Physical sciences:** Chemistry, geology, physics, planetary. **Protective services:** Police science. **Psychology:** General. **Social sciences:** Anthropology, economics, geography, political science, sociology. **Visual/performing arts:** Art, dramatic, interior design, photography.

Computing on campus. 100 workstations in computer center.

Student life. Activities: Bands, choral groups, dance, drama, film society, literary magazine, music ensembles, musical theater, radio station, student government, student newspaper, symphony orchestra, Ahora, Indian club, Vietnamese club, Black Student Union.

Athletics. NJCAA. **Intercollegiate:** Baseball M, basketball, cross-country, diving, football (tackle) M, golf M, soccer M, softball W, swimming, tennis, track and field, volleyball W, water polo M, wrestling M.

Student services. Adult student services, career counseling, financial aid counseling, health services, on-campus daycare, personal counseling, veterans' counselor, women's services. **Physically disabled:** Services for visually, speech, hearing impaired. **Transfer:** Special adviser, orientation for new students. Transfer adviser, college fairs on campus for students transferring to 4-year colleges.

Contact. Phone: (562) 860-2451 Fax: (562) 860-9680
Stephanie Murguia, Dean, Admissions and Records, Cerritos Community College, 11110 Alondra Boulevard, Norwalk, CA 90650

Cerro Coso Community College

Ridgecrest, California
www.cerrocoso.edu **CB code: 4027**

- Public 2-year community college
- Commuter campus in large town

General. Founded in 1973. Regionally accredited. **Enrollment:** 560 full-time, degree-seeking students. **Degrees:** 251 associate awarded. **Location:** 120 miles from Bakersfield. **Calendar:** Semester, limited summer session. **Full-time faculty:** 55 total; 27% have terminal degrees. **Part-time faculty:** 140 total. **Class size:** 44% < 20, 52% 20-39, 3% 40-49, 1% 50-99. **Special facilities:** Nature preserve, sculpture garden.

Student profile. Among full-time, degree-seeking students, 88% enrolled in a transfer program, 5% enrolled in a vocational program, 11% already have a bachelor's degree or higher, 254 enrolled as first-time, first-year students.

Out-of-state:	2%	**25 or older:**	63%

Basis for selection. Open admission. Interview required of nursing majors.

2005-2006 Annual costs. Tuition/fees: $780; $5,790 out-of-state. Per-credit charge: $26 in-state; $191 out-of-state. Books/supplies: $882. Personal expenses: $1,656.

Financial aid. Need-based: Need-based aid available for part-time students. Work study available nights and for part-time students.

Application procedures. Admission: No deadline. No application fee. Application may be submitted online. Admission notification on a rolling basis. **Financial aid:** Priority date 5/15; no closing date. FAFSA required. Applicants notified on a rolling basis starting 6/1; must reply within 2 week(s) of notification.

Academics. Special study options: Cooperative education, distance learning, double major, dual enrollment of high school students, ESL, honors, independent study, internships, study abroad. License preparation in nursing. **Credit/placement by examination:** AP, CLEP. 30 credit hours maximum toward associate degree. **Support services:** GED preparation and test center, learning center, remedial instruction, study skills assistance, tutoring.

Majors. Business: General, administrative services, business admin, office management, office technology, office/clerical. **Computer sciences:** General. **Education:** Early childhood. **Engineering technology:** General, drafting, electrical. **Family/consumer sciences:** Child care. **Health:** Licensed practical nurse. **Interdisciplinary:** Biological/physical sciences. **Liberal arts:** Arts/sciences. **Mechanic/repair:** Auto body, heating/ac/refrig. **Parks/recreation:** Facilities management. **Physical sciences:** General. **Protective services:** Fire safety technology, police science. **Social sciences:** General. **Visual/performing arts:** Art.

Most popular majors. Business/marketing 20%, liberal arts 49%, social sciences 13%.

Computing on campus. Online course registration, online library available.

Student life. Freshman orientation: Available. **Activities:** Bands, choral groups, drama, literary magazine, student government, student newspaper, symphony orchestra.

Athletics. Intercollegiate: Baseball M, basketball W, softball W, volleyball W. **Team name:** Coyotes.

Student services. Career counseling, student employment services, financial aid counseling, on-campus daycare, personal counseling, placement for graduates, veterans' counselor. **Physically disabled:** Services for visually, speech, hearing impaired. **Learning disabled:** Comprehensive services available. **Transfer:** Special adviser, orientation for new students. Transfer adviser, college fairs on campus for students transferring to 4-year colleges.

Contact. E-mail: jboard@cerrocoso.edu
Phone: (760) 384-6357 Fax: (760) 384-6377
Jill Board, Vice President, Cerro Coso Community College, 3000 College Heights Boulevard, Ridgecrest, CA 93555-7777

Chabot College

Hayward, California
www.chabotcollege.edu **CB code: 4725**

- Public 2-year community college
- Commuter campus in large city

General. Founded in 1961. Regionally accredited. **Enrollment:** 7,313 degree-seeking undergraduates; 7,586 non-degree-seeking students. **Degrees:** 610 associate awarded. **ROTC:** Army, Air Force. **Location:** 30 miles from San Francisco, 15 miles from Berkeley. **Calendar:** Semester, extensive summer session. **Full-time faculty:** 175 total; 27% minority, 46% women. **Part-time faculty:** 350 total; 29% minority, 44% women. **Special facilities:** Planetarium, theater. **Partnerships:** Formal partnership with Lawrence Livermore National Lab.

Student profile. Among degree-seeking undergraduates, 10% already have a bachelor's degree or higher, 1,174 enrolled as first-time, first-year students, 2,862 transferred in from other institutions.

Part-time:	62%	**Women:**	58%
Out-of-state:	1%	**25 or older:**	35%

Transfer out. Colleges most students transferred to 2005: California State University at Hayward, California State University at San Jose, University of California at Berkeley, California State University at San Francisco, University of California at Davis.

Basis for selection. Open admission. All applicants must be 18 years of age or high school graduates. Selective admission to nursing, dental hygiene, and paramedic programs.

2005-2006 Annual costs. Tuition/fees: $808; $5,488 out-of-state. Per-credit charge: $26 in-state; $182 out-of-state. Books/supplies: $1,206. Personal expenses: $2,340.

Financial aid. Need-based: Work study available nights, weekends and for part-time students. **Additional information:** Tuition and/or fee waivers for low-income students.

Application procedures. Admission: No deadline. No application fee. Application may be submitted online. Admission notification on a rolling basis. Early action available for local high school students only. **Financial aid:** Priority date 8/1; no closing date. FAFSA, institutional form required. Applicants notified on a rolling basis.

Academics. Special study options: Cooperative education, cross-registration, distance learning, double major, dual enrollment of high school students, ESL, independent study, internships, liberal arts/career combination, student-designed major, study abroad, weekend college. License preparation in nursing. **Credit/placement by examination:** CLEP, institutional tests. 15 credit hours maximum toward associate degree. English and math tests required for placement. **Support services:** Learning center, pre-admission summer program, reduced course load, remedial instruction, study skills assistance, tutoring, writing center.

Majors. Biology: General. **Business:** General, accounting, administrative services, banking/financial services, logistics, management information systems, management science, office management, office technology, office/clerical, real estate, sales/distribution, tourism/travel. **Communications:** Broadcast journalism, journalism. **Communications technology:** General, radio/tv. **Computer sciences:** General, applications programming, computer science, data processing, information systems, programming. **Construction:** Maintenance, power transmission. **Education:** Early childhood, teacher assistance. **Engineering:** General. **Engineering technology:** Architectural, civil, drafting, electrical, surveying. **English:** Speech/rhetoric. **Family/consumer**

sciences: Child care, clothing/textiles. **Foreign languages:** French, German, Italian, Portuguese, Spanish. **Health:** Clinical lab technology, dental hygiene, medical assistant, medical records admin, medical records technology, nursing (RN), predentistry, premedicine, prepharmacy, preveterinary. **History:** General. **Legal studies:** Court reporting, legal secretary, prelaw. **Liberal arts:** Arts/sciences, library assistant. **Math:** General, statistics. **Mechanic/repair:** Auto body, automotive, electronics/electrical. **Parks/ recreation:** General. **Personal/culinary services:** General. **Philosophy/ religion:** Philosophy. **Physical sciences:** Physics. **Production:** Welding. **Protective services:** Firefighting, police science. **Psychology:** General. **Social sciences:** General, criminology, geography, political science, sociology. **Transportation:** Aviation, flight attendant. **Visual/performing arts:** Art, ceramics, commercial/advertising art, dance, dramatic, drawing, music performance, painting, photography, sculpture, studio arts.

Most popular majors. Business/marketing 10%, health sciences 15%, liberal arts 50%.

Student life. **Freshman orientation:** Available. Introduction to college experience, programs, services, and registration process. **Activities:** Bands, choral groups, drama, film society, literary magazine, musical theater, radio station, student government, student newspaper, TV station, various religious, political, ethnic, and social service organizations.

Athletics. NJCAA. **Intercollegiate:** Baseball M, basketball, cross-country, football (tackle) M, golf M, soccer, softball W, swimming, tennis, track and field, volleyball W, water polo W, wrestling M. **Intramural:** Archery, badminton, basketball, bowling, handball, racquetball, soccer, softball, table tennis, tennis, volleyball. **Team name:** Gladiators.

Student services. Adult student services, career counseling, student employment services, on-campus daycare, personal counseling, placement for graduates. **Physically disabled:** Services for visually, speech, hearing impaired. **Transfer:** Special adviser, orientation, re-entry adviser for new students. Transfer center, college fairs on campus for students transferring to 4-year colleges.

Contact. E-mail: jyoung@chabotcollege.edu
Phone: (510) 723-6700 Fax: (510) 723-7510
Judy Young, Registrar, Chabot College, 25555 Hesperian Boulevard, Hayward, CA 94545

Chaffey Community College

Rancho Cucamonga, California — **CB member**
www.chaffey.cc.ca.us — **CB code: 4046**

- Public 2-year community college
- Commuter campus in small city

General. Founded in 1883. Regionally accredited. **Enrollment:** 5,776 full-time, degree-seeking students. **Degrees:** 1,116 associate awarded. **Location:** 50 miles from Los Angeles. **Calendar:** Semester, limited summer session. **Special facilities:** Nature preserve, natural history collection, planetarium, 2 swimming pools, children's center, museum/gallery, theater.

Basis for selection. Open admission. Assessment testing is recommended.

2005-2006 Annual costs. Tuition/fees: $802; $5,332 out-of-state. Per-credit charge: $26 in-state; $177 out-of-state. Books/supplies: $650. Personal expenses: $1,710.

Financial aid. **Need-based:** Need-based aid available for part-time students. Work study available for part-time students. **Non-need-based:** Scholarships awarded for academics. **Additional information:** State of California Board of Governors fee waivers to qualified state residents. Criteria for eligibility: households which receive public assistance, meet state's low income guidelines, and demonstrate need as defined by Title IV programs.

Application procedures. **Admission:** No deadline. No application fee. Admission notification on a rolling basis. **Financial aid:** No deadline. FAFSA required. Applicants notified on a rolling basis starting 7/15; must reply within 2 week(s) of notification.

Academics. **Special study options:** Accelerated study, cooperative education, dual enrollment of high school students, ESL, honors, independent study, internships, liberal arts/career combination, study abroad, weekend college. License preparation in aviation, nursing. **Credit/placement by examination:** CLEP, institutional tests. **Support services:** GED preparation, learning center, remedial instruction, tutoring, writing center.

Majors. **Biology:** General. **Business:** Accounting, administrative services, business admin, fashion, office management, sales/distribution. **Communications:** General, broadcast journalism. **Computer sciences:** General, applications programming. **Conservation:** Environmental studies. **Education:** General, early childhood, physical. **Engineering:** General. **Engineering technology:** Architectural, drafting. **Family/consumer sciences:** General, child care. **Foreign languages:** French, German, Spanish. **Health:** Dental assistant, medical radiologic technology/radiation therapy, nursing (RN). **History:** General. **Interdisciplinary:** Gerontology, science/society. **Liberal arts:** Arts/sciences. **Math:** General. **Mechanic/repair:** Aircraft, auto body, automotive, electronics/electrical. **Philosophy/religion:** Philosophy, religion. **Physical sciences:** Chemistry, geology, physics, planetary. **Psychology:** General. **Social sciences:** General, anthropology, economics, geography, political science, sociology. **Visual/performing arts:** Art, commercial/advertising art, dance, design, dramatic, fashion design, graphic design, interior design, multimedia, photography, studio arts.

Computing on campus. 950 workstations in library, computer center. Repair service available.

Student life. **Freshman orientation:** Mandatory. 3-hour session covers registration procedures, fees, financial aid, programs and services, counseling, course descriptions. **Activities:** Bands, choral groups, dance, drama, film society, music ensembles, musical theater, student government, student newspaper, multicultural organizations, Model United Nations, Vietnamese club, MECHA, Alpha Gamma Sigma, Black Student Union, ski club, religious organizations, French club, German club, Spanish club, Lambda.

Athletics. **Intercollegiate:** Baseball M, basketball, diving, football (tackle) M, softball W, swimming, volleyball W, water polo M. **Team name:** Panthers.

Student services. Alcohol/substance abuse counseling, career counseling, services for economically disadvantaged, student employment services, financial aid counseling, health services, on-campus daycare, personal counseling, veterans' counselor. **Physically disabled:** Services for visually, speech, hearing impaired. **Transfer:** Special adviser, orientation, pre-admission transcript evaluation for new students. Transfer center, transfer adviser, college fairs on campus for students transferring to 4-year colleges.

Contact. Phone: (909) 941-2483 Fax: (909) 941-2783
Cecilia Carrera, Director of Admissions, Chaffey Community College, 5885 Haven Avenue, Rancho Cucamonga, CA 91701-3002

Citrus College

Glendora, California
www.citruscollege.edu — **CB code: 4051**

- Public 2-year community college
- Commuter campus in large town

General. Founded in 1915. Regionally accredited. **Enrollment:** 9,909 degree-seeking undergraduates. **Degrees:** 902 associate awarded. **Location:** 25 miles from Los Angeles. **Calendar:** Semester, limited summer session. **Full-time faculty:** 162 total. **Part-time faculty:** 255 total. **Special facilities:** Performing arts center, golf driving range.

Student profile.

Out-of-state:	3%	**25 or older:**	29%

Basis for selection. Open admission.

2005-2006 Annual costs. Tuition/fees: $808; $5,338 out-of-state. Per-credit charge: $26 in-state; $177 out-of-state. Books/supplies: $1,260. Personal expenses: $2,340.

2005-2006 Financial aid. **Need-based:** 3% of total undergraduate aid awarded as scholarships/grants, 97% as loans/jobs. Need-based aid available for part-time students. Work study available nights, weekends and for part-time students.

Application procedures. **Admission:** No deadline. No application fee. Application must be submitted on paper. Admission notification on a rolling basis. **Financial aid:** Priority date 3/1; no closing date. FAFSA required. Applicants notified on a rolling basis; must reply within 2 week(s) of notification.

Academics. **Special study options:** Cooperative education, distance learning, double major, dual enrollment of high school students, ESL, honors, independent study, study abroad. License preparation in nursing. **Credit/ placement by examination:** AP, CLEP. 30 credit hours maximum toward associate degree. **Support services:** Learning center, remedial instruction, tutoring.

Majors. **Biology:** Botany, zoology. **Business:** General, management information systems, office management, office/clerical. **Computer sciences:** General, data processing. **Conservation:** Forestry. **Engineering:** General. **Engineering technology:** Drafting. **Foreign languages:** French, German, Japanese,

Spanish. **Health:** Dental assistant, licensed practical nurse, medical assistant. **Interdisciplinary:** Biological/physical sciences. **Liberal arts:** Arts/sciences, library assistant, library science. **Math:** General. **Mechanic/repair:** Automotive, diesel, electronics/electrical, heating/ac/refrig. **Parks/recreation:** Health/fitness. **Personal/culinary services:** Cosmetic. **Physical sciences:** Chemistry, physics. **Protective services:** Criminal justice, law enforcement admin. **Psychology:** General. **Social sciences:** General. **Visual/performing arts:** Art, photography, studio arts.

Most popular majors. Business/marketing 17%, English 6%, interdisciplinary studies 13%, liberal arts 17%, social sciences 35%, visual/performing arts 9%.

Computing on campus. 1,100 workstations in library, computer center. Online course registration available.

Student life. **Freshman orientation:** Available. **Policies:** Freshmen permitted cars on campus. **Activities:** Jazz band, dance, drama, literary magazine, music ensembles, musical theater, student government, student newspaper, African American Student Alliance, European Heritage Club, Get Real Christian Fellowship, International Students Club, Latinos Unidos Student Association, Latter Day Saints Students Association, Natives of the Americas Student Association, Students United for Societal Change.

Athletics. **Intercollegiate:** Baseball M, basketball, cross-country, football (tackle) M, golf, soccer, softball W, swimming, tennis, track and field, volleyball W, water polo. **Team name:** Owls.

Student services. Career counseling, services for economically disadvantaged, student employment services, financial aid counseling, health services, legal services, minority student services, on-campus daycare, personal counseling, placement for graduates, veterans' counselor. **Physically disabled:** Services for visually, speech, hearing impaired.

Contact. E-mail: admissions@citruscollege.edu
Phone: (626) 914-8511 Fax: (626) 914-8613
Lois Papner, Associate Dean of Admissions & Financial Aid, Citrus College, 1000 West Foothill Boulevard, Glendora, CA 91741-1899

City College of San Francisco

San Francisco, California CB member
www.ccsf.edu CB code: 4052

- Public 2-year community college
- Commuter campus in very large city

General. Founded in 1935. Regionally accredited. **Enrollment:** 12,391 degree-seeking undergraduates. **Degrees:** 1,236 associate awarded. **Location:** Downtown. **Calendar:** Semester, extensive summer session. **Full-time faculty:** 720 total. **Part-time faculty:** 1,300 total. **Special facilities:** Observatory.

Transfer out. **Colleges most students transferred to 2005:** San Francisco State College, California State University-Hayward, San Jose State College, University of California-Berkeley, University of California-Davis.

Basis for selection. Open admission. If applicant lacks high school diploma, must be 18 or older and demonstrate ability to benefit. All students entering the credit program are tested for placement into English, Mathematics, and ESL courses. **Adult students:** Entrance exam policies same as for first-time freshmen.

2005-2006 Annual costs. Tuition/fees: $806; $5,126 out-of-state. Per-credit charge: $26 in-state; $170 out-of-state. Books/supplies: $648. Personal expenses: $2,000.

Financial aid. **Need-based:** Work study available nights, weekends and for part-time students.

Application procedures. **Admission:** No deadline. No application fee. Application may be submitted online. Admission notification on a rolling basis. **Financial aid:** Priority date 3/1; no closing date. FAFSA required. Applicants notified on a rolling basis starting 7/1.

Academics. **Special study options:** Accelerated study, cooperative education, distance learning, dual enrollment of high school students, ESL, independent study, internships, liberal arts/career combination, study abroad, weekend college. License preparation in dental hygiene, nursing, paramedic, radiology. **Credit/placement by examination:** AP, CLEP, institutional tests. 45 credit hours maximum toward associate degree. **Support services:** GED preparation and test center, learning center, pre-admission summer program, remedial instruction, study skills assistance, tutoring, writing center.

Majors. **Agriculture:** Ornamental horticulture. **Architecture:** Environmental design, landscape. **Area/ethnic studies:** African-American, Chinese, gay/lesbian, Hispanic-American/Latino/Chicano. **Biology:** General. **Business:** Accounting, administrative services, business admin, fashion, hospitality/recreation, human resources, management information systems, marketing, office technology, office/clerical, operations, real estate, tourism promotion, tourism/travel. **Communications:** Broadcast journalism, journalism. **Communications technology:** General, graphic/printing. **Computer sciences:** General, applications programming, programming. **Construction:** Maintenance. **Education:** Teacher assistance. **Engineering:** General, civil, electrical, mechanical, mechanics. **Engineering technology:** Architectural, civil, drafting, electrical. **Family/consumer sciences:** General, food/nutrition. **Health:** Clinical lab science, dental assistant, dental lab technology, medical assistant, medical radiologic technology/radiation therapy, medical records admin, medical records technology, medical secretary, physician assistant, predentistry, premedicine, prepharmacy. **Legal studies:** Court reporting, legal secretary, paralegal. **Liberal arts:** Arts/sciences, library assistant, library science. **Mechanic/repair:** Aircraft. **Physical sciences:** Chemistry. **Protective services:** Fire safety technology, police science. **Transportation:** Aviation. **Visual/performing arts:** Cinematography, commercial/advertising art, interior design, photography, printmaking, studio arts.

Computing on campus. 656 workstations in library, computer center, student center. Commuter students can connect to campus network. Online library available.

Student life. **Freshman orientation:** Available. Mandatory for degree-seeking students taking 9 or more credit units. **Activities:** Jazz band, choral groups, dance, drama, film society, music ensembles, musical theater, opera, radio station, student government, student newspaper, TV station, Intervarsity Christian Fellowship, Newman Center, Baptist Campus Ministry, Black Students' Union, La Raza Unida, Chinese culture club, UPASA Filipino cub, Gay and Lesbian Alliance, campus police service organization.

Athletics. NJCAA. **Intercollegiate:** Badminton W, baseball M, basketball, cross-country, football (tackle) M, judo, soccer M, softball W, swimming, tennis, track and field, volleyball W. **Intramural:** Fencing W.

Student services. Career counseling, services for economically disadvantaged, student employment services, financial aid counseling, health services, minority student services, on-campus daycare, personal counseling, placement for graduates, veterans' counselor. **Physically disabled:** Services for visually, hearing impaired. **Transfer:** Special adviser, orientation for new students. Transfer adviser, college fairs on campus for students transferring to 4-year colleges.

Contact. E-mail: applications@ccsf.edu
Phone: (415) 239-3285 Fax: (415) 239-3936
Robert Balestreri, Dean of Admissions and Records, City College of San Francisco, 50 Phelan Avenue, San Francisco, CA 94112

Coastline Community College

Fountain Valley, California
www.coastline.cccd.edu CB code: 0933

- Public 2-year community college
- Commuter campus in small city

General. Founded in 1976. Regionally accredited. Classes held at community-based sites during the daytime, evenings, weekends, and through extensive distance learning education. **Enrollment:** 5,167 degree-seeking undergraduates. **Degrees:** 682 associate awarded. **Location:** 30 miles from Los Angeles. **Calendar:** Semester, limited summer session. **Full-time faculty:** 44 total. **Part-time faculty:** 217 total. **Class size:** 45% < 20, 40% 20-39, 6% 40-49, 6% 50-99, 2% >100. **Special facilities:** Computer commons at Garden Grove center for all students. One-stop center in Costa Mesa prepares and gears students to the workplace.

Student profile.

Out-of-state:	1%	**25 or older:**	73%

Transfer out. **Colleges most students transferred to 2005:** California State University: Long Beach, University of California: Irvine, California State University: Fullerton, National University.

Basis for selection. Open admission. College administered English and math tests used for placement.

2005-2006 Annual costs. Tuition/fees: $806; $5,366 out-of-state. Per-credit charge: $26 in-state; $178 out-of-state. Books/supplies: $648. Personal expenses: $1,566.

2004-2005 Financial aid. All financial aid based on need. Need-based aid available for part-time students. **Additional information:** Board of Governor's Grant: statewide fee waiver program for students or dependents receiving HFOL/TANF, SSI, General Relief, or whose income meets set standards or who are considered eligible through Federal needs analysis.

Application procedures. Admission: No deadline. No application fee. Application may be submitted online. Admission notification on a rolling basis. **Financial aid:** Priority date 3/2; no closing date. FAFSA, institutional form required. Applicants notified on a rolling basis starting 8/1; must reply within 2 week(s) of notification.

Academics. Special study options: Accelerated study, cooperative education, distance learning, dual enrollment of high school students, ESL, independent study, liberal arts/career combination, study abroad, weekend college. Midnight college via telecourse delivery. License preparation in physical therapy, real estate. **Credit/placement by examination:** AP, CLEP. 30 credit hours maximum toward associate degree. If submitted, SAT/ACT used for placement and counseling. **Support services:** GED preparation, reduced course load, remedial instruction, tutoring.

Majors. Business: General, accounting, business admin, entrepreneurial studies, management science, office technology, real estate. **Computer sciences:** General. **Liberal arts:** Arts/sciences. **Mechanic/repair:** Electronics/electrical.

Computing on campus. 100 workstations in computer center.

Student life. Freshman orientation: Available. Preregistration for classes offered. **Activities:** Choral groups, dance, student government.

Student services. Career counseling, services for economically disadvantaged, student employment services, financial aid counseling, health services, personal counseling, veterans' counselor. **Physically disabled:** Services for hearing impaired. **Transfer:** Special adviser, orientation for new students. Transfer center for students transferring to 4-year colleges.

Contact. E-mail: jmcdonald@cccd.edu
Phone: (714) 241-6176 Fax: (714) 241-6288
Jennifer McDonald, Director of Admissions and Records, Coastline Community College, 11460 Warner Avenue, Fountain Valley, CA 92708

Coleman College: San Marcos

San Marcos, California
www.coleman.edu

- For-profit 2-year technical college
- Small city

General. Accredited by ACICS. **Calendar:** Continuous.

Annual costs/financial aid. Tuition costs range from $11,760-$26,460.

Contact. Phone: (760) 747-3990
1284 West San Marcos Boulevard, Suite 110, San Marcos, CA 92069

College of Alameda

Alameda, California
alameda.peralta.edu **CB code: 4118**

- Public 2-year community college
- Commuter campus in small city

General. Founded in 1970. Regionally accredited. **Enrollment:** 5,168 undergraduates. **Degrees:** 267 associate awarded. **Calendar:** Semester, limited summer session. **Full-time faculty:** 55 total. **Part-time faculty:** 95 total.

Student profile.

Out-of-state:	2%	**25 or older:**	54%

Basis for selection. Open admission.

2005-2006 Annual costs. Tuition/fees: $784; $5,704 out-of-state. Per-credit charge: $26 in-state; $190 out-of-state. Books/supplies: $630. Personal expenses: $1,584.

Application procedures. Admission: No deadline. No application fee. Application may be submitted online. Admission notification on a rolling basis. **Financial aid:** Priority date 3/2; no closing date. FAFSA required. Applicants notified on a rolling basis starting 7/1; must reply within 2 week(s) of notification.

Academics. Special study options: Cooperative education, cross-registration, dual enrollment of high school students, honors, independent study, liberal arts/career combination. License preparation in aviation. **Credit/placement by examination:** CLEP, institutional tests. **Support services:** Learning center, remedial instruction, tutoring.

Majors. Area/ethnic studies: African-American. **Biology:** General. **Business:** General, accounting, administrative services, business admin, entrepreneurial studies, fashion, marketing, office/clerical. **Education:** Teacher assistance. **Foreign languages:** Spanish. **Health:** Dental assistant, health aide. **History:** General. **Liberal arts:** Arts/sciences. **Math:** General. **Mechanic/repair:** Aircraft. **Philosophy/religion:** Philosophy. **Psychology:** General. **Social sciences:** General, anthropology, economics, geography, political science, sociology, urban studies. **Transportation:** Aviation management. **Visual/performing arts:** General, studio arts.

Computing on campus. Online course registration available.

Student life. Freshman orientation: Available. **Activities:** Jazz band, choral groups, dance, drama, student government, student newspaper.

Athletics. Intercollegiate: Basketball, bowling, cross-country M, fencing, golf, soccer M, tennis, track and field, volleyball. **Intramural:** Golf, sailing, softball W.

Student services. Adult student services, career counseling, services for economically disadvantaged, student employment services, health services, on-campus daycare, personal counseling, placement for graduates, veterans' counselor. **Physically disabled:** Services for visually, speech, hearing impaired. **Transfer:** Special adviser, orientation for new students. Transfer adviser, college fairs on campus for students transferring to 4-year colleges.

Contact. Phone: (510) 748-2227
Howard Perdue, Associate Vice Chancellor, Admissions, Records and Student Services, College of Alameda, 555 Ralph Appezzato Memorial Parkway, Alameda, CA 94501

College of Marin: Kentfield

Kentfield, California
www.marin.cc.ca.us **CB code: 4061**

- Public 2-year community college
- Commuter campus in small town

General. Founded in 1926. Regionally accredited. Additional campus at Indian Valley. **Enrollment:** 2,903 degree-seeking undergraduates. **Degrees:** 320 associate awarded. **Location:** 25 miles from San Francisco. **Calendar:** Semester. **Full-time faculty:** 135 total. **Part-time faculty:** 160 total.

Basis for selection. Open admission, but selective for some programs. Limited admissions to nursing programs.

2005-2006 Annual costs. Tuition/fees: $808; $5,938 out-of-state. Per-credit charge: $26 in-state; $197 out-of-state. Books/supplies: $650. Personal expenses: $2,021.

Financial aid. Need-based: Need-based aid available for part-time students.

Application procedures. Admission: No deadline. No application fee. Admission notification on a rolling basis. **Financial aid:** Priority date 3/1; no closing date. FAFSA required. Applicants notified on a rolling basis starting 5/15.

Academics. Credit/placement by examination: CLEP, institutional tests.

Majors. Biology: General, environmental. **Business:** General, accounting, entrepreneurial studies, human resources, real estate. **Communications:** General, broadcast journalism, public relations. **Computer sciences:** General, programming, systems analysis. **Education:** ESL. **Legal studies:** Court reporting. **Liberal arts:** Arts/sciences. **Math:** General. **Mechanic/repair:** Auto body. **Visual/performing arts:** Studio arts.

Student life. Activities: Student government, student newspaper.

Athletics. Intercollegiate: Baseball M, basketball, cross-country, diving, football (tackle) M, soccer, softball, squash, tennis, track and field. **Intramural:** Cross-country, softball, swimming.

Contact. Phone: (415) 485-9412
Pamela Mize-Kurzman, Dean of Enrollment Services, College of Marin: Kentfield, 835 College Avenue, Kentfield, CA 94904

College of Oceaneering
Wilmington, California
www.natpoly.edu **CB code: 1243**

- For-profit 2-year technical and maritime college
- Commuter campus in small city

General. Founded in 1969. Regionally accredited. Provides underwater training for offshore oil industry, coastal and inland water and harbors. All classes near or on water. **Enrollment:** 485 full-time, degree-seeking students. **Degrees:** 10 associate awarded. **Location:** 30 miles from Los Angeles, 5 miles from Long Beach. **Calendar:** Continuous. **Full-time faculty:** 15 total. **Special facilities:** Bell saturation barge, welding pier, hemidome.

Basis for selection. Must be medically approved to dive. Applicants who do not have high school diploma or GED must prove their ability to benefit from program. Students expected to have mechanical aptitude and, if possible, experience in construction-related field. Interviews recommended.

2006-2007 Annual costs. Tuition/fees (projected): $16,100.

Application procedures. Admission: No deadline. $60 fee. Admission notification on a rolling basis. **Financial aid:** No deadline. FAFSA, institutional form required. Applicants notified on a rolling basis; must reply within 3 week(s) of notification.

Academics. Special programs prepare students for work as underwater welders, diver medical technicians, and topside/underwater nondestructive testing/inspection personnel. **Credit/placement by examination:** CLEP, institutional tests. 20 credit hours maximum toward associate degree. **Support services:** Remedial instruction, tutoring.

Majors. Engineering technology: General.

Student life. Activities: Film society, student newspaper.

Student services. Career counseling, student employment services, personal counseling, placement for graduates, veterans' counselor. **Transfer:** Special adviser, orientation for new students. Transfer adviser for students transferring to 4-year colleges.

Contact. Phone: (310) 834-2501 Fax: (310) 834-7132
Deborah Montgomery, Director of Admissions, College of Oceaneering, 272 South Fries Avenue, Wilmington, CA 90744

College of San Mateo
San Mateo, California
www.collegeofsanmateo.edu **CB code: 4070**

- Public 2-year community college
- Commuter campus in small city

General. Founded in 1922. Regionally accredited. **Enrollment:** 6,891 degree-seeking undergraduates. **Degrees:** 372 associate awarded. **ROTC:** Army, Air Force. **Location:** 15 miles from San Francisco. **Calendar:** Semester, limited summer session. **Full-time faculty:** 350 total. **Part-time faculty:** 200 total. **Special facilities:** Planetarium.

Student profile. Among degree-seeking undergraduates, 75% enrolled in a transfer program, 25% enrolled in a vocational program, 19% already have a bachelor's degree or higher.

Out-of-state:	2%	**25 or older:**	51%

Basis for selection. Open admission, but selective for some programs. Nursing program has separate requirements and is selective.

2005-2006 Annual costs. Tuition/fees: $806; $5,876 out-of-state. Per-credit charge: $26 in-state; $195 out-of-state. Books/supplies: $630. Personal expenses: $1,674.

Application procedures. Admission: No deadline. No application fee. Application may be submitted online. Admission notification on a rolling basis. Completion of CSM Placement tests for English, reading and mathematics recommmended prior to counseling session. **Financial aid:** Priority date 3/2; no closing date. FAFSA, institutional form required. Applicants notified on a rolling basis starting 6/15.

Academics. Special study options: Cooperative education, cross-registration, distance learning, double major, dual enrollment of high school students, ESL, honors, independent study, liberal arts/career combination, study abroad, weekend college. License preparation in dental hygiene, nursing, real estate. **Credit/placement by examination:** AP, CLEP, IB, institutional tests. 12 credit hours maximum toward associate degree. **Support services:** Learning center, reduced course load, remedial instruction, study skills assistance, tutoring, writing center.

Majors. Agriculture: Horticulture, ornamental horticulture. **Biology:** General, biomedical sciences. **Business:** General, accounting, entrepreneurial studies, fashion, logistics, management information systems, office/clerical, real estate. **Communications:** Advertising, broadcast journalism. **Communications technology:** General. **Computer sciences:** General, web page design. **Construction:** Pipefitting. **Engineering:** General. **Engineering technology:** Drafting, electrical. **English:** Speech/rhetoric. **Foreign languages:** French, German, Spanish. **Health:** Dental assistant, medical assistant, nursing (RN), substance abuse counseling. **Legal studies:** Legal secretary. **Liberal arts:** Arts/sciences. **Math:** General. **Mechanic/repair:** Aircraft, heating/ac/refrig. **Personal/culinary services:** General. **Physical sciences:** Chemistry, geology, physics. **Protective services:** Fire safety technology. **Social sciences:** General. **Transportation:** Airline/commercial pilot, aviation. **Visual/performing arts:** Cinematography, commercial/advertising art, painting, photography, studio arts.

Computing on campus. 150 workstations in library, computer center, student center. Online course registration, wireless network available.

Student life. Freshman orientation: Available. **Policies:** Freshmen permitted cars on campus. **Activities:** Bands, choral groups, dance, literary magazine, radio station, student government, student newspaper, symphony orchestra, TV station, Asian student union, Christian Fellowship, ethnic studies society, international students union, Latin American student organization, Arts in Recovery, Ballet Folklorico de CSM, Earth Preservation Committee, Peace Action, Unity Among Brothers.

Athletics. NCAA. **Intercollegiate:** Baseball M, basketball W, cross-country, football (tackle) M, softball W, swimming, tennis W, track and field, water polo. **Team name:** Bulldogs.

Student services. Adult student services, alcohol/substance abuse counseling, career counseling, services for economically disadvantaged, student employment services, financial aid counseling, health services, minority student services, on-campus daycare, personal counseling, veterans' counselor. **Physically disabled:** Services for visually, speech, hearing impaired. **Learning disabled:** Comprehensive services available. **Transfer:** Pre-admission transcript evaluation for new students. Transfer center, transfer adviser, college fairs on campus for students transferring to 4-year colleges.

Contact. E-mail: villarealh@smccd.net
Phone: (650) 574-6165 Fax: (650) 574-6506
Henry Villareal, Dean of Admissions and Records, College of San Mateo, 1700 West Hillsdale Boulevard, San Mateo, CA 94402-3784

College of the Canyons
Santa Clarita, California
www.canyons.edu **CB code: 4117**

- Public 2-year community college
- Commuter campus in small city

General. Founded in 1967. Regionally accredited. **Enrollment:** 4,512 full-time, degree-seeking students. **Degrees:** 866 associate awarded. **Location:** 15 miles from Los Angeles. **Calendar:** Semester, extensive summer session. **Full-time faculty:** 165 total. **Part-time faculty:** 350 total. **Special facilities:** Child development center.

Transfer out. Colleges most students transferred to 2005: California State University - Northridge, UCLA, California State University - San Diego, UC - Santa Barbara, California State University - Long Beach.

Basis for selection. Open admission, but selective for some programs. Limited admission to nursing program.

2005-2006 Annual costs. Tuition/fees: $816; $5,166 out-of-state. Per-credit charge: $26 in-state; $171 out-of-state. Personal expenses: $2,250.

Financial aid. Need-based: Need-based aid available for part-time students. Work study available nights and for part-time students. **Non-need-based:** Scholarships awarded for academics, alumni affiliation, art, athletics, leadership, music/drama, state residency. **Additional information:** Enrollment fees waived for students enrolled concurrently in high school and COC. School has own payment plan.

Application procedures. Admission: No deadline. No application fee. Admission notification on a rolling basis. **Financial aid:** Closing date 3/2. FAFSA required. Applicants notified on a rolling basis starting 6/1; must reply within 4 week(s) of notification.

Academics. **Special study options:** Accelerated study, cooperative education, distance learning, dual enrollment of high school students, ESL, honors, independent study, internships, liberal arts/career combination, study abroad, weekend college. Bachelor's degree programs available on campus. License preparation in nursing, real estate. **Credit/placement by examination:** AP, CLEP, institutional tests. 18 credit hours maximum toward associate degree. Applicants must take institutional English and mathematics placement tests. **Support services:** Learning center, remedial instruction, study skills assistance, tutoring.

Majors. **Business:** Accounting, administrative services, business admin, real estate. **Communications:** Broadcast journalism, journalism. **Communications technology:** General. **Computer sciences:** General, computer graphics, computer science, data processing, information systems, programming, systems analysis. **Engineering technology:** Drafting, quality control, water quality. **English:** English lit. **Family/consumer sciences:** Child care. **Foreign languages:** French, German, Spanish. **Health:** Licensed practical nurse, nursing (RN). **Interdisciplinary:** Biological/physical sciences. **Liberal arts:** Arts/sciences, library assistant. **Math:** General. **Mechanic/repair:** General, electronics/electrical. **Parks/recreation:** Health/fitness. **Production:** Welding. **Protective services:** Fire safety technology, law enforcement admin. **Social sciences:** General. **Visual/performing arts:** Commercial/advertising art, multimedia, photography.

Computing on campus. 800 workstations in library, computer center, student center. Online course registration, online library, helpline available.

Student life. **Freshman orientation:** Mandatory. **Policies:** Freshmen permitted cars on campus. **Activities:** Jazz band, choral groups, dance, drama, music ensembles, student government, student newspaper, symphony orchestra, Quest Campus Crusade for Christ, COC Bible Study club, Latter-day Saint Student Association.

Athletics. **Intercollegiate:** Baseball M, basketball, cross-country, football (tackle) M, golf, soccer W, softball W, swimming, track and field, volleyball W, water polo W. **Team name:** Cougars.

Student services. Adult student services, career counseling, services for economically disadvantaged, student employment services, financial aid counseling, health services, on-campus daycare, personal counseling, placement for graduates, veterans' counselor. **Physically disabled:** Services for visually, speech, hearing impaired. **Learning disabled:** Comprehensive services available. **Transfer:** Special adviser, orientation, pre-admission transcript evaluation for new students. Transfer center, transfer adviser, college fairs on campus for students transferring to 4-year colleges.

Contact. E-mail: rio_d@canyons.edu
Phone: (661) 362-3280 Fax: (661) 259-8302
Debbie Rio, Director, Admissions and Records, College of the Canyons, 26455 Rockwell Canyon Road, Santa Clarita, CA 91355

College of the Desert

Palm Desert, California — **CB member**
www.collegeofthedesert.edu — **CB code: 4085**

- Public 2-year community college
- Commuter campus in large town

General. Founded in 1958. Regionally accredited. **Enrollment:** 5,156 degree-seeking undergraduates; 2,782 non-degree-seeking students. **Degrees:** 421 associate awarded. **Location:** 20 miles from Palm Springs, 120 miles from Los Angeles. **Calendar:** Semester, limited summer session. **Full-time faculty:** 109 total; 14% have terminal degrees, 15% minority, 44% women. **Part-time faculty:** 329 total; 5% have terminal degrees, 18% minority, 52% women. **Special facilities:** Performing arts center, theater, college-operated art museum, golf institute, public safety academy.

Student profile. Among degree-seeking undergraduates, 1,194 enrolled as first-time, first-year students.

Part-time:	59%	**Asian American:**	4%
Out-of-state:	3%	**Hispanic American:**	50%
Women:	58%	**Native American:**	1%
African American:	3%	**25 or older:**	40%

Basis for selection. Open admission, but selective for some programs. Separate application requirements for nursing and golf management and public safety academy. Interviews required for nursing/allied health majors. **Adult students:** Entrance exam policies same as for first-time freshmen. SAT/ACT scores not required. **Learning Disabled:** Participation is voluntary. Interested students must meet with the appropriate Disabled Students Programs and Services counselor to apply for these programs.

2005-2006 Annual costs. Tuition/fees: $814; $5,344 out-of-state. Per-credit charge: $26 in-state; $177 out-of-state. Books/supplies: $1,254. Personal expenses: $1,584.

2004-2005 Financial aid. All financial aid based on need. 91% of total undergraduate aid awarded as scholarships/grants, 9% as loans/jobs. Need-based aid available for part-time students. Work study available weekends and for part-time students.

Application procedures. **Admission:** Priority date 5/2; deadline 8/19 (receipt date). No application fee. Application may be submitted online. Admission notification on a rolling basis. **Financial aid:** Priority date 3/2; no closing date. FAFSA, institutional form required. Applicants notified on a rolling basis starting 7/1.

Academics. **Special study options:** Cooperative education, distance learning, double major, dual enrollment of high school students, ESL, honors, independent study, liberal arts/career combination, weekend college. License preparation in nursing. **Credit/placement by examination:** CLEP, institutional tests. **Support services:** GED preparation and test center, learning center, remedial instruction, study skills assistance, tutoring, writing center.

Majors. **Agriculture:** Business, ornamental horticulture, plant sciences, turf management. **Architecture:** Technology. **Biology:** General. **Business:** Business admin, construction management, hotel/motel admin, managerial economics, office management, restaurant/food services. **Communications:** General, journalism, media studies, organizational. **Computer sciences:** General, computer science. **Conservation:** General, environmental science, environmental studies. **Engineering technology:** Architectural, architectural drafting, drafting, heat/ac/refrig. **English:** American lit, composition, speech/rhetoric. **Family/consumer sciences:** Child care, food/nutrition, human nutrition. **Foreign languages:** Comparative lit, French, German, Italian, Spanish. **Health:** Dietetic technician, licensed practical nurse, nursing (RN). **History:** General. **Interdisciplinary:** Biological/physical sciences. **Liberal arts:** Arts/sciences. **Math:** General. **Mechanic/repair:** Heating/ac/refrig. **Parks/recreation:** General, facilities management. **Personal/culinary services:** Restaurant/catering. **Philosophy/religion:** Philosophy. **Physical sciences:** Chemistry, geology, physics. **Protective services:** Fire safety technology, law enforcement admin. **Psychology:** General. **Social sciences:** General, anthropology, economics, geography, political science, sociology. **Visual/performing arts:** Acting, art, art history/conservation, dance, dramatic, drawing, graphic design, painting, photography, printmaking, studio arts, theater history.

Computing on campus. 125 workstations in library, computer center, student center. Online course registration, online library, wireless network available.

Student life. **Freshman orientation:** Mandatory. **Activities:** Choral groups, dance, drama, music ensembles, musical theater, opera, student government, student newspaper.

Athletics. **Intercollegiate:** Baseball M, basketball, cheerleading, cross-country, fencing, football (tackle) M, golf, soccer, softball W, tennis, volleyball W. **Team name:** Roadrunners.

Student services. Adult student services, career counseling, services for economically disadvantaged, student employment services, financial aid counseling, health services, minority student services, on-campus daycare, personal counseling, placement for graduates, veterans' counselor. **Physically disabled:** Services for visually, speech, hearing impaired. **Learning disabled:** Comprehensive services available. **Transfer:** Special adviser, orientation, re-entry adviser, pre-admission transcript evaluation for new students. Transfer center, transfer adviser, college fairs on campus for students transferring to 4-year colleges.

Contact. Phone: (760) 773-2516 Fax: (760) 776-0136
John Loera, Dean of Enrollment Services, College of the Desert, 43-500 Monterey Avenue, Palm Desert, CA 92260

College of the Redwoods

Eureka, California — **CB member**
www.redwoods.edu — **CB code: 4100**

- Public 2-year community college
- Commuter campus in large town

General. Founded in 1964. Regionally accredited. Centers at Fort Bragg and Crescent City; instructional sites in Hoopa, downtown Eureka, and Arcata. **Enrollment:** 4,677 degree-seeking undergraduates. **Degrees:** 550 associate awarded. **Location:** 275 miles from San Francisco. **Calendar:** Semester, limited summer session. **Full-time faculty:** 100 total. **Part-time faculty:** 310 total. **Class size:** 19% < 20, 64% 20-39, 12% 40-49, 5% 50-99. **Special facilities:** Observatories, fish hatchery.

Student profile.

Out-of-state:	4%	**Live on campus:**	1%
25 or older:	52%		

Transfer out. Colleges most students transferred to 2005: Humboldt State University, Chico State University.

Basis for selection. Open admission, but selective for some programs. Admission for nursing applicants based on school record and test scores. **Homeschooled:** Students under 18 years of age and home-schooled must submit a copy of their affidavit filed with County Office of Education.

2005-2006 Annual costs. Tuition/fees: $806; $6,296 out-of-state. Per-credit charge: $26 in-state; $209 out-of-state. Room/board: $5,700. Books/supplies: $1,224. Personal expenses: $1,476.

Financial aid. Need-based: Need-based aid available for part-time students. Work study available for part-time students.

Application procedures. Admission: Priority date 8/14; no deadline. No application fee. Admission notification on a rolling basis. **Financial aid:** Priority date 4/15; no closing date. FAFSA, institutional form required. Applicants notified on a rolling basis starting 5/1; must reply within 6 week(s) of notification.

Academics. Special study options: Cooperative education, cross-registration, distance learning, double major, dual enrollment of high school students, ESL, honors, independent study, teacher certification program. License preparation in nursing. **Credit/placement by examination:** CLEP, institutional tests. **Support services:** GED preparation and test center, learning center, pre-admission summer program, remedial instruction, tutoring, writing center.

Majors. Agriculture: Agribusiness operations, animal sciences, plant sciences. **Business:** General, administrative services, hospitality admin, managerial economics, office technology, real estate. **Communications:** Journalism. **Computer sciences:** General. **Conservation:** Fisheries, forestry. **Construction:** Maintenance. **Education:** Early childhood. **Engineering:** Electrical. **Engineering technology:** Construction, drafting. **Legal studies:** Legal secretary, paralegal. **Liberal arts:** Arts/sciences. **Physical sciences:** Planetary. **Protective services:** Law enforcement admin. **Visual/performing arts:** Commercial/advertising art.

Computing on campus. 578 workstations in dormitories, library, computer center, student center. Dormitories wired for high-speed internet access. Online course registration, online library available.

Student life. Freshman orientation: Available. Preregistration for classes offered. **Policies:** Freshmen permitted cars on campus. **Housing:** Coed dorms available. Limited housing also available for police academy students. **Activities:** Jazz band, choral groups, dance, student government, Native American club, international students club, apologetics club, Bible study, Latter-day Saints club, veterans club, EOPS club.

Athletics. Intercollegiate: Baseball M, basketball, cross-country, football (tackle) M, golf M, soccer W, track and field, volleyball W. **Intramural:** Badminton, bowling, diving, golf, gymnastics, soccer, volleyball, water polo. **Team name:** Corsairs.

Student services. Career counseling, services for economically disadvantaged, student employment services, financial aid counseling, health services, on-campus daycare, personal counseling, placement for graduates, veterans' counselor. **Physically disabled:** Services for visually, speech, hearing impaired. **Transfer:** Special adviser, orientation for new students. Transfer center, transfer adviser, college fairs on campus for students transferring to 4-year colleges.

Contact. E-mail: admissions@redwoods.edu
Phone: (707) 476-4200 Toll-free number: (800) 641-0400
Fax: (707) 476-4406
Sue Bailey, Director Enrollment Services, College of the Redwoods, 7351 Tompkins Hill Road, Eureka, CA 95501-9300

College of the Sequoias

Visalia, California
www.cos.edu **CB code: 4071**

- Public 2-year agricultural and community college
- Commuter campus in small city

General. Founded in 1925. Regionally accredited. **Enrollment:** 4,633 full-time, degree-seeking students. **Degrees:** 690 associate awarded. **ROTC:** Air Force. **Location:** 45 miles from Fresno. **Calendar:** Semester, limited summer session. **Full-time faculty:** 157 total. **Part-time faculty:** 291 total. **Special facilities:** Self-sufficient farm; affiliation with University of California at Davis School of Veterinary Medicine in Tulare.

Student profile.

Out-of-state:	3%	**25 or older:**	39%

Transfer out. Colleges most students transferred to 2005: California State University-Fresno, California State University-Bakersfield, California Polytechnic State University: San Luis Obispo, California State University-Long Beach.

Basis for selection. Open admission, but selective for some programs. Limited admission to nursing program. Interviews required for work program, nursing majors. Auditions required for music majors.

2005-2006 Annual costs. Tuition/fees: $816; $5,526 out-of-state. Per-credit charge: $26 in-state; $183 out-of-state. Books/supplies: $846.

Application procedures. Admission: No deadline. No application fee. Admission notification on a rolling basis. **Financial aid:** Priority date 3/2; no closing date. FAFSA, institutional form required. Applicants notified on a rolling basis starting 6/1; must reply within 2 week(s) of notification.

Academics. Special study options: Dual enrollment of high school students, ESL, honors, independent study, internships, student-designed major, study abroad. License preparation in nursing. **Credit/placement by examination:** CLEP, institutional tests. 12 credit hours maximum toward associate degree. **Support services:** Learning center, pre-admission summer program, reduced course load, remedial instruction, study skills assistance, tutoring, writing center.

Majors. Agriculture: Agribusiness operations, landscaping, ornamental horticulture. **Business:** General, accounting, administrative services, management information systems, office/clerical, real estate, sales/distribution. **Communications:** General, journalism. **Computer sciences:** Computer science. **Construction:** Carpentry, maintenance. **Education:** Adult/continuing, physical. **Engineering:** General. **Engineering technology:** Architectural, construction, drafting, electrical, industrial, manufacturing. **English:** Speech/rhetoric. **Family/consumer sciences:** General, child care. **Foreign languages:** General, French. **Health:** Nursing (RN). **Interdisciplinary:** Biological/physical sciences. **Legal studies:** Paralegal. **Liberal arts:** Arts/sciences. **Math:** General. **Mechanic/repair:** Electronics/electrical. **Parks/recreation:** Facilities management. **Personal/culinary services:** Cosmetic. **Protective services:** Fire safety technology, law enforcement admin. **Public administration:** Human services. **Social sciences:** General. **Visual/performing arts:** Art, commercial/advertising art, dramatic, multimedia, studio arts, theater design.

Computing on campus. 325 workstations in library, computer center. Online course registration available.

Student life. Freshman orientation: Mandatory. **Activities:** Bands, choral groups, dance, drama, music ensembles, musical theater, student government, student newspaper, symphony orchestra.

Athletics. Intercollegiate: Baseball M, basketball, cross-country, diving, football (tackle) M, golf M, soccer W, softball W, swimming, tennis, track and field, volleyball W. **Team name:** Giants.

Student services. Adult student services, alcohol/substance abuse counseling, career counseling, services for economically disadvantaged, student employment services, financial aid counseling, health services, minority student services, on-campus daycare, personal counseling, veterans' counselor. **Physically disabled:** Services for visually, speech, hearing impaired. **Transfer:** Special adviser, orientation for new students. Transfer adviser, college fairs on campus for students transferring to 4-year colleges.

Contact. Phone: (559) 730-3727 Fax: (559) 730-3894
Don Mast, Dean of Student Services, College of the Sequoias, 915 South Mooney Boulevard, Visalia, CA 93277

College of the Siskiyous

Weed, California
www.siskiyous.edu **CB code: 4087**

- Public 2-year community and junior college
- Commuter campus in small town

General. Founded in 1957. Regionally accredited. **Enrollment:** 920 full-time, degree-seeking students. **Degrees:** 178 associate awarded. **Location:** 270 miles from Sacramento, 80 miles from Medford, Oregon. **Calendar:** Semester, limited summer session. **Full-time faculty:** 50 total. **Part-time faculty:** 120 total. **Class size:** 57% < 20, 35% 20-39, 3% 40-49, 4% 50-99, less than 1% >100. **Special facilities:** Process technology laboratory, firearms training simulator, flashover burn unit, driver operator simulator.

Student profile.

Out-of-state:	27%	**Live on campus:**	14%
25 or older:	39%		

Transfer out. Colleges most students transferred to 2005: California State University at Chico, Southern Oregon University, University of California at Davis, Simpson College, Humboldt University.

Basis for selection. Open admission.

2005-2006 Annual costs. Tuition/fees: $806; $6,026 out-of-state. Per-credit charge: $26 in-state; $200 out-of-state. Room/board: $6,350. Books/supplies: $846. Personal expenses: $1,500.

Financial aid. All financial aid based on need. Need-based aid available for part-time students. Work study available nights, weekends and for part-time students.

Application procedures. Admission: No deadline. No application fee. **Financial aid:** Priority date 4/30; no closing date. FAFSA required. Applicants notified on a rolling basis starting 6/1; must reply within 2 week(s) of notification.

Academics. Special study options: Cooperative education, distance learning, dual enrollment of high school students, ESL, exchange student, independent study, internships, liberal arts/career combination, student-designed major, study abroad. License preparation in nursing, paramedic. **Credit/placement by examination:** AP, CLEP, institutional tests. **Support services:** Learning center, pre-admission summer program, reduced course load, remedial instruction, study skills assistance, tutoring, writing center.

Majors. Agriculture: Animal sciences, plant sciences. **Biology:** General. **Business:** Accounting, administrative services, business admin, management information systems, office/clerical. **Communications:** General. **Computer sciences:** General, applications programming, computer science. **Education:** General, physical. **Family/consumer sciences:** Child care. **Foreign languages:** Spanish. **Health:** EMT paramedic, licensed practical nurse, predentistry, premedicine, prepharmacy, preveterinary. **Interdisciplinary:** Biological/physical sciences. **Legal studies:** Prelaw. **Liberal arts:** Arts/sciences, humanities. **Math:** General. **Physical sciences:** Chemistry, geology, physics. **Protective services:** Firefighting, police science. **Social sciences:** General. **Visual/performing arts:** Crafts, dramatic, photography, theater history.

Most popular majors. Liberal arts 93%, security/protective services 10%.

Computing on campus. 260 workstations in dormitories, library, computer center. Dormitories linked to campus network. Online library, helpline, repair service, wireless network available.

Student life. Freshman orientation: Available. 1-day orientation held the day before classes start. **Policies:** Freshmen permitted cars on campus. **Housing:** Coed dorms available. $100 deposit. **Activities:** Bands, choral groups, dance, drama, music ensembles, musical theater, student government, student newspaper, symphony orchestra, TV station, Latino Student Union, Black Student Union, Phi Theta Kappa, Intercultural club, American Indian Alliance, Intervarsity club, Associated Student Board, speech club, chess club, disabled student alliance, speech and forensics club.

Athletics. Intercollegiate: Baseball M, basketball, cross-country, football (tackle) M, golf W, skiing, softball W, track and field, volleyball W. **Intramural:** Basketball M, softball, volleyball. **Team name:** Eagles.

Student services. Adult student services, alcohol/substance abuse counseling, career counseling, services for economically disadvantaged, student employment services, financial aid counseling, health services, on-campus daycare, personal counseling, veterans' counselor. **Physically disabled:** Services for visually, speech, hearing impaired. **Learning disabled:** Comprehensive services available. **Transfer:** Special adviser, orientation, re-entry adviser, pre-admission transcript evaluation for new students. Transfer center, transfer adviser, college fairs on campus for students transferring to 4-year colleges.

Contact. E-mail: registration@siskiyous.edu
Phone: (530) 938-5555 Toll-free number: (888) 397-4339
Fax: (530) 938-5367
Teresa Winkelman, Director of Admissions & Records, College of the Siskiyous, 800 College Avenue, Weed, CA 96094

Columbia College

Sonora, California
www.gocolumbia.org **CB code: 4108**

- Public 2-year community college
- Commuter campus in small town

General. Founded in 1968. Regionally accredited. **Enrollment:** 988 degree-seeking undergraduates. **Degrees:** 172 associate awarded. **Location:** 150 miles from Sacramento. **Calendar:** Semester, limited summer session. **Full-time faculty:** 45 total. **Part-time faculty:** 80 total. **Special facilities:** Jogging/fitness trail, arboretum, astronomy dome, seismograph.

Basis for selection. Open admission. Institution uses own assessment test for placement only.

2005-2006 Annual costs. Tuition/fees: $818; $5,348 out-of-state. Per-credit charge: $26 in-state; $177 out-of-state. Books/supplies: $882. Personal expenses: $1,656.

Financial aid. Need-based: Need-based aid available for part-time students. **Non-need-based:** Scholarships awarded for academics.

Application procedures. Admission: No deadline. No application fee. Application may be submitted online. Admission notification on a rolling basis. Matriculation procedures required before new or returning students may register. Early application assures accommodation to new student priority registration periods. **Financial aid:** Priority date 3/2, closing date 12/15. FAFSA, institutional form required. Applicants notified on a rolling basis starting 6/15; must reply within 2 week(s) of notification.

Academics. Special study options: Cooperative education, double major, ESL, independent study, internships, liberal arts/career combination. License preparation in paramedic. **Credit/placement by examination:** AP, CLEP, institutional tests. 12 credit hours maximum toward associate degree. **Support services:** GED preparation and test center, learning center, remedial instruction, study skills assistance, tutoring, writing center.

Majors. Biology: General. **Business:** General, administrative services, business admin, hospitality admin. **Computer sciences:** General, programming. **Conservation:** General, forestry, management/policy. **English:** Speech/rhetoric. **Family/consumer sciences:** Child development. **Interdisciplinary:** Natural sciences. **Liberal arts:** Arts/sciences. **Math:** General. **Mechanic/repair:** Automotive. **Parks/recreation:** Health/fitness. **Personal/culinary services:** Culinary arts. **Physical sciences:** Chemistry, physics, planetary. **Protective services:** Fire safety technology. **Social sciences:** General. **Visual/performing arts:** Art, photography.

Computing on campus. 60 workstations in library, computer center.

Student life. Freshman orientation: Mandatory. 1-hour session prior to registration. **Housing:** Coed dorms, special housing for disabled, apartments available. Privately owned apartments on campus available to single students. **Activities:** Bands, choral groups, dance, music ensembles, student government, student newspaper, symphony orchestra.

Athletics. Intercollegiate: Basketball M, volleyball W. **Team name:** Claim Jumpers.

Student services. Adult student services, alcohol/substance abuse counseling, career counseling, services for economically disadvantaged, student employment services, financial aid counseling, health services, on-campus daycare, personal counseling, placement for graduates, veterans' counselor. **Physically disabled:** Services for visually, speech, hearing impaired. **Transfer:** Special adviser, orientation, re-entry adviser for new students. Transfer center, transfer adviser, college fairs on campus for students transferring to 4-year colleges.

Contact. Phone: (209) 588-5250 Fax: (209) 588-5337
Kathy Smith, Director of Student Success/Matriculation, Columbia College, 11600 Columbia College Drive, Sonora, CA 95370

Concorde Career College

North Hollywood, California
www.concordecareercolleges.com

- For-profit 2-year health science college
- Large city

General. Accredited by ACCSCT. **Enrollment:** 595 degree-seeking undergraduates. **Degrees:** 53 associate awarded. **Calendar:** Continuous. **Full-time faculty:** 34 total. **Part-time faculty:** 11 total.

Basis for selection. Institutional exam scores important. CPAT, Wonderlic used.

2005-2006 Annual costs. Cost of full programs: associate degree programs $21,000, diploma programs $8,000-9,000; includes fees, books, uniforms.

Application procedures. Admission: No deadline. No application fee. Admission notification on a rolling basis.

Academics. Credit/placement by examination: CLEP.

Majors. Health: Respiratory therapy technology.

Contact. Phone: (818) 766-8151 Toll-free number: (800) 464-1212
Fax: (818) 766-1587
Concorde Career College, 12412 Victory Boulevard, North Hollywood, CA 91606

Contra Costa College
San Pablo, California
www.contracosta.edu **CB code: 4943**

- Public 2-year community college
- Large town

General. Founded in 1948. Regionally accredited. **Enrollment:** 1,315 full-time, degree-seeking students. **Degrees:** 276 associate awarded. **ROTC:** Navy. **Location:** 20 miles from San Francisco. **Calendar:** Semester, limited summer session. **Full-time faculty:** 115 total. **Part-time faculty:** 220 total. **Special facilities:** Center for scientific excellence.

Basis for selection. Open admission.

2005-2006 Annual costs. Tuition/fees: $780; $5,310 out-of-state. Per-credit charge: $26 in-state; $177 out-of-state. Books/supplies: $680. Personal expenses: $1,620.

Application procedures. Admission: No deadline. No application fee. Admission notification on a rolling basis. **Financial aid:** Priority date 3/2; no closing date. Applicants notified on a rolling basis; must reply within 2 week(s) of notification.

Academics. Special study options: Cross-registration, dual enrollment of high school students, honors, independent study. **Credit/placement by examination:** CLEP, institutional tests. 12 credit hours maximum toward associate degree. **Support services:** Learning center, remedial instruction, tutoring.

Majors. Area/ethnic studies: African-American, Hispanic-American/Latino/Chicano. **Biology:** General. **Business:** Administrative services, office/clerical, real estate. **Computer sciences:** General, applications programming. **Education:** Bilingual, teacher assistance. **Engineering:** General. **Engineering technology:** Architectural, drafting. **Family/consumer sciences:** Institutional food production. **Health:** Dental assistant, medical assistant, nursing (RN). **History:** General. **Liberal arts:** Arts/sciences. **Math:** General. **Mechanic/repair:** Auto body. **Personal/culinary services:** Cosmetic. **Physical sciences:** Chemistry, physics. **Protective services:** Police science. **Psychology:** General. **Social sciences:** Geography, sociology. **Visual/performing arts:** Dramatic, interior design.

Student life. Activities: Jazz band, TV station.

Athletics. Intercollegiate: Baseball M, basketball, football (tackle) M, tennis, track and field.

Student services. Career counseling, student employment services, health services, personal counseling.

Contact. Phone: (510) 235-7800 ext. 4210 Fax: (510) 236-6768
Frank Hernandez, Dean of Enrollment Services, Contra Costa College, 2600 Mission Bell Drive, San Pablo, CA 94806

Copper Mountain College
Joshua Tree, California
www.cmccd.edu **CB code: 3889**

- Public 2-year community college
- Commuter campus in small town

General. Regionally accredited. **Enrollment:** 1,018 degree-seeking undergraduates. **Degrees:** 112 associate awarded. **Location:** 120 miles from Los Angeles, 45 miles from Palm Springs. **Calendar:** Semester, limited summer session. **Full-time faculty:** 36 total. **Part-time faculty:** 111 total.

Transfer out. Colleges most students transferred to 2005: California State University, San Bernardino.

Basis for selection. Open admission. Limited admission to some allied health programs.

2005-2006 Annual costs. Tuition/fees: $780; $5,310 out-of-state. Per-credit charge: $26 in-state; $177 out-of-state.

2004-2005 Financial aid. Need-based: 115 full-time freshmen applied for aid; 105 were judged to have need; 100 of these received aid. Average need met was 37%. Average scholarship/grant was $2,954; average loan $2,423. 69% of total undergraduate aid awarded as scholarships/grants, 31% as loans/jobs. Need-based aid available for part-time students. **Non-need-based:** Awarded to 6 full-time undergraduates, including 6 freshmen.

Application procedures. Admission: No deadline. No application fee. Application must be submitted online. Admission notification on a rolling basis. **Financial aid:** Priority date 3/2; no closing date. FAFSA required.

Academics. Special study options: Distance learning, dual enrollment of high school students, ESL, independent study, study abroad. License preparation in nursing, paramedic. **Credit/placement by examination:** AP, CLEP. **Support services:** GED preparation and test center, remedial instruction, study skills assistance, tutoring.

Majors. Business: Business admin. **Communications:** General. **Computer sciences:** General, computer science. **Foreign languages:** Spanish. **Health:** Licensed practical nurse. **History:** General. **Liberal arts:** Arts/sciences. **Math:** General. **Mechanic/repair:** Automotive. **Philosophy/religion:** Philosophy. **Protective services:** Fire safety technology, law enforcement admin. **Psychology:** General. **Social sciences:** General, anthropology, economics, political science. **Visual/performing arts:** Art.

Computing on campus. 40 workstations in library, computer center.

Student life. Freshman orientation: Mandatory. Preregistration for classes offered. 1.5 hour group orientation offered about 16 times prior to each semester. **Activities:** Literary magazine, student government.

Student services. Adult student services, career counseling, services for economically disadvantaged, student employment services, financial aid counseling, veterans' counselor. **Physically disabled:** Services for visually, speech, hearing impaired. **Transfer:** Special adviser, orientation for new students. Transfer center, transfer adviser, college fairs on campus for students transferring to 4-year colleges.

Contact. E-mail: lturk@cmccd.edu
Phone: (760) 366-3791 ext. 4232 Toll-free number: (866) 366-3791 ext. 4232 Fax: (760) 366-5257
Laraine Turk, Associate Dean of Student Services, Copper Mountain College, 6162 Rotary Way, Joshua Tree, CA 92252

Cosumnes River College
Sacramento, California
www.crc.losrios.edu **CB code: 4121**

- Public 2-year junior college
- Commuter campus in large city

General. Founded in 1970. Regionally accredited. Classes offered at Folsom Lake Center, El Dorado Center, Folsom Prison and locations along highway 50 corridor going east to Lake Tahoe. **Enrollment:** 11,500 full-time, degree-seeking students. **Degrees:** 540 associate awarded. **Location:** 12 miles from downtown. **Calendar:** Semester, limited summer session. **Full-time faculty:** 175 total. **Part-time faculty:** 200 total.

Basis for selection. Open admission.

2005-2006 Annual costs. Tuition/fees: $812; $5,342 out-of-state. Per-credit charge: $26 in-state; $177 out-of-state. Books/supplies: $716. Personal expenses: $1,302.

Application procedures. Admission: No deadline. No application fee. Admission notification on a rolling basis beginning on or about 3/1. First-time students encouraged to participate in orientation and matriculation sessions. English and mathematics tests for placement recommended. **Financial aid:** Priority date 5/1; no closing date. FAFSA required. Applicants notified on a rolling basis starting 7/20; must reply within 4 week(s) of notification.

Academics. **Special study options:** Cooperative education, distance learning, double major, dual enrollment of high school students, ESL, honors, independent study, internships, study abroad. **Credit/placement by examination:** CLEP. 15 credit hours maximum toward associate degree. **Support services:** Learning center, reduced course load, remedial instruction, tutoring.

Majors. **Agriculture:** Animal sciences, business, equestrian studies, horticultural science, plant sciences. **Architecture:** Environmental design, interior, landscape. **Area/ethnic studies:** American, women's. **Business:** General, accounting, business admin, entrepreneurial studies, finance, real estate. **Communications:** Advertising, broadcast journalism, journalism, public relations. **Communications technology:** General. **Computer sciences:** Information systems, programming. **Construction:** Maintenance. **Education:** Early childhood. **Engineering technology:** Drafting. **Health:** Medical assistant, medical records technology. **Interdisciplinary:** Gerontology. **Liberal arts:** Arts/sciences. **Protective services:** Fire safety technology, law enforcement admin. **Social sciences:** Sociology. **Visual/performing arts:** Art, art history/conservation, cinematography, commercial photography, dramatic, interior design, photography, studio arts.

Student life. **Activities:** Bands, choral groups, drama, radio station, student government, student newspaper, TV station, African-American Students Association, Hispanic/Latino Scholars, Asian American Club, Christian Club, earth club.

Athletics. **Intercollegiate:** Baseball M, basketball, soccer, softball W, tennis, track and field, volleyball W. **Intramural:** Badminton, bowling, fencing, golf, racquetball, skiing, swimming, tennis, track and field, volleyball.

Student services. Adult student services, career counseling, student employment services, health services, on-campus daycare, personal counseling, placement for graduates, veterans' counselor. **Physically disabled:** Services for hearing impaired. **Transfer:** Special adviser, orientation for new students. Transfer adviser for students transferring to 4-year colleges.

Contact. Phone: (916) 691-7410 Fax: (916) 691-7467
Celia Esposito-Noy, Dean of Student and Administrative Service,
Cosumnes River College, 8401 Center Parkway, Sacramento, CA 95823

Crafton Hills College

Yucaipa, California
www.craftonhills.edu **CB code: 4126**

- Public 2-year community college
- Commuter campus in large town

General. Founded in 1972. Regionally accredited. **Enrollment:** 3,257 degree-seeking undergraduates. **Degrees:** 333 associate awarded. **Location:** 12 miles from San Bernardino. **Calendar:** Semester, limited summer session. **Full-time faculty:** 60 total. **Part-time faculty:** 160 total. **Special facilities:** Golf course, walking trails.

Basis for selection. Open admission.

2005-2006 Annual costs. Tuition/fees: $818; $5,348 out-of-state. Per-credit charge: $26 in-state; $177 out-of-state. Books/supplies: $630. Personal expenses: $1,440.

Financial aid. All financial aid based on need. Need-based aid available for part-time students. Work study available nights and for part-time students.

Application procedures. **Admission:** No deadline. No application fee. Admission notification on a rolling basis. Students under 18 admitted with special permission. **Financial aid:** Priority date 4/15, closing date 6/2. FAFSA, institutional form required. Applicants notified on a rolling basis starting 7/31; must reply within 2 week(s) of notification.

Academics. **Special study options:** Cooperative education, cross-registration, distance learning, dual enrollment of high school students, weekend college. **Credit/placement by examination:** CLEP, institutional tests. 36 credit hours maximum toward associate degree. **Support services:** Learning center, remedial instruction, study skills assistance, tutoring.

Majors. **Biology:** General, anatomy, bacteriology. **Business:** Administrative services, business admin, office/clerical. **Computer sciences:** General, programming. **Education:** Early childhood, health occupations. **Foreign languages:** General, French, Spanish. **Health:** EMT paramedic, medical radiologic technology/radiation therapy, respiratory therapy technology. **History:** General. **Liberal arts:** Arts/sciences. **Math:** General. **Physical sciences:** Chemistry, geology, physics. **Protective services:** Firefighting, law enforcement admin. **Psychology:** General. **Social sciences:** General, anthropology, economics, geography, political science, sociology. **Visual/performing arts:** Art, dramatic.

Computing on campus. 172 workstations in library, computer center.

Student life. **Freshman orientation:** Mandatory. **Activities:** Jazz band, drama, music ensembles, musical theater, student government.

Athletics. **Intercollegiate:** Golf, tennis, volleyball, weight lifting.

Student services. Career counseling, student employment services, health services, on-campus daycare, personal counseling, placement for graduates, veterans' counselor. **Physically disabled:** Services for visually, speech, hearing impaired. **Transfer:** Special adviser, orientation, pre-admission transcript evaluation for new students. Transfer center, transfer adviser, college fairs on campus for students transferring to 4-year colleges.

Contact. E-mail: admissions@craftonhills.edu
Phone: (909) 389-3372 Fax: (909) 389-9141
Joe Cabrales, Director of Admissions and Records, Crafton Hills College, 11711 Sand Canyon Road, Yucaipa, CA 92399-1799

Cuesta College

San Luis Obispo, California
www.cuesta.org **CB code: 4101**

- Public 2-year community college
- Commuter campus in large town

General. Founded in 1964. Regionally accredited. Additional North County Campus in Paso Robles and South County Center (s) in Arroyo Grande and Nipomo. **Enrollment:** 4,706 degree-seeking undergraduates. **Degrees:** 622 associate awarded. **Location:** 200 miles from Los Angeles, 6 miles from San Luis Obispo. **Calendar:** Semester, extensive summer session. **Full-time faculty:** 145 total. **Part-time faculty:** 315 total. **Special facilities:** Adobe museum (Chumash Indian).

Student profile.

Out-of-state:	3%	**25 or older:**	33%

Transfer out. **Colleges most students transferred to 2005:** California Polytechnic State University: San Luis Obispo, Chico State University, San Francisco State University, California State Polytechnic University: Pomona.

Basis for selection. Open admission, but selective for some programs. Nursing program requires critical thinking and math assessments. Prerequisite courses evaluated. **Learning Disabled:** No special admission but must be assessed and qualified to receive services.

2005-2006 Annual costs. Tuition/fees: $818; $5,618 out-of-state. Per-credit charge: $26 in-state; $186 out-of-state. Books/supplies: $810. Personal expenses: $1,625.

Financial aid. **Need-based:** Work study available for part-time students.

Application procedures. **Admission:** No deadline. No application fee. Admission notification on a rolling basis. **Financial aid:** Priority date 3/2; no closing date. FAFSA required. Applicants notified on a rolling basis starting 4/15.

Academics. **Special study options:** Cooperative education, distance learning, double major, ESL, honors, independent study, student-designed major, study abroad, weekend college. Bachelor's degree programs available on campus. **Credit/placement by examination:** CLEP, institutional tests. 12 credit hours maximum toward associate degree. **Support services:** Learning center, remedial instruction, study skills assistance, tutoring, writing center.

Majors. **Biology:** General. **Business:** General, real estate. **Communications:** General, broadcast journalism, journalism. **Computer sciences:** Computer science. **Education:** Art, early childhood, mathematics, physical, special. **Engineering:** Electrical. **Health:** Nursing (RN). **Liberal arts:** Arts/sciences, library assistant. **Math:** General. **Mechanic/repair:** Auto body. **Physical sciences:** Chemistry, physics. **Protective services:** Law enforcement admin. **Visual/performing arts:** Interior design.

Computing on campus. 300 workstations in library, computer center, student center. Online course registration, online library available.

Student life. **Freshman orientation:** Available. **Activities:** Jazz band, choral groups, dance, drama, music ensembles, musical theater, radio station, student government, student newspaper, TV station, Alpha Gamma Sigma (honor society).

Athletics. **Intercollegiate:** Baseball M, basketball, cross-country, diving, soccer W, softball W, swimming, tennis W, track and field, volleyball W, water polo, wrestling M.

Student services. Adult student services, career counseling, student employment services, financial aid counseling, health services, legal services, on-campus daycare, personal counseling, veterans' counselor. **Physically disabled:** Services for visually, speech, hearing impaired. **Transfer:** Special adviser, orientation, re-entry adviser for new students. Transfer center, transfer adviser, college fairs on campus for students transferring to 4-year colleges.

Contact. E-mail: admit@bass.cuesta.cc.ca.us
Phone: (805) 546-3140 Fax: (805) 546-3975
Joy Chambers, Director of Admissions and Records, Cuesta College, Box 8106, San Luis Obispo, CA 93403

Cuyamaca College

El Cajon, California
www.cuyamaca.net **CB code: 4252**

- Public 2-year community college
- Small city

General. Founded in 1978. Regionally accredited. **Enrollment:** 1,217 degree-seeking undergraduates. **Degrees:** 364 associate awarded. **ROTC:** Army, Air Force. **Location:** 18 miles from San Diego. **Calendar:** Semester, limited summer session. **Full-time faculty:** 85 total. **Part-time faculty:** 331 total. **Special facilities:** Museum, automotive technology facility, water gardens.

Transfer out. Colleges most students transferred to 2005: San Diego State University, National University.

Basis for selection. Open admission.

2005-2006 Annual costs. Tuition/fees: $818; $5,348 out-of-state. Per-credit charge: $26 in-state; $177 out-of-state. Books/supplies: $1,200. Personal expenses: $1,500.

Financial aid. Need-based: Work study available nights, weekends and for part-time students.

Application procedures. Admission: Closing date 8/18. No application fee in-state; $152 out-of-state. Application may be submitted online. Admission notification on a rolling basis. **Financial aid:** Priority date 7/21; no closing date. FAFSA required. Applicants notified on a rolling basis; must reply within 2 week(s) of notification.

Academics. Special study options: Cooperative education, cross-registration, distance learning, double major, dual enrollment of high school students, ESL, honors, independent study, internships, study abroad, weekend college. License preparation in real estate. **Credit/placement by examination:** AP, CLEP, institutional tests. **Support services:** Remedial instruction, tutoring.

Majors. Agriculture: Ornamental horticulture. **Business:** Accounting, business admin, real estate. **Engineering technology:** Architectural, computer systems, drafting, electrical, surveying. **Family/consumer sciences:** Child care. **Liberal arts:** Arts/sciences.

Most popular majors. Business/marketing 15%, computer/information sciences 6%, education 7%, liberal arts 48%.

Computing on campus. Online course registration available.

Student life. Freshman orientation: Available. **Policies:** Freshmen permitted cars on campus. **Activities:** Dance, student government, student newspaper, African American student union, Christian club, Cuyamaca College Spanish club, MECHA, Phi Theta Kappa.

Athletics. Intercollegiate: Basketball, cross-country, golf M, soccer, tennis W, track and field, volleyball W. **Team name:** Coyotes.

Student services. Adult student services, career counseling, student employment services, financial aid counseling, health services, on-campus daycare, personal counseling, veterans' counselor. **Physically disabled:** Services for visually, speech, hearing impaired. **Transfer:** Special adviser, orientation, pre-admission transcript evaluation for new students. Transfer center, transfer adviser, college fairs on campus for students transferring to 4-year colleges.

Contact. Phone: (619) 660-4275 Fax: (619) 660-4575
Beth Appenzeller, Dean of Admissions and Records, Cuyamaca College, 900 Rancho San Diego Parkway, El Cajon, CA 92019-4304

Cypress College

Cypress, California
www.cypress.cc.ca.us **CB code: 4104**

- Public 2-year community college
- Commuter campus in small city

General. Founded in 1966. Regionally accredited. **Enrollment:** 12,900 undergraduates. **Degrees:** 764 associate awarded. **Location:** 30 miles from Los Angeles. **Calendar:** Semester, limited summer session. **Full-time faculty:** 190 total. **Part-time faculty:** 220 total.

Student profile.

Out-of-state:	5%	**25 or older:**	44%

Basis for selection. Open admission. College administered English and math placement exams used for placement.

2005-2006 Annual costs. Tuition/fees: $806; $5,336 out-of-state. Per-credit charge: $26 in-state; $177 out-of-state. Books/supplies: $630. Personal expenses: $1,898.

Application procedures. Admission: Closing date 8/28. No application fee. Admission notification on a rolling basis beginning on or about 8/1. **Financial aid:** Priority date 5/31; no closing date. FAFSA required. Applicants notified on a rolling basis starting 8/1; must reply within 2 week(s) of notification.

Academics. Special study options: Distance learning, dual enrollment of high school students, ESL, honors, independent study, internships, liberal arts/career combination, study abroad. License preparation in aviation, dental hygiene, nursing, real estate. **Credit/placement by examination:** CLEP, institutional tests. 12 credit hours maximum toward associate degree. **Support services:** Learning center, reduced course load, remedial instruction, study skills assistance, tutoring, writing center.

Majors. Area/ethnic studies: Asian, Latin American. **Business:** General, accounting, administrative services, business admin, hospitality/recreation, management information systems, management science, office technology, office/clerical, tourism promotion. **Communications:** Journalism. **Computer sciences:** General, data processing, information systems. **Conservation:** Forestry. **Education:** General, elementary, physical, secondary, technology/industrial arts. **Engineering:** General. **English:** Speech/rhetoric. **Family/consumer sciences:** Institutional food production. **Foreign languages:** French, German, Spanish. **Health:** Dental assistant, dental hygiene, dental lab technology, health services, medical assistant, medical radiologic technology/radiation therapy, medical records admin, medical records technology, nursing (RN), predentistry, premedicine, prepharmacy, preveterinary. **History:** General. **Legal studies:** Court reporting, legal secretary, prelaw. **Liberal arts:** Arts/sciences. **Math:** General. **Mechanic/repair:** Aircraft, auto body, automotive, electronics/electrical, heating/ac/refrig. **Parks/recreation:** General. **Personal/culinary services:** Culinary arts, mortuary science. **Philosophy/religion:** Philosophy. **Physical sciences:** Chemistry, geology, physics. **Psychology:** General. **Public administration:** Human services. **Social sciences:** Anthropology, economics, geography, political science, sociology. **Transportation:** Airline/commercial pilot, aviation, aviation management, flight attendant. **Visual/performing arts:** General, art, commercial/advertising art, dance, dramatic, music performance, theater design.

Computing on campus. 800 workstations in library, computer center, student center.

Student life. Activities: Bands, choral groups, dance, drama, literary magazine, music ensembles, musical theater, student government, student newspaper.

Athletics. NJCAA. **Intercollegiate:** Baseball M, basketball, diving, golf, soccer, softball W, swimming, tennis, volleyball W, water polo, wrestling M. **Intramural:** Badminton, baseball M, basketball, softball, volleyball.

Student services. Career counseling, student employment services, health services, on-campus daycare, personal counseling, veterans' counselor. **Physically disabled:** Services for visually, speech, hearing impaired. **Transfer:** Special adviser, orientation, re-entry adviser, pre-admission transcript evaluation for new students. Transfer center, transfer adviser, college fairs on campus for students transferring to 4-year colleges.

Contact. Phone: (714) 826-2220 Fax: (714) 826-4224
Dave Wassenaar, Dean of Admissions and Records, Cypress College, 9200 Valley View Street, Cypress, CA 90630

De Anza College
Cupertino, California
www.deanza.edu
CB member
CB code: 4286

- Public 2-year community college
- Commuter campus in large town

General. Founded in 1967. Regionally accredited. **Enrollment:** 14,880 degree-seeking undergraduates. **Degrees:** 1,140 associate awarded. **ROTC:** Army, Air Force. **Location:** 5 miles from San Jose, 40 miles from San Francisco. **Calendar:** Quarter, extensive summer session. **Full-time faculty:** 300 total. **Part-time faculty:** 540 total. **Special facilities:** Planetarium, California history center, environmental studies area, advanced technology center.

Transfer out. Colleges most students transferred to 2005: University of California: Davis, San Jose State, San Francisco State, University of California: Berkeley, University of California: Santa Cruz.

Basis for selection. Open admission, but selective for some programs. Limited admission for nursing and physical therapist assistant applicants.

2005-2006 Annual costs. Tuition/fees: $798; $5,343 out-of-state. Per-credit charge: $17 in-state; $118 out-of-state. Books/supplies: $846. Personal expenses: $1,719.

Financial aid. All financial aid based on need. Need-based aid available for part-time students.

Application procedures. Admission: No deadline. No application fee. Application may be submitted online. Admission notification on a rolling basis. **Financial aid:** Priority date 3/2; no closing date. FAFSA required. Applicants notified on a rolling basis starting 5/15; must reply within 2 week(s) of notification.

Academics. Special study options: Cooperative education, cross-registration, distance learning, dual enrollment of high school students, ESL, honors, independent study, internships, study abroad, weekend college. License preparation in nursing. **Credit/placement by examination:** CLEP, institutional tests. 45 credit hours maximum toward associate degree. **Support services:** Learning center, pre-admission summer program, remedial instruction, tutoring.

Majors. Area/ethnic studies: African-American, Asian-American, Hispanic-American/Latino/Chicano, Latin American, Native American. **Biology:** General. **Business:** Accounting, administrative services, business admin, marketing, purchasing, real estate, taxation. **Communications:** General. **Computer sciences:** General, applications programming, computer science, programming, systems analysis. **Education:** Early childhood. **Engineering:** General, computer, electrical, mechanical. **Engineering technology:** Drafting. **English:** Technical writing. **Foreign languages:** French, German, Russian, Spanish. **Health:** Medical assistant, nursing (RN). **History:** General. **Legal studies:** Paralegal. **Liberal arts:** Arts/sciences. **Math:** General. **Philosophy/religion:** Philosophy. **Physical sciences:** Astronomy, chemistry, geology, physics. **Protective services:** Law enforcement admin, security services. **Psychology:** General. **Science technology:** Biological. **Social sciences:** Anthropology, economics, geography, political science, sociology. **Visual/performing arts:** Art, art history/conservation, ceramics, cinematography, commercial/advertising art, painting, photography, printmaking, sculpture.

Computing on campus. 300 workstations in library, computer center, student center. Online course registration available.

Student life. Freshman orientation: Available. **Activities:** Bands, choral groups, dance, drama, literary magazine, music ensembles, student government, student newspaper, symphony orchestra, TV station.

Athletics. Intercollegiate: Baseball M, basketball, cross-country, diving, football (tackle) M, golf, soccer, softball W, swimming, tennis, track and field, volleyball, water polo M. **Intramural:** Badminton, baseball M, basketball, bowling, fencing, gymnastics, racquetball, soccer W, swimming, tennis, volleyball. **Team name:** Dons.

Student services. Adult student services, alcohol/substance abuse counseling, career counseling, services for economically disadvantaged, student employment services, financial aid counseling, health services, legal services, minority student services, on-campus daycare, personal counseling, placement for graduates, veterans' counselor. **Physically disabled:** Services for visually, speech, hearing impaired. **Transfer:** Special adviser, orientation, re-entry adviser for new students. Transfer center, transfer adviser, college fairs on campus for students transferring to 4-year colleges.

Contact. E-mail: webreg@fhda.edu
Phone: (408) 864-5300 Fax: (408) 864-8329
Kathleen Kyne, Dean of Admissions and Records, De Anza College, 21250 Stevens Creek Boulevard, Cupertino, CA 95014

Deep Springs College
Dyer, Nevada
www.deepsprings.edu
CB code: 4281

- Private 2-year liberal arts college for men
- Residential campus in rural community
- SAT or ACT (ACT writing recommended), application essay, interview required

General. Founded in 1917. Regionally accredited. Located in isolated high-desert valley of over 60 square miles. **Enrollment:** 27 degree-seeking undergraduates. **Location:** 45 miles from Bishop, California. **Calendar:** 6 terms of 7 weeks each. Limited summer session. **Full-time faculty:** 3 total; 100% have terminal degrees, 33% women. **Part-time faculty:** 3 total; 100% have terminal degrees. **Class size:** 100% < 20. **Special facilities:** Student-operated 2,600-acre cattle and alfalfa ranch, dairy.

Student profile.

Out-of-state:	100%	**Live on campus:**	100%

Transfer out. 92% of students enrolled in the transfer program go on to 4-year colleges. **Colleges most students transferred to 2005:** Harvard University, University of Chicago, Oxford University.

Basis for selection. School achievement record, interview, assessment of altruistic interests, and essays most important. Extracurricular activities and recommendations strongly considered. Student body has central role in admission decisions. SAT Subject Tests recommended. 2-round application process: in first round, student fills out application form, writes 3 essays, and sends HS transcript. If admitted to second round, he writes additional 4 essays and visits college for a 3-day interview.

2005-2006 Annual costs. All students receive full scholarship (typically renewed for second year) covering tuition, room, and board. Books/supplies: $1,500.

Financial aid. Need-based: Work study available nights and weekends. **Non-need-based:** Scholarships awarded for academics.

Application procedures. Admission: Closing date 11/15 (postmark date). No application fee. Admission notification 4/15. Must reply by 5/1. Approximately 40 applicants are invited to complete part II of application process between January and March. This includes a 3-day campus visit, interview, and writing four additional essays. Foreign students and those with economic hardship may be exempt from the visit upon request. **Financial aid:** No deadline.

Academics. Students required to take three classes: English Composition, Public Speaking and the Summer Seminar, an interdisciplinary course broadly oriented around questions of political theory. Deep Springs also consistently offers courses in the humanities, social sciences and natural sciences. **Special study options:** Independent study. **Credit/placement by examination:** CLEP. **Support services:** Reduced course load.

Majors. Liberal arts: Arts/sciences.

Computing on campus. 6 workstations in library, computer center. Helpline, repair service available.

Student life. Freshman orientation: Mandatory. **Policies:** All students required to work at least 20 hours per week on jobs related to operation of college and ranch. Student committees organize all community events as well as handle admissions, public relations, and review/reinvitation process. Alcohol and drugs forbidden. Students may not leave campus during term. Freshmen permitted cars on campus. **Housing:** Guaranteed on-campus for all undergraduates. Pets allowed in dorm rooms. **Activities:** Drama, film society, literary magazine, music ensembles, student government, student newspaper.

Athletics. Intramural: Basketball M, boxing M, cross-country M, equestrian M, football (tackle) M, rifle M, rodeo M, soccer M, swimming M, table tennis M, track and field M, weight lifting M, wrestling M.

Student services. Career counseling, health services, personal counseling, placement for graduates. **Transfer:** Special adviser, orientation for new students. Transfer adviser for students transferring to 4-year colleges.

Contact. E-mail: apcom@deepsprings.edu
Phone: (760) 872-2000 Fax: (760) 872-4466
Mike Zaletel, Chair, Applications Committee, Deep Springs College, HC 72, Box 45001, Dyer, NV 89010-9803

Diablo Valley College
Pleasant Hill, California
www.dvc.edu **CB code: 4295**

- Public 2-year community college
- Commuter campus in large town

General. Founded in 1948. Regionally accredited. **Enrollment:** 7,536 full-time, degree-seeking students. **Degrees:** 774 associate awarded. **ROTC:** Army, Navy. **Location:** 25 miles from San Francisco. **Calendar:** Semester, extensive summer session. **Full-time faculty:** 260 total. **Part-time faculty:** 570 total. **Class size:** 24% < 20, 57% 20-39, 17% 40-49, 3% 50-99, less than 1% >100. **Partnerships:** Formal partnerships with Wells Fargo, Chevron, Pacific Bell, City of San Ramon, Telecommunication Incubator.

Student profile.

Out-of-state:	1%	25 or older:	38%

Transfer out. Colleges most students transferred to 2005: University of California at Berkeley, San Francisco State University, University of California at Hayward, Sacramento State University, University of California at Davis.

Basis for selection. Open admission. Open to all applicants with high school diploma (or equivalent) or no longer in high school and over 18 years of age. **Adult students:** SAT/ACT scores not required. **Home-schooled:** Applicants must supply a copy of their private school affidavit.

2005-2006 Annual costs. Tuition/fees: $790; $5,320 out-of-state. Per-credit charge: $26 in-state; $177 out-of-state. Books/supplies: $882. Personal expenses: $1,656.

Financial aid. Need-based: Need-based aid available for part-time students.

Application procedures. Admission: Priority date 4/1; no deadline. No application fee. Application may be submitted online. Admission notification on a rolling basis beginning on or about 4/1. **Financial aid:** Priority date 3/2, closing date 5/1. FAFSA, institutional form required. Applicants notified on a rolling basis starting 6/1; must reply within 2 week(s) of notification.

Academics. The college offers a comprehensive educational program that includes courses in general education, transfer, vocational, basic skills, and life-long learning. These courses are offered in flexible formats that include different hours, days, term length, and a variety of instructional delivery methods (classroom and on-line). **Special study options:** Accelerated study, cooperative education, cross-registration, distance learning, dual enrollment of high school students, ESL, honors, independent study, internships, liberal arts/career combination, study abroad, weekend college. License preparation in dental hygiene. **Credit/placement by examination:** AP, CLEP, institutional tests. **Support services:** Learning center, pre-admission summer program, reduced course load, remedial instruction, study skills assistance, tutoring, writing center.

Majors. Computer sciences: General, computer science, networking. **Education:** Physical, special. **Health:** Athletic training. **Liberal arts:** Arts/sciences.

Computing on campus. 1,000 workstations in library, computer center, student center. Commuter students can connect to campus network. Online course registration, online library, helpline, repair service available.

Student life. Freshman orientation: Mandatory. **Policies:** No smoking except in designated areas. Freshmen permitted cars on campus. **Activities:** Bands, choral groups, dance, drama, film society, literary magazine, music ensembles, musical theater, student government, student newspaper, symphony orchestra, TV station, Afghan club, Alpha Gamma Sigma, Asian student union, DVC Republicans, student health improvement project, Black student union, Latino students' alliance, Muslim student association, Christian Science organization, horticulture club.

Athletics. NJCAA. **Intercollegiate:** Baseball M, basketball, cross-country, football (tackle) M, soccer W, softball W, swimming, tennis, track and field, volleyball W, water polo. **Team name:** Vikings.

Student services. Adult student services, career counseling, services for economically disadvantaged, student employment services, financial aid counseling, on-campus daycare, personal counseling, placement for graduates, women's services. **Physically disabled:** Services for visually, speech, hearing impaired. **Learning disabled:** Comprehensive services available. **Transfer:** Special adviser, orientation, re-entry adviser for new students. Transfer center, transfer adviser, college fairs on campus for students transferring to 4-year colleges.

Contact. E-mail: informationcenter@dvc.edu
Phone: (925) 685-1310 Fax: (925) 685-1551
Gary Fincher, Director of Admissions and Records, Diablo Valley College, 321 Golf Club Road, Pleasant Hill, CA 94523

East Los Angeles College
Monterey Park, California **CB member**
www.elac.edu **CB code: 4296**

- Public 2-year community college
- Commuter campus in small city

General. Founded in 1945. Regionally accredited. **Enrollment:** 4,807 full-time, degree-seeking students. **Degrees:** 1,254 associate awarded. **Location:** 5 miles from Los Angeles. **Calendar:** Semester, limited summer session. **Full-time faculty:** 266 total. **Part-time faculty:** 400 total.

Student profile.

Out-of-state:	2%	25 or older:	47%

Basis for selection. Open admission, but selective for some programs. Limited admission to nursing and allied health associate programs. Institution uses Assessment Placement Test for English and mathematics placement. Interview required for nursing, respiratory technology majors.

2005-2006 Annual costs. Tuition/fees: $804; $5,424 out-of-state. Per-credit charge: $26 in-state; $180 out-of-state. Books/supplies: $500. Personal expenses: $1,300.

Financial aid. Need-based: Need-based aid available for part-time students. **Non-need-based:** Scholarships awarded for academics. **Additional information:** Need-based enrollment fee waivers available through a state aid program.

Application procedures. Admission: Closing date 8/15. No application fee. **Financial aid:** Closing date 3/2. FAFSA required. Applicants notified on a rolling basis; must reply within 2 week(s) of notification.

Academics. Plan A major requires 18 credits in major; Plan B major requires 36 credits in major. **Special study options:** Accelerated study, cooperative education, cross-registration, distance learning, double major, dual enrollment of high school students, ESL, honors, independent study, study abroad, weekend college. PACE Program (TV and Saturday classes). **Credit/placement by examination:** CLEP. 15 credit hours maximum toward associate degree. **Support services:** Learning center, pre-admission summer program, reduced course load, remedial instruction, study skills assistance, tutoring.

Majors. Architecture: Landscape, urban/community planning. **Area/ethnic studies:** African-American. **Business:** Accounting, administrative services, business admin, international marketing, managerial economics, office technology, office/clerical, real estate. **Communications:** Journalism. **Computer sciences:** General, programming. **Engineering:** General, architectural, civil, electrical, mechanics. **Engineering technology:** Architectural. **Health:** Electrocardiograph technology, medical assistant, nursing (RN), respiratory therapy technology. **History:** General. **Legal studies:** Legal secretary. **Mechanic/repair:** Automotive. **Parks/recreation:** Health/fitness. **Philosophy/religion:** Philosophy. **Physical sciences:** Chemistry, geology, physics. **Protective services:** Police science. **Psychology:** General. **Social sciences:** General, anthropology, economics, geography, political science, sociology. **Visual/performing arts:** Art, dramatic, photography.

Computing on campus. 200 workstations in library, computer center, student center. Online course registration available.

Student life. Activities: Jazz band, choral groups, dance, drama, music ensembles, student government, student newspaper, Associated Students Organization, engineering club, Spanish club, Chicanos for Creative Medicine, MESA, American Society of Engineers and Architects.

Athletics. NJCAA. **Intercollegiate:** Baseball M, basketball, cross-country, diving, football (tackle) M, soccer M, softball W, swimming, track and field, volleyball W, wrestling M.

Student services. Adult student services, career counseling, student employment services, health services, on-campus daycare, personal counseling. **Physically disabled:** Services for visually, hearing impaired. **Transfer:** Special adviser, orientation, pre-admission transcript evaluation for new students. Transfer center, transfer adviser, college fairs on campus for students transferring to 4-year colleges.

Contact. Phone: (323) 265-8712 Fax: (323) 265-8688
Jeremy Allred, Associate Dean of Admissions, East Los Angeles College, 1301 Avenida Cesar Chavez, Monterey Park, CA 91754

El Camino College
Torrance, California
www.elcamino.edu **CB code: 4302**

- Public 2-year community college
- Commuter campus in very large city
- Interview required

General. Founded in 1947. Regionally accredited. **Enrollment:** 7,502 full-time, degree-seeking students. **Degrees:** 1,390 associate awarded. **ROTC:** Army. **Location:** 15 miles from Los Angeles. **Calendar:** Semester, limited summer session. **Full-time faculty:** 340 total. **Part-time faculty:** 530 total. **Special facilities:** Anthropology museum, planetarium, conference center, computer/media center, child development center.

Transfer out. Colleges most students transferred to 2005: California State University: Long Beach, California State University: Dominguez Hills, California State University: Northridge, University of California at Los Angeles.

Basis for selection. Open admission, but selective for some programs. Allied health programs require completion of preparatory courses (anatomy, microbiology, college-level English and mathematics). Interview required for nursing, honors program, x-ray technician, respiratory care majors. **Homeschooled:** Home school must be registered with state of California.

2005-2006 Annual costs. Tuition/fees: $800; $5,330 out-of-state. Per-credit charge: $26 in-state; $177 out-of-state. Books/supplies: $630. Personal expenses: $2,160.

Financial aid. Need-based: Work study available for part-time students. **Non-need-based:** Scholarships awarded for academics, art, leadership, music/drama. **Additional information:** Students may apply for Pell grants until May 1.

Application procedures. Admission: Priority date 5/1; no deadline. Admission notification on a rolling basis beginning on or about 8/20. **Financial aid:** Closing date 5/1. FAFSA, institutional form required. Applicants notified on a rolling basis starting 7/15.

Academics. Special study options: Cooperative education, cross-registration, distance learning, double major, dual enrollment of high school students, ESL, honors, independent study, liberal arts/career combination, study abroad, weekend college. **Credit/placement by examination:** CLEP, IB, institutional tests. 15 credit hours maximum toward associate degree. **Support services:** Learning center, remedial instruction, study skills assistance, tutoring, writing center.

Majors. Agriculture: Ornamental horticulture. **Area/ethnic studies:** African-American, American, Asian-American, Hispanic-American/Latino/Chicano, Native American. **Biology:** General, botany, zoology. **Business:** General, administrative services, business admin, office management, real estate, sales/distribution. **Communications:** Journalism. **Communications technology:** General. **Computer sciences:** General, computer science. **Construction:** Maintenance. **Education:** Early childhood. **Engineering:** General. **Engineering technology:** Architectural, construction, drafting. **English:** Speech/rhetoric. **Family/consumer sciences:** General. **Foreign languages:** French, German, Japanese, Russian, Spanish. **Health:** Licensed practical nurse, medical radiologic technology/radiation therapy, nursing (RN), predentistry, premedicine, prepharmacy, respiratory therapy technology. **History:** General. **Legal studies:** Paralegal. **Math:** General. **Mechanic/repair:** Auto body, automotive, electronics/electrical, heating/ac/refrig. **Parks/recreation:** Health/fitness. **Personal/culinary services:** Cosmetic. **Philosophy/religion:** Philosophy. **Physical sciences:** Astronomy, chemistry, geology, physics. **Protective services:** Fire safety technology, law enforcement admin, police science. **Psychology:** General. **Social sciences:** Anthropology, economics, geography, political science, sociology. **Visual/performing arts:** Art, dance, dramatic, photography, studio arts.

Student life. Freshman orientation: Available. **Activities:** Bands, choral groups, dance, drama, literary magazine, music ensembles, musical theater, student government, student newspaper, symphony orchestra, approximately 60 service, special interest, activist and religious clubs.

Athletics. NJCAA. **Intercollegiate:** Baseball M, basketball, cross-country, fencing M, football (tackle) M, golf M, soccer, softball W, swimming, tennis, track and field, volleyball, water polo, wrestling M.

Student services. Adult student services, career counseling, student employment services, health services, on-campus daycare, personal counseling, placement for graduates, veterans' counselor. **Physically disabled:** Services for visually, speech, hearing impaired. **Transfer:** Special adviser, orientation, re-entry adviser, pre-admission transcript evaluation for new students. Transfer center, transfer adviser, college fairs on campus for students transferring to 4-year colleges.

Contact. E-mail: admissionshelp@elcamino.edu
Phone: (310) 532-3670 Toll-free number: (866) 352-2646
Bill Mulrooney, Director of Admissions and Records, El Camino College, 16007 Crenshaw Boulevard, Torrance, CA 90506

Empire College
Santa Rosa, California
www.empcol.edu **CB code: 4275**

- For-profit 2-year business college
- Commuter campus in small city
- Interview required

General. Accredited by ACICS. **Enrollment:** 644 degree-seeking undergraduates. **Degrees:** 112 associate awarded. **Location:** 55 miles from San Francisco. **Calendar:** Continuous. **Full-time faculty:** 30 total; 63% women. **Part-time faculty:** 6 total; 50% women. **Special facilities:** Law library.

Student profile. Among degree-seeking undergraduates, 100% enrolled in a vocational program, 164 enrolled as first-time, first-year students.

Part-time:	3%	**25 or older:**	50%
Women:	81%		

Transfer out. Colleges most students transferred to 2005: Santa Rosa Junior College.

Basis for selection. Open admission. Scholastic Level Exam (SLE) administered during admission process. Some programs also have typing speed requirement for entrance.

High school preparation. Recommended units include English 10 and mathematics 5.

2005-2006 Annual costs. Books/supplies: $1,500. Personal expenses: $189.

2005-2006 Financial aid. All financial aid based on need. Average need met was 55%. Average scholarship/grant was $4,000; average loan $2,625. 30% of total undergraduate aid awarded as scholarships/grants, 70% as loans/jobs.

Application procedures. Admission: No deadline. $75 fee. Admission notification on a rolling basis. No fall term, ongoing 5-week application/entry. **Financial aid:** No deadline. FAFSA required. Applicants notified on a rolling basis.

Academics. Special study options: Accelerated study, double major. **Credit/placement by examination:** CLEP. **Support services:** Tutoring.

Majors. Business: Accounting, administrative services. **Computer sciences:** Information systems. **Health:** Medical secretary. **Legal studies:** Paralegal.

Computing on campus. 375 workstations in computer center. Online library, student web hosting, wireless network available.

Student life. Freshman orientation: Mandatory.

Student services. Student employment services, financial aid counseling, placement for graduates. **Transfer:** Orientation, re-entry adviser, pre-admission transcript evaluation for new students.

Contact. E-mail: dahnja@empirecollege.com
Phone: (707) 546-4000 ext. 238 Fax: (707) 546-4058
Dahnja Straub, Director of Admissions, Empire College, 3035 Cleveland Avenue, Santa Rosa, CA 95403-2100

Evergreen Valley College
San Jose, California
www.evc.edu **CB code: 4273**

- Public 2-year community and junior college
- Commuter campus in very large city

General. Founded in 1975. Regionally accredited. **Enrollment:** 9,000 undergraduates. **Degrees:** 401 associate awarded. **Location:** 7 miles from downtown. **Calendar:** Semester, extensive summer session. **Full-time faculty:** 100 total; 40% have terminal degrees. **Special facilities:** Library/technology building with large open-access computer labs, hiking trails, parks, observatory, natural habitat (used in natural science and biology course work), cross-country course.

Transfer out. Colleges most students transferred to 2005: San Jose University.

Basis for selection. Open admission, but selective for some programs. Limited admission for nursing and criminal justice programs. **Adult students:** Entrance exam policies same as for first-time freshmen. **Home-schooled:** Interview required. Must complete form R-42 and state affidavit.

2005-2006 Annual costs. Tuition/fees: $808; $5,878 out-of-state. Per-credit charge: $26 in-state; $195 out-of-state. Books/supplies: $700. Personal expenses: $1,550.

Application procedures. Admission: No deadline. No application fee. Application may be submitted online. Admission notification on a rolling basis. **Financial aid:** Priority date 5/31; no closing date. FAFSA required. Applicants notified on a rolling basis.

Academics. Special study options: Accelerated study, cooperative education, cross-registration, distance learning, double major, dual enrollment of high school students, ESL, honors, independent study, internships, liberal arts/career combination, weekend college. License preparation in nursing, paramedic. **Credit/placement by examination:** AP, CLEP, institutional tests. 12 credit hours maximum toward associate degree. Assessment testing as prescribed by California law required for placement in English and mathematics. **Support services:** Learning center, reduced course load, remedial instruction, study skills assistance, tutoring, writing center.

Majors. Business: Administrative services, fashion, management information systems, office technology, office/clerical. **Computer sciences:** General, applications programming. **Engineering technology:** Drafting. **Health:** Nursing (RN). **Liberal arts:** Arts/sciences. **Protective services:** Police science. **Visual/performing arts:** Commercial/advertising art.

Computing on campus. 800 workstations in library, computer center, student center.

Student life. Freshman orientation: Mandatory. Preregistration for classes offered. **Policies:** Freshmen permitted cars on campus. **Activities:** Choral groups, dance, drama, literary magazine, music ensembles, musical theater, student government, student newspaper, Black Students Union, ASPIRE, Enlace, AFFIRM.

Athletics. NJCAA. **Intercollegiate:** Soccer, track and field, volleyball W, wrestling M. **Intramural:** Basketball, football (non-tackle) M. **Team name:** Hawks.

Student services. Alcohol/substance abuse counseling, career counseling, services for economically disadvantaged, student employment services, financial aid counseling, health services, minority student services, on-campus daycare, personal counseling, veterans' counselor. **Physically disabled:** Services for visually, speech, hearing impaired. **Transfer:** Special adviser, orientation for new students. Transfer center, transfer adviser, college fairs on campus for students transferring to 4-year colleges.

Contact. E-mail: lynn.gulkin@evc.edu
Phone: (408) 270-6441 Fax: (408) 223-9351
Kathleen Moberg, Director of Admissions and Records, Evergreen Valley College, 3095 Yerba Buena Road, San Jose, CA 95135

Fashion Careers College

San Diego, California
www.fashioncareerscollege.com **CB code: 3494**

- Private 2-year business college
- Very large city
- Application essay, interview required

General. Accredited by ACICS. **Enrollment:** 100 degree-seeking undergraduates. **Degrees:** 28 associate awarded. **Calendar:** Quarter. **Full-time faculty:** 10 total. **Part-time faculty:** 20 total.

Basis for selection. Exam score, essay, interview important. Wonderlic test used for admission.

2006-2007 Annual costs. Tuition/fees: $17,150. $13,950 for fashion merchandising, $15,900 for fashion design. $300 fees.

Application procedures. Admission: No deadline. $25 fee. Admission notification on a rolling basis. **Financial aid:** No deadline. FAFSA required.

Academics. Credit/placement by examination: CLEP.

Majors. Business: Fashion. **Visual/performing arts:** Fashion design.

Student life. Freshman orientation: Available. Held 1 week before classes start.

Contact. E-mail: info@fashioncareerscollege.com
Phone: (619) 275-4700 Toll-free number: (888) 322-2999
Fax: (619) 275-0635
Fashion Careers College, 1923 Morena Boulevard, San Diego, CA 92110

Fashion Institute of Design and Merchandising

Los Angeles, California **CB member**
www.fidm.edu **CB code: 4457**

- For-profit 2-year visual arts and business college
- Commuter campus in very large city
- Application essay required

General. Founded in 1969. Regionally accredited. Branch campuses in Orange County, San Francisco and San Diego. **Enrollment:** 3,522 degree-seeking undergraduates. **Degrees:** 1,436 associate awarded. **Calendar:** Quarter, extensive summer session. **Full-time faculty:** 52 total; 21% minority, 62% women. **Part-time faculty:** 162 total; 24% minority, 64% women. **Class size:** 77% < 20, 23% 20-39. **Special facilities:** Hollywood costume collection, costume museum, textile museum, fragrance bottle collection, fashion library.

Student profile. Among degree-seeking undergraduates, 895 enrolled as first-time, first-year students.

Part-time:	21%	**Women:**	90%
Out-of-state:	32%	**25 or older:**	19%

Basis for selection. Open admission. High school record, institutional test scores, references, and evidence of interest in major area through work experience, high school preparation, or extracurricular activities considered. Portfolio required for fashion design, interior design, and visual presentation majors. Out-of-state applicants interviewed by telephone. **Adult students:** Entrance exam policies same as for first-time freshmen.

2005-2006 Annual costs. Tuition/fees: $16,775. Per-credit charge: $362. Tuition and fees may vary depending on program. Books/supplies: $1,900.

Financial aid. Non-need-based: Scholarships awarded for academics. **Additional information:** Tuition/fee expenses may be reduced by applying for admission by December 31 of year before student plans to attend.

Application procedures. Admission: No deadline. $25 fee. Application may be submitted online. Admission notification on a rolling basis. **Financial aid:** Priority date 3/1; no closing date. FAFSA, institutional form required. Applicants notified on a rolling basis starting 3/15; must reply within 3 week(s) of notification.

Academics. Faculty and staff come from related industries. Project-oriented courses give students hands-on experience. **Special study options:** Exchange student, independent study, internships, study abroad. **Credit/placement by examination:** AP, CLEP, IB, institutional tests. 15 credit hours maximum toward associate degree. **Support services:** Learning center, reduced course load, remedial instruction, study skills assistance, tutoring, writing center.

Majors. Business: Fashion, marketing, operations, sales/distribution. **Family/consumer sciences:** Apparel marketing, clothing/textiles, fashion consultant, merchandising, textile manufacture, textile science. **Visual/performing arts:** Design, fashion design, fiber arts, graphic design, interior design, theater design.

Most popular majors. Business/marketing 36%, visual/performing arts 14%.

Computing on campus. 120 workstations in library, computer center, student center. Commuter students can connect to campus network. Online course registration, online library, wireless network available.

Student life. Freshman orientation: Mandatory. **Policies:** Freshmen permitted cars on campus. **Activities:** Student government, student newspaper, honor society, international club, Association of Manufacturing Students, Visual Design Forum, student activities committee, ASID, design council, Phi Theta Kappa.

Student services. Adult student services, career counseling, student employment services, personal counseling, placement for graduates. **Physically disabled:** Services for visually, hearing impaired. **Transfer:** Special adviser, orientation, pre-admission transcript evaluation for new students. Transfer adviser for students transferring to 4-year colleges.

Contact. E-mail: admissionsdirector@fidm.edu
Phone: (213) 624-1200 Toll-free number: (800) 624-1200
Fax: (213) 624-4799
Susan Aronson, Director of Admission, Fashion Institute of Design and Merchandising, 919 South Grand Avenue, Los Angeles, CA 90015

Fashion Institute of Design and Merchandising: San Diego

San Diego, California
www.fidm.edu **CB code: 2949**

- For-profit 2-year visual arts and business college
- Commuter campus in very large city
- Application essay, interview required

General. Regionally accredited. **Enrollment:** 272 degree-seeking undergraduates. **Degrees:** 37 associate awarded. **Calendar:** Quarter, extensive summer session. **Full-time faculty:** 3 total; 67% women. **Part-time faculty:** 32 total; 22% minority, 78% women. **Class size:** 76% < 20, 22% 20-39. **Special facilities:** Branch level access to one of largest historical costume collection and fashion libraries in United States.

Student profile. Among degree-seeking undergraduates, 150 enrolled as first-time, first-year students.

Part-time:	14%	**Hispanic American:**	23%
Women:	95%	**International:**	1%
African American:	4%	**25 or older:**	19%
Asian American:	11%		

Basis for selection. Open admission. Out-of-state applicants interviewed by telephone. Portfolio required for fashion design, interior design and visual presentation majors. **Adult students:** Entrance exam policies same as for first-time freshmen.

2005-2006 Annual costs. Tuition/fees: $16,775. Tuition and fees vary by program. Books/supplies: $1,900.

Financial aid. Non-need-based: Scholarships awarded for academics.

Application procedures. Admission: No deadline. $25 fee. Application may be submitted online. Admission notification on a rolling basis. **Financial aid:** No deadline. FAFSA, institutional form required. Applicants notified on a rolling basis; must reply within 3 week(s) of notification.

Academics. Special study options: Distance learning, ESL, independent study. **Credit/placement by examination:** AP, CLEP, IB, institutional tests. 15 credit hours maximum toward associate degree. **Support services:** Learning center, reduced course load, remedial instruction, study skills assistance, tutoring, writing center.

Majors. Business: Fashion, marketing. **Family/consumer sciences:** Apparel marketing, clothing/textiles, fashion consultant, merchandising, textile manufacture, textile science. **Visual/performing arts:** Design, fashion design, fiber arts, graphic design, interior design, theater design.

Computing on campus. 25 workstations in computer center, student center.

Student life. Freshman orientation: Mandatory. **Activities:** Honor students society, international club, Association of Manufacturing Students, alumni association, ASID student chapter, Design Council, Phi Theta Kappa, student activities committee.

Student services. Adult student services, career counseling, student employment services, financial aid counseling, personal counseling, placement for graduates. **Physically disabled:** Services for visually, hearing impaired. **Transfer:** Special adviser, orientation for new students. Transfer adviser for students transferring to 4-year colleges.

Contact. E-mail: admissionsdirector@fidm.com
Phone: (619) 235-2049 Toll-free number: (800) 243-3436
Fax: (619) 232-4322
Susan Aronson, Director of Admissions, Fashion Institute of Design and Merchandising: San Diego, 1010 Second Avenue, Suite 2000, San Diego, CA 92101

Fashion Institute of Design and Merchandising: San Francisco

San Francisco, California
www.fidm.com **CB code: 4988**

- For-profit 2-year visual arts and business college
- Commuter campus in very large city
- Application essay, interview required

General. Founded in 1969. Regionally accredited. **Enrollment:** 936 degree-seeking undergraduates. **Degrees:** 305 associate awarded. **Calendar:** Quarter, extensive summer session. **Full-time faculty:** 13 total; 8% minority, 69% women. **Part-time faculty:** 57 total; 18% minority, 68% women. **Class size:** 77% < 20, 23% 20-39.

Student profile. Among degree-seeking undergraduates, 289 enrolled as first-time, first-year students.

Part-time:	20%	**Women:**	93%
Out-of-state:	8%	**25 or older:**	14%

Transfer out. 10% of students enrolled in the transfer program go on to 4-year colleges.

Basis for selection. Open admission. Out-of-state applicants interviewed by telephone. Portfolio required for fashion design, interior design, design and visual presentation majors. **Adult students:** Entrance exam policies same as for first-time freshmen.

2006-2007 Annual costs. Tuition/fees: $16,775. Tuition and fees vary by program. Books/supplies: $1,900.

Financial aid. Non-need-based: Scholarships awarded for academics.

Application procedures. Admission: No deadline. $25 fee. Application may be submitted online. Admission notification on a rolling basis. **Financial aid:** No deadline. FAFSA, institutional form required. Applicants notified on a rolling basis starting 3/15; must reply within 3 week(s) of notification.

Academics. Faculty and staff come from related industries. Project-oriented courses give students hands-on experience. **Special study options:** Distance learning, exchange student, internships, study abroad. **Credit/placement by examination:** AP, CLEP, IB, institutional tests. 15 credit hours maximum toward associate degree. **Support services:** Learning center, reduced course load, remedial instruction, study skills assistance, tutoring, writing center.

Majors. Business: Fashion. **Computer sciences:** Computer graphics. **Family/consumer sciences:** Apparel marketing, clothing/textiles, fashion consultant, merchandising, textile manufacture, textile science. **Visual/performing arts:** General, commercial/advertising art, design, fashion design, graphic design, interior design, theater design.

Most popular majors. Business/marketing 36%, visual/performing arts 64%.

Computing on campus. 40 workstations in library, computer center.

Student life. Freshman orientation: Mandatory. **Activities:** Student newspaper, Honor students society, international club, Association of Manufacturing Students, alumni association, ASID student chapter, DECA, Visual Design Forum, student activities committee, Design Council, Phi Theta Kappa.

Student services. Adult student services, career counseling, student employment services, personal counseling, placement for graduates. **Physically disabled:** Services for visually, hearing impaired. **Transfer:** Special adviser, orientation for new students. Transfer adviser for students transferring to 4-year colleges.

Contact. E-mail: admissionsdirector@fidm.edu
Phone: (415) 675-5200 Toll-free number: (800) 422-3436
Fax: (415) 394-9700
Sheryl Badalamente, Director of Admissions, Fashion Institute of Design and Merchandising: San Francisco, 55 Stockton Street, San Francisco, CA 94108-5805

Feather River College

Quincy, California
www.frc.edu **CB code: 4318**

- Public 2-year community and liberal arts college
- Residential campus in small town

General. Founded in 1968. Regionally accredited. **Enrollment:** 634 degree-seeking undergraduates; 993 non-degree-seeking students. **Degrees:** 110 associate awarded. **Location:** 150 miles from Sacramento, 80 miles from Reno, Nevada. **Calendar:** Semester, limited summer session. **Full-time faculty:** 27 total; 15% have terminal degrees, 15% minority, 30% women. **Part-time faculty:** 91 total. **Class size:** 54% < 20, 46% 20-39. **Special facilities:** Fish hatchery, horse boarding facility, state wildlife preserve.

Two-Year Colleges

Student profile. Among degree-seeking undergraduates, 40% enrolled in a transfer program, 60% enrolled in a vocational program, 141 enrolled as first-time, first-year students.

Part-time:	34%	**Hispanic American:**	7%
Out-of-state:	30%	**Native American:**	3%
Women:	48%	**International:**	1%
African American:	9%	**25 or older:**	35%
Asian American:	2%	**Live on campus:**	10%

Transfer out. 83% of students enrolled in the transfer program go on to 4-year colleges. **Colleges most students transferred to 2005:** CUS: Chico, CSU: Humboldt, University of Nevada: Reno, California Polytechnic State University: San Luis Obispo, University of California: Davis.

Basis for selection. Open admission. Institute's own test required of all students for placement purposes. **Adult students:** Entrance exam policies same as for first-time freshmen. **Learning Disabled:** Placement tests in English and Math are required for new students with no college experience.

2005-2006 Annual costs. Tuition/fees: $836; $6,086 out-of-state. Per-credit charge: $26 in-state; $201 out-of-state. Costs for Nevada residents: $42 per unit with good neighbor policy. Room only: $3,825. Books/supplies: $800.

2005-2006 Financial aid. Need-based: Need-based aid available for part-time students. Work study available nights, weekends and for part-time students.

Application procedures. Admission: No deadline. No application fee. Application may be submitted online. **Financial aid:** No deadline. FAFSA required. Applicants notified on a rolling basis starting 7/30; must reply within 3 week(s) of notification.

Academics. General education/core courses are offered that satisfy all lower division requirements of California State University, University of California, and University of Nevada system. **Special study options:** Cooperative education, cross-registration, distance learning, double major, dual enrollment of high school students, ESL, honors, independent study, liberal arts/career combination. License preparation in nursing, paramedic. **Credit/placement by examination:** AP, CLEP, IB, institutional tests. 12 credit hours maximum toward associate degree. **Support services:** GED preparation and test center, learning center, reduced course load, remedial instruction, study skills assistance, tutoring.

Majors. Agriculture: Equestrian studies. **Biology:** General, wildlife. **Business:** Business admin, office/clerical. **Computer sciences:** Computer science. **Conservation:** General, environmental studies, fisheries, forest technology, forestry, management/policy, wildlife. **Construction:** Carpentry, maintenance. **Education:** General. **Engineering technology:** Construction. **Family/consumer sciences:** Child care. **Health:** Licensed practical nurse. **History:** General. **Liberal arts:** Arts/sciences. **Math:** General. **Protective services:** Law enforcement admin. **Social sciences:** General, criminology. **Visual/performing arts:** Art.

Most popular majors. Agriculture 30%, biological/life sciences 33%, business/marketing 10%, security/protective services 9%.

Computing on campus. 120 workstations in dormitories, library, computer center, student center. Dormitories wired for high-speed internet access. Online library available.

Student life. Freshman orientation: Mandatory, $26 fee. 2-day, 1-night orientation held in fall and spring. **Policies:** Freshmen permitted cars on campus. **Housing:** Apartments available. **Activities:** Choral groups, drama, literary magazine, musical theater, student government, Phi Theta Kappa.

Athletics. NJCAA. **Intercollegiate:** Baseball M, basketball, football (tackle) M, rodeo, soccer, softball W, volleyball W. **Intramural:** Basketball, equestrian, skiing, softball, volleyball. **Team name:** Golden Eagles.

Student services. Adult student services, career counseling, services for economically disadvantaged, student employment services, financial aid counseling, health services, on-campus daycare, personal counseling, placement for graduates, veterans' counselor. **Physically disabled:** Services for visually, speech, hearing impaired. **Transfer:** Special adviser, orientation, reentry adviser, pre-admission transcript evaluation for new students. Transfer center, transfer adviser, college fairs on campus for students transferring to 4-year colleges.

Contact. E-mail: khayden@frc.edu
Phone: (530) 283-0202 ext. 285 Toll-free number: (800) 442-9799 ext. 285
Fax: (530) 283-3757
Karen Hayden, Registrar, Feather River College, 570 Golden Eagle Avenue, Quincy, CA 95971

Folsom Lake College

Folsom, California
www.flc.losrios.edu

- Public 2-year community college
- Large town

General. Regionally accredited. **Calendar:** Semester.

Contact. Phone: (916) 608-6500
100 Scholar Way, Folsom, CA 95630

Foothill College

Los Altos Hills, California
www.foothill.edu **CB code: 4315**

- Public 2-year community college
- Commuter campus in large town

General. Founded in 1958. Regionally accredited. Travel careers computer lab, Math Center, NASA Ames internship program. **Enrollment:** 6,437 degree-seeking undergraduates. **Degrees:** 658 associate awarded. **ROTC:** Army, Navy, Air Force. **Calendar:** Quarter, limited summer session. **Full-time faculty:** 193 total; 60% women. **Part-time faculty:** 452 total. **Special facilities:** Center for Innovation, Japanese Cultural Center, observatory, bamboo garden, theater, dental health clinic.

Student profile. Among degree-seeking undergraduates, 80% enrolled in a transfer program, 20% enrolled in a vocational program, 30% already have a bachelor's degree or higher, 3,284 transferred in from other institutions.

Transfer out. Colleges most students transferred to 2005: CSU: San Jose, UC: Berkeley, UC: Santa Cruz, UC: Los Angeles, UC: Davis.

Basis for selection. Open admission, but selective for some programs. Allied health programs have special prerequisites: using point system to rank required college-level and general education classes, top 20-40 students selected for admission. Must be 2-year transfer.

2005-2006 Annual costs. Tuition/fees: $798; $5,343 out-of-state. Per-credit charge: $17 in-state; $118 out-of-state. Books/supplies: $1,287.

Financial aid. All financial aid based on need. Need-based aid available for part-time students.

Application procedures. Admission: No deadline. No application fee. Application may be submitted online. Admission notification on a rolling basis. **Financial aid:** Priority date 3/30; no closing date. FAFSA, institutional form required. Applicants notified on a rolling basis; must reply within 2 week(s) of notification.

Academics. NASA Ames Research Center internships available. **Special study options:** Cooperative education, cross-registration, distance learning, ESL, exchange student, honors, independent study, internships, liberal arts/career combination, study abroad, weekend college. License preparation in dental hygiene, paramedic, radiology, real estate. **Credit/placement by examination:** AP, CLEP, institutional tests. 20 credit hours maximum toward associate degree. **Support services:** Learning center, remedial instruction, tutoring, writing center.

Majors. Agriculture: Landscaping, nursery operations, ornamental horticulture. **Area/ethnic studies:** American, women's. **Biology:** General, bioinformatics, biotechnology. **Business:** Accounting, business admin, international, office technology, real estate, tourism promotion. **Communications:** General, broadcast journalism, media studies, radio/tv. **Computer sciences:** General, computer graphics, computer science, database management, information technology, LAN/WAN management, programming. **Education:** Early childhood. **Engineering:** General, software. **Engineering technology:** Electrical. **English:** Creative writing, speech/rhetoric. **Family/consumer sciences:** Child development. **Foreign languages:** Chinese, French, Japanese, linguistics, Spanish. **Health:** Athletic training, dental assistant, dental hygiene, medical radiologic technology/radiation therapy, pharmacy assistant, physician assistant, predentistry, premedicine, prepharmacy, preveterinary, radiologic technology/medical imaging, respiratory therapy assistant, respiratory therapy technology, sonography, veterinary technology/assistant. **History:** General. **Interdisciplinary:** Intercultural. **Legal studies:** Prelaw. **Liberal arts:** Arts/sciences, library assistant. **Math:** General. **Mechanic/repair:** Aircraft. **Philosophy/religion:** Philosophy. **Physical sciences:** Chemistry, geology, physics. **Psychology:** General. **Science technology:** Biological. **Social sciences:** General, anthropology, economics, geography, political science, sociology. **Visual/performing arts:** Art, art history/

conservation, commercial/advertising art, dramatic, photography, studio arts, theater design.

Computing on campus. 200 workstations in library, computer center, student center. Commuter students can connect to campus network. Online course registration available.

Student life. Freshman orientation: Available. **Activities:** Bands, choral groups, dance, drama, film society, music ensembles, musical theater, radio station, student government, student newspaper, symphony orchestra, TV station, 32 different multicultural/ethnic campus clubs.

Athletics. Intercollegiate: Basketball, diving, football (tackle) M, golf, soccer, softball W, swimming, tennis, volleyball W, water polo. **Team name:** Owls.

Student services. Adult student services, alcohol/substance abuse counseling, career counseling, services for economically disadvantaged, student employment services, financial aid counseling, health services, legal services, minority student services, personal counseling, placement for graduates, veterans' counselor. **Physically disabled:** Services for visually, speech, hearing impaired. **Transfer:** Special adviser, orientation for new students. Transfer adviser, college fairs on campus for students transferring to 4-year colleges.

Contact. Phone: (650) 949-7325 Fax: (650) 949-7048
Penelope Johnson, Dean of Counseling and Student Services, Foothill College, 12345 El Monte Road, Los Altos Hills, CA 94022

Fresno City College

Fresno, California — **CB member**
www.fresnocitycollege.edu — **CB code: 4311**

- Public 2-year community college
- Commuter campus in large city

General. Founded in 1910. Regionally accredited. **Enrollment:** 12,610 degree-seeking undergraduates. **Degrees:** 1,357 associate awarded. **ROTC:** Army, Air Force. **Location:** 185 miles from San Francisco. **Calendar:** Semester, extensive summer session. **Full-time faculty:** 420 total. **Class size:** 28% < 20, 59% 20-39, 7% 40-49, 4% 50-99, 3% >100. **Special facilities:** Anthropology museum, high-tech laboratory for disabled students.

Student profile.

Out-of-state:	2%	**25 or older:**	39%

Transfer out. Colleges most students transferred to 2005: CSU: Fresno, University of Phoenix, National University, Fresno Pacific.

Basis for selection. Open admission, but selective for some programs. Limited admission to allied health programs, police academy, and apprenticeship programs.

2005-2006 Annual costs. Tuition/fees: $808; $5,338 out-of-state. Per-credit charge: $26 in-state; $177 out-of-state. Books/supplies: $1,206. Personal expenses: $1,710.

Financial aid. All financial aid based on need. Need-based aid available for part-time students. Work study available for part-time students. **Additional information:** Board of Governors Grant Program to offset enrollment fees based on untaxed income, low income, or calculated need. Students qualifying for program also automatically exempt from health fees. March 2 application deadline for California grants.

Application procedures. Admission: No deadline. No application fee. Application may be submitted online. Admission notification on a rolling basis. **Financial aid:** Priority date 4/15; no closing date. FAFSA required. Applicants notified on a rolling basis starting 4/1.

Academics. Special study options: Accelerated study, cross-registration, distance learning, double major, dual enrollment of high school students, ESL, honors, independent study, internships, study abroad, weekend college. License preparation in dental hygiene, nursing, radiology. **Credit/placement by examination:** AP, CLEP, institutional tests. 48 credit hours maximum toward associate degree. **Support services:** Learning center, pre-admission summer program, reduced course load, remedial instruction, tutoring, writing center.

Majors. Agriculture: General, food science. **Area/ethnic studies:** African-American, Hispanic-American/Latino/Chicano, Native American, women's. **Business:** General, accounting, administrative services, banking/financial services, business admin, fashion, insurance, office/clerical, purchasing, real estate. **Communications:** General, journalism. **Communications technology:** Graphic/printing. **Computer sciences:** General, computer science, data processing, information systems, programming. **Conservation:** General. **Construction:** Carpentry, electrician, maintenance, pipefitting, power transmission. **Education:** Bilingual, early childhood, multi-level teacher. **Engineering:** General. **Engineering technology:** Drafting. **English:** Speech/rhetoric. **Family/consumer sciences:** General, child care, clothing/textiles, food/nutrition, institutional food production. **Foreign languages:** General, Spanish. **Health:** Clinical lab technology, dental hygiene, medical assistant, medical radiologic technology/radiation therapy, medical records technology, medical secretary, medical transcription, nursing (RN), respiratory therapy technology, substance abuse counseling. **History:** General. **Interdisciplinary:** Biological/physical sciences. **Legal studies:** Legal secretary, paralegal. **Liberal arts:** Arts/sciences, library science. **Math:** General. **Mechanic/repair:** General, auto body, automotive, electronics/electrical, heating/ac/refrig, industrial. **Parks/recreation:** General, facilities management. **Physical sciences:** Chemistry. **Protective services:** Corrections, firefighting, law enforcement admin, police science. **Psychology:** General. **Public administration:** General, social work. **Social sciences:** General, anthropology, criminology, geography, sociology. **Transportation:** General. **Visual/performing arts:** General, art, crafts, dance, dramatic, music management, photography, piano/organ, printmaking, theater design, voice/opera.

Most popular majors. Health sciences 30%, liberal arts 55%.

Computing on campus. 400 workstations in library, computer center. Commuter students can connect to campus network. Online course registration available.

Student life. Freshman orientation: Available. **Policies:** Freshmen permitted cars on campus. **Activities:** Bands, choral groups, dance, drama, film society, literary magazine, music ensembles, musical theater, student government, student newspaper, symphony orchestra, TV station, Christian Athletes in Acting, MECHA, Pan American Association, Alpha Gamma Sigma, International Club, Phi Theta Kappa.

Athletics. NJCAA. **Intercollegiate:** Badminton, baseball M, basketball, cheerleading, cross-country, football (tackle) M, golf, soccer, softball W, tennis, track and field, volleyball W, wrestling M. **Intramural:** Basketball, football (non-tackle), soccer, softball, table tennis, volleyball, weight lifting. **Team name:** Rams.

Student services. Adult student services, career counseling, services for economically disadvantaged, student employment services, health services, minority student services, on-campus daycare, personal counseling, placement for graduates, veterans' counselor. **Physically disabled:** Services for visually, speech, hearing impaired. **Transfer:** Special adviser, orientation for new students. Transfer center, transfer adviser, college fairs on campus for students transferring to 4-year colleges.

Contact. E-mail: info@scccd.com
Phone: (559) 442-4600 Toll-free number: (866) 245-3276
Fax: (559) 237-4232
John Cummings, District Dean of Admissions, Records and Institutional Research, Fresno City College, 1101 East University Avenue, Fresno, CA 93741

Fullerton College

Fullerton, California
www.fullcoll.edu — **CB code: 4314**

- Public 2-year community, junior and technical college
- Commuter campus in small city

General. Founded in 1913. Regionally accredited. **Enrollment:** 13,471 degree-seeking undergraduates. **Degrees:** 1,126 associate awarded. **ROTC:** Navy. **Location:** 35 miles from Los Angeles. **Calendar:** Semester, extensive summer session. **Full-time faculty:** 315 total. **Part-time faculty:** 480 total.

Basis for selection. Open admission. College-administered English, reading, and math exams used for placement.

2005-2006 Annual costs. Tuition/fees: $806; $5,336 out-of-state. Per-credit charge: $26 in-state; $177 out-of-state. Books/supplies: $648. Personal expenses: $1,818.

Application procedures. Admission: No deadline. No application fee. Admission notification on a rolling basis. **Financial aid:** No deadline. FAFSA required. Applicants notified on a rolling basis.

Academics. Special study options: Distance learning, double major, dual enrollment of high school students, ESL, independent study, internships, study abroad. **Credit/placement by examination:** AP, CLEP, institutional tests. 15 credit hours maximum toward associate degree. **Support services:** Learning center, remedial instruction, tutoring.

Majors. **Agriculture:** Horticulture, nursery operations. **Architecture:** Landscape. **Area/ethnic studies:** Latin American. **Biology:** General, bacteriology, zoology. **Business:** Accounting, administrative services, business admin, fashion, international, management information systems, purchasing, real estate, tourism promotion. **Communications:** General, broadcast journalism, journalism. **Communications technology:** Graphic/printing. **Computer sciences:** General, applications programming, data processing. **Conservation:** General, fisheries, forestry. **Construction:** Carpentry, maintenance. **Education:** Business, trade/industrial. **Engineering:** General. **Engineering technology:** Drafting, electrical. **English:** Speech/rhetoric. **Family/consumer sciences:** General, child care, family studies. **Foreign languages:** General. **Health:** Clinical lab science, prenursing. **History:** General. **Legal studies:** Legal secretary, paralegal. **Liberal arts:** Arts/sciences, library assistant. **Math:** General. **Mechanic/repair:** Auto body. **Parks/recreation:** General. **Personal/culinary services:** Cosmetic. **Philosophy/religion:** Philosophy. **Physical sciences:** Astronomy, chemistry, geology, physics. **Protective services:** Police science. **Psychology:** General. **Social sciences:** Anthropology, economics, geography, political science, sociology. **Visual/performing arts:** General, art, commercial/advertising art, dance, design, dramatic, fashion design.

Student life. **Activities:** Bands, choral groups, dance, drama, film society, literary magazine, music ensembles, musical theater, radio station, student government, student newspaper, symphony orchestra, TV station, volunteer bureau, Movimiento Estudiantil Chicano de Aztlan.

Athletics. **Intercollegiate:** Badminton, baseball M, basketball, cross-country, diving, football (tackle) M, golf M, gymnastics, soccer, softball W, swimming, tennis, track and field, volleyball, water polo M. **Team name:** Hornets.

Student services. Adult student services, career counseling, student employment services, health services, on-campus daycare, personal counseling, placement for graduates, veterans' counselor. **Physically disabled:** Services for visually, speech, hearing impaired. **Transfer:** Special adviser for new students. Transfer adviser for students transferring to 4-year colleges.

Contact. E-mail: admissions@fullcoll.edu
Phone: (714) 992-7568
Peter Fong, Dean of Admissions and Records, Fullerton College, 321 East Chapman Avenue, Fullerton, CA 92832-2095

Gavilan Community College

Gilroy, California
www.gavilan.edu **CB code: 4678**

- Public 2-year community college
- Large town

General. Founded in 1919. Regionally accredited. **Enrollment:** 4,550 undergraduates. **Degrees:** 237 associate awarded. **Location:** 35 miles from San Jose. **Calendar:** Semester, limited summer session. **Full-time faculty:** 71 total; 11% have terminal degrees. **Part-time faculty:** 116 total; 3% have terminal degrees. **Special facilities:** Golf course, hiking trails.

Transfer out. **Colleges most students transferred to 2005:** San Jose State University, California State University-Monterey Bay, University of California-Santa Cruz.

Basis for selection. Open admission. **Adult students:** Entrance exam policies same as for first-time freshmen.

2005-2006 Annual costs. Tuition/fees: $817; $5,827 out-of-state. Per-credit charge: $26 in-state; $193 out-of-state. Books/supplies: $1,206. Personal expenses: $2,250.

Application procedures. **Admission:** No deadline. No application fee. Admission notification on a rolling basis. **Financial aid:** Priority date 6/30; no closing date. FAFSA required. Applicants notified on a rolling basis starting 7/15; must reply within 2 week(s) of notification.

Academics. **Special study options:** Distance learning, dual enrollment of high school students, ESL, honors, independent study, internships, liberal arts/career combination, study abroad. License preparation in aviation, nursing. **Credit/placement by examination:** AP, CLEP, institutional tests. **Support services:** Learning center, reduced course load, remedial instruction, study skills assistance, tutoring, writing center.

Majors. **Biology:** General, ecology. **Business:** General. **Communications:** General, journalism. **Computer sciences:** General, computer graphics. **Foreign languages:** Spanish. **Health:** Nursing (RN). **History:** General. **Liberal arts:** Arts/sciences. **Math:** General. **Mechanic/repair:** Aircraft. **Personal/culinary services:** Cosmetic. **Philosophy/religion:** Philosophy. **Physical sciences:** Astronomy, chemistry, geology. **Protective services:** Corrections. **Psychology:** General. **Social sciences:** General, anthropology, economics, geography, political science, sociology. **Visual/performing arts:** Art, art history/conservation, dramatic, music performance, studio arts, theater design.

Most popular majors. Business/marketing 12%, foreign language 6%, health sciences 24%, liberal arts 35%, social sciences 6%, visual/performing arts 7%.

Computing on campus. 600 workstations in library, computer center.

Student life. **Freshman orientation:** Mandatory. **Activities:** Choral groups, drama, literary magazine, music ensembles, musical theater, student government, student newspaper, symphony orchestra, TV station.

Athletics. **Intercollegiate:** Baseball M, basketball, football (tackle) M, golf, soccer W, softball W, tennis, volleyball W. **Team name:** Rams.

Student services. Adult student services, career counseling, services for economically disadvantaged, financial aid counseling, health services, on-campus daycare, personal counseling, veterans' counselor. **Physically disabled:** Services for visually, speech, hearing impaired. **Learning disabled:** Comprehensive services available. **Transfer:** Special adviser, orientation for new students. Transfer center, transfer adviser, college fairs on campus for students transferring to 4-year colleges.

Contact. Phone: (408) 848-4735 Fax: (408) 848-4940
Joy Parker, Director of Admissions and Records, Gavilan Community College, 5055 Santa Teresa Boulevard, Gilroy, CA 95020

Glendale Community College

Glendale, California **CB member**
www.glendale.edu **CB code: 4327**

- Public 2-year community college
- Commuter campus in small city

General. Founded in 1927. Regionally accredited. **Enrollment:** 7,640 degree-seeking undergraduates; 6,625 non-degree-seeking students. **Degrees:** 547 associate awarded. **Location:** 10 miles from downtown Los Angeles. **Calendar:** Semester, limited summer session. **Full-time faculty:** 241 total; 21% minority, 50% women. **Part-time faculty:** 464 total; 22% minority, 49% women. **Class size:** 37% < 20, 49% 20-39, 9% 40-49, 4% 50-99, less than 1% >100. **Special facilities:** Science center with planetarium, Baja California (Mexico) field station.

Student profile. Among degree-seeking undergraduates, 68% enrolled in a transfer program, 8% enrolled in a vocational program, 7% already have a bachelor's degree or higher, 1,568 enrolled as first-time, first-year students, 599 transferred in from other institutions.

Part-time:	61%	**Asian American:**	10%
Out-of-state:	1%	**Hispanic American:**	22%
Women:	60%	**International:**	26%
African American:	3%	**25 or older:**	42%

Transfer out. **Colleges most students transferred to 2005:** California State University-Northridge, University of California at Los Angeles, California State University-Los Angeles, University of Southern California.

Basis for selection. Open admission, but selective for some programs. Nursing program has special requirements. **Adult students:** Entrance exam policies same as for first-time freshmen.

2005-2006 Annual costs. Tuition/fees: $808; $5,308 out-of-state. Per-credit charge: $26 in-state; $176 out-of-state. Books/supplies: $810. Personal expenses: $1,548.

Financial aid. All financial aid based on need. Need-based aid available for part-time students. Work study available nights, weekends and for part-time students.

Application procedures. **Admission:** Priority date 4/15; no deadline. No application fee. Application may be submitted online. Admission notification on a rolling basis. **Financial aid:** Priority date 4/15; no closing date. FAFSA, institutional form required. Applicants notified on a rolling basis starting 6/15; must reply within 2 week(s) of notification.

Academics. **Special study options:** Cooperative education, distance learning, dual enrollment of high school students, ESL, honors, independent study, internships, study abroad. License preparation in aviation, nursing, real estate. **Credit/placement by examination:** AP, CLEP, institutional tests. 12 credit hours maximum toward associate degree. **Support services:** GED preparation and test center, learning center, remedial instruction, study skills assistance, tutoring, writing center.

Honors college/program. Scholars program admits academically accomplished students and offers priority transfer opportunites at UCLA, USC, Pepperdine, and others.

Majors. Biology: General. **Business:** General, accounting, administrative services, hospitality/recreation, office management, real estate. **Communications:** Broadcast journalism, journalism. **Computer sciences:** General. **Education:** Early childhood, multi-level teacher. **Engineering technology:** Drafting. **English:** Composition. **Family/consumer sciences:** General, child care, clothing/textiles, food/nutrition. **Foreign languages:** General, comparative lit, French, Spanish. **Health:** Licensed practical nurse, medical assistant, medical secretary, nursing (RN). **History:** General. **Interdisciplinary:** Biological/physical sciences. **Legal studies:** Legal secretary, paralegal. **Liberal arts:** Arts/sciences, humanities. **Math:** General. **Mechanic/repair:** Aircraft. **Parks/recreation:** General. **Personal/culinary services:** Cosmetic, culinary arts. **Philosophy/religion:** Philosophy. **Physical sciences:** Chemistry, physics. **Protective services:** Fire safety technology, law enforcement admin, police science. **Psychology:** General. **Social sciences:** General, anthropology, economics, sociology. **Visual/performing arts:** General, commercial/advertising art, dance, theater design.

Most popular majors. Business/marketing 15%, English 7%, health sciences 11%, liberal arts 52%, social sciences 6%.

Computing on campus. 1,000 workstations in library, computer center. Helpline, repair service, wireless network available.

Student life. Freshman orientation: Available. **Policies:** Freshmen permitted cars on campus. **Activities:** Bands, choral groups, dance, drama, literary magazine, music ensembles, musical theater, radio station, student government, student newspaper, TV station, International Student Association, Armenian Student Association, Korean Christian Club, Organization of Latin for Higher Education, Association of Latin American Students.

Athletics. Intercollegiate: Baseball M, basketball, cross-country, football (tackle) M, soccer M, tennis, track and field, volleyball W. **Team name:** Vaqueros.

Student services. Adult student services, career counseling, services for economically disadvantaged, student employment services, financial aid counseling, health services, on-campus daycare, personal counseling, placement for graduates, veterans' counselor. **Physically disabled:** Services for visually, speech, hearing impaired. **Learning disabled:** Comprehensive services available. **Transfer:** Re-entry adviser for new students. Transfer center, transfer adviser, college fairs on campus for students transferring to 4-year colleges.

Contact. E-mail: info@glendale.edu
Phone: (818) 240-1000 ext. 5901 Fax: (818) 549-9436
Sharon Combs, Dean of Admissions and Records, Glendale Community College, 1500 North Verdugo Road, Glendale, CA 91208-2809

Golden West College

Huntington Beach, California
www.gwc.info **CB code: 4339**

- Public 2-year community and junior college
- Commuter campus in small city

General. Founded in 1966. Regionally accredited. **Enrollment:** 4,865 full-time, degree-seeking students. **Degrees:** 798 associate awarded. **Location:** 40 miles from Los Angeles. **Calendar:** Semester, extensive summer session. **Full-time faculty:** 260 total. **Part-time faculty:** 165 total. **Special facilities:** Natural history museum, outdoor amphitheatre.

Transfer out. Colleges most students transferred to 2005: California State University-Long Beach, California State University-Dominguez Hills, California State University-Fullerton, University of California-Irvine, University of California-Los Angeles.

Basis for selection. Open admission, but selective for some programs. Any student at least 18 years of age eligible for admission. Selective admission to police academy and nursing program. Nursing applicants accepted on basis of prerequisite courses completed and GPA. SAT or ACT scores can be used for counseling and placement in lieu of institutional placement exams.

2005-2006 Annual costs. Tuition/fees: $805; $5,365 out-of-state. Per-credit charge: $26 in-state; $178 out-of-state. Books/supplies: $810. Personal expenses: $1,530.

Financial aid. Non-need-based: Scholarships awarded for academics.

Application procedures. Admission: Priority date 4/1; no deadline. No application fee. Admission notification on a rolling basis. **Financial aid:** Priority date 6/1; no closing date. FAFSA, institutional form required. Applicants notified on a rolling basis starting 7/1; must reply within 3 week(s) of notification.

Academics. Special study options: Accelerated study, cooperative education, cross-registration, distance learning, double major, dual enrollment of high school students, ESL, honors, independent study, study abroad, weekend college. License preparation in nursing, real estate. **Credit/placement by examination:** AP, CLEP, institutional tests. 6 credit hours maximum toward associate degree. **Support services:** Learning center, pre-admission summer program, remedial instruction, tutoring, writing center.

Majors. Agriculture: Horticultural science. **Biology:** General. **Business:** General, accounting, administrative services, business admin, office management, office technology, office/clerical, real estate, sales/distribution. **Communications:** Broadcast journalism, journalism, public relations. **Computer sciences:** General. **Education:** Physical. **Engineering technology:** Architectural, drafting. **English:** Speech/rhetoric. **Foreign languages:** General, French, German, sign language interpretation, Spanish. **Health:** Nursing (RN), predentistry, premedicine, prepharmacy, preveterinary. **History:** General. **Interdisciplinary:** Biological/physical sciences. **Legal studies:** Legal secretary, prelaw. **Liberal arts:** Arts/sciences. **Math:** General. **Mechanic/repair:** Auto body, automotive, diesel. **Personal/culinary services:** Cosmetic. **Philosophy/religion:** Philosophy. **Physical sciences:** Astronomy, chemistry, geology. **Protective services:** Criminal justice, law enforcement admin. **Psychology:** General. **Social sciences:** General, anthropology, economics, political science, sociology. **Visual/performing arts:** Art, commercial/advertising art, dance, dramatic, music performance, music theory/composition, photography, studio arts.

Student life. Freshman orientation: Mandatory. Preregistration for classes offered. Program held prior to enrollment. **Activities:** Bands, choral groups, dance, drama, film society, literary magazine, music ensembles, musical theater, radio station, student government, student newspaper, symphony orchestra, TV station, honor society, student nurses, cosmetology club, French club, international club, Circle K, Women of Action.

Athletics. NJCAA. **Intercollegiate:** Baseball M, basketball, cross-country, football (tackle) M, golf M, soccer, softball W, swimming, tennis, track and field, volleyball, water polo M, wrestling M. **Team name:** Rustlers.

Student services. Adult student services, career counseling, services for economically disadvantaged, student employment services, health services, on-campus daycare, personal counseling, placement for graduates, veterans' counselor. **Physically disabled:** Services for visually, speech, hearing impaired. **Transfer:** Special adviser, orientation for new students. Transfer center, transfer adviser, college fairs on campus for students transferring to 4-year colleges.

Contact. Phone: (714) 892-7711 Fax: (714) 895-8960
Shirley Donnelly, Director of Admissions and Records, Golden West College, 15744 Golden West Street, Box 2748, Huntington Beach, CA 92647-2748

Golf Academy of San Diego

Vista, California
www.sdgagolf.com **CB code: 3495**

- For-profit 2-year college of golf course management
- Small city

General. Accredited by ACICS. **Calendar:** Semester.

Annual costs/financial aid. $4050 per semester for 4 semesters (16 months); $40 one-time computer lab fee; $90 per semester activities fee; $50 one-time club repair lab fee. Books/supplies: $900.

Contact. Phone: (760) 734-1208
1910 Shadowridge Drive, Suite 111, Vista, CA 92081

Grossmont Community College

El Cajon, California
www.grossmont.edu **CB code: 4334**

- Public 2-year community college
- Commuter campus in small city

General. Founded in 1961. Regionally accredited. **Enrollment:** 16,450 undergraduates. **Degrees:** 1,087 associate awarded. **Location:** 25 miles from San Diego. **Calendar:** Semester, extensive summer session. **Full-time faculty:** 180 total. **Part-time faculty:** 550 total.

Two-Year Colleges

Transfer out. **Colleges most students transferred to 2005:** San Diego State University.

Basis for selection. Open admission, but selective for some programs. Limited admission to health professions programs. **Adult students:** Entrance exam policies same as for first-time freshmen.

2005-2006 Annual costs. Tuition/fees: $818; $5,348 out-of-state. Per-credit charge: $26 in-state; $177 out-of-state. Books/supplies: $850. Personal expenses: $1,100.

Financial aid. All financial aid based on need. Need-based aid available for part-time students. Work study available nights, weekends and for part-time students.

Application procedures. **Admission:** Priority date 8/22; no deadline. No application fee. Application may be submitted online. Admission notification on a rolling basis. **Financial aid:** Priority date 2/1; no closing date. FAFSA required. Applicants notified on a rolling basis starting 7/15; must reply within 2 week(s) of notification.

Academics. **Special study options:** Accelerated study, cross-registration, distance learning, double major, dual enrollment of high school students, ESL, independent study, internships, student-designed major, study abroad. License preparation in nursing. **Credit/placement by examination:** AP, CLEP. Students may earn a maximum of 18 units on the CLEP general examinations. **Support services:** Learning center, reduced course load, remedial instruction, tutoring, writing center.

Majors. **Area/ethnic studies:** Native American. **Biology:** General. **Business:** General, administrative services, business admin, executive assistant, hospitality admin, international, management science, marketing, sales/distribution, tourism promotion, tourism/travel. **Communications:** Broadcast journalism, digital media, journalism. **Computer sciences:** General, applications programming, computer science, LAN/WAN management, programming, webmaster. **English:** Speech/rhetoric. **Family/consumer sciences:** Child care, child development. **Foreign languages:** Arabic, French, German, Japanese, Russian, Spanish. **Health:** Athletic training, cardiovascular technology, nursing (RN), respiratory therapy technology. **History:** General. **Legal studies:** General. **Liberal arts:** Arts/sciences. **Math:** General. **Parks/recreation:** Exercise sciences. **Personal/culinary services:** Baking, culinary arts, restaurant/catering. **Philosophy/religion:** Philosophy. **Physical sciences:** Chemistry, geology, physics. **Protective services:** Corrections, forensics, police science, security services. **Social sciences:** Economics, geography, political science. **Visual/performing arts:** Acting, art history/conservation, ceramics, cinematography, dance, dramatic, drawing, painting, photography, sculpture, theater design.

Computing on campus. 500 workstations in library, computer center. Online course registration available.

Student life. **Freshman orientation:** Available. **Policies:** Freshmen permitted cars on campus. **Activities:** Bands, choral groups, dance, drama, music ensembles, musical theater, radio station, student government, student newspaper, symphony orchestra.

Athletics. **Intercollegiate:** Baseball M, basketball, football (tackle) M, soccer W, softball W, swimming, tennis, volleyball, water polo. **Team name:** Griffins.

Student services. Adult student services, alcohol/substance abuse counseling, career counseling, services for economically disadvantaged, student employment services, financial aid counseling, health services, on-campus daycare, personal counseling, placement for graduates. **Physically disabled:** Services for visually, speech, hearing impaired. **Transfer:** Special adviser, orientation for new students. Transfer center, transfer adviser, college fairs on campus for students transferring to 4-year colleges.

Contact. Phone: (619) 644-7186 Fax: (619) 644-7933
Brad Tiffany, Dean of Admissions and Records, Grossmont Community College, 8800 Grossmont College Drive, El Cajon, CA 92020

Hartnell College

Salinas, California
www.hartnell.edu **CB code: 4340**

- Public 2-year community college
- Commuter campus in small city

General. Founded in 1920. Regionally accredited. **Enrollment:** 3,907 degree-seeking undergraduates. **Degrees:** 553 associate awarded. **Location:** 110 miles from San Francisco, 65 miles from San Jose. **Calendar:** Semester, limited summer session. **Full-time faculty:** 115 total. **Part-time faculty:** 250 total.

Basis for selection. Open admission, but selective for some programs. Limited admission to nursing programs and animal health technology. Interview required for nursing, physician's assistant, animal health technician majors.

2005-2006 Annual costs. Tuition/fees: $788; $5,498 out-of-state. Per-credit charge: $26 in-state; $183 out-of-state. Books/supplies: $800. Personal expenses: $1,800.

Application procedures. **Admission:** No deadline. No application fee. Admission notification on a rolling basis. **Financial aid:** Priority date 8/1; no closing date. FAFSA required. Applicants notified on a rolling basis.

Academics. **Special study options:** Cooperative education. **Credit/placement by examination:** CLEP. **Support services:** Learning center, remedial instruction, tutoring.

Student life. **Activities:** Bands, choral groups, drama, music ensembles, musical theater, student government, student newspaper.

Athletics. **Intercollegiate:** Baseball M, basketball, cross-country M, football (tackle) M, soccer M.

Student services. Career counseling, student employment services, personal counseling, placement for graduates.

Contact. Phone: (831) 755-6711 Fax: (831) 759-6014
Cheryl Gray, Director of Matriculation and Enrollment Services, Hartnell College, 156 Homestead Avenue, Salinas, CA 93901

Heald College: Concord

Concord, California
www.heald.edu **CB code: 0235**

- Private 2-year business college
- Commuter campus in small city
- Interview required

General. Founded in 1863. Regionally accredited. **Enrollment:** 648 degree-seeking undergraduates. **Degrees:** 221 associate awarded. **Location:** 25 miles from San Francisco. **Calendar:** Quarter. **Full-time faculty:** 33 total. **Part-time faculty:** 4 total.

Basis for selection. Institutional admissions examination and personal interview. Institutionally designed test used for admissions. **Adult students:** Entrance exam policies same as for first-time freshmen.

2006-2007 Annual costs. Tuition/fees: $9,900. Books/supplies: $1,200.

Financial aid. All financial aid based on need. Need-based aid available for part-time students. Work study available nights, weekends and for part-time students.

Application procedures. **Admission:** No deadline. $100 fee. Admission notification on a rolling basis. **Financial aid:** No deadline. FAFSA required. Applicants notified on a rolling basis.

Academics. **Special study options:** Cooperative education, internships. **Credit/placement by examination:** CLEP. **Support services:** Learning center, remedial instruction, study skills assistance, tutoring.

Computing on campus. Online library available.

Student services. Placement for graduates, veterans' counselor. **Transfer:** Special adviser, orientation for new students.

Contact. E-mail: info@heald.edu
Phone: (925) 288-5800 Toll-free number: (800) 755-3550
Fax: (925) 288-5896
Lily Woo, Admissions Director, Heald College: Concord, 5130 Commercial Circle, Concord, CA 94520

Heald College: Fresno

Fresno, California
www.heald.edu **CB code: 2119**

- Private 2-year business and technical college
- Commuter campus in small city
- Interview required

General. Founded in 1863. Regionally accredited. **Enrollment:** 729 degree-seeking undergraduates. **Degrees:** 240 associate awarded. **Location:** 200

miles from San Francisco. **Calendar:** Quarter. **Full-time faculty:** 27 total. **Part-time faculty:** 11 total. **Class size:** 46% < 20, 54% 20-39.

Transfer out. Colleges most students transferred to 2005: Fresno State University, Fresno City College, National University.

Basis for selection. CPAT entrance exam.

2006-2007 Annual costs. Tuition/fees: $9,900. Books/supplies: $900.

Application procedures. Admission: No deadline. $40 fee. Admission notification on a rolling basis. **Financial aid:** No deadline. FAFSA required. Applicants notified on a rolling basis.

Academics. Special study options: Liberal arts/career combination. **Credit/placement by examination:** CLEP. **Support services:** Tutoring.

Majors. Business: Accounting, business admin, management information systems, office technology, office/clerical. **Computer sciences:** Data processing. **Legal studies:** Legal secretary.

Most popular majors. Business/marketing 60%, computer/information sciences 40%.

Student life. Freshman orientation: Mandatory.

Student services. Adult student services, career counseling, student employment services, placement for graduates.

Contact. E-mail: info@heald.edu
Phone: (559) 438-4222 Toll-free number: (800) 755-3550
Fax: (559) 438-0948
Carolyn Kovalski, Registrar, Heald College: Fresno, 255 West Bullard, Fresno, CA 93704-1706

Heald College: Hayward

Hayward, California
www.heald.edu **CB code: 7106**

- Private 2-year technical college
- Commuter campus in small city

General. Regionally accredited. **Enrollment:** 865 degree-seeking undergraduates. **Degrees:** 360 associate awarded. **Calendar:** Quarter. **Full-time faculty:** 27 total. **Part-time faculty:** 7 total.

Basis for selection. Admission based on high school diploma/GED equivalent, entrance placement assessment, recommendation of admissions adviser.

2006-2007 Annual costs. Tuition/fees: $9,900.

Financial aid. All financial aid based on need. Need-based aid available for part-time students. Work study available nights, weekends and for part-time students.

Application procedures. Admission: No deadline. $100 fee. **Financial aid:** FAFSA required.

Academics. Special study options: Cooperative education, internships. **Credit/placement by examination:** CLEP. **Support services:** Learning center, remedial instruction, study skills assistance, tutoring.

Computing on campus. Online library available.

Student services. Career counseling, student employment services, financial aid counseling, placement for graduates.

Contact. Phone: (510) 783-2100 Toll-free number: (800) 755-3550
Fax: (510) 783-3287
Sandi Galan, Registrar, Heald College: Hayward, 25500 Industrial Boulevard, Hayward, CA 94545

Heald College: Rancho Cordova

Rancho Cordova, California
www.heald.edu **CB code: 7105**

- Private 2-year technical college
- Commuter campus in large city
- Interview required

General. Regionally accredited. **Enrollment:** 471 degree-seeking undergraduates. **Degrees:** 130 associate awarded. **Calendar:** Quarter. **Full-time faculty:** 24 total. **Part-time faculty:** 9 total.

Basis for selection. Institutional admissions test and interview very important. **Adult students:** Entrance exam policies same as for first-time freshmen.

2006-2007 Annual costs. Tuition/fees: $9,900.

Financial aid. All financial aid based on need. Need-based aid available for part-time students. Work study available nights, weekends and for part-time students.

Application procedures. Admission: No deadline. $100 fee. Application may be submitted online. **Financial aid:** FAFSA required.

Academics. Special study options: Cooperative education, internships. **Credit/placement by examination:** CLEP. **Support services:** Learning center, remedial instruction, study skills assistance, tutoring.

Majors. Business: Accounting, hospitality admin, office technology. **Computer sciences:** Networking. **Health:** Medical secretary. **Legal studies:** Legal secretary.

Computing on campus. Online library available.

Student services. Career counseling, student employment services, financial aid counseling, placement for graduates.

Contact. E-mail: info@heald.edu
Phone: (916) 638-1616 Toll-free number: (800) 88H-EALD
Fax: (916) 638-1580
Cindi Stevens, Director of Admissions, Heald College: Rancho Cordova, 2910 Prospect Park Drive, Rancho Cordova, CA 95670

Heald College: Roseville

Roseville, California
www.heald.edu **CB code: 4145**

- Private 2-year business and junior college
- Commuter campus in small city
- Interview required

General. Regionally accredited. **Enrollment:** 528 degree-seeking undergraduates. **Degrees:** 147 associate awarded. **Calendar:** Quarter. **Full-time faculty:** 26 total. **Part-time faculty:** 2 total.

2006-2007 Annual costs. Tuition/fees: $9,900.

Financial aid. All financial aid based on need. Need-based aid available for part-time students. Work study available nights, weekends and for part-time students.

Application procedures. Admission: No deadline. $100 fee. Application may be submitted online. **Financial aid:** FAFSA required.

Academics. Special study options: Cooperative education, internships. **Credit/placement by examination:** CLEP. **Support services:** Learning center, remedial instruction, study skills assistance, tutoring.

Majors. Business: Accounting, business admin.

Computing on campus. Online library available.

Student services. Career counseling, student employment services, financial aid counseling, placement for graduates.

Contact. E-mail: rosevilleinfo@heald.edu
Phone: (916) 789-8600 Toll-free number: (800) 755-3550
Fax: (916) 789-8616
Marci Vistro, Registrar, Heald College: Roseville, 7 Sierra Gate Plaza, Roseville, CA 95678

Heald College: Salinas

Salinas, California
www.heald.edu **CB code: 7107**

- Private 2-year business college
- Commuter campus in small city
- Interview required

General. Regionally accredited. **Enrollment:** 414 degree-seeking undergraduates. **Degrees:** 174 associate awarded. **Location:** 62 miles from San Jose. **Calendar:** Quarter. **Full-time faculty:** 25 total. **Part-time faculty:** 8 total.

Basis for selection. Adult students: Entrance exam policies same as for first-time freshmen.

2006-2007 Annual costs. Tuition/fees: $9,900. Books/supplies: $900. Personal expenses: $1,400.

Financial aid. All financial aid based on need. Need-based aid available for part-time students. Work study available nights, weekends and for part-time students.

Application procedures. Admission: No deadline. $100 fee. **Financial aid:** FAFSA required.

Academics. Special study options: Cooperative education, internships. **Credit/placement by examination:** CLEP. **Support services:** Learning center, remedial instruction, study skills assistance, tutoring.

Majors. Business: General, accounting, administrative services. **Health:** Medical secretary.

Computing on campus. Online library available.

Student services. Career counseling, student employment services, financial aid counseling, placement for graduates.

Contact. Phone: (831) 443-1700 Toll-free number: (800) 755-3550
Fax: (831) 443-1050
Angelica Hernandez, Registrar, Heald College: Salinas, 1450 North Main Street, Salinas, CA 93906

Heald College: San Francisco

San Francisco, California
www.heald.edu **CB code: 7109**

- Private 2-year business college
- Commuter campus in very large city
- Interview required

General. Regionally accredited. **Enrollment:** 389 degree-seeking undergraduates. **Degrees:** 181 associate awarded. **Calendar:** Quarter. **Full-time faculty:** 30 total. **Part-time faculty:** 5 total.

Basis for selection. Admission based on high school diploma/GED equivalent, entrance placement assessment, recommendation of admissions adviser. **Adult students:** Entrance exam policies same as for first-time freshmen.

2006-2007 Annual costs. Tuition/fees: $9,900.

Financial aid. All financial aid based on need. Need-based aid available for part-time students. Work study available nights, weekends and for part-time students.

Application procedures. Admission: No deadline. $100 fee. **Financial aid:** No deadline. FAFSA required.

Academics. Special study options: Cooperative education, internships. **Credit/placement by examination:** CLEP. **Support services:** Learning center, remedial instruction, study skills assistance, tutoring.

Computing on campus. Online library available.

Student services. Career counseling, student employment services, financial aid counseling, placement for graduates.

Contact. Phone: (415) 808-3000 Toll-free number: (800) 755-3550
Fax: (418) 808-3005
Azawent Tadesse, Registrar, Heald College: San Francisco, 350 Mission Street, San Francisco, CA 94103

Heald College: San Jose

Milpitas, California
www.heald.edu **CB code: 0405**

- Private 2-year business college
- Commuter campus in very large city
- Interview required

General. Founded in 1863. Regionally accredited. **Enrollment:** 639 degree-seeking undergraduates. **Degrees:** 178 associate awarded. **Location:** 45 miles from San Francisco. **Calendar:** Quarter. **Full-time faculty:** 33 total. **Part-time faculty:** 6 total.

Basis for selection. Institutional admissions test and personal interview most important. **Adult students:** Entrance exam policies same as for first-time freshmen.

2006-2007 Annual costs. Tuition/fees: $9,900. Books/supplies: $1,200.

Financial aid. All financial aid based on need. Need-based aid available for part-time students. Work study available nights, weekends and for part-time students.

Application procedures. Admission: No deadline. $100 fee. Admission notification on a rolling basis. **Financial aid:** Priority date 6/1; no closing date. FAFSA required. Applicants notified on a rolling basis starting 6/15; must reply within 2 week(s) of notification.

Academics. Special study options: Cooperative education, internships. **Credit/placement by examination:** CLEP, institutional tests. 45 credit hours maximum toward associate degree. **Support services:** Learning center, reduced course load, remedial instruction, tutoring.

Majors. Business: Accounting, business admin, office management. **Health:** Office admin. **Legal studies:** Legal secretary.

Computing on campus. Online library available.

Student life. Policies: Freshmen permitted cars on campus.

Student services. Career counseling, student employment services, financial aid counseling, placement for graduates.

Contact. E-mail: sanjoseinfo@heald.edu
Phone: (408) 934-4900 Toll-free number: (800) 755-3550
Fax: (415) 934-7777
Cathy Sousa, Registrar, Heald College: San Jose, 341 Great Mall Parkway, Milpitas, CA 95035

Heald College: Stockton

Stockton, California
www.heald.edu **CB code: 7108**

- Private 2-year business college
- Large city

General. Regionally accredited. **Enrollment:** 530 degree-seeking undergraduates. **Degrees:** 213 associate awarded. **Calendar:** Quarter. **Full-time faculty:** 19 total. **Part-time faculty:** 12 total.

Basis for selection. Open admission.

2006-2007 Annual costs. Tuition/fees: $9,900.

Financial aid. Need-based: Work study available for part-time students.

Application procedures. Admission: No deadline. $100 fee. **Financial aid:** FAFSA required.

Academics. Credit/placement by examination: CLEP.

Majors. Business: Accounting, office technology. **Computer sciences:** Data entry, vendor certification.

Contact. Phone: (209) 473-5200 Toll-free number: (800) 755-3550
Fax: (209) 477-2739
Ronald Guider, Registrar, Heald College: Stockton, 1605 East March Lane, Stockton, CA 95210

High-Tech Institute

Sacramento, California
www.hightechinstitute.edu **CB code: 3041**

- For-profit 2-year technical college
- Commuter campus in very large city

General. Accredited by ACCSCT. **Calendar:** Continuous.

Annual costs/financial aid. $17,700 for medical assistant program, $21,110 for dental assistant program, $37,300 for surgical technologist program, $32,500 for computer networking and information technology program, $19,900 for medical billing and coding program, $18,500 for massage therapy, $20,700 for pharmacy technician. Includes tuition, fees, book, supplies, and uniform. Need-based financial aid available for full-time students.

Contact. Phone: (916) 929-9700
Admissions Director, 9738 Lincoln Village Drive, Sacramento, CA 95827

Imperial Valley College
Imperial, California
www.imperial.edu
CB member
CB code: 4358

- Public 2-year community college
- Commuter campus in rural community

General. Founded in 1922. Regionally accredited. **Enrollment:** 3,300 full-time, degree-seeking students. **Degrees:** 328 associate awarded. **Location:** 6 miles from El Centro. **Calendar:** Semester, limited summer session. **Full-time faculty:** 95 total. **Part-time faculty:** 180 total. **Class size:** 36% < 20, 54% 20-39, 8% 40-49, 2% 50-99.

Transfer out. Colleges most students transferred to 2005: San Diego State University, California State Polytechnic University: Pomona, California State University: San Marcos, CSU: San Bernadino, California State University: Long Beach.

Basis for selection. Open admission, but selective for some programs. Limited admission for nursing programs. **Adult students:** Entrance exam policies same as for first-time freshmen.

2005-2006 Annual costs. Tuition/fees: $810; $5,340 out-of-state. Per-credit charge: $26 in-state; $177 out-of-state. Books/supplies: $1,206. Personal expenses: $2,250.

Application procedures. Admission: Priority date 5/1; no deadline. No application fee. **Financial aid:** Priority date 3/2; no closing date. FAFSA required. Applicants notified on a rolling basis starting 5/1.

Academics. Special study options: Double major, dual enrollment of high school students, ESL, honors, independent study, liberal arts/career combination. License preparation in nursing, paramedic, real estate. **Credit/placement by examination:** CLEP, institutional tests. 25 credit hours maximum toward associate degree. **Support services:** GED test center, learning center, pre-admission summer program, reduced course load, remedial instruction, study skills assistance, tutoring, writing center.

Majors. Agriculture: Business. **Business:** Administrative services, banking/financial services, business admin, office management, office technology, office/clerical, real estate. **Communications:** Journalism. **Computer sciences:** General. **Education:** Bilingual, early childhood, elementary. **Engineering:** General, agricultural. **Family/consumer sciences:** Child care. **Foreign languages:** General, French, Spanish. **Health:** Health care admin, licensed practical nurse, nursing (RN), substance abuse counseling. **Legal studies:** Paralegal. **Liberal arts:** Arts/sciences. **Math:** General. **Mechanic/repair:** General, auto body. **Parks/recreation:** Health/fitness. **Protective services:** Corrections, firefighting, law enforcement admin. **Psychology:** General. **Social sciences:** General, anthropology. **Visual/performing arts:** Art.

Most popular majors. Business/marketing 12%, education 20%, family/consumer sciences 6%, health sciences 13%, liberal arts 10%, psychology 8%, security/protective services 12%, social sciences 8%.

Computing on campus. 90 workstations in library, computer center.

Student life. Freshman orientation: Available, $20 fee. **Policies:** Freshmen permitted cars on campus. **Activities:** Jazz band, choral groups, drama, music ensembles, student government, student newspaper, Christian club, Movimiento Estudiantil Chicano de Aztlan, Upward Bound club, French club, spirit club.

Athletics. Intercollegiate: Baseball M, basketball, soccer M, softball W, tennis, volleyball W. **Team name:** Arabs.

Student services. Career counseling, services for economically disadvantaged, student employment services, financial aid counseling, minority student services, on-campus daycare, personal counseling, veterans' counselor. **Physically disabled:** Services for visually, speech, hearing impaired. **Transfer:** Special adviser, orientation for new students. Transfer center, transfer adviser, college fairs on campus for students transferring to 4-year colleges.

Contact. Phone: (760) 352-8320 Fax: (760) 355-2663
Kathie Westerfield, Director of Admissions, Imperial Valley College, Box 158, Imperial, CA 92251-0158

Irvine Valley College
Irvine, California
www.ivc.edu
CB code: 3356

- Public 2-year community college
- Commuter campus in small city

General. Regionally accredited. **Enrollment:** 5,133 degree-seeking undergraduates. **Degrees:** 462 associate awarded. **ROTC:** Air Force. **Location:** 50 miles from Los Angeles. **Calendar:** Semester, extensive summer session. **Full-time faculty:** 115 total. **Part-time faculty:** 304 total. **Special facilities:** Dance studio, Microsoft Office user specialist testing site, telescope.

Student profile. Among degree-seeking undergraduates, 437 transferred in from other institutions.

Transfer out. Colleges most students transferred to 2005: University of California-Irvine, California State University-Fullerton.

Basis for selection. Open admission. **Adult students:** Entrance exam policies same as for first-time freshmen.

2005-2006 Annual costs. Tuition/fees: $806; $5,336 out-of-state. Per-credit charge: $26 in-state; $177 out-of-state. Books/supplies: $1,260. Personal expenses: $3,708.

2004-2005 Financial aid. All financial aid based on need. 65% of total undergraduate aid awarded as scholarships/grants, 35% as loans/jobs. Need-based aid available for part-time students. Work study available nights and for part-time students.

Application procedures. Admission: No deadline. No application fee. Application may be submitted online. Admission notification on a rolling basis. **Financial aid:** No deadline. FAFSA, institutional form required. Applicants notified on a rolling basis starting 4/30.

Academics. Special study options: Accelerated study, cooperative education, cross-registration, distance learning, double major, dual enrollment of high school students, ESL, honors, independent study, internships, study abroad, weekend college. **Credit/placement by examination:** CLEP, institutional tests. 12 credit hours maximum toward associate degree. Minimum 2.0 GPA in at least 12 units completed at IVC required to enroll in credit by examination. **Support services:** Learning center, remedial instruction, study skills assistance, tutoring, writing center.

Majors. Area/ethnic studies: Women's. **Biology:** General, ecology. **Business:** General, accounting, business admin, office management, office technology, real estate. **Communications:** Advertising. **Computer sciences:** General, applications programming, networking, programming, systems analysis. **Conservation:** General. **Education:** Early childhood, physical. **Engineering technology:** Drafting, electrical, manufacturing. **English:** British lit, composition, speech/rhetoric. **Foreign languages:** French, Spanish. **History:** General. **Liberal arts:** Arts/sciences. **Math:** General. **Parks/recreation:** Health/fitness. **Philosophy/religion:** Philosophy. **Physical sciences:** Chemistry, geology. **Protective services:** Law enforcement admin, police science. **Psychology:** General. **Social sciences:** Anthropology, economics, geography, political science, sociology. **Visual/performing arts:** General, art, dance, dramatic, photography, studio arts, theater design.

Most popular majors. Business/marketing 9%, liberal arts 77%.

Computing on campus. 250 workstations in library, computer center. Commuter students can connect to campus network. Online course registration, online library, helpline available.

Student life. Freshman orientation: Mandatory. **Housing:** Homestay referral for international students. **Activities:** Bands, choral groups, dance, drama, literary magazine, music ensembles, musical theater, student government, student newspaper, symphony orchestra, administration of justice club, Phi Theta Kappa honor society, Muslim Student Association, biology society, dance club, geology club, health sciences society, journalism club, Phi Theta Kappa, Psi Beta, student liberties club, computer science society.

Athletics. Intercollegiate: Badminton W, baseball M, basketball, cross-country, golf, soccer, softball W, tennis, volleyball. **Intramural:** Basketball, soccer, tennis, volleyball. **Team name:** Lasers.

Student services. Adult student services, career counseling, services for economically disadvantaged, student employment services, financial aid counseling, health services, on-campus daycare, personal counseling, placement for graduates, veterans' counselor, women's services. **Physically disabled:** Services for visually, speech, hearing impaired. **Transfer:** Special adviser, orientation, re-entry adviser for new students. Transfer center, transfer adviser, college fairs on campus for students transferring to 4-year colleges.

Contact. E-mail: admissions@ivc.edu
Phone: (949) 451-5416 Fax: (949) 451-5443
John Edwards, Director of Admissions and Records, Irvine Valley College, 5500 Irvine Center Drive, Irvine, CA 92618-4399

Lake Tahoe Community College
South Lake Tahoe, California
www.ltcc.edu **CB code: 4420**

- Public 2-year community college
- Commuter campus in large town

General. Founded in 1975. Regionally accredited. **Enrollment:** 1,130 degree-seeking undergraduates. **Degrees:** 159 associate awarded. **Location:** 55 miles from Reno, Nevada, 110 miles from Sacramento. **Calendar:** Quarter, limited summer session. **Full-time faculty:** 46 total. **Part-time faculty:** 180 total.

Transfer out. Colleges most students transferred to 2005: California State University; University of California; University of Nevada, Reno.

Basis for selection. Open admission.

2005-2006 Annual costs. Tuition/fees: $777; $5,907 out-of-state. Per-credit charge: $17 in-district; $28 out-of-district; $131 out-of-state. $28 per credit hour for Nevada residents. Books/supplies: $670. Personal expenses: $1,386.

Application procedures. Admission: No deadline. No application fee. Application may be submitted online. Admission notification on a rolling basis. **Financial aid:** Priority date 5/1; no closing date. FAFSA required. Applicants notified on a rolling basis starting 7/1; must reply within 2 week(s) of notification.

Academics. Special study options: Cooperative education, distance learning, double major, dual enrollment of high school students, ESL, internships, study abroad. License preparation in real estate. **Credit/placement by examination:** CLEP, institutional tests. 4 credit hours maximum toward associate degree. **Support services:** GED preparation, learning center, remedial instruction, study skills assistance, tutoring, writing center.

Majors. Business: General, accounting, administrative services, entrepreneurial studies, finance, marketing, office management, office/clerical, real estate. **Education:** Early childhood. **Foreign languages:** Spanish. **Health:** Medical assistant, medical records admin. **Interdisciplinary:** Natural sciences. **Legal studies:** Legal secretary. **Liberal arts:** Arts/sciences. **Parks/recreation:** Health/fitness. **Personal/culinary services:** Culinary arts. **Protective services:** Firefighting, law enforcement admin. **Psychology:** General. **Social sciences:** General. **Visual/performing arts:** Art, dance, dramatic, studio arts.

Most popular majors. Business/marketing 16%, liberal arts 34%, security/protective services 12%, social sciences 38%.

Computing on campus. 135 workstations in library, computer center, student center. Online course registration, online library available.

Student life. Freshman orientation: Available. **Activities:** Choral groups, dance, drama, music ensembles, musical theater, student government, Alpha Gamma Sigma, associated student council, international club.

Athletics. NJCAA. **Intercollegiate:** Cross-country, volleyball W.

Student services. Career counseling, services for economically disadvantaged, student employment services, financial aid counseling, on-campus daycare, personal counseling, placement for graduates, veterans' counselor. **Physically disabled:** Services for visually, speech, hearing impaired. **Learning disabled:** Comprehensive services available. **Transfer:** Special adviser, orientation for new students. Transfer center, transfer adviser, college fairs on campus for students transferring to 4-year colleges.

Contact. E-mail: admissions@ltcc.edu
Phone: (530) 541-4660 ext. 211 Fax: (530) 542-1781
Cheri Jones, Director of Admissions & Records, Lake Tahoe Community College, One College Drive, South Lake Tahoe, CA 96150-4524

Laney College
Oakland, California
www.peralta.cc.ca.us **CB code: 4406**

- Public 2-year community college
- Commuter campus in large city

General. Founded in 1953. Regionally accredited. **Enrollment:** 4,840 degree-seeking undergraduates. **Degrees:** 427 associate awarded. **Location:** 10 miles from San Francisco. **Calendar:** Semester, extensive summer session. **Full-time faculty:** 123 total; 48% minority. **Part-time faculty:** 325 total; 44% minority. **Special facilities:** CAD laboratory.

Student profile.

Out-of-state:	2%	**25 or older:**	61%

Transfer out. Colleges most students transferred to 2005: California State University: Hayward, San Francisco, Berkeley.

Basis for selection. Open admission.

2005-2006 Annual costs. Tuition/fees: $784; $5,704 out-of-state. Per-credit charge: $26 in-state; $190 out-of-state. Books/supplies: $648. Personal expenses: $1,620.

Application procedures. Admission: No deadline. No application fee. Application may be submitted online. Admission notification on a rolling basis. **Financial aid:** Priority date 4/1; no closing date. FAFSA, institutional form required. Applicants notified on a rolling basis; must reply within 2 week(s) of notification.

Academics. Special study options: Cooperative education, distance learning, dual enrollment of high school students, ESL, honors, independent study, liberal arts/career combination, weekend college. **Credit/placement by examination:** CLEP, institutional tests. **Support services:** Learning center, remedial instruction, study skills assistance, tutoring.

Majors. Area/ethnic studies: African-American, Asian, Latin American. **Business:** General, accounting, administrative services, banking/financial services, management information systems, office technology, office/clerical, operations, sales/distribution. **Communications:** Broadcast journalism, journalism. **Communications technology:** General, graphic/printing. **Computer sciences:** General, information systems. **Construction:** Carpentry, maintenance. **Education:** General. **Engineering technology:** Architectural. **Interdisciplinary:** Biological/physical sciences. **Liberal arts:** Arts/sciences. **Math:** General. **Mechanic/repair:** Heating/ac/refrig. **Personal/culinary services:** Cosmetic, culinary arts. **Production:** Woodworking. **Social sciences:** General. **Visual/performing arts:** Art, ceramics, commercial/advertising art, dance, design, dramatic.

Computing on campus. 400 workstations in library, computer center, student center. Online course registration, online library available.

Student life. Freshman orientation: Mandatory. Preregistration for classes offered. **Activities:** Pep band, dance, drama, literary magazine, musical theater, student government, student newspaper, TV station.

Athletics. Intercollegiate: Baseball M, basketball M, football (tackle) M, softball W, swimming. **Team name:** Eagles.

Student services. Adult student services, career counseling, services for economically disadvantaged, student employment services, financial aid counseling, health services, minority student services, on-campus daycare, personal counseling, placement for graduates. **Physically disabled:** Services for visually, speech, hearing impaired. **Transfer:** Special adviser, orientation, re-entry adviser for new students. Transfer center, transfer adviser, college fairs on campus for students transferring to 4-year colleges.

Contact. Phone: (510) 464-3121 Fax: (510) 464-3240
Howard Perdue, Director of Admissions and Records, Laney College, 900 Fallon Street, Oakland, CA 94607

Las Positas College
Livermore, California
www.laspositas.cc.ca.us **CB code: 6507**

- Public 2-year community college
- Commuter campus in small city

General. Founded in 1991. Regionally accredited. **Enrollment:** 2,392 full-time, degree-seeking students. **Degrees:** 449 associate awarded. **Location:** 43 miles from San Francisco, 39 miles from San Jose. **Calendar:** Semester, limited summer session. **Full-time faculty:** 95 total. **Part-time faculty:** 250 total.

Basis for selection. Open admission. Open admissions policy. High school diploma or GED required for student under 18 years.

2005-2006 Annual costs. Tuition/fees: $808; $5,488 out-of-state. Per-credit charge: $26 in-state; $182 out-of-state. Books/supplies: $810. Personal expenses: $1,548.

Application procedures. **Admission:** No deadline. No application fee. Admission notification on a rolling basis. **Financial aid:** Priority date 5/1; no closing date. Institutional form required. Applicants notified on a rolling basis starting 7/1; must reply within 2 week(s) of notification.

Academics. **Special study options:** Accelerated study, distance learning, dual enrollment of high school students, ESL, independent study, internships, student-designed major. **Credit/placement by examination:** CLEP. **Support services:** Learning center, remedial instruction, tutoring.

Majors. **Agriculture:** Ornamental horticulture. **Biology:** General. **Business:** Office management, sales/distribution. **Communications technology:** Graphic/printing. **Computer sciences:** General, computer science. **Engineering technology:** Drafting. **English:** Speech/rhetoric. **Family/consumer sciences:** Child care. **Health:** Environmental health. **Liberal arts:** Arts/sciences. **Mechanic/repair:** Electronics/electrical. **Physical sciences:** Chemistry, physics. **Protective services:** Firefighting. **Social sciences:** General, international relations, sociology. **Visual/performing arts:** Commercial/advertising art, dramatic, interior design, studio arts.

Most popular majors. Business/marketing 26%, computer/information sciences 10%, liberal arts 55%.

Computing on campus. 285 workstations in library, computer center.

Student life. **Freshman orientation:** Available. **Activities:** Choral groups, dance, drama, literary magazine, music ensembles, musical theater, student government, student newspaper, TV station.

Athletics. **Intercollegiate:** Cross-country, soccer. **Intramural:** Basketball, bowling, fencing, handball M, racquetball, skin diving, soccer, volleyball.

Student services. Adult student services, career counseling, student employment services, financial aid counseling, health services, personal counseling, veterans' counselor. **Learning disabled:** Comprehensive services available. **Transfer:** Special adviser, orientation for new students. Transfer adviser, college fairs on campus for students transferring to 4-year colleges.

Contact. Phone: (925) 424-1000 Fax: (925) 443-0742
Sylvia Rodriguez, Registrar, Las Positas College, 3033 Collier Canyon Road, Livermore, CA 94551

Lassen College
Susanville, California
www.lassencollege.edu **CB code: 4383**

- Public 2-year community college
- Small town

General. Founded in 1925. Regionally accredited. **Enrollment:** 857 degree-seeking undergraduates. **Degrees:** 122 associate awarded. **Location:** 100 miles from Chico, 84 miles from Reno, Nevada. **Calendar:** Semester, limited summer session. **Full-time faculty:** 40 total. **Part-time faculty:** 120 total.

Student profile.

Out-of-state:	7%	Live on campus:	3%

Basis for selection. Open admission, but selective for some programs. Limited admission to nursing program.

2005-2006 Annual costs. Tuition/fees: $795; $6,285 out-of-state. Per-credit charge: $26 in-state; $209 out-of-state. Nevada residents pay $42 per-credit-hour with good neighbor policy. Room/board: $4,100. Books/supplies: $648. Personal expenses: $1,314.

Financial aid. **Additional information:** Board of Governors Grant: low-income California residents can have registration fees waived.

Application procedures. **Admission:** No application fee. Admission notification on a rolling basis. Institutional placement tests recommended. **Financial aid:** Priority date 7/1; no closing date. FAFSA required. Applicants notified on a rolling basis starting 7/1; must reply within 2 week(s) of notification.

Academics. Gunsmithing and summer NRA programs offered. **Special study options:** Cooperative education, distance learning, dual enrollment of high school students, honors, independent study, internships. **Credit/placement by examination:** AP, CLEP, institutional tests. 15 credit hours maximum toward associate degree. **Support services:** Learning center, pre-admission summer program, reduced course load, remedial instruction, tutoring.

Majors. **Business:** General, accounting, administrative services, business admin, management information systems, office technology, office/clerical, real estate. **Communications:** Journalism. **Computer sciences:** General, applications programming. **Construction:** Maintenance. **Education:** General, early childhood, physical. **Health:** Nursing (RN), nursing assistant. **Interdisciplinary:** Biological/physical sciences. **Liberal arts:** Arts/sciences. **Math:** General. **Mechanic/repair:** Auto body, automotive. **Protective services:** Corrections, law enforcement admin, police science. **Social sciences:** General. **Visual/performing arts:** Art.

Computing on campus. 40 workstations in computer center.

Student life. **Housing:** Coed dorms available. **Activities:** Choral groups, drama, film society, student government, student newspaper, over 20 student organizations and clubs.

Athletics. NJCAA. **Intercollegiate:** Baseball M, basketball, cross-country, golf, rifle, softball W, track and field, volleyball W, wrestling M. **Intramural:** Skiing.

Student services. Career counseling, health services, on-campus daycare, personal counseling, veterans' counselor. **Physically disabled:** Services for visually, speech, hearing impaired. **Transfer:** Special adviser, orientation for new students. Transfer adviser, college fairs on campus for students transferring to 4-year colleges.

Contact. Phone: (530) 251-8808 Fax: (530) 257-8964
Chris Alberico, Registrar and Admissions Director, Lassen College, Box 3000, Susanville, CA 96130

Long Beach City College
Long Beach, California
www.lbcc.edu **CB code: 4388**

- Public 2-year community college
- Commuter campus in large city

General. Founded in 1927. Regionally accredited. **Enrollment:** 11,226 degree-seeking undergraduates. **Degrees:** 875 associate awarded. **Location:** 20 miles from downtown Los Angeles. **Calendar:** Semester, limited summer session. **Full-time faculty:** 340 total. **Part-time faculty:** 650 total. **Class size:** 35% < 20, 47% 20-39, 10% 40-49, 7% 50-99, 1% >100.

Student profile. Among degree-seeking undergraduates, 60% enrolled in a transfer program, 40% enrolled in a vocational program, 5% already have a bachelor's degree or higher.

Out-of-state:	1%	25 or older:	51%

Transfer out. **Colleges most students transferred to 2005:** California State University-Long Beach, California State University-Dominguez Hills, California State University-Fullerton, University of California-Irvine.

Basis for selection. Open admission.

2005-2006 Annual costs. Tuition/fees: $806; $5,336 out-of-state. Per-credit charge: $26 in-state; $177 out-of-state. Books/supplies: $1,560. Personal expenses: $1,955.

Financial aid. All financial aid based on need. Need-based aid available for part-time students. Work study available for part-time students.

Application procedures. **Admission:** No deadline. No application fee. Admission notification on a rolling basis. **Financial aid:** Priority date 5/6; no closing date. FAFSA, institutional form required. Applicants notified on a rolling basis starting 7/6; must reply within 2 week(s) of notification.

Academics. **Special study options:** Accelerated study, cooperative education, cross-registration, distance learning, dual enrollment of high school students, ESL, honors, independent study, internships, liberal arts/career combination, study abroad, weekend college. License preparation in aviation, nursing, radiology, real estate. **Credit/placement by examination:** AP, CLEP, IB, institutional tests. 40 credit hours maximum toward associate degree. Students must first complete 12 units in residence. **Support services:** GED preparation and test center, learning center, pre-admission summer program, remedial instruction, study skills assistance, tutoring, writing center.

Majors. **Agriculture:** Ornamental horticulture. **Biology:** General. **Business:** General, accounting, administrative services, business admin, fashion, hotel/motel admin, office technology, office/clerical, real estate, restaurant/food services, sales/distribution, tourism promotion, tourism/travel. **Communications:** Advertising, broadcast journalism, journalism, public relations, publishing. **Communications technology:** General, desktop publishing, graphic/printing. **Computer sciences:** Applications programming, data processing, word processing. **Construction:** Carpentry. **Education:** Teacher assistance. **Engineering:** General. **Engineering technology:** Architectural, architectural drafting, drafting, heat/ac/refrig. **English:** English lit, speech/rhetoric. **Family/consumer sciences:** General, child care, child development, consumer economics, family resources, institutional food production. **Foreign languages:** General, Spanish. **Health:** Dietetic technician, licensed practical nurse, medical assistant, medical radiologic technology/radiation therapy, nursing (RN). **Legal studies:** Legal secretary. **Liberal arts:** Arts/sciences. **Math:** General. **Mechanic/repair:** General, aircraft powerplant, alternative fuel vehicle, auto body, automotive, diesel, electronics/electrical. **Parks/recreation:** Health/fitness. **Personal/culinary services:** Baking, culinary arts, restaurant/catering. **Physical sciences:** General. **Production:** Cabinetmaking/millwright, machine shop technology, machine tool, welding. **Protective services:** Fire safety technology, law enforcement admin. **Public administration:** General, human services. **Social sciences:** General. **Transportation:** Aviation. **Visual/performing arts:** Art, commercial photography, commercial/advertising art, dance, design, dramatic, drawing, fashion design, film/cinema, interior design, multimedia, printmaking, sculpture, theater design.

Most popular majors. Business/marketing 7%, health sciences 19%, liberal arts 44%, security/protective services 7%.

Computing on campus. 500 workstations in library, computer center, student center. Helpline available.

Student life. **Freshman orientation:** Available. Preregistration for classes offered. **Activities:** Bands, choral groups, dance, drama, literary magazine, music ensembles, musical theater, radio station, student government, student newspaper, symphony orchestra, TV station, College Republicans, Students for a Democratic Society, religious clubs, Cambodian, Vietnamese, Hispanic, international clubs.

Athletics. NJCAA. **Intercollegiate:** Baseball M, basketball, cross-country, football (tackle) M, golf, soccer, softball W, swimming, tennis, track and field, volleyball, water polo. **Intramural:** Archery, badminton, basketball, bowling, golf, racquetball, soccer, softball, swimming, table tennis, tennis, track and field, volleyball, wrestling M. **Team name:** Vikings.

Student services. Career counseling, student employment services, health services, on-campus daycare, personal counseling, veterans' counselor. **Physically disabled:** Services for visually, speech, hearing impaired. **Transfer:** Re-entry adviser for new students. Transfer center, transfer adviser, college fairs on campus for students transferring to 4-year colleges.

Contact. Phone: (562) 938-4139 Fax: (562) 938-4858
Ross Miyashiro, Dean of Admissions and Records, Long Beach City College, 4901 East Carson Street, Long Beach, CA 90808

Los Angeles City College

Los Angeles, California
www.lacitycollege.edu **CB code: 4391**

- Public 2-year community college
- Very large city

General. Founded in 1929. Regionally accredited. **Enrollment:** 5,544 full-time, degree-seeking students. **Degrees:** 823 associate awarded. **ROTC:** Army, Navy, Air Force. **Location:** 5 miles from downtown. **Calendar:** Semester, limited summer session. **Full-time faculty:** 186 total. **Part-time faculty:** 372 total.

Basis for selection. Open admission. Auditions required of theater academy, music majors.

2005-2006 Annual costs. Tuition/fees: $804; $5,424 out-of-state. Per-credit charge: $26 in-state; $180 out-of-state. Books/supplies: $840. Personal expenses: $2,040.

2004-2005 Financial aid. **Need-based:** 89% of total undergraduate aid awarded as scholarships/grants, 11% as loans/jobs. **Additional information:** Fee waivers available for public assistance and Social Security insurance recipients; fee credits available for low income families.

Application procedures. **Admission:** Closing date 9/1. No application fee. Admission notification on a rolling basis beginning on or about 4/30. **Financial aid:** Priority date 3/2; no closing date. FAFSA required. Applicants notified on a rolling basis; must reply within 2 week(s) of notification.

Academics. **Special study options:** Cross-registration, dual enrollment of high school students, ESL, honors, independent study, study abroad, weekend college. **Credit/placement by examination:** CLEP, institutional tests. 15 credit hours maximum toward associate degree. **Support services:** Learning center, remedial instruction, tutoring.

Majors. **Area/ethnic studies:** African-American, Asian-American. **Biology:** General. **Business:** Accounting, administrative services, banking/financial services, business admin, entrepreneurial studies, management information systems, office technology, office/clerical, real estate, tourism promotion, tourism/travel. **Communications:** Advertising, broadcast journalism, journalism, public relations. **Communications technology:** General. **Computer sciences:** General, applications programming. **Engineering:** General, software. **Engineering technology:** Biomedical, drafting, electrical. **Family/consumer sciences:** General, child care. **Foreign languages:** Chinese, French, German, Italian, Japanese, Spanish. **Health:** Dental lab technology, health services, medical radiologic technology/radiation therapy, medical records technology, medical secretary. **Legal studies:** Legal secretary, paralegal. **Liberal arts:** Arts/sciences. **Math:** General. **Mechanic/repair:** Electronics/electrical. **Physical sciences:** Chemistry, physics. **Protective services:** Police science. **Psychology:** General. **Visual/performing arts:** Art, cinematography, commercial/advertising art, dramatic, film/cinema, photography.

Computing on campus. 200 workstations in library, computer center.

Student life. **Activities:** Bands, choral groups, dance, drama, film society, literary magazine, music ensembles, musical theater, radio station, student government, student newspaper, TV station, religious, political, ethnic, and foreign student clubs.

Athletics. NJCAA. **Intercollegiate:** Baseball M, basketball M, cross-country, track and field.

Student services. Career counseling, student employment services, health services, on-campus daycare, personal counseling, veterans' counselor. **Physically disabled:** Services for visually, speech, hearing impaired. **Transfer:** Special adviser, orientation for new students. Transfer adviser, college fairs on campus for students transferring to 4-year colleges.

Contact. Phone: (323) 953-4381 Fax: (323) 953-4013
William Marmolejo, Dean of Admissions, Los Angeles City College, 855 North Vermont Avenue, Los Angeles, CA 90029-3589

Los Angeles Harbor College

Wilmington, California
www.lahc.edu **CB code: 4395**

- Public 2-year community college
- Commuter campus in small city

General. Founded in 1949. Regionally accredited. **Enrollment:** 2,467 full-time, degree-seeking students. **Degrees:** 506 associate awarded. **Location:** 15 miles from downtown Los Angeles. **Calendar:** Semester, limited summer session. **Full-time faculty:** 130 total. **Part-time faculty:** 145 total. **Special facilities:** Observatory, nature museum.

Transfer out. **Colleges most students transferred to 2005:** California State University-Long Beach, California State University-Dominguez Hills.

Basis for selection. Open admission, but selective for some programs.

High school preparation. Recommended units include mathematics 2, social studies 2, science 5 and foreign language 2. Nursing program requires high school diploma with chemistry and algebra, or college equivalent.

2005-2006 Annual costs. Tuition/fees: $804; $5,424 out-of-state. Per-credit charge: $26 in-state; $180 out-of-state. Books/supplies: $1,260. Personal expenses: $2,304.

Financial aid. All financial aid based on need. Need-based aid available for part-time students. Work study available nights, weekends and for part-time students.

Application procedures. **Admission:** No deadline. No application fee. Application may be submitted online. Admission notification on a rolling basis. High school students accepted on part-time basis. **Financial aid:** Priority date 3/2; no closing date. FAFSA, institutional form required. Applicants notified on a rolling basis; must reply within 2 week(s) of notification.

Academics. Transfer-Alliance Honors Program with UCLA. **Special study options:** Accelerated study, cooperative education, cross-registration, distance learning, double major, dual enrollment of high school students, ESL, honors, independent study, liberal arts/career combination, study abroad, weekend college. License preparation in nursing, paramedic, physical therapy, real estate. **Credit/placement by examination:** CLEP. **Support services:** GED preparation, learning center, remedial instruction, study skills assistance, tutoring, writing center.

Majors. **Business:** General, accounting, administrative services, business admin, management information systems, office management, office technology, office/clerical, real estate. **Computer sciences:** General, applications programming, information systems. **Engineering:** Electrical. **Engineering technology:** Architectural, drafting, electrical. **Family/consumer sciences:** Child care. **Health:** Medical secretary, nursing (RN). **Legal studies:** Legal secretary. **Liberal arts:** Arts/sciences, library science. **Mechanic/repair:** Automotive, electronics/electrical. **Protective services:** Firefighting, police science. **Psychology:** General. **Visual/performing arts:** Art, interior design.

Most popular majors. Computer/information sciences 8%, health sciences 11%, liberal arts 77%.

Computing on campus. 528 workstations in library, computer center, student center. Commuter students can connect to campus network. Online course registration, online library available.

Student life. **Freshman orientation:** Available. **Policies:** Freshmen permitted cars on campus. **Activities:** Bands, choral groups, dance, drama, literary magazine, music ensembles, musical theater, student government, Equal Opportunity Program Student Association.

Athletics. NJCAA. **Intercollegiate:** Baseball M, basketball, football (tackle) M, golf, soccer M, track and field W. **Intramural:** Baseball, basketball, football (tackle) M, soccer, tennis W. **Team name:** Seahawks.

Student services. Adult student services, career counseling, student employment services, health services, legal services, on-campus daycare, personal counseling, placement for graduates, veterans' counselor. **Physically disabled:** Services for visually, speech, hearing impaired. **Transfer:** Special adviser, orientation for new students. Transfer center, transfer adviser, college fairs on campus for students transferring to 4-year colleges.

Contact. Phone: (310) 233-5090 Fax: (310) 233-4223
David Ching, Dean of Admissions and Records, Los Angeles Harbor College, 1111 Figueroa Place, Wilmington, CA 90744-2397

Los Angeles Mission College

Sylmar, California
www.lamission.cc.ca.us **CB code: 4404**

- Public 2-year community college
- Large town

General. Founded in 1974. Regionally accredited. College serves nontraditional student body. **Enrollment:** 1,842 full-time, degree-seeking students. **Degrees:** 367 associate awarded. **ROTC:** Army, Air Force. **Location:** 20 miles from Los Angeles. **Calendar:** Semester, limited summer session. **Full-time faculty:** 60 total. **Part-time faculty:** 50 total.

Basis for selection. Open admission.

2005-2006 Annual costs. Tuition/fees: $804; $5,424 out-of-state. Per-credit charge: $26 in-state; $180 out-of-state. Books/supplies: $846. Personal expenses: $1,719.

Financial aid. **Additional information:** Board of Governors Grant available to those in receipt of AFDC, Social Security Insurance, or General Relief. If not in receipt of program, may qualify based on income.

Application procedures. **Admission:** Priority date 4/20; no deadline. No application fee. Admission notification on a rolling basis. **Financial aid:** Priority date 8/1; no closing date. FAFSA required. Applicants notified on a rolling basis starting 8/15.

Academics. Bilingual instruction available. **Special study options:** Accelerated study, cooperative education, dual enrollment of high school students, independent study. **Credit/placement by examination:** CLEP, institutional tests. 15 credit hours maximum toward associate degree. **Support services:** Learning center, remedial instruction, tutoring.

Majors. **Business:** Accounting, administrative services, business admin, management science, market research, office management, office/clerical, real estate. **Computer sciences:** General. **Education:** Teacher assistance. **Family/consumer sciences:** Clothing/textiles, food/nutrition, institutional food production. **Foreign languages:** Spanish. **Legal studies:** Paralegal. **Liberal arts:** Arts/sciences. **Math:** General. **Mechanic/repair:** Electronics/electrical. **Personal/culinary services:** Culinary arts. **Philosophy/religion:** Philosophy. **Protective services:** Criminal justice. **Psychology:** General. **Visual/performing arts:** Art, interior design.

Computing on campus. 10 workstations in library.

Student life. **Activities:** Choral groups, drama, student government.

Athletics. **Intercollegiate:** Baseball M, cross-country, golf M, soccer M.

Student services. Career counseling, on-campus daycare, personal counseling, placement for graduates, veterans' counselor. **Physically disabled:** Services for speech, hearing impaired.

Contact. Phone: (818) 364-7661
David Green, Vice President, Los Angeles Mission College, 13356 Eldridge Avenue, Sylmar, CA 91342-3245

Los Angeles Pierce College

Woodland Hills, California
www.piercecollege.edu **CB code: 4398**

- Public 2-year community college
- Commuter campus in very large city

General. Founded in 1947. Regionally accredited. **Enrollment:** 4,731 full-time, degree-seeking students. **Degrees:** 1,092 associate awarded. **Location:** 27 miles from downtown Los Angeles. **Calendar:** Semester, extensive summer session. **Full-time faculty:** 160 total. **Part-time faculty:** 395 total. **Special facilities:** Braille nature trail, life science museum, nature center, weather station, working farm, botanical garden.

Transfer out. **Colleges most students transferred to 2005:** California State University-Northridge, University of California-Los Angeles.

Basis for selection. Open admission, but selective for some programs. Limited admission to nursing and animal health technology programs. All students required to take English and math placement tests prior to course registration. **Adult students:** Entrance exam policies same as for first-time freshmen.

2005-2006 Annual costs. Tuition/fees: $804; $5,424 out-of-state. Per-credit charge: $26 in-state; $180 out-of-state. Books/supplies: $1,200.

Financial aid. All financial aid based on need. Need-based aid available for part-time students.

Application procedures. **Admission:** Closing date 9/10 (receipt date). No application fee. Application may be submitted online. Admission notification on a rolling basis. **Financial aid:** Priority date 5/1; no closing date. FAFSA, institutional form required. Applicants notified on a rolling basis starting 8/1.

Academics. **Special study options:** Cooperative education, distance learning, dual enrollment of high school students, honors, student-designed major, study abroad. **Credit/placement by examination:** CLEP, institutional tests. 15 credit hours maximum toward associate degree. **Support services:** GED preparation, learning center, remedial instruction, tutoring.

Majors. **Agriculture:** Animal health, animal sciences, business, dairy, equestrian studies, equine science, greenhouse operations, horticultural science, horticulture, landscaping, ornamental horticulture. **Area/ethnic studies:** Latin American. **Business:** General, accounting, business admin, management science, marketing. **Communications:** Journalism. **Computer sciences:** General, applications programming, computer science, programming. **Conservation:** Management/policy. **Engineering:** General. **Engineering technology:** Construction, drafting. **Foreign languages:** French, Italian, sign language interpretation, Spanish. **Health:** Nursing (RN), preveterinary. **Liberal arts:** Arts/sciences. **Mechanic/repair:** Auto body, automotive. **Philosophy/religion:** Religion. **Visual/performing arts:** Commercial/advertising art, industrial design, photography, studio arts.

Most popular majors. Health sciences 8%, liberal arts 78%.

Computing on campus. Online course registration available.

Student life. **Policies:** Freshmen permitted cars on campus. **Activities:** Bands, choral groups, dance, drama, literary magazine, music ensembles, student government, student newspaper, symphony orchestra, international students association, Bible Fellowship, Alpha Gamma Sigma honor society, Phi Theta Kappa honor society, Phi Beta Lambda business association, Hillel, Union of African American Students, Muslim students association.

Athletics. NJCAA. **Intercollegiate:** Baseball M, basketball W, cheerleading, diving, football (tackle) M, soccer W, softball W, swimming, tennis, volleyball. **Team name:** Brahmas.

Student services. Adult student services, career counseling, services for economically disadvantaged, student employment services, health services, on-campus daycare, personal counseling, placement for graduates, veterans' counselor. **Physically disabled:** Services for visually, speech, hearing impaired. **Transfer:** Special adviser, orientation for new students. Transfer center, transfer adviser, college fairs on campus for students transferring to 4-year colleges.

Contact. Phone: (818) 719-6448 Fax: (818) 716-1087
Shelley Gerstl, Dean of Admissions and Records, Los Angeles Pierce College, 6201 Winnetka Avenue, Woodland Hills, CA 91371

Los Angeles Southwest College

Los Angeles, California
www.lasc.cc.ca.us **CB code: 4409**

- Public 2-year community college
- Commuter campus in very large city

General. Founded in 1967. Regionally accredited. **Enrollment:** 1,436 full-time, degree-seeking students. **Degrees:** 390 associate awarded. **Calendar:** Semester, limited summer session. **Full-time faculty:** 75 total. **Part-time faculty:** 180 total.

Basis for selection. Open admission, but selective for some programs. Limited admission to nursing and allied health programs.

2005-2006 Annual costs. Tuition/fees: $804; $5,424 out-of-state. Per-credit charge: $26 in-state; $180 out-of-state. Books/supplies: $630. Personal expenses: $1,530.

Financial aid. Need-based: Need-based aid available for part-time students. **Additional information:** Board of Governors Enrollment Fee Waiver available to students receiving AFDC, SSI/SSP, or General Assistance. May also qualify on basis of income.

Application procedures. Admission: No deadline. No application fee. Late registration allowed through third week of classes, if permitted by instructor. **Financial aid:** No deadline. FAFSA required. Applicants notified on a rolling basis; must reply within 2 week(s) of notification.

Academics. Special study options: Accelerated study, cooperative education, cross-registration, double major, dual enrollment of high school students, ESL, honors, independent study, liberal arts/career combination, study abroad, weekend college. **Credit/placement by examination:** CLEP, institutional tests. 15 credit hours maximum toward associate degree. **Support services:** Learning center, reduced course load, remedial instruction, tutoring.

Majors. Area/ethnic studies: African-American. **Biology:** General, molecular. **Business:** General, accounting, administrative services, banking/financial services, business admin, insurance, management information systems, office technology, office/clerical, real estate. **Communications:** Advertising, journalism. **Communications technology:** General. **Computer sciences:** General, applications programming, computer graphics, computer science, programming. **Education:** General, early childhood, English, foreign languages, mathematics, music, teacher assistance. **Engineering:** General, electrical. **Engineering technology:** Drafting, electrical. **Family/consumer sciences:** Child care. **Foreign languages:** General, French, Spanish. **Health:** Clinical lab technology, nursing (RN), respiratory therapy technology. **History:** General. **Legal studies:** Paralegal. **Liberal arts:** Arts/sciences. **Math:** General. **Parks/recreation:** General. **Philosophy/religion:** Philosophy. **Physical sciences:** Chemistry, geology, physics. **Psychology:** General. **Social sciences:** Geography, political science, sociology. **Visual/performing arts:** Art, art history/conservation, commercial/advertising art, dramatic, fashion design, photography.

Computing on campus. Helpline, repair service available.

Student life. Activities: Bands, choral groups, dance, drama, literary magazine, musical theater, student government, student newspaper.

Athletics. NJCAA. **Intercollegiate:** Basketball M, cross-country, football (tackle) M, tennis W, track and field. **Intramural:** Baseball M, basketball, bowling, golf, softball, tennis, track and field, volleyball.

Student services. Career counseling, student employment services, on-campus daycare, personal counseling, placement for graduates. **Transfer:** Orientation for new students. Transfer adviser for students transferring to 4-year colleges.

Contact. Phone: (323) 241-5320
Linda Daniels, Associate Dean of Admissions, Los Angeles Southwest College, 1600 West Imperial Highway, Los Angeles, CA 90047

Los Angeles Trade and Technical College

Los Angeles, California
www.lattc.edu **CB code: 4400**

- Public 2-year community and technical college
- Commuter campus in very large city

General. Founded in 1925. Regionally accredited. Specialized culinary arts program, fashion, cosmetology, nursing programs. **Enrollment:** 3,300 full-time, degree-seeking students. **Degrees:** 541 associate awarded. **Location:** 23 blocks from downtown. **Calendar:** Semester, limited summer session. **Full-time faculty:** 185 total. **Part-time faculty:** 285 total. **Class size:** 46% < 20, 38% 20-39, 9% 40-49, 4% 50-99, 4% >100.

Student profile.

Out-of-state:	8%	**25 or older:**	60%

Transfer out. Colleges most students transferred to 2005: UCLA, California State University: Los Angeles, Dominguez Hills, USC.

Basis for selection. Open admission, but selective for some programs. Limited admission to nursing program. Portfolio recommended of commercial art majors.

2005-2006 Annual costs. Tuition/fees: $804; $5,424 out-of-state. Per-credit charge: $26 in-state; $180 out-of-state. Books/supplies: $708. Personal expenses: $1,620.

Financial aid. All financial aid based on need. Need-based aid available for part-time students. Work study available nights, weekends and for part-time students.

Application procedures. Admission: No deadline. No application fee. Application may be submitted online. Admission notification on a rolling basis. **Financial aid:** Priority date 5/1; no closing date. FAFSA required. Applicants notified on a rolling basis.

Academics. Special study options: Accelerated study, cooperative education, distance learning, dual enrollment of high school students, ESL, independent study, liberal arts/career combination, study abroad, weekend college. License preparation in nursing. **Credit/placement by examination:** CLEP, institutional tests. 15 credit hours maximum toward associate degree. **Support services:** GED preparation, learning center, pre-admission summer program, reduced course load, remedial instruction, study skills assistance, tutoring, writing center.

Majors. Business: General, accounting, administrative services, business admin, entrepreneurial studies, fashion, hospitality/recreation, labor relations, office/clerical, real estate. **Communications:** Journalism. **Communications technology:** General, graphic/printing. **Computer sciences:** General, computer science. **Construction:** Carpentry, electrician, maintenance, pipefitting, power transmission. **Engineering:** General. **Engineering technology:** Architectural, drafting, electrical. **Family/consumer sciences:** Clothing/textiles, institutional food production. **Health:** Health services, licensed practical nurse. **Liberal arts:** Arts/sciences. **Mechanic/repair:** Auto body, diesel, electronics/electrical, heating/ac/refrig. **Personal/culinary services:** Culinary arts. **Public administration:** Community org/advocacy. **Visual/performing arts:** Commercial/advertising art, fashion design, photography.

Most popular majors. Computer/information sciences 11%, health sciences 11%, liberal arts 34%, trade and industry 30%, visual/performing arts 8%.

Computing on campus. 550 workstations in library, computer center. Commuter students can connect to campus network. Online course registration, wireless network available.

Student life. Freshman orientation: Available. **Policies:** Freshmen permitted cars on campus. **Activities:** Dance, student government, student newspaper, political organizations.

Athletics. NJCAA. **Intercollegiate:** Basketball, cross-country, tennis, track and field. **Intramural:** Golf, swimming.

Student services. Adult student services, career counseling, services for economically disadvantaged, student employment services, financial aid counseling, health services, minority student services, on-campus daycare, personal counseling, placement for graduates, veterans' counselor. **Physically disabled:** Services for visually, speech, hearing impaired. **Transfer:** Special adviser, orientation for new students. Transfer adviser, college fairs on campus for students transferring to 4-year colleges.

Contact. Phone: (213) 763-7000
Ester Usaha, Registrar, Los Angeles Trade and Technical College, 400 West Washington Boulevard, Los Angeles, CA 90015-4181

Los Angeles Valley College

Valley Glen, California
www.lavc.edu **CB code: 4401**

- Public 2-year community college
- Commuter campus in very large city

General. Founded in 1949. Regionally accredited. **Enrollment:** 4,731 full-time, degree-seeking students. **Degrees:** 893 associate awarded. **Location:** 15 miles from downtown Los Angeles. **Calendar:** Semester, limited summer session. **Full-time faculty:** 241 total; 29% minority, 47% women. **Part-time faculty:** 285 total; 21% minority, 39% women. **Special facilities:** Planetarium.

Student profile.

Out-of-state:	2%	**25 or older:**	69%

Basis for selection. Open admission, but selective for some programs. Registered nursing program has competitive admission based on points accumulated for prerequisite courses, grades, and placement test scores. Institutional placement tests required of all students.

2005-2006 Annual costs. Tuition/fees: $804; $5,424 out-of-state. Per-credit charge: $26 in-state; $180 out-of-state. Books/supplies: $648. Personal expenses: $1,620.

Financial aid. All financial aid based on need. Need-based aid available for part-time students.

Application procedures. Admission: No deadline. No application fee. Application may be submitted online. Admission notification on a rolling basis. **Financial aid:** Priority date 6/12; no closing date. FAFSA required. Applicants notified on a rolling basis.

Academics. Special study options: Cooperative education, dual enrollment of high school students, honors, independent study. License preparation in nursing, paramedic. **Credit/placement by examination:** AP, CLEP, IB, institutional tests. 15 credit hours maximum toward associate degree. **Support services:** Learning center, remedial instruction, study skills assistance, tutoring, writing center.

Majors. Area/ethnic studies: American. **Biology:** General. **Business:** General, administrative services, fashion, hospitality/recreation, management information systems, office technology, office/clerical. **Communications:** Broadcast journalism, journalism. **Computer sciences:** Applications programming, data processing. **Engineering technology:** Electrical. **Family/consumer sciences:** General. **Foreign languages:** French, German, Italian, Spanish. **Health:** Nursing (RN), respiratory therapy technology. **History:** General. **Liberal arts:** Arts/sciences. **Math:** General. **Parks/recreation:** General. **Philosophy/religion:** Philosophy. **Physical sciences:** Chemistry, geology, physics, planetary. **Protective services:** Police science. **Psychology:** General. **Social sciences:** Economics, geography, political science, sociology. **Visual/performing arts:** Art, art history/conservation, commercial/advertising art.

Computing on campus. 300 workstations in library, computer center, student center. Online course registration, wireless network available.

Student life. Freshman orientation: Available. Preregistration for classes offered. **Activities:** Bands, choral groups, dance, drama, film society, literary magazine, music ensembles, musical theater, radio station, student government, student newspaper, symphony orchestra.

Athletics. NJCAA. **Intercollegiate:** Baseball M, basketball, cross-country, diving, football (tackle) M, soccer W, softball W, swimming, track and field, water polo M. **Team name:** Monarchs.

Student services. Career counseling, student employment services, health services, on-campus daycare, personal counseling, placement for graduates, veterans' counselor. **Physically disabled:** Services for visually, speech, hearing impaired. **Learning disabled:** Comprehensive services available. **Transfer:** Special adviser, orientation for new students. Transfer adviser, college fairs on campus for students transferring to 4-year colleges.

Contact. Phone: (818) 947-2553 Fax: (818) 947-2501
Florentino Manzano, Dean of Enrollment Management, Los Angeles Valley College, 5800 Fulton Avenue, Valley Glen, CA 91401-4096

Los Medanos College
Pittsburg, California
www.losmedanos.edu **CB code: 4396**

- Public 2-year community college
- Commuter campus in small city

General. Founded in 1973. Regionally accredited. **Enrollment:** 2,496 full-time, degree-seeking students. **Degrees:** 267 associate awarded. **Location:** 45 miles from San Francisco. **Calendar:** Semester. **Full-time faculty:** 103 total. **Part-time faculty:** 199 total.

Student profile.

Out-of-state:	1%	**25 or older:**	53%

Basis for selection. Open admission.

2005-2006 Annual costs. Tuition/fees: $790; $5,320 out-of-state. Per-credit charge: $26 in-state; $177 out-of-state. Books/supplies: $648. Personal expenses: $1,485.

Application procedures. Admission: No deadline. Admission notification on a rolling basis. **Financial aid:** Priority date 3/2; no closing date. FAFSA required. Applicants notified on a rolling basis starting 7/1; must reply within 2 week(s) of notification.

Academics. Special study options: Cooperative education, cross-registration, independent study, study abroad. **Credit/placement by examination:** CLEP, institutional tests. 20 credit hours maximum toward associate degree. **Support services:** Learning center, remedial instruction, tutoring.

Majors. Biology: General. **Business:** Accounting, entrepreneurial studies, labor relations, office management, real estate, tourism promotion. **Communications:** Journalism. **Family/consumer sciences:** Child care. **Health:** EMT paramedic, nursing (RN). **Liberal arts:** Arts/sciences. **Math:** General. **Mechanic/repair:** Electronics/electrical, small engine. **Physical sciences:** Chemistry. **Protective services:** Firefighting. **Psychology:** General. **Social sciences:** Anthropology, sociology. **Visual/performing arts:** Commercial/advertising art, music performance, studio arts.

Most popular majors. Business/marketing 8%, health sciences 20%, liberal arts 56%.

Computing on campus. 150 workstations in computer center.

Student life. Activities: Bands, choral groups, drama, music ensembles, student government, student newspaper.

Athletics. Intercollegiate: Baseball M, basketball, football (tackle) M, soccer M, softball W, volleyball W. **Intramural:** Basketball, softball, tennis.

Student services. Career counseling, student employment services, on-campus daycare, personal counseling, placement for graduates. **Physically disabled:** Services for visually, speech, hearing impaired. **Transfer:** Special adviser, orientation for new students. Transfer adviser, college fairs on campus for students transferring to 4-year colleges.

Contact. Phone: (925) 439-2181 ext. 7500 Fax: (925) 427-1599
Gail Newman, Director of Admissions, Los Medanos College, 2700 East Leland Road, Pittsburg, CA 94565

Maric College
San Diego, California
www.mariccollege.edu **CB code: 3064**

- For-profit 2-year business and health science college
- Very large city

General. Accredited by ACCSCT. **Calendar:** Continuous.

Annual costs/financial aid. Tuition varies by program and ranges from $172 per unit to $400 per unit. Program lengths vary.

Contact. Phone: (858) 279-4500
3666 Kearny Villa Road, Suite 100, San Diego, CA 92123-1995

Maric College: Anaheim
Anaheim, California
www.mariccollege.edu **CB code: 3533**

- For-profit 2-year business college
- Very large city

General. Accredited by ACICS. **Enrollment:** 140 degree-seeking undergraduates. **Degrees:** 41 associate awarded. **Calendar:** Continuous. **Full-time faculty:** 8 total. **Part-time faculty:** 3 total.

Basis for selection. Open admission.

Application procedures. Admission: No deadline. $20 fee. Admission notification on a rolling basis. **Financial aid:** No deadline. Applicants notified on a rolling basis.

Academics. **Credit/placement by examination:** CLEP.

Majors. **Business:** Business admin. **Engineering technology:** General. **Legal studies:** General.

Contact. Phone: (714) 758-1500 Fax: (714) 758-1220
Roger Cranmer, Admissions Director, Maric College: Anaheim, 1360 South Anaheim Boulevard, Anaheim, CA 92805

Maric College: Panorama City

Panorama City, California
www.mariccollege.edu **CB code: 3541**

- For-profit 2-year junior and technical college
- Commuter campus in very large city
- Interview required

General. Accredited by ACICS. **Enrollment:** 89 degree-seeking undergraduates. **Degrees:** 49 associate awarded. **Location:** 15 miles from Los Angeles. **Calendar:** Continuous. **Full-time faculty:** 21 total. **Part-time faculty:** 2 total. **Class size:** 76% < 20, 24% 20-39.

Basis for selection. Open admission. **Adult students:** Entrance exam policies same as for first-time freshmen.

2006-2007 Annual costs. Tuition/fees (projected): $11,385. Books/supplies: $1,600. Personal expenses: $2,520.

2005-2006 Financial aid. All financial aid based on need. 56% of total undergraduate aid awarded as scholarships/grants, 44% as loans/jobs. Work study available nights.

Application procedures. **Admission:** No deadline. No application fee. Application must be submitted on paper. **Financial aid:** No deadline. FAFSA, institutional form required.

Academics. **Special study options:** Internships, liberal arts/career combination. **Credit/placement by examination:** AP, CLEP. **Support services:** Learning center, study skills assistance, tutoring.

Majors. **Business:** Accounting, accounting technology, accounting/business management, business admin, office management. **Computer sciences:** Information technology, LAN/WAN management, system admin. **Legal studies:** Court reporting, paralegal.

Most popular majors. Business/marketing 17%, computer/information sciences 35%, legal studies 46%.

Computing on campus. 20 workstations in library, computer center. Online library available.

Student life. **Freshman orientation:** Mandatory. **Activities:** Student newspaper.

Student services. Career counseling, student employment services, financial aid counseling, placement for graduates.

Contact. E-mail: kschepps@mariccollege.edu
Phone: (818) 672-3000 Toll-free number: (800) 206-0095
Fax: (818) 672-8919
Kristine Schepps, Director of Admissions, Maric College: Panorama City, 14355 Roscoe Boulevard, Panorama City, CA 91402

Maric College: Sacramento

Sacramento, California
www.mariccollege.edu

- For-profit 2-year business and technical college
- Large city

General. Accredited by ACICS. **Enrollment:** 365 degree-seeking undergraduates. **Degrees:** 61 associate awarded. **Calendar:** Continuous. **Full-time faculty:** 12 total. **Part-time faculty:** 28 total.

Basis for selection. Open admission.

Application procedures. **Admission:** No deadline. $20 fee.

Academics. **Credit/placement by examination:** CLEP.

Majors. **Legal studies:** Paralegal.

Contact. E-mail: admissions@mariccollege.edu
Phone: (916) 649-8168
Eric Lopez, Admissions Director, Maric College: Sacramento, 4330 Watt Avenue, Suite 400, Sacramento, CA 95821

Maric College: Vista

Vista, California
www.mariccollege.edu

- For-profit 2-year technical college
- Commuter campus in small city

General. Accredited by ACCSCT. **Enrollment:** 800 degree-seeking undergraduates. **Degrees:** 24 associate awarded. **Calendar:** Continuous. **Full-time faculty:** 66 total. **Part-time faculty:** 22 total.

Basis for selection. Institutional entrance exam important. High school diploma/GED required for some programs. Timed institutional examination administered onsite.

Application procedures. **Admission:** No deadline. $20 fee.

Academics. **Credit/placement by examination:** CLEP.

Majors. **Computer sciences:** LAN/WAN management. **Legal studies:** Paralegal. **Protective services:** Criminal justice.

Contact. Phone: (760) 630-1555 Fax: (760) 630-1656
Nancie Froning, Director of Admissions, Maric College: Vista, 2022 University Drive, Vista, CA 92083

Marymount College

Rancho Palos Verdes, California **CB member**
www.marymountpv.edu **CB code: 4515**

- Private 2-year junior and liberal arts college affiliated with Roman Catholic Church
- Residential campus in large town

General. Founded in 1933. Regionally accredited. **Enrollment:** 726 degree-seeking undergraduates. **Degrees:** 154 associate awarded. **Location:** 30 miles from Los Angeles. **Calendar:** Semester, limited summer session. **Full-time faculty:** 33 total; 67% have terminal degrees. **Part-time faculty:** 47 total; 21% have terminal degrees, 8% minority, 55% women. **Class size:** 61% < 20, 36% 20-39, 3% 40-49.

Student profile. Among degree-seeking undergraduates, 366 enrolled as first-time, first-year students.

Part-time:	2%	**Asian American:**	8%
Out-of-state:	13%	**Hispanic American:**	18%
Women:	52%	**International:**	11%
African American:	4%	**Live on campus:**	58%

Transfer out. 90% of students enrolled in the transfer program go on to 4-year colleges. **Colleges most students transferred to 2005:** University of Southern California, Loyola Marymount University, University of California, California State University, University of San Diego.

Basis for selection. High school record, quality of academic preparation, recommendations, student's personal statement all considered. SAT and SAT Subject Tests or ACT recommended. ACCUPLACER used for placement. Interview and essay recommended. **Homeschooled:** Transcript of courses and grades, letter of recommendation (nonparent) required. General syllabus of all coursework completed or private tutoring received, statement explaining why family chose home schooling and its advantages and disadvantages required. SAT or ACT scores and state H.S. equivalency certificate recommended.

High school preparation. College-preparatory program recommended. 13 units recommended. Recommended units include English 4, mathematics 3, social studies 2, science 2 (laboratory 1) and foreign language 2.

2005-2006 Annual costs. Tuition/fees: $18,785. Room/board: $9,400. Books/supplies: $1,242. Personal expenses: $2,903.

Financial aid. **Non-need-based:** Scholarships awarded for academics, athletics, leadership.

Application procedures. **Admission:** Priority date 3/2; no deadline. $35 fee, may be waived for applicants with need. Application may be submitted online. Admission notification on a rolling basis beginning on or about 12/

15. Must reply by May 1 or within 4 week(s) if notified thereafter. **Financial aid:** Priority date 3/2; no closing date. FAFSA, institutional form required. Applicants notified on a rolling basis starting 4/30; must reply by 5/1 or within 2 week(s) of notification.

Academics. Special study options: Dual enrollment of high school students, ESL, honors, independent study, internships, study abroad, weekend college. **Credit/placement by examination:** AP, CLEP, IB, institutional tests. 15 credit hours maximum toward associate degree. **Support services:** Learning center, pre-admission summer program, reduced course load, remedial instruction, study skills assistance, tutoring.

Majors. Liberal arts: Arts/sciences.

Computing on campus. 60 workstations in library, computer center. Dormitories linked to campus network. Commuter students can connect to campus network. Online library, helpline, wireless network available.

Student life. Freshman orientation: Mandatory, $125 fee. Preregistration for classes offered. **Policies:** Freshmen permitted cars on campus. **Housing:** Guaranteed on-campus for freshmen. Apartments available. $400 fully refundable deposit, deadline 7/1. Housing available through volunteers in the community. **Activities:** Choral groups, dance, drama, music ensembles, musical theater, student government, campus ministry, Marymount opportunities for volunteer experience, philosophy discussion club, pre-med club, student integrity council, yoga/meditation cub, Phi Theta Kappa, Latinos Unidos, international peers, Black Student Union.

Athletics. NJCAA. **Intercollegiate:** Tennis. **Intramural:** Basketball, golf, skiing, soccer, softball, swimming, tennis. **Team name:** Mariners.

Student services. Adult student services, alcohol/substance abuse counseling, campus ministries, career counseling, student employment services, financial aid counseling, health services, personal counseling. **Physically disabled:** Services for hearing impaired. **Transfer:** Special adviser, orientation, pre-admission transcript evaluation for new students. Transfer center, transfer adviser, college fairs on campus for students transferring to 4-year colleges.

Contact. E-mail: admissions@marymountpv.edu
Phone: (310) 377-5501 ext. 208 Fax: (310) 265-0962
Nina Lococo, Dean of Admissions, Marymount College, 30800 Palos Verdes Drive East, Rancho Palos Verdes, CA 90275-6299

Mendocino College
Ukiah, California
www.mendocino.edu **CB code: 4517**

- Public 2-year community college
- Large town

General. Founded in 1973. Regionally accredited. **Enrollment:** 1,134 full-time, degree-seeking students. **Degrees:** 305 associate awarded. **Location:** 60 miles from Santa Rosa, 110 miles from San Francisco. **Calendar:** Semester, limited summer session. **Full-time faculty:** 50 total. **Part-time faculty:** 170 total. **Special facilities:** Fine arts facility.

Student profile.

Out-of-state:	5%	**25 or older:**	60%

Basis for selection. Open admission.

2005-2006 Annual costs. Tuition/fees: $799; $6,049 out-of-state. Per-credit charge: $26 in-state; $201 out-of-state. Books/supplies: $630. Personal expenses: $1,584.

Financial aid. Need-based: Need-based aid available for part-time students.

Application procedures. Admission: Priority date 5/1; no deadline. No application fee. Admission notification on a rolling basis beginning on or about 7/1. **Financial aid:** Priority date 5/31; no closing date. FAFSA required. Applicants notified on a rolling basis starting 7/1; must reply within 2 week(s) of notification.

Academics. Special study options: Accelerated study, cooperative education, distance learning, double major, dual enrollment of high school students, independent study, student-designed major. **Credit/placement by examination:** AP, CLEP, institutional tests. 12 credit hours maximum toward associate degree. **Support services:** Learning center, remedial instruction, tutoring.

Majors. Agriculture: Plant sciences. **Biology:** General. **Business:** General, accounting, administrative services, business admin, entrepreneurial studies. **Computer sciences:** General. **English:** Speech/rhetoric. **Foreign languages:** French, Spanish. **Health:** Substance abuse counseling. **Liberal arts:** Arts/sciences. **Math:** General. **Mechanic/repair:** Auto body, electronics/electrical. **Parks/recreation:** Sports admin. **Protective services:** Law enforcement admin. **Psychology:** General. **Social sciences:** General. **Visual/performing arts:** Art, dramatic.

Computing on campus. 40 workstations in library, computer center.

Student life. Activities: Bands, choral groups, dance, drama, music ensembles, musical theater, student government, student newspaper, symphony orchestra.

Athletics. NJCAA. **Intercollegiate:** Baseball M, basketball, football (tackle) M, softball W, track and field, volleyball W. **Intramural:** Basketball, bowling, softball, volleyball.

Student services. Career counseling, student employment services, on-campus daycare, personal counseling, placement for graduates, veterans' counselor. **Physically disabled:** Services for visually, speech, hearing impaired. **Transfer:** Special adviser, orientation for new students. Transfer adviser, college fairs on campus for students transferring to 4-year colleges.

Contact. Phone: (707) 468-3101 Fax: (707) 468-3120
Kristie Anderson, Director of Admissions and Records, Mendocino College, 1000 Hensley Creek/Box 3000, Ukiah, CA 95482

Merced College
Merced, California
www.merced.cc.ca.us **CB code: 4500**

- Public 2-year community college
- Commuter campus in small city

General. Founded in 1962. Regionally accredited. Off-campus centers at Los Banos. **Enrollment:** 8,887 undergraduates. **Degrees:** 428 associate awarded. **Location:** 50 miles from Fresno. **Calendar:** Semester, limited summer session. **Full-time faculty:** 120 total. **Part-time faculty:** 300 total.

Basis for selection. Open admission. Institutional placement tests used.

2005-2006 Annual costs. Tuition/fees: $806; $5,336 out-of-state. Per-credit charge: $26 in-state; $177 out-of-state. Books/supplies: $650. Personal expenses: $1,750.

Financial aid. Non-need-based: Scholarships awarded for academics.

Application procedures. Admission: No deadline. No application fee. Admission notification on a rolling basis. Must reply by May 1 or within 4 week(s) if notified thereafter. **Financial aid:** Priority date 6/1; no closing date. FAFSA required. Applicants notified on a rolling basis starting 1/2; must reply within 3 week(s) of notification.

Academics. Special study options: Dual enrollment of high school students, honors, internships, study abroad. **Credit/placement by examination:** AP, CLEP, institutional tests. 12 credit hours maximum toward associate degree. **Support services:** Learning center, pre-admission summer program, remedial instruction, tutoring.

Majors. Agriculture: Agronomy, animal sciences, business, equestrian studies, horticulture, ornamental horticulture, soil science. **Biology:** General. **Business:** General, accounting, administrative services, banking/financial services, business admin, entrepreneurial studies, management information systems, office management, office/clerical, real estate. **Communications:** General, journalism. **Computer sciences:** General, applications programming, computer science, information systems, programming. **Education:** General, early childhood. **Engineering:** General, aerospace. **Engineering technology:** Drafting, electrical. **English:** Speech/rhetoric. **Family/consumer sciences:** General, family studies, institutional food production. **Foreign languages:** French, German, Spanish. **Health:** Licensed practical nurse, medical assistant, medical radiologic technology/radiation therapy, medical secretary, nursing (RN), substance abuse counseling. **History:** General. **Legal studies:** Legal secretary. **Liberal arts:** Arts/sciences. **Math:** General. **Mechanic/repair:** Auto body, diesel, industrial. **Parks/recreation:** Health/fitness. **Philosophy/religion:** Philosophy. **Physical sciences:** Chemistry, physics. **Protective services:** Firefighting, police science. **Psychology:** General. **Public administration:** Social work. **Social sciences:** General, anthropology, archaeology, economics, geography, political science, sociology. **Visual/performing arts:** General, commercial/advertising art, dramatic, photography, studio arts.

Computing on campus. 80 workstations in library, computer center.

Student life. **Freshman orientation:** Available. **Activities:** Bands, choral groups, dance, drama, music ensembles, musical theater, student government, student newspaper, symphony orchestra, black student union, Movimiento Estudiantil Chicano de Aztlan, Intervarsity Christian group, Rotaract.

Athletics. NJCAA. **Intercollegiate:** Baseball M, basketball, cross-country, diving, football (tackle) M, golf, soccer M, softball W, swimming, tennis, track and field, volleyball W, water polo M. **Team name:** Blue Devils.

Student services. Career counseling, student employment services, health services, on-campus daycare, personal counseling, placement for graduates, veterans' counselor. **Physically disabled:** Services for visually, speech, hearing impaired. **Transfer:** Orientation for new students. Transfer adviser, college fairs on campus for students transferring to 4-year colleges.

Contact. Phone: (209) 384-6042
Robert Lenz, Dean of Student Services, Merced College, Administration Building Box #14, Merced, CA 95348

Merritt College
Oakland, California
www.merritt.edu **CB code: 4502**

- Public 2-year community college
- Large city

General. Founded in 1953. Regionally accredited. **Enrollment:** 7,301 undergraduates. **Degrees:** 347 associate awarded. **Location:** 15 miles from San Francisco. **Calendar:** Semester, extensive summer session. **Full-time faculty:** 92 total. **Part-time faculty:** 90 total. **Special facilities:** Anthropology museum, landscape/horticulture complex.

Student profile.

Out-of-state:	5%	**25 or older:**	60%

Basis for selection. Open admission.

2005-2006 Annual costs. Tuition/fees: $784; $5,704 out-of-state. Per-credit charge: $26 in-state; $190 out-of-state. Books/supplies: $846. Personal expenses: $1,800.

Financial aid. **Need-based:** Need-based aid available for part-time students.

Application procedures. **Admission:** No deadline. No application fee. Admission notification on a rolling basis. **Financial aid:** Priority date 4/1, closing date 6/30. FAFSA, institutional form required. Applicants notified on a rolling basis starting 6/1.

Academics. **Special study options:** Cooperative education, cross-registration, distance learning, dual enrollment of high school students, honors, independent study. **Credit/placement by examination:** CLEP, institutional tests. 15 credit hours maximum toward associate degree. **Support services:** Learning center, pre-admission summer program, reduced course load, remedial instruction, tutoring.

Majors. **Agriculture:** Horticultural science, landscaping. **Area/ethnic studies:** African-American. **Business:** General, real estate. **Computer sciences:** General. **Education:** General, business, early childhood. **Engineering:** Electrical. **Family/consumer sciences:** Child care, family/community services. **Foreign languages:** French, Spanish. **Health:** Licensed practical nurse, medical radiologic technology/radiation therapy, nursing (RN). **Legal studies:** Paralegal. **Liberal arts:** Arts/sciences. **Math:** General. **Parks/recreation:** General. **Public administration:** Community org/advocacy. **Social sciences:** General.

Computing on campus. 200 workstations in library, computer center, student center.

Student life. **Activities:** Choral groups, dance, student government, student newspaper, Merritt Christian Fellowship, LaRaza Student Union, Native American Association, Black Student Union, Asian Student Union, Ecology Action Club, Disabled Students Coalition.

Athletics. **Intercollegiate:** Basketball, cross-country, track and field. **Intramural:** Badminton, golf, tennis, volleyball.

Student services. Adult student services, career counseling, student employment services, health services, on-campus daycare, personal counseling, placement for graduates, veterans' counselor. **Physically disabled:** Services for visually, speech, hearing impaired. **Transfer:** Special adviser for new students. Transfer adviser, college fairs on campus for students transferring to 4-year colleges.

Contact. Phone: (510) 466-7368
Howard Perdue, Dean of Admissions and Records, Merritt College, 12500 Campus Drive, Oakland, CA 94619

MiraCosta College
Oceanside, California
www.miracosta.edu **CB code: 4582**

- Public 2-year community college
- Commuter campus in large city

General. Founded in 1934. Regionally accredited. Study abroad programs in Japan, Mexico, Costa Rica and several countries in Europe. **Enrollment:** 6,085 degree-seeking undergraduates; 4,206 non-degree-seeking students. **Degrees:** 486 associate awarded. **Location:** 35 miles from San Diego. **Calendar:** Semester, limited summer session. **Full-time faculty:** 120 total. **Part-time faculty:** 280 total. **Class size:** 29% < 20, 62% 20-39, 7% 40-49, 1% 50-99, less than 1% >100. **Special facilities:** Bioprocessing training facility, music recording studios. **Partnerships:** Formal partnerships with local high schools providing tech-prep programs, Cisco Academy providing network and router training.

Student profile. Among degree-seeking undergraduates, 88% enrolled in a transfer program, 4% enrolled in a vocational program, 10% already have a bachelor's degree or higher, 1,263 enrolled as first-time, first-year students.

Part-time:	59%	**Asian American:**	10%
Out-of-state:	2%	**Hispanic American:**	21%
Women:	56%	**Native American:**	1%
African American:	5%		

Transfer out. **Colleges most students transferred to 2005:** San Diego State University, CSU San Marcos, UC San Diego.

Basis for selection. Open admission. Locally administered tests may be used for placement and counseling.

2005-2006 Annual costs. Tuition/fees: $816; $5,346 out-of-state. Per-credit charge: $26 in-state; $177 out-of-state. Books/supplies: $1,332. Personal expenses: $2,340.

2004-2005 Financial aid. **Need-based:** 79% of total undergraduate aid awarded as scholarships/grants, 21% as loans/jobs. Need-based aid available for part-time students. **Additional information:** Waiver of in-state fees for eligible low-income students.

Application procedures. **Admission:** No deadline. No application fee. Application may be submitted online. Admission notification on a rolling basis. **Financial aid:** Priority date 3/3; no closing date. FAFSA required. Applicants notified on a rolling basis.

Academics. **Special study options:** Accelerated study, cooperative education, distance learning, double major, dual enrollment of high school students, ESL, exchange student, honors, independent study, internships, liberal arts/career combination, student-designed major, study abroad, teacher certification program, weekend college. **Credit/placement by examination:** AP, CLEP, IB, institutional tests. 15 credit hours maximum toward associate degree. **Support services:** GED preparation and test center, learning center, pre-admission summer program, reduced course load, remedial instruction, study skills assistance, tutoring, writing center.

Honors college/program. Students wanting to study at the honors level contract for an honors option in designated courses.

Majors. **Agriculture:** Business, floriculture, landscaping, nursery operations, turf management. **Architecture:** Landscape. **Biology:** General. **Business:** Accounting, administrative services, business admin, hospitality admin, office management, office/clerical, real estate, tourism/travel. **Communications:** General. **Computer sciences:** General, computer graphics, computer science, LAN/WAN management, programming. **Education:** Early childhood. **Engineering technology:** Drafting. **Family/consumer sciences:** Child care. **Foreign languages:** General, French, German, Japanese, Spanish. **Health:** Licensed practical nurse, premedicine, preveterinary. **History:** General. **Interdisciplinary:** Behavioral sciences, gerontology. **Legal studies:** Prelaw. **Liberal arts:** Arts/sciences. **Math:** General. **Mechanic/repair:** Auto body, automotive. **Personal/culinary services:** Cosmetic. **Philosophy/religion:** Philosophy. **Physical sciences:** Chemistry, geology, physics. **Protective services:** Police science. **Psychology:** General. **Science technology:** Biological. **Social sciences:** General, economics, geography, political science, sociology. **Visual/performing arts:** Art, art history/conservation, commercial/advertising art, dance, dramatic, theater design.

Most popular majors. Business/marketing 8%, liberal arts 60%, visual/performing arts 8%.

Computing on campus. 1,000 workstations in library, computer center, student center. Online course registration, online library, student web hosting available.

Student life. **Freshman orientation:** Available. One-hour session offered 9 times prior to classes each semester. **Policies:** Freshmen permitted cars on campus. **Activities:** Bands, choral groups, dance, drama, music ensembles, musical theater, student government, student newspaper, symphony orchestra, MECHA/Latina organization, Black Student Union, women's issues and studies group, Phi Theta Kappa, Future Educators, international club, National Science club, Allied Health club, Behavioral Science club, Creative Entertainers, Japanese club, Intervarsity Christian Fellowship, Latina Leadership Network.

Athletics. NJCAA. **Intercollegiate:** Basketball M, cross-country, soccer W, track and field W. **Intramural:** Soccer. **Team name:** Spartans.

Student services. Career counseling, services for economically disadvantaged, student employment services, financial aid counseling, health services, on-campus daycare, personal counseling, placement for graduates. **Physically disabled:** Services for visually, speech, hearing impaired. **Learning disabled:** Comprehensive services available. **Transfer:** Special adviser, orientation for new students. Transfer center, transfer adviser, college fairs on campus for students transferring to 4-year colleges.

Contact. E-mail: admissions@miracosta.edu
Phone: (760) 795-6620 Toll-free number: (888) 201-8480
Fax: (760) 795-6626
Alicia Terry, Director of Admissions and Records, MiraCosta College, One Barnard Drive, Oceanside, CA 92056-3899

Mission College

Santa Clara, California
www.missioncollege.org **CB code: 7587**

- Public 2-year community college
- Small city

General. Founded in 1975. Regionally accredited. **Enrollment:** 1,991 full-time, degree-seeking students. **Degrees:** 563 associate awarded. **ROTC:** Navy, Air Force. **Location:** 8 miles from San Jose. **Calendar:** Semester, limited summer session. **Full-time faculty:** 149 total. **Part-time faculty:** 270 total.

Basis for selection. Open admission, but selective for some programs. Limited admission to vocational nursing and allied health. Interviews required of nursing, psychiatric technician majors.

2005-2006 Annual costs. Tuition/fees: $816; $5,346 out-of-state. Per-credit charge: $26 in-state; $177 out-of-state. Books/supplies: $648. Personal expenses: $1,630.

Application procedures. **Admission:** No deadline. No application fee. Admission notification on a rolling basis. **Financial aid:** Priority date 5/1; no closing date. Applicants notified on a rolling basis starting 8/1; must reply within 2 week(s) of notification.

Academics. **Special study options:** Cooperative education, dual enrollment of high school students, honors, independent study, weekend college. **Credit/placement by examination:** CLEP, institutional tests. 12 credit hours maximum toward associate degree. **Support services:** Learning center, remedial instruction, tutoring.

Majors. **Agriculture:** Food science. **Biology:** General. **Business:** General, accounting, administrative services, banking/financial services, business admin, management information systems, management science, office management, office/clerical, real estate. **Communications technology:** Graphic/printing. **Computer sciences:** Applications programming, computer science, information systems. **Engineering:** General. **Engineering technology:** Drafting. **Health:** Health services, licensed practical nurse, nursing (RN). **Liberal arts:** Arts/sciences. **Math:** General. **Physical sciences:** Chemistry, physics. **Protective services:** Fire safety technology. **Social sciences:** General. **Visual/performing arts:** Art, commercial/advertising art.

Student life. **Activities:** Bands, music ensembles, musical theater, TV station.

Athletics. **Intercollegiate:** Baseball M, soccer M, softball W, tennis. **Team name:** Saints.

Student services. Adult student services, career counseling, student employment services, health services, on-campus daycare, personal counseling, placement for graduates, veterans' counselor. **Transfer:** Orientation for new students. College fairs on campus for students transferring to 4-year colleges.

Contact. Phone: (408) 988-2200 Fax: (408) 980-8980
Arlene Atondo, Director of Admissions, Mission College, 3000 Mission College Boulevard, Santa Clara, CA 95054-1897

Modesto Junior College

Modesto, California
www.mjc.edu **CB code: 4486**

- Public 2-year community college
- Commuter campus in small city

General. Founded in 1921. Regionally accredited. **Enrollment:** 11,385 degree-seeking undergraduates. **Degrees:** 1,131 associate awarded. **Location:** 90 miles from San Francisco. **Calendar:** Semester, limited summer session. **Full-time faculty:** 283 total. **Part-time faculty:** 251 total. **Special facilities:** Natural history museum.

Transfer out. **Colleges most students transferred to 2005:** California State University: Stanislaus, California State University: Fresno, California State University: Sacramento, University of California: Davis, University of California: San Diego.

Basis for selection. Open admission, but selective for some programs. Selective admission offered to some programs such as nursing (RN), dental assisting, medical assisting, and related majors. Also selective for police academy and fire academy.

High school preparation. Certain programs require specific courses.

2005-2006 Annual costs. Tuition/fees: $818; $5,348 out-of-state. Per-credit charge: $26 in-state; $177 out-of-state. Books/supplies: $1,224. Personal expenses: $1,844.

2004-2005 Financial aid. All financial aid based on need. 96% of total undergraduate aid awarded as scholarships/grants, 4% as loans/jobs. Need-based aid available for part-time students. Work study available nights, weekends and for part-time students. **Additional information:** Modesto Junior College scholarship priority deadline 12/15.

Application procedures. **Admission:** Priority date 8/3; no deadline. No application fee. Application may be submitted online. Admission notification on a rolling basis beginning on or about 3/1. **Financial aid:** Priority date 3/2; no closing date. FAFSA, institutional form required. Applicants notified on a rolling basis starting 5/1; must reply within 2 week(s) of notification.

Academics. **Special study options:** Cooperative education, distance learning, double major, dual enrollment of high school students, ESL, honors, independent study, internships, liberal arts/career combination, study abroad, weekend college. License preparation in nursing, real estate. **Credit/placement by examination:** AP, CLEP, institutional tests. 30 credit hours maximum toward associate degree. **Support services:** GED preparation, learning center, pre-admission summer program, remedial instruction, study skills assistance, tutoring, writing center.

Majors. **Agriculture:** Agronomy, animal breeding, animal sciences, business, dairy, food science, landscaping, ornamental horticulture, plant sciences, poultry, soil science, supplies. **Architecture:** Landscape, urban/community planning. **Business:** General, accounting, administrative services, business admin, fashion, finance, management information systems, marketing, real estate. **Communications:** General, broadcast journalism, journalism. **Communications technology:** Graphic/printing. **Computer sciences:** General, computer graphics, computer science, programming. **Conservation:** General, forestry, wildlife. **Construction:** Electrician, maintenance, pipefitting. **Engineering:** General, electrical. **Engineering technology:** Architectural, drafting. **English:** Speech/rhetoric. **Family/consumer sciences:** General, child care, clothing/textiles, family/community services, food/nutrition. **Foreign languages:** General, French, German, Spanish. **Health:** Dental assistant, licensed practical nurse, medical assistant, nursing (RN), nursing assistant, respiratory therapy technology. **Liberal arts:** Arts/sciences. **Math:** General. **Mechanic/repair:** General, auto body, automotive, electronics/electrical, heating/ac/refrig. **Parks/recreation:** General, health/fitness. **Protective services:** Criminal justice, firefighting, law enforcement admin, police science. **Public administration:** Human services. **Social sciences:** General. **Visual/performing arts:** General, art, cinematography, commercial photography, commercial/advertising art, dramatic, fashion design, interior design, photography, studio arts.

Computing on campus. 95 workstations in library, computer center, student center. Commuter students can connect to campus network. Online course registration available.

Student life. Freshman orientation: Available. One hour, held during registration. **Policies:** Freshmen permitted cars on campus. **Activities:** Bands, choral groups, dance, drama, film society, music ensembles, opera, radio station, student government, student newspaper, symphony orchestra, TV station, Christian Collegiate Fellowship; Able-Disabled Association; foreign, ethnic, minority student and women re-entry clubs; Young Farmers; other special interest and concern groups.

Athletics. NJCAA. **Intercollegiate:** Baseball M, basketball, cross-country, diving, football (tackle) M, golf, soccer, softball W, swimming, tennis, track and field, volleyball W, water polo, wrestling M. **Intramural:** Basketball, football (tackle) M, softball W, table tennis, tennis, volleyball. **Team name:** Pirates.

Student services. Adult student services, career counseling, services for economically disadvantaged, student employment services, financial aid counseling, health services, minority student services, on-campus daycare, personal counseling, placement for graduates, veterans' counselor. **Physically disabled:** Services for visually, speech, hearing impaired. **Learning disabled:** Comprehensive services available. **Transfer:** Special adviser, orientation, re-entry adviser for new students. Transfer center, transfer adviser, college fairs on campus for students transferring to 4-year colleges.

Contact. Phone: (209) 575-6013 Fax: (209) 575-6859
Susie Agostini, Dean, Matriculation and Enrollment Services, Modesto Junior College, 435 College Avenue, Modesto, CA 95350-5800

Monterey Peninsula College

Monterey, California
www.mpc.edu **CB code: 4490**

- Public 2-year community college
- Commuter campus in large town

General. Founded in 1947. Regionally accredited. **Enrollment:** 1,808 full-time, degree-seeking students. **Degrees:** 377 associate awarded. **Location:** 120 miles from San Francisco. **Calendar:** Semester, limited summer session. **Full-time faculty:** 120 total. **Part-time faculty:** 170 total.

Basis for selection. Open admission, but selective for some programs. Additional requirements, including interview, for dental assistant, nursing, administrative justice and police academy programs.

2005-2006 Annual costs. Tuition/fees: $826; $5,356 out-of-state. Per-credit charge: $26 in-state; $177 out-of-state. Books/supplies: $846. Personal expenses: $1,719.

Financial aid. Need-based: Need-based aid available for part-time students.

Application procedures. Admission: No deadline. No application fee. Application may be submitted online. Admission notification on a rolling basis. **Financial aid:** Priority date 3/2; no closing date. FAFSA, institutional form required. Applicants notified on a rolling basis starting 6/1.

Academics. Special study options: Cooperative education, cross-registration, distance learning, double major, dual enrollment of high school students, ESL, independent study, weekend college. **Credit/placement by examination:** CLEP, institutional tests. 30 credit hours maximum toward associate degree. **Support services:** Learning center, remedial instruction, tutoring.

Majors. Agriculture: Ornamental horticulture. **Area/ethnic studies:** Women's. **Biology:** General. **Business:** General, accounting, business admin, hospitality admin, hospitality/recreation, international, office/clerical, real estate. **Communications:** General. **Computer sciences:** General, data processing, LAN/WAN management, programming, web page design, word processing. **Engineering technology:** Drafting. **Family/consumer sciences:** General, child development, clothing/textiles, family/community services, fashion consultant, institutional food production. **Foreign languages:** General. **Health:** Dental assistant, medical assistant, nursing (RN), predentistry, premedicine, prepharmacy, preveterinary. **History:** General. **Liberal arts:** Arts/sciences. **Math:** General. **Philosophy/religion:** Philosophy. **Physical sciences:** Chemistry, physics. **Protective services:** Fire safety technology, law enforcement admin. **Psychology:** General. **Social sciences:** Anthropology, economics, political science, sociology. **Visual/performing arts:** Acting, art, art history/conservation, ceramics, dance, directing/producing, dramatic, drawing, graphic design, interior design, metal/jewelry, painting, photography, printmaking, sculpture, studio arts.

Student life. Activities: Bands, choral groups, dance, drama, music ensembles, musical theater, opera, student government.

Athletics. NJCAA. **Intercollegiate:** Baseball M, basketball, cross-country, football (tackle) M, golf, softball W, swimming, tennis W, track and field, volleyball W. **Team name:** Lobos.

Student services. Career counseling, student employment services, health services, on-campus daycare, personal counseling. **Physically disabled:** Services for visually, speech, hearing impaired. **Transfer:** Special adviser, orientation for new students. Transfer center, transfer adviser, college fairs on campus for students transferring to 4-year colleges.

Contact. Phone: (831) 646-4002 Fax: (831) 646-4015
Vera Coleman, Director of Admissions and Records, Monterey Peninsula College, 980 Fremont Street, Monterey, CA 93940-4799

Moorpark College

Moorpark, California
www.moorpark.net **CB code: 4512**

- Public 2-year community college
- Commuter campus in large town

General. Founded in 1963. Regionally accredited. **Enrollment:** 9,031 degree-seeking undergraduates. **Degrees:** 1,255 associate awarded. **Location:** 50 miles from Los Angeles. **Calendar:** Semester, limited summer session. **Full-time faculty:** 175 total; 21% have terminal degrees. **Part-time faculty:** 446 total. **Special facilities:** Exotic animal compound and teaching zoo, observatory.

Transfer out. Colleges most students transferred to 2005: CSU, USC, UCLA.

Basis for selection. Open admission, but selective for some programs. Limited admission to nursing program, exotic animal training management program, radiologic technology.

2005-2006 Annual costs. Tuition/fees: $818; $5,468 out-of-state. Per-credit charge: $26 in-state; $181 out-of-state. Books/supplies: $882. Personal expenses: $1,656.

Application procedures. Admission: Priority date 7/30; no deadline. No application fee. Application may be submitted online. Admission notification on a rolling basis. **Financial aid:** Priority date 5/16; no closing date. FAFSA required. Applicants notified on a rolling basis starting 6/15; must reply within 2 week(s) of notification.

Academics. Special study options: Cooperative education, distance learning, honors, independent study, internships, study abroad. **Credit/placement by examination:** AP, CLEP. 12 credit hours maximum toward associate degree. **Support services:** Learning center, remedial instruction, tutoring.

Majors. Agriculture: Animal sciences. **Biology:** General. **Business:** Accounting, administrative services, business admin, management information systems, office management, real estate. **Communications:** General, broadcast journalism. **Communications technology:** General, graphic/printing. **Computer sciences:** General, applications programming, information systems. **Engineering technology:** Electrical. **Family/consumer sciences:** General, child care, family studies. **Health:** Medical radiologic technology/radiation therapy, nursing (RN). **Liberal arts:** Arts/sciences. **Math:** General. **Physical sciences:** Chemistry, geology, physics. **Protective services:** Police science. **Social sciences:** General. **Visual/performing arts:** General, cinematography, commercial/advertising art, dramatic, interior design, photography, studio arts.

Computing on campus. 75 workstations in computer center. Online course registration, wireless network available.

Student life. Freshman orientation: Available. Online orientation. **Activities:** Bands, choral groups, dance, drama, film society, music ensembles, musical theater, opera, radio station, student government, student newspaper, TV station, Mexican-American club, Black student Union, Alpha Gamma Sigma, Muslim Student Association.

Athletics. Intercollegiate: Baseball M, basketball, cheerleading M, cross-country, football (tackle) M, golf M, softball W, tennis W, track and field, volleyball, wrestling M. **Team name:** Raiders.

Student services. Career counseling, services for economically disadvantaged, student employment services, financial aid counseling, health services, legal services, on-campus daycare, personal counseling, veterans' counselor. **Physically disabled:** Services for visually, speech, hearing impaired.

Transfer: Special adviser, orientation for new students. Transfer center, transfer adviser, college fairs on campus for students transferring to 4-year colleges.

Contact. E-mail: mcadmissions@vcccd.net
Phone: (805) 378-1429 Fax: (805) 378-1499
Katherine Colborn, Registrar, Moorpark College, 7075 Campus Road, Moorpark, CA 93021

Mount San Antonio College

Walnut, California
www.mtsac.edu **CB code: 4494**

- Public 2-year community college
- Commuter campus in small city

General. Founded in 1946. Regionally accredited. **Enrollment:** 20,587 degree-seeking undergraduates. **Degrees:** 1,265 associate awarded. **ROTC:** Air Force. **Location:** 30 miles from Los Angeles. **Calendar:** Semester, extensive summer session. **Full-time faculty:** 360 total. **Part-time faculty:** 750 total. **Special facilities:** Planetarium, wildlife sanctuary.

Transfer out. Colleges most students transferred to 2005: California State Polytechnic University: Pomona, California State University: Los Angeles, California State University: Fullerton.

Basis for selection. Open admission.

2005-2006 Annual costs. Tuition/fees: $806; $5,336 out-of-state. Per-credit charge: $26 in-state; $177 out-of-state. Books/supplies: $1,280. Personal expenses: $2,200.

Financial aid. All financial aid based on need. Need-based aid available for part-time students.

Application procedures. Admission: No deadline. No application fee. Admission notification on a rolling basis. **Financial aid:** No deadline. FAFSA, institutional form required. Applicants notified on a rolling basis starting 6/1; must reply within 4 week(s) of notification.

Academics. Special study options: Cooperative education, cross-registration, distance learning, dual enrollment of high school students, ESL, honors, internships, study abroad, teacher certification program, weekend college. License preparation in aviation, nursing, paramedic, radiology, real estate. **Credit/placement by examination:** CLEP. 12 credit hours maximum toward associate degree. **Support services:** GED preparation, learning center, pre-admission summer program, remedial instruction, study skills assistance, tutoring.

Majors. Agriculture: Animal sciences, business, horticulture. **Biology:** General, marine. **Business:** General, accounting, administrative services, banking/financial services, business admin, entrepreneurial studies, fashion, office/clerical, real estate. **Communications:** Advertising, broadcast journalism, journalism. **Communications technology:** General. **Computer sciences:** Data processing. **Conservation:** General, forestry. **Engineering:** General. **Engineering technology:** Architectural, drafting, electrical. **Family/consumer sciences:** General, clothing/textiles. **Foreign languages:** Sign language interpretation. **Health:** EMT paramedic, health services, medical radiologic technology/radiation therapy, medical secretary, nursing (RN), respiratory therapy technology. **Legal studies:** Paralegal. **Liberal arts:** Arts/sciences. **Mechanic/repair:** Aircraft, electronics/electrical, heating/ac/refrig. **Parks/recreation:** General, facilities management. **Protective services:** Firefighting, police science. **Transportation:** Air traffic control, aviation, flight attendant. **Visual/performing arts:** Design, interior design, photography.

Computing on campus. 600 workstations in library, computer center, student center. Commuter students can connect to campus network. Online course registration, helpline available.

Student life. Freshman orientation: Mandatory. Preregistration for classes offered. **Policies:** Freshmen permitted cars on campus. **Activities:** Bands, choral groups, dance, drama, film society, literary magazine, music ensembles, musical theater, radio station, student government, student newspaper, symphony orchestra, TV station, Asian student association, Chinese club, Black student alliance, Indo-Pak club, Democratic club, Republican club, sign language club, MECHA, Muslim student association.

Athletics. Intercollegiate: Badminton W, baseball M, basketball, cross-country, diving, football (tackle) M, golf, soccer, softball W, swimming, tennis, track and field, volleyball, water polo M, wrestling M. **Team name:** Mounties.

Student services. Adult student services, alcohol/substance abuse counseling, career counseling, services for economically disadvantaged, student employment services, financial aid counseling, health services, minority student services, on-campus daycare, personal counseling, placement for graduates, veterans' counselor. **Physically disabled:** Services for visually, speech, hearing impaired. **Transfer:** Special adviser, orientation, re-entry adviser, pre-admission transcript evaluation for new students. Transfer center, transfer adviser, college fairs on campus for students transferring to 4-year colleges.

Contact. Phone: (909) 594-5611 ext. 4415 Fax: (909) 468-4068
Patty Montoya, Director of Admissions and Records, Mount San Antonio College, 1100 North Grand Avenue, Walnut, CA 91789

Mount San Jacinto College

San Jacinto, California
www.msjc.edu **CB code: 4501**

- Public 2-year community college
- Commuter campus in small city

General. Founded in 1962. Regionally accredited. **Enrollment:** 5,717 degree-seeking undergraduates. **Degrees:** 1,062 associate awarded. **ROTC:** Army, Air Force. **Location:** 35 miles from Riverside, 45 miles from Palm Springs. **Calendar:** Semester, limited summer session. **Full-time faculty:** 110 total. **Part-time faculty:** 400 total. **Class size:** 38% < 20, 54% 20-39, 7% 40-49, less than 1% 50-99.

Transfer out. Colleges most students transferred to 2005: California State University: San Bernardino, University of California: Riverside, California State University: San Marcos, Azusa Pacific University.

Basis for selection. Open admission, but selective for some programs. Special requirements for nursing program. Interview required of nursing majors. Audition recommended of performing arts majors.

2005-2006 Annual costs. Tuition/fees: $780; $5,310 out-of-state. Per-credit charge: $26 in-state; $177 out-of-state. Books/supplies: $1,206. Personal expenses: $2,250.

Financial aid. All financial aid based on need. Need-based aid available for part-time students. Work study available nights and for part-time students. **Additional information:** Board of Governors Grant Program for state residents to defray cost of enrollment fee.

Application procedures. Admission: Closing date 8/20. No application fee. Application may be submitted online. Admission notification on a rolling basis beginning on or about 4/1. All students admitted, but nursing students have additional admissions policies. **Financial aid:** Priority date 3/2; no closing date. FAFSA, institutional form required. Applicants notified on a rolling basis starting 5/1; must reply within 3 week(s) of notification.

Academics. Special study options: Cooperative education, cross-registration, distance learning, double major, dual enrollment of high school students, ESL, honors, independent study, internships, weekend college. License preparation in nursing, paramedic, real estate. **Credit/placement by examination:** AP, CLEP, institutional tests. 12 credit hours maximum toward associate degree. **Support services:** Learning center, reduced course load, remedial instruction, study skills assistance, tutoring, writing center.

Majors. Agriculture: Turf management. **Business:** Business admin, real estate. **Computer sciences:** General. **Education:** Early childhood, physical. **Health:** Nursing (RN), substance abuse counseling. **Interdisciplinary:** Behavioral sciences. **Liberal arts:** Arts/sciences. **Math:** General. **Mechanic/repair:** Automotive. **Protective services:** Police science. **Social sciences:** General. **Visual/performing arts:** Art, dance, dramatic, photography.

Computing on campus. 120 workstations in library, computer center, student center. Commuter students can connect to campus network. Online course registration available.

Student life. Freshman orientation: Mandatory. 2-hour orientation. **Activities:** Bands, dance, drama, musical theater, student government, Campus Crusade, MECHA, Black Students Union.

Athletics. Intercollegiate: Baseball M, basketball, football (tackle) M, golf, soccer W, softball W, tennis, volleyball W. **Intramural:** Volleyball W. **Team name:** Eagles.

Student services. Adult student services, career counseling, services for economically disadvantaged, student employment services, financial aid counseling, on-campus daycare, personal counseling, veterans' counselor. **Physically disabled:** Services for visually, speech, hearing impaired. **Transfer:** Special adviser, orientation, pre-admission transcript evaluation for new students. Transfer center, transfer adviser, college fairs on campus for students transferring to 4-year colleges.

Contact. Phone: (951) 487-6752 ext. 1410 Fax: (951) 654-6738
Susan Loomis, Director, Enrollment Services, Mount San Jacinto College, 1499 North State Street, San Jacinto, CA 92583

MTI College

Sacramento, California
www.mticollege.edu **CB code: 3543**

- For-profit 2-year business and technical college
- Commuter campus in large city
- Interview required

General. Regionally accredited. **Enrollment:** 396 degree-seeking undergraduates; 295 non-degree-seeking students. **Degrees:** 125 associate awarded. **Calendar:** Continuous, extensive summer session. **Full-time faculty:** 9 total. **Part-time faculty:** 61 total.

Student profile. Among degree-seeking undergraduates, 100% enrolled in a vocational program, 261 enrolled as first-time, first-year students.

Transfer out. Colleges most students transferred to 2005: University of Phoenix, Golden Gate University.

Basis for selection. Interview, talent, ability, character and personal qualities important. **Adult students:** Entrance exam policies same as for first-time freshmen.

High school preparation. College-preparatory program required.

2005-2006 Annual costs. Tuition/fees: $9,050. Books/supplies: $1,100. Personal expenses: $246.

Financial aid. Need-based: Work study available nights.

Application procedures. Admission: No deadline. $50 fee. Admission notification on a rolling basis.

Academics. Special study options: Cooperative education, distance learning, internships, liberal arts/career combination. **Credit/placement by examination:** CLEP, institutional tests. **Support services:** GED preparation, learning center, reduced course load, remedial instruction, study skills assistance, tutoring.

Majors. Business: Business admin. **Computer sciences:** System admin, systems analysis. **Legal studies:** Paralegal.

Most popular majors. Business/marketing 9%, computer/information sciences 27%, legal studies 64%.

Computing on campus. 300 workstations in library, computer center.

Student life. Freshman orientation: Mandatory.

Student services. Adult student services, career counseling, financial aid counseling, placement for graduates, veterans' counselor. **Transfer:** Special adviser, orientation, pre-admission transcript evaluation for new students. College fairs on campus for students transferring to 4-year colleges.

Contact. E-mail: webmaster@mticollege.edu
Phone: (916) 339-1500 Fax: (916) 339-0305
Marije Miller, Director of Admissions, MTI College, 5221 Madison Avenue, Sacramento, CA 95841

Napa Valley College

Napa, California
www.napavalley.edu **CB code: 4530**

- Public 2-year community college
- Commuter campus in small city

General. Founded in 1940. Regionally accredited. **Enrollment:** 2,074 degree-seeking undergraduates. **Degrees:** 685 associate awarded. **Location:** 50 miles from San Francisco. **Calendar:** Semester, limited summer session. **Full-time faculty:** 106 total. **Part-time faculty:** 210 total. **Special facilities:** Nature preserve, working vineyard, telecommunications laboratory.

Basis for selection. Open admission, but selective for some programs. Special admission requirements for health occupations programs and athletic program applicants.

2005-2006 Annual costs. Tuition/fees: $804; $5,334 out-of-state. Per-credit charge: $26 in-state; $177 out-of-state. Books/supplies: $630. Personal expenses: $1,476.

Application procedures. Admission: No deadline. No application fee. Admission notification on a rolling basis. College-administered placement tests recommended for students enrolling in English or mathematics. **Financial aid:** Priority date 4/1; no closing date. FAFSA required. Applicants notified on a rolling basis starting 6/1; must reply within 3 week(s) of notification.

Academics. Culinary arts program available. **Special study options:** Cooperative education, distance learning, double major, dual enrollment of high school students, ESL, honors, independent study, internships, study abroad, weekend college. Exchange program with Tafe College, Tasmania. **Credit/placement by examination:** CLEP, institutional tests. 12 credit hours maximum toward associate degree. **Support services:** Learning center, remedial instruction, tutoring, writing center.

Majors. Agriculture: General. **Business:** General, accounting, administrative services, real estate. **Communications technology:** General. **Computer sciences:** General. **Conservation:** Wildlife. **Education:** General, early childhood. **Engineering technology:** Biomedical, drafting, electrical. **Health:** Health services, licensed practical nurse, nursing (RN), respiratory therapy technology. **Legal studies:** Paralegal. **Liberal arts:** Arts/sciences. **Protective services:** Police science. **Social sciences:** General.

Computing on campus. 30 workstations in library, computer center.

Student life. Activities: Bands, choral groups, dance, drama, music ensembles, musical theater, student government, student newspaper, symphony orchestra, various religious, ethnic, social service, and special interest organizations including International Student Club, Amnesty International, Hispano-Americano Club.

Athletics. NJCAA. **Intercollegiate:** Baseball M, basketball, diving, golf, soccer M, softball W, swimming, tennis, volleyball W. **Intramural:** Volleyball. **Team name:** Storm.

Student services. Adult student services, career counseling, student employment services, on-campus daycare, personal counseling, veterans' counselor. **Physically disabled:** Services for visually, speech, hearing impaired. **Transfer:** Special adviser, orientation, re-entry adviser for new students. Transfer center, transfer adviser, college fairs on campus for students transferring to 4-year colleges.

Contact. Phone: (707) 253-3000 Fax: (707) 253-3064
Beth Hauscarriague, Director of Admissions, Napa Valley College, 2277 Napa-Vallejo Highway, Napa, CA 94558

National Institute of Technology

Long Beach, California
www.nitschools.com **CB code: 3162**

- For-profit 2-year health science and technical college
- Commuter campus in large city

General. Accredited by ACCSCT. **Enrollment:** 1,600 degree-seeking undergraduates. **Degrees:** 4 associate awarded. **Calendar:** Continuous. **Full-time faculty:** 140 total. **Part-time faculty:** 10 total.

Basis for selection. Institutional placement assessment examination, interview important. Institutional career placement assessment examination used.

Application procedures. Admission: No deadline. Application fee varies by program.

Academics. Credit/placement by examination: CLEP.

Contact. Phone: (562) 437-0501 Toll-free number: (888) 741-4271
Fax: (562) 432-3721
Claudia Fimbres, Senior Admissions Representative, National Institute of Technology, 2161 Technology Place, Long Beach, CA 90810

Northwestern College

Gold River, California
www.ntcollege.com

- For-profit 2-year technical college
- Very large city
- Interview required

General. Accredited by ACCSCT. **Enrollment:** 175 degree-seeking undergraduates. **Degrees:** 38 associate awarded. **Location:** 10 miles from downtown Sacramento. **Calendar:** Continuous, limited summer session. **Full-time faculty:** 7 total. **Part-time faculty:** 3 total. **Special facilities:** Massage therapy students get hands-on experience in public massage clinic. Personal training students work with fitness professionals to gain field experience.

Basis for selection. Interview, interest important.

Application procedures. Admission: No deadline. $35 fee.

Academics. Credit/placement by examination: CLEP.

Majors. Health: Massage therapy.

Contact. E-mail: admissions@ntcollege.com
Phone: (916) 649-2400 Toll-free number: (866) 649-2400
Fax: (916) 641-8649
Northwestern College, 2317 Gold Meadow Way, Gold River, CA 95670

Ohlone College
Fremont, California
www.ohlone.cc.ca.us **CB code: 4579**

- Public 2-year community college
- Commuter campus in large city

General. Founded in 1966. Regionally accredited. **Enrollment:** 2,261 degree-seeking undergraduates. **Degrees:** 493 associate awarded. **ROTC:** Air Force. **Location:** 15 miles from San Jose, 40 miles from San Francisco. **Calendar:** Semester, extensive summer session. **Full-time faculty:** 150 total. **Part-time faculty:** 470 total. **Class size:** 54% < 20, 40% 20-39, 2% 40-49, 2% 50-99, less than 1% >100. **Special facilities:** Fine and performing arts center, business and technology center. **Partnerships:** Formal partnerships with Sun Microsystems, Metatec Inc., Washington Hospital, Fremont Unified School District, Newark Unified School District.

Student profile.

Out-of-state:	1%	**25 or older:**	45%

Transfer out. Colleges most students transferred to 2005: California State University at Hayward, San Jose State University.

Basis for selection. Open admission, but selective for some programs. Nursing, respiratory therapy and physical therapy assisting programs require basic competence in reading comprehension and English skills, basic knowledge of related sciences. All candidates who achieve minimum standards selected by lottery. High school diploma or equivalent not required if applicant is 18 years of age or older.

High school preparation. Nursing and physical therapy assisting programs require anatomy and physiology. Respiratory therapy program requires algebra and physics 103.

2005-2006 Annual costs. Tuition/fees: $816; $5,346 out-of-state. Per-credit charge: $26 in-state; $177 out-of-state. Books/supplies: $810. Personal expenses: $2,616.

Financial aid. Need-based: Need-based aid available for part-time students. Work study available for part-time students. **Non-need-based:** Scholarships awarded for academics.

Application procedures. Admission: Priority date 6/25; no deadline. No application fee. **Financial aid:** Priority date 7/1; no closing date. FAFSA, institutional form required. Applicants notified on a rolling basis starting 7/30; must reply within 2 week(s) of notification.

Academics. Special study options: Cooperative education, cross-registration, distance learning, double major, dual enrollment of high school students, ESL, independent study, internships, liberal arts/career combination, study abroad, weekend college. License preparation in nursing, physical therapy. **Credit/placement by examination:** CLEP, IB, institutional tests. 10 credit hours maximum toward associate degree. **Support services:** Learning center, pre-admission summer program, reduced course load, remedial instruction, study skills assistance, tutoring, writing center.

Majors. Biology: General. **Business:** General, accounting, administrative services, business admin, marketing, office management, office technology, office/clerical, real estate, receptionist, small business admin. **Communications:** Broadcast journalism, digital media, journalism. **Communications technology:** Desktop publishing. **Computer sciences:** Computer graphics, information systems, LAN/WAN management, programming, system admin. **Education:** Early childhood. **Engineering technology:** CAD/CADD, electrical, electromechanical. **Family/consumer sciences:** Child care, food/nutrition, institutional food production. **Foreign languages:** American Sign Language. **Health:** Medical assistant, nursing (RN), physical therapy assistant, respiratory therapy technology. **Interdisciplinary:** Biological/physical sciences, natural sciences. **Liberal arts:** Arts/sciences. **Mechanic/repair:** Electronics/electrical. **Protective services:** Law enforcement admin. **Social sciences:** General. **Visual/performing arts:** Commercial/advertising art, graphic design, interior design, multimedia, studio arts, theater design.

Most popular majors. Biological/life sciences 21%, business/marketing 10%, health sciences 18%, liberal arts 38%.

Computing on campus. 450 workstations in library, computer center. Online library available.

Student life. Freshman orientation: Mandatory. **Activities:** Bands, choral groups, dance, drama, literary magazine, music ensembles, musical theater, radio station, student government, student newspaper, symphony orchestra, TV station, Abundant Life Christian Fellowship, Afghan Students Association, Asian Pacific Islanders Club, Chinese Culture Club, Muslim Student Association, Alpha Gamma Sigma Honor Society, Ohlone Women Engineers and Physical Scientists, Theater and Dance Alliance.

Athletics. Intercollegiate: Baseball M, basketball, soccer, softball W, swimming, volleyball, water polo. **Team name:** Renegades.

Student services. Adult student services, career counseling, services for economically disadvantaged, student employment services, financial aid counseling, health services, on-campus daycare, personal counseling, placement for graduates, veterans' counselor. **Physically disabled:** Services for visually, hearing impaired. **Transfer:** Special adviser, orientation, pre-admission transcript evaluation for new students. Transfer center, transfer adviser, college fairs on campus for students transferring to 4-year colleges.

Contact. E-mail: registration@ohlone.cc.ca.us
Phone: (510) 659-6100 Fax: (510) 659-7231
Kimberly Robbie, Dean of Enrollment Management, Ohlone College, 43600 Mission Boulevard, Fremont, CA 94539-0390

Orange Coast College
Costa Mesa, California
www.orangecoastcollege.edu **CB code: 4584**

- Public 2-year community college
- Commuter campus in small city

General. Founded in 1947. Regionally accredited. **Enrollment:** 17,411 degree-seeking undergraduates; 5,783 non-degree-seeking students. **Degrees:** 1,320 associate awarded. **Location:** 40 miles from Los Angeles. **Calendar:** Semester, extensive summer session. **Full-time faculty:** 298 total; 21% have terminal degrees, 16% minority, 49% women. **Part-time faculty:** 642 total; 17% minority, 47% women. **Class size:** 28% < 20, 51% 20-39, 11% 40-49, 7% 50-99, 4% >100. **Special facilities:** Planetarium, plastination lab, sailing academy, international center.

Student profile. Among degree-seeking undergraduates, 3,037 enrolled as first-time, first-year students.

Part-time:	53%	**Hispanic American:**	18%
Out-of-state:	2%	**Native American:**	1%
Women:	51%	**International:**	2%
African American:	2%	**25 or older:**	30%
Asian American:	26%		

Transfer out. Colleges most students transferred to 2005: University of California at Irvine, California State University at Fullerton, California State University at Long Beach.

Basis for selection. Open admission.

2005-2006 Annual costs. Tuition/fees: $806; $5,366 out-of-state. Per-credit charge: $26 in-state; $178 out-of-state. Books/supplies: $1,287. Personal expenses: $2,700.

2005-2006 Financial aid. Need-based: 76% of total undergraduate aid awarded as scholarships/grants, 24% as loans/jobs. Need-based aid available for part-time students. Work study available for part-time students. **Non-need-based:** Scholarships awarded for academics.

Application procedures. Admission: No deadline. No application fee. Admission notification on a rolling basis. Admission opens first working day in April for fall semester, first working day in October for spring semester; dates establish registration priority. **Financial aid:** Priority date 3/2, closing date 5/31. FAFSA, institutional form required. Applicants notified on a rolling basis; must reply within 2 week(s) of notification.

Academics. Special study options: Cooperative education, cross-registration, distance learning, ESL, honors, independent study, internships, liberal arts/career combination, student-designed major, study abroad, weekend college. License preparation in aviation, radiology, real estate. **Credit/placement by examination:** AP, CLEP, institutional tests. 12 credit hours maximum toward associate degree. **Support services:** Learning center, pre-admission summer program, reduced course load, remedial instruction, study skills assistance, tutoring, writing center.

Honors college/program. Students complete a minimum of 18 units in honors courses for program certification.

Majors. Agriculture: Ornamental horticulture. **Biology:** General, ecology. **Business:** General, accounting, administrative services, fashion, hospitality/recreation, international, management information systems, office technology, office/clerical. **Communications:** Advertising, broadcast journalism. **Computer sciences:** General, computer graphics, data entry, information systems. **Construction:** Maintenance, pipefitting, power transmission. **Education:** Early childhood. **Engineering technology:** Architectural, drafting, electrical. **English:** Speech/rhetoric, technical writing. **Family/consumer sciences:** General, child care, food/nutrition. **Foreign languages:** French, German, Italian, Japanese, Spanish. **Health:** Athletic training, cardiovascular technology, dental assistant, electroencephalograph technology, medical assistant, medical radiologic technology/radiation therapy, medical records technology, respiratory therapy technology, sonography. **History:** General. **Liberal arts:** Arts/sciences. **Math:** General. **Mechanic/repair:** Aircraft, electronics/electrical, heating/ac/refrig. **Parks/recreation:** Exercise sciences. **Personal/culinary services:** Culinary arts. **Philosophy/religion:** Philosophy, religion. **Physical sciences:** Astronomy, chemistry, geology, physics. **Psychology:** General. **Social sciences:** Anthropology, economics, geography, political science, sociology. **Transportation:** Aviation, flight attendant. **Visual/performing arts:** Art, cinematography, commercial/advertising art, dance, dramatic, fashion design, film/cinema, interior design, photography, studio arts.

Computing on campus. 1,500 workstations in library, computer center. Wireless network available.

Student life. Freshman orientation: Available. 3-hour sessions given year round. **Activities:** Bands, choral groups, dance, drama, film society, music ensembles, musical theater, student government, student newspaper, symphony orchestra, Buddhists Crusade for Christ, Christian Fellowship, COPTIC, Hillel.

Athletics. Intercollegiate: Badminton W, baseball M, basketball, cross-country, diving, football (tackle) M, golf, rowing (crew), soccer, softball W, swimming, tennis, track and field, volleyball, water polo. **Team name:** Pirates.

Student services. Adult student services, alcohol/substance abuse counseling, career counseling, services for economically disadvantaged, student employment services, financial aid counseling, health services, minority student services, on-campus daycare, personal counseling, placement for graduates, veterans' counselor. **Physically disabled:** Services for visually, speech, hearing impaired. **Learning disabled:** Comprehensive services available. **Transfer:** Special adviser, orientation, re-entry adviser for new students. Transfer center, transfer adviser, college fairs on campus for students transferring to 4-year colleges.

Contact. E-mail: nkidder@cccd.edu
Phone: (714) 432-5072
Nancy Kidder, Dean of Enrollment Services, Orange Coast College, 2701 Fairview Road, Costa Mesa, CA 92628-5005

Oxnard College
Oxnard, California
www.oxnard.cc.ca.us **CB code: 4591**

- Public 2-year community college
- Small city

General. Founded in 1975. Regionally accredited. **Enrollment:** 3,799 degree-seeking undergraduates. **Degrees:** 511 associate awarded. **Location:** 60 miles from Los Angeles. **Calendar:** Semester, limited summer session. **Full-time faculty:** 85 total. **Part-time faculty:** 250 total.

Basis for selection. Open admission.

2005-2006 Annual costs. Tuition/fees: $818; $5,468 out-of-state. Per-credit charge: $26 in-state; $181 out-of-state. Books/supplies: $600. Personal expenses: $1,300.

Application procedures. Admission: No deadline. No application fee. Admission notification on a rolling basis. **Financial aid:** Priority date 7/1; no closing date. Applicants notified on a rolling basis; must reply within 2 week(s) of notification.

Academics. Special study options: Distance learning, dual enrollment of high school students, external degree, honors, independent study, study abroad. First 2 years of bilingual (English-Spanish) teacher preparatory program. **Credit/placement by examination:** CLEP, institutional tests. 12 credit hours maximum toward associate degree. **Support services:** Learning center, remedial instruction, tutoring.

Majors. Biology: Bacteriology, marine. **Computer sciences:** General. **Health:** Medical records admin. **Liberal arts:** Arts/sciences.

Student life. Activities: Jazz band, choral groups, drama, student government, student newspaper, TV station, veterans club, Mini Corps Club, Vietnamese Club, Latino Club, ceramics club, Black Student Union, international students club.

Athletics. Intercollegiate: Baseball M, basketball, cross-country, soccer, track and field.

Student services. Career counseling, student employment services, health services, on-campus daycare, personal counseling, veterans' counselor. **Physically disabled:** Services for visually, speech, hearing impaired. **Transfer:** Special adviser, orientation for new students. Transfer adviser, college fairs on campus for students transferring to 4-year colleges.

Contact. Phone: (805) 986-5810
Leo Orange, Dean of Student Services, Oxnard College, 4000 South Rose Avenue, Oxnard, CA 93033

Palo Verde College
Blythe, California
www.paloverde.edu **CB code: 4603**

- Public 2-year community college
- Commuter campus in large town

General. Founded in 1947. Regionally accredited. **Enrollment:** 1,027 degree-seeking undergraduates. **Degrees:** 111 associate awarded. **Location:** 160 miles from Riverside. **Calendar:** Semester. **Full-time faculty:** 37 total; 40% minority, 51% women. **Part-time faculty:** 94 total; 26% minority, 49% women.

Student profile. Among degree-seeking undergraduates, 3% already have a bachelor's degree or higher, 192 enrolled as first-time, first-year students, 81 transferred in from other institutions.

Part-time:	50%	**Women:**	38%
Out-of-state:	5%		

Transfer out. Colleges most students transferred to 2005: Coastline CC, College of the Desert, Mohave CC, Fresno Pacific College, Riverside CC.

Basis for selection. Open admission, but selective for some programs. Limited admission to nursing program.

2005-2006 Annual costs. Tuition/fees: $780; $5,310 out-of-state. Per-credit charge: $26 in-state; $177 out-of-state. Books/supplies: $1,260. Personal expenses: $2,000.

2004-2005 Financial aid. All financial aid based on need. 98% of total undergraduate aid awarded as scholarships/grants, 2% as loans/jobs. Need-based aid available for part-time students. Work study available nights and for part-time students.

Application procedures. Admission: No deadline. No application fee. Application must be submitted on paper. Admission notification on a rolling basis. SAT or ACT recommended for placement. **Financial aid:** No deadline. FAFSA, institutional form required. Applicants notified on a rolling basis starting 7/1; must reply within 4 week(s) of notification.

Academics. Special study options: Cooperative education, distance learning, dual enrollment of high school students, ESL, independent study. **Credit/placement by examination:** AP, CLEP, institutional tests. 12 credit hours maximum toward associate degree. **Support services:** GED test center, learning center, remedial instruction, study skills assistance, tutoring, writing center.

Majors. Agriculture: General. **Business:** Accounting, business admin, office/clerical, real estate. **History:** General. **Liberal arts:** Arts/sciences. **Mechanic/repair:** Automotive. **Protective services:** Firefighting, law enforcement admin.

Most popular majors. Business/marketing 17%, liberal arts 79%.

Computing on campus. 125 workstations in library, computer center.

Student life. Freshman orientation: Mandatory. Preregistration for classes offered. **Activities:** Literary magazine, student government.

Athletics. Intramural: Soccer.

Student services. Career counseling, services for economically disadvantaged, student employment services, financial aid counseling, personal counseling, placement for graduates. **Physically disabled:** Services for visually, speech, hearing impaired. **Transfer:** Special adviser, orientation for new students. Transfer center, transfer adviser, college fairs on campus for students transferring to 4-year colleges.

Contact. E-mail: mwalnoha@paloverde.edu
Phone: (760) 921-5500
Melinda Walnoha, Registrar, Palo Verde College, One College Drive, Blythe, CA 92225

Palomar College

San Marcos, California
www.palomar.edu **CB code: 4602**

- Public 2-year community college
- Commuter campus in large town

General. Founded in 1946. Regionally accredited. Off-campus sites located throughout North County area. **Enrollment:** 14,693 degree-seeking undergraduates. **Degrees:** 1,189 associate awarded. **Location:** 40 miles from San Diego. **Calendar:** Semester, limited summer session. **Full-time faculty:** 300 total. **Part-time faculty:** 960 total. **Special facilities:** Nature preserve, observatory.

Basis for selection. Open admission, but selective for some programs. ASSET mathematics and English tests required for nursing applicants.

2005-2006 Annual costs. Tuition/fees: $814; $5,344 out-of-state. Per-credit charge: $26 in-state; $177 out-of-state. Books/supplies: $648. Personal expenses: $1,620.

Financial aid. All financial aid based on need. Need-based aid available for part-time students. Work study available nights and for part-time students.

Application procedures. Admission: Priority date 3/12; deadline 8/25. No application fee. Application may be submitted online. Admission notification on a rolling basis. Application deadlines for nursing program April 1 for fall semester, November 1 for spring semester. **Financial aid:** Priority date 4/1; no closing date. FAFSA, institutional form required. Applicants notified on a rolling basis starting 6/1.

Academics. Special study options: Cooperative education, distance learning, dual enrollment of high school students, ESL, internships, liberal arts/career combination, study abroad, weekend college. **Credit/placement by examination:** CLEP, institutional tests. 15 credit hours maximum toward associate degree. **Support services:** Learning center, pre-admission summer program, reduced course load, remedial instruction, tutoring.

Majors. Biology: General, zoology. **Business:** General, accounting, administrative services, banking/financial services, business admin, fashion, international, management science, office/clerical, operations, real estate, tourism promotion. **Communications:** Advertising, journalism. **Communications technology:** General, graphic/printing. **Computer sciences:** General, computer science, information systems. **Construction:** Carpentry, maintenance, masonry, pipefitting, power transmission. **Education:** Early childhood. **Engineering:** General. **Engineering technology:** Drafting, surveying. **English:** Speech/rhetoric. **Family/consumer sciences:** Child care, institutional food production. **Foreign languages:** Sign language interpretation. **Health:** Dental assistant, EMT paramedic, medical assistant, medical records admin, medical secretary, nursing (RN). **Legal studies:** Legal secretary, paralegal. **Liberal arts:** Arts/sciences, library science. **Math:** General. **Mechanic/repair:** General, auto body, diesel, electronics/electrical. **Parks/recreation:** General, facilities management, health/fitness. **Physical sciences:** Astronomy, chemistry, geology. **Production:** Woodworking. **Protective services:** Firefighting, law enforcement admin, police science, security services. **Public administration:** General. **Social sciences:** Archaeology, economics. **Transportation:** Aviation. **Visual/performing arts:** Art, ceramics, commercial/advertising art, crafts, dance, dramatic, fashion design, film/cinema, interior design, metal/jewelry, painting, photography, printmaking, sculpture.

Most popular majors. Health sciences 7%, liberal arts 76%, trade and industry 6%.

Computing on campus. 922 workstations in library, computer center, student center. Online library available.

Student life. Freshman orientation: Available. **Activities:** Bands, choral groups, dance, drama, literary magazine, music ensembles, musical theater, radio station, student government, student newspaper, symphony orchestra, TV station.

Athletics. NJCAA. **Intercollegiate:** Baseball M, basketball, football (tackle) M, golf M, soccer, softball W, swimming, tennis, volleyball, water polo M, wrestling M. **Intramural:** Volleyball W. **Team name:** Comets.

Student services. Career counseling, student employment services, financial aid counseling, health services, on-campus daycare, personal counseling, placement for graduates, veterans' counselor. **Physically disabled:** Services for visually, speech, hearing impaired. **Transfer:** Special adviser, orientation for new students. Transfer center, transfer adviser, college fairs on campus for students transferring to 4-year colleges.

Contact. E-mail: admissions@palomar.edu
Phone: (760) 744-1150 ext. 2160 Fax: (760) 761-3536
Herman Lee, Director of Enrollment Services, Palomar College, 1140 West Mission Road, San Marcos, CA 92069

Pasadena City College

Pasadena, California
www.pasadena.edu **CB code: 4604**

- Public 2-year community college
- Commuter campus in small city

General. Founded in 1924. Regionally accredited. **Enrollment:** 24,516 undergraduates. **Degrees:** 1,844 associate awarded. **Location:** 10 miles from downtown Los Angeles. **Calendar:** Semester, limited summer session. **Full-time faculty:** 320 total; 30% have terminal degrees. **Part-time faculty:** 740 total; 14% have terminal degrees. **Class size:** 6% < 20, 66% 20-39, 25% 40-49, 2% 50-99, 1% >100. **Special facilities:** Observatory.

Student profile.

Out-of-state:	3%	**25 or older:**	36%

Transfer out. Colleges most students transferred to 2005: California State University: Los Angeles, Long Beach, Northridge; California State Polytechnic Institute: Pomona.

Basis for selection. Open admission, but selective for some programs. Admission to RN, LVN, dental hygiene programs based on test scores, interview, high school record; minimum 2.0 high school GPA required. School and College Ability Tests, SAT, ACT, or California Achievement Test scores used for admission to some programs. Interview required of dental hygiene majors. Audition required of music majors.

2005-2006 Annual costs. Tuition/fees: $808; $5,338 out-of-state. Per-credit charge: $26 in-state; $177 out-of-state. Books/supplies: $860. Personal expenses: $1,719.

Financial aid. All financial aid based on need.

Application procedures. Admission: Closing date 8/11. No application fee. Admission notification on a rolling basis beginning on or about 3/1. **Financial aid:** Priority date 5/13; no closing date. FAFSA required. Applicants notified on a rolling basis starting 6/1; must reply within 2 week(s) of notification.

Academics. Special study options: Accelerated study, distance learning, dual enrollment of high school students, honors, independent study, internships, liberal arts/career combination, study abroad. **Credit/placement by examination:** CLEP, institutional tests. 12 credit hours maximum toward associate degree. **Support services:** Learning center, pre-admission summer program, reduced course load, remedial instruction, study skills assistance, tutoring, writing center.

Majors. Biology: General. **Business:** General, accounting, administrative services, banking/financial services, entrepreneurial studies, fashion, hospitality/recreation, management information systems, office/clerical, real estate, sales/distribution, tourism promotion. **Communications:** General, broadcast journalism, journalism. **Communications technology:** General. **Computer sciences:** Applications programming, data processing, programming. **Construction:** Carpentry, maintenance. **Education:** Early childhood. **Engineering technology:** Drafting. **English:** Speech/rhetoric. **Health:** Clinical lab technology, dental assistant, dental hygiene, dental lab technology, licensed practical nurse, medical assistant, medical radiologic technology/radiation therapy, medical secretary, nursing (RN). **Legal studies:** Legal secretary, paralegal. **Liberal arts:** Arts/sciences, library assistant. **Mechanic/repair:**

Auto body. **Parks/recreation:** General. **Protective services:** Firefighting, police science. **Psychology:** General. **Social sciences:** General. **Visual/performing arts:** Ceramics, commercial photography, commercial/advertising art, crafts, drawing, painting, printmaking, sculpture, studio arts.

Computing on campus. 300 workstations in computer center, student center.

Student life. **Freshman orientation:** Available. **Activities:** Bands, choral groups, dance, drama, film society, literary magazine, music ensembles, musical theater, radio station, student government, student newspaper, symphony orchestra, TV station, wide variety of religious, political, ethnic, and social service organizations.

Athletics. **Intercollegiate:** Badminton W, baseball M, basketball, cross-country, football (tackle) M, soccer, softball W, swimming, tennis W, track and field, volleyball W, water polo W. **Team name:** Lancers.

Student services. Career counseling, student employment services, health services, personal counseling, placement for graduates. **Physically disabled:** Services for visually, speech, hearing impaired. **Transfer:** Orientation for new students. Transfer center, transfer adviser, college fairs on campus for students transferring to 4-year colleges.

Contact. Phone: (626) 578-7396 Fax: (626) 585-7912
Margaret Ramey, Associate Dean of Admissions and Records, Pasadena City College, 1570 East Colorado Boulevard, Pasadena, CA 91106

Platt College: Cerritos

Cerritos, California
www.westerncollegesocal.com **CB code: 3007**

- For-profit 2-year visual arts and business college
- Commuter campus in very large city
- Application essay, interview required

General. Accredited by ACCSCT. Year-round program with starts every 8 weeks. **Enrollment:** 150 degree-seeking undergraduates. **Degrees:** 73 associate awarded. **Calendar:** Continuous. **Full-time faculty:** 3 total. **Part-time faculty:** 19 total. **Class size:** 67% < 20, 33% 20-39.

Basis for selection. High school diploma or GED and successful completion of Wonderlic Testing required.

2006-2007 Annual costs. $18,000 for 18-month Paralegal program; $12,000 for Massage Therapy program. Books/supplies: $584.

Financial aid. All financial aid based on need.

Application procedures. **Admission:** No deadline. $75 fee. Admission notification on a rolling basis. **Financial aid:** FAFSA, institutional form required.

Academics. **Special study options:** Accelerated study, internships. **Credit/placement by examination:** CLEP, IB. **Support services:** Tutoring.

Majors. **Business:** General, office/clerical. **Computer sciences:** Computer graphics. **English:** Composition. **Legal studies:** General, paralegal. **Psychology:** General. **Visual/performing arts:** General, art, art history/conservation, commercial/advertising art.

Computing on campus. 50 workstations in library, computer center.

Student services. Financial aid counseling, placement for graduates. **Transfer:** Orientation, pre-admission transcript evaluation for new students.

Contact. Phone: (562) 809-5100 Toll-free number: (800) 807-5288
Fax: (562) 809-7100
Jameela Woods, Admissions Director, Platt College: Cerritos, 10900 East 183rd Street, Suite 290, Cerritos, CA 90703-5342

Platt College: Los Angeles

Alhambra, California
www.plattcollege.edu **CB code: 3014**

- For-profit 2-year visual arts and technical college
- Commuter campus in very large city
- Application essay, interview required

General. Accredited by ACCSCT. **Enrollment:** 125 degree-seeking undergraduates. **Degrees:** 9 bachelor's, 96 associate awarded. **Calendar:** Continuous. **Full-time faculty:** 24 total. **Class size:** 85% < 20, 15% 20-39.

Transfer out. **Colleges most students transferred to 2005:** University of LaVerne, University of Phoenix.

Basis for selection. Must score at least 126 on CPAT for admissions. Multimedia program requires degree. MCSE program requires computer background. CPAT examination used. **Adult students:** Entrance exam policies same as for first-time freshmen. **Learning Disabled:** Students with learning disabilities allowed 30 extra minutes on CPAT examination.

2006-2007 Annual costs. Varies by program: associate degree cost range $26,780 (paralegal) to $28,370 (information technology).

Financial aid. **Need-based:** Need-based aid available for part-time students. Work study available nights.

Application procedures. **Admission:** No deadline. $75 fee. Application may be submitted online. Admission notification on a rolling basis. **Financial aid:** Priority date 3/2; no closing date. FAFSA, institutional form required. Applicants notified on a rolling basis starting 1/1.

Academics. **Special study options:** Accelerated study, cooperative education, internships. Bachelor's degree programs available on campus. **Credit/placement by examination:** CLEP, institutional tests. 48 credit hours maximum toward associate degree. **Support services:** Tutoring.

Majors. **Computer sciences:** General, computer graphics. **Visual/performing arts:** General, commercial/advertising art.

Computing on campus. 10 workstations in library.

Student life. **Freshman orientation:** Mandatory. Preregistration for classes offered. 2-hour program on or around first day of classes. **Policies:** Freshmen permitted cars on campus.

Student services. Adult student services, career counseling, student employment services, financial aid counseling, placement for graduates. **Transfer:** Special adviser, orientation, re-entry adviser, pre-admission transcript evaluation for new students. Transfer adviser for students transferring to 4-year colleges.

Contact. Phone: (626) 300-5444 Toll-free number: (866) 752-8852
Fax: (626) 300-3978
Admissions Director, Platt College: Los Angeles, 1000 South Fremont Avenue A9W, Alhambra, CA 91803

Platt College: Newport Beach

Huntington Beach, California
www.plattcollege.edu **CB code: 3004**

- For-profit 2-year visual arts and technical college
- Commuter campus in large city
- Application essay, interview required

General. Accredited by ACCSCT. **Enrollment:** 122 degree-seeking undergraduates. **Degrees:** 95 associate awarded. **Calendar:** Continuous. **Full-time faculty:** 10 total. **Part-time faculty:** 15 total. **Class size:** 86% < 20, 14% 20-39.

Basis for selection. Standardized test scores, essay, interview most important. Talent, personal qualities, work experience may also be admissions criteria. **Adult students:** Entrance exam policies same as for first-time freshmen.

2005-2006 Annual costs. Full academic program tuition ranges from $8,300 to $22,000.

Financial aid. **Need-based:** Need-based aid available for part-time students. Work study available nights.

Application procedures. **Admission:** No deadline. $75 fee. Admission notification on a rolling basis. **Financial aid:** Priority date 3/2; no closing date. FAFSA, institutional form required. Applicants notified on a rolling basis starting 1/1.

Academics. **Special study options:** Accelerated study, cooperative education, internships. **Credit/placement by examination:** CLEP, institutional tests. 48 credit hours maximum toward associate degree. **Support services:** Tutoring.

Majors. **Computer sciences:** Computer graphics, information technology. **Visual/performing arts:** General, commercial/advertising art.

Most popular majors. Computer/information sciences 22%, visual/performing arts 78%.

Computing on campus. 10 workstations in library.

Student life. Freshman orientation: Mandatory. Preregistration for classes offered. Two-hour orientation held on or around first day of classes. **Policies:** Freshmen permitted cars on campus.

Student services. Adult student services, career counseling, student employment services, financial aid counseling, placement for graduates. **Transfer:** Special adviser, orientation, re-entry adviser, pre-admission transcript evaluation for new students. Transfer adviser for students transferring to 4-year colleges.

Contact. Phone: (949) 833-2300 Toll-free number: (866) 752-8848
Fax: (949) 833-0269
Tyka Burton, Platt College: Newport Beach, 7755 Center Avenue, Suite 400, Huntington Beach, CA 92647

Porterville College
Porterville, California
www.portervillecollege.edu **CB code: 4608**

- Public 2-year community college
- Commuter campus in large town

General. Founded in 1927. Regionally accredited. **Enrollment:** 1,795 full-time, degree-seeking students. **Degrees:** 248 associate awarded. **Location:** 75 miles from Fresno, 50 miles from Bakersfield. **Calendar:** Semester, limited summer session. **Full-time faculty:** 81 total. **Part-time faculty:** 151 total.

Basis for selection. Open admission.

2005-2006 Annual costs. Tuition/fees: $818; $5,768 out-of-state. Per-credit charge: $26 in-state; $191 out-of-state. Books/supplies: $882. Personal expenses: $1,656.

Application procedures. Admission: No deadline. No application fee. Admission notification on a rolling basis. **Financial aid:** Priority date 3/1; no closing date. FAFSA required. Applicants notified on a rolling basis; must reply within 2 week(s) of notification.

Academics. Special study options: Double major, dual enrollment of high school students. **Credit/placement by examination:** CLEP, institutional tests. 30 credit hours maximum toward associate degree. **Support services:** Learning center, reduced course load, remedial instruction, tutoring.

Majors. Biology: General. **Business:** General, administrative services, banking/financial services, business admin, office/clerical, real estate. **Computer sciences:** General. **Construction:** Carpentry. **Education:** General. **Engineering technology:** Drafting. **Family/consumer sciences:** Child care. **Health:** Licensed practical nurse. **Interdisciplinary:** Biological/physical sciences. **Liberal arts:** Arts/sciences. **Math:** General. **Mechanic/repair:** Auto body. **Physical sciences:** Chemistry. **Protective services:** Police science. **Social sciences:** General, criminology. **Visual/performing arts:** General, commercial/advertising art, studio arts.

Computing on campus. 25 workstations in library, computer center.

Student life. Activities: Choral groups, drama, music ensembles, musical theater, student government, Mexican-American Student Association.

Athletics. NJCAA. **Intercollegiate:** Baseball M, basketball, tennis, volleyball W.

Student services. Career counseling, student employment services, health services, on-campus daycare, personal counseling, placement for graduates, veterans' counselor. **Physically disabled:** Services for visually, speech, hearing impaired. **Transfer:** Special adviser, orientation for new students. Transfer adviser for students transferring to 4-year colleges.

Contact. Phone: (209) 791-2220 Fax: (209) 784-4779
Virginia Gurrola, Vice President Student Services and Enrollment, Porterville College, 100 East College Avenue, Porterville, CA 93257

Professional Golfers Career College
Temecula, California
www.progolfed.com **CB code: 3548**

- For-profit 2-year golf course academy
- Large town

General. Accredited by ACICS. **Enrollment:** 160 degree-seeking undergraduates. **Degrees:** 96 associate awarded. **Calendar:** Semester. **Part-time faculty:** 26 total.

Basis for selection. Handicap of 20 or below, 3 letters of personal character reference, 1 letter of recommendation attesting to golf ability required.

2006-2007 Annual costs. Tuition $4,910/semester; program lasts 4 semesters. Books/supplies: $600.

Application procedures. Admission: No deadline. $75 fee. Admission notification on a rolling basis.

Academics. Credit/placement by examination: CLEP.

Majors. Parks/recreation: Facilities management.

Contact. E-mail: admissions@progolfed.com
Phone: (951) 719-2994 Toll-free number: (800) 877-4380
Fax: (951) 693-2863
Arnold Maravilla, Admissions Director, Professional Golfers Career College, PO Box 892319, Temecula, CA 92591-2319

Queen of the Holy Rosary College
Fremont, California
www.msjdominicans.org/college.html **CB code: 0228**

- Private 2-year junior and seminary college affiliated with Roman Catholic Church
- Residential campus in small city
- Interview required

General. Founded in 1930. Regionally accredited. College dedicated to religious formation. Full-time students are members of Dominican Order or other candidates for religious life. **Enrollment:** 60 undergraduates. **Degrees:** 1 associate awarded. **Location:** 40 miles from San Francisco, 22 miles from San Jose. **Calendar:** Semester, limited summer session. **Full-time faculty:** 1 total. **Part-time faculty:** 6 total. **Class size:** 100% < 20.

Transfer out. Colleges most students transferred to 2005: California State University: Hayward, San Francisco City College.

Basis for selection. Interview and religious commitment very important, followed by essay and recommendations. SAT Subject Tests recommended. ESL testing required for all students whose first language is other than English.

High school preparation. 20 units recommended. Recommended units include English 3, mathematics 2, social studies 3, science 2, foreign language 2 and academic electives 8. Religion courses desirable.

2006-2007 Annual costs. Tuition/fees: $3,000. Per-credit charge: $100. Books/supplies: $150.

Financial aid. Additional information: Full-time students receive financial aid based on need.

Application procedures. Admission: Closing date 7/1 (postmark date). No application fee. Admission notification 8/1. **Financial aid:** No deadline.

Academics. Special emphasis on preparation of religious sisters for educational apostolate. **Special study options:** ESL. **Credit/placement by examination:** CLEP, institutional tests. **Support services:** Reduced course load, remedial instruction, study skills assistance, tutoring.

Majors. Philosophy/religion: Religion.

Computing on campus. 3 workstations in dormitories, library, student center. Dormitories linked to campus network. Online library, helpline available.

Student life. Freshman orientation: Available. Preregistration for classes offered. **Policies:** Religious observance required. **Housing:** Single-sex dorms available. College-affiliated housing available for candidates to religious life only. Full-time students live at convent. **Activities:** Choral groups.

Student services. Career counseling, health services, personal counseling, placement for graduates. **Transfer:** Special adviser, orientation, pre-admission transcript evaluation for new students. Transfer adviser for students transferring to 4-year colleges.

Contact. Phone: (510) 657-2468
Sr. Katherine Cowan, Dean, Queen of the Holy Rosary College, 43326 Mission Boulevard, Fremont, CA 94539

Reedley College
Reedley, California
www.reedleycollege.edu **CB code: 4655**

- Public 2-year community college
- Commuter campus in large town

General. Founded in 1926. Regionally accredited. Courses also offered at community campus sites in Madera, Clovis, Sanger, Easton, Selma, Kerman, Oakhurst, Parlier, Fowler, Orange Cove, Dinuba, Kingsburg, and Sunnyside. **Enrollment:** 4,812 degree-seeking undergraduates; 5,099 non-degree-seeking students. **Degrees:** 582 associate awarded. **Location:** 25 miles from Fresno. **Calendar:** Semester, extensive summer session. **Full-time faculty:** 80 total. **Part-time faculty:** 190 total.

Student profile. Among degree-seeking undergraduates, 980 enrolled as first-time, first-year students.

Part-time:	61%	**Hispanic American:**	47%
Women:	59%	**Native American:**	1%
African American:	3%	**25 or older:**	35%
Asian American:	4%	**Live on campus:**	4%

Transfer out. Colleges most students transferred to 2005: California State University: Fresno, California State University: Long Beach.

Basis for selection. Open admission. **Adult students:** Entrance exam policies same as for first-time freshmen. **Homeschooled:** If under 18, a letter from parent required.

2005-2006 Annual costs. Tuition/fees: $808; $5,338 out-of-state. Per-credit charge: $26 in-state; $177 out-of-state. Room/board: $4,520. Books/supplies: $1,260. Personal expenses: $1,550.

Financial aid. All financial aid based on need. Need-based aid available for part-time students. Work study available for part-time students. **Additional information:** Board of Governors fee waiver available for low-income students. Book voucher available for EOPS students.

Application procedures. Admission: No deadline. No application fee. Application may be submitted online. Admission notification on a rolling basis. **Financial aid:** Priority date 3/2; no closing date. FAFSA required. Applicants notified on a rolling basis starting 3/2; must reply within 3 week(s) of notification.

Academics. Special study options: Cooperative education, cross-registration, distance learning, double major, dual enrollment of high school students, ESL, honors, independent study, study abroad, weekend college. License preparation in aviation, dental hygiene. **Credit/placement by examination:** AP, CLEP. 48 credit hours maximum toward associate degree. **Support services:** Learning center, pre-admission summer program, reduced course load, remedial instruction, study skills assistance, tutoring, writing center.

Majors. Agriculture: Business, plant sciences. **Biology:** General. **Business:** Accounting. **Computer sciences:** General, computer science, information systems. **Conservation:** Forestry. **Education:** Early childhood, physical. **Foreign languages:** General. **Health:** Dental assistant. **Liberal arts:** Arts/sciences. **Math:** General. **Social sciences:** General. **Visual/performing arts:** Art, dramatic.

Most popular majors. Interdisciplinary studies 80%.

Computing on campus. 140 workstations in dormitories, library, computer center. Dormitories wired for high-speed internet access and linked to campus network. Commuter students can connect to campus network. Online course registration, online library available.

Student life. Freshman orientation: Available. Preregistration for classes offered. **Policies:** Freshmen permitted cars on campus. **Housing:** Single-sex dorms available. $125 deposit. **Activities:** Bands, choral groups, drama, music ensembles, musical theater, student government, student newspaper, symphony orchestra.

Athletics. NJCAA. **Intercollegiate:** Baseball M, basketball, equestrian, football (tackle) M, golf, softball W, tennis, track and field, volleyball W. **Team name:** Tigers.

Student services. Adult student services, alcohol/substance abuse counseling, career counseling, services for economically disadvantaged, student employment services, financial aid counseling, health services, minority student services, on-campus daycare, personal counseling, placement for graduates, veterans' counselor, women's services. **Physically disabled:** Services for visually, speech, hearing impaired. **Transfer:** Special adviser, orientation for new students. Transfer adviser, college fairs on campus for students transferring to 4-year colleges.

Contact. Phone: (559) 638-0323 Fax: (559) 638-5040
John Cummings, District Dean of Admissions and Records, Reedley College, 995 North Reed Avenue, Reedley, CA 93654

Rio Hondo College
Whittier, California
www.riohondo.edu **CB code: 4663**

- Public 2-year community college
- Commuter campus in small city

General. Founded in 1960. Regionally accredited. **Enrollment:** 4,754 full-time, degree-seeking students. **Degrees:** 736 associate awarded. **Location:** 15 miles from Los Angeles. **Calendar:** Semester, extensive summer session. **Full-time faculty:** 184 total; 40% minority, 47% women. **Part-time faculty:** 288 total; 36% minority, 46% women. **Special facilities:** Observatory.

Basis for selection. Open admission, but selective for some programs. Nursing program has special requirements.

2005-2006 Annual costs. Tuition/fees: $808; $4,528 out-of-state. Per-credit charge: $26 in-state; $150 out-of-state. Books/supplies: $1,206. Personal expenses: $2,250.

Application procedures. Admission: No deadline. No application fee. Admission notification on a rolling basis. **Financial aid:** Priority date 7/15; no closing date. FAFSA required. Applicants notified on a rolling basis.

Academics. Special study options: Dual enrollment of high school students, honors, independent study, study abroad, weekend college. **Credit/placement by examination:** CLEP, institutional tests. 12 credit hours maximum toward associate degree. **Support services:** Learning center, remedial instruction, tutoring.

Majors. Business: Accounting, administrative services, office/clerical, real estate. **Communications technology:** General, graphic/printing. **Engineering technology:** Drafting. **Health:** Dental assistant, health services, licensed practical nurse, nursing (RN), respiratory therapy technology. **Liberal arts:** Arts/sciences, library assistant. **Mechanic/repair:** Automotive. **Protective services:** Fire safety technology, police science.

Student life. Activities: Jazz band, choral groups, dance, drama, film society, literary magazine, music ensembles, musical theater, radio station, student government, student newspaper, TV station.

Athletics. NJCAA. **Intercollegiate:** Baseball M, basketball, diving, golf, softball W, swimming, tennis, volleyball W, water polo, wrestling M.

Student services. Career counseling, student employment services, health services, on-campus daycare, personal counseling, veterans' counselor. **Physically disabled:** Services for visually, speech, hearing impaired.

Contact. Phone: (562) 908-3415 Fax: (562) 692-8318
Mary Becerril, Supervisor of Admissions and Records, Rio Hondo College, 3600 Workman Mill Road, Whittier, CA 90601-1699

Riverside Community College
Riverside, California
www.rcc.edu **CB member**
CB code: 4658

- Public 2-year community college
- Commuter campus in large city

General. Founded in 1916. Regionally accredited. **Enrollment:** 32,228 undergraduates. **Degrees:** 2,133 associate awarded. **ROTC:** Army, Navy, Air Force. **Location:** 60 miles from Los Angeles. **Calendar:** Semester, limited summer session. **Full-time faculty:** 231 total; 29% minority, 52% women. **Part-time faculty:** 1,145 total; 26% minority, 43% women. **Class size:** 34% < 20, 53% 20-39, 8% 40-49, 5% 50-99. **Special facilities:** Planetarium.

Student profile.

Out-of-state:	1%	**25 or older:**	40%

Transfer out. Colleges most students transferred to 2005: University of California: Riverside, California State University: San Bernardino.

Basis for selection. Open admission, but selective for some programs. Limited admission to nursing programs.

2005-2006 Annual costs. Tuition/fees: $820; $5,350 out-of-state. Per-credit charge: $26 in-state; $177 out-of-state. Books/supplies: $1,224. Personal expenses: $2,286.

2004-2005 Financial aid. Need-based: 88% of total undergraduate aid awarded as scholarships/grants, 12% as loans/jobs. Need-based aid available for part-time students. Work study available nights, weekends and for part-time students. **Non-need-based:** Scholarships awarded for academics, alumni affiliation, art, leadership, minority status, music/drama, state residency.

Application procedures. Admission: No deadline. No application fee. Application may be submitted online. Admission notification on a rolling basis. **Financial aid:** Priority date 3/2; no closing date. FAFSA, institutional form required. Applicants notified on a rolling basis starting 7/1.

Academics. Honor Society (Alpha Gamma Sigma) for freshmen with 3.0 GPA. **Special study options:** Cooperative education, distance learning, double major, dual enrollment of high school students, ESL, honors, internships, study abroad, weekend college. License preparation in nursing. **Credit/placement by examination:** AP, CLEP, institutional tests. 30 credit hours maximum toward associate degree. **Support services:** GED preparation, learning center, remedial instruction, tutoring, writing center.

Majors. Business: General, accounting, administrative services, business admin, marketing, office technology, real estate. **Communications technology:** Graphic/printing. **Computer sciences:** General, programming. **Construction:** Maintenance. **Education:** Early childhood. **Engineering:** General. **Engineering technology:** Construction, drafting, electrical. **Family/consumer sciences:** General, food/nutrition. **Foreign languages:** Sign language interpretation. **Health:** Dental lab technology, licensed practical nurse, medical assistant, medical secretary, medical transcription, nursing (RN). **Legal studies:** Legal secretary. **Mechanic/repair:** General, auto body, automotive, heating/ac/refrig. **Personal/culinary services:** Cosmetic. **Protective services:** Fire safety technology. **Public administration:** Human services. **Social sciences:** Cartography. **Visual/performing arts:** Commercial/advertising art, photography.

Computing on campus. 200 workstations in library, computer center. Online library, helpline, repair service available.

Student life. Freshman orientation: Available. **Activities:** Bands, choral groups, dance, drama, literary magazine, music ensembles, musical theater, student government, student newspaper, College Democrats, MECHA, Latter Day Saints Student Association, Multicultural Advisory Council, African American Student Union.

Athletics. Intercollegiate: Baseball M, basketball, cross-country, diving, football (tackle) M, golf, soccer, softball W, swimming, tennis, track and field, volleyball W, water polo. **Intramural:** Badminton, baseball M, basketball, bowling, golf, racquetball, soccer, tennis, volleyball. **Team name:** Tigers.

Student services. Adult student services, career counseling, services for economically disadvantaged, student employment services, financial aid counseling, health services, on-campus daycare, personal counseling, placement for graduates, veterans' counselor. **Physically disabled:** Services for visually, speech, hearing impaired. **Transfer:** Special adviser for new students. Transfer center, transfer adviser, college fairs on campus for students transferring to 4-year colleges.

Contact. E-mail: webmstr@rcc.edu
Phone: (951) 222-8600 Fax: (951) 222-8028
Lorraine Anderson, District Dean, Admissions and Records, Riverside Community College, 4800 Magnolia Avenue, Riverside, CA 92506

Sacramento City College

Sacramento, California
www.scc.losrios.edu **CB code: 4670**

- Public 2-year community college
- Commuter campus in large city

General. Founded in 1916. Regionally accredited. **Enrollment:** 13,710 degree-seeking undergraduates. **Degrees:** 2,774 associate awarded. **ROTC:** Army, Navy, Air Force. **Location:** 75 miles from San Francisco. **Calendar:** Semester, extensive summer session. **Full-time faculty:** 286 total. **Part-time faculty:** 138 total. **Special facilities:** Observatory, theater.

Student profile.

Out-of-state:	5%	**25 or older:**	68%

Basis for selection. Open admission.

2005-2006 Annual costs. Tuition/fees: $812; $5,342 out-of-state. Per-credit charge: $26 in-state; $177 out-of-state. Books/supplies: $1,260. Personal expenses: $1,376.

Financial aid. Need-based: Need-based aid available for part-time students. Work study available nights, weekends and for part-time students.

Application procedures. Admission: Priority date 7/28; no deadline. No application fee. Admission notification on a rolling basis. **Financial aid:** Priority date 3/2; no closing date. FAFSA required. Applicants notified on a rolling basis starting 7/1; must reply within 2 week(s) of notification.

Academics. Special study options: Accelerated study, cooperative education, cross-registration, distance learning, double major, dual enrollment of high school students, ESL, honors, independent study, internships, study abroad, weekend college. License preparation in aviation, dental hygiene, nursing, physical therapy, real estate. **Credit/placement by examination:** CLEP, institutional tests. 15 credit hours maximum toward associate degree. **Support services:** Learning center, remedial instruction, study skills assistance, tutoring, writing center.

Majors. Area/ethnic studies: Women's. **Business:** General, accounting, administrative services, international marketing, management information systems, office/clerical, real estate. **Communications:** Journalism. **Communications technology:** Graphic/printing. **Computer sciences:** General. **Education:** Bilingual, special. **Engineering technology:** Drafting. **Family/consumer sciences:** General, child care, clothing/textiles, family/community services. **Health:** Dental assistant, dental hygiene, licensed practical nurse, medical secretary, nursing (RN), occupational therapy assistant, physical therapy assistant. **Legal studies:** Legal secretary. **Liberal arts:** Arts/sciences, library assistant. **Math:** General. **Mechanic/repair:** Aircraft, electronics/electrical, heating/ac/refrig. **Personal/culinary services:** Cosmetic. **Protective services:** Corrections, police science. **Social sciences:** General. **Visual/performing arts:** General, commercial photography, dramatic, music management, studio arts.

Computing on campus. 350 workstations in library, computer center. Online course registration available.

Student life. Freshman orientation: Available. **Activities:** Bands, choral groups, dance, drama, literary magazine, music ensembles, musical theater, student government, student newspaper, minority groups, professional associations, Bible club, gay and lesbian student alliance, special interest groups.

Athletics. Intercollegiate: Baseball M, basketball, cross-country, football (tackle) M, golf W, soccer W, softball W, swimming, tennis, track and field, volleyball W, water polo W, wrestling M. **Intramural:** Badminton, baseball M, basketball, bowling, boxing M, fencing, football (tackle) M, golf, handball, racquetball, softball, swimming, table tennis, tennis, volleyball. **Team name:** Panthers.

Student services. Adult student services, career counseling, services for economically disadvantaged, student employment services, financial aid counseling, health services, on-campus daycare, personal counseling, placement for graduates, veterans' counselor. **Physically disabled:** Services for visually, speech, hearing impaired. **Transfer:** Special adviser for new students. Transfer center, transfer adviser, college fairs on campus for students transferring to 4-year colleges.

Contact. E-mail: sccaeinfo@scc.losrios.edu
Phone: (916) 558-2351 Fax: (916) 558-2190
Sam Sandusky, Dean of Admissions, Sacramento City College, 3835 Freeport Boulevard, Sacramento, CA 95822

Saddleback College

Mission Viejo, California
www.saddleback.edu **CB code: 4747**

- Public 2-year community college
- Commuter campus in small city

General. Founded in 1967. Regionally accredited. **Enrollment:** 9,879 degree-seeking undergraduates. **Degrees:** 805 associate awarded. **Location:** 55 miles from Los Angeles and San Diego. **Calendar:** Semester, limited summer session. **Full-time faculty:** 214 total. **Part-time faculty:** 565 total. **Special facilities:** Solar observatory, theaters, Olympic-size pool, outdoor environmental laboratory, golf driving range, computer/technology centers, greenhouse.

Student profile. Among degree-seeking undergraduates, 500 transferred in from other institutions.

Basis for selection. Open admission, but selective for some programs. Nursing candidates must complete core curriculum with 2.0 GPA or better before screening process. SAT/ACT recommended for placement and counseling.

High school preparation. 10 units recommended. Recommended units include English 3, mathematics 2, social studies 3 and science 2.

2005-2006 Annual costs. Tuition/fees: $806; $5,336 out-of-state. Per-credit charge: $26 in-state; $177 out-of-state. Books/supplies: $1,260. Personal expenses: $3,708.

Financial aid. All financial aid based on need. Need-based aid available for part-time students.

Application procedures. Admission: Priority date 5/1; no deadline. No application fee. Application may be submitted online. Admission notification on a rolling basis. **Financial aid:** Closing date 5/1. FAFSA required. Applicants notified on a rolling basis; must reply within 2 week(s) of notification.

Academics. Special study options: Cooperative education, cross-registration, distance learning, double major, dual enrollment of high school students, ESL, honors, independent study, internships, student-designed major, study abroad, weekend college. License preparation in nursing, paramedic, real estate. **Credit/placement by examination:** CLEP, institutional tests. 30 credit hours maximum toward associate degree. **Support services:** Learning center, pre-admission summer program, reduced course load, remedial instruction, study skills assistance, tutoring, writing center.

Honors college/program. Overall GPA of 3.25 in all academic work required.

Majors. Agriculture: Ornamental horticulture. **Area/ethnic studies:** Women's. **Biology:** General. **Business:** General, accounting, administrative services, business admin, fashion, marketing, office management, real estate, tourism/travel. **Communications:** Broadcast journalism, journalism. **Computer sciences:** General, computer science, programming. **Conservation:** General, environmental studies. **Education:** Early childhood, family/consumer sciences, mathematics, music, physical, social science. **Engineering:** General. **Engineering technology:** Drafting. **English:** British lit, speech/rhetoric. **Family/consumer sciences:** General, food/nutrition. **Foreign languages:** General, sign language interpretation. **Health:** Medical assistant, nursing (RN), surgical technology. **History:** General. **Interdisciplinary:** Natural sciences. **Legal studies:** Legal secretary, paralegal. **Liberal arts:** Arts/sciences. **Math:** General. **Parks/recreation:** Health/fitness. **Philosophy/religion:** Philosophy. **Physical sciences:** Astronomy, chemistry, geology, physics. **Psychology:** General. **Social sciences:** General, anthropology, economics, geography, international relations, political science, sociology. **Visual/performing arts:** Art, commercial photography, commercial/advertising art, dance, design, dramatic, fashion design, interior design, photography, studio arts.

Most popular majors. Business/marketing 10%, health sciences 23%, liberal arts 43%.

Computing on campus. 253 workstations in library, computer center. Commuter students can connect to campus network.

Student life. Policies: Freshmen permitted cars on campus. **Activities:** Bands, choral groups, dance, drama, literary magazine, music ensembles, musical theater, radio station, student government, student newspaper, symphony orchestra, TV station, Democratic Club, Republican Club, Christian Club, Black United Students, Hillel, Gay and Lesbian Club, Amnesty International, Muslim Student Union, environmental awareness, sign language club.

Athletics. NJCAA. **Intercollegiate:** Baseball M, basketball, cross-country, diving, football (tackle) M, golf, soccer W, softball W, swimming, tennis, track and field, volleyball W, water polo. **Team name:** Gauchos.

Student services. Adult student services, alcohol/substance abuse counseling, career counseling, services for economically disadvantaged, student employment services, health services, on-campus daycare, personal counseling, placement for graduates, veterans' counselor, women's services. **Physically disabled:** Services for visually, speech, hearing impaired. **Transfer:** Special adviser, orientation, re-entry adviser for new students. Transfer center, transfer adviser, college fairs on campus for students transferring to 4-year colleges.

Contact. E-mail: scadmissions@saddleback.edu
Phone: (949) 582-4555 Fax: (949) 347-8315
Jane Rosenkrans, Director, Admissions, Records and Enrollment Services, Saddleback College, 28000 Marguerite Parkway, Mission Viejo, CA 92692

Sage College
Moreno Valley, California
www.sagecollege.edu

- For-profit 2-year technical college
- Large city

General. Accredited by ACICS. **Enrollment:** 392 degree-seeking undergraduates. **Calendar:** Quarter. **Full-time faculty:** 9 total. **Part-time faculty:** 15 total.

Basis for selection. Satisfactory performance on institutional examination required.

Application procedures. Admission: No deadline. $100 fee. Admission notification on a rolling basis.

Academics. Credit/placement by examination: CLEP.

Majors. Legal studies: Court reporting, paralegal.

Contact. E-mail: admissions@sagecollege.edu
Phone: (951) 781-2727
Lauren Somma, Executive Director, Sage College, 12125 Day Street, Building L, Moreno Valley, CA 92557-6720

Salvation Army Crestmont College
Rancho Palos Verdes, California
www.crestmont.edu **CB code: 3890**

- Private 2-year seminary college
- Small city

General. Regionally accredited. Christian education for Salvation Army officer candidates and others. Officers are ordained ministers who manage human service programs and ministries in western US and overseas. **Enrollment:** 27 degree-seeking undergraduates. **Degrees:** 24 associate awarded. **Calendar:** Semester. **Full-time faculty:** 23 total. **Part-time faculty:** 20 total. **Special facilities:** Salvation Army musuem.

2005-2006 Annual costs. Tuition/fees: $3,000.

Application procedures. Admission: No deadline. No application fee.

Academics. Credit/placement by examination: CLEP.

Majors. Theology: Missionary.

Contact. Phone: (310) 377-0481
Capt. Kevin Jackson, Director of Admissions, Salvation Army Crestmont College, 30840 Hawthorne Boulevard, Rancho Palos Verdes, CA 90275

San Bernardino Valley College
San Bernardino, California
www.valleycollege.edu **CB code: 4679**

- Public 2-year community college
- Small city

General. Founded in 1926. Regionally accredited. **Enrollment:** 3,582 full-time, degree-seeking students. **Degrees:** 716 associate awarded. **Location:** 60 miles from Los Angeles. **Calendar:** Semester, limited summer session. **Full-time faculty:** 225 total; 34% minority. **Part-time faculty:** 450 total; 37% minority. **Special facilities:** Planetarium.

Basis for selection. Open admission, but selective for some programs. Special requirements for nursing program. **Homeschooled:** Transcript of courses and grades required.

2005-2006 Annual costs. Tuition/fees: $818; $5,348 out-of-state. Per-credit charge: $26 in-state; $177 out-of-state. Books/supplies: $1,113. Personal expenses: $2,250.

Application procedures. Admission: No deadline. No application fee. **Financial aid:** Priority date 4/15; no closing date. Applicants notified on a rolling basis starting 5/1; must reply within 2 week(s) of notification.

Academics. Special study options: Cooperative education, cross-registration, distance learning, double major, dual enrollment of high school students, ESL, honors, independent study, internships, liberal arts/career combination, weekend college. Service Members Opportunity College. **Credit/**

placement by examination: AP, CLEP, institutional tests. **Support services:** GED preparation, learning center, pre-admission summer program, reduced course load, remedial instruction, study skills assistance, tutoring, writing center.

Majors. Biology: General. **Business:** Accounting, business admin, real estate. **Communications:** General. **Computer sciences:** Computer science, systems analysis. **Engineering technology:** Electrical. **Liberal arts:** Arts/sciences, library science. **Math:** General. **Mechanic/repair:** Automotive, diesel, electronics/electrical, heating/ac/refrig. **Physical sciences:** Astronomy, chemistry, geology, physics. **Protective services:** Law enforcement admin. **Psychology:** General. **Public administration:** Social work. **Social sciences:** Geography. **Transportation:** Aviation management. **Visual/performing arts:** Commercial/advertising art.

Computing on campus. 180 workstations in library, computer center, student center.

Student life. Freshman orientation: Available. **Activities:** Bands, choral groups, drama, literary magazine, music ensembles, musical theater, radio station, student government, student newspaper, TV station, Campus Crusade for Christ, Newman Club, Baptist Student Union, Movimiento Estudiantil Chicano de Aztlan, Black Student Union, Young Democrats, Young Republicans.

Athletics. NCAA. **Intercollegiate:** Baseball M, basketball, cross-country M, football (tackle) M, golf M, softball W, swimming, tennis, track and field, volleyball W, wrestling M. **Team name:** Wolverines.

Student services. Adult student services, career counseling, services for economically disadvantaged, student employment services, financial aid counseling, health services, on-campus daycare, personal counseling, placement for graduates, veterans' counselor. **Physically disabled:** Services for visually, speech, hearing impaired.

Contact. E-mail: admissions@valleycollege.edu
Phone: (909) 384-4400
Helena Johnson, Director of Admissions and Records, San Bernardino Valley College, 701 South Mount Vernon Avenue, San Bernardino, CA 92410

San Diego City College

San Diego, California
www.sdccd.edu **CB code: 4681**

- Public 2-year community college
- Commuter campus in very large city

General. Founded in 1914. Regionally accredited. **Enrollment:** 7,822 degree-seeking undergraduates. **Degrees:** 620 associate awarded. **ROTC:** Army, Air Force. **Location:** Downtown. **Calendar:** Semester, extensive summer session. **Full-time faculty:** 160 total. **Part-time faculty:** 325 total. **Special facilities:** Computerized independent study and learning laboratories, vocational training centers and theater.

Student profile. Among degree-seeking undergraduates, 9% already have a bachelor's degree or higher, 5,142 transferred in from other institutions.

Out-of-state:	4%	**25 or older:**	50%

Basis for selection. Open admission. High school students seeking admission to simultaneous high school/college program must provide approval documents from principal, registrar, or school district official. **Adult students:** Entrance exam policies same as for first-time freshmen.

2005-2006 Annual costs. Tuition/fees: $806; $5,606 out-of-state. Per-credit charge: $26 in-state; $186 out-of-state. Books/supplies: $1,242. Personal expenses: $2,700.

2004-2005 Financial aid. All financial aid based on need. 81% of total undergraduate aid awarded as scholarships/grants, 19% as loans/jobs. Need-based aid available for part-time students. Work study available for part-time students.

Application procedures. Admission: No deadline. No application fee. Application may be submitted online. Admission notification on a rolling basis. **Financial aid:** Priority date 4/1; no closing date. FAFSA required. Applicants notified on a rolling basis starting 7/1; must reply within 4 week(s) of notification.

Academics. Special study options: Accelerated study, cooperative education, cross-registration, double major, dual enrollment of high school students, honors, independent study, internships, liberal arts/career combination, student-designed major, study abroad, teacher certification program, weekend college. **Credit/placement by examination:** AP, CLEP, institutional tests. 15 credit hours maximum toward associate degree. **Support services:** Learning center, pre-admission summer program, reduced course load, remedial instruction, tutoring, writing center.

Majors. Area/ethnic studies: African, African-American, Latin American. **Biology:** General. **Business:** General, accounting, administrative services, business admin, labor relations, management information systems, management science, office technology, office/clerical, operations, purchasing, real estate, tourism promotion. **Communications:** Broadcast journalism. **Communications technology:** General. **Computer sciences:** General, applications programming, data entry, data processing, information systems, systems analysis. **Construction:** Pipefitting, power transmission. **Education:** Bilingual. **Engineering:** General. **Engineering technology:** Drafting, electrical, manufacturing. **English:** Speech/rhetoric. **Family/consumer sciences:** Child care. **Foreign languages:** General, French, Italian, Spanish. **Health:** Nursing (RN), substance abuse counseling. **History:** General. **Interdisciplinary:** Behavioral sciences. **Legal studies:** Paralegal, prelaw. **Liberal arts:** Arts/sciences. **Math:** General, applied. **Mechanic/repair:** Heating/ac/refrig. **Parks/recreation:** Health/fitness. **Philosophy/religion:** Philosophy. **Physical sciences:** Chemistry, geology, physics. **Psychology:** General. **Science technology:** Biological. **Social sciences:** General, anthropology, geography, political science. **Visual/performing arts:** General, art history/conservation, commercial/advertising art, dramatic, photography, studio arts.

Most popular majors. Business/marketing 8%, health sciences 8%, interdisciplinary studies 9%, liberal arts 40%.

Computing on campus. 121 workstations in library, computer center, student center. Online course registration, online library, helpline, repair service available.

Student life. Freshman orientation: Available. **Policies:** Freshmen permitted cars on campus. **Activities:** Jazz band, choral groups, dance, drama, film society, musical theater, radio station, student government, student newspaper, symphony orchestra, TV station, Arabic club, Italian club, MECHA, National Society of Black Engineers, Society of Hispanic Professional Engineers, California Coalition Against Poverty, students for labor and solidarity, lesbian, gay, bisexual and transsexual student union.

Athletics. Intercollegiate: Baseball, basketball M, cross-country, football (tackle) M, golf, soccer, softball W, tennis, track and field, volleyball. **Intramural:** Archery, badminton, baseball M, basketball, bowling, racquetball, soccer, tennis, track and field, volleyball, weight lifting. **Team name:** Knights.

Student services. Adult student services, career counseling, student employment services, health services, on-campus daycare, personal counseling, placement for graduates, veterans' counselor. **Physically disabled:** Services for visually, speech, hearing impaired. **Transfer:** Special adviser, orientation, pre-admission transcript evaluation for new students. Transfer center, transfer adviser, college fairs on campus for students transferring to 4-year colleges.

Contact. Phone: (619) 388-3475 Fax: (619) 388-3505
Lou Humphries, Director, Admissions and Records, San Diego City College, 1313 Park Boulevard, San Diego, CA 92101-4787

San Diego Mesa College

San Diego, California
www.sandiegomesacollege.net **CB code: 4735**

- Public 2-year community college
- Commuter campus in very large city

General. Founded in 1964. Regionally accredited. **Enrollment:** 3,490 full-time, degree-seeking students. **Degrees:** 1,120 associate awarded. **Calendar:** Semester, limited summer session. **Full-time faculty:** 280 total. **Part-time faculty:** 620 total. **Special facilities:** Anthropology museum, art museum.

Student profile.

Out-of-state:	1%	**25 or older:**	43%

Transfer out. Colleges most students transferred to 2005: San Diego State University, University of California-San Diego.

Basis for selection. Open admission. Students without high school diploma or equivalent admitted provisionally. **Adult students:** Entrance exam policies same as for first-time freshmen. **Learning Disabled:** Disabled Student Service Program (DSPS) available.

2005-2006 Annual costs. Tuition/fees: $806; $5,606 out-of-state. Per-credit charge: $26 in-state; $186 out-of-state. Books/supplies: $1,206. Personal expenses: $1,584.

Application procedures. Admission: No deadline. No application fee. Application may be submitted online. Admission notification on a rolling basis. Applications not accepted by mail. **Financial aid:** Priority date 3/2; no closing date. FAFSA required. Applicants notified on a rolling basis starting 6/15; must reply within 3 week(s) of notification.

Academics. Special study options: Accelerated study, distance learning, double major, dual enrollment of high school students, honors, independent study, internships, liberal arts/career combination, student-designed major, study abroad, teacher certification program. License preparation in dental hygiene, physical therapy, real estate. **Credit/placement by examination:** CLEP, institutional tests. 15 credit hours maximum toward associate degree. Institutional test required for placement and counseling. **Support services:** Learning center, reduced course load, remedial instruction, study skills assistance, tutoring.

Majors. Agriculture: Animal health. **Architecture:** Landscape. **Area/ethnic studies:** African, African-American, Hispanic-American/Latino/Chicano. **Biology:** General. **Business:** General, accounting, business admin, fashion, hotel/motel admin, real estate, tourism/travel. **Computer sciences:** Programming, web page design. **Education:** Physical, sales/marketing, speech. **Engineering:** General. **Engineering technology:** Construction, water quality. **Family/consumer sciences:** Child development. **Foreign languages:** American Sign Language, French, Spanish. **Health:** Dental assistant, dental lab technology, medical assistant, medical radiologic technology/radiation therapy, physical therapy assistant. **Liberal arts:** Arts/sciences. **Math:** General. **Personal/culinary services:** Culinary arts. **Philosophy/religion:** Philosophy. **Physical sciences:** Chemistry, physics. **Psychology:** General. **Social sciences:** General, anthropology, sociology. **Visual/performing arts:** Art, dramatic, interior design, studio arts.

Most popular majors. Business/marketing 10%, liberal arts 20%.

Computing on campus. Commuter students can connect to campus network. Online library available.

Student life. Freshman orientation: Available. **Policies:** Freshmen permitted cars on campus. **Activities:** Concert band, choral groups, dance, drama, music ensembles, student government, student newspaper.

Athletics. Intercollegiate: Badminton W, baseball M, basketball, cross-country, diving, football (tackle) M, soccer, softball W, swimming, tennis, track and field, volleyball, water polo. **Team name:** Olympians.

Student services. Adult student services, career counseling, health services, on-campus daycare, personal counseling, placement for graduates, veterans' counselor. **Physically disabled:** Services for visually, speech, hearing impaired. **Transfer:** Special adviser, orientation for new students. Transfer center, transfer adviser, college fairs on campus for students transferring to 4-year colleges.

Contact. E-mail: csawyer@sdccd.net
Phone: (619) 388-2682 Fax: (619) 388-2960
Ivonne Alvarez, Director of Admissions and Records, San Diego Mesa College, 7250 Mesa College Drive, San Diego, CA 92111

San Diego Miramar College

San Diego, California
www.miramarcollege.net **CB code: 4728**

- Public 2-year community college
- Commuter campus in very large city

General. Founded in 1969. Regionally accredited. **Enrollment:** 1,404 full-time, degree-seeking students. **Degrees:** 591 associate awarded. **Location:** 9 miles from downtown. **Calendar:** Semester, limited summer session.

Student profile.

Out-of-state:	1%	**25 or older:**	64%

Basis for selection. Open admission.

2005-2006 Annual costs. Tuition/fees: $806; $5,606 out-of-state. Per-credit charge: $26 in-state; $186 out-of-state. Books/supplies: $648. Personal expenses: $1,503.

Financial aid. Need-based: Need-based aid available for part-time students. **Additional information:** Private scholarships available.

Application procedures. Admission: No deadline. No application fee. Admission notification on a rolling basis. **Financial aid:** Priority date 3/2; no closing date. FAFSA required. Applicants notified on a rolling basis; must reply within 3 week(s) of notification.

Academics. Special study options: Accelerated study, cross-registration, dual enrollment of high school students, honors, independent study, weekend college. **Credit/placement by examination:** CLEP. Institutional placement tests required. **Support services:** Learning center, remedial instruction, tutoring.

Majors. Biology: General, biomedical sciences. **Business:** Accounting, administrative services, business admin, marketing, office/clerical. **Computer sciences:** General. **Education:** Early childhood. **English:** Speech/rhetoric. **Foreign languages:** French, Spanish. **Health:** Occupational health. **History:** General. **Legal studies:** Paralegal. **Liberal arts:** Arts/sciences. **Math:** General, applied. **Mechanic/repair:** Aircraft. **Parks/recreation:** Health/fitness. **Philosophy/religion:** Philosophy. **Physical sciences:** Chemistry, physics. **Protective services:** Criminal justice, law enforcement admin. **Psychology:** General. **Social sciences:** General, anthropology, geography, political science, sociology. **Visual/performing arts:** Art, studio arts.

Most popular majors. Business/marketing 14%, legal studies 6%, liberal arts 29%, security/protective services 30%.

Computing on campus. 10 workstations in library, computer center.

Student life. Activities: Student government, student newspaper, international club, Filipino-American association.

Student services. Career counseling, services for economically disadvantaged, on-campus daycare, personal counseling, veterans' counselor. **Physically disabled:** Services for visually, hearing impaired. **Transfer:** Special adviser, orientation for new students. Transfer adviser, college fairs on campus for students transferring to 4-year colleges.

Contact. Phone: (858) 536-7844
Dana Andras, Vice President of Student Services, San Diego Miramar College, 10440 Black Mountain Road, San Diego, CA 92126-2999

San Joaquin Delta College

Stockton, California
www.deltacollege.edu **CB code: 4706**

- Public 2-year community college
- Commuter campus in large city

General. Founded in 1935. Regionally accredited. 14 off-campus sites located in service district. **Enrollment:** 6,839 full-time, degree-seeking students. **Degrees:** 1,467 associate awarded. **Location:** 45 miles from Sacramento. **Calendar:** Semester, extensive summer session. **Full-time faculty:** 214 total; 28% minority, 48% women. **Part-time faculty:** 351 total; 18% minority, 43% women. **Class size:** 48% < 20, 40% 20-39, 7% 40-49, 5% 50-99, less than 1% >100. **Special facilities:** Planetarium, electron microscopy laboratory, farm laboratory, natural resources laboratory, 3 theaters. **Partnerships:** Nissan, General Motors, Caterpillar.

Transfer out. Colleges most students transferred to 2005: California State University: Stanislaus, California State University: Sacramento, University of the Pacific, California State Polytechnic University, University of California: Davis.

Basis for selection. Open admission, but selective for some programs. Limited admission to registered nursing, psychiatric technician, licensed vocational nursing, radiological technician, and police academy programs.

2005-2006 Annual costs. Tuition/fees: $780; $5,310 out-of-state. Per-credit charge: $26 in-state; $177 out-of-state. Books/supplies: $1,200. Personal expenses: $2,000.

2004-2005 Financial aid. Need-based: 4,328 full-time freshmen applied for aid; 3,182 were judged to have need; 2,693 of these received aid. Average need met was 32%. Average scholarship/grant was $3,453; average loan $1,389. 91% of total undergraduate aid awarded as scholarships/grants, 9% as loans/jobs. Need-based aid available for part-time students. Work study available nights, weekends and for part-time students. **Non-need-based:** Awarded to 32 full-time undergraduates, including 5 freshmen. Scholarships awarded for academics, athletics. **Additional information:** Enrollment fee waivers available for low-income California residents.

Application procedures. Admission: No deadline. No application fee. Admission notification on a rolling basis beginning on or about 6/1. **Financial aid:** Priority date 4/15; no closing date. FAFSA, institutional form required. Applicants notified on a rolling basis starting 5/1; must reply within 3 week(s) of notification.

Academics. Special study options: Cooperative education, distance learning, dual enrollment of high school students, ESL, internships, liberal arts/career combination, study abroad, weekend college. License preparation in nursing, real estate. **Credit/placement by examination:** AP, CLEP, IB, institutional tests. 15 credit hours maximum toward associate degree. All students taking more than one course must take ASSET for placement. AP and CLEP credit granted after 12 semester hours in residence completed. **Support services:** GED preparation, learning center, reduced course load, remedial instruction, study skills assistance, tutoring, writing center.

Majors. Agriculture: Agribusiness operations, agronomy, animal sciences, business, economics, food science, horticulture, ornamental horticulture, plant protection, plant sciences, soil science. **Architecture:** Landscape. **Biology:** General, botany, zoology. **Business:** General, accounting, administrative services, business admin, fashion, management information systems, managerial economics, office technology, office/clerical, real estate. **Communications:** Broadcast journalism, journalism. **Communications technology:** Graphic/printing. **Computer sciences:** General, computer science, data processing, database management, programming. **Conservation:** General, wildlife. **Construction:** Carpentry, maintenance, power transmission. **Engineering:** General, architectural. **Engineering technology:** Architectural, drafting, electrical, software. **English:** American lit, speech/rhetoric. **Family/consumer sciences:** General, child care, food/nutrition, institutional food production. **Foreign languages:** French, German, Spanish. **Health:** EMT paramedic, medical radiologic technology/radiation therapy, mental health services, nursing (RN). **Interdisciplinary:** Natural sciences. **Legal studies:** Prelaw. **Liberal arts:** Arts/sciences. **Math:** General. **Mechanic/repair:** Heavy equipment, locksmithing. **Personal/culinary services:** Culinary arts. **Physical sciences:** Astronomy, chemistry, geology, physics. **Production:** Woodworking. **Protective services:** Fire safety technology, police science. **Psychology:** General. **Public administration:** General. **Social sciences:** General, anthropology. **Visual/performing arts:** General, crafts, fashion design, interior design, photography, studio arts.

Computing on campus. 220 workstations in library, computer center. Online course registration, online library, wireless network available.

Student life. Freshman orientation: Available. **Activities:** Bands, choral groups, dance, drama, literary magazine, music ensembles, musical theater, radio station, student government, student newspaper, symphony orchestra, African-American Student Union, Movimiento Estudiantil Chicano de Aztlan, Vietnamese and Asian student clubs, International Student Association.

Athletics. NJCAA. **Intercollegiate:** Baseball M, basketball, cross-country, diving, football (tackle) M, golf M, soccer, softball W, swimming, tennis, track and field, volleyball W, water polo, wrestling M. **Intramural:** Baseball M, basketball, bowling, diving, fencing, golf, softball, swimming, tennis, track and field, volleyball. **Team name:** Mustangs.

Student services. Adult student services, alcohol/substance abuse counseling, career counseling, services for economically disadvantaged, student employment services, financial aid counseling, health services, legal services, minority student services, on-campus daycare, personal counseling, placement for graduates, veterans' counselor. **Physically disabled:** Services for visually, hearing impaired. **Transfer:** Special adviser, orientation, reentry adviser for new students. Transfer center, transfer adviser, college fairs on campus for students transferring to 4-year colleges.

Contact. Phone: (209) 954-5635 Fax: (209) 954-5644
Catherine Mooney, Registrar, San Joaquin Delta College, 5151 Pacific Avenue, Stockton, CA 95207-6370

San Joaquin Valley College Inc.

Visalia, California
www.sjvc.edu **CB code: 2052**

- For-profit 2-year junior college
- Commuter campus in small city
- Application essay, interview required

General. Regionally accredited. Additional campuses in Bakersfield, Fresno, Hanford, Modesto, Sacramento and Rancho Cucamonga. Aviation campus located in Fresno. **Enrollment:** 875 degree-seeking undergraduates. **Degrees:** 508 associate awarded. **Calendar:** Semester, extensive summer session. **Full-time faculty:** 80 total. **Part-time faculty:** 40 total.

Basis for selection. Open admission, but selective for some programs. Limited admission to nursing and some health related programs. ACCUPLACER for placement in Math and English.

2005-2006 Annual costs. Tuition/fees: $10,753. Per-credit charge: $348. Costs may vary with program, annual tuition includes textbooks and supplies.

Application procedures. Admission: No deadline. No application fee. Admission notification on a rolling basis. **Financial aid:** No deadline. FAFSA, institutional form required.

Academics. Special study options: Independent study, internships, liberal arts/career combination. License preparation in aviation, dental hygiene, nursing. **Credit/placement by examination:** CLEP. **Support services:** Learning center, remedial instruction, study skills assistance, tutoring.

Majors. Business: Administrative services, business admin, hospitality admin. **Computer sciences:** General, applications programming, information systems, information technology, networking, programming. **Engineering technology:** Electrical. **Health:** Dental assistant, dental hygiene, EMT paramedic, health care admin, insurance coding, licensed practical nurse, medical assistant, medical records admin, medical secretary, office assistant, pharmacy assistant, surgical technology, veterinary technology/assistant. **Mechanic/repair:** Aircraft, heating/ac/refrig. **Protective services:** Corrections.

Computing on campus. 100 workstations in library, computer center.

Student life. Freshman orientation: Mandatory. Preregistration for classes offered. Full day on Friday prior to start of classes, continues through first week. **Activities:** Student government, student newspaper.

Student services. Adult student services, career counseling, services for economically disadvantaged, student employment services, financial aid counseling, personal counseling, placement for graduates. **Transfer:** Special adviser, orientation, pre-admission transcript evaluation for new students.

Contact. Phone: (559) 651-2500 Fax: (559) 651-0574
Susie Topjian, Admissions Director, San Joaquin Valley College Inc., 8400 West Mineral King Avenue, Visalia, CA 93291-9283

San Jose City College

San Jose, California
www.sjcc.edu **CB code: 4686**

- Public 2-year community college
- Commuter campus in very large city

General. Founded in 1921. Regionally accredited. **Enrollment:** 5,006 degree-seeking undergraduates. **Degrees:** 295 associate awarded. **Location:** 55 miles from San Francisco. **Calendar:** Semester, limited summer session. **Full-time faculty:** 170 total. **Part-time faculty:** 230 total. **Partnerships:** Formal partnerships with Intel (Manufacturing Technology program), Laser Electro-Optics Manufacturing Association (Laser Technology program), IntelSemiconductor (Mask Design Technology program).

Transfer out. Colleges most students transferred to 2005: San Jose State University.

Basis for selection. Open admission.

2005-2006 Annual costs. Tuition/fees: $808; $5,878 out-of-state. Per-credit charge: $26 in-state; $195 out-of-state. Books/supplies: $712.

Financial aid. All financial aid based on need. **Additional information:** Board of Governors Grant (fee waivers) available to all qualified applicants.

Application procedures. Admission: No deadline. No application fee. Application may be submitted online. **Financial aid:** Priority date 5/31; no closing date. FAFSA required. Applicants notified on a rolling basis; must reply within 4 week(s) of notification.

Academics. Special study options: Accelerated study, cooperative education, dual enrollment of high school students, honors, independent study, weekend college. License preparation in real estate. **Credit/placement by examination:** CLEP, IB, institutional tests. 30 credit hours maximum toward associate degree. **Support services:** Learning center, pre-admission summer program, reduced course load, remedial instruction, tutoring.

Majors. Business: Accounting, administrative services, banking/financial services, entrepreneurial studies, labor studies, marketing, office technology, office/clerical, real estate. **Communications technology:** General. **Computer sciences:** General, applications programming, data entry, networking, programming. **Construction:** General, power transmission. **Education:** Early childhood. **Engineering technology:** Drafting, electrical, heat/ac/refrig, laser/optical. **Health:** Dental assistant, substance abuse counseling. **Liberal arts:** Arts/sciences. **Mechanic/repair:** Electronics/electrical, heating/ac/refrig. **Personal/culinary services:** Cosmetic, hair styling. **Production:** Machine tool. **Protective services:** Law enforcement admin. **Psychology:** General. **Social sciences:** General. **Visual/performing arts:** Studio arts.

Computing on campus. 250 workstations in library, computer center. Commuter students can connect to campus network. Online course registration available.

Student life. **Freshman orientation:** Available. **Activities:** Bands, choral groups, dance, drama, music ensembles, musical theater, radio station, student government, student newspaper, symphony orchestra.

Athletics. **Intercollegiate:** Baseball M, basketball, cross-country, football (tackle) M, golf M, softball W, track and field, volleyball W. **Team name:** Jaguars.

Student services. Career counseling, services for economically disadvantaged, student employment services, health services, minority student services, on-campus daycare, personal counseling, veterans' counselor. **Physically disabled:** Services for visually, speech, hearing impaired. **Transfer:** Special adviser for new students. Transfer adviser, college fairs on campus for students transferring to 4-year colleges.

Contact. Phone: (408) 288-3700 Fax: (408) 298-1935
Carlo Santos, District Director of Admissions and Records, San Jose City College, 2100 Moorpark Avenue, San Jose, CA 95128-2798

Santa Ana College

Santa Ana, California
www.sac.edu
CB member
CB code: 4689

- Public 2-year community college
- Commuter campus in large city

General. Founded in 1915. Regionally accredited. **Enrollment:** 4,433 full-time, degree-seeking students. **Degrees:** 1,386 associate awarded. **Location:** 40 miles from Los Angeles. **Calendar:** Semester, extensive summer session. **Full-time faculty:** 344 total. **Part-time faculty:** 2,210 total. **Special facilities:** Planetarium.

Student profile.

Out-of-state:	2%	**25 or older:**	51%

Transfer out. **Colleges most students transferred to 2005:** California State University - Fullerton, California State University - Long Beach, California State University - Irvine.

Basis for selection. Open admission.

2005-2006 Annual costs. Tuition/fees: $808; $5,338 out-of-state. Per-credit charge: $26 in-state; $177 out-of-state. Books/supplies: $1,206. Personal expenses: $2,000.

Application procedures. **Admission:** Priority date 4/1; no deadline. No application fee. Admission notification on a rolling basis. **Financial aid:** Priority date 6/30; no closing date. FAFSA required. Applicants notified on a rolling basis starting 6/1; must reply within 2 week(s) of notification.

Academics. **Special study options:** Cooperative education, distance learning, double major, dual enrollment of high school students, ESL, honors, independent study, internships, liberal arts/career combination, study abroad, weekend college. **Credit/placement by examination:** CLEP, institutional tests. 30 credit hours maximum toward associate degree. **Support services:** GED preparation, learning center, pre-admission summer program, reduced course load, remedial instruction, study skills assistance, tutoring.

Majors. **Area/ethnic studies:** African-American, Hispanic-American/Latino/Chicano, women's. **Biology:** General, botany. **Business:** General, accounting, business admin, fashion, insurance, real estate, tourism promotion. **Communications:** General, advertising, broadcast journalism, journalism. **Computer sciences:** General, computer science, data processing, programming. **Construction:** Carpentry, power transmission. **Education:** Early childhood. **Engineering:** General, civil, computer. **Engineering technology:** Civil, drafting, surveying. **Family/consumer sciences:** Family/community services, food/nutrition. **Foreign languages:** General. **Health:** Medical assistant, nursing (RN), occupational therapy assistant. **History:** General. **Liberal arts:** Library science. **Math:** General. **Mechanic/repair:** Automotive. **Parks/recreation:** Exercise sciences. **Personal/culinary services:** Cosmetic. **Philosophy/religion:** Philosophy. **Physical sciences:** Chemistry, geology, physics. **Protective services:** Fire safety technology, fire services admin, firefighting, police science. **Psychology:** General. **Social sciences:** General, anthropology, economics, geography, political science, sociology. **Visual/performing arts:** Commercial/advertising art, dance, dramatic, photography.

Computing on campus. 66 workstations in library, computer center.

Student life. **Freshman orientation:** Available. **Activities:** Bands, choral groups, dance, drama, literary magazine, music ensembles, musical theater, student government, student newspaper, TV station.

Athletics. NJCAA. **Intercollegiate:** Baseball M, basketball, cross-country, football (tackle) M, golf M, soccer M, softball W, swimming, tennis, track and field, volleyball W, water polo M, wrestling M. **Team name:** Dons.

Student services. Adult student services, career counseling, student employment services, health services, on-campus daycare, personal counseling, veterans' counselor. **Physically disabled:** Services for visually, speech, hearing impaired. **Transfer:** Special adviser, orientation, re-entry adviser, pre-admission transcript evaluation for new students. Transfer center, transfer adviser, college fairs on campus for students transferring to 4-year colleges.

Contact. E-mail: adm_records@rsccd.org
Phone: (714) 564-6015
Dean of Admissions and Enrollment Services, Santa Ana College, 1530 West 17th Street, Santa Ana, CA 92706

Santa Barbara Business College

Santa Barbara, California
www.sbbcollege.edu

- For-profit 2-year business college
- Large city
- Interview required

General. Accredited by ACICS. **Enrollment:** 100 degree-seeking undergraduates. **Degrees:** 25 associate awarded. **Calendar:** Modules begin every 6 weeks. **Full-time faculty:** 5 total. **Part-time faculty:** 8 total.

Basis for selection. Admissions decisions based on Wonderlic assessment and interview to determine interest and motivation of prospective student.

2006-2007 Annual costs. Costs for full programs as follows: administrative business systems diploma $11,065; medical/dental diploma $13,000; medical assistant diploma $12,355; medical assistant associate degree $21,600; business administration diploma $12,785; business administration associate degree $22,030; criminal justice associate degree $20,525; paralegal diploma for students with 4-year degree in field $14,075; paralegal associate degree $22,245; pharmacy technician diploma $13,215; pharmacy technician associate degree $19,880.

Application procedures. **Financial aid:** FAFSA required. Applicants notified on a rolling basis.

Academics. **Credit/placement by examination:** CLEP.

Majors. **Business:** General. **Health:** Office assistant, pharmacy assistant. **Legal studies:** Paralegal. **Protective services:** Criminal justice.

Contact. Phone: (866) 749-7222
Holly Ortiz, Director of Admissions, Santa Barbara Business College, 5266 Hollister Avenue, Santa Barbara, CA 93111

Santa Barbara Business College: Bakersfield

Bakersfield, California
www.sbbcollege.edu

- For-profit 2-year business college
- Large city

General. Accredited by ACICS. **Enrollment:** 300 degree-seeking undergraduates. **Degrees:** 37 associate awarded. **Calendar:** Modules begin every 6 weeks. **Full-time faculty:** 15 total. **Part-time faculty:** 10 total.

Basis for selection. Admissions decisions based on Wonderlic assessment and interview to determine interest and motivation of prospective student. **Adult students:** Entrance exam policies same as for first-time freshmen.

2006-2007 Annual costs. Costs for full programs as follows: administrative business systems diploma $11,065; medical/dental diploma $13,000; medical assistant diploma $12,355; medical assistant associate degree $21,600; business administration diploma $12,785; business administration associate degree $22,030; criminal justice associate degree $20,525; network systems administration diploma $13,000; network systems administration associate degree $19,880; paralegal diploma for students with 4-year degree in field $14,075; paralegal associate degree $22,245; pharmacy technician diploma $13,215; pharmacy technician associate degree $19,880.

Application procedures. Admission: No deadline. No application fee. **Financial aid:** FAFSA required. Applicants notified on a rolling basis.

Academics. Credit/placement by examination: CLEP.

Majors. Business: General. **Computer sciences:** LAN/WAN management. **Health:** Office assistant, pharmacy assistant. **Legal studies:** Paralegal. **Protective services:** Criminal justice.

Contact. Phone: (866) 749-7222
Holly Ortiz, Director of Admissions, Santa Barbara Business College: Bakersfield, 211 South Real Road, Bakersfield, CA 93309

Santa Barbara Business College: Santa Maria

Santa Maria, California
www.sbbcollege.com

- For-profit 2-year business college
- Small city

General. Accredited by ACICS. **Enrollment:** 200 degree-seeking undergraduates. **Degrees:** 12 associate awarded. **Calendar:** Modules begin every 6 weeks. **Full-time faculty:** 8 total. **Part-time faculty:** 12 total.

Basis for selection. Admissions decisions based on Wonderlic assessment and interview to determine interest and motivation of prospective student.

2006-2007 Annual costs. Costs for full programs as follows: administrative business systems diploma $11,065; medical/dental diploma $13,000; medical assistant diploma $12,355; medical assistant associate degree $21,600; business administration diploma $12,785; business administration associate degree $22,030; criminal justice associate degree $20,525; paralegal diploma for students with 4-year degree in field $14,075; paralegal associate degree $22,245; pharmacy technician diploma $13,215; pharmacy technician associate degree $19,880.

Application procedures. Admission: No deadline. $75 fee. **Financial aid:** Applicants notified on a rolling basis.

Academics. Credit/placement by examination: CLEP.

Majors. Business: General. **Health:** Office assistant, pharmacy assistant. **Legal studies:** Paralegal. **Protective services:** Criminal justice.

Contact. E-mail: infosm@sbbcollege.net
Phone: (805) 922-8256
Holly Ortiz, Director of Admissions, Santa Barbara Business College: Santa Maria, 303 East Plaza Drive, Santa Maria, CA 93454

Santa Barbara Business College: Ventura

Santa Barbara, California
www.sbbcollege.edu

- For-profit 2-year business college
- Commuter campus
- Interview required

General. Accredited by ACICS. **Enrollment:** 170 degree-seeking undergraduates. **Degrees:** 24 associate awarded. **Calendar:** Continuous. **Full-time faculty:** 4 total. **Part-time faculty:** 27 total.

Basis for selection. Wonderlic Basic Skills Test required.

2006-2007 Annual costs. Costs for full programs as follows: administrative business systems diploma $11,065; medical/dental diploma $13,000; medical assistant diploma $12,355; medical assistant associate degree $21,600; business administration diploma $12,785; business administration associate degree $22,030; criminal justice associate degree $20,525; paralegal diploma for students with 4-year degree in field $14,075; paralegal associate degree $22,245; pharmacy technician diploma $13,215; pharmacy technician associate degree $19,880.

Application procedures. Admission: No deadline. No application fee.

Academics. Credit/placement by examination: CLEP.

Majors. Business: Business admin. **Health:** Office assistant, pharmacy assistant. **Legal studies:** Paralegal. **Protective services:** Criminal justice.

Contact. Phone: (866) 749-7222
Holly Ortiz, Director of Admissions, Santa Barbara Business College: Ventura, 4839 Market Street, Santa Barbara, CA 93003

Santa Barbara City College

Santa Barbara, California
www.sbcc.edu **CB code: 4690**

- Public 2-year community college
- Commuter campus in small city

General. Founded in 1908. Regionally accredited. **Enrollment:** 7,655 degree-seeking undergraduates; 8,085 non-degree-seeking students. **Degrees:** 1,309 associate awarded. **Location:** 90 miles from Los Angeles. **Calendar:** Semester, limited summer session. **Full-time faculty:** 259 total; 18% minority, 56% women. **Part-time faculty:** 479 total; 16% minority, 57% women. **Class size:** 21% < 20, 64% 20-39, 7% 40-49, 6% 50-99, 2% >100.

Student profile. Among degree-seeking undergraduates, 81% enrolled in a transfer program, 7% enrolled in a vocational program, 12% already have a bachelor's degree or higher, 1,731 enrolled as first-time, first-year students, 902 transferred in from other institutions.

Part-time:	44%	**Hispanic American:**	23%
Out-of-state:	6%	**Native American:**	1%
Women:	51%	**International:**	6%
African American:	3%	**25 or older:**	25%
Asian American:	5%		

Transfer out. Colleges most students transferred to 2005: University of California: Santa Barbara, California State University: Northridge, San Francisco State University, San Diego State University, University of California: Los Angeles.

Basis for selection. Open admission, but selective for some programs. Special requirements for hotel/restaurant/culinary, nursing, radiography, early childhood education, cosmetology, marine diving technology programs. Criteria vary by program. Interview required of nursing, hotel and restaurant management, marine technology majors. Audition required of some music and theater majors. **Adult students:** English assessment test required for placement.

2005-2006 Annual costs. Tuition/fees: $831; $5,361 out-of-state. Per-credit charge: $26 in-state; $177 out-of-state. Books/supplies: $1,242. Personal expenses: $2,340.

Financial aid. Need-based: Need-based aid available for part-time students. **Additional information:** California residents may qualify for Board of Governor's Financial Assistance Program, which will allow institutions to waive enrollment fee.

Application procedures. Admission: Priority date 2/1; deadline 8/26 (receipt date). No application fee. Application may be submitted online. Admission notification on a rolling basis beginning on or about 3/1. **Financial aid:** No deadline. FAFSA required. Applicants notified on a rolling basis starting 5/1; must reply within 2 week(s) of notification.

Academics. Special study options: Cooperative education, cross-registration, distance learning, double major, dual enrollment of high school students, ESL, honors, independent study, internships, study abroad. License preparation in nursing, paramedic, radiology, real estate. **Credit/placement by examination:** AP, CLEP, IB, institutional tests. 12 credit hours maximum toward associate degree. **Support services:** Learning center, pre-admission summer program, reduced course load, remedial instruction, study skills assistance, tutoring, writing center.

Majors. Agriculture: Horticulture, landscaping, ornamental horticulture. **Area/ethnic studies:** African-American, Hispanic-American/Latino/Chicano, Native American. **Biology:** General. **Business:** General, accounting, accounting technology, administrative services, banking/financial services, business admin, finance, hospitality/recreation, international, marketing, office management, real estate, sales/distribution, selling, small business admin. **Communications:** General, digital media. **Communications technology:** General, computer typography. **Computer sciences:** General, computer science, data processing. **Conservation:** Environmental studies. **Education:** Early childhood, kindergarten/preschool, physical. **Engineering:** General, computer, marine. **Engineering technology:** General, automotive, biomedical, computer, drafting, electrical. **English:** English lit, speech/rhetoric. **Family/consumer sciences:** Child care, institutional food production. **Foreign languages:** French, Spanish. **Health:** Athletic training, licensed practical nurse, medical radiologic technology/radiation therapy, nursing (RN), recreational therapy, sonography, substance abuse counseling. **History:** General. **Legal studies:** General. **Liberal arts:** Arts/sciences. **Math:** General.

Mechanic/repair: Automotive, electronics/electrical. **Parks/recreation:** General, exercise sciences, health/fitness. **Personal/culinary services:** Cosmetic, culinary arts, institutional food service. **Philosophy/religion:** Philosophy. **Physical sciences:** Chemistry, geology, physics. **Protective services:** Law enforcement admin. **Psychology:** General. **Public administration:** General. **Science technology:** Biological. **Social sciences:** Anthropology, economics, geography, political science, sociology. **Transportation:** Diver. **Visual/performing arts:** Art, art history/conservation, commercial/advertising art, dramatic, film/cinema, interior design, multimedia, studio arts, theater design.

Most popular majors. Health sciences 8%, liberal arts 61%, social sciences 7%.

Computing on campus. 1,465 workstations in library, computer center, student center. Commuter students can connect to campus network. Online library, helpline, wireless network available.

Student life. **Freshman orientation:** Mandatory. Preregistration for classes offered. 2-hour on-campus or on-line orientation. **Policies:** Freshmen permitted cars on campus. **Activities:** Bands, choral groups, dance, drama, literary magazine, music ensembles, musical theater, student government, student newspaper, symphony orchestra, Black Student Union, College Republicans, EOPS, Hillel Club, Latter Day Saint Student Association, Phi Theta Kappa, Shodo Japanese Calligraphy Club, Special Abilities Club, Students Left Alliance Party, Student Sustainability Club, Vaquero Christian Fellowship.

Athletics. **Intercollegiate:** Baseball M, basketball, cross-country, football (tackle) M, golf, soccer, softball W, tennis, track and field, volleyball. **Team name:** Vaqueros.

Student services. Adult student services, alcohol/substance abuse counseling, career counseling, services for economically disadvantaged, student employment services, financial aid counseling, health services, minority student services, on-campus daycare, personal counseling, placement for graduates, veterans' counselor, women's services. **Physically disabled:** Services for visually, speech, hearing impaired. **Learning disabled:** Comprehensive services available. **Transfer:** Special adviser, orientation for new students. Transfer center, transfer adviser, college fairs on campus for students transferring to 4-year colleges.

Contact. E-mail: admissions@sbcc.edu
Phone: (805) 965-0581 ext. 2200 Fax: (805) 963-7222
Allison Curtis, Director of Admissions and Records, Santa Barbara City College, 721 Cliff Drive, Santa Barbara, CA 93109-2394

Santa Monica College

Santa Monica, California — **CB member**
www.smc.edu — **CB code: 4691**

- Public 2-year community college
- Commuter campus in small city

General. Founded in 1929. Regionally accredited. Off-campus program at Santa Monica College of Design. **Enrollment:** 16,751 degree-seeking undergraduates. **Degrees:** 1,413 associate awarded. **Location:** 18 miles from Los Angeles. **Calendar:** Semester, extensive summer session. **Full-time faculty:** 318 total; 23% minority, 55% women. **Part-time faculty:** 900 total; 15% minority, 54% women. **Special facilities:** Planetarium, photo gallery, humanities center, entertainment technology academy. **Partnerships:** Formal partnerships with DreamWorks, Disney Channel, Sony, 20th Century Fox, and other entertainment industry leaders (for Academy of Entertainment Technology students).

Student profile. Among degree-seeking undergraduates, 58% enrolled in a transfer program, 16% already have a bachelor's degree or higher.

Transfer out. **Colleges most students transferred to 2005:** University of California at Los Angeles, California State University-Northridge, University of Southern California.

Basis for selection. Open admission, but selective for some programs. Music, theater arts, entertainment technology are selective with various requirements. Nursing program has course requirements for admission. Audition and portfolio required for music, theater arts.

2005-2006 Annual costs. Tuition/fees: $804; $5,454 out-of-state. Per-credit charge: $26 in-state; $181 out-of-state. Students may also pay annual $16 identity card fee, $20 associated student fee. Books/supplies: $670.

2004-2005 Financial aid. **Need-based:** 93% of total undergraduate aid awarded as scholarships/grants, 7% as loans/jobs. Need-based aid available for part-time students.

Application procedures. **Admission:** No deadline. No application fee. Admission notification on a rolling basis. **Financial aid:** No deadline. FAFSA, institutional form required. Applicants notified on a rolling basis starting 7/1; must reply within 2 week(s) of notification.

Academics. **Special study options:** Accelerated study, cooperative education, distance learning, dual enrollment of high school students, ESL, honors, independent study, internships, study abroad, weekend college. License preparation in nursing. **Credit/placement by examination:** AP, CLEP, institutional tests. 30 credit hours maximum toward associate degree. Math and English placement tests required for some students. **Support services:** Learning center, pre-admission summer program, remedial instruction, study skills assistance, tutoring, writing center.

Majors. **Business:** General, accounting, business admin, entrepreneurial studies, office/clerical, real estate. **Communications:** Journalism. **Communications technology:** General. **Computer sciences:** Data processing, information systems, programming. **Construction:** Maintenance. **Engineering technology:** Architectural, drafting, electrical. **Family/consumer sciences:** General. **History:** General. **Liberal arts:** Arts/sciences. **Mechanic/repair:** Auto body. **Parks/recreation:** General. **Physical sciences:** Chemistry, geology, physics. **Protective services:** Firefighting, law enforcement admin, police science. **Social sciences:** General, political science. **Visual/performing arts:** Commercial photography, commercial/advertising art, dance, dramatic, photography, studio arts.

Most popular majors. Business/marketing 20%, liberal arts 56%.

Computing on campus. 600 workstations in library, computer center, student center. Commuter students can connect to campus network. Helpline available.

Student life. **Freshman orientation:** Mandatory. **Activities:** Concert band, choral groups, dance, drama, literary magazine, music ensembles, musical theater, opera, radio station, student government, student newspaper.

Athletics. NJCAA. **Intercollegiate:** Basketball, cross-country M, diving, football (tackle) M, swimming, tennis, track and field, volleyball, water polo M. **Intramural:** Badminton. **Team name:** Corsairs.

Student services. Adult student services, career counseling, services for economically disadvantaged, student employment services, financial aid counseling, health services, minority student services, on-campus daycare, personal counseling, placement for graduates, veterans' counselor. **Physically disabled:** Services for visually, speech, hearing impaired. **Learning disabled:** Comprehensive services available. **Transfer:** Special adviser, orientation for new students. Transfer center, transfer adviser, college fairs on campus for students transferring to 4-year colleges.

Contact. Phone: (310) 434-4380 Fax: (310) 434-3645
Teresita Rodriguez, Dean of Enrollment Services, Santa Monica College, 1900 Pico Boulevard, Santa Monica, CA 90405-1628

Santa Rosa Junior College

Santa Rosa, California
www.santarosa.edu — **CB code: 4692**

- Public 2-year community college
- Commuter campus in small city

General. Founded in 1918. Regionally accredited. **Enrollment:** 16,510 degree-seeking undergraduates. **Degrees:** 1,132 associate awarded. **Location:** 55 miles from San Francisco. **Calendar:** Semester, extensive summer session. **Full-time faculty:** 309 total; 56% women. **Part-time faculty:** 1,117 total; 57% women. **Special facilities:** Native American art museum, farm, summer repertory theater, planetarium.

Student profile.

Out-of-state:	2%	**25 or older:**	53%

Transfer out. **Colleges most students transferred to 2005:** Sonoma State University, San Francisco State University, University of California-Davis, Chico State University, Sacramento State University.

Basis for selection. Open admission. Audition recommended of music performance, some physical education, some communications majors.

2005-2006 Annual costs. Tuition/fees: $808; $6,118 out-of-state. Per-credit charge: $26 in-state; $203 out-of-state. Books/supplies: $1,206. Personal expenses: $2,250.

Financial aid. **Need-based:** Need-based aid available for part-time students. Work study available nights, weekends and for part-time students. **Non-need-based:** Scholarships awarded for academics, art, music/drama.

Additional information: California's Board of Governors Program (BOG) provides fee waivers for applicants with need, welfare recipients, and families with low income.

Application procedures. Admission: Priority date 4/15; no deadline. No application fee. Application may be submitted online. Admission notification on a rolling basis beginning on or about 4/15. **Financial aid:** Priority date 3/1; no closing date. FAFSA required. Applicants notified on a rolling basis starting 3/28; must reply within 4 week(s) of notification.

Academics. Special study options: Cooperative education, cross-registration, distance learning, dual enrollment of high school students, ESL, independent study, internships, liberal arts/career combination, study abroad. License preparation in dental hygiene, nursing, paramedic, real estate. **Credit/placement by examination:** AP, CLEP, IB, institutional tests. **Support services:** GED preparation and test center, learning center, pre-admission summer program, reduced course load, remedial instruction, study skills assistance, tutoring.

Majors. Agriculture: Agribusiness operations, equestrian studies, equine science. **Business:** Business admin. **Computer sciences:** Computer science. **Conservation:** General, environmental studies. **Education:** General, early childhood. **Engineering:** General. **Engineering technology:** Civil, electrical. **Foreign languages:** Portuguese. **Health:** Dental assistant, dental hygiene, EMT paramedic, licensed practical nurse, medical radiologic technology/radiation therapy, mental health services, nursing (RN), nursing assistant, pharmacy assistant. **Interdisciplinary:** Natural sciences. **Liberal arts:** Arts/sciences. **Math:** General. **Parks/recreation:** General. **Physical sciences:** Chemistry, physics. **Protective services:** Firefighting, police science. **Psychology:** General. **Social sciences:** Anthropology, economics, geography, political science, sociology. **Visual/performing arts:** Art, commercial/advertising art, dramatic, fashion design.

Computing on campus. 1,325 workstations in library, computer center. Commuter students can connect to campus network.

Student life. Freshman orientation: Available. Preregistration for classes offered. **Policies:** Freshmen permitted cars on campus. **Activities:** Jazz band, choral groups, dance, drama, film society, music ensembles, musical theater, student government, student newspaper, symphony orchestra, various clubs and organizations.

Athletics. Intercollegiate: Badminton W, baseball M, basketball, cross-country, diving, football (tackle) M, golf M, soccer, softball W, swimming, tennis, track and field, volleyball W, water polo, wrestling M. **Team name:** Bear Cubs.

Student services. Adult student services, career counseling, student employment services, financial aid counseling, health services, on-campus daycare, personal counseling, placement for graduates, veterans' counselor. **Physically disabled:** Services for visually, speech, hearing impaired. **Transfer:** Special adviser, orientation, re-entry adviser, pre-admission transcript evaluation for new students. Transfer center, transfer adviser, college fairs on campus for students transferring to 4-year colleges.

Contact. Phone: (707) 527-4685 Fax: (707) 527-4798
Ricardo Navarette, Vice President of Student Services, Santa Rosa Junior College, 1501 Mendocino Avenue, Santa Rosa, CA 95401

Santiago Canyon College

Orange, California
www.sccollege.edu **CB code: 2830**

- Public 2-year community college
- Commuter campus in large city

General. Regionally accredited. **Enrollment:** 5,269 degree-seeking undergraduates; 5,187 non-degree-seeking students. **Degrees:** 650 associate awarded. **Calendar:** Semester, limited summer session. **Full-time faculty:** 90 total. **Part-time faculty:** 300 total.

Student profile. Among degree-seeking undergraduates, 39% enrolled in a vocational program, 7% already have a bachelor's degree or higher, 1,011 enrolled as first-time, first-year students, 384 transferred in from other institutions.

Part-time:	51%	**Women:**	52%

Transfer out. Colleges most students transferred to 2005: CSU Fullerton, CSU Long Beach, Chapman University, UCI.

Basis for selection. Open admission. **Adult students:** SAT/ACT scores not required. Placement tests for English, math, reading, and chemistry.

Homeschooled: Statement describing homeschool structure and mission required. Must show private school affidavit confirmation from the California Department of Education.

2005-2006 Annual costs. Tuition/fees: $808; $5,338 out-of-state. Per-credit charge: $26 in-state; $177 out-of-state. Books/supplies: $850.

2004-2005 Financial aid. Need-based: 80% of total undergraduate aid awarded as scholarships/grants, 20% as loans/jobs.

Application procedures. Admission: No application fee. Application may be submitted online.

Academics. Special study options: Accelerated study, cooperative education, distance learning, double major, dual enrollment of high school students, ESL, honors, weekend college. License preparation in real estate. **Credit/placement by examination:** CLEP. **Support services:** GED test center, learning center, study skills assistance, tutoring, writing center.

Majors. Biology: General. **Business:** Accounting, business admin, managerial economics, marketing, selling, tourism/travel. **Communications:** General. **Communications technology:** Graphics, photo/film/video. **Computer sciences:** Computer science, information systems, web page design. **Construction:** Carpentry, electrician. **Engineering:** General. **Engineering technology:** Drafting. **English:** Speech/rhetoric. **Family/consumer sciences:** General. **Health:** Medical assistant. **History:** General. **Legal studies:** Paralegal. **Liberal arts:** Arts/sciences, library science. **Math:** General. **Mechanic/repair:** Automotive. **Parks/recreation:** Exercise sciences. **Personal/culinary services:** Cosmetic. **Philosophy/religion:** Philosophy. **Physical sciences:** Chemistry, geology, hydrology, physics. **Protective services:** Fire safety technology. **Psychology:** General. **Social sciences:** General, anthropology, economics, geography, political science, sociology. **Visual/performing arts:** Commercial/advertising art, crafts, dance, fashion design, metal/jewelry.

Most popular majors. Liberal arts 87%.

Computing on campus. Online course registration available.

Student life. Freshman orientation: Available. **Policies:** Freshmen permitted cars on campus. **Activities:** Choral groups, dance, music ensembles, student government, student newspaper, TV station.

Athletics. Intercollegiate: Cross-country, golf, soccer, track and field. **Team name:** Hawks.

Student services. Adult student services, alcohol/substance abuse counseling, career counseling, services for economically disadvantaged, student employment services, financial aid counseling, health services, minority student services, on-campus daycare, personal counseling, placement for graduates, veterans' counselor, women's services. **Physically disabled:** Services for visually, hearing impaired. **Learning disabled:** Comprehensive services available. **Transfer:** Special adviser, orientation, re-entry adviser, pre-admission transcript evaluation for new students. Transfer center, transfer adviser, college fairs on campus for students transferring to 4-year colleges.

Contact. Phone: (714) 628-4978 Fax: (714) 628-4723
Linda Miskovic, Director, Admissions & Records, Santiago Canyon College, 8045 East Chapman Avenue, Orange, CA 92869

Shasta College

Redding, California
www.shastacollege.edu **CB code: 4696**

- Public 2-year community college
- Commuter campus in small city

General. Founded in 1948. Regionally accredited. **Enrollment:** 3,540 degree-seeking undergraduates. **Degrees:** 513 associate awarded. **Location:** 160 miles from Sacramento. **Calendar:** Semester, limited summer session. **Full-time faculty:** 130 total. **Part-time faculty:** 370 total. **Class size:** 58% < 20, 38% 20-39, 2% 40-49, 2% 50-99, less than 1% >100. **Special facilities:** Museum.

Student profile.

Out-of-state:	3%	**Live on campus:**	1%
25 or older:	46%		

Basis for selection. Open admission, but selective for some programs. Applicants to nursing program must be high school graduates, take National League for Nursing examination, and complete series of courses outlined in college catalog. **Adult students:** Entrance exam policies same as for first-time freshmen.

Two-Year Colleges

2005-2006 Annual costs. Tuition/fees: $847; $5,977 out-of-state. Per-credit charge: $26 in-state; $197 out-of-state. Room only: $2,525. Books/supplies: $810. Personal expenses: $1,350.

Financial aid. All financial aid based on need. Need-based aid available for part-time students.

Application procedures. Admission: No deadline. No application fee. Admission notification on a rolling basis. **Financial aid:** Priority date 3/2; no closing date. FAFSA, institutional form required. Applicants notified on a rolling basis starting 7/1.

Academics. On-campus programs leading to bachelor's degree from California State University: Chico offered. **Special study options:** Cooperative education, distance learning, double major, dual enrollment of high school students, ESL, honors, independent study, internships, weekend college. License preparation in dental hygiene, nursing, occupational therapy, paramedic, physical therapy, real estate. **Credit/placement by examination:** CLEP, institutional tests. 12 credit hours maximum toward associate degree. **Support services:** Learning center, reduced course load, remedial instruction, tutoring, writing center.

Majors. Agriculture: General, agribusiness operations, business, equestrian studies, ornamental horticulture. **Business:** General, accounting, administrative services, business admin, entrepreneurial studies, executive assistant, fashion, management information systems, office management, office technology, office/clerical, sales/distribution. **Communications:** General, journalism. **Computer sciences:** General, applications programming. **Construction:** Carpentry. **Education:** Early childhood, teacher assistance. **Engineering:** General, civil. **Engineering technology:** Architectural drafting, civil, construction, electrical. **Family/consumer sciences:** General, child care, institutional food production. **Health:** Nursing (RN). **Legal studies:** Legal secretary, paralegal. **Mechanic/repair:** General, aircraft, automotive, diesel, heating/ac/refrig. **Personal/culinary services:** Culinary arts. **Production:** Welding. **Protective services:** Fire safety technology, police science. **Public administration:** Human services. **Visual/performing arts:** Art, commercial/advertising art, dramatic, studio arts.

Computing on campus. 141 workstations in library, computer center. Online library available.

Student life. Freshman orientation: Mandatory. **Policies:** Freshmen permitted cars on campus. **Housing:** Single-sex dorms available. **Activities:** Bands, choral groups, dance, drama, literary magazine, music ensembles, musical theater, student government, student newspaper, symphony orchestra, Environmental Resources Leadership Club, LEAF, Ornamental Horticulture club, jazz choir, science club, Veteran's Club, dorm club.

Athletics. NJCAA. **Intercollegiate:** Baseball M, basketball, cross-country, football (tackle) M, golf, soccer, softball W, swimming, tennis, track and field, volleyball W, wrestling M. **Team name:** Knights.

Student services. Adult student services, career counseling, services for economically disadvantaged, student employment services, financial aid counseling, health services, minority student services, on-campus daycare, personal counseling, veterans' counselor. **Physically disabled:** Services for visually, speech, hearing impaired. **Transfer:** Special adviser, orientation for new students. Transfer center, transfer adviser, college fairs on campus for students transferring to 4-year colleges.

Contact. E-mail: cryan@shastacollege.edu
Phone: (530) 225-4841 Fax: (530) 225-4995
Don Gray, Dean of Admissions, Shasta College, Box 496006, Redding, CA 96049-6006

Sierra College
Rocklin, California
www.sierracollege.edu **CB code: 4697**

- Public 2-year community college
- Commuter campus in large town

General. Founded in 1914. Regionally accredited. **Enrollment:** 9,934 degree-seeking undergraduates. **Degrees:** 2,426 associate awarded. **Location:** 25 miles from Sacramento. **Calendar:** Semester, extensive summer session. **Full-time faculty:** 210 total; 14% minority, 59% women. **Part-time faculty:** 769 total. **Class size:** 30% < 20, 58% 20-39, 10% 40-49, 2% 50-99, less than 1% >100. **Special facilities:** Nature trail, planetarium, science center displays, learning resource center.

Student profile.

Out-of-state:	1%	**Live on campus:**	6%

Transfer out. Colleges most students transferred to 2005: California State University-Sacramento, University of California-Davis, California State University-Chico, University of California-Berkeley.

Basis for selection. Open admission.

2005-2006 Annual costs. Tuition/fees: $816; $5,346 out-of-state. Per-credit charge: $26 in-state; $177 out-of-state. Room/board: $6,890. Books/supplies: $1,206. Personal expenses: $1,574.

2004-2005 Financial aid. Need-based: 76% of total undergraduate aid awarded as scholarships/grants, 24% as loans/jobs. Need-based aid available for part-time students. Work study available nights, weekends and for part-time students.

Application procedures. Admission: No deadline. No application fee. Applicants notified within 4 working days. **Financial aid:** Priority date 3/1, closing date 4/22. FAFSA required. Applicants notified on a rolling basis starting 4/15.

Academics. Special study options: Cooperative education, cross-registration, distance learning, double major, dual enrollment of high school students, ESL, honors, independent study, internships, study abroad, weekend college. License preparation in nursing, real estate. **Credit/placement by examination:** AP, CLEP, institutional tests. 15 credit hours maximum toward associate degree. **Support services:** Learning center, remedial instruction, study skills assistance, tutoring, writing center.

Majors. Agriculture: General, animal husbandry, equestrian studies, horticulture. **Biology:** General. **Business:** General, accounting, administrative services, business admin, real estate, sales/distribution, small business admin. **Communications:** Digital media. **Computer sciences:** Data entry, information technology, networking, programming, system admin, web page design, webmaster. **Conservation:** Forestry. **Construction:** Carpentry, maintenance. **Education:** Early childhood, teacher assistance. **Engineering:** General. **Engineering technology:** Architectural drafting, hazardous materials, mechanical drafting. **English:** Speech/rhetoric. **Family/consumer sciences:** General, child care, institutional food production. **Foreign languages:** American Sign Language. **Health:** Licensed practical nurse, medical secretary, nursing (RN). **Legal studies:** Legal secretary. **Liberal arts:** Arts/sciences, library assistant, library science. **Math:** General. **Mechanic/repair:** Automotive, electronics/electrical. **Parks/recreation:** Health/fitness. **Philosophy/religion:** Philosophy. **Physical sciences:** Chemistry, geology. **Production:** Woodworking. **Protective services:** Criminal justice, fire safety technology, firefighting, police science, security services. **Visual/performing arts:** Art, music performance, photography, studio arts.

Computing on campus. 300 workstations in dormitories, library, computer center. Dormitories linked to campus network. Commuter students can connect to campus network. Online course registration, online library, wireless network available.

Student life. Freshman orientation: Mandatory. **Policies:** Freshmen permitted cars on campus. **Housing:** Coed dorms available. **Activities:** Concert band, choral groups, drama, music ensembles, student government, student newspaper.

Athletics. Intercollegiate: Baseball M, basketball, cross-country W, diving, football (tackle) M, golf, soccer W, softball W, swimming, tennis, track and field W, volleyball W, water polo W, wrestling M. **Intramural:** Archery, badminton, basketball, cheerleading W, football (non-tackle), golf, softball, tennis, volleyball. **Team name:** Wolverines.

Student services. Adult student services, alcohol/substance abuse counseling, career counseling, services for economically disadvantaged, student employment services, financial aid counseling, health services, on-campus daycare, personal counseling, veterans' counselor. **Physically disabled:** Services for visually, speech, hearing impaired. **Transfer:** Special adviser, orientation, pre-admission transcript evaluation for new students. Transfer center, transfer adviser, college fairs on campus for students transferring to 4-year colleges.

Contact. Phone: (916) 781-0430 Toll-free number: (800) 242-4004
Fax: (916) 781-0403
Sierra College, 5000 Rocklin Road, Rocklin, CA 95677

Silicon Valley College
Fremont, California
www.svcollege.com **CB code: 3032**

- For-profit 2-year health science and technical college
- Small city

General. Accredited by ACCSCT. **Calendar:** Continuous.

Annual costs/financial aid. Computer-aided design and graphic arts programs: $24,000 for 18 months. Information technology networking programs: $28,200 for 18 months. Books/supplies: $1,125.

Contact. Phone: (510) 623-9966
41350 Christy Street, Fremont, CA 94538

Skyline College
San Bruno, California
skylinecollege.net **CB code: 4746**

- Public 2-year community college
- Commuter campus in small city

General. Founded in 1969. Regionally accredited. **Enrollment:** 5,290 degree-seeking undergraduates. **Degrees:** 370 associate awarded. **Location:** 15 miles from San Francisco. **Calendar:** Semester, limited summer session. **Full-time faculty:** 105 total. **Part-time faculty:** 200 total.

Student profile.

Out-of-state:	1%	**25 or older:**	49%

Transfer out. Colleges most students transferred to 2005: San Francisco State University, San Jose State University, California State University: Hayward.

Basis for selection. Open admission, but selective for some programs. Additional requirements for applicants to automotive technology, cosmetology, and respiratory therapy programs, and for participants in concurrent enrollment. SAT/ACT may be substituted for institutional placement tests. Interview required of respiratory therapy majors. Essay required of full-time international student applicants.

2005-2006 Annual costs. Tuition/fees: $806; $5,876 out-of-state. Per-credit charge: $26 in-state; $195 out-of-state. Personal expenses: $1,818.

Financial aid. Need-based: Need-based aid available for part-time students.

Application procedures. Admission: Priority date 7/1; deadline 8/1 (receipt date). No application fee. Admission notification on a rolling basis. **Financial aid:** Priority date 3/2; no closing date. FAFSA, institutional form required. Applicants notified on a rolling basis starting 5/1; must reply within 2 week(s) of notification.

Academics. Classes given on Sundays. **Special study options:** Cooperative education, cross-registration, dual enrollment of high school students, ESL, honors, study abroad. **Credit/placement by examination:** CLEP, institutional tests. 12 credit hours maximum toward associate degree. **Support services:** Learning center, study skills assistance, tutoring.

Majors. Business: Accounting, administrative services, business admin, hospitality admin, management information systems, office/clerical. **Communications technology:** General. **Computer sciences:** General, computer science, data processing, information systems, webmaster. **Education:** Early childhood. **English:** Speech/rhetoric. **Family/consumer sciences:** General, business. **Foreign languages:** Spanish. **Health:** Medical secretary, medical transcription, respiratory therapy technology, surgical technology. **Interdisciplinary:** Global studies. **Legal studies:** Legal secretary, paralegal. **Liberal arts:** Arts/sciences. **Math:** General. **Mechanic/repair:** Automotive. **Personal/culinary services:** Cosmetic. **Protective services:** Law enforcement admin. **Psychology:** General. **Science technology:** Biological. **Visual/performing arts:** General, art, dance.

Computing on campus. 220 workstations in library, computer center, student center. Online course registration, helpline, repair service available.

Student life. Freshman orientation: Available. **Activities:** Bands, choral groups, dance, literary magazine, student government, student newspaper.

Athletics. NJCAA. **Intercollegiate:** Baseball M, basketball M, cross-country, soccer M, softball W, track and field, volleyball W, wrestling M. **Team name:** Trojans.

Student services. Career counseling, services for economically disadvantaged, student employment services, health services, minority student services, on-campus daycare, personal counseling, veterans' counselor, women's services. **Physically disabled:** Services for visually, speech, hearing impaired. **Transfer:** Special adviser, orientation for new students. Transfer center, transfer adviser, college fairs on campus for students transferring to 4-year colleges.

Contact. E-mail: skyadmissions@smccd.net
Phone: (650) 738-4252 Fax: (650) 738-4200
Sherri Hancock, Dean of Enrollment Services, Skyline College, 3300 College Drive, San Bruno, CA 94066

Solano Community College
Fairfield, California
www.solano.edu **CB code: 4930**

- Public 2-year community college
- Commuter campus in small city

General. Founded in 1945. Regionally accredited. Classes offered in Vallejo and Vacaville. **Enrollment:** 6,810 degree-seeking undergraduates; 4,877 non-degree-seeking students. **Degrees:** 901 associate awarded. **ROTC:** Air Force. **Location:** 11 miles from Vallejo. **Calendar:** Semester, extensive summer session. **Full-time faculty:** 156 total; 22% minority, 54% women. **Part-time faculty:** 273 total; 19% minority, 46% women.

Student profile. Among degree-seeking undergraduates, 7% already have a bachelor's degree or higher, 1,107 enrolled as first-time, first-year students.

Part-time:	60%	**Asian American:**	21%
Out-of-state:	2%	**Hispanic American:**	14%
Women:	59%	**Native American:**	1%
African American:	18%		

Basis for selection. Open admission, but selective for some programs. Special requirements for nursing program.

2005-2006 Annual costs. Tuition/fees: $807; $5,337 out-of-state. Per-credit charge: $26 in-state; $177 out-of-state. Books/supplies: $810. Personal expenses: $2,599.

Application procedures. Admission: No deadline. No application fee. Application may be submitted online. Admission notification on a rolling basis. **Financial aid:** Priority date 3/1; no closing date. FAFSA required. Applicants notified on a rolling basis starting 7/1.

Academics. Special study options: Cooperative education, cross-registration, distance learning, double major, dual enrollment of high school students, honors, independent study, internships, study abroad, weekend college. **Credit/placement by examination:** AP, CLEP, institutional tests. 15 credit hours maximum toward associate degree. **Support services:** Reduced course load, remedial instruction, tutoring, writing center.

Majors. Agriculture: Landscaping, ornamental horticulture. **Area/ethnic studies:** African-American, Asian-American, Hispanic-American/Latino/Chicano, Native American. **Biology:** General. **Business:** Accounting, administrative services, banking/financial services, business admin, office management, real estate. **Communications:** General, journalism. **Computer sciences:** General, programming. **Education:** Early childhood. **Engineering technology:** Aerospace, drafting, electrical, water quality. **Family/consumer sciences:** General. **Foreign languages:** General, French, German, Spanish. **Health:** Medical secretary, nursing (RN). **History:** General. **Interdisciplinary:** Biological/physical sciences. **Legal studies:** Legal secretary. **Liberal arts:** Arts/sciences. **Math:** General. **Mechanic/repair:** Aircraft, appliance, auto body, computer. **Parks/recreation:** Health/fitness, sports admin. **Personal/culinary services:** Cosmetic. **Physical sciences:** Chemistry, physics. **Production:** Welding. **Protective services:** Firefighting, police science. **Psychology:** General. **Public administration:** Human services. **Science technology:** Biological. **Social sciences:** General, international relations, political science. **Visual/performing arts:** Commercial photography, commercial/advertising art, dramatic, drawing, interior design, painting, sculpture, studio arts.

Computing on campus. 240 workstations in library, computer center.

Student life. Freshman orientation: Available. **Activities:** Bands, choral groups, drama, musical theater, student government, student newspaper, symphony orchestra, Black Student Union, women's change, veterans organization, Sierra club, student nurses, Filipino club, Democratic club, Mathematics, Engineering & Science Achievement club, Asian-Pacific Islander club.

Athletics. Intercollegiate: Baseball M, basketball, cross-country, diving, football (tackle) M, soccer W, softball W, swimming, track and field, volleyball W, water polo M. **Intramural:** Table tennis, tennis. **Team name:** Falcons.

Student services. Career counseling, student employment services, financial aid counseling, health services, on-campus daycare, personal counseling, placement for graduates, veterans' counselor. **Physically disabled:**

Services for visually, speech, hearing impaired. **Transfer:** Transfer center for students transferring to 4-year colleges.

Contact. E-mail: admissions@solano.edu
Phone: (707) 864-7171 Fax: (707) 864-7175
Catherine Fites-Chavis, Dean of Admissions and Records, Solano Community College, 4000 Suisun Valley Road, Fairfield, CA 94534-3197

South Coast College
Orange, California
www.southcoastcollege.com

- For-profit 2-year business college
- Small city

General. Accredited by ACICS. **Calendar:** Quarter.

Contact. Phone: (714) 867-5009
2011 West Chapman Avenue, Orange, CA 92868

Southwestern College
Chula Vista, California
www.swc.cc.ca.us **CB code: 4726**

- Public 2-year community college
- Commuter campus in small city

General. Founded in 1961. Regionally accredited. Medical occupation programs accredited by the National League for Nursing Accrediting Commission Inc. (NLNAC). **Enrollment:** 10,226 degree-seeking undergraduates. **Degrees:** 1,074 associate awarded. **Location:** 10 miles from San Diego. **Calendar:** Semester, extensive summer session. **Full-time faculty:** 80 total. **Part-time faculty:** 120 total. **Class size:** 36% < 20, 49% 20-39, 13% 40-49, 3% 50-99.

Student profile. Among degree-seeking undergraduates, 45% enrolled in a transfer program, 16% enrolled in a vocational program, 4% already have a bachelor's degree or higher.

Part-time:	60%	**Women:**	55%
Out-of-state:	1%		

Transfer out. Colleges most students transferred to 2005: San Diego State University, University of California: San Diego.

Basis for selection. Open admission, but selective for some programs. Limited admission to nursing and dental hygiene programs.

2005-2006 Annual costs. Tuition/fees: $816; $5,346 out-of-state. Per-credit charge: $26 in-state; $177 out-of-state. Books/supplies: $1,224.

Financial aid. Need-based: Need-based aid available for part-time students. Work study available nights, weekends and for part-time students.

Application procedures. Admission: No deadline. No application fee. Application may be submitted online. Admission notification on a rolling basis. **Financial aid:** Closing date 3/2. FAFSA required. Applicants notified on a rolling basis starting 7/1.

Academics. Broad offerings of online and traditional courses. Online credit and non-credit courses available. **Special study options:** Cooperative education, cross-registration, distance learning, double major, dual enrollment of high school students, ESL, honors, independent study, internships, study abroad, weekend college. License preparation in dental hygiene, nursing, paramedic, real estate. **Credit/placement by examination:** AP, CLEP, IB, institutional tests. 15 credit hours maximum toward associate degree. In-house placement test required for some. **Support services:** Learning center, pre-admission summer program, remedial instruction, study skills assistance, tutoring, writing center.

Majors. Agriculture: Floriculture, greenhouse operations, landscaping, nursery operations, ornamental horticulture, turf management. **Architecture:** Landscape, technology. **Area/ethnic studies:** African-American, American, Asian-American, Hispanic-American/Latino/Chicano, women's. **Biology:** General, biotechnology. **Business:** Accounting, business admin, construction management, entrepreneurial studies, finance, financial planning, international, market research, office management, office/clerical, real estate, tourism promotion, tourism/travel. **Communications:** General, broadcast journalism, journalism. **Communications technology:** General, radio/tv, recording arts. **Computer sciences:** General, applications programming, computer science, information systems, information technology, networking, programming, web page design, webmaster. **Conservation:** Environmental studies. **Construction:** Building inspection, maintenance. **Education:** General, early childhood, elementary, kindergarten/preschool, physical. **Engineering:** General. **Engineering technology:** CAD/CADD, computer, drafting, occupational safety, telecommunications. **English:** English lit. **Family/consumer sciences:** Child care, child development. **Foreign languages:** Comparative lit, French, Spanish. **Health:** Dental hygiene, EMT paramedic, insurance coding, licensed practical nurse, medical records admin, medical records technology, medical transcription, nursing (RN), prenursing, surgical technology. **History:** General. **Legal studies:** General, legal secretary, paralegal. **Liberal arts:** Arts/sciences, humanities. **Math:** General. **Mechanic/repair:** Automotive, electronics/electrical, small engine. **Parks/recreation:** General, health/fitness. **Philosophy/religion:** Philosophy. **Physical sciences:** Astronomy, chemistry, geology, physics. **Protective services:** Criminal justice, firefighting, forensics, law enforcement admin. **Psychology:** General. **Public administration:** Social work. **Social sciences:** Anthropology, economics, geography, political science, sociology. **Visual/performing arts:** Art, cinematography, dance, dramatic, graphic design, photography.

Computing on campus. 1,360 workstations in library, computer center. Online course registration, online library, helpline, repair service, student web hosting, wireless network available.

Student life. Freshman orientation: Available. Preregistration for classes offered. **Policies:** Freshmen permitted cars on campus. **Activities:** Jazz band, choral groups, dance, drama, literary magazine, music ensembles, musical theater, student government, student newspaper, over 40 student clubs and organizations available.

Athletics. Intercollegiate: Baseball M, basketball, cross-country, football (tackle) M, soccer, softball W, tennis, track and field, volleyball W, water polo. **Team name:** Jaguars.

Student services. Career counseling, services for economically disadvantaged, student employment services, financial aid counseling, health services, legal services, on-campus daycare, personal counseling, veterans' counselor, women's services. **Physically disabled:** Services for visually, speech, hearing impaired. **Transfer:** Special adviser, orientation, pre-admission transcript evaluation for new students. Transfer center, transfer adviser, college fairs on campus for students transferring to 4-year colleges.

Contact. E-mail: gcopeland@swc.cc.ca.us
Phone: (619) 421-6700 ext. 5215 Fax: (619) 482-6489
Georgia Copeland, Director of Admissions and Records, Southwestern College, 900 Otay Lakes Road, Chula Vista, CA 91910-7297

Taft College
Taft, California
www.taft.cc.ca.us **CB code: 4820**

- Public 2-year community college
- Commuter campus in small town

General. Founded in 1922. Regionally accredited. **Enrollment:** 803 full-time, degree-seeking students. **Degrees:** 173 associate awarded. **Location:** 35 miles from Bakersfield. **Calendar:** Semester, limited summer session. **Full-time faculty:** 41 total; 20% have terminal degrees, 15% minority, 42% women. **Part-time faculty:** 53 total; 4% have terminal degrees, 8% minority, 40% women. **Class size:** 71% < 20, 27% 20-39, 1% 40-49, less than 1% 50-99.

Transfer out. Colleges most students transferred to 2005: California State University: Bakersfield, California State University: Fresno, California Polytechnic State University: San Luis Obispo, University of La Verne.

Basis for selection. Open admission. **Adult students:** SAT/ACT scores not required.

2005-2006 Annual costs. Tuition/fees: $780; $5,310 out-of-state. Per-credit charge: $26 in-state; $177 out-of-state. Room/board: $3,148. Books/supplies: $1,260. Personal expenses: $220.

2004-2005 Financial aid. Need-based: 81% of total undergraduate aid awarded as scholarships/grants, 19% as loans/jobs. Need-based aid available for part-time students. Work study available nights and for part-time students. **Non-need-based:** Scholarships awarded for academics.

Application procedures. Admission: No deadline. No application fee. Application may be submitted online. Admission notification on a rolling basis. **Financial aid:** No deadline. FAFSA, institutional form required. Applicants notified on a rolling basis; must reply within 4 week(s) of notification.

Academics. Special study options: Distance learning, ESL, independent study. License preparation in dental hygiene. **Credit/placement by examination:** AP, CLEP, institutional tests. 12 credit hours maximum toward associate degree. **Support services:** GED preparation and test center, learning center, pre-admission summer program, reduced course load, remedial instruction, study skills assistance, tutoring.

Majors. Business: General, accounting, administrative services, business admin, management information systems, office/clerical. **Communications:** Journalism. **Computer sciences:** General, computer science, information systems. **Education:** General, early childhood, physical, social science. **Engineering:** General. **Engineering technology:** Automotive, CAD/CADD, electrical, petroleum. **Health:** Dental hygiene. **Liberal arts:** Arts/sciences. **Math:** General. **Mechanic/repair:** Automotive, industrial. **Parks/recreation:** General. **Physical sciences:** General. **Protective services:** Corrections, criminal justice. **Social sciences:** General. **Visual/performing arts:** Art.

Most popular majors. Business/marketing 13%, health sciences 14%, liberal arts 60%, security/protective services 10%.

Computing on campus. 121 workstations in dormitories, library, computer center, student center. Dormitories wired for high-speed internet access. Online course registration, online library, helpline available.

Student life. Freshman orientation: Available. Offered online or by video. **Policies:** Freshmen permitted cars on campus. **Housing:** Single-sex dorms, special housing for disabled available. $125 deposit. **Activities:** Student government, student newspaper, International club, rotary club, MECHA club, Best Buddies.

Athletics. Intercollegiate: Baseball M, basketball W, soccer M, softball W, volleyball W. **Team name:** Cougars.

Student services. Adult student services, career counseling, student employment services, on-campus daycare, personal counseling, veterans' counselor. **Physically disabled:** Services for visually, speech, hearing impaired. **Learning disabled:** Comprehensive services available. **Transfer:** Special adviser, orientation, re-entry adviser for new students. Transfer center, transfer adviser, college fairs on campus for students transferring to 4-year colleges.

Contact. E-mail: ldobbs@taft.org
Phone: (661) 763-7741 Toll-free number: (800) 379-6784
Fax: (661) 763-7758
Gayle Roberts, Director of Financial Aid and Admissions, Taft College, 29 Emmons Park Drive, Taft, CA 93268

Ventura College
Ventura, California
www.venturacollege.edu **CB code: 4931**

- Public 2-year community college
- Small city

General. Founded in 1925. Regionally accredited. **Enrollment:** 6,257 degree-seeking undergraduates. **Degrees:** 511 associate awarded. **ROTC:** Air Force. **Location:** 60 miles from Los Angeles. **Calendar:** Semester, limited summer session. **Full-time faculty:** 133 total. **Part-time faculty:** 386 total. **Special facilities:** Theater, 2 art galleries.

Basis for selection. Open admission, but selective for some programs. Limited admission to nursing program.

2005-2006 Annual costs. Tuition/fees: $818; $5,468 out-of-state. Per-credit charge: $26 in-state; $181 out-of-state. Books/supplies: $600. Personal expenses: $1,300.

Application procedures. Admission: No deadline. No application fee. Admission notification on a rolling basis. **Financial aid:** Priority date 3/2; no closing date. FAFSA required. Applicants notified on a rolling basis.

Academics. Special study options: Cross-registration, dual enrollment of high school students, ESL, honors, independent study, study abroad. **Credit/placement by examination:** CLEP, institutional tests. 12 credit hours maximum toward associate degree. **Support services:** Learning center, reduced course load, remedial instruction, tutoring.

Majors. Agriculture: Agribusiness operations, agronomy, animal sciences, horticulture, ornamental horticulture, plant protection, plant sciences, soil science. **Area/ethnic studies:** African-American, Hispanic-American/Latino/Chicano. **Biology:** General, botany, zoology. **Business:** General, accounting, administrative services, business admin, fashion, human resources, management information systems, management science, managerial economics, marketing, office/clerical, real estate. **Communications:** General, journalism. **Communications technology:** General, graphic/printing. **Computer sciences:** General, applications programming, data processing, information systems, programming. **Construction:** Maintenance, masonry, pipefitting. **Education:** General, bilingual, early childhood. **Engineering:** General. **Engineering technology:** Architectural, civil, drafting, electrical. **English:** Speech/rhetoric. **Family/consumer sciences:** General, child care, food/nutrition. **Foreign languages:** French, German, Spanish. **Health:** EMT paramedic, health services, licensed practical nurse, medical records technology, medical secretary, nursing (RN), predentistry, premedicine, prepharmacy, preveterinary. **History:** General. **Legal studies:** Legal secretary, prelaw. **Liberal arts:** Arts/sciences. **Math:** General. **Mechanic/repair:** Automotive. **Parks/recreation:** Facilities management. **Philosophy/religion:** Philosophy. **Physical sciences:** Chemistry, geology, physics. **Production:** Welding. **Protective services:** Criminal justice, police science. **Psychology:** General. **Social sciences:** General, anthropology, economics, geography, political science, sociology. **Visual/performing arts:** Ceramics, commercial photography, dramatic, fashion design, interior design, photography, studio arts.

Student life. Housing: Student housing available off-campus at nearby apartments. **Activities:** Religious, ethnic, political, special interest organizations, international student club.

Athletics. Intercollegiate: Baseball M, basketball, cross-country, diving, football (tackle) M, golf M, rifle M, softball W, swimming, tennis, track and field, volleyball M, water polo M.

Student services. Adult student services, career counseling, student employment services, health services, on-campus daycare, personal counseling, placement for graduates, veterans' counselor. **Transfer:** Special adviser, orientation for new students. Transfer adviser, college fairs on campus for students transferring to 4-year colleges.

Contact. Phone: (805) 654-6457 Fax: (805) 654-6357
Susan Bricker, Registrar, Ventura College, 4667 Telegraph Road, Ventura, CA 93003

Victor Valley College
Victorville, California
www.vvc.edu **CB code: 4932**

- Public 2-year community college
- Small city

General. Founded in 1960. Regionally accredited. **Enrollment:** 6,946 degree-seeking undergraduates. **Degrees:** 1,013 associate awarded. **Location:** 38 from San Bernardino. **Calendar:** Semester, limited summer session. **Full-time faculty:** 135 total. **Part-time faculty:** 325 total. **Special facilities:** Planetarium, mock archaeological dig site.

Student profile.

Out-of-state:	1%	**25 or older:**	40%

Transfer out. Colleges most students transferred to 2005: California State University: San Bernardino.

Basis for selection. Open admission, but selective for some programs. **Adult students:** SAT/ACT scores not required. **Homeschooled:** Must complete concurrent enrollment form with parent signature.

2005-2006 Annual costs. Tuition/fees: $790; $5,500 out-of-state. Per-credit charge: $26 in-state; $183 out-of-state. Nevada residents pay $49 per credit hour. Books/supplies: $648. Personal expenses: $1,566.

Financial aid. Need-based: Need-based aid available for part-time students. Work study available for part-time students. **Additional information:** Board of Governors grant pays enrollment fee in full for low-income students.

Application procedures. Admission: No deadline. No application fee. Application may be submitted online. Admission notification on a rolling basis. **Financial aid:** Priority date 3/2; no closing date. FAFSA, institutional form, CSS PROFILE required. Applicants notified on a rolling basis starting 8/1; must reply within 4 week(s) of notification.

Academics. Special study options: Cooperative education, distance learning, double major, dual enrollment of high school students, ESL, honors, independent study, semester at sea, study abroad. License preparation in nursing, paramedic. **Credit/placement by examination:** CLEP, institutional tests. 32 credit hours maximum toward associate degree. **Support services:** Learning center, pre-admission summer program, reduced course load, remedial instruction, study skills assistance, tutoring, writing center.

Majors. **Agriculture:** Ornamental horticulture. **Business:** General, administrative services, business admin, real estate. **Construction:** Carpentry. **Health:** EMT paramedic, medical assistant, nursing (RN), respiratory therapy technology. **Liberal arts:** Arts/sciences. **Math:** General. **Mechanic/repair:** Automotive, electronics/electrical, industrial electronics. **Production:** Welding. **Protective services:** Fire safety technology, law enforcement admin. **Visual/performing arts:** Art.

Most popular majors. Business/marketing 10%, health sciences 8%, interdisciplinary studies 16%, liberal arts 43%.

Computing on campus. 350 workstations in computer center, student center. Online course registration, online library, helpline available.

Student life. **Freshman orientation:** Available. **Policies:** Freshmen permitted cars on campus. **Activities:** Jazz band, choral groups, dance, drama, music ensembles, musical theater, student government, student newspaper, symphony orchestra.

Athletics. NJCAA. **Intercollegiate:** Baseball M, basketball, cross-country, football (tackle) M, golf M, soccer, softball W, tennis, track and field, volleyball W, wrestling M. **Team name:** Rams.

Student services. Career counseling, services for economically disadvantaged, student employment services, financial aid counseling, health services, on-campus daycare, personal counseling, placement for graduates, veterans' counselor. **Physically disabled:** Services for visually, speech, hearing impaired. **Transfer:** Special adviser, orientation, re-entry adviser, preadmission transcript evaluation for new students. College fairs on campus for students transferring to 4-year colleges.

Contact. Phone: (760) 245-4271 ext. 2280 Fax: (760) 843-7707
Mary Marble, Director, Admissions and Records, Victor Valley College, 18422 Bear Valley Road, Victorville, CA 92392-5849

Vista Community College

Berkeley, California
www.peralta.cc.ca.us **CB code: 7711**

- Public 2-year community college
- Commuter campus in small city

General. Founded in 1974. Regionally accredited. Noncampus college in 125 locations located in 6 cities adjacent to Berkeley. Access to other Peralta community college district libraries, as well as Berkeley Public Library and University of California at Berkeley libraries. **Enrollment:** 1,530 degree-seeking undergraduates. **Degrees:** 116 associate awarded. **Location:** 15 miles from San Francisco. **Calendar:** Semester, limited summer session. **Full-time faculty:** 30 total. **Part-time faculty:** 140 total.

Student profile.

Out-of-state:	1%	**25 or older:**	18%

Basis for selection. Open admission.

2005-2006 Annual costs. Tuition/fees: $784; $5,704 out-of-state. Per-credit charge: $26 in-state; $190 out-of-state. Books/supplies: $630. Personal expenses: $1,584.

Financial aid. All financial aid based on need. Need-based aid available for part-time students. Work study available for part-time students.

Application procedures. **Admission:** No deadline. No application fee. Application may be submitted online. Admission notification on a rolling basis. **Financial aid:** No deadline. Applicants notified on a rolling basis.

Academics. **Special study options:** Accelerated study, cross-registration, dual enrollment of high school students, ESL, independent study, liberal arts/career combination, study abroad, weekend college. **Credit/placement by examination:** CLEP, institutional tests. 6 credit hours maximum toward associate degree. **Support services:** Learning center, remedial instruction, tutoring.

Majors. **Biology:** Biotechnology. **Business:** Business admin, small business admin. **Computer sciences:** General. **Education:** Art, Spanish. **Foreign languages:** Sign language interpretation. **Visual/performing arts:** Art.

Computing on campus. Online course registration available.

Student life. **Freshman orientation:** Mandatory. Preregistration for classes offered. Assessments and orientations scheduled several times before the beginning of the semester. **Policies:** Freshmen permitted cars on campus. **Activities:** Literary magazine, student government, Phi Theta Kappa, Spanish club, X Club, Bahai Club.

Student services. Adult student services, career counseling, services for economically disadvantaged, student employment services, financial aid counseling, veterans' counselor. **Physically disabled:** Services for visually, speech, hearing impaired. **Learning disabled:** Comprehensive services available. **Transfer:** Special adviser, orientation for new students. Transfer center, transfer adviser, college fairs on campus for students transferring to 4-year colleges.

Contact. Phone: (510) 841-8431 Fax: (510) 841-7333
Loretta Newsom, Admissions and Records Specialist, Vista Community College, 2020 Milvia Street, Berkeley, CA 94704-1183

West Hills Community College

Coalinga, California
www.westhillscollege.com **CB code: 4056**

- Public 2-year community college
- Commuter campus in small town

General. Founded in 1932. Regionally accredited. **Enrollment:** 4,545 undergraduates. **Degrees:** 431 associate awarded. **Location:** 60 miles from Fresno. **Calendar:** Semester, limited summer session. **Full-time faculty:** 45 total. **Part-time faculty:** 70 total.

Student profile. 20% enrolled in a transfer program, 80% enrolled in a vocational program, 2% already have a bachelor's degree or higher.

Out-of-state:	15%	**25 or older:**	48%

Transfer out. **Colleges most students transferred to 2005:** California State University Fresno, California Polytechnical University.

Basis for selection. Open admission. K-12 students admitted with parental permission and principal of the educational insitution recommendation as special admit students. **Homeschooled:** Students must petition President of College in writing for admittance.

2005-2006 Annual costs. Tuition/fees: $780; $5,310 out-of-state. Per-credit charge: $26 in-state; $177 out-of-state. Additional housing fee for cable, computer access and other services: $185.50/semester. Room/board: $4,010. Books/supplies: $630. Personal expenses: $1,602.

Financial aid. **Need-based:** Need-based aid available for part-time students.

Application procedures. **Admission:** No deadline. No application fee. Application must be submitted online. Admission notification on a rolling basis. **Financial aid:** Priority date 3/2; no closing date. Applicants notified on a rolling basis starting 6/1.

Academics. **Special study options:** Cooperative education, distance learning, dual enrollment of high school students, ESL, honors, independent study, study abroad. **Credit/placement by examination:** AP, CLEP, institutional tests. 15 credit hours maximum toward associate degree. **Support services:** Learning center, reduced course load, remedial instruction, tutoring.

Majors. **Agriculture:** General, animal sciences, business. **Business:** General, accounting, administrative services, business admin, management information systems, office technology, office/clerical. **Computer sciences:** General, applications programming. **Education:** Early childhood. **Health:** Medical secretary. **Liberal arts:** Arts/sciences. **Mechanic/repair:** Diesel. **Physical sciences:** Chemistry, geology, physics. **Protective services:** Police science. **Psychology:** General. **Social sciences:** General, criminology, geography. **Visual/performing arts:** Art, commercial/advertising art, studio arts.

Most popular majors. Business/marketing 9%, health sciences 7%, liberal arts 65%.

Computing on campus. 40 workstations in dormitories, library, computer center. Dormitories wired for high-speed internet access. Online course registration, helpline available.

Student life. **Freshman orientation:** Mandatory. Preregistration for classes offered. **Policies:** Freshmen permitted cars on campus. **Housing:** Single-sex dorms, substance-free housing available. $500 fully refundable deposit. **Activities:** Dance, drama, musical theater, student government.

Athletics. NJCAA. **Intercollegiate:** Baseball M, basketball M, football (tackle) M, golf, rodeo, soccer, softball W, tennis W, volleyball W. **Team name:** Falcons and Eagles.

Student services. Adult student services, career counseling, services for economically disadvantaged, student employment services, on-campus daycare, personal counseling, veterans' counselor. **Physically disabled:** Services for visually, speech, hearing impaired. **Transfer:** Special adviser, orientation for new students. Transfer center, transfer adviser for students transferring to 4-year colleges.

Contact. E-mail: sandradagnino@westhillscollege.com
Phone: (559) 934-2302 Toll-free number: (800) 266-1114
Fax: (559) 935-2788
Sandra Dagnino, District Director, Enrollment Services, West Hills Community College, 300 Cherry Lane, Coalinga, CA 93210

West Los Angeles College

Culver City, California
www.wlac.edu **CB code: 4964**

- Public 2-year community college
- Large town

General. Founded in 1968. Regionally accredited. **Enrollment:** 1,746 full-time, degree-seeking students. **Degrees:** 322 associate awarded. **Location:** 10 miles from Civic Center. **Calendar:** Semester, limited summer session. **Full-time faculty:** 105 total. **Part-time faculty:** 200 total.

Basis for selection. Open admission.

2005-2006 Annual costs. Tuition/fees: $804; $5,424 out-of-state. Per-credit charge: $26 in-state; $180 out-of-state. Books/supplies: $810. Personal expenses: $1,548.

2005-2006 Financial aid. All financial aid based on need. 22% of total undergraduate aid awarded as scholarships/grants, 78% as loans/jobs. Need-based aid available for part-time students. Work study available for part-time students. **Additional information:** California residents may qualify for Board of Governor's Grant Program.

Application procedures. Admission: No deadline. No application fee. Admission notification on a rolling basis. **Financial aid:** No deadline. FAFSA required. Applicants notified on a rolling basis; must reply within 4 week(s) of notification.

Academics. Special study options: Cooperative education, dual enrollment of high school students, honors, independent study, student-designed major, study abroad. **Credit/placement by examination:** CLEP, institutional tests. 15 credit hours maximum toward associate degree. **Support services:** Learning center, remedial instruction, tutoring.

Majors. Biology: General. **Business:** General, accounting, administrative services, business admin, real estate. **Engineering:** General. **English:** Speech/rhetoric. **Foreign languages:** French, Spanish. **Health:** Dental hygiene. **History:** General. **Legal studies:** Paralegal. **Liberal arts:** Arts/sciences. **Mechanic/repair:** Aircraft. **Parks/recreation:** Health/fitness. **Philosophy/religion:** Philosophy. **Physical sciences:** Chemistry, geology, physics. **Psychology:** General. **Social sciences:** Anthropology, economics, geography, political science, sociology. **Visual/performing arts:** Art, ceramics.

Student life. Freshman orientation: Available. 2 hour session prior to start of each semester. **Activities:** Bands, choral groups, dance, drama, film society, student government, student newspaper, TV station.

Athletics. Intercollegiate: Baseball M, basketball M, football (tackle) M, tennis, track and field. **Team name:** Oilers.

Student services. Adult student services, career counseling, services for economically disadvantaged, student employment services, financial aid counseling, health services, on-campus daycare, personal counseling, placement for graduates, veterans' counselor. **Physically disabled:** Services for visually, speech, hearing impaired.

Contact. Phone: (310) 287-4501
Lawrence Jarmon, Dean of Student Affairs, West Los Angeles College, 9000 Overland Ave, Culver City, CA 90230

West Valley College

Saratoga, California
www.westvalley.edu **CB code: 4958**

- Public 2-year community college
- Large town

General. Founded in 1963. Regionally accredited. **Enrollment:** 3,500 degree-seeking undergraduates. **Degrees:** 679 associate awarded. **ROTC:** Army, Air Force. **Location:** 13 miles from San Jose. **Calendar:** Semester, limited summer session. **Full-time faculty:** 200 total. **Part-time faculty:** 250 total. **Special facilities:** Planetarium.

Student profile. Among degree-seeking undergraduates, 15% enrolled in a transfer program, 8% enrolled in a vocational program, 7% already have a bachelor's degree or higher.

Basis for selection. Open admission.

2005-2006 Annual costs. Tuition/fees: $830; $5,360 out-of-state. Per-credit charge: $26 in-state; $177 out-of-state. Books/supplies: $612. Personal expenses: $1,566.

Financial aid. All financial aid based on need. Need-based aid available for part-time students.

Application procedures. Admission: Priority date 4/21; no deadline. No application fee. Admission notification on a rolling basis. **Financial aid:** Priority date 5/31; no closing date. FAFSA required. Applicants notified on a rolling basis starting 7/1.

Academics. Special study options: Distance learning, double major, dual enrollment of high school students, ESL, honors, independent study, teacher certification program. **Credit/placement by examination:** CLEP, institutional tests. 12 credit hours maximum toward associate degree. **Support services:** Learning center, pre-admission summer program, remedial instruction, tutoring.

Majors. Architecture: Landscape. **Area/ethnic studies:** Women's. **Biology:** General. **Business:** General, accounting, administrative services, business admin, fashion, office management, office technology, office/clerical, real estate. **Computer sciences:** General, programming. **Construction:** Maintenance. **Education:** Early childhood. **Engineering:** General. **Engineering technology:** Drafting, electrical. **English:** Speech/rhetoric. **Family/consumer sciences:** Child care. **Foreign languages:** General. **Health:** Medical assistant. **History:** General. **Legal studies:** Court reporting, paralegal. **Liberal arts:** Arts/sciences. **Math:** General. **Parks/recreation:** Facilities management. **Physical sciences:** Chemistry, geology, physics. **Protective services:** Criminal justice. **Psychology:** General. **Social sciences:** General, sociology. **Visual/performing arts:** Art, dramatic, fashion design, interior design.

Computing on campus. 150 workstations in library, computer center. Commuter students can connect to campus network. Online course registration, online library, repair service available.

Student life. Freshman orientation: Available. **Activities:** Bands, choral groups, drama, music ensembles, student government, student newspaper, symphony orchestra, TV station, Vietnamese student association, Unlimited Horizons (handicapped), Descendants of Africa, Latin American student association, Alpha Gamma Sigma, Latter-Day Saints, fashion design, Puente, JC Ministries (Christian).

Athletics. Intercollegiate: Baseball M, basketball, cross-country, field hockey W, football (tackle) M, gymnastics W, soccer M, softball W, swimming, tennis, track and field, volleyball, water polo M, wrestling M. **Intramural:** Badminton, basketball, bowling, swimming, tennis, volleyball. **Team name:** Vikings.

Student services. Adult student services, career counseling, student employment services, health services, on-campus daycare, personal counseling, veterans' counselor. **Physically disabled:** Services for visually, speech, hearing impaired. **Transfer:** Special adviser, orientation, re-entry adviser for new students. Transfer center, transfer adviser, college fairs on campus for students transferring to 4-year colleges.

Contact. Phone: (408) 741-2001 Fax: (408) 867-5033
Paula Prichett, Director of Admissions, West Valley College, 14000 Fruitvale Avenue, Saratoga, CA 95070-5698

Western Career College

Sacramento, California
www.westerncollege.com **CB code: 2917**

- For-profit 2-year health science and technical college
- Large city

General. Accredited by ACCSCT. **Calendar:** Continuous.

Annual costs/financial aid. Tuition for 15-month associate science degree program: veterinary technology $20,251; dental assisting $18,918; medical assisting $19,204; medical billing $19,446; medical administrative assisting $19,091; pharmacy tech $20,425; massage therapy $19,616; vocational nursing $30,533. Tuition for 10-month certificate program: dental assisting

$11,717; medical assisting $12,003; massage therapy $12,414; vocational nursing $24,852. Books, supplies, uniform, fees included. Books/supplies: $448. Personal expenses: $1,686.

Contact. Phone: (916) 361-1660
8909 Folsom Boulevard, Sacramento, CA 95826-9823

Western Career College: Pleasant Hill

Pleasant Hill, California
www.westerncollege.com **CB code: 2922**

- For-profit 2-year health science and technical college
- Small city

General. Accredited by ACCSCT. **Enrollment:** 350 degree-seeking undergraduates. **Degrees:** 206 associate awarded. **Calendar:** Continuous. **Full-time faculty:** 5 total. **Part-time faculty:** 53 total.

Basis for selection. CPAT examination important.

2005-2006 Annual costs. Tuition $18,830; books, supplies, uniform expenses for medical billing $1,727, medical administrative assistant $1,402, medical assisting $1,515, dental assisting program $1,229, massage therapy $1,927. Tuition for pharmacy technology $20,125; books, supplies, uniform expenses $1,468. Program length ranges from 15 to 19 months. Registration fee $100.

Application procedures. **Admission:** No deadline. $100 fee. Admission notification on a rolling basis. **Financial aid:** No deadline. Applicants notified on a rolling basis.

Academics. **Credit/placement by examination:** CLEP.

Majors. **Health:** Dental assistant, medical assistant.

Contact. Phone: (925) 609-6650 Toll-free number: (800) 584-4520
Fax: (925) 609-6666
Lashon Wells, Admissions Director, Western Career College: Pleasant Hill, 380 Civic Drive, Suite 300, Pleasant Hill, CA 94523

Western Career College: San Jose

San Jose, California
www.svcollege.com

- For-profit 2-year technical college
- Very large city

General. Accredited by ACCSCT. **Enrollment:** 350 degree-seeking undergraduates. **Degrees:** 185 associate awarded. **Calendar:** Continuous. **Full-time faculty:** 13 total. **Part-time faculty:** 10 total.

Basis for selection. Open admission, but selective for some programs. Limited admission to dental programs.

Application procedures. **Admission:** No deadline. $75 fee. Admission notification on a rolling basis.

Academics. **Credit/placement by examination:** CLEP.

Majors. **Computer sciences:** Computer graphics. **Engineering technology:** Architectural drafting. **Health:** Dental assistant, dental hygiene, massage therapy, medical assistant, medical records technology, pharmacy assistant, surgical technology, veterinary technology/assistant.

Contact. Phone: (408) 360-0840 Fax: (408) 360-0848
Indy Decroos, Admissions Director, Western Career College: San Jose, 6201 San Ignacio Avenue, San Jose, CA 95119

Western Career College: San Leandro

San Leandro, California
www.westerncollege.edu **CB code: 2918**

- For-profit 2-year health science and technical college
- Small city

General. Accredited by ACCSCT. **Enrollment:** 562 degree-seeking undergraduates. **Degrees:** 104 associate awarded. **Calendar:** Continuous. **Full-time faculty:** 26 total. **Part-time faculty:** 26 total.

Basis for selection. CPAT score, interest important. CPAT required.

2005-2006 Annual costs. Books/supplies: $448. Personal expenses: $1,686.

Application procedures. **Admission:** No deadline. $100 fee. Admission notification on a rolling basis. **Financial aid:** No deadline. Applicants notified on a rolling basis.

Academics. **Credit/placement by examination:** CLEP.

Majors. **Health:** Licensed practical nurse, pharmacy assistant, veterinary technology/assistant.

Contact. Phone: (510) 276-3888 Toll-free number: (800) 584-4553
Fax: (510) 276-3854
Western Career College: San Leandro, 1555 East 14th Street Suite 500, San Leandro, CA 94578

Western Career College: Walnut Creek

Antioch, California
www.westerncollege.edu **CB code: 3033**

- For-profit 2-year technical college
- Small city

General. Accredited by ACCSCT. **Enrollment:** 240 degree-seeking undergraduates. **Degrees:** 58 associate awarded. **Calendar:** Continuous. **Full-time faculty:** 11 total. **Part-time faculty:** 7 total.

Basis for selection. CPAT results important.

2005-2006 Annual costs. Tuition and fees range from $7,000 to $44,050 depending on program; certificate program length 30 weeks to 2 years, bachelor's slightly over 2 years.

Application procedures. **Admission:** No deadline. $100 fee. Admission notification on a rolling basis.

Academics. **Credit/placement by examination:** CLEP.

Majors. **Computer sciences:** General.

Contact. Phone: (925) 280-0235 Fax: (925) 280-0267
Western Career College: Walnut Creek, 2157 Country Hills Road, Antioch, CA 94531

Westwood College: Los Angeles

Los Angeles, California
www.westwood.edu

- For-profit 2-year technical college
- Very large city

General. Accredited by ACICS. **Enrollment:** 851 degree-seeking undergraduates. **Degrees:** 51 associate awarded. **Calendar:** 10-week terms throughout year. **Full-time faculty:** 12 total. **Part-time faculty:** 47 total.

Basis for selection. High school record and standardized test codes most important. Accuplacer required.

2005-2006 Annual costs. Total cost of tuition plus fees for 17-month, 7-term associate degree program: $24,855. Cost of tuition plus fees for 14-term, 34-month bachelor program: $49,635. Cost of books, supplies will vary with program.

Application procedures. **Admission:** No deadline. $100 fee. Admission notification on a rolling basis. **Financial aid:** FAFSA required. Applicants notified on a rolling basis.

Academics. **Credit/placement by examination:** CLEP.

Majors. **Computer sciences:** Computer graphics, programming.

Contact. Phone: (213) 739-9999
Guy Lopatin, Director of Admissions, Westwood College: Los Angeles, 3250 Wilshire Boulevard, Suite 400, Los Angeles, CA 90010

WyoTech Institute: Fremont

Fremont, California
www.wyotech.com **CB code: 3030**

- For-profit 2-year technical college
- Small city

General. Accredited by ACCSCT. **Enrollment:** 1,364 full-time, degree-seeking students. **Degrees:** 287 associate awarded. **Calendar:** Continuous. **Full-time faculty:** 75 total.

2005-2006 Annual costs. 14-month diploma tuition and fees $21,950 ; 18-month associate degree tuition and fees $27,725 - $28,200.

Academics. Credit/placement by examination: CLEP. **Support services:** Learning center.

Majors. Mechanic/repair: General.

Contact. Phone: (510) 490-6900 Toll-free number: (800) 248-8585
WyoTech Institute: Fremont, 200 Whitney Place, Fremont, CA 94539

Yuba Community College District

Marysville, California
www.yccd.edu **CB code: 4994**

- Public 2-year community college
- Commuter campus in small city

General. Founded in 1927. Regionally accredited. **Enrollment:** 5,156 degree-seeking undergraduates. **Degrees:** 783 associate awarded. **Location:** 56 miles from Sacramento. **Calendar:** Semester, limited summer session. **Full-time faculty:** 135 total. **Part-time faculty:** 375 total. **Special facilities:** Veterinary technical training clinic, manufacturing technology facilities (factory), measurement science/scale repair training facilities. **Partnerships:** Formal partnerships with numerous local businesses.

Transfer out. Colleges most students transferred to 2005: California State University-Sacramento, California State University-Chico, University of California-Davis.

Basis for selection. Open admission, but selective for some programs. Selective admission to allied health programs. CPT tests recommended for counseling. **Adult students:** Entrance exam policies same as for first-time freshmen.

2005-2006 Annual costs. Tuition/fees: $792; $5,322 out-of-state. Per-credit charge: $26 in-state; $177 out-of-state. Books/supplies: $1,260.

Financial aid. Need-based: Need-based aid available for part-time students. Work study available for part-time students. **Non-need-based:** Scholarships awarded for academics, athletics, job skills, minority status, music/drama. **Additional information:** Tuition fee waiver based on Board of Governors Grant.

Application procedures. Admission: No deadline. No application fee. Admission notification on a rolling basis beginning on or about 6/1. **Financial aid:** Closing date 3/1. FAFSA required. Applicants notified on a rolling basis starting 4/1.

Academics. Special study options: Cooperative education, distance learning, ESL. License preparation in nursing, radiology. **Credit/placement by examination:** CLEP, institutional tests. **Support services:** Learning center, remedial instruction, tutoring.

Majors. Agriculture: Business, landscaping, mechanization, ornamental horticulture. **Business:** Accounting, administrative services, business admin, entrepreneurial studies, human resources, taxation. **Communications:** Journalism, media studies. **Computer sciences:** General, computer science. **Education:** Early childhood, physical. **Engineering technology:** Electrical, water quality. **Family/consumer sciences:** Family/community services. **Health:** Medical radiologic technology/radiation therapy, medical transcription, nursing (RN), substance abuse counseling, veterinary technology/assistant. **History:** General. **Liberal arts:** Arts/sciences. **Math:** General. **Mechanic/repair:** General, automotive, electronics/electrical. **Personal/culinary services:** Cosmetology. **Production:** General, sheet metal. **Protective services:** Criminal justice, fire safety technology, police science. **Social sciences:** General. **Visual/performing arts:** Art, dramatic, photography, studio arts.

Most popular majors. Education 31%.

Computing on campus. 300 workstations in library.

Student life. Freshman orientation: Available. **Policies:** Freshmen permitted cars on campus. **Activities:** Bands, choral groups, drama, music ensembles, musical theater, student government, student newspaper, symphony orchestra, AD Nursing Students Association, Care Club, EOP&S Club DECA/Marketing Club, Christian Students Association, Green Society, Future Teachers of America, Speech Team, Photography Guild, Veterinary Technicians Association.

Athletics. Intercollegiate: Baseball M, basketball, cross-country, football (tackle) M, soccer, softball W, tennis, track and field, volleyball W. **Team name:** 49'ers.

Student services. Adult student services, career counseling, services for economically disadvantaged, student employment services, financial aid counseling, health services, minority student services, on-campus daycare, personal counseling, placement for graduates, veterans' counselor, women's services. **Physically disabled:** Services for visually, speech, hearing impaired. **Transfer:** Special adviser, orientation for new students. Transfer adviser, college fairs on campus for students transferring to 4-year colleges.

Contact. E-mail: kpope@yccd.edu
Phone: (530) 741-6720 Fax: (530) 741-6872
Connie Elder, Admissions Registrar, Yuba Community College District, 2088 North Beale Road, Marysville, CA 95901

Colorado

Aims Community College

Greeley, Colorado
www.aims.edu
CB member
CB code: 4204

- Public 2-year community college
- Commuter campus in small city

General. Founded in 1967. Regionally accredited. **Enrollment:** 3,750 degree-seeking undergraduates. **Degrees:** 340 associate awarded. **ROTC:** Air Force. **Location:** 55 miles from Denver. **Calendar:** Quarter, extensive summer session. **Full-time faculty:** 115 total. **Part-time faculty:** 135 total.

Student profile.

Out-of-state:	2%	**25 or older:**	80%

Basis for selection. Open admission, but selective for some programs. Special requirements for radiologic technology, police academy and biofeedback programs based on test scores. All students must meet assessment requirement by taking computerized placement test, submitting ACT/SAT scores or showing proof of previous college experience. Interview required of radiologic technology, police academy, biofeedback majors.

2005-2006 Annual costs. Tuition/fees: $1,890; $2,970 out-of-district; $9,390 out-of-state. Per-credit charge: $50 in-district; $86 out-of-district; $300 out-of-state. Books/supplies: $600. Personal expenses: $450.

Application procedures. Admission: No deadline. No application fee. Admission notification on a rolling basis. **Financial aid:** Priority date 4/1, closing date 4/15. FAFSA required. Applicants notified on a rolling basis starting 6/1.

Academics. Special study options: Cooperative education, double major, dual enrollment of high school students, independent study, internships, weekend college. **Credit/placement by examination:** AP, CLEP, institutional tests. 48 credit hours maximum toward associate degree. **Support services:** Learning center, remedial instruction, tutoring.

Majors. Agriculture: General, supplies. **Business:** Accounting, administrative services, management information systems, marketing. **Communications technology:** Graphic/printing. **Engineering technology:** Electrical. **Family/consumer sciences:** Child care. **Health:** Medical radiologic technology/radiation therapy. **Liberal arts:** Arts/sciences. **Mechanic/repair:** Auto body. **Protective services:** Fire safety technology, law enforcement admin. **Transportation:** Aviation.

Most popular majors. Business/marketing 18%, liberal arts 62%, trade and industry 7%.

Computing on campus. 500 workstations in computer center, student center.

Student life. Activities: Concert band, dance, drama, literary magazine, musical theater, student government, student newspaper.

Athletics. Intramural: Basketball, volleyball.

Student services. Career counseling, student employment services, on-campus daycare, placement for graduates, veterans' counselor. **Physically disabled:** Services for visually, speech, hearing impaired. **Transfer:** Special adviser, orientation for new students. Transfer adviser, college fairs on campus for students transferring to 4-year colleges.

Contact. E-mail: admissions.records@aims.edu
Phone: (970) 339-6440 Toll-free number: (800) 301-5388
Stewart Thomas, Director of Admissions, Aims Community College, 5401 West 20th Street PO Box 69, Greeley, CO 80632

Arapahoe Community College

Littleton, Colorado
www.arapahoe.edu
CB code: 4014

- Public 2-year community college
- Commuter campus in small city

General. Founded in 1965. Regionally accredited. **Enrollment:** 4,707 degree-seeking undergraduates. **Degrees:** 525 associate awarded. **ROTC:** Army, Air Force. **Location:** 10 miles from Denver. **Calendar:** Semester, limited summer session. **Full-time faculty:** 94 total. **Part-time faculty:** 444 total. **Class size:** 61% < 20, 112% 20-39, 2% 40-49, less than 1% 50-99. **Partnerships:** Formal partnerships with National Cable Communications Institute, Swedish Medical Center, Porter Adventist Hospital.

Student profile.

Out-of-state:	4%	**25 or older:**	55%

Transfer out. Colleges most students transferred to 2005: University of Colorado at Denver, Colorado State University, University of Northern Colorado, Colorado School of Mines, Adams State College.

Basis for selection. Open admission, but selective for some programs. Selective admission to allied health, automotive, legal assistant, and law enforcement programs, requiring personal interviews and/or certain test scores. SAT or ACT scores considered for placement if submitted. Interview required of health occupation programs, legal assistant, automotive services, and police academy majors.

2005-2006 Annual costs. Tuition/fees: $2,351; $10,523 out-of-state. Per-credit charge: $73 in-state; $345 out-of-state. In-state tuition based upon assumption of Colorado Oppurtunity Fund waiver of $80 per-credit-hour. Books/supplies: $850.

Financial aid. Need-based: Need-based aid available for part-time students. Work study available nights, weekends and for part-time students. **Non-need-based:** Scholarships awarded for academics, athletics, leadership, state residency.

Application procedures. Admission: No deadline. No application fee. Application may be submitted online. Admission notification on a rolling basis. Closing date for nursing applicants February 4. **Financial aid:** Priority date 5/1, closing date 6/1. FAFSA, institutional form required. Applicants notified on a rolling basis starting 5/1; must reply within 3 week(s) of notification.

Academics. Special study options: Accelerated study, cooperative education, cross-registration, distance learning, dual enrollment of high school students, ESL, honors, independent study, internships, liberal arts/career combination, student-designed major, weekend college. License preparation in nursing, occupational therapy, paramedic, physical therapy, real estate. **Credit/placement by examination:** AP, CLEP, institutional tests. No more than half of required credit can be fulfilled through credit for prior learning. **Support services:** GED preparation and test center, learning center, reduced course load, remedial instruction, study skills assistance, tutoring, writing center.

Majors. Architecture: Technology. **Business:** Accounting technology, administrative services, banking/financial services, hospitality admin, international, management information systems, marketing, office management, selling. **Communications technology:** General. **Computer sciences:** Data entry, LAN/WAN management, networking, web page design. **Construction:** General, building inspection. **Engineering technology:** General, architectural, computer, electrical, manufacturing. **Family/consumer sciences:** Child development. **Health:** Clinical lab technology, medical records technology, nursing (RN), occupational therapy assistant, office admin, physical therapy assistant. **Legal studies:** Paralegal. **Liberal arts:** Arts/sciences. **Mechanic/repair:** Automotive. **Parks/recreation:** Health/fitness. **Personal/culinary services:** Mortuary science. **Protective services:** Law enforcement admin. **Visual/performing arts:** Graphic design, interior design.

Most popular majors. Business/marketing 9%, health sciences 26%, legal studies 7%, liberal arts 32%, visual/performing arts 13%.

Computing on campus. 110 workstations in library, computer center. Commuter students can connect to campus network. Online course registration, online library, helpline, student web hosting available.

Student life. Freshman orientation: Mandatory. Preregistration for classes offered. **Activities:** Concert band, choral groups, dance, drama, student government, student newspaper, Phi Theta Kappa, ADA-Council, UMOJA, Latino Task-Force, diversity council.

Athletics. NJCAA. **Intercollegiate:** Baseball M, softball W. **Intramural:** Basketball, soccer, table tennis, tennis, volleyball. **Team name:** Coyotes.

Student services. Adult student services, alcohol/substance abuse counseling, career counseling, services for economically disadvantaged, student employment services, financial aid counseling, minority student services, on-campus daycare, personal counseling, placement for graduates, veterans' counselor. **Physically disabled:** Services for visually, speech, hearing impaired. **Learning disabled:** Comprehensive services available. **Transfer:**

Special adviser, orientation, pre-admission transcript evaluation for new students. Transfer adviser, college fairs on campus for students transferring to 4-year colleges.

Contact. Phone: (303) 797-4222 Fax: (303) 797-5970
Matt Jamison, Director of Admissions and Records, Arapahoe Community College, PO Box 9002, Littleton, CO 80160-9002

Bel-Rea Institute of Animal Technology

Denver, Colorado
www.bel-rea.com **CB code: 0928**

- For-profit 2-year technical college
- Commuter campus in very large city

General. Accredited by ACCSCT. Students intern at college-affiliated emergency veterinary hospital. **Enrollment:** 600 degree-seeking undergraduates. **Degrees:** 290 associate awarded. **Calendar:** Continuous. **Full-time faculty:** 22 total. **Part-time faculty:** 3 total.

Transfer out. Colleges most students transferred to 2005: University of Denver.

Basis for selection. Interview most important, followed by school achievement record. Recommendations considered. Minimum 2.5 high school GPA or GED required. Applicants with GPA below 2.5 or without GED must take entrance exam.

High school preparation. As much science and math as possible recommended. Algebra and chemistry recommended.

2006-2007 Annual costs. Tuition for full associate program $20,750 including fees. Books/supplies: $1,500. Personal expenses: $1,100.

Financial aid. All financial aid based on need.

Application procedures. Admission: No deadline. No application fee. Admission notification on a rolling basis. **Financial aid:** Priority date 8/31; no closing date. FAFSA required. Applicants notified on a rolling basis starting 8/15.

Academics. Special study options: Internships. **Credit/placement by examination:** CLEP. **Support services:** Reduced course load, study skills assistance, tutoring.

Majors. Health: Veterinary technology/assistant.

Computing on campus. PC or laptop required. 20 workstations in student center.

Student life. Freshman orientation: Available. **Activities:** Student government.

Student services. Career counseling, student employment services, personal counseling, placement for graduates, veterans' counselor. **Transfer:** Special adviser, orientation for new students.

Contact. E-mail: kaufman@bel-rea.com
Phone: (303) 751-8700 Toll-free number: (800) 950-8001
Fax: (303) 751-9969
Paulette Kaufman, Director, Bel-Rea Institute of Animal Technology, 1681 South Dayton Street, Denver, CO 80247

Blair College

Colorado Springs, Colorado
www.cci.edu **CB code: 0934**

- For-profit 2-year business and junior college
- Commuter campus in large city
- Interview required

General. Founded in 1897. Accredited by ACICS. **Enrollment:** 700 degree-seeking undergraduates. **Degrees:** 138 associate awarded. **Location:** 70 miles from Denver. **Calendar:** Quarter, extensive summer session. **Full-time faculty:** 15 total. **Part-time faculty:** 30 total.

Basis for selection. Open admission.

2005-2006 Annual costs. For linear programs: $260 per credit hour for all other linear programs; $25 registration fee and tech fee. For modular programs: (Medical Administrative Assistant; 8 modules, 47 credits) - tuition: $9765 plus $900 for text/materials; (Homeland Security Specialist; 7 modules, 48 credits) - tuition: $8451, plus $1500 for text/matrials and uniform; (Medical Insurance Billing & Coding; 6 modules, 35 credits) - tuition: $8657, plus $900 for text/materials. Books/supplies: $1,025.

Financial aid. Need-based: Need-based aid available for part-time students. Work study available nights and for part-time students.

Application procedures. Admission: No deadline. No application fee. Application must be submitted on paper. Admission notification on a rolling basis. **Financial aid:** No deadline. FAFSA, institutional form required. Applicants notified on a rolling basis starting 7/1.

Academics. Special study options: Distance learning, double major, dual enrollment of high school students, independent study, internships, liberal arts/career combination. **Credit/placement by examination:** AP, CLEP, institutional tests. **Support services:** Tutoring.

Majors. Business: Accounting, business admin. **Computer sciences:** General, LAN/WAN management, networking. **Health:** Medical assistant, medical secretary. **Legal studies:** Legal secretary, paralegal. **Protective services:** Criminal justice.

Most popular majors. Business/marketing 42%, computer/information sciences 15%, health sciences 27%, legal studies 16%.

Computing on campus. PC or laptop required. 174 workstations in library, computer center.

Student life. Freshman orientation: Mandatory. Preregistration for classes offered. **Activities:** Student newspaper.

Student services. Career counseling, student employment services, financial aid counseling, personal counseling, placement for graduates, veterans' counselor. **Transfer:** Orientation, pre-admission transcript evaluation for new students.

Contact. E-mail: afi@cci.edu
Phone: (719) 638-6580 Fax: (719) 574-4493
Alexandra Fi, Director of Admissions, Blair College, 1815 Jet Wing Drive, Colorado Springs, CO 80916

Boulder College of Massage Therapy

Boulder, Colorado
www.bcmt.org

- Private 1-year health science and community college
- Residential campus in small city
- Application essay, interview required

General. Accredited by ACCSCT. **Enrollment:** 220 undergraduates. **Degrees:** 29 associate awarded. **Location:** 30 miles from Denver. **Calendar:** Quarter, extensive summer session. **Full-time faculty:** 6 total; 50% have terminal degrees, 67% women. **Part-time faculty:** 39 total; 15% have terminal degrees, 10% minority, 69% women. **Special facilities:** Student massage therapy clinic, wellness bookstore.

Basis for selection. Open admission, but selective for some programs. Interview by a staff or faculty member required. Health history form required.

2006-2007 Annual costs. Programs range from $13,160-$16,450.

Financial aid. All financial aid based on need. Need-based aid available for part-time students.

Application procedures. Admission: No deadline. $75 fee, may be waived for applicants with need. Application must be submitted on paper. Admission notification on a rolling basis. **Financial aid:** No deadline. FAFSA required.

Academics. Special study options: Honors, internships. **Credit/placement by examination:** CLEP. **Support services:** Learning center, reduced course load, study skills assistance, tutoring.

Majors. Health: Massage therapy.

Computing on campus. 10 workstations in library, computer center. Online library, wireless network available.

Student life. Freshman orientation: Mandatory. Preregistration for classes offered. Held the Monday prior to start of quarter. **Policies:** Freshmen permitted cars on campus. **Activities:** Student government.

Student services. Adult student services, alcohol/substance abuse counseling, career counseling, services for economically disadvantaged, student employment services, financial aid counseling, health services, personal counseling, placement for graduates, veterans' counselor. **Physically disabled:** Services for visually, speech, hearing impaired.

Contact. Phone: (303) 530-2100 Toll-free number: (303) 442-5131
Fax: (303) 530-2204
Director of Marketing and Admissions, Boulder College of Massage Therapy, 6255 Longbow Drive, Boulder, CO 80301

Cambridge College
Aurora, Colorado
www.hightechschools.edu **CB code: 3201**

- For-profit 2-year technical college
- Commuter campus in small city
- Interview required

General. Accredited by ACCSCT. **Enrollment:** 415 degree-seeking undergraduates. **Degrees:** 233 associate awarded. **Calendar:** Continuous, extensive summer session. **Full-time faculty:** 35 total.

Basis for selection. Interview most important. Entrance exam required for students out of high school more than 6 months. **Adult students:** Entrance exam policies same as for first-time freshmen.

2005-2006 Annual costs. Tuition for full associate degree programs ranges from $16,550 to $24,500 depending on program; tuition for diploma programs ranges from $7,950 to $10,150. Books and supplies included. Housing provided by private company.

Financial aid. All financial aid based on need.

Application procedures. Admission: No deadline. $50 fee ($150 out-of-state). Admission notification on a rolling basis. **Financial aid:** No deadline. FAFSA, institutional form required. Applicants notified on a rolling basis.

Academics. Special study options: License preparation in radiology. **Credit/placement by examination:** CLEP. **Support services:** GED preparation.

Majors. Computer sciences: General. **Health:** Massage therapy, medical assistant, radiologic technology/medical imaging, surgical technology.

Student life. Freshman orientation: Mandatory. **Policies:** Freshmen permitted cars on campus. **Housing:** Apartments available through private company.

Student services. Adult student services, career counseling, student employment services, financial aid counseling, placement for graduates. **Transfer:** Orientation for new students.

Contact. Phone: (720) 859-7900 Toll-free number: (800) 322-4132
Fax: (303) 338-9701
Stacey Keele, Director of Admissions, Cambridge College, 350 Blackhawk Street, Aurora, CO 80011

CollegeAmerica-Denver
Denver, Colorado
www.collegeamerica.com

- For-profit 2-year technical college
- Commuter campus in very large city

General. Accredited by ACCSCT. **Enrollment:** 439 degree-seeking undergraduates. **Degrees:** 5 bachelor's, 131 associate awarded. **Calendar:** Continuous. **Full-time faculty:** 5 total; 20% have terminal degrees, 40% minority, 40% women. **Part-time faculty:** 22 total; 4% have terminal degrees, 14% minority, 36% women. **Class size:** 89% < 20, 11% 20-39.

Student profile. Among degree-seeking undergraduates, 100% enrolled in a vocational program, 74 enrolled as first-time, first-year students, 110 transferred in from other institutions.

Women:	73%	**Hispanic American:**	19%
African American:	14%	**Native American:**	1%
Asian American:	3%	**25 or older:**	70%

Basis for selection. Open admission. High school diploma or GED required of all students. **Adult students:** Entrance exam policies same as for first-time freshmen. **Homeschooled:** Transcript of courses and grades, state high school equivalency certificate required.

2005-2006 Annual costs. Tuition and fees: $27,950. Off-campus room and board: $12,525; other expenses: $7348. Books and supplies are provided for students. Books/supplies: $101. Personal expenses: $1,000.

2005-2006 Financial aid. All financial aid based on need. 74 full-time freshmen applied for aid; 74 were judged to have need; 74 of these received aid. Average need met was 50%. Average loan was $8,100.

Application procedures. Admission: No deadline. No application fee. **Financial aid:** No deadline. FAFSA, institutional form required. Applicants notified on a rolling basis; must reply within 4 week(s) of notification.

Academics. Special study options: Accelerated study, distance learning. Bachelor's degree programs available on campus. License preparation in radiology. **Credit/placement by examination:** AP, CLEP. **Support services:** Tutoring.

Majors. Business: Accounting/business management, business admin. **Computer sciences:** Computer graphics, networking, programming. **Health:** Health services.

Most popular majors. Business/marketing 10%, computer/information sciences 10%, health sciences 70%.

Computing on campus. 50 workstations in library, computer center. Commuter students can connect to campus network. Online course registration, online library available.

Student life. Freshman orientation: Mandatory. **Policies:** Freshmen permitted cars on campus.

Student services. Career counseling, student employment services, financial aid counseling, placement for graduates. **Transfer:** Orientation for new students.

Contact. Phone: (303) 691-9756 Toll-free number: (800) 977-5455
Mary Nebel, Director of Admissions, CollegeAmerica-Denver, 1385 South Colorado Boulevard, Suite A512, Denver, CO 80222-1912

Colorado Mountain College: Alpine Campus
Steamboat Springs, Colorado
www.coloradomtn.edu **CB code: 4140**

- Public 2-year community and liberal arts college
- Residential campus in small town

General. Founded in 1981. Regionally accredited. Part of 3 residential-campus system in the Colorado Rocky Mountains. **Enrollment:** 750 degree-seeking undergraduates. **Degrees:** 355 associate awarded. **Location:** 190 miles from Denver. **Calendar:** Semester, limited summer session. **Full-time faculty:** 82 total. **Part-time faculty:** 270 total.

Transfer out. Colleges most students transferred to 2005: University of Colorado-Boulder, Colorado State University, Western State College, Mesa State College, Fort Lewis College.

Basis for selection. Open admission. SAT or ACT recommended for placement and counseling. Institutional test available in place of SAT or ACT.

2005-2006 Annual costs. Tuition/fees: $1,490; $2,360 out-of-district; $7,130 out-of-state. Per-credit charge: $43 in-district; $72 out-of-district; $231 out-of-state. Room/board: $6,392. Books/supplies: $700. Personal expenses: $2,050.

Financial aid. Need-based: Need-based aid available for part-time students. Work study available nights, weekends and for part-time students. **Non-need-based:** Scholarships awarded for academics, athletics, state residency.

Application procedures. Admission: No deadline. No application fee. Admission notification on a rolling basis. **Financial aid:** Priority date 3/31; no closing date. FAFSA required. Applicants notified on a rolling basis starting 5/15; must reply within 4 week(s) of notification.

Academics. Ski industry training programs available. **Special study options:** Distance learning, dual enrollment of high school students, independent study, internships, liberal arts/career combination, study abroad. **Credit/placement by examination:** AP, CLEP, institutional tests. 30 credit hours maximum toward associate degree. Also recognize and accept exam results for DANTES, PEP, Institutional Challenge Exams and credit for life experience. **Support services:** GED preparation and test center, learning center, reduced course load, remedial instruction, study skills assistance, tutoring.

Majors. Biology: General. **Business:** General, accounting, business admin, hospitality admin, hospitality/recreation, management information systems. **Communications:** Journalism. **Computer sciences:** Information systems. **Education:** General, early childhood. **Interdisciplinary:** Biological/physical sciences. **Liberal arts:** Arts/sciences. **Math:** General. **Parks/recreation:** Facilities management. **Psychology:** General. **Social sciences:** General. **Visual/performing arts:** General, art, studio arts.

Computing on campus. 43 workstations in dormitories, library, computer center. Dormitories linked to campus network.

Student life. Freshman orientation: Mandatory. Preregistration for classes offered. **Housing:** Coed dorms available. $300 deposit, deadline 7/1. **Activities:** Dance, drama, student government, student newspaper, international student club.

Athletics. NAIA. **Intercollegiate:** Skiing. **Intramural:** Basketball, soccer, volleyball.

Student services. Adult student services, career counseling, student employment services, personal counseling, placement for graduates, veterans' counselor. **Physically disabled:** Services for visually, speech, hearing impaired. **Transfer:** Special adviser, orientation for new students. Transfer adviser, college fairs on campus for students transferring to 4-year colleges.

Contact. E-mail: joinus@coloradomtn.edu
Phone: (970) 870-4417 Toll-free number: (800) 621-8559
Fax: (970) 870-0485
Bill Sommers, Dean of Enrollment Services, Colorado Mountain College: Alpine Campus, 1330 Bob Adams Drive, Steamboat Springs, CO 80487

Colorado Mountain College: Spring Valley Campus

Glenwood Springs, Colorado
www.coloradomtn.edu **CB code: 4112**

- Public 2-year community and liberal arts college
- Residential campus in small town

General. Founded in 1965. Regionally accredited. Part of 3 residential-campus system in the Colorado Rocky Mountains. **Enrollment:** 3,737 degree-seeking undergraduates. **Degrees:** 355 associate awarded. **Location:** 160 miles from Denver. **Calendar:** Semester, limited summer session. **Full-time faculty:** 79 total. **Part-time faculty:** 272 total. **Special facilities:** Outdoor education center, farm for veterinarian technician program, hot springs, climbing wall.

Transfer out. Colleges most students transferred to 2005: University of Colorado-Boulder, Colorado State University, Mesa State University, Western State College, Fort Lewis College.

Basis for selection. Open admission, but selective for some programs. Special requirements for nursing applicants. Testing requirements for veterinary technology students. Testing requirements for photography students. SAT or ACT recommended for placement and counseling. College placement test may be used in place of SAT or ACT.

2005-2006 Annual costs. Tuition/fees: $1,490; $2,360 out-of-district; $7,130 out-of-state. Per-credit charge: $43 in-district; $72 out-of-district; $231 out-of-state. Room/board: $6,392. Books/supplies: $650. Personal expenses: $2,050.

Financial aid. All financial aid based on need. Need-based aid available for part-time students. Work study available nights, weekends and for part-time students.

Application procedures. Financial aid: Priority date 3/31; no closing date. FAFSA required. Applicants notified on a rolling basis starting 5/15; must reply within 4 week(s) of notification.

Academics. Special study options: Distance learning, dual enrollment of high school students, independent study, internships, liberal arts/career combination, study abroad. License preparation in nursing. **Credit/placement by examination:** AP, CLEP, institutional tests. 30 credit hours maximum toward associate degree. Also recognize and accept exam results for DANTES, PEP, Institutional Challenge Exams and credit for life experiences. **Support services:** GED preparation and test center, learning center, reduced course load, remedial instruction, study skills assistance, tutoring.

Majors. Agriculture: Animal health. **Biology:** General. **Business:** General, accounting, business admin, management information systems, real estate. **Computer sciences:** Networking. **Education:** General, bilingual. **Health:** Nursing (RN), veterinary technology/assistant. **Interdisciplinary:** Biological/physical sciences. **Legal studies:** Prelaw. **Liberal arts:** Arts/sciences. **Military:** General. **Physical sciences:** Chemistry, geology. **Protective services:** Criminal justice. **Social sciences:** General. **Visual/performing arts:** General, art, commercial photography, commercial/advertising art, design, dramatic, photography.

Computing on campus. 30 workstations in dormitories, library, computer center. Dormitories linked to campus network.

Student life. Freshman orientation: Mandatory, $40 fee. Preregistration for classes offered. **Policies:** All students living on-campus must follow housing policies. Freshmen permitted cars on campus. **Housing:** Coed dorms available. $300 deposit, deadline 7/1. **Activities:** Dance, drama, musical theater, student government, student newspaper, World Awareness Society (WAS).

Athletics. Intercollegiate: Skiing. **Intramural:** Basketball, skiing, soccer, softball, volleyball.

Student services. Adult student services, career counseling, student employment services, personal counseling, placement for graduates, veterans' counselor. **Physically disabled:** Services for visually, speech, hearing impaired. **Transfer:** Special adviser, orientation for new students. Transfer center, transfer adviser, college fairs on campus for students transferring to 4-year colleges.

Contact. E-mail: admspring@coloradomtn.edu
Phone: (970) 947-8276 Toll-free number: (800) 621-8559
Bill Sommers, Director of Pre-Enrollment Services, Collegewide, Colorado Mountain College: Spring Valley Campus, 3000 County Road 114, Department CB, Glenwood Springs, CO 81601

Colorado Mountain College: Timberline Campus

Leadville, Colorado
www.coloradomtn.edu **CB code: 4113**

- Public 2-year community and liberal arts college
- Residential campus in small town

General. Founded in 1965. Regionally accredited. Part of 3 residential-campus system in the Colorado Rocky Mountains. **Enrollment:** 400 degree-seeking undergraduates. **Degrees:** 355 associate awarded. **Location:** 100 miles from Denver, 120 miles from Colorado Springs. **Calendar:** Semester, limited summer session. **Full-time faculty:** 82 total. **Part-time faculty:** 270 total. **Special facilities:** Ski hill outdoor lab.

Transfer out. Colleges most students transferred to 2005: Colorado State University, University of Northern Colorado, Western State College, Fort Lewis College, University of Colorado.

Basis for selection. Open admission.

2005-2006 Annual costs. Tuition/fees: $1,490; $2,360 out-of-district; $7,130 out-of-state. Per-credit charge: $43 in-district; $72 out-of-district; $231 out-of-state. Room/board: $6,392. Books/supplies: $650. Personal expenses: $2,050.

Financial aid. Need-based: Work study available nights, weekends and for part-time students. **Non-need-based:** Scholarships awarded for academics, athletics, state residency.

Application procedures. Admission: No deadline. No application fee. Application must be submitted on paper. Admission notification on a rolling basis. **Financial aid:** Priority date 3/31; no closing date. FAFSA required. Applicants notified on a rolling basis starting 5/15; must reply within 4 week(s) of notification.

Academics. Outdoor semester in the Rockies: academic liberal arts program balanced with outdoor learning experiences. Other environmental and ski industry programs available. **Special study options:** Distance learning, dual enrollment of high school students, independent study, internships, liberal arts/career combination, study abroad. **Credit/placement by examination:** AP, CLEP, institutional tests. 30 credit hours maximum toward associate degree. Accept exam results for DANTES, CLEP, Institutional Challenge Exams, and credit for life experience. **Support services:** GED preparation and test center, learning center, reduced course load, remedial instruction, study skills assistance, tutoring.

Majors. Agriculture: Soil science. **Biology:** General. **Business:** General, accounting, business admin, real estate. **Communications:** Photojournalism. **Communications technology:** Photo/film/video. **Computer sciences:** Systems analysis. **Conservation:** General, environmental studies, management/policy. **Education:** General, bilingual. **Interdisciplinary:** Biological/

physical sciences, natural sciences. **Legal studies:** Prelaw. **Liberal arts:** Arts/sciences. **Math:** General. **Parks/recreation:** General, facilities management, health/fitness. **Personal/culinary services:** Culinary arts. **Social sciences:** General. **Visual/performing arts:** Art.

Computing on campus. 30 workstations in library, computer center. Dormitories wired for high-speed internet access and linked to campus network.

Student life. **Freshman orientation:** Mandatory, $40 fee. Preregistration for classes offered. **Policies:** Freshmen permitted cars on campus. **Housing:** Coed dorms available. $300 deposit, deadline 7/1. **Activities:** Student government, student newspaper, environmental clubs and organizations.

Athletics. **Intercollegiate:** Skiing. **Intramural:** Basketball M, skiing, soccer M, volleyball.

Student services. Adult student services, career counseling, student employment services, personal counseling, placement for graduates, veterans' counselor. **Physically disabled:** Services for visually, speech, hearing impaired. **Transfer:** Special adviser, orientation for new students. Transfer adviser, college fairs on campus for students transferring to 4-year colleges.

Contact. E-mail: espinoza@coloradomtn.edu
Phone: (719) 486-4291 Toll-free number: (800) 621-8559
Fax: (719) 486-3212
Bill Sommers, Dean of Enrollment Services, Colorado Mountain College: Timberline Campus, 901 South Highway 24, Dept. CB, Leadville, CO 80461

Colorado Northwestern Community College
Rangely, Colorado
www.cncc.edu **CB code: 4665**

- Public 2-year community college
- Residential campus in small town

General. Founded in 1962. Regionally accredited. Courses also offered at campus in Craig and 3 off-campus sites (Meeker, Hayden, Oak Creek). **Enrollment:** 701 degree-seeking undergraduates; 1,500 non-degree-seeking students. **Degrees:** 99 associate awarded. **Location:** 300 miles from Denver, 90 miles from Grand Junction. **Calendar:** Semester, limited summer session. **Full-time faculty:** 50 total. **Part-time faculty:** 150 total. **Class size:** 87% < 20, 13% 20-39. **Special facilities:** Flight simulator, firearms training simulator, cadaver lab.

Student profile. Among degree-seeking undergraduates, 110 enrolled as first-time, first-year students.

Part-time:	40%	**25 or older:**	25%
Out-of-state:	16%	**Live on campus:**	45%
Women:	67%		

Transfer out. **Colleges most students transferred to 2005:** University of Northern Colorado, Colorado State University, Mesa State College.

Basis for selection. Open admission, but selective for some programs. Students not submitting ACT/SAT must take institutional placement tests in English, math, reading. Interview required of dental hygiene majors. **Adult students:** Entrance exam policies same as for first-time freshmen.

High school preparation. Biological science and/or chemistry required for dental hygiene. Mathematics/science desirable for aviation technology and aviation maintenance.

2005-2006 Annual costs. Tuition/fees: $2,373; $8,473 out-of-state. Per-credit charge: $73 in-state; $276 out-of-state. In-state tuition based upon assumption of Colorado Oppurtunity Fund waiver of $80 per-credit-hour. Room/board: $5,650. Books/supplies: $750. Personal expenses: $1,650.

Financial aid. **Need-based:** Need-based aid available for part-time students. Work study available nights, weekends and for part-time students. **Non-need-based:** Scholarships awarded for academics, athletics, state residency.

Application procedures. **Admission:** No deadline. No application fee. Application may be submitted online. Admission notification on a rolling basis. Application closing date for dental hygiene program February 15. **Financial aid:** Priority date 4/15; no closing date. FAFSA, institutional form required. Applicants notified on a rolling basis starting 5/15; must reply within 4 week(s) of notification.

Academics. **Special study options:** Distance learning, dual enrollment of high school students, independent study, internships, student-designed major. Bachelor's degree programs available on campus. License preparation in aviation, dental hygiene. **Credit/placement by examination:** AP, CLEP, institutional tests. 30 credit hours maximum toward associate degree. **Support services:** GED preparation and test center, learning center, remedial instruction, study skills assistance, tutoring, writing center.

Majors. **Business:** Entrepreneurial studies, management information systems, office management. **Family/consumer sciences:** Child care. **Health:** Dental hygiene. **Legal studies:** Paralegal. **Liberal arts:** Arts/sciences. **Mechanic/repair:** Aircraft. **Protective services:** Law enforcement admin. **Transportation:** Aviation.

Computing on campus. 54 workstations in dormitories, library, computer center. Dormitories linked to campus network. Online course registration, online library, wireless network available.

Student life. **Freshman orientation:** Mandatory, $30 fee. Preregistration for classes offered. 2 sessions in July, 1 in August. January session for spring semester. **Policies:** Freshmen permitted cars on campus. **Housing:** Guaranteed on-campus for freshmen. Coed dorms, special housing for disabled, apartments available. $100 deposit. **Activities:** Concert band, choral groups, drama, music ensembles, musical theater, student government, student newspaper.

Athletics. NJCAA. **Intercollegiate:** Baseball M, basketball, cross-country, softball W, volleyball W. **Intramural:** Basketball, football (non-tackle), golf, racquetball, soccer, softball, table tennis, tennis, track and field, volleyball. **Team name:** Spartans.

Student services. Adult student services, alcohol/substance abuse counseling, career counseling, student employment services, financial aid counseling, personal counseling, placement for graduates, veterans' counselor. **Physically disabled:** Services for visually, hearing impaired. **Transfer:** Special adviser, orientation, pre-admission transcript evaluation for new students. Transfer adviser, college fairs on campus for students transferring to 4-year colleges.

Contact. E-mail: lynn.rusher@cncc.edu
Phone: (970) 675-3218 Toll-free number: (800) 562-1105
Fax: (970) 975-3343
Gene Bilodeau, Registrar, Colorado Northwestern Community College, 500 Kennedy Drive, Rangely, CO 81648

Colorado School of Healing Arts
Lakewood, Colorado
www.csha.net

- For-profit 2-year health science college
- Commuter campus in small city
- Application essay, interview required

General. Accredited by ACCSCT. **Enrollment:** 256 degree-seeking undergraduates. **Degrees:** 29 associate awarded. **Calendar:** Quarter, extensive summer session. **Full-time faculty:** 4 total. **Part-time faculty:** 35 total.

Student profile. Among degree-seeking undergraduates, 100% enrolled in a vocational program, 7 transferred in from other institutions. Of all enrolled students, 30% already have a bachelor's degree or higher.

Basis for selection. Open admission. **Homeschooled:** Interview required.

2005-2006 Annual costs. Costs range from 9433 to 15,000 for entire programs, depending on program.

2004-2005 Financial aid. All financial aid based on need. 39% of total undergraduate aid awarded as scholarships/grants, 61% as loans/jobs. Need-based aid available for part-time students.

Application procedures. **Admission:** No deadline. $50 fee. Application must be submitted on paper. **Financial aid:** No deadline. FAFSA required.

Academics. **Special study options:** Accelerated study. **Credit/placement by examination:** CLEP.

Majors. **Health:** Massage therapy.

Student life. **Freshman orientation:** Mandatory. Preregistration for classes offered.

Contact. E-mail: amy@csha.net
Phone: (303) 986-2320 Toll-free number: (800) 233-7114
Fax: (303) 980-6594
Amy Nelson, Director of Admissions, Colorado School of Healing Arts, 7655 West Mississippi, Suite 100, Lakewood, CO 80226

Colorado School of Trades
Lakewood, Colorado
www.schooloftrades.com **CB code: 3211**

- For-profit 2-year technical college
- Small city

General. Accredited by ACCSCT. **Enrollment:** 115 degree-seeking undergraduates. **Degrees:** 52 associate awarded. **Calendar:** Continuous. **Full-time faculty:** 10 total. **Part-time faculty:** 3 total.

Basis for selection. Open admission.

2005-2006 Annual costs. For gunsmithing program: tuition and fees, $16,200; books and supplies, $2,500; off-campus room/board, $4,200; other expenses, $180. For farrier science program: tuition and fees, $6,150. Books/supplies: $2,500. Personal expenses: $1,260.

Application procedures. Admission: No deadline. $25 fee. Admission notification on a rolling basis. **Financial aid:** FAFSA, institutional form required.

Academics. Credit/placement by examination: CLEP.

Majors. Education: Trade/industrial. **Mechanic/repair:** General.

Contact. Phone: (303) 233-4697 Toll-free number: (800) 234-4594
Sunny Duvont-Holt, Director of Admissions, Colorado School of Trades, 1575 Hoyt Street, Lakewood, CO 80215

Community College of Aurora
Aurora, Colorado
www.ccaurora.edu **CB code: 0969**

- Public 2-year community college
- Commuter campus in large city

General. Founded in 1983. Regionally accredited. **Enrollment:** 2,650 degree-seeking undergraduates. **Degrees:** 500 associate awarded. **Calendar:** Semester, extensive summer session. **Full-time faculty:** 40 total. **Part-time faculty:** 300 total.

Student profile.

Out-of-state:	3%	**Live on campus:**	2%
25 or older:	60%		

Transfer out. Colleges most students transferred to 2005: Metropolitan State University, University of Colorado Denver, Colorado State University, University of Northern Colorado.

Basis for selection. Open admission. **Adult students:** Entrance exam policies same as for first-time freshmen.

2005-2006 Annual costs. Tuition/fees: $2,309; $10,481 out-of-state. Per-credit charge: $73 in-state; $345 out-of-state. In-state tuition based upon assumption of Colorado Oppurtunity Fund waiver of $80 per-credit-hour. Books/supplies: $400.

Financial aid. Need-based: Need-based aid available for part-time students. Work study available nights and for part-time students.

Application procedures. Admission: No deadline. No application fee. Application may be submitted online. Admission notification on a rolling basis. **Financial aid:** Priority date 6/1; no closing date. FAFSA, institutional form required. Applicants notified on a rolling basis starting 7/15.

Academics. Special study options: Cooperative education, cross-registration, distance learning, ESL, internships, study abroad, weekend college. License preparation in paramedic. **Credit/placement by examination:** CLEP, IB. 30 credit hours maximum toward associate degree. **Support services:** GED preparation, learning center, remedial instruction, tutoring.

Majors. Business: General, accounting, administrative services, banking/financial services, business admin, management information systems, marketing, office technology, sales/distribution. **Communications technology:** Graphic/printing. **Computer sciences:** General, information systems. **Construction:** Carpentry, power transmission. **Education:** Early childhood. **Engineering technology:** Drafting, electrical. **Family/consumer sciences:** Child care. **Health:** Medical secretary. **Legal studies:** Legal secretary, paralegal. **Mechanic/repair:** Heating/ac/refrig. **Personal/culinary services:** Culinary arts. **Protective services:** Criminal justice, law enforcement admin.

Computing on campus. 210 workstations in dormitories, library, computer center, student center. Dormitories wired for high-speed internet access and linked to campus network. Commuter students can connect to campus network. Online course registration, online library, repair service available.

Student life. Freshman orientation: Available. Preregistration for classes offered. **Policies:** Freshmen permitted cars on campus. **Housing:** Guaranteed on-campus for freshmen. Coed dorms available. $150 deposit. **Activities:** Dance, drama, music ensembles, musical theater, student government, student newspaper, black student alliance, Lazos Culturales, Phi Theta Kappa, Phi Alpha Omega, Campus Crusade for Christ.

Athletics. Intramural: Basketball, softball, tennis, volleyball.

Student services. Career counseling, student employment services, financial aid counseling, personal counseling, veterans' counselor. **Physically disabled:** Services for visually, speech, hearing impaired. **Transfer:** Special adviser, orientation for new students. Transfer adviser, college fairs on campus for students transferring to 4-year colleges.

Contact. E-mail: connie.simpson@cca.cccoes.edu
Phone: (303) 360-4700 Fax: (303) 361-7432
Kristen Cusack, Registrar, Community College of Aurora, 16000 East CentreTech Parkway, Aurora, CO 80011-9036

Community College of Denver
Denver, Colorado
http://ccd.rightchoice.org **CB code: 4137**

- Public 2-year community college
- Commuter campus in very large city

General. Founded in 1970. Regionally accredited. Library, student center and physical education facilities shared with Metropolitan State College and University of Colorado at Denver. **Enrollment:** 1,922 full-time, degree-seeking students. **Degrees:** 413 associate awarded. **ROTC:** Army. **Location:** Downtown. **Calendar:** Semester, limited summer session. **Full-time faculty:** 64 total. **Part-time faculty:** 377 total. **Class size:** 53% < 20, 46% 20-39, less than 1% 40-49, less than 1% 50-99. **Partnerships:** Formal partnership with U.S. West Alliance; Beta test site for Microsoft.

Student profile.

Out-of-state:	5%	**25 or older:**	51%

Transfer out. Colleges most students transferred to 2005: Metropolitan State College of Denver, University of Colorado at Denver.

Basis for selection. Open admission, but selective for some programs. Special requirements for health occupations and computer information systems programs. State of Colorado requires ACT of high school juniors, but institution does not require or recommend it. ACT used for placement if submitted. **Adult students:** Entrance exam policies same as for first-time freshmen.

2005-2006 Annual costs. Tuition/fees: $2,795; $10,967 out-of-state. In-state tuition based upon assumption of Colorado Oppurtunity Fund waiver of $80 per-credit-hour. Books/supplies: $1,163. Personal expenses: $2,547.

Financial aid. Need-based: Need-based aid available for part-time students.

Application procedures. Admission: Priority date 8/1; no deadline. No application fee. Application may be submitted online. Admission notification on a rolling basis. **Financial aid:** Priority date 1/1; no closing date. FAFSA, institutional form required. Applicants notified on a rolling basis starting 5/15; must reply within 3 week(s) of notification.

Academics. Special study options: Accelerated study, cooperative education, cross-registration, distance learning, double major, dual enrollment of high school students, ESL, independent study, internships, liberal arts/career combination, study abroad, weekend college. On-campus license preparation for psychiatric technician. **Credit/placement by examination:** AP, CLEP, institutional tests. 45 credit hours maximum toward associate degree. **Support services:** GED preparation and test center, learning center, pre-admission summer program, reduced course load, remedial instruction, study skills assistance, tutoring, writing center.

Majors. Biology: Biomedical sciences. **Business:** Accounting, administrative services, business admin, management information systems. **Communications technology:** Graphic/printing. **Engineering technology:** Drafting, electrical. **Family/consumer sciences:** Child care, family studies. **Health:** Dental hygiene, electroencephalograph technology, medical radiologic technology/radiation therapy, nursing (RN). **Legal studies:** Paralegal. **Liberal arts:** Arts/sciences. **Parks/recreation:** General, health/fitness. **Visual/**

performing arts: Commercial photography, commercial/advertising art, design.

Most popular majors. Business/marketing 16%, health sciences 26%, liberal arts 46%.

Computing on campus. 1,032 workstations in computer center. Commuter students can connect to campus network. Online course registration available.

Student life. **Freshman orientation:** Available. **Policies:** Freshmen permitted cars on campus. **Housing:** Dormitory housing available at Lowry campus through cooperative agreement. **Activities:** Choral groups, drama, student government, student newspaper, Mexican-American student organization, black student organization, Amnesty International, Ad Hoc nursing club.

Student services. Adult student services, career counseling, services for economically disadvantaged, student employment services, financial aid counseling, health services, legal services, minority student services, on-campus daycare, personal counseling, placement for graduates, veterans' counselor, women's services. **Physically disabled:** Services for visually, hearing impaired. **Transfer:** Special adviser, orientation, re-entry adviser, preadmission transcript evaluation for new students. Transfer center, transfer adviser, college fairs on campus for students transferring to 4-year colleges.

Contact. E-mail: admission@ccd.edu
Phone: (303) 556-2430 Fax: (303) 556-2431
Emita Samuels, Director of Registration and Records, Community College of Denver, Campus Box 201, PO Box 173363, Denver, CO 80217-3363

Concorde Career College

Aurora, Colorado
www.concorde.edu/denver/

- For-profit 2-year health science college
- Large city

General. Accredited by ACCSCT. **Enrollment:** 478 degree-seeking undergraduates. **Calendar:** Continuous. **Full-time faculty:** 40 total. **Part-time faculty:** 15 total.

Application procedures. **Admission:** No deadline. No application fee. Admission notification on a rolling basis.

Academics. **Credit/placement by examination:** CLEP.

Majors. **Health:** Medical radiologic technology/radiation therapy, nursing (RN), respiratory therapy technology.

Contact. Phone: (303) 861-1151
Paul Ochoa, Director of Admissions, Concorde Career College, 111 North Havana Street, Aurora, CO 80010

Denver Academy of Court Reporting

Denver, Colorado
www.dacr.org **CB code: 3561**

- For-profit 2-year college of court reporting
- Large city

General. Accredited by ACICS. **Enrollment:** 230 undergraduates. **Degrees:** 9 associate awarded. **Calendar:** Continuous. **Full-time faculty:** 10 total. **Part-time faculty:** 10 total.

2005-2006 Annual costs. Day program tuition $2,100 per quarter, evening program $1,900 per quarter. One-time $150 required fees. Books/supplies: $450.

Application procedures. **Admission:** No deadline. $100 fee.

Academics. **Credit/placement by examination:** CLEP.

Majors. **Legal studies:** Court reporting.

Contact. E-mail: info@dacr.org
Phone: (303) 427-5292 Fax: (303) 427-5383
Director of Admissions, Denver Academy of Court Reporting, 9051 Harlan Street, Unit #20, Westminster, CO 80031

Denver Automotive & Diesel College

Denver, Colorado
www.dadc.com **CB code: 3133**

- For-profit 2-year technical college
- Very large city

General. Accredited by ACCSCT. **Enrollment:** 1,240 degree-seeking undergraduates. **Degrees:** 338 associate awarded. **Calendar:** Continuous, extensive summer session. **Full-time faculty:** 41 total. **Part-time faculty:** 1 total. **Special facilities:** Full automotive and diesel lab shops.

Basis for selection. Open admission.

2005-2006 Annual costs. 18-month automotive technology program $16,650. 19.5-month diesel technology program $18,000. One time $75 uniform cost required of all students. Books/supplies: $360. Personal expenses: $1,967.

Application procedures. **Admission:** No deadline. $100 fee. Admission notification on a rolling basis.

Academics. **Credit/placement by examination:** CLEP.

Majors. **Mechanic/repair:** General, automotive, diesel.

Contact. Phone: (303) 722-5724 Toll-free number: (866) 647-3232
Dan Michalec, Director of Admissions, Denver Automotive & Diesel College, 460 South Lipan Street, Denver, CO 80223-9366

Front Range Community College

Westminster, Colorado **CB member**
www.frcc.cc.co.us **CB code: 4119**

- Public 2-year community college
- Commuter campus in large city

General. Founded in 1968. Regionally accredited. **Enrollment:** 11,495 degree-seeking undergraduates. **Degrees:** 1,081 associate awarded. **ROTC:** Army, Air Force. **Location:** 12 miles from Denver. **Calendar:** Semester, limited summer session. **Full-time faculty:** 175 total; 10% minority, 62% women. **Part-time faculty:** 829 total; 6% minority. **Class size:** 41% < 20, 57% 20-39, 1% 40-49, 1% 50-99. **Special facilities:** Observatory (Larimer campus). **Partnerships:** Formal partnerships with local workforce centers for career training or retraining.

Student profile.

Out-of-state:	1%	**25 or older:**	45%

Transfer out. **Colleges most students transferred to 2005:** University of Northern Colorado, University of Colorado at Denver, University of Colorado at Boulder, Metropolitan State College, Colorado State University.

Basis for selection. Open admission.

High school preparation. 13 units recommended. Recommended units include English 4, mathematics 3, history 3, science 2 (laboratory 1).

2005-2006 Annual costs. Tuition/fees: $2,452; $10,624 out-of-state. Per-credit charge: $73 in-state; $345 out-of-state. In-state tuition based upon assumption of Colorado Oppurtunity Fund waiver of $80 per-credit-hour. Books/supplies: $1,100.

2004-2005 Financial aid. **Need-based:** 47% of total undergraduate aid awarded as scholarships/grants, 53% as loans/jobs. Need-based aid available for part-time students. Work study available nights, weekends and for part-time students. **Non-need-based:** Scholarships awarded for academics, job skills, leadership, state residency.

Application procedures. **Admission:** No deadline. No application fee. Application may be submitted online. Admission notification on a rolling basis. **Financial aid:** Priority date 5/1; no closing date. FAFSA, institutional form required. Applicants notified on a rolling basis starting 7/1; must reply within 3 week(s) of notification.

Academics. **Special study options:** Cooperative education, cross-registration, distance learning, double major, dual enrollment of high school students, ESL, honors, independent study, internships, liberal arts/career combination, study abroad, teacher certification program, weekend college. License preparation in dental hygiene, nursing, paramedic, real estate. **Credit/placement by examination:** CLEP, institutional tests. 30 credit hours maximum toward associate degree. **Support services:** GED preparation and test center, learning center, remedial instruction, study skills assistance, tutoring.

Majors. Agriculture: Horticulture. **Business:** Accounting, business admin, management information systems. **Engineering technology:** Architectural, drafting, electrical. **Family/consumer sciences:** Child care, institutional food production. **Foreign languages:** Sign language interpretation. **Health:** Nursing (RN), respiratory therapy technology. **Liberal arts:** Arts/sciences. **Mechanic/repair:** Automotive. **Parks/recreation:** Sports admin.

Most popular majors. Business/marketing 11%, health sciences 22%, liberal arts 58%.

Computing on campus. 175 workstations in library, computer center. Online course registration, helpline available.

Student life. Freshman orientation: Available. Preregistration for classes offered. **Activities:** Jazz band, choral groups, drama, literary magazine, student government, student newspaper, Student Colorado Registry of Interpreters for the Deaf, Hispanic club, black student alliance club.

Athletics. Intramural: Volleyball.

Student services. Career counseling, student employment services, financial aid counseling, minority student services, on-campus daycare, personal counseling, placement for graduates, veterans' counselor, women's services. **Physically disabled:** Services for visually, speech, hearing impaired. **Transfer:** Special adviser, orientation for new students. Transfer center, college fairs on campus for students transferring to 4-year colleges.

Contact. Phone: (303) 404-5471 Fax: (303) 439-2614
Front Range Community College, 3645 West 112th Avenue, Westminster, CO 80031

Heritage College

Denver, Colorado
www.heritage-education.com

- For-profit 2-year health science college
- Very large city
- Application essay, interview required

General. Accredited by ACCSCT. Web-based classes meet once a week. **Enrollment:** 480 degree-seeking undergraduates. **Degrees:** 226 associate awarded. **Calendar:** Continuous. **Full-time faculty:** 25 total. **Part-time faculty:** 5 total.

Basis for selection. Open admission, but selective for some programs. Special requirements for some health programs. **Adult students:** Entrance exam policies same as for first-time freshmen.

Financial aid. All financial aid based on need. Work study available nights and weekends.

Application procedures. Admission: No deadline. No application fee. Admission notification on a rolling basis. **Financial aid:** No deadline. FAFSA required. Applicants notified on a rolling basis.

Academics. Special study options: Distance learning, liberal arts/career combination, student-designed major, weekend college. **Credit/placement by examination:** CLEP. 52 credit hours maximum toward associate degree. **Support services:** Learning center, study skills assistance, tutoring.

Majors. Computer sciences: General, computer science. **Health:** Massage therapy, radiologic technology/medical imaging.

Computing on campus. PC or laptop required. 6 workstations in student center. Helpline available.

Student life. Freshman orientation: Mandatory. Preregistration for classes offered.

Student services. Adult student services, career counseling. **Transfer:** Orientation for new students. Transfer adviser for students transferring to 4-year colleges.

Contact. Phone: (303) 477-7240
Heidi McDonald, Director of Admissions, Heritage College, 12 Lakeside Lane, Denver, CO 80212-7413

Institute of Business & Medical Careers

Fort Collins, Colorado
www.ibmc.edu **CB code: 3566**

- For-profit 2-year business and health science college
- Residential campus in small city
- Application essay, interview required

General. Accredited by ACICS. **Enrollment:** 312 degree-seeking undergraduates. **Degrees:** 72 associate awarded. **Calendar:** Continuous. **Full-time faculty:** 20 total; 15% minority, 85% women. **Part-time faculty:** 55 total; 6% minority, 73% women.

Student profile. Among degree-seeking undergraduates, 100% enrolled in a vocational program, 2% already have a bachelor's degree or higher, 306 enrolled as first-time, first-year students.

Transfer out. Colleges most students transferred to 2005: Colorado Christian University, Front Range Community College, Aims Community College.

Basis for selection. Open admission, but selective for some programs. Institutional entrance exam required. **Homeschooled:** State high school equivalency certificate required.

2005-2006 Annual costs. Per-credit charge: $250. Books/supplies: $1,400.

Application procedures. Admission: No deadline. $75 fee. Admission notification on a rolling basis.

Academics. Credit/placement by examination: AP, CLEP, institutional tests. Up to 50% of total progam credits may be obtained through transfer or test out. **Support services:** Learning center, reduced course load, study skills assistance, tutoring.

Majors. Business: Business admin.

Computing on campus. 4 workstations in library, student center. Commuter students can connect to campus network. Wireless network available.

Student life. Freshman orientation: Available.

Student services. Career counseling, student employment services, financial aid counseling, placement for graduates. **Transfer:** Special adviser, orientation, pre-admission transcript evaluation for new students.

Contact. E-mail: info@ibmc.edu
Phone: (970) 223-2669 Toll-free number: (800) 495-2669
Steven Steele, Vice President of Operations, Institute of Business & Medical Careers, 1609 Oakridge Drive, Suite 102, Fort Collins, CO 80525

IntelliTec College

Colorado Springs, Colorado
www.intelliteccollege.com **CB code: 2500**

- For-profit 2-year technical college
- Commuter campus in large city

General. Founded in 1965. Accredited by ACCSCT. **Location:** 68 miles from Denver. **Calendar:** 6-week cycle.

Annual costs/financial aid. Tuition/fees (2005-2006): $8,910. Average certification program tuition is $8500. Books/supplies: $1,200. Need-based financial aid available to full-time and part-time students.

Contact. Phone: (719) 632-7626
Director of Admissions, 2315 East Pikes Peak Avenue, Colorado Springs, CO 80909

IntelliTec College: Grand Junction

Grand Junction, Colorado
www.intelliteccollege.com **CB code: 2489**

- For-profit 2-year technical college
- Commuter campus in small city
- Interview required

General. Accredited by ACCSCT. **Enrollment:** 243 degree-seeking undergraduates. **Degrees:** 92 associate awarded. **Location:** 250 miles from Denver, 300 miles from Salt Lake City. **Calendar:** Continuous, extensive summer session. **Full-time faculty:** 19 total. **Part-time faculty:** 9 total.

Basis for selection. Open admission.

2005-2006 Annual costs. Lab fees vary per program; average $242. Books/supplies: $1,500.

Financial aid. All financial aid based on need.

Application procedures. Admission: No deadline. No application fee. Admission notification on a rolling basis. **Financial aid:** No deadline. FAFSA required. Applicants notified on a rolling basis.

Academics. Special study options: Cooperative education. **Credit/placement by examination:** CLEP. **Support services:** Tutoring.

Majors. Business: Accounting/business management. **Engineering:** Electrical. **Engineering technology:** Architectural drafting, computer hardware, mechanical drafting, software. **Health:** Medical assistant. **Mechanic/repair:** Automotive.

Computing on campus. 64 workstations in library, computer center.

Student services. Career counseling, student employment services, on-campus daycare, placement for graduates. **Transfer:** Orientation for new students.

Contact. Phone: (970) 245-8101 Fax: (970) 243-8074
Analisa Watson, Director of Admissions, IntelliTec College: Grand Junction, 772 Horizon Drive, Grand Junction, CO 81506

Lamar Community College

Lamar, Colorado
www.lamarcc.edu **CB code: 4382**

- Public 2-year community college
- Commuter campus in large town

General. Founded in 1937. Regionally accredited. **Location:** 117 miles from Pueblo. **Calendar:** Semester.

Annual costs/financial aid. Tuition/fees (2005-2006): $2,556; $8,656 out-of-state. In-state tuition based upon assumption of Colorado Oppurtunity Fund waiver of $80 per-credit-hour. Room/board: $4,470. Books/supplies: $1,163. Personal expenses: $420. Need-based financial aid available to full-time and part-time students.

Contact. Phone: (719) 336-1590
Director of Admissions, 2401 South Main Street, Lamar, CO 81052-3999

Morgan Community College

Fort Morgan, Colorado
www.morgancc.edu **CB code: 0444**

- Public 2-year community college
- Commuter campus in large town

General. Founded in 1967. Regionally accredited. **Enrollment:** 360 full-time, degree-seeking students. **Degrees:** 131 associate awarded. **Location:** 81 miles from Denver. **Calendar:** Semester, limited summer session. **Full-time faculty:** 42 total. **Part-time faculty:** 161 total.

Basis for selection. Open admission, but selective for some programs. Special requirements for physical therapist assistant, occupational therapy assistant, and nursing programs. Interview required of allied health majors.

2005-2006 Annual costs. Tuition/fees: $2,359; $10,531 out-of-state. Per-credit charge: $73 in-state; $345 out-of-state. In-state tuition based upon assumption of Colorado Oppurtunity Fund waiver of $80 per-credit-hour. Books/supplies: $675.

Financial aid. Need-based: Need-based aid available for part-time students. Work study available nights, weekends and for part-time students. **Non-need-based:** Scholarships awarded for academics, state residency.

Application procedures. Admission: No deadline. No application fee. Admission notification on a rolling basis. **Financial aid:** Priority date 6/1; no closing date. FAFSA required. Applicants notified on a rolling basis.

Academics. Special study options: Distance learning, double major, dual enrollment of high school students, ESL, independent study, internships, liberal arts/career combination, student-designed major, teacher certification program, weekend college. **Credit/placement by examination:** AP, CLEP, institutional tests. 31 credit hours maximum toward associate degree. **Support services:** GED preparation and test center, learning center, reduced course load, remedial instruction, study skills assistance, tutoring.

Majors. Business: General, accounting. **Education:** General. **Health:** Nursing (RN), occupational therapy assistant, physical therapy assistant. **Interdisciplinary:** Biological/physical sciences. **Liberal arts:** Arts/sciences. **Mechanic/repair:** Auto body, automotive. **Visual/performing arts:** Art.

Most popular majors. Business/marketing 10%, health sciences 20%, liberal arts 20%, trade and industry 45%.

Computing on campus. 50 workstations in library, computer center, student center. Commuter students can connect to campus network. Online course registration available.

Student life. Activities: Student government, student newspaper, occupational therapy association, vocational industrial collusion association, Phi Theta Kappa, science club, history club, student nursing association, Phi Beta Lambda, health occupation student organization, physical therapy association.

Student services. Career counseling. **Transfer:** Special adviser, orientation, pre-admission transcript evaluation for new students.

Contact. Phone: (970) 542-3156 Fax: (970) 867-6608
Sally Nestor, Director of Admissions, Morgan Community College, 920 Barlow Road, Fort Morgan, CO 80701

Northeastern Junior College

Sterling, Colorado **CB member**
www.njc.edu **CB code: 4537**

- Public 2-year junior college
- Commuter campus in large town

General. Founded in 1941. Regionally accredited. **Enrollment:** 1,095 degree-seeking undergraduates. **Degrees:** 233 associate awarded. **Location:** 125 miles from Denver. **Calendar:** Semester, limited summer session. **Full-time faculty:** 60 total. **Part-time faculty:** 200 total. **Class size:** 81% < 20, 17% 20-39, less than 1% 40-49, 2% 50-99. **Special facilities:** Equine center, greenhouse, college farm.

Student profile.

Out-of-state:	4%	**Live on campus:**	40%

Transfer out. Colleges most students transferred to 2005: Colorado State University, University of Northern Colorado, University of Colorado, University of Wyoming, Oklahoma State University.

Basis for selection. Open admission, but selective for some programs. Qualifications for programs with limited space, such as licensed practical nursing program, set individually by department. Cooperative admission program with Colorado State University. SAT or ACT required for some technical vocational programs. Assessment required by ACCUPLACER, minimum ACT or SAT scores in subject areas, or proof of previous successful college experience.

2005-2006 Annual costs. Tuition/fees: $2,776; $8,876 out-of-state. Per-credit charge: $73 in-state; $345 out-of-state. In-state tuition based upon assumption of Colorado Oppurtunity Fund waiver of $80 per-credit-hour. Room/board: $5,162. Books/supplies: $1,163. Personal expenses: $2,529.

Financial aid. Need-based: Need-based aid available for part-time students. **Non-need-based:** Scholarships awarded for academics, athletics. **Additional information:** Need-based financial aid available to part-time students taking 6 credits or more per semester.

Application procedures. Admission: No deadline. No application fee. Application may be submitted online. Admission notification on a rolling basis. **Financial aid:** Priority date 3/1; no closing date. FAFSA, institutional form required. Applicants notified on a rolling basis starting 4/15; must reply within 4 week(s) of notification.

Academics. Special study options: Cooperative education, distance learning, dual enrollment of high school students, ESL, independent study, internships. License preparation in nursing. **Credit/placement by examination:** AP, CLEP, institutional tests. 30 credit hours maximum toward associate degree. **Support services:** GED preparation and test center, learning center, tutoring.

Majors. Agriculture: Equestrian studies, farm/ranch, ornamental horticulture. **Biology:** General, botany. **Business:** Accounting, administrative services, business admin, entrepreneurial studies, tourism/travel. **Communications:** General, broadcast journalism, journalism. **Communications technology:**

General. **Computer sciences:** General, computer graphics, computer science, data processing, information systems, programming. **Education:** Agricultural, art, business, early childhood, elementary, middle, physical, secondary, special. **Health:** EMT paramedic, medical secretary, nursing (RN). **Legal studies:** Legal secretary. **Mechanic/repair:** Automotive, diesel.

Most popular majors. Agriculture 27%, liberal arts 63%.

Computing on campus. 130 workstations in library, computer center.

Student life. Freshman orientation: Mandatory. Preregistration for classes offered. **Housing:** Coed dorms, single-sex dorms available. $125 deposit. **Activities:** Bands, choral groups, dance, drama, literary magazine, music ensembles, musical theater, student government, student newspaper, campus Christian fellowship.

Athletics. NJCAA. **Intercollegiate:** Baseball M, basketball, rodeo, softball W, volleyball W. **Intramural:** Baseball M, basketball, bowling, field hockey W, golf, handball, racquetball, soccer M, swimming, table tennis. **Team name:** Plainswomen, Plainsmen.

Student services. Adult student services, alcohol/substance abuse counseling, career counseling, student employment services, financial aid counseling, health services, on-campus daycare, personal counseling, placement for graduates, veterans' counselor. **Physically disabled:** Services for hearing impaired. **Transfer:** Special adviser, orientation for new students. Transfer adviser, college fairs on campus for students transferring to 4-year colleges.

Contact. Phone: (970) 521-6600 Fax: (970) 521-6801
Director of Admissions, Northeastern Junior College, 100 College Avenue, Sterling, CO 80751

Otero Junior College
La Junta, Colorado
www.ojc.edu **CB code: 4588**

- Public 2-year community and junior college
- Commuter campus in small town

General. Founded in 1941. Regionally accredited. **Enrollment:** 1,120 degree-seeking undergraduates. **Degrees:** 199 associate awarded. **Location:** 60 miles from Pueblo, 100 miles from Colorado Springs. **Calendar:** Semester, limited summer session. **Full-time faculty:** 32 total. **Part-time faculty:** 10 total. **Class size:** 74% < 20, 21% 20-39, 2% 40-49, 3% 50-99. **Special facilities:** Koshare Indian kiva museum.

Student profile.

Out-of-state:	7%	**Live on campus:**	10%
25 or older:	33%		

Basis for selection. Open admission, but selective for some programs. Special admission requirements for nursing program.

2005-2006 Annual costs. Tuition/fees: $2,354; $8,454 out-of-state. Per-credit charge: $73 in-state; $276 out-of-state. In-state tuition based upon assumption of Colorado Oppurtunity Fund waiver of $80 per-credit-hour. Room/board: $4,302. Books/supplies: $1,100. Personal expenses: $2,500.

Financial aid. Need-based: Need-based aid available for part-time students. **Non-need-based:** Scholarships awarded for academics, athletics, state residency.

Application procedures. Admission: No deadline. No application fee. Admission notification on a rolling basis. **Financial aid:** Priority date 4/15; no closing date. FAFSA required. Applicants notified on a rolling basis; must reply within 2 week(s) of notification.

Academics. Special study options: Dual enrollment of high school students. Bachelor's degree programs available on campus. **Credit/placement by examination:** AP, CLEP, institutional tests. 30 credit hours maximum toward associate degree. **Support services:** GED preparation and test center, learning center, reduced course load, remedial instruction, study skills assistance, tutoring.

Majors. Biology: General. **Business:** Administrative services, business admin. **Computer sciences:** General. **Education:** General, early childhood, elementary, secondary, teacher assistance. **Health:** Medical secretary, nursing (RN), pharmacy assistant, predentistry, premedicine, prepharmacy, preveterinary, veterinary technology/assistant. **History:** General. **Legal studies:** Legal secretary, prelaw. **Liberal arts:** Arts/sciences. **Math:** General. **Physical sciences:** Chemistry. **Psychology:** General. **Social sciences:** Political science. **Visual/performing arts:** Dramatic.

Computing on campus. 70 workstations in library, computer center, student center. Dormitories linked to campus network.

Student life. Freshman orientation: Available. **Housing:** Single-sex dorms available. **Activities:** Dance, drama, student government.

Athletics. NJCAA. **Intercollegiate:** Baseball M, basketball, golf, softball W, volleyball W. **Intramural:** Basketball, bowling, softball, volleyball. **Team name:** Rattlers.

Student services. Career counseling, student employment services, on-campus daycare, personal counseling, placement for graduates, veterans' counselor. **Physically disabled:** Services for visually, hearing impaired. **Transfer:** Special adviser, orientation, pre-admission transcript evaluation for new students. Transfer adviser, college fairs on campus for students transferring to 4-year colleges.

Contact. E-mail: jan.schiro@ojc.edu
Phone: (719) 384-6831 Fax: (719) 384-6933
Jan Schiro, Admissions Coordinator, Otero Junior College, 1802 Colorado Avenue, La Junta, CO 81050

Parks College
Denver, Colorado
www.cci.edu **CB code: 0349**

- For-profit 2-year junior college
- Commuter campus in large town
- Interview required

General. Founded in 1895. Accredited by ACICS. Branch campus in Aurora. **Enrollment:** 719 degree-seeking undergraduates. **Degrees:** 109 associate awarded. **Location:** 7 miles from downtown. **Calendar:** Quarter, extensive summer session. **Full-time faculty:** 20 total. **Part-time faculty:** 55 total.

Basis for selection. Score on institution's entrance examination, personal qualities, preliminary and qualifying interview important. Institutional examination (CPAT) required for admissions and placement.

Financial aid. Need-based: Need-based aid available for part-time students.

Application procedures. Admission: No deadline. $25 fee, may be waived for applicants with need. Admission notification on a rolling basis. **Financial aid:** No deadline. FAFSA, institutional form required. Applicants notified on a rolling basis starting 8/1.

Academics. Special study options: Internships. **Credit/placement by examination:** CLEP, institutional tests. **Support services:** Reduced course load, tutoring.

Majors. Business: Accounting, business admin, tourism/travel. **Computer sciences:** General, networking. **Engineering technology:** Computer systems. **Health:** Medical assistant, medical records technology, medical secretary. **Legal studies:** Paralegal.

Most popular majors. Business/marketing 56%, computer/information sciences 13%, health sciences 12%, legal studies 19%.

Computing on campus. 75 workstations in library, computer center.

Student life. Activities: Student government, student newspaper.

Student services. Career counseling, student employment services, placement for graduates.

Contact. E-mail: jmira@cci.edu
Phone: (303) 457-2757 Fax: (303) 457-4030
Jimmy Henig, Director of Admissions, Parks College, 9065 Grant Street, Denver, CO 80229

Parks College: Aurora
Aurora, Colorado
www.cci.edu **CB code: 3568**

- For-profit 2-year branch campus and technical college
- Commuter campus in large city
- Interview required

General. Accredited by ACICS. **Enrollment:** 332 degree-seeking undergraduates. **Degrees:** 80 associate awarded. **Location:** 15 miles from Denver. **Calendar:** Continuous, extensive summer session. **Full-time faculty:** 10 total. **Part-time faculty:** 25 total.

Student profile. Among degree-seeking undergraduates, 100% enrolled in a vocational program.

Transfer out. Colleges most students transferred to 2005: University of Phoenix, Florida Metropolitan University.

Basis for selection. Open admission. **Homeschooled:** Students without a high school diploma or equivalent may enroll, but must receive a specific score on an admissions test. **Learning Disabled:** Must provide documentation of disability.

2005-2006 Annual costs. Tuition for homeland security program (48 credit hours) - $8048; tuition for medical administrative assistant/medical assistant (47 credit hours) - $9300; tuition for medical insurance billing and coding (35 credit hours) - $8244. Books/supplies: $900.

2004-2005 Financial aid. All financial aid based on need. Average need met was 48%. Average scholarship/grant was $1,532; average loan $4,560. 34% of total undergraduate aid awarded as scholarships/grants, 66% as loans/jobs. Need-based aid available for part-time students. Work study available nights and for part-time students.

Application procedures. Admission: No deadline. $25 fee, may be waived for applicants with need. Application may be submitted online. Admission notification on a rolling basis. **Financial aid:** No deadline. FAFSA, institutional form required. Applicants notified on a rolling basis; must reply within 4 week(s) of notification.

Academics. Special study options: Accelerated study, cooperative education, distance learning, double major, honors, independent study, internships, liberal arts/career combination. **Credit/placement by examination:** AP, CLEP. 48 credit hours maximum toward associate degree. **Support services:** Learning center, reduced course load, remedial instruction, study skills assistance, tutoring.

Majors. Business: Accounting, business admin. **Computer sciences:** General. **Legal studies:** General, paralegal. **Protective services:** Criminal justice.

Most popular majors. Business/marketing 48%, computer/information sciences 14%, legal studies 39%.

Computing on campus. 6 workstations in library. Commuter students can connect to campus network. Online library, repair service available.

Student life. Freshman orientation: Mandatory. Preregistration for classes offered. **Policies:** Freshmen permitted cars on campus.

Student services. Career counseling, student employment services, financial aid counseling, placement for graduates. **Physically disabled:** Services for speech, hearing impaired. **Transfer:** Special adviser, orientation, re-entry adviser, pre-admission transcript evaluation for new students. Transfer adviser for students transferring to 4-year colleges.

Contact. E-mail: jrosenthal@cci.edu
Phone: (303) 745-6244 Fax: (303) 745-6245
Julie Rosenthal, Director of Admissions, Parks College: Aurora, 14280 East Jewell Suite 100, Aurora, CO 80012

Pikes Peak Community College

Colorado Springs, Colorado
www.ppcc.edu **CB code: 4291**

- Public 2-year community college
- Commuter campus in large city

General. Founded in 1967. Regionally accredited. **Enrollment:** 9,300 degree-seeking undergraduates. **Degrees:** 975 associate awarded. **Location:** 70 miles from Denver. **Calendar:** Semester, extensive summer session. **Full-time faculty:** 150 total. **Part-time faculty:** 525 total. **Class size:** 70% < 20, 30% 20-39, less than 1% 40-49, less than 1% 50-99, less than 1% >100.

Student profile.

Out-of-state:	12%	**25 or older:**	49%

Basis for selection. Open admission, but selective for some programs.

2005-2006 Annual costs. Tuition/fees: $2,339; $10,511 out-of-state. Per-credit charge: $73 in-state; $345 out-of-state. In-state tuition based upon assumption of Colorado Oppurtunity Fund waiver of $80 per-credit-hour. Books/supplies: $1,163. Personal expenses: $2,547.

Financial aid. Need-based: Need-based aid available for part-time students. **Non-need-based:** Scholarships awarded for state residency.

Application procedures. Admission: No deadline. No application fee. Application may be submitted online. Admission notification on a rolling basis. **Financial aid:** Priority date 7/1; no closing date. FAFSA required. Applicants notified on a rolling basis starting 8/1; must reply within 2 week(s) of notification.

Academics. Special study options: Cooperative education, distance learning, double major, dual enrollment of high school students, ESL, external degree, independent study, internships, study abroad, weekend college. License preparation in nursing, real estate. **Credit/placement by examination:** CLEP, IB, institutional tests. **Support services:** GED test center, learning center, remedial instruction, study skills assistance, tutoring, writing center.

Majors. Agriculture: Landscaping. **Business:** Accounting technology, business admin, management information systems. **Communications technology:** Graphics. **Computer sciences:** LAN/WAN management. **Conservation:** Management/policy. **Construction:** Maintenance. **Engineering technology:** Architectural, electrical, robotics. **Family/consumer sciences:** Child development. **Foreign languages:** Sign language interpretation. **Health:** Dental assistant, EMT paramedic, mental health services, nursing (RN), office admin. **Legal studies:** Paralegal. **Liberal arts:** Arts/sciences. **Mechanic/repair:** Auto body, automotive. **Personal/culinary services:** Culinary arts. **Production:** Machine shop technology, welding. **Protective services:** Fire safety technology, law enforcement admin. **Visual/performing arts:** Interior design.

Most popular majors. Business/marketing 12%, health sciences 12%, liberal arts 51%, security/protective services 10%.

Computing on campus. 180 workstations in library, computer center. Commuter students can connect to campus network. Online course registration available.

Student life. Freshman orientation: Available. **Policies:** Freshmen permitted cars on campus. **Activities:** Dance, drama, student government, student newspaper, Phi Theta Kappa.

Student services. Services for economically disadvantaged, student employment services, financial aid counseling, on-campus daycare, placement for graduates, veterans' counselor. **Physically disabled:** Services for visually, speech, hearing impaired. **Learning disabled:** Comprehensive services available. **Transfer:** Special adviser, orientation for new students. Transfer adviser, college fairs on campus for students transferring to 4-year colleges.

Contact. E-mail: admissions@ppcc.edu
Phone: (719) 540-7722 Toll-free number: (866) 411-7722
Fax: (719) 540-7092
Assistat Director of Enrollment Services and Admissions, Pikes Peak Community College, 5675 South Academy Boulevard, Colorado Springs, CO 80906-5498

Platt College: Aurora

Aurora, Colorado
www.plattcolorado.edu **CB code: 3012**

- For-profit 2-year art and technical college
- Small city

General. Accredited by ACCSCT. **Calendar:** Continuous.

Annual costs/financial aid. Total cost of typical associate degree program: $29,000; bachelor's degree program: $46,000. Costs include tuition, registration fee, lab fees, supplies. Cost of books, art kit vary with program. Need-based financial aid available for full-time students.

Contact. Phone: (303) 369-5151
Admissions Coordinator, 3100 South Parker Road, Aurora, CO 80014

Pueblo Community College

Pueblo, Colorado
www.pueblocc.edu **CB code: 4634**

- Public 2-year community college
- Commuter campus in small city

General. Founded in 1933. Regionally accredited. **Enrollment:** 4,600 degree-seeking undergraduates. **Degrees:** 499 associate awarded. **Location:** 50 miles

from Colorado Springs, 100 miles from Denver. **Calendar:** Semester, extensive summer session. **Full-time faculty:** 75 total. **Part-time faculty:** 293 total. **Special facilities:** Advanced technology centers.

Student profile. Among degree-seeking undergraduates, 204 transferred in from other institutions.

Out-of-state:	2%	**25 or older:**	55%

Basis for selection. Open admission, but selective for some programs. Admission to health programs based on GPA, high school courses, and test scores. ACT required of dental hygiene applicants; score report by May 1. Interview required of allied health majors.

2005-2006 Annual costs. Tuition/fees: $2,408; $10,580 out-of-state. Per-credit charge: $83 in-state; $345 out-of-state. In-state tuition based upon assumption of Colorado Oppurtunity Fund waiver of $80 per-credit-hour. Books/supplies: $1,162. Personal expenses: $1,600.

Financial aid. Need-based: Need-based aid available for part-time students. Work study available for part-time students. **Non-need-based:** Scholarships awarded for academics, state residency.

Application procedures. Admission: Priority date 8/1; no deadline. No application fee. Application may be submitted online. Admission notification on a rolling basis. Foreign applicants must pay for 1 full academic year before acceptance. Application closing date for allied health programs, April 1. **Financial aid:** Priority date 3/15; no closing date. FAFSA, institutional form required. Applicants notified on a rolling basis starting 4/15.

Academics. Special study options: Accelerated study, cooperative education, distance learning, double major, dual enrollment of high school students, independent study, internships, liberal arts/career combination. License preparation in dental hygiene, nursing, paramedic, physical therapy, radiology, real estate. **Credit/placement by examination:** CLEP, institutional tests. All but 15 hours residence requirement for either certificate or associate degree may be from credit for prior learning. **Support services:** GED preparation, learning center, reduced course load, remedial instruction, study skills assistance, tutoring, writing center.

Majors. Business: Accounting, administrative services, banking/financial services, business admin, office technology, office/clerical, tourism promotion, tourism/travel. **Communications:** Broadcast journalism. **Computer sciences:** General, computer graphics. **Education:** Early childhood. **Engineering technology:** Architectural, civil, drafting, electrical, manufacturing. **Family/consumer sciences:** Child care, institutional food production. **Health:** Dental assistant, dental hygiene, EMT paramedic, medical radiologic technology/radiation therapy, medical secretary, nursing (RN), occupational therapy assistant, optician, physical therapy assistant, respiratory therapy technology, surgical technology. **Legal studies:** Legal secretary, paralegal. **Liberal arts:** Arts/sciences, library assistant. **Mechanic/repair:** Auto body, automotive, industrial, watch/jewelry. **Personal/culinary services:** Culinary arts. **Production:** Machine tool, welding. **Protective services:** Corrections, law enforcement admin, police science. **Visual/performing arts:** Design, metal/jewelry.

Most popular majors. Business/marketing 12%, health sciences 41%, liberal arts 34%, security/protective services 6%.

Student life. Freshman orientation: Available. Preregistration for classes offered. **Activities:** Choral groups, drama, radio station, student government, student newspaper, TV station.

Athletics. Team name: Panthers.

Student services. Adult student services, career counseling, student employment services, financial aid counseling, on-campus daycare, personal counseling, placement for graduates, veterans' counselor. **Physically disabled:** Services for visually, speech, hearing impaired. **Transfer:** Special adviser, orientation for new students. Transfer adviser, college fairs on campus for students transferring to 4-year colleges.

Contact. E-mail: admissions@pueblocc.edu
Phone: (719) 549-3010 Toll-free number: (888) 642-6017
Fax: (719) 549-3012
Mary Santoro, Director of Admissions and Records, Pueblo Community College, 900 West Orman Avenue, Pueblo, CO 81004-1499

Red Rocks Community College

Lakewood, Colorado
www.rrcc.cccoes.edu **CB code: 4130**

- Public 2-year community college
- Large city

General. Founded in 1969. Regionally accredited. **Enrollment:** 4,510 degree-seeking undergraduates. **Degrees:** 394 associate awarded. **ROTC:** Army. **Location:** 10 miles from Denver. **Calendar:** Semester, extensive summer session. **Full-time faculty:** 80 total. **Part-time faculty:** 350 total. **Class size:** 74% < 20, 21% 20-39, 1% 40-49, 4% 50-99. **Partnerships:** Formal partnerships with Coors, Microsoft, Apple, Oracle.

Transfer out. Colleges most students transferred to 2005: University of Colorado at Denver, Metropolitan State College of Denver, University of Colorado at Boulder, Colorado State University.

Basis for selection. Open admission. Degree-seeking students can fulfill asessment requirement by providing test scores.

2005-2006 Annual costs. Tuition/fees: $2,398; $10,580 out-of-state. Per-credit charge: $73 in-state; $345 out-of-state. In-state tuition based upon assumption of Colorado Oppurtunity Fund waiver of $80 per-credit-hour. Books/supplies: $873.

Financial aid. Need-based: Need-based aid available for part-time students. Work study available nights, weekends and for part-time students.

Application procedures. Admission: No deadline. No application fee. Application may be submitted online. Admission notification on a rolling basis. **Financial aid:** Priority date 4/1; no closing date. FAFSA, institutional form required. Applicants notified on a rolling basis starting 6/1; must reply within 2 week(s) of notification.

Academics. Students in advanced ESL classes may begin some college level courses early. Scholarships offered for outstanding ESL performance when funds are available. **Special study options:** Accelerated study, cooperative education, cross-registration, distance learning, double major, dual enrollment of high school students, ESL, honors, independent study, internships, liberal arts/career combination, semester at sea, student-designed major, study abroad, weekend college. License preparation in paramedic, radiology, real estate. **Credit/placement by examination:** AP, CLEP, institutional tests. 45 credit hours maximum toward associate degree. **Support services:** Learning center, reduced course load, remedial instruction, study skills assistance, tutoring, writing center.

Majors. Biology: General, biotechnology. **Business:** General, accounting, accounting technology, administrative services, business admin, management information systems, office technology, tourism promotion. **Communications:** General. **Computer sciences:** General, data processing, programming. **Conservation:** Forest technology. **Construction:** General, carpentry, masonry, pipefitting, power transmission. **Education:** Early childhood. **Engineering technology:** Construction, drafting, electrical, manufacturing, water quality. **Family/consumer sciences:** Child development. **Foreign languages:** French, German, Spanish. **Health:** EMT paramedic, medical secretary, office admin, prenursing, radiologic technology/medical imaging. **History:** General. **Legal studies:** Legal secretary. **Liberal arts:** Arts/sciences. **Mechanic/repair:** General, auto body, automotive, electronics/electrical, heating/ac/refrig. **Physical sciences:** Chemistry, geology, physics. **Production:** Woodworking. **Protective services:** Criminal justice, fire safety technology, law enforcement admin. **Psychology:** General. **Public administration:** General. **Social sciences:** Economics, political science, sociology. **Visual/performing arts:** Art, cinematography, commercial/advertising art, dramatic, theater design.

Most popular majors. Business/marketing 8%, liberal arts 59%, security/protective services 11%, trade and industry 10%, visual/performing arts 9%.

Computing on campus. 175 workstations in library, computer center, student center.

Student life. Freshman orientation: Available. **Activities:** Drama, student government, student newspaper, Phi Theta Kappa, environment club, international club.

Athletics. NJCAA.

Student services. Adult student services, career counseling, student employment services, health services, on-campus daycare, personal counseling, placement for graduates, veterans' counselor. **Physically disabled:** Services for visually, speech, hearing impaired. **Transfer:** Special adviser, orientation for new students. Transfer adviser, college fairs on campus for students transferring to 4-year colleges.

Contact. Phone: (303) 914-6351 Fax: (303) 989-6919
Dean Rathe, Director of Enrollment Services, Red Rocks Community College, 13300 West Sixth Avenue, Lakewood, CO 80228-1255

Remington College: Colorado Springs

Colorado Springs, Colorado
www.remingtoncollege.com **CB code: 3565**

- For-profit 2-year branch campus and technical college
- Commuter campus in very large city
- Interview required

General. Accredited by ACICS. **Enrollment:** 186 degree-seeking undergraduates. **Degrees:** 23 bachelor's, 96 associate awarded. **Location:** 60 miles from Denver. **Calendar:** Quarter, extensive summer session. **Full-time faculty:** 4 total; 75% women. **Part-time faculty:** 13 total; 8% minority, 46% women.

Student profile. Among degree-seeking undergraduates, 166 enrolled as first-time, first-year students.

Women:	69%	**25 or older:**	60%

Basis for selection. Open admission, but selective for some programs.

2005-2006 Annual costs. $30,480 for all 2-year associate programs. Tuition covers costs of all books, lab fees, laptop computer.

2005-2006 Financial aid. All financial aid based on need. 35% of total undergraduate aid awarded as scholarships/grants, 65% as loans/jobs. Need-based aid available for part-time students. Work study available nights and for part-time students.

Application procedures. **Admission:** No deadline. $50 fee. Admission notification on a rolling basis. **Financial aid:** No deadline. FAFSA required. Applicants notified on a rolling basis; must reply within 3 week(s) of notification.

Academics. **Special study options:** Accelerated study. Bachelor's degree programs available on campus. **Credit/placement by examination:** AP, CLEP. **Support services:** Tutoring.

Majors. **Protective services:** Criminal justice.

Computing on campus. PC or laptop required. 34 workstations in library, computer center. Online library, helpline, repair service available.

Student life. **Freshman orientation:** Available.

Student services. Career counseling, student employment services, financial aid counseling, personal counseling, placement for graduates, veterans' counselor. **Transfer:** Orientation, pre-admission transcript evaluation for new students.

Contact. E-mail: Shirley.McCray@remingtoncollege.edu
Phone: (719) 532-1234 Fax: (719) 264-1234
Larry Schafer, Director of Recruitment, Remington College: Colorado Springs, 6050 Erin Park Drive, Colorado Springs, CO 80918

Trinidad State Junior College
Trinidad, Colorado
www.trinidadstate.edu **CB code: 4821**

- Public 2-year community and junior college
- Commuter campus in small town

General. Founded in 1925. Regionally accredited. **Enrollment:** 1,327 degree-seeking undergraduates; 504 non-degree-seeking students. **Degrees:** 222 associate awarded. **Location:** 90 miles from Pueblo. **Calendar:** Semester, limited summer session. **Full-time faculty:** 40 total. **Part-time faculty:** 72 total. **Class size:** 93% < 20, 7% 20-39, less than 1% 40-49. **Special facilities:** Museum of anthropology and geology, gunsmithing laboratory, gun range.

Student profile. Among degree-seeking undergraduates, 431 enrolled as first-time, first-year students, 38 transferred in from other institutions.

Part-time:	42%	**25 or older:**	57%
Out-of-state:	8%	**Live on campus:**	30%
Women:	61%		

Transfer out. **Colleges most students transferred to 2005:** University of Southern Colorado, Adams State College, Colorado State University, Northern Colorado University.

Basis for selection. Open admission, but selective for some programs. Interview recommended for nursing majors.

2005-2006 Annual costs. Tuition/fees: $2,733; $8,833 out-of-state. Per-credit charge: $73 in-state; $276 out-of-state. In-state tuition based upon assumption of Colorado Oppurtunity Fund waiver of $80 per-credit-hour. Room/board: $4,248. Books/supplies: $800. Personal expenses: $972.

Financial aid. **Need-based:** Need-based aid available for part-time students. Work study available nights and for part-time students. **Non-need-based:** Scholarships awarded for academics, athletics, state residency.

Application procedures. **Admission:** No deadline. No application fee. Application may be submitted online. Admission notification on a rolling basis. **Financial aid:** Priority date 5/1; no closing date. FAFSA, institutional form required. Applicants notified on a rolling basis starting 6/15.

Academics. **Special study options:** Accelerated study, cooperative education, distance learning, double major, dual enrollment of high school students, ESL, independent study, liberal arts/career combination. Bachelor's degree programs available on campus. License preparation in nursing. **Credit/placement by examination:** AP, CLEP, institutional tests. 45 credit hours maximum toward associate degree. **Support services:** GED preparation and test center, learning center, pre-admission summer program, reduced course load, remedial instruction, study skills assistance, tutoring, writing center.

Majors. **Biology:** General. **Business:** General, accounting, business admin. **Communications:** Advertising, journalism. **Computer sciences:** General, computer science, programming, word processing. **Conservation:** General, fisheries. **Education:** General, physical, social studies. **Engineering:** General. **Engineering technology:** Civil, construction, drafting. **Foreign languages:** Spanish. **Legal studies:** Prelaw. **Liberal arts:** Arts/sciences. **Math:** General. **Mechanic/repair:** Auto body, automotive, diesel. **Parks/recreation:** Health/fitness. **Personal/culinary services:** Cosmetic. **Philosophy/religion:** Philosophy. **Physical sciences:** Chemistry. **Protective services:** Criminal justice, law enforcement admin, police science. **Psychology:** General. **Social sciences:** Criminology. **Visual/performing arts:** Commercial/advertising art.

Most popular majors. Business/marketing 11%, education 10%, health sciences 26%, liberal arts 35%, trade and industry 6%.

Computing on campus. 260 workstations in dormitories, library. Dormitories wired for high-speed internet access and linked to campus network. Online course registration, wireless network available.

Student life. **Freshman orientation:** Available. Preregistration for classes offered. **Policies:** Freshmen permitted cars on campus. **Housing:** Single-sex dorms available. $100 deposit. **Activities:** Pep band, choral groups, drama, music ensembles, student government, student newspaper, TV station, MECHA (for students of Chicano and Hispanic descent), Black Student Alliance, campus ministries.

Athletics. NJCAA. **Intercollegiate:** Baseball M, basketball M, golf, volleyball W. **Intramural:** Baseball M, basketball, rifle, softball, table tennis, tennis, volleyball. **Team name:** Trojans.

Student services. Adult student services, alcohol/substance abuse counseling, career counseling, student employment services, financial aid counseling, on-campus daycare, personal counseling, placement for graduates, veterans' counselor. **Physically disabled:** Services for visually, speech, hearing impaired. **Transfer:** Special adviser, orientation for new students. Transfer adviser, college fairs on campus for students transferring to 4-year colleges.

Contact. E-mail: alex.borja@trinidadstate.edu
Phone: (719) 846-5622 Toll-free number: (800) 621-8752
Fax: (719) 846-5050
Sandra Veltri, Dean of Student Services, Trinidad State Junior College, 600 Prospect Street, Trinidad, CO 81082

Westwood College of Aviation Technology
Broomfield, Colorado
www.aviation.westwood.edu **CB code: 2230**

- For-profit 2-year technical college
- Commuter campus in small city

General. Accredited by ACCSCT. **Location:** 15 miles from Denver and Boulder. **Calendar:** Continuous.

Annual costs/financial aid. Tuition for full associate program $26,808; includes books. Tools $720 for airframe/powerplant program; $669 for advanced electronics program. Need-based financial aid available for full-time students.

Contact. Phone: (303) 466-1714
Director of Admissions, 10851 West 120th Avenue, Broomfield, CO 80021-3401

Connecticut

Asnuntuck Community College

Enfield, Connecticut — **CB member**
www.acc.commnet.edu — **CB code: 3656**

- Public 2-year community and technical college
- Commuter campus in large town

General. Founded in 1972. Regionally accredited. **Enrollment:** 918 degree-seeking undergraduates; 565 non-degree-seeking students. **Degrees:** 137 associate awarded. **Location:** 15 miles from Hartford, 10 miles from Springfield, Massachusetts. **Calendar:** Semester, extensive summer session. **Full-time faculty:** 25 total; 44% women. **Part-time faculty:** 90 total; 38% women. **Class size:** 47% < 20, 52% 20-39, less than 1% 40-49.

Student profile. Among degree-seeking undergraduates, 199 enrolled as first-time, first-year students, 217 transferred in from other institutions.

Part-time:	52%	**Asian American:**	2%
Out-of-state:	4%	**Hispanic American:**	3%
Women:	63%	**25 or older:**	45%
African American:	5%		

Transfer out. Colleges most students transferred to 2005: Eastern Connecticut State University, Central Connecticut State University, University of Connecticut, Western New England College.

Basis for selection. Open admission. **Adult students:** Entrance exam policies same as for first-time freshmen.

2005-2006 Annual costs. Tuition/fees: $2,536; $7,872 out-of-state. Per-credit charge: $93 in-state; $279 out-of-state. New England Regional Student Program: $3,998 annual tuition/fees, $231.50 per credit-hour. Books/supplies: $1,000. Personal expenses: $1,230.

Financial aid. All financial aid based on need. Need-based aid available for part-time students. Work study available nights, weekends and for part-time students.

Application procedures. Admission: No deadline. $20 fee, may be waived for applicants with need. Application may be submitted online. Admission notification on a rolling basis. **Financial aid:** Priority date 6/1; no closing date. FAFSA, institutional form required. Applicants notified on a rolling basis starting 7/1; must reply within 2 week(s) of notification.

Academics. On-line tutoring available. **Special study options:** Cooperative education, cross-registration, distance learning, double major, dual enrollment of high school students, independent study, internships, liberal arts/career combination, weekend college. License preparation in paramedic, real estate. **Credit/placement by examination:** AP, CLEP, institutional tests. 48 credit hours maximum toward associate degree. **Support services:** Learning center, remedial instruction, study skills assistance, tutoring.

Majors. Business: Accounting technology, administrative services, business admin, fashion, management information systems. **Communications technology:** General, radio/tv. **Engineering technology:** Industrial, manufacturing. **Family/consumer sciences:** Child care. **Health:** Mental health services. **Liberal arts:** Arts/sciences. **Protective services:** Police science.

Most popular majors. Business/marketing 31%, family/consumer sciences 7%, liberal arts 47%, security/protective services 7%.

Computing on campus. 111 workstations in library, computer center. Online course registration, online library available.

Student life. Freshman orientation: Available. **Policies:** Freshmen permitted cars on campus. **Activities:** Drama, literary magazine, radio station, student government, human services club, Phi Theta Kappa.

Student services. Career counseling, student employment services, financial aid counseling, on-campus daycare, personal counseling, placement for graduates, veterans' counselor. **Physically disabled:** Services for visually, speech, hearing impaired. **Transfer:** Special adviser, orientation, pre-admission transcript evaluation for new students. Transfer adviser, college fairs on campus for students transferring to 4-year colleges.

Contact. E-mail: dshaw@acc.commnet.edu
Phone: (860) 253-3010 Toll-free number: (800) 501-3967
Fax: (860) 253-3014
Donna Shaw, Director of Admissions and Marketing, Asnuntuck Community College, 170 Elm Street, Enfield, CT 06082

Capital Community College

Hartford, Connecticut
www.ccc.commnet.edu — **CB code: 3421**

- Public 2-year community and technical college
- Commuter campus in small city

General. Founded in 1946. Regionally accredited. **Enrollment:** 2,912 degree-seeking undergraduates; 661 non-degree-seeking students. **Degrees:** 287 associate awarded. **ROTC:** Army, Navy, Air Force. **Calendar:** Semester, limited summer session. **Full-time faculty:** 63 total. **Part-time faculty:** 150 total. **Special facilities:** Mathematics development center, computerized English as a Second Language laboratory, interactive videodisc instruction for nursing students, learning/writing center. **Partnerships:** Formal partnerships with high schools for Tech Prep program.

Student profile. Among degree-seeking undergraduates, 693 enrolled as first-time, first-year students.

Part-time:	70%	**25 or older:**	57%
Women:	74%		

Transfer out. Colleges most students transferred to 2005: University of Connecticut, Central Connecticut State University, University of Hartford, Eastern Connecticut State University.

Basis for selection. Open admission, but selective for some programs. SAT scores used to satisfy admission criteria for nursing, physical therapist assistant, and radiologic technology programs. **Adult students:** Entrance exam policies same as for first-time freshmen.

High school preparation. Algebra, biology, and chemistry required for nursing program. Physical therapy assistant, radiologic technology, and pre-nursing programs also have specific course requirements. Paramedic program has specific educational and training requirements.

2005-2006 Annual costs. Tuition/fees: $2,536; $7,568 out-of-state. Per-credit charge: $93 in-state; $279 out-of-state. Out-of-state tuition includes an additional $568 in required fees. New England Regional Student Program: $5,286 annual tuition/fees, $220 per credit-hour. Books/supplies: $850. Personal expenses: $1,965.

Financial aid. All financial aid based on need. Need-based aid available for part-time students. Work study available nights and for part-time students.

Application procedures. Admission: No deadline. $20 fee, may be waived for applicants with need. Application may be submitted online. Admission notification on a rolling basis. **Financial aid:** Closing date 7/15. FAFSA required. Applicants notified on a rolling basis starting 7/15; must reply within 2 week(s) of notification.

Academics. Special study options: Accelerated study, cross-registration, distance learning, double major, dual enrollment of high school students, ESL, independent study, internships, weekend college. Interdisciplinary summer program with Smith College. License preparation in nursing, paramedic, radiology. **Credit/placement by examination:** AP, CLEP, institutional tests. **Support services:** GED preparation, learning center, pre-admission summer program, remedial instruction, study skills assistance, tutoring, writing center.

Majors. Business: Accounting, administrative services, business admin. **Computer sciences:** General. **Education:** Early childhood. **Engineering:** Electrical. **Engineering technology:** Architectural. **Health:** EMT paramedic, medical assistant, medical radiologic technology/radiation therapy, mental health services, nursing (RN), physical therapy assistant. **Liberal arts:** Arts/sciences, library assistant. **Protective services:** Fire safety technology.

Computing on campus. 500 workstations in library, computer center, student center. Online course registration, online library available.

Student life. Freshman orientation: Available. Preregistration for classes offered. Three-day program held prior to start of semester. **Policies:** Policies against drugs and alcohol, violence, weapons, and sexual harassment on campus. Freshmen permitted cars on campus. **Activities:** Choral groups, dance, drama, literary magazine, student government, TV station, Latin American students association, senior renewal club, early childhood club, preprofessional club, Phi Theta Kappa, nursing club, Black student union, student senate, drama club.

Student services. Campus ministries, career counseling, services for economically disadvantaged, student employment services, financial aid counseling, minority student services, on-campus daycare, personal counseling, placement for graduates, veterans' counselor, women's services. **Physically disabled:** Services for visually, speech, hearing impaired. **Learning disabled:** Comprehensive services available. **Transfer:** Special adviser, orientation for new students. College fairs on campus for students transferring to 4-year colleges.

Contact. E-mail: MBall-davis@ccc.commnet.edu
Phone: (860) 906-5126 Toll-free number: (800) 894-6126
Marsha Ball-Davis, Director of Admissions, Capital Community College, 950 Main Street, Hartford, CT 06103-1207

Two-Year Colleges

Gateway Community College
New Haven, Connecticut — **CB member**
www.gwcc.commnet.edu — **CB code: 3425**

- Public 2-year community college
- Commuter campus in small city

General. Founded in 1992. Regionally accredited. **Enrollment:** 4,487 degree-seeking undergraduates; 1,252 non-degree-seeking students. **Degrees:** 415 associate awarded. **Location:** 75 miles from New York City, 130 miles from Boston. **Calendar:** Semester, limited summer session. **Full-time faculty:** 72 total; 21% have terminal degrees, 18% minority, 53% women. **Part-time faculty:** 231 total; 6% have terminal degrees, 21% minority, 54% women. **Class size:** 12% < 20, 78% 20-39, 9% 40-49, less than 1% 50-99. **Special facilities:** Early childhood learning center.

Student profile. Among degree-seeking undergraduates, 1,487 enrolled as first-time, first-year students, 818 transferred in from other institutions.

Part-time:	62%	**Women:**	63%
Out-of-state:	1%	**25 or older:**	51%

Transfer out. Colleges most students transferred to 2005: Southern Connecticut State University, University of New Haven, Quinnipiac College.

Basis for selection. Open admission, but selective for some programs. Special requirements for radiology, pharmacy technician, nuclear medicine technology, diagnostic medical sonography, drug and alcohol rehabilitation counselor. ACCUPLACER/LOPE required for placement. Interview required of radiology, drug and alcohol counseling, nuclear medicine technology, diagnostic medical sonography, pharmacy technician majors.

2005-2006 Annual costs. Tuition/fees: $2,536; $7,568 out-of-state. Per-credit charge: $93 in-state; $279 out-of-state. Out-of-state tuition includes additional $920 in required fees. New England Regional Student Program: $3998.00 annual tuition/fees, $231.50 per credit-hour. Books/supplies: $1,200. Personal expenses: $1,100.

Financial aid. All financial aid based on need. Need-based aid available for part-time students. Work study available nights, weekends and for part-time students.

Application procedures. Admission: Priority date 6/1; deadline 9/1. $20 fee, may be waived for applicants with need. Admission notification on a rolling basis beginning on or about 2/1. **Financial aid:** No deadline. FAFSA, institutional form required. Applicants notified on a rolling basis; must reply within 2 week(s) of notification.

Academics. Special study options: Accelerated study, cross-registration, distance learning, dual enrollment of high school students, ESL, independent study, internships, liberal arts/career combination. **Credit/placement by examination:** AP, CLEP, institutional tests. 30 credit hours maximum toward associate degree. **Support services:** GED preparation, learning center, pre-admission summer program, reduced course load, remedial instruction, study skills assistance, tutoring, writing center.

Majors. Business: Accounting, administrative services, business admin, fashion, office/clerical, sales/distribution. **Computer sciences:** Information systems. **Conservation:** General. **Education:** Early childhood, special. **Engineering:** Science. **Engineering technology:** Electrical, manufacturing. **Family/consumer sciences:** Aging, food/nutrition, institutional food production. **Health:** Medical radiologic technology/radiation therapy, medical secretary, nuclear medical technology, nursing (RN), pharmacy assistant, sonography, substance abuse counseling. **Legal studies:** Legal secretary. **Liberal arts:** Arts/sciences. **Mechanic/repair:** General, automotive. **Protective services:** Fire services admin. **Transportation:** Air traffic control. **Visual/performing arts:** Graphic design, studio arts.

Most popular majors. Business/marketing 17%, engineering/engineering technologies 9%, family/consumer sciences 14%, health sciences 31%, liberal arts 24%.

Computing on campus. 650 workstations in library, computer center. Online library available.

Student life. Freshman orientation: Available. **Activities:** Choral groups, drama, literary magazine, music ensembles, student government, student newspaper, Spanish-American club, international students club, math/science club, Phi Theta Kappa, art club, athletic club, veteran's club, biology club, Theater Goer's, Black Student Union.

Athletics. NJCAA. **Intercollegiate:** Baseball M, basketball. **Team name:** Ravens.

Student services. Adult student services, career counseling, student employment services, financial aid counseling, health services, on-campus daycare, personal counseling, placement for graduates, veterans' counselor, women's services. **Physically disabled:** Services for visually, speech, hearing impaired. **Transfer:** Special adviser, orientation for new students. Transfer adviser for students transferring to 4-year colleges.

Contact. E-mail: csurface@gwcc.commnet.edu
Phone: (203) 285-2010 Toll-free number: (800) 390-7723
Fax: (203) 285-2018
Catherine Surface, Director of Admissions and Counseling, Gateway Community College, 60 Sargent Drive, New Haven, CT 06511-5970

Gibbs College
Norwalk, Connecticut
www.gibbscollege.com — **CB code: 3470**

- For-profit 2-year business and junior college
- Commuter campus in small city
- Interview required

General. Founded in 1974. Accredited by ACICS. **Enrollment:** 1,000 degree-seeking undergraduates. **Degrees:** 300 associate awarded. **Location:** 15 miles from Bridgeport, 10 miles from Stamford. **Calendar:** Quarter. **Full-time faculty:** 10 total. **Part-time faculty:** 50 total.

Basis for selection. Students must score 850 on SAT (exclusive of writing), or 17 on ACT, or 500 on TOEFL.

2005-2006 Annual costs. Tuition/fees: $19,200. Books/supplies: $900.

Application procedures. Admission: No deadline, $50 fee. Admission notification on a rolling basis. **Financial aid:** No deadline. FAFSA, institutional form required. Applicants notified on a rolling basis.

Academics. Special study options: Cooperative education, internships. **Credit/placement by examination:** CLEP. **Support services:** Tutoring.

Majors. Business: General, administrative services, office management.

Computing on campus. 90 workstations in library, computer center.

Student life. Activities: Student newspaper.

Student services. Career counseling, student employment services, personal counseling, placement for graduates. **Transfer:** Special adviser, orientation, re-entry adviser for new students.

Contact. E-mail: info@gibbsnorwalk.com
Phone: (203) 838-4173 Toll-free number: (800) 845-5333
Fax: (203) 899-0788
Ted Havelka, Director of Admissions, Gibbs College, 10 Norden Place, Norwalk, CT 06855

Goodwin College
East Hartford, Connecticut
www.goodwin.edu — **CB member**

- Private 2-year health science and junior college
- Commuter campus in small city

General. Accredited by ACICS. **Enrollment:** 1,161 degree-seeking undergraduates; 58 non-degree-seeking students. **Degrees:** 56 associate awarded.

Location: 5 miles from Hartford. **Calendar:** Semester, extensive summer session. **Full-time faculty:** 16 total. **Part-time faculty:** 49 total.

Student profile. Among degree-seeking undergraduates, 100% enrolled in a vocational program, 196 enrolled as first-time, first-year students, 208 transferred in from other institutions.

Part-time:	89%	**Asian American:**	1%
Women:	89%	**Hispanic American:**	14%
African American:	31%		

Transfer out. Colleges most students transferred to 2005: Manchester Community College, Capital Community College, University of Connecticut, Central Connecticut State University, Tunxis Community College.

Basis for selection. Open admission, but selective for some programs. Applicants to the nursing, respiratory therapist, and histology technician programs must have successfully completed pre-requisite courses prior to application and submit a completed application to program desired. Interviews may be required for some programs. **Adult students:** Entrance exam policies same as for first-time freshmen. **Homeschooled:** State high school equivalency certificate required.

2005-2006 Annual costs. Tuition/fees: $12,300. Per-credit charge: $375.

Application procedures. Admission: No deadline. $50 fee, may be waived for applicants with need. Admission notification on a rolling basis.

Academics. Special study options: Cooperative education, distance learning, ESL. License preparation in nursing. **Credit/placement by examination:** AP, CLEP. **Support services:** Remedial instruction, tutoring.

Majors. Business: General. **Computer sciences:** General. **Health:** Histologic assistant, medical assistant, nursing (RN), respiratory therapy assistant.

Computing on campus. Online library, repair service available.

Student life. Freshman orientation: Mandatory. **Activities:** Student government, student newspaper.

Athletics. Intramural: Bowling, golf.

Student services. Career counseling, student employment services, financial aid counseling. **Transfer:** Special adviser, orientation for new students.

Contact. E-mail: dnoonan@goodwin.edu
Phone: (860) 528-4111 Toll-free number: (800) 889-3282
Fax: (860) 291-9550
Daniel Noonan, Director of Enrollment, Goodwin College, 745 Burnside Avenue, East Hartford, CT 06108

Housatonic Community College
Bridgeport, Connecticut
www.hcc.commnet.edu **CB code: 3446**

- Public 2-year community college
- Commuter campus in small city

General. Founded in 1966. Regionally accredited. **Enrollment:** 3,738 degree-seeking undergraduates. **Degrees:** 342 associate awarded. **Location:** 60 miles from Hartford, 60 miles from New York City. **Calendar:** Semester, extensive summer session. **Full-time faculty:** 75 total. **Part-time faculty:** 200 total. **Class size:** 45% < 20, 53% 20-39, 2% 40-49, less than 1% 50-99. **Special facilities:** Art museum.

Basis for selection. Open admission, but selective for some programs. Special requirements for clinical lab science, physical therapist assistant, occupational therapy assistant, nursing programs. Interview required of allied health, computer program majors.

2005-2006 Annual costs. Tuition/fees: $2,536; $7,568 out-of-state. Per-credit charge: $93 in-state; $279 out-of-state. Out-of-state tuition includes additional $568 in required fees. New England Regional Student Program: $5,286 annual tuition/fees, $220 per credit-hour. Books/supplies: $700.

2004-2005 Financial aid. All financial aid based on need. 90% of total undergraduate aid awarded as scholarships/grants, 10% as loans/jobs. Need-based aid available for part-time students.

Application procedures. Admission: No deadline. $20 fee, may be waived for applicants with need. Admission notification on a rolling basis. Application period ends one week after start of classes. **Financial aid:** Priority date 11/1, closing date 5/1. FAFSA required. Applicants notified on a rolling basis starting 6/1.

Academics. Special study options: Cooperative education, distance learning, double major, dual enrollment of high school students, ESL, honors, independent study, internships, weekend college. **Credit/placement by examination:** CLEP, institutional tests. 30 credit hours maximum toward associate degree. New Jersey Basic Skills Placement Test and/or ACCUPLACER used for advising and placement. **Support services:** GED preparation, learning center, reduced course load, remedial instruction, study skills assistance, tutoring, writing center.

Majors. Business: General, accounting, administrative services, business admin. **Computer sciences:** General. **Education:** Early childhood. **Family/consumer sciences:** Child care. **Health:** Clinical lab technology, mental health services, nursing (RN), physical therapy assistant, substance abuse counseling. **Liberal arts:** Arts/sciences. **Mechanic/repair:** Aircraft. **Protective services:** Police science. **Public administration:** Human services. **Visual/performing arts:** Commercial/advertising art, studio arts.

Computing on campus. 140 workstations in library, computer center.

Student life. Freshman orientation: Available. Preregistration for classes offered. **Activities:** Drama, literary magazine, student government, student newspaper.

Student services. Adult student services, career counseling, services for economically disadvantaged, student employment services, financial aid counseling, health services, on-campus daycare, personal counseling, placement for graduates, veterans' counselor. **Transfer:** Special adviser for new students. Transfer adviser, college fairs on campus for students transferring to 4-year colleges.

Contact. Phone: (203) 332-5100 Fax: (203) 332-5123
Deloris Curtis, Director of Admissions, Housatonic Community College, 900 Lafayette Boulevard, Bridgeport, CT 06604-4704

International College of Hospitality Management
Suffield, Connecticut
www.ichm.edu **CB code: 3615**

- For-profit 2-year culinary school and business college
- Residential campus in small town
- Application essay, interview required

General. Regionally accredited. Transfer to sister schools in Switzerland or Australia for second year possible. **Enrollment:** 76 degree-seeking undergraduates. **Degrees:** 37 associate awarded. **Location:** 50 miles from Hartford. **Calendar:** Quarter, limited summer session. **Full-time faculty:** 6 total; 33% have terminal degrees, 50% minority, 50% women. **Part-time faculty:** 5 total; 20% have terminal degrees, 40% minority, 60% women. **Class size:** 95% < 20, 5% 20-39.

Student profile.

Out-of-state:	90%	**Live on campus:**	90%
25 or older:	40%		

Transfer out. Colleges most students transferred to 2005: University Center Cesar Ritz (Switzerland), Institut Hotelier Cesar Ritz (Switzerland).

Basis for selection. Recommendations and interview are important. Visa required for international students. **Adult students:** Entrance exam policies same as for first-time freshmen.

2006-2007 Annual costs. Tuition/fees: $17,800. International students who have no health insurance are required to purchase it for $62 per month. Room/board: $4,978.

Financial aid. Need-based: Need-based aid available for part-time students. Work study available nights, weekends and for part-time students. **Non-need-based:** Scholarships awarded for academics.

Application procedures. Admission: No deadline. $100 fee, may be waived for applicants with need. Application may be submitted online. Admission notification on a rolling basis. **Financial aid:** No deadline. Applicants notified on a rolling basis starting 1/1.

Academics. Special study options: Accelerated study, cooperative education, internships, liberal arts/career combination, study abroad. **Credit/placement by examination:** AP, CLEP, institutional tests. 18 credit hours maximum toward associate degree. **Support services:** Learning center, remedial instruction, study skills assistance, tutoring, writing center.

Majors. Business: Hospitality admin. **Personal/culinary services:** Culinary arts.

Computing on campus. 38 workstations in dormitories, library, computer center, student center. Dormitories wired for high-speed internet access and linked to campus network. Online library, helpline, wireless network available.

Student life. Freshman orientation: Mandatory. Preregistration for classes offered. Half of the first week is devoted to orientation. **Policies:** Freshmen permitted cars on campus. **Housing:** Guaranteed on-campus for freshmen. Coed dorms, substance-free housing available. $500 deposit. **Activities:** Film society, student government, Ritz Guild.

Athletics. Intramural: Basketball, soccer, table tennis, tennis, volleyball, weight lifting.

Student services. Adult student services, alcohol/substance abuse counseling, career counseling, student employment services, financial aid counseling, health services, placement for graduates. **Transfer:** Special adviser, orientation, pre-admission transcript evaluation for new students.

Contact. E-mail: admissions@ichm.edu
Phone: (860) 668-3515 ext. 228 Toll-free number: (800) 955-0809
Fax: (860) 668-7369
Tina Merullo, Director of Admissions, International College of Hospitality Management, 1760 Mapleton Avenue, Suffield, CT 06078

Manchester Community College

Manchester, Connecticut
www.mcc.commnet.edu **CB code: 3544**

- Public 2-year community college
- Commuter campus in small city

General. Founded in 1963. Regionally accredited. **Enrollment:** 4,995 degree-seeking undergraduates. **Degrees:** 490 associate awarded. **Location:** 8 miles from Hartford. **Calendar:** Semester, extensive summer session. **Full-time faculty:** 95 total. **Part-time faculty:** 282 total. **Class size:** 25% < 20, 65% 20-39, 10% 40-49, less than 1% 50-99.

Student profile.

Out-of-state:	1%	**25 or older:**	35%

Transfer out. Colleges most students transferred to 2005: Central Connecticut State University, University of Connecticut, Eastern Connecticut State University.

Basis for selection. Open admission, but selective for some programs. 2.0 school GPA, minimum SAT combined score of 800 (exclusive of writing), rank in top half of class considered for admission to allied health programs. SAT required for admission to allied health programs. Interview required of allied health, drug and alcohol rehabilitation counselor majors.

High school preparation. 2 units mathematics and 1 unit laboratory science required of allied health applicants.

2005-2006 Annual costs. Tuition/fees: $2,536; $7,568 out-of-state. Per-credit charge: $93 in-state; $279 out-of-state. Out-of-state tuition includes additional $568 in required fees. New England Regional Student Program: $5,286 annual tuition/fees, $220 per credit-hour. Books/supplies: $800. Personal expenses: $1,596.

Financial aid. Need-based: Need-based aid available for part-time students.

Application procedures. Admission: No deadline. $20 fee. Application may be submitted online. Admission notification on a rolling basis beginning on or about 5/1. **Financial aid:** Priority date 5/15; no closing date. FAFSA required. Applicants notified on a rolling basis starting 5/1; must reply within 2 week(s) of notification.

Academics. Special study options: Cooperative education, cross-registration, distance learning, double major, dual enrollment of high school students, ESL, independent study, internships, semester at sea, student-designed major, weekend college. **Credit/placement by examination:** AP, CLEP, institutional tests. 45 credit hours maximum toward associate degree. **Support services:** Learning center, reduced course load, remedial instruction, study skills assistance, tutoring, writing center.

Majors. Area/ethnic studies: Women's. **Business:** Accounting, administrative services, business admin, hospitality/recreation, management information systems. **Communications:** Digital media, journalism. **Computer sciences:** Data entry, information systems, networking. **Education:** Early childhood, teacher assistance. **Engineering:** Science. **Engineering technology:** Manufacturing. **Family/consumer sciences:** Institutional food production. **Health:** Clinical lab technology, occupational therapy assistant, pharmacy assistant, physical therapy assistant, respiratory therapy technology, substance abuse counseling, surgical technology. **Legal studies:** Paralegal. **Liberal arts:** Arts/sciences. **Math:** General. **Parks/recreation:** Exercise sciences. **Public administration:** Community org/advocacy. **Visual/performing arts:** Commercial/advertising art.

Most popular majors. Business/marketing 19%, health sciences 9%, liberal arts 43%, security/protective services 8%.

Computing on campus. 310 workstations in library, computer center. Online course registration available.

Student life. Freshman orientation: Available. **Activities:** Choral groups, dance, drama, student government, student newspaper, minority student alliance, Hispanic cultural club, Upper Room Christian Fellowship, voluntary action program.

Athletics. NJCAA. **Intercollegiate:** Baseball, basketball M, soccer. **Intramural:** Softball M. **Team name:** Cougars.

Student services. Adult student services, career counseling, student employment services, health services, on-campus daycare, personal counseling, placement for graduates, veterans' counselor. **Physically disabled:** Services for visually impaired. **Transfer:** Special adviser for new students. Transfer adviser, college fairs on campus for students transferring to 4-year colleges.

Contact. Phone: (860) 512-3210 Fax: (860) 512-3221
Peter Harris, Director of Admissions, Manchester Community College, Great Path PO Box 1046, MS 12, Manchester, CT 06040-1046

Middlesex Community College

Middletown, Connecticut **CB member**
www.mxcc.commnet.edu **CB code: 3551**

- Public 2-year community college
- Commuter campus in large town

General. Founded in 1966. **Enrollment:** 1,562 degree-seeking undergraduates; 724 non-degree-seeking students. **Degrees:** 201 associate awarded. **Location:** 20 miles from Hartford and New Haven. **Calendar:** Semester, limited summer session. **Full-time faculty:** 39 total; 15% minority, 54% women. **Part-time faculty:** 131 total; 16% minority, 54% women.

Student profile. Among degree-seeking undergraduates, 55% enrolled in a transfer program, 45% enrolled in a vocational program, .2% already have a bachelor's degree or higher, 432 enrolled as first-time, first-year students, 161 transferred in from other institutions.

Part-time:	52%	**Asian American:**	3%
Out-of-state:	1%	**Hispanic American:**	10%
Women:	66%	**25 or older:**	65%
African American:	9%		

Transfer out. 45% of students enrolled in the transfer program go on to 4-year colleges.

Basis for selection. Open admission, but selective for some programs. Special requirements for radiology technician, broadcast communications, human services, and drug and alcohol rehabilitation counselor programs. Interview recommended of mental health, radiology, drug and alcohol counseling program majors. **Adult students:** Entrance exam policies same as for first-time freshmen.

2005-2006 Annual costs. Tuition/fees: $2,536; $7,568 out-of-state. Per-credit charge: $93 in-state; $279 out-of-state. Out-of-state students pay additional $568 required fees. New England Regional Student Program: $3,794 annual tuition/fees, $139.50 per credit-hour. Books/supplies: $400. Personal expenses: $700.

Financial aid. All financial aid based on need. Need-based aid available for part-time students. Work study available for part-time students. **Additional information:** Tuition and/or fee waiver for veterans.

Application procedures. Admission: Priority date 7/1; deadline 8/1 (postmark date). $20 fee, may be waived for applicants with need. Application may be submitted online. Admission notification on a rolling basis beginning on or about 1/1. **Financial aid:** Priority date 6/1; no closing date. FAFSA, institutional form required. Applicants notified on a rolling basis starting 7/1; must reply within 2 week(s) of notification.

Academics. **Special study options:** Cross-registration, dual enrollment of high school students, ESL, independent study, internships, student-designed major. License preparation in radiology. **Credit/placement by examination:** CLEP, institutional tests. 48 credit hours maximum toward associate degree. **Support services:** Pre-admission summer program, reduced course load, remedial instruction, tutoring.

Majors. **Business:** Accounting, administrative services, business admin, marketing. **Communications:** General, broadcast journalism. **Computer sciences:** Information systems. **Conservation:** General. **Education:** Early childhood. **Health:** Medical radiologic technology/radiation therapy, medical secretary, nuclear medical technology, ophthalmic lab technology, optician, substance abuse counseling. **Legal studies:** Legal secretary. **Liberal arts:** Arts/sciences. **Public administration:** Human services. **Visual/performing arts:** Metal/jewelry, studio arts.

Most popular majors. Business/marketing 30%, health sciences 25%, liberal arts 35%.

Computing on campus. Online library, helpline available.

Student life. **Freshman orientation:** Available. **Activities:** Concert band, drama, literary magazine, radio station, student government, student newspaper, TV station, Black Student Alliance, national scholastic honor society, student guild, radio/TV club, Collegiate Secretaries International, Minority Opportunities in Education Club, art club, human services organization.

Student services. Career counseling, student employment services, on-campus daycare, personal counseling, placement for graduates, veterans' counselor. **Physically disabled:** Services for visually, hearing impaired. **Transfer:** Special adviser for new students. Transfer adviser, college fairs on campus for students transferring to 4-year colleges.

Contact. E-mail: mshabazz@mxcc.commnet.edu
Phone: (860) 343-5719 Toll-free number: (800) 818-5501
Fax: (860) 344-7488
Mensimah Shabazz, Director of Admissions, Middlesex Community College, 100 Training Hill Road, Middletown, CT 06457

Naugatuck Valley Community College

Waterbury, Connecticut — **CB member**
www.nvcc.commnet.edu — **CB code: 3550**

- Public 2-year community and technical college
- Commuter campus in small city

General. Founded in 1992. Regionally accredited. **Enrollment:** 4,685 degree-seeking undergraduates; 982 non-degree-seeking students. **Degrees:** 479 associate awarded. **Location:** 32 miles from Hartford, 2 miles from Waterbury. **Calendar:** Semester, limited summer session. **Full-time faculty:** 100 total. **Part-time faculty:** 371 total. **Special facilities:** Observatory, fine arts center, automotive technology center, culinary arts facility. **Partnerships:** Cooperative education, Tech Prep, Disney internships.

Student profile. Among degree-seeking undergraduates, 15% enrolled in a transfer program, 5% enrolled in a vocational program, 15% already have a bachelor's degree or higher, 1,169 enrolled as first-time, first-year students, 2,014 transferred in from other institutions.

Part-time:	56%	**Asian American:**	2%
Out-of-state:	1%	**Hispanic American:**	12%
Women:	60%	**25 or older:**	41%
African American:	8%		

Transfer out. 50% of students enrolled in the transfer program go on to 4-year colleges. **Colleges most students transferred to 2005:** Western Connecticut State University, Southern Connecticut State University, Central Connecticut State University, University of Connecticut, Post University.

Basis for selection. Open admission, but selective for some programs. Admission to nursing, physical therapy assistant, radiology, respiratory care programs based on school achievement, recommendations, test scores, maturity of student, motivation. Levels of English Proficiency (LOEP) used for ESL population. Interview required of physical therapy majors. Audition recommended of music majors. Portfolio recommended of art majors. **Adult students:** Entrance exam policies same as for first-time freshmen. **Homeschooled:** Statement describing homeschool structure and mission, interview required. Placement test and interview required.

High school preparation. Recommended units include English 4, mathematics 3, social studies 2, history 2 and science 1. Most allied health programs require high school algebra, biology, chemistry. Engineering technologies require 2 years algebra, 1 year laboratory science (preferably physics or chemistry), and some computer literacy.

2005-2006 Annual costs. Tuition/fees: $2,536; $7,568 out-of-state. Per-credit charge: $93 in-state; $279 out-of-state. Books/supplies: $1,200. Personal expenses: $1,970.

2004-2005 Financial aid. All financial aid based on need. 92% of total undergraduate aid awarded as scholarships/grants, 8% as loans/jobs. Need-based aid available for part-time students. Work study available for part-time students.

Application procedures. **Admission:** Priority date 6/1; no deadline. $20 fee, may be waived for applicants with need. Application may be submitted online. Admission notification on a rolling basis beginning on or about 9/1. **Financial aid:** Priority date 4/1; no closing date. FAFSA required. Applicants notified on a rolling basis starting 6/1.

Academics. Composition, technical writing, computer information systems, math, business, psychology, astronomy , biology and introduction to multimedia courses available through distance learning. **Special study options:** Cooperative education, cross-registration, distance learning, double major, dual enrollment of high school students, ESL, independent study, internships, study abroad. License preparation in aviation, nursing, physical therapy, radiology, real estate. **Credit/placement by examination:** AP, CLEP, institutional tests. 45 credit hours maximum toward associate degree. **Support services:** Learning center, reduced course load, remedial instruction, study skills assistance, tutoring, writing center.

Majors. **Agriculture:** Horticulture. **Business:** Accounting technology, administrative services, banking/financial services, business admin, hotel/motel admin, merchandising, selling. **Communications:** Digital media. **Engineering:** Science. **Engineering technology:** General, CAD/CADD, electrical, energy systems, industrial management, manufacturing, mechanical, plastics, quality control. **Family/consumer sciences:** Child care, institutional food production. **Health:** Medical radiologic technology/radiation therapy, mental health services, nursing (RN), physical therapy assistant, respiratory therapy technology, substance abuse counseling. **Legal studies:** Legal secretary, paralegal. **Liberal arts:** Arts/sciences. **Mechanic/repair:** Automotive. **Protective services:** Fire services admin, police science. **Transportation:** Aviation. **Visual/performing arts:** Art, dance, dramatic, multimedia.

Most popular majors. Business/marketing 14%, engineering/engineering technologies 15%, health sciences 22%, liberal arts 19%, security/protective services 20%.

Computing on campus. 1,000 workstations in library, computer center. Online course registration, helpline, repair service available.

Student life. **Freshman orientation:** Available. Preregistration for classes offered. **Activities:** Jazz band, choral groups, dance, drama, literary magazine, music ensembles, musical theater, student government, student newspaper, symphony orchestra, Black student union, Hispanic student union, human services club, Phi Theta Kappa, Alpha Beta Gamma, IEEE, Association of Facilities Engineers, international students, Agro-Bio Club, student nurses clubs.

Athletics. **Team name:** The Wave.

Student services. Adult student services, career counseling, student employment services, financial aid counseling, health services, personal counseling, placement for graduates, veterans' counselor. **Physically disabled:** Services for visually, speech, hearing impaired. **Learning disabled:** Comprehensive services available. **Transfer:** Special adviser, orientation, pre-admission transcript evaluation for new students. Transfer adviser, college fairs on campus for students transferring to 4-year colleges.

Contact. E-mail: nvcc@nvcc.commnet.edu
Phone: (203) 575-8151 Fax: (203) 596-8766
Lucretia Sveda, Director of Enrollment Service, Naugatuck Valley Community College, 750 Chase Parkway, Waterbury, CT 06708-3089

Northwestern Connecticut Community College

Winsted, Connecticut — **CB member**
www.nwctc.commnet.edu — **CB code: 3652**

- Public 2-year community and technical college
- Commuter campus in large town

General. Founded in 1965. Regionally accredited. **Enrollment:** 1,127 degree-seeking undergraduates; 442 non-degree-seeking students. **Degrees:** 123 associate awarded. **Location:** 25 miles from Hartford, 25 miles from Waterbury. **Calendar:** Semester, limited summer session. **Full-time faculty:** 27 total. **Part-time faculty:** 86 total. **Class size:** 53% < 20, 44% 20-39, 2% 40-49, less than 1% 50-99. **Special facilities:** Computer graphics multimedia laboratory.

Student profile. Among degree-seeking undergraduates, 296 enrolled as first-time, first-year students, 139 transferred in from other institutions.

Part-time:	54%	**Women:**	68%
Out-of-state:	1%	**25 or older:**	35%

Basis for selection. Open admission, but selective for some programs. Special requirements for drug and alcohol rehabilitation counseling, adventure education, physical therapy assistant, and dialysis patient care programs. New Jersey Placement Test required of all first-time freshmen.

2005-2006 Annual costs. Tuition/fees: $2,536; $7,568 out-of-state. Per-credit charge: $93 in-state; $279 out-of-state. New England Regional Student Program: $5,286 annual tuition/fees, $220 per credit-hour. Books/supplies: $600. Personal expenses: $1,000.

Financial aid. Non-need-based: Scholarships awarded for academics, art, state residency.

Application procedures. Admission: No deadline. $20 fee, may be waived for applicants with need. Admission notification on a rolling basis. **Financial aid:** Priority date 6/1; no closing date. FAFSA required. Applicants notified on a rolling basis starting 6/1.

Academics. Career education for the deaf program offers full range of services and participation in all majors by deaf and hearing impaired students. Interpreting major prepares hearing students for National Registry test for interpreters for the deaf. **Special study options:** Cooperative education, cross-registration, distance learning, double major, dual enrollment of high school students, ESL, independent study, internships. **Credit/placement by examination:** AP, CLEP, institutional tests. 48 credit hours maximum toward associate degree. **Support services:** Learning center, reduced course load, remedial instruction, tutoring.

Majors. Business: Accounting, administrative services, business admin, management information systems, marketing. **Computer sciences:** Information systems, programming. **Education:** General, early childhood. **Foreign languages:** Sign language interpretation. **Health:** Medical assistant, physical therapy assistant, recreational therapy, substance abuse counseling, veterinary technology/assistant. **Interdisciplinary:** Behavioral sciences. **Liberal arts:** Arts/sciences. **Math:** General. **Parks/recreation:** General, facilities management. **Protective services:** Law enforcement admin. **Public administration:** Human services. **Social sciences:** General. **Visual/performing arts:** Commercial/advertising art, design, studio arts.

Most popular majors. Business/marketing 12%, engineering/engineering technologies 7%, foreign language 9%, health sciences 24%, liberal arts 26%, security/protective services 7%, visual/performing arts 9%.

Computing on campus. 80 workstations in library, computer center.

Student life. Housing: Dormitory for hearing impaired and interpreting students available in Winsted. **Activities:** Literary magazine, student government, student newspaper, Spectrum (minority), community service club, Signs of our Times (Hearing Impaired and Interpretory Students).

Student services. Career counseling, student employment services, on-campus daycare, personal counseling, veterans' counselor. **Physically disabled:** Services for hearing impaired. **Transfer:** Special adviser, orientation for new students. Transfer adviser, college fairs on campus for students transferring to 4-year colleges.

Contact. E-mail: bchrzah@nwcc.commnet.edu
Phone: (860) 738-6330 Fax: (860) 379-4465
Beverly Chrzan, Director of Admissions, Northwestern Connecticut Community College, Park Place East, Winsted, CT 06098

Norwalk Community College

Norwalk, Connecticut
www.ncc.commnet.edu **CB code: 3677**

- Public 2-year community and technical college
- Commuter campus in small city

General. Founded in 1961. Regionally accredited. Non-credit courses offered through continuing education department. Lifetime Learners Institute for senior citizens. **Enrollment:** 6,036 undergraduates. **Degrees:** 600 associate awarded. **Location:** 50 miles from New York City. **Calendar:** Semester, extensive summer session. **Full-time faculty:** 100 total. **Part-time faculty:** 250 total. **Special facilities:** Theater, rotating art and cultural exhibits, culinary arts facility, early childhood education lab/preschool.

Student profile.

Out-of-state:	1%	**25 or older:**	52%

Basis for selection. Open admission, but selective for some programs. Special requirements for nursing, legal assistant, respiratory care programs. ACCUPLACER placement test required of all entering, first-time students in English and math. ESL test required of non-native English speakers. **Adult students:** Entrance exam policies same as for first-time freshmen.

High school preparation. Recommended units include English 4, mathematics 3 and science 2. Chemistry, biology and algebra required for nursing and respiratory therapy applicants. Nursing applicants must have taken chemistry within past 5 years.

2005-2006 Annual costs. Tuition/fees: $2,536; $7,568 out-of-state. Per-credit charge: $93 in-state; $279 out-of-state. Out-of-state tuition includes additional $568 required fees. New England Regional Student Program: $5,286 annual tuition/fees, $220 per credit-hour. Books/supplies: $800. Personal expenses: $2,000.

Financial aid. Need-based: Need-based aid available for part-time students. Work study available for part-time students. **Non-need-based:** Scholarships awarded for academics, alumni affiliation.

Application procedures. Admission: No deadline. $20 fee, may be waived for applicants with need. Admission notification on a rolling basis beginning on or about 1/1. Applicants to nursing program should apply by February 1. **Financial aid:** Priority date 4/1; no closing date. FAFSA, institutional form required. Applicants notified on a rolling basis starting 7/1; must reply within 2 week(s) of notification.

Academics. Special 10-week sessions with longer class hours per day let students finish courses more quickly during fall and spring. **Special study options:** Cooperative education, cross-registration, double major, dual enrollment of high school students, ESL, honors, internships, liberal arts/career combination, weekend college. Early childhood education credential training program. License preparation in nursing, paramedic, real estate. **Credit/placement by examination:** AP, CLEP, IB, institutional tests. 45 credit hours maximum toward associate degree. **Support services:** Learning center, pre-admission summer program, reduced course load, remedial instruction, study skills assistance, tutoring, writing center.

Majors. Business: Accounting, business admin, finance, hospitality admin, hospitality/recreation, management information systems, marketing, office management, office technology. **Communications:** Journalism. **Communications technology:** General. **Computer sciences:** General, applications programming, data processing, information systems, programming, systems analysis. **Education:** Early childhood. **Engineering:** General, architectural, science. **Engineering technology:** Architectural, construction. **Health:** Nursing (RN), recreational therapy, respiratory therapy technology, substance abuse counseling. **Legal studies:** Legal secretary, paralegal. **Liberal arts:** Arts/sciences. **Math:** General. **Parks/recreation:** General. **Protective services:** Fire safety technology, fire services admin, law enforcement admin. **Public administration:** Human services. **Visual/performing arts:** Art, commercial/advertising art, studio arts.

Computing on campus. 500 workstations in library, computer center, student center. Commuter students can connect to campus network. Online library, helpline available.

Student life. Freshman orientation: Available. One-day orientation for new students before start of semester. **Policies:** Freshmen permitted cars on campus. **Activities:** Choral groups, dance, drama, music ensembles, musical theater, student government, student newspaper, TV station, African culture club, Hay Motivo, Phi Theta Kappa, legal assistants club, early childhood education club, global development club, French club, Haitian student association, Asian club, criminal justice club.

Student services. Adult student services, career counseling, services for economically disadvantaged, student employment services, financial aid counseling, on-campus daycare, placement for graduates, veterans' counselor, women's services. **Physically disabled:** Services for visually, speech, hearing impaired. **Transfer:** Special adviser, orientation, re-entry adviser, pre-admission transcript evaluation for new students. Transfer adviser, college fairs on campus for students transferring to 4-year colleges.

Contact. E-mail: admissions@ncc.commnet.edu
Phone: (203) 857-7060 Fax: (203) 857-3335
Kimberlee Csapo-Ebert, Director of Enrollment Management, Norwalk Community College, 188 Richards Avenue, Norwalk, CT 06854-1655

Quinebaug Valley Community College

Danielson, Connecticut **CB member**
www.qvcc.commnet.edu **CB code: 3716**

- Public 2-year community and technical college
- Commuter campus in large town

General. Founded in 1971. Regionally accredited. **Enrollment:** 1,473 degree-seeking undergraduates; 241 non-degree-seeking students. **Degrees:** 130 associate awarded. **Location:** 50 miles from Hartford, 25 miles from Providence, Rhode Island. **Calendar:** Semester, limited summer session. **Full-time faculty:** 22 total; 23% have terminal degrees, 4% minority, 59% women. **Part-time faculty:** 102 total; 5% have terminal degrees, 2% minority, 71% women. **Special facilities:** Plastics laboratory.

Student profile. Among degree-seeking undergraduates, 30% enrolled in a transfer program, 60% enrolled in a vocational program, 1% already have a bachelor's degree or higher, 338 enrolled as first-time, first-year students, 155 transferred in from other institutions.

Part-time:	58%	**Asian American:**	1%
Out-of-state:	8%	**Hispanic American:**	10%
Women:	68%	**Native American:**	1%
African American:	2%	**25 or older:**	32%

Transfer out. Colleges most students transferred to 2005: Eastern Connecticut State University, University of Connecticut, Worcester State College.

Basis for selection. Open admission. Drug and alcohol counseling degree candidates must file special application after completing general education component. Interview recommended.

2005-2006 Annual costs. Tuition/fees: $2,536; $7,568 out-of-state. Per-credit charge: $93 in-state; $279 out-of-state. Out-of-state tution includes additional $568 required fees. New England Regional Student Program: $5,286 annual tuition/fees, $220 per credit-hour. Books/supplies: $900. Personal expenses: $1,000.

2005-2006 Financial aid. All financial aid based on need. 99% of total undergraduate aid awarded as scholarships/grants, 1% as loans/jobs. Need-based aid available for part-time students. Work study available nights, weekends and for part-time students.

Application procedures. Admission: No deadline. $20 fee, may be waived for applicants with need. Application may be submitted online. Admission notification on a rolling basis. **Financial aid:** Closing date 10/1. FAFSA required. Applicants notified on a rolling basis starting 5/1.

Academics. Special study options: Distance learning, double major, dual enrollment of high school students, ESL. License preparation in real estate. **Credit/placement by examination:** AP, CLEP, institutional tests. 30 credit hours maximum toward associate degree. **Support services:** Learning center, pre-admission summer program, reduced course load, remedial instruction, study skills assistance, tutoring.

Majors. Business: Accounting, administrative services, business admin, office management, office technology. **Computer sciences:** General. **Education:** Early childhood. **Engineering:** Polymer. **Engineering technology:** Plastics. **Health:** Medical assistant. **Liberal arts:** Arts/sciences. **Mechanic/repair:** Aircraft. **Public administration:** Human services. **Visual/performing arts:** Studio arts.

Most popular majors. Business/marketing 15%, health sciences 6%, liberal arts 70%, visual/performing arts 6%.

Computing on campus. 110 workstations in library, computer center. Commuter students can connect to campus network. Online course registration, online library, wireless network available.

Student life. Freshman orientation: Available. **Policies:** Freshmen permitted cars on campus. **Activities:** Student government, medical assisting association, Phi Theta Kappa, Alpha Beta Gamma, book club.

Student services. Career counseling, student employment services, financial aid counseling, on-campus daycare, placement for graduates, veterans' counselor. **Physically disabled:** Services for visually, speech, hearing impaired. **Transfer:** Special adviser, orientation, pre-admission transcript evaluation for new students. Transfer adviser, college fairs on campus for students transferring to 4-year colleges.

Contact. E-mail: qv_lsd@commnet.edu
Phone: (860) 774-1130 Fax: (860) 774-7768
Toni Moumouris, Enrollment and Transition Counselor, Quinebaug Valley Community College, 742 Upper Maple Street, Danielson, CT 06239-1440

St. Vincent's College

Bridgeport, Connecticut
www.stvincentscollege.edu

- Private 2-year health science and junior college
- Small city

General. Regionally accredited. **Enrollment:** 337 degree-seeking undergraduates. **Degrees:** 81 associate awarded. **Calendar:** Semester. **Full-time faculty:** 11 total. **Part-time faculty:** 30 total.

Application procedures. Admission: Closing date 7/1. $35 fee. Application fee for certificate programs is $15.

Academics. Credit/placement by examination: CLEP.

Majors. Health: Cardiovascular technology, medical assistant, nursing (RN), radiologic technology/medical imaging.

Student life. Freshman orientation: Mandatory.

Contact. E-mail: admissions@stvincentscollege.edu
Phone: (203) 576-5513
Joseph Marrone, Admissions Director, St. Vincent's College, 2800 Main Street, Bridgeport, CT 06606

Three Rivers Community College

Norwich, Connecticut **CB member**
www.trcc.commnet.edu **CB code: 3558**

- Public 2-year community and technical college
- Commuter campus in large town

General. Founded in 1969. Regionally accredited. **Enrollment:** 3,253 degree-seeking undergraduates. **Degrees:** 357 associate awarded. **Location:** 45 miles from Hartford. **Calendar:** Semester, limited summer session. **Full-time faculty:** 77 total; 9% have terminal degrees, 6% minority, 54% women. **Part-time faculty:** 122 total; 12% minority, 47% women. **Special facilities:** Nuclear reactor simulator.

Student profile.

Out-of-state:	1%	**25 or older:**	52%

Transfer out. Colleges most students transferred to 2005: Eastern Connecticut State University, University of Connecticut, Central Connecticut State University, Southern Illinois University, Sacred Heart University.

Basis for selection. Open admission, but selective for some programs. Selective admission for nursing, drug and alcohol rehabilitation counselor, and paramedic applicants. Admission to these programs based on recommendations, admission test, and applicant's grades in mathematics and natural sciences. **Adult students:** Basic skills placement tests in Math and English required unless students have completed a college level Math and English course. **Homeschooled:** Applicants advised to submit GED or demonstrate ability to benefit through the Accuplacer test administered by the college.

High school preparation. One unit chemistry, biology, and algebra required for nursing program.

2005-2006 Annual costs. Tuition/fees: $2,536; $7,568 out-of-state. Per-credit charge: $93 in-state; $279 out-of-state. Out-of-state tuition includes additional $568 required fees. New England Regional Student Program: $5,286 annual tuition/fees, $220 per credit hour. Books/supplies: $700.

2005-2006 Financial aid. All financial aid based on need. 252 full-time freshmen applied for aid; 144 were judged to have need; 144 of these received aid. Average need met was 64%. Average scholarship/grant was $1,963; average loan $1,540. 77% of total undergraduate aid awarded as scholarships/grants, 23% as loans/jobs. Need-based aid available for part-time students.

Application procedures. Admission: No deadline. $20 fee. Application may be submitted online. Admission notification on a rolling basis beginning on or about 3/30. **Financial aid:** Priority date 7/15; no closing date. FAFSA required. Applicants notified on a rolling basis; must reply within 2 week(s) of notification.

Academics. Special study options: Cooperative education, cross-registration, double major, dual enrollment of high school students, ESL, independent study, internships, liberal arts/career combination, study abroad. License preparation in nursing. **Credit/placement by examination:** AP, CLEP, institutional tests. 45 credit hours maximum toward associate degree. **Support services:** Reduced course load, remedial instruction, study skills assistance, tutoring, writing center.

Majors. Business: Accounting, business admin, hospitality admin, management information systems, office technology, tourism/travel. **Computer sciences:** General, applications programming, information systems. **Education:** Early childhood, special. **Engineering technology:** Architectural, civil, drafting, electrical, manufacturing, water quality. **Health:** Medical secretary, mental health services, substance abuse counseling. **Legal studies:** Legal secretary. **Liberal arts:** Arts/sciences. **Mechanic/repair:** General. **Physical sciences:** General. **Protective services:** Criminal justice, fire safety technology, police science. **Public administration:** General, human services, policy analysis. **Transportation:** Aviation.

Most popular majors. Business/marketing 12%, education 6%, health sciences 10%, liberal arts 49%.

Computing on campus. 200 workstations in library, computer center. Online course registration available.

Student life. Freshman orientation: Available. **Policies:** Student government controls student activity fees. Freshmen permitted cars on campus. **Activities:** Drama, literary magazine, student government, student newspaper, Spanish American Association, Afro-American Association, student chapters of professional organizations.

Athletics. NJCAA. **Intercollegiate:** Golf. **Intramural:** Basketball, bowling, skiing, table tennis, volleyball.

Student services. Adult student services, career counseling, student employment services, on-campus daycare, personal counseling, placement for graduates, veterans' counselor. **Physically disabled:** Services for visually, hearing impaired. **Transfer:** Special adviser, re-entry adviser for new students. Transfer adviser, college fairs on campus for students transferring to 4-year colleges.

Contact. E-mail: info3rivers@trcc.commnet.edu
Phone: (860) 383-5260 Fax: (860) 886-0691
Dan Zaneski, Director of Financial Aid and Admissions, Three Rivers Community College, 7 Mahan Drive, Norwich, CT 06360-2479

Tunxis Community College

Farmington, Connecticut — **CB member**
www.tunxis.commnet.edu — **CB code: 3897**

- Public 2-year community college
- Commuter campus in large town

General. Founded in 1970. Regionally accredited. **Enrollment:** 2,774 degree-seeking undergraduates; 1,120 non-degree-seeking students. **Degrees:** 266 associate awarded. **ROTC:** Army, Navy, Air Force. **Location:** 15 miles from Hartford. **Calendar:** Semester, limited summer session. **Full-time faculty:** 62 total. **Part-time faculty:** 186 total. **Class size:** 29% < 20, 71% 20-39, less than 1% 40-49. **Special facilities:** Early childhood center.

Student profile. Among degree-seeking undergraduates, 604 enrolled as first-time, first-year students.

Part-time:	52%	**25 or older:**	27%
Women:	61%		

Transfer out. Colleges most students transferred to 2005: Central Connecticut State University, Charter Oak College, St. Joseph College.

Basis for selection. Open admission, but selective for some programs. Selective admission for dental hygiene, drug and alcohol rehabilitation counselor, physical therapist assistant, technological studies: television operations option, dental assisting, criminal justice command institute: supervisory leadership programs, and correction pre-service certification. ESL placement test required on non-native English speakers. Interview required of dental hygiene, drug and alcohol rehabilitation counselor majors. **Adult students:** Entrance exam policies same as for first-time freshmen. **Homeschooled:** Contact admissions office for enrollment information. **Learning Disabled:** Contact Academic Support Center prior to placement testing if accommodations are necessary.

2005-2006 Annual costs. Tuition/fees: $2,536; $7,568 out-of-state. Per-credit charge: $93 in-state; $279 out-of-state. Out-of-state tuition includes additional $568 required fees. New England Regional Student Program: $5,286 annual tuition/fees, $220 per credit hour. Books/supplies: $420. Personal expenses: $1,210.

2004-2005 Financial aid. Need-based: 84% of total undergraduate aid awarded as scholarships/grants, 16% as loans/jobs. Need-based aid available for part-time students. Work study available nights, weekends and for part-time students. **Non-need-based:** Scholarships awarded for academics, leadership. **Additional information:** Financial aid available to all students showing need. Part-time students encouraged to apply.

Application procedures. Admission: No deadline. $20 fee, may be waived for applicants with need. Application may be submitted online. Admission notification on a rolling basis. Dental hygiene program closing date 01/01, notification by 03/01. Drug and alcohol rehabilitation counselor program closing date 02/01. **Financial aid:** Priority date 6/1; no closing date. FAFSA required. Applicants notified on a rolling basis starting 3/1.

Academics. Special study options: Cross-registration, distance learning, double major, dual enrollment of high school students, ESL, independent study, internships, liberal arts/career combination. License preparation in dental hygiene, physical therapy. **Credit/placement by examination:** CLEP, institutional tests. 30 credit hours maximum toward associate degree. **Support services:** Learning center, pre-admission summer program, reduced course load, remedial instruction, tutoring.

Majors. Business: Accounting, administrative services, business admin, fashion, finance, office/clerical. **Computer sciences:** Applications programming, computer graphics. **Education:** Early childhood. **Engineering:** Science. **Engineering technology:** Manufacturing. **Health:** Dental hygiene, medical secretary, substance abuse counseling. **Legal studies:** Legal secretary. **Liberal arts:** Arts/sciences. **Public administration:** Human services. **Visual/performing arts:** General, commercial/advertising art.

Most popular majors. Business/marketing 34%, health sciences 18%, liberal arts 25%, security/protective services 11%, visual/performing arts 7%.

Computing on campus. 200 workstations in computer center. Commuter students can connect to campus network.

Student life. Freshman orientation: Available. Preregistration for classes offered. Held once a week during the month before start of classes. **Policies:** Freshmen permitted cars on campus. **Activities:** Choral groups, student government, student newspaper, Minority Student Alliance, human services club, criminal justice club, dental hygiene group.

Student services. Career counseling, student employment services, financial aid counseling, health services, minority student services, on-campus daycare, personal counseling, placement for graduates. **Physically disabled:** Services for visually impaired. **Transfer:** Special adviser for new students. Transfer adviser, college fairs on campus for students transferring to 4-year colleges.

Contact. E-mail: tx-admissions@txcc.commnet.edu
Phone: (860) 679-9521 Fax: (860) 676-8906
Peter McCluskey, Director of Admissions, Tunxis Community College, 271 Scott Swamp Road, Farmington, CT 06032-3187

Delaware

Delaware College of Art and Design

Wilmington, Delaware
www.dcad.edu

- Private 2-year visual arts college
- Large city

General. Regionally accredited. **Enrollment:** 176 degree-seeking undergraduates. **Degrees:** 46 associate awarded. **Calendar:** Semester. **Part-time faculty:** 54 total.

Application procedures. Admission: Closing date 3/31. $25 fee. Admission notification on a rolling basis.

Academics. Credit/placement by examination: CLEP.

Majors. Communications technology: Animation/special effects. **Visual/performing arts:** Graphic design, illustration, interior design, photography, studio arts.

Contact. E-mail: admissions@dcad.edu
Phone: (302) 622-8867 ext. 118
Lynda Schmid, Director of Admissions, Delaware College of Art and Design, 600 North Market Street, Wilmington, DE 19801

Delaware Technical and Community College: Owens Campus

Georgetown, Delaware
www.dtcc.edu **CB code: 5169**

- Public 2-year community and technical college
- Commuter campus in rural community
- Interview required

General. Founded in 1967. Regionally accredited. **Enrollment:** 1,604 full-time, degree-seeking students. **Degrees:** 345 associate awarded. **Location:** 80 miles from Wilmington. **Calendar:** Semester, limited summer session. **Full-time faculty:** 100 total. **Part-time faculty:** 175 total. **Class size:** 69% < 20, 31% 20-39.

Student profile.

Out-of-state:	6%	25 or older:	50%

Basis for selection. Open admission. Interview required of health technology majors.

2005-2006 Annual costs. Tuition/fees: $2,166; $5,100 out-of-state. Per-credit charge: $82 in-state; $204 out-of-state. Books/supplies: $800. Personal expenses: $400.

Financial aid. Non-need-based: Scholarships awarded for academics, athletics.

Application procedures. Admission: Priority date 8/1; no deadline. $10 fee, may be waived for applicants with need. Admission notification on a rolling basis. **Financial aid:** Priority date 6/15; no closing date. FAFSA required. Applicants notified on a rolling basis; must reply within 2 week(s) of notification.

Academics. Special study options: Cooperative education, cross-registration, distance learning, double major, dual enrollment of high school students, internships. License preparation in nursing, paramedic, physical therapy. **Credit/placement by examination:** CLEP, institutional tests. **Support services:** GED preparation, learning center, reduced course load, remedial instruction, tutoring.

Majors. Agriculture: Agribusiness operations, horticulture, poultry. **Business:** General, accounting, administrative services, banking/financial services, business admin, hospitality admin, human resources, marketing, office technology, office/clerical. **Communications:** Journalism. **Computer sciences:** General, data processing, information systems, programming, systems analysis. **Engineering technology:** Architectural, civil, electrical. **Family/consumer sciences:** Child care. **Health:** Clinical lab assistant, clinical lab technology, EMT paramedic, medical assistant, medical radiologic technology/radiation therapy, medical secretary, medical transcription, mental health services, nursing (RN), occupational therapy assistant, ophthalmic lab technology, respiratory therapy technology, veterinary technology/assistant. **Legal studies:** Paralegal. **Mechanic/repair:** Heating/ac/refrig. **Protective services:** Criminal justice.

Computing on campus. 400 workstations in library, computer center. Commuter students can connect to campus network.

Student life. Freshman orientation: Mandatory. **Activities:** Radio station, student government, student newspaper.

Athletics. NJCAA. **Intercollegiate:** Baseball M, softball W.

Student services. Adult student services, career counseling, student employment services, on-campus daycare, personal counseling, placement for graduates, veterans' counselor. **Physically disabled:** Services for visually, hearing impaired. **Transfer:** Special adviser, orientation for new students. Transfer adviser for students transferring to 4-year colleges.

Contact. Phone: (302) 856-5400
Claire MacDonald, Admissions Coordinator, Delaware Technical and Community College: Owens Campus, Box 610, Georgetown, DE 19947

Delaware Technical and Community College: Stanton/Wilmington Campus

Newark, Delaware
www.dtcc.edu **CB code: 5154**

- Public 2-year community and technical college
- Commuter campus in small city

General. Founded in 1967. Regionally accredited. Multilocation institution. **Enrollment:** 2,779 full-time, degree-seeking students. **Degrees:** 508 associate awarded. **Location:** 30 miles from Philadelphia. **Calendar:** Semester, limited summer session. **Full-time faculty:** 165 total. **Part-time faculty:** 338 total. **Class size:** 77% < 20, 22% 20-39, less than 1% 40-49, less than 1% 50-99.

Student profile.

Out-of-state:	11%	25 or older:	47%

Basis for selection. Open admission, but selective for some programs and for out-of-state students. Admission to health technologies program restricted to state residents. Restricted admission to dental hygiene, nursing, and culinary arts programs. Interview required for all technology programs.

2005-2006 Annual costs. Tuition/fees: $2,166; $5,100 out-of-state. Per-credit charge: $82 in-state; $204 out-of-state. Books/supplies: $800. Personal expenses: $400.

Financial aid. Need-based: Need-based aid available for part-time students. **Non-need-based:** Scholarships awarded for academics, athletics. **Additional information:** Male Delaware residents must be registered for Selective Service to be eligible for state financial aid.

Application procedures. Admission: Priority date 8/1; no deadline. $10 fee, may be waived for applicants with need. Admission notification on a rolling basis. **Financial aid:** Priority date 7/1; no closing date. FAFSA, institutional form required. Applicants notified on a rolling basis; must reply within 2 week(s) of notification.

Academics. Special study options: Cooperative education, cross-registration, distance learning, double major, dual enrollment of high school students, ESL, internships. **Credit/placement by examination:** AP, CLEP, IB, institutional tests. **Support services:** Learning center, pre-admission summer program, reduced course load, remedial instruction, study skills assistance, tutoring, writing center.

Majors. Business: General, accounting, administrative services, banking/financial services, marketing, office technology, office/clerical. **Computer sciences:** General, data processing, information systems, networking, programming, systems analysis. **Education:** Early childhood. **Engineering technology:** Architectural, civil, drafting, electrical. **Family/consumer sciences:** Child care. **Foreign languages:** Sign language interpretation. **Health:** Clinical lab technology, dental hygiene, EMT paramedic, histologic assistant, medical assistant, medical radiologic technology/radiation therapy, medical secretary, mental health services, nuclear medical technology, nursing (RN), occupational therapy assistant, physical therapy assistant, respiratory therapy technology, sonography, substance abuse counseling. **Interdisciplinary:** Gerontology. **Mechanic/repair:** Heating/ac/refrig. **Personal/culinary services:** Culinary arts. **Physical sciences:** General. **Protective**

services: Fire safety technology, law enforcement admin. **Science technology:** Biological, chemical.

Computing on campus. 339 workstations in library, computer center. Commuter students can connect to campus network.

Student life. Activities: Student government, student newspaper.

Athletics. NJCAA. **Intercollegiate:** Baseball M, basketball, soccer. **Intramural:** Baseball M, basketball, soccer, softball, tennis, volleyball.

Student services. Adult student services, career counseling, student employment services, health services, personal counseling, placement for graduates, veterans' counselor. **Physically disabled:** Services for visually, speech, hearing impaired. **Transfer:** Special adviser, orientation for new students. Transfer adviser for students transferring to 4-year colleges.

Contact. Phone: (302) 454-3954 Fax: (302) 453-3029
Rebecca Bailey, Admissions Representative, Delaware Technical and Community College: Stanton/Wilmington Campus, 400 Stanton-Christiana Road, Newark, DE 19713

Two-Year Colleges

Delaware Technical and Community College: Terry Campus

Dover, Delaware — **CB member**
www.dtcc.edu — **CB code: 5201**

- Public 2-year community and technical college
- Commuter campus in large town

General. Founded in 1972. Regionally accredited. **Enrollment:** 874 full-time, degree-seeking students. **Degrees:** 178 associate awarded. **Location:** 90 miles from Baltimore, 75 miles from Philadelphia. **Calendar:** Semester, limited summer session. **Full-time faculty:** 61 total. **Part-time faculty:** 106 total. **Class size:** 87% < 20, 13% 20-39.

Student profile.

Out-of-state:	3%	25 or older:	54%

Basis for selection. Open admission, but selective for some programs. Special requirements for health/nursing programs. Interview required of technology majors.

2005-2006 Annual costs. Tuition/fees: $2,166; $5,100 out-of-state. Per-credit charge: $82 in-state; $204 out-of-state. Books/supplies: $800. Personal expenses: $400.

Financial aid. Need-based: Need-based aid available for part-time students.

Application procedures. Admission: No deadline. $10 fee, may be waived for applicants with need. Admission notification on a rolling basis. **Financial aid:** No deadline. FAFSA required. Applicants notified on a rolling basis starting 7/1; must reply within 2 week(s) of notification.

Academics. Special study options: Cooperative education, cross-registration, distance learning, double major, dual enrollment of high school students, internships. **Credit/placement by examination:** AP, CLEP, institutional tests. **Support services:** Learning center, reduced course load, remedial instruction, tutoring.

Majors. Business: General, accounting, administrative services, banking/financial services, business admin, human resources, management information systems, marketing, office technology. **Communications:** Advertising. **Computer sciences:** General, computer science, data processing, information systems, programming, systems analysis. **Construction:** Maintenance. **Engineering technology:** Architectural, civil, construction, electrical, surveying. **Family/consumer sciences:** Child care. **Health:** Dental hygiene, EMT paramedic, medical assistant, medical transcription, mental health services, nursing (RN), substance abuse counseling. **Mechanic/repair:** Industrial. **Protective services:** Criminal justice. **Visual/performing arts:** Interior design.

Computing on campus. 125 workstations in library, computer center. Commuter students can connect to campus network.

Student life. Freshman orientation: Mandatory. **Activities:** Student government, Students of Color, Phi Theta Kappa, Alpha Beta Gamma, human services organization.

Student services. Adult student services, career counseling, student employment services, personal counseling, placement for graduates, veterans' counselor. **Physically disabled:** Services for visually, hearing impaired. **Transfer:** Special adviser, orientation for new students. Transfer adviser for students transferring to 4-year colleges.

Contact. Phone: (302) 857-1020 Fax: (302) 739-6169
Maria Harris, Admissions Coordinator, Delaware Technical and Community College: Terry Campus, 100 Campus Drive, Dover, DE 19901

Florida

Angley College
Deland, Florida
www.angley.edu

- For-profit 2-year health science college
- Commuter campus

General. Accredited by ACICS. **Enrollment:** 74 degree-seeking undergraduates. **Degrees:** 13 associate awarded. **Calendar:** Semester. **Full-time faculty:** 11 total. **Part-time faculty:** 4 total.

2006-2007 Annual costs. Tuition/fees: $13,050.

Academics. Credit/placement by examination: CLEP.

Majors. Health: Medical assistant, office assistant.

Contact. E-mail: admissions@angley.edu
Phone: (386) 740-1215 Toll-free number: (866) 639-1215
Angley College, 230 North Woodland Boulevard, Suite 310, Deland, FL 32720

ATI Career Training Center
Oakland Park, Florida
www.aticareertraining.edu **CB code: 3182**

- For-profit 2-year technical college
- Large town

General. Accredited by ACCSCT. **Calendar:** Continuous.

Annual costs/financial aid. Tuition and fees entire AC/refrigeration program $17,776; for entire automotive service technician program $18,000.

Contact. Phone: (954) 563-5899
Director of Admission, 3501 NW 9th Avenue, Oakland Park, FL 33309

ATI Career Training Center: Ft. Lauderdale
Ft. Lauderdale, Florida
www.aticareertraining.edu **CB code: 2945**

- For-profit 2-year technical college
- Small city

General. Accredited by ACCSCT. **Calendar:** Continuous.

Annual costs/financial aid. Full program costs: $21,795 for electronics, $15,996 for drafting, $13,995 for medical.

Contact. Phone: (954) 973-4760
2890 NW 62nd Street, Fort Lauderdale, FL 33309-9731

ATI College of Health
Miami, Florida
www.aticareertraining.edu **CB code: 3183**

- For-profit 2-year health science and technical college
- Very large city

General. Accredited by ACCSCT. **Calendar:** Semester.

Annual costs/financial aid. $15,895 tuition for medical assistant program and pharmacy technician program; $32,895 tuition for diagnostic ultrasound program and respiratory therapist program. Personal expenses: $2,064. Need-based financial aid available to full-time and part-time students.

Contact. Phone: (305) 628-1000
1395 NW 167th Street, Miami, FL 33169-5745

Brevard Community College
Cocoa, Florida **CB member**
www.brevard.cc.fl.us **CB code: 5073**

- Public 2-year community college
- Commuter campus in large town

General. Founded in 1960. Regionally accredited. 4 campuses: Cocoa, Titusville, Melbourne, Palm Bay. **Enrollment:** 12,985 degree-seeking undergraduates. **Degrees:** 1,952 associate awarded. **Location:** 50 miles from Orlando. **Calendar:** Semester, extensive summer session. **Full-time faculty:** 210 total. **Part-time faculty:** 676 total. **Special facilities:** Planetarium, solar observatory.

Student profile.

Out-of-state:	2%	25 or older:	52%

Basis for selection. Open admission, but selective for some programs. Special requirements for allied health, human services, law enforcement, cosmetology programs. CPT required for admission but scores not used. SAT or ACT may be submitted instead of CPT. California Achievement Tests, Stanford Test of Academic Skills, Test of Adult Basic Education required for health program applicants. Interview required of allied health, cosmetology majors.

2005-2006 Annual costs. Tuition/fees: $1,927; $6,755 out-of-state. Per-credit charge: $53 in-state; $214 out-of-state. Books/supplies: $640. Personal expenses: $1,024.

2004-2005 Financial aid. Need-based: Need-based aid available for part-time students. **Non-need-based:** Scholarships awarded for academics, athletics.

Application procedures. Admission: No deadline. $20 fee, may be waived for applicants with need. Application may be submitted online. Admission notification on a rolling basis. **Financial aid:** Priority date 4/15, closing date 6/30. FAFSA required. Applicants notified on a rolling basis starting 6/1; must reply within 2 week(s) of notification.

Academics. Special study options: Accelerated study, cooperative education, cross-registration, distance learning, double major, dual enrollment of high school students, honors, independent study, internships, student-designed major, study abroad. Bachelor's degree programs available on campus. License preparation in dental hygiene, nursing, paramedic. **Credit/placement by examination:** AP, CLEP, IB, institutional tests. 45 credit hours maximum toward associate degree. **Support services:** Learning center, reduced course load, remedial instruction, study skills assistance, tutoring, writing center.

Majors. Business: Administrative services, business admin, fashion, hospitality admin, hospitality/recreation, international, international marketing, logistics, management information systems, marketing, office management, real estate. **Communications:** Broadcast journalism. **Computer sciences:** Programming, systems analysis. **Construction:** Maintenance. **Education:** Early childhood. **Engineering:** General, chemical, computer. **Engineering technology:** Drafting, electrical. **Health:** Clinical lab technology, dental hygiene, EMT paramedic, medical radiologic technology/radiation therapy, nursing (RN), physical therapy assistant, respiratory therapy technology. **Legal studies:** Court reporting, legal secretary, paralegal. **Mechanic/repair:** Heating/ac/refrig. **Protective services:** Firefighting. **Public administration:** Human services. **Visual/performing arts:** Commercial/advertising art, photography.

Computing on campus. 1,800 workstations in library, computer center. Online course registration, helpline available.

Student life. Freshman orientation: Mandatory. **Activities:** Concert band, choral groups, drama, literary magazine, music ensembles, musical theater, student government, student newspaper, TV station, Circle-K, Distributive Education Clubs of America, international students club, Student Nurses Association of Florida, Phi Theta Kappa, African-American student association, Phi Mu Alpha (music fraternity), Terraphile Club.

Athletics. NJCAA. **Intercollegiate:** Baseball M, basketball, golf, softball W, volleyball W. **Intramural:** Basketball, bowling, cross-country, racquetball, tennis. **Team name:** Titans.

Student services. Adult student services, career counseling, student employment services, financial aid counseling, health services, on-campus daycare, personal counseling, placement for graduates, veterans' counselor. **Physically disabled:** Services for visually, speech, hearing impaired. **Transfer:** Special adviser for new students. College fairs on campus for students transferring to 4-year colleges.

Contact. Phone: (321) 632-1111 ext. 63700 Fax: (321) 433-7357
Brenda Fettrow, Vice President of Student Services, Brevard Community College, 1519 Clearlake Road Building #12, Cocoa, FL 32922-9987

Broward Community College

Ft. Lauderdale, Florida — **CB member**
www.broward.edu — **CB code: 5074**

- Public 2-year community college
- Commuter campus in small city

General. Founded in 1959. Regionally accredited. Multilocation institution. North campus located in Coconut Creek, central campus in Davie, south campus in Pembroke Pines. Credit courses also offered at corporate sites (Ft. Lauderdale Center). **Enrollment:** 25,513 degree-seeking undergraduates; 6,322 non-degree-seeking students. **Degrees:** 3,128 associate awarded. **ROTC:** Army, Air Force. **Location:** 20 miles from Miami. **Calendar:** Semester, extensive summer session. **Full-time faculty:** 360 total; 14% minority, 49% women. **Part-time faculty:** 983 total; 32% minority, 48% women. **Class size:** 37% < 20, 61% 20-39, 1% 40-49, less than 1% 50-99, less than 1% >100. **Special facilities:** Concert hall, planetarium, golf course, sailing.

Student profile. Among degree-seeking undergraduates, 92% enrolled in a transfer program, 8% enrolled in a vocational program, 4,356 enrolled as first-time, first-year students, 1,535 transferred in from other institutions.

Part-time:	65%	**Women:**	63%
Out-of-state:	2%	**25 or older:**	39%

Transfer out. Colleges most students transferred to 2005: Florida Atlantic University, Florida International University.

Basis for selection. Open admission, but selective for some programs. Limited access programs require a secondary application process. SAT or ACT may be used for placement in lieu of Florida CPT. **Adult students:** Entrance exam policies same as for first-time freshmen. **Homeschooled:** Transcript of courses and grades required.

2005-2006 Annual costs. Tuition/fees: $1,892; $6,857 out-of-state. Per-credit charge: $52 in-state; $218 out-of-state.

2004-2005 Financial aid. Need-based: 70% of total undergraduate aid awarded as scholarships/grants, 30% as loans/jobs. Need-based aid available for part-time students. Work study available nights, weekends and for part-time students. **Non-need-based:** Scholarships awarded for academics, athletics, leadership, state residency.

Application procedures. Admission: No deadline. $35 fee, may be waived for applicants with need. Application may be submitted online. Admission notification on a rolling basis beginning on or about 2/15. **Financial aid:** Priority date 4/15, closing date 7/1. FAFSA, institutional form required. Applicants notified on a rolling basis starting 7/15.

Academics. Special study options: Accelerated study, cooperative education, distance learning, dual enrollment of high school students, exchange student, honors, independent study, internships, study abroad, weekend college. License preparation in aviation, dental hygiene, nursing, paramedic, physical therapy, real estate. **Credit/placement by examination:** AP, CLEP, IB, institutional tests. 30 credit hours maximum toward associate degree. **Support services:** Learning center, pre-admission summer program, remedial instruction, study skills assistance, tutoring, writing center.

Majors. Architecture: Landscape. **Biology:** General, anatomy. **Business:** General, accounting, business admin, finance, hospitality admin, international, international marketing, management science, office/clerical, tourism/travel. **Communications:** Broadcast journalism, journalism. **Computer sciences:** General, computer graphics, computer science, data processing, information systems, programming, systems analysis. **Conservation:** Environmental science. **Education:** General, early childhood, elementary, mathematics, music, science, special. **Engineering:** General, civil, computer, electrical, software. **Engineering technology:** Civil. **Family/consumer sciences:** Child care, food/nutrition. **Foreign languages:** General. **Health:** Athletic training, cardiovascular technology, clinical lab assistant, clinical lab technology, dental hygiene, EMT paramedic, health care admin, medical radiologic technology/radiation therapy, medical records admin, nuclear medical technology, nursing (RN), ophthalmic lab technology, physical therapy assistant, predentistry, premedicine, prenursing, prepharmacy, preveterinary, recreational therapy, respiratory therapy technology, sonography. **History:** General. **Legal studies:** Court reporting, legal secretary, paralegal, prelaw. **Liberal arts:** Arts/sciences. **Math:** General. **Mechanic/repair:** Automotive. **Parks/recreation:** General. **Philosophy/religion:** Religion. **Physical sciences:** Chemistry, physics. **Protective services:** Criminal justice, firefighting, security services. **Psychology:** General. **Public administration:** Social work. **Social sciences:** Anthropology, economics, geography, political science, sociology. **Transportation:** Aviation, aviation management. **Visual/performing arts:** Art, dramatic, interior design, music history.

Most popular majors. Health sciences 19%, liberal arts 69%.

Computing on campus. 4,000 workstations in library, computer center, student center. Online course registration, online library available.

Student life. Freshman orientation: Available. Preregistration for classes offered. **Activities:** Bands, choral groups, dance, drama, literary magazine, music ensembles, musical theater, opera, student government, student newspaper, symphony orchestra, Phi Theta Kappa (honors), Phi Beta Lambda (business), African American Student Union, American Institute of Architecture Students, Catholic club, chess club, HIV Peer educators, film club, French club.

Athletics. NCAA. **Intercollegiate:** Baseball M, basketball, diving M, softball W, tennis W, volleyball W. **Intramural:** Basketball, bowling, football (non-tackle) M, soccer M, swimming, tennis. **Team name:** Seahawks.

Student services. Adult student services, alcohol/substance abuse counseling, career counseling, student employment services, financial aid counseling, health services, on-campus daycare, personal counseling, placement for graduates, veterans' counselor. **Physically disabled:** Services for visually, speech, hearing impaired. **Transfer:** Special adviser, orientation for new students.

Contact. Phone: (954) 201-6500 Fax: (954) 201-7466
Barbara Bryan, Associate Vice President for Student Affairs and Registrar, Broward Community College, 225 East Las Olas Boulevard, Fort Lauderdale, FL 33301

Brown Mackie College: Miami

Miami, Florida
www.cbcaec.com

- For-profit 2-year business and health science college
- Very large city

General. Accredited by ACICS. **Calendar:** Quarter.

Annual costs/financial aid. Tuition/fees (projected): $8,604.

Contact. Phone: (305) 341-6600
1501 Biscayne Boulevard, Miami, FL 33132

Central Florida College

Winter Park, Florida
www.centralfloridacollege.edu

- For-profit 2-year technical college
- Very large city
- Interview required

General. Accredited by ACCSCT. **Enrollment:** 349 degree-seeking undergraduates. **Degrees:** 20 associate awarded. **Calendar:** Continuous, extensive summer session. **Full-time faculty:** 15 total. **Part-time faculty:** 20 total.

Student profile. Among degree-seeking undergraduates, 100% enrolled in a vocational program, 1% already have a bachelor's degree or higher, 254 enrolled as first-time, first-year students.

Basis for selection. Open admission. **Adult students:** SAT/ACT scores not required.

2006-2007 Annual costs. Certificate and Diploma programs range fron $4,995 to $12,995. Associate of Science Degrees range from $19,995 to $22,995; including books.

Financial aid. All financial aid based on need.

Application procedures. Admission: No deadline. $50 fee. Admission notification on a rolling basis. **Financial aid:** No deadline. FAFSA required.

Academics. Special study options: Liberal arts/career combination. **Credit/placement by examination:** CLEP. **Support services:** Study skills assistance.

Majors. Health: Insurance specialist, medical assistant, medical records technology.

Computing on campus. 64 workstations in library, computer center. Online library available.

Student services. Transfer: Special adviser, orientation for new students.

Contact. E-mail: admissions@centralfloridacollege.edu
Phone: (407) 843-3984
Roger Buck, Coporate Operations Director, Central Florida College, 1573 West Fairbanks Avenue, Winter Park, FL 32789

Central Florida Community College
Ocala, Florida
www.gocfcc.com **CB code: 5127**

- Public 2-year community college
- Commuter campus in small city

General. Founded in 1957. Regionally accredited. Bachelor's degrees available through University Center. Corporate University available in conjunction with Emergency One Corporation. **Enrollment:** 5,199 degree-seeking undergraduates; 779 non-degree-seeking students. **Degrees:** 653 associate awarded. **Location:** 72 miles from Orlando. **Calendar:** Semester, extensive summer session. **Full-time faculty:** 118 total; 7% minority, 51% women. **Part-time faculty:** 487 total; 14% minority, 51% women. **Special facilities:** Art museum. **Partnerships:** Formal partnership with Emergency One Corporation.

Student profile. Among degree-seeking undergraduates, 64% enrolled in a transfer program, 36% enrolled in a vocational program, 991 enrolled as first-time, first-year students.

Part-time:	55%	**Hispanic American:**	7%
Out-of-state:	2%	**Native American:**	1%
Women:	66%	**International:**	1%
African American:	11%	**25 or older:**	42%
Asian American:	2%		

Transfer out. Colleges most students transferred to 2005: University of Florida, University of Central Florida, Florida State University.

Basis for selection. Open admission, but selective for some programs. Special requirements for registered nursing, physical therapy assistant, criminal justice, practical nursing, surgical technology programs. **Adult students:** Entrance exam policies same as for first-time freshmen.

High school preparation. Recommended units include English 4, mathematics 3, social studies 3 and science 3.

2005-2006 Annual costs. Tuition/fees: $1,843; $6,015 out-of-state. Per-credit charge: $54 in-state; $228 out-of-state. Books/supplies: $1,230. Personal expenses: $3,386.

Financial aid. Need-based: Need-based aid available for part-time students. **Non-need-based:** Scholarships awarded for academics, athletics, minority status, music/drama, state residency.

Application procedures. Admission: No deadline. $20 fee, may be waived for applicants with need. Application must be submitted on paper. Admission notification on a rolling basis. **Financial aid:** No deadline. FAFSA required.

Academics. Special study options: Accelerated study, cooperative education, distance learning, dual enrollment of high school students, ESL, honors, independent study, internships, liberal arts/career combination, teacher certification program. Bachelor's degree programs available on campus. License preparation in real estate. **Credit/placement by examination:** AP, CLEP, IB, institutional tests. 21 credit hours maximum toward associate degree. ACT, SAT I, CPT are authorized placement tests for community colleges in state of Florida. **Support services:** GED preparation and test center, learning center, pre-admission summer program, reduced course load, remedial instruction, study skills assistance, tutoring, writing center.

Majors. Agriculture: Ornamental horticulture. **Business:** Accounting, accounting technology, business admin, executive assistant, restaurant/food services. **Computer sciences:** Information technology, LAN/WAN management, systems analysis. **Education:** Early childhood, elementary. **Health:** EMT paramedic, licensed practical nurse, medical records technology, nursing (RN), physical therapy assistant, veterinary technology/assistant. **Legal studies:** Paralegal. **Liberal arts:** Arts/sciences. **Mechanic/repair:** Automotive. **Personal/culinary services:** Chef training, restaurant/catering. **Protective services:** Fire safety technology, law enforcement admin. **Public administration:** Human services.

Most popular majors. Health sciences 15%, liberal arts 71%.

Computing on campus. 737 workstations in library, computer center.

Student life. Freshman orientation: Mandatory. Preregistration for classes offered. Program prior to beginning of term; also available online. **Policies:** Freshmen permitted cars on campus. **Housing:** College Square Student Residence Center owned and operated by Central Florida Community College Foundation near campus. **Activities:** Bands, choral groups, dance, drama, literary magazine, music ensembles, musical theater, student government, student newspaper, symphony orchestra, Afro-Student Union, Hispanic club, Phi Theta Kappa, Community of Scholars, Brain Bowl, Phi Beta Lambda, Gay Straight Alliance, campus ministry, peer educators.

Athletics. NJCAA. **Intercollegiate:** Baseball M, basketball, softball W, tennis W. **Team name:** Patriots.

Student services. Adult student services, career counseling, services for economically disadvantaged, student employment services, financial aid counseling, on-campus daycare, personal counseling, placement for graduates, veterans' counselor. **Physically disabled:** Services for visually, speech, hearing impaired. **Transfer:** Special adviser, orientation for new students. Transfer adviser, college fairs on campus for students transferring to 4-year colleges.

Contact. Phone: (352) 873-5801 Fax: (352) 237-0510
Lyn Powell, Director of Admissions and Records, Central Florida Community College, 3001 SW College Road, Ocala, FL 34478

City College: Casselberry
Casselberry, Florida

- For-profit 2-year community college
- Large town
- Interview required

General. Accredited by ACICS. **Enrollment:** 260 undergraduates. **Degrees:** 125 associate awarded. **Calendar:** Semester. **Full-time faculty:** 4 total. **Part-time faculty:** 21 total.

Basis for selection. Applicant must pass the college's entrance examination and interview.

2005-2006 Annual costs. Tuition/fees: $7,425. Per-credit charge: $165.

Application procedures. Admission: No deadline. $25 fee. **Financial aid:** No deadline.

Academics. Credit/placement by examination: CLEP.

Majors. Business: Business admin, marketing. **Computer sciences:** General. **Health:** Health services. **Protective services:** Security management.

Contact. Phone: (407) 831-8466 Fax: (407) 831-1147
John Wright, Director of Admissions, City College: Casselberry, 853 Semoran Boulevard, Suite 200, Casselberry, FL 32707-5353

City College: Gainesville
Gainesville, Florida
www.citycollege.edu **CB code: 3579**

- For-profit 2-year business and health science college
- Small city

General. Accredited by ACICS. **Calendar:** Continuous.

Annual costs/financial aid. Books/supplies: $1,044. Personal expenses: $1,692.

Contact. Phone: (352) 335-4000
Registrar, 2400 S.W. 13th Street, Gainesville, FL 32608

City College: Miami
Miami, Florida
www.citycollege.edu **CB code: 3580**

- For-profit 2-year business and health science college
- Large city

General. Accredited by ACICS. **Enrollment:** 280 degree-seeking undergraduates. **Degrees:** 106 associate awarded. **Calendar:** Continuous. **Full-time faculty:** 3 total. **Part-time faculty:** 27 total.

Basis for selection. TABE is required. SAT or ACT considered if submitted.

2005-2006 Annual costs. Tuition/fees: $8,100. Per-credit charge: $165. Books/supplies: $1,044. Personal expenses: $1,692.

Financial aid. All financial aid based on need. Need-based aid available for part-time students.

Application procedures. Admission: No deadline. $25 fee. Admission notification on a rolling basis. **Financial aid:** No deadline. FAFSA, institutional form required. Applicants notified on a rolling basis.

Academics. Credit/placement by examination: CLEP.

Contact. E-mail: tkretschmer@citycollege.edu
Phone: (305) 666-9242 Fax: (305) 666-9243
Thomas Kretschmer, Director of Admissions, City College: Miami, 9300 South Dadeland Boulevard, Miami, FL 33156

College of Business and Technology: Flagler

Miami, Florida
www.cbt.edu

- Private 2-year junior and technical college
- Very large city

General. Accredited by ACICS. **Calendar:** Continuous.

Contact. Phone: (305) 273-4499 ext. 2203
8230 W. Flagler St., Miami, FL 33176

College of Business and Technology: Kendall

Miami, Florida

- Private 2-year health science and junior college
- Very large city

General. Accredited by ACICS. **Calendar:** Semester.

Annual costs/financial aid. Tuition/fees (projected): $6,240.

Contact. Phone: (305) 273-4499
8991 S.W. 107 Avenue, Suite 200, Miami, FL 33176

Daytona Beach Community College

Daytona Beach, Florida — **CB member**
www.dbcc.edu — **CB code: 5159**

- Public 2-year community and technical college
- Residential campus in large city

General. Founded in 1958. Regionally accredited. **Enrollment:** 10,469 degree-seeking undergraduates; 944 non-degree-seeking students. **Degrees:** 1,352 associate awarded. **ROTC:** Army, Air Force. **Location:** 90 miles from Jacksonville, 65 miles from Orlando. **Calendar:** Semester, limited summer session. **Full-time faculty:** 279 total; 22% have terminal degrees, 16% minority, 46% women. **Part-time faculty:** 600 total; 9% have terminal degrees, 50% minority, 43% women. **Special facilities:** Museum of photography, interactive TV system.

Student profile. Among degree-seeking undergraduates, 41% enrolled in a transfer program, 59% enrolled in a vocational program, 1% already have a bachelor's degree or higher, 1,787 enrolled as first-time, first-year students, 676 transferred in from other institutions.

Part-time:	51%	**Asian American:**	2%
Out-of-state:	10%	**Hispanic American:**	7%
Women:	63%	**International:**	1%
African American:	13%	**25 or older:**	26%

Transfer out. 75% of students enrolled in the transfer program go on to 4-year colleges. **Colleges most students transferred to 2005:** University of Central Florida.

Basis for selection. Open admission, but selective for some programs. Special requirements for nursing, allied health, and public service programs. **Adult students:** Entrance exam policies same as for first-time freshmen.

High school preparation. Recommended units include mathematics 3 and science 3.

2005-2006 Annual costs. Tuition/fees: $2,003; $7,760 out-of-state. Per-credit charge: $53 in-state; $245 out-of-state. Books/supplies: $800. Personal expenses: $2,624.

Financial aid. Need-based: Need-based aid available for part-time students. Work study available for part-time students. **Non-need-based:** Scholarships awarded for athletics, leadership, music/drama.

Application procedures. Admission: No deadline. No application fee. Application may be submitted online. Admission notification on a rolling basis. **Financial aid:** No deadline. FAFSA required. Applicants notified on a rolling basis starting 2/15.

Academics. Special study options: Cooperative education, distance learning, dual enrollment of high school students, ESL, honors, independent study, internships, liberal arts/career combination, study abroad, weekend college. License preparation in dental hygiene, nursing, paramedic, physical therapy. **Credit/placement by examination:** AP, CLEP, IB, institutional tests. 45 credit hours maximum toward associate degree. **Support services:** GED preparation and test center, learning center, pre-admission summer program, remedial instruction, tutoring.

Majors. Business: Accounting, banking/financial services, business admin, hospitality admin, marketing, office management, office technology, tourism/travel. **Computer sciences:** General, information systems, programming. **Education:** General. **Engineering:** General, computer. **Engineering technology:** Architectural, civil, construction, drafting, electrical. **Family/consumer sciences:** Child care. **Health:** EMT paramedic, health services, medical radiologic technology/radiation therapy, medical records technology, medical secretary, respiratory therapy technology. **Legal studies:** Court reporting, legal secretary, paralegal. **Liberal arts:** Arts/sciences. **Protective services:** Firefighting, police science. **Visual/performing arts:** Commercial/advertising art, interior design, photography.

Most popular majors. Business/marketing 6%, engineering/engineering technologies 7%, health sciences 15%, liberal arts 64%.

Computing on campus. 752 workstations in library, computer center. Online course registration available.

Student life. Freshman orientation: Available. **Housing:** Assistance in locating off-campus housing available to international students. **Activities:** Bands, choral groups, dance, drama, music ensembles, musical theater, opera, student government, student newspaper, symphony orchestra, TV station, Amnesty International, Baptist campus ministry, human services paraprofessional organization, African-American Student Union.

Athletics. NJCAA. **Intercollegiate:** Baseball M, basketball, golf W, softball W. **Intramural:** Basketball, bowling, fencing, racquetball, soccer, table tennis, tennis, volleyball. **Team name:** Falcons.

Student services. Career counseling, student employment services, on-campus daycare, personal counseling, placement for graduates, veterans' counselor, women's services. **Physically disabled:** Services for visually, speech, hearing impaired. **Transfer:** Special adviser, orientation for new students. Transfer adviser, college fairs on campus for students transferring to 4-year colleges.

Contact. E-mail: admissions@dbcc.edu
Phone: (386) 506-3000 ext. 3059 Fax: (386) 506-4489
Thomas Lobasso, Dean, Enrollment Management, Daytona Beach Community College, DBCC Admissions Office, Daytona Beach, FL 32114

Edison College

Fort Myers, Florida — **CB member**
www.edison.edu — **CB code: 5191**

- Public 2-year community college
- Commuter campus in very large city

General. Founded in 1961. Regionally accredited. **Enrollment:** 4,210 degree-seeking undergraduates. **Degrees:** 1,133 associate awarded. **Location:** 35 miles from Naples, 120 miles from Tampa. **Calendar:** Semester, limited summer session. **Full-time faculty:** 94 total. **Part-time faculty:** 320 total. **Class size:** 31% < 20, 35% 20-39, 3% 40-49, 1% 50-99. **Special facilities:** Performing arts hall, observatory, art gallery, 3-hole instructional golf course.

Student profile.

Out-of-state:	3%	25 or older:	33%

Transfer out. Colleges most students transferred to 2005: University of South Florida, Florida Gulf Coast University, University of Central Florida, Florida State University, University of Florida.

Basis for selection. Open admission, but selective for some programs. Special requirements for allied health programs. TOEFL scores required for non-native speakers of English. **Adult students:** Entrance exam policies same as for first-time freshmen. **Homeschooled:** Applicants must submit an affidavit of completion.

High school preparation. 21 units required. Required units include English 4, mathematics 3, social studies 3 and science 3.

2005-2006 Annual costs. Tuition/fees: $1,983; $6,611 out-of-state. Per-credit charge: $55 in-state; $209 out-of-state. Books/supplies: $626. Personal expenses: $1,060.

Financial aid. Need-based: Need-based aid available for part-time students. Work study available nights, weekends and for part-time students. **Non-need-based:** Scholarships awarded for art, music/drama.

Application procedures. Admission: Closing date 8/15 (receipt date). $20 fee. Application may be submitted online. Admission notification on a rolling basis. **Financial aid:** Priority date 5/1; no closing date. FAFSA required. Applicants notified on a rolling basis starting 6/1; must reply within 2 week(s) of notification.

Academics. Special study options: Accelerated study, cooperative education, cross-registration, distance learning, double major, dual enrollment of high school students, ESL, honors, independent study, internships, liberal arts/career combination. Bachelor's degree programs available on campus. License preparation in real estate. **Credit/placement by examination:** CLEP, IB, institutional tests. 45 credit hours maximum toward associate degree. Credit by exam not available. **Support services:** Learning center, reduced course load, remedial instruction, tutoring.

Majors. Business: Accounting, business admin, finance, hospitality admin, international, marketing, tourism/travel. **Computer sciences:** General, programming. **Engineering:** General, civil. **Health:** Cardiovascular technology, dental hygiene, EMT paramedic, medical radiologic technology/radiation therapy, nursing (RN), respiratory therapy technology. **Legal studies:** Paralegal. **Liberal arts:** Arts/sciences. **Parks/recreation:** Facilities management. **Protective services:** Criminal justice, firefighting, forensics, law enforcement admin.

Most popular majors. Health sciences 10%, liberal arts 75%.

Computing on campus. 80 workstations in library, computer center.

Student life. Freshman orientation: Mandatory. Preregistration for classes offered. **Policies:** Freshmen permitted cars on campus. **Activities:** Bands, choral groups, drama, music ensembles, student government, Black Student Union, Intervarsity Christian Fellowship, Young Republicans, environmental club, foreign student club, Young Democrats, Rotaract, Latin American Student Association, Student Nurses Association.

Student services. Career counseling, services for economically disadvantaged, student employment services, financial aid counseling, minority student services, on-campus daycare, placement for graduates, veterans' counselor. **Physically disabled:** Services for visually, speech, hearing impaired. **Transfer:** Special adviser, orientation for new students. Transfer adviser, college fairs on campus for students transferring to 4-year colleges.

Contact. E-mail: registrar@edison.edu
Phone: (239) 489-9121 Toll-free number: (800) 749-2322
Fax: (239) 489-9094
Edison College, Box 60210, Fort Myers, FL 33906-6210

Florida Career College: Hialeah

Miramar, Florida
www.careercollege.edu

- For-profit 2-year junior and technical college
- Commuter campus in very large city
- Interview required

General. Accredited by ACICS. **Enrollment:** 368 degree-seeking undergraduates. **Degrees:** 19 associate awarded. **Calendar:** Quarter, limited summer session. **Full-time faculty:** 12 total. **Part-time faculty:** 7 total. **Class size:** 69% < 20, 31% 20-39.

Basis for selection. Open admission, but selective for some programs. High school diploma or GED requried. Interview with admissions representative required. **Adult students:** Entrance exam policies same as for first-time freshmen.

2005-2006 Annual costs. Tuition/fees: $11,660. Per-credit charge: $310. Books/supplies: $1,000.

Application procedures. Admission: No deadline. No application fee. Application must be submitted on paper. Admission notification on a rolling basis.

Academics. Special study options: Accelerated study, internships. **Credit/placement by examination:** CLEP. Up to 50% of program credits can be earned through a combination of transfer and/or credit by examination. **Support services:** Learning center, tutoring.

Majors. Computer sciences: Programming, webmaster. **Engineering:** Computer. **Health:** Office admin.

Computing on campus. 250 workstations in library, computer center. Commuter students can connect to campus network. Online course registration, online library available.

Student life. Freshman orientation: Available.

Student services. Financial aid counseling, placement for graduates.

Contact. Phone: (954) 499-8888 Fax: (954) 499-7274
Robert Lopez, Director of Admissions, Florida Career College: Hialeah, 3750 West 18th Avenue, Hialeah, FL 33012

Florida Career College: Miami

Miami, Florida
www.careercollege.edu **CB code: 3581**

- For-profit 2-year business and technical college
- Large city

General. Accredited by ACICS. **Enrollment:** 354 degree-seeking undergraduates. **Degrees:** 132 associate awarded. **Calendar:** Continuous. **Full-time faculty:** 12 total. **Part-time faculty:** 7 total.

Application procedures. Admission: No deadline. No application fee.

Academics. Credit/placement by examination: CLEP.

Majors. Computer sciences: General, webmaster. **Engineering:** Computer. **Health:** Office admin. **Mechanic/repair:** General.

Contact. Phone: (305) 553-6065
Marcel Sopena, msopena@careercollege.edu, Florida Career College: Miami, 1321 S.W. 107 Avenue, Suite 201B, Miami, FL 3317-521

Florida Career College: Pembroke Pines

Pembroke Pines, Florida
www.careercollege.edu

- For-profit 2-year business and technical college
- Small city

General. Accredited by ACICS. **Enrollment:** 492 degree-seeking undergraduates. **Degrees:** 135 associate awarded. **Calendar:** Continuous.

Application procedures. Admission: No deadline. No application fee.

Academics. Credit/placement by examination: CLEP.

Majors. Computer sciences: Programming, webmaster. **Engineering:** Computer. **Health:** Office admin.

Contact. E-mail: info@careercollege.edu
Phone: (954) 965-7272 Fax: (954) 983-2707
Florida Career College: Pembroke Pines, 7891 Pines Boulevard, Pembroke Pines, FL 33024

Florida Career College: West Palm Beach

West Palm Beach, Florida

- For-profit 2-year technical college
- Commuter campus

General. Accredited by ACICS. **Enrollment:** 516 degree-seeking undergraduates. **Degrees:** 61 associate awarded. **Full-time faculty:** 16 total. **Part-time faculty:** 12 total.

Basis for selection. Open admission, but selective for some programs.

Application procedures. Admission: No deadline. No application fee.

Academics. Credit/placement by examination: CLEP.

Majors. Computer sciences: General. **Engineering:** Computer. **Health:** Office admin.

Contact. Phone: (561) 689-0550 Toll-free number: (888) 852-7272
Fax: (561) 689-0739
Florida Career College: West Palm Beach, 6065 Okeechobee Boulevard West, West Palm Beach, FL 33417

Florida College of Natural Health
Pompano Beach, Florida
www.fcnh.com **CB code: 5238**

- For-profit 2-year junior college
- Very large city

General. Accredited by ACCSCT. **Enrollment:** 114 degree-seeking undergraduates. **Degrees:** 60 associate awarded. **Calendar:** Continuous. **Full-time faculty:** 8 total. **Part-time faculty:** 3 total.

Basis for selection. Open admission, but selective for some programs. Must take OLSAT for placement if SAT or ACT not submitted.

2005-2006 Annual costs. Tuition varies per program. Books/supplies: $1,340. Personal expenses: $1,647.

Financial aid. All financial aid based on need.

Application procedures. Admission: No deadline. No application fee. Admission notification on a rolling basis. **Financial aid:** No deadline. FAFSA required. Applicants notified on a rolling basis.

Academics. Credit/placement by examination: CLEP.

Majors. Health: Massage therapy.

Contact. E-mail: ftlauderdale@fcnh.com
Phone: (954) 975-6400 Toll-free number: (800) 541-9299
Fax: (954) 975-9633
Leonore Barfield, Director of Marketing, Florida College of Natural Health, 2001 West Sample Road, Suite 100, Pompano Beach, FL 33064

Florida College of Natural Health: Bradenton
Bradenton, Florida
www.fcnh.com **CB code: 5024**

- For-profit 2-year health science college
- Large town

General. Accredited by ACCSCT. **Enrollment:** 88 degree-seeking undergraduates. **Degrees:** 46 associate awarded. **Calendar:** Continuous. **Full-time faculty:** 4 total. **Part-time faculty:** 7 total.

Basis for selection. Open admission, but selective for some programs. Passing score on college entrance exam (OLSAT) or minimum 800 SAT (exclusive of Writing), or 17 ACT composite required of degree-seeking applicants.

2005-2006 Annual costs. 3 degree programs with $236 per-credit-hour charge. 2 diploma programs with flat rate: therapeutic massage 6-month training program, $6100; skincare 4 to 5-month training program, $3250. Books/supplies: $1,340. Personal expenses: $1,647.

Financial aid. All financial aid based on need.

Application procedures. Admission: No deadline. No application fee. Admission notification on a rolling basis. **Financial aid:** No deadline. FAFSA required. Applicants notified on a rolling basis.

Academics. Credit/placement by examination: CLEP.

Majors. Health: Massage therapy.

Contact. E-mail: sarasota@fcnh.com
Phone: (941) 744-1244 Toll-free number: (800) 966-7117
Fax: (941) 954-8991
Leonore Barfield, Director of Marketing, Florida College of Natural Health: Bradenton, 616 67th Street Circle East, Bradenton, FL 34208

Florida College of Natural Health: Maitland
Maitland, Florida
www.fcnh.com **CB code: 5239**

- For-profit 2-year health science and junior college
- Large town
- SAT or ACT required

General. Accredited by ACCSCT. **Enrollment:** 177 degree-seeking undergraduates. **Degrees:** 84 associate awarded. **Calendar:** Continuous. **Full-time faculty:** 8 total. **Part-time faculty:** 11 total.

Basis for selection. Passing score on college entrance exam (OLSAT) or minimum 800 SAT (exclusive of Writing) or 17 ACT composite required of degree-seeking applicants.

2006-2007 Annual costs. Tuition for paramedical skin care program: $18,600. 5-month therapeutic massage training diploma program: $8,100. Books/supplies: $1,340. Personal expenses: $1,647.

Financial aid. All financial aid based on need.

Application procedures. Admission: No deadline. No application fee. Admission notification on a rolling basis. **Financial aid:** No deadline. FAFSA required. Applicants notified on a rolling basis.

Academics. Credit/placement by examination: CLEP.

Majors. Health: Massage therapy. **Personal/culinary services:** Cosmetic.

Contact. E-mail: orlando@fcnh.com
Phone: (407) 261-0319 Toll-free number: (800) 393-7337
Fax: (407) 261-0342
Leonore Barfield, Director of Marketing, Florida College of Natural Health: Maitland, 2600 Lake Lucien Drive; Suite 140, Maitland, FL 32751

Florida College of Natural Health: Miami
Miami, Florida
www.fcnh.com **CB code: 5231**

- For-profit 2-year branch campus and community college
- Very large city
- SAT or ACT (ACT writing optional) required

General. Accredited by ACCSCT. **Enrollment:** 114 degree-seeking undergraduates. **Degrees:** 60 associate awarded. **Calendar:** Continuous. **Full-time faculty:** 8 total. **Part-time faculty:** 3 total.

Basis for selection. Passing score on college entrance exam (OLSAT) or minimum 800 SAT (exclusive of Writing) or 17 ACT composite required of degree-seeking applicants. Must take OLSAT if SAT or ACT not submitted.

2006-2007 Annual costs. Tuition for paramedical skin care program: $18,600. 5-month therapeutic massage training diploma program: $8,100. Books/supplies: $1,340. Personal expenses: $1,647.

Financial aid. All financial aid based on need.

Application procedures. Admission: No deadline. No application fee. Admission notification on a rolling basis. **Financial aid:** No deadline. FAFSA required. Applicants notified on a rolling basis.

Academics. Credit/placement by examination: CLEP.

Majors. Health: Massage therapy.

Contact. E-mail: miami@fcnh.com
Phone: (305) 597-9599 Toll-free number: (800) 599-9599
Fax: (305) 597-9110
Leonore Barfield, Director of Marketing, Florida College of Natural Health: Miami, 7925 Northwest 12th Street, Suite 201, Miami, FL 33126

Florida Community College at Jacksonville

Jacksonville, Florida
www.fccj.org **CB code: 5232**

- Public 2-year community college
- Commuter campus in very large city

General. Founded in 1963. Regionally accredited. 4 campus locations and 6 center sites. **Enrollment:** 4,974 degree-seeking undergraduates; 24,847 non-degree-seeking students. **Degrees:** 2,746 associate awarded. **ROTC:** Navy. **Location:** Downtown Jacksonville. **Calendar:** Semester, limited summer session. **Full-time faculty:** 365 total; 20% have terminal degrees, 20% minority, 52% women. **Part-time faculty:** 769 total; 6% have terminal degrees, 21% minority, 47% women. **Class size:** 51% < 20, 49% 20-39, less than 1% 40-49, less than 1% 50-99. **Special facilities:** Performing arts theater, computer support wing, allied health building, criminal justice center, Nassau center. **Partnerships:** Formal partnerships with Florida Construction Institute, Florida Home Builders Association, Navy Contracts, GM/ASEP contracts for non-credit (Education-To-Go), NE Florida Credit Union Association, Aviation Professional/Pilot Contract, Cisco Agreement with 2 schools in midwest.

Student profile. Among degree-seeking undergraduates, 700 enrolled as first-time, first-year students, 334 transferred in from other institutions.

Part-time:	73%	**Asian American:**	4%
Out-of-state:	23%	**Hispanic American:**	6%
Women:	60%	**25 or older:**	47%
African American:	28%		

Transfer out. Colleges most students transferred to 2005: University of North Florida, Jacksonville University, University of Florida, Florida State University, Central Florida University.

Basis for selection. Open admission, but selective for some programs. Special requirements for some associate of science degree programs. Some require specific application in addition to school application. SAT or ACT can be used to satisfy CPT test requirement for placement. **Adult students:** CPT or CPTL required. **Homeschooled:** Student required to fill out form (home-school letter) and provide high school transcript. **Learning Disabled:** Medical documentation required.

High school preparation. 24 units recommended. Recommended units include English 4, mathematics 3, social studies 3, science 3 (laboratory 2), foreign language 2 and academic electives 9. One algebra strongly recommended. 3 social studies recommended include .5 American government, .5 economics, 1 American history, 1 world history.

2005-2006 Annual costs. Tuition/fees: $1,897; $7,176 out-of-state. Per-credit charge: $55 in-state; $231 out-of-state. Books/supplies: $900. Personal expenses: $812.

2004-2005 Financial aid. Need-based: 54% of total undergraduate aid awarded as scholarships/grants, 46% as loans/jobs. Need-based aid available for part-time students. Work study available nights, weekends and for part-time students. **Non-need-based:** Scholarships awarded for academics, alumni affiliation, art, athletics, job skills, leadership, minority status, music/drama.

Application procedures. Admission: Priority date 8/17; no deadline. $15 fee. Application may be submitted online. Admission notification on a rolling basis. **Financial aid:** Priority date 8/1; no closing date. FAFSA, institutional form required.

Academics. Associate of arts degree requires 60 credit hours for graduation, associate of science requires 60 to 88 credit hours. **Special study options:** Accelerated study, cooperative education, cross-registration, distance learning, double major, dual enrollment of high school students, ESL, exchange student, external degree, honors, independent study, internships, liberal arts/career combination, study abroad, weekend college. License preparation in aviation, dental hygiene, nursing, paramedic, physical therapy, radiology, real estate. **Credit/placement by examination:** AP, CLEP, institutional tests. 45 credit hours maximum toward associate degree. **Support services:** GED preparation and test center, learning center, reduced course load, remedial instruction, study skills assistance, tutoring.

Majors. Architecture: Environmental design, interior. **Biology:** Biomedical sciences. **Business:** Accounting, administrative services, banking/financial services, business admin, fashion, financial planning, hospitality admin, insurance, management information systems, office management, office technology, sales/distribution, tourism/travel. **Communications technology:** Graphic/printing. **Computer sciences:** General, applications programming, computer graphics, data processing, information systems, networking, programming, systems analysis. **Construction:** Maintenance. **Education:** Elementary. **Engineering:** General, biomedical, civil, computer. **Engineering technology:** Architectural, civil, construction, drafting, electrical. **Family/consumer sciences:** Clothing/textiles. **Foreign languages:** Sign language interpretation. **Health:** Clinical lab technology, dental hygiene, EMT paramedic, medical radiologic technology/radiation therapy, medical records technology, medical secretary, nursing (RN), physical therapy assistant, respiratory therapy technology, sonography, substance abuse counseling. **Legal studies:** Legal secretary, paralegal. **Mechanic/repair:** Automotive. **Military:** General. **Personal/culinary services:** Culinary arts, mortuary science. **Protective services:** Criminal justice, fire safety technology, fire services admin, firefighting, law enforcement admin. **Public administration:** Human services. **Transportation:** Air traffic control, aviation, aviation management. **Visual/performing arts:** General, cinematography, commercial/advertising art, design, dramatic, interior design, theater design.

Computing on campus. 2,500 workstations in library, computer center, student center. Commuter students can connect to campus network. Online course registration, online library, helpline, repair service, student web hosting, wireless network available.

Student life. Freshman orientation: Mandatory. Preregistration for classes offered. Program is for degree seeking students only. **Policies:** Freshmen permitted cars on campus. **Housing:** Housing assistance available to qualified Talent Grant students. **Activities:** Bands, choral groups, dance, drama, literary magazine, music ensembles, musical theater, radio station, student government, student newspaper, TV station, forensic team, brain bowl team, international student association, Phi Theta Kappa.

Athletics. NJCAA. **Intercollegiate:** Baseball M, basketball, softball W, tennis W, volleyball W. **Intramural:** Badminton, basketball, bowling, football (non-tackle), golf, soccer, softball, table tennis, tennis, volleyball. **Team name:** Stars.

Student services. Adult student services, career counseling, services for economically disadvantaged, student employment services, financial aid counseling, minority student services, on-campus daycare, personal counseling, placement for graduates, veterans' counselor, women's services. **Physically disabled:** Services for visually, speech, hearing impaired. **Transfer:** Special adviser, orientation for new students. Transfer adviser, college fairs on campus for students transferring to 4-year colleges.

Contact. E-mail: admissions@fccj.org
Phone: (904) 632-3100 Fax: (904) 632-5105
Kevin Cotton, Associate Director of Admissions, Florida Community College at Jacksonville, 501 West State Street, Jacksonville, FL 32202

Florida Keys Community College

Key West, Florida
www.fkcc.edu **CB code: 5236**

- Public 2-year community college
- Commuter campus in large town

General. Founded in 1965. Regionally accredited. 2-year transfer programs offered at main campus, Coral Shores and Marathon branch campuses. **Enrollment:** 832 degree-seeking undergraduates. **Degrees:** 130 associate awarded. **Location:** 154 miles from Miami. **Calendar:** Semester, extensive summer session. **Full-time faculty:** 25 total. **Part-time faculty:** 70 total. **Special facilities:** Fine arts center, marine propulsion technology center, welding lab, aquatic center.

Student profile.

Out-of-state:	4%	**25 or older:**	55%

Transfer out. Colleges most students transferred to 2005: University of Florida, Florida State University, University of Central Florida, Florida International University, St. Leo's College.

Basis for selection. Open admission, but selective for some programs. Special application, placement examination, physical examination, and interview required for nursing technology applicants. Admission based on objective points system.

High school preparation. Recommended units include English 4, mathematics 3, social studies 3 and science 3.

2005-2006 Annual costs. Tuition/fees: $2,016; $7,864 out-of-state. Per-credit charge: $53 in-state; $248 out-of-state. Books/supplies: $2,300. Personal expenses: $1,000.

Financial aid. Need-based: Need-based aid available for part-time students. Work study available nights and for part-time students. **Non-need-based:** Scholarships awarded for academics, art, leadership, minority status.

Two-Year Colleges

Application procedures. Admission: No deadline. $20 fee. Admission notification on a rolling basis. **Financial aid:** Priority date 5/1; no closing date. FAFSA, institutional form required. Applicants notified on a rolling basis starting 6/15; must reply within 2 week(s) of notification.

Academics. Special study options: Cooperative education, distance learning, double major, dual enrollment of high school students, ESL, independent study. License preparation in nursing, real estate. **Credit/placement by examination:** AP, CLEP, IB, institutional tests. 45 credit hours maximum toward associate degree. Students taking Florida College Entry Level Placement Test prior to registering do not need SAT I or ACT. **Support services:** Learning center, reduced course load, remedial instruction, tutoring.

Majors. Biology: Marine. **Business:** Business admin. **Computer sciences:** Programming. **Health:** Nursing (RN). **Liberal arts:** Arts/sciences. **Mechanic/repair:** Marine. **Visual/performing arts:** Commercial/advertising art.

Computing on campus. 25 workstations in library, computer center.

Student life. Freshman orientation: Available. Preregistration for classes offered. **Activities:** Choral groups, literary magazine, student government, nurses pinning club, Florida Nurses Student Association, Keys Chorale, Mud-Pi ceramics club, Phi Theta Kappa, Cyber League, Photo Guild club, wreckers club, swim club, scuba club, propmasters club, literary club.

Student services. Career counseling, student employment services, personal counseling, placement for graduates, veterans' counselor. **Physically disabled:** Services for visually, speech, hearing impaired. **Transfer:** Special adviser, orientation, pre-admission transcript evaluation for new students. Transfer adviser, college fairs on campus for students transferring to 4-year colleges.

Contact. Phone: (305) 809-3188 Fax: (305) 292-5163
Cheryl Malsheimer, Director of Admissions and Records, Florida Keys Community College, 5901 College Road, Key West, FL 33040

Florida National College

Hialeah, Florida
www.fnc.edu **CB code: 2057**

- For-profit 2-year community and junior college
- Commuter campus in very large city

General. Regionally accredited. **Enrollment:** 2,000 degree-seeking undergraduates. **Degrees:** 228 associate awarded. **Location:** 12 miles from Miami. **Calendar:** Semester. **Full-time faculty:** 50 total. **Part-time faculty:** 27 total. **Class size:** 100% 20-39.

Transfer out. Colleges most students transferred to 2005: Nova Southeastern University, Florida International University, American Intercontinental University, Miami Institute of Psychology.

Basis for selection. Open admission.

2006-2007 Annual costs. Tuition/fees: $10,616. Per-credit charge: $340. Books/supplies: $850.

2005-2006 Financial aid. All financial aid based on need. 37% of total undergraduate aid awarded as scholarships/grants, 63% as loans/jobs. Need-based aid available for part-time students.

Application procedures. Admission: No deadline. No application fee. Admission notification on a rolling basis beginning on or about 7/15. **Financial aid:** No deadline. FAFSA, institutional form required.

Academics. Special study options: Cooperative education, dual enrollment of high school students, ESL, student-designed major. **Credit/placement by examination:** AP, CLEP. 9 credit hours maximum toward associate degree. **Support services:** GED preparation, reduced course load, remedial instruction, tutoring.

Majors. Business: Accounting, business admin, tourism promotion, tourism/travel. **Computer sciences:** General, programming, system admin, web page design. **Education:** General. **Engineering technology:** Computer hardware. **Health:** Dental lab technology, medical assistant. **Legal studies:** Paralegal. **Protective services:** Criminal justice.

Most popular majors. Business/marketing 37%, computer/information sciences 18%, health sciences 29%, legal studies 16%.

Student life. Freshman orientation: Available. **Activities:** Student government, student newspaper.

Student services. Career counseling, student employment services, financial aid counseling, personal counseling. **Transfer:** Special adviser, orientation for new students.

Contact. E-mail: admissions@fnc.edu
Phone: (305) 821-3333 Fax: (305) 362-0595
Maria Regueiro, Vice President/Assistant CEO, Florida National College, 4425 West 20th Avenue, Hialeah, FL 33012

Florida Technical College

Orlando, Florida
www.flatech.edu **CB code: 3588**

- For-profit 2-year technical college
- Commuter campus in large city

General. Accredited by ACICS. **Calendar:** Continuous.

Annual costs/financial aid. Network administration/programming $14,664 annually. Tuition includes cost of books and supplies. Need-based financial aid available to full-time and part-time students.

Contact. Phone: (407) 447-7300
Director, 12689 Challenger Parkway, #130, Orlando, FL 32826-2707

Florida Technical College: Auburndale

Auburndale, Florida
www.flatech.edu **CB code: 3432**

- For-profit 2-year business and junior college
- Small city

General. Accredited by ACICS. **Calendar:** Continuous.

Annual costs/financial aid. Tuition, including cost of books and supplies, ranges from $3,333 to $3,666 per quarter. Fees, $490. Need-based financial aid available to full-time and part-time students.

Contact. Phone: (863) 967-8822
School Director, 298 Havendale Boulevard, Auburndale, FL 33823

Florida Technical College: Deland

Deland, Florida
www.flatech.edu **CB code: 3589**

- For-profit 2-year junior and technical college
- Small city
- Interview required

General. Accredited by ACICS. **Enrollment:** 258 degree-seeking undergraduates. **Degrees:** 138 associate awarded. **Location:** 30 miles from Orlando, 20 miles from Daytona Beach. **Calendar:** Quarter, extensive summer session. **Full-time faculty:** 13 total; 38% minority, 23% women. **Class size:** 100% < 20. **Partnerships:** Formal partnerships with Microsoft, Pearson Vue testing center, NCCT testing center.

Basis for selection. Open admission.

2005-2006 Annual costs. $4,347 tuition per quarter for paralegal, medical administrative assistant, business, computer drafting & design, electronics/computer technology; $4,713 tuition per quarter for medical assistant, network hardware, network administration/programming, web-design and graphics design program. Required fees $100. Tuition includes cost of books and supplies.

Financial aid. All financial aid based on need. Need-based aid available for part-time students. Work study available nights and for part-time students.

Application procedures. Admission: No deadline. $25 fee. Admission notification on a rolling basis. **Financial aid:** No deadline. FAFSA required. Applicants notified on a rolling basis.

Academics. Credit/placement by examination: CLEP, institutional tests. Credit by examination will be charged $50 per quarter credit not covered by financial aid. Tests must be passed with 70% or higher percentile. May not test out of lab-based classes.

Majors. Business: Business admin. **Computer sciences:** General, networking, programming, systems analysis. **Engineering technology:** Drafting.

Health: Medical assistant, medical secretary, office admin. **Legal studies:** Paralegal. **Mechanic/repair:** Electronics/electrical.

Computing on campus. 90 workstations in library, computer center. Online library, wireless network available.

Student life. Freshman orientation: Mandatory. **Policies:** Freshmen permitted cars on campus.

Student services. Career counseling, financial aid counseling, placement for graduates.

Contact. E-mail: ddesk@flatech.edu
Phone: (386) 734-3303 Toll-free number: (888) 724-6441
Fax: (386) 734-5150
Dane Boothe, Director of Admissions, Florida Technical College: Deland, 1199 South Woodland Boulevard, Deland, FL 32720

Florida Technical College: Jacksonville

Jacksonville, Florida
www.flatech.edu **CB code: 3590**

- For-profit 2-year technical college
- Very large city

General. Accredited by ACICS. **Calendar:** Continuous.

Annual costs/financial aid. Network administration/programming $12,100 annually. Tuition includes cost of books and supplies.

Contact. Phone: (904) 724-2229
Campus Director, 8711 Lone Star Road, Jacksonville, FL 32211

Full Sail Real World Education

Winter Park, Florida
www.fullsail.com **CB code: 3164**

- For-profit 2-year visual arts and technical college
- Commuter campus in very large city

General. Accredited by ACCSCT. **Enrollment:** 5,060 degree-seeking undergraduates. **Degrees:** 224 bachelor's, 2,935 associate awarded. **Location:** 8 miles from Orlando. **Calendar:** Continuous. **Full-time faculty:** 415 total. **Part-time faculty:** 30 total. **Special facilities:** Recording studios, production suites, sound stages.

Student profile.

Out-of-state:	75%	**25 or older:**	20%
Women:	11%		

Basis for selection. Open admission, but selective for some programs. Applicants for Game Design and Development bachelor's degree program must have an "A" average in Algebra II. Geometry, physics and programming experience also recommended. **Adult students:** Entrance exam policies same as for first-time freshmen. **Homeschooled:** Diplomas recognized if applicant's state board of education recognizes them. **Learning Disabled:** Require documentation, not more than 3 years old, describing learning disabilities.

2005-2006 Annual costs. Tuition for associate degree programs range between $40,005 to $41,660. Tuition for bachelor degree programs range between $61,775 and $69,460. Books and supplies included in tuition.

Financial aid. Need-based: Work study available nights and weekends.

Application procedures. Admission: No deadline. $150 fee. Application may be submitted online. Admission notification on a rolling basis. **Financial aid:** No deadline. FAFSA required. Applicants notified on a rolling basis; must reply within 2 week(s) of notification.

Academics. Cognitive development course offered at no charge. Tutoring offered through federal work study program. **Special study options:** Cooperative education, internships. Bachelor's degree programs available on campus. **Credit/placement by examination:** AP, CLEP, institutional tests. Students may take a test-out exam in each course for which credit is being sought. If credit is earned, the tuition and program hours are reduced accordingly. A minimum of 25% of a degree program's semester hours or equivalent must be earned in residence to receive a degree. **Support services:** Study skills assistance, tutoring.

Majors. Computer sciences: Web page design.

Computing on campus. 56 workstations in library, computer center. Online library, wireless network available.

Student life. Freshman orientation: Mandatory. **Policies:** Alcohol and drug free facility. Freshmen permitted cars on campus.

Student services. Financial aid counseling, placement for graduates.

Contact. E-mail: admissions@fullsail.com
Phone: (407) 679-6333 Toll-free number: (800) 226-7625
Fax: (407) 678-0070
MaryBeth Plank-Mezo, Director of Admission, Full Sail Real World Education, 3300 University Boulevard, Winter Park, FL 32792-7429

Golf Academy of the South

Scottsdale, Arizona
www.sdgagolf.com

- For-profit 2-year community college
- Large town

General. Accredited by ACICS. **Calendar:** Semester.

Contact. Phone: (480) 905-9288
7373 North Scottsdale Road, Suite B-100, Scottsdale, AZ 85253

Gulf Coast College

Tampa, Florida
www.gulfcoastcollege.com **CB code: 3448**

- For-profit 2-year technical college
- Large city

General. Accredited by ACICS. **Calendar:** Quarter.

Annual costs/financial aid. Educational resource fee includes cost of books. Personal expenses: $2,856.

Contact. Phone: (813) 620-1446
Director of Admissions, 3910 U.S. Highway 301 North, Suite 200, Tampa, FL 33619-1290

Gulf Coast Community College

Panama City, Florida
www.gulfcoast.edu **CB code: 5271**

- Public 2-year community college
- Commuter campus in small city

General. Founded in 1957. Regionally accredited. **Enrollment:** 7,223 degree-seeking undergraduates. **Degrees:** 529 associate awarded. **Location:** 100 miles from Tallahassee, 100 miles from Pensacola. **Calendar:** Semester, limited summer session. **Full-time faculty:** 120 total. **Part-time faculty:** 375 total. **Partnerships:** Training programs with local businesses, high school teacher training.

Student profile.

Part-time:	70%	**Women:**	58%
Out-of-state:	6%	**25 or older:**	42%

Transfer out. Colleges most students transferred to 2005: Florida State University, University of Florida, University of Central Florida, University of West Florida.

Basis for selection. Open admission, but selective for some programs. Admission to health science programs determined through high school transcripts, placement test performance and other admissions criteria. Interview required of allied health applicants. Audition recommended for music majors.

High school preparation. 13 units recommended. Recommended units include English 4, mathematics 3, social studies 3 and science 3.

2005-2006 Annual costs. Tuition/fees: $1,871; $6,489 out-of-state. Per-credit charge: $51 in-state; $205 out-of-state. Books/supplies: $800. Personal expenses: $1,500.

Financial aid. Need-based: Need-based aid available for part-time students. Work study available nights, weekends and for part-time students. **Non-need-based:** Scholarships awarded for academics, athletics, job skills, leadership, minority status, music/drama, state residency.

Application procedures. **Admission:** No deadline. No application fee. Admission notification on a rolling basis. Application deadline for nursing program February 28; dental hygiene April 1; EMT and paramedic June 1; radiography May 15; physical therapist assistant April 1; surgical technology October 21. **Financial aid:** Priority date 4/1, closing date 7/1. FAFSA required. Applicants notified on a rolling basis starting 7/1.

Academics. **Special study options:** Accelerated study, cooperative education, distance learning, dual enrollment of high school students, honors, independent study, internships, teacher certification program, weekend college. License preparation in dental hygiene, nursing, paramedic, radiology, real estate. **Credit/placement by examination:** AP, CLEP, IB, institutional tests. 45 credit hours maximum toward associate degree. **Support services:** GED preparation, learning center, reduced course load, remedial instruction, study skills assistance, tutoring.

Majors. **Agriculture:** Landscaping, ornamental horticulture. **Biology:** General, marine. **Business:** Accounting, banking/financial services, business admin, communications, marketing, office/clerical, real estate. **Communications:** General, advertising, broadcast journalism, journalism, public relations. **Computer sciences:** General, applications programming, computer science, programming, systems analysis. **Conservation:** General, forestry. **Education:** Biology, chemistry, elementary, family/consumer sciences, health, mathematics, physics, sales/marketing, science, social studies, special. **Engineering:** General, electrical, marine. **Engineering technology:** Architectural, civil, construction, electrical. **English:** Speech/rhetoric. **Family/consumer sciences:** General, institutional food production. **Foreign languages:** General, translation. **Health:** Dental hygiene, EMT paramedic, health services, medical radiologic technology/radiation therapy, medical records admin, nursing (RN), optician, physical therapy assistant, physics/radiologic health, predentistry, premedicine, prepharmacy, preveterinary, respiratory therapy technology. **History:** General. **Legal studies:** General, paralegal, prelaw. **Liberal arts:** Arts/sciences, library science. **Math:** General. **Parks/recreation:** General, health/fitness. **Personal/culinary services:** Culinary arts. **Philosophy/religion:** Philosophy, religion. **Physical sciences:** Atmospheric science, chemistry, geology, oceanography, physics. **Protective services:** Criminal justice, fire safety technology, firefighting, law enforcement admin. **Psychology:** General. **Public administration:** Human services, social work. **Social sciences:** Anthropology, archaeology, criminology, economics, political science, sociology. **Visual/performing arts:** Art, dramatic.

Most popular majors. Health sciences 26%, liberal arts 63%.

Computing on campus. 550 workstations in library, computer center. Commuter students can connect to campus network. Online library available.

Student life. **Freshman orientation:** Available. Orientation programs also available on the Internet. **Activities:** Bands, choral groups, dance, drama, literary magazine, music ensembles, musical theater, radio station, student government, student newspaper, African-American student union, Baptist campus ministry, international student organization.

Athletics. NJCAA. **Intercollegiate:** Baseball M, basketball, softball W, volleyball W. **Intramural:** Basketball. **Team name:** Commodores.

Student services. Adult student services, career counseling, services for economically disadvantaged, student employment services, financial aid counseling, minority student services, personal counseling, veterans' counselor, women's services. **Physically disabled:** Services for visually, speech, hearing impaired. **Learning disabled:** Comprehensive services available. **Transfer:** Special adviser, orientation, pre-admission transcript evaluation for new students. Transfer adviser, college fairs on campus for students transferring to 4-year colleges.

Contact. E-mail: jkuczenski@gulfcoast.edu
Phone: (850) 872-3892 Toll-free number: (800) 311-3685
Fax: (850) 913-3308
Sharon Todd, Director of Enrollment Services and Institutional Research, Gulf Coast Community College, 5230 West Highway 98, Panama City, FL 32401-1041

Heritage Institute: Jacksonville

Jacksonville, Florida
www.heritage-education.com

- Private 2-year technical college
- Very large city

General. Accredited by ACCSCT. **Calendar:** Continuous.

Contact. Phone: (904) 332-0910 ext. 121
4130 Salisbury Road North, Suite 1100, Jacksonville, FL 32216

Herzing College: Orlando

Winter Park, Florida
www.herzing.edu **CB code: 3438**

- For-profit 2-year business and health science college
- Commuter campus in very large city
- Interview required

General. Accredited by ACICS. **Enrollment:** 171 degree-seeking undergraduates. **Degrees:** 2 bachelor's, 20 associate awarded. **Calendar:** Semester, extensive summer session. **Full-time faculty:** 7 total; 14% have terminal degrees, 29% minority. **Part-time faculty:** 4 total; 25% have terminal degrees, 50% minority.

Student profile. Among degree-seeking undergraduates, 39 enrolled as first-time, first-year students.

Part-time:	52%	**Women:**	73%

Basis for selection. Open admission, but selective for some programs. Entrance test and evaluation for all applicants. SAT or ACT considered if submitted. **Adult students:** Entrance exam policies same as for first-time freshmen.

2005-2006 Annual costs. Tuition is $1,080 per class. Students typically take 3 to 4 classes per semester.

Application procedures. **Admission:** No deadline. No application fee. Application may be submitted online. Admission notification on a rolling basis.

Academics. **Special study options:** Distance learning. Bachelor's degree programs available on campus. **Credit/placement by examination:** AP, CLEP, IB, institutional tests. 52 credit hours maximum toward associate degree, 97 toward bachelor's. **Support services:** Reduced course load, remedial instruction, study skills assistance, tutoring.

Majors. **Business:** General, business admin. **Computer sciences:** Information technology, LAN/WAN management, programming. **Health:** Insurance coding, insurance specialist.

Computing on campus. 120 workstations in library, computer center. Online library, wireless network available.

Student life. **Freshman orientation:** Mandatory. Preregistration for classes offered.

Student services. Adult student services, student employment services, financial aid counseling. **Transfer:** Orientation, pre-admission transcript evaluation for new students.

Contact. E-mail: info@orl.herzing.edu
Phone: (407) 478-0500 Toll-free number: (800) 574-4446
Fax: (401) 418-0501
John Wright, Director of Admissions, Herzing College: Orlando, 1595 South Semoran Boulevard, Suite 1501, Winter Park, FL 32792-5509

High-Tech Institute

Orlando, Florida
www.hightechinstitute.edu

- For-profit 2-year health science and technical college
- Commuter campus

General. Accredited by ACCSCT.

Contact. Phone: (407) 893-7400
Admissions Director, 3710 Maguire Boulevard, Orlando, FL 32803

Hillsborough Community College

Tampa, Florida **CB member**
www.hccfl.edu **CB code: 5304**

- Public 2-year community college
- Commuter campus in large city

General. Founded in 1968. Regionally accredited. Four campuses and two education centers in county. **Enrollment:** 22,125 degree-seeking undergraduates. **Degrees:** 1,937 associate awarded. **ROTC:** Army, Air Force. **Location:** 2 miles from downtown. **Calendar:** Semester, limited summer session. **Full-time faculty:** 240 total. **Part-time faculty:** 600 total. **Class size:**

50% < 20, 48% 20-39, less than 1% 40-49, less than 1% 50-99, less than 1% >100. **Special facilities:** Environmental study centers, Florida Studies Center (site of International Wetlands Conference).

Student profile.

Out-of-state:	4%	25 or older:	37%

Transfer out. Colleges most students transferred to 2005: University of South Florida, Florida State University, University of Florida, University of Central Florida.

Basis for selection. Open admission. **Adult students:** Entrance exam policies same as for first-time freshmen.

High school preparation. 24 units recommended. Recommended units include English 4, mathematics 3, science 3, foreign language 2 and academic electives 8. Performing arts recommended.

2005-2006 Annual costs. Tuition/fees: $1,983; $6,924 out-of-state. Per-credit charge: $55 in-state; $220 out-of-state. Books/supplies: $800. Personal expenses: $2,375.

2004-2005 Financial aid. Need-based: 60% of total undergraduate aid awarded as scholarships/grants, 40% as loans/jobs. Work study available nights, weekends and for part-time students.

Application procedures. Admission: No deadline. $20 fee. Admission notification on a rolling basis. **Financial aid:** Closing date 6/30. FAFSA required. Applicants notified on a rolling basis starting 7/1; must reply within 2 week(s) of notification.

Academics. Special study options: Accelerated study, cross-registration, distance learning, double major, dual enrollment of high school students, ESL, honors, internships, liberal arts/career combination, study abroad, teacher certification program, weekend college. License preparation in dental hygiene, nursing, paramedic. **Credit/placement by examination:** AP, CLEP, IB, institutional tests. Approval required. **Support services:** GED preparation, learning center, remedial instruction, study skills assistance, tutoring, writing center.

Majors. Agriculture: Business, ornamental horticulture. **Biology:** Biomedical sciences. **Business:** General, accounting, business admin, customer service, office management. **Communications:** Broadcast journalism, digital media, journalism, radio/tv. **Computer sciences:** General, computer graphics, computer science, information systems, networking, programming, web page design, webmaster. **Conservation:** Environmental science, fisheries. **Education:** General, elementary, physical, secondary, technology/industrial arts. **Engineering:** General, computer, electrical, environmental, software. **Engineering technology:** Architectural, biomedical, electrical, industrial management. **Family/consumer sciences:** Child care, food/nutrition. **Foreign languages:** Sign language interpretation. **Health:** Dental hygiene, EMT paramedic, health services, medical radiologic technology/radiation therapy, nuclear medical technology, nursing (RN), occupational therapy assistant, optician, premedicine, radiologic technology/medical imaging, respiratory therapy technology, sonography. **Legal studies:** Paralegal. **Liberal arts:** Arts/sciences. **Mechanic/repair:** Heating/ac/refrig. **Personal/culinary services:** General, chef training, culinary arts, restaurant/catering. **Protective services:** Criminal justice, firefighting, law enforcement admin. **Public administration:** Human services. **Visual/performing arts:** Art, dance, theater history.

Most popular majors. Health sciences 13%, liberal arts 79%.

Computing on campus. 1,840 workstations in library, computer center, student center. Commuter students can connect to campus network. Online course registration, online library, helpline available.

Student life. Freshman orientation: Mandatory. Preregistration for classes offered. Held approximately 2 hours prior to registration. **Policies:** Freshmen permitted cars on campus. **Activities:** Bands, choral groups, dance, drama, literary magazine, music ensembles, radio station, student government, student newspaper, African-American student union, international club, Latin American student club, Intervarsity Christian Fellowship.

Athletics. NJCAA. **Intercollegiate:** Baseball M, basketball, softball W, tennis W, volleyball W. **Intramural:** Bowling, soccer M. **Team name:** Hawks.

Student services. Career counseling, services for economically disadvantaged, student employment services, financial aid counseling, on-campus daycare, personal counseling, placement for graduates, veterans' counselor. **Physically disabled:** Services for visually, speech, hearing impaired. **Learning disabled:** Comprehensive services available. **Transfer:** Special adviser, orientation for new students. Transfer center, transfer adviser, college fairs on campus for students transferring to 4-year colleges.

Contact. Phone: (813) 253-7004 Fax: (813) 253-7196
Kathy Cecil, Director of Admissions, Hillsborough Community College, Box 31127, Tampa, FL 33631-3127

Indian River Community College

Fort Pierce, Florida — **CB member**
www.ircc.edu — **CB code: 5322**

- Public 2-year community college
- Commuter campus in small city

General. Founded in 1960. Regionally accredited. Branch campuses in Vero Beach, Stuart, Okeechobee, Port St. Lucie; Criminal Justice Academy, Marine Center in Fort Pierce. **Enrollment:** 6,862 degree-seeking undergraduates. **Degrees:** 1,143 associate awarded. **Location:** 65 miles from West Palm Beach. **Calendar:** Semester, limited summer session. **Full-time faculty:** 170 total. **Part-time faculty:** 700 total. **Special facilities:** Olympic-size pool complex, fine arts center, planetarium.

Student profile.

Out-of-state:	2%	25 or older:	42%

Transfer out. Colleges most students transferred to 2005: University of Central Florida, University of South Florida, University of Florida, Florida State University, Florida Atlantic University.

Basis for selection. Open admission, but selective for some programs. Testing and academic records determine admission to health science programs. SAT or ACT recommended for placement.

High school preparation. 24 units recommended. Recommended units include English 4, mathematics 3, social studies 3, history 2, science 3, foreign language 2 and academic electives 7.

2005-2006 Annual costs. Tuition/fees: $1,872; $6,990 out-of-state. Per-credit charge: $52 in-state; $223 out-of-state. Books/supplies: $700. Personal expenses: $856.

2004-2005 Financial aid. Need-based: 77% of total undergraduate aid awarded as scholarships/grants, 23% as loans/jobs. Need-based aid available for part-time students. Work study available for part-time students. **Non-need-based:** Scholarships awarded for academics, athletics, minority status, music/drama, state residency.

Application procedures. Admission: No deadline. No application fee. Admission notification on a rolling basis. **Financial aid:** Priority date 7/18; no closing date. FAFSA, institutional form required. Applicants notified on a rolling basis starting 5/15.

Academics. Special study options: Accelerated study, distance learning, dual enrollment of high school students, weekend college. License preparation in paramedic, real estate. **Credit/placement by examination:** AP, CLEP, IB, institutional tests. 45 credit hours maximum toward associate degree. Degree-seeking students must achieve state-designated cutoff scores on placement test to enter college-level programs, or complete sequence of developmental courses. **Support services:** GED preparation and test center, learning center, pre-admission summer program, reduced course load, remedial instruction, study skills assistance, tutoring.

Majors. Agriculture: Business technology, turf management. **Biology:** General. **Business:** Accounting, administrative services, business admin, hospitality admin, management information systems, office management, sales/distribution. **Communications:** Public relations. **Communications technology:** Graphic/printing. **Computer sciences:** General, applications programming, computer graphics, information technology, programming, systems analysis, web page design. **Conservation:** Environmental studies. **Education:** General, early childhood, elementary, secondary. **Engineering:** General. **Engineering technology:** Architectural drafting, civil, construction, electrical. **Foreign languages:** General. **Health:** Clinical lab technology, dental hygiene, dental lab technology, EMT paramedic, medical radiologic technology/radiation therapy, medical records admin, medical records technology, medical transcription, nursing (RN), physical therapy assistant, predentistry, premedicine, prepharmacy, preveterinary, respiratory therapy technology. **History:** General. **Legal studies:** Legal secretary, paralegal, prelaw. **Liberal arts:** Arts/sciences, library assistant. **Math:** General. **Mechanic/repair:** Automotive, heating/ac/refrig. **Personal/culinary services:** Restaurant/catering. **Philosophy/religion:** Philosophy. **Physical sciences:** Chemistry, physics. **Protective services:** Criminal justice, fire safety technology. **Psychology:** General. **Public administration:** Human services. **Social sciences:** Anthropology, economics, political science, sociology. **Visual/performing arts:** Art, commercial/advertising art, dance, dramatic, interior design.

Computing on campus. Online course registration, online library available.

Student life. Freshman orientation: Available. **Policies:** Freshmen permitted cars on campus. **Housing:** Apartments available. **Activities:** Bands, choral groups, dance, drama, literary magazine, music ensembles, musical theater, radio station, student government, symphony orchestra, Distributive Education Clubs of America, international club, Vocational International Clubs of America, cultural exchange club, human services club, ambassador club, Bacchus Club, Phi Beta Lambda.

Athletics. NJCAA. **Intercollegiate:** Baseball M, basketball, cheerleading W, diving, softball W, swimming, volleyball W. **Team name:** Pioneers.

Student services. Alcohol/substance abuse counseling, career counseling, services for economically disadvantaged, student employment services, financial aid counseling, health services, minority student services, on-campus daycare, placement for graduates, veterans' counselor, women's services. **Physically disabled:** Services for visually, speech, hearing impaired. **Transfer:** Special adviser, orientation for new students. Transfer adviser, college fairs on campus for students transferring to 4-year colleges.

Contact. Phone: (772) 462-4740 Toll-free number: (866) 866-4722
Fax: (772) 462-4699
Karen Chapdelaine, Director of Admissions, Indian River Community College, 3209 Virginia Avenue, Fort Pierce, FL 34981-5596

Two-Year Colleges

Keiser Career College: Pembroke Pines

Pembroke Pines, Florida

- For-profit 2-year business and health science college
- Commuter campus

General. Accredited by ACCSCT.

Contact. Phone: (954) 431-4300
12520 Pines Boulevard, Pembroke Pines, FL 33027

Keiser Career College: Port St. Lucie

Port St. Lucie, Florida

CB code: 5355

- For-profit 2-year business and health science college
- Commuter campus

General. Accredited by ACCSCT.

Contact. Phone: (772) 398-9990
9468 South US I, Port St. Lucie, FL 34952

Keiser Career College: West Palm Beach

West Palm Beach, Florida

- For-profit 2-year business and health science college
- Commuter campus

General. Accredited by ACCSCT.

Contact. Phone: (561) 471-6000
2085 Vista Parkway, West Palm Beach, FL 33411

Keiser College

Ft. Lauderdale, Florida
www.keisercollege.edu

CB code: 7004

- For-profit 2-year junior and technical college
- Commuter campus in large city

General. Founded in 1977. Regionally accredited. **Location:** 35 miles from Miami. **Calendar:** Semester.

Annual costs/financial aid. Students in business, health services administration, accounting, and computer technology programs pay additional $600 fee per year for lease of computer. Books/supplies: $1,200. Personal expenses: $1,900. Need-based financial aid available to full-time and part-time students.

Contact. Phone: (954) 776-4456
Director of Admissions, 1500 Northwest 49th Street, Fort Lauderdale, FL 33309

Key College

Dania Beach, Florida
www.keycollege.edu

CB code: 3577

- For-profit 2-year business and technical college
- Commuter campus in very large city
- Interview required

General. Accredited by ACICS. **Enrollment:** 187 degree-seeking undergraduates. **Degrees:** 32 associate awarded. **Calendar:** Quarter, extensive summer session. **Full-time faculty:** 9 total. **Part-time faculty:** 4 total.

Student profile. Among degree-seeking undergraduates, 75% enrolled in a vocational program. Of all enrolled students, 16% already have a bachelor's degree or higher.

Out-of-state:	6%	**International:**	2%
African American:	33%	**25 or older:**	67%
Hispanic American:	15%		

Basis for selection. Entrance exam required. SAT or ACT recommended. **Adult students:** Entrance exam policies same as for first-time freshmen. **Homeschooled:** State high school equivalency certificate required.

High school preparation. College-preparatory program recommended.

2006-2007 Annual costs. Tuition/fees (projected): $9,220. Books/supplies: $1,050.

Financial aid. Need-based: Work study available nights and for part-time students. **Additional information:** Federal Supplemental Educational Opportunities Grant (FSEOG), PELL grant, FFEL (federal loan program) available; direct loans offered.

Application procedures. Admission: No deadline. $35 fee. Application must be submitted on paper. Admission notification on a rolling basis. **Financial aid:** No deadline.

Academics. Credit/placement by examination: CLEP, institutional tests. **Support services:** Remedial instruction, study skills assistance.

Majors. Computer sciences: General. **Engineering technology:** Drafting. **Health:** Medical transcription. **Legal studies:** Court reporting, paralegal.

Computing on campus. 65 workstations in library, computer center.

Student life. Freshman orientation: Mandatory. Held one week prior to beginning of classes for approximately 3 hours. **Policies:** Freshmen permitted cars on campus. **Activities:** Student newspaper.

Student services. Career counseling, financial aid counseling, personal counseling, veterans' counselor.

Contact. E-mail: admissions@keycollege.edu
Phone: (954) 923-4440 Toll-free number: (800) 581-8292
Fax: (954) 583-9458
Ann Charleus, Director of Admissions, Key College, 225 Dania Beach Boulevard, Dania Beach, FL 33004

Lake City Community College

Lake City, Florida
www.lakecitycc.edu

CB member
CB code: 5377

- Public 2-year community college
- Commuter campus in large town

General. Founded in 1947. Regionally accredited. **Enrollment:** 2,736 degree-seeking undergraduates. **Degrees:** 297 associate awarded. **Location:** 60 miles from Jacksonville, 45 miles from Gainesville. **Calendar:** Semester, limited summer session. **Full-time faculty:** 54 total. **Part-time faculty:** 110 total. **Special facilities:** Performing arts center, arboretum.

Student profile.

Out-of-state:	3%	**Live on campus:**	1%
25 or older:	30%		

Basis for selection. Open admission, but selective for some programs. Locally administered CPT test may be used in place of SAT or ACT. Interview recommended for most allied health programs and all golf course operations programs.

High school preparation. 13 units recommended. Recommended units include English 4, mathematics 3, social studies 3 and science 3. Applicants to forest management should have good mathematics background.

2005-2006 Annual costs. Tuition/fees: $1,887; $7,050 out-of-state. Per-credit charge: $51 in-state; $223 out-of-state. Books/supplies: $800. Personal expenses: $750.

2004-2005 Financial aid. Need-based: 79% of total undergraduate aid awarded as scholarships/grants, 21% as loans/jobs. Need-based aid available for part-time students. Work study available for part-time students. **Non-need-based:** Scholarships awarded for academics, athletics.

Application procedures. Admission: Priority date 8/1; no deadline. $15 fee. Application may be submitted online. Admission notification on a rolling basis. Some technical programs reach maximum enrollment and are closed prior to August 1. **Financial aid:** Priority date 6/1; no closing date. FAFSA, institutional form required. Applicants notified on a rolling basis starting 6/1; must reply within 2 week(s) of notification.

Academics. Special study options: Accelerated study, cooperative education, distance learning, dual enrollment of high school students, exchange student, independent study, internships, study abroad, weekend college. Bachelor's degree programs available on campus. License preparation in nursing, paramedic, physical therapy. **Credit/placement by examination:** CLEP, IB, institutional tests. 30 credit hours maximum toward associate degree. **Support services:** GED preparation and test center, learning center, reduced course load, remedial instruction, study skills assistance, tutoring.

Majors. Agriculture: Landscaping. **Architecture:** Landscape. **Business:** General, administrative services, business admin, office/clerical. **Communications:** General. **Computer sciences:** General, information systems, programming. **Conservation:** Forestry. **Education:** General. **Health:** Clinical lab assistant, clinical lab technology, EMT paramedic, nursing (RN), physical therapy assistant. **Legal studies:** Prelaw. **Liberal arts:** Arts/sciences. **Math:** General. **Parks/recreation:** Facilities management. **Protective services:** Criminal justice. **Social sciences:** Criminology.

Most popular majors. Agriculture 14%, health sciences 22%, liberal arts 57%.

Computing on campus. 350 workstations in library, computer center.

Student life. Freshman orientation: Available. **Policies:** Freshmen permitted cars on campus. **Housing:** Coed dorms available. $100 deposit. **Activities:** Bands, choral groups, dance, drama, literary magazine, music ensembles, student government, TV station, Florida Turf Grass Association, Florida Student Nurses Association, Phi Theta Kappa, Baptist Student Union, Granger Hall Council, medical lab technology club, physical therapy assistant club, Practical Nurses Association.

Athletics. NJCAA. **Intercollegiate:** Baseball M, golf W, softball W. **Intramural:** Basketball, racquetball, softball, table tennis, volleyball. **Team name:** Timberwolves.

Student services. Alcohol/substance abuse counseling, career counseling, student employment services, financial aid counseling, personal counseling, placement for graduates, veterans' counselor. **Physically disabled:** Services for visually, speech, hearing impaired. **Transfer:** Special adviser, orientation for new students. Transfer adviser, college fairs on campus for students transferring to 4-year colleges.

Contact. E-mail: admissions@lakecitycc.edu
Phone: (386) 754-4287 Fax: (386) 754-4787
Vince Rice, Director of Post-secondary Transition, Lake City Community College, 149 SE College Place, Lake City, FL 32025-8703

Lake-Sumter Community College

Leesburg, Florida
www.lscc.edu **CB code: 5376**

- Public 2-year community college
- Commuter campus in small city

General. Founded in 1962. Regionally accredited. **Enrollment:** 2,773 degree-seeking undergraduates; 586 non-degree-seeking students. **Degrees:** 431 associate awarded. **Location:** 35 miles from Orlando. **Calendar:** Semester, limited summer session. **Full-time faculty:** 48 total; 21% have terminal degrees, 4% minority, 65% women. **Part-time faculty:** 120 total; 8% have terminal degrees, 15% minority, 53% women. **Class size:** 52% < 20, 46% 20-39, less than 1% 40-49, less than 1% 50-99.

Student profile. Among degree-seeking undergraduates, 74% enrolled in a transfer program, 26% enrolled in a vocational program, 1% already have a bachelor's degree or higher, 609 enrolled as first-time, first-year students, 105 transferred in from other institutions.

Part-time:	60%	**Asian American:**	2%
Out-of-state:	1%	**Hispanic American:**	9%
Women:	66%	**International:**	1%
African American:	11%	**25 or older:**	34%

Transfer out. Colleges most students transferred to 2005: University of Central Florida, University of Florida, Florida State University, University of South Florida.

Basis for selection. Open admission, but selective for some programs. Special requirements for nursing program. **Adult students:** Entrance exam policies same as for first-time freshmen. **Homeschooled:** In lieu of a high school diploma or GED, a home-schooled affidavit will be accepted.

High school preparation. All Florida high school diplomas are accepted; units vary depending on diploma.

2005-2006 Annual costs. Tuition/fees: $1,932; $7,108 out-of-state. Per-credit charge: $52 in-state; $225 out-of-state. Books/supplies: $850. Personal expenses: $1,000.

2004-2005 Financial aid. Need-based: 3% of total undergraduate aid awarded as scholarships/grants, 97% as loans/jobs. Need-based aid available for part-time students. Work study available nights, weekends and for part-time students. **Non-need-based:** Scholarships awarded for academics, art, athletics, leadership, minority status, music/drama.

Application procedures. Admission: No deadline. $25 fee. Application must be submitted on paper. Admission notification on a rolling basis. **Financial aid:** Priority date 4/15; no closing date. FAFSA, institutional form required. Applicants notified on a rolling basis starting 7/1.

Academics. Nursing program requires at least one semester of college with cumulative GPA of 2.5, completion of specific courses, score of 50 on NLN pre-admission exam, math placement, CPR certification. **Special study options:** Cooperative education, distance learning, dual enrollment of high school students, independent study, internships, liberal arts/career combination. Bachelor's degree programs available on campus. License preparation in nursing, real estate. **Credit/placement by examination:** AP, CLEP, institutional tests. 39 credit hours maximum toward associate degree. **Support services:** Learning center, reduced course load, remedial instruction, study skills assistance, tutoring, writing center.

Majors. Business: Business admin. **Computer sciences:** Information technology, webmaster. **Education:** Early childhood. **Engineering:** Software. **Health:** EMT paramedic, medical records technology, nursing (RN). **Legal studies:** Paralegal. **Liberal arts:** Arts/sciences. **Parks/recreation:** Sports admin. **Protective services:** Firefighting, law enforcement admin. **Visual/performing arts:** Commercial/advertising art.

Most popular majors. Health sciences 16%, liberal arts 73%.

Computing on campus. 500 workstations in library, computer center, student center. Commuter students can connect to campus network. Online course registration, online library, wireless network available.

Student life. Freshman orientation: Mandatory. Both day and evening sessions are scheduled as well as online orientation. **Policies:** Freshmen permitted cars on campus. **Activities:** Bands, choral groups, drama, literary magazine, music ensembles, student government, student newspaper, TV station, Baptist Collegiate Ministry, College Democrats, College Republicans, environmental society, Fellowship of Christian Athletes, Health Explorers, Lion's Club.

Athletics. NJCAA. **Intercollegiate:** Baseball M, softball W, volleyball W. **Intramural:** Basketball, softball, volleyball. **Team name:** Lakers.

Student services. Adult student services, career counseling, student employment services, financial aid counseling, personal counseling, placement for graduates, veterans' counselor, women's services. **Physically disabled:** Services for visually, speech, hearing impaired. **Transfer:** Special adviser, orientation, pre-admission transcript evaluation for new students. Transfer adviser, college fairs on campus for students transferring to 4-year colleges.

Contact. E-mail: admissinquiry@lscc.edu
Phone: (352) 323-3665 Fax: (352) 365-3553
Tabitha Richards, Director, Admissions/ Registrar, Lake-Sumter Community College, 9501 U.S. Highway 441, Leesburg, FL 34788-8751

Manatee Community College

Bradenton, Florida **CB member**
www.mccfl.edu **CB code: 5427**

- Public 2-year community college
- Commuter campus in small city

Two-Year Colleges

General. Founded in 1957. Regionally accredited. **Enrollment:** 8,984 degree-seeking undergraduates; 783 non-degree-seeking students. **Degrees:** 1,207 associate awarded. **Location:** 40 miles from Tampa, 20 miles from St. Petersburg. **Calendar:** Semester, extensive summer session. **Full-time faculty:** 129 total; 22% have terminal degrees, 8% minority, 57% women. **Part-time faculty:** 382 total; 5% have terminal degrees, 9% minority, 51% women.

Student profile. Among degree-seeking undergraduates, 67% enrolled in a transfer program, 33% enrolled in a vocational program, 2,281 enrolled as first-time, first-year students.

Part-time:	58%	**Asian American:**	2%
Out-of-state:	4%	**Hispanic American:**	7%
Women:	62%	**International:**	2%
African American:	11%	**25 or older:**	39%

Basis for selection. Open admission, but selective for some programs. Limited enrollment in health programs. TOEFL required of non-native speakers of English. Interview recommended for nursing, radiologic technology, respiratory therapy, occupational therapy assistant, physical therapist assistant, dental hygiene majors.

High school preparation. Recommended units include English 4, mathematics 3, social studies 2, history 1, science 3 and foreign language 2.

2005-2006 Annual costs. Tuition/fees: $1,983; $7,352 out-of-state. Per-credit charge: $55 in-state; $234 out-of-state. Books/supplies: $1,127. Personal expenses: $1,790.

Financial aid. Need-based: Need-based aid available for part-time students. Work study available nights, weekends and for part-time students. **Non-need-based:** Scholarships awarded for academics, art, athletics, music/drama, state residency.

Application procedures. Admission: No deadline. $40 fee. Admission notification on a rolling basis. **Financial aid:** Priority date 6/1; no closing date. FAFSA required. Applicants notified on a rolling basis starting 3/15.

Academics. Special study options: Accelerated study, cooperative education, distance learning, dual enrollment of high school students, honors, independent study. License preparation in dental hygiene, nursing, occupational therapy, physical therapy, radiology. **Credit/placement by examination:** AP, CLEP. 30 credit hours maximum toward associate degree. Scores on SAT I or ACT or CPT (Florida Placement Test) used for placement only. **Support services:** GED preparation, learning center, remedial instruction, study skills assistance, tutoring.

Majors. Area/ethnic studies: African, African-American, American, Latin American, women's. **Biology:** General, bacteriology, marine. **Business:** General, accounting, administrative services, business admin. **Communications:** General, advertising, broadcast journalism, digital media, journalism, media studies, public relations, radio/tv. **Communications technology:** Radio/tv. **Computer sciences:** General, information systems, networking, programming, systems analysis. **Education:** General, biology, chemistry, early childhood, elementary, English, foreign languages, health, kindergarten/preschool, mathematics, music, physics, science, secondary, social studies, trade/industrial. **Engineering:** General, civil, computer, science. **Engineering technology:** Automotive, civil, construction, drafting, electrical. **English:** English lit, speech/rhetoric. **Foreign languages:** French, German, Spanish. **Health:** Clinical lab science, clinical lab technology, community health services, dental hygiene, health care admin, medical radiologic technology/radiation therapy, nuclear medical technology, nursing (RN), occupational therapy assistant, physical therapy assistant, respiratory therapy technology, veterinary technology/assistant. **History:** General. **Legal studies:** General, paralegal, prelaw. **Liberal arts:** Arts/sciences, humanities. **Math:** General, statistics. **Parks/recreation:** Sports admin. **Personal/culinary services:** General. **Philosophy/religion:** Philosophy, religion. **Physical sciences:** Atmospheric science, chemistry, physics. **Protective services:** Criminal justice, firefighting. **Psychology:** General. **Public administration:** General, social work. **Social sciences:** General, economics. **Visual/performing arts:** General, art, art history/conservation, commercial/advertising art, dramatic, fashion design, jazz, music theory/composition, studio arts, theater history.

Most popular majors. Health sciences 14%, liberal arts 76%.

Computing on campus. 2,275 workstations in library, computer center. Online course registration, online library, helpline, repair service available.

Student life. Freshman orientation: Mandatory. Preregistration for classes offered. **Policies:** Freshmen permitted cars on campus. **Activities:** Bands, drama, film society, literary magazine, music ensembles, musical theater, opera, student government, student newspaper, symphony orchestra, African-American Student Union, multicultural student club, art club, student Bible club, Manasota Geographic and Anthropological Society, American Chemical Society, student film club, Hispanic-American club.

Athletics. NJCAA. **Intercollegiate:** Baseball M, basketball M, softball W, volleyball W. **Intramural:** Basketball, golf, soccer, softball, volleyball, weight lifting. **Team name:** Lancers.

Student services. Campus ministries, career counseling, student employment services, financial aid counseling, health services, personal counseling, placement for graduates, veterans' counselor. **Physically disabled:** Services for visually, speech, hearing impaired. **Transfer:** Special adviser, orientation for new students. Transfer adviser for students transferring to 4-year colleges.

Contact. Phone: (941) 752-5031 Fax: (941) 727-6380
Marilynn Paro, Registrar, Manatee Community College, Box 1849, Bradenton, FL 34206-1849

Miami Dade College

Miami, Florida **CB member**
www.mdc.edu **CB code: 5458**

- Public 2-year community college
- Commuter campus in very large city
- SAT or ACT required

General. Founded in 1959. Regionally accredited. Multilocation institution consisting of campuses and outreach centers. **Enrollment:** 47,878 degree-seeking undergraduates; 6,291 non-degree-seeking students. **Degrees:** 4 bachelor's, 6,152 associate awarded. **ROTC:** Army, Air Force. **Calendar:** Semester, limited summer session. **Full-time faculty:** 723 total; 23% have terminal degrees, 52% minority, 50% women. **Part-time faculty:** 1,354 total; 12% have terminal degrees, 64% minority, 47% women. **Class size:** 29% < 20, 61% 20-39, 9% 40-49, less than 1% 50-99, less than 1% >100. **Special facilities:** Art galleries; environmental demonstration center; bilingual center; greenhouse; fire science tower; fire science burn building; emerging technologies center of the Americas; center for the environment; horticulture center; firearms demonstration lab; earth science museum; studio theater; human patient simulator lab; flight simulator lab; child care labs.

Student profile. Among degree-seeking undergraduates, 72% enrolled in a transfer program, 28% enrolled in a vocational program, 1% already have a bachelor's degree or higher, 8,058 enrolled as first-time, first-year students, 1,271 transferred in from other institutions.

Part-time:	63%	**Asian American:**	1%
Out-of-state:	5%	**Hispanic American:**	65%
Women:	62%	**International:**	3%
African American:	20%	**25 or older:**	42%

Transfer out. 75% of students enrolled in the transfer program go on to 4-year colleges. **Colleges most students transferred to 2005:** Florida International University.

Basis for selection. Open admission, but selective for some programs. Special requirements for visual and performing arts, Honors College, allied health programs, and Bachelor's in Education programs. Audition required of performing arts majors. Portfolio required of visual arts majors. **Home-schooled:** Parental verification statement required.

High school preparation. 24 units recommended. 18 credits with a 3-year high school option or 24 credits with a 4-year high school option.

2005-2006 Annual costs. Tuition/fees: $1,921; $6,298 out-of-state. Per-credit charge: $54 in-state; $200 out-of-state. Additional fees of $290 are required for Out-of-State students. Books/supplies: $1,500. Personal expenses: $1,168.

2005-2006 Financial aid. Need-based: Average need met was 68%. Average scholarship/grant was $3,245; average loan $1,074. 74% of total undergraduate aid awarded as scholarships/grants, 26% as loans/jobs. Need-based aid available for part-time students. Work study available nights, weekends and for part-time students. **Non-need-based:** Scholarships awarded for academics, art, athletics, music/drama, state residency.

Application procedures. Admission: No deadline. $20 fee. Application may be submitted online. Admission notification on a rolling basis. **Financial aid:** Priority date 3/15; no closing date. FAFSA required. Applicants notified on a rolling basis starting 5/15.

Academics. Special study options: Accelerated study, cooperative education, cross-registration, distance learning, dual enrollment of high school students, ESL, honors, independent study, internships, study abroad, weekend college. Bachelor's degree programs available on campus. License preparation in aviation, dental hygiene, nursing, physical therapy, radiology, real estate. **Credit/placement by examination:** AP, CLEP, IB, institutional tests. 45 credit hours maximum toward associate degree, 45 toward bachelor's.

Support services: GED preparation, learning center, reduced course load, remedial instruction, study skills assistance, tutoring, writing center.

Honors college/program. Admission requirements include application package, interview, minimum 3.7 high school GPA, and College Level Entrance Exam or 1200 SAT (exclusive of Writing) or 26 ACT; 225 freshmen admitted; rigorous and comprehensive curriculum, honors classes with certified faculty, seminars and enrichment activities.

Majors. Agriculture: Agribusiness operations, landscaping. **Area/ethnic studies:** American, Asian, Latin American. **Biology:** General. **Business:** Accounting, administrative services, banking/financial services, business admin, management science, office management, office/clerical, real estate, tourism promotion, tourism/travel. **Communications:** Broadcast journalism, journalism. **Communications technology:** General, animation/special effects, graphic/printing, graphics. **Computer sciences:** General, applications programming, information systems, information technology, web page design. **Conservation:** Environmental science, forestry. **Construction:** Maintenance. **Education:** Early childhood, elementary, mathematics, physical, science, secondary, special, technology/industrial arts. **Engineering:** Architectural, chemical, civil, electrical. **Engineering technology:** Architectural, civil, electrical, electrical drafting. **English:** American lit, English lit, speech/rhetoric. **Family/consumer sciences:** Child development, food/nutrition. **Foreign languages:** General, sign language interpretation, translation. **Health:** Clinical lab technology, dental hygiene, EMT paramedic, histologic technology, medical assistant, medical radiologic technology/radiation therapy, medical records admin, medical secretary, midwifery, nursing (RN), optician, predentistry, premedicine, prepharmacy, preveterinary, respiratory therapy technology, veterinary technology/assistant. **History:** General. **Legal studies:** Court reporting, legal secretary, paralegal, prelaw. **Liberal arts:** Arts/sciences. **Math:** General. **Mechanic/repair:** Heating/ac/refrig, industrial. **Parks/recreation:** Exercise sciences. **Personal/culinary services:** Mortuary science. **Philosophy/religion:** Philosophy, religion. **Physical sciences:** Atmospheric science, chemistry, geology, physics. **Protective services:** Criminal justice, fire services admin. **Psychology:** General. **Public administration:** General, human services, social work. **Social sciences:** Anthropology, economics, international relations, political science, sociology. **Transportation:** Aviation, aviation management. **Visual/performing arts:** Cinematography, commercial/advertising art, dance, dramatic, studio arts.

Most popular majors. Health sciences 12%, liberal arts 78%.

Computing on campus. 7,400 workstations in library, computer center. Online course registration, helpline available.

Student life. Freshman orientation: Available. **Policies:** Freshmen permitted cars on campus. **Activities:** Bands, choral groups, dance, drama, film society, literary magazine, music ensembles, musical theater, radio station, student government, student newspaper, Newman Club.

Athletics. NJCAA. **Intercollegiate:** Baseball M, basketball, softball W, volleyball W. **Intramural:** Basketball, soccer, softball, table tennis, tennis. **Team name:** Sharks.

Student services. Adult student services, career counseling, services for economically disadvantaged, student employment services, financial aid counseling, personal counseling, placement for graduates, veterans' counselor. **Physically disabled:** Services for visually, speech, hearing impaired. **Transfer:** Special adviser, orientation for new students. Transfer center, transfer adviser, college fairs on campus for students transferring to 4-year colleges.

Contact. Phone: (305) 237-2222 Fax: (305) 237-2964
Steven Kelly, College Director, Admissions and Registration Services, Miami Dade College, 11011 Southwest 104th Street, Miami, FL 33176

New England Institute of Technology
West Palm Beach, Florida
www.newenglandtech.com **CB code: 0529**

- For-profit 2-year technical college
- Commuter campus in small city

General. Founded in 1982. Accredited by ACICS. **Enrollment:** 1,300 degree-seeking undergraduates. **Degrees:** 630 associate awarded. **Location:** 75 miles from Miami. **Calendar:** Quarter, extensive summer session. **Full-time faculty:** 61 total; 8% have terminal degrees, 5% minority, 38% women. **Part-time faculty:** 20 total; 20% have terminal degrees, 10% minority, 45% women. **Class size:** 75% < 20, 24% 20-39, 1% 40-49.

Basis for selection. Open admission. Applicants who do not have a high school diploma or GED may be admitted if they pass a standardized test approved by the Department Of Education. Interview recommended. **Adult students:** Entrance exam policies same as for first-time freshmen.

2005-2006 Annual costs. Tuition and lab fees range from $11,700 to $36,900. Registration fee $125. Books/supplies: $900. Personal expenses: $1,998.

2004-2005 Financial aid. Need-based: 52% of total undergraduate aid awarded as scholarships/grants, 48% as loans/jobs. Work study available nights, weekends and for part-time students.

Application procedures. Admission: No deadline. $25 fee. Application may be submitted online. Admission notification on a rolling basis. **Financial aid:** No deadline. FAFSA, institutional form required. Applicants notified on a rolling basis.

Academics. Courses are designed to provide a combination of theory and instruction that simulates real world experiences. **Special study options:** Double major, dual enrollment of high school students, internships. Bachelor's degree programs available on campus. **Credit/placement by examination:** AP, CLEP, institutional tests. **Support services:** GED preparation, learning center, remedial instruction, study skills assistance, tutoring.

Majors. Business: General, administrative services. **Computer sciences:** Information systems, networking, programming, system admin, web page design. **Engineering technology:** Architectural drafting, mechanical drafting. **Legal studies:** Paralegal. **Mechanic/repair:** Automotive, heating/ac/refrig. **Parks/recreation:** Exercise sciences. **Personal/culinary services:** Baking, chef training, restaurant/catering.

Most popular majors. Personal/culinary services 57%, trade and industry 31%.

Computing on campus. 479 workstations in library, computer center, student center. Online library, helpline, repair service, student web hosting, wireless network available.

Student life. Freshman orientation: Mandatory.

Student services. Adult student services, career counseling, student employment services, financial aid counseling, personal counseling, placement for graduates, veterans' counselor. **Physically disabled:** Services for visually, hearing impaired.

Contact. E-mail: info@newenglandtech.com
Phone: (561) 842-8324 Toll-free number: (800) 826-9986
Fax: (561) 842-9503
Kevin Cassidy, Admissions Director, New England Institute of Technology, 2410 Metrocentre Boulevard, West Palm Beach, FL 33407

North Florida Community College
Madison, Florida
www.nfcc.edu **CB code: 5503**

- Public 2-year community college
- Commuter campus in small town

General. Founded in 1958. Regionally accredited. **Enrollment:** 1,443 degree-seeking undergraduates. **Degrees:** 192 associate awarded. **Location:** 56 miles from Tallahassee. **Calendar:** Semester, limited summer session. **Full-time faculty:** 32 total. **Part-time faculty:** 108 total. **Special facilities:** Nature center. **Partnerships:** Articulation for dual enrollment/testing/remediation.

Transfer out. Colleges most students transferred to 2005: Florida State University, Florida A&M University, Valdasta State University, University of Florida.

Basis for selection. Open admission, but selective for some programs. Limited enrollment for nursing program, criminal justice, EMT. Background checks completed by Florida Department of Law Enforcement. Florida College Entry-Level Placement Tests required for all students. Students with satisfactory ACT or SAT scores are exempt from taking the FCELPT. **Homeschooled:** Submit affidavit stating that home education complies with Florida law. **Learning Disabled:** Disabilities must have documentation.

High school preparation. 24 units recommended. Recommended units include English 4, mathematics 4, social studies 3, science 2 (laboratory 1) and foreign language 2. Algebra 1 recommended.

2005-2006 Annual costs. Tuition/fees: $1,860; $4,920 out-of-state. Per-credit charge: $51 in-state; $153 out-of-state. $510 required fees for out-of-state students. Books/supplies: $500. Personal expenses: $475.

2004-2005 Financial aid. All financial aid based on need. 98% of total undergraduate aid awarded as scholarships/grants, 2% as loans/jobs. Need-based aid available for part-time students. Work study available nights, weekends and for part-time students.

Application procedures. Admission: Priority date 7/1; no deadline. $20 fee. Application must be submitted on paper. Admission notification on a rolling basis. **Financial aid:** Priority date 5/15; no closing date. FAFSA required. Applicants notified on a rolling basis starting 6/20; must reply within 2 week(s) of notification.

Academics. Special study options: Accelerated study, distance learning, dual enrollment of high school students, independent study, teacher certification program. Bachelor's degree programs available on campus. License preparation in nursing, paramedic, real estate. **Credit/placement by examination:** AP, CLEP, IB, institutional tests. 45 credit hours maximum toward associate degree. **Support services:** GED preparation and test center, reduced course load, remedial instruction, study skills assistance, tutoring, writing center.

Majors. Liberal arts: Arts/sciences.

Computing on campus. 39 workstations in library, computer center, student center. Online course registration, online library, wireless network available.

Student life. Freshman orientation: Available. Six week program of 1 hour sessions 2 or 3 days per week, emphasizing academic success skills. **Activities:** Jazz band, choral groups, drama, music ensembles, musical theater, student government, student newspaper, environmental awareness group (SOAR), African-American Association, veterans club, ASL.

Athletics. NJCAA. **Intercollegiate:** Baseball M, basketball W, softball W. **Team name:** Sentinels.

Student services. Adult student services, career counseling, student employment services, health services, personal counseling, placement for graduates, veterans' counselor. **Physically disabled:** Services for hearing impaired. **Transfer:** Special adviser, orientation, pre-admission transcript evaluation for new students. Transfer adviser, college fairs on campus for students transferring to 4-year colleges.

Contact. E-mail: wallerd@nfcc.edu
Phone: (850) 973-1622 Toll-free number: (866) 937-6322
Fax: (850) 973-1697
Mary Wheeler, Dean of Enrollment Services, North Florida Community College, 325 NW Turner Davis Drive, Madison, FL 32340

Orlando Culinary Academy

Orlando, Florida
www.orlandoculinary.com

- For-profit 2-year culinary school
- Very large city
- Application essay, interview required

General. Accredited by ACICS. **Enrollment:** 1,171 degree-seeking undergraduates. **Degrees:** 568 associate awarded. **Location:** Downtown Orlando. **Calendar:** Continuous. **Full-time faculty:** 35 total. **Part-time faculty:** 3 total. **Special facilities:** 14 teaching kitchens, one open-to-the-public restaurant and cafe.

Student profile. Among degree-seeking undergraduates, 100% enrolled in a vocational program, 724 enrolled as first-time, first-year students.

Women:	37%	**25 or older:**	42%

Basis for selection. Open admission. Prospective students must complete the Application for Admission, attest to High School Diploma or its equivalent, complete and sign the Enrollment Agreement, write a 150 word essay, be interviewed by the Admissions Representative and the Director of Admissions. **Adult students:** Entrance exam policies same as for first-time freshmen.

Application procedures. Admission: No deadline. $50 fee. Application must be submitted online. Admission notification on a rolling basis.

Academics. Credit/placement by examination: CLEP. **Support services:** Learning center, study skills assistance, tutoring.

Majors. Personal/culinary services: General, baking, chef training, restaurant/catering.

Computing on campus. 60 workstations in computer center. Online library, wireless network available.

Contact. Phone: (407) 888-4000 Toll-free number: (866) 622-2433
Fax: (407) 888-4019
Orlando Culinary Academy, 8511 Commodity Circle, Suite 100, Orlando, FL 32819

Palm Beach Community College

Lake Worth, Florida — **CB member**
www.pbcc.edu — **CB code: 5531**

- Public 2-year community college
- Commuter campus in large town

General. Founded in 1933. Regionally accredited. Multilocation institution with 4 campuses, numerous other locations throughout service area. **Enrollment:** 13,683 degree-seeking undergraduates; 8,003 non-degree-seeking students. **Degrees:** 1,823 associate awarded. **Location:** 30 miles from Ft. Lauderdale. **Calendar:** Semester. Two 16-week terms and third term consisting of two 6-week sessions and one 12-week session. Limited summer session. **Full-time faculty:** 231 total; 22% have terminal degrees, 24% minority, 54% women. **Part-time faculty:** 562 total; 22% have terminal degrees, 13% minority, 43% women. **Special facilities:** Performing arts centers at 3 campuses. **Partnerships:** Tech prep programs with Palm Beach County school district.

Student profile. Among degree-seeking undergraduates, 2,377 enrolled as first-time, first-year students.

Part-time:	59%	**Women:**	60%
Out-of-state:	6%	**25 or older:**	40%

Transfer out. Colleges most students transferred to 2005: Florida Atlantic University, University of Florida, Florida State University, University of South Florida.

Basis for selection. Open admission, but selective for some programs. Special requirements for dental, nursing, dietetic, occupational therapy assistant programs. Admission to paramedic, radiography, respiratory care programs based on test scores and GPA. SAT or ACT required for admission to nursing and dental programs. CPT, SAT or ACT used for placement for all incoming freshmen. Interview required for nursing, dental, radiography, respiratory care, paramedic majors. Audition required of music majors.

High school preparation. Special requirements for health program applicants.

2005-2006 Annual costs. Tuition/fees: $1,890; $6,614 out-of-state. Per-credit charge: $52 in-state; $210 out-of-state. $279 in required fees for out-of-state students. Books/supplies: $600. Personal expenses: $400.

2005-2006 Financial aid. Need-based: 74% of total undergraduate aid awarded as scholarships/grants, 26% as loans/jobs. Work study available nights, weekends and for part-time students. **Non-need-based:** Scholarships awarded for academics, alumni affiliation, athletics, leadership, state residency.

Application procedures. Admission: Closing date 8/23. $20 fee. Admission notification on a rolling basis beginning on or about 3/1. **Financial aid:** Priority date 7/1; no closing date. FAFSA, institutional form required. Applicants notified on a rolling basis; must reply within 2 week(s) of notification.

Academics. Center for Personalized Instruction offers full assistance in all academic areas for students. **Special study options:** Cooperative education, distance learning, double major, dual enrollment of high school students, ESL, honors, independent study, internships, study abroad, weekend college. License preparation in dental hygiene, nursing, paramedic, real estate. **Credit/placement by examination:** AP, CLEP, IB, institutional tests. 45 credit hours maximum toward associate degree. **Support services:** Learning center, pre-admission summer program, reduced course load, remedial instruction, study skills assistance, tutoring, writing center.

Majors. Agriculture: Ornamental horticulture. **Architecture:** Interior. **Biology:** General, zoology. **Business:** General, accounting, business admin, finance, hospitality admin, management information systems, marketing, sales/distribution. **Communications:** Broadcast journalism, journalism. **Communications technology:** Graphic/printing. **Computer sciences:** General, applications programming, information systems, programming, systems analysis. **Construction:** Maintenance. **Education:** Art, early childhood, elementary, health, health occupations, music, physical, sales/marketing, science, secondary, social science, voc/tech. **Engineering:** General, electrical. **Engineering technology:** Construction, drafting, electrical, industrial management, surveying. **Family/consumer sciences:** General, child care. **Health:** Clinical lab technology, dental hygiene, dietetics, EMT paramedic, health services, massage therapy, medical radiologic technology/radiation therapy, nursing (RN), occupational therapy assistant, premedicine, respiratory therapy technology. **History:** General. **Interdisciplinary:** Biological/physical sciences. **Legal studies:** Paralegal. **Liberal arts:** Arts/sciences. **Math:** General. **Mechanic/repair:** Automotive, marine. **Parks/recreation:** General, health/fitness. **Philosophy/religion:** Philosophy. **Physical sciences:** Chemistry, physics. **Protective services:** Fire services admin, firefighting. **Psychology:** General. **Public administration:** Human services, social work. **Social sciences:**

General, anthropology, geography, international relations, political science, sociology. **Transportation:** Aviation. **Visual/performing arts:** General, art history/conservation, cinematography, commercial/advertising art, dance, dramatic, interior design, jazz, photography, studio arts.

Most popular majors. Biological/life sciences 10%, health sciences 10%, liberal arts 75%.

Computing on campus. 1,485 workstations in library, computer center. Online course registration available.

Student life. **Freshman orientation:** Mandatory. Preregistration for classes offered. **Activities:** Bands, choral groups, dance, drama, literary magazine, music ensembles, student government, student newspaper, black student union, Students for International Understanding.

Athletics. NJCAA. **Intercollegiate:** Baseball M, basketball, softball W, volleyball W. **Intramural:** Basketball, soccer, softball, tennis, volleyball. **Team name:** Panthers.

Student services. Career counseling, student employment services, personal counseling, placement for graduates, veterans' counselor. **Physically disabled:** Services for visually, speech, hearing impaired. **Transfer:** Special adviser, orientation for new students. Transfer adviser, college fairs on campus for students transferring to 4-year colleges.

Contact. E-mail: muellere@pbcc.edu
Phone: (561) 868-3300 Fax: (561) 868-3584
Edward Mueller, Admissions Coordinator, Palm Beach Community College, 4200 Congress Avenue, Lake Worth, FL 33461

Pasco-Hernando Community College
New Port Richey, Florida
www.phcc.edu **CB code: 5562**

- Public 2-year community college
- Commuter campus in large town

General. Founded in 1972. Regionally accredited. District covers counties of Pasco and Hernando; 4 college locations. Distance learning courses are offered for a variety of courses. **Enrollment:** 7,346 degree-seeking undergraduates. **Degrees:** 781 associate awarded. **ROTC:** Army, Navy. **Location:** 35 miles from Tampa. **Calendar:** Semester, limited summer session. **Full-time faculty:** 98 total; 22% have terminal degrees, 65% women. **Part-time faculty:** 217 total; 52% women.

Student profile. Among degree-seeking undergraduates, 1,766 enrolled as first-time, first-year students.

Part-time:	64%	**Women:**	66%
Out-of-state:	1%	**25 or older:**	35%

Transfer out. **Colleges most students transferred to 2005:** University of South Florida, St. Leo University, University of Florida, University of Central Florida, St. Petersburg College.

Basis for selection. Open admission, but selective for some programs. Special requirements for nursing, paramedic, dental, radiography. TOEFL required of non-natives entering on F visas. Most placement is based on Florida College Entry Level Placement Test (FCELPT), that is administered locally. **Adult students:** Entrance exam policies same as for first-time freshmen. **Learning Disabled:** Completed no-fee application and appropriate documentation to Office of Disabilities Services required.

High school preparation. 24 units recommended. Recommended units include English 4, mathematics 3, social studies 3, science 3 and foreign language 2.

2005-2006 Annual costs. Tuition/fees: $1,872; $7,222 out-of-state. Per-credit charge: $50 in-state; $199 out-of-state. $863 required fees for out-of-state students. Books/supplies: $1,100. Personal expenses: $1,850.

Financial aid. **Need-based:** Need-based aid available for part-time students. Work study available nights, weekends and for part-time students. **Non-need-based:** Scholarships awarded for academics, athletics, minority status. **Additional information:** Childcare assistance grants available to eligible students.

Application procedures. **Admission:** No deadline. $20 fee. Application may be submitted online. Admission notification on a rolling basis. **Financial aid:** Priority date 4/1; no closing date. FAFSA required. Applicants notified on a rolling basis starting 3/1.

Academics. License preparation in radiography. **Special study options:** Accelerated study, combined bachelor's/graduate degree, cross-registration, distance learning, double major, dual enrollment of high school students, ESL, honors, independent study, internships, weekend college. Bachelor's degree programs available on campus. License preparation in dental hygiene, nursing, paramedic, radiology. **Credit/placement by examination:** AP, CLEP, IB, institutional tests. 45 credit hours maximum toward associate degree. **Support services:** GED preparation and test center, learning center, reduced course load, remedial instruction, study skills assistance, tutoring.

Majors. **Business:** Business admin, marketing, office management. **Computer sciences:** Applications programming, information technology, networking, programming, systems analysis, vendor certification. **Health:** Dental hygiene, EMT paramedic, nursing (RN), radiologic technology/medical imaging. **Legal studies:** Paralegal. **Liberal arts:** Arts/sciences. **Protective services:** Law enforcement admin. **Public administration:** Human services.

Most popular majors. Computer/information sciences 6%, health sciences 20%, liberal arts 66%.

Computing on campus. 1,595 workstations in library, computer center. Online course registration, online library available.

Student life. **Freshman orientation:** Mandatory. 3- to 4-hour program held on variety of days, nights, Saturdays. **Policies:** Freshmen permitted cars on campus. **Activities:** Choral groups, drama, literary magazine, music ensembles, student government, human services club, drama club, student nursing club, writers' club, Phi Beta Lambda (business), Phi Theta Kappa, Delta Epsilon Chi, Psi Beta (psychology club), STRIKE (Student Tobacco Reform Initiative), computer club.

Athletics. NJCAA. **Intercollegiate:** Baseball M, basketball M, softball W, tennis W, volleyball W. **Team name:** Conquistadors.

Student services. Career counseling, services for economically disadvantaged, financial aid counseling, minority student services, on-campus daycare, personal counseling, placement for graduates, veterans' counselor. **Physically disabled:** Services for visually, speech, hearing impaired. **Transfer:** Special adviser, orientation for new students. College fairs on campus for students transferring to 4-year colleges.

Contact. E-mail: bullard@phcc.edu
Phone: (727) 816-3261 Toll-free number: (877) 879-7422
Fax: (727) 816-3389
Debra Bullard, Director of Admissions and Student Records, Pasco-Hernando Community College, 10230 Ridge Road, New Port Richey, FL 34654-5199

Pensacola Junior College
Pensacola, Florida **CB member**
www.pjc.edu **CB code: 5535**

- Public 2-year community college
- Commuter campus in small city

General. Founded in 1948. Regionally accredited. Additional campuses: Milton, Warrington, Downtown Center, NAS Center. **Enrollment:** 9,715 degree-seeking undergraduates. **Degrees:** 1,830 associate awarded. **ROTC:** Army. **Location:** 60 miles from Mobile, Alabama. **Calendar:** Semester, extensive summer session. **Full-time faculty:** 230 total. **Part-time faculty:** 570 total. **Special facilities:** Science and space theater.

Student profile.

Out-of-state:	2%	**25 or older:**	50%

Basis for selection. Open admission, but selective for some programs. Special requirements for health programs. Florida Entry Level Placement Test must be taken for admission; student may submit SAT or ACT in its place. Scores used for placement only.

High school preparation. 24 units recommended. Recommended units include English 4, mathematics 3, social studies 3, science 3, foreign language 2 and academic electives 11. College preparatory program required for associate of arts program: 13 academic units including 4 English, 3 science, 3 mathematics, and 3 social science.

2005-2006 Annual costs. Tuition/fees: $1,871; $6,588 out-of-state. Per-credit charge: $52 in-state; $200 out-of-state. Books/supplies: $800. Personal expenses: $1,100.

Financial aid. **Non-need-based:** Scholarships awarded for academics, athletics, state residency.

Application procedures. **Admission:** No deadline. $30 fee. Admission notification on a rolling basis. **Financial aid:** Priority date 4/1; no closing date. FAFSA, institutional form required. Applicants notified on a rolling basis starting 7/1; must reply within 2 week(s) of notification.

Academics. **Special study options:** Accelerated study, cooperative education, cross-registration, distance learning, double major, dual enrollment of high school students, ESL, honors, independent study, internships, study abroad, weekend college. License preparation in dental hygiene, nursing, paramedic, radiology. **Credit/placement by examination:** AP, CLEP, IB, institutional tests. 39 credit hours maximum toward associate degree. **Support services:** GED preparation and test center, learning center, reduced course load, remedial instruction, study skills assistance, tutoring, writing center.

Majors. **Agriculture:** General, ornamental horticulture. **Biology:** General, biochemistry, botany, zoology. **Business:** General, accounting, administrative services, banking/financial services, business admin, hospitality/recreation, management information systems, management science, office management. **Communications:** General, journalism. **Communications technology:** General. **Computer sciences:** General, computer science, information systems, programming. **Conservation:** Forest resources, forestry, management/policy. **Construction:** Maintenance. **Education:** General, art, early childhood, elementary, music, physical, special. **Engineering:** General, chemical, civil, computer, electrical. **Engineering technology:** Civil, construction, electrical, hazardous materials, manufacturing. **Family/consumer sciences:** Advocacy, child care, food/nutrition, institutional food production. **Health:** Dental hygiene, EMT paramedic, health care admin, medical radiologic technology/radiation therapy, medical records admin, nursing (RN), physical therapy assistant, predentistry, premedicine, prenursing, prepharmacy, preveterinary, sonography. **History:** General. **Legal studies:** Legal secretary, paralegal, prelaw. **Liberal arts:** Arts/sciences. **Math:** General. **Mechanic/repair:** Automotive. **Personal/culinary services:** Culinary arts. **Philosophy/religion:** Philosophy, religion. **Physical sciences:** Chemistry, geology, physics. **Protective services:** Firefighting, law enforcement admin. **Psychology:** General. **Science technology:** Chemical. **Social sciences:** Sociology. **Visual/performing arts:** Art, commercial/advertising art, dramatic.

Computing on campus. 1,437 workstations in library, computer center.

Student life. **Freshman orientation:** Mandatory. **Activities:** Bands, choral groups, dance, drama, literary magazine, music ensembles, musical theater, student government, student newspaper, symphony orchestra, TV station, Baptist campus ministry, Florida African-American Student Association, Wesley Foundation, International Club, Phi Theta Kappa, Campus Activities Board, Students for Multi-Cultural Society.

Athletics. NJCAA. **Intercollegiate:** Baseball M, basketball, cheerleading, softball W, volleyball W. **Intramural:** Archery, badminton, basketball, bowling, racquetball, skin diving, soccer, softball W, table tennis, tennis, volleyball, water polo, weight lifting. **Team name:** Pirates.

Student services. Adult student services, alcohol/substance abuse counseling, campus ministries, career counseling, services for economically disadvantaged, student employment services, financial aid counseling, health services, minority student services, on-campus daycare, personal counseling, placement for graduates, veterans' counselor, women's services. **Physically disabled:** Services for visually, speech, hearing impaired. **Transfer:** Special adviser, orientation, pre-admission transcript evaluation for new students. Transfer adviser, college fairs on campus for students transferring to 4-year colleges.

Contact. Phone: (850) 484-1601 Fax: (850) 484-1829
Martha Coughey, Registrar, Pensacola Junior College, 1000 College Boulevard, Pensacola, FL 32504-8998

Polk Community College

Winter Haven, Florida
www.polk.edu

CB member
CB code: 5548

- Public 2-year community college
- Commuter campus in large town

General. Founded in 1963. Regionally accredited. Branch campus in Lakeland shared with University of South Florida. **Enrollment:** 6,018 degree-seeking undergraduates; 1,051 non-degree-seeking students. **Degrees:** 731 associate awarded. **ROTC:** Army. **Location:** 60 miles from Tampa, 60 miles from Orlando. **Calendar:** Semester, extensive summer session. **Full-time faculty:** 133 total; 18% have terminal degrees, 16% minority, 51% women. **Part-time faculty:** 465 total; 4% have terminal degrees, 12% minority, 55% women. **Class size:** 35% < 20, 64% 20-39, less than 1% 50-99, less than 1% >100.

Student profile. Among degree-seeking undergraduates, 26% enrolled in a vocational program, 1,118 enrolled as first-time, first-year students, 230 transferred in from other institutions.

Part-time:	68%	**Asian American:**	2%
Out-of-state:	1%	**Hispanic American:**	8%
Women:	67%	**International:**	4%
African American:	14%	**25 or older:**	35%

Transfer out. **Colleges most students transferred to 2005:** University of South Florida, University of Central Florida, University of Florida, Florida State University, Florida Southern College.

Basis for selection. Open admission, but selective for some programs. Limited access to nursing, radiology, physical therapy assistant, occupational therapy assistant, and paramedic programs. Require Levels of English Proficiency (LOEP) for placement of non-native English speakers. Audition recommended for theater, music majors. Portfolio recommended for graphic arts majors. **Adult students:** Entrance exam policies same as for first-time freshmen. **Homeschooled:** PCC adheres to FLDOE policy and Florida state statute: Only an affidavit signed by the guardian attesting to home school applicant completion is required in place of the high school diploma.

High school preparation. Recommended units include English 4, mathematics 4, social studies 3, science 3 and foreign language 2.

2005-2006 Annual costs. Tuition/fees: $1,841; $7,043 out-of-state. Per-credit charge: $52 in-state; $210 out-of-state. Books/supplies: $1,200. Personal expenses: $800.

2004-2005 Financial aid. **Need-based:** 79% of total undergraduate aid awarded as scholarships/grants, 21% as loans/jobs. Need-based aid available for part-time students. Work study available nights, weekends and for part-time students. **Non-need-based:** Scholarships awarded for academics, athletics, leadership, state residency.

Application procedures. **Admission:** No deadline. $20 fee. Application may be submitted online. Admission notification on a rolling basis. **Financial aid:** Priority date 5/15; no closing date. FAFSA required. Applicants notified on a rolling basis.

Academics. **Special study options:** Accelerated study, cross-registration, distance learning, double major, dual enrollment of high school students, ESL, honors, independent study, internships. License preparation in nursing, occupational therapy, paramedic, physical therapy, radiology. **Credit/placement by examination:** AP, CLEP, IB, institutional tests. 45 credit hours maximum toward associate degree. CPT required of all without college credit in Mathematics, English, Reading. **Support services:** Learning center, reduced course load, remedial instruction, study skills assistance, tutoring.

Honors college/program. High School grads who have a 3.5 GPA from high school may apply for honors program and designated courses.

Majors. **Business:** Accounting, administrative services, banking/financial services, business admin, marketing, office management, office/clerical. **Computer sciences:** General, computer graphics, information systems, programming. **Construction:** Power transmission. **Education:** General. **Engineering technology:** Electrical. **Family/consumer sciences:** Child care. **Health:** EMT paramedic, medical records admin, medical records technology, nursing (RN), occupational therapy assistant, physical therapy assistant, respiratory therapy technology. **Liberal arts:** Arts/sciences. **Mechanic/repair:** Computer. **Protective services:** Criminal justice, firefighting, police science.

Most popular majors. Health sciences 18%, liberal arts 69%.

Computing on campus. 171 workstations in library, computer center, student center. Online course registration available.

Student life. **Freshman orientation:** Available. Preregistration for classes offered. **Activities:** Bands, choral groups, drama, music ensembles, musical theater, student government.

Athletics. NJCAA. **Intercollegiate:** Baseball M, basketball M, soccer W, softball W, volleyball W. **Intramural:** Basketball, bowling, football (non-tackle), table tennis, volleyball W. **Team name:** Vikings.

Student services. Adult student services, career counseling, services for economically disadvantaged, student employment services, financial aid counseling, veterans' counselor. **Physically disabled:** Services for visually, speech, hearing impaired. **Transfer:** Special adviser, orientation, re-entry adviser for new students. Transfer adviser, college fairs on campus for students transferring to 4-year colleges.

Contact. E-mail: StudentServices@polk.edu
Phone: (863) 297-1010 ext. 5225 Fax: (863) 297-1060
Barbara Guthrie, College Registrar/Admission Director, Polk Community College, 999 Avenue H NE, Winter Haven, FL 33881-4299

Professional Golfers Career College: Orlando

Winter Garden, Florida
www.golfcollege.edu

- For-profit 2-year branch campus and junior college
- Very large city

General. Accredited by ACICS. **Calendar:** Semester.

Annual costs/financial aid. Tuition/fees: $15,795.

Contact. Phone: (407) 905-2200
26109 Ynez Road, Temecula, CA 92591

St. Johns River Community College

Palatka, Florida **CB member**
www.sjrcc.cc.fl.us **CB code: 5641**

- Public 2-year community college
- Commuter campus in large town

General. Founded in 1957. Regionally accredited. **Enrollment:** 3,268 degree-seeking undergraduates. **Degrees:** 521 associate awarded. **Location:** 55 miles from Jacksonville and Daytona Beach. **Calendar:** Trimester, limited summer session. **Full-time faculty:** 106 total. **Part-time faculty:** 153 total.

Basis for selection. Open admission, but selective for some programs. Interview, audition, and portfolio required of applicants to Florida School of Arts program.

High school preparation. 24 units recommended. Recommended units include English 4, mathematics 3, social studies 3 and science 3.

2005-2006 Annual costs. Tuition/fees: $2,006; $6,920 out-of-state. Per-credit charge: $55 in-state; $218 out-of-state. $614 required fees for out-of-state students. Books/supplies: $752. Personal expenses: $87.

2005-2006 Financial aid. Need-based: 70% of total undergraduate aid awarded as scholarships/grants, 30% as loans/jobs. Need-based aid available for part-time students.

Application procedures. Admission: Priority date 7/15; no deadline. $20 fee. Admission notification on a rolling basis. **Financial aid:** Priority date 5/15; no closing date. FAFSA required. Applicants notified on a rolling basis.

Academics. Special study options: Dual enrollment of high school students. **Credit/placement by examination:** AP, CLEP. 45 credit hours maximum toward associate degree. **Support services:** Remedial instruction, tutoring.

Majors. Business: Accounting, accounting technology, administrative services, business admin. **Computer sciences:** Programming, systems analysis. **Engineering technology:** Electrical. **Health:** EMT paramedic. **Liberal arts:** Arts/sciences. **Protective services:** Fire safety technology. **Visual/performing arts:** General.

Student life. Activities: Student government, student newspaper, Black Student Union, Circle-K, Compass Club, future educators, Phi Beta Lamba, Mathematical Association of America.

Athletics. NJCAA. **Intercollegiate:** Baseball M, basketball M, softball W. **Intramural:** Table tennis.

Student services. Career counseling, personal counseling, placement for graduates, veterans' counselor. **Physically disabled:** Services for speech impaired.

Contact. Phone: (386) 312-4030 Fax: (386) 312-4048
O'Neal Williams, Admission and Records, St. Johns River Community College, 5001 St. Johns Avenue, Palatka, FL 32177-3897

St. Petersburg College

St. Petersburg, Florida **CB member**
www.spcollege.edu **CB code: 5606**

- Public 2-year community college
- Commuter campus in large city

General. Founded in 1927. Regionally accredited. Campuses include Clearwater, Seminole, St. Petersburg, Tarpon Springs. Health education center in Pinellas Park. Criminal justice/computer complex in St. Petersburg. Corporate training and Cisco at the Epicenter. **Enrollment:** 19,822 degree-seeking undergraduates; 4,560 non-degree-seeking students. **Degrees:** 223 bachelor's, 2,521 associate awarded. **Location:** 20 miles from Tampa. **Calendar:** Semester, extensive summer session. **Full-time faculty:** 313 total; 14% minority, 58% women. **Part-time faculty:** 1,599 total; 6% have terminal degrees. **Special facilities:** Observatory, planetarium, firing range. **Partnerships:** Formal agreements with 14 colleges and universities through University Partnership Program.

Student profile. Among degree-seeking undergraduates, 3,347 enrolled as first-time, first-year students.

Part-time:	65%	**Hispanic American:**	5%
Out-of-state:	4%	**Native American:**	1%
Women:	63%	**International:**	1%
African American:	12%	**25 or older:**	47%
Asian American:	3%		

Transfer out. 80% of students enrolled in the transfer program go on to 4-year colleges.

Basis for selection. Open admission, but selective for some programs. Limited enrollment to health-related programs. Florida CPT required for all degree-seeking students. Interview recommended for allied health applicants. Essay required for B.S. College of Education applicants. **Homeschooled:** Transcript of courses and grades, state high school equivalency certificate required.

2005-2006 Annual costs. Tuition/fees: $1,983; $6,924 out-of-state. Per-credit charge: $55 in-state; $219 out-of-state. Books/supplies: $1,000. Personal expenses: $2,780.

Financial aid. Need-based: Need-based aid available for part-time students. Work study available nights and for part-time students. **Non-need-based:** Scholarships awarded for academics, art, athletics, minority status, music/drama.

Application procedures. Admission: No deadline. $35 fee. Application may be submitted online. Admission notification on a rolling basis. **Financial aid:** Priority date 4/15; no closing date. FAFSA, institutional form required. Applicants notified on a rolling basis starting 5/15; must reply within 2 week(s) of notification.

Academics. Special study options: Accelerated study, cooperative education, cross-registration, distance learning, dual enrollment of high school students, ESL, exchange student, honors, independent study, internships, liberal arts/career combination, study abroad, teacher certification program, weekend college. 2-year associate degree program in business and computer science for deaf students. Bachelor's degree programs available on campus. License preparation in dental hygiene, nursing, paramedic, physical therapy, radiology. **Credit/placement by examination:** AP, CLEP, IB, institutional tests. 45 credit hours maximum toward associate degree, 45 toward bachelor's. Florida CPT required for placement. **Support services:** Learning center, reduced course load, remedial instruction, study skills assistance, tutoring.

Majors. Business: General, accounting technology, business admin, hospitality admin, marketing. **Computer sciences:** Computer science, database management, information technology, networking, programming, web page design, webmaster. **Education:** Early childhood. **Engineering technology:** Architectural drafting, computer, drafting, electrical, industrial, manufacturing, telecommunications. **Foreign languages:** Sign language interpretation. **Health:** Clinical lab technology, dental hygiene, EMT paramedic, health services, medical records admin, nursing (RN), physical therapy assistant, radiologic technology/medical imaging, respiratory therapy technology, substance abuse counseling, veterinary technology/assistant. **Legal studies:** Paralegal. **Liberal arts:** Arts/sciences. **Mechanic/repair:** Automotive. **Personal/culinary services:** Mortuary science. **Protective services:** Correctional facilities, criminalistics, fire safety technology, forensics, law enforcement admin, security management, security services. **Public administration:** Human services. **Transportation:** Aviation management. **Visual/performing arts:** Graphic design.

Most popular majors. Health sciences 17%, liberal arts 79%.

Computing on campus. 4,129 workstations in library, computer center, student center. Commuter students can connect to campus network. Online course registration, online library, helpline, student web hosting, wireless network available.

Student life. Freshman orientation: Mandatory. Preregistration for classes offered. **Policies:** Freshmen permitted cars on campus. **Activities:** Jazz band, choral groups, dance, drama, literary magazine, music ensembles, student government, student newspaper, Phi Theta Kappa, Harambee Black culture club, student government association, ethics club, math and science Club, Silent Titans (American Sign Language), international friendship society.

Athletics. NJCAA. **Intercollegiate:** Baseball M, basketball, softball W, volleyball. **Intramural:** Basketball, bowling, golf, table tennis, tennis, volleyball W, water polo M. **Team name:** Titans.

Student services. Career counseling, services for economically disadvantaged, student employment services, financial aid counseling, health services, minority student services, personal counseling, placement for graduates, veterans' counselor, women's services. **Physically disabled:** Services for visually, speech, hearing impaired. **Transfer:** Special adviser, orientation for new students. College fairs on campus for students transferring to 4-year colleges.

Contact. Phone: (727) 341-4792
Martyn Clay, College Registrar, St. Petersburg College, Box 13489, St. Petersburg, FL 33733

Sanford-Brown Institute: Jacksonville

Jacksonville, Florida
www.sbjacksonville.com

- For-profit 2-year health science college
- Commuter campus in large city
- Application essay, interview required

General. Accredited by ACICS. **Enrollment:** 330 undergraduates. **Degrees:** 10 associate awarded. **Calendar:** Continuous. **Full-time faculty:** 7 total. **Part-time faculty:** 30 total.

Basis for selection. Homeschooled: Statement describing homeschool structure and mission, transcript of courses and grades, state high school equivalency certificate, interview, letter of recommendation (nonparent) required.

Application procedures. Admission: No deadline. $25 fee. Application may be submitted online. Admission notification on a rolling basis.

Academics. Credit/placement by examination: CLEP. **Support services:** Learning center, reduced course load, study skills assistance, tutoring.

Majors. Health: Cardiovascular technology.

Computing on campus. 60 workstations in library, computer center, student center. Commuter students can connect to campus network.

Student life. Freshman orientation: Mandatory. Preregistration for classes offered. **Policies:** Freshmen permitted cars on campus.

Student services. Adult student services, career counseling, student employment services, financial aid counseling, health services, personal counseling, placement for graduates. **Physically disabled:** Services for speech, hearing impaired. **Transfer:** Orientation for new students.

Contact. E-mail: tahmed@sbjacksonville.com
Phone: (904) 363-6221
Tanveer Ahmed, Director of Admissions, Sanford-Brown Institute: Jacksonville, 10255 Fortune Parkway, Suite 501, Jacksonville, FL 32256

Sanford-Brown Institute: Tampa

Tampa, Florida
www.sbtampa.edu

- For-profit 2-year health science and community college
- Large city

General. Accredited by ACICS. **Calendar:** Continuous.

Contact. Phone: (813) 621-0072
Director of Admissions, 5701 East Hillsboro Avenue, Tampa, FL 33610

Santa Fe Community College

Gainesville, Florida — **CB member**
www.santafe.sfcc.edu — **CB code: 5653**

- Public 2-year community college
- Commuter campus in small city

General. Founded in 1965. Regionally accredited. Branch campuses located downtown and in Starke. **Enrollment:** 6,880 degree-seeking undergraduates. **Degrees:** 2,340 associate awarded. **ROTC:** Army, Navy, Air Force. **Location:** 80 miles from Jacksonville, 80 miles from Orlando. **Calendar:** Semester, extensive summer session. **Full-time faculty:** 266 total. **Part-time faculty:** 374 total. **Special facilities:** Teaching zoo.

Student profile.

Out-of-state:	3%	**25 or older:**	28%

Basis for selection. Open admission, but selective for some programs. Nursing program requires 5 prerequisite courses. Radiologic technology and dental hygiene applicants selected by admissions committee. Radiation therapy students must have X-ray or nuclear medicine license and experience. Computerized Placement Tests may be submitted in place of SAT or ACT.

High school preparation. Recommended units include foreign language 2.

2005-2006 Annual costs. Tuition/fees: $1,900; $7,041 out-of-state. Per-credit charge: $52 in-state; $210 out-of-state. Books/supplies: $700. Personal expenses: $1,008.

Financial aid. Need-based: Need-based aid available for part-time students. **Non-need-based:** Scholarships awarded for academics, art, athletics, leadership, minority status, music/drama, state residency.

Application procedures. Admission: No deadline. $30 fee. Application may be submitted online. Admission notification on a rolling basis. High school diploma not required of applicants to most vocational programs. **Financial aid:** Priority date 3/15, closing date 6/30. FAFSA required. Applicants notified by 8/1.

Academics. Special study options: Cooperative education, cross-registration, distance learning, dual enrollment of high school students, ESL, honors, independent study, weekend college. **Credit/placement by examination:** AP, CLEP, institutional tests. 30 credit hours maximum toward associate degree. **Support services:** GED preparation, learning center, remedial instruction, tutoring.

Majors. Agriculture: Ornamental horticulture. **Biology:** Botany. **Business:** Accounting, administrative services, banking/financial services, business admin, fashion, marketing, office technology, office/clerical. **Computer sciences:** Data processing, programming. **Construction:** Maintenance. **Education:** Early childhood. **Engineering technology:** Drafting, electrical. **Family/consumer sciences:** Child care. **Health:** Dental hygiene, EMT paramedic, medical radiologic technology/radiation therapy, medical secretary, nuclear medical technology, nursing (RN), predentistry, premedicine, prepharmacy, respiratory therapy technology. **Legal studies:** Legal secretary, paralegal. **Liberal arts:** Arts/sciences. **Parks/recreation:** Exercise sciences, facilities management. **Physical sciences:** Astronomy, chemistry. **Protective services:** Fire safety technology, forensics. **Social sciences:** Anthropology. **Visual/performing arts:** Commercial/advertising art, fashion design.

Most popular majors. Health sciences 10%, liberal arts 77%.

Student life. Freshman orientation: Available. **Activities:** Choral groups, dance, drama, music ensembles, musical theater, radio station, student government, student newspaper, TV station, Black Student Union, Phi Theta Kappa.

Athletics. NJCAA. **Intercollegiate:** Baseball M, basketball, softball W. **Intramural:** Basketball, racquetball. **Team name:** Saints.

Student services. Career counseling, student employment services, health services, on-campus daycare, personal counseling, placement for graduates, veterans' counselor. **Physically disabled:** Services for visually, speech, hearing impaired. **Transfer:** Special adviser, orientation for new students. Transfer adviser for students transferring to 4-year colleges.

Contact. E-mail: information@sfcc.edu
Phone: (352) 395-7322 Fax: (352) 395-5581
Margaret Karrh, Director of Enrollment Services, Santa Fe Community College, 3000 NW 83rd Street, Gainesville, FL 32606

Seminole Community College

Sanford, Florida
www.scc-fl.edu **CB code: 5662**

- Public 2-year community college
- Commuter campus in large town

General. Founded in 1965. Regionally accredited. **Enrollment:** 9,951 degree-seeking undergraduates; 1,456 non-degree-seeking students. **Degrees:** 1,246 associate awarded. **Location:** 21 miles from Orlando. **Calendar:** Semester, limited summer session. **Full-time faculty:** 678 total; 6% have terminal degrees, 28% minority, 63% women. **Part-time faculty:** 944 total; 6% have terminal degrees, 22% minority, 56% women. **Special facilities:** Planetarium, art museum. **Partnerships:** Formal partnerships with Siemens/Stromberg, local businesses.

Student profile. Among degree-seeking undergraduates, 2,110 enrolled as first-time, first-year students, 2,718 transferred in from other institutions.

Part-time:	59%	**Women:**	60%
Out-of-state:	3%	**25 or older:**	48%

Basis for selection. Open admission, but selective for some programs. Limited access to associate of science degrees including nursing, physical therapy, and respiratory care. English competency required of non-native speakers. Students may provide TOEFL or LOEP scores or certificate of completion of ESOL/ESL training or SCC will test to determine placement. College credit entry students need ACT or SAT scores less than 2 years old, or must take a state placement test, CPT, for placement purposes. Interview recommended for respiratory therapy, nursing, physical therapy majors, international students. **Adult students:** Entrance exam policies same as for first-time freshmen.

High school preparation. 24 units required. Required units include English 4, mathematics 3, social studies 3, science 3 and academic electives 11.

2005-2006 Annual costs. Tuition/fees: $2,080; $7,351 out-of-state. Per-credit charge: $53 in-state; $214 out-of-state. Books/supplies: $1,200. Personal expenses: $900.

2004-2005 Financial aid. Need-based: 54% of total undergraduate aid awarded as scholarships/grants, 46% as loans/jobs. Need-based aid available for part-time students. Work study available for part-time students. **Non-need-based:** Scholarships awarded for academics, art, athletics, leadership, minority status, music/drama, state residency.

Application procedures. Admission: Closing date 9/24 (receipt date). No application fee. Admission notification on a rolling basis. **Financial aid:** No deadline. FAFSA required. Applicants notified on a rolling basis starting 4/1.

Academics. Special study options: Accelerated study, cooperative education, cross-registration, distance learning, dual enrollment of high school students, ESL, honors, independent study, study abroad, teacher certification program, weekend college. **Credit/placement by examination:** AP, CLEP, IB, institutional tests. 45 credit hours maximum toward associate degree. **Support services:** GED preparation and test center, learning center, reduced course load, remedial instruction, study skills assistance, tutoring.

Majors. Architecture: Interior. **Business:** Administrative services, banking/financial services. **Communications:** General. **Communications technology:** General. **Computer sciences:** General, applications programming, computer graphics, computer science, data processing, information systems, networking, programming, systems analysis. **Conservation:** General. **Education:** Kindergarten/preschool. **Engineering:** Electrical, software. **Engineering technology:** Architectural, construction, electrical. **Family/consumer sciences:** Child care. **Health:** EMT paramedic, medical secretary, nursing (RN), physical therapy assistant, respiratory therapy technology. **Legal studies:** Legal secretary, paralegal. **Liberal arts:** Arts/sciences. **Mechanic/repair:** Automotive. **Protective services:** Firefighting, law enforcement admin. **Visual/performing arts:** Interior design.

Computing on campus. 100 workstations in library, computer center. Commuter students can connect to campus network. Online course registration, online library, student web hosting, wireless network available.

Student life. Freshman orientation: Mandatory. Preregistration for classes offered. **Policies:** Freshmen permitted cars on campus. **Activities:** Bands, choral groups, drama, film society, literary magazine, music ensembles, musical theater, student government, student newspaper, symphony orchestra, African American cultural forum, College Republicans, disabled students lead, Hispanic student associations, international student organization, Muslim student association, Unity Organization, Fellowship of Christian Athletes, Latter-day Saint student association.

Athletics. NJCAA. **Intercollegiate:** Baseball M, basketball, softball W. **Team name:** Raider.

Student services. Adult student services, alcohol/substance abuse counseling, career counseling, services for economically disadvantaged, student employment services, financial aid counseling, personal counseling, placement for graduates, veterans' counselor. **Physically disabled:** Services for visually, speech, hearing impaired. **Transfer:** Special adviser, orientation for new students. Transfer adviser for students transferring to 4-year colleges.

Contact. E-mail: admissions@scc-fl.edu
Phone: (407) 708-2580 Fax: (407) 708-2395
Pamela Mennechey, Director of Admissions, Seminole Community College, 100 Weldon Boulevard, Sanford, FL 32773-6199

South Florida Community College

Avon Park, Florida **CB member**
www.southflorida.edu **CB code: 5666**

- Public 2-year community and technical college
- Commuter campus in small town

General. Founded in 1965. Regionally accredited. **Enrollment:** 1,689 degree-seeking undergraduates; 692 non-degree-seeking students. **Degrees:** 267 associate awarded. **Location:** 90 miles from Orlando. **Calendar:** Semester, limited summer session. **Full-time faculty:** 63 total; 21% have terminal degrees, 8% minority, 54% women. **Part-time faculty:** 163 total; 5% have terminal degrees, 17% minority, 50% women. **Class size:** 69% < 20, 30% 20-39, 1% 40-49. **Special facilities:** Museum of Florida Art and Culture.

Student profile. Among degree-seeking undergraduates, 60% enrolled in a transfer program, 40% enrolled in a vocational program, 365 enrolled as first-time, first-year students, 127 transferred in from other institutions.

Part-time:	65%	**Hispanic American:**	17%
Out-of-state:	2%	**Native American:**	1%
Women:	66%	**International:**	1%
African American:	10%	**25 or older:**	25%
Asian American:	2%	**Live on campus:**	2%

Basis for selection. Open admission. Some selected programs have additional test and pre-requisite requirements. Additional requirements include health screening and financial ability. SAT or ACT recommended. FCELPT can be used in place of SAT or ACT. Interview recommended for selected programs. **Adult students:** Entrance exam policies same as for first-time freshmen. TABE, FCELPT. **Homeschooled:** Students must meet with Registrar prior to admission. **Learning Disabled:** Recommend that students seek assistance from campus disabilities specialist.

High school preparation. College-preparatory program recommended. 13 units required. Required and recommended units include English 4, mathematics 3, social studies 3 and science 3.

2005-2006 Annual costs. Tuition/fees: $1,933; $7,257 out-of-state. Per-credit charge: $52 in-state; $210 out-of-state. $ 660 required fees for out-of-state students. Room/board: $2,654. Books/supplies: $882. Personal expenses: $1,577.

Financial aid. Need-based: Need-based aid available for part-time students. Work study available for part-time students. **Non-need-based:** Scholarships awarded for academics, athletics, leadership, minority status, music/drama, state residency.

Application procedures. Admission: No deadline. No application fee. Admission notification on a rolling basis. **Financial aid:** Priority date 3/15; no closing date. FAFSA required. Applicants notified on a rolling basis starting 4/1.

Academics. Special study options: Accelerated study, cooperative education, distance learning, double major, dual enrollment of high school students, ESL, external degree, honors, independent study, internships. Bachelor's degree programs available on campus. **Credit/placement by examination:** AP, CLEP, IB, institutional tests. 30 credit hours maximum toward associate degree. **Support services:** GED preparation and test center, learning center, reduced course load, remedial instruction, study skills assistance, tutoring, writing center.

Majors. Agriculture: General, agribusiness operations, horticultural science, ornamental horticulture. **Business:** Accounting, administrative services, business admin, hospitality admin. **Computer sciences:** LAN/WAN management, programming. **Construction:** General, power transmission. **Education:** Teacher assistance. **Engineering technology:** Biomedical, computer hardware, drafting, electrical. **Family/consumer sciences:** Child care.

Health: Dental hygiene, EMT paramedic, medical secretary, nursing (RN). **Liberal arts:** Arts/sciences. **Protective services:** Law enforcement admin.

Most popular majors. Health sciences 11%, liberal arts 77%.

Computing on campus. 100 workstations in library, computer center, student center. Online course registration, online library, helpline, repair service, wireless network available.

Student life. Freshman orientation: Mandatory. Preregistration for classes offered. **Policies:** Freshmen permitted cars on campus. **Housing:** Coed dorms, substance-free housing available. **Activities:** Concert band, music ensembles, student government, student newspaper, symphony orchestra, Adventist social club, Hispanic student organization, African American association.

Athletics. NJCAA. **Intercollegiate:** Baseball M, softball W, volleyball W. **Team name:** Panthers.

Student services. Adult student services, career counseling, services for economically disadvantaged, student employment services, financial aid counseling, minority student services, personal counseling, placement for graduates, veterans' counselor, women's services. **Physically disabled:** Services for visually, speech, hearing impaired. **Transfer:** Special adviser, orientation for new students. Transfer adviser, college fairs on campus for students transferring to 4-year colleges.

Contact. E-mail: laura.white@southflorida.edu
Phone: (863) 453-6661 ext. 7408 Fax: (863) 453-2365
Laura White, Associate Dean, Admissions, Enrollment Management, University Relations, South Florida Community College, 600 West College Drive, Avon Park, FL 33825

Southwest Florida College

Ft. Myers, Florida
www.swfc.edu **CB code: 3445**

- Private 2-year junior college
- Residential campus in small city
- Interview required

General. Accredited by ACICS. Additional campus in Tampa. **Enrollment:** 1,198 degree-seeking undergraduates; 44 non-degree-seeking students. **Degrees:** 361 associate awarded. **Location:** 130 miles from Tampa. **Calendar:** Quarter, extensive summer session. **Full-time faculty:** 38 total; 16% have terminal degrees, 8% minority, 55% women. **Part-time faculty:** 69 total; 7% have terminal degrees, 7% minority, 49% women.

Student profile. Among degree-seeking undergraduates, 184 enrolled as first-time, first-year students, 16 transferred in from other institutions.

Part-time:	36%	**Hispanic American:**	21%
Women:	74%	**Native American:**	1%
African American:	19%	**International:**	1%
Asian American:	1%	**25 or older:**	52%

Transfer out. Colleges most students transferred to 2005: International College.

Basis for selection. Open admission, but selective for some programs. Microsoft Network Engineer program requires passing scores in technical and scholastic exam pior to acceptance. **Adult students:** Entrance exam policies same as for first-time freshmen.

2005-2006 Annual costs. Expenses vary with programs. Books/ supplies: $1,725. Personal expenses: $1,551.

Financial aid. Need-based: Need-based aid available for part-time students. Work study available nights and for part-time students.

Application procedures. Admission: No deadline. $25 fee. Application must be submitted on paper. Admission notification on a rolling basis. **Financial aid:** Priority date 4/15; no closing date. FAFSA required. Applicants notified on a rolling basis.

Academics. Special study options: Cooperative education, distance learning, double major, liberal arts/career combination, weekend college. **Credit/ placement by examination:** AP, CLEP, institutional tests. 24 credit hours maximum toward associate degree. **Support services:** Learning center, reduced course load, remedial instruction, study skills assistance, tutoring.

Majors. Business: Accounting, business admin, hospitality/recreation. **Computer sciences:** General, computer graphics, security. **Education:** Early childhood. **Engineering:** Computer. **Engineering technology:** Drafting. **Health:** Medical assistant, medical secretary, medical transcription, pharmacy assistant, surgical technology. **Legal studies:** General, paralegal. **Protective services:** Criminal justice.

Computing on campus. 194 workstations in library, computer center, student center. Online library, wireless network available.

Student life. Freshman orientation: Mandatory. **Policies:** Freshmen permitted cars on campus.

Student services. Adult student services, career counseling, student employment services, financial aid counseling, placement for graduates. **Physically disabled:** Services for visually, speech, hearing impaired. **Learning disabled:** Comprehensive services available. **Transfer:** Special adviser, orientation, pre-admission transcript evaluation for new students.

Contact. E-mail: ccordisco@swfc.edu
Phone: (239) 939-4766 Toll-free number: (866) 793-2669
Fax: (239) 936-4040
CarmenJean Cordisco, Director of Admissions, Southwest Florida College, 1685 Medical Lane, Ft. Myers, FL 33907-1108

Southwest Florida College: Tampa

Tampa, Florida
www.swfc.edu

- Private 2-year branch campus and junior college
- Commuter campus in very large city

General. Accredited by ACICS. Institution is a branch campus of Southwest Florida College, Ft. Myers. **Enrollment:** 649 degree-seeking undergraduates; 3 non-degree-seeking students. **Degrees:** 167 associate awarded. **Location:** 15 miles from downtown. **Calendar:** Quarter, extensive summer session. **Full-time faculty:** 15 total; 20% minority, 60% women. **Part-time faculty:** 22 total; 18% minority, 23% women. **Class size:** 77% < 20, 23% 20-39.

Student profile. Among degree-seeking undergraduates, 103 enrolled as first-time, first-year students.

Part-time:	28%	**Hispanic American:**	22%
Women:	68%	**Native American:**	1%
African American:	27%	**25 or older:**	49%
Asian American:	2%		

Basis for selection. Open admission.

2005-2006 Annual costs. Expenses vary by program.

Application procedures. Admission: No deadline. $25 fee, may be waived for applicants with need. Admission notification on a rolling basis.

Academics. Special study options: Cooperative education, distance learning, double major, dual enrollment of high school students, internships. **Credit/ placement by examination:** CLEP, institutional tests. 24 credit hours maximum toward associate degree. **Support services:** Learning center, reduced course load, remedial instruction, study skills assistance, tutoring, writing center.

Majors. Business: Accounting, marketing. **Computer sciences:** Computer graphics, information systems. **Education:** Early childhood. **Engineering technology:** Computer, drafting. **Health:** Medical assistant, office admin, pharmacy assistant, surgical technology. **Legal studies:** Paralegal. **Protective services:** Criminal justice.

Most popular majors. Business/marketing 8%, computer/information sciences 12%, engineering/engineering technologies 11%, health sciences 57%, legal studies 6%, security/protective services 6%.

Computing on campus. Online library, wireless network available.

Student life. Freshman orientation: Mandatory. Preregistration for classes offered. **Activities:** Student newspaper.

Student services. Career counseling, student employment services, financial aid counseling, placement for graduates, veterans' counselor.

Contact. Phone: (813) 630-4401 Toll-free number: (877) 907-2456
Patrick McDermott, Vice President of Admissions, Southwest Florida College: Tampa, 3910 Riga Boulevard, Tampa, FL 33619

Stenotype Institute: Jacksonville

Jacksonville, Florida
www.thestenotypeinstitute.com

- For-profit 2-year business and community college
- Very large city

General. Accredited by ACICS. **Calendar:** Continuous.

Contact. Phone: (904) 398-4141
Director Of Admissions, 3986 Boulevard Center Drive, Jacksonville, FL 32207

Stenotype Institute: Orlando

Orlando, Florida

- Private 2-year technical college
- Very large city

General. Accredited by ACICS. **Calendar:** Semester.

Annual costs/financial aid. Tuition/fees (projected): $12,000.

Contact. Phone: (407) 816-5573
1636 West Oakridge Road, Orlando, FL 32809

Tallahassee Community College

Tallahassee, Florida — **CB member**
www.tcc.fl.edu — **CB code: 5794**

- Public 2-year community college
- Commuter campus in small city

General. Founded in 1965. Regionally accredited. **Enrollment:** 12,348 degree-seeking undergraduates; 1,385 non-degree-seeking students. **Degrees:** 1,958 associate awarded. **ROTC:** Army, Navy, Air Force. **Location:** 230 miles from Tampa, 200 miles from Pensacola. **Calendar:** Semester, extensive summer session. **Full-time faculty:** 170 total; 26% have terminal degrees, 19% minority, 56% women. **Part-time faculty:** 514 total; 27% minority, 43% women. **Class size:** 19% < 20, 62% 20-39, 15% 40-49, 4% 50-99.

Student profile. Among degree-seeking undergraduates, 2,534 enrolled as first-time, first-year students.

Part-time:	63%	**Women:**	55%
Out-of-state:	3%	**25 or older:**	24%

Transfer out. Colleges most students transferred to 2005: Florida State University.

Basis for selection. Open admission, but selective for some programs. Special requirements for nursing, dental hygiene, emergency medical technology, and respiratory therapy programs. Each program requires specific course prerequisites or test scores or required GPA in addition to letters of recommendation. SAT/ACT may substitute for Florida CPT for placement. Placement test score required of degree-seeking applicants before enrolling in classes. **Homeschooled:** Present affidavit verifying completion of high school requirements. **Learning Disabled:** If service or accommodations are needed, documentation required.

2005-2006 Annual costs. Tuition/fees: $1,680; $6,330 out-of-state. Per-credit charge: $48 in-state; $195 out-of-state. Books/supplies: $800. Personal expenses: $1,800.

Financial aid. Need-based: Need-based aid available for part-time students. **Non-need-based:** Scholarships awarded for academics, art, athletics, leadership, music/drama, state residency.

Application procedures. Admission: Priority date 7/31; deadline 8/21 (receipt date). No application fee. Admission notification on a rolling basis. Separate application procedure for health programs. **Financial aid:** Priority date 5/1; no closing date. FAFSA, institutional form required. Applicants notified on a rolling basis starting 5/15.

Academics. Special study options: Cooperative education, cross-registration, distance learning, double major, dual enrollment of high school students, ESL, honors, independent study, liberal arts/career combination, study abroad. Bachelor's degree programs available on campus. License preparation in dental hygiene, nursing, paramedic, real estate. **Credit/placement by examination:** AP, CLEP, IB, institutional tests. 45 credit hours maximum toward associate degree. **Support services:** GED preparation, learning center, pre-admission summer program, reduced course load, remedial instruction, study skills assistance, tutoring, writing center.

Majors. Business: General, accounting, administrative services, banking/financial services, business admin, management information systems, sales/distribution. **Computer sciences:** Computer graphics, networking, programming. **Construction:** Maintenance. **Education:** Early childhood, health. **Engineering:** General, civil, software. **Engineering technology:** Civil, construction, drafting, industrial management. **Health:** Dental hygiene, EMT paramedic, nursing (RN), respiratory therapy technology. **Legal studies:** Paralegal. **Liberal arts:** Arts/sciences. **Parks/recreation:** Facilities management. **Protective services:** Criminal justice, law enforcement admin. **Public administration:** General. **Social sciences:** General. **Visual/performing arts:** General, film/cinema.

Most popular majors. Liberal arts 87%.

Computing on campus. 320 workstations in library, computer center, student center. Commuter students can connect to campus network. Online course registration, online library, helpline, wireless network available.

Student life. Freshman orientation: Mandatory. Preregistration for classes offered. All-day event held a few days prior to start of term; includes small group meetings and advising. Online orientation also available. **Activities:** Bands, choral groups, dance, drama, literary magazine, music ensembles, musical theater, student government, student newspaper, TV station, Phi Theta Kappa, Black Student Union, Returning Adults Valuing Education, international students club, Baptist campus ministries, Future Educators of America, Students Interested in Legal Careers, College Democrats, BACCHUS, student environmental action coalition.

Athletics. NJCAA. **Intercollegiate:** Baseball M, basketball, softball W. **Intramural:** Basketball, golf, soccer, softball, table tennis, tennis. **Team name:** Eagles.

Student services. Adult student services, career counseling, services for economically disadvantaged, financial aid counseling, minority student services, on-campus daycare, personal counseling, placement for graduates, veterans' counselor. **Physically disabled:** Services for visually, speech, hearing impaired. **Transfer:** Special adviser, orientation for new students. Transfer adviser, college fairs on campus for students transferring to 4-year colleges.

Contact. E-mail: enroll@tcc.fl.edu
Phone: (850) 201-8555 Fax: (850) 201-8474
Sheri Rowland, Director of Enrollment Services and Testing, Tallahassee Community College, 444 Appleyard Drive, Tallahassee, FL 32304

Valencia Community College

Orlando, Florida — **CB member**
www.valenciacc.edu — **CB code: 5869**

- Public 2-year community college
- Commuter campus in very large city

General. Founded in 1967. Regionally accredited. **Enrollment:** 23,865 degree-seeking undergraduates; 5,679 non-degree-seeking students. **Degrees:** 3,996 associate awarded. **ROTC:** Army. **Location:** 90 miles from Tampa, 145 miles from Jacksonville. **Calendar:** Semester, extensive summer session. **Full-time faculty:** 392 total; 23% have terminal degrees, 17% minority, 56% women. **Part-time faculty:** 767 total; 12% have terminal degrees, 21% minority, 51% women. **Class size:** 26% < 20, 72% 20-39, 1% 40-49, less than 1% 50-99, less than 1% >100.

Student profile. Among degree-seeking undergraduates, 97% enrolled in a transfer program, 3% enrolled in a vocational program, 5,009 enrolled as first-time, first-year students, 1,997 transferred in from other institutions.

Part-time:	55%	**Hispanic American:**	23%
Out-of-state:	4%	**Native American:**	1%
Women:	58%	**International:**	2%
African American:	15%	**25 or older:**	27%
Asian American:	5%		

Transfer out. Colleges most students transferred to 2005: University of Central Florida.

Basis for selection. Open admission, but selective for some programs. Admission to Criminal Justice Institute based on minimum score on required entry assessment test. Applicants must be at least 19 years of age, must be U.S. citizen, must not have misdemeanor or felony convictions or dishonorable discharge from military. **Adult students:** SAT/ACT scores not required. **Homeschooled:** Home school diplomas accepted with official Home School Verification Affidavit.

High school preparation. Recommended units include English 4, mathematics 3, social studies 3 and science 3.

2005-2006 Annual costs. Tuition/fees: $1,983; $7,441 out-of-state. Per-credit charge: $55 in-state; $219 out-of-state. $854 required fees for out-of-state students. Books/supplies: $1,000. Personal expenses: $4,300.

Financial aid. Need-based: Need-based aid available for part-time students. Work study available nights and for part-time students.

Application procedures. Admission: Closing date 8/1 (postmark date). $25 fee. Application may be submitted online. Admission notification on a rolling basis beginning on or about 3/31. **Financial aid:** Closing date 5/15. FAFSA, institutional form required. Applicants notified on a rolling basis starting 4/2; must reply within 2 week(s) of notification.

Academics. Special study options: Cooperative education, distance learning, double major, dual enrollment of high school students, ESL, honors, independent study, internships, student-designed major, study abroad, weekend college. License preparation in dental hygiene, nursing, paramedic, physical therapy, radiology, real estate. **Credit/placement by examination:** AP, CLEP, IB, institutional tests. 45 credit hours maximum toward associate degree. **Support services:** Learning center, remedial instruction, study skills assistance, tutoring, writing center.

Majors. Agriculture: Horticultural science, ornamental horticulture. **Biology:** General, marine. **Business:** Accounting, accounting technology, administrative services, business admin, hospitality admin, human resources, office management, office technology, office/clerical. **Communications:** Journalism, public relations. **Computer sciences:** Computer science, data entry, information technology, programming, systems analysis. **Conservation:** Environmental science. **Education:** General. **Engineering:** General, computer, electrical. **Engineering technology:** Civil, construction, drafting, electrical. **English:** English lit. **Family/consumer sciences:** Institutional food production. **Foreign languages:** French, German, Portuguese, Spanish. **Health:** Cardiovascular technology, clinical lab technology, dental hygiene, EMT ambulance attendant, EMT paramedic, health care admin, medical radiologic technology/radiation therapy, medical records technology, medical secretary, nursing (RN), office admin, respiratory therapy technology, sonography. **History:** General. **Legal studies:** Paralegal. **Liberal arts:** Arts/sciences, humanities. **Math:** General, statistics. **Personal/culinary services:** Chef training, culinary arts, restaurant/catering. **Philosophy/religion:** Philosophy. **Physical sciences:** Chemistry. **Protective services:** Fire safety technology, law enforcement admin, police science. **Psychology:** General. **Public administration:** General. **Social sciences:** General, economics, political science, sociology. **Visual/performing arts:** Art, commercial/advertising art, dance, dramatic, theater arts management.

Computing on campus. 2,500 workstations in library, computer center, student center. Commuter students can connect to campus network. Online course registration, helpline available.

Student life. Freshman orientation: Mandatory. Preregistration for classes offered. 2-hour program. **Policies:** Freshmen permitted cars on campus. **Activities:** Bands, choral groups, dance, drama, literary magazine, music ensembles, musical theater, student government, student newspaper, symphony orchestra, VISA (foreign students club), A2CS (African American cultural society), Brain Bowl, Latin American student organization, student nurses association, Valencia Volunteers (community service), Phi Beta Lambda (business), Earth Club (environmental), Muslim student organization, Black high achievers club.

Student services. Career counseling, student employment services, financial aid counseling, health services, personal counseling, placement for graduates, veterans' counselor. **Physically disabled:** Services for visually, hearing impaired. **Transfer:** Special adviser, orientation for new students. College fairs on campus for students transferring to 4-year colleges.

Contact. Phone: (407) 582-1507 Fax: (407) 582-1403
Renee Simpson, Director of Admissions and Records, Valencia Community College, PO Box 3028, Orlando, FL 32802-3028

Virginia College at Pensacola

Pensacola, Florida
www.vc.edu/pensacola

- For-profit 2-year technical college
- Commuter campus

General. Accredited by ACICS.

Contact. Phone: (850) 436-8444
Associate Director of Admissions, 19 West Garden Street, Pensacola, FL 32502

Georgia

Abraham Baldwin Agricultural College
Tifton, Georgia **CB member**
www.abac.edu **CB code: 5001**

- Public 2-year agricultural and community college
- Commuter campus in large town
- SAT or ACT required

General. Founded in 1924. Regionally accredited. Students may pursue programs of study at 3 off-campus sites: Valdosta State College (associate in nursing), Ben-Hill Irwin Technical Institute (associate in applied science), and Moultrie Area Technical Institute. **Enrollment:** 3,423 degree-seeking undergraduates. **Degrees:** 519 associate awarded. **Location:** 100 miles from Macon, 50 miles from Albany. **Calendar:** Semester. **Full-time faculty:** 90 total. **Part-time faculty:** 35 total. **Special facilities:** 200-acre farm.

Student profile.

Out-of-state:	7%	**Live on campus:**	28%
25 or older:	12%		

Basis for selection. Minimum 1.8 GPA and SAT verbal score of 330 and math score of 310 or ACT English of 12 and math of 14 necessary to get calculated required Freshman Index of 1830. Interview recommended for nursing majors.

High school preparation. 16 units required. Required units include English 4, mathematics 3, social studies 3, science 3 and foreign language 2. College-preparatory program not required for students pursuing AAS degree.

2005-2006 Annual costs. Tuition/fees: $2,026; $6,650 out-of-state. Per-credit charge: $65 in-state; $257 out-of-state. Various block meal plans available. Minimum $300 block meal plan required for campus apartment residents. Room only: $4,260. Books/supplies: $775. Personal expenses: $1,500.

Application procedures. Admission: No deadline. $20 fee. Admission notification on a rolling basis. **Financial aid:** Priority date 5/1; no closing date. FAFSA, institutional form required. Applicants notified on a rolling basis starting 5/15; must reply within 2 week(s) of notification.

Academics. Special study options: Dual enrollment of high school students, external degree, honors, independent study, internships, study abroad. **Credit/placement by examination:** AP, CLEP, institutional tests. **Support services:** Learning center, remedial instruction, tutoring.

Majors. Agriculture: Animal sciences, business, ornamental horticulture, plant sciences, poultry. **Biology:** General. **Business:** Accounting, business admin, fashion, hospitality admin, office technology, office/clerical. **Communications:** General, journalism. **Computer sciences:** General, applications programming, data processing. **Conservation:** Forestry, wildlife. **Education:** General. **Engineering:** Agricultural. **Family/consumer sciences:** General, child care, institutional food production. **Health:** Athletic training, dental hygiene, medical records technology, predentistry, premedicine, prepharmacy. **History:** General. **Legal studies:** Prelaw. **Liberal arts:** Arts/sciences. **Math:** General. **Parks/recreation:** Facilities management. **Physical sciences:** Chemistry. **Protective services:** Police science. **Psychology:** General. **Social sciences:** General, sociology. **Visual/performing arts:** General, studio arts.

Computing on campus. 158 workstations in library, computer center.

Student life. Housing: Coed dorms, single-sex dorms available. **Activities:** Bands, choral groups, dance, drama, literary magazine, radio station, student government, student newspaper.

Athletics. NJCAA. **Intercollegiate:** Badminton W, baseball M, basketball M, golf M, softball W, tennis, volleyball W. **Intramural:** Softball, volleyball.

Student services. Adult student services, career counseling, student employment services, health services, personal counseling, placement for graduates, veterans' counselor. **Transfer:** Transfer adviser, college fairs on campus for students transferring to 4-year colleges.

Contact. Phone: (229) 386-3230 Fax: (229) 386-7481
Beth Saxon, Director of Admissions, Abraham Baldwin Agricultural College, ABAC Station, Box 4, Tifton, GA 31794-2693

Albany Technical College
Albany, Georgia
www.albanytech.edu **CB code: 3921**

- Public 2-year technical college
- Commuter campus in small city

General. Regionally accredited. **Enrollment:** 2,543 degree-seeking undergraduates; 240 non-degree-seeking students. **Degrees:** 28 associate awarded. **Location:** 225 miles from Atlanta. **Calendar:** Quarter, extensive summer session. **Full-time faculty:** 90 total; 2% have terminal degrees, 50% minority, 50% women. **Part-time faculty:** 103 total; 1% have terminal degrees, 53% minority, 79% women.

Student profile. Among degree-seeking undergraduates, 100% enrolled in a vocational program, 591 enrolled as first-time, first-year students.

Part-time:	47%	**Hispanic American:**	1%
Women:	64%	**25 or older:**	50%
African American:	68%		

Transfer out. Colleges most students transferred to 2005: Wallace Community College, Bainbridge College, Darton College.

Basis for selection. Open admission. ASSET, COMPASS, SAT/ACT must be submitted for placement. **Adult students:** SAT/ACT scores not required. ASSET or COMPASS used for DTAE schools; SAT, ACT or CPE exam scores also accepted.

2005-2006 Annual costs. Tuition/fees: $1,359; $2,475 out-of-state. Per-credit charge: $31 in-state; $62 out-of-state.

2004-2005 Financial aid. Need-based: 96% of total undergraduate aid awarded as scholarships/grants, 4% as loans/jobs. Need-based aid available for part-time students. Work study available nights and for part-time students. **Non-need-based:** Scholarships awarded for academics, state residency.

Application procedures. Admission: Closing date 10/1 (postmark date). $15 fee, may be waived for applicants with need. Application may be submitted online. Admission notification 10/1. Admission notification on a rolling basis beginning on or about 8/1. **Financial aid:** No deadline. FAFSA required. Applicants notified on a rolling basis starting 5/1.

Academics. Special study options: Cooperative education, distance learning, dual enrollment of high school students, internships, liberal arts/career combination. License preparation in nursing, paramedic, radiology. **Credit/placement by examination:** AP, CLEP, institutional tests. **Support services:** GED preparation and test center, remedial instruction, tutoring.

Majors. Business: Sales/distribution. **Computer sciences:** Data processing, networking. **Conservation:** Forestry. **Construction:** Carpentry. **Education:** Early childhood. **Engineering technology:** Drafting. **Health:** Pharmacy assistant. **Mechanic/repair:** Electronics/electrical, industrial. **Personal/culinary services:** Chef training. **Protective services:** Criminal justice.

Computing on campus. Online library available.

Student life. Freshman orientation: Available. Preregistration for classes offered. Students contact advisor to register for classes. Advisor registers students via Internet. **Activities:** Choral groups, student government.

Student services. Adult student services, career counseling, services for economically disadvantaged, student employment services, financial aid counseling, on-campus daycare, personal counseling, placement for graduates, veterans' counselor. **Physically disabled:** Services for visually, speech, hearing impaired. **Transfer:** Special adviser, orientation, pre-admission transcript evaluation for new students.

Contact. E-mail: albanytech.edu
Phone: (229) 430-3520 Fax: (229) 430-6180
Director of Admissions, Albany Technical College, 1704 South Slappy Boulevard, Albany, GA 31701-3514

Andrew College
Cuthbert, Georgia
www.andrewcollege.edu **CB code: 5009**

- Private 2-year junior and liberal arts college affiliated with United Methodist Church
- Residential campus in small town
- SAT or ACT (ACT writing recommended) required

General. Founded in 1854. Regionally accredited. **Enrollment:** 307 degree-seeking undergraduates. **Degrees:** 65 associate awarded. **Location:** 60 miles from Columbus, 40 miles from Albany. **Calendar:** Semester, limited summer session. **Full-time faculty:** 23 total. **Part-time faculty:** 2 total. **Class size:** 75% < 20, 25% 20-39.

Student profile.

Out-of-state:	13%	**Live on campus:**	85%
25 or older:	4%		

Transfer out. **Colleges most students transferred to 2005:** Georgia Southwestern State University, Valdosta State University, Georgia Southern University, Columbus State University.

Basis for selection. High school academic record, test scores, school and community activities important. Standardized test scores in writing not required for Fall 2007 admissions. Essay recommended. Interview required of the academically weak. Audition required of music majors. Portfolio recommended for art majors. **Adult students:** Entrance exam policies same as for first-time freshmen.

High school preparation. 18 units recommended.

2005-2006 Annual costs. Tuition/fees: $9,192. Per-credit charge: $400. Room/board: $5,790. Books/supplies: $600. Personal expenses: $1,200.

Financial aid. **Need-based:** Need-based aid available for part-time students. **Non-need-based:** Scholarships awarded for academics, art, athletics, leadership, music/drama, religious affiliation, state residency.

Application procedures. **Admission:** Priority date 6/1; deadline 8/1 (receipt date). $20 fee, may be waived for applicants with need. Application may be submitted online. Admission notification on a rolling basis. **Financial aid:** Priority date 4/1, closing date 8/1. FAFSA, institutional form required. Applicants notified on a rolling basis starting 4/15.

Academics. **Special study options:** Double major, dual enrollment of high school students, ESL. **Credit/placement by examination:** AP, CLEP, institutional tests. 24 credit hours maximum toward associate degree. **Support services:** Pre-admission summer program, remedial instruction, study skills assistance, tutoring.

Majors. **Agriculture:** General. **Business:** General. **Communications:** General, journalism. **Computer sciences:** Computer science. **Conservation:** Forestry. **Education:** General. **Engineering:** General. **Health:** Predentistry, premedicine, prenursing, prepharmacy, preveterinary. **History:** General. **Legal studies:** Prelaw. **Liberal arts:** Arts/sciences. **Math:** General. **Physical sciences:** General. **Psychology:** General. **Social sciences:** General, sociology. **Visual/performing arts:** General, dramatic.

Most popular majors. Business/marketing 11%, education 21%, health sciences 8%, legal studies 10%, liberal arts 8%, social sciences 10%, visual/performing arts 10%.

Computing on campus. 100 workstations in dormitories, library, computer center, student center. Dormitories wired for high-speed internet access and linked to campus network. Commuter students can connect to campus network.

Student life. **Freshman orientation:** Mandatory. Preregistration for classes offered. Selected weekends during summer and beginning of fall term, 3-4 days. **Policies:** No alcohol/illegal drugs allowed on campus. Freshmen permitted cars on campus. **Housing:** Guaranteed on-campus for all undergraduates. Coed dorms, single-sex dorms available. **Activities:** Choral groups, drama, literary magazine, musical theater, student government, student newspaper, Baptist Student Union, Wesley Fellowship, Unity, community service group, interdenominational Christian group.

Athletics. NJCAA. **Intercollegiate:** Baseball M, cross-country, golf, soccer, softball W. **Intramural:** Badminton, basketball, cheerleading W, cross-country, football (non-tackle) M, golf, racquetball, soccer, softball, swimming, table tennis, volleyball, weight lifting M. **Team name:** Tigers.

Student services. Alcohol/substance abuse counseling, campus ministries, career counseling, services for economically disadvantaged, financial aid counseling, health services, veterans' counselor. **Transfer:** Special adviser, orientation for new students. Transfer adviser, college fairs on campus for students transferring to 4-year colleges.

Contact. E-mail: admissions@andrewcollege.edu
Phone: (800) 664-9250 Toll-free number: (800) 664-9250
Fax: (229) 732-2176
Janna Brown, Director of Admissions and Financial Aid, Andrew College, 413 College Street, Cuthbert, GA 39840-1395

Ashworth College
Norcross, Georgia
www.ashworthcollege.com **CB code: 3912**

- For-profit 2-year community college

General. Accredited by DETC. **Calendar:** Semester.

Annual costs/financial aid. All-inclusive programs range from $1578 to $2178 per year.

Contact. Phone: (770) 729-8400
Registrar, 430 Technology Parkway, Norcross, GA 30092-3406

Athens Technical College
Athens, Georgia
www.athenstech.edu **CB code: 0462**

- Public 2-year technical college
- Commuter campus in small city

General. Founded in 1959. Regionally accredited. **Enrollment:** 2,721 degree-seeking undergraduates. **Degrees:** 252 associate awarded. **Location:** 65 miles from Atlanta. **Calendar:** Quarter, extensive summer session. **Full-time faculty:** 79 total. **Part-time faculty:** 5 total. **Class size:** 61% < 20, 36% 20-39, 1% 40-49, 2% 50-99.

Student profile. Among degree-seeking undergraduates, 100% enrolled in a vocational program, 3% already have a bachelor's degree or higher.

Out-of-state:	1%	**25 or older:**	38%

Transfer out. **Colleges most students transferred to 2005:** University of Georgia.

Basis for selection. Open admission, but selective for some programs. Special requirements for radiology, respiratory therapy, nursing, physical therapy assistant, dental hygiene, surgical technology, veterinary technology dental assisting, medical assisting, practical nursing and diagnostic medical sonography. School record, recommendations, standardized test scores, essay, and interview required or recommended depending on program. Applicants to nursing program must submit SAT or ACT scores by April 1, radiation technology and respiratory therapy applicants by April 30. Interview required of radiology, respiratory therapy, nursing, physical therapy assistant, dental assisting, and dental hygiene majors. **Adult students:** Entrance exam policies same as for first-time freshmen. **Homeschooled:** Must provide documentation of designated home study program activities.

2006-2007 Annual costs. Tuition/fees (projected): $1,359; $2,475 out-of-state. Per-credit charge: $31 in-state; $62 out-of-state. Books/supplies: $800. Personal expenses: $1,000.

2004-2005 Financial aid. **Need-based:** 60 full-time freshmen applied for aid; 39 were judged to have need; 38 of these received aid. Average need met was 9%. Average scholarship/grant was $869. 93% of total undergraduate aid awarded as scholarships/grants, 7% as loans/jobs. Need-based aid available for part-time students. Work study available for part-time students. **Non-need-based:** Awarded to 57 full-time undergraduates, including 25 freshmen. Scholarships awarded for academics, leadership.

Application procedures. **Admission:** Priority date 8/1; no deadline. $15 fee. Application may be submitted online. Admission notification on a rolling basis. February 1 deadline for applicants to nursing and dental hygiene programs. March 1 deadline for dental assistance program. April 1 deadline for radiography, surgical technology, diagnostic medical sonography, nursing accelerated, and veterinary technology programs. May 1 deadline for physical therapist assistant, and practical nursing programs. July 1 deadline for respiratory therapy. August 1 deadline for medical assistance program. **Financial aid:** No deadline. FAFSA required. Applicants notified on a rolling basis starting 6/15; must reply within 2 week(s) of notification.

Academics. **Special study options:** Distance learning, dual enrollment of high school students, ESL, internships, weekend college. License preparation in real estate. **Credit/placement by examination:** AP, CLEP, institutional tests. **Support services:** GED preparation and test center, learning center, reduced course load, remedial instruction, study skills assistance, tutoring.

Majors. **Business:** Accounting technology, administrative services, sales/distribution. **Computer sciences:** Applications programming, data processing, networking, programming. **Education:** Early childhood. **Health:** Dental assistant, dental hygiene, nursing (RN), physical therapy assistant, radiologic technology/medical imaging, respiratory therapy technology, sonography, veterinary technology/assistant. **Legal studies:** Paralegal. **Science technology:** Biological.

Most popular majors. Business/marketing 17%, computer/information sciences 19%, health sciences 39%, trade and industry 13%.

Computing on campus. 346 workstations in computer center. Commuter students can connect to campus network. Online course registration, online library, wireless network available.

Student life. Freshman orientation: Mandatory. Preregistration for classes offered. **Policies:** Freshmen permitted cars on campus. **Activities:** Student government.

Student services. Adult student services, career counseling, student employment services, financial aid counseling, personal counseling, placement for graduates, veterans' counselor. **Physically disabled:** Services for visually, speech, hearing impaired. **Transfer:** Special adviser, orientation for new students. Transfer adviser for students transferring to 4-year colleges.

Contact. Phone: (706) 355-5004 Fax: (706) 369-5756
Daniel Smith, Vice President for Student Development Services, Athens Technical College, 800 U.S. Highway 29 North, Athens, GA 30601-1500

Atlanta Metropolitan College

Atlanta, Georgia — **CB member**
www.atlm.edu — **CB code: 5725**

- Public 2-year junior college
- Commuter campus in very large city

General. Founded in 1974. Regionally accredited. **Enrollment:** 1,689 degree-seeking undergraduates. **Degrees:** 157 associate awarded. **Location:** 4 miles from downtown. **Calendar:** Semester, limited summer session. **Full-time faculty:** 43 total; 44% have terminal degrees, 79% minority, 54% women. **Part-time faculty:** 28 total; 64% have terminal degrees, 93% minority, 46% women. **Partnerships:** Formal partnerships with several high schools to offer college-level courses to high school seniors.

Student profile. Among degree-seeking undergraduates, 88% enrolled in a transfer program, 3% enrolled in a vocational program, 1% already have a bachelor's degree or higher, 156 transferred in from other institutions.

Basis for selection. Applicants must have 2.0 GPA and be current on all vaccinations. SAT or ACT scores not required, but considered if submitted. Applicants with an SAT verbal score of 430 or an ACT English Score of 17 and completion of the college preparatory curriculum in English, are exempted from taking the COMPASS Placement Test in English and Reading. Applicants with an SAT math score of 400 or an ACT math score of 17 and completion of the college preparatory curriculum in math, are exempt from taking the COMPASS Placement Test in math. **Adult students:** Entrance exam policies same as for first-time freshmen. SAT/ACT scores not required if out of high school 5 year(s) or more. For placement purposes, students out of high school for five years or more must take the COMPASS Placement Test.

High school preparation. 16 units required. Required units include English 4, mathematics 4, social studies 1, history 2, science 3 and foreign language 2.

2005-2006 Annual costs. Tuition/fees: $1,772; $6,396 out-of-state. Per-credit charge: $65 in-state; $257 out-of-state.

2004-2005 Financial aid. All financial aid based on need. Average need met was 31%. Average scholarship/grant was $3,322; average loan $2,051. 71% of total undergraduate aid awarded as scholarships/grants, 29% as loans/jobs. Need-based aid available for part-time students. Work study available nights, weekends and for part-time students.

Application procedures. Admission: Closing date 7/15 (receipt date). $20 fee. Application may be submitted online. Admission notification on a rolling basis. **Financial aid:** Closing date 6/1. FAFSA required. Applicants notified on a rolling basis.

Academics. Various workshops are provided to enhance students' academic and technological skills. Math tutorial services are also available. **Special study options:** Cooperative education, distance learning, dual enrollment of high school students, honors, independent study, study abroad, teacher certification program, weekend college. **Credit/placement by examination:** AP, CLEP, ACT. **Support services:** Learning center, remedial instruction, study skills assistance, tutoring, writing center.

Majors. Area/ethnic studies: African-American. **Biology:** General. **Business:** Business admin, office management. **Communications:** General. **Computer sciences:** General, computer science. **Education:** Multi-level teacher. **Engineering technology:** General. **English:** Speech/rhetoric. **Foreign languages:** General. **Health:** Medical records admin. **History:** General. **Math:** General. **Parks/recreation:** Health/fitness. **Physical sciences:** Chemistry, physics. **Protective services:** Law enforcement admin. **Psychology:** General. **Public administration:** Social work. **Social sciences:** Political science. **Visual/performing arts:** Art.

Most popular majors. Liberal arts 91%.

Computing on campus. 512 workstations in library, computer center, student center. Online course registration, online library, helpline, repair service, wireless network available.

Student life. Freshman orientation: Available. Preregistration for classes offered. 1 daytime and 1 evening session held each semester. **Policies:** Freshmen permitted cars on campus. **Activities:** Choral groups, dance, drama, student government, student newspaper, International Students Organization.

Athletics. NJCAA. **Intercollegiate:** Basketball, cheerleading. **Team name:** Panthers.

Student services. Adult student services, alcohol/substance abuse counseling, career counseling, services for economically disadvantaged, student employment services, financial aid counseling, minority student services, personal counseling, veterans' counselor. **Physically disabled:** Services for visually, speech, hearing impaired. **Transfer:** Special adviser, orientation, pre-admission transcript evaluation for new students. College fairs on campus for students transferring to 4-year colleges.

Contact. E-mail: areid@atlm.edu
Phone: (404) 756-4004 Fax: (404) 756-4407
Audrey Reid, Director of Admissions, Atlanta Metropolitan College, 1630 Metropolitan Parkway, SW, Atlanta, GA 30310-4498

Atlanta Technical College

Atlanta, Georgia
www.atlantatech.org/

- Public 2-year technical college
- Very large city

General. Regionally accredited. **Calendar:** Quarter.

Annual costs/financial aid. Tuition/fees (projected): $1,362.

Contact. Phone: (404) 225-4447
1560 Metropolitan Parkway, S.W., Atlanta, GA 30310

Augusta Technical Institute

Augusta, Georgia
www.augustatech.edu — **CB code: 2620**

- Public 2-year technical college
- Commuter campus in large city

General. Founded in 1961. Regionally accredited. 3 campus locations: Augusta, Thomson, Waynesboro. **Enrollment:** 4,390 degree-seeking undergraduates. **Degrees:** 214 associate awarded. **Location:** 145 miles from Atlanta, 75 miles from Columbia, South Carolina. **Calendar:** Quarter, extensive summer session. **Full-time faculty:** 90 total. **Part-time faculty:** 100 total.

Basis for selection. Test scores most important. High school diploma or GED required for all medical and associate degree programs. ASSET accepted in place of SAT or ACT. **Adult students:** Entrance exam policies same as for first-time freshmen.

High school preparation. Recommended units include English 4, mathematics 2, science 4 (laboratory 2). Highly recommended that math units include algebra and trigonometry.

2006-2007 Annual costs. Tuition/fees (projected): $1,828; $3,316 out-of-state. Per-credit charge: $31 in-state; $62 out-of-state. Books/supplies: $450.

Financial aid. Non-need-based: Scholarships awarded for state residency.

Application procedures. Admission: $15 fee, may be waived for applicants with need. Application deadlines exist for competitive healthcare programs and vary by major. **Financial aid:** No deadline. FAFSA, institutional form required. Must reply within 2 week(s) of notification.

Academics. **Special study options:** Distance learning, double major, dual enrollment of high school students, ESL, internships. **Credit/placement by examination:** CLEP, institutional tests. **Support services:** GED preparation and test center, learning center, reduced course load, remedial instruction, tutoring.

Majors. **Business:** Accounting, administrative services, sales/distribution. **Computer sciences:** Applications programming. **Engineering technology:** Electrical. **Health:** Cardiovascular technology, clinical lab technology, EMT paramedic, pharmacy assistant, respiratory therapy technology.

Computing on campus. Commuter students can connect to campus network. Online course registration, online library available.

Student life. **Freshman orientation:** Available. Preregistration for classes offered. **Activities:** Student government.

Student services. Career counseling, student employment services, financial aid counseling, on-campus daycare, placement for graduates, veterans' counselor. **Physically disabled:** Services for visually, speech, hearing impaired. **Transfer:** Special adviser, orientation, pre-admission transcript evaluation for new students.

Contact. Phone: (706) 771-4000 Fax: (706) 771-4034
Brian Roberts, Director of Admissions, Augusta Technical Institute, 3200 Augusta Tech Drive, Augusta, GA 30906

Bainbridge College
Bainbridge, Georgia
www.bainbridge.edu **CB code: 5062**

- Public 2-year community and technical college
- Commuter campus in large town
- SAT or ACT required

General. Founded in 1973. Regionally accredited. **Enrollment:** 2,475 degree-seeking undergraduates. **Degrees:** 94 associate awarded. **Location:** 43 miles from Tallahassee, Florida. **Calendar:** Semester, limited summer session. **Full-time faculty:** 57 total; 33% have terminal degrees, 7% minority, 49% women. **Part-time faculty:** 69 total; 10% have terminal degrees, 10% minority, 61% women. **Class size:** 60% < 20, 39% 20-39, less than 1% 50-99. **Special facilities:** Nature trail.

Student profile. Among degree-seeking undergraduates, 45% enrolled in a transfer program, 55% enrolled in a vocational program, 960 enrolled as first-time, first-year students, 85 transferred in from other institutions.

Part-time:	61%	**Women:**	70%
Out-of-state:	1%	**25 or older:**	38%

Transfer out. 65% of students enrolled in the transfer program go on to 4-year colleges. **Colleges most students transferred to 2005:** Valdosta State University, Albany State University.

Basis for selection. Open admission, but selective for some programs. Minimum score of 330 on SAT verbal or 13 on ACT English or 310 on SAT math or 14 on ACT math, or 1.8 high school GPA required. College preparatory curriculum required for associate of arts degree-seeking students. Limited number admitted who do not meet admission standards. **Adult students:** SAT/ACT scores not required if out of high school 5 year(s) or more.

High school preparation. 16 units required. Required units include English 4, mathematics 4, social studies 3, science 3 and foreign language 2.

2005-2006 Annual costs. Tuition/fees: $1,670; $6,294 out-of-state. Per-credit charge: $65 in-state; $257 out-of-state. Books/supplies: $600. Personal expenses: $450.

2005-2006 Financial aid. All financial aid based on need. 43% of total undergraduate aid awarded as scholarships/grants, 57% as loans/jobs. Need-based aid available for part-time students. **Additional information:** 30-day loans available for tuition and fees.

Application procedures. **Admission:** Closing date 8/1. No application fee. Application may be submitted online. Admission notification on a rolling basis. **Financial aid:** Priority date 6/1, closing date 8/1. FAFSA, institutional form required. Applicants notified on a rolling basis starting 6/1; must reply within 2 week(s) of notification.

Academics. **Special study options:** Distance learning, double major, dual enrollment of high school students, honors, independent study, study abroad, weekend college. 2-year registered nursing program. Bachelor's degree programs available on campus. License preparation in nursing, real estate. **Credit/placement by examination:** AP, CLEP, institutional tests. 18 credit hours maximum toward associate degree. **Support services:** GED preparation, learning center, reduced course load, remedial instruction, study skills assistance, tutoring.

Majors. **Business:** General, accounting, administrative services, management information systems, marketing. **Communications:** General. **Computer sciences:** General. **Construction:** Electrician. **Education:** General, early childhood, health, middle, physical, secondary. **Engineering technology:** Drafting, electrical. **English:** English lit. **Foreign languages:** General. **Health:** Nursing (RN). **History:** General. **Math:** General. **Mechanic/repair:** Industrial. **Protective services:** Law enforcement admin. **Psychology:** General. **Social sciences:** Political science.

Most popular majors. Business/marketing 29%, liberal arts 61%.

Computing on campus. 295 workstations in library, computer center, student center.

Student life. **Freshman orientation:** Mandatory. Preregistration for classes offered. Held prior to the semester; on-line orientation. **Policies:** Freshmen permitted cars on campus. **Activities:** Concert band, choral groups, drama, music ensembles, student government, student newspaper, Delta club, service organizations, Phi Theta Kappa, Sigma Kappa Delta.

Athletics. **Intramural:** Basketball M, football (non-tackle), softball, table tennis, tennis, volleyball.

Student services. Adult student services, career counseling, services for economically disadvantaged, student employment services, financial aid counseling, minority student services, personal counseling, placement for graduates, veterans' counselor. **Physically disabled:** Services for visually, speech, hearing impaired. **Transfer:** Special adviser for new students. Transfer adviser, college fairs on campus for students transferring to 4-year colleges.

Contact. E-mail: csnyder@bainbridge.edu
Phone: (229) 248-2504 Fax: (229) 248-2623
Connie Snyder, Director of Admissions and Records, Bainbridge College, 2500 East Shotwell Street, Bainbridge, GA 39818-0990

Brown Mackie College: Atlanta
Atlanta, Georgia

- For-profit 2-year business, health science and technical college
- Very large city

General. Accredited by ACICS. **Enrollment:** 200 degree-seeking undergraduates. **Degrees:** 75 associate awarded. **Calendar:** Quarter. **Full-time faculty:** 5 total. **Part-time faculty:** 3 total.

2005-2006 Annual costs. Tuition/fees: $6,444. Per-credit charge: $179. Full-time cost is based on maximum courseload of 12 hours.

Academics. **Credit/placement by examination:** CLEP.

Majors. **Business:** Accounting, business admin. **Health:** Medical assistant. **Legal studies:** Paralegal.

Contact. E-mail: bmcatadm@amedcts.com
Phone: (770) 638-0121 Toll-free number: (888) 301-3670
Brown Mackie College: Atlanta, 6600 Peachtree Dunwoody NE, Atlanta, GA 30328

Central Georgia Technical College
Macon, Georgia
www.cgtcollege.org **CB code: 1709**

- Public 2-year community and technical college
- Commuter campus in small city

General. Regionally accredited. **Enrollment:** 5,530 degree-seeking undergraduates. **Degrees:** 227 associate awarded. **Location:** 80 miles from Atlanta. **Calendar:** Quarter, extensive summer session. **Full-time faculty:** 109 total. **Part-time faculty:** 375 total. **Class size:** 87% < 20, 13% 20-39, less than 1% 40-49. **Partnerships:** Formal partnerships with Cisco and local industries.

Student profile.

Out-of-state:	1%	**25 or older:**	35%

Basis for selection. Open admission, but selective for some programs. Requirements vary according to program of study. **Adult students:** Entrance exam policies same as for first-time freshmen.

2005-2006 Annual costs. Tuition/fees: $1,359; $2,475 out-of-state. Per-credit charge: $31 in-state; $62 out-of-state. Books/supplies: $750.

2004-2005 Financial aid. Need-based: Need-based aid available for part-time students.

Application procedures. Admission: $15 fee, may be waived for applicants with need. Admission notification on a rolling basis. Application closing date is one month prior to first day of attendance. **Financial aid:** Closing date 7/14. FAFSA, institutional form required.

Academics. Special study options: Distance learning, dual enrollment of high school students, ESL, liberal arts/career combination. License preparation in dental hygiene, nursing, paramedic, radiology, real estate. **Credit/placement by examination:** CLEP, institutional tests. Dependent on department. **Support services:** GED preparation and test center, reduced course load, remedial instruction, study skills assistance, tutoring.

Majors. Business: Accounting technology, administrative services, logistics, operations. **Computer sciences:** Data processing, networking, web page design. **Education:** Early childhood. **Engineering technology:** Drafting. **Health:** Clinical lab technology, dental hygiene, medical assistant. **Protective services:** Criminal justice.

Most popular majors. Business/marketing 25%, computer/information sciences 37%, education 16%, health sciences 15%.

Computing on campus. 400 workstations in library, computer center. Commuter students can connect to campus network. Online course registration, online library, repair service, wireless network available.

Student life. Freshman orientation: Mandatory. Preregistration for classes offered. Held prior to each quarterly registration period. **Policies:** Freshmen permitted cars on campus. **Activities:** Student government.

Student services. Adult student services, career counseling, services for economically disadvantaged, financial aid counseling, on-campus daycare, placement for graduates, veterans' counselor. **Physically disabled:** Services for visually, speech, hearing impaired. **Transfer:** Special adviser for new students. College fairs on campus for students transferring to 4-year colleges.

Contact. E-mail: info@cgtcollege.org
Phone: (478) 757-3403 Fax: (478) 757-3454
Tammy Carter, Director of Admissions, Central Georgia Technical College, 3300 Macon Tech Drive, Macon, GA 31206

Chattahoochee Technical College

Marietta, Georgia
www.chattcollege.com **CB code: 5441**

- Public 2-year technical college
- Commuter campus in large city

General. Founded in 1961. Regionally accredited. **Enrollment:** 5,060 degree-seeking undergraduates. **Degrees:** 258 associate awarded. **Location:** 20 miles from Atlanta. **Calendar:** Quarter, extensive summer session. **Full-time faculty:** 75 total. **Part-time faculty:** 120 total.

Student profile.

Out-of-state:	5%	**25 or older:**	50%

Basis for selection. Open admission, but selective for some programs. Special requirements for allied health programs.

2005-2006 Annual costs. Tuition/fees: $1,380; $2,496 out-of-state. Per-credit charge: $31 in-state; $62 out-of-state. Books/supplies: $1,020. Personal expenses: $1,300.

Financial aid. Need-based: Need-based aid available for part-time students. Work study available nights, weekends and for part-time students. **Non-need-based:** Scholarships awarded for state residency.

Application procedures. Admission: No deadline. $15 fee. Admission notification on a rolling basis. **Financial aid:** Priority date 7/15; no closing date. FAFSA, institutional form required. Applicants notified on a rolling basis starting 6/15.

Academics. Special study options: Distance learning, dual enrollment of high school students, ESL, honors, internships. License preparation in nursing. **Credit/placement by examination:** CLEP, institutional tests. 15 credit hours maximum toward associate degree. **Support services:** Learning center, reduced course load, remedial instruction, study skills assistance, tutoring.

Majors. Business: General, accounting, administrative services, marketing, office management. **Computer sciences:** General, applications programming. **Engineering technology:** Electrical. **Family/consumer sciences:** Child care. **Mechanic/repair:** Automotive. **Personal/culinary services:** Culinary arts. **Protective services:** Criminal justice.

Most popular majors. Business/marketing 73%.

Computing on campus. 857 workstations in library, computer center, student center. Commuter students can connect to campus network. Online course registration, repair service available.

Student life. Policies: Freshmen permitted cars on campus. **Activities:** Student government.

Student services. Career counseling, student employment services, personal counseling, placement for graduates, veterans' counselor. **Physically disabled:** Services for visually, hearing impaired. **Transfer:** Special adviser, orientation, pre-admission transcript evaluation for new students. College fairs on campus for students transferring to 4-year colleges.

Contact. E-mail: info@chattcollege.com
Phone: (770) 528-4465 Fax: (770) 528-5818
Nichole Kennedy, Director of Admissions, Chattahoochee Technical College, 980 South Cobb Drive, Marietta, GA 30060

Coastal Georgia Community College

Brunswick, Georgia **CB member**
www.cgcc.edu **CB code: 5078**

- Public 2-year community college
- Commuter campus in large town

General. Founded in 1961. Regionally accredited. Students may take courses at Camden Center in Kingsland. **Enrollment:** 2,144 full-time, degree-seeking students. **Degrees:** 184 associate awarded. **Location:** 70 miles from Savannah, 60 miles from Jacksonville, Florida. **Calendar:** Semester, limited summer session. **Full-time faculty:** 73 total; 8% minority, 62% women. **Part-time faculty:** 68 total. **Class size:** 53% < 20, 47% 20-39, less than 1% >100.

Student profile. Among full-time, degree-seeking students, 65% enrolled in a transfer program, 35% enrolled in a vocational program.

Transfer out. Colleges most students transferred to 2005: Armstrong Atlantic State University, Georgia Southern University.

Basis for selection. Open admission, but selective for some programs. Must be graduate of a regionally accredited high school or GED program. Tests are not required, but will be used to exempt students from placement testing. Interviews required of those applying for registered nursing and allied health programs. **Adult students:** SAT/ACT scores not required. SAT will be considered if taken. Otherwise adult students new to college will be given a placement exam. **Homeschooled:** Statement describing homeschool structure and mission, transcript of courses and grades, letter of recommendation (nonparent) required. Must take SAT or ACT and score at the average of last year's Freshman class. **Learning Disabled:** Students must go through an accreditation process with system agency on learning disabilities to receive accommodations.

High school preparation. 16 units recommended. Recommended units include English 4, mathematics 4, social studies 3, science 2 (laboratory 1) and foreign language 2. College-preparatory program recommended only of prebaccalaureate transfer program applicants.

2005-2006 Annual costs. Tuition/fees: $1,754; $6,378 out-of-state. Per-credit charge: $65 in-state; $257 out-of-state. Books/supplies: $600. Personal expenses: $500.

Financial aid. Non-need-based: Scholarships awarded for academics, leadership, state residency.

Application procedures. Admission: $20 fee, may be waived for applicants with need. Application may be submitted online. Admission notification on a rolling basis. **Financial aid:** Priority date 5/1; no closing date. FAFSA required. Applicants notified on a rolling basis starting 7/1.

Academics. Special study options: Cooperative education, distance learning, dual enrollment of high school students, independent study, liberal arts/career combination, study abroad, teacher certification program. Bachelor's degree programs available on campus. **Credit/placement by examination:** AP, CLEP, SAT, ACT, institutional tests. 30 credit hours maximum toward associate degree. **Support services:** GED preparation and test center, learning center, reduced course load, remedial instruction, study skills assistance, tutoring.

Majors. Agriculture: Agribusiness operations. **Biology:** General. **Business:** Accounting, administrative services, management information systems, marketing. **Communications:** General. **Computer sciences:** Computer science. **Education:** General, elementary, middle, secondary, special. **Engineering:** General. **Engineering technology:** Drafting. **English:** English lit. **Foreign languages:** General. **Health:** Clinical lab technology, medical radiologic technology/radiation therapy, nursing (RN). **History:** General. **Legal studies:** Prelaw. **Liberal arts:** Arts/sciences. **Math:** General. **Mechanic/repair:** Electronics/electrical. **Parks/recreation:** General. **Physical sciences:** Chemistry, physics. **Protective services:** Law enforcement admin. **Psychology:** General. **Social sciences:** Sociology. **Visual/performing arts:** Art.

Computing on campus. 300 workstations in library, computer center, student center. Commuter students can connect to campus network. Online course registration, online library, helpline available.

Student life. Freshman orientation: Mandatory. Preregistration for classes offered. **Activities:** Literary magazine, student government, student newspaper, minority club, Baptist student union.

Athletics. NJCAA. **Intercollegiate:** Basketball M, softball W. **Intramural:** Archery, badminton, basketball, bowling, cross-country, golf, handball, racquetball, softball, swimming, table tennis, tennis, volleyball. **Team name:** Mariners.

Student services. Adult student services, career counseling, student employment services, minority student services, personal counseling, placement for graduates, veterans' counselor. **Physically disabled:** Services for visually, hearing impaired. **Transfer:** Special adviser, orientation for new students. College fairs on campus for students transferring to 4-year colleges.

Contact. E-mail: admiss@cgcc.edu
Phone: (912) 264-7253 Fax: (912) 262-3072
Lisa Lesseig, Registrar/Director of Admissions, Coastal Georgia Community College, 3700 Altama Avenue, Brunswick, GA 31520

Columbus Technical College

Columbus, Georgia
www.columbustech.org **CB code: 7005**

- Public 2-year technical college
- Commuter campus in small city
- Interview required

General. Founded in 1961. Regionally accredited. **Enrollment:** 3,450 undergraduates. **Degrees:** 97 associate awarded. **Location:** 110 miles from Atlanta, 86 miles from Albany. **Calendar:** Quarter, extensive summer session. **Full-time faculty:** 74 total; 4% have terminal degrees, 23% minority, 60% women.

Student profile. 100% enrolled in a vocational program.

Basis for selection. Open admission, but selective for some programs. Special requirements for health programs. ASSET, SAT required for some programs.

2006-2007 Annual costs. Tuition/fees (projected): $1,807; $3,295 out-of-state. Per-credit charge: $31 in-state; $62 out-of-state. Books/supplies: $1,600. Personal expenses: $1,100.

Financial aid. Need-based: Need-based aid available for part-time students.

Application procedures. Admission: Closing date 9/16. $15 fee. Application may be submitted online. Notification before registration date. **Financial aid:** No deadline. FAFSA required. Applicants notified on a rolling basis.

Academics. Special study options: Distance learning, dual enrollment of high school students, honors, internships. License preparation in dental hygiene, nursing, paramedic, radiology, real estate. **Credit/placement by examination:** AP, CLEP. **Support services:** Learning center, remedial instruction, study skills assistance, tutoring.

Majors. Agriculture: Horticultural science. **Business:** Accounting, administrative services, business admin. **Education:** Early childhood. **Engineering technology:** Electrical. **Health:** Cardiovascular technology, dental hygiene, nursing (RN), surgical technology. **Mechanic/repair:** Automotive, industrial.

Computing on campus. 40 workstations in library, computer center. Online library available.

Student life. Freshman orientation: Mandatory. Preregistration for classes offered. 3-hour orientation held the day before the start of classes. **Policies:** Freshmen permitted cars on campus. **Activities:** Student government.

Student services. Career counseling, student employment services, financial aid counseling, personal counseling, placement for graduates, veterans' counselor. **Physically disabled:** Services for speech, hearing impaired. **Transfer:** Special adviser, orientation for new students.

Contact. Phone: (706) 649-1800 Fax: (404) 649-1885
Nicole Kennedy, Director of Admissions, Columbus Technical College, 928 Manchester Expressway, Columbus, GA 31904-6572

Darton College

Albany, Georgia **CB member**
www.darton.edu **CB code: 5026**

- Public 2-year community college
- Commuter campus in small city
- SAT or ACT (ACT writing recommended) required

General. Founded in 1963. Regionally accredited. **Enrollment:** 4,578 degree-seeking undergraduates. **Degrees:** 467 associate awarded. **ROTC:** Army. **Location:** 175 miles from Atlanta. **Calendar:** Semester, limited summer session. **Full-time faculty:** 85 total. **Part-time faculty:** 120 total. **Class size:** 52% < 20, 43% 20-39, 3% 40-49, 1% 50-99. **Special facilities:** 50-foot Carolina Tower and climbing wall, nature trail.

Student profile.

Out-of-state:	37%	**25 or older:**	40%

Transfer out. Colleges most students transferred to 2005: Georgia Southwestern State University, Albany State University, Florida State University, Valdosta State University.

Basis for selection. Traditional students must have 1.8 high school GPA, 330 verbal SAT, 310 math SAT, or GED minimum score of 2750 for acceptance. Interview, portfolios and essays are considered when students do not meet minimum admission requirements but still show promise. **Adult students:** SAT/ACT scores not required.

High school preparation. 16 units required. Required units include English 4, mathematics 4, social studies 3, science 3 and foreign language 2.

2005-2006 Annual costs. Tuition/fees: $1,842; $6,466 out-of-state. Per-credit charge: $65 in-state; $257 out-of-state. Books/supplies: $1,100. Personal expenses: $1,200.

Financial aid. Need-based: Need-based aid available for part-time students. Work study available nights, weekends and for part-time students. **Non-need-based:** Scholarships awarded for academics, alumni affiliation, art, athletics, music/drama, state residency. **Additional information:** Auditions, portfolios, essays, extracurricular activities impact scholarship decisions.

Application procedures. Admission: No deadline. $20 fee. Application may be submitted online. Admission notification on a rolling basis. Applications must be received 10 days prior to registration. **Financial aid:** No deadline. FAFSA, institutional form required. Applicants notified on a rolling basis; must reply within 3 week(s) of notification.

Academics. Career and transfer programs available. Career graduates aggressively recruited. **Special study options:** Cooperative education, cross-registration, distance learning, double major, dual enrollment of high school students, ESL, honors, independent study, liberal arts/career combination, study abroad, weekend college. License preparation in dental hygiene, nursing, occupational therapy, paramedic, physical therapy. **Credit/placement by examination:** AP, CLEP, institutional tests. 18-hours residence courses required. **Support services:** Learning center, reduced course load, remedial instruction, study skills assistance, tutoring, writing center.

Majors. Agriculture: General, horticulture. **Biology:** General. **Business:** General, accounting, administrative services, business admin, entrepreneurial studies, management information systems, office management. **Communications:** Journalism. **Computer sciences:** General, applications programming, computer science, data processing, information systems, networking, programming. **Conservation:** Environmental studies, forestry. **Education:** General, art, business, English, foreign languages, kindergarten/preschool, mathematics, middle, multi-level teacher, music, physical, secondary, social science, social studies, speech, teacher assistance, technology/industrial arts, trade/industrial. **Engineering:** General, agricultural. **Engineering technology:** General, drafting, industrial. **English:** English lit, speech/rhetoric. **Family/consumer sciences:** Child care, institutional food production. **Foreign languages:** General. **Health:** Cardiovascular technology, clinical lab science, clinical lab technology, community health services, dental hygiene, EMT paramedic, histologic assistant, licensed practical nurse, medical assistant, medical radiologic technology/radiation therapy, medical records admin, medical records technology, mental health services, nuclear medical technology, nursing (RN), occupational therapy assistant, office admin, ophthalmic lab technology, physical therapy assistant, physician assistant, predentistry, premedicine, prepharmacy, preveterinary, public health ed, respiratory therapy assistant, respiratory therapy technology, sonography, surgical technology. **History:** General. **Legal studies:** Paralegal. **Liberal arts:** Arts/sciences, humanities. **Math:** General. **Mechanic/repair:** Electronics/electrical, heating/ac/refrig. **Parks/recreation:** General, exercise sciences, health/fitness. **Philosophy/religion:** Philosophy. **Physical sciences:** Chemistry, physics. **Protective services:** Criminal justice, forensics. **Psychology:** General. **Public administration:** General, human services, social work. **Social sciences:** General, anthropology, criminology, economics, geography, political science, sociology. **Visual/performing arts:** General, art, commercial/advertising art, dramatic.

Computing on campus. 400 workstations in library, computer center. Commuter students can connect to campus network. Online course registration, helpline, wireless network available.

Student life. Freshman orientation: Available. Preregistration for classes offered. Held every semester, required of all students enrolled in learning support classes. **Activities:** Bands, choral groups, drama, literary magazine, music ensembles, musical theater, student government, student newspaper, symphony orchestra.

Athletics. NJCAA. **Intercollegiate:** Baseball M, basketball W, golf, soccer, softball W, swimming. **Intramural:** Basketball, bowling, golf, softball, table tennis, tennis, volleyball. **Team name:** Cavaliers.

Student services. Alcohol/substance abuse counseling, career counseling, student employment services, financial aid counseling, minority student services, personal counseling, placement for graduates. **Physically disabled:** Services for visually, speech, hearing impaired. **Transfer:** Special adviser, pre-admission transcript evaluation for new students. Transfer adviser, college fairs on campus for students transferring to 4-year colleges.

Contact. E-mail: info@darton.edu
Phone: (229) 430-6740 Toll-free number: (866) 775-1214
Fax: (229) 430-2926
Terri Carroll, Director of Admission, Darton College, 2400 Gillionville Road, Albany, GA 31707-3098

DeKalb Technical College

Clarkston, Georgia
www.dekalbtech.edu **CB code: 3226**

- Public 2-year technical college
- Commuter campus in large city

General. Founded in 1961. Regionally accredited. Second campus located in Covington. **Enrollment:** 4,063 degree-seeking undergraduates. **Degrees:** 223 associate awarded. **Location:** 17 miles from Atlanta. **Calendar:** Quarter, extensive summer session. **Full-time faculty:** 86 total; 2% have terminal degrees, 30% minority, 44% women. **Part-time faculty:** 193 total; 49% minority, 66% women. **Class size:** 88% < 20, 12% 20-39. **Partnerships:** Formal partnerships wtih MARTA (Employee Training); Fulton County Government (Employee training); DeKalb , Rockdale, Newton, Morgan County Schools and Decatur City Schools (Articulation Agreements).

Student profile. Among degree-seeking undergraduates, 2% enrolled in a transfer program, 100% enrolled in a vocational program, 3% already have a bachelor's degree or higher, 1,147 enrolled as first-time, first-year students.

Part-time:	65%	**25 or older:**	40%
Women:	63%		

Transfer out. Colleges most students transferred to 2005: Georgia State University, Southern Polytechnic State University, DeVry University, Clayton College and State University, Georgia Perimeter College.

Basis for selection. Open admission, but selective for some programs. ASSET or COMPASS test required for placement. Test scores most important for placement into specific study programs. Interview recommended. **Adult students:** Entrance exam policies same as for first-time freshmen.

2005-2006 Annual costs. Tuition/fees: $1,407; $2,523 out-of-state. Per-credit charge: $31 in-state; $62 out-of-state. Books/supplies: $1,200. Personal expenses: $900.

2005-2006 Financial aid. Need-based: 342 full-time freshmen applied for aid; 280 were judged to have need; 257 of these received aid. Average need met was 43%. Average scholarship/grant was $3,048. Need-based aid available for part-time students. Work study available nights, weekends and for part-time students.

Application procedures. Admission: Closing date 8/22 (receipt date). $15 fee. Application must be submitted on paper. Admission notification on a rolling basis. **Financial aid:** Priority date 7/15, closing date 8/20. FAFSA required. Applicants notified on a rolling basis starting 6/1.

Academics. Special study options: Distance learning, dual enrollment of high school students, ESL, internships. License preparation in nursing, paramedic, real estate. **Credit/placement by examination:** AP, CLEP, institutional tests. 35 credit hours maximum toward associate degree. **Support services:** GED preparation and test center, learning center, reduced course load, remedial instruction, study skills assistance, tutoring.

Majors. Business: Accounting, business admin, marketing. **Computer sciences:** General, programming. **Engineering:** Computer, electrical. **Engineering technology:** Electrical, instrumentation. **Health:** Ophthalmic lab technology, optician. **Mechanic/repair:** Automotive.

Most popular majors. Business/marketing 29%, computer/information sciences 35%, education 10%, legal studies 8%.

Computing on campus. 500 workstations in computer center. Online course registration, online library available.

Student life. Freshman orientation: Available. **Policies:** Freshmen permitted cars on campus. **Activities:** Student government, student newspaper, Delta Epsilon Chi, Collegiate Secretaries International, Noon Net-Working of New Connections, Phi Beta Lambda, Student Optical Society, GA Licensed Practical Nurses Association, Inc., Vocational Industrial Clubs of America, Epsilon Delta Phi Honorary Society, Phi Theta Kappa Honor Society.

Student services. Adult student services, career counseling, services for economically disadvantaged, student employment services, financial aid counseling, minority student services, placement for graduates, veterans' counselor, women's services. **Physically disabled:** Services for visually, speech, hearing impaired. **Transfer:** Special adviser, orientation, pre-admission transcript evaluation for new students.

Contact. E-mail: admissionsclark@dekalbtech.org
Phone: (404) 297-9522 ext. 1602 Fax: (404) 294-3424
Terry Richardson, Coordinator of Admissions and Special Services, DeKalb Technical College, 495 North Indian Creek Drive, Clarkston, GA 30021-2397

East Georgia College

Swainsboro, Georgia **CB member**
www.ega.edu **CB code: 5200**

- Public 2-year community and junior college
- Commuter campus in small town

General. Founded in 1973. Regionally accredited. **Enrollment:** 1,511 degree-seeking undergraduates. **Degrees:** 105 associate awarded. **Location:** 80 miles from Savannah, Augusta, and Macon. **Calendar:** Semester, limited summer session. **Full-time faculty:** 33 total; 42% have terminal degrees, 6% minority, 21% women. **Part-time faculty:** 26 total; 15% have terminal degrees, 31% minority, 77% women. **Class size:** 37% < 20, 60% 20-39, 3% 40-49. **Special facilities:** Nature trail, outdoor exercise trail, fitness/wellness center.

Student profile.

Out-of-state:	1%	**25 or older:**	20%

Transfer out. Colleges most students transferred to 2005: Georgia Southern University.

Basis for selection. Minimum SAT verbal 330, math 310 or ACT English 12, math 14, or 1.8 high school GPA in college preparatory courses. Incoming freshmen must take collegiate placement examination. **Adult students:** SAT/ACT scores not required if out of high school 5 year(s) or more. **Homeschooled:** SAT scores equal to or greater than previous year's SAT average for first-time entering freshmen and validation with a portfolio of each CPC area.

High school preparation. 16 units recommended. Recommended units include English 4, mathematics 4, social studies 3, science 3 and foreign language 2.

2005-2006 Annual costs. Tuition/fees: $1,674; $6,298 out-of-state. Per-credit charge: $65 in-state; $257 out-of-state. Books/supplies: $600. Personal expenses: $900.

Financial aid. Need-based: Need-based aid available for part-time students. **Non-need-based:** Scholarships awarded for academics, leadership, state residency.

Application procedures. Admission: No deadline. $20 fee, may be waived for applicants with need. Application may be submitted online. Admission notification on a rolling basis beginning on or about 2/1. **Financial aid:** Priority date 6/15; no closing date. FAFSA, institutional form required. Applicants notified on a rolling basis starting 6/15; must reply within 2 week(s) of notification.

Academics. Special study options: Cross-registration, distance learning, double major, dual enrollment of high school students, honors, independent study, study abroad. License preparation in nursing. **Credit/placement by examination:** CLEP, institutional tests. 30 credit hours maximum toward associate degree. **Support services:** Learning center, reduced course load, remedial instruction, study skills assistance, tutoring, writing center.

Majors. Agriculture: General. **Biology:** General. **Business:** Business admin. **Computer sciences:** General, computer science, information technology. **Education:** General, business, multi-level teacher. **Family/consumer sciences:** General. **Foreign languages:** Translation. **Health:** Prenursing. **History:** General. **Liberal arts:** Arts/sciences. **Math:** General. **Parks/recreation:** General, exercise sciences, health/fitness. **Physical sciences:** Chemistry, geology. **Protective services:** Criminal justice. **Psychology:** General. **Social sciences:** Anthropology, criminology, political science, sociology. **Visual/performing arts:** Art.

Computing on campus. 120 workstations in library, computer center, student center. Commuter students can connect to campus network. Online course registration, online library, wireless network available.

Student life. Freshman orientation: Mandatory. Preregistration for classes offered. Combined 1-day orientation/registration. **Policies:** Substance-free campus. Freshmen permitted cars on campus. **Activities:** Choral groups, drama, literary magazine, student government, student newspaper, Baptist Student Union, Afro-American Union, earth club, Students in Free Enterprise, Student Professional Association of Georgia Educators, art club, international club, Quiz Bowl, Circle K, Non-Traditonal Club.

Athletics. Intramural: Basketball M, football (non-tackle) M, soccer M, softball, table tennis, tennis, volleyball, weight lifting. **Team name:** Renegades.

Student services. Adult student services, career counseling, financial aid counseling, minority student services, personal counseling, veterans' counselor. **Transfer:** Special adviser, orientation, pre-admission transcript evaluation for new students. Transfer adviser, college fairs on campus for students transferring to 4-year colleges.

Contact. E-mail: davery@ega.edu
Phone: (478) 289-2017 Fax: (478) 289-2038
Donald Avery, Director of Enrollment Services, East Georgia College, 131 College Circle, Swainsboro, GA 30401-2699

Gainesville State College

Gainesville, Georgia
www.gsc.edu **CB code: 5273**

- Public 2-year community and junior college
- Commuter campus in large town

General. Founded in 1964. Regionally accredited. **Enrollment:** 4,985 degree-seeking undergraduates. **Degrees:** 566 associate awarded. **Location:** 45 miles from Atlanta, 40 miles from Athens. **Calendar:** Semester, extensive summer session. **Full-time faculty:** 131 total. **Part-time faculty:** 171 total. **Class size:** 22% < 20, 78% 20-39, less than 1% 40-49, less than 1% 50-99.

Student profile. Among degree-seeking undergraduates, 95% enrolled in a transfer program, 5% enrolled in a vocational program, 2% already have a bachelor's degree or higher, 2,519 transferred in from other institutions.

Transfer out. 85% of students enrolled in the transfer program go on to 4-year colleges. **Colleges most students transferred to 2005:** North Georgia College and State University, University of Georgia, Brenau University, Georgia State University, Athens Technical College.

Basis for selection. Minimum high school GPA of 2.0 for applicants with college prep curriculum diploma. Minimum high school GPA of 2.2 for applicants with technical prep curriculum diploma. **Adult students:** SAT/ACT scores not required if out of high school 5 year(s) or more.

High school preparation. 16 units required. Required units include English 4, mathematics 4, social studies 3, science 3 (laboratory 3) and foreign language 2.

2005-2006 Annual costs. Tuition/fees: $1,686; $6,310 out-of-state. Per-credit charge: $65 in-state; $257 out-of-state. Books/supplies: $630. Personal expenses: $1,000.

2004-2005 Financial aid. Need-based: Average need met was 22%. Average scholarship/grant was $2,760; average loan $2,154. 69% of total undergraduate aid awarded as scholarships/grants, 31% as loans/jobs. Need-based aid available for part-time students. **Non-need-based:** Scholarships awarded for academics, art, leadership, music/drama.

Application procedures. Admission: Priority date 7/1; deadline 3/15 (postmark date). $25 fee, may be waived for applicants with need. Application may be submitted online. Admission notification on a rolling basis. Must reply by 7/1. **Financial aid:** Priority date 6/1; no closing date. FAFSA required. Applicants notified on a rolling basis starting 5/1; must reply within 2 week(s) of notification.

Academics. Special study options: Distance learning, dual enrollment of high school students, ESL, honors, study abroad. Bachelor's degree programs available on campus. License preparation in dental hygiene, paramedic. **Credit/placement by examination:** AP, CLEP, institutional tests. 30 credit hours maximum toward associate degree. **Support services:** Learning center, remedial instruction, study skills assistance, tutoring, writing center.

Majors. Agriculture: General, business. **Business:** General, accounting, administrative services, business admin. **Communications:** Journalism. **Computer sciences:** General. **Conservation:** Forestry. **Education:** General, art, early childhood, elementary, English, mathematics, music, physical, science, secondary, social science. **Engineering:** General. **Engineering technology:** Electrical. **Family/consumer sciences:** Child care. **Health:** Dental hygiene, EMT paramedic. **History:** General. **Legal studies:** Paralegal. **Liberal arts:** Arts/sciences. **Math:** General. **Physical sciences:** Chemistry, geology, physics. **Protective services:** Criminal justice. **Psychology:** General. **Public administration:** Social work. **Social sciences:** Anthropology, political science, sociology. **Visual/performing arts:** Dramatic, music performance, studio arts.

Computing on campus. 600 workstations in library, computer center, student center. Commuter students can connect to campus network. Online course registration, online library, helpline, wireless network available.

Student life. Freshman orientation: Mandatory. Preregistration for classes offered. **Activities:** Bands, choral groups, drama, literary magazine, music ensembles, musical theater, student government, student newspaper.

Athletics. Intramural: Basketball, bowling, football (non-tackle), golf, softball, tennis, volleyball.

Student services. Adult student services, alcohol/substance abuse counseling, career counseling, student employment services, financial aid counseling, minority student services, personal counseling, placement for graduates, veterans' counselor. **Physically disabled:** Services for visually, speech, hearing impaired. **Transfer:** Special adviser, orientation for new students. Transfer adviser, college fairs on campus for students transferring to 4-year colleges.

Contact. E-mail: admissions@gsc.edu
Phone: (770) 718-3641 Fax: (770) 718-3643
Mack Palmour, Director of Admissions, Gainesville State College, PO Box 1358, Gainesville, GA 30503

Georgia Highlands College

Rome, Georgia **CB member**
www.highlands.edu **CB code: 5237**

- Public 2-year community and liberal arts college
- Commuter campus in small city

General. Founded in 1968. Regionally accredited. Classes offered at Cartersville, Acworth, Marietta, Rome. **Enrollment:** 3,666 degree-seeking undergraduates; 151 non-degree-seeking students. **Degrees:** 363 associate awarded. **Location:** 75 miles from Atlanta. **Calendar:** Semester, limited summer session. **Full-time faculty:** 85 total. **Part-time faculty:** 110 total. **Special facilities:** Observatory, wetland preserve. **Partnerships:** Formal partnership with Georgia Department of Labor.

Student profile. Among degree-seeking undergraduates, 85% enrolled in a transfer program, 15% enrolled in a vocational program, 1% already have

a bachelor's degree or higher, 1,021 enrolled as first-time, first-year students.

Part-time:	44%	**Asian American:**	2%
Women:	65%	**Hispanic American:**	3%
African American:	11%	**International:**	1%

Transfer out. Colleges most students transferred to 2005: Kennesaw State, State University of West Georgia, Berry College, Shorter College, University of Georgia.

Basis for selection. No longer require the SAT or ACT exam. A 2.0 CP or 2.2 TP HSGPA required. TOEFL, SAT, or ACT required of non-native English speakers. COMPASS placement examinations required for some. **Adult students:** SAT/ACT scores not required if out of high school 5 year(s) or more. COMPASS placement exam required. **Homeschooled:** Statement describing homeschool structure and mission, transcript of courses and grades, state high school equivalency certificate required. Must submit SAT scores that are equal to or greater than last year's freshman class and a completed Home School CPC Evaluation Form; portfolio required. **Learning Disabled:** Foreign language college preparatory curriculum may be waived through Georgia Board of Regents Center of Learning Disabilities.

High school preparation. 16 units recommended. Recommended units include English 4, mathematics 4, social studies 3, science 3 (laboratory 2) and foreign language 2. College preparatory program required for students planning to transfer to 4-year school.

2005-2006 Annual costs. Tuition/fees: $1,740; $6,364 out-of-state. Per-credit charge: $65 in-state; $257 out-of-state. Books/supplies: $450. Personal expenses: $250.

Financial aid. Need-based: Work study available nights and for part-time students. **Non-need-based:** Scholarships awarded for academics, art.

Application procedures. Admission: Priority date 7/1; no deadline. $20 fee. Application may be submitted online. Admission notification on a rolling basis. **Financial aid:** Closing date 4/1. FAFSA required. Applicants notified on a rolling basis starting 4/1; must reply within 2 week(s) of notification.

Academics. All classrooms and many common areas wired for computer usage. **Special study options:** Distance learning, double major, dual enrollment of high school students, independent study, liberal arts/career combination, study abroad. License preparation in dental hygiene, nursing, physical therapy. **Credit/placement by examination:** AP, CLEP, SAT, ACT, institutional tests. College placement examination required for applicants with SAT I verbal score below 480, SAT I math score below 440. **Support services:** Remedial instruction, study skills assistance, tutoring.

Majors. Agriculture: Horticultural science, landscaping. **Biology:** General. **Business:** General, administrative services, hospitality/recreation. **Communications:** General, journalism. **Computer sciences:** General. **Education:** General, multi-level teacher. **Foreign languages:** Sign language interpretation. **Health:** Dental hygiene, EMT paramedic, health services, medical radiologic technology/radiation therapy, medical records admin, nursing (RN), premedicine, prepharmacy, preveterinary, respiratory therapy technology. **Legal studies:** Paralegal. **Liberal arts:** Arts/sciences. **Math:** General. **Mechanic/repair:** Auto body. **Physical sciences:** Chemistry. **Protective services:** Police science. **Psychology:** General. **Social sciences:** General, urban studies.

Computing on campus. Commuter students can connect to campus network. Online library, helpline, repair service, student web hosting, wireless network available.

Student life. Freshman orientation: Mandatory. **Policies:** New Access program tracks all student involvement in school and community activities. Transcripts available for resume use or transferring to another institution. Freshmen permitted cars on campus. **Housing:** Housing available through Southern Poly Tech University for Marietta Campus. **Activities:** Literary magazine, student government, student newspaper, TV station, Baptist Student Union, College Bowl Team, volunteer opportunity center, Black Student Awareness, Insiders, Phi Theta Kappa.

Athletics. Intramural: Archery, badminton, basketball, bowling, field hockey W, football (tackle) M, golf, sailing, skiing, soccer, softball, table tennis, tennis, volleyball, wrestling M. **Team name:** Chargers.

Student services. Adult student services, alcohol/substance abuse counseling, career counseling, student employment services, financial aid counseling, minority student services, personal counseling, placement for graduates, veterans' counselor. **Physically disabled:** Services for visually, speech, hearing impaired. **Transfer:** Special adviser, orientation, re-entry adviser, pre-admission transcript evaluation for new students. College fairs on campus for students transferring to 4-year colleges.

Contact. E-mail: admitme@highlands.edu
Phone: (706) 295-6339 Toll-free number: (800) 332-2406 ext. 6339
Fax: (706) 295-6341
Todd Jones, Director of Admissons, Georgia Highlands College, 3175 Cedartown Highway, SE, Rome, GA 30161

Georgia Military College
Milledgeville, Georgia
www.gmc.cc.ga.us **CB code: 5249**

- Public 2-year junior and military college
- Commuter campus in large town

General. Founded in 1879. Regionally accredited. Multilocation institution. 2-year ROTC commissioning program on main campus. Military base programs and degree programs for civilians. **Enrollment:** 4,724 degree-seeking undergraduates. **Degrees:** 697 associate awarded. **ROTC:** Army. **Location:** 90 miles from Atlanta, 30 miles from Macon. **Calendar:** Quarter, limited summer session. **Full-time faculty:** 96 total; 15% have terminal degrees, 50% women. **Part-time faculty:** 232 total; 21% have terminal degrees, 61% women. **Class size:** 66% < 20, 34% 20-39.

Student profile. Among degree-seeking undergraduates, 1,042 enrolled as first-time, first-year students.

Part-time:	37%	**Asian American:**	1%
Out-of-state:	9%	**Hispanic American:**	3%
Women:	60%	**25 or older:**	37%
African American:	39%	**Live on campus:**	5%

Basis for selection. Open admission, but selective for some programs. ROTC applicants for early commissioning must have SAT combined score of 920 (exclusive of Writing) or ACT composite score of 19 and minimum 2.0 high school GPA. ROTC contract students must have combined SAT score of 920 (exclusive of Writing) or ACT composite score of 19. Interview recommended for ROTC cadets. **Homeschooled:** A list of courses completed and bibliography of textbooks and/or assigned readings used. Must also submit a writing sample or show successful GED completion.

2006-2007 Annual costs. Tuition/fees (projected): $13,214. Quoted full-time tuition and fees are for cadet students. Additional $1,150 for uniforms. Room/board: $3,840. Books/supplies: $1,050. Personal expenses: $900.

2004-2005 Financial aid. Need-based: Average scholarship/grant was $1,011. 75% of total undergraduate aid awarded as scholarships/grants, 25% as loans/jobs. Need-based aid available for part-time students. Work study available nights and for part-time students. **Non-need-based:** Scholarships awarded for athletics, leadership, ROTC, state residency. **Additional information:** Institutional aid offered to those enrolled in Cadet Corps who reside on campus.

Application procedures. Admission: Priority date 8/1; deadline 9/1 (receipt date). $35 fee, may be waived for applicants with need. Application may be submitted online. Admission notification on a rolling basis. August 1 closing date for cadets; September 1 closing date for civilians. Students interested in attending ROTC Basic Camp must apply by May 1. **Financial aid:** No deadline. FAFSA required. Applicants notified on a rolling basis starting 3/1.

Academics. Special study options: Cross-registration, double major, external degree, independent study. **Credit/placement by examination:** AP, CLEP, institutional tests. 45 credit hours maximum toward associate degree. **Support services:** Learning center, reduced course load, remedial instruction, study skills assistance, tutoring.

Majors. Business: Business admin, logistics, office management. **Communications:** Digital media. **Computer sciences:** General. **Education:** General, early childhood. **Engineering technology:** Electrical. **Family/consumer sciences:** Family studies. **Health:** Prenursing. **Mechanic/repair:** Aircraft powerplant. **Philosophy/religion:** Religion. **Protective services:** Criminal justice.

Most popular majors. Business/marketing 15%, education 16%, health sciences 7%, legal studies 8%, psychology 6%.

Computing on campus. 75 workstations in library, computer center, student center. Online library available.

Student life. Freshman orientation: Available. Preregistration for classes offered. 2 summer orientation sessions, college athlete orientation, early commissioning orientation, state service scholarship orientation, one final orientation each quarter. **Policies:** Resident programs are only available to members of the Corps of Cadets. Freshmen permitted cars on campus. **Housing:** Single-sex dorms, substance-free housing available. $75 deposit, deadline 9/1. **Activities:** Marching band, choral groups, drama, literary magazine, student government, student newspaper, Circle-K,,Phi Theta Kappa,,Alpha Phi Omega, Ranger Challenge, drill team, drama club, officer Christians' fellowship, business club, math club, student government association, debate/speech organization.

Athletics. NJCAA. **Intercollegiate:** Cross-country, football (tackle) M, golf, rifle, soccer, track and field. **Intramural:** Badminton, basketball, bowling, golf, softball, volleyball. **Team name:** Bulldogs.

Student services. Alcohol/substance abuse counseling, career counseling, financial aid counseling, health services, personal counseling, veterans' counselor. **Physically disabled:** Services for visually, speech, hearing impaired. **Transfer:** Special adviser, orientation for new students.

Contact. E-mail: Admissionsinfo@gmc.cc.ga.us
Phone: (478) 445-2707 Toll-free number: (800) 342-0413
Fax: (478) 445-2688
Donna Findley, Director of Admissions and Enrollments, Georgia Military College, 201 East Greene Street, Milledgeville, GA 31061

Georgia Perimeter College

Clarkston, Georgia — **CB member**
www.gpc.edu — **CB code: 5711**

- Public 2-year junior and liberal arts college
- Commuter campus in very large city

General. Founded in 1964. Regionally accredited. 4 campuses; Clarkston, Dunwoody, Decatur, Lawrenceville; educational center in Rockdale County; educational site in Alpharetta. **Enrollment:** 20,461 degree-seeking undergraduates. **Degrees:** 1,310 associate awarded. **Calendar:** Semester, extensive summer session. **Full-time faculty:** 379 total; 28% have terminal degrees, 28% minority, 58% women. **Part-time faculty:** 1,341 total; 16% have terminal degrees, 37% minority, 54% women. **Class size:** 38% < 20, 59% 20-39, 2% 40-49, less than 1% 50-99, less than 1% >100. **Special facilities:** Botanical gardens.

Student profile. Among degree-seeking undergraduates, 100% enrolled in a transfer program, 4% enrolled in a vocational program, 3,801 enrolled as first-time, first-year students, 1,219 transferred in from other institutions.

Part-time:	55%	**Women:**	62%
Out-of-state:	22%	**25 or older:**	36%

Transfer out. Colleges most students transferred to 2005: Georgia State University, University of Georgia.

Basis for selection. Admission is based on high school GPA. Any college preparatory curriculum deficiencies must be satisfied by placement testing or substituting college coursework. COMPASS is used for placement in English, reading, and mathematics. SAT or ACT scores are used as supplements to the COMPASS results for English and reading. Satisfactory SAT or ACT scores may exempt some students from English and reading placement testing. If scores are submitted, they will be used for advisement and/or placement, but not used in admission decision. Interview required of nursing and dental hygiene majors. **Adult students:** SAT/ACT scores not required. **Homeschooled:** Transcript of courses and grades required. A detailed portfolio must be submitted.

High school preparation. 16 units required. Required units include English 4, mathematics 4, social studies 3, science 3 (laboratory 2) and foreign language 2.

2005-2006 Annual costs. Tuition/fees: $1,822; $6,446 out-of-state. Per-credit charge: $65 in-state; $257 out-of-state. Books/supplies: $1,000. Personal expenses: $1,200.

2004-2005 Financial aid. Need-based: 77% of total undergraduate aid awarded as scholarships/grants, 23% as loans/jobs. Need-based aid available for part-time students. Work study available nights, weekends and for part-time students.

Application procedures. Admission: Closing date 7/1 (postmark date). $20 fee, may be waived for applicants with need. Application may be submitted online. Admission notification on a rolling basis. **Financial aid:** Closing date 6/1. FAFSA required. Applicants notified on a rolling basis; must reply within 3 week(s) of notification.

Academics. Special study options: Accelerated study, distance learning, double major, ESL, honors, liberal arts/career combination, study abroad, weekend college. Bachelor's degree programs available on campus. License preparation in dental hygiene, nursing. **Credit/placement by examination:** AP, CLEP, institutional tests. **Support services:** Learning center, remedial instruction, study skills assistance, tutoring.

Majors. Biology: General. **Business:** Business admin. **Communications:** General, journalism. **Computer sciences:** Computer science, information technology. **Education:** General, health, physical. **Engineering:** General. **Foreign languages:** General, sign language interpretation. **Health:** Dental hygiene, nursing (RN), predentistry, premedicine, prepharmacy. **History:** General. **Math:** General. **Philosophy/religion:** Philosophy. **Physical sciences:** Chemistry, geology, physics. **Protective services:** Fire services admin, law enforcement admin. **Psychology:** General. **Social sciences:** Anthropology, political science, sociology. **Visual/performing arts:** Art, dramatic.

Most popular majors. Health sciences 7%, liberal arts 92%.

Computing on campus. Online course registration, online library, helpline available.

Student life. Freshman orientation: Mandatory. Preregistration for classes offered. Six hour program. **Activities:** Jazz band, choral groups, drama, literary magazine, music ensembles, musical theater, student government, student newspaper, symphony orchestra, international student club, Campus Crusade for Christ, Muslim student association, student government association, math club, drama club, computer club.

Athletics. NJCAA. **Intercollegiate:** Baseball M, basketball, soccer, softball W, tennis. **Team name:** Jaguars.

Student services. Adult student services, career counseling, services for economically disadvantaged, financial aid counseling, minority student services, on-campus daycare, personal counseling, veterans' counselor. **Physically disabled:** Services for visually, hearing impaired. **Transfer:** Special adviser, orientation for new students. Transfer adviser, college fairs on campus for students transferring to 4-year colleges.

Contact. Phone: (678) 891-3250 Toll-free number: (888) 696-2780
Fax: (404) 299-4574
Douglas Ruch, Director for Admissions and Records, Georgia Perimeter College, 555 North Indian Creek Drive, Clarkston, GA 30021-2361

Gordon College

Barnesville, Georgia — **CB member**
www.gdn.edu — **CB code: 5256**

- Public 2-year junior college
- Commuter campus in small town

General. Founded in 1852. Regionally accredited. **Enrollment:** 3,473 degree-seeking undergraduates; 27 non-degree-seeking students. **Degrees:** 409 associate awarded. **Location:** 57 miles from Atlanta. **Calendar:** Semester, limited summer session. **Full-time faculty:** 102 total; 93% have terminal degrees, 47% women. **Part-time faculty:** 53 total; 8% have terminal degrees, 47% women. **Class size:** 17% < 20, 80% 20-39, 1% 40-49, 1% 50-99, less than 1% >100. **Special facilities:** Library room housing Gordon memorabilia dating from 1852, Georgia book collection, performance theater, indoor pool, ropes course, walking trail, ampitheatre.

Student profile. Among degree-seeking undergraduates, 1,261 enrolled as first-time, first-year students.

Part-time:	33%	**Hispanic American:**	2%
Out-of-state:	1%	**International:**	1%
Women:	64%	**25 or older:**	19%
African American:	31%	**Live on campus:**	16%
Asian American:	1%		

Transfer out. 75% of students enrolled in the transfer program go on to 4-year colleges.

Basis for selection. Test scores, GPA considered in admission decisions. SAT or ACT recommended. Interview required for nursing program. **Adult students:** SAT/ACT scores not required if out of high school 5 year(s) or more. Placement test required. **Homeschooled:** Statement describing homeschool structure and mission required.

High school preparation. College-preparatory program recommended. 16 units recommended. Recommended units include English 4, mathematics 4, social studies 3, science 3 and foreign language 2. Foreign language units must be in same language.

2005-2006 Annual costs. Tuition/fees: $1,742; $6,366 out-of-state. Per-credit charge: $65 in-state; $257 out-of-state. Room/board: $3,990. Books/supplies: $950. Personal expenses: $903.

2004-2005 Financial aid. Need-based: 98% of total undergraduate aid awarded as scholarships/grants, 2% as loans/jobs. Need-based aid available for part-time students. Work study available nights, weekends and for part-time students. **Non-need-based:** Scholarships awarded for academics, athletics, music/drama, state residency.

Application procedures. **Admission:** No deadline. $20 fee. Application may be submitted online. Admission notification on a rolling basis. **Financial aid:** Priority date 5/1; no closing date. Institutional form required. Applicants notified on a rolling basis starting 5/1.

Academics. **Special study options:** Distance learning, dual enrollment of high school students, liberal arts/career combination, study abroad. Bachelor's degree programs available on campus. **Credit/placement by examination:** AP, CLEP, institutional tests. 45 credit hours maximum toward associate degree. **Support services:** Learning center, remedial instruction, study skills assistance, tutoring, writing center.

Majors. **Agriculture:** Horticultural science. **Biology:** General. **Business:** Administrative services, business admin. **Computer sciences:** Computer science, information systems, information technology, networking. **Conservation:** Forestry. **Education:** General, multi-level teacher. **Foreign languages:** General. **Health:** Dental hygiene, medical records admin, nuclear medical technology, nursing (RN), physician assistant, prepharmacy, radiologic technology/medical imaging, respiratory therapy assistant, sonography. **History:** General. **Liberal arts:** Arts/sciences. **Math:** General. **Parks/recreation:** Health/fitness. **Physical sciences:** General, astronomy, chemistry, physics. **Protective services:** Criminal justice. **Psychology:** General. **Public administration:** Social work. **Social sciences:** Political science, sociology. **Visual/performing arts:** Art, dramatic.

Most popular majors. Business/marketing 14%, education 24%, health sciences 29%, psychology 6%.

Computing on campus. 125 workstations in dormitories, library, computer center, student center. Dormitories wired for high-speed internet access and linked to campus network. Commuter students can connect to campus network. Online course registration, online library, helpline available.

Student life. **Freshman orientation:** Mandatory. Preregistration for classes offered. Presentation for student and parents, 5-6 hour duration. Students are given an advisor and their academic standing is reviewed. **Policies:** Freshmen permitted cars on campus. **Housing:** Coed dorms, single-sex dorms, apartments, substance-free housing available. $100 deposit. **Activities:** Choral groups, dance, drama, literary magazine, music ensembles, musical theater, student government, student newspaper, Baptist student union, art club, Fellowship of Christian Athletes, minority advising program, Phi Beta Lambda (business), eplorers club, GA Association of Nursing Students, Draftwood, theater club.

Athletics. NJCAA. **Intercollegiate:** Baseball M, soccer, softball W, tennis W. **Intramural:** Badminton, basketball, football (non-tackle), handball, racquetball, soccer, softball, table tennis, tennis, volleyball. **Team name:** Highlanders.

Student services. Adult student services, alcohol/substance abuse counseling, career counseling, student employment services, financial aid counseling, health services, minority student services, personal counseling, placement for graduates, veterans' counselor. **Physically disabled:** Services for visually impaired. **Transfer:** Special adviser, orientation for new students. College fairs on campus for students transferring to 4-year colleges.

Contact. E-mail: gordon@eagle.gdn.edu
Phone: (770) 358-5000 Fax: (770) 358-3031
Patricia Lemmons, Director of Enrollment Services, Gordon College, 419 College Drive, Barnesville, GA 30204

Griffin Technical College

Griffin, Georgia
www.griftec.org **CB code: 5670**

- Public 2-year technical college
- Small city

General. Regionally accredited. **Enrollment:** 3,408 degree-seeking undergraduates. **Degrees:** 183 associate awarded. **Calendar:** Quarter. **Full-time faculty:** 52 total. **Part-time faculty:** 123 total.

Basis for selection. ASSET test required for admission to associate degree, diploma, and most certificate programs.

2005-2006 Annual costs. Tuition/fees: $1,359; $2,475 out-of-state. Per-credit charge: $31 in-state; $62 out-of-state. Books/supplies: $150. Personal expenses: $587.

Application procedures. **Admission:** No deadline. $15 fee. **Financial aid:** FAFSA, institutional form required. Applicants notified on a rolling basis.

Academics. **Credit/placement by examination:** CLEP.

Majors. **Business:** Accounting, administrative services, business admin, management science. **Computer sciences:** General, information systems. **Engineering technology:** Electrical. **Health:** Radiologic technology/medical imaging. **Protective services:** Law enforcement admin.

Contact. Phone: (770) 228-7348
Christine James-Brown, Vice President of Student Services, Griffin Technical College, 501 Varsity Road, Griffin, GA 30223

Gupton Jones College of Funeral Service

Decatur, Georgia
www.gupton-jones.edu **CB code: 6200**

- Private 2-year technical college
- Commuter campus in very large city

General. Founded in 1920. Accredited by American Board of Funeral Service Education. **Enrollment:** 185 degree-seeking undergraduates. **Degrees:** 116 associate awarded. **Location:** 18 miles from Atlanta. **Calendar:** Quarter. **Full-time faculty:** 7 total; 14% women. **Part-time faculty:** 1 total; 100% women.

Student profile. Among degree-seeking undergraduates, 100% enrolled in a vocational program. Of all enrolled students, 15% already have a bachelor's degree or higher.

Out-of-state:	65%	**25 or older:**	50%
Women:	52%		

Basis for selection. Open admission. **Adult students:** Entrance exam policies same as for first-time freshmen.

2005-2006 Annual costs. Tuition/fees: $7,550. Per-credit charge: $175. Personal expenses: $500.

Financial aid. All financial aid based on need. Need-based aid available for part-time students.

Application procedures. **Admission:** No deadline. $50 fee. Application may be submitted online. Admission notification on a rolling basis. **Financial aid:** No deadline. FAFSA required. Applicants notified on a rolling basis.

Academics. **Credit/placement by examination:** CLEP.

Majors. **Personal/culinary services:** Mortuary science.

Computing on campus. 23 workstations in library, computer center.

Student life. **Freshman orientation:** Mandatory. Preregistration for classes offered. **Policies:** Freshmen permitted cars on campus.

Student services. Career counseling, student employment services, personal counseling, placement for graduates.

Contact. E-mail: gjcfs@mindspring.com
Phone: (770) 593-2257 Fax: (770) 593-1891
Patty Hutcheson, President, Gupton Jones College of Funeral Service, 5141 Snapfinger Woods Drive, Decatur, GA 30035

Gwinnett College

Lilburn, Georgia
www.gwinnettcollege.edu

- For-profit 2-year junior college
- Commuter campus in large city

General. Accredited by ACICS. **Enrollment:** 245 undergraduates. **Degrees:** 82 associate awarded. **Location:** 20 miles from Atlanta. **Calendar:** Quarter, extensive summer session.

Transfer out. **Colleges most students transferred to 2005:** DeVry University, American Intercontinental University, University of Phoenix.

Basis for selection. Open admission, but selective for some programs. **Homeschooled:** Transcript of courses and grades required.

2005-2006 Annual costs. 2005 Tuition is $475 per class. Required number of classes varies by program. No out-of-state tuition applicable.

Financial aid. Need-based: Need-based aid available for part-time students.

Application procedures. Admission: No deadline. No application fee. Application must be submitted on paper. **Financial aid:** FAFSA required.

Academics. Special study options: Double major, internships. **Credit/placement by examination:** CLEP.

Majors. Business: Business admin. **Computer sciences:** Information technology. **Health:** Medical assistant, medical secretary. **Legal studies:** Paralegal.

Student services. Adult student services, financial aid counseling, placement for graduates. **Transfer:** Special adviser, orientation, re-entry adviser, pre-admission transcript evaluation for new students.

Contact. E-mail: admissions@gwinnettcollege.edu
Phone: (770) 381-7200 Fax: (770) 381-0454
Lee Cates, Director of Admissions, Gwinnett College, 4230 Highway 29, Lilburn, GA 30047

Gwinnett Technical College

Lawrenceville, Georgia
www.gwinnetttech.edu
CB member
CB code: 5168

- Public 2-year technical college
- Commuter campus in large town
- SAT or ACT required

General. Founded in 1984. Regionally accredited. Internships available with several manufacturers and companies, including Toyota, Nissan, Chrysler, and General Motors. **Enrollment:** 1,663 degree-seeking undergraduates. **Degrees:** 349 associate awarded. **Location:** 25 miles from Atlanta. **Calendar:** Quarter, extensive summer session. **Full-time faculty:** 70 total. **Part-time faculty:** 130 total. **Class size:** 55% < 20, 44% 20-39, less than 1% 40-49. **Special facilities:** Media center, studio, seminar room containing microcomputers and multimedia compilers.

Student profile. Among degree-seeking undergraduates, 100% enrolled in a vocational program, 10% already have a bachelor's degree or higher.

Basis for selection. School achievement record and test scores most important, followed by interview and state residency. Competitive screening process for some health science programs. Interview required of carpentry, automotive, machine tools, drafting majors and health science program applicants. **Adult students:** Entrance exam policies same as for first-time freshmen.

2005-2006 Annual costs. Tuition/fees: $1,425; $2,541 out-of-state. Per-credit charge: $31 in-state; $62 out-of-state. Books/supplies: $600.

Financial aid. Need-based: Need-based aid available for part-time students.

Application procedures. Admission: Closing date 8/15. $20 fee. Application may be submitted online. Admission notification on a rolling basis. Application closing date for some health sciences programs January 15. Call for information. **Financial aid:** Closing date 7/1. FAFSA required.

Academics. Special study options: Cooperative education, distance learning, double major, dual enrollment of high school students, ESL, internships, study abroad. License preparation in nursing, paramedic, physical therapy, radiology, real estate. **Credit/placement by examination:** AP, CLEP, institutional tests. **Support services:** GED preparation and test center, learning center, remedial instruction, study skills assistance, tutoring, writing center.

Majors. Biology: Biotechnology. **Business:** Accounting, administrative services, construction management, fashion, human resources, marketing, office management, office technology, restaurant/food services, tourism/travel. **Computer sciences:** Programming. **Construction:** General, site management. **Engineering technology:** Drafting. **Health:** Dental lab technology, EMT paramedic, medical radiologic technology/radiation therapy, respiratory therapy technology, veterinary technology/assistant. **Mechanic/repair:** Automotive. **Personal/culinary services:** Culinary arts. **Production:** Woodworking. **Protective services:** Police science. **Visual/performing arts:** Commercial photography, interior design, photography.

Computing on campus. 120 workstations in library, computer center, student center. Commuter students can connect to campus network. Online course registration, helpline, repair service, wireless network available.

Student life. Freshman orientation: Mandatory. Preregistration for classes offered. One-hour mandatory session, 4 30-minute breakout sessions on advisement, financial aid, registration, and online classes. **Activities:** Student government, student newspaper.

Student services. Adult student services, career counseling, student employment services, financial aid counseling, placement for graduates, veterans' counselor. **Physically disabled:** Services for visually, speech, hearing impaired. **Transfer:** Special adviser for new students.

Contact. Phone: (770) 962-7580 ext. 116 Fax: (770) 338-9217
Michelle McIntire, Director of Admissions, Gwinnett Technical College, 5150 Sugarloaf Parkway, Lawrenceville, GA 30243

High-Tech Institute: Atlanta

Marietta, Georgia
www.high-techinstitute.com

- For-profit 2-year technical college
- Commuter campus

General. Accredited by ACCSCT. **Enrollment:** 645 degree-seeking undergraduates. **Degrees:** 165 associate awarded. **Calendar:** Continuous. **Full-time faculty:** 20 total.

Basis for selection. Open admission.

2005-2006 Annual costs. Total costs of associate degree programs including books and supplies range from $18,450 to $27,350.

Application procedures. Admission: $50 fee.

Academics. Credit/placement by examination: CLEP.

Majors. Health: Medical assistant.

Contact. Phone: (770) 988-9877 Fax: (770) 988-9843
Ron Brandt, Director of Admissions, High-Tech Institute: Atlanta, 1090 Northchase Parkway, Marietta, GA 30067

Le Cordon Bleu College of Culinary Arts

Tucker, Georgia
www.atlantaculinary.ciom

- For-profit 2-year branch campus and technical college
- Commuter campus in very large city
- Interview required

General. Accredited by ACCSCT. **Enrollment:** 683 degree-seeking undergraduates. **Degrees:** 135 associate awarded. **Location:** 10 miles from Atlanta. **Calendar:** Continuous.

Student profile. Among degree-seeking undergraduates, 100% enrolled in a vocational program, 4% already have a bachelor's degree or higher, 273 enrolled as first-time, first-year students.

Basis for selection. Open admission. Documentation of high school graduation or GED only requirement. **Adult students:** Entrance exam policies same as for first-time freshmen.

2006-2007 Annual costs. Total cost of associate degree program is $36,300.

Application procedures. Admission: No deadline. $50 fee. Application must be submitted on paper. Admission notification on a rolling basis.

Academics. Credit/placement by examination: AP, CLEP. **Support services:** Study skills assistance, tutoring.

Majors. Personal/culinary services: Culinary arts.

Computing on campus. Online library available.

Student life. Freshman orientation: Mandatory.

Student services. Adult student services, career counseling, student employment services, financial aid counseling, placement for graduates. **Transfer:** Orientation, re-entry adviser for new students.

Contact. Phone: (770) 938-4711 Toll-free number: (866) 315-2433
Fax: (773) 938-4571
Terri Holte, Vice President of Admissions, Le Cordon Bleu College of Culinary Arts, 1927 Lakeside Parkway, Tucker, GA 30084

Middle Georgia College
Cochran, Georgia
www.mgc.edu **CB code: 5411**

- Public 2-year junior college
- Commuter campus in small town

General. Founded in 1884. Regionally accredited. **Enrollment:** 2,677 degree-seeking undergraduates. **Degrees:** 412 associate awarded. **Location:** 39 miles from Macon. **Calendar:** Semester, limited summer session. **Full-time faculty:** 77 total; 35% have terminal degrees, 6% minority, 47% women. **Part-time faculty:** 52 total; 8% have terminal degrees, 17% minority, 58% women. **Class size:** 38% < 20, 59% 20-39, less than 1% 40-49, 2% 50-99.

Student profile. Among degree-seeking undergraduates, 95% enrolled in a transfer program, 5% enrolled in a vocational program, 890 enrolled as first-time, first-year students, 125 transferred in from other institutions.

Part-time:	32%	**Asian American:**	1%
Out-of-state:	6%	**Hispanic American:**	1%
Women:	59%	**25 or older:**	25%
African American:	34%	**Live on campus:**	30%

Transfer out. Colleges most students transferred to 2005: Georgia College and State University, Macon College, Valdosta State University, Georgia Military College.

Basis for selection. Students graduating with a college prep diploma must have a minimum 2.0 academic core GPA. Students graduating with a tech prep/vocational/general diploma must have a minimum 2.2 academic core GPA. SAT or ACT not required. Students with college preparatory deficiencies may submit SAT Subject Tests scores in the area of their deficiencies. Interview and essay required for applicants to Georgia Academy of Mathematics, Engineering, and Science Program only. **Adult students:** SAT/ACT scores not required if out of high school 5 year(s) or more. **Homeschooled:** Transcript of courses and grades required. Students must submit a home-schooled application and submit minimum SAT score of 920 (exclusive of writing) or minimum 19 ACT composite.

High school preparation. 13 units required; 16 recommended. Required and recommended units include English 4, mathematics 3-4, social studies 1, history 2, science 3 (laboratory 2) and foreign language 2.

2005-2006 Annual costs. Tuition/fees: $1,966; $6,590 out-of-state. Per-credit charge: $65 in-state; $257 out-of-state. Room/board: $4,200. Books/supplies: $800. Personal expenses: $600.

2004-2005 Financial aid. Need-based: Average need met was 95%. Average scholarship/grant was $2,904; average loan $1,923. 64% of total undergraduate aid awarded as scholarships/grants, 36% as loans/jobs. Need-based aid available for part-time students. Work study available nights, weekends and for part-time students. **Non-need-based:** Scholarships awarded for academics, alumni affiliation, art, athletics, job skills, leadership, minority status, music/drama, state residency.

Application procedures. Admission: No deadline. $20 fee, may be waived for applicants with need. Application may be submitted online. Admission notification on a rolling basis. **Financial aid:** Priority date 4/1; no closing date. FAFSA required. Applicants notified on a rolling basis starting 5/1.

Academics. Special study options: Accelerated study, cooperative education, distance learning, double major, exchange student, honors, independent study, study abroad, weekend college. Weekend college at Dublin campus only; Georgia Academy of Mathematics, Engineering and Science is 2-year residential joint enrollment program for gifted high school juniors and seniors to pursue associate degree utilizing dual credits. Bachelor's degree programs available on campus. **Credit/placement by examination:** AP, CLEP, SAT, ACT, institutional tests. 30 credit hours maximum toward associate degree. **Support services:** Learning center, remedial instruction, study skills assistance, tutoring, writing center.

Majors. Agriculture: General. **Architecture:** Environmental design. **Biology:** General. **Business:** Accounting, business admin, human resources, merchandising, office technology, sales/distribution. **Communications:** Journalism. **Computer sciences:** General, applications programming, computer science, data entry, information technology, programming. **Conservation:** Forestry. **Education:** Early childhood, elementary, health, middle, secondary, special. **Engineering:** General, civil, computer, electrical. **Engineering technology:** Aerospace, civil, computer, drafting, manufacturing, surveying. **Family/consumer sciences:** Family studies. **Foreign languages:** General. **Health:** Dental assistant, dental hygiene, licensed practical nurse, medical assistant, medical radiologic technology/radiation therapy, medical records admin, medical records technology, nursing (RN), occupational therapy assistant, pharmacy assistant, physical therapy assistant, predentistry, premedicine, prenursing, prepharmacy, preveterinary, respiratory therapy technology, surgical technology. **History:** General. **Legal studies:** Prelaw. **Liberal arts:** Arts/sciences. **Math:** General. **Mechanic/repair:** Aircraft, auto body, automotive, electronics/electrical, heating/ac/refrig, industrial. **Parks/recreation:** General, health/fitness. **Physical sciences:** Chemistry, geology, physics. **Protective services:** Criminal justice, police science. **Psychology:** General. **Public administration:** General, social work. **Social sciences:** Economics, political science, sociology. **Visual/performing arts:** Art, dramatic.

Most popular majors. Health sciences 24%, liberal arts 67%.

Computing on campus. 464 workstations in dormitories, library. Dormitories wired for high-speed internet access and linked to campus network. Commuter students can connect to campus network. Online course registration, online library, helpline available.

Student life. Freshman orientation: Available. Preregistration for classes offered. Spring and summer, 1-day orientation. **Policies:** Alcohol not allowed on campus. Students must live with their immediate families or live in college housing unless given permission to live off-campus. Freshmen permitted cars on campus. **Housing:** Guaranteed on-campus for all undergraduates. Single-sex dorms, substance-free housing available. $100 nonrefundable deposit, deadline 7/1. **Activities:** Choral groups, dance, drama, literary magazine, music ensembles, musical theater, student government, student newspaper, Baptist student union, Wesley Foundation, minority alliance club, Rotaract, cultural relations club, Young Republicans, Young Democrats, Joyful Ministries, Fellowship of Christian Athletes.

Athletics. NJCAA. **Intercollegiate:** Baseball M, basketball, cross-country, soccer, softball W. **Intramural:** Badminton, basketball, football (tackle), golf, handball M, rifle M, softball, tennis, volleyball, weight lifting. **Team name:** Warriors.

Student services. Adult student services, alcohol/substance abuse counseling, career counseling, services for economically disadvantaged, student employment services, financial aid counseling, health services, minority student services, personal counseling, veterans' counselor, women's services. **Physically disabled:** Services for visually, hearing impaired. **Learning disabled:** Comprehensive services available. **Transfer:** Special adviser for new students. College fairs on campus for students transferring to 4-year colleges.

Contact. E-mail: admissions@mgc.edu
Phone: (478) 934-3103 Fax: (478) 934-3403
Jennifer Brannon, Director of Admissions, Middle Georgia College, 1100 Second Street SE, Cochran, GA 31014

Middle Georgia Technical College
Warner Robins, Georgia
www.mgtc.org **CB code: 5035**

- Public 2-year technical college
- Commuter campus in small town

General. Regionally accredited. Associate of Applied Technology degrees are terminal degrees. Courses cannot be transferred to a higher degree level. **Enrollment:** 2,345 degree-seeking undergraduates; 101 non-degree-seeking students. **Degrees:** 33 associate awarded. **Location:** 105 miles from Atlanta. **Calendar:** Quarter. **Full-time faculty:** 65 total. **Part-time faculty:** 70 total.

Student profile. Among degree-seeking undergraduates, 957 enrolled as first-time, first-year students.

Part-time:	48%	**Women:**	57%

Basis for selection. Open admission. ACT, SAT, CPE, ASSET, COMPASS scores used for placement.

2005-2006 Annual costs. Tuition/fees: $1,197; $2,313 out-of-state. Per-credit charge: $31 in-state; $62 out-of-state.

Application procedures. Admission: No deadline. $15 fee. **Financial aid:** FAFSA required.

Academics. Special study options: License preparation in aviation, dental hygiene, radiology. **Credit/placement by examination:** AP, CLEP. **Support services:** GED preparation and test center, learning center, remedial instruction, tutoring.

Majors. Business: Office technology.

Student life. Freshman orientation: Mandatory.

Student services. Career counseling, financial aid counseling.

Two-Year Colleges

Contact. Phone: (478) 988-6850 Toll-free number: (800) 474-1031
Fax: (478) 988-6813
Craig Jackson, Director of Admissions, Middle Georgia Technical College, 80 Cohen Walker Drive, Warner Robins, GA 31088

North Metro Technical College
Acworth, Georgia
www.northmetrotech.edu/

- Public 2-year technical college
- Large town

General. Regionally accredited. **Calendar:** Quarter.

Annual costs/financial aid. Tuition/fees (projected): $1,359.

Contact. Phone: (770) 975-4000
5198 Ross Road, Acworth, GA 30102

Northwestern Technical College
Rock Spring, Georgia
www.nwtcollege.org **CB code: 2860**

- Public 2-year technical college
- Commuter campus in small town

General. Regionally accredited. **Enrollment:** 1,550 degree-seeking undergraduates. **Degrees:** 134 associate awarded. **Calendar:** Quarter. **Full-time faculty:** 50 total. **Part-time faculty:** 125 total.

Basis for selection. Open admission, but selective for some programs. Special requirements for nursing, emergency medical technician, licensed practical nursing, medical assistant, cccupational therapy assistant, and surgical technology programs. SAT, ACT, COMPASS, CPE, or ASSET required for placement. **Adult students:** Entrance exam policies same as for first-time freshmen.

2005-2006 Annual costs. Tuition/fees: $1,359; $2,475 out-of-state. Per-credit charge: $31 in-state; $62 out-of-state.

Financial aid. Need-based: Need-based aid available for part-time students.

Application procedures. Admission: No deadline. $15 fee. Admission notification on a rolling basis. **Financial aid:** No deadline. FAFSA, institutional form required.

Academics. Special study options: Distance learning, double major, dual enrollment of high school students, liberal arts/career combination. License preparation in nursing, occupational therapy. **Credit/placement by examination:** CLEP, institutional tests. **Support services:** GED preparation and test center, remedial instruction, study skills assistance, tutoring, writing center.

Majors. Architecture: Technology. **Business:** Accounting, business admin, executive assistant, office/clerical. **Communications:** Organizational. **Computer sciences:** General, data entry, data processing, information systems, information technology, LAN/WAN management, networking, programming, web page design, webmaster, word processing. **Education:** Early childhood. **Engineering technology:** Architectural, computer systems, drafting, electrical, industrial, mechanical drafting. **Health:** Cardiovascular technology, medical assistant, nursing (RN), occupational therapy assistant, pharmacy assistant, surgical technology. **Protective services:** Law enforcement admin, police science.

Computing on campus. 300 workstations in library, computer center.

Student life. Freshman orientation: Mandatory. Preregistration for classes offered. **Activities:** Student government.

Student services. Adult student services, career counseling, services for economically disadvantaged, student employment services, financial aid counseling, placement for graduates, veterans' counselor, women's services.

Contact. E-mail: csolomon@nwtcollege.org
Phone: (706) 764-3511 Toll-free number: (800) 735-5726
Fax: (706) 764-3707
Carolyn Solmon, Director of Admissions and Career Counseling, Northwestern Technical College, 265 Bicentennial Trail, Rock Spring, GA 30739

Oxford College of Emory University
Oxford, Georgia **CB member**
www.emory.edu/OXFORD **CB code: 5186**

- Private 2-year branch campus and liberal arts college affiliated with United Methodist Church
- Residential campus in large town
- SAT or ACT (ACT writing optional), application essay required

General. Founded in 1836. Regionally accredited. One of nine schools of Emory University. Students who successfully complete two years at Oxford automatically continue to Emory College to complete bachelor's degree. Selective continuation to Emory School of Business and Emory School of Nursing is also available. **Enrollment:** 680 degree-seeking undergraduates. **Degrees:** 234 associate awarded. **Location:** 38 miles from Atlanta. **Calendar:** Semester, extensive summer session. **Full-time faculty:** 47 total; 89% have terminal degrees, 11% minority, 53% women. **Part-time faculty:** 6 total; 33% have terminal degrees, 33% women. **Class size:** 60% < 20, 40% 20-39. **Special facilities:** Center for international studies, two hospitals, regional primate center, Center for Disease Control.

Student profile. Among degree-seeking undergraduates, 100% enrolled in a transfer program.

Out-of-state:	42%	**Native American:**	1%
African American:	13%	**International:**	5%
Asian American:	24%	**Live on campus:**	94%
Hispanic American:	5%		

Transfer out. 100% of students enrolled in the transfer program go on to 4-year colleges.

Basis for selection. High school curriculum and transcript most important, standardized test scores, letters of recommendation, extracurricular activities, and essays also important. Students who took the ACT prior to the administration of the "new" ACT will be allowed to submit scores without writing component. All others submitting ACT scores must include results of ACT Writing. SAT Subject Tests are required for students applying with GED and those who were homeschooled. **Adult students:** SAT/ACT scores not required if out of high school 1 year(s) or more. **Homeschooled:** Transcript of courses and grades, state high school equivalency certificate required. SAT Subject Tests and portfolio are required.

High school preparation. 16 units recommended. Recommended units include English 4, mathematics 4, social studies 3, science 3 (laboratory 3) and foreign language 2. Mathematics units should include geometry and algebra II.

2006-2007 Annual costs. Tuition/fees: $24,970. Per-credit charge: $1,025. Room/board: $7,436. Books/supplies: $1,000. Personal expenses: $1,448.

2004-2005 Financial aid. Need-based: 81% of total undergraduate aid awarded as scholarships/grants, 19% as loans/jobs. Need-based aid available for part-time students. Work study available nights and weekends. **Non-need-based:** Scholarships awarded for academics, leadership, religious affiliation, state residency. **Additional information:** Deadline of November 15 to apply for Oxford College Scholars Program.

Application procedures. Admission: Priority date 2/1; no deadline. $40 fee, may be waived for applicants with need. Application may be submitted online. Admission notification on a rolling basis beginning on or about 3/15. Must reply by May 1 or within 3 week(s) if notified thereafter. November 15 is also the deadline for academic scholars program. **Financial aid:** Priority date 2/15, closing date 4/1. FAFSA, CSS PROFILE required. Applicants notified by 4/1; must reply by 5/1 or within 2 week(s) of notification.

Academics. Special study options: Cooperative education, cross-registration, distance learning, double major, dual enrollment of high school students, independent study, internships, liberal arts/career combination, study abroad, Washington semester. **Credit/placement by examination:** AP, CLEP, IB, institutional tests. 16 credit hours maximum toward associate degree. **Support services:** Reduced course load, study skills assistance, tutoring, writing center.

Majors. Liberal arts: Arts/sciences.

Computing on campus. 80 workstations in dormitories, library, computer center, student center. Dormitories wired for high-speed internet access and linked to campus network. Commuter students can connect to campus network. Online course registration, online library, helpline, student web hosting, wireless network available.

Student life. **Freshman orientation:** Mandatory, $100 fee. 6-day program held prior to start of school year; includes registration. **Policies:** Freshmen permitted cars on campus. **Housing:** Guaranteed on-campus for all undergraduates. Coed dorms, single-sex dorms, special housing for disabled, substance-free housing available. $75 deposit, deadline 5/1. Themed housing for healthy living is available. **Activities:** Choral groups, dance, drama, film society, literary magazine, music ensembles, student government, student newspaper, Volunteer Oxford, Oxford Fellowship, Outdoor Oxford, College Republicans, Circle K, Jewish student union, Catholic student union, Muslim student association, Young Democrats, Hindu student council.

Athletics. NJCAA. **Intercollegiate:** Basketball M, soccer W, tennis. **Intramural:** Badminton, basketball, football (non-tackle), soccer, softball, swimming, tennis, volleyball. **Team name:** Eagles.

Student services. Alcohol/substance abuse counseling, campus ministries, career counseling, financial aid counseling, health services, minority student services, personal counseling, placement for graduates. **Physically disabled:** Services for visually, speech, hearing impaired. **Transfer:** Special adviser, orientation for new students.

Contact. E-mail: oxadmission@learnlink.emory.edu
Phone: (770) 784-8328 Toll-free number: (800) 723-8328
Fax: (770) 784-8359
Jennifer Taylor, Associate Dean of Admission and Financial Aid, Oxford College of Emory University, 100 Hamill Street, Oxford, GA 30054-1418

Savannah Technical College

Savannah, Georgia
www.savannahtech.edu **CB code: 3741**

- Public 2-year technical college
- Commuter campus in small city

General. Regionally accredited. Classes offered at satellite campus in Hinesville. **Enrollment:** 3,867 degree-seeking undergraduates. **Degrees:** 257 associate awarded. **Location:** 250 miles from Atlanta. **Calendar:** Quarter, extensive summer session. **Full-time faculty:** 46 total. **Part-time faculty:** 148 total.

Student profile. Among degree-seeking undergraduates, 2% enrolled in a transfer program, 79% enrolled in a vocational program, 1% already have a bachelor's degree or higher, 1,359 enrolled as first-time, first-year students, 96 transferred in from other institutions.

Part-time:	60%	**Women:**	68%
Out-of-state:	1.4%	**25 or older:**	57%

Transfer out. **Colleges most students transferred to 2005:** Savannah State University.

Basis for selection. Open admission. **Adult students:** Entrance exam policies same as for first-time freshmen. **Learning Disabled:** Must meet with disability coordinator.

High school preparation. Recommended units include English 4 and mathematics 3.

2005-2006 Annual costs. Tuition/fees: $1,359; $2,475 out-of-state. Per-credit charge: $31 in-state; $62 out-of-state. Books/supplies: $1,500.

2004-2005 Financial aid. **Need-based:** 98% of total undergraduate aid awarded as scholarships/grants, 2% as loans/jobs. Need-based aid available for part-time students. **Non-need-based:** Scholarships awarded for academics, leadership, minority status, state residency.

Application procedures. **Admission:** No deadline. $15 fee. Application may be submitted online. Admission notification on a rolling basis. **Financial aid:** No deadline. FAFSA required. Applicants notified on a rolling basis.

Academics. **Special study options:** Dual enrollment of high school students, ESL, internships, liberal arts/career combination. License preparation in nursing, paramedic. **Credit/placement by examination:** AP, CLEP, institutional tests. **Support services:** GED test center, learning center, reduced course load, remedial instruction, study skills assistance, tutoring.

Majors. **Business:** Accounting technology, administrative services, human resources, marketing, operations, sales/distribution. **Computer sciences:** General, data processing, networking, programming. **Construction:** Electrician. **Engineering technology:** Computer, drafting, electrical. **Health:** Dental assistant, EMT paramedic, licensed practical nurse, medical assistant, surgical technology. **Mechanic/repair:** Auto body, automotive, heating/ac/refrig, industrial. **Personal/culinary services:** Chef training, cosmetic. **Production:** Machine shop technology, welding. **Protective services:** Criminal justice, fire safety technology.

Computing on campus. 100 workstations in library, computer center. Online course registration, online library available.

Student life. **Freshman orientation:** Available. Preregistration for classes offered. **Policies:** Freshmen permitted cars on campus. **Activities:** Student government.

Student services. Career counseling, services for economically disadvantaged, student employment services, financial aid counseling, on-campus daycare, personal counseling, placement for graduates. **Transfer:** Special adviser, orientation, re-entry adviser, pre-admission transcript evaluation for new students.

Contact. Phone: (912) 443-5517 Toll-free number: (800) 769-6362
Fax: (912) 443-5879
Verlene Lampley, Vice President of Student Services, Savannah Technical College, 5717 White Bluff Road, Savannah, GA 31405

South Georgia College

Douglas, Georgia
www.sga.edu **CB code: 5619**

- Public 2-year community and junior college
- Commuter campus in large town
- SAT or ACT required

General. Founded in 1906. Regionally accredited. **Enrollment:** 1,500 degree-seeking undergraduates. **Degrees:** 209 associate awarded. **Location:** 200 miles from Atlanta, 120 miles from Jacksonville, Florida. **Calendar:** Semester, limited summer session. **Full-time faculty:** 45 total. **Part-time faculty:** 15 total. **Class size:** 39% < 20, 55% 20-39, 6% 40-49, less than 1% 50-99. **Special facilities:** Mobile nursing clinic.

Transfer out. **Colleges most students transferred to 2005:** Valdosta State University, Georgia Southern University, University of Georgia.

Basis for selection. Minimum SAT verbal score of 330 or ACT English of 10 and SAT math score of 310 or ACT math of 5 required. Students who score below 400 on SAT math (ACT math 16) or 430 on SAT verbal (ACT English 18) required to take College Placement Exam in English, reading, and/or math. Interview required of nursing majors. **Adult students:** SAT/ACT scores not required if out of high school 5 year(s) or more.

High school preparation. 16 units recommended. Recommended units include English 4, mathematics 4, social studies 3, science 3 (laboratory 3) and foreign language 2.

2005-2006 Annual costs. Tuition/fees: $1,840; $6,464 out-of-state. Per-credit charge: $65 in-state; $257 out-of-state. Room only: $2,550. Books/supplies: $660. Personal expenses: $825.

Financial aid. **Need-based:** Need-based aid available for part-time students. **Non-need-based:** Scholarships awarded for academics.

Application procedures. **Admission:** Priority date 5/31; deadline 7/28. $20 fee, may be waived for applicants with need. Application may be submitted online. Admission notification on a rolling basis. **Financial aid:** Priority date 6/1; no closing date. FAFSA, institutional form required. Applicants notified on a rolling basis starting 7/6; must reply within 2 week(s) of notification.

Academics. Students may pursue associate in nursing through South Georgia College/Waycross College campus. **Special study options:** Distance learning, dual enrollment of high school students, independent study, study abroad. **Credit/placement by examination:** AP, CLEP, IB, institutional tests. 30 credit hours maximum toward associate degree. **Support services:** Learning center, reduced course load, remedial instruction, tutoring.

Majors. **Agriculture:** General, agribusiness operations, business. **Biology:** General. **Business:** General, accounting, administrative services, banking/financial services, business admin, communications, finance, management information systems, managerial economics, marketing, office management, office technology, office/clerical, operations, statistics. **Communications:** General, journalism. **Computer sciences:** General, applications programming, programming. **Education:** General, business, health, physical. **Foreign languages:** General, French, German, Spanish. **Health:** Nursing (RN), predentistry, premedicine, prepharmacy. **History:** General. **Legal studies:** Prelaw. **Liberal arts:** Arts/sciences. **Math:** General. **Parks/recreation:** General, facilities management, health/fitness, sports admin. **Philosophy/religion:** Philosophy. **Physical sciences:** Chemistry, physics. **Protective services:** Criminal justice, law enforcement admin, police science. **Psychology:**

General. **Social sciences:** General, criminology, economics, political science, sociology.

Most popular majors. Health sciences 26%, liberal arts 68%.

Computing on campus. 80 workstations in library, computer center.

Student life. Freshman orientation: Mandatory. Preregistration for classes offered. **Policies:** Freshmen permitted cars on campus. **Housing:** Guaranteed on-campus for all undergraduates. Coed dorms available. $30 deposit, deadline 7/28. **Activities:** Drama, literary magazine, student government, student newspaper, Baptist Student Union, Georgia Association of Student Nurses, Students for Multicultural Unity, Phi Beta Lambda.

Athletics. NJCAA. **Intercollegiate:** Baseball M, softball W, tennis W. **Intramural:** Basketball, softball, swimming, synchronized swimming, table tennis, tennis, volleyball. **Team name:** Tigers.

Student services. Career counseling, student employment services, financial aid counseling, personal counseling, veterans' counselor. **Learning disabled:** Comprehensive services available. **Transfer:** Special adviser, orientation for new students. Transfer adviser, college fairs on campus for students transferring to 4-year colleges.

Contact. E-mail: admissions@sga.edu
Phone: (912) 389-4510 Toll-free number: (800) 342-6364
Fax: (912) 389-4388
Randy Braswell, Director, Admissions, Records and Research, South Georgia College, 100 West College Park Drive, Douglas, GA 31533-5098

Southeastern Technical College

Vidalia, Georgia
www.southeasterntech.org/

- Public 2-year technical college
- Large town

General. Regionally accredited. **Calendar:** Quarter.

Annual costs/financial aid. Tuition/fees (projected): $1,359.

Contact. Phone: (912) 538-3121
3001 East First Street, Vidalia, GA 30474

Southwest Georgia Technical College

Thomasville, Georgia
www.southwestgatech.edu **CB code: 3627**

- Public 2-year technical college
- Commuter campus in large town

General. Regionally accredited. **Enrollment:** 1,419 degree-seeking undergraduates. **Degrees:** 159 associate awarded. **Location:** 35 miles from Tallahassee, Florida. **Calendar:** Quarter, extensive summer session. **Full-time faculty:** 62 total. **Part-time faculty:** 89 total. **Partnerships:** John Deere sponsors associates degrees for agricultural technology, construction equipment technology.

Basis for selection. Open admission, but selective for some programs. Most health programs selective due to limited enrollment. Selection process can include required certifications, additional standardized testing, prerequisite courses and physical exam. **Adult students:** All students able to take Asset in lieu of SAT/ACT for admissions. **Learning Disabled:** Students seeking accomodations should provide documentation of learning disability.

2005-2006 Annual costs. Tuition/fees: $1,359; $2,475 out-of-state. Per-credit charge: $31 in-state; $62 out-of-state. Books/supplies: $800. Personal expenses: $4,400.

2004-2005 Financial aid. Need-based: Need-based aid available for part-time students. Work study available nights. **Non-need-based:** Scholarships awarded for state residency.

Application procedures. Admission: No deadline. $20 fee. Admission notification on a rolling basis. **Financial aid:** No deadline. FAFSA, institutional form required. Applicants notified on a rolling basis starting 7/1.

Academics. Special study options: Cooperative education, distance learning, double major, dual enrollment of high school students, internships, liberal arts/career combination. License preparation in nursing, paramedic, physical therapy, radiology, real estate. **Credit/placement by examination:** CLEP, institutional tests. **Support services:** GED preparation and test center, remedial instruction, tutoring.

Majors. Agriculture: Equipment technology, power machinery. **Business:** Accounting technology, administrative services, business admin, office/clerical, operations. **Computer sciences:** Data entry, data processing, networking. **Education:** Early childhood. **Health:** Clinical lab technology, medical assistant, medical radiologic technology/radiation therapy, nursing (RN), pharmacy assistant, radiologic technology/medical imaging, respiratory therapy technology, surgical technology. **Mechanic/repair:** Heavy equipment. **Protective services:** Criminal justice, police science.

Most popular majors. Business/marketing 36%, health sciences 60%.

Computing on campus. 42 workstations in library. Online course registration, online library available.

Student life. Freshman orientation: Mandatory. Preregistration for classes offered. Held quarterly. **Policies:** Freshmen permitted cars on campus. **Activities:** Student government, Student Council, National Vocational Honor Society, Phi Beta Lambda, SkillsUSA.

Student services. Adult student services, career counseling, services for economically disadvantaged, student employment services, financial aid counseling, personal counseling, placement for graduates. **Physically disabled:** Services for visually, hearing impaired. **Transfer:** Special adviser, orientation, pre-admission transcript evaluation for new students.

Contact. E-mail: info@southwestgatech.edu
Phone: (229) 225-5060 Fax: (229) 227-2666
Deborah Gray, Registrar, Southwest Georgia Technical College, 15689 US Highway 19N, Thomasville, GA 31792

Waycross College

Waycross, Georgia
www.waycross.edu **CB code: 5889**

- Public 2-year community and liberal arts college
- Commuter campus in small town
- SAT or ACT required

General. Founded in 1976. Regionally accredited. **Enrollment:** 754 degree-seeking undergraduates. **Degrees:** 118 associate awarded. **Location:** 70 miles from Jacksonville, Florida. **Calendar:** Semester, limited summer session. **Full-time faculty:** 20 total; 20% have terminal degrees. **Part-time faculty:** 27 total. **Special facilities:** Repository of materials about the Okefenokee Swamp.

Student profile.

Out-of-state:	10%	**25 or older:**	28%

Transfer out. Colleges most students transferred to 2005: Valdosta State University, Armstrong Atlantic University, Georgia Southern University, University of Georgia.

Basis for selection. Minimum SAT score of 330 verbal or 310 math required. Open for all students out of school for over 5 years with high school diploma or GED. Essay required of low-scoring SAT-verbal or ACT-English applicants and those who have not completed 4 years high school English. **Adult students:** SAT/ACT scores not required if out of high school 5 year(s) or more. COMPASS placement exams required.

High school preparation. 16 units required. Required units include English 4, mathematics 4, social studies 3, science 3 and foreign language 2.

2005-2006 Annual costs. Tuition/fees: $1,696; $6,320 out-of-state. Per-credit charge: $65 in-state; $257 out-of-state. Books/supplies: $500. Personal expenses: $900.

Financial aid. Need-based: Work study available nights, weekends and for part-time students. **Non-need-based:** Scholarships awarded for academics, alumni affiliation, leadership.

Application procedures. Admission: No deadline. $20 fee, may be waived for applicants with need. Application may be submitted online. Admission notification on a rolling basis. **Financial aid:** Priority date 5/1; no closing date. FAFSA, institutional form required. Applicants notified on a rolling basis; must reply within 2 week(s) of notification.

Academics. Special study options: Dual enrollment of high school students, independent study, liberal arts/career combination, study abroad. Cooperative nursing programs (RN) with South Georgia College, Valdosta State College. Bachelor's degree programs available on campus. **Credit/placement by examination:** CLEP, institutional tests. 20 credit hours maximum toward associate degree. SAT Subject Tests used to replace courses students did not take in high school. **Support services:** Learning center, reduced course load, remedial instruction, study skills assistance, tutoring, writing center.

Majors. Biology: General. **Business:** Accounting, business admin. **Computer sciences:** General, programming. **Conservation:** Environmental science. **Education:** General, physical. **Family/consumer sciences:** Child care. **Health:** Clinical lab technology, dental hygiene, EMT paramedic, medical radiologic technology/radiation therapy, surgical technology. **History:** General. **Math:** General. **Mechanic/repair:** Automotive, electronics/electrical, heating/ac/refrig, industrial. **Parks/recreation:** Health/fitness. **Personal/culinary services:** Cosmetic. **Physical sciences:** Chemistry. **Psychology:** General. **Social sciences:** Political science, sociology.

Computing on campus. 100 workstations in library, computer center, student center. Online course registration available.

Student life. Freshman orientation: Mandatory. Preregistration for classes offered. **Activities:** Drama, literary magazine, student government, student newspaper, Baptist student union, multicultural student alliance, Circle-K.

Athletics. Intramural: Baseball M, basketball, football (non-tackle), softball. **Team name:** Swamp Fox.

Student services. Adult student services, alcohol/substance abuse counseling, career counseling, student employment services, financial aid counseling, minority student services, personal counseling, placement for graduates, veterans' counselor. **Physically disabled:** Services for visually, speech, hearing impaired. **Transfer:** Special adviser, pre-admission transcript evaluation for new students. Transfer adviser, college fairs on campus for students transferring to 4-year colleges.

Contact. E-mail: admiss@waycross.edu
Phone: (912) 285-6133 Fax: (912) 285-6158
Robert Stewart, Director of Student Services, Waycross College, 2001 South Georgia Parkway, Waycross, GA 31503

West Georgia Technical College

LaGrange, Georgia
www.westgatech.org **CB code: 3632**

- Public 2-year technical college
- Commuter campus in small city

General. Regionally accredited. **Enrollment:** 1,834 degree-seeking undergraduates; 28 non-degree-seeking students. **Degrees:** 67 associate awarded. **Location:** 60 miles from Atlanta. **Calendar:** Quarter, limited summer session. **Full-time faculty:** 44 total; 9% minority, 46% women. **Part-time faculty:** 67 total; 8% minority, 48% women. **Class size:** 80% < 20, 20% 20-39.

Student profile. Among degree-seeking undergraduates, 554 enrolled as first-time, first-year students.

Part-time:	59%	**Women:**	64%
Out-of-state:	1%		

Basis for selection. Open admission, but selective for some programs. Admission to radiology and nursing programs based on examination, interview and space availability. ASSET used for placement when scores required. **Adult students:** Entrance exam policies same as for first-time freshmen. Applicants must take the ACT Asset test for placement when required by program if no SAT/ACT scores available, or if acceptable college credit for math or English not available. **Homeschooled:** Must provide satisfactory documentation indicating the home school is approved. Must provide official high school transcript and meet all other admission requirements. **Learning Disabled:** Disabilities must be documented with the on-site coordinator to receive consideration for accommodation.

2005-2006 Annual costs. Tuition/fees: $1,359; $2,475 out-of-state. Per-credit charge: $31 in-state; $62 out-of-state. Tuition reciprocity with bordering states. CDL program is $2012. Basic welding and EMT programs are $37 per-credit-hour. Books/supplies: $945. Personal expenses: $1,300.

2004-2005 Financial aid. Need-based: 1,228 full-time freshmen applied for aid; 954 were judged to have need; 954 of these received aid. Average need met was 75%. Average scholarship/grant was $535. 92% of total undergraduate aid awarded as scholarships/grants, 8% as loans/jobs. Need-based aid available for part-time students. Work study available nights and for part-time students. **Non-need-based:** Scholarships awarded for state residency.

Application procedures. Admission: No deadline. $15 fee. Application may be submitted online. Admission notification on a rolling basis. **Financial aid:** No deadline. FAFSA, institutional form required. Applicants notified on a rolling basis; must reply within 1 week(s) of notification.

Academics. Tutorial program available. **Special study options:** Distance learning, dual enrollment of high school students, liberal arts/career combination. License preparation in paramedic, radiology, real estate. **Credit/placement by examination:** AP, CLEP. 15 credit hours maximum toward associate degree. **Support services:** GED preparation and test center, learning center, study skills assistance, tutoring.

Majors. Business: Accounting, administrative services, business admin, executive assistant, management science. **Computer sciences:** General, data entry, networking, web page design. **Education:** Early childhood. **Health:** Medical records technology, pharmacy assistant. **Mechanic/repair:** General, electronics/electrical, industrial. **Protective services:** Criminal justice, firefighting.

Computing on campus. 100 workstations in library, computer center. Online library available.

Student life. Freshman orientation: Mandatory. Preregistration for classes offered. **Activities:** Student government, TV station, Phi Beta Lambda.

Student services. Adult student services, career counseling, student employment services, financial aid counseling, on-campus daycare, placement for graduates, veterans' counselor, women's services. **Physically disabled:** Services for visually, hearing impaired. **Transfer:** Special adviser, orientation for new students.

Contact. E-mail: lbasham@westgatech.org
Phone: (706) 845-4323 ext. 5722 Fax: (706) 845-4340
Lori Basham, Director of Admission, West Georgia Technical College, 303 Fort Drive, LaGrange, GA 30240

Young Harris College

Young Harris, Georgia
www.yhc.edu **CB code: 5990**

- Private 2-year junior and liberal arts college affiliated with United Methodist Church
- Residential campus in rural community
- SAT or ACT (ACT writing optional) required

General. Founded in 1886. Regionally accredited. **Enrollment:** 532 degree-seeking undergraduates. **Degrees:** 120 associate awarded. **Location:** 120 miles from Atlanta. **Calendar:** Semester, limited summer session. **Full-time faculty:** 34 total. **Part-time faculty:** 17 total. **Class size:** 69% < 20, 31% 20-39. **Special facilities:** Planetarium, black box theater, observatory.

Student profile. Among degree-seeking undergraduates, 281 enrolled as first-time, first-year students, 14 transferred in from other institutions.

Part-time:	5%	**25 or older:**	1%
Out-of-state:	11%	**Live on campus:**	80%
Women:	54%		

Transfer out. 84% of students enrolled in the transfer program go on to 4-year colleges. **Colleges most students transferred to 2005:** University of Georgia, Georgia College & State University, University of West Georgia, North Georgia College & State University, Kennesaw State University.

Basis for selection. Heavy emphasis on academic GPA and SAT or ACT scores. High school record, interview considered. Conditional admission possible. **Adult students:** SAT/ACT scores not required if out of high school 5 year(s) or more. Must be part time, at least 22 years of age, must commute. **Homeschooled:** Transcript of courses and grades required. SAT or ACT required, possible GED requirement dependent upon SAT and/or ACT scores. **Learning Disabled:** Psycho-educational analysis required.

High school preparation. Recommended units include English 4, mathematics 4, social studies 3, science 3 and foreign language 2.

2006-2007 Annual costs. Tuition/fees (projected): $14,690. Per-credit charge: $500. Room/board: $4,780. Books/supplies: $750. Personal expenses: $1,050.

2004-2005 Financial aid. Need-based: 82% of total undergraduate aid awarded as scholarships/grants, 18% as loans/jobs. Need-based aid available for part-time students. Work study available nights. **Non-need-based:** Scholarships awarded for academics, art, athletics, job skills, music/drama, state residency.

Application procedures. Admission: Priority date 1/1; no deadline. $30 fee, may be waived for applicants with need. Application may be submitted online. Admission notification on a rolling basis beginning on or about 9/1. **Financial aid:** Priority date 4/1; no closing date. FAFSA, institutional form required. Applicants notified on a rolling basis starting 3/1; must reply within 2 week(s) of notification.

Academics. Special study options: Dual enrollment of high school students, internships, study abroad. **Credit/placement by examination:** AP, CLEP, IB, institutional tests. Student may exempt computer science 101 but receives no credit. **Support services:** Pre-admission summer program, reduced course load, remedial instruction, study skills assistance, tutoring, writing center.

Majors. Biology: General. **Business:** General, hospitality admin. **Communications:** General. **Conservation:** Forestry. **Education:** General, art, music. **Engineering:** General. **English:** Speech/rhetoric. **Foreign languages:** General, French, Spanish. **Health:** Predentistry, premedicine, prenursing, prepharmacy, preveterinary. **History:** General. **Interdisciplinary:** Biological/physical sciences. **Legal studies:** Prelaw. **Liberal arts:** Arts/sciences. **Math:** General. **Parks/recreation:** Health/fitness. **Philosophy/religion:** Religion. **Physical sciences:** Astronomy, chemistry, physics. **Protective services:** Criminal justice. **Psychology:** General. **Social sciences:** General. **Visual/performing arts:** General, art, dramatic, studio arts.

Most popular majors. Business/marketing 11%, education 26%, health sciences 12%, liberal arts 22%, physical sciences 13%, visual/performing arts 16%.

Computing on campus. 100 workstations in dormitories, library, computer center. Dormitories wired for high-speed internet access and linked to campus network. Commuter students can connect to campus network. Online library, helpline, wireless network available.

Student life. Freshman orientation: Mandatory, $75 fee. Preregistration for classes offered. 2 day, 1 night program held during the summer prior to fall enrollment. **Policies:** All single freshmen and sophomores under age 22 not living with family must reside in college dormitories. Freshmen permitted cars on campus. **Housing:** Guaranteed on-campus for all undergraduates. Coed dorms, single-sex dorms, substance-free housing available. $200 fully refundable deposit. **Activities:** Choral groups, dance, drama, literary magazine, music ensembles, musical theater, student government, student newspaper, Wesley Fellowship, Baptist Student Union, Newman Club, honorary service organizations, Pi Sigma Omega (political science).

Athletics. NJCAA. **Intercollegiate:** Baseball M, cross-country, golf, soccer, softball W, tennis W. **Intramural:** Badminton, basketball, bowling, football (non-tackle), soccer, softball, swimming, table tennis, tennis, volleyball. **Team name:** Mountain Lions.

Student services. Campus ministries, career counseling, financial aid counseling, health services, personal counseling. **Transfer:** Special adviser, orientation, pre-admission transcript evaluation for new students. Transfer center, transfer adviser, college fairs on campus for students transferring to 4-year colleges.

Contact. E-mail: admissions@yhc.edu
Phone: (706) 379-3111 Toll-free number: (800) 241-3754
Fax: (706) 379-3108
Clinton Hobbs, Vice President for Enrollment Management, Young Harris College, PO Box 116, Young Harris, GA 30582-0116

Hawaii

Hawaii Business College
Honolulu, Hawaii
www.hbc.edu **CB code: 3520**

- For-profit 2-year business and health science college
- Commuter campus in large city
- Interview required

General. Accredited by ACICS. **Enrollment:** 350 degree-seeking undergraduates. **Degrees:** 53 associate awarded. **Calendar:** Quarter, extensive summer session. **Full-time faculty:** 10 total. **Part-time faculty:** 20 total. **Class size:** 82% < 20, 18% 20-39. **Partnerships:** Formal partnerships with local businesses.

Basis for selection. Open admission. Wonderlic test required for placement.

2005-2006 Annual costs. Books/supplies: $900. Personal expenses: $1,665.

Financial aid. All financial aid based on need. Need-based aid available for part-time students. Work study available nights, weekends and for part-time students.

Application procedures. Admission: No deadline. $50 fee. Application may be submitted online. Admission notification on a rolling basis. **Financial aid:** No deadline. FAFSA required. Applicants notified on a rolling basis; must reply within 3 week(s) of notification.

Academics. Special study options: Double major, independent study, internships, liberal arts/career combination, weekend college. **Credit/placement by examination:** CLEP, institutional tests. **Support services:** Learning center, remedial instruction, study skills assistance, tutoring, writing center.

Majors. Business: Accounting, business admin, tourism/travel. **Computer sciences:** Networking, web page design. **Health:** Medical secretary.

Most popular majors. Business/marketing 66%, computer/information sciences 24%, health sciences 10%.

Computing on campus. 100 workstations in library, computer center. Repair service available.

Student life. Freshman orientation: Mandatory. Half-day program. **Policies:** Freshmen permitted cars on campus. **Activities:** Student government, student council association, computer club, Polynesian club, Sife club, MOP club, accounting club.

Student services. Adult student services, career counseling, student employment services, financial aid counseling, personal counseling, placement for graduates, veterans' counselor. **Transfer:** Special adviser, orientation, re-entry adviser, pre-admission transcript evaluation for new students.

Contact. E-mail: admin@hbc.edu
Phone: (808) 524-4014 Fax: (808) 524-0284
Jason Reyes, Director of Admissions, Hawaii Business College, 33 South King Street, 4th Floor, Honolulu, HI 96813

Hawaii Tokai International College
Honolulu, Hawaii
www.hawaiitokai.edu **CB code: 2588**

- Private 2-year junior and liberal arts college
- Residential campus in large city
- Application essay, interview required

General. Regionally accredited. **Enrollment:** 110 degree-seeking undergraduates. **Degrees:** 45 associate awarded. **Calendar:** Quarter, limited summer session. **Full-time faculty:** 7 total; 43% have terminal degrees, 29% women. **Class size:** 100% < 20.

Student profile.

Out-of-state:	100%	**Live on campus:**	67%
Women:	47%		

Transfer out. 97% of students enrolled in the transfer program go on to 4-year colleges. **Colleges most students transferred to 2005:** University of Hawaii at Manoa.

Basis for selection. Essay, academic GPA, recommendations, character, interview, and level of interest most important. **Adult students:** Entrance exam policies same as for first-time freshmen. **Homeschooled:** Transcript of courses and grades, interview, letter of recommendation (nonparent) required.

2005-2006 Annual costs. Tuition varies by program. Typical annual tuition is $9,150. Books/supplies: $800.

Application procedures. Admission: Closing date 8/2 (postmark date). $50 fee. Application must be submitted on paper. Admission notification on a rolling basis. Must reply by May 1 or within 3 week(s) if notified thereafter. **Financial aid:** Institutional form required.

Academics. Special study options: ESL. **Credit/placement by examination:** CLEP, institutional tests. 12 credit hours maximum toward associate degree. **Support services:** Study skills assistance, tutoring.

Majors. Liberal arts: Arts/sciences.

Computing on campus. 60 workstations in library, computer center. Dormitories wired for high-speed internet access and linked to campus network. Online library, wireless network available.

Student life. Freshman orientation: Mandatory. Preregistration for classes offered. **Policies:** Freshmen permitted cars on campus. **Housing:** Guaranteed on-campus for all undergraduates. Coed dorms, substance-free housing available. $20 deposit. **Activities:** Dance, music ensembles, student government, student newspaper.

Athletics. Intercollegiate: Judo. **Intramural:** Baseball M, basketball M, soccer M. **Team name:** T-Wave.

Student services. Adult student services, alcohol/substance abuse counseling, career counseling, services for economically disadvantaged, student employment services, financial aid counseling, personal counseling. **Physically disabled:** Services for visually impaired. **Transfer:** Special adviser, orientation, re-entry adviser, pre-admission transcript evaluation for new students. Transfer center, transfer adviser, college fairs on campus for students transferring to 4-year colleges.

Contact. E-mail: htic@tokai.edu
Phone: (808) 983-4187 Fax: (808) 983-4173
Derrick Kerr, Director, Student Services, Hawaii Tokai International College, 2241 Kapiolani Boulevard, Honolulu, HI 96826

Heald College: Honolulu
Honolulu, Hawaii
www.heald.edu **CB code: 4324**

- Private 2-year business and technical college
- Commuter campus in very large city

General. Founded in 1863. Regionally accredited. **Enrollment:** 807 degree-seeking undergraduates. **Degrees:** 429 associate awarded. **Calendar:** Quarter. **Full-time faculty:** 32 total. **Part-time faculty:** 22 total.

Basis for selection. Open admission. Career Program Assessment Test (CPAT) administered prior to application. **Adult students:** Entrance exam policies same as for first-time freshmen.

2006-2007 Annual costs. Tuition/fees: $9,900.

Financial aid. All financial aid based on need. Need-based aid available for part-time students. Work study available nights, weekends and for part-time students.

Application procedures. Admission: No deadline. $40 fee. Application may be submitted online. Admission notification on a rolling basis. **Financial aid:** No deadline. FAFSA required.

Academics. Special study options: Cooperative education, internships. **Credit/placement by examination:** CLEP, institutional tests. **Support services:** Learning center, reduced course load, remedial instruction, tutoring.

Majors. Business: Accounting, business admin, hospitality admin, tourism/travel. **Computer sciences:** General, vendor certification. **Engineering technology:** Electrical. **Health:** Medical assistant, medical secretary. **Legal studies:** Legal secretary.

Computing on campus. Online library available.

Student life. Policies: Freshmen permitted cars on campus.

Student services. Career counseling, student employment services, financial aid counseling, placement for graduates. **Transfer:** Special adviser, orientation, pre-admission transcript evaluation for new students. Transfer adviser for students transferring to 4-year colleges.

Contact. Phone: (808) 955-1500 Toll-free number: (800) 755-3550
Fax: (808) 955-6964
Phyllis Miyamura, Registrar, Heald College: Honolulu, 1500 Kapiolani Boulevard, Honolulu, HI 96814-3715

Remington College: Honolulu

Honolulu, Hawaii
www.remingtoncollege.edu **CB code: 3507**

- For-profit 2-year branch campus college
- Commuter campus in very large city
- Interview required

General. Accredited by ACICS. **Enrollment:** 538 degree-seeking undergraduates. **Degrees:** 30 bachelor's, 237 associate awarded. **Calendar:** Quarter. **Full-time faculty:** 35 total. **Part-time faculty:** 20 total.

Basis for selection. Interview most important; CPAT assessment test score also important. CPAT entrance examination required. **Adult students:** Entrance exam policies same as for first-time freshmen.

2005-2006 Annual costs. Per-credit charge: $334. Associate degree program $32,010; Computer Networking Technology program $32,810; Bachelor programs $29,070. Personal expenses: $1,764.

Financial aid. All financial aid based on need.

Application procedures. Admission: No deadline. $50 fee. Admission notification on a rolling basis. **Financial aid:** No deadline. FAFSA required. Applicants notified on a rolling basis.

Academics. Special study options: Bachelor's degree programs available on campus. **Credit/placement by examination:** CLEP. **Support services:** Tutoring.

Majors. Business: International. **Computer sciences:** General, networking. **Health:** Medical assistant. **Protective services:** Criminal justice.

Most popular majors. Business/marketing 10%, computer/information sciences 20%, health sciences 40%, security/protective services 30%.

Computing on campus. 170 workstations in library, computer center. Online library available.

Student life. Freshman orientation: Mandatory. **Activities:** International club.

Student services. Student employment services, financial aid counseling, placement for graduates. **Transfer:** Orientation, pre-admission transcript evaluation for new students.

Contact. E-mail: kheinema@remingtoncollege.edu
Phone: (808) 942-1000 Fax: (808) 533-3064
Kenneth Heinemann, Campus President, Remington College: Honolulu, 1111 Bishop Street, Suite 400, Honolulu, HI 96813-2811

TransPacific Hawaii College

Honolulu, Hawaii
www.transpacific.org **CB code: 4429**

- Private 2-year liberal arts college
- Commuter campus in large city

General. Regionally accredited. **Location:** 6 miles from Honolulu. **Calendar:** Continuous.

Annual costs/financial aid. Tuition/fees (2005-2006): $16,150. Books/supplies: $600.

Contact. Phone: (808) 377-5402
Director of International Admissions, 5257 Kalanianaole Highway, Honolulu, HI 96821

University of Hawaii: Hawaii Community College

Hilo, Hawaii
www.hawcc.hawaii.edu **CB code: 1801**

- Public 2-year community college
- Small city

General. Founded in 1969. Regionally accredited. **Enrollment:** 2,440 degree-seeking undergraduates. **Degrees:** 255 associate awarded. **ROTC:** Navy. **Location:** 200 miles from Honolulu. **Calendar:** Semester, limited summer session. **Full-time faculty:** 87 total. **Part-time faculty:** 7 total.

Student profile.

25 or older:	32%	**Live on campus:**	35%

Basis for selection. Open admission.

2005-2006 Annual costs. Tuition/fees: $1,594; $7,384 out-of-state. Per-credit charge: $49 in-state; $242 out-of-state. Books/supplies: $672. Personal expenses: $953.

Financial aid. All financial aid based on need. Need-based aid available for part-time students. **Additional information:** Hawaii student incentive grants and tuition waivers (merit and need-based) available to Hawaii residents.

Application procedures. Admission: Closing date 7/30. No application fee in-state; $25 out-of-state. Admission notification on a rolling basis. **Financial aid:** Priority date 4/1; no closing date. FAFSA required. Applicants notified on a rolling basis starting 5/1; must reply within 2 week(s) of notification.

Academics. Special study options: Cooperative education, cross-registration, distance learning, double major, dual enrollment of high school students, ESL, honors, independent study. **Credit/placement by examination:** CLEP. 15 credit hours maximum toward associate degree. **Support services:** Learning center, pre-admission summer program, reduced course load, remedial instruction, tutoring.

Majors. Agriculture: General. **Business:** Accounting, administrative services, market research, marketing, operations. **Construction:** Carpentry, power transmission. **Education:** Early childhood. **Engineering technology:** Drafting, electrical. **Family/consumer sciences:** Food/nutrition. **Health:** Nursing (RN). **Liberal arts:** Arts/sciences. **Mechanic/repair:** Auto body, automotive, diesel, electronics/electrical. **Protective services:** Criminal justice, law enforcement admin.

Most popular majors. Business/marketing 15%, education 6%, health sciences 6%, liberal arts 36%, trade and industry 31%.

Student life. Housing: Coed dorms, apartments available. **Activities:** Choral groups, music ensembles, TV station, Phi Theta Kappa honors society.

Student services. Adult student services, career counseling, student employment services, health services, personal counseling, veterans' counselor. **Transfer:** Special adviser, orientation for new students. Transfer adviser, college fairs on campus for students transferring to 4-year colleges.

Contact. E-mail: hawccinf@hawaii.edu
Phone: (808) 974-7661 Fax: (808) 974-7692
David Loeding, Registrar, University of Hawaii: Hawaii Community College, 200 West Kawili Street, Hilo, HI 96720-4091

University of Hawaii: Honolulu Community College

Honolulu, Hawaii
www.hcc.hawaii.edu **CB code: 4350**

- Public 2-year community and technical college
- Commuter campus in very large city

General. Founded in 1920. Regionally accredited. **Enrollment:** 3,307 degree-seeking undergraduates. **Degrees:** 529 associate awarded. **ROTC:** Army, Air Force. **Calendar:** Semester, limited summer session. **Full-time faculty:** 140 total. **Part-time faculty:** 75 total.

Student profile.

Out-of-state:	7%	25 or older:	43%

Transfer out. **Colleges most students transferred to 2005:** University of Hawaii at Manoa, University of Hawaii at Hilo, Chaminade University, Hawaii Pacific University.

Basis for selection. Open admission, but selective for out-of-state students. Out of state and foreign applicants subject to non-resident quota. High school diploma required for cosmetology program.

2005-2006 Annual costs. Tuition/fees: $1,500; $7,290 out-of-state. Per-credit charge: $49 in-state; $242 out-of-state. Books/supplies: $773. Personal expenses: $1,166.

Financial aid. **Need-based:** Need-based aid available for part-time students. Work study available for part-time students. **Non-need-based:** Scholarships awarded for academics, state residency. **Additional information:** Hawaii student incentive grants and tuition waivers (merit and need-based) available to Hawaii residents at participating institutions.

Application procedures. **Admission:** Priority date 7/1; no deadline. No application fee in-state; $25 out-of-state. Admission notification on a rolling basis beginning on or about 3/1. **Financial aid:** Priority date 4/1; no closing date. FAFSA required. Applicants notified on a rolling basis starting 7/1; must reply within 3 week(s) of notification.

Academics. **Special study options:** Cooperative education, cross-registration, distance learning, dual enrollment of high school students, ESL, independent study, internships, student-designed major. License preparation in aviation. **Credit/placement by examination:** CLEP, institutional tests. 30 credit hours maximum toward associate degree. **Support services:** Learning center, remedial instruction, study skills assistance, tutoring.

Majors. **Business:** Fashion. **Communications technology:** Graphic/printing. **Computer sciences:** General, computer graphics, information systems. **Construction:** Carpentry, electrician. **Education:** Early childhood, technology/industrial arts, voc/tech. **Engineering:** Aerospace, architectural, computer, polymer. **Engineering technology:** Drafting, electrical, occupational safety. **Family/consumer sciences:** Child care, institutional food production. **Health:** Occupational health. **Liberal arts:** Arts/sciences. **Mechanic/repair:** General, aircraft, auto body, automotive, diesel, electronics/electrical, heating/ac/refrig, marine. **Personal/culinary services:** Cosmetic. **Protective services:** Criminal justice, fire safety technology, fire services admin, firefighting, law enforcement admin, police science. **Public administration:** Community org/advocacy, human services, social work. **Transportation:** Airline/commercial pilot, aviation management. **Visual/performing arts:** Commercial/advertising art, fashion design.

Computing on campus. 97 workstations in library, computer center, student center. Commuter students can connect to campus network. Online course registration available.

Student life. **Housing:** Dorms and apartments available at University of Hawaii at Manoa campus. **Activities:** Literary magazine, student government, student newspaper, Pacific Islander association, Filipino club.

Student services. Career counseling, student employment services, financial aid counseling, health services, on-campus daycare, placement for graduates, veterans' counselor. **Physically disabled:** Services for visually, speech, hearing impaired. **Transfer:** Special adviser, orientation, pre-admission transcript evaluation for new students. Transfer center, transfer adviser, college fairs on campus for students transferring to 4-year colleges.

Contact. E-mail: admissions@hcc.hawaii.edu
Phone: (808) 845-9129 Fax: (808) 847-9829
Frank Fenlon, Admissions Counselor, University of Hawaii: Honolulu Community College, 874 Dillingham Boulevard, Honolulu, HI 96817

University of Hawaii: Kapiolani Community College

Honolulu, Hawaii
www.kcc.hawaii.edu **CB code: 4377**

- Public 2-year community college
- Commuter campus in very large city

General. Founded in 1957. Regionally accredited. **Enrollment:** 4,341 degree-seeking undergraduates. **Degrees:** 676 associate awarded. **Calendar:** Semester, limited summer session. **Full-time faculty:** 245 total. **Part-time faculty:** 150 total. **Class size:** 55% < 20, 45% 20-39, less than 1% 40-49, less than 1% 50-99.

Student profile.

Out-of-state:	7%	25 or older:	41%

Transfer out. **Colleges most students transferred to 2005:** University of Hawaii at Manoa.

Basis for selection. Open admission, but selective for some programs. High school diploma required for allied health and nursing programs and for students under age 18. Essay recommended. Interview required of allied health, legal assistant, and nursing programs.

2005-2006 Annual costs. Tuition/fees: $1,555; $7,320 out-of-state. Per-credit charge: $49 in-state; $242 out-of-state. Books/supplies: $725. Personal expenses: $1,143.

Financial aid. All financial aid based on need. Need-based aid available for part-time students. **Additional information:** Hawaii student incentive grants and tuition waivers (merit and need-based) available to Hawaii residents.

Application procedures. **Admission:** Closing date 7/1 (postmark date). $25 fee. Application must be submitted on paper. Admission notification on a rolling basis. Application deadline April 1 for allied health and legal assistant programs; deadline February 1 for registered nursing program. **Financial aid:** Priority date 4/1; no closing date. FAFSA required. Applicants notified on a rolling basis; must reply within 2 week(s) of notification.

Academics. **Special study options:** Cross-registration, distance learning, double major, dual enrollment of high school students, ESL, exchange student, external degree, honors, independent study, internships, study abroad, teacher certification program, weekend college. Service learning. License preparation in nursing, paramedic. **Credit/placement by examination:** CLEP, institutional tests. **Support services:** Learning center, remedial instruction, tutoring.

Majors. **Business:** General, accounting, hospitality/recreation, office technology, sales/distribution. **Computer sciences:** Data processing. **Family/consumer sciences:** Institutional food production. **Health:** Clinical lab technology, dental assistant, dental hygiene, EMT paramedic, licensed practical nurse, medical assistant, medical radiologic technology/radiation therapy, nursing (RN), nursing assistant, occupational therapy assistant, physical therapy assistant, physician assistant, respiratory therapy technology, sonography. **Legal studies:** Legal secretary, paralegal. **Liberal arts:** Arts/sciences. **Personal/culinary services:** Culinary arts.

Most popular majors. Business/marketing 30%, computer/information sciences 6%, health sciences 21%, liberal arts 38%.

Computing on campus. 150 workstations in library, computer center.

Student life. **Freshman orientation:** Available. 15 two-hour sessions, any one of which may be attended by a new student. **Policies:** Freshmen permitted cars on campus. **Housing:** Coed dorms available. Housing available through University of Hawaii system. **Activities:** Choral groups, drama, literary magazine, student government, student newspaper, international students club, marketing association, music club, Phi Theta Kappa, nursing association, Japanese, Chinese and Korean club, Catholic Ministry Association, pre-engineering club.

Student services. Career counseling, services for economically disadvantaged, student employment services, financial aid counseling, minority student services, on-campus daycare, personal counseling, placement for graduates, veterans' counselor. **Physically disabled:** Services for visually, speech, hearing impaired. **Transfer:** Orientation for new students.

Contact. Phone: (808) 734-9559 Fax: (808) 734-9456
Terri Ota, Coordinator of Enrollment Services, University of Hawaii: Kapiolani Community College, 4303 Diamond Head Road, Honolulu, HI 96816

University of Hawaii: Kauai Community College

Lihue, Hawaii
www.kauai.hawaii.edu **CB code: 4378**

- Public 2-year community college
- Commuter campus in large town

General. Founded in 1928. Regionally accredited. **Enrollment:** 1,059 undergraduates. **Degrees:** 126 associate awarded. **Location:** 100 miles from Honolulu. **Calendar:** Semester, limited summer session. **Full-time faculty:** 66 total. **Part-time faculty:** 29 total.

Basis for selection. Open admission, but selective for out-of-state students. Special requirements for out-of-state residents in nursing, electrical installation and maintenance technology, facilities engineering technology, nurse's aide, electronics technology programs, culinary arts.

2005-2006 Annual costs. Tuition/fees: $1,500; $7,290 out-of-state. Per-credit charge: $49 in-state; $242 out-of-state. Books/supplies: $750. Personal expenses: $1,000.

Financial aid. Need-based: Work study available nights and for part-time students. **Additional information:** Hawaii student incentive grants and tuition waivers (merit and need-based) available to Hawaii residents.

Application procedures. Admission: Priority date 8/1; no deadline. Admission notification on a rolling basis beginning on or about 3/1. Institutional placement test. **Financial aid:** Priority date 3/1, closing date 5/1. FAFSA, institutional form required. Applicants notified on a rolling basis starting 5/1.

Academics. Special study options: Cooperative education, cross-registration, distance learning, dual enrollment of high school students, ESL, internships, study abroad. **Credit/placement by examination:** AP, CLEP, institutional tests. **Support services:** Learning center, tutoring, writing center.

Majors. Business: Accounting, hospitality admin, office/clerical. **Construction:** Carpentry, electrician. **Education:** Early childhood. **Engineering technology:** Electrical. **Health:** Nursing (RN). **Liberal arts:** Arts/sciences. **Mechanic/repair:** Auto body, automotive. **Personal/culinary services:** Culinary arts.

Computing on campus. 150 workstations in computer center.

Student life. Freshman orientation: Available. **Activities:** Concert band, choral groups, music ensembles, student government, international club, Hawaiian club, Pamantasan club, Hawaiian performing arts club, Japanese club, environmental club.

Athletics. Intramural: Basketball.

Student services. Adult student services, career counseling, student employment services, health services, on-campus daycare, personal counseling, placement for graduates, veterans' counselor. **Physically disabled:** Services for visually, speech, hearing impaired. **Transfer:** Special adviser, orientation for new students. Transfer adviser, college fairs on campus for students transferring to 4-year colleges.

Contact. E-mail: arkauai@hawaii.edu
Phone: (808) 245-8225 Fax: (808) 245-8297
Leighton Oride, Admissions Officer and Registrar, University of Hawaii: Kauai Community College, 3-1901 Kaumualii Highway, Lihue, HI 96766-9500

University of Hawaii: Leeward Community College

Pearl City, Hawaii
www.lcc.hawaii.edu **CB code: 4410**

- Public 2-year community college
- Commuter campus in large town

General. Founded in 1968. Regionally accredited. **Enrollment:** 4,598 degree-seeking undergraduates. **Degrees:** 465 associate awarded. **ROTC:** Army, Air Force. **Location:** 10 miles from Honolulu. **Calendar:** Semester, limited summer session. **Full-time faculty:** 180 total. **Part-time faculty:** 80 total. **Special facilities:** Observatory.

Student profile.

Out-of-state:	10%	**25 or older:**	34%

Basis for selection. Open admission.

2005-2006 Annual costs. Tuition/fees: $1,495; $7,285 out-of-state. Per-credit charge: $49 in-state; $242 out-of-state. Books/supplies: $672. Personal expenses: $953.

Financial aid. Need-based: Need-based aid available for part-time students. **Additional information:** Leveraging Educational Assistance Partnership (LEAP) funds or tuition waivers available to students with financial need.

Application procedures. Admission: Closing date 7/15 (postmark date). No application fee in-state; $25 out-of-state. Admission notification on a rolling basis beginning on or about 12/1. **Financial aid:** Priority date 4/15; no closing date. FAFSA required. Applicants notified on a rolling basis starting 6/1; must reply within 2 week(s) of notification.

Academics. Special study options: Cross-registration, distance learning, dual enrollment of high school students, honors, independent study, internships, liberal arts/career combination, weekend college. **Credit/placement by examination:** CLEP, IB, institutional tests. 21 credit hours maximum toward associate degree. **Support services:** Learning center, pre-admission summer program, remedial instruction, study skills assistance, tutoring.

Majors. Business: Accounting, office/clerical. **Communications:** Broadcast journalism. **Computer sciences:** General. **Liberal arts:** Arts/sciences.

Computing on campus. 200 workstations in library, computer center. Commuter students can connect to campus network. Helpline available.

Student life. Policies: Freshmen permitted cars on campus. **Activities:** Bands, choral groups, dance, drama, film society, literary magazine, music ensembles, musical theater, student government, student newspaper, TV station, Filipino ethnic organization, club for physically handicapped, Campus Crusade for Christ, human services club.

Athletics. Intramural: Bowling, golf, soccer, tennis, volleyball.

Student services. Adult student services, career counseling, student employment services, health services, on-campus daycare, personal counseling, placement for graduates, veterans' counselor. **Physically disabled:** Services for visually, speech, hearing impaired. **Transfer:** Special adviser, orientation for new students. Transfer adviser, college fairs on campus for students transferring to 4-year colleges.

Contact. E-mail: lccar@hawaii.edu
Phone: (808) 455-0217 Fax: (808) 454-8804
Warren Mau, Registrar, University of Hawaii: Leeward Community College, 96-045 Ala Ike, Pearl City, HI 96782

University of Hawaii: Maui Community College

Kahului, Hawaii
www.maui.hawaii.edu **CB code: 4510**

- Public 2-year community college
- Commuter campus in small city

General. Founded in 1931. Regionally accredited. Branch campuses on Molokai, Lanai and Hana. **Enrollment:** 2,368 degree-seeking undergraduates. **Degrees:** 210 associate awarded. **Location:** 150 miles from Honolulu. **Calendar:** Semester, limited summer session. **Full-time faculty:** 93 total. **Part-time faculty:** 6 total.

Student profile.

Out-of-state:	1%	**Live on campus:**	1%

Basis for selection. Open admission, but selective for some programs. Special requirements for nursing program. Interview required of nursing majors. **Adult students:** Entrance exam policies same as for first-time freshmen.

2005-2006 Annual costs. Tuition/fees: $1,508; $7,298 out-of-state. Per-credit charge: $49 in-state; $242 out-of-state. Books/supplies: $820.

2004-2005 Financial aid. Need-based: 48% of total undergraduate aid awarded as scholarships/grants, 52% as loans/jobs. Need-based aid available for part-time students. Work study available nights and for part-time students.

Application procedures. Admission: Priority date 7/31; no deadline. No application fee in-state; $25 out-of-state. Application may be submitted online. Admission notification on a rolling basis. **Financial aid:** Priority date 4/1; no closing date. FAFSA, institutional form required. Must reply within 4 week(s) of notification.

Academics. Special study options: Cooperative education, distance learning, double major, dual enrollment of high school students, ESL, independent study, liberal arts/career combination, weekend college. **Credit/placement by examination:** CLEP, institutional tests. 30 credit hours maximum toward associate degree. **Support services:** Learning center, pre-admission summer program, reduced course load, remedial instruction, tutoring.

Majors. Agriculture: General. **Business:** General, accounting, tourism/travel. **Construction:** Carpentry. **Engineering technology:** Drafting. **Liberal arts:** Arts/sciences. **Mechanic/repair:** Auto body, automotive. **Public administration:** Human services.

Computing on campus. Dormitories wired for high-speed internet access and linked to campus network. Commuter students can connect to campus network. Online course registration, helpline available.

Student life. Freshman orientation: Available. **Policies:** Freshmen permitted cars on campus. **Housing:** Coed dorms available. $160 deposit, deadline 6/1. **Activities:** Student government, student newspaper, TV station.

Student services. Career counseling, student employment services, health services, on-campus daycare, personal counseling, veterans' counselor. **Physically disabled:** Services for visually, speech, hearing impaired. **Transfer:** Special adviser, orientation for new students. Transfer adviser for students transferring to 4-year colleges.

Contact. E-mail: tanakag@hawaii.edu
Phone: (808) 984-3500 Toll-free number: (800) 479-6692
Fax: (808) 242-9618
Stephen Kameda, Admissions Officer/Registrar, University of Hawaii: Maui Community College, 310 West Kaahumanu Avenue, Kahului, HI 96732-1617

University of Hawaii: Windward Community College

Kaneohe, Hawaii
www.wcc.hawaii.edu **CB code: 4976**

- Public 2-year community college
- Commuter campus in small city

General. Founded in 1972. Regionally accredited. **Enrollment:** 1,357 degree-seeking undergraduates. **Degrees:** 110 associate awarded. **ROTC:** Army. **Location:** 10 miles from Honolulu. **Calendar:** Semester, limited summer session. **Full-time faculty:** 40 total. **Part-time faculty:** 32 total. **Special facilities:** Planetarium, greenhouse.

Student profile.

Out-of-state:	9%	**25 or older:**	38%

Basis for selection. Open admission. Students under 18 must have high school diploma. **Adult students:** SAT/ACT scores not required.

2005-2006 Annual costs. Tuition/fees: $1,510; $7,300 out-of-state. Per-credit charge: $49 in-state; $242 out-of-state. Books/supplies: $987. Personal expenses: $1,730.

2005-2006 Financial aid. Need-based: 72% of total undergraduate aid awarded as scholarships/grants, 28% as loans/jobs. Need-based aid available for part-time students. **Additional information:** Hawaii student incentive grants and tuition waivers (merit and need-based) available to Hawaii residents.

Application procedures. Admission: Priority date 8/1; no deadline. No application fee in-state; $25 out-of-state. Admission notification on a rolling basis. Out-of-state military dependents not required to pay application fee. **Financial aid:** Priority date 4/1; no closing date. FAFSA required. Applicants notified on a rolling basis starting 3/15; must reply within 2 week(s) of notification.

Academics. Special study options: Cooperative education, distance learning, double major, independent study, student-designed major. **Credit/placement by examination:** CLEP, institutional tests. **Support services:** Learning center, reduced course load, remedial instruction, tutoring.

Majors. Liberal arts: Arts/sciences.

Computing on campus. 30 workstations in computer center.

Student life. Freshman orientation: Available. Preregistration for classes offered. **Policies:** Freshmen permitted cars on campus. **Activities:** Choral groups, drama, student government, student newspaper.

Student services. Adult student services, career counseling, services for economically disadvantaged, student employment services, financial aid counseling, minority student services, personal counseling, placement for graduates, veterans' counselor. **Transfer:** Special adviser, orientation, pre-admission transcript evaluation for new students. Transfer adviser, college fairs on campus for students transferring to 4-year colleges.

Contact. E-mail: mcastana@hawaii.edu
Phone: (808) 235-7432 Fax: (808) 235-9148
Russell Chan, Registrar, University of Hawaii: Windward Community College, 45-720 Keaahala Road, Kaneohe, HI 96744

Idaho

College of Southern Idaho

Twin Falls, Idaho
www.csi.edu **CB code: 4114**

- Public 2-year community and junior college
- Commuter campus in large town

General. Founded in 1964. Regionally accredited. **Enrollment:** 5,145 degree-seeking undergraduates. **Degrees:** 656 associate awarded. **Location:** 130 miles from Boise. **Calendar:** Semester, limited summer session. **Full-time faculty:** 160 total. **Part-time faculty:** 270 total. **Special facilities:** Museum and planetarium including anthropology, archeology, fine arts collections.

Student profile.

Out-of-state:	5%	**Live on campus:**	5%
25 or older:	52%		

Transfer out. Colleges most students transferred to 2005: Boise State University, University of Idaho, Idaho State University, Utah State University.

Basis for selection. Open admission, but selective for some programs. For applicants to registered nursing program, ACT recommended; letters of reference, letter of intent, special tests required. Interview required of registered nursing, technical majors.

2005-2006 Annual costs. Tuition/fees: $1,900; $5,300 out-of-state. Per-credit charge: $95 in-state; $265 out-of-state. Room/board: $4,300. Books/supplies: $800. Personal expenses: $1,900.

2004-2005 Financial aid. Need-based: 59% of total undergraduate aid awarded as scholarships/grants, 41% as loans/jobs. Need-based aid available for part-time students. **Additional information:** Out-of-state tuition waivers based on GPA and activities.

Application procedures. Admission: No deadline. No application fee. Admission notification on a rolling basis. **Financial aid:** Priority date 3/1; no closing date. FAFSA required. Applicants notified on a rolling basis starting 4/30; must reply within 3 week(s) of notification.

Academics. Special study options: Cooperative education, distance learning, dual enrollment of high school students, ESL, honors, internships. License preparation in real estate. **Credit/placement by examination:** CLEP, institutional tests. 21 credit hours maximum toward associate degree. **Support services:** GED preparation and test center, learning center, pre-admission summer program, reduced course load, remedial instruction, study skills assistance, tutoring, writing center.

Majors. Agriculture: Aquaculture, business, equestrian studies, food science, horticultural science, range science. **Biology:** General, botany, zoology. **Business:** General, accounting, hospitality/recreation, marketing, office technology, real estate, tourism promotion. **Communications:** General. **Computer sciences:** Computer graphics, computer science, LAN/WAN management. **Conservation:** General, forestry, water/wetlands/marine, wildlife. **Education:** Bilingual, early childhood, elementary, physical, secondary. **Engineering:** Civil, computer, electrical. **Engineering technology:** Computer systems, drafting. **Foreign languages:** General, sign language interpretation. **Health:** Dental hygiene, EMT paramedic, nursing (RN), pharmacy assistant, predentistry, premedicine, prepharmacy, preveterinary, respiratory therapy technology, veterinary technology/assistant. **History:** General. **Interdisciplinary:** Natural sciences. **Legal studies:** Prelaw. **Liberal arts:** Arts/sciences, library science. **Math:** General. **Mechanic/repair:** Auto body, automotive, diesel, heating/ac/refrig. **Parks/recreation:** Health/fitness. **Personal/culinary services:** Culinary arts. **Physical sciences:** Chemistry, geology, physics. **Production:** Welding, woodworking. **Protective services:** Fire safety technology, law enforcement admin, police science. **Psychology:** General. **Public administration:** Human services. **Social sciences:** Anthropology, economics, geography, political science, sociology. **Visual/performing arts:** Art, commercial/advertising art, dramatic, photography.

Computing on campus. 350 workstations in dormitories, library, computer center. Dormitories wired for high-speed internet access. Online course registration, online library, helpline, student web hosting available.

Student life. Freshman orientation: Available. Half-day program at end of first week of fall semester. **Policies:** Freshmen permitted cars on campus. **Housing:** Coed dorms, apartments available. $100 deposit. **Activities:** Bands, choral groups, drama, music ensembles, radio station, student government, symphony orchestra, Christian Fellowship, international students, Latter Day Saints student association, Ambassadors, Latinos Unidos, Baptist campus ministries, Golden Eagle Native Americans, Chi Alpha, Accent club.

Athletics. NJCAA. **Intercollegiate:** Baseball M, basketball, equestrian, rodeo, volleyball W. **Intramural:** Basketball, bowling, football (non-tackle), golf, racquetball, skiing, soccer, softball, tennis, volleyball. **Team name:** Eagles.

Student services. Adult student services, alcohol/substance abuse counseling, career counseling, services for economically disadvantaged, student employment services, financial aid counseling, health services, minority student services, on-campus daycare, personal counseling, veterans' counselor. **Physically disabled:** Services for visually, speech, hearing impaired. **Transfer:** Special adviser, re-entry adviser, pre-admission transcript evaluation for new students. College fairs on campus for students transferring to 4-year colleges.

Contact. Phone: (208) 732-6231 Fax: (208) 736-3014
John Martin, Director of Admissions, College of Southern Idaho, Box 1238, Twin Falls, ID 83303-1238

Eastern Idaho Technical College

Idaho Falls, Idaho
www.eitc.edu **CB code: 0975**

- Public 2-year technical college
- Commuter campus in large town

General. Founded in 1969. Regionally accredited. **Enrollment:** 638 degree-seeking undergraduates; 117 non-degree-seeking students. **Degrees:** 86 associate awarded. **Location:** 280 miles from Boise, 230 miles from Salt Lake City. **Calendar:** Semester, limited summer session. **Full-time faculty:** 40 total; 60% women. **Part-time faculty:** 51 total; 57% women. **Class size:** 77% < 20, 19% 20-39, 4% 40-49. **Partnerships:** Customized work-force training and Tech Prep agreements available. Professional technical high school programs for 7 area high schools taught on campus.

Student profile. Among degree-seeking undergraduates, 141 enrolled as first-time, first-year students, 141 transferred in from other institutions.

Part-time:	65%	**Women:**	71%

Transfer out. Colleges most students transferred to 2005: Idaho State University, Brigham Young University-Idaho, University of Idaho, Boise State University.

Basis for selection. Open admission, but selective for some programs. Entrance exam, essay required for nursing. COMPASS required of all applicants. Students who score below acceptable level must take developmental classes before enrolling in degree program. **Adult students:** Entrance exam policies same as for first-time freshmen.

High school preparation. Recommended units include English 8, mathematics 6 and science 6.

2005-2006 Annual costs. Tuition/fees: $1,646; $5,730 out-of-state. Per-credit charge: $76 in-state; $152 out-of-state. Fees may vary according to the program of study. Books/supplies: $808. Personal expenses: $1,276.

2004-2005 Financial aid. Need-based: 48% of total undergraduate aid awarded as scholarships/grants, 52% as loans/jobs. Need-based aid available for part-time students. Work study available for part-time students. **Non-need-based:** Scholarships awarded for academics, job skills, state residency.

Application procedures. Admission: Closing date 8/23. $10 fee, may be waived for applicants with need. Application must be submitted on paper. Admission notification on a rolling basis. **Financial aid:** Priority date 6/1; no closing date. FAFSA, institutional form required. Applicants notified on a rolling basis starting 6/6; must reply by 6/5 or within 4 week(s) of notification.

Academics. Special study options: Dual enrollment of high school students, ESL, internships, weekend college. License preparation in nursing, real estate. **Credit/placement by examination:** AP, CLEP. **Support services:** GED preparation and test center, learning center, pre-admission summer program, reduced course load, remedial instruction, study skills assistance, tutoring, writing center.

Majors. Business: Accounting, administrative services, marketing. **Computer sciences:** Networking. **Engineering technology:** Electrical. **Health:**

Medical assistant, surgical technology. **Legal studies:** Paralegal. **Mechanic/repair:** General, automotive, diesel. **Production:** Welding.

Most popular majors. Business/marketing 33%, computer/information sciences 9%, engineering/engineering technologies 6%, health sciences 29%, legal studies 7%, trade and industry 12%.

Computing on campus. 209 workstations in library, computer center. Online library available.

Student life. Freshman orientation: Mandatory. **Activities:** Student government.

Student services. Adult student services, alcohol/substance abuse counseling, career counseling, student employment services, financial aid counseling, personal counseling, placement for graduates, veterans' counselor, women's services. **Physically disabled:** Services for visually, speech, hearing impaired. **Transfer:** Special adviser, orientation for new students. Transfer adviser for students transferring to 4-year colleges.

Contact. E-mail: salbisto@eitc.edu
Phone: (208) 524-3000 ext. 3371 Toll-free number: (800) 662-0261 ext. 3371 Fax: (208) 525-7026
Steven Albiston, Dean of Students, Eastern Idaho Technical College, 1600 South 25th East, Idaho Falls, ID 83404-5788

North Idaho College

Coeur d'Alene, Idaho — **CB member**
www.nic.edu — **CB code: 4539**

- Public 2-year community college
- Commuter campus in large town

General. Founded in 1933. Regionally accredited. **Enrollment:** 3,853 degree-seeking undergraduates; 246 non-degree-seeking students. **Degrees:** 478 associate awarded. **Location:** 30 miles from Spokane, Washington. **Calendar:** Semester, limited summer session. **Full-time faculty:** 155 total; 1% have terminal degrees, 3% minority, 52% women. **Part-time faculty:** 142 total; 1% have terminal degrees, 6% minority, 50% women. **Special facilities:** Museum. **Partnerships:** Formal partnerships with local businesses.

Student profile. Among degree-seeking undergraduates, 1,015 enrolled as first-time, first-year students.

Part-time:	36%	**25 or older:**	36%
Out-of-state:	8%	**Live on campus:**	4%
Women:	62%		

Transfer out. Colleges most students transferred to 2005: University of Idaho, Lewis-Clark State College, Boise State University, Eastern Washington University, Spokane Community College.

Basis for selection. Open admission, but selective for some programs. RN, LPN and other allied health program applicants must submit 3 references and supplemental statement. Professional technical applicants should be interviewed by counselor. ACT, SAT, or Compass used for placement; scores must not be more than 2 years old. TOEFL scores used for placement of international students. Interview recommended for professional technical majors. **Adult students:** Entrance exam policies same as for first-time freshmen. **Homeschooled:** GED highly recommended. **Learning Disabled:** Contact Disability Support Services at time of application.

High school preparation. Recommended units include English 4, mathematics 3, social studies 2, science 3 (laboratory 1). Algebra, biology, 2 years chemistry with laboratory, or 1 year chemistry and 1 year physics, with cumulative 2.50 GPA required for registered nursing applicants. Physics, advanced algebra recommended for nursing applicants.

2005-2006 Annual costs. Tuition/fees: $1,888; $2,888 out-of-district; $6,440 out-of-state. Per-credit charge: $117 in-district; $180 out-of-district; $401 out-of-state. Room/board: $5,410. Books/supplies: $700. Personal expenses: $926.

2004-2005 Financial aid. Need-based: 57% of total undergraduate aid awarded as scholarships/grants, 43% as loans/jobs. Need-based aid available for part-time students. Work study available weekends and for part-time students. **Non-need-based:** Scholarships awarded for academics, art, athletics, leadership, minority status, music/drama, state residency.

Application procedures. Admission: Closing date 8/21 (receipt date). $25 fee, may be waived for applicants with need. Application may be submitted online. Admission notification on a rolling basis beginning on or about 2/1. **Financial aid:** Priority date 3/15; no closing date. FAFSA, institutional form required. Applicants notified on a rolling basis starting 4/1; must reply within 2 week(s) of notification.

Academics. Special study options: Cooperative education, distance learning, double major, dual enrollment of high school students, ESL, independent study, internships, liberal arts/career combination, semester at sea. Lewis Clark State College and University of Idaho upper division and graduate classes on campus. Bachelor's degree programs available on campus. License preparation in nursing. **Credit/placement by examination:** CLEP, institutional tests. 24 credit hours maximum toward associate degree. **Support services:** GED preparation and test center, learning center, reduced course load, remedial instruction, study skills assistance, tutoring, writing center.

Majors. Area/ethnic studies: Native American. **Biology:** General, botany, zoology. **Business:** Administrative services, business admin. **Communications:** General, journalism, public relations. **Computer sciences:** General, applications programming, programming. **Conservation:** Fisheries, forestry, wildlife. **Construction:** Carpentry. **Education:** General, business, early childhood, elementary, secondary. **Engineering:** General, chemical, civil, electrical. **Engineering technology:** Drafting. **Foreign languages:** General. **Health:** Clinical lab assistant, health services, medical assistant, medical secretary, medical transcription, mental health services, nursing (RN), pharmacy assistant, physical therapy assistant, predentistry, premedicine, prepharmacy, preveterinary. **History:** General. **Legal studies:** Legal secretary, prelaw. **Liberal arts:** Arts/sciences. **Math:** General. **Mechanic/repair:** Auto body, automotive, diesel, heating/ac/refrig, industrial. **Parks/recreation:** Health/fitness. **Philosophy/religion:** Philosophy. **Physical sciences:** Astronomy, chemistry, geology, physics. **Protective services:** Criminal justice, police science. **Psychology:** General. **Public administration:** Human services. **Social sciences:** General, anthropology, political science, sociology. **Visual/performing arts:** Commercial/advertising art, music performance, music theory/composition, studio arts.

Most popular majors. Business/marketing 22%, education 10%, health sciences 14%, liberal arts 22%.

Computing on campus. 150 workstations in library, computer center, student center. Dormitories wired for high-speed internet access. Commuter students can connect to campus network. Online course registration, helpline available.

Student life. Freshman orientation: Available. Usually half-day program held Friday before start of classes. **Policies:** Freshmen permitted cars on campus. **Housing:** Coed dorms, special housing for disabled available. $150 deposit, deadline 6/1. Apartment complex adjacent to campus. **Activities:** Bands, choral groups, dance, drama, literary magazine, music ensembles, student government, student newspaper, symphony orchestra, Students for Human Equality, creative writers club, nursing student association, veterans club, International Student Relations, Baptist Student Ministry, Latter-Day Saints Student Association, Campus Crusade for Christ.

Athletics. NJCAA. **Intercollegiate:** Basketball, cheerleading, soccer, softball W, volleyball W, wrestling M. **Intramural:** Basketball, bowling, football (non-tackle), golf, softball, table tennis, tennis, volleyball. **Team name:** Cardinals.

Student services. Adult student services, alcohol/substance abuse counseling, career counseling, services for economically disadvantaged, student employment services, financial aid counseling, health services, legal services, minority student services, on-campus daycare, personal counseling, placement for graduates, veterans' counselor, women's services. **Physically disabled:** Services for visually, speech, hearing impaired. **Transfer:** Special adviser, orientation for new students. Transfer adviser, college fairs on campus for students transferring to 4-year colleges.

Contact. E-mail: admit@nic.edu
Phone: (208) 769-3311 Toll-free number: (877) 404-4536
Fax: (208) 769-3399
Maxine Gish, Director of Admissions, North Idaho College, 1000 West Garden Avenue, Coeur d'Alene, ID 83814-2199

Stevens-Henager College: Boise

Boise, Idaho
www.stevenshenager.edu/shc/campus/boise.cfm

- Private 2-year business and technical college
- Large city

General. Accredited by ACCSCT. **Calendar:** Continuous.

Annual costs/financial aid. Tuition/fees (projected): $5,901.

Contact. Phone: (208) 345-0700
700 Americana Boulevard, Boise, ID 83702

Illinois

Black Hawk College
Moline, Illinois
www.bhc.edu
CB code: 1483

- Public 2-year community college
- Commuter campus in large town

General. Founded in 1946. Regionally accredited. **Enrollment:** 5,246 degree-seeking undergraduates; 1,161 non-degree-seeking students. **Degrees:** 573 associate awarded. **Location:** 160 miles from Chicago, 60 miles from Iowa City. **Calendar:** Semester, limited summer session. **Full-time faculty:** 134 total; 16% have terminal degrees, 10% minority, 50% women. **Part-time faculty:** 220 total; 12% have terminal degrees, 9% minority, 55% women. **Class size:** 65% < 20, 33% 20-39, less than 1% 40-49, less than 1% 50-99, less than 1% >100. **Special facilities:** Local PBS station on campus.

Student profile. Among degree-seeking undergraduates, 57% enrolled in a transfer program, 43% enrolled in a vocational program, 5% already have a bachelor's degree or higher, 915 enrolled as first-time, first-year students, 325 transferred in from other institutions.

Part-time:	46%	**Asian American:**	1%
Out-of-state:	4%	**Hispanic American:**	7%
Women:	62%	**Native American:**	1%
African American:	7%	**25 or older:**	40%

Transfer out. 65% of students enrolled in the transfer program go on to 4-year colleges. **Colleges most students transferred to 2005:** Western Illinois University, Illinois State University, St. Ambrose University, University of Illinois, University of Iowa.

Basis for selection. Open admission, but selective for some programs. Special requirements for health care-related programs, such as nursing and physical therapy assistant. Applicants must submit ACT test scores within 2 years of admission or course placement. **Adult students:** Entrance exam policies same as for first-time freshmen. SAT/ACT scores not required.

High school preparation. 15 units recommended. Recommended units include English 4, mathematics 3, social studies 3, science 3 and foreign language 2.

2005-2006 Annual costs. Tuition/fees: $2,070; $4,410 out-of-district; $7,980 out-of-state. Per-credit charge: $62 in-district; $140 out-of-district; $259 out-of-state. Agreement with 5 contiguous Iowa counties for special tuition rate of $100 per credit plus required fees. Books/supplies: $950. Personal expenses: $3,750.

2004-2005 Financial aid. Need-based: 390 full-time freshmen applied for aid; 367 were judged to have need; 343 of these received aid. Average need met was 69%. Average scholarship/grant was $3,160; average loan $1,740. 83% of total undergraduate aid awarded as scholarships/grants, 17% as loans/jobs. Need-based aid available for part-time students. Work study available for part-time students. **Non-need-based:** Awarded to 349 full-time undergraduates, including 125 freshmen. Scholarships awarded for academics, art, athletics, leadership, music/drama, state residency. **Additional information:** Application deadlines for scholarships: 5/15 fall semester, 12/1 spring semester.

Application procedures. Admission: No deadline. No application fee. Application may be submitted online. Admission notification on a rolling basis beginning on or about 3/1. **Financial aid:** Priority date 5/15; no closing date. FAFSA required. Applicants notified on a rolling basis starting 5/1.

Academics. Special study options: Accelerated study, cooperative education, cross-registration, distance learning, dual enrollment of high school students, ESL, independent study, internships, study abroad, weekend college. License preparation in nursing, physical therapy. **Credit/placement by examination:** AP, CLEP, institutional tests. 30 credit hours maximum toward associate degree. Most CLEP credit awarded to students pursuing associate degree in liberal studies. **Support services:** GED preparation, learning center, reduced course load, remedial instruction, study skills assistance, tutoring.

Majors. Agriculture: Animal husbandry, business, crop production, equestrian studies, horticulture, mechanization, production. **Business:** Accounting, accounting technology, administrative services, banking/financial services, business admin, human resources, international, office management, office technology, small business admin. **Communications technology:** Radio/tv. **Computer sciences:** Programming. **Construction:** Carpentry. **Education:** Mathematics. **Engineering technology:** Civil, electromechanical, environmental, manufacturing, robotics. **English:** Technical writing. **Family/consumer sciences:** Home furnishings. **Foreign languages:** Sign language interpretation. **Health:** Electroencephalograph technology, medical records technology, nursing (RN), physical therapy assistant, radiologic technology/medical imaging. **Interdisciplinary:** Biological/physical sciences. **Legal studies:** Legal secretary, paralegal. **Liberal arts:** Arts/sciences. **Mechanic/repair:** Auto body, automotive, diesel, heating/ac/refrig. **Personal/culinary services:** Restaurant/catering. **Protective services:** Fire services admin, police science. **Visual/performing arts:** Design.

Most popular majors. Agriculture 7%, business/marketing 7%, health sciences 16%, interdisciplinary studies 13%, liberal arts 44%.

Computing on campus. 822 workstations in library, computer center. Commuter students can connect to campus network. Online course registration available.

Student life. Freshman orientation: Mandatory. Preregistration for classes offered. Most students required to attend orientation if they enroll in or accumulate 6 or more credit hours. **Policies:** Freshmen permitted cars on campus. **Activities:** Jazz band, choral groups, drama, music ensembles, student government, student newspaper, TV station, African-American Student Union, Alpha Beta Gamma, Association of Latin America, Brotherhood On Campus, College Democrats of America, College Republicans, International Student Association, Student Government Association, Sisterhood On Campus, Social Action Connection.

Athletics. NJCAA. **Intercollegiate:** Baseball M, basketball, golf M, softball W, volleyball W. **Team name:** Braves.

Student services. Career counseling, services for economically disadvantaged, student employment services, financial aid counseling, minority student services, on-campus daycare, personal counseling, placement for graduates, women's services. **Physically disabled:** Services for visually, speech, hearing impaired. **Transfer:** Special adviser for new students. Transfer center, transfer adviser, college fairs on campus for students transferring to 4-year colleges.

Contact. Phone: (309) 796-5300 Fax: (309) 792-5976
Kim Armstrong, Dean of Student Support Services, Black Hawk College, 6600 34th Avenue, Moline, IL 61265-5899

Black Hawk College: East Campus
Kewanee, Illinois
www.bhc.edu
CB code: 0690

- Public 2-year community college
- Commuter campus in small town

General. Founded in 1967. Regionally accredited. **Enrollment:** 780 degree-seeking undergraduates. **Degrees:** 182 associate awarded. **Location:** 45 miles from Peoria. **Calendar:** Semester, extensive summer session. **Full-time faculty:** 28 total. **Part-time faculty:** 34 total.

Transfer out. Colleges most students transferred to 2005: Western Illinois University, Illinois State University, University of Illinois.

Basis for selection. Open admission, but selective for some programs. Special requirements for physical therapy assistant and nursing programs, limited enrollment in practical nursing and truck driving certificates. SAT or ACT may be used in lieu of placement exam. Interview required of nursing and physical therapy assistant majors.

2005-2006 Annual costs. Tuition/fees: $2,070; $4,410 out-of-district; $7,980 out-of-state. Per-credit charge: $62 in-district; $140 out-of-district; $259 out-of-state. Agreement with 5 contiguous Iowa counties for special tuition rate of $100 per credit plus required fees. Books/supplies: $600.

Application procedures. Admission: No deadline. No application fee. Admission notification on a rolling basis. **Financial aid:** Priority date 6/1; no closing date. FAFSA required. Applicants notified on a rolling basis; must reply within 2 week(s) of notification.

Academics. Special study options: Cooperative education, cross-registration, distance learning, double major, dual enrollment of high school students, independent study, internships, study abroad. **Credit/placement by examination:** CLEP, institutional tests. 40 credit hours maximum toward associate degree. **Support services:** GED preparation and test center, learning center, pre-admission summer program, reduced course load, remedial instruction, tutoring.

Majors. Agriculture: Business, equestrian studies, horticulture. **Biology:** General, zoology. **Business:** General, accounting, administrative services, office technology. **Communications:** Journalism, public relations. **Computer sciences:** General, data processing, programming. **Education:** Elementary, secondary. **Health:** Predentistry, premedicine, prepharmacy. **History:** General. **Interdisciplinary:** Natural sciences. **Legal studies:** Paralegal, prelaw. **Liberal arts:** Arts/sciences. **Math:** General. **Mechanic/repair:** Automotive. **Physical sciences:** Chemistry, planetary. **Psychology:** General. **Social sciences:** Anthropology, economics, political science, sociology. **Visual/performing arts:** Art.

Computing on campus. 82 workstations in computer center.

Student life. Housing: Foundation-owned apartments available next to college. **Activities:** Student government.

Athletics. NJCAA. **Intercollegiate:** Basketball. **Team name:** Warriors (M)/ Lady Warriors (F).

Student services. Career counseling, student employment services, personal counseling, placement for graduates, veterans' counselor. **Physically disabled:** Services for visually, speech, hearing impaired. **Transfer:** Special adviser for new students. Transfer adviser, college fairs on campus for students transferring to 4-year colleges.

Contact. E-mail: recruiter@bhc.edu
Phone: (309) 852-5671 ext. 6220 Toll-free number: (800) 233-5671 ext. 6220 Fax: (309) 856-6005
Patricia Varner, Director of Educational Services, Black Hawk College: East Campus, 1501 State Highway 78, Kewanee, IL 61443-0630

Career Colleges of Chicago

Chicago, Illinois
www.careerchi.com **CB code: 2227**

- For-profit 2-year business college
- Commuter campus in very large city
- Interview required

General. Founded in 1950. Regionally accredited; also accredited by ACICS. **Enrollment:** 162 degree-seeking undergraduates. **Location:** Downtown. **Calendar:** Quarter, extensive summer session. **Part-time faculty:** 20 total. **Class size:** 96% < 20, 4% 20-39.

Student profile.

Out-of-state:	1%	25 or older:	69%

Basis for selection. Minimum GPA 2.0, keyboarding speed 25 WPM required; interview, resume required, school/office experience helpful. Wonderlic Scholastic Level Examination required - score of 21 or above required for regular admission, score of 16-20 for conditional admission. **Adult students:** Entrance exam policies same as for first-time freshmen.

2005-2006 Annual costs. Per-credit-hour charge is either $240 or $270, depending on whether technology or non-technology course is selected. Books/supplies: $600.

Financial aid. All financial aid based on need.

Application procedures. Admission: No deadline. $50 fee, may be waived for applicants with need. Admission notification on a rolling basis. **Financial aid:** No deadline. FAFSA, institutional form required. Applicants notified on a rolling basis.

Academics. Special study options: Internships. **Credit/placement by examination:** CLEP, institutional tests. 15 credit hours maximum toward associate degree.

Majors. Health: Medical secretary. **Legal studies:** Court reporting, legal secretary, paralegal.

Computing on campus. 65 workstations in computer center. Online library available.

Student life. Freshman orientation: Mandatory. Preregistration for classes offered.

Student services. Student employment services, financial aid counseling, placement for graduates. **Transfer:** Orientation, pre-admission transcript evaluation for new students.

Contact. E-mail: admissions@careerchi.com
Phone: (312) 895-6317 Toll-free number: (877) 854-6300
Fax: (312) 895-6317
Bonnie Kirincic-Reyburn, Director of Admissions, Career Colleges of Chicago, 11 East Adams Street, Chicago, IL 60603

Carl Sandburg College

Galesburg, Illinois
www.sandburg.edu **CB code: 1982**

- Public 2-year community college
- Commuter campus in large town

General. Founded in 1966. Regionally accredited. Branch center in Carthage, extension center in Bushnell. **Enrollment:** 3,400 undergraduates. **Degrees:** 306 associate awarded. **ROTC:** Army. **Location:** 200 miles from Chicago, 40 miles from Peoria. **Calendar:** Semester, limited summer session. **Full-time faculty:** 75 total. **Part-time faculty:** 230 total. **Special facilities:** Greenhouse, 22-acre agriculture experience plot.

Student profile.

Out-of-state:	1%	25 or older:	60%

Transfer out. Colleges most students transferred to 2005: Western Illinois University, Illinois State University.

Basis for selection. Open admission, but selective for some programs. Special requirements for allied health programs. ACT required of nursing program applicants; score report by February 1. Interview recommended for radiologic technology, mortuary science, and physical therapy assistant majors.

High school preparation. 15 units recommended. Recommended units include English 4, mathematics 3, social studies 2, science 2 (laboratory 2) and academic electives 2.

2005-2006 Annual costs. Tuition/fees: $2,595; $3,915 out-of-district; $4,335 out-of-state. Per-credit charge: $72 in-district; $116 out-of-district; $130 out-of-state. Books/supplies: $710. Personal expenses: $880.

Financial aid. Need-based: Work study available for part-time students. **Non-need-based:** Scholarships awarded for academics, art, athletics.

Application procedures. Admission: No deadline. No application fee. Admission notification on a rolling basis. **Financial aid:** Priority date 5/1; no closing date. FAFSA, institutional form required. Applicants notified on a rolling basis starting 6/15; must reply within 2 week(s) of notification.

Academics. Special study options: Cross-registration, dual enrollment of high school students, ESL, honors, independent study, internships, student-designed major, study abroad. License preparation in dental hygiene, nursing, paramedic, radiology. **Credit/placement by examination:** AP, CLEP, institutional tests. 20 credit hours maximum toward associate degree. **Support services:** GED preparation and test center, learning center, remedial instruction, tutoring.

Majors. Agriculture: Business. **Business:** Accounting, administrative services, banking/financial services, business admin, operations. **Computer sciences:** General. **Engineering technology:** Drafting. **Family/consumer sciences:** Child care. **Health:** Nursing (RN). **Mechanic/repair:** Auto body. **Personal/culinary services:** Mortuary science. **Protective services:** Firefighting, law enforcement admin.

Most popular majors. Business/marketing 12%, health sciences 26%, liberal arts 45%, trade and industry 12%.

Computing on campus. 69 workstations in library, computer center.

Student life. Activities: Bands, choral groups, drama, literary magazine, music ensembles, student government.

Athletics. NJCAA. **Intercollegiate:** Baseball M, basketball, softball W, volleyball W. **Team name:** Chargers.

Student services. Career counseling, student employment services, on-campus daycare, personal counseling, placement for graduates, veterans' counselor. **Physically disabled:** Services for visually, hearing impaired. **Transfer:** Special adviser for new students. Transfer adviser, college fairs on campus for students transferring to 4-year colleges.

Contact. Phone: (309) 344-2518 Fax: (309) 344-3526
Carol Kreider, Director of Admissions and Records, Carl Sandburg College, 2400 Tom L. Wilson Boulevard, Galesburg, IL 61401

Two-Year Colleges

City Colleges of Chicago: Harold Washington College

Chicago, Illinois
www.ccc.edu **CB code: 1089**

- Public 2-year community college
- Commuter campus in very large city

General. Founded in 1962. Regionally accredited. **Enrollment:** 6,830 degree-seeking undergraduates. **Degrees:** 350 associate awarded. **Calendar:** Semester, limited summer session. **Full-time faculty:** 104 total; 52% women. **Part-time faculty:** 292 total; 48% women. **Partnerships:** Formal partnerships with McDonalds, Dominicks, and Chicago public schools.

Transfer out. Colleges most students transferred to 2005: Chicago State University, Northeastern Illinois University, University of Illinois-Chicago, De Paul University, Roosevelt University.

Basis for selection. Open admission, but selective for some programs. Special requirements for physicians assistant and police programs. All incoming freshmen required to test with this institution.

High school preparation. 20 units required. Required units include English 4, mathematics 4, social studies 4, science 3 and academic electives 3. 2 additional units in foreign language, art, music, computer science, or other electives required.

2005-2006 Annual costs. Tuition/fees: $2,260; $5,130 out-of-district; $8,236 out-of-state. Per-credit charge: $67 in-district; $163 out-of-district; $266 out-of-state. Books/supplies: $600. Personal expenses: $1,761.

Financial aid. All financial aid based on need. Need-based aid available for part-time students. Work study available nights and for part-time students.

Application procedures. Admission: No deadline. No application fee. Application may be submitted online. **Financial aid:** Priority date 5/1, closing date 6/30. FAFSA required. Applicants notified on a rolling basis starting 7/1; must reply within 2 week(s) of notification.

Academics. Special study options: Cooperative education, cross-registration, distance learning, double major, dual enrollment of high school students, ESL, honors, independent study, internships, liberal arts/career combination. Courses by videocassette at Chicago public libraries; offer license preparation in taxi, limousine, foodservice and sanitation, and substance abuse counseling. **Credit/placement by examination:** AP, CLEP, institutional tests. **Support services:** GED preparation, learning center, reduced course load, remedial instruction, study skills assistance, tutoring.

Majors. Biology: General. **Business:** Accounting, administrative services, banking/financial services, business admin, hospitality admin, international, tourism/travel. **Communications:** Journalism. **Computer sciences:** General, data processing, information systems. **Education:** Early childhood, elementary, secondary, teacher assistance. **Engineering:** General. **English:** Speech/rhetoric. **Family/consumer sciences:** Family studies. **Foreign languages:** General, French, German, Japanese, Spanish. **Health:** Predentistry, premedicine, prepharmacy, substance abuse counseling. **Legal studies:** General, prelaw. **Liberal arts:** Arts/sciences. **Math:** General. **Philosophy/religion:** Philosophy. **Physical sciences:** Chemistry, physics. **Protective services:** Corrections, firefighting, law enforcement admin, police science. **Public administration:** Social work. **Social sciences:** General. **Visual/performing arts:** Art, commercial/advertising art, design, dramatic.

Most popular majors. Business/marketing 9%, education 7%, health sciences 6%, liberal arts 66%.

Computing on campus. 180 workstations in computer center. Online library available.

Student life. Freshman orientation: Mandatory. Preregistration for classes offered. 1 hour overview. **Activities:** Jazz band, choral groups, drama, literary magazine, music ensembles, student government, student newspaper, Black Student Union, Organization of Latin American Students, Berean Bible Club, Circle K Club.

Student services. Adult student services, career counseling, services for economically disadvantaged, student employment services, financial aid counseling, minority student services, personal counseling, placement for graduates, veterans' counselor. **Physically disabled:** Services for visually, speech, hearing impaired. **Learning disabled:** Comprehensive services available. **Transfer:** Special adviser, orientation for new students. Transfer adviser, college fairs on campus for students transferring to 4-year colleges.

Contact. Phone: (312) 553-6000 Fax: (312) 553-6007
Robert Brown, Registrar, City Colleges of Chicago: Harold Washington College, 30 East Lake Street, Chicago, IL 60601

City Colleges of Chicago: Harry S. Truman College

Chicago, Illinois
www.ccc.edu **CB code: 1111**

- Public 2-year community college
- Commuter campus in very large city

General. Founded in 1956. Regionally accredited. **Enrollment:** 4,884 degree-seeking undergraduates. **Degrees:** 193 associate awarded. **Location:** In northeast section of Chicago. **Calendar:** Semester, limited summer session. **Full-time faculty:** 83 total; 55% women. **Part-time faculty:** 174 total; 53% women. **Special facilities:** Art gallery for Chicago artists, theater for performing arts. **Partnerships:** Formal partnerships with Chamber of Commerce and aldermanic representative for our ward.

Transfer out. Colleges most students transferred to 2005: University of Illinois, Loyola University of Chicago, Roosevelt University, Northeastern Illinois University.

Basis for selection. Open admission, but selective for some programs. Test scores, essay considered for nursing and certain allied health programs. Applicants without high school diploma must obtain GED prior to graduation. ACT required of nursing applicants.

2005-2006 Annual costs. Tuition/fees: $2,260; $5,130 out-of-district; $8,236 out-of-state. Per-credit charge: $67 in-district; $163 out-of-district; $266 out-of-state. Books/supplies: $800. Personal expenses: $1,530.

Financial aid. All financial aid based on need. Need-based aid available for part-time students. Work study available nights and weekends.

Application procedures. Admission: No deadline. No application fee. Application may be submitted online. Admission notification on a rolling basis. **Financial aid:** No deadline. FAFSA required. Applicants notified on a rolling basis starting 7/1; must reply within 3 week(s) of notification.

Academics. Special study options: Cooperative education, cross-registration, dual enrollment of high school students, honors, independent study, internships, liberal arts/career combination, weekend college. License preparation in nursing. **Credit/placement by examination:** AP, CLEP, institutional tests. 30 credit hours maximum toward associate degree. **Support services:** GED preparation and test center, learning center, reduced course load, remedial instruction, tutoring.

Majors. Business: Business admin. **Computer sciences:** General. **Health:** Nursing (RN).

Computing on campus. 86 workstations in library, computer center.

Student life. Freshman orientation: Available. **Activities:** Drama, student government, student newspaper, TV station, Latin American center, refugee center, Native American center.

Athletics. NJCAA.

Student services. Adult student services, career counseling, student employment services, health services, on-campus daycare, personal counseling, placement for graduates, veterans' counselor. **Transfer:** Special adviser, orientation for new students. Transfer adviser for students transferring to 4-year colleges.

Contact. Phone: (773) 878-1700 Fax: (773) 907-4464
Cathryn Battle, Admissions, City Colleges of Chicago: Harry S. Truman College, 1145 West Wilson Avenue, Chicago, IL 60640

City Colleges of Chicago: Kennedy-King College

Chicago, Illinois
www.ccc.edu **CB code: 1910**

- Public 2-year community college
- Commuter campus in very large city

General. Founded in 1935. Regionally accredited. **Enrollment:** 3,355 degree-seeking undergraduates. **Degrees:** 255 associate awarded. **Calendar:** Semester, limited summer session. **Full-time faculty:** 61 total; 49% women. **Part-time faculty:** 115 total; 59% women. **Class size:** 19% < 20, 77% 20-39, 3% 40-49, less than 1% 50-99.

Student profile.

Out-of-state:	1%	25 or older:	65%

Transfer out. **Colleges most students transferred to 2005:** University of Illinois at Chicago, Chicago State University.

Basis for selection. Open admission. Applicants admitted without high school diploma must pass GED by end of first school year. **Adult students:** Entrance exam policies same as for first-time freshmen.

2005-2006 Annual costs. Tuition/fees: $2,260; $5,130 out-of-district; $8,236 out-of-state. Per-credit charge: $67 in-district; $163 out-of-district; $266 out-of-state. Lab fees for technical and vocational courses. Books/supplies: $1,000. Personal expenses: $2,000.

Financial aid. All financial aid based on need. Need-based aid available for part-time students.

Application procedures. **Admission:** No deadline. No application fee. Application may be submitted online. **Financial aid:** Priority date 8/1; no closing date. FAFSA required. Applicants notified on a rolling basis starting 8/15; must reply within 2 week(s) of notification.

Academics. **Special study options:** Cooperative education, cross-registration, distance learning, dual enrollment of high school students, honors, independent study, internships, liberal arts/career combination, weekend college. License preparation in dental hygiene, nursing. **Credit/placement by examination:** AP, CLEP, institutional tests. 15 credit hours maximum toward associate degree. Interview recommended for placement and counseling. **Support services:** GED preparation, learning center, pre-admission summer program, reduced course load, remedial instruction, study skills assistance, tutoring, writing center.

Majors. **Area/ethnic studies:** African-American. **Business:** Accounting, administrative services, business admin. **Communications:** Broadcast journalism, journalism. **Communications technology:** Graphics, printing press operator. **Computer sciences:** General. **Education:** General, early childhood, elementary, middle, voc/tech. **Engineering technology:** Heat/ac/refrig. **Family/consumer sciences:** Child development. **Foreign languages:** General. **Health:** Dental hygiene, health services, nursing (RN), predentistry, premedicine, prepharmacy. **History:** General. **Legal studies:** Prelaw. **Liberal arts:** Arts/sciences. **Math:** General. **Mechanic/repair:** Automotive, heating/ac/refrig. **Physical sciences:** Chemistry, physics. **Psychology:** General. **Public administration:** Social work. **Social sciences:** General. **Visual/performing arts:** General, commercial/advertising art, dramatic, studio arts.

Computing on campus. 100 workstations in library, computer center.

Student life. **Freshman orientation:** Available. Preregistration for classes offered. **Activities:** Choral groups, drama, musical theater, radio station, student government, student newspaper, TV station, Phi Theta Kappa, Student Nursing Association, broadcasting club, math club, Future Teachers of Chicago.

Athletics. NJCAA. **Intercollegiate:** Basketball. **Intramural:** Basketball M, softball, swimming, volleyball. **Team name:** Statesman, Lady Statesman.

Student services. Adult student services, career counseling, student employment services, on-campus daycare, personal counseling, placement for graduates, veterans' counselor. **Physically disabled:** Services for visually, hearing impaired. **Transfer:** Special adviser, orientation, re-entry adviser, pre-admission transcript evaluation for new students. Transfer center, transfer adviser, college fairs on campus for students transferring to 4-year colleges.

Contact. E-mail: wmurphy@ccc.edu
Phone: (773) 602-5062 Fax: (773) 602-5247
Welton Murphy, Director of Recruitment and Admissions, City Colleges of Chicago: Kennedy-King College, 6800 South Wentworth Avenue, Chicago, IL 60621

City Colleges of Chicago: Malcolm X College

Chicago, Illinois
malcolmx.ccc.edu **CB code: 1144**

- Public 2-year community and junior college
- Commuter campus in very large city

General. Founded in 1911. Regionally accredited. **Enrollment:** 3,830 degree-seeking undergraduates. **Degrees:** 296 associate awarded. **Location:** 3 miles from downtown. **Calendar:** Semester, limited summer session. **Full-time faculty:** 60 total; 47% women. **Part-time faculty:** 145 total; 56% women. **Class size:** 53% < 20, 47% 20-39. **Partnerships:** Formal partnerships with three middle and six high schools to provide TRIO Talent Search and Upward Bound programs.

Student profile.

Out-of-state:	1%	25 or older:	58%

Transfer out. **Colleges most students transferred to 2005:** University of Illinois at Chicago, Chicago State University, Northeastern Illinois University, Robert Morris College, National-Louis University.

Basis for selection. Open admission, but selective for some programs. Interview recommended for nursing and allied health applicants. Adults out of high school 5 years or more may be concurrently registered while obtaining GED.

2005-2006 Annual costs. Tuition/fees: $2,260; $5,130 out-of-district; $8,236 out-of-state. Per-credit charge: $67 in-district; $163 out-of-district; $266 out-of-state. Some courses require a $20 lab fee. Books/supplies: $800.

Financial aid. All financial aid based on need. Need-based aid available for part-time students. Work study available nights, weekends and for part-time students.

Application procedures. **Admission:** No deadline. No application fee. Admission notification on a rolling basis. **Financial aid:** Priority date 7/1; no closing date. FAFSA, institutional form required. Applicants notified on a rolling basis starting 7/1; must reply within 2 week(s) of notification.

Academics. **Special study options:** Cooperative education, cross-registration, distance learning, dual enrollment of high school students, ESL, internships, liberal arts/career combination, weekend college. License preparation in nursing, paramedic, radiology. **Credit/placement by examination:** AP, CLEP, institutional tests. 30 credit hours maximum toward associate degree. **Support services:** GED preparation, learning center, pre-admission summer program, reduced course load, remedial instruction, study skills assistance, tutoring.

Majors. **Agriculture:** Food science. **Biology:** General. **Business:** General, accounting, administrative services, business admin, office technology. **Education:** Teacher assistance. **Family/consumer sciences:** Child care, institutional food production. **Health:** Clinical lab technology, dialysis technology, EMT paramedic, medical radiologic technology/radiation therapy, nursing (RN), respiratory therapy technology, surgical technology. **Liberal arts:** Arts/sciences. **Personal/culinary services:** Culinary arts, mortuary science.

Most popular majors. Biological/life sciences 9%, health sciences 63%, liberal arts 25%.

Computing on campus. 275 workstations in library, computer center. Online course registration, online library, repair service, wireless network available.

Student life. **Freshman orientation:** Available. Preregistration for classes offered. **Activities:** Dance, drama, literary magazine, student government, student newspaper.

Athletics. NJCAA. **Intercollegiate:** Basketball, cheerleading M, track and field. **Intramural:** Basketball, cheerleading W, table tennis, track and field, volleyball. **Team name:** Hawks.

Student services. Adult student services, career counseling, student employment services, financial aid counseling, minority student services, on-campus daycare, personal counseling, placement for graduates, veterans' counselor. **Physically disabled:** Services for visually, speech, hearing impaired. **Learning disabled:** Comprehensive services available. **Transfer:** Special adviser, orientation, pre-admission transcript evaluation for new students. Transfer center, transfer adviser, college fairs on campus for students transferring to 4-year colleges.

Contact. E-mail: mmarsh@ccc.edu
Phone: (312) 850-7055 Fax: (312) 850-7092
Mary Marsh, Registrar, City Colleges of Chicago: Malcolm X College, 1900 West Van Buren Street, Chicago, IL 60612

City Colleges of Chicago: Olive-Harvey College

Chicago, Illinois
www.ccc.edu **CB code: 1584**

- Public 2-year community college
- Commuter campus in very large city

General. Founded in 1970. Regionally accredited. **Enrollment:** 2,718 degree-seeking undergraduates. **Degrees:** 232 associate awarded. **Location:** 16 miles from downtown. **Calendar:** Semester, limited summer session. **Full-time faculty:** 54 total; 54% women. **Part-time faculty:** 115 total; 56% women. **Special facilities:** Child development, high technology centers.

Basis for selection. Open admission, but selective for some programs. Special requirements for nursing, electronics, respiratory care, and local area networking programs.

High school preparation. 15 units recommended. Recommended units include English 4, mathematics 3, social studies 3, science 3 and foreign language 2.

2005-2006 Annual costs. Tuition/fees: $2,260; $5,130 out-of-district; $8,236 out-of-state. Per-credit charge: $67 in-district; $163 out-of-district; $266 out-of-state. Books/supplies: $600.

Financial aid. Need-based: Need-based aid available for part-time students.

Application procedures. Admission: No deadline. No application fee. Admission notification on a rolling basis. **Financial aid:** Priority date 8/15; no closing date. FAFSA required. Applicants notified on a rolling basis; must reply within 3 week(s) of notification.

Academics. Special study options: Cooperative education, cross-registration, distance learning, dual enrollment of high school students, honors, independent study, internships, student-designed major, study abroad. **Credit/placement by examination:** AP, CLEP, institutional tests. 30 credit hours maximum toward associate degree. **Support services:** Learning center, reduced course load, remedial instruction, tutoring.

Majors. Area/ethnic studies: African-American. **Biology:** General. **Business:** General, accounting, administrative services, business admin, management information systems. **Computer sciences:** General, data processing, programming. **Education:** Art. **Engineering:** General, architectural, electrical. **Family/consumer sciences:** Child care, child development. **Foreign languages:** General. **Legal studies:** General. **Liberal arts:** Arts/sciences. **Math:** General. **Philosophy/religion:** Philosophy. **Physical sciences:** Chemistry, physics, planetary. **Social sciences:** General. **Visual/performing arts:** Drawing, painting, photography, studio arts.

Computing on campus. 517 workstations in library, computer center.

Student life. Activities: Student government, student newspaper, African-American and Latino student groups.

Athletics. NJCAA. **Intercollegiate:** Basketball M, volleyball W. **Intramural:** Basketball, volleyball.

Student services. Adult student services, career counseling, student employment services, on-campus daycare, placement for graduates, veterans' counselor. **Transfer:** Special adviser, orientation for new students. Transfer center, transfer adviser, college fairs on campus for students transferring to 4-year colleges.

Contact. Phone: (773) 291-6349 Fax: (773) 291-6185
Ernestine Taylor, Director of Admissions, City Colleges of Chicago: Olive-Harvey College, 10001 South Woodlawn Avenue, Chicago, IL 60628

City Colleges of Chicago: Richard J. Daley College

Chicago, Illinois
daley.ccc.edu — **CB code: 1093**

- Public 2-year community college
- Commuter campus in very large city

General. Founded in 1960. Regionally accredited. **Enrollment:** 4,566 degree-seeking undergraduates. **Degrees:** 362 associate awarded. **Calendar:** Semester, limited summer session. **Full-time faculty:** 56 total; 45% women. **Part-time faculty:** 180 total; 52% women.

Basis for selection. Open admission, but selective for some programs. Special requirements for nursing program.

High school preparation. 15 units recommended. Recommended units include English 4, mathematics 3, social studies 3, science 3 and academic electives 2.

2005-2006 Annual costs. Tuition/fees: $2,260; $5,130 out-of-district; $8,236 out-of-state. Per-credit charge: $67 in-district; $163 out-of-district; $266 out-of-state. Books/supplies: $800. Personal expenses: $320.

Application procedures. Admission: No deadline. No application fee. Admission notification on a rolling basis. **Financial aid:** No deadline. FAFSA required. Applicants notified on a rolling basis.

Academics. Cross-registration with other City Colleges of Chicago. **Special study options:** Cooperative education, cross-registration, distance learning, dual enrollment of high school students, honors, independent study, internships, weekend college. **Credit/placement by examination:** AP, CLEP, institutional tests. 30 credit hours maximum toward associate degree. **Support services:** Learning center, reduced course load, remedial instruction, tutoring.

Majors. Business: General. **Liberal arts:** Arts/sciences. **Social sciences:** General.

Computing on campus. 250 workstations in library, computer center.

Student life. Activities: Student government, student newspaper, TV station.

Athletics. NJCAA.

Student services. Adult student services, career counseling, student employment services, on-campus daycare, personal counseling, placement for graduates, veterans' counselor. **Physically disabled:** Services for visually, speech, hearing impaired. **Transfer:** Special adviser, orientation for new students. Transfer adviser, college fairs on campus for students transferring to 4-year colleges.

Contact. Phone: (773) 838-7599 Fax: (773) 838-7524
Saundra Listenbee, Registrar, City Colleges of Chicago: Richard J. Daley College, 7500 South Pulaski Road, Chicago, IL 60652

City Colleges of Chicago: Wright College

Chicago, Illinois
www.ccc.edu — **CB code: 1925**

- Public 2-year community college
- Commuter campus in very large city

General. Founded in 1934. Regionally accredited. **Enrollment:** 6,798 degree-seeking undergraduates. **Degrees:** 438 associate awarded. **Location:** 15 miles from downtown. **Calendar:** Semester, limited summer session. **Full-time faculty:** 103 total; 53% women. **Part-time faculty:** 248 total; 46% women. **Class size:** 100% 20-39.

Transfer out. Colleges most students transferred to 2005: Northeastern Illinois University, University of Illinois at Chicago, DePaul University.

Basis for selection. Open admission.

2005-2006 Annual costs. Tuition/fees: $2,260; $5,130 out-of-district; $8,236 out-of-state. Per-credit charge: $67 in-district; $163 out-of-district; $266 out-of-state. Books/supplies: $630. Personal expenses: $1,280.

Financial aid. Need-based: Need-based aid available for part-time students. Work study available nights, weekends and for part-time students.

Application procedures. Admission: No deadline. No application fee. Application may be submitted online. Admission notification on a rolling basis. **Financial aid:** Priority date 6/1; no closing date. FAFSA, institutional form required. Applicants notified on a rolling basis starting 7/15.

Academics. Special study options: Cross-registration, distance learning, dual enrollment of high school students, ESL, honors, independent study, internships, weekend college. License preparation in nursing, occupational therapy. **Credit/placement by examination:** AP, CLEP, IB, institutional tests. 10 credit hours maximum toward associate degree. **Support services:** GED preparation and test center, learning center, reduced course load, remedial instruction, tutoring.

Majors. Business: Accounting, administrative services, business admin, sales/distribution. **Computer sciences:** General, applications programming. **Engineering technology:** Mechanical drafting. **Health:** Licensed practical nurse, medical radiologic technology/radiation therapy, occupational therapy assistant, radiologic technology/medical imaging, sonography. **Interdisciplinary:** Gerontology. **Liberal arts:** Arts/sciences, library assistant. **Mechanic/repair:** Electronics/electrical. **Visual/performing arts:** Design.

Computing on campus. 534 workstations in computer center.

Student life. Freshman orientation: Available. Preregistration for classes offered. **Policies:** Freshmen permitted cars on campus. **Activities:** Concert band, choral groups, drama, film society, literary magazine, music ensembles, student government, student newspaper, symphony orchestra, Circle-K, service organization, honor society, various ethnic clubs.

Athletics. NJCAA. **Intercollegiate:** Basketball, wrestling M. **Team name:** Rams.

Student services. Adult student services, campus ministries, career counseling, student employment services, financial aid counseling, health services, legal services, on-campus daycare, personal counseling, placement for graduates, veterans' counselor. **Physically disabled:** Services for visually, speech, hearing impaired. **Transfer:** Special adviser, orientation for new students. Transfer center, transfer adviser, college fairs on campus for students transferring to 4-year colleges.

Contact. E-mail: aaiello@ccc.edu
Phone: (773) 481-8200 Fax: (773) 481-8205
Amy Aiello, Assistant Dean, Student Services, City Colleges of Chicago: Wright College, 4300 N. Narragansett Avenue, Chicago, IL 60634-4276

College of DuPage
Glen Ellyn, Illinois — **CB member**
www.cod.edu — **CB code: 1083**

- Public 2-year community college
- Commuter campus in large town

General. Founded in 1966. Regionally accredited. Continuing Education division offers courses at more than 50 off-campus locations. Selected courses available through the Internet. Adult fast-track program for highly motivated, self-disciplined students 24 years and older. **Enrollment:** 22,582 degree-seeking undergraduates; 4,535 non-degree-seeking students. **Degrees:** 1,784 associate awarded. **Location:** 25 miles from Chicago. **Calendar:** Semester, extensive summer session. **Full-time faculty:** 306 total; 26% have terminal degrees, 12% minority, 54% women. **Part-time faculty:** 1,268 total; 10% have terminal degrees, 11% minority, 56% women. **Class size:** 48% < 20, 51% 20-39, less than 1% 40-49, less than 1% 50-99, less than 1% >100. **Special facilities:** Older adult institute, prairie-marsh nature preserve, arts center, community recreation center.

Student profile. Among degree-seeking undergraduates, 44% enrolled in a transfer program, 28% enrolled in a vocational program, 14% already have a bachelor's degree or higher, 3,158 enrolled as first-time, first-year students.

Part-time:	63%	**Asian American:**	11%
Women:	55%	**Hispanic American:**	8%
African American:	6%	**25 or older:**	53%

Transfer out. 74% of students enrolled in the transfer program go on to 4-year colleges. **Colleges most students transferred to 2005:** Northern Illinois University, Illinois State University, University of Illinois-Chicago, Elmhurst College, North Central College.

Basis for selection. Open admission, but selective for some programs. Special requirements for allied health programs. **Adult students:** Entrance exam policies same as for first-time freshmen.

2006-2007 Annual costs. Tuition/fees (projected): $2,881; $6,691 out-of-district; $8,401 out-of-state. Per-credit charge: $75 in-district; $231 out-of-district; $265 out-of-state. Books/supplies: $1,172. Personal expenses: $1,365.

2004-2005 Financial aid. Need-based: 763 full-time freshmen applied for aid; 553 were judged to have need; 485 of these received aid. Average need met was 56%. Average scholarship/grant was $3,477; average loan $2,132. 55% of total undergraduate aid awarded as scholarships/grants, 45% as loans/jobs. Need-based aid available for part-time students. Work study available nights, weekends and for part-time students. **Non-need-based:** Awarded to 425 full-time undergraduates, including 121 freshmen. Scholarships awarded for academics, art, leadership, minority status, music/drama, state residency.

Application procedures. Admission: No deadline. $10 fee, may be waived for applicants with need. Application must be submitted on paper. Admission notification on a rolling basis. **Financial aid:** Priority date 4/8; no closing date. FAFSA, institutional form required. Applicants notified on a rolling basis starting 6/1; must reply within 2 week(s) of notification.

Academics. Special study options: Accelerated study, cooperative education, cross-registration, distance learning, double major, dual enrollment of high school students, ESL, honors, independent study, internships, student-designed major, study abroad, weekend college. License preparation in dental hygiene, nursing, paramedic, real estate. **Credit/placement by examination:** AP, CLEP, institutional tests. 65 credit hours maximum toward associate degree. **Support services:** GED preparation and test center, learning center, pre-admission summer program, reduced course load, remedial instruction, study skills assistance, tutoring, writing center.

Honors college/program. Students may take individual honors courses or join honors scholar program. Entering freshmen must have at least 2 of the following: 3.5 GPA, composite ACT score greater than 24, or top 20% high school class rank.

Majors. Agriculture: Horticulture. **Business:** Accounting, accounting technology, administrative services, business admin, fashion, office management, real estate, sales/distribution, tourism promotion. **Communications technology:** General, graphic/printing. **Computer sciences:** Applications programming. **Construction:** Maintenance. **Engineering:** General. **Engineering technology:** Drafting, electrical, plastics, robotics. **Family/consumer sciences:** Child care. **Health:** Dental hygiene, EMT paramedic, medical radiologic technology/radiation therapy, medical records technology, nursing (RN), occupational therapy assistant, physical therapy assistant, respiratory therapy technology, substance abuse counseling, surgical technology. **Interdisciplinary:** Biological/physical sciences. **Legal studies:** Legal secretary. **Liberal arts:** Arts/sciences, library assistant. **Mechanic/repair:** Automotive, communications systems, electronics/electrical, heating/ac/refrig, industrial electronics. **Personal/culinary services:** Chef training, cosmetic, culinary arts, restaurant/catering. **Protective services:** Fire safety technology, police science. **Public administration:** Social work. **Visual/performing arts:** Art, commercial photography, design.

Most popular majors. Business/marketing 9%, health sciences 12%, interdisciplinary studies 7%, liberal arts 53%.

Computing on campus. 2,403 workstations in library, computer center. Commuter students can connect to campus network. Online library, helpline, repair service available.

Student life. Freshman orientation: Available. Campus tour and general session explaining what students need to know. **Housing:** Housing available in cooperation with nearby private college. **Activities:** Bands, choral groups, dance, drama, literary magazine, music ensembles, opera, radio station, student government, student newspaper, symphony orchestra, InterVarsity Christian Fellowship, international students organization, Endowment for Future Generations, BASIC (Brothers and Sisters in Christ), Black Student Union, Latino Ethnic Awareness Association, Japanese culture club, Model United Nations Club, La Rencontre Francaise, Muslim student association.

Athletics. NJCAA. **Intercollegiate:** Baseball M, basketball, cross-country, diving, football (tackle) M, golf M, soccer, softball W, swimming, tennis, track and field, volleyball W. **Intramural:** Basketball, bowling, diving, football (non-tackle), golf, racquetball, soccer, softball, swimming, tennis, volleyball, weight lifting. **Team name:** Chaparrels.

Student services. Adult student services, career counseling, services for economically disadvantaged, student employment services, financial aid counseling, health services, minority student services, on-campus daycare, personal counseling, placement for graduates. **Physically disabled:** Services for visually, speech, hearing impaired. **Transfer:** Special adviser, orientation for new students. Transfer center, transfer adviser, college fairs on campus for students transferring to 4-year colleges.

Contact. E-mail: admissions@cdnet.cod.edu
Phone: (630) 942-2482 Fax: (630) 790-2686
Cris Legner, Coordinator of Admission Services, College of DuPage, 425 Fawell Boulevard, Glen Ellyn, IL 60137-6599

College of Lake County
Grayslake, Illinois — **CB member**
www.clcillinois.edu — **CB code: 1983**

- Public 2-year community college
- Commuter campus in large town

General. Founded in 1967. Regionally accredited. The largest campus is located on 226 acres in Grayslake. **Enrollment:** 12,431 degree-seeking undergraduates; 3,314 non-degree-seeking students. **Degrees:** 890 associate awarded. **Location:** 40 miles from Chicago, 45 miles from Milwaukee. **Calendar:** Semester, extensive summer session. **Full-time faculty:** 178 total; 21% have terminal degrees, 21% minority, 52% women. **Part-time faculty:** 616 total; 7% have terminal degrees, 11% minority, 52% women. **Class size:** 39% < 20, 61% 20-39, less than 1% 40-49, less than 1% 50-99. **Special facilities:** CAD/CAM center, automated industrial center, performing arts center, nationally accredited child care center, lake.

Student profile. Among degree-seeking undergraduates, 59% enrolled in a transfer program, 41% enrolled in a vocational program, 8% already have

a bachelor's degree or higher, 1,959 enrolled as first-time, first-year students.

Part-time:	66%	**Asian American:**	6%
Out-of-state:	1%	**Hispanic American:**	16%
Women:	56%	**International:**	2%
African American:	9%	**25 or older:**	49%

Transfer out. 63% of students enrolled in the transfer program go on to 4-year colleges. **Colleges most students transferred to 2005:** University of Wisconsin at Parkside, Northern Illinois University.

Basis for selection. Open admission for certificate and associate of applied science degree. College-preparatory high school program required for associate of arts and science degrees. Selective admission for health career programs: academic record, class rank, test scores important; recommendations, interview considered. TOEFL is accepted for international students that are non-native speakers of English. **Adult students:** Entrance exam policies same as for first-time freshmen. **Learning Disabled:** The admissions process is the same for all students, except accommodations when taking proficiency exams. Students with learning disabilities may also qualify for extra time or readers. Other accommodations and assistance may be available once admitted.

High school preparation. 15 units recommended. Recommended units include English 4, mathematics 3, social studies 3, (laboratory 3) and academic electives 2. 2 biology and 1 chemistry required for nursing program, mathematics for medical laboratory technician program, and chemistry for radiology program. Recommended electives include foreign language, music, vocational education, or art.

2006-2007 Annual costs. Tuition/fees (projected): $2,400; $6,150 out-of-district; $8,280 out-of-state. Per-credit charge: $71 in-district; $196 out-of-district; $267 out-of-state. Books/supplies: $900. Personal expenses: $1,225.

2004-2005 Financial aid. Need-based: 88% of total undergraduate aid awarded as scholarships/grants, 12% as loans/jobs. Need-based aid available for part-time students. Work study available nights and for part-time students. **Non-need-based:** Scholarships awarded for academics, alumni affiliation, art, athletics, leadership, minority status, music/drama.

Application procedures. Admission: No deadline. No application fee. Application may be submitted online. Admission notification on a rolling basis. Application deadlines vary for health career programs. **Financial aid:** Priority date 6/5; no closing date. FAFSA required. Applicants notified on a rolling basis starting 6/15; must reply within 2 week(s) of notification.

Academics. High school distribution requirement for associate degree applicants may be fulfilled at college. **Special study options:** Accelerated study, cooperative education, cross-registration, distance learning, dual enrollment of high school students, ESL, honors, independent study, internships, student-designed major, study abroad. License preparation in dental hygiene, nursing, paramedic, radiology, real estate. **Credit/placement by examination:** AP, CLEP, institutional tests. 30 credit hours maximum toward associate degree. **Support services:** GED preparation and test center, learning center, reduced course load, remedial instruction, study skills assistance, tutoring, writing center.

Majors. Agriculture: Landscaping, ornamental horticulture, turf management. **Business:** Accounting technology, administrative services, business admin, office technology. **Conservation:** Management/policy. **Construction:** Electrician. **Education:** Music. **Engineering:** General. **Engineering technology:** Civil, construction, electrical, mechanical. **English:** Technical writing. **Health:** Dental hygiene, medical radiologic technology/radiation therapy, nursing (RN), office admin, substance abuse counseling. **Interdisciplinary:** Biological/physical sciences. **Legal studies:** Paralegal. **Liberal arts:** Arts/sciences, library assistant. **Mechanic/repair:** Automotive, computer, heating/ac/refrig, industrial, industrial electronics. **Personal/culinary services:** Restaurant/catering. **Production:** Machine shop technology. **Protective services:** Fire safety technology, police science. **Public administration:** Social work. **Visual/performing arts:** Art.

Most popular majors. Health sciences 16%, interdisciplinary studies 9%, liberal arts 53%.

Computing on campus. 800 workstations in library, computer center. Online course registration, wireless network available.

Student life. Freshman orientation: Available. **Policies:** Alcohol free campus, smoking allowed only outside the building. Freshmen permitted cars on campus. **Activities:** Bands, choral groups, dance, drama, literary magazine, music ensembles, musical theater, radio station, student government, student newspaper, 11 academic organizations, 6 ethnic organizations, 4 religious organizations, 6 health and fitness organizations.

Athletics. NJCAA. **Intercollegiate:** Baseball M, basketball, cross-country, golf, soccer, softball W, tennis, volleyball W. **Intramural:** Basketball, golf, soccer, table tennis, tennis, volleyball. **Team name:** Lancers.

Student services. Alcohol/substance abuse counseling, campus ministries, career counseling, services for economically disadvantaged, student employment services, financial aid counseling, health services, minority student services, on-campus daycare, personal counseling, placement for graduates, veterans' counselor, women's services. **Physically disabled:** Services for visually, speech, hearing impaired. **Transfer:** Special adviser, orientation, re-entry adviser for new students. Transfer center, transfer adviser, college fairs on campus for students transferring to 4-year colleges.

Contact. E-mail: info@clcillinois.edu
Phone: (847) 543-2061 Fax: (847) 543-3061
Karen Hlavin, Director, College of Lake County, 19351 West Washington Street, Grayslake, IL 60030-1198

College of Office Technology

Chicago, Illinois
www.cot.edu **CB code: 3527**

- For-profit 2-year business college
- Commuter campus in very large city

General. Accredited by ACICS. **Enrollment:** 388 undergraduates. **Degrees:** 8 associate awarded. **Calendar:** Continuous, limited summer session. **Full-time faculty:** 18 total; 28% have terminal degrees, 83% minority, 28% women. **Part-time faculty:** 12 total; 92% minority, 67% women.

Basis for selection. Open admission. **Adult students:** Entrance exam policies same as for first-time freshmen.

2005-2006 Annual costs. Tuition/fees: $15,705. Personal expenses: $4,574.

2004-2005 Financial aid. All financial aid based on need. 38% of total undergraduate aid awarded as scholarships/grants, 62% as loans/jobs. Need-based aid available for part-time students.

Application procedures. Admission: No deadline. $50 fee. Admission notification on a rolling basis. **Financial aid:** No deadline. FAFSA required. Applicants notified on a rolling basis.

Academics. Credit/placement by examination: AP, CLEP. **Support services:** Tutoring.

Majors. Computer sciences: Data entry.

Computing on campus. 20 workstations in library.

Student life. Freshman orientation: Mandatory.

Contact. E-mail: info@cotedu.com
Phone: (773) 278-0042 Toll-free number: (800) 953-6161
Fax: (773) 278-0143
Greg Brown, Director of Admissions, College of Office Technology, 1520 West Division Street, Chicago, IL 60622-3312

Cooking & Hospitality Institute of Chicago

Chicago, Illinois
www.chicnet.org **CB code: 2564**

- For-profit 2-year culinary school
- Commuter campus in very large city

General. Regionally accredited. **Location:** Downtown. **Calendar:** Semester.

Annual costs/financial aid. Tuition for 16-month Le Cordon Bleu associate in applied science program in Culinary Arts is $38,250; Patisserie and Baking is $32,950. Books/supplies: $3,200. Personal expenses: $1,446. Need-based financial aid available to full-time and part-time students.

Contact. Phone: (312) 944-0882
Director of Admissions, 361 West Chestnut, Chicago, IL 60610-3050

Danville Area Community College

Danville, Illinois
www.dacc.cc.il.us **CB code: 1160**

- Public 2-year community college
- Commuter campus in large town

General. Founded in 1946. Regionally accredited. **Enrollment:** 2,575 degree-seeking undergraduates. **Degrees:** 105 associate awarded. **Location:** 150

miles from Chicago, 90 miles from Indianapolis. **Calendar:** Semester, limited summer session. **Full-time faculty:** 51 total. **Part-time faculty:** 103 total. **Class size:** 63% < 20, 35% 20-39, less than 1% 40-49, less than 1% 50-99.

Student profile.

Out-of-state:	7%	**25 or older:**	50%

Basis for selection. Open admission.

High school preparation. 15 units recommended. Recommended units include English 4, mathematics 3, social studies 2, science 2 and academic electives 2. 2 additional electives recommended.

2005-2006 Annual costs. Tuition/fees: $1,920; $4,680 out-of-state. Per-credit charge: $58 in-state; $150 out-of-state. Books/supplies: $700. Personal expenses: $1,575.

2004-2005 Financial aid. Need-based: 96% of total undergraduate aid awarded as scholarships/grants, 4% as loans/jobs. Need-based aid available for part-time students. Work study available nights, weekends and for part-time students. **Non-need-based:** Scholarships awarded for academics, athletics, minority status.

Application procedures. Admission: No deadline. No application fee. Admission notification on a rolling basis. **Financial aid:** Priority date 7/1; no closing date. FAFSA, institutional form required. Applicants notified on a rolling basis starting 6/1.

Academics. Special study options: Distance learning, double major, dual enrollment of high school students, ESL, independent study, internships, liberal arts/career combination. License preparation in nursing, real estate. **Credit/placement by examination:** CLEP, institutional tests. 30 credit hours maximum toward associate degree. **Support services:** GED preparation and test center, learning center, remedial instruction, study skills assistance, tutoring, writing center.

Majors. Agriculture: Agribusiness operations, horticultural science. **Biology:** General. **Business:** Accounting, administrative services, finance, management information systems, tourism promotion. **Communications:** General, advertising, journalism. **Computer sciences:** General, information systems, programming. **Education:** General. **Engineering:** General. **Health:** Medical secretary, medical transcription, nursing (RN). **History:** General. **Legal studies:** Prelaw. **Liberal arts:** Arts/sciences. **Math:** General. **Mechanic/repair:** General, diesel, electronics/electrical, industrial. **Personal/culinary services:** Cosmetic. **Physical sciences:** Chemistry. **Protective services:** Law enforcement admin. **Psychology:** General. **Public administration:** Human services. **Social sciences:** Political science, sociology.

Computing on campus. 400 workstations in library, computer center. Helpline, repair service available.

Student life. Freshman orientation: Mandatory. Preregistration for classes offered. **Activities:** Choral groups, student government, symphony orchestra, Fellowship of Christian Athletes, Black Student Association, Hispanic Student Association.

Athletics. NJCAA. **Intercollegiate:** Baseball M, basketball, cross-country, golf, soccer M, softball W, track and field, volleyball W. **Team name:** Jaguars.

Student services. Adult student services, career counseling, student employment services, health services, on-campus daycare, personal counseling, placement for graduates, veterans' counselor. **Physically disabled:** Services for visually, speech, hearing impaired. **Transfer:** Special adviser, orientation for new students. Transfer adviser, college fairs on campus for students transferring to 4-year colleges.

Contact. Phone: (217) 443-8800 Fax: (217) 443-8560
Stacy Ehmen, Director of Admissions and Records, Danville Area Community College, 2000 East Main Street, Danville, IL 61832

Elgin Community College
Elgin, Illinois
www.elgin.edu **CB code: 1203**

- Public 2-year community college
- Commuter campus in small city

General. Founded in 1949. Regionally accredited. **Enrollment:** 8,315 degree-seeking undergraduates; 2,134 non-degree-seeking students. **Degrees:** 735 associate awarded. **Location:** 35 miles from Chicago. **Calendar:** Semester, extensive summer session. **Full-time faculty:** 116 total. **Part-time faculty:** 347 total. **Special facilities:** Greenhouse, business conference center, visual and performing arts center, culinary arts program, student-run gourmet restaurant.

Student profile. Among degree-seeking undergraduates, 51% enrolled in a transfer program, 49% enrolled in a vocational program, 4% already have a bachelor's degree or higher, 1,127 enrolled as first-time, first-year students.

Part-time:	61%	**Asian American:**	7%
Out-of-state:	1%	**Hispanic American:**	17%
Women:	55%	**25 or older:**	43%
African American:	5%		

Transfer out. Colleges most students transferred to 2005: Northern Illinois University, Illinois State University, Southern Illinois University-Carbondale, University of Illinois, University of Illinois at Chicago.

Basis for selection. Open admission, but selective for some programs. Additional requirements for nursing and some health professions programs.

2005-2006 Annual costs. Tuition/fees: $2,260; $7,676 out-of-district; $9,957 out-of-state. Per-credit charge: $75 in-district; $256 out-of-district; $332 out-of-state. Books/supplies: $700.

Financial aid. Need-based: Need-based aid available for part-time students. Work study available nights and weekends. **Non-need-based:** Scholarships awarded for academics, alumni affiliation, art, athletics, job skills, leadership, minority status, music/drama, religious affiliation, ROTC, state residency.

Application procedures. Admission: No deadline. No application fee. Application may be submitted online. Admission notification on a rolling basis. **Financial aid:** Priority date 5/15; no closing date. FAFSA, institutional form required. Applicants notified on a rolling basis starting 4/7; must reply within 3 week(s) of notification.

Academics. Special study options: Accelerated study, cooperative education, distance learning, double major, dual enrollment of high school students, ESL, honors, independent study, internships, study abroad, weekend college. Dual admission with selected 4-year schools. Bachelor's degree programs available on campus. License preparation in aviation, nursing, paramedic, real estate. **Credit/placement by examination:** AP, CLEP, institutional tests. 30 credit hours maximum toward associate degree. **Support services:** GED preparation and test center, learning center, reduced course load, remedial instruction, study skills assistance, tutoring.

Majors. Business: Accounting, administrative services, business admin, sales/distribution. **Computer sciences:** Applications programming, computer graphics. **Engineering technology:** Electrical. **Health:** Clinical lab technology, medical secretary, medical transcription, nursing (RN), physical therapy assistant. **Legal studies:** Legal secretary, paralegal. **Liberal arts:** Arts/sciences. **Math:** Applied. **Mechanic/repair:** Automotive, heating/ac/refrig. **Personal/culinary services:** Culinary arts. **Protective services:** Corrections, fire safety technology, police science. **Public administration:** Social work. **Visual/performing arts:** Art, design.

Most popular majors. Health sciences 10%, interdisciplinary studies 14%, liberal arts 53%, personal/culinary services 14%.

Computing on campus. 800 workstations in library, computer center, student center.

Student life. Freshman orientation: Available. **Activities:** Bands, choral groups, drama, literary magazine, music ensembles, musical theater, student government, student newspaper, symphony orchestra, Phi Theta Kappa, Alpha Beta Gamma, Organization of Latin American Students, United Students of All Cultures, Black student association, single parents student group, Advocacy for Disabled and Abled Persons Together, Amnesty International, gay/lesbian/bi-sexual, Earth First.

Athletics. NJCAA. **Intercollegiate:** Baseball M, basketball, cross-country, golf M, soccer M, softball W, tennis, volleyball W. **Team name:** Spartans.

Student services. Adult student services, career counseling, services for economically disadvantaged, student employment services, financial aid counseling, minority student services, on-campus daycare, personal counseling, placement for graduates, veterans' counselor. **Physically disabled:** Services for visually, speech, hearing impaired. **Transfer:** Special adviser, orientation for new students. Transfer center, transfer adviser, college fairs on campus for students transferring to 4-year colleges.

Contact. E-mail: admissions@elgin.edu
Phone: (847) 214-7385 Fax: (847) 608-5458
Susan Smith, Associate Dean of Registration and Testing, Elgin Community College, 1700 Spartan Drive, Elgin, IL 60123-7193

Fox College
Oak Lawn, Illinois
www.foxcollege.edu **CB code: 2670**

- For-profit 2-year junior and technical college
- Very large city

General. Accredited by ACICS. **Enrollment:** 200 degree-seeking undergraduates. **Degrees:** 96 associate awarded. **Calendar:** Semester. **Full-time faculty:** 8 total. **Part-time faculty:** 7 total.

Basis for selection. Open admission, but selective for some programs. GED/High school academic record, writing sample, and interview considered.

2006-2007 Annual costs. Tuition/fees: $13,240. $450 lab fee for Medical Assistant program. Books/supplies: $1,680.

Application procedures. **Admission:** No deadline. $50 fee, may be waived for applicants with need. **Financial aid:** No deadline.

Academics. **Credit/placement by examination:** CLEP.

Majors. **Business:** Accounting, administrative services. **Health:** Medical assistant.

Contact. E-mail: admissions@foxcollege.edu
Phone: (708) 636-7700 Toll-free number: (708) 636-7700
Fax: (708) 636-8078
Fox College, 4201 West 93rd Street, Oak Lawn, IL 60453

Heartland Community College
Normal, Illinois
www.heartland.edu **CB code: 1361**

- Public 2-year community college
- Commuter campus in small city

General. Regionally accredited. **Enrollment:** 4,628 degree-seeking undergraduates; 108 non-degree-seeking students. **Degrees:** 528 associate awarded. **Calendar:** Semester, extensive summer session. **Full-time faculty:** 75 total. **Part-time faculty:** 183 total. **Class size:** 44% < 20, 56% 20-39.

Student profile. Among degree-seeking undergraduates, 80% enrolled in a transfer program, 20% enrolled in a vocational program, 2% already have a bachelor's degree or higher, 2,276 enrolled as first-time, first-year students.

Part-time:	58%	**Asian American:**	2%
Out-of-state:	1%	**Hispanic American:**	2%
Women:	57%	**25 or older:**	38%
African American:	9%		

Transfer out. **Colleges most students transferred to 2005:** Illinois State University.

Basis for selection. Open admission, but selective for some programs. Special requirements for associate degree in nursing. All students must take COMPASS, basic skills assessment. **Adult students:** Entrance exam policies same as for first-time freshmen.

High school preparation. Recommended units include English 4, mathematics 3, social studies 2, science 2 and foreign language 2. Social studies units should include history and government.

2005-2006 Annual costs. Tuition/fees: $1,890; $3,780 out-of-district; $5,670 out-of-state. Per-credit charge: $63 in-district; $126 out-of-district; $189 out-of-state. Books/supplies: $800. Personal expenses: $910.

Financial aid. All financial aid based on need. Need-based aid available for part-time students. Work study available nights, weekends and for part-time students.

Application procedures. **Admission:** No deadline. No application fee. Application may be submitted online. Admission notification on a rolling basis. **Financial aid:** No deadline. FAFSA, institutional form required.

Academics. **Special study options:** Distance learning, double major, dual enrollment of high school students, ESL, independent study, internships, liberal arts/career combination, study abroad. License preparation in nursing, paramedic. **Credit/placement by examination:** CLEP. 15 credit hours maximum toward associate degree. **Support services:** GED preparation, learning center, remedial instruction, study skills assistance, tutoring, writing center.

Majors. **Business:** Insurance. **Computer sciences:** Data entry, information technology, networking. **Construction:** Electrician. **Education:** Mathematics, teacher assistance. **Engineering:** General. **Engineering technology:** CAD/CADD, electrical, manufacturing. **Health:** Nursing (RN), radiologic technology/medical imaging. **Interdisciplinary:** Biological/physical sciences. **Liberal arts:** Arts/sciences. **Mechanic/repair:** Industrial. **Production:** Welding. **Protective services:** Criminal justice. **Visual/performing arts:** Design.

Most popular majors. Business/marketing 6%, interdisciplinary studies 10%, liberal arts 76%.

Computing on campus. 1,500 workstations in library, computer center. Commuter students can connect to campus network. Online library available.

Student life. **Freshman orientation:** Available. **Policies:** Freshmen permitted cars on campus. **Activities:** Jazz band, drama, student government, student newspaper, Alpha Beta Gamma, Christian life club, cine' club, environmental club.

Student services. Adult student services, alcohol/substance abuse counseling, career counseling, services for economically disadvantaged, student employment services, financial aid counseling, minority student services, on-campus daycare, personal counseling, placement for graduates, veterans' counselor. **Physically disabled:** Services for visually, speech, hearing impaired. **Transfer:** Special adviser for new students. Transfer adviser, college fairs on campus for students transferring to 4-year colleges.

Contact. Phone: (309) 268-8000 Fax: (309) 268-7992
Fred Peterson, Dean of Student Services, Heartland Community College, 1500 West Raab Road, Normal, IL 61761

Highland Community College
Freeport, Illinois
www.highland.edu **CB code: 1233**

- Public 2-year community college
- Commuter campus in large town

General. Founded in 1961. Regionally accredited. **Enrollment:** 1,899 degree-seeking undergraduates; 507 non-degree-seeking students. **Degrees:** 271 associate awarded. **Location:** 100 miles from Chicago, 38 miles from Rockford. **Calendar:** Semester, limited summer session. **Full-time faculty:** 48 total; 10% have terminal degrees, 2% minority, 29% women. **Part-time faculty:** 142 total; 4% have terminal degrees, 2% minority, 65% women. **Class size:** 71% < 20, 25% 20-39, 3% 40-49, less than 1% 50-99. **Special facilities:** Regional arboretum, YMCA on campus.

Student profile. Among degree-seeking undergraduates, 47% enrolled in a transfer program, 51% enrolled in a vocational program, 1% already have a bachelor's degree or higher, 508 enrolled as first-time, first-year students, 134 transferred in from other institutions.

Part-time:	44%	**Asian American:**	1%
Women:	63%	**Hispanic American:**	2%
African American:	9%		

Transfer out. **Colleges most students transferred to 2005:** Illinois State University, University of Wisconsin-Platteville, Northern Illinois University, Western Illinois University, Columbia College (HCC Campus).

Basis for selection. Open admission, but selective for some programs. Special criteria for acceptance into nursing program: based on points accumulated by taking prerequisite courses, class rank, test scores considered. **Adult students:** Entrance exam policies same as for first-time freshmen. SAT/ACT scores not required. **Homeschooled:** Transcript of courses and grades required.

High school preparation. College-preparatory program recommended. 15 units recommended. Recommended units include English 4, mathematics 3, social studies 2, science 2 (laboratory 2) and academic electives 4.

2005-2006 Annual costs. Tuition/fees: $2,010; $3,480 out-of-district; $3,480 out-of-state. Per-credit charge: $62 in-district; $111 out-of-district; $111 out-of-state. Books/supplies: $900. Personal expenses: $1,300.

2004-2005 Financial aid. **Need-based:** 81% of total undergraduate aid awarded as scholarships/grants, 19% as loans/jobs. Need-based aid available for part-time students. Work study available nights and for part-time students. **Non-need-based:** Scholarships awarded for academics, athletics.

Application procedures. **Admission:** No deadline. No application fee. Application may be submitted online. Admission notification on a rolling basis. **Financial aid:** No deadline. FAFSA, institutional form required. Applicants notified on a rolling basis starting 8/1; must reply within 2 week(s) of notification.

Academics. **Special study options:** Distance learning, dual enrollment of high school students, ESL, independent study, internships, student-designed major. Bachelor's degree programs available on campus. **Credit/placement by examination:** AP, CLEP, institutional tests. 21 credit hours maximum toward associate degree. ACT or COMPASS scores can be used for placement. **Support services:** GED preparation and test center, learning center, remedial instruction, tutoring, writing center.

Majors. **Agriculture:** General, business. **Biology:** General. **Business:** General, accounting, business admin, management information systems, office management. **Computer sciences:** General, computer science, data processing, information systems, programming. **Education:** General, early childhood. **Engineering:** General. **Engineering technology:** Electrical. **Family/consumer sciences:** Child care. **Health:** Medical transcription, nursing (RN). **History:** General. **Legal studies:** Prelaw. **Liberal arts:** Arts/sciences. **Math:** General. **Mechanic/repair:** Auto body, automotive. **Physical sciences:** Chemistry, geology, physics. **Psychology:** General. **Social sciences:** General, political science, sociology. **Visual/performing arts:** General, art, commercial/advertising art.

Most popular majors. Business/marketing 13%, health sciences 11%, liberal arts 45%, parks/recreation 21%.

Computing on campus. 366 workstations in library, computer center, student center. Commuter students can connect to campus network. Online course registration, helpline, repair service, wireless network available.

Student life. **Freshman orientation:** Available. Semester-long, 2-credit class. **Activities:** Bands, choral groups, dance, drama, literary magazine, music ensembles, musical theater, student government, student newspaper, current issues club, environmental awareness, religious fellowship, international club, People of Color, Pride Club, student senate.

Athletics. NJCAA. **Intercollegiate:** Baseball M, basketball, golf M, softball W, volleyball W. **Intramural:** Basketball, volleyball. **Team name:** Cougars.

Student services. Adult student services, career counseling, veterans' counselor. **Physically disabled:** Services for visually, speech, hearing impaired. **Transfer:** Special adviser, orientation, pre-admission transcript evaluation for new students. Transfer center, transfer adviser, college fairs on campus for students transferring to 4-year colleges.

Contact. E-mail: karl.richards@highland.edu
Phone: (815) 235-6121 ext. 3414 Fax: (815) 235-6130
Karl Richards, Dean of Enrollment Services, Highland Community College, 2998 West Pearl City Road, Freeport, IL 61032-9341

Illinois Central College

East Peoria, Illinois
www.icc.edu **CB code: 1312**

- Public 2-year community college
- Commuter campus in large town

General. Founded in 1966. Regionally accredited. **Enrollment:** 12,343 degree-seeking undergraduates. **Degrees:** 1,147 associate awarded. **Location:** 150 miles from Chicago, 5 miles from Peoria. **Calendar:** Semester, extensive summer session. **Full-time faculty:** 170 total. **Part-time faculty:** 570 total.

Basis for selection. Open admission, but selective for some programs. Special requirements for health occupation programs. ACT required for admissions and placement in certain programs. Audition required of music majors.

High school preparation. 15 units recommended. Recommended units include English 4, mathematics 3, social studies 2 and science 2.

2005-2006 Annual costs. Tuition/fees: $1,920; $4,200 out-of-district; $4,200 out-of-state. Per-credit charge: $64 in-district; $140 out-of-district; $140 out-of-state. Books/supplies: $600. Personal expenses: $2,335.

Financial aid. **Non-need-based:** Scholarships awarded for athletics.

Application procedures. **Admission:** No deadline. No application fee. Admission notification on a rolling basis. **Financial aid:** Priority date 4/15; no closing date. FAFSA, institutional form required. Applicants notified on a rolling basis starting 6/1; must reply within 2 week(s) of notification.

Academics. QUEST (Quality Undergraduate Education for Transfer Students) provides team-taught, multidisciplinary program for transfers. **Special study options:** Distance learning, honors, internships, weekend college. Bachelor's degree programs available on campus. **Credit/placement by examination:** AP, CLEP, institutional tests. 30 credit hours maximum toward associate degree. **Support services:** Learning center, remedial instruction, study skills assistance, tutoring, writing center.

Majors. **Agriculture:** Business, horticulture. **Architecture:** Interior. **Business:** General, accounting, administrative services, banking/financial services, business admin, international, real estate. **Communications:** Broadcast journalism, journalism. **Computer sciences:** General, applications programming, programming. **Conservation:** General. **Education:** Elementary, physical, secondary, special. **Engineering:** General, agricultural, electrical. **Engineering technology:** Robotics. **English:** Speech/rhetoric. **Family/consumer sciences:** General, child care, food/nutrition. **Foreign languages:** General. **Health:** Clinical lab technology, dental hygiene, health care admin, medical radiologic technology/radiation therapy, medical records technology, occupational therapy assistant, physical therapy assistant, predentistry, premedicine, prepharmacy, preveterinary, respiratory therapy technology. **Legal studies:** Court reporting, paralegal, prelaw. **Liberal arts:** Arts/sciences, library assistant. **Math:** General. **Physical sciences:** Chemistry, geology, physics, planetary. **Protective services:** Criminal justice, fire safety technology. **Visual/performing arts:** Dance, dramatic, studio arts.

Computing on campus. 500 workstations in library, computer center.

Student life. **Activities:** Bands, choral groups, dance, drama, music ensembles, student government, student newspaper, Tomorrow's Black Leaders, College Republicans, College Democrats, Inter-Varsity Christian Fellowship, international student organization.

Athletics. NJCAA. **Intercollegiate:** Baseball M, basketball, golf M, softball W, volleyball W. **Intramural:** Badminton, basketball, golf, table tennis, tennis, volleyball. **Team name:** Cougars.

Student services. Adult student services, career counseling, student employment services, health services, on-campus daycare, personal counseling, placement for graduates, veterans' counselor. **Physically disabled:** Services for visually, speech, hearing impaired. **Transfer:** Special adviser for new students. Transfer center, transfer adviser, college fairs on campus for students transferring to 4-year colleges.

Contact. Phone: (309) 694-5354 Fax: (309) 694-8461
Guy Goodman, Director of Enrollment Management, Illinois Central College, One College Drive, East Peoria, IL 61635-0001

Illinois Eastern Community Colleges: Frontier Community College

Fairfield, Illinois
www.iecc.edu/fcc **CB code: 1894**

- Public 2-year community college
- Commuter campus in small town

General. Founded in 1976. Regionally accredited. **Enrollment:** 1,169 degree-seeking undergraduates. **Degrees:** 60 associate awarded. **Location:** 110 miles from St. Louis. **Calendar:** Semester, extensive summer session. **Full-time faculty:** 5 total. **Part-time faculty:** 230 total.

Student profile. Among degree-seeking undergraduates, 44% enrolled in a transfer program, 56% enrolled in a vocational program.

Basis for selection. Open admission.

High school preparation. Recommended units include English 3, mathematics 2 and science 1.

2005-2006 Annual costs. Tuition/fees: $1,680; $5,629 out-of-district; $6,947 out-of-state. Per-credit charge: $53 in-district; $185 out-of-district; $229 out-of-state. Students in qualifying Indiana districts pay per-credit-hour rate of $96. Books/supplies: $800. Personal expenses: $1,120.

Financial aid. **Need-based:** Need-based aid available for part-time students. **Non-need-based:** Scholarships awarded for academics, state residency.

Application procedures. **Admission:** No deadline. $10 fee. Application may be submitted online. Admission notification on a rolling basis beginning on or about 8/1. **Financial aid:** No deadline. FAFSA, institutional form required. Applicants notified on a rolling basis starting 8/1; must reply within 2 week(s) of notification.

Academics. Students, with counselors' aid, design own academic programs through nontraditional alternatives to classroom study. **Special study**

options: Distance learning, double major, dual enrollment of high school students, ESL, honors, independent study, student-designed major, study abroad, teacher certification program, weekend college. License preparation in nursing. **Credit/placement by examination:** AP, CLEP, institutional tests. 32 credit hours maximum toward associate degree. **Support services:** GED preparation, learning center, remedial instruction, study skills assistance, tutoring.

Majors. Business: Administrative services, office technology. **Computer sciences:** General. **Health:** Mental health services. **Liberal arts:** Arts/sciences.

Most popular majors. Business/marketing 23%, engineering/engineering technologies 12%, interdisciplinary studies 23%, liberal arts 40%.

Computing on campus. 40 workstations in library, computer center. Commuter students can connect to campus network.

Student life. Freshman orientation: Available. Preregistration for classes offered. **Policies:** Freshmen permitted cars on campus.

Student services. Adult student services, career counseling, services for economically disadvantaged, financial aid counseling, minority student services, personal counseling, placement for graduates, veterans' counselor. **Physically disabled:** Services for visually, speech, hearing impaired. **Transfer:** Special adviser, orientation, pre-admission transcript evaluation for new students. Transfer adviser, college fairs on campus for students transferring to 4-year colleges.

Contact. Phone: (618) 842-3711 Toll-free number: (877) 464-3687
Fax: (618) 842-6340
Suzanne Brooks, Coordinator of Admissions and Records, Illinois Eastern Community Colleges: Frontier Community College, Frontier Drive, Fairfield, IL 62837-9801

Illinois Eastern Community Colleges: Lincoln Trail College

Robinson, Illinois
www.iecc.edu/ltc **CB code: 0758**

- Public 2-year community college
- Commuter campus in small town

General. Founded in 1969. Regionally accredited. **Enrollment:** 1,002 degree-seeking undergraduates. **Degrees:** 189 associate awarded. **Location:** 200 miles from Indianapolis, 110 miles from St. Louis. **Calendar:** Semester, extensive summer session. **Full-time faculty:** 26 total. **Part-time faculty:** 60 total.

Student profile. Among degree-seeking undergraduates, 66% enrolled in a transfer program, 34% enrolled in a vocational program.

Out-of-state:	2%	**25 or older:**	54%

Basis for selection. Open admission.

High school preparation. Recommended units include English 3, mathematics 2 and science 1.

2005-2006 Annual costs. Tuition/fees: $1,680; $5,629 out-of-district; $6,947 out-of-state. Per-credit charge: $53 in-district; $185 out-of-district; $229 out-of-state. Students in qualifying Indiana districts pay per-credit-hour rate of $96. Books/supplies: $800. Personal expenses: $1,120.

Financial aid. Need-based: Need-based aid available for part-time students. **Non-need-based:** Scholarships awarded for academics, athletics, state residency.

Application procedures. Admission: No deadline. $10 fee. Application may be submitted online. Admission notification on a rolling basis beginning on or about 8/1. **Financial aid:** No deadline. FAFSA, institutional form required. Applicants notified on a rolling basis starting 8/1; must reply within 2 week(s) of notification.

Academics. Students (with counselors' aid) design academic programs through nontraditional alternatives to classroom study. **Special study options:** Distance learning, double major, dual enrollment of high school students, ESL, honors, independent study, internships, student-designed major, study abroad, weekend college. License preparation in nursing. **Credit/placement by examination:** AP, CLEP, institutional tests. 32 credit hours maximum toward associate degree. **Support services:** GED preparation, learning center, remedial instruction, study skills assistance, tutoring.

Majors. Agriculture: Horticulture. **Business:** Administrative services, banking/financial services, office technology. **Computer sciences:** General. **Education:** Music, teacher assistance. **Engineering technology:** Drafting. **Interdisciplinary:** Biological/physical sciences. **Liberal arts:** Arts/sciences. **Mechanic/repair:** Electronics/electrical, heating/ac/refrig.

Most popular majors. Engineering/engineering technologies 10%, interdisciplinary studies 23%, liberal arts 57%.

Computing on campus. 91 workstations in library, computer center. Commuter students can connect to campus network.

Student life. Freshman orientation: Available. Preregistration for classes offered. **Policies:** Freshmen permitted cars on campus. **Activities:** Bands, choral groups, drama, music ensembles, musical theater, student government, student newspaper.

Athletics. NJCAA. **Intercollegiate:** Baseball M, basketball, softball W. **Intramural:** Basketball, softball. **Team name:** Statesmen.

Student services. Career counseling, services for economically disadvantaged, student employment services, financial aid counseling, minority student services, personal counseling, placement for graduates, veterans' counselor. **Physically disabled:** Services for visually, speech, hearing impaired. **Transfer:** Special adviser, orientation, pre-admission transcript evaluation for new students. Transfer adviser, college fairs on campus for students transferring to 4-year colleges.

Contact. Phone: (618) 544-8657 Toll-free number: (866) 582-4322
Fax: (618) 544-3957
Becky Mikeworth, Director of Admissions, Illinois Eastern Community Colleges: Lincoln Trail College, 11220 State Highway 1, Robinson, IL 62454-5707

Illinois Eastern Community Colleges: Olney Central College

Olney, Illinois
www.iecc.edu/occ **CB code: 0827**

- Public 2-year community college
- Commuter campus in small town

General. Founded in 1962. Regionally accredited. **Enrollment:** 1,022 degree-seeking undergraduates; 643 non-degree-seeking students. **Degrees:** 358 associate awarded. **Location:** 200 miles from St. Louis. **Calendar:** Semester, extensive summer session. **Full-time faculty:** 48 total. **Part-time faculty:** 70 total.

Student profile. Among degree-seeking undergraduates, 55% enrolled in a transfer program, 45% enrolled in a vocational program, 119 enrolled as first-time, first-year students.

Part-time:	31%	**25 or older:**	39%
Women:	59%		

Basis for selection. Open admission, but selective for some programs. Special requirements for nursing, radiology programs. Preference given to Illinois Eastern Community College region residents. Interview recommended for nursing, radiology technology majors.

High school preparation. Recommended units include English 3, mathematics 2 and science 1.

2005-2006 Annual costs. Tuition/fees: $1,680; $5,629 out-of-district; $6,947 out-of-state. Per-credit charge: $53 in-district; $185 out-of-district; $229 out-of-state. Students in qualifying Indiana districts pay per-credit-hour rate of $96. Books/supplies: $800. Personal expenses: $1,120.

Financial aid. Need-based: Need-based aid available for part-time students. **Non-need-based:** Scholarships awarded for academics, athletics, state residency.

Application procedures. Admission: No deadline. $10 fee. Application may be submitted online. Admission notification on a rolling basis beginning on or about 8/1. **Financial aid:** No deadline. FAFSA, institutional form required. Applicants notified on a rolling basis starting 8/1; must reply within 2 week(s) of notification.

Academics. Students with aid of counselors design academic programs through nontraditional alternatives to classroom study. **Special study options:** Distance learning, double major, dual enrollment of high school students, ESL, honors, independent study, internships, student-designed major, study abroad, weekend college. License preparation in nursing, radiology, real estate. **Credit/placement by examination:** AP, CLEP, institutional tests.

32 credit hours maximum toward associate degree. **Support services:** GED preparation, learning center, remedial instruction, study skills assistance, tutoring.

Majors. Business: Accounting, administrative services, office technology. **Education:** Music. **Health:** Medical radiologic technology/radiation therapy, medical secretary, nursing (RN). **Liberal arts:** Arts/sciences. **Mechanic/repair:** Auto body, industrial. **Production:** Woodworking. **Protective services:** Police science.

Most popular majors. Health sciences 35%, interdisciplinary studies 6%, liberal arts 46%, trade and industry 8%.

Computing on campus. 125 workstations in library, computer center. Commuter students can connect to campus network.

Student life. Freshman orientation: Available. **Policies:** Freshmen permitted cars on campus. **Activities:** Bands, choral groups, drama, music ensembles, musical theater, student government, student newspaper.

Athletics. NJCAA. **Intercollegiate:** Baseball M, basketball, softball W. **Intramural:** Basketball, softball. **Team name:** Blue Knights.

Student services. Career counseling, services for economically disadvantaged, student employment services, financial aid counseling, minority student services, on-campus daycare, personal counseling, placement for graduates, veterans' counselor. **Physically disabled:** Services for visually, speech, hearing impaired. **Transfer:** Special adviser, orientation, preadmission transcript evaluation for new students. Transfer adviser, college fairs on campus for students transferring to 4-year colleges.

Contact. Phone: (618) 395-7777 Toll-free number: (866) 622-4322
Fax: (618) 392-5212
Chris Webber, Assistant Dean of Student Services, Illinois Eastern Community Colleges: Olney Central College, 305 North West Street, Olney, IL 62450

Illinois Eastern Community Colleges: Wabash Valley College

Mount Carmel, Illinois
www.iecc.edu/wvc **CB code: 1936**

- Public 2-year community college
- Commuter campus in small town

General. Founded in 1960. Regionally accredited. **Enrollment:** 631 degree-seeking undergraduates. **Degrees:** 232 associate awarded. **Location:** 40 miles from Evansville, Indiana. **Calendar:** Semester, extensive summer session. **Full-time faculty:** 43 total. **Part-time faculty:** 148 total.

Student profile. Among degree-seeking undergraduates, 35% enrolled in a transfer program, 65% enrolled in a vocational program.

Out-of-state:	3%	**25 or older:**	65%

Basis for selection. Open admission.

High school preparation. Recommended units include English 3, mathematics 2 and science 1.

2005-2006 Annual costs. Tuition/fees: $1,680; $5,629 out-of-district; $6,947 out-of-state. Per-credit charge: $53 in-district; $185 out-of-district; $229 out-of-state. Students in qualifying Indiana districts pay per-credit-hour rate of $96. Books/supplies: $800. Personal expenses: $1,120.

Financial aid. Need-based: Need-based aid available for part-time students. **Non-need-based:** Scholarships awarded for academics, athletics, state residency.

Application procedures. Admission: No deadline. $10 fee. Application may be submitted online. Admission notification on a rolling basis beginning on or about 8/1. **Financial aid:** No deadline. FAFSA, institutional form required. Applicants notified on a rolling basis starting 8/1; must reply within 2 week(s) of notification.

Academics. Students, with counselor's aid, design own academic programs through nontraditional alternatives to classroom study. **Special study options:** Distance learning, double major, dual enrollment of high school students, ESL, honors, independent study, internships, student-designed major, study abroad, weekend college. License preparation in nursing, real estate. **Credit/placement by examination:** AP, CLEP, institutional tests. 32 credit hours maximum toward associate degree. **Support services:** GED preparation, learning center, remedial instruction, study skills assistance, tutoring.

Majors. Agriculture: Business, horticulture, production. **Business:** Accounting technology, administrative services, office technology. **Communications:** Broadcast journalism. **Engineering technology:** Electrical, manufacturing. **Family/consumer sciences:** Child care. **Liberal arts:** Arts/sciences. **Mechanic/repair:** Diesel, industrial. **Production:** Machine shop technology. **Public administration:** Social work.

Most popular majors. Agriculture 6%, business/marketing 11%, interdisciplinary studies 21%, liberal arts 38%, public administration/social services 6%, trade and industry 9%.

Computing on campus. 100 workstations in library, computer center. Commuter students can connect to campus network.

Student life. Freshman orientation: Available. Preregistration for classes offered. **Policies:** Freshmen permitted cars on campus. **Activities:** Bands, choral groups, drama, music ensembles, musical theater, radio station, student government, student newspaper, TV station.

Athletics. NJCAA. **Intercollegiate:** Baseball M, basketball, softball W. **Intramural:** Basketball, softball. **Team name:** Warriors.

Student services. Career counseling, services for economically disadvantaged, student employment services, financial aid counseling, minority student services, on-campus daycare, personal counseling, placement for graduates, veterans' counselor. **Physically disabled:** Services for visually, speech, hearing impaired. **Transfer:** Special adviser, orientation, preadmission transcript evaluation for new students. Transfer adviser, college fairs on campus for students transferring to 4-year colleges.

Contact. Phone: (618) 262-8641 Toll-free number: (866) 982-4322
Fax: (618) 262-5347
Diana Spear, Assistant Dean for Student Services, Illinois Eastern Community Colleges: Wabash Valley College, 2200 College Drive, Mount Carmel, IL 62863-2657

Illinois Valley Community College

Oglesby, Illinois **CB member**
www.ivcc.edu **CB code: 1397**

- Public 2-year community college
- Commuter campus in small town

General. Founded in 1966. Regionally accredited. **Enrollment:** 4,027 degree-seeking undergraduates. **Degrees:** 429 associate awarded. **Location:** 60 miles from Peoria, 95 miles from Chicago. **Calendar:** Semester, extensive summer session. **Full-time faculty:** 75 total. **Part-time faculty:** 100 total. **Special facilities:** Federal and state nuclear regulatory commission document depositories.

Transfer out. Colleges most students transferred to 2005: Illinois State University, Northern Illinois University, Western Illinois University, University of Illinois/Urbana-Champaign, Eastern Illinois University.

Basis for selection. Open admission, but selective for some programs. Applicants to nursing programs must have minimum 2.0 GPA and background in laboratory science; minimum 2.0 GPA required for dental assisting. **Adult students:** Entrance exam policies same as for first-time freshmen.

2005-2006 Annual costs. Tuition/fees: $1,742; $5,977 out-of-district; $7,237 out-of-state. Per-credit charge: $60 in-district; $192 out-of-district; $234 out-of-state. Books/supplies: $650. Personal expenses: $1,107.

Application procedures. Admission: No deadline. No application fee. Application may be submitted online. Admission notification on a rolling basis. **Financial aid:** Priority date 5/1; no closing date. FAFSA required. Applicants notified on a rolling basis starting 5/1.

Academics. Special study options: Cross-registration, distance learning, dual enrollment of high school students, honors, internships, study abroad. License preparation in nursing, real estate. **Credit/placement by examination:** AP, CLEP, institutional tests. 16 credit hours maximum toward associate degree. **Support services:** GED preparation and test center, learning center, pre-admission summer program, reduced course load, remedial instruction, study skills assistance, tutoring, writing center.

Majors. Agriculture: General. **Biology:** General. **Business:** Management science. **Communications:** General, journalism. **Computer sciences:** General, applications programming, information systems. **Education:** General. **Engineering:** General. **Engineering technology:** Drafting. **English:** American lit, British lit, composition, speech/rhetoric. **Family/consumer sciences:** General, child care. **Foreign languages:** General, comparative lit. **Health:** Athletic training, nursing (RN). **History:** General. **Legal studies:** General. **Math:** General, applied. **Parks/recreation:** Health/fitness, sports admin. **Physical sciences:** Astronomy, chemistry, geology, oceanography, physics, planetary. **Protective services:** Law enforcement admin, police science. **Psychology:** General. **Public administration:** Social work. **Social sciences:** General, political science, sociology. **Visual/performing arts:** General, art, art history/conservation, dramatic, music history, music performance, studio arts.

Computing on campus. Online course registration, wireless network available.

Student life. Freshman orientation: Available. Sessions held in spring and fall. **Policies:** Freshmen permitted cars on campus. **Activities:** Bands, choral groups, drama, literary magazine, musical theater, student government, student newspaper, Amnesty International, gay/straight alliance, People of the World End Racism (POWER), student nurses association.

Athletics. NJCAA. **Intercollegiate:** Baseball M, basketball, golf M, softball W, tennis, volleyball W. **Intramural:** Basketball, softball, volleyball. **Team name:** Eagles.

Student services. Career counseling, student employment services, financial aid counseling, on-campus daycare, personal counseling, placement for graduates, veterans' counselor. **Physically disabled:** Services for visually, hearing impaired. **Transfer:** Transfer adviser for students transferring to 4-year colleges.

Contact. E-mail: tracy_morris@ivcc.edu
Phone: (815) 224-0439 Fax: (815) 224-6091
Tracy Morris, Director of Admissions and Records, Illinois Valley Community College, 815 North Orlando Smith Avenue, Oglesby, IL 61348-9693

John A. Logan College

Carterville, Illinois
www.jalc.edu **CB code: 1357**

- Public 2-year community college
- Commuter campus in small town

General. Founded in 1967. Regionally accredited. **Enrollment:** 2,632 full-time, degree-seeking students. **Degrees:** 584 associate awarded. **ROTC:** Army, Air Force. **Location:** 10 miles from Carbondale. **Calendar:** Semester, limited summer session. **Full-time faculty:** 101 total. **Part-time faculty:** 14 total. **Class size:** 53% < 20, 44% 20-39, less than 1% 40-49, less than 1% 50-99, less than 1% >100. **Special facilities:** Museum/art gallery.

Student profile.

Out-of-state:	1%	**25 or older:**	21%

Transfer out. Colleges most students transferred to 2005: Southern Illinois University at Carbondale.

Basis for selection. Open admission, but selective for some programs. Admission to allied health program is competitive. Criteria are unique to each program. ASSET and/or COMPASS accepted in place of SAT or ACT. **Adult students:** Entrance exam policies same as for first-time freshmen.

High school preparation. College preparatory program required of 2-year transfer degree applicants. Must have 15 high school course units: 4 English, 3 math, 3 laboratory science, 3 social science, 2 electives.

2005-2006 Annual costs. Tuition/fees: $1,830. Per-credit charge: $61. Books/supplies: $1,030. Personal expenses: $601.

Financial aid. All financial aid based on need. Need-based aid available for part-time students. Work study available for part-time students.

Application procedures. Admission: No deadline. No application fee. Application may be submitted online. Admission notification on a rolling basis. **Financial aid:** Priority date 5/1; no closing date. FAFSA, institutional form required. Applicants notified on a rolling basis starting 5/1.

Academics. Special study options: Distance learning, dual enrollment of high school students, liberal arts/career combination. Bachelor's degree programs available on campus. License preparation in dental hygiene, nursing, occupational therapy, paramedic, real estate. **Credit/placement by examination:** CLEP, institutional tests. 30 credit hours maximum toward associate degree. **Support services:** GED preparation and test center, study skills assistance, tutoring, writing center.

Majors. Agriculture: Business. **Biology:** General. **Business:** Accounting technology, business admin, executive assistant, office management. **Communications:** Journalism. **Computer sciences:** General. **Construction:** Carpentry. **Education:** Art, early childhood, elementary, history, mathematics, physical, secondary, social studies, special, teacher assistance. **Engineering:** General. **Engineering technology:** Drafting. **English:** English lit. **Health:** Clinical lab technology, dental hygiene, medical records technology, nursing (RN), occupational therapy assistant, prepharmacy, sonography. **Interdisciplinary:** Biological/physical sciences. **Liberal arts:** Arts/sciences. **Math:** General. **Mechanic/repair:** Auto body, automotive, electronics/electrical, industrial. **Personal/culinary services:** Cosmetic. **Physical sciences:** Chemistry, physics. **Production:** Machine shop technology, tool and die, welding. **Protective services:** Corrections, criminal justice. **Psychology:** General. **Public administration:** Social work. **Social sciences:** Economics, international relations, political science, sociology. **Visual/performing arts:** Art, dramatic.

Computing on campus. 651 workstations in library, computer center. Online course registration available.

Student life. Freshman orientation: Available. **Policies:** Freshmen permitted cars on campus. **Housing:** Housing at Southern Illinois University - Carbondale. **Activities:** Concert band, choral groups, drama, music ensembles, musical theater, student government, student newspaper.

Athletics. NJCAA. **Intercollegiate:** Baseball M, basketball, golf, softball W, volleyball W. **Team name:** Volunteers.

Student services. Adult student services, career counseling, student employment services, financial aid counseling, minority student services, on-campus daycare, placement for graduates, veterans' counselor. **Physically disabled:** Services for visually, hearing impaired. **Transfer:** Transfer center, college fairs on campus for students transferring to 4-year colleges.

Contact. E-mail: terrycrain@jalc.edu
Phone: (618) 985-3741 Fax: (618) 985-4433
Terry Crain, Dean of Student Services, John A. Logan College, 700 Logan College Road, Carterville, IL 62918

John Wood Community College

Quincy, Illinois
www.jwcc.edu **CB code: 1374**

- Public 2-year community college
- Commuter campus in large town

General. Founded in 1974. Regionally accredited. **Enrollment:** 1,845 degree-seeking undergraduates; 685 non-degree-seeking students. **Degrees:** 283 associate awarded. **Location:** 140 miles from St. Louis, 100 miles from Springfield. **Calendar:** Semester, extensive summer session. **Full-time faculty:** 51 total; 2% have terminal degrees, 4% minority, 55% women. **Part-time faculty:** 139 total; 7% have terminal degrees, 1% minority, 50% women. **Class size:** 68% < 20, 32% 20-39. **Special facilities:** Greenhouse, truck driver training facility.

Student profile. Among degree-seeking undergraduates, 71% enrolled in a transfer program, 29% enrolled in a vocational program, 2% already have a bachelor's degree or higher, 545 enrolled as first-time, first-year students, 148 transferred in from other institutions.

Part-time:	41%	**Asian American:**	1%
Out-of-state:	9%	**Hispanic American:**	1%
Women:	62%	**25 or older:**	32%
African American:	4%		

Transfer out. Colleges most students transferred to 2005: Western Illinois University, Eastern Illinois University, University of Illinois-Springfield,Quincy University.

Basis for selection. Open admission, but selective for some programs. Limited enrollment in certificate degree programs in dietary management, practical nursing, nurse assistant and in associate degree program in nursing and truck driver training. **Adult students:** Entrance exam policies same as for first-time freshmen.

High school preparation. Recommended units include English 4, mathematics 3, social studies 3 and science 4.

2005-2006 Annual costs. Tuition/fees: $2,430; $5,430 out-of-state. Per-credit charge: $76 in-state; $176 out-of-state. Books/supplies: $1,152. Personal expenses: $720.

Financial aid. Need-based: Need-based aid available for part-time students. Work study available nights and weekends.

Application procedures. Admission: No deadline. No application fee. Application may be submitted online. Admission notification on a rolling

basis. **Financial aid:** No deadline. FAFSA required. Applicants notified on a rolling basis starting 3/1.

Academics. Special study options: Distance learning, dual enrollment of high school students, ESL, independent study, internships, liberal arts/career combination, student-designed major, study abroad. License preparation in nursing, paramedic, real estate. **Credit/placement by examination:** AP, CLEP, institutional tests. 30 credit hours maximum toward associate degree. **Support services:** GED preparation and test center, learning center, reduced course load, remedial instruction, study skills assistance, tutoring, writing center.

Majors. Agriculture: General, animal husbandry, animal sciences, business, horticulture. **Biology:** General. **Business:** General, accounting, accounting technology, administrative services, business admin, executive assistant, sales/distribution. **Communications:** General. **Computer sciences:** General, applications programming. **Construction:** Electrician. **Education:** General, early childhood. **Engineering:** General. **Engineering technology:** Mechanical drafting. **Family/consumer sciences:** Child care. **Foreign languages:** Spanish. **Health:** Clinical lab technology, EMT paramedic, medical radiologic technology/radiation therapy, medical secretary, nursing (RN). **History:** General. **Interdisciplinary:** Biological/physical sciences. **Legal studies:** Legal secretary, prelaw. **Liberal arts:** Arts/sciences. **Math:** General. **Mechanic/repair:** Industrial. **Parks/recreation:** Health/fitness. **Personal/culinary services:** Restaurant/catering. **Physical sciences:** General, physics. **Protective services:** Fire safety technology, police science. **Psychology:** General. **Social sciences:** Economics, sociology. **Visual/performing arts:** Art.

Most popular majors. Business/marketing 10%, health sciences 14%, interdisciplinary studies 35%, liberal arts 25%, security/protective services 6%.

Computing on campus. 266 workstations in library, computer center. Online course registration, helpline available.

Student life. Freshman orientation: Mandatory. **Activities:** Jazz band, choral groups, drama, music ensembles, musical theater, student government, service organizations, honor society, Phi Theta Kappa.

Athletics. NJCAA. **Intercollegiate:** Baseball M, basketball, golf M, softball W, volleyball W. **Intramural:** Basketball M, bowling, volleyball. **Team name:** Trail Blazers.

Student services. Adult student services, career counseling, services for economically disadvantaged, student employment services, financial aid counseling, minority student services, veterans' counselor. **Physically disabled:** Services for visually, speech, hearing impaired. **Transfer:** Special adviser, orientation for new students. Transfer adviser, college fairs on campus for students transferring to 4-year colleges.

Contact. E-mail: admissions@jwcc.edu
Phone: (217) 641-4338 Fax: (217) 224-4208
Mark McNett, Director of Admissions, John Wood Community College, 1301 South 48th Street, Quincy, IL 62305-8736

Joliet Junior College

Joliet, Illinois
www.jjc.cc.il.us **CB code: 1346**

- Public 2-year community college
- Commuter campus in small city

General. Founded in 1901. Regionally accredited. **Enrollment:** 13,022 degree-seeking undergraduates. **Degrees:** 787 associate awarded. **Location:** 35 miles from Chicago. **Calendar:** Semester, extensive summer session. **Full-time faculty:** 184 total. **Part-time faculty:** 500 total. **Class size:** 63% < 20, 37% 20-39, less than 1% 40-49, less than 1% >100. **Special facilities:** Planetarium, nature trail, arboretum, working farm, fitness center.

Student profile.

Out-of-state:	1%	**25 or older:**	26%

Transfer out. Colleges most students transferred to 2005: Northern Illinois University, Illinois State University, University of St. Francis, Lewis University, Governors State University.

Basis for selection. Open admission, but selective for some programs and for out-of-state students. Preference given to cooperative programs and in-district applicants. For admission to nursing program, applicant must have ACT score of 20 if in top third of high school class, 21 if in top half. ACT, interview recommended for some applicants. **Learning Disabled:** Students with disabilities are encouraged to utilize services provided by Students Accomodations and Resources (StAR).

High school preparation. 15 units recommended. Recommended units include English 4, mathematics 3, social studies 3, science 3 and academic electives 2.

2005-2006 Annual costs. Tuition/fees: $2,130; $6,210 out-of-district; $7,140 out-of-state. Per-credit charge: $56 in-district; $194 out-of-district; $225 out-of-state. Additional course fees range from $3 to $90. Personal expenses: $1,500.

Financial aid. Need-based: Need-based aid available for part-time students. Work study available nights, weekends and for part-time students. **Non-need-based:** Scholarships awarded for academics.

Application procedures. Admission: No deadline. No application fee. Application may be submitted online. Admission notification on a rolling basis. **Financial aid:** Priority date 6/1; no closing date. FAFSA, institutional form required. Applicants notified on a rolling basis starting 5/15.

Academics. Special study options: Cooperative education, distance learning, dual enrollment of high school students, ESL, honors, independent study, internships, study abroad. License preparation in nursing, paramedic, radiology, real estate. **Credit/placement by examination:** AP, CLEP, institutional tests. 45 credit hours maximum toward associate degree. **Support services:** GED preparation, learning center, pre-admission summer program, reduced course load, remedial instruction, study skills assistance, tutoring.

Majors. Agriculture: General, greenhouse operations, horticulture, landscaping, nursery operations, ornamental horticulture, supplies, turf management. **Biology:** General. **Business:** Accounting, administrative services, business admin, fashion, office management, office technology, office/clerical. **Computer sciences:** General, information systems, programming. **Education:** Early childhood, elementary, secondary, special, teacher assistance. **Engineering:** Electrical. **Engineering technology:** Architectural, construction, drafting, electrical. **Family/consumer sciences:** Clothing/textiles. **Health:** Medical secretary, nursing (RN), veterinary technology/assistant. **History:** General. **Legal studies:** Legal secretary. **Liberal arts:** Arts/sciences. **Math:** General. **Mechanic/repair:** Auto body. **Personal/culinary services:** Culinary arts. **Physical sciences:** Chemistry. **Protective services:** Law enforcement admin. **Psychology:** General. **Social sciences:** Political science, sociology. **Visual/performing arts:** Art, interior design.

Computing on campus. Helpline, repair service available.

Student life. Freshman orientation: Available. **Activities:** Bands, choral groups, drama, literary magazine, music ensembles, musical theater, student government, student newspaper, campus ministry, Black Student Organization, Intervarsity Christian Fellowship, Latinos Unidos, Latter Day Saints Association, Unity.

Athletics. NJCAA. **Intercollegiate:** Baseball M, basketball, football (tackle) M, softball W, tennis, volleyball W. **Team name:** Wolves.

Student services. Career counseling, services for economically disadvantaged, student employment services, financial aid counseling, on-campus daycare, personal counseling, placement for graduates, veterans' counselor, women's services. **Physically disabled:** Services for visually, speech, hearing impaired. **Transfer:** Special adviser, orientation for new students. Transfer center, transfer adviser for students transferring to 4-year colleges.

Contact. E-mail: ktillman@jjc.edu
Phone: (815) 729-9020 Fax: (815) 744-5507
Jennifer Kloberdanz, Director of Admissions and Financial Aid, Joliet Junior College, 1215 Houbolt Road, Joliet, IL 60431-8938

Kankakee Community College

Kankakee, Illinois
www.kcc.edu **CB code: 1380**

- Public 2-year community college
- Commuter campus in large town

General. Founded in 1966. Regionally accredited. **Enrollment:** 2,488 degree-seeking undergraduates. **Degrees:** 325 associate awarded. **Location:** 60 miles from Chicago. **Calendar:** Semester, extensive summer session. **Full-time faculty:** 55 total. **Part-time faculty:** 125 total.

Student profile. Among degree-seeking undergraduates, 30% enrolled in a transfer program, 70% enrolled in a vocational program.

Transfer out. Colleges most students transferred to 2005: Illinois State University, Governors State University, Olivet Nazarene University.

Two-Year Colleges

Basis for selection. Open admission, but selective for some programs. Criteria for health career programs may include prerequisite coursework, high school record and test scores. Separate application and ASSET required for admission to health career programs. ASSET required of all students for placement. **Adult students:** Adult students take our ASSET or COMPASS exam.

High school preparation. 15 units recommended. Recommended units include English 4, mathematics 3, social studies 2, science 2 and academic electives 4.

2005-2006 Annual costs. Tuition/fees: $1,800; $4,312 out-of-district; $9,697 out-of-state. Per-credit charge: $55 in-district; $139 out-of-district; $318 out-of-state. Books/supplies: $648. Personal expenses: $720.

Financial aid. Need-based: Need-based aid available for part-time students. **Non-need-based:** Scholarships awarded for athletics.

Application procedures. Admission: No deadline. No application fee. Application must be submitted on paper. Admission notification on a rolling basis. **Financial aid:** Priority date 7/1; no closing date. FAFSA, institutional form required. Applicants notified on a rolling basis; must reply within 4 week(s) of notification.

Academics. Prerequisite courses for those in health career programs. **Special study options:** Cross-registration, distance learning, dual enrollment of high school students, ESL, honors, independent study, internships, study abroad, teacher certification program. License preparation in nursing, paramedic, radiology. **Credit/placement by examination:** AP, CLEP, institutional tests. 16 credit hours maximum toward associate degree. **Support services:** GED preparation and test center, learning center, pre-admission summer program, reduced course load, remedial instruction, study skills assistance, tutoring, writing center.

Majors. Biology: General. **Business:** Accounting, administrative services, business admin, construction management. **Computer sciences:** Applications programming. **Education:** General, art, early childhood, elementary, mathematics, multi-level teacher, secondary. **Engineering:** General. **Engineering technology:** Drafting, manufacturing. **Health:** Clinical lab technology, EMT paramedic, insurance coding, medical radiologic technology/radiation therapy, medical secretary, nursing (RN), predentistry, premedicine, prepharmacy, preveterinary, radiologic technology/medical imaging, respiratory therapy technology. **Interdisciplinary:** Biological/physical sciences. **Legal studies:** Legal secretary. **Liberal arts:** Arts/sciences. **Math:** General. **Mechanic/repair:** General, automotive, electronics/electrical, heating/ac/refrig, industrial. **Protective services:** Police science. **Psychology:** General. **Social sciences:** General. **Visual/performing arts:** Art, graphic design, studio arts.

Computing on campus. 500 workstations in library, computer center. Commuter students can connect to campus network. Online library available.

Student life. Freshman orientation: Available, $80 fee. Preregistration for classes offered. **Activities:** Student government.

Athletics. NJCAA. **Intercollegiate:** Baseball M, basketball, soccer M, softball W, volleyball W. **Intramural:** Basketball, golf. **Team name:** Cavaliers.

Student services. Adult student services, career counseling, student employment services, financial aid counseling, minority student services, on-campus daycare, placement for graduates. **Physically disabled:** Services for visually, speech, hearing impaired. **Transfer:** Special adviser, pre-admission transcript evaluation for new students. Transfer center, transfer adviser, college fairs on campus for students transferring to 4-year colleges.

Contact. Phone: (815) 802-8520 Fax: (815) 802-8101
Michelle Driscoll, Director, Admissions and Registration, Kankakee Community College, PO Box 888, Kankakee, IL 60901

Kaskaskia College

Centralia, Illinois
www.kaskaskia.edu **CB code: 1108**

- Public 2-year community college
- Commuter campus in large town

General. Founded in 1966. Regionally accredited. **Enrollment:** 3,371 degree-seeking undergraduates; 1,393 non-degree-seeking students. **Degrees:** 591 associate awarded. **Location:** 60 miles from St. Louis. **Calendar:** Semester, limited summer session. **Full-time faculty:** 73 total; 10% have terminal degrees, 3% minority, 42% women. **Part-time faculty:** 174 total; 5% have terminal degrees, 7% minority, 55% women. **Class size:** 81% < 20, 17% 20-39, 1% 40-49, less than 1% 50-99. **Partnerships:** Formal partnerships with local businesses, hospitals, factories/industries, and correctional institutions that participate in training, apprenticeship, and safety features in major ongoing programs.

Student profile. Among degree-seeking undergraduates, 43% enrolled in a transfer program, 40% enrolled in a vocational program, 4% already have a bachelor's degree or higher, 662 enrolled as first-time, first-year students.

Part-time:	44%	**African American:**	8%
Out-of-state:	1%	**Hispanic American:**	2%
Women:	61%		

Transfer out. Colleges most students transferred to 2005: Southern Illinois University at Carbondale, Southern Illinois University at Edwardsville, Eastern Illinois University.

Basis for selection. Open admission, but selective for some programs. Special requirements for health-related programs. ASSET recommended for practical nursing, cosmetology, dental, radiologic technology, physical therapy assistant program applicants. Nelson-Denny Reading Test recommended and ASSET required for nursing assistant, diagnostic medical sonography, respiratory therapy applicants. Interview required of allied health majors. **Adult students:** Entrance exam policies same as for first-time freshmen. **Home-schooled:** ASSET/ACT required. **Learning Disabled:** As soon as students are identified, they meet with the accommodations coordinator. The coordinator provides specialized counseling, orientation, and referral to other campus programs and outside agencies when appropriate.

High school preparation. 15 units recommended. Recommended units include English 4, mathematics 3, social studies 3, science 3, foreign language 2 and academic electives 2. Specific requirements for allied health.

2005-2006 Annual costs. Tuition/fees: $1,800; $3,240 out-of-district; $7,260 out-of-state. Per-credit charge: $53 in-district; $101 out-of-district; $235 out-of-state.

2004-2005 Financial aid. Need-based: 88% of total undergraduate aid awarded as scholarships/grants, 12% as loans/jobs. Need-based aid available for part-time students. Work study available for part-time students. **Non-need-based:** Scholarships awarded for academics, athletics, state residency.

Application procedures. Admission: No deadline. No application fee. Application must be submitted on paper. Admission notification on a rolling basis. Allied health programs have specific closing dates. **Financial aid:** Priority date 5/15; no closing date. FAFSA required. Applicants notified on a rolling basis starting 4/1; must reply within 2 week(s) of notification.

Academics. Learning communities. **Special study options:** Accelerated study, cooperative education, cross-registration, distance learning, double major, dual enrollment of high school students, ESL, honors, independent study, internships, liberal arts/career combination, student-designed major, study abroad, weekend college. License preparation in nursing, paramedic, physical therapy, radiology. **Credit/placement by examination:** CLEP, institutional tests. 30 credit hours maximum toward associate degree. **Support services:** GED preparation and test center, learning center, reduced course load, remedial instruction, study skills assistance, tutoring.

Majors. Agriculture: General, horticulture. **Business:** General, accounting, executive assistant, office technology. **Computer sciences:** Information systems, system admin. **Construction:** Carpentry. **Education:** Teacher assistance. **Engineering technology:** Architectural drafting, electrical. **Health:** EMT paramedic, nursing (RN), physical therapy assistant, radiologic technology/medical imaging, respiratory therapy technology. **Interdisciplinary:** Biological/physical sciences. **Liberal arts:** Arts/sciences. **Mechanic/repair:** Auto body, automotive, industrial. **Personal/culinary services:** Chef training. **Protective services:** Juvenile corrections, law enforcement admin.

Most popular majors. Business/marketing 10%, health sciences 27%, liberal arts 39%.

Computing on campus. 40 workstations in library, student center. Helpline, repair service available.

Student life. Freshman orientation: Available, $65 fee. Preregistration for classes offered. One-day session on campus, the other half of assignments done online. Usually held prior to each semester. **Policies:** Freshmen permitted cars on campus. **Activities:** Bands, choral groups, drama, film society, music ensembles, student government, student newspaper, Brothers and Sisters in Christ, Black student association.

Athletics. NJCAA. **Intercollegiate:** Baseball M, basketball, cheerleading, golf, softball W, volleyball W. **Team name:** Blue Devils.

Student services. Adult student services, career counseling, services for economically disadvantaged, student employment services, financial aid counseling, minority student services, on-campus daycare, personal counseling, placement for graduates, veterans' counselor. **Physically disabled:** Services for visually, speech, hearing impaired. **Transfer:** Special adviser, orientation, pre-admission transcript evaluation for new students. Transfer center, transfer adviser, college fairs on campus for students transferring to 4-year colleges.

Contact. Phone: (618) 545-3040 Fax: (618) 532-1135
Sharon Conners, Director of Admissions, Kaskaskia College, 27210 College Road, Centralia, IL 62801

Kishwaukee College

Malta, Illinois
www.kishwaukeecollege.edu **CB code: 0511**

- Public 2-year community college
- Commuter campus in rural community

General. Founded in 1967. Regionally accredited. **Enrollment:** 3,258 degree-seeking undergraduates. **Degrees:** 478 associate awarded. **ROTC:** Army. **Location:** 7 miles from DeKalb. **Calendar:** Semester, limited summer session. **Full-time faculty:** 83 total. **Part-time faculty:** 144 total.

Student profile.

Out-of-state:	1%	25 or older:	32%

Transfer out. Colleges most students transferred to 2005: Northern Illinois University.

Basis for selection. Open admission, but selective for some programs. Special requirements for nursing, radiologic technology and therapeutic massage programs. Interview required of nursing, radiologic technology, therapeutic massage majors. Portfolio recommended for art majors. **Adult students:** Entrance exam policies same as for first-time freshmen. **Learning Disabled:** Students with learning disabilities should contact disabilities service office at least 30 days before enrollment to assist student with reasonable accommodations.

High school preparation. 15 units recommended. Recommended units include English 4, mathematics 3, social studies 3, science 3 and foreign language 2. High school diploma or equivalency required for nursing, radiologic technology, and therapeutic massage applicants.

2005-2006 Annual costs. Tuition/fees: $2,100; $6,750 out-of-district; $7,590 out-of-state. Per-credit charge: $63 in-district; $218 out-of-district; $246 out-of-state. Books/supplies: $800. Personal expenses: $1,020.

Financial aid. Need-based: Need-based aid available for part-time students. Work study available nights, weekends and for part-time students. **Non-need-based:** Scholarships awarded for academics, athletics, leadership, music/drama, state residency.

Application procedures. Admission: No deadline. No application fee. Admission notification on a rolling basis. **Financial aid:** Priority date 5/1; no closing date. FAFSA, institutional form required. Applicants notified on a rolling basis starting 5/1; must reply within 2 week(s) of notification.

Academics. Cross-registration with Northern Illinois University and nearby community colleges. Distance Learning Consortium, member Illinois Virtual College (IVC). **Special study options:** Cross-registration, distance learning, double major, dual enrollment of high school students, ESL, independent study, internships, study abroad. License preparation in aviation, nursing, radiology, real estate. **Credit/placement by examination:** AP, CLEP, institutional tests. 48 credit hours maximum toward associate degree. Must complete 15 hours residency prior to posting proficiency credit. **Support services:** GED preparation and test center, learning center, pre-admission summer program, reduced course load, remedial instruction, study skills assistance, tutoring.

Majors. Agriculture: Agribusiness operations, animal breeding, business, greenhouse operations, horticultural science, horticulture, landscaping, nursery operations, ornamental horticulture, supplies. **Architecture:** Landscape. **Business:** General, accounting, human resources, management information systems, office management, office/clerical, operations. **Communications:** General, journalism. **Computer sciences:** Applications programming. **Education:** General, early childhood, elementary, physical, secondary, special. **Engineering:** General. **Engineering technology:** Drafting, electrical, manufacturing. **Family/consumer sciences:** General, child care. **Foreign languages:** General, French, Spanish. **Health:** Medical radiologic technology/radiation therapy, nursing (RN), predentistry, premedicine, prenursing, prepharmacy, preveterinary. **History:** General. **Interdisciplinary:** Biological/physical sciences. **Legal studies:** Prelaw. **Liberal arts:** Arts/sciences. **Math:** General. **Mechanic/repair:** Auto body, automotive, diesel. **Parks/recreation:** Health/fitness. **Physical sciences:** Astronomy, chemistry, physics. **Protective services:** Fire safety technology, firefighting, police science. **Psychology:** General. **Public administration:** Social work. **Social sciences:** General, criminology, economics, political science, sociology. **Visual/performing arts:** General, art, dramatic.

Most popular majors. Agriculture 7%, health sciences 10%, interdisciplinary studies 51%, liberal arts 29%.

Computing on campus. 376 workstations in library, computer center. Online library, helpline available.

Student life. Freshman orientation: Available. Preregistration for classes offered. 5 sessions held during summer. **Policies:** Freshmen permitted cars on campus. **Activities:** Choral groups, drama, literary magazine, music ensembles, musical theater, student government, student newspaper, international student club, Nurses Christian Fellowship, Phi Theta Kappa, Black Student Union, Vocational Industrial Clubs of America, Christian Fellowship, agriculture club, horticulture club, student nurses organization, student radiographers association.

Athletics. NJCAA. **Intercollegiate:** Baseball M, basketball, golf, soccer M, softball W, volleyball W. **Intramural:** Badminton, basketball, softball, volleyball. **Team name:** Kougars.

Student services. Adult student services, career counseling, services for economically disadvantaged, student employment services, financial aid counseling, health services, minority student services, on-campus daycare, personal counseling, placement for graduates, veterans' counselor, women's services. **Physically disabled:** Services for visually, speech, hearing impaired. **Learning disabled:** Comprehensive services available. **Transfer:** Special adviser, re-entry adviser, pre-admission transcript evaluation for new students. Transfer center, transfer adviser, college fairs on campus for students transferring to 4-year colleges.

Contact. E-mail: arr@kishwaukeecollege.edu
Phone: (815) 825-2086 ext. 218 Fax: (815) 825-2306
Jill Bier, Director of Admissions, Registration and Records, Kishwaukee College, 21193 Malta Road, Malta, IL 60150-9699

Lake Land College

Mattoon, Illinois
www.lakelandcollege.edu **CB code: 1424**

- Public 2-year community college
- Commuter campus in large town

General. Founded in 1966. Regionally accredited. **Enrollment:** 5,277 degree-seeking undergraduates. **Degrees:** 789 associate awarded. **Location:** 45 miles from Decatur, 45 miles from Champaign. **Calendar:** Semester, extensive summer session. **Full-time faculty:** 119 total; 74% have terminal degrees, 2% minority, 44% women. **Part-time faculty:** 248 total; 60% have terminal degrees, less than 1% minority, 56% women. **Class size:** 55% < 20, 45% 20-39.

Student profile. Among degree-seeking undergraduates, 40% enrolled in a transfer program, 60% enrolled in a vocational program.

Out-of-state:	3%	25 or older:	46%

Transfer out. Colleges most students transferred to 2005: Eastern Illinois University, Southern Illinois University, University of Illinois.

Basis for selection. Open admission, but selective for some programs. Special requirements for dental hygiene, nursing, physical therapist assistant, John Deere agricultural technology, massage therapy, and cosmetology programs. ACT required of dental hygiene applicants. **Adult students:** SAT/ACT scores not required. LLC Assessment Battery.

High school preparation. Recommended units include English 4, mathematics 3, social studies 3, history 3, science 3 (laboratory 3), foreign language 2 and academic electives 2. Mathematics and biology required for dental hygiene and nursing applicants.

2005-2006 Annual costs. Tuition/fees: $1,919; $4,015 out-of-district; $7,927 out-of-state. Per-credit charge: $54 in-district; $120 out-of-district; $252 out-of-state. Books/supplies: $318.

2004-2005 Financial aid. Need-based: 76% of total undergraduate aid awarded as scholarships/grants, 24% as loans/jobs. Need-based aid available for part-time students. Work study available nights, weekends and for part-time students. **Non-need-based:** Scholarships awarded for academics, athletics.

Application procedures. Admission: No deadline. No application fee. Application may be submitted online. Admission notification on a rolling basis. **Financial aid:** Closing date 5/1. FAFSA, institutional form required.

Applicants notified on a rolling basis starting 6/1; must reply within 2 week(s) of notification.

Academics. Special study options: Accelerated study, cooperative education, distance learning, dual enrollment of high school students, ESL, honors, independent study, internships, study abroad, weekend college. License preparation in real estate. **Credit/placement by examination:** AP, CLEP, institutional tests. 32 credit hours maximum toward associate degree. **Support services:** GED preparation, learning center, reduced course load, remedial instruction, study skills assistance, tutoring.

Majors. Agriculture: General. **Business:** General, administrative services, human resources. **Communications:** Broadcast journalism, journalism. **Computer sciences:** LAN/WAN management, networking. **Conservation:** Fisheries, wildlife. **Education:** General, biology, mathematics, social science. **Engineering:** General, civil. **English:** Speech/rhetoric. **Family/consumer sciences:** General, child care. **Health:** Dental hygiene, nursing (RN), physical therapy assistant, premedicine, prepharmacy, preveterinary. **Legal studies:** Legal secretary, prelaw. **Liberal arts:** Arts/sciences. **Math:** General. **Protective services:** Police science. **Psychology:** General. **Social sciences:** General, economics. **Visual/performing arts:** Studio arts.

Computing on campus. 400 workstations in library, computer center. Online course registration available.

Student life. Freshman orientation: Mandatory. Preregistration for classes offered. Mandatory for degree-seeking students only. Approximately 4 hours in length. **Activities:** Choral groups, radio station, student government, student newspaper, Phi Theta Kappa.

Athletics. NJCAA. **Intercollegiate:** Baseball M, basketball, soccer M, softball W, tennis, volleyball W. **Intramural:** Bowling, golf, softball, volleyball. **Team name:** Lakers.

Student services. Career counseling, student employment services, health services, on-campus daycare, personal counseling, placement for graduates, veterans' counselor. **Physically disabled:** Services for visually, speech, hearing impaired. **Transfer:** Special adviser for new students. Transfer adviser, college fairs on campus for students transferring to 4-year colleges.

Contact. E-mail: admissions@lakeland.cc.il.us
Phone: (217) 234-5434 Fax: (217) 234-5390
Jon VanDyke, Dean, Admission Services, Lake Land College, 5001 Lake Land Boulevard, Mattoon, IL 61938-9366

Lewis and Clark Community College

Godfrey, Illinois — **CB member**
www.lc.edu — **CB code: 0623**

- Public 2-year community college
- Commuter campus in large town

General. Founded in 1970. Regionally accredited. **Enrollment:** 5,222 degree-seeking undergraduates. **Degrees:** 509 associate awarded. **ROTC:** Army. **Location:** 30 miles from St. Louis. **Calendar:** Semester, limited summer session. **Full-time faculty:** 85 total. **Part-time faculty:** 225 total.

Basis for selection. Open admission, but selective for some programs. Special requirements for nursing and other Allied Health programs. Interview required for radio broadcasting, music majors. Audition required for music majors.

2005-2006 Annual costs. Tuition/fees: $2,220; $6,120 out-of-district; $8,070 out-of-state. Per-credit charge: $65 in-district; $195 out-of-district; $260 out-of-state. Out-of-state, out-of-district on-line tuition is $95 per credit including fees. Books/supplies: $435. Personal expenses: $1,100.

Financial aid. Need-based: Need-based aid available for part-time students.

Application procedures. Admission: No deadline. No application fee. Admission notification on a rolling basis. **Financial aid:** Priority date 6/1; no closing date. FAFSA required. Applicants notified on a rolling basis starting 8/1; must reply within 3 week(s) of notification.

Academics. Cross-registration with Blackburn College, cooperative agreements with Southwestern Junior Community College, Illinois Eastern Community College, John Wood College and Lincoln Land Community College. **Special study options:** Cooperative education, cross-registration, distance learning, double major, dual enrollment of high school students, internships, liberal arts/career combination, student-designed major. Bachelor's degree programs available on campus. License preparation in dental hygiene, nursing, occupational therapy, paramedic, real estate. **Credit/placement by examination:** CLEP, institutional tests. 32 credit hours maximum toward associate degree. **Support services:** GED preparation and test center, learning center, remedial instruction, study skills assistance, tutoring, writing center.

Majors. Business: General, accounting, banking/financial services, business admin, office/clerical. **Communications:** Radio/tv. **Computer sciences:** General, computer graphics, computer science, data processing, information technology, LAN/WAN management, web page design, webmaster. **Education:** General, early childhood, teacher assistance. **Engineering technology:** Drafting. **Family/consumer sciences:** Child care. **Health:** Dental hygiene, nursing (RN), occupational therapy assistant, predentistry, premedicine, prenursing, prepharmacy. **Legal studies:** Legal secretary, prelaw. **Liberal arts:** Arts/sciences. **Mechanic/repair:** Automotive. **Protective services:** Criminal justice, firefighting. **Visual/performing arts:** Studio arts.

Computing on campus. 300 workstations in library, computer center.

Student life. Freshman orientation: Available. **Policies:** Freshmen permitted cars on campus. **Activities:** Bands, choral groups, dance, drama, music ensembles, radio station, student government, student newspaper, TV station, veterans organization, Christian Campus Fellowship, disabled students organization, Black Students Association, political action club.

Athletics. NJCAA. **Intercollegiate:** Baseball M, basketball, golf M, soccer, softball W, tennis, volleyball W. **Intramural:** Basketball, bowling, softball, tennis, volleyball. **Team name:** Trailblazers.

Student services. Adult student services, career counseling, student employment services, health services, on-campus daycare, personal counseling, placement for graduates, veterans' counselor. **Physically disabled:** Services for visually, hearing impaired. **Transfer:** Special adviser, orientation, pre-admission transcript evaluation for new students. Transfer center, transfer adviser, college fairs on campus for students transferring to 4-year colleges.

Contact. E-mail: enroll@lc.edu
Phone: (618) 468-2222 Toll-free number: (800) 500-5222
Fax: (618) 468-2310
Peggy Hudson, Director Enrollment Center for Admissions Services, Lewis and Clark Community College, 5800 Godfrey Road, Godfrey, IL 62035-2466

Lincoln College

Lincoln, Illinois
www.lincolncollege.edu — **CB code: 1406**

- Private 2-year junior college
- Residential campus in large town

General. Founded in 1865. Regionally accredited. **Location:** 185 miles from Chicago, 125 miles from St. Louis. **Calendar:** Semester.

Annual costs/financial aid. Tuition/fees (2005-2006): $15,126. Room/board: $5,600. Books/supplies: $240. Personal expenses: $1,000. Need-based financial aid available to full-time and part-time students.

Contact. Phone: (800) 569-0556
Director of Enrollment Management, 300 Keokuk Street, Lincoln, IL 62656

Lincoln Land Community College

Springfield, Illinois
www.llcc.edu — **CB code: 1428**

- Public 2-year community and junior college
- Commuter campus in small city

General. Founded in 1967. Regionally accredited. **Enrollment:** 5,235 degree-seeking undergraduates; 1,612 non-degree-seeking students. **Degrees:** 599 associate awarded. **ROTC:** Army, Navy, Air Force. **Location:** 180 miles from Chicago, 96 miles from St. Louis. **Calendar:** Semester, extensive summer session. **Full-time faculty:** 125 total; 90% have terminal degrees, 8% minority, 50% women. **Part-time faculty:** 263 total; 3% minority, 52% women. **Class size:** 65% < 20, 35% 20-39, less than 1% 40-49. **Special facilities:** Museum.

Student profile. Among degree-seeking undergraduates, 41% enrolled in a transfer program, 59% enrolled in a vocational program, 4% already have

a bachelor's degree or higher, 753 enrolled as first-time, first-year students, 49 transferred in from other institutions.

Part-time:	58%	**Asian American:**	1%
Women:	60%	**Hispanic American:**	2%
African American:	8%	**25 or older:**	39%

Transfer out. Colleges most students transferred to 2005: University of Illinois: Springfield, Southern Illinois University: Carbondale, Eastern Illinois University, Western Illinois University, Illinois State University.

Basis for selection. Open admission, but selective for some programs. Applicants to nursing and allied health programs must rank in top half of high school graduating class and have minimum ACT score of 20. ACT required for nursing, respiratory therapy, and radiologic technology applicants. Admissions assessment not required for students with ACT composite score of 22 or above. **Adult students:** Entrance exam policies same as for first-time freshmen.

High school preparation. College-preparatory program recommended. Recommended units include English 4, mathematics 3, social studies 3, science 3 and foreign language 2.

2005-2006 Annual costs. Tuition/fees: $1,986; $8,104 out-of-district; $9,687 out-of-state. Per-credit charge: $63 in-district; $266 out-of-district; $317 out-of-state. Books/supplies: $750. Personal expenses: $990.

2004-2005 Financial aid. Need-based: 77% of total undergraduate aid awarded as scholarships/grants, 23% as loans/jobs. Need-based aid available for part-time students. Work study available nights. **Non-need-based:** Scholarships awarded for academics, athletics, minority status, state residency.

Application procedures. Admission: No deadline. No application fee. Application may be submitted online. Admission notification on a rolling basis. **Financial aid:** Priority date 5/1; no closing date. FAFSA, institutional form required. Applicants notified on a rolling basis starting 4/15; must reply within 2 week(s) of notification.

Academics. Special study options: Accelerated study, cooperative education, cross-registration, distance learning, double major, dual enrollment of high school students, ESL, honors, independent study, internships, liberal arts/career combination, study abroad, United Nations semester, weekend college. License preparation in nursing, occupational therapy, paramedic, physical therapy, radiology, real estate. **Credit/placement by examination:** AP, CLEP, institutional tests. 30 credit hours maximum toward associate degree. **Support services:** GED preparation, learning center, reduced course load, remedial instruction, study skills assistance, tutoring, writing center.

Majors. Agriculture: Landscaping, production. **Business:** General, accounting, administrative services, hospitality admin, office technology. **Computer sciences:** Networking, programming. **Construction:** Maintenance. **Education:** General. **Engineering:** General. **Engineering technology:** Architectural drafting, construction, electrical. **Health:** Nursing (RN), occupational therapy assistant, office assistant, radiologic technology/medical imaging. **Interdisciplinary:** Biological/physical sciences. **Legal studies:** Legal secretary. **Liberal arts:** Arts/sciences. **Mechanic/repair:** Aircraft, auto body, automotive, industrial electronics. **Protective services:** Firefighting, police science. **Transportation:** Aviation management. **Visual/performing arts:** Graphic design, studio arts.

Most popular majors. Health sciences 15%, interdisciplinary studies 26%, liberal arts 47%.

Computing on campus. 300 workstations in library, computer center, student center. Commuter students can connect to campus network. Online course registration, online library, helpline, wireless network available.

Student life. Freshman orientation: Available. Preregistration for classes offered. Half-day program offered at beginning of each semester. **Activities:** Bands, choral groups, dance, drama, literary magazine, music ensembles, musical theater, student government, student newspaper.

Athletics. NJCAA. **Intercollegiate:** Baseball M, basketball, soccer M, softball W, volleyball W. **Intramural:** Basketball, bowling, softball, table tennis, tennis, volleyball M. **Team name:** Loggers.

Student services. Adult student services, career counseling, services for economically disadvantaged, student employment services, financial aid counseling, minority student services, on-campus daycare, personal counseling, placement for graduates, veterans' counselor, women's services. **Physically disabled:** Services for visually, speech, hearing impaired. **Learning disabled:** Comprehensive services available. **Transfer:** Special adviser, orientation for new students, pre-admission transcript evaluation for new students. Transfer adviser, college fairs on campus for students transferring to 4-year colleges.

Contact. E-mail: ron.gregoire@llcc.cc.il.us
Phone: (217) 786-2290 Toll-free number: (800) 727-4161
Fax: (217) 786-2492
Ron Gregoire, Director of Admissions and Records, Lincoln Land Community College, 5250 Shepherd Road, Springfield, IL 62794-9256

MacCormac College

Chicago, Illinois
www.maccormac.edu — **CB code: 1520**

- Private 2-year junior college
- Commuter campus in very large city
- Interview required

General. Founded in 1904. Regionally accredited. **Enrollment:** 264 degree-seeking undergraduates. **Degrees:** 57 associate awarded. **Calendar:** Semester, limited summer session. **Full-time faculty:** 5 total. **Part-time faculty:** 21 total.

Student profile.

Out-of-state:	1%	**25 or older:**	30%

Transfer out. Colleges most students transferred to 2005: Loyola University, DePaul University, Roosevelt University.

Basis for selection. Open admission, but selective for some programs. Test scores and class rank most important. ACT recommended.

High school preparation. 13 units required; 15 recommended. Required and recommended units include English 4, mathematics 2-3, social studies 3-4, history 1, science 2 (laboratory 1).

2005-2006 Annual costs. Tuition/fees: $9,960. Per-credit charge: $415. Books/supplies: $600. Personal expenses: $1,200.

2005-2006 Financial aid. Non-need-based: Scholarships awarded for academics, leadership.

Application procedures. Admission: No deadline. $20 fee, may be waived for applicants with need. Admission notification on a rolling basis. **Financial aid:** Closing date 8/15. FAFSA required. Must reply within 2 week(s) of notification.

Academics. Special study options: ESL, internships. Bachelor's degree programs available on campus. **Credit/placement by examination:** CLEP, IB. 36 credit hours maximum toward associate degree. **Support services:** Learning center, study skills assistance, tutoring.

Majors. Business: General, accounting, administrative services, business admin, hospitality admin, international, international marketing, management information systems, marketing, office management, tourism promotion, tourism/travel. **Computer sciences:** General, computer science, information systems. **Education:** Teacher assistance. **Health:** Medical transcription. **Legal studies:** Court reporting, legal secretary, paralegal.

Most popular majors. Business/marketing 80%, legal studies 15%.

Computing on campus. 118 workstations in library, computer center.

Student life. Freshman orientation: Mandatory. **Activities:** Student government, student activities committee, Phi Theta Kappa.

Student services. Career counseling, student employment services, financial aid counseling, personal counseling, placement for graduates, veterans' counselor. **Transfer:** Special adviser, orientation for new students. Transfer adviser for students transferring to 4-year colleges.

Contact. E-mail: admissions@maccormac.edu
Phone: (312) 922-1884 Fax: (312) 922-3196
Adam Schauer, Admissions Counselor, MacCormac College, 29 East Madison Avenue, Chicago, IL 60607

McHenry County College

Crystal Lake, Illinois — **CB member**
www.mchenry.edu — **CB code: 1525**

- Public 2-year community college
- Commuter campus in large town

General. Founded in 1967. Regionally accredited. **Enrollment:** 5,416 degree-seeking undergraduates; 28 non-degree-seeking students. **Degrees:** 459 associate awarded. **Location:** 50 miles from Chicago. **Calendar:** Semester, limited summer session. **Full-time faculty:** 89 total; 10% minority, 46% women. **Part-time faculty:** 203 total; 7% minority, 54% women. **Special facilities:** Planetarium, art galleries, weather cam.

Student profile. Among degree-seeking undergraduates, 72% enrolled in a transfer program, 28% enrolled in a vocational program, 905 enrolled as first-time, first-year students.

Part-time:	62%	**Asian American:**	2%
Women:	58%	**Hispanic American:**	7%
African American:	1%	**International:**	2%

Transfer out. Colleges most students transferred to 2005: Northern Illinois University, Illinois State University, University of Illinois at Chicago, Southern Illinois University, Columbia College.

Basis for selection. Open admission. **Adult students:** Entrance exam policies same as for first-time freshmen.

High school preparation. 18 units recommended. Recommended units include English 4, mathematics 3, social studies 3, science 3 (laboratory 3) and academic electives 2. 2 units among any of the following: foreign language, music, vocational education, or art recommended.

2005-2006 Annual costs. Tuition/fees: $2,174; $7,885 out-of-district; $9,236 out-of-state. Per-credit charge: $63 in-district; $253 out-of-district; $298 out-of-state. Books/supplies: $800. Personal expenses: $1,362.

Financial aid. Need-based: Need-based aid available for part-time students. Work study available nights, weekends and for part-time students. **Non-need-based:** Scholarships awarded for academics, athletics, leadership, music/drama, state residency. **Additional information:** Students can apply throughout the award year for federal and state aid. Students with physical handicaps or learning disabilities may apply for special needs scholarship.

Application procedures. Admission: No deadline. $15 fee. Application may be submitted online. Admission notification on a rolling basis. **Financial aid:** Priority date 6/1; no closing date. FAFSA, institutional form required. Applicants notified on a rolling basis starting 5/1.

Academics. Special study options: Accelerated study, distance learning, dual enrollment of high school students, ESL, honors, independent study, internships, liberal arts/career combination, study abroad. Cooperative programs (tech prep) with Education for Employment. License preparation in paramedic, real estate. **Credit/placement by examination:** AP, CLEP, institutional tests. 30 credit hours maximum toward associate degree. Local proficiency exams available for occupational course credit, DANTES exams accepted. **Support services:** GED preparation and test center, learning center, pre-admission summer program, reduced course load, remedial instruction, study skills assistance, tutoring, writing center.

Majors. Agriculture: Horticulture. **Business:** Accounting technology, administrative services, business admin, operations, real estate, selling. **Computer sciences:** Applications programming. **Construction:** Building inspection. **Engineering:** General. **Engineering technology:** Electrical, mechanical. **Health:** EMT paramedic. **Interdisciplinary:** Biological/physical sciences. **Liberal arts:** Arts/sciences. **Mechanic/repair:** Automotive. **Protective services:** Firefighting, police science. **Visual/performing arts:** Art.

Most popular majors. Business/marketing 6%, interdisciplinary studies 68%, liberal arts 12%.

Computing on campus. 153 workstations in library, computer center, student center. Commuter students can connect to campus network. Online course registration, online library available.

Student life. Freshman orientation: Mandatory. Preregistration for classes offered. Admitted students from local high schools are invited to participate in orientation and preregistration during April and May. **Policies:** Freshmen permitted cars on campus. **Activities:** Bands, choral groups, drama, literary magazine, music ensembles, student government, student newspaper, Latinos Unidos, Phi Theta Kappa, campus activities board, campus Christian fellowship, Club Concordia, Pride Alliance, Black Student Alliance, Latter-day Saint student association, Special Needs Action Program (SNAP), student leadership team.

Athletics. NJCAA. **Intercollegiate:** Baseball M, basketball, soccer M, softball W, tennis, volleyball W. **Intramural:** Basketball. **Team name:** Fighting Scots.

Student services. Adult student services, career counseling, student employment services, financial aid counseling, minority student services, on-campus daycare, personal counseling, placement for graduates, veterans' counselor. **Physically disabled:** Services for visually, speech, hearing impaired. **Transfer:** Special adviser, orientation, pre-admission transcript evaluation for new students. Transfer center, transfer adviser, college fairs on campus for students transferring to 4-year colleges.

Contact. E-mail: admissions@mchenry.edu
Phone: (815) 455-8530 Toll-free number: (866) 743-6667
Fax: (815) 455-3766
Marilyn Weniger, Director of Admissions and Advising, McHenry County College, 8900 U.S. Highway 14, Crystal Lake, IL 60012-2761

Moraine Valley Community College

Palos Hills, Illinois
www.morainevalley.edu **CB code: 1524**

- Public 2-year community college
- Commuter campus in large town

General. Founded in 1967. Regionally accredited. **Enrollment:** 10,738 degree-seeking undergraduates; 5,191 non-degree-seeking students. **Degrees:** 1,168 associate awarded. **Location:** 25 miles from downtown Chicago. **Calendar:** Semester, extensive summer session. **Full-time faculty:** 165 total; 6% minority, 56% women. **Part-time faculty:** 596 total; 52% women. **Class size:** 37% < 20, 61% 20-39, 1% 40-49, less than 1% 50-99. **Special facilities:** Nature study area, center for contemporary technology, fine and performing arts center.

Student profile. Among degree-seeking undergraduates, 52% enrolled in a transfer program, 37% enrolled in a vocational program, 5% already have a bachelor's degree or higher, 2,009 enrolled as first-time, first-year students, 705 transferred in from other institutions.

Part-time:	48%	**Hispanic American:**	10%
Women:	58%	**International:**	2%
African American:	9%	**25 or older:**	29%
Asian American:	2%		

Transfer out. 85% of students enrolled in the transfer program go on to 4-year colleges. **Colleges most students transferred to 2005:** Governors State University, St. Xavier University, University of Illinois-Chicago, Illinois State University, Eastern Illinois University.

Basis for selection. Open admission, but selective for some programs. Some health science programs have special admission requirements and limited enrollment. Placement tests may be waived for students with specified ACT scores. COMPASS tests required of all full-time students. **Adult students:** SAT/ACT scores not required. COMPASS placement test required. **Learning Disabled:** Students should register with the Center for Disability Services before May 1 for the fall semester, before Oct. 1 for the spring semester, before March 1 for the summer session.

High school preparation. 15 units required. Required units include English 4, mathematics 2, social studies 2, science 2 (laboratory 2) and academic electives 5.

2006-2007 Annual costs. Tuition/fees (projected): $2,070; $6,120 out-of-district; $7,410 out-of-state. Per-credit charge: $64 in-district; $199 out-of-district; $242 out-of-state. Books/supplies: $1,440. Personal expenses: $1,572.

2004-2005 Financial aid. Need-based: 89% of total undergraduate aid awarded as scholarships/grants, 11% as loans/jobs. Need-based aid available for part-time students. Work study available nights and for part-time students. **Non-need-based:** Scholarships awarded for academics, athletics, leadership.

Application procedures. Admission: No deadline. No application fee. Application may be submitted online. Admission notification on a rolling basis. **Financial aid:** Priority date 5/1; no closing date. FAFSA, institutional form required. Applicants notified on a rolling basis starting 3/1; must reply within 4 week(s) of notification.

Academics. Special study options: Accelerated study, cooperative education, distance learning, double major, dual enrollment of high school students, ESL, honors, independent study, internships, liberal arts/career combination, study abroad, weekend college. License preparation in nursing, paramedic, radiology. **Credit/placement by examination:** AP, CLEP, institutional tests. **Support services:** GED preparation and test center, learning center, reduced course load, remedial instruction, study skills assistance, tutoring, writing center.

Majors. Business: General, administrative services, business admin, entrepreneurial studies, human resources, management information systems, retailing, selling, travel services. **Computer sciences:** Applications programming, data processing, information technology, LAN/WAN management, networking. **Engineering technology:** CAD/CADD, instrumentation, quality control. **Health:** Clinical lab technology, medical radiologic technology/radiation therapy, medical records technology, nursing (RN), recreational therapy, respiratory therapy technology. **Interdisciplinary:** Biological/

physical sciences. **Liberal arts:** Arts/sciences. **Mechanic/repair:** Automotive. **Parks/recreation:** Facilities management. **Personal/culinary services:** Restaurant/catering. **Protective services:** Corrections, fire safety technology, police science. **Visual/performing arts:** General, design.

Most popular majors. Health sciences 13%, interdisciplinary studies 36%, liberal arts 34%, security/protective services 6%.

Computing on campus. 800 workstations in library, computer center, student center. Online course registration, online library available.

Student life. Freshman orientation: Mandatory. Students registering for 12 or more credit hours are required to participate in an orientation program prior to their first registration. **Policies:** Freshmen permitted cars on campus. **Housing:** Assistance given to foreign students looking for housing. **Activities:** Bands, choral groups, dance, drama, literary magazine, music ensembles, musical theater, student government, student newspaper, community service volunteer program, forensics team, international student club, inter-club council, peers educating peers, student entertainment board, Muslim student association, Alliance for African-American students, Latin and Arab student groups.

Athletics. NJCAA. **Intercollegiate:** Baseball M, basketball, cross-country, golf M, soccer, softball W, tennis, volleyball W. **Intramural:** Badminton, basketball, volleyball W. **Team name:** Cyclones.

Student services. Adult student services, campus ministries, career counseling, services for economically disadvantaged, student employment services, financial aid counseling, minority student services, on-campus daycare, personal counseling, placement for graduates, women's services. **Physically disabled:** Services for visually, speech, hearing impaired. **Transfer:** Special adviser, orientation for new students. Transfer center, transfer adviser, college fairs on campus for students transferring to 4-year colleges.

Contact. E-mail: manser@morainevalley.edu
Phone: (708) 974-2110 Fax: (708) 974-0974
Wendy Manser, Dean of Enrollment Services, Moraine Valley Community College, 9000 West College Parkway, Palos Hills, IL 60465-0937

Morrison Institute of Technology
Morrison, Illinois
www.morrison.tec.il.us **CB code: 1269**

- Private 2-year junior and technical college
- Residential campus in small town

General. Founded in 1973. Accredited by Technology Accreditation Commission of Accreditation Board of Engineering and Technology. **Enrollment:** 125 degree-seeking undergraduates. **Degrees:** 57 associate awarded. **Location:** 100 miles from Chicago, 50 miles from Davenport, Iowa. **Calendar:** Semester, limited summer session. **Full-time faculty:** 9 total; 33% women. **Part-time faculty:** 1 total; 100% women. **Class size:** 43% < 20, 57% 20-39. **Special facilities:** 4 computer-aided design (CAD) laboratories.

Student profile. Among degree-seeking undergraduates, 5 transferred in from other institutions.

Out-of-state:	15%	**Live on campus:**	70%
25 or older:	5%		

Transfer out. Colleges most students transferred to 2005: Bradley University, Southern Illinois University.

Basis for selection. Open admission. Interview recommended.

High school preparation. Recommended units include mathematics 2 and science 1. Algebra and geometry, drafting recommended.

2006-2007 Annual costs. Tuition/fees (projected): $12,380. Per-credit charge: $481. Room only: $2,600. Books/supplies: $850. Personal expenses: $900.

2004-2005 Financial aid. Need-based: Need-based aid available for part-time students. Work study available nights and weekends. **Non-need-based:** Scholarships awarded for academics.

Application procedures. Admission: Priority date 8/1; no deadline. $100 fee. Admission notification on a rolling basis. **Financial aid:** No deadline. FAFSA, institutional form required. Applicants notified on a rolling basis; must reply within 2 week(s) of notification.

Academics. Special study options: Double major. **Credit/placement by examination:** AP, CLEP, IB, institutional tests. 25 credit hours maximum toward associate degree. SOC approved guidelines. **Support services:** Reduced course load, tutoring.

Majors. Computer sciences: LAN/WAN management. **Engineering technology:** Architectural, civil, construction, manufacturing, surveying.

Computing on campus. 80 workstations in library, computer center. Dormitories wired for high-speed internet access and linked to campus network. Wireless network available.

Student life. Freshman orientation: Mandatory. Preregistration for classes offered. Orientation program consists of five one hour presentations given during the course of the first five weeks of each semester. **Policies:** Freshmen permitted cars on campus. **Housing:** Guaranteed on-campus for all undergraduates. Coed dorms, special housing for disabled, substance-free housing available. $100 deposit. **Activities:** Student government, student newspaper, professional societies, student chapters.

Athletics. Intramural: Basketball M, bowling, volleyball.

Student services. Career counseling, student employment services, personal counseling, placement for graduates. **Transfer:** Special adviser, orientation for new students. Transfer adviser, college fairs on campus for students transferring to 4-year colleges.

Contact. Phone: (815) 772-7218 ext. 11 Fax: (815) 772-7548
Richard Parkinson, Vice President of Academic Affairs and Finance, Morrison Institute of Technology, 701 Portland Avenue, Morrison, IL 61270-2959

Two-Year Colleges

Morton College
Cicero, Illinois
www.morton.edu **CB code: 1489**

- Public 2-year community college
- Commuter campus in small city

General. Founded in 1924. Regionally accredited. **Enrollment:** 2,310 degree-seeking undergraduates; 2,434 non-degree-seeking students. **Degrees:** 295 associate awarded. **Location:** 9 miles from Chicago. **Calendar:** Semester, limited summer session. **Full-time faculty:** 52 total; 12% have terminal degrees, 15% minority, 48% women. **Part-time faculty:** 200 total; 10% have terminal degrees, 20% minority, 54% women. **Class size:** 37% < 20, 55% 20-39, 3% 40-49, 4% 50-99, less than 1% >100. **Special facilities:** Planetarium, museum.

Student profile. Among degree-seeking undergraduates, 49% enrolled in a transfer program, 48% enrolled in a vocational program, 2% already have a bachelor's degree or higher, 371 enrolled as first-time, first-year students.

Part-time:	59%	**Hispanic American:**	71%
Women:	60%	**International:**	2%
African American:	4%	**25 or older:**	48%
Asian American:	2%		

Basis for selection. Open admission, but selective for some programs and for out-of-state students. Nursing and physical therapist assistant programs have limited space. Preference given to in-district applicants using class rank, mathematics and science course prerequisites, and placement tests as guides. **Adult students:** Entrance exam policies same as for first-time freshmen.

High school preparation. 15 units recommended. Recommended units include English 4, mathematics 3, social studies 3, science 3 and foreign language 2.

2005-2006 Annual costs. Tuition/fees: $2,090; $5,570 out-of-district; $7,310 out-of-state. Per-credit charge: $58 in-district; $174 out-of-district; $232 out-of-state. Books/supplies: $875. Personal expenses: $1,875.

Financial aid. Need-based: Need-based aid available for part-time students. Work study available nights, weekends and for part-time students.

Application procedures. Admission: No deadline. $10 fee. Admission notification on a rolling basis. **Financial aid:** Priority date 6/1; no closing date. FAFSA, institutional form required. Applicants notified on a rolling basis starting 8/1.

Academics. Special study options: Distance learning, double major, dual enrollment of high school students, ESL, internships, weekend college. License preparation in nursing, physical therapy. **Credit/placement by examination:** AP, CLEP, institutional tests. 30 credit hours maximum toward associate degree. **Support services:** GED preparation, learning center, preadmission summer program, remedial instruction, tutoring, writing center.

Majors. Business: Accounting, administrative services, business admin. **Computer sciences:** Information technology. **Engineering technology:** CAD/CADD. **Health:** Nursing (RN), physical therapy assistant. **Interdisciplinary:** Biological/physical sciences. **Liberal arts:** Arts/sciences. **Mechanic/repair:** Automotive, heating/ac/refrig. **Protective services:** Police science. **Visual/performing arts:** Studio arts.

Computing on campus. 265 workstations in library, computer center, student center. Wireless network available.

Student life. Freshman orientation: Available. Preregistration for classes offered. **Activities:** Jazz band, choral groups, dance, drama, music ensembles, musical theater, student government, student newspaper, art club, nursing students association, Phi Theta Kappa, HALO, College Bowl, film club, Yes We Can!-Si Se Puede!, open options, student success club, automotive club.

Athletics. NJCAA. **Intercollegiate:** Baseball M, basketball, cross-country, soccer M, softball W, volleyball W. **Team name:** Panthers.

Student services. Career counseling, services for economically disadvantaged, student employment services, financial aid counseling, on-campus daycare, personal counseling, placement for graduates. **Physically disabled:** Services for visually, speech, hearing impaired. **Transfer:** Special adviser, orientation for new students. Transfer center, transfer adviser, college fairs on campus for students transferring to 4-year colleges.

Contact. Phone: (708) 656-8000 ext. 346 Fax: (708) 656-9592
Roslyn Wolz, Director of Enrollment Management, Morton College, 3801 South Central Avenue, Cicero, IL 60804

Northwestern Business College

Chicago, Illinois
northwesternbc.edu **CB code: 2433**

- For-profit 2-year technical college
- Commuter campus in very large city

General. Founded in 1902. Regionally accredited. Additional campuses in Bridgeview and Naperville. **Enrollment:** 1,922 degree-seeking undergraduates; 314 non-degree-seeking students. **Degrees:** 258 associate awarded. **Calendar:** Quarter, extensive summer session. **Full-time faculty:** 41 total; 20% minority, 61% women. **Part-time faculty:** 88 total; 27% minority, 67% women. **Class size:** 78% < 20, 22% 20-39, less than 1% 40-49. **Special facilities:** Health sciences laboratories.

Student profile. Among degree-seeking undergraduates, 669 enrolled as first-time, first-year students.

Part-time:	59%	**Asian American:**	2%
Women:	80%	**Hispanic American:**	32%
African American:	40%	**25 or older:**	31%

Basis for selection. Students must have a minimum ACT score of 15 or SAT score of 550 (exclusive of writing) or pass college's admission test administered on campus. COMPASS or ASSET is used for placement. **Adult students:** Entrance exam policies same as for first-time freshmen.

2006-2007 Annual costs. Tuition/fees (projected): $16,340. Per-credit charge: $330. Tuition may be higher for some classes. Books/supplies: $875. Personal expenses: $1,000.

2004-2005 Financial aid. All financial aid based on need. 44% of total undergraduate aid awarded as scholarships/grants, 56% as loans/jobs. Need-based aid available for part-time students. Work study available nights and for part-time students. **Additional information:** State grant programs for Illinois residents and alternative loans offered.

Application procedures. Admission: No deadline. $25 fee. Application may be submitted online. Admission notification on a rolling basis. **Financial aid:** Priority date 6/30; no closing date. FAFSA, institutional form required. Applicants notified on a rolling basis starting 8/15; must reply within 4 week(s) of notification.

Academics. Students wishing to graduate early may attend summer quarter. **Special study options:** Double major, internships. License preparation in real estate. **Credit/placement by examination:** AP, CLEP, IB, institutional tests. 50 credit hours maximum toward associate degree. Maximum credit awarded by examination is 25% of major, 50% of program. **Support services:** Learning center, reduced course load, remedial instruction, study skills assistance, tutoring.

Majors. Business: Accounting, administrative services, business admin, entrepreneurial studies, hospitality admin, tourism/travel. **Computer sciences:** General, applications programming, programming. **Health:** Medical assistant, medical records technology, medical secretary. **Legal studies:** Paralegal.

Most popular majors. Business/marketing 43%, computer/information sciences 16%, health sciences 9%, legal studies 32%.

Computing on campus. 413 workstations in library, computer center.

Student life. Freshman orientation: Mandatory. Preregistration for classes offered. Orientation is about 3 hours in length offered at all campuses day and evening. **Activities:** Honor society, clubs related to majors, Junior Achievement.

Student services. Alcohol/substance abuse counseling, career counseling, student employment services, financial aid counseling, personal counseling, placement for graduates. **Physically disabled:** Services for visually, speech, hearing impaired. **Transfer:** Special adviser, orientation, pre-admission transcript evaluation for new students. Transfer center, transfer adviser, college fairs on campus for students transferring to 4-year colleges.

Contact. Phone: (773) 481-3730 Toll-free number: (800) 396-5613
Fax: (773) 481-3738
Mark Sliz, Director of Admissions, Northwestern Business College, 4839 North Milwaukee Avenue, Chicago, IL 60630

Oakton Community College

Des Plaines, Illinois
www.oakton.edu **CB code: 1573**

- Public 2-year community college
- Commuter campus in small city

General. Founded in 1969. Regionally accredited. **Enrollment:** 4,895 degree-seeking undergraduates. **Degrees:** 407 associate awarded. **Location:** 15 miles from Chicago. **Calendar:** Semester, limited summer session. **Full-time faculty:** 156 total; 25% have terminal degrees, 10% minority, 57% women. **Part-time faculty:** 509 total; 13% have terminal degrees, 9% minority, 43% women. **Special facilities:** Campus located within wildlife preserve, visual arts center at Des Plaines campus.

Student profile.

Out-of-state:	7%	**25 or older:**	45%

Transfer out. Colleges most students transferred to 2005: University of Illinois-Chicago, Northeastern Illinois University, DePaul University, Loyola University-Chicago.

Basis for selection. Open admission, but selective for some programs. Special requirements for health career programs. ACT recommended for placement and counseling; SAT accepted. Scores must be received prior to enrolling in an English course. Interview required of health career (except nursing) majors. **Learning Disabled:** Following completion of admission application, students arrange meetings to provide documentation of disability, and for testing and registration.

2006-2007 Annual costs. Tuition/fees (projected): $2,085; $6,159 out-of-district; $7,920 out-of-state. Books/supplies: $800. Personal expenses: $1,000.

2004-2005 Financial aid. Need-based: 92% of total undergraduate aid awarded as scholarships/grants, 8% as loans/jobs. Need-based aid available for part-time students. Work study available nights, weekends and for part-time students. **Non-need-based:** Scholarships awarded for academics, art, leadership, minority status, music/drama, state residency. **Additional information:** Foundation Scholarships application available January through mid-March.

Application procedures. Admission: No deadline. $25 fee. Application may be submitted online. Admission notification on a rolling basis. **Financial aid:** Closing date 5/1. FAFSA, institutional form required. Applicants notified on a rolling basis starting 6/1; must reply within 2 week(s) of notification.

Academics. Special study options: Accelerated study, distance learning, dual enrollment of high school students, exchange student, honors, independent study, internships, study abroad, teacher certification program, weekend college. License preparation in nursing, real estate. **Credit/placement by examination:** AP, CLEP, institutional tests. 30 credit hours maximum toward associate degree. **Support services:** GED preparation, learning center, remedial instruction, study skills assistance, tutoring, writing center.

Honors college/program. Eligibility for honors program requires ACT score of 25, SAT score of 1200 (exclusive of Writing), graduation in top 20% of high school class or GED of 300+.

Majors. Business: Accounting, business admin, international, office management, real estate. **Computer sciences:** General, data processing. **Construction:** Maintenance. **Education:** Early childhood. **Engineering:** General. **Engineering technology:** Architectural, construction, drafting, electrical, electrical drafting, robotics. **Health:** Clinical lab assistant, medical records technology, nursing (RN), physical therapy assistant. **Liberal arts:** Arts/sciences. **Mechanic/repair:** Automotive. **Production:** Machine shop technology. **Protective services:** Firefighting, police science. **Visual/performing arts:** Commercial/advertising art.

Computing on campus. 800 workstations in library, computer center, student center. Commuter students can connect to campus network. Online course registration, online library, helpline, wireless network available.

Student life. Freshman orientation: Available. Preregistration for classes offered. **Policies:** Freshmen permitted cars on campus. **Activities:** Jazz band, choral groups, drama, literary magazine, music ensembles, student government, student newspaper, Christian student association, Indian student association, political science forum, Black student union, Hillel, Japanese club, desktop publishing club.

Athletics. NJCAA. **Intercollegiate:** Baseball M, basketball, cross-country, golf M, soccer, softball W, tennis, track and field, volleyball W. **Intramural:** Basketball, volleyball. **Team name:** Raiders.

Student services. Adult student services, alcohol/substance abuse counseling, career counseling, student employment services, financial aid counseling, health services, minority student services, on-campus daycare, personal counseling, placement for graduates, veterans' counselor. **Transfer:** Special adviser, orientation for new students. Transfer center, transfer adviser, college fairs on campus for students transferring to 4-year colleges.

Contact. E-mail: admiss@oakton.edu
Phone: (847) 635-1629 Fax: (847) 635-1890
Michele Brown, Director of Admission and Enrollment Management, Oakton Community College, 1600 East Golf Road, Des Plaines, IL 60016

Parkland College
Champaign, Illinois
www.parkland.edu **CB code: 1619**

- Public 2-year community college
- Commuter campus in small city
- Interview required

General. Founded in 1966. Regionally accredited. Students have access to resources at University of Illinois and within certain guidelines may enroll in University of Illinois classes. **Enrollment:** 9,552 degree-seeking undergraduates; 200 non-degree-seeking students. **Degrees:** 849 associate awarded. **ROTC:** Army, Navy, Air Force. **Location:** 150 miles from Chicago, 120 miles from Indianapolis. **Calendar:** Semester, extensive summer session. **Full-time faculty:** 164 total; 17% have terminal degrees, 12% minority, 46% women. **Part-time faculty:** 371 total; 10% have terminal degrees, 8% minority, 52% women. **Class size:** 59% < 20, 41% 20-39, less than 1% 50-99, less than 1% >100. **Special facilities:** Planetarium, nature preserve, art gallery, agricultural technology applications center, land laboratory. **Partnerships:** Formal partnerships with local businesses including CISCO Systems, Case Corporation, Microsoft, Ford ASSET, LINUX Professional Institute.

Student profile. Among degree-seeking undergraduates, 1,519 enrolled as first-time, first-year students, 581 transferred in from other institutions.

Part-time:	53%	**Women:**	54%
Out-of-state:	1%	**25 or older:**	31%

Transfer out. Colleges most students transferred to 2005: University of Illinois at Urbana-Champaign.

Basis for selection. Open admission, but selective for some programs. ACT required for health programs. **Adult students:** Entrance exam policies same as for first-time freshmen. **Homeschooled:** Recommended that students meet with admissions adviser. **Learning Disabled:** Students with learning disabilities encouraged to contact Learning Disabilities specialist prior to enrolling.

High school preparation. 15 units required. Required units include English 4, mathematics 3, social studies 2, science 2, foreign language 2 and academic electives 2.

2006-2007 Annual costs. Tuition/fees (projected): $2,220; $6,360 out-of-district; $9,450 out-of-state. Per-credit charge: $72 in-district; $212 out-of-district; $315 out-of-state. For internet classes, in-district students pay $72 per-credit-hour, all others pay $112 per-credit-hour. Books/supplies: $1,000. Personal expenses: $1,000.

2004-2005 Financial aid. Need-based: 437 full-time freshmen applied for aid; 389 were judged to have need; 389 of these received aid. Average need met was 62%. Average scholarship/grant was $3,594. 56% of total undergraduate aid awarded as scholarships/grants, 44% as loans/jobs. Work study available nights. **Non-need-based:** Awarded to 90 full-time undergraduates, including 33 freshmen. Scholarships awarded for academics, art, athletics, leadership, minority status, music/drama, state residency.

Application procedures. Admission: No deadline. No application fee. Admission notification on a rolling basis. **Financial aid:** Priority date 3/1; no closing date. FAFSA, institutional form required. Applicants notified on a rolling basis starting 6/1; must reply within 2 week(s) of notification.

Academics. Special study options: Accelerated study, cooperative education, cross-registration, distance learning, double major, dual enrollment of high school students, ESL, honors, independent study, internships, student-designed major, study abroad, weekend college. Bachelor's degree programs available on campus. License preparation in dental hygiene, nursing, paramedic. **Credit/placement by examination:** AP, CLEP, SAT, ACT, institutional tests. 25 credit hours maximum toward associate degree. Institutionally-prepared proficiency exams are available. **Support services:** GED preparation and test center, learning center, reduced course load, remedial instruction, study skills assistance, tutoring, writing center.

Honors college/program. Students take 4 honors survey courses, complete an honors research project. Must maintain a cumulative GPA of 3.5 or better.

Majors. Agriculture: General, animal husbandry, business, landscaping, mechanization. **Business:** General, accounting technology, business admin, executive assistant, hotel/motel admin, marketing, selling. **Communications:** Radio/tv. **Communications technology:** Radio/tv. **Computer sciences:** Applications programming, networking. **Construction:** General, electrician. **Education:** Art, music. **Engineering:** General. **Engineering technology:** Computer systems, industrial, surveying. **Health:** Dental hygiene, nursing (RN), occupational therapy assistant, radiologic technology/medical imaging, respiratory therapy technology, surgical technology, veterinary technology/assistant. **Interdisciplinary:** Biological/physical sciences. **Liberal arts:** Arts/sciences. **Mechanic/repair:** Auto body, automotive, diesel. **Personal/culinary services:** Restaurant/catering. **Protective services:** Fire safety technology, police science. **Public administration:** Social work. **Visual/performing arts:** Art, commercial/advertising art.

Most popular majors. Biological/life sciences 21%, business/marketing 14%, education 7%, health sciences 16%, liberal arts 14%.

Computing on campus. 1,425 workstations in library, computer center. Online course registration available.

Student life. Freshman orientation: Mandatory. Preregistration for classes offered. Held at beginning of each semester. **Policies:** Students may also take part in activities at the University of Illinois. Freshmen permitted cars on campus. **Housing:** Students may reside at University of Illinois or use privately-owned dormitories in town. **Activities:** Bands, choral groups, dance, drama, literary magazine, music ensembles, musical theater, radio station, student government, student newspaper, TV station, Black Student Association, international student association, Phi Theta Kappa, student nurses association, veterinary technology association, Parkland Christian Fellowship, Colours, dental assisting association, dental hygienists association.

Athletics. NJCAA. **Intercollegiate:** Baseball M, basketball, golf M, soccer, softball W, volleyball W. **Intramural:** Basketball, bowling, softball, tennis, volleyball. **Team name:** Cobras.

Student services. Adult student services, career counseling, services for economically disadvantaged, student employment services, financial aid counseling, minority student services, on-campus daycare, personal counseling, placement for graduates, veterans' counselor, women's services. **Physically disabled:** Services for visually, speech, hearing impaired. **Learning disabled:** Comprehensive services available. **Transfer:** Special adviser, orientation for new students. Transfer center, transfer adviser, college fairs on campus for students transferring to 4-year colleges.

Contact. E-mail: mhenry@parkland.edu
Phone: (217) 351-2208 Toll-free number: (800) 346-8089
Fax: (217) 353-2640
Micheal Henry, Director of Admissions and Records, Parkland College, 2400 West Bradley Avenue, Champaign, IL 61821-1899

Prairie State College
Chicago Heights, Illinois
www.prairiestate.edu **CB code: 1077**

- Public 2-year community college
- Commuter campus in large town

General. Founded in 1957. Regionally accredited. **Enrollment:** 5,083 undergraduates. **Degrees:** 342 associate awarded. **Location:** 30 miles from Chicago. **Calendar:** Semester, limited summer session. **Full-time faculty:** 81 total. **Part-time faculty:** 203 total. **Special facilities:** Art Gallery, fitness center.

Transfer out. Colleges most students transferred to 2005: Governors State University, University of Illinois - Chicago.

Basis for selection. Open admission, but selective for some programs. Admission to nursing and dental hygiene programs based on GPA in required courses and test scores.

High school preparation. One unit each of chemistry and algebra required for nursing and dental programs, plus 1 unit biology for nursing.

2005-2006 Annual costs. Tuition/fees: $2,300; $6,620 out-of-district; $9,020 out-of-state. Per-credit charge: $76 in-district; $220 out-of-district; $300 out-of-state. Books/supplies: $750. Personal expenses: $1,700.

Financial aid. Need-based: Need-based aid available for part-time students. Work study available nights, weekends and for part-time students.

Application procedures. Admission: No deadline. $10 fee, may be waived for applicants with need. Admission notification on a rolling basis. **Financial aid:** Priority date 7/1; no closing date. FAFSA, institutional form required. Applicants notified on a rolling basis; must reply within 2 week(s) of notification.

Academics. Students completing an Associate in Arts or Science degree are guaranteed their classes will transfer to other Illinois colleges. **Special study options:** Cross-registration, distance learning, dual enrollment of high school students, ESL, honors, independent study, internships, study abroad, weekend college. License preparation in dental hygiene, nursing. **Credit/placement by examination:** CLEP, institutional tests. 45 credit hours maximum toward associate degree. **Support services:** GED preparation and test center, learning center, pre-admission summer program, reduced course load, remedial instruction, study skills assistance, tutoring.

Majors. Business: Administrative services, operations. **Computer sciences:** Applications programming, programming. **Construction:** Electrician. **Engineering technology:** Electrical. **Family/consumer sciences:** Child care. **Health:** Dental hygiene, mental health services, nursing (RN), substance abuse counseling. **Interdisciplinary:** Biological/physical sciences. **Liberal arts:** Arts/sciences. **Mechanic/repair:** Automotive. **Protective services:** Fire safety technology, police science. **Visual/performing arts:** Commercial photography, design, interior design, photography.

Most popular majors. Business/marketing 12%, education 12%, health sciences 27%, liberal arts 17%, psychology 8%.

Computing on campus. 248 workstations in library, computer center, student center. Helpline available.

Student life. Freshman orientation: Available. **Activities:** Jazz band, choral groups, dance, drama, musical theater, student government, student newspaper, symphony orchestra, All Latin Alliance, Black Student Union.

Athletics. Intercollegiate: Baseball M, basketball M, golf M, soccer M. **Team name:** Pioneers.

Student services. Student employment services, financial aid counseling, minority student services, on-campus daycare, personal counseling, placement for graduates. **Physically disabled:** Services for visually, speech, hearing impaired. **Transfer:** Special adviser, orientation for new students. Transfer center, transfer adviser, college fairs on campus for students transferring to 4-year colleges.

Contact. Phone: (708) 709-3516
Mary Welsh, Coordinator of Admissions and Records, Prairie State College, 202 South Halsted Street, Chicago Heights, IL 60411

Rend Lake College

Ina, Illinois
www.rlc.edu **CB code: 1673**

- Public 2-year community college
- Commuter campus in rural community

General. Founded in 1955. Regionally accredited. **Enrollment:** 4,913 degree-seeking undergraduates. **Degrees:** 594 associate awarded. **Location:** 45 miles from Carbondale, 85 miles from St. Louis. **Calendar:** Semester, limited summer session. **Full-time faculty:** 60 total. **Part-time faculty:** 180 total. **Class size:** 68% < 20, 29% 20-39, 2% 40-49, less than 1% 50-99. **Special facilities:** Two satellite campuses located in Mt. Vernon and Pinckneyville where students can take courses toward an associate degree. **Partnerships:** Formal partnerships to provide technical training for employees of General Tire (Mt. Vernon) and Matsushita Universal; mandated federal training provided to Department of Natural Resources-Mines and Minerals; authorized training provided for Cisco curriculum.

Student profile.

Out-of-state:	1%	**Live on campus:**	1%
25 or older:	70%		

Transfer out. Colleges most students transferred to 2005: Southern Illinois University-Carbondale, Southern Illinois University-Edwardsville, Eastern Illinois University, Southeast Missouri State University, Murray State University.

Basis for selection. Open admission, but selective for some programs. Special requirements for allied health programs. SAT, ACT, ASSET, or COMPASS scores required for degree-seeking students, including international students. **Adult students:** Entrance exam policies same as for first-time freshmen.

High school preparation. 15 units recommended. Recommended units include English 4, mathematics 3, social studies 3, science 3 (laboratory 3) and academic electives 2. Social studies units should include history and government. Electives may include foreign language, vocational education, music, or art. Lowest level math accepted is algebra 1.

2005-2006 Annual costs. Tuition/fees: $1,860; $2,880 out-of-district; $4,500 out-of-state. Per-credit charge: $62 in-district; $96 out-of-district; $150 out-of-state. Books/supplies: $900. Personal expenses: $1,636.

2004-2005 Financial aid. Need-based: Need-based aid available for part-time students. **Non-need-based:** Scholarships awarded for academics, art, athletics, leadership, music/drama, state residency.

Application procedures. Admission: No deadline. No application fee. Application may be submitted online. Admission notification on a rolling basis. **Financial aid:** No deadline. FAFSA required. Applicants notified on a rolling basis starting 3/15; must reply within 4 week(s) of notification.

Academics. Special study options: Cooperative education, distance learning, dual enrollment of high school students, ESL, honors, independent study, internships, study abroad. Bachelor's degree programs available on campus. License preparation in nursing, occupational therapy, paramedic, real estate. **Credit/placement by examination:** AP, CLEP, institutional tests. 16 credit hours maximum toward associate degree. Credits awarded for CLEP, proficiency exams and AP scores. **Support services:** GED preparation, learning center, remedial instruction, study skills assistance, tutoring.

Majors. Agriculture: Business, horticulture, mechanization, production. **Architecture:** Technology. **Business:** Administrative services, business admin. **Computer sciences:** Applications programming, LAN/WAN management. **Engineering:** General. **Engineering technology:** Manufacturing, surveying. **Family/consumer sciences:** Child development. **Health:** Clinical lab technology, EMT paramedic, medical records technology, nursing (RN), occupational therapy assistant. **Interdisciplinary:** Biological/physical sciences. **Liberal arts:** Arts/sciences. **Mechanic/repair:** Automotive, diesel, heavy equipment, industrial. **Personal/culinary services:** Chef training. **Protective services:** Corrections, fire services admin, police science. **Visual/performing arts:** Art, commercial/advertising art.

Computing on campus. 472 workstations in library, computer center. Commuter students can connect to campus network. Online library available.

Student life. Freshman orientation: Mandatory. **Housing:** Apartments available. **Activities:** Bands, choral groups, dance, drama, music ensembles, musical theater, student government, student newspaper, symphony orchestra, culinary arts club, Rend Lake College Active College Christians, Practical Nursing club, automotive club, horticulture club, Art League, criminal justice club.

Athletics. NJCAA. **Intercollegiate:** Baseball M, basketball, cheerleading M, cross-country M, golf, softball W, tennis W, track and field M, volleyball W. **Team name:** Warriors.

Student services. Adult student services, career counseling, services for economically disadvantaged, student employment services, financial aid counseling, on-campus daycare, personal counseling, placement for graduates, veterans' counselor. **Physically disabled:** Services for visually, speech, hearing impaired. **Transfer:** Special adviser, orientation, pre-admission transcript evaluation for new students. Transfer adviser, college fairs on campus for students transferring to 4-year colleges.

Contact. E-mail: admiss@rlc.edu
Phone: (618) 437-5321 ext. 1230 Fax: (618) 437-5677
Tammy Tadlock, Director of Student Records, Rend Lake College, 468 North Ken Gray Parkway, Ina, IL 62846

Richland Community College

Decatur, Illinois
www.richland.edu **CB code: 0738**

- Public 2-year community college
- Commuter campus in small city

General. Founded in 1971. Regionally accredited. **Enrollment:** 3,034 degree-seeking undergraduates. **Degrees:** 308 associate awarded. **Location:** 180 miles from Chicago, 120 miles from St. Louis. **Calendar:** Semester, limited summer session. **Full-time faculty:** 71 total; 6% have terminal degrees, 6% minority, 52% women. **Part-time faculty:** 171 total; 3% have terminal degrees, 8% minority, 53% women. **Class size:** 76% < 20, 24% 20-39, less than 1% 40-49. **Special facilities:** Human patient simulator for allied health students.

Transfer out. Colleges most students transferred to 2005: Illinois State University, Millikin University, Southern Illinois University-Carbondale, Eastern Illinois University, University of Illinois-Springfield.

Basis for selection. Open admission, but selective for some programs. All allied health programs have a separate admission process. **Adult students:** Entrance exam policies same as for first-time freshmen.

High school preparation. Required units include English 4, mathematics 3, social studies 3, science 3 and foreign language 2.

2005-2006 Annual costs. Tuition/fees: $1,870; $6,551 out-of-district; $8,642 out-of-state. Per-credit charge: $58 in-district; $214 out-of-district; $341 out-of-state. Books/supplies: $1,000.

2004-2005 Financial aid. Need-based: 125 full-time freshmen applied for aid; 79 were judged to have need; 66 of these received aid. Average need met was 59%. Average scholarship/grant was $3,336; average loan $2,288. 94% of total undergraduate aid awarded as scholarships/grants, 6% as loans/jobs. Need-based aid available for part-time students. Work study available nights and for part-time students. **Non-need-based:** Awarded to 131 full-time undergraduates, including 20 freshmen. Scholarships awarded for academics.

Application procedures. Admission: No deadline. No application fee. Application may be submitted online. Admission notification on a rolling basis. **Financial aid:** No deadline. FAFSA required. Applicants notified on a rolling basis starting 3/20.

Academics. Special study options: Distance learning, dual enrollment of high school students, ESL, honors, independent study, internships, liberal arts/career combination, teacher certification program. License preparation in nursing, paramedic, radiology. **Credit/placement by examination:** AP, CLEP, institutional tests. **Support services:** GED preparation, learning center, reduced course load, remedial instruction, study skills assistance, tutoring, writing center.

Majors. Agriculture: Business, horticultural science, horticulture. **Biology:** General. **Business:** General, accounting, hospitality admin, management information systems. **Communications:** Journalism. **Computer sciences:** General, computer graphics, computer science, data entry, programming. **Construction:** Electrician. **Education:** General. **Engineering:** General. **Engineering technology:** Drafting. **English:** American lit, British lit, composition, speech/rhetoric. **Foreign languages:** French, German, Spanish. **Health:** EMT paramedic, nursing (RN), radiologic technology/medical imaging, surgical technology. **History:** General. **Legal studies:** Prelaw. **Liberal arts:** Arts/sciences. **Math:** General. **Mechanic/repair:** General, automotive, electronics/electrical, heating/ac/refrig, industrial. **Philosophy/religion:** Philosophy. **Physical sciences:** Planetary. **Protective services:** Criminal justice, firefighting, police science. **Psychology:** General. **Social sciences:** General, anthropology, archaeology, economics, geography, political science, sociology. **Visual/performing arts:** General, art, art history/conservation, ceramics, drawing, painting, sculpture.

Computing on campus. 245 workstations in library, computer center. Commuter students can connect to campus network. Online course registration, online library, helpline available.

Student life. Freshman orientation: Mandatory. Preregistration for classes offered. 2 hours, includes registering for courses, variety of times available. **Policies:** Freshmen permitted cars on campus. **Activities:** Drama, student government, student newspaper.

Athletics. Team name: Knights.

Student services. Adult student services, career counseling, services for economically disadvantaged, student employment services, financial aid counseling, minority student services, on-campus daycare, personal counseling, placement for graduates, veterans' counselor, women's services. **Physically disabled:** Services for visually, speech, hearing impaired. **Transfer:** Special adviser, orientation, pre-admission transcript evaluation for new students. Transfer center, transfer adviser, college fairs on campus for students transferring to 4-year colleges.

Contact. Phone: (217) 875-7200 ext. 284 Fax: (217) 875-7783
JoAnn Wirey, Director, Admissions & Records, Richland Community College, One College Park, Decatur, IL 62521

Rock Valley College

Rockford, Illinois
www.rockvalleycollege.edu **CB code: 1674**

- Public 2-year community college
- Commuter campus in small city

General. Founded in 1964. Regionally accredited. **Enrollment:** 2,959 degree-seeking undergraduates; 652 non-degree-seeking students. **Degrees:** 1,297 associate awarded. **Location:** 85 miles from Chicago. **Calendar:** Semester, limited summer session. **Full-time faculty:** 138 total; 17% have terminal degrees, 9% minority, 46% women. **Part-time faculty:** 172 total; 9% have terminal degrees, 5% minority, 45% women. **Special facilities:** Outdoor theater. **Partnerships:** Formal partnership with CISCO.

Student profile. Among degree-seeking undergraduates, 650 enrolled as first-time, first-year students.

Women:	54%	**25 or older:**	43%

Transfer out. Colleges most students transferred to 2005: Northern Illinois University, Illinois State University, Western Illinois University.

Basis for selection. Open admission, but selective for some programs. Special requirements for nursing and respiratory therapy programs. Test scores used for nursing students only. Interview required of respiratory therapy, nursing, aviation maintenance majors. Audition required of music majors. **Adult students:** SAT/ACT scores not required.

High school preparation. Recommended units include English 4, mathematics 3, social studies 2 and science 2. One chemistry required for nursing applicants, 1 chemistry and 1 algebra for respiratory therapy applicants.

2006-2007 Annual costs. Tuition/fees (projected): $2,012; $6,122 out-of-district; $8,972 out-of-state. Per-credit charge: $54 in-district; $194 out-of-district; $417 out-of-state. Costs vary by program. Books/supplies: $900.

Financial aid. Need-based: Need-based aid available for part-time students. Work study available nights and for part-time students. **Non-need-based:** Scholarships awarded for academics, ROTC.

Application procedures. Admission: No deadline. No application fee. Application must be submitted on paper. Admission notification on a rolling basis. **Financial aid:** No deadline. FAFSA required. Applicants notified on a rolling basis starting 4/1; must reply within 2 week(s) of notification.

Academics. Special study options: Cooperative education, dual enrollment of high school students, ESL, external degree, independent study, internships, liberal arts/career combination, student-designed major, study abroad. License preparation in aviation, dental hygiene, nursing. **Credit/placement by examination:** AP, CLEP, institutional tests. 39 credit hours maximum toward associate degree. **Support services:** GED preparation, learning center, reduced course load, remedial instruction, study skills assistance, tutoring, writing center.

Majors. Business: General, accounting, administrative services, business admin, logistics, marketing. **Computer sciences:** General. **Engineering technology:** Construction, electrical, manufacturing. **Family/consumer sciences:** Child care. **Health:** Medical records technology, nursing (RN), respiratory therapy technology. **Legal studies:** Paralegal. **Liberal arts:** Arts/sciences. **Mechanic/repair:** Aircraft, automotive. **Protective services:** Firefighting, law enforcement admin. **Public administration:** Human services.

Computing on campus. 130 workstations in library, computer center, student center. Commuter students can connect to campus network. Online course registration, online library, helpline, wireless network available.

Student life. Freshman orientation: Available. Preregistration for classes offered. **Activities:** Bands, choral groups, dance, drama, literary magazine, music ensembles, musical theater, student government, student newspaper, 21 student interest groups.

Athletics. NJCAA. **Intercollegiate:** Baseball M, basketball, football (tackle) M, golf M, soccer, softball W, squash W, tennis, volleyball W. **Intramural:** Basketball M, skiing. **Team name:** Eagles.

Student services. Adult student services, career counseling, student employment services, financial aid counseling, personal counseling, placement for graduates, veterans' counselor. **Physically disabled:** Services for visually, speech, hearing impaired. **Transfer:** Special adviser, orientation for new students. Transfer adviser, college fairs on campus for students transferring to 4-year colleges.

Contact. Phone: (815) 921-4250 Fax: (815) 921-4269
Steve Ullrick, Dean of Student Support Services, Rock Valley College, 3301 North Mulford Road, Rockford, IL 61114-5699

Rockford Business College

Rockford, Illinois
www.rbcsuccess.com **CB code: 2459**

- For-profit 2-year business and technical college
- Commuter campus in small city
- Interview required

General. Founded in 1862. Accredited by ACICS. **Enrollment:** 471 degree-seeking undergraduates. **Degrees:** 127 associate awarded. **Location:** 90 miles from Chicago, 75 miles from Madison, Wisconsin. **Calendar:** Quarter, extensive summer session. **Full-time faculty:** 8 total. **Part-time faculty:** 30 total. **Class size:** 88% < 20, 11% 20-39, 1% 40-49.

Basis for selection. Interview very important. High school record, recommendations, personal statement important. TABE (Adult Basic Education) exam used to determine academic ability. **Adult students:** Entrance exam policies same as for first-time freshmen.

2006-2007 Annual costs. Tuition/fees (projected): $7,200. Per-credit charge: $160. Per-credit-hour charge for computer courses is $285. Books/supplies: $2,000. Personal expenses: $2,880.

Financial aid. Need-based: Need-based aid available for part-time students. Work study available nights.

Application procedures. Admission: No deadline. $150 fee. Application must be submitted on paper. Admission notification on a rolling basis. **Financial aid:** No deadline. FAFSA required. Applicants notified on a rolling basis.

Academics. Special study options: Dual enrollment of high school students, independent study, internships. **Credit/placement by examination:** AP, CLEP, IB, institutional tests. **Support services:** Remedial instruction, tutoring.

Majors. Business: General, accounting, business admin, marketing, office/clerical. **Computer sciences:** General, data processing, information systems. **Health:** Medical assistant, medical secretary, medical transcription. **Legal studies:** Legal secretary, paralegal.

Computing on campus. 75 workstations in library, computer center. Online library available.

Student life. Freshman orientation: Mandatory. Preregistration for classes offered. **Activities:** Student government.

Student services. Career counseling, student employment services, financial aid counseling, placement for graduates. **Physically disabled:** Services for visually impaired. **Transfer:** Orientation, pre-admission transcript evaluation for new students.

Contact. E-mail: bholliman@rbcsuccess.com
Phone: (815) 967-7322 Toll-free number: (866) 722-4632
Fax: (815) 965-0360
Randy Plunkett, Director of Enrollment Services, Rockford Business College, 730 North Church Street, Rockford, IL 61103

Sanford-Brown College: Collinsville

Collinsville, Illinois

- For-profit 2-year college

General. Accredited by ACICS.

Annual costs/financial aid. Certificate programs range from $19,400 to $20,655.

Contact. Phone: (618) 931-0300
1101 Eastport Drive, Collinsville, IL 62234

Sauk Valley Community College

Dixon, Illinois
www.svcc.edu **CB code: 1780**

- Public 2-year community college
- Commuter campus in large town

General. Founded in 1965. Regionally accredited. **Enrollment:** 2,085 degree-seeking undergraduates. **Degrees:** 257 associate awarded. **Location:** 110 miles from Chicago. **Calendar:** Semester, limited summer session. **Full-time faculty:** 54 total; 13% have terminal degrees, 4% minority, 37% women. **Part-time faculty:** 105 total; 8% have terminal degrees, 8% minority, 51% women. **Class size:** 54% < 20, 42% 20-39, 4% 40-49, less than 1% 50-99. **Special facilities:** Observatory, prairie plots.

Student profile. Among degree-seeking undergraduates, 56% enrolled in a transfer program, 44% enrolled in a vocational program, 3% already have a bachelor's degree or higher.

Out-of-state:	1%	**Live on campus:**	1%
25 or older:	44%		

Transfer out. Colleges most students transferred to 2005: Northern Illinois University, Illinois State University, Western Illinois University, University of Illinois, Southern Illinois University.

Basis for selection. Open admission, but selective for some programs. Special requirements for allied health programs: academic record, state residency important; class rank, test scores considered. New York placement test, BEST (Basic English Skills Test) and CELSA used for applicants not native speakers of English. Placement exam required of all full- and part-time students who intend to enroll in English or math course. **Adult students:** Entrance exam policies same as for first-time freshmen. **Homeschooled:** Transcript of courses and grades required.

High school preparation. 15 units recommended. Recommended units include English 4, mathematics 3, social studies 2, science 2 (laboratory 2) and academic electives 4. Special course requirements for allied health programs.

2005-2006 Annual costs. Tuition/fees: $2,190; $7,740 out-of-district; $8,760 out-of-state. Per-credit charge: $71 in-district; $256 out-of-district; $290 out-of-state. Books/supplies: $500. Personal expenses: $900.

2005-2006 Financial aid. Need-based: 201 full-time freshmen applied for aid; 90 were judged to have need; 90 of these received aid. Average need met was 81%. Average scholarship/grant was $4,313; average loan $2,540. 86% of total undergraduate aid awarded as scholarships/grants, 14% as loans/jobs. Need-based aid available for part-time students. Work study available nights and for part-time students. **Non-need-based:** Awarded to 242 full-time undergraduates, including 68 freshmen. Scholarships awarded for academics, athletics, leadership, minority status, state residency.

Application procedures. Admission: No deadline. No application fee. Application may be submitted online. Admission notification on a rolling basis. **Financial aid:** Priority date 3/1; no closing date. FAFSA, institutional form required. Applicants notified on a rolling basis starting 5/1.

Academics. Special study options: Cooperative education, distance learning, dual enrollment of high school students, ESL, honors, independent study, internships. License preparation in nursing, paramedic, radiology, real estate. **Credit/placement by examination:** AP, CLEP, institutional tests. 30 credit hours maximum toward associate degree. **Support services:** GED preparation and test center, learning center, remedial instruction, study skills assistance, tutoring, writing center.

Majors. Biology: General. **Business:** General, accounting, administrative services, business admin, management information systems, marketing, office management, office technology, office/clerical. **Communications:** General, journalism, public relations. **Computer sciences:** General, applications programming, data processing, programming. **Education:** General, art, bilingual, biology, chemistry, early childhood, elementary, English, family/consumer sciences, French, German, gifted/talented, health, history, learning disabled, mathematics, middle, multi-level teacher, music, physical, physically handicapped, physics, sales/marketing, science, secondary, social science, social studies, Spanish, special, speech, technology/industrial arts, voc/tech. **Engineering:** General, civil, electrical, physics. **Engineering technology:** Drafting, manufacturing, solar energy. **English:** Composition. **Family/consumer sciences:** Child care. **Foreign languages:** General, French, German, Spanish. **Health:** Athletic training, medical radiologic technology/radiation therapy, medical secretary, nursing (RN), predentistry, premedicine, prenursing, prepharmacy, preveterinary. **History:** General. **Interdisciplinary:** Math/computer science. **Legal studies:** Legal secretary, prelaw. **Liberal arts:** Arts/sciences. **Math:** General. **Mechanic/repair:** Diesel, heating/ac/refrig. **Parks/recreation:** Exercise sciences, sports admin. **Philosophy/religion:** Philosophy. **Physical sciences:** Chemistry, physics. **Protective services:** Criminal justice, law enforcement admin, police science. **Psychology:** General. **Public administration:** Human services, social work. **Social sciences:** General, economics, political science, sociology. **Visual/performing arts:** Art, art history/conservation, commercial/advertising art, dramatic, fashion design, music performance, studio arts, voice/opera.

Most popular majors. Business/marketing 10%, engineering/engineering technologies 7%, health sciences 22%, interdisciplinary studies 33%, liberal arts 22%.

Computing on campus. 120 workstations in library, computer center. Commuter students can connect to campus network.

Student life. **Freshman orientation:** Mandatory, $53 fee. Preregistration for classes offered. 15 hours held throughout first semester or prior to start of semester. **Policies:** Freshmen permitted cars on campus. **Housing:** Apartments available. **Activities:** Bands, choral groups, drama, music ensembles, musical theater, student government, student newspaper, symphony orchestra.

Athletics. NJCAA. **Intercollegiate:** Baseball M, basketball, cheerleading M, cross-country, golf M, softball W, tennis, volleyball W. **Team name:** Skyhawks.

Student services. Adult student services, career counseling, services for economically disadvantaged, student employment services, financial aid counseling, on-campus daycare, personal counseling, placement for graduates, veterans' counselor. **Physically disabled:** Services for visually, speech, hearing impaired. **Transfer:** Special adviser, orientation, pre-admission transcript evaluation for new students. Transfer center, transfer adviser, college fairs on campus for students transferring to 4-year colleges.

Contact. Phone: (815) 288-5511 ext. 273 Fax: (815) 288-3190
Thomas Breed, Director of Admissions, Records, and Placement, Sauk Valley Community College, 173 Illinois Route 2, Dixon, IL 61021-9110

Shawnee Community College

Ullin, Illinois
www.shawneecc.edu **CB code: 0882**

- Public 2-year community college
- Commuter campus in rural community

General. Founded in 1967. Regionally accredited. **Location:** 40 miles from Paducah, Kentucky. **Calendar:** Semester.

Annual costs/financial aid. Tuition/fees (2005-2006): $1,500; $2,580 out-of-state. Reduced tuition of $68 for some neighboring Kentucky counties. Books/supplies: $500. Personal expenses: $680. Need-based financial aid available to full-time and part-time students.

Contact. Phone: (618) 634-3200 ext. 3247
Director of Admissions and Counseling, 8364 Shawnee College Road, Ullin, IL 62992

South Suburban College of Cook County

South Holland, Illinois
www.southsuburbancollege.edu **CB code: 1806**

- Public 2-year community college
- Commuter campus in large town

General. Founded in 1927. Regionally accredited. **Enrollment:** 6,625 degree-seeking undergraduates. **Degrees:** 483 associate awarded. **Location:** 20 miles from the Chicago Loop. **Calendar:** Semester, limited summer session. **Full-time faculty:** 210 total. **Part-time faculty:** 270 total. **Special facilities:** Art galleries.

Student profile. Among degree-seeking undergraduates, 39% enrolled in a transfer program, 61% enrolled in a vocational program, 150 transferred in from other institutions.

Out-of-state:	7%	**Hispanic American:**	8%
African American:	64%	**25 or older:**	49%
Asian American:	1%		

Transfer out. **Colleges most students transferred to 2005:** Governors State University, University of Illinois-Chicago, Purdue University-Calumet, Chicago State University.

Basis for selection. Open admission, but selective for some programs. Separate requirements for health career programs and transfer-seeking students. Audition recommended for music majors. **Adult students:** Entrance exam policies same as for first-time freshmen. **Learning Disabled:** Students need to self-declare with counseling center. Accommodations as needed provided.

High school preparation. 15 units required. Required units include English 4, mathematics 3, social studies 2, science 2 (laboratory 1) and academic electives 4.

2006-2007 Annual costs. Tuition/fees (projected): $2,880; $7,890 out-of-district; $9,540 out-of-state. Per-credit charge: $87 in-district; $254 out-of-district; $309 out-of-state. Some students in nearby states may qualify for tuition rate of $99 per-credit-hour under regional tuition plan. Books/supplies: $500. Personal expenses: $1,000.

Financial aid. **Need-based:** Need-based aid available for part-time students. Work study available nights and for part-time students. **Non-need-based:** Scholarships awarded for academics, art, athletics, music/drama, state residency.

Application procedures. **Admission:** No deadline. No application fee. Application must be submitted on paper. Admission notification on a rolling basis. **Financial aid:** Priority date 6/1; no closing date. FAFSA required. Applicants notified on a rolling basis starting 7/1.

Academics. **Special study options:** Distance learning, double major, dual enrollment of high school students, ESL, honors, internships, liberal arts/career combination, study abroad. License preparation in nursing, occupational therapy, paramedic, radiology, real estate. **Credit/placement by examination:** AP, CLEP, institutional tests. 15 credit hours maximum toward associate degree. **Support services:** GED preparation and test center, learning center, reduced course load, remedial instruction, study skills assistance, tutoring.

Majors. **Biology:** General, biomedical sciences. **Business:** General, accounting, administrative services, fashion, finance, marketing, office management. **Computer sciences:** General. **Construction:** Maintenance. **Education:** General, early childhood, special, teacher assistance. **Engineering:** General, science. **Engineering technology:** Construction, drafting, electrical. **English:** English lit. **Foreign languages:** Spanish. **Health:** Medical radiologic technology/radiation therapy, nursing (RN), occupational therapy assistant, pharmacy assistant. **History:** General. **Legal studies:** Court reporting, paralegal. **Liberal arts:** Arts/sciences. **Math:** General. **Parks/recreation:** Health/fitness, sports admin. **Philosophy/religion:** Philosophy. **Physical sciences:** Astronomy, chemistry, geology, physics. **Protective services:** Criminal justice. **Psychology:** General. **Public administration:** Human services. **Social sciences:** Anthropology, economics, geography, political science, sociology. **Visual/performing arts:** Dramatic, studio arts.

Computing on campus. 622 workstations in library, computer center, student center. Online course registration, online library available.

Student life. **Freshman orientation:** Mandatory. Preregistration for classes offered. Continuous Orientation program as well as specialized High School Student Success program in the summers. **Policies:** Freshmen permitted cars on campus. **Activities:** Bands, choral groups, drama, literary magazine, music ensembles, opera, student government, Business Professionals, veterans organization, paralegal association, student government association, occupational therapy organization, human service club, Creative Dimensions, nursing club.

Athletics. NJCAA. **Intercollegiate:** Baseball M, basketball, soccer M, softball W, volleyball W. **Intramural:** Baseball M, basketball, softball, volleyball. **Team name:** Bulldogs.

Student services. Career counseling, student employment services, financial aid counseling, on-campus daycare, personal counseling, veterans' counselor. **Physically disabled:** Services for visually, speech, hearing impaired. **Learning disabled:** Comprehensive services available. **Transfer:** Special adviser, orientation for new students. Transfer center, transfer adviser, college fairs on campus for students transferring to 4-year colleges.

Contact. E-mail: admissions@southsuburbancollege.edu
Phone: (708) 596-2000 ext. 2329 Fax: (708) 225-5806
Robin Rihacek, Manager of Admissions and Records, South Suburban College of Cook County, 15800 South State Street, South Holland, IL 60473

Two-Year Colleges

Southeastern Illinois College
Harrisburg, Illinois
www.sic.edu **CB code: 1777**

- Public 2-year community college
- Commuter campus in small town

General. Founded in 1960. Regionally accredited. **Enrollment:** 1,207 degree-seeking undergraduates. **Degrees:** 259 associate awarded. **Location:** 45 miles from Carbondale, 65 miles from Evansville, Indiana. **Calendar:** Semester, extensive summer session. **Full-time faculty:** 54 total. **Part-time faculty:** 119 total. **Special facilities:** Game preserve management facility. **Partnerships:** Formal partnership with Cummins Corporation for Deisel Technology.

Transfer out. Colleges most students transferred to 2005: Southern Illinois University at Carbondale.

Basis for selection. Open admission, but selective for some programs. Special requirements for nursing, medical records, health information technology, surgical nurse, occupational therapy assistant, and conservation game management programs. Admission to health programs based on test scores. Psychological Services Bureau-Health Occupations Examination for medical laboratory technician, ASSET for health information systems. NET test required for Associate degree nursing program and practical nursing program.

High school preparation. 15 units required. Required units include English 4, mathematics 3, social studies 3, science 3 and academic electives 2. Applicants to vocational programs exempted from high school requirements.

2005-2006 Annual costs. Tuition/fees: $1,920; $2,790 out-of-district; $3,210 out-of-state. Per-credit charge: $64 in-district; $93 out-of-district; $107 out-of-state. Books/supplies: $450. Personal expenses: $1,357.

2004-2005 Financial aid. Need-based: Need-based aid available for part-time students. Work study available for part-time students. **Non-need-based:** Scholarships awarded for academics, alumni affiliation, art, athletics, music/drama.

Application procedures. Admission: No deadline. No application fee. Application may be submitted online. Admission notification on a rolling basis beginning on or about 5/1. **Financial aid:** No deadline. FAFSA required. Applicants notified on a rolling basis starting 4/15; must reply within 2 week(s) of notification.

Academics. Special study options: Cross-registration, distance learning, double major, dual enrollment of high school students, independent study, internships, student-designed major, study abroad. Bachelor's degree programs available on campus. License preparation in nursing, paramedic, real estate. **Credit/placement by examination:** AP, CLEP, institutional tests. 29 credit hours maximum toward associate degree. **Support services:** GED preparation and test center, learning center, pre-admission summer program, reduced course load, remedial instruction, tutoring.

Majors. Business: Administrative services, business admin, office technology. **Computer sciences:** Information systems, LAN/WAN management. **Conservation:** Wildlife. **Education:** General. **Family/consumer sciences:** Child care. **Health:** Clinical lab technology, medical records technology, nursing (RN), occupational therapy assistant, office assistant. **Interdisciplinary:** Behavioral sciences, math/computer science, natural sciences. **Legal studies:** Prelaw. **Liberal arts:** Arts/sciences. **Math:** General. **Mechanic/repair:** Diesel. **Protective services:** Police science. **Public administration:** Human services.

Computing on campus. 75 workstations in library, computer center.

Student life. Freshman orientation: Available. Preregistration for classes offered. Individual student orientation/advisement/registration appointment with new freshmen degree seeking students. **Activities:** Bands, choral groups, drama, literary magazine, music ensembles, musical theater, student government, student newspaper, art club, math and science club, BASIC, Students in Free Enterprise, Phi Theta Kappa, Phi Beta Lambda, Theta Sigma Phi, Student Association of Family and Consumer Sciences, Theta Sigma Phi.

Athletics. NJCAA. **Intercollegiate:** Baseball M, basketball, softball W. **Intramural:** Basketball. **Team name:** Falcons.

Student services. Career counseling, student employment services, financial aid counseling, on-campus daycare, personal counseling, placement for graduates, veterans' counselor. **Physically disabled:** Services for visually, hearing impaired. **Transfer:** Special adviser for new students. Transfer adviser, college fairs on campus for students transferring to 4-year colleges.

Contact. E-mail: registrar@sic.cc.il.us
Phone: (618) 252-5400 ext. 2441 Toll-free number: (866) 338-2742
Fax: (618) 252-3062
Tyra Taylor, Director of Enrollment Services, Southeastern Illinois College, 3575 College Road, Harrisburg, IL 62946

Southwestern Illinois College
Belleville, Illinois
www.swic.edu **CB code: 1057**

- Public 2-year community college
- Commuter campus in large town

General. Founded in 1946. Regionally accredited. Campuses at Belleville, Granite City, and Red Bud and extension centers in 22 locations throughout the district. **Enrollment:** 8,841 degree-seeking undergraduates. **Degrees:** 1,065 associate awarded. **ROTC:** Air Force. **Location:** 20 miles from St. Louis. **Calendar:** Semester, limited summer session. **Full-time faculty:** 133 total. **Part-time faculty:** 665 total. **Special facilities:** Largest greenhouse solar collector in North America; native tree arboretum, interactive video classrooms.

Student profile.

Out-of-state:	1%	25 or older:	59%

Basis for selection. Open admission, but selective for some programs. Special requirements for health career programs. All applicants required to take COMPASS and ASSET tests. Applicants to allied health programs to contact college advisor.

High school preparation. 15 units recommended. Recommended units include English 4, mathematics 2, social studies 3 and science 3. 1 unit of foreign language, music, art, or vocational education.

2005-2006 Annual costs. Tuition/fees: $1,740; $4,710 out-of-district; $7,470 out-of-state. Per-credit charge: $58 in-district; $157 out-of-district; $249 out-of-state. Required fees vary by courses taken. Those 60 and over pay a reduced rate of $50 per-credit-hour. Books/supplies: $500. Personal expenses: $1,320.

2004-2005 Financial aid. Need-based: 80% of total undergraduate aid awarded as scholarships/grants, 20% as loans/jobs. Need-based aid available for part-time students. **Non-need-based:** Scholarships awarded for academics, athletics.

Application procedures. Admission: No deadline. $10 fee. Admission notification on a rolling basis beginning on or about 4/16. **Financial aid:** Priority date 5/31; no closing date. FAFSA required. Applicants notified on a rolling basis starting 7/1; must reply within 2 week(s) of notification.

Academics. Special study options: Accelerated study, distance learning, double major, dual enrollment of high school students, ESL, independent study, internships, study abroad, weekend college. **Credit/placement by examination:** CLEP, institutional tests. 30 credit hours maximum toward associate degree. **Support services:** Learning center, reduced course load, remedial instruction, study skills assistance, tutoring, writing center.

Majors. Agriculture: Greenhouse operations, horticulture, landscaping, nursery operations, turf management. **Biology:** General. **Business:** General, accounting, banking/financial services, business admin, hospitality admin, management information systems, management science, office/clerical, sales/distribution. **Communications:** General. **Communications technology:** General. **Computer sciences:** General, applications programming, computer science, data processing, information systems, programming. **Construction:** Carpentry, electrician, maintenance, masonry, power transmission. **Education:** General, early childhood, elementary, middle, secondary. **Engineering:** General. **Engineering technology:** Construction, drafting. **English:** Speech/rhetoric. **Family/consumer sciences:** Child care. **Foreign languages:** General. **Health:** Clinical lab assistant, clinical lab technology, EMT paramedic, medical assistant, medical radiologic technology/radiation therapy, medical records technology, nursing (RN), physical therapy assistant, premedicine, prepharmacy, preveterinary, respiratory therapy technology. **History:** General. **Legal studies:** Paralegal, prelaw. **Liberal arts:** Arts/sciences. **Math:** General. **Mechanic/repair:** General, aircraft, electronics/electrical, heating/ac/refrig, industrial. **Parks/recreation:** Health/fitness. **Personal/culinary services:** Culinary arts. **Philosophy/religion:** Philosophy. **Physical sciences:** Astronomy, chemistry, physics. **Protective services:** Firefighting, police science, security services. **Psychology:** General. **Social sciences:** Anthropology, archaeology, economics, geography, political science, sociology. **Visual/performing arts:** Art, dramatic, photography, studio arts.

Computing on campus. 250 workstations in library, computer center.

Student life. **Activities:** Bands, choral groups, drama, literary magazine, music ensembles, student government, student newspaper, Minority Transfer Center, Black Affairs Council, Physically Challenged Organization, Campus Christian Fellowship, International Student Organization.

Athletics. NJCAA. **Intercollegiate:** Baseball M, basketball, soccer M, softball W, tennis, volleyball W. **Intramural:** Badminton, basketball M, bowling, softball, table tennis, volleyball.

Student services. Adult student services, career counseling, student employment services, on-campus daycare, personal counseling, placement for graduates, veterans' counselor. **Physically disabled:** Services for visually, speech, hearing impaired. **Transfer:** Special adviser, orientation for new students. Transfer adviser, college fairs on campus for students transferring to 4-year colleges.

Contact. Phone: (618) 235-2700 ext. 5400 Fax: (618) 235-1578
Michelle Birk, Director of Admissions, Southwestern Illinois College, 2500 Carlyle Avenue, Belleville, IL 62221-9989

Spoon River College
Canton, Illinois
www.spoonrivercollege.net **CB code: 1154**

- Public 2-year community college
- Commuter campus in large town

General. Founded in 1959. Regionally accredited. **Enrollment:** 2,955 degree-seeking undergraduates. **Degrees:** 281 associate awarded. **ROTC:** Army. **Location:** 35 miles from Peoria. **Calendar:** Semester, limited summer session. **Full-time faculty:** 41 total. **Part-time faculty:** 101 total.

Student profile.

Out-of-state:	1%	**25 or older:**	42%

Transfer out. Colleges most students transferred to 2005: Western Illinois University.

Basis for selection. Open admission, but selective for some programs. Special requirements for nursing program. College-preparatory program recommended for transfer degree programs. Vocational students not required to have specific high school courses. All students must take COMPASS exam; if score indicates, student must be remediated before taking college-level courses.

High school preparation. 15 units recommended. Recommended units include English 4, mathematics 3, social studies 3, science 3 and academic electives 2.

2006-2007 Annual costs. Tuition/fees (projected): $2,250; $4,050 out-of-district; $5,160 out-of-state. Per-credit charge: $65 in-district; $125 out-of-district; $162 out-of-state. Books/supplies: $600.

Financial aid. Non-need-based: Scholarships awarded for academics, athletics.

Application procedures. Admission: No deadline. No application fee. Admission notification on a rolling basis. **Financial aid:** Closing date 7/2. FAFSA required. Applicants notified on a rolling basis starting 3/15.

Academics. Special study options: Distance learning, dual enrollment of high school students, honors, internships. License preparation in nursing. **Credit/placement by examination:** AP, CLEP, institutional tests. 32 credit hours maximum toward associate degree. Maximum of 50% credit hours toward degree may be awarded through CLEP. **Support services:** GED preparation, learning center, reduced course load, remedial instruction, tutoring.

Honors college/program. Must have at least a 3.25 GPA, at least 22 on ACT, top 20% of graduating high school class. Program includes leadership course and at least 1 honors course per semester. Articulation with 4-year college Honors Program.

Majors. Agriculture: Business. **Business:** General, administrative services. **Computer sciences:** Data processing. **Education:** Adult/continuing, early childhood, ESL. **Health:** Nursing assistant. **History:** General. **Legal studies:** Prelaw. **Liberal arts:** Arts/sciences. **Mechanic/repair:** Automotive, diesel, electronics/electrical. **Protective services:** Law enforcement admin. **Visual/performing arts:** Art, dramatic.

Computing on campus. 100 workstations in library, computer center.

Student life. Freshman orientation: Available. **Activities:** Drama, literary magazine, student government, Alpha Gamma Tau (agriculture fraternity), Phi Theta Kappa (honors fraternity), Peer Ambassador Program, Phi Mu Tau (diesel fraternity).

Athletics. NJCAA. **Intercollegiate:** Baseball M, basketball, softball W, track and field.

Student services. Adult student services, career counseling, on-campus daycare, personal counseling, placement for graduates. **Physically disabled:** Services for visually, hearing impaired. **Transfer:** Special adviser for new students. Transfer adviser, college fairs on campus for students transferring to 4-year colleges.

Contact. E-mail: info@src.cc.il.us
Phone: (309) 649-7020 Toll-free number: (800) 334-7337
Fax: (309) 649-6235
Missy Wilkinson, Director of Admissions, Spoon River College, 23235 North County Road 22, Canton, IL 61520

Springfield College in Illinois
Springfield, Illinois
www.sci.edu **CB code: 1734**

- Private 2-year junior and liberal arts college affiliated with Roman Catholic Church
- Commuter campus in small city
- SAT or ACT (ACT writing optional) required

General. Founded in 1929. Regionally accredited. **Enrollment:** 551 degree-seeking undergraduates. **Degrees:** 100 associate awarded. **Location:** 200 miles from Chicago, 100 miles from St. Louis. **Calendar:** 4-4-1. Limited summer session. **Full-time faculty:** 21 total. **Part-time faculty:** 24 total.

Student profile. Among degree-seeking undergraduates, 130 enrolled as first-time, first-year students, 21 transferred in from other institutions.

Part-time:	51%	**Women:**	68%

Transfer out. Colleges most students transferred to 2005: University of Illinois Urbana-Champaign, Illinois State University, Southern Illinois University.

Basis for selection. High school course work, test scores, GPA, class rank required criteria. If GED, test scores, certification required, interview may be recommended. Require TOEFL, academic transcripts, and/or recommendations to determine English language proficiency. If students do not meet automatic transfer or re-entry admission criteria, additional institutional testing required in English, reading skills, and math. Interview may be recommended for academically weak applicants. Portfolio recommended for art majors. **Adult students:** SAT/ACT scores not required if applicant over 24. **Homeschooled:** Transcript of courses and grades, state high school equivalency certificate required. GED required to qualify for federal and state financial aid. **Learning Disabled:** Admission requirements for students with learning disabilities are handled on a case by case basis.

High school preparation. Recommended units include English 4, mathematics 3, social studies 2, science 2 and academic electives 2. Mathematics and physical science recommended for all applicants, foreign language for some.

2005-2006 Annual costs. Tuition/fees: $7,844. Per-credit charge: $312. Room only: $2,650. Books/supplies: $700. Personal expenses: $1,210.

Financial aid. Need-based: Need-based aid available for part-time students. Work study available nights, weekends and for part-time students. **Non-need-based:** Scholarships awarded for academics, art, athletics, leadership, religious affiliation.

Application procedures. Admission: No deadline. $20 fee, may be waived for applicants with need. Application may be submitted online. Admission notification on a rolling basis. **Financial aid:** Priority date 3/1; no closing date. FAFSA, institutional form required. Applicants notified on a rolling basis starting 3/15; must reply within 2 week(s) of notification.

Academics. Special study options: Cross-registration, double major, dual enrollment of high school students, honors, independent study, internships, study abroad. **Credit/placement by examination:** AP, CLEP, ACT, institutional tests. 30 credit hours maximum toward associate degree. **Support services:** Learning center, reduced course load, remedial instruction, study skills assistance, tutoring.

Majors. Business: General, business admin. **Education:** Elementary, secondary. **Health:** Clinical lab science, predentistry, premedicine, prenursing, prepharmacy, preveterinary. **Legal studies:** Prelaw. **Liberal arts:** Arts/

sciences. **Math:** General. **Philosophy/religion:** Religion. **Public administration:** Social work. **Transportation:** Aviation. **Visual/performing arts:** Art.

Most popular majors. Business/marketing 16%, education 7%, health sciences 20%, liberal arts 39%.

Computing on campus. 45 workstations in library, computer center.

Student life. Freshman orientation: Mandatory. Preregistration for classes offered. Held Friday before classes begin. **Policies:** Alcohol and other drugs prohibited. Freshmen permitted cars on campus. **Housing:** Apartments available. $300 nonrefundable deposit, deadline 7/1. **Activities:** Literary magazine, student government, campus ministry, Student Ambassadors, Phi Theta Kappa, arts and cultural events club, international club, Alpha Sigma Lambda.

Athletics. NJCAA. **Intercollegiate:** Baseball M, golf M, soccer, softball W, volleyball W. **Team name:** Bulldogs.

Student services. Campus ministries, financial aid counseling, personal counseling, veterans' counselor. **Transfer:** Special adviser, orientation, preadmission transcript evaluation for new students. Transfer adviser, college fairs on campus for students transferring to 4-year colleges.

Contact. E-mail: admissions@sci.edu
Phone: (217) 525-1420 ext. 210 Toll-free number: (800) 635-7289
Fax: (217) 789-1698
Terri Hinrichs, Director of Admissions, Springfield College in Illinois, 1500 North Fifth Street, Springfield, IL 62702-2694

Taylor Business Institute

Chicago, Illinois
www.tbiil.org **CB code: 2488**

- For-profit 2-year business college
- Very large city

General. Accredited by ACICS. **Enrollment:** 225 degree-seeking undergraduates. **Degrees:** 129 associate awarded. **Calendar:** Continuous. **Full-time faculty:** 29 total. **Part-time faculty:** 15 total.

Basis for selection. Open admission. CPAT required for placement and assessment after admission.

2005-2006 Annual costs. Costs vary by program. Tuition for nondegree programs is $15,425-$18,325; associate degree programs are $23,725-$18,325. Fees and book estimates are included in tuition charges.

Financial aid. Need-based: Work study available nights.

Application procedures. Admission: No deadline. $25 fee, may be waived for applicants with need. **Financial aid:** FAFSA, institutional form required.

Academics. Credit/placement by examination: CLEP.

Majors. Business: Accounting.

Student life. Freshman orientation: Available.

Student services. Alcohol/substance abuse counseling, career counseling, services for economically disadvantaged, student employment services, financial aid counseling, minority student services, personal counseling, placement for graduates, veterans' counselor, women's services.

Contact. Phone: (312) 658-5100
Ken Hatcher, Director of Admissions, Taylor Business Institute, 200 North Michigan Avenue, Suite 301, Chicago, IL 60601

Triton College

River Grove, Illinois **CB member**
www.triton.edu **CB code: 1821**

- Public 2-year community and junior college
- Commuter campus in large town

General. Founded in 1964. Regionally accredited. **Enrollment:** 9,754 degree-seeking undergraduates; 6,091 non-degree-seeking students. **Degrees:** 753 associate awarded. **Location:** 3 miles from Chicago. **Calendar:** Semester, extensive summer session. **Full-time faculty:** 109 total. **Part-time faculty:** 498 total. **Special facilities:** Earth and space center with planetarium and theater, performing arts center, botanical gardens, educational technology resource center.

Student profile. Among degree-seeking undergraduates, 2,089 enrolled as first-time, first-year students.

Part-time:	64%	Asian American:	5%
Women:	55%	Hispanic American:	18%
African American:	23%		

Basis for selection. Open admission, but selective for some programs. Applicants to allied health program must attend information session. Special requirements for court reporting, two manufacturer-related automotive programs, and most health programs. Internal placement test required for all students. **Adult students:** SAT/ACT scores not required. **Learning Disabled:** Students must self identify.

High school preparation. Biology, chemistry, or algebra required for most allied health programs. 15 specified units required for university transfer programs.

2006-2007 Annual costs. Tuition/fees (projected): $1,980; $5,550 out-of-district; $6,960 out-of-state. Per-credit charge: $56 in-district; $175 out-of-district; $222 out-of-state. Books/supplies: $700. Personal expenses: $1,500.

2004-2005 Financial aid. Need-based: 81% of total undergraduate aid awarded as scholarships/grants, 19% as loans/jobs. Need-based aid available for part-time students. Work study available nights, weekends and for part-time students. **Non-need-based:** Scholarships awarded for academics, athletics.

Application procedures. Admission: No deadline. No application fee. Application may be submitted online. Admission notification on a rolling basis. **Financial aid:** Priority date 4/15; no closing date. FAFSA, institutional form required. Applicants notified on a rolling basis starting 4/1; must reply within 2 week(s) of notification.

Academics. Special study options: Accelerated study, cooperative education, cross-registration, distance learning, dual enrollment of high school students, ESL, exchange student, honors, independent study, internships, liberal arts/career combination, teacher certification program, weekend college. License preparation in paramedic, radiology, real estate. **Credit/placement by examination:** AP, CLEP, institutional tests. 30 credit hours maximum toward associate degree. **Support services:** GED preparation, learning center, reduced course load, remedial instruction, study skills assistance, tutoring.

Honors college/program. ACT of 25 and/or minimum high school GPA of 3.35; about 25 admitted each year.

Majors. Agriculture: Greenhouse operations, landscaping, ornamental horticulture. **Architecture:** Interior. **Biology:** General. **Business:** Accounting, administrative services, business admin, hospitality admin, human resources, international, management information systems, marketing, office technology. **Communications:** Journalism. **Communications technology:** Graphic/printing. **Computer sciences:** General, applications programming, computer graphics, computer science, data processing. **Construction:** Carpentry, maintenance. **Education:** General, early childhood. **Engineering:** General. **Engineering technology:** Construction, drafting. **English:** Speech/rhetoric. **Family/consumer sciences:** Child care. **Foreign languages:** General, French, Italian, Spanish. **Health:** Medical radiologic technology/radiation therapy, nuclear medical technology, nursing (RN), ophthalmic lab technology, respiratory therapy technology, sonography, substance abuse counseling. **History:** General. **Interdisciplinary:** Biological/physical sciences. **Legal studies:** Court reporting. **Liberal arts:** Arts/sciences. **Math:** General. **Mechanic/repair:** Automotive, electronics/electrical, heating/ac/refrig, industrial. **Personal/culinary services:** Culinary arts. **Philosophy/religion:** Philosophy. **Physical sciences:** Chemistry, geology, physics. **Protective services:** Firefighting, police science. **Psychology:** General. **Public administration:** Community org/advocacy. **Social sciences:** General, anthropology, economics, geography, political science. **Transportation:** General. **Visual/performing arts:** Art, commercial/advertising art, dramatic, interior design.

Computing on campus. 500 workstations in library, computer center. Online course registration, online library, helpline available.

Student life. Freshman orientation: Available. Sessions held throughout summer months and in December. **Policies:** Freshmen permitted cars on campus. **Activities:** Jazz band, choral groups, drama, music ensembles, musical theater, radio station, student government, student newspaper, 30 clubs and organizations available.

Athletics. NJCAA. **Intercollegiate:** Baseball M, basketball, diving W, soccer, softball W, volleyball W, wrestling M. **Team name:** Trojans.

Student services. Career counseling, financial aid counseling, health services, minority student services, on-campus daycare, personal counseling, placement for graduates, veterans' counselor. **Physically disabled:** Services for visually, speech, hearing impaired. **Transfer:** Special adviser, orientation for new students. Transfer center, transfer adviser, college fairs on campus for students transferring to 4-year colleges.

Contact. E-mail: triton@triton.edu
Phone: (708) 456-0300 ext. 3130 Fax: (708) 583-3162
Mary-Rita Moore, Dean, Enrollment Services, Triton College, 2000 North Fifth Avenue, River Grove, IL 60171

Waubonsee Community College

Sugar Grove, Illinois
www.waubonsee.edu **CB code: 1938**

- Public 2-year community college
- Commuter campus in small town

General. Founded in 1966. Regionally accredited. **Enrollment:** 6,014 degree-seeking undergraduates; 2,820 non-degree-seeking students. **Degrees:** 458 associate awarded. **ROTC:** Army. **Location:** 9 miles from Aurora. **Calendar:** 4-4-1 semester system. Extensive summer session. **Full-time faculty:** 85 total; 13% have terminal degrees, 16% minority, 52% women. **Part-time faculty:** 850 total; 8% have terminal degrees, 23% minority, 58% women. **Special facilities:** Observatory, nature trail.

Student profile. Among degree-seeking undergraduates, 57% enrolled in a transfer program, 43% enrolled in a vocational program, 11% already have a bachelor's degree or higher, 916 enrolled as first-time, first-year students, 244 transferred in from other institutions.

Part-time:	58%	**Asian American:**	2%
Women:	60%	**Hispanic American:**	17%
African American:	7%	**25 or older:**	49%

Transfer out. 65% of students enrolled in the transfer program go on to 4-year colleges. **Colleges most students transferred to 2005:** Northern Illinois University, Illinois State University, Aurora University-Illinois, University of Illinois at Urbana-Champaign, University of Illinois at Chicago.

Basis for selection. Open admission, but selective for some programs. Admission to limited enrollment programs based on specific assessment testing and/or successful completion of prerequisite coursework. **Adult students:** Entrance exam policies same as for first-time freshmen.

High school preparation. College-preparatory program recommended. 15 units recommended. Recommended units include English 4, mathematics 3, social studies 3, science 3 and academic electives 2.

2006-2007 Annual costs. Tuition/fees (projected): $1,920; $6,360 out-of-district; $7,170 out-of-state. Per-credit charge: $62 in-district; $210 out-of-district; $237 out-of-state. Books/supplies: $1,188. Personal expenses: $1,099.

2004-2005 Financial aid. Need-based: 81% of total undergraduate aid awarded as scholarships/grants, 19% as loans/jobs. Need-based aid available for part-time students. Work study available nights and for part-time students. **Non-need-based:** Scholarships awarded for academics, art, athletics, leadership, minority status, music/drama.

Application procedures. Admission: No deadline. No application fee. Application must be submitted on paper. Admission notification on a rolling basis. **Financial aid:** Closing date 12/2. FAFSA, institutional form required. Applicants notified on a rolling basis starting 5/1.

Academics. Special study options: Accelerated study, distance learning, dual enrollment of high school students, ESL, honors, independent study, internships, liberal arts/career combination, study abroad, weekend college. License preparation in nursing, real estate. **Credit/placement by examination:** AP, CLEP, institutional tests. 30 credit hours maximum toward associate degree. Student must be enrolled before scores can be recorded on transcript. A recording fee may apply. **Support services:** GED preparation and test center, learning center, remedial instruction, study skills assistance, tutoring, writing center.

Majors. Business: Accounting technology, administrative services, banking/financial services, business admin, construction management, executive assistant, logistics, office technology, operations, retailing, small business admin. **Communications:** General. **Construction:** Electrician. **Education:** Art, mathematics, multi-level teacher, music, teacher assistance. **Engineering:** General. **Engineering technology:** Electrical, quality control, robotics. **Foreign languages:** Sign language interpretation, translation. **Health:** Massage therapy, nursing (RN). **Interdisciplinary:** Biological/physical sciences. **Liberal arts:** Arts/sciences. **Mechanic/repair:** Auto body, automotive, heating/ac/refrig, industrial. **Production:** Machine shop technology, machine tool. **Protective services:** Fire safety technology, police science. **Public administration:** Social work. **Transportation:** Airline/commercial pilot. **Visual/performing arts:** Design, graphic design, studio arts.

Most popular majors. Business/marketing 6%, health sciences 8%, interdisciplinary studies 40%, liberal arts 34%.

Computing on campus. 160 workstations in computer center, student center. Online course registration, helpline available.

Student life. Freshman orientation: Available. Optional 1-day. **Policies:** Freshmen permitted cars on campus. **Activities:** Bands, choral groups, dance, drama, literary magazine, music ensembles, musical theater, opera, student government, student newspaper, Latino Unidos, Christian fellowship, Amnesty International, African cultural alliance, model Illinois government, Students for a Diverse Society.

Athletics. NJCAA. **Intercollegiate:** Baseball M, basketball, cross-country, golf M, soccer, softball W, tennis, volleyball W, wrestling M. **Intramural:** Basketball, bowling, golf, table tennis. **Team name:** Chiefs.

Student services. Career counseling, services for economically disadvantaged, student employment services, financial aid counseling, minority student services, on-campus daycare, personal counseling, placement for graduates, veterans' counselor. **Physically disabled:** Services for visually, speech, hearing impaired. **Transfer:** Special adviser for new students. Transfer adviser, college fairs on campus for students transferring to 4-year colleges.

Contact. E-mail: recruitment@waubonsee.edu
Phone: (630) 466-7900 ext. 2370 Fax: (630) 466-4964
Faith Marston, Recruitment and Retention Manager, Waubonsee Community College, Route 47 at Waubonsee Drive, Sugar Grove, IL 60554-9454

William Rainey Harper College

Palatine, Illinois
www.harpercollege.edu **CB code: 1932**

- Public 2-year community college
- Commuter campus in small city

General. Founded in 1965. Regionally accredited. Program for hearing-impaired offered. Bachelor completion program with Indiana University. **Enrollment:** 13,421 degree-seeking undergraduates; 1,605 non-degree-seeking students. **Degrees:** 1,052 associate awarded. **Location:** 30 miles from Chicago. **Calendar:** Semester, limited summer session. **Full-time faculty:** 195 total; 70% have terminal degrees, 9% minority, 58% women. **Part-time faculty:** 635 total; 8% minority, 53% women. **Class size:** 57% < 20, 41% 20-39, less than 1% 40-49, less than 1% 50-99, less than 1% >100. **Special facilities:** Observatory.

Student profile. Among degree-seeking undergraduates, 51% enrolled in a transfer program, 49% enrolled in a vocational program, 8% already have a bachelor's degree or higher, 2,494 enrolled as first-time, first-year students.

Part-time:	55%	**Asian American:**	12%
Out-of-state:	1%	**Hispanic American:**	9%
Women:	57%	**International:**	1%
African American:	4%	**25 or older:**	39%

Transfer out. Colleges most students transferred to 2005: Northern Illinois University, Illinois State University, Roosevelt University, University of Illinois, University of Illinois-Chicago.

Basis for selection. Open admission, but selective for some programs. Selective admission to cardiac technology, dental hygiene, emergency medical technician, certified nursing assistant, electrocardiograph technology, emergency medical service paramedic, and diagnostic medical sonography. Pre-nursing examinations for nursing applicants. Critical thinking test for legal technology applicants. Assessment Test Battery for full-time students and for placement in English and mathematics for part-time students.

High school preparation. College-preparatory program recommended. 17 units recommended. Recommended units include English 4, mathematics 4, social studies 2 and science 2.

2006-2007 Annual costs. Tuition/fees (projected): $2,868; $9,048 out-of-district; $11,180 out-of-state. Per-credit charge: $77 in-district; $284 out-of-district; $354 out-of-state. In-district tuition rates available to employees of in-district companies who reside outside college district. Rates based on 30 credit hours per academic year. Full-time is considered to be 12 credit hours per semester. Books/supplies: $800. Personal expenses: $2,250.

2004-2005 Financial aid. Need-based: 66% of total undergraduate aid awarded as scholarships/grants, 34% as loans/jobs. Need-based aid available for part-time students. Work study available nights and weekends. **Non-need-based:** Scholarships awarded for academics, art, leadership, minority status, music/drama, state residency.

Application procedures. Admission: No deadline. $25 fee, may be waived for applicants with need. Application may be submitted online. Admission notification on a rolling basis. Priority given to applications to nursing program received by December 1. Priority given to applications received by February 1 for all other limited-enrollment programs. **Financial aid:** Priority date 5/1; no closing date. FAFSA, institutional form required. Applicants notified on a rolling basis starting 3/1; must reply within 2 week(s) of notification.

Academics. Cooperative career program with in-district high schools. Students begin specialized training in high school and continue in colleges. Team-taught interdisciplinary courses and courseloads offered each semester. **Special study options:** Accelerated study, cooperative education, distance learning, dual enrollment of high school students, ESL, honors, independent study, internships, study abroad, weekend college. License preparation in dental hygiene, nursing, paramedic, radiology, real estate. **Credit/placement by examination:** AP, CLEP, institutional tests. 30 credit hours maximum toward associate degree. Maximum of 50% total hours in any degree program may be earned through credit by examination. **Support services:** GED preparation and test center, learning center, reduced course load, remedial instruction, study skills assistance, tutoring, writing center.

Majors. Agriculture: Horticultural science, horticulture, turf management. **Business:** General, accounting, administrative services, banking/financial services, entrepreneurial studies, executive assistant, fashion, finance, hospitality admin, hospitality/recreation, human resources, insurance, international, logistics, management information systems, marketing, office management, operations, real estate, sales/distribution. **Communications:** Journalism. **Computer sciences:** General, applications programming, computer science, data processing, information systems, programming, systems analysis, web page design. **Education:** General, early childhood, teacher assistance. **Engineering:** General. **Engineering technology:** Architectural, electrical, manufacturing. **Family/consumer sciences:** Child care, food/nutrition, home furnishings, institutional food production. **Foreign languages:** Sign language interpretation. **Health:** Cardiovascular technology, dental hygiene, EMT paramedic, medical assistant, medical secretary, nursing (RN). **Legal studies:** Legal secretary, paralegal. **Liberal arts:** Arts/sciences. **Math:** General. **Mechanic/repair:** Electronics/electrical, heating/ac/refrig. **Parks/recreation:** Exercise sciences, facilities management. **Personal/culinary services:** Culinary arts, restaurant/catering. **Philosophy/religion:** Philosophy. **Physical sciences:** General. **Protective services:** Firefighting, police science. **Psychology:** General. **Social sciences:** General. **Visual/performing arts:** General, art, fashion design, interior design, studio arts.

Most popular majors. Health sciences 15%, liberal arts 60%, physical sciences 9%.

Computing on campus. 206 workstations in library, computer center, student center. Online course registration, online library, wireless network available.

Student life. Freshman orientation: Mandatory. Preregistration for classes offered. Two-day program includes tour, assessment tests, academic advising, registration. Orientation is optional but encouraged for part-time students. **Policies:** Freshmen permitted cars on campus. **Activities:** Bands, choral groups, dance, drama, literary magazine, music ensembles, musical theater, radio station, student government, student newspaper, international student club, religious organizations, service organizations, professional organizations, student ambassadors.

Athletics. NJCAA. **Intercollegiate:** Baseball M, basketball, cross-country, football (tackle) M, soccer, softball W, track and field, volleyball W, wrestling M. **Intramural:** Baseball M, basketball M, football (non-tackle) M, racquetball, skiing, softball, table tennis, tennis, volleyball. **Team name:** Hawks.

Student services. Adult student services, career counseling, services for economically disadvantaged, student employment services, financial aid counseling, health services, legal services, minority student services, on-campus daycare, personal counseling, veterans' counselor, women's services. **Physically disabled:** Services for visually, speech, hearing impaired. **Transfer:** Special adviser, orientation for new students. Transfer adviser, college fairs on campus for students transferring to 4-year colleges.

Contact. E-mail: admissions@harpercollege.edu
Phone: (847) 925-6707 Fax: (847) 925-6044
Michael Held, Director of Admissions Outreach, William Rainey Harper College, 1200 West Algonquin Road, Palatine, IL 60067-7398

Indiana

Ancilla College

Donaldson, Indiana
www.ancilla.edu **CB code: 1015**

- Private 2-year community and liberal arts college affiliated with Roman Catholic Church
- Commuter campus in rural community

General. Founded in 1937. Regionally accredited. **Enrollment:** 600 degree-seeking undergraduates. **Degrees:** 52 associate awarded. **Location:** 30 miles from South Bend, 7 miles from Plymouth. **Calendar:** Semester, limited summer session. **Full-time faculty:** 20 total. **Part-time faculty:** 40 total. **Class size:** 67% < 20, 33% 20-39.

Student profile.

Out-of-state:	1%	**25 or older:**	40%

Transfer out. Colleges most students transferred to 2005: Indiana University-South Bend, Purdue North Central, Bethel College.

Basis for selection. Open admission, but selective for some programs. Special requirements for Nursing program. **Adult students:** No admissions test (SAT or ACT) needed for students out of high school more than 3 years. **Homeschooled:** Official instructor-notarized homeschooled transcript required with full description of courses taken and grades received, registration number of home school. ACT or SAT required for students who have graduated within past 3 years.

High school preparation. 21 units recommended. Recommended units include English 4, mathematics 4, social studies 2, history 3, science 3 (laboratory 3) and foreign language 2.

2005-2006 Annual costs. Tuition/fees: $9,830. Per-credit charge: $320. Books/supplies: $812. Personal expenses: $612.

Financial aid. Need-based: Need-based aid available for part-time students. Work study available for part-time students. **Non-need-based:** Scholarships awarded for academics, athletics, job skills, leadership.

Application procedures. Admission: No deadline. $25 fee, may be waived for applicants with need. Application may be submitted online. Admission notification on a rolling basis. **Financial aid:** Closing date 3/1. FAFSA, institutional form required. Applicants notified on a rolling basis starting 3/1; must reply within 2 week(s) of notification.

Academics. Special study options: Accelerated study, cooperative education, double major, dual enrollment of high school students, independent study, liberal arts/career combination. License preparation in real estate. **Credit/placement by examination:** CLEP, institutional tests. 12 credit hours maximum toward associate degree. **Support services:** Learning center, reduced course load, remedial instruction, study skills assistance, tutoring.

Majors. Biology: General. **Business:** Business admin. **Communications:** Media studies. **Computer sciences:** General. **Education:** Early childhood, elementary, secondary. **English:** English lit. **Health:** Nursing (RN), prenursing. **History:** General. **Interdisciplinary:** Behavioral sciences. **Liberal arts:** Arts/sciences. **Math:** General. **Physical sciences:** Chemistry. **Protective services:** Criminal justice. **Visual/performing arts:** Graphic design, studio arts.

Computing on campus. 53 workstations in library, computer center. Online library available.

Student life. Freshman orientation: Mandatory. Preregistration for classes offered. **Policies:** Freshmen permitted cars on campus. **Activities:** Literary magazine, student government, student newspaper, Student Ambassadors, Phi Theta Kappa.

Athletics. NJCAA. **Intercollegiate:** Baseball M, basketball, cheerleading M, golf M, softball W, volleyball W. **Team name:** Chargers.

Student services. Campus ministries, career counseling, student employment services, financial aid counseling, personal counseling. **Transfer:** Special adviser, orientation for new students. Transfer adviser, college fairs on campus for students transferring to 4-year colleges.

Contact. E-mail: admissions@ancilla.edu
Phone: (574) 936-8898 ext. 330 Fax: (574) 935-1773
Jim Bastis, Director of Enrollment Management, Ancilla College, 9001 Union Road, Donaldson, IN 46513

Aviation Institute of Maintenance: Indianapolis

Indianapolis, Indiana
www.aviationmaintenance.edu/aviation-indianapolis.asp
CB code: 3192

- For-profit 2-year technical college
- Commuter campus in very large city

General. Accredited by ACCSCT. **Location:** 10 miles from downtown. **Calendar:** Continuous.

Annual costs/financial aid. Tuition for 18-month associate program $31,050. Need-based financial aid available for full-time students.

Contact. Phone: (317) 243-4519
Managing Director, 7251 West McCarty Street, Indianapolis, IN 46241-1445

Brown Mackie College: Fort Wayne

Fort Wayne, Indiana
www.brownmackie.com **CB code: 3379**

- For-profit 2-year branch campus and business college
- Large city

General. Accredited by ACICS. **Enrollment:** 670 degree-seeking undergraduates. **Degrees:** 181 associate awarded. **Calendar:** Quarter. **Full-time faculty:** 25 total. **Part-time faculty:** 40 total.

Basis for selection. Open admission, but selective for some programs.

2005-2006 Annual costs. Nursing program tuition $300 per credit hour. Occupational therapy courses $300 per credit hour, with general education courses for Occupational therapy $179 per credit hour. $10 per credit hour fee for all courses. Books/supplies: $1,100.

Application procedures. Admission: No deadline. $20 fee.

Academics. Credit/placement by examination: CLEP.

Majors. Business: Accounting, business admin. **Computer sciences:** General. **Health:** Medical assistant, occupational therapy assistant. **Legal studies:** Paralegal.

Contact. E-mail: btaylor@brownmackie.edu
Phone: (260) 484-4400 Fax: (260) 484-2678
Ken Taboh, Director of Admissions, Brown Mackie College: Fort Wayne, 3000 Coliseum Boulevard, Suite 100, Fort Wayne, IN 46805

Brown Mackie College: Merrillville

Merrillville, Indiana
www.brownmackie.edu **CB code: 7115**

- For-profit 2-year business college
- Small city

General. Accredited by ACICS. **Calendar:** Continuous.

Annual costs/financial aid. Books/supplies: $720. Personal expenses: $845.

Contact. Phone: (219) 769-3321
Director of Admissions, 1000 East 80th Place, Suite 101N, Merrillville, IN 46410

Brown Mackie College: Michigan City

Michigan City, Indiana
www.cbcaec.com **CB code: 3345**

- For-profit 2-year branch campus college
- Large town
- Interview required

General. Accredited by ACICS. **Enrollment:** 300 degree-seeking undergraduates. **Degrees:** 135 associate awarded. **Calendar:** Continuous. **Full-time faculty:** 5 total. **Part-time faculty:** 15 total.

Transfer out. Colleges most students transferred to 2005: Tri-State University.

Basis for selection. Open admission. **Homeschooled:** GED or equivalent required.

2005-2006 Annual costs. Tuition/fees: $6,804. Per-credit charge: $179. Books/supplies: $630. Personal expenses: $2,664.

Application procedures. Admission: No deadline. $20 fee.

Academics. Credit/placement by examination: CLEP.

Majors. Business: Accounting, business admin. **Computer sciences:** General. **Health:** Medical secretary. **Legal studies:** Paralegal.

Contact. Phone: (219) 877-3100
Sheryl Elston, Director of Admissions, Brown Mackie College: Michigan City, 325 East US Highway 20, Michigan City, IN 46360-7362

Brown Mackie College: South Bend

South Bend, Indiana
www.brownmackie.edu **CB code: 3140**

- For-profit 2-year community and technical college
- Commuter campus in small city

General. Founded in 1882. Accredited by ACICS. **Location:** 90 miles from Chicago, 150 miles from Indianapolis. **Calendar:** Quarter.

Annual costs/financial aid. Books/supplies: $1,200. Need-based financial aid available to full-time and part-time students.

Contact. Phone: (574) 237-0774
Campus President, 1030 East Jefferson Boulevard, South Bend, IN 46617

Indiana Business College

Indianapolis, Indiana
www.ibcschools.edu **CB code: 2317**

- For-profit 2-year business and health science college
- Commuter campus in very large city

General. Founded in 1902. Accredited by ACICS. **Enrollment:** 670 degree-seeking undergraduates. **Degrees:** 200 associate awarded. **Calendar:** Quarter, extensive summer session.

Basis for selection. Interview and Wonderlic evaluation are main admission criteria.

Financial aid. Need-based: Need-based aid available for part-time students. **Additional information:** Work-study programs are available.

Application procedures. Admission: No deadline. $50 fee. Admission notification on a rolling basis. **Financial aid:** FAFSA required. Applicants notified on a rolling basis.

Academics. Special study options: Cooperative education, distance learning, dual enrollment of high school students, internships. **Credit/placement by examination:** CLEP, institutional tests. Free test-out program is available to high school seniors. Test-outs are available to all other students for a $30 fee per exam.

Majors. Business: Accounting, administrative services, business admin, fashion. **Computer sciences:** Information technology, networking, security. **Health:** Medical assistant. **Protective services:** Law enforcement admin.

Computing on campus. Repair service available.

Student life. Policies: Freshmen permitted cars on campus. **Activities:** Student government.

Athletics. Intramural: Basketball, softball.

Student services. Career counseling, student employment services, financial aid counseling, placement for graduates.

Contact. Phone: (317) 264-5656 Toll-free number: (800) 422-4723
Fax: (317) 264-5650
Jim Schuld, Director of Admissions, Indiana Business College, 550 East Washington Street, Indianapolis, IN 46204

Indiana Business College: Anderson

Anderson, Indiana
www.ibcschools.edu **CB code: 3364**

- For-profit 2-year business and health science college
- Commuter campus in small city
- Interview required

General. Accredited by ACICS. **Enrollment:** 235 degree-seeking undergraduates. **Degrees:** 60 associate awarded. **Location:** 45 miles from Indianapolis. **Calendar:** Quarter, extensive summer session.

Basis for selection. Interview and Wonderlic evaluation are main admission criteria.

Financial aid. Need-based: Need-based aid available for part-time students. **Additional information:** Work-study programs available.

Application procedures. Admission: No deadline. $50 fee. Admission notification on a rolling basis. **Financial aid:** FAFSA required. Applicants notified on a rolling basis.

Academics. Special study options: Cooperative education, distance learning, dual enrollment of high school students, internships. **Credit/placement by examination:** CLEP, institutional tests. Free test-out program is available to high school seniors. Test-outs are available to all other students for a $30 fee.

Majors. Business: Accounting, administrative services, business admin, nonprofit/public. **Health:** Medical assistant, medical claims examiner, medical records technology.

Student life. Activities: Student government.

Student services. Career counseling, student employment services, financial aid counseling, placement for graduates.

Contact. Phone: (765) 644-7514 Toll-free number: (800) 422-4723
Fax: (765) 644-5724
Troy Robertson, Associate Director of Admissions, Indiana Business College: Anderson, 140 East 53rd Street, Anderson, IN 46013

Indiana Business College: Columbus

Columbus, Indiana
www.ibcschools.edu **CB code: 3349**

- For-profit 2-year business and health science college
- Commuter campus in small city
- Interview required

General. Accredited by ACICS. **Enrollment:** 273 degree-seeking undergraduates. **Degrees:** 85 associate awarded. **Location:** 50 miles from Indianapolis. **Calendar:** Quarter, extensive summer session.

Basis for selection. Interview and Wonderlic evaluation are main admission criteria.

Financial aid. Need-based: Need-based aid available for part-time students. **Additional information:** Work-study programs are available.

Application procedures. Admission: No deadline. $50 fee. Admission notification on a rolling basis. **Financial aid:** FAFSA required. Applicants notified on a rolling basis.

Academics. Special study options: Cooperative education, distance learning, dual enrollment of high school students, internships. **Credit/placement by examination:** CLEP, institutional tests. Free test-out program is available to high school seniors. Test-outs are available to other students for a $30 fee.

Majors. Business: Accounting, administrative services, business admin. **Computer sciences:** Information technology. **Health:** Medical assistant, medical claims examiner.

Student life. Policies: Freshmen permitted cars on campus.

Student services. Career counseling, student employment services, financial aid counseling, placement for graduates.

Contact. Phone: (812) 379-9000 Toll-free number: (800) 422-4723
Fax: (812) 375-0414
Gina Pate, Associate Director of Admissions, Indiana Business College: Columbus, 2222 Poshard Drive, Columbus, IN 47203

Indiana Business College: Evansville

Evansville, Indiana
www.ibcschools.edu **CB code: 3346**

- For-profit 2-year business and health science college
- Commuter campus in small city
- Interview required

General. Accredited by ACICS. **Enrollment:** 295 degree-seeking undergraduates. **Degrees:** 54 associate awarded. **Calendar:** Quarter, extensive summer session.

Basis for selection. Interview and Wonderlic evaluation are main admission criteria. **Adult students:** Entrance exam policies same as for first-time freshmen.

Financial aid. Need-based: Need-based aid available for part-time students. **Additional information:** Work-study programs are available.

Application procedures. Admission: No deadline. $50 fee. Admission notification on a rolling basis. **Financial aid:** FAFSA required. Applicants notified on a rolling basis.

Academics. Special study options: Cooperative education, distance learning, dual enrollment of high school students, internships. **Credit/placement by examination:** CLEP, institutional tests. A free test-out program is available to high school seniors. Test-outs are available to all other students for a $30 fee.

Majors. Business: Accounting, administrative services, business admin. **Computer sciences:** Information technology. **Health:** Medical assistant, medical claims examiner, medical records technology.

Student services. Career counseling, student employment services, financial aid counseling, placement for graduates.

Contact. Phone: (812) 476-6000 Toll-free number: (800) 422-4723
Fax: (812) 471-8576
Starlet Gupton, Associate Director of Admissions, Indiana Business College: Evansville, 4601 Theater Drive, Evansville, IN 47715

Indiana Business College: Fort Wayne

Fort Wayne, Indiana
www.ibcschools.edu **CB code: 3867**

- For-profit 2-year business and health science college
- Commuter campus in large city
- Interview required

General. Accredited by ACICS. **Enrollment:** 384 degree-seeking undergraduates. **Degrees:** 62 associate awarded. **Calendar:** Quarter, extensive summer session.

Basis for selection. Interview and Wonderlic evaluation are main admission criteria.

Financial aid. Need-based: Need-based aid available for part-time students. **Additional information:** Work-Study programs are available.

Application procedures. Admission: No deadline. $50 fee. Admission notification on a rolling basis. **Financial aid:** FAFSA required.

Academics. Special study options: Cooperative education, distance learning, dual enrollment of high school students, internships. **Credit/placement by examination:** CLEP, institutional tests. Free test-out program is vailable to high school seniors. Test-outs are available to all other students for a $30 fee.

Majors. Business: Accounting, administrative services, business admin. **Health:** Medical assistant, medical claims examiner, surgical technology.

Student life. Policies: Freshmen permitted cars on campus.

Student services. Career counseling, student employment services, financial aid counseling, placement for graduates.

Contact. Phone: (260) 471-7667 Toll-free number: (800) 422-4723
Fax: (260) 471-6918
Janet Hein-Herman, Executive Director, Indiana Business College: Fort Wayne, 6413 North Clinton St., Fort Wayne, IN 46825

Indiana Business College: Lafayette

Lafayette, Indiana
www.ibcschools.edu **CB code: 3353**

- For-profit 2-year business and health science college
- Commuter campus in small city
- Interview required

General. Accredited by ACICS. **Enrollment:** 215 degree-seeking undergraduates. **Degrees:** 66 associate awarded. **Location:** 60 miles from Indianapolis. **Calendar:** Quarter, extensive summer session.

Basis for selection. Interview and Wonderlic evaluation are main admission criteria.

Financial aid. Need-based: Need-based aid available for part-time students. **Additional information:** Work-Study Programs are available.

Application procedures. Admission: No deadline. $50 fee. Admission notification on a rolling basis. **Financial aid:** FAFSA required. Applicants notified on a rolling basis.

Academics. Special study options: Cooperative education, distance learning, dual enrollment of high school students, internships. **Credit/placement by examination:** CLEP, institutional tests. Free test-out program is available to high school seniors. Test-outs are available to all other students for a $30 fee.

Majors. Business: Accounting, administrative services, business admin. **Computer sciences:** Information technology. **Health:** Medical assistant, medical claims examiner, medical records technology.

Student life. Policies: Freshmen permitted cars on campus.

Student services. Career counseling, student employment services, financial aid counseling, placement for graduates.

Contact. Phone: (765) 447-9550 Toll-free number: (800) 422-4723
Fax: (765) 447-0868
Stacy Golleher, Interim Associate Director of Admissions, Indiana Business College: Lafayette, 4705 Meijer Court, Lafayette, IN 47905

Indiana Business College: Marion

Marion, Indiana
www.ibcschools.edu **CB code: 3360**

- For-profit 2-year business and health science college
- Commuter campus in large town
- Interview required

General. Accredited by ACICS. **Enrollment:** 120 degree-seeking undergraduates. **Degrees:** 45 associate awarded. **Location:** 70 miles from Indianapolis, 40 miles from Fort Wayne. **Calendar:** Quarter, extensive summer session.

Basis for selection. Interview and Wonderlic evaluation are main admission criteria.

Financial aid. Need-based: Need-based aid available for part-time students. **Additional information:** Work-Study Programs are available.

Application procedures. Admission: No deadline. $50 fee. Admission notification on a rolling basis. **Financial aid:** FAFSA required. Applicants notified on a rolling basis.

Academics. Special study options: Cooperative education, distance learning, dual enrollment of high school students, internships. **Credit/placement by examination:** CLEP, institutional tests. Free test-out program available to high school seniors. Test-outs are available to all other students for a $30 fee per exam.

Majors. Business: Accounting, administrative services, business admin. **Health:** Medical assistant, medical records technology.

Student life. **Policies:** Freshmen permitted cars on campus.

Student services. Career counseling, student employment services, financial aid counseling, placement for graduates.

Contact. Phone: (765) 662-7497 Toll-free number: (800) 422-4723
Fax: (765) 651-9421
Richard Herman, Executive Director, Indiana Business College: Marion, 830 North Miller Avenue, Marion, IN 46952

Indiana Business College: Medical

Indianapolis, Indiana
www.ibcschools.edu **CB code: 3370**

- For-profit 2-year health science college
- Commuter campus in very large city
- Interview required

General. Accredited by ACICS. **Enrollment:** 584 degree-seeking undergraduates. **Degrees:** 190 associate awarded. **Calendar:** Quarter, extensive summer session.

Basis for selection. Interview and Wonderlic evaluation are main admission criteria. **Adult students:** Wonderlic Scholastic Level Exam.

Financial aid. Need-based: Need-based aid available for part-time students. **Additional information:** Work-study programs are available.

Application procedures. Admission: No deadline. $50 fee. Admission notification on a rolling basis. **Financial aid:** FAFSA required. Applicants notified on a rolling basis.

Academics. Special study options: Cooperative education, distance learning, dual enrollment of high school students, internships. **Credit/placement by examination:** CLEP, institutional tests. Free test-out program available to high school seniors. Test-outs are available to all other students for a $30 fee per exam. **Support services:** Reduced course load, study skills assistance, tutoring.

Majors. Health: Clinical lab assistant, massage therapy, medical assistant, medical claims examiner, medical records technology, surgical technology.

Student life. Freshman orientation: Available. One-hour orientation held quarterly on first day of classes. **Policies:** Freshmen permitted cars on campus.

Student services. Career counseling, student employment services, financial aid counseling, placement for graduates.

Contact. Phone: (317) 375-8000 Toll-free number: (800) 422-4723
Fax: (317) 351-1871
Carlos Irizarry, Director of Admissions, Indiana Business College: Medical, 8150 Brookville Road, Indianapolis, IN 46239

Indiana Business College: Muncie

Muncie, Indiana
www.ibcschools.edu **CB code: 3347**

- For-profit 2-year business and health science college
- Commuter campus in small city
- Interview required

General. Accredited by ACICS. **Enrollment:** 310 degree-seeking undergraduates. **Degrees:** 80 associate awarded. **Calendar:** Quarter, extensive summer session.

Basis for selection. Interview and Wonderlic evaluation are main admission criteria.

Financial aid. Need-based: Need-based aid available for part-time students. **Additional information:** Work-Study Programs are available.

Application procedures. Admission: No deadline. $50 fee. Admission notification on a rolling basis. **Financial aid:** FAFSA required. Applicants notified on a rolling basis.

Academics. Special study options: Cooperative education, distance learning, dual enrollment of high school students, internships. **Credit/placement by examination:** CLEP, institutional tests. Free test-out program available to high school seniors. Test-outs are available to all other students for a $30 fee per exam. **Support services:** Study skills assistance, tutoring.

Majors. Business: Accounting, administrative services, business admin, nonprofit/public. **Computer sciences:** Information technology, networking. **Health:** Medical assistant, medical records technology. **Protective services:** Law enforcement admin.

Student life. Freshman orientation: Mandatory. **Policies:** Freshmen permitted cars on campus.

Student services. Career counseling, student employment services, financial aid counseling, placement for graduates.

Contact. Phone: (765) 288-8681 Toll-free number: (800) 422-4723
Fax: (765) 288-8797
Nikki Adams, Associate Director of Admissions, Indiana Business College: Muncie, 411 West Riggin Road, Muncie, IN 47303

Indiana Business College: Terre Haute

Terre Haute, Indiana
www.ibcschools.edu **CB code: 3348**

- For-profit 2-year business and health science college
- Commuter campus in small city
- Interview required

General. Accredited by ACICS. **Enrollment:** 220 degree-seeking undergraduates. **Degrees:** 69 associate awarded. **Calendar:** Quarter, extensive summer session.

Basis for selection. Interview and Wonderlic evaluation are main admission criteria.

Financial aid. Need-based: Need-based aid available for part-time students. **Additional information:** Work-study programs are available.

Application procedures. Admission: No deadline. $50 fee. Admission notification on a rolling basis. **Financial aid:** FAFSA required. Applicants notified on a rolling basis.

Academics. Special study options: Cooperative education, distance learning, dual enrollment of high school students, internships. **Credit/placement by examination:** CLEP, institutional tests. Free test-out program available to high school seniors. Test-outs are available to all other students for a fee of $30 per test. **Support services:** Study skills assistance, tutoring.

Majors. Business: Accounting, administrative services, business admin. **Health:** Insurance coding, medical assistant, medical claims examiner.

Student life. Policies: Freshmen permitted cars on campus.

Student services. Career counseling, student employment services, financial aid counseling, placement for graduates.

Contact. Phone: (812) 232-4458 Toll-free number: (800) 422-4723
Fax: (812) 234-2361
Jan Holtz, Associate Director of Admissions, Indiana Business College: Terre Haute, 3175 South Third Place, Terre Haute, IN 47802

International Business College: Indianapolis

Indianapolis, Indiana
www.intlbusinesscollege.com **CB code: 3374**

- For-profit 2-year business college
- Commuter campus in very large city

General. Accredited by ACICS. Branch campus of International Business College. **Enrollment:** 300 degree-seeking undergraduates. **Degrees:** 128 associate awarded. **Calendar:** Continuous. **Full-time faculty:** 10 total. **Part-time faculty:** 3 total.

Basis for selection. Interview and Wonderlic evaluation are main admission criteria.

2005-2006 Annual costs. Room only: $5,400. Books/supplies: $1,400.

Application procedures. Admission: No deadline. $50 fee.

Academics. Credit/placement by examination: CLEP.

Majors. Business: Business admin. **Computer sciences:** General. **Legal studies:** Paralegal.

Contact. Phone: (317) 841-6400
International Business College: Indianapolis, 7205 Shadeland Station, Indianapolis, IN 46256

Ivy Tech Community College: Bloomington

Bloomington, Indiana
www.ivytech.edu **CB code: 1455**

- Public 2-year community college
- Commuter campus in small city

General. **Enrollment:** 3,204 degree-seeking undergraduates; 361 non-degree-seeking students. **Degrees:** 241 associate awarded. **Calendar:** Semester, extensive summer session. **Full-time faculty:** 48 total. **Part-time faculty:** 227 total.

Student profile. Among degree-seeking undergraduates, 62% enrolled in a transfer program, 38% enrolled in a vocational program, 618 enrolled as first-time, first-year students, 278 transferred in from other institutions.

Part-time:	51%	**Asian American:**	1%
Women:	62%	**Hispanic American:**	1%
African American:	3%	**25 or older:**	47%

Transfer out. **Colleges most students transferred to 2005:** Indiana University - Bloomington.

Basis for selection. Open admission, but selective for some programs. Special requirements for human services and health technology programs based on test scores and prior academic work. **Adult students:** SAT/ACT scores not required.

2005-2006 Annual costs. Tuition/fees: $2,590; $5,178 out-of-state. Per-credit charge: $84 in-state; $170 out-of-state. Books/supplies: $956. Personal expenses: $2,151.

2004-2005 Financial aid. **Need-based:** 50% of total undergraduate aid awarded as scholarships/grants, 50% as loans/jobs. Need-based aid available for part-time students. Work study available nights and for part-time students.

Application procedures. **Admission:** No deadline. No application fee. Admission notification on a rolling basis. Application closing date for international students at least 60 days prior to start of semester. **Financial aid:** Priority date 3/1; no closing date. FAFSA required. Applicants notified on a rolling basis starting 7/1.

Academics. **Special study options:** Combined bachelor's/graduate degree, distance learning, dual enrollment of high school students, internships, liberal arts/career combination, teacher certification program, weekend college. License preparation in nursing. **Credit/placement by examination:** AP, CLEP, institutional tests. 45 credit hours maximum toward associate degree. 15 credits must be earned in residence. **Support services:** Learning center, reduced course load, remedial instruction, tutoring.

Majors. **Business:** General, accounting technology, executive assistant. **Computer sciences:** General. **Construction:** Electrician, maintenance, pipefitting, plumbing. **Engineering technology:** Drafting, electrical, industrial. **Family/consumer sciences:** Child care. **Health:** EMT paramedic, medical radiologic technology/radiation therapy, mental health services, nursing (RN), respiratory therapy technology. **Legal studies:** Paralegal. **Liberal arts:** Arts/sciences, library assistant. **Mechanic/repair:** General, heating/ac/refrig. **Production:** Cabinetmaking/millwright, machine tool, sheet metal, tool and die. **Protective services:** Criminal justice.

Most popular majors. Business/marketing 34%, computer/information sciences 15%, engineering/engineering technologies 10%, health sciences 21%, security/protective services 10%, trade and industry 6%.

Computing on campus. 904 workstations in library, computer center, student center. Online course registration, online library, helpline, repair service, student web hosting available.

Student life. **Freshman orientation:** Mandatory. **Activities:** Student government, Phi Theta Kappa, College Democrats, student leadership academy, Christian Challenge, computer club, cultural awareness.

Student services. Adult student services, career counseling, student employment services, financial aid counseling, minority student services, placement for graduates, veterans' counselor. **Physically disabled:** Services for visually, speech, hearing impaired. **Transfer:** Special adviser for new students. Transfer center, transfer adviser, college fairs on campus for students transferring to 4-year colleges.

Contact. E-mail: nfrederi@ivytech.edu
Phone: (812) 330-6026 Toll-free number: (800) 447-0700 ext. 6350
Fax: (812) 330-6200
Neil Frederick, Assistant Director of Admissions, Ivy Tech Community College: Bloomington, 200 Daniels Way, Bloomington, IN 47404-1511

Ivy Tech Community College: Central Indiana

Indianapolis, Indiana
www.ivytech.edu **CB code: 1311**

- Public 2-year community college
- Commuter campus in very large city

General. Founded in 1966. Regionally accredited. Branch location at Lawrence. **Enrollment:** 10,266 degree-seeking undergraduates; 1,324 non-degree-seeking students. **Degrees:** 735 associate awarded. **Location:** 2 miles from downtown. **Calendar:** Semester, extensive summer session. **Full-time faculty:** 137 total. **Part-time faculty:** 525 total.

Student profile. Among degree-seeking undergraduates, 49% enrolled in a transfer program, 51% enrolled in a vocational program, 1,846 enrolled as first-time, first-year students, 598 transferred in from other institutions.

Part-time:	68%	**Asian American:**	1%
Women:	60%	**Hispanic American:**	2%
African American:	25%	**25 or older:**	53%

Transfer out. **Colleges most students transferred to 2005:** Indiana University-Purdue University Indianapolis, Vincennes University, Indiana University-Bloomington, Purdue University-West Lafayette, Ball State University.

Basis for selection. Open admission, but selective for some programs. Special requirements for human services and health technology programs based on test scores and prior academic work. **Adult students:** SAT/ACT scores not required.

2005-2006 Annual costs. Tuition/fees: $2,590; $5,178 out-of-state. Per-credit charge: $84 in-state; $170 out-of-state. Books/supplies: $956. Personal expenses: $2,151.

2004-2005 Financial aid. **Need-based:** 51% of total undergraduate aid awarded as scholarships/grants, 49% as loans/jobs. Need-based aid available for part-time students. Work study available nights, weekends and for part-time students.

Application procedures. **Admission:** No deadline. No application fee. Admission notification on a rolling basis. Application closing date for undergraduate international students at least 60 days prior to start of semester. **Financial aid:** Priority date 3/1; no closing date. FAFSA required. Applicants notified on a rolling basis starting 7/1.

Academics. **Special study options:** Combined bachelor's/graduate degree, cooperative education, distance learning, dual enrollment of high school students, ESL, internships, liberal arts/career combination, teacher certification program, weekend college. License preparation in nursing, radiology. **Credit/placement by examination:** AP, CLEP, institutional tests. 45 credit hours maximum toward associate degree. 15 credits must be earned in residence. **Support services:** GED preparation and test center, learning center, reduced course load, remedial instruction, tutoring.

Majors. **Biology:** Biotechnology. **Business:** Accounting technology, business admin, executive assistant. **Computer sciences:** General. **Construction:** Carpentry, electrician, maintenance, masonry, painting, pipefitting, plumbing. **Engineering technology:** Electrical, industrial, occupational safety. **Family/consumer sciences:** Child care. **Health:** Medical assistant, medical radiologic technology/radiation therapy, mental health services, nursing (RN), respiratory therapy technology, surgical technology. **Legal studies:** Paralegal. **Liberal arts:** Arts/sciences. **Mechanic/repair:** General, automotive, heating/ac/refrig, industrial, industrial electronics. **Personal/culinary services:** Mortuary science. **Production:** Cabinetmaking/millwright, ironworking, machine shop technology, machine tool, sheet metal, tool and die. **Protective services:** Criminal justice. **Visual/performing arts:** Design.

Most popular majors. Business/marketing 18%, computer/information sciences 11%, engineering/engineering technologies 7%, health sciences 23%, trade and industry 30%.

Computing on campus. 1,135 workstations in library, computer center, student center. Online course registration, online library, helpline, repair service, student web hosting, wireless network available.

Two-Year Colleges

Student life. Freshman orientation: Available. **Activities:** Radio station, student government, Phi Theta Kappa, accounting association, human service club, radiology technology club, student leadership academy, Black Student Union, Veterans Association.

Athletics. Intramural: Basketball, football (non-tackle), soccer M, softball.

Student services. Adult student services, career counseling, student employment services, financial aid counseling, minority student services, placement for graduates, veterans' counselor. **Physically disabled:** Services for visually, speech, hearing impaired. **Transfer:** Special adviser for new students. Transfer center, transfer adviser, college fairs on campus for students transferring to 4-year colleges.

Contact. E-mail: tfunk@ivytech.edu
Phone: (317) 921-4371 Toll-free number: (800) 732-1470
Fax: (317) 917-5919
Tracy Funk, Counselor, Ivy Tech Community College: Central Indiana, 50 West Fall Creek Parkway North Drive, Indianapolis, IN 46208-5752

Ivy Tech Community College: Columbus

Columbus, Indiana
www.ivytech.edu **CB code: 1286**

- Public 2-year community college
- Commuter campus in large town

General. Founded in 1963. Regionally accredited. **Enrollment:** 1,887 degree-seeking undergraduates; 329 non-degree-seeking students. **Degrees:** 131 associate awarded. **Location:** 40 miles from Indianapolis. **Calendar:** Semester, extensive summer session. **Full-time faculty:** 39 total. **Part-time faculty:** 154 total. **Special facilities:** Visual communications gallery.

Student profile. Among degree-seeking undergraduates, 43% enrolled in a transfer program, 57% enrolled in a vocational program, 283 enrolled as first-time, first-year students, 142 transferred in from other institutions.

Part-time:	61%	**Asian American:**	1%
Women:	74%	**Hispanic American:**	1%
African American:	2%	**25 or older:**	54%

Transfer out. Colleges most students transferred to 2005: Indiana University-Purdue University Indianapolis, Indiana University-Bloomington, Purdue University, Vincennes University, Indiana State University.

Basis for selection. Open admission, but selective for some programs. Special requirements for human services and health technology programs based on test scores and prior academic work. **Adult students:** SAT/ACT scores not required.

2005-2006 Annual costs. Tuition/fees: $2,590; $5,178 out-of-state. Per-credit charge: $84 in-state; $170 out-of-state. Books/supplies: $956. Personal expenses: $2,151.

2004-2005 Financial aid. Need-based: 61% of total undergraduate aid awarded as scholarships/grants, 39% as loans/jobs. Need-based aid available for part-time students. Work study available nights and for part-time students.

Application procedures. Admission: No deadline. No application fee. Admission notification on a rolling basis. Application closing date for international students at least 60 days prior to start of semester. **Financial aid:** Priority date 3/1; no closing date. FAFSA required. Applicants notified on a rolling basis starting 7/1.

Academics. Special study options: Combined bachelor's/graduate degree, distance learning, dual enrollment of high school students, internships, liberal arts/career combination, teacher certification program, weekend college. License preparation in dental hygiene, nursing, paramedic, radiology. **Credit/placement by examination:** AP, CLEP, institutional tests. 45 credit hours maximum toward associate degree. 15 credits must be earned in residence. **Support services:** Learning center, reduced course load, remedial instruction, tutoring.

Majors. Business: Accounting technology, business admin, executive assistant. **Computer sciences:** General. **Construction:** Electrician, maintenance, masonry, pipefitting, power transmission. **Engineering technology:** Drafting, electrical, industrial, robotics. **Family/consumer sciences:** Child care. **Health:** EMT paramedic, medical assistant, medical radiologic technology/radiation therapy, mental health services, nursing (RN), surgical technology. **Legal studies:** Paralegal. **Liberal arts:** Arts/sciences, library assistant. **Mechanic/repair:** General, automotive, heating/ac/refrig. **Production:** Cabinetmaking/millwright, machine tool, sheet metal, tool and die. **Visual/performing arts:** Design.

Most popular majors. Business/marketing 22%, computer/information sciences 10%, engineering/engineering technologies 14%, health sciences 39%, visual/performing arts 10%.

Computing on campus. 880 workstations in library, computer center. Online course registration, online library, helpline, repair service, student web hosting available.

Student life. Freshman orientation: Available. **Activities:** Student government, Phi Theta Kappa, Student Leadership Academy.

Athletics. Intramural: Softball, volleyball.

Student services. Adult student services, career counseling, student employment services, financial aid counseling, minority student services, personal counseling, placement for graduates, veterans' counselor. **Physically disabled:** Services for visually, hearing impaired. **Transfer:** Special adviser for new students. Transfer adviser, college fairs on campus for students transferring to 4-year colleges.

Contact. E-mail: nbagadio@ivytech.edu
Phone: (812) 374-5129 Toll-free number: (800) 922-4838
Fax: (812) 372-0311
Neil Bagadiong, Director of Admissions/Assistant Director of Student Affairs, Ivy Tech Community College: Columbus, 4475 Central Avenue, Columbus, IN 47203-1868

Ivy Tech Community College: East Central

Muncie, Indiana
www.ivytech.edu **CB code: 1279**

- Public 2-year community college
- Commuter campus in small city

General. Founded in 1968. Regionally accredited. Campuses also at Anderson and Marion. **Enrollment:** 5,460 degree-seeking undergraduates; 483 non-degree-seeking students. **Degrees:** 347 associate awarded. **Location:** 50 miles from Indianapolis. **Calendar:** Semester, extensive summer session. **Full-time faculty:** 87 total. **Part-time faculty:** 358 total.

Student profile. Among degree-seeking undergraduates, 53% enrolled in a transfer program, 47% enrolled in a vocational program, 899 enrolled as first-time, first-year students, 347 transferred in from other institutions.

Part-time:	55%	**Hispanic American:**	1%
Women:	67%	**25 or older:**	53%
African American:	8%		

Transfer out. Colleges most students transferred to 2005: Ball State University, Purdue University-West Lafayette, Indiana University-Kokomo.

Basis for selection. Open admission, but selective for some programs. Special requirements for human services and health technology programs based on test scores and prior academic work. **Adult students:** SAT/ACT scores not required.

2005-2006 Annual costs. Tuition/fees: $2,590; $5,178 out-of-state. Per-credit charge: $84 in-state; $170 out-of-state. Books/supplies: $956. Personal expenses: $2,151.

2004-2005 Financial aid. Need-based: 62% of total undergraduate aid awarded as scholarships/grants, 38% as loans/jobs. Need-based aid available for part-time students. Work study available nights and for part-time students. **Additional information:** Higher Education Aid (HEA), Child of Disabled/Deceased Veterans (CDV), Ivy Tech Scholarships (IVTC) and grants, vocational rehabilitation and veteran's assistance available. None require repayment.

Application procedures. Admission: No deadline. No application fee. Admission notification on a rolling basis. Application closing date for international students at least 60 days prior to start of semester. **Financial aid:** Priority date 3/1; no closing date. FAFSA required. Applicants notified on a rolling basis starting 7/1.

Academics. Special study options: Combined bachelor's/graduate degree, distance learning, dual enrollment of high school students, internships, liberal arts/career combination, teacher certification program, weekend college. License preparation in dental hygiene, nursing, physical therapy, radiology. **Credit/placement by examination:** AP, CLEP, institutional tests. 45 credit hours maximum toward associate degree. 15 credits must be earned in residence. **Support services:** GED preparation and test center, learning center, reduced course load, remedial instruction, tutoring.

Majors. **Business:** Accounting technology, business admin, executive assistant, hospitality admin. **Computer sciences:** General. **Construction:** General, carpentry, electrician, maintenance, masonry, painting, pipefitting, plumbing. **Engineering technology:** Electrical, industrial, robotics. **Family/consumer sciences:** Child care. **Health:** Medical assistant, mental health services, nursing (RN), physical therapy assistant, surgical technology. **Legal studies:** Paralegal. **Liberal arts:** Arts/sciences, library assistant. **Mechanic/repair:** General, automotive, heating/ac/refrig. **Production:** Cabinetmaking/millwright, machine tool, sheet metal, tool and die. **Protective services:** Criminal justice.

Most popular majors. Business/marketing 25%, computer/information sciences 9%, engineering/engineering technologies 10%, family/consumer sciences 6%, health sciences 41%.

Computing on campus. 1,219 workstations in library, computer center, student center. Online course registration, online library, helpline, repair service, student web hosting available.

Student life. **Freshman orientation:** Available. **Activities:** Student government, Phi Theta Kappa, Skills USA-VICA, early childhood education club, human services club, Student Leadership Academy.

Student services. Adult student services, career counseling, student employment services, financial aid counseling, minority student services, placement for graduates, veterans' counselor. **Physically disabled:** Services for visually, speech, hearing impaired. **Transfer:** Special adviser, orientation for new students. Transfer center, transfer adviser, college fairs on campus for students transferring to 4-year colleges.

Contact. E-mail: mlewelle@ivytech.edu
Phone: (765) 289-2291 ext. 391 Toll-free number: (800) 589-8324
Fax: (765) 289-2292 ext. 502
Mary Lewellen, Recruitement/Outreach Specialist, Ivy Tech Community College: East Central, 4301 South Cowan Road, Muncie, IN 47302-9448

Ivy Tech Community College: Kokomo

Kokomo, Indiana
www.ivytech.edu **CB code: 1329**

- Public 2-year community college
- Commuter campus in large town

General. Founded in 1968. Regionally accredited. Campus also at Logansport. Branch location at Wabash. **Enrollment:** 2,701 degree-seeking undergraduates; 547 non-degree-seeking students. **Degrees:** 166 associate awarded. **Location:** 50 miles from Indianapolis. **Calendar:** Semester, extensive summer session. **Full-time faculty:** 58 total. **Part-time faculty:** 197 total.

Student profile. Among degree-seeking undergraduates, 39% enrolled in a transfer program, 61% enrolled in a vocational program, 588 enrolled as first-time, first-year students, 27 transferred in from other institutions.

Part-time:	63%	**Hispanic American:**	2%
Women:	67%	**Native American:**	1%
African American:	4%	**25 or older:**	57%

Transfer out. **Colleges most students transferred to 2005:** Indiana University-Kokomo, Purdue University-West Lafayette, Ball State University.

Basis for selection. Open admission, but selective for some programs. Special requirements for human services and health technology programs based on test scores and prior academic work. **Adult students:** SAT/ACT scores not required.

2005-2006 Annual costs. Tuition/fees: $2,590; $5,178 out-of-state. Per-credit charge: $84 in-state; $170 out-of-state. Books/supplies: $956. Personal expenses: $2,151.

2004-2005 Financial aid. **Need-based:** 55% of total undergraduate aid awarded as scholarships/grants, 45% as loans/jobs. Need-based aid available for part-time students. Work study available nights and for part-time students.

Application procedures. **Admission:** Priority date 8/1; no deadline. No application fee. Admission notification on a rolling basis. Application closing date for international students at least 60 days prior to start of semester. **Financial aid:** Priority date 3/1; no closing date. FAFSA required. Applicants notified on a rolling basis starting 7/1.

Academics. **Special study options:** Combined bachelor's/graduate degree, distance learning, dual enrollment of high school students, independent study, internships, liberal arts/career combination, teacher certification program, weekend college. License preparation in nursing, paramedic, physical therapy. **Credit/placement by examination:** AP, CLEP, institutional tests. 45 credit hours maximum toward associate degree. 15 credits must be earned in residence. **Support services:** Learning center, reduced course load, remedial instruction, tutoring.

Majors. **Business:** Accounting technology, business admin, executive assistant. **Computer sciences:** General. **Construction:** General, electrician, maintenance, pipefitting, plumbing, site management. **Engineering technology:** Drafting, industrial, occupational safety. **Family/consumer sciences:** Child care. **Health:** EMT paramedic, medical assistant, mental health services, nursing (RN), physical therapy assistant, surgical technology. **Liberal arts:** Arts/sciences, library assistant. **Mechanic/repair:** General, automotive, heating/ac/refrig. **Production:** Cabinetmaking/millwright, machine tool, sheet metal, tool and die. **Protective services:** Criminal justice. **Visual/performing arts:** Design.

Most popular majors. Business/marketing 30%, computer/information sciences 6%, engineering/engineering technologies 9%, family/consumer sciences 9%, health sciences 17%, trade and industry 18%.

Computing on campus. 777 workstations in library, computer center, student center. Online course registration, online library, helpline, repair service, student web hosting available.

Student life. **Freshman orientation:** Available. **Activities:** Student government, student newspaper, Phi Theta Kappa, student leadership academy, business administration student organization, professional and trade organization.

Student services. Adult student services, career counseling, student employment services, financial aid counseling, minority student services, placement for graduates, veterans' counselor. **Physically disabled:** Services for visually, speech, hearing impaired. **Transfer:** Special adviser, orientation for new students. Transfer adviser, college fairs on campus for students transferring to 4-year colleges.

Contact. E-mail: sdillman@ivytech.edu
Phone: (765) 459-0561 ext. 318 Toll-free number: (800) 459-0561
Fax: (765) 454-5111
Suzanne Dillman, Director of Admissions, Ivy Tech Community College: Kokomo, 1815 East Morgan Street, Kokomo, IN 46903-1373

Ivy Tech Community College: Lafayette

Lafayette, Indiana
www.ivytech.edu **CB code: 1282**

- Public 2-year community college
- Commuter campus in large town

General. Founded in 1968. Regionally accredited. **Enrollment:** 4,359 degree-seeking undergraduates; 1,611 non-degree-seeking students. **Degrees:** 365 associate awarded. **Location:** 60 miles from Indianapolis. **Calendar:** Semester, extensive summer session. **Full-time faculty:** 68 total. **Part-time faculty:** 246 total. **Special facilities:** Multimedia laboratory.

Student profile. Among degree-seeking undergraduates, 38% enrolled in a transfer program, 62% enrolled in a vocational program, 685 enrolled as first-time, first-year students, 344 transferred in from other institutions.

Part-time:	50%	**Asian American:**	1%
Women:	56%	**Hispanic American:**	4%
African American:	3%	**25 or older:**	46%

Transfer out. **Colleges most students transferred to 2005:** Purdue University - West Lafayette, Indiana University - Purdue University Indianapolis.

Basis for selection. Open admission, but selective for some programs. Special requirements for human services and health technology programs based on test scores and prior academic work. **Adult students:** SAT/ACT scores not required.

2005-2006 Annual costs. Tuition/fees: $2,590; $5,178 out-of-state. Per-credit charge: $84 in-state; $170 out-of-state. Books/supplies: $956. Personal expenses: $2,151.

2004-2005 Financial aid. **Need-based:** 44% of total undergraduate aid awarded as scholarships/grants, 56% as loans/jobs. Need-based aid available for part-time students. Work study available nights and for part-time students.

Application procedures. **Admission:** No deadline. No application fee. Admission notification on a rolling basis. Application closing date for international students at least 60 days prior to start of semester. **Financial aid:**

Priority date 3/1; no closing date. FAFSA required. Applicants notified on a rolling basis starting 7/1.

Academics. **Special study options:** Combined bachelor's/graduate degree, distance learning, dual enrollment of high school students, internships, liberal arts/career combination, teacher certification program, weekend college. License preparation in dental hygiene, nursing. **Credit/placement by examination:** AP, CLEP, institutional tests. 45 credit hours maximum toward associate degree. 15 credits must be earned in residence. **Support services:** Learning center, reduced course load, remedial instruction, tutoring.

Majors. Biology: Biotechnology. **Business:** Accounting technology, business admin, executive assistant. **Computer sciences:** General. **Construction:** Carpentry, electrician, lineworker, maintenance, masonry, painting, plumbing. **Engineering technology:** Drafting, electrical, industrial, quality control, robotics. **Family/consumer sciences:** Child care. **Health:** Medical assistant, medical records technology, mental health services, nursing (RN), respiratory therapy technology, surgical technology. **Liberal arts:** Arts/sciences, library assistant. **Mechanic/repair:** General, automotive, heating/ac/refrig. **Production:** Cabinetmaking/millwright, ironworking, machine tool, sheet metal, tool and die. **Protective services:** Criminal justice.

Most popular majors. Business/marketing 23%, computer/information sciences 12%, engineering/engineering technologies 9%, family/consumer sciences 6%, health sciences 33%, trade and industry 15%.

Computing on campus. 1,464 workstations in library, computer center. Online course registration, online library, helpline, repair service, student web hosting available.

Student life. Freshman orientation: Available. **Activities:** Student government, student newspaper, Phi Theta Kappa, American Chemical Society, Dental Assistant Society, Respiratory Care Society, student leadership academy, culture club.

Student services. Adult student services, career counseling, student employment services, financial aid counseling, minority student services, personal counseling, placement for graduates, veterans' counselor. **Physically disabled:** Services for visually, hearing impaired. **Transfer:** Special adviser, orientation for new students. Transfer center, transfer adviser for students transferring to 4-year colleges.

Contact. E-mail: jdoppelf@ivytech.edu
Phone: (765) 269-5116 Toll-free number: (800) 715-1058
Fax: (765) 772-9293
Judy Doppelfeld, Director of Admissions, Ivy Tech Community College: Lafayette, 3101 South Creasy Lane, Lafayette, IN 47905-6299

Ivy Tech Community College: North Central

South Bend, Indiana
www.ivytech.edu **CB code: 1280**

- Public 2-year community college
- Commuter campus in small city

General. Founded in 1968. Regionally accredited. Campuses also at Warsaw and Elkhart. Distance learning through computer. **Enrollment:** 4,404 degree-seeking undergraduates; 824 non-degree-seeking students. **Degrees:** 366 associate awarded. **Location:** 100 miles from Chicago. **Calendar:** Semester, extensive summer session. **Full-time faculty:** 72 total. **Part-time faculty:** 239 total.

Student profile. Among degree-seeking undergraduates, 30% enrolled in a transfer program, 70% enrolled in a vocational program, 821 enrolled as first-time, first-year students, 138 transferred in from other institutions.

Part-time:	74%	**Asian American:**	1%
Out-of-state:	2%	**Hispanic American:**	5%
Women:	59%	**25 or older:**	58%
African American:	14%		

Transfer out. Colleges most students transferred to 2005: Indiana University - South Bend, Indiana University - Purdue University Fort Wayne, Purdue University - West Lafayette, Purdue University - North Central.

Basis for selection. Open admission, but selective for some programs. Special requirements for human services and health technology programs based on test scores and prior academic work. Comparative Guidance and Placement Program required for admission of allied health applicants. Interview required of allied health majors. Portfolio recommended for photographic technology and graphic arts technology majors. **Adult students:** SAT/ACT scores not required.

High school preparation. Medical laboratory assistant program requires 1 chemistry and 1 algebra.

2005-2006 Annual costs. Tuition/fees: $2,590; $5,178 out-of-state. Per-credit charge: $84 in-state; $170 out-of-state. Books/supplies: $956. Personal expenses: $2,151.

2005-2006 Financial aid. Need-based: 58% of total undergraduate aid awarded as scholarships/grants, 42% as loans/jobs. Need-based aid available for part-time students. Work study available nights and for part-time students.

Application procedures. Admission: No deadline. No application fee. Admission notification on a rolling basis. **Financial aid:** Priority date 3/1; no closing date. FAFSA required. Applicants notified on a rolling basis starting 7/1.

Academics. Industrial training division offers customized courses and seminars to companies and corporations in surrounding community. **Special study options:** Combined bachelor's/graduate degree, distance learning, dual enrollment of high school students, ESL, internships, liberal arts/career combination, teacher certification program, weekend college. License preparation in nursing. **Credit/placement by examination:** AP, CLEP, institutional tests. 45 credit hours maximum toward associate degree. 15 credits must be earned in residence. **Support services:** Learning center, reduced course load, remedial instruction, tutoring.

Majors. Business: Accounting technology, business admin, executive assistant, hospitality admin. **Computer sciences:** General. **Construction:** Carpentry, electrician, maintenance, masonry, painting, pipefitting, plumbing, roofing. **Engineering technology:** Electrical, industrial, robotics, telecommunications. **Family/consumer sciences:** Child care. **Health:** Clinical lab technology, EMT paramedic, medical assistant, mental health services, nursing (RN). **Legal studies:** Paralegal. **Liberal arts:** Arts/sciences, library assistant. **Mechanic/repair:** General, automotive, heating/ac/refrig. **Production:** Cabinetmaking/millwright, ironworking, machine tool, sheet metal, tool and die. **Protective services:** Criminal justice. **Visual/performing arts:** Design, interior design.

Most popular majors. Business/marketing 16%, computer/information sciences 8%, engineering/engineering technologies 6%, health sciences 19%, trade and industry 42%.

Computing on campus. 923 workstations in library, computer center. Online course registration, online library, helpline, repair service, student web hosting available.

Student life. Freshman orientation: Available. **Activities:** Student government, Phi Theta Kappa, culinary club, student leadership academy, student ad club.

Student services. Adult student services, career counseling, student employment services, financial aid counseling, minority student services, placement for graduates, veterans' counselor. **Physically disabled:** Services for visually, speech, hearing impaired. **Transfer:** Special adviser, orientation for new students. Transfer adviser, college fairs on campus for students transferring to 4-year colleges.

Contact. E-mail: pdecker@ivytech.edu
Phone: (574) 289-7001 Toll-free number: (888) 489-5463
Fax: (574) 236-7177
Pam Decker, Director of Admissions, Ivy Tech Community College: North Central, 220 Dean Johnson Boulevard, South Bend, IN 46601-3415

Ivy Tech Community College: Northeast

Fort Wayne, Indiana
www.ivytech.edu **CB code: 1278**

- Public 2-year community college
- Commuter campus in small city

General. Founded in 1963. Regionally accredited. **Enrollment:** 4,733 degree-seeking undergraduates; 1,349 non-degree-seeking students. **Degrees:** 456 associate awarded. **Location:** 120 miles from Indianapolis. **Calendar:** Semester, extensive summer session. **Full-time faculty:** 87 total. **Part-time faculty:** 348 total.

Student profile. Among degree-seeking undergraduates, 35% enrolled in a transfer program, 65% enrolled in a vocational program, 608 enrolled as first-time, first-year students, 250 transferred in from other institutions.

Part-time:	62%	**Asian American:**	1%
Out-of-state:	1%	**Hispanic American:**	2%
Women:	65%	**Native American:**	1%
African American:	15%	**25 or older:**	57%

Transfer out. Colleges most students transferred to 2005: Indiana University, Purdue University-Ft. Wayne, Ball State University.

Basis for selection. Open admission, but selective for some programs. Special requirements for human services and health technology programs based on test scores and prior academic work. **Adult students:** SAT/ACT scores not required.

2005-2006 Annual costs. Tuition/fees: $2,590; $5,178 out-of-state. Per-credit charge: $84 in-state; $170 out-of-state. Books/supplies: $956. Personal expenses: $2,151.

2004-2005 Financial aid. Need-based: 46% of total undergraduate aid awarded as scholarships/grants, 54% as loans/jobs. Need-based aid available for part-time students. Work study available nights and for part-time students.

Application procedures. Admission: No deadline. No application fee. Admission notification on a rolling basis. Application closing dates for international students at least 60 days prior to start of semester. **Financial aid:** Priority date 3/1; no closing date. FAFSA required. Applicants notified on a rolling basis starting 7/1.

Academics. Special study options: Combined bachelor's/graduate degree, distance learning, dual enrollment of high school students, ESL, internships, liberal arts/career combination, teacher certification program, weekend college. License preparation in nursing. **Credit/placement by examination:** AP, CLEP, institutional tests. 45 credit hours maximum toward associate degree. 15 credits must be completed in residence. **Support services:** GED preparation and test center, learning center, reduced course load, remedial instruction, tutoring.

Majors. Business: Accounting technology, administrative services, business admin, executive assistant, hospitality admin. **Computer sciences:** General. **Construction:** General, electrician, maintenance, masonry, painting, pipefitting, plumbing, site management. **Engineering technology:** Industrial, occupational safety, robotics, telecommunications. **Family/consumer sciences:** Child care. **Health:** EMT paramedic, massage therapy, medical assistant, medical records technology, mental health services, nursing (RN), respiratory therapy technology. **Liberal arts:** Arts/sciences, library assistant. **Mechanic/repair:** General, automotive, heating/ac/refrig. **Production:** Cabinetmaking/millwright, ironworking, machine tool, sheet metal, tool and die. **Protective services:** Criminal justice.

Most popular majors. Business/marketing 30%, computer/information sciences 8%, engineering/engineering technologies 12%, family/consumer sciences 6%, health sciences 24%, legal studies 8%, trade and industry 12%.

Computing on campus. 1,187 workstations in library, computer center, student center. Online course registration, online library, helpline, repair service, student web hosting available.

Student life. Freshman orientation: Available. **Activities:** Student government, student newspaper, Phi Theta Kappa, multi-cultural organization, Society of Manufacturing Engineers, student leadership academy, Association of Construction Technology Students.

Student services. Adult student services, career counseling, student employment services, financial aid counseling, minority student services, placement for graduates, veterans' counselor. **Physically disabled:** Services for visually, speech, hearing impaired. **Transfer:** Special adviser for new students. Transfer center, transfer adviser, college fairs on campus for students transferring to 4-year colleges.

Contact. E-mail: sscheer@ivytech.edu
Phone: (260) 480-4221 Toll-free number: (800) 859-4882
Fax: (260) 480-2053
Steve Scheer, Director of Admissions, Ivy Tech Community College: Northeast, 3800 North Anthony Boulevard, Fort Wayne, IN 46805-1489

Ivy Tech Community College: Northwest

Gary, Indiana
www.ivytech.edu **CB code: 1281**

- Public 2-year community college
- Commuter campus in small city

General. Founded in 1968. Regionally accredited. Campuses also at East Chicago, Valparaiso, and Michigan City. **Enrollment:** 4,024 degree-seeking undergraduates; 791 non-degree-seeking students. **Degrees:** 318 associate awarded. **Location:** 30 miles from Chicago. **Calendar:** Semester, extensive summer session. **Full-time faculty:** 91 total. **Part-time faculty:** 328 total.

Student profile. Among degree-seeking undergraduates, 37% enrolled in a transfer program, 63% enrolled in a vocational program, 585 enrolled as first-time, first-year students, 285 transferred in from other institutions.

Part-time:	66%	**Asian American:**	1%
Women:	71%	**Hispanic American:**	9%
African American:	30%	**25 or older:**	60%

Transfer out. Colleges most students transferred to 2005: Purdue University- Calumet, Indiana University-Northwest, Purdue University-North Central.

Basis for selection. Open admission, but selective for some programs. Special requirements for human services and health technology programs based on test scores and prior academic work. **Adult students:** SAT/ACT scores not required.

2005-2006 Annual costs. Tuition/fees: $2,590; $5,178 out-of-state. Per-credit charge: $84 in-state; $170 out-of-state. Books/supplies: $956. Personal expenses: $2,151.

2004-2005 Financial aid. Need-based: 78% of total undergraduate aid awarded as scholarships/grants, 22% as loans/jobs. Need-based aid available for part-time students. Work study available nights and for part-time students.

Application procedures. Admission: No deadline. No application fee. Admission notification on a rolling basis. Application closing date for international students at least 60 days prior to start of semester. **Financial aid:** Priority date 3/1; no closing date. FAFSA required. Applicants notified on a rolling basis starting 7/1.

Academics. Special study options: Combined bachelor's/graduate degree, distance learning, dual enrollment of high school students, internships, liberal arts/career combination, teacher certification program, weekend college. License preparation in nursing, physical therapy, real estate. **Credit/placement by examination:** AP, CLEP, institutional tests. 45 credit hours maximum toward associate degree. 15 credits must be earned in residence. **Support services:** Learning center, reduced course load, remedial instruction, tutoring.

Majors. Business: Accounting technology, administrative services, business admin, executive assistant, hospitality admin. **Computer sciences:** General. **Construction:** General, carpentry, electrician, maintenance, masonry, painting, pipefitting, site management. **Engineering technology:** Electrical, industrial, occupational safety, telecommunications. **Family/consumer sciences:** Child care. **Health:** Medical assistant, mental health services, nursing (RN), physical therapy assistant, radiologic technology/medical imaging, respiratory therapy technology, surgical technology. **Legal studies:** Paralegal. **Liberal arts:** Arts/sciences, library assistant. **Mechanic/repair:** General, automotive, heating/ac/refrig. **Personal/culinary services:** Mortuary science. **Production:** Cabinetmaking/millwright, ironworking, machine tool, sheet metal, tool and die. **Protective services:** Criminal justice.

Most popular majors. Business/marketing 30%, computer/information sciences 12%, engineering/engineering technologies 17%, health sciences 25%.

Computing on campus. 498 workstations in library, computer center. Online course registration, online library, helpline, repair service, student web hosting available.

Student life. Freshman orientation: Available. **Activities:** Student government, Phi Theta Kappa,computer club, business club, culinary arts club, medical assistants, mortuary science club, student leadership academy, early childhood development club, nursing club.

Athletics. Intramural: Softball M.

Student services. Adult student services, career counseling, student employment services, financial aid counseling, minority student services, placement for graduates, veterans' counselor. **Physically disabled:** Services for visually, speech, hearing impaired. **Transfer:** Special adviser for new students. Transfer adviser, college fairs on campus for students transferring to 4-year colleges.

Contact. E-mail: tlewis@ivytech.edu
Phone: (219) 981-1111 ext. 273 Toll-free number: (800) 843-4882
Fax: (219) 981-4415
Twilla Lewis, Associate Dean of Student Affairs, Ivy Tech Community College: Northwest, 1440 East 35th Avenue, Gary, IN 46409-1499

Two-Year Colleges

Ivy Tech Community College: South Central
Sellersburg, Indiana
www.ivytech.edu **CB code: 1273**

- Public 2-year community college
- Commuter campus in small town

General. Founded in 1968. Regionally accredited. **Enrollment:** 2,783 degree-seeking undergraduates; 329 non-degree-seeking students. **Degrees:** 200 associate awarded. **Location:** 10 miles from Louisville, KY. **Calendar:** Semester, extensive summer session. **Full-time faculty:** 47 total. **Part-time faculty:** 126 total.

Student profile. Among degree-seeking undergraduates, 28% enrolled in a transfer program, 72% enrolled in a vocational program, 493 enrolled as first-time, first-year students, 104 transferred in from other institutions.

Part-time:	69%	**Hispanic American:**	1%
Out-of-state:	19%	**Native American:**	1%
Women:	52%	**25 or older:**	55%
African American:	5%		

Transfer out. Colleges most students transferred to 2005: Indiana University - Southeast.

Basis for selection. Open admission, but selective for some programs. Special requirements for human services and health technology programs based on test scores and prior academic work. **Adult students:** Entrance exam policies same as for first-time freshmen.

2005-2006 Annual costs. Tuition/fees: $2,590; $5,178 out-of-state. Per-credit charge: $84 in-state; $170 out-of-state. Books/supplies: $956. Personal expenses: $2,151.

2004-2005 Financial aid. Need-based: 62% of total undergraduate aid awarded as scholarships/grants, 38% as loans/jobs. Need-based aid available for part-time students. Work study available nights and for part-time students.

Application procedures. Admission: No deadline. No application fee. Admission notification on a rolling basis. Application closing date for international students at least 60 days prior to start of semester. **Financial aid:** Priority date 3/1; no closing date. FAFSA required. Applicants notified on a rolling basis starting 7/1.

Academics. Special study options: Combined bachelor's/graduate degree, cooperative education, distance learning, dual enrollment of high school students, internships, liberal arts/career combination, teacher certification program, weekend college. License preparation in nursing, real estate. **Credit/placement by examination:** AP, CLEP, institutional tests. 45 credit hours maximum toward associate degree. 15 credits must be earned in residence. **Support services:** GED preparation and test center, learning center, reduced course load, remedial instruction, tutoring.

Majors. Business: Accounting technology, business admin, executive assistant. **Computer sciences:** General. **Construction:** Carpentry, electrician, maintenance, masonry, pipefitting, plumbing. **Engineering technology:** Drafting, electrical, industrial, robotics, telecommunications. **Family/consumer sciences:** Child care. **Health:** Medical assistant, mental health services, nursing (RN), respiratory therapy technology. **Legal studies:** Paralegal. **Liberal arts:** Arts/sciences, library assistant. **Mechanic/repair:** General, automotive, heating/ac/refrig. **Production:** Cabinetmaking/millwright, machine tool, sheet metal, tool and die. **Visual/performing arts:** Design.

Most popular majors. Business/marketing 25%, computer/information sciences 12%, engineering/engineering technologies 9%, health sciences 39%, trade and industry 9%.

Computing on campus. 634 workstations in library, computer center. Online course registration, online library, helpline, repair service, student web hosting available.

Student life. Freshman orientation: Available. **Activities:** Student government, student newspaper, Phi Theta Kappa, art club, Christian Student Fellowship, C.A.R.E. club, ASN club, Business Professionals of America, human services club, Computer Information Club, Student Leadership Academy.

Athletics. Intramural: Baseball M.

Student services. Career counseling, student employment services, financial aid counseling, minority student services, placement for graduates, veterans' counselor. **Transfer:** Special adviser for new students. Transfer center, transfer adviser, college fairs on campus for students transferring to 4-year colleges.

Contact. E-mail: msteinbe@ivytech.edu
Phone: (812) 246-3301 ext. 4136 Toll-free number: (800) 321-9021
Fax: (812) 246-9905
Mindy Steinberg, Director of Admissions, Ivy Tech Community College: South Central, 8204 Highway 311, Sellersburg, IN 47172-1897

Ivy Tech Community College: Southeast
Madison, Indiana
www.ivytech.edu **CB code: 1334**

- Public 2-year community college
- Commuter campus in large town

General. Founded in 1968. Regionally accredited. Branch in Lawrenceburg. **Enrollment:** 1,520 degree-seeking undergraduates; 246 non-degree-seeking students. **Degrees:** 123 associate awarded. **Location:** 46 miles from Columbus, Ohio, 88 miles from Indianapolis. **Calendar:** Semester, extensive summer session. **Full-time faculty:** 35 total. **Part-time faculty:** 113 total. **Special facilities:** Gaming training center in Aurora, Indiana.

Student profile. Among degree-seeking undergraduates, 28% enrolled in a transfer program, 72% enrolled in a vocational program, 266 enrolled as first-time, first-year students, 22 transferred in from other institutions.

Part-time:	59%	**African American:**	1%
Out-of-state:	2%	**Hispanic American:**	1%
Women:	74%	**25 or older:**	51%

Transfer out. Colleges most students transferred to 2005: Indiana University - Southeast.

Basis for selection. Open admission, but selective for some programs. Special requirements for human services and health technology programs based on test scores and prior academic work. **Adult students:** SAT/ACT scores not required.

2005-2006 Annual costs. Tuition/fees: $2,590; $5,178 out-of-state. Per-credit charge: $84 in-state; $170 out-of-state. Books/supplies: $956. Personal expenses: $2,151.

2004-2005 Financial aid. Need-based: 55% of total undergraduate aid awarded as scholarships/grants, 45% as loans/jobs. Need-based aid available for part-time students. Work study available nights and for part-time students.

Application procedures. Admission: No deadline. No application fee. Admission notification on a rolling basis. Application closing date for international students at least 60 days prior to start of semester. **Financial aid:** Priority date 3/1; no closing date. FAFSA required. Applicants notified on a rolling basis starting 7/1.

Academics. Special study options: Combined bachelor's/graduate degree, distance learning, dual enrollment of high school students, internships, liberal arts/career combination, teacher certification program, weekend college. License preparation in nursing. **Credit/placement by examination:** AP, CLEP, institutional tests. 45 credit hours maximum toward associate degree. 15 credit hours must be earned in residence. **Support services:** Learning center, reduced course load, remedial instruction, tutoring.

Majors. Business: Accounting technology, business admin, executive assistant. **Computer sciences:** General. **Engineering technology:** Drafting, electrical, industrial, robotics. **Family/consumer sciences:** Child care. **Health:** Medical assistant, mental health services, nursing (RN). **Legal studies:** Paralegal. **Liberal arts:** Arts/sciences, library assistant.

Most popular majors. Business/marketing 56%, computer/information sciences 21%, engineering/engineering technologies 7%, health sciences 7%.

Computing on campus. 805 workstations in library, computer center. Online course registration, online library, helpline, repair service, student web hosting available.

Student life. Freshman orientation: Available. **Activities:** Student government, Phi Theta Kappa, student leadership academy, computer club, fitness club.

Student services. Career counseling, student employment services, financial aid counseling, minority student services, personal counseling, placement for graduates, veterans' counselor. **Physically disabled:** Services for visually, hearing impaired. **Transfer:** Special adviser for new students. Transfer adviser, college fairs on campus for students transferring to 4-year colleges.

Contact. E-mail: chutcher@ivytech.edu
Phone: (812) 265-2580 ext. 4142 Toll-free number: (800) 403-2190
Fax: (812) 265-4028
Cindy Hutcherson, Assistant Director of Admission/Career Counselor, Ivy Tech Community College: Southeast, 590 Ivy Tech Drive, Madison, IN 47250-1881

Ivy Tech Community College: Southwest

Evansville, Indiana
www.ivytech.edu **CB code: 1277**

- Public 2-year community college
- Commuter campus in small city

General. Founded in 1968. Regionally accredited. Branch location at Tell City. **Enrollment:** 4,095 degree-seeking undergraduates; 763 non-degree-seeking students. **Degrees:** 428 associate awarded. **Location:** 180 miles from Indianapolis, 112 miles from Louisville, Kentucky. **Calendar:** Semester, extensive summer session. **Full-time faculty:** 71 total. **Part-time faculty:** 237 total. **Special facilities:** Plastics lab, computer integrated manufacturing lab.

Student profile. Among degree-seeking undergraduates, 27% enrolled in a transfer program, 73% enrolled in a vocational program, 606 enrolled as first-time, first-year students, 223 transferred in from other institutions.

Part-time:	64%	**African American:**	8%
Out-of-state:	3%	**Hispanic American:**	1%
Women:	55%	**25 or older:**	49%

Transfer out. Colleges most students transferred to 2005: University of Southern Indiana, Vincennes University, Indiana State University.

Basis for selection. Open admission, but selective for some programs. Special requirements for human services and health technology programs based on test scores and prior academic work. **Adult students:** SAT/ACT scores not required.

2005-2006 Annual costs. Tuition/fees: $2,590; $5,178 out-of-state. Per-credit charge: $84 in-state; $170 out-of-state. Books/supplies: $956. Personal expenses: $2,151.

2004-2005 Financial aid. Need-based: 52% of total undergraduate aid awarded as scholarships/grants, 48% as loans/jobs. Need-based aid available for part-time students. Work study available nights and for part-time students.

Application procedures. Admission: No deadline. No application fee. Admission notification on a rolling basis. Application closing date for international students at least 60 days prior to start of semester. **Financial aid:** Priority date 3/1; no closing date. FAFSA required. Applicants notified on a rolling basis starting 7/1.

Academics. Special study options: Combined bachelor's/graduate degree, cooperative education, distance learning, dual enrollment of high school students, independent study, internships, liberal arts/career combination, teacher certification program, weekend college. License preparation in nursing, paramedic. **Credit/placement by examination:** AP, CLEP, institutional tests. 45 credit hours maximum toward associate degree. 15 credit hours must be earned in residence. **Support services:** Learning center, reduced course load, remedial instruction, tutoring.

Majors. Biology: Biotechnology. **Business:** Accounting technology, business admin, executive assistant. **Computer sciences:** General. **Construction:** Carpentry, electrician, maintenance, masonry, painting, pipefitting, plumbing, site management. **Engineering technology:** Drafting, electrical, industrial, robotics, telecommunications. **Family/consumer sciences:** Child care. **Health:** EMT paramedic, medical assistant, mental health services, nursing (RN), surgical technology. **Legal studies:** Paralegal. **Liberal arts:** Arts/sciences, library assistant. **Mechanic/repair:** General, automotive, heating/ac/refrig. **Production:** Boilermaking, cabinetmaking/millwright, ironworking, machine tool, sheet metal, tool and die. **Protective services:** Criminal justice. **Transportation:** Heavy/earthmoving equipment. **Visual/performing arts:** Design, interior design.

Most popular majors. Business/marketing 21%, computer/information sciences 11%, engineering/engineering technologies 12%, health sciences 19%, trade and industry 25%, visual/performing arts 9%.

Computing on campus. 756 workstations in library, computer center. Online course registration, online library, helpline, repair service, student web hosting available.

Student life. Freshman orientation: Available. **Housing:** Housing available at University of Southern Indiana. **Activities:** Student government, Phi Theta Kappa, American Institute of Architectural Students, National Association of Industrial Technicians, International Association Of Administrative Professionals, human services club, student leadership academy, art & design club.

Athletics. Intramural: Softball.

Student services. Adult student services, career counseling, student employment services, financial aid counseling, minority student services, placement for graduates, veterans' counselor. **Physically disabled:** Services for visually, speech, hearing impaired. **Transfer:** Special adviser for new students. Transfer adviser, college fairs on campus for students transferring to 4-year colleges.

Contact. E-mail: ajohnson@ivytech.edu
Phone: (812) 429-1430 Toll-free number: (888) 489-5463
Fax: (812) 429-9878
Denise Johnson-Kincaid, Director of Admissions, Ivy Tech Community College: Southwest, 3501 First Avenue, Evansville, IN 47710-3398

Ivy Tech Community College: Wabash Valley

Terre Haute, Indiana
www.ivytech.edu **CB code: 1284**

- Public 2-year community college
- Commuter campus in small city

General. Founded in 1966. Regionally accredited. Branch location at Greencastle. **Enrollment:** 4,148 degree-seeking undergraduates; 844 non-degree-seeking students. **Degrees:** 396 associate awarded. **Location:** 80 miles from Indianapolis. **Calendar:** Semester, extensive summer session. **Full-time faculty:** 78 total. **Part-time faculty:** 235 total. **Special facilities:** Plastics productivity center.

Student profile. Among degree-seeking undergraduates, 27% enrolled in a transfer program, 73% enrolled in a vocational program, 710 enrolled as first-time, first-year students, 304 transferred in from other institutions.

Part-time:	50%	**African American:**	3%
Out-of-state:	3%	**Native American:**	1%
Women:	63%	**25 or older:**	50%

Transfer out. Colleges most students transferred to 2005: Indiana State University, Vincennes University, Purdue University - West Lafayette.

Basis for selection. Open admission, but selective for some programs. Special requirements for human services and health technology programs based on test scores and prior academic work. **Adult students:** SAT/ACT scores not required.

2005-2006 Annual costs. Tuition/fees: $2,590; $5,178 out-of-state. Per-credit charge: $84 in-state; $170 out-of-state. Books/supplies: $956. Personal expenses: $2,151.

2004-2005 Financial aid. Need-based: 46% of total undergraduate aid awarded as scholarships/grants, 54% as loans/jobs. Need-based aid available for part-time students. Work study available nights and for part-time students.

Application procedures. Admission: No deadline. No application fee. Admission notification on a rolling basis. Application closing date for international students is at least 60 days prior to start of semester. **Financial aid:** Priority date 3/1; no closing date. FAFSA required. Applicants notified on a rolling basis starting 7/1.

Academics. Special study options: Combined bachelor's/graduate degree, distance learning, dual enrollment of high school students, internships, liberal arts/career combination, teacher certification program, weekend college. License preparation in aviation, nursing, paramedic, radiology. **Credit/placement by examination:** AP, CLEP, institutional tests. 45 credit hours maximum toward associate degree. 15 credits must be earned in residence. **Support services:** Learning center, reduced course load, remedial instruction, tutoring.

Majors. Biology: Biotechnology. **Business:** Accounting technology, business admin, executive assistant. **Computer sciences:** General. **Construction:** Carpentry, electrician, maintenance, masonry, painting, pipefitting, plumbing. **Engineering technology:** Electrical, occupational safety, robotics. **Family/consumer sciences:** Child care. **Health:** Clinical lab technology, EMT paramedic, medical assistant, medical radiologic technology/radiation therapy, mental health services, nursing (RN), respiratory therapy technology, surgical technology. **Liberal arts:** Arts/sciences, library assistant. **Mechanic/repair:** General, aircraft, automotive, heating/ac/refrig. **Production:** Cabinetmaking/millwright, ironworking, machine tool, sheet metal, tool and die.

Protective services: Criminal justice. **Transportation:** Heavy/earthmoving equipment. **Visual/performing arts:** Design.

Most popular majors. Business/marketing 20%, computer/information sciences 6%, engineering/engineering technologies 7%, health sciences 33%, trade and industry 23%.

Computing on campus. 1,608 workstations in library, computer center, student center. Online course registration, online library, helpline, repair service, student web hosting, wireless network available.

Student life. Freshman orientation: Available. **Activities:** Student government, Phi Theta Kappa, Student Leadership Academy, Practical Nurses Class Organization.

Athletics. Intramural: Basketball M, volleyball.

Student services. Adult student services, career counseling, student employment services, financial aid counseling, minority student services, on-campus daycare, personal counseling, placement for graduates, veterans' counselor. **Physically disabled:** Services for visually, speech, hearing impaired. **Transfer:** Special adviser, orientation for new students. Transfer center, transfer adviser, college fairs on campus for students transferring to 4-year colleges.

Contact. E-mail: mfisher@ivytech.edu
Phone: (812) 298-2300 Toll-free number: (800) 377-4882
Fax: (812) 298-2291
Michael Fisher, Director of Admissions, Ivy Tech Community College: Wabash Valley, 7999 US Highway 41 South, Terre Haute, IN 47802-4898

Ivy Tech Community College: Whitewater

Richmond, Indiana
www.ivytech.edu **CB code: 1283**

- Public 2-year community college
- Commuter campus in large town

General. Founded in 1968. Regionally accredited. Branch location at Connersville. **Enrollment:** 1,588 degree-seeking undergraduates; 244 non-degree-seeking students. **Degrees:** 127 associate awarded. **Location:** 70 miles from Indianapolis, 45 miles from Dayton, Ohio. **Calendar:** Semester, extensive summer session. **Full-time faculty:** 29 total. **Part-time faculty:** 146 total. **Special facilities:** Student-operated restaurant.

Student profile. Among degree-seeking undergraduates, 12% enrolled in a transfer program, 88% enrolled in a vocational program, 221 enrolled as first-time, first-year students, 77 transferred in from other institutions.

Part-time:	65%	**African American:**	5%
Out-of-state:	6%	**Hispanic American:**	1%
Women:	76%	**25 or older:**	61%

Transfer out. Colleges most students transferred to 2005: Indiana University East, Purdue University-West Lafayette.

Basis for selection. Open admission, but selective for some programs. Special requirements for human services and health technology programs based on test scores and prior academic work. **Adult students:** SAT/ACT scores not required.

2005-2006 Annual costs. Tuition/fees: $2,590; $5,178 out-of-state. Per-credit charge: $84 in-state; $170 out-of-state. Books/supplies: $956. Personal expenses: $2,151.

2004-2005 Financial aid. Need-based: 52% of total undergraduate aid awarded as scholarships/grants, 48% as loans/jobs. Need-based aid available for part-time students. Work study available nights and for part-time students.

Application procedures. Admission: No deadline. No application fee. Admission notification on a rolling basis. Application closing date for international students at least 60 days prior to start of semester. **Financial aid:** Priority date 3/1; no closing date. FAFSA required. Applicants notified on a rolling basis starting 7/1; must reply within 3 week(s) of notification.

Academics. Special study options: Combined bachelor's/graduate degree, distance learning, dual enrollment of high school students, independent study, internships, liberal arts/career combination, teacher certification program, weekend college. License preparation in nursing. **Credit/placement by examination:** AP, CLEP, institutional tests. 45 credit hours maximum toward associate degree. 15 credits must be earned in residence. **Support services:** Learning center, reduced course load, remedial instruction, tutoring.

Majors. Business: Accounting technology, business admin, executive assistant. **Computer sciences:** General. **Construction:** General, electrician, maintenance, plumbing. **Engineering technology:** Electrical, robotics. **Family/consumer sciences:** Child care. **Health:** Medical assistant, mental health services, nursing (RN). **Legal studies:** Paralegal. **Liberal arts:** Arts/sciences, library assistant. **Mechanic/repair:** General, automotive, heating/ac/refrig. **Production:** Cabinetmaking/millwright, machine tool, sheet metal, tool and die.

Most popular majors. Business/marketing 34%, computer/information sciences 8%, engineering/engineering technologies 10%, family/consumer sciences 9%, health sciences 33%.

Computing on campus. 462 workstations in library, computer center, student center. Online course registration, online library, helpline, repair service, student web hosting available.

Student life. Freshman orientation: Available. **Activities:** Student government, student newspaper, Phi Theta Kappa, Business Professionals of America, student computer association, Student Chapter of the Institute of Management Accounts, Refrigeration service engineers society, student leadership academy, multicultural student organization.

Athletics. Intramural: Softball.

Student services. Adult student services, career counseling, student employment services, financial aid counseling, minority student services, on-campus daycare, personal counseling, placement for graduates, veterans' counselor. **Physically disabled:** Services for visually, speech, hearing impaired. **Transfer:** Special adviser, orientation for new students. Transfer adviser for students transferring to 4-year colleges.

Contact. E-mail: jplaster@ivytech.edu
Phone: (765) 966-2656 ext. 1212 Toll-free number: (800) 659-4562
Fax: (765) 962-8741
Jeff Plasterer, Director of Admissions, Ivy Tech Community College: Whitewater, 2325 Chester Boulevard, Richmond, IN 47374-1298

Lincoln Technical Institute

Indianapolis, Indiana
www.lincolntech.com **CB code: 3058**

- For-profit 2-year technical college
- Very large city

General. Accredited by ACCSCT. **Enrollment:** 610 degree-seeking undergraduates. **Degrees:** 860 associate awarded. **Calendar:** Continuous. **Full-time faculty:** 75 total. **Part-time faculty:** 15 total.

Basis for selection. Open admission.

2005-2006 Annual costs. Tuition $20,000 for auto-diesel management program, $16,000 for technology programs, $16,000 for drafting program. Books/supplies: $1,815.

Application procedures. Admission: No deadline. No application fee.

Academics. Credit/placement by examination: AP, CLEP.

Majors. Mechanic/repair: General.

Contact. Phone: (317) 632-5553 Toll-free number: (800) 554-4465
Fax: (317) 634-1089
Lincoln Technical Institute, 7225 Winton Drive, Building 128, Indianapolis, IN 46268

Mid-America College of Funeral Service

Jeffersonville, Indiana
www.mid-america.edu **CB code: 0644**

- For-profit 2-year school of mortuary science
- Commuter campus in large town

General. Founded in 1905. **Enrollment:** 100 degree-seeking undergraduates. **Degrees:** 74 associate awarded. **Location:** 5 miles from Louisville, Kentucky. **Calendar:** Quarter. **Full-time faculty:** 6 total.

Basis for selection. Open admission.

2005-2006 Annual costs. Cost of AAS degree program (including tuition, books, fees) is $14,100; cost per online course $700. Personal expenses: $2,520.

Application procedures. Admission: No deadline. $50 fee. Admission notification on a rolling basis. **Financial aid:** No deadline. FAFSA required. Applicants notified on a rolling basis.

Academics. Credit/placement by examination: CLEP.

Majors. Personal/culinary services: Mortuary science.

Computing on campus. 15 workstations in library, computer center.

Student life. Activities: Student government.

Student services. Student employment services, personal counseling, placement for graduates. **Transfer:** Pre-admission transcript evaluation for new students.

Contact. E-mail: macfs@mindspring.com
Phone: (812) 288-8878 Fax: (812) 288-5942
Cathy Denison, Director of Admissions, Mid-America College of Funeral Service, 3111 Hamburg Pike, Jeffersonville, IN 47130

Professional Careers Institute
Indianapolis, Indiana
www.pcicareers.com **CB code: 7700**

- For-profit 2-year business and health science college
- Commuter campus in very large city
- Application essay, interview required

General. Accredited by ACCSCT. **Enrollment:** 600 degree-seeking undergraduates. **Degrees:** 5 associate awarded. **Calendar:** Continuous. **Full-time faculty:** 50 total.

Basis for selection. Interview most important. Class rank, school record, recommendations, standardized test scores, and essay also important. **Adult students:** Entrance exam policies same as for first-time freshmen.

2006-2007 Annual costs. Tuition/fees: $9,900. Books/supplies: $500. Personal expenses: $1,472.

Financial aid. All financial aid based on need.

Application procedures. Admission: No deadline. $100 fee. Admission notification on a rolling basis.

Academics. Special study options: Accelerated study, internships. **Credit/placement by examination:** CLEP.

Majors. Business: Administrative services, business admin. **Computer sciences:** General, applications programming, data entry, information technology. **Health:** Dental assistant, massage therapy, medical assistant, medical secretary, office admin. **Legal studies:** Legal secretary, paralegal.

Computing on campus. 30 workstations in library, computer center.

Student life. Policies: Freshmen permitted cars on campus.

Student services. Financial aid counseling, placement for graduates.

Contact. E-mail: pclay@khec.com
Phone: (317) 299-6001
Paulette Clay, Director of Admissions, Professional Careers Institute, 7302 Woodland Drive, Indianapolis, IN 46278-1736

Sawyer College
Hammond, Indiana
www.sawyercollege.com **CB code: 2461**

- For-profit 2-year business and technical college
- Commuter campus in small city
- Interview required

General. Founded in 1969. Accredited by ACICS. Branch campus in Merrillville. **Enrollment:** 315 degree-seeking undergraduates. **Degrees:** 45 associate awarded. **Location:** 30 miles from Chicago, 15 miles from Merrillville. **Calendar:** Quarter, extensive summer session. **Full-time faculty:** 11 total. **Part-time faculty:** 30 total.

Basis for selection. Personal interview with admissions representative and passing score on entrance examination required.

Application procedures. Admission: No deadline. No application fee. Admission notification on a rolling basis. **Financial aid:** FAFSA required. Applicants notified on a rolling basis.

Academics. Special study options: Internships. **Credit/placement by examination:** CLEP, institutional tests. 24 credit hours maximum toward associate degree. Institutional placement test score must be at least 81%. **Support services:** Remedial instruction, study skills assistance, tutoring.

Majors. Business: Accounting, administrative services. **Computer sciences:** General. **Health:** Massage therapy, medical assistant, medical secretary. **Legal studies:** Legal secretary.

Most popular majors. Business/marketing 48%, computer/information sciences 52%.

Computing on campus. 70 workstations in computer center.

Student life. Activities: Student newspaper.

Student services. Career counseling, student employment services, personal counseling, placement for graduates. **Transfer:** Orientation, pre-admission transcript evaluation for new students.

Contact. E-mail: info@sawyercollege.com
Phone: (219) 844-0100 Fax: (219) 933-1239
Melissa Ovanin, Admissions Director, Sawyer College, 6040 Hohman Avenue, Hammond, IN 46320

Sawyer College: Merrillville
Merrillville, Indiana
www.sawyercollege.edu **CB code: 3381**

- For-profit 2-year technical college
- Commuter campus in large town
- Interview required

General. Accredited by ACICS. Branch campus of Sawyer College. **Enrollment:** 375 undergraduates. **Degrees:** 125 associate awarded. **Location:** 35 miles from Chicago. **Calendar:** Quarter. **Full-time faculty:** 18 total.

Basis for selection. Personal interview with admissions representative and passing score on entrance examination required. **Adult students:** Entrance exam policies same as for first-time freshmen. SAT/ACT scores not required.

2005-2006 Annual costs. Programs costs: $21,100 for 2 year programs, $12,100 for 9-month certificate programs. Books/supplies: $1,292.

Financial aid. Need-based: Need-based aid available for part-time students.

Application procedures. Admission: No deadline. $20 fee. Admission notification on a rolling basis. **Financial aid:** No deadline. FAFSA required. Applicants notified on a rolling basis.

Academics. Special study options: Liberal arts/career combination. **Credit/placement by examination:** CLEP, institutional tests. 50 credit hours maximum toward associate degree. **Support services:** Reduced course load, study skills assistance, tutoring.

Majors. Business: Accounting, accounting/business management, administrative services, business admin, executive assistant. **Communications technology:** Graphic/printing, graphics. **Computer sciences:** General, computer graphics, data processing, networking, programming, systems analysis, web page design, webmaster, word processing. **Engineering:** Computer hardware. **Engineering technology:** Computer, computer hardware, computer systems, software. **Health:** Massage therapy, medical assistant, medical transcription, office admin, office computer specialist. **Legal studies:** Legal secretary.

Computing on campus. PC or laptop required. 72 workstations in library, computer center. Online library, wireless network available.

Student life. Freshman orientation: Mandatory. Preregistration for classes offered. **Policies:** Freshmen permitted cars on campus.

Student services. Adult student services, career counseling, student employment services, financial aid counseling, placement for graduates. **Transfer:** Orientation, pre-admission transcript evaluation for new students.

Contact. E-mail: info@sawyercollege.edu
Phone: (219) 736-0436 Toll-free number: (800) 964-0218
Fax: (219) 942-3762
Linda Yednak, Executive Director, Sawyer College: Merrillville, 3803 East Lincoln Highway, Merrillville, IN 46410

Vincennes University

Vincennes, Indiana — **CB member**
www.vinu.edu — **CB code: 1877**

- Public 2-year junior and technical college
- Residential campus in large town

General. Founded in 1801. Regionally accredited. Oldest institution of higher education in Indiana. **Enrollment:** 4,700 degree-seeking undergraduates. **Degrees:** 4,115 associate awarded. **ROTC:** Army, Air Force. **Location:** 120 miles from Indianapolis, 55 miles from Evansville. **Calendar:** Semester, extensive summer session. **Full-time faculty:** 320 total. **Part-time faculty:** 120 total. **Special facilities:** 2 college-owned airports.

Student profile.

Out-of-state:	9%	**Live on campus:**	40%
25 or older:	20%		

Transfer out. Colleges most students transferred to 2005: Indiana University, Indiana State University, Purdue University, University of Southern Indiana, Ball State University.

Basis for selection. Open admission, but selective for some programs. Admission to health occupation programs based primarily on school achievement records, test scores, school and community activities, special talents/skills. SAT or ACT (SAT preferred) required for health occupation programs. Essay recommended. Audition required of music majors. Portfolio recommended for fine arts, commercial art, design majors. **Adult students:** Entrance exam policies same as for first-time freshmen. **Learning Disabled:** Separate application required for STEP program, psychometric testing required for students with learning disabilities.

High school preparation. Recommended units include English 4, mathematics 3, social studies 2, history 2, science 3 (laboratory 2) and foreign language 2.

2005-2006 Annual costs. Tuition/fees: $3,376; $8,200 out-of-state. Per-credit charge: $108 in-state; $268 out-of-state. Students from Crawford, Richland, Lawrence and Wabash counties in Illinois pay tuition of $5131, $171 per credit. Room/board: $6,402. Books/supplies: $500. Personal expenses: $550.

Financial aid. Need-based: Need-based aid available for part-time students. Work study available nights, weekends and for part-time students. **Non-need-based:** Scholarships awarded for academics, art, athletics, leadership, music/drama, state residency.

Application procedures. Admission: Priority date 7/14; deadline 8/20. $20 fee, may be waived for applicants with need. Application may be submitted online. Admission notification on a rolling basis. **Financial aid:** Priority date 3/1, closing date 5/1. FAFSA required. Applicants notified on a rolling basis starting 5/1; must reply by 8/24.

Academics. Special study options: Distance learning, dual enrollment of high school students, ESL, external degree, honors, independent study, internships, student-designed major, weekend college. License preparation in aviation, dental hygiene, nursing, paramedic, physical therapy, real estate. **Credit/placement by examination:** AP, CLEP, IB, institutional tests. 18 credit hours maximum toward associate degree. **Support services:** Learning center, pre-admission summer program, reduced course load, remedial instruction, study skills assistance, tutoring.

Honors college/program. 1100 SAT (exclusive of Writing), 25 ACT, leadership qualities, writing sample, 3 references. 20 students admitted for fall.

Majors. Agriculture: General, agribusiness operations, business, horticultural science, horticulture, products processing. **Area/ethnic studies:** American. **Biology:** General, botany. **Business:** General, accounting, administrative services, banking/financial services, business admin, fashion, hospitality admin, hospitality/recreation, hotel/motel admin, management information systems, marketing, office management, office technology, office/clerical, restaurant/food services, sales/distribution. **Communications:** General, advertising, broadcast journalism, digital media, journalism, media studies, public relations. **Communications technology:** Desktop publishing, graphic/printing, graphics, printing press operator, radio/tv. **Computer sciences:** General, applications programming, computer graphics, computer science, data processing, information systems, LAN/WAN management, networking, programming, web page design, webmaster. **Conservation:** General, environmental science, forestry. **Construction:** General, carpentry, maintenance. **Education:** General, art, biology, chemistry, computer, early childhood, elementary, English, family/consumer sciences, foreign languages, French, health, history, mathematics, middle, multi-level teacher, music, physical, physics, sales/marketing, science, secondary, social science, social studies, Spanish, special, speech, technology/industrial arts, trade/industrial, voc/tech. **Engineering:** General, chemical, civil, construction, electrical, environmental, mechanical, physics, surveying. **Engineering technology:** General, architectural drafting, civil, construction, drafting, electrical, manufacturing, robotics, surveying. **English:** Speech/rhetoric. **Family/consumer sciences:** General, child care, clothing/textiles, food/nutrition, institutional food production. **Foreign languages:** General, American Sign Language, French, German, sign language interpretation, Spanish. **Health:** Athletic training, dental hygiene, dietician assistant, EMT ambulance attendant, EMT paramedic, licensed practical nurse, medical records admin, medical records technology, medical secretary, medical transcription, nursing (RN), pharmacy assistant, physical therapy assistant, predentistry, premedicine, prepharmacy, preveterinary, recreational therapy. **History:** General. **Interdisciplinary:** Gerontology. **Legal studies:** Legal secretary, paralegal, prelaw. **Liberal arts:** Arts/sciences. **Math:** General. **Mechanic/repair:** General, aircraft, auto body, automotive, diesel, electronics/electrical, industrial. **Parks/recreation:** General, exercise sciences, facilities management, health/fitness, sports admin. **Personal/culinary services:** Cosmetic, culinary arts, funeral direction, mortuary science, restaurant/catering. **Philosophy/religion:** Philosophy. **Physical sciences:** General, chemistry, geology, physics, planetary. **Protective services:** Corrections, fire safety technology, firefighting, law enforcement admin, police science, security services. **Psychology:** General. **Public administration:** Social work. **Social sciences:** General, anthropology, economics, geography, political science, sociology. **Transportation:** Airline/commercial pilot, aviation management. **Visual/performing arts:** General, art, ceramics, commercial/advertising art, design, dramatic, drawing, fashion design, fiber arts, graphic design, interior design, music performance, music theory/composition, painting, piano/organ, printmaking, sculpture, studio arts, theater design, voice/opera.

Computing on campus. 350 workstations in dormitories, library, computer center, student center. Dormitories wired for high-speed internet access and linked to campus network. Online library, helpline, repair service, student web hosting available.

Student life. Freshman orientation: Mandatory. Preregistration for classes offered. Held the weekend prior to first day of classes; includes study skills, social activities, parent orientation. **Policies:** Freshmen permitted cars on campus. **Housing:** Guaranteed on-campus for freshmen. Coed dorms, single-sex dorms, special housing for disabled, fraternity/sorority housing available. $150 deposit. **Activities:** Bands, choral groups, dance, drama, film society, literary magazine, music ensembles, musical theater, radio station, student government, student newspaper, TV station, Latter Day Saints Student Association, Black Male Initiative, international students club, College Republicans, Christian Campus Fellowship, Catholic Campus Ministries, Baptist Collegiate Ministries, Democrat Club.

Athletics. NJCAA. **Intercollegiate:** Baseball M, basketball, bowling, cheerleading, cross-country, diving, golf M, swimming, tennis M, track and field, volleyball W. **Intramural:** Baseball M, basketball, bowling, cross-country, golf, gymnastics, handball, racquetball, skiing, softball, swimming, table tennis, tennis, track and field, volleyball, wrestling M. **Team name:** Trailblazers.

Student services. Adult student services, alcohol/substance abuse counseling, campus ministries, career counseling, student employment services, financial aid counseling, health services, minority student services, on-campus daycare, personal counseling, placement for graduates, veterans' counselor. **Physically disabled:** Services for visually, hearing impaired. **Learning disabled:** Comprehensive services available. **Transfer:** Special adviser, orientation for new students. Transfer adviser for students transferring to 4-year colleges.

Contact. E-mail: vuadmit@indian.vinu.edu
Phone: (812) 888-4313 Toll-free number: (800) 742-9198
Fax: (812) 888-5707
Phyllis Carling, Director of Admissions, Vincennes University, 1002 North First Street, Vincennes, IN 47591

Iowa

AIB College of Business

Des Moines, Iowa
www.aib.edu **CB code: 7302**

- Private 2-year business and junior college
- Residential campus in large city
- Interview required

General. Founded in 1921. Regionally accredited. Realtime reporting program approved by National Court Reporters Association. **Enrollment:** 811 degree-seeking undergraduates. **Degrees:** 226 associate awarded. **Location:** 2 miles from downtown. **Calendar:** Quarter, extensive summer session. **Full-time faculty:** 23 total; 4% have terminal degrees, 61% women. **Part-time faculty:** 45 total; 9% have terminal degrees, 2% minority, 49% women. **Class size:** 59% < 20, 41% 20-39. **Special facilities:** Dictation tape library for realtime reporting speed development, video collection, lab developed for CISCO classes, two labs developed for MCSE classes as part of Microsoft IT Academy. **Partnerships:** Formal partnerships with IBM, Microsoft certification AATP, high schools.

Student profile.

Out-of-state:	4%	**Live on campus:**	50%
25 or older:	29%		

Transfer out. Colleges most students transferred to 2005: Graceland College, Simpson College, Upper Iowa University.

Basis for selection. High school record, interview, and test scores important. All students required to take standardized test (ACT or institution's own). ACT recommended. If ACT score is below 18 or if ACT is not submitted, institution's own test is administered. **Adult students:** Testing not required if student has proof of previous college degree.

2005-2006 Annual costs. Tuition/fees: $11,889. Per-credit charge: $330. Room/board: $3,957. Books/supplies: $840. Personal expenses: $1,135.

Financial aid. Need-based: Need-based aid available for part-time students. Work study available nights, weekends and for part-time students. **Non-need-based:** Scholarships awarded for academics, alumni affiliation, leadership.

Application procedures. Admission: No deadline. $25 fee, may be waived for applicants with need. Application may be submitted online. Admission notification on a rolling basis. **Financial aid:** Closing date 4/1. FAFSA, institutional form required. Applicants notified on a rolling basis starting 3/1; must reply within 3 week(s) of notification.

Academics. Special study options: Cross-registration, distance learning, double major, dual enrollment of high school students, internships, liberal arts/career combination. **Credit/placement by examination:** AP, CLEP, institutional tests. **Support services:** Reduced course load, remedial instruction, study skills assistance, tutoring.

Majors. Business: General, accounting, accounting/business management, accounting/finance, administrative services, banking/financial services, business admin, finance, marketing, office management, selling, tourism/travel. **Computer sciences:** Information technology, networking, programming, system admin. **Legal studies:** Court reporting.

Most popular majors. Business/marketing 63%, computer/information sciences 18%.

Computing on campus. 340 workstations in dormitories, library, student center. Dormitories linked to campus network. Online course registration, online library, helpline available.

Student life. Freshman orientation: Mandatory. One-day to 1-week program. **Policies:** Freshmen permitted cars on campus. **Housing:** Coed dorms, special housing for disabled, apartments, fraternity/sorority housing available. $150 deposit. Housing available for single-parent, married students, families. **Activities:** Student government.

Athletics. Intramural: Badminton, basketball, bowling, football (non-tackle) M, golf, softball, table tennis, tennis, volleyball.

Student services. Adult student services, alcohol/substance abuse counseling, career counseling, student employment services, financial aid counseling, personal counseling, placement for graduates. **Physically disabled:** Services for visually, speech, hearing impaired. **Transfer:** Special adviser, orientation, pre-admission transcript evaluation for new students. Transfer adviser for students transferring to 4-year colleges.

Contact. E-mail: info@aib.edu
Phone: (515) 244-4221 Toll-free number: (800) 444-1921
Fax: (515) 244-6773
Bindel Joan, Vice President for Enrollment, AIB College of Business, 2500 Fleur Drive, Des Moines, IA 50321-1799

Clinton Community College

Clinton, Iowa
www.eicc.edu **CB code: 6100**

- Public 2-year community college
- Commuter campus in large town

General. Founded in 1946. Regionally accredited. **Degrees:** 168 associate awarded. **Location:** 40 miles from Davenport. **Calendar:** Semester, limited summer session. **Full-time faculty:** 30 total. **Part-time faculty:** 40 total.

Basis for selection. Open admission, but selective for some programs. Special requirements for nursing program. Interview recommended.

2005-2006 Annual costs. Tuition/fees: $2,700; $4,050 out-of-state. Per-credit charge: $90 in-state; $135 out-of-state. Books/supplies: $900. Personal expenses: $900.

Application procedures. Admission: No deadline. No application fee. Admission notification on a rolling basis beginning on or about 9/1. **Financial aid:** Priority date 4/20; no closing date. FAFSA, institutional form required. Applicants notified on a rolling basis starting 5/15; must reply within 2 week(s) of notification.

Academics. Special study options: Accelerated study, cooperative education, cross-registration, distance learning, double major, dual enrollment of high school students, ESL, honors, independent study, study abroad. **Credit/placement by examination:** CLEP. 30 credit hours maximum toward associate degree. **Support services:** Learning center, reduced course load, remedial instruction, tutoring.

Majors. Business: Administrative services. **Communications technology:** Graphic/printing. **Engineering technology:** Drafting, electrical, occupational safety. **Health:** Nursing (RN). **Liberal arts:** Arts/sciences.

Computing on campus. 70 workstations in library, computer center.

Student life. Activities: Drama, student government, student newspaper, Circle-K, Phi Beta Lambda, skiing, drafting, art.

Athletics. NJCAA. **Intercollegiate:** Baseball M, basketball M, golf, soccer, softball W, volleyball W. **Intramural:** Basketball, bowling, softball, table tennis, tennis, volleyball.

Student services. Career counseling, student employment services, personal counseling, placement for graduates, veterans' counselor. **Physically disabled:** Services for visually, speech, hearing impaired. **Transfer:** Special adviser, orientation for new students. Transfer adviser, college fairs on campus for students transferring to 4-year colleges.

Contact. Phone: (319) 244-7001 Fax: (563) 242-7868
Susan Carmody, Assistant Dean for Enrollment Services, Clinton Community College, 1000 Lincoln Boulevard, Clinton, IA 52732

Des Moines Area Community College

Ankeny, Iowa **CB member**
www.dmacc.edu **CB code: 6177**

- Public 2-year community college
- Commuter campus in large town

General. Founded in 1966. Regionally accredited. Multilocation institution with campuses at Boone, Des Moines, West Des Moines, Carroll, and Newton. Ankeny campus is primary location and administrative center. **Enrollment:** 16,046 degree-seeking undergraduates. **Degrees:** 1,420 associate awarded. **Location:** 15 miles from downtown Des Moines, 25 miles from Ames. **Calendar:** Semester, extensive summer session. **Full-time faculty:** 289 total; 11% have terminal degrees, 5% minority, 52% women. **Part-time faculty:** 765 total; 13% have terminal degrees, 6% minority, 48% women. **Special facilities:** Wireless computer technology campus.

Two-Year Colleges

Student profile. Among degree-seeking undergraduates, 4,901 enrolled as first-time, first-year students.

Part-time:	60%	**Hispanic American:**	3%
Women:	56%	**International:**	1%
African American:	5%	**25 or older:**	28%
Asian American:	3%		

Transfer out. Colleges most students transferred to 2005: Iowa State University, Grand View College, University of Northern Iowa.

Basis for selection. Open admission, but selective for some programs. Special requirements for dental hygiene, commercial art, nursing, CAP programs. Interview required of dental hygiene, commercial art majors. Portfolio required of commercial art majors. **Adult students:** Entrance exam policies same as for first-time freshmen.

High school preparation. Recommended units include English 3, mathematics 3, social studies 1 and science 1.

2005-2006 Annual costs. Tuition/fees: $2,850; $5,700 out-of-state. Per-credit charge: $95 in-state; $190 out-of-state. Books/supplies: $860. Personal expenses: $1,568.

Financial aid. Need-based: Need-based aid available for part-time students. Work study available nights, weekends and for part-time students. **Non-need-based:** Scholarships awarded for academics, athletics, state residency.

Application procedures. Admission: No deadline. No application fee. Application may be submitted online. Admission notification on a rolling basis. **Financial aid:** Priority date 4/1; no closing date. FAFSA required. Applicants notified on a rolling basis starting 4/1; must reply within 2 week(s) of notification.

Academics. Special study options: Cooperative education, cross-registration, distance learning, dual enrollment of high school students, ESL, honors, independent study, internships, liberal arts/career combination, study abroad, weekend college. License preparation in dental hygiene, nursing, paramedic, real estate. **Credit/placement by examination:** AP, CLEP, institutional tests. 28 credit hours maximum toward associate degree. **Support services:** GED preparation and test center, learning center, preadmission summer program, reduced course load, remedial instruction, study skills assistance, tutoring, writing center.

Majors. Agriculture: Horticulture, supplies. **Biology:** Biotechnology. **Business:** Accounting, accounting technology, apparel, business admin, hospitality admin, marketing, office management, sales/distribution. **Communications technology:** Desktop publishing. **Computer sciences:** General, applications programming, information technology. **Construction:** Carpentry. **Engineering:** Surveying. **Engineering technology:** Architectural drafting, civil, electrical, mechanical drafting. **Health:** Clinical lab technology, dental hygiene, health care admin, medical secretary, nursing (RN), respiratory therapy technology, veterinary technology/assistant. **Legal studies:** Paralegal. **Liberal arts:** Arts/sciences. **Mechanic/repair:** Auto body, automotive, communications systems, diesel, heating/ac/refrig, industrial, industrial electronics. **Parks/recreation:** Sports admin. **Personal/culinary services:** Chef training. **Production:** Machine tool, tool and die, welding. **Protective services:** Fire safety technology, police science. **Public administration:** Community org/advocacy. **Visual/performing arts:** Commercial/advertising art.

Most popular majors. Business/marketing 13%, health sciences 14%, liberal arts 45%, trade and industry 8%.

Computing on campus. 200 workstations in library, computer center. Commuter students can connect to campus network. Online course registration, online library, helpline, wireless network available.

Student life. Freshman orientation: Available. Preregistration for classes offered. Half-day program offered. **Policies:** Student Action Board responsible for many on-campus activities: professional and social. Freshmen permitted cars on campus. **Activities:** Choral groups, drama, literary magazine, student government, student newspaper.

Athletics. NJCAA. **Intercollegiate:** Baseball M, basketball, volleyball W. **Intramural:** Badminton, basketball, bowling, football (non-tackle), golf, softball, table tennis, tennis, volleyball. **Team name:** Bears (Boone campus only).

Student services. Adult student services, career counseling, student employment services, financial aid counseling, health services, on-campus daycare, personal counseling, placement for graduates, veterans' counselor. **Physically disabled:** Services for visually, speech, hearing impaired. **Transfer:** Special adviser, orientation for new students. Transfer adviser, college fairs on campus for students transferring to 4-year colleges.

Contact. Phone: (515) 964-6241 Toll-free number: (800) 362-2127 ext. 6241 Fax: (515) 964-6391
Keith Knowles, Director of Admissions and Assessment, Des Moines Area Community College, 2006 South Ankeny Boulevard, Ankeny, IA 50021

Ellsworth Community College

Iowa Falls, Iowa
www.ellsworthcollege.edu **CB code: 5528**

- Public 2-year community college
- Residential campus in small town

General. Founded in 1890. Regionally accredited. **Enrollment:** 1,000 degree-seeking undergraduates. **Degrees:** 197 associate awarded. **Location:** 70 miles from Des Moines. **Calendar:** Semester, limited summer session. **Full-time faculty:** 35 total. **Special facilities:** 80-acre wildlife area.

Transfer out. Colleges most students transferred to 2005: University of Northern Iowa, Buena Vista University, Iowa State University, Wartburg College, University of Iowa.

Basis for selection. Open admission, but selective for some programs. Special requirements for some nursing programs. **Adult students:** Entrance exam policies same as for first-time freshmen.

2005-2006 Annual costs. Tuition/fees: $3,705; $4,455 out-of-state. Per-credit charge: $101 in-state; $126 out-of-state. Books/supplies: $700. Personal expenses: $1,400.

2004-2005 Financial aid. Need-based: 39% of total undergraduate aid awarded as scholarships/grants, 61% as loans/jobs. Need-based aid available for part-time students. Work study available nights, weekends and for part-time students. **Non-need-based:** Scholarships awarded for academics, art, athletics, leadership, minority status, music/drama.

Application procedures. Admission: No deadline. No application fee. Application may be submitted online. Admission notification on a rolling basis. COMPASS required of applicants without SAT or ACT. **Financial aid:** Priority date 4/1; no closing date. FAFSA, institutional form required. Applicants notified on a rolling basis starting 2/15; must reply within 4 week(s) of notification.

Academics. Special study options: Cooperative education, cross-registration, distance learning, double major, dual enrollment of high school students, ESL, honors, independent study, internships, liberal arts/career combination. Bachelor's degree programs available on campus. License preparation in nursing. **Credit/placement by examination:** AP, CLEP, institutional tests. 24 credit hours maximum toward associate degree. **Support services:** GED preparation and test center, learning center, remedial instruction, study skills assistance, tutoring, writing center.

Majors. Agriculture: Business, equestrian studies, farm/ranch. **Biology:** General, biotechnology. **Business:** General, accounting, administrative services, fashion, insurance, office technology, office/clerical. **Communications:** General. **Computer sciences:** General, computer graphics, computer science, data processing, information systems, LAN/WAN management, programming. **Conservation:** General, wildlife. **Construction:** Carpentry. **Education:** General, agricultural, biology, business, chemistry, elementary, family/consumer sciences, history, mathematics, middle, multi-level teacher, physical, physically handicapped, physics, science, secondary, social science, social studies, teacher assistance. **Engineering:** General. **Family/consumer sciences:** General, clothing/textiles, family/community services. **Health:** Athletic training, medical secretary, nursing (RN), predentistry, premedicine, prepharmacy, preveterinary. **History:** General. **Interdisciplinary:** Behavioral sciences, natural sciences. **Legal studies:** Legal secretary, prelaw. **Liberal arts:** Arts/sciences. **Math:** General. **Parks/recreation:** Health/fitness. **Physical sciences:** Chemistry, physics. **Protective services:** Criminal justice, law enforcement admin. **Psychology:** General. **Public administration:** Human services, social work. **Science technology:** Biological. **Social sciences:** General, criminology, sociology. **Visual/performing arts:** Art, commercial/advertising art, dramatic, studio arts.

Most popular majors. Business/marketing 10%, health sciences 10%, liberal arts 59%, trade and industry 7%.

Computing on campus. 100 workstations in dormitories, library, computer center, student center. Dormitories wired for high-speed internet access and linked to campus network. Commuter students can connect to campus network. Online library, repair service, wireless network available.

Student life. Freshman orientation: Mandatory. Preregistration for classes offered. 6 to 8 dates set for orientation, advising, and preregistration. **Policies:** Freshmen permitted cars on campus. **Housing:** Guaranteed on-campus for freshmen. Single-sex dorms available. $200 deposit. **Activities:** Bands, choral groups, dance, drama, literary magazine, music ensembles, musical theater, student government, student newspaper, Young Democrats, Young Republicans, minority student organization, human services club, ag science club, criminal justice club, international club.

Athletics. NJCAA. **Intercollegiate:** Baseball M, basketball, cross-country, football (tackle) M, golf, softball W, volleyball W, wrestling M. **Intramural:** Badminton, basketball, bowling, football (non-tackle), handball, racquetball, swimming, tennis, volleyball. **Team name:** Panthers.

Student services. Adult student services, alcohol/substance abuse counseling, career counseling, services for economically disadvantaged, student employment services, financial aid counseling, health services, personal counseling, placement for graduates, veterans' counselor. **Transfer:** Special adviser, orientation, pre-admission transcript evaluation for new students. Transfer adviser, college fairs on campus for students transferring to 4-year colleges.

Contact. Phone: (641) 648-4611 ext. 431 Toll-free number: (800) 322-9253 Fax: (641) 648-3128
Annie Stelow, Director of Admissions, Ellsworth Community College, 1100 College Avenue, Iowa Falls, IA 50126

Hawkeye Community College

Waterloo, Iowa
www.hawkeyecollege.edu **CB code: 6288**

- Public 2-year community and technical college
- Commuter campus in small city

General. Founded in 1966. Regionally accredited. **Enrollment:** 4,822 degree-seeking undergraduates. **Degrees:** 849 associate awarded. **ROTC:** Army, Navy, Air Force. **Location:** 120 miles from Des Moines, 90 miles from Cedar Rapids, South Dakota. **Calendar:** Semester, limited summer session. **Full-time faculty:** 112 total; 8% have terminal degrees, 4% minority, 44% women. **Part-time faculty:** 231 total; 4% have terminal degrees, 6% minority, 64% women.

Student profile. Among degree-seeking undergraduates, 52% enrolled in a transfer program, 48% enrolled in a vocational program.

Out-of-state:	1%	**25 or older:**	26%

Transfer out. Colleges most students transferred to 2005: University of Northern Iowa, University of Iowa, Iowa State University.

Basis for selection. Open admission, but selective for some programs. Program requirements and basic skills required for all programs. ACT required for admission to medical laboratory technician and dental hygiene programs only. **Adult students:** Entrance exam policies same as for first-time freshmen.

High school preparation. One year biology required for nursing and medical laboratory technicians. One year chemistry required for respiratory care and nursing. Two semesters of studio art and one computer course required for graphic communications.

2005-2006 Annual costs. Tuition/fees: $3,255; $6,195 out-of-state. Per-credit charge: $98 in-state; $196 out-of-state. Books/supplies: $850. Personal expenses: $4,304.

2004-2005 Financial aid. Need-based: 32% of total undergraduate aid awarded as scholarships/grants, 68% as loans/jobs. Work study available nights, weekends and for part-time students. **Non-need-based:** Scholarships awarded for academics, state residency.

Application procedures. Admission: No deadline. No application fee. Application may be submitted online. Admission notification on a rolling basis. Accepted students asked to pay first-semester tuition in August to confirm fall enrollment or enter into a tuition payment plan. **Financial aid:** Priority date 3/15; no closing date. FAFSA, institutional form required. Applicants notified on a rolling basis starting 4/25; must reply within 2 week(s) of notification.

Academics. Special study options: Cooperative education, distance learning, dual enrollment of high school students, external degree, honors, independent study, internships, liberal arts/career combination, study abroad, weekend college. License preparation in dental hygiene, nursing. **Credit/placement by examination:** AP, CLEP, institutional tests. 30 credit hours maximum toward associate degree. **Support services:** GED preparation and test center, learning center, reduced course load, remedial instruction, study skills assistance, tutoring.

Majors. Agriculture: Animal husbandry, horticulture, power machinery, supplies. **Business:** General, accounting, executive assistant, marketing. **Communications technology:** Graphics. **Computer sciences:** Networking, web page design. **Conservation:** Management/policy. **Engineering technology:** Architectural drafting, civil, electrical, manufacturing, mechanical drafting. **Health:** Clinical lab technology, dental hygiene, medical secretary, nursing (RN), preop/surgical nursing, respiratory therapy technology. **Liberal arts:** Arts/sciences. **Mechanic/repair:** Auto body, automotive, avionics, diesel. **Production:** Machine tool, tool and die. **Protective services:** Police science. **Visual/performing arts:** Commercial photography, interior design.

Most popular majors. Engineering/engineering technologies 6%, health sciences 12%, liberal arts 48%, security/protective services 6%, trade and industry 6%, visual/performing arts 6%.

Computing on campus. 300 workstations in library, computer center. Commuter students can connect to campus network. Online course registration available.

Student life. Freshman orientation: Available. Preregistration for classes offered. Held week before classes begin. **Policies:** Freshmen permitted cars on campus. **Activities:** Student government.

Athletics. Intramural: Basketball, bowling, football (non-tackle), softball, volleyball.

Student services. Career counseling, student employment services, financial aid counseling, on-campus daycare, personal counseling, placement for graduates, veterans' counselor. **Physically disabled:** Services for visually, hearing impaired. **Transfer:** Special adviser, orientation, pre-admission transcript evaluation for new students. Transfer center, transfer adviser, college fairs on campus for students transferring to 4-year colleges.

Contact. E-mail: admission@hawkeyecollege.edu
Phone: (319) 296-4000 Toll-free number: (800) 670-4769 ext. 4000
Fax: (319) 296-2505
David Ball, Director of Admissions & Recruiting, Hawkeye Community College, Box 8015, Waterloo, IA 50704-8015

Indian Hills Community College

Ottumwa, Iowa
www.indianhills.edu **CB code: 6312**

- Public 2-year community college
- Commuter campus in large town

General. Founded in 1966. Regionally accredited. **Enrollment:** 3,007 degree-seeking undergraduates; 670 non-degree-seeking students. **Degrees:** 805 associate awarded. **Location:** 90 miles from Des Moines. **Calendar:** Quarter, limited summer session. **Full-time faculty:** 127 total; 46% women. **Part-time faculty:** 21 total; 52% women. **Class size:** 66% < 20, 27% 20-39, 4% 40-49, 4% 50-99. **Special facilities:** Nature preserve, outdoor amphitheater.

Student profile. Among degree-seeking undergraduates, 27% enrolled in a transfer program, 73% enrolled in a vocational program, 840 enrolled as first-time, first-year students, 155 transferred in from other institutions.

Part-time:	24%	**Hispanic American:**	1%
Out-of-state:	7%	**Native American:**	1%
Women:	58%	**International:**	1%
African American:	1%	**25 or older:**	29%
Asian American:	1%	**Live on campus:**	15%

Basis for selection. Open admission, but selective for some programs. GPA, any prior college credit, test scores considered for limited enrollment programs. ACT required for technology programs and for counseling. College Qualification Test required for some health occupation program applicants. **Adult students:** Entrance exam policies same as for first-time freshmen. SAT/ACT scores not required. **Homeschooled:** Students admitted without a high school diploma or equivalent but must have either one before receiving degree.

High school preparation. Recommended units include English 2, mathematics 2, science 2 (laboratory 2).

2006-2007 Annual costs. Tuition/fees (projected): $3,195; $4,755 out-of-state. Per-credit charge: $104 in-state; $156 out-of-state. Room/board: $4,300. Books/supplies: $675. Personal expenses: $750.

2004-2005 Financial aid. Need-based: 55% of total undergraduate aid awarded as scholarships/grants, 45% as loans/jobs. Need-based aid available for part-time students. **Non-need-based:** Scholarships awarded for athletics, state residency.

Application procedures. Admission: Priority date 7/1; no deadline. No application fee. Application may be submitted online. Admission notification on a rolling basis. **Financial aid:** Priority date 4/1; no closing date. FAFSA, institutional form required. Applicants notified on a rolling basis starting 6/1; must reply within 2 week(s) of notification.

Academics. **Special study options:** Cooperative education, distance learning, dual enrollment of high school students, ESL, honors, independent study, internships, liberal arts/career combination. License preparation in aviation, nursing, paramedic, physical therapy, radiology, real estate. **Credit/placement by examination:** CLEP, institutional tests. 16 credit hours maximum toward associate degree. **Support services:** GED preparation and test center, learning center, reduced course load, remedial instruction, study skills assistance, tutoring.

Majors. **Agriculture:** Production. **Computer sciences:** Applications programming, networking, security. **Construction:** General. **Engineering:** Agricultural. **Engineering technology:** Electrical, laser/optical, mechanical drafting, robotics. **Health:** Clinical lab technology, EMT paramedic, medical records technology, nursing (RN), physical therapy assistant, radiologic technology/medical imaging. **Liberal arts:** Arts/sciences. **Mechanic/repair:** Auto body, automotive, avionics, diesel. **Personal/culinary services:** Chef training. **Production:** Machine tool. **Protective services:** Police science. **Science technology:** Biological. **Transportation:** Airline/commercial pilot.

Computing on campus. 150 workstations in library, computer center, student center. Dormitories wired for high-speed internet access. Commuter students can connect to campus network. Online course registration, wireless network available.

Student life. **Freshman orientation:** Available. **Housing:** Coed dorms, single-sex dorms available. $50 deposit. **Activities:** Jazz band, choral groups, dance, drama, music ensembles, musical theater, student government, symphony orchestra.

Athletics. NJCAA. **Intercollegiate:** Baseball M, basketball M, golf M, softball W, volleyball W. **Intramural:** Basketball, bowling, fencing, racquetball, softball, tennis, volleyball. **Team name:** Warriors.

Student services. Adult student services, career counseling, student employment services, health services, on-campus daycare, personal counseling, placement for graduates, veterans' counselor. **Physically disabled:** Services for visually, hearing impaired. **Transfer:** Special adviser for new students. Transfer adviser, college fairs on campus for students transferring to 4-year colleges.

Contact. E-mail: enrollment_services@ihcc.cc
Phone: (641) 683-5153 Toll-free number: (800) 726-2585 ext. 5153
Fax: (641) 683-5184
Jane Sapp, Admissions Officer, Indian Hills Community College, 623 Indian Hills Drive, Building 12, Ottumwa, IA 52501

Iowa Central Community College

Fort Dodge, Iowa
www.iccc.cc.ia.us **CB code: 6217**

- Public 2-year community college
- Commuter campus in large town

General. Founded in 1966. Regionally accredited. College courses available at 3 branch campuses: Webster City, Eagle Grove, Storm Lake. **Enrollment:** 5,352 degree-seeking undergraduates. **Degrees:** 641 associate awarded. **Location:** 90 miles from Des Moines. **Calendar:** Semester, limited summer session. **Full-time faculty:** 70 total. **Part-time faculty:** 200 total. **Special facilities:** Audio/video studio, broadcasting suite.

Student profile.

Out-of-state:	5%	Live on campus:	20%

Transfer out. **Colleges most students transferred to 2005:** Buena Vista University, Iowa State University, University of Northern Iowa.

Basis for selection. Open admission, but selective for some programs. **Adult students:** Entrance exam policies same as for first-time freshmen.

2005-2006 Annual costs. Tuition/fees: $3,090; $4,485 out-of-state. Per-credit charge: $93 in-state; $140 out-of-state. Room/board: $4,400. Books/supplies: $750. Personal expenses: $1,240.

Financial aid. All financial aid based on need. Need-based aid available for part-time students. Work study available nights, weekends and for part-time students.

Application procedures. **Admission:** No deadline. No application fee. Admission notification on a rolling basis. **Financial aid:** No deadline. FAFSA required. Applicants notified on a rolling basis starting 4/15; must reply within 2 week(s) of notification.

Academics. **Special study options:** Accelerated study, cooperative education, cross-registration, distance learning, dual enrollment of high school students, external degree, honors, independent study, internships, study abroad. Semester in England. License preparation in aviation, nursing, paramedic, radiology. **Credit/placement by examination:** AP, CLEP. 30 credit hours maximum toward associate degree. ACT may be submitted for placement in lieu of COMPASS or ASSET. **Support services:** GED preparation and test center, learning center, pre-admission summer program, reduced course load, remedial instruction, study skills assistance, tutoring.

Majors. **Business:** Accounting, administrative services, business admin, office management. **Communications:** Broadcast journalism. **Communications technology:** General. **Computer sciences:** Networking. **Construction:** Electrician. **Engineering technology:** Drafting, manufacturing. **Health:** Clinical lab technology, EMT paramedic, medical assistant, medical radiologic technology/radiation therapy, nursing (RN), occupational therapy assistant, physical therapy assistant, premedicine, prepharmacy, preveterinary. **Legal studies:** Prelaw. **Liberal arts:** Arts/sciences. **Mechanic/repair:** Automotive. **Protective services:** Police science. **Psychology:** General. **Public administration:** Community org/advocacy. **Transportation:** Aviation.

Computing on campus. 500 workstations in library, computer center. Dormitories wired for high-speed internet access and linked to campus network. Commuter students can connect to campus network. Online course registration, helpline available.

Student life. **Freshman orientation:** Available. Preregistration for classes offered. One-day program. **Housing:** Coed dorms, single-sex dorms, special housing for disabled, apartments available. $100 deposit. **Activities:** Bands, choral groups, dance, drama, music ensembles, musical theater, radio station, student government, student newspaper, symphony orchestra.

Athletics. NJCAA. **Intercollegiate:** Baseball M, basketball, cross-country, football (tackle) M, golf, rodeo, soccer, softball W, track and field, volleyball W, wrestling M. **Intramural:** Basketball, bowling, golf, volleyball. **Team name:** Tritons.

Student services. Career counseling, services for economically disadvantaged, student employment services, financial aid counseling, health services, minority student services, personal counseling, placement for graduates, veterans' counselor. **Physically disabled:** Services for visually, speech, hearing impaired. **Transfer:** Special adviser, orientation for new students. Transfer adviser, college fairs on campus for students transferring to 4-year colleges.

Contact. Phone: (515) 576-7201 ext. 2400 Toll-free number: (800) 362-2793 Fax: (515) 576-7724
Patty Harrison, Director of Admissions, Iowa Central Community College, 330 Avenue M, Fort Dodge, IA 50501

Iowa Lakes Community College

Estherville, Iowa
www.iowalakes.edu **CB code: 6196**

- Public 2-year community college
- Commuter campus in small town

General. Founded in 1967. Regionally accredited. 2 campuses operating in Estherville and Emmetsburg. Classes also offered at centers located in Spencer, Algona, and Spirit Lake. **Enrollment:** 3,046 degree-seeking undergraduates. **Degrees:** 411 associate awarded. **Location:** 100 miles from Mason City, 100 miles from Sioux Falls, South Dakota. **Calendar:** Semester, limited summer session. **Full-time faculty:** 65 total. **Part-time faculty:** 20 total. **Special facilities:** 360-acre farm, print collection.

Transfer out. **Colleges most students transferred to 2005:** University of Northern Iowa, Iowa State University, University of Iowa, Minnesota State University-Mankato, Buena Vista University.

Basis for selection. Open admission, but selective for some programs. Special requirements for nursing, aviation/airport management, and computer-aided drafting and design programs. ACT required for nursing students. Interview required of career programs. Audition recommended for music majors. Portfolio recommended for advertising design majors.

2005-2006 Annual costs. Tuition/fees: $3,522; $3,582 out-of-state. Per-credit charge: $103 in-state; $105 out-of-state. Room/board: $4,120. Books/supplies: $600. Personal expenses: $500.

Application procedures. **Admission:** No deadline. No application fee. Admission notification on a rolling basis. **Financial aid:** Priority date 4/22; no closing date. FAFSA, institutional form required. Applicants notified on a rolling basis starting 4/15.

Academics. **Special study options:** Cooperative education, cross-registration, distance learning, dual enrollment of high school students, honors, internships, weekend college. Evening college. License preparation in aviation, nursing, paramedic, real estate. **Credit/placement by examination:** CLEP, institutional tests. 30 credit hours maximum toward associate degree. **Support services:** GED preparation and test center, learning center, pre-admission summer program, reduced course load, remedial instruction, study skills assistance, tutoring.

Majors. Agriculture: Landscaping, power machinery, production, supplies. **Business:** Accounting, business admin, office management, sales/distribution, tourism promotion. **Communications:** Broadcast journalism, journalism. **Computer sciences:** Applications programming, networking, security. **Conservation:** Environmental studies. **Engineering:** Agricultural. **Engineering technology:** Drafting, energy systems, environmental, mechanical drafting. **Health:** EMT paramedic, health care admin, nursing (RN). **Legal studies:** Paralegal. **Liberal arts:** Arts/sciences. **Parks/recreation:** Facilities management. **Protective services:** Police science. **Social sciences:** Cartography. **Transportation:** Aviation. **Visual/performing arts:** Commercial/advertising art, photography.

Computing on campus. 800 workstations in library, computer center, student center. Dormitories wired for high-speed internet access. Online course registration, helpline, wireless network available.

Student life. Freshman orientation: Available. Preregistration for classes offered. **Policies:** Freshmen permitted cars on campus. **Housing:** Coed dorms, apartments available. **Activities:** Bands, choral groups, literary magazine, music ensembles, musical theater, student government, student newspaper.

Athletics. NJCAA. **Intercollegiate:** Baseball M, basketball, golf, softball W, track and field, volleyball W. **Intramural:** Basketball, bowling, golf, racquetball, skiing, softball, table tennis, volleyball. **Team name:** Lakers.

Student services. Adult student services, alcohol/substance abuse counseling, career counseling, services for economically disadvantaged, financial aid counseling, personal counseling, placement for graduates, veterans' counselor, women's services. **Transfer:** Special adviser, orientation for new students. Transfer adviser, college fairs on campus for students transferring to 4-year colleges.

Contact. E-mail: info@iowalakes.edu
Phone: (712) 362-2604 ext. 145 Toll-free number: (800) 521-5054
Fax: (712) 362-3969
Julie Carlson, Admissions Counselor, Iowa Lakes Community College, 300 South 18th Street, Estherville, IA 51334-2725

Iowa Western Community College

Council Bluffs, Iowa
www.iwcc.edu **CB code: 6302**

- Public 2-year community and technical college
- Commuter campus in small city
- Interview required

General. Founded in 1966. Regionally accredited. Branch campus at Clarinda offers liberal arts and vocational programs in practical nursing, secretarial, mechanical technology, and electromechanical technology. Centers in Harlan and Atlantic offer evening programs in liberal arts and business administration. Practical nursing offered at Harlan. **Enrollment:** 5,092 degree-seeking undergraduates. **Degrees:** 532 associate awarded. **ROTC:** Army, Air Force. **Location:** 10 miles from Omaha. **Calendar:** Semester, extensive summer session. **Full-time faculty:** 100 total. **Part-time faculty:** 67 total. **Partnerships:** College courses offered through us to several high schools in our area.

Student profile.

Out-of-state:	10%	**Live on campus:**	21%

Transfer out. Colleges most students transferred to 2005: University of Iowa, Iowa State University, Northwest Missouri State University, University of Nebraska at Omaha, Buena Vista University.

Basis for selection. Open admission, but selective for some programs. Academic enrichment courses available to help gain proficiency needed for admission to specific programs. The COMPASS or ACT/SAT is required for all new students. Interview required of vocational-technical applicants. **Adult students:** Entrance exam policies same as for first-time freshmen.

High school preparation. Specific subject requirements for some career programs.

2005-2006 Annual costs. Tuition/fees: $3,620; $5,270 out-of-state. Room/board: $5,490. Books/supplies: $800. Personal expenses: $1,440.

Financial aid. Need-based: Need-based aid available for part-time students. **Non-need-based:** Scholarships awarded for athletics, music/drama.

Application procedures. Admission: No deadline. No application fee. Application may be submitted online. Admission notification on a rolling basis. Applicants for limited-enrollment programs considered on first applied, first accepted basis. **Financial aid:** Priority date 5/1; no closing date. FAFSA required. Applicants notified on a rolling basis starting 3/1; must reply within 3 week(s) of notification.

Academics. Special study options: Cooperative education, distance learning, ESL, independent study, internships, weekend college. License preparation in aviation, dental hygiene, nursing. **Credit/placement by examination:** CLEP, institutional tests. 40 credit hours maximum toward associate degree. **Support services:** GED preparation and test center, learning center, reduced course load, remedial instruction, study skills assistance, tutoring, writing center.

Majors. Agriculture: General, agribusiness operations, business. **Biology:** General. **Business:** Administrative services, sales/distribution. **Communications technology:** Graphic/printing. **Computer sciences:** Programming. **Education:** General. **Engineering technology:** Architectural, civil, electrical. **Family/consumer sciences:** Child care, institutional food production. **Foreign languages:** Sign language interpretation. **Health:** Dental hygiene, medical secretary, nursing (RN), substance abuse counseling. **Legal studies:** Legal secretary, paralegal. **Liberal arts:** Arts/sciences. **Math:** General. **Mechanic/repair:** General, aircraft. **Personal/culinary services:** Culinary arts. **Protective services:** Firefighting, forensics. **Psychology:** General. **Public administration:** Human services, social work.

Computing on campus. 250 workstations in dormitories, library, computer center, student center. Dormitories wired for high-speed internet access.

Student life. Freshman orientation: Mandatory. Preregistration for classes offered. **Policies:** Freshmen permitted cars on campus. **Housing:** Coed dorms, apartments available. **Activities:** Bands, choral groups, dance, drama, literary magazine, musical theater, radio station, student government, student newspaper, TV station, Christian Fellowship, special interest clubs, Phi Theta Kappa.

Athletics. NJCAA. **Intercollegiate:** Baseball M, basketball, softball W, volleyball W. **Intramural:** Basketball, bowling, football (non-tackle), softball, tennis, volleyball. **Team name:** Reivers.

Student services. Career counseling, services for economically disadvantaged, student employment services, financial aid counseling, health services, on-campus daycare, placement for graduates, veterans' counselor. **Physically disabled:** Services for visually, speech, hearing impaired. **Transfer:** Special adviser, orientation, pre-admission transcript evaluation for new students. Transfer center, transfer adviser, college fairs on campus for students transferring to 4-year colleges.

Contact. E-mail: admissions@iwcc.edu
Phone: (712) 325-3277 Toll-free number: (800) 432-5852
Fax: (712) 325-3720
Tammy Young, Director of Admissions, Iowa Western Community College, 2700 College Road, Council Bluffs, IA 51502-3004

Kirkwood Community College

Cedar Rapids, Iowa
www.kirkwood.cc.ia.us **CB code: 6027**

- Public 2-year community college
- Commuter campus in small city

General. Founded in 1966. Regionally accredited. Off-campus sites in Iowa City, Vinton, Tipton, Williamsburg, Monticello, Washington, Belle Plaine, Marion, Cedar Rapids. **Enrollment:** 14,700 degree-seeking undergraduates. **Degrees:** 1,908 associate awarded. **Location:** 128 miles from Des Moines. **Calendar:** Semester, extensive summer session. **Full-time faculty:** 275 total. **Part-time faculty:** 550 total. **Special facilities:** Telecommunications center, raptor center, equestrian center. **Partnerships:** With CISCO LAN Management.

Student profile.

Out-of-state:	2%	**25 or older:**	26%

Transfer out. Colleges most students transferred to 2005: University of Iowa, University of Northern Iowa, Iowa State University, Mount Mercy College, Coe College.

Basis for selection. Open admission, but selective for some programs. ACT/COMPASS test used for placement decisions. Interview required of vocational-technical, career option applicants.

Two-Year Colleges

2005-2006 Annual costs. Tuition/fees: $2,850; $5,700 out-of-state. Per-credit charge: $95 in-state; $190 out-of-state. Books/supplies: $500. Personal expenses: $900.

Financial aid. Need-based: Need-based aid available for part-time students. Work study available nights, weekends and for part-time students. **Non-need-based:** Scholarships awarded for art, athletics, leadership, music/drama.

Application procedures. Admission: Priority date 3/15; no deadline. No application fee. Application may be submitted online. Admission notification on a rolling basis. **Financial aid:** Priority date 7/1; no closing date. FAFSA required. Applicants notified on a rolling basis starting 4/1.

Academics. Special study options: Accelerated study, cooperative education, cross-registration, distance learning, dual enrollment of high school students, ESL, exchange student, external degree, honors, independent study, internships, liberal arts/career combination, student-designed major, study abroad, weekend college. License preparation in dental hygiene, nursing, paramedic, physical therapy, real estate. **Credit/placement by examination:** CLEP, IB, institutional tests. 21 credit hours maximum toward associate degree. **Support services:** GED preparation and test center, learning center, pre-admission summer program, reduced course load, remedial instruction, study skills assistance, tutoring, writing center.

Majors. Agriculture: Equestrian studies, nursery operations, supplies, turf management. **Biology:** Biotechnology. **Business:** Accounting, administrative services, business admin, fashion, finance, office technology, sales/distribution. **Communications technology:** General, graphic/printing. **Computer sciences:** Applications programming. **Conservation:** General. **Construction:** Maintenance, power transmission. **Engineering:** General. **Engineering technology:** Drafting, electrical, surveying. **Family/consumer sciences:** Child care, institutional food production. **Foreign languages:** Sign language interpretation. **Health:** Dental assistant, dental hygiene, dental lab technology, electroencephalograph technology, EMT ambulance attendant, EMT paramedic, medical assistant, medical records technology, medical secretary, nursing (RN), occupational therapy assistant, physical therapy assistant, respiratory therapy technology, surgical technology, veterinary technology/assistant. **Legal studies:** Legal secretary, paralegal. **Liberal arts:** Arts/sciences. **Mechanic/repair:** Automotive, diesel, electronics/electrical. **Personal/culinary services:** Culinary arts. **Protective services:** Fire services admin, firefighting, police science. **Public administration:** Community org/advocacy.

Computing on campus. 1,000 workstations in library, computer center, student center. Commuter students can connect to campus network. Online course registration, online library, helpline available.

Student life. Freshman orientation: Available. Preregistration for classes offered. Various group sessions throughout year. One credit hour session over two days, week before fall classes start. **Policies:** Freshmen permitted cars on campus. **Activities:** Bands, choral groups, drama, film society, literary magazine, music ensembles, musical theater, radio station, student government, student newspaper, symphony orchestra, TV station, Over 50 organizations.

Athletics. NJCAA. **Intercollegiate:** Baseball M, basketball, golf M, softball W, volleyball W. **Intramural:** Basketball, cheerleading, handball, racquetball, soccer, volleyball. **Team name:** Eagles.

Student services. Adult student services, alcohol/substance abuse counseling, campus ministries, career counseling, services for economically disadvantaged, student employment services, financial aid counseling, health services, minority student services, on-campus daycare, personal counseling, placement for graduates, veterans' counselor. **Physically disabled:** Services for visually, speech, hearing impaired. **Learning disabled:** Comprehensive services available. **Transfer:** Special adviser, orientation, pre-admission transcript evaluation for new students. Transfer center, transfer adviser, college fairs on campus for students transferring to 4-year colleges.

Contact. E-mail: info@kirkwood.cc.ia.us
Phone: (319) 398-5517 Toll-free number: (800) 332-2055 ext. 5517
Fax: (319) 398-1244
Doug Bannon, Director of Admissions Services, Kirkwood Community College, 6301 Kirkwood Boulevard SW, Cedar Rapids, IA 52406

Marshalltown Community College

Marshalltown, Iowa
www.marshalltowncommunitycollege.com CB code: 6394

- Public 2-year community college
- Residential campus in large town

General. Founded in 1927. Regionally accredited. **Enrollment:** 1,610 degree-seeking undergraduates. **Degrees:** 264 associate awarded. **Location:** 50 miles from Des Moines. **Calendar:** Semester, limited summer session. **Full-time faculty:** 43 total. **Part-time faculty:** 68 total. **Special facilities:** Prairie, Challenge course.

Transfer out. Colleges most students transferred to 2005: Iowa State University, University of Northern Iowa, University of Iowa.

Basis for selection. Open admission, but selective for some programs. Special requirements for health career programs. Interview recommended for health careers majors.

2006-2007 Annual costs. Tuition/fees (projected): $3,810. Per-credit charge: $105. Room/board: $3,400. Books/supplies: $425.

2005-2006 Financial aid. Need-based: 57% of total undergraduate aid awarded as scholarships/grants, 43% as loans/jobs.

Application procedures. Admission: No deadline. No application fee. Admission notification on a rolling basis. **Financial aid:** Priority date 3/1; no closing date. Institutional form required. Applicants notified on a rolling basis starting 6/1; must reply within 2 week(s) of notification.

Academics. Special study options: Accelerated study, cooperative education, cross-registration, distance learning, dual enrollment of high school students, ESL, honors, independent study, internships, liberal arts/career combination, study abroad. Bachelor's degree programs available on campus. License preparation in nursing, real estate. **Credit/placement by examination:** AP, CLEP, institutional tests. 30 credit hours maximum toward associate degree. **Support services:** GED preparation and test center, learning center, reduced course load, remedial instruction, study skills assistance, tutoring, writing center.

Majors. Agriculture: Business. **Biology:** General, botany, zoology. **Business:** General, accounting, administrative services, business admin. **Communications:** Journalism. **Communications technology:** General. **Computer sciences:** General, networking, systems analysis. **Conservation:** Forestry. **Education:** General, elementary, physical, secondary. **Engineering:** General. **Engineering technology:** Drafting. **English:** British lit. **Family/consumer sciences:** General, child care. **Foreign languages:** Spanish. **Health:** Health services, nursing (RN), predentistry, premedicine, prenursing, prepharmacy, preveterinary, surgical technology. **Legal studies:** Prelaw. **Liberal arts:** Arts/sciences. **Math:** General. **Mechanic/repair:** Heating/ac/refrig, industrial. **Personal/culinary services:** Embalming, mortuary science. **Protective services:** Law enforcement admin, police science. **Psychology:** General. **Public administration:** Community org/advocacy. **Social sciences:** General. **Visual/performing arts:** General, studio arts.

Most popular majors. Computer/information sciences 7%, education 8%, health sciences 10%, liberal arts 65%.

Computing on campus. 250 workstations in dormitories, library, computer center. Commuter students can connect to campus network. Online library, helpline available.

Student life. Freshman orientation: Available. Preregistration for classes offered. **Policies:** Freshmen permitted cars on campus. **Housing:** Special housing for disabled, apartments available. $300 deposit. **Activities:** Concert band, choral groups, drama, radio station, student government, student newspaper, TV station, international student organization.

Athletics. NJCAA. **Intercollegiate:** Baseball M, basketball, golf, soccer M, softball W. **Intramural:** Basketball, racquetball. **Team name:** Tigers.

Student services. Adult student services, career counseling, services for economically disadvantaged, student employment services, financial aid counseling, health services, on-campus daycare, personal counseling, placement for graduates, veterans' counselor. **Physically disabled:** Services for visually, speech, hearing impaired. **Learning disabled:** Comprehensive services available. **Transfer:** Special adviser, orientation for new students. College fairs on campus for students transferring to 4-year colleges.

Contact. E-mail: dtrawny@iavalley.edu
Phone: (641) 752-7106 ext. 216 Fax: (641) 752-8149
Deana Inman, Director of Admissions, Marshalltown Community College, 3700 South Center Street, Marshalltown, IA 50158

Muscatine Community College

Muscatine, Iowa
www.eicc.edu CB code: 6422

- Public 2-year community college
- Commuter campus in large town

General. Founded in 1929. Regionally accredited. **Degrees:** 166 associate awarded. **Location:** 30 miles from Davenport. **Calendar:** Semester, limited summer session. **Full-time faculty:** 30 total. **Part-time faculty:** 60 total.

Basis for selection. Open admission, but selective for some programs. Special requirements for nursing program.

2005-2006 Annual costs. Tuition/fees: $2,700; $4,050 out-of-state. Per-credit charge: $90 in-state; $135 out-of-state. Room only: $3,390. Books/supplies: $900.

Application procedures. Admission: No deadline. No application fee. Admission notification on a rolling basis beginning on or about 9/1. **Financial aid:** Priority date 4/20; no closing date. FAFSA required. Applicants notified on a rolling basis starting 5/15; must reply within 2 week(s) of notification.

Academics. Special study options: Accelerated study, cooperative education, cross-registration, distance learning, double major, dual enrollment of high school students, ESL, honors, independent study, internships, study abroad. **Credit/placement by examination:** CLEP, institutional tests. 30 credit hours maximum toward associate degree. **Support services:** Learning center, reduced course load, remedial instruction, tutoring.

Majors. Agriculture: Supplies. **Business:** Accounting, administrative services. **Conservation:** General. **Liberal arts:** Arts/sciences. **Mechanic/repair:** Industrial.

Student life. Activities: Choral groups, drama, music ensembles, student government, student newspaper, TV station.

Athletics. NJCAA. **Intercollegiate:** Baseball M, basketball M, golf, soccer, softball W, volleyball W. **Intramural:** Basketball, bowling, softball, table tennis, volleyball.

Student services. Career counseling, student employment services, on-campus daycare, personal counseling, placement for graduates, veterans' counselor. **Physically disabled:** Services for visually, speech, hearing impaired. **Transfer:** Special adviser, orientation for new students. Transfer adviser, college fairs on campus for students transferring to 4-year colleges.

Contact. Phone: (563) 288-6000 Fax: (563) 264-8341
Katie Watson, Coordinator of Admissions, Muscatine Community College, 152 Colorado Street, Muscatine, IA 52761-5396

North Iowa Area Community College

Mason City, Iowa
www.niacc.edu **CB code: 6400**

- Public 2-year community college
- Commuter campus in large town

General. Founded in 1918. Regionally accredited. **Enrollment:** 2,515 degree-seeking undergraduates; 489 non-degree-seeking students. **Degrees:** 538 associate awarded. **Location:** 120 miles from Des Moines, 120 miles from Minneapolis-St. Paul. **Calendar:** Semester, limited summer session. **Full-time faculty:** 84 total; 7% have terminal degrees, 37% women. **Part-time faculty:** 111 total; 4% have terminal degrees, 50% women. **Class size:** 51% < 20, 45% 20-39, 2% 40-49, 2% 50-99, less than 1% >100. **Special facilities:** Manufacturing technology center, entrepreneurial center.

Student profile. Among degree-seeking undergraduates, 62% enrolled in a transfer program, 38% enrolled in a vocational program, 855 enrolled as first-time, first-year students.

Part-time:	32%	**25 or older:**	25%
Women:	56%	**Live on campus:**	11%

Transfer out. Colleges most students transferred to 2005: University of Northern Iowa, Iowa State University, University of Iowa.

Basis for selection. Open admission, but selective for some programs. Special admission requirements for nursing and physical therapist assistants. **Adult students:** Entrance exam policies same as for first-time freshmen.

2005-2006 Annual costs. Tuition/fees: $3,138; $4,533 out-of-state. Per-credit charge: $93 in-state; $140 out-of-state. Room/board: $3,920. Books/supplies: $746. Personal expenses: $1,508.

2004-2005 Financial aid. Need-based: 54% of total undergraduate aid awarded as scholarships/grants, 46% as loans/jobs. Need-based aid available for part-time students. Work study available nights and for part-time students. **Non-need-based:** Scholarships awarded for academics, alumni affiliation, art, athletics, leadership, music/drama.

Application procedures. Admission: No deadline. No application fee. Application may be submitted online. Admission notification on a rolling basis. **Financial aid:** Priority date 3/1; no closing date. FAFSA, institutional form required. Applicants notified on a rolling basis starting 4/1; must reply within 2 week(s) of notification.

Academics. Special study options: Cooperative education, distance learning, honors, independent study, internships, liberal arts/career combination, study abroad. Bachelor's degree programs available on campus. License preparation in real estate. **Credit/placement by examination:** AP, CLEP, institutional tests. 30 credit hours maximum toward associate degree. **Support services:** GED preparation and test center, learning center, remedial instruction, study skills assistance, tutoring, writing center.

Majors. Agriculture: General, agribusiness operations, business, farm/ranch, production, supplies. **Business:** Accounting, administrative services, business admin, entrepreneurial studies, hospitality admin. **Computer sciences:** System admin. **Education:** General, early childhood, physical, secondary. **Engineering technology:** Electrical. **Family/consumer sciences:** General. **Health:** Clinical lab technology, EMT paramedic, nursing (RN), physical therapy assistant. **Liberal arts:** Arts/sciences. **Mechanic/repair:** Automotive, heating/ac/refrig, industrial electronics. **Parks/recreation:** Sports admin. **Personal/culinary services:** Mortuary science. **Production:** Machine tool, tool and die. **Protective services:** Fire services admin, police science. **Social sciences:** General, criminology, geography, political science, sociology.

Most popular majors. Liberal arts 71%.

Computing on campus. 350 workstations in dormitories, library, computer center. Dormitories wired for high-speed internet access and linked to campus network. Commuter students can connect to campus network. Online library, wireless network available.

Student life. Freshman orientation: Mandatory, $25 fee. 5 week class that will also be available on-line in the future. **Policies:** Freshmen permitted cars on campus. **Housing:** Coed dorms, apartments, substance-free housing available. $50 fully refundable deposit. **Activities:** Bands, choral groups, dance, drama, music ensembles, student government, student newspaper, symphony orchestra, OK House.

Athletics. NJCAA. **Intercollegiate:** Baseball M, basketball, cross-country, football (tackle) M, golf, soccer, softball W, track and field, volleyball W. **Intramural:** Basketball, bowling, football (non-tackle), soccer, softball, volleyball. **Team name:** Trojans.

Student services. Adult student services, alcohol/substance abuse counseling, career counseling, student employment services, financial aid counseling, health services, personal counseling, placement for graduates, veterans' counselor. **Physically disabled:** Services for visually, speech, hearing impaired. **Transfer:** Special adviser, orientation for new students. Transfer adviser, college fairs on campus for students transferring to 4-year colleges.

Contact. E-mail: request@niacc.cc.ia.us
Phone: (641) 422-4245 Toll-free number: (888) 466-4222 ext. 4245
Fax: (641) 422-4385
Rachel McGuire, Director of Admissions, North Iowa Area Community College, 500 College Drive, Mason City, IA 50401

Northeast Iowa Community College

Calmar, Iowa **CB member**
www.nicc.edu **CB code: 6751**

- Public 2-year community college
- Commuter campus in rural community

General. Founded in 1966. Regionally accredited. Branch campus at Peosta, 10 miles from Dubuque. **Enrollment:** 1,914 degree-seeking undergraduates; 2,919 non-degree-seeking students. **Degrees:** 523 associate awarded. **Location:** 60 miles from Waterloo. **Calendar:** Semester, extensive summer session. **Full-time faculty:** 115 total. **Part-time faculty:** 75 total.

Student profile. Among degree-seeking undergraduates, 32% enrolled in a transfer program, 63% enrolled in a vocational program, 284 enrolled as first-time, first-year students, 32 transferred in from other institutions.

Part-time:	34%	**African American:**	1%
Out-of-state:	5%	**Hispanic American:**	1%
Women:	66%		

Transfer out. Colleges most students transferred to 2005: University of Northern Iowa-Cedar Fall, Loras College, Clarke College, University of Dubuque.

Two-Year Colleges

Two-Year Colleges

Basis for selection. Open admission.

2006-2007 Annual costs. Tuition/fees (projected): $3,894. Books/supplies: $1,200. Personal expenses: $1,604.

Financial aid. Need-based: Need-based aid available for part-time students. Work study available nights and for part-time students. **Non-need-based:** Scholarships awarded for academics, leadership.

Application procedures. Admission: No deadline. No application fee. Application may be submitted online. Admission notification on a rolling basis. **Financial aid:** Priority date 7/1; no closing date. FAFSA required. Applicants notified on a rolling basis starting 5/1.

Academics. Dental assisting certification exam given on-campus. **Special study options:** Cooperative education, distance learning, double major, dual enrollment of high school students, ESL, independent study, internships, student-designed major, study abroad. **Credit/placement by examination:** AP, CLEP. **Support services:** GED preparation and test center, learning center, reduced course load, remedial instruction, study skills assistance, tutoring, writing center.

Majors. Agriculture: Business, landscaping. **Business:** General, accounting, banking/financial services, business admin, management information systems, marketing, office management. **Computer sciences:** Applications programming, data processing, networking, programming, systems analysis. **Construction:** Power transmission. **Education:** General. **Engineering:** Electrical, metallurgical. **Engineering technology:** Electrical. **Health:** Clinical lab assistant, clinical lab technology, EMT paramedic, medical radiologic technology/radiation therapy, medical records admin, medical records technology, medical secretary, nursing (RN), respiratory therapy technology. **Legal studies:** Legal secretary. **Mechanic/repair:** Automotive, electronics/electrical. **Personal/culinary services:** General. **Protective services:** Firefighting. **Public administration:** Human services.

Computing on campus. 1,300 workstations in library, computer center. Helpline, repair service available.

Student life. Freshman orientation: Available. One day program with different interest sessions available. **Activities:** Student government, student newspaper.

Athletics. Intramural: Basketball, bowling, golf, skiing, softball, volleyball.

Student services. Adult student services, alcohol/substance abuse counseling, career counseling, services for economically disadvantaged, student employment services, financial aid counseling, health services, on-campus daycare, personal counseling, placement for graduates, veterans' counselor, women's services. **Physically disabled:** Services for visually, speech, hearing impaired. **Transfer:** Special adviser, orientation, pre-admission transcript evaluation for new students. Transfer adviser, college fairs on campus for students transferring to 4-year colleges.

Contact. Phone: (563) 562-3263 ext. 234 Toll-free number: (800) 728-2256 ext. 234 Fax: (563) 562-4369
Martha Keune, Student Enrollment Manager, Northeast Iowa Community College, Box 400, Calmar, IA 52132

Northwest Iowa Community College

Sheldon, Iowa
www.nwicc.edu **CB code: 1359**

- Public 2-year community college
- Commuter campus in small town

General. Founded in 1966. Regionally accredited. **Enrollment:** 780 degree-seeking undergraduates. **Degrees:** 140 associate awarded. **Location:** 60 miles from Sioux City, 65 miles from Sioux Falls. **Calendar:** Semester, extensive summer session. **Full-time faculty:** 38 total; 34% women. **Part-time faculty:** 84 total; 7% have terminal degrees, 1% minority, 50% women. **Class size:** 85% < 20, 15% 20-39. **Special facilities:** Natural prairie preserve.

Student profile.

Out-of-state:	4%	**Live on campus:**	4%
25 or older:	19%		

Basis for selection. Open admission, but selective for some programs. 2.0 GPA and 2 science required for LPN program. Algebra required for some technical programs. Minimum COMPASS scores for ADN and Powerline programs. **Adult students:** Entrance exam policies same as for first-time freshmen.

2005-2006 Annual costs. Tuition/fees: $3,630; $5,115 out-of-state. Per-credit charge: $99 in-state; $148 out-of-state. Room only: $1,900. Books/supplies: $716. Personal expenses: $854.

Financial aid. Need-based: Need-based aid available for part-time students.

Application procedures. Admission: No deadline. $10 fee. Application may be submitted online. Admission notification on a rolling basis. **Financial aid:** Priority date 4/1; no closing date. FAFSA, institutional form required. Applicants notified on a rolling basis starting 5/1.

Academics. Special study options: Cooperative education, distance learning, dual enrollment of high school students, ESL, independent study, liberal arts/career combination. Bachelor's degree programs available on campus. License preparation in nursing, paramedic, radiology. **Credit/placement by examination:** AP, CLEP, institutional tests. 30 credit hours maximum toward associate degree. **Support services:** GED preparation, learning center, pre-admission summer program, reduced course load, remedial instruction, study skills assistance, tutoring.

Majors. Business: Accounting, business admin. **Computer sciences:** Networking, system admin. **Construction:** Carpentry, lineworker. **Engineering technology:** Electrical, manufacturing. **Health:** EMT paramedic, medical records technology, nursing (RN), radiologic technology/medical imaging. **Liberal arts:** Arts/sciences. **Mechanic/repair:** Auto body, automotive, diesel, industrial electronics. **Production:** Tool and die.

Most popular majors. Business/marketing 43%, health sciences 25%, liberal arts 32%.

Computing on campus. 110 workstations in library, computer center, student center. Commuter students can connect to campus network. Online course registration, online library, helpline, wireless network available.

Student life. Freshman orientation: Available. Preregistration for classes offered. **Policies:** Freshmen permitted cars on campus. **Housing:** Apartments available. $175 deposit. **Activities:** Student government, student newspaper, Campus Crusade for Christ.

Athletics. Intramural: Basketball, bowling, football (non-tackle), racquetball, softball, swimming, volleyball.

Student services. Career counseling, student employment services, financial aid counseling, personal counseling, placement for graduates, veterans' counselor. **Physically disabled:** Services for visually, speech, hearing impaired. **Transfer:** Special adviser, orientation, pre-admission transcript evaluation for new students. Transfer adviser, college fairs on campus for students transferring to 4-year colleges.

Contact. E-mail: lstory@nwicc.edu
Phone: (712) 324-5061 Toll-free number: (800) 352-4907
Fax: (712) 324-4136
Lisa Story, Director of Admissions, Northwest Iowa Community College, 603 West Park Street, Sheldon, IA 51201

St. Luke's College

Sioux City, Iowa
www.stlukes.org **CB code: 3625**

- Private 2-year health science and nursing college affiliated with Lutheran and Methodist churches
- Commuter campus in small city
- ACT (writing optional), application essay, interview required

General. Regionally accredited. **Enrollment:** 155 degree-seeking undergraduates; 9 non-degree-seeking students. **Degrees:** 58 associate awarded. **Location:** 90 miles from Omaha. **Calendar:** Semester, limited summer session. **Full-time faculty:** 16 total; 94% women. **Part-time faculty:** 9 total; 67% have terminal degrees, 78% women. **Class size:** 69% < 20, 19% 20-39, 6% 40-49, 6% 50-99. **Special facilities:** Hospital-based health care provider programs.

Student profile. Among degree-seeking undergraduates, 22% enrolled in a transfer program, 2% already have a bachelor's degree or higher, 23 enrolled as first-time, first-year students, 80 transferred in from other institutions.

Part-time:	15%	**Women:**	91%
Out-of-state:	23%	**25 or older:**	30%

Transfer out. 75% of students enrolled in the transfer program go on to 4-year colleges. **Colleges most students transferred to 2005:** Morningside College, Briar Cliff College, Creighton University, Dordt College.

Basis for selection. Professional programs require minimum 2.5 high school GPA, or GED, 19 ACT or transfer credits with minimum 2.3 GPA. Pre-professional programs require only one of criteria listed above. ACT or SAT required of students who have been out of high school 5 years or more. ASSET test required of all enrolled students. **Adult students:** Entrance exam policies same as for first-time freshmen. **Learning Disabled:** Job shadowing recommended.

High school preparation. 8 units recommended. Recommended units include English 4, mathematics 2 and science 2. Electives recommended include psychology, computer operations, typing, or keyboarding.

2006-2007 Annual costs. Tuition/fees (projected): $12,500. Per-credit charge: $340. Summer general fee: $125. Books/supplies: $1,200. Personal expenses: $1,188.

2004-2005 Financial aid. Need-based: 18 full-time freshmen applied for aid; 16 were judged to have need; 16 of these received aid. Average scholarship/grant was $2,300; average loan $1,688. 53% of total undergraduate aid awarded as scholarships/grants, 47% as loans/jobs. Need-based aid available for part-time students. Work study available nights, weekends and for part-time students. **Non-need-based:** Awarded to 4 full-time undergraduates, including 1 freshmen. Scholarships awarded for academics, job skills, leadership.

Application procedures. Admission: Priority date 11/1; deadline 8/15 (receipt date). $100 fee. Application may be submitted online. **Financial aid:** Priority date 3/1; no closing date. FAFSA required. Applicants notified on a rolling basis starting 4/1; must reply within 2 week(s) of notification.

Academics. Students can attend any bachelor's nursing program in Iowa after graduating with associate degree in nursing. Local college offers students access to learning and writing center. **Special study options:** Combined bachelor's/graduate degree, internships, liberal arts/career combination. License preparation in nursing, radiology. **Credit/placement by examination:** AP, CLEP, institutional tests. 22 credit hours maximum toward associate degree. Must have score of 38 in math portion of ASSET or will be placed in math review program. **Support services:** Learning center, reduced course load, study skills assistance, tutoring.

Majors. Health: Medical radiologic technology/radiation therapy, nursing (RN), respiratory therapy technology.

Computing on campus. 12 workstations in library, computer center, student center. Commuter students can connect to campus network. Online library, helpline, repair service available.

Student life. Freshman orientation: Mandatory, $20 fee. Preregistration for classes offered. Orientation held week prior to classes. Additional orientation sessions held during first semester for freshmen. **Policies:** Alcohol and drug-free campus. Freshmen permitted cars on campus. **Activities:** Student government, community service.

Student services. Campus ministries, student employment services, financial aid counseling, health services, on-campus daycare, personal counseling. **Transfer:** Special adviser, orientation, pre-admission transcript evaluation for new students.

Contact. E-mail: mccartsj@stlukes.org
Phone: (712) 279-3158 Toll-free number: (800) 352-4660 ext. 3158
Fax: (712) 233-8017
Sherry McCarthy, Enrollment Coordinator, St. Luke's College, 2720 Stone Park Boulevard, Sioux City, IA 51104

Scott Community College
Bettendorf, Iowa
www.eicc.edu **CB code: 0282**

- Public 2-year community college
- Commuter campus in small city

General. Founded in 1966. Regionally accredited. **Degrees:** 513 associate awarded. **Location:** 3 miles from Davenport. **Calendar:** Semester, extensive summer session. **Full-time faculty:** 90 total. **Part-time faculty:** 250 total.

Student profile.

Out-of-state:	10%	**25 or older:**	46%

Basis for selection. Open admission, but selective for some programs. Admission to some programs, particularly health occupations, based on academic achievement and previous courses. Interview required for radiologic technology and medical laboratory technician; recommended for nursing, electroneuro diagnostic technology and pharmacy technician.

2005-2006 Annual costs. Tuition/fees: $2,700; $4,050 out-of-state. Per-credit charge: $90 in-state; $135 out-of-state. Books/supplies: $900. Personal expenses: $900.

Application procedures. Admission: No deadline. No application fee. Admission notification on a rolling basis beginning on or about 9/1. **Financial aid:** Priority date 4/20; no closing date. FAFSA required. Applicants notified on a rolling basis starting 5/15; must reply within 2 week(s) of notification.

Academics. Special study options: Accelerated study, cooperative education, cross-registration, distance learning, double major, dual enrollment of high school students, ESL, honors, independent study, internships, study abroad. **Credit/placement by examination:** CLEP. 30 credit hours maximum toward associate degree. **Support services:** Learning center, reduced course load, remedial instruction, tutoring.

Majors. Business: Accounting, administrative services. **Communications technology:** General. **Computer sciences:** Applications programming. **Foreign languages:** Sign language interpretation. **Health:** Clinical lab technology, medical radiologic technology/radiation therapy, nursing (RN), pharmacy assistant. **Mechanic/repair:** Auto body, automotive, diesel, heating/ac/refrig. **Personal/culinary services:** Culinary arts.

Student life. Activities: Drama, literary magazine, student government.

Athletics. Intercollegiate: Baseball M, basketball M, golf, soccer, softball W, volleyball W. **Intramural:** Basketball, bowling, racquetball, skiing, softball, table tennis, tennis, volleyball, wrestling M.

Student services. Career counseling, student employment services, on-campus daycare, personal counseling, placement for graduates, veterans' counselor. **Physically disabled:** Services for visually, speech, hearing impaired. **Transfer:** Special adviser, orientation for new students. Transfer adviser, college fairs on campus for students transferring to 4-year colleges.

Contact. Phone: (563) 441-4004 Fax: (563) 359-8139
Scott Kashmarek, Admissions Officer, Scott Community College, 500 Belmont Road, Bettendorf, IA 52722-6804

Southeastern Community College: North Campus
West Burlington, Iowa
www.scciowa.edu **CB code: 6048**

- Public 2-year community and junior college
- Commuter campus in large town

General. Founded in 1966. Regionally accredited. Associated with Southeastern Community College: South Campus, Mt. Pleasant Center and Ft. Madison Center. **Enrollment:** 4,115 degree-seeking undergraduates. **Degrees:** 520 associate awarded. **Location:** 200 miles from Des Moines, 300 miles from Chicago. **Calendar:** Semester, limited summer session. **Full-time faculty:** 75 total. **Part-time faculty:** 10 total. **Special facilities:** Greenhouse.

Student profile.

Out-of-state:	14%	**Live on campus:**	5%
25 or older:	35%		

Transfer out. Colleges most students transferred to 2005: The University of Iowa, Western Illinois University, Iowa State University, The University of Northern Iowa, Iowa Wesleyan College.

Basis for selection. Open admission, but selective for some programs. Special requirements for nursing, computer programming, electronic technology, automated manufacturing, medical assistant, design engineering technology programs, and respiratory care. Interview required of nursing, medical assistant majors. **Adult students:** Entrance exam policies same as for first-time freshmen. Placement testing required for full-time students. SCC will accept current (taken within the last two years) ACT, ASSET, or COMPASS test scores.

High school preparation. 12 units recommended. Recommended units include English 3, mathematics 3, social studies 3 and science 3.

2005-2006 Annual costs. Tuition/fees: $2,910; $3,270 out-of-state. Per-credit charge: $97 in-state; $109 out-of-state.

Financial aid. All financial aid based on need. Need-based aid available for part-time students.

Application procedures. Admission: No deadline. No application fee. Application may be submitted online. Admission notification on a rolling basis. **Financial aid:** Priority date 6/5; no closing date. FAFSA, institutional form required. Applicants notified on a rolling basis starting 6/5; must reply within 4 week(s) of notification.

Academics. Special study options: Combined bachelor's/graduate degree, cooperative education, cross-registration, distance learning, dual enrollment of high school students, ESL, independent study, internships, liberal arts/career combination. License preparation in dental hygiene, nursing, paramedic, radiology. **Credit/placement by examination:** AP, CLEP, institutional tests. 30 credit hours maximum toward associate degree. **Support services:** GED preparation and test center, learning center, pre-admission summer program, reduced course load, remedial instruction, study skills assistance, tutoring.

Majors. Agriculture: General, business, supplies. **Business:** General, accounting, administrative services, business admin, construction management, executive assistant, office management, office technology, office/clerical, receptionist. **Computer sciences:** Computer graphics, data processing, networking, programming, web page design. **Construction:** Carpentry, maintenance. **Engineering:** Electrical, mechanics. **Engineering technology:** Construction, drafting, electrical, robotics. **Family/consumer sciences:** Child care. **Health:** EMT paramedic, medical assistant, medical radiologic technology/radiation therapy, nursing (RN), substance abuse counseling. **Legal studies:** Legal secretary. **Liberal arts:** Arts/sciences. **Mechanic/repair:** General. **Production:** General, machine tool, tool and die. **Protective services:** Law enforcement admin.

Computing on campus. 100 workstations in library, computer center. Helpline available.

Student life. Freshman orientation: Mandatory. Preregistration for classes offered. One time, two hour session offered both day and evening before each term begins. **Policies:** Freshmen permitted cars on campus. **Housing:** Coed dorms, single-sex dorms, substance-free housing available. $300 deposit. **Activities:** Choral groups, student government, Campus Crusade for Christ, multicultural club.

Athletics. NJCAA. **Intercollegiate:** Baseball M, basketball, golf M, softball W, volleyball W. **Intramural:** Basketball, cheerleading, football (tackle), softball, volleyball. **Team name:** Black Hawks.

Student services. Career counseling, services for economically disadvantaged, student employment services, financial aid counseling, minority student services, on-campus daycare, personal counseling, placement for graduates, veterans' counselor. **Physically disabled:** Services for visually, speech, hearing impaired. **Learning disabled:** Comprehensive services available. **Transfer:** Special adviser, orientation, pre-admission transcript evaluation for new students. Transfer adviser, college fairs on campus for students transferring to 4-year colleges.

Contact. E-mail: admoff@secc.cc.ia.us
Phone: (319) 752-2731 ext. 8123 Toll-free number: (866) 722-4692 ext. 8123 Fax: (319) 758-6725
Dana Chrisman, Senior Enrollment Officer, Southeastern Community College: North Campus, 1500 West Agency Road, West Burlington, IA 52655-0605

Southeastern Community College: South Campus

Keokuk, Iowa
www.scciowa.edu **CB code: 6340**

- Public 2-year community college
- Commuter campus in large town

General. Founded in 1966. Regionally accredited. **Location:** 45 miles from Burlington, 45 miles from Quincy, Illinois. **Calendar:** Semester.

Annual costs/financial aid. Tuition/fees (2005-2006): $2,910; $3,270 out-of-state. Books/supplies: $600. Need-based financial aid available to full-time and part-time students.

Contact. Phone: (319) 524-3221 ext. 8416
Senior Enrollment Officer, Box 6007, Keokuk, IA 52632-6007

Southwestern Community College

Creston, Iowa
www.swcciowa.edu **CB code: 6122**

- Public 2-year community college
- Commuter campus in small town

General. Founded in 1966. Regionally accredited. **Enrollment:** 860 degree-seeking undergraduates. **Degrees:** 223 associate awarded. **Location:** 75 miles from Des Moines, 110 miles from Omaha, Nebraska. **Calendar:** Semester, limited summer session. **Full-time faculty:** 49 total. **Part-time faculty:** 60 total. **Class size:** 39% < 20, 58% 20-39, less than 1% 40-49, 3% 50-99. **Special facilities:** Recording studio.

Student profile.

Out-of-state:	5%	**Live on campus:**	2%
25 or older:	30%		

Transfer out. Colleges most students transferred to 2005: Northwest Missouri State University, Buena Vista University, Iowa State University, Graceland College, University of Northern Iowa.

Basis for selection. Open admission, but selective for some programs. Special requirements for nursing. LPN criteria includes date nursing application is received and date COMPASS test scores are achieved. ADN requirements are contingent on the application, COMPASS test scores, and a ranking selection process. **Adult students:** Students must take COMPASS test for placement.

High school preparation. One chemistry required for health programs.

2006-2007 Annual costs. Tuition/fees (projected): $3,420. Room/board: $3,800. Books/supplies: $600. Personal expenses: $1,500.

2004-2005 Financial aid. Need-based: 51% of total undergraduate aid awarded as scholarships/grants, 49% as loans/jobs. Work study available nights, weekends and for part-time students. **Non-need-based:** Scholarships awarded for academics, athletics, leadership, music/drama, state residency.

Application procedures. Admission: Priority date 8/1; no deadline. No application fee. Application may be submitted online. Admission notification on a rolling basis. **Financial aid:** Priority date 7/1; no closing date. FAFSA, institutional form required. Applicants notified on a rolling basis starting 6/1; must reply within 2 week(s) of notification.

Academics. Special study options: Cooperative education, distance learning, double major, dual enrollment of high school students, independent study, internships, liberal arts/career combination. License preparation in nursing. **Credit/placement by examination:** AP, CLEP. 30 credit hours maximum toward associate degree. Arts and science students without ACT composite score of 19 or above required to take ASSET exam. **Support services:** GED preparation and test center, learning center, reduced course load, remedial instruction, tutoring.

Majors. Agriculture: Business, plant protection. **Business:** General, accounting, administrative services, marketing. **Computer sciences:** Applications programming, information systems, programming, webmaster. **Education:** General. **Engineering technology:** Drafting, electrical. **Health:** Medical transcription, nursing (RN). **Liberal arts:** Arts/sciences. **Mechanic/repair:** Electronics/electrical. **Visual/performing arts:** Music performance.

Computing on campus. 140 workstations in dormitories, library, computer center, student center. Dormitories wired for high-speed internet access and linked to campus network. Helpline, repair service, wireless network available.

Student life. Freshman orientation: Mandatory. Preregistration for classes offered. **Policies:** Freshmen permitted cars on campus. **Housing:** Single-sex dorms available. $100 deposit. **Activities:** Bands, choral groups, music ensembles, student government, student newspaper.

Athletics. NJCAA. **Intercollegiate:** Baseball M, basketball, golf M, softball W, volleyball W. **Intramural:** Basketball, table tennis, tennis, volleyball. **Team name:** Spartans.

Student services. Adult student services, career counseling, services for economically disadvantaged, student employment services, health services, legal services, personal counseling, placement for graduates, veterans' counselor. **Physically disabled:** Services for visually, speech, hearing impaired. **Transfer:** Special adviser, orientation, pre-admission transcript evaluation for new students. Transfer adviser, college fairs on campus for students transferring to 4-year colleges.

Contact. E-mail: carstens@swcciowa.edu
Phone: (641) 782-7081 ext. 421 Toll-free number: (800) 247-4023
Fax: (641) 782-3312
Lisa Carstens, Director of Admissions, Southwestern Community College, 1501 West Townline Street, Creston, IA 50801

Vatterott College

Des Moines, Iowa
www.vatterott-college.edu **CB code: 2909**

- For-profit 2-year health science and technical college
- Commuter campus in large city
- Interview required

General. Accredited by ACCSCT. **Enrollment:** 172 degree-seeking undergraduates. **Degrees:** 29 associate awarded. **Calendar:** Continuous, extensive summer session. **Full-time faculty:** 13 total. **Part-time faculty:** 3 total.

Basis for selection. Open admission. School tour, interview with admissions representative, financial clearance, completion of placement evaluation, application, and enrollment forms required.

2005-2006 Annual costs. Tuition ranges from $8,569 to $11,135. Costs vary depending on program for each campus. Fees included in costs.

Financial aid. All financial aid based on need.

Application procedures. Admission: No deadline. No application fee. Application may be submitted online. Admission notification on a rolling basis. **Financial aid:** No deadline. FAFSA required. Applicants notified on a rolling basis.

Academics. Credit/placement by examination: CLEP, institutional tests. 24 credit hours maximum toward associate degree. Maximum number of credit hours is 24 by examination. Credits may be counted toward a diploma if a student passes and is awarded credit for previous training.

Majors. Computer sciences: Networking, programming. **Engineering technology:** Drafting.

Computing on campus. 125 workstations in library, computer center.

Student life. Freshman orientation: Mandatory. **Policies:** Freshmen permitted cars on campus.

Student services. Financial aid counseling, placement for graduates. **Transfer:** Orientation, pre-admission transcript evaluation for new students.

Contact. E-mail: desmoines@vatterott-college.edu
Phone: (515) 309-9000 Toll-free number: (800) 353-7264
Fax: (515) 309-0366
JoAnne Ward, Director of Admissions, Vatterott College, 6100 Thornton, Suite 290, Des Moines, IA 50321

Western Iowa Tech Community College

Sioux City, Iowa **CB member**
www.witcc.com **CB code: 6950**

- Public 2-year community college
- Commuter campus in small city

General. Founded in 1966. Regionally accredited. Most programs require attendance for at least 4 semester terms. **Enrollment:** 2,481 degree-seeking undergraduates. **Degrees:** 406 associate awarded. **Location:** 200 miles from Des Moines, 90 miles from Omaha, Nebraska. **Calendar:** Semester, extensive summer session. **Full-time faculty:** 88 total. **Part-time faculty:** 218 total. **Class size:** 73% < 20, 25% 20-39, 1% 40-49, less than 1% 50-99.

Student profile.

Out-of-state:	10%	**Live on campus:**	2%
25 or older:	30%		

Transfer out. Colleges most students transferred to 2005: Iowa State University, Briar Cliff College, Morningside College, University of Northern Iowa, Bellevue University.

Basis for selection. Open admission, but selective for some programs. Special requirements for nursing, surgical technician, dental assistant, physical therapy assistant, childcare supervision and management, emergency medical technician, police science, and business. LOPE used for placement. Computerized placement test (CPT or ACT) required of all diploma and degree-seeking students and of all students taking English composition and mathematics courses. **Adult students:** Entrance exam policies same as for first-time freshmen.

High school preparation. Recommended units include English 3, mathematics 2 and science 2.

2005-2006 Annual costs. Tuition/fees: $3,240; $4,440 out-of-state. Per-credit charge: $93 in-state; $133 out-of-state. Room only: $2,655. Books/supplies: $800. Personal expenses: $990.

2004-2005 Financial aid. Need-based: Need-based aid available for part-time students. Work study available nights, weekends and for part-time students. **Non-need-based:** Scholarships awarded for academics, leadership.

Application procedures. Admission: No deadline. $20 fee. Application may be submitted online. Admission notification on a rolling basis. We have an open enrollment policy. Any person who has a high school diploma or equivalent, or who is 18 years of age and can benefit from a program of study may be admitted to our college. **Financial aid:** No deadline. FAFSA required. Applicants notified on a rolling basis starting 4/1.

Academics. Special study options: Accelerated study, distance learning, double major, dual enrollment of high school students, ESL, honors, independent study, internships. License preparation in paramedic. **Credit/placement by examination:** AP, CLEP, institutional tests. **Support services:** GED preparation and test center, learning center, pre-admission summer program, reduced course load, remedial instruction, study skills assistance, tutoring.

Majors. Agriculture: Turf management. **Business:** Accounting, business admin, executive assistant, human resources, office technology. **Communications technology:** Desktop publishing. **Computer sciences:** Data entry. **Construction:** Lineworker. **Engineering technology:** Architectural, biomedical, computer hardware, electrical. **Family/consumer sciences:** Child care. **Health:** Clinical lab technology, dental hygiene, EMT paramedic, medical secretary, nursing (RN), office admin, physical therapy assistant. **Legal studies:** Legal secretary. **Liberal arts:** Arts/sciences. **Mechanic/repair:** Auto body, automotive, industrial, musical instruments. **Production:** Machine tool, tool and die. **Protective services:** Law enforcement admin.

Computing on campus. 612 workstations in dormitories, library, computer center. Commuter students can connect to campus network. Online course registration, online library, helpline, wireless network available.

Student life. Freshman orientation: Available. Preregistration for classes offered. **Policies:** Freshmen permitted cars on campus. **Housing:** Apartments available. $100 deposit. **Activities:** Choral groups, student government, celebrations, multicultural group.

Student services. Adult student services, career counseling, services for economically disadvantaged, student employment services, health services, personal counseling, placement for graduates. **Physically disabled:** Services for visually, speech, hearing impaired. **Transfer:** Special adviser, orientation for new students. Transfer center, transfer adviser, college fairs on campus for students transferring to 4-year colleges.

Contact. Phone: (712) 274-6403 Toll-free number: (800) 352-4649 ext. 6403 Fax: (712) 274-6441
Lora VanderZwaag, Director of Admissions, Western Iowa Tech Community College, Box 5199, Sioux City, IA 51102-5199

Two-Year Colleges

Two-Year Colleges

Kansas

Allen County Community College

Iola, Kansas
www.allencc.edu **CB code: 6305**

- Public 2-year community college
- Commuter campus in small town

General. Founded in 1923. Regionally accredited. Two campuses available to serve students in rural or metropolitan area. **Enrollment:** 2,800 degree-seeking undergraduates. **Degrees:** 240 associate awarded. **Location:** 100 miles from Wichita and Kansas City, Missouri. **Calendar:** Semester, limited summer session. **Full-time faculty:** 33 total. **Part-time faculty:** 139 total. **Special facilities:** College-operated farm, technology building.

Student profile.

Out-of-state:	3%	**Live on campus:**	20%
25 or older:	31%		

Transfer out. Colleges most students transferred to 2005: Pittsburg State University, Kansas State University, Emporia State University, University of Kansas, Washburn University.

Basis for selection. Open admission. TOEFL score of 520 or higher required for admission of non-English-speaking students. Placement test required. **Adult students:** Entrance exam policies same as for first-time freshmen. **Homeschooled:** Placement test required (ACT, COMPASS or ASSET). **Learning Disabled:** Copies of a high school IEP are helpful, but not necessary.

2005-2006 Annual costs. Tuition/fees: $1,530; $1,620 out-of-district; $1,620 out-of-state. Per-credit charge: $35 in-district; $38 out-of-district; $38 out-of-state. Room/board: $3,500. Books/supplies: $300. Personal expenses: $1,620.

2004-2005 Financial aid. Need-based: 66% of total undergraduate aid awarded as scholarships/grants, 34% as loans/jobs. Need-based aid available for part-time students. Work study available nights and weekends. **Non-need-based:** Scholarships awarded for academics, art, athletics, music/drama, state residency. **Additional information:** Scholarships for livestock judging, cheerleading, choir, dance, drama, art, academic challenge, and student ambassadors.

Application procedures. Admission: No deadline. No application fee. Application may be submitted online. Admission notification on a rolling basis. **Financial aid:** Priority date 6/1, closing date 8/1. FAFSA required. Applicants notified on a rolling basis starting 6/1; must reply within 2 week(s) of notification.

Academics. Special study options: Cooperative education, distance learning, double major, dual enrollment of high school students, independent study, internships, liberal arts/career combination, student-designed major, weekend college. Bachelor's degree programs available on campus. **Credit/placement by examination:** AP, CLEP, institutional tests. 12 credit hours maximum toward associate degree. **Support services:** GED preparation and test center, learning center, reduced course load, remedial instruction, study skills assistance, tutoring, writing center.

Majors. Agriculture: Farm/ranch. **Biology:** General. **Business:** Accounting, administrative services, business admin, office management, sales/distribution. **Computer sciences:** General, computer science. **Education:** Mathematics, music, secondary. **Engineering:** Electrical. **Engineering technology:** Drafting. **Health:** EMT paramedic, nursing assistant. **History:** General. **Liberal arts:** Library science. **Math:** General. **Mechanic/repair:** Electronics/electrical. **Physical sciences:** Chemistry, physics. **Production:** Woodworking. **Protective services:** Police science. **Social sciences:** Economics, geography, sociology. **Visual/performing arts:** Art, ceramics, crafts, drawing, painting, studio arts, voice/opera.

Most popular majors. Business/marketing 28%, communications/journalism 16%, education 12%, health sciences 12%, liberal arts 13%.

Computing on campus. 100 workstations in dormitories, library, computer center, student center. Dormitories wired for high-speed internet access. Online library, repair service, wireless network available.

Student life. Freshman orientation: Mandatory. Preregistration for classes offered. **Policies:** Freshmen permitted cars on campus. **Housing:** Coed dorms, apartments available. $125 deposit, deadline 7/1. **Activities:** Bands, choral groups, dance, drama, music ensembles, musical theater, student government, student newspaper, Aggie Club, biology club, Phi Theta Kappa.

Athletics. NJCAA. **Intercollegiate:** Baseball M, basketball, cheerleading, cross-country, golf, soccer, softball W, track and field, volleyball W. **Intramural:** Basketball, football (non-tackle), softball, table tennis, tennis, volleyball. **Team name:** Red Devils.

Student services. Adult student services, alcohol/substance abuse counseling, career counseling, services for economically disadvantaged, student employment services, financial aid counseling, minority student services, personal counseling, placement for graduates, veterans' counselor, women's services. **Physically disabled:** Services for visually, hearing impaired. **Transfer:** Special adviser, orientation, pre-admission transcript evaluation for new students. Transfer adviser, college fairs on campus for students transferring to 4-year colleges.

Contact. Phone: (620) 365-5116 ext. 268 Fax: (620) 365-3284
Randy Weber, Admissions Director, Allen County Community College, 1801 North Cottonwood, Iola, KS 66749

Barton County Community College

Great Bend, Kansas
www.bartonccc.edu **CB code: 0784**

- Public 2-year community college
- Commuter campus in large town

General. Founded in 1965. Regionally accredited. **Enrollment:** 3,258 degree-seeking undergraduates; 563 non-degree-seeking students. **Degrees:** 476 associate awarded. **Location:** 125 miles from Wichita. **Calendar:** Semester, limited summer session. **Full-time faculty:** 72 total; 8% have terminal degrees, 4% minority, 42% women. **Part-time faculty:** 108 total; 2% have terminal degrees, 4% minority, 59% women. **Class size:** 77% < 20, 22% 20-39, 1% 40-49, less than 1% 50-99. **Special facilities:** Planetarium, natatorium.

Student profile. Among degree-seeking undergraduates, 28% enrolled in a transfer program, 15% enrolled in a vocational program, 1,487 enrolled as first-time, first-year students, 135 transferred in from other institutions.

Part-time:	71%	**Hispanic American:**	6%
Out-of-state:	17%	**Native American:**	1%
Women:	52%	**International:**	2%
African American:	13%	**25 or older:**	39%
Asian American:	2%	**Live on campus:**	8%

Transfer out. Colleges most students transferred to 2005: Fort Hays State University, Kansas State University, University of Kansas, Wichita State University, Emporia State University.

Basis for selection. Open admission, but selective for some programs. Special requirements for medical laboratory technician, nursing, and mobile intensive care technician programs. ACT, SAT or ASSET scores accepted for placement; ACT, SAT, ASSET or ACCUPLACER required for placement in math or English courses. Interview required of nursing majors. **Adult students:** Entrance exam policies same as for first-time freshmen.

2005-2006 Annual costs. Tuition/fees: $1,950; $2,580 out-of-state. Per-credit charge: $47 in-state; $68 out-of-state. Room/board: $3,619. Books/supplies: $1,000. Personal expenses: $3,200.

2004-2005 Financial aid. Need-based: 64% of total undergraduate aid awarded as scholarships/grants, 36% as loans/jobs. Need-based aid available for part-time students. **Non-need-based:** Scholarships awarded for academics, athletics.

Application procedures. Admission: No deadline. No application fee. Application must be submitted on paper. Admission notification on a rolling basis. **Financial aid:** Priority date 3/1; no closing date. FAFSA required. Applicants notified on a rolling basis starting 6/1; must reply within 4 week(s) of notification.

Academics. Special study options: Accelerated study, cooperative education, distance learning, dual enrollment of high school students, ESL, independent study, internships. License preparation in nursing, paramedic, real estate. **Credit/placement by examination:** AP, CLEP, IB, institutional tests. ACT, SAT, ASSET, or ACCUPLACER is required for enrollment in Math or English coursework. **Support services:** GED preparation and test center, learning center, remedial instruction, tutoring.

Majors. **Agriculture:** General, production. **Biology:** General, wildlife. **Business:** General, accounting, administrative services, human resources, operations. **Communications:** General, journalism. **Computer sciences:** Computer science, data processing, information systems. **Conservation:** Forestry. **Education:** General. **Engineering:** General. **Engineering technology:** Computer systems, hazardous materials. **English:** English lit. **Family/consumer sciences:** Child care. **Foreign languages:** General. **Health:** Athletic training, clinical lab science, clinical lab technology, dietician assistant, EMT paramedic, medical assistant, medical records admin, nursing (RN), predentistry, premedicine, prenursing, prepharmacy, preveterinary. **History:** General. **Legal studies:** Prelaw. **Liberal arts:** Arts/sciences. **Math:** General. **Mechanic/repair:** Automotive. **Military:** General. **Parks/recreation:** Exercise sciences, health/fitness, sports admin. **Personal/culinary services:** Mortuary science. **Philosophy/religion:** Philosophy. **Physical sciences:** General, chemistry, physics. **Protective services:** Firefighting, police science. **Psychology:** General. **Public administration:** General, social work. **Social sciences:** Anthropology, economics, political science, sociology. **Visual/performing arts:** Art, dance, dramatic, graphic design.

Most popular majors. Business/marketing 10%, health sciences 14%, liberal arts 55%.

Computing on campus. 350 workstations in dormitories, library, computer center, student center. Dormitories wired for high-speed internet access and linked to campus network. Commuter students can connect to campus network. Online course registration, online library, helpline available.

Student life. **Freshman orientation:** Mandatory. Preregistration for classes offered. **Policies:** Freshmen permitted cars on campus. **Housing:** Guaranteed on-campus for freshmen. Coed dorms, substance-free housing available. $100 fully refundable deposit. **Activities:** Bands, choral groups, dance, drama, literary magazine, music ensembles, musical theater, student government, student newspaper, Newman Club, Fellowship of Christian Athletes, Campus Christian Fellowship, Student Ambassadors.

Athletics. NJCAA. **Intercollegiate:** Baseball M, basketball, cheerleading, cross-country, golf, soccer, softball W, tennis, track and field, volleyball W. **Intramural:** Baseball M, basketball, football (non-tackle), softball, table tennis, tennis, volleyball. **Team name:** Cougars.

Student services. Adult student services, alcohol/substance abuse counseling, career counseling, services for economically disadvantaged, student employment services, financial aid counseling, health services, on-campus daycare, personal counseling, placement for graduates, veterans' counselor. **Physically disabled:** Services for hearing impaired. **Transfer:** Special adviser, orientation, pre-admission transcript evaluation for new students. Transfer adviser, college fairs on campus for students transferring to 4-year colleges.

Contact. E-mail: admissions@bartonccc.edu
Phone: (620) 792-2701 ext. 241 Toll-free number: (800) 722-6842
Fax: (620) 786-1160
Todd Moore, Director of Marketing, Barton County Community College, 245 NE 30th Road, Great Bend, KS 67530-9283

Brown Mackie College
Salina, Kansas
www.brownmackie.edu/sa **CB code: 3366**

- For-profit 2-year junior college
- Large town
- Interview required

General. Regionally accredited. Branch campus in Kansas City. **Enrollment:** 361 degree-seeking undergraduates. **Degrees:** 82 associate awarded. **Location:** 90 miles from Wichita, 108 miles from Topeka. **Calendar:** Quarter, extensive summer session. **Full-time faculty:** 11 total; 91% have terminal degrees, 73% women. **Part-time faculty:** 10 total; 80% have terminal degrees, 50% women.

Student profile.

African American:	21%	**Hispanic American:**	7%
Asian American:	1%		

Transfer out. **Colleges most students transferred to 2005:** Kansas Wesleyan University, Kansas State University.

Basis for selection. Open admission.

2005-2006 Annual costs. Tuition/fees: $9,168. Per-credit charge: $179. Computer networking: $300 per-credit-hour; required fees: $26.25 per-credit-hour. Books/supplies: $1,440. Personal expenses: $1,520.

Application procedures. **Admission:** No deadline. No application fee. Application must be submitted on paper. Admission notification on a rolling basis. **Financial aid:** No deadline. Applicants notified on a rolling basis.

Academics. **Special study options:** Internships. **Credit/placement by examination:** CLEP, institutional tests. **Support services:** Remedial instruction, study skills assistance, tutoring.

Majors. **Business:** Accounting, business admin, selling. **Computer sciences:** Information technology, networking. **Engineering technology:** CAD/CADD. **Health:** Office admin. **Legal studies:** Paralegal. **Protective services:** Law enforcement admin.

Computing on campus. 134 workstations in library, computer center.

Student life. **Freshman orientation:** Mandatory. Part-day program held prior to start of classes. **Activities:** Student government, student newspaper.

Athletics. NJCAA. **Intercollegiate:** Baseball M, basketball, softball W. **Intramural:** Softball. **Team name:** Lions.

Student services. Career counseling, student employment services, placement for graduates. **Transfer:** Special adviser, orientation for new students.

Contact. E-mail: dheath@brownmackie.edu
Phone: (785) 825-5422
Diann Heath, Director of Admissions, Brown Mackie College, 2106 South Ninth Street, Salina, KS 67401

Butler County Community College
El Dorado, Kansas
www.butlercc.edu **CB code: 6191**

- Public 2-year community college
- Commuter campus in large town

General. Founded in 1927. Regionally accredited. Off-campus sites at Andover, McConnell, Augusta, Flint Hills, Rose Hill and 20 other smaller locations. **Enrollment:** 5,859 degree-seeking undergraduates; 3,011 non-degree-seeking students. **Degrees:** 762 associate awarded. **Location:** 25 miles from Wichita. **Calendar:** Semester, extensive summer session. **Full-time faculty:** 140 total; 4% minority, 58% women. **Part-time faculty:** 473 total; 10% minority, 58% women. **Class size:** 71% < 20, 29% 20-39, less than 1% 40-49, less than 1% 50-99.

Student profile. Among degree-seeking undergraduates, 65% enrolled in a transfer program, 35% enrolled in a vocational program, 1,443 enrolled as first-time, first-year students.

Part-time:	51%	**Hispanic American:**	6%
Out-of-state:	1%	**Native American:**	2%
Women:	62%	**International:**	2%
African American:	11%	**25 or older:**	38%
Asian American:	2%	**Live on campus:**	2%

Transfer out. **Colleges most students transferred to 2005:** Wichita State University, Kansas State University, Emporia State University, University of Kansas, Kansas Newman College.

Basis for selection. Open admission, but selective for some programs. Nursing applicants admitted based on GPA in prerequisite courses. **Adult students:** Entrance exam policies same as for first-time freshmen.

2005-2006 Annual costs. Tuition/fees: $1,770; $2,070 out-of-district; $3,390 out-of-state. Per-credit charge: $45 in-district; $55 out-of-district; $99 out-of-state. Room/board: $4,335. Books/supplies: $1,000. Personal expenses: $1,350.

Financial aid. **Need-based:** Need-based aid available for part-time students. Work study available nights, weekends and for part-time students. **Non-need-based:** Scholarships awarded for academics, athletics.

Application procedures. **Admission:** No deadline. No application fee. Application may be submitted online. Admission notification on a rolling basis. **Financial aid:** Priority date 4/1; no closing date. FAFSA, institutional form required. Applicants notified on a rolling basis starting 5/1; must reply within 2 week(s) of notification.

Academics. **Special study options:** Accelerated study, cooperative education, distance learning, dual enrollment of high school students, ESL, honors, independent study, internships, liberal arts/career combination, weekend college. License preparation in nursing, paramedic. **Credit/placement by examination:** AP, CLEP, institutional tests. 30 credit hours maximum toward associate degree. **Support services:** GED preparation, learning center, reduced course load, remedial instruction, study skills assistance, tutoring, writing center.

Majors. **Agriculture:** Animal sciences, farm/ranch. **Business:** Accounting, business admin, hospitality admin, hospitality/recreation, office/clerical. **Communications:** Journalism. **Computer sciences:** General, computer science. **Education:** Business, early childhood, elementary, physical, secondary, teacher assistance. **Engineering:** General. **Engineering technology:** Drafting. **English:** Composition, speech/rhetoric. **Family/consumer sciences:** Child care. **Foreign languages:** General, French, Japanese, Spanish. **Health:** Licensed practical nurse, nursing (RN), premedicine. **History:** General. **Legal studies:** Prelaw. **Liberal arts:** Arts/sciences. **Math:** General. **Mechanic/repair:** General, auto body, automotive, electronics/electrical. **Physical sciences:** Chemistry, physics. **Protective services:** Criminal justice, firefighting, police science. **Psychology:** General. **Public administration:** Social work. **Social sciences:** Economics, political science. **Visual/performing arts:** Art, dramatic.

Most popular majors. Health sciences 24%, liberal arts 68%.

Computing on campus. 130 workstations in dormitories, library, computer center, student center. Dormitories wired for high-speed internet access and linked to campus network. Commuter students can connect to campus network. Online course registration, online library, helpline, repair service available.

Student life. **Freshman orientation:** Available. Preregistration for classes offered. **Policies:** Freshmen permitted cars on campus. **Housing:** Coed dorms, single-sex dorms, special housing for disabled, substance-free housing available. $75 deposit. **Activities:** Bands, choral groups, dance, drama, literary magazine, music ensembles, musical theater, radio station, student government, student newspaper, TV station, international student association, Campus Crusade for Christ.

Athletics. NJCAA. **Intercollegiate:** Baseball M, basketball, cross-country, football (tackle) M, softball W, tennis, track and field, volleyball W. **Intramural:** Badminton, basketball, bowling, soccer M, softball, table tennis, tennis, volleyball. **Team name:** Grizzlies.

Student services. Adult student services, career counseling, student employment services, financial aid counseling, health services, on-campus daycare, personal counseling, placement for graduates, veterans' counselor. **Physically disabled:** Services for visually, speech, hearing impaired. **Transfer:** Special adviser, orientation, pre-admission transcript evaluation for new students. Transfer adviser, college fairs on campus for students transferring to 4-year colleges.

Contact. E-mail: pkyle@butlercc.edu
Phone: (316) 322-3255 Fax: (316) 322-3316
Paul Kyle, Director of Enrollment Management, Butler County Community College, 901 South Haverhill Road, El Dorado, KS 67042-3280

Cloud County Community College
Concordia, Kansas
www.cloud.edu **CB code: 6137**

- Public 2-year community college
- Commuter campus in small town

General. Founded in 1965. Regionally accredited. **Enrollment:** 1,543 degree-seeking undergraduates. **Degrees:** 223 associate awarded. **Location:** 200 miles from Kansas City, 140 miles from Topeka. **Calendar:** Semester, limited summer session. **Full-time faculty:** 40 total. **Part-time faculty:** 200 total. **Class size:** 68% < 20, 30% 20-39, 1% 40-49, less than 1% 50-99. **Special facilities:** Theater, observatory, children's center, human cadaver lab. **Partnerships:** Formal partnerships with Tallgrass TechPrep Consortium.

Student profile.

Out-of-state:	5%	**Live on campus:**	4%
25 or older:	35%		

Transfer out. **Colleges most students transferred to 2005:** Kansas State University, Fort Hays State University, Wichita State University, Kansas Wesleyan University, Kansas University.

Basis for selection. Open admission. **Adult students:** Entrance exam policies same as for first-time freshmen.

High school preparation. 18 units recommended. Recommended units include English 4, mathematics 3, social studies 2 and science 4.

2005-2006 Annual costs. Tuition/fees: $2,100; $4,110 out-of-state. Per-credit charge: $52 in-state; $119 out-of-state. Room/board: $3,780. Books/supplies: $650. Personal expenses: $1,650.

Financial aid. **Need-based:** Need-based aid available for part-time students. Work study available nights, weekends and for part-time students.

Application procedures. **Admission:** No deadline. No application fee. Admission notification on a rolling basis. **Financial aid:** Priority date 4/1; no closing date. FAFSA required. Applicants notified on a rolling basis starting 5/1; must reply within 4 week(s) of notification.

Academics. **Special study options:** Cooperative education, distance learning, dual enrollment of high school students, ESL, independent study, internships, teacher certification program. License preparation in nursing. **Credit/placement by examination:** AP, CLEP, institutional tests. 30 credit hours maximum toward associate degree. **Support services:** GED preparation and test center, learning center, remedial instruction, study skills assistance, tutoring, writing center.

Majors. **Agriculture:** Production. **Biology:** General. **Business:** General, business admin, office management, tourism promotion. **Communications:** General. **Computer sciences:** General, networking, programming. **Education:** General. **Engineering:** General. **Engineering technology:** Civil. **Family/consumer sciences:** General, child care. **Foreign languages:** General. **Health:** Nursing (RN). **Legal studies:** Paralegal. **Liberal arts:** Arts/sciences. **Math:** General. **Physical sciences:** General. **Protective services:** Firefighting, law enforcement admin, police science. **Psychology:** General. **Social sciences:** General. **Transportation:** Aviation. **Visual/performing arts:** General, commercial/advertising art.

Most popular majors. Agriculture 9%, business/marketing 25%, computer/information sciences 6%, education 26%, health sciences 13%, liberal arts 8%.

Computing on campus. 100 workstations in dormitories, library, computer center. Dormitories wired for high-speed internet access and linked to campus network. Online library available.

Student life. **Freshman orientation:** Mandatory. Preregistration for classes offered. Held one day prior to registration each Fall semester, from 9am to 3pm. Offers a variety of activities to acquaint students with services available both at the college and in the community. **Policies:** Freshmen permitted cars on campus. **Housing:** Special housing for disabled, apartments available. $100 deposit. **Activities:** Jazz band, choral groups, dance, drama, music ensembles, radio station, student government, student newspaper, Fellowship of Christian Athletes.

Athletics. NJCAA. **Intercollegiate:** Baseball M, basketball, cross-country, soccer, softball W, track and field, volleyball W. **Intramural:** Basketball, football (non-tackle), soccer, softball, volleyball. **Team name:** Thunderbirds.

Student services. Alcohol/substance abuse counseling, career counseling, services for economically disadvantaged, student employment services, financial aid counseling, health services, on-campus daycare, personal counseling, placement for graduates, veterans' counselor. **Physically disabled:** Services for visually, speech, hearing impaired. **Transfer:** Special adviser for new students.

Contact. E-mail: admit@cloud.edu
Phone: (785) 243-1435 ext. 212 Toll-free number: (800) 729-5101
Fax: (785) 243-9380
Chris Burlew, Director of Admissions, Cloud County Community College, 2221 Campus Drive, Concordia, KS 66901-1002

Coffeyville Community College
Coffeyville, Kansas
www.coffeyville.edu **CB code: 6102**

- Public 2-year community college
- Commuter campus in large town

General. Founded in 1923. Regionally accredited. **Enrollment:** 2,035 degree-seeking undergraduates. **Degrees:** 231 associate awarded. **Location:** 75 miles from Tulsa, Oklahoma, 137 miles from Wichita. **Calendar:** Semester, limited summer session. **Full-time faculty:** 50 total. **Part-time faculty:** 25 total. **Class size:** 64% < 20, 33% 20-39, less than 1% 40-49, 3% 50-99. **Special facilities:** Greenhouse, commercial television station, agriculture farm. **Partnerships:** Formal partnership with Wal-Mart.

Student profile. Among degree-seeking undergraduates, 10% enrolled in a vocational program.

Out-of-state:	15%	**Live on campus:**	31%

Transfer out. 60% of students enrolled in the transfer program go on to 4-year colleges. **Colleges most students transferred to 2005:** Pittsburg State University, Kansas State University, University of Kansas.

Basis for selection. Open admission. **Adult students:** SAT/ACT scores not required. **Homeschooled:** ACT or placement test required for placement.

High school preparation. 15 units recommended.

2005-2006 Annual costs. Tuition/fees: $1,500; $2,700 out-of-state. Per-credit charge: $25 in-state; $65 out-of-state. Oklahoma border county resident tuition: $32.50 per-credit-hour, $975 full-time. International students pay $2,610 in required fees. Room/board: $3,380. Books/supplies: $500. Personal expenses: $1,200.

2005-2006 Financial aid. Need-based: 89% of total undergraduate aid awarded as scholarships/grants, 11% as loans/jobs. Need-based aid available for part-time students. Work study available nights, weekends and for part-time students. **Non-need-based:** Scholarships awarded for academics, alumni affiliation, art, athletics, leadership, music/drama. **Additional information:** Provide aid to unemployed women.

Application procedures. Admission: No deadline. No application fee. Application may be submitted online. Admission notification on a rolling basis beginning on or about 4/1. **Financial aid:** No deadline. FAFSA required. Applicants notified on a rolling basis starting 6/20.

Academics. Special study options: Distance learning, double major, dual enrollment of high school students, ESL, honors, independent study, internships, liberal arts/career combination, student-designed major. License preparation in paramedic, real estate. **Credit/placement by examination:** AP, CLEP, institutional tests. **Support services:** GED preparation and test center, learning center, reduced course load, remedial instruction, study skills assistance, tutoring.

Honors college/program. Application for Presidential Scholarship, minimum ACT score of 24, minimum 3.5 high school GPA, essay required. Top 12-15 applicants accepted each fall.

Majors. Agriculture: General, business, horticulture, supplies. **Biology:** General. **Business:** General, accounting, administrative services, business admin, entrepreneurial studies, management information systems, office management, office/clerical, retailing. **Communications:** General, broadcast journalism, journalism. **Communications technology:** General. **Computer sciences:** General, networking. **Education:** General, early childhood, elementary, multi-level teacher, physical, secondary, speech. **Engineering:** General. **English:** Speech/rhetoric. **Family/consumer sciences:** General, institutional food production. **Foreign languages:** General, Spanish. **Health:** Athletic training, EMT paramedic, predentistry, premedicine, prenursing, prepharmacy, preveterinary. **History:** General. **Legal studies:** Prelaw. **Liberal arts:** Arts/sciences. **Math:** General. **Parks/recreation:** Health/fitness. **Physical sciences:** Chemistry, physics. **Psychology:** General. **Public administration:** Social work. **Social sciences:** General, demography, economics, political science, sociology. **Visual/performing arts:** General, art, dramatic, studio arts.

Most popular majors. Agriculture 6%, business/marketing 17%, education 8%, liberal arts 58%.

Computing on campus. 100 workstations in dormitories, library, computer center, student center. Dormitories wired for high-speed internet access. Commuter students can connect to campus network.

Student life. Freshman orientation: Mandatory. Preregistration for classes offered. **Policies:** Freshmen permitted cars on campus. **Housing:** Coed dorms, single-sex dorms available. $100 fully refundable deposit. **Activities:** Bands, choral groups, dance, drama, film society, music ensembles, musical theater, student government, TV station, international club, Phi Theta Kappa, agriculture club.

Athletics. NJCAA. **Intercollegiate:** Baseball M, basketball, cheerleading, cross-country, football (tackle) M, golf M, rodeo, soccer, softball W, track and field, volleyball W. **Intramural:** Basketball, bowling, golf, table tennis, volleyball. **Team name:** Red Ravens.

Student services. Adult student services, career counseling, student employment services, financial aid counseling, health services, personal counseling, veterans' counselor. **Physically disabled:** Services for visually, speech, hearing impaired. **Learning disabled:** Comprehensive services available. **Transfer:** Special adviser for new students. Transfer adviser, college fairs on campus for students transferring to 4-year colleges.

Contact. E-mail: admiss@coffeyville.edu
Phone: (620) 252-7155 Toll-free number: (800) 782-4732
Fax: (316) 252-7098
Kelli Bauer, Coordinator, Admissions and Recruiting, Coffeyville Community College, 400 West 11th Street, Coffeyville, KS 67337-5064

Colby Community College
Colby, Kansas
www.colbycc.edu **CB code: 6129**

- Public 2-year community college
- Commuter campus in small town
- Interview required

General. Founded in 1964. Regionally accredited. **Enrollment:** 1,175 degree-seeking undergraduates. **Degrees:** 281 associate awarded. **Location:** 100 miles from Hays, 200 miles from Denver. **Calendar:** Semester, limited summer session. **Full-time faculty:** 40 total. **Part-time faculty:** 35 total. **Special facilities:** 64-acre farm, cultural arts center, fitness laboratory.

Student profile.

Out-of-state:	30%	**Live on campus:**	30%
25 or older:	12%		

Transfer out. Colleges most students transferred to 2005: Fort Hays State University, Kansas State University, University of Kansas.

Basis for selection. Open admission, but selective for some programs. Interview required for physical therapist assistant, veterinary technology, horse production, dental hygiene, and nursing programs. Audition recommended for music majors. Portfolios recommended for art majors. **Adult students:** SAT/ACT scores not required. COMPASS is required if it has been 2 or more years since ACT/SAT was taken. **Homeschooled:** Transcript of courses and grades, state high school equivalency certificate required.

2005-2006 Annual costs. Tuition/fees: $2,100; $3,270 out-of-state. Per-credit charge: $43 in-state; $82 out-of-state. Nebraska and Colorado border county residents pay $53 per-credit-hour. Room/board: $3,542. Books/supplies: $700. Personal expenses: $670.

Financial aid. Need-based: Need-based aid available for part-time students. Work study available nights, weekends and for part-time students. **Non-need-based:** Scholarships awarded for academics, athletics, music/drama.

Application procedures. Admission: No deadline. No application fee. Application may be submitted online. Admission notification on a rolling basis. **Financial aid:** Priority date 6/1; no closing date. FAFSA required. Applicants notified on a rolling basis starting 5/1.

Academics. Special study options: Cooperative education, distance learning, dual enrollment of high school students, honors, independent study, internships, liberal arts/career combination. License preparation in nursing. **Credit/placement by examination:** AP, CLEP, institutional tests. 30 credit hours maximum toward associate degree. **Support services:** GED preparation and test center, learning center, pre-admission summer program, reduced course load, remedial instruction, study skills assistance, tutoring, writing center.

Majors. Agriculture: Agribusiness operations, agronomy, animal sciences, equestrian studies, farm/ranch. **Biology:** General. **Business:** General, accounting, office technology. **Communications:** Broadcast journalism, journalism. **Computer sciences:** Data processing. **Conservation:** Forestry, wildlife. **Education:** General, agricultural, art, biology, business, chemistry, elementary, English, family/consumer sciences, mathematics, music, physical, science, secondary. **Engineering:** General. **Family/consumer sciences:** General, child care. **Health:** Dental hygiene, nursing (RN), physical therapy assistant, premedicine, prenursing, prepharmacy, preveterinary, veterinary technology/assistant. **History:** General. **Legal studies:** Prelaw. **Liberal arts:** Arts/sciences. **Math:** General. **Physical sciences:** Chemistry. **Psychology:** General. **Public administration:** Social work. **Social sciences:** Sociology. **Visual/performing arts:** General, dramatic.

Computing on campus. 100 workstations in dormitories, library, computer center, student center. Dormitories linked to campus network. Online library, helpline, repair service available.

Student life. Freshman orientation: Mandatory, $15 fee. Preregistration for classes offered. **Policies:** Freshmen permitted cars on campus. **Housing:** Coed dorms, single-sex dorms, special housing for disabled, substance-free housing available. $100 fully refundable deposit. **Activities:** Bands, choral groups, drama, literary magazine, music ensembles, musical theater, radio station, student government, student newspaper, TV station.

Athletics. NJCAA. **Intercollegiate:** Baseball M, basketball, cross-country, equestrian, golf, rodeo, softball W, track and field, volleyball W, wrestling M. **Intramural:** Basketball, softball, volleyball. **Team name:** Trojans.

Student services. Adult student services, alcohol/substance abuse counseling, career counseling, student employment services, financial aid counseling, health services, personal counseling, placement for graduates, veterans' counselor. **Physically disabled:** Services for visually, speech, hearing impaired. **Transfer:** Special adviser for new students. Transfer adviser, college fairs on campus for students transferring to 4-year colleges.

Contact. E-mail: bobbi@colbycc.edu
Phone: (785) 460-4690 Toll-free number: (888) 634-9350
Fax: (785) 460-4691
Nikol Nolan, Director of Admissions, Colby Community College, 1255 South Range Avenue, Colby, KS 67701

Cowley County Community College
Arkansas City, Kansas
www.cowley.edu **CB code: 6008**

- Public 2-year community and technical college
- Commuter campus in large town

General. Founded in 1922. Regionally accredited. Area vocational-technical school programs available. **Enrollment:** 3,272 degree-seeking undergraduates; 1,400 non-degree-seeking students. **Degrees:** 643 associate awarded. **Location:** 50 miles from Wichita. **Calendar:** Semester, limited summer session. **Full-time faculty:** 46 total; 2% minority, 48% women. **Part-time faculty:** 185 total; 22% minority, 57% women. **Class size:** 69% <20, 31% 20-39, less than 1% 40-49, less than 1% 50-99, less than 1% >100.

Student profile. Among degree-seeking undergraduates, 41% enrolled in a transfer program, 12% enrolled in a vocational program, 2% already have a bachelor's degree or higher, 815 enrolled as first-time, first-year students.

Part-time:	36%	**Hispanic American:**	4%
Out-of-state:	4%	**Native American:**	1%
Women:	57%	**International:**	1%
African American:	7%	**Live on campus:**	10%
Asian American:	4%		

Basis for selection. Open admission, but selective for some programs. Special requirements for mobile intensive care and interpreter training programs. **Adult students:** Entrance exam policies same as for first-time freshmen. **Homeschooled:** Transcript of courses and grades required.

2005-2006 Annual costs. Tuition/fees: $1,800; $1,950 out-of-district; $3,510 out-of-state. Per-credit charge: $42 in-district; $47 out-of-district; $99 out-of-state. Oklahoma border county resident tuition: $47 per-credit-hour. Room/board: $3,450. Books/supplies: $600. Personal expenses: $900.

2005-2006 Financial aid. Need-based: 413 full-time freshmen applied for aid; 413 were judged to have need; 413 of these received aid. Average need met was 100%. Average scholarship/grant was $1,407; average loan $1,193. 52% of total undergraduate aid awarded as scholarships/grants, 48% as loans/jobs. Need-based aid available for part-time students. **Non-need-based:** Awarded to 1,911 full-time undergraduates, including 536 freshmen. Scholarships awarded for academics, athletics.

Application procedures. Admission: No deadline. No application fee. Application may be submitted online. Admission notification on a rolling basis. **Financial aid:** Priority date 4/15; no closing date. FAFSA, institutional form required. Applicants notified on a rolling basis starting 1/15; must reply within 2 week(s) of notification.

Academics. Special study options: Cooperative education, double major, dual enrollment of high school students, independent study, internships, student-designed major, teacher certification program. **Credit/placement by examination:** AP, CLEP. 15 credit hours maximum toward associate degree. Students with ACT scores of 21 on verbal and math not required to take placement test. **Support services:** GED preparation and test center, learning center, reduced course load, remedial instruction, study skills assistance, tutoring.

Majors. Agriculture: General, agribusiness operations, business, farm/ranch. **Business:** General, business admin, office technology, office/clerical. **Communications:** General, journalism. **Computer sciences:** Networking. **Education:** General. **Engineering:** General. **Engineering technology:** Drafting. **Family/consumer sciences:** General, child care. **Foreign languages:** General, sign language interpretation. **Health:** EMT paramedic, nursing (RN). **Math:** General. **Mechanic/repair:** Aircraft, automotive. **Personal/culinary services:** Cosmetic. **Production:** Machine shop technology, welding. **Protective services:** Corrections, law enforcement admin. **Social sciences:** General. **Visual/performing arts:** General, art, commercial/advertising art, design.

Most popular majors. Liberal arts 79%, trade and industry 6%.

Computing on campus. 125 workstations in dormitories, library, computer center, student center. Dormitories wired for high-speed internet access and linked to campus network. Commuter students can connect to campus network.

Student life. Freshman orientation: Available. Preregistration for classes offered. **Policies:** Freshmen permitted cars on campus. **Housing:** Single-sex dorms, substance-free housing available. $150 nonrefundable deposit. **Activities:** Bands, choral groups, drama, literary magazine, music ensembles, student government, student newspaper, academic civic engagement through services, Campus Christian Fellowship, Black Student Union, Young Democrats, College Republicans.

Athletics. NJCAA. **Intercollegiate:** Baseball M, basketball, golf M, softball W, tennis, volleyball W. **Intramural:** Basketball, softball, table tennis, volleyball. **Team name:** Tigers.

Student services. Career counseling, student employment services, health services, personal counseling, placement for graduates, veterans' counselor. **Transfer:** Special adviser for new students.

Contact. Phone: (620) 442-0430 Toll-free number: (800) 593-2222
Fax: (620) 441-5350
Pam Doyle, Dean of Student Learning, Cowley County Community College, Box 1147, Arkansas City, KS 67005-1147

Dodge City Community College
Dodge City, Kansas
www.dccc.cc.ks.us **CB code: 6166**

- Public 2-year community and technical college
- Commuter campus in large town

General. Founded in 1935. Regionally accredited. **Enrollment:** 1,805 degree-seeking undergraduates. **Degrees:** 157 associate awarded. **Location:** 150 miles from Wichita. **Calendar:** Semester, limited summer session. **Full-time faculty:** 60 total. **Part-time faculty:** 110 total. **Class size:** 25% < 20, 75% 20-39. **Special facilities:** Federal depository of books and documents, horse barn, rodeo practice arena, astronomy center.

Student profile.

Out-of-state:	5%	**Live on campus:**	33%
25 or older:	45%		

Transfer out. Colleges most students transferred to 2005: Kansas State University, Fort Hays State University, University of Kansas, Pittsburg State University, Wichita State University.

Basis for selection. Open admission, but selective for some programs. Special requirements for nursing program. Students without GED or high school diploma must take test to demonstrate ability to benefit. Michigan test given to ESL students. ASSET used as placement test. Interview recommended for nursing majors. Audition recommended for music majors. Portfolio recommended for art majors. **Adult students:** Entrance exam policies same as for first-time freshmen.

High school preparation. Recommended units include English 4, mathematics 3, social studies 3 and science 3.

2005-2006 Annual costs. Tuition/fees: $1,740; $1,950 out-of-state. Per-credit charge: $35 in-state; $35 out-of-state. Room/board: $4,060. Books/supplies: $600. Personal expenses: $1,000.

Financial aid. Need-based: Need-based aid available for part-time students. Work study available nights, weekends and for part-time students. **Non-need-based:** Scholarships awarded for academics, athletics, state residency.

Application procedures. Admission: No deadline. No application fee. Admission notification on a rolling basis. **Financial aid:** Priority date 6/1; no closing date. FAFSA, institutional form required. Applicants notified on a rolling basis; must reply within 2 week(s) of notification.

Academics. Special study options: Cross-registration, distance learning, double major, dual enrollment of high school students, ESL, independent study, internships. License preparation in nursing, paramedic. **Credit/placement by examination:** CLEP. 30 credit hours maximum toward associate degree. ASSET required for placement. **Support services:** GED preparation and test center, learning center, reduced course load, remedial instruction, tutoring, writing center.

Majors. Agriculture: Agribusiness operations, business, equestrian studies, farm/ranch, horticulture. **Biology:** General. **Business:** General, banking/financial services, management information systems, office management. **Communications:** Broadcast journalism, journalism. **Computer sciences:** General, computer science, data processing. **Education:** General, elementary, secondary. **Engineering:** General. **Family/consumer sciences:** Child care. **Health:** Athletic training, dental assistant, licensed practical nurse, medical records technology, nursing (RN), nursing assistant, premedicine, prepharmacy, preveterinary, substance abuse counseling. **Legal studies:** Legal secretary, prelaw. **Math:** General. **Mechanic/repair:** Electronics/electrical. **Parks/recreation:** Health/fitness. **Physical sciences:** Chemistry. **Protective services:** Firefighting. **Social sciences:** General, economics, sociology. **Visual/performing arts:** Art.

Computing on campus. 125 workstations in library, computer center.

Student life. Freshman orientation: Available, $50 fee. Preregistration for classes offered. 2 days before class begins for fall term. **Housing:** Guaranteed on-campus for freshmen. Coed dorms, single-sex dorms available. **Activities:** Bands, choral groups, drama, film society, literary magazine, music ensembles, radio station, student government, student newspaper, TV station, Black Student Union, Fellowship of Christian Athletes, Hispanic American Leadership Organization, Newman Club.

Athletics. NJCAA. **Intercollegiate:** Baseball M, basketball, cross-country, football (tackle) M, golf, softball W, track and field, volleyball W. **Intramural:** Basketball, handball, racquetball, softball, table tennis.

Student services. Adult student services, career counseling, student employment services, health services, on-campus daycare, personal counseling, placement for graduates, veterans' counselor. **Physically disabled:** Services for visually, speech, hearing impaired. **Transfer:** Special adviser for new students. Transfer adviser, college fairs on campus for students transferring to 4-year colleges.

Contact. Phone: (620) 227-9207 Toll-free number: (800) 367-3222
Fax: (620) 227-9277
Tammy Tabor, Director of Admissions, Dodge City Community College, 2501 North 14th Avenue, Dodge City, KS 67801-2399

Donnelly College
Kansas City, Kansas
www.donnelly.edu **CB code: 6167**

- Private 2-year community and liberal arts college affiliated with Roman Catholic Church
- Commuter campus in large city

General. Founded in 1949. Regionally accredited. **Enrollment:** 462 degree-seeking undergraduates; 12 non-degree-seeking students. **Degrees:** 37 associate awarded. **Location:** 5 miles from downtown. **Calendar:** Semester, limited summer session. **Full-time faculty:** 7 total; 14% have terminal degrees, 14% minority, 71% women. **Part-time faculty:** 32 total; 9% have terminal degrees, 41% minority, 47% women. **Class size:** 92% < 20, 8% 20-39.

Student profile. Among degree-seeking undergraduates, 89 enrolled as first-time, first-year students, 45 transferred in from other institutions.

Part-time:	40%	**Asian American:**	6%
Out-of-state:	8%	**Hispanic American:**	35%
Women:	68%	**International:**	11%
African American:	36%	**25 or older:**	39%

Transfer out. 35% of students enrolled in the transfer program go on to 4-year colleges. **Colleges most students transferred to 2005:** University of Kansas, University of Missouri-Kansas City, Kansas City Kansas Community College, Kansas State, Johnson County Community College.

Basis for selection. Open admission. Michigan Proficiency Test required of foreign applicants.

2005-2006 Annual costs. Tuition/fees: $4,536. Per-credit charge: $162. Books/supplies: $764. Personal expenses: $1,800.

2004-2005 Financial aid. Need-based: 65 full-time freshmen applied for aid; 58 were judged to have need; 58 of these received aid. Average need met was 28%. Average scholarship/grant was $2,518; average loan $1,784. 88% of total undergraduate aid awarded as scholarships/grants, 12% as loans/jobs. Need-based aid available for part-time students. Work study available for part-time students. **Non-need-based:** Awarded to 39 full-time undergraduates, including 18 freshmen. Scholarships awarded for academics.

Application procedures. Admission: No deadline. No application fee. Admission notification on a rolling basis. **Financial aid:** Priority date 6/1; no closing date. FAFSA required. Applicants notified on a rolling basis starting 7/1.

Academics. Special study options: Distance learning, dual enrollment of high school students, ESL, weekend college. **Credit/placement by examination:** CLEP, institutional tests. 20 credit hours maximum toward associate degree. **Support services:** GED preparation, learning center, reduced course load, remedial instruction, study skills assistance, tutoring.

Majors. Biology: General. **Business:** General, accounting, office/clerical. **Computer sciences:** Data processing, programming. **Education:** Early childhood, elementary. **Engineering:** General. **English:** Speech/rhetoric. **Health:** Prenursing. **Math:** General. **Physical sciences:** General. **Psychology:** General. **Social sciences:** General.

Most popular majors. Business/marketing 14%, computer/information sciences 8%, education 8%, engineering/engineering technologies 14%, health sciences 30%, physical sciences 8%.

Computing on campus. 40 workstations in library, computer center.

Student life. Freshman orientation: Available. Preregistration for classes offered. **Activities:** Literary magazine, student newspaper.

Student services. Career counseling, services for economically disadvantaged, student employment services, financial aid counseling, personal counseling, placement for graduates, veterans' counselor, women's services. **Physically disabled:** Services for visually, speech, hearing impaired. **Transfer:** Special adviser, orientation for new students. Transfer adviser, college fairs on campus for students transferring to 4-year colleges.

Contact. E-mail: keving@donnelly.edu
Phone: (913) 621-8700 Fax: (913) 621-8719
Kevin Kelley, Vice President Marketing, Enrollmentg Management and Community Services, Donnelly College, 608 North 18th Street, Kansas City, KS 66102-4210

Fort Scott Community College
Fort Scott, Kansas
www.ftscott.cc.ks.us **CB code: 6219**

- Public 2-year community college
- Commuter campus in small town

General. Founded in 1919. Regionally accredited. **Enrollment:** 1,835 degree-seeking undergraduates. **Degrees:** 232 associate awarded. **Location:** 25 miles north of Pittsburg. **Calendar:** Semester, limited summer session. **Full-time faculty:** 46 total. **Part-time faculty:** 94 total. **Special facilities:** Indoor and outdoor rodeo training facilities.

Student profile.

Out-of-state:	14%	**Live on campus:**	14%
25 or older:	34%		

Basis for selection. Open admission.

2005-2006 Annual costs. Tuition/fees: $1,774; $3,454 out-of-state. Per-credit charge: $36 in-state; $92 out-of-state. Students from bordering states of Oklahoma, Nebraska, Missouri, and Colorado pay $1,920 annual full-time tuition or $64 per-credit-hour. Room/board: $3,820. Books/supplies: $550. Personal expenses: $1,020.

Application procedures. Admission: No deadline. No application fee. Admission notification on a rolling basis. **Financial aid:** Priority date 5/1; no closing date. Applicants notified on a rolling basis starting 10/1.

Academics. Special study options: Cooperative education, distance learning, dual enrollment of high school students, ESL, independent study, internships, study abroad, teacher certification program, weekend college. **Credit/placement by examination:** AP, CLEP. 18 credit hours maximum toward associate degree. **Support services:** Learning center, pre-admission summer program, remedial instruction, tutoring.

Majors. Agriculture: Animal sciences, business. **Business:** General, administrative services, business admin, management information systems. **Communications:** General, public relations. **Communications technology:** Graphic/printing. **Computer sciences:** General. **Conservation:** General. **Education:** General. **Health:** Licensed practical nurse. **History:** General. **Liberal arts:** Arts/sciences. **Physical sciences:** Chemistry, physics. **Protective services:** Law enforcement admin. **Psychology:** General. **Social sciences:** General, criminology.

Student life. Freshman orientation: Available. Preregistration for classes offered. **Policies:** Freshmen permitted cars on campus. **Housing:** Coed dorms available. **Activities:** Bands, choral groups, dance, drama, literary magazine, music ensembles, musical theater, student government, student newspaper, symphony orchestra, Christians on Campus.

Athletics. NJCAA. **Intercollegiate:** Baseball M, basketball, cheerleading M, cross-country, football (tackle) M, rodeo, softball W, volleyball W. **Intramural:** Basketball, bowling, racquetball. **Team name:** Greyhounds.

Student services. Adult student services, services for economically disadvantaged, student employment services, financial aid counseling. **Transfer:** Special adviser for new students. Transfer adviser, college fairs on campus for students transferring to 4-year colleges.

Contact. Phone: (620) 223-2700 ext. 87 Fax: (620) 223-6530
Mert Barrows, Director of Admissions, Fort Scott Community College, 2108 South Horton Street, Fort Scott, KS 66701

Garden City Community College

Garden City, Kansas
www.gcccks.edu **CB code: 6246**

- Public 2-year community college
- Commuter campus in large town

General. Founded in 1919. Regionally accredited. **Enrollment:** 2,257 degree-seeking undergraduates. **Degrees:** 137 associate awarded. **Location:** 200 miles from Wichita. **Calendar:** Semester, limited summer session. **Full-time faculty:** 64 total. **Part-time faculty:** 127 total. **Class size:** 80% < 20, 19% 20-39, less than 1% 40-49, less than 1% 50-99, less than 1% >100. **Special facilities:** Cadaver lab, art gallery, fire arms training system. **Partnerships:** John Deere Agricultural technical program is a cooperative program with the John Deere Company and dealers. Centers of excellence in automotive, cosmetology and broadcasting offered in cooperation with area high schools; also with Ford Motor Company.

Student profile.

Part-time:	56%	**25 or older:**	40%
Out-of-state:	7%	**Live on campus:**	15%
Women:	50%		

Basis for selection. Open admission, but selective for some programs. Special requirements for nursing program and John Deere agricultural technical program. Michigan English Placement Test required. Compass/ESL Assessment required for placement. Scores valid for one year. Audition recommended for music majors. Portfolio recommended for art and photography majors. **Adult students:** Entrance exam policies same as for first-time freshmen.

High school preparation. Recommended units include English 4, mathematics 2, social studies 2 and science 2.

2005-2006 Annual costs. Tuition/fees: $1,800; $2,580 out-of-state. Per-credit charge: $39 in-state; $65 out-of-state. Room/board: $4,050. Books/supplies: $780. Personal expenses: $1,550.

2005-2006 Financial aid. Need-based: 65% of total undergraduate aid awarded as scholarships/grants, 35% as loans/jobs. Need-based aid available for part-time students. Work study available nights, weekends and for part-time students. **Non-need-based:** Scholarships awarded for academics, art, athletics, leadership, minority status, music/drama, state residency.

Application procedures. Admission: No deadline. No application fee. Application must be submitted on paper. Admission notification on a rolling basis. **Financial aid:** Priority date 4/1; no closing date. FAFSA, institutional form required. Applicants notified on a rolling basis starting 4/15; must reply within 2 week(s) of notification.

Academics. Special study options: Cooperative education, cross-registration, distance learning, dual enrollment of high school students, ESL, internships, liberal arts/career combination, student-designed major. Bachelor's degree programs available on campus. License preparation in nursing, paramedic. **Credit/placement by examination:** AP, CLEP, IB, institutional tests. 30 credit hours maximum toward associate degree. **Support services:** GED test center, learning center, reduced course load, remedial instruction, study skills assistance, tutoring.

Majors. Agriculture: General, agronomy, animal sciences, business, economics, farm/ranch. **Biology:** General. **Business:** General. **Communications:** General, journalism. **Computer sciences:** General, computer science, networking. **Conservation:** Forestry, management/policy, wildlife. **Education:** General, art, business, chemistry, early childhood, elementary, health, history, mathematics, middle, music, physical, physics, reading, science, secondary, social science, social studies. **Engineering:** General, science. **Engineering technology:** Drafting. **Family/consumer sciences:** General, child care. **Health:** Athletic training, nursing (RN). **Interdisciplinary:** Behavioral sciences, natural sciences. **Legal studies:** Prelaw. **Liberal arts:** Arts/sciences. **Math:** General. **Parks/recreation:** Health/fitness. **Physical sciences:** General, chemistry. **Protective services:** Firefighting, law enforcement admin, police science. **Psychology:** General. **Social sciences:** General. **Visual/performing arts:** General, art, dramatic.

Most popular majors. Agriculture 6%, biological/life sciences 8%, business/marketing 14%, education 15%, health sciences 12%, liberal arts 16%.

Computing on campus. 150 workstations in dormitories, library, computer center, student center. Dormitories wired for high-speed internet access and linked to campus network.

Student life. Freshman orientation: Available. Held prior to start of classes. **Policies:** Freshmen permitted cars on campus. **Housing:** Coed dorms, apartments, substance-free housing available. $300 deposit, deadline 8/1. **Activities:** Bands, choral groups, dance, drama, literary magazine, music ensembles, musical theater, student government, student newspaper, Newman Club, Hispanic American Leadership Organization, Black student union.

Athletics. NJCAA. **Intercollegiate:** Baseball M, basketball, cheerleading, cross-country, football (tackle) M, rodeo, soccer, softball W, track and field, volleyball W. **Intramural:** Archery, basketball, bowling, racquetball, rifle, softball, swimming, table tennis, tennis, track and field, volleyball. **Team name:** Broncbusters.

Student services. Career counseling, services for economically disadvantaged, student employment services, financial aid counseling, health services, on-campus daycare, personal counseling, veterans' counselor. **Physically disabled:** Services for visually, speech, hearing impaired. **Transfer:** Special adviser, orientation for new students. Transfer adviser, college fairs on campus for students transferring to 4-year colleges.

Contact. E-mail: nikki.geier@gcccks.edu
Phone: (620) 276-7611 Toll-free number: (800) 658-1696
Fax: (620) 276-9573
Nikki Geier, Director of Admissions, Garden City Community College, 801 Campus Drive, Garden City, KS 67846-6333

Hesston College

Hesston, Kansas
www.hesston.edu **CB code: 6274**

- Private 2-year junior college affiliated with Mennonite Church
- Residential campus in small town

General. Founded in 1909. Regionally accredited. **Enrollment:** 456 degree-seeking undergraduates; 21 non-degree-seeking students. **Degrees:** 178 associate awarded. **Location:** 35 miles north of Wichita. **Calendar:** Semester, limited summer session. **Full-time faculty:** 19 total; 32% have terminal degrees, 32% women. **Part-time faculty:** 23 total; 9% have terminal degrees, 13% minority, 52% women. **Class size:** 56% < 20, 36% 20-39, 7% 40-49, less than 1% 50-99. **Special facilities:** Arboretum, retreat center.

Student profile. Among degree-seeking undergraduates, 60% enrolled in a transfer program, 40% enrolled in a vocational program, 1% already have a bachelor's degree or higher, 195 enrolled as first-time, first-year students, 77 transferred in from other institutions.

Part-time:	9%	**Hispanic American:**	3%
Out-of-state:	58%	**Native American:**	1%
Women:	51%	**International:**	9%
African American:	6%	**25 or older:**	17%
Asian American:	1%	**Live on campus:**	71%

Transfer out. Colleges most students transferred to 2005: Eastern Mennonite College, Goshen College.

Basis for selection. Open admission, but selective for some programs. Special requirements for nursing and pastoral ministries programs. ASSET required for placement if ACT/SAT scores not submitted. **Adult students:** Entrance exam policies same as for first-time freshmen. **Homeschooled:** Must provide ACT, SAT, ASSET, or COMPASS scores.

High school preparation. Recommended units include English 4, mathematics 3, social studies 3 and science 3.

2005-2006 Annual costs. Tuition/fees: $15,370. $315 per-credit-hour charge for 1-5 credits; $630 per-credit-hour charge for 6-11 credits; special rates apply for high school students and senior citizens. Room/board: $5,620. Books/supplies: $1,000. Personal expenses: $1,500.

2004-2005 Financial aid. Need-based: 183 full-time freshmen applied for aid; 163 were judged to have need; 163 of these received aid. Average need met was 80%. Average scholarship/grant was $8,760; average loan $5,495. 62% of total undergraduate aid awarded as scholarships/grants, 38% as loans/jobs. Need-based aid available for part-time students. Work study available nights, weekends and for part-time students. **Non-need-based:** Awarded to 220 full-time undergraduates, including 117 freshmen. Scholarships awarded for academics, alumni affiliation, athletics, job skills, music/drama.

Application procedures. Admission: Priority date 5/1; no deadline. $15 fee. Application may be submitted online. Admission notification on a rolling basis. **Financial aid:** Priority date 4/1; no closing date. FAFSA required. Applicants notified on a rolling basis starting 2/1; must reply within 4 week(s) of notification.

Academics. Special study options: Cooperative education, ESL, independent study, internships, liberal arts/career combination. License preparation in aviation, nursing. **Credit/placement by examination:** AP, CLEP, institutional tests. 12 credit hours maximum toward associate degree. **Support services:** Learning center, reduced course load, remedial instruction, study skills assistance, tutoring, writing center.

Majors. Business: General. **Computer sciences:** General. **Education:** Early childhood. **Health:** Nursing (RN). **Liberal arts:** Arts/sciences. **Theology:** Theology. **Transportation:** Aviation.

Most popular majors. Health sciences 26%, liberal arts 64%.

Computing on campus. 90 workstations in library, computer center, student center. Dormitories wired for high-speed internet access and linked to campus network. Online library available.

Student life. Freshman orientation: Mandatory. Preregistration for classes offered. **Policies:** Use of alcohol, drugs, smoking and possession of firearms/fireworks prohibited. Decency in dress and appearance is expected. Chapel attendance is required. Religious observance required. Freshmen permitted cars on campus. **Housing:** Guaranteed on-campus for all undergraduates. Single-sex dorms, substance-free housing available. $50 deposit. **Activities:** Pep band, choral groups, drama, music ensembles, musical theater, student newspaper, peace and service club, prison ministries, International Christian Fellowship, Students for Responsible Citizenship.

Athletics. NJCAA. **Intercollegiate:** Baseball M, basketball, soccer M, softball W, tennis, volleyball W. **Intramural:** Basketball, soccer, volleyball. **Team name:** Larks.

Student services. Alcohol/substance abuse counseling, campus ministries, career counseling, financial aid counseling, minority student services, personal counseling, veterans' counselor. **Learning disabled:** Comprehensive services available. **Transfer:** Special adviser, orientation, preadmission transcript evaluation for new students. Transfer adviser, college fairs on campus for students transferring to 4-year colleges.

Contact. E-mail: admissions@hesston.edu
Phone: (620) 327-8222 Toll-free number: (800) 995-2757
Fax: (620) 327-8300
Clark Roth, Director of Admissions, Hesston College, Box 3000, Hesston, KS 67062-2093

Highland Community College

Highland, Kansas
www.highlandcc.edu **CB code: 6276**

- Public 2-year community college
- Residential campus in rural community

General. Founded in 1857. Regionally accredited. **Enrollment:** 2,821 degree-seeking undergraduates. **Degrees:** 117 associate awarded. **Location:** 26 miles from St. Joseph, Missouri. **Calendar:** Semester, limited summer session. **Full-time faculty:** 34 total. **Part-time faculty:** 185 total. **Special facilities:** Photography studio, sports medicine/athletic trainer facilities, learning skills center, communication technology complex.

Student profile.

Out-of-state:	6%	**Live on campus:**	15%

Transfer out. Colleges most students transferred to 2005: Kansas State University, Emporia State University, University of Kansas, Washburn University, Missouri Western State College.

Basis for selection. Open admission, but selective for out-of-state students. Out-of-state applicants must be in top two-thirds of graduating class or have ACT composite score of 14 or SAT combined score of 660 (exclusive of Writing). Placement tests determine program eligibility.

High school preparation. 11 units recommended. Recommended units include English 3, mathematics 2, social studies 2 and science 4.

2005-2006 Annual costs. Tuition/fees: $1,830; $2,070 out-of-district; $3,570 out-of-state. Per-credit charge: $37 in-district; $45 out-of-district; $95 out-of-state. Out-of-state within 150 miles: $57 per-credit-hour. Room/board: $3,986. Books/supplies: $275. Personal expenses: $845.

Financial aid. Need-based: Work study available nights, weekends and for part-time students. **Non-need-based:** Scholarships awarded for academics, alumni affiliation, art, athletics, leadership, minority status, music/drama. **Additional information:** Auditions and portfolios important for certain scholarship candidates.

Application procedures. Admission: Priority date 7/1; no deadline. Admission notification on a rolling basis beginning on or about 4/1. Application deadline for out-of-state applicants August 1, must reply within 2 weeks. SAT or ACT recommended, ACT preferred. Score report by August 1. **Financial aid:** Priority date 4/1; no closing date. FAFSA required. Applicants notified on a rolling basis starting 4/15.

Academics. Special study options: Cooperative education, double major, dual enrollment of high school students, independent study, student-designed major. 5 non-credit classes given through website. **Credit/placement by examination:** AP, CLEP, institutional tests. 15 credit hours maximum toward associate degree. **Support services:** GED preparation and test center, learning center, pre-admission summer program, reduced course load, remedial instruction, study skills assistance, tutoring.

Majors. Business: General. **Education:** General.

Computing on campus. 96 workstations in library, computer center. Dormitories linked to campus network.

Student life. Freshman orientation: Mandatory. **Policies:** Freshmen permitted cars on campus. **Housing:** Coed dorms, single-sex dorms, apartments, substance-free housing available. **Activities:** Bands, choral groups, drama, music ensembles, musical theater, student government, student newspaper, campus Christian fellowship, Christian athletes association.

Athletics. NJCAA. **Intercollegiate:** Baseball M, basketball, cross-country, football (tackle) M, softball W, track and field, volleyball W. **Intramural:** Badminton, basketball, softball, table tennis, tennis, volleyball. **Team name:** Scotties.

Student services. Adult student services, career counseling, student employment services, placement for graduates, veterans' counselor. **Transfer:** Special adviser, orientation for new students. Transfer adviser, college fairs on campus for students transferring to 4-year colleges.

Contact. Phone: (785) 442-6020 Fax: (785) 442-6100
Cheryl Rasmussen, Vice President for Student Services, Highland Community College, 606 West Main Street, Highland, KS 66035-0068

Hutchinson Community College

Hutchinson, Kansas
www.hutchcc.edu **CB code: 6281**

- Public 2-year community college
- Commuter campus in large town

General. Founded in 1928. Regionally accredited. 2 campuses and 2 centers (Newton, McPherson). **Enrollment:** 3,480 degree-seeking undergraduates; 1,389 non-degree-seeking students. **Degrees:** 536 associate awarded. **Location:** 45 miles from Wichita, 200 miles from Kansas City. **Calendar:** Semester, limited summer session. **Full-time faculty:** 113 total; 11% have terminal degrees, 4% minority, 45% women. **Part-time faculty:** 220 total; 2% have terminal degrees, 1% minority, 50% women. **Class size:** 81% < 20, 18% 20-39, 1% 40-49, less than 1% 50-99. **Special facilities:** Kansas Cosmosphere and Space Center, Kansas State Fair.

Student profile. Among degree-seeking undergraduates, 60% enrolled in a transfer program, 40% enrolled in a vocational program, 5% already have a bachelor's degree or higher, 1,059 enrolled as first-time, first-year students, 268 transferred in from other institutions.

Part-time:	44%	**Hispanic American:**	5%
Out-of-state:	6%	**Native American:**	1%
Women:	56%	**25 or older:**	38%
African American:	6%	**Live on campus:**	11%
Asian American:	1%		

Transfer out. 70% of students enrolled in the transfer program go on to 4-year colleges. **Colleges most students transferred to 2005:** Kansas State University, University of Kansas, Wichita State University, Emporia State University, Fort Hays State University.

Basis for selection. Open admission, but selective for some programs. Special requirements for associate degree programs in nursing, radiology, emergency medical sciences paramedic, health information technology, and to diploma program in licensed practical nursing and surgical technology. C-NET exam required for nursing program applicants. Interview required for nursing, radiology, paramedic, health information technology, surgical technology programs. **Homeschooled:** Provide home-school/high school diploma or GED.

2005-2006 Annual costs. Tuition/fees: $1,950; $3,090 out-of-state. Per-credit charge: $50 in-state; $88 out-of-state. International students pay $750 required fees for academic year. Room/board: $4,020. Books/supplies: $900. Personal expenses: $1,000.

2004-2005 Financial aid. Need-based: 570 full-time freshmen applied for aid; 424 were judged to have need; 401 of these received aid. Average need met was 31%. Average scholarship/grant was $1,423; average loan $1,016. 65% of total undergraduate aid awarded as scholarships/grants, 35% as loans/jobs. Need-based aid available for part-time students. **Non-need-based:** Awarded to 1,034 full-time undergraduates, including 718 freshmen. Scholarships awarded for academics, athletics, minority status, state residency.

Application procedures. Admission: No deadline. No application fee. Admission notification on a rolling basis. Priority application dates: 1/15 practical nursing, 2/1 nursing, 5/1 paramedic, 6/1 health information. **Financial aid:** Priority date 2/1; no closing date. FAFSA, institutional form required. Applicants notified on a rolling basis starting 4/1; must reply within 2 week(s) of notification.

Academics. Special study options: Cooperative education, distance learning, double major, dual enrollment of high school students, ESL, honors, independent study, internships, weekend college. **Credit/placement by examination:** AP, CLEP, institutional tests. 16 credit hours maximum toward associate degree. **Support services:** GED preparation and test center, learning center, remedial instruction, study skills assistance, tutoring, writing center.

Majors. Agriculture: General, farm/ranch, power machinery. **Biology:** General. **Business:** General, administrative services, management information systems, personal/financial services, retailing. **Communications:** General. **Communications technology:** General. **Computer sciences:** General. **Construction:** Carpentry. **Education:** General. **Engineering:** General. **Engineering technology:** Drafting, manufacturing. **English:** English lit. **Family/consumer sciences:** General, child care. **Foreign languages:** General. **Health:** EMT paramedic, medical radiologic technology/radiation therapy, medical records technology, nursing (RN). **Legal studies:** Paralegal. **Liberal arts:** Arts/sciences. **Math:** General. **Mechanic/repair:** Auto body, automotive, electronics/electrical. **Physical sciences:** General. **Production:** Machine tool, welding. **Protective services:** Fire safety technology, police science. **Psychology:** General. **Social sciences:** General. **Visual/performing arts:** General.

Most popular majors. Biological/life sciences 9%, business/marketing 17%, education 6%, health sciences 16%, liberal arts 18%, security/protective services 10%.

Computing on campus. 550 workstations in dormitories, library, computer center, student center. Dormitories wired for high-speed internet access. Helpline, wireless network available.

Student life. Freshman orientation: Available. Preregistration for classes offered. **Policies:** Freshmen permitted cars on campus. **Housing:** Single-sex dorms available. $100 deposit, deadline 7/15. **Activities:** Bands, choral groups, dance, drama, literary magazine, music ensembles, student government, student newspaper, symphony orchestra, Black Cultural Society, Hispanic American leadership organization, Hutchinson Christian Fellowship, Campus Crusade for Christ, Right to Life.

Athletics. NJCAA. **Intercollegiate:** Baseball M, basketball, cross-country, football (tackle) M, golf M, soccer W, softball W, tennis, track and field, volleyball W. **Intramural:** Badminton, basketball, bowling, racquetball, soccer, softball, table tennis, tennis, track and field, volleyball. **Team name:** Blue Dragons.

Student services. Adult student services, career counseling, student employment services, financial aid counseling, health services, on-campus daycare, personal counseling, placement for graduates, veterans' counselor. **Physically disabled:** Services for visually, speech, hearing impaired. **Transfer:** Special adviser, pre-admission transcript evaluation for new students. Transfer adviser, college fairs on campus for students transferring to 4-year colleges.

Contact. E-mail: info@hutchcc.edu
Phone: (620) 665-3536 Toll-free number: (800) 289-3501
Fax: (620) 665-3301
Corbin Strobel, Director of Admissions, Hutchinson Community College, 1300 North Plum, Hutchinson, KS 67501

Independence Community College
Independence, Kansas
www.indycc.edu **CB code: 6304**

- Public 2-year community and junior college
- Commuter campus in large town

General. Founded in 1925. Regionally accredited. **Location:** 90 miles from Tulsa, Oklahoma. **Calendar:** Semester.

Annual costs/financial aid. Tuition/fees (2005-2006): $1,680; $1,830 out-of-district; $1,830 out-of-state. Room/board: $4,100. Books/supplies: $500. Need-based financial aid available to full-time and part-time students.

Contact. Phone: (620) 331-4100
Enrollment Coordinator, Box 708, Independence, KS 67301

Johnson County Community College
Overland Park, Kansas
www.jccc.edu **CB code: 6325**

- Public 2-year community college
- Commuter campus in large city

General. Founded in 1967. Regionally accredited. **Enrollment:** 6,231 full-time, degree-seeking students. **Degrees:** 1,100 associate awarded. **Location:** 20 miles from Kansas City. **Calendar:** Semester, extensive summer session. **Full-time faculty:** 220 total. **Part-time faculty:** 500 total.

Student profile.

Out-of-state:	6%	**25 or older:**	37%

Transfer out. Colleges most students transferred to 2005: Kansas University, Kansas State University.

Basis for selection. Open admission, but selective for some programs. Special requirements for some allied health programs. ACT required for admission for nursing and dental hygiene applicants. Interview required for nursing, dental hygiene, emergency medical intensive care technician, respiratory therapy, paralegal programs. Portfolio required of art majors.

2005-2006 Annual costs. Tuition/fees: $1,920; $2,370 out-of-district; $4,350 out-of-state. Per-credit charge: $50 in-district; $65 out-of-district; $131 out-of-state. Books/supplies: $840. Personal expenses: $1,170.

2005-2006 Financial aid. Need-based: Need-based aid available for part-time students. **Non-need-based:** Scholarships awarded for academics.

Application procedures. Admission: No deadline. No application fee. Application may be submitted online. Admission notification on a rolling basis. **Financial aid:** Priority date 4/1; no closing date. FAFSA required. Applicants notified on a rolling basis starting 4/15; must reply within 2 week(s) of notification.

Academics. Wide variety of telecourses and courses offered by special arrangement. **Special study options:** Cooperative education, cross-registration, distance learning, double major, dual enrollment of high school students, exchange student, honors, independent study, internships, study abroad, weekend college. **Credit/placement by examination:** AP, CLEP, institutional tests. 30 credit hours maximum toward associate degree. **Support services:** GED preparation and test center, learning center, reduced course load, remedial instruction, tutoring, writing center.

Majors. **Business:** Accounting, administrative services, business admin, sales/distribution. **Computer sciences:** Applications programming, networking. **Construction:** Power transmission. **Engineering technology:** Civil, drafting, electrical. **Family/consumer sciences:** Child care, institutional food production. **Foreign languages:** Sign language interpretation. **Health:** Dental hygiene, EMT paramedic, medical radiologic technology/radiation therapy, medical records technology, nursing (RN), occupational therapy assistant, physical therapy assistant, respiratory therapy technology, surgical technology, veterinary technology/assistant. **Legal studies:** Paralegal. **Liberal arts:** Arts/sciences. **Mechanic/repair:** Automotive, electronics/electrical. **Protective services:** Firefighting, police science. **Visual/performing arts:** Commercial/advertising art.

Most popular majors. Business/marketing 7%, family/consumer sciences 8%, health sciences 12%, liberal arts 60%.

Computing on campus. 800 workstations in computer center. Online course registration available.

Student life. **Freshman orientation:** Available. **Activities:** Bands, choral groups, drama, student government, student newspaper.

Athletics. NJCAA. **Intercollegiate:** Baseball M, basketball, cross-country, golf M, soccer M, softball W, tennis, track and field, volleyball W. **Intramural:** Basketball M, bowling, handball, racquetball, softball M, table tennis M, tennis M, volleyball M. **Team name:** Cavaliers.

Student services. Adult student services, career counseling, student employment services, on-campus daycare, personal counseling, placement for graduates, veterans' counselor. **Physically disabled:** Services for visually, hearing impaired. **Transfer:** Special adviser, orientation for new students. Transfer adviser, college fairs on campus for students transferring to 4-year colleges.

Contact. E-mail: pbelk@jccc.edu
Phone: (913) 469-8500 Fax: (913) 469-2524
Pete Belk, Director of Admission, Johnson County Community College, 12345 College Boulevard, Overland Park, KS 66210-1299

Kansas City Kansas Community College

Kansas City, Kansas — **CB member**
www.kckcc.edu — **CB code: 6333**

- Public 2-year community and junior college
- Commuter campus in very large city

General. Founded in 1923. Regionally accredited. **Enrollment:** 3,933 degree-seeking undergraduates; 1,486 non-degree-seeking students. **Degrees:** 484 associate awarded. **Calendar:** Semester, extensive summer session. **Full-time faculty:** 108 total; 32% have terminal degrees, 16% minority, 47% women. **Part-time faculty:** 244 total; 46% women. **Class size:** 76% < 20, 23% 20-39, less than 1% 40-49.

Student profile. Among degree-seeking undergraduates, 43% enrolled in a transfer program, 56% enrolled in a vocational program, 7% already have a bachelor's degree or higher, 690 enrolled as first-time, first-year students, 399 transferred in from other institutions.

Part-time:	58%	**Hispanic American:**	7%
Out-of-state:	5%	**Native American:**	1%
Women:	65%	**International:**	2%
African American:	25%	**25 or older:**	50%
Asian American:	2%		

Basis for selection. Open admission, but selective for some programs. Special requirements for nursing program. **Homeschooled:** Interview required. Admission based on ACT, SAT, or GED scores and interview.

High school preparation. 21 units recommended. Recommended units include English 4, mathematics 4, social studies 4, history 4, science 3 and foreign language 2.

2005-2006 Annual costs. Tuition/fees: $1,770; $4,710 out-of-state. Per-credit charge: $49 in-state; $147 out-of-state. Fees vary by program. Books/supplies: $812. Personal expenses: $2,250.

2004-2005 Financial aid. **Need-based:** 55% of total undergraduate aid awarded as scholarships/grants, 45% as loans/jobs. Need-based aid available for part-time students. Work study available nights, weekends and for part-time students. **Non-need-based:** Scholarships awarded for academics, art, athletics, music/drama.

Application procedures. **Admission:** No deadline. No application fee. Application may be submitted online. Admission notification on a rolling basis. **Financial aid:** Priority date 4/15; no closing date. FAFSA required. Applicants notified on a rolling basis starting 5/1; must reply within 4 week(s) of notification.

Academics. Extensive online classes. **Special study options:** Cooperative education, distance learning, dual enrollment of high school students, ESL, external degree, honors, independent study, internships, liberal arts/career combination, weekend college. PACE (Program for Adult College Education). **Credit/placement by examination:** AP, CLEP, IB, institutional tests. 15 credit hours maximum toward associate degree. **Support services:** GED preparation and test center, learning center, reduced course load, remedial instruction, study skills assistance, tutoring, writing center.

Majors. **Business:** Administrative services, business admin, international. **Communications technology:** Desktop publishing, recording arts. **Computer sciences:** Data processing, web page design. **Engineering technology:** Computer, drafting, hazardous materials. **Family/consumer sciences:** Child care. **Health:** EMT paramedic, nursing (RN), physical therapy assistant, respiratory therapy assistant, respiratory therapy technology, substance abuse counseling. **Legal studies:** Paralegal. **Liberal arts:** Arts/sciences. **Personal/culinary services:** Mortuary science. **Protective services:** Firefighting, police science.

Most popular majors. Health sciences 20%, liberal arts 52%, personal/culinary services 10%.

Computing on campus. 800 workstations in library, computer center. Commuter students can connect to campus network. Online course registration, online library, helpline, wireless network available.

Student life. **Freshman orientation:** Mandatory. Preregistration for classes offered. Semester long 3 credit hour course in student's first semester. **Policies:** Freshmen permitted cars on campus. **Activities:** Bands, choral groups, drama, music ensembles, musical theater, student government, student newspaper, TV station, African American Student Union, international student organization, campus forum, Christian Student Union, Phi Theta Kappa, student senate, Out Questioning & Straight Diversity Club, student organization of Latinos, economics club, students in free enterprise.

Athletics. NJCAA. **Intercollegiate:** Baseball M, basketball, cross-country, golf M, soccer M, softball W, track and field, volleyball W. **Team name:** Blue Devils.

Student services. Adult student services, alcohol/substance abuse counseling, career counseling, services for economically disadvantaged, student employment services, financial aid counseling, health services, on-campus daycare, personal counseling, placement for graduates, veterans' counselor, women's services. **Physically disabled:** Services for visually, speech, hearing impaired. **Learning disabled:** Comprehensive services available. **Transfer:** Special adviser for new students. Transfer adviser, college fairs on campus for students transferring to 4-year colleges.

Contact. E-mail: admiss@toto.net
Phone: (913) 288-7600 Fax: (913) 288-7648
Denise McDowell, Dean of Enrollment Management and Registrar, Kansas City Kansas Community College, 7250 State Avenue, Kansas City, KS 66112

Labette Community College

Parsons, Kansas
www.labette.edu — **CB code: 6576**

- Public 2-year community college
- Commuter campus in large town

General. Founded in 1923. Regionally accredited. **Enrollment:** 915 degree-seeking undergraduates. **Degrees:** 168 associate awarded. **Location:** 130 miles from Kansas City, 50 miles from Tulsa, Oklahoma. **Calendar:** Semester, extensive summer session. **Full-time faculty:** 30 total. **Part-time faculty:** 150 total. **Class size:** 84% < 20, 15% 20-39, less than 1% 40-49. **Special facilities:** Commercial music program and equipment, health science facilities. **Partnerships:** With local business, schools.

Student profile.

Out-of-state:	5%	**Live on campus:**	3%
25 or older:	41%		

Transfer out. **Colleges most students transferred to 2005:** Pittsburg State, Emporia State, Wichita State, Kansas University, Kansas State University.

Basis for selection. Open admission, but selective for some programs. Special requirements for health and commercial music programs. COMPASS also used to measure language proficiency. ACT, school and College

Ability Tests required of nursing applicants. Interview required for nursing, radiology, respiratory therapy programs and commercial music programs. **Adult students:** Entrance exam policies same as for first-time freshmen. **Homeschooled:** GED and ACT scores may be considered. Placement testing available. **Learning Disabled:** Student must notify campus ADA coordinator at least 30 days prior to first day of classes (earlier in special circumstances).

2005-2006 Annual costs. Tuition/fees: $2,070; $3,690 out-of-state. Per-credit charge: $41 in-state; $95 out-of-state. Residents of neighboring states (MO, AR, OK) pay per-credit-hour rate of $62. Books/supplies: $550. Personal expenses: $2,000.

Financial aid. Need-based: Need-based aid available for part-time students. Work study available nights. **Non-need-based:** Scholarships awarded for academics, leadership.

Application procedures. Admission: No deadline. No application fee. Admission notification on a rolling basis. **Financial aid:** No deadline. FAFSA required. Applicants notified on a rolling basis starting 4/4; must reply within 2 week(s) of notification.

Academics. Extensive PLATO learning system available. **Special study options:** Distance learning, dual enrollment of high school students, ESL, internships, liberal arts/career combination. Open entry/open exit, competency-based courses. License preparation in nursing, radiology. **Credit/placement by examination:** AP, CLEP, institutional tests. 12 credit hours maximum toward associate degree. **Support services:** GED preparation and test center, learning center, reduced course load, remedial instruction, study skills assistance, tutoring, writing center.

Majors. Biology: General. **Business:** Accounting, business admin, office/clerical. **Communications:** Journalism. **Computer sciences:** General, data processing, LAN/WAN management, networking, programming. **Education:** General, business, early childhood, elementary, music, secondary. **Health:** Medical secretary, nursing (RN), radiologic technology/medical imaging, respiratory therapy technology. **History:** General. **Legal studies:** Legal secretary, prelaw. **Liberal arts:** Arts/sciences. **Protective services:** Corrections, firefighting, law enforcement admin. **Psychology:** General. **Social sciences:** General, political science. **Visual/performing arts:** Commercial/advertising art, music management, studio arts.

Most popular majors. Business/marketing 12%, education 15%, health sciences 43%, psychology 6%.

Computing on campus. 200 workstations in library, computer center, student center. Online library, student web hosting available.

Student life. Freshman orientation: Mandatory. **Policies:** Freshmen permitted cars on campus. **Activities:** Bands, choral groups, dance, drama, music ensembles, student government, Christian Club, Phi Beta Lambda, Phi Theta Kappa.

Athletics. NJCAA. **Intercollegiate:** Baseball M, basketball, cheerleading, softball W, tennis W, volleyball W, wrestling M. **Team name:** Cardinals.

Student services. Adult student services, career counseling, services for economically disadvantaged, student employment services, financial aid counseling, personal counseling, placement for graduates, veterans' counselor. **Physically disabled:** Services for visually, speech, hearing impaired. **Transfer:** Special adviser, orientation for new students. Transfer adviser, college fairs on campus for students transferring to 4-year colleges.

Contact. Phone: (620) 421-6700 Toll-free number: (888) 522-3883
Fax: (620) 421-0180
Jeff Almond, Director of Admissions, Labette Community College, 200 South 14th Street, Parsons, KS 67357

Manhattan Area Technical College

Manhattan, Kansas
www.matc.net

- Public 2-year technical college
- Commuter campus in large town

General. Enrollment: 386 degree-seeking undergraduates; 16 non-degree-seeking students. **Degrees:** 107 associate awarded. **Calendar:** Semester, limited summer session. **Full-time faculty:** 27 total; 48% women. **Part-time faculty:** 5 total; 80% women.

Student profile. Among degree-seeking undergraduates, 100% enrolled in a vocational program, 1% already have a bachelor's degree or higher, 126 enrolled as first-time, first-year students.

Part-time:	16%	**Hispanic American:**	4%
Women:	34%	**Native American:**	2%
African American:	5%	**25 or older:**	31%
Asian American:	1%		

Basis for selection. Open admission, but selective for some programs. Practical Nursing applicants must meet testing requirements and be KS licensed Certified Nurse Aide; Associate Degree/Registered Nurse applicants must be KS licensed Practical Nurses; Electric Power & Distribution applicants must be 18 years of age prior to June 1 of their year of enrollment and have or be eligible to receive a Commercial Drivers License by the same date. WorkKeys testing is required for Practical Nursing applicants.

2005-2006 Annual costs. Tuition/fees: $1,950. Per-credit charge: $55.

2004-2005 Financial aid. Need-based: 10% of total undergraduate aid awarded as scholarships/grants, 90% as loans/jobs. Need-based aid available for part-time students. **Non-need-based:** Scholarships awarded for academics, leadership.

Application procedures. Admission: No deadline. $40 fee. Application must be submitted on paper. Admission notification on a rolling basis. Varies by program. **Financial aid:** No deadline. FAFSA, institutional form required. Applicants notified on a rolling basis.

Academics. Special study options: Cooperative education. License preparation in nursing. **Credit/placement by examination:** AP, CLEP, institutional tests. 9 credit hours maximum toward associate degree. **Support services:** Learning center, reduced course load, study skills assistance, tutoring.

Majors. Business: Executive assistant. **Computer sciences:** General. **Construction:** Carpentry, power transmission. **Engineering technology:** CAD/CADD, industrial. **Health:** Nursing (RN). **Mechanic/repair:** Auto body, automotive, heating/ac/refrig. **Production:** Welding.

Most popular majors. Business/marketing 10%, communication technologies 15%, computer/information sciences 20%, engineering/engineering technologies 20%, health sciences 9%, trade and industry 17%.

Computing on campus. 16 workstations in library, student center. Commuter students can connect to campus network. Online library, wireless network available.

Student life. Freshman orientation: Mandatory. Preregistration for classes offered. Approximately 6-8 weeks prior to beginning of semester. Half day sessions include pre-enrollment, and pre-testing. **Policies:** Freshmen permitted cars on campus.

Student services. Career counseling, financial aid counseling, personal counseling, placement for graduates. **Transfer:** Special adviser, orientation, pre-admission transcript evaluation for new students.

Contact. E-mail: rsmith@matc.net
Phone: (785) 587-2800 ext. 104 Toll-free number: (800) 352-7575 ext. 104
Fax: (785) 587-2804
Rick Smith, Director of Admissions, Manhattan Area Technical College, 3136 Dickens Avenue, Manhattan, KS 66503-2499

Neosho County Community College

Chanute, Kansas
www.neosho.cc.ks.us **CB code: 6093**

- Public 2-year community college
- Commuter campus in small town

General. Founded in 1936. Regionally accredited. **Enrollment:** 1,019 degree-seeking undergraduates. **Degrees:** 187 associate awarded. **Location:** 110 miles from Kansas City, Missouri, 100 miles from Wichita. **Calendar:** Semester, limited summer session. **Full-time faculty:** 30 total. **Part-time faculty:** 135 total. **Partnerships:** Partners in Change work preparation program in association with Job Training Partnership Act, social and rehabilitative services and local business.

Student profile.

Out-of-state:	14%	**Live on campus:**	28%

Transfer out. Colleges most students transferred to 2005: Pittsburg State University, Emporia State University, Kansas State University, University of Kansas, Wichita State University.

Basis for selection. Open admission, but selective for some programs. Selective admission to nursing program, nursing entrance test (NET) required. Students not submitting ACT scores take college-administered placement exam. **Adult students:** Entrance exam policies same as for first-time freshmen. **Homeschooled:** Must take GED.

2005-2006 Annual costs. Tuition/fees: $1,710; $2,010 out-of-district; $2,460 out-of-state. Per-credit charge: $37 in-district; $37 out-of-district; $37 out-of-state. Room/board: $3,800. Books/supplies: $350. Personal expenses: $360.

Financial aid. Need-based: Need-based aid available for part-time students. **Non-need-based:** Scholarships awarded for academics, art, athletics, music/drama.

Application procedures. Admission: Priority date 8/15; no deadline. No application fee. Application may be submitted online. Admission notification on a rolling basis. **Financial aid:** Priority date 7/15; no closing date. FAFSA required. Applicants notified on a rolling basis; must reply within 4 week(s) of notification.

Academics. Special study options: Cooperative education, distance learning, dual enrollment of high school students, ESL, honors, independent study, liberal arts/career combination, weekend college. License preparation in nursing, real estate. **Credit/placement by examination:** CLEP, institutional tests. 15 credit hours maximum toward associate degree. **Support services:** GED preparation and test center, learning center, reduced course load, remedial instruction, study skills assistance, tutoring, writing center.

Majors. Biology: General. **Business:** Accounting, administrative services, banking/financial services, business admin, office management. **Communications:** General. **Computer sciences:** General. **Education:** General, secondary. **Engineering technology:** Drafting. **Family/consumer sciences:** General. **Foreign languages:** General. **Health:** Athletic training, licensed practical nurse. **Interdisciplinary:** Natural sciences. **Liberal arts:** Arts/sciences. **Math:** General. **Parks/recreation:** Exercise sciences. **Physical sciences:** Chemistry. **Psychology:** General. **Public administration:** Social work. **Social sciences:** General. **Visual/performing arts:** Art, dramatic, studio arts.

Computing on campus. 120 workstations in dormitories, library, computer center, student center. Dormitories wired for high-speed internet access. Online library, helpline available.

Student life. Freshman orientation: Mandatory. Preregistration for classes offered. **Policies:** Freshmen permitted cars on campus. **Housing:** Guaranteed on-campus for freshmen. Coed dorms available. $100 deposit. Home stays with host families for international students. **Activities:** Choral groups, dance, drama, music ensembles, musical theater, student government.

Athletics. NJCAA. **Intercollegiate:** Baseball M, basketball, cheerleading, cross-country, soccer, softball W, track and field, volleyball W, wrestling M. **Team name:** Panthers.

Student services. Adult student services, career counseling, student employment services, financial aid counseling, personal counseling, placement for graduates, veterans' counselor. **Physically disabled:** Services for visually, speech, hearing impaired. **Transfer:** Special adviser, pre-admission transcript evaluation for new students. Transfer center, transfer adviser, college fairs on campus for students transferring to 4-year colleges.

Contact. E-mail: sciufulescu@neosho.edu
Phone: (620) 431-2820 ext. 280 Toll-free number: (800) 729-6222
Fax: (316) 431-6056
Lisa Last, Dean of Student Development/Registrar, Neosho County Community College, 800 West 14th Street, Chanute, KS 66720

North Central Kansas Technical College

Beloit, Kansas
www.ncktc.tec.ks.us **CB code: 2616**

- Public 2-year technical college
- Small town

General. Regionally accredited. Multicampus institution. **Enrollment:** 135 degree-seeking undergraduates. **Degrees:** 51 associate awarded. **Location:** 107 miles from Hays, 175 miles from Topeka. **Calendar:** Semester. **Full-time faculty:** 40 total. **Part-time faculty:** 4 total.

Basis for selection. Open admission. **Learning Disabled:** Students must present written documentation from certified professional identifying disability with recommendations for accommodations.

2005-2006 Annual costs. Tool expenses $350-$4,000 depending on program. Books/supplies: $800.

Financial aid. All financial aid based on need. Need-based aid available for part-time students. Work study available nights and for part-time students.

Application procedures. Admission: No deadline. $50 fee. Admission notification on a rolling basis. **Financial aid:** FAFSA required.

Academics. Credit/placement by examination: CLEP.

Majors. Agriculture: Equipment technology. **Engineering technology:** Electrical. **Health:** Nursing (RN). **Mechanic/repair:** Automotive, diesel, electronics/electrical.

Student life. Freshman orientation: Available. Preregistration for classes offered. **Housing:** Coed dorms available. **Activities:** Student government.

Athletics. Intramural: Basketball M, football (non-tackle) M, volleyball, wrestling M.

Student services. Career counseling, financial aid counseling, placement for graduates.

Contact. Phone: (800) 658-4655 Toll-free number: (800) 658-4655
Fax: (785) 738-2903
Clark Coco, Director of Student Services, North Central Kansas Technical College, P.O. Box 507, Beloit, KS 67420

Pratt Community College

Pratt, Kansas
www.prattcc.edu **CB code: 6581**

- Public 2-year community and technical college
- Residential campus in small town

General. Founded in 1938. Regionally accredited. **Enrollment:** 662 degree-seeking undergraduates; 884 non-degree-seeking students. **Degrees:** 149 associate awarded. **Location:** 70 miles from Wichita. **Calendar:** Semester, limited summer session. **Full-time faculty:** 41 total; 7% have terminal degrees, 51% women. **Part-time faculty:** 124 total; 8% have terminal degrees, 8% minority, 52% women. **Class size:** 64% < 20, 33% 20-39, 2% 40-49, less than 1% 50-99. **Special facilities:** Indoor and outdoor rodeo facilities, electrical powerlineman training facility.

Student profile. Among degree-seeking undergraduates, 258 enrolled as first-time, first-year students.

Part-time:	20%	**Hispanic American:**	5%
Out-of-state:	16%	**Native American:**	1%
Women:	49%	**International:**	2%
African American:	5%	**25 or older:**	21%
Asian American:	1%	**Live on campus:**	37%

Transfer out. Colleges most students transferred to 2005: Fort Hays State University, Emporia State University, Kansas State University.

Basis for selection. Open admission, but selective for some programs. Special requirements for nursing, agriculture power technology and electrical power distribution programs. ACT scores used if they are high enough for course placement; if not, ASSET administered. Interview required of nursing majors. Audition required of music and drama majors. Portfolio recommended for art majors. **Adult students:** Entrance exam policies same as for first-time freshmen. **Homeschooled:** Transcript of courses and grades required.

2005-2006 Annual costs. Tuition/fees: $2,070; $2,070 out-of-state. Per-credit charge: $40 in-state; $40 out-of-state. Out-of-district Kansas residents have additional fee of $100; out-of-state $200, and international students $300 for the year. Room/board: $4,168. Books/supplies: $800. Personal expenses: $1,000.

2004-2005 Financial aid. Need-based: 59% of total undergraduate aid awarded as scholarships/grants, 41% as loans/jobs. Need-based aid available for part-time students. Work study available for part-time students. **Non-need-based:** Scholarships awarded for academics, art, athletics, leadership, music/drama, state residency.

Application procedures. Admission: No deadline. No application fee. Application may be submitted online. Admission notification on a rolling basis beginning on or about 1/1. **Financial aid:** Priority date 5/1, closing date 8/1. FAFSA, institutional form required. Applicants notified on a rolling basis starting 2/1; must reply within 2 week(s) of notification.

Academics. Special study options: Distance learning, dual enrollment of high school students, honors, independent study, internships, liberal arts/career combination, weekend college. Bachelor's degree programs available on campus. License preparation in nursing. **Credit/placement by examination:** AP, CLEP, IB, institutional tests. 15 credit hours maximum toward associate degree. **Support services:** Learning center, remedial instruction, tutoring.

Majors. Agriculture: General, animal sciences, business, farm/ranch, range science. **Biology:** General, botany, zoology. **Business:** Accounting, business admin, entrepreneurial studies, office management, office technology, office/clerical, operations. **Communications:** General, journalism. **Computer sciences:** General. **Conservation:** Wildlife. **Education:** General, early childhood, elementary, secondary. **Engineering:** General. **English:** Speech/rhetoric. **Health:** Licensed practical nurse, medical secretary, nursing (RN), predentistry, premedicine, prepharmacy, preveterinary. **History:** General. **Interdisciplinary:** Biological/physical sciences. **Legal studies:** Legal secretary, prelaw. **Liberal arts:** Arts/sciences. **Math:** General. **Mechanic/repair:** Automotive. **Physical sciences:** Chemistry, inorganic chemistry, physics. **Psychology:** General. **Social sciences:** General, political science, sociology. **Visual/performing arts:** General, ceramics, commercial/advertising art, dramatic, drawing, painting, studio arts.

Most popular majors. Agriculture 8%, biological/life sciences 6%, business/marketing 7%, health sciences 18%, liberal arts 21%, trade and industry 16%.

Computing on campus. 125 workstations in dormitories, library, computer center. Dormitories wired for high-speed internet access and linked to campus network. Commuter students can connect to campus network. Online course registration, online library, wireless network available.

Student life. Freshman orientation: Mandatory. Preregistration for classes offered. Held preceding each fall and spring semester. One to 2 days before classes begin. **Policies:** Meningitis inoculations required for dorm students. Freshmen permitted cars on campus. **Housing:** Coed dorms, single-sex dorms, substance-free housing available. $200 fully refundable deposit. **Activities:** Bands, choral groups, drama, literary magazine, music ensembles, musical theater, student government, student newspaper, Christian Challenge, Student Senate, Student Ambassadors.

Athletics. NJCAA. **Intercollegiate:** Baseball M, basketball, cheerleading, cross-country, golf, rodeo, softball W, track and field, volleyball W. **Intramural:** Basketball, rodeo, softball, table tennis, volleyball. **Team name:** Beavers.

Student services. Adult student services, career counseling, student employment services, financial aid counseling, health services, on-campus daycare, personal counseling, placement for graduates, veterans' counselor. **Physically disabled:** Services for visually, speech, hearing impaired. **Transfer:** Special adviser, orientation for new students. College fairs on campus for students transferring to 4-year colleges.

Contact. E-mail: lynnp@prattcc.edu
Phone: (620) 672-5641 ext. 217 Toll-free number: (800) 794-3091 ext. 217
Fax: (620) 672-5288
Lynn Perez, Director of Admissions, Pratt Community College, 348 NE SR 61, Pratt, KS 67124-8317

Seward County Community College
Liberal, Kansas
www.sccc.edu **CB code: 0286**

- Public 2-year community college
- Commuter campus in large town

General. Founded in 1967. Regionally accredited. Off-campus classes offered in 7 locations, adult learning center with ESL classes, interactive television classrooms to off-site locations, adult basic education classes, GED testing available. **Enrollment:** 1,912 undergraduates. **Degrees:** 150 associate awarded. **Location:** 210 miles from Wichita, 150 miles from Amarillo, Texas. **Calendar:** Semester, limited summer session. **Full-time faculty:** 47 total; 4% have terminal degrees, 6% minority, 53% women. **Part-time faculty:** 98 total; 1% have terminal degrees, 6% minority, 61% women. **Class size:** 83% < 20, 16% 20-39, less than 1% 40-49, less than 1% 50-99. **Special facilities:** Wellness center.

Student profile.

Out-of-state:	19%	**Live on campus:**	15%
25 or older:	34%		

Transfer out. Colleges most students transferred to 2005: Kansas State University, Texas Christian University, University of Texas-Arlington, University of Central Oklahoma, Fort Hays State University.

Basis for selection. Open admission, but selective for some programs and for out-of-state students.

High school preparation. 20 units recommended. Recommended units include English 4, mathematics 3, social studies 2, science 2 and foreign language 1.

2005-2006 Annual costs. Tuition/fees: $1,860; $2,550 out-of-state. Per-credit charge: $40 in-state; $63 out-of-state. Residents of neighboring counties in OK, TX and CO pay per-credit-hour rate of $50. Room/board: $3,900. Books/supplies: $700. Personal expenses: $1,000.

Financial aid. Need-based: Need-based aid available for part-time students. **Non-need-based:** Scholarships awarded for academics, athletics.

Application procedures. Admission: No deadline. No application fee. Admission notification on a rolling basis. **Financial aid:** Priority date 5/1; no closing date. FAFSA, institutional form required. Applicants notified on a rolling basis starting 6/15; must reply within 4 week(s) of notification.

Academics. Special study options: Cooperative education, cross-registration, distance learning, double major, dual enrollment of high school students, ESL, external degree, honors, independent study, internships, liberal arts/career combination. Bachelor's degree programs available on campus. License preparation in nursing, paramedic. **Credit/placement by examination:** AP, CLEP, institutional tests. 24 credit hours maximum toward associate degree. **Support services:** GED preparation and test center, learning center, remedial instruction, study skills assistance, tutoring, writing center.

Majors. Agriculture: General, animal sciences, business, economics, farm/ranch. **Biology:** General. **Business:** General, accounting, administrative services, business admin, fashion, finance, hospitality admin, office management, office technology, office/clerical, sales/distribution. **Communications:** General, journalism. **Computer sciences:** General, applications programming, computer graphics, computer science, data entry, data processing, information technology, programming. **Conservation:** Forestry, wildlife. **Education:** General, teacher assistance. **Engineering:** General. **Health:** Athletic training, clinical lab assistant, clinical lab technology, dental hygiene, medical secretary, nursing (RN), predentistry, premedicine, prenursing, prepharmacy, preveterinary, respiratory therapy technology. **History:** General. **Interdisciplinary:** Biological/physical sciences, math/computer science, natural sciences. **Legal studies:** Legal secretary, prelaw. **Liberal arts:** Arts/sciences, library assistant. **Math:** General. **Military:** General. **Parks/recreation:** General, exercise sciences, health/fitness. **Personal/culinary services:** Cosmetology. **Philosophy/religion:** Religion. **Physical sciences:** Chemistry, physics. **Protective services:** Law enforcement admin, police science. **Psychology:** General. **Public administration:** Social work. **Social sciences:** General, economics, sociology. **Visual/performing arts:** General, art, ceramics, dramatic, music performance, painting, studio arts, theater history, voice/opera.

Computing on campus. 450 workstations in dormitories, library, computer center, student center. Dormitories wired for high-speed internet access. Commuter students can connect to campus network. Online course registration, online library, wireless network available.

Student life. Freshman orientation: Mandatory. Preregistration for classes offered. **Policies:** Freshmen permitted cars on campus. **Housing:** Coed dorms available. $100 deposit, deadline 6/30. **Activities:** Bands, choral groups, drama, film society, literary magazine, music ensembles, musical theater, student government, student newspaper, symphony orchestra, TV station.

Athletics. NJCAA. **Intercollegiate:** Baseball M, basketball, softball W, tennis, volleyball W. **Intramural:** Basketball, bowling, football (non-tackle), golf, soccer, swimming, table tennis, volleyball. **Team name:** Saints.

Student services. Adult student services, career counseling, student employment services, financial aid counseling, personal counseling, veterans' counselor. **Learning disabled:** Comprehensive services available. **Transfer:** Special adviser, orientation for new students. Transfer adviser, college fairs on campus for students transferring to 4-year colleges.

Contact. E-mail: gokane@sccc.edu
Phone: (620) 269-2710 Toll-free number: (800) 373-9951 ext. 710
Fax: (620) 626-3016
Jon Armstrong, Director of Admissions, Seward County Community College, 1801 North Kansas Avenue, Liberal, KS 67905-1137

Kentucky

Ashland Community and Technical College
Ashland, Kentucky
www.ashland.kctcs.edu **CB code: 0703**

- Public 2-year community college
- Commuter campus in large town

General. Founded in 1957. Regionally accredited. Off-campus classes in surrounding counties. **Enrollment:** 3,000 degree-seeking undergraduates. **Degrees:** 188 associate awarded. **Location:** 120 miles from Lexington; 15 miles from Huntington, West Virginia. **Calendar:** Semester, limited summer session. **Full-time faculty:** 60 total. **Part-time faculty:** 65 total. **Special facilities:** 3 open computer labs with Internet and e-mail access learning assistance center, early intervention program for students at risk.

Student profile.

Out-of-state:	26%	**25 or older:**	43%

Transfer out. Colleges most students transferred to 2005: Morehead State University, Marshall University, Shawnee State University.

Basis for selection. Open admission, but selective for some programs. Admission to nursing program based on test scores and academic record. COMPASS test used for placement. Interview recommended.

High school preparation. 11 units recommended. Recommended units include English 4, mathematics 3, social studies 2, science 2 (laboratory 2).

2005-2006 Annual costs. Tuition/fees: $2,940; $8,820 out-of-state. Per-credit charge: $98 in-state; $294 out-of-state. Books/supplies: $450. Personal expenses: $920.

Financial aid. Non-need-based: Scholarships awarded for academics, job skills, leadership, minority status, music/drama. **Additional information:** In-state 100% disabled or deceased veterans' children receive tuition waiver from state.

Application procedures. Admission: No deadline. No application fee. Application may be submitted online. Admission notification on a rolling basis. Nursing applications due by March 1. **Financial aid:** Priority date 3/15; no closing date. FAFSA, institutional form required. Applicants notified on a rolling basis starting 5/1; must reply within 3 week(s) of notification.

Academics. Special study options: Cooperative education, cross-registration, distance learning, dual enrollment of high school students, honors, internships, liberal arts/career combination, weekend college. **Credit/placement by examination:** AP, CLEP, institutional tests. 40 credit hours maximum toward associate degree. **Support services:** GED test center, learning center, pre-admission summer program, reduced course load, remedial instruction, study skills assistance, tutoring.

Honors college/program. Participants have option of taking selected honors courses.

Majors. Business: Accounting, banking/financial services, business admin, management information systems, office/clerical, real estate. **Computer sciences:** Information systems, vendor certification. **Health:** Medical secretary, nursing (RN), physical therapy assistant, respiratory therapy technology. **Legal studies:** Legal secretary. **Liberal arts:** Arts/sciences. **Protective services:** Police science.

Most popular majors. Biological/life sciences 14%, business/marketing 16%, health sciences 49%, liberal arts 16%.

Computing on campus. 138 workstations in library, computer center. Commuter students can connect to campus network. Online course registration, helpline available.

Student life. Freshman orientation: Mandatory. Preregistration for classes offered. **Activities:** Choral groups, drama, literary magazine, music ensembles, musical theater, student government, student newspaper, Baptist Student Union/Students for Christ, Circle K, drama club, multicultural student affairs, Phi Theta Kappa, students in free enterprise.

Athletics. Intramural: Basketball, bowling, fencing, softball, table tennis, tennis, volleyball.

Student services. Adult student services, career counseling, student employment services, financial aid counseling, health services, minority student services, on-campus daycare, personal counseling, placement for graduates, veterans' counselor. **Physically disabled:** Services for visually, speech, hearing impaired. **Transfer:** Special adviser, orientation, re-entry adviser for new students. Transfer center, transfer adviser for students transferring to 4-year colleges.

Contact. E-mail: willie.mccullough@kctcs.net
Phone: (606) 326-2000 Toll-free number: (800) 370-7191
Fax: (606) 325-8124
Willie McCullough, Dean for Student Affairs, Ashland Community and Technical College, 1400 College Drive, Ashland, KY 41101-3683

Big Sandy Community and Technical College
Prestonsburg, Kentucky
www.bigsandy.kctcs.edu **CB code: 0869**

- Public 2-year community and technical college
- Commuter campus in small town

General. Founded in 1964. Regionally accredited. Four campuses in Hager Hill, Paintsville, Pikeville, and Prestonsburg. **Enrollment:** 3,589 degree-seeking undergraduates. **Degrees:** 276 associate awarded. **Location:** 120 miles from Lexington. **Calendar:** Semester, limited summer session. **Full-time faculty:** 70 total. **Part-time faculty:** 65 total.

Student profile.

Out-of-state:	1%	**25 or older:**	40%

Basis for selection. Open admission, but selective for some programs. Special requirements for nursing, respiratory care and dental hygiene programs. Nursing and dental hygiene programs require minimum ACT score of 20 for admission. All others required to submit COMPASS or ASSET scores for placement, but ACT or SAT will be considered if submitted. **Adult students:** Entrance exam policies same as for first-time freshmen.

2005-2006 Annual costs. Tuition/fees: $2,940; $8,820 out-of-state. Per-credit charge: $98 in-state; $294 out-of-state. Books/supplies: $450. Personal expenses: $3,000.

Financial aid. Need-based: Need-based aid available for part-time students. **Non-need-based:** Scholarships awarded for academics.

Application procedures. Admission: No deadline. No application fee. Application must be submitted on paper. Admission notification on a rolling basis. Must have completed junior year of high school prior to enrolling full-time; may audit courses if junior or sophomore, except English 101/102. **Financial aid:** Priority date 4/1; no closing date. FAFSA, institutional form required. Applicants notified on a rolling basis; must reply within 2 week(s) of notification.

Academics. Special study options: Cooperative education, distance learning, dual enrollment of high school students, independent study, internships, liberal arts/career combination, weekend college. Bachelor's degree programs available on campus. **Credit/placement by examination:** AP, CLEP, institutional tests. 36 credit hours maximum toward associate degree. **Support services:** GED preparation and test center, learning center, remedial instruction, study skills assistance, tutoring, writing center.

Majors. Business: Accounting, administrative services, management information systems, management science, real estate. **Computer sciences:** Information technology, networking, programming, webmaster. **Health:** Dental hygiene, nursing (RN). **Liberal arts:** Arts/sciences. **Mechanic/repair:** Automotive, heating/ac/refrig. **Protective services:** Police science. **Public administration:** Human services.

Computing on campus. 575 workstations in library, computer center, student center. Online course registration, online library, wireless network available.

Student life. Freshman orientation: Mandatory. Preregistration for classes offered. **Activities:** Choral groups, dance, drama, literary magazine, student government, Baptist Student Union, Phi Theta Kappa, Phi Beta Lambda, Kentucky Association of Nursing Students, CARE, law enforcement club.

Student services. Financial aid counseling, personal counseling, placement for graduates, veterans' counselor. **Physically disabled:** Services for visually, speech, hearing impaired. **Transfer:** Special adviser, pre-admission transcript evaluation for new students.

Contact. E-mail: gia.potter@kctcs.edu
Phone: (606) 886-3863 ext. 67366 Toll-free number: (888) 641-4132 ext. 67366 Fax: (606) 886-6943
Gia Potte, Associate Dean of Students, Big Sandy Community and Technical College, One Bert T. Combs Drive, Prestonsburg, KY 41653

Bluegrass Community and Technical College

Lexington, Kentucky **CB member**
www.bluegrass.kctcs.edu **CB code: 0645**

- Public 2-year community and technical college
- Commuter campus in large city

General. Founded in 1965. Regionally accredited. In Fall 2005, Lexington Community College merged with Central Kentucky Technical College to form Bluegrass Community & Technical College. Locations now include Danville, Lawrenceburg, Lexington, Nicholasville, and Winchester. **Enrollment:** 10,128 degree-seeking undergraduates. **Degrees:** 717 associate awarded. **Location:** 90 miles from Cincinnati. **Calendar:** Semester, limited summer session. **Full-time faculty:** 267 total; 4% minority, 50% women. **Part-time faculty:** 420 total; 8% minority, 54% women.

Student profile.

Out-of-state:	5%	25 or older:	32%

Transfer out. Colleges most students transferred to 2005: University of Kentucky.

Basis for selection. Open admission, but selective for some programs. Special requirements for computer information systems, health technologies, nursing, nuclear medicine, radiography, respiratory care, dental hygiene, dental laboratory technology. ACT required for admission to some health programs. NLN preadmission test may be used for nursing rather than ACT. **Adult students:** Entrance exam policies same as for first-time freshmen. **Homeschooled:** ACT/SAT scores (or COMPASS) and transcript including grading scale required.

High school preparation. Students strongly encouraged to follow state pre-college curriculum.

2005-2006 Annual costs. Tuition/fees: $3,002; $7,706 out-of-state. Per-credit charge: $114 in-state; $310 out-of-state. Room/board: $5,840. Books/supplies: $800. Personal expenses: $800.

2004-2005 Financial aid. Need-based: 39% of total undergraduate aid awarded as scholarships/grants, 61% as loans/jobs. Need-based aid available for part-time students. Work study available nights and for part-time students. **Non-need-based:** Scholarships awarded for academics, minority status, state residency.

Application procedures. Admission: Closing date 8/1 (postmark date). $20 fee. Application may be submitted online. Admission notification on a rolling basis. **Financial aid:** Priority date 4/15; no closing date. FAFSA, institutional form required. Applicants notified on a rolling basis starting 6/5; must reply within 3 week(s) of notification.

Academics. Six nationally accredited programs offered in allied health and nursing. **Special study options:** Cooperative education, distance learning, double major, dual enrollment of high school students, ESL, exchange student, internships, study abroad, weekend college. License preparation in dental hygiene, nursing, radiology, real estate. **Credit/placement by examination:** AP, CLEP, institutional tests. **Support services:** Remedial instruction, study skills assistance, tutoring, writing center.

Majors. Business: Administrative services, business admin. **Computer sciences:** Information technology. **Conservation:** Environmental studies. **Education:** Early childhood. **Engineering technology:** Architectural, civil, electrical. **Health:** Dental hygiene, dental lab technology, medical radiologic technology/radiation therapy, nuclear medical technology, nursing (RN), respiratory therapy technology. **Liberal arts:** Arts/sciences.

Most popular majors. Business/marketing 12%, computer/information sciences 6%, engineering/engineering technologies 6%, health sciences 21%, liberal arts 51%.

Computing on campus. 400 workstations in library, computer center. Commuter students can connect to campus network. Online course registration, helpline, repair service available.

Student life. Freshman orientation: Mandatory. Preregistration for classes offered. 4-hour session held periodically throughout summer. **Policies:** Freshmen permitted cars on campus. **Housing:** Coed dorms, single-sex dorms, apartments available. $300 deposit. Students apply for and are assigned housing at University of Kentucky. Applications submitted to Office of Student Housing, University of Kentucky. **Activities:** Radio station, student government, student newspaper, Athena's Club.

Student services. Adult student services, alcohol/substance abuse counseling, career counseling, services for economically disadvantaged, student employment services, financial aid counseling, health services, minority student services, personal counseling, placement for graduates, veterans' counselor. **Physically disabled:** Services for visually, speech, hearing impaired. **Transfer:** Special adviser, orientation, pre-admission transcript evaluation for new students. Transfer adviser, college fairs on campus for students transferring to 4-year colleges.

Contact. E-mail: shelbie.hugle@kctcs.edu
Phone: (859) 246-6210 Toll-free number: (866) 774-4872 ext. 56210
Fax: (859) 246-4666
Shelbie Hugle, Director of Admissions, Bluegrass Community and Technical College, 200 Oswald Building, Cooper Drive, Lexington, KY 40506-0235

Brown Mackie College: Hopkinsville

Hopkinsville, Kentucky
www.brownmackie.edu **CB code: 5375**

- For-profit 2-year business and junior college
- Large town

General. Accredited by ACICS. **Enrollment:** 180 degree-seeking undergraduates. **Degrees:** 40 associate awarded. **Calendar:** Quarter. **Full-time faculty:** 3 total. **Part-time faculty:** 7 total.

Basis for selection. Open admission.

2005-2006 Annual costs. Required fees are $40 per class. Books/supplies: $500.

Application procedures. Admission: No deadline. $20 fee. Admission notification on a rolling basis. High school diploma not required for those entering certificate/diploma programs. **Financial aid:** No deadline. FAFSA required. Applicants notified on a rolling basis.

Academics. Credit/placement by examination: CLEP.

Majors. Business: Accounting, business admin, management information systems. **Health:** Medical assistant.

Contact. Phone: (270) 886-1302 Toll-free number: (800) 359-4753
Fax: (270) 886-3544
Brown Mackie College: Hopkinsville, 4001 Fort Campbell Boulevard, Hopkinsville, KY 42240

Brown Mackie College: Louisville

Louisville, Kentucky
www.brownmackie.edu **CB code: 0305**

- For-profit 2-year technical college
- Commuter campus in large city
- Interview required

General. Founded in 1972. Accredited by ACICS. **Enrollment:** 400 degree-seeking undergraduates. **Degrees:** 90 associate awarded. **Calendar:** Quarter, extensive summer session. **Full-time faculty:** 8 total. **Part-time faculty:** 11 total.

Student profile.

Out-of-state:	9%	25 or older:	59%

Basis for selection. Open admission. All students must take CPAT. **Adult students:** Entrance exam policies same as for first-time freshmen.

2005-2006 Annual costs. Cost of 23-month associate degree programs $14,720 ($640 per month). Cost of books and supplies varies with program. Personal expenses: $896.

Financial aid. All financial aid based on need.

Application procedures. Admission: No deadline. No application fee. Admission notification on a rolling basis. **Financial aid:** No deadline. FAFSA required. Applicants notified on a rolling basis.

Academics. Credit/placement by examination: CLEP. 16 hours of credit by CLEP Engineering Technologies examination may be counted toward associate degree. **Support services:** Tutoring.

Majors. **Computer sciences:** General. **Engineering technology:** Electrical.

Computing on campus. 12 workstations in library, computer center.

Student life. **Freshman orientation:** Mandatory. **Activities:** Student government, student newspaper.

Athletics. **Intercollegiate:** Softball M.

Student services. Career counseling, student employment services, personal counseling, placement for graduates.

Contact. Phone: (502) 968-7191 Toll-free number: (888) 476-1266
Fax: (502) 968-1727
Kathleen Belanger, Brown Mackie College: Louisville, 300 High Rise Drive, Louisville, KY 40213-3206

Brown Mackie College: North Kentucky

Fort Mitchell, Kentucky
www.brownmackie.edu **CB code: 3419**

- For-profit 2-year business and health science college
- Small town

General. Accredited by ACICS. **Enrollment:** 465 degree-seeking undergraduates. **Degrees:** 130 associate awarded. **Calendar:** Continuous. **Full-time faculty:** 4 total. **Part-time faculty:** 22 total.

Basis for selection. Open admission, but selective for some programs.

2006-2007 Annual costs. Tuition/fees (projected): $2,158. Per-credit charge: $179. Books/supplies: $1,116. Personal expenses: $1,764.

Application procedures. **Admission:** No deadline. No application fee. Admission notification on a rolling basis.

Academics. **Credit/placement by examination:** CLEP.

Majors. **Business:** Accounting technology, business admin. **Computer sciences:** General. **Health:** Health services.

Contact. Phone: (859) 341-5627
Joanne Dellefield, Director of Admissions, Brown Mackie College: North Kentucky, 309 Buttermilk Pike, Fort Mitchell, KY 41017

Daymar College

Owensboro, Kentucky
www.daymarcollege.edu **CB code: 0772**

- For-profit 2-year business and junior college
- Commuter campus in small city
- Interview required

General. Founded in 1963. Accredited by ACICS. Provides hands-on training with practical theory. In Medical Assisting - Clinical Track, students have 3 classes at Owensboro Medical Health System. **Enrollment:** 289 degree-seeking undergraduates; 56 non-degree-seeking students. **Degrees:** 71 associate awarded. **Location:** 120 miles from Louisville; 35 miles from Evansville, Indiana. **Calendar:** Quarter, extensive summer session. **Full-time faculty:** 12 total. **Part-time faculty:** 15 total.

Student profile. Among degree-seeking undergraduates, 25% enrolled in a transfer program, 289 enrolled as first-time, first-year students, 84 transferred in from other institutions.

Part-time:	37%	**Women:**	80%
Out-of-state:	5%		

Basis for selection. Open admission. Must have high school diploma or GED, admissions interview, Wonderlic Scholastic assessment. SAT, ACT, or Wonderlic Scholastic Level Exam required for placement. **Adult students:** Entrance exam policies same as for first-time freshmen. **Home-schooled:** Interview required. **Learning Disabled:** Copy of IEP from high school required.

High school preparation. Recommended units include English 3, mathematics 1, social studies 1 and science 1. One human relations also recommended.

2005-2006 Annual costs. Books/supplies: $933.

Financial aid. All financial aid based on need. Need-based aid available for part-time students. Work study available for part-time students.

Application procedures. **Admission:** No deadline. , may be waived for applicants with need. No application fee. Application may be submitted online. Admission notification on a rolling basis. **Financial aid:** No deadline. FAFSA required. Applicants notified on a rolling basis.

Academics. **Special study options:** Cooperative education, distance learning, double major, dual enrollment of high school students, honors, independent study, internships. **Credit/placement by examination:** AP, CLEP, institutional tests. 12 credit hours maximum toward associate degree. **Support services:** GED preparation, remedial instruction, tutoring.

Majors. **Business:** Administrative services, business admin, office management, office technology, office/clerical, operations. **Computer sciences:** General, data processing, information systems, networking, systems analysis. **Health:** Medical assistant, medical secretary, pharmacy assistant. **Legal studies:** Legal secretary, paralegal.

Most popular majors. Business/marketing 14%, computer/information sciences 36%, health sciences 32%, legal studies 19%.

Computing on campus. 115 workstations in library, computer center.

Student life. **Freshman orientation:** Mandatory. **Activities:** Student newspaper, Phi Beta Lambda.

Student services. Alcohol/substance abuse counseling, career counseling, student employment services, financial aid counseling, on-campus daycare, personal counseling, placement for graduates. **Physically disabled:** Services for visually, hearing impaired. **Transfer:** Special adviser, orientation, re-entry adviser, pre-admission transcript evaluation for new students. Transfer adviser for students transferring to 4-year colleges.

Contact. E-mail: vmcdougal@daymarcollege.edu
Phone: (270) 926-4040 Toll-free number: (800) 960-4090
Fax: (270) 685-4090
Vickie McDougal, Director of Admissions, Daymar College, 3361 Buckland Square, Owensboro, KY 42301

Daymar College: Louisville

Louisville, Kentucky
CB code: 3407

- For-profit 2-year business college
- Large city

General. Accredited by ACICS. **Enrollment:** 300 degree-seeking undergraduates. **Degrees:** 50 associate awarded. **Calendar:** Quarter. **Full-time faculty:** 5 total. **Part-time faculty:** 30 total.

Basis for selection. Open admission. SAT, ACT, or Wonderlic Scholastic Level Exam required for placement.

2005-2006 Annual costs. Books/supplies: $950.

Application procedures. **Admission:** No deadline. $20 fee.

Academics. **Credit/placement by examination:** AP, CLEP.

Student life. **Freshman orientation:** Available.

Contact. Phone: (502) 495-1040
Shawn McDaniel, Director of Admissions, Daymar College: Louisville, 4400 Breckinridge Lane, Suite 415, Louisville, KY 40218

Draughons Junior College

Bowling Green, Kentucky
www.draughons.org **CB code: 3399**

- For-profit 2-year branch campus and junior college
- Commuter campus in large town

General. Accredited by ACICS. **Enrollment:** 515 degree-seeking undergraduates. **Degrees:** 100 associate awarded. **Location:** 120 miles from Louisville; 60 miles from Nashville, Tennessee. **Calendar:** Semester, extensive summer session. **Full-time faculty:** 13 total. **Part-time faculty:** 17 total. **Class size:** 92% < 20, 8% 20-39.

Transfer out. **Colleges most students transferred to 2005:** Western Kentucky University, Lindsey Wilson College, Kentuky Advanced Technology Institute.

Basis for selection. Open admission. SAT and ACT scores used for placement and counseling in remedial work.

2005-2006 Annual costs. Books/supplies: $700.

Financial aid. All financial aid based on need. Need-based aid available for part-time students. Work study available nights.

Application procedures. Admission: No deadline. $20 fee, may be waived for applicants with need. **Financial aid:** No deadline. FAFSA required.

Academics. Special study options: Cooperative education, double major, internships. **Credit/placement by examination:** AP, CLEP, institutional tests. 15 credit hours maximum toward associate degree. **Support services:** Learning center, reduced course load, remedial instruction, tutoring.

Majors. Business: Administrative services, business admin. **Computer sciences:** General. **Health:** Medical secretary. **Legal studies:** Legal secretary.

Most popular majors. Business/marketing 25%, computer/information sciences 15%, health sciences 45%, legal studies 15%.

Computing on campus. 45 workstations in library, computer center. Online library, wireless network available.

Student life. Freshman orientation: Mandatory. Preregistration for classes offered. One-day session held 1 week prior to begining of semester. **Policies:** Freshmen permitted cars on campus.

Student services. Adult student services, career counseling, financial aid counseling, personal counseling, placement for graduates. **Transfer:** Special adviser, orientation, re-entry adviser, pre-admission transcript evaluation for new students. Transfer adviser for students transferring to 4-year colleges.

Contact. E-mail: kathye@draughons.org
Phone: (270) 843-6750
Traci Henderson, Admissions, Draughons Junior College, 2421 Fitzgerald Industrial Drive, Bowling Green, KY 42101

Elizabethtown Community and Technical College

Elizabethtown, Kentucky
www.elizabethtown.kctcs.edu **CB code: 1211**

- Public 2-year community and technical college
- Commuter campus in large town

General. Founded in 1964. Regionally accredited. Off-campus locations at Fort Knox, Bardstown, Leitchfield, Hardinsburg, and Brandenburg. **Enrollment:** 3,130 degree-seeking undergraduates. **Degrees:** 338 associate awarded. **Location:** 40 miles from Louisville. **Calendar:** Semester. Bi-term. Limited summer session. **Special facilities:** Regional Home for the Arts center.

Student profile.

Out-of-state:	1%	**25 or older:**	52%

Transfer out. Colleges most students transferred to 2005: Western Kentucky University, University of Louisville, University of Kentucky.

Basis for selection. Open admission, but selective for some programs. All nursing, radiography and dental hygiene programs have specific criteria to each that is available upon request. Enrolled freshmen must take ACT or ACT/Career Planning Profile or ASSET by start of second semester. **Adult students:** Entrance exam policies same as for first-time freshmen.

2005-2006 Annual costs. Tuition/fees: $2,940; $8,820 out-of-state. Per-credit charge: $98 in-state; $294 out-of-state. Books/supplies: $400.

Financial aid. All financial aid based on need. Need-based aid available for part-time students. Work study available nights, weekends and for part-time students.

Application procedures. Admission: No deadline. No application fee. Application may be submitted online. Admission notification on a rolling basis beginning on or about 4/1. Early admission available for specially qualified high school students on part-time basis. **Financial aid:** Priority date 4/1; no closing date. FAFSA required. Applicants notified on a rolling basis starting 6/1; must reply within 2 week(s) of notification.

Academics. Special study options: Cooperative education, distance learning, dual enrollment of high school students, honors, internships, liberal arts/career combination, weekend college. Bachelor's degree programs available on campus. License preparation in dental hygiene, nursing. **Credit/placement by examination:** AP, CLEP, institutional tests. 6 credit hours maximum toward associate degree. **Support services:** GED test center, learning center, remedial instruction, study skills assistance, tutoring, writing center.

Majors. Business: Business admin, executive assistant, real estate. **Computer sciences:** General. **Construction:** Electrician. **Education:** Early childhood, teacher assistance. **Engineering technology:** General, quality control. **Health:** Dental hygiene, medical radiologic technology/radiation therapy, medical secretary, nursing (RN). **Liberal arts:** Arts/sciences. **Mechanic/repair:** Appliance, automotive, diesel, locksmithing. **Production:** Machine shop technology, welding. **Protective services:** Firefighting, law enforcement admin. **Public administration:** Human services, social work.

Computing on campus. 87 workstations in library, computer center, student center. Online library, helpline available.

Student life. Freshman orientation: Available. Preregistration for classes offered. **Policies:** Freshmen permitted cars on campus. **Activities:** Choral groups, drama, literary magazine, student government, student newspaper, Baptist Campus Ministry, Association of Nursing Students, Phi Theta Kappa, Phi Beta Lambda, Gay Straight Alliance, students in free enterprise, student's government association, Skills USA, Young Republican's Club.

Student services. Adult student services, career counseling, services for economically disadvantaged, student employment services, financial aid counseling, personal counseling, placement for graduates, veterans' counselor, women's services. **Transfer:** Special adviser, orientation for new students. Transfer adviser, college fairs on campus for students transferring to 4-year colleges.

Contact. Phone: (270) 769-1632 Toll-free number: (877) 246-2322
Fax: (270) 769-1618
Cristy Null, Coordinator of Admissions, Elizabethtown Community and Technical College, 600 College Street Road, Elizabethtown, KY 42701

Hazard Community College

Hazard, Kentucky
www.hazard.kctcs.edu **CB code: 0815**

- Public 2-year community college
- Commuter campus in small town

General. Founded in 1968. Regionally accredited. **Enrollment:** 3,885 undergraduates. **Degrees:** 336 associate awarded. **Location:** 100 miles from Lexington. **Calendar:** Semester, limited summer session. **Full-time faculty:** 105 total. **Part-time faculty:** 110 total. **Class size:** 69% < 20, 30% 20-39, less than 1% 40-49, less than 1% 50-99.

Student profile.

Out-of-state:	1%	**Live on campus:**	1%

Transfer out. Colleges most students transferred to 2005: Morehead State University, Eastern Kentucky University, University of Kentucky, Lindsey Wilson College.

Basis for selection. Open admission, but selective for some programs. Out-of-state applicants must rank in top half of high school class or have 3.0 GPA. Interview required of nursing, radiology, and physical therapy assistant majors.

High school preparation. 11 units recommended. Recommended units include English 4, mathematics 3, social studies 1, history 1 and science 2.

2005-2006 Annual costs. Tuition/fees: $2,940; $8,820 out-of-state. Per-credit charge: $98 in-state; $294 out-of-state. Books/supplies: $800. Personal expenses: $800.

Financial aid. All financial aid based on need. Need-based aid available for part-time students.

Application procedures. Admission: Priority date 8/1; no deadline. No application fee. Admission notification on a rolling basis beginning on or about 6/15. **Financial aid:** Priority date 4/1; no closing date. FAFSA required. Applicants notified on a rolling basis starting 6/15; must reply within 2 week(s) of notification.

Academics. Special study options: Cooperative education, distance learning, dual enrollment of high school students, honors, liberal arts/career combination. 2+2 bachelor's degree programs in business administration, elementary education and University Studies with Morehead State University; 2+2 bachelor's degree program in criminal justice, Individualized Studies, nursing and social work with Eastern Kentucky University; 2+2 bachelor's degree in Arts/Human Services and Counseling with Lindsey Wilson and a Master of Education in Mental Health Counseling with Lindsey Wilson. **Credit/placement by examination:** CLEP, institutional tests. **Support services:** GED preparation and test center, learning center, remedial instruction, tutoring, writing center.

Majors. Business: Marketing. **Computer sciences:** General. **Conservation:** Forestry. **Education:** Early childhood. **Health:** Clinical lab science, medical radiologic technology/radiation therapy, nursing (RN), physical therapy assistant. **Interdisciplinary:** Science/society. **Liberal arts:** Arts/sciences. **Mechanic/repair:** Automotive. **Public administration:** Human services.

Computing on campus. 494 workstations in dormitories, library, computer center.

Student life. Freshman orientation: Available. **Policies:** Freshmen permitted cars on campus. **Housing:** Single-sex dorms available. **Activities:** Student government.

Student services. Career counseling. **Physically disabled:** Services for visually, hearing impaired. **Transfer:** Special adviser, pre-admission transcript evaluation for new students. College fairs on campus for students transferring to 4-year colleges.

Contact. E-mail: nena.eddington@kctcs.edu
Phone: (606) 436-5721 Toll-free number: (800) 246-7521
Germaine Shaffer, Enrollment Services Director, Hazard Community College, One Community College Drive, Hazard, KY 41701

Henderson Community College

Henderson, Kentucky
www.hencc.kctcs.edu **CB code: 1307**

- Public 2-year community college
- Large town

General. Founded in 1960. Regionally accredited. **Enrollment:** 1,990 undergraduates. **Degrees:** 165 associate awarded. **Location:** 10 miles from Evansville, Indiana. **Calendar:** Semester, limited summer session. **Full-time faculty:** 50 total. **Part-time faculty:** 55 total. **Special facilities:** Fine arts center hosting variety of social and cultural activities in visual and performing arts.

Transfer out. Colleges most students transferred to 2005: Western Kentucky University, Murray State University, University of Kentucky, University of Southern Indiana, Wesley University.

Basis for selection. Open admission, but selective for some programs. Dental hygiene, nursing and clinical lab technician programs selective; test scores and high school GPA important admissions criteria. Though ACT is required, there is no minimum score except in dental hygiene, nursing and clinical technician programs. Interview required for nursing program.

2005-2006 Annual costs. Tuition/fees: $2,940; $8,820 out-of-state. Per-credit charge: $98 in-state; $294 out-of-state. Books/supplies: $500.

Application procedures. Admission: No deadline. No application fee. Admission notification on a rolling basis beginning on or about 3/1. **Financial aid:** No deadline. FAFSA required. Applicants notified on a rolling basis starting 5/1.

Academics. Special study options: Cooperative education, cross-registration, distance learning, double major, dual enrollment of high school students, honors, independent study, liberal arts/career combination, weekend college. License preparation in dental hygiene, nursing. **Credit/placement by examination:** AP, CLEP. **Support services:** GED preparation and test center, learning center, pre-admission summer program, reduced course load, remedial instruction, study skills assistance, tutoring, writing center.

Majors. Agriculture: Business technology. **Business:** Administrative services, business admin, management information systems. **Communications:** General. **Computer sciences:** Data processing. **Education:** Early childhood. **Engineering technology:** Electrical. **Health:** Clinical lab technology. **Liberal arts:** Arts/sciences. **Public administration:** Community org/advocacy, social work.

Computing on campus. 99 workstations in library, computer center, student center. Commuter students can connect to campus network. Online course registration, online library, repair service available.

Student life. Freshman orientation: Available. Preregistration for classes offered. **Activities:** Choral groups, literary magazine, student government, student newspaper, Baptist Student Union.

Student services. Career counseling, financial aid counseling, minority student services, personal counseling, placement for graduates, veterans' counselor. **Transfer:** Special adviser, orientation, re-entry adviser, pre-admission transcript evaluation for new students. Transfer center, transfer adviser, college fairs on campus for students transferring to 4-year colleges.

Contact. Phone: (270) 830-5256
Patricia Mitchell, Dean for Student Affairs, Henderson Community College, 2660 South Green Street, Henderson, KY 42420

Hopkinsville Community College

Hopkinsville, Kentucky
www.hopkinsville.kctcs.edu **CB code: 1274**

- Public 2-year community college
- Commuter campus in small city

General. Founded in 1965. Regionally accredited. **Enrollment:** 2,980 degree-seeking undergraduates. **Degrees:** 327 associate awarded. **Location:** 70 miles from Nashville, Tennessee; 25 miles from Clarksville, Tennessee. **Calendar:** Semester, limited summer session. **Full-time faculty:** 68 total. **Part-time faculty:** 101 total. **Class size:** 57% < 20, 39% 20-39, 4% 40-49, less than 1% >100.

Student profile.

Out-of-state:	12%	25 or older:	51%

Transfer out. Colleges most students transferred to 2005: Murray State University, Austin Peay University, Western Kentucky University.

Basis for selection. Open admission. ACT scores below 19 require COMPASS for placement.

2005-2006 Annual costs. Tuition/fees: $2,940; $8,820 out-of-state. Per-credit charge: $98 in-state; $294 out-of-state. Books/supplies: $450. Personal expenses: $1,840.

Financial aid. Need-based: Need-based aid available for part-time students. **Non-need-based:** Scholarships awarded for academics, leadership, minority status, state residency. **Additional information:** ACT required for academic scholarships.

Application procedures. Admission: No deadline. No application fee. Application must be submitted on paper. Admission notification on a rolling basis. **Financial aid:** No deadline. FAFSA required. Applicants notified on a rolling basis starting 7/1.

Academics. Special study options: Cooperative education, distance learning, double major, dual enrollment of high school students, ESL, honors. Bachelor's degree programs available on campus. License preparation in nursing. **Credit/placement by examination:** AP, CLEP, institutional tests. **Support services:** GED preparation and test center, learning center, reduced course load, remedial instruction, study skills assistance, tutoring.

Majors. Agriculture: General. **Business:** Administrative services, business admin, management information systems. **Computer sciences:** LAN/WAN management, networking, programming, webmaster. **Education:** Early childhood, teacher assistance. **Engineering technology:** General, industrial. **Family/consumer sciences:** Child care. **Health:** Nursing (RN). **Liberal arts:** Arts/sciences. **Protective services:** Corrections, criminal justice, law enforcement admin, security services.

Most popular majors. Health sciences 16%, liberal arts 65%.

Computing on campus. 400 workstations in library, computer center. Commuter students can connect to campus network. Online course registration, online library, helpline available.

Student life. Freshman orientation: Available. Preregistration for classes offered. **Policies:** Freshmen permitted cars on campus. **Activities:** Choral groups, drama, literary magazine, student government, student newspaper, Black Student Union, Baptist Student Organization, Returning Students Group, Student Nurses Organization, Circle-K, Phi Theta Kappa, Scholars Club.

Athletics. Intramural: Basketball, table tennis, volleyball.

Student services. Adult student services, career counseling, services for economically disadvantaged, student employment services, financial aid counseling, personal counseling, placement for graduates, veterans' counselor.

Physically disabled: Services for visually, speech, hearing impaired. **Transfer:** Special adviser for new students. Transfer adviser, college fairs on campus for students transferring to 4-year colleges.

Contact. E-mail: admit.record@kctcs.edu
Phone: (270) 886-3921 ext. 6195 Fax: (270) 886-0237
Ruth Rettie, Registrar, Hopkinsville Community College, PO Box 2100, Hopkinsville, KY 42241

Jefferson Community College
Louisville, Kentucky
www.jefferson.kctcs.edu **CB code: 1328**

- Public 2-year community and technical college
- Commuter campus in large city
- Interview required

General. Founded in 1968. Regionally accredited. 3 other campuses: southwestern Jefferson County, Shelby County and Carrollton. Courses also offered off-campus and online. **Enrollment:** 10,600 degree-seeking undergraduates. **Degrees:** 696 associate awarded. **ROTC:** Army. **Location:** Downtown. **Calendar:** Semester, extensive summer session. **Full-time faculty:** 250 total. **Part-time faculty:** 274 total. **Class size:** 43% < 20, 55% 20-39, 1% 40-49, less than 1% 50-99, less than 1% >100. **Special facilities:** Horticultural center within Sawyer State Park, classes taught at local zoo, local pottery, local truck manufacturing plant, multimedia allied health lab, machine shop lab. **Partnerships:** Formal partnerships with United Parcel Service, Ford Motor Company, Norton Hospital, Jewish Hospital, St. Mary's Health Care System and Local Area Technology Centers.

Student profile. Among degree-seeking undergraduates, 6% enrolled in a transfer program, 41% enrolled in a vocational program.

Out-of-state:	2%	**25 or older:**	37%

Transfer out. Colleges most students transferred to 2005: University of Louisville, Spalding University, University of Kentucky, Bellarmine University.

Basis for selection. Open admission, but selective for some programs. Students required to sit for ESL Compass Assessment Test after application for admission to determine appropriate course placement. Entering freshmen required to take ACT for placement before start of second semester. Interview required for selective admissions allied health programs: nursing, respiratory therapy, radiology, nuclear medicine, health information technology, occupational therapy, physical therapy, surgical technology, and practical nursing. **Adult students:** Entrance exam policies same as for first-time freshmen.

2005-2006 Annual costs. Tuition/fees: $2,940; $8,820 out-of-state. Per-credit charge: $98 in-state; $294 out-of-state. Books/supplies: $800. Personal expenses: $848.

Financial aid. Need-based: Need-based aid available for part-time students. Work study available for part-time students. **Non-need-based:** Scholarships awarded for academics, art, minority status.

Application procedures. Admission: No deadline. No application fee. Application may be submitted online. Admission notification on a rolling basis. **Financial aid:** Priority date 3/15; no closing date. FAFSA, institutional form required. Applicants notified on a rolling basis starting 6/15; must reply within 3 week(s) of notification.

Academics. Special study options: Cooperative education, cross-registration, distance learning, dual enrollment of high school students, ESL, honors, independent study, internships, teacher certification program, weekend college. License preparation in aviation, nursing, occupational therapy, physical therapy, radiology, real estate. **Credit/placement by examination:** AP, CLEP, IB, institutional tests. STEP test, challenge exams available. **Support services:** GED preparation and test center, learning center, reduced course load, remedial instruction, study skills assistance, tutoring, writing center.

Majors. Agriculture: Horticulture. **Business:** Accounting technology, business admin, executive assistant, real estate. **Communications technology:** General. **Computer sciences:** General, data processing. **Education:** Teacher assistance. **Engineering technology:** General, electromechanical. **Health:** Medical records technology, nuclear medical technology, nursing (RN), occupational therapy assistant, physical therapy assistant, respiratory therapy technology. **Liberal arts:** Arts/sciences. **Mechanic/repair:** Automotive. **Personal/culinary services:** Chef training. **Production:** Welding. **Protective services:** Firefighting. **Public administration:** Social work.

Computing on campus. 1,442 workstations in library, computer center, student center. Commuter students can connect to campus network. Online course registration, online library, helpline available.

Student life. Freshman orientation: Mandatory. Preregistration for classes offered. **Policies:** Freshmen permitted cars on campus. **Activities:** Drama, literary magazine, student government, student newspaper, Black Student Union, Baptist Student Union, Earth-Ecology club, Aspire, International Student Club, WOW.

Student services. Adult student services, career counseling, services for economically disadvantaged, student employment services, financial aid counseling, health services, minority student services, on-campus daycare, personal counseling, placement for graduates, veterans' counselor, women's services. **Physically disabled:** Services for visually, speech, hearing impaired. **Transfer:** Special adviser, orientation, re-entry adviser, pre-admission transcript evaluation for new students. Transfer adviser, college fairs on campus for students transferring to 4-year colleges.

Contact. Phone: (502) 213-5333
Denise Gray, Dean of Student Affairs, Jefferson Community College, 109 East Broadway, Louisville, KY 40202

Louisville Technical Institute
Louisville, Kentucky
www.louisvilletech.edu **CB code: 1501**

- For-profit 2-year technical college
- Commuter campus in very large city
- Interview required

General. Founded in 1961. Accredited by ACICS. **Enrollment:** 611 degree-seeking undergraduates. **Degrees:** 192 associate awarded. **Location:** 7 miles from downtown. **Calendar:** Quarter, extensive summer session. **Full-time faculty:** 32 total. **Part-time faculty:** 31 total. **Class size:** 91% < 20, 9% 20-39. **Special facilities:** Laboratories for computer-aided graphics, computer-aided drafting; robotics, interior design resource centers, computer networking labs, marine mechanics labs, computer repair labs.

Student profile. Among degree-seeking undergraduates, 100% enrolled in a vocational program, 5% already have a bachelor's degree or higher, 53 transferred in from other institutions.

Out-of-state:	19%	**Live on campus:**	9%
25 or older:	33%		

Transfer out. 5% of students enrolled in the transfer program go on to 4-year colleges. **Colleges most students transferred to 2005:** Sullivan University.

Basis for selection. Test scores most important. School achievement record also important. Interview with admissions representative important. CPAT exam used for entrance evaluation. **Adult students:** Entrance exam policies same as for first-time freshmen. **Homeschooled:** Statement describing homeschool structure and mission, transcript of courses and grades, state high school equivalency certificate required. **Learning Disabled:** Student must provide documentation from professional analysis indicating the level of disability and recommendation of type of accomodations that may be required.

2005-2006 Annual costs. Tuition/fees: $16,584. Computer graphic design program tuition: $12,285; fees: $1,400. Room only: $3,690. Books/supplies: $950. Personal expenses: $1,830.

Financial aid. Need-based: Need-based aid available for part-time students. Work study available nights. **Non-need-based:** Scholarships awarded for academics, art, job skills.

Application procedures. Admission: No deadline. $90 fee. Application must be submitted on paper. Admission notification on a rolling basis. **Financial aid:** No deadline. FAFSA required. Applicants notified on a rolling basis; must reply within 2 week(s) of notification.

Academics. Special study options: Accelerated study, cooperative education, double major, internships. **Credit/placement by examination:** AP, CLEP, institutional tests. 51 credit hours maximum toward associate degree. **Support services:** Learning center, study skills assistance, tutoring.

Majors. Architecture: Interior. **Communications technology:** Animation/special effects, desktop publishing, graphics. **Computer sciences:** Computer graphics, information systems, information technology, LAN/WAN management, security, system admin, vendor certification, web page design. **Engineering:** Architectural. **Engineering technology:** Architectural, architectural drafting, CAD/CADD, computer, computer hardware, drafting, electrical, mechanical drafting, robotics. **Mechanic/repair:** Computer. **Visual/performing arts:** Commercial/advertising art, drawing, graphic design, illustration, interior design.

Most popular majors. Communications/journalism 21%, computer/information sciences 14%, engineering/engineering technologies 49%, family/consumer sciences 16%.

Computing on campus. 207 workstations in library, computer center. Online library available.

Student life. Freshman orientation: Mandatory. Preregistration for classes offered. **Policies:** Freshmen permitted cars on campus. **Housing:** Coed dorms, apartments, substance-free housing available. $95 nonrefundable deposit, deadline 9/1.

Athletics. Intramural: Basketball M, bowling, softball M.

Student services. Career counseling, student employment services, financial aid counseling, placement for graduates, veterans' counselor. **Transfer:** Special adviser, orientation, pre-admission transcript evaluation for new students.

Contact. E-mail: gwright@louisvilletech.com
Phone: (502) 456-6509 Toll-free number: (800) 844-6528
Fax: (502) 456-2341
George Wright, Director of Admissions, Louisville Technical Institute, 3901 Atkinson Square Drive, Louisville, KY 40218-4524

Madisonville Community College

Madisonville, Kentucky
www.madisonville.kctcs.edu **CB code: 1606**

- Public 2-year community college
- Commuter campus in large town

General. Founded in 1968. Regionally accredited. Campuses include: North Campus, Health Campus, Technology Campus and Muhlenberg County Campus. Classes also offered at area high schools and other off-campus locations, including KET telecourses and online. **Enrollment:** 3,720 undergraduates. **Degrees:** 348 associate awarded. **Location:** 50 miles from Evansville, Indiana. **Calendar:** Semester, extensive summer session. **Full-time faculty:** 100 total. **Part-time faculty:** 80 total.

Student profile. 1,030 transferred in from other institutions.

Out-of-state:	1%	**25 or older:**	41%

Transfer out. Colleges most students transferred to 2005: Murray State University, Western Kentucky University, University of Kentucky.

Basis for selection. Open admission, but selective for some programs. Special requirements for health programs (nursing, physical therapy assistant, radiography, resipiratory, biomedical, occupational therapy assistant, clinical lab technology). ACT or CAPS scores required for placement/counseling. Interview recommended for nursing and physical therapy assistant applicants. **Adult students:** Entrance exam policies same as for first-time freshmen. ACT or COMPASS test scores required of all students; scores must be less than 5 years old to be considered. **Homeschooled:** Encouraged to apply for early admissions status prior to completion of high school credential. **Learning Disabled:** Disability resources provided for qualified students.

High school preparation. 14 units recommended. Recommended units include English 4, mathematics 3, social studies 2, history 2, science 2 (laboratory 1).

2005-2006 Annual costs. Tuition/fees: $2,940; $8,820 out-of-state. Per-credit charge: $98 in-state; $294 out-of-state. Books/supplies: $500. Personal expenses: $1,000.

Financial aid. Need-based: Need-based aid available for part-time students. Work study available nights, weekends and for part-time students. **Non-need-based:** Scholarships awarded for minority status.

Application procedures. Admission: Priority date 7/1; no deadline. No application fee. Application may be submitted online. Admission notification on a rolling basis. **Financial aid:** Priority date 3/15; no closing date. FAFSA, institutional form required. Applicants notified on a rolling basis; must reply within 3 week(s) of notification.

Academics. Adult and continuing education programs available both on and off-campus. Tech prep and school-to-work programs available. **Special study options:** Combined bachelor's/graduate degree, cooperative education, distance learning, double major, dual enrollment of high school students, honors, independent study, internships, liberal arts/career combination, weekend college. Bachelor's degree programs available on campus. License preparation in nursing, occupational therapy, physical therapy, radiology, real estate. **Credit/placement by examination:** AP, CLEP, institutional tests. **Support services:** GED preparation and test center, learning center, remedial instruction, study skills assistance, tutoring, writing center.

Majors. Business: Accounting, administrative services, business admin, finance, management information systems, real estate, sales/distribution. **Computer sciences:** Information systems. **Education:** General, early childhood. **Engineering technology:** Drafting, electrical. **Health:** Clinical lab science, clinical lab technology, medical radiologic technology/radiation therapy, nursing (RN), occupational therapy assistant, physical therapy assistant, respiratory therapy technology. **Liberal arts:** Arts/sciences. **Protective services:** Police science.

Most popular majors. Business/marketing 14%, health sciences 39%, liberal arts 36%.

Computing on campus. 200 workstations in library, computer center, student center. Commuter students can connect to campus network. Online course registration, online library, helpline available.

Student life. Freshman orientation: Mandatory. Preregistration for classes offered. **Activities:** Choral groups, drama, literary magazine, musical theater, student government, student newspaper, multicultural student organization, Lions Club, Student Ambassadors, Socratic Society, Phi Theta Kappa, student government association, Baptist Student Union.

Athletics. Intramural: Basketball.

Student services. Adult student services, career counseling, services for economically disadvantaged, student employment services, financial aid counseling, health services, minority student services, placement for graduates, veterans' counselor. **Physically disabled:** Services for visually, speech, hearing impaired. **Transfer:** Special adviser, orientation, pre-admission transcript evaluation for new students. Transfer adviser, college fairs on campus for students transferring to 4-year colleges.

Contact. E-mail: aimee.bullock@kctcs.edu
Phone: (270) 821-2250 Toll-free number: (866) 227-4812
Fax: (270) 825-8553
Aimee Bullock, Director of Admissions, Madisonville Community College, 2000 College Drive, Madisonville, KY 42431

Maysville Community College

Maysville, Kentucky
www.maysville.kctcs.edu **CB code: 0693**

- Public 2-year community and technical college
- Commuter campus in small town

General. Founded in 1968. Regionally accredited. Access to University of Kentucky library through automated system (KYVU). **Enrollment:** 1,636 degree-seeking undergraduates. **Degrees:** 157 associate awarded. **Location:** 60 miles from Lexington, 60 miles from Cincinnati. **Calendar:** Semester, limited summer session. **Full-time faculty:** 85 total. **Part-time faculty:** 61 total. **Class size:** 73% < 20, 26% 20-39, less than 1% 40-49, less than 1% 50-99.

Student profile.

Out-of-state:	8%	**25 or older:**	54%

Basis for selection. Open admission, but selective for some programs. High school diploma required and ACT scores considered for nursing program. ACT or COMPASS may be required for placement in degree-seeking programs. Interview required of nursing majors.

High school preparation. Recommended units include English 4, mathematics 3, social studies 2, science 2 and foreign language 2.

2005-2006 Annual costs. Tuition/fees: $2,940; $8,820 out-of-state. Per-credit charge: $98 in-state; $294 out-of-state. Books/supplies: $1,500. Personal expenses: $1,100.

2004-2005 Financial aid. Need-based: 81% of total undergraduate aid awarded as scholarships/grants, 19% as loans/jobs. Need-based aid available for part-time students. Work study available nights. **Non-need-based:** Scholarships awarded for academics.

Application procedures. Admission: No deadline. $5 fee. Application may be submitted online. Admission notification on a rolling basis. March 1st priority date for nursing applicants. **Financial aid:** Priority date 4/1; no closing date. FAFSA, institutional form required. Applicants notified on a rolling basis starting 3/1; must reply within 3 week(s) of notification.

Academics. **Special study options:** Cooperative education, distance learning, double major, dual enrollment of high school students, honors, independent study, internships, teacher certification program. License preparation in nursing, real estate. **Credit/placement by examination:** AP, CLEP, institutional tests. **Support services:** GED preparation and test center, learning center, reduced course load, remedial instruction, study skills assistance, tutoring.

Majors. **Agriculture:** Horticultural science. **Business:** General, accounting, business admin, e-commerce, executive assistant, office management. **Computer sciences:** General, computer science, data processing, database management, information systems, programming, security, system admin, web page design. **Conservation:** Environmental studies. **Construction:** Carpentry. **Education:** Early childhood. **Engineering:** Industrial, manufacturing. **Engineering technology:** Electrical, electromechanical, industrial, manufacturing. **Health:** Licensed practical nurse, medical secretary, nursing (RN), surgical technology. **Liberal arts:** Arts/sciences. **Mechanic/repair:** General, auto body, automotive, diesel, industrial.

Computing on campus. 375 workstations in library, computer center. Commuter students can connect to campus network.

Student life. **Freshman orientation:** Mandatory. Preregistration for classes offered. **Policies:** Freshmen permitted cars on campus. **Activities:** Drama, student government, Phi Theta Kappa, student education association, society of manufacturing student engineers, association of nursing students.

Student services. Adult student services, alcohol/substance abuse counseling, career counseling, services for economically disadvantaged, student employment services, financial aid counseling, personal counseling, placement for graduates, veterans' counselor. **Physically disabled:** Services for hearing impaired. **Transfer:** Special adviser, orientation for new students. Transfer adviser, college fairs on campus for students transferring to 4-year colleges.

Contact. E-mail: patee.massie@kctcs.edu
Phone: (606) 759-5818 ext. 6186 Fax: (606) 759-5818
Patricia Massie, Registrar/Admissions Officer, Maysville Community College, 1755 US 68, Maysville, KY 41056

National College of Business & Technology: Danville

Danville, Kentucky
www.ncbt.edu **CB code: 3413**

- For-profit 2-year business college
- Commuter campus in large town

General. Accredited by ACICS. **Enrollment:** 311 degree-seeking undergraduates. **Degrees:** 38 associate awarded. **Calendar:** Quarter, extensive summer session. **Full-time faculty:** 1 total. **Part-time faculty:** 32 total.

Basis for selection. Open admission. Interviews highly recommended.

2006-2007 Annual costs. Tuition/fees: $8,976. Per-credit charge: $187. Books/supplies: $1,200.

Financial aid. All financial aid based on need. Need-based aid available for part-time students.

Application procedures. **Admission:** No deadline. $30 fee, may be waived for applicants with need. Application may be submitted online. Admission notification on a rolling basis. **Financial aid:** No deadline. FAFSA required. Applicants notified on a rolling basis.

Academics. **Special study options:** Double major, internships, liberal arts/career combination. **Credit/placement by examination:** CLEP, institutional tests. **Support services:** Learning center, remedial instruction, tutoring.

Majors. **Business:** Accounting, administrative services, business admin. **Computer sciences:** Computer science. **Health:** Medical assistant, medical secretary, physician assistant.

Computing on campus. 35 workstations in library, computer center.

Student life. **Freshman orientation:** Mandatory. Preregistration for classes offered. **Activities:** Student government.

Student services. Career counseling, student employment services, financial aid counseling, personal counseling, placement for graduates, veterans' counselor. **Transfer:** Special adviser, orientation for new students.

Contact. E-mail: market@educorp.edu
Phone: (859) 236-6991 Toll-free number: (800) 664-1886
Fax: (859) 236-1063
Larry Steele, Vice President of Admissions, National College of Business & Technology: Danville, PO Box 6400, Roanoke, VA 24017

National College of Business & Technology: Florence

Florence, Kentucky
www.ncbt.edu **CB code: 3408**

- For-profit 2-year business college
- Commuter campus in large town

General. Accredited by ACICS. **Enrollment:** 237 degree-seeking undergraduates. **Degrees:** 29 associate awarded. **Calendar:** Quarter, limited summer session. **Full-time faculty:** 2 total. **Part-time faculty:** 45 total.

Basis for selection. Open admission. Interview highly recommended.

2006-2007 Annual costs. Tuition/fees: $8,976. Per-credit charge: $187. Books/supplies: $1,200.

Financial aid. All financial aid based on need. Need-based aid available for part-time students.

Application procedures. **Admission:** No deadline. $30 fee. Application may be submitted online. Admission notification on a rolling basis. **Financial aid:** No deadline. FAFSA required. Applicants notified on a rolling basis.

Academics. **Special study options:** Double major, internships. **Credit/placement by examination:** CLEP, institutional tests. **Support services:** Learning center, remedial instruction, tutoring.

Majors. **Business:** Accounting, administrative services, business admin. **Computer sciences:** Computer science. **Health:** Medical assistant, medical secretary.

Computing on campus. 35 workstations in library, computer center.

Student life. **Freshman orientation:** Mandatory. Preregistration for classes offered. **Activities:** Student government.

Student services. Career counseling, student employment services, financial aid counseling, personal counseling, placement for graduates, veterans' counselor. **Transfer:** Special adviser, orientation for new students.

Contact. E-mail: market@educorp.edu
Phone: (606) 525-6510 Fax: (606) 525-8961
Larry Steele, Director of Admissions, National College of Business & Technology: Florence, PO Box 6400, Roanoke, VA 24017

National College of Business & Technology: Lexington

Lexington, Kentucky
www.ncbt.edu **CB code: 0987**

- For-profit 2-year business and junior college
- Commuter campus in small city

General. Founded in 1941. Accredited by ACICS. **Enrollment:** 369 degree-seeking undergraduates. **Degrees:** 57 associate awarded. **Location:** 100 miles from Cincinnati. **Calendar:** Quarter, limited summer session. **Full-time faculty:** 4 total. **Part-time faculty:** 46 total.

Basis for selection. Open admission. Interview recommended.

2006-2007 Annual costs. Tuition/fees: $8,976. Per-credit charge: $187. Books/supplies: $1,200.

Financial aid. All financial aid based on need. Need-based aid available for part-time students.

Application procedures. **Admission:** No deadline. $30 fee, may be waived for applicants with need. Application may be submitted online. Admission notification on a rolling basis. **Financial aid:** No deadline. FAFSA required. Applicants notified on a rolling basis.

Academics. **Special study options:** Double major, internships. **Credit/placement by examination:** CLEP, institutional tests. **Support services:** Learning center, remedial instruction, tutoring.

Majors. **Business:** Accounting, administrative services, business admin, office management, office/clerical. **Computer sciences:** Computer science. **Health:** Medical assistant, medical secretary, physician assistant. **Legal studies:** Legal secretary.

Computing on campus. 35 workstations in library, computer center.

Student life. **Freshman orientation:** Mandatory. Preregistration for classes offered. **Activities:** Student government.

Student services. Career counseling, student employment services, personal counseling, placement for graduates, veterans' counselor. **Transfer:** Special adviser, orientation for new students.

Contact. E-mail: market@educorp.edu
Phone: (859) 253-0621 Toll-free number: (800) 664-1886
Fax: (859) 233-3054
Larry Steele, Vice President of Admissions, National College of Business & Technology: Lexington, PO Box 6400, Roanoke, VA 24017

National College of Business & Technology: Louisville

Louisville, Kentucky
www.ncbt.edu **CB code: 3415**

- For-profit 2-year business college
- Commuter campus in large city

General. Accredited by ACICS. **Enrollment:** 771 degree-seeking undergraduates. **Degrees:** 105 associate awarded. **Calendar:** Quarter, limited summer session. **Full-time faculty:** 5 total. **Part-time faculty:** 39 total.

Basis for selection. Open admission. Interviews highly recommended.

2006-2007 Annual costs. Tuition/fees: $8,976. Per-credit charge: $187. Books/supplies: $1,200.

Financial aid. All financial aid based on need. Need-based aid available for part-time students.

Application procedures. **Admission:** No deadline. $30 fee, may be waived for applicants with need. Application may be submitted online. Admission notification on a rolling basis. **Financial aid:** No deadline. FAFSA required. Applicants notified on a rolling basis.

Academics. **Special study options:** Internships. **Credit/placement by examination:** CLEP, institutional tests. **Support services:** Learning center, remedial instruction, tutoring.

Majors. **Business:** Accounting, administrative services, business admin. **Computer sciences:** Computer science. **Health:** Medical assistant, medical secretary. **Legal studies:** Legal secretary.

Computing on campus. 35 workstations in library, computer center.

Student life. **Freshman orientation:** Mandatory. Preregistration for classes offered. **Activities:** Student government.

Student services. Career counseling, student employment services, personal counseling, placement for graduates, veterans' counselor. **Transfer:** Special adviser, orientation for new students.

Contact. E-mail: market@educorp.edu
Phone: (502) 447-7634 Toll-free number: (800) 664-1886
Fax: (502) 447-7665
Larry Steele, Vice President of Admissions, National College of Business & Technology: Louisville, PO Box 6400, Roanoke, VA 24017

National College of Business & Technology: Pikeville

Pikeville, Kentucky
www.ncbt.edu **CB code: 3412**

- For-profit 2-year business college
- Commuter campus in large town

General. Accredited by ACICS. **Enrollment:** 194 degree-seeking undergraduates. **Degrees:** 45 associate awarded. **Calendar:** Quarter, extensive summer session. **Full-time faculty:** 2 total. **Part-time faculty:** 15 total.

Basis for selection. Open admission. Interviews highly recommended.

2006-2007 Annual costs. Tuition/fees: $8,976. Per-credit charge: $187. Books/supplies: $1,200.

Financial aid. All financial aid based on need. Need-based aid available for part-time students.

Application procedures. **Admission:** No deadline. $30 fee, may be waived for applicants with need. Application may be submitted online. Admission notification on a rolling basis. **Financial aid:** No deadline. FAFSA required.

Academics. **Special study options:** Double major, internships. **Credit/placement by examination:** CLEP, institutional tests. **Support services:** Learning center, remedial instruction, tutoring.

Majors. **Business:** Accounting, administrative services, business admin. **Health:** Medical assistant, medical secretary. **Legal studies:** Legal secretary.

Computing on campus. 35 workstations in library, computer center.

Student life. **Freshman orientation:** Mandatory. Preregistration for classes offered. **Activities:** Student government.

Student services. Career counseling, student employment services, financial aid counseling, personal counseling, placement for graduates, veterans' counselor. **Transfer:** Special adviser, orientation for new students.

Contact. E-mail: market@educorp.edu
Phone: (606) 432-5477 Toll-free number: (800) 664-1886
Fax: (606) 437-4952
Larry Steele, Vice Presidnet of Admissions, National College of Business & Technology: Pikeville, PO Box 6400, Roanoke, VA 24017

National College of Business & Technology: Richmond

Richmond, Kentucky
www.ncbt.edu **CB code: 3414**

- For-profit 2-year business college
- Commuter campus in large town

General. Accredited by ACICS. **Enrollment:** 312 degree-seeking undergraduates. **Degrees:** 43 associate awarded. **Calendar:** Quarter, limited summer session. **Full-time faculty:** 1 total. **Part-time faculty:** 32 total.

Basis for selection. Open admission. Interviews highly recommended.

2006-2007 Annual costs. Tuition/fees: $8,976. Per-credit charge: $187. Books/supplies: $1,200.

Financial aid. All financial aid based on need. Need-based aid available for part-time students.

Application procedures. **Admission:** No deadline. $30 fee, may be waived for applicants with need. Application may be submitted online. Admission notification on a rolling basis. **Financial aid:** No deadline. FAFSA required. Applicants notified on a rolling basis.

Academics. **Special study options:** Double major, internships. **Credit/placement by examination:** CLEP, institutional tests. **Support services:** Learning center, remedial instruction, tutoring.

Majors. **Business:** Accounting, administrative services, business admin. **Computer sciences:** Computer science. **Health:** Medical assistant, medical secretary.

Computing on campus. 35 workstations in library, computer center.

Student life. **Freshman orientation:** Mandatory. Preregistration for classes offered. **Activities:** Student government.

Student services. Career counseling, student employment services, financial aid counseling, personal counseling, placement for graduates, veterans' counselor. **Transfer:** Special adviser, orientation for new students.

Contact. E-mail: market@educorp.edu
Phone: (859) 623-8956 Toll-free number: (800) 664-1886
Fax: (859) 624-5544
Larry Steele, Vice President of Admissions, National College of Business & Technology: Richmond, PO Box 6400, Roanoke, VA 24017

Owensboro Community College
Owensboro, Kentucky
www.octc.kctcs.edu **CB code: 0613**

- Public 2-year community college
- Commuter campus in small city

General. Founded in 1986. Regionally accredited. **Enrollment:** 4,084 degree-seeking undergraduates. **Degrees:** 350 associate awarded. **Location:** 120 miles from Louisville; 40 miles from Evansville, Indiana. **Calendar:** Semester, extensive summer session. **Full-time faculty:** 290 total. **Part-time faculty:** 64 total. **Class size:** 45% < 20, 53% 20-39, 2% 40-49. **Special facilities:** Outdoor classroom/nature area, early Headstart program.

Student profile.

Out-of-state:	5%	25 or older:	32%

Transfer out. Colleges most students transferred to 2005: Western Kentucky University, Kentucky Wesleyan College, Brescia University, University of Southern Indiana, University of Kentucky.

Basis for selection. Open admission, but selective for some programs. ACT scores required for nursing, radiography, and early childhood education programs. Placement test required for all new degree-seeking students, although ACT scores may be used in lieu of this requirement. **Homeschooled:** Documentation of courses required.

High school preparation. 11 units recommended. Recommended units include English 4, mathematics 3, history 2, science 2 (laboratory 1).

2005-2006 Annual costs. Tuition/fees: $2,940; $8,820 out-of-state. Per-credit charge: $98 in-state; $294 out-of-state. Books/supplies: $600. Personal expenses: $1,040.

2004-2005 Financial aid. Need-based: 83% of total undergraduate aid awarded as scholarships/grants, 17% as loans/jobs. Need-based aid available for part-time students. Work study available for part-time students. **Non-need-based:** Scholarships awarded for academics, state residency.

Application procedures. Admission: No deadline. No application fee. Admission notification on a rolling basis beginning on or about 3/1. **Financial aid:** Priority date 3/16; no closing date. FAFSA required. Applicants notified by 6/1; must reply within 2 week(s) of notification.

Academics. Special study options: Cooperative education, distance learning, double major, dual enrollment of high school students, independent study, study abroad. License preparation in nursing, radiology, real estate. **Credit/placement by examination:** CLEP, IB, institutional tests. **Support services:** Learning center, remedial instruction, study skills assistance, tutoring.

Majors. Agriculture: Business. **Business:** General, accounting, administrative services, business admin, management information systems, office/clerical. **Computer sciences:** Information systems. **Education:** Early childhood. **Engineering technology:** Electrical. **Health:** Medical radiologic technology/radiation therapy, nursing (RN). **Liberal arts:** Arts/sciences. **Protective services:** Police science. **Public administration:** Social work.

Computing on campus. 90 workstations in library, computer center, student center. Online library available.

Student life. Freshman orientation: Mandatory. Preregistration for classes offered. Half-day session conducted a month before classes begin. **Policies:** Freshmen permitted cars on campus. **Activities:** Choral groups, drama, literary magazine, radio station, student government, student newspaper, TV station.

Athletics. Intramural: Basketball, softball.

Student services. Career counseling, services for economically disadvantaged, student employment services, financial aid counseling, on-campus daycare, personal counseling, placement for graduates, veterans' counselor. **Physically disabled:** Services for visually, speech, hearing impaired. **Transfer:** Special adviser, orientation, pre-admission transcript evaluation for new students. Transfer adviser, college fairs on campus for students transferring to 4-year colleges.

Contact. Phone: (270) 686-4412 Toll-free number: (877) 734-0694
Fax: (270) 686-4648
Kevin Beardmore, Dean of Enrollment, Owensboro Community College, 4800 New Hartford Road, Owensboro, KY 42303-1899

Paducah Technical College
Paducah, Kentucky
www.paducahtech.edu **CB code: 0669**

- For-profit 2-year technical college
- Commuter campus in small city
- Interview required

General. Founded in 1964. Accredited by ACCSCT. Associate program completes 3 academic years in 2 calendar years. **Enrollment:** 150 degree-seeking undergraduates. **Degrees:** 50 associate awarded. **Location:** 150 miles from Nashville, Tennessee and St. Louis. **Calendar:** Trimester, extensive summer session. **Full-time faculty:** 20 total. **Part-time faculty:** 10 total.

Basis for selection. Open admission.

2005-2006 Annual costs. $18,975 for 3-year program includes books, fees, tools. Personal expenses: $2,000.

Application procedures. Admission: No deadline. $75 fee, may be waived for applicants with need. Admission notification on a rolling basis. **Financial aid:** No deadline. CSS PROFILE required. Applicants notified on a rolling basis; must reply within 3 week(s) of notification.

Academics. Credit/placement by examination: AP, CLEP. **Support services:** Tutoring.

Majors. Engineering: Electrical. **Engineering technology:** Electrical. **Math:** Applied.

Computing on campus. 18 workstations in library, computer center.

Student life. Freshman orientation: Mandatory. Preregistration for classes offered. **Policies:** Freshmen permitted cars on campus.

Student services. Alcohol/substance abuse counseling, career counseling, student employment services, financial aid counseling, personal counseling, placement for graduates, veterans' counselor. **Transfer:** Special adviser, orientation, pre-admission transcript evaluation for new students.

Contact. Phone: (270) 444-9676 Toll-free number: (800) 995-4438
Fax: (270) 441-7202
Kathy Baird, Director of Admission, Paducah Technical College, 509 South 30th Street, Paducah, KY 42001

Somerset Community College
Somerset, Kentucky
www.somerset.kctcs.edu **CB code: 1779**

- Public 2-year community and technical college
- Commuter campus in large town

General. Founded in 1965. Regionally accredited. One of 15 community colleges and 12 technical colleges consolidated under one administration. **Enrollment:** 4,100 degree-seeking undergraduates. **Degrees:** 435 associate awarded. **Location:** 70 miles from Lexington. **Calendar:** Semester, limited summer session. **Full-time faculty:** 148 total; 6% have terminal degrees, 3% minority. **Part-time faculty:** 161 total; 5% have terminal degrees, 4% minority. **Class size:** 71% < 20, 28% 20-39, less than 1% 40-49, less than 1% 50-99.

Student profile. Among degree-seeking undergraduates, 332 transferred in from other institutions.

Out-of-state:	1%	25 or older:	45%

Transfer out. Colleges most students transferred to 2005: Morehead State University, University of Kentucky, Western Kentucky University, Eastern Kentucky University.

Basis for selection. Open admission, but selective for some programs. Test scores, letters of recommendation, and interview required for limited enrollment programs in allied health. ACT required in admissions process but not ordinarily used as selective criterion. **Adult students:** Entrance exam policies same as for first-time freshmen.

High school preparation. College-preparatory program recommended. 20 units recommended. Recommended units include English 4, mathematics 3, social studies 2, science 2 and academic electives 9.

2005-2006 Annual costs. Tuition/fees: $2,940; $8,820 out-of-state. Per-credit charge: $98 in-state; $294 out-of-state. Books/supplies: $500.

2005-2006 Financial aid. All financial aid based on need. 80% of total undergraduate aid awarded as scholarships/grants, 20% as loans/jobs. Need-based aid available for part-time students. Work study available nights and for part-time students.

Application procedures. Admission: No deadline. No application fee. Application must be submitted on paper. Admission notification on a rolling basis. Admitted students in nursing, clinical laboratory techniques, and physical therapy assisting must reply within 10 days. **Financial aid:** Priority date 3/1; no closing date. FAFSA required. Applicants notified on a rolling basis starting 6/30; must reply within 2 week(s) of notification.

Academics. Special study options: Cooperative education, distance learning, dual enrollment of high school students, internships, liberal arts/career combination. Bachelor's degree programs available on campus. License preparation in aviation, dental hygiene, nursing, physical therapy, radiology, real estate. **Credit/placement by examination:** AP, CLEP. 12 credit hours maximum toward associate degree. **Support services:** GED preparation and test center, learning center, reduced course load, remedial instruction, study skills assistance, tutoring, writing center.

Majors. Business: Business admin, executive assistant. **Communications technology:** Graphics, printing management. **Computer sciences:** General. **Construction:** Carpentry, electrician, masonry, pipefitting, plumbing. **Education:** General, teacher assistance. **Family/consumer sciences:** Child care. **Health:** Clinical lab assistant, clinical lab technology, licensed practical nurse, medical assistant, medical secretary, nursing (RN), physical therapy assistant. **Liberal arts:** Arts/sciences. **Mechanic/repair:** Aircraft powerplant, auto body, automotive, diesel, industrial, industrial electronics. **Personal/culinary services:** Cosmetology. **Production:** Machine shop technology, welding. **Protective services:** Law enforcement admin, police science.

Computing on campus. 947 workstations in library, computer center, student center. Commuter students can connect to campus network. Online course registration, online library, repair service available.

Student life. Freshman orientation: Mandatory. Preregistration for classes offered. **Policies:** Freshmen permitted cars on campus. **Activities:** Choral groups, drama, film society, music ensembles, student government, student newspaper, Baptist Student Union, student government association, Students for Free Enterprise, Phi Beta Lambda, Phi Theta Kappa, criminal justice student organization.

Athletics. Intramural: Basketball, football (non-tackle), racquetball, softball, volleyball. **Team name:** Cougars.

Student services. Adult student services, career counseling, services for economically disadvantaged, student employment services, financial aid counseling, minority student services, personal counseling, placement for graduates, veterans' counselor. **Physically disabled:** Services for visually, speech, hearing impaired. **Transfer:** Special adviser, orientation, pre-admission transcript evaluation for new students. Transfer adviser, college fairs on campus for students transferring to 4-year colleges.

Contact. E-mail: tracy.casada@kctcs.edu
Phone: (606) 679-8501 Toll-free number: (877) 629-9722
Fax: (606) 677-9658
Tracy Casada, Dean of Student Affairs, Somerset Community College, 808 Monticello Street, Somerset, KY 42501

Southeast Kentucky Community and Technical College

Cumberland, Kentucky
www.secc.kctcs.net **CB code: 1770**

- Public 2-year community college
- Commuter campus in small town

General. Founded in 1960. Regionally accredited. Branch campuses at Middlesboro and Whitesburg. **Enrollment:** 1,700 degree-seeking undergraduates. **Degrees:** 414 associate awarded. **Location:** 150 miles from Lexington. **Calendar:** Semester, limited summer session. **Full-time faculty:** 115 total. **Part-time faculty:** 69 total. **Special facilities:** Appalachian archives.

Student profile.

Out-of-state:	4%	**25 or older:**	30%

Transfer out. Colleges most students transferred to 2005: Lincoln Memorial University, University of Louisville, Eastern Kentucky University.

Basis for selection. Open admission, but selective for some programs. Interview required for nursing, radiography, respiratory care and physical therapy programs.

High school preparation. 12 units recommended. Recommended units include English 4, mathematics 3, history 2, science 2 (laboratory 1).

2005-2006 Annual costs. Tuition/fees: $2,940; $8,820 out-of-state. Per-credit charge: $98 in-state; $294 out-of-state. Books/supplies: $450. Personal expenses: $1,100.

Financial aid. All financial aid based on need. Need-based aid available for part-time students. Work study available for part-time students. **Additional information:** March 15 deadline for state financial aid.

Application procedures. Admission: No deadline. No application fee. Application may be submitted online. Admission notification on a rolling basis. **Financial aid:** Priority date 3/15; no closing date. FAFSA required. Applicants notified by 6/15; must reply within 2 week(s) of notification.

Academics. Special study options: Cross-registration, distance learning, dual enrollment of high school students, internships, liberal arts/career combination. License preparation in nursing. **Credit/placement by examination:** AP, CLEP, institutional tests. 30 credit hours maximum toward associate degree. **Support services:** GED preparation and test center, learning center, pre-admission summer program, reduced course load, remedial instruction, study skills assistance, tutoring, writing center.

Majors. Business: Administrative services, banking/financial services, business admin, finance, management information systems. **Computer sciences:** General, data processing. **Engineering technology:** Computer. **Health:** Clinical lab assistant, medical radiologic technology/radiation therapy, nursing (RN), physical therapy assistant, respiratory therapy technology. **Liberal arts:** Arts/sciences. **Protective services:** Police science.

Most popular majors. Business/marketing 15%, education 10%, health sciences 20%, liberal arts 52%.

Computing on campus. 46 workstations in library, computer center.

Student life. Freshman orientation: Mandatory. Eight-week orientation class earns one credit hour. **Activities:** Choral groups, dance, drama, student government, student newspaper, Christian student union, black student union, Professional Business Leaders, wilderness club, nursing club, student government association.

Athletics. Intramural: Basketball, golf, table tennis, volleyball.

Student services. Adult student services, career counseling, financial aid counseling, personal counseling, placement for graduates, veterans' counselor. **Physically disabled:** Services for visually impaired. **Transfer:** Special adviser for new students. Transfer adviser, college fairs on campus for students transferring to 4-year colleges.

Contact. E-mail: cookie.baker@kctcs.edu
Phone: (606) 589-2145 Toll-free number: (888) 274-7332
Fax: (606) 589-5423
Veria Baker, Director of Admissions, Southeast Kentucky Community and Technical College, 700 College Road, Cumberland, KY 40823

Southwestern College: Florence

Florence, Kentucky
www.swcollege.net **CB code: 2482**

- For-profit 2-year health science and junior college
- Residential campus in small city
- Interview required

General. Accredited by ACICS. **Enrollment:** 235 degree-seeking undergraduates. **Degrees:** 4 associate awarded. **Location:** 5 miles from Cincinnati. **Calendar:** Quarter, extensive summer session. **Full-time faculty:** 4 total. **Part-time faculty:** 8 total.

Student profile. Among degree-seeking undergraduates, 100% enrolled in a vocational program.

Basis for selection. Open admission. **Adult students:** Entrance exam policies same as for first-time freshmen. **Homeschooled:** State high school equivalency certificate required.

Application procedures. Admission: No deadline. $20 fee. Application must be submitted on paper. Admission notification on a rolling basis. **Financial aid:** No deadline. FAFSA required.

Academics. Special study options: Liberal arts/career combination. **Credit/placement by examination:** CLEP. **Support services:** GED preparation, study skills assistance, tutoring.

Majors. Computer sciences: General. **Health:** Medical assistant.

Computing on campus. 35 workstations in library, computer center. Online library available.

Student life. Freshman orientation: Mandatory. Preregistration for classes offered. Held on campus before each quarter in mornings and evenings. **Policies:** Freshmen permitted cars on campus. **Activities:** Student government, student newspaper.

Student services. Career counseling, services for economically disadvantaged, student employment services, financial aid counseling, placement for graduates. **Transfer:** Special adviser, orientation, pre-admission transcript evaluation for new students.

Contact. E-mail: lpaletta@swcollege.net
Phone: (859) 282-9999 Fax: (859) 282-7940
Laura Paletta, Director of Admissions, Southwestern College: Florence, 8095 Connector Drive, Florence, KY 41042

Spencerian College
Louisville, Kentucky
www.spencerian.edu **CB code: 3422**

- For-profit 2-year business and nursing college
- Commuter campus in large city

General. Accredited by ACICS. **Enrollment:** 1,327 degree-seeking undergraduates. **Degrees:** 183 associate awarded. **Location:** 10 miles from Louisville. **Calendar:** Quarter, extensive summer session. **Full-time faculty:** 48 total. **Part-time faculty:** 39 total. **Special facilities:** Radiology labs, mock operating room.

Basis for selection. Open admission, but selective for some programs. Practical Nursing students must attain 50+ on the NET, ADN students must attain 63+ on the NET, ACT scores of 16+; or for non-nursing, a passing score on the CPAT. Only 40 students accepted into the nursing program per quarter; 25 surg techs. For nursing and surg tech, we reserve the right to interview. **Adult students:** Entrance exam policies same as for first-time freshmen. **Homeschooled:** State high school equivalency certificate required.

2005-2006 Annual costs. Tuition/fees: $12,655. Room/board: $3,960. Books/supplies: $900. Personal expenses: $2,619.

Application procedures. Admission: No deadline. $90 fee. Application may be submitted online. Admission notification on a rolling basis.

Academics. Fridays are set aside for catch-up, make-up, and acceleration opportunites for all students whose programs do not require Friday classes or clinicals. **Special study options:** Distance learning, independent study, internships. License preparation in nursing, radiology. **Credit/placement by examination:** CLEP, institutional tests. 75 credit hours maximum toward associate degree. **Support services:** Learning center, tutoring.

Majors. Business: Accounting, business admin. **Health:** Medical assistant, medical radiologic technology/radiation therapy, medical records admin, medical transcription, nursing (RN).

Most popular majors. Business/marketing 10%, health sciences 90%.

Computing on campus. 67 workstations in library, computer center.

Student life. Freshman orientation: Mandatory. One-day session held week before classes begin. **Policies:** Freshmen permitted cars on campus. **Housing:** Apartments available. $95 nonrefundable deposit. **Activities:** Student newspaper.

Student services. Career counseling, student employment services, financial aid counseling, personal counseling, placement for graduates, veterans' counselor. **Transfer:** Special adviser, orientation, pre-admission transcript evaluation for new students.

Contact. E-mail: tthomas@spencerian.edu
Phone: (502) 447-1000 Toll-free number: (800) 264-1799
Fax: (502) 447-4574
Terri Thomas, Director of Admissions, Spencerian College, 4627 Dixie Highway, Louisville, KY 40216

Spencerian College: Lexington
Lexington, Kentucky
www.spencerian.edu **CB code: 3424**

- For-profit 2-year branch campus and technical college
- Commuter campus in small city

General. Accredited by ACICS. **Enrollment:** 400 degree-seeking undergraduates; 181 non-degree-seeking students. **Degrees:** 101 associate awarded. **Calendar:** Quarter, limited summer session. **Full-time faculty:** 15 total. **Part-time faculty:** 25 total. **Class size:** 100% < 20. **Partnerships:** Tech Prep scholarship program with area high schools.

Student profile. Among degree-seeking undergraduates, 100% enrolled in a vocational program, 5% already have a bachelor's degree or higher, 83 enrolled as first-time, first-year students.

Part-time:	28%	**Asian American:**	1%
Women:	22%	**Hispanic American:**	1%
African American:	7%	**Native American:**	1%

Transfer out. Colleges most students transferred to 2005: Lexington Community College, University of Kentucky, Eastern Kentucky University, KCTCS.

Basis for selection. Open admission. **Adult students:** Entrance exam policies same as for first-time freshmen. **Homeschooled:** Transcript of courses and grades, state high school equivalency certificate required.

2005-2006 Annual costs. Tuition for full 18-month associate programs ranges from $21,840 to $23,400; tuition for diploma programs ranges from $10,920 to $14,560. General fee $415; additional $1,770 fee for computer graphic design program. On-campus housing $6,750 for full associate program. Room only: $3,690. Books/supplies: $1,200. Personal expenses: $2,313.

2005-2006 Financial aid. All financial aid based on need. Average need met was 100%. Average scholarship/grant was $1,500; average loan $5,000. 40% of total undergraduate aid awarded as scholarships/grants, 60% as loans/jobs. Need-based aid available for part-time students.

Application procedures. Admission: No deadline. $90 fee. Admission notification on a rolling basis. **Financial aid:** No deadline. FAFSA, institutional form required. Applicants notified on a rolling basis starting 1/1.

Academics. No classes on Fridays, labs and teachers available to assist. **Special study options:** Cooperative education, double major, independent study. **Credit/placement by examination:** AP, CLEP. 23 credit hours maximum toward associate degree. **Support services:** Reduced course load, study skills assistance, tutoring.

Majors. Computer sciences: Computer graphics. **Engineering:** Electrical. **Engineering technology:** Drafting, electrical. **Health:** Health services. **Mechanic/repair:** Electronics/electrical. **Visual/performing arts:** Commercial/advertising art.

Most popular majors. Architecture 22%, engineering/engineering technologies 27%, trade and industry 22%, visual/performing arts 22%.

Computing on campus. 170 workstations in library, computer center. Online library available.

Student life. Freshman orientation: Mandatory. Preregistration for classes offered. **Policies:** Freshmen permitted cars on campus. **Housing:** Single-sex dorms, special housing for disabled, apartments, substance-free housing available. $95 nonrefundable deposit. **Activities:** Student newspaper, Baptist Student Union, Healing Hands student organization.

Athletics. Intramural: Football (non-tackle), volleyball.

Student services. Campus ministries, career counseling, student employment services, financial aid counseling, placement for graduates. **Transfer:** Special adviser, orientation, pre-admission transcript evaluation for new students.

Contact. Phone: (859) 223-9608 ext. 5460 Toll-free number: (800) 456-3253 ext. 5460 Fax: (859) 224-7744
Victor Adcock, Director of Admissions, Spencerian College: Lexington, 1575 Winchester Rd., Lexington, KY 40505

West Kentucky Community and Technical College
Paducah, Kentucky
www.pccky.com **CB code: 1620**

- Public 2-year community college
- Commuter campus in large town

General. Founded in 1932. Regionally accredited. **Enrollment:** 6,726 degree-seeking undergraduates. **Degrees:** 325 associate awarded. **Location:** 140 miles from Nashville, Tennessee. **Calendar:** Semester, limited summer session. **Full-time faculty:** 140 total. **Part-time faculty:** 100 total.

Student profile.

Out-of-state: 4% **25 or older:** 51%

Basis for selection. Open admission, but selective for some programs. ACT score of 19 required for nursing and physical therapist assistant applicants. CPP placement test required for non-traditional students. ACT required for some applicants and must be received by August 25. Interview required of nursing applicants.

High school preparation. 20 units recommended. Recommended units include English 4, mathematics 3, social studies 2 and science 2.

2005-2006 Annual costs. Tuition/fees: $2,940; $8,820 out-of-state. Per-credit charge: $98 in-state; $294 out-of-state. Books/supplies: $400. Personal expenses: $425.

Financial aid. Need-based: Need-based aid available for part-time students.

Application procedures. Admission: Priority date 4/15; no deadline. No application fee. Admission notification on a rolling basis beginning on or about 4/1. Must reply by 6/1. **Financial aid:** Priority date 4/1; no closing date. FAFSA required. Applicants notified on a rolling basis starting 7/15; must reply within 4 week(s) of notification.

Academics. Special study options: Distance learning, dual enrollment of high school students, honors, weekend college. **Credit/placement by examination:** CLEP. **Support services:** Learning center, reduced course load, remedial instruction, tutoring.

Majors. Business: Accounting, administrative services, banking/financial services, business admin, management information systems, office technology, real estate. **Communications:** General. **Computer sciences:** General, applications programming. **Health:** Physical therapy assistant. **Liberal arts:** Arts/sciences. **Personal/culinary services:** Culinary arts.

Computing on campus. 70 workstations in library, computer center.

Student life. Freshman orientation: Mandatory. **Activities:** Choral groups, drama, musical theater, radio station, student government, student newspaper, TV station.

Athletics. Intramural: Golf, volleyball.

Student services. Adult student services, career counseling, student employment services, personal counseling, placement for graduates, veterans' counselor. **Physically disabled:** Services for visually, speech, hearing impaired. **Transfer:** Special adviser, orientation for new students. Transfer adviser for students transferring to 4-year colleges.

Contact. Phone: (270) 554-9200 Fax: (270) 554-6218
Nancy McMurtry, Career Counselor and Student Service Officer, West Kentucky Community and Technical College, 4810 Alben Barkley Drive, Paducah, KY 42002

Louisiana

American School of Business
Shreveport, Louisiana
www.americanschoolofbusiness.com **CB code: 3426**

- For-profit 1-year business college
- Small city

General. Accredited by ACICS. **Calendar:** Continuous.

Annual costs/financial aid. Tuition varies by program and ranges from $8,200 to $9,100. Personal expenses: $2,429.

Contact. Phone: (318) 798-3333
702 Professional Drive North, Shreveport, LA 71105

Baton Rouge Community College
Baton Rouge, Louisiana
www.mybr.cc **CB code: 6023**

- Public 2-year community college
- Commuter campus in large city

General. Regionally accredited. **Enrollment:** 4,291 degree-seeking undergraduates. **Degrees:** 191 associate awarded. **Calendar:** Semester, extensive summer session. **Full-time faculty:** 92 total. **Part-time faculty:** 151 total. **Class size:** 24% < 20, 71% 20-39, 5% 40-49.

Basis for selection. Open admission. **Adult students:** Entrance exam policies same as for first-time freshmen. SAT/ACT scores not required.

2005-2006 Annual costs. Tuition/fees: $1,776; $4,584 out-of-state.

2004-2005 Financial aid. Need-based: 96% of total undergraduate aid awarded as scholarships/grants, 4% as loans/jobs.

Application procedures. Admission: No deadline. $7 fee. Application may be submitted online. Admission notification on a rolling basis. **Financial aid:** Priority date 4/15; no closing date.

Academics. Special study options: Cross-registration, dual enrollment of high school students, ESL, honors, internships. **Credit/placement by examination:** CLEP, institutional tests.

Majors. Business: General, office technology. **Liberal arts:** Arts/sciences.

Computing on campus. Online course registration, online library, wireless network available.

Student life. Freshman orientation: Available. Preregistration for classes offered. **Policies:** Freshmen permitted cars on campus. **Activities:** Dance, student government, student newspaper.

Athletics. Team name: Bears.

Student services. Career counseling, financial aid counseling, personal counseling, veterans' counselor. **Physically disabled:** Services for visually, speech, hearing impaired. **Learning disabled:** Comprehensive services available. **Transfer:** Special adviser for new students.

Contact. E-mail: hillm@mybr.cc
Phone: (225) 216-8700
Michelle Hill, Associate Dean of Enrollment Services, Baton Rouge Community College, 5310 Florida Boulevard, Baton Rouge, LA 70806

Baton Rouge School of Computers
Baton Rouge, Louisiana
www.brsc.net **CB code: 3197**

- For-profit 2-year technical college
- Small city

General. Accredited by ACCSCT. **Calendar:** Continuous.

Annual costs/financial aid. $10,500 tuition for certificate program, $21,000 for associate degree; includes cost of textbooks. $150 registration fee. Books/supplies: $500. Personal expenses: $2,400.

Contact. Phone: (225) 923-2525
Director of Admissions, 10425 Plaza Americana, Baton Rouge, LA 70816

Bossier Parish Community College
Bossier City, Louisiana
www.bpcc.edu **CB code: 0787**

- Public 2-year community college
- Commuter campus in small city

General. Founded in 1966. Regionally accredited. **Enrollment:** 4,008 degree-seeking undergraduates; 837 non-degree-seeking students. **Degrees:** 283 associate awarded. **Location:** 6 miles from downtown Shreveport. **Calendar:** Semester, limited summer session. **Full-time faculty:** 106 total; 8% have terminal degrees, 10% minority, 68% women. **Part-time faculty:** 186 total; 2% have terminal degrees, 16% minority, 51% women. **Class size:** 42% < 20, 57% 20-39, less than 1% 40-49. **Partnerships:** Formal partnerships with General Motors, Libby Glass.

Student profile. Among degree-seeking undergraduates, 959 enrolled as first-time, first-year students, 258 transferred in from other institutions.

Part-time:	43%	**Asian American:**	1%
Out-of-state:	2%	**Hispanic American:**	2%
Women:	66%	**25 or older:**	40%
African American:	29%		

Transfer out. Colleges most students transferred to 2005: Louisiana State University-Shreveport, Northwestern State University of Louisiana, Louisiana Tech University, Southern Arkansas University, Grambling State University.

Basis for selection. Open admission, but selective for out-of-state students. ACT scores required for admission for out-of-state students. **Adult students:** Entrance exam policies same as for first-time freshmen. **Home-schooled:** Students generally expected to complete requirements for GED.

2005-2006 Annual costs. Tuition/fees: $1,720; $3,860 out-of-state. Books/supplies: $1,000. Personal expenses: $1,533.

2005-2006 Financial aid. Need-based: 603 full-time freshmen applied for aid; 489 were judged to have need; 454 of these received aid. Average need met was 25%. Average scholarship/grant was $3,428; average loan $1,226. 56% of total undergraduate aid awarded as scholarships/grants, 44% as loans/jobs. Need-based aid available for part-time students. Work study available nights and for part-time students. **Non-need-based:** Scholarships awarded for academics, alumni affiliation, athletics, minority status, music/drama.

Application procedures. Admission: Closing date 8/8 (receipt date). $15 fee. Admission notification on a rolling basis. **Financial aid:** Closing date 7/1. FAFSA required. Applicants notified on a rolling basis.

Academics. Special study options: Distance learning, double major, dual enrollment of high school students, honors, internships. **Credit/placement by examination:** AP, CLEP, institutional tests. 30 credit hours maximum toward associate degree. **Support services:** GED preparation, learning center, remedial instruction, study skills assistance, tutoring.

Majors. Business: General. **Communications technology:** Recording arts. **Computer sciences:** Information systems, web page design. **Engineering technology:** CAD/CADD, industrial. **Health:** EMT paramedic, medical assistant, pharmacy assistant, physical therapy assistant, respiratory therapy technology. **Liberal arts:** Arts/sciences. **Mechanic/repair:** Industrial. **Protective services:** Criminal justice. **Visual/performing arts:** Dramatic.

Computing on campus. 120 workstations in library. Online library available.

Student life. Policies: Freshmen permitted cars on campus. **Activities:** Bands, choral groups, dance, drama, literary magazine, music ensembles, musical theater, radio station, student government, student newspaper, TV station, Baptist Collegiate Ministries, campus ministries, College Republicans, gospel choir, ADAPTS, Maroon Jackets, NAACP, FCA, SGA.

Athletics. NJCAA. **Intercollegiate:** Baseball M, basketball M, cheerleading, soccer W, softball W. **Team name:** Cavaliers.

Student services. Career counseling, services for economically disadvantaged, student employment services, financial aid counseling, minority student services, personal counseling, veterans' counselor. **Physically disabled:** Services for visually, speech, hearing impaired. **Transfer:** Special adviser, orientation, pre-admission transcript evaluation for new students. College fairs on campus for students transferring to 4-year colleges.

Contact. E-mail: Admissions@bpcc.edu
Phone: (318) 678-6004 Fax: (318) 678-6390
Ann Jampole, Admissions Officer, Bossier Parish Community College, 6220 East Texas Street, Bossier City, LA 71111-6922

Camelot College
Baton Rouge, Louisiana
www.camelotcollege.com **CB code: 3427**

- For-profit 2-year health science and technical college
- Small city

General. Accredited by ACICS. **Calendar:** Continuous.

Annual costs/financial aid. Annual tuition $9,340 for computer data processing and medical assistant programs, $10,900 for paralegal and cosmetology programs, $8,141 for cosmetology instructor's training program.

Contact. Phone: (225) 928-3005
Admissions Representative, 2618 Wooddale Boulevard, Suite A, Baton Rouge, LA 70805

Delgado Community College
New Orleans, Louisiana **CB member**
www.dcc.edu **CB code: 6176**

- Public 2-year community college
- Commuter campus in very large city

General. Founded in 1921. Regionally accredited. Because of higher priorities in the aftermath of Hurricane Katrina, the information in this profile has not been updated for the 2006-2007 academic year. **Enrollment:** 15,539 degree-seeking undergraduates. **Degrees:** 1,124 associate awarded. **ROTC:** Army, Air Force. **Calendar:** Semester, extensive summer session. **Full-time faculty:** 379 total; 10% have terminal degrees, 21% minority, 67% women. **Part-time faculty:** 383 total; 33% minority, 55% women. **Class size:** 45% < 20, 50% 20-39, 4% 40-49, 1% 50-99, less than 1% >100. **Special facilities:** Ship simulator, fine arts gallery.

Student profile.

Out-of-state:	2%	**25 or older:**	49%

Transfer out. Colleges most students transferred to 2005: University of New Orleans, Southern University at New Orleans, Louisiana State University, Nicholls State University, Southeastern Louisiana University.

Basis for selection. Open admission, but selective for some programs. ACT scores may be submitted before or during student's first semester of enrollment. ACT without writing component accepted. **Adult students:** SAT/ACT scores not required if applicant over 25. Adult students without high school diploma or GED required to pass Ability to Benefit Exam. **Homeschooled:** Applicants who have not completed a state or regionally approved program are required to have a GED or successfully pass the Ability to Benefit Exam.

2005-2006 Annual costs. Tuition/fees: $1,757; $4,737 out-of-state. Books/supplies: $100. Personal expenses: $1,533.

2004-2005 Financial aid. Need-based: 935 full-time freshmen applied for aid; 780 were judged to have need; 758 of these received aid. Average need met was 54%. Average scholarship/grant was $3,405; average loan $2,404. 57% of total undergraduate aid awarded as scholarships/grants, 43% as loans/jobs. Need-based aid available for part-time students. Work study available nights, weekends and for part-time students. **Non-need-based:** Awarded to 451 full-time undergraduates, including 177 freshmen. Scholarships awarded for academics, athletics, leadership, music/drama, state residency.

Application procedures. Admission: No deadline. $15 fee. Application may be submitted online. Admission notification on a rolling basis. **Financial aid:** Priority date 5/1, closing date 7/15. FAFSA, institutional form required. Applicants notified on a rolling basis starting 4/1; must reply within 2 week(s) of notification.

Academics. Special study options: Cooperative education, cross-registration, distance learning, double major, dual enrollment of high school students, ESL, honors, independent study, internships, liberal arts/career combination, student-designed major, weekend college. License preparation in nursing, paramedic, physical therapy, real estate. **Credit/placement by examination:** AP, CLEP, institutional tests. 24 credit hours maximum toward associate degree. **Support services:** Learning center, pre-admission summer program, remedial instruction, tutoring.

Majors. Agriculture: Horticulture. **Architecture:** Interior. **Business:** Accounting, administrative services, business admin, hospitality admin. **Computer sciences:** Data processing. **Construction:** Maintenance. **Education:** Early childhood. **Engineering technology:** Architectural, biomedical, civil, electrical, occupational safety. **Family/consumer sciences:** Institutional food production. **Foreign languages:** Sign language interpretation. **Health:** Clinical lab technology, dental hygiene, dental lab technology, EMT paramedic, medical radiologic technology/radiation therapy, medical records technology, nursing (RN), occupational therapy assistant, physical therapy assistant, respiratory therapy technology. **Interdisciplinary:** Biological/physical sciences. **Liberal arts:** Arts/sciences. **Mechanic/repair:** Automotive, computer, electronics/electrical. **Personal/culinary services:** Mortuary science. **Production:** Machine shop technology. **Protective services:** Fire safety technology, police science. **Visual/performing arts:** Art, commercial/advertising art, design.

Computing on campus. 800 workstations in library, computer center, student center. Online library available.

Student life. Freshman orientation: Available. Preregistration for classes offered. **Policies:** Freshmen permitted cars on campus. **Activities:** Concert band, choral groups, dance, drama, film society, music ensembles, musical theater, student government, student newspaper, TV station, religious organizations available.

Athletics. NJCAA. **Intercollegiate:** Baseball M, basketball M, cheerleading. **Intramural:** Archery, badminton, baseball M, basketball, golf, soccer, softball, swimming, table tennis, tennis, volleyball. **Team name:** Dolphins.

Student services. Adult student services, career counseling, services for economically disadvantaged, student employment services, financial aid counseling, health services, on-campus daycare, personal counseling, placement for graduates, veterans' counselor. **Physically disabled:** Services for visually, speech, hearing impaired. **Transfer:** Special adviser, orientation, reentry adviser for new students. Transfer center, transfer adviser, college fairs on campus for students transferring to 4-year colleges.

Contact. E-mail: vsmith@dcc.edu
Phone: (504) 483-4822 Fax: (504) 483-1895
Attn: Admissions, Delgado Community College, 615 City Park Avenue, New Orleans, LA 70119

Delta College of Arts & Technology
Baton Rouge, Louisiana
www.deltacollege.com **CB code: 3131**

- For-profit 2-year art and technical college
- Large city

General. Accredited by ACCSCT. **Calendar:** Continuous.

Annual costs/financial aid. Tuition for full programs ranges from $6,695 to $15,400 and includes books and supplies. Registration fee $100. Books/supplies: $775. Personal expenses: $250.

Contact. Phone: (225) 928-7770
Director of Admissions, 7380 Exchange Place, Baton Rouge, LA 70806

Delta School of Business & Technology
Lake Charles, Louisiana
www.deltatech.edu **CB code: 2252**

- For-profit 2-year business and technical college
- Small city

General. Founded in 1970. Accredited by ACICS. **Location:** 128 miles from Baton Rouge. **Calendar:** Continuous.

Annual costs/financial aid. Books/supplies: $800.

Contact. Phone: (337) 439-5765
Vice President, 517 Broad Street, Lake Charles, LA 70601

Gretna Career College
Gretna, Louisiana
www.gretnacareercollege.edu

- For-profit 2-year technical college
- Commuter campus

General. Accredited by ACCSCT. Because of higher priorities in the aftermath of Hurricane Katrina, the information in this profile has not been updated for the 2006-2007 academic year. **Enrollment:** 150 degree-seeking undergraduates. **Calendar:** Semester. **Full-time faculty:** 35 total.

Basis for selection. Open admission.

2005-2006 Annual costs. Tuition varies by program and ranges from $5,350 - $16,000. Books and supplies approximately $1,525.

Application procedures. Admission: No deadline. $50 fee. Admission notification on a rolling basis.

Academics. Credit/placement by examination: CLEP.

Majors. Health: Nursing assistant, office assistant. **Mechanic/repair:** Auto body.

Contact. E-mail: admissions@gretnacareercollege.edu
Phone: (504) 366-5409 ext. 23
Ana Heimes, Director of Admissions, Gretna Career College, 1415 Whitney Avenue, Gretna, LA 70053

ITI Technical College
Baton Rouge, Louisiana
www.iticollege.edu

- For-profit 2-year technical college
- Commuter campus in large city
- Interview required

General. Accredited by ACCSCT. **Enrollment:** 349 degree-seeking undergraduates. **Degrees:** 130 associate awarded. **Calendar:** Differs by program. **Full-time faculty:** 22 total; 54% have terminal degrees, 4% women. **Part-time faculty:** 17 total; 29% have terminal degrees.

Student profile.

African American:	32%	**Hispanic American:**	1%
Asian American:	1%	**Native American:**	1%

Basis for selection. Open admission. All applicants must pass an entrance examination. Applicant completes application, must interview and tour campus, complete entrance evaluation, settle funding, sign enrollment agreement. School administers an entrance exam. **Adult students:** Entrance exam policies same as for first-time freshmen. **Homeschooled:** Students must have an acceptable certificate or diploma at the time of enrollment. **Learning Disabled:** Students must meet with school director regarding special needs and referral for assistance.

2006-2007 Annual costs. Tuition varies by program from $5,000 to $22,000.

2004-2005 Financial aid. All financial aid based on need. 227 full-time freshmen applied for aid; 202 were judged to have need; 202 of these received aid. Average need met was 42%. Average scholarship/grant was $1,950; average loan $2,526. 29% of total undergraduate aid awarded as scholarships/grants, 71% as loans/jobs. Need-based aid available for part-time students.

Application procedures. Admission: No deadline. No application fee. Admission notification on a rolling basis. **Financial aid:** No deadline. FAFSA required.

Academics. Credit/placement by examination: AP, CLEP. **Support services:** Study skills assistance, tutoring.

Majors. Business: Administrative services, business admin, executive assistant, office management, office technology. **Computer sciences:** Data processing, information systems. **Engineering technology:** Drafting, electrical, instrumentation. **Health:** Insurance coding, insurance specialist, medical records admin, medical records technology, medical secretary, medical transcription, office admin, office assistant, office computer specialist, receptionist.

Computing on campus. 4 workstations in library.

Student life. Freshman orientation: Mandatory.

Student services. Career counseling, financial aid counseling, placement for graduates.

Contact. E-mail: admissions@iticollege.edu
Phone: (225) 752-4233 Toll-free number: (800) 467-4484
Fax: (225) 756-0903
Joe Martin, Director of Admissions, ITI Technical College, 13944 Airline Highway, Baton Rouge, LA 70817-5998

Louisiana State University at Eunice
Eunice, Louisiana
www.lsue.edu **CB code: 6386**

- Public 2-year branch campus and community college
- Commuter campus in large town

General. Founded in 1964. Regionally accredited. **Location:** 40 miles from Lafayette, 90 miles from Baton Rouge. **Calendar:** Semester.

Annual costs/financial aid. Tuition/fees (2005-2006): $2,096; $5,096 out-of-state. Books/supplies: $1,000. Need-based financial aid available to full-time and part-time students.

Contact. Phone: (337) 550-1305
Admissions Director, Box 1129, Eunice, LA 70535

New Orleans School of Urban Missions
Gretna, Louisiana
www.sumonline.org

- Private 2-year Bible college affiliated with Assemblies of God, Church of God in Christ
- Commuter campus in very large city
- Application essay, interview required

General. Accredited by ABHE. **Enrollment:** 129 degree-seeking undergraduates. **Degrees:** 12 associate awarded. **Location:** 2 miles from New Orleans. **Calendar:** Trimester, limited summer session. **Full-time faculty:** 8 total; 25% have terminal degrees, 38% minority, 12% women. **Part-time faculty:** 15 total; 27% have terminal degrees, 27% minority, 20% women.

Student profile. Among degree-seeking undergraduates, 27% enrolled in a transfer program, 5% already have a bachelor's degree or higher, 81 enrolled as first-time, first-year students, 5 transferred in from other institutions.

Part-time:	73%	**Women:**	51%

Transfer out. 30% of students enrolled in the transfer program go on to 4-year colleges. **Colleges most students transferred to 2005:** Southwestern University of the Assemblies of God.

Basis for selection. Phone interview and personal written testimony of call to ministry and salvation required. **Homeschooled:** State high school equivalency certificate required.

2006-2007 Annual costs. Average tuition is $6000 per trimester, but most students receive scholarships/grants/student loans/church donations; thus, out-of-pocket costs range from $600 to $1,400 per trimester. Books/supplies: $600.

2004-2005 Financial aid. Need-based: Need-based aid available for part-time students. **Non-need-based:** Scholarships awarded for academics, leadership, religious affiliation.

Application procedures. Admission: Closing date 7/31. $20 fee. **Financial aid:** No deadline. FAFSA, institutional form required.

Academics. Special study options: Distance learning. **Credit/placement by examination:** CLEP. **Support services:** Remedial instruction, tutoring.

Majors. Theology: Bible, pastoral counseling, youth ministry.

Computing on campus. 40 workstations in dormitories, library, computer center. Dormitories wired for high-speed internet access and linked to campus network. Online library, wireless network available.

Student life. Freshman orientation: Mandatory. Preregistration for classes offered. **Policies:** Morning devotions and chapel attendance are required; full-time students are required to participate in practicum ministries. Religious observance required. Freshmen permitted cars on campus. **Housing:**

Guaranteed on-campus for all undergraduates. Single-sex dorms, apartments, substance-free housing available. **Activities:** Student government, Assemblies of God, Church of God in Christ.

Student services. Adult student services, career counseling, financial aid counseling, health services, personal counseling, placement for graduates, veterans' counselor. **Transfer:** Special adviser, orientation, preadmission transcript evaluation for new students.

Contact. E-mail: sum@sumonline.org
Phone: (800) 385-6364 Fax: (504) 362-4895
Rev. Jonathan Logan, Admissions Counselor and Alumni Director, New Orleans School of Urban Missions, 511 Westbank Expressway, Gretna, LA 70053

Nunez Community College

Chalmette, Louisiana
www.nunez.edu **CB code: 0295**

- Public 2-year community and technical college
- Commuter campus in large town

General. Founded in 1992. Regionally accredited. Because of higher priorities in the aftermath of Hurricane Katrina, the information in this profile has not been updated for the 2006-2007 academic year. **Enrollment:** 1,960 degree-seeking undergraduates. **Degrees:** 193 associate awarded. **Location:** 11 miles from New Orleans. **Calendar:** Semester, limited summer session. **Full-time faculty:** 59 total; 8% have terminal degrees, 17% minority, 63% women. **Part-time faculty:** 69 total; 7% have terminal degrees, 19% minority, 49% women. **Class size:** 52% < 20, 47% 20-39, 1% 40-49.

Transfer out. Colleges most students transferred to 2005: University of New Orleans, Southern University of New Orleans, Louisiana State University-Baton Rouge, Our Lady of Holy Cross College, Loyola University of New Orleans.

Basis for selection. Open admission, but selective for some programs. Additional requirements for the Practical Nursing Certificate program and Emergency Medical Technician Basic courses. **Adult students:** Entrance exam policies same as for first-time freshmen.

High school preparation. 12 units recommended. Recommended units include English 4, mathematics 4, social studies 1, history 1, science 2 (laboratory 1).

2005-2006 Annual costs. Tuition/fees: $1,770; $4,290 out-of-state. Books/supplies: $1,700.

2005-2006 Financial aid. Need-based: Average scholarship/grant was $1,741. 60% of total undergraduate aid awarded as scholarships/grants, 40% as loans/jobs. Need-based aid available for part-time students. **Additional information:** Pell Grants, Stafford Loans, campus workstudy, and tuition waiver scholarships available. Louisiana National Guard tuition exemption, teacher tuition exemption, dependents of injured fire-police tuition waivers.

Application procedures. Admission: Priority date 8/1; no deadline. $10 fee ($20 out-of-state). **Financial aid:** Priority date 4/1, closing date 7/1. FAFSA, institutional form required. Applicants notified by 8/1; must reply by 8/15.

Academics. Special study options: Accelerated study, cooperative education, cross-registration, distance learning, double major, dual enrollment of high school students, ESL, honors, independent study, internships, liberal arts/career combination, student-designed major, weekend college. License preparation in nursing, paramedic. **Credit/placement by examination:** AP, CLEP, institutional tests. 24 credit hours maximum toward associate degree. **Support services:** Learning center, reduced course load, remedial instruction, tutoring.

Majors. Business: Accounting, business admin, office technology. **Computer sciences:** Computer science, information systems. **Education:** Early childhood. **Engineering technology:** Computer, drafting. **Health:** EMT paramedic, office admin. **Legal studies:** Paralegal. **Liberal arts:** Arts/sciences. **Mechanic/repair:** Heating/ac/refrig. **Personal/culinary services:** Culinary arts. **Social sciences:** General.

Computing on campus. 200 workstations in library, computer center, student center. Online library, helpline available.

Student life. Freshman orientation: Mandatory. Preregistration for classes offered. 2-hour orientation offered during registration period. **Policies:** Freshmen permitted cars on campus. **Activities:** Drama, film society, literary magazine, student government, student newspaper.

Athletics. Intramural: Football (non-tackle) M. **Team name:** Pelicans.

Student services. Career counseling, financial aid counseling, personal counseling, placement for graduates, veterans' counselor. **Physically disabled:** Services for visually, hearing impaired. **Transfer:** Special adviser, orientation for new students. Transfer adviser, college fairs on campus for students transferring to 4-year colleges.

Contact. E-mail: dclark@nunez.edu
Phone: (504) 680-2467 Toll-free number: (866) 825-1954
Donna Clark, Vice Chancellor of Student Affairs, Nunez Community College, 3710 Paris Road, Chalmette, LA 70043

Remington College: Baton Rouge

Baton Rouge, Louisiana
www.remingtoncollege.edu/batonrouge/index.html
CB code: 3428

- For-profit 2-year technical college
- Commuter campus in large city

General. Accredited by ACICS. **Calendar:** Quarter.

Annual costs/financial aid. Tuition/fees (2005-2006): $15,745. Need-based financial aid available for full-time students.

Contact. Phone: (225) 922-3990
Director of Admissions, 10551 Coursey Boulevard, Baton Rouge, LA 70816

Remington College: Lafayette

Lafayette, Louisiana
www.educationamerica.com **CB code: 7117**

- For-profit 2-year junior college
- Commuter campus in small city
- Interview required

General. Founded in 1940. Accredited by ACICS. **Enrollment:** 400 degree-seeking undergraduates. **Degrees:** 102 associate awarded. **Location:** 50 miles from Baton Rouge. **Calendar:** Quarter, extensive summer session. **Full-time faculty:** 15 total; 73% have terminal degrees, 27% minority, 40% women. **Part-time faculty:** 9 total; 78% have terminal degrees, 44% minority, 67% women.

Basis for selection. Applicants must test with Wonderlic.

2005-2006 Annual costs. Tuition/fees: $15,745.

Financial aid. All financial aid based on need. Work study available nights.

Application procedures. Admission: No deadline. $50 fee. Application must be submitted on paper. Admission notification on a rolling basis. **Financial aid:** No deadline. FAFSA, institutional form required.

Academics. Each student is provided with a laptop computer. **Special study options:** Accelerated study, independent study, liberal arts/career combination. **Credit/placement by examination:** CLEP. **Support services:** GED preparation, tutoring.

Majors. Business: Business admin. **Computer sciences:** General. **Engineering technology:** Electrical. **Health:** Medical assistant.

Computing on campus. 110 workstations in library, computer center. Online library, helpline, repair service available.

Student life. Freshman orientation: Mandatory. Preregistration for classes offered. **Policies:** Freshmen permitted cars on campus. **Activities:** National Vocational Technical Society (honors society).

Student services. Student employment services, financial aid counseling, placement for graduates. **Transfer:** Special adviser, orientation, preadmission transcript evaluation for new students.

Contact. Phone: (337) 981-4010 Fax: (337) 983-7130
Gary Schwartz, Director of Recruitment, Remington College: Lafayette, 303 Rue Louis XIV, Lafayette, LA 70508

Remington College: New Orleans

Metairie, Louisiana
www.remingtoncollege.edu/neworleans/index.html
CB code: 3156

- For-profit 2-year technical college

General. Accredited by ACCSCT. Because of higher priorities in the aftermath of Hurricane Katrina, the information in this profile has not been updated for the 2006-2007 academic year. **Enrollment:** 500 degree-seeking undergraduates. **Degrees:** 112 associate awarded. **Calendar:** Quarter. **Full-time faculty:** 25 total. **Part-time faculty:** 10 total.

Basis for selection. Wonderlic test used for admissions.

Application procedures. Admission: No deadline. No application fee. Admission notification on a rolling basis.

Academics. Credit/placement by examination: CLEP.

Majors. Computer sciences: Computer graphics, information systems, networking. **Engineering technology:** Drafting, electrical.

Student life. Freshman orientation: Mandatory.

Contact. Phone: (504) 831-8889 Fax: (504) 831-6803
Attn: Admissions, Remington College: New Orleans, 321 Veterans Memorial Boulevard, Metairie, LA 70005

River Parishes Community College
Sorrento, Louisiana
http://rpcc.cc.la.us/

- Public 2-year community college
- Rural community

General. Regionally accredited. **Calendar:** Semester.

Contact. Phone: (225) 675-8270
PO Box 310, Sorrento, LA 70778

South Louisiana Community College
Lafayette, Louisiana
www.slcc.cc.la.us

- Public 2-year community college
- Small city

General. Regionally accredited. **Calendar:** Semester.

Annual costs/financial aid. Tuition/fees (projected): $1,852.

Contact. Phone: (337) 521-8923
320 Devalcourt, Lafayette, LA 70506-4124

Southern University in Shreveport
Shreveport, Louisiana
www.susla.edu **CB code: 0322**

- Public 2-year community college
- Commuter campus in small city

General. Founded in 1964. Regionally accredited. **Enrollment:** 2,538 degree-seeking undergraduates. **Degrees:** 251 associate awarded. **Calendar:** Semester, limited summer session. **Full-time faculty:** 82 total. **Part-time faculty:** 115 total.

Basis for selection. Open admission.

High school preparation. 15 units recommended. Recommended units include English 3, mathematics 2, social studies 2 and science 5.

2005-2006 Annual costs. Tuition/fees: $2,252; $3,382 out-of-state. Books/supplies: $600. Personal expenses: $1,420.

Application procedures. Admission: No deadline. $5 fee ($15 out-of-state). Admission notification on a rolling basis. **Financial aid:** No deadline. FAFSA required. Applicants notified on a rolling basis.

Academics. Special study options: Cross-registration, internships. License preparation in dental hygiene, nursing, radiology. **Credit/placement by examination:** CLEP, institutional tests. 3 credit hours maximum toward associate degree. **Support services:** GED preparation, remedial instruction, study skills assistance, tutoring, writing center.

Majors. Biology: General. **Business:** Accounting, banking/financial services, business admin. **Computer sciences:** General, applications programming, computer science. **Education:** Early childhood. **Engineering technology:** Electrical. **Health:** Clinical lab technology, dental hygiene, health services, medical radiologic technology/radiation therapy, medical records technology, respiratory therapy technology, surgical technology. **Liberal arts:** Arts/sciences. **Physical sciences:** Chemistry. **Protective services:** Law enforcement admin. **Public administration:** Human services. **Social sciences:** General, sociology. **Transportation:** Aviation management.

Computing on campus. 50 workstations in library, computer center. Commuter students can connect to campus network. Online course registration, online library available.

Student life. Freshman orientation: Mandatory. Preregistration for classes offered. **Activities:** Choral groups, dance, student government, student newspaper, Baptist Student Union, Afro-American Society.

Athletics. NJCAA. **Intercollegiate:** Basketball. **Team name:** Jaguars.

Student services. Health services, personal counseling, placement for graduates, veterans' counselor. **Transfer:** Special adviser, orientation for new students.

Contact. Phone: (318) 674-3342 Fax: (318) 674-3489
Teresa Jones, Associate Vice Chancellor Enrollment Management, Southern University in Shreveport, 3050 Martin Luther King, Jr. Drive, Shreveport, LA 71107

Maine

Andover College
Portland, Maine
www.andovercollege.edu **CB code: 0688**

- For-profit 2-year business and junior college
- Commuter campus in small city
- Interview required

General. Founded in 1966. Regionally accredited. **Enrollment:** 570 degree-seeking undergraduates. **Degrees:** 175 associate awarded. **Location:** 115 miles from Boston. **Calendar:** Six 8-week terms. Extensive summer session. **Full-time faculty:** 16 total; 69% women. **Part-time faculty:** 9 total; 11% have terminal degrees, 78% women.

Student profile. Among degree-seeking undergraduates, 158 enrolled as first-time, first-year students.

Out-of-state:	4%	**25 or older:**	90%
Women:	78%		

Transfer out. Colleges most students transferred to 2005: University of Southern Maine.

Basis for selection. Open admission. **Adult students:** Entrance exam policies same as for first-time freshmen.

2005-2006 Annual costs. Tuition/fees: $7,200. Books/supplies: $1,200. Personal expenses: $1,115.

Financial aid. All financial aid based on need. **Additional information:** Work-study positions available.

Application procedures. Admission: No deadline. $20 fee, may be waived for applicants with need. Admission notification on a rolling basis. **Financial aid:** No deadline. FAFSA required. Applicants notified on a rolling basis.

Academics. Special study options: Accelerated study, cooperative education, double major, dual enrollment of high school students, independent study, internships, liberal arts/career combination, teacher certification program. **Credit/placement by examination:** AP, CLEP, institutional tests. 12 credit hours maximum toward associate degree. **Support services:** Learning center, reduced course load, remedial instruction, study skills assistance, tutoring, writing center.

Majors. Business: Accounting, administrative services, business admin, hospitality admin, hospitality/recreation, office management, office technology, office/clerical, tourism promotion, tourism/travel. **Computer sciences:** General, computer science, data processing, programming. **Education:** Early childhood. **Family/consumer sciences:** Child care. **Health:** Medical assistant, medical records admin, medical records technology, medical secretary, medical transcription. **Legal studies:** Legal secretary, paralegal. **Protective services:** Criminal justice, law enforcement admin, police science.

Most popular majors. Business/marketing 21%, computer/information sciences 9%, health sciences 17%, legal studies 12%.

Computing on campus. 90 workstations in library, computer center. Helpline available.

Student life. Freshman orientation: Mandatory. Preregistration for classes offered. **Policies:** Freshmen permitted cars on campus. **Activities:** Student government, student newspaper, Phi Beta Lambda, C.O.P.S. (criminal justice), medical assistants, paralegal professionals, college student advisers.

Student services. Adult student services, career counseling, student employment services, financial aid counseling, personal counseling, placement for graduates. **Physically disabled:** Services for hearing impaired. **Transfer:** Special adviser, orientation for new students.

Contact. E-mail: enroll@andovercollege.edu
Phone: (207) 774-6126 Toll-free number: (800) 639-3110
Fax: (207) 774-1715
David Blessing, Director of Enrollment Management, Andover College, 901 Washington Avenue, Portland, ME 04103

Beal College
Bangor, Maine
www.bealcollege.edu **CB code: 3114**

- For-profit 2-year business and junior college
- Commuter campus in large town

General. Founded in 1891. Accredited by ACICS. Extensive business-oriented, continuing education evening program. **Enrollment:** 360 degree-seeking undergraduates. **Degrees:** 46 associate awarded. **Location:** 250 miles from Boston. **Calendar:** Six 8-week modules per year. Extensive summer session. **Full-time faculty:** 7 total. **Part-time faculty:** 8 total. **Class size:** 59% < 20, 41% 20-39.

Basis for selection. Open admission. Non-resident alien applicants required to submit high school transcript from American school or TOEFL score of at least 500 or complete 1 year of ESL training to satisfy admission criteria. Interview recommended. **Homeschooled:** Students who earned high school diploma through home-school education must provide passing GED scores.

High school preparation. Recommended units include English 4, mathematics 4 and science 1.

2005-2006 Annual costs. Tuition/fees: $5,860. Per-credit charge: $155. Books/supplies: $900. Personal expenses: $700.

Application procedures. Admission: No deadline. $25 fee, may be waived for applicants with need. Admission notification on a rolling basis. Mathematics and English pre-admission tests required to determine possible need for remedial coursework. **Financial aid:** Priority date 5/1; no closing date. FAFSA, institutional form required. Applicants notified on a rolling basis starting 6/15; must reply within 2 week(s) of notification.

Academics. Students in travel and tourism programs required to complete travel requirements and 80-hour externship. Students in medical assisting program must complete 160-hour practicum. **Special study options:** Accelerated study, double major, independent study. Externships. **Credit/placement by examination:** CLEP, institutional tests. 30 credit hours maximum toward associate degree. **Support services:** Reduced course load, remedial instruction, tutoring.

Majors. Business: Accounting, administrative services, business admin, office management, sales/distribution, tourism promotion. **Computer sciences:** General. **Education:** Early childhood. **Health:** Medical assistant, medical secretary. **Legal studies:** Legal secretary, paralegal. **Protective services:** Police science.

Computing on campus. 45 workstations in library, computer center.

Student life. Freshman orientation: Available. **Activities:** Student newspaper.

Student services. Adult student services, career counseling, student employment services, placement for graduates, veterans' counselor. **Transfer:** Special adviser, orientation, pre-admission transcript evaluation for new students.

Contact. E-mail: admissions@bealcollege.edu
Phone: (207) 947-4591 Fax: (207) 947-0208
Catherine Haskell, Admissions Director, Beal College, 99 Farm Road, Bangor, ME 04401

Central Maine Community College
Auburn, Maine **CB member**
www.cmcc.edu **CB code: 3309**

- Public 2-year community and technical college
- Commuter campus in small city

General. Founded in 1964. Regionally accredited. **Enrollment:** 1,644 degree-seeking undergraduates. **Degrees:** 235 associate awarded. **Location:** 1 mile from downtown. **Calendar:** Semester, limited summer session. **Full-time faculty:** 53 total. **Part-time faculty:** 82 total. **Class size:** 75% < 20, 22% 20-39, 2% 40-49, less than 1% 50-99. **Partnerships:** Formal partnership with the Verizon Telecommunications Technology program.

Student profile.

Out-of-state:	2%	**Live on campus:**	8%
25 or older:	35%		

Transfer out. Colleges most students transferred to 2005: University of Maine System.

Basis for selection. Open admission, but selective for some programs. Special requirements for nursing and radiologic technology. Many other academic programs have specific academic prerequisites but are not selective in terms of admission to the program. Institutional placement test required for all applicants unless SAT scores submitted. **Adult students:** Entrance exam policies same as for first-time freshmen. **Homeschooled:** A copy of the state department of education correspondence granting approval of homeschooling program and the most recent teacher certification recognizing student's grade level and/or appropriate test results required. **Learning Disabled:** Applicants with documented disabilities should contact college's disability coordinator.

High school preparation. Recommended units include English 4, mathematics 2, social studies 1, history 1 and science 2.

2005-2006 Annual costs. Tuition/fees: $3,096; $5,556 out-of-state. Per-credit charge: $74 in-state; $156 out-of-state. New England Regional tuition: $111 per- credit-hour. Room/board: $5,050. Books/supplies: $800. Personal expenses: $1,300.

2004-2005 Financial aid. All financial aid based on need. 606 full-time freshmen applied for aid; 514 were judged to have need; 382 of these received aid. Average need met was 56%. Average scholarship/grant was $2,639; average loan $1,396. 50% of total undergraduate aid awarded as scholarships/grants, 50% as loans/jobs. Need-based aid available for part-time students. Work study available nights, weekends and for part-time students. **Additional information:** Tuition and/or fee waivers may be available to orphans, Native Americans, fire fighters, police, disabled veterans, dependents or survivors of veterans killed in line of duty.

Application procedures. Admission: No deadline. $20 fee, may be waived for applicants with need. Application may be submitted online. Admission notification on a rolling basis. **Financial aid:** Priority date 5/1; no closing date. FAFSA, institutional form required. Applicants notified on a rolling basis starting 3/15; must reply within 2 week(s) of notification.

Academics. Special study options: Distance learning, ESL, independent study, internships, liberal arts/career combination. License preparation in nursing, radiology, real estate. **Credit/placement by examination:** AP, CLEP, IB, institutional tests. **Support services:** Learning center, reduced course load, remedial instruction, study skills assistance, tutoring, writing center.

Majors. Business: Accounting, business admin, hospitality admin, office technology. **Communications technology:** Graphic/printing. **Computer sciences:** Data entry, LAN/WAN management. **Construction:** Maintenance. **Education:** Early childhood. **Engineering technology:** Civil, drafting. **Health:** Clinical lab technology, medical radiologic technology/radiation therapy, nursing (RN), occupational health. **Interdisciplinary:** Accounting/computer science. **Liberal arts:** Arts/sciences. **Mechanic/repair:** Automotive, electronics/electrical.

Most popular majors. Architecture 13%, business/marketing 40%, computer/information sciences 43%.

Computing on campus. 400 workstations in library, computer center. Dormitories wired for high-speed internet access and linked to campus network. Online library, helpline, wireless network available.

Student life. Freshman orientation: Available. Preregistration for classes offered. **Policies:** Student code of conduct observed. Freshmen permitted cars on campus. **Housing:** Single-sex dorms, apartments available. $50 nonrefundable deposit. **Activities:** Drama, literary magazine, student government, TV station.

Athletics. USCAA. **Intercollegiate:** Baseball M, basketball. **Intramural:** Basketball, skiing. **Team name:** Mustangs.

Student services. Career counseling, services for economically disadvantaged, student employment services, financial aid counseling, personal counseling, placement for graduates, women's services. **Physically disabled:** Services for visually, speech, hearing impaired. **Transfer:** Special adviser, orientation for new students. Transfer adviser, college fairs on campus for students transferring to 4-year colleges.

Contact. E-mail: enroll@cmcc.edu
Phone: (207) 755-5273 Toll-free number: (800) 891-2002
Fax: (207) 755-5493
Elizabeth Oken, Director of Admissions, Central Maine Community College, 1250 Turner Street, Auburn, ME 04210

Central Maine Medical Center School of Nursing

Lewiston, Maine — **CB member**
www.cmmcson.edu — **CB code: 3302**

- Private 2-year nursing college
- Commuter campus in large town
- SAT, application essay, interview required

General. Founded in 1891. Regionally accredited. **Enrollment:** 124 degree-seeking undergraduates. **Degrees:** 42 associate awarded. **Location:** 35 miles from Portland. **Calendar:** Semester. **Full-time faculty:** 11 total; 9% have terminal degrees, 91% women. **Part-time faculty:** 4 total; 100% women. **Class size:** 100% 50-99.

Student profile. Among degree-seeking undergraduates, 16% already have a bachelor's degree or higher, 5 enrolled as first-time, first-year students.

Part-time:	85%	**African American:**	1%
Women:	78%	**Hispanic American:**	1%

Basis for selection. Test scores required. Recommendations, essay very important. SAT may be waived if applicant has completed 12 academic college credits with minimum grade of 2.0. **Adult students:** Entrance exam policies same as for first-time freshmen. **Homeschooled:** High school diploma or GED required.

High school preparation. Required units include science 1. Biology course required.

2005-2006 Annual costs. Tuition/fees: $5,345. Per-credit charge: $138. Room/board: $3,350.

2004-2005 Financial aid. All financial aid based on need. 89 full-time freshmen applied for aid; 89 were judged to have need; 89 of these received aid. Average need met was 34%. Average scholarship/grant was $3,400; average loan $2,625. 33% of total undergraduate aid awarded as scholarships/grants, 67% as loans/jobs. Need-based aid available for part-time students.

Application procedures. Admission: Priority date 1/1; deadline 3/1 (receipt date). $40 fee, may be waived for applicants with need. Admission notification 3/15. Must reply by 5/1. **Financial aid:** Priority date 5/1, closing date 7/1. FAFSA, institutional form required. Applicants notified on a rolling basis starting 4/1; must reply within 2 week(s) of notification.

Academics. Special study options: Distance learning, internships, liberal arts/career combination. License preparation in nursing. **Credit/placement by examination:** AP, CLEP. 15 credit hours maximum toward associate degree. **Support services:** Learning center, remedial instruction, study skills assistance.

Majors. Health: Nursing (RN).

Computing on campus. PC or laptop required. 11 workstations in computer center.

Student life. Freshman orientation: Mandatory. Preregistration for classes offered. Held for 2 days the week before fall classes begin. **Policies:** Entire campus is smoke-free; zero tolerance for alcohol, drugs, weapons, etc. Freshmen permitted cars on campus. **Housing:** Coed dorms, substance-free housing available. $50 nonrefundable deposit, deadline 8/15. Single rooms available at extra cost. **Activities:** Student government.

Student services. Financial aid counseling, health services, personal counseling, veterans' counselor. **Transfer:** Special adviser, orientation, preadmission transcript evaluation for new students. College fairs on campus for students transferring to 4-year colleges.

Contact. E-mail: djenison@cmhc.org
Phone: (207) 795-2843 Fax: (207) 795-2849
Peter Miller, Admissions Committee Chairperson, Central Maine Medical Center School of Nursing, 70 Middle Street, Lewiston, ME 04240

Eastern Maine Community College

Bangor, Maine — **CB member**
www.emcc.edu — **CB code: 3372**

- Public 2-year community and technical college
- Commuter campus in large town
- Application essay required

General. Founded in 1966. Regionally accredited. **Enrollment:** 1,458 degree-seeking undergraduates. **Degrees:** 221 associate awarded. **Location:** 250

miles from Boston, 130 miles from Portland. **Calendar:** Semester, limited summer session. **Full-time faculty:** 57 total. **Part-time faculty:** 88 total.

Student profile. Among degree-seeking undergraduates, 544 enrolled as first-time, first-year students.

Part-time:	34%	**Asian American:**	1%
Women:	47%	**Native American:**	2%
African American:	1%	**Live on campus:**	20%

Transfer out. Colleges most students transferred to 2005: University of Maine-Orono, Husson College.

Basis for selection. Open admission, but selective for some programs. School record, recommendations, and essays most important. Entrance requirements vary by program. SAT required for engineering technologies, registered nursing, and medical radiography applicants; score report preferred by April 30. Interview recommended for some majors.

High school preparation. Recommended units include English 4, mathematics 3 and science 2. Academic requirements vary by program.

2005-2006 Annual costs. Tuition/fees: $2,730; $5,190 out-of-state. Per-credit charge: $74 in-state; $156 out-of-state. New England Regional tuition: $110 per credit hour. Laboratory and technology fees vary with program. Room/board: $5,588. Books/supplies: $800. Personal expenses: $1,500.

2004-2005 Financial aid. All financial aid based on need. 66% of total undergraduate aid awarded as scholarships/grants, 34% as loans/jobs. Need-based aid available for part-time students. Work study available nights, weekends and for part-time students.

Application procedures. Admission: No deadline. $20 fee, may be waived for applicants with need. Admission notification on a rolling basis. Must reply by May 1 or within 4 week(s) if notified thereafter. Deposit refundable up to 60 days before program begins. **Financial aid:** Priority date 5/1; no closing date. FAFSA, institutional form required. Applicants notified on a rolling basis starting 5/1; must reply within 3 week(s) of notification.

Academics. Special study options: External degree, internships, student-designed major. **Credit/placement by examination:** CLEP, institutional tests. Maximum of 40% of required credit total in student's field of study may be obtained through credit by examination. **Support services:** Learning center, reduced course load, remedial instruction, study skills assistance, tutoring.

Majors. Agriculture: Food science. **Business:** General, administrative services, banking/financial services, business admin, office management. **Construction:** Carpentry, pipefitting, power transmission. **Education:** Early childhood. **Engineering technology:** Construction, electrical. **Health:** Medical radiologic technology/radiation therapy, nursing (RN), preop/surgical nursing. **Liberal arts:** Arts/sciences. **Mechanic/repair:** Automotive, heating/ac/refrig. **Personal/culinary services:** Culinary arts. **Production:** Machine tool, welding. **Protective services:** Firefighting.

Most popular majors. Business/marketing 26%, communications/journalism 8%, computer/information sciences 12%, engineering/engineering technologies 10%, health sciences 16%, interdisciplinary studies 8%, personal/culinary services 10%, trade and industry 10%.

Computing on campus. 75 workstations in dormitories, library, computer center. Repair service available.

Student life. Freshman orientation: Mandatory. Preregistration for classes offered. **Policies:** Freshmen permitted cars on campus. **Housing:** Guaranteed on-campus for all undergraduates. Coed dorms available. $50 deposit, deadline 7/1. **Activities:** Student government, student newspaper.

Athletics. Intercollegiate: Basketball M, golf, soccer. **Intramural:** Badminton, basketball, bowling, ice hockey M, skiing, softball, table tennis, volleyball. **Team name:** Golden Eagles.

Student services. Adult student services, career counseling, student employment services, personal counseling, placement for graduates, veterans' counselor. **Transfer:** Special adviser, orientation for new students.

Contact. E-mail: admissions@emcc.edu
Phone: (207) 974-4680 Toll-free number: (800) 286-9357
Fax: (207) 974-4683
Gregory Swett, Director of Admissions, Eastern Maine Community College, 354 Hogan Road, Bangor, ME 04401

Kennebec Valley Community College

Fairfield, Maine
www.kvcc.me.edu **CB code: 3475**

- Public 2-year community and technical college
- Commuter campus in small town

General. Founded in 1969. Regionally accredited. **Enrollment:** 1,316 degree-seeking undergraduates; 466 non-degree-seeking students. **Degrees:** 267 associate awarded. **Location:** 24 miles from Augusta, 75 miles from Portland. **Calendar:** Semester, limited summer session. **Full-time faculty:** 37 total. **Part-time faculty:** 200 total.

Student profile. Among degree-seeking undergraduates, 303 enrolled as first-time, first-year students.

Part-time:	60%	**Women:**	71%

Basis for selection. Open admission, but selective for some programs. Special requirements for nursing and allied health programs.

2005-2006 Annual costs. Tuition/fees: $2,595; $5,055 out-of-state. Per-credit charge: $74 in-state; $156 out-of-state. New England Regional tuition: $3,060 full-time, $102 per credit hour. Health insurance required if student does not have own insurance. Lab fees vary depending on course. Books/supplies: $730.

Financial aid. Need-based: Need-based aid available for part-time students.

Application procedures. Admission: No deadline. $20 fee. Admission notification on a rolling basis. Only allied health programs have application deadline. **Financial aid:** Priority date 3/1; no closing date. FAFSA, institutional form required. Applicants notified on a rolling basis starting 5/1.

Academics. Special study options: Cooperative education, cross-registration, distance learning, internships, liberal arts/career combination. **Credit/placement by examination:** AP, CLEP.

Majors. Biology: Biomedical sciences. **Business:** Business admin, office management. **Education:** Teacher assistance. **Engineering:** Electrical. **Engineering technology:** Electrical, manufacturing. **Health:** EMT paramedic, medical assistant, occupational therapy assistant, physical therapy assistant, radiologic technology/medical imaging, respiratory therapy technology. **Liberal arts:** Arts/sciences.

Student life. Activities: Student government, student newspaper.

Athletics. Intercollegiate: Basketball. **Intramural:** Basketball, volleyball.

Student services. Career counseling, student employment services, on-campus daycare, personal counseling, placement for graduates. **Transfer:** Transfer adviser, college fairs on campus for students transferring to 4-year colleges.

Contact. E-mail: jbourgoin@kvcc.me.edu
Phone: (207) 453-5131 Toll-free number: (800) 528-5882
Fax: (207) 453-5011
Kathleen Moore, Dean of Student Affairs, Kennebec Valley Community College, 92 Western Avenue, Fairfield, ME 04937-1367

Northern Maine Community College

Presque Isle, Maine
www.nmcc.edu **CB code: 3631**

- Public 2-year technical college
- Commuter campus in small town
- Application essay, interview required

General. Founded in 1961. Regionally accredited. **Enrollment:** 839 degree-seeking undergraduates. **Degrees:** 129 associate awarded. **Location:** 165 miles from Bangor. **Calendar:** Semester, limited summer session. **Full-time faculty:** 43 total. **Part-time faculty:** 35 total.

Basis for selection. School achievement record and test scores important.

High school preparation. Required units include English 4 and mathematics 2.

2005-2006 Annual costs. Tuition/fees: $2,582; $5,042 out-of-state. Per-credit charge: $74 in-state; $156 out-of-state. New England Regional Student Program tuition: $3,060 full-time, $102 per credit hour. Room/board: $4,490. Books/supplies: $1,200. Personal expenses: $1,200.

Financial aid. Need-based: Need-based aid available for part-time students.

Application procedures. Admission: No deadline. $20 fee, may be waived for applicants with need. Application may be submitted online. Admission notification on a rolling basis. **Financial aid:** Priority date 5/1; no

closing date. FAFSA, institutional form required. Applicants notified on a rolling basis starting 4/15; must reply within 2 week(s) of notification.

Academics. Special study options: Cross-registration, double major, internships, liberal arts/career combination. **Credit/placement by examination:** CLEP. 15 credit hours maximum toward associate degree. **Support services:** Learning center, pre-admission summer program, reduced course load, remedial instruction, tutoring.

Majors. Agriculture: Business. **Business:** Accounting, administrative services, business admin, management information systems, office management, office technology, operations. **Computer sciences:** Applications programming, data processing, programming. **Construction:** Carpentry, electrician, pipefitting, power transmission. **Education:** Early childhood. **Engineering technology:** Drafting, electrical. **Health:** Medical secretary, nursing (RN). **Legal studies:** Legal secretary. **Mechanic/repair:** Auto body, automotive, diesel, electronics/electrical, heating/ac/refrig, industrial. **Production:** Woodworking.

Computing on campus. Commuter students can connect to campus network.

Student life. Freshman orientation: Mandatory. Preregistration for classes offered. Held both in fall and spring semester. **Policies:** Freshmen permitted cars on campus. **Housing:** Coed dorms, apartments available. $25 deposit. **Activities:** Student government, student newspaper.

Athletics. Intercollegiate: Basketball M, golf, ice hockey, soccer. **Intramural:** Archery, badminton, baseball M, basketball M, racquetball, softball, table tennis, tennis, volleyball.

Student services. Adult student services, alcohol/substance abuse counseling, career counseling, student employment services, financial aid counseling, health services, personal counseling, placement for graduates, veterans' counselor. **Transfer:** Special adviser, orientation for new students. Transfer adviser for students transferring to 4-year colleges.

Contact. E-mail: nbcasava@nmcc.edu
Phone: (207) 768-2700 Fax: (207) 768-2831
William Casavant, Director of Admissions, Northern Maine Community College, 33 Edgemont Drive, Presque Isle, ME 04769

Southern Maine Community College

South Portland, Maine — **CB member**
www.smccme.edu — **CB code: 3535**

- Public 2-year community and technical college
- Commuter campus in large town

General. Founded in 1946. Regionally accredited. **Enrollment:** 3,720 degree-seeking undergraduates; 767 non-degree-seeking students. **Degrees:** 448 associate awarded. **Location:** 3 miles from Portland, 120 miles from Boston. **Calendar:** Semester, limited summer session. **Full-time faculty:** 92 total. **Part-time faculty:** 170 total.

Student profile.

Part-time:	40%	**Women:**	49%

Basis for selection. Open admission, but selective for some programs. Psychological Services Bureau exam for Allied Health programs. Require ERI/NET exam for nursing applicants.

High school preparation. Recommended units include English 4, mathematics 3, science 1 (laboratory 1). Academic subject requirements vary by program.

2005-2006 Annual costs. Tuition/fees: $2,870; $5,330 out-of-state. Per-credit charge: $74 in-state; $156 out-of-state. Room/board: $5,824. Books/supplies: $900.

Financial aid. All financial aid based on need. Need-based aid available for part-time students. Work study available nights, weekends and for part-time students.

Application procedures. Admission: Priority date 7/15; no deadline. $20 fee, may be waived for applicants with need. Application may be submitted online. Admission notification on a rolling basis. Must reply by May 1 or within 4 week(s) if notified thereafter. **Financial aid:** Priority date 3/30; no closing date. FAFSA required. Applicants notified on a rolling basis; must reply by 5/1 or within 2 week(s) of notification.

Academics. Special study options: Cross-registration, distance learning, double major, dual enrollment of high school students, independent study, internships, liberal arts/career combination. License preparation in nursing, paramedic, radiology. **Credit/placement by examination:** CLEP, institutional tests. **Support services:** Learning center, reduced course load, remedial instruction, study skills assistance, tutoring.

Majors. Agriculture: Greenhouse operations, landscaping, plant sciences, soil science. **Biology:** Marine. **Business:** Business admin, hospitality admin, office management, office technology. **Computer sciences:** General, computer graphics, computer science. **Construction:** Carpentry, maintenance, power transmission. **Engineering:** Computer, electrical, metallurgical. **Engineering technology:** Construction, drafting, electrical. **Family/consumer sciences:** Child care, food/nutrition, institutional food production. **Health:** Cardiovascular technology, dietetics, medical radiologic technology/radiation therapy, nursing (RN), respiratory therapy technology, surgical technology. **Liberal arts:** Arts/sciences. **Mechanic/repair:** General, electronics/electrical, heating/ac/refrig. **Personal/culinary services:** Culinary arts. **Physical sciences:** Oceanography. **Production:** Woodworking. **Protective services:** Fire safety technology, fire services admin, firefighting, law enforcement admin, police science. **Visual/performing arts:** Cinematography.

Computing on campus. 300 workstations in library, computer center, student center. Dormitories wired for high-speed internet access and linked to campus network. Commuter students can connect to campus network.

Student life. Freshman orientation: Available. Preregistration for classes offered. **Policies:** Freshmen permitted cars on campus. **Housing:** Coed dorms available. $50 deposit. **Activities:** Choral groups, student government, student newspaper, Phi Theta Kappa.

Athletics. Intercollegiate: Baseball M, basketball, golf, soccer, softball W. **Intramural:** Softball, volleyball. **Team name:** Seawolves.

Student services. Adult student services, alcohol/substance abuse counseling, career counseling, student employment services, financial aid counseling, on-campus daycare, personal counseling, placement for graduates, veterans' counselor. **Physically disabled:** Services for visually, speech, hearing impaired. **Transfer:** Special adviser, orientation, pre-admission transcript evaluation for new students. College fairs on campus for students transferring to 4-year colleges.

Contact. Phone: (207) 741-5800 Toll-free number: (877) 282-2182
Fax: (207) 741-5670
Staci Graski, Associate Dean for Information and Enrollment Services / Registrar, Southern Maine Community College, 2 Fort Road, South Portland, ME 04106

Washington County Community College

Calais, Maine
www.wccc.me.edu — **CB code: 3961**

- Public 2-year community and technical college
- Commuter campus in small town

General. Founded in 1969. Regionally accredited. **Enrollment:** 400 degree-seeking undergraduates. **Degrees:** 85 associate awarded. **Location:** 98 miles from Bangor, 75 miles from St. John, Canada. **Calendar:** Semester, limited summer session. **Full-time faculty:** 26 total.

Student profile.

Out-of-state:	5%	**Live on campus:**	25%
25 or older:	34%		

Transfer out. Colleges most students transferred to 2005: University of Maine at Machias, University of Maine at Augusta, Husson College.

Basis for selection. Open admission, but selective for some programs. Algebra I and college-preparatory biology required for aquaculture program. Algebra I required for computer support technician program. Algebra I, college-preparatory biology, general chemistry, and college-preparatory English required for dietetic technician program. ASSET used for placement. **Homeschooled:** Applicants required to take GED exam or equivalent.

High school preparation. 20 units recommended. Recommended units include English 4, mathematics 2, social studies 1, history 2 and science 2. Program-specific requirements apply in some areas.

2005-2006 Annual costs. Tuition/fees: $2,745; $5,205 out-of-state. Per-credit charge: $74 in-state; $156 out-of-state. New England Regional Student Program tuition: $111 per-credit-hour. Room only: $2,216. Books/supplies: $700. Personal expenses: $500.

Financial aid. Need-based: Need-based aid available for part-time students. Work study available for part-time students. **Non-need-based:** Scholarships awarded for academics.

Application procedures. **Admission:** Closing date 8/14. $20 fee, may be waived for applicants with need. Application may be submitted online. Admission notification on a rolling basis. **Financial aid:** Priority date 5/1; no closing date. FAFSA, institutional form required. Applicants notified on a rolling basis starting 6/1; must reply within 2 week(s) of notification.

Academics. **Special study options:** Cooperative education, double major, independent study, internships, liberal arts/career combination, student-designed major. Offer license preparation program in heating and plumbing. **Credit/placement by examination:** CLEP, IB. **Support services:** Learning center, reduced course load, remedial instruction, study skills assistance, tutoring, writing center.

Majors. **Business:** Office management, small business admin. **Education:** Early childhood. **Family/consumer sciences:** Food/nutrition, institutional food production. **Liberal arts:** Arts/sciences. **Mechanic/repair:** General.

Most popular majors. Business/marketing 19%, computer/information sciences 33%, liberal arts 13%, trade and industry 35%.

Computing on campus. 117 workstations in library, computer center, student center. Dormitories linked to campus network. Helpline available.

Student life. **Freshman orientation:** Mandatory. Preregistration for classes offered. **Housing:** Guaranteed on-campus for all undergraduates. Special housing for disabled, apartments available. $100 deposit. **Activities:** Student government, Gender Equity, Native American club.

Athletics. **Intramural:** Baseball M, basketball, cross-country, golf, skiing, volleyball.

Student services. Adult student services, career counseling, student employment services, on-campus daycare, personal counseling, placement for graduates, veterans' counselor. **Physically disabled:** Services for visually, speech, hearing impaired. **Transfer:** Special adviser, pre-admission transcript evaluation for new students. College fairs on campus for students transferring to 4-year colleges.

Contact. E-mail: admissions@wccc.me.edu
Phone: (207) 454-1049 Toll-free number: (800) 210-6932
Fax: (207) 454-1026
Kent Lyons, Director of Admissions, Washington County Community College, One College Drive, Calais, ME 04619

York County Community College

Wells, Maine
www.yccc.edu **CB code: 3990**

- Public 2-year community and technical college
- Commuter campus in small town

General. Regionally accredited. **Enrollment:** 670 degree-seeking undergraduates. **Degrees:** 46 associate awarded. **Location:** 30 miles from Portland, 30 miles from Portsmouth, New Hampshire. **Calendar:** Semester, extensive summer session. **Full-time faculty:** 13 total. **Part-time faculty:** 70 total. **Partnerships:** Formal partnership with a local high school.

Transfer out. **Colleges most students transferred to 2005:** University of Southern Maine.

Basis for selection. Open admission.

2005-2006 Annual costs. Tuition/fees: $2,760; $5,220 out-of-state. Per-credit charge: $74 in-state; $156 out-of-state. New England Regional tuition:$111 per credit hour. Lecture and lab fees may vary per class. Books/supplies: $714. Personal expenses: $1,915.

2004-2005 Financial aid. **Need-based:** 78 full-time freshmen applied for aid; 61 were judged to have need; 61 of these received aid. Average need met was 62%. Average scholarship/grant was $3,101; average loan $1,629. 67% of total undergraduate aid awarded as scholarships/grants, 33% as loans/jobs. Need-based aid available for part-time students. Work study available nights, weekends and for part-time students. **Non-need-based:** Awarded to 19 full-time undergraduates, including 11 freshmen. Scholarships awarded for academics, art, leadership.

Application procedures. **Admission:** No deadline. $20 fee, may be waived for applicants with need. **Financial aid:** Priority date 5/1; no closing date. FAFSA required. Applicants notified by 3/1; must reply within 2 week(s) of notification.

Academics. **Special study options:** Distance learning, honors. **Credit/placement by examination:** CLEP. **Support services:** Remedial instruction, tutoring.

Majors. **Business:** Accounting, business admin, hospitality admin. **Family/consumer sciences:** General. **Personal/culinary services:** General, culinary arts.

Computing on campus. 50 workstations in library, student center. Wireless network available.

Student life. **Freshman orientation:** Available. Preregistration for classes offered. **Activities:** Student government, student newspaper.

Student services. Career counseling, financial aid counseling. **Transfer:** Special adviser for new students. Transfer adviser, college fairs on campus for students transferring to 4-year colleges.

Contact. Phone: (207) 646-9282 ext. 304
Fred Quistgard, Director of Admissions, York County Community College, 112 College Drive, Wells, ME 04090

Two-Year Colleges

Maryland

Allegany College of Maryland
Cumberland, Maryland
www.allegany.edu **CB code: 5028**

- Public 2-year community college
- Commuter campus in large town

General. Founded in 1961. Regionally accredited. Tri-state service region. **Enrollment:** 2,903 degree-seeking undergraduates; 763 non-degree-seeking students. **Degrees:** 520 associate awarded. **ROTC:** Army. **Location:** 150 miles from Baltimore and Washington, DC. **Calendar:** Semester, limited summer session. **Full-time faculty:** 111 total; 16% have terminal degrees, 54% women. **Part-time faculty:** 119 total; 6% have terminal degrees, less than 1% minority, 65% women. **Class size:** 73% < 20, 26% 20-39, 2% 40-49, less than 1% >100. **Special facilities:** Greenhouse, arboretum, wetlands, Appalachian Room.

Student profile. Among degree-seeking undergraduates, 33% enrolled in a transfer program, 67% enrolled in a vocational program, 3% already have a bachelor's degree or higher, 865 enrolled as first-time, first-year students, 218 transferred in from other institutions.

Part-time:	29%	**Asian American:**	1%
Out-of-state:	42%	**Hispanic American:**	1%
Women:	69%	**25 or older:**	33%
African American:	8%		

Transfer out. **Colleges most students transferred to 2005:** Frostburg State University, Shippensburg University, University of Pittsburgh at Johnstown.

Basis for selection. Open admission, but selective for some programs. Admission to allied health programs based on high school records, test scores. ACT required for allied health applicants. **Adult students:** Entrance exam policies same as for first-time freshmen.

2005-2006 Annual costs. Tuition/fees: $3,005; $5,465 out-of-district; $6,365 out-of-state. Per-credit charge: $90 in-district; $172 out-of-district; $202 out-of-state. Books/supplies: $700. Personal expenses: $1,200.

2004-2005 Financial aid. **Need-based:** 661 full-time freshmen applied for aid; 510 were judged to have need; 493 of these received aid. Average need met was 65%. Average scholarship/grant was $3,266; average loan $2,135. 69% of total undergraduate aid awarded as scholarships/grants, 31% as loans/jobs. Need-based aid available for part-time students. Work study available nights and for part-time students. **Non-need-based:** Awarded to 548 full-time undergraduates, including 218 freshmen. Scholarships awarded for academics, athletics, leadership, state residency.

Application procedures. **Admission:** No deadline. No application fee. Application may be submitted online. Admission notification on a rolling basis. High school and/or college transcript and placement tests in English, reading, and mathematics required. **Financial aid:** Priority date 3/15; no closing date. FAFSA required. Applicants notified on a rolling basis starting 5/15; must reply within 2 week(s) of notification.

Academics. **Special study options:** Cooperative education, distance learning, double major, dual enrollment of high school students, ESL, honors, independent study, internships, liberal arts/career combination. Bachelor's degree programs available on campus. License preparation in dental hygiene, nursing, occupational therapy, physical therapy, radiology, real estate. **Credit/placement by examination:** AP, CLEP, SAT, ACT, institutional tests. 30 credit hours maximum toward associate degree. **Support services:** Learning center, reduced course load, remedial instruction, study skills assistance, tutoring.

Majors. **Biology:** General. **Business:** General, accounting, accounting technology, administrative services, business admin, hospitality admin, hospitality/recreation, management information systems, managerial economics, marketing. **Communications:** General. **Communications technology:** General. **Computer sciences:** General, computer science, information systems. **Conservation:** Forest management. **Education:** Early childhood, elementary, health, physical, secondary. **Engineering:** General. **Foreign languages:** Spanish. **Health:** Clinical lab technology, dental hygiene, health services, massage therapy, medical assistant, medical radiologic technology/radiation therapy, medical secretary, medical transcription, mental health services, nursing (RN), occupational therapy assistant, physical therapy assistant, prepharmacy, respiratory therapy technology. **History:** General. **Liberal arts:** Arts/sciences. **Math:** General. **Mechanic/repair:** Automotive. **Parks/recreation:** Facilities management. **Personal/culinary services:** General, chef training. **Physical sciences:** Chemistry, physics. **Protective services:** Police science. **Psychology:** General. **Public administration:** Social work. **Social sciences:** General, economics, political science, sociology. **Visual/performing arts:** Art.

Most popular majors. Business/marketing 20%, health sciences 39%, liberal arts 27%.

Computing on campus. 450 workstations in library, computer center. Online course registration, online library, student web hosting, wireless network available.

Student life. **Freshman orientation:** Available, $4 fee. Preregistration for classes offered. **Policies:** Freshmen permitted cars on campus. **Housing:** Substance-free housing available. Private apartments accommodating 240 students available near campus. **Activities:** Choral groups, dance, literary magazine, student government, forestry club, Older and Wiser Club, Phi Theta Kappa-Honors Society, Christian Fellowship, chess club, respiratory therapy club, dental hygiene club, medical laboratory technology club.

Athletics. NJCAA. **Intercollegiate:** Baseball M, basketball, soccer, softball W, tennis, volleyball W. **Team name:** Trojans.

Student services. Career counseling, student employment services, financial aid counseling, on-campus daycare, personal counseling, placement for graduates, veterans' counselor, women's services. **Physically disabled:** Services for visually, speech, hearing impaired. **Transfer:** Special adviser, orientation, pre-admission transcript evaluation for new students. Transfer adviser, college fairs on campus for students transferring to 4-year colleges.

Contact. E-mail: cnolan@allegany.edu
Phone: (301) 784-5199 Fax: (301) 784-5027
Cathy Nolan, Director of Admissions and Registration, Allegany College of Maryland, 12401 Willowbrook Road, SE, Cumberland, MD 21502

Anne Arundel Community College
Arnold, Maryland **CB member**
www.aacc.edu **CB code: 5019**

- Public 2-year community college
- Commuter campus in large town

General. Founded in 1964. Regionally accredited. 3 off-campus degree centers: Fort Meade Army Education Center, Glen Burnie Town Center and Arundel Mills. 3 literacy centers available. **Enrollment:** 10,793 degree-seeking undergraduates; 3,836 non-degree-seeking students. **Degrees:** 1,148 associate awarded. **Location:** 20 miles from Baltimore, 8 miles from Annapolis. **Calendar:** Semester, limited summer session. **Full-time faculty:** 245 total; 33% have terminal degrees, 12% minority, 56% women. **Part-time faculty:** 660 total; 1% have terminal degrees, 13% minority, 52% women. **Special facilities:** Environmental center, astronomy laboratory, center for performing arts, fine arts academic center, allied health/public services center.

Student profile. Among degree-seeking undergraduates, 42% enrolled in a transfer program, 18% enrolled in a vocational program, 2% already have a bachelor's degree or higher, 2,632 enrolled as first-time, first-year students.

Part-time:	57%	**Hispanic American:**	3%
Women:	62%	**Native American:**	1%
African American:	14%	**International:**	1%
Asian American:	4%		

Transfer out. **Colleges most students transferred to 2005:** University of Maryland-Baltimore County, Towson University, University of Maryland-College Park, Salisbury University, University of Maryland University College.

Basis for selection. Open admission, but selective for some programs. Special requirements for certain allied health programs. International students must provide certification of finances. Interview recommended for applicants to nursing, human services, radiologic technology, physician's assistant programs.

2005-2006 Annual costs. Tuition/fees: $2,770; $5,050 out-of-district; $8,740 out-of-state. Per-credit charge: $83 in-district; $159 out-of-district; $282 out-of-state. Books/supplies: $900. Personal expenses: $1,300.

2004-2005 Financial aid. **Need-based:** 42% of total undergraduate aid awarded as scholarships/grants, 58% as loans/jobs. Need-based aid available for part-time students. Work study available nights, weekends and for part-time students.

Application procedures. **Admission:** No deadline. No application fee. Application may be submitted online. Admission notification on a rolling basis. **Financial aid:** Priority date 5/15; no closing date. FAFSA, institutional form required. Applicants notified on a rolling basis starting 7/1; must reply within 2 week(s) of notification.

Academics. **Special study options:** Combined bachelor's/graduate degree, cooperative education, distance learning, double major, dual enrollment of high school students, ESL, honors, independent study, internships, liberal arts/career combination, student-designed major, weekend college. Bachelor's degree programs available on campus. License preparation in nursing, paramedic, radiology, real estate. **Credit/placement by examination:** AP, CLEP, institutional tests. 15 credit hours maximum toward associate degree. **Support services:** GED preparation, learning center, reduced course load, remedial instruction, study skills assistance, tutoring, writing center.

Majors. **Business:** General, accounting. **Computer sciences:** General. **Education:** General, elementary, secondary. **Engineering:** General. **Engineering technology:** Drafting, electrical. **Family/consumer sciences:** Child care. **Health:** Dental assistant, EMT paramedic, health services, medical assistant, medical radiologic technology/radiation therapy, nursing (RN), pharmacy assistant, physical therapy assistant. **Legal studies:** Paralegal. **Liberal arts:** Arts/sciences. **Math:** General. **Mechanic/repair:** Electronics/electrical. **Parks/recreation:** Health/fitness. **Personal/culinary services:** Baking, chef training, culinary arts, restaurant/catering. **Protective services:** Forensics, law enforcement admin. **Visual/performing arts:** Commercial/advertising art, interior design.

Most popular majors. Business/marketing 16%, health sciences 13%, liberal arts 56%.

Computing on campus. Wireless network available.

Student life. **Freshman orientation:** Mandatory. One day orientation program required for all first-time, full-time students. **Policies:** Freshmen permitted cars on campus. **Activities:** Bands, choral groups, dance, drama, literary magazine, music ensembles, musical theater, opera, student government, student newspaper, symphony orchestra, black student union, international student association, Lambda Pioneers, Baptist campus minstry, Fellowship of Christian Athletes, BAACHU chapter.

Athletics. NJCAA. **Intercollegiate:** Baseball M, basketball, cross-country, golf M, lacrosse, soccer, softball W, volleyball W. **Intramural:** Basketball, softball, swimming, table tennis, tennis, volleyball, weight lifting. **Team name:** Pioneers.

Student services. Adult student services, alcohol/substance abuse counseling, career counseling, student employment services, financial aid counseling, health services, minority student services, on-campus daycare, personal counseling, placement for graduates, veterans' counselor. **Physically disabled:** Services for visually, speech, hearing impaired. **Transfer:** Special adviser, orientation for new students. Transfer center, transfer adviser, college fairs on campus for students transferring to 4-year colleges.

Contact. E-mail: admissions@aacc.edu
Phone: (410) 777-2246 Fax: (410) 777-2827
Thomas McGinn, Director of Enrollment Development and Admissions, Anne Arundel Community College, 101 College Parkway, Arnold, MD 21012-1895

Baltimore City Community College

Baltimore, Maryland — **CB member**
www.bccc.edu — **CB code: 5051**

- Public 2-year community college
- Commuter campus in very large city

General. Founded in 1947. Regionally accredited. Sites throughout Baltimore City. **Enrollment:** 7,160 degree-seeking undergraduates. **Degrees:** 154 associate awarded. **Location:** 50 miles from Washington, DC, 75 miles from Philadelphia. **Calendar:** Semester, extensive summer session. **Full-time faculty:** 120 total. **Part-time faculty:** 305 total. **Special facilities:** Greenhouse, planetarium.

Student profile. Among degree-seeking undergraduates, 1,596 enrolled as first-time, first-year students.

Part-time:	63%	**Asian American:**	2%
Out-of-state:	1%	**Hispanic American:**	1%
Women:	73%	**25 or older:**	58%
African American:	81%		

Transfer out. **Colleges most students transferred to 2005:** Coppin State University, Morgan State University, University of Baltimore, Towson University, University of Maryland Baltimore County.

Basis for selection. Open admission, but selective for some programs. Applicants in health sciences must have 2.5 GPA. SAT and ACT scores may be used in place of reading, math, and English proficiency tests required of all first students. Interview recommended for applicants to allied health, paralegal, emergency medical services programs. Portfolio recommended for art, fashion design majors. **Adult students:** Entrance exam policies same as for first-time freshmen.

2005-2006 Annual costs. Tuition/fees: $2,575; $5,275 out-of-state. Per-credit charge: $78 in-state; $168 out-of-state. Books/supplies: $500.

Financial aid. All financial aid based on need. Need-based aid available for part-time students. Work study available nights, weekends and for part-time students.

Application procedures. **Admission:** No deadline. $10 fee, may be waived for applicants with need. Application may be submitted online. Admission notification on a rolling basis. **Financial aid:** Priority date 6/1; no closing date. FAFSA, institutional form required. Applicants notified on a rolling basis starting 7/1; must reply within 2 week(s) of notification.

Academics. Adults without diploma or GED become eligible for degree programs after successfully completing 15 college-level credits. **Special study options:** Cooperative education, distance learning, double major, dual enrollment of high school students, ESL, honors, independent study, internships, liberal arts/career combination, study abroad, teacher certification program, weekend college. License preparation in dental hygiene, nursing, paramedic, physical therapy, real estate. **Credit/placement by examination:** CLEP, IB, institutional tests. 15 credit hours maximum toward associate degree. **Support services:** GED preparation, learning center, pre-admission summer program, reduced course load, remedial instruction, study skills assistance, tutoring, writing center.

Majors. **Biology:** Biotechnology. **Business:** General, accounting, administrative services, business admin, fashion, hospitality admin, management information systems, marketing, office management, office technology. **Computer sciences:** General, computer graphics, computer science, information systems, systems analysis. **Education:** General, early childhood, multi-level teacher. **Engineering:** General. **Engineering technology:** Drafting, electrical. **Family/consumer sciences:** Clothing/textiles. **Health:** Dental hygiene, EMT paramedic, health care admin, health services, licensed practical nurse, medical records admin, medical records technology, medical secretary, nursing (RN), physical therapy assistant, respiratory therapy technology. **Interdisciplinary:** Biological/physical sciences. **Legal studies:** Legal secretary, paralegal. **Liberal arts:** Arts/sciences. **Protective services:** Corrections, law enforcement admin, police science. **Public administration:** Social work. **Visual/performing arts:** Art, fashion design.

Most popular majors. Business/marketing 14%, computer/information sciences 7%, health sciences 30%, liberal arts 26%, security/protective services 9%.

Computing on campus. 200 workstations in library, computer center, student center. Online library available.

Student life. **Freshman orientation:** Mandatory. Preregistration for classes offered. **Activities:** Choral groups, drama, musical theater, radio station, student government, student newspaper, fashion club, human services club, media club, civic organizations, computer club, international student club.

Athletics. NJCAA. **Intercollegiate:** Baseball M, basketball, volleyball W. **Team name:** Panthers.

Student services. Career counseling, student employment services, financial aid counseling, health services, on-campus daycare, personal counseling, placement for graduates, veterans' counselor. **Physically disabled:** Services for visually, speech, hearing impaired. **Learning disabled:** Comprehensive services available. **Transfer:** Special adviser, orientation, pre-admission transcript evaluation for new students. Transfer adviser, college fairs on campus for students transferring to 4-year colleges.

Contact. E-mail: admissions@bccc.edu
Phone: (410) 462-8300 Toll-free number: (888) 203-1261
Fax: (410) 462-8345
Nicole Cameron, Director Admissions and Outreach, Baltimore City Community College, 2901 Liberty Heights Avenue, Baltimore, MD 21215-7893

Carroll Community College
Westminster, Maryland
www.carrollcc.edu **CB code: 5797**

- Public 2-year community college
- Commuter campus in large town

General. Founded in 1993. Regionally accredited. **Enrollment:** 3,102 degree-seeking undergraduates; 13 non-degree-seeking students. **Degrees:** 304 associate awarded. **Location:** 30 miles from Baltimore. **Calendar:** Semester, extensive summer session. **Full-time faculty:** 60 total; 15% have terminal degrees, 2% minority, 63% women. **Part-time faculty:** 150 total; 6% minority, 55% women. **Class size:** 55% < 20, 45% 20-39, less than 1% 40-49. **Special facilities:** Theater, amphitheatre.

Student profile. Among degree-seeking undergraduates, 80% enrolled in a transfer program, 20% enrolled in a vocational program, 711 enrolled as first-time, first-year students.

Part-time:	57%	**Asian American:**	2%
Out-of-state:	1%	**Hispanic American:**	2%
Women:	64%	**25 or older:**	30%
African American:	3%		

Transfer out. Colleges most students transferred to 2005: Towson University, McDaniel College, University of Maryland Baltimore County, Villa Julie College, University of Maryland College Park.

Basis for selection. Open admission, but selective for some programs.

2005-2006 Annual costs. Tuition/fees: $3,234; $4,476 out-of-district; $6,788 out-of-state. Per-credit charge: $92 in-district; $128 out-of-district; $195 out-of-state. Books/supplies: $800. Personal expenses: $1,000.

2004-2005 Financial aid. Need-based: 96% of total undergraduate aid awarded as scholarships/grants, 4% as loans/jobs. Need-based aid available for part-time students. Work study available nights, weekends and for part-time students. **Non-need-based:** Scholarships awarded for academics.

Application procedures. Admission: No deadline. No application fee. Application must be submitted on paper. Admission notification on a rolling basis. **Financial aid:** Priority date 3/1; no closing date. FAFSA required. Applicants notified by 6/1; must reply within 2 week(s) of notification.

Academics. Special study options: Distance learning, dual enrollment of high school students, ESL, honors, independent study, internships, liberal arts/career combination, weekend college. **Credit/placement by examination:** AP, CLEP, institutional tests. 30 credit hours maximum toward associate degree. **Support services:** Learning center, remedial instruction, study skills assistance, tutoring, writing center.

Majors. Business: General, accounting, administrative services, management information systems. **Computer sciences:** General, computer graphics, networking. **Education:** General, early childhood, multi-level teacher. **Engineering technology:** Drafting. **Family/consumer sciences:** Child care. **Health:** Physical therapy assistant. **Liberal arts:** Arts/sciences. **Visual/performing arts:** Commercial/advertising art.

Most popular majors. Business/marketing 13%, education 9%, health sciences 10%, liberal arts 64%.

Computing on campus. 686 workstations in library, computer center, student center. Commuter students can connect to campus network. Online library, wireless network available.

Student life. Freshman orientation: Available. Preregistration for classes offered. 1-day program in late August. **Policies:** Freshmen permitted cars on campus. **Activities:** Choral groups, drama, film society, literary magazine, student government, student newspaper, BACCHUS, Carroll Community Chorus, Christian club, LGBTA, World Watch.

Student services. Career counseling, student employment services, financial aid counseling, on-campus daycare, personal counseling. **Physically disabled:** Services for visually, speech, hearing impaired. **Transfer:** Special adviser for new students. Transfer center, transfer adviser, college fairs on campus for students transferring to 4-year colleges.

Contact. E-mail: cedwards@carrollcc.edu
Phone: (410) 386-8430 Toll-free number: (888) 221-9748
Fax: (410) 386-8446
Candace Edwards, Coordinator of Admissions, Carroll Community College, 1601 Washington Road, Westminster, MD 21157

Cecil Community College
North East, Maryland
www.cecilcc.edu **CB code: 5091**

- Public 2-year community college
- Commuter campus in small town

General. Founded in 1968. Regionally accredited. **Enrollment:** 1,729 degree-seeking undergraduates; 187 non-degree-seeking students. **Degrees:** 111 associate awarded. **Location:** 50 miles from Baltimore, 50 miles from Philadelphia. **Calendar:** Semester, limited summer session. **Full-time faculty:** 41 total; 22% have terminal degrees, 7% minority, 63% women. **Part-time faculty:** 151 total; 3% have terminal degrees, 9% minority, 55% women. **Class size:** 81% < 20, 17% 20-39, less than 1% 40-49, 1% 50-99.

Student profile. Among degree-seeking undergraduates, 50% enrolled in a transfer program, 50% enrolled in a vocational program, 475 enrolled as first-time, first-year students, 11 transferred in from other institutions.

Part-time:	63%	**Asian American:**	1%
Out-of-state:	9%	**Hispanic American:**	2%
Women:	65%	**25 or older:**	31%
African American:	8%		

Basis for selection. Open admission, but selective for some programs. Admission to nursing programs based on high school record, test scores, required interview. All students must take Cecil Community College placement tests.

2005-2006 Annual costs. Tuition/fees: $2,730; $5,430 out-of-district; $6,780 out-of-state. Per-credit charge: $80 in-district; $170 out-of-district; $215 out-of-state. Books/supplies: $810. Personal expenses: $1,760.

2004-2005 Financial aid. Need-based: 62% of total undergraduate aid awarded as scholarships/grants, 38% as loans/jobs. **Non-need-based:** Scholarships awarded for academics, alumni affiliation, athletics, job skills, state residency.

Application procedures. Admission: No deadline. No application fee. Application may be submitted online. Admission notification on a rolling basis. Application deadline for nursing program March 1. **Financial aid:** Priority date 8/1; no closing date. FAFSA required. Applicants notified on a rolling basis; must reply within 2 week(s) of notification.

Academics. Special study options: Cooperative education, distance learning, double major, dual enrollment of high school students, ESL, independent study, internships, teacher certification program, weekend college. License preparation in nursing. **Credit/placement by examination:** AP, CLEP, institutional tests. 45 credit hours maximum toward associate degree. **Support services:** Learning center, reduced course load, remedial instruction, tutoring, writing center.

Majors. Biology: General. **Business:** General, accounting, administrative services, business admin, communications, finance, management science, office management. **Computer sciences:** Data processing, information systems. **Education:** Elementary, secondary. **Engineering technology:** Electrical. **Health:** Nursing (RN). **Liberal arts:** Arts/sciences. **Math:** General. **Physical sciences:** Chemistry, physics. **Protective services:** Law enforcement admin. **Visual/performing arts:** Design, drawing, photography.

Most popular majors. Business/marketing 6%, education 6%, health sciences 37%, liberal arts 26%, visual/performing arts 8%.

Computing on campus. 85 workstations in library, computer center, student center. Commuter students can connect to campus network. Online course registration, online library available.

Student life. Freshman orientation: Available. Preregistration for classes offered. **Activities:** Dance, drama, musical theater, student government, student newspaper.

Athletics. NJCAA. **Intercollegiate:** Baseball M, basketball, bowling, cheerleading W, golf M, soccer M, softball W, tennis, volleyball W. **Team name:** Seahawks.

Student services. Adult student services, alcohol/substance abuse counseling, career counseling, student employment services, financial aid counseling, legal services, minority student services, personal counseling, placement for graduates, veterans' counselor. **Transfer:** Special adviser, orientation for new students. Transfer adviser, college fairs on campus for students transferring to 4-year colleges.

Contact. E-mail: dlane@cecilcc.edu
Phone: (410) 287-6060 Fax: (410) 287-1026
Diane Lane, Vice President of Student Services, Cecil Community College, One Seahawk Drive, North East, MD 21901

Chesapeake College

Wye Mills, Maryland — CB member
www.chesapeake.edu — CB code: 5143

- Public 2-year community college
- Commuter campus in rural community

General. Founded in 1965. Regionally accredited. **Enrollment:** 1,895 degree-seeking undergraduates. **Degrees:** 194 associate awarded. **Location:** 50 miles from Washington DC., 50 miles from Baltimore. **Calendar:** Semester, limited summer session. **Full-time faculty:** 55 total. **Part-time faculty:** 87 total. **Special facilities:** Performing arts center/theater.

Student profile.

Out-of-state:	1%	25 or older:	47%

Transfer out. Colleges most students transferred to 2005: Salisbury State College, Towson University, Frostburg State College, University of Maryland.

Basis for selection. Open admission, but selective for some programs. Selective admission to radiological technology, surgical technology, physical therapist assistant and nursing programs based on specific high school courses, cumulative grade point averages, and/or test scores.

2005-2006 Annual costs. Tuition/fees: $2,924; $4,814 out-of-district; $6,974 out-of-state. Per-credit charge: $84 in-district; $147 out-of-district; $219 out-of-state. Additional capital improvement fee per semester is $10 in-district and $25 out-of-district. Books/supplies: $1,200. Personal expenses: $1,000.

Financial aid. Need-based: Need-based aid available for part-time students. **Non-need-based:** Scholarships awarded for academics, art, athletics, state residency.

Application procedures. Admission: No deadline. No application fee. Admission notification on a rolling basis. Early application advised for radiologic technology and nursing programs. **Financial aid:** Priority date 5/1; no closing date. FAFSA, institutional form required. Applicants notified on a rolling basis starting 5/1; must reply within 2 week(s) of notification.

Academics. Special study options: Cooperative education, cross-registration, distance learning, dual enrollment of high school students, ESL, honors, independent study, internships, student-designed major, teacher certification program, weekend college. License preparation in nursing, paramedic, physical therapy. **Credit/placement by examination:** CLEP, institutional tests. 32 credit hours maximum toward associate degree. **Support services:** Learning center, reduced course load, remedial instruction, study skills assistance, tutoring, writing center.

Majors. Business: General, accounting, administrative services, management information systems, tourism promotion. **Computer sciences:** General. **Education:** General, elementary, secondary. **Engineering technology:** Drafting, manufacturing. **Family/consumer sciences:** Child care. **Health:** Medical radiologic technology/radiation therapy, medical records technology, mental health services, nursing (RN), physical therapy assistant. **Legal studies:** Paralegal. **Liberal arts:** Arts/sciences. **Mechanic/repair:** Aircraft. **Protective services:** Criminal justice, police science. **Psychology:** General. **Social sciences:** General.

Computing on campus. Commuter students can connect to campus network. Helpline available.

Student life. Freshman orientation: Available. Preregistration for classes offered. **Activities:** Choral groups, drama, student government, action teams, peer associates, African American student union, Phi Theta Kappa honor society, Best Buddies.

Athletics. NJCAA. **Intercollegiate:** Baseball M, basketball, soccer, softball W. **Intramural:** Basketball, soccer. **Team name:** Skipjacks.

Student services. Adult student services, career counseling, student employment services, financial aid counseling, minority student services, on-campus daycare, personal counseling, placement for graduates, veterans' counselor. **Physically disabled:** Services for visually, speech, hearing impaired. **Transfer:** Special adviser, orientation for new students. Transfer adviser, college fairs on campus for students transferring to 4-year colleges.

Contact. E-mail: kpetrichenko@chesapeake.edu
Phone: (410) 822-5400 ext. 287 Fax: (410) 827-5878
Kathy Petrichenko, Director of Admissions, Chesapeake College, PO Box 8, Wye Mills, MD 21679-0008

College of Southern Maryland

La Plata, Maryland
www.csmd.edu — CB code: 5144

- Public 2-year community college
- Commuter campus in large town

General. Founded in 1958. Regionally accredited. Other campuses are located in Charles, Calvert, and St. Mary's counties. **Enrollment:** 5,987 degree-seeking undergraduates. **Degrees:** 658 associate awarded. **Location:** 30 miles from Washington, DC. **Calendar:** Semester, limited summer session. **Full-time faculty:** 114 total; 22% have terminal degrees, 17% minority, 52% women. **Part-time faculty:** 312 total; 8% have terminal degrees, 13% minority, 54% women. **Class size:** 42% < 20, 57% 20-39, less than 1% 40-49, less than 1% 50-99. **Partnerships:** Formal partnership with Charles, Calvert, or St. Mary's County high schools.

Transfer out. Colleges most students transferred to 2005: University of MD - University College, Towson University, Salisbury University, St. Mary's College of Maryland, University of MD - Baltimore County.

Basis for selection. Open admission, but selective for some programs. 2.5 GPA and special testing required of nursing applicants. Must have graduated from high school, earned high school equivalency or have met the criteria of one of the college's special admission programs. Students must take the college skills assessment test unless they have taken the SAT, scored 550 in English and math or the ACT, scored 21 or higher. Interview required of early admission and nursing applicants. **Adult students:** SAT/ACT scores not required.

High school preparation. Biology (with laboratory) required for nursing majors.

2005-2006 Annual costs. Tuition/fees: $3,312; $5,352 out-of-district; $6,582 out-of-state. Per-credit charge: $92 in-district; $160 out-of-district; $201 out-of-state. In-state, out-of-district fees, $960; out-of-state, $1206. Books/supplies: $650. Personal expenses: $900.

2004-2005 Financial aid. Need-based: 94% of total undergraduate aid awarded as scholarships/grants, 6% as loans/jobs. Need-based aid available for part-time students. Work study available nights, weekends and for part-time students. **Non-need-based:** Scholarships awarded for academics, athletics, state residency.

Application procedures. Admission: No deadline. No application fee. Application may be submitted online. Admission notification on a rolling basis. **Financial aid:** Priority date 3/1; no closing date. FAFSA required. Applicants notified on a rolling basis starting 5/15; must reply within 2 week(s) of notification.

Academics. Students must successfully complete any required remedial courses before registering for regular courses. **Special study options:** Accelerated study, cooperative education, distance learning, dual enrollment of high school students, honors, independent study, liberal arts/career combination, weekend college. Bachelor's degree programs available on campus. License preparation in nursing, paramedic, physical therapy, radiology. **Credit/placement by examination:** AP, CLEP, institutional tests. 30 credit hours maximum toward associate degree. **Support services:** Learning center, reduced course load, remedial instruction, study skills assistance, tutoring.

Majors. Biology: General. **Business:** General, accounting technology, business admin, management information systems. **Computer sciences:** Programming. **Education:** General, elementary, secondary. **Engineering:** General. **Engineering technology:** Electrical, environmental, manufacturing. **Family/consumer sciences:** Child care. **Health:** EMT paramedic, licensed practical nurse, massage therapy, medical records technology, nursing (RN), physical therapy assistant. **Interdisciplinary:** Biological/physical sciences. **Legal studies:** Paralegal. **Liberal arts:** Arts/sciences. **Math:** General. **Philosophy/religion:** Philosophy. **Protective services:** Firefighting, law enforcement admin, police science. **Social sciences:** General.

Most popular majors. Business/marketing 21%, computer/information sciences 15%, engineering/engineering technologies 10%, health sciences 10%, liberal arts 37%.

Computing on campus. 639 workstations in library, computer center. Commuter students can connect to campus network. Online course registration, helpline available.

Student life. **Freshman orientation:** Available. Preregistration for classes offered. **Activities:** Choral groups, drama, literary magazine, music ensembles, musical theater, student government, Association for Information Technology, BAACHUD Peer Education Network, Black student union, Campus Crusade for Christ, The Hawkeye, nursing student association, Phi Theta Kappa.

Athletics. NJCAA. **Intercollegiate:** Baseball M, basketball, cheerleading, golf, soccer, softball W, tennis, volleyball W. **Team name:** Hawks.

Student services. Adult student services, career counseling, student employment services, personal counseling, placement for graduates, veterans' counselor. **Physically disabled:** Services for visually, speech, hearing impaired. **Transfer:** Special adviser, orientation, re-entry adviser for new students. Transfer adviser, college fairs on campus for students transferring to 4-year colleges.

Contact. E-mail: info@csmd.edu
Phone: (301) 934-7530 Fax: (301) 934-7698
Julia Pittman, Director of Admissions, College of Southern Maryland, 8730 Mitchell Road, La Plata, MD 20646-0910

Community College of Baltimore County

Baltimore, Maryland — **CB member**
www.ccbcmd.edu — **CB code: 5137**

- Public 2-year community college
- Commuter campus in very large city

General. Founded in 1956. Regionally accredited. Affiliated with Dundalk and Essex campuses of the Community College of Baltimore County. Courses also offered at Hunt Valley, Owings Mills, and White Marsh. **Enrollment:** 17,051 degree-seeking undergraduates; 2,571 non-degree-seeking students. **Degrees:** 1,357 associate awarded. **Location:** 8 miles from Baltimore. **Calendar:** Semester, limited summer session. **Full-time faculty:** 353 total; 22% have terminal degrees, 15% minority, 56% women. **Part-time faculty:** 711 total; 2% have terminal degrees, 27% minority, 53% women. **Special facilities:** Planetarium, occupational training center, performing arts theater, computer integrated manufacturing center. **Partnerships:** Formal partnership with the Baltimore County Public Schools for the Early Assessment and Intervention Project.

Student profile. Among degree-seeking undergraduates, 3,212 enrolled as first-time, first-year students.

Part-time:	61%	**25 or older:**	45%
Women:	63%		

Transfer out. **Colleges most students transferred to 2005:** University of Baltimore, University of Maryland Baltimore County, Towson University, Morgan State University.

Basis for selection. Open admission, but selective for some programs. Special requirements for nursing, automotive technology, honors, and occupational therapy assistant programs. In-house placement tests required of applicants not presenting SAT or ACT scores. Score reports preferred by July 1. Interview recommended for applicants under age 16 and early admission applicants. **Adult students:** Entrance exam policies same as for first-time freshmen.

High school preparation. 21 units recommended. Recommended units include English 4, mathematics 3, social studies 3.5, science 3, foreign language 2, academic electives 5.5.

2005-2006 Annual costs. Tuition/fees: $2,925; $4,815 out-of-district; $6,465 out-of-state. Per-credit charge: $87 in-district; $150 out-of-district; $205 out-of-state. Books/supplies: $1,000. Personal expenses: $1,200.

Financial aid. **Need-based:** Need-based aid available for part-time students. **Additional information:** On-campus employment typically available.

Application procedures. **Admission:** No deadline. $15 fee, may be waived for applicants with need. Application may be submitted online. Admission notification on a rolling basis. Early application encouraged. **Financial aid:** Priority date 4/15; no closing date. FAFSA required. Applicants notified on a rolling basis starting 7/1; must reply within 2 week(s) of notification.

Academics. **Special study options:** Cooperative education, cross-registration, distance learning, dual enrollment of high school students, ESL, honors, independent study, internships, liberal arts/career combination, study abroad, teacher certification program, weekend college. License preparation in nursing. **Credit/placement by examination:** AP, CLEP, institutional tests. 30 credit hours maximum toward associate degree. **Support services:** GED preparation, learning center, reduced course load, remedial instruction, tutoring.

Majors. **Agriculture:** Business, farm/ranch, horticulture. **Architecture:** Interior, landscape. **Business:** General, accounting, administrative services, business admin, hospitality admin, labor relations, office management, office technology, office/clerical, real estate. **Communications:** General, journalism. **Computer sciences:** General, applications programming, computer graphics, computer science, data entry, data processing, information systems, programming, web page design, webmaster. **Education:** General, art, drama/dance, early childhood, elementary, health, music, secondary, special. **Engineering:** General. **Engineering technology:** CAD/CADD, civil, construction, drafting, electrical, hydraulics, mechanical, occupational safety, surveying. **Family/consumer sciences:** Child care. **Foreign languages:** French, German, sign language interpretation, Spanish. **Health:** Athletic training, clinical lab technology, EMT paramedic, health services, massage therapy, medical radiologic technology/radiation therapy, medical secretary, mental health services, nursing (RN), occupational health, occupational therapy assistant, predentistry, premedicine, prepharmacy, preveterinary, respiratory therapy technology, substance abuse counseling, veterinary technology/assistant. **Interdisciplinary:** Math/computer science. **Legal studies:** Legal secretary, paralegal, prelaw. **Liberal arts:** Arts/sciences. **Math:** General. **Mechanic/repair:** Automotive, heating/ac/refrig, industrial. **Parks/recreation:** General, exercise sciences, facilities management, health/fitness, sports admin. **Personal/culinary services:** Mortuary science. **Philosophy/religion:** Philosophy. **Physical sciences:** Chemistry, physics. **Protective services:** Corrections, fire safety technology, law enforcement admin, police science, security services. **Psychology:** General. **Science technology:** Chemical. **Social sciences:** Anthropology, economics, geography, political science. **Transportation:** Aviation, aviation management. **Visual/performing arts:** Commercial photography, commercial/advertising art, dramatic, interior design, studio arts.

Most popular majors. Business/marketing 13%, health sciences 18%, liberal arts 46%.

Computing on campus. 2,359 workstations in library, computer center, student center. Online course registration, online library available.

Student life. **Freshman orientation:** Available. Preregistration for classes offered. One-day program. **Activities:** Choral groups, dance, drama, literary magazine, music ensembles, musical theater, radio station, student government, student newspaper, TV station, black student union, international club, Adventure Society, Christian fellowship.

Athletics. NJCAA. **Intercollegiate:** Baseball M, basketball, lacrosse, soccer, softball W, tennis, volleyball W. **Intramural:** Track and field.

Student services. Career counseling, services for economically disadvantaged, student employment services, financial aid counseling, minority student services, on-campus daycare, personal counseling, placement for graduates, veterans' counselor. **Physically disabled:** Services for visually, speech, hearing impaired. **Transfer:** Special adviser, orientation, pre-admission transcript evaluation for new students. Transfer adviser, college fairs on campus for students transferring to 4-year colleges.

Contact. E-mail: ringrassia@ccbcmd.edu
Phone: (410) 455-4304 Fax: (410) 719-6546
Diane Drake, Director of Admissions, Community College of Baltimore County, 800 South Rolling Road, Baltimore, MD 21228

Frederick Community College

Frederick, Maryland — **CB member**
www.frederick.edu — **CB code: 5230**

- Public 2-year community college
- Commuter campus in small city

General. Founded in 1957. Regionally accredited. **Enrollment:** 3,922 degree-seeking undergraduates; 655 non-degree-seeking students. **Degrees:** 545 associate awarded. **Location:** 40 miles from Washington, DC, 40 miles from Baltimore. **Calendar:** Semester, extensive summer session. **Full-time faculty:** 82 total. **Part-time faculty:** 260 total. **Partnerships:** Formal partnership with ESS to offer high-end computer networking/security courses.

Student profile. Among degree-seeking undergraduates, 61% enrolled in a transfer program, 29% enrolled in a vocational program, 1,143 enrolled as first-time, first-year students, 166 transferred in from other institutions.

Part-time:	55%	**Women:**	63%
Out-of-state:	1%	**25 or older:**	50%

Transfer out. **Colleges most students transferred to 2005:** Hood College, Mount St. Mary's University, Towson University, University of Maryland: College Park, Frostburg University.

Basis for selection. Open admission, but selective for some programs. All nursing programs, respiratory therapy, and surgical technology have special requirements. Students must show successful completion of appropriate general education requirements. Score of 550 or higher on either SAT math or verbal will exempt student from appropriate assessment. Interview required of nursing, respiratory therapy applicants. **Adult students:** Entrance exam policies same as for first-time freshmen. **Learning Disabled:** Meet with Office of Services for Students with Disabilities staff prior to testing/registration.

2005-2006 Annual costs. Tuition/fees: $2,889; $5,949 out-of-district; $7,959 out-of-state. Per-credit charge: $85 in-district; $187 out-of-district; $254 out-of-state. Books/supplies: $800. Personal expenses: $850.

Financial aid. **Need-based:** Need-based aid available for part-time students. Work study available for part-time students. **Non-need-based:** Scholarships awarded for academics, athletics, state residency.

Application procedures. **Admission:** No deadline. No application fee. Application may be submitted online. Admission notification on a rolling basis beginning on or about 1/1. Application deadline for nursing applicants December 15, surgical technology and emergency medical services applicants February 1. **Financial aid:** Priority date 6/15; no closing date. FAFSA, institutional form required. Applicants notified on a rolling basis starting 5/15; must reply within 2 week(s) of notification.

Academics. **Special study options:** Cooperative education, distance learning, dual enrollment of high school students, ESL, honors, independent study, internships, liberal arts/career combination, study abroad, teacher certification program, weekend college. License preparation in nursing, paramedic, real estate. **Credit/placement by examination:** AP, CLEP, institutional tests. 30 credit hours maximum toward associate degree. **Support services:** Learning center, pre-admission summer program, reduced course load, remedial instruction, study skills assistance, tutoring, writing center.

Majors. **Biology:** General. **Business:** Accounting, banking/financial services, business admin, hospitality admin, international. **Communications:** General. **Communications technology:** General. **Computer sciences:** General, applications programming, computer science, information systems, information technology, system admin, systems analysis. **Construction:** General. **Education:** General, early childhood, multi-level teacher, physical. **Engineering:** General. **English:** Speech/rhetoric. **Family/consumer sciences:** Child care. **Health:** EMT paramedic, nuclear medical technology, nursing (RN), prenursing, prepharmacy, respiratory therapy technology. **History:** General. **Legal studies:** Legal secretary, paralegal. **Liberal arts:** Arts/sciences. **Math:** General. **Personal/culinary services:** Culinary arts. **Philosophy/religion:** Philosophy. **Physical sciences:** Chemistry. **Protective services:** Criminal justice. **Psychology:** General. **Public administration:** Human services. **Science technology:** Biological. **Social sciences:** Economics, political science, sociology. **Visual/performing arts:** Art, dramatic.

Computing on campus. 150 workstations in library, computer center. Commuter students can connect to campus network. Online course registration, online library available.

Student life. **Freshman orientation:** Mandatory. Preregistration for classes offered. Held throughout summer; include advisement and pre-registration. **Policies:** Freshmen permitted cars on campus. **Activities:** Jazz band, choral groups, drama, film society, literary magazine, music ensembles, student government, student newspaper, multicultural student union, Christian students club, chess club, community service club, environmental awareness club, honors student association, international students club, gay/lesbian/bisexual group, nursing club, young Democrats and Republicans.

Athletics. NJCAA. **Intercollegiate:** Baseball M, basketball, golf, soccer, softball W, volleyball W. **Team name:** Cougars.

Student services. Adult student services, alcohol/substance abuse counseling, career counseling, student employment services, financial aid counseling, minority student services, on-campus daycare, personal counseling, placement for graduates, veterans' counselor, women's services. **Physically disabled:** Services for visually, speech, hearing impaired. **Transfer:** Special adviser for new students. Transfer center, transfer adviser, college fairs on campus for students transferring to 4-year colleges.

Contact. E-mail: kfrawley@frederick.edu
Phone: (301) 846-2431 Fax: (301) 624-2799
Kathy Frawley, Associate Vice President/Registrar, Frederick Community College, 7932 Opossumtown Pike, Frederick, MD 21702

Garrett College
McHenry, Maryland
www.garrettcollege.edu **CB code: 5279**

- Public 2-year community college
- Commuter campus in rural community

General. Founded in 1971. Regionally accredited. **Enrollment:** 509 degree-seeking undergraduates. **Degrees:** 82 associate awarded. **Location:** 45 miles from Cumberland, 40 miles from Morgantown, West Virginia. **Calendar:** Semester, limited summer session. **Full-time faculty:** 16 total. **Part-time faculty:** 39 total. **Class size:** 79% < 20, 18% 20-39, 2% 40-49, less than 1% 50-99.

Student profile.

Out-of-state:	18%	**Live on campus:**	10%
25 or older:	18%		

Transfer out. **Colleges most students transferred to 2005:** Frostburg State University.

Basis for selection. Open admission. Applicants without high school diploma must earn diploma or GED before completing 20 credit hours when enrolling in certificate program, and complete 30 credit hours when enrolling in degree program.

2005-2006 Annual costs. Tuition/fees: $2,880; $6,000 out-of-district; $7,080 out-of-state. Per-credit charge: $78 in-district; $182 out-of-district; $218 out-of-state. Room/board: $3,850. Books/supplies: $2,000. Personal expenses: $1,000.

2005-2006 Financial aid. **Need-based:** Need-based aid available for part-time students. Work study available for part-time students. **Non-need-based:** Scholarships awarded for academics, athletics, leadership. **Additional information:** Many local scholarships both merit and need based.

Application procedures. **Admission:** No deadline. No application fee. Admission notification on a rolling basis. **Financial aid:** Priority date 3/1; no closing date. FAFSA required. Applicants notified on a rolling basis starting 5/15; must reply within 2 week(s) of notification.

Academics. **Special study options:** Distance learning, double major, dual enrollment of high school students, honors, independent study. Bachelor's degree programs available on campus. **Credit/placement by examination:** CLEP, institutional tests. 30 credit hours maximum toward associate degree. **Support services:** GED preparation and test center, learning center, pre-admission summer program, reduced course load, remedial instruction, tutoring.

Majors. **Agriculture:** Business. **Business:** General, business admin. **Conservation:** Fisheries, wildlife. **Education:** General, elementary, physical, secondary. **Interdisciplinary:** Behavioral sciences. **Liberal arts:** Arts/sciences. **Math:** General. **Parks/recreation:** General. **Psychology:** General. **Visual/performing arts:** General.

Most popular majors. Business/marketing 22%, education 12%, liberal arts 35%, natural resources/environmental science 7%, parks/recreation 16%.

Computing on campus. 80 workstations in library, computer center. Online library available.

Student life. **Freshman orientation:** Available. Preregistration for classes offered. **Policies:** Freshmen permitted cars on campus. **Housing:** Coed dorms, special housing for disabled, apartments available. **Activities:** Concert band, choral groups, drama, literary magazine, music ensembles, musical theater, student government, student newspaper, TV station, agriculture club, math club, pottery club, wildlife club, Christian club.

Athletics. NJCAA. **Intercollegiate:** Baseball M, basketball, golf M, skiing M, volleyball W. **Intramural:** Softball W, volleyball W. **Team name:** Lakers.

Student services. Adult student services, career counseling, student employment services, personal counseling, placement for graduates, veterans' counselor. **Physically disabled:** Services for visually, speech, hearing impaired. **Transfer:** Special adviser for new students. Transfer adviser, college fairs on campus for students transferring to 4-year colleges.

Contact. E-mail: admissions@garrettcollege.edu
Phone: (301) 387-3010 Fax: (301) 387-3038
Nancy Priselac, Director of Enrollment Development, Garrett College, 687 Mosser Road, McHenry, MD 21541

Hagerstown Business College
Hagerstown, Maryland
www.hagerstownbusinesscol.org **CB code: 0804**

- For-profit 2-year business and junior college
- Commuter campus in large town
- Interview required

General. Founded in 1938. Accredited by ACICS. College includes allied health, legal, business, criminal justice, computer forensics and information technology divisions. Several bachelor's programs offered in online courses. **Enrollment:** 850 degree-seeking undergraduates. **Degrees:** 250 associate awarded. **Location:** 70 miles from Baltimore, 70 miles from Washington, DC. **Calendar:** Quarter, limited summer session. **Full-time faculty:** 25 total. **Part-time faculty:** 50 total. **Special facilities:** Firearms training simulator, Forensic Recovery and Evidence Detection (FRED) lab.

Student profile.

Out-of-state:	60%	**Live on campus:**	3%
25 or older:	55%		

Basis for selection. Open admission, but selective for some programs.

2005-2006 Annual costs. Tuition and fees vary from $10,608-$26,391for entire program. Room only: $3,360. Books/supplies: $875. Personal expenses: $1,260.

Financial aid. Need-based: Need-based aid available for part-time students.

Application procedures. Admission: No deadline. $20 fee. Admission notification on a rolling basis. **Financial aid:** No deadline. FAFSA, institutional form required. Applicants notified on a rolling basis starting 6/1; must reply within 2 week(s) of notification.

Academics. Special study options: Distance learning, double major, internships. **Credit/placement by examination:** AP, CLEP, institutional tests. 15 credit hours maximum toward associate degree. **Support services:** Reduced course load, remedial instruction, tutoring.

Majors. Business: Accounting, administrative services, business admin, office technology. **Computer sciences:** Computer graphics, data processing, LAN/WAN management, programming, system admin, webmaster. **Health:** Medical assistant, medical records technology, medical secretary, medical transcription. **Legal studies:** Paralegal. **Protective services:** Criminal justice, forensics, law enforcement admin.

Most popular majors. Business/marketing 22%, computer/information sciences 28%, health sciences 39%, legal studies 11%.

Computing on campus. 85 workstations in library, computer center.

Student life. Freshman orientation: Mandatory. **Policies:** Freshmen permitted cars on campus. **Housing:** Coed dorms available. $150 deposit. **Activities:** Student government.

Student services. Career counseling, student employment services, financial aid counseling, personal counseling, placement for graduates. **Transfer:** Orientation for new students.

Contact. E-mail: info@hagerstownbusinesscol.edu
Phone: (301) 739-2670 Toll-free number: (800) 422-2670
Fax: (301) 791-7661
Jim Klein, Director of Admissions, Hagerstown Business College, 18618 Crestwood Drive, Hagerstown, MD 21742

Hagerstown Community College
Hagerstown, Maryland
www.hagerstowncc.edu **CB code: 5290**

- Public 2-year community college
- Commuter campus in small city

General. Founded in 1946. Regionally accredited. **Enrollment:** 3,018 degree-seeking undergraduates; 503 non-degree-seeking students. **Degrees:** 348 associate awarded. **Location:** 70 miles from Baltimore. **Calendar:** Semester, extensive summer session. **Full-time faculty:** 69 total; 19% have terminal degrees, 1% minority, 64% women. **Part-time faculty:** 158 total; 3% minority, 51% women. **Special facilities:** Technology center, distance learning classrooms, amphitheater.

Student profile. Among degree-seeking undergraduates, 70% enrolled in a transfer program, 30% enrolled in a vocational program, 874 enrolled as first-time, first-year students, 261 transferred in from other institutions.

Part-time:	62%	**Asian American:**	1%
Out-of-state:	23%	**Hispanic American:**	2%
Women:	63%	**Native American:**	1%
African American:	7%	**25 or older:**	36%

Transfer out. Colleges most students transferred to 2005: Frostburg State University, Towson State University, Shepherd University, Shippensburg University, University of Maryland.

Basis for selection. Open admission, but selective for some programs. Admission to nursing and radiography programs based on 2.0 GPA, ACT composite score of 21, 1 laboratory chemistry and algebra. SAT/ACT (ACT preferred) and interview required for nursing and radiography program. **Adult students:** Entrance exam policies same as for first-time freshmen.

High school preparation. 16 units recommended. Recommended units include English 4, mathematics 3, social studies 1, history 1, science 3 (laboratory 2) and academic electives 2. One chemistry, 1 biology, 2 algebra required of nursing applicants; 1 physics, 1 chemistry, 2 algebra required of radiologic technologies applicants.

2005-2006 Annual costs. Tuition/fees: $2,950; $4,540 out-of-district; $5,860 out-of-state. Per-credit charge: $89 in-district; $142 out-of-district; $186 out-of-state. Books/supplies: $1,000. Personal expenses: $200.

Financial aid. All financial aid based on need. Need-based aid available for part-time students. Work study available nights, weekends and for part-time students.

Application procedures. Admission: No deadline. No application fee. Application may be submitted online. Admission notification on a rolling basis. **Financial aid:** No deadline. FAFSA required. Applicants notified on a rolling basis starting 5/1.

Academics. Special study options: Accelerated study, cooperative education, cross-registration, distance learning, double major, dual enrollment of high school students, ESL, honors, independent study, internships, liberal arts/career combination. License preparation in nursing, paramedic, radiology, real estate. **Credit/placement by examination:** AP, CLEP, institutional tests. 30 credit hours maximum toward associate degree. **Support services:** GED preparation and test center, learning center, pre-admission summer program, remedial instruction, study skills assistance, tutoring.

Majors. Business: General, accounting technology, banking/financial services, business admin, management information systems. **Communications technology:** Animation/special effects. **Computer sciences:** General, web page design. **Education:** General, early childhood, elementary. **Engineering:** General. **Engineering technology:** Electromechanical, industrial, mechanical. **Family/consumer sciences:** Child care. **Health:** EMT paramedic, medical radiologic technology/radiation therapy, medical secretary, mental health services, nursing (RN). **Liberal arts:** Arts/sciences. **Protective services:** Police science. **Visual/performing arts:** Commercial/advertising art.

Most popular majors. Business/marketing 22%, health sciences 23%, liberal arts 40%.

Computing on campus. 500 workstations in library, computer center, student center. Online course registration, online library, helpline, repair service available.

Student life. Freshman orientation: Available. **Policies:** Freshmen permitted cars on campus. **Activities:** Jazz band, choral groups, drama, literary magazine, musical theater, student government, student newspaper, Intervarsity Christian Fellowship, international club.

Athletics. NJCAA. **Intercollegiate:** Baseball M, basketball, cheerleading, cross-country, golf, soccer, softball W, tennis, track and field, volleyball W. **Team name:** Hawks.

Student services. Adult student services, career counseling, services for economically disadvantaged, student employment services, financial aid counseling, health services, on-campus daycare, personal counseling, placement for graduates, veterans' counselor. **Physically disabled:** Services for visually, speech, hearing impaired. **Transfer:** Special adviser, orientation, pre-admission transcript evaluation for new students. Transfer adviser, college fairs on campus for students transferring to 4-year colleges.

Contact. E-mail: admissions@hagerstowncc.edu
Phone: (301) 790-2800 ext. 238 Fax: (301) 791-9165
Jennifer Fisher, Director of Admissions, Records and Registration, Hagerstown Community College, 11400 Robinwood Drive, Hagerstown, MD 21742-6590

Harford Community College

Bel Air, Maryland
www.harford.cc.md.us **CB code: 5303**

- Public 2-year community college
- Commuter campus in small city

General. Founded in 1957. Regionally accredited. **Enrollment:** 4,568 degree-seeking undergraduates. **Degrees:** 496 associate awarded. **Location:** 25 miles from Baltimore. **Calendar:** Semester, limited summer session. **Full-time faculty:** 104 total. **Part-time faculty:** 204 total. **Special facilities:** Observatory.

Student profile.

Out-of-state:	1%	25 or older:	47%

Transfer out. Colleges most students transferred to 2005: Essex Community College, Towson University, Catonsville Community College, Baltimore City Community College, University of Maryland at College Park.

Basis for selection. Open admission, but selective for some programs. Some restrictions apply for applicants under 16 years old and international students. Nursing program has specific selection criteria. Students not meeting basic requirements must complete transitional courses. Students with minimum SAT scores of 500 each on math and verbal (exclusive of writing) exempt from academic assessment exams in English, reading, and math.

High school preparation. 12 units recommended. Recommended units include English 4, mathematics 3, social studies 2 and science 3. Several degree programs require additional preparation.

2005-2006 Annual costs. Tuition/fees: $2,475; $4,725 out-of-district; $6,975 out-of-state. Per-credit charge: $75 in-district; $150 out-of-district; $225 out-of-state. Books/supplies: $500. Personal expenses: $500.

Financial aid. Need-based: Work study available for part-time students.

Application procedures. Admission: No deadline. No application fee. Admission notification on a rolling basis. Application deadline for nursing June 1. Notification within 30 days. **Financial aid:** Priority date 3/1; no closing date. FAFSA, institutional form required. Applicants notified on a rolling basis starting 4/1; must reply within 2 week(s) of notification.

Academics. Special study options: Cooperative education, distance learning, double major, dual enrollment of high school students, independent study, internships, liberal arts/career combination, weekend college. License preparation in nursing. **Credit/placement by examination:** AP, CLEP, institutional tests. 30 credit hours maximum toward associate degree. **Support services:** Learning center, reduced course load, remedial instruction, study skills assistance, tutoring, writing center.

Majors. Architecture: Interior. **Biology:** General. **Business:** General, accounting, administrative services, business admin, management information systems, sales/distribution. **Communications technology:** General. **Computer sciences:** General, computer science. **Conservation:** General. **Education:** General, multi-level teacher, secondary. **Engineering:** General. **Engineering technology:** Electrical. **Health:** Electroencephalograph technology, health services, nursing (RN). **Legal studies:** Paralegal. **Liberal arts:** Arts/sciences. **Math:** General. **Philosophy/religion:** Philosophy. **Physical sciences:** Chemistry, physics. **Protective services:** Police science. **Social sciences:** Sociology. **Visual/performing arts:** Interior design, photography.

Most popular majors. Business/marketing 21%, health sciences 22%, liberal arts 31%.

Computing on campus. 350 workstations in library, computer center, student center.

Student life. Freshman orientation: Mandatory. **Activities:** Bands, choral groups, dance, drama, film society, literary magazine, music ensembles, musical theater, radio station, student government, student newspaper, TV station, Black Student Union, multinational Hispanic student association, Student Environmental Action Coalition, paralegal studies association, Future Teachers, Future Interior Designers, political science club, WHFC radio club, Phi Theta Kappa.

Athletics. NJCAA. **Intercollegiate:** Baseball M, basketball, cross-country M, field hockey W, lacrosse, soccer M, softball W, tennis.

Student services. Career counseling, student employment services, on-campus daycare, personal counseling, placement for graduates, veterans' counselor. **Physically disabled:** Services for visually, speech, hearing impaired. **Transfer:** Special adviser for new students. Transfer adviser, college fairs on campus for students transferring to 4-year colleges.

Contact. Phone: (410) 836-4223 Fax: (410) 836-4169
Lynne LaCalle, Associate Dean of Enrollment Services, Harford Community College, 401 Thomas Run Road, Bel Air, MD 21015

Howard Community College

Columbia, Maryland
www.howardcc.edu **CB code: 5308**

- Public 2-year community college
- Commuter campus in small city

General. Founded in 1966. Regionally accredited. **Enrollment:** 5,932 degree-seeking undergraduates; 909 non-degree-seeking students. **Degrees:** 452 associate awarded. **Location:** 20 miles from Baltimore, 30 miles from Washington, DC. **Calendar:** Semester, extensive summer session. **Full-time faculty:** 115 total; 26% have terminal degrees, 20% minority, 62% women. **Part-time faculty:** 382 total; 14% have terminal degrees, 22% minority, 61% women. **Class size:** 60% < 20, 37% 20-39, 1% 40-49, less than 1% 50-99. **Partnerships:** Formal partnerships with Novell Education Academic Partner, Microsoft Authorized Academic Training Program, Sylvan/Prometric Authorized Testing/Academic Center, Comp Tia Authorized Education Partner, Regional Cisco Networking Academy.

Student profile. Among degree-seeking undergraduates, 72% enrolled in a transfer program, 28% enrolled in a vocational program, 11% already have a bachelor's degree or higher, 1,339 enrolled as first-time, first-year students, 1,068 transferred in from other institutions.

Part-time:	57%	Hispanic American:	4%
Women:	59%	Native American:	1%
African American:	21%	International:	6%
Asian American:	9%	25 or older:	44%

Transfer out. 68% of students enrolled in the transfer program go on to 4-year colleges. **Colleges most students transferred to 2005:** University of Maryland-College Park, University of Maryland-Baltimore County, Towson University.

Basis for selection. Open admission, but selective for some programs. Special requirements for clinical nursing, emergency medical services, cardiovascular technology applicants. Selective admission to James W. Rouse Scholars and Silas Craft Collegians programs. SAT or ACT required for admission to James W. Rouse Scholars Program. Mandatory assessment policy. Most students must complete placement testing before completing 12 credits. Placement test exemptions allowed based on SAT/ACT scores. Interview and portfolio recommended for some selective admissions programs. **Homeschooled:** Transcripts, recommendations, test scores, interview with admissions officer required. Social and emotional maturity also required.

High school preparation. Recommended units include English 4, mathematics 4, social studies 4, history 3, science 3 (laboratory 2) and foreign language 3. Computer related course involving skills such as word-processing, databases and spreadsheets, as well as the Internet.

2006-2007 Annual costs. Tuition/fees (projected): $3,300; $5,790 out-of-district; $7,140 out-of-state. Per-credit charge: $110 in-district; $193 out-of-district; $238 out-of-state. Books/supplies: $1,000. Personal expenses: $1,000.

2004-2005 Financial aid. Need-based: 74% of total undergraduate aid awarded as scholarships/grants, 26% as loans/jobs. Need-based aid available for part-time students. Work study available nights and for part-time students.

Application procedures. Admission: No deadline. $25 fee, may be waived for applicants with need. Application must be submitted on paper. Admission notification on a rolling basis. Specific deadlines apply for applications to James W. Rouse Scholars program and clinical nursing program. **Financial aid:** Priority date 3/1; no closing date. FAFSA, institutional form required. Applicants notified on a rolling basis starting 4/1.

Academics. Pre-admission summer program for disabled students only. **Special study options:** Accelerated study, cooperative education, distance learning, dual enrollment of high school students, external degree, honors, independent study, internships, liberal arts/career combination, study abroad, teacher certification program, weekend college. Online courses, Maryland Community College Teleconsortium, joint programs with other community colleges. License preparation in nursing, paramedic. **Credit/placement by examination:** AP, CLEP, IB, institutional tests. 30 credit hours maximum toward associate degree. **Support services:** GED preparation, learning center, pre-admission summer program, reduced course load, remedial instruction, study skills assistance, tutoring, writing center.

Majors. **Agriculture:** Horticultural science. **Area/ethnic studies:** American, women's. **Biology:** Biomedical sciences. **Business:** Business admin, financial planning, hospitality admin, management information systems, office management, retailing, sales/distribution. **Communications:** Digital media. **Communications technology:** Desktop publishing. **Computer sciences:** Computer graphics, computer science, information technology, networking, security. **Conservation:** General. **Education:** Early childhood, elementary, secondary. **Engineering:** General. **Engineering technology:** Biomedical, CAD/CADD, electrical, laser/optical, telecommunications. **Family/consumer sciences:** Child development. **Health:** Athletic training, cardiovascular technology, clinical lab technology, EMT paramedic, health services admin, licensed practical nurse, massage therapy, music therapy, nursing (RN), physical therapy assistant, predentistry, premedicine, prepharmacy, preveterinary, radiologic technology/medical imaging, respiratory therapy assistant, substance abuse counseling, surgical technology. **Interdisciplinary:** Global studies, intercultural. **Legal studies:** Legal secretary. **Liberal arts:** Arts/sciences. **Math:** General. **Mechanic/repair:** Electronics/electrical. **Parks/recreation:** Exercise sciences, health/fitness. **Physical sciences:** General. **Protective services:** Criminal justice. **Psychology:** General. **Social sciences:** General, anthropology, criminology, international economics. **Visual/performing arts:** Art, cinematography, commercial/advertising art, dance, design, dramatic, photography, studio arts, theater design.

Most popular majors. Business/marketing 13%, education 8%, health sciences 16%, liberal arts 55%.

Computing on campus. 106 workstations in library, computer center, student center. Commuter students can connect to campus network. Online course registration, online library, helpline, repair service, student web hosting, wireless network available.

Student life. **Freshman orientation:** Available. Preregistration for classes offered. One day or evening program 3-4 hours in length the week before start of fall and spring semesters. **Policies:** Drug and alcohol free campus. Freshmen permitted cars on campus. **Activities:** Jazz band, choral groups, dance, drama, literary magazine, music ensembles, musical theater, student government, student newspaper, TV station, Christian fellowship, African-American student union, environmental club, cultural club, Jewish student union, nursing club, Japanese animation club, Muslim student association, Global Student Union, Gay, Lesbian & Bisexual Alliance.

Athletics. NJCAA. **Intercollegiate:** Cross-country, lacrosse, soccer, track and field, volleyball W. **Team name:** Dragons.

Student services. Adult student services, career counseling, services for economically disadvantaged, student employment services, financial aid counseling, on-campus daycare, personal counseling, placement for graduates, veterans' counselor, women's services. **Physically disabled:** Services for visually, speech, hearing impaired. **Learning disabled:** Comprehensive services available. **Transfer:** Special adviser, orientation, pre-admission transcript evaluation for new students. Transfer center, transfer adviser, college fairs on campus for students transferring to 4-year colleges.

Contact. E-mail: adm-adv@howardcc.edu
Phone: (410) 772-4856 Fax: (410) 772-4589
Christy Thomson, Assistant Director of Admissions, Howard Community College, 10901 Little Patuxent Parkway, Columbia, MD 21044-3197

Montgomery College

Rockville, Maryland — **CB member**
www.montgomerycollege.edu — **CB code: 5440**

- Public 2-year community college
- Commuter campus in very large city

General. Founded in 1946. Regionally accredited. 3 campus institution in suburban Washington, DC. Takoma Park/Silver Spring campus is directly adjacent to Washington, DC. Rockville campus is 12 miles from Washington, DC, and Germantown campus is 20 miles from Washington, DC. **Enrollment:** 16,412 degree-seeking undergraduates; 5,851 non-degree-seeking students. **Degrees:** 1,491 associate awarded. **Location:** 5 miles from Washington, DC. **Calendar:** Semester, extensive summer session. **Full-time faculty:** 468 total; 34% have terminal degrees, 27% minority, 54% women. **Part-time faculty:** 769 total; 25% minority, 55% women. **Class size:** 41% < 20, 58% 20-39, less than 1% 40-49, less than 1% 50-99. **Special facilities:** Performing arts center, child care center, career search center, the learning center program, disability support services. **Partnerships:** Formal partnership with two local high schools through the College Institute.

Student profile. Among degree-seeking undergraduates, 73% enrolled in a transfer program, 27% enrolled in a vocational program, 5% already have a bachelor's degree or higher, 2,895 enrolled as first-time, first-year students, 1,166 transferred in from other institutions.

Part-time:	59%	**Women:**	46%
Out-of-state:	6%	**25 or older:**	39%

Transfer out. 60% of students enrolled in the transfer program go on to 4-year colleges. **Colleges most students transferred to 2005:** University of Maryland-College Park, University of Maryland-Baltimore County, Towson State University, University of Maryland-University College.

Basis for selection. Open admission, but selective for some programs. Admission to medical health programs considers standardized test scores, secondary school record, geographical residence, and state residence. Montgomery County residents get first priority; GPA rank within residency category important. Audition required for music majors. **Adult students:** Entrance exam policies same as for first-time freshmen.

High school preparation. Recommended units include English 4, mathematics 3 and science 2.

2005-2006 Annual costs. Tuition/fees: $3,708; $7,236 out-of-district; $9,612 out-of-state. Per-credit charge: $93 in-district; $191 out-of-district; $257 out-of-state. Books/supplies: $800. Personal expenses: $1,000.

2004-2005 Financial aid. **Need-based:** 76% of total undergraduate aid awarded as scholarships/grants, 24% as loans/jobs. Need-based aid available for part-time students. Work study available nights, weekends and for part-time students. **Non-need-based:** Scholarships awarded for academics, alumni affiliation, art, music/drama, state residency.

Application procedures. **Admission:** No deadline. $25 fee, may be waived for applicants with need. Application may be submitted online. Admission notification on a rolling basis beginning on or about 4/1. **Financial aid:** Priority date 5/15; no closing date. FAFSA, institutional form required. Applicants notified on a rolling basis starting 5/30.

Academics. **Special study options:** Accelerated study, cooperative education, distance learning, double major, dual enrollment of high school students, ESL, honors, independent study, internships, student-designed major, study abroad, weekend college. License preparation in nursing, physical therapy, radiology. **Credit/placement by examination:** AP, CLEP, institutional tests. 45 credit hours maximum toward associate degree. **Support services:** GED preparation, learning center, pre-admission summer program, remedial instruction, study skills assistance, tutoring, writing center.

Majors. **Architecture:** Interior. **Business:** Accounting, business admin, hospitality admin, hospitality/recreation, international marketing, management science, merchandising, sales/distribution. **Communications:** Advertising, broadcast journalism. **Communications technology:** Desktop publishing, graphic/printing, graphics. **Computer sciences:** General, computer graphics, computer science, information systems, programming. **Construction:** Maintenance. **Education:** General, early childhood, science. **Engineering:** General, civil. **Engineering technology:** Architectural, biomedical, civil, drafting, electrical. **Family/consumer sciences:** Child care, institutional food production. **Health:** Medical radiologic technology/radiation therapy, medical records technology, nursing (RN), physical therapy assistant, predentistry, premedicine, prepharmacy, sonography. **Interdisciplinary:** Biological/physical sciences. **Legal studies:** Paralegal. **Liberal arts:** Arts/sciences. **Mechanic/repair:** Automotive, electronics/electrical. **Personal/culinary services:** Food service. **Protective services:** Criminal justice, fire safety technology, firefighting, law enforcement admin, police science. **Visual/performing arts:** General, art history/conservation, commercial photography, commercial/advertising art, dance, interior design, photography, studio arts, theater design.

Most popular majors. Business/marketing 21%, computer/information sciences 6%, health sciences 10%, liberal arts 48%.

Computing on campus. 400 workstations in library, computer center. Commuter students can connect to campus network. Online course registration, online library, helpline available.

Student life. **Freshman orientation:** Available. Preregistration for classes offered. **Policies:** Freshmen permitted cars on campus. **Activities:** Concert band, choral groups, dance, drama, musical theater, radio station, student government, student newspaper, TV station, Jewish student association, progressive student alliance, Christian fellowship, international student association, lesbian student alliance, Students Against Driving Drunk, international student organizations, African-American student organization, Hispanic student organization, Asian student organization.

Athletics. NJCAA. **Intercollegiate:** Baseball M, basketball, cross-country, field hockey W, golf M, lacrosse M, soccer, softball W, tennis, track and field, volleyball W, wrestling M. **Intramural:** Basketball.

Student services. Adult student services, career counseling, services for economically disadvantaged, student employment services, financial aid counseling, minority student services, on-campus daycare, personal counseling, placement for graduates, veterans' counselor. **Physically disabled:** Services for visually, speech, hearing impaired. **Learning disabled:** Comprehensive services available. **Transfer:** Special adviser, orientation, re-entry adviser for new students. Transfer center, transfer adviser, college fairs on campus for students transferring to 4-year colleges.

Contact. Phone: (301) 279-5034 Fax: (301) 279-5037
Sherman Helberg, Director of Enrollment Management, Montgomery College, 51 Mannakee Street, Room 105, Rockville, MD 20850

Prince George's Community College

Largo, Maryland — **CB member**
www.pgcc.edu — **CB code: 5545**

- Public 2-year community college
- Commuter campus in very large city

General. Founded in 1958. Regionally accredited. Extension center at Andrews Air Force Base serves both military and civilian personnel. **Enrollment:** 11,011 degree-seeking undergraduates; 1,381 non-degree-seeking students. **Degrees:** 727 associate awarded. **ROTC:** Army, Air Force. **Location:** 10 miles from Washington, DC. **Calendar:** Semester, limited summer session. **Full-time faculty:** 263 total; 27% have terminal degrees, 31% minority, 59% women. **Part-time faculty:** 387 total; 57% minority, 51% women. **Class size:** 58% < 20, 41% 20-39, less than 1% 40-49, less than 1% 50-99. **Special facilities:** Natatorium, art gallery.

Student profile. Among degree-seeking undergraduates, 2,107 enrolled as first-time, first-year students, 1,025 transferred in from other institutions.

Part-time:	73%	**Asian American:**	4%
Out-of-state:	4%	**Hispanic American:**	4%
Women:	65%	**International:**	5%
African American:	79%	**25 or older:**	47%

Transfer out. Colleges most students transferred to 2005: University of Maryland-College Park, Bowie State University, University of Maryland-University College, Morgan State University.

Basis for selection. Open admission, but selective for some programs. Special requirements for health technology programs and for international students. Health technology program requires high school diploma or GED. For some scholarship awards or honors program consideration, SAT combined score of 1050 or above (exclusive of writing) required. SAT or ACT scores may be used in place of college's placement tests.

High school preparation. Recommended units include English 4, mathematics 4, social studies 3, history 3, science 3 (laboratory 2) and academic electives 4. One computer literacy recommended.

2005-2006 Annual costs. Tuition/fees: $3,710; $5,840 out-of-district; $8,480 out-of-state. Per-credit charge: $94 in-district; $165 out-of-district; $263 out-of-state. Instructional services fees range from $22 to $32 per credit depending on course. Books/supplies: $700.

Financial aid. All financial aid based on need. Need-based aid available for part-time students. Work study available for part-time students.

Application procedures. Admission: No deadline. $25 fee. Admission notification on a rolling basis. **Financial aid:** Priority date 6/1; no closing date. FAFSA, institutional form required. Applicants notified on a rolling basis starting 6/1; must reply within 2 week(s) of notification.

Academics. Special study options: Cooperative education, distance learning, double major, dual enrollment of high school students, ESL, honors, independent study, liberal arts/career combination, teacher certification program, weekend college. Bachelor's degree programs available on campus. License preparation in nursing, paramedic, real estate. **Credit/placement by examination:** AP, CLEP, institutional tests. 30 credit hours maximum toward associate degree. **Support services:** Learning center, reduced course load, remedial instruction, study skills assistance, tutoring, writing center.

Majors. Area/ethnic studies: African-American, American, women's. **Biology:** General. **Business:** Accounting, administrative services, business admin, marketing, office management, office technology. **Computer sciences:** General, computer science, information systems, programming, systems analysis. **Education:** Business, early childhood, elementary, health, mathematics, physical, science, secondary. **Engineering:** General, aerospace. **Engineering technology:** Drafting, electrical. **Family/consumer sciences:** Child care. **Health:** EMT paramedic, medical radiologic technology/radiation therapy, medical records admin, medical records technology, medical secretary, nuclear medical technology, nursing (RN), premedicine, prepharmacy, respiratory therapy technology. **Legal studies:** Legal secretary, paralegal. **Liberal arts:** Arts/sciences. **Physical sciences:** Chemistry. **Protective services:** Criminal justice, forensics. **Psychology:** General. **Visual/performing arts:** Commercial/advertising art, studio arts.

Most popular majors. Business/marketing 21%, computer/information sciences 18%, health sciences 20%, liberal arts 25%, security/protective services 8%.

Computing on campus. 950 workstations in library, computer center, student center. Commuter students can connect to campus network. Helpline, repair service available.

Student life. Freshman orientation: Available. Preregistration for classes offered. **Policies:** Freshmen permitted cars on campus. **Activities:** Choral groups, drama, film society, literary magazine, music ensembles, musical theater, opera, student government, student newspaper, TV station, Union of Black Scholars, Active Seniors (for senior citizens), student program board, Spanish club, international students society, French club, Caribbean students club, Muslim society, women's Bible study.

Athletics. NJCAA. **Intercollegiate:** Baseball M, basketball, bowling, golf, soccer, softball W, tennis M, volleyball W. **Intramural:** Basketball, bowling, golf, racquetball, soccer, table tennis, volleyball. **Team name:** Owls.

Student services. Adult student services, career counseling, services for economically disadvantaged, student employment services, financial aid counseling, health services, minority student services, on-campus daycare, personal counseling, placement for graduates, veterans' counselor. **Physically disabled:** Services for visually, speech, hearing impaired. **Learning disabled:** Comprehensive services available. **Transfer:** Special adviser, orientation, re-entry adviser for new students. Transfer center, transfer adviser, college fairs on campus for students transferring to 4-year colleges.

Contact. Phone: (301) 322-0801 Fax: (301) 322-0119
Vera Bagley, Director of Admissions and Records, Prince George's Community College, 301 Largo Road, Largo, MD 20774

TESST College of Technology: Baltimore

Baltimore, Maryland
www.retstraining.com

- For-profit 2-year technical college
- Very large city

General. Accredited by ACCSCT. **Enrollment:** 1,000 undergraduates. **Degrees:** 33 associate awarded. **Calendar:** Semester. **Full-time faculty:** 40 total. **Part-time faculty:** 30 total.

Basis for selection. Open admission, but selective for some programs. Institutional evaluation test may be accepted in lieu of SAT/ACT.

2006-2007 Annual costs. Cost for complete program is $11,300-$26,000, depending on field of study.

Application procedures. Admission: No deadline. $20 fee. Admission notification on a rolling basis. **Financial aid:** No deadline.

Academics. Credit/placement by examination: AP, CLEP.

Majors. Computer sciences: Information systems. **Engineering technology:** Electrical, telecommunications.

Contact. Phone: (410) 644-6400 Fax: (410) 644-6481
William Scott, Director of Admissions, TESST College of Technology: Baltimore, 1520 South Caton Avenue, Baltimore, MD 21227-1063

TESST College of Technology: Beltsville

Beltsville, Maryland
www.tesst.com

- For-profit 2-year technical college
- Large town

General. Accredited by ACCSCT. **Calendar:** Semester.

Annual costs/financial aid. Comprehensive fee for complete program is $10,700-$25,500, depending on field of study.

Contact. Phone: (301) 937-8448
President, 4600 Powder Mill Road, Beltsville, MD 20705

Two-Year Colleges

TESST College of Technology: Towson
Towson, Maryland
www.tesst.com

- For-profit 2-year technical college
- Interview required

General. Accredited by ACCSCT. **Enrollment:** 422 undergraduates. **Degrees:** 41 associate awarded. **Location:** 15 miles from Baltimore. **Calendar:** Semester. **Full-time faculty:** 15 total. **Part-time faculty:** 20 total.

Basis for selection. Open admission, but selective for some programs. **Adult students:** CPAT for all students.

2005-2006 Annual costs. 2 year associate degree program, including books, fees and tuition, \$21,600 - \$26,750; certificate program, \$10,580 - \$23,400.

Application procedures. Admission: No deadline. \$20 fee. Admission notification on a rolling basis.

Academics. Credit/placement by examination: CLEP. **Support services:** Tutoring.

Majors. Computer sciences: Information systems. **Engineering technology:** Electrical, telecommunications. **Protective services:** Law enforcement admin.

Student life. Freshman orientation: Mandatory. Preregistration for classes offered.

Student services. Career counseling, student employment services, financial aid counseling, placement for graduates, veterans' counselor.

Contact. Phone: (410) 296-5350 Fax: (410) 296-5356
Alicia Hayman, Director of Admissions, TESST College of Technology: Towson, 803 Glen Eagles Court, Towson, MD 21286

Wor-Wic Community College
Salisbury, Maryland — **CB member**
www.worwic.edu — **CB code: 1613**

- Public 2-year community college
- Commuter campus in large town

General. Founded in 1975. Regionally accredited. **Enrollment:** 2,785 degree-seeking undergraduates; 258 non-degree-seeking students. **Degrees:** 261 associate awarded. **Location:** 110 miles from Baltimore, 120 miles from Washington, DC. **Calendar:** Semester, limited summer session. **Full-time faculty:** 56 total; 23% have terminal degrees, 7% minority, 61% women. **Part-time faculty:** 112 total; 4% have terminal degrees, 9% minority, 61% women. **Class size:** 42% < 20, 50% 20-39, 5% 40-49, 3% 50-99. **Partnerships:** Formal partnership with local medical center to provide financial and clinical support to the college's health programs.

Student profile. Among degree-seeking undergraduates, 41% enrolled in a transfer program, 59% enrolled in a vocational program, 678 enrolled as first-time, first-year students, 277 transferred in from other institutions.

Part-time:	67%	**Asian American:**	2%
Out-of-state:	3%	**Hispanic American:**	2%
Women:	67%	**25 or older:**	43%
African American:	25%		

Transfer out. 65% of students enrolled in the transfer program go on to 4-year colleges. **Colleges most students transferred to 2005:** Salisbury University, University of Maryland Eastern Shore.

Basis for selection. Open admission, but selective for some programs. Special requirements for emergency medical services, nursing and radiologic technology programs. **Adult students:** Entrance exam policies same as for first-time freshmen.

High school preparation. Recommended units include English 4 and mathematics 2.

2006-2007 Annual costs. Tuition/fees (projected): \$2,336; \$5,816 out-of-district; \$6,776 out-of-state. Per-credit charge: \$76 in-district; \$192 out-of-district; \$224 out-of-state. Books/supplies: \$1,200. Personal expenses: \$1,000.

2005-2006 Financial aid. Need-based: 203 full-time freshmen applied for aid; 184 were judged to have need; 148 of these received aid. Average need met was 19%. Average scholarship/grant was \$1,953; average loan \$1,173. 80% of total undergraduate aid awarded as scholarships/grants, 20% as loans/jobs. Need-based aid available for part-time students. Work study available nights, weekends and for part-time students. **Non-need-based:** Awarded to 7 full-time undergraduates, including 3 freshmen. Scholarships awarded for academics, state residency.

Application procedures. Admission: No deadline. No application fee. Application must be submitted on paper. Admission notification on a rolling basis. **Financial aid:** Priority date 6/1; no closing date. FAFSA, institutional form required. Applicants notified on a rolling basis starting 4/1.

Academics. Special study options: Distance learning, double major, dual enrollment of high school students, ESL, honors, internships. License preparation in nursing, paramedic, radiology. **Credit/placement by examination:** AP, CLEP, institutional tests. 30 credit hours maximum toward associate degree. **Support services:** Learning center, reduced course load, remedial instruction, tutoring, writing center.

Majors. Business: General, accounting technology, administrative services, business admin, hospitality admin. **Computer sciences:** General, systems analysis. **Education:** General, early childhood, elementary. **Engineering technology:** Drafting, electrical. **Family/consumer sciences:** Child care. **Health:** EMT paramedic, medical radiologic technology/radiation therapy, nursing (RN), substance abuse counseling. **Protective services:** Police science.

Most popular majors. Business/marketing 20%, education 6%, health sciences 31%, liberal arts 29%, security/protective services 6%.

Computing on campus. 494 workstations in library, computer center, student center. Commuter students can connect to campus network. Online library available.

Student life. Freshman orientation: Available. Preregistration for classes offered. **Activities:** Choral groups, drama, literary magazine, student government, student newspaper.

Student services. Career counseling, student employment services, financial aid counseling, personal counseling, placement for graduates, veterans' counselor. **Physically disabled:** Services for visually, speech, hearing impaired. **Transfer:** Orientation for new students.

Contact. E-mail: admissions@worwic.edu
Phone: (410) 334-2895 Fax: (410) 334-2954
Richard Webster, Director of Admissions, Wor-Wic Community College, 32000 Campus Drive, Salisbury, MD 21804

Massachusetts

Bay State College
Boston, Massachusetts
www.baystate.edu **CB code: 3120**

- Private 2-year junior college
- Commuter campus in very large city
- Application essay, interview required

General. Founded in 1946. Regionally accredited. **Enrollment:** 938 degree-seeking undergraduates. **Degrees:** 211 associate awarded. **Calendar:** Semester, limited summer session. **Full-time faculty:** 20 total. **Part-time faculty:** 25 total.

Student profile.

25 or older:	12%	**Live on campus:**	19%

Basis for selection. Special consideration to students with lower than minimum 2.0 GPA; interview and 2 recommendations from guidance counselors. Writing sample and second interview may be requested.

High school preparation. Recommended units include English 4, mathematics 2, social studies 1, history 1, science 2 (laboratory 1).

2005-2006 Annual costs. Tuition/fees: $15,650. Per-credit charge: $510. Room/board: $9,825. Books/supplies: $810.

Financial aid. Need-based: Need-based aid available for part-time students. Work study available nights, weekends and for part-time students.

Application procedures. Admission: No deadline. $40 fee, may be waived for applicants with need. Application may be submitted online. Admission notification on a rolling basis. **Financial aid:** Closing date 4/15. FAFSA, institutional form required. Applicants notified on a rolling basis starting 3/15; must reply within 3 week(s) of notification.

Academics. Special study options: Cooperative education, ESL, honors, independent study, internships. License preparation in occupational therapy, physical therapy. **Credit/placement by examination:** CLEP, IB, institutional tests. 9 credit hours maximum toward associate degree. **Support services:** Learning center, reduced course load, study skills assistance, tutoring.

Majors. Business: Accounting, administrative services, business admin, fashion, hospitality/recreation, office management, sales/distribution, tourism promotion. **Computer sciences:** General. **Education:** Early childhood. **Health:** Medical assistant, medical secretary, occupational therapy assistant, physical therapy assistant. **Legal studies:** Legal secretary, paralegal. **Visual/performing arts:** Fashion design.

Most popular majors. Business/marketing 73%, health sciences 27%.

Computing on campus. 62 workstations in computer center, student center.

Student life. Freshman orientation: Mandatory. Preregistration for classes offered. **Housing:** Coed dorms, single-sex dorms available. $200 deposit, deadline 3/1. **Activities:** Literary magazine, clubs associated with majors, student activities club, international club.

Student services. Adult student services, career counseling, student employment services, financial aid counseling, health services, personal counseling, placement for graduates, veterans' counselor. **Transfer:** Special adviser, orientation, pre-admission transcript evaluation for new students. Transfer adviser, college fairs on campus for students transferring to 4-year colleges.

Contact. E-mail: admissions@baystate.edu
Phone: (617) 236-8000 Toll-free number: (800) 815-3276
Fax: (617) 536-1735
Pamela DellaPorta, Dean of Admissions, Bay State College, 122 Commonwealth Avenue, Boston, MA 02116

Benjamin Franklin Institute of Technology
Boston, Massachusetts
www.bfit.edu **CB code: 3394**

- Private 2-year technical college
- Commuter campus in very large city

General. Founded in 1908. Regionally accredited. Founded under provisions of will of Benjamin Franklin and managed by Franklin Foundation. **Enrollment:** 380 degree-seeking undergraduates. **Degrees:** 1 bachelor's, 56 associate awarded. **Calendar:** Semester, limited summer session. **Full-time faculty:** 30 total. **Part-time faculty:** 20 total. **Special facilities:** Extensive labs for automotive, architecture, computer, electronic, electrical and mechanized engineering technologies.

Student profile.

Out-of-state:	5%	**25 or older:**	13%

Transfer out. Colleges most students transferred to 2005: Northeastern University, University of Massachusetts at Lowell, Worcester Polytech, Wentworth Institute.

Basis for selection. School achievement record, particularly in mathematics and science, most important. SAT or ACT recommended. Interview and essay recommended.

High school preparation. 8 units required. Required and recommended units include English 4, mathematics 3-5 and science 1-3. Level of math and science required varies by program.

2005-2006 Annual costs. Tuition/fees: $12,500. Per-credit charge: $521. Books/supplies: $600.

2004-2005 Financial aid. Need-based: Need-based aid available for part-time students. **Non-need-based:** Scholarships awarded for academics.

Application procedures. Admission: Priority date 5/1; no deadline. $25 fee, may be waived for applicants with need. Application may be submitted online. **Financial aid:** Priority date 4/1; no closing date. FAFSA required. Applicants notified on a rolling basis starting 3/1; must reply within 4 week(s) of notification.

Academics. Special study options: ESL, liberal arts/career combination. Bachelor's degree programs available on campus. **Credit/placement by examination:** CLEP, IB, institutional tests. **Support services:** Learning center, pre-admission summer program, reduced course load, remedial instruction, study skills assistance, tutoring.

Majors. Architecture: Technology. **Biology:** Biomedical sciences. **Computer sciences:** General, programming. **Construction:** Electrician. **Engineering technology:** Architectural, automotive, biomedical, computer, computer hardware, computer systems, electrical, mechanical, mechanical drafting. **Mechanic/repair:** General, automotive.

Computing on campus. 120 workstations in library, computer center.

Student life. Freshman orientation: Mandatory. Preregistration for classes offered. Half-day program held in August. **Housing:** Student housing available at Boston University. **Activities:** Student government, student newspaper.

Athletics. NJCAA. **Intercollegiate:** Basketball M, soccer M. **Intramural:** Basketball M. **Team name:** Shockers.

Student services. Career counseling, student employment services, financial aid counseling, personal counseling, placement for graduates, veterans' counselor. **Transfer:** Special adviser, orientation, pre-admission transcript evaluation for new students. Transfer adviser, college fairs on campus for students transferring to 4-year colleges.

Contact. E-mail: admis@bfit.edu
Phone: (617) 423-4630 ext. 121 Fax: (617) 482-3706
Norman Kraft, Dean of Enrollment Management, Benjamin Franklin Institute of Technology, 41 Berkeley Street, Boston, MA 02116

Berkshire Community College
Pittsfield, Massachusetts
www.berkshirecc.edu **CB code: 3102**

- Public 2-year community college
- Commuter campus in small city

General. Founded in 1960. Regionally accredited. Elderhostel program site, children's circus, site for Berkshire Opera. **Enrollment:** 1,772 degree-seeking undergraduates; 556 non-degree-seeking students. **Degrees:** 273 associate awarded. **Location:** 40 miles from Albany, New York. **Calendar:** Semester, limited summer session. **Full-time faculty:** 53 total; 72% have terminal degrees, 66% women. **Part-time faculty:** 107 total; 58% have terminal degrees, 2% minority, 46% women. **Special facilities:** Global positioning laboratory, nature trail. **Partnerships:** Formal partnerships with Plastics Network, Applied Technology Council, Berkshire Works, Tech-Prep programs, service learning programs.

Student profile. Among degree-seeking undergraduates, 44% enrolled in a transfer program, 56% enrolled in a vocational program, 399 enrolled as first-time, first-year students, 105 transferred in from other institutions.

Part-time:	50%	**Hispanic American:**	3%
Out-of-state:	4%	**Native American:**	1%
Women:	65%	**International:**	2%
African American:	4%	**25 or older:**	45%
Asian American:	2%		

Transfer out. Colleges most students transferred to 2005: Massachusetts College of Liberal Arts, Westfield State College, University of Massachusetts-Amherst, Framingham College, SUNY Albany.

Basis for selection. Open admission, but selective for some programs. Special requirements for nursing and allied health programs. Fall-only admission to nursing and allied health programs. **Adult students:** Entrance exam policies same as for first-time freshmen.

High school preparation. 1 chemistry, 1 biology, 1 algebra, with demonstrated college level English skills required for nursing and health program applicants.

2005-2006 Annual costs. Tuition/fees: $3,600; $10,620 out-of-state. Per-credit charge: $26 in-state; $260 out-of-state. $133 per-credit-hour (tuition/fees): New England Regional tuition, New York residents. All part-time students pay $120 per-credit-hour. Books/supplies: $720. Personal expenses: $2,038.

2004-2005 Financial aid. Need-based: 77% of total undergraduate aid awarded as scholarships/grants, 23% as loans/jobs. Need-based aid available for part-time students. Work study available nights, weekends and for part-time students. **Additional information:** Tuition waivers available to students who are Massachusetts residents and fall into one of the following categories: adopted or foster children, Massachusetts Rehabilitation Commission clients, high-scoring MCAS students, National Guard members, Native Americans, state employees and their dependents, and veterans.

Application procedures. Admission: No deadline. $10 fee ($35 out-of-state), may be waived for applicants with need. Application must be submitted on paper. Admission notification on a rolling basis. **Financial aid:** Priority date 5/1; no closing date. FAFSA required. Applicants notified on a rolling basis starting 6/1; must reply within 2 week(s) of notification.

Academics. Special study options: Combined bachelor's/graduate degree, cooperative education, cross-registration, distance learning, double major, dual enrollment of high school students, ESL, honors, independent study, internships, liberal arts/career combination, student-designed major, study abroad. Bachelor's degree programs available on campus. License preparation in nursing, occupational therapy, physical therapy. **Credit/placement by examination:** AP, CLEP, IB, institutional tests. 30 credit hours maximum toward associate degree. **Support services:** GED test center, learning center, pre-admission summer program, reduced course load, remedial instruction, study skills assistance, tutoring, writing center.

Majors. Business: General, business admin, hospitality admin, hotel/motel admin, office technology. **Computer sciences:** General. **Conservation:** Environmental science. **Engineering:** General. **Engineering technology:** Electrical. **Health:** Health services, nursing (RN), physical therapy assistant, respiratory therapy technology. **Liberal arts:** Arts/sciences. **Protective services:** Criminal justice, firefighting. **Public administration:** Community org/advocacy. **Visual/performing arts:** General.

Most popular majors. Business/marketing 22%, health sciences 22%, liberal arts 34%, security/protective services 8%.

Computing on campus. 350 workstations in library, computer center, student center. Online library, helpline available.

Student life. Freshman orientation: Mandatory. Preregistration for classes offered. Variety of options, including 1-day orientation/registration and 2-week summer transition program. **Policies:** Alcohol-free campus. Freshmen permitted cars on campus. **Activities:** Bands, choral groups, dance, drama, literary magazine, music ensembles, musical theater, student government, student newspaper, TV station, Phi Theta Kappa honor society.

Student services. Adult student services, alcohol/substance abuse counseling, career counseling, services for economically disadvantaged, student employment services, financial aid counseling, minority student services, on-campus daycare, personal counseling, veterans' counselor, women's services. **Physically disabled:** Services for visually, speech, hearing impaired. **Learning disabled:** Comprehensive services available. **Transfer:** Special adviser, orientation, re-entry adviser, pre-admission transcript evaluation for new students. Transfer adviser, college fairs on campus for students transferring to 4-year colleges.

Contact. E-mail: admissions@berkshirecc.edu
Phone: (413) 499-4660 ext. 242 Toll-free number: (800) 816-1233 ext. 242
Fax: (413) 496-9511
Michael Bullock, Director of Enrollment Services, Berkshire Community College, 1350 West Street, Pittsfield, MA 01201-5786

Bristol Community College

Fall River, Massachusetts — **CB member**
www.bristolcommunitycollege.edu — **CB code: 3110**

- Public 2-year community college
- Commuter campus in small city

General. Founded in 1965. Regionally accredited. **Enrollment:** 5,608 degree-seeking undergraduates; 1,265 non-degree-seeking students. **Degrees:** 745 associate awarded. **Location:** 48 miles from Boston, 17 miles from Providence, Rhode Island. **Calendar:** Semester, extensive summer session. **Full-time faculty:** 100 total. **Part-time faculty:** 330 total. **Special facilities:** Planetarium, greenhouse, robotics laboratory, aquaculture laboratory. **Partnerships:** Formal partnerships with local businesses and non-profit organizations.

Student profile. Among degree-seeking undergraduates, 1,491 enrolled as first-time, first-year students.

Part-time:	49%	**Women:**	64%
Out-of-state:	15%	**25 or older:**	49%

Basis for selection. Open admission, but selective for some programs. Special requirements for allied health and culinary arts programs. SAT scores required for allied health programs. **Homeschooled:** Letter of approval from student's school district which authenticates homeschool education required.

High school preparation. Specific programs have varying course requirements.

2005-2006 Annual costs. Tuition/fees: $3,720; $9,900 out-of-state. Per-credit charge: $24 in-state; $230 out-of-state. Books/supplies: $500. Personal expenses: $1,175.

Financial aid. Need-based: Need-based aid available for part-time students. Work study available nights, weekends and for part-time students. **Non-need-based:** Scholarships awarded for academics, art, leadership, minority status, music/drama.

Application procedures. Admission: Priority date 1/15; no deadline. $10 fee ($35 out-of-state), may be waived for applicants with need. Application must be submitted on paper. Admission notification on a rolling basis beginning on or about 12/1. Must reply by May 1 or within 2 week(s) if notified thereafter. **Financial aid:** Priority date 5/1; no closing date. FAFSA, institutional form required. Applicants notified on a rolling basis starting 5/1; must reply within 2 week(s) of notification.

Academics. Students must complete general education requirement core curriculum prior to graduation. **Special study options:** Cooperative education, cross-registration, distance learning, dual enrollment of high school students, ESL, honors, independent study, internships, student-designed major, weekend college. **Credit/placement by examination:** CLEP, institutional tests. 30 credit hours maximum toward associate degree. **Support services:** GED preparation and test center, learning center, pre-admission summer program, reduced course load, remedial instruction, tutoring, writing center.

Majors. Business: Accounting, administrative services, banking/financial services, business admin. **Communications:** General. **Computer sciences:** General, computer science, data processing, information systems, programming. **Conservation:** Environmental studies. **Education:** General, business, early childhood, elementary, kindergarten/preschool. **Engineering:** General, environmental, manufacturing, mechanical, science, structural. **Engineering technology:** General, civil, computer systems, electrical, electromechanical, environmental, mechanical, water quality. **Family/consumer sciences:** Child care. **Foreign languages:** American Sign Language. **Health:** Clinical lab technology, dental hygiene, medical records technology, medical secretary, nursing (RN), occupational therapy assistant. **Legal studies:** Paralegal.

Liberal arts: Arts/sciences. **Personal/culinary services:** Chef training. **Protective services:** Criminal justice, firefighting. **Public administration:** Human services. **Visual/performing arts:** Art, dramatic.

Computing on campus. Dormitories linked to campus network. Commuter students can connect to campus network. Online course registration, online library, helpline available.

Student life. **Freshman orientation:** Available. Preregistration for classes offered. **Policies:** Freshmen permitted cars on campus. **Activities:** Drama, radio station, student government, student newspaper, TV station, Catholic student association, Christian Fellowship, water watch, international club, Portuguese club, Latino club, Cambodian association, human services club, coalition for social justice.

Student services. Adult student services, alcohol/substance abuse counseling, campus ministries, career counseling, student employment services, financial aid counseling, health services, minority student services, on-campus daycare, personal counseling, placement for graduates, veterans' counselor. **Physically disabled:** Services for visually, speech, hearing impaired. **Learning disabled:** Comprehensive services available. **Transfer:** Special adviser, orientation for new students. Transfer adviser, college fairs on campus for students transferring to 4-year colleges.

Contact. Phone: (508) 678-2811 ext. 2516 Toll-free number: (800) 462-0035 Fax: (508) 730-3265
Rodney Clark, Director of Admissions, Bristol Community College, 777 Elsbree Street, Fall River, MA 02720-7395

Bunker Hill Community College

Boston, Massachusetts — **CB member**
www.bhcc.mass.edu — **CB code: 3123**

- Public 2-year community college
- Commuter campus in very large city

General. Founded in 1973. Regionally accredited. **Enrollment:** 5,723 degree-seeking undergraduates; 2,114 non-degree-seeking students. **Degrees:** 505 associate awarded. **Location:** 5 miles from downtown. **Calendar:** Semester, extensive summer session. **Full-time faculty:** 123 total; 60% women. **Part-time faculty:** 325 total; 50% women. **Class size:** 52% < 20, 48% 20-39, less than 1% 40-49, less than 1% 50-99. **Special facilities:** Adaptive computer laboratory.

Student profile. Among degree-seeking undergraduates, 62% enrolled in a transfer program, 38% enrolled in a vocational program, 1,356 enrolled as first-time, first-year students, 348 transferred in from other institutions.

Part-time:	62%	**Hispanic American:**	14%
Women:	60%	**Native American:**	1%
African American:	29%	**International:**	6%
Asian American:	14%	**25 or older:**	45%

Transfer out. **Colleges most students transferred to 2005:** University of Massachusetts Boston, Salem State College, Northeastern University, Bentley College, Suffolk University.

Basis for selection. Open admission, but selective for some programs. Special requirements for nursing, medical radiography, surgical technology, ultrasound, overhead electrical line worker programs. Allied Health Aptitude Test required for allied health programs; school-administered exam required for nursing and medical imaging programs. **Adult students:** Entrance exam policies same as for first-time freshmen.

2005-2006 Annual costs. Tuition/fees: $3,000; $9,180 out-of-state. Per-credit charge: $24 in-state; $230 out-of-state. New England Regional Tuition: $112 per-credit-hour. Books/supplies: $1,000. Personal expenses: $1,150.

2004-2005 Financial aid. **Need-based:** 88% of total undergraduate aid awarded as scholarships/grants, 12% as loans/jobs. Need-based aid available for part-time students. Work study available for part-time students. **Non-need-based:** Scholarships awarded for academics.

Application procedures. **Admission:** Priority date 5/1; deadline 9/2. $10 fee ($35 out-of-state), may be waived for applicants with need. Application must be submitted on paper. Admission notification on a rolling basis. Must reply by May 1 or within 2 week(s) if notified thereafter. **Financial aid:** Priority date 4/15; no closing date. FAFSA required. Applicants notified on a rolling basis starting 6/1; must reply within 2 week(s) of notification.

Academics. Some courses taught off-campus in the community. **Special study options:** Cross-registration, distance learning, double major, dual enrollment of high school students, ESL, external degree, honors, independent study, internships, liberal arts/career combination, study abroad, weekend college. License preparation in nursing, paramedic, radiology, real estate. **Credit/placement by examination:** AP, CLEP, institutional tests. 45 credit hours maximum toward associate degree. **Support services:** GED preparation, learning center, pre-admission summer program, reduced course load, remedial instruction, study skills assistance, tutoring, writing center.

Majors. **Biology:** General. **Business:** Accounting, business admin, finance, hospitality admin, international, office/clerical, operations, tourism/travel. **Communications:** General, media studies. **Computer sciences:** Applications programming, computer science, data entry, database management, networking, system admin, web page design. **Education:** General, early childhood. **Engineering technology:** Computer systems, software. **English:** English lit. **Foreign languages:** General. **Health:** Cardiovascular technology, medical radiologic technology/radiation therapy, medical secretary, nursing (RN), sonography. **History:** General. **Math:** General. **Personal/culinary services:** Chef training. **Physical sciences:** Chemistry, physics. **Protective services:** Corrections, fire safety technology, law enforcement admin, security management. **Psychology:** General. **Public administration:** Human services. **Social sciences:** Sociology. **Visual/performing arts:** Art, design, dramatic.

Most popular majors. Business/marketing 31%, computer/information sciences 9%, education 6%, health sciences 18%, liberal arts 10%, security/protective services 6%.

Computing on campus. 640 workstations in library, computer center. Commuter students can connect to campus network. Online course registration, online library, helpline available.

Student life. **Freshman orientation:** Available. Preregistration for classes offered. **Activities:** Jazz band, choral groups, drama, literary magazine, music ensembles, musical theater, radio station, student government, student newspaper, African American cultural society, Alpha Kappa Mu honor society, Amnesty International, Arab students association, Asian students association, Brazilian cultural club, criminal justice society, gay, lesbian, bisexual and transgender student union, multicultural club, student government association.

Athletics. NJCAA. **Intercollegiate:** Baseball M, basketball, golf, soccer, softball W. **Intramural:** Basketball, table tennis, tennis. **Team name:** Bulldogs.

Student services. Adult student services, career counseling, services for economically disadvantaged, student employment services, financial aid counseling, health services, on-campus daycare, personal counseling, placement for graduates, veterans' counselor. **Physically disabled:** Services for visually, speech, hearing impaired. **Transfer:** Special adviser, orientation, reentry adviser, pre-admission transcript evaluation for new students. Transfer center, transfer adviser, college fairs on campus for students transferring to 4-year colleges.

Contact. E-mail: enrollment@bhcc.mass.edu
Phone: (617) 228-2420 Fax: (617) 228-2082
Debra Boyer, Registrar/Director of Enrollment Services, Bunker Hill Community College, 250 New Rutherford Avenue, Boston, MA 02129-2925

Cape Cod Community College

West Barnstable, Massachusetts — **CB member**
www.capecod.edu — **CB code: 3289**

- Public 2-year community college
- Commuter campus in small town

General. Founded in 1961. Regionally accredited. **Enrollment:** 3,209 degree-seeking undergraduates. **Degrees:** 345 associate awarded. **Location:** 79 miles from Boston, 80 miles from Providence, Rhode Island. **Calendar:** Semester, limited summer session. **Full-time faculty:** 62 total; 16% minority, 64% women. **Part-time faculty:** 227 total; 4% minority, 62% women. **Special facilities:** Source collection for Cape Cod history, marshland nature preserve, maritime studies collection. **Partnerships:** Formal partnerships with Tech Prep, School-to-Career, Cape Cod Technology Council Apprenticeship Program.

Student profile. Among degree-seeking undergraduates, 207 transferred in from other institutions.

Transfer out. **Colleges most students transferred to 2005:** Bridgewater State College, University of Massachusetts (Amherst, Boston, Dartmouth), Suffolk University.

Basis for selection. Open admission, but selective for some programs. Special requirements for dental hygiene and nursing programs; priority given to Massachusetts residents. Interview recommended for dental hygiene and nursing programs. **Adult students:** Entrance exam policies same as for first-time freshmen.

High school preparation. Chemistry with lab and algebra required for dental hygiene and nursing programs. Nursing also requires biology with anatomy and physiology unit labs.

2005-2006 Annual costs. Tuition/fees: $3,660; $9,840 out-of-state. Per-credit charge: $24 in-state; $230 out-of-state. Books/supplies: $800. Personal expenses: $1,072.

2004-2005 Financial aid. Need-based: 203 full-time freshmen applied for aid; 139 were judged to have need; 132 of these received aid. Average need met was 55%. Average scholarship/grant was $3,252; average loan $1,549. 79% of total undergraduate aid awarded as scholarships/grants, 21% as loans/jobs. Need-based aid available for part-time students. Work study available for part-time students. **Non-need-based:** Awarded to 68 full-time undergraduates, including 32 freshmen. Scholarships awarded for academics, art, job skills, leadership, music/drama, state residency.

Application procedures. Admission: Priority date 8/10; no deadline. $10 fee ($35 out-of-state), may be waived for applicants with need. Admission notification on a rolling basis. Must reply by May 1 or within 4 week(s) if notified thereafter. January 5 application priority date for nursing, February 1 for dental hygiene. **Financial aid:** Priority date 4/1; no closing date. FAFSA required. Applicants notified on a rolling basis starting 5/1.

Academics. Special study options: Accelerated study, cooperative education, cross-registration, distance learning, dual enrollment of high school students, ESL, honors, independent study, internships, study abroad. Bachelor's degree programs available on campus. License preparation in dental hygiene, nursing, paramedic, real estate. **Credit/placement by examination:** AP, CLEP, institutional tests. 30 credit hours maximum toward associate degree. **Support services:** GED preparation and test center, learning center, reduced course load, remedial instruction, study skills assistance, tutoring, writing center.

Majors. Business: Accounting, accounting/business management, administrative services, business admin, executive assistant, hotel/motel admin, management science, marketing, office management, office/clerical. **Communications:** General, journalism, media studies, public relations. **Computer sciences:** General, applications programming, computer science, information systems, information technology, LAN/WAN management, networking, web page design, webmaster. **Conservation:** General, environmental science, environmental studies. **Education:** General, early childhood, kindergarten/preschool. **Engineering:** General. **Foreign languages:** General. **Health:** Dental hygiene, EMT paramedic, medical secretary, nursing (RN), predentistry, premedicine, prenursing, prepharmacy. **Interdisciplinary:** Behavioral sciences, global studies, natural sciences. **Legal studies:** Legal secretary. **Liberal arts:** Arts/sciences. **Math:** General. **Parks/recreation:** General, health/fitness. **Philosophy/religion:** Philosophy. **Physical sciences:** General. **Protective services:** Criminal justice, fire safety technology, firefighting, law enforcement admin. **Psychology:** General. **Public administration:** Human services. **Social sciences:** General, sociology. **Visual/performing arts:** General, commercial/advertising art, dance, dramatic, graphic design.

Most popular majors. Business/marketing 9%, health sciences 28%, liberal arts 49%, security/protective services 7%.

Computing on campus. 240 workstations in library, computer center, student center. Commuter students can connect to campus network. Helpline, wireless network available.

Student life. Freshman orientation: Mandatory. Preregistration for classes offered. Half-day program includes meeting with assigned adviser. **Policies:** Freshmen permitted cars on campus. **Activities:** Choral groups, dance, drama, literary magazine, music ensembles, musical theater, radio station, student government, student newspaper, TV station, Phi Theta Kappa, Earth Workers club, cultural affairs club, diversity club, learning disability support group, gay-bi-lesbian club.

Athletics. Intramural: Badminton, basketball, racquetball, tennis, volleyball. **Team name:** Helmsmen.

Student services. Adult student services, alcohol/substance abuse counseling, career counseling, services for economically disadvantaged, student employment services, financial aid counseling, health services, minority student services, on-campus daycare, personal counseling, placement for graduates, veterans' counselor, women's services. **Physically disabled:** Services for visually, speech, hearing impaired. **Transfer:** Special adviser, orientation, re-entry adviser, pre-admission transcript evaluation for new students. Transfer adviser, college fairs on campus for students transferring to 4-year colleges.

Contact. E-mail: admiss@capecod.mass.edu
Phone: (508) 362-2131 ext. 4311 Toll-free
number: (877) 846-3672 ext. 4311 Fax: (508) 375-4089
Susan Kline-Symington, Director of Admissions, Cape Cod Community College, 2240 Iyanough Road, West Barnstable, MA 02668-1599

Dean College

Franklin, Massachusetts **CB member**
www.dean.edu **CB code: 3352**

- Private 2-year junior and liberal arts college
- Residential campus in large town
- SAT or ACT (ACT writing optional), application essay required

General. Founded in 1865. Regionally accredited. **Enrollment:** 1,249 degree-seeking undergraduates. **Degrees:** 22 bachelor's, 246 associate awarded. **Location:** 30 miles from Boston, 30 miles from Providence, Rhode Island. **Calendar:** Semester, limited summer session. **Full-time faculty:** 30 total. **Part-time faculty:** 67 total. **Special facilities:** Telecommunication center. **Partnerships:** Formal partnerships with Putnam Investments (students may earn associate's degree while working) and Suffolk University (offers baccalaureate degrees in criminology, business, communications, information technology, and psychology that may be earned entirely in residence).

Student profile.

Out-of-state:	55%	Live on campus:	84%

Basis for selection. School achievement record, recommendations most important. Interview recommended.

High school preparation. Recommended units include English 4, mathematics 3, history 3, science 2 (laboratory 1).

2006-2007 Annual costs. Tuition/fees (projected): $23,783. Per-credit charge: $452. Room/board: $10,253. Books/supplies: $1,500.

2005-2006 Financial aid. Need-based: 65% of total undergraduate aid awarded as scholarships/grants, 35% as loans/jobs. Need-based aid available for part-time students. **Non-need-based:** Scholarships awarded for academics, athletics, leadership, music/drama.

Application procedures. Admission: No deadline. $35 fee, may be waived for applicants with need. Application may be submitted online. Admission notification on a rolling basis beginning on or about 12/15. Must reply by May 1 or within 2 week(s) if notified thereafter. **Financial aid:** Priority date 3/1; no closing date. FAFSA required. Applicants notified on a rolling basis starting 4/1; must reply within 3 week(s) of notification.

Academics. Special study options: ESL, honors, independent study, student-designed major. Bachelor's degree programs available on campus. **Credit/placement by examination:** AP, CLEP, IB. **Support services:** Learning center, pre-admission summer program, reduced course load, remedial instruction, study skills assistance, tutoring, writing center.

Majors. Business: General, business admin. **Communications:** General. **Computer sciences:** General. **Education:** Early childhood, physical. **Health:** Athletic training. **History:** General. **Liberal arts:** Arts/sciences. **Math:** General. **Parks/recreation:** Health/fitness, sports admin. **Physical sciences:** General. **Protective services:** Criminal justice, law enforcement admin. **Psychology:** General. **Visual/performing arts:** Dance, dramatic.

Computing on campus. Wireless network available.

Student life. Freshman orientation: Mandatory, $200 fee. Preregistration for classes offered. **Housing:** Guaranteed on-campus for all undergraduates. Coed dorms, single-sex dorms available. $400 deposit, deadline 5/1. **Activities:** Jazz band, choral groups, dance, drama, literary magazine, music ensembles, musical theater, radio station, student government, TV station, Hillel, Christian Fellowship.

Athletics. NJCAA. **Intercollegiate:** Baseball M, basketball, football (tackle) M, golf M, lacrosse, soccer, softball W, volleyball W. **Intramural:** Basketball, soccer, softball W, volleyball. **Team name:** Bulldogs.

Student services. Adult student services, career counseling, financial aid counseling, health services. **Physically disabled:** Services for visually, speech, hearing impaired. **Learning disabled:** Comprehensive services available. **Transfer:** Special adviser, orientation for new students. Transfer center, transfer adviser, college fairs on campus for students transferring to 4-year colleges.

Contact. E-mail: admission@dean.edu
Phone: (508) 541-1508 Toll-free number: (877) 879-3326
Fax: (508) 541-8726
Paul Vaccaro, Dean of Admissions, Dean College, 99 Main Street, Franklin, MA 02038-1994

Fisher College
Boston, Massachusetts
www.fisher.edu **CB code: 3391**

- Private 2-year liberal arts college
- Residential campus in very large city

General. Founded in 1903. Regionally accredited. Branch campuses in Boston, North Attleboro and New Bedford. **Enrollment:** 507 degree-seeking undergraduates. **Degrees:** 19 bachelor's, 91 associate awarded. **Location:** Downtown. **Calendar:** Semester, limited summer session. **Full-time faculty:** 21 total; 33% have terminal degrees, 5% minority, 67% women. **Part-time faculty:** 24 total; 12% minority, 50% women. **Class size:** 53% < 20, 47% 20-39. **Partnerships:** Formal agreements with TechPrep programs in Massachusetts.

Student profile. Among degree-seeking undergraduates, 219 enrolled as first-time, first-year students, 33 transferred in from other institutions.

Part-time:	1%	**Hispanic American:**	16%
Out-of-state:	29%	**International:**	5%
Women:	66%	**25 or older:**	4%
African American:	19%	**Live on campus:**	51%
Asian American:	4%		

Transfer out. 24% of students enrolled in the transfer program go on to 4-year colleges.

Basis for selection. High school GPA, test scores, personal essays and recommendation letters reviewed. Essay recommended. **Adult students:** Entrance exam policies same as for first-time freshmen. **Learning Disabled:** Accommodation review available upon request. Students requesting review should submit latest individualized education plan (IEP) as well as current psychoeducational testing.

High school preparation. Recommended units include English 4, mathematics 3, social studies 3 and science 2.

2005-2006 Annual costs. Tuition/fees: $18,450. Room/board: $11,210. Books/supplies: $1,200. Personal expenses: $1,200.

2005-2006 Financial aid. Need-based: Average need met was 44%. Average scholarship/grant was $9,046; average loan $2,959. 94% of total undergraduate aid awarded as scholarships/grants, 6% as loans/jobs. Need-based aid available for part-time students. Work study available nights, weekends and for part-time students. **Non-need-based:** Scholarships awarded for academics, alumni affiliation, state residency.

Application procedures. Admission: No deadline. $25 fee, may be waived for applicants with need. Application may be submitted online. Admission notification on a rolling basis. **Financial aid:** Priority date 3/1; no closing date. FAFSA required. Applicants notified on a rolling basis starting 3/1; must reply within 2 week(s) of notification.

Academics. Special study options: Cross-registration, distance learning, double major, ESL, honors, internships, liberal arts/career combination. Bachelor's degree programs available on campus. **Credit/placement by examination:** AP, CLEP, IB, institutional tests. 30 credit hours maximum toward associate degree, 75 toward bachelor's. Institution follows ACE guide for credit by examination. **Support services:** Learning center, reduced course load, remedial instruction, study skills assistance, tutoring, writing center.

Majors. Business: Business admin, fashion, hospitality admin, tourism/travel. **Education:** Early childhood. **Family/consumer sciences:** Clothing/textiles. **Liberal arts:** Arts/sciences. **Psychology:** General.

Most popular majors. Business/marketing 47%, education 9%, liberal arts 25%, visual/performing arts 7%.

Computing on campus. 60 workstations in dormitories, library, computer center, student center. Dormitories wired for high-speed internet access and linked to campus network. Helpline, repair service available.

Student life. Freshman orientation: Mandatory. Preregistration for classes offered. Several 1-day preregistration days scheduled throughout summer with full 2-day orientation program prior to start of classes. **Housing:** Coed dorms, single-sex dorms available. $400 deposit. **Activities:** Drama, film society, literary magazine, student government.

Athletics. NAIA. **Intercollegiate:** Baseball M, basketball, softball W. **Team name:** Falcons.

Student services. Adult student services, alcohol/substance abuse counseling, career counseling, student employment services, financial aid counseling, health services, personal counseling, placement for graduates, veterans' counselor. **Transfer:** Special adviser, orientation, re-entry adviser, pre-admission transcript evaluation for new students. Transfer adviser, college fairs on campus for students transferring to 4-year colleges.

Contact. E-mail: admissions@fisher.edu
Phone: (617) 236-8818 Toll-free number: (866) 266-6007
Fax: (617) 236-5473
Rober Melaragni, Director of Admissions, Fisher College, 118 Beacon Street, Boston, MA 02116

Gibbs College
Boston, Massachusetts
www.gibbsboston.edu **CB code: 3473**

- For-profit 2-year junior college
- Commuter campus in very large city
- Interview required

General. Founded in 1911. Accredited by ACICS. Ongoing placement assistance for graduates. **Enrollment:** 900 degree-seeking undergraduates. **Degrees:** 302 associate awarded. **Location:** Downtown. **Calendar:** Quarter, extensive summer session. **Special facilities:** Learning assistance center.

Basis for selection. Open admission. ACCUPLACER required for placement.

2005-2006 Annual costs. Tuition/fees: $15,000.

Financial aid. All financial aid based on need. Need-based aid available for part-time students.

Application procedures. Admission: No deadline. $25 fee. Application may be submitted online. Admission notification on a rolling basis. **Financial aid:** No deadline. FAFSA, institutional form required. Applicants notified on a rolling basis.

Academics. Special study options: Cooperative education, internships, liberal arts/career combination, study abroad. **Credit/placement by examination:** CLEP. **Support services:** Learning center, tutoring.

Majors. Business: Administrative services, business admin, hospitality admin. **Communications:** Digital media. **Communications technology:** Desktop publishing, graphics. **Computer sciences:** Networking. **Health:** Management/clinical assistant, medical assistant, medical secretary, office admin, office assistant, receptionist. **Legal studies:** Legal secretary. **Visual/performing arts:** Design.

Computing on campus. 135 workstations in library. Commuter students can connect to campus network. Online library available.

Student life. Freshman orientation: Mandatory. **Activities:** Student government.

Student services. Career counseling, student employment services, financial aid counseling, placement for graduates. **Transfer:** Special adviser, orientation, re-entry adviser for new students. Transfer adviser for students transferring to 4-year colleges.

Contact. E-mail: jtyler@gibbsboston.edu
Phone: (617) 578-7100 Toll-free number: (800) 675-4557
Fax: (617) 578-7163
Jaimee Tyler, Director of High School Admissions, Gibbs College, 126 Newbury Street, Boston, MA 02116

Greenfield Community College
Greenfield, Massachusetts
www.gcc.mass.edu **CB code: 3420**

- Public 2-year community college
- Commuter campus in large town

General. Founded in 1962. Regionally accredited. Students may enroll in credit courses taught at Smith College and Veterans Hospital, Northampton. **Enrollment:** 1,958 degree-seeking undergraduates; 259 non-degree-seeking students. **Degrees:** 262 associate awarded. **Location:** 40 miles from Springfield. **Calendar:** Semester, limited summer session. **Full-time faculty:** 56

total. **Part-time faculty:** 139 total. **Class size:** 28% < 20, 70% 20-39, 1% 40-49, less than 1% 50-99.

Student profile. Among degree-seeking undergraduates, 325 enrolled as first-time, first-year students.

Part-time:	51%	**Women:**	63%
Out-of-state:	11%	**25 or older:**	46%

Transfer out. Colleges most students transferred to 2005: University of Massachusetts-Amherst, Elms College, Westfield State College, Smith College, Massachusetts College of Liberal Arts.

Basis for selection. Open admission, but selective for some programs. Special entrance requirements for occupational technology, nursing, paramedic, massage therapy, outdoor leadership programs. Students whose native language is not English must take institutional ESOL test. **Adult students:** Entrance exam policies same as for first-time freshmen.

High school preparation. Students from public high schools in the Commonwealth must be MCAS graduates, or demonstrate an ability to benefit.

2005-2006 Annual costs. Tuition/fees: $4,007; $11,657 out-of-state. Per-credit charge: $26 in-state; $260 out-of-state. Books/supplies: $850. Personal expenses: $1,560.

Financial aid. All financial aid based on need. Need-based aid available for part-time students. Work study available nights, weekends and for part-time students.

Application procedures. Admission: No deadline. $10 fee ($35 out-of-state), may be waived for applicants with need. Admission notification on a rolling basis. Limited space available in nursing and outdoor leadership programs. Application priority date February 1. **Financial aid:** Priority date 4/15; no closing date. FAFSA, institutional form required. Applicants notified on a rolling basis starting 5/1; must reply within 2 week(s) of notification.

Academics. Special study options: Cooperative education, cross-registration, distance learning, dual enrollment of high school students, ESL, honors, independent study, internships, liberal arts/career combination. License preparation in nursing, paramedic, real estate. **Credit/placement by examination:** AP, CLEP, institutional tests. 15 credit hours maximum toward associate degree. **Support services:** GED test center, learning center, reduced course load, remedial instruction, study skills assistance, tutoring.

Majors. Business: General, accounting, administrative services, business admin. **Computer sciences:** General. **Education:** Early childhood. **Engineering:** Science. **Health:** Nursing (RN), occupational therapy assistant. **Liberal arts:** Arts/sciences. **Personal/culinary services:** Cosmetic. **Protective services:** Police science. **Visual/performing arts:** Commercial/advertising art.

Most popular majors. Business/marketing 18%, health sciences 15%, liberal arts 46%, visual/performing arts 8%.

Computing on campus. 212 workstations in library, computer center. Commuter students can connect to campus network. Helpline, repair service, wireless network available.

Student life. Freshman orientation: Available. Preregistration for classes offered. **Activities:** Jazz band, choral groups, dance, drama, music ensembles, student government.

Student services. Adult student services, career counseling, services for economically disadvantaged, student employment services, financial aid counseling, health services, personal counseling, placement for graduates, veterans' counselor, women's services. **Physically disabled:** Services for visually, speech, hearing impaired. **Transfer:** Special adviser, orientation, reentry adviser, pre-admission transcript evaluation for new students. Transfer adviser, college fairs on campus for students transferring to 4-year colleges.

Contact. E-mail: admissions@gcc.mass.edu
Phone: (413) 775-1809 Fax: (413) 773-5129
Herbert Hentz, Director of Admissions, Greenfield Community College, One College Drive, Greenfield, MA 01301

Holyoke Community College

Holyoke, Massachusetts — **CB member**
www.hcc.mass.edu — **CB code: 3437**

- Public 2-year community college
- Commuter campus in large town

General. Founded in 1946. Regionally accredited. **Enrollment:** 5,580 degree-seeking undergraduates; 678 non-degree-seeking students. **Degrees:** 791 associate awarded. **ROTC:** Army, Air Force. **Location:** 8 miles from Springfield. **Calendar:** Semester, extensive summer session. **Full-time faculty:** 112 total; 7% minority, 56% women. **Part-time faculty:** 283 total. **Class size:** 48% < 20, 51% 20-39, less than 1% 40-49.

Student profile. Among degree-seeking undergraduates, 1,524 enrolled as first-time, first-year students, 358 transferred in from other institutions.

Part-time:	46%	**Asian American:**	2%
Out-of-state:	1%	**Hispanic American:**	14%
Women:	65%	**Native American:**	1%
African American:	6%	**25 or older:**	35%

Transfer out. Colleges most students transferred to 2005: University of Massachusetts-Amherst, Western New England College, American International College, Westfield State College, Elms College.

Basis for selection. Open admission, but selective for some programs. Special requirements for nursing, radiography, animal sciences, practical nursing programs. Audition required of music majors. Portfolio required of fine arts majors.

2005-2006 Annual costs. Tuition/fees: $3,188; $9,368 out-of-state. Per-credit charge: $24 in-state; $230 out-of-state. Books/supplies: $800. Personal expenses: $2,400.

2004-2005 Financial aid. Need-based: 80% of total undergraduate aid awarded as scholarships/grants, 20% as loans/jobs. Need-based aid available for part-time students. Work study available nights and for part-time students. **Non-need-based:** Scholarships awarded for academics, art, leadership, music/drama.

Application procedures. Admission: No deadline. $10 fee, may be waived for applicants with need. Admission notification on a rolling basis. **Financial aid:** Priority date 5/1; no closing date. FAFSA required. Applicants notified on a rolling basis starting 5/1; must reply within 2 week(s) of notification.

Academics. Special study options: Cooperative education, cross-registration, distance learning, double major, dual enrollment of high school students, ESL, honors, independent study, internships, liberal arts/career combination, student-designed major, study abroad, teacher certification program, weekend college. License preparation in nursing. **Credit/placement by examination:** AP, CLEP, institutional tests. 30 credit hours maximum toward associate degree. **Support services:** GED preparation and test center, learning center, reduced course load, remedial instruction, study skills assistance, tutoring, writing center.

Majors. Business: Accounting technology, administrative services, business admin, human resources, restaurant/food services, retailing. **Computer sciences:** Applications programming. **Conservation:** Environmental science. **Engineering:** General. **Family/consumer sciences:** Child care. **Health:** Medical radiologic technology/radiation therapy, nursing (RN), optician, pharmacy assistant, veterinary technology/assistant. **Liberal arts:** Arts/sciences. **Parks/recreation:** Health/fitness, sports admin. **Protective services:** Criminal justice. **Public administration:** Social work. **Social sciences:** Geography. **Visual/performing arts:** Art.

Most popular majors. Business/marketing 19%, family/consumer sciences 6%, health sciences 13%, liberal arts 43%, security/protective services 8%.

Computing on campus. 434 workstations in library, computer center, student center. Commuter students can connect to campus network. Online course registration, online library, helpline, wireless network available.

Student life. Freshman orientation: Mandatory. Preregistration for classes offered. **Activities:** Jazz band, choral groups, drama, literary magazine, music ensembles, musical theater, radio station, student government, student newspaper, symphony orchestra, more than 30 clubs and organizations.

Athletics. NJCAA. **Intercollegiate:** Baseball M, basketball, golf, soccer, softball W, tennis, volleyball W. **Intramural:** Basketball, soccer, softball, tennis, volleyball. **Team name:** Cougars.

Student services. Adult student services, alcohol/substance abuse counseling, campus ministries, career counseling, services for economically disadvantaged, student employment services, financial aid counseling, health services, minority student services, on-campus daycare, personal counseling, placement for graduates, veterans' counselor, women's services. **Physically disabled:** Services for visually, speech, hearing impaired. **Transfer:** Special adviser, orientation for new students. Transfer adviser, college fairs on campus for students transferring to 4-year colleges.

Contact. E-mail: admission@hcc.mass.edu
Phone: (413) 552-2850 Toll-free number: (888) 530-8855
Fax: (413) 552-2045
Mark Broadbent, Director of Admissions and Transfer Affairs, Holyoke Community College, 303 Homestead Avenue, Holyoke, MA 01040

ITT Technical Institute: Norwood

Norwood, Massachusetts
www.itt-tech.edu **CB code: 2699**

- For-profit 2-year technical college
- Commuter campus in small city

General. Accredited by ACICS. **Calendar:** Quarter.

Annual costs/financial aid. Tuition varies by program, $260-$368 per credit hour.

Contact. Phone: (781) 278-7200
Director of Recruitment, 333 Providence Highway, Norwood, MA 02062

ITT Technical Institute: Woburn

Woburn, Massachusetts
www.itt-tech.edu

- For-profit 2-year technical college
- Small city

General. Accredited by ACICS. **Calendar:** Quarter.

Annual costs/financial aid. Tuition varies by program, $260-$368 per credit hour.

Contact. Phone: (781) 937-8324
Director of Recruitment, 10 Forbes Road, Woburn, MA 01801

Laboure College

Boston, Massachusetts
www.laboure.edu **CB code: 3287**

- Private 2-year health science and junior college affiliated with Roman Catholic Church
- Commuter campus in very large city
- Interview required

General. Founded in 1971. Regionally accredited. Affiliated with more than 100 health care agencies in Greater Boston area. **Enrollment:** 450 degree-seeking undergraduates. **Degrees:** 94 associate awarded. **Location:** 5 miles from downtown. **Calendar:** Semester, limited summer session. **Full-time faculty:** 15 total. **Part-time faculty:** 10 total. **Class size:** 87% < 20, 13% 20-39.

Student profile.

Out-of-state:	1%	**25 or older:**	70%

Basis for selection. School achievement record, recommendations, interview important, work experience considered.

High school preparation. 10 units required; 16 recommended. Required and recommended units include English 4, mathematics 3, science 1-2 (laboratory 1).

2005-2006 Annual costs. Tuition/fees: $12,680. Per-credit charge: $410. Books/supplies: $800. Personal expenses: $1,000.

Financial aid. Need-based: Need-based aid available for part-time students. Work study available nights and for part-time students. **Non-need-based:** Scholarships awarded for academics, alumni affiliation, leadership, religious affiliation. **Additional information:** Allied Health Scholarship: covers cost of general education courses for students enrolled in electroneurodiagnostic technology, health information technology, and nutrition and food management programs; constitutes significant reduction in tuition. Caritas Christi Scholarship: for students who work 16 hours per week at a Caritas Christi healthcare agency; covers 25% of tuition for nursing and radiation therapy courses; also covers 50% of cost of nursing courses for students with LPN credential. Evening LPN Scholarship: discounts tuition 75% for evening nursing majors with LPN credential.

Application procedures. Admission: No deadline. $25 fee, may be waived for applicants with need. Admission notification on a rolling basis. **Financial aid:** Priority date 4/1; no closing date. FAFSA, institutional form required. Applicants notified on a rolling basis starting 5/15; must reply within 2 week(s) of notification.

Academics. Special study options: Accelerated study, independent study, liberal arts/career combination. License preparation in nursing. **Credit/placement by examination:** CLEP, institutional tests. 23 credit hours maximum toward associate degree. **Support services:** Learning center, preadmission summer program, reduced course load, remedial instruction, tutoring.

Majors. Health: Clinical lab science, dietetics, medical radiologic technology/radiation therapy, medical records technology, nuclear medical technology, nursing (RN), radiologic technology/medical imaging.

Most popular majors. Family/consumer sciences 8%, health sciences 92%.

Computing on campus. 20 workstations in library, computer center.

Student life. Freshman orientation: Available. Preregistration for classes offered. One day information session and tour prior to fall term. **Activities:** Student government.

Student services. Campus ministries, career counseling, financial aid counseling, personal counseling.

Contact. E-mail: admit@laboure.edu
Phone: (617) 296-8300 ext. 4016 Fax: (617) 296-7947
Stephanie McCormick, Director of Admissions, Laboure College, 2120 Dorchester Avenue, Boston, MA 02124-5698

Marian Court College

Swampscott, Massachusetts **CB member**
www.mariancourt.edu **CB code: 9100**

- Private 2-year junior college affiliated with Roman Catholic Church
- Commuter campus in large town
- Application essay, interview required

General. Founded in 1964. Regionally accredited. Evening division on quarter system. **Enrollment:** 220 full-time, degree-seeking students. **Degrees:** 54 associate awarded. **Location:** 5 miles from Lynn, 20 miles from Boston. **Calendar:** Semester, limited summer session. **Full-time faculty:** 7 total. **Part-time faculty:** 20 total.

Basis for selection. High school grades, recommendations, interview important. Institutional English and math tests used for placement.

2005-2006 Annual costs. Tuition/fees: $12,000. Evening program: $675 for 3 credit course. Books/supplies: $600. Personal expenses: $1,957.

Financial aid. Need-based: Need-based aid available for part-time students. **Non-need-based:** Scholarships awarded for academics.

Application procedures. Admission: No deadline. No application fee. Admission notification on a rolling basis. Must reply by May 1 or within 2 week(s) if notified thereafter. **Financial aid:** Priority date 4/1; no closing date. FAFSA, institutional form required. Applicants notified on a rolling basis starting 4/15.

Academics. Freshman Seminar required of all freshmen. Also special Adult Learner Freshman Seminars available. Writing lab available evenings for extra assistance. **Special study options:** Cross-registration, double major, honors, independent study, internships, weekend college. Member Northeast Consortium of Colleges and Universities in Massachusetts. **Credit/placement by examination:** CLEP, institutional tests. 15 credit hours maximum toward associate degree. **Support services:** Reduced course load, tutoring.

Majors. Business: Accounting, administrative services, business admin, hospitality admin, human resources, management information systems, marketing, tourism/travel. **Computer sciences:** Data entry, web page design. **Health:** Medical secretary, medical transcription. **Legal studies:** Legal secretary, paralegal. **Liberal arts:** Arts/sciences. **Protective services:** Law enforcement admin, security services.

Computing on campus. 53 workstations in library, computer center, student center.

Student life. Activities: Literary magazine, student government, Mercy Outreach, travel club, campus ministry, student life organization.

Student services. Adult student services, career counseling, student employment services, health services, personal counseling, placement for graduates. **Transfer:** Special adviser for new students. Transfer adviser, college fairs on campus for students transferring to 4-year colleges.

Contact. E-mail: lparker@mariancourt.edu
Phone: (781) 595-6768 Fax: (781) 595-3560
Maureen Sanphy, Director of Admissions, Marian Court College, 35 Little's Point Road, Swampscott, MA 01907-2896

Massachusetts Bay Community College
Wellesley Hills, Massachusetts
www.massbay.edu **CB code: 3294**

- Public 2-year community college
- Commuter campus in large town

General. Founded in 1961. Regionally accredited. **Enrollment:** 4,512 degree-seeking undergraduates; 503 non-degree-seeking students. **Degrees:** 420 associate awarded. **Location:** 13 miles from Boston. **Calendar:** Semester, extensive summer session. **Full-time faculty:** 73 total; 15% minority, 58% women. **Part-time faculty:** 263 total; 11% minority, 48% women. **Class size:** 40% < 20, 58% 20-39, less than 1% 40-49, 1% 50-99. **Special facilities:** Advanced technology center (technology and health science laboratories). **Partnerships:** Formal partnerships with Toyota, Chrysler, General Motors, EMC2.

Student profile. Among degree-seeking undergraduates, 1,353 enrolled as first-time, first-year students, 396 transferred in from other institutions.

Part-time:	54%	**Asian American:**	4%
Out-of-state:	1%	**Hispanic American:**	7%
Women:	57%	**International:**	2%
African American:	12%	**25 or older:**	42%

Transfer out. Colleges most students transferred to 2005: Framingham State College, University of Massachusetts-Boston, Northeastern University, Bentley College.

Basis for selection. Open admission, but selective for some programs. Special requirements for nursing, occupational therapy, radiologic technology, paramedic, respiratory therapy programs.

High school preparation. Some programs require special academic preparation.

2005-2006 Annual costs. Tuition/fees: $3,570; $9,750 out-of-state. Per-credit charge: $24 in-state; $230 out-of-state. Books/supplies: $800. Personal expenses: $2,966.

2004-2005 Financial aid. Need-based: 72% of total undergraduate aid awarded as scholarships/grants, 28% as loans/jobs. Need-based aid available for part-time students.

Application procedures. Admission: No deadline. $35 fee ($35 out-of-state), may be waived for applicants with need. Application may be submitted online. Admission notification on a rolling basis. **Financial aid:** Priority date 8/30; no closing date. FAFSA, institutional form required. Applicants notified on a rolling basis starting 4/1.

Academics. Special study options: Cooperative education, distance learning, dual enrollment of high school students, honors, internships, liberal arts/career combination, study abroad. **Credit/placement by examination:** AP, CLEP, IB, institutional tests. 30 credit hours maximum toward associate degree. **Support services:** Learning center, reduced course load, remedial instruction, study skills assistance, tutoring, writing center.

Majors. Biology: Marine. **Business:** Accounting, business admin, hospitality admin. **Communications:** General. **Computer sciences:** General, computer science, information systems. **Engineering technology:** Automotive, computer, electrical, laser/optical. **Family/consumer sciences:** Child care. **Health:** Medical informatics, medical radiologic technology/radiation therapy, nursing (RN), occupational therapy assistant, physical therapy assistant, respiratory therapy technology. **Legal studies:** Paralegal. **Liberal arts:** Arts/sciences. **Protective services:** Forensics, law enforcement admin. **Public administration:** Human services. **Science technology:** Biological, chemical. **Social sciences:** General. **Visual/performing arts:** Dramatic.

Computing on campus. 550 workstations in library, computer center, student center. Commuter students can connect to campus network.

Student life. Freshman orientation: Available. **Activities:** Drama, student government, student newspaper, volunteer service corps, Christian Fellowship, Hillel, New World club, Latino club, sexual orientation support group.

Athletics. NJCAA. **Intercollegiate:** Baseball M, basketball, cross-country, golf, soccer M, softball W, tennis. **Intramural:** Ice hockey M, soccer.

Student services. Adult student services, career counseling, student employment services, health services, personal counseling, placement for graduates, veterans' counselor. **Transfer:** Special adviser, orientation, pre-admission transcript evaluation for new students. Transfer adviser, college fairs on campus for students transferring to 4-year colleges.

Contact. E-mail: info@massbay.edu
Phone: (781) 239-2500 Fax: (781) 239-1047
Donna Raposa, Director for Admissions, Massachusetts Bay Community College, 50 Oakland Street, Wellesley Hills, MA 02481

Massasoit Community College
Brockton, Massachusetts **CB member**
www.massasoit.mass.edu **CB code: 3549**

- Public 2-year community college
- Commuter campus in small city

General. Founded in 1966. Regionally accredited. Second campus located in Canton, 10 miles from Boston. **Enrollment:** 4,960 degree-seeking undergraduates; 1,746 non-degree-seeking students. **Degrees:** 635 associate awarded. **Location:** 25 miles from Boston. **Calendar:** Semester, extensive summer session. **Full-time faculty:** 125 total; 56% women. **Part-time faculty:** 363 total; 52% women. **Special facilities:** Theater, conference center.

Student profile. Among degree-seeking undergraduates, 47% enrolled in a transfer program, 53% enrolled in a vocational program, 1,319 enrolled as first-time, first-year students.

Part-time:	41%	**Asian American:**	2%
Out-of-state:	1%	**Hispanic American:**	3%
Women:	56%	**Native American:**	1%
African American:	17%	**25 or older:**	45%

Transfer out. 75% of students enrolled in the transfer program go on to 4-year colleges. **Colleges most students transferred to 2005:** Bridgewater State College, University of Massachusetts Boston, University of Massachusetts Amherst, Stonehill College, Northeastern University.

Basis for selection. Open admission, but selective for some programs. Special requirements for allied health programs. Interview recommended for allied health applicants. **Adult students:** Entrance exam policies same as for first-time freshmen.

2005-2006 Annual costs. Tuition/fees: $3,330; $9,510 out-of-state. Per-credit charge: $24 in-state; $230 out-of-state. Books/supplies: $725. Personal expenses: $1,000.

Financial aid. All financial aid based on need.

Application procedures. Admission: No deadline. No application fee. Application must be submitted on paper. Admission notification on a rolling basis. Application priority date of 02/01 for nursing and radiology programs. **Financial aid:** Priority date 4/15; no closing date. FAFSA required. Applicants notified on a rolling basis starting 6/1.

Academics. Special study options: Accelerated study, cooperative education, cross-registration, distance learning, dual enrollment of high school students, ESL, honors, independent study, internships, liberal arts/career combination, weekend college. License preparation in dental hygiene, nursing, radiology, real estate. **Credit/placement by examination:** CLEP, institutional tests. 30 credit hours maximum toward associate degree. **Support services:** GED preparation and test center, learning center, pre-admission summer program, reduced course load, remedial instruction, study skills assistance, tutoring, writing center.

Majors. Business: Accounting, administrative services, business admin, hospitality admin, management information systems, marketing, office management, operations, tourism/travel. **Communications:** Media studies. **Computer sciences:** General, programming. **Education:** Teacher assistance. **Engineering technology:** Architectural, electrical, heat/ac/refrig, telecommunications. **Family/consumer sciences:** Child care. **Health:** Medical radiologic technology/radiation therapy, nursing (RN), respiratory therapy technology. **Legal studies:** Legal secretary, paralegal. **Liberal arts:** Arts/sciences. **Mechanic/repair:** Diesel. **Personal/culinary services:** Chef training. **Protective services:** Firefighting, police science. **Public administration:** Human services. **Visual/performing arts:** Commercial/advertising art, dramatic, studio arts.

Most popular majors. Business/marketing 18%, engineering/engineering technologies 6%, health sciences 17%, liberal arts 33%, security/protective services 10%.

Computing on campus. 280 workstations in library, computer center, student center. Commuter students can connect to campus network. Helpline, repair service, student web hosting, wireless network available.

Student life. Freshman orientation: Available. Preregistration for classes offered. **Policies:** Freshmen permitted cars on campus. **Activities:** Jazz band, choral groups, dance, drama, literary magazine, music ensembles, musical theater, opera, radio station, student government, student newspaper, TV station, Phi Theta Kappa, art and museum association, Helping Hands, International Touch, senior center, women's resource center, Top of the Rainbow.

Athletics. NJCAA. **Intercollegiate:** Baseball M, basketball, soccer, softball W. **Intramural:** Swimming, weight lifting. **Team name:** Warriors.

Student services. Adult student services, alcohol/substance abuse counseling, career counseling, services for economically disadvantaged, student employment services, financial aid counseling, health services, minority student services, on-campus daycare, personal counseling, placement for graduates, veterans' counselor, women's services. **Physically disabled:** Services for visually, speech, hearing impaired. **Transfer:** Orientation for new students. Transfer adviser, college fairs on campus for students transferring to 4-year colleges.

Contact. Phone: (508) 588-9100 ext. 1411 Fax: (508) 427-1255
Michelle Hughes, Director of Admissions, Massasoit Community College, One Massasoit Boulevard, Brockton, MA 02302-3996

Middlesex Community College

Bedford, Massachusetts **CB member**
www.middlesex.mass.edu **CB code: 3554**

- Public 2-year community college
- Commuter campus in small city

General. Founded in 1969. Regionally accredited. Second main campus located in Lowell. **Enrollment:** 3,400 full-time, degree-seeking students. **Degrees:** 867 associate awarded. **ROTC:** Air Force. **Location:** 16 miles from Boston. **Calendar:** Semester, limited summer session. **Full-time faculty:** 115 total. **Part-time faculty:** 429 total. **Special facilities:** Dental clinic, law center. **Partnerships:** Formal partnerships with business and industry links.

Student profile.

Out-of-state:	1%	**25 or older:**	49%

Basis for selection. Open admission, but selective for some programs. Admission to some health programs based on prerequisite courses in mathematics and science and placement test scores. Some health, counseling, business honors and biotechnology programs require essays, letters of reference and interview.

High school preparation. For some health programs, 1 unit each of biology and chemistry required in addition to 2 units of mathematics at the Algebra I level and above.

2005-2006 Annual costs. Tuition/fees: $3,600; $9,780 out-of-state. Per-credit charge: $24 in-state; $230 out-of-state. New England resident tuition $123 per-credit-hour. Books/supplies: $600. Personal expenses: $600.

Financial aid. Need-based: Need-based aid available for part-time students. Work study available nights, weekends and for part-time students. **Additional information:** Application priority date 5/1 for Massachusetts state funds.

Application procedures. Admission: No deadline. No application fee. Application may be submitted online. Admission notification on a rolling basis. Closing date 02/01 for dental hygiene, 04/01for diagnostic medical sonography. Applications received later considered on space-available basis. Applicants must reply within 2 weeks of acceptance. **Financial aid:** No deadline. FAFSA, institutional form required. Applicants notified on a rolling basis starting 6/1; must reply within 2 week(s) of notification.

Academics. Special study options: Accelerated study, cooperative education, cross-registration, distance learning, dual enrollment of high school students, ESL, exchange student, honors, independent study, internships, liberal arts/career combination, study abroad, weekend college. **Credit/placement by examination:** AP, CLEP, institutional tests. 45 credit hours maximum toward associate degree. **Support services:** GED preparation, learning center, pre-admission summer program, reduced course load, remedial instruction, study skills assistance, tutoring, writing center.

Majors. Biology: Biotechnology. **Business:** Accounting, administrative services, business admin, fashion, hospitality admin, office management, office technology, sales/distribution. **Communications:** General. **Communications technology:** Desktop publishing. **Computer sciences:** Computer science, networking. **Education:** Early childhood. **Engineering:** Science. **Engineering technology:** Drafting. **Health:** Clinical lab technology, dental assistant, dental hygiene, dental lab technology, health services, medical assistant, medical radiologic technology/radiation therapy, nursing (RN), sonography. **Legal studies:** Paralegal. **Liberal arts:** Arts/sciences. **Mechanic/repair:** Aircraft, automotive. **Protective services:** Fire safety technology, law enforcement admin. **Science technology:** Biological. **Visual/performing arts:** General, commercial/advertising art, dramatic, studio arts.

Most popular majors. Business/marketing 24%, health sciences 19%, liberal arts 32%, security/protective services 10%, trade and industry 10%.

Computing on campus. 350 workstations in library, computer center. Helpline available.

Student life. Freshman orientation: Available. **Housing:** Dorm rooms contractable on space-available basis at University of Massachusetts-Lowell. **Activities:** Drama, student government, student newspaper, international club, student activities, mental health club, early childhood education club, art club, MassPIRG.

Athletics. Intramural: Table tennis, volleyball.

Student services. Adult student services, career counseling, student employment services, health services, on-campus daycare, personal counseling, placement for graduates, veterans' counselor. **Physically disabled:** Services for visually, speech, hearing impaired. **Transfer:** Special adviser, orientation, pre-admission transcript evaluation for new students. Transfer adviser, college fairs on campus for students transferring to 4-year colleges.

Contact. E-mail: admissions@middlesex.mass.edu
Phone: (978) 656-3207 Toll-free number: (800) 818-3434
Fax: (978) 656-3322
Laurie Dimitrov, Director of Admissions and Recruitment, Middlesex Community College, 33 Kearney Square, Lowell, MA 01852-1987

Mount Wachusett Community College

Gardner, Massachusetts **CB member**
www.mwcc.mass.edu **CB code: 3545**

- Public 2-year community college
- Commuter campus in large town

General. Founded in 1963. Regionally accredited. **Enrollment:** 3,696 degree-seeking undergraduates; 474 non-degree-seeking students. **Degrees:** 442 associate awarded. **Location:** 59 miles from Boston. **Calendar:** Semester, extensive summer session. **Full-time faculty:** 71 total; 14% have terminal degrees, 4% minority, 65% women. **Part-time faculty:** 150 total; 5% minority, 65% women. **Class size:** 55% < 20, 45% 20-39, less than 1% 40-49, less than 1% 50-99. **Partnerships:** Formal partnership with Tech Prep (high school articulation programs).

Student profile. Among degree-seeking undergraduates, 1,028 enrolled as first-time, first-year students, 267 transferred in from other institutions.

Part-time:	48%	**Hispanic American:**	8%
Out-of-state:	5%	**Native American:**	2%
Women:	67%	**International:**	1%
African American:	4%	**25 or older:**	43%
Asian American:	2%		

Transfer out. Colleges most students transferred to 2005: Fitchburg State College, University of Massachusetts-Amherst, Worcester State College, University of Massachusetts-Lowell.

Basis for selection. Open admission, but selective for some programs. Special requirements for all health science programs with emphasis on college level academic programs, other academic preparation and work/volunteer experience. Interview required for early admission of high school students. Portfolio recommended for art programs. **Adult students:** Entrance exam policies same as for first-time freshmen. **Homeschooled:** Applicants must submit copies of their curriculum approvals from their local secondary school district.

High school preparation. 16 units recommended. Recommended units include English 4, mathematics 3, social studies 1, history 1, science 2 (laboratory 2), foreign language 2 and academic electives 3.

2005-2006 Annual costs. Tuition/fees: $4,080; $10,230 out-of-state. Per-credit charge: $25 in-state; $230 out-of-state. New England resident tuition is $1,150. Books/supplies: $800. Personal expenses: $1,700.

2005-2006 Financial aid. All financial aid based on need. 74% of total undergraduate aid awarded as scholarships/grants, 26% as loans/jobs. Need-based aid available for part-time students. Work study available nights and for part-time students.

Application procedures. **Admission:** Priority date 4/1; no deadline. $10 fee, may be waived for applicants with need. Application may be submitted online. Admission notification on a rolling basis beginning on or about 2/1. Nursing program applicants must apply by March 1. **Financial aid:** Priority date 4/15; no closing date. FAFSA, institutional form required. Applicants notified on a rolling basis starting 5/1.

Academics. **Special study options:** Cooperative education, distance learning, double major, dual enrollment of high school students, ESL, honors, independent study, internships, liberal arts/career combination, study abroad, weekend college. License preparation in dental hygiene, nursing, physical therapy. **Credit/placement by examination:** AP, CLEP, IB, institutional tests. 30 credit hours maximum toward associate degree. **Support services:** GED preparation and test center, learning center, pre-admission summer program, reduced course load, remedial instruction, study skills assistance, tutoring, writing center.

Majors. **Business:** Business admin, executive assistant. **Communications technology:** Radio/tv. **Computer sciences:** General, computer graphics, data processing, information systems, web page design. **Conservation:** Environmental studies. **Engineering technology:** Computer, manufacturing, plastics. **Family/consumer sciences:** Child care, child development. **Health:** Dental hygiene, medical assistant, mental health services, nursing (RN), physical therapy assistant. **Legal studies:** Paralegal. **Liberal arts:** Arts/sciences. **Mechanic/repair:** Automotive. **Protective services:** Corrections, criminal justice, fire safety technology, law enforcement admin. **Public administration:** Human services. **Visual/performing arts:** Art.

Computing on campus. 415 workstations in library, computer center. Commuter students can connect to campus network. Online library, helpline, wireless network available.

Student life. **Freshman orientation:** Available. Preregistration for classes offered. One-day session week before start of classes. **Policies:** Freshmen permitted cars on campus. **Housing:** Limited housing available on campus of Fitchburg State College. **Activities:** Drama, literary magazine, musical theater, student government, student newspaper, nursing clubs, sign language club, student government association.

Student services. Adult student services, alcohol/substance abuse counseling, campus ministries, career counseling, services for economically disadvantaged, student employment services, financial aid counseling, health services, minority student services, on-campus daycare, personal counseling, placement for graduates, veterans' counselor, women's services. **Physically disabled:** Services for visually, speech, hearing impaired. **Learning disabled:** Comprehensive services available. **Transfer:** Special adviser, orientation, pre-admission transcript evaluation for new students. Transfer adviser, college fairs on campus for students transferring to 4-year colleges.

Contact. E-mail: admissions@mwcc.mass.edu
Phone: (978) 632-6600 ext. 110 Fax: (978) 630-9554
John Walsh, Director of Admissions, Mount Wachusett Community College, 444 Green Street, Gardner, MA 01440-1000

New England College of Finance

Boston, Massachusetts
www.finance.edu **CB code: 3376**

- Public 2-year college of banking, finance and insurance
- Very large city
- Interview required

General. Founded in 1909. Regionally accredited. Access to libraries in major Boston banks and local colleges and universities. 70% of faculty come from banking industry. Branch campuses in Rhode Island, Connecticut, and New Hampshire. **Enrollment:** 1,212 degree-seeking undergraduates. **Degrees:** 61 associate awarded. **Calendar:** Continuous, limited summer session. **Part-time faculty:** 180 total. **Partnerships:** Formal partnerships with several financial services companies.

Basis for selection. Open admission. Academic background, professional recommendation, demonstrated commitment to program and banking, and interview considered.

2005-2006 Annual costs. Per-credit-hour charges vary by program, location, membership, and partnership. Member per-credit-hour charges range from $543 to $795; partner per-credit-hour charges range from $669 to $915; non-member per-credit-hour charges range from $795 to $1,041. Additional $35 registration fee per registrant.

Financial aid. **Additional information:** No college-administered financial aid. 90% of students receive tuition reimbursement from employer.

Application procedures. **Admission:** No deadline. No application fee. Admission notification on a rolling basis. **Financial aid:** No deadline.

Academics. **Special study options:** Accelerated study, dual enrollment of high school students, independent study, student-designed major. **Credit/placement by examination:** CLEP. 9 credit hours maximum toward associate degree. **Support services:** Remedial instruction, tutoring.

Majors. **Business:** General, banking/financial services, business admin.

Computing on campus. 24 workstations in computer center.

Student life. **Activities:** Film society, literary magazine.

Student services. Personal counseling. **Transfer:** Special adviser, orientation, pre-admission transcript evaluation for new students. Transfer adviser for students transferring to 4-year colleges.

Contact. Phone: (617) 951-2350 Fax: (617) 951-2533
Diane Monaghan, Vice President for Academic Affairs, New England College of Finance, 10 High Street, Suite 204, Boston, MA 02110

North Shore Community College

Danvers, Massachusetts **CB member**
www.northshore.edu **CB code: 3651**

- Public 2-year community college
- Commuter campus in small city

General. Founded in 1965. Regionally accredited. Additional campus in Lynn and Corporate Training Center in Beverly. **Enrollment:** 5,800 degree-seeking undergraduates; 804 non-degree-seeking students. **Degrees:** 562 associate awarded. **Location:** 25 miles from Boston. **Calendar:** Semester, limited summer session. **Full-time faculty:** 135 total; 87% have terminal degrees, 13% minority, 64% women. **Part-time faculty:** 269 total; 4% have terminal degrees, 2% minority, 59% women. **Class size:** 49% < 20, 51% 20-39, less than 1% 40-49, less than 1% 50-99. **Special facilities:** Agricultural facility for horticulture. **Partnerships:** Formal partnerships with area high schools for Tech Prep, consortium providing distance learning opportunities and partnerships with Verizon.

Student profile. Among degree-seeking undergraduates, 42% enrolled in a transfer program, 58% enrolled in a vocational program, 1,470 enrolled as first-time, first-year students, 521 transferred in from other institutions.

Part-time:	54%	**Asian American:**	3%
Women:	62%	**Hispanic American:**	12%
African American:	8%	**25 or older:**	48%

Transfer out. **Colleges most students transferred to 2005:** Salem State College, University of Massachusetts-Boston, University of Massachusetts-Lowell, Suffolk University, Northeastern University, Lesley College.

Basis for selection. Open admission, but selective for some programs. School achievement record considered for health, engineering, computer science programs; some prerequisite course requirements exist. Pre-Nursing Assessment Test required for pre-nursing program; Nurse Entrance Exam required for LPN program. Essay and/or interview may be required in some programs, including health and human services. **Adult students:** Entrance exam policies same as for first-time freshmen. **Homeschooled:** Home program must be affiliated with accredited agency or local school system. **Learning Disabled:** Students must identify disability, individual test administration available.

High school preparation. One algebra, 1 biology, and 1 chemistry required for some health programs and for biotechnology. Trigonometry, physics, chemistry required for engineering. Trigonometry, computer literacy required for computer science.

2005-2006 Annual costs. Tuition/fees: $3,480; $10,440 out-of-state. Per-credit charge: $25 in-state; $257 out-of-state. New England Regional tuition: $125.50 per-credit-hour. Books/supplies: $800. Personal expenses: $1,300.

2004-2005 Financial aid. All financial aid based on need. 618 full-time freshmen applied for aid; 553 were judged to have need; 486 of these received aid. Average need met was 18%. Average scholarship/grant was $1,869; average loan $1,542. 92% of total undergraduate aid awarded as scholarships/grants, 8% as loans/jobs. Need-based aid available for part-time students. Work study available for part-time students.

Application procedures. **Admission:** No deadline. No application fee. Admission notification on a rolling basis. Rolling admission. **Financial aid:** Priority date 5/1; no closing date. FAFSA required. Applicants notified on a rolling basis starting 6/1; must reply within 2 week(s) of notification.

Academics. Participation in state dual enrollment program which allows high school juniors and seniors to take credit courses contingent upon approval of high school principal. Tuition and fees paid by state. **Special study**

options: Accelerated study, cross-registration, distance learning, double major, dual enrollment of high school students, ESL, honors, independent study, internships, student-designed major, study abroad, weekend college. License preparation in aviation, nursing, occupational therapy, physical therapy, radiology, real estate. **Credit/placement by examination:** AP, CLEP, institutional tests. 45 credit hours maximum toward associate degree. DANTES, Excelsior, CLEP tests accepted. CLEP tests in Freshman Composition and Analyzing and Interpreting Literature must be accompanied by essay; lab credit not awarded for Biology and Chemistry tests. **Support services:** GED preparation and test center, learning center, remedial instruction, study skills assistance, tutoring, writing center.

Majors. Agriculture: Animal grooming, floriculture, horticulture. **Business:** Accounting technology, business admin, executive assistant, hospitality admin, hotel/motel admin, marketing, office technology, tourism/travel. **Computer sciences:** General, computer science, programming. **Conservation:** Urban forestry. **Education:** Early childhood, kindergarten/preschool, teacher assistance. **Engineering:** General. **Engineering technology:** Telecommunications. **Family/consumer sciences:** Aging. **Health:** Dietetic technician, medical secretary, mental health services, nursing (RN), occupational therapy assistant, physical therapy assistant, radiologic technology/medical imaging, respiratory therapy technology, substance abuse counseling, veterinary technology/assistant. **Legal studies:** Legal secretary, paralegal. **Liberal arts:** Arts/sciences. **Personal/culinary services:** Chef training. **Protective services:** Criminal justice, fire safety technology. **Science technology:** Biological. **Transportation:** Airline/commercial pilot. **Visual/performing arts:** Graphic design.

Most popular majors. Business/marketing 9%, family/consumer sciences 6%, health sciences 24%, liberal arts 28%, security/protective services 13%.

Computing on campus. 300 workstations in library, computer center, student center. Commuter students can connect to campus network. Online course registration, online library, helpline available.

Student life. Freshman orientation: Available. Preregistration for classes offered. All day event includes placement testing, adviser assistance. **Activities:** Drama, student government, student newspaper, Club Soda (students against drug abuse), early childhood club, marketing club, engineering club, Harvard Model UN, Women in Transition club, multicultural society, poets and writers club, gerontology club, occupational therapy assistant club.

Athletics. Team name: Seahawks.

Student services. Career counseling, student employment services, health services, on-campus daycare, personal counseling, placement for graduates, veterans' counselor. **Physically disabled:** Services for visually, speech, hearing impaired. **Learning disabled:** Comprehensive services available. **Transfer:** Special adviser, orientation, pre-admission transcript evaluation for new students. Transfer adviser, college fairs on campus for students transferring to 4-year colleges.

Contact. Phone: (978) 762-4188 Fax: (978) 762-4015
Jennifer Kirk, Director of Recruitment, North Shore Community College, One Ferncroft Road, Danvers, MA 01923-0840

Northern Essex Community College

Haverhill, Massachusetts — **CB member**
www.necc.mass.edu — **CB code: 3674**

- Public 2-year community college
- Commuter campus in small city

General. Founded in 1960. Regionally accredited. Additional campus in Lawrence. **Enrollment:** 5,509 degree-seeking undergraduates; 853 non-degree-seeking students. **Degrees:** 615 associate awarded. **Location:** 40 miles from Boston. **Calendar:** Semester, extensive summer session. **Full-time faculty:** 94 total; 5% minority, 57% women. **Part-time faculty:** 360 total; 3% minority, 57% women. **Class size:** 38% < 20, 62% 20-39.

Student profile. Among degree-seeking undergraduates, 40% enrolled in a transfer program, 60% enrolled in a vocational program, 10% already have a bachelor's degree or higher, 1,489 enrolled as first-time, first-year students, 352 transferred in from other institutions.

Part-time:	60%	**Asian American:**	2%
Out-of-state:	16%	**Hispanic American:**	22%
Women:	66%	**International:**	1%
African American:	3%		

Basis for selection. Open admission, but selective for some programs. Special requirements for technology studies (engineering, computer, computer maintenance, electronics) and health and human services. Entrance examination required for schools of practical/vocational nursing. Interview required of health and human services majors.

High school preparation. Health and technologies programs have specific math and/or science requirements.

2005-2006 Annual costs. Tuition/fees: $3,150; $10,380 out-of-state. Per-credit charge: $25 in-state; $266 out-of-state. New England residents pay $122 per-credit-hour. Books/supplies: $800. Personal expenses: $850.

Financial aid. Need-based: Need-based aid available for part-time students. **Non-need-based:** Scholarships awarded for academics.

Application procedures. Admission: Priority date 2/1; no deadline. $25 fee. Admission notification on a rolling basis. **Financial aid:** Priority date 5/1; no closing date. FAFSA required. Applicants notified on a rolling basis starting 3/1; must reply within 2 week(s) of notification.

Academics. Special study options: Accelerated study, combined bachelor's/graduate degree, cooperative education, cross-registration, distance learning, double major, dual enrollment of high school students, ESL, exchange student, honors, internships, liberal arts/career combination, study abroad, weekend college. Bachelor's degree programs available on campus. License preparation in dental hygiene, nursing, paramedic, radiology, real estate. **Credit/placement by examination:** AP, CLEP, institutional tests. 36 credit hours maximum toward associate degree. **Support services:** GED preparation and test center, learning center, pre-admission summer program, reduced course load, remedial instruction, study skills assistance, tutoring, writing center.

Majors. Business: General, accounting, administrative services, business admin, finance, international, logistics, marketing, office management, office technology, tourism promotion, tourism/travel. **Communications technology:** General. **Computer sciences:** General, computer graphics, computer science, information systems, programming. **Education:** Business, early childhood. **Engineering:** Science. **Engineering technology:** Biomedical, electrical. **Family/consumer sciences:** Child care. **Foreign languages:** Sign language interpretation. **Health:** Medical records admin, medical secretary, mental health services, nursing (RN), physics/radiologic health, respiratory therapy technology. **Legal studies:** Paralegal. **Liberal arts:** Arts/sciences. **Parks/recreation:** Sports admin. **Protective services:** Criminal justice. **Public administration:** Social work. **Visual/performing arts:** Commercial/advertising art, design.

Computing on campus. 400 workstations in library, computer center, student center. Commuter students can connect to campus network. Online library, wireless network available.

Student life. Freshman orientation: Mandatory. Preregistration for classes offered. **Activities:** Choral groups, dance, drama, literary magazine, student government, student newspaper, American Sign Language club, Hispanic cultural club, Women's Resource Network, social club (students with disabilities), Agape Fellowship (Bible club).

Athletics. NJCAA. **Intercollegiate:** Baseball M, basketball, golf, soccer M, softball W. **Intramural:** Basketball, cross-country, golf, skiing, softball, table tennis, volleyball. **Team name:** Scarlet Knights.

Student services. Adult student services, career counseling, services for economically disadvantaged, student employment services, financial aid counseling, health services, on-campus daycare, personal counseling, placement for graduates, veterans' counselor, women's services. **Physically disabled:** Services for visually, speech, hearing impaired. **Learning disabled:** Comprehensive services available. **Transfer:** Special adviser, orientation for new students. Transfer adviser, college fairs on campus for students transferring to 4-year colleges.

Contact. Phone: (978) 556-3600
Nora Sheridan, Director of Admissions, Northern Essex Community College, 100 Elliott Street, Haverhill, MA 01830-2399

Quincy College

Quincy, Massachusetts
www.quincycollege.com — **CB code: 3713**

- Public 2-year community college
- Commuter campus in small city

General. Founded in 1956. Regionally accredited. Branch campus in Plymouth. **Enrollment:** 4,000 degree-seeking undergraduates. **Degrees:** 770 associate awarded. **Location:** 10 miles from downtown Boston. **Calendar:** Semester, extensive summer session. **Full-time faculty:** 35 total. **Part-time faculty:** 288 total.

Student profile.

Out-of-state:	1%	**25 or older:**	51%

Basis for selection. Open admission, but selective for some programs. Admission to health career programs based on test scores and high school record.

High school preparation. College-preparatory program with biology and chemistry required for registered nursing program.

2005-2006 Annual costs. Tuition/fees: $4,470. Per-credit charge: $149. Tuition varies among different programs. Additional charges for international students. Books/supplies: $400. Personal expenses: $400.

Application procedures. Admission: Priority date 5/1; no deadline. $20 fee, may be waived for applicants with need. Admission notification on a rolling basis beginning on or about 4/1. **Financial aid:** Priority date 4/1, closing date 5/15. FAFSA required. Applicants notified on a rolling basis starting 5/1; must reply within 2 week(s) of notification.

Academics. Special study options: Accelerated study, dual enrollment of high school students, independent study, internships. **Credit/placement by examination:** CLEP, institutional tests. 30 credit hours maximum toward associate degree. College administers MAPS and Michigan exam for placement upon enrollment. **Support services:** Learning center, preadmission summer program, reduced course load, remedial instruction, tutoring.

Majors. Business: General, office technology, tourism/travel. **Computer sciences:** Computer science. **Conservation:** General. **Education:** Early childhood. **Health:** Nursing (RN). **Legal studies:** Paralegal. **Liberal arts:** Arts/sciences. **Protective services:** Criminal justice.

Most popular majors. Business/marketing 30%, communications/journalism 6%, computer/information sciences 6%, health sciences 30%, liberal arts 13%, security/protective services 6%.

Student life. Activities: Student government, student newspaper.

Student services. Adult student services, career counseling, student employment services, on-campus daycare, veterans' counselor. **Transfer:** Special adviser, orientation for new students. College fairs on campus for students transferring to 4-year colleges.

Contact. E-mail: apruchnicki@quincycollege.com
Phone: (617) 984-1700 Toll-free number: (800) 698-1700
Fax: (617) 984-1669
Admissions Director, Quincy College, 34 Coddington Street, Quincy, MA 02169

Quinsigamond Community College

Worcester, Massachusetts — **CB member**
www.qcc.mass.edu — **CB code: 3714**

- Public 2-year community college
- Commuter campus in small city

General. Founded in 1963. Regionally accredited. **Enrollment:** 4,772 degree-seeking undergraduates; 1,182 non-degree-seeking students. **Degrees:** 579 associate awarded. **ROTC:** Army, Air Force. **Location:** 45 miles from Boston. **Calendar:** Semester, extensive summer session. **Full-time faculty:** 106 total. **Part-time faculty:** 292 total. **Special facilities:** Dental hygiene clinic.

Student profile. Among degree-seeking undergraduates, 1,227 enrolled as first-time, first-year students, 454 transferred in from other institutions.

Part-time:	47%	**Hispanic American:**	10%
Out-of-state:	2%	**Native American:**	1%
Women:	60%	**International:**	1%
African American:	8%	**25 or older:**	50%
Asian American:	3%		

Transfer out. Colleges most students transferred to 2005: Worcester State College, Unviersity of Massachusetts-Amherst, Assumption College, Anna Maria College, Framingham State College.

Basis for selection. Open admission, but selective for some programs. Special requirements for health programs.

High school preparation. English, college math, and laboratory sciences required for health programs. English and math required for business, technology, engineering, and early childhood education.

2005-2006 Annual costs. Tuition/fees: $3,820; $10,000 out-of-state. Per-credit charge: $24 in-state; $230 out-of-state. Books/supplies: $900. Personal expenses: $1,240.

2005-2006 Financial aid. All financial aid based on need. 83% of total undergraduate aid awarded as scholarships/grants, 17% as loans/jobs. Need-based aid available for part-time students. Work study available nights, weekends and for part-time students.

Application procedures. Admission: No deadline. $20 fee ($50 out-of-state), may be waived for applicants with need. Application may be submitted online. Admission notification on a rolling basis beginning on or about 10/1. Must reply by May 1 or within 2 week(s) if notified thereafter. **Financial aid:** Priority date 4/1; no closing date. FAFSA required. Applicants notified on a rolling basis starting 4/1.

Academics. Special study options: Accelerated study, cooperative education, cross-registration, distance learning, double major, dual enrollment of high school students, ESL, honors, independent study, internships, liberal arts/career combination, weekend college. Member 10-school Worcester consortium. **Credit/placement by examination:** AP, CLEP, IB, institutional tests. Unlimited number of hours of credit by examination may be counted toward degree. **Support services:** GED preparation and test center, learning center, reduced course load, remedial instruction, tutoring, writing center.

Majors. Business: Administrative services, business admin, office/clerical. **Computer sciences:** Programming. **Education:** Early childhood. **Engineering:** General. **Engineering technology:** Computer, electrical, electromechanical, manufacturing, telecommunications. **Health:** Dental hygiene, EMT paramedic, medical assistant, medical radiologic technology/radiation therapy, medical secretary, nursing (RN), occupational therapy assistant, respiratory therapy technology, substance abuse counseling. **Liberal arts:** Arts/sciences. **Mechanic/repair:** Automotive, electronics/electrical. **Protective services:** Criminal justice. **Public administration:** Human services. **Visual/performing arts:** Commercial/advertising art.

Computing on campus. 400 workstations in library, computer center. Helpline available.

Student life. Freshman orientation: Available. **Policies:** Freshmen permitted cars on campus. **Activities:** Choral groups, drama, film society, student government, student newspaper, multicultural club, several occupational groups, academic clubs.

Athletics. NJCAA. **Intercollegiate:** Baseball M, basketball, field hockey W, softball W. **Intramural:** Badminton, golf, racquetball, swimming, table tennis, volleyball. **Team name:** Chiefs.

Student services. Campus ministries, career counseling, student employment services, financial aid counseling, health services, on-campus daycare, personal counseling, placement for graduates, veterans' counselor. **Physically disabled:** Services for visually, hearing impaired. **Learning disabled:** Comprehensive services available. **Transfer:** Special adviser, orientation for new students. Transfer adviser, college fairs on campus for students transferring to 4-year colleges.

Contact. E-mail: qccadm@qcc.mass.edu
Phone: (508) 854-4262 Fax: (508) 854-4357
Ronald Smith, Director of Admissions, Quinsigamond Community College, 670 West Boylston Street, Worcester, MA 01606

Roxbury Community College

Roxbury Crossing, Massachusetts — **CB member**
www.rcc.mass.edu — **CB code: 3740**

- Public 2-year community college
- Commuter campus in very large city

General. Founded in 1973. Regionally accredited. **Enrollment:** 2,015 degree-seeking undergraduates; 221 non-degree-seeking students. **Degrees:** 190 associate awarded. **ROTC:** Army. **Calendar:** Semester, extensive summer session. **Full-time faculty:** 50 total. **Part-time faculty:** 120 total. **Class size:** 86% < 20, 14% 20-39. **Special facilities:** Indoor track and field facilities. **Partnerships:** Formal partnerships with local employers.

Student profile. Among degree-seeking undergraduates, 55% enrolled in a transfer program, 45% enrolled in a vocational program, 639 enrolled as first-time, first-year students.

Part-time:	57%	**Hispanic American:**	13%
Women:	69%	**International:**	4%
African American:	49%	**25 or older:**	63%
Asian American:	2%		

Basis for selection. Open admission, but selective for some programs. Nursing program has specific admissions criteria. **Adult students:** Entrance exam policies same as for first-time freshmen.

2005-2006 Annual costs. Tuition/fees: $3,510; $10,140 out-of-state. Per-credit charge: $26 in-state; $247 out-of-state. New England Regional per-credit-hour charge is $105. Books/supplies: $800. Personal expenses: $1,800.

Financial aid. All financial aid based on need. Need-based aid available for part-time students.

Application procedures. Admission: No deadline. $10 fee ($35 out-of-state), may be waived for applicants with need. Admission notification on a rolling basis. **Financial aid:** Priority date 5/1; no closing date. FAFSA, institutional form required. Applicants notified on a rolling basis starting 6/15; must reply within 2 week(s) of notification.

Academics. Special study options: Cross-registration, double major, dual enrollment of high school students, ESL, honors, independent study, internships, liberal arts/career combination. License preparation in nursing. **Credit/placement by examination:** CLEP, institutional tests. **Support services:** GED preparation and test center, learning center, remedial instruction, tutoring.

Majors. Architecture: Technology. **Biology:** General. **Business:** Accounting, administrative services, business admin, hospitality/recreation, management information systems, office management, office technology. **Communications technology:** Radio/tv. **Computer sciences:** General, applications programming. **Conservation:** General. **Education:** Early childhood. **Engineering technology:** CAD/CADD, drafting. **English:** British lit. **Family/consumer sciences:** Child care. **Foreign languages:** French. **Health:** Medical secretary, nursing (RN), prenursing. **Legal studies:** Legal secretary, paralegal. **Liberal arts:** Arts/sciences, humanities. **Math:** General. **Physical sciences:** General. **Protective services:** Law enforcement admin. **Social sciences:** General. **Visual/performing arts:** General.

Computing on campus. 52 workstations in library, computer center.

Student life. Freshman orientation: Available. Preregistration for classes offered. **Activities:** Choral groups, dance, drama, student government, student newspaper, Union Estudiantil Latina, international student association, Christian ministry.

Athletics. NJCAA. **Intercollegiate:** Basketball, soccer M.

Student services. Career counseling, student employment services, financial aid counseling, health services, on-campus daycare, personal counseling, placement for graduates. **Transfer:** Special adviser, orientation for new students. Transfer adviser, college fairs on campus for students transferring to 4-year colleges.

Contact. Phone: (617) 541-5310 Fax: (617) 541-5316
Walter Clark, Director of Admissions, Roxbury Community College, 1234 Columbus Avenue, Roxbury Crossing, MA 02120-3400

Springfield Technical Community College

Springfield, Massachusetts **CB member**
www.stcc.edu **CB code: 3791**

- Public 2-year community and technical college
- Commuter campus in small city

General. Founded in 1967. Regionally accredited. **Enrollment:** 4,751 degree-seeking undergraduates; 1,072 non-degree-seeking students. **Degrees:** 765 associate awarded. **Location:** 90 miles from Boston, 30 miles from Hartford, Connecticut. **Calendar:** Semester, limited summer session. **Full-time faculty:** 155 total. **Part-time faculty:** 370 total. **Special facilities:** Armory museum (national historic site). **Partnerships:** Formal partnerships with Verizon, Microsoft, Novell, A+, Cisco, Ford Asset, and IBM.

Student profile. Among degree-seeking undergraduates, 1,093 enrolled as first-time, first-year students.

Part-time:	47%	**Asian American:**	2%
Out-of-state:	4%	**Hispanic American:**	16%
Women:	58%	**International:**	1%
African American:	15%	**25 or older:**	43%

Transfer out. Colleges most students transferred to 2005: University of Massachusetts-Amherst, Westfield State College, Elms College, American International College, Springfield College.

Basis for selection. Open admission, but selective for some programs. Special requirements for certain health, engineering and science programs. SAT required for selective health and engineering programs.

High school preparation. Course prerequisites vary with program. Mathematics, chemistry, biology and/or physics required for many competitive programs.

2005-2006 Annual costs. Tuition/fees: $3,354; $9,864 out-of-state. Per-credit charge: $25 in-state; $242 out-of-state. New England reciprocal rate is $220 per credit-hour, including fees. Books/supplies: $800. Personal expenses: $1,200.

2004-2005 Financial aid. All financial aid based on need. 80% of total undergraduate aid awarded as scholarships/grants, 20% as loans/jobs. Need-based aid available for part-time students. Work study available for part-time students.

Application procedures. Admission: No deadline. $10 fee ($35 out-of-state), may be waived for applicants with need. Application may be submitted online. Admission notification on a rolling basis beginning on or about 3/1. Applicants must reply within 3 weeks of notification of admission. **Financial aid:** Priority date 4/1; no closing date. FAFSA, institutional form required. Applicants notified on a rolling basis starting 7/1.

Academics. Special study options: Cooperative education, cross-registration, distance learning, dual enrollment of high school students, ESL, honors, independent study, internships, liberal arts/career combination. **Credit/placement by examination:** AP, CLEP, institutional tests. 45 credit hours maximum toward associate degree. **Support services:** GED preparation and test center, learning center, reduced course load, remedial instruction, study skills assistance, tutoring, writing center.

Majors. Agriculture: Landscaping. **Biology:** General, biotechnology. **Business:** General, accounting, business admin, executive assistant, finance, logistics, marketing, small business admin. **Communications technology:** Animation/special effects, desktop publishing, radio/tv. **Computer sciences:** Applications programming, computer science, data processing, security, system admin, web page design. **Education:** Elementary. **Engineering:** General. **Engineering technology:** Automotive, civil, computer, electrical, electromechanical, heat/ac/refrig, laser/optical, mechanical, quality control, telecommunications. **Health:** Clinical lab technology, dental hygiene, insurance coding, massage therapy, medical assistant, medical secretary, nuclear medical technology, nursing (RN), occupational therapy assistant, physical therapy assistant, premedicine, radiologic technology/medical imaging, respiratory therapy technology, sonography, surgical technology. **Liberal arts:** Arts/sciences. **Math:** General. **Physical sciences:** Chemistry, physics. **Protective services:** Fire safety technology, police science. **Visual/performing arts:** Commercial/advertising art, studio arts.

Most popular majors. Business/marketing 13%, engineering/engineering technologies 17%, health sciences 27%, liberal arts 19%, security/protective services 8%.

Computing on campus. 1,320 workstations in library, computer center, student center. Commuter students can connect to campus network. Online course registration, online library, helpline, student web hosting, wireless network available.

Student life. Freshman orientation: Available. Half-day session three weeks before start of classes. **Policies:** No alcohol permitted. **Activities:** Drama, student government, student newspaper, TV station, business club, gay/lesbian/bisexual alliance, Christian Fellowship, Phi Theta Kappa, Campus Civitan, computer club, gallery players, engineering club, criminal justice club, massage therapy club.

Athletics. NJCAA. **Intercollegiate:** Basketball, golf, soccer, tennis, wrestling. **Intramural:** Volleyball, weight lifting. **Team name:** Rams.

Student services. Adult student services, alcohol/substance abuse counseling, career counseling, services for economically disadvantaged, student employment services, financial aid counseling, health services, on-campus daycare, personal counseling, placement for graduates, veterans' counselor, women's services. **Physically disabled:** Services for visually, speech, hearing impaired. **Learning disabled:** Comprehensive services available. **Transfer:** Special adviser, pre-admission transcript evaluation for new students. Transfer center, transfer adviser, college fairs on campus for students transferring to 4-year colleges.

Contact. E-mail: admissions@stcc.edu
Phone: (413) 755-4202
Louisa Davis-Freeman, Assistant Vice President: Admissions, Recruitment, Career Services, Springfield Technical Community College, One Armory Square, Springfield, MA 01102-9000

Urban College of Boston

Boston, Massachusetts
www.urbancollege.edu **CB code: 3630**

- Private 2-year community college
- Commuter campus in very large city

General. Regionally accredited. **Enrollment:** 521 degree-seeking undergraduates; 272 non-degree-seeking students. **Degrees:** 37 associate awarded. **Calendar:** Semester, limited summer session. **Full-time faculty:** 3 total. **Part-time faculty:** 35 total. **Class size:** 57% < 20, 43% 20-39.

Student profile. Among degree-seeking undergraduates, 54 enrolled as first-time, first-year students.

Part-time:	97%	Women:	96%

Transfer out. Colleges most students transferred to 2005: Lesley College, Springfield College, Cambridge College.

Basis for selection. Open admission.

2006-2007 Annual costs. Tuition/fees (projected): $3,780. Per-credit charge: $125. Books/supplies: $1,000. Personal expenses: $2,340.

2004-2005 Financial aid. All financial aid based on need. Need-based aid available for part-time students.

Application procedures. Admission: No deadline. $10 fee, may be waived for applicants with need. Admission notification on a rolling basis. **Financial aid:** No deadline. FAFSA required. Applicants notified on a rolling basis starting 4/15.

Academics. Special study options: Independent study, internships. **Credit/placement by examination:** AP, CLEP, IB. **Support services:** Learning center, study skills assistance, tutoring.

Majors. Education: Early childhood. **Liberal arts:** Arts/sciences. **Public administration:** Human services.

Computing on campus. 2 workstations in library, computer center.

Student life. Policies: Drug and alcohol use prohibited. Freshmen permitted cars on campus.

Student services. Career counseling, services for economically disadvantaged, financial aid counseling, minority student services, personal counseling, placement for graduates. **Transfer:** Special adviser for new students. Transfer adviser for students transferring to 4-year colleges.

Contact. Phone: (617) 292-4723 Fax: (617) 423-4758
Henry Johnson, Director of Enrollment Services and Registrar, Urban College of Boston, 178 Tremont Street, Seventh Floor, Boston, MA 02111

Two-Year Colleges

Michigan

Alpena Community College

Alpena, Michigan
www.alpenacc.edu **CB code: 1011**

- Public 2-year community college
- Commuter campus in large town

General. Founded in 1952. Regionally accredited. **Enrollment:** 1,853 degree-seeking undergraduates. **Degrees:** 284 associate awarded. **Location:** 240 miles from Detroit. **Calendar:** Semester, limited summer session. **Full-time faculty:** 52 total. **Part-time faculty:** 85 total. **Special facilities:** Museum, planetarium.

Student profile.

Out-of-state:	1%	**Live on campus:**	3%
25 or older:	48%		

Transfer out. Colleges most students transferred to 2005: Lake Superior State University, Central Michigan University, Michigan State University, Ferris State University, Spring Arbor University.

Basis for selection. Open admission, but selective for some programs. Special requirements for practical nursing, registered nursing, and utility technician programs. ACT may be used for scholarship consideration or as basis for corroboration of institutional placement exam results. Placement test requirement waived for applicants with ACT composite score of 20 or higher. **Adult students:** Entrance exam policies same as for first-time freshmen.

High school preparation. High school diploma or equivalent required for nursing applicants.

2005-2006 Annual costs. Tuition/fees: $2,660; $3,740 out-of-district; $4,820 out-of-state. Per-credit charge: $72 in-district; $108 out-of-district; $144 out-of-state. Books/supplies: $500. Personal expenses: $600.

2005-2006 Financial aid. Need-based: 66% of total undergraduate aid awarded as scholarships/grants, 34% as loans/jobs. Need-based aid available for part-time students. Work study available for part-time students. **Non-need-based:** Scholarships awarded for academics, art, athletics, job skills, leadership, music/drama.

Application procedures. Admission: Priority date 6/15; no deadline. No application fee. Application may be submitted online. Admission notification on a rolling basis beginning on or about 2/15. **Financial aid:** Priority date 8/1; no closing date. FAFSA required. Applicants notified on a rolling basis starting 5/15; must reply within 3 week(s) of notification.

Academics. Special study options: Distance learning, double major, dual enrollment of high school students, internships, liberal arts/career combination. Bachelor's degree programs available on campus. License preparation in nursing. **Credit/placement by examination:** AP, CLEP, institutional tests. 30 credit hours maximum toward associate degree. **Support services:** Learning center, reduced course load, remedial instruction, study skills assistance, tutoring, writing center.

Majors. Business: Accounting, business admin, management information systems. **Communications technology:** Graphic/printing. **Computer sciences:** General, information systems, LAN/WAN management, networking. **Education:** General. **Engineering:** General. **Engineering technology:** Construction, drafting, manufacturing. **Health:** Medical assistant, nursing (RN). **Liberal arts:** Arts/sciences. **Mechanic/repair:** Automotive. **Protective services:** Corrections, law enforcement admin.

Computing on campus. 75 workstations in library, computer center. Commuter students can connect to campus network. Online library available.

Student life. Freshman orientation: Available. Preregistration for classes offered. One-day program during week prior to start of each semester. **Policies:** Freshmen permitted cars on campus. **Housing:** Apartments available. $250 deposit, deadline 7/1. **Activities:** Jazz band, dance, drama, literary magazine, musical theater, student government, student newspaper.

Athletics. NJCAA. **Intercollegiate:** Basketball, golf M, softball W, volleyball W. **Intramural:** Basketball, bowling, softball, volleyball. **Team name:** Lumberjacks.

Student services. Adult student services, alcohol/substance abuse counseling, career counseling, student employment services, financial aid counseling, personal counseling, placement for graduates, veterans' counselor, women's services. **Transfer:** Special adviser, orientation, pre-admission transcript evaluation for new students. Transfer adviser, college fairs on campus for students transferring to 4-year colleges.

Contact. E-mail: kollienm@alpena.cc.mi.us
Phone: (989) 358-7339 Toll-free number: (888) 468-6222
Fax: (989) 358-7561
Max Lindsay, Dean of Students, Alpena Community College, 666 Johnson Street, Alpena, MI 49707

Bay de Noc Community College

Escanaba, Michigan
www.baycollege.edu **CB code: 1049**

- Public 2-year community college
- Commuter campus in large town

General. Founded in 1962. Regionally accredited. **Enrollment:** 2,033 degree-seeking undergraduates; 221 non-degree-seeking students. **Degrees:** 354 associate awarded. **Location:** 110 miles from Green Bay, Wisconsin. **Calendar:** Semester, limited summer session. **Full-time faculty:** 40 total. **Part-time faculty:** 95 total. **Class size:** 64% < 20, 34% 20-39, less than 1% 40-49, less than 1% 50-99. **Special facilities:** Reading, writing, mathematics and computer-assisted instructional laboratories.

Student profile. Among degree-seeking undergraduates, 42% enrolled in a transfer program, 48% enrolled in a vocational program, 508 enrolled as first-time, first-year students.

Part-time:	39%	**Native American:**	4%
Out-of-state:	4%	**25 or older:**	17%
Women:	62%	**Live on campus:**	4%
Hispanic American:	1%		

Transfer out. Colleges most students transferred to 2005: Northern Michigan University, Lake Superior State University, Michigan Technological University.

Basis for selection. Open admission. Nursing program has own set of admissions criteria. **Adult students:** Students over age 22 may take ASSET in place of ACT.

2005-2006 Annual costs. Tuition/fees: $2,120; $3,035 out-of-district; $4,655 out-of-state. Per-credit charge: $65 in-district; $95 out-of-district; $149 out-of-state. Tuition and instructional fees charged on per contact hour basis. Room/board: $3,840. Books/supplies: $350. Personal expenses: $500.

Financial aid. Need-based: Need-based aid available for part-time students. Work study available nights, weekends and for part-time students. **Non-need-based:** Scholarships awarded for academics.

Application procedures. Admission: Closing date 8/15. No application fee. Application may be submitted online. Admission notification on a rolling basis. **Financial aid:** Priority date 4/1; no closing date. FAFSA required. Applicants notified on a rolling basis starting 2/1; must reply within 2 week(s) of notification.

Academics. Special study options: Cooperative education, distance learning, dual enrollment of high school students, internships, liberal arts/career combination, weekend college. Bachelor's degree programs available on campus. License preparation in nursing. **Credit/placement by examination:** AP, CLEP, institutional tests. 40 credit hours maximum toward associate degree. **Support services:** Pre-admission summer program, reduced course load, remedial instruction, study skills assistance, tutoring, writing center.

Majors. Architecture: Landscape. **Business:** Accounting, administrative services, business admin, sales/distribution. **Conservation:** Wood science. **Engineering technology:** Drafting, electrical, water quality. **Family/consumer sciences:** Child care. **Health:** Nursing (RN). **Legal studies:** Prelaw. **Liberal arts:** Arts/sciences. **Mechanic/repair:** General, automotive. **Physical sciences:** Astronomy.

Computing on campus. 220 workstations in library, computer center. Commuter students can connect to campus network. Online course registration, online library, helpline, wireless network available.

Student life. Freshman orientation: Mandatory. Students meet with counselors, financial aid officers, student services representatives to determine course of study and expenses. **Policies:** Freshmen permitted cars on campus. **Housing:** Apartments available. $353 deposit, deadline 8/15. **Activities:** Choral groups, drama, literary magazine, student government, student newspaper, Bay Area Campus Ministries, student volunteer association, nurses association, student activities board, United Nations club, history club, water tech club, art club.

Athletics. Intramural: Basketball, bowling, golf, skiing, softball, swimming, table tennis, volleyball.

Student services. Adult student services, career counseling, student employment services, financial aid counseling, on-campus daycare, personal counseling, veterans' counselor. **Physically disabled:** Services for visually, hearing impaired. **Transfer:** Special adviser, orientation for new students. Transfer adviser, college fairs on campus for students transferring to 4-year colleges.

Contact. E-mail: airdc@baycollege.edu
Phone: (906) 786-5802 ext. 1276 Toll-free number: (800) 221-2001 ext. 1276 Fax: (906) 786-8515
Cynthia Carter, Director of Admissions, Bay de Noc Community College, 2001 North Lincoln Road, Escanaba, MI 49829-2511

Bay Mills Community College

Brimley, Michigan
www.bmcc.edu **CB code: 2101**

- Public 2-year community college
- Residential campus in rural community

General. Regionally accredited. **Enrollment:** 175 full-time, degree-seeking students. **Degrees:** 26 associate awarded. **Location:** 20 miles from Sault Ste. Marie. **Calendar:** Semester. **Full-time faculty:** 10 total. **Part-time faculty:** 35 total.

Transfer out. Colleges most students transferred to 2005: Lake Superior State University, Northern Michigan University.

Basis for selection. Open admission.

2005-2006 Annual costs. Tuition/fees: $2,910. Per-credit charge: $85. Books/supplies: $200.

Financial aid. Need-based: Work study available nights and for part-time students.

Application procedures. Admission: Closing date 8/24. No application fee. Application may be submitted online. **Financial aid:** Institutional form required.

Academics. Special study options: Cooperative education, distance learning, double major, dual enrollment of high school students, independent study, internships. **Credit/placement by examination:** CLEP, institutional tests. **Support services:** GED preparation, learning center, remedial instruction, study skills assistance, tutoring.

Majors. Business: Business admin. **Computer sciences:** General, computer science. **Construction:** General. **Education:** Early childhood.

Computing on campus. Online library, repair service available.

Student life. Freshman orientation: Available. Preregistration for classes offered. **Policies:** Freshmen permitted cars on campus. **Housing:** $125 deposit. **Activities:** Student government.

Student services. Career counseling, financial aid counseling. **Transfer:** Special adviser, orientation, pre-admission transcript evaluation for new students. College fairs on campus for students transferring to 4-year colleges.

Contact. E-mail: elehre@bmcc.org
Phone: (906) 248-3354 Toll-free number: (800) 844-2622
Fax: (906) 248-3351
Elaine Lehre, Admissions Officer, Bay Mills Community College, 12214 West Lakeshore Drive, Brimley, MI 49715

Delta College

University Center, Michigan
www.delta.edu **CB code: 1816**

- Public 2-year community and junior college
- Commuter campus in small city

General. Founded in 1957. Regionally accredited. Classes offered at 21 off-campus sites; 4 major off-campus facilities in operation. **Enrollment:** 10,184 degree-seeking undergraduates. **Degrees:** 1,149 associate awarded. **Location:** 10 miles from Saginaw, 12 miles from Midland. **Calendar:** Trimester, limited summer session. **Full-time faculty:** 211 total. **Part-time faculty:** 285 total. **Class size:** 44% < 20, 55% 20-39, less than 1% 40-49, less than 1% 50-99. **Special facilities:** Planetarium, on-site dental clinic. **Partnerships:** Formal partnership with General Motors (ASEP program for automotive students).

Student profile. Among degree-seeking undergraduates, 374 transferred in from other institutions.

Part-time:	62%	**Women:**	56%
Out-of-state:	2%	**25 or older:**	43%

Transfer out. Colleges most students transferred to 2005: Central Michigan University, Saginaw Valley State University, Northwood University, University of Michigan, Michigan State University.

Basis for selection. Open admission. ACT, ASSET or COMPASS required of all students for counseling purposes. **Adult students:** Entrance exam policies same as for first-time freshmen.

2005-2006 Annual costs. Tuition/fees: $2,400; $3,345 out-of-district; $4,680 out-of-state. Per-credit charge: $73 in-district; $104 out-of-district; $149 out-of-state. Books/supplies: $767. Personal expenses: $690.

Financial aid. Need-based: Need-based aid available for part-time students. Work study available nights and for part-time students. **Non-need-based:** Scholarships awarded for academics, athletics.

Application procedures. Admission: No deadline. $20 fee, may be waived for applicants with need. Application may be submitted online. Admission notification on a rolling basis. **Financial aid:** Priority date 8/1; no closing date. FAFSA required. Applicants notified on a rolling basis; must reply within 2 week(s) of notification.

Academics. Special study options: Cooperative education, distance learning, double major, dual enrollment of high school students, honors, independent study, internships, liberal arts/career combination, student-designed major, study abroad, weekend college. Bachelor's in business with Northwood University (3+1 program). License preparation in aviation, dental hygiene, nursing, occupational therapy, physical therapy, radiology, real estate. **Credit/placement by examination:** AP, CLEP, IB, institutional tests. 38 credit hours maximum toward associate degree. **Support services:** GED test center, learning center, reduced course load, remedial instruction, study skills assistance, tutoring.

Majors. Agriculture: Business. **Architecture:** Technology. **Biology:** General, biotechnology. **Business:** General, accounting, administrative services, business admin, construction management, international, marketing, merchandising, office management, office technology, small business admin. **Communications:** Journalism. **Communications technology:** General, graphic/printing. **Computer sciences:** General, computer science, information systems, information technology, networking, programming, web page design, webmaster. **Conservation:** General, environmental science, forestry, water/wetlands/marine. **Construction:** General, carpentry, electrician, maintenance, pipefitting, plumbing. **Education:** Art, business, elementary, kindergarten/preschool, music, physical, secondary, special, technology/industrial arts. **Engineering:** General, architectural, mechanical. **Engineering technology:** Drafting, electrical, heat/ac/refrig, industrial, manufacturing. **Family/consumer sciences:** Child development. **Foreign languages:** General. **Health:** Clinical lab science, dental assistant, dental hygiene, dietetics, licensed practical nurse, medical assistant, medical radiologic technology/radiation therapy, medical secretary, nursing (RN), office assistant, optometric assistant, pharmacy assistant, physical therapy assistant, physics/radiologic health, predentistry, premedicine, prenursing, prepharmacy, preveterinary, respiratory therapy assistant, respiratory therapy technology, sonography, surgical technology. **Legal studies:** Legal secretary, paralegal, prelaw. **Liberal arts:** Arts/sciences. **Math:** General. **Mechanic/repair:** Automotive, electronics/electrical, heating/ac/refrig. **Parks/recreation:** Health/fitness. **Personal/culinary services:** Mortuary science. **Physical sciences:** General, chemistry, geology. **Production:** Machine tool, welding. **Protective services:** Corrections, fire safety technology, fire services admin, firefighting, law enforcement admin, police science. **Psychology:** General. **Public administration:** Human services, social work. **Science technology:** Biological, chemical. **Social sciences:** Economics, geography, sociology. **Transportation:** Aviation. **Visual/performing arts:** Art, dramatic, graphic design, interior design, photography.

Computing on campus. 350 workstations in library, computer center, student center. Commuter students can connect to campus network. Online course registration, online library, helpline, wireless network available.

Student life. Freshman orientation: Mandatory. General campus overview and individual academic counseling/advising assessment required prior to orientation. **Policies:** Freshmen permitted cars on campus. **Activities:** Drama, radio station, student government, student newspaper, TV station, black student union, Chi Alpha, Delta Collegiate, Delta Epsilon Chi, health care organizations, InterVarsity Christian Fellowship, Phi Theta Kappa International, Society of Hispanic Leaders, student senate, trilogy club.

Athletics. NJCAA. **Intercollegiate:** Basketball, cross-country M, golf, soccer M, softball W, volleyball W. **Team name:** Pioneers.

Student services. Adult student services, career counseling, services for economically disadvantaged, student employment services, financial aid counseling, minority student services, placement for graduates, veterans' counselor. **Physically disabled:** Services for visually, speech, hearing impaired. **Transfer:** Special adviser, orientation for new students. Transfer adviser, college fairs on campus for students transferring to 4-year colleges.

Contact. E-mail: admit@delta.edu
Phone: (989) 686-9093 Toll-free number: (800) 285-1704
Fax: (989) 667-2202
Duff Zube, Director of Admissions, Records & Assesment, Delta College, 1961 Delta Road, University Center, MI 48710

Glen Oaks Community College

Centreville, Michigan
www.glenoaks.cc.mi.us **CB code: 1261**

- Public 2-year community college
- Commuter campus in rural community

General. Founded in 1965. Regionally accredited. **Enrollment:** 950 degree-seeking undergraduates. **Degrees:** 159 associate awarded. **Location:** 35 miles from Kalamazoo. **Calendar:** Semester, limited summer session. **Full-time faculty:** 28 total. **Part-time faculty:** 80 total.

Student profile.

Out-of-state:	18%	**25 or older:**	82%

Transfer out. Colleges most students transferred to 2005: Western Michigan University, Grand Valley State University, Kalamazoo Valley Community College, Kellogg Community College, Michigan State University.

Basis for selection. Open admission, but selective for some programs. Admission to nursing program based on pre-admission test, high school grades, and health form. ACCUPLACER test requested for certain programs. ACT or SAT may be considered in lieu of ACCUPLACER.

2006-2007 Annual costs. Tuition/fees (projected): $2,281; $3,211 out-of-district; $4,111 out-of-state. Per-credit charge: $64 in-district; $95 out-of-district; $125 out-of-state. Books/supplies: $480. Personal expenses: $775.

2004-2005 Financial aid. Need-based: 99% of total undergraduate aid awarded as scholarships/grants, 1% as loans/jobs. Need-based aid available for part-time students. Work study available nights and for part-time students. **Non-need-based:** Scholarships awarded for academics, art, athletics, leadership, minority status, music/drama.

Application procedures. Admission: No deadline. No application fee. Admission notification on a rolling basis. **Financial aid:** No deadline. FAFSA, institutional form required. Applicants notified on a rolling basis.

Academics. Special study options: Accelerated study, distance learning, double major, dual enrollment of high school students, independent study, internships, liberal arts/career combination. Bachelor's degree programs available on campus. License preparation in paramedic. **Credit/placement by examination:** AP, CLEP, institutional tests. 47 credit hours maximum toward associate degree. **Support services:** Learning center, remedial instruction, study skills assistance, tutoring.

Majors. Business: General. **Education:** Early childhood. **Engineering:** Science. **Family/consumer sciences:** Child care. **Health:** Nursing (RN). **Liberal arts:** Arts/sciences.

Most popular majors. Business/marketing 35%, health sciences 16%, liberal arts 41%.

Computing on campus. 85 workstations in library, computer center. Online library, wireless network available.

Student life. Freshman orientation: Available. **Policies:** Freshmen permitted cars on campus. **Activities:** Choral groups, literary magazine, music ensembles, student government, student newspaper, academic honorary society, Phi Theta Kappa.

Athletics. NJCAA. **Intercollegiate:** Baseball M, basketball, golf M, softball W, tennis W, volleyball W. **Intramural:** Table tennis. **Team name:** Vikings.

Student services. Career counseling, services for economically disadvantaged, student employment services, financial aid counseling, on-campus daycare, personal counseling, women's services. **Physically disabled:** Services for visually, speech, hearing impaired. **Transfer:** Special adviser, orientation for new students. Transfer adviser, college fairs on campus for students transferring to 4-year colleges.

Contact. E-mail: jbower@glenoaks.edu
Phone: (269) 467-9945 ext. 320 Toll-free number: (888) 994-7818 ext. 320
Fax: (269) 467-9068
Beverly Andrews, Director of Admissions/Registrar, Glen Oaks Community College, 62249 Shimmel Road, Centreville, MI 49032-9719

Gogebic Community College

Ironwood, Michigan
www.gogebic.edu **CB code: 1250**

- Public 2-year community college
- Commuter campus in small town

General. Founded in 1932. Regionally accredited. **Enrollment:** 525 full-time, degree-seeking students. **Degrees:** 140 associate awarded. **Location:** 100 miles from Duluth, Minnesota, 150 miles from Marquette. **Calendar:** Semester, limited summer session. **Full-time faculty:** 29 total. **Part-time faculty:** 60 total. **Class size:** 72% < 20, 27% 20-39, less than 1% 40-49, less than 1% 50-99. **Special facilities:** Arboretum, ski hill, tubing park, cross-country ski trails.

Transfer out. Colleges most students transferred to 2005: Northern Michigan University, University of Wisconsin-Superior, Northland College, Michigan Technological University.

Basis for selection. Open admission, but selective for some programs. Students applying to nursing programs required to show competency in biology and chemistry. Admission based on assessment test scores and academic achievement. Interview recommended. **Adult students:** Entrance exam policies same as for first-time freshmen.

High school preparation. Nursing applicants must have background in chemistry, math, and biology.

2005-2006 Annual costs. Tuition/fees: $2,568; $3,168 out-of-district; $3,948 out-of-state. Per-credit charge: $74 in-district; $94 out-of-district; $120 out-of-state. Reciprocity tuition is the same as in-state, out-of-district tuition, $94 per-credit-hour. Books/supplies: $700. Personal expenses: $700.

Financial aid. Need-based: Need-based aid available for part-time students. Work study available nights, weekends and for part-time students. **Non-need-based:** Scholarships awarded for academics, art, athletics, job skills, leadership, music/drama, state residency.

Application procedures. Admission: No deadline. $10 fee, may be waived for applicants with need. Application may be submitted online. Admission notification on a rolling basis. **Financial aid:** Priority date 5/1; no closing date. FAFSA required. Applicants notified on a rolling basis starting 3/15; must reply within 2 week(s) of notification.

Academics. Special study options: Cooperative education, distance learning, double major, dual enrollment of high school students, honors, independent study, internships, student-designed major. License preparation in nursing, paramedic. **Credit/placement by examination:** AP, CLEP, institutional tests. 12 credit hours maximum toward associate degree. AP exam scores not listed in policy evaluated on individual basis. **Support services:** GED test center, learning center, reduced course load, remedial instruction, study skills assistance, tutoring.

Majors. Biology: General. **Business:** General, accounting, administrative services, business admin, entrepreneurial studies, office management, office technology. **Communications technology:** Graphics. **Computer sciences:** General, data processing, programming. **Conservation:** General, forestry. **Construction:** General, carpentry. **Education:** General, early childhood, elementary, secondary, special, teacher assistance. **Engineering:** General. **Engineering technology:** Automotive, CAD/CADD, construction. **Health:** Clinical lab science, EMT paramedic, insurance coding, medical transcription, nursing (RN), predentistry, premedicine, prenursing, prepharmacy, preveterinary. **Legal studies:** Prelaw. **Liberal arts:** Arts/sciences. **Math:** General. **Mechanic/repair:** Automotive. **Parks/recreation:** Facilities management. **Personal/culinary services:** Mortuary science. **Physical sciences:** General, chemistry, physics. **Protective services:** Law enforcement admin. **Psychology:** General. **Public administration:** Social work. **Social sciences:** General. **Visual/performing arts:** Art, commercial/advertising art.

Computing on campus. 240 workstations in library, computer center. Online library available.

Student life. **Freshman orientation:** Mandatory. Preregistration for classes offered. Early orientation held in April for all accepted who have completed their assessment. Other orientation programs in August and June. **Policies:** Freshmen permitted cars on campus. **Activities:** Concert band, choral groups, drama, music ensembles, student government, student newspaper, Intervarsity Christian Fellowship, Phi Theta Kappa, drama club, student senate.

Athletics. NJCAA. **Intercollegiate:** Basketball. **Intramural:** Basketball, bowling, cheerleading, football (non-tackle) M, golf, skiing, soccer, softball, tennis, volleyball. **Team name:** Samsons.

Student services. Alcohol/substance abuse counseling, career counseling, services for economically disadvantaged, student employment services, financial aid counseling, personal counseling, placement for graduates, veterans' counselor. **Physically disabled:** Services for visually, hearing impaired. **Transfer:** Special adviser, orientation, re-entry adviser for new students. Transfer adviser, college fairs on campus for students transferring to 4-year colleges.

Contact. E-mail: nancyg@gogebic.edu
Phone: (906) 932-4231 ext. 207 Toll-free number: (800) 682-5910 ext. 207
Fax: (906) 932-2339
Jeanne Graham, Director of Admissions and Public Information, Gogebic Community College, E4946 Jackson Road, Ironwood, MI 49938

Grand Rapids Community College

Grand Rapids, Michigan
www.grcc.edu
CB member
CB code: 1254

- Public 2-year community college
- Commuter campus in small city

General. Founded in 1914. Regionally accredited. Evening courses offered at 9 off-campus sites in Western Michigan. **Enrollment:** 13,193 degree-seeking undergraduates; 1,605 non-degree-seeking students. **Degrees:** 1,289 associate awarded. **Location:** 30 miles from Holland, 70 miles from Lansing. **Calendar:** Semester, extensive summer session. **Full-time faculty:** 224 total; 12% have terminal degrees, 12% minority, 49% women. **Part-time faculty:** 424 total; 6% have terminal degrees, 9% minority, 46% women.

Student profile. Among degree-seeking undergraduates, 53% enrolled in a transfer program, 47% enrolled in a vocational program, 3,334 enrolled as first-time, first-year students.

Part-time:	52%	**Hispanic American:**	6%
Out-of-state:	1%	**Native American:**	1%
Women:	52%	**International:**	1%
African American:	10%	**25 or older:**	29%
Asian American:	2%		

Transfer out. **Colleges most students transferred to 2005:** Grand Valley State University, Ferris State University, Western Michigan University, Aquinas College, Michigan State University.

Basis for selection. Open admission, but selective for some programs. Occupational health program applicants must be high school graduates, have GPAs and completed specific classes with a 2.0 grade or better. **Adult students:** Entrance exam policies same as for first-time freshmen. GED; previous college transfer credit. **Homeschooled:** Assessment exam required.

High school preparation. Recommended units include English 4, mathematics 3, social studies 2 and science 3.

2005-2006 Annual costs. Tuition/fees: $2,185; $3,750 out-of-district; $5,350 out-of-state. Per-credit charge: $70 in-district; $125 out-of-district; $175 out-of-state. Tuition charged per contact hour. Books/supplies: $1,470. Personal expenses: $548.

2005-2006 Financial aid. **Need-based:** 1,839 full-time freshmen applied for aid; 1,406 were judged to have need; 1,309 of these received aid. Average scholarship/grant was $2,572; average loan $1,859. 61% of total undergraduate aid awarded as scholarships/grants, 39% as loans/jobs. Need-based aid available for part-time students. Work study available nights, weekends and for part-time students. **Non-need-based:** Awarded to 2,335 full-time undergraduates, including 1,056 freshmen. Scholarships awarded for academics, alumni affiliation, art, athletics, leadership, minority status, music/drama, state residency. **Additional information:** Tuition reimbursement and/or child-care services for single parents and displaced homemakers who meet Perkins guidelines.

Application procedures. **Admission:** Closing date 8/30 (receipt date). $20 fee, may be waived for applicants with need. Application may be submitted online. Admission notification on a rolling basis. **Financial aid:** Priority date 4/1; no closing date. FAFSA required. Applicants notified on a rolling basis starting 5/1; must reply within 3 week(s) of notification.

Academics. Liberal arts and pre-professional curricula along with extensive work-force training and technical seminars offered. **Special study options:** Cooperative education, distance learning, dual enrollment of high school students, ESL, independent study, internships, study abroad, weekend college. License preparation in dental hygiene, nursing, occupational therapy, radiology. **Credit/placement by examination:** AP, CLEP, institutional tests. 30 credit hours maximum toward associate degree. **Support services:** Learning center, reduced course load, remedial instruction, study skills assistance, tutoring, writing center.

Majors. **Agriculture:** Landscaping. **Architecture:** Technology. **Business:** General, accounting, business admin, executive assistant, fashion, management information systems, marketing. **Communications technology:** Graphic/printing. **Computer sciences:** General, webmaster. **Conservation:** Fisheries, forestry, management/policy, wildlife. **Engineering technology:** General, automotive, electrical, heat/ac/refrig, plastics, quality control, water quality. **Family/consumer sciences:** Child care, child development, home furnishings, institutional food production. **Health:** Dental assistant, dental hygiene, licensed practical nurse, medical radiologic technology/radiation therapy, medical secretary, nursing (RN), occupational therapy assistant. **Legal studies:** General, legal secretary. **Liberal arts:** Arts/sciences. **Mechanic/repair:** Electronics/electrical, heating/ac/refrig. **Personal/culinary services:** Chef training, restaurant/catering. **Production:** General, machine shop technology, welding. **Protective services:** Corrections, firefighting, police science. **Science technology:** Chemical. **Visual/performing arts:** Commercial/advertising art, interior design.

Most popular majors. Business/marketing 7%, education 8%, health sciences 18%, liberal arts 30%, personal/culinary services 9%, public administration/social services 6%.

Computing on campus. 1,042 workstations in library, computer center. Commuter students can connect to campus network. Online course registration, online library, wireless network available.

Student life. **Freshman orientation:** Available. Preregistration for classes offered. Provides campus tours and general information about the college. **Policies:** Freshmen permitted cars on campus. **Activities:** Bands, choral groups, dance, drama, film society, literary magazine, music ensembles, musical theater, student government, student newspaper, symphony orchestra, black student organization, Hispanic student organization, Native American student organization, Vietnamese student organization, Christian Fellowship, content area student organizations, service learning.

Athletics. NJCAA. **Intercollegiate:** Baseball M, basketball, cross-country, diving, football (tackle) M, golf M, softball W, swimming, tennis, track and field, volleyball W, wrestling M. **Intramural:** Basketball, racquetball, skiing, soccer M, swimming. **Team name:** Raiders.

Student services. Adult student services, career counseling, student employment services, on-campus daycare, personal counseling, placement for graduates. **Physically disabled:** Services for visually, speech, hearing impaired. **Transfer:** Special adviser, orientation, pre-admission transcript evaluation for new students. Transfer adviser, college fairs on campus for students transferring to 4-year colleges.

Contact. E-mail: jhartman@grcc.edu
Phone: (616) 234-7623 Fax: (616) 234-4107
Diane Patrick, Director of Admissions, Grand Rapids Community College, 143 Bostwick Northeast, Grand Rapids, MI 49503-3295

Henry Ford Community College

Dearborn, Michigan
www.hfcc.edu
CB code: 1293

- Public 2-year community college
- Commuter campus in small city

General. Founded in 1938. Regionally accredited. **Enrollment:** 5,250 full-time, degree-seeking students. **Degrees:** 1,117 associate awarded. **Location:** 8 miles from Detroit. **Calendar:** Semester, limited summer session. **Full-time faculty:** 195 total. **Part-time faculty:** 600 total.

Student profile.

Out-of-state:	2%	**25 or older:**	47%

Basis for selection. Open admission, but selective for some programs. Special requirements for specific allied health programs.

High school preparation. For allied health programs: 1 year high school biology, chemistry, and algebra.

2005-2006 Annual costs. Tuition/fees: $2,112; $3,762 out-of-district; $4,002 out-of-state. Per-credit charge: $57 in-district; $112 out-of-district; $120 out-of-state. Books/supplies: $500. Personal expenses: $585.

Financial aid. Need-based: Work study available nights, weekends and for part-time students.

Application procedures. Admission: No deadline. $30 fee, may be waived for applicants with need. Application may be submitted online. Admission notification on a rolling basis. **Financial aid:** Priority date 4/1; no closing date. FAFSA required. Applicants notified on a rolling basis starting 3/1.

Academics. Special study options: Cooperative education, distance learning, dual enrollment of high school students, honors, independent study. **Credit/placement by examination:** CLEP. 20 credit hours maximum toward associate degree. **Support services:** Learning center, pre-admission summer program, reduced course load, remedial instruction, tutoring.

Majors. Area/ethnic studies: Women's. **Business:** General, accounting, management science, office management, office/clerical, real estate. **Communications:** General, broadcast journalism. **Communications technology:** Graphic/printing. **Computer sciences:** General. **Engineering technology:** Drafting, electrical. **Family/consumer sciences:** Institutional food production. **Health:** EMT paramedic, licensed practical nurse, medical records technology, nursing (RN), physical therapy assistant, respiratory therapy technology. **Legal studies:** Legal secretary, paralegal. **Liberal arts:** Arts/sciences. **Mechanic/repair:** Automotive, heating/ac/refrig. **Parks/recreation:** Exercise sciences, health/fitness. **Personal/culinary services:** Culinary arts. **Protective services:** Firefighting, police science, security services. **Transportation:** General. **Visual/performing arts:** Art, ceramics, commercial/advertising art, dramatic, industrial design, interior design.

Student life. Freshman orientation: Available. **Activities:** Bands, choral groups, drama, film society, literary magazine, music ensembles, radio station, student government, student newspaper.

Athletics. NJCAA. **Intercollegiate:** Baseball M, basketball, golf M, softball W, tennis, volleyball W. **Intramural:** Basketball, bowling, sailing, table tennis.

Student services. Adult student services, career counseling, student employment services, on-campus daycare, personal counseling, placement for graduates, veterans' counselor. **Physically disabled:** Services for visually, hearing impaired. **Transfer:** Special adviser, orientation for new students. Transfer adviser, college fairs on campus for students transferring to 4-year colleges.

Contact. Phone: (313) 845-9613 Toll-free number: (800) 585-4322
Fax: (313) 845-9891
Mark Ulseth, Director of Admissions/Registrar, Henry Ford Community College, 5101 Evergreen Road, Dearborn, MI 48128

ITT Technical Institute: Grand Rapids

Grand Rapids, Michigan
www.itt-tech.edu **CB code: 2705**

- For-profit 2-year technical college
- Commuter campus in small city

General. Accredited by ACICS. **Calendar:** Quarter.

Annual costs/financial aid. Tuition varies by program, $260-$368 per credit hour.

Contact. Phone: (616) 956-1060
Director of Recruitment, 4020 Sparks Drive S.E., Grand Rapids, MI 49546

ITT Technical Institute: Troy

Troy, Michigan
www.itt-tech.edu **CB code: 2784**

- For-profit 2-year technical college
- Commuter campus in small city

General. Accredited by ACICS. **Calendar:** Quarter.

Annual costs/financial aid. Tuition varies by program, $260-$368 per credit hour.

Contact. Phone: (248) 524-1800
Director of Recruitment, 1522 E. Big Beaver Road, Troy, MI 48083-1905

Jackson Community College

Jackson, Michigan **CB member**
www.jccmi.edu **CB code: 1340**

- Public 2-year community college
- Commuter campus in small city

General. Founded in 1928. Regionally accredited. Off-campus locations in Hillsdale County, Lenawee County; extensive on-line offerings. Students may also complete bachelor's degrees on-campus from partner universities. **Enrollment:** 5,151 degree-seeking undergraduates; 719 non-degree-seeking students. **Degrees:** 523 associate awarded. **Location:** 6 miles from downtown. **Calendar:** Semester, limited summer session. **Full-time faculty:** 93 total; 4% minority, 52% women. **Part-time faculty:** 242 total; 6% minority, 48% women. **Class size:** 65% < 20, 34% 20-39, 1% 40-49. **Partnerships:** Formal partnership with Foote Health University to provide education and training for employees.

Student profile. Among degree-seeking undergraduates, 39% enrolled in a transfer program, 61% enrolled in a vocational program, 267 enrolled as first-time, first-year students.

Part-time:	60%	**Hispanic American:**	4%
Women:	64%	**Native American:**	1%
African American:	5%	**25 or older:**	44%
Asian American:	1%		

Transfer out. Colleges most students transferred to 2005: Michigan State University, Spring Arbor University, Eastern Michigan University, Siena Heights University, Western Michigan University.

Basis for selection. Open admission, but selective for some programs. Special requirements for allied health programs and nursing program. ACT scores used for placement, if submitted. Student not submitting ACT scores must take college-administered placement tests. Second admit programs require interviews and specific academic prerequisites. **Adult students:** Entrance exam policies same as for first-time freshmen.

2005-2006 Annual costs. Tuition/fees: $2,691; $3,591 out-of-district; $4,461 out-of-state. Per-credit charge: $74 in-district; $104 out-of-district; $133 out-of-state. Books/supplies: $672. Personal expenses: $720.

Financial aid. Need-based: Need-based aid available for part-time students. Work study available nights, weekends and for part-time students. **Non-need-based:** Scholarships awarded for academics, art, leadership, music/drama, state residency.

Application procedures. Admission: No deadline. No application fee. Application may be submitted online. Admission notification on a rolling basis. **Financial aid:** Priority date 4/1; no closing date. FAFSA, institutional form required. Applicants notified on a rolling basis starting 3/1.

Academics. Special study options: Distance learning, dual enrollment of high school students, ESL, independent study, internships, liberal arts/career combination. Bachelor's degree programs available on campus. License preparation in aviation, nursing, paramedic, radiology. **Credit/placement by examination:** AP, CLEP, IB, institutional tests. 30 credit hours maximum toward associate degree. **Support services:** GED preparation and test center, learning center, pre-admission summer program, remedial instruction, study skills assistance, tutoring, writing center.

Majors. Business: General, accounting, business admin, finance. **Computer sciences:** Applications programming, computer graphics, data processing, programming, web page design. **Construction:** Electrician. **Education:** Early childhood. **Engineering technology:** Electrical, heat/ac/refrig. **Health:** EMT paramedic, medical assistant, medical transcription, nursing (RN), radiologic technology/medical imaging, sonography. **Liberal arts:** Arts/sciences. **Mechanic/repair:** Automotive, electronics/electrical, heating/ac/refrig. **Protective services:** Criminal justice. **Visual/performing arts:** Graphic design.

Most popular majors. Business/marketing 12%, health sciences 28%, liberal arts 39%, physical sciences 6%, security/protective services 7%.

Computing on campus. 356 workstations in library, computer center, student center. Online course registration, helpline available.

Student life. Freshman orientation: Available. 2- to 3-hour program prior to each semester. **Activities:** Bands, choral groups, dance, drama, music ensembles, musical theater, student government, student newspaper.

Athletics. **Intramural:** Basketball M, football (non-tackle) M, soccer M. **Team name:** Golden Jets.

Student services. Adult student services, career counseling, services for economically disadvantaged, financial aid counseling, minority student services, on-campus daycare. **Physically disabled:** Services for visually, speech, hearing impaired. **Transfer:** Special adviser, orientation, pre-admission transcript evaluation for new students. Transfer center, transfer adviser, college fairs on campus for students transferring to 4-year colleges.

Contact. E-mail: admissions@jccmi.edu
Phone: (517) 796-8425 Toll-free number: (888) 522-7344
Fax: (517) 796-8631
Julie Hand, Enrollment Services Team Leader, Jackson Community College, 2111 Emmons Road, Jackson, MI 49201-8399

Kalamazoo Valley Community College

Kalamazoo, Michigan
www.kvcc.edu **CB code: 1378**

- Public 2-year community college
- Commuter campus in small city

General. Founded in 1966. Regionally accredited. Additional campus downtown. **Enrollment:** 9,210 degree-seeking undergraduates; 1,375 non-degree-seeking students. **Degrees:** 649 associate awarded. **Location:** 130 miles from Detroit, 150 miles from Chicago. **Calendar:** Semester, limited summer session. **Full-time faculty:** 118 total; 7% have terminal degrees, 7% minority, 44% women. **Part-time faculty:** 317 total; 1% have terminal degrees, 7% minority, 50% women. **Class size:** 30% < 20, 59% 20-39, 10% 40-49, less than 1% 50-99. **Special facilities:** Museum.

Student profile. Among degree-seeking undergraduates, 1,921 enrolled as first-time, first-year students.

Part-time:	58%	**Hispanic American:**	3%
Out-of-state:	1%	**Native American:**	1%
Women:	54%	**International:**	1%
African American:	8%	**25 or older:**	50%
Asian American:	1%		

Transfer out. **Colleges most students transferred to 2005:** Western Michigan University.

Basis for selection. Open admission. **Adult students:** Entrance exam policies same as for first-time freshmen.

2005-2006 Annual costs. Tuition/fees: $1,650; $2,820 out-of-district; $3,840 out-of-state. Per-credit charge: $55 in-district; $94 out-of-district; $128 out-of-state. Books/supplies: $912. Personal expenses: $1,282.

Financial aid. **Need-based:** Need-based aid available for part-time students. Work study available nights, weekends and for part-time students. **Non-need-based:** Scholarships awarded for academics, athletics.

Application procedures. **Admission:** No deadline. No application fee. Application may be submitted online. Admission notification on a rolling basis. **Financial aid:** Priority date 6/1; no closing date. FAFSA, institutional form required. Applicants notified on a rolling basis starting 5/1; must reply within 2 week(s) of notification.

Academics. **Special study options:** Cooperative education, cross-registration, distance learning, dual enrollment of high school students, ESL, honors, independent study, internships, liberal arts/career combination, weekend college. License preparation in dental hygiene, nursing. **Credit/placement by examination:** CLEP, institutional tests. 32 credit hours maximum toward associate degree. Michigan Language Assessment Battery (MiLAB) may be used for placement. **Support services:** Learning center, reduced course load, remedial instruction, tutoring, writing center.

Majors. **Business:** Accounting, administrative services, business admin, management information systems. **Communications technology:** General. **Computer sciences:** Computer graphics, data processing, programming. **Education:** General. **Engineering:** General. **Engineering technology:** Drafting, electrical. **Family/consumer sciences:** Family studies. **Health:** Dental hygiene, licensed practical nurse, medical assistant, medical secretary, nursing (RN), respiratory therapy technology. **Legal studies:** Legal secretary. **Liberal arts:** Arts/sciences. **Mechanic/repair:** Automotive. **Physical sciences:** General. **Protective services:** Firefighting, law enforcement admin, police science. **Visual/performing arts:** Commercial/advertising art.

Most popular majors. Business/marketing 11%, education 11%, engineering/engineering technologies 8%, health sciences 12%, liberal arts 43%, security/protective services 8%.

Computing on campus. 1,000 workstations in library, computer center, student center. Online course registration, wireless network available.

Student life. **Freshman orientation:** Available. **Policies:** Freshmen permitted cars on campus. **Activities:** Choral groups, student newspaper, Fellowship of Christian Athletes, international student club, Student American Dental Hygiene Association, data processing association, African American association, Latino student association, Native American association, Deaf student association.

Athletics. NJCAA. **Intercollegiate:** Baseball M, basketball, golf M, softball W, tennis, volleyball W. **Intramural:** Basketball M, softball M, tennis W, volleyball W. **Team name:** Cougars.

Student services. Career counseling, student employment services, on-campus daycare, personal counseling, placement for graduates. **Physically disabled:** Services for visually, speech, hearing impaired. **Transfer:** Special adviser, orientation for new students. Transfer adviser, college fairs on campus for students transferring to 4-year colleges.

Contact. E-mail: admissions@kvcc.edu
Phone: (269) 488-4400 Fax: (269) 488-4161
Michael McCall, Director of Admissions, Registration and Records, Kalamazoo Valley Community College, 6767 West O Avenue, P.O. Box 4070, Kalamazoo, MI 49003-4070

Kellogg Community College

Battle Creek, Michigan
www.kellogg.edu **CB code: 1375**

- Public 2-year community college
- Commuter campus in small city

General. Founded in 1956. Regionally accredited. Academic centers in Coldwater, Hastings and Albion. Regional manufacturing technical center with open entry/open exit programs in 7 different technical areas. **Enrollment:** 4,357 degree-seeking undergraduates; 1,843 non-degree-seeking students. **Degrees:** 624 associate awarded. **Location:** 20 miles from Kalamazoo, 80 miles from Grand Rapids. **Calendar:** Semester, limited summer session. **Full-time faculty:** 90 total. **Part-time faculty:** 290 total.

Student profile. Among degree-seeking undergraduates, 910 enrolled as first-time, first-year students, 197 transferred in from other institutions.

Part-time:	62%	**25 or older:**	42%
Women:	64%		

Transfer out. **Colleges most students transferred to 2005:** Western Michigan University, Michigan State University, Ferris State University, Grand Valley State University, Central Michigan University.

Basis for selection. Open admission, but selective for some programs. Allied health and nursing program applicants must supply high school record, ACT scores, any previous college record. ACT or SAT used in consideration of allied health and nursing applicants admission decisions. **Adult students:** Entrance exam policies same as for first-time freshmen.

High school preparation. College-preparatory program recommended. Recommended units include English 4, mathematics 4, social studies 1, history 3, science 4 (laboratory 1), foreign language 1 and academic electives 6.

2005-2006 Annual costs. Tuition/fees: $2,010; $3,180 out-of-district; $4,710 out-of-state. Per-credit charge: $62 in-district; $101 out-of-district; $152 out-of-state. Books/supplies: $750. Personal expenses: $4,190.

2004-2005 Financial aid. **Need-based:** 83% of total undergraduate aid awarded as scholarships/grants, 17% as loans/jobs. Need-based aid available for part-time students. Work study available nights and for part-time students. **Non-need-based:** Scholarships awarded for academics, alumni affiliation, athletics.

Application procedures. **Admission:** Priority date 8/10; no deadline. No application fee. Application may be submitted online. Admission notification on a rolling basis. **Financial aid:** Priority date 4/1; no closing date. FAFSA, institutional form required. Applicants notified on a rolling basis starting 4/1.

Academics. **Special study options:** Accelerated study, cooperative education, distance learning, double major, dual enrollment of high school students, honors, independent study, internships, liberal arts/career combination, weekend college. Bachelor's degree programs available on campus. License preparation in dental hygiene, nursing, paramedic, physical therapy, radiology. **Credit/placement by examination:** AP, CLEP, IB, institutional tests. Must be 2.0 or above for credit. **Support services:** Learning center, reduced course load, remedial instruction, study skills assistance, tutoring, writing center.

Majors. Biology: General. **Business:** Accounting, administrative services, business admin. **Communications:** Journalism, public relations. **Communications technology:** General. **Computer sciences:** Programming. **Construction:** Electrician, pipefitting. **Education:** Art, elementary, physical, secondary, special. **Engineering technology:** Drafting, electrical. **English:** Technical writing. **Family/consumer sciences:** Child care. **Health:** Clinical lab technology, dental hygiene, EMT paramedic, health services, medical radiologic technology/radiation therapy, medical secretary, nursing (RN), physical therapy assistant, premedicine, prepharmacy, preveterinary. **History:** General. **Legal studies:** Legal secretary, paralegal, prelaw. **Liberal arts:** Arts/sciences. **Math:** General. **Mechanic/repair:** Heating/ac/refrig, industrial. **Philosophy/religion:** Philosophy. **Physical sciences:** General, chemistry, physics. **Protective services:** Corrections, fire safety technology, police science. **Psychology:** General. **Public administration:** Social work. **Social sciences:** Anthropology, political science, sociology. **Visual/performing arts:** Art, commercial/advertising art, dramatic.

Most popular majors. Business/marketing 8%, health sciences 27%, legal studies 8%, liberal arts 41%.

Computing on campus. 350 workstations in library, computer center. Commuter students can connect to campus network. Online course registration, online library, helpline, wireless network available.

Student life. Freshman orientation: Available. **Activities:** Bands, choral groups, drama, literary magazine, music ensembles, student newspaper, Christian fellowship, African American Cultural Enhancement Association, human services club, Phi Theta Kappa, international students organization, literary/photography magazine, art league, crude arts club, tech club.

Athletics. NJCAA. **Intercollegiate:** Baseball M, basketball, soccer M, softball W, volleyball W. **Team name:** Bruins.

Student services. Student employment services, financial aid counseling, personal counseling, placement for graduates, veterans' counselor. **Physically disabled:** Services for visually, speech, hearing impaired. **Transfer:** Special adviser, orientation, pre-admission transcript evaluation for new students. Transfer adviser, college fairs on campus for students transferring to 4-year colleges.

Contact. Phone: (269) 365-4153 Fax: (269) 966-4089
Sedgwick Harris, Director of Admissions, Kellogg Community College, 450 North Avenue, Battle Creek, MI 49017-3397

Kirtland Community College
Roscommon, Michigan
www.kirtland.edu **CB code: 1382**

- Public 2-year community college
- Residential campus in rural community

General. Founded in 1966. Regionally accredited. **Enrollment:** 1,386 degree-seeking undergraduates. **Degrees:** 139 associate awarded. **Location:** 192 miles from Detroit, 150 miles from Grand Rapids. **Calendar:** Semester, extensive summer session. **Full-time faculty:** 35 total; 54% women. **Part-time faculty:** 112 total. **Special facilities:** Fitness and nature trail.

Student profile. Among degree-seeking undergraduates, 309 enrolled as first-time, first-year students.

Part-time:	57%	**25 or older:**	55%
Women:	66%	**Live on campus:**	5%

Transfer out. Colleges most students transferred to 2005: Central Michigan University, Saginaw Valley State University.

Basis for selection. Open admission, but selective for some programs. Special requirements for nursing (levels I and II), precorrections, criminal justice administration, criminal justice pre-services, and corrections administration programs.

High school preparation. 10 units recommended. Recommended units include English 4, mathematics 2, social studies 2 and science 2.

2005-2006 Annual costs. Tuition/fees: $2,276; $4,100 out-of-district; $4,815 out-of-state. Per-credit charge: $67 in-district; $128 out-of-district; $152 out-of-state. Books/supplies: $450.

Financial aid. Need-based: Need-based aid available for part-time students. **Additional information:** Federal Work Study available.

Application procedures. Admission: No deadline. No application fee. Admission notification on a rolling basis. **Financial aid:** Priority date 5/15; no closing date. FAFSA required. Applicants notified on a rolling basis.

Academics. Special study options: Accelerated study, cooperative education, distance learning, double major, dual enrollment of high school students, ESL, honors, independent study, internships. **Credit/placement by examination:** AP, CLEP, institutional tests. 45 credit hours maximum toward associate degree. **Support services:** Learning center, reduced course load, remedial instruction, tutoring.

Majors. Agriculture: Landscaping, plant breeding, turf management. **Business:** Accounting technology, administrative services, business admin, management information systems, marketing, real estate. **Computer sciences:** Systems analysis, webmaster, word processing. **Construction:** Carpentry. **Education:** Teacher assistance. **Engineering:** Computer. **Engineering technology:** Automotive, drafting, electrical, industrial, manufacturing. **Health:** EMT paramedic, massage therapy, medical assistant, medical secretary, medical transcription, nursing (RN), predentistry, premedicine, prepharmacy, preveterinary. **Legal studies:** Legal secretary. **Liberal arts:** Arts/sciences, humanities, library assistant. **Mechanic/repair:** Automotive, heating/ac/refrig, industrial, small engine. **Personal/culinary services:** Aesthetician, cosmetic, cosmetology, manicurist, salon management. **Production:** Machine tool, welding. **Protective services:** Correctional facilities, corrections, criminal justice, law enforcement admin, police science. **Visual/performing arts:** Graphic design.

Most popular majors. Engineering/engineering technologies 10%, health sciences 28%, liberal arts 35%, security/protective services 15%.

Computing on campus. 90 workstations in library, computer center. Dormitories linked to campus network. Online course registration, online library, helpline, wireless network available.

Student life. Freshman orientation: Available. **Policies:** Freshmen permitted cars on campus. **Activities:** Choral groups, drama, literary magazine, student government, student newspaper, student senate, Phi Theta Kappa, Christian Fellowship, criminal justice club.

Athletics. NJCAA. **Intercollegiate:** Basketball, cross-country, golf M. **Team name:** Firebirds.

Student services. Adult student services, career counseling, student employment services, financial aid counseling, on-campus daycare, personal counseling, placement for graduates, veterans' counselor. **Physically disabled:** Services for visually, hearing impaired. **Transfer:** Special adviser, orientation for new students. Transfer adviser, college fairs on campus for students transferring to 4-year colleges.

Contact. E-mail: allens@kirtland.edu
Phone: (989) 275-5121 ext. 284 Fax: (989) 275-6727
Susie Allen, Coordinator of Admissions, Kirtland Community College, 10775 North St. Helen Road, Roscommon, MI 48653

Lake Michigan College
Benton Harbor, Michigan
www.lakemichigancollege.edu **CB code: 1137**

- Public 2-year community college
- Large town

General. Founded in 1946. Regionally accredited. Full-service campus located in Niles with additional off-campus offerings at Van Buren Voc-Tech center, South Haven River Valley and Berren Springs high schools. **Enrollment:** 4,041 degree-seeking undergraduates. **Degrees:** 329 associate awarded. **Location:** 40 miles from South Bend, Indiana, 90 miles from Chicago. **Calendar:** Semester, limited summer session. **Full-time faculty:** 65 total. **Part-time faculty:** 180 total. **Special facilities:** Video production facility, nature area.

Basis for selection. Open admission, but selective for some programs. Admission to health sciences programs based on 2.5 high school GPA in academic subjects. Interview required for dental assistant, radiologic technology, nursing majors.

2005-2006 Annual costs. Tuition/fees: $2,330; $2,696 out-of-district; $3,480 out-of-state. Per-credit charge: $67 in-district; $79 out-of-district; $105 out-of-state. Books/supplies: $800. Personal expenses: $1,260.

2004-2005 Financial aid. Need-based: 94% of total undergraduate aid awarded as scholarships/grants, 6% as loans/jobs.

Application procedures. Admission: No deadline. No application fee. Admission notification on a rolling basis. **Financial aid:** Priority date 3/1;

no closing date. FAFSA required. Applicants notified on a rolling basis; must reply within 2 week(s) of notification.

Academics. **Special study options:** Cooperative education, distance learning, dual enrollment of high school students, honors, weekend college. **Credit/placement by examination:** AP, CLEP, institutional tests. 30 credit hours maximum toward associate degree. **Support services:** Learning center, remedial instruction, tutoring.

Majors. **Biology:** General. **Business:** Accounting, administrative services, business admin, finance, hospitality admin, office/clerical, operations, sales/distribution. **Communications:** Journalism. **Computer sciences:** Information systems, word processing. **Education:** General. **Engineering:** General. **Engineering technology:** Drafting, electrical, manufacturing. **English:** Speech/rhetoric. **Foreign languages:** General. **Health:** Dental assistant, medical radiologic technology/radiation therapy, medical secretary, nursing (RN), occupational therapy assistant. **History:** General. **Interdisciplinary:** Biological/physical sciences. **Legal studies:** Legal secretary. **Liberal arts:** Arts/sciences, humanities. **Math:** General. **Parks/recreation:** Health/fitness. **Philosophy/religion:** Philosophy. **Physical sciences:** Chemistry, geology, physics. **Production:** Machine tool. **Protective services:** Corrections, police science. **Psychology:** General. **Social sciences:** Geography, political science, sociology. **Visual/performing arts:** Art, dramatic.

Computing on campus. 100 workstations in computer center.

Student life. **Freshman orientation:** Mandatory. Freshman seminar for first-time college students. **Activities:** Bands, choral groups, drama, music ensembles, student government, student newspaper.

Athletics. NJCAA. **Intercollegiate:** Baseball M, basketball, golf M, softball W, volleyball W. **Intramural:** Badminton, baseball M, basketball, bowling, softball, table tennis, tennis, volleyball.

Student services. Career counseling, student employment services, health services, personal counseling, placement for graduates, veterans' counselor. **Physically disabled:** Services for visually, hearing impaired. **Transfer:** Orientation for new students. College fairs on campus for students transferring to 4-year colleges.

Contact. E-mail: dail@lakemichigancollege.edu
Phone: (269) 927-8128 Toll-free number: (800) 252-1562
Ann Liska, Registrar, Lake Michigan College, 2755 East Napier Avenue, Benton Harbor, MI 49022-1899

Lansing Community College

Lansing, Michigan — **CB member**
www.lansing.cc.mi.us — **CB code: 1414**

- Public 2-year community college
- Commuter campus in small city

General. Founded in 1957. Regionally accredited. Several 4-year degree course studies available, students complete 3 years at LCC and 4th year at a 4-year degree institution. **Enrollment:** 9,730 degree-seeking undergraduates; 9,077 non-degree-seeking students. **Degrees:** 1,278 associate awarded. **ROTC:** Army, Air Force. **Location:** 90 miles from Detroit. **Calendar:** Semester, extensive summer session. **Full-time faculty:** 231 total; 16% minority, 52% women. **Part-time faculty:** 1,160 total; 12% minority, 50% women. **Class size:** 67% < 20, 33% 20-39, less than 1% 40-49, less than 1% 50-99, less than 1% >100. **Special facilities:** Planetarium, observatory, science concepts laboratory, computer-integrated manufacturing institute, in-depth photography institute, truck driver training range, technical library.

Student profile. Among degree-seeking undergraduates, 30% enrolled in a transfer program, 30% enrolled in a vocational program, 10% already have a bachelor's degree or higher, 2,071 enrolled as first-time, first-year students.

Part-time:	68%	**25 or older:**	38%
Women:	55%		

Transfer out. **Colleges most students transferred to 2005:** Michigan State University, Central Michigan University.

Basis for selection. Open admission, but selective for some programs. Special requirements for health, aviation, music, police academy programs, fire academy. MELAB required of foreign students. TOEFL also accepted. Interview required of health program applicants and international applicants. Audition recommended for music, dance, theater majors. Portfolio recommended for art majors.

2006-2007 Annual costs. Tuition/fees (projected): $2,000; $3,200 out-of-district; $4,400 out-of-state. Per-credit charge: $65 in-district; $105 out-of-district; $145 out-of-state. Books/supplies: $660. Personal expenses: $1,020.

Financial aid. **Need-based:** Need-based aid available for part-time students. Work study available nights, weekends and for part-time students. **Non-need-based:** Scholarships awarded for academics, athletics.

Application procedures. **Admission:** No deadline. No application fee. Application may be submitted online. Admission notification on a rolling basis. SAT or ACT recommended for assessment waivers and counseling. **Financial aid:** Priority date 7/5; no closing date. FAFSA required. Applicants notified on a rolling basis starting 4/3.

Academics. **Special study options:** Accelerated study, cooperative education, cross-registration, distance learning, double major, dual enrollment of high school students, exchange student, honors, independent study, internships, study abroad, teacher certification program, weekend college. External bachelor's degree with Northwood Institute, 3+1 degree program, 2+2 degree program. Bachelor's degree programs available on campus. License preparation in aviation, dental hygiene, nursing, paramedic, real estate. **Credit/placement by examination:** AP, CLEP, IB, institutional tests. 40 credit hours maximum toward associate degree. **Support services:** Learning center, pre-admission summer program, reduced course load, remedial instruction, study skills assistance, tutoring, writing center.

Majors. **Architecture:** Interior, landscape. **Area/ethnic studies:** African. **Biology:** General. **Business:** General, accounting, administrative services, business admin, fashion, hospitality/recreation, human resources, insurance, international, management information systems, marketing, office management, office technology, real estate, sales/distribution, tourism promotion, tourism/travel. **Communications:** General, advertising, broadcast journalism, journalism. **Communications technology:** General, graphic/printing. **Computer sciences:** General, applications programming, data processing, networking, programming, systems analysis, vendor certification. **Conservation:** General. **Construction:** Carpentry, maintenance, masonry, pipefitting, power transmission. **Education:** General, art, elementary, English, mathematics, music, physical, science, secondary, social science, special, speech, trade/industrial. **Engineering:** General. **Engineering technology:** Civil, drafting, electrical, environmental, hydraulics. **English:** American lit. **Family/consumer sciences:** General, child care, institutional food production. **Foreign languages:** General, French, German, sign language interpretation, Spanish. **Health:** Clinical lab science, dental hygiene, EMT paramedic, health care admin, licensed practical nurse, medical assistant, medical radiologic technology/radiation therapy, medical secretary, nuclear medical technology, physician assistant, predentistry, respiratory therapy technology, sonography, surgical technology. **History:** General. **Interdisciplinary:** Biological/physical sciences, gerontology. **Legal studies:** Court reporting, legal secretary, paralegal, prelaw. **Liberal arts:** Arts/sciences. **Math:** General, applied. **Mechanic/repair:** General, aircraft, avionics, electronics/electrical, heating/ac/refrig, industrial. **Parks/recreation:** Facilities management. **Personal/culinary services:** Cosmetic, culinary arts. **Philosophy/religion:** Philosophy, religion. **Physical sciences:** Chemistry. **Protective services:** Criminal justice, firefighting, law enforcement admin, police science. **Psychology:** General. **Public administration:** Social work. **Social sciences:** General, anthropology, geography, political science, sociology. **Transportation:** Aviation. **Visual/performing arts:** General, art, cinematography, commercial/advertising art, dance, dramatic, drawing, music performance, music theory/composition, painting, photography.

Most popular majors. Business/marketing 8%, health sciences 14%, liberal arts 51%.

Computing on campus. 200 workstations in library, computer center. Commuter students can connect to campus network. Online course registration, helpline, wireless network available.

Student life. **Freshman orientation:** Available. Preregistration for classes offered. Occurs first 5 days of open registration. **Policies:** Freshmen permitted cars on campus. **Activities:** Bands, choral groups, dance, drama, film society, music ensembles, musical theater, radio station, student government, student newspaper, symphony orchestra, TV station, Newman Club, black student delegates, Hispanic club, Campus Disciples, Baptist Student Union, international club, Maranatha Christian Fellowship, student adviser club, substance abuse association.

Athletics. NJCAA. **Intercollegiate:** Basketball, cross-country, golf, track and field, volleyball W. **Intramural:** Basketball, bowling, boxing M. **Team name:** Stars.

Student services. Adult student services, career counseling, services for economically disadvantaged, student employment services, financial aid counseling, minority student services, personal counseling, placement for graduates, veterans' counselor, women's services. **Physically disabled:** Services for visually, speech, hearing impaired. **Transfer:** Special adviser, orientation for new students. Transfer adviser, college fairs on campus for students transferring to 4-year colleges.

Contact. Phone: (517) 483-1200 Toll-free number: (800) 644-4522
Fax: (517) 483-9668
Sandra Putkamer, Director of Admissions, Lansing Community College, 422 North Washington Square, Lansing, MI 48901

Lewis College of Business
Detroit, Michigan
www.lewiscollege.edu **CB code: 1425**

- Private 2-year business and junior college
- Commuter campus in very large city
- Interview required

General. Founded in 1920. Regionally accredited. **Enrollment:** 250 full-time, degree-seeking students. **Degrees:** 38 associate awarded. **Location:** 50 miles from Ann Arbor, 90 miles from Lansing. **Calendar:** Semester, extensive summer session. **Full-time faculty:** 10 total. **Part-time faculty:** 30 total. **Special facilities:** Slave trade special collections.

Basis for selection. Open admission.

2005-2006 Annual costs. Tuition/fees: $10,080. Per-credit charge: $325. Books/supplies: $500.

Application procedures. Admission: No deadline. $20 fee. Admission notification on a rolling basis beginning on or about 8/30. **Financial aid:** No deadline. FAFSA required.

Academics. Special study options: Double major, honors, independent study. GED program. **Credit/placement by examination:** CLEP. 30 credit hours maximum toward associate degree. **Support services:** Learning center, reduced course load, remedial instruction, tutoring.

Majors. Business: Business admin, office technology. **Computer sciences:** General, information technology. **Liberal arts:** Arts/sciences.

Computing on campus. 50 workstations in library, computer center, student center.

Student life. Activities: Choral groups, drama, student government, student newspaper, business club, Sister to Sister, office information systems club.

Student services. Adult student services, career counseling, student employment services, on-campus daycare, placement for graduates. **Transfer:** Special adviser, orientation for new students. Transfer adviser for students transferring to 4-year colleges.

Contact. E-mail: sukowal@aol.com
Phone: (313) 862-6300 ext. 501 Fax: (313) 862-1027
Carl King, Director of Admissions, Lewis College of Business, 17370 Meyers Road, Detroit, MI 48235

Macomb Community College
Warren, Michigan **CB member**
www.macomb.edu **CB code: 1722**

- Public 2-year community college
- Commuter campus in small city

General. Founded in 1954. Regionally accredited. **Enrollment:** 11,815 degree-seeking undergraduates; 8,781 non-degree-seeking students. **Degrees:** 2,109 associate awarded. **Location:** 20 miles from Detroit. **Calendar:** Semester, extensive summer session. **Full-time faculty:** 227 total; 14% have terminal degrees, 4% minority, 40% women. **Part-time faculty:** 708 total; 10% have terminal degrees, 5% minority, 40% women. **Special facilities:** Nature preserves, center for performing arts.

Student profile. Among degree-seeking undergraduates, 2,031 enrolled as first-time, first-year students.

Part-time:	64%	**Hispanic American:**	1%
Women:	51%	**International:**	1%
African American:	6%	**25 or older:**	39%
Asian American:	4%		

Transfer out. Colleges most students transferred to 2005: Central Michigan University, Oakland University, Walsh College, Wayne State University, Michigan State University.

Basis for selection. Open admission, but selective for some programs. Special requirements for nursing, physical therapy assistant, occupational therapy assistant, respiratory therapy assistant, veterinarian technician programs; combination of GPA and test scores considered.

2006-2007 Annual costs. Tuition/fees (projected): $2,055; $3,109 out-of-district; $4,039 out-of-state. Per-credit charge: $65 in-district; $99 out-of-district; $129 out-of-state. Books/supplies: $578. Personal expenses: $791.

2005-2006 Financial aid. Need-based: Need-based aid available for part-time students. Work study available nights, weekends and for part-time students. **Non-need-based:** Scholarships awarded for academics, athletics, leadership, music/drama, state residency.

Application procedures. Admission: No deadline. No application fee. Admission notification on a rolling basis. January 31 closing date for nursing and physical therapy assistant programs. **Financial aid:** Priority date 4/15; no closing date. FAFSA, institutional form required. Applicants notified on a rolling basis starting 5/15; must reply within 2 week(s) of notification.

Academics. Courses toward bachelor's degrees offered on campus by University of Detroit, Walsh College of Accountancy and Business Administration, Wayne State University, Central Michigan University, Oakland University, University of Detroit Mercy, Davenport University, and Rochester College. On-line degree program with Franklin University. **Special study options:** Cooperative education, cross-registration, distance learning, dual enrollment of high school students, ESL, independent study, internships, liberal arts/career combination, study abroad, weekend college. **Credit/placement by examination:** AP, CLEP, institutional tests. 47 credit hours maximum toward associate degree. **Support services:** Learning center, reduced course load, remedial instruction, tutoring.

Majors. Biology: General. **Business:** General, accounting, administrative services, business admin, marketing, office technology, operations. **Communications:** General, broadcast journalism, public relations. **Communications technology:** Graphic/printing. **Computer sciences:** General, data entry, networking, programming, web page design. **Engineering technology:** Civil, construction, drafting, electrical, manufacturing, surveying. **Family/consumer sciences:** Child care. **Health:** EMT paramedic, health services, medical assistant, medical secretary, nursing (RN), occupational therapy assistant, physical therapy assistant, respiratory therapy technology, surgical technology, veterinary technology/assistant. **Legal studies:** Paralegal. **Liberal arts:** Arts/sciences. **Math:** General. **Mechanic/repair:** Automotive, electronics/electrical, heating/ac/refrig. **Personal/culinary services:** Culinary arts. **Physical sciences:** Chemistry. **Protective services:** Fire safety technology, firefighting, forensics, police science. **Visual/performing arts:** Commercial/advertising art.

Most popular majors. Business/marketing 12%, engineering/engineering technologies 6%, health sciences 13%, liberal arts 50%.

Computing on campus. 1,800 workstations in library, computer center. Commuter students can connect to campus network.

Student life. Freshman orientation: Available. Occurs beginning of each semester. **Activities:** Bands, choral groups, dance, drama, music ensembles, musical theater, symphony orchestra, student activities board, College Republicans, service learning and volunteerism, Newman Club, Campus Crusade for Christ, Young Democrats, African American alliance, international culture club, Phi Theta Kappa.

Athletics. NJCAA. **Intercollegiate:** Baseball M, basketball, cross-country, soccer M, softball W, volleyball W.

Student services. Campus ministries, career counseling, student employment services, financial aid counseling, health services, personal counseling, placement for graduates. **Physically disabled:** Services for visually, speech, hearing impaired. **Transfer:** Special adviser, orientation for new students. Transfer adviser, college fairs on campus for students transferring to 4-year colleges.

Contact. Phone: (586) 445-7999 Toll-free number: (866) 622-6621
Fax: (586) 445-7157
Ronald Hughes, Director of Enrollment Services, Macomb Community College, 14500 East Twelve Mile Road, Warren, MI 48088-3896

Mid Michigan Community College
Harrison, Michigan
www.midmich.edu **CB code: 1523**

- Public 2-year community college
- Commuter campus in small town

General. Founded in 1965. Regionally accredited. Branch campus in Mt. Pleasant. **Enrollment:** 3,276 degree-seeking undergraduates. **Degrees:** 159 associate awarded. **Location:** 30 miles from Mount Pleasant, 100 miles from Lansing. **Calendar:** Semester, limited summer session. **Full-time faculty:** 40 total; 12% have terminal degrees, 40% women. **Part-time faculty:** 150 total; 2% have terminal degrees, 7% minority, 33% women. **Class size:** 55% < 20, 42% 20-39, 2% 40-49, less than 1% 50-99.

Student profile. Among degree-seeking undergraduates, 66% enrolled in a transfer program, 34% enrolled in a vocational program, 1% already have

a bachelor's degree or higher, 1,126 enrolled as first-time, first-year students.

Part-time:	54%	**Asian American:**	1%
Out-of-state:	5%	**Hispanic American:**	2%
Women:	62%	**Native American:**	2%
African American:	2%	**25 or older:**	65%

Transfer out. **Colleges most students transferred to 2005:** Central Michigan University, Ferris State University, Saginaw Valley State University.

Basis for selection. Open admission, but selective for some programs. Admission for health occupations majors based on prerequisite course completion and grades. High school diploma or GED recommended. Interview required of health program applicants. **Adult students:** SAT/ACT scores not required. **Learning Disabled:** Students referred to counselor to address special needs.

High school preparation. Recommended units include English 4, mathematics 4, social studies 2, history 1, science 3 (laboratory 2) and foreign language 1. One unit chemistry, 1 algebra, 1 biology required for health occupations majors.

2006-2007 Annual costs. Tuition/fees (projected): $2,023; $3,620 out-of-district; $6,410 out-of-state. Books/supplies: $766. Personal expenses: $698.

Financial aid. **Need-based:** Need-based aid available for part-time students. Work study available for part-time students. **Non-need-based:** Scholarships awarded for academics.

Application procedures. **Admission:** No deadline. No application fee. Application may be submitted online. Admission notification on a rolling basis. **Financial aid:** Priority date 5/1; no closing date. FAFSA, institutional form required. Applicants notified on a rolling basis starting 4/1; must reply within 2 week(s) of notification.

Academics. **Special study options:** Cooperative education, distance learning, double major, dual enrollment of high school students, independent study, internships, liberal arts/career combination. License preparation in nursing, paramedic, radiology. **Credit/placement by examination:** AP, CLEP, institutional tests. 15 credit hours maximum toward associate degree. **Support services:** Learning center, reduced course load, remedial instruction, study skills assistance, tutoring, writing center.

Majors. **Biology:** General, biotechnology. **Business:** Accounting, administrative services, banking/financial services, business admin, entrepreneurial studies, marketing. **Communications:** General. **Computer sciences:** General, applications programming, computer science. **Conservation:** General, fisheries. **Education:** Elementary, secondary, teacher assistance. **Engineering:** General. **Engineering technology:** Manufacturing. **English:** Speech/rhetoric. **Family/consumer sciences:** Child care. **Health:** EMT paramedic, medical assistant, medical radiologic technology/radiation therapy, medical secretary, medical transcription, nursing (RN), prepharmacy. **Legal studies:** Legal secretary. **Liberal arts:** Arts/sciences. **Math:** General. **Mechanic/repair:** Heating/ac/refrig. **Physical sciences:** Chemistry. **Protective services:** Firefighting, police science. **Psychology:** General. **Social sciences:** Sociology. **Visual/performing arts:** General, commercial/advertising art, dramatic.

Computing on campus. 450 workstations in library, computer center. Commuter students can connect to campus network. Online library, helpline available.

Student life. **Freshman orientation:** Available. Preregistration for classes offered. Scheduled before each semester. **Housing:** Community-wide housing bulletin available on request. **Activities:** Drama, musical theater, student government, student newspaper, Phi Theta Kappa.

Student services. Adult student services, alcohol/substance abuse counseling, career counseling, services for economically disadvantaged, student employment services, financial aid counseling, personal counseling, placement for graduates, veterans' counselor. **Physically disabled:** Services for visually, speech, hearing impaired. **Transfer:** Special adviser, orientation, pre-admission transcript evaluation for new students. Transfer adviser, college fairs on campus for students transferring to 4-year colleges.

Contact. E-mail: kbarnes@midmich.edu
Phone: (989) 386-6661 Fax: (989) 386-6613
Kim Barnes, Director of Admissions and Placement, Mid Michigan Community College, 1375 South Clare Avenue, Harrison, MI 48625

Monroe County Community College

Monroe, Michigan
www.monroeccc.edu **CB code: 1514**

- Public 2-year community college
- Commuter campus in large town

General. Founded in 1964. Regionally accredited. Off-campus site at Whitman Center. **Enrollment:** 4,180 undergraduates. **Degrees:** 370 associate awarded. **Location:** 45 miles from Detroit, 20 miles from Toledo, Ohio. **Calendar:** Semester, limited summer session. **Full-time faculty:** 62 total. **Part-time faculty:** 125 total.

Student profile.

Out-of-state:	1%	**25 or older:**	40%

Transfer out. **Colleges most students transferred to 2005:** Eastern Michigan University, University of Toledo, Sierra Heights University, Western Michigan University, University of Michigan.

Basis for selection. Open admission, but selective for some programs. Admission for nursing, respiratory therapy and medical assistance applicants based on 2.5 high school GPA, 21 ACT preferred. Completion of biological and chemistry courses, and completion of college math required. Culinary skills program also selective and requires interview. ACT required for nursing and respiratory therapy applicants. Test scores required by March 31. Interview required of respiratory therapy and culinary program applicants.

High school preparation. Recommended units include English 4, mathematics 3, social studies 3, history 1 and science 3. Nursing and respiratory therapy applicants must have 1 unit chemistry and 1 biology. Strong science background highly recommended.

2005-2006 Annual costs. Tuition/fees: $2,030; $3,230 out-of-district; $3,530 out-of-state. Per-credit charge: $62 in-district; $102 out-of-district; $112 out-of-state. Books/supplies: $700. Personal expenses: $560.

Financial aid. **Need-based:** Need-based aid available for part-time students. Work study available nights, weekends and for part-time students. **Non-need-based:** Scholarships awarded for academics, alumni affiliation, art, leadership, music/drama, state residency.

Application procedures. **Admission:** Priority date 5/1; no deadline. No application fee. Application may be submitted online. Admission notification on a rolling basis. Closing date for nursing applications March 31, respiratory therapy April 30. **Financial aid:** Priority date 4/1; no closing date. FAFSA, institutional form required. Applicants notified on a rolling basis starting 4/1; must reply within 2 week(s) of notification.

Academics. **Special study options:** Accelerated study, cooperative education, dual enrollment of high school students, independent study. License preparation in nursing, paramedic, real estate. **Credit/placement by examination:** AP, CLEP, institutional tests. 30 credit hours maximum toward associate degree. **Support services:** Learning center, reduced course load, remedial instruction, tutoring.

Majors. **Business:** Accounting, administrative services, banking/financial services, business admin, office technology, office/clerical. **Computer sciences:** General, applications programming, programming. **Education:** Early childhood. **Engineering:** Electrical. **Engineering technology:** Architectural, drafting, electrical, manufacturing. **Family/consumer sciences:** Child care. **Health:** Medical secretary, nursing (RN), respiratory therapy technology. **Legal studies:** Legal secretary. **Liberal arts:** Arts/sciences. **Personal/culinary services:** Culinary arts. **Visual/performing arts:** Studio arts.

Computing on campus. 90 workstations in computer center.

Student life. **Freshman orientation:** Available. **Activities:** Concert band, choral groups, drama, student government, student newspaper, respiratory therapy club, nursing club, Society of Automotive Engineers, campus Bible study.

Student services. Career counseling, student employment services, on-campus daycare, personal counseling, placement for graduates. **Physically disabled:** Services for visually, speech, hearing impaired. **Transfer:** Special adviser, orientation for new students. Transfer adviser, college fairs on campus for students transferring to 4-year colleges.

Contact. E-mail: rdaniels@monroeccc.edu
Phone: (734) 384-4104 Toll-free number: (877) 937-6222
Fax: (734) 242-9711
Randell Daniels, Director of Admissions and Guidance Services, Monroe County Community College, 1555 South Raisinville Road, Monroe, MI 48161

Montcalm Community College

Sidney, Michigan
www.montcalm.edu **CB code: 1522**

- Public 2-year community and liberal arts college
- Commuter campus in rural community

General. Founded in 1965. Regionally accredited. Off-campus centers in Ionia, Howard City, Greenville and Alma. **Enrollment:** 1,796 degree-seeking undergraduates; 401 non-degree-seeking students. **Degrees:** 124 associate awarded. **Location:** 50 miles from Grand Rapids, 65 miles from Lansing. **Calendar:** Semester, limited summer session. **Full-time faculty:** 25 total. **Part-time faculty:** 108 total. **Class size:** 77% < 20, 22% 20-39, less than 1% 40-49, less than 1% 50-99. **Special facilities:** Marked nature preserves and trails, barn theatre.

Student profile. Among degree-seeking undergraduates, 322 enrolled as first-time, first-year students.

Part-time:	61%	**Hispanic American:**	2%
Women:	70%	**Native American:**	1%

Transfer out. Colleges most students transferred to 2005: Central Michigan University, Ferris State University, Grand Valley State University, Davenport University.

Basis for selection. Open admission, but selective for some programs. Applicants to nursing program must have a score of 41 on ASSET Reading Skills Test and 41 on Numerical Skills Test or 18 or above in corresponding ACT subscores. **Adult students:** Entrance exam policies same as for first-time freshmen.

2005-2006 Annual costs. Tuition/fees: $2,085; $3,105 out-of-district; $3,975 out-of-state. Per-credit charge: $64 in-district; $98 out-of-district; $127 out-of-state. Personal expenses: $1,912.

Financial aid. Need-based: Need-based aid available for part-time students. Work study available for part-time students. **Non-need-based:** Scholarships awarded for academics, state residency.

Application procedures. Admission: No deadline. No application fee. Application must be submitted on paper. Admission notification on a rolling basis. **Financial aid:** Priority date 2/15; no closing date. FAFSA, institutional form required. Applicants notified on a rolling basis starting 6/15; must reply within 2 week(s) of notification.

Academics. Special study options: Cooperative education, distance learning, dual enrollment of high school students, independent study, internships, liberal arts/career combination. License preparation in nursing, paramedic. **Credit/placement by examination:** AP, CLEP, institutional tests. **Support services:** GED test center, learning center, reduced course load, remedial instruction, study skills assistance, tutoring.

Majors. Business: Accounting, administrative services, business admin, entrepreneurial studies, executive assistant, management information systems, office technology. **Computer sciences:** General, data processing. **Engineering technology:** Drafting, electrical, surveying. **Family/consumer sciences:** Child care. **Health:** EMT paramedic, medical radiologic technology/radiation therapy, medical secretary, nursing (RN). **Liberal arts:** Arts/sciences. **Mechanic/repair:** Computer, electronics/electrical. **Personal/culinary services:** Cosmetic. **Protective services:** Criminal justice.

Most popular majors. Business/marketing 13%, family/consumer sciences 6%, health sciences 40%, liberal arts 33%.

Computing on campus. 450 workstations in library, computer center. Helpline available.

Student life. Freshman orientation: Mandatory. **Activities:** Jazz band, choral groups, drama, music ensembles, musical theater, Phi Theta Kappa, future business professionals club, Native American club, nursing club, judo club.

Athletics. Intramural: Volleyball.

Student services. Career counseling, student employment services, financial aid counseling, placement for graduates. **Physically disabled:** Services for visually, speech, hearing impaired. **Transfer:** Special adviser, orientation, pre-admission transcript evaluation for new students. Transfer adviser, college fairs on campus for students transferring to 4-year colleges.

Contact. E-mail: admissions@montcalm.edu
Phone: (989) 328-1250 Toll-free number: (877) 328-2111
Fax: (989) 328-2950
Debra Alexander, Director of Admissions, Montcalm Community College, 2800 College Drive, Sidney, MI 48885

Mott Community College

Flint, Michigan — **CB member**
www.mcc.edu — **CB code: 1225**

- Public 2-year community college
- Commuter campus in large city

General. Founded in 1923. Regionally accredited. Branch campuses located in Fenton, Lapeer, Livingston, and Clio. **Enrollment:** 7,337 degree-seeking undergraduates; 2,962 non-degree-seeking students. **Degrees:** 787 associate awarded. **Location:** 65 miles from Detroit. **Calendar:** Semester, extensive summer session. **Full-time faculty:** 147 total; 22% have terminal degrees, 17% minority, 56% women. **Part-time faculty:** 362 total; 4% have terminal degrees, 16% minority, 54% women. **Special facilities:** Geology museum, regional technology center, dental clinic, visual arts and design center, greenhouse, student-operated cosmetology/nail technology salon.

Student profile. Among degree-seeking undergraduates, 14% enrolled in a transfer program, 73% enrolled in a vocational program, 1,101 enrolled as first-time, first-year students, 312 transferred in from other institutions.

Part-time:	67%	**Hispanic American:**	2%
Women:	65%	**Native American:**	1%
African American:	18%	**25 or older:**	40%
Asian American:	1%		

Transfer out. Colleges most students transferred to 2005: University of Michigan-Flint, Ferris State University, Central Michigan University, Saginaw Valley State University, MIchigan State University.

Basis for selection. Open admission, but selective for some programs. Special requirements for nursing and allied health programs. Audition recommended for music majors. **Adult students:** Entrance exam policies same as for first-time freshmen. **Learning Disabled:** MCC provides supportive services to students with documented disabilities. Students must request assistance, provide documentation of disabilities, and register with Disability Services before classes begin.

2006-2007 Annual costs. Tuition/fees (projected): $2,508; $3,638 out-of-district; $4,776 out-of-state. Per-credit charge: $76 in-district; $113 out-of-district; $151 out-of-state. Books/supplies: $746. Personal expenses: $779.

2004-2005 Financial aid. Need-based: 75% of total undergraduate aid awarded as scholarships/grants, 25% as loans/jobs. Need-based aid available for part-time students. Work study available nights, weekends and for part-time students. **Non-need-based:** Scholarships awarded for academics, alumni affiliation, art, athletics, leadership, minority status, music/drama, state residency.

Application procedures. Admission: No deadline. No application fee. Application may be submitted online. Admission notification on a rolling basis. **Financial aid:** No deadline. FAFSA required. Applicants notified on a rolling basis starting 5/1.

Academics. Distance learning and open entry/open exit modular courses being expanded in Regional Technology Center. **Special study options:** Cooperative education, distance learning, double major, dual enrollment of high school students, ESL, honors, independent study, internships, liberal arts/career combination. Bachelor's degree programs available on campus. License preparation in dental hygiene, nursing, occupational therapy, physical therapy, real estate. **Credit/placement by examination:** AP, CLEP, institutional tests. 16 credit hours maximum toward associate degree. **Support services:** Learning center, reduced course load, remedial instruction, study skills assistance, tutoring, writing center.

Majors. Business: General, accounting technology, administrative services, business admin, entrepreneurial studies, executive assistant, information resources management, international, management information systems, marketing, office management, office technology. **Communications technology:** General. **Computer sciences:** Networking. **Education:** Early childhood, teacher assistance. **Engineering technology:** Architectural, drafting, electrical, heat/ac/refrig, industrial, manufacturing, mechanical, mechanical drafting, quality control, surveying. **Family/consumer sciences:** Institutional food production. **Foreign languages:** Sign language interpretation. **Health:** Community health services, dental assistant, dental hygiene, EMT paramedic, histologic assistant, medical radiologic technology/radiation therapy, medical secretary, nursing (RN), occupational therapy assistant, physical therapy assistant, respiratory therapy technology. **Legal studies:** Legal secretary. **Liberal arts:** Arts/sciences. **Mechanic/repair:** Auto body, automotive. **Personal/culinary services:** Chef training, salon management. **Protective services:** Fire safety technology, police science. **Visual/performing arts:** Graphic design, photography.

Most popular majors. Business/marketing 8%, health sciences 22%, liberal arts 47%, security/protective services 7%.

Computing on campus. 1,290 workstations in library, computer center, student center. Commuter students can connect to campus network. Online course registration, helpline, student web hosting, wireless network available.

Student life. Freshman orientation: Mandatory. **Policies:** Freshmen permitted cars on campus. **Activities:** Bands, choral groups, music ensembles, student government, law enforcement resource network, connoisseur club, environmental club, Phi Theta Kappa (Alpha Omicron Iota Chapter), student nurses association, dental assisting, gardening association, social work club, travel club.

Athletics. NJCAA. **Intercollegiate:** Baseball M, basketball, cross-country, golf M, softball W, volleyball W. **Team name:** Bears.

Student services. Career counseling, services for economically disadvantaged, student employment services, financial aid counseling, health services, on-campus daycare, personal counseling, placement for graduates. **Physically disabled:** Services for visually, speech, hearing impaired. **Transfer:** Special adviser, orientation, pre-admission transcript evaluation for new students. Transfer adviser, college fairs on campus for students transferring to 4-year colleges.

Contact. E-mail: Inquiry@mcc.edu
Phone: (810) 762-0315 Toll-free number: (800) 852-8614
Fax: (810) 232-9442
Marc Payne, Executive Director, Admissions & Recruitment, Mott Community College, 1401 East Court Street, Flint, MI 48503-2089

Muskegon Community College

Muskegon, Michigan
www.muskegon.edu **CB code: 1495**

- Public 2-year community college
- Commuter campus in small city

General. Founded in 1926. Regionally accredited. Bachelor's and graduate programs offered on-campus with participating 4-year institutions. **Enrollment:** 1,900 full-time, degree-seeking students. **Degrees:** 386 associate awarded. **Location:** 45 miles from Grand Rapids. **Calendar:** Two 15-week terms followed by two 7 1/2-week terms. Limited summer session. **Full-time faculty:** 110 total. **Part-time faculty:** 150 total. **Special facilities:** Planetarium, nature preserve.

Basis for selection. Open admission, but selective for some programs. Nursing applicants must have math (level 35) and basic college chemistry. High school diploma, GED, 10th-grade reading level on Nelson Denny, or ACT composite score of at least 22 required for select programs and courses. High school diploma, GED or completion of 15 credits with at least a C average required for degree-seeking candidates.

2005-2006 Annual costs. Tuition/fees: $1,970; $2,870 out-of-district; $3,620 out-of-state. Per-credit charge: $60 in-district; $90 out-of-district; $115 out-of-state. Students also assessed contact hour fees, which vary according to residency status, and course fees, which vary. Books/supplies: $700. Personal expenses: $800.

Application procedures. Admission: Priority date 5/1; no deadline. No application fee. Admission notification on a rolling basis. **Financial aid:** Priority date 5/1; no closing date. FAFSA, institutional form required. Applicants notified on a rolling basis starting 6/1; must reply within 2 week(s) of notification.

Academics. Special study options: Cooperative education, cross-registration, distance learning, double major, dual enrollment of high school students, honors, independent study, internships. **Credit/placement by examination:** CLEP, institutional tests. 30 credit hours maximum toward associate degree. **Support services:** Learning center, remedial instruction, tutoring.

Majors. Business: Accounting, administrative services, international, marketing. **Communications technology:** Graphic/printing. **Computer sciences:** General, data processing. **Engineering technology:** Drafting, electrical. **Health:** Licensed practical nurse, medical secretary, nursing (RN), respiratory therapy technology. **Legal studies:** Legal secretary. **Mechanic/repair:** General. **Protective services:** Law enforcement admin. **Visual/performing arts:** Commercial/advertising art.

Student life. Activities: Bands, choral groups, dance, drama, music ensembles, musical theater, student government, student newspaper, TV station, interdenominational religious group, black student alliance, Students Again Gaining Enlightenment, study opportunities for adults and mature citizens.

Athletics. NJCAA. **Intercollegiate:** Baseball M, basketball, golf, softball W, tennis W, volleyball W, wrestling M. **Intramural:** Baseball M, basketball, golf, softball W.

Student services. Career counseling, student employment services, health services, personal counseling, placement for graduates, veterans' counselor. **Physically disabled:** Services for visually, speech, hearing impaired. **Transfer:** Special adviser, orientation for new students. College fairs on campus for students transferring to 4-year colleges.

Contact. E-mail: bamfiej@muskegon.edu
Phone: (231) 777-0363 Fax: (231) 777-0209
John Bamfield, Associate Dean, Muskegon Community College, 221 South Quarterline Road, Muskegon, MI 49442

North Central Michigan College

Petoskey, Michigan
www.ncmc.cc.mi.us **CB code: 1569**

- Public 2-year community college
- Commuter campus in small town

General. Founded in 1958. Regionally accredited. **Enrollment:** 1,935 degree-seeking undergraduates. **Degrees:** 215 associate awarded. **Location:** 40 miles from Mackinaw City, 60 miles from Traverse City. **Calendar:** Semester, limited summer session. **Full-time faculty:** 35 total. **Part-time faculty:** 130 total. **Class size:** 100% 20-39. **Special facilities:** Nature preserve.

Student profile.

Out-of-state:	5%	**Live on campus:**	5%
25 or older:	57%		

Transfer out. Colleges most students transferred to 2005: Lake Superior State University, Grand Valley State University, Central Michigan University, Northern Michigan University, Ferris State University.

Basis for selection. Open admission, but selective for some programs. Special requirements for nursing program. All degree-seeking students must provide ACT, SAT or COMPASS scores for mandatory placement. **Adult students:** Entrance exam policies same as for first-time freshmen.

High school preparation. Recommended units include English 3, mathematics 3 and science 3. Chemistry recommended for nursing applicants.

2005-2006 Annual costs. Tuition/fees: $2,175; $3,294 out-of-district; $4,037 out-of-state. Per-credit charge: $64 in-district; $101 out-of-district; $126 out-of-state. Room only: $2,300. Books/supplies: $750.

Financial aid. Need-based: Need-based aid available for part-time students. Work study available nights, weekends and for part-time students.

Application procedures. Admission: No deadline. No application fee. Application must be submitted online. Admission notification on a rolling basis. **Financial aid:** Priority date 4/15; no closing date. FAFSA, institutional form required. Applicants notified on a rolling basis starting 4/30.

Academics. Special study options: Cooperative education, cross-registration, distance learning, dual enrollment of high school students, independent study, internships. Bachelor's degree programs available on campus. **Credit/placement by examination:** AP, CLEP, IB. 15 credit hours maximum toward associate degree. **Support services:** Learning center, remedial instruction, tutoring.

Majors. Business: General, accounting, administrative services, business admin, office/clerical. **Computer sciences:** General. **Education:** Early childhood. **Health:** EMT paramedic, nursing (RN). **Legal studies:** Paralegal. **Liberal arts:** Arts/sciences.

Most popular majors. Health sciences 21%, liberal arts 71%.

Computing on campus. 133 workstations in dormitories, library, computer center, student center. Dormitories wired for high-speed internet access and linked to campus network. Commuter students can connect to campus network. Online course registration available.

Student life. Freshman orientation: Available. Preregistration for classes offered. Held in summer before classes begin. **Policies:** Freshmen permitted cars on campus. **Housing:** Coed dorms available. $50 deposit. **Activities:** Student government, student newspaper, sports clubs, nursing student association, Phi Theta Kappa, Campus Crusade.

Athletics. Intramural: Basketball, volleyball.

Student services. Career counseling, services for economically disadvantaged, financial aid counseling, personal counseling, veterans' counselor, women's services. **Physically disabled:** Services for visually, speech, hearing impaired. **Learning disabled:** Comprehensive services available. **Transfer:** Special adviser, orientation for new students. Transfer adviser, college fairs on campus for students transferring to 4-year colleges.

Contact. E-mail: advisor@ncmc.cc.mi.us
Phone: (231) 348-6600 Toll-free number: (888) 298-6605
Fax: (231) 348-6672
Julieanne Tobin, Director Enrollment Management, North Central Michigan College, 1515 Howard Street, Petoskey, MI 49770

Northwestern Michigan College

Traverse City, Michigan
www.nmc.edu **CB code: 1564**

- Public 2-year community college
- Commuter campus in small city

General. Founded in 1951. Regionally accredited. **Enrollment:** 3,949 degree-seeking undergraduates; 631 non-degree-seeking students. **Degrees:** 400 associate awarded. **Location:** 180 miles from Lansing, 265 miles from Detroit. **Calendar:** Semester, extensive summer session. **Full-time faculty:** 90 total. **Part-time faculty:** 120 total. **Special facilities:** Great Lakes Maritime Academy, pilot training center, observatory, Dennos Museum.

Student profile. Among degree-seeking undergraduates, 49% enrolled in a transfer program, 51% enrolled in a vocational program, 997 enrolled as first-time, first-year students, 248 transferred in from other institutions.

Part-time:	52%	**25 or older:**	64%
Out-of-state:	5%	**Live on campus:**	3%
Women:	58%		

Transfer out. Colleges most students transferred to 2005: Michigan State University, Grand Valley State University, Ferris State University, Central Michigan University.

Basis for selection. Open admission, but selective for some programs. Admission for maritime and nursing programs based on school GPA, recommendation and test scores. ACT required for maritime program. **Homeschooled:** Provide transcript of records.

High school preparation. One year of algebra and chemistry required for nursing and maritime programs. Nursing applicants also need 1 year biology.

2005-2006 Annual costs. Tuition/fees: $2,564; $4,200 out-of-district; $5,151 out-of-state. Per-credit charge: $79 in-district; $130 out-of-district; $160 out-of-state. Room/board: $6,285. Books/supplies: $690. Personal expenses: $690.

2004-2005 Financial aid. Need-based: 53% of total undergraduate aid awarded as scholarships/grants, 47% as loans/jobs. Need-based aid available for part-time students. Work study available nights, weekends and for part-time students. **Non-need-based:** Scholarships awarded for academics, art, job skills, leadership, minority status, music/drama, ROTC, state residency.

Application procedures. Admission: No deadline. $15 fee. Application may be submitted online. Admission notification on a rolling basis. **Financial aid:** Priority date 4/1; no closing date. FAFSA required. Applicants notified on a rolling basis starting 5/1; must reply within 2 week(s) of notification.

Academics. Great Lakes Maritime Academy (4-year deck officer and marine engineer training program) for service in shipping industry on campus. 9 months spent aboard commercial vessels. Bachelor's degree awarded to maritime academy graduates in conjunction with Ferris State University. **Special study options:** Cooperative education, distance learning, dual enrollment of high school students, ESL, honors, independent study, internships, liberal arts/career combination. Bachelor's degree programs available on campus. **Credit/placement by examination:** AP, CLEP, institutional tests. 32 credit hours maximum toward associate degree. **Support services:** Learning center, pre-admission summer program, reduced course load, remedial instruction, study skills assistance, tutoring, writing center.

Majors. Agriculture: Crop production, landscaping, nursery operations, turf management. **Biology:** General. **Business:** General, accounting, accounting technology, business admin, management information systems, office technology. **Communications:** General. **Computer sciences:** Information systems. **Education:** General. **Engineering:** General. **Engineering technology:** Drafting, electrical. **English:** English lit. **Health:** Dental assistant, medical assistant, nursing (RN). **Liberal arts:** Arts/sciences. **Math:** General. **Mechanic/repair:** Automotive, electronics/electrical. **Personal/culinary services:** Chef training, culinary arts. **Physical sciences:** General. **Protective services:** Law enforcement admin, police science. **Social sciences:** General. **Transportation:** Airline/commercial pilot, aviation, marine science/Merchant Marine. **Visual/performing arts:** Art, commercial/advertising art, dramatic, piano/organ, studio arts, voice/opera.

Most popular majors. Business/marketing 12%, health sciences 18%, liberal arts 44%, trade and industry 6%.

Computing on campus. 625 workstations in dormitories, library, computer center, student center. Dormitories wired for high-speed internet access and linked to campus network. Commuter students can connect to campus network. Online course registration, online library, helpline, wireless network available.

Student life. Freshman orientation: Mandatory. Preregistration for classes offered. One-day sessions include placement testing, orientation, and registration. Multiple sessions prior to the start of each semester. **Policies:** Freshmen permitted cars on campus. **Housing:** Guaranteed on-campus for freshmen. Coed dorms, special housing for disabled, apartments available. $100 deposit. **Activities:** Bands, choral groups, dance, drama, literary magazine, music ensembles, musical theater, radio station, student government, student newspaper, symphony orchestra, student government association, residence hall council, propeller club, international student club, Phi Theta Kappa, engineer club, botany club, law cnforcement club, diverse student body group, Native American student group, Campus Green.

Student services. Adult student services, career counseling, student employment services, health services, minority student services, personal counseling, placement for graduates, veterans' counselor. **Physically disabled:** Services for visually, speech, hearing impaired. **Transfer:** Special adviser, orientation, re-entry adviser, pre-admission transcript evaluation for new students. Transfer adviser, college fairs on campus for students transferring to 4-year colleges.

Contact. E-mail: jbensley@nmc.edu
Phone: (231) 995-1054 Toll-free number: (800) 748-0566
Fax: (231) 995-1339
James Bensley, Coordinator for Admissions, Northwestern Michigan College, 1701 East Front Street, Traverse City, MI 49686

Oakland Community College

Bloomfield Hills, Michigan **CB member**
www.oaklandcc.edu **CB code: 1607**

- Public 2-year community college
- Commuter campus in large city

General. Founded in 1964. Regionally accredited. Multicampus institution with locations in Auburn Hills, Farmington Hills, Southfield, Royal Oak, Waterford. CREST (Combined Regional Emergency Services Training Center) in Auburn Hills. **Enrollment:** 13,047 degree-seeking undergraduates; 11,240 non-degree-seeking students. **Degrees:** 1,908 associate awarded. **Location:** 30 miles from downtown Detroit. **Calendar:** Semester, limited summer session. **Full-time faculty:** 275 total; 10% minority, 52% women. **Part-time faculty:** 670 total; 8% minority, 48% women. **Class size:** 27% < 20, 73% 20-39, less than 1% 40-49.

Student profile. Among degree-seeking undergraduates, 11% enrolled in a transfer program, 57% enrolled in a vocational program, 2% already have a bachelor's degree or higher, 1,704 enrolled as first-time, first-year students, 603 transferred in from other institutions.

Part-time:	69%	**Hispanic American:**	2%
Out-of-state:	1%	**Native American:**	1%
Women:	62%	**International:**	8%
African American:	16%	**25 or older:**	47%
Asian American:	2%		

Transfer out. 18% of students enrolled in the transfer program go on to 4-year colleges. **Colleges most students transferred to 2005:** Oakland University, Wayne State University, Walsh College, Eastern Michigan University, University of Michigan-Dearborn.

Basis for selection. Open admission. Interview recommended. **Adult students:** Entrance exam policies same as for first-time freshmen. **Homeschooled:** English and math placement testing mandatory.

2005-2006 Annual costs. Tuition/fees: $1,725; $2,871 out-of-district; $3,997 out-of-state. Per-credit charge: $55 in-district; $93 out-of-district; $131 out-of-state. Books/supplies: $900. Personal expenses: $620.

2005-2006 Financial aid. Need-based: 64% of total undergraduate aid awarded as scholarships/grants, 36% as loans/jobs. Need-based aid available for part-time students. Work study available for part-time students. **Non-need-based:** Scholarships awarded for academics, athletics.

Application procedures. Admission: No deadline. No application fee. Application must be submitted on paper. Admission notification on a rolling

basis. **Financial aid:** Priority date 4/15; no closing date. FAFSA required. Applicants notified on a rolling basis starting 4/15.

Academics. Special study options: Cooperative education, distance learning, dual enrollment of high school students, ESL, internships, study abroad. Saturday classes offered. License preparation in dental hygiene, nursing, occupational therapy, paramedic, physical therapy, radiology. **Credit/placement by examination:** AP, CLEP, institutional tests. Last 15 credit hours toward degree program must be satisfied with institution's coursework, not credit by exam. **Support services:** Learning center, reduced course load, remedial instruction, study skills assistance, tutoring, writing center.

Majors. Agriculture: Landscaping. **Business:** Accounting, business admin, construction management, entrepreneurial studies, hotel/motel admin, international, office management, office technology, restaurant/food services. **Communications technology:** Radio/tv. **Computer sciences:** Programming, security, systems analysis. **Construction:** Carpentry, electrician, pipefitting. **Engineering:** General. **Engineering technology:** Architectural, computer hardware, electrical, electromechanical, heat/ac/refrig, industrial, manufacturing, mechanical drafting, robotics. **Family/consumer sciences:** Aging, child care. **Foreign languages:** Sign language interpretation. **Health:** Dental hygiene, EMT paramedic, health care admin, histologic technology, massage therapy, medical assistant, medical radiologic technology/radiation therapy, medical transcription, nuclear medical technology, nursing (RN), pharmacy assistant, respiratory therapy technology, sonography, surgical technology. **Legal studies:** Court reporting, paralegal. **Liberal arts:** Arts/sciences, library assistant. **Mechanic/repair:** General, automotive, industrial electronics, medium/heavy vehicle. **Parks/recreation:** Exercise sciences. **Personal/culinary services:** Chef training, cosmetic, salon management. **Production:** Tool and die, welding. **Protective services:** Corrections, criminalistics, firefighting, law enforcement admin, police science. **Visual/performing arts:** Art, ceramics, graphic design, interior design, music performance, music theory/composition, photography, voice/opera.

Most popular majors. Business/marketing 16%, engineering/engineering technologies 6%, health sciences 19%, liberal arts 44%.

Computing on campus. 2,337 workstations in library, computer center. Online course registration, online library, helpline available.

Student life. Freshman orientation: Available. **Policies:** Freshmen permitted cars on campus. **Activities:** Bands, choral groups, dance, drama, literary magazine, music ensembles, symphony orchestra, Association of Black Students, Students in Free Enterprise, Human Enrichment Center, Students Against Hunger, Phi Theta Kappa, women's center, international club, Jewish student association, student optimist club, Student Michigan Education Association.

Athletics. NJCAA. **Intercollegiate:** Basketball, cross-country, golf M, softball W, tennis W, volleyball W. **Intramural:** Basketball, cross-country, golf, racquetball, tennis, volleyball. **Team name:** Raiders.

Student services. Career counseling, services for economically disadvantaged, student employment services, financial aid counseling, on-campus daycare, personal counseling, placement for graduates, veterans' counselor, women's services. **Physically disabled:** Services for visually, speech, hearing impaired. **Transfer:** Special adviser, orientation, pre-admission transcript evaluation for new students. Transfer center, transfer adviser, college fairs on campus for students transferring to 4-year colleges.

Contact. Phone: (248) 341-2200 Fax: (248) 341-2099
Maurice McCall, Director of Enrollment Services/Registrar, Oakland Community College, 2480 Opdyke Road, Bloomfield Hills, MI 48304-2266

Saginaw Chippewa Tribal College
Mount Pleasant, Michigan
www.sagchip.org/tribalcollege

- Public 2-year community college

General. Enrollment: 40 full-time, degree-seeking students. **Degrees:** 14 associate awarded. **Calendar:** Semester. **Full-time faculty:** 4 total. **Part-time faculty:** 10 total.

Basis for selection. Open admission.

2005-2006 Annual costs. Tuition/fees: $1,786. Per-credit charge: $.

Application procedures. Admission: No deadline. No application fee. Admission notification on a rolling basis.

Academics. Credit/placement by examination: CLEP.

Majors. Area/ethnic studies: Native American. **Business:** Business admin.

Contact. Phone: (989) 775-4123
Tracy Reed, Director of Admissions, Saginaw Chippewa Tribal College, 7070 East Broadway, Mount Pleasant, MI 48858

St. Clair County Community College
Port Huron, Michigan
www.sc4.edu **CB code: 1628**

- Public 2-year community college
- Commuter campus in large town

General. Founded in 1923. Regionally accredited. **Enrollment:** 4,400 undergraduates. **Degrees:** 542 associate awarded. **Location:** 55 miles from Detroit. **Calendar:** Semester, limited summer session. **Full-time faculty:** 90 total. **Part-time faculty:** 180 total. **Special facilities:** Fine arts facility, natural history museum.

Student profile.

Out-of-state:	2%	25 or older:	44%

Basis for selection. Open admission.

2005-2006 Annual costs. Tuition/fees: $2,327; $3,591 out-of-district; $4,775 out-of-state. Per-credit charge: $69 in-district; $108 out-of-district; $145 out-of-state. Residents of Lambton County, Canada pay in-state, out-of-district rate for tuition. Lambton County residents pay in-district tuition rate if enrolled in program of study not offered at Lambton College. Books/supplies: $850. Personal expenses: $439.

Application procedures. Admission: Closing date 9/1. No application fee. Application may be submitted online. Admission notification on a rolling basis. **Financial aid:** Priority date 6/1; no closing date. FAFSA required. Applicants notified on a rolling basis starting 5/15; must reply within 2 week(s) of notification.

Academics. Special study options: Accelerated study, cooperative education, distance learning, double major, dual enrollment of high school students, honors, internships, weekend college. Bachelor's degree programs available on campus. **Credit/placement by examination:** AP, CLEP, institutional tests. 45 credit hours maximum toward associate degree. **Support services:** Learning center, reduced course load, remedial instruction, study skills assistance, tutoring.

Majors. Agriculture: Horticultural science, supplies. **Business:** General, accounting, administrative services, business admin, office technology, office/clerical. **Communications:** Broadcast journalism, journalism. **Computer sciences:** Data processing. **Education:** General. **Engineering:** General. **Engineering technology:** Architectural drafting, drafting, electrical, manufacturing. **Family/consumer sciences:** Child care. **Health:** Medical secretary, nursing (RN). **Legal studies:** Legal secretary. **Liberal arts:** Arts/sciences. **Production:** Machine tool, welding. **Protective services:** Law enforcement admin. **Visual/performing arts:** Commercial/advertising art, studio arts.

Computing on campus. 229 workstations in library, computer center, student center.

Student life. Freshman orientation: Mandatory. Online orientation for all new students. On-campus orientation option available, but limited in dates and times. **Activities:** Concert band, choral groups, drama, music ensembles, radio station, student government, student newspaper, symphony orchestra, TV station, global awareness club.

Athletics. NJCAA. **Intercollegiate:** Baseball M, basketball, golf, softball W, volleyball W. **Intramural:** Volleyball M. **Team name:** Skippers.

Student services. Career counseling, student employment services, financial aid counseling, on-campus daycare, personal counseling, placement for graduates, veterans' counselor. **Physically disabled:** Services for visually, speech, hearing impaired. **Transfer:** Special adviser, orientation for new students. Transfer adviser, college fairs on campus for students transferring to 4-year colleges.

Contact. E-mail: enrollment@sc4.edu
Phone: (810) 989-5500 Fax: (810) 984-4730
Pete Lacey, Registrar, St. Clair County Community College, 323 Erie Street, Port Huron, MI 48061-5015

Schoolcraft College
Livonia, Michigan **CB member**
www.schoolcraft.cc.mi.us **CB code: 1764**

- Public 2-year community college
- Commuter campus in small city

General. Founded in 1961. Regionally accredited. **Enrollment:** 3,380 full-time, degree-seeking students. **Degrees:** 908 associate awarded. **Location:** 20 miles from Detroit. **Calendar:** Semester, limited summer session. **Full-time faculty:** 99 total; 18% have terminal degrees, 44% women. **Part-time faculty:** 336 total; 42% women. **Class size:** 35% < 20, 64% 20-39, less than 1% 40-49, less than 1% 50-99.

Transfer out. **Colleges most students transferred to 2005:** Henry Ford Community College, Oakland Community College, Eastern Michigan University, Michigan State University, Wayne State University.

Basis for selection. Open admission. International students advised to start application process 3 months prior to start date of semester.

High school preparation. 12 units recommended. Recommended units include English 4, mathematics 4 and science 4.

2005-2006 Annual costs. Tuition/fees: $2,080; $3,040 out-of-district; $4,420 out-of-state. Per-credit charge: $65 in-district; $97 out-of-district; $143 out-of-state. Books/supplies: $680. Personal expenses: $648.

2004-2005 Financial aid. **Need-based:** 74% of total undergraduate aid awarded as scholarships/grants, 26% as loans/jobs. Work study available nights, weekends and for part-time students. **Non-need-based:** Scholarships awarded for academics, athletics, leadership, music/drama, state residency.

Application procedures. **Admission:** No deadline. No application fee. Admission notification on a rolling basis. **Financial aid:** No deadline. FAFSA required. Applicants notified on a rolling basis starting 6/1.

Academics. **Special study options:** Accelerated study, cooperative education, distance learning, double major, dual enrollment of high school students, external degree, honors, liberal arts/career combination, weekend college. **Credit/placement by examination:** AP, CLEP, institutional tests. 30 credit hours maximum toward associate degree. **Support services:** GED preparation and test center, learning center, remedial instruction, tutoring.

Honors college/program. Minimum high school GPA of 3.5, ACT 25 or SAT 1100 (exclusive of Writing), writing sample, personal interview and 2 letters of recommendation required.

Majors. **Business:** General, accounting, administrative services, business admin, entrepreneurial studies. **Communications:** General, advertising, broadcast journalism, journalism. **Communications technology:** General. **Computer sciences:** Information systems, programming. **Conservation:** General. **Education:** Elementary, physical, special. **Engineering:** General, biomedical. **Engineering technology:** Drafting, electrical, laser/optical. **Family/consumer sciences:** Child care. **Health:** Medical records technology, nursing (RN), occupational therapy assistant, predentistry, premedicine, prepharmacy, preveterinary. **Legal studies:** Prelaw. **Liberal arts:** Arts/sciences. **Personal/culinary services:** Culinary arts, mortuary science. **Protective services:** Corrections, criminal justice, firefighting, police science. **Public administration:** Social work. **Visual/performing arts:** Commercial/advertising art, dramatic, studio arts.

Computing on campus. 775 workstations in library, computer center.

Student life. **Freshman orientation:** Available. **Activities:** Bands, choral groups, drama, literary magazine, music ensembles, musical theater, student newspaper, symphony orchestra, music club, beekeepers club, international students club, quilting club, student activities board, Phi Theta Kappa, honors society, gourmet club, occupational therapy club.

Athletics. NJCAA. **Intercollegiate:** Basketball, cross-country W, golf, soccer, volleyball W.

Student services. Career counseling, student employment services, health services, on-campus daycare, personal counseling, placement for graduates, veterans' counselor. **Physically disabled:** Services for visually, speech, hearing impaired. **Transfer:** Orientation for new students. College fairs on campus for students transferring to 4-year colleges.

Contact. E-mail: admissions@schoolcraft.cc.mi.us
Phone: (734) 462-4426 Fax: (734) 462-4553
Julieanne Tobin, Director of Enrollment Management, Schoolcraft College, 18600 Haggerty Road, Livonia, MI 48152-2696

Southwestern Michigan College

Dowagiac, Michigan
www.swmich.edu **CB code: 1783**

- Public 2-year community college
- Commuter campus in small town

General. Founded in 1964. Regionally accredited. Two traditional semesters (fall and winter) and one optional spring term. Bachelor's degree programs offered in agreement with four-year colleges and universities including Bethel College, Ferris State University and Western Michigan University. **Enrollment:** 2,016 degree-seeking undergraduates; 660 non-degree-seeking students. **Degrees:** 267 associate awarded. **Location:** 30 miles from South Bend, Indiana. **Calendar:** Semester, extensive summer session. **Full-time faculty:** 46 total; 24% have terminal degrees, 46% women. **Part-time faculty:** 115 total; 13% have terminal degrees, 8% minority, 53% women. **Special facilities:** Running/walking trails, museum.

Student profile. Among degree-seeking undergraduates, 449 enrolled as first-time, first-year students.

Part-time:	52%	**Hispanic American:**	4%
Out-of-state:	9%	**Native American:**	1%
Women:	68%	**International:**	4%
African American:	9%	**25 or older:**	40%
Asian American:	1%		

Transfer out. **Colleges most students transferred to 2005:** Western Michigan University, Ferris State University, Bethel College, Indiana University of South Bend, Michigan State University.

Basis for selection. Open admission, but selective for some programs. Special requirements for nursing programs. Assessment tests in reading, writing, and mathematics administered prior to registration for classes. Students may be exempted based upon ACT/SAT scores. Interview required for nursing applicants.

2006-2007 Annual costs. Tuition/fees (projected): $2,860; $3,451 out-of-district; $3,676 out-of-state. Per-credit charge: $75 in-district; $94 out-of-district; $101 out-of-state. Books/supplies: $800. Personal expenses: $900.

Financial aid. **Need-based:** Need-based aid available for part-time students. Work study available nights, weekends and for part-time students. **Non-need-based:** Scholarships awarded for academics, art, leadership, music/drama.

Application procedures. **Admission:** No deadline. No application fee. Application may be submitted online. Admission notification on a rolling basis. **Financial aid:** Priority date 8/1; no closing date. FAFSA, institutional form required. Applicants notified on a rolling basis starting 4/1; must reply within 4 week(s) of notification.

Academics. **Special study options:** Accelerated study, cooperative education, distance learning, double major, dual enrollment of high school students, ESL, independent study, internships, weekend college. Bachelor's degree programs available on campus. License preparation in nursing. **Credit/placement by examination:** AP, CLEP, institutional tests. 30 credit hours maximum toward associate degree. **Support services:** Learning center, pre-admission summer program, reduced course load, remedial instruction, study skills assistance, tutoring, writing center.

Majors. **Business:** General, accounting technology, administrative services, business admin. **Communications technology:** Graphic/printing. **Computer sciences:** General, programming. **Education:** Teacher assistance. **Engineering technology:** General, drafting, electrical. **Family/consumer sciences:** Child care. **Health:** EMT paramedic, health services, medical records technology, nursing (RN). **Liberal arts:** Arts/sciences. **Mechanic/repair:** General, automotive, industrial. **Production:** Machine tool, tool and die, welding. **Public administration:** Social work. **Science technology:** Chemical.

Most popular majors. Business/marketing 7%, family/consumer sciences 8%, health sciences 12%, liberal arts 57%, trade and industry 7%.

Computing on campus. 200 workstations in library, computer center, student center. Commuter students can connect to campus network. Online library, helpline available.

Student life. **Freshman orientation:** Available. Preregistration for classes offered. Several half-day sessions available. **Activities:** Bands, choral groups, dance, drama, literary magazine, music ensembles, musical theater, student newspaper, Phi Theta Kappa.

Athletics. **Intramural:** Archery, badminton, basketball, cross-country, football (non-tackle), handball, racquetball, skiing, soccer, softball, track and field, volleyball.

Student services. Career counseling, student employment services, financial aid counseling, placement for graduates, veterans' counselor. **Physically disabled:** Services for visually, speech, hearing impaired. **Transfer:** Special adviser, orientation for new students. Transfer adviser, college fairs on campus for students transferring to 4-year colleges.

Contact. E-mail: nmyers@swmich.edu
Phone: (269) 782-1000 Toll-free number: (800) 456-8675
Fax: (269) 782-1331
Margaret Hay, Dean of Academic Support, Southwestern Michigan College, 58900 Cherry Grove Road, Dowagiac, MI 49047-9793

Washtenaw Community College
Ann Arbor, Michigan
www.wccnet.edu **CB code: 1935**

- Public 2-year community college
- Commuter campus in small city

General. Founded in 1965. Regionally accredited. Classes taught in Brighton, Saline, Chelsea, Ypsilanti and Hartland. **Enrollment:** 9,268 degree-seeking undergraduates. **Degrees:** 914 associate awarded. **ROTC:** Army. **Location:** 40 miles from Detroit. **Calendar:** Trimester, extensive summer session. **Full-time faculty:** 201 total. **Part-time faculty:** 620 total.

Basis for selection. Open admission, but selective for some programs. Special requirements for health service technologies programs and some computer technology programs.

High school preparation. 15 units recommended. Recommended units include English 4, mathematics 4, social studies 2, science 4 and foreign language 1. Biology, chemistry and algebra for health programs. Trigonometry and drafting for technical programs.

2005-2006 Annual costs. Tuition/fees: $2,310; $3,600 out-of-district; $4,650 out-of-state. Books/supplies: $600. Personal expenses: $2,000.

Financial aid. Non-need-based: Scholarships awarded for academics.

Application procedures. Admission: Priority date 8/12; no deadline. No application fee. Application may be submitted online. Admission notification on a rolling basis beginning on or about 2/20. Rolling admission, no deadline. **Financial aid:** Priority date 6/1, closing date 7/1. FAFSA, institutional form required. Applicants notified on a rolling basis.

Academics. Special study options: Cooperative education, cross-registration, distance learning, dual enrollment of high school students, ESL, honors, independent study, internships, liberal arts/career combination, weekend college. Bachelor's degree programs available on campus. **Credit/placement by examination:** AP, CLEP, institutional tests. 45 credit hours maximum toward associate degree. **Support services:** GED preparation and test center, learning center, remedial instruction, study skills assistance, tutoring, writing center.

Majors. Architecture: Technology. **Business:** Accounting, administrative services, business admin. **Communications technology:** Graphic/printing. **Computer sciences:** General, applications programming, computer graphics, computer science, data processing, information systems, LAN/WAN management, networking, programming, security, web page design. **Construction:** Maintenance. **Education:** Early childhood, elementary, secondary. **Engineering:** General, mechanics, science. **Engineering technology:** Construction, drafting, electrical. **English:** Technical writing. **Health:** Medical radiologic technology/radiation therapy, medical records admin, nursing (RN), premedicine, respiratory therapy technology, substance abuse counseling. **Liberal arts:** Arts/sciences. **Mechanic/repair:** Auto body, automotive, electronics/electrical, heating/ac/refrig. **Personal/culinary services:** Culinary arts. **Protective services:** Corrections, law enforcement admin, police science. **Social sciences:** General. **Visual/performing arts:** Commercial photography, photography.

Computing on campus. 211 workstations in library, computer center, student center. Commuter students can connect to campus network. Online course registration, online library, helpline, repair service, student web hosting available.

Student life. Freshman orientation: Mandatory. **Activities:** Jazz band, choral groups, dance, drama, literary magazine, musical theater, student government, student newspaper, African-American student association, Christian Challenge Student Advisory Council, international student association, Phi Theta Kappa, student assembly.

Student services. Adult student services, alcohol/substance abuse counseling, career counseling, services for economically disadvantaged, student employment services, financial aid counseling, minority student services, on-campus daycare, personal counseling, placement for graduates, veterans' counselor, women's services. **Physically disabled:** Services for visually, speech, hearing impaired. **Transfer:** Special adviser, orientation, pre-admission transcript evaluation for new students. Transfer center, transfer adviser, college fairs on campus for students transferring to 4-year colleges.

Contact. E-mail: studrec@wccnet.org
Phone: (734) 973-3543 Fax: (734) 677-5414
Sukanya Jett, Assistant Director of Admissions, Washtenaw Community College, 4800 East Huron River Drive, Ann Arbor, MI 48106-1610

Wayne County Community College
Detroit, Michigan
www.wcccd.edu **CB code: 1937**

- Public 2-year community college
- Commuter campus in very large city

General. Founded in 1967. Regionally accredited. 5 campuses. **Enrollment:** 14,258 degree-seeking undergraduates; 506 non-degree-seeking students. **Degrees:** 991 associate awarded. **Calendar:** Semester, extensive summer session. **Full-time faculty:** 100 total. **Part-time faculty:** 500 total. **Class size:** 46% < 20, 53% 20-39, less than 1% 40-49, less than 1% 50-99. **Partnerships:** Formal partnerships with corporations and high schools.

Student profile. Among degree-seeking undergraduates, 4,031 enrolled as first-time, first-year students, 14,698 transferred in from other institutions.

Part-time:	78%	**25 or older:**	58%
Women:	72%		

Basis for selection. Open admission, but selective for some programs. High school students may need parental, principal's approval for dual enrollment. Nursing applicants must have high school diploma or GED, 2.0 GPA or higher in prerequisite courses and must take Nursing School Aptitude Examination. International students must submit results from TOEFL or MELAB (Michigan English Language Assessment Battery). Other nonnative speakers of English must complete COMPASS ESL examination for placement purposes. **Adult students:** Entrance exam policies same as for first-time freshmen. **Learning Disabled:** ACCESS Program provides support services such as interpreters, note takers, readers, tutors and other assistance for students with special needs.

2006-2007 Annual costs. Tuition/fees (projected): $2,055; $2,543 out-of-district; $3,120 out-of-state. Per-credit charge: $56 in-district; $72 out-of-district; $91 out-of-state. Books/supplies: $1,330.

2004-2005 Financial aid. Need-based: 87% of total undergraduate aid awarded as scholarships/grants, 13% as loans/jobs. Need-based aid available for part-time students. Work study available nights, weekends and for part-time students. **Additional information:** High school diploma, GED, or passing grade on ABT required for financial aid.

Application procedures. Admission: No deadline. $10 fee ($10 out-of-state), may be waived for applicants with need. Application may be submitted online. Admission notification on a rolling basis. **Financial aid:** Priority date 6/1; no closing date. FAFSA required. Applicants notified on a rolling basis starting 5/1.

Academics. Special study options: Accelerated study, cooperative education, distance learning, double major, dual enrollment of high school students, honors, independent study, internships, liberal arts/career combination. License preparation in dental hygiene, nursing, occupational therapy, paramedic. **Credit/placement by examination:** AP, CLEP, IB. Recommendation of CAO or program chair. **Support services:** GED preparation, learning center, remedial instruction, study skills assistance, tutoring.

Majors. Agriculture: Landscaping. **Business:** Accounting technology, administrative services, business admin, executive assistant, labor relations. **Computer sciences:** Programming. **Construction:** Masonry. **Education:** General, elementary, secondary. **Engineering:** General. **Engineering technology:** Architectural, computer, electrical, electromechanical, metallurgical, telecommunications. **Family/consumer sciences:** Aging, child care, institutional food production. **Health:** Dental hygiene, EMT paramedic, environmental health, mental health services, nursing (RN), occupational therapy assistant, pharmacy assistant, respiratory therapy technology, surgical technology, veterinary technology/assistant. **Legal studies:** Paralegal. **Liberal arts:** Arts/sciences. **Mechanic/repair:** Aircraft, aircraft powerplant, auto body, automotive, diesel, heating/ac/refrig. **Philosophy/religion:** Islamic, religion. **Production:** Machine tool, tool and die, welding. **Protective services:** Corrections, fire safety technology, law enforcement admin. **Public administration:** Social work. **Social sciences:** General.

Most popular majors. Health sciences 21%, liberal arts 65%.

Computing on campus. 1,500 workstations in library, computer center. Online course registration, online library, helpline, wireless network available.

Student life. Freshman orientation: Available. Preregistration for classes offered. **Policies:** Students must follow the student code of conduct. Freshmen permitted cars on campus. **Activities:** Choral groups, dance, drama, film society, student government, student newspaper.

Athletics. NJCAA. **Intramural:** Basketball, cross-country M, golf M, volleyball W. **Team name:** Wild Cats.

Student services. Adult student services, career counseling, services for economically disadvantaged, student employment services, financial aid counseling, on-campus daycare, personal counseling, placement for graduates, veterans' counselor, women's services. **Physically disabled:** Services for visually, speech, hearing impaired. **Learning disabled:** Comprehensive services available. **Transfer:** Special adviser, orientation, re-entry adviser, pre-admission transcript evaluation for new students. Transfer adviser, college fairs on campus for students transferring to 4-year colleges.

Contact. Phone: (313) 496-2600 Fax: (313) 962-1643
Carol Wells, Executive Dean of Student Services, Wayne County Community College, 801 West Fort Street, Detroit, MI 48226

West Shore Community College

Scottville, Michigan
www.westshore.edu **CB code: 1941**

- Public 2-year community college
- Commuter campus in rural community

General. Founded in 1967. Regionally accredited. **Enrollment:** 1,097 degree-seeking undergraduates. **Degrees:** 113 associate awarded. **Location:** 54 miles from Muskegon. **Calendar:** Semester, limited summer session. **Full-time faculty:** 26 total. **Part-time faculty:** 69 total. **Special facilities:** Modern fitness center.

Transfer out. Colleges most students transferred to 2005: Grand Valley State University, Ferris State University, Davenport College, Central Michigan University.

Basis for selection. Open admission, but selective for some programs. Applicants to nursing programs must complete prerequisite course work with minimum 2.0 GPA.

2005-2006 Annual costs. Tuition/fees: $2,103; $3,333 out-of-district; $4,383 out-of-state. Per-credit charge: $65 in-district; $106 out-of-district; $141 out-of-state. Books/supplies: $700. Personal expenses: $650.

2005-2006 Financial aid. Need-based: 77% of total undergraduate aid awarded as scholarships/grants, 23% as loans/jobs. Need-based aid available for part-time students. Work study available nights, weekends and for part-time students.

Application procedures. Admission: No deadline. $15 fee. Admission notification on a rolling basis. Applicants for associate degree in nursing must apply by January 1, practical nursing applicants by June 1. **Financial aid:** Priority date 3/15; no closing date. FAFSA required. Applicants notified on a rolling basis starting 5/15; must reply within 2 week(s) of notification.

Academics. Special study options: Distance learning, dual enrollment of high school students, independent study, internships. Bachelor's degree programs available on campus. License preparation in nursing. **Credit/placement by examination:** AP, CLEP, institutional tests. 10 credit hours maximum toward associate degree. **Support services:** GED test center, learning center, reduced course load, remedial instruction, study skills assistance, tutoring.

Majors. Business: General, accounting, administrative services, management information systems, marketing, office technology, office/clerical. **Computer sciences:** Data processing. **Education:** General. **Engineering technology:** CAD/CADD, electrical. **Health:** EMT paramedic, nursing (RN), nursing assistant, prepharmacy. **Legal studies:** Prelaw. **Liberal arts:** Arts/sciences. **Math:** General. **Production:** Welding. **Protective services:** Law enforcement admin.

Computing on campus. 300 workstations in library, computer center, student center. Commuter students can connect to campus network. Helpline available.

Student life. Freshman orientation: Mandatory. Preregistration for classes offered. No group orientation for first-year students; each student meets one-on-one with academic counselor during registration period before classes begin. **Activities:** Choral groups, drama, music ensembles, musical theater, student government, student newspaper, Phi Theta Kappa honor society, law enforcement club, art club, science club, additional special interest clubs.

Athletics. Intramural: Basketball, racquetball, softball, volleyball.

Student services. Career counseling, student employment services, personal counseling, placement for graduates, veterans' counselor. **Physically disabled:** Services for visually, speech, hearing impaired. **Transfer:** Special adviser, orientation, pre-admission transcript evaluation for new students. Transfer adviser, college fairs on campus for students transferring to 4-year colleges.

Contact. E-mail: admissions@westshore.edu
Phone: (231) 845-6211 ext. 3117 Fax: (231) 845-3944
Tom Bell, Director of Admissions, West Shore Community College, 3000 North Stiles Road, Scottville, MI 49454-0277

Minnesota

Academy College
Bloomington, Minnesota
www.academycollege.edu CB code: 3311

- For-profit 2-year junior and technical college
- Large city
- Interview required

General. Accredited by ACICS. **Enrollment:** 290 degree-seeking undergraduates. **Degrees:** 5 bachelor's, 50 associate awarded. **Calendar:** Quarter. **Full-time faculty:** 5 total. **Part-time faculty:** 50 total.

Student profile. Among degree-seeking undergraduates, 50 enrolled as first-time, first-year students.

Part-time:	28%	Women:	21%

Basis for selection. Open admission.

2005-2006 Annual costs. Tuition ranges from $215 to $369 per-credit-hour depending on program. Books/supplies: $700. Personal expenses: $2,200.

Financial aid. Need-based: Need-based aid available for part-time students. Work study available nights and for part-time students.

Application procedures. Admission: No deadline. $30 fee. Application must be submitted on paper. Admission notification on a rolling basis. **Financial aid:** FAFSA, institutional form required.

Academics. Special study options: Distance learning, internships. Bachelor's degree programs available on campus. **Credit/placement by examination:** CLEP.

Majors. Business: Accounting, business admin, finance, sales/distribution, training/development. **Communications technology:** General, animation/special effects. **Computer sciences:** General, computer graphics, programming, system admin, web page design. **Transportation:** Airline/commercial pilot, aviation, aviation management. **Visual/performing arts:** General, commercial/advertising art.

Computing on campus. 100 workstations in computer center. Online library available.

Student life. Freshman orientation: Mandatory.

Student services. Placement for graduates.

Contact. E-mail: admissions@academycollege.edu
Phone: (952) 851-0066 Toll-free number: (800) 292-9149
Fax: (952) 851-0094
Char Drechen, Director of Admissions, Academy College, 1101 East 78th Street, Bloomington, MN 55420

Alexandria Technical College
Alexandria, Minnesota
www.alextech.edu CB code: 0771

- Public 2-year technical college
- Commuter campus in large town
- Interview required

General. Founded in 1961. Regionally accredited. **Enrollment:** 1,725 degree-seeking undergraduates. **Degrees:** 550 associate awarded. **Location:** 135 miles from Minneapolis-St. Paul. **Calendar:** Semester, limited summer session. **Full-time faculty:** 85 total. **Part-time faculty:** 35 total.

Student profile.

Out-of-state:	4%	25 or older:	21%

Basis for selection. Open admission, but selective for some programs. School achievement record, test scores, and interview considered for course placement. Selective admission to law enforcement program. Applicants considered in order of applications received. Minnesota Multiphasic Personality Inventory required. ACT recommended and physical agility test required for law enforcement applicants. NET test for practical nursing examination required for practical nursing applicants. Mechanical reasoning tests required for marine and small engine mechanics and diesel mechanics applicants. Portfolio required for communications art and design students. **Adult students:** Entrance exam policies same as for first-time freshmen.

2005-2006 Annual costs. Tuition/fees: $3,857; $7,419 out-of-state. Per-credit charge: $119 in-state; $238 out-of-state. Books/supplies: $800. Personal expenses: $1,800.

Financial aid. All financial aid based on need. Need-based aid available for part-time students. Work study available for part-time students.

Application procedures. Admission: Priority date 8/1; no deadline. $20 fee. Application may be submitted online. Admission notification on a rolling basis. **Financial aid:** Priority date 5/1; no closing date. FAFSA, institutional form required. Applicants notified on a rolling basis starting 6/30; must reply within 2 week(s) of notification.

Academics. Special study options: Distance learning, double major, independent study, internships. Bachelor's degree programs available on campus. License preparation in nursing, real estate. **Credit/placement by examination:** CLEP, institutional tests. No separate limits on CLEP and credit by exam. **Support services:** Pre-admission summer program, reduced course load, remedial instruction, study skills assistance, tutoring, writing center.

Majors. Business: Accounting, banking/financial services, business admin, fashion, hotel/motel admin, marketing, office management, operations. **Computer sciences:** General, networking, programming, web page design. **Engineering technology:** Computer systems, hydraulics, industrial, manufacturing, mechanical drafting, telecommunications. **Family/consumer sciences:** Child care. **Health:** Clinical lab technology, medical secretary. **Legal studies:** Legal secretary, paralegal. **Mechanic/repair:** Diesel. **Parks/recreation:** Health/fitness. **Protective services:** Police science. **Visual/performing arts:** Commercial/advertising art, interior design.

Most popular majors. Business/marketing 35%, computer/information sciences 16%, family/consumer sciences 6%, health sciences 13%, visual/performing arts 27%.

Computing on campus. 1,100 workstations in library, computer center. Commuter students can connect to campus network. Online course registration, online library, helpline, repair service, wireless network available.

Student life. Freshman orientation: Available. Preregistration for classes offered. **Policies:** Freshmen permitted cars on campus. **Activities:** Choral groups, student government, Phi Theta Kappa, Business Professionals of America, Delta Epsilon Chi, Skills USA.

Athletics. Intercollegiate: Basketball M, volleyball. **Intramural:** Basketball, football (non-tackle), softball, volleyball.

Student services. Adult student services, alcohol/substance abuse counseling, career counseling, services for economically disadvantaged, student employment services, financial aid counseling, health services, personal counseling, placement for graduates, veterans' counselor, women's services. **Physically disabled:** Services for visually, speech, hearing impaired. **Transfer:** Special adviser, orientation, pre-admission transcript evaluation for new students. Transfer adviser for students transferring to 4-year colleges.

Contact. E-mail: admissionsrep@alextech.edu
Phone: (320) 762-4520 Toll-free number: (888) 234-1222
Fax: (320) 762-4603
Doug Tatge, Vice President of Academic & Student Affairs, Alexandria Technical College, 1601 Jefferson Street, Alexandria, MN 56308-3799

Anoka Technical College
Anoka, Minnesota
www.anokatech.edu CB code: 6084

- Public 2-year technical college
- Commuter campus in large town

General. Regionally accredited. **Enrollment:** 2,020 undergraduates. **Degrees:** 175 associate awarded. **Location:** 25 miles from Minneapolis-St. Paul. **Calendar:** Semester, limited summer session. **Full-time faculty:** 75 total. **Part-time faculty:** 30 total.

Basis for selection. Open admission.

2005-2006 Annual costs. Tuition/fees: $4,309; $8,195 out-of-state. Per-credit charge: $130 in-state; $259 out-of-state. Various reciprocity agreements with some neighboring states provide tuition reduction to out-of-state students.

Financial aid. All financial aid based on need. Need-based aid available for part-time students.

Application procedures. Admission: Closing date 8/1. $20 fee. Application may be submitted online. Admission notification on a rolling basis. **Financial aid:** No deadline. FAFSA, institutional form required. Applicants notified on a rolling basis starting 5/1.

Academics. Special study options: Internships, liberal arts/career combination. License preparation in aviation, nursing. **Credit/placement by examination:** CLEP, institutional tests. 72 credit hours maximum toward associate degree. **Support services:** GED preparation and test center, reduced course load, remedial instruction, study skills assistance, tutoring.

Majors. Agriculture: Horticulture, landscaping, nursery operations, turf management. **Computer sciences:** Information systems. **Engineering technology:** Drafting, electrical. **Family/consumer sciences:** Child care. **Health:** Licensed practical nurse, medical secretary, occupational therapy assistant, physical therapy assistant. **Mechanic/repair:** Automotive. **Parks/recreation:** Facilities management. **Transportation:** Air traffic control, aviation, aviation management.

Computing on campus. 250 workstations in library, computer center.

Student life. Freshman orientation: Mandatory. **Policies:** Freshmen permitted cars on campus. **Activities:** Student government.

Student services. Career counseling, student employment services, health services, on-campus daycare, personal counseling, placement for graduates, veterans' counselor. **Physically disabled:** Services for visually, speech, hearing impaired. **Transfer:** Special adviser, orientation for new students.

Contact. E-mail: admissions@anokatech.edu
Phone: (763) 576-4850 Fax: (763) 576-4756
Bob Hoenie, Director of Admissions, Anoka Technical College, 1355 West Highway 10, Anoka, MN 55303

Anoka-Ramsey Community College

Coon Rapids, Minnesota
www.anokaramsey.edu **CB code: 6024**

- Public 2-year community college
- Commuter campus in small city

General. Founded in 1965. Regionally accredited. Extension sites at Elk River and Fridley. **Enrollment:** 7,230 degree-seeking undergraduates. **Degrees:** 618 associate awarded. **ROTC:** Army, Navy, Air Force. **Location:** 20 miles from Minneapolis-St. Paul. **Calendar:** Semester, limited summer session. **Full-time faculty:** 100 total. **Part-time faculty:** 235 total. **Special facilities:** Glass-blowing studio, native prairie ground.

Transfer out. Colleges most students transferred to 2005: University of Minnesota-Twin Cities, St. Cloud State University.

Basis for selection. Open admission, but selective for some programs and for out-of-state students. Special requirements for nursing, biomedical technology, computer networking, and telecommunications programs. National League of Nursing Pre-admissions Test required for nursing applicants.

High school preparation. One year laboratory chemistry and 1 year laboratory biology required for nursing applicants out of high school less than 5 years.

2005-2006 Annual costs. Tuition/fees: $3,582; $6,780 out-of-state. Per-credit charge: $107 in-state; $213 out-of-state. Various reciprocity agreements with some neighboring states provide tuition reduction to out-of-state students. Books/supplies: $600. Personal expenses: $600.

Financial aid. All financial aid based on need. Work study available nights, weekends and for part-time students.

Application procedures. Admission: No deadline. $20 fee, may be waived for applicants with need. Admission notification on a rolling basis. **Financial aid:** Priority date 6/1; no closing date. FAFSA, institutional form required. Applicants notified on a rolling basis; must reply within 2 week(s) of notification.

Academics. Special study options: Cross-registration, distance learning, dual enrollment of high school students, independent study, internships, study abroad, weekend college. Joint admission with Colleges of Science and Engineering at Duluth and Mankato State University, University of Minnesota, St. Cloud State University, and University of Minnesota-Twin Cities in agriculture, natural resources, human ecology, and liberal arts. **Credit/placement by examination:** AP, CLEP, institutional tests. 30 credit hours maximum toward associate degree. **Support services:** Learning center, reduced course load, remedial instruction, study skills assistance, tutoring, writing center.

Majors. Agriculture: Landscaping, nursery operations, turf management. **Business:** Accounting, administrative services, business admin, marketing. **Computer sciences:** Information systems. **Conservation:** Environmental science. **Engineering:** General. **Engineering technology:** Architectural, electrical. **Family/consumer sciences:** Child care. **Health:** Medical secretary, nursing (RN), occupational therapy assistant, optician, physical therapy assistant. **Legal studies:** Legal secretary. **Liberal arts:** Arts/sciences. **Mechanic/repair:** Automotive. **Parks/recreation:** General.

Most popular majors. Business/marketing 11%, health sciences 27%, liberal arts 56%.

Computing on campus. 300 workstations in library, computer center.

Student life. Freshman orientation: Mandatory. **Activities:** Bands, choral groups, drama, literary magazine, music ensembles, musical theater, student government, student newspaper, symphony orchestra, Phi Theta Kappa, humanities club, Intervarsity Christian Fellowship, international student club.

Athletics. NJCAA. **Intercollegiate:** Baseball M, basketball, volleyball W. **Intramural:** Archery M, baseball M, basketball, bowling, golf, ice hockey, soccer, softball, volleyball.

Student services. Adult student services, career counseling, student employment services, personal counseling, veterans' counselor. **Physically disabled:** Services for visually, speech, hearing impaired. **Transfer:** Special adviser, orientation for new students. Transfer adviser, college fairs on campus for students transferring to 4-year colleges.

Contact. Phone: (763) 422-3333 Fax: (763) 422-3636
Matthew Crawford, New Student Services, Anoka-Ramsey Community College, 11200 Mississippi Boulevard NW, Coon Rapids, MN 55433

Central Lakes College

Brainerd, Minnesota
www.clcmn.edu **CB code: 6045**

- Public 2-year community and technical college
- Commuter campus in large town

General. Founded in 1938. Regionally accredited. Access to 1.5 million book titles through participation in online catalog system with 28 other libraries. **Enrollment:** 2,768 undergraduates. **Degrees:** 394 associate awarded. **Location:** 125 miles from Minneapolis-St. Paul. **Calendar:** Semester, limited summer session. **Full-time faculty:** 102 total; 2% have terminal degrees, 3% minority, 37% women. **Part-time faculty:** 69 total; 46% women. **Class size:** 50% < 20, 48% 20-39, 1% 40-49. **Special facilities:** Conservatory, American Indian studies center.

Student profile. 49% enrolled in a transfer program, 51% enrolled in a vocational program, 134 transferred in from other institutions.

Basis for selection. Open admission, but selective for some programs. Applicants to mobility nursing program must have graduate license in practical nursing (LPN). Practical nurse program grades and college grades considered. Instructor and employer references, practical to registered nursing mobility profile, and mathematics test scores also considered.

2005-2006 Annual costs. Tuition/fees: $3,940. Per-credit charge: $116. Books/supplies: $800. Personal expenses: $1,500.

2005-2006 Financial aid. Need-based: 43% of total undergraduate aid awarded as scholarships/grants, 57% as loans/jobs. Need-based aid available for part-time students. Work study available for part-time students.

Application procedures. Admission: No deadline. $20 fee. Application may be submitted online. Admission notification on a rolling basis. **Financial aid:** Priority date 6/1; no closing date. FAFSA, institutional form required. Applicants notified on a rolling basis starting 6/10; must reply within 2 week(s) of notification.

Academics. Special study options: Combined bachelor's/graduate degree, distance learning, dual enrollment of high school students, independent study, internships, liberal arts/career combination. 2+2 management program with College of St. Scholastica, 2+2 programs with Southwest State in organizational management and teacher education, 2+2 natural resources with University of Minnesota: Crookston. Bachelor's degree programs available on campus. License preparation in nursing. **Credit/placement by examination:** AP, CLEP, IB, institutional tests. **Support services:** Learning center, remedial instruction, study skills assistance, tutoring.

Majors. Agriculture: Horticulture. **Business:** Accounting, administrative services, business admin, tourism/travel. **Communications technology:** Photo/film/video. **Computer sciences:** Data processing, networking, programming. **Conservation:** General. **Education:** Teacher assistance. **Engineering:** General. **Engineering technology:** Computer systems, robotics. **Family/consumer sciences:** Child care. **Health:** Medical secretary, nursing (RN). **Liberal arts:** Arts/sciences. **Mechanic/repair:** Automotive, heavy equipment, industrial electronics, marine. **Production:** Welding. **Protective services:** Criminal justice, criminalistics, police science. **Visual/performing arts:** Commercial/advertising art, theater design.

Most popular majors. Business/marketing 8%, health sciences 11%, liberal arts 57%, security/protective services 6%.

Computing on campus. 150 workstations in library, computer center. Commuter students can connect to campus network. Online course registration, online library, repair service, wireless network available.

Student life. Freshman orientation: Mandatory. Mandatory online orientation. Orientations also held in-person throughout spring and summer. **Activities:** Bands, choral groups, drama, music ensembles, musical theater, student government, student newspaper, Anishinabe Student Association, campus ambassadors, law enforcement club, mentoring, theater club, Phi Theta Kappa, Spanish club, minority student forum.

Athletics. NJCAA. **Intercollegiate:** Baseball M, basketball, football (tackle) M, golf, soccer W, softball W, volleyball W. **Intramural:** Baseball M, basketball, bowling, golf, softball, volleyball. **Team name:** Raiders.

Student services. Adult student services, career counseling, services for economically disadvantaged, financial aid counseling, health services, minority student services, on-campus daycare, personal counseling, placement for graduates, veterans' counselor, women's services. **Physically disabled:** Services for visually, speech, hearing impaired. **Transfer:** Special adviser, orientation, pre-admission transcript evaluation for new students. Transfer adviser, college fairs on campus for students transferring to 4-year colleges.

Contact. E-mail: rtretter@clcmn.edu
Phone: (218) 855-8037 Toll-free number: (800) 933-0346
Fax: (218) 855-8230
Charlotte Daniels, Director of Admissions, Central Lakes College, 501 West College Drive, Brainerd, MN 56401

Century Community and Technical College

White Bear Lake, Minnesota
www.century.edu **CB code: 6388**

- Public 2-year community and technical college
- Commuter campus in large town

General. Founded in 1967. Regionally accredited. **Enrollment:** 7,527 degree-seeking undergraduates; 1,026 non-degree-seeking students. **Degrees:** 780 associate awarded. **ROTC:** Army. **Location:** 9 miles from Minneapolis-St. Paul. **Calendar:** Semester, limited summer session. **Full-time faculty:** 174 total; 16% have terminal degrees, 8% minority, 54% women. **Part-time faculty:** 144 total; 10% minority, 57% women. **Class size:** 35% < 20, 52% 20-39, 8% 40-49, 5% 50-99. **Special facilities:** 92-acre nature area.

Student profile. Among degree-seeking undergraduates, 34% enrolled in a transfer program, 66% enrolled in a vocational program, 1% already have a bachelor's degree or higher, 1,491 enrolled as first-time, first-year students, 541 transferred in from other institutions.

Part-time:	52%	**Hispanic American:**	2%
Women:	59%	**Native American:**	1%
African American:	8%	**International:**	1%
Asian American:	10%	**25 or older:**	32%

Transfer out. Colleges most students transferred to 2005: Metropolitan State University, University of Minnesota, University of Wisconsin-River Falls, St. Cloud State University, Concordia University.

Basis for selection. Open admission, but selective for some programs. Special requirements for nursing, medical imaging orthotics, prosthetics, paramedic, dental assist and dental hygiene programs. CELT/CELSA used to determine English proficiency. **Learning Disabled:** Documentation of disability must be provided within the first semester of service.

2005-2006 Annual costs. Tuition/fees: $3,858; $7,338 out-of-state. Per-credit charge: $116 in-state; $232 out-of-state. Various reciprocity agreements with some neighboring states provide tuition reduction to out-of-state students. Books/supplies: $1,000.

2005-2006 Financial aid. All financial aid based on need. 39% of total undergraduate aid awarded as scholarships/grants, 61% as loans/jobs. Need-based aid available for part-time students. Work study available for part-time students. **Additional information:** Minnesota resident out of high school or not enrolled in college for 7 years without bachelor's or other higher degree offered cost of tuition and books for 1 course in 1 semester up to maximum of 5 credits.

Application procedures. Admission: No deadline. $20 fee, may be waived for applicants with need. Application may be submitted online. Admission notification on a rolling basis. **Financial aid:** No deadline. FAFSA, institutional form required. Applicants notified on a rolling basis starting 5/15.

Academics. Special study options: Dual enrollment of high school students, ESL, honors, internships, liberal arts/career combination. License preparation in dental hygiene, nursing, paramedic, radiology. **Credit/placement by examination:** AP, CLEP, IB. **Support services:** Learning center, remedial instruction, study skills assistance, tutoring, writing center.

Majors. Agriculture: Horticulture. **Business:** Accounting, administrative services, business admin, management information systems, marketing. **Communications technology:** General. **Computer sciences:** Data processing. **Engineering:** General. **Engineering technology:** Drafting. **Health:** Dental assistant, dental hygiene, EMT paramedic, medical radiologic technology/radiation therapy, medical secretary, nursing (RN), orthotics/prosthetics, pharmacy assistant, substance abuse counseling. **Liberal arts:** Arts/sciences. **Mechanic/repair:** Auto body, automotive, heating/ac/refrig. **Parks/recreation:** Sports admin. **Protective services:** Criminal justice, police science. **Public administration:** Social work.

Most popular majors. Business/marketing 10%, health sciences 26%, liberal arts 44%, security/protective services 10%.

Computing on campus. 1,048 workstations in library, computer center. Commuter students can connect to campus network. Online course registration, wireless network available.

Student life. Freshman orientation: Mandatory. Preregistration for classes offered. 4-hour session preceding semester start. Online orientation also available. **Policies:** Freshmen permitted cars on campus. **Activities:** Bands, choral groups, drama, literary magazine, music ensembles, student government, symphony orchestra, Alpha & Omega, Asian student association, parliamentary debate, Democrats club, drama club, French club, Phi Theta Kappa, Republicans club, Spanish club, Q & S, creative arts alliance.

Athletics. Intercollegiate: Golf. **Intramural:** Badminton, basketball, cross-country, golf, soccer, softball, table tennis, tennis, volleyball.

Student services. Career counseling, student employment services, financial aid counseling, health services, on-campus daycare, personal counseling. **Physically disabled:** Services for visually, speech, hearing impaired. **Transfer:** Special adviser, orientation for new students. Transfer adviser, college fairs on campus for students transferring to 4-year colleges.

Contact. E-mail: admissions@century.edu
Phone: (651) 779-1700 Toll-free number: (800) 228-1978
Fax: (651) 779-1796
Christine Paulos, Director of Admissions, Century Community and Technical College, 3300 Century Avenue North, White Bear Lake, MN 55110

Dakota County Technical College

Rosemount, Minnesota
www.dctc.edu **CB code: 7149**

- Public 2-year technical college
- Commuter campus in large town

General. Regionally accredited. **Enrollment:** 2,281 degree-seeking undergraduates; 350 non-degree-seeking students. **Degrees:** 264 associate awarded. **Location:** 20 miles from Minneapolis-St. Paul. **Calendar:** Semester, limited summer session. **Full-time faculty:** 86 total; 37% women. **Part-time faculty:** 73 total; 6% minority, 55% women. **Class size:** 63% < 20, 35% 20-39, 2% 40-49. **Special facilities:** Greenhouse, truck driving rodeo, skid pad. **Partnerships:** Formal partnership with General Motors for Automotive Service Education Program/Body Service Education Program.

Student profile. Among degree-seeking undergraduates, 100% enrolled in a vocational program, 1,143 enrolled as first-time, first-year students.

Part-time:	38%	**Hispanic American:**	2%
Women:	51%	**Native American:**	1%
African American:	6%	**25 or older:**	46%
Asian American:	3%		

Basis for selection. Open admission, but selective for some programs. Some programs are selective based on test scores. Require the TOEFL for international students and the CELSA for ESL students. Require an admissions visit that includes meeting with the program instructor(s). **Adult students:** Entrance exam policies same as for first-time freshmen. **Home-schooled:** Transcript of courses and grades required.

2005-2006 Annual costs. Tuition/fees: $4,218; $7,932 out-of-state. Per-credit charge: $124 in-state; $248 out-of-state. Various reciprocity agreements with neighboring states provides tuition reduction to some out-of-state students. Books/supplies: $1,525. Personal expenses: $1,710.

2004-2005 Financial aid. Need-based: 33% of total undergraduate aid awarded as scholarships/grants, 67% as loans/jobs. Need-based aid available for part-time students. Work study available nights, weekends and for part-time students. **Non-need-based:** Scholarships awarded for academics, leadership.

Application procedures. Admission: No deadline. $20 fee, may be waived for applicants with need. Application may be submitted online. Admission notification on a rolling basis. **Financial aid:** No deadline. FAFSA required. Applicants notified on a rolling basis starting 3/15.

Academics. Special study options: Accelerated study, cooperative education, cross-registration, distance learning, double major, ESL, internships, liberal arts/career combination. Bachelor's degree programs available on campus. License preparation in nursing, real estate. **Credit/placement by examination:** AP, CLEP, institutional tests. **Support services:** Learning center, pre-admission summer program, remedial instruction, study skills assistance, tutoring, writing center.

Majors. Agriculture: Landscaping. **Business:** Accounting, business admin, executive assistant, marketing, real estate, travel services. **Computer sciences:** Applications programming, database management, networking, programming, web page design, webmaster. **Construction:** Electrician, lineworker, masonry. **Engineering technology:** Architectural drafting, manufacturing, telecommunications. **Health:** Dental assistant, medical assistant, medical secretary. **Mechanic/repair:** Auto body, automotive, communications systems, heavy equipment, medium/heavy vehicle. **Parks/recreation:** Exercise sciences. **Transportation:** Aviation management. **Visual/performing arts:** Commercial/advertising art, graphic design, interior design, photography.

Most popular majors. Business/marketing 18%, computer/information sciences 12%, trade and industry 21%, visual/performing arts 31%.

Computing on campus. 200 workstations in library, computer center, student center. Online course registration, online library available.

Student life. Freshman orientation: Mandatory. Preregistration for classes offered. Sessions available 2-3 months prior to semester. **Policies:** Freshmen permitted cars on campus. **Activities:** Student government, student newspaper.

Athletics. NJCAA. **Intercollegiate:** Baseball M, soccer, softball W, wrestling M. **Intramural:** Basketball, ice hockey M, volleyball. **Team name:** Blue Knights.

Student services. Career counseling, student employment services, financial aid counseling, health services, minority student services, personal counseling, placement for graduates. **Physically disabled:** Services for visually, hearing impaired. **Learning disabled:** Comprehensive services available. **Transfer:** Special adviser, orientation, re-entry adviser, pre-admission transcript evaluation for new students. Transfer adviser, college fairs on campus for students transferring to 4-year colleges.

Contact. E-mail: admissions@dctc.mnsu.edu
Phone: (651) 423-8301 Toll-free number: (877) 937-3282
Fax: (651) 423-8775
Patrick Lair, Director of Admissions, Dakota County Technical College, 1300 145th Street East, Rosemount, MN 55068

Duluth Business University

Duluth, Minnesota
www.dbumn.edu **CB code: 3312**

- For-profit 2-year business college
- Small city
- Interview required

General. Accredited by ACICS. **Enrollment:** 295 degree-seeking undergraduates. **Degrees:** 35 associate awarded. **Location:** 150 miles from Minneapolis-St. Paul. **Calendar:** Quarter, extensive summer session. **Full-time faculty:** 13 total. **Part-time faculty:** 19 total. **Class size:** 96% < 20, 4% 20-39.

Student profile. Among degree-seeking undergraduates, 104 enrolled as first-time, first-year students.

Part-time:	16%	**Asian American:**	1%
Women:	84%	**Hispanic American:**	2%
African American:	1%	**Native American:**	2%

Basis for selection. High school diploma or GED and interview required.

Application procedures. Admission: No deadline. $35 fee. Application must be submitted on paper. Admission notification on a rolling basis.

Academics. Special study options: Distance learning, internships. **Credit/placement by examination:** AP, CLEP. **Support services:** Remedial instruction, tutoring.

Majors. Business: Business admin.

Most popular majors. Business/marketing 12%, health sciences 88%.

Computing on campus. Helpline, repair service, wireless network available.

Student life. Freshman orientation: Mandatory.

Student services. Career counseling. **Transfer:** Special adviser, orientation, re-entry adviser, pre-admission transcript evaluation for new students.

Contact. E-mail: info@dbumn.edu
Phone: (218) 722-4000 Toll-free number: (800) 777-8406
Fax: (218) 628-2127
Mark Truax, Director of Marketing, Duluth Business University, 4727 Mike Colalillo Drive, Duluth, MN 55807

Dunwoody College of Technology

Minneapolis, Minnesota
www.dunwoody.edu **CB code: 2265**

- Private 2-year technical college
- Commuter campus in very large city
- Application essay, interview required

General. Founded in 1914. Regionally accredited. **Enrollment:** 1,292 degree-seeking undergraduates; 112 non-degree-seeking students. **Degrees:** 127 associate awarded. **Calendar:** Quarter, limited summer session. **Full-time faculty:** 71 total; 11% minority, 16% women. **Part-time faculty:** 14 total; 29% minority, 21% women. **Class size:** 67% < 20, 30% 20-39, 1% 40-49, less than 1% 50-99. **Partnerships:** Formal partnerships with Printing Industry of Minnesota to provide instruction, with area high schools to design and deliver school-to-work programs, and with industries for donations of the most advanced equipment and other forms of support.

Student profile. Among degree-seeking undergraduates, 275 enrolled as first-time, first-year students.

Part-time:	7%	**Asian American:**	5%
Out-of-state:	5%	**Hispanic American:**	2%
Women:	7%	**Native American:**	1%
African American:	6%	**25 or older:**	28%

Transfer out. Colleges most students transferred to 2005: Minneapolis Community and Technical College, Normandale Community College, University of Minnesota-Twin Cities.

Basis for selection. Institutional entrance test required. Rank in upper-half of high school class preferred. Essay or personal statement required at time of admissions testing. **Adult students:** Entrance exam policies same as for first-time freshmen. **Learning Disabled:** Students must submit official documentation.

High school preparation. 8 units required; 20 recommended. Required and recommended units include English 3-4, mathematics 3-4, social studies 2, history 2, science 1-2 (laboratory 1-2) and academic electives 4.

2005-2006 Annual costs. Tuition/fees: $13,185. Books/supplies: $1,500. Personal expenses: $1,035.

2005-2006 Financial aid. Need-based: Average need met was 38%. Average scholarship/grant was $4,518; average loan $3,409. 38% of total undergraduate aid awarded as scholarships/grants, 62% as loans/jobs. Need-based aid available for part-time students. **Non-need-based:** Scholarships awarded for academics.

Application procedures. Admission: No deadline. $50 fee. Application may be submitted online. Admission notification on a rolling basis. Applicants to architecture, computer and electrical programs should apply at least 6 months prior to beginning of quarter. **Financial aid:** Priority date 6/1; no closing date. FAFSA, institutional form required. Applicants notified on a rolling basis starting 6/15.

Academics. Special study options: Independent study, internships. Bachelor's degree programs available on campus. **Credit/placement by examination:** CLEP, IB, institutional tests. **Support services:** Pre-admission summer program, reduced course load, remedial instruction, study skills assistance, tutoring.

Majors. Architecture: Technology. **Business:** Accounting, construction management. **Communications technology:** Graphic/printing. **Computer sciences:** Applications programming, information technology, networking. **Construction:** Electrician. **Engineering:** Manufacturing. **Engineering technology:** Electrical, electrical drafting, heat/ac/refrig, instrumentation, robotics. **Mechanic/repair:** Auto body, automotive, heating/ac/refrig. **Production:** Machine tool.

Computing on campus. PC or laptop required. 1,900 workstations in library, computer center. Commuter students can connect to campus network. Helpline, repair service, wireless network available.

Student life. Freshman orientation: Mandatory. One-day program, offered 4 times. **Policies:** Freshmen permitted cars on campus. **Activities:** Student government.

Student services. Career counseling, student employment services, financial aid counseling, minority student services, personal counseling, placement for graduates, veterans' counselor, women's services. **Transfer:** Special adviser, orientation, re-entry adviser, pre-admission transcript evaluation for new students.

Contact. E-mail: info@dunwoody.edu
Phone: (612) 374-5800 Toll-free number: (800) 292-4625
Fax: (612) 374-4128
Alan Wimes, Director of Admission, Dunwoody College of Technology, 818 Dunwoody Blvd, Minneapolis, MN 55403-1192

Fond du Lac Tribal and Community College

Cloquet, Minnesota
www.fdltcc.edu **CB code: 7119**

- Public 2-year community college
- Commuter campus in large town

General. Founded in 1987. Regionally accredited. Institution is the only combined state community college and tribal college in the United States. **Enrollment:** 1,950 degree-seeking undergraduates. **Degrees:** 178 associate awarded. **Location:** 16 miles from Duluth. **Calendar:** Semester, limited summer session. **Full-time faculty:** 37 total. **Part-time faculty:** 30 total. **Special facilities:** 21,000 acre environmental study area.

Student profile.

Out-of-state:	3%	**Live on campus:**	8%
25 or older:	34%		

Basis for selection. Open admission. ACT or SAT may be substituted for ASSET.

High school preparation. Recommended units include English 4, mathematics 3 and foreign language 4.

2005-2006 Annual costs. Tuition/fees: $3,976; $7,499 out-of-state. Per-credit charge: $117 in-state; $235 out-of-state. Cost for double room is $10.18 per day. Books/supplies: $600. Personal expenses: $1,050.

Financial aid. Need-based: Need-based aid available for part-time students. **Non-need-based:** Scholarships awarded for academics.

Application procedures. Admission: No deadline. $20 fee, may be waived for applicants with need. Admission notification on a rolling basis. **Financial aid:** Priority date 3/15; no closing date. FAFSA, institutional form required. Applicants notified on a rolling basis starting 4/15.

Academics. Special study options: Cooperative education, distance learning. Bachelor's degree programs available on campus. License preparation in nursing. **Credit/placement by examination:** CLEP, IB, institutional tests. 24 credit hours maximum toward associate degree. **Support services:** Learning center, remedial instruction, study skills assistance, tutoring.

Majors. Business: Administrative services, finance. **Computer sciences:** Information technology, security. **Conservation:** Environmental science. **Construction:** Power transmission. **Family/consumer sciences:** Food/nutrition. **Liberal arts:** Arts/sciences. **Protective services:** Corrections, forensics, police science. **Public administration:** Human services. **Social sciences:** Cartography.

Computing on campus. 100 workstations in dormitories, library, computer center, student center. Dormitories linked to campus network.

Student life. Freshman orientation: Mandatory. **Housing:** Coed dorms, special housing for disabled, apartments available. $150 deposit, deadline 6/15. **Activities:** Choral groups, drama, student government, student newspaper, Phi Theta Kappa Honor Society, law enforcement club, human services club, science club, volunteer information program, Anishinaabe Congress, math club, veterans club, American Indian Business Leaders.

Athletics. Intramural: Bowling, softball, volleyball.

Student services. Adult student services, career counseling, student employment services, financial aid counseling, health services, minority student services, on-campus daycare, personal counseling, placement for graduates, veterans' counselor. **Physically disabled:** Services for visually, speech, hearing impaired. **Transfer:** Special adviser, orientation, pre-admission transcript evaluation for new students. Transfer adviser, college fairs on campus for students transferring to 4-year colleges.

Contact. E-mail: admissions@fdltcc.edu
Phone: (218) 879-0808 Toll-free number: (800) 657-3712
Fax: (218) 879-0814
Nancy Gordon, Admissions Representative, Fond du Lac Tribal and Community College, 2101 14th Street, Cloquet, MN 55720

Hennepin Technical College

Brooklyn Park, Minnesota
www.htc.mnscu.edu **CB code: 6290**

- Public 2-year technical college
- Commuter campus in small city

General. Regionally accredited. **Enrollment:** 28 full-time, degree-seeking students. **Degrees:** 465 associate awarded. **Calendar:** Semester, limited summer session. **Full-time faculty:** 142 total. **Part-time faculty:** 173 total.

Student profile. Among full-time, degree-seeking students, 3,210 transferred in from other institutions.

Basis for selection. Open admission. **Adult students:** Entrance exam policies same as for first-time freshmen.

2005-2006 Annual costs. Tuition/fees: $3,707; $7,232 out-of-state. Per-credit charge: $118 in-state; $235 out-of-state. Reciprocity agreements for in-state tuition rates with some neighboring states. Books/supplies: $800.

Financial aid. All financial aid based on need.

Application procedures. Admission: No deadline. $20 fee, may be waived for applicants with need. Admission notification on a rolling basis. **Financial aid:** No deadline. FAFSA, institutional form required. Applicants notified on a rolling basis starting 3/1.

Academics. Special study options: Cooperative education, distance learning, double major, dual enrollment of high school students, ESL, independent study, internships, weekend college. License preparation in dental hygiene, nursing, paramedic, real estate. **Credit/placement by examination:** AP, CLEP. **Support services:** Learning center, pre-admission summer program, reduced course load, remedial instruction, study skills assistance, tutoring.

Majors. Agriculture: Floriculture, landscaping, nursery operations. **Business:** Accounting, accounting technology, office technology, office/clerical. **Communications:** Advertising, digital media, publishing. **Communications technology:** General, desktop publishing, graphic/printing, graphics, photo/film/video, printing press operator, recording arts. **Computer sciences:** General, applications programming, computer graphics, data processing, information systems, programming, security, systems analysis, web page design. **Construction:** Carpentry, electrician, maintenance. **Engineering technology:** Architectural drafting, automotive, construction, drafting, electrical, heat/ac/refrig, hydraulics, industrial, manufacturing, mechanical, plastics. **Family/consumer sciences:** Child development. **Health:** Dental assistant, EMT paramedic, licensed practical nurse, medical secretary, office admin, ward clerk. **Mechanic/repair:** General, auto body, automotive, diesel, electronics/electrical, heating/ac/refrig, industrial, marine, medium/heavy vehicle, motorcycle, small engine. **Personal/culinary services:** Chef training, culinary arts, food prep, restaurant/catering. **Production:** Ironworking, machine shop technology, machine tool, sheet metal, tool and die, welding, woodworking.

Computing on campus. 75 workstations in library, computer center, student center.

Student life. **Freshman orientation:** Available. 1.5 hours before school starts. **Policies:** Freshmen permitted cars on campus. **Activities:** Student government.

Athletics. NAIA.

Student services. Career counseling, student employment services, financial aid counseling, personal counseling, placement for graduates, veterans' counselor. **Physically disabled:** Services for visually, speech, hearing impaired. **Transfer:** Special adviser, orientation, pre-admission transcript evaluation for new students. Transfer adviser for students transferring to 4-year colleges.

Contact. E-mail: info@hennepintech.edu
Phone: (763) 488-2500 Toll-free number: (800) 345-4655
Fax: (763) 488-2944
Joy Bodin, Director of Admissions, Hennepin Technical College, 9000 Brooklyn Boulevard, Brooklyn Park, MN 55455

Hibbing Community College

Hibbing, Minnesota
www.hibbing.edu **CB code: 6275**

- Public 2-year community and technical college
- Commuter campus in large town

General. Founded in 1916. Regionally accredited. **Enrollment:** 1,820 degree-seeking undergraduates. **Degrees:** 240 associate awarded. **Location:** 75 miles from Duluth. **Calendar:** Semester, limited summer session. **Full-time faculty:** 65 total. **Part-time faculty:** 45 total. **Special facilities:** Space planetarium.

Student profile.

Out-of-state:	13%	**Live on campus:**	7%
25 or older:	40%		

Transfer out. **Colleges most students transferred to 2005:** Bemidji State University, University of Minnesota-Duluth, College of St. Scholastica, University of Wisconsin-Superior.

Basis for selection. Open admission, but selective for some programs. Special requirements for nursing and law enforcement programs. Academic placement test required. **Adult students:** Entrance exam policies same as for first-time freshmen.

2005-2006 Annual costs. Tuition/fees: $3,957; $4,832 out-of-state. Per-credit charge: $117 in-state; $146 out-of-state. Books/supplies: $800.

Application procedures. **Admission:** Priority date 4/15; no deadline. $20 fee, may be waived for applicants with need. Application may be submitted online. Admission notification on a rolling basis. **Financial aid:** Priority date 7/1; no closing date. Institutional form required. Applicants notified on a rolling basis starting 6/30; must reply within 2 week(s) of notification.

Academics. **Special study options:** Cooperative education, cross-registration, distance learning, dual enrollment of high school students, honors, independent study, internships, liberal arts/career combination, study abroad. Bachelor's degree programs available on campus. License preparation in real estate. **Credit/placement by examination:** CLEP, institutional tests. 17 credit hours maximum toward associate degree. **Support services:** Learning center, reduced course load, remedial instruction, study skills assistance, tutoring.

Majors. **Business:** Administrative services, business admin, office/clerical. **Computer sciences:** General, security, web page design. **Health:** Clinical lab technology, dental assistant, medical secretary, nursing (RN). **Legal studies:** Legal secretary. **Liberal arts:** Arts/sciences. **Personal/culinary services:** Culinary arts. **Protective services:** Police science.

Computing on campus. 100 workstations in dormitories, library, computer center. Commuter students can connect to campus network. Online course registration, online library available.

Student life. **Freshman orientation:** Available. Preregistration for classes offered. Registration orientation held throughout the summer; All-student orientation held day before classes begin. **Policies:** Freshmen permitted cars on campus. **Housing:** Coed dorms available. $250 deposit. City-owned housing available to students. **Activities:** Bands, choral groups, drama, music ensembles, musical theater, student government, student newspaper, Phi Theta Kappa (honor society).

Athletics. NJCAA. **Intercollegiate:** Baseball M, basketball, football (tackle) M, golf, softball W, volleyball W. **Intramural:** Baseball M, basketball, bowling, skiing, volleyball. **Team name:** Cardinals.

Student services. Adult student services, career counseling, services for economically disadvantaged, student employment services, financial aid counseling, minority student services, personal counseling, placement for graduates, veterans' counselor. **Physically disabled:** Services for visually, speech, hearing impaired. **Transfer:** Special adviser, orientation, pre-admission transcript evaluation for new students. Transfer adviser, college fairs on campus for students transferring to 4-year colleges.

Contact. E-mail: admissions@hibbing.edu
Phone: (218) 262-7207 Toll-free number: (800) 224-4422
Fax: (218) 263-2992
Holly Bigelow, Director of Enrollment Services, Hibbing Community College, 1515 East 25th Street, Hibbing, MN 55746

High-Tech Institute

St. Louis Park, Minnesota
www.hightechschools.com **CB code: 3042**

- For-profit 2-year technical college
- Small city

General. Accredited by ACCSCT. **Enrollment:** 550 full-time, degree-seeking students. **Degrees:** 259 associate awarded. **Calendar:** Continuous. **Full-time faculty:** 70 total.

Basis for selection. Open admission.

2005-2006 Annual costs. Costs for full associate programs range from $21,950 to $31,250; diploma programs range from $10,650 to $24,550. Fees, books, uniforms and tools included. Estimated cost of other supplies $50.

Application procedures. **Admission:** No deadline. $50 fee. Admission notification on a rolling basis. Application/registration fee $150 for non-residents of Anoka, Carver, Dakota, Hennepin, Ramsey and Scott Counties.

Academics. **Credit/placement by examination:** CLEP.

Majors. **Computer sciences:** Networking. **Health:** Health care admin, medical assistant, medical radiologic technology/radiation therapy, surgical technology.

Contact. Phone: (952) 417-2200
High-Tech Institute, 5100 Gamble Drive, St. Louis Park, MN 55416

Inver Hills Community College

Inver Grove Heights, Minnesota
www.inverhills.edu **CB code: 6300**

- Public 2-year community college
- Commuter campus in large town

General. Founded in 1967. Regionally accredited. **Enrollment:** 4,166 degree-seeking undergraduates; 685 non-degree-seeking students. **Degrees:** 499 associate awarded. **ROTC:** Air Force. **Location:** 6 miles from Minneapolis-St. Paul. **Calendar:** Semester, limited summer session. **Full-time faculty:** 84 total; 7% minority, 60% women. **Part-time faculty:** 127 total; 6% minority, 45% women. **Class size:** 39% < 20, 58% 20-39, 4% 40-49, less than 1% 50-99.

Student profile. Among degree-seeking undergraduates, 52% enrolled in a transfer program, 35% enrolled in a vocational program, 1,280 enrolled as first-time, first-year students, 441 transferred in from other institutions.

Part-time:	59%	**Women:**	60%
Out-of-state:	3%	**25 or older:**	43%

Transfer out. **Colleges most students transferred to 2005:** University of Minnesota, Metro State University, St. Thomas/St. Catherine's University, University of Wisconsin-River Falls, Minnesota State University-Mankato.

Basis for selection. Open admission, but selective for some programs. Special requirements for nursing and emergency health service programs, Computer and Networking Technology and international students. **Adult students:** SAT/ACT scores not required. **Homeschooled:** Transcript of courses and grades, state high school equivalency certificate required.

2005-2006 Annual costs. Tuition/fees: $4,179; $7,953 out-of-state. Per-credit charge: $126 in-state; $252 out-of-state. Reciprocity agreements for in-state tuition rates with some neighboring states. Books/supplies: $900. Personal expenses: $900.

2005-2006 Financial aid. All financial aid based on need. Average need met was 67%. Average scholarship/grant was $1,500; average loan $2,625. 32% of total undergraduate aid awarded as scholarships/grants, 68% as loans/jobs. Need-based aid available for part-time students. Work study available nights, weekends and for part-time students.

Application procedures. Admission: Priority date 8/1; no deadline. $20 fee, may be waived for applicants with need. Application may be submitted online. Admission notification on a rolling basis. **Financial aid:** No deadline. FAFSA required. Applicants notified on a rolling basis starting 6/1.

Academics. Special study options: Accelerated study, distance learning, dual enrollment of high school students, honors, independent study, internships, liberal arts/career combination, student-designed major, study abroad, weekend college. License preparation in aviation, nursing, paramedic. **Credit/placement by examination:** AP, CLEP, IB, institutional tests. 30 credit hours maximum toward associate degree. **Support services:** GED test center, learning center, pre-admission summer program, reduced course load, remedial instruction, study skills assistance, tutoring, writing center.

Majors. Business: Accounting, business admin, construction management. **Computer sciences:** Computer science, networking, programming. **Construction:** Building inspection. **Health:** EMT paramedic, nursing (RN). **Legal studies:** Legal secretary, paralegal. **Liberal arts:** Arts/sciences. **Parks/recreation:** Health/fitness. **Protective services:** Law enforcement admin, police science. **Public administration:** Social work. **Transportation:** Air traffic control, airline/commercial pilot, aviation management.

Most popular majors. Business/marketing 12%, health sciences 25%, legal studies 17%, liberal arts 21%, security/protective services 14%.

Computing on campus. 141 workstations in library, computer center, student center. Commuter students can connect to campus network. Online course registration, helpline, repair service, wireless network available.

Student life. Freshman orientation: Mandatory. Preregistration for classes offered. Three hour session before start of semester. **Policies:** Freshmen permitted cars on campus. **Activities:** Concert band, choral groups, drama, literary magazine, music ensembles, musical theater, student government, student newspaper, French club, German club, Spanish club, student senate, Christian Fellowship, international club, Black student union, Progressive Student Alliance, GLBT (Gay-Straight Alliance).

Athletics. Intramural: Basketball, football (non-tackle) M, golf, ice hockey, soccer M, softball, table tennis, volleyball.

Student services. Alcohol/substance abuse counseling, career counseling, student employment services, financial aid counseling, health services, on-campus daycare, personal counseling, placement for graduates, veterans' counselor. **Physically disabled:** Services for visually, speech, hearing impaired. **Transfer:** Special adviser, orientation, pre-admission transcript evaluation for new students. Transfer adviser, college fairs on campus for students transferring to 4-year colleges.

Contact. E-mail: iseekinfo@inverhills.edu
Phone: (651) 450-8503 Fax: (651) 450-8677
Landon Pirius, Director of Enrollment Services, Inver Hills Community College, 2500 East 80th Street, Inver Grove Heights, MN 55076-3224

Itasca Community College

Grand Rapids, Minnesota
www.itascacc.edu **CB code: 6309**

- Public 2-year community college
- Commuter campus in large town

General. Founded in 1922. Regionally accredited. **Enrollment:** 1,137 degree-seeking undergraduates. **Degrees:** 191 associate awarded. **Location:** 78 miles from Duluth, 180 miles from Minneapolis-St. Paul. **Calendar:** Semester, limited summer session. **Full-time faculty:** 50 total. **Part-time faculty:** 40 total. **Special facilities:** Educational wetland habitat, University of Minnesota agricultural station and U.S. Forest Service share campus, 500 acres experimental forest. **Partnerships:** Formal partnerships with local businesses for training, partnership council with area high schools.

Student profile.

Out-of-state:	7%	**Live on campus:**	14%
25 or older:	20%		

Transfer out. Colleges most students transferred to 2005: Bemidji State University, The College of St. Scholastica, University of Minnesota-Duluth, St. Cloud State University, Moorhead State University, University of Minnesota-Minneapolis.

Basis for selection. Open admission, but selective for some programs. College-level reading and English testing required for class act teacher education program.

High school preparation. College-preparatory program recommended. 12 units recommended. Recommended units include English 4, mathematics 2, social studies 2, science 2 and foreign language 2. Computer skills recommended.

2005-2006 Annual costs. Tuition/fees: $4,148; $5,072 out-of-state. Per-credit charge: $123 in-state; $154 out-of-state. Different reciprocity agreements for Wisconsin, North Dakota, and South Dakota. Books/supplies: $900. Personal expenses: $1,350.

2004-2005 Financial aid. Need-based: 48% of total undergraduate aid awarded as scholarships/grants, 52% as loans/jobs. Need-based aid available for part-time students. Work study available nights and for part-time students. **Non-need-based:** Scholarships awarded for academics, leadership.

Application procedures. Admission: Priority date 8/1; deadline 9/7 (postmark date). $20 fee, may be waived for applicants with need. Application may be submitted online. Admission notification on a rolling basis. **Financial aid:** Priority date 5/1; no closing date. FAFSA required. Applicants notified on a rolling basis starting 4/1.

Academics. Special study options: Cooperative education, dual enrollment of high school students, independent study, internships, liberal arts/career combination, study abroad. Bachelor's degree programs available on campus. License preparation in nursing, real estate. **Credit/placement by examination:** AP, CLEP, IB, institutional tests. 10 credit hours maximum toward associate degree. **Support services:** GED test center, learning center, pre-admission summer program, reduced course load, remedial instruction, study skills assistance, tutoring.

Majors. Area/ethnic studies: Native American. **Business:** Accounting, business admin, management information systems. **Conservation:** General, forestry. **Education:** General. **Engineering:** General. **Engineering technology:** General. **Health:** Prenursing. **Liberal arts:** Arts/sciences. **Protective services:** Firefighting. **Psychology:** General. **Public administration:** Human services, social work. **Social sciences:** Geography.

Most popular majors. Liberal arts 55%.

Computing on campus. 275 workstations in dormitories, library, computer center, student center. Dormitories wired for high-speed internet access and linked to campus network. Commuter students can connect to campus network. Online course registration, wireless network available.

Student life. Freshman orientation: Available. Preregistration for classes offered. Orientation held before classes begin. **Policies:** Freshmen permitted cars on campus. **Housing:** Coed dorms available. **Activities:** Literary magazine, student government, Circle-K, business club, Student Ambassadors, Panarama, Global Ed, engineering club, psychology club, STARS.

Athletics. NJCAA. **Intercollegiate:** Baseball M, basketball, football (tackle) M, softball W, volleyball W, wrestling M. **Intramural:** Basketball M, bowling, softball, table tennis, volleyball. **Team name:** Vikings.

Student services. Adult student services, career counseling, student employment services, financial aid counseling, minority student services, personal counseling. **Physically disabled:** Services for visually, speech, hearing impaired. **Learning disabled:** Comprehensive services available. **Transfer:** Special adviser, orientation for new students. Transfer adviser for students transferring to 4-year colleges.

Contact. E-mail: info@itascacc.edu
Phone: (218) 327-4468 ext. 4468 Toll-free number: (800) 996-6422
Fax: (218) 327-4350
Candace Perry, Director of Enrollment Services, Itasca Community College, 1851 Highway 169 East, Grand Rapids, MN 55744

ITT Technical Institute: Eden Prairie

Eden Prairie, Minnesota
www.itt-tech.edu/campus/school.cfm?lloc_num=27

- Private 2-year technical college
- Small city

General. Accredited by ACICS. **Calendar:** Quarter.

Contact. Phone: (952) 914-5300
8911 Columbine Road, Eden Prairie, MN 55347

Lake Superior College

Duluth, Minnesota
www.lsc.edu **CB code: 6352**

- Public 2-year community and technical college
- Commuter campus in small city

General. Regionally accredited. **Enrollment:** 3,511 degree-seeking undergraduates; 385 non-degree-seeking students. **Degrees:** 594 associate awarded. **ROTC:** Army, Navy. **Location:** 150 miles from Minneapolis-St. Paul. **Calendar:** Semester, limited summer session. **Full-time faculty:** 97 total. **Part-time faculty:** 142 total. **Class size:** 60% < 20, 39% 20-39, 2% 40-49, less than 1% 50-99. **Special facilities:** Aircraft rescue and fire fighting training center, emergency response training center, technology center.

Student profile. Among degree-seeking undergraduates, 42% enrolled in a transfer program, 58% enrolled in a vocational program, 789 enrolled as first-time, first-year students, 466 transferred in from other institutions.

Part-time:	38%	**Women:**	58%
Out-of-state:	11%	**25 or older:**	33%

Transfer out. Colleges most students transferred to 2005: University of Minnesota-Duluth, University of Minnesota-Twin Cities.

Basis for selection. Open admission, but selective for some programs. Special requirements for radiology and dental hygiene with minimum 2.6 GPA and nursing with a minimum 2.8 GPA. The Academic Skills Assessment Program Computerized Placement Test required for all students unless transcript shows completion of college level math and English composition. **Adult students:** Entrance exam policies same as for first-time freshmen.

2005-2006 Annual costs. Tuition/fees: $3,702; $6,927 out-of-state. Per-credit charge: $108 in-state; $215 out-of-state. Various reciprocity plans for residents of neighboring states may reduce tuition for out-of-state students. Books/supplies: $800. Personal expenses: $2,162.

2004-2005 Financial aid. Need-based: 36% of total undergraduate aid awarded as scholarships/grants, 64% as loans/jobs. Need-based aid available for part-time students. Work study available nights, weekends and for part-time students. **Non-need-based:** Scholarships awarded for academics, leadership.

Application procedures. Admission: Closing date 8/22 (postmark date). $20 fee, may be waived for applicants with need. Application must be submitted on paper. Admission notification on a rolling basis. **Financial aid:** Priority date 5/1; no closing date. FAFSA required. Applicants notified on a rolling basis starting 5/1.

Academics. Special study options: Accelerated study, cooperative education, distance learning, double major, dual enrollment of high school students, ESL, honors, independent study, internships, liberal arts/career combination, study abroad. License preparation in aviation, dental hygiene, nursing, paramedic, physical therapy, radiology, real estate. **Credit/placement by examination:** AP, CLEP, institutional tests. 30 credit hours maximum toward associate degree. **Support services:** Learning center, reduced course load, remedial instruction, study skills assistance, tutoring, writing center.

Majors. Architecture: Technology. **Business:** Accounting, business admin, executive assistant, management information systems. **Computer sciences:** Applications programming, information technology, programming. **Construction:** Carpentry, electrician. **Engineering technology:** Architectural, CAD/CADD, civil, computer systems, electrical. **Health:** Dental hygiene, massage therapy, medical radiologic technology/radiation therapy, medical secretary, nursing (RN), occupational therapy assistant, office admin, physical therapy assistant, radiologic technology/medical imaging, respiratory therapy technology, surgical technology. **Legal studies:** Legal secretary, paralegal. **Liberal arts:** Arts/sciences. **Mechanic/repair:** Automotive. **Production:** Machine tool. **Protective services:** Fire services admin. **Transportation:** Airline/commercial pilot.

Most popular majors. Business/marketing 10%, engineering/engineering technologies 6%, health sciences 38%, liberal arts 34%, trade and industry 7%.

Computing on campus. 304 workstations in library, computer center, student center. Commuter students can connect to campus network. Online course registration, online library, helpline, wireless network available.

Student life. Freshman orientation: Available. Preregistration for classes offered. Half day each semester prior to start of term. **Policies:** Policy describes the student role in the allocation of student activity fees. Freshmen permitted cars on campus. **Activities:** Drama, student government, Intervarsity Christian Fellowship, Phi Theta Kappa, Teachers of Tomorrow, United Multicultural Group, art club, Gus Gus Players (theater), VICA, nursing, dental hygiene club, radiology club.

Athletics. Intramural: Baseball, basketball, ice hockey, softball, volleyball. **Team name:** Huskies.

Student services. Adult student services, alcohol/substance abuse counseling, career counseling, services for economically disadvantaged, student employment services, financial aid counseling, health services, minority student services, on-campus daycare, personal counseling, placement for graduates, veterans' counselor, women's services. **Physically disabled:** Services for visually, speech, hearing impaired. **Transfer:** Special adviser, orientation, pre-admission transcript evaluation for new students. Transfer center, transfer adviser, college fairs on campus for students transferring to 4-year colleges.

Contact. E-mail: enroll@lsc.edu
Phone: (218) 733-7601 Toll-free number: (800) 432-2884
Fax: (218) 733-5945
Melissa Leno, Director of Admissions, Lake Superior College, 2101 Trinity Road, Duluth, MN 55811

Lakeland Academy Division of Herzing College

Crystal, Minnesota
www.herzing.edu **CB code: 3051**

- For-profit 2-year health science college
- Large city

General. Accredited by ACCSCT. **Enrollment:** 341 degree-seeking undergraduates. **Degrees:** 51 associate awarded. **Calendar:** Continuous. **Full-time faculty:** 18 total. **Part-time faculty:** 12 total.

2006-2007 Annual costs. Cost of full programs ranges from $13,360 to $43,585, including fees and books.

2004-2005 Financial aid. Need-based: 38% of total undergraduate aid awarded as scholarships/grants, 62% as loans/jobs.

Application procedures. Admission: No deadline. No application fee. Admission notification on a rolling basis. **Financial aid:** FAFSA required.

Academics. Credit/placement by examination: CLEP.

Majors. Business: General.

Contact. E-mail: info@mpls.herzing.edu
Phone: (763) 535-3000
Shelly Larson, Director of Admissions, Lakeland Academy Division of Herzing College, 5700 West Broadway, Crystal, MN 55428

Le Cordon Bleu College of Culinary Arts

Mendota Heights, Minnesota
www.twincitiesculinary.com

- For-profit 2-year technical college
- Very large city

General. Accredited by ACCSCT. **Calendar:** Quarter.

Contact. Phone: (651) 675-4700
1315 Mendota Heights Road, Mendota Heights, MN 55120

Leech Lake Tribal College
Cass Lake, Minnesota
www.lltc.org **CB code: 3931**

- Private 2-year community college
- Commuter campus in small town

General. Regionally accredited. Chartered by the Leech Lake Band of Ojibwe. Grounded in Anishinaabe knowledge and culture. **Enrollment:** 170 degree-seeking undergraduates. **Degrees:** 7 associate awarded. **Location:** 15 miles from Bemidji. **Calendar:** Semester, limited summer session. **Full-time faculty:** 15 total. **Class size:** 100% < 20.

Basis for selection. Secondary school record important. Elders (55 years and older) who do not meet college requirements and do not qualify for financial aid will be admitted under special status. **Adult students:** Entrance exam policies same as for first-time freshmen. **Homeschooled:** Documentation of high school classes required.

2005-2006 Annual costs. Tuition/fees: $3,330. Per-credit charge: $100. Books/supplies: $600.

Financial aid. All financial aid based on need. Need-based aid available for part-time students.

Application procedures. Admission: $15 fee. Admission notification on a rolling basis. **Financial aid:** FAFSA required.

Academics. Special study options: Cooperative education, double major, independent study, internships, liberal arts/career combination, teacher certification program. **Credit/placement by examination:** CLEP, institutional tests. **Support services:** Reduced course load, remedial instruction, study skills assistance, tutoring.

Majors. Area/ethnic studies: Native American. **Business:** Business admin. **Education:** Early childhood. **Health:** Clinical nutrition. **Liberal arts:** Arts/sciences. **Protective services:** Police science.

Computing on campus. 31 workstations in library, computer center, student center.

Student life. Freshman orientation: Available. Preregistration for classes offered. **Activities:** Choral groups, student government.

Student services. Adult student services, financial aid counseling, personal counseling. **Transfer:** Special adviser, orientation for new students. Transfer adviser for students transferring to 4-year colleges.

Contact. E-mail: chrisf@lltc.org
Phone: (218) 335-4222 Toll-free number: (888) 829-4240
Fax: (218) 335-4209
Delina White, Director of Admissions, Leech Lake Tribal College, PO Box 180, Cass Lake, MN 56633

Mesabi Range Community and Technical College
Virginia, Minnesota
www.mr.mnscu.edu **CB code: 6432**

- Public 2-year community and technical college
- Commuter campus in large town

General. Founded in 1918. Regionally accredited. Career/technical programs offered at Eveleth campus. **Enrollment:** 1,374 degree-seeking undergraduates. **Degrees:** 160 associate awarded. **Location:** 60 miles from Duluth. **Calendar:** Semester, limited summer session. **Full-time faculty:** 50 total. **Part-time faculty:** 20 total.

Student profile.

Out-of-state:	9%	**Live on campus:**	8%
25 or older:	26%		

Transfer out. Colleges most students transferred to 2005: University of Minnesota-Duluth, Bemidji State University, St. Cloud State University, Mankato State University, University of Minnesota-Minneapolis.

Basis for selection. Open admission.

2005-2006 Annual costs. Tuition/fees: $4,028; $4,928 out-of-state. Per-credit charge: $120 in-state; $150 out-of-state. Room only: $2,750. Books/supplies: $600. Personal expenses: $1,000.

Financial aid. Need-based: Need-based aid available for part-time students. Work study available nights, weekends and for part-time students. **Non-need-based:** Scholarships awarded for state residency.

Application procedures. Admission: No deadline. $20 fee, may be waived for applicants with need. Admission notification on a rolling basis beginning on or about 1/1. **Financial aid:** Priority date 4/22; no closing date. FAFSA, institutional form required. Applicants notified on a rolling basis starting 5/1; must reply within 2 week(s) of notification.

Academics. Special study options: Dual enrollment of high school students, independent study, internships, liberal arts/career combination, study abroad. Bachelor's degree programs available on campus. License preparation in nursing. **Credit/placement by examination:** CLEP, institutional tests. **Support services:** Learning center, reduced course load, remedial instruction, study skills assistance, tutoring.

Majors. Biology: General. **Business:** General, administrative services, marketing, office technology. **Communications technology:** Graphic/printing. **Computer sciences:** General, programming, systems analysis. **Construction:** Carpentry. **Education:** General. **Engineering:** Computer. **Engineering technology:** Robotics. **Health:** Substance abuse counseling. **Liberal arts:** Arts/sciences. **Mechanic/repair:** General, automotive, industrial electronics. **Public administration:** Human services.

Computing on campus. Online course registration available.

Student life. Freshman orientation: Mandatory. **Policies:** Freshmen permitted cars on campus. **Housing:** Apartments available. $300 deposit, deadline 9/1. **Activities:** Bands, choral groups, dance, drama, literary magazine, music ensembles, musical theater, student government, student newspaper, symphony orchestra.

Athletics. NJCAA. **Intercollegiate:** Baseball M, basketball, football (tackle) M, softball W, volleyball W. **Intramural:** Badminton, basketball, bowling, field hockey W, ice hockey, racquetball, softball, table tennis, volleyball. **Team name:** Norseman.

Student services. Career counseling, student employment services, minority student services, on-campus daycare, personal counseling, placement for graduates. **Physically disabled:** Services for visually, hearing impaired. **Transfer:** Special adviser, orientation, pre-admission transcript evaluation for new students.

Contact. Phone: (218) 749-0315 Fax: (218) 749-0318
Brenda Kochevar, Director of Enrollment Services, Mesabi Range Community and Technical College, 1001 Chestnut Street West, Virginia, MN 55792-3448

Minneapolis Business College
Roseville, Minnesota
www.mplsbusinesscollege.com **CB code: 7126**

- For-profit 2-year business and technical college
- Very large city

General. Founded in 1874. Accredited by ACICS. **Enrollment:** 350 undergraduates. **Degrees:** 82 associate awarded. **Location:** 10 miles from Minneapolis-St. Paul. **Calendar:** Semester, limited summer session.

Student profile. 100% enrolled in a vocational program, 350 enrolled as first-time, first-year students.

Out-of-state:	20%	**Live on campus:**	12%

Basis for selection. Open admission. Interview recommended.

2005-2006 Annual costs. Tuition/fees: $12,240. Fees for books and supplies vary from $40 to $1,320 per academic year depending on program. Lab fee for medical assistant program $1,160. Room only: $6,040.

Financial aid. Additional information: Individual financial planning available for all students to meet the cost of education.

Application procedures. Admission: No deadline. $50 fee. Admission notification on a rolling basis beginning on or about 7/1. **Financial aid:** No deadline. Applicants notified on a rolling basis.

Academics. Externships related to career available. 14-month associate of applied science degree options. **Credit/placement by examination:** CLEP.

Majors. Business: Accounting, administrative services, hospitality admin, management information systems, office management, tourism/travel. **Computer sciences:** Applications programming. **Health:** Medical assistant. **Legal studies:** Legal secretary. **Visual/performing arts:** Commercial/advertising art.

Student life. **Housing:** Single-sex dorms available. **Activities:** Student government, student newspaper.

Student services. Career counseling, placement for graduates.

Contact. Phone: (651) 636-7406 Toll-free number: (800) 279-5200
Fax: (651) 636-8185
Minneapolis Business College, 1711 West County Road B, Roseville, MN 55113

Minneapolis Community and Technical College

Minneapolis, Minnesota **CB member**
www.minneapolis.edu **CB code: 6434**

- Public 2-year community and technical college
- Commuter campus in large city

General. Founded in 1965. Regionally accredited. **Enrollment:** 7,546 undergraduates. **Degrees:** 483 associate awarded. **Location:** Downtown Minneapolis. **Calendar:** Semester, limited summer session. **Full-time faculty:** 156 total; 97% have terminal degrees, 10% minority, 53% women. **Part-time faculty:** 228 total; 22% have terminal degrees, 14% minority, 50% women. **Class size:** 25% < 20, 55% 20-39, 6% 40-49, 14% 50-99, less than 1% >100.

Student profile. 57% enrolled in a vocational program, 400 transferred in from other institutions.

Out-of-state:	7%	**Hispanic American:**	4%
African American:	30%	**Native American:**	3%
Asian American:	6%	**25 or older:**	46%

Transfer out. **Colleges most students transferred to 2005:** University of Minnesota, Metro State University.

Basis for selection. Open admission, but selective for some programs. The following programs has additional requirements for admission (please consult the MCTC website for details): Nursing, Air Traffic Control, Film, Video, Screenwriting, Sound Arts, Law Enforcement, and Urban Teacher Program. **Adult students:** Entrance exam policies same as for first-time freshmen.

2005-2006 Annual costs. Tuition/fees: $4,028; $7,694 out-of-state. Per-credit charge: $122 in-state; $244 out-of-state. Books/supplies: $1,200. Personal expenses: $2,026.

2004-2005 Financial aid. All financial aid based on need. 38% of total undergraduate aid awarded as scholarships/grants, 62% as loans/jobs. Need-based aid available for part-time students. Work study available nights, weekends and for part-time students.

Application procedures. **Admission:** No deadline. $20 fee, may be waived for applicants with need. Application may be submitted online. Admission notification on a rolling basis. **Financial aid:** Priority date 6/1; no closing date. FAFSA required. Applicants notified on a rolling basis starting 7/15; must reply within 2 week(s) of notification.

Academics. **Special study options:** Accelerated study, cross-registration, distance learning, dual enrollment of high school students, ESL, honors, independent study, internships, liberal arts/career combination, weekend college. License preparation in aviation, dental hygiene, nursing, paramedic. **Credit/placement by examination:** AP, CLEP, IB, institutional tests. **Support services:** Learning center, remedial instruction, tutoring.

Majors. **Business:** Accounting, accounting technology, administrative services, business admin, office technology. **Communications:** Digital media. **Communications technology:** Photo/film/video, recording arts. **Computer sciences:** Networking, programming, security, web page design. **Education:** General. **Family/consumer sciences:** Child care. **Health:** Insurance coding, nursing (RN), preop/surgical nursing, substance abuse counseling. **Liberal arts:** Arts/sciences, library assistant. **Mechanic/repair:** Aircraft, aircraft powerplant, heating/ac/refrig, watch/jewelry. **Personal/culinary services:** Chef training. **Physical sciences:** Acoustics. **Production:** Cabinetmaking/millwright. **Protective services:** Criminal justice, police science. **Public administration:** Human services. **Visual/performing arts:** Cinematography, play/screenwriting.

Most popular majors. Computer/information sciences 14%, health sciences 36%, liberal arts 46%.

Computing on campus. 235 workstations in library, computer center. Online course registration, online library available.

Student life. **Freshman orientation:** Mandatory. Preregistration for classes offered. **Activities:** Jazz band, choral groups, drama, literary magazine, musical theater, student government, student newspaper, International Student Association, Phi Theta Kappa Honor Society, Vocational Industrial Clubs of America, Association of Black Collegiates, Student Nurses Association, Business Professionals of America, Chess Club, Education Club, United Nations of Indian Tribes for Education, Out Campus Alliance.

Athletics. NJCAA. **Intercollegiate:** Basketball, golf. **Team name:** Marauders.

Student services. Adult student services, career counseling, services for economically disadvantaged, student employment services, financial aid counseling, minority student services, personal counseling, placement for graduates, veterans' counselor. **Physically disabled:** Services for visually, speech, hearing impaired. **Learning disabled:** Comprehensive services available. **Transfer:** Special adviser, orientation for new students. Transfer adviser, college fairs on campus for students transferring to 4-year colleges.

Contact. E-mail: admissions@minneapolis.edu
Phone: (612) 659-6200 Toll-free number: (800) 247-0911
Fax: (612) 659-6210
Dena Russell, Director of Admissions, Minneapolis Community and Technical College, 1501 Hennepin Avenue, Minneapolis, MN 55403-1779

Minneapolis Drafting School Division of Herzing College

Minneapolis, Minnesota
www.herzing.edu

- For-profit 2-year technical college

General. Accredited by ACCSCT. **Calendar:** Semester.

Annual costs/financial aid. Cost of full programs ranges from $13,360 to $43,585, including fees and books.

Contact. Phone: (763) 535-3000
Director of Admissions, 5700 West Broadway, Minneapolis, MN 55428

Minnesota School of Business: Brooklyn Center

Brooklyn Center, Minnesota
www.msbcollege.edu **CB code: 3314**

- For-profit 2-year business college
- Large town
- SAT or ACT (ACT writing optional), interview required

General. Accredited by ACICS. **Enrollment:** 600 degree-seeking undergraduates. **Degrees:** 29 bachelor's, 102 associate awarded. **Calendar:** Continuous. **Full-time faculty:** 5 total. **Part-time faculty:** 45 total.

Basis for selection. Personal interview and assessment examination most important. Applicants must submit ACT scores of 17 or above, SAT equivalent, or take an entrance exam.

2005-2006 Annual costs. Tuition/fees: $14,900. Per-credit charge: $330. Books/supplies: $1,800.

Financial aid. All financial aid based on need. Need-based aid available for part-time students.

Application procedures. **Admission:** No deadline. $50 fee. Admission notification on a rolling basis. **Financial aid:** FAFSA required.

Academics. **Special study options:** Bachelor's degree programs available on campus. **Credit/placement by examination:** CLEP.

Majors. **Business:** Business admin. **Legal studies:** General. **Visual/performing arts:** General.

Contact. Phone: (763) 566-7777
Jeff Georgeson, Director of Admissions, Minnesota School of Business: Brooklyn Center, 5910 Shingle Creek Parkway, Brooklyn Center, MN 55430

Two-Year Colleges

Minnesota State College - Southeast Technical

Winona, Minnesota
www.southeastmn.edu **CB code: 7123**

- Public 2-year technical college
- Commuter campus in large town

General. Founded in 1949. Regionally accredited. One campus in Red Wind and two in Winona. **Enrollment:** 1,702 degree-seeking undergraduates; 220 non-degree-seeking students. **Degrees:** 192 associate awarded. **Location:** 50 miles from Minneapolis-St. Paul. **Calendar:** Semester, limited summer session. **Full-time faculty:** 53 total; 91% have terminal degrees, 2% minority, 40% women. **Part-time faculty:** 40 total; 100% have terminal degrees, 5% minority, 68% women. **Partnerships:** Formal partnerships with School-to-Work and Tech Prep programs.

Student profile. Among degree-seeking undergraduates, 546 enrolled as first-time, first-year students.

Part-time:	34%	**Women:**	56%
Out-of-state:	10%		

Basis for selection. Open admission. Interview recommended. **Adult students:** Accuplacer. **Learning Disabled:** Documentation of disability recommended.

High school preparation. Recommended units include English 4, mathematics 2 and science 1.

2005-2006 Annual costs. Tuition/fees: $4,055; $7,753 out-of-state. Per-credit charge: $123 in-state; $247 out-of-state. Various reciprocity agreements with neighboring states provide tuition reduction to some out-of-state students. Books/supplies: $600. Personal expenses: $1,800.

2005-2006 Financial aid. Need-based: Average need met was 60%. Average scholarship/grant was $4,050; average loan $2,625. 37% of total undergraduate aid awarded as scholarships/grants, 63% as loans/jobs. Need-based aid available for part-time students. Work study available nights, weekends and for part-time students. **Non-need-based:** Scholarships awarded for academics, state residency.

Application procedures. Admission: No deadline. $20 fee, may be waived for applicants with need. Application may be submitted online. Admission notification on a rolling basis. **Financial aid:** No deadline. FAFSA, institutional form required. Applicants notified on a rolling basis; must reply within 3 week(s) of notification.

Academics. Special study options: Accelerated study, cooperative education, distance learning, ESL, internships, liberal arts/career combination. License preparation in aviation, nursing. **Credit/placement by examination:** AP, CLEP, institutional tests. **Support services:** GED preparation, learning center, reduced course load, remedial instruction, study skills assistance, tutoring.

Majors. Business: Accounting, administrative services, business admin, management information systems, sales/distribution. **Computer sciences:** Networking, web page design. **Construction:** Carpentry. **Engineering technology:** Drafting, electrical. **Family/consumer sciences:** Child care. **Health:** Medical secretary, nursing (RN). **Legal studies:** Legal secretary. **Mechanic/repair:** Aircraft, auto body, electronics/electrical, heating/ac/refrig, musical instruments. **Personal/culinary services:** Cosmetic.

Most popular majors. Business/marketing 33%, health sciences 41%, trade and industry 15%.

Computing on campus. 298 workstations in library, computer center, student center. Commuter students can connect to campus network. Online course registration, online library available.

Student life. Freshman orientation: Mandatory. Program combined with new student registration. **Policies:** Freshmen permitted cars on campus. **Housing:** Privately-owned dormitory near college available for Red Wing campus, cooperative arrangement with Winona State University for Winona campus. **Activities:** Student government.

Student services. Career counseling, student employment services, financial aid counseling, minority student services, personal counseling, placement for graduates, veterans' counselor. **Physically disabled:** Services for visually, speech, hearing impaired. **Transfer:** Special adviser, orientation, pre-admission transcript evaluation for new students. Transfer adviser for students transferring to 4-year colleges.

Contact. E-mail: enrollmentservices@southeastmn.edu
Phone: (507) 453-2700 Toll-free number: (877) 853-8324
Fax: (507) 453-2715
Al Ducett, Director of Admissions, Minnesota State College - Southeast Technical, 1250 Homer Road, Winona, MN 55987-0409

Minnesota State Community and Technical College - Fergus Falls

Fergus Falls, Minnesota
www.minnesota.edu **CB code: 2110**

- Public 2-year community and technical college
- Commuter campus in large town

General. Founded in 1960. Regionally accredited. Campuses in Detroit Lakes, Wadena, Moorhead. **Enrollment:** 4,734 degree-seeking undergraduates; 504 non-degree-seeking students. **Degrees:** 760 associate awarded. **Location:** 180 miles from Minneapolis-St. Paul, 60 miles from Fargo, North Dakota. **Calendar:** Semester, limited summer session. **Full-time faculty:** 160 total. **Part-time faculty:** 147 total. **Partnerships:** Formal partnerships with local high schools; juniors and seniors can enroll in specially designed courses for college credit at their high school.

Student profile. Among degree-seeking undergraduates, 27% enrolled in a transfer program, 73% enrolled in a vocational program, 1% already have a bachelor's degree or higher, 1,884 enrolled as first-time, first-year students, 345 transferred in from other institutions.

Part-time:	26%	**25 or older:**	15%
Out-of-state:	10%	**Live on campus:**	10%
Women:	57%		

Transfer out. 80% of students enrolled in the transfer program go on to 4-year colleges. **Colleges most students transferred to 2005:** Moorhead State University, St. Cloud State University, Bemidji State University, Minnesota State University - Mankato, University of Minnesota-Minneapolis.

Basis for selection. Open admission. Academic Skills Assessment Program (ASAP) required for English and math. **Adult students:** Entrance exam policies same as for first-time freshmen. **Learning Disabled:** Special accommodations available for students during placement assessment tests.

2005-2006 Annual costs. Tuition/fees: $4,364; $8,201 out-of-state. Per-credit charge: $128 in-state; $256 out-of-state. Various reciprocity agreements provide tuition reduction to some out-of-state students. Room/board: $2,750.

Financial aid. Need-based: Need-based aid available for part-time students. Work study available nights and weekends.

Application procedures. Admission: No deadline. $20 fee. Application may be submitted online. Admission notification on a rolling basis. **Financial aid:** Priority date 6/1; no closing date. FAFSA, institutional form required. Applicants notified on a rolling basis starting 7/1.

Academics. Special study options: Distance learning, dual enrollment of high school students, ESL, honors, internships, liberal arts/career combination, study abroad, weekend college. Bachelor's degree programs available on campus. License preparation in nursing. **Credit/placement by examination:** AP, CLEP, IB, institutional tests. **Support services:** Learning center, reduced course load, remedial instruction, study skills assistance, tutoring, writing center.

Majors. Business: Accounting, administrative services, banking/financial services, business admin, fashion, human resources, management information systems, marketing, office technology, sales/distribution, selling. **Computer sciences:** Networking, programming, security, web page design. **Construction:** Carpentry, site management. **Education:** Teacher assistance. **Engineering technology:** Architectural drafting, computer, computer systems, electrical, manufacturing, mechanical drafting, telecommunications. **Health:** Clinical lab technology, dental hygiene, histologic assistant, licensed practical nurse, medical records technology, medical secretary, nursing (RN), pharmacy assistant, radiologic technology/medical imaging. **Legal studies:** Legal secretary, paralegal. **Liberal arts:** Arts/sciences. **Mechanic/repair:** Auto body, automotive, diesel, industrial, marine. **Protective services:** Criminal justice. **Visual/performing arts:** Graphic design.

Most popular majors. Business/marketing 13%, computer/information sciences 6%, engineering/engineering technologies 7%, health sciences 37%, liberal arts 17%, trade and industry 15%.

Computing on campus. 200 workstations in library, computer center, student center. Dormitories wired for high-speed internet access and linked

to campus network. Online course registration, online library, helpline, wireless network available.

Student life. Freshman orientation: Mandatory. Preregistration for classes offered. 5-8 hour session held in summer. **Policies:** Freshmen permitted cars on campus. **Housing:** Apartments, substance-free housing available. Privately owned dormitories within walking distance of the college. **Activities:** Bands, choral groups, drama, music ensembles, musical theater, student government, student newspaper, organizations in music, drama, athletics, journalism, government, honors and public relations.

Athletics. NJCAA. **Intercollegiate:** Baseball M, basketball, football (tackle) M, golf, softball W, volleyball W. **Intramural:** Basketball, bowling, football (non-tackle), football (tackle) M, golf, softball, volleyball. **Team name:** Spartans.

Student services. Adult student services, career counseling, student employment services, financial aid counseling, minority student services, personal counseling, placement for graduates, veterans' counselor. **Physically disabled:** Services for visually, speech, hearing impaired. **Transfer:** Special adviser, orientation, pre-admission transcript evaluation for new students. Transfer adviser, college fairs on campus for students transferring to 4-year colleges.

Contact. E-mail: enroll@minnesota.edu
Phone: (218) 736-1525 Toll-free number: (877) 450-3322
Fax: (218) 736-1510
Carrie Brimhall, Director of Enrollment Management, Minnesota State Community and Technical College - Fergus Falls, 1414 College Way, Fergus Falls, MN 56537-1000

Minnesota West Community and Technical College: Worthington Campus

Worthington, Minnesota
www.mnwest.mnscu.edu **CB code: 6945**

- Public 2-year community and technical college
- Commuter campus in large town

General. Founded in 1936. Regionally accredited. **Enrollment:** 2,180 full-time, degree-seeking students. **Degrees:** 270 associate awarded. **Location:** 200 miles from Minneapolis-St. Paul, 60 miles from Sioux Falls, South Dakota. **Calendar:** Semester, limited summer session. **Full-time faculty:** 95 total. **Part-time faculty:** 190 total.

Basis for selection. Open admission. Test scores not required for continuing education students. PSB-Aptitude for Practical Nursing Examination required of nursing applicants. Interview recommended.

2005-2006 Annual costs. Tuition/fees: $4,174; $8,001 out-of-state. Per-credit charge: $128 in-state; $255 out-of-state. Tuition is the same for in-state and out-of-state students. Books/supplies: $600.

Financial aid. Need-based: Need-based aid available for part-time students.

Application procedures. Admission: No deadline. $20 fee. Admission notification on a rolling basis. Priority deadline for practical nursing applicants 01/15. **Financial aid:** Priority date 6/1; no closing date. FAFSA required. Applicants notified on a rolling basis starting 7/1; must reply within 2 week(s) of notification.

Academics. Special study options: Cooperative education, cross-registration, distance learning, dual enrollment of high school students, independent study, internships, student-designed major, study abroad. **Credit/placement by examination:** AP, CLEP, institutional tests. 60 credit hours maximum toward associate degree. **Support services:** Learning center, reduced course load, remedial instruction, tutoring.

Majors. Agriculture: General. **Business:** General. **Computer sciences:** General. **Health:** Nursing (RN). **Liberal arts:** Arts/sciences.

Most popular majors. Agriculture 10%, business/marketing 15%, liberal arts 68%.

Student life. Housing: Subsidized apartments adjacent to campus. **Activities:** Jazz band, choral groups, drama, music ensembles, musical theater, radio station, student government, student newspaper, TV station, non-traditional student club, student senate, Phi Beta Kappa.

Athletics. NJCAA. **Intercollegiate:** Basketball, football (tackle) M, golf, softball, volleyball W, wrestling M. **Intramural:** Basketball, bowling, golf, skiing, softball, tennis. **Team name:** Blue Jays.

Student services. Adult student services, career counseling, student employment services, personal counseling, veterans' counselor. **Physically disabled:** Services for visually, speech, hearing impaired. **Transfer:** Special adviser, orientation for new students. Transfer adviser, college fairs on campus for students transferring to 4-year colleges.

Contact. E-mail: jheidelberger@wr.mnwest.mnscu.edu
Phone: (507) 372-3402 Toll-free number: (800) 657-3966
Fax: (507) 372-5803
Mike Fury, Director, Student Services, Minnesota West Community and Technical College: Worthington Campus, 1450 Collegeway, Worthington, MN 56187

Normandale Community College

Bloomington, Minnesota
www.normandale.edu **CB code: 6501**

- Public 2-year community college
- Commuter campus in very large city

General. Founded in 1968. Regionally accredited. **Enrollment:** 8,304 degree-seeking undergraduates. **Degrees:** 796 associate awarded. **ROTC:** Army, Navy, Air Force. **Location:** 12 miles from Minneapolis-St. Paul. **Calendar:** Semester, extensive summer session. **Full-time faculty:** 178 total; 12% minority, 46% women. **Part-time faculty:** 53 total. **Class size:** 29% < 20, 56% 20-39, 13% 40-49, 2% 50-99. **Special facilities:** Japanese garden, marshland area, Career and Academic Planning Center.

Student profile. Among degree-seeking undergraduates, 872 transferred in from other institutions.

Part-time:	50%	**Women:**	59%
Out-of-state:	2%	**25 or older:**	34%

Transfer out. Colleges most students transferred to 2005: University of Minnesota, University of St. Thomas, Minnesota State University-Mankato, St. Cloud State University, Metropolitan State University, Concordia College-St. Paul.

Basis for selection. Open admission, but selective for some programs. Admission to health-related programs (dental hygiene, nursing, dietetic technology, radiologic technology) based on high school GPA and completion of specific course requirements. In-house placement tests in English, mathematics, reading administered before registration. **Adult students:** Entrance exam policies same as for first-time freshmen.

High school preparation. Chemistry required for nursing and dental hygiene programs.

2005-2006 Annual costs. Tuition/fees: $3,976; $7,589 out-of-state. Per-credit charge: $120 in-state; $241 out-of-state. Various reciprocity agreements with some neighboring states provide tuition reduction to out-of-state students. Books/supplies: $1,060. Personal expenses: $2,000.

2004-2005 Financial aid. Need-based: 57% of total undergraduate aid awarded as scholarships/grants, 43% as loans/jobs. Need-based aid available for part-time students. Work study available nights, weekends and for part-time students.

Application procedures. Admission: Priority date 7/1; no deadline. $20 fee, may be waived for applicants with need. Admission notification on a rolling basis. **Financial aid:** Priority date 4/1; no closing date. FAFSA required. Applicants notified on a rolling basis starting 4/15.

Academics. Special study options: Accelerated study, combined bachelor's/graduate degree, cooperative education, distance learning, double major, dual enrollment of high school students, ESL, independent study, internships, liberal arts/career combination, study abroad, weekend college. Bachelor's degree programs available on campus. License preparation in dental hygiene, nursing, radiology, real estate. **Credit/placement by examination:** AP, CLEP, IB, institutional tests. 20 credit hours maximum toward associate degree. **Support services:** Learning center, reduced course load, remedial instruction, study skills assistance, tutoring, writing center.

Majors. Business: General, accounting technology, hospitality admin, marketing, office management, office/clerical. **Computer sciences:** General, computer science, data entry, information technology, programming. **Education:** Elementary, special. **Engineering:** General. **Engineering technology:** Biomedical. **Health:** Dental hygiene, dietetics, medical radiologic technology/radiation therapy, nursing (RN). **Liberal arts:** Arts/sciences. **Protective services:** Criminal justice, police science. **Visual/performing arts:** Art.

Most popular majors. Business/marketing 8%, health sciences 16%, liberal arts 66%.

Computing on campus. 575 workstations in library, computer center, student center. Commuter students can connect to campus network. Online course registration, online library, helpline, repair service, wireless network available.

Student life. Freshman orientation: Mandatory, $25 fee. Preregistration for classes offered. **Activities:** Bands, choral groups, drama, literary magazine, music ensembles, musical theater, student government, student newspaper, Christian Fellowship club, Black student alliance, ASIA, single parents, wellness support group, Phi Theta Kappa, Somali student association, Ethiopian student association, Club Latino.

Athletics. Intramural: Archery, badminton, basketball, bowling, football (non-tackle), golf, ice hockey, racquetball, soccer, softball, table tennis, tennis, volleyball.

Student services. Adult student services, career counseling, services for economically disadvantaged, student employment services, financial aid counseling, on-campus daycare, personal counseling, placement for graduates, veterans' counselor. **Physically disabled:** Services for visually, speech, hearing impaired. **Transfer:** Special adviser, orientation, re-entry adviser, preadmission transcript evaluation for new students. Transfer adviser, college fairs on campus for students transferring to 4-year colleges.

Contact. E-mail: information@normandale.edu
Phone: (952) 487-8201 Toll-free number: (866) 880-8740
Fax: (952) 487-8230
Rick Smith, Director of Admissions, Normandale Community College, 9700 France Avenue South, Bloomington, MN 55431

North Hennepin Community College

Minneapolis, Minnesota
www.nh.cc.edu **CB code: 6498**

- Public 2-year community college
- Commuter campus in large city

General. Founded in 1966. Regionally accredited. **Enrollment:** 2,464 full-time, degree-seeking students. **Degrees:** 655 associate awarded. **ROTC:** Air Force. **Location:** 12 miles from downtown. **Calendar:** Semester, limited summer session. **Full-time faculty:** 88 total. **Part-time faculty:** 125 total. **Special facilities:** Dark room and laboratory, super circuit training course.

Student profile. Among full-time, degree-seeking students, 2% already have a bachelor's degree or higher, 2,200 transferred in from other institutions.

Basis for selection. Open admission, but selective for some programs. Competitive admission for medical programs. Must show proof of immunization to be enrolled in classes.

High school preparation. One unit chemistry and 1 algebra required for nursing program.

2005-2006 Annual costs. Tuition/fees: $4,070; $7,271 out-of-state. Per-credit charge: $125 in-state; $232 out-of-state. Various reciprocity agreements with some neighboring states provide tuition reduction to out-of-state students. Books/supplies: $639. Personal expenses: $1,000.

Financial aid. Non-need-based: Scholarships awarded for academics. **Additional information:** Computerized financial aid application.

Application procedures. Admission: No deadline. $20 fee. Admission notification on a rolling basis. **Financial aid:** Priority date 4/15; no closing date. FAFSA, institutional form required. Applicants notified on a rolling basis starting 6/1.

Academics. Special study options: Cross-registration, distance learning, dual enrollment of high school students, ESL, honors, independent study, internships, study abroad, weekend college. **Credit/placement by examination:** AP, CLEP, institutional tests. **Support services:** Learning center, reduced course load, remedial instruction, study skills assistance, tutoring, writing center.

Majors. Business: Accounting, administrative services, business admin, office management, sales/distribution. **Computer sciences:** General. **Education:** General. **Engineering technology:** Electrical. **Health:** Electrocardiograph technology, medical radiologic technology/radiation therapy, nursing (RN). **Legal studies:** Paralegal. **Liberal arts:** Arts/sciences. **Mechanic/repair:** Automotive. **Protective services:** Police science. **Visual/performing arts:** Commercial/advertising art.

Computing on campus. 200 workstations in library, computer center, student center. Online course registration, helpline available.

Student life. Activities: Choral groups, drama, literary magazine, musical theater, student government, student newspaper.

Athletics. NJCAA. **Intercollegiate:** Baseball M, softball W. **Intramural:** Basketball, bowling, soccer, softball, tennis, volleyball.

Student services. Career counseling, student employment services, on-campus daycare, personal counseling, placement for graduates. **Physically disabled:** Services for visually, speech, hearing impaired. **Transfer:** Special adviser, orientation, pre-admission transcript evaluation for new students. Transfer adviser, college fairs on campus for students transferring to 4-year colleges.

Contact. Phone: (763) 424-0719
Lori Kirkeby, Registrar, North Hennepin Community College, 7411 85th Avenue North, Minneapolis, MN 55445

Northland Community & Technical College

Thief River Falls, Minnesota
www.northlandcollege.edu **CB code: 6500**

- Public 2-year community and technical college
- Commuter campus in small town

General. Founded in 1965. Regionally accredited. **Enrollment:** 2,017 degree-seeking undergraduates. **Degrees:** 543 associate awarded. **Location:** 55 miles from Grand Forks, North Dakota. **Calendar:** Semester, limited summer session. **Full-time faculty:** 72 total. **Part-time faculty:** 29 total. **Special facilities:** Campuses in East Grand Forks and Thief River Falls.

Student profile. Among degree-seeking undergraduates, 1,363 transferred in from other institutions.

Out-of-state:	18%	**Hispanic American:**	2%
African American:	3%	**Native American:**	3%
Asian American:	1%		

Transfer out. Colleges most students transferred to 2005: University of North Dakota, North Dakota State University, Bemidji State University, University of Minnesota: Crookston, Moorhead State University, St. Cloud State University.

Basis for selection. Open admission. Students are required to go through the ACCUPLACER assessment program to determine level of mathematics, reading and english skills. **Adult students:** Entrance exam policies same as for first-time freshmen. **Homeschooled:** Transcript of courses and grades required.

2005-2006 Annual costs. Tuition/fees: $4,209. Per-credit charge: $128. Tuition is the same for both in-state and out-of-state students. Books/supplies: $600. Personal expenses: $1,350.

2005-2006 Financial aid. Need-based: 43% of total undergraduate aid awarded as scholarships/grants, 57% as loans/jobs. Need-based aid available for part-time students. Work study available nights. **Non-need-based:** Scholarships awarded for academics.

Application procedures. Admission: No deadline. $20 fee. Application may be submitted online. Admission notification on a rolling basis. **Financial aid:** Priority date 5/1; no closing date. FAFSA required. Applicants notified on a rolling basis starting 5/15.

Academics. Special study options: Distance learning, internships, liberal arts/career combination. License preparation in aviation, nursing. **Credit/placement by examination:** AP, CLEP. 44 credit hours maximum toward associate degree. **Support services:** GED test center, learning center, reduced course load, remedial instruction, study skills assistance, tutoring, writing center.

Majors. Agriculture: Business, economics, farm/ranch. **Architecture:** Environmental design, interior, technology. **Biology:** General. **Business:** General, accounting, administrative services. **Communications:** General, broadcast journalism, journalism. **Computer sciences:** General, information systems. **Conservation:** Environmental science, management/policy. **Construction:** General. **Education:** General, biology, business, elementary, health, history, mathematics, middle, music, physical, sales/marketing, science, secondary, social studies, special. **Engineering:** General, electrical. **Engineering technology:** Drafting. **Foreign languages:** General, Spanish. **Health:** Athletic training, cardiovascular technology, clinical lab science, clinical lab technology, EMT paramedic, health services, insurance coding, medical assistant, medical secretary, medical transcription, nursing (RN), occupational therapy assistant, pharmacy assistant, radiologic technology/medical imaging, respiratory therapy technology, surgical technology. **Interdisciplinary:** Math/computer science. **Legal studies:** Paralegal, prelaw. **Liberal arts:** Arts/

sciences. **Math:** General. **Mechanic/repair:** Aircraft, auto body, automotive, avionics, electronics/electrical. **Parks/recreation:** General. **Production:** Welding. **Protective services:** Corrections, criminal justice, law enforcement admin, police science. **Psychology:** General. **Public administration:** Human services. **Social sciences:** General. **Transportation:** Aviation management. **Visual/performing arts:** General, art, studio arts.

Computing on campus. 228 workstations in library, computer center, student center. Online course registration, online library, helpline, repair service available.

Student life. **Freshman orientation:** Available. **Policies:** Freshmen permitted cars on campus. **Housing:** Coed dorms, single-sex dorms, apartments available. Housing differs by campus. **Activities:** Bands, choral groups, dance, drama, music ensembles, radio station, student government, student newspaper, Phi Theta Kappa honor society.

Athletics. NJCAA. **Intercollegiate:** Baseball M, basketball, football (tackle) M, golf, softball W, volleyball W. **Intramural:** Badminton, basketball, bowling, golf, racquetball, softball, tennis, volleyball. **Team name:** Pioneers.

Student services. Adult student services, career counseling, services for economically disadvantaged, student employment services, financial aid counseling, minority student services, on-campus daycare, personal counseling, placement for graduates, veterans' counselor. **Physically disabled:** Services for visually, speech, hearing impaired. **Transfer:** Special adviser, orientation, re-entry adviser, pre-admission transcript evaluation for new students. Transfer adviser, college fairs on campus for students transferring to 4-year colleges.

Contact. E-mail: admissions@northlandcollege.edu
Phone: (218) 773-3441 Toll-free number: (800) 959-6282
Fax: (218) 681-0774
Eugene Klinke, Enrollment Management Coordinator, Northland Community & Technical College, 1101 Highway 1 East, Thief River Falls, MN 56701

Northwest Technical College

Bemidji, Minnesota
www.ntcmn.edu **CB code: 3626**

- Public 2-year technical college
- Commuter campus in large town

General. Regionally accredited. **Enrollment:** 833 degree-seeking undergraduates; 43 non-degree-seeking students. **Degrees:** 100 associate awarded. **Location:** 229 miles from Minneapolis-St. Paul, 152 miles from Duluth. **Calendar:** Semester, limited summer session. **Full-time faculty:** 31 total; 6% minority, 68% women. **Part-time faculty:** 25 total; 64% women. **Class size:** 44% < 20, 55% 20-39, less than 1% 40-49. **Special facilities:** American Indian resource center, lake, 3D Hologram technology. **Partnerships:** Formal partnerships with 41 high schools allowing for college credit. Over 71,000 hours of training for 350 corporations.

Student profile. Among degree-seeking undergraduates, 100% enrolled in a vocational program, 1% already have a bachelor's degree or higher, 225 enrolled as first-time, first-year students, 79 transferred in from other institutions.

Part-time:	30%	**25 or older:**	37%
Out-of-state:	5%	**Live on campus:**	5%
Women:	70%		

Transfer out. **Colleges most students transferred to 2005:** Northland Community and Technical College, Bemidji State University, University of North Dakota.

Basis for selection. Open admission. **Adult students:** Entrance exam policies same as for first-time freshmen.

2005-2006 Annual costs. Tuition/fees: $4,125; $4,125 out-of-state. Per-credit charge: $129 in-state; $129 out-of-state. Residence halls available at Bemidji State University. Books/supplies: $1,600.

2005-2006 Financial aid. All financial aid based on need. 46% of total undergraduate aid awarded as scholarships/grants, 54% as loans/jobs. Need-based aid available for part-time students. Work study available nights and for part-time students.

Application procedures. **Admission:** No deadline. $20 fee, may be waived for applicants with need. Application must be submitted online. Admission notification on a rolling basis. **Financial aid:** Priority date 7/1; no closing date. FAFSA, institutional form required. Applicants notified on a rolling basis.

Academics. **Special study options:** Combined bachelor's/graduate degree, cooperative education, cross-registration, distance learning, double major, dual enrollment of high school students, ESL, external degree, honors, independent study, internships, liberal arts/career combination, study abroad. License preparation in nursing. **Credit/placement by examination:** AP, CLEP, IB, institutional tests. **Support services:** Learning center, pre-admission summer program, reduced course load, remedial instruction, study skills assistance, tutoring.

Majors. **Business:** Accounting, administrative services, business admin, sales/distribution, selling. **Education:** Teacher assistance. **Engineering technology:** Industrial, manufacturing. **Family/consumer sciences:** Child care. **Health:** Clinical lab technology, licensed practical nurse, medical secretary. **Mechanic/repair:** Engine machinist, industrial.

Most popular majors. Business/marketing 22%, computer/information sciences 6%, health sciences 61%, trade and industry 8%.

Computing on campus. PC or laptop required. 75 workstations in dormitories, library, computer center, student center. Dormitories wired for high-speed internet access. Commuter students can connect to campus network. Online course registration, online library, helpline, repair service, wireless network available.

Student life. **Freshman orientation:** Mandatory. Preregistration for classes offered. All-day event sessions held throughout the year. **Policies:** Freshmen permitted cars on campus. **Housing:** Coed dorms, special housing for disabled, apartments, substance-free housing available. $150 deposit. **Activities:** Student government, campus government, Phi Theta Kappa, SkillsUSA.

Student services. Adult student services, alcohol/substance abuse counseling, campus ministries, career counseling, services for economically disadvantaged, student employment services, financial aid counseling, health services, minority student services, personal counseling, placement for graduates, veterans' counselor, women's services. **Physically disabled:** Services for visually, speech, hearing impaired. **Learning disabled:** Comprehensive services available. **Transfer:** Special adviser, orientation, re-entry adviser, pre-admission transcript evaluation for new students. Transfer adviser, college fairs on campus for students transferring to 4-year colleges.

Contact. E-mail: richard.lehmann@ntcmn.edu
Phone: (218) 333-6647 Toll-free number: (800) 942-8324
Fax: (218) 333-6697
Richard Lehmann, Admissions Specialist, Northwest Technical College, 905 Grant Avenue Southeast, Bemidji, MN 56601-4907

Northwest Technical Institute

Eden Prairie, Minnesota
www.nti.edu **CB code: 1388**

- For-profit 2-year technical college
- Commuter campus in small city
- Application essay, interview required

General. Founded in 1957. Accredited by ACCSCT. **Enrollment:** 85 degree-seeking undergraduates. **Degrees:** 50 associate awarded. **Location:** 10 miles from Minneapolis-St. Paul. **Calendar:** Semester, extensive summer session. **Full-time faculty:** 6 total; 17% have terminal degrees, 17% women. **Class size:** 100% < 20.

Basis for selection. School achievement record most important, followed by interview, test scores and recommendations.

High school preparation. Recommended units include English 2, mathematics 3 and science 2.

2005-2006 Annual costs. Tuition/fees: $14,185. Per-credit charge: $443. Books/supplies: $650. Personal expenses: $3,192.

Financial aid. **Need-based:** Need-based aid available for part-time students.

Application procedures. **Admission:** No deadline. $25 fee. Admission notification on a rolling basis. **Financial aid:** No deadline. FAFSA, institutional form required. Applicants notified on a rolling basis; must reply within 2 week(s) of notification.

Academics. **Special study options:** Honors, liberal arts/career combination. **Credit/placement by examination:** AP, CLEP. **Support services:** Tutoring.

Majors. **Architecture:** Technology. **Engineering:** General, mechanical. **Engineering technology:** General, architectural, architectural drafting, drafting, mechanical, mechanical drafting.

Computing on campus. 120 workstations in student center.

Student life. Freshman orientation: Mandatory. **Policies:** Freshmen permitted cars on campus.

Student services. Career counseling, student employment services, placement for graduates. **Transfer:** Special adviser, orientation, re-entry adviser, pre-admission transcript evaluation for new students.

Contact. E-mail: info@nti.edu
Phone: (952) 944-0080 Toll-free number: (800) 443-4223
Fax: (952) 944-9274
John Hartman, Director of Admissions, Northwest Technical Institute, 11995 Singletree Lane, Eden Prairie, MN 55344-5351

Pine Technical College

Pine City, Minnesota
www.pinetech.edu **CB code: 7118**

- Public 2-year technical college
- Commuter campus in small town

General. Regionally accredited. **Enrollment:** 456 degree-seeking undergraduates; 270 non-degree-seeking students. **Degrees:** 13 associate awarded. **Location:** 60 miles from Minneapolis-St. Paul. **Calendar:** Semester, limited summer session. **Full-time faculty:** 10 total; 60% have terminal degrees, 10% minority. **Part-time faculty:** 34 total; 62% have terminal degrees, 3% minority, 76% women. **Class size:** 77% < 20, 18% 20-39, 2% 40-49, 2% 50-99.

Student profile. Among degree-seeking undergraduates, 7% enrolled in a transfer program, 100% enrolled in a vocational program, 89 enrolled as first-time, first-year students, 3 transferred in from other institutions.

Part-time:	53%	**Asian American:**	2%
Out-of-state:	11%	**Native American:**	1%
Women:	69%	**25 or older:**	35%
African American:	1%		

Transfer out. 1% of students enrolled in the transfer program go on to 4-year colleges. **Colleges most students transferred to 2005:** St. Cloud Technical College, Anoka-Ramsey Community College, Lake Superior Community College, Mesabi Community College, North Hennepin College.

Basis for selection. Open admission, but selective for some programs. Additional requirements for some majors. Criminal history check. **Adult students:** Entrance exam policies same as for first-time freshmen. **Home-schooled:** State high school equivalency certificate required.

2005-2006 Annual costs. Tuition/fees: $3,726; $7,026 out-of-state. Per-credit charge: $110 in-state; $220 out-of-state. Various reciprocity agreements with some neighboring states provide tuition reduction to out-of-state students. Books/supplies: $800. Personal expenses: $600.

2004-2005 Financial aid. Need-based: 63% of total undergraduate aid awarded as scholarships/grants, 37% as loans/jobs. Need-based aid available for part-time students. Work study available for part-time students. **Non-need-based:** Scholarships awarded for academics, state residency.

Application procedures. Admission: No deadline. $20 fee, may be waived for applicants with need. Application may be submitted online. Admission notification on a rolling basis. **Financial aid:** Priority date 5/5; no closing date. FAFSA, institutional form required. Applicants notified on a rolling basis starting 6/5.

Academics. Special study options: Cross-registration, distance learning, double major, dual enrollment of high school students, honors, independent study, internships, liberal arts/career combination. License preparation in nursing. **Credit/placement by examination:** AP, CLEP, institutional tests. 35 credit hours maximum toward associate degree. **Support services:** Learning center, reduced course load, remedial instruction, study skills assistance, tutoring.

Majors. Business: Accounting, business admin. **Computer sciences:** Data processing, information systems, programming. **Engineering technology:** Manufacturing. **Family/consumer sciences:** Child care. **Health:** Insurance coding, medical transcription. **Mechanic/repair:** Automotive, gunsmithing, locksmithing. **Production:** Machine tool. **Public administration:** Human services.

Most popular majors. Business/marketing 62%, family/consumer sciences 31%.

Computing on campus. 100 workstations in library, computer center. Commuter students can connect to campus network. Online course registration, online library, helpline, wireless network available.

Student life. Freshman orientation: Mandatory. **Policies:** Freshmen permitted cars on campus. **Activities:** Student government.

Athletics. Intercollegiate: Rifle. **Intramural:** Rifle, tennis.

Student services. Career counseling, services for economically disadvantaged, student employment services, financial aid counseling, on-campus daycare, personal counseling, placement for graduates. **Physically disabled:** Services for visually, hearing impaired. **Transfer:** Special adviser, orientation, pre-admission transcript evaluation for new students. Transfer adviser, college fairs on campus for students transferring to 4-year colleges.

Contact. E-mail: information@pinetech.edu
Phone: (320) 629-5100 Toll-free number: (800) 521-7463
Fax: (320) 629-5101
Nancy Mach, Dean of Student Affairs, Pine Technical College, 900 Fourth Street SE, Pine City, MN 55063

Rainy River Community College

International Falls, Minnesota
www.rrcc.mnscu.edu **CB code: 1637**

- Public 2-year community and technical college
- Commuter campus in small town

General. Founded in 1967. Regionally accredited. **Enrollment:** 390 degree-seeking undergraduates. **Degrees:** 49 associate awarded. **Location:** 300 miles from Minneapolis-St. Paul, 150 miles from Duluth. **Calendar:** Semester, limited summer session. **Full-time faculty:** 20 total.

Transfer out. Colleges most students transferred to 2005: St. Cloud State University, Bemidji State University, University of Minnesota-Duluth.

Basis for selection. Open admission.

2005-2006 Annual costs. Tuition/fees: $4,178; $5,096 out-of-state. Per-credit charge: $122 in-state; $153 out-of-state. Books/supplies: $600. Personal expenses: $900.

Financial aid. Need-based: Need-based aid available for part-time students. Work study available nights, weekends and for part-time students. **Non-need-based:** Scholarships awarded for academics, alumni affiliation, minority status, state residency. **Additional information:** Many scholarship and employment opportunities for applicants showing little or no need.

Application procedures. Admission: No deadline. $20 fee. Application may be submitted online. Admission notification on a rolling basis. **Financial aid:** Priority date 6/1; no closing date. FAFSA, institutional form required. Applicants notified on a rolling basis starting 5/1; must reply within 3 week(s) of notification.

Academics. Special study options: Distance learning, dual enrollment of high school students, ESL, honors, independent study, internships, liberal arts/career combination. Bachelor's degree programs available on campus. License preparation in aviation, nursing. **Credit/placement by examination:** CLEP, IB, institutional tests. **Support services:** GED preparation, learning center, pre-admission summer program, reduced course load, remedial instruction, study skills assistance, tutoring, writing center.

Majors. Area/ethnic studies: Native American. **Business:** Office technology. **Computer sciences:** General. **Conservation:** General. **Liberal arts:** Arts/sciences.

Most popular majors. Computer/information sciences 10%, health sciences 16%, liberal arts 65%.

Computing on campus. 100 workstations in dormitories, library, computer center. Online course registration available.

Student life. Freshman orientation: Mandatory. **Policies:** Freshmen permitted cars on campus. **Housing:** Guaranteed on-campus for all undergraduates. Special housing for disabled, apartments available. $200 deposit. Student apartments equipped with computers. **Activities:** Choral groups, drama, literary magazine, music ensembles, musical theater, student government, Black Student Association club, Native Student club, environment club.

Athletics. NJCAA. **Intercollegiate:** Basketball, football (tackle) M, golf, softball W, volleyball W. **Intramural:** Archery, badminton, bowling, cross-country, golf, racquetball, skiing, softball, table tennis, tennis, volleyball. **Team name:** Voyageurs.

Student services. Adult student services, career counseling, services for economically disadvantaged, student employment services, financial aid counseling, minority student services, personal counseling, placement for graduates, veterans' counselor. **Physically disabled:** Services for visually, speech, hearing impaired. **Transfer:** Special adviser, orientation, re-entry adviser, pre-admission transcript evaluation for new students. Transfer adviser, college fairs on campus for students transferring to 4-year colleges.

Contact. E-mail: admissions@rrcc.mnscu.edu
Phone: (218) 285-2213 Toll-free number: (800) 456-3996
Fax: (218) 285-2239
Berta Hagen, Registrar, Rainy River Community College, 1501 Highway 71, International Falls, MN 56649

Rasmussen College-Eagan

Eagan, Minnesota
www.rasmussen.edu **CB code: 2449**

- For-profit 2-year business college
- Small city

General. Accredited by ACICS. **Enrollment:** 475 degree-seeking undergraduates. **Degrees:** 79 associate awarded. **Calendar:** Continuous. **Full-time faculty:** 15 total. **Part-time faculty:** 30 total.

Basis for selection. Open admission.

2005-2006 Annual costs. Regular courses: $275/credit; networking classes: $370/credit; child care classes: $175/credit. Books/supplies: $1,200.

Financial aid. All financial aid based on need. Need-based aid available for part-time students.

Application procedures. Admission: No deadline. $60 fee. Admission notification on a rolling basis. **Financial aid:** No deadline. FAFSA, institutional form required. Applicants notified on a rolling basis.

Academics. Credit/placement by examination: CLEP.

Majors. Business: Business admin, international marketing, training/development. **Education:** Early childhood. **Health:** Medical assistant, ward clerk.

Student life. Freshman orientation: Mandatory.

Contact. Phone: (651) 687-9000 Toll-free number: (800) 852-6367
Fax: (651) 687-0507
Jeannie Lindgren, Director of Admissions, Rasmussen College-Eagan, 3500 Federal Drive, Eagan, MN 55122

Rasmussen College-Mankato

Mankato, Minnesota
www.rasmussen.edu **CB code: 2453**

- For-profit 2-year business college
- Commuter campus in large town
- Interview required

General. Founded in 1983. Accredited by ACICS. **Enrollment:** 490 degree-seeking undergraduates. **Degrees:** 64 associate awarded. **Location:** 60 miles from Minneapolis-St. Paul. **Calendar:** Quarter. **Full-time faculty:** 15 total. **Part-time faculty:** 25 total.

Basis for selection. Open admission.

2005-2006 Annual costs. Regular courses: $275/credit; networking classes: $370/credit; child care classes: $175/credit. Books/supplies: $450. Personal expenses: $1,575.

Financial aid. Non-need-based: Scholarships awarded for academics.

Application procedures. Admission: No deadline. $60 fee. Admission notification on a rolling basis. **Financial aid:** No deadline. FAFSA, institutional form required.

Academics. Special study options: Cooperative education, internships. **Credit/placement by examination:** CLEP. **Support services:** Tutoring.

Majors. Business: General, accounting, business admin, fashion, hospitality admin, sales/distribution, tourism promotion, tourism/travel. **Health:** Licensed practical nurse, massage therapy, medical assistant, medical records technology. **Legal studies:** Court reporting.

Computing on campus. PC or laptop required. Helpline, repair service available.

Student life. Freshman orientation: Mandatory. **Housing:** Apartments locally owned in Mankato located directly behind Rasmussen College. **Activities:** Student government, student newspaper.

Athletics. Intramural: Volleyball.

Student services. Career counseling, student employment services, on-campus daycare, placement for graduates. **Transfer:** Special adviser, orientation, pre-admission transcript evaluation for new students. Transfer adviser, college fairs on campus for students transferring to 4-year colleges.

Contact. E-mail: rascoll@ic.mankato.mn.us
Phone: (507) 625-6556 Fax: (507) 625-6557
Kathleen Clifford, Director of Admissions, Rasmussen College-Mankato, 501 Holly Lane, Mankato, MN 56001

Rasmussen College-Minnetonka

Minnetonka, Minnesota
www.rasmussen.edu **CB code: 2448**

- For-profit 2-year business and junior college
- Commuter campus in very large city

General. Accredited by ACICS. 4 campuses: Minnetonka, St. Cloud, Eagan, Mankato. **Enrollment:** 336 degree-seeking undergraduates. **Degrees:** 77 associate awarded. **Location:** 5 miles from Minneapolis-St. Paul. **Calendar:** Quarter, extensive summer session. **Full-time faculty:** 15 total. **Part-time faculty:** 15 total.

Basis for selection. Open admission.

2005-2006 Annual costs. Regular courses: $275/credit; networking classes: $370/credit; child care classes: $175/credit.

Financial aid. Need-based: Need-based aid available for part-time students.

Application procedures. Admission: No deadline. $60 fee. Admission notification on a rolling basis. **Financial aid:** No deadline. FAFSA, institutional form required. Applicants notified on a rolling basis.

Academics. Special study options: Distance learning. **Credit/placement by examination:** CLEP. 12 credit hours maximum toward associate degree. **Support services:** Pre-admission summer program, reduced course load, study skills assistance, tutoring.

Majors. Business: Accounting, administrative services, business admin, hospitality admin, international marketing, marketing, office management, office/clerical, operations, tourism/travel. **Health:** Medical assistant, medical records admin, medical records technology, medical secretary. **Legal studies:** Court reporting, legal secretary.

Computing on campus. PC or laptop required. Helpline, repair service available.

Student life. Freshman orientation: Mandatory.

Student services. Career counseling, student employment services, placement for graduates. **Transfer:** Special adviser, orientation, pre-admission transcript evaluation for new students.

Contact. Phone: (952) 545-2000
Jeff Hagy, Director of Admisson, Rasmussen College-Minnetonka, 12450 Wayzata Boulevard, Minnetonka, MN 55305-9845

Rasmussen College-St. Cloud

St. Cloud, Minnesota
www.rasmussen.edu **CB code: 3315**

- For-profit 2-year community and junior college
- Commuter campus in small city
- Interview required

General. Regionally accredited; also accredited by ACICS. **Enrollment:** 456 degree-seeking undergraduates. **Degrees:** 91 associate awarded. **Location:** 60 miles from Minneapolis. **Calendar:** Quarter, extensive summer session. **Full-time faculty:** 12 total. **Part-time faculty:** 17 total. **Class size:** 61% < 20, 39% 20-39.

Basis for selection. Open admission. **Adult students:** Entrance exam policies same as for first-time freshmen.

2005-2006 Annual costs. Regular courses: $275/credit; networking classes: $370/credit; child care classes: $175/credit. Books/supplies: $1,200. Personal expenses: $1,575.

2005-2006 Financial aid. Need-based: 34% of total undergraduate aid awarded as scholarships/grants, 66% as loans/jobs. Need-based aid available for part-time students. Work study available nights, weekends and for part-time students. **Non-need-based:** Scholarships awarded for academics.

Application procedures. Admission: No deadline. $60 fee. Application may be submitted online. Admission notification on a rolling basis. The college has two early enrollment deadlines. Dates are available from the admissions department. **Financial aid:** No deadline. FAFSA, institutional form required. Applicants notified on a rolling basis starting 1/4.

Academics. Special study options: Distance learning, double major. **Credit/placement by examination:** CLEP, institutional tests. **Support services:** Learning center, reduced course load, remedial instruction, study skills assistance, tutoring.

Majors. Business: Accounting, business admin, office management. **Computer sciences:** General, information systems, information technology, LAN/WAN management, system admin, web page design, webmaster, word processing. **Education:** Early childhood. **Family/consumer sciences:** Child care. **Health:** Insurance coding, medical records admin, medical records technology, medical transcription, office assistant, receptionist. **Legal studies:** Legal secretary. **Social sciences:** Criminology.

Most popular majors. Business/marketing 65%, health sciences 32%.

Computing on campus. 135 workstations in library, computer center. Commuter students can connect to campus network. Online library available.

Student life. Freshman orientation: Mandatory. **Activities:** Student senate, Student Ambassadors.

Student services. Career counseling, student employment services, financial aid counseling, placement for graduates. **Transfer:** Special adviser, orientation, pre-admission transcript evaluation for new students.

Contact. E-mail: jeffh@rasmussen.edu
Phone: (320) 251-5600 Toll-free number: (800) 852-0460
Fax: (320) 251-3702
Andrea Peters, Director of Admissions, Rasmussen College-St. Cloud, 226 Park Avenue South, St. Cloud, MN 56301-3713

Ridgewater College
Willmar, Minnesota
www.ridgewater.edu **CB code: 6949**

- Public 2-year community and technical college
- Commuter campus in large town

General. Founded in 1961. Regionally accredited. Two campuses: Willmar and Hutchinson. **Enrollment:** 3,617 degree-seeking undergraduates. **Degrees:** 433 associate awarded. **Location:** 100 miles from Minneapolis-St. Paul, (Willmar campus), 60 miles from Minneapolis-St. Paul (Hutchinson campus). **Calendar:** Semester, limited summer session. **Special facilities:** Natural wooded prairie and wetlands areas for biological study; nursing simulation centers; art galleries.

Student profile. Among degree-seeking undergraduates, 49% enrolled in a transfer program, 51% enrolled in a vocational program, 1,420 enrolled as first-time, first-year students, 396 transferred in from other institutions.

African American:	1%	**Hispanic American:**	3%
Asian American:	1%		

Basis for selection. Open admission, but selective for some programs. Special requirements for practical nursing, registered nursing, radiologic technology, chemical dependency counseling, veterinary technology, and post-secondary programs. Interview recommended for law enforcement, nursing, radiologic technology, and veterinary technology. **Adult students:** Entrance exam policies same as for first-time freshmen.

High school preparation. Chemistry and mathematics recommended for mathematics, science, and health science majors.

2005-2006 Annual costs. Tuition/fees: $4,134; $4,134 out-of-state. Per-credit charge: $123 in-state; $123 out-of-state. Some courses may carry higher per credit hour charge. Reciprocity agreements for in-state tuition rates with some neighboring states. Books/supplies: $800. Personal expenses: $1,660.

2005-2006 Financial aid. Need-based: 54% of total undergraduate aid awarded as scholarships/grants, 46% as loans/jobs. Need-based aid available for part-time students. **Additional information:** Special funds are available for adult transfer students returning or continuing education after a 7-year absence from academic training. ALLISS grants provide reimbursement for one class, up to five credits for one semester.

Application procedures. Admission: Priority date 8/1; no deadline. $20 fee. Application must be submitted on paper. Admission notification on a rolling basis. **Financial aid:** No deadline. FAFSA, institutional form required. Applicants notified on a rolling basis.

Academics. 4-year baccalaureate degrees including business administration, psychology, sociology, speech communications taught by state universities available on campus. **Special study options:** Cooperative education, cross-registration, distance learning, dual enrollment of high school students, internships, liberal arts/career combination, student-designed major, study abroad. Bachelor's degree programs available on campus. License preparation in nursing, paramedic. **Credit/placement by examination:** AP, CLEP, institutional tests. 20 credit hours maximum toward associate degree. **Support services:** GED test center, learning center, pre-admission summer program, reduced course load, remedial instruction, study skills assistance, tutoring.

Majors. Agriculture: General, agribusiness operations, agronomy, business, dairy, economics, farm/ranch, production. **Biology:** General, conservation. **Business:** General, accounting, management information systems, marketing, retailing, sales/distribution. **Communications:** General, journalism, media studies, publishing. **Communications technology:** Desktop publishing. **Computer sciences:** General, computer science, networking, web page design, webmaster. **Construction:** Carpentry, electrician. **Education:** General, adult/continuing, art, business, elementary, English, health, instructional media, mathematics, middle, multi-level teacher, music, physical, science, secondary, special, teacher assistance, voc/tech. **Engineering technology:** General, CAD/CADD, drafting, electrical, instrumentation, metallurgical. **English:** Speech/rhetoric. **Family/consumer sciences:** Family studies. **Health:** Athletic training, health care admin, medical assistant, medical radiologic technology/radiation therapy, medical records technology, medical secretary, nursing (RN), substance abuse counseling, veterinary technology/assistant. **History:** General. **Interdisciplinary:** Math/computer science. **Legal studies:** Legal secretary, prelaw. **Liberal arts:** Arts/sciences. **Math:** General. **Mechanic/repair:** Auto body, automotive. **Parks/recreation:** General, health/fitness. **Personal/culinary services:** Cosmetic. **Physical sciences:** Chemistry, geology. **Production:** Machine tool, tool and die, welding. **Protective services:** Criminal justice, police science. **Psychology:** General. **Public administration:** Social work. **Social sciences:** General, criminology, economics, political science, sociology, urban studies. **Visual/performing arts:** Art, commercial photography, photography, studio arts.

Computing on campus. 1,000 workstations in library, computer center. Commuter students can connect to campus network. Online course registration, repair service, wireless network available.

Student life. Freshman orientation: Mandatory. Held on Advising and Registration day. **Policies:** Freshmen permitted cars on campus. **Housing:** Apartment buildings are adjacent to campus. **Activities:** Choral groups, drama, music ensembles, musical theater, student government, student newspaper, symphony orchestra, Christian Students Together, connections club, first responders, multicultural club, Phi Theta Kappa.

Athletics. NJCAA. **Intercollegiate:** Baseball M, basketball, football (tackle) M, golf, softball W, volleyball W, wrestling M. **Intramural:** Basketball, football (non-tackle) M, skiing, softball, volleyball, weight lifting. **Team name:** Warriors.

Student services. Adult student services, alcohol/substance abuse counseling, campus ministries, career counseling, services for economically disadvantaged, student employment services, financial aid counseling, health services, minority student services, on-campus daycare, personal counseling, placement for graduates. **Physically disabled:** Services for visually, speech, hearing impaired. **Transfer:** Special adviser, orientation for new students. Transfer adviser, college fairs on campus for students transferring to 4-year colleges.

Contact. E-mail: info@ridgewater.edu
Phone: (320) 231-2906 Toll-free number: (800) 722-1151
Fax: (320) 231-7677
Sally Kerfeld, Director of Admissions, Ridgewater College, 2101 15th Avenue NW, Willmar, MN 56201

Riverland Community College
Austin, Minnesota
www.riverland.cc.mn.us **CB code: 6017**

- Public 2-year community and technical college
- Commuter campus in large town

General. Founded in 1996. Regionally accredited. **Enrollment:** 3,563 degree-seeking undergraduates. **Degrees:** 255 associate awarded. **Location:** 90 miles from Minneapolis-St. Paul. **Calendar:** Semester, limited summer session. **Full-time faculty:** 97 total; 7% have terminal degrees, 3% minority, 41% women. **Part-time faculty:** 125 total; 6% have terminal degrees, 4% minority, 46% women.

Student profile. Among degree-seeking undergraduates, 49% enrolled in a transfer program, 51% enrolled in a vocational program, 2% already have a bachelor's degree or higher, 1,700 enrolled as first-time, first-year students.

Part-time:	58%	**25 or older:**	32%
Out-of-state:	2%	**Live on campus:**	3%
Women:	55%		

Transfer out. Colleges most students transferred to 2005: Mankato State University, Winona State University, Southwest Minnesota State University.

Basis for selection. Open admission, but selective for some programs. Special requirements for human services, nursing, corrections, networking communications, radiography, and construction electrician. **Adult students:** Entrance exam policies same as for first-time freshmen.

High school preparation. Chemistry required of nursing applicants.

2005-2006 Annual costs. Tuition/fees: $4,109; $7,968 out-of-state. Per-credit charge: $121 in-state; $121 out-of-state. Some courses carry a higher per-credit-hour charge. Various reciprocity agreements with some neighboring states provide tuition reduction to out-of-state students. Books/supplies: $650. Personal expenses: $1,800.

2004-2005 Financial aid. All financial aid based on need. Average scholarship/grant was $3,053; average loan $4,294. 47% of total undergraduate aid awarded as scholarships/grants, 53% as loans/jobs. Need-based aid available for part-time students. Work study available for part-time students. **Additional information:** One class tuition-free for Minnesota residents over 25 who have not attended college for at least 7 years.

Application procedures. Admission: Closing date 8/25. $20 fee, may be waived for applicants with need. Application may be submitted online. Admission notification on a rolling basis. **Financial aid:** Priority date 5/15; no closing date. FAFSA required. Applicants notified on a rolling basis; must reply within 5 week(s) of notification.

Academics. Special study options: Cross-registration, distance learning, double major, dual enrollment of high school students, ESL, internships, liberal arts/career combination, study abroad, weekend college. Bachelor's degree programs available on campus. License preparation in nursing, radiology, real estate. **Credit/placement by examination:** CLEP, institutional tests. 20 credit hours maximum toward associate degree. **Support services:** GED test center, learning center, reduced course load, remedial instruction, study skills assistance, tutoring.

Majors. Agriculture: Farm/ranch. **Business:** Accounting, administrative services, management science, marketing. **Computer sciences:** General, LAN/WAN management. **Engineering:** Software. **Engineering technology:** Electrical. **Health:** Medical radiologic technology/radiation therapy, medical records technology, medical secretary, nursing (RN), occupational therapy assistant, physical therapy assistant. **Legal studies:** Legal secretary. **Liberal arts:** Arts/sciences. **Protective services:** Police science. **Public administration:** Human services.

Most popular majors. Liberal arts 98%.

Computing on campus. 250 workstations in library, computer center, student center. Online course registration, helpline available.

Student life. Freshman orientation: Mandatory. **Policies:** Freshmen permitted cars on campus. **Housing:** Coed dorms available. $350 deposit, deadline 8/1. College foundation-owned student housing. **Activities:** Concert band, choral groups, drama, music ensembles, musical theater, student government, student newspaper, various organizations.

Athletics. NJCAA. **Intercollegiate:** Baseball M, basketball, golf, softball W, volleyball W. **Intramural:** Baseball, basketball, bowling, skiing, softball, volleyball, weight lifting. **Team name:** Blue Devils.

Student services. Career counseling, services for economically disadvantaged, student employment services, minority student services, on-campus daycare, personal counseling, placement for graduates, veterans' counselor, women's services. **Physically disabled:** Services for visually, speech, hearing impaired. **Transfer:** Special adviser, orientation for new students. Transfer adviser, college fairs on campus for students transferring to 4-year colleges.

Contact. E-mail: d.heiny@river.cc.mn.us
Phone: (507) 433-0517 Fax: (507) 433-0515
Dani Heiny, Admissions, Riverland Community College, 1900 Eighth Avenue Northwest, Austin, MN 55912-1407

Rochester Community and Technical College
Rochester, Minnesota
www.roch.edu **CB code: 6610**

- Public 2-year community and technical college
- Commuter campus in small city

General. Founded in 1915. Regionally accredited. University Center offers extension courses from Winona State University, University of Minnesota, Rochester Community and Technical College. **Enrollment:** 5,277 degree-seeking undergraduates. **Degrees:** 690 associate awarded. **Location:** 80 miles from Minneapolis-St. Paul. **Calendar:** Semester, limited summer session. **Full-time faculty:** 125 total. **Part-time faculty:** 185 total. **Special facilities:** Observatory, dental clinic, horticulture lab.

Student profile.

Part-time:	41%	**Women:**	63%
Out-of-state:	5%	**25 or older:**	40%

Transfer out. Colleges most students transferred to 2005: Winona State University, Minnesota State College: Mankato, Unniversity of Minnesota.

Basis for selection. Open admission, but selective for some programs. Admission to allied health and technology programs based on course work, class rank, institutional placement test scores.

High school preparation. Biology, chemistry, algebra and/or English required for some programs.

2005-2006 Annual costs. Tuition/fees: $4,268; $8,011 out-of-state. Per-credit charge: $125 in-state; $250 out-of-state. Various reciprocity agreements with some neighboring states provide tuition reduction to out-of-state students. Personal expenses: $1,860.

Application procedures. Admission: Priority date 6/1; no deadline. $20 fee. Admission notification on a rolling basis. **Financial aid:** No deadline. FAFSA, institutional form required.

Academics. Special study options: Distance learning, dual enrollment of high school students, honors, independent study, internships. Bachelor's degree programs available on campus. License preparation in dental hygiene, nursing, paramedic. **Credit/placement by examination:** AP, CLEP, institutional tests. **Support services:** Learning center, reduced course load, remedial instruction, study skills assistance, tutoring, writing center.

Majors. Agriculture: Equine science, greenhouse operations, horticultural science, turf management. **Biology:** Biomedical sciences. **Business:** Accounting, administrative services, business admin, customer service, management information systems, retailing, special products marketing. **Communications:** Digital media. **Communications technology:** General. **Computer sciences:** General, computer science, web page design. **Education:** Teacher assistance. **Engineering:** General. **Engineering technology:** CAD/CADD, drafting, electrical, manufacturing, mechanical. **Family/consumer sciences:** Child care. **Health:** Cardiovascular technology, clinical lab technology, dental assistant, dental hygiene, electroencephalograph technology, EMT paramedic, medical records technology, medical secretary, mental health services, nursing (RN), premedicine, radiologic technology/medical imaging, surgical technology, veterinary technology/assistant. **Interdisciplinary:** Natural sciences. **Legal studies:** Legal secretary. **Liberal arts:** Arts/sciences. **Protective services:** Criminal justice, police science. **Visual/performing arts:** Graphic design, music theory/composition.

Most popular majors. Business/marketing 9%, health sciences 30%, liberal arts 42%.

Computing on campus. 90 workstations in library, computer center, student center. Online course registration available.

Student life. **Freshman orientation:** Available. Preregistration for classes offered. **Policies:** Freshmen permitted cars on campus. **Housing:** Non-college-affiliated student-only housing available near campus. **Activities:** Bands, choral groups, drama, music ensembles, musical theater, student government, student newspaper, International Student Association, Asian club, Intervarsity Christian Fellowship.

Athletics. NJCAA. **Intercollegiate:** Baseball M, basketball, football (tackle) M, golf, soccer W, softball W, volleyball W, wrestling M. **Intramural:** Badminton, basketball, football (non-tackle), golf, softball, volleyball. **Team name:** Yellowjackets.

Student services. Career counseling, financial aid counseling, health services, on-campus daycare, personal counseling. **Physically disabled:** Services for visually, speech, hearing impaired. **Transfer:** Special adviser, orientation, pre-admission transcript evaluation for new students. Transfer adviser, college fairs on campus for students transferring to 4-year colleges.

Contact. Phone: (507) 285-7265 Fax: (507) 280-3529
Troy Tynsky, Director of Admissions, Rochester Community and Technical College, 851 30th Avenue SE, Rochester, MN 55904-4999

St. Cloud Technical College

St. Cloud, Minnesota
www.sctc.edu **CB code: 1986**

- Public 2-year technical college
- Commuter campus in small city

General. Founded in 1948. Regionally accredited. **Enrollment:** 3,017 degree-seeking undergraduates; 331 non-degree-seeking students. **Degrees:** 418 associate awarded. **Location:** 65 miles from Minneapolis-St. Paul. **Calendar:** Semester, limited summer session. **Full-time faculty:** 112 total; 4% have terminal degrees, 3% minority, 39% women. **Part-time faculty:** 139 total; 2% have terminal degrees, 1% minority, 45% women.

Student profile. Among degree-seeking undergraduates, 833 enrolled as first-time, first-year students.

Part-time:	29%	**Asian American:**	2%
Out-of-state:	4%	**Native American:**	1%
Women:	51%	**25 or older:**	24%
African American:	2%		

Transfer out. **Colleges most students transferred to 2005:** St. Cloud State University, Bemidji State University, University of Minnesota.

Basis for selection. Open admission, but selective for some programs. Paramedicine applicants must complete EMT basic and emergency cardiac care courses prior to acceptance. Echocardiogrpy, Sonography, Cardiovascular Technician, Practical Nursing and Dental Hygiene all require prerequisite courses to be completed prior to admission to the major. **Homeschooled:** Proof of high school graduation required. **Learning Disabled:** Students with developmental disabilities may take the course placement test with accomodations.

High school preparation. Recommended units include English 2, mathematics 2, science 1 (laboratory 1). Mathematics and science classes recommended for technical programs; algebra required for civil engineering; dental hygiene applicants must have all science and nutrition coursework completed; anatomy and physiology, college algebra and physics required for echocardiography and sonography.

2005-2006 Annual costs. Tuition/fees: $3,968; $7,646 out-of-state. Per-credit charge: $123 in-state; $245 out-of-state. Higher per-credit-hour charges may apply to some programs. Various reciprocity agreements with some neighboring states provide tuition reduction to out-of-state students. Books/supplies: $900. Personal expenses: $950.

2004-2005 Financial aid. **Need-based:** 45% of total undergraduate aid awarded as scholarships/grants, 55% as loans/jobs. Need-based aid available for part-time students. Work study available nights, weekends and for part-time students. **Non-need-based:** Scholarships awarded for academics, leadership.

Application procedures. **Admission:** Closing date 8/5 (postmark date). $20 fee. Application must be submitted on paper. Admission notification on a rolling basis beginning on or about 10/5. **Financial aid:** Priority date 5/15; no closing date. FAFSA, institutional form required. Applicants notified on a rolling basis starting 6/1.

Academics. **Special study options:** Accelerated study, cooperative education, cross-registration, distance learning, double major, dual enrollment of high school students, independent study, internships. Bachelor's degree programs available on campus. License preparation in dental hygiene, nursing, paramedic, real estate. **Credit/placement by examination:** AP, CLEP, institutional tests. **Support services:** Learning center, pre-admission summer program, reduced course load, remedial instruction, tutoring.

Majors. **Business:** Accounting, banking/financial services, business admin, executive assistant, sales/distribution. **Communications:** Advertising. **Computer sciences:** Applications programming, database management, networking, programming, web page design. **Construction:** Carpentry, electrician, plumbing. **Education:** Teacher assistance. **Engineering technology:** Architectural drafting, CAD/CADD, civil, electrical, instrumentation, mechanical drafting, water quality. **Family/consumer sciences:** Child care. **Health:** Cardiovascular technology, dental assistant, dental hygiene, EMT paramedic, licensed practical nurse, medical records technology, sonography, surgical technology. **Legal studies:** Legal secretary. **Mechanic/repair:** Auto body, automotive, heating/ac/refrig, medium/heavy vehicle. **Production:** Machine tool.

Most popular majors. Business/marketing 32%, communications/journalism 8%, computer/information sciences 11%, engineering/engineering technologies 14%, family/consumer sciences 9%, health sciences 25%.

Computing on campus. PC or laptop required. 500 workstations in library, computer center, student center. Commuter students can connect to campus network. Online course registration, helpline, repair service available.

Student life. **Freshman orientation:** Mandatory. **Policies:** Freshmen permitted cars on campus. **Housing:** Privately-owned dormitory next to campus. Housing also available at St. Cloud State University. **Activities:** Student government, student newspaper, TV station, Campus Crusade for Christ, Newman Center, Delta Kappa Phi.

Athletics. NJCAA. **Intercollegiate:** Baseball M, basketball, softball W, volleyball W. **Intramural:** Basketball, football (non-tackle), football (tackle), golf, ice hockey, racquetball, soccer, softball, volleyball. **Team name:** Cyclones.

Student services. Adult student services, career counseling, student employment services, financial aid counseling, on-campus daycare, personal counseling, placement for graduates, veterans' counselor. **Physically disabled:** Services for visually, speech, hearing impaired. **Transfer:** Special adviser, orientation, pre-admission transcript evaluation for new students. Transfer adviser for students transferring to 4-year colleges.

Contact. E-mail: enroll@sctc.edu
Phone: (320) 308-5089 Toll-free number: (800) 222-1009 ext. 5089
Fax: (320) 308-5981
Jodi Elness, Director of Enrollment Management, St. Cloud Technical College, 1540 Northway Drive, St. Cloud, MN 56303

St. Paul College

Saint Paul, Minnesota
www.saintpaul.edu **CB code: 0534**

- Public 2-year community and technical college
- Commuter campus in large city

General. Founded in 1919. Regionally accredited. **Enrollment:** 3,431 degree-seeking undergraduates. **Degrees:** 264 associate awarded. **Calendar:** Semester, limited summer session. **Full-time faculty:** 108 total; 7% have terminal degrees, 10% minority, 49% women. **Part-time faculty:** 185 total; 5% minority, 39% women. **Class size:** 69% < 20, 31% 20-39, less than 1% 40-49.

Student profile. Among degree-seeking undergraduates, 2,991 enrolled as first-time, first-year students.

Part-time:	56%	**Women:**	45%
Out-of-state:	1%	**25 or older:**	70%

Transfer out. **Colleges most students transferred to 2005:** Metropoltian State University, Century Community and Technical College, Inver Hills Community College.

Basis for selection. Open admission. ACT considered for placement if submitted; scores must be received by July 1. Interview recommended for selected programs. **Adult students:** Entrance exam policies same as for first-time freshmen. **Homeschooled:** Transcript of courses and grades required.

High school preparation. College-preparatory program recommended. Recommended units include English 3, mathematics 2, social studies 3 and history 3.

2005-2006 Annual costs. Tuition/fees: $3,791; $7,283 out-of-state. Per-credit charge: $116 in-state; $233 out-of-state. Various reciprocity agreements with some neighboring states provide tuition reduction to out-of-state students. Books/supplies: $700. Personal expenses: $1,485.

2004-2005 Financial aid. Need-based: 60% of total undergraduate aid awarded as scholarships/grants, 40% as loans/jobs. Need-based aid available for part-time students. Work study available nights and for part-time students. **Non-need-based:** Scholarships awarded for leadership.

Application procedures. Admission: Priority date 7/1; no deadline. $20 fee. Application must be submitted online. Admission notification on a rolling basis. **Financial aid:** No deadline. FAFSA required. Applicants notified on a rolling basis starting 6/1.

Academics. Special study options: Distance learning, ESL, internships. License preparation in nursing. **Credit/placement by examination:** AP, CLEP, IB, institutional tests. **Support services:** Learning center, reduced course load, remedial instruction, tutoring.

Majors. Business: General, accounting, administrative services, entrepreneurial studies, human resources, international, international marketing, logistics, management information systems, office management, office technology. **Communications technology:** Animation/special effects. **Computer sciences:** Applications programming, computer science, programming. **Construction:** Site management. **Engineering:** Software. **Engineering technology:** Architectural drafting, drafting, electrical, manufacturing, mechanical drafting, surveying. **Family/consumer sciences:** Child care. **Foreign languages:** Sign language interpretation. **Health:** Clinical lab technology, massage therapy, office assistant, respiratory therapy technology. **Liberal arts:** Arts/sciences. **Personal/culinary services:** Aesthetician, chef training, cosmetic. **Science technology:** Chemical.

Most popular majors. Business/marketing 10%, computer/information sciences 8%, family/consumer sciences 12%, foreign language 30%, health sciences 20%, liberal arts 10%.

Computing on campus. 600 workstations in library, computer center. Online course registration, helpline, wireless network available.

Student life. Freshman orientation: Available. Preregistration for classes offered. **Activities:** Student government, Business Professionals of America, Vocational-Industrial Clubs of America, Student Senate, African Heritage student association, Hispanic student association, Asian student association.

Student services. Adult student services, career counseling, student employment services, financial aid counseling, on-campus daycare, personal counseling, placement for graduates, veterans' counselor. **Physically disabled:** Services for visually, speech, hearing impaired. **Learning disabled:** Comprehensive services available. **Transfer:** Special adviser, pre-admission transcript evaluation for new students. Transfer center, transfer adviser, college fairs on campus for students transferring to 4-year colleges.

Contact. E-mail: admissions@saintpaul.edu
Phone: (651) 846-1555 Toll-free number: (800) 227-6029
Fax: (651) 221-1416
Thomas Matos, Director of Office of Enrollment Services, St. Paul College, 235 Marshall Avenue, St. Paul, MN 55102-1800

South Central College
North Mankato, Minnesota
www.southcentral.edu **CB code: 7124**

- Public 2-year technical college
- Large town

General. Founded in 1946. Regionally accredited. Additional campus in Faribault. **Enrollment:** 5,000 degree-seeking undergraduates. **Degrees:** 370 associate awarded. **Location:** 80 miles from Minneapolis-St. Paul. **Calendar:** Semester, limited summer session. **Full-time faculty:** 120 total. **Part-time faculty:** 35 total.

Basis for selection. Open admission.

2005-2006 Annual costs. Tuition/fees: $3,818. Per-credit charge: $114. Out-of-state students pay same rate as in-state students. Books/supplies: $650. Personal expenses: $1,050.

Financial aid. Need-based: Need-based aid available for part-time students.

Application procedures. Admission: No deadline. $20 fee. Admission notification on a rolling basis. **Financial aid:** No deadline. FAFSA, institutional form required. Applicants notified on a rolling basis.

Academics. Special study options: Internships. **Credit/placement by examination:** AP, CLEP. **Support services:** GED test center, pre-admission summer program, remedial instruction, study skills assistance, tutoring.

Majors. Agriculture: General, animal sciences. **Business:** Accounting, administrative services, restaurant/food services. **Communications technology:** Graphic/printing. **Computer sciences:** Computer graphics, programming. **Engineering:** Electrical. **Engineering technology:** Civil, drafting, electrical. **Family/consumer sciences:** Child development. **Health:** Clinical lab assistant, clinical lab technology, dental assistant, EMT paramedic, insurance coding, licensed practical nurse, medical secretary, medical transcription, nursing (RN). **Legal studies:** Legal secretary. **Mechanic/repair:** Auto body, automotive, electronics/electrical, heating/ac/refrig, marine. **Personal/culinary services:** Culinary arts, restaurant/catering. **Public administration:** Human services. **Visual/performing arts:** Commercial/advertising art, graphic design.

Student life. Activities: Student government, student newspaper.

Student services. Career counseling, student employment services, on-campus daycare, personal counseling, placement for graduates, veterans' counselor. **Physically disabled:** Services for visually, speech, hearing impaired.

Contact. E-mail: admissions@southcentral.edu
Phone: (507) 389-7218 Toll-free number: (800) 722-9359
Fax: (507) 388-9951
Linda Beer, Registrar, South Central College, 1920 Lee Boulevard, North Mankato, MN 56003

Vermilion Community College
Ely, Minnesota
www.vcc.edu **CB code: 6194**

- Public 2-year community and technical college
- Residential campus in small town

General. Founded in 1922. Regionally accredited. **Enrollment:** 800 degree-seeking undergraduates. **Degrees:** 119 associate awarded. **Location:** 100 miles from Duluth. **Calendar:** Semester, limited summer session. **Full-time faculty:** 35 total. **Part-time faculty:** 25 total. **Special facilities:** 40-acre outdoor learning center near Boundary Waters Canoe Area.

Student profile.

Out-of-state:	5%	**Live on campus:**	40%
25 or older:	18%		

Basis for selection. Open admission. Interview required for law enforcement, natural resources, parks and recreation students.

2005-2006 Annual costs. Tuition/fees: $4,188; $5,117 out-of-state. Per-credit charge: $124 in-state; $155 out-of-state. Various reciprocity agreements with some neighboring states provide tuition reduction to out-of-state students. Room/board: $4,630. Books/supplies: $600. Personal expenses: $1,500.

Financial aid. Need-based: Need-based aid available for part-time students. Work study available nights and weekends. **Non-need-based:** Scholarships awarded for academics.

Application procedures. Admission: No deadline. $20 fee. Admission notification on a rolling basis beginning on or about 1/1. **Financial aid:** No deadline. FAFSA, institutional form required. Applicants notified on a rolling basis starting 4/1.

Academics. Special study options: Cooperative education, cross-registration, dual enrollment of high school students, honors, independent study, internships, liberal arts/career combination. **Credit/placement by examination:** CLEP. **Support services:** Learning center, pre-admission summer program, reduced course load, remedial instruction, tutoring.

Majors. Biology: General. **Business:** General, accounting, business admin. **Communications:** General, journalism. **Conservation:** General, environmental studies, fisheries, forest resources, forestry, management/policy, wildlife. **Education:** General, art, biology, business, chemistry, computer, elementary, geography, health, history, kindergarten/preschool, mathematics, middle, physics, science, secondary, social studies. **Engineering:** Chemical, civil. **Family/consumer sciences:** General, consumer economics. **Health:** Environmental health, predentistry, premedicine, preveterinary. **History:** General. **Legal studies:** Prelaw. **Parks/recreation:** General, facilities management. **Physical sciences:** General, astronomy, chemistry, geology, physics.

Protective services: Criminal justice, law enforcement admin, police science. **Psychology:** General. **Social sciences:** General, criminology, geography, political science. **Transportation:** Aviation, aviation management. **Visual/performing arts:** Dramatic.

Computing on campus. Dormitories linked to campus network.

Student life. Freshman orientation: Mandatory. 6 different programs from April through start of classes. **Housing:** Guaranteed on-campus for all undergraduates. Coed dorms available. **Activities:** Choral groups, drama, student government.

Athletics. NJCAA. **Intercollegiate:** Baseball M, basketball, football (tackle) M, softball W, volleyball W. **Intramural:** Basketball, bowling, ice hockey M, skiing, softball, tennis, track and field, volleyball, wrestling M. **Team name:** Ironmen, Ironwomen.

Student services. Career counseling, student employment services, personal counseling, placement for graduates, veterans' counselor. **Physically disabled:** Services for visually, speech, hearing impaired. **Transfer:** Special adviser, orientation for new students. Transfer adviser, college fairs on campus for students transferring to 4-year colleges.

Contact. E-mail: admissions@vcc.edu
Phone: (218) 365-7200 Toll-free number: (800) 657-3608 ext. 7215
Fax: (218) 365-7218
Todd Heiman, Director of Enrollment Services, Vermilion Community College, 1900 East Camp Street, Ely, MN 55731-9989

Mississippi

Antonelli College: Hattiesburg

Hattiesburg, Mississippi
www.antonellic.com **CB code: 3195**

- For-profit 2-year health science and technical college
- Large town

General. Accredited by ACCSCT. **Enrollment:** 295 degree-seeking undergraduates. **Degrees:** 50 associate awarded. **Calendar:** Continuous. **Full-time faculty:** 18 total. **Part-time faculty:** 10 total.

Basis for selection. Open admission.

2005-2006 Annual costs. Total cost of tuition for 2-year associate degree program in medical assisting $16,400, additional required fees $600, part-time per credit hour charge $175; for 2-year associate degree program in graphic design $19,960, additional required fees $965, part-time per credit hour charge $210; for 2-year associate degree program in health information technology $17,040, additional required fees $600, part-time per credit hour charge $180. Books/supplies: $900.

Academics. Credit/placement by examination: CLEP.

Majors. Computer sciences: General.

Contact. E-mail: gautreau@antonellic.com
Phone: (601) 583-4100
Karen Gautreau, Director, Antonelli College: Hattiesburg, 1500 North 31st Avenue, Hattiesburg, MS 39401

Antonelli College: Jackson

Jackson, Mississippi
www.antonellicollege.edu **CB code: 3193**

- For-profit 2-year technical college
- Commuter campus in small city

General. Accredited by ACCSCT. **Enrollment:** 303 degree-seeking undergraduates. **Degrees:** 61 associate awarded. **Calendar:** Quarter. **Full-time faculty:** 15 total. **Part-time faculty:** 22 total.

Basis for selection. Open admission.

2005-2006 Annual costs. Books/supplies: $1,200.

Application procedures. Admission: No deadline. $75 fee. **Financial aid:** No deadline.

Academics. Credit/placement by examination: CLEP, institutional tests. 14 credit hours maximum toward associate degree. **Support services:** Study skills assistance, tutoring.

Majors. Business: Accounting, office technology. **Computer sciences:** Computer graphics, data entry, networking, security, web page design, webmaster. **Health:** Insurance coding, massage therapy, medical assistant, medical transcription. **Legal studies:** General. **Visual/performing arts:** Graphic design, interior design.

Computing on campus. 100 workstations in library, computer center. Wireless network available.

Student life. Freshman orientation: Mandatory. Preregistration for classes offered. Held 2 days prior to start of class. **Policies:** Freshmen permitted cars on campus. **Activities:** Student newspaper.

Student services. Student employment services, financial aid counseling, placement for graduates.

Contact. Phone: (601) 362-9991
Debbie More, Admissions Director, Antonelli College: Jackson, 2323 Lakeland Drive, Jackson, MS 39232

Coahoma Community College

Clarksdale, Mississippi
www.coahomacc.edu **CB code: 1126**

- Public 2-year community college
- Residential campus in rural community

General. Founded in 1949. Regionally accredited. **Enrollment:** 1,946 degree-seeking undergraduates. **Degrees:** 232 associate awarded. **Location:** 65 miles from Memphis, Tennessee. **Calendar:** Semester, limited summer session. **Full-time faculty:** 73 total; 58% women. **Part-time faculty:** 17 total; 18% women.

Student profile. Among degree-seeking undergraduates, 74% enrolled in a transfer program, 26% enrolled in a vocational program.

Out-of-state:	20%	**25 or older:**	25%
African American:	94%	**Live on campus:**	23%

Transfer out. Colleges most students transferred to 2005: Alcorn State University, Delta State University, Jackson State University, Mississippi Valley State University, University of Mississippi.

Basis for selection. Open admission, but selective for some programs. High school record most important for admission to degree programs. Open admissions to vocational programs. Selective admission to licensed practical nursing and respiratory therapy. ACT/SAT required for nursing. Interview required for nursing students; audition required for music students. **Homeschooled:** Transcript of courses and grades, letter of recommendation (nonparent) required.

High school preparation. Recommended units include English 4, mathematics 3, social studies 2, science 3 (laboratory 3) and foreign language 1.

2005-2006 Annual costs. Tuition/fees: $1,800; $3,100 out-of-state. Per-credit charge: $90. Room/board: $2,914. Books/supplies: $800. Personal expenses: $700.

Financial aid. All financial aid based on need. Need-based aid available for part-time students.

Application procedures. Admission: No deadline. No application fee. Admission notification on a rolling basis. **Financial aid:** Priority date 4/1; no closing date. FAFSA, institutional form required. Applicants notified on a rolling basis starting 7/1.

Academics. Special study options: Distance learning, dual enrollment of high school students. **Credit/placement by examination:** CLEP. **Support services:** GED preparation, reduced course load, remedial instruction, tutoring, writing center.

Majors. Biology: General. **Business:** General, accounting, hotel/motel admin, office technology. **Communications:** Broadcast journalism, journalism. **Computer sciences:** General, computer science. **Education:** General, art, business, early childhood, elementary, English, health, mathematics, music, physical, science, social science. **Engineering technology:** Electrical. **Family/consumer sciences:** Child care. **Health:** Clinical lab science, medical records admin, nursing (RN), predentistry, premedicine, prenursing, prepharmacy, preveterinary, respiratory therapy technology. **Legal studies:** Prelaw. **Math:** General. **Mechanic/repair:** Industrial. **Parks/recreation:** Sports admin. **Physical sciences:** Chemistry. **Protective services:** Criminal justice. **Public administration:** Social work. **Social sciences:** General. **Visual/performing arts:** General.

Most popular majors. Business/marketing 16%, education 41%, health sciences 15%, public administration/social services 11%, security/protective services 8%.

Computing on campus. Online course registration, online library available.

Student life. Freshman orientation: Mandatory. **Housing:** Single-sex dorms available. $100 deposit, deadline 8/1. **Activities:** Bands, choral groups, student government, student newspaper, Baptist student union, Wesley Foundation, Black literary society.

Athletics. NJCAA. **Intercollegiate:** Baseball M, basketball, football (tackle) M, softball W. **Intramural:** Badminton, basketball, cheerleading W, football (tackle) M, softball, table tennis, volleyball. **Team name:** Tigers.

Student services. Career counseling, services for economically disadvantaged, financial aid counseling, health services, on-campus daycare, personal counseling. **Physically disabled:** Services for visually, speech, hearing impaired. **Transfer:** Pre-admission transcript evaluation for new students.

Transfer adviser, college fairs on campus for students transferring to 4-year colleges.

Contact. E-mail: wholmes@coahoma.cc.edu
Phone: (662) 621-4205 Toll-free number: (800) 844-1222
Fax: (800) 844-1222
Wanda Holmes, Director of Admissions, Coahoma Community College, 3240 Friars Point Road, Clarksdale, MS 38614-9799

Copiah-Lincoln Community College

Wesson, Mississippi
www.colin.edu **CB code: 1142**

- Public 2-year community college
- Commuter campus in small town

General. Founded in 1928. Regionally accredited. Branch campus in Natchez and Simpson County Mississippi. **Enrollment:** 3,010 undergraduates; 3,010 non-degree-seeking students. **Degrees:** 441 associate awarded. **Location:** 45 miles from Jackson. **Calendar:** Semester, limited summer session. **Full-time faculty:** 122 total; 5% have terminal degrees, 8% minority, 57% women. **Part-time faculty:** 75 total; 4% have terminal degrees, 7% minority, 67% women. **Special facilities:** Chapel, walking trail, golf course.

Student profile.

Out-of-state:	2%	**Live on campus:**	30%
25 or older:	21%		

Transfer out. Colleges most students transferred to 2005: University of Southern Mississippi, Alcorn State University, University of Mississippi, Mississippi State University, Jackson State University.

Basis for selection. Open admission, but selective for some programs. ACT required for certain technology and health occupation professions programs. **Homeschooled:** Transcript of courses and grades required. ACT required.

2006-2007 Annual costs. Tuition/fees (projected): $1,750; $3,350 out-of-state. Per-credit charge: $100 in-state; $175 out-of-state. Parking Fee: 20.00. Room/board: $3,400. Books/supplies: $600.

Financial aid. Need-based: Need-based aid available for part-time students. Work study available nights, weekends and for part-time students. **Non-need-based:** Scholarships awarded for academics, art, athletics, job skills, leadership, music/drama, state residency.

Application procedures. Admission: No deadline. No application fee. Admission notification on a rolling basis. **Financial aid:** Priority date 4/1; no closing date. FAFSA required. Applicants notified on a rolling basis starting 4/1; must reply within 2 week(s) of notification.

Academics. Special study options: Dual enrollment of high school students, honors. License preparation in nursing, paramedic. **Credit/placement by examination:** AP, CLEP, institutional tests. 12 credit hours maximum toward associate degree. **Support services:** GED preparation and test center, learning center, remedial instruction, study skills assistance, tutoring.

Majors. Business: Accounting, administrative services, business admin, hospitality admin, office technology. **Computer sciences:** Data processing, networking. **Conservation:** Wood science. **Engineering technology:** Drafting, electrical. **Health:** Clinical lab science, clinical lab technology, medical radiologic technology/radiation therapy, nursing (RN), respiratory therapy technology. **Liberal arts:** Arts/sciences. **Mechanic/repair:** Automotive, diesel, electronics/electrical. **Personal/culinary services:** Food service. **Production:** Machine tool.

Computing on campus. 200 workstations in library, computer center. Dormitories linked to campus network. Online course registration, online library, helpline available.

Student life. Freshman orientation: Mandatory. Preregistration for classes offered. **Policies:** Freshmen permitted cars on campus. **Housing:** Guaranteed on-campus for all undergraduates. Single-sex dorms, special housing for disabled, apartments, substance-free housing available. $50 fully refundable deposit. **Activities:** Bands, choral groups, drama, literary magazine, music ensembles, radio station, student government, student newspaper.

Athletics. NJCAA. **Intercollegiate:** Baseball M, basketball, football (tackle) M, golf, softball W, tennis, track and field M. **Intramural:** Basketball, softball, volleyball. **Team name:** Wolves.

Student services. Career counseling, financial aid counseling, health services, on-campus daycare, personal counseling, veterans' counselor. **Physically disabled:** Services for visually, speech, hearing impaired. **Transfer:** Special adviser, orientation, pre-admission transcript evaluation for new students. College fairs on campus for students transferring to 4-year colleges.

Contact. Phone: (601) 643-8307 Fax: (601) 643-8225
Phil Broome, Director of Admissions and Records, Copiah-Lincoln Community College, Box 649, Wesson, MS 39191

East Central Community College

Decatur, Mississippi
www.eccc.cc.ms.us **CB code: 1196**

- Public 2-year community college
- Commuter campus in rural community

General. Founded in 1928. Regionally accredited. **Enrollment:** 2,410 degree-seeking undergraduates. **Degrees:** 404 associate awarded. **Location:** 30 miles from Meridian. **Calendar:** Semester, limited summer session. **Full-time faculty:** 73 total. **Part-time faculty:** 64 total.

Student profile.

Out-of-state:	2%	**Live on campus:**	30%
25 or older:	32%		

Basis for selection. Open admission, but selective for some programs. Special requirements for nursing program. All applicants must submit ACT. No minimum score required.

2005-2006 Annual costs. Tuition/fees: $1,400; $3,500 out-of-state. Per-credit charge: $65 in-state; $153 out-of-state. Room/board: $2,540. Books/supplies: $800. Personal expenses: $900.

Financial aid. Non-need-based: Scholarships awarded for academics, athletics, state residency.

Application procedures. Admission: No deadline. No application fee. **Financial aid:** No deadline. FAFSA, institutional form required. Applicants notified on a rolling basis starting 7/31; must reply within 2 week(s) of notification.

Academics. Special study options: Distance learning, dual enrollment of high school students, honors. **Credit/placement by examination:** CLEP, institutional tests. 6 credit hours maximum toward associate degree. **Support services:** GED preparation and test center, remedial instruction, study skills assistance, tutoring.

Majors. Biology: General. **Business:** General. **Computer sciences:** General, applications programming, data processing, programming. **Education:** General. **Engineering:** General. **Engineering technology:** Drafting, electrical. **English:** Composition. **Health:** Predentistry, premedicine, prepharmacy, preveterinary. **Interdisciplinary:** Gerontology. **Liberal arts:** Arts/sciences. **Math:** General. **Physical sciences:** Chemistry. **Psychology:** General. **Visual/performing arts:** Studio arts.

Student life. Housing: Guaranteed on-campus for freshmen. Single-sex dorms, apartments available. **Activities:** Bands, choral groups, drama, student government, student newspaper.

Athletics. NJCAA. **Intercollegiate:** Baseball M, basketball, football (tackle) M, golf, soccer, softball W, tennis. **Intramural:** Basketball, softball, table tennis.

Student services. Career counseling, health services, on-campus daycare, personal counseling, veterans' counselor. **Transfer:** Special adviser, orientation for new students. College fairs on campus for students transferring to 4-year colleges.

Contact. Phone: (601) 635-2111 ext. 206 Toll-free number: (877) 462-3222 Fax: (601) 635-4060
Donna Luke, Director of Admissions, East Central Community College, Box 129, Decatur, MS 39327

East Mississippi Community College

Scooba, Mississippi
www.eastms.edu **CB code: 1197**

- Public 2-year community college
- Residential campus in rural community

General. Founded in 1927. Regionally accredited. **Location:** 37 miles from Meridian. **Calendar:** Semester.

Annual costs/financial aid. Tuition/fees (2005-2006): $1,760; $3,510 out-of-state. $50 health fee for on-campus residents. Room/board: $2,550. Books/supplies: $900. Personal expenses: $2,200. Need-based financial aid available to full-time and part-time students.

Contact. Phone: (662) 476-8442
Director of Admissions, Admissions Office, Scooba, MS 39358

Hinds Community College

Raymond, Mississippi
www.hindscc.edu **CB code: 1296**

- Public 2-year branch campus and community college
- Commuter campus in small town

General. Founded in 1917. Regionally accredited. 6 off-campus credit bearing locations: Raymond, Utica, Rankin, Academic/Technical Center, Nursing/Allied Health Center, Vicksburg Warren County Center. **Enrollment:** 10,552 degree-seeking undergraduates. **Degrees:** 884 associate awarded. **ROTC:** Army. **Location:** 10 miles from Jackson. **Calendar:** Semester, extensive summer session. **Full-time faculty:** 390 total. **Part-time faculty:** 530 total. **Class size:** 45% < 20, 48% 20-39, 5% 40-49, less than 1% 50-99, less than 1% >100.

Student profile.

Out-of-state:	1%	**Live on campus:**	16%
25 or older:	43%		

Transfer out. Colleges most students transferred to 2005: Mississippi State University, University of Southern Mississippi, Jackson State, University of Mississippi, Mississippi College.

Basis for selection. Open admission, but selective for some programs. Special requirements for allied health, data processing programs. 19 high school units, ACT composite score of 18 may be substituted for diploma. ACT not required for placement in vocational programs. Interview required for allied health, vocational majors.

High school preparation. 19 units recommended. Recommended units include English 4, mathematics 2, social studies 2 and science 2.

2005-2006 Annual costs. Tuition/fees: $1,740; $3,946 out-of-state. Per-credit charge: $85 in-state; $170 out-of-state. Room/board: $2,240. Books/supplies: $420. Personal expenses: $1,500.

Financial aid. Need-based: Need-based aid available for part-time students. **Non-need-based:** Scholarships awarded for academics, art, athletics, job skills, leadership, minority status, music/drama, state residency.

Application procedures. Admission: Closing date 8/19 (postmark date). $40 fee. Application may be submitted online. Admission notification on a rolling basis beginning on or about 3/1. **Financial aid:** Priority date 4/1; no closing date. FAFSA required. Applicants notified on a rolling basis starting 5/15; must reply within 2 week(s) of notification.

Academics. Special study options: Accelerated study, cooperative education, distance learning, double major, dual enrollment of high school students, honors, independent study, internships, liberal arts/career combination, study abroad. License preparation in nursing. **Credit/placement by examination:** CLEP, institutional tests. 18 credit hours maximum toward associate degree. **Support services:** GED preparation and test center, learning center, remedial instruction, tutoring.

Majors. Agriculture: General, agribusiness operations, animal breeding, food science, landscaping. **Biology:** General. **Business:** Administrative services, fashion, finance, management information systems, office management, operations, sales/distribution, tourism promotion. **Communications:** Journalism. **Communications technology:** General, graphic/printing. **Computer sciences:** General, data processing. **Education:** Business, elementary, physical, secondary, trade/industrial. **Engineering:** General. **Engineering technology:** Civil, drafting, electrical. **English:** Speech/rhetoric. **Family/consumer sciences:** General, child care, institutional food production. **Foreign languages:** Sign language interpretation. **Health:** Clinical lab assistant, clinical lab technology, dental assistant, EMT paramedic, licensed practical nurse, medical records technology, nursing assistant, respiratory therapy technology, surgical technology, veterinary technology/assistant. **History:** General. **Legal studies:** Legal secretary, paralegal, prelaw. **Liberal arts:** Arts/sciences. **Math:** General. **Mechanic/repair:** Electronics/electrical. **Personal/culinary services:** Culinary arts. **Physical sciences:** Chemistry, geology, physics. **Protective services:** Criminal justice, fire safety technology. **Psychology:** General. **Social sciences:** Political science, sociology. **Visual/performing arts:** Art, commercial/advertising art, dramatic.

Most popular majors. Business/marketing 12%, health sciences 28%, liberal arts 45%.

Computing on campus. 55 workstations in library, computer center. Online course registration, helpline, repair service available.

Student life. Freshman orientation: Available. Preregistration for classes offered. **Policies:** Freshmen permitted cars on campus. **Housing:** Single-sex dorms available. $50 deposit. **Activities:** Bands, choral groups, dance, drama, music ensembles, musical theater, student government, student newspaper, Baptist Student Union, Afro-American Cultural Society, Catholic Student Organization, College Independents, College Republicans, Fellowship of Christian Athletes, Class/Leadership/Authority and Womanhood, Campus Christian Fellowship.

Athletics. NJCAA. **Intercollegiate:** Baseball M, basketball, football (tackle) M, golf M, soccer M, softball W, tennis, track and field M. **Intramural:** Basketball, football (tackle) M, softball M, volleyball. **Team name:** Eagles.

Student services. Career counseling, student employment services, personal counseling, placement for graduates. **Physically disabled:** Services for visually, hearing impaired. **Transfer:** Special adviser, orientation for new students. Transfer adviser, college fairs on campus for students transferring to 4-year colleges.

Contact. E-mail: records@hindscc.edu
Phone: (601) 857-3212 Toll-free number: (800) 446-3722
Fax: (601) 857-3539
Jay Allen, Director of Admissions and Records, Hinds Community College, 505 East Main Street, Raymond, MS 39154-1100

Holmes Community College

Goodman, Mississippi
www.holmes.cc.ms.us **CB code: 1299**

- Public 2-year community college
- Residential campus in rural community

General. Founded in 1925. Regionally accredited. Because of higher priorities in the aftermath of Hurricane Katrina, the information in this profile has not been updated for the 2006-2007 academic year. **Enrollment:** 4,494 degree-seeking undergraduates. **Degrees:** 369 associate awarded. **Location:** 45 miles from Jackson. **Calendar:** Semester, limited summer session. **Full-time faculty:** 83 total. **Special facilities:** Observatory, planetarium.

Student profile.

Out-of-state:	5%	**Live on campus:**	25%
25 or older:	33%		

Transfer out. Colleges most students transferred to 2005: Mississippi State University, University of Mississippi, Delta State University, University of Southern Mississippi.

Basis for selection. School record and test scores very important. ACT preferred for placement.

High school preparation. 19 units required. Required units include English 4, mathematics 2, social studies 2, science 2 and academic electives 9.

2005-2006 Annual costs. Tuition/fees: $1,430; $3,130 out-of-state. Per-credit charge: $65. Room/board: $1,900. Books/supplies: $600. Personal expenses: $1,600.

Financial aid. Non-need-based: Scholarships awarded for academics, athletics.

Application procedures. Admission: No deadline. No application fee. Admission notification on a rolling basis. **Financial aid:** Priority date 6/1; no closing date. FAFSA, institutional form required. Applicants notified on a rolling basis.

Academics. Special study options: Cooperative education, distance learning, dual enrollment of high school students, honors, internships, liberal arts/career combination, weekend college. License preparation in nursing, paramedic. **Credit/placement by examination:** AP, CLEP, institutional tests. 30 credit hours maximum toward associate degree. **Support services:** GED test center, learning center, reduced course load, remedial instruction, tutoring.

Majors. **Business:** Administrative services, business admin, fashion. **Computer sciences:** General, computer science, programming. **Conservation:** Forestry. **Education:** Elementary, secondary. **Engineering:** General, architectural, electrical. **Engineering technology:** Drafting. **Health:** Predentistry, premedicine, prepharmacy, preveterinary. **Liberal arts:** Arts/sciences. **Math:** General. **Mechanic/repair:** Heating/ac/refrig.

Computing on campus. 400 workstations in library, computer center. Repair service available.

Student life. **Freshman orientation:** Available. **Policies:** Freshmen permitted cars on campus. **Housing:** Single-sex dorms available. **Activities:** Bands, choral groups, dance, drama, literary magazine, music ensembles, musical theater, student government, student newspaper, Baptist Student Union, Wesley Foundation, College Republican Club, Fellowship of Christian Athletes.

Athletics. NJCAA. **Intercollegiate:** Baseball M, basketball, football (tackle) M, golf M, soccer, softball W, tennis, track and field. **Intramural:** Basketball, football (tackle) M, soccer M, softball, track and field M, volleyball. **Team name:** Bulldogs.

Student services. Adult student services, career counseling, personal counseling, veterans' counselor. **Physically disabled:** Services for visually, speech, hearing impaired. **Transfer:** Special adviser, orientation, pre-admission transcript evaluation for new students. Transfer adviser, college fairs on campus for students transferring to 4-year colleges.

Contact. E-mail: grichardson@holmes.cc.ms.us
Phone: (662) 472-9023 Toll-free number: (800) 465-6374
Fax: (662) 472-9152
Lynn Wright, Dean of Admissions, Holmes Community College, Box 369, Goodman, MS 39079

Itawamba Community College
Fulton, Mississippi
www.iccms.edu **CB code: 1326**

- Public 2-year community college
- Commuter campus in small town

General. Founded in 1948. Regionally accredited. ICC has campuses in Fulton, Mississippi and Tupelo, Mississippi, in addition to a comprehensive online distance learning program. **Enrollment:** 6,000 undergraduates. **Degrees:** 478 associate awarded. **Location:** 115 miles from Memphis, Tennessee, 135 miles from Birmingham, Alabama. **Calendar:** Semester, limited summer session. **Full-time faculty:** 123 total; 6% have terminal degrees, 3% minority, 57% women. **Part-time faculty:** 17 total; 6% minority, 41% women. **Class size:** 51% < 20, 43% 20-39, 5% 40-49, 1% 50-99.

Student profile. 75% enrolled in a transfer program, 25% enrolled in a vocational program.

Transfer out. **Colleges most students transferred to 2005:** Mississippi State University, University of Mississippi.

Basis for selection. Open admission, but selective for some programs. Special requirements for health science programs. Minimum test scores generally required on ACT or other discipline-specific tests, and program prerequisites must be met and grade of at least 2.0 earned. **Adult students:** Entrance exam policies same as for first-time freshmen. **Homeschooled:** Home schooled must complete GED or appeal to Admissions and Guidance Committee. **Learning Disabled:** Developmental courses recommended. Assistance provided by special needs counselor.

2005-2006 Annual costs. Tuition/fees: $1,480; $3,230 out-of-state. Per-credit charge: $75. Room/board: $2,554. Books/supplies: $900. Personal expenses: $180.

Financial aid. **Need-based:** Need-based aid available for part-time students. Work study available for part-time students. **Non-need-based:** Scholarships awarded for academics, art, athletics, leadership, music/drama, state residency.

Application procedures. **Admission:** No deadline. No application fee. Admission notification on a rolling basis. **Financial aid:** Priority date 4/30; no closing date. FAFSA, institutional form required. Applicants notified on a rolling basis starting 4/15.

Academics. **Special study options:** Accelerated study, cooperative education, distance learning, double major, dual enrollment of high school students, ESL, honors, independent study, internships. License preparation in nursing, paramedic, physical therapy, radiology, real estate. **Credit/placement by examination:** CLEP, institutional tests. 15 credit hours maximum toward associate degree. **Support services:** GED preparation and test center, reduced course load, remedial instruction, study skills assistance, tutoring.

Majors. **Agriculture:** Business. **Business:** General, accounting, administrative services, management information systems, office/clerical. **Communications:** Broadcast journalism, journalism, public relations. **Computer sciences:** General, computer science, data processing, programming. **Conservation:** Forestry. **Construction:** Electrician. **Education:** Art, biology, business, chemistry, elementary, English, French, health, history, mathematics, music, physical, physics, science, secondary, social studies, Spanish, special, speech. **Engineering:** General, electrical. **Engineering technology:** Electrical. **Family/consumer sciences:** General, child care. **Foreign languages:** French, sign language interpretation, Spanish. **Health:** EMT paramedic, medical radiologic technology/radiation therapy, medical records admin, medical records technology, nursing (RN), occupational health, physical therapy assistant, predentistry, premedicine, prepharmacy, preveterinary, respiratory therapy technology, sonography, surgical technology. **History:** General. **Legal studies:** Paralegal, prelaw. **Liberal arts:** Arts/sciences, library science. **Math:** General. **Mechanic/repair:** Automotive, diesel, electronics/electrical. **Philosophy/religion:** Philosophy. **Physical sciences:** Chemistry, geology, physics. **Production:** Tool and die. **Protective services:** Criminal justice. **Psychology:** General. **Public administration:** Social work. **Social sciences:** Economics, sociology. **Visual/performing arts:** Art.

Most popular majors. Business/marketing 9%, health sciences 29%, liberal arts 34%, trade and industry 15%.

Computing on campus. 300 workstations in dormitories, library, computer center. Dormitories wired for high-speed internet access and linked to campus network. Commuter students can connect to campus network. Online course registration, online library, helpline, wireless network available.

Student life. **Freshman orientation:** Available. Preregistration for classes offered. **Policies:** Freshmen permitted cars on campus. **Housing:** Single-sex dorms, substance-free housing available. $50 deposit. **Activities:** Bands, choral groups, dance, drama, literary magazine, music ensembles, musical theater, student government, student newspaper.

Athletics. NJCAA. **Intercollegiate:** Baseball M, basketball, cheerleading, football (tackle) M, golf M, soccer M, softball W. **Intramural:** Basketball. **Team name:** Indians.

Student services. Alcohol/substance abuse counseling, campus ministries, career counseling, services for economically disadvantaged, student employment services, financial aid counseling, minority student services, on-campus daycare, placement for graduates, veterans' counselor, women's services. **Physically disabled:** Services for visually, hearing impaired. **Transfer:** Special adviser for new students. Transfer adviser, college fairs on campus for students transferring to 4-year colleges.

Contact. E-mail: hgjefcoat@iccms.edu
Phone: (662) 862-8031 Fax: (662) 862-8036
Gregg Jefcoat, Director of Admissions, Itawamba Community College, 602 West Hill Street, Fulton, MS 38843

Jones County Junior College
Ellisville, Mississippi
www.jcjc.cc.ms.us **CB code: 1347**

- Public 2-year junior college
- Commuter campus in small town

General. Founded in 1927. Regionally accredited. **Enrollment:** 4,791 degree-seeking undergraduates. **Degrees:** 770 associate awarded. **ROTC:** Air Force. **Location:** 7 miles from Laurel, 20 miles from Hattiesburg. **Calendar:** Semester, limited summer session. **Full-time faculty:** 180 total. **Part-time faculty:** 17 total. **Special facilities:** Visual arts center, advanced technology center.

Student profile.

Out-of-state:	2%	**Live on campus:**	20%

Transfer out. **Colleges most students transferred to 2005:** University of Southern Mississippi, Mississippi State University, University of Mississippi, William Carey College.

Basis for selection. Open admission, but selective for some programs. Minimum ACT composite score of 16 required for practical nursing program, 17 for radiologic technology program, and 18 for AD nursing program. Interview required for health majors; audition required for band, music majors; portfolio required for art majors.

High school preparation. College-preparatory program required for admission to selective programs.

Two-Year Colleges

2005-2006 Annual costs. Tuition/fees: $1,720; $3,620 out-of-state. Per-credit charge: $75 in-state; $160 out-of-state. Room/board: $2,712. Books/supplies: $600. Personal expenses: $1,299.

2004-2005 Financial aid. Need-based: 98% of total undergraduate aid awarded as scholarships/grants, 2% as loans/jobs. Need-based aid available for part-time students. Work study available nights, weekends and for part-time students. **Non-need-based:** Scholarships awarded for academics, athletics, state residency.

Application procedures. Admission: No deadline. No application fee. Application may be submitted online. Admission notification on a rolling basis beginning on or about 2/1. **Financial aid:** Priority date 5/1; no closing date. FAFSA, institutional form required. Applicants notified on a rolling basis starting 6/1; must reply within 2 week(s) of notification.

Academics. Special study options: Cooperative education, dual enrollment of high school students. **Credit/placement by examination:** CLEP, institutional tests. 30 credit hours maximum toward associate degree. **Support services:** GED preparation and test center, learning center, reduced course load, remedial instruction, tutoring.

Majors. Liberal arts: Arts/sciences.

Computing on campus. 500 workstations in library, computer center. Dormitories wired for high-speed internet access and linked to campus network. Commuter students can connect to campus network. Online library available.

Student life. Freshman orientation: Available. Preregistration for classes offered. **Policies:** Freshmen permitted cars on campus. **Housing:** Single-sex dorms available. $100 deposit. **Activities:** Bands, choral groups, dance, drama, music ensembles, musical theater, student government, student newspaper, symphony orchestra, Wesley Foundation, Association of African-American Students.

Athletics. NJCAA. **Intercollegiate:** Baseball M, basketball, football (tackle) M, golf, gymnastics, soccer, softball W, tennis. **Intramural:** Basketball, bowling, handball, racquetball, softball, swimming, tennis, volleyball. **Team name:** Bobcats.

Student services. Career counseling, health services, on-campus daycare, personal counseling, placement for graduates, veterans' counselor. **Physically disabled:** Services for visually, speech, hearing impaired. **Transfer:** Special adviser, orientation for new students. Transfer adviser, college fairs on campus for students transferring to 4-year colleges.

Contact. E-mail: admissions@jcjc.edu
Phone: (601) 477-4025 Fax: (601) 477-4017
Dianne Speed, Director of Admissions & Records, Jones County Junior College, 900 South Court Street, Ellisville, MS 39437

Meridian Community College

Meridian, Mississippi **CB member**
www.meridiancc.edu **CB code: 1461**

- Public 2-year community college
- Commuter campus in large town

General. Founded in 1937. Regionally accredited. **Enrollment:** 3,435 degree-seeking undergraduates. **Degrees:** 540 associate awarded. **Location:** 90 miles from Jackson, 90 miles from Tuscaloosa, Alabama. **Calendar:** Semester, limited summer session. **Full-time faculty:** 148 total. **Part-time faculty:** 92 total. **Special facilities:** Fitness center with enclosed swimming pool.

Student profile. Among degree-seeking undergraduates, 1,577 enrolled as first-time, first-year students, 2,402 transferred in from other institutions.

Part-time:	27%	**25 or older:**	50%
Out-of-state:	4%	**Live on campus:**	7%
Women:	70%		

Basis for selection. Open admission, but selective for some programs. Test scores, recommendations considered for health education applicants. Interview recommended for broadcast technology, data processing, graphic communication technology, and health programs majors.

High school preparation. Recommended units include English 4, mathematics 3, social studies 3, science 3 and academic electives 2. .5 unit computer applications recommended.

2005-2006 Annual costs. Tuition/fees: $1,630; $2,920 out-of-state. Per-credit charge: $80 in-state; $137 out-of-state. Room/board: $3,350. Books/supplies: $1,300. Personal expenses: $1,400.

2004-2005 Financial aid. Need-based: 77% of total undergraduate aid awarded as scholarships/grants, 23% as loans/jobs. Need-based aid available for part-time students. **Non-need-based:** Scholarships awarded for academics, art, athletics, leadership, music/drama, state residency.

Application procedures. Admission: Closing date 9/6. No application fee. Admission notification on a rolling basis. **Financial aid:** Priority date 6/1; no closing date. FAFSA, institutional form required. Applicants notified on a rolling basis starting 5/15; must reply within 2 week(s) of notification.

Academics. Special study options: Accelerated study, cooperative education, distance learning, dual enrollment of high school students, independent study, internships, weekend college. **Credit/placement by examination:** CLEP. 45 credit hours maximum toward associate degree. **Support services:** GED preparation and test center, learning center, remedial instruction, study skills assistance, tutoring.

Majors. Agriculture: Horticulture. **Business:** Administrative services, management information systems. **Communications:** General, broadcast journalism. **Communications technology:** General. **Computer sciences:** General, computer graphics, programming. **Engineering technology:** Drafting. **Family/consumer sciences:** Child care. **Health:** Clinical lab technology, dental hygiene, licensed practical nurse, medical radiologic technology/radiation therapy, medical records technology, medical secretary, physical therapy assistant, respiratory therapy technology. **Legal studies:** Prelaw. **Mechanic/repair:** Electronics/electrical. **Protective services:** Firefighting.

Computing on campus. 83 workstations in library, computer center. Dormitories wired for high-speed internet access and linked to campus network. Commuter students can connect to campus network. Online course registration, online library, helpline, repair service available.

Student life. Freshman orientation: Mandatory. Orientation sessions specific to certain programs. **Policies:** Freshmen permitted cars on campus. **Housing:** Coed dorms, single-sex dorms, apartments, substance-free housing available. $50 deposit. **Activities:** Bands, choral groups, drama, literary magazine, music ensembles, musical theater, radio station, student government, student newspaper, TV station, Baptist Student Union, T.J. Harris Organization, Wesley Foundation, Fellowship of Christian Athletes, Phi Theta Kappa, multicultural student association.

Athletics. NJCAA. **Intercollegiate:** Baseball M, basketball, golf M, soccer M, softball W, tennis. **Intramural:** Basketball, bowling, softball W, swimming, tennis, volleyball. **Team name:** Eagles.

Student services. Career counseling, student employment services, personal counseling, placement for graduates, veterans' counselor. **Physically disabled:** Services for visually, speech, hearing impaired. **Transfer:** Pre-admission transcript evaluation for new students. Transfer adviser, college fairs on campus for students transferring to 4-year colleges.

Contact. E-mail: dwalton@mcc.cc.ms.us
Phone: (601) 484-8895 Toll-free number: (800) 622-8431
Fax: (601) 484-8838
Dianne Walton, Associate Dean, Enrollment Services, Meridian Community College, 910 Highway 19, North, Meridian, MS 39307-5890

Mississippi Delta Community College

Moorhead, Mississippi
www.msdelta.edu **CB code: 1742**

- Public 2-year community college
- Commuter campus in rural community

General. Founded in 1926. Regionally accredited. **Enrollment:** 925 degree-seeking undergraduates. **Degrees:** 325 associate awarded. **Location:** 20 miles from Greenwood. **Calendar:** Semester, limited summer session. **Full-time faculty:** 122 total. **Part-time faculty:** 35 total.

Student profile.

Out-of-state:	3%	**Live on campus:**	25%

Transfer out. Colleges most students transferred to 2005: Delta State University, Mississippi State University, University of Mississippi, University of Southern Mississippi.

Basis for selection. Open admission, but selective for some programs. Test scores most important. Open admission to vocational programs. Selective admission to health occupations and computer technology curriculum.

High school preparation. 19 units recommended. Recommended units include English 3, mathematics 3, social studies 3, science 3, foreign language 3 and academic electives 4. 12 of the recommended units may be distributed in any combination in mathematics, science, foreign language, social studies, and history.

2005-2006 Annual costs. Tuition/fees: $1,850; $3,458 out-of-state. Room/board: $2,130. Books/supplies: $450. Personal expenses: $400.

Financial aid. Non-need-based: Scholarships awarded for academics, athletics, state residency.

Application procedures. Admission: Priority date 7/1; no deadline. No application fee. Admission notification on a rolling basis beginning on or about 5/30. **Financial aid:** Priority date 8/1; no closing date. FAFSA, institutional form required. Applicants notified on a rolling basis; must reply within 2 week(s) of notification.

Academics. Special study options: Distance learning. License preparation in nursing. **Credit/placement by examination:** CLEP. 15 credit hours maximum toward associate degree. **Support services:** GED preparation and test center, reduced course load, remedial instruction.

Majors. Agriculture: Business, economics, farm/ranch, horticulture. **Area/ethnic studies:** American. **Biology:** General. **Business:** Accounting, administrative services. **Communications:** General, advertising. **Computer sciences:** Programming. **Conservation:** Forestry. **Construction:** Maintenance. **Education:** General, art, business, elementary, English, health, physical, secondary, special, speech. **Engineering:** General. **Engineering technology:** Architectural, electrical. **Family/consumer sciences:** General. **Health:** Clinical lab technology, dental hygiene, EMT paramedic, medical radiologic technology/radiation therapy, medical records admin, predentistry, prepharmacy, preveterinary. **History:** General. **Legal studies:** Prelaw. **Liberal arts:** Arts/sciences. **Mechanic/repair:** Heating/ac/refrig. **Protective services:** Law enforcement admin. **Psychology:** General. **Public administration:** Social work. **Social sciences:** General, sociology. **Visual/performing arts:** Studio arts.

Student life. Freshman orientation: Available. **Housing:** Single-sex dorms available. **Activities:** Bands, choral groups, dance, drama, student government, student newspaper, Baptist Student Union, Wesley Foundation, Vocational Industrial Clubs of America.

Athletics. NJCAA. **Intercollegiate:** Baseball M, basketball, football (tackle) M, golf M, soccer M, softball W, tennis, track and field M. **Intramural:** Basketball, softball, tennis, track and field, volleyball.

Student services. Career counseling, student employment services, personal counseling, placement for graduates, veterans' counselor. **Transfer:** Special adviser, orientation for new students. Transfer adviser for students transferring to 4-year colleges.

Contact. E-mail: admissions@msdelta.edu
Phone: (662) 246-6306 Fax: (662) 246-6321
Joe Ray, Chief Admissions Officer, Mississippi Delta Community College, Box 668, Moorhead, MS 38761

Mississippi Gulf Coast Community College: Jefferson Davis Campus

Perkinston, Mississippi — **CB member**
www.mgccc.edu — **CB code: 1353**

- Public 2-year community college
- Commuter campus in large city

General. Founded in 1965. Regionally accredited. Instruction is available at our 3 campuses and 4 centers. **Enrollment:** 10,315 degree-seeking undergraduates; 109 non-degree-seeking students. **Degrees:** 1,366 associate awarded. **Location:** 30 miles from Biloxi, 90 miles from New Orleans. **Calendar:** Semester, limited summer session. **Full-time faculty:** 335 total. **Part-time faculty:** 260 total.

Student profile. Among degree-seeking undergraduates, 2,363 enrolled as first-time, first-year students.

Part-time:	37%	**25 or older:**	39%
Out-of-state:	2%	**Live on campus:**	6%
Women:	62%		

Transfer out. Colleges most students transferred to 2005: University of Southern MS; Mississippi State University; University of South Alabama.

Basis for selection. Open admission, but selective for some programs. Special requirements for health occupations programs. **Adult students:** Entrance exam policies same as for first-time freshmen.

High school preparation. 19 units recommended. Recommended units include English 3, mathematics 3 and science 3.

2005-2006 Annual costs. Tuition/fees: $1,602; $3,448 out-of-state. Per-credit charge: $75 in-state; $152 out-of-state. $15 rental fee required per book. Books/supplies: $280. Personal expenses: $600.

Financial aid. All financial aid based on need.

Application procedures. Admission: No deadline. No application fee. **Financial aid:** Priority date 6/1; no closing date. Institutional form required. Applicants notified on a rolling basis starting 7/1.

Academics. Special study options: Accelerated study, cooperative education, distance learning, dual enrollment of high school students, honors, weekend college. License preparation in nursing, paramedic. **Credit/placement by examination:** CLEP. 32 credit hours maximum toward associate degree. **Support services:** GED preparation and test center, learning center, reduced course load, remedial instruction, study skills assistance, tutoring.

Majors. Agriculture: General, food science, landscaping, ornamental horticulture, turf management. **Biology:** General, biotechnology. **Business:** General, accounting, administrative services, banking/financial services, business admin, fashion, management information systems, marketing, office technology. **Communications:** General. **Computer sciences:** General. **Conservation:** Fisheries, forestry. **Construction:** Lineworker, pipefitting, power transmission. **Education:** General, art, business, elementary, mathematics, multi-level teacher, science, secondary, trade/industrial. **Engineering:** General. **Engineering technology:** CAD/CADD, drafting. **Health:** Clinical lab science, clinical lab technology, EMT paramedic, medical radiologic technology/radiation therapy, medical records admin, medical secretary, nursing (RN), optician, orthotics/prosthetics, prepharmacy, respiratory therapy technology, veterinary technology/assistant. **Legal studies:** Court reporting, paralegal, prelaw. **Liberal arts:** Arts/sciences. **Math:** General. **Mechanic/repair:** Electronics/electrical. **Personal/culinary services:** Cosmetic, funeral direction. **Protective services:** Criminal justice, fire safety technology. **Psychology:** General. **Public administration:** Social work. **Visual/performing arts:** Art, commercial/advertising art, interior design, sculpture.

Most popular majors. Business/marketing 20%, education 19%, health sciences 24%, liberal arts 16%.

Computing on campus. 325 workstations in library, computer center, student center. Dormitories wired for high-speed internet access and linked to campus network. Commuter students can connect to campus network. Online course registration available.

Student life. Freshman orientation: Mandatory. Preregistration for classes offered. **Policies:** Freshmen permitted cars on campus. **Housing:** Single-sex dorms, special housing for disabled available. **Activities:** Bands, choral groups, dance, drama, music ensembles, musical theater, student government, student newspaper, Baptist student union, United Ministries for Higher Education, Wesley Foundation, Newman Club, A.D.U.L.T.

Athletics. NJCAA. **Intercollegiate:** Baseball M, basketball, cheerleading, football (tackle) M, golf M, softball, tennis. **Intramural:** Baseball, basketball, football (tackle), softball, tennis. **Team name:** Bulldogs.

Student services. Adult student services, career counseling, student employment services, financial aid counseling, health services, on-campus daycare, personal counseling, placement for graduates, veterans' counselor. **Physically disabled:** Services for visually, hearing impaired. **Transfer:** Special adviser for new students. Transfer adviser, college fairs on campus for students transferring to 4-year colleges.

Contact. E-mail: michelle.sekul@mgccc.edu
Phone: (601) 928-6333 Toll-free number: (866) 735-1122
Fax: (601) 928-6345
Michelle Sekul, Director of Admissions, Mississippi Gulf Coast Community College: Jefferson Davis Campus, PO Box 548, Perkinston, MS 39573

Northeast Mississippi Community College

Booneville, Mississippi
www.necc.cc.ms.us — **CB code: 1557**

- Public 2-year community college
- Commuter campus in small town

General. Founded in 1948. Regionally accredited. **Location:** 30 miles from Tupelo, 110 miles from Memphis, Tennessee. **Calendar:** Semester.

Annual costs/financial aid. Tuition/fees (2005-2006): $1,806; $3,526 out-of-state. Room/board: $2,768. Books/supplies: $840. Personal expenses: $1,989.

Contact. Phone: (662) 720-7290
Director of Admissions, 101 Cunningham Boulevard, Booneville, MS 38829

Northwest Mississippi Community College

Senatobia, Mississippi
www.northwestms.edu **CB code: 1562**

- Public 2-year community college
- Commuter campus in small town

General. Founded in 1927. Regionally accredited. **Location:** 30 miles from Memphis, Tennessee. **Calendar:** Semester.

Annual costs/financial aid. Tuition/fees (2005-2006): $1,700; $3,700 out-of-state. Lab fees range from $15 to $25 per course. Room/board: $2,700. Books/supplies: $600. Personal expenses: $375. Need-based financial aid available for full-time students.

Contact. Phone: (601) 562-3200 ext. 3219
Registrar, 4975 Highway 51 North, Senatobia, MS 38668

Pearl River Community College

Poplarville, Mississippi
www.prcc.edu **CB code: 1622**

- Public 2-year community college
- Commuter campus in small town

General. Founded in 1921. Regionally accredited. **Enrollment:** 3,679 degree-seeking undergraduates. **Degrees:** 435 associate awarded. **Location:** 35 miles from Hattiesburg, 70 miles from New Orleans. **Calendar:** Semester, limited summer session. **Full-time faculty:** 135 total. **Part-time faculty:** 50 total.

Student profile.

Out-of-state:	9%	**Live on campus:**	25%
25 or older:	23%		

Basis for selection. Open admission, but selective for some programs. Special requirements for health occupation programs. ACT required for placement and counseling. Interview recommended for nursing majors.

2005-2006 Annual costs. Tuition/fees: $1,726; $4,124 out-of-state. Per-credit charge: $86 in-state; $186 out-of-state. Room/board: $2,718. Books/supplies: $500.

2004-2005 Financial aid. Need-based: 98% of total undergraduate aid awarded as scholarships/grants, 2% as loans/jobs. Need-based aid available for part-time students. **Non-need-based:** Scholarships awarded for academics, alumni affiliation, athletics, leadership, music/drama, state residency.

Application procedures. Admission: No deadline. No application fee. Application may be submitted online. Admission notification on a rolling basis. **Financial aid:** Priority date 4/17; no closing date. FAFSA, institutional form required. Applicants notified on a rolling basis.

Academics. Special study options: Cooperative education, dual enrollment of high school students. License preparation in dental hygiene, nursing, occupational therapy, physical therapy, radiology. **Credit/placement by examination:** CLEP. 30 credit hours maximum toward associate degree. **Support services:** GED preparation and test center, learning center, reduced course load, remedial instruction, tutoring.

Majors. Business: Business admin, management information systems, office technology. **Computer sciences:** Applications programming, data processing. **Construction:** Carpentry, masonry, power transmission. **Education:** Multi-level teacher. **Engineering technology:** Drafting, electrical. **Health:** Licensed practical nurse, medical secretary, respiratory therapy technology. **Legal studies:** Legal secretary. **Liberal arts:** Arts/sciences. **Mechanic/repair:** Auto body, heating/ac/refrig.

Computing on campus. 150 workstations in library, computer center.

Student life. Freshman orientation: Available, $25 fee. Preregistration for classes offered. **Housing:** Single-sex dorms, special housing for disabled available. $50 deposit. **Activities:** Bands, choral groups, drama, music ensembles, student government, student newspaper, Black Student Union, Wesley and Newman Clubs, Phi Theta Kappa, Afro-American Club, Baptist Student Union.

Athletics. NJCAA. **Intercollegiate:** Baseball M, basketball, football (tackle) M, golf M, softball W, tennis. **Intramural:** Badminton, basketball, softball, table tennis, tennis, volleyball. **Team name:** Wildcats.

Student services. Career counseling, student employment services, health services, personal counseling, placement for graduates, veterans' counselor. **Transfer:** Special adviser, orientation for new students.

Contact. E-mail: dford@prcc.edu
Phone: (601) 403-1214 Fax: (601) 403-1339
Dow Ford, Registrar, Pearl River Community College, 101 Highway 11 North, Poplarville, MS 39470

Southwest Mississippi Community College

Summit, Mississippi
www.smcc.edu **CB code: 1729**

- Public 2-year community college
- Commuter campus in rural community

General. Founded in 1918. Regionally accredited. Rotary drilling program for oil-well drilling available. **Enrollment:** 1,865 degree-seeking undergraduates. **Degrees:** 313 associate awarded. **Location:** 76 miles from Jackson, 100 miles from New Orleans. **Calendar:** Semester, limited summer session. **Full-time faculty:** 84 total. **Part-time faculty:** 16 total. **Class size:** 67% < 20, 26% 20-39, 4% 40-49, 2% 50-99, less than 1% >100. **Special facilities:** Observatory.

Student profile. Among degree-seeking undergraduates, 71% enrolled in a transfer program, 29% enrolled in a vocational program, 660 enrolled as first-time, first-year students.

Part-time:	22%	**African American:**	39%
Out-of-state:	9%	**Asian American:**	1%
Women:	65%	**Live on campus:**	40%

Transfer out. Colleges most students transferred to 2005: The University of Southern Mississippi, Southeastern Louisiana University, Mississippi State University, The University of Mississippi, Jackson State University.

Basis for selection. Open admission.

High school preparation. College-preparatory program recommended. For ability to benefit from vocational programs, high school graduation or GED preferred.

2005-2006 Annual costs. Tuition/fees: $1,800; $3,600 out-of-state. Per-credit charge: $75 in-state; $165 out-of-state. Room/board: $2,180. Books/supplies: $600. Personal expenses: $2,840.

Financial aid. Need-based: Need-based aid available for part-time students.

Application procedures. Admission: Priority date 8/1; no deadline. No application fee. Application must be submitted on paper. Admission notification on a rolling basis. **Financial aid:** Priority date 8/6; no closing date. Applicants notified on a rolling basis.

Academics. Special study options: Distance learning, dual enrollment of high school students. License preparation in nursing. **Credit/placement by examination:** AP, CLEP. 12 credit hours maximum toward associate degree. **Support services:** GED preparation and test center, learning center, reduced course load, remedial instruction, tutoring.

Majors. Business: Office/clerical. **Computer sciences:** Data processing. **Liberal arts:** Arts/sciences. **Protective services:** Police science.

Computing on campus. 150 workstations in library, computer center. Commuter students can connect to campus network.

Student life. Freshman orientation: Mandatory. Preregistration for classes offered. Orientation sessions are offered during the month of June, and the week before the first day of class. The sessions last approximately 4 hours. **Policies:** Freshmen permitted cars on campus. **Housing:** Single-sex dorms, apartments available. $30 deposit, deadline 8/1. **Activities:** Bands, choral groups, student government, student newspaper.

Athletics. NJCAA. **Intercollegiate:** Baseball M, basketball, football (tackle) M, golf M, softball W, tennis. **Intramural:** Basketball, tennis, volleyball. **Team name:** Bears.

Student services. Career counseling, health services, personal counseling, placement for graduates, veterans' counselor. **Transfer:** Special adviser for new students. Transfer adviser, college fairs on campus for students transferring to 4-year colleges.

Contact. E-mail: mattc@smcc.edu
Phone: (601) 276-2001 Fax: (601) 276-3888
Matthew Calhoun, Dean of Admissions, Southwest Mississippi Community College, 1156 College Drive, Summit, MS 39666

Virginia College
Jackson, Mississippi
www.vc.edu

- For-profit 2-year community college
- Small city

General. Accredited by ACICS. **Calendar:** Quarter.

Contact. Phone: (601) 977-0960
Director, 5360 I-55 North, Jackson, MS 39211

Virginia College Gulf Coast
Biloxi, Mississippi
www.vc.edu/gulfcoast/index.cfm

- For-profit 2-year business and health science college
- Small city

General. Accredited by ACICS. **Calendar:** Quarter.

Annual costs/financial aid. Tuition/fees (projected): $11,575.

Contact. Phone: (228) 392-2994
920 Cedar Lake Road, BIloxi, MS 39532

Missouri

Blue River Community College

Independence, Missouri
www.mcckc.edu **CB code: 6060**

- Public 2-year community college
- Commuter campus in small city

General. Regionally accredited. **Enrollment:** 1,811 degree-seeking undergraduates; 851 non-degree-seeking students. **Degrees:** 199 associate awarded. **Location:** 25 miles from Kansas City. **Calendar:** Semester, limited summer session. **Full-time faculty:** 31 total; 6% minority, 61% women. **Part-time faculty:** 273 total; 6% minority, 36% women. **Class size:** 35% < 20, 64% 20-39, less than 1% 40-49, less than 1% 50-99.

Student profile. Among degree-seeking undergraduates, 53% enrolled in a transfer program, 21% enrolled in a vocational program, 1% already have a bachelor's degree or higher, 487 enrolled as first-time, first-year students, 425 transferred in from other institutions.

Part-time:	50%	**Asian American:**	1%
Out-of-state:	1%	**Hispanic American:**	2%
Women:	61%	**Native American:**	1%
African American:	2%	**25 or older:**	31%

Basis for selection. Open admission. **Homeschooled:** Statement describing homeschool structure and mission, transcript of courses and grades, interview required. Provide proof of graduation requirements. Applicants under age 16 must meet with dean of student services and bring student portfolio.

High school preparation. 16 units recommended. Recommended units include English 4, mathematics 3, social studies 3, science 3 and foreign language 2. 1 visual/performing arts recommended.

2006-2007 Annual costs. Tuition/fees (projected): $2,190; $3,990 out-of-district; $5,400 out-of-state. Per-credit charge: $73 in-district; $133 out-of-district; $180 out-of-state. Books/supplies: $700. Personal expenses: $1,500.

2004-2005 Financial aid. Need-based: 181 full-time freshmen applied for aid; 126 were judged to have need; 106 of these received aid. Average scholarship/grant was $2,474; average loan $1,962. 67% of total undergraduate aid awarded as scholarships/grants, 33% as loans/jobs. Need-based aid available for part-time students. Work study available nights and for part-time students. **Non-need-based:** Awarded to 125 full-time undergraduates, including 30 freshmen. Scholarships awarded for academics, athletics, leadership.

Application procedures. Admission: No deadline. No application fee. Application may be submitted online. Admission notification on a rolling basis. **Financial aid:** Priority date 5/30, closing date 8/20. FAFSA, institutional form required. Applicants notified on a rolling basis starting 4/8.

Academics. Special study options: Accelerated study, cooperative education, cross-registration, distance learning, dual enrollment of high school students, honors, independent study, internships, weekend college. **Credit/placement by examination:** AP, CLEP, institutional tests. 30 credit hours maximum toward associate degree. **Support services:** GED test center, learning center, remedial instruction, tutoring.

Majors. Business: General, business admin. **Computer sciences:** Computer science. **Engineering:** General. **Engineering technology:** Software. **Liberal arts:** Arts/sciences. **Protective services:** Firefighting, law enforcement admin, police science.

Most popular majors. Liberal arts 90%.

Computing on campus. 373 workstations in library, computer center. Online course registration, online library available.

Student life. Freshman orientation: Available. Preregistration for classes offered. **Policies:** Freshmen permitted cars on campus. **Activities:** Choral groups, student government, student newspaper.

Student services. Adult student services, career counseling, student employment services, personal counseling, placement for graduates, veterans' counselor. **Physically disabled:** Services for visually, hearing impaired. **Transfer:** Special adviser, orientation for new students. Transfer adviser for students transferring to 4-year colleges.

Contact. Phone: (816) 220-6577
Chris Henson, Registrar, Blue River Community College, 3200 Broadway, Kansas City, MO 64111-2429

Bolivar Technical College

Bolivar, Missouri

- Private 2-year nursing and technical college
- Small town

General. Calendar: Semester.

Annual costs/financial aid. Tuition varies by program, $145-$310 per credit-hour.

Contact. Phone: (417) 777-5062
PO Box 592, Bolivar, MO 65613

Branson Technical College

Branson, Missouri

- Private 2-year nursing and technical college
- Small town

General. Accredited by ACICS. **Calendar:** Semester.

Annual costs/financial aid. Tuition varies by program, $145 to $310 per credit-hour.

Contact. Phone: (417) 239-1500
1756 Bee Creek Road, Branson, MO 65616

Colorado Technical University: North Kansas City

North Kansas City, Missouri
www.ctukansascity.com **CB code: 3322**

- For-profit 2-year health science and technical college
- Rural community

General. Accredited by ACICS. **Calendar:** Continuous.

Annual costs/financial aid. Tuition programs range from $14,000-$32,000. Fees vary depending on program. Books/supplies: $1,620.

Contact. Phone: (816) 472-7400
Admissions Director, 520 East 19th Avenue, North Kansas City, MO 64116

Concorde Career College

Kansas City, Missouri
www.concorde.edu/kansas **CB code: 3126**

- For-profit 2-year business and health science college
- Large city

General. Accredited by ACCSCT. **Calendar:** Continuous.

Annual costs/financial aid. Cost of full programs: associate degree programs $16,000, diploma programs $8,000 to $9,000; includes fees, books, uniforms. Books/supplies: $348.

Contact. Phone: (816) 531-5223
Campus Director, 3239 Broadway, Kansas City, MO 64111

Cottey College

Nevada, Missouri **CB member**
www.cottey.edu **CB code: 6120**

- Private 2-year junior and liberal arts college for women
- Residential campus in small town
- SAT or ACT required

General. Founded in 1884. Regionally accredited. Sponsored and supported by P.E.O. Sisterhood, nonsectarian philanthropic educational organization. Only college in United States owned and supported by women for women. **Enrollment:** 290 degree-seeking undergraduates. **Degrees:** 97 associate awarded. **Location:** 100 miles from Kansas City, 60 miles from Joplin. **Calendar:** Semester. **Full-time faculty:** 31 total; 90% have terminal degrees, 3% minority, 55% women. **Part-time faculty:** 12 total; 50% have terminal degrees, 75% women. **Special facilities:** 33-acre wooded area with lodge for outings and nature laboratory, women's leadership center.

Student profile.

Out-of-state:	90%	**Live on campus:**	99%

Transfer out. Colleges most students transferred to 2005: Smith College, Hood College, Truman State University, Boston University, Mount Holyoke College.

Basis for selection. High school course of study most important; rank in top half of graduating class, test scores, essay also important. Recommendations and interviews considered when other criteria not met. Interview recommended for all students. Audition recommended for music students; portfolio recommended for art students. Essay requested sometimes. **Homeschooled:** Students should take GED examination.

High school preparation. 18 units required. Required units include English 4, mathematics 3, social studies 2, science 3 (laboratory 2) and foreign language 2. Mathematics should include algebra I, algebra II, geometry.

2005-2006 Annual costs. Tuition/fees: $12,310. Room/board: $5,200. Books/supplies: $800. Personal expenses: $900.

Financial aid. Need-based: Need-based aid available for part-time students. **Non-need-based:** Scholarships awarded for academics, alumni affiliation, art, athletics, music/drama.

Application procedures. Admission: Priority date 5/1; no deadline. $20 fee, may be waived for applicants with need. Application may be submitted online. Admission notification on a rolling basis. Must reply by May 1 or within 2 week(s) if notified thereafter. **Financial aid:** Priority date 3/30; no closing date. FAFSA required. Applicants notified on a rolling basis starting 3/15; must reply by 5/1.

Academics. Special study options: Dual enrollment of high school students, independent study. **Credit/placement by examination:** AP, CLEP, IB, institutional tests. **Support services:** Tutoring.

Majors. Liberal arts: Arts/sciences.

Computing on campus. 62 workstations in dormitories, library, computer center.

Student life. Freshman orientation: Mandatory, $25 fee. **Policies:** Freshmen permitted cars on campus. **Housing:** Guaranteed on-campus for all undergraduates. **Activities:** Jazz band, choral groups, dance, drama, literary magazine, music ensembles, student government, student newspaper, 32 campus service and social organizations available.

Athletics. NJCAA. **Intercollegiate:** Basketball W, volleyball W. **Intramural:** Archery W, badminton W, basketball W, fencing W, field hockey W, golf W, soccer W, softball W, swimming W, synchronized swimming W, tennis W, volleyball W, water polo W. **Team name:** Comets.

Student services. Campus ministries, career counseling, student employment services, financial aid counseling, health services, personal counseling. **Transfer:** Special adviser, orientation for new students. Transfer center, transfer adviser, college fairs on campus for students transferring to 4-year colleges.

Contact. E-mail: enrollmgt@cottey.edu
Phone: (417) 667-8181 Toll-free number: (888) 526-8839
Fax: (417) 667-8103
Dean of Enrollment Management, Cottey College, 1000 West Austin Boulevard, Nevada, MO 64772

Crowder College

Neosho, Missouri
www.crowder.edu **CB code: 6138**

- Public 2-year community and liberal arts college
- Commuter campus in small town

General. Founded in 1963. Regionally accredited. Internationally recognized water resource school and active/passive solar program. **Enrollment:** 2,290 degree-seeking undergraduates; 325 non-degree-seeking students. **Degrees:** 338 associate awarded. **Location:** 70 miles from Springfield, 28 miles from Joplin. **Calendar:** Semester, limited summer session. **Full-time faculty:** 62 total. **Part-time faculty:** 137 total. **Class size:** 59% < 20, 41% 20-39.

Student profile. Among degree-seeking undergraduates, 566 enrolled as first-time, first-year students, 926 transferred in from other institutions.

Part-time:	43%	**Live on campus:**	10%
Women:	66%		

Transfer out. Colleges most students transferred to 2005: Missouri Southern State College, Pittsburg State University, Southwest Missouri State University.

Basis for selection. Open admission, but selective for some programs. For nursing program: interview, 2.75 GPA and minimum 19 ACT score required. **Adult students:** Entrance exam policies same as for first-time freshmen. **Homeschooled:** Must pass GED.

High school preparation. Recommended units include English 4, mathematics 3 and science 3.

2005-2006 Annual costs. Tuition/fees: $2,220; $3,000 out-of-district; $3,810 out-of-state. Per-credit charge: $62 in-district; $88 out-of-district; $115 out-of-state. Room/board: $3,870. Books/supplies: $700. Personal expenses: $1,100.

Financial aid. All financial aid based on need. Need-based aid available for part-time students. Work study available nights, weekends and for part-time students.

Application procedures. Admission: No deadline. $25 fee, may be waived for applicants with need. Application may be submitted online. Admission notification on a rolling basis. **Financial aid:** Priority date 7/1; no closing date. FAFSA, institutional form required. Applicants notified on a rolling basis starting 5/15.

Academics. Special study options: Distance learning, dual enrollment of high school students, ESL, honors, independent study, internships, liberal arts/career combination, study abroad, weekend college. License preparation in nursing. **Credit/placement by examination:** AP, CLEP, institutional tests. 15 credit hours maximum toward associate degree. **Support services:** GED preparation and test center, learning center, reduced course load, remedial instruction, study skills assistance, tutoring.

Majors. Agriculture: Agribusiness operations, farm/ranch, poultry, production. **Biology:** General. **Business:** General, administrative services, office/clerical. **Communications:** Journalism, public relations. **Computer sciences:** General, system admin. **Education:** Elementary, physical, secondary. **Engineering:** General. **Engineering technology:** Electrical, solar energy. **Foreign languages:** Spanish. **Health:** Environmental health, nursing (RN), office assistant. **History:** General. **Interdisciplinary:** Math/computer science. **Liberal arts:** Arts/sciences. **Math:** General. **Mechanic/repair:** Automotive, diesel, industrial electronics. **Physical sciences:** General, chemistry, physics. **Psychology:** General. **Social sciences:** General. **Visual/performing arts:** Art, theater arts management.

Most popular majors. Business/marketing 14%, health sciences 12%, liberal arts 47%.

Computing on campus. 1,000 workstations in dormitories, library, computer center. Dormitories wired for high-speed internet access. Online library, helpline, wireless network available.

Student life. Freshman orientation: Mandatory. Preregistration for classes offered. **Policies:** Freshmen permitted cars on campus. **Housing:** Guaranteed on-campus for all undergraduates. Single-sex dorms, substance-free housing available. $150 deposit. **Activities:** Bands, choral groups, dance, drama, literary magazine, music ensembles, musical theater, student government, student newspaper, Aggies (agricultural club), art club, Baptist student union, Students in Free Enterprise, Student-Missouri State Teacher's Association, Phi Theta Kappa, Latino union, Habitat for Humanity.

Athletics. NJCAA. **Intercollegiate:** Baseball M, basketball W, softball W. **Team name:** Roughriders.

Student services. Career counseling, student employment services, financial aid counseling, personal counseling, placement for graduates. **Transfer:** Special adviser, orientation for new students. Transfer adviser, college fairs on campus for students transferring to 4-year colleges.

Contact. E-mail: admissions@crowder.edu
Phone: (417) 455-5718 Toll-free number: (866) 238-7788
Fax: (417) 455-2439
Jim Riggs, Director of Admission, Crowder College, 601 LaClede Avenue, Neosho, MO 64850

East Central College

Union, Missouri
www.eastcentral.edu **CB code: 0845**

- Public 2-year community college
- Commuter campus in small town

General. Founded in 1968. Regionally accredited. **Enrollment:** 2,709 degree-seeking undergraduates; 777 non-degree-seeking students. **Degrees:** 388 associate awarded. **Location:** 45 miles from St. Louis. **Calendar:** Semester, limited summer session. **Full-time faculty:** 55 total; 13% have terminal degrees, 6% minority, 40% women. **Part-time faculty:** 109 total; 3% have terminal degrees, 5% minority, 41% women. **Class size:** 60% < 20, 37% 20-39, 2% 40-49, less than 1% 50-99, less than 1% >100. **Special facilities:** Learning and assessment center, outdoor laboratory.

Student profile. Among degree-seeking undergraduates, 42% enrolled in a transfer program, 58% enrolled in a vocational program, 899 enrolled as first-time, first-year students, 429 transferred in from other institutions.

Part-time:	51%	**Asian American:**	1%
Women:	60%	**Hispanic American:**	1%
African American:	1%	**25 or older:**	25%

Transfer out. Colleges most students transferred to 2005: University of Missouri - Columbia, Missouri State University, University of Missouri - St. Louis, St. Louis Community College - Meramec.

Basis for selection. Open admission, but selective for some programs. Special requirements for nursing program. ASSET required for placement for degree seeking students but not required for all certificate programs. **Homeschooled:** GED or ACT composite score of 21 required.

2006-2007 Annual costs. Tuition/fees (projected): $2,130; $2,910 out-of-district; $4,230 out-of-state. Per-credit charge: $61 in-district; $87 out-of-district; $131 out-of-state. Books/supplies: $700. Personal expenses: $600.

2004-2005 Financial aid. Need-based: 72% of total undergraduate aid awarded as scholarships/grants, 28% as loans/jobs. Need-based aid available for part-time students. Work study available nights, weekends and for part-time students. **Non-need-based:** Scholarships awarded for academics, alumni affiliation, art, athletics, music/drama, state residency.

Application procedures. Admission: No deadline. No application fee. Application may be submitted online. Admission notification on a rolling basis. **Financial aid:** Priority date 3/30; no closing date. FAFSA required. Applicants notified on a rolling basis starting 3/15.

Academics. Special study options: Distance learning, dual enrollment of high school students, ESL, honors, independent study, internships, liberal arts/career combination. Central Methodist College classes offered on campus and may count toward 4-year degree. Bachelor's degree programs available on campus. License preparation in nursing, paramedic, radiology. **Credit/placement by examination:** AP, CLEP, institutional tests. 15 credit hours maximum toward associate degree. **Support services:** GED preparation and test center, learning center, reduced course load, remedial instruction, study skills assistance, tutoring, writing center.

Majors. Business: Accounting technology. **Computer sciences:** Networking. **Construction:** General. **Engineering:** Ceramic, chemical, civil, computer, electrical, geological, mechanical, metallurgical, mining, nuclear, petroleum. **Engineering technology:** Aerospace, drafting, industrial management, manufacturing. **Health:** EMT paramedic, medical radiologic technology/radiation therapy, medical secretary, nursing (RN), respiratory therapy technology. **Legal studies:** Legal secretary. **Mechanic/repair:** Automotive, heating/ac/refrig. **Personal/culinary services:** Chef training. **Production:** Machine tool, welding. **Protective services:** Firefighting, police science. **Visual/performing arts:** Commercial/advertising art.

Most popular majors. Business/marketing 12%, health sciences 18%, liberal arts 48%, trade and industry 9%.

Computing on campus. 315 workstations in library, computer center, student center. Online course registration, online library, wireless network available.

Student life. Freshman orientation: Mandatory. Preregistration for classes offered. Held prior to start of classes, includes tours, seminars, adviser activities, social activities. **Activities:** Jazz band, choral groups, dance, drama, music ensembles, musical theater, student government, student newspaper, Phi Theta Kappa honor society, student government, variety of religious and social clubs.

Athletics. NJCAA. **Intercollegiate:** Soccer M, softball W. **Team name:** Rebels.

Student services. Adult student services, career counseling, student employment services, financial aid counseling, personal counseling, placement for graduates, veterans' counselor. **Physically disabled:** Services for visually, hearing impaired. **Transfer:** Special adviser, orientation, pre-admission transcript evaluation for new students. Transfer adviser, college fairs on campus for students transferring to 4-year colleges.

Contact. E-mail: wiedaks@eastcentral.edu
Phone: (636) 583-5193 Fax: (636) 583-1897
Karen Wieda, Registrar, East Central College, 1964 Prairie Dell Road, Union, MO 63084-0529

Everest College: Springfield

Springfield, Missouri
www.springfield-college.com **CB code: 1478**

- For-profit 2-year junior college
- Commuter campus in small city
- SAT or ACT, interview required

General. Founded in 1979. Accredited by ACICS. **Enrollment:** 550 degree-seeking undergraduates. **Degrees:** 4 bachelor's, 118 associate awarded. **Location:** 250 miles from St. Louis, 190 miles from Kansas City. **Calendar:** Quarter, extensive summer session. **Full-time faculty:** 16 total. **Part-time faculty:** 15 total. **Class size:** 91% < 20, 9% 20-39. **Special facilities:** Learning center.

Student profile. Among degree-seeking undergraduates, 100 transferred in from other institutions.

Basis for selection. 15 ACT or 700 SAT (exclusive of Writing) required.

2005-2006 Annual costs. Tuition/fees: $12,425. Per-credit charge: $265. Books/supplies: $1,000. Personal expenses: $1,260.

Financial aid. All financial aid based on need. Need-based aid available for part-time students.

Application procedures. Admission: No deadline. $25 fee. Admission notification on a rolling basis. **Financial aid:** No deadline. FAFSA required. Applicants notified on a rolling basis.

Academics. Special study options: Accelerated study, cooperative education, distance learning, internships. Bachelor's degree programs available on campus. **Credit/placement by examination:** CLEP, institutional tests. 32 credit hours maximum toward associate degree, 64 toward bachelor's. **Support services:** GED preparation, learning center, reduced course load, remedial instruction, study skills assistance, tutoring.

Majors. Business: Accounting, administrative services, business admin, hospitality admin. **Computer sciences:** General, data processing. **Health:** Medical assistant, medical secretary. **Legal studies:** Legal secretary, paralegal.

Most popular majors. Business/marketing 28%, computer/information sciences 24%, health sciences 26%, legal studies 26%.

Computing on campus. 140 workstations in library, computer center.

Student life. Freshman orientation: Mandatory. Preregistration for classes offered. Held week prior to start of classes. **Activities:** Student government, student newspaper, Phi Beta Lambda.

Student services. Adult student services, career counseling, student employment services, personal counseling, placement for graduates, veterans' counselor.

Contact. E-mail: slester@cci.edu
Phone: (417) 864-7220 Toll-free number: (800) 475-2669
Fax: (417) 864-5697
Scott Lester, Director of Admissions, Everest College: Springfield, 1010 West Sunshine, Springfield, MO 65807

Two-Year Colleges

High-Tech Institute
Kansas City, Missouri
www.hightechinstitute.edu

- For-profit 2-year technical college
- Very large city

General. Accredited by ACCSCT. **Calendar:** Continuous.

Basis for selection. Open admission.

Academics. Credit/placement by examination: CLEP.

Contact. Phone: (816) 444-4300
Barbette Hatcher, Director of Admissions, High-Tech Institute, 9001 State Line Road, Kansas City, MO 64114

Jefferson College
Hillsboro, Missouri
www.jeffco.edu **CB code: 6320**

- Public 2-year community and technical college
- Commuter campus in rural community

General. Founded in 1963. Regionally accredited. College also serves as area vocational school, continuing education program, adult basic education center and business and technology customized training center. **Enrollment:** 3,900 degree-seeking undergraduates; 455 non-degree-seeking students. **Degrees:** 465 associate awarded. **Location:** 30 miles from St. Louis. **Calendar:** Semester, limited summer session. **Full-time faculty:** 89 total; 16% have terminal degrees, 3% minority, 52% women. **Part-time faculty:** 179 total; 4% have terminal degrees, 3% minority, 46% women. **Class size:** 50% < 20, 46% 20-39, 1% 40-49, 2% 50-99, less than 1% >100. **Special facilities:** Outdoor theater, facility for computer-related technologies.

Student profile. Among degree-seeking undergraduates, 53% enrolled in a transfer program, 37% enrolled in a vocational program, 1% already have a bachelor's degree or higher, 1,071 enrolled as first-time, first-year students, 319 transferred in from other institutions.

Part-time:	43%	**25 or older:**	32%
Out-of-state:	2%	**Live on campus:**	2%
Women:	60%		

Transfer out. Colleges most students transferred to 2005: University of Missouri - St. Louis, Missouri Baptist University, Southeast Missouri State University.

Basis for selection. Open admission, but selective for some programs. Special requirements for nursing, veterinary technology programs and police training institute. Interview required for health services technologies students. **Adult students:** Entrance exam policies same as for first-time freshmen. **Homeschooled:** Minimum placement test scores if high school transcript is not from an approved accrediting body. **Learning Disabled:** Suggested that students with disabilities meet with the campus Assessment Counselor prior to enrollment.

High school preparation. Elementary algebra required for electronics; chemistry required for nursing and veterinary technology.

2006-2007 Annual costs. Tuition/fees (projected): $1,980; $2,790 out-of-district; $3,570 out-of-state. Per-credit charge: $53 in-district; $80 out-of-district; $106 out-of-state. Room/board: $5,794. Books/supplies: $1,000. Personal expenses: $1,000.

2004-2005 Financial aid. Need-based: 655 full-time freshmen applied for aid; 454 were judged to have need; 411 of these received aid. Average need met was 40%. Average scholarship/grant was $1,817; average loan $1,920. 60% of total undergraduate aid awarded as scholarships/grants, 40% as loans/jobs. Need-based aid available for part-time students. Work study available nights and for part-time students. **Non-need-based:** Awarded to 477 full-time undergraduates, including 268 freshmen. Scholarships awarded for academics, art, athletics, leadership, music/drama, state residency.

Application procedures. Admission: Priority date 5/3; no deadline. $20 fee, may be waived for applicants with need. Application may be submitted online. Admission notification on a rolling basis. **Financial aid:** Priority date 4/1; no closing date. FAFSA required. Applicants notified on a rolling basis starting 4/15.

Academics. Student Support Services (TRIO) program available for at-risk students. **Special study options:** Distance learning, double major, dual enrollment of high school students, ESL, honors, independent study, internships, liberal arts/career combination, study abroad. Cooperative agreement with 2 neighboring community colleges. Bachelor's degree programs available on campus. License preparation in nursing, paramedic. **Credit/placement by examination:** AP, CLEP, institutional tests. 30 credit hours maximum toward associate degree. **Support services:** GED preparation and test center, learning center, reduced course load, remedial instruction, study skills assistance, tutoring, writing center.

Majors. Business: General, administrative services, office/clerical. **Computer sciences:** General, security. **Education:** Early childhood. **Engineering:** General. **Engineering technology:** Architectural drafting, drafting, electrical. **Health:** EMT paramedic, medical secretary, nursing (RN), veterinary technology/assistant. **Liberal arts:** Arts/sciences. **Mechanic/repair:** Automotive, heating/ac/refrig, industrial. **Personal/culinary services:** Chef training, culinary arts, food prep, food service, restaurant/catering. **Production:** Machine tool, welding. **Protective services:** Fire safety technology, law enforcement admin, police science. **Science technology:** Biological.

Most popular majors. Business/marketing 7%, engineering/engineering technologies 7%, health sciences 14%, liberal arts 60%.

Computing on campus. 250 workstations in dormitories, library, computer center, student center. Dormitories wired for high-speed internet access and linked to campus network. Commuter students can connect to campus network. Online course registration, online library, helpline available.

Student life. Freshman orientation: Mandatory. 90-minute program held prior to the start of each semester. **Policies:** Freshmen permitted cars on campus. **Housing:** Apartments, substance-free housing available. $200 partly refundable deposit. **Activities:** Bands, choral groups, drama, literary magazine, music ensembles, musical theater, student government, student newspaper, TV station, Phi Theta Kappa, College Ambassadors, Habitat for Humanity, academic clubs, student senate, cultural club, creative writers.

Athletics. NJCAA. **Intercollegiate:** Baseball M, basketball W, soccer M, softball W, volleyball W. **Team name:** Vikings.

Student services. Adult student services, alcohol/substance abuse counseling, career counseling, services for economically disadvantaged, student employment services, financial aid counseling, on-campus daycare, personal counseling, placement for graduates, veterans' counselor. **Physically disabled:** Services for visually, speech, hearing impaired. **Learning disabled:** Comprehensive services available. **Transfer:** Special adviser, orientation for new students. Transfer adviser, college fairs on campus for students transferring to 4-year colleges.

Contact. E-mail: admissions@jeffco.edu
Phone: (636) 797-3000 ext. 217 Fax: (636) 789-5103
Julie Pierce, Director of Admissions and Financial Aid, Jefferson College, 1000 Viking Drive, Hillsboro, MO 63050-2441

Linn State Technical College
Linn, Missouri
www.linnstate.edu

- Public 2-year technical college
- Residential campus

Contact. Phone: (573) 897-5000
One Technology Drive, Linn, MO 65051

Longview Community College
Lee's Summit, Missouri
www.mcckc.edu **CB code: 6359**

- Public 2-year community college
- Commuter campus in small city

General. Founded in 1968. Regionally accredited. **Enrollment:** 3,651 degree-seeking undergraduates; 2,016 non-degree-seeking students. **Degrees:** 462 associate awarded. **Location:** 10 miles from Kansas City. **Calendar:** Semester, extensive summer session. **Full-time faculty:** 83 total; 6% minority, 47% women. **Part-time faculty:** 297 total; 7% minority, 54% women. **Class size:** 35% < 20, 57% 20-39, less than 1% 40-49.

Student profile. Among degree-seeking undergraduates, 51% enrolled in a transfer program, 17% enrolled in a vocational program, 2% already have

a bachelor's degree or higher, 963 enrolled as first-time, first-year students, 811 transferred in from other institutions.

Part-time:	48%	**Asian American:**	1%
Out-of-state:	1%	**Hispanic American:**	2%
Women:	60%	**25 or older:**	34%
African American:	11%		

Basis for selection. Open admission, but selective for some programs. **Homeschooled:** Statement describing homeschool structure and mission, transcript of courses and grades, interview required. Provide proof of graduation requirements. Applicants under the age of 16 must meet with Dean of Student Services and bring student portfolio.

High school preparation. 16 units recommended. Recommended units include English 4, mathematics 3, social studies 3, science 3 and foreign language 2. One unit in visual/performing arts recommended.

2005-2006 Annual costs. Tuition/fees: $2,280; $4,170 out-of-district; $5,550 out-of-state. Per-credit charge: $76 in-district; $134 out-of-district; $180 out-of-state. Books/supplies: $700. Personal expenses: $1,500.

2004-2005 Financial aid. Need-based: 358 full-time freshmen applied for aid; 247 were judged to have need; 210 of these received aid. Average scholarship/grant was $2,707; average loan $1,943. 73% of total undergraduate aid awarded as scholarships/grants, 27% as loans/jobs. Work study available nights and for part-time students. **Non-need-based:** Awarded to 327 full-time undergraduates, including 95 freshmen. Scholarships awarded for academics, athletics, leadership.

Application procedures. Admission: No deadline. No application fee. Application may be submitted online. Admission notification on a rolling basis. **Financial aid:** Priority date 5/30, closing date 8/20. FAFSA, institutional form required. Applicants notified on a rolling basis starting 4/8.

Academics. Special study options: Accelerated study, cooperative education, cross-registration, distance learning, dual enrollment of high school students, honors, independent study, internships, weekend college. **Credit/placement by examination:** AP, CLEP, institutional tests. 30 credit hours maximum toward associate degree. **Support services:** GED test center, learning center, remedial instruction, tutoring.

Majors. Agriculture: Turf management. **Business:** General, accounting, administrative services, business admin, office management, office technology, sales/distribution. **Computer sciences:** General, applications programming. **Engineering:** General. **Engineering technology:** Surveying. **Liberal arts:** Arts/sciences. **Mechanic/repair:** Auto body, automotive. **Protective services:** Corrections, criminal justice.

Most popular majors. Business/marketing 8%, engineering/engineering technologies 7%, liberal arts 81%.

Computing on campus. 693 workstations in library, computer center.

Student life. Freshman orientation: Available. Preregistration for classes offered. **Activities:** Choral groups, drama, literary magazine, student government, student newspaper.

Athletics. NJCAA. **Intercollegiate:** Baseball M, volleyball W. **Intramural:** Basketball, swimming, volleyball. **Team name:** Lakers.

Student services. Adult student services, career counseling, student employment services, on-campus daycare, personal counseling, placement for graduates, veterans' counselor. **Physically disabled:** Services for visually, hearing impaired. **Transfer:** Special adviser, orientation for new students. Transfer adviser for students transferring to 4-year colleges.

Contact. Phone: (816) 672-2000 Fax: (816) 672-2025
Kathy Hale, Registrar, Longview Community College, 500 Longview Road, Lee's Summit, MO 64081-2105

Maple Woods Community College

Kansas City, Missouri
www.mcckc.edu **CB code: 6436**

- Public 2-year community college
- Commuter campus in large city

General. Founded in 1968. Regionally accredited. **Enrollment:** 2,913 degree-seeking undergraduates; 1,529 non-degree-seeking students. **Degrees:** 368 associate awarded. **Location:** 15 miles from downtown. **Calendar:** Semester, limited summer session. **Full-time faculty:** 53 total; 11% minority, 51% women. **Part-time faculty:** 293 total; 4% minority, 50% women. **Class size:** 41% < 20, 55% 20-39, less than 1% 40-49, less than 1% 50-99.

Student profile. Among degree-seeking undergraduates, 53% enrolled in a transfer program, 15% enrolled in a vocational program, 2% already have a bachelor's degree or higher, 856 enrolled as first-time, first-year students, 755 transferred in from other institutions.

Part-time:	47%	**Asian American:**	1%
Out-of-state:	1%	**Hispanic American:**	2%
Women:	59%	**25 or older:**	33%
African American:	3%		

Basis for selection. Open admission, but selective for some programs. Special requirements for animal health technology program. **Homeschooled:** Provide proof of high school graduation. If under 16 years old must meet with Dean of Student Services and bring student portfolio.

High school preparation. 16 units recommended. Recommended units include English 4, mathematics 3, social studies 3, science 3 and foreign language 2. One unit in visual/performing arts recommended.

2006-2007 Annual costs. Tuition/fees (projected): $2,340; $4,140 out-of-district; $5,550 out-of-state. Per-credit charge: $73 in-district; $133 out-of-district; $180 out-of-state. Books/supplies: $700. Personal expenses: $1,500.

2004-2005 Financial aid. Need-based: 343 full-time freshmen applied for aid; 211 were judged to have need; 181 of these received aid. Average scholarship/grant was $2,481; average loan $1,917. 73% of total undergraduate aid awarded as scholarships/grants, 27% as loans/jobs. Need-based aid available for part-time students. Work study available nights and for part-time students. **Non-need-based:** Awarded to 276 full-time undergraduates, including 82 freshmen. Scholarships awarded for academics, athletics, leadership.

Application procedures. Admission: No deadline. No application fee. Application may be submitted online. Admission notification on a rolling basis. Separate application required for animal health technology; deadline March 1. **Financial aid:** Priority date 5/30; no closing date. FAFSA, institutional form required. Applicants notified on a rolling basis.

Academics. Special study options: Cross-registration, distance learning, dual enrollment of high school students, exchange student, honors, internships. **Credit/placement by examination:** AP, CLEP, institutional tests. 30 credit hours maximum toward associate degree. **Support services:** GED test center, learning center, reduced course load, remedial instruction, tutoring.

Majors. Business: General, administrative services, business admin, office technology, sales/distribution. **Computer sciences:** General, applications programming. **Engineering:** General. **Foreign languages:** Sign language interpretation. **Health:** Nursing (RN), veterinary technology/assistant. **Liberal arts:** Arts/sciences. **Physical sciences:** General. **Protective services:** Criminal justice, law enforcement admin.

Most popular majors. Health sciences 7%, liberal arts 80%.

Computing on campus. 369 workstations in computer center. Online course registration, online library available.

Student life. Freshman orientation: Available. Preregistration for classes offered. **Activities:** Choral groups, student government, student newspaper.

Athletics. NJCAA. **Intercollegiate:** Baseball M, softball W. **Intramural:** Softball, volleyball W. **Team name:** Centaurs.

Student services. Adult student services, career counseling, student employment services, personal counseling, placement for graduates, veterans' counselor. **Physically disabled:** Services for visually, speech, hearing impaired. **Transfer:** Special adviser for new students. Transfer adviser, college fairs on campus for students transferring to 4-year colleges.

Contact. Phone: (816) 437-3100 Fax: (816) 437-3049
Dawn Hatterman, Registrar, Maple Woods Community College, 2601 NE Barry Road, Kansas City, MO 64156-1299

Metro Business College

Cape Girardeau, Missouri
www.metrobusinesscollege.edu **CB code: 3316**

- For-profit 2-year business college
- Large town

General. Accredited by ACICS. **Calendar:** Continuous.

Annual costs/financial aid. Full program costs range from $8,085 to $16,170; book rental included. Required fees $100.

Contact. Phone: (573) 334-9181
Assistant to the President, 1732 North Kingshighway, Cape Girardeau, MO 36701

Metro Business College: Jefferson City
Jefferson City, Missouri
www.metrobusinesscollege.edu **CB code: 3318**

- For-profit 2-year business and health science college
- Commuter campus in large town
- Interview required

General. Accredited by ACICS. **Enrollment:** 157 degree-seeking undergraduates. **Degrees:** 31 associate awarded. **Location:** 35 miles from Columbia. **Calendar:** Quarter, extensive summer session. **Full-time faculty:** 8 total; 75% women. **Part-time faculty:** 3 total; 67% have terminal degrees, 33% women. **Class size:** 100% 40-49.

Student profile. Among degree-seeking undergraduates, 1% already have a bachelor's degree or higher, 32 enrolled as first-time, first-year students.

Part-time:	9%	**Asian American:**	1%
Women:	90%	**25 or older:**	61%
African American:	18%		

Transfer out. 1% of students enrolled in the transfer program go on to 4-year colleges.

Basis for selection. Open admission, but selective for some programs. Students must take entrance exam. Required scores vary by program. **Adult students:** Entrance exam policies same as for first-time freshmen.

2005-2006 Annual costs. $2,695 per quarter;book rental included. Required fee $100.

Financial aid. Need-based: Need-based aid available for part-time students.

Application procedures. Admission: No deadline. $25 fee. Application must be submitted on paper. Admission notification on a rolling basis. **Financial aid:** No deadline. FAFSA, institutional form required. Applicants notified on a rolling basis.

Academics. Credit/placement by examination: CLEP. **Support services:** Reduced course load, remedial instruction, study skills assistance, tutoring.

Majors. Business: Business admin. **Health:** Office assistant.

Most popular majors. Computer/information sciences 57%, health sciences 43%.

Computing on campus. 7 workstations in library. Online library, repair service, wireless network available.

Student life. Freshman orientation: Mandatory. **Activities:** Student government.

Student services. Adult student services, alcohol/substance abuse counseling, services for economically disadvantaged, student employment services, financial aid counseling, personal counseling, placement for graduates. **Transfer:** Orientation, pre-admission transcript evaluation for new students.

Contact. E-mail: infojeff@metrobusinesscollege.edu
Phone: (573) 635-6600 Toll-free number: (800) 467-0786
Fax: (573) 635-6999
Patti Sander, Admissions Representative, Metro Business College: Jefferson City, 1407 Southwest Boulevard, Jefferson City, MO 65109

Metro Business College: Rolla
Rolla, Missouri
www.metrobusinesscollege.edu **CB code: 3317**

- For-profit 2-year business college
- Large town

General. Accredited by ACICS. **Calendar:** Continuous.

Annual costs/financial aid. Costs vary per program. Tuition ranges from $2,495 to $2,695 per quarter; full program costs range from $7,485 to $16,170; book rental included. Required fee $100.

Contact. Phone: (573) 364-8464
Director, 1202 East Highway 72, Rolla, MO 65401

Mineral Area College
Park Hills, Missouri
www.mineralarea.edu **CB code: 6323**

- Public 2-year community college
- Commuter campus in small town

General. Founded in 1922. Regionally accredited. **Enrollment:** 2,342 degree-seeking undergraduates. **Degrees:** 435 associate awarded. **Location:** 60 miles from St. Louis. **Calendar:** Semester, limited summer session. **Full-time faculty:** 75 total. **Part-time faculty:** 100 total. **Class size:** 49% < 20, 51% 20-39.

Student profile.

Out-of-state:	1%	**Live on campus:**	4%
25 or older:	34%		

Transfer out. Colleges most students transferred to 2005: Central Methodist College at Park Hills, Southeast Missouri State University, Southwest Missouri State University, University of Missouri - St. Louis, University of Missouri - Columbia.

Basis for selection. Open admission, but selective for some programs. Interview required for health majors and law enforcement academy. **Adult students:** Entrance exam policies same as for first-time freshmen. **Home-schooled:** Must submit documentation as required by Missouri State Statute 167.031 concerning home-school graduates.

2005-2006 Annual costs. Tuition/fees: $2,160; $2,880 out-of-district; $3,540 out-of-state. Per-credit charge: $72 in-district; $96 out-of-district; $118 out-of-state. Room/board: $2,475. Books/supplies: $1,200.

Financial aid. Need-based: Need-based aid available for part-time students. Work study available for part-time students. **Non-need-based:** Scholarships awarded for academics, alumni affiliation, art, athletics, leadership, music/drama, state residency.

Application procedures. Admission: Priority date 8/1; no deadline. $15 fee. Application may be submitted online. Admission notification on a rolling basis beginning on or about 2/15. **Financial aid:** Priority date 4/1; no closing date. FAFSA required. Applicants notified on a rolling basis starting 2/15; must reply within 4 week(s) of notification.

Academics. Special study options: Cross-registration, distance learning, dual enrollment of high school students, honors, independent study, internships, liberal arts/career combination, study abroad. Bachelor's degree programs available on campus. License preparation in nursing. **Credit/placement by examination:** AP, CLEP, institutional tests. 30 credit hours maximum toward associate degree. Credit held in escrow for 1 semester. **Support services:** GED test center, learning center, pre-admission summer program, reduced course load, remedial instruction, study skills assistance, tutoring, writing center.

Majors. Agriculture: Horticulture, production. **Business:** General, accounting, administrative services, banking/financial services, business admin. **Communications technology:** Graphic/printing. **Computer sciences:** Networking, programming. **Education:** Voc/tech. **Engineering technology:** CAD/CADD, civil, construction, electrical, manufacturing, occupational safety. **Family/consumer sciences:** Child development. **Health:** Clinical lab technology, health services, nursing (RN), respiratory therapy technology. **Liberal arts:** Arts/sciences. **Mechanic/repair:** Auto body, automotive, heating/ac/refrig, industrial. **Production:** General, machine tool, welding. **Protective services:** Firefighting, police science. **Social sciences:** General.

Computing on campus. Dormitories wired for high-speed internet access. Online course registration, helpline available.

Student life. Freshman orientation: Mandatory. Preregistration for classes offered. One-day program for students and parents. **Policies:** Freshmen permitted cars on campus. **Housing:** Coed dorms, substance-free housing available. $200 deposit. Privatized housing available. **Activities:** Bands, choral groups, drama, music ensembles, musical theater, student government, Young Democrats, Young Republicans, Baptist Youth.

Athletics. NJCAA. **Intercollegiate:** Baseball M, basketball, volleyball W. **Team name:** Cardinals.

Student services. Adult student services, career counseling, student employment services, financial aid counseling, personal counseling, placement for graduates, veterans' counselor. **Physically disabled:** Services for visually, speech, hearing impaired. **Transfer:** Special adviser, orientation, preadmission transcript evaluation for new students. Transfer adviser, college fairs on campus for students transferring to 4-year colleges.

Contact. E-mail: admissions@mineralarea.edu
Phone: (573) 518-2206 Fax: (573) 518-2166
Julie Sheets, Admissions Officer, Mineral Area College, PO Box 1000, Park Hills, MO 63601-1000

Missouri College

St. Louis, Missouri
www.missouricollege.com **CB code: 3074**

- For-profit 2-year technical college
- Commuter campus in very large city
- Interview required

General. Accredited by ACCSCT. **Enrollment:** 750 undergraduates. **Degrees:** 62 associate awarded. **Calendar:** Continuous. **Full-time faculty:** 14 total. **Part-time faculty:** 20 total. **Class size:** 59% < 20, 41% 20-39.

Basis for selection. All applicants required to take personnel test.

2005-2006 Annual costs. Books/supplies: $1,409.

Financial aid. Need-based: Need-based aid available for part-time students. Work study available nights.

Application procedures. Admission: No deadline. $100 fee. Admission notification on a rolling basis. **Financial aid:** No deadline. FAFSA required.

Academics. Credit/placement by examination: CLEP.

Student life. Freshman orientation: Mandatory.

Student services. Career counseling, financial aid counseling, personal counseling, placement for graduates. **Physically disabled:** Services for visually impaired.

Contact. E-mail: cmerrell@missouricollege.com
Phone: (314) 821-7700 Toll-free number: (800) 216-6732
Charles Merrell, Dean of Academics, Missouri College, 10121 Manchester Road, St. Louis, MO 63122-1583

Missouri State University: West Plains

West Plains, Missouri
www.wp.missouristate.edu **CB code: 6662**

- Public 2-year university and branch campus college
- Commuter campus in small town

General. Regionally accredited. **Enrollment:** 1,264 degree-seeking undergraduates; 411 non-degree-seeking students. **Degrees:** 224 associate awarded. **Location:** 110 miles from Springfield. **Calendar:** Semester, limited summer session. **Full-time faculty:** 29 total. **Part-time faculty:** 88 total. **Class size:** 13% < 20, 79% 20-39, 8% 40-49.

Student profile. Among degree-seeking undergraduates, 391 enrolled as first-time, first-year students, 92 transferred in from other institutions.

Part-time:	31%	**Native American:**	1%
Women:	67%	**International:**	1%
African American:	1%	**25 or older:**	45%
Asian American:	1%	**Live on campus:**	4%
Hispanic American:	2%		

Transfer out. Colleges most students transferred to 2005: Missouri State University: Springfield.

Basis for selection. Open admission, but selective for some programs. Separate application required for selective respiratory therapy program by September 30; for selective nursing program by March 1. **Homeschooled:** Must submit ACT score (minimum 18) or official GED transcript.

2005-2006 Annual costs. Tuition/fees: $3,124; $6,034 out-of-state. Per-credit charge: $97 in-state; $194 out-of-state. Room/board: $4,558. Books/supplies: $870.

Financial aid. Need-based: Work study available nights, weekends and for part-time students.

Application procedures. Admission: Closing date 8/18 (postmark date). $15 fee. Admission notification on a rolling basis. Nursing program requires separate application; deadline March 1. **Financial aid:** Priority date 3/31; no closing date.

Academics. Special study options: Distance learning, dual enrollment of high school students, honors, independent study, internships, liberal arts/career combination, student-designed major, study abroad. Bachelor's degree programs available on campus. License preparation in nursing. **Credit/placement by examination:** AP, CLEP, IB, ACT, institutional tests. 15 credit hours maximum toward associate degree. **Support services:** GED test center, learning center, remedial instruction, study skills assistance, tutoring, writing center.

Majors. Agriculture: Business. **Business:** General. **Computer sciences:** General. **Engineering technology:** Drafting. **Family/consumer sciences:** Child care. **Health:** Nursing (RN). **Liberal arts:** Arts/sciences. **Protective services:** Police science.

Most popular majors. Health sciences 19%, liberal arts 71%.

Computing on campus. 94 workstations in dormitories, library, computer center, student center. Dormitories wired for high-speed internet access and linked to campus network. Commuter students can connect to campus network. Online library, helpline, repair service, wireless network available.

Student life. Freshman orientation: Mandatory. Preregistration for classes offered. Half-day sessions held throughout summer. **Policies:** Freshmen permitted cars on campus. **Housing:** Coed dorms, substance-free housing available. $100 fully refundable deposit. **Activities:** Choral groups, drama, student government.

Athletics. NJCAA. **Intercollegiate:** Basketball M, cheerleading, volleyball W. **Team name:** Grizzlies.

Student services. Career counseling, student employment services, financial aid counseling, health services, minority student services, personal counseling, placement for graduates, veterans' counselor. **Physically disabled:** Services for visually, hearing impaired. **Transfer:** Special adviser, orientation for new students. Transfer adviser for students transferring to 4-year colleges.

Contact. E-mail: wpadmissions@missouristate.edu
Phone: (417) 255-7955 Toll-free number: (888) 466-7897
Fax: (417) 255-7959
Melissa Jett, Coordinator of Admissions, Missouri State University: West Plains, 128 Garfield, West Plains, MO 65775

Moberly Area Community College

Moberly, Missouri
www.macc.edu **CB code: 6414**

- Public 2-year community college
- Commuter campus in large town

General. Founded in 1927. Regionally accredited. **Enrollment:** 2,776 degree-seeking undergraduates; 1,059 non-degree-seeking students. **Degrees:** 370 associate awarded. **Location:** 35 miles from Columbia. **Calendar:** Semester, extensive summer session. **Full-time faculty:** 57 total. **Part-time faculty:** 182 total. **Special facilities:** Multimedia/instructional television center, graphic arts/fine arts gallery.

Student profile. Among degree-seeking undergraduates, 65% enrolled in a transfer program, 35% enrolled in a vocational program, 2% already have a bachelor's degree or higher, 906 enrolled as first-time, first-year students, 160 transferred in from other institutions.

Part-time:	38%	**25 or older:**	25%
Out-of-state:	2%	**Live on campus:**	1%
Women:	64%		

Transfer out. Colleges most students transferred to 2005: Central Missouri State University, Columbia College, University of Missouri, Truman State University.

Basis for selection. Open admission, but selective for some programs. Special requirements for nursing and law enforcement programs. ACT scores required for admission to nursing programs. Degree-seeking students, or those taking 14 or more credits, must have ACT or ASSET score for placement purposes; tests also required for students enrolling in English or mathematics courses. **Adult students:** Entrance exam policies same as for first-time freshmen. **Homeschooled:** Applicants must provide transcript outlining educational process or take GED. **Learning Disabled:** No special admission requirements. Formal process exists to identify students with special needs. Extensive effort made to provide assistance.

2005-2006 Annual costs. Tuition/fees: $1,890; $2,670 out-of-district; $4,080 out-of-state. Per-credit charge: $55 in-district; $81 out-of-district; $128 out-of-state. Room only: $1,800. Books/supplies: $800. Personal expenses: $1,500.

2004-2005 Financial aid. **Need-based:** 518 full-time freshmen applied for aid; 376 were judged to have need; 376 of these received aid. Average need met was 50%. Average scholarship/grant was $2,277; average loan $2,634. 68% of total undergraduate aid awarded as scholarships/grants, 32% as loans/jobs. Need-based aid available for part-time students. Work study available nights, weekends and for part-time students. **Non-need-based:** Awarded to 432 full-time undergraduates, including 129 freshmen. Scholarships awarded for academics, alumni affiliation, art, athletics, leadership, music/drama.

Application procedures. **Admission:** No deadline. No application fee. Application may be submitted online. Admission notification on a rolling basis. **Financial aid:** Priority date 4/1; no closing date. FAFSA required. Applicants notified on a rolling basis starting 4/1; must reply by 7/15 or within 2 week(s) of notification.

Academics. **Special study options:** Cooperative education, distance learning, dual enrollment of high school students, honors, internships, study abroad, teacher certification program. License preparation in nursing, paramedic. **Credit/placement by examination:** AP, CLEP, IB, institutional tests. 30 credit hours maximum toward associate degree. **Support services:** GED preparation, learning center, remedial instruction, study skills assistance, tutoring.

Majors. **Business:** Accounting technology, marketing, office/clerical. **Communications:** Journalism. **Communications technology:** Graphic/printing. **Computer sciences:** Programming. **Education:** Voc/tech. **Engineering:** General. **Engineering technology:** Drafting, electrical, manufacturing. **Family/consumer sciences:** Child care. **Health:** Nursing (RN). **Liberal arts:** Arts/sciences. **Production:** Welding. **Protective services:** Criminal justice.

Most popular majors. Business/marketing 23%, education 10%, engineering/engineering technologies 7%, health sciences 9%, liberal arts 29%.

Computing on campus. 750 workstations in library, computer center. Commuter students can connect to campus network. Online library, repair service available.

Student life. **Freshman orientation:** Available. Preregistration for classes offered. Half-day program held during late summer. **Policies:** Freshmen permitted cars on campus. **Housing:** Single-sex dorms, substance-free housing available. $100 deposit, deadline 8/23. Limited housing available. **Activities:** Choral groups, drama, literary magazine, student government, student newspaper, Phi Theta Kappa, Association for the Education of Young Children, Brothers OX, NGN (service organizations), multicultural club.

Athletics. NJCAA. **Intercollegiate:** Basketball, cheerleading. **Intramural:** Basketball, volleyball. **Team name:** Greyhounds.

Student services. Adult student services, career counseling, services for economically disadvantaged, student employment services, financial aid counseling, personal counseling, placement for graduates. **Physically disabled:** Services for visually, hearing impaired. **Transfer:** Special adviser, orientation, pre-admission transcript evaluation for new students. Transfer adviser, college fairs on campus for students transferring to 4-year colleges.

Contact. E-mail: info@macc.edu
Phone: (660) 263-4110 ext. 270 Toll-free number: (800) 622-2070 ext. 270
Fax: (660) 263-2406
James Grant, Dean of Student Services, Moberly Area Community College, 101 College Avenue, Moberly, MO 65270-1304

North Central Missouri College

Trenton, Missouri
www.ncmissouri.edu **CB code: 6830**

- Public 2-year community college
- Commuter campus in small town

General. Founded in 1925. Regionally accredited. Evening classes offered at outreach sites in many area communities. **Enrollment:** 946 degree-seeking undergraduates; 396 non-degree-seeking students. **Degrees:** 229 associate awarded. **Location:** 90 miles from Kansas City. **Calendar:** Semester, limited summer session. **Full-time faculty:** 29 total; 21% have terminal degrees, 48% women. **Part-time faculty:** 79 total; 1% have terminal degrees. **Special facilities:** Academic reinforcement center.

Student profile. Among degree-seeking undergraduates, 282 enrolled as first-time, first-year students.

Part-time:	27%	**Hispanic American:**	1%
Out-of-state:	1%	**Native American:**	1%
Women:	74%	**25 or older:**	30%
African American:	3%	**Live on campus:**	11%

Transfer out. **Colleges most students transferred to 2005:** Missouri Western State College, Northwest Missouri State University, Southwest Missouri State University, Central Missouri State University.

Basis for selection. Open admission, but selective for some programs. Special requirements for associate and certificate programs in nursing. ACT preferred. ASSET scores may be substituted for ACT. Interview required for nursing students. **Adult students:** Entrance exam policies same as for first-time freshmen. **Homeschooled:** GED required.

2005-2006 Annual costs. Tuition/fees: $2,130; $3,000 out-of-district; $4,020 out-of-state. Per-credit charge: $56 in-district; $85 out-of-district; $119 out-of-state. Room/board: $4,404. Books/supplies: $600. Personal expenses: $1,278.

Financial aid. **Need-based:** Need-based aid available for part-time students. Work study available nights, weekends and for part-time students. **Non-need-based:** Scholarships awarded for academics, athletics, minority status, music/drama.

Application procedures. **Admission:** No deadline. No application fee. Admission notification on a rolling basis beginning on or about 2/1. **Financial aid:** Priority date 3/15; no closing date. FAFSA, institutional form required. Applicants notified on a rolling basis starting 3/15.

Academics. **Special study options:** Cooperative education, distance learning, double major, dual enrollment of high school students, internships, liberal arts/career combination. Bachelor's degree programs available on campus. License preparation in nursing, paramedic. **Credit/placement by examination:** AP, CLEP, SAT, ACT, institutional tests. 30 credit hours maximum toward associate degree. **Support services:** GED preparation and test center, learning center, reduced course load, remedial instruction, study skills assistance, tutoring.

Majors. **Agriculture:** Agribusiness operations, farm/ranch. **Business:** Accounting, business admin, office technology, office/clerical. **Computer sciences:** General. **Conservation:** Environmental science. **Construction:** Maintenance. **Education:** Voc/tech. **Engineering technology:** Electrical, industrial. **Health:** Nursing (RN), office assistant. **Liberal arts:** Arts/sciences. **Mechanic/repair:** General, auto body, electronics/electrical. **Protective services:** Criminal justice. **Public administration:** Human services.

Most popular majors. Business/marketing 10%, computer/information sciences 6%, health sciences 17%, liberal arts 55%.

Computing on campus. 159 workstations in dormitories, library, computer center, student center. Dormitories wired for high-speed internet access.

Student life. **Freshman orientation:** Available. **Policies:** Freshmen permitted cars on campus. **Housing:** Single-sex dorms available. $100 deposit. **Activities:** Drama, student government, Baptist Student Union.

Athletics. NJCAA. **Intercollegiate:** Baseball M, basketball, softball W. **Intramural:** Volleyball. **Team name:** Pirates.

Student services. Alcohol/substance abuse counseling, career counseling, student employment services, financial aid counseling, personal counseling, placement for graduates. **Physically disabled:** Services for visually, speech, hearing impaired. **Transfer:** Special adviser, orientation for new students. Transfer adviser, college fairs on campus for students transferring to 4-year colleges.

Contact. E-mail: admissions@mail.ncmissouri.edu
Phone: (660) 359-3948 ext. 401 Toll-free number: (800) 880-6180 ext. 401
Fax: (660) 359-2211
Blair Birdsong, Admission Director, North Central Missouri College, 1301 Main Street, Trenton, MO 64683

Ozarks Technical Community College

Springfield, Missouri
www.otc.edu **CB code: 2583**

- Public 2-year community and technical college
- Commuter campus in small city

General. Regionally accredited. **Enrollment:** 7,999 degree-seeking undergraduates; 1,382 non-degree-seeking students. **Degrees:** 888 associate awarded. **Location:** 160 miles from Kansas City, 250 miles from St. Louis. **Calendar:** Semester, extensive summer session. **Full-time faculty:** 130 total. **Part-time faculty:** 350 total.

Student profile. Among degree-seeking undergraduates, 47% enrolled in a transfer program, 38% enrolled in a vocational program, 1% already have a bachelor's degree or higher, 2,223 enrolled as first-time, first-year students.

Part-time:	43%	**Asian American:**	2%
Out-of-state:	1%	**Hispanic American:**	2%
Women:	56%	**Native American:**	1%
African American:	2%	**25 or older:**	29%

Transfer out. Colleges most students transferred to 2005: Drury University, Evangel University, Southwest Missouri State University.

Basis for selection. Open admission, but selective for some programs. Special requirements for some allied health programs. **Adult students:** Entrance exam policies same as for first-time freshmen.

2005-2006 Annual costs. Tuition/fees: $2,700; $3,300 out-of-district; $4,200 out-of-state. Per-credit charge: $78 in-district; $98 out-of-district; $128 out-of-state. Books/supplies: $600. Personal expenses: $1,100.

Financial aid. All financial aid based on need. Need-based aid available for part-time students. Work study available for part-time students.

Application procedures. Admission: No deadline. No application fee. Admission notification on a rolling basis. **Financial aid:** Priority date 5/1, closing date 7/1. FAFSA, institutional form required. Applicants notified on a rolling basis starting 5/16.

Academics. Special study options: Cooperative education, distance learning, dual enrollment of high school students, ESL, independent study, internships. License preparation in dental hygiene, nursing, paramedic. **Credit/placement by examination:** CLEP, IB, institutional tests. **Support services:** GED preparation, learning center, reduced course load, remedial instruction, study skills assistance, tutoring, writing center.

Majors. Agriculture: Turf management. **Business:** Accounting, business admin, hospitality admin, hotel/motel admin, office technology. **Communications:** Digital media. **Communications technology:** Graphic/printing. **Computer sciences:** Information technology, LAN/WAN management, web page design. **Engineering:** Electrical. **Engineering technology:** CAD/CADD, construction, electrical, industrial. **Family/consumer sciences:** Child development. **Health:** Dental hygiene, EMT paramedic, medical records technology, occupational therapy assistant, physical therapy assistant, respiratory therapy technology. **Liberal arts:** Arts/sciences. **Mechanic/repair:** Auto body, automotive, diesel, heating/ac/refrig, industrial. **Personal/culinary services:** Culinary arts. **Production:** Machine tool, welding. **Protective services:** Fire safety technology. **Visual/performing arts:** Graphic design.

Most popular majors. Business/marketing 19%, computer/information sciences 6%, health sciences 7%, liberal arts 50%, trade and industry 8%.

Computing on campus. 250 workstations in library, computer center. Online course registration, online library, helpline, wireless network available.

Student life. Freshman orientation: Available, $81 fee. Preregistration for classes offered. **Policies:** Freshmen permitted cars on campus. **Activities:** Student government, student newspaper, Phi Theta Kappa, National Honor Society, Women in Construction, nursing students groups, Phi Beta Lambda, national business organizations, electronics club, Society of Manufacturing Engineers.

Athletics. Team name: Eagles.

Student services. Career counseling, student employment services, financial aid counseling, on-campus daycare, personal counseling, placement for graduates. **Physically disabled:** Services for visually, speech, hearing impaired. **Transfer:** Special adviser for new students. Transfer adviser, college fairs on campus for students transferring to 4-year colleges.

Contact. Phone: (417) 447-6900 Fax: (417) 447-6906
Peter Sullivan, Director of Admissions, Ozarks Technical Community College, 1001 East Chestnut Expressway, Springfield, MO 65802

Patricia Stevens College

St. Louis, Missouri
www.patriciastevenscollege.edu **CB code: 3319**

- For-profit 2-year business and junior college
- Commuter campus in very large city
- Application essay, interview required

General. Accredited by ACICS. **Enrollment:** 177 degree-seeking undergraduates. **Degrees:** 89 associate awarded. **Location:** Downtown. **Calendar:** Quarter, extensive summer session. **Full-time faculty:** 6 total. **Part-time faculty:** 18 total. **Class size:** 95% < 20, 5% 20-39.

Student profile. Among degree-seeking undergraduates, 177 enrolled as first-time, first-year students.

Part-time:	27%	**Women:**	96%
Out-of-state:	26%	**25 or older:**	39%

Transfer out. Colleges most students transferred to 2005: Fontbonne University, Lindenwood University, Maryville University, University of Phoenix, Webster University.

Basis for selection. Open admission. **Adult students:** Entrance exam policies same as for first-time freshmen.

2006-2007 Annual costs. Tuition/fees (projected): $10,150. Per-credit charge: $195. Books included in tuition.

Financial aid. All financial aid based on need. Need-based aid available for part-time students.

Application procedures. Admission: No deadline. $15 fee. Application must be submitted on paper. Admission notification on a rolling basis. **Financial aid:** No deadline. FAFSA required. Applicants notified on a rolling basis.

Academics. Special study options: Accelerated study, double major, internships. **Credit/placement by examination:** CLEP. **Support services:** Reduced course load, study skills assistance, tutoring.

Majors. Business: Retailing. **Health:** Office assistant. **Legal studies:** Paralegal. **Visual/performing arts:** Interior design.

Most popular majors. Business/marketing 26%, health sciences 7%, legal studies 24%.

Computing on campus. 38 workstations in computer center.

Student life. Freshman orientation: Mandatory. Preregistration for classes offered. Held each quarter before start of classes. **Policies:** Dress code and attendance policies enforced. Freshmen permitted cars on campus.

Student services. Adult student services, alcohol/substance abuse counseling, career counseling, student employment services, financial aid counseling, placement for graduates. **Transfer:** Special adviser, orientation, preadmission transcript evaluation for new students.

Contact. E-mail: admissions@patriciastevenscollege.edu
Phone: (314) 421-0949 ext. 10 Toll-free number: (800) 871-0949
Fax: (314) 421-0304
John Willmon, Director of Admissions, Patricia Stevens College, 330 North Fourth Street, Suite 306, St. Louis, MO 63102

Penn Valley Community College

Kansas City, Missouri
www.mcckc.edu **CB code: 6324**

- Public 2-year community college
- Commuter campus in large city

General. Regionally accredited. **Enrollment:** 3,550 degree-seeking undergraduates; 1,077 non-degree-seeking students. **Degrees:** 369 associate awarded. **Location:** 2 miles from downtown. **Calendar:** Semester, extensive summer session. **Full-time faculty:** 101 total; 24% minority, 70% women. **Part-time faculty:** 336 total; 24% minority, 66% women. **Class size:** 59% < 20, 29% 20-39, less than 1% 40-49, less than 1% 50-99.

Student profile. Among degree-seeking undergraduates, 40% enrolled in a transfer program, 35% enrolled in a vocational program, 5% already have a bachelor's degree or higher, 785 enrolled as first-time, first-year students, 776 transferred in from other institutions.

Part-time:	64%	**Asian American:**	3%
Out-of-state:	2%	**Hispanic American:**	5%
Women:	75%	**Native American:**	1%
African American:	29%	**25 or older:**	50%

Basis for selection. Open admission, but selective for some programs. Special requirements for allied health programs. ACT or ASSET required for placement and counseling. **Homeschooled:** Statement describing home-school structure and mission, transcript of courses and grades, interview required. Students under 16 must bring portfolio to Dean of Student Services.

High school preparation. 16 units recommended. Recommended units include English 4, mathematics 3, social studies 3, science 3 and foreign language 2. One unit visual/performing arts recommended.

2006-2007 Annual costs. Tuition/fees (projected): $2,190; $3,990 out-of-district; $5,400 out-of-state. Per-credit charge: $73 in-district; $133 out-of-district; $180 out-of-state. Books/supplies: $700. Personal expenses: $1,500.

2004-2005 Financial aid. **Need-based:** 261 full-time freshmen applied for aid; 243 were judged to have need; 226 of these received aid. Average scholarship/grant was $3,060; average loan $2,253. 63% of total undergraduate aid awarded as scholarships/grants, 37% as loans/jobs. Work study available nights and for part-time students. **Non-need-based:** Awarded to 131 full-time undergraduates, including 24 freshmen. Scholarships awarded for academics, athletics, leadership.

Application procedures. **Admission:** No deadline. No application fee. Application may be submitted online. Admission notification on a rolling basis. **Financial aid:** Priority date 5/30; no closing date. FAFSA, institutional form required. Applicants notified on a rolling basis starting 4/8.

Academics. **Special study options:** Cross-registration, distance learning, dual enrollment of high school students, ESL, honors, internships, liberal arts/career combination, weekend college. Cooperative programs in allied health with Johnson County Community College. License preparation in dental hygiene, nursing, occupational therapy, paramedic, physical therapy, radiology. **Credit/placement by examination:** AP, CLEP, institutional tests. 30 credit hours maximum toward associate degree. **Support services:** GED test center, learning center, reduced course load, remedial instruction, tutoring.

Majors. **Business:** General, accounting, administrative services, business admin, fashion, office management, office technology, sales/distribution. **Computer sciences:** General. **Engineering:** General. **Family/consumer sciences:** Child care. **Health:** Dental assistant, EMT paramedic, medical radiologic technology/radiation therapy, mental health services, nursing (RN), occupational therapy assistant, physical therapy assistant, respiratory therapy technology. **Legal studies:** Paralegal. **Liberal arts:** Arts/sciences. **Mechanic/repair:** Heating/ac/refrig. **Protective services:** Corrections, criminal justice, law enforcement admin. **Visual/performing arts:** Commercial/advertising art, fashion design, graphic design, music.

Most popular majors. Health sciences 46%, liberal arts 30%, visual/performing arts 6%.

Computing on campus. 1,101 workstations in library, computer center.

Student life. **Freshman orientation:** Available. **Policies:** Freshmen permitted cars on campus. **Activities:** Jazz band, drama, music ensembles, opera, student government, student newspaper, Black student association, Los Americanos.

Athletics. NJCAA. **Intercollegiate:** Basketball M, golf M. **Team name:** Scouts.

Student services. Career counseling, student employment services, on-campus daycare, personal counseling, placement for graduates, veterans' counselor. **Physically disabled:** Services for visually, speech, hearing impaired. **Transfer:** Special adviser for new students.

Contact. Phone: (816) 759-4100 Fax: (816) 759-4161
Carroll O'Neal, Registrar, Penn Valley Community College, 3201 Southwest Trafficway, Kansas City, MO 64111-2429

Pinnacle Career Institute: Kansas City

Kansas City, Missouri
www.pcitraining.edu **CB code: 2271**

- For-profit 2-year technical college
- Large city

General. Accredited by ACCSCT. **Enrollment:** 204 degree-seeking undergraduates. **Degrees:** 138 associate awarded. **Calendar:** Quarter, limited summer session. **Full-time faculty:** 4 total. **Part-time faculty:** 17 total.

Student profile. Among degree-seeking undergraduates, 50 enrolled as first-time, first-year students.

Basis for selection. Open admission.

2005-2006 Annual costs. Tuition/fees: $7,223. Books/supplies: $965.

Application procedures. **Admission:** No deadline. $50 fee. Admission notification on a rolling basis. **Financial aid:** No deadline.

Academics. **Credit/placement by examination:** CLEP.

Contact. E-mail: Bricks@pcitraining.edu
Phone: (816) 331-5700 Fax: (816) 331-2026
John Walsh, Admissions Director, Pinnacle Career Institute: Kansas City, 1001 East 101st Terrace, Suite 325, Kansas City, MO 64131-3367

St. Charles Community College

Cottleville, Missouri
www.stchas.edu **CB code: 0168**

- Public 2-year community college
- Commuter campus in small city

General. Founded in 1986. Regionally accredited. **Enrollment:** 5,746 degree-seeking undergraduates; 1,124 non-degree-seeking students. **Degrees:** 578 associate awarded. **Location:** 35 miles from St. Louis. **Calendar:** Semester, limited summer session. **Full-time faculty:** 81 total; 20% have terminal degrees, 2% minority, 54% women. **Part-time faculty:** 348 total; 5% minority, 60% women.

Student profile. Among degree-seeking undergraduates, 83% enrolled in a transfer program, 17% enrolled in a vocational program, 1,428 enrolled as first-time, first-year students.

Part-time:	46%	**Asian American:**	2%
Women:	60%	**Hispanic American:**	2%
African American:	4%	**25 or older:**	70%

Transfer out. **Colleges most students transferred to 2005:** University of Missouri: St. Louis, Lindenwood University, University of Missouri: Columbia, Southwest Missouri State University, Maryville University.

Basis for selection. Open admission, but selective for some programs. Special requirements for nursing and allied health programs. Only 100 nursing applicants admitted every year; in-state applicants preferred. ACT scores required for admission to nursing and allied health programs; deadline August 20. ACT scores required of full-time students for placement. **Adult students:** SAT/ACT scores not required. **Homeschooled:** Transcript of courses and grades required.

High school preparation. 16 units recommended. Recommended units include English 4, mathematics 3, social studies 3, science 2, foreign language 2 and academic electives 1. One visual or performing arts recommended.

2006-2007 Annual costs. Tuition/fees (projected): $2,280; $3,360 out-of-district; $4,980 out-of-state. Per-credit charge: $76 in-district; $112 out-of-district; $166 out-of-state. Books/supplies: $900. Personal expenses: $1,500.

2004-2005 Financial aid. **Need-based:** 68% of total undergraduate aid awarded as scholarships/grants, 32% as loans/jobs. Need-based aid available for part-time students. Work study available for part-time students. **Non-need-based:** Scholarships awarded for academics, art, athletics, leadership, music/drama.

Application procedures. **Admission:** No deadline. No application fee. Application must be submitted on paper. Admission notification on a rolling basis. **Financial aid:** Priority date 6/1; no closing date. FAFSA, institutional form required. Applicants notified on a rolling basis starting 3/1; must reply within 3 week(s) of notification.

Academics. **Special study options:** Combined bachelor's/graduate degree, cross-registration, distance learning, double major, dual enrollment of high school students, ESL, independent study, internships, liberal arts/career combination, study abroad. License preparation in nursing, occupational therapy, paramedic. **Credit/placement by examination:** AP, CLEP, IB, institutional tests. 49 credit hours maximum toward associate degree. **Support services:** GED preparation and test center, learning center, preadmission summer program, remedial instruction, study skills assistance, tutoring, writing center.

Majors. **Business:** Accounting, administrative services, business admin, marketing. **Computer sciences:** General, computer graphics, programming. **Education:** Teacher assistance. **Engineering:** General. **Engineering technology:** Architectural, drafting. **Health:** Medical records technology, nursing (RN), occupational therapy assistant, substance abuse counseling. **Liberal arts:** Arts/sciences. **Protective services:** Law enforcement admin. **Public administration:** Human services. **Visual/performing arts:** Commercial/advertising art.

Most popular majors. Health sciences 14%, liberal arts 72%.

Computing on campus. 131 workstations in library, computer center, student center. Online library available.

Student life. **Freshman orientation:** Available. **Policies:** Freshmen permitted cars on campus. **Activities:** Choral groups, drama, literary magazine, music ensembles, student government, criminal justice student organization, education of young children club, math club, Phi Theta Kappa, art club, human services student organization, returning learners club, health info club, sociology & anthropology club.

Athletics. NJCAA. **Intercollegiate:** Baseball M, softball W. **Intramural:** Basketball, football (tackle) M, golf M, soccer, softball, volleyball. **Team name:** Cougars.

Student services. Adult student services, career counseling, student employment services, financial aid counseling, on-campus daycare, placement for graduates, veterans' counselor. **Physically disabled:** Services for visually, speech, hearing impaired. **Transfer:** Special adviser, orientation, pre-admission transcript evaluation for new students. Transfer adviser, college fairs on campus for students transferring to 4-year colleges.

Contact. E-mail: adm-reg@stchas.edu
Phone: (636) 922-8237 Fax: (636) 922-8236
Kathy Brockgreitens-Gober, Director of Admissions and Financial Assistance, St. Charles Community College, 4601 Mid Rivers Mall Drive, Cottleville, MO 63376

St. Louis Community College at Florissant Valley

St. Louis, Missouri
www.stlcc.edu **CB code: 6225**

- Public 2-year branch campus and community college
- Commuter campus in large city

General. Founded in 1962. Regionally accredited. **Enrollment:** 6,442 degree-seeking undergraduates. **Degrees:** 121 associate awarded. **ROTC:** Army. **Location:** 17 miles from downtown. **Calendar:** Semester, extensive summer session. **Full-time faculty:** 140 total. **Part-time faculty:** 250 total. **Special facilities:** Observatory, child development center.

Student profile.

Out-of-state:	2%	25 or older:	48%

Basis for selection. Open admission, but selective for some programs. Nursing program applicants required to pass institutional test.

2005-2006 Annual costs. Tuition/fees: $2,340; $3,090 out-of-district; $4,140 out-of-state. Per-credit charge: $78 in-district; $103 out-of-district; $138 out-of-state. Books/supplies: $800. Personal expenses: $2,000.

Application procedures. **Admission:** No deadline. No application fee. Admission notification on a rolling basis. **Financial aid:** Priority date 8/1; no closing date. FAFSA required. Applicants notified on a rolling basis starting 5/1.

Academics. **Special study options:** Cooperative education, cross-registration, distance learning, dual enrollment of high school students, ESL, exchange student, honors, independent study, internships, study abroad, teacher certification program, weekend college. **Credit/placement by examination:** CLEP, institutional tests. 49 credit hours maximum toward associate degree. **Support services:** Learning center, remedial instruction, tutoring.

Majors. **Biology:** General. **Business:** Administrative services, banking/financial services, business admin, fashion, management information systems, office technology. **Communications:** General, advertising, broadcast journalism, journalism, public relations. **Communications technology:** Graphic/printing. **Computer sciences:** General, applications programming, data processing, programming, systems analysis. **Education:** Early childhood, teacher assistance. **Engineering:** General. **Engineering technology:** Civil, computer hardware, drafting, electrical, manufacturing, mechanical. **English:** Speech/rhetoric, technical writing. **Family/consumer sciences:** Child care. **Foreign languages:** Sign language interpretation. **Health:** Predentistry, premedicine, prepharmacy. **Liberal arts:** Arts/sciences. **Math:** General. **Personal/culinary services:** Culinary arts. **Physical sciences:** Chemistry, physics. **Protective services:** Fire safety technology, police science. **Psychology:** General. **Social sciences:** General. **Visual/performing arts:** General, commercial/advertising art, dramatic, studio arts.

Student life. **Activities:** Concert band, drama, musical theater, radio station, student government, student newspaper, TV station, Black student association.

Athletics. NJCAA. **Intercollegiate:** Baseball M, basketball, cross-country, soccer, softball W, track and field, volleyball W.

Student services. Career counseling, student employment services, health services, on-campus daycare, personal counseling, placement for graduates. **Physically disabled:** Services for visually, speech, hearing impaired. **Transfer:** Special adviser, orientation for new students. Transfer adviser, college fairs on campus for students transferring to 4-year colleges.

Contact. Phone: (314) 513-4244 Fax: (314) 513-4724
Laura Sterman, Associate Dean of Admissions, St. Louis Community College at Florissant Valley, 3400 Pershall Road, St. Louis, MO 63135

St. Louis Community College at Forest Park

St. Louis, Missouri
www.stlcc.edu **CB code: 6226**

- Public 2-year community and junior college
- Commuter campus in large city

General. Founded in 1962. Regionally accredited. **Calendar:** Semester.

Annual costs/financial aid. Tuition/fees (2005-2006): $2,340; $3,090 out-of-district; $4,140 out-of-state. Books/supplies: $800. Personal expenses: $2,100. Need-based financial aid available to full-time and part-time students.

Contact. Phone: (314) 644-9127
Manager, Admissions/Registration, 5600 Oakland, St. Louis, MO 63110-1393

St. Louis Community College at Meramec

St. Louis, Missouri
www.stlcc.edu **CB code: 6430**

- Public 2-year community college
- Commuter campus in large city

General. Founded in 1963. Regionally accredited. Two off-campus sites at South County Education Center and West County Education Center. **Enrollment:** 12,130 undergraduates. **Degrees:** 912 associate awarded. **ROTC:** Army, Air Force. **Location:** 15 miles from St. Louis. **Calendar:** Semester, extensive summer session. **Full-time faculty:** 190 total. **Part-time faculty:** 500 total. **Special facilities:** Center for advanced imaging.

Student profile.

Out-of-state:	1%	25 or older:	42%

Basis for selection. Open admission, but selective for some programs. Nursing, occupational therapy assistant, physical therapist assistant, paramedic technology programs have specific admission requirements. SAT or ACT score used to waive Accuplacer Test. Interview required for some health programs.

High school preparation. 22 units recommended. Recommended units include English 4, mathematics 2, social studies 3 and science 2.

2005-2006 Annual costs. Tuition/fees: $2,340; $3,090 out-of-district; $4,140 out-of-state. Per-credit charge: $78 in-district; $103 out-of-district; $138 out-of-state. Books/supplies: $800. Personal expenses: $2,100.

Financial aid. **Need-based:** Need-based aid available for part-time students.

Application procedures. **Admission:** Priority date 8/1; no deadline. No application fee. Application may be submitted online. Admission notification on a rolling basis beginning on or about 3/1. **Financial aid:** Closing date 6/30. FAFSA, institutional form required. Applicants notified on a rolling basis starting 2/1.

Academics. **Special study options:** Accelerated study, cross-registration, distance learning, dual enrollment of high school students, honors, independent study, internships, study abroad. **Credit/placement by examination:** AP, CLEP, institutional tests. 49 credit hours maximum toward associate degree. **Support services:** Learning center, pre-admission summer program, reduced course load, remedial instruction, tutoring.

Majors. **Agriculture:** Horticultural science, ornamental horticulture. **Architecture:** Interior. **Business:** General, accounting, administrative services, banking/financial services, management information systems, office technology, office/clerical, real estate. **Communications:** General. **Computer sciences:** General, applications programming, data processing. **Education:** General, elementary, secondary. **Engineering:** General. **Engineering technology:** Architectural, electrical. **Health:** EMT paramedic, occupational therapy assistant, physical therapy assistant. **Interdisciplinary:** Biological/

physical sciences. **Legal studies:** Court reporting, legal secretary, paralegal. **Liberal arts:** Arts/sciences. **Math:** General. **Protective services:** Criminal justice, police science. **Public administration:** Social work. **Social sciences:** General. **Transportation:** Air traffic control. **Visual/performing arts:** Commercial/advertising art, photography, studio arts.

Computing on campus. 420 workstations in library, computer center.

Student life. Freshman orientation: Mandatory. Preregistration for classes offered. **Activities:** Bands, choral groups, drama, literary magazine, music ensembles, musical theater, student government, student newspaper, symphony orchestra, Phi Theta Kappa, international club, Intervarsity Christian Fellowship, horticulture club, bridge club, engineering club, photo club, scuba club, Student Ambassadors.

Athletics. NJCAA. **Intercollegiate:** Baseball M, basketball M, soccer, softball W, volleyball W, wrestling M. **Intramural:** Basketball, volleyball. **Team name:** Magic.

Student services. Career counseling, student employment services, financial aid counseling, health services, on-campus daycare, personal counseling, placement for graduates, veterans' counselor. **Physically disabled:** Services for visually, speech, hearing impaired. **Learning disabled:** Comprehensive services available. **Transfer:** Special adviser for new students. Transfer adviser, college fairs on campus for students transferring to 4-year colleges.

Contact. Phone: (314) 984-7601 Fax: (314) 984-7051
Jean Campbell, Associate Dean of Admission, St. Louis Community College at Meramec, 11333 Big Bend Boulevard, Kirkwood, MO 63122-5799

Sanford-Brown College
Fenton, Missouri
www.sbcfenton.com **CB code: 3320**

- For-profit 2-year business and health science college
- Commuter campus in small town

General. Accredited by ACICS. **Calendar:** Continuous.

Annual costs/financial aid. Tuition programs range from $14,000-$32,000. Fees vary depending on program. Books/supplies: $1,714. Need-based financial aid available to full-time and part-time students.

Contact. Phone: (636) 349-4900
Dean, 1345 Smizer Mill Road, Fenton, MO 63026-1583

Sanford-Brown College: Hazelwood
Hazelwood, Missouri
www.sanford-brown.edu **CB code: 3321**

- For-profit 2-year business and technical college
- Large town

General. Accredited by ACICS. **Calendar:** Continuous.

Annual costs/financial aid. Tuition programs range from $14,000-$32,000. Fees vary depending on program. Books/supplies: $909.

Contact. Phone: (314) 731-1101
Director of Admissions, 75 Village Square, Hazelwood, MO 63042

Sanford-Brown College: St. Charles
St. Charles, Missouri
www.sbcstcharles.com **CB code: 3323**

- For-profit 2-year business and technical college
- Small city

General. Accredited by ACICS. **Calendar:** Continuous.

Annual costs/financial aid. Tuition programs range from $14,000-$32,000. Fees vary depending on program. Books/supplies: $972.

Contact. Phone: (636) 949-2620
Director of Admissions, 3555 Franks Drive, St. Charles, MO 63301

Southeast Missouri Hospital College of Nursing and Health Sciences
Cape Girardeau, Missouri
www.sehosp.org **CB code: 4459**

- Private 2-year health science and nursing college
- Large town

General. Enrollment: 150 degree-seeking undergraduates. **Degrees:** 35 associate awarded. **Calendar:** Semester.

Basis for selection. Open admission, but selective for some programs.

Application procedures. Admission: Closing date 2/15. $40 fee.

Academics. Credit/placement by examination: AP, CLEP.

Contact. E-mail: dpugh@sehosp.org
Phone: (573) 334-6825 ext. 23
Don Pugh, Registrar/Enrollment Counselor, Southeast Missouri Hospital College of Nursing and Health Sciences, 2001 William Street, Second Floor, Cape Girardeau, MO 63703

State Fair Community College
Sedalia, Missouri
www.sfccmo.edu **CB code: 6709**

- Public 2-year community college
- Commuter campus in large town

General. Founded in 1966. Regionally accredited. **Enrollment:** 2,652 degree-seeking undergraduates; 263 non-degree-seeking students. **Degrees:** 418 associate awarded. **Location:** 78 miles from Kansas City. **Calendar:** Semester, limited summer session. **Full-time faculty:** 63 total; 100% have terminal degrees, 5% minority, 51% women. **Part-time faculty:** 136 total; 100% have terminal degrees, 4% minority, 64% women. **Special facilities:** Museum.

Student profile. Among degree-seeking undergraduates, 69% enrolled in a transfer program, 31% enrolled in a vocational program, 732 enrolled as first-time, first-year students, 186 transferred in from other institutions.

Part-time:	41%	**Asian American:**	1%
Out-of-state:	2%	**Hispanic American:**	3%
Women:	59%	**Native American:**	1%
African American:	6%	**Live on campus:**	3%

Transfer out. Colleges most students transferred to 2005: Central Missouri State University, Southwest Missouri State University.

Basis for selection. Open admission, but selective for some programs. Some health programs have special requirements. ASSET may be accepted. Mechanical knowledge test required of all auto mechanics program students. Interview for radiologic technology program applicants. **Adult students:** ACT, ASSET, or COMPASS score(s) that are current within the last five years required of full-time students and all degree seeking students whether full or part-time. **Learning Disabled:** Students are encouraged to establish documentation at least two weeks prior to the first day of each semester in order to receive accommodations.

2005-2006 Annual costs. Tuition/fees: $2,100; $2,910 out-of-district; $4,500 out-of-state. Per-credit charge: $60 in-district; $87 out-of-district; $140 out-of-state. Books/supplies: $900. Personal expenses: $750.

2004-2005 Financial aid. All financial aid based on need. 47% of total undergraduate aid awarded as scholarships/grants, 53% as loans/jobs. Need-based aid available for part-time students. Work study available nights and weekends.

Application procedures. Admission: No deadline. $25 fee, may be waived for applicants with need. Application must be submitted on paper. Admission notification on a rolling basis. **Financial aid:** Priority date 7/1; no closing date. FAFSA required. Applicants notified on a rolling basis starting 7/15; must reply within 3 week(s) of notification.

Academics. Special study options: Cooperative education, cross-registration, distance learning, dual enrollment of high school students, ESL, internships, study abroad. License preparation in dental hygiene, nursing, paramedic, radiology, real estate. **Credit/placement by examination:** AP, CLEP, institutional tests. 30 credit hours maximum toward associate degree. Students may earn a maximum of 30 hours in combination from credit by exam or nontraditional credit. **Support services:** GED preparation, learning center, reduced course load, remedial instruction, study skills assistance, tutoring, writing center.

Majors. **Agriculture:** Business, horticulture. **Business:** Accounting, administrative services, banking/financial services, business admin, management information systems, special products marketing. **Communications:** Journalism. **Computer sciences:** General, applications programming, networking, programming, web page design. **Construction:** Site management. **Education:** Voc/tech. **Engineering technology:** CAD/CADD, electrical. **Family/consumer sciences:** Child care. **Health:** Dental hygiene, medical secretary, nursing (RN), office admin, radiologic technology/medical imaging. **Interdisciplinary:** Accounting/computer science. **Legal studies:** Court reporting, legal secretary. **Liberal arts:** Arts/sciences. **Mechanic/repair:** Automotive, electronics/electrical, industrial, industrial electronics. **Production:** Machine tool. **Protective services:** Firefighting, police science.

Most popular majors. Business/marketing 10%, computer/information sciences 10%, health sciences 14%, liberal arts 53%.

Computing on campus. 85 workstations in dormitories, library, computer center, student center. Dormitories linked to campus network. Commuter students can connect to campus network. Online course registration, helpline, repair service, wireless network available.

Student life. **Freshman orientation:** Available. Preregistration for classes offered. **Policies:** Freshmen permitted cars on campus. **Housing:** Coed dorms, substance-free housing available. $100 fully refundable deposit, deadline 7/15. **Activities:** Jazz band, choral groups, dance, drama, music ensembles, student government.

Athletics. NJCAA. **Intercollegiate:** Basketball, volleyball W. **Intramural:** Bowling, softball, volleyball. **Team name:** Roadrunners.

Student services. Career counseling, services for economically disadvantaged, student employment services, financial aid counseling, minority student services, personal counseling, placement for graduates, veterans' counselor, women's services. **Physically disabled:** Services for visually, speech, hearing impaired. **Transfer:** Special adviser, orientation, preadmission transcript evaluation for new students. Transfer adviser, college fairs on campus for students transferring to 4-year colleges.

Contact. E-mail: mheck@sfccmo.edu
Phone: (660) 530-5800 ext. 221 Toll-free number: (877) 311-7322
Fax: (660) 530-5546
Matthew Heck, Director of Admissions, State Fair Community College, 3201 West 16th Street, Sedalia, MO 65301-2199

Texas County Technical Institute
Houston, Missouri

- Private 2-year nursing and technical college
- Small town

General. **Calendar:** Semester.

Annual costs/financial aid. Tuition varies by program, $145 to $310 per credit-hour.

Contact. Phone: (417) 967-5466
6915 South Hwy 63, Houston, MO 65483

Three Rivers Community College
Poplar Bluff, Missouri
www.trcc.edu **CB code: 6836**

- Public 2-year community college
- Commuter campus in large town

General. Founded in 1966. Regionally accredited. Selected courses offered at area high schools, vocational schools and other off-campus facilities. **Enrollment:** 2,597 degree-seeking undergraduates; 342 non-degree-seeking students. **Degrees:** 395 associate awarded. **Location:** 160 miles from St. Louis. **Calendar:** Semester, limited summer session. **Full-time faculty:** 56 total. **Part-time faculty:** 72 total.

Student profile. Among degree-seeking undergraduates, 73% enrolled in a transfer program, 27% enrolled in a vocational program, 1,599 enrolled as first-time, first-year students.

Part-time:	39%	**25 or older:**	36%
Out-of-state:	2%	**Live on campus:**	6%
Women:	67%		

Transfer out. **Colleges most students transferred to 2005:** Southeast Missouri State University, Arkansas State University, Southwest Missouri State University.

Basis for selection. Open admission, but selective for some programs. Special requirements for allied health programs and nursing. **Adult students:** Entrance exam policies same as for first-time freshmen.

2005-2006 Annual costs. Tuition/fees: $2,080; $3,190 out-of-district; $3,910 out-of-state. Per-credit charge: $61 in-district; $98 out-of-district; $122 out-of-state. Book rental $12 per book. Refundable book deposit fee $25 per semester. Lab fees vary per course. Books/supplies: $400. Personal expenses: $1,040.

Financial aid. **Need-based:** Need-based aid available for part-time students. Work study available for part-time students. **Non-need-based:** Scholarships awarded for academics, athletics, state residency.

Application procedures. **Admission:** No deadline. $20 fee. Application may be submitted online. Admission notification on a rolling basis. **Financial aid:** Priority date 5/1; no closing date. FAFSA, institutional form required. Applicants notified on a rolling basis starting 6/1; must reply within 2 week(s) of notification.

Academics. **Special study options:** Accelerated study, distance learning, dual enrollment of high school students, independent study, internships, liberal arts/career combination. Bachelor's degree programs available on campus. License preparation in nursing, paramedic. **Credit/placement by examination:** AP, CLEP. 30 credit hours maximum toward associate degree. **Support services:** GED test center, learning center, remedial instruction, study skills assistance, tutoring, writing center.

Majors. **Agriculture:** Business. **Biology:** General. **Business:** Accounting, administrative services, entrepreneurial studies, management information systems, marketing. **Education:** General. **Engineering technology:** Civil, drafting. **English:** Speech/rhetoric. **Foreign languages:** General. **Health:** Clinical lab technology, nursing (RN), premedicine, prepharmacy, preveterinary. **History:** General. **Legal studies:** Prelaw. **Liberal arts:** Arts/sciences, library science. **Math:** General. **Parks/recreation:** Health/fitness. **Philosophy/religion:** Philosophy. **Physical sciences:** Chemistry. **Protective services:** Police science. **Psychology:** General. **Social sciences:** Economics, geography, political science, sociology. **Visual/performing arts:** Studio arts.

Most popular majors. Business/marketing 26%, health sciences 12%, liberal arts 49%.

Computing on campus. 100 workstations in dormitories, library, computer center. Dormitories wired for high-speed internet access.

Student life. **Freshman orientation:** Available. Preregistration for classes offered. Mini orientation activities are held for incoming freshmen during the registration process. Orientation for new students is offered at the beginning of each semester for students, family and friends. **Policies:** Freshmen permitted cars on campus. **Housing:** Apartments, substance-free housing available. **Activities:** Concert band, choral groups, drama, music ensembles, student government, Student Senate, Phi Theta Kappa, Marketing Management Association,.

Athletics. NJCAA. **Intercollegiate:** Baseball M, basketball, softball W, volleyball W. **Intramural:** Baseball M, basketball, volleyball W. **Team name:** Raiders.

Student services. Career counseling, student employment services, on-campus daycare, placement for graduates, veterans' counselor. **Transfer:** Special adviser, orientation for new students. Transfer adviser, college fairs on campus for students transferring to 4-year colleges.

Contact. E-mail: mfields@trcc.edu
Phone: (573) 840-9605 ext. 605 Toll-free number: (877) 879-8722
Fax: (573) 840-9058
Marcia Fields, Director of Admissions, Three Rivers Community College, 2080 Three Rivers Boulevard, Poplar Bluff, MO 63901-1308

Vatterott College
St. Ann, Missouri
www.vatterott-college.edu **CB code: 2507**

- For-profit 2-year technical college
- Large city
- Interview required

General. Accredited by ACCSCT. Technical/business college for adults emphasizing hands-on training. **Enrollment:** 669 undergraduates. **Degrees:** 17 bachelor's, 137 associate awarded. **Location:** 20 miles from St. Louis, 310 miles from Chicago. **Calendar:** Continuous. **Full-time faculty:** 15 total. **Part-time faculty:** 5 total.

Basis for selection. High school achievement, interview, and institutional testing used to determine admission.

2005-2006 Annual costs. Costs vary per program. 170-week bachelor's degree: tuition $50,713, required fees $3,240, books and supplies $2,229; total cost $56,295 including taxes. Associate degree programs (90 weeks): tuition $25,913; required fees range from $1,250 to $1,850; books and supplies range from $752 to $1,548; total costs up to $28,847 including taxes. Diploma programs (60 weeks): tuition $16,935; required fees range from $900 to $1,450; books and supplies range from $587 to $1,400; total costs up to $19,196 including taxes.

Application procedures. Admission: No deadline. No application fee. Admission notification on a rolling basis. **Financial aid:** No deadline. Institutional form required.

Academics. Credit/placement by examination: CLEP. **Support services:** Remedial instruction, tutoring.

Majors. Computer sciences: Programming, system admin. **Construction:** Electrician. **Engineering technology:** Drafting. **Mechanic/repair:** Heating/ac/refrig. **Production:** Welding.

Student life. Activities: Literary magazine, TV station.

Contact. E-mail: adm@vatterot-college.edu
Phone: (314) 428-5900 Toll-free number: (888) 370-7955
Fax: (314) 428-5956
Jennifer Commuso, Director of Admissions, Vatterott College, 3925 Industrial Drive, St. Ann, MO 63074-1807

Vatterott College: Kansas City

Kansas City, Missouri
www.vatterott-college.edu **CB code: 2893**

- For-profit 2-year technical college
- Large city

General. Accredited by ACCSCT. **Calendar:** Continuous.

Contact. Phone: (816) 252-3997
Campus Co-Director, 8955 East 38th Terrace, Kansas City, MO 64129

Vatterott College: O'Fallon

O'Fallon, Missouri

- Private 2-year branch campus and technical college
- Large city

General. Accredited by ACCSCT. **Calendar:** Quarter.

Contact. Phone: (636) 978-9488
927 East Terra Lane, O'Fallon, MO 63366

Vatterott College: St. Joseph

St. Joseph, Missouri
www.vatterott-college.edu **CB code: 2896**

- For-profit 2-year branch campus and technical college
- Commuter campus in small city

General. Accredited by ACCSCT. **Enrollment:** 240 degree-seeking undergraduates. **Degrees:** 57 associate awarded. **Location:** 50 miles from Kansas City. **Calendar:** Quarter, extensive summer session. **Full-time faculty:** 18 total; 67% women. **Part-time faculty:** 3 total; 100% women.

Basis for selection. Open admission.

2005-2006 Annual costs. Personal expenses: $1,288.

Financial aid. Need-based: Need-based aid available for part-time students.

Application procedures. Admission: No deadline. No application fee. Application may be submitted online. **Financial aid:** No deadline. FAFSA required.

Academics. Credit/placement by examination: CLEP, institutional tests. 36 credit hours maximum toward associate degree. **Support services:** Tutoring.

Majors. Computer sciences: General. **Engineering technology:** Drafting. **Health:** Medical secretary.

Student life. Freshman orientation: Mandatory. Preregistration for classes offered. Held first day of classes. Students are briefed on policies and procedures and are introduced to the directors, career services, instructors and financial aid paperwork. **Policies:** Freshmen permitted cars on campus.

Student services. Career counseling, student employment services, financial aid counseling, placement for graduates, veterans' counselor.

Contact. E-mail: sarah.griffin@vatterott-college.edu
Phone: (816) 364-5399 Toll-free number: (800) 282-5327
Fax: (816) 364-1593
Maggie Franz, Admissions Representative, Vatterott College: St. Joseph, 3131 Frederick Avenue, St. Joseph, MO 64506

Vatterott College: Springfield

Springfield, Missouri
www.vatterott-college.edu **CB code: 2895**

- For-profit 2-year branch campus and technical college
- Commuter campus in small city
- Application essay, interview required

General. Accredited by ACCSCT. **Enrollment:** 64 degree-seeking undergraduates. **Degrees:** 25 associate awarded. **Calendar:** Quarter. **Full-time faculty:** 15 total. **Part-time faculty:** 6 total.

Student profile. Among degree-seeking undergraduates, 100% enrolled in a vocational program, 1% already have a bachelor's degree or higher.

Basis for selection. Open admission, but selective for some programs. **Adult students:** SAT/ACT scores not required. **Homeschooled:** Transcript of courses and grades required.

2006-2007 Annual costs. Tuition/fees (projected): $9,410. Books/supplies: $752. Personal expenses: $2,289.

Financial aid. All financial aid based on need.

Application procedures. Admission: No deadline. No application fee. Application must be submitted on paper. Admission notification on a rolling basis. **Financial aid:** No deadline. FAFSA required.

Academics. Credit/placement by examination: CLEP, institutional tests. 36 credit hours maximum toward associate degree. **Support services:** Tutoring.

Majors. Computer sciences: System admin, web page design. **Engineering technology:** CAD/CADD. **Health:** Medical assistant, pharmacy assistant. **Legal studies:** Paralegal.

Most popular majors. Computer/information sciences 75%, engineering/engineering technologies 20%.

Computing on campus. 2 workstations in library.

Student life. Freshman orientation: Mandatory. Preregistration for classes offered. Held the week before class term is scheduled to start.

Student services. Adult student services, student employment services, financial aid counseling, placement for graduates, veterans' counselor.

Contact. E-mail: kevin.asberry@vatterott-college.edu
Phone: (417) 831-8116 Toll-free number: (800) 766-5829
Fax: (417) 831-5099
Kevin Asberry, Director of Admissions, Vatterott College: Springfield, 3850 South Campbell, Springfield, MO 65807

Vatterott College: Sunset Hills

Sunset Hills, Missouri
www.vatterott-college.com **CB code: 2898**

- For-profit 2-year branch campus and technical college
- Very large city

General. Accredited by ACCSCT. **Calendar:** Continuous.

Annual costs/financial aid. Costs vary per program. 170-week bachelor's degree: tuition $53,742, required fees $2,100, books and supplies $2,931; total cost $58,846 including taxes. Associate degree programs (90 weeks): tuition ranges from $19,800 to $26,950; required fees $1,375; books and supplies range from $842 to $1,696; total costs up to $28,797 including taxes. Diploma programs (60 weeks): tuition ranges from $13,200 to $17,612; required fees $900; books and supplies range from $532 to $1,438; total costs up to $19,755 including taxes.

Contact. Phone: (314) 843-4200
Director, 12970 Maurer Industrial Drive, Sunset Hills, MO 63127

Wentworth Military Junior College

Lexington, Missouri
www.wma1880.org **CB code: 6934**

- Private 2-year junior and military college
- Commuter campus in small town

General. Founded in 1880. Regionally accredited. **Location:** 40 miles from Independence. **Calendar:** Semester.

Annual costs/financial aid. Tuition/fees (2005-2006): $11,500. Uniform: $2,150 for men and women. Room/board: $4,700. Books/supplies: $450.

Contact. Phone: (660) 259-2221
Director of Admissions, 1880 Washington Avenue, Lexington, MO 64067-1799

Montana

Blackfeet Community College
Browning, Montana
www.bfcc.org **CB code: 0379**

- Public 2-year community college
- Small town

General. Founded in 1976. Regionally accredited. Tribally controlled college located on Blackfeet Indian reservation. **Enrollment:** 490 degree-seeking undergraduates. **Degrees:** 80 associate awarded. **Location:** 126 miles from Great Falls. **Calendar:** Semester, limited summer session. **Full-time faculty:** 20 total. **Part-time faculty:** 10 total.

Student profile. Among degree-seeking undergraduates, 99 enrolled as first-time, first-year students.

Part-time:	14%	**Women:**	59%
Out-of-state:	2%		

Basis for selection. Open admission. **Homeschooled:** State high school equivalency certificate required.

2005-2006 Annual costs. Tuition/fees: $2,000. Per-credit charge: $69. Books/supplies: $600. Personal expenses: $1,200.

Financial aid. Need-based: Need-based aid available for part-time students.

Application procedures. Admission: No deadline. $20 fee. Application must be submitted on paper. Admission notification on a rolling basis. **Financial aid:** No deadline. FAFSA, institutional form required.

Academics. Special study options: Distance learning, internships. 2-2 teacher training program with University of Montana. **Credit/placement by examination:** CLEP. **Support services:** GED preparation and test center, pre-admission summer program, remedial instruction, tutoring.

Majors. Business: Business admin. **Education:** General, early childhood. **Health:** Health services. **Liberal arts:** Humanities.

Computing on campus. 5 workstations in library, computer center, student center.

Student life. Activities: Literary magazine, student newspaper.

Athletics. Intramural: Basketball.

Student services. Career counseling, student employment services, personal counseling, placement for graduates. **Transfer:** Special adviser, orientation for new students. Transfer adviser for students transferring to 4-year colleges.

Contact. Phone: (406) 338-5421 ext. 243 Toll-free number: (800) 549-7457 Fax: (406) 338-3272
Deana McNabb, Registrar/Admissions Officer, Blackfeet Community College, Highway 2 & 89, PO Box 819, Browning, MT 59417

Chief Dull Knife College
Lame Deer, Montana
www.cdkc.edu **CB code: 5938**

- Public 2-year junior college
- Rural community

General. Regionally accredited. **Enrollment:** 110 full-time, degree-seeking students. **Degrees:** 26 associate awarded. **Location:** 110 miles from Billings. **Calendar:** Semester, limited summer session. **Full-time faculty:** 13 total. **Part-time faculty:** 31 total.

Basis for selection. Open admission.

2005-2006 Annual costs. Tuition/fees: $2,610. Per-credit charge: $90. Books/supplies: $850. Personal expenses: $800.

Financial aid. Need-based: Need-based aid available for part-time students. Work study available nights and for part-time students.

Application procedures. Admission: No deadline. No application fee. Admission notification on a rolling basis. **Financial aid:** No deadline. FAFSA, institutional form required. Applicants notified on a rolling basis; must reply within 2 week(s) of notification.

Academics. Special study options: Cooperative education, double major, internships. **Credit/placement by examination:** CLEP, institutional tests. 9 credit hours maximum toward associate degree. **Support services:** Learning center, remedial instruction.

Computing on campus. 25 workstations in computer center.

Student life. Activities: Student government, student newspaper.

Athletics. Intramural: Basketball.

Student services. Career counseling, on-campus daycare, personal counseling, veterans' counselor. **Transfer:** Special adviser, orientation for new students. Transfer adviser for students transferring to 4-year colleges.

Contact. Phone: (406) 477-6215 Fax: (406) 477-6219
Brooke Gondara, Dean of Student Affairs, Chief Dull Knife College, Box 98, Lame Deer, MT 59043

Dawson Community College
Glendive, Montana
www.dawson.edu **CB code: 4280**

- Public 2-year community college
- Commuter campus in small town

General. Founded in 1940. Regionally accredited. **Enrollment:** 436 degree-seeking undergraduates; 113 non-degree-seeking students. **Degrees:** 90 associate awarded. **Location:** 220 miles from Billings, 100 miles from Dickinson, North Dakota. **Calendar:** Semester, limited summer session. **Full-time faculty:** 33 total. **Part-time faculty:** 25 total.

Student profile. Among degree-seeking undergraduates, 55% enrolled in a transfer program, 45% enrolled in a vocational program, 3% already have a bachelor's degree or higher, 125 enrolled as first-time, first-year students.

Part-time:	14%	**Hispanic American:**	1%
Out-of-state:	15%	**Native American:**	5%
Women:	53%	**International:**	1%
African American:	2%	**Live on campus:**	48%

Transfer out. Colleges most students transferred to 2005: Dickinson State University, Montana State University-Bozeman, Montana State University-Billings, University of Montana.

Basis for selection. Open admission.

2005-2006 Annual costs. Tuition/fees: $2,324; $3,195 out-of-district; $6,854 out-of-state. Per-credit charge: $44 in-district; $75 out-of-district; $205 out-of-state. Western Undergraduate Exchange tuition: $112 per credit hour, $3,155 full-time. Books/supplies: $660. Personal expenses: $1,048.

Financial aid. Need-based: Work study available nights, weekends and for part-time students. **Non-need-based:** Scholarships awarded for academics, art, athletics, music/drama.

Application procedures. Admission: No deadline. $30 fee. Admission notification on a rolling basis. **Financial aid:** Priority date 3/1; no closing date. FAFSA required. Applicants notified on a rolling basis starting 5/15; must reply within 2 week(s) of notification.

Academics. Special study options: Distance learning, double major, dual enrollment of high school students, independent study, internships. **Credit/placement by examination:** CLEP, institutional tests. 15 credit hours maximum toward associate degree. **Support services:** GED preparation and test center, learning center, reduced course load, remedial instruction, study skills assistance, tutoring.

Majors. Agriculture: Business, equestrian studies, farm/ranch, power machinery. **Business:** General, administrative services. **Computer sciences:** General, vendor certification. **Education:** Early childhood. **Health:** Medical transcription, substance abuse counseling. **Liberal arts:** Arts/sciences. **Mechanic/repair:** Automotive. **Protective services:** Police science.

Computing on campus. 70 workstations in dormitories, library, computer center. Dormitories wired for high-speed internet access and linked to campus network.

Student life. Freshman orientation: Mandatory. Preregistration for classes offered. Held during June and July. **Policies:** Freshmen permitted cars on campus. **Housing:** Coed dorms available. $150 deposit. Student dormitories include kitchen facilities. **Activities:** Bands, choral groups, drama, music ensembles, musical theater, student government, human services club, law enforcement club, Intervarsity Christian Fellowship.

Athletics. NJCAA. **Intercollegiate:** Baseball M, basketball, rodeo, softball W. **Intramural:** Basketball, bowling, golf, racquetball, softball, table tennis, tennis, volleyball. **Team name:** Buccaneers.

Student services. Adult student services, career counseling, student employment services, placement for graduates, veterans' counselor. **Physically disabled:** Services for visually, speech, hearing impaired. **Transfer:** Special adviser, orientation, pre-admission transcript evaluation for new students. College fairs on campus for students transferring to 4-year colleges.

Contact. E-mail: myers@dawson.edu
Phone: (406) 377-9410 Toll-free number: (800) 821-8320
Fax: (406) 377-8132
Jolene Myers, Director of Admissions, Dawson Community College, 300 College Drive, Glendive, MT 59330

Flathead Valley Community College

Kalispell, Montana
www.fvcc.edu **CB code: 4317**

- Public 2-year community college
- Commuter campus in large town

General. Founded in 1967. Regionally accredited. **Enrollment:** 1,337 degree-seeking undergraduates. **Degrees:** 298 associate awarded. **Location:** 250 miles from Spokane, Washington. **Calendar:** Semester, limited summer session. **Full-time faculty:** 42 total. **Part-time faculty:** 100 total. **Class size:** 78% < 20, 22% 20-39. **Partnerships:** Formal partnerships with Tech Prep and Running Start programs with area high schools.

Student profile. Among degree-seeking undergraduates, 60% enrolled in a transfer program, 40% enrolled in a vocational program, 270 enrolled as first-time, first-year students, 126 transferred in from other institutions.

Out-of-state:	2%	**Native American:**	2%
Asian American:	1%	**International:**	1%
Hispanic American:	2%	**25 or older:**	49%

Transfer out. Colleges most students transferred to 2005: University of Montana, Montana State University - Bozeman.

Basis for selection. Open admission. ASSET and COMPASS used for placement purposes. **Adult students:** Entrance exam policies same as for first-time freshmen. **Homeschooled:** Applicants must have GED or ASSET test scores.

2005-2006 Annual costs. Tuition/fees: $2,349; $3,466 out-of-district; $7,755 out-of-state. Per-credit charge: $82 in-district; $130 out-of-district; $283 out-of-state. Books/supplies: $600. Personal expenses: $900.

2004-2005 Financial aid. Need-based: 76% of total undergraduate aid awarded as scholarships/grants, 24% as loans/jobs. Need-based aid available for part-time students. Work study available for part-time students. **Non-need-based:** Scholarships awarded for academics, athletics.

Application procedures. Admission: No deadline. $15 fee. Application must be submitted on paper. Admission notification on a rolling basis. **Financial aid:** Priority date 3/1; no closing date. FAFSA required. Applicants notified by 4/15; must reply within 2 week(s) of notification.

Academics. Special study options: Distance learning, dual enrollment of high school students, independent study, internships, liberal arts/career combination. **Credit/placement by examination:** CLEP, institutional tests. 12 AP credits allowed toward associate degree. **Support services:** GED preparation and test center, learning center, reduced course load, remedial instruction, study skills assistance, tutoring, writing center.

Majors. Business: General, accounting, management information systems, marketing, office technology. **Conservation:** Management/policy. **Engineering:** General. **Engineering technology:** Surveying. **Health:** Health care admin, health services, medical assistant, medical records technology, medical secretary, medical transcription, office admin, office assistant, office computer specialist, receptionist, substance abuse counseling. **Legal studies:** Legal secretary. **Liberal arts:** Arts/sciences, humanities. **Mechanic/repair:** Watch/jewelry. **Protective services:** Law enforcement admin. **Public administration:** Human services.

Computing on campus. 175 workstations in library, computer center.

Student life. Freshman orientation: Available, $10 fee. 4 half-day summer advising and registration programs. **Activities:** Drama, student government, student newspaper, Phi Theta Kappa, veterans organization, forestry club, campus ministry group, Bitta Club (Native American), human service club, international student association.

Athletics. NJCAA. **Intercollegiate:** Cross-country, soccer M. **Intramural:** Badminton, basketball, football (tackle) M, softball, table tennis, tennis, volleyball.

Student services. Adult student services, career counseling, student employment services, financial aid counseling, health services, personal counseling, placement for graduates, veterans' counselor. **Physically disabled:** Services for visually, hearing impaired. **Transfer:** Special adviser, orientation, pre-admission transcript evaluation for new students. Transfer adviser for students transferring to 4-year colleges.

Contact. E-mail: mstoltz@fvcc.edu
Phone: (406) 756-3846 Toll-free number: (800) 313-3822
Fax: (406) 756-3965
Marlene Stoltz, Admissions and Records Coordinator, Flathead Valley Community College, 777 Grandview Drive, Kalispell, MT 59901

Fort Belknap College

Harlem, Montana
www.fbcc.edu **CB code: 5971**

- Public 2-year community college
- Commuter campus in rural community

General. Regionally accredited. **Enrollment:** 144 degree-seeking undergraduates; 14 non-degree-seeking students. **Degrees:** 11 associate awarded. **Location:** On Fort Belknap Reservation. **Calendar:** Semester. **Full-time faculty:** 8 total. **Part-time faculty:** 10 total. **Special facilities:** Native American cultural center.

Student profile. Among degree-seeking undergraduates, 6% enrolled in a transfer program, 38 enrolled as first-time, first-year students, 4 transferred in from other institutions.

Part-time:	45%	**Women:**	26%

Transfer out. 20% of students enrolled in the transfer program go on to 4-year colleges.

Basis for selection. Open admission. **Adult students:** Test for Adult Basic Education (TABE) required. **Homeschooled:** Transcript of courses and grades, state high school equivalency certificate required.

2006-2007 Annual costs. Tuition/fees (projected): $2,410. Per-credit charge: $70. Books/supplies: $910. Personal expenses: $960.

Application procedures. Admission: No deadline. $10 fee. Admission notification on a rolling basis. **Financial aid:** No deadline. Applicants notified on a rolling basis.

Academics. Special study options: Combined bachelor's/graduate degree, dual enrollment of high school students. **Credit/placement by examination:** CLEP. **Support services:** GED preparation, learning center, tutoring.

Majors. Area/ethnic studies: Native American. **Business:** General. **Computer sciences:** Data processing. **Conservation:** Management/policy. **Education:** Elementary. **Health:** Substance abuse counseling. **Liberal arts:** Arts/sciences. **Public administration:** Human services.

Student life. Freshman orientation: Mandatory. **Activities:** Student government.

Student services. Career counseling, financial aid counseling.

Contact. Phone: (406) 353-2607 Fax: (406) 353-2898
Dixie Brockie, Registrar/Admissions Officer, Fort Belknap College, Box 159, Harlem, MT 59526-0159

Fort Peck Community College

Poplar, Montana
www.fpcc.edu **CB code: 5972**

- Public 2-year community college
- Commuter campus in small town

General. Regionally accredited. Tribally controlled college. **Enrollment:** 416 degree-seeking undergraduates. **Degrees:** 35 associate awarded. **Location:** 70 miles from Williston, North Dakota, 300 miles from Billings. **Calendar:** Semester, limited summer session. **Full-time faculty:** 19 total. **Part-time faculty:** 12 total. **Special facilities:** Individual student science lab stations.

Transfer out. Colleges most students transferred to 2005: Rocky Mountain College.

Basis for selection. Open admission. Interview recommended.

2005-2006 Annual costs. Tuition/fees: $1,840. Per-credit charge: $60. Books/supplies: $500. Personal expenses: $2,000.

Financial aid. Need-based: Need-based aid available for part-time students. Work study available nights and for part-time students.

Application procedures. Admission: Closing date 9/16. $15 fee, may be waived for applicants with need. Admission notification on a rolling basis. **Financial aid:** No deadline. FAFSA, institutional form required. Applicants notified on a rolling basis; must reply within 2 week(s) of notification.

Academics. Special study options: Distance learning, double major, dual enrollment of high school students, independent study, internships, teacher certification program. **Credit/placement by examination:** CLEP. **Support services:** GED preparation and test center, learning center, remedial instruction, study skills assistance, tutoring.

Majors. Area/ethnic studies: Native American. **Biology:** Biomedical sciences. **Business:** General, administrative services, business admin. **Computer sciences:** Computer graphics, data processing. **Conservation:** General, management/policy. **Education:** General, science. **Health:** Substance abuse counseling. **Mechanic/repair:** Automotive. **Public administration:** Human services. **Visual/performing arts:** Studio arts.

Computing on campus. 65 workstations in library, computer center.

Student life. Freshman orientation: Available. **Activities:** Student government, student newspaper, American Indian Business Leaders.

Student services. Adult student services, career counseling, student employment services, on-campus daycare, personal counseling, placement for graduates, veterans' counselor. **Transfer:** Special adviser, orientation, preadmission transcript evaluation for new students. Transfer adviser, college fairs on campus for students transferring to 4-year colleges.

Contact. Phone: (406) 768-5553 Fax: (406) 768-5552
Alleigh Melbourne, Director of Admissions, Fort Peck Community College, Box 398 605 Indian, Poplar, MT 59255-0398

Helena College of Technology of the University of Montana

Helena, Montana
www.hct.umontana.edu **CB code: 2022**

- Public 2-year technical college
- Commuter campus in large town

General. Founded in 1939. Regionally accredited. **Enrollment:** 525 full-time, degree-seeking students. **Degrees:** 147 associate awarded. **Location:** 90 miles from Great Falls. **Calendar:** Semester. **Full-time faculty:** 42 total. **Part-time faculty:** 30 total.

Basis for selection. Open admission. Interview recommended.

High school preparation. Recommended units include English 3 and mathematics 3.

2005-2006 Annual costs. Tuition/fees: $2,874; $7,506 out-of-state. Books/supplies: $600. Personal expenses: $710.

Financial aid. Need-based: Need-based aid available for part-time students.

Application procedures. Admission: No deadline. $30 fee. Admission notification on a rolling basis beginning on or about 2/15. **Financial aid:** Priority date 4/1; no closing date. FAFSA, institutional form required. Applicants notified on a rolling basis starting 5/1.

Academics. Special study options: Independent study, internships. **Credit/placement by examination:** CLEP. **Support services:** Learning center, preadmission summer program, remedial instruction, tutoring, writing center.

Majors. Business: Accounting, administrative services, office technology. **Computer sciences:** Programming. **Health:** Medical secretary. **Legal studies:** Legal secretary, paralegal. **Liberal arts:** Arts/sciences. **Mechanic/repair:** Aircraft, automotive, diesel, electronics/electrical. **Protective services:** Firefighting.

Student life. Freshman orientation: Mandatory. **Activities:** Student government.

Athletics. Intramural: Basketball, volleyball.

Student services. Adult student services, career counseling, student employment services, placement for graduates, veterans' counselor. **Physically disabled:** Services for visually, speech, hearing impaired. **Transfer:** Special adviser, orientation for new students. Transfer adviser for students transferring to 4-year colleges.

Contact. E-mail: info@umh.umt.edu
Phone: (406) 444-6800 Toll-free number: (800) 241-4882
Fax: (406) 444-6892
Vicky Lorenz, Director of Admissions, Helena College of Technology of the University of Montana, 1115 North Roberts Street, Helena, MT 59601-3098

Little Big Horn College

Crow Agency, Montana
www.lbhc.cc.mt.us **CB code: 0536**

- Private 2-year community college
- Commuter campus in rural community

General. Founded in 1980. Regionally accredited. Provides education for Crow Indian community. Crow lifeways, economic environment, history, language, and culture emphasized with standard curriculum. **Enrollment:** 225 full-time, degree-seeking students. **Degrees:** 16 associate awarded. **Location:** 60 miles from Billings. **Calendar:** Quarter. **Full-time faculty:** 12 total. **Part-time faculty:** 12 total.

Basis for selection. Open admission.

2005-2006 Annual costs. Tuition/fees: $2,700. Per-credit charge: $75. Books/supplies: $600. Personal expenses: $600.

Financial aid. Need-based: Need-based aid available for part-time students.

Application procedures. Admission: No deadline. No application fee. Admission notification on a rolling basis. **Financial aid:** No deadline. Applicants notified on a rolling basis.

Academics. Bilingual methodologies approach in some course work. **Special study options:** Distance learning, exchange student, internships. **Credit/placement by examination:** CLEP, institutional tests. **Support services:** Remedial instruction, tutoring.

Majors. Area/ethnic studies: Native American. **Biology:** General. **Business:** General, business admin, management information systems. **Computer sciences:** Data processing, information systems. **Family/consumer sciences:** General, child care. **Health:** Substance abuse counseling. **Liberal arts:** Arts/sciences. **Math:** General. **Psychology:** General. **Social sciences:** General.

Most popular majors. Business/marketing 10%, liberal arts 90%.

Student life. Policies: Native religious ceremonies offered. **Activities:** Student government.

Athletics. Intercollegiate: Basketball.

Student services. Career counseling, student employment services, personal counseling. **Transfer:** Special adviser, orientation for new students. Transfer adviser, college fairs on campus for students transferring to 4-year colleges.

Contact. Phone: (406) 638-3116 Fax: (406) 638-3169
Tina Pretty On Top, Admissions Clerk, Little Big Horn College, Box 370, Crow Agency, MT 59022

Miles Community College

Miles City, Montana
www.milescc.edu **CB code: 4081**

- Public 2-year community college
- Commuter campus in small town

General. Founded in 1939. Regionally accredited. **Enrollment:** 460 degree-seeking undergraduates; 31 non-degree-seeking students. **Degrees:** 171 associate awarded. **Location:** 150 miles from Billings. **Calendar:** Semester, limited summer session. **Full-time faculty:** 26 total; 54% women. **Part-time faculty:** 13 total; 46% women. **Class size:** 77% < 20, 17% 20-39, 4% 40-49, 3% 50-99.

Student profile. Among degree-seeking undergraduates, 60% enrolled in a transfer program, 40% enrolled in a vocational program, 136 enrolled as first-time, first-year students, 15 transferred in from other institutions.

Part-time:	22%	**25 or older:**	45%
Out-of-state:	1%	**Live on campus:**	25%
Women:	63%		

Transfer out. Colleges most students transferred to 2005: Montana State University-Billings, Montana State University-Bozeman, Dickinson State University, University of Montana, South Dakota State University.

Basis for selection. Open admission, but selective for some programs. Special requirements for nursing program: National League for Nursing Pre-Admission Examination required, Certified Nurse's Aide required. COMPASS required for all students. **Adult students:** Entrance exam policies same as for first-time freshmen. **Homeschooled:** Minimum COMPASS scores: Writing, 32; Reading, 62; Pre-Algebra/Number Skills, 25; may be used in lieu of high school diploma or GED.

2006-2007 Annual costs. Tuition/fees (projected): $2,835; $3,705 out-of-district; $5,895 out-of-state. Per-credit charge: $56 in-district; $85 out-of-district; $158 out-of-state. Room/board: $4,250. Books/supplies: $800. Personal expenses: $630.

Financial aid. Need-based: Need-based aid available for part-time students. Work study available nights, weekends and for part-time students. **Non-need-based:** Scholarships awarded for academics, athletics, leadership.

Application procedures. Admission: No deadline. $30 fee. Admission notification on a rolling basis. **Financial aid:** Priority date 3/1; no closing date. FAFSA required. Applicants notified on a rolling basis starting 4/15; must reply within 4 week(s) of notification.

Academics. Special study options: Cooperative education, cross-registration, distance learning, dual enrollment of high school students, ESL, independent study, internships. License preparation in nursing. **Credit/placement by examination:** AP, CLEP, IB, institutional tests. 15 credit hours maximum toward associate degree. **Support services:** GED preparation and test center, learning center, pre-admission summer program, reduced course load, remedial instruction, study skills assistance, tutoring, writing center.

Majors. Agriculture: Business. **Biology:** General. **Business:** Administrative services, business admin, office management, office/clerical. **Communications:** Journalism. **Computer sciences:** General, computer graphics, data processing. **Conservation:** General, forestry, wildlife. **Construction:** Carpentry, maintenance, power transmission. **Education:** General. **Engineering:** General. **English:** American lit, British lit, English lit, speech/rhetoric. **Family/consumer sciences:** General. **Foreign languages:** General. **Health:** Medical secretary, nursing (RN), prenursing. **Liberal arts:** Arts/sciences. **Math:** General. **Parks/recreation:** Health/fitness. **Physical sciences:** General. **Psychology:** General. **Public administration:** General, human services, social work. **Social sciences:** General, economics, political science. **Visual/performing arts:** Art, crafts, dramatic, photography.

Computing on campus. 90 workstations in library, computer center. Dormitories wired for high-speed internet access. Commuter students can connect to campus network. Online course registration available.

Student life. Freshman orientation: Mandatory. Preregistration for classes offered. **Policies:** Freshmen permitted cars on campus. **Housing:** Coed dorms available. $200 deposit. **Activities:** Choral groups, dance, drama, student government, campus ministry, multicultural club, Phi Theta Kappa, rodeo club, student senate, student ambassadors.

Athletics. NJCAA. **Intercollegiate:** Baseball M, basketball, cheerleading M, golf, rodeo, volleyball W. **Intramural:** Basketball, bowling, fencing, golf, handball, ice hockey, racquetball, soccer, tennis, volleyball, weight lifting. **Team name:** Pioneers.

Student services. Adult student services, career counseling, student employment services, financial aid counseling, personal counseling, placement for graduates, veterans' counselor. **Transfer:** Special adviser, orientation, pre-admission transcript evaluation for new students. College fairs on campus for students transferring to 4-year colleges.

Contact. E-mail: bluntl@milescc.edu
Phone: (406) 874-6217 Toll-free number: (800) 541-9281
Fax: (406) 874-6283
Darren Pitcher, Director of Student Services, Miles Community College, 2715 Dickinson Street, Miles City, MT 59301

Montana State University College of Technology-Great Falls

Great Falls, Montana
www.msugf.edu **CB code: 4482**

- Public 2-year community and technical college
- Commuter campus in small city

General. Founded in 1969. Regionally accredited. **Enrollment:** 1,268 degree-seeking undergraduates. **Degrees:** 144 associate awarded. **Location:** 200 miles from Billings, 300 miles from Calgary, Alberta, Canada. **Calendar:** Semester, limited summer session. **Full-time faculty:** 46 total. **Part-time faculty:** 72 total.

Student profile.

Out-of-state:	1%	**25 or older:**	50%

Basis for selection. Open admission, but selective for some programs. Special requirements for dental hygiene and physical therapy assistant programs.

2005-2006 Annual costs. Tuition/fees: $2,877; $8,181 out-of-state. Books/supplies: $660. Personal expenses: $1,800.

2004-2005 Financial aid. Need-based: 55% of total undergraduate aid awarded as scholarships/grants, 45% as loans/jobs. Need-based aid available for part-time students. Work study available nights, weekends and for part-time students.

Application procedures. Admission: No deadline. $30 fee. Admission notification on a rolling basis. **Financial aid:** Priority date 3/1; no closing date. FAFSA, institutional form required. Applicants notified on a rolling basis starting 4/1; must reply within 3 week(s) of notification.

Academics. Special study options: Distance learning, dual enrollment of high school students, honors, independent study, internships, liberal arts/career combination. Bachelor's degree programs available on campus. License preparation in nursing, paramedic. **Credit/placement by examination:** CLEP, institutional tests. **Support services:** Learning center, remedial instruction, tutoring.

Majors. Biology: Biotechnology. **Business:** Accounting, administrative services, business admin, office/clerical. **Computer sciences:** General. **Education:** Elementary. **Health:** EMT paramedic, licensed practical nurse, medical assistant, medical records admin, medical secretary, medical transcription, occupational therapy assistant, physical therapy assistant, respiratory therapy technology. **Legal studies:** Legal secretary. **Science technology:** Biological. **Visual/performing arts:** Interior design.

Computing on campus. 200 workstations in library, computer center. Online course registration available.

Student life. Freshman orientation: Mandatory. Preregistration for classes offered. **Activities:** Student government, student newspaper, Phi Theta Kappa.

Athletics. Intramural: Basketball.

Student services. Career counseling, student employment services, financial aid counseling, placement for graduates. **Physically disabled:** Services for visually, hearing impaired. **Transfer:** Special adviser, orientation for new students. College fairs on campus for students transferring to 4-year colleges.

Contact. E-mail: information@msugf.edu
Phone: (406) 771-4420 Toll-free number: (800) 446-2698
Fax: (406) 771-4317
Carol Schopfer, Dean of Admissions, Montana State University College of Technology-Great Falls, 2100 16th Avenue South, Great Falls, MT 59405

Stone Child College

Box Elder, Montana
www.montana.edu/wwwscc/ **CB code: 7044**

- Public 2-year community and junior college
- Commuter campus in rural community

General. Founded in 1984. Regionally accredited. Tribally-controlled college located on the Rocky Boys Indian Reservation. **Enrollment:** 200 full-time, degree-seeking students. **Degrees:** 27 associate awarded. **Location:** 26 miles from Havre, 100 miles from Great Falls. **Calendar:** Semester, limited summer session. **Full-time faculty:** 12 total. **Part-time faculty:** 6 total; 83% have terminal degrees, 67% minority, 67% women.

Student profile.

Out-of-state:	2%	**25 or older:**	56%

Transfer out. Colleges most students transferred to 2005: Montana State University-Northern, Montana State University-Billings, University of Montana, University of Great Falls.

Basis for selection. Open admission.

High school preparation. 22 units recommended. Recommended units include English 4, mathematics 3, social studies 3, history 4, science 3, foreign language 1 and academic electives 4.

2005-2006 Annual costs. Books/supplies: $400.

Financial aid. Need-based: Need-based aid available for part-time students. Work study available for part-time students. **Non-need-based:** Scholarships awarded for academics. **Additional information:** Scholarships available to high school and GED graduates who apply for college admission during the first term after graduation.

Application procedures. Admission: No deadline. $10 fee. Admission notification on a rolling basis. **Financial aid:** Priority date 3/1, closing date 6/30. FAFSA, institutional form required. Applicants notified on a rolling basis.

Academics. Special study options: Cooperative education, distance learning, double major, dual enrollment of high school students, independent study, liberal arts/career combination. Hosts distance learning programs from 4-year institutions, bachelors available in computer science, counseling, psychology, criminal justice, health care administration, human services management, marketing, paralegal studies, sociology, theology and religion. **Credit/placement by examination:** CLEP, institutional tests. 12 credit hours maximum toward associate degree. **Support services:** GED preparation, learning center, remedial instruction, tutoring.

Majors. Area/ethnic studies: Native American. **Business:** General, management information systems, office/clerical. **Computer sciences:** Data processing, information systems. **Education:** Elementary. **Health:** Substance abuse counseling. **Interdisciplinary:** Biological/physical sciences. **Liberal arts:** Arts/sciences. **Public administration:** Human services.

Computing on campus. 64 workstations in library, computer center, student center.

Student life. Freshman orientation: Mandatory. **Activities:** Student government, student newspaper.

Athletics. Intercollegiate: Basketball. **Intramural:** Basketball.

Student services. Career counseling, on-campus daycare, personal counseling. **Transfer:** Special adviser, orientation for new students. Transfer adviser, college fairs on campus for students transferring to 4-year colleges.

Contact. Phone: (406) 395-4313 Fax: (406) 395-4836
Theodore Whitford, Director of Admissions, Stone Child College, RR1 Box 1082, Box Elder, MT 59521-9796

Nebraska

Central Community College

Grand Island, Nebraska
www.cccneb.edu **CB code: 6136**

- Public 2-year community and technical college
- Commuter campus in large town

General. Founded in 1966. Regionally accredited. Multilocation institution with campuses at Columbus, Grand Island, and Hastings. Centers located in Holdrege, Kearney, and Lexington. Multiple starting dates for most programs and courses. **Enrollment:** 3,263 degree-seeking undergraduates; 3,301 non-degree-seeking students. **Degrees:** 579 associate awarded. **Location:** 100 miles from Lincoln. **Calendar:** Semester, extensive summer session. **Full-time faculty:** 145 total. **Part-time faculty:** 150 total.

Student profile. Among degree-seeking undergraduates, 10% enrolled in a transfer program, 35% enrolled in a vocational program, 466 enrolled as first-time, first-year students, 117 transferred in from other institutions.

Part-time:	49%	**Asian American:**	1%
Out-of-state:	1%	**Hispanic American:**	8%
Women:	61%	**25 or older:**	63%
African American:	1%	**Live on campus:**	20%

Transfer out. Colleges most students transferred to 2005: University of Nebraska-Kearney, University of Nebraska-Lincoln, University of Nebraska-Omaha, Bellevue University.

Basis for selection. Open admission, but selective for some programs and for out-of-state students. Special requirements for dental hygiene, dental assisting, medical assisting, medical laboratory technician, practical nursing, associate degree nursing, health information management services, truck driving programs. ACT or Dental Hygiene Aptitude Test required for dental hygiene program, ACT or ASSET required for nursing programs. Interview recommended for health information management services.

2005-2006 Annual costs. Tuition/fees: $1,860; $2,730 out-of-state. Per-credit charge: $62 in-state; $91 out-of-state. Room/board: $3,744. Books/supplies: $800. Personal expenses: $1,380.

2005-2006 Financial aid. Need-based: 76% of total undergraduate aid awarded as scholarships/grants, 24% as loans/jobs. Need-based aid available for part-time students. Work study available nights and for part-time students. **Non-need-based:** Scholarships awarded for academics, art, athletics, job skills, leadership, music/drama.

Application procedures. Admission: No deadline. No application fee. Application may be submitted online. Admission notification on a rolling basis. Score report for dental hygiene applicants due by September 2. Application deadlines: March 1 for practical nursing, January 15 for dental hygiene, February 15 for associate degree nursing and practical nursing. **Financial aid:** Priority date 6/1; no closing date. FAFSA, institutional form required. Applicants notified on a rolling basis starting 3/1; must reply within 1 week(s) of notification.

Academics. Open entry/open exit, self-paced, flexible scheduling for most programs. **Special study options:** Accelerated study, cooperative education, distance learning, double major, dual enrollment of high school students, ESL, honors, independent study, internships, weekend college. Bachelor's degree programs available on campus. License preparation in dental hygiene, nursing, real estate. **Credit/placement by examination:** AP, CLEP, institutional tests. 48 credit hours maximum toward associate degree. **Support services:** GED preparation and test center, learning center, reduced course load, remedial instruction, study skills assistance, tutoring.

Majors. Agriculture: Business, horticulture. **Business:** Administrative services, business admin, vehicle parts marketing. **Communications:** Digital media. **Computer sciences:** General. **Construction:** Electrician. **Engineering technology:** Drafting, electrical, quality control. **Family/consumer sciences:** General, child care. **Health:** Dental assistant, dental hygiene, licensed practical nurse, medical assistant, nursing (RN). **Legal studies:** Paralegal. **Liberal arts:** Arts/sciences. **Mechanic/repair:** Auto body, automotive, diesel, heating/ac/refrig, industrial. **Production:** General, machine tool, welding. **Protective services:** Criminal justice. **Visual/performing arts:** Commercial/advertising art.

Most popular majors. Business/marketing 18%, computer/information sciences 8%, engineering/engineering technologies 10%, health sciences 17%, liberal arts 17%, trade and industry 13%.

Computing on campus. Dormitories linked to campus network. Commuter students can connect to campus network. Online course registration, helpline available.

Student life. Freshman orientation: Available. Preregistration for classes offered. **Policies:** Freshmen permitted cars on campus. **Housing:** Coed dorms, single-sex dorms, apartments, substance-free housing available. $150 deposit. **Activities:** Jazz band, choral groups, dance, drama, music ensembles, musical theater, radio station, student government, student newspaper.

Athletics. NJCAA. **Intercollegiate:** Basketball M, volleyball W. **Intramural:** Basketball, bowling, golf, softball, table tennis, volleyball, weight lifting.

Student services. Adult student services, career counseling, services for economically disadvantaged, student employment services, financial aid counseling, health services, on-campus daycare, personal counseling, placement for graduates, veterans' counselor, women's services. **Physically disabled:** Services for visually, speech, hearing impaired. **Transfer:** Special adviser, orientation, pre-admission transcript evaluation for new students. Transfer adviser, college fairs on campus for students transferring to 4-year colleges.

Contact. E-mail: lkohout@cccneb.edu
Phone: (308) 398-7406 Toll-free number: (800) 652-9177
Fax: (308) 398-7398
Liz Kohout, Admissions Director, Central Community College, 3134 West Highway 34, Grand Island, NE 68802-4903

Creative Center

Omaha, Nebraska
www.creativecenter.edu

- For-profit 2-year visual arts and technical college
- Commuter campus in large city
- Application essay, interview required

General. Accredited by ACCSCT. **Enrollment:** 81 degree-seeking undergraduates. **Degrees:** 39 associate awarded. **Calendar:** Semester, limited summer session. **Full-time faculty:** 3 total; 33% women. **Part-time faculty:** 12 total; 33% women.

Student profile. Among degree-seeking undergraduates, 100% enrolled in a vocational program, 28 enrolled as first-time, first-year students.

Out-of-state:	16%	**25 or older:**	1%
Women:	48%		

Basis for selection. Students must provide a letter of recommendation, a letter of intent, a high school transcript and a portfolio to be reviewed and approved. Portfolio, recommendation required. **Adult students:** Entrance exam policies same as for first-time freshmen.

2005-2006 Annual costs. Tuition/fees: $16,900.

Financial aid. Need-based: Need-based aid available for part-time students. **Non-need-based:** Scholarships awarded for academics, art.

Application procedures. Admission: No deadline. $100 fee. Application must be submitted on paper. Admission notification on a rolling basis. **Financial aid:** No deadline. Applicants notified on a rolling basis starting 1/1.

Academics. Credit/placement by examination: CLEP.

Majors. Computer sciences: Computer graphics. **Visual/performing arts:** Commercial/advertising art, graphic design.

Computing on campus. PC or laptop required. 8 workstations in library. Online library, wireless network available.

Student life. Freshman orientation: Mandatory. Held throughout the first week of class. **Policies:** Freshmen permitted cars on campus. **Housing:** The Creative Center has made arrangements with a nearby apartment complex to assist with student housing.

Student services. Career counseling, financial aid counseling, placement for graduates. **Transfer:** Orientation for new students.

Contact. E-mail: admissions@creativecenter.edu
Phone: (402) 898-1000 ext. 224 Toll-free number: (888) 898-1789 ext. 224
Fax: (402) 898-1301
Sandy LaRocca, Admissions and Placement Coordinator, Creative Center, 10850 Emmet Street, Omaha, NE 68164

Hamilton College: Lincoln

Lincoln, Nebraska
www.hamiltonlincoln.edu **CB code: 3385**

- For-profit 2-year business and junior college
- Commuter campus in large city

General. Founded in 1884. Accredited by ACICS. **Enrollment:** 629 degree-seeking undergraduates. **Degrees:** 130 associate awarded. **Calendar:** Quarter, extensive summer session. **Full-time faculty:** 9 total. **Part-time faculty:** 37 total. **Class size:** 70% < 20, 30% 20-39.

Transfer out. Colleges most students transferred to 2005: Southeast Community College.

Basis for selection. Open admission, but selective for some programs. Students must pass entrance exam. CPAT required of all applicants.

2005-2006 Annual costs. Tuition/fees: $11,575. Room only: $2,100.

Financial aid. All financial aid based on need. Need-based aid available for part-time students.

Application procedures. Admission: No deadline. $25 fee. Admission notification on a rolling basis. **Financial aid:** No deadline. FAFSA, institutional form required. Applicants notified on a rolling basis.

Academics. Special study options: Internships, liberal arts/career combination. Bachelor's degree programs available on campus. License preparation in nursing. **Credit/placement by examination:** CLEP. **Support services:** Learning center, reduced course load, study skills assistance, tutoring.

Majors. Business: Accounting, administrative services, business admin, marketing, tourism promotion, tourism/travel. **Computer sciences:** Applications programming, information systems, programming. **Health:** Medical assistant, medical secretary. **Legal studies:** Legal secretary, paralegal.

Computing on campus. 130 workstations in library, computer center. Online library, repair service available.

Student life. Freshman orientation: Mandatory. Orientation held on first day of classes for all new students. **Policies:** Freshmen permitted cars on campus. **Housing:** Apartments, substance-free housing available. $150 deposit. **Activities:** Student government, tour and travel club, medical club, association of information technology professionals, business club, legal assisting club.

Athletics. NJCAA. **Intercollegiate:** Basketball. **Team name:** Aliens.

Student services. Adult student services, alcohol/substance abuse counseling, career counseling, student employment services, financial aid counseling, personal counseling, placement for graduates, veterans' counselor. **Physically disabled:** Services for visually impaired. **Transfer:** Special adviser, orientation, re-entry adviser, pre-admission transcript evaluation for new students. Transfer adviser for students transferring to 4-year colleges.

Contact. Phone: (402) 474-5315 Toll-free number: (800) 742-7738
Fax: (402) 474-0896
Jill Mathers, Director of Admissions, Hamilton College: Lincoln, 1821 K Street, Lincoln, NE 68508

Hamilton College: Omaha

Omaha, Nebraska
www.hamiltonomaha.edu **CB code: 3326**

- For-profit 2-year business and technical college
- Very large city

General. Accredited by ACICS. **Calendar:** Quarter.

Annual costs/financial aid. Books/supplies: $100. Need-based financial aid available to full-time and part-time students.

Contact. Phone: (402) 572-8500
President, 3350 North 90th Street, Omaha, NE 68134

Little Priest Tribal College

Winnebago, Nebraska
www.lptc.bia.edu **CB code: 3616**

- Private 2-year community college
- Commuter campus in rural community

General. Regionally accredited. **Enrollment:** 150 undergraduates. **Degrees:** 5 associate awarded. **Location:** 30 miles from Sioux City, Iowa. **Calendar:** Semester, limited summer session. **Full-time faculty:** 4 total; 25% minority, 25% women. **Part-time faculty:** 12 total; 8% minority, 67% women. **Class size:** 82% < 20, 18% 20-39.

Transfer out. Colleges most students transferred to 2005: Wayne State College, Haskell Indian Nations University.

Basis for selection. Open admission.

High school preparation. 11 units recommended. Recommended units include English 3, mathematics 3, social studies 3 and science 2.

2005-2006 Annual costs. Tuition/fees: $2,985. Per-credit charge: $80. Books/supplies: $700.

Financial aid. Need-based: Need-based aid available for part-time students. Work study available for part-time students.

Application procedures. Admission: No deadline. $10 fee. **Financial aid:** No deadline. FAFSA, institutional form required.

Academics. Special study options: Dual enrollment of high school students, independent study, liberal arts/career combination. **Credit/placement by examination:** CLEP. **Support services:** GED preparation and test center, learning center, reduced course load, remedial instruction, study skills assistance, tutoring.

Majors. Area/ethnic studies: Native American. **Business:** General. **Computer sciences:** General. **Conservation:** General. **Education:** General. **Health:** Health services, substance abuse counseling. **Liberal arts:** Arts/sciences. **Math:** General.

Most popular majors. Area/ethnic studies 20%, business/marketing 20%, health sciences 20%, liberal arts 40%.

Computing on campus. 20 workstations in library, computer center, student center.

Student life. Freshman orientation: Available. Preregistration for classes offered. **Policies:** Freshmen permitted cars on campus. **Activities:** Student government, student newspaper.

Student services. Adult student services, financial aid counseling, personal counseling. **Transfer:** Special adviser, orientation, pre-admission transcript evaluation for new students. College fairs on campus for students transferring to 4-year colleges.

Contact. Phone: (402) 878-2380 ext. 103 Fax: (402) 878-2355
Karen Kemling, Dean of Admissions, Little Priest Tribal College, PO Box 270, Winnebago, NE 68071

Metropolitan Community College

Omaha, Nebraska **CB member**
www.mccneb.edu **CB code: 5755**

- Public 2-year community and technical college
- Commuter campus in large city

General. Founded in 1974. Regionally accredited. Multilocation institution: Fort Omaha campus and South Campus in Omaha, Elkhorn Valley campus 6 miles west of Omaha, Fremont site 35 miles northwest of Omaha, Sarpy Center in La Vista. **Enrollment:** 6,244 degree-seeking undergraduates; 6,993 non-degree-seeking students. **Degrees:** 815 associate awarded. **Location:** 50 miles from Lincoln. **Calendar:** Quarter, extensive summer session. **Full-time faculty:** 187 total; 11% minority, 46% women. **Part-time faculty:** 560 total; 10% minority, 49% women. **Class size:** 65% < 20, 34% 20-39, less than 1% 40-49, less than 1% 50-99. **Special facilities:** CAD/CAM and electronic graphics facilities.

Student profile. Among degree-seeking undergraduates, 28% enrolled in a transfer program, 48% enrolled in a vocational program, 1,509 enrolled as first-time, first-year students, 2,086 transferred in from other institutions.

Part-time:	55%	**Hispanic American:**	5%
Out-of-state:	2%	**Native American:**	1%
Women:	58%	**International:**	1%
African American:	15%	**25 or older:**	46%
Asian American:	3%		

Transfer out. **Colleges most students transferred to 2005:** University of Nebraska-Omaha, Bellevue University.

Basis for selection. Open admission, but selective for some programs. Admission to nursing and allied health programs based on test scores and references. Assessment testing and standardized RN entrance examination required for nursing associate degree programs. Human services programs require a "C" and approval from Human Services Faculty Review Committee. Admission to college does not mean admission to all programs. Students may be required to take preparatory work before attending classes. Interview required for nursing and allied health programs.

High school preparation. High school diploma or GED required of nursing and allied health applicants.

2006-2007 Annual costs. Tuition/fees (projected): $1,992; $3,072 out-of-state. Per-credit charge: $41 in-state; $63 out-of-state. Books/supplies: $1,050. Personal expenses: $1,053.

2005-2006 Financial aid. **Need-based:** 87% of total undergraduate aid awarded as scholarships/grants, 13% as loans/jobs. Need-based aid available for part-time students. **Non-need-based:** Scholarships awarded for academics.

Application procedures. **Admission:** No deadline. No application fee. Admission notification on a rolling basis. **Financial aid:** Priority date 3/15; no closing date. FAFSA, institutional form required. Applicants notified on a rolling basis starting 4/15.

Academics. Individualized, self-paced instruction. Degree through telecourses available. **Special study options:** Cooperative education, distance learning, double major, dual enrollment of high school students, ESL, honors, independent study, internships, weekend college. License preparation in nursing. **Credit/placement by examination:** AP, CLEP, institutional tests. 81 credit hours maximum toward associate degree. **Support services:** GED preparation and test center, learning center, remedial instruction, tutoring, writing center.

Majors. **Agriculture:** Horticulture, nursery operations. **Architecture:** Interior. **Business:** General, accounting, administrative services, business admin, management information systems. **Communications technology:** Graphic/printing, graphics. **Computer sciences:** Data entry, information systems, programming. **Construction:** Maintenance, power transmission. **Engineering technology:** Civil, drafting, electrical, software. **Family/consumer sciences:** Child care, institutional food production. **Foreign languages:** Sign language interpretation. **Health:** Nursing (RN), respiratory therapy technology, surgical technology. **Legal studies:** Paralegal. **Liberal arts:** Arts/sciences. **Mechanic/repair:** Auto body, automotive, heating/ac/refrig, industrial. **Personal/culinary services:** Culinary arts. **Protective services:** Police science. **Public administration:** Social work. **Visual/performing arts:** Commercial photography, commercial/advertising art, studio arts.

Most popular majors. Business/marketing 22%, computer/information sciences 13%, health sciences 8%, liberal arts 22%, security/protective services 6%, trade and industry 7%, visual/performing arts 9%.

Computing on campus. 1,550 workstations in library, computer center. Commuter students can connect to campus network. Online course registration, helpline available.

Student life. **Freshman orientation:** Available. **Policies:** Freshmen permitted cars on campus. **Activities:** Phi Theta Kappa scholastic honor society.

Student services. Career counseling, services for economically disadvantaged, student employment services, financial aid counseling, minority student services, personal counseling, placement for graduates, veterans' counselor, women's services. **Physically disabled:** Services for visually, speech, hearing impaired. **Transfer:** Special adviser, orientation for new students. Transfer adviser for students transferring to 4-year colleges.

Contact. E-mail: bnicks@mccneb.edu
Phone: (402) 457-2422 Toll-free number: (800) 228-9553
Fax: (402) 457-2616
Becky Nicks, Director of Admissions and Records, Metropolitan Community College, Box 3777, Omaha, NE 68103-0777

Mid-Plains Community College Area

North Platte, Nebraska
www.mpcc.edu **CB code: 6497**

- Public 2-year community and technical college
- Commuter campus in large town

General. Founded in 1964. Regionally accredited. Two major sites, North Platte and McCook; four other extended campus sites in Broken Bow, Imperial, Ogallala, and Valentine. **Enrollment:** 1,209 degree-seeking undergraduates; 1,398 non-degree-seeking students. **Degrees:** 240 associate awarded. **Location:** 230 miles from Lincoln, 270 miles from Denver. **Calendar:** Semester, limited summer session. **Full-time faculty:** 61 total. **Part-time faculty:** 182 total. **Partnerships:** Formal partnership with Union Pacific Railroad for apprenticeships, technical training, continuing education.

Student profile. Among degree-seeking undergraduates, 17% enrolled in a transfer program, 8% enrolled in a vocational program, 345 enrolled as first-time, first-year students.

Part-time:	30%	**Hispanic American:**	3%
Out-of-state:	5%	**Native American:**	1%
Women:	63%	**25 or older:**	75%
African American:	2%	**Live on campus:**	12%
Asian American:	1%		

Transfer out. **Colleges most students transferred to 2005:** University of Nebraska at Lincoln, University of Nebraska at Kearney, Chadron State College.

Basis for selection. Open admission, but selective for some programs. Special requirements for nursing and laboratory technology programs. Psychological Corporation Pre-Nursing Examination required of applicants to nursing program. Minimum ACT score of 17 required for licensed practical nursing and 21 for associate degree nursing. Minimum ASSET score of 40 in all areas required for medical laboratory technology program. Interview required for nursing and medical laboratory technology programs.

2005-2006 Annual costs. Tuition/fees: $1,950; $2,460 out-of-state. Per-credit charge: $57 in-state; $74 out-of-state. Room/board: $3,900. Books/supplies: $900. Personal expenses: $750.

2004-2005 Financial aid. **Need-based:** 63% of total undergraduate aid awarded as scholarships/grants, 37% as loans/jobs. Need-based aid available for part-time students. Work study available nights. **Non-need-based:** Scholarships awarded for academics, art, athletics, music/drama.

Application procedures. **Admission:** No deadline. No application fee. Admission notification on a rolling basis. **Financial aid:** Priority date 5/1; no closing date. FAFSA, institutional form required. Applicants notified on a rolling basis starting 5/1; must reply within 3 week(s) of notification.

Academics. **Special study options:** Cooperative education, distance learning, dual enrollment of high school students, exchange student, honors, independent study, internships, liberal arts/career combination. Bachelor's degree programs available on campus. License preparation in dental hygiene, nursing, paramedic, real estate. **Credit/placement by examination:** CLEP. 20 credit hours maximum toward associate degree. **Support services:** GED preparation and test center, remedial instruction, study skills assistance, tutoring.

Majors. **Business:** Business admin, office management. **Computer sciences:** Information technology. **Construction:** Electrician, maintenance. **Engineering technology:** Electrical. **Family/consumer sciences:** Child care. **Health:** Clinical lab technology, dental assistant, nursing (RN). **Liberal arts:** Arts/sciences. **Mechanic/repair:** General, auto body, automotive, diesel, electronics/electrical, heating/ac/refrig. **Production:** Welding. **Protective services:** Firefighting, police science.

Most popular majors. Business/marketing 14%, health sciences 16%, liberal arts 58%, trade and industry 8%.

Computing on campus. 100 workstations in dormitories, library, computer center, student center. Dormitories wired for high-speed internet access. Commuter students can connect to campus network. Online library, wireless network available.

Student life. **Freshman orientation:** Available. Preregistration for classes offered. **Policies:** Drugs, alcohol, tobacco strictly prohibited. Freshmen permitted cars on campus. **Housing:** Coed dorms, single-sex dorms, special housing for disabled, apartments available. $200 fully refundable deposit, deadline 8/15. **Activities:** Bands, choral groups, drama, music ensembles, student government, student newspaper.

Athletics. NJCAA. **Intercollegiate:** Baseball M, basketball, golf M, softball W, volleyball W. **Intramural:** Volleyball.

Student services. Career counseling, financial aid counseling, on-campus daycare, placement for graduates. **Transfer:** Special adviser for new students. Transfer adviser for students transferring to 4-year colleges.

Contact. E-mail: rippenk@mpcc.edu
Phone: (308) 535-3609 Toll-free number: (800) 658-4308 ext. 3609
Fax: (308) 534-5767
Kelly Rippen, Area Admissions Coordinator, Mid-Plains Community College Area, 1101 Halligan Drive, North Platte, NE 69101

Myotherapy Institute
Lincoln, Nebraska
www.myotherapy.edu

- For-profit 2-year health science and community college
- Small city

General. Accredited by ACCSCT. **Calendar:** Continuous.

Contact. Phone: (402) 421-7410
Director, 6020 South 58th Street, Lincoln, NE 68516

Nebraska College of Technical Agriculture
Curtis, Nebraska
www.ncta.unl.edu **CB code: 1305**

- Public 2-year agricultural college
- Residential campus in rural community

General. Founded in 1965. Regionally accredited. **Enrollment:** 244 degree-seeking undergraduates. **Degrees:** 85 associate awarded. **Location:** 47 miles from North Platte and McCook. **Calendar:** Semester, limited summer session. **Full-time faculty:** 15 total. **Part-time faculty:** 5 total. **Special facilities:** Farm, community golf course, land lab, cattle working facilities, indoor arena, horticulture greenhouse, extensive vet tech surgery and lab facilities.

Student profile. Among degree-seeking undergraduates, 15% enrolled in a transfer program, 1% already have a bachelor's degree or higher, 154 enrolled as first-time, first-year students.

Out-of-state:	36%	**25 or older:**	7%
Women:	47%	**Live on campus:**	58%

Basis for selection. Open admission. ACT scores are criterion in awarding scholarships. **Adult students:** Entrance exam policies same as for first-time freshmen. **Homeschooled:** State high school equivalency certificate required.

High school preparation. 11 units recommended. Recommended units include English 3, mathematics 3, social studies 1 and science 4.

2005-2006 Annual costs. Tuition/fees: $2,926; $5,431 out-of-state. Per-credit charge: $84 in-state; $167 out-of-state. Room/board: $4,150. Books/supplies: $1,000. Personal expenses: $1,375.

2004-2005 Financial aid. All financial aid based on need. 50% of total undergraduate aid awarded as scholarships/grants, 50% as loans/jobs. Need-based aid available for part-time students.

Application procedures. **Admission:** Closing date 8/15. $25 fee. Application may be submitted online. Admission notification on a rolling basis. **Financial aid:** Priority date 4/1; no closing date. FAFSA required. Applicants notified on a rolling basis starting 5/1; must reply within 2 week(s) of notification.

Academics. **Special study options:** Distance learning, double major, internships. Bachelor's degree programs available on campus. **Credit/placement by examination:** AP, CLEP, institutional tests. **Support services:** Reduced course load, remedial instruction, study skills assistance, tutoring.

Majors. **Agriculture:** General, agribusiness operations, animal health, business, equestrian studies, greenhouse operations, horticultural science, horticulture, landscaping, nursery operations, ornamental horticulture, turf management. **Computer sciences:** Information systems. **Conservation:** Management/policy. **Health:** Veterinary technology/assistant. **Mechanic/repair:** General, diesel.

Computing on campus. 75 workstations in dormitories, library, computer center. Dormitories wired for high-speed internet access and linked to campus network. Online course registration, online library, repair service available.

Student life. **Freshman orientation:** Mandatory. 2-day program. **Policies:** Freshmen permitted cars on campus. **Housing:** Guaranteed on-campus for freshmen. Single-sex dorms, substance-free housing available. $200 fully refundable deposit. **Activities:** Drama, student government, student newspaper.

Athletics. **Intercollegiate:** Basketball, equestrian, golf, rodeo, volleyball. **Intramural:** Basketball, cross-country, football (non-tackle), golf, softball, volleyball, wrestling M. **Team name:** Aggies.

Student services. Alcohol/substance abuse counseling, campus ministries, career counseling, student employment services, financial aid counseling, health services, personal counseling, placement for graduates, veterans' counselor. **Transfer:** Special adviser, orientation, pre-admission transcript evaluation for new students. Transfer adviser, college fairs on campus for students transferring to 4-year colleges.

Contact. Phone: (308) 367-4124 Toll-free number: (800) 328-7847
Fax: (308) 367-5203
Jill Koslosky, Admissions/Recruiting, Nebraska College of Technical Agriculture, Route 3, Box 23A, Curtis, NE 69025-0069

Nebraska Indian Community College
Macy, Nebraska
www.thenicc.edu **CB code: 1431**

- Public 2-year community college
- Commuter campus in rural community

General. Founded in 1979. Regionally accredited. Tribal college. **Enrollment:** 90 degree-seeking undergraduates. **Degrees:** 7 associate awarded. **Location:** 70 miles from Omaha, 30 miles from Sioux City, Iowa. **Calendar:** Semester, limited summer session. **Full-time faculty:** 5 total. **Part-time faculty:** 9 total. **Class size:** 100% < 20.

Student profile.

Out-of-state:	20%	**25 or older:**	66%

Basis for selection. Open admission.

High school preparation. Strong background in english, mathematics, and science recommended.

2006-2007 Annual costs. Tuition/fees: $3,200. Per-credit charge: $80. Books/supplies: $600. Personal expenses: $450.

Financial aid. All financial aid based on need. Need-based aid available for part-time students. Work study available for part-time students.

Application procedures. **Admission:** No deadline. $50 fee, may be waived for applicants with need. Admission notification on a rolling basis. **Financial aid:** Priority date 7/15; no closing date. FAFSA, institutional form required. Applicants notified on a rolling basis starting 8/30; must reply within 2 week(s) of notification.

Academics. **Special study options:** Double major, dual enrollment of high school students, independent study, internships. **Credit/placement by examination:** CLEP, institutional tests. 15 credit hours maximum toward associate degree. **Support services:** GED preparation and test center, remedial instruction, study skills assistance, tutoring.

Majors. **Area/ethnic studies:** Native American. **Business:** Business admin. **Computer sciences:** General, data entry. **Conservation:** General. **Construction:** Carpentry. **Education:** Early childhood. **Liberal arts:** Arts/sciences. **Protective services:** Police science. **Public administration:** Social work.

Most popular majors. Business/marketing 36%, computer/information sciences 9%, education 27%, liberal arts 27%.

Computing on campus. 40 workstations in library, computer center.

Student life. **Freshman orientation:** Available. Preregistration for classes offered. **Activities:** Student government, student newspaper.

Student services. Adult student services, career counseling, financial aid counseling. **Transfer:** Special adviser, orientation, pre-admission transcript evaluation for new students. Transfer adviser, college fairs on campus for students transferring to 4-year colleges.

Contact. E-mail: estevens@thenicc.edu
Phone: (402) 344-8428 ext. 14 Toll-free number: (888) 843-6422
Fax: (402) 344-8358
Ed Stevens, Director of Admissions, Nebraska Indian Community College, 2451 St. Mary's Avenue, Omaha, NE 68105

Northeast Community College
Norfolk, Nebraska
www.northeastcollege.com **CB code: 6473**

- Public 2-year community college
- Commuter campus in large town

General. Founded in 1973. Regionally accredited. Off-campus credit classes available. Lifelong Learning Center offers students opportunity to earn advanced degrees on NECC campus. **Enrollment:** 2,542 degree-seeking undergraduates; 2,559 non-degree-seeking students. **Degrees:** 595 associate awarded. **Location:** 110 miles from Omaha. **Calendar:** Semester, limited summer session. **Full-time faculty:** 103 total; 2% have terminal degrees, 1% minority, 36% women. **Part-time faculty:** 292 total; 66% women. **Class size:** 74% < 20, 26% 20-39, less than 1% >100. **Special facilities:** College farm.

Student profile. Among degree-seeking undergraduates, 49% enrolled in a transfer program, 51% enrolled in a vocational program, 836 enrolled as first-time, first-year students.

Part-time:	18%	**Hispanic American:**	3%
Out-of-state:	3%	**Native American:**	1%
Women:	51%	**25 or older:**	12%
African American:	2%	**Live on campus:**	18%

Transfer out. Colleges most students transferred to 2005: Wayne State College, University of Nebraska-Lincoln, University of Nebraska-Omaha, University of Nebraska-Kearney, University of South Dakota.

Basis for selection. Open admission, but selective for some programs. Special requirements for nursing programs, physical therapy assistant program, and veterinary technician program. ACT or ASSET scores required for placement for students enrolling in 6 or more credit hours. **Adult students:** Entrance exam policies same as for first-time freshmen.

2005-2006 Annual costs. Tuition/fees: $1,965; $2,393 out-of-state. Per-credit charge: $57 in-state; $71 out-of-state. Room/board: $3,642. Books/supplies: $800. Personal expenses: $900.

2004-2005 Financial aid. Need-based: 584 full-time freshmen applied for aid; 476 were judged to have need; 473 of these received aid. Average need met was 51%. Average scholarship/grant was $2,865; average loan $2,019. 48% of total undergraduate aid awarded as scholarships/grants, 52% as loans/jobs. Need-based aid available for part-time students. Work study available nights, weekends and for part-time students. **Non-need-based:** Awarded to 763 full-time undergraduates, including 405 freshmen. Scholarships awarded for academics, athletics, music/drama.

Application procedures. Admission: No deadline. No application fee. Application may be submitted online. Admission notification on a rolling basis. **Financial aid:** No deadline. FAFSA, institutional form required. Applicants notified on a rolling basis; must reply within 2 week(s) of notification.

Academics. Special study options: Accelerated study, cooperative education, cross-registration, distance learning, dual enrollment of high school students, ESL, independent study, internships, liberal arts/career combination. Bachelor's degree programs available on campus. License preparation in nursing, paramedic, real estate. **Credit/placement by examination:** AP, CLEP, institutional tests. 16 credit hours maximum toward associate degree. **Support services:** GED preparation and test center, learning center, reduced course load, remedial instruction, study skills assistance, tutoring, writing center.

Majors. Agriculture: General, agribusiness operations, agronomy, animal sciences, business, crop production, farm/ranch, horticultural science, horticulture, livestock, mechanization, production. **Biology:** General. **Business:** Accounting, administrative services, banking/financial services, business admin, entrepreneurial studies, international marketing, marketing, real estate, retailing. **Communications:** Journalism, radio/tv. **Communications technology:** Recording arts. **Computer sciences:** General, applications programming, computer science, programming. **Construction:** Carpentry, electrician, lineworker. **Education:** General, early childhood, elementary, secondary. **Engineering:** General. **Engineering technology:** Architectural drafting, electrical, electromechanical, heat/ac/refrig. **English:** English lit, speech/rhetoric. **Health:** Chiropractic assistant, clinical lab science, dietetics, EMT paramedic, nursing (RN), physician assistant, predentistry, premedicine, prenursing, prepharmacy, preveterinary, radiologic technology/medical imaging, surgical technology, veterinary technology/assistant. **Interdisciplinary:** Behavioral sciences. **Legal studies:** Legal secretary, paralegal, prelaw. **Liberal arts:** Arts/sciences. **Math:** General. **Mechanic/repair:** Auto body, automotive, diesel, electronics/electrical, heating/ac/refrig, industrial. **Parks/recreation:** Health/fitness. **Physical sciences:** Chemistry, physics. **Protective services:** Corrections, law enforcement admin. **Social sciences:** General. **Visual/performing arts:** Art, dramatic, music management, music performance.

Most popular majors. Agriculture 7%, business/marketing 17%, health sciences 19%, liberal arts 9%, social sciences 6%, trade and industry 19%.

Computing on campus. 225 workstations in dormitories, library, computer center, student center. Dormitories linked to campus network. Online course registration, online library, helpline available.

Student life. Freshman orientation: Mandatory. **Policies:** Freshmen permitted cars on campus. **Housing:** Coed dorms, special housing for disabled, apartments, substance-free housing available. $25 nonrefundable deposit. **Activities:** Bands, choral groups, dance, drama, music ensembles, musical theater, radio station, student government, student newspaper, symphony orchestra, TV station, student government association, Habitat for Humanity, HOPE, multicultural club, Campus Crusade for Christ, Christian Student Fellowship.

Athletics. NJCAA. **Intercollegiate:** Basketball. **Intramural:** Basketball, soccer, softball. **Team name:** Hawks.

Student services. Adult student services, career counseling, student employment services, financial aid counseling, health services, minority student services, on-campus daycare, personal counseling, placement for graduates, veterans' counselor. **Physically disabled:** Services for visually, speech, hearing impaired. **Learning disabled:** Comprehensive services available. **Transfer:** Special adviser, orientation, pre-admission transcript evaluation for new students. Transfer adviser for students transferring to 4-year colleges.

Contact. E-mail: admission@northeastcollege.com
Phone: (402) 844-7260 Toll-free number: (800) 348-9033
Fax: (402) 844-7400
Maureen Baker, Dean of Enrollment Management, Northeast Community College, 801 East Benjamin Avenue, Norfolk, NE 68702-0469

Southeast Community College: Beatrice Campus
Beatrice, Nebraska
www.southeast.edu **CB code: 6795**

- Public 2-year community and liberal arts college
- Commuter campus in large town

General. Founded in 1986. Regionally accredited. **Location:** 40 miles from Lincoln, 98 miles from Omaha. **Calendar:** Quarter.

Annual costs/financial aid. Tuition/fees (2005-2006): $1,795; $2,183 out-of-state. Room: $2,646. Books/supplies: $600. Personal expenses: $2,538.

Contact. Phone: (402) 228-3468 ext. 214
Dean of Student Services, Milford Campus, 4771 West Scott Road, Beatrice, NE 68310

Southeast Community College: Lincoln Campus
Lincoln, Nebraska
www.southeast.edu **CB code: 1189**

- Public 2-year community college
- Commuter campus in small city

General. Founded in 1973. Regionally accredited. Extensive adult and continuing education programs, both credit and noncredit. **Enrollment:** 10,500 undergraduates. **Degrees:** 1,344 associate awarded. **Location:** 50 miles from Omaha. **Calendar:** Quarter, extensive summer session. **Full-time faculty:** 190 total. **Part-time faculty:** 222 total. **Special facilities:** Fire service training facility.

Transfer out. Colleges most students transferred to 2005: University of Nebraska, Doane-Lincoln, College of St. Mary, Nebraska Wesleyan, University of Nebraska-Kearney.

Basis for selection. Open admission.

2005-2006 Annual costs. Tuition/fees: $1,800; $2,183 out-of-state. Per-credit charge: $39 in-state; $48 out-of-state. Books/supplies: $1,000. Personal expenses: $1,200.

Financial aid. Need-based: Need-based aid available for part-time students. Work study available nights, weekends and for part-time students. **Non-need-based:** Scholarships awarded for academics.

Application procedures. Admission: No deadline. No application fee. Admission notification on a rolling basis. **Financial aid:** No deadline. FAFSA, institutional form required. Applicants notified on a rolling basis; must reply within 2 week(s) of notification.

Academics. Academic transfer courses (liberal arts) offered on Saturdays and Sundays. **Special study options:** Cooperative education, distance learning, dual enrollment of high school students, independent study, internships, liberal arts/career combination, weekend college. License preparation in nursing, radiology. **Credit/placement by examination:** CLEP, institutional tests. 32 credit hours maximum toward associate degree. Most applicants required to take COMPASS or ASSET for placement purposes. ACT may be substituted for ASSET. **Support services:** GED preparation and test center, learning center, remedial instruction, study skills assistance, tutoring, writing center.

Majors. Business: Accounting, business admin, marketing, office/clerical, purchasing. **Computer sciences:** Information systems. **Engineering technology:** Architectural, drafting, electrical. **Family/consumer sciences:** Child care, institutional food production. **Health:** Clinical lab technology, health services, medical radiologic technology/radiation therapy, nursing (RN), respiratory therapy technology, surgical technology. **Liberal arts:** Arts/sciences. **Personal/culinary services:** Culinary arts. **Production:** Welding. **Protective services:** Fire safety technology.

Computing on campus. 300 workstations in library, computer center.

Student life. Freshman orientation: Mandatory. **Activities:** Student government, student newspaper, multicultural student organization.

Athletics. Intercollegiate: Rowing (crew) W. **Intramural:** Basketball, softball, table tennis, tennis, volleyball.

Student services. Career counseling, student employment services, on-campus daycare, personal counseling, placement for graduates, veterans' counselor. **Physically disabled:** Services for visually, speech, hearing impaired. **Transfer:** Special adviser, orientation for new students. Transfer adviser, college fairs on campus for students transferring to 4-year colleges.

Contact. Phone: (402) 437-2600 Toll-free number: (800) 642-4075
Fax: (402) 437-2402
David Sonenberg, Dean of Student Services, Southeast Community College: Lincoln Campus, 8800 O Street, Lincoln, NE 68520

Southeast Community College: Milford Campus

Milford, Nebraska
www.southeast.edu **CB code: 6502**

- Public 2-year community and technical college
- Commuter campus in rural community

General. Founded in 1941. Regionally accredited. **Location:** 20 miles from Lincoln. **Calendar:** Quarter.

Annual costs/financial aid. Tuition/fees (2005-2006): $1,800; $2,183 out-of-state. Room/board: $3,393. Books/supplies: $750. Personal expenses: $900. Need-based financial aid available to full-time and part-time students.

Contact. Phone: (402) 761-2131 ext. 8243
Dean of Students, 600 State Street, Milford, NE 68405-8498

Vatterott College: Spring Valley

Omaha, Nebraska
www.vatterott-college.com

- For-profit 2-year community and technical college
- Large city

General. Accredited by ACCSCT. **Enrollment:** 400 undergraduates. **Degrees:** 15 associate awarded. **Calendar:** Quarter. **Full-time faculty:** 17 total; 6% have terminal degrees, 53% women. **Part-time faculty:** 5 total; 80% women.

Basis for selection. Interview most important. High school record also important.

2005-2006 Annual costs. Associate degree programs range in cost from $31,427 to $33,595. Diploma programs range in cost from $18,299 to $21,847.

Application procedures. Admission: No application fee.

Academics. Credit/placement by examination: CLEP.

Majors. Business: Accounting. **Health:** Medical assistant, medical secretary, pharmacy assistant, substance abuse counseling, veterinary technology/assistant. **Mechanic/repair:** Heating/ac/refrig. **Visual/performing arts:** Graphic design.

Contact. Phone: (402) 891-9411 Toll-free number: (888) 886-3856
Fax: (402) 891-9413
Maria Palmershien, Director of Admissions, Vatterott College: Spring Valley, 11818 I Street, Omaha, NE 68137

Western Nebraska Community College

Scottsbluff, Nebraska
www.wncc.net **CB code: 6648**

- Public 2-year community college
- Commuter campus in large town

General. Founded in 1926. Regionally accredited. Additional enters at Sidney and Alliance, centers for business and individual training located in Scottsbluff. **Enrollment:** 1,488 degree-seeking undergraduates; 794 non-degree-seeking students. **Degrees:** 224 associate awarded. **Location:** 100 miles from Cheyenne, Wyoming, 190 miles from Denver. **Calendar:** Semester, limited summer session. **Full-time faculty:** 69 total; 9% have terminal degrees, 4% minority, 44% women. **Part-time faculty:** 150 total; 7% have terminal degrees, 2% minority, 59% women. **Class size:** 82% < 20, 17% 20-39, less than 1% 40-49.

Student profile. Among degree-seeking undergraduates, 72% enrolled in a transfer program, 28% enrolled in a vocational program, 477 enrolled as first-time, first-year students, 46 transferred in from other institutions.

Part-time:	42%	**Native American:**	1%
Out-of-state:	10%	**International:**	3%
Women:	62%	**25 or older:**	38%
African American:	2%	**Live on campus:**	7%
Hispanic American:	13%		

Transfer out. 38% of students enrolled in the transfer program go on to 4-year colleges. **Colleges most students transferred to 2005:** Agreements with Chadron State College, University of Nebraska Lincoln, University of Wyoming.

Basis for selection. Open admission, but selective for some programs. Special requirements for practical nursing and radiologic technologies programs. ASSET or COMPASS required unless SAT or ACT scores submitted. **Adult students:** ECOMPASS used for proper course placement in writing, mathematics, and classes with a reading prerequisite; ACT, SAT, or ASSET accepted in lieu of eCOMPASS.

High school preparation. Recommended units include English 4, mathematics 4, social studies 3, history 3, science 4 (laboratory 2) and foreign language 1.

2005-2006 Annual costs. Tuition/fees: $1,860; $2,160 out-of-state. Per-credit charge: $52 in-state; $62 out-of-state. Room/board: $3,770. Books/supplies: $840. Personal expenses: $1,872.

2005-2006 Financial aid. Need-based: 203 full-time freshmen applied for aid; 170 were judged to have need; 163 of these received aid. Average need met was 80%. Average scholarship/grant was $3,383; average loan $2,164. 76% of total undergraduate aid awarded as scholarships/grants, 24% as loans/jobs. Need-based aid available for part-time students. Work study available nights, weekends and for part-time students. **Non-need-based:** Awarded to 319 full-time undergraduates, including 155 freshmen. Scholarships awarded for academics, art, athletics, leadership, music/drama, state residency.

Application procedures. Admission: No deadline. No application fee. Application may be submitted online. Admission notification on a rolling

basis. **Financial aid:** Priority date 3/1; no closing date. FAFSA required. Applicants notified on a rolling basis starting 4/1.

Academics. Special study options: Cooperative education, cross-registration, distance learning, double major, dual enrollment of high school students, ESL, independent study, internships, liberal arts/career combination, student-designed major. Radiological technology program at Regional West Medical Center, respiratory therapy technician and surgical technician in partnership with Southeast Community College. License preparation in aviation, nursing, paramedic, real estate. **Credit/placement by examination:** AP, CLEP, IB, institutional tests. 25 credit hours maximum toward associate degree. **Support services:** GED preparation and test center, learning center, pre-admission summer program, reduced course load, remedial instruction, study skills assistance, tutoring, writing center.

Majors. Biology: General, ecology. **Business:** General, accounting, administrative services, business admin, office/clerical. **Communications:** Journalism. **Computer sciences:** General, computer science, programming. **Conservation:** Forestry. **Construction:** Lineworker. **Education:** General, art, early childhood, elementary, music, physical, secondary. **Engineering:** General. **Engineering technology:** Electrical. **English:** English lit. **Family/consumer sciences:** Food/nutrition. **Foreign languages:** French, German, Spanish. **Health:** Athletic training, medical radiologic technology/radiation therapy, medical records technology, nursing (RN), predentistry, premedicine, prenursing, prepharmacy, preveterinary. **History:** General. **Legal studies:** Prelaw. **Liberal arts:** Arts/sciences. **Math:** General. **Mechanic/repair:** Aircraft, aircraft powerplant, auto body, automotive. **Parks/recreation:** Health/fitness. **Personal/culinary services:** Cosmetic. **Physical sciences:** Chemistry, physics. **Production:** Welding. **Protective services:** Criminal justice. **Psychology:** General. **Public administration:** Social work. **Social sciences:** Anthropology, economics, geography, political science, sociology. **Visual/performing arts:** Art.

Computing on campus. 454 workstations in dormitories, library, computer center. Dormitories wired for high-speed internet access and linked to campus network. Commuter students can connect to campus network. Online course registration, online library, helpline, wireless network available.

Student life. Freshman orientation: Available. Preregistration for classes offered. 6 hours held the weekday before classes begin. **Policies:** Freshmen permitted cars on campus. **Housing:** Coed dorms, substance-free housing available. $100 fully refundable deposit, deadline 8/15. **Activities:** Bands, choral groups, drama, literary magazine, music ensembles, musical theater, student government, student newspaper.

Athletics. NJCAA. **Intercollegiate:** Baseball M, basketball, soccer, volleyball W. **Intramural:** Basketball, football (non-tackle), table tennis, volleyball. **Team name:** Cougars.

Student services. Adult student services, alcohol/substance abuse counseling, career counseling, student employment services, financial aid counseling, minority student services, on-campus daycare, personal counseling, placement for graduates, veterans' counselor. **Physically disabled:** Services for visually, speech, hearing impaired. **Transfer:** Special adviser, orientation, pre-admission transcript evaluation for new students. Transfer adviser, college fairs on campus for students transferring to 4-year colleges.

Contact. E-mail: martinh@wncc.net
Phone: (308) 635-6010 Toll-free number: (800) 348-4435 ext. 6010
Fax: (308) 635-6100
Heath Martin, Admisssions Director, Western Nebraska Community College, 1601 East 27th Street, Scottsbluff, NE 69361

Two-Year Colleges

Nevada

Career College of Northern Nevada
Reno, Nevada
www.ccnn.edu
CB code: 3202

- For-profit 2-year business and technical college
- Commuter campus in large city

General. Accredited by ACCSCT. **Enrollment:** 303 degree-seeking undergraduates. **Degrees:** 70 associate awarded. **Calendar:** Quarter. 6-week cycles. **Full-time faculty:** 10 total. **Part-time faculty:** 12 total.

Student profile. Among degree-seeking undergraduates, 100% enrolled in a vocational program, 6% already have a bachelor's degree or higher, 303 enrolled as first-time, first-year students.

Out-of-state:	2%	**Asian American:**	6%
Women:	77%	**Hispanic American:**	16%
African American:	3%	**Native American:**	8%

Basis for selection. Open admission. **Adult students:** Entrance exam policies same as for first-time freshmen.

2005-2006 Annual costs. Tuition/fees: $7,964. Per-credit charge: $175. Tuition for associate programs ranges from $14,830 to $18,813; diploma programs $9,887 to $11,085. Fees and books range from $120 to $624. Books/supplies: $1,500. Personal expenses: $1,832.

Financial aid. All financial aid based on need.

Application procedures. Admission: No deadline. $25 fee. Admission notification on a rolling basis. **Financial aid:** Closing date 5/30. FAFSA required. Applicants notified on a rolling basis.

Academics. Special study options: Accelerated study, cooperative education, internships, liberal arts/career combination. **Credit/placement by examination:** CLEP. **Support services:** Remedial instruction, study skills assistance, tutoring.

Majors. Business: Business admin.

Computing on campus. 78 workstations in computer center, student center.

Student life. Freshman orientation: Mandatory. Preregistration for classes offered. Held Saturday morning before classes begin. **Policies:** Freshmen permitted cars on campus.

Student services. Adult student services, career counseling, financial aid counseling, placement for graduates.

Contact. E-mail: lgoldhammer@ccnn4u.com
Phone: (775) 856-2266
Career College of Northern Nevada, 1195 A Corporate Boulevard, Reno, NV 89502-2331

Community College of Southern Nevada
Las Vegas, Nevada
www.ccsn.nevada.edu
CB member
CB code: 4136

- Public 2-year community college
- Commuter campus in very large city

General. Founded in 1971. Regionally accredited. Branch campuses at Henderson and North Las Vegas. Health science center in West Las Vegas. **Enrollment:** 21,188 degree-seeking undergraduates. **Degrees:** 1,333 associate awarded. **ROTC:** Army. **Location:** 6 miles from downtown. **Calendar:** Semester, limited summer session. **Full-time faculty:** 460 total. **Part-time faculty:** 1,050 total. **Special facilities:** Planetarium, ornamental horticulture demonstration facilities, culinary facilities, telecommunications/multimedia center, automotive technology center.

Student profile. Among degree-seeking undergraduates, 4,729 enrolled as first-time, first-year students.

Out-of-state:	2%	**25 or older:**	54%

Transfer out. Colleges most students transferred to 2005: University of Nevada Las Vegas.

Basis for selection. Open admission, but selective for some programs. Special requirements for nursing and dental hygiene programs. Associate degree and certification required for BS dental hygiene program. **Adult students:** Entrance exam policies same as for first-time freshmen.

2005-2006 Annual costs. Tuition/fees: $1,643; $6,557 out-of-state. Per-credit charge: $51 in-state; $215 out-of-state. Reduced tuition for nonresidents who are within 50 miles of Nevada border. Books/supplies: $600. Personal expenses: $1,480.

2004-2005 Financial aid. Need-based: 72% of total undergraduate aid awarded as scholarships/grants, 28% as loans/jobs. Work study available nights, weekends and for part-time students. **Non-need-based:** Scholarships awarded for state residency.

Application procedures. Admission: No deadline. $5 fee, may be waived for applicants with need. Application may be submitted online. Admission notification on a rolling basis. **Financial aid:** Priority date 5/1, closing date 6/30. FAFSA required. Applicants notified on a rolling basis starting 7/15; must reply within 2 week(s) of notification.

Academics. Special study options: Cross-registration, distance learning, double major, dual enrollment of high school students, ESL, honors, independent study, internships, liberal arts/career combination, student-designed major, weekend college. Bachelor's degree programs available on campus. License preparation in aviation, dental hygiene, nursing, occupational therapy, paramedic, physical therapy, radiology, real estate. **Credit/placement by examination:** CLEP, institutional tests. 15 credit hours maximum toward associate degree. **Support services:** GED preparation and test center, learning center, remedial instruction, study skills assistance, tutoring, writing center.

Majors. Agriculture: Landscaping, ornamental horticulture. **Biology:** General, anatomy. **Business:** General, accounting, administrative services, banking/financial services, business admin, hospitality admin, hospitality/recreation, management information systems, office management, real estate, sales/distribution. **Communications:** General. **Communications technology:** Animation/special effects, computer typography, graphic/printing. **Computer sciences:** Computer graphics, data processing, database management, information systems, LAN/WAN management, networking, programming, systems analysis, webmaster. **Education:** Deaf/hearing impaired, early childhood, kindergarten/preschool. **Engineering:** Electrical, software. **Engineering technology:** General, CAD/CADD, drafting, electrical, environmental, mechanical, surveying, water quality. **English:** English lit. **Health:** Acupuncture, clinical lab assistant, clinical lab technology, dental hygiene, EMT paramedic, medical records technology, nursing (RN), optician, orthotics/prosthetics, physical therapy assistant. **Legal studies:** Legal secretary, paralegal. **Liberal arts:** Arts/sciences. **Mechanic/repair:** Automotive, heating/ac/refrig. **Personal/culinary services:** Chef training. **Production:** Welding. **Protective services:** Corrections, criminal justice, fire safety technology, firefighting, police science, security services. **Psychology:** General. **Social sciences:** General. **Visual/performing arts:** Art, commercial photography, commercial/advertising art, studio arts.

Computing on campus. 550 workstations in library, computer center. Online course registration, helpline available.

Student life. Freshman orientation: Mandatory. Orientation is mandatory for degree-seeking students only. **Policies:** Freshmen permitted cars on campus. **Activities:** Jazz band, choral groups, dance, drama, literary magazine, music ensembles, musical theater, student government, student newspaper.

Athletics. NJCAA. **Intercollegiate:** Baseball M, softball W. **Team name:** Coyotes.

Student services. Adult student services, career counseling, student employment services, financial aid counseling, on-campus daycare, personal counseling, placement for graduates, veterans' counselor, women's services. **Physically disabled:** Services for visually, hearing impaired. **Transfer:** Special adviser, orientation, re-entry adviser for new students. College fairs on campus for students transferring to 4-year colleges.

Contact. E-mail: admrec@ccsn.nevada.edu
Phone: (702) 651-4060 Fax: (702) 651-4811
Patricia Zozaya, Admissions Director, Community College of Southern Nevada, 6375 West Charleston Boulevard, Las Vegas, NV 89146-1164

Heritage College

Las Vegas, Nevada
www.heritagecollege.com **CB code: 3167**

- For-profit 2-year business and health science college
- Large city

General. Accredited by ACCSCT. **Enrollment:** 165 degree-seeking undergraduates. **Degrees:** 19 associate awarded. **Calendar:** Continuous. **Full-time faculty:** 15 total. **Part-time faculty:** 15 total.

Basis for selection. Open admission. Pharmacy program requires clean legal record. CPAT required only for applicants with no high school diploma and no GED; can only apply for selected diploma programs.

2005-2006 Annual costs. Cost of full programs: associate degree programs $20,404, diploma programs $10,204, including fees and books. Personal expenses: $380.

Application procedures. Admission: No deadline. No application fee. **Financial aid:** No deadline. FAFSA, institutional form required.

Academics. Credit/placement by examination: CLEP.

Majors. Legal studies: General.

Contact. Phone: (702) 368-2338 Fax: (702) 368-3853
Director of Admissions, Heritage College, 3315 Spring Mountain Road, Las Vegas, NV 89102

High-Tech Institute

Las Vegas, Nevada
www.hightechinstitute.edu

- For-profit 2-year technical college
- Commuter campus in very large city
- Interview required

General. Accredited by ACCSCT. **Enrollment:** 550 degree-seeking undergraduates. **Degrees:** 164 associate awarded. **Calendar:** Semester, extensive summer session. **Full-time faculty:** 23 total; 26% have terminal degrees, 44% minority, 91% women. **Class size:** 100% 20-39.

Basis for selection. Open admission, but selective for some programs.

2005-2006 Annual costs. Tuition/fees: $25,550. Tuition costs vary by program.

Financial aid. All financial aid based on need.

Application procedures. Admission: No deadline. $50 fee, may be waived for applicants with need. Application must be submitted on paper. Admission notification on a rolling basis. **Financial aid:** FAFSA, institutional form required.

Academics. Special study options: Accelerated study, distance learning. Bachelor's degree programs available on campus. **Credit/placement by examination:** CLEP. **Support services:** GED preparation, learning center, study skills assistance, tutoring.

Majors. Health: Dental assistant, insurance coding, massage therapy, medical assistant, pharmacy assistant, surgical technology. **Protective services:** Law enforcement admin.

Computing on campus. 65 workstations in library, computer center. Online library, helpline available.

Student life. Freshman orientation: Mandatory.

Student services. Career counseling, student employment services, financial aid counseling, personal counseling, placement for graduates. **Physically disabled:** Services for visually impaired.

Contact. Phone: (702) 385-6700 Toll-free number: (866) 385-6700
Fax: (702) 388-4463
Amy Tu, Director of Admissions, High-Tech Institute, 2320 South Rancho Drive, Las Vegas, NV 89102

Las Vegas College

Las Vegas, Nevada
lasvegas-college.com **CB code: 2149**

- For-profit 2-year business and health science college
- Commuter campus in very large city
- Interview required

General. Founded in 1979. Accredited by ACICS. **Enrollment:** 680 degree-seeking undergraduates. **Degrees:** 101 associate awarded. **Calendar:** Quarter, extensive summer session. **Full-time faculty:** 10 total. **Part-time faculty:** 40 total. **Special facilities:** Court reporting laboratory.

Basis for selection. Open admission.

2005-2006 Annual costs. Books/supplies: $300. Personal expenses: $124.

Financial aid. All financial aid based on need. Need-based aid available for part-time students. Work study available nights and weekends.

Application procedures. Admission: No deadline. No application fee. Admission notification on a rolling basis. **Financial aid:** FAFSA required. Applicants notified on a rolling basis; must reply within 2 week(s) of notification.

Academics. Special study options: Accelerated study, independent study. **Credit/placement by examination:** CLEP. **Support services:** Reduced course load, study skills assistance, tutoring.

Majors. Business: Administrative services, business admin. **Health:** Medical assistant. **Legal studies:** Court reporting, paralegal.

Most popular majors. Business/marketing 40%, legal studies 60%.

Computing on campus. 55 workstations in library, computer center.

Student life. Freshman orientation: Available. **Activities:** Student government.

Student services. Adult student services, career counseling, services for economically disadvantaged, student employment services, financial aid counseling, placement for graduates, veterans' counselor. **Transfer:** Orientation, re-entry adviser, pre-admission transcript evaluation for new students.

Contact. E-mail: spetty@cci.edu
Phone: (702) 368-6200 Fax: (702) 368-6464
Kristen Weiss, Director of Admissions, Las Vegas College, 4100 West Flamingo Road, Las Vegas, NV 89103

Le Cordon Bleu College of Culinary Arts

Las Vegas, Nevada
www.VegasCulinary.com

- For-profit 2-year culinary school
- Commuter campus in very large city

General. Accredited by ACCSCT. **Enrollment:** 500 full-time, degree-seeking students. **Degrees:** 308 associate awarded. **Calendar:** Continuous. **Full-time faculty:** 50 total. **Part-time faculty:** 10 total. **Special facilities:** 10 kitchens, student-run restaurant open to general public.

Basis for selection. Open admission.

Application procedures. Admission: No deadline. $50 fee. Application may be submitted online. Admission notification on a rolling basis.

Academics. Special study options: Accelerated study. **Credit/placement by examination:** CLEP. **Support services:** Learning center, tutoring.

Majors. Personal/culinary services: Chef training.

Student life. Freshman orientation: Mandatory. **Policies:** Freshmen permitted cars on campus. **Housing:** Apartments, substance-free housing available. **Activities:** Student newspaper.

Student services. Career counseling, student employment services, financial aid counseling. **Transfer:** Special adviser, orientation, re-entry adviser, pre-admission transcript evaluation for new students. Transfer center for students transferring to 4-year colleges.

Contact. E-mail: akirsh@vegasculinary.com
Phone: (702) 851-5300 Toll-free number: (866) 450-2433
John Hayet, Vice President of Admissions, Le Cordon Bleu College of Culinary Arts, 1451 Center Crossing Road, Las Vegas, NV 89144

Truckee Meadows Community College

Reno, Nevada
www.tmcc.edu **CB code: 1096**

- Public 2-year community and technical college
- Commuter campus in large city

General. Founded in 1971. Regionally accredited. Classes offered at over 30 sites in Reno-Sparks area and Lake Tahoe. **Enrollment:** 8,400 degree-seeking undergraduates. **Degrees:** 544 associate awarded. **ROTC:** Army. **Location:** 9 miles from downtown. **Calendar:** Semester, limited summer session. **Full-time faculty:** 150 total. **Part-time faculty:** 350 total.

Transfer out. Colleges most students transferred to 2005: University of Nevada-Reno, University of Nevada-Las Vegas.

Basis for selection. Open admission, but selective for some programs. High school diploma or GED required if student under 18 years of age. Selective admission to nursing, dental assistant, and radiological technician programs. **Learning Disabled:** Applicants must contact Disabled Students Office. Accommodations provided according to documentation.

High school preparation. Special course unit requirements for allied health programs (nursing, dental assistant, radiological technician).

2005-2006 Annual costs. Tuition/fees: $1,643; $6,558 out-of-state. Per-credit charge: $51 in-state; $215 out-of-state. Good Neighbor tuition: $30 per-credit-hour in addition to registration costs. Books/supplies: $800. Personal expenses: $1,000.

Financial aid. Need-based: Work study available nights, weekends and for part-time students. **Non-need-based:** Scholarships awarded for academics, art, leadership, minority status, music/drama, state residency. **Additional information:** Institutional grants to state residents, short-term emergency loans available. Work-study applications must reply within 10 days of notification.

Application procedures. Admission: No deadline. $10 fee. Application may be submitted online. Admission notification on a rolling basis. Application fee is paid at time of registration for first class. **Financial aid:** No deadline. FAFSA, institutional form required. Applicants notified by 5/15.

Academics. Special study options: Cooperative education, distance learning, dual enrollment of high school students, ESL, honors, internships, liberal arts/career combination, weekend college. Bachelor's degree programs available on campus. License preparation in dental hygiene, nursing, radiology, real estate. **Credit/placement by examination:** CLEP, institutional tests. 15 credit hours maximum toward associate degree. **Support services:** GED preparation and test center, learning center, reduced course load, remedial instruction, study skills assistance, tutoring, writing center.

Majors. Architecture: Landscape. **Business:** General, accounting, administrative services, business admin, office management, office technology, real estate. **Computer sciences:** General, data processing, programming. **Conservation:** Environmental studies. **Construction:** Carpentry, maintenance, masonry, pipefitting, power transmission. **Education:** Early childhood, elementary, secondary. **Engineering technology:** Architectural, drafting, solar energy. **Family/consumer sciences:** Child care, institutional food production. **Health:** Dental assistant, dental hygiene, medical radiologic technology/radiation therapy, medical secretary, nursing (RN), radiologic technology/medical imaging, substance abuse counseling. **Legal studies:** Legal secretary, paralegal. **Mechanic/repair:** Automotive, diesel, heating/ac/refrig. **Military:** General. **Parks/recreation:** Facilities management. **Protective services:** Corrections, criminal justice, firefighting, juvenile corrections, law enforcement admin, police science. **Social sciences:** Anthropology. **Visual/performing arts:** Design, dramatic.

Most popular majors. Health sciences 13%, liberal arts 55%.

Computing on campus. 558 workstations in library, computer center. Helpline, repair service available.

Student life. Freshman orientation: Available. Preregistration for classes offered. **Housing:** Housing available 2 miles away at University of Nevada: Reno, for students enrolled for 12 or more credits. **Activities:** Concert band, choral groups, drama, literary magazine, music ensembles, student government, student newspaper, symphony orchestra, social organization for handicapped students.

Student services. Adult student services, career counseling, student employment services, financial aid counseling, health services, on-campus daycare, personal counseling, placement for graduates, veterans' counselor. **Physically disabled:** Services for visually, speech, hearing impaired. **Transfer:** Special adviser, orientation, re-entry adviser for new students. Transfer adviser, college fairs on campus for students transferring to 4-year colleges.

Contact. E-mail: admrec@scs.unr.edu/tmcc
Phone: (775) 673-7042 Fax: (775) 673-7028
Dave Harbeck, Director of Admissions and Records, Truckee Meadows Community College, 7000 Dandini Boulevard, Reno, NV 89512

Western Nevada Community College

Carson City, Nevada
www.wncc.edu **CB code: 1141**

- Public 2-year community college
- Commuter campus in small city

General. Founded in 1971. Regionally accredited. 9 teaching centers in western Nevada. **Enrollment:** 3,244 degree-seeking undergraduates; 1,696 non-degree-seeking students. **Degrees:** 345 associate awarded. **Location:** 30 miles from Reno. **Calendar:** Semester, limited summer session. **Full-time faculty:** 77 total; 21% have terminal degrees, 4% minority, 46% women. **Part-time faculty:** 288 total; 8% minority, 47% women. **Special facilities:** Observatory. **Partnerships:** Formal partnerships with selected high schools for dual credit.

Student profile. Among degree-seeking undergraduates, 751 enrolled as first-time, first-year students.

Part-time:	74%	**Hispanic American:**	9%
Women:	60%	**Native American:**	4%
African American:	2%	**25 or older:**	59%
Asian American:	3%		

Transfer out. Colleges most students transferred to 2005: University of Nevada-Reno.

Basis for selection. Open admission, but selective for some programs. Special requirements for nursing and surgical tech programs. SAT and ACT scores accepted, but not required, for math and English placement. **Adult students:** Entrance exam policies same as for first-time freshmen.

2005-2006 Annual costs. Tuition/fees: $1,643; $6,558 out-of-state. Per-credit charge: $51 in-state; $215 out-of-state. Good Neighbor tuition: $81 per-credit-hour for student living within 50 miles of the Nevada border for one year or more or, graduates of specifically designated high schools or community colleges from neighboring states. Books/supplies: $1,000. Personal expenses: $1,200.

Financial aid. Need-based: Need-based aid available for part-time students. Work study available nights and weekends. **Non-need-based:** Scholarships awarded for academics, state residency.

Application procedures. Admission: No deadline. $15 fee. Application may be submitted online. No notification sent to applicants except by request. **Financial aid:** Priority date 4/15; no closing date. FAFSA required. Applicants notified on a rolling basis.

Academics. Special study options: Accelerated study, cooperative education, distance learning, double major, dual enrollment of high school students, ESL, honors, independent study, internships. License preparation in nursing, paramedic, real estate. **Credit/placement by examination:** AP, CLEP, institutional tests. 30 credit hours maximum toward associate degree. **Support services:** GED preparation and test center, learning center, remedial instruction, study skills assistance, tutoring.

Majors. Biology: Biophysics. **Business:** Accounting, business admin, management science, office technology, real estate. **Communications technology:** Graphics. **Computer sciences:** General, LAN/WAN management, webmaster. **Conservation:** General. **Education:** Early childhood. **Engineering:** General. **Engineering technology:** Drafting, electrical. **Health:** Nursing (RN). **Legal studies:** Paralegal. **Liberal arts:** Arts/sciences. **Math:** General. **Mechanic/repair:** Automotive. **Physical sciences:** Chemistry, physics. **Production:** Machine tool, welding. **Protective services:** Corrections, police science.

Most popular majors. Business/marketing 12%, health sciences 12%, liberal arts 55%.

Computing on campus. 678 workstations in library, computer center, student center. Commuter students can connect to campus network. Online course registration, online library available.

Student life. Freshman orientation: Available. Preregistration for classes offered. **Policies:** Freshmen permitted cars on campus. **Activities:** Choral groups, drama, musical theater, student government, student newspaper.

Athletics. NJCAA. **Intercollegiate:** Baseball M, rodeo, soccer W. **Team name:** Wildcats.

Student services. Career counseling, student employment services, financial aid counseling, on-campus daycare, personal counseling, placement for graduates, veterans' counselor. **Physically disabled:** Services for visually, hearing impaired. **Transfer:** Special adviser, orientation, preadmission transcript evaluation for new students. Transfer center, transfer adviser for students transferring to 4-year colleges.

Contact. E-mail: wncc_aro@wncc.edu
Phone: (775) 445-3277 Fax: (775) 887-3147
Dianne Hilliard, Director, Admissions and Records, Western Nevada Community College, 2201 West College Parkway, Carson City, NV 89703-7399

New Hampshire

McIntosh College

Dover, New Hampshire
www.mcintoshcollege.edu **CB code: 3553**

- For-profit 2-year community college
- Commuter campus in large town
- Interview required

General. Founded in 1896. Regionally accredited. **Enrollment:** 1,402 degree-seeking undergraduates. **Degrees:** 268 associate awarded. **Location:** 5 miles from Durham, 75 miles from Boston. **Calendar:** Quarter, extensive summer session. **Full-time faculty:** 19 total. **Part-time faculty:** 21 total. **Class size:** 59% < 20, 41% 20-39.

Student profile. Among degree-seeking undergraduates, 12% enrolled in a transfer program, 1% already have a bachelor's degree or higher.

Transfer out. Colleges most students transferred to 2005: Southern New Hampshire University, University of New Hampshire.

Basis for selection. Open admission. **Adult students:** Entrance exam policies same as for first-time freshmen. **Homeschooled:** Proof of accreditation of school required.

2006-2007 Annual costs. Cost of full associate programs vary from $26,500 to $39,500. Cost of room and board for length of program: $13,200. Books/supplies: $950.

Financial aid. All financial aid based on need. Need-based aid available for part-time students. Work study available nights and weekends.

Application procedures. Admission: No deadline. $25 fee. Application may be submitted online. Admission notification on a rolling basis. **Financial aid:** No deadline. FAFSA required. Applicants notified on a rolling basis; must reply within 4 week(s) of notification.

Academics. Special study options: Accelerated study, combined bachelor's/graduate degree, internships, liberal arts/career combination, study abroad. **Credit/placement by examination:** AP, CLEP, IB, institutional tests. 50% of credits must be earned in residence. **Support services:** Learning center, pre-admission summer program, reduced course load, remedial instruction, study skills assistance, tutoring, writing center.

Majors. Business: General, accounting, accounting/business management, accounting/finance, administrative services, apparel, business admin, communications, finance, managerial economics, market research, marketing, office management, office/clerical, operations, sales/distribution, taxation. **Health:** Clinical lab assistant, health aide, health care admin, health services, home attendant, medical assistant, medical records technology, medical secretary, office admin, office assistant, receptionist, staff services technology. **Legal studies:** General, legal secretary, paralegal. **Protective services:** Correctional facilities, corrections, criminal justice, criminalistics, forensics, juvenile corrections, law enforcement admin, police science, security management, security services. **Visual/performing arts:** Art, commercial photography, commercial/advertising art, design, drawing, graphic design, illustration, photography.

Computing on campus. 225 workstations in dormitories, library, computer center. Dormitories wired for high-speed internet access and linked to campus network. Commuter students can connect to campus network. Online course registration, online library, helpline, repair service, student web hosting, wireless network available.

Student life. Freshman orientation: Mandatory. Preregistration for classes offered. **Policies:** Freshmen permitted cars on campus. **Housing:** Guaranteed on-campus for freshmen. Coed dorms, substance-free housing available. $100 deposit. **Activities:** Drama, student government, student newspaper, Student Activities Committee, Criminal Justice Association, Paralegal Association, Collegiate Secretaries International, liberal arts club, drama club, Delta Epsilon Chi.

Student services. Career counseling, student employment services, financial aid counseling, personal counseling, placement for graduates. **Physically disabled:** Services for visually, speech, hearing impaired. **Transfer:** Special adviser, orientation, re-entry adviser, pre-admission transcript evaluation for new students. Transfer adviser, college fairs on campus for students transferring to 4-year colleges.

Contact. E-mail: admissions@mcintoshcollege.edu
Phone: (888) 262-1111 Toll-free number: (800) 624-6867
Fax: (603) 743-0060
Jody LaBrie, Vice President of Admissions, McIntosh College, 23 Cataract Avenue, Dover, NH 03820-3990

New Hampshire Community Technical College: Berlin

Berlin, New Hampshire
www.berlin.nhctc.edu **CB code: 3646**

- Public 2-year community and technical college
- Commuter campus in large town

General. Founded in 1966. Regionally accredited. **Enrollment:** 587 degree-seeking undergraduates. **Degrees:** 294 associate awarded. **Location:** 110 miles from Concord, 100 miles from Portland, Maine. **Calendar:** Semester, limited summer session. **Full-time faculty:** 31 total. **Part-time faculty:** 59 total.

Basis for selection. School record, class rank, counselor recommendations, test results, interview considered. NLN PreAdmission Exam-RN required for nursing students. All others participate in ASSET test. Interview recommended.

2005-2006 Annual costs. Tuition/fees: $5,040; $11,400 out-of-state. Per-credit charge: $164 in-state; $376 out-of-state. New England Regional Plan $246 per credit hour. Books/supplies: $500. Personal expenses: $1,500.

Financial aid. All financial aid based on need. Need-based aid available for part-time students.

Application procedures. Admission: Priority date 5/1; no deadline. $10 fee, may be waived for applicants with need. Admission notification on a rolling basis beginning on or about 12/1. **Financial aid:** Priority date 5/1; no closing date. FAFSA, institutional form required. Applicants notified on a rolling basis starting 5/1; must reply within 2 week(s) of notification.

Academics. Special study options: Cooperative education, distance learning, double major, dual enrollment of high school students, independent study, internships, student-designed major. **Credit/placement by examination:** CLEP, institutional tests. 32 credit hours maximum toward associate degree. **Support services:** Learning center, reduced course load, remedial instruction, study skills assistance, tutoring.

Majors. Business: Accounting, administrative services, business admin, hospitality admin, office technology, office/clerical, restaurant/food services. **Communications technology:** Graphic/printing. **Computer sciences:** General. **Conservation:** Environmental studies, forestry, management/policy. **Construction:** Electrician. **Education:** Early childhood, multi-level teacher. **Engineering technology:** Computer systems, drafting, manufacturing, surveying, water quality. **Health:** Nursing (RN). **Liberal arts:** Arts/sciences. **Mechanic/repair:** Automotive, diesel, electronics/electrical. **Personal/culinary services:** Chef training, restaurant/catering. **Protective services:** Fire safety technology, firefighting, law enforcement admin. **Public administration:** Human services. **Visual/performing arts:** Graphic design.

Computing on campus. 45 workstations in library, computer center. Online course registration, online library available.

Student life. Freshman orientation: Mandatory, $25 fee. **Activities:** Student government, student newspaper.

Athletics. Intercollegiate: Basketball, ice hockey M, soccer. **Intramural:** Basketball, ice hockey M, volleyball.

Student services. Adult student services, career counseling, student employment services, financial aid counseling, on-campus daycare, personal counseling, veterans' counselor. **Physically disabled:** Services for visually, hearing impaired. **Transfer:** Special adviser, orientation for new students. Transfer adviser for students transferring to 4-year colleges.

Contact. E-mail: berlin4u@nhctc.edu
Phone: (603) 752-1113 Toll-free number: (800) 445-4525
Fax: (603) 752-6335
Mark Desmarais, Admissions Director, New Hampshire Community Technical College: Berlin, 2020 Riverside Drive, Berlin, NH 03570

New Hampshire Community Technical College: Claremont

Claremont, New Hampshire
www.ncctc.edu **CB code: 3684**

- Public 2-year technical college
- Large town

General. Founded in 1967. Regionally accredited. Restaurant mangement program includes one year in Switzerland with study at Les Roches. **Enrollment:** 1,200 degree-seeking undergraduates. **Degrees:** 123 associate awarded. **Location:** 50 miles from Concord. **Calendar:** Semester, limited summer session. **Full-time faculty:** 41 total. **Part-time faculty:** 5 total.

Basis for selection. Open admission, but selective for some programs. Special requirements for nursing program. Accuplacer test used for placement.

High school preparation. Typing required for medical assistant, chemistry required for nursing and medical laboratory programs. Algebra recommended for all applicants.

2005-2006 Annual costs. Tuition/fees: $5,010; $11,370 out-of-state. Per-credit charge: $164 in-state; $376 out-of-state. New England Regional tuition: $246 per credit hour. Books/supplies: $550. Personal expenses: $1,100.

Financial aid. All financial aid based on need. Need-based aid available for part-time students.

Application procedures. Admission: No deadline. $10 fee. Admission notification on a rolling basis. **Financial aid:** Priority date 5/1; no closing date. FAFSA required. Applicants notified on a rolling basis; must reply within 2 week(s) of notification.

Academics. Special study options: Accelerated study, cooperative education, double major, independent study, internships. Joint associate degree program in restaurant management with Les Roches, 2-2 program in teacher education with Keene State College. **Credit/placement by examination:** CLEP, institutional tests. 16 credit hours maximum toward associate degree. **Support services:** Learning center, reduced course load, tutoring.

Majors. Business: General, accounting, office technology. **Engineering technology:** Computer systems, manufacturing. **Health:** Clinical lab technology, nursing (RN), occupational therapy assistant, physical therapy assistant, respiratory therapy technology. **Liberal arts:** Arts/sciences. **Parks/recreation:** General. **Public administration:** Human services.

Most popular majors. Health sciences 87%.

Computing on campus. 45 workstations in library, computer center.

Student life. Activities: Student government.

Student services. Student employment services, health services, on-campus daycare, personal counseling, placement for graduates, veterans' counselor. **Transfer:** Special adviser, orientation for new students.

Contact. Phone: (603) 542-7744 Fax: (603) 543-1844
Chuck Kusselow, Director of Admissions, New Hampshire Community Technical College: Claremont, One College Drive, Claremont, NH 03743-9707

New Hampshire Community Technical College: Manchester

Manchester, New Hampshire **CB member**
www.manchester.nhctc.edu **CB code: 3660**

- Public 2-year community and technical college
- Commuter campus in small city

General. Founded in 1945. Regionally accredited. Many opportunities for internships (paid and unpaid) and clinicals; strong support for immigrants, first generation college students. **Enrollment:** 3,000 undergraduates. **Degrees:** 141 associate awarded. **Location:** 50 miles from Boston. **Calendar:** Semester, limited summer session. **Full-time faculty:** 70 total. **Part-time faculty:** 125 total. **Partnerships:** On-site programs with local businesses. Established articulation agreements with a select number of high school technical programs.

Student profile.

Out-of-state:	10%	25 or older:	35%

Basis for selection. Open admission, but selective for some programs. Ford automotive program students must be sponsored by Ford dealership. Selective admission to nursing program. NLN pre-admission test required for nursing applicants. ACCUPLACER required for all other applicants. Interview recommended for all; portfolio recommended for commercial design and illustration. Essay required for exercise science and nursing programs.

High school preparation. Recommended units include English 4, mathematics 3 and science 2. Chemistry, algebra, geometry and biology required for some programs.

2005-2006 Annual costs. Tuition/fees: $5,070; $11,430 out-of-state. Per-credit charge: $164 in-state; $376 out-of-state. New England Regional tuition: $246 per credit hour. Books/supplies: $550. Personal expenses: $1,770.

Financial aid. All financial aid based on need. Work study available nights, weekends and for part-time students. **Additional information:** 100% of direct educational expenses met for all financial aid applicants.

Application procedures. Admission: No deadline. $10 fee, may be waived for applicants with need. Admission notification on a rolling basis. **Financial aid:** Priority date 5/1; no closing date. FAFSA, institutional form required. Applicants notified on a rolling basis starting 4/15; must reply within 2 week(s) of notification.

Academics. Special study options: Cooperative education, distance learning, double major, ESL, independent study, internships, liberal arts/career combination, student-designed major. **Credit/placement by examination:** CLEP, institutional tests. 32 credit hours maximum toward associate degree. **Support services:** Learning center, reduced course load, remedial instruction, study skills assistance, tutoring, writing center.

Majors. Business: Accounting, administrative services, business admin, management science, marketing, office management. **Computer sciences:** General. **Construction:** Maintenance. **Education:** Early childhood. **Engineering technology:** Construction, drafting, electrical. **Health:** Medical assistant, medical records technology, medical secretary, nursing (RN). **Liberal arts:** Arts/sciences. **Mechanic/repair:** Automotive, heating/ac/refrig. **Parks/recreation:** Exercise sciences. **Production:** Welding. **Public administration:** Human services. **Visual/performing arts:** Commercial/advertising art, interior design.

Computing on campus. 75 workstations in library, computer center. Online library available.

Student life. Freshman orientation: Available, $25 fee. Preregistration for classes offered. **Activities:** Literary magazine, student government, honor society, community service club, Alternative Spring Break (service), International Club, Student Senate.

Athletics. Intercollegiate: Basketball M, volleyball. **Intramural:** Basketball, skiing, soccer, volleyball.

Student services. Career counseling, services for economically disadvantaged, financial aid counseling, minority student services, on-campus daycare. **Physically disabled:** Services for visually, hearing impaired. **Transfer:** Special adviser, orientation for new students. Transfer adviser for students transferring to 4-year colleges.

Contact. Phone: (603) 668-6706 ext. 208 Toll-free number: (800) 924-3445 Fax: (603) 668-5354
Jaquelyn Poirier, Director of Admissions, New Hampshire Community Technical College: Manchester, 1066 Front Street, Manchester, NH 03102-8518

New Hampshire Community Technical College: Nashua

Nashua, New Hampshire **CB member**
www.nashua.nhctc.edu **CB code: 3643**

- Public 2-year community and technical college
- Commuter campus in small city
- Interview required

General. Founded in 1967. Regionally accredited. Small class size; free parking; online classes available. **Enrollment:** 1,386 degree-seeking undergraduates. **Degrees:** 155 associate awarded. **Location:** 20 miles from Lowell, Massachusetts. **Calendar:** Semester, limited summer session. **Full-time faculty:** 40 total. **Part-time faculty:** 65 total. **Class size:** 82% < 20, 18% 20-39. **Special facilities:** Clinical labs and classrooms for nursing students

Two-Year Colleges

off campus at Southern New Hampshire Medical Center, a short distance from campus.

Transfer out. Colleges most students transferred to 2005: University of Southern New Hampshire, University of New Hampshire, Keene State College, Plymouth State College.

Basis for selection. Open admission, but selective for some programs. Prerequisite courses, references, interview, exam required to apply for Nursing program. **Adult students:** Entrance exam policies same as for first-time freshmen. **Homeschooled:** Must meet ability-to-benefit rules for admission.

High school preparation. One unit algebra required for business and technical programs, 2 for computer/engineering technology.

2005-2006 Annual costs. Tuition/fees: $5,023; $11,383 out-of-state. Per-credit charge: $164 in-state; $376 out-of-state. New England Regional tuition: $246 per credit hour. Books/supplies: $500. Personal expenses: $500.

2004-2005 Financial aid. All financial aid based on need. 51% of total undergraduate aid awarded as scholarships/grants, 49% as loans/jobs. Need-based aid available for part-time students. Work study available nights and for part-time students.

Application procedures. Admission: No deadline. $10 fee, may be waived for applicants with need. Admission notification on a rolling basis. Priority given to applicants for full-time study. Application priority date of 12/31 for Nursing applicants. **Financial aid:** Priority date 5/1; no closing date. FAFSA required. Applicants notified on a rolling basis starting 3/1; must reply within 2 week(s) of notification.

Academics. Special study options: Distance learning, dual enrollment of high school students, ESL, independent study, internships, student-designed major, weekend college. Bachelor's degree programs available on campus. License preparation in aviation. **Credit/placement by examination:** CLEP, institutional tests. 48 credit hours maximum toward associate degree. **Support services:** Learning center, pre-admission summer program, reduced course load, remedial instruction, study skills assistance, tutoring, writing center.

Majors. Business: Accounting, business admin. **Computer sciences:** General, applications programming, computer science, data entry, data processing, information systems, networking, webmaster. **Education:** Early childhood. **Engineering:** Electrical. **Engineering technology:** Drafting, electrical, manufacturing, robotics. **Health:** Nursing (RN). **Legal studies:** Paralegal. **Liberal arts:** Arts/sciences. **Mechanic/repair:** Aircraft, auto body, automotive, electronics/electrical, industrial. **Public administration:** Human services.

Computing on campus. 150 workstations in library, computer center. Student web hosting available.

Student life. Freshman orientation: Mandatory, $25 fee. Preregistration for classes offered. One-day session includes college adjustment seminars and academic advising. **Housing:** Student housing available near campus; partnership with local college for residence hall space. **Activities:** Drama, literary magazine, student government, student newspaper, Phi Theta Kappa, Rotoract.

Athletics. Intramural: Soccer.

Student services. Adult student services, career counseling, student employment services, financial aid counseling, personal counseling, placement for graduates, veterans' counselor. **Transfer:** Special adviser, orientation, pre-admission transcript evaluation for new students. Transfer adviser, college fairs on campus for students transferring to 4-year colleges.

Contact. E-mail: nashua@nhctc.edu
Phone: (603) 882-6923 ext. 1520 Fax: (603) 882-8690
Patricia Goodman, Director of Admissions, New Hampshire Community Technical College: Nashua, 505 Amherst Street, Nashua, NH 03063

New Hampshire Community Technical College: Stratham

Stratham, New Hampshire
www.stratham.nhctc.edu **CB code: 3661**

- Public 2-year community and technical college
- Commuter campus in small town

General. Founded in 1945. Regionally accredited. **Enrollment:** 2,000 undergraduates. **Degrees:** 142 associate awarded. **Location:** 45 miles from Boston. **Calendar:** Semester, limited summer session. **Full-time faculty:** 32 total. **Part-time faculty:** 41 total. **Special facilities:** Biotechnology lab.

Basis for selection. Open admission, but selective for some programs and for out-of-state students. Rank in top three-fifths of class preferred for nursing programs. Out-of-state applicants must rank in top half. National League for Nursing Pre-Admission Assessment for Registered Nursing required for applicants to RN program. ACT-PEP Nursing Fundamentals Test required for admission to associate degree nursing program as advanced standing students. Career Guidance Placement Test given to technical majors on selected basis. Interview required for allied health applicants, recommended for all technical applicants. **Adult students:** SAT/ACT scores not required.

High school preparation. Recommended units include English 4, mathematics 2, social studies 2 and science 2. High school vocational and college-preparatory courses recommended. For mechanical-technical majors, algebra I and II and geometry recommended. For associate nursing applicants, biology, chemistry, algebra I required. For business management, typing or keyboarding skills required.

2005-2006 Annual costs. Tuition/fees: $5,070; $11,430 out-of-state. Per-credit charge: $164 in-state; $376 out-of-state. New England Regional tuition: $246 per credit hour. Books/supplies: $600. Personal expenses: $1,000.

Application procedures. Admission: No deadline. $10 fee, may be waived for applicants with need. Application may be submitted online. Admission notification on a rolling basis. Out-of-state students encouraged to apply in early fall of senior year but not before completion of 1 marking period. **Financial aid:** Priority date 5/1; no closing date. FAFSA, institutional form required. Applicants notified on a rolling basis; must reply within 2 week(s) of notification.

Academics. Part-time day study available to matriculated and nonmatriculated students. **Special study options:** Accelerated study, distance learning, double major, dual enrollment of high school students, ESL, independent study, internships, liberal arts/career combination. License preparation in nursing, real estate. **Credit/placement by examination:** CLEP, institutional tests. **Support services:** GED preparation, learning center, pre-admission summer program, reduced course load, remedial instruction, study skills assistance, tutoring.

Majors. Biology: Biotechnology. **Business:** General, accounting, administrative services, business admin. **Computer sciences:** Information systems, programming, web page design. **Education:** Social science. **Engineering technology:** Drafting. **Family/consumer sciences:** Child care. **Health:** Nursing (RN), surgical technology, veterinary technology/assistant. **Interdisciplinary:** Gerontology. **Mechanic/repair:** Automotive.

Computing on campus. 140 workstations in computer center. Online library available.

Student life. Freshman orientation: Available. **Activities:** Literary magazine, student government, student senate, Phi Theta Kappa.

Athletics. Intercollegiate: Baseball M, basketball, soccer, softball, volleyball.

Student services. Career counseling, student employment services, placement for graduates. **Transfer:** Special adviser, orientation, pre-admission transcript evaluation for new students. Transfer adviser, college fairs on campus for students transferring to 4-year colleges.

Contact. E-mail: lshennett@nhctc.edu
Phone: (603) 772-1194 Toll-free number: (800) 522-1194
Fax: (603) 772-1198
Laurilee Shennett, Admissions Coordinator, New Hampshire Community Technical College: Stratham, 277 Portsmouth Avenue, Stratham, NH 03885

New Hampshire Technical Institute

Concord, New Hampshire
www.nhti.edu **CB code: 3647**

- Public 2-year community and technical college
- Commuter campus in large town

General. Founded in 1965. Regionally accredited. **Enrollment:** 2,729 degree-seeking undergraduates. **Degrees:** 506 associate awarded. **Location:** 75 miles from Boston. **Calendar:** Semester, extensive summer session. **Full-time faculty:** 100 total; 12% have terminal degrees, 60% women. **Part-time faculty:** 100 total; 70% women. **Special facilities:** Planetarium, wellness center.

Student profile.

Out-of-state:	2%	**Hispanic American:**	1%
African American:	2%	**25 or older:**	50%
Asian American:	1%	**Live on campus:**	23%

Transfer out. Colleges most students transferred to 2005: University of NH, Southern NH University, Plymouth State College, Keene State College, Granite State College.

Basis for selection. Requirements vary by program. Nursing and allied health programs require special testing and interviews. National League for Nursing Pre-Nursing Test, special challenge test for practical nursing required. Interview required for health program applicants, recommended for others. **Adult students:** Institutional assessment test is required of all students. **Homeschooled:** Transcript of courses and grades required. Must submit portfolio of work approved by school district.

High school preparation. College-preparatory program recommended. Recommended units include English 4, mathematics 3 and science 2. High school academic subject requirements vary according to program. Strong background in mathematics and natural sciences recommended.

2005-2006 Annual costs. Tuition/fees: $5,400; $11,760 out-of-state. Per-credit charge: $164 in-state; $376 out-of-state. New England Regional tuition: $246 per credit hour. Room/board: $6,110. Books/supplies: $600. Personal expenses: $1,600.

2005-2006 Financial aid. All financial aid based on need. Need-based aid available for part-time students. Work study available nights, weekends and for part-time students. **Additional information:** 60% of students who apply receive some form of financial aid. State school; all financial aid need-based, primarily from federal sources. No scholarships awarded.

Application procedures. Admission: No deadline. $10 fee, may be waived for applicants with need. Application may be submitted online. Admission notification on a rolling basis. Must reply by May 1 or within 4 week(s) if notified thereafter. Applicants must make a $100 deposit within 30 days of acceptance. **Financial aid:** Priority date 5/1; no closing date. FAFSA, institutional form required. Applicants notified on a rolling basis starting 6/1; must reply within 2 week(s) of notification.

Academics. Special study options: Distance learning, double major, ESL, internships. License preparation in dental hygiene, nursing, paramedic, radiology, real estate. **Credit/placement by examination:** AP, CLEP, IB, institutional tests. **Support services:** Learning center, pre-admission summer program, reduced course load, remedial instruction, study skills assistance, tutoring, writing center.

Majors. Business: Accounting, business admin, hospitality admin, hospitality/recreation, marketing, real estate, tourism promotion, tourism/travel. **Communications technology:** General. **Computer sciences:** General. **Education:** General, early childhood. **Engineering technology:** Architectural, civil, computer, electrical, manufacturing. **Health:** Dental hygiene, EMT paramedic, medical radiologic technology/radiation therapy, mental health services, nursing (RN), substance abuse counseling. **Legal studies:** Paralegal. **Liberal arts:** Arts/sciences. **Parks/recreation:** Sports admin. **Protective services:** Law enforcement admin. **Public administration:** Human services. **Social sciences:** General.

Most popular majors. Business/marketing 15%, computer/information sciences 7%, engineering/engineering technologies 14%, health sciences 39%, liberal arts 8%, security/protective services 7%.

Computing on campus. 225 workstations in dormitories, library, computer center. Wireless network available.

Student life. Freshman orientation: Mandatory, $25 fee. Preregistration for classes offered. Held before start of fall and spring semesters. **Policies:** Freshmen permitted cars on campus. **Housing:** Coed dorms, single-sex dorms, substance-free housing available. $50 fully refundable deposit. **Activities:** Drama, literary magazine, student government, student newspaper, student senate, campus pride, outing club, Phi Theta Kappa, student nurses association, Roentga Ray society, alternative spring break, criminal justice club, Christian Fellowship.

Athletics. Intercollegiate: Baseball M, basketball, soccer, softball W, volleyball. **Intramural:** Basketball, football (non-tackle) M, volleyball. **Team name:** Capitals.

Student services. Career counseling, financial aid counseling, health services, on-campus daycare, personal counseling, placement for graduates, veterans' counselor. **Physically disabled:** Services for visually, speech, hearing impaired. **Learning disabled:** Comprehensive services available. **Transfer:** Special adviser, orientation, pre-admission transcript evaluation for new students. Transfer adviser, college fairs on campus for students transferring to 4-year colleges.

Contact. E-mail: nhtiadm@nhctc.edu
Phone: (603) 271-7134 Toll-free number: (800) 247-0179
Fax: (603) 271-7139
Francis Meyer, Director of Admissions, New Hampshire Technical Institute, 31 College Drive, Concord, NH 03301

Two-Year Colleges

New Jersey

Assumption College for Sisters
Mendham, New Jersey
www.acscollegeforsisters.org **CB code: 2009**

- Private 2-year junior and liberal arts college for women affiliated with Roman Catholic Church
- Commuter campus in small town
- Interview required

General. Founded in 1953. Regionally accredited. **Enrollment:** 31 degree-seeking undergraduates; 6 non-degree-seeking students. **Degrees:** 6 associate awarded. **Location:** 35 miles from New York City. **Calendar:** Semester, limited summer session. **Full-time faculty:** 1 total; 100% women. **Part-time faculty:** 16 total; 12% have terminal degrees, 81% women. **Class size:** 100% < 20.

Student profile. Among degree-seeking undergraduates, 16 enrolled as first-time, first-year students.

Part-time:	6%	**Women:**	100%
Out-of-state:	60%	**International:**	84%

Basis for selection. Interview, recommendations, school achievement record, test scores, commitment to obligations of religious vocation as well as acceptance of applicant by a religious community important.

High school preparation. 16 units required. Required units include English 4, mathematics 2, social studies 2, science 1 and foreign language 2.

2005-2006 Annual costs. Tuition/fees: $3,350. Per-credit charge: $100. Books/supplies: $400.

Application procedures. Admission: No deadline. No application fee. Admission notification on a rolling basis. **Financial aid:** No deadline.

Academics. Special study options: ESL. **Credit/placement by examination:** AP, CLEP. **Support services:** Reduced course load, remedial instruction, tutoring.

Majors. Liberal arts: Arts/sciences.

Computing on campus. 16 workstations in library, computer center, student center.

Student life. Freshman orientation: Mandatory. **Policies:** Religious observance required. **Housing:** Students reside with their religious congregations or with the Sisters of Christian Charity. **Activities:** Choral groups.

Student services. Personal counseling. **Transfer:** Special adviser, orientation, pre-admission transcript evaluation for new students. Transfer adviser for students transferring to 4-year colleges.

Contact. E-mail: srgerardine@scceast.org
Phone: (973) 543-6528 ext. 228 Fax: (973) 543-1738
Sr. Gerardine Tantsits, Academic Dean, Assumption College for Sisters, 350 Bernardsville Road, Mendham, NJ 07945-2923

Atlantic Cape Community College
Mays Landing, New Jersey **CB member**
www.atlantic.edu **CB code: 2024**

- Public 2-year community college
- Commuter campus in small town

General. Founded in 1964. Regionally accredited. Instruction and student/academic support services are delivered at a main campus (Mays Landing) and at 2 extension centers located in Atlantic City and Cape May. **Enrollment:** 6,845 degree-seeking undergraduates. **Degrees:** 634 associate awarded. **Location:** 15 miles from Atlantic City, 30 miles from Philadelphia. **Calendar:** Semester, limited summer session. **Full-time faculty:** 80 total. **Part-time faculty:** 200 total.

Transfer out. Colleges most students transferred to 2005: Richard Stockton State College of New Jersey, Rowan University, Rutgers University.

Basis for selection. Open admission, but selective for some programs. Admission to allied health and nursing programs based upon entrance exam scores and GPA. Deposit required for culinary arts program. All students must take college basic skills exam after completing their 12th credit or when they officially matriculate. Students who score 500 and above on Verbal section, and 470 on Math section of SAT are exempt from basic skills testing. **Adult students:** Entrance exam policies same as for first-time freshmen. **Homeschooled:** Students must be in certified home schooling program. A letter from the certifying school district approving the courses is required.

2005-2006 Annual costs. Tuition/fees: $2,610; $4,800 out-of-district; $8,100 out-of-state. Per-credit charge: $73 in-district; $146 out-of-district; $256 out-of-state. Books/supplies: $800.

Financial aid. Need-based: Need-based aid available for part-time students. Work study available for part-time students. **Additional information:** Installment plan available for culinary arts majors. Employees of Atlantic City casinos may attend ACCC at in-county rates regardless of where they live.

Application procedures. Admission: Closing date 9/1 (postmark date). $35 fee, may be waived for applicants with need. Application may be submitted online. Admission notification on a rolling basis. Applicants must make arrangements to take the College Basic Skills Placement Test unless SAT scores qualify them for exemption. **Financial aid:** Priority date 5/1; no closing date. FAFSA, institutional form required. Applicants notified on a rolling basis starting 5/1.

Academics. 8 associate degrees available through distance education: in liberal arts, history, psychology, business, computer information systems, humanities, general studies, and literature. **Special study options:** Cooperative education, distance learning, double major, dual enrollment of high school students, ESL, independent study, internships, liberal arts/career combination. License preparation in nursing, real estate. **Credit/placement by examination:** CLEP, institutional tests. 32 credit hours maximum toward associate degree. Total of 32 transfer credits may be awarded through combination of: college course transfer, articulation agreements, CLEP, Ponsi/ACE and/or Tech-Prep. **Support services:** GED test center, learning center, pre-admission summer program, reduced course load, remedial instruction, study skills assistance, tutoring, writing center.

Majors. Biology: General. **Business:** Accounting, business admin, hospitality admin, management information systems, tourism/travel. **Computer sciences:** General, data processing, programming. **Education:** General. **Family/consumer sciences:** Child care. **Health:** Nursing (RN), occupational therapy assistant, physical therapy assistant, respiratory therapy technology. **History:** General. **Legal studies:** Paralegal. **Math:** General. **Personal/culinary services:** Culinary arts. **Physical sciences:** Chemistry. **Psychology:** General. **Public administration:** Social work. **Social sciences:** General, sociology. **Visual/performing arts:** Studio arts.

Most popular majors. Business/marketing 23%, health sciences 11%, interdisciplinary studies 22%, liberal arts 30%.

Computing on campus. 430 workstations in library, computer center, student center. Online course registration, online library, helpline available.

Student life. Freshman orientation: Available. Preregistration for classes offered. **Housing:** Reserved housing program available. **Activities:** Choral groups, drama, literary magazine, music ensembles, radio station, student government, student newspaper, Human Services club, African American Coalition, international club, Jewish Association of Students, Phi Theta Kappa, Alpha & Omega Christian clubs, Shades of Brown of Atlantic City, special interest clubs.

Athletics. NJCAA. **Intercollegiate:** Archery, basketball M, golf, softball W. **Intramural:** Basketball, volleyball. **Team name:** Buccaneers.

Student services. Adult student services, career counseling, student employment services, health services, on-campus daycare, personal counseling, placement for graduates, veterans' counselor. **Physically disabled:** Services for visually, speech, hearing impaired. **Transfer:** Special adviser, orientation, pre-admission transcript evaluation for new students. Transfer adviser, college fairs on campus for students transferring to 4-year colleges.

Contact. E-mail: accadmit@atlantic.edu
Phone: (609) 343-5000 Fax: (609) 343-4921
Regina Skinner, Director, Admission and College Enrollment, Atlantic Cape Community College, 5100 Black Horse Pike, Mays Landing, NJ 08330

Bergen Community College
Paramus, New Jersey **CB member**
www.bergen.edu **CB code: 2032**

- Public 2-year community college
- Commuter campus in large town

General. Founded in 1965. Regionally accredited. **Enrollment:** 12,443 degree-seeking undergraduates. **Degrees:** 1,228 associate awarded. **Location:** 12 miles from New York City. **Calendar:** Semester, extensive summer session. **Full-time faculty:** 297 total. **Part-time faculty:** 459 total. **Special facilities:** Center for deaf education.

Student profile.

Out-of-state:	1%	25 or older:	37%

Transfer out. Colleges most students transferred to 2005: Montclair State College, William Paterson University, Rutgers University, Ramapo College.

Basis for selection. Open admission, but selective for some programs. Admission to allied health programs based on academic record and specific courses taken. Priority given to county residents. High school diploma not required for students over 18 years old.

High school preparation. Mathematics, biology, and chemistry required for most allied health programs.

2005-2006 Annual costs. Tuition/fees: $3,023; $5,790 out-of-district; $6,090 out-of-state. Per-credit charge: $87 in-district; $179 out-of-district; $189 out-of-state.

Application procedures. Admission: No deadline. $25 fee, may be waived for applicants with need. Admission notification on a rolling basis. Application closing date for nursing and dental hygiene is April 1. **Financial aid:** Priority date 5/15; no closing date. FAFSA required. Applicants notified on a rolling basis starting 6/1.

Academics. Special study options: Cooperative education, distance learning, dual enrollment of high school students, ESL, honors, internships, study abroad. Semester at Disney World for selected students. **Credit/placement by examination:** AP, CLEP, institutional tests. 45 credit hours maximum toward associate degree. **Support services:** Learning center, pre-admission summer program, reduced course load, remedial instruction, tutoring, writing center.

Majors. Agriculture: Horticulture. **Area/ethnic studies:** American. **Business:** Accounting technology, administrative services, banking/financial services, hotel/motel admin, marketing, sales/distribution, special products marketing, travel services. **Computer sciences:** Applications programming, information technology. **Education:** Early childhood. **Engineering technology:** General, electrical, manufacturing, mechanical drafting. **Health:** Clinical lab technology, dental hygiene, health services, medical assistant, medical radiologic technology/radiation therapy, nursing (RN), physical therapy assistant, respiratory therapy technology, sonography, veterinary technology/assistant. **Legal studies:** Paralegal. **Liberal arts:** Arts/sciences. **Protective services:** Police science. **Visual/performing arts:** Commercial/advertising art.

Most popular majors. Health sciences 17%, liberal arts 61%.

Student life. Activities: Choral groups, dance, drama, literary magazine, music ensembles, musical theater, student government, student newspaper.

Athletics. NJCAA. **Intercollegiate:** Baseball M, basketball, cross-country, golf M, soccer M, softball W, tennis M, track and field, volleyball W, wrestling M.

Student services. Career counseling, student employment services, financial aid counseling, health services, on-campus daycare, personal counseling, placement for graduates, veterans' counselor. **Physically disabled:** Services for visually, speech, hearing impaired. **Transfer:** Orientation for new students. Transfer adviser, college fairs on campus for students transferring to 4-year colleges.

Contact. E-mail: admsoffice@bergen.edu
Phone: (201) 447-7195 Fax: (201) 670-7973
Priscilla Klymenko, Director of Enrollment Services, Bergen Community College, 400 Paramus Road, Paramus, NJ 07652-1595

Brookdale Community College

Lincroft, New Jersey — **CB member**
www.brookdalecc.edu — **CB code: 2181**

- Public 2-year community college
- Commuter campus in small city

General. Founded in 1967. Regionally accredited. **Enrollment:** 11,438 degree-seeking undergraduates. **Degrees:** 1,498 associate awarded. **ROTC:** Army, Air Force. **Location:** 5 miles from Red Bank, 25 miles from New Brunswick. **Calendar:** Semester, extensive summer session. **Full-time faculty:** 233 total. **Part-time faculty:** 488 total.

Student profile.

Out-of-state:	1%	25 or older:	38%

Transfer out. Colleges most students transferred to 2005: Monmouth University, Rutgers University, Kean University.

Basis for selection. Open admission, but selective for some programs. Special requirements for health sciences programs and automative technology programs. Applicants without high school diploma or GED may be admitted. Must take equivalent of GED after specific number of credits in specific distribution. ACCUPLACER used for placement for all degree-seeking students who have reached their 12th credit. Group interview required for nursing, medical laboratory technology, respiratory therapy applicants, radiologic technology.

High school preparation. One unit high school or college algebra, 1 chemistry, 1 biology required for allied health programs.

2005-2006 Annual costs. Tuition/fees: $3,331; $6,083 out-of-district; $7,328 out-of-state. Per-credit charge: $92 in-district; $184 out-of-district; $225 out-of-state. Books/supplies: $1,000. Personal expenses: $1,195.

Financial aid. Need-based: Need-based aid available for part-time students. **Non-need-based:** Scholarships awarded for athletics.

Application procedures. Admission: No deadline. $25 fee. Application may be submitted online. Admission notification on a rolling basis. **Financial aid:** Priority date 5/1; no closing date. FAFSA, institutional form required. Applicants notified on a rolling basis starting 5/1; must reply within 2 week(s) of notification.

Academics. Special study options: Cooperative education, distance learning, ESL, honors, independent study, internships, study abroad, weekend college. License preparation in dental hygiene, nursing. **Credit/placement by examination:** AP, CLEP, institutional tests. **Support services:** GED preparation and test center, learning center, pre-admission summer program, reduced course load, remedial instruction, tutoring, writing center.

Majors. Business: General, accounting, administrative services, business admin, fashion, marketing. **Communications technology:** General, graphic/printing. **Computer sciences:** General. **Education:** General, teacher assistance. **Engineering:** General. **Engineering technology:** Electrical. **Health:** Clinical lab technology, dental hygiene, medical radiologic technology/radiation therapy, nursing (RN), respiratory therapy technology. **Legal studies:** Paralegal. **Liberal arts:** Arts/sciences. **Personal/culinary services:** Culinary arts. **Protective services:** Police science. **Public administration:** Social work. **Social sciences:** General. **Visual/performing arts:** Art, interior design, photography, studio arts.

Most popular majors. Business/marketing 28%, education 8%, health sciences 10%, liberal arts 23%, security/protective services 7%, social sciences 12%.

Computing on campus. 1,100 workstations in library, computer center. Commuter students can connect to campus network. Helpline available.

Student life. Freshman orientation: Available. Preregistration for classes offered. **Policies:** Freshmen permitted cars on campus. **Activities:** Dance, drama, film society, literary magazine, musical theater, radio station, student government, student newspaper, TV station.

Athletics. NJCAA. **Intercollegiate:** Baseball M, basketball, cross-country, soccer, softball W, tennis. **Intramural:** Basketball, golf M, volleyball. **Team name:** Blues.

Student services. Career counseling, student employment services, health services, on-campus daycare, personal counseling, placement for graduates, veterans' counselor. **Physically disabled:** Services for visually, speech, hearing impaired. **Transfer:** Special adviser for new students. Transfer adviser for students transferring to 4-year colleges.

Contact. Phone: (732) 224-2375 Fax: (732) 224-2271
Kim Toomey, Registrar, Brookdale Community College, 765 Newman Springs Road, Lincroft, NJ 07738

Burlington County College

Pemberton, New Jersey — **CB member**
www.bcc.edu — **CB code: 2180**

- Public 2-year community college
- Commuter campus in small town

General. Founded in 1966. Regionally accredited. Credit courses offered at 11 high schools, 2 military bases, Mount Laurel Campus, and extension centers in Willingboro and Mount Holly. **Enrollment:** 6,534 degree-seeking undergraduates; 1,354 non-degree-seeking students. **Degrees:** 694 associate awarded. **Location:** 30 miles from Philadelphia, 80 miles from New York City. **Calendar:** Semester, limited summer session. **Full-time faculty:** 65 total. **Part-time faculty:** 400 total. **Class size:** 33% < 20, 62% 20-39, 2% 40-49, 3% 50-99. **Partnerships:** Formal partnership with police academy.

Student profile. Among degree-seeking undergraduates, 66% enrolled in a transfer program, 34% enrolled in a vocational program, 1,895 enrolled as first-time, first-year students.

Part-time:	46%	**25 or older:**	37%
Women:	62%		

Transfer out. Colleges most students transferred to 2005: Rutgers University (Camden), Rutgers University (Newark), Rowan University, College of New Jersey, New Jersey Institute of Technology.

Basis for selection. Open admission, but selective for some programs. Academic high school background required of nursing program applicants.

2005-2006 Annual costs. Tuition/fees: $2,116; $2,950 out-of-district; $4,900 out-of-state. Per-credit charge: $66 in-district; $85 out-of-district; $150 out-of-state. Books/supplies: $1,000.

Financial aid. All financial aid based on need. Need-based aid available for part-time students.

Application procedures. Admission: No deadline. $20 fee, may be waived for applicants with need. Admission notification on a rolling basis. **Financial aid:** No deadline. FAFSA, institutional form required. Applicants notified on a rolling basis starting 7/1; must reply within 3 week(s) of notification.

Academics. Special study options: Cooperative education, distance learning, double major, dual enrollment of high school students, ESL, independent study, internships, study abroad, weekend college. Bachelor's degree programs available on campus. License preparation in dental hygiene, nursing, radiology. **Credit/placement by examination:** AP, CLEP, institutional tests. 30 credit hours maximum toward associate degree. **Support services:** GED preparation and test center, learning center, pre-admission summer program, reduced course load, remedial instruction, study skills assistance, tutoring, writing center.

Majors. Biology: Biotechnology. **Business:** General, accounting, accounting technology, business admin, fashion, management information systems, restaurant/food services, sales/distribution. **Communications technology:** Animation/special effects. **Computer sciences:** Computer graphics, computer science, data processing, information systems. **Engineering technology:** Automotive, CAD/CADD, civil, construction, drafting, electrical. **Foreign languages:** Sign language interpretation. **Health:** Dental hygiene, medical radiologic technology/radiation therapy, medical records technology, nursing (RN). **Legal studies:** Paralegal. **Liberal arts:** Arts/sciences. **Mechanic/repair:** Automotive. **Physical sciences:** General. **Protective services:** Firefighting, police science. **Public administration:** Human services. **Science technology:** Chemical. **Visual/performing arts:** Fashion design.

Most popular majors. Health sciences 14%, liberal arts 63%, security/protective services 8%.

Computing on campus. 1,600 workstations in library, computer center, student center. Wireless network available.

Student life. Freshman orientation: Available. Preregistration for classes offered. **Activities:** Concert band, choral groups, dance, drama, literary magazine, music ensembles, musical theater, radio station, student government, minority student union, veterans club, Phi Theta Kappa, Student Nurses Association, Collegiate Republicans, Young Democrats, Circle K, Students for Ecological Action, international student club, Christian student club.

Athletics. NJCAA. **Intercollegiate:** Baseball M, basketball, golf M, soccer, softball W. **Team name:** Barons.

Student services. Adult student services, alcohol/substance abuse counseling, career counseling, services for economically disadvantaged, student employment services, financial aid counseling, health services, minority student services, on-campus daycare, personal counseling, placement for graduates, veterans' counselor. **Physically disabled:** Services for visually, speech, hearing impaired. **Transfer:** Special adviser, orientation for new students. Transfer adviser, college fairs on campus for students transferring to 4-year colleges.

Contact. Phone: (609) 894-9311 ext. 1282 Fax: (609) 894-0764
Elva DeJesus-Lopez, Admissions Coordinator, Burlington County College, 601 Pemberton-Browns Mills Road, Pemberton, NJ 08068-1599

Camden County College

Blackwood, New Jersey — **CB member**
www.camdencc.edu — **CB code: 2121**

- Public 2-year community college
- Commuter campus in large town

General. Founded in 1966. Regionally accredited. Strong program in robotics, laser/electro optics technology, and computer graphics. **Enrollment:** 7,249 full-time, degree-seeking students. **Degrees:** 1,189 associate awarded. **Location:** 15 miles from Philadelphia, 13 miles from Camden. **Calendar:** Semester, extensive summer session. **Full-time faculty:** 141 total. **Part-time faculty:** 613 total. **Special facilities:** Integrated manufacturing building, laser technology institute for education and research, computer graphics laboratories.

Student profile.

Out-of-state:	2%	**25 or older:**	41%

Transfer out. Colleges most students transferred to 2005: Rowan University, Rutgers University-Camden, Temple University, Widener University.

Basis for selection. Open admission, but selective for some programs. Special requirements for allied health, dental, and nursing programs. SAT or ACT required for admission to certain selective programs. Psychological Corporation Pre-Nursing examination, entrance examination for School of Nursing or National League for Nursing, Pre-Nursing and Guidance examination required of nursing applicants. Mechanical aptitude test required for General Motors automotive service education program applicants. Dental Hygiene Aptitude Test required of students entering dental hygiene program. Interview recommended for various health and the General Motors programs.

2005-2006 Annual costs. Tuition/fees: $2,580; $2,700 out-of-state. Per-credit charge: $73 in-state; $77 out-of-state. Books/supplies: $650.

Financial aid. Need-based: Need-based aid available for part-time students. Work study available for part-time students.

Application procedures. Admission: No deadline. No application fee. Application may be submitted online. Admission notification on a rolling basis beginning on or about 2/3. **Financial aid:** Closing date 7/1. FAFSA, institutional form required. Applicants notified on a rolling basis starting 7/1.

Academics. Special study options: Cooperative education, cross-registration, distance learning, dual enrollment of high school students, ESL, honors, independent study, internships, liberal arts/career combination, weekend college. General Motors automotive service education program. **Credit/placement by examination:** CLEP, institutional tests. 30 credit hours maximum toward associate degree. New Jersey College Basic Skills placement test required. **Support services:** Learning center, pre-admission summer program, reduced course load, remedial instruction, study skills assistance, tutoring.

Majors. Business: Accounting, banking/financial services, business admin, management information systems, marketing, sales/distribution. **Computer sciences:** General, computer graphics. **Engineering:** Science. **Engineering technology:** Drafting, electrical. **Foreign languages:** Sign language interpretation. **Health:** Clinical lab technology, dental assistant, dental hygiene, nursing (RN), optician, respiratory therapy technology, veterinary technology/assistant. **Liberal arts:** Arts/sciences. **Protective services:** Fire safety technology, police science. **Public administration:** Social work. **Visual/performing arts:** Photography.

Computing on campus. 800 workstations in library, computer center.

Student life. Freshman orientation: Available. **Activities:** Concert band, choral groups, drama, literary magazine, radio station, student government, student newspaper.

Athletics. NJCAA. **Intercollegiate:** Baseball M, basketball, soccer, softball W. **Intramural:** Racquetball W.

Student services. Career counseling, student employment services, health services, on-campus daycare, placement for graduates, veterans' counselor. **Physically disabled:** Services for visually, speech, hearing impaired. **Transfer:** Special adviser for new students. Transfer adviser, college fairs on campus for students transferring to 4-year colleges.

Contact. Phone: (856) 227-7200 ext. 4200 Toll-free number: (888) 228-2466 Fax: (856) 374-4917
Dennis Ferry, Director of Admissions/Recruitment, Camden County College, Box 200, Blackwood, NJ 08012

County College of Morris

Randolph, New Jersey **CB member**
www.ccm.edu **CB code: 2124**

- Public 2-year community college
- Commuter campus in large town

General. Founded in 1965. Regionally accredited. Courses available at off-campus sites. **Enrollment:** 6,288 degree-seeking undergraduates. **Degrees:** 1,043 associate awarded. **Location:** 40 miles from New York City. **Calendar:** Semester, extensive summer session. **Full-time faculty:** 170 total. **Part-time faculty:** 335 total. **Special facilities:** Planetarium.

Student profile.

Out-of-state:	1%	25 or older:	25%

Transfer out. Colleges most students transferred to 2005: Montclair State University, William Paterson University of New Jersey, Rutgers University, Kean University, Fairleigh Dickinson University, New Jersey Institute of Technology.

Basis for selection. Open admission, but selective for some programs. Restricted admissions to nursing, medical lab technology, radiography, respiratory therapy, and veterinary technology on space-available basis. Applicants who are not native speakers of English are required to take the LOEP test (Levels of English Proficiency) for placement. SAT required for honors programs. Students who submit SAT scores of 500 (exclusive of writing) and over are exempt from basic skills placement test. Audition required for music programs. **Learning Disabled:** Learning-disabled students may apply to Horizons program if they want accomodations. This is in addition to application for admission.

High school preparation. 16 units recommended. Some programs require 2 to 4 units mathematics and 1 to 2 units laboratory science.

2005-2006 Annual costs. Tuition/fees: $3,045; $5,685 out-of-district; $7,815 out-of-state. Per-credit charge: $88 in-district; $176 out-of-district; $247 out-of-state. Tuition reciprocity agreements with neighboring counties allow some out-of-county residents to pay in-county rates. Books/supplies: $750. Personal expenses: $1,120.

Financial aid. Need-based: Need-based aid available for part-time students. Work study available for part-time students. **Non-need-based:** Scholarships awarded for athletics.

Application procedures. Admission: No deadline. $25 fee. Application may be submitted online. Admission notification on a rolling basis. **Financial aid:** Priority date 3/1; no closing date. FAFSA required. Applicants notified on a rolling basis starting 5/1.

Academics. Special study options: Cooperative education, distance learning, double major, dual enrollment of high school students, ESL, exchange student, external degree, honors, independent study, internships, liberal arts/career combination, study abroad, weekend college. Bachelor's degree programs available on campus. License preparation in aviation, nursing. **Credit/placement by examination:** AP, CLEP, institutional tests. **Support services:** GED preparation, learning center, pre-admission summer program, reduced course load, remedial instruction, study skills assistance, tutoring, writing center.

Majors. Agriculture: Business. **Business:** Administrative services, business admin, management information systems. **Communications technology:** General. **Education:** Early childhood. **Engineering:** Science. **Engineering technology:** Electrical. **Health:** Clinical lab technology, medical radiologic technology/radiation therapy, nursing (RN), respiratory therapy technology, veterinary technology/assistant. **Liberal arts:** Arts/sciences. **Parks/recreation:** Health/fitness. **Physical sciences:** General. **Protective services:** Police science. **Public administration:** General. **Science technology:** Biological. **Transportation:** Aviation. **Visual/performing arts:** General, commercial/advertising art.

Most popular majors. Business/marketing 29%, health sciences 10%, liberal arts 33%, security/protective services 7%, visual/performing arts 8%.

Computing on campus. 450 workstations in library, computer center. Commuter students can connect to campus network. Online course registration, online library, helpline available.

Student life. Freshman orientation: Available. Preregistration for classes offered. Half-day sessions held one week prior to start of academic year. **Activities:** Bands, choral groups, dance, drama, literary magazine, music ensembles, musical theater, radio station, student government, student newspaper, symphony orchestra, Phi Theta Kappa, united Latino organization, international students association, CCM ambassadors, black student union, Asian students association, Catholic campus ministry, Jewish students association, campus Christian fellowship, I.E.E.E.

Athletics. NJCAA. **Intercollegiate:** Baseball M, basketball, golf, ice hockey M, soccer, softball W, tennis. **Intramural:** Badminton, basketball, bowling, soccer W, softball, tennis, volleyball. **Team name:** Titans.

Student services. Adult student services, alcohol/substance abuse counseling, career counseling, services for economically disadvantaged, student employment services, financial aid counseling, health services, minority student services, on-campus daycare, personal counseling, placement for graduates, veterans' counselor, women's services. **Physically disabled:** Services for visually, hearing impaired. **Transfer:** Special adviser, orientation, pre-admission transcript evaluation for new students. Transfer adviser, college fairs on campus for students transferring to 4-year colleges.

Contact. E-mail: admis@ccm.edu
Phone: (973) 328-5100 Toll-free number: (888) 226-8001
Fax: (973) 328-5199
James McCarthy, Director of Admissions, County College of Morris, 214 Center Grove Road, Randolph, NJ 07869-2086

Cumberland County College

Vineland, New Jersey
www.cccnj.net **CB code: 2118**

- Public 2-year community college
- Commuter campus in small city

General. Founded in 1963. Regionally accredited. **Enrollment:** 3,256 degree-seeking undergraduates. **Degrees:** 380 associate awarded. **Location:** 35 miles from Philadelphia. **Calendar:** Semester, extensive summer session. **Full-time faculty:** 43 total. **Part-time faculty:** 170 total. **Class size:** 47% < 20, 46% 20-39, 6% 40-49, less than 1% 50-99. **Special facilities:** Fine and performing arts center.

Transfer out. Colleges most students transferred to 2005: Rowan University, Stockton State College, Rutgers University, University of Delaware.

Basis for selection. Open admission, but selective for some programs. Special requirements for nursing program. National League for Nursing pre-entrance examination required of nursing applicants.

2006-2007 Annual costs. Tuition/fees (projected): $2,940; $5,340 out-of-district; $10,140 out-of-state. $9 per-credit-hour technology fee in addition to the comprehensive fee included above. Tuition data are based on 30 credits for a full academic year. Books/supplies: $1,100. Personal expenses: $1,802.

2004-2005 Financial aid. Need-based: 66% of total undergraduate aid awarded as scholarships/grants, 34% as loans/jobs. Need-based aid available for part-time students. Work study available for part-time students. **Non-need-based:** Scholarships awarded for academics.

Application procedures. Admission: No deadline. $25 fee, may be waived for applicants with need. Application may be submitted online. Admission notification on a rolling basis. **Financial aid:** No deadline. FAFSA required. Applicants notified on a rolling basis; must reply within 3 week(s) of notification.

Academics. Special study options: Accelerated study, distance learning, double major, dual enrollment of high school students, ESL, honors, independent study. Regional program for students with learning disabilities. License preparation in nursing, radiology. **Credit/placement by examination:** CLEP, institutional tests. 32 credit hours maximum toward associate degree. **Support services:** GED preparation and test center, learning center, pre-admission summer program, reduced course load, remedial instruction, study skills assistance, tutoring, writing center.

Majors. Agriculture: General, aquaculture, ornamental horticulture. **Business:** Accounting, administrative services, business admin, hospitality/recreation, management information systems, marketing, office management, operations, tourism/travel. **Communications:** Journalism, radio/tv. **Computer sciences:** Computer science, networking, vendor certification. **Construction:** Site management. **Education:** Art, early childhood, multi-level teacher. **Engineering:** General. **Engineering technology:** Construction, electrical. **Health:** Medical radiologic technology/radiation therapy, nursing (RN), respiratory therapy assistant. **Interdisciplinary:** Biological/physical sciences, math/computer science. **Legal studies:** Paralegal. **Liberal arts:** Arts/sciences. **Math:** General. **Mechanic/repair:** Aircraft, industrial. **Protective services:** Criminal justice, police science. **Public**

Two-Year Colleges

Two-Year Colleges

administration: Social work. **Visual/performing arts:** Art, ceramics, cinematography, commercial/advertising art, dramatic, graphic design, studio arts.

Most popular majors. Business/marketing 7%, health sciences 18%, liberal arts 51%, public administration/social services 9%.

Computing on campus. 150 workstations in library, computer center. Online library, helpline available.

Student life. Freshman orientation: Mandatory. Preregistration for classes offered. **Policies:** Comprehensive support center for learning disabled students. **Activities:** Choral groups, drama, literary magazine, student government, student newspaper, symphony orchestra, multicultural club, Latin American club, African American club.

Athletics. NJCAA. **Intercollegiate:** Baseball M, basketball, cross-country, softball W, track and field. **Intramural:** Cross-country. **Team name:** Dukes, Lady Dukes.

Student services. Career counseling, services for economically disadvantaged, student employment services, financial aid counseling, personal counseling, placement for graduates. **Physically disabled:** Services for visually, speech, hearing impaired. **Learning disabled:** Comprehensive services available. **Transfer:** Special adviser for new students. Transfer adviser, college fairs on campus for students transferring to 4-year colleges.

Contact. Phone: (609) 691-8600 Fax: (609) 691-6157
Maud Fried-Goodnight, Executive Director of Enrollment and Student Support Services, Cumberland County College, PO Box 1500, Vineland, NJ 08362-9912

Essex County College
Newark, New Jersey
www.essex.edu **CB code: 2237**

- Public 2-year community college
- Commuter campus in large city

General. Founded in 1966. Regionally accredited. Classes also given at West Caldwell campus and several locations in Essex County and Newark. **Enrollment:** 9,359 degree-seeking undergraduates; 1,076 non-degree-seeking students. **Degrees:** 713 associate awarded. **Location:** 12 miles from New York City. **Calendar:** Semester, limited summer session. **Full-time faculty:** 158 total; 46% minority, 44% women. **Part-time faculty:** 436 total; 71% minority, 45% women. **Special facilities:** Theater, police academy, Africana Institute.

Student profile. Among degree-seeking undergraduates, 75% enrolled in a transfer program, 25% enrolled in a vocational program, 1% already have a bachelor's degree or higher, 2,314 enrolled as first-time, first-year students, 251 transferred in from other institutions.

Part-time:	42%	**Asian American:**	.3%
Out-of-state:	2%	**Hispanic American:**	19%
Women:	63%	**International:**	8%
African American:	51%	**25 or older:**	48%

Transfer out. 75% of students enrolled in the transfer program go on to 4-year colleges. **Colleges most students transferred to 2005:** Rutgers University at Newark, Montclair University, Kean University, New Jersey Institute of Technology.

Basis for selection. Open admission, but selective for some programs. Special requirements for allied health programs. Priority given to allied health program applications received by April 15. National League for nursing test required of nursing students. TOEFL recommended for international students. Interview recommended for nursing, ophthalmic science, physical therapy programs. **Adult students:** Companion Placement Test required.

2006-2007 Annual costs. Tuition/fees (projected): $3,165; $5,550 out-of-district; $5,550 out-of-state. Per-credit charge: $80 in-district; $159 out-of-district; $159 out-of-state. Books/supplies: $1,000. Personal expenses: $1,061.

Financial aid. Need-based: Need-based aid available for part-time students.

Application procedures. Admission: No deadline. $25 fee, may be waived for applicants with need. Admission notification on a rolling basis. **Financial aid:** Priority date 6/30; no closing date. FAFSA, institutional form required. Applicants notified on a rolling basis starting 6/15; must reply within 3 week(s) of notification.

Academics. Special study options: Cooperative education, cross-registration, double major, dual enrollment of high school students, ESL, honors, independent study, internships, teacher certification program. Cross-registration with other institutions in Council of Higher Education in Newark; civil construction engineering program with New Jersey Institute of Technology; criminal justice program with Rutgers: State University of New Jersey. License preparation in nursing, physical therapy, radiology. **Credit/placement by examination:** AP, CLEP, institutional tests. 30 credit hours maximum toward associate degree. Maximum credits accepted must be 30 credits less than number required for degree at Essex County College; may not include more than half credits required in major field. **Support services:** GED preparation and test center, learning center, reduced course load, remedial instruction, study skills assistance, tutoring, writing center.

Majors. Biology: General. **Business:** Accounting, accounting technology, administrative services, business admin, hospitality admin, office technology, tourism/travel. **Communications:** Journalism, media studies. **Computer sciences:** General, programming. **Education:** General, elementary, kindergarten/preschool, music, physical, secondary. **Engineering:** General, chemical, civil, electrical. **Engineering technology:** Architectural, civil, construction, electrical, manufacturing, surveying. **Health:** Dental hygiene, EMT paramedic, health care admin, health services, medical radiologic technology/radiation therapy, medical secretary, nursing (RN), optician, physical therapy assistant, premedicine, respiratory therapy technology. **Legal studies:** Paralegal. **Liberal arts:** Arts/sciences. **Math:** General. **Physical sciences:** Chemistry. **Protective services:** Criminal justice, firefighting, law enforcement admin, police science. **Public administration:** Human services, social work. **Science technology:** Chemical. **Social sciences:** General. **Visual/performing arts:** Art, commercial/advertising art, dramatic, studio arts, theater design.

Most popular majors. Business/marketing 24%, education 12%, health sciences 15%, liberal arts 14%, social sciences 10%.

Computing on campus. 750 workstations in library, computer center. Commuter students can connect to campus network. Online course registration available.

Student life. Freshman orientation: Available. Preregistration for classes offered. **Activities:** Choral groups, drama, music ensembles, musical theater, student government, student newspaper, Circle Francophone (French club), Islamic student organization, Latin student union, DECA (Distributive Education Club of America), criminal justice organization, Black student association, social science club, fashion entertainment board, Phi Theta Kappa.

Athletics. NJCAA. **Intercollegiate:** Basketball, soccer M, track and field. **Intramural:** Basketball, table tennis, volleyball. **Team name:** Wolverines.

Student services. Alcohol/substance abuse counseling, career counseling, student employment services, financial aid counseling, health services, on-campus daycare, personal counseling, placement for graduates, veterans' counselor, women's services. **Physically disabled:** Services for visually, speech, hearing impaired. **Transfer:** Special adviser for new students. Transfer center, transfer adviser, college fairs on campus for students transferring to 4-year colleges.

Contact. Phone: (973) 877-3100 Fax: (973) 623-6449
Marva Mack, Director of Admissions, Essex County College, 303 University Avenue, Newark, NJ 07102

Gibbs College
Livingston, New Jersey
www.gibbsnj.edu **CB code: 4914**

- For-profit 2-year business and junior college
- Commuter campus in large town

General. Founded in 1911. Accredited by ACICS. **Location:** 12 miles from New York City. **Calendar:** Quarter.

Annual costs/financial aid. Tuition for full 18-month associate programs ranges from $25,850 to $32,095; books $1,900-$2,000. Tuition for certificate programs ranges from $15,995 to $17,995; books $950-$2,000. Need-based financial aid available for full-time students.

Contact. Phone: (973) 369-1360
President, 630 West Mount Pleasant Avenue, Route 10, Livingston, NJ 07039

Gloucester County College
Sewell, New Jersey
www.gccnj.edu **CB member** **CB code: 2281**

- Public 2-year community college
- Commuter campus in large town

General. Founded in 1966. Regionally accredited. **Enrollment:** 3,205 full-time, degree-seeking students. **Degrees:** 482 associate awarded. **Location:** 12 miles from Camden, 16 miles from Philadelphia. **Calendar:** Semester, limited summer session. **Full-time faculty:** 60 total. **Part-time faculty:** 165 total. **Special facilities:** Satellite downlink dish, learning resource center, 60-station computer room for multimedia course delivery and Internet access, interactive television (ITV) distance learning classroom.

Student profile.

Out-of-state:	1%	**25 or older:**	55%

Transfer out. Colleges most students transferred to 2005: Rowan University, Rutgers University, Richard Stockton College of New Jersey, Drexel University (PA).

Basis for selection. Open admission, but selective for some programs. Special requirements for certain programs including allied health and automotive technology programs. Special-need students, deaf or hearing-impaired evaluated for support college can offer. Institutional placement tests may be used. **Homeschooled:** Eligible, but admission determined on individual basis.

High school preparation. Biology and chemistry required for nursing applicants. Algebra also required for respiratory therapy, nuclear medicine, and diagnostic medical sonography applicants.

2005-2006 Annual costs. Tuition/fees: $2,760; $2,790 out-of-district; $4,980 out-of-state. Per-credit charge: $74 in-district; $75 out-of-district; $148 out-of-state. On-line courses per-credit-hour charge: $90. Books/supplies: $750.

Financial aid. All financial aid based on need. Need-based aid available for part-time students. Work study available nights and for part-time students.

Application procedures. Admission: No deadline. $20 fee, may be waived for applicants with need. Application may be submitted online. Admission notification on a rolling basis beginning on or about 2/28. Application closing dates for selective admission programs vary per program. **Financial aid:** Priority date 5/1; no closing date. FAFSA, institutional form required. Applicants notified on a rolling basis starting 3/20.

Academics. Through New Jersey Virtual Community College Consortium, students can take online courses from any New Jersey community college and receive GCC credit at no extra cost. **Special study options:** Cooperative education, distance learning, dual enrollment of high school students, internships. License preparation in nursing. **Credit/placement by examination:** CLEP, institutional tests. 16 credit hours maximum toward associate degree. **Support services:** GED preparation and test center, learning center, pre-admission summer program, reduced course load, study skills assistance, tutoring.

Majors. Biology: General. **Business:** General, accounting, administrative services, business admin, finance, hospitality admin, marketing, office management, office technology, office/clerical, sales/distribution. **Communications:** General, journalism. **Computer sciences:** General, computer graphics, computer science, data processing, LAN/WAN management, web page design. **Education:** General, early childhood, multi-level teacher, multiple handicapped, physical, special. **Engineering:** General, science. **Engineering technology:** Civil, drafting, surveying. **Health:** Medical secretary, nuclear medical technology, nursing (RN), respiratory therapy technology, sonography. **History:** General. **Interdisciplinary:** Biological/physical sciences, math/computer science. **Legal studies:** Legal secretary, paralegal. **Liberal arts:** Arts/sciences. **Math:** General. **Mechanic/repair:** Automotive. **Parks/recreation:** Exercise sciences, health/fitness. **Physical sciences:** General, chemistry. **Protective services:** Police science. **Psychology:** General. **Social sciences:** Political science, sociology. **Visual/performing arts:** Art, commercial/advertising art, dramatic.

Most popular majors. Business/marketing 17%, education 16%, health sciences 17%, liberal arts 27%, security/protective services 6%.

Computing on campus. 750 workstations in library, computer center. Online course registration, online library available.

Student life. Freshman orientation: Available. **Activities:** Choral groups, drama, literary magazine, musical theater, radio station, student government, student newspaper, student activities board, student government association, human services club, Equal Opportunity club, Phi Theta Kappa, paralegal club.

Athletics. NJCAA. **Intercollegiate:** Baseball M, basketball, cross-country, soccer, softball W, tennis, track and field, wrestling M. **Intramural:** Golf, volleyball.

Student services. Career counseling, services for economically disadvantaged, student employment services, financial aid counseling, health services, on-campus daycare, veterans' counselor. **Physically disabled:** Services for visually, speech, hearing impaired. **Transfer:** Special adviser, pre-admission transcript evaluation for new students. Transfer adviser, college fairs on campus for students transferring to 4-year colleges.

Contact. Phone: (856) 415-2209 Fax: (856) 468-8498
Kimberly Momballou, Registrar, Gloucester County College, 1400 Tanyard Road, Sewell, NJ 08080

Hudson County Community College

Jersey City, New Jersey — **CB member**
www.hccc.edu — **CB code: 2291**

- Public 2-year community college
- Commuter campus in large city
- Application essay required

General. Founded in 1974. Regionally accredited. **Enrollment:** 6,336 degree-seeking undergraduates. **Degrees:** 335 associate awarded. **Location:** 10 miles from New York City. **Calendar:** Semester, limited summer session. **Full-time faculty:** 90 total. **Part-time faculty:** 295 total. **Special facilities:** Center for Academic Student Success.

Student profile. Among degree-seeking undergraduates, 1,921 enrolled as first-time, first-year students.

Part-time:	41%	**Women:**	64%
Out-of-state:	2%	**25 or older:**	45%

Transfer out. Colleges most students transferred to 2005: New Jersey City University, St. Peter's College.

Basis for selection. Open admission. High school diploma required if applicant is less than 18 years of age.

2005-2006 Annual costs. Tuition/fees: $3,213; $5,553 out-of-district; $7,893 out-of-state. Per-credit charge: $78 in-district; $156 out-of-district; $234 out-of-state. Books/supplies: $800. Personal expenses: $1,500.

Financial aid. All financial aid based on need. Need-based aid available for part-time students.

Application procedures. Admission: No deadline. $15 fee, may be waived for applicants with need. Admission notification on a rolling basis. **Financial aid:** Priority date 7/15; no closing date. FAFSA required. Applicants notified on a rolling basis starting 6/1; must reply within 1 week(s) of notification.

Academics. Students may earn second degree by completing 24 additional credits, including all requirements for second major. **Special study options:** Cross-registration, distance learning, dual enrollment of high school students, ESL, independent study, internships, liberal arts/career combination, weekend college. License preparation in nursing, real estate. **Credit/placement by examination:** CLEP, IB, institutional tests. 12 credit hours maximum toward associate degree. **Support services:** GED preparation and test center, pre-admission summer program, remedial instruction, tutoring, writing center.

Majors. Business: Accounting, administrative services, business admin, hospitality admin, management information systems. **Computer sciences:** Computer science, data processing. **Education:** Early childhood. **Engineering:** Science. **Engineering technology:** Computer systems, electrical. **Family/consumer sciences:** Child care. **Health:** Medical assistant, medical records technology, respiratory therapy technology. **History:** General. **Legal studies:** Paralegal. **Liberal arts:** Arts/sciences. **Math:** General. **Personal/culinary services:** Chef training, culinary arts, mortuary science. **Physical sciences:** Chemistry. **Protective services:** Criminal justice. **Social sciences:** Sociology.

Most popular majors. Business/marketing 14%, computer/information sciences 6%, health sciences 18%, legal studies 8%, liberal arts 54%.

Computing on campus. 645 workstations in library, computer center. Online library available.

Student life. Freshman orientation: Mandatory. Preregistration for classes offered. **Policies:** Freshmen permitted cars on campus. **Activities:** Drama, student government, student newspaper, South Asian society, black history and art society, law club, French club, international students' organization, Hispanos Unidos para el Progreso, women's awareness organization, hospitality club, health information and technology club, medical assisting club.

Student services. Adult student services, career counseling, student employment services, personal counseling, placement for graduates, veterans' counselor. **Physically disabled:** Services for visually, speech, hearing impaired. **Transfer:** Special adviser, orientation, pre-admission transcript evaluation for new students. Transfer center, college fairs on campus for students transferring to 4-year colleges.

Contact. Phone: (201) 714-7100 Fax: (201) 714-2136
Robert Martin, Associate Dean of Enrollment Management, Hudson County Community College, 70 Sip Avenue, Jersey City, NJ 07306

Mercer County Community College

Trenton, New Jersey **CB member**
www.mccc.edu **CB code: 2444**

- Public 2-year community college
- Commuter campus in small city

General. Founded in 1966. Regionally accredited. Courses also available at downtown Trenton location. External degree program for military service members. **Enrollment:** 7,805 degree-seeking undergraduates; 1,123 non-degree-seeking students. **Degrees:** 771 associate awarded. **Location:** 35 miles from Philadelphia, 60 miles from New York City. **Calendar:** Semester, extensive summer session. **Full-time faculty:** 137 total; 17% have terminal degrees, 13% minority, 52% women. **Part-time faculty:** 480 total; 8% have terminal degrees, 16% minority, 52% women. **Class size:** 57% < 20, 41% 20-39, less than 1% 40-49, 1% 50-99. **Special facilities:** CAD laboratory, computer graphics laboratory, greenhouse complex, mortuary science lab.

Student profile. Among degree-seeking undergraduates, 60% enrolled in a transfer program, 40% enrolled in a vocational program, 1% already have a bachelor's degree or higher, 2,082 enrolled as first-time, first-year students, 224 transferred in from other institutions.

Part-time:	59%	**Asian American:**	4%
Out-of-state:	2%	**Hispanic American:**	8%
Women:	58%	**International:**	5%
African American:	26%	**25 or older:**	30%

Transfer out. Colleges most students transferred to 2005: The College of New Jersey, Rider University, Rutgers University, Rowan University, Thomas Edison State College.

Basis for selection. Open admission. Applicants without high school diploma or GED must be 18 or older and have completed the New Jersey Basic Skills Placement Examination. Designation of provisional status dependent on skills scores and/or high school units. Interview required for nursing and funeral service programs; recommended for all others.

2005-2006 Annual costs. Tuition/fees: $2,730; $3,645 out-of-district; $5,657 out-of-state. Per-credit charge: $91 in-district; $122 out-of-district; $189 out-of-state. Books/supplies: $770. Personal expenses: $1,610.

2004-2005 Financial aid. Need-based: 72% of total undergraduate aid awarded as scholarships/grants, 28% as loans/jobs. Need-based aid available for part-time students. Work study available nights and for part-time students. **Non-need-based:** Scholarships awarded for academics, athletics, state residency.

Application procedures. Admission: No deadline. No application fee. Application may be submitted online. Admission notification on a rolling basis. **Financial aid:** No deadline. FAFSA required. Applicants notified on a rolling basis.

Academics. Cross-registration with area hospitals for nursing. **Special study options:** Cooperative education, cross-registration, distance learning, double major, dual enrollment of high school students, ESL, external degree, independent study, internships, liberal arts/career combination, weekend college. License preparation in aviation, nursing, occupational therapy, physical therapy, radiology. **Credit/placement by examination:** AP, CLEP, institutional tests. 45 credit hours maximum toward associate degree. **Support services:** GED preparation and test center, learning center, preadmission summer program, reduced course load, remedial instruction, study skills assistance, tutoring, writing center.

Majors. Agriculture: Ornamental horticulture, plant sciences. **Architecture:** Technology. **Biology:** General. **Business:** General, accounting, administrative services, business admin, management information systems. **Communications technology:** General. **Computer sciences:** Networking. **Engineering technology:** Architectural, civil, electrical. **Health:** Clinical lab technology, medical radiologic technology/radiation therapy, nursing (RN), physical therapy assistant, respiratory therapy technology. **Legal studies:** Paralegal. **Liberal arts:** Arts/sciences. **Math:** General. **Mechanic/repair:** Aircraft, automotive. **Personal/culinary services:** Culinary arts, mortuary science. **Protective services:** Fire safety technology, police science. **Public administration:** Human services. **Science technology:** Biological. **Transportation:** Aviation, aviation management, flight attendant. **Visual/performing arts:** General, commercial/advertising art.

Most popular majors. Business/marketing 20%, health sciences 22%, liberal arts 29%, psychology 6%, visual/performing arts 7%.

Computing on campus. 1,100 workstations in library, computer center. Commuter students can connect to campus network. Online course registration, online library, helpline, wireless network available.

Student life. Freshman orientation: Available. Preregistration for classes offered. **Activities:** Bands, choral groups, dance, drama, literary magazine, music ensembles, musical theater, radio station, student government, student newspaper, TV station, Christian Fellowship, bilingual club, African-American student organization, international student organization, Fuerza Latina, ecology club, Educational Opportunity Fund club, gay/straight alliance.

Athletics. NJCAA. **Intercollegiate:** Baseball M, basketball, soccer, softball W, tennis, track and field. **Intramural:** Basketball, softball, volleyball. **Team name:** Vikings.

Student services. Adult student services, career counseling, services for economically disadvantaged, student employment services, financial aid counseling, minority student services, personal counseling, placement for graduates, veterans' counselor. **Physically disabled:** Services for visually, speech, hearing impaired. **Transfer:** Special adviser, orientation for new students. Transfer center, transfer adviser, college fairs on campus for students transferring to 4-year colleges.

Contact. E-mail: admiss@mccc.edu
Phone: (609) 586-0505 Fax: (609) 588-3778
Joan Guggenheim, Dean, Enrollment Services, Mercer County Community College, Box B, Trenton, NJ 08690-1099

Middlesex County College

Edison, New Jersey **CB member**
www.middlesexcc.edu **CB code: 2441**

- Public 2-year community college
- Commuter campus in small city

General. Founded in 1964. Regionally accredited. **Enrollment:** 9,943 degree-seeking undergraduates. **Degrees:** 1,012 associate awarded. **ROTC:** Army. **Location:** 5 miles from New Brunswick, 30 miles from New York City. **Calendar:** Semester, extensive summer session. **Full-time faculty:** 208 total; 53% women. **Class size:** 23% < 20, 77% 20-39, less than 1% 40-49, less than 1% >100. **Special facilities:** Ecological walking path.

Student profile.

Out-of-state:	2%	**25 or older:**	35%

Transfer out. Colleges most students transferred to 2005: Rutgers State University, New Jersey Institute of Technology, Montclair State University, Kean University, Farleigh Dickinson University.

Basis for selection. Open admission, but selective for some programs. Special requirements for dental hygiene, nursing, radiography, respiratory care, psychosocial rehabilitation and treatment, medical laboratory technology, automotive technology programs. Allied Health Aptitude Test required for radiography education, dental hygiene and respiratory care applicants. National League of Nursing Exam (NLN) required for nursing applicants. **Learning Disabled:** Must submit separate application to Project Connections Office to be eligible for learning disabilities program.

High school preparation. Recommended units include English 4, mathematics 3, social studies 2, history 2, science 3 (laboratory 3) and foreign language 2. Mathematics and science units required for some programs.

2005-2006 Annual costs. Tuition/fees: $3,180; $5,557 out-of-district; $5,557 out-of-state. Per-credit charge: $79 in-district; $158 out-of-district; $158 out-of-state. Out-of-county and out-of-state students pay additional $675 in required fees. Books/supplies: $1,162. Personal expenses: $1,643.

Financial aid. Need-based: Need-based aid available for part-time students. Work study available for part-time students.

Application procedures. Admission: Priority date 8/1; no deadline. $25 fee, may be waived for applicants with need. Admission notification on a rolling basis. **Financial aid:** Priority date 4/1; no closing date. FAFSA, institutional form required. Applicants notified on a rolling basis starting 5/4.

Academics. Special study options: Cooperative education, cross-registration, distance learning, double major, dual enrollment of high school students, ESL, independent study, internships, study abroad. License preparation in dental hygiene, nursing. **Credit/placement by examination:** CLEP, institutional tests. 45 credit hours maximum toward associate degree. **Support services:** Learning center, pre-admission summer program, reduced course load, remedial instruction, tutoring.

Majors. Business: Accounting, business admin, fashion, office management. **Communications:** General, journalism. **Computer sciences:** General, computer graphics, programming. **Education:** General, teacher assistance. **Engineering:** Civil, science. **Engineering technology:** Civil, electrical, manufacturing, surveying. **Health:** Clinical lab technology, dental hygiene, nursing (RN), pharmacy assistant, respiratory therapy technology. **Legal studies:** Paralegal. **Mechanic/repair:** Automotive. **Parks/recreation:** Health/fitness. **Physical sciences:** Astronomy, chemistry, physics. **Protective services:** Corrections, firefighting, law enforcement admin. **Science technology:** Biological. **Social sciences:** Political science, sociology. **Visual/performing arts:** Commercial photography, commercial/advertising art, dance, dramatic, music performance, studio arts.

Computing on campus. 1,255 workstations in library, computer center. Commuter students can connect to campus network. Online library, helpline available.

Student life. Freshman orientation: Available. Preregistration for classes offered. One day program scheduled 1 week prior to start of classes. **Policies:** Freshmen permitted cars on campus. **Activities:** Jazz band, choral groups, dance, drama, literary magazine, music ensembles, musical theater, radio station, student government, student newspaper, Third World student association, Hispanic club, foreign student association.

Athletics. NJCAA. **Intercollegiate:** Baseball M, basketball, cross-country, golf, soccer, softball W, track and field, wrestling M. **Team name:** Blue Colts.

Student services. Alcohol/substance abuse counseling, career counseling, student employment services, financial aid counseling, health services, minority student services, on-campus daycare, personal counseling, placement for graduates, veterans' counselor. **Physically disabled:** Services for visually, speech, hearing impaired. **Transfer:** Special adviser, orientation for new students. Transfer adviser, college fairs on campus for students transferring to 4-year colleges.

Contact. E-mail: admissions@middlesexcc.edu
Phone: (732) 906-4243 Toll-free number: (888) 968-4622
Fax: (732) 956-7728
Peter Rice, Director of Admissions and Recruitment, Middlesex County College, 2600 Woodbridge Avenue, Edison, NJ 08818-3050

Ocean County College

Toms River, New Jersey
www.ocean.edu **CB code: 2630**

- Public 2-year community college
- Commuter campus in small city

General. Founded in 1964. Regionally accredited. Off-campus sites at 13 locations in Ocean County. **Enrollment:** 6,635 degree-seeking undergraduates; 1,814 non-degree-seeking students. **Degrees:** 32 associate awarded. **Location:** 60 miles from Philadelphia, 80 miles from New York City. **Calendar:** Semester, extensive summer session. **Full-time faculty:** 119 total; 9% minority, 56% women. **Part-time faculty:** 291 total; 6% minority, 45% women. **Special facilities:** Planetarium, arboretum, fine arts theater. **Partnerships:** Formal partnerships through Jump Start program that allows high school juniors/seniors to enroll for college credits.

Student profile. Among degree-seeking undergraduates, 80% enrolled in a transfer program, 20% enrolled in a vocational program, 1% already have a bachelor's degree or higher, 1,876 enrolled as first-time, first-year students.

Part-time:	42%	**25 or older:**	22%
Women:	55%		

Transfer out. 85% of students enrolled in the transfer program go on to 4-year colleges. **Colleges most students transferred to 2005:** Georgian Court College, Stockton State College of New Jersey, Rutgers University.

Basis for selection. Open admission, but selective for some programs. Admission to nursing, medical laboratory technology, honors programs based on test scores and academic record. SAT or ACT required of nursing and honors program applicants. Score report by May 30. **Adult students:** SAT/ACT scores not required. **Learning Disabled:** Students are invited to share their learning disability needs with the Disability Resource Center, which then makes the appropriate accommodations.

High school preparation. Algebra, chemistry, biology required of nursing applicants.

2005-2006 Annual costs. Tuition/fees: $3,180; $4,080 out-of-district; $6,240 out-of-state. Per-credit charge: $82 in-district; $112 out-of-district; $184 out-of-state. Books/supplies: $700. Personal expenses: $1,000.

Financial aid. All financial aid based on need. Need-based aid available for part-time students.

Application procedures. Admission: No deadline. No application fee. Admission notification on a rolling basis beginning on or about 11/1. **Financial aid:** Priority date 5/31; no closing date. FAFSA required. Applicants notified on a rolling basis starting 7/15; must reply within 1 week(s) of notification.

Academics. Special study options: Combined bachelor's/graduate degree, distance learning, dual enrollment of high school students, ESL, honors, independent study, internships, liberal arts/career combination, study abroad. License preparation in nursing, real estate. **Credit/placement by examination:** AP, CLEP, institutional tests. 30 credit hours maximum toward associate degree. **Support services:** GED test center, learning center, reduced course load, remedial instruction, study skills assistance, tutoring, writing center.

Honors college/program. For liberal arts students only; admission based on GPA, test scores, class rank, interview.

Majors. Agriculture: Horticulture. **Business:** General, business admin. **Communications:** Journalism. **Communications technology:** General, photo/film/video. **Computer sciences:** General, computer science, LAN/WAN management. **Conservation:** General. **Engineering:** General. **Engineering technology:** Civil, surveying. **Family/consumer sciences:** Child care. **Health:** Clinical lab technology, histologic assistant, medical assistant, nursing (RN). **Interdisciplinary:** Gerontology. **Liberal arts:** Arts/sciences. **Protective services:** Fire safety technology, police science. **Psychology:** General. **Public administration:** Human services, social work. **Science technology:** Biological. **Transportation:** Airline/commercial pilot. **Visual/performing arts:** Art, dramatic.

Most popular majors. Business/marketing 18%, health sciences 18%, liberal arts 54%, security/protective services 6%.

Computing on campus. 500 workstations in library, computer center. Commuter students can connect to campus network. Online library, helpline available.

Student life. Freshman orientation: Available. Preregistration for classes offered. **Activities:** Bands, choral groups, dance, drama, literary magazine, musical theater, radio station, student government, student newspaper, Circle K, Student Life Program Board, Phi Theta Kappa, veterans club, student health organization, disabled students service club, Organization for Black Unity, Women's Network, South Asian American Student Association.

Athletics. NJCAA. **Intercollegiate:** Baseball M, basketball, cross-country, diving, field hockey W, golf, soccer M, softball W, swimming, tennis. **Intramural:** Basketball, bowling, cross-country, swimming, track and field, volleyball. **Team name:** Vikings.

Student services. Alcohol/substance abuse counseling, career counseling, services for economically disadvantaged, student employment services, financial aid counseling, health services, minority student services, personal counseling, placement for graduates, veterans' counselor. **Physically disabled:** Services for visually, speech, hearing impaired. **Learning disabled:** Comprehensive services available. **Transfer:** Re-entry adviser, pre-admission transcript evaluation for new students. Transfer adviser, college fairs on campus for students transferring to 4-year colleges.

Contact. E-mail: mfennessy@ocean.edu
Phone: (732) 255-0304 Fax: (732) 255-0444
Mary Fennessy, Director of Admissions and Records, Ocean County College, College Drive, Toms River, NJ 08754-2001

Passaic County Community College

Paterson, New Jersey **CB member**
www.pccc.cc.nj.us **CB code: 2694**

- Public 2-year community college
- Commuter campus in small city

General. Founded in 1968. Regionally accredited. **Enrollment:** 7,000 degree-seeking undergraduates. **Degrees:** 403 associate awarded. **Location:** 15 miles

from New York City. **Calendar:** Semester, limited summer session. **Full-time faculty:** 85 total. **Part-time faculty:** 350 total. **Class size:** 59% < 20, 40% 20-39, less than 1% 40-49. **Special facilities:** 2 art galleries, playhouse, poetry center.

Transfer out. Colleges most students transferred to 2005: William Paterson University, Rutgers University, Montclair State University, Bergen County College, Kean University.

Basis for selection. Open admission, but selective for some programs. Special requirements for nursing and other allied health programs. Interview recommended.

2005-2006 Annual costs. Tuition/fees: $2,748; $4,938 out-of-state. Per-credit charge: $73 in-state; $146 out-of-state. Additional course fees up to maximum of $600 per year. Books/supplies: $839. Personal expenses: $978.

Financial aid. Need-based: Need-based aid available for part-time students. **Non-need-based:** Scholarships awarded for academics. **Additional information:** Limited scholarship funds available for low income students eligible for federal or state aid.

Application procedures. Admission: No deadline. No application fee. Application may be submitted online. Admission notification on a rolling basis. Early admissions available to high school students based on decisions made by high school guidance counselor and college's director of admissions. **Financial aid:** Priority date 8/1; no closing date. FAFSA, CSS PROFILE required. Applicants notified on a rolling basis starting 8/1; must reply within 2 week(s) of notification.

Academics. Special study options: Cooperative education, cross-registration, distance learning, double major, dual enrollment of high school students, ESL, honors, independent study, internships, liberal arts/career combination, student-designed major, study abroad, weekend college. License preparation in nursing. **Credit/placement by examination:** AP, CLEP, institutional tests. 12 credit hours maximum toward associate degree. New Jersey Basic Skills test required for placement. **Support services:** Learning center, reduced course load, remedial instruction, study skills assistance, tutoring, writing center.

Majors. Business: General, accounting, administrative services, management information systems, marketing, sales/distribution. **Communications:** General. **Computer sciences:** General, applications programming. **Education:** Early childhood. **Engineering:** Science. **Engineering technology:** Electrical. **Health:** Medical radiologic technology/radiation therapy, nursing (RN), respiratory therapy technology. **Liberal arts:** Arts/sciences. **Math:** General. **Protective services:** Police science. **Psychology:** General. **Public administration:** Human services. **Social sciences:** Sociology.

Most popular majors. Business/marketing 21%, computer/information sciences 14%, health sciences 22%, liberal arts 28%, security/protective services 25%.

Computing on campus. 900 workstations in computer center.

Student life. Freshman orientation: Mandatory. Preregistration for classes offered. **Policies:** Freshmen permitted cars on campus. **Activities:** Student government, student newspaper, Latin American club, Newman Club, international club, Organization of African Ancestry, earth awareness, fashion awareness, veterans club, Phi Theta Kappa, photography club, Arabic club, poetry club.

Athletics. NJCAA. **Intercollegiate:** Basketball, soccer M. **Intramural:** Basketball M, volleyball W. **Team name:** Panthers.

Student services. Adult student services, career counseling, services for economically disadvantaged, student employment services, financial aid counseling, minority student services, on-campus daycare, personal counseling, placement for graduates, veterans' counselor, women's services. **Transfer:** Special adviser, orientation for new students. Transfer adviser, college fairs on campus for students transferring to 4-year colleges.

Contact. Phone: (973) 684-6868 Fax: (973) 684-6778
Patrick Noonan, Director of Admission, Passaic County Community College, One College Boulevard, Paterson, NJ 07505-1179

Raritan Valley Community College

Somerville, New Jersey — **CB member**
www.raritanval.edu — **CB code: 2867**

- Public 2-year community college
- Commuter campus in large town

General. Founded in 1966. Regionally accredited. **Enrollment:** 4,945 degree-seeking undergraduates; 1,306 non-degree-seeking students. **Degrees:** 507 associate awarded. **ROTC:** Army, Air Force. **Location:** 36 miles from New York City. **Calendar:** Semester, extensive summer session. **Full-time faculty:** 101 total; 31% have terminal degrees, 9% minority, 56% women. **Part-time faculty:** 300 total; 20% have terminal degrees, 6% minority, 49% women. **Special facilities:** Planetarium, professional theater. **Partnerships:** Formal partnership with area high schools for articulated credit program.

Student profile. Among degree-seeking undergraduates, 61% enrolled in a transfer program, 39% enrolled in a vocational program, 3% already have a bachelor's degree or higher, 1,018 enrolled as first-time, first-year students, 498 transferred in from other institutions.

Part-time:	50%	**Asian American:**	7%
Out-of-state:	7%	**Hispanic American:**	9%
Women:	57%	**International:**	4%
African American:	9%	**25 or older:**	40%

Transfer out. 63% of students enrolled in the transfer program go on to 4-year colleges. **Colleges most students transferred to 2005:** Rutgers State University, Kean University, Montclair State University, Rider University, Fairleigh Dickinson University.

Basis for selection. Open admission, but selective for some programs. Special requirements for nursing program; interview recommended. Matriculated students must take New Jersey Basic Skills Placement Test. **Adult students:** SAT/ACT scores are not required; however, based on their scores, students may be exempt from taking the College's placement test.

High school preparation. 16 units recommended. Recommended units include English 4, mathematics 2 and science 2.

2005-2006 Annual costs. Tuition/fees: $3,080. Per-credit charge: $78. Books/supplies: $800. Personal expenses: $1,000.

2004-2005 Financial aid. Need-based: 319 full-time freshmen applied for aid; 209 were judged to have need; 196 of these received aid. Average need met was 65%. Average scholarship/grant was $1,723; average loan $1,482. 87% of total undergraduate aid awarded as scholarships/grants, 13% as loans/jobs. Need-based aid available for part-time students. Work study available for part-time students. **Non-need-based:** Awarded to 128 full-time undergraduates, including 29 freshmen. Scholarships awarded for academics.

Application procedures. Admission: No deadline. $25 fee, may be waived for applicants with need. Application may be submitted online. Admission notification on a rolling basis. **Financial aid:** No deadline. FAFSA required. Applicants notified on a rolling basis starting 7/1; must reply within 12 week(s) of notification.

Academics. Special study options: Accelerated study, cooperative education, distance learning, double major, dual enrollment of high school students, ESL, honors, independent study. Service learning. Bachelor's degree programs available on campus. License preparation in nursing. **Credit/placement by examination:** AP, CLEP, institutional tests. 45 credit hours maximum toward associate degree. **Support services:** GED test center, learning center, pre-admission summer program, remedial instruction, study skills assistance, tutoring, writing center.

Majors. Biology: General. **Business:** Accounting, real estate. **Computer sciences:** General, computer science, programming, web page design. **Conservation:** General. **Construction:** Maintenance. **Education:** Early childhood, elementary. **Engineering:** Science. **Engineering technology:** Manufacturing, mechanical. **Health:** Licensed practical nurse, nursing (RN), optician. **Legal studies:** Paralegal. **Liberal arts:** Arts/sciences. **Math:** General. **Mechanic/repair:** General, diesel, electronics/electrical, heating/ac/refrig. **Physical sciences:** Chemistry. **Social sciences:** General. **Transportation:** Aviation. **Visual/performing arts:** Commercial/advertising art, dramatic, studio arts.

Most popular majors. Business/marketing 31%, communications/journalism 17%, engineering/engineering technologies 9%, health sciences 17%, social sciences 7%, visual/performing arts 9%.

Computing on campus. 844 workstations in library, computer center, student center. Commuter students can connect to campus network. Online course registration, online library, helpline, wireless network available.

Student life. Freshman orientation: Available. **Policies:** Freshmen permitted cars on campus. **Activities:** Dance, drama, student government, student newspaper, Black students association, international student club, Students for Environmental Awareness, BLGT Club, Christian Fellowship, Islamic Culture Association, Performing Artist Club, Orgullo Latino/Latin Pride Club, Social Justice Club.

Athletics. NJCAA. **Intercollegiate:** Baseball M, basketball M, golf, softball W. **Team name:** Golden Lions.

Student services. Adult student services, alcohol/substance abuse counseling, career counseling, student employment services, financial aid counseling, on-campus daycare, personal counseling, placement for graduates, veterans' counselor. **Physically disabled:** Services for visually, hearing impaired. **Transfer:** Special adviser, orientation, re-entry adviser, pre-admission transcript evaluation for new students. Transfer center, transfer adviser, college fairs on campus for students transferring to 4-year colleges.

Contact. E-mail: registrar@raritanval.edu
Phone: (908) 526-1200 Fax: (908) 704-3442
Charles Chulvick, Vice President of Learning and Technology Services, Raritan Valley Community College, PO Box 3300, Somerville, NJ 08876-1265

Salem Community College

Carneys Point, New Jersey — **CB member**
www.salemcc.edu — **CB code: 2868**

- Public 2-year community college
- Commuter campus in small town

General. Founded in 1972. Regionally accredited. **Enrollment:** 990 degree-seeking undergraduates; 232 non-degree-seeking students. **Degrees:** 78 associate awarded. **Location:** 25 miles from Philadelphia. **Calendar:** Semester, limited summer session. **Full-time faculty:** 22 total; 23% have terminal degrees, 9% minority, 50% women. **Part-time faculty:** 44 total; 9% minority, 59% women. **Class size:** 76% < 20, 24% 20-39. **Special facilities:** Glass art and scientific glass technology laboratories, chemical process technology simulation laboratories, computer graphic arts lab.

Student profile. Among degree-seeking undergraduates, 84% enrolled in a transfer program, 16% enrolled in a vocational program, 284 enrolled as first-time, first-year students, 2 transferred in from other institutions.

Part-time:	44%	**Hispanic American:**	4%
Out-of-state:	19%	**Native American:**	1%
Women:	65%	**International:**	5%
African American:	22%	**25 or older:**	43%
Asian American:	1%		

Transfer out. Colleges most students transferred to 2005: Rowan University, Wilmington College, Gloucester County College, Rutgers University, Cumberland County College.

Basis for selection. Open admission, but selective for some programs. Licensed Practical Nursing applicants must complete six prerequisite courses with a C+ or higher grade in each course. Registered Nursing applicants must complete four prerequisite courses with a C+ or higher grade in each course. Both programs require a high school diploma or GED. Interview recommended for scientific glassblowing and glass art programs. **Adult students:** Entrance exam policies same as for first-time freshmen. **Learning Disabled:** Students must file a release form and documentation of their disability to be granted special accommodations.

2005-2006 Annual costs. Tuition/fees: $3,305; $3,605 out-of-state. Per-credit charge: $80 in-state; $90 out-of-state. Books/supplies: $1,000. Personal expenses: $600.

2004-2005 Financial aid. All financial aid based on need. 83% of total undergraduate aid awarded as scholarships/grants, 17% as loans/jobs. Need-based aid available for part-time students. Work study available for part-time students.

Application procedures. Admission: No deadline. $25 fee, may be waived for applicants with need. Application must be submitted on paper. Admission notification on a rolling basis. **Financial aid:** Priority date 6/1; no closing date. FAFSA, institutional form required. Applicants notified on a rolling basis starting 4/1; must reply within 2 week(s) of notification.

Academics. Special study options: Cooperative education, distance learning, double major, dual enrollment of high school students, ESL, honors, independent study, internships, teacher certification program. License preparation in nursing. **Credit/placement by examination:** AP, CLEP, institutional tests. 30 credit hours maximum toward associate degree. **Support services:** GED preparation and test center, learning center, pre-admission summer program, reduced course load, remedial instruction, study skills assistance, tutoring, writing center.

Majors. Biology: General. **Business:** Accounting, business admin, human resources, management information systems, marketing. **Communications:** Journalism. **Computer sciences:** Computer graphics, computer science, webmaster. **Education:** General, early childhood. **Health:** Nursing (RN). **History:** General. **Liberal arts:** Arts/sciences, humanities. **Math:** General. **Parks/recreation:** Health/fitness. **Physical sciences:** Chemistry, physics. **Psychology:** General. **Public administration:** Community org/advocacy. **Social sciences:** General, criminology, political science, sociology.

Most popular majors. Business/marketing 17%, liberal arts 63%.

Computing on campus. 300 workstations in library, computer center. Commuter students can connect to campus network. Online library, helpline available.

Student life. Freshman orientation: Available. Preregistration for classes offered. Given at beginning of both the fall and spring semesters. **Activities:** Choral groups, student government, Chi Alpha Epsilon, Educational Opportunity Fund (EOF) Students, institutional diversity committee, Phi Theta Kappa, multicultural club.

Athletics. NJCAA. **Intercollegiate:** Baseball M, basketball, golf M, softball W. **Team name:** Oaks.

Student services. Adult student services, career counseling, services for economically disadvantaged, student employment services, financial aid counseling, minority student services, personal counseling, veterans' counselor. **Physically disabled:** Services for visually, speech, hearing impaired. **Transfer:** Special adviser, orientation, re-entry adviser, pre-admission transcript evaluation for new students. Transfer center, transfer adviser, college fairs on campus for students transferring to 4-year colleges.

Contact. E-mail: sccinfo@salemcc.edu
Phone: (856) 351-2703 Fax: (856) 299-9193
Scott Hendrickson, Director of Enrollment Services, Salem Community College, 460 Hollywood Avenue, Carneys Point, NJ 08069-2799

Somerset Christian College

Zarephath, New Jersey
www.somerset.edu — **CB code: 3933**

- Private 2-year Bible college affiliated with Pillar of Fire International
- Commuter campus in small town
- Application essay required

General. Accredited by ABHE. **Enrollment:** 126 degree-seeking undergraduates; 13 non-degree-seeking students. **Degrees:** 23 associate awarded. **Location:** 10 miles from New Brunswick. **Calendar:** Semester, limited summer session. **Full-time faculty:** 3 total; 67% have terminal degrees, 33% women. **Part-time faculty:** 6 total; 33% have terminal degrees, 17% minority, 17% women.

Student profile. Among degree-seeking undergraduates, 11% already have a bachelor's degree or higher, 24 enrolled as first-time, first-year students.

Part-time:	80%	**25 or older:**	80%
Women:	56%		

Transfer out. Colleges most students transferred to 2005: Philadelphia Biblical University, Nyack College, Eastern University.

Basis for selection. Recommendations most important. High school record, standardized test scores, essay also important. SAT or ACT recommended. **Adult students:** English placement test if no SAT or ACT test scores. **Homeschooled:** Interview, letter of recommendation (nonparent) required. Education portfolio required.

2005-2006 Annual costs. Tuition/fees: $5,750. Per-credit charge: $185. Personal expenses: $1,120.

Financial aid. All financial aid based on need. Need-based aid available for part-time students.

Application procedures. Admission: No deadline. $25 fee, may be waived for applicants with need. Application may be submitted online. Admission notification on a rolling basis. **Financial aid:** No deadline. FAFSA required. Applicants notified on a rolling basis starting 1/31.

Academics. Special study options: Dual enrollment of high school students, independent study, internships, weekend college. **Credit/placement by examination:** AP, CLEP, IB, SAT, ACT, institutional tests. 12 credit hours maximum toward associate degree. **Support services:** Learning center, reduced course load, remedial instruction, study skills assistance, tutoring, writing center.

Majors. Theology: Bible.

Computing on campus. 5 workstations in library. Online library, wireless network available.

Student life. Freshman orientation: Available. Preregistration for classes offered. **Policies:** Religious observance required. Freshmen permitted cars on campus. **Activities:** Student government.

Student services. Campus ministries, financial aid counseling. **Transfer:** Special adviser, orientation for new students.

Contact. E-mail: info@somerset.edu
Phone: (732) 356-1595 Toll-free number: (800) 234-9305
Fax: (732) 356-4846
Tony Viscioni, Vice President Communications/Enrollment Management, Somerset Christian College, 10 Liberty Square, Zarephath, NJ 08890

Sussex County Community College

Newton, New Jersey
www.sussex.edu
CB member
CB code: 2711

- Public 2-year community college
- Commuter campus in small town

General. Founded in 1981. Regionally accredited. Extension sites at Sussex County Technical School and various high school sites. **Enrollment:** 2,573 degree-seeking undergraduates; 888 non-degree-seeking students. **Degrees:** 248 associate awarded. **Location:** 70 miles from New York City. **Calendar:** Semester, limited summer session. **Full-time faculty:** 41 total. **Part-time faculty:** 204 total. **Class size:** 68% < 20, 32% 20-39, less than 1% 40-49. **Special facilities:** 10 computer laboratories (including graphic design). **Partnerships:** Formal partnerships with Oracle database administration training program, Unix operating system training program, Cisco network training program.

Student profile. Among degree-seeking undergraduates, 629 enrolled as first-time, first-year students, 203 transferred in from other institutions.

Part-time:	41%	**Asian American:**	1%
Out-of-state:	11%	**Hispanic American:**	6%
Women:	61%	**25 or older:**	31%
African American:	2%		

Transfer out. Colleges most students transferred to 2005: Montclair State University, William Paterson University of New Jersey, Rutgers University, Ramapo College of New Jersey, Centenary College.

Basis for selection. Open admission, but selective for some programs. Special requirements for the nursing program. SAT test scores of 500 or above in either verbal or math and 550 on the Sentence Skills portion can be used in lieu of college placement test. Incoming freshmen must pass ACCUPLACER placement test for admission to program of study; those failing any part of test must satisfactorily complete remedial study in appropriate areas before being admitted to program. **Adult students:** Entrance exam policies same as for first-time freshmen.

2005-2006 Annual costs. Tuition/fees: $2,670; $4,860 out-of-state. Per-credit charge: $73 in-district; $146 out-of-district; $146 out-of-state. Residents of Pike County (PA): $104 per credit hour. Books/supplies: $900. Personal expenses: $1,244.

Financial aid. All financial aid based on need. Need-based aid available for part-time students.

Application procedures. Admission: No deadline. $15 fee, may be waived for applicants with need. Application must be submitted on paper. Admission notification on a rolling basis. **Financial aid:** Closing date 6/1. FAFSA, institutional form required. Applicants notified on a rolling basis; must reply within 2 week(s) of notification.

Academics. Special study options: Distance learning, double major, dual enrollment of high school students, ESL, honors, independent study, internships, teacher certification program. Bachelor's degree programs available on campus. License preparation in nursing, paramedic. **Credit/placement by examination:** CLEP, IB, institutional tests. 30 credit hours maximum toward associate degree. **Support services:** GED preparation and test center, learning center, reduced course load, remedial instruction, study skills assistance, tutoring, writing center.

Majors. Biology: General. **Business:** Accounting, business admin. **Communications:** Journalism. **Computer sciences:** General, applications programming. **Conservation:** Environmental studies. **Education:** Early childhood, elementary, secondary. **Engineering:** General. **Engineering technology:** Automotive. **Health:** Clinical lab technology, health services, predentistry, premedicine, prepharmacy, respiratory therapy technology, veterinary technology/assistant. **Interdisciplinary:** Biological/physical sciences. **Legal studies:** Paralegal. **Liberal arts:** Arts/sciences. **Math:** General. **Mechanic/repair:** Automotive. **Physical sciences:** Chemistry. **Protective services:** Criminal justice, firefighting. **Psychology:** General. **Public administration:** Social work. **Social sciences:** General. **Visual/performing arts:** Art, commercial/advertising art, studio arts.

Most popular majors. Business/marketing 15%, liberal arts 53%, visual/performing arts 11%.

Computing on campus. 250 workstations in library, computer center, student center.

Student life. Freshman orientation: Mandatory. Preregistration for classes offered. Half-day program held 2 days before regular classes each semester. **Policies:** Freshmen permitted cars on campus. **Activities:** Choral groups, drama, literary magazine, musical theater, student government, student newspaper, TV station, Student Ambassadors, humanities club, arts club, broadcasting club, criminal justice club, Law and Justice Society, Phi Theta Kappa (honor society), AIDS Brigade, lifestyles and diversity group, psychology club.

Athletics. NJCAA. **Intercollegiate:** Baseball M, basketball M, soccer, softball W. **Intramural:** Archery, badminton, basketball, soccer, softball, table tennis, volleyball. **Team name:** Skylanders.

Student services. Adult student services, career counseling, student employment services, financial aid counseling, personal counseling, placement for graduates, veterans' counselor, women's services. **Physically disabled:** Services for visually, speech, hearing impaired. **Transfer:** Special adviser, orientation, pre-admission transcript evaluation for new students. Transfer adviser, college fairs on campus for students transferring to 4-year colleges.

Contact. E-mail: jdonohue@sussex.edu
Phone: (973) 300-2216 Fax: (973) 579-5226
James Donohue, Director of Admissions, Sussex County Community College, One College Hill, Newton, NJ 07860

Union County College

Cranford, New Jersey
www.ucc.edu
CB code: 2921

- Public 2-year community college
- Commuter campus in large town

General. Founded in 1933. Regionally accredited. Branch campuses in Elizabeth, Plainfield, and Scotch Plains. **Enrollment:** 8,998 degree-seeking undergraduates; 1,978 non-degree-seeking students. **Degrees:** 616 associate awarded. **ROTC:** Air Force. **Location:** 20 miles from New York City. **Calendar:** Semester, limited summer session. **Full-time faculty:** 184 total; 29% have terminal degrees, 17% minority, 59% women. **Part-time faculty:** 304 total; 16% have terminal degrees, 24% minority, 44% women. **Special facilities:** Observatory, art gallery.

Student profile. Among degree-seeking undergraduates, 81% enrolled in a transfer program, 19% enrolled in a vocational program, 1,134 enrolled as first-time, first-year students, 657 transferred in from other institutions.

Part-time:	46%	**Asian American:**	6%
Out-of-state:	1%	**Hispanic American:**	25%
Women:	67%	**International:**	2%
African American:	24%		

Transfer out. Colleges most students transferred to 2005: Kean University, Rutgers University, Montclair State University, Fairleigh Dickinson University.

Basis for selection. Open admission, but selective for some programs. Special requirements for allied health and nursing programs. SAT required of dental hygiene program applicants; score report required by April. Essay, interview recommended for nursing, interpreter for the deaf programs. **Adult students:** Entrance exam policies same as for first-time freshmen.

High school preparation. 19 units recommended. Recommended units include English 4, mathematics 3, history 3, science 2 (laboratory 2), foreign language 2 and academic electives 5. Chemistry and biology required of health program applicants. Trigonometry, geometry, algebra, physics and chemistry required of engineering and physical science applicants. Level 3 proficiency in American Sign Language required of interpreter for the deaf program applicants. Algebra and geometry recommended for business majors.

2005-2006 Annual costs. Tuition/fees: $3,009; $5,349 out-of-district; $5,349 out-of-state. Per-credit charge: $78 in-district; $156 out-of-district; $156 out-of-state. Books/supplies: $840. Personal expenses: $1,210.

2004-2005 Financial aid. All financial aid based on need. 81% of total undergraduate aid awarded as scholarships/grants, 19% as loans/jobs. Need-based aid available for part-time students.

Application procedures. Admission: No deadline. $25 fee. Application may be submitted online. Admission notification on a rolling basis. Must reply by May 1 or within 3 week(s) if notified thereafter. **Financial aid:** Priority date 5/1; no closing date. FAFSA, institutional form required. Must reply within 2 week(s) of notification.

Academics. Special study options: Accelerated study, cross-registration, distance learning, dual enrollment of high school students, ESL, internships, liberal arts/career combination, weekend college. License preparation in dental hygiene, nursing, paramedic, radiology. **Credit/placement by examination:** AP, CLEP, institutional tests. 32 credit hours maximum toward associate degree. **Support services:** GED preparation, learning center, reduced course load, remedial instruction, study skills assistance, tutoring.

Majors. Biology: General, biotechnology. **Business:** General, accounting technology, administrative services, business admin, marketing, restaurant/food services. **Communications:** Media studies. **Computer sciences:** Computer science, information technology. **Engineering:** General. **Engineering technology:** Civil, electromechanical, manufacturing, mechanical. **Foreign languages:** American Sign Language, sign language interpretation, translation. **Health:** Dental hygiene, EMT paramedic, health services, medical radiologic technology/radiation therapy, nuclear medical technology, nursing (RN), physical therapy assistant, radiologic technology/medical imaging, respiratory therapy technology, vocational rehab counseling. **Interdisciplinary:** Gerontology. **Legal studies:** Paralegal. **Liberal arts:** Arts/sciences. **Physical sciences:** General, chemistry. **Protective services:** Fire safety technology, law enforcement admin. **Visual/performing arts:** Music.

Computing on campus. 868 workstations in library, computer center, student center. Commuter students can connect to campus network. Helpline available.

Student life. Freshman orientation: Available. **Policies:** Freshmen permitted cars on campus. **Activities:** Literary magazine, radio station, student government, student newspaper, Catholic student organization, UCC Christian Fellowship, International Cultural Exchange, student volunteer organization, Phi Theta Kappa, Phi Beta, Union of African Students, gerontology club, French club, Spanish club.

Athletics. NJCAA. **Intercollegiate:** Baseball M, basketball, golf, soccer M, volleyball W. **Team name:** Owls; Lady Owls.

Student services. Alcohol/substance abuse counseling, campus ministries, career counseling, services for economically disadvantaged, student employment services, financial aid counseling, minority student services, personal counseling, placement for graduates, veterans' counselor. **Physically disabled:** Services for visually, speech, hearing impaired. **Transfer:** Special adviser, orientation, re-entry adviser, pre-admission transcript evaluation for new students. Transfer adviser, college fairs on campus for students transferring to 4-year colleges.

Contact. Phone: (908) 709-7500 Fax: (908) 709-7125
JoAnn Davis-Wayne, Registrar, Union County College, 1033 Springfield Avenue, Cranford, NJ 07016-1599

Warren County Community College

Washington, New Jersey
www.warren.edu **CB code: 2722**

- Public 2-year community college
- Commuter campus in small town

General. Founded in 1981. Regionally accredited. **Enrollment:** 1,732 undergraduates. **Degrees:** 106 associate awarded. **Location:** 12 miles from Easton, Pennsylvania. **Calendar:** Semester, limited summer session. **Full-time faculty:** 20 total. **Part-time faculty:** 70 total. **Special facilities:** Audio-visual tutorial laboratory, small business collection, extensive video tape collection. **Partnerships:** Tech prep; 2+2.

Student profile. 60% enrolled in a transfer program, 35% enrolled in a vocational program, 3% already have a bachelor's degree or higher, 704 transferred in from other institutions.

Out-of-state:	3%	**25 or older:**	40%

Transfer out. 80% of students enrolled in the transfer program go on to 4-year colleges. **Colleges most students transferred to 2005:** Centenary College, Rutgers-New Brunswick, East Strousburg University.

Basis for selection. Open admission, but selective for some programs. Interview recommended.

High school preparation. High school diploma or GED strongly recommended.

2005-2006 Annual costs. Tuition/fees: $2,925; $3,225 out-of-district; $3,825 out-of-state. Per-credit charge: $75 in-district; $85 out-of-district; $105 out-of-state. Books/supplies: $700. Personal expenses: $900.

Financial aid. Need-based: Work study available nights, weekends and for part-time students. **Non-need-based:** Scholarships awarded for academics, state residency.

Application procedures. Admission: No deadline. $25 fee, may be waived for applicants with need. Admission notification on a rolling basis. Early admission students ages 16-18 must provide written permission from parent/guardian and high school official. **Financial aid:** Closing date 7/1. FAFSA, institutional form required. Applicants notified on a rolling basis starting 4/1; must reply within 2 week(s) of notification.

Academics. Special study options: Cooperative education, cross-registration, distance learning, double major, dual enrollment of high school students, ESL, independent study, internships, liberal arts/career combination, weekend college. Bachelor's degree programs available on campus. **Credit/placement by examination:** CLEP, IB, institutional tests. 30 credit hours maximum toward associate degree. Challenge exams. **Support services:** GED preparation, learning center, pre-admission summer program, reduced course load, remedial instruction, tutoring, writing center.

Majors. Biology: General. **Business:** General, accounting, entrepreneurial studies. **Computer sciences:** General. **Conservation:** Environmental studies. **Education:** General, early childhood. **Health:** Health services, nursing (RN). **Interdisciplinary:** Natural sciences. **Legal studies:** General, paralegal, prelaw. **Liberal arts:** Arts/sciences. **Physical sciences:** Chemistry. **Protective services:** Criminal justice. **Social sciences:** General. **Visual/performing arts:** Studio arts.

Computing on campus. 100 workstations in library, computer center.

Student life. Freshman orientation: Available. Preregistration for classes offered. **Activities:** Literary magazine, student government, student newspaper, Phi Theta Kappa Honor Society, Criminal Justice Association, legal studies club.

Athletics. Team name: Golden Eagles.

Student services. Career counseling, student employment services, personal counseling, placement for graduates, veterans' counselor. **Physically disabled:** Services for visually, speech, hearing impaired. **Transfer:** Special adviser, orientation for new students. Transfer adviser, college fairs on campus for students transferring to 4-year colleges.

Contact. Phone: (908) 835-9222 Fax: (908) 689-5824
Laurel Attanasio, Director of Admissions, Warren County Community College, Route 57 West, Washington, NJ 07882-4343

Two-Year Colleges

New Mexico

Albuquerque Technical-Vocational Institute

Albuquerque, New Mexico **CB member**
www.tvi.edu **CB code: 3387**

- Public 2-year community and technical college
- Commuter campus in very large city

General. Founded in 1965. Regionally accredited. **Enrollment:** 18,557 degree-seeking undergraduates; 4,255 non-degree-seeking students. **Degrees:** 1,079 associate awarded. **ROTC:** Army, Navy, Air Force. **Calendar:** Trimester, extensive summer session. **Full-time faculty:** 340 total. **Part-time faculty:** 695 total. **Class size:** 39% < 20, 59% 20-39, 2% 40-49, less than 1% 50-99.

Student profile. Among degree-seeking undergraduates, 2,804 enrolled as first-time, first-year students, 952 transferred in from other institutions.

Part-time:	64%	**Asian American:**	2%
Out-of-state:	1%	**Hispanic American:**	43%
Women:	61%	**Native American:**	8%
African American:	3%	**25 or older:**	51%

Basis for selection. Open admission. Submitting test scores for placement is optional. **Adult students:** Entrance exam policies same as for first-time freshmen.

2005-2006 Annual costs. Tuition/fees: $1,045; $1,224 out-of-district; $5,223 out-of-state. Per-credit charge: $40 in-district; $48 out-of-district; $214 out-of-state. In-district students do not pay tuition for technical courses, only arts and sciences courses.

2004-2005 Financial aid. Need-based: 44% of total undergraduate aid awarded as scholarships/grants, 56% as loans/jobs. Need-based aid available for part-time students. Work study available for part-time students. **Non-need-based:** Scholarships awarded for academics, state residency.

Application procedures. Admission: No deadline. No application fee. Application may be submitted online. Admission notification on a rolling basis. **Financial aid:** Priority date 3/1; no closing date. FAFSA required. Applicants notified by 5/1.

Academics. Special study options: Cooperative education, distance learning, double major, dual enrollment of high school students, ESL, internships, liberal arts/career combination, weekend college. Apprenticeships. License preparation in aviation, dental hygiene, nursing, paramedic, radiology, real estate. **Credit/placement by examination:** AP, CLEP, institutional tests. **Support services:** GED preparation and test center, learning center, remedial instruction, study skills assistance, tutoring, writing center.

Majors. Biology: Biotechnology. **Business:** Accounting, administrative services, banking/financial services, business admin, hospitality admin. **Computer sciences:** Data processing, information systems, systems analysis. **Education:** Elementary. **Engineering:** General, environmental. **Engineering technology:** Architectural drafting, electrical, electrical drafting, laser/optical, manufacturing, surveying. **Family/consumer sciences:** Child care. **Health:** Clinical lab technology, medical radiologic technology/radiation therapy, medical records admin, nursing (RN), respiratory therapy technology, sonography, veterinary technology/assistant. **Legal studies:** Paralegal. **Liberal arts:** Arts/sciences. **Personal/culinary services:** Chef training, cosmetic. **Protective services:** Criminal justice, fire safety technology. **Transportation:** Airline/commercial pilot.

Most popular majors. Business/marketing 21%, computer/information sciences 6%, engineering/engineering technologies 9%, health sciences 15%, liberal arts 27%, trade and industry 6%.

Computing on campus. Commuter students can connect to campus network. Online course registration, online library available.

Student life. Freshman orientation: Mandatory. Preregistration for classes offered. **Policies:** Freshmen permitted cars on campus. **Activities:** Literary magazine, student government, student newspaper.

Student services. Adult student services, career counseling, services for economically disadvantaged, student employment services, financial aid counseling, health services, minority student services, placement for graduates. **Physically disabled:** Services for visually, speech, hearing impaired. **Transfer:** Special adviser, orientation for new students. Transfer adviser for students transferring to 4-year colleges.

Contact. Phone: (505) 224-3160 Fax: (505) 224-3237
Jane Campbell, Registrar/Director of Enrollment Services, Albuquerque Technical-Vocational Institute, 525 Buena Vista Southeast, Albuquerque, NM 87106

Art Center Design College

Albuquerque, New Mexico
www.theartcenter.edu **CB code: 3039**

- For-profit 2-year visual arts college
- Large city

General. Accredited by ACCSCT. **Enrollment:** 275 degree-seeking undergraduates. **Degrees:** 11 bachelor's, 4 associate awarded. **Calendar:** Continuous. **Full-time faculty:** 8 total. **Part-time faculty:** 25 total.

Basis for selection. ACT test score required if student does not have 3.0 high school or college GPA.

2005-2006 Annual costs. Costs per calendar year: tuition $15,921; required fees $100 (one-time registration fee); estimated cost of books and supplies $1,200.

Application procedures. Admission: No deadline. $25 fee.

Academics. Credit/placement by examination: CLEP.

Majors. Visual/performing arts: Commercial/advertising art, interior design.

Contact. E-mail: inquie@theartcenter.edu
Phone: (505) 254-7575
Colleen Gimbel-Froebe, Director of Admissions, Art Center Design College, 5000 Marble Avenue NE, Albuquerque, NM 87119

Clovis Community College

Clovis, New Mexico **CB member**
www.clovis.edu **CB code: 4921**

- Public 2-year community and junior college
- Commuter campus in large town

General. Founded in 1990. Regionally accredited. **Enrollment:** 2,048 degree-seeking undergraduates; 1,879 non-degree-seeking students. **Degrees:** 257 associate awarded. **Location:** 200 miles from Albuquerque, 100 miles from Lubbock, Texas. **Calendar:** Semester, limited summer session. **Full-time faculty:** 51 total; 8% have terminal degrees, 8% minority, 53% women. **Part-time faculty:** 232 total; 10% have terminal degrees, 8% minority, 66% women. **Class size:** 58% < 20, 42% 20-39, less than 1% 40-49, less than 1% 50-99. **Special facilities:** Art collection representing multiple cultures of New Mexico. **Partnerships:** Formal partnerships with 12 high schools for Instructional Television Consortium.

Student profile. Among degree-seeking undergraduates, 59% enrolled in a transfer program, 41% enrolled in a vocational program, 242 enrolled as first-time, first-year students, 158 transferred in from other institutions.

Part-time:	68%	**Asian American:**	2%
Out-of-state:	14%	**Hispanic American:**	36%
Women:	73%	**Native American:**	1%
African American:	5%	**25 or older:**	51%

Transfer out. Colleges most students transferred to 2005: Eastern New Mexico University, New Mexico State University, University of New Mexico, Texas Tech University, West Texas A&M University.

Basis for selection. Open admission, but selective for some programs. Nursing and radiologic technology are selective-criteria include GPA, performance in related science courses. Test of Adult Basic Education (TABE) required for vocational programs, has been replaced with ACCUPLACER for some programs. **Adult students:** Entrance exam policies same as for first-time freshmen.

2006-2007 Annual costs. Tuition/fees (projected): $784; $832 out-of-district; $1,504 out-of-state. Books/supplies: $600. Personal expenses: $1,500.

2005-2006 Financial aid. Need-based: 94% of total undergraduate aid awarded as scholarships/grants, 6% as loans/jobs. Need-based aid available for part-time students. Work study available nights, weekends and for part-time students. **Non-need-based:** Scholarships awarded for academics, state residency.

Application procedures. Admission: No deadline. No application fee. Application may be submitted online. Admission notification on a rolling basis. **Financial aid:** Priority date 9/1; no closing date. FAFSA required. Applicants notified on a rolling basis starting 4/15.

Academics. Special study options: Cooperative education, distance learning, double major, dual enrollment of high school students, ESL, honors, independent study, internships, weekend college. License preparation in aviation, nursing, paramedic, radiology. **Credit/placement by examination:** AP, CLEP, institutional tests. 32 credit hours maximum toward associate degree. **Support services:** GED preparation and test center, learning center, remedial instruction, study skills assistance, tutoring, writing center.

Majors. Business: General, accounting, administrative services, banking/financial services, business admin, management information systems, office management, office technology, sales/distribution. **Computer sciences:** General, computer graphics, computer science, information technology, networking, programming, systems analysis. **Education:** General, early childhood, teacher assistance. **Engineering:** Electrical. **Engineering technology:** Drafting. **Health:** Medical radiologic technology/radiation therapy, medical secretary. **Interdisciplinary:** Natural sciences. **Legal studies:** General, legal secretary. **Math:** General. **Mechanic/repair:** Automotive, electronics/electrical, heating/ac/refrig. **Personal/culinary services:** Cosmetic. **Protective services:** Criminal justice. **Psychology:** General. **Transportation:** Aviation. **Visual/performing arts:** Commercial/advertising art, studio arts.

Most popular majors. Business/marketing 10%, health sciences 28%, liberal arts 46%.

Computing on campus. 160 workstations in library, computer center. Online course registration, wireless network available.

Student life. Freshman orientation: Available. Preregistration for classes offered. 3 hours prior to semester. **Policies:** Freshmen permitted cars on campus. **Activities:** Choral groups, drama, literary magazine, musical theater, student government, student newspaper, Hispanic Advisory Council, Phi Theta Kappa, social commmittee, International Awareness Organization, student ambassadors, black student union, pre-legal society, psychology club.

Athletics. Intramural: Basketball, racquetball.

Student services. Adult student services, career counseling, services for economically disadvantaged, student employment services, financial aid counseling, minority student services, on-campus daycare, personal counseling, placement for graduates, veterans' counselor. **Physically disabled:** Services for visually, speech, hearing impaired. **Transfer:** Special adviser, orientation, re-entry adviser for new students. Transfer adviser, college fairs on campus for students transferring to 4-year colleges.

Contact. E-mail: admissions@clovis.edu
Phone: (505) 769-4025 Fax: (505) 769-4190
Rosie Corrie, Director of Admissions/Registrar, Clovis Community College, 417 Schepps Boulevard, Clovis, NM 88101-8381

Crownpoint Institute of Technology

Crownpoint, New Mexico
www.citech.edu

- Public 2-year technical college
- Commuter campus in small town

General. Enrollment: 315 undergraduates. **Degrees:** 44 associate awarded. **Calendar:** Semester. **Full-time faculty:** 44 total. **Part-time faculty:** 2 total.

Basis for selection. Open admission.

Application procedures. Admission: No deadline. No application fee. Admission notification on a rolling basis. **Financial aid:** No deadline.

Academics. Credit/placement by examination: CLEP.

Contact. Phone: (505) 786-4100
Delores Becenti, Registrar, Crownpoint Institute of Technology, PO Box 849, Crownpoint, NM 87313

Dona Ana Branch Community College of New Mexico State University

Las Cruces, New Mexico
www.nmsu.edu **CB code: 6296**

- Public 2-year branch campus and community college
- Commuter campus in small city

General. Founded in 1973. Regionally accredited. Access to New Mexico State University facilities and activities. **Enrollment:** 2,224 full-time, degree-seeking students. **Degrees:** 448 associate awarded. **ROTC:** Army, Air Force. **Location:** 42 miles from El Paso, Texas. **Calendar:** Semester, limited summer session. **Full-time faculty:** 91 total. **Part-time faculty:** 333 total.

Basis for selection. Open admission, but selective for some programs. Applicants to radiology technology, EMT-paramedic, and respiratory care programs selected on basis of COMPASS scores, Health Occupations Aptitude Test scores, resume, 3 letters of recommendation, clinical observation, and interview. Applicants to nursing program selected on basis of Nursing Entrance Exam scores and completion of requirements. COMPASS required for placement if ACT or SAT not taken.

2005-2006 Annual costs. Tuition/fees: $1,080; $1,320 out-of-district; $3,024 out-of-state. Per-credit charge: $45 in-district; $55 out-of-district; $126 out-of-state. Room/board: $5,332. Books/supplies: $664. Personal expenses: $1,215.

2004-2005 Financial aid. Need-based: Need-based aid available for part-time students.

Application procedures. Admission: No deadline. $15 fee, may be waived for applicants with need. Admission notification on a rolling basis. February 15th application deadline for radiology technology, EMT-paramedic, nursing, and respiratory care programs. **Financial aid:** Priority date 3/1; no closing date. FAFSA required. Applicants notified on a rolling basis starting 5/1.

Academics. Special study options: Cooperative education, cross-registration, double major, dual enrollment of high school students, ESL, independent study, internships. **Credit/placement by examination:** CLEP, institutional tests. 30 credit hours maximum toward associate degree. **Support services:** Learning center, pre-admission summer program, remedial instruction, study skills assistance, tutoring.

Majors. Agriculture: Landscaping. **Business:** Administrative services, business admin, fashion, hospitality admin, office management. **Computer sciences:** Computer graphics, computer science, data processing. **Construction:** Electrician, maintenance. **Engineering:** Electrical. **Engineering technology:** Drafting, electrical. **Health:** EMT paramedic, medical radiologic technology/radiation therapy, medical secretary, nursing (RN), respiratory therapy technology. **Legal studies:** Legal secretary, paralegal. **Liberal arts:** Library assistant. **Mechanic/repair:** Automotive, electronics/electrical, heating/ac/refrig. **Protective services:** Firefighting.

Computing on campus. 425 workstations in library, computer center. Commuter students can connect to campus network. Online course registration, helpline, repair service available.

Student life. Freshman orientation: Available. **Housing:** Coed dorms, single-sex dorms, special housing for disabled, apartments available. Housing available on adjacent New Mexico State University campus. **Activities:** Student government, student newspaper, Vocational Industrial Clubs of America, Distributive Education Clubs of America, Phi Theta Kappa, fraternities and sororities available to students through New Mexico State University.

Student services. Adult student services, career counseling, student employment services, health services, personal counseling, placement for graduates, veterans' counselor. **Physically disabled:** Services for visually, speech, hearing impaired. **Transfer:** Special adviser, orientation for new students. Transfer adviser, college fairs on campus for students transferring to 4-year colleges.

Contact. Phone: (505) 527-7710 Fax: (505) 527-7515
Ike Ledesma, Coordinator, Admissions, Dona Ana Branch Community College of New Mexico State University, MSC-3DA, Las Cruces, NM 88003-8001

Eastern New Mexico University: Roswell Campus

Roswell, New Mexico **CB member**
www.roswell.enmu.edu **CB code: 4662**

- Public 2-year branch campus and community college
- Commuter campus in large town

General. Founded in 1958. Regionally accredited. **Enrollment:** 2,501 degree-seeking undergraduates; 1,651 non-degree-seeking students. **Degrees:** 244 associate awarded. **Location:** 200 miles from Albuquerque. **Calendar:** Semester, limited summer session. **Full-time faculty:** 67 total; 4% have terminal degrees, 15% minority, 57% women. **Part-time faculty:** 200 total; 14% minority, 54% women. **Class size:** 80% < 20, 18% 20-39, less than 1% 40-49, less than 1% 50-99, less than 1% >100. **Special facilities:** Instructional television, online and on-site classes available from main campus, allowing students to continue upper-division classes without travel.

Student profile. Among degree-seeking undergraduates, 21% enrolled in a transfer program, 40% enrolled in a vocational program, 1% already have a bachelor's degree or higher, 503 enrolled as first-time, first-year students, 422 transferred in from other institutions.

Part-time:	56%	**Hispanic American:**	45%
Out-of-state:	12%	**Native American:**	2%
Women:	61%	**25 or older:**	58%
African American:	2%	**Live on campus:**	3%
Asian American:	1%		

Transfer out. 33% of students enrolled in the transfer program go on to 4-year colleges. **Colleges most students transferred to 2005:** Eastern New Mexico University-Portales, New Mexico State University, University of New Mexico New Mexico Highlands University.

Basis for selection. Open admission, but selective for some programs. Some Health Services programs require completion of a pre-admission series of courses, have minimum course grades and GPAs. Students must pass university skills placement test to enroll in math or English courses. Remedial reading course required if test not passed. Student may be exempt based on ACT scores. **Adult students:** Some programs require completion of placement testing as prerequisite. **Homeschooled:** ACT score of 15 or more and high school transcript with graduation date required. **Learning Disabled:** No special admission requirements for students with learning disabilities; services based on need and disability documentation. Students requiring special services asked to provide information on needs as soon as possible to avoid delays in receiving service.

2006-2007 Annual costs. Tuition/fees (projected): $1,128; $1,164 out-of-district; $4,394 out-of-state. Per-credit charge: $41 in-district; $43 out-of-district; $177 out-of-state. Room/board: $4,439. Books/supplies: $731. Personal expenses: $2,177.

2004-2005 Financial aid. Need-based: 288 full-time freshmen applied for aid; 260 were judged to have need; 255 of these received aid. Average need met was 15%. Average scholarship/grant was $2,141; average loan $614. 75% of total undergraduate aid awarded as scholarships/grants, 25% as loans/jobs. Need-based aid available for part-time students. Work study available nights, weekends and for part-time students. **Non-need-based:** Awarded to 110 full-time undergraduates, including 56 freshmen.

Application procedures. Admission: No deadline. No application fee. Application may be submitted online. Admission notification on a rolling basis. **Financial aid:** Priority date 4/1; no closing date. FAFSA required. Applicants notified on a rolling basis starting 7/1; must reply within 3 week(s) of notification.

Academics. Special study options: Distance learning, dual enrollment of high school students, independent study, internships, liberal arts/career combination. License preparation in aviation, nursing, occupational therapy, paramedic. **Credit/placement by examination:** CLEP, IB, institutional tests. 30 credit hours maximum toward associate degree. Credits earned through CLEP and Advanced Placement must be mutually exclusive. **Support services:** GED preparation and test center, learning center, remedial instruction, study skills assistance, tutoring.

Majors. Business: General, accounting, administrative services. **Communications technology:** Animation/special effects. **Computer sciences:** General. **Education:** General, teacher assistance. **Engineering technology:** Architectural, drafting. **Family/consumer sciences:** Child care. **Health:** EMT paramedic, medical assistant, medical records technology, occupational therapy assistant, phlebotomy, respiratory therapy assistant. **Legal studies:** Paralegal. **Liberal arts:** Arts/sciences. **Mechanic/repair:** Automotive, avionics, electronics/electrical. **Production:** Welding. **Protective services:** Criminal justice, fire safety technology, police science. **Public administration:** Social work. **Transportation:** Aviation, aviation management.

Most popular majors. Business/marketing 12%, health sciences 22%, liberal arts 19%, trade and industry 31%.

Computing on campus. 50 workstations in library, computer center. Online course registration, wireless network available.

Student life. Freshman orientation: Available. Preregistration for classes offered. One-day program before classes commence. **Policies:** Freshmen permitted cars on campus. **Housing:** Coed dorms, apartments available. $50 deposit, deadline 8/1. **Activities:** Drama, student government, student newspaper, art club, ski club, computer club, Spanish club, science club, Student Nurses Association, residence hall council, psychology club, electronics club, occupational therapy assistants.

Athletics. Intramural: Basketball M, football (non-tackle) M, racquetball, softball W, tennis, volleyball, weight lifting M.

Student services. Career counseling, services for economically disadvantaged, student employment services, financial aid counseling, health services, on-campus daycare, personal counseling, placement for graduates, veterans' counselor. **Physically disabled:** Services for visually, speech, hearing impaired. **Transfer:** Special adviser, orientation for new students. College fairs on campus for students transferring to 4-year colleges.

Contact. E-mail: admissions@roswell.enmu.edu
Phone: (505) 624-7149 Toll-free number: (800) 243-6687 ext. 149
Fax: (505) 624-7144
Ida Stover, Director of Admissions and Records, Eastern New Mexico University: Roswell Campus, Box 6000, Roswell, NM 88202-6000

Luna Community College

Las Vegas, New Mexico
www.luna.edu **CB code: 2591**

- Public 2-year community and technical college
- Large town

General. Regionally accredited. **Enrollment:** 888 degree-seeking undergraduates. **Degrees:** 87 associate awarded. **Calendar:** Semester. **Full-time faculty:** 34 total. **Part-time faculty:** 34 total.

Basis for selection. Open admission, but selective for some programs and for out-of-state students.

2005-2006 Annual costs. Tuition/fees: $718; $1,006 out-of-district; $1,942 out-of-state. Per-credit charge: $28 in-district; $40 out-of-district; $79 out-of-state. Books/supplies: $500. Personal expenses: $572.

Application procedures. Admission: No deadline. No application fee. Admission notification on a rolling basis.

Academics. Credit/placement by examination: CLEP.

Majors. Business: General, accounting, business admin, office management. **Computer sciences:** General. **Education:** Early childhood. **Engineering:** Electrical. **Engineering technology:** Drafting. **Health:** Clinical lab technology.

Student life. Freshman orientation: Mandatory. Preregistration for classes offered.

Contact. E-mail: tmares@luna.edu
Phone: (505) 454-2550
Henrietta Griego, Director of Admissions, Luna Community College, 366 Luna Drive, Las Vegas, NM 87701

Mesalands Community College

Tucumcari, New Mexico
www.mesalands.edu **CB code: 3618**

- Public 2-year community and technical college
- Commuter campus in small town

General. Regionally accredited. **Enrollment:** 312 degree-seeking undergraduates; 221 non-degree-seeking students. **Degrees:** 12 associate awarded. **Location:** 175 miles from Albuquerque, 110 miles from Amarillo, Texas. **Calendar:** Semester, extensive summer session. **Full-time faculty:** 12 total. **Part-time faculty:** 20 total. **Special facilities:** Museum, foundry.

Student profile. Among degree-seeking undergraduates, 84% enrolled in a transfer program, 16% enrolled in a vocational program, 92 enrolled as first-time, first-year students.

Part-time:	31%	**Women:**	60%
Out-of-state:	10%		

Basis for selection. Open admission. **Homeschooled:** Ability to Benefit Test or GED required.

2005-2006 Annual costs. Tuition/fees: $1,394; $2,264 out-of-state. Per-credit charge: $37 in-state; $66 out-of-state. Books/supplies: $564. Personal expenses: $1,427.

2004-2005 Financial aid. Need-based: 32 full-time freshmen applied for aid; 32 were judged to have need; 32 of these received aid. Average need met was 21%. Average scholarship/grant was $1,713. 98% of total undergraduate aid awarded as scholarships/grants, 2% as loans/jobs. Need-based aid available for part-time students. Work study available nights and for part-time students. **Non-need-based:** Awarded to 33 full-time undergraduates, including 8 freshmen. Scholarships awarded for academics, athletics, leadership, minority status, music/drama, state residency.

Application procedures. Admission: No deadline. No application fee. Admission notification on a rolling basis. **Financial aid:** Priority date 4/1; no closing date. FAFSA required. Applicants notified on a rolling basis starting 4/1; must reply within 3 week(s) of notification.

Academics. Special study options: Distance learning, internships. Bachelor's degree programs available on campus. **Credit/placement by examination:** AP, CLEP. 18 credit hours maximum toward associate degree. **Support services:** GED preparation and test center, learning center, remedial instruction, study skills assistance, tutoring.

Majors. Agriculture: General. **Business:** Business admin. **Computer sciences:** General.

Computing on campus. 75 workstations in library, computer center. Online course registration, wireless network available.

Student life. Freshman orientation: Available. Preregistration for classes offered. **Policies:** Freshmen permitted cars on campus. **Activities:** Student government.

Athletics. Intercollegiate: Rodeo.

Student services. Adult student services, career counseling, financial aid counseling. **Physically disabled:** Services for visually, hearing impaired. **Transfer:** Special adviser, orientation for new students.

Contact. Phone: (505) 461-4413
Mesalands Community College, 911 South Tenth Street, Tucumcari, NM 88401

New Mexico Junior College

Hobbs, New Mexico
www.nmjc.cc.nm.us **CB code: 4553**

- Public 2-year community and technical college
- Commuter campus in large town

General. Founded in 1965. Regionally accredited. **Enrollment:** 2,600 degree-seeking undergraduates. **Degrees:** 210 associate awarded. **Location:** 110 miles from Roswell, 100 miles from Lubbock, Texas. **Calendar:** Semester, extensive summer session. **Full-time faculty:** 73 total. **Part-time faculty:** 120 total. **Special facilities:** Cowboy Hall of Fame.

Student profile.

Out-of-state:	10%	**Live on campus:**	8%
25 or older:	51%		

Basis for selection. Open admission, but selective for some programs. Special requirements for nursing, law enforcement, and automotive service education programs. Applicants admitted without high school diploma or GED must pass GED before completion of degree program. Interview required for nursing, medical laboratory technician, automotive service education programs.

High school preparation. 18 units recommended. Recommended units include English 4, mathematics 3, social studies 4, science 2 and academic electives 5.

2005-2006 Annual costs. Tuition/fees: $730; $1,138 out-of-district; $1,258 out-of-state. Per-credit charge: $22 in-district; $39 out-of-district; $44 out-of-state. Room/board: $3,200. Books/supplies: $700. Personal expenses: $1,575.

Financial aid. Need-based: Need-based aid available for part-time students.

Application procedures. Admission: No deadline. No application fee. Admission notification on a rolling basis. **Financial aid:** Priority date 6/1; no closing date. FAFSA required. Applicants notified on a rolling basis; must reply within 2 week(s) of notification.

Academics. Special study options: Cooperative education, cross-registration, distance learning, dual enrollment of high school students, ESL, honors, internships, weekend college. **Credit/placement by examination:** AP, CLEP, institutional tests. 30 credit hours maximum toward associate degree. **Support services:** Learning center, pre-admission summer program, reduced course load, remedial instruction, study skills assistance, tutoring.

Majors. Biology: General. **Business:** General, accounting, administrative services, banking/financial services, business admin, office management, office technology, real estate. **Communications:** General. **Computer sciences:** General, applications programming, computer graphics, programming. **Education:** General, elementary, middle, physical, secondary. **Engineering:** General. **Engineering technology:** Drafting, hazardous materials. **Foreign languages:** Spanish. **Health:** Athletic training, clinical lab assistant, clinical lab technology, EMT paramedic, medical radiologic technology/radiation therapy, predentistry, premedicine, prepharmacy. **Legal studies:** Legal secretary, paralegal, prelaw. **Liberal arts:** Arts/sciences. **Math:** General. **Mechanic/repair:** Automotive. **Personal/culinary services:** Cosmetic. **Physical sciences:** Chemistry, physics. **Protective services:** Criminal justice, police science. **Psychology:** General. **Social sciences:** General. **Visual/performing arts:** Commercial/advertising art, studio arts.

Most popular majors. Agriculture 6%, business/marketing 11%, education 13%, health sciences 24%, liberal arts 10%, mathematics 7%, trade and industry 13%.

Computing on campus. 275 workstations in dormitories, library, computer center, student center. Commuter students can connect to campus network.

Student life. Freshman orientation: Mandatory. **Housing:** Guaranteed on-campus for freshmen. Single-sex dorms, special housing for disabled available. **Activities:** Bands, choral groups, drama, music ensembles, musical theater, student government, Young Republicans, Young Democrats, student nurses.

Athletics. NJCAA. **Intercollegiate:** Baseball M, basketball, golf M. **Intramural:** Badminton, basketball, bowling, golf, handball, racquetball, skiing, softball, swimming, table tennis, tennis, volleyball.

Student services. Career counseling, student employment services, health services, personal counseling, placement for graduates, veterans' counselor. **Physically disabled:** Services for visually, speech, hearing impaired. **Transfer:** Special adviser, orientation for new students. Transfer adviser, college fairs on campus for students transferring to 4-year colleges.

Contact. Phone: (505) 392-5113 Fax: (505) 392-2526
Robert Bensing, Dean of Enrollment Management, New Mexico Junior College, 1 Thunderbird Circle, Hobbs, NM 88240

New Mexico Military Institute Junior College

Roswell, New Mexico **CB member**
www.nmmi.edu **CB code: 4534**

- Public 2-year junior and military college
- Residential campus in large town
- SAT or ACT (ACT writing optional) required

General. Founded in 1891. Regionally accredited. **Enrollment:** 450 degree-seeking undergraduates. **Degrees:** 90 associate awarded. **ROTC:** Army. **Location:** 200 miles from Albuquerque, 200 miles from El Paso, Texas. **Calendar:** Semester, limited summer session. **Full-time faculty:** 67 total. **Class size:** 59% < 20, 40% 20-39, 1% 40-49. **Special facilities:** Museum, television production, ropes course.

Student profile.

Out-of-state:	59%	**Live on campus:**	100%

Transfer out. Colleges most students transferred to 2005: University of New Mexico, New Mexico State University, Texas A&M University, University of Colorado.

Basis for selection. 2.0 minimum high school GPA, ACT composite score of 19 or SAT 920 (exclusive of writing) for participation in Advanced Army ROTC. Minimum ACT composite score of 17 or SAT combined score (exclusive of writing) of 800 for Basic Army ROTC program. Preference given to in-state applicants. Maximum age of 22 for enrollment. Students cannot be married or have children. Interview recommended for all applicants.

High school preparation. 21 units recommended. Recommended units include English 4, mathematics 3, social studies 1, history 2, science 2 (laboratory 2), foreign language 2 and academic electives 5. Computer science 0.5 unit recommended.

2005-2006 Annual costs. Tuition/fees: $7,670; $10,166 out-of-state. Tuition costs include room and board, uniform, supplies, and fees. Books/supplies: $700.

Financial aid. Non-need-based: Scholarships awarded for academics, athletics, ROTC, state residency.

Application procedures. Admission: No deadline. $60 fee, may be waived for applicants with need. Admission notification on a rolling basis beginning on or about 9/1. Advanced Army ROTC applicants must pass Army physical examination. **Financial aid:** Priority date 4/1; no closing date. FAFSA required. Applicants notified on a rolling basis starting 5/1; must reply within 3 week(s) of notification.

Academics. Special study options: Dual enrollment of high school students. Bachelor's degree programs available on campus. **Credit/placement by examination:** CLEP, institutional tests. 30 credit hours maximum toward associate degree. **Support services:** Learning center, remedial instruction, tutoring.

Majors. Liberal arts: Arts/sciences.

Computing on campus. 100 workstations in dormitories, library, computer center, student center. Dormitories linked to campus network. Helpline, repair service available.

Student life. Freshman orientation: Mandatory. **Housing:** Guaranteed on-campus for all undergraduates. Single-sex dorms available. $100 deposit. All students must live in college housing. **Activities:** Bands, choral groups, film society, music ensembles, student government, student newspaper, symphony orchestra, TV station.

Athletics. NJCAA. **Intercollegiate:** Baseball M, basketball M, fencing, football (tackle) M, golf, rifle, tennis, track and field. **Intramural:** Fencing, football (tackle) M, handball, racquetball, skiing, soccer, softball, swimming, tennis, track and field, volleyball. **Team name:** Broncos.

Student services. Career counseling, health services, personal counseling. **Transfer:** Special adviser, pre-admission transcript evaluation for new students.

Contact. E-mail: admissions@nmmi.edu
Phone: (505) 624-8050 Toll-free number: (800) 421-5376
Fax: (505) 624-8058
Director of Admissions, New Mexico Military Institute Junior College, 101 West College Boulevard, Roswell, NM 88201-5173

New Mexico State University at Alamogordo

Alamogordo, New Mexico
www.alamo.nmsu.edu **CB code: 4012**

- Public 2-year branch campus college
- Commuter campus in large town

General. Founded in 1958. Regionally accredited. **Enrollment:** 1,445 degree-seeking undergraduates. **Degrees:** 197 associate awarded. **ROTC:** Air Force. **Location:** 65 miles from Las Cruces, 85 miles from El Paso, Texas. **Calendar:** Semester, limited summer session. **Full-time faculty:** 52 total; 10% have terminal degrees, 15% minority, 42% women. **Part-time faculty:** 75 total; 8% have terminal degrees, 12% minority, 55% women. **Special facilities:** Planetarium.

Student profile. Among degree-seeking undergraduates, 80% enrolled in a transfer program, 20% enrolled in a vocational program, 199 transferred in from other institutions. Of all enrolled students, 1% already have a bachelor's degree or higher.

Out-of-state:	6%	**25 or older:**	55%

Transfer out. Colleges most students transferred to 2005: New Mexico State University.

Basis for selection. Open admission, but selective for some programs. Special requirements for nursing and medical technologies programs; essay and interview required.

2005-2006 Annual costs. Tuition/fees: $1,260; $1,404 out-of-district; $4,020 out-of-state. Per-credit charge: $50 in-district; $56 out-of-district; $165 out-of-state. Books/supplies: $664. Personal expenses: $1,458.

Financial aid. Need-based: Need-based aid available for part-time students. **Non-need-based:** Scholarships awarded for academics, state residency.

Application procedures. Admission: No deadline. $15 fee. Admission notification on a rolling basis. **Financial aid:** FAFSA, institutional form required. Applicants notified by 6/1.

Academics. Special study options: Combined bachelor's/graduate degree, cooperative education, cross-registration, distance learning, double major, dual enrollment of high school students, honors, independent study, liberal arts/career combination, weekend college. License preparation in nursing, paramedic. **Credit/placement by examination:** AP, CLEP, institutional tests. 30 credit hours maximum toward associate degree. **Support services:** GED preparation and test center, learning center, reduced course load, remedial instruction, study skills assistance, tutoring, writing center.

Majors. Business: General, administrative services, management information systems. **Communications technology:** Photo/film/video. **Computer sciences:** Data processing, information systems, web page design. **Education:** General, early childhood, teacher assistance. **Engineering:** General, computer. **Engineering technology:** Electrical. **Health:** Clinical lab assistant, clinical lab technology. **Legal studies:** Paralegal. **Liberal arts:** Arts/sciences. **Protective services:** Criminal justice, firefighting, forensics. **Public administration:** Social work. **Visual/performing arts:** Art, commercial/advertising art, design.

Most popular majors. Business/marketing 17%, education 6%, health sciences 11%, liberal arts 52%.

Computing on campus. 203 workstations in library, computer center, student center. Commuter students can connect to campus network. Online course registration, online library, helpline, repair service available.

Student life. Freshman orientation: Available. **Policies:** Freshmen permitted cars on campus. **Activities:** Jazz band, choral groups, drama, music ensembles, student government.

Athletics. Intramural: Softball, table tennis, volleyball.

Student services. Career counseling, student employment services, financial aid counseling, personal counseling, placement for graduates, veterans' counselor. **Physically disabled:** Services for visually, speech, hearing impaired. **Transfer:** Special adviser, orientation for new students. Transfer adviser, college fairs on campus for students transferring to 4-year colleges.

Contact. Phone: (505) 439-3700
Kathy Fuller, Admissions Coordinator, New Mexico State University at Alamogordo, 2400 North Scenic Drive, Alamogordo, NM 88310

New Mexico State University at Carlsbad

Carlsbad, New Mexico
cavern.nmsu.edu **CB code: 4547**

- Public 2-year branch campus and community college
- Commuter campus in large town

General. Founded in 1950. Regionally accredited. **Enrollment:** 1,600 undergraduates. **Degrees:** 130 associate awarded. **Location:** 165 miles from El Paso, Texas. **Calendar:** Semester, limited summer session. **Full-time faculty:** 28 total. **Part-time faculty:** 55 total. **Special facilities:** Computer/electronics center.

Basis for selection. Open admission, but selective for some programs. Special admission requirements for nursing applicants; ACT required. Interview required for nursing, radiological technology programs. **Home-schooled:** Copy of document verifying registration as home-schooled student and academic transcript outlining 9th-12th grade courses and grades required.

High school preparation. 10 units recommended. Recommended units include English 4, mathematics 3, science 2 and foreign language 1. Required science units must be beyond general science.

2005-2006 Annual costs. Tuition/fees: $1,128; $1,248 out-of-district; $2,544 out-of-state. Per-credit charge: $45 in-district; $50 out-of-district; $104 out-of-state. Books/supplies: $580. Personal expenses: $1,300.

Financial aid. Need-based: Need-based aid available for part-time students. **Non-need-based:** Scholarships awarded for academics, state residency.

Application procedures. Admission: No deadline. $15 fee, may be waived for applicants with need. Application may be submitted online. Admission notification on a rolling basis. **Financial aid:** Priority date 3/1; no

closing date. FAFSA required. Applicants notified on a rolling basis starting 5/3; must reply within 4 week(s) of notification.

Academics. Special study options: Cooperative education, distance learning, double major, dual enrollment of high school students, ESL, honors, independent study, internships, student-designed major, weekend college. License preparation in nursing. **Credit/placement by examination:** CLEP, institutional tests. 30 credit hours maximum toward associate degree. **Support services:** GED preparation and test center, learning center, remedial instruction, study skills assistance, tutoring.

Majors. Business: General, administrative services. **Computer sciences:** General, computer science, information systems. **Education:** General. **Engineering:** General. **Engineering technology:** Electrical, manufacturing. **Health:** Nursing (RN). **Liberal arts:** Arts/sciences. **Production:** Welding. **Protective services:** Firefighting. **Social sciences:** General.

Most popular majors. Business/marketing 10%, health sciences 13%, liberal arts 69%.

Computing on campus. 300 workstations in library, computer center. Commuter students can connect to campus network.

Student life. Freshman orientation: Available. **Activities:** Choral groups, drama, student government, business club, Student Nursing Association, Vocational Trade Association, NMSU-C Ambassadors, Phi Theta Kappa, computer science club.

Student services. Career counseling, student employment services, personal counseling, veterans' counselor. **Physically disabled:** Services for visually, speech, hearing impaired. **Transfer:** Special adviser, orientation for new students. Transfer adviser, college fairs on campus for students transferring to 4-year colleges.

Contact. E-mail: mgutierrez@cavern.nmsu.edu
Phone: (505) 234-9223 Fax: (505) 885-4951
Michael Cleary, Director of Admissions, New Mexico State University at Carlsbad, 1500 University Drive, Carlsbad, NM 88220

New Mexico State University at Grants

Grants, New Mexico
www.grants.nmsu.edu **CB code: 0461**

- Public 2-year branch campus and community college
- Commuter campus in small town

General. Founded in 1968. Regionally accredited. **Enrollment:** 700 undergraduates. **Degrees:** 65 associate awarded. **Location:** 75 miles from Albuquerque. **Calendar:** Semester, limited summer session. **Full-time faculty:** 16 total. **Part-time faculty:** 46 total. **Special facilities:** Judicial district law library.

Basis for selection. Open admission.

High school preparation. 15 units recommended. Recommended units include English 3, mathematics 3, social studies 1 and science 1.

2005-2006 Annual costs. Tuition/fees: $1,152; $1,272 out-of-district; $2,664 out-of-state. Per-credit charge: $47 in-district; $52 out-of-district; $110 out-of-state. Books/supplies: $400.

Financial aid. Need-based: Need-based aid available for part-time students. Work study available nights, weekends and for part-time students.

Application procedures. Admission: Closing date 8/28. $15 fee, may be waived for applicants with need. Application may be submitted online. Admission notification on a rolling basis beginning on or about 8/3. **Financial aid:** Priority date 3/5; no closing date. FAFSA, institutional form required. Applicants notified on a rolling basis starting 6/15; must reply by 8/28.

Academics. Special study options: Distance learning, double major, dual enrollment of high school students, student-designed major, weekend college. Bachelor's degree programs available on campus. License preparation in nursing. **Credit/placement by examination:** CLEP, institutional tests. 30 credit hours maximum toward associate degree. **Support services:** GED preparation and test center, learning center, reduced course load, remedial instruction, tutoring.

Majors. Business: General, office management. **Computer sciences:** Programming. **Education:** General. **Engineering technology:** Electrical. **Legal studies:** Paralegal. **Mechanic/repair:** Automotive. **Protective services:** Law enforcement admin. **Public administration:** Human services. **Visual/performing arts:** Art.

Computing on campus. 230 workstations in computer center. Online library available.

Student life. Freshman orientation: Available. Preregistration for classes offered. **Activities:** Student government, student newspaper.

Athletics. Team name: Aggies.

Student services. Adult student services, career counseling, student employment services, personal counseling, veterans' counselor. **Transfer:** Special adviser, orientation, pre-admission transcript evaluation for new students. Transfer adviser, college fairs on campus for students transferring to 4-year colleges.

Contact. E-mail: ilutz@grants.nmsu.edu
Phone: (505) 287-7981 Toll-free number: (888) 450-6678
Fax: (505) 287-2329
Ms. Irene Lutz, Campus Student Services Officer, New Mexico State University at Grants, 1500 North Third Street, Grants, NM 87020

San Juan College

Farmington, New Mexico **CB member**
www.sanjuancollege.edu **CB code: 4732**

- Public 2-year community college
- Commuter campus in large town

General. Founded in 1956. Regionally accredited. **Enrollment:** 4,345 degree-seeking undergraduates; 719 non-degree-seeking students. **Degrees:** 429 associate awarded. **Location:** 183 miles from Albuquerque. **Calendar:** Semester, limited summer session. **Full-time faculty:** 101 total. **Part-time faculty:** 275 total. **Class size:** 28% < 20, 72% 20-39, less than 1% >100. **Special facilities:** Planetarium, special collection of Southwestern books and materials, geographic information system, art gallery and 800-seat performance hall, fire tower for specialized training, commercial truck driving training range, drilling rig, clean room for instrumentation training, plant operations equipment, jet simulator for pilot training.

Student profile. Among degree-seeking undergraduates, 35% enrolled in a transfer program, 30% enrolled in a vocational program, 1% already have a bachelor's degree or higher, 838 enrolled as first-time, first-year students.

Part-time:	42%	**Asian American:**	1%
Out-of-state:	7%	**Hispanic American:**	12%
Women:	63%	**Native American:**	33%
African American:	1%		

Basis for selection. Open admission. **Adult students:** Entrance exam policies same as for first-time freshmen.

High school preparation. College-preparatory program recommended. 13 units recommended. Recommended units include English 4, mathematics 3, social studies 3, science 2 and foreign language 1.

2006-2007 Annual costs. Tuition/fees (projected): $600; $840 out-of-state. Per-credit charge: $25 in-state; $35 out-of-state. Books/supplies: $600.

2004-2005 Financial aid. Need-based: 54% of total undergraduate aid awarded as scholarships/grants, 46% as loans/jobs. Need-based aid available for part-time students. Work study available nights, weekends and for part-time students. **Non-need-based:** Scholarships awarded for academics, state residency.

Application procedures. Admission: No deadline. No application fee. Application may be submitted online. Admission notification on a rolling basis. **Financial aid:** No deadline. FAFSA required. Applicants notified on a rolling basis starting 7/1; must reply within 2 week(s) of notification.

Academics. Special study options: Combined bachelor's/graduate degree, cooperative education, distance learning, dual enrollment of high school students, ESL, external degree, honors, independent study, internships, liberal arts/career combination, teacher certification program. Bachelor's degree programs available on campus. License preparation in aviation, dental hygiene, nursing, physical therapy, real estate. **Credit/placement by examination:** CLEP, institutional tests. 30 credit hours maximum toward associate degree. **Support services:** GED preparation and test center, learning center, reduced course load, remedial instruction, study skills assistance, tutoring, writing center.

Majors. Agriculture: Business. **Area/ethnic studies:** Regional. **Biology:** General. **Business:** Accounting technology, administrative services, business admin, office technology, real estate. **Communications:** General. **Computer sciences:** General, computer graphics, data processing, information systems. **Conservation:** General. **Construction:** Carpentry, well drilling.

Education: General, early childhood. **Engineering:** General. **Engineering technology:** Civil drafting, drafting, electrical, industrial, instrumentation, mechanical drafting, solar energy, surveying. **English:** English lit. **Foreign languages:** General. **Health:** Dental hygiene, medical records technology, nursing (RN), office admin, physical therapy assistant, premedicine. **History:** General. **Legal studies:** Legal secretary. **Liberal arts:** Arts/sciences. **Math:** General. **Mechanic/repair:** Auto body, automotive, diesel. **Personal/culinary services:** Cosmetic. **Philosophy/religion:** Philosophy. **Physical sciences:** General, chemistry, geology, physics. **Production:** Machine shop technology, welding. **Protective services:** Firefighting, police science. **Psychology:** General. **Public administration:** General, social work. **Social sciences:** Anthropology, archaeology, economics, political science, sociology. **Transportation:** Airline/commercial pilot. **Visual/performing arts:** Art, commercial/advertising art, dramatic, theater design.

Most popular majors. Business/marketing 6%, engineering/engineering technologies 12%, health sciences 16%, liberal arts 36%, trade and industry 18%.

Computing on campus. 802 workstations in library, computer center, student center. Commuter students can connect to campus network. Online course registration, wireless network available.

Student life. Freshman orientation: Available. Preregistration for classes offered. One-day session held prior to beginning of semester. **Activities:** Bands, choral groups, dance, drama, film society, music ensembles, musical theater, radio station, student government, student newspaper, TV station, Native American club, Student Ambassadors, Phi Theta Kappa (honor society).

Athletics. Intramural: Archery, badminton, baseball M, basketball, bowling, cross-country, golf, handball, racquetball, skiing, softball, table tennis, tennis, volleyball.

Student services. Career counseling, student employment services, financial aid counseling, minority student services, on-campus daycare, personal counseling, placement for graduates, veterans' counselor. **Physically disabled:** Services for visually, speech, hearing impaired. **Transfer:** Special adviser for new students. Transfer adviser, college fairs on campus for students transferring to 4-year colleges.

Contact. E-mail: drangc@sanjuancollege.edu
Phone: (505) 566-3300 Fax: (505) 566-3500
Cheryl Drangmeister, Associate Vice President for Student Services, San Juan College, 4601 College Boulevard, Farmington, NM 87402-4699

Santa Fe Community College

Santa Fe, New Mexico
www.sfccnm.edu **CB code: 4816**

- Public 2-year community college
- Commuter campus in small city

General. Founded in 1983. Regionally accredited. **Enrollment:** 1,729 degree-seeking undergraduates. **Degrees:** 182 associate awarded. **Location:** 50 miles from Albuquerque. **Calendar:** Semester, limited summer session. **Full-time faculty:** 65 total. **Part-time faculty:** 294 total. **Class size:** 74% < 20, 24% 20-39, less than 1% 40-49, 1% 50-99, less than 1% >100. **Special facilities:** Planetarium, art galleries, child development center. **Partnerships:** Formal partnerships with businesses, including Intel, and state agencies.

Transfer out. Colleges most students transferred to 2005: University of New Mexico, New Mexico State University, College of Santa Fe.

Basis for selection. Open admission. Essay and interview required for international students; interview required for concurrent high school/college students. **Adult students:** Entrance exam policies same as for first-time freshmen.

2005-2006 Annual costs. Tuition/fees: $1,050; $1,364 out-of-district; $2,368 out-of-state. Per-credit charge: $31 in-district; $42 out-of-district; $75 out-of-state. Books/supplies: $500. Personal expenses: $1,500.

2004-2005 Financial aid. Need-based: 14% of total undergraduate aid awarded as scholarships/grants, 86% as loans/jobs. Need-based aid available for part-time students. Work study available nights, weekends and for part-time students.

Application procedures. Admission: No deadline. No application fee. Admission notification on a rolling basis. **Financial aid:** Priority date 3/1; no closing date. FAFSA, institutional form required. Applicants notified on a rolling basis starting 7/15; must reply within 4 week(s) of notification.

Academics. Special study options: Cooperative education, distance learning, dual enrollment of high school students, ESL, honors, independent study, internships, liberal arts/career combination, weekend college. Bachelor's degree programs available on campus. License preparation in nursing, real estate. **Credit/placement by examination:** CLEP, institutional tests. 30 credit hours maximum toward associate degree. Maximum of 9 hours credit can be earned through challenge examinations; also accept DANTES. **Support services:** GED preparation and test center, learning center, reduced course load, remedial instruction, study skills assistance, tutoring, writing center.

Majors. Area/ethnic studies: Regional. **Biology:** General. **Business:** General, accounting, administrative services, business admin, entrepreneurial studies, restaurant/food services. **Computer sciences:** General. **Education:** General, kindergarten/preschool. **Engineering:** General. **Engineering technology:** Construction, drafting. **Foreign languages:** Sign language interpretation, Spanish. **Health:** Nursing (RN). **Legal studies:** Paralegal. **Parks/recreation:** Health/fitness. **Personal/culinary services:** Chef training. **Physical sciences:** General. **Protective services:** Criminal justice. **Public administration:** Human services, social work. **Visual/performing arts:** Art, dance, design, interior design.

Most popular majors. Business/marketing 26%, engineering/engineering technologies 7%, health sciences 11%, liberal arts 10%, security/protective services 14%, visual/performing arts 14%.

Computing on campus. 200 workstations in library, computer center, student center. Commuter students can connect to campus network. Online library, helpline, wireless network available.

Student life. Freshman orientation: Available. Preregistration for classes offered. **Policies:** Freshmen permitted cars on campus. **Activities:** Choral groups, dance, drama, music ensembles, radio station, student government, student newspaper, TV station, Phi Theta Kappa, Native American student association, Student Nursing Association, student council, MEChA (Movimiento Estudiantil Chiemo de Aztlan), fine arts club, Access club, Los Tournants, sign language interpreters club.

Student services. Adult student services, career counseling, student employment services, financial aid counseling, on-campus daycare, personal counseling, placement for graduates, veterans' counselor, women's services. **Physically disabled:** Services for visually, speech, hearing impaired. **Transfer:** Special adviser, orientation for new students. Transfer adviser, college fairs on campus for students transferring to 4-year colleges.

Contact. E-mail: enroll@sfccnm.edu
Phone: (505) 428-1278
Amy Tilley, Director of Admissions, Santa Fe Community College, 6401 Richards Avenue, Santa Fe, NM 87508-4887

Southwestern Indian Polytechnic Institute

Albuquerque, New Mexico
www.sipi.bia.edu **CB code: 7047**

- Public 2-year community and technical college
- Residential campus in large city

General. Founded in 1971. Regionally accredited. National Indian community college serving American Indians from federally recognized Indian tribes from across the United States. **Enrollment:** 614 degree-seeking undergraduates. **Degrees:** 79 associate awarded. **Calendar:** Trimester, extensive summer session. **Full-time faculty:** 24 total; 25% have terminal degrees, 58% minority, 29% women. **Part-time faculty:** 1 total; 100% minority.

Student profile. Among degree-seeking undergraduates, 216 enrolled as first-time, first-year students.

Part-time:	24%	**Native American:**	100%
Women:	56%		

Transfer out. Colleges most students transferred to 2005: University of New Mexico, New Mexico State University, New Mexico Highlands University, Fort Lewis College.

Basis for selection. Open admission. Applicants must have valid membership in U.S. federally recognized Indian tribe. ACT, COMPASS, and TABE required for placement. **Adult students:** Entrance exam policies same as for first-time freshmen.

2006-2007 Annual costs. Students with valid membership in U.S. federally recognized Indian tribe attend tuition-free. Required fees: full-time Lodge student $280.00, full-time commuter $225.00, part-time $150.00. Books/supplies: $800. Personal expenses: $1,400.

2004-2005 Financial aid. Need-based: 231 full-time freshmen applied for aid; 231 were judged to have need; 231 of these received aid. Average

scholarship/grant was $500. Need-based aid available for part-time students. Work study available nights and weekends. **Non-need-based:** Scholarships awarded for academics, leadership, minority status.

Application procedures. Admission: Closing date 9/1 (postmark date). No application fee. Admission notification on a rolling basis. **Financial aid:** Closing date 3/1. FAFSA required. Applicants notified on a rolling basis starting 9/30.

Academics. Special study options: Cooperative education, distance learning, double major, honors, liberal arts/career combination. **Credit/ placement by examination:** AP, CLEP, institutional tests. **Support services:** GED preparation, learning center, remedial instruction, study skills assistance, tutoring.

Majors. Agriculture: Agribusiness operations, agronomy, soil science. **Business:** General, accounting technology, business admin, hospitality admin, hospitality/recreation, office technology. **Communications technology:** Graphic/ printing. **Computer sciences:** General, computer science, LAN/WAN management. **Conservation:** General, environmental science, management/ policy. **Education:** Early childhood. **Engineering technology:** Electrical, environmental, manufacturing, surveying. **Family/consumer sciences:** Institutional food production. **Health:** Optician, optometric assistant. **Liberal arts:** Arts/sciences. **Personal/culinary services:** General, culinary arts. **Social sciences:** Cartography.

Computing on campus. 15 workstations in dormitories, library, computer center, student center. Dormitories linked to campus network.

Student life. Freshman orientation: Mandatory. Held week prior to start of classes. **Policies:** Zero tolerance policy on alcohol and drugs. Freshmen permitted cars on campus. **Housing:** Single-sex dorms available. $55 deposit. **Activities:** Dance, student government, New Optical Image, Natural Resources Club, Native American Political Action Council, Phi theta Kappa, Student Senate, Dance Club, AISES, Inter-tribal Pow-wow club, Music & Art Club, Four Winds and Golden Eagle Lodge Council.

Athletics. Intramural: Basketball, softball, volleyball, weight lifting. **Team name:** Eagles.

Student services. Alcohol/substance abuse counseling, campus ministries, career counseling, student employment services, financial aid counseling, health services, personal counseling, placement for graduates. **Transfer:** Special adviser, orientation for new students. Transfer adviser, college fairs on campus for students transferring to 4-year colleges.

Contact. E-mail: jcarpio@sipi.bia.edu
Phone: (505) 346-2324 Toll-free number: (800) 586-7474
Fax: (505) 346-2373
Joseph Carpio, Registrar, Southwestern Indian Polytechnic Institute, 9169 Coors Road Northwest, Albuquerque, NM 87184

New York

Adirondack Community College

Queensbury, New York
www.sunyacc.edu **CB code: 2017**

- Public 2-year community college
- Commuter campus in large town

General. Founded in 1960. Regionally accredited. **Enrollment:** 2,903 degree-seeking undergraduates; 590 non-degree-seeking students. **Degrees:** 477 associate awarded. **Location:** 50 miles from Albany, 200 miles from New York City. **Calendar:** Semester, limited summer session. **Full-time faculty:** 98 total; 22% have terminal degrees, 49% women. **Part-time faculty:** 145 total. **Special facilities:** Solar botany laboratory, fitness trail, pond preserve, arboretum, weather station, forensic science lab.

Student profile. Among degree-seeking undergraduates, 65% enrolled in a transfer program, 35% enrolled in a vocational program, 806 enrolled as first-time, first-year students, 73 transferred in from other institutions.

Part-time:	32%	**Women:**	61%
Out-of-state:	1%	**25 or older:**	29%

Transfer out. Colleges most students transferred to 2005: State University of New York at Plattsburgh, Siena College, State University of New York at Albany, College of St. Rose, State University of New York at Oneonta.

Basis for selection. Open admission, but selective for some programs. Minimum high school average of 80 or minimum GPA of 2.5 for entry into nursing. If submitted, SAT or ACT and SAT Subject Tests used for placement and counseling. Essay and interview recommended. **Homeschooled:** Must take and pass GED or successfuly complete ability to benefit test.

High school preparation. College-preparatory program recommended. 22 units recommended. Recommended units include English 4, mathematics 3, social studies 4, history 2, science 3, foreign language 1 and academic electives 5. Allied health programs require Regents biology, chemistry examinations. Engineering requires Regents biology, chemistry and mathematics through pre-calculus. Computer science, mechanical and electrical technology require mathematics through advanced algebra. Forestry requires Regents biology, chemistry, and mathematics through intermediate algebra.

2005-2006 Annual costs. Tuition/fees: $3,062; $5,932 out-of-state. Per-credit charge: $120 in-state; $240 out-of-state. Books/supplies: $800. Personal expenses: $785.

Financial aid. All financial aid based on need. Need-based aid available for part-time students.

Application procedures. Admission: Priority date 3/15; deadline 8/1. $40 fee, may be waived for applicants with need. Application must be submitted on paper. Admission notification on a rolling basis beginning on or about 1/15. **Financial aid:** Priority date 4/15; no closing date. FAFSA, institutional form required. Applicants notified on a rolling basis starting 5/1.

Academics. Special study options: Distance learning, double major, dual enrollment of high school students, independent study, internships, liberal arts/career combination, study abroad. Bachelor's degree programs available on campus. License preparation in nursing. **Credit/placement by examination:** AP, CLEP, IB, institutional tests. 34 credit hours maximum toward associate degree. **Support services:** GED preparation, learning center, reduced course load, remedial instruction, study skills assistance, tutoring, writing center.

Majors. Biology: General. **Business:** General, accounting, administrative services, banking/financial services, business admin, marketing, office/clerical, tourism promotion, tourism/travel. **Communications:** Broadcast journalism, media studies. **Computer sciences:** General, computer science, data processing, information systems, programming. **Engineering:** General, science. **Engineering technology:** Drafting, electrical. **Health:** Nursing (RN). **History:** General. **Interdisciplinary:** Math/computer science. **Liberal arts:** Arts/sciences. **Math:** General. **Personal/culinary services:** Culinary arts. **Physical sciences:** Chemistry, geology, physics. **Protective services:** Corrections, police science. **Psychology:** General. **Social sciences:** General, political science, sociology. **Visual/performing arts:** General, art, dramatic, photography.

Most popular majors. Business/marketing 17%, health sciences 17%, liberal arts 49%, security/protective services 6%.

Computing on campus. 350 workstations in library, computer center, student center. Online library available.

Student life. Freshman orientation: Available. **Policies:** Freshmen permitted cars on campus. **Activities:** Concert band, choral groups, dance, drama, literary magazine, music ensembles, musical theater, radio station, student government, TV station.

Athletics. NJCAA. **Intercollegiate:** Baseball M, basketball, bowling, golf M, soccer, softball W, volleyball W. **Intramural:** Badminton, basketball, football (non-tackle), skiing, softball, volleyball. **Team name:** Timberwolves.

Student services. Adult student services, career counseling, student employment services, financial aid counseling, on-campus daycare, personal counseling, placement for graduates, veterans' counselor. **Physically disabled:** Services for visually, speech, hearing impaired. **Transfer:** Special adviser, orientation for new students. Transfer adviser, college fairs on campus for students transferring to 4-year colleges.

Contact. E-mail: info@acc.sunyacc.edu
Phone: (518) 743-2264 Fax: (518) 743-2317
Sara Jane Linehan, Director of Enrollment Management, Adirondack Community College, 640 Bay Road, Queensbury, NY 12804

American Academy McAllister Institute of Funeral Service

New York, New York
www.funeraleducation.org **CB code: 0774**

- Private 2-year school of mortuary science
- Commuter campus in very large city

General. Founded in 1926. **Enrollment:** 105 degree-seeking undergraduates. **Degrees:** 21 associate awarded. **Calendar:** Semester, extensive summer session. **Full-time faculty:** 3 total. **Part-time faculty:** 22 total. **Class size:** 67% 20-39, 33% 40-49.

Student profile.

Out-of-state:	26%	**25 or older:**	39%

Basis for selection. Open admission. Interview recommended.

2006-2007 Annual costs. Tuition/fees: $9,975. Books/supplies: $709. Personal expenses: $2,635.

Financial aid. All financial aid based on need.

Application procedures. Admission: Closing date 8/27. $35 fee. Admission notification on a rolling basis. **Financial aid:** FAFSA required. Applicants notified on a rolling basis starting 7/1; must reply by 9/1 or within 3 week(s) of notification.

Academics. Special study options: Cross-registration. **Credit/placement by examination:** CLEP. **Support services:** Tutoring.

Majors. Personal/culinary services: Mortuary science.

Computing on campus. 12 workstations in library.

Student life. Activities: Student government.

Student services. Personal counseling, placement for graduates. **Transfer:** Special adviser, orientation for new students. Transfer adviser for students transferring to 4-year colleges.

Contact. E-mail: info@funeraleducation.org
Phone: (212) 757-1190 Fax: (212) 765-5923
Norman Provost, Director of Admissions/Bursar, American Academy McAllister Institute of Funeral Service, 619 West 54th Street, New York, NY 10019-3602

American Academy of Dramatic Arts

New York, New York
www.aada.org **CB code: 2603**

- Private 2-year junior and performing arts college
- Commuter campus in very large city
- Application essay, interview required

General. Founded in 1884. Regionally accredited. Offers practical conservatory and training. Additional campus in Hollywood, CA. **Enrollment:** 220 degree-seeking undergraduates. **Degrees:** 81 associate awarded. **Location:** Midtown Manhattan. **Calendar:** Semester, limited summer session. **Full-time faculty:** 7 total; 29% have terminal degrees, 57% women. **Part-time faculty:** 12 total; 67% women. **Class size:** 100% < 20. **Special facilities:** 3 theaters, dance studio, costume department, property/production areas, audio/visual center.

Student profile. Among degree-seeking undergraduates, 6% already have a bachelor's degree or higher, 56 enrolled as first-time, first-year students, 64 transferred in from other institutions.

Out-of-state:	87%	**25 or older:**	14%
Women:	66%		

Basis for selection. Dramatic ability or potential, academic qualifications, maturity and motivation very important. Audition required; regional audition/interview may be arranged.

2006-2007 Annual costs. Tuition/fees: $17,400. Books/supplies: $1,542. Personal expenses: $1,000.

2005-2006 Financial aid. All financial aid based on need. Average need met was 57%. Average scholarship/grant was $5,400; average loan $2,800. 40% of total undergraduate aid awarded as scholarships/grants, 60% as loans/jobs. **Additional information:** Need-based incentive grants of $200-$500 for first-year students available. Merit awards of $500-$1,500. Scholarships of $500-$3,000 available for second year. Scholarships of $500-$5,000 available for post-degree third year.

Application procedures. Admission: No deadline. $50 fee. Application may be submitted online. Admission notification on a rolling basis. **Financial aid:** No deadline. FAFSA, institutional form required. Applicants notified on a rolling basis.

Academics. 2-year professional actor training program offered with associate of occupational studies degree. Third year, available by faculty invitation, forms showcase Academy Company. **Special study options:** Students may study 1 year at each of 2 campuses. **Credit/placement by examination:** CLEP. **Support services:** Tutoring.

Majors. Visual/performing arts: Acting.

Computing on campus. 6 workstations in library.

Student life. Freshman orientation: Mandatory. Assembly meeting with administration, question-and-answer with senior students, social events, orientation to city held. **Activities:** Drama, student government, student newspaper, all student activities arts-related, including student productions.

Student services. Career counseling, student employment services, placement for graduates.

Contact. E-mail: admissions-ny@aada.org
Phone: (212) 686-9244 Toll-free number: (800) 463-8990
Fax: (212) 685-8093
Karen Higginbotham, Director of Admissions, American Academy of Dramatic Arts, 120 Madison Avenue, New York, NY 10016

Art Institute of New York City

New York, New York
www.ainyc.artinstitutes.edu **CB code: 3106**

- For-profit 2-year culinary school and technical college
- Commuter campus in very large city
- Application essay, interview required

General. Accredited by ACICS. **Enrollment:** 1,477 undergraduates. **Degrees:** 88 associate awarded. **Calendar:** Quarter, extensive summer session. **Full-time faculty:** 86 total. **Part-time faculty:** 15 total.

Student profile. 4 transferred in from other institutions.

Basis for selection. Open admission. COMPASS may be used in placement for certain programs of study.

2005-2006 Annual costs. Tuition/fees: $20,418. Per-credit charge: $431. Books/supplies: $650.

Application procedures. Admission: No deadline. $50 fee. Application may be submitted online. Admission notification on a rolling basis.

Academics. Special study options: Cooperative education, internships. **Credit/placement by examination:** AP, CLEP. **Support services:** Learning center, remedial instruction, study skills assistance.

Majors. Communications technology: Animation/special effects, photo/film/video. **Personal/culinary services:** Culinary arts. **Visual/performing arts:** Graphic design, interior design.

Computing on campus. 40 workstations in library, computer center. Online library, helpline, repair service available.

Student life. Freshman orientation: Mandatory. Preregistration for classes offered. Scheduled prior to class start or in first week. **Activities:** Film society, student newspaper.

Student services. Adult student services, career counseling, student employment services, financial aid counseling, personal counseling, placement for graduates. **Transfer:** Special adviser, orientation, re-entry adviser, preadmission transcript evaluation for new students.

Contact. E-mail: lmalone@edmc.edu
Phone: (212) 226-5500 Toll-free number: (800) 654-2433
Fax: (212) 625-6065
Lauren Malone, Director of Admissions, Art Institute of New York City, 75 Varick Street, 16th Floor, New York, NY 10013-1917

ASA Institute of Business and Computer Technology

Brooklyn, New York
www.asa.edu

- For-profit 2-year business and junior college
- Commuter campus in very large city
- ACT with writing, interview required

General. Accredited by ACICS. **Enrollment:** 2,961 degree-seeking undergraduates; 16 non-degree-seeking students. **Degrees:** 1,014 associate awarded. **Calendar:** Semester, extensive summer session. **Full-time faculty:** 46 total; 22% have terminal degrees, 46% minority, 41% women. **Part-time faculty:** 150 total; 17% have terminal degrees, 43% minority, 47% women. **Class size:** 55% < 20, 45% 20-39, less than 1% 40-49.

Student profile. Among degree-seeking undergraduates, 926 enrolled as first-time, first-year students, 52 transferred in from other institutions.

Part-time:	2%	**Hispanic American:**	37%
Women:	81%	**International:**	2%
African American:	43%	**25 or older:**	64%
Asian American:	7%		

Basis for selection. Candidates accorded individual consideration through comprehensive evaluation of prior scholastic records and assessment testing results. **Adult students:** Entrance exam policies same as for first-time freshmen.

2005-2006 Annual costs. Tuition/fees: $9,430.

2005-2006 Financial aid. Need-based: 926 full-time freshmen applied for aid; 833 were judged to have need; 833 of these received aid. Average need met was 90%. Average scholarship/grant was $6,575; average loan $2,625. 99% of total undergraduate aid awarded as scholarships/grants, 1% as loans/jobs. Need-based aid available for part-time students. Work study available nights and weekends. **Non-need-based:** Awarded to 163 full-time undergraduates, including 155 freshmen. Scholarships awarded for academics, alumni affiliation, state residency. **Additional information:** Tuition at time of enrollment guaranteed to all students until graduation, provided no break in enrollment.

Application procedures. Admission: No deadline. $25 fee. Application must be submitted on paper. **Financial aid:** No deadline. FAFSA required. Applicants notified on a rolling basis starting 7/5; must reply by 10/5.

Academics. Special study options: Accelerated study, cooperative education, distance learning, ESL, internships. **Credit/placement by examination:** AP, CLEP, ACT, institutional tests. 29 credit hours maximum toward associate degree. Must have acceptable score on CLEP, MCSE, MOS, CISCO. **Support services:** GED preparation, learning center, reduced course load, remedial instruction, study skills assistance, tutoring, writing center.

Majors. Business: Business admin. **Computer sciences:** Networking, programming. **Health:** Office assistant, pharmacy assistant.

Most popular majors. Business/marketing 18%, computer/information sciences 7%, health sciences 75%.

Computing on campus. 1,000 workstations in library, computer center. Commuter students can connect to campus network. Online library, helpline available.

Student life. **Freshman orientation:** Available. **Activities:** Drama, literary magazine, student government.

Student services. Adult student services, career counseling, services for economically disadvantaged, student employment services, financial aid counseling, personal counseling, placement for graduates.

Contact. E-mail: admissions@asa.edu
Phone: (718) 522-9073 Toll-free number: (877) 867-5327
Fax: (718) 532-1430
Victoria Kostyukov, Vice President of Marketing and Admissions, ASA Institute of Business and Computer Technology, 151 Lawrence Street, Brooklyn, NY 11201-9805

Bramson ORT College
Forest Hills, New York
www.bramsonort.org **CB code: 0944**

- Private 2-year junior and technical college affiliated with Jewish faith
- Commuter campus in very large city

General. Founded in 1977. Regionally accredited. Extensions in Brooklyn and Manhattan. **Enrollment:** 582 undergraduates. **Degrees:** 116 associate awarded. **Calendar:** Semester, extensive summer session. **Part-time faculty:** 89 total. **Special facilities:** Ophthalmic laboratory.

Basis for selection. High school diploma and placement examination required. English and mathematics placement tests required. Interview recommended.

2006-2007 Annual costs. Tuition/fees: $9,040. Per-credit charge: $365.

Application procedures. **Admission:** No deadline. $50 fee. Admission notification on a rolling basis. **Financial aid:** No deadline. Institutional form required. Applicants notified on a rolling basis; must reply within 3 week(s) of notification.

Academics. **Special study options:** Accelerated study, double major, ESL, internships. **Credit/placement by examination:** CLEP, institutional tests. 50% of total hours needed for degree may be maximum of earned by examination. **Support services:** Learning center, pre-admission summer program, reduced course load, remedial instruction, tutoring.

Majors. **Business:** Accounting, administrative services, business admin, financial planning, management information systems. **Computer sciences:** General, applications programming, data processing, programming. **Engineering:** Electrical.

Computing on campus. 87 workstations in library, computer center.

Student life. **Activities:** Student government, student newspaper.

Student services. Adult student services, career counseling, student employment services, personal counseling, placement for graduates, veterans' counselor. **Physically disabled:** Services for visually, speech, hearing impaired. **Transfer:** Orientation for new students.

Contact. Phone: (718) 261-5800 Fax: (718) 575-5118
Aleksandra Kagan, Admissions Coordinator, Bramson ORT College, 6930 Austin Street, Forest Hills, NY 11375

Broome Community College
Binghamton, New York
www.sunybroome.edu **CB code: 2048**

- Public 2-year community college
- Commuter campus in small city

General. Founded in 1946. Regionally accredited. SUNY institution. **Enrollment:** 5,008 degree-seeking undergraduates. **Degrees:** 1,011 associate awarded. **Location:** 3 miles from downtown. **Calendar:** Semester, extensive summer session. **Full-time faculty:** 146 total. **Part-time faculty:** 248 total. **Class size:** 71% < 20, 28% 20-39, less than 1% 40-49, less than 1% 50-99, less than 1% >100. **Special facilities:** College-operated ice rink.

Student profile.

Out-of-state:	4%	**25 or older:**	31%

Transfer out. **Colleges most students transferred to 2005:** Binghamton University, Rochester Institute of Technology, State University of New York Cortland, State University of New York Utica-Rome, Ithaca College.

Basis for selection. Open admission. Some Health Sciences programs have waiting lists for clinical component of program. Interview recommended for computer science and health science programs.

High school preparation. High school subject recommendations vary by program.

2005-2006 Annual costs. Tuition/fees: $3,046; $5,860 out-of-state. Per-credit charge: $118 in-state; $236 out-of-state. Books/supplies: $800. Personal expenses: $820.

2004-2005 Financial aid. All financial aid based on need. 74% of total undergraduate aid awarded as scholarships/grants, 26% as loans/jobs. Need-based aid available for part-time students.

Application procedures. **Admission:** No deadline. No application fee. Application may be submitted online. Admission notification on a rolling basis. **Financial aid:** Priority date 3/1; no closing date. FAFSA required. Applicants notified on a rolling basis starting 3/15; must reply within 2 week(s) of notification.

Academics. **Special study options:** Cooperative education, distance learning, dual enrollment of high school students, ESL, exchange student, honors, independent study, internships, student-designed major, study abroad, weekend college. License preparation in dental hygiene, nursing, paramedic, physical therapy, radiology, real estate. **Credit/placement by examination:** AP, CLEP, institutional tests. **Support services:** Learning center, pre-admission summer program, reduced course load, remedial instruction, study skills assistance, tutoring, writing center.

Majors. **Business:** Accounting technology, business admin, executive assistant, financial planning, hotel/motel admin, international finance. **Communications:** General. **Computer sciences:** General, information systems. **Engineering:** General, science. **Engineering technology:** Civil, computer, electrical, mechanical, quality control. **Family/consumer sciences:** Child care. **Health:** Clinical lab technology, dental hygiene, EMT paramedic, medical assistant, medical radiologic technology/radiation therapy, medical records technology, nursing (RN), physical therapy assistant, substance abuse counseling. **Interdisciplinary:** Gerontology. **Legal studies:** Paralegal. **Liberal arts:** Arts/sciences. **Mechanic/repair:** Communications systems. **Protective services:** Corrections, fire services admin, police science. **Public administration:** Human services.

Computing on campus. 500 workstations in library, computer center. Commuter students can connect to campus network. Online course registration, helpline, wireless network available.

Student life. **Freshman orientation:** Available. Preregistration for classes offered. **Policies:** Freshmen permitted cars on campus. **Activities:** Bands, choral groups, dance, drama, music ensembles, musical theater, student government, student newspaper, international student organization, black student union, political science club, Latino Chi Alpha, Vietnamese student club.

Athletics. NJCAA. **Intercollegiate:** Baseball M, basketball, cross-country, golf M, ice hockey M, soccer, softball W, tennis M, volleyball W. **Intramural:** Basketball, cross-country, volleyball. **Team name:** Hornets.

Student services. Adult student services, career counseling, services for economically disadvantaged, student employment services, financial aid counseling, health services, on-campus daycare, personal counseling, placement for graduates, veterans' counselor. **Physically disabled:** Services for visually, speech, hearing impaired. **Transfer:** Special adviser, orientation for new students. Transfer adviser, college fairs on campus for students transferring to 4-year colleges.

Contact. Phone: (607) 778-5001 Fax: (607) 778-5310
Anthony Fiorelli, Director of Admissions, Broome Community College, Box 1017, Binghamton, NY 13902

Bryant & Stratton College: Albany
Albany, New York
www.bryantstratton.edu **CB code: 2018**

- For-profit 2-year business college
- Commuter campus in small city
- Application essay, interview required

General. Founded in 1854. Regionally accredited. **Enrollment:** 469 degree-seeking undergraduates; 1 non-degree-seeking students. **Degrees:** 104 associate awarded. **Location:** 2 miles from Albany, 28 miles from Saratoga. **Calendar:** Semester, extensive summer session. **Full-time faculty:** 10 total; 30% have terminal degrees, 40% women. **Part-time faculty:** 29 total; 21% have terminal degrees, 10% minority, 62% women.

Student profile. Among degree-seeking undergraduates, 109 enrolled as first-time, first-year students.

Part-time:	25%	**Hispanic American:**	7%
Women:	78%	**Native American:**	1%
African American:	48%	**25 or older:**	51%
Asian American:	2%		

Basis for selection. High school record, entrance examination score, personal interview and personal essay considered. Portfolio recommended.

High school preparation. Business courses recommended. Mathematics concentration preferred.

2006-2007 Annual costs. Tuition/fees: $12,450.

2004-2005 Financial aid. All financial aid based on need. 57% of total undergraduate aid awarded as scholarships/grants, 43% as loans/jobs. Need-based aid available for part-time students. Work study available nights, weekends and for part-time students.

Application procedures. Admission: No deadline. $25 fee. Admission notification on a rolling basis. Must reply by May 1 or within 4 week(s) if notified thereafter. **Financial aid:** No deadline. FAFSA required. Applicants notified on a rolling basis.

Academics. Special study options: Distance learning, double major, independent study, internships. **Credit/placement by examination:** CLEP. 31 credit hours maximum toward associate degree. **Support services:** Learning center, reduced course load, remedial instruction, tutoring.

Majors. Business: Accounting, administrative services, business admin, human resources. **Computer sciences:** General. **Health:** Medical assistant. **Legal studies:** Paralegal.

Most popular majors. Business/marketing 46%, computer/information sciences 16%, health sciences 15%, legal studies 24%.

Computing on campus. 100 workstations in library, computer center.

Student life. Freshman orientation: Mandatory.

Student services. Alcohol/substance abuse counseling, career counseling, student employment services, financial aid counseling, personal counseling, placement for graduates, veterans' counselor. **Physically disabled:** Services for visually impaired. **Transfer:** Special adviser, orientation, preadmission transcript evaluation for new students. Transfer adviser, college fairs on campus for students transferring to 4-year colleges.

Contact. Phone: (518) 437-1802 ext. 203 Fax: (518) 437-1048
Robert Ferrell, Director of Admissions, Bryant & Stratton College: Albany, 1259 Central Avenue, Albany, NY 12205

Bryant & Stratton College: Buffalo
Buffalo, New York
www.bryantstratton.edu **CB code: 2058**

- For-profit 2-year business college
- Large city
- Interview required

General. Founded in 1854. Regionally accredited. Branch campuses in Amherst and Orchard Park. **Enrollment:** 625 degree-seeking undergraduates. **Degrees:** 108 associate awarded. **Calendar:** Semester, extensive summer session. **Full-time faculty:** 20 total. **Part-time faculty:** 25 total.

Basis for selection. Open admission. IBM Aptitude Test for Programmer Personnel required of computer and data processing program applicants. Turse Shorthand Aptitude and Cloze tests required of court reporting program applicants. CPAT for all others.

2005-2006 Annual costs. Tuition/fees: $11,820. Books/supplies: $1,200. Personal expenses: $1,350.

Application procedures. Admission: No deadline. $25 fee, may be waived for applicants with need. Admission notification on a rolling basis. **Financial aid:** No deadline. Applicants notified on a rolling basis.

Academics. Special study options: Internships. Bachelor's degree programs available on campus. **Credit/placement by examination:** CLEP, institutional tests. 45 credit hours maximum toward associate degree. **Support services:** Learning center, remedial instruction, tutoring.

Majors. Business: General, administrative services. **Computer sciences:** General. **Engineering technology:** Electrical. **Health:** Medical assistant.

Computing on campus. 130 workstations in library, computer center.

Student life. Activities: Radio station, student government, student newspaper, numerous special interest clubs.

Athletics. Intramural: Bowling, skiing, softball, swimming.

Student services. Career counseling, student employment services, personal counseling, placement for graduates. **Physically disabled:** Services for visually, hearing impaired. **Transfer:** Special adviser, orientation for new students. Transfer adviser for students transferring to 4-year colleges.

Contact. Phone: (716) 884-9120 Fax: (716) 884-0091
Philip Struebel, Director of Admissions, Bryant & Stratton College: Buffalo, 465 Main Street Suite 400, Buffalo, NY 14203

Bryant & Stratton College: Henrietta
Rochester, New York
www.bryantstratton.edu

- For-profit 2-year business college
- Commuter campus

General. Enrollment: 290 degree-seeking undergraduates. **Degrees:** 121 associate awarded. **Calendar:** Semester. **Full-time faculty:** 88 total.

Basis for selection. Interview, entrance evaluation important.

2005-2006 Annual costs. Tuition/fees: $11,820. Per-credit charge: $394.

Application procedures. Admission: No deadline. No application fee.

Academics. Credit/placement by examination: CLEP.

Majors. Business: Accounting, administrative services, human resources. **Computer sciences:** Information technology. **Health:** Medical assistant, medical secretary. **Legal studies:** Paralegal. **Protective services:** Law enforcement admin. **Visual/performing arts:** Graphic design.

Contact. Phone: (585) 292-5627
Maria Scalise, Admissions Director, Bryant & Stratton College: Henrietta, 1225 Jefferson Road, Rochester, NY 14623

Bryant & Stratton College: Lackawanna
Orchard Park, New York
www.bryantstratton.edu **CB code: 3328**

- For-profit 2-year business college
- Commuter campus in large town

General. Regionally accredited. **Enrollment:** 269 degree-seeking undergraduates. **Degrees:** 67 associate awarded. **Calendar:** Continuous, extensive summer session. **Full-time faculty:** 7 total. **Part-time faculty:** 25 total.

Student profile. Among degree-seeking undergraduates, 94 transferred in from other institutions.

Basis for selection. Open admission.

2005-2006 Annual costs. Tuition/fees: $11,820. Per-credit charge: $394. Books/supplies: $1,200.

Application procedures. Admission: No deadline. $25 fee. Application may be submitted online.

Academics. Special study options: Distance learning, double major. **Credit/placement by examination:** CLEP. **Support services:** Learning center, study skills assistance, tutoring.

Majors. Business: Business admin. **Computer sciences:** General.

Computing on campus. Online library available.

Student life. **Freshman orientation:** Mandatory. Preregistration for classes offered. **Activities:** Student government, student newspaper.

Student services. Career counseling, student employment services, financial aid counseling. **Physically disabled:** Services for visually, hearing impaired. **Transfer:** Special adviser, orientation, pre-admission transcript evaluation for new students.

Contact. E-mail: dedwards@bryantstratton.edu
Phone: (716) 677-9500 Fax: (716) 677-9599
Dee Edwards, Director of Admissions, Bryant & Stratton College: Lackawanna, 200 Redtail, Orchard Park, NY 14127

Bryant & Stratton College: Rochester

Rochester, New York
www.bryantstratton.edu **CB code: 7327**

- For-profit 2-year business college
- Commuter campus in large city
- Interview required

General. Founded in 1973. Regionally accredited. Second campus in Rochester. Degree program runs 4 consecutive semesters. **Enrollment:** 482 degree-seeking undergraduates. **Degrees:** 218 associate awarded. **Calendar:** Semester, extensive summer session. **Full-time faculty:** 21 total. **Part-time faculty:** 70 total.

Basis for selection. Character, previous scholastic record, and counselor recommendation important. CPAT required for admission. **Adult students:** Entrance exam policies same as for first-time freshmen.

2005-2006 Annual costs. Tuition/fees: $11,820. Per-credit charge: $394. Books/supplies: $1,000.

Application procedures. **Admission:** No deadline. $25 fee, may be waived for applicants with need. Admission notification on a rolling basis. **Financial aid:** No deadline. FAFSA required. Applicants notified on a rolling basis.

Academics. **Special study options:** Accelerated study, distance learning, double major, internships. **Credit/placement by examination:** CLEP. **Support services:** Learning center, reduced course load, study skills assistance, tutoring.

Majors. **Business:** Accounting, administrative services, business admin, customer service, office technology. **Computer sciences:** Information technology, webmaster. **Health:** Office admin. **Legal studies:** Legal secretary, paralegal. **Visual/performing arts:** Design.

Computing on campus. 10 workstations in computer center. Commuter students can connect to campus network.

Student life. **Freshman orientation:** Available. Preregistration for classes offered. **Activities:** Student government, professional interest clubs.

Student services. Career counseling, financial aid counseling, personal counseling, placement for graduates. **Transfer:** Special adviser, orientation, pre-admission transcript evaluation for new students. Transfer adviser for students transferring to 4-year colleges.

Contact. Phone: (585) 292-5627
Maria Scalise, Director of Admissions, Bryant & Stratton College: Rochester, 1225 Jefferson Road, Rochester, NY 14623

Bryant & Stratton College: Syracuse

Syracuse, New York
www.bryantstratton.edu **CB code: 0654**

- For-profit 2-year business college
- Commuter campus in small city
- Interview required

General. Founded in 1854. Regionally accredited. **Enrollment:** 633 degree-seeking undergraduates. **Degrees:** 132 associate awarded. **Location:** 75 miles from Rochester. **Calendar:** Trimester, extensive summer session. **Full-time faculty:** 15 total. **Part-time faculty:** 41 total. **Class size:** 54% < 20, 46% 20-39.

Student profile.

Out-of-state:	2%	**Live on campus:**	20%
25 or older:	32%		

Basis for selection. High school record, interview, guidance counselor recommendation, admissions evaluation test, or SAT combined score of 956 (500 verbal, 460 math) or 20 ACT, and essay important. SAT Subject Tests considered if submitted. **Adult students:** Entrance exam policies same as for first-time freshmen.

2006-2007 Annual costs. Tuition/fees: $12,450. Per-credit charge: $415. Books/supplies: $1,000. Personal expenses: $1,350.

Financial aid. All financial aid based on need. Work study available nights, weekends and for part-time students.

Application procedures. **Admission:** No deadline. $25 fee. Application must be submitted on paper. Admission notification on a rolling basis. **Financial aid:** No deadline. FAFSA required. Applicants notified on a rolling basis starting 10/1.

Academics. **Special study options:** Cooperative education, cross-registration, distance learning, double major, honors, internships. **Credit/placement by examination:** AP, CLEP. **Support services:** Learning center, reduced course load, remedial instruction, study skills assistance, tutoring.

Majors. **Business:** Accounting, administrative services, business admin, hotel/motel admin, marketing, office management, sales/distribution, tourism promotion, tourism/travel. **Computer sciences:** General. **Health:** Medical assistant, medical secretary. **Legal studies:** Legal secretary.

Most popular majors. Business/marketing 68%, computer/information sciences 12%, health sciences 20%.

Computing on campus. 170 workstations in dormitories, library, computer center, student center. Dormitories wired for high-speed internet access and linked to campus network. Online library available.

Student life. **Freshman orientation:** Mandatory. **Policies:** Freshmen permitted cars on campus. **Housing:** Coed dorms, special housing for disabled available. $50 deposit. **Activities:** Choral groups, student newspaper.

Athletics. NJCAA. **Intercollegiate:** Soccer. **Team name:** Bobcats.

Student services. Career counseling, student employment services, financial aid counseling, personal counseling, placement for graduates. **Physically disabled:** Services for visually, speech, hearing impaired. **Transfer:** Special adviser, orientation, re-entry adviser, pre-admission transcript evaluation for new students. Transfer adviser, college fairs on campus for students transferring to 4-year colleges.

Contact. Phone: (315) 472-6603 Fax: (315) 474-4383
Dawn Rajkowski, Director of Admissions, Bryant & Stratton College: Syracuse, 953 James Street, Syracuse, NY 13203

Bryant & Stratton College: Syracuse North

Liverpool, New York
www.bryantstratton.edu

- For-profit 2-year business college
- Commuter campus

General. **Enrollment:** 450 degree-seeking undergraduates. **Degrees:** 152 associate awarded. **Calendar:** Semester, extensive summer session. **Full-time faculty:** 9 total.

Basis for selection. Accuplacer used for placement/counseling; students with minimum SAT (exclusive of Writing) 956 or 20 ACT not required to take Accuplacer.

2005-2006 Annual costs. Tuition/fees: $11,820. Per-credit charge: $394.

Academics. **Credit/placement by examination:** AP, CLEP.

Majors. **Business:** General, accounting, administrative services. **Computer sciences:** Information technology. **Legal studies:** Paralegal. **Visual/performing arts:** Graphic design.

Athletics. **Team name:** Bobcats.

Contact. Phone: (315) 652-6500
Bryant & Stratton College: Syracuse North, 8687 Carling Road, Liverpool, NY 13090

Bryant & Stratton College: Williamsville
Amherst, New York
www.bryantstratton.edu **CB code: 3331**

- For-profit 2-year business college
- Small town

General. Regionally accredited. **Calendar:** Continuous.

Annual costs/financial aid. Tuition/fees (2005-2006): $11,820. Books/supplies: $1,200.

Contact. Phone: (716) 691-0012
40 Hazelwood Drive, Amherst, NY 14228-2230

Business Informatics Center
Valley Stream, New York
www.thecollegeforbusiness.com

- For-profit 2-year business and community college
- Commuter campus in large town
- Interview required

General. Accredited by ACCSCT. **Enrollment:** 200 degree-seeking undergraduates. **Degrees:** 150 associate awarded. **Calendar:** Quarter. **Full-time faculty:** 20 total. **Part-time faculty:** 10 total. **Class size:** 92% < 20, 8% 20-39.

Transfer out. Colleges most students transferred to 2005: Briarcliff, Katherine Gibbs.

Basis for selection. Open admission. **Adult students:** Entrance exam policies same as for first-time freshmen.

2005-2006 Annual costs. Tuition/fees: $10,050. Per-credit charge: $215.

Application procedures. Admission: No deadline. $50 fee, may be waived for applicants with need. Admission notification on a rolling basis.

Academics. Credit/placement by examination: AP, CLEP, institutional tests. **Support services:** Tutoring.

Majors. Business: Office technology. **Legal studies:** Court reporting.

Most popular majors. Business/marketing 77%, legal studies 23%.

Computing on campus. 50 workstations in library, computer center.

Student life. Freshman orientation: Mandatory. **Activities:** Student government.

Student services. Financial aid counseling, placement for graduates. **Transfer:** Orientation for new students. Transfer center for students transferring to 4-year colleges.

Contact. Phone: (516) 561-0050
Hank Meaney, Admissions Director, Business Informatics Center, 134 South Central Avenue, Valley Stream, NY 11580-5431

Cayuga County Community College
Auburn, New York
www.cayuga-cc.edu **CB code: 2010**

- Public 2-year community college
- Commuter campus in large town

General. Founded in 1953. Regionally accredited. **Enrollment:** 2,825 degree-seeking undergraduates. **Degrees:** 585 associate awarded. **Location:** 30 miles from Syracuse. **Calendar:** Semester, limited summer session. **Full-time faculty:** 53 total. **Part-time faculty:** 189 total. **Class size:** 43% < 20, 55% 20-39, 1% 40-49, less than 1% 50-99. **Special facilities:** Nature trail, multitrack recording studio and video-editing suites, NASA regional application center.

Student profile.

Out-of-state:	15%	**25 or older:**	37%

Transfer out. Colleges most students transferred to 2005: SUNY Oswego, SUNY Cortland, SUNY Brockport, Rochester Institute of Technology, SUNY Institute of Technology.

Basis for selection. Open admission, but selective for some programs. Special requirements for nursing; interview required. All new students with no prior college credits must take placement test in English and math. **Adult students:** Entrance exam policies same as for first-time freshmen. **Home-schooled:** Must be able to document completion of high school or equivalent through: 1) official final high school transcript from student's school district indicating graduation or 2) letter on district letterhead from relevant district superintendent certifying that student has documented satisfactory completion of equivalent of 4-year high school program of study or 3) GED achieved by the State Education Department written exam or 4) taking college's placement test; and if Ability to Benefit scores set by college met/exceeded, may matriculate and be considered for financial aid and work toward satisfying 24-credit option prescribed by New York State Education Department.

High school preparation. Recommended units include English 4, mathematics 2, social studies 3 and science 1.

2005-2006 Annual costs. Tuition/fees: $3,327; $6,227 out-of-state. Per-credit charge: $105 in-state; $210 out-of-state. Books/supplies: $1,000. Personal expenses: $789.

Financial aid. All financial aid based on need. Need-based aid available for part-time students. Work study available nights, weekends and for part-time students.

Application procedures. Admission: No deadline. No application fee. Application may be submitted online. Admission notification on a rolling basis. **Financial aid:** Closing date 5/1. FAFSA required. Applicants notified on a rolling basis starting 6/1.

Academics. Special study options: Accelerated study, distance learning, double major, dual enrollment of high school students, honors, internships, liberal arts/career combination, study abroad, weekend college. License preparation in nursing, real estate. **Credit/placement by examination:** AP, CLEP, institutional tests. 32 credit hours maximum toward associate degree. **Support services:** Learning center, pre-admission summer program, reduced course load, remedial instruction, study skills assistance, tutoring, writing center.

Majors. Biology: General. **Business:** General, accounting, business admin. **Communications:** Broadcast journalism, radio/tv. **Communications technology:** General, photo/film/video, recording arts. **Computer sciences:** General, computer science, data processing, web page design. **Education:** Early childhood. **Engineering technology:** Computer hardware, electrical, electrical drafting, mechanical, mechanical drafting, telecommunications. **Health:** Nursing (RN). **Liberal arts:** Arts/sciences, humanities. **Math:** General. **Physical sciences:** Chemistry, geology. **Protective services:** Corrections, criminal justice, police science. **Social sciences:** Cartography. **Visual/performing arts:** Art, studio arts.

Computing on campus. 600 workstations in library, computer center. Online library available.

Student life. Freshman orientation: Available. Held week before classes begin. **Policies:** Freshmen permitted cars on campus. **Activities:** Choral groups, drama, film society, musical theater, radio station, student government, student newspaper, TV station, honor fraternity, business society, nursing club, multicultural association, criminal justice club, alumni association, diversity club.

Athletics. NJCAA. **Intercollegiate:** Basketball, cheerleading M, cross-country, lacrosse, soccer. **Intramural:** Basketball, football (non-tackle), racquetball, skiing, soccer, softball, tennis, volleyball. **Team name:** Spartans.

Student services. Campus ministries, career counseling, student employment services, financial aid counseling, health services, on-campus daycare, personal counseling, placement for graduates, veterans' counselor. **Learning disabled:** Comprehensive services available. **Transfer:** Special adviser, orientation, pre-admission transcript evaluation for new students. Transfer adviser, college fairs on campus for students transferring to 4-year colleges.

Contact. E-mail: admissions@cayuga-cc.edu
Phone: (315) 255-1743 ext. 2241 Fax: (315) 255-2117
Bruce Blodgett, Director of Admissions, Cayuga County Community College, 197 Franklin Street, Auburn, NY 13021-3099

City University of New York: Borough of Manhattan Community College
New York, New York **CB member**
www.bmcc.cuny.edu **CB code: 2063**

- Public 2-year community college
- Commuter campus in very large city

Two-Year Colleges

General. Founded in 1963. Regionally accredited. **Enrollment:** 17,998 degree-seeking undergraduates. **Degrees:** 2,156 associate awarded. **Calendar:** Semester, limited summer session. **Full-time faculty:** 379 total. **Part-time faculty:** 678 total. **Special facilities:** 2 theaters, media center, gymnasium with intercollegiate-size swimming pool. **Partnerships:** Formal partnerships with local businesses/corporations to provide courses to their employees.

Student profile.

Out-of-state:	1%	**25 or older:**	40%

Transfer out. Colleges most students transferred to 2005: Baruch College, Hunter College, City College, Brooklyn College, New York City College of Technology.

Basis for selection. Open admission, but selective for some programs. Special requirements for associate degree programs in nursing; admission to clinical sequence of AAS degree programs competitive, based on college GPA. High school academic units recommended for admission must be acquired before graduation.

High school preparation. 16 units recommended. Recommended units include English 4, mathematics 3, social studies 4, science 2 (laboratory 2) and foreign language 2. One unit of fine arts recommended.

2005-2006 Annual costs. Tuition/fees: $3,066; $5,966 out-of-state. Per-credit charge: $120 in-state; $190 out-of-state. Books/supplies: $759. Personal expenses: $1,656.

2004-2005 Financial aid. All financial aid based on need. 89% of total undergraduate aid awarded as scholarships/grants, 11% as loans/jobs. Need-based aid available for part-time students.

Application procedures. Admission: Priority date 4/1; no deadline. $65 fee, may be waived for applicants with need. Admission notification on a rolling basis beginning on or about 3/1. **Financial aid:** Priority date 4/15, closing date 5/1. FAFSA, institutional form required. Applicants notified on a rolling basis starting 8/1; must reply within 2 week(s) of notification.

Academics. Special study options: Cooperative education, cross-registration, distance learning, dual enrollment of high school students, ESL, exchange student, honors, independent study, internships, study abroad, weekend college. License preparation in nursing. **Credit/placement by examination:** CLEP. 32 credit hours maximum toward associate degree. **Support services:** GED preparation and test center, learning center, pre-admission summer program, remedial instruction, study skills assistance, tutoring, writing center.

Majors. Business: Accounting, administrative services, business admin, office management. **Communications technology:** General. **Computer sciences:** Data processing, networking, programming. **Education:** Early childhood. **Engineering:** General, science. **Health:** EMT paramedic, health care admin, nursing (RN), respiratory therapy technology. **Liberal arts:** Arts/sciences. **Math:** General. **Public administration:** Human services. **Visual/performing arts:** Multimedia.

Computing on campus. 1,200 workstations in library, computer center, student center. Commuter students can connect to campus network. Online course registration, online library, wireless network available.

Student life. Freshman orientation: Mandatory. **Activities:** Jazz band, choral groups, dance, drama, music ensembles, musical theater, student government, student newspaper, numerous organizations.

Athletics. NJCAA. **Intercollegiate:** Baseball, basketball, soccer M, volleyball. **Intramural:** Basketball, cricket, football (non-tackle), soccer, table tennis, triathlon, volleyball. **Team name:** Panthers.

Student services. Alcohol/substance abuse counseling, career counseling, student employment services, financial aid counseling, health services, on-campus daycare, personal counseling, placement for graduates, veterans' counselor, women's services. **Physically disabled:** Services for visually, speech, hearing impaired. **Transfer:** Special adviser, orientation, pre-admission transcript evaluation for new students. Transfer center, transfer adviser, college fairs on campus for students transferring to 4-year colleges.

Contact. E-mail: ebarrios@bmcc.cuny.edu
Phone: (212) 220-1265 Fax: (212) 220-2366
Eugenio Barrios, Director of Admissions, City University of New York: Borough of Manhattan Community College, 199 Chambers Street, New York, NY 10007-1097

City University of New York: Bronx Community College

Bronx, New York — **CB member**
www.bcc.cuny.edu — **CB code: 2051**

- Public 2-year community college
- Commuter campus in very large city

General. Founded in 1957. Regionally accredited. **Enrollment:** 8,186 degree-seeking undergraduates; 284 non-degree-seeking students. **Degrees:** 942 associate awarded. **Calendar:** Semester, limited summer session. **Full-time faculty:** 222 total; 39% minority, 44% women. **Part-time faculty:** 325 total; 46% minority, 40% women. **Special facilities:** Hall of Fame for Great Americans.

Student profile. Among degree-seeking undergraduates, 43% enrolled in a transfer program, 53% enrolled in a vocational program, 1,457 enrolled as first-time, first-year students.

Part-time:	38%	**Asian American:**	3%
Out-of-state:	9%	**Hispanic American:**	48%
Women:	64%	**International:**	11%
African American:	35%		

Transfer out. 54% of students enrolled in the transfer program go on to 4-year colleges. **Colleges most students transferred to 2005:** Lehman College, City College, Baruch College, Hunter College, John Jay College of Criminal Justice.

Basis for selection. Units recommended for admission must be acquired before graduation from any CUNY community college.

High school preparation. 9 units recommended. Recommended units include English 3, mathematics 2 and science 1.

2005-2006 Annual costs. Tuition/fees: $3,102; $6,002 out-of-state. Per-credit charge: $120 in-state; $190 out-of-state. Books/supplies: $759. Personal expenses: $2,100.

Application procedures. Admission: Priority date 1/15; deadline 8/15. $60 fee. Admission notification on a rolling basis. **Financial aid:** Closing date 7/15. FAFSA required. Applicants notified on a rolling basis starting 8/1.

Academics. Special study options: Cooperative education, cross-registration, dual enrollment of high school students, ESL, external degree, honors, independent study, internships, liberal arts/career combination, weekend college. License preparation in nursing. **Credit/placement by examination:** CLEP, ACT, institutional tests. 30 credit hours maximum toward associate degree. **Support services:** GED preparation, learning center, pre-admission summer program, reduced course load, remedial instruction, study skills assistance, tutoring, writing center.

Majors. Agriculture: Horticultural science. **Business:** General, accounting, administrative services, management information systems, office technology. **Computer sciences:** Computer science, data processing. **Education:** Teacher assistance. **Engineering:** Aerospace, chemical. **Engineering technology:** Electrical. **Health:** Clinical lab technology, medical assistant, medical radiologic technology/radiation therapy, nuclear medical technology, nursing (RN). **Legal studies:** Paralegal. **Liberal arts:** Arts/sciences. **Visual/performing arts:** Commercial/advertising art.

Most popular majors. Business/marketing 21%, computer/information sciences 6%, health sciences 14%, liberal arts 27%, public administration/social services 15%.

Computing on campus. 490 workstations in library, computer center. Commuter students can connect to campus network. Online course registration available.

Student life. Activities: Choral groups, dance, drama, literary magazine, music ensembles, radio station, student government, student newspaper.

Athletics. Intercollegiate: Baseball M, basketball, soccer M, track and field.

Student services. Career counseling, student employment services, health services, on-campus daycare, personal counseling, placement for graduates, veterans' counselor. **Physically disabled:** Services for visually, speech impaired. **Transfer:** Special adviser for new students. Transfer adviser, college fairs on campus for students transferring to 4-year colleges.

Contact. Phone: (718) 289-5889 Fax: (718) 289-6352
Alba Cancetty, Director of Admissions, City University of New York: Bronx Community College, West 181st Street and University Avenue, Bronx, NY 10453

City University of New York: Hostos Community College

Bronx, New York — **CB member**
www.hostos.cuny.edu — **CB code: 2303**

- Public 2-year community college
- Commuter campus in very large city

General. Founded in 1970. Regionally accredited. Bilingual Spanish/English liberal arts program. **Enrollment:** 4,059 degree-seeking undergraduates; 421 non-degree-seeking students. **Degrees:** 369 associate awarded. **Calendar:** Semester, limited summer session. **Full-time faculty:** 158 total; 54% have terminal degrees, 57% minority, 50% women. **Part-time faculty:** 174 total; 25% have terminal degrees, 73% minority, 41% women. **Class size:** 33% < 20, 61% 20-39, 5% 40-49. **Special facilities:** Theater.

Student profile. Among degree-seeking undergraduates, 36% enrolled in a transfer program, 64% enrolled in a vocational program, 2% already have a bachelor's degree or higher, 721 enrolled as first-time, first-year students, 410 transferred in from other institutions.

Part-time:	32%	**Women:**	73%
Out-of-state:	1%	**25 or older:**	52%

Transfer out. Colleges most students transferred to 2005: CUNY Lehman College, CUNY City College, CUNY John Jay College.

Basis for selection. Open admission, but selective for some programs. Admission to allied health programs based on Freshman Skills Assessment. **Adult students:** Entrance exam policies same as for first-time freshmen.

High school preparation. 16 units recommended. Recommended units include English 4, mathematics 3, social studies 4, science 2 and foreign language 2. 2 fine arts required. High school biology, chemistry, mathematics required of allied health applicants.

2005-2006 Annual costs. Tuition/fees: $3,104; $6,004 out-of-state. Per-credit charge: $120 in-state; $190 out-of-state. Books/supplies: $692. Personal expenses: $2,667.

2005-2006 Financial aid. Need-based: Need-based aid available for part-time students. Work study available for part-time students.

Application procedures. Admission: Closing date 8/15 (postmark date). $50 fee, may be waived for applicants with need. Application may be submitted online. Admission notification on a rolling basis. **Financial aid:** Priority date 7/1; no closing date. FAFSA, institutional form required. Applicants notified on a rolling basis; must reply within 3 week(s) of notification.

Academics. Special study options: Cooperative education, distance learning, dual enrollment of high school students, ESL, honors, independent study, internships, liberal arts/career combination, study abroad, weekend college. Serrano scholars program. License preparation in dental hygiene, nursing, radiology. **Credit/placement by examination:** CLEP, institutional tests. **Support services:** GED preparation and test center, learning center, pre-admission summer program, remedial instruction, study skills assistance, tutoring, writing center.

Majors. Business: General, accounting, administrative services, business admin, office technology. **Computer sciences:** Data processing. **Education:** Early childhood. **Engineering technology:** Civil, electrical. **Health:** Dental hygiene, medical radiologic technology/radiation therapy, medical secretary, nursing (RN). **Interdisciplinary:** Gerontology. **Legal studies:** Paralegal. **Liberal arts:** Arts/sciences. **Public administration:** General.

Most popular majors. Business/marketing 14%, computer/information sciences 6%, education 11%, health sciences 17%, legal studies 8%, liberal arts 39%.

Computing on campus. 1,000 workstations in library, computer center, student center. Commuter students can connect to campus network. Online course registration, online library, helpline, wireless network available.

Student life. Freshman orientation: Mandatory. Preregistration for classes offered. Held once a week each semester. **Activities:** Marching band, dance, drama, student government, student newspaper, TV station, Puerto Rican club, Christian club, black student union, Dominican association, South American student union, Ecuadorian student association, dental hygiene club, nursing club, Mexican club, Cuban club.

Athletics. NJCAA. **Intercollegiate:** Baseball M, basketball, soccer, volleyball W. **Intramural:** Basketball, volleyball W. **Team name:** Caimans.

Student services. Campus ministries, career counseling, services for economically disadvantaged, student employment services, financial aid counseling, health services, on-campus daycare, personal counseling, placement for graduates, veterans' counselor, women's services. **Physically disabled:** Services for visually, speech, hearing impaired. **Transfer:** Special adviser, orientation, re-entry adviser, pre-admission transcript evaluation for new students. Transfer adviser, college fairs on campus for students transferring to 4-year colleges.

Contact. E-mail: admissions@hostos.cuny.edu
Phone: (718) 518-4405 Fax: (718) 518-6643
Roland Velez, Director of Admissions/Recruitment, City University of New York: Hostos Community College, 120 East 149th Street, Room D210, Bronx, NY 10451

City University of New York: Kingsborough Community College

Brooklyn, New York — **CB member**
www.kbcc.cuny.edu — **CB code: 2358**

- Public 2-year community college
- Commuter campus in very large city

General. Founded in 1963. Regionally accredited. **Enrollment:** 10,751 degree-seeking undergraduates. **Degrees:** 1,772 associate awarded. **Location:** 10 miles from midtown. **Calendar:** Semester. Semester academic year calendar with a 12-week and a 6-week nodule. Extensive summer session. **Full-time faculty:** 284 total. **Part-time faculty:** 387 total. **Class size:** 35% < 20, 57% 20-39, 8% 40-49. **Special facilities:** Private beach on campus. **Partnerships:** Formal partnership with College Now program for high school seniors.

Student profile.

Out-of-state:	1%	**25 or older:**	28%

Transfer out. Colleges most students transferred to 2005: City University of New York: Brooklyn College, Long Island University, Pace University, City University of New York: College of Staten Island, City University of New York: Baruch College.

Basis for selection. Open admission. Units recommended for admission must be acquired before graduation from any CUNY community college. Students who achieve high scores on SAT exempted from basic skills remediation.

High school preparation. 16 units recommended. Recommended units include English 4, mathematics 3, social studies 4, science 2 and foreign language 2. One unit fine arts.

2005-2006 Annual costs. Tuition/fees: $3,098; $5,998 out-of-state. Per-credit charge: $120 in-state; $190 out-of-state. Books/supplies: $832. Personal expenses: $2,679.

Financial aid. All financial aid based on need. Need-based aid available for part-time students.

Application procedures. Admission: Closing date 8/15. $50 fee, may be waived for applicants with need. Application may be submitted online. Admission notification on a rolling basis beginning on or about 3/31. **Financial aid:** Closing date 4/30. FAFSA required. Applicants notified on a rolling basis; must reply within 2 week(s) of notification.

Academics. Special study options: Accelerated study, cross-registration, dual enrollment of high school students, ESL, honors, independent study, internships. My Turn Program for senior citizens, New Start Program for students academically dismissed from 4-year institutions. License preparation in nursing. **Credit/placement by examination:** AP, CLEP, institutional tests. 16 credit hours maximum toward associate degree. **Support services:** GED preparation, learning center, pre-admission summer program, reduced course load, remedial instruction, tutoring, writing center.

Majors. Biology: General. **Business:** Accounting, business admin, fashion, marketing, office management, tourism promotion, tourism/travel. **Communications:** Broadcast journalism, journalism. **Computer sciences:** Computer science, data processing. **Education:** Early childhood, elementary, teacher assistance. **Engineering:** General. **Health:** Community health services, mental health services, nursing (RN), physical therapy assistant. **Legal studies:** Legal secretary. **Liberal arts:** Arts/sciences. **Math:** General. **Parks/recreation:** General, exercise sciences. **Physical sciences:** Chemistry, physics. **Visual/performing arts:** General, commercial/advertising art, studio arts.

Most popular majors. Business/marketing 30%, computer/information sciences 6%, education 9%, health sciences 10%, liberal arts 32%.

Computing on campus. 900 workstations in library, computer center. Online course registration available.

Student life. Freshman orientation: Available. **Activities:** Bands, choral groups, dance, drama, film society, literary magazine, music ensembles, musical theater, opera, radio station, student government, student newspaper, symphony orchestra, over 60 ethnic, academic, religious, and political groups.

Athletics. NJCAA. **Intercollegiate:** Baseball M, basketball, soccer M, softball W, tennis, track and field, volleyball W. **Intramural:** Basketball, bowling, football (non-tackle), racquetball, soccer, softball, swimming, table tennis, tennis, volleyball, weight lifting.

Student services. Adult student services, career counseling, student employment services, health services, on-campus daycare, personal counseling, placement for graduates, veterans' counselor. **Physically disabled:** Services for visually, speech, hearing impaired. **Transfer:** Special adviser, orientation for new students. Transfer adviser for students transferring to 4-year colleges.

Contact. E-mail: info@kbcc.cuny.edu
Phone: (718) 368-4600 Fax: (718) 368-5356
Robert Ingenito, Admissions Information Center Director, City University of New York: Kingsborough Community College, 2001 Oriental Boulevard, Brooklyn, NY 11235

City University of New York: LaGuardia Community College

Long Island City, New York
www.lagcc.cuny.edu **CB code: 2246**

- Public 2-year community college
- Commuter campus in very large city

General. Founded in 1970. Regionally accredited. **Enrollment:** 11,285 degree-seeking undergraduates; 2,092 non-degree-seeking students. **Degrees:** 1,384 associate awarded. **Calendar:** Semester, limited summer session. **Full-time faculty:** 270 total; 52% have terminal degrees, 38% minority, 57% women. **Part-time faculty:** 503 total; 13% have terminal degrees, 41% minority, 49% women. **Class size:** 20% < 20, 79% 20-39, less than 1% 40-49, less than 1% >100. **Special facilities:** LaGuardia and Wagner archives.

Student profile. Among degree-seeking undergraduates, 67% enrolled in a transfer program, 33% enrolled in a vocational program, 2,082 enrolled as first-time, first-year students, 1,140 transferred in from other institutions.

Part-time:	40%	**Asian American:**	12%
Out-of-state:	1%	**Hispanic American:**	34%
Women:	64%	**International:**	18%
African American:	20%	**25 or older:**	40%

Transfer out. 36% of students enrolled in the transfer program go on to 4-year colleges. **Colleges most students transferred to 2005:** Baruch College, Hunter College, NYC Technical College, Queens College.

Basis for selection. Open admission. Units recommended for admission must be acquired before graduation from any CUNY community college.

High school preparation. 13 units recommended. Recommended units include English 4, mathematics 2, social studies 2, science 1 and academic electives 4.

2005-2006 Annual costs. Tuition/fees: $3,090; $5,990 out-of-state. Per-credit charge: $120 in-state; $190 out-of-state. Books/supplies: $832. Personal expenses: $1,659.

2005-2006 Financial aid. All financial aid based on need. 83% of total undergraduate aid awarded as scholarships/grants, 17% as loans/jobs. Need-based aid available for part-time students. Work study available nights, weekends and for part-time students.

Application procedures. Admission: Priority date 1/15; no deadline. $50 fee, may be waived for applicants with need. Application may be submitted online. Admission notification on a rolling basis. **Financial aid:** No deadline. FAFSA required. Applicants notified on a rolling basis starting 8/1; must reply within 4 week(s) of notification.

Academics. Special study options: Cooperative education, cross-registration, dual enrollment of high school students, independent study, internships, liberal arts/career combination, student-designed major. Summer program with Vassar College. License preparation in nursing, paramedic. **Credit/placement by examination:** AP, CLEP, institutional tests. 10 credit hours maximum toward associate degree. **Support services:** GED preparation and test center, learning center, pre-admission summer program, reduced course load, remedial instruction, tutoring, writing center.

Majors. Business: Accounting, administrative services, business admin, tourism promotion. **Computer sciences:** General, computer science, data processing, programming. **Education:** Bilingual. **Engineering:** General, civil, electrical, mechanical. **Family/consumer sciences:** Child care, institutional food production. **Health:** EMT paramedic, health services, occupational therapy assistant, physical therapy assistant, veterinary technology/assistant. **Interdisciplinary:** Gerontology. **Legal studies:** Legal secretary, paralegal. **Liberal arts:** Arts/sciences. **Personal/culinary services:** Mortuary science. **Visual/performing arts:** Commercial photography, studio arts.

Most popular majors. Business/marketing 30%, computer/information sciences 14%, education 8%, health sciences 11%, liberal arts 19%, personal/culinary services 11%.

Computing on campus. 909 workstations in library, computer center. Helpline available.

Student life. Freshman orientation: Available. Preregistration for classes offered. **Activities:** Bands, choral groups, dance, drama, music ensembles, radio station, student government, student newspaper, TV station.

Athletics. Intramural: Basketball, bowling, football (non-tackle) M, football (tackle) M, handball, soccer, softball, swimming, table tennis, volleyball.

Student services. Adult student services, career counseling, student employment services, health services, on-campus daycare, personal counseling, placement for graduates, veterans' counselor. **Physically disabled:** Services for visually, speech, hearing impaired. **Transfer:** Special adviser, orientation for new students. Transfer adviser, college fairs on campus for students transferring to 4-year colleges.

Contact. E-mail: admissions@lagcc.cuny.edu
Phone: (718) 482-7206 Fax: (718) 609-2023
Reine Sarmiento, Senior Director of Admissions, City University of New York: LaGuardia Community College, 31-10 Thomson Avenue, Long Island City, NY 11101

City University of New York: Queensborough Community College

Bayside, New York
www.qcc.cuny.edu **CB code: 2751**

- Public 2-year community college
- Commuter campus in very large city

General. Founded in 1958. Regionally accredited. **Enrollment:** 10,695 degree-seeking undergraduates; 2,143 non-degree-seeking students. **Degrees:** 1,833 associate awarded. **Location:** 10 miles from midtown Manhattan. **Calendar:** Semester, limited summer session. **Full-time faculty:** 293 total. **Part-time faculty:** 517 total. **Special facilities:** Resource center for Holocaust studies, observatory, art museum. **Partnerships:** Formal partnership with Verizon for Next Step associate degree program in telecommunication technology for Verizon employees.

Student profile. Among degree-seeking undergraduates, 48% enrolled in a transfer program, 32% enrolled in a vocational program, 2,464 enrolled as first-time, first-year students.

Part-time:	42%	**Asian American:**	17%
Out-of-state:	1%	**Hispanic American:**	21%
Women:	58%	**International:**	12%
African American:	25%	**25 or older:**	32%

Transfer out. 51% of students enrolled in the transfer program go on to 4-year colleges. **Colleges most students transferred to 2005:** CUNY Queens College, St. John's University.

Basis for selection. Open admission. Units recommended for admission must be acquired before graduation from CUNY. **Adult students:** Entrance exam policies same as for first-time freshmen.

High school preparation. 15 units recommended. Recommended units include English 4, mathematics 3, social studies 2, science 2 (laboratory 2) and academic electives 4.

2005-2006 Annual costs. Tuition/fees: $3,084; $5,984 out-of-state. Per-credit charge: $120 in-state; $190 out-of-state. Books/supplies: $500. Personal expenses: $2,100.

Application procedures. Admission: No deadline. $50 fee, may be waived for applicants with need. Application may be submitted online. Admission notification on a rolling basis. **Financial aid:** No deadline. FAFSA, institutional form required. Applicants notified on a rolling basis starting 7/15.

Academics. Special study options: Cooperative education, dual enrollment of high school students, ESL, independent study, internships, liberal arts/career combination. External education for homebound students, honors program for high school seniors. License preparation in nursing. **Credit/placement by examination:** AP, CLEP, institutional tests. **Support services:** Learning center, pre-admission summer program, remedial instruction, tutoring.

Majors. Biology: General. **Business:** General, accounting, administrative services, business admin, office management. **Communications technology:** General, recording arts. **Computer sciences:** General, data processing, information systems, programming. **Engineering:** Computer. **Engineering technology:** Drafting, electrical. **Health:** Clinical lab technology, environmental health, nursing (RN). **History:** General. **Liberal arts:** Arts/sciences. **Physical sciences:** Chemistry. **Psychology:** General. **Social sciences:** Political science, sociology. **Visual/performing arts:** General, art, dance, dramatic, music history, photography.

Computing on campus. 104 workstations in library, computer center. Online course registration available.

Student life. Freshman orientation: Available. Preregistration for classes offered. **Activities:** Bands, choral groups, dance, drama, film society, music ensembles, musical theater, radio station, student government, student newspaper, symphony orchestra, numerous ethnic, religious, social, political, and special interest clubs.

Athletics. NJCAA. **Intercollegiate:** Baseball M, basketball, cross-country, soccer M, softball W, tennis, track and field, volleyball. **Intramural:** Badminton, basketball, soccer, softball, swimming, table tennis, tennis, track and field, volleyball.

Student services. Adult student services, career counseling, student employment services, health services, on-campus daycare, personal counseling, placement for graduates, veterans' counselor. **Physically disabled:** Services for visually, speech, hearing impaired. **Transfer:** Special adviser, orientation for new students. Transfer adviser, college fairs on campus for students transferring to 4-year colleges.

Contact. Phone: (718) 631-6236 Fax: (718) 281-5208
Winston Yarde, Director of Admissions, City University of New York: Queensborough Community College, Springfield Boulevard & 56th Avenue, Bayside, NY 11364-1497

Clinton Community College

Plattsburgh, New York

www.clinton.edu **CB code: 2135**

- Public 2-year community college
- Commuter campus in large town

General. Founded in 1966. Regionally accredited. SUNY institution. **Enrollment:** 1,494 full-time, degree-seeking students. **Degrees:** 351 associate awarded. **Location:** 60 miles from Montreal, Canada; 30 miles from Burlington, Vermont. **Calendar:** Semester, limited summer session. **Full-time faculty:** 54 total. **Part-time faculty:** 93 total. **Class size:** 15% < 20, 83% 20-39, 2% 50-99. **Special facilities:** Science and technology center, special equipment and facilities for clean water research, forensic science. **Partnerships:** Formal partnership with area high schools in collaboration with College Advancement Program (CAP).

Student profile. Among full-time, degree-seeking students, 5 transferred in from other institutions.

Transfer out. Colleges most students transferred to 2005: SUNY at Plattsburgh.

Basis for selection. Open admission, but selective for some programs. Special requirements for nursing. Test scores may exempt students from taking placement test. Essay required for nursing. **Adult students:** Entrance exam policies same as for first-time freshmen. **Homeschooled:** State high school equivalency certificate required. Recommend completing GED, must take ability to benefit test.

High school preparation. Recommended units include English 4, mathematics 3, social studies 4, history 4, science 2 (laboratory 2) and foreign language 2. Chemistry required for nursing and medical laboratory technology.

2005-2006 Annual costs. Tuition/fees: $3,236; $7,766 out-of-state. Per-credit charge: $125 in-state; $312 out-of-state. Books/supplies: $675. Personal expenses: $870.

2005-2006 Financial aid. All financial aid based on need. 65% of total undergraduate aid awarded as scholarships/grants, 35% as loans/jobs. Need-based aid available for part-time students. Work study available for part-time students.

Application procedures. Admission: No deadline. No application fee. Application may be submitted online. Admission notification on a rolling basis. Early application recommended for selective admission programs and financial aid. **Financial aid:** Priority date 6/2; no closing date. FAFSA required. Applicants notified on a rolling basis starting 5/1; must reply within 2 week(s) of notification.

Academics. Special study options: Cross-registration, distance learning, dual enrollment of high school students, independent study, internships, liberal arts/career combination, New York semester, student-designed major. Semester in Albany, basic skills program. License preparation in nursing. **Credit/placement by examination:** AP, CLEP, IB, institutional tests. 30 credit hours maximum toward associate degree. **Support services:** GED preparation, reduced course load, remedial instruction, study skills assistance, tutoring, writing center.

Majors. Business: Accounting, administrative services, business admin, office management, office technology. **Computer sciences:** General, computer science. **Health:** Clinical lab technology, nursing (RN). **Liberal arts:** Arts/sciences. **Math:** General. **Public administration:** Human services.

Computing on campus. 350 workstations in library, computer center. Dormitories wired for high-speed internet access and linked to campus network. Commuter students can connect to campus network. Online library, wireless network available.

Student life. Freshman orientation: Mandatory. Preregistration for classes offered. Held day before classes begin each semester. **Policies:** Freshmen permitted cars on campus. **Housing:** Guaranteed on-campus for freshmen. Coed dorms, special housing for disabled available. $200 fully refundable deposit. **Activities:** Choral groups, drama, student government, student newspaper, nursing, laboratory technology, art clubs, business club, Native American club, Global Awareness, criminal justice, student activities board, student senate.

Athletics. NJCAA. **Intercollegiate:** Baseball M, basketball, soccer, softball W. **Intramural:** Volleyball. **Team name:** Cougars.

Student services. Alcohol/substance abuse counseling, career counseling, student employment services, financial aid counseling, health services, on-campus daycare, personal counseling, placement for graduates, veterans' counselor, women's services. **Physically disabled:** Services for visually, speech, hearing impaired. **Learning disabled:** Comprehensive services available. **Transfer:** Special adviser, orientation, pre-admission transcript evaluation for new students. Transfer adviser, college fairs on campus for students transferring to 4-year colleges.

Contact. E-mail: admissions@clinton.edu
Phone: (518) 562-4170 Toll-free number: (800) 552-1160
Fax: (518) 562-4380
Karen Burnam, Director of Admissions/Financial Aid, Clinton Community College, 136 Clinton Point Drive, Plattsburgh, NY 12901-4297

Cochran School of Nursing-St. John's Riverside Hospital

Yonkers, New York

www.riversidehealth.org **CB code: 2894**

- Private 2-year nursing college
- Commuter campus in small city
- Application essay, interview required

General. Founded in 1894. Access to all clinical facilities at St. John's Riverside Hospital. **Enrollment:** 309 degree-seeking undergraduates. **Degrees:** 61 associate awarded. **Location:** 20 miles from New York City. **Calendar:** Differs by program, limited summer session. **Full-time faculty:** 18 total; 17% minority, 94% women. **Class size:** 20% < 20, 73% 20-39, 7% 40-49.

Student profile. Among degree-seeking undergraduates, 100% enrolled in a transfer program, 15% already have a bachelor's degree or higher, 147 transferred in from other institutions.

Part-time:	52%	**Asian American:**	20%
Women:	84%	**Hispanic American:**	7%
African American:	37%		

Transfer out. **Colleges most students transferred to 2005:** Mercy College, College of New Rochelle, College of Mount St. Vincent.

Basis for selection. School achievement record, test scores, interview most important. Completion of prerequisite with C+ grade or better. **Adult students:** SAT/ACT scores not required. **Learning Disabled:** Must submit necessary documentation of disabilities at time of admission to disability officer.

High school preparation. 16 units required. Required and recommended units include English 4, mathematics 4, social studies 2, history 2, science 2 and foreign language 2. Mathematics units should include 1 algebra, science units should include 1 biology and 1 chemistry. 2 units of laboratory recommended.

2006-2007 Annual costs. Tuition and fees for full 2-year AAS program $20,149. Books/supplies: $1,800.

2005-2006 Financial aid. All financial aid based on need. 27% of total undergraduate aid awarded as scholarships/grants, 73% as loans/jobs. Need-based aid available for part-time students.

Application procedures. **Admission:** No deadline. $25 fee. Application must be submitted on paper. Admission notification on a rolling basis. **Financial aid:** No deadline. FAFSA required. Applicants notified on a rolling basis.

Academics. Special testing program facilitates career goals of LPNs who want to become RNs. **Special study options:** Accelerated study, combined bachelor's/graduate degree, liberal arts/career combination. License preparation in nursing. **Credit/placement by examination:** AP, CLEP, institutional tests. 27 credit hours maximum toward associate degree. **Support services:** Learning center, tutoring.

Majors. **Health:** Nursing (RN).

Computing on campus. 22 workstations in library, computer center. Online library available.

Student life. **Freshman orientation:** Mandatory. **Policies:** Freshmen permitted cars on campus. **Activities:** Student government.

Student services. Adult student services, career counseling, health services, personal counseling. **Transfer:** Special adviser, orientation, pre-admission transcript evaluation for new students. College fairs on campus for students transferring to 4-year colleges.

Contact. E-mail: pmclean@riversidehealth.org
Phone: (914) 964-4296 Fax: (914) 964-4796
Paulette McLean, Admissions Coordinator, Cochran School of Nursing-St. John's Riverside Hospital, 967 North Broadway, Yonkers, NY 10701

College of Westchester

White Plains, New York
www.cw.edu **CB code: 1023**

- For-profit 2-year business college
- Commuter campus in large town
- Application essay, interview required

General. Founded in 1915. Candidate for regional accreditation; also accredited by ACICS. **Enrollment:** 1,034 degree-seeking undergraduates; 16 non-degree-seeking students. **Degrees:** 292 associate awarded. **Location:** 30 miles from New York City. **Calendar:** Differs by program, extensive summer session. **Full-time faculty:** 25 total; 4% have terminal degrees, 24% minority, 52% women. **Part-time faculty:** 57 total; 4% have terminal degrees, 23% minority, 33% women. **Class size:** 68% < 20, 32% 20-39. **Partnerships:** Formal partnerships with local corporations and business for co-op work experience programs.

Student profile. Among degree-seeking undergraduates, 233 enrolled as first-time, first-year students.

Part-time:	20%	**Asian American:**	2%
Out-of-state:	4%	**Hispanic American:**	29%
Women:	58%	**Native American:**	1%
African American:	26%	**25 or older:**	56%

Basis for selection. Interview, prior academic performance, recommendations most important. Activities considered. Test scores considered when available. Institution-administered assessments used for both admissions and academic placement. **Adult students:** Entrance exam policies same as for first-time freshmen.

2005-2006 Annual costs. Tuition/fees: $17,955. Books/supplies: $990.

Financial aid. **Need-based:** Need-based aid available for part-time students. Work study available nights and weekends. **Non-need-based:** Scholarships awarded for academics, alumni affiliation.

Application procedures. **Admission:** No deadline. $40 fee, may be waived for applicants with need. Application may be submitted online. Admission notification on a rolling basis. **Financial aid:** No deadline. FAFSA, institutional form required. Applicants notified on a rolling basis starting 1/6; must reply within 2 week(s) of notification.

Academics. 100 credit hours required for graduation in day (quarterly) program, 66 in evening (semester) program. **Special study options:** Accelerated study, cooperative education, distance learning, double major, honors, internships, weekend college. **Credit/placement by examination:** AP, CLEP, institutional tests. **Support services:** GED preparation, learning center, reduced course load, remedial instruction, study skills assistance, tutoring.

Majors. **Business:** Accounting, administrative services, business admin, e-commerce, management information systems, office management, office technology, office/clerical, purchasing. **Computer sciences:** General, applications programming, computer graphics, computer science, data processing, information systems, LAN/WAN management, programming, systems analysis, web page design. **Engineering:** Software. **Health:** Office admin. **Visual/performing arts:** Commercial/advertising art.

Most popular majors. Business/marketing 64%, computer/information sciences 36%.

Computing on campus. 240 workstations in library, computer center, student center. Online library, helpline available.

Student life. **Freshman orientation:** Mandatory. **Activities:** Student government, student newspaper, accounting society, management and marketing club, office technology club, computer club, multimedia club, Alpha Beta honor society, women's business issues club, public speaking club.

Student services. Adult student services, career counseling, student employment services, financial aid counseling, personal counseling, placement for graduates. **Transfer:** Special adviser, orientation, pre-admission transcript evaluation for new students. Transfer adviser for students transferring to 4-year colleges.

Contact. E-mail: admissions@cw.edu
Phone: (914) 948-4442 ext. 318 Fax: (914) 948-5441
Kevin Tice, Director of Admissions, College of Westchester, 325 Central Park Avenue, White Plains, NY 10602

Columbia-Greene Community College

Hudson, New York
www.sunycgcc.edu **CB code: 2138**

- Public 2-year community college
- Commuter campus in small town

General. Founded in 1966. Regionally accredited. SUNY institution. **Enrollment:** 963 full-time, degree-seeking students. **Degrees:** 300 associate awarded. **Location:** 40 miles from Albany. **Calendar:** Semester, limited summer session. **Full-time faculty:** 48 total. **Part-time faculty:** 65 total. **Class size:** 57% < 20, 41% 20-39, 1% 40-49, less than 1% 50-99. **Special facilities:** 4 art galleries, Hudson River biological field station.

Student profile. Among full-time, degree-seeking students, 59% enrolled in a transfer program, 41% enrolled in a vocational program.

Out-of-state:	1%	**25 or older:**	31%

Transfer out. 44% of students enrolled in the transfer program go on to 4-year colleges.

Basis for selection. Open admission, but selective for some programs. Admission to some programs based on school achievement record, test scores, and recommendations. Interview recommended. **Adult students:** SAT/ACT scores not required. **Homeschooled:** Transcript of courses and grades, interview required.

High school preparation. Recommended units include English 3, mathematics 3, science 3 and foreign language 3.

2005-2006 Annual costs. Tuition/fees: $3,042; $5,874 out-of-state. Per-credit charge: $118 in-state; $236 out-of-state. Books/supplies: $550. Personal expenses: $950.

Financial aid. Need-based: Need-based aid available for part-time students. Work study available nights, weekends and for part-time students. **Non-need-based:** Scholarships awarded for academics, state residency.

Application procedures. Admission: No deadline. $30 fee, may be waived for applicants with need. Admission notification on a rolling basis. **Financial aid:** Priority date 5/1; no closing date. FAFSA, institutional form required. Applicants notified on a rolling basis starting 7/1; must reply within 2 week(s) of notification.

Academics. Special study options: Combined bachelor's/graduate degree, cooperative education, cross-registration, distance learning, dual enrollment of high school students, honors, independent study, internships, student-designed major. License preparation in aviation, nursing. **Credit/placement by examination:** AP, CLEP, institutional tests. 30 credit hours maximum toward associate degree. **Support services:** Learning center, pre-admission summer program, remedial instruction, study skills assistance, tutoring.

Honors college/program. Program offers the opportunity to work closely with faculty, conduct research, and participate in seminars and conferences with an interdisciplinary focus.

Majors. Biology: General. **Business:** Accounting, administrative services, business admin, office management, office technology. **Computer sciences:** General, applications programming, computer science, LAN/WAN management. **Conservation:** Environmental science. **Education:** Multi-level teacher, physical. **Engineering:** Science. **Health:** Massage therapy, nursing (RN). **Liberal arts:** Arts/sciences. **Math:** General. **Mechanic/repair:** Automotive. **Protective services:** Criminal justice, law enforcement admin. **Public administration:** Social work. **Social sciences:** General. **Visual/performing arts:** Studio arts.

Most popular majors. Business/marketing 14%, computer/information sciences 6%, health sciences 28%, liberal arts 37%.

Computing on campus. 150 workstations in library, computer center. Commuter students can connect to campus network. Online library available.

Student life. Freshman orientation: Available. Preregistration for classes offered. Held 1 week prior to start of fall classes. **Activities:** Choral groups, dance, drama, music ensembles, musical theater, student government, International Rotary Club, minority alliance group, College Union Board.

Athletics. NJCAA. **Intercollegiate:** Baseball M, basketball, bowling, soccer, softball W. **Intramural:** Basketball, bowling, fencing, table tennis, tennis, volleyball. **Team name:** Twins.

Student services. Adult student services, alcohol/substance abuse counseling, career counseling, student employment services, health services, on-campus daycare, personal counseling, placement for graduates, veterans' counselor. **Physically disabled:** Services for visually, hearing impaired. **Transfer:** Special adviser, orientation for new students. Transfer adviser, college fairs on campus for students transferring to 4-year colleges.

Contact. E-mail: garafalo@sunycgcc.edu
Phone: (518) 828-4181 ext. 5513 Fax: (518) 828-8543
Berne Bendel, Director of Admissions, Columbia-Greene Community College, 4400 Route 23, Hudson, NY 12534

Corning Community College

Corning, New York
www.corning-cc.edu **CB code: 2106**

- Public 2-year community college
- Commuter campus in large town

General. Founded in 1956. Regionally accredited. SUNY institution. **Enrollment:** 3,500 degree-seeking undergraduates. **Degrees:** 674 associate awarded. **ROTC:** Army, Navy, Air Force. **Location:** 50 miles from Binghamton. **Calendar:** Semester, limited summer session. **Full-time faculty:** 98 total. **Part-time faculty:** 155 total. **Class size:** 67% < 20, 31% 20-39, less than 1% 40-49, less than 1% 50-99, less than 1% >100. **Special facilities:** 200-acre nature center, criminal justice complex, observatory with historic working model of Hale telescope, planetarium.

Student profile.

Out-of-state:	4%	**25 or older:**	43%

Transfer out. Colleges most students transferred to 2005: Elmira College, Mansfield University, SUNY Cortland, SUNY Binghamton, SUNY Buffalo.

Basis for selection. Open admission, but selective for some programs. Applicants without diploma or GED evaluated on individual basis. **Homeschooled:** Ability to Benefit testing required. **Learning Disabled:** Students should contact disability services to arrange accommodations, including accommodations for placement tests.

High school preparation. Recommended units include English 4, mathematics 1, social studies 4, science 1 (laboratory 1). 4 mathematics and 4 science required of engineering science applicants; 1 algebra and 1 biology required of nursing applicants.

2005-2006 Annual costs. Tuition/fees: $3,448; $6,548 out-of-state. Per-credit charge: $129 in-state; $258 out-of-state. Personal expenses: $550.

Financial aid. All financial aid based on need. Need-based aid available for part-time students. Work study available weekends and for part-time students.

Application procedures. Admission: No deadline. $25 fee, may be waived for applicants with need. Admission notification on a rolling basis. **Financial aid:** Priority date 4/1; no closing date. FAFSA required. Applicants notified on a rolling basis starting 4/15; must reply within 2 week(s) of notification.

Academics. Special study options: Distance learning, double major, dual enrollment of high school students, honors, independent study, internships, study abroad, weekend college. License preparation in nursing, paramedic, real estate. **Credit/placement by examination:** AP, CLEP, institutional tests. 30 credit hours maximum toward associate degree. **Support services:** Learning center, reduced course load, remedial instruction, study skills assistance, tutoring, writing center.

Majors. Business: Accounting, administrative services, business admin, tourism promotion, tourism/travel. **Computer sciences:** General, computer graphics, computer science, programming. **Education:** Early childhood, elementary, health, physical. **Engineering:** Science. **Engineering technology:** Electrical, manufacturing. **Health:** EMT paramedic, nursing (RN), substance abuse counseling. **Interdisciplinary:** Biological/physical sciences. **Legal studies:** Paralegal. **Liberal arts:** Arts/sciences. **Math:** General. **Mechanic/repair:** Automotive, computer. **Parks/recreation:** Health/fitness. **Physical sciences:** General, optics. **Production:** Machine tool. **Protective services:** Corrections, criminal justice, fire safety technology, law enforcement admin. **Public administration:** Human services. **Science technology:** Chemical. **Social sciences:** General.

Computing on campus. 360 workstations in library, computer center. Wireless network available.

Student life. Freshman orientation: Available, $56 fee. One-day transition course offered in January, end of August. **Policies:** Freshmen permitted cars on campus. **Activities:** Choral groups, drama, literary magazine, music ensembles, radio station, student government, student newspaper, human services club, law society, Christian club, College Republicans, Phi Theta Kappa, nursing society, multicultural society.

Athletics. NJCAA. **Intercollegiate:** Baseball M, basketball, soccer, softball W, volleyball W. **Intramural:** Archery, badminton, basketball, bowling, golf, soccer, softball, table tennis, volleyball, weight lifting. **Team name:** Red Barons.

Student services. Alcohol/substance abuse counseling, campus ministries, career counseling, student employment services, financial aid counseling, health services, minority student services, personal counseling, placement for graduates. **Physically disabled:** Services for visually, speech, hearing impaired. **Transfer:** Special adviser, orientation for new students. Transfer center, transfer adviser, college fairs on campus for students transferring to 4-year colleges.

Contact. E-mail: admissions@corning-cc.edu
Phone: (607) 962-9220 Toll-free number: (800) 358-7171 ext. 220
Fax: (607) 962-9122
Karen McCarthy, Director of Admissions, Corning Community College, One Academic Drive, Corning, NY 14830

Dutchess Community College
Poughkeepsie, New York **CB member**
www.sunydutchess.edu **CB code: 2198**

- Public 2-year community college
- Commuter campus in large town

General. Founded in 1957. Regionally accredited. Extension programs at 6 sites. **Enrollment:** 6,807 degree-seeking undergraduates. **Degrees:** 805 associate awarded. **Location:** 70 miles from New York City. **Calendar:** Semester, limited summer session. **Full-time faculty:** 136 total; 23% have terminal degrees, 11% minority, 53% women. **Part-time faculty:** 316 total; 46% women. **Special facilities:** Biological experimentation site on Hudson River. **Partnerships:** Formal partnership with Verizon.

Student profile. Among degree-seeking undergraduates, 59% enrolled in a transfer program, 41% enrolled in a vocational program, 192 transferred in from other institutions.

Out-of-state:	1%	**25 or older:**	31%

Transfer out. 67% of students enrolled in the transfer program go on to 4-year colleges. **Colleges most students transferred to 2005:** State University of New York at Paltz, Marist College, Mount St. Mary's College, State University of New York at Albany.

Basis for selection. Open admission, but selective for some programs. Special requirements for nursing and engineering programs. **Adult students:** Entrance exam policies same as for first-time freshmen. **Homeschooled:** Students must pass entrance test unless they have local diploma or diploma from accredited school.

High school preparation. Recommended units include English 4, mathematics 3, social studies 4, science 3 and foreign language 2.

2005-2006 Annual costs. Tuition/fees: $2,986; $5,586 out-of-state. Per-credit charge: $105 in-state; $210 out-of-state. Books/supplies: $1,000. Personal expenses: $1,000.

Financial aid. Need-based: Need-based aid available for part-time students. Work study available for part-time students.

Application procedures. Admission: No deadline. No application fee. Application may be submitted online. Admission notification on a rolling basis. **Financial aid:** Priority date 5/1; no closing date. FAFSA, institutional form required. Applicants notified on a rolling basis starting 5/15; must reply within 2 week(s) of notification.

Academics. Special study options: Cooperative education, cross-registration, distance learning, dual enrollment of high school students, ESL, honors, independent study, internships, liberal arts/career combination, study abroad, weekend college. Combined degree in education with SUNY at New Paltz. License preparation in dental hygiene, nursing, paramedic. **Credit/placement by examination:** AP, CLEP, institutional tests. 40 credit hours maximum toward associate degree. **Support services:** GED preparation and test center, learning center, pre-admission summer program, reduced course load, remedial instruction, study skills assistance, tutoring, writing center.

Majors. Business: Accounting, administrative services, business admin, office technology, sales/distribution, tourism promotion, tourism/travel, travel services. **Communications:** General. **Computer sciences:** General, computer science. **Education:** Biology, chemistry, early childhood, elementary, English, French, German, kindergarten/preschool, mathematics, middle, science, secondary, social studies, Spanish, teacher assistance. **Engineering:** Electrical, science. **Engineering technology:** Architectural, construction, electrical, manufacturing. **Family/consumer sciences:** Child care. **Health:** Clinical lab technology, EMT paramedic, health services, mental health services, nursing (RN), physical therapy assistant. **Legal studies:** Legal secretary, paralegal. **Liberal arts:** Arts/sciences, humanities. **Math:** General. **Parks/recreation:** General, exercise sciences, facilities management. **Physical sciences:** General. **Protective services:** Criminal justice. **Visual/performing arts:** Commercial/advertising art, dramatic.

Most popular majors. Business/marketing 22%, education 9%, health sciences 12%, liberal arts 33%, security/protective services 6%.

Computing on campus. 1,000 workstations in library, computer center. Online course registration, online library, helpline, repair service available.

Student life. Freshman orientation: Available. Preregistration for classes offered. **Activities:** Jazz band, choral groups, dance, drama, film society, literary magazine, music ensembles, musical theater, radio station, student government, student newspaper, TV station, foreign student organization, special interest clubs.

Athletics. NJCAA. **Intercollegiate:** Baseball M, basketball M, bowling M, golf M, soccer M, softball W, tennis, volleyball W. **Intramural:** Archery, badminton, basketball, bowling, fencing, racquetball, soccer, softball, tennis, volleyball, weight lifting. **Team name:** Falcons.

Student services. Adult student services, career counseling, services for economically disadvantaged, student employment services, financial aid counseling, health services, minority student services, on-campus daycare, personal counseling, placement for graduates, veterans' counselor. **Physically disabled:** Services for visually, speech, hearing impaired. **Transfer:** Special adviser, orientation, pre-admission transcript evaluation for new students. Transfer adviser, college fairs on campus for students transferring to 4-year colleges.

Contact. E-mail: admissions@sunydutchess.edu
Phone: (845) 431-8010 Toll-free number: (800) 378-9707
Fax: (845) 431-8605
Rita Banner, Director of Admissions, Dutchess Community College, 53 Pendell Road, Poughkeepsie, NY 12601-1595

Elmira Business Institute
Elmira, New York
www.ebi-college.com **CB code: 3332**

- For-profit 2-year business and technical college
- Commuter campus in large town
- Interview required

General. Accredited by ACICS. **Enrollment:** 265 degree-seeking undergraduates; 96 non-degree-seeking students. **Degrees:** 64 associate awarded. **Calendar:** Trimester. **Full-time faculty:** 7 total; 71% women. **Part-time faculty:** 11 total; 73% women.

Student profile. Among degree-seeking undergraduates, 94 enrolled as first-time, first-year students, 94 transferred in from other institutions.

Part-time:	16%	**Women:**	89%
Out-of-state:	30%	**25 or older:**	80%

Basis for selection. Open admission. **Homeschooled:** State high school equivalency certificate required.

2005-2006 Annual costs. Program cost for 16 month associate degree in office technology (medical or legal) $19,520. Includes tuition, fees, books, graduation costs. Costs of other programs vary.

Financial aid. All financial aid based on need. Need-based aid available for part-time students.

Application procedures. Admission: No deadline. No application fee. Application may be submitted online. **Financial aid:** Closing date 5/1. FAFSA, institutional form required.

Academics. Special study options: Internships, weekend college. **Credit/placement by examination:** CLEP, institutional tests. **Support services:** Reduced course load, remedial instruction, tutoring.

Majors. Business: Accounting. **Health:** Clinical lab assistant, insurance coding, medical assistant, medical records admin, medical records technology, medical secretary, medical transcription. **Legal studies:** Legal secretary, paralegal.

Computing on campus. 100 workstations in library, computer center.

Student life. Freshman orientation: Mandatory. Preregistration for classes offered.

Student services. Career counseling, financial aid counseling, personal counseling, placement for graduates. **Transfer:** Special adviser, orientation, pre-admission transcript evaluation for new students. College fairs on campus for students transferring to 4-year colleges.

Contact. E-mail: lroan@ebi-college.com
Phone: (607) 733-7177 Toll-free number: (800) 843-1812
Fax: (607) 733-7178
Lisa Roan, Director, Elmira Business Institute, 303 North Main Street, Elmira, NY 14901

Elmira Business Institute: Vestal
Vestal, New York

- For-profit 2-year business and technical college
- Commuter campus

General. Accredited by ACICS.

Annual costs/financial aid. Program cost for 16 month associate degree in office technology (medical or legal) $19,520. Includes tuition, fees, books, graduation costs. Costs of other programs vary.

Contact. Phone: (607) 729-8915
4100 Vestal Road, Vestal, NY 13850

Erie Community College: City Campus

Buffalo, New York — **CB member**
www.ecc.edu — **CB code: 2213**

- Public 2-year community college
- Commuter campus in large city

General. Founded in 1971. Regionally accredited. SUNY institution. Additional campuses in Williamsville and Orchard Park. **Enrollment:** 2,685 degree-seeking undergraduates; 264 non-degree-seeking students. **Degrees:** 380 associate awarded. **ROTC:** Army. **Calendar:** Semester, limited summer session. **Full-time faculty:** 345 total; 11% minority, 50% women. **Part-time faculty:** 938 total; 6% minority, 43% women. **Special facilities:** Child care centers, vehicle training technology center, corporate training facility. **Partnerships:** Formal partnerships with Ford Motor Company, Daimler Chrysler, Verizon.

Student profile. Among degree-seeking undergraduates, 45% enrolled in a transfer program, 55% enrolled in a vocational program, 1% already have a bachelor's degree or higher, 632 enrolled as first-time, first-year students, 129 transferred in from other institutions.

Part-time:	21%	**Hispanic American:**	8%
Women:	64%	**Native American:**	1%
African American:	42%	**25 or older:**	44%
Asian American:	2%		

Transfer out. Colleges most students transferred to 2005: SUNY College at Buffalo, SUNY College at Fredonia, SUNY College at Brockport.

Basis for selection. Open admission, but selective for some programs. Special requirements for nursing and radiologic technology programs; interview required. Minimum age is 17 for international students. Students who receive 500 or higher on SAT Critical Reading and/or Math Sections are waived from the placement test. **Adult students:** Entrance exam policies same as for first-time freshmen. **Homeschooled:** Applicants follow same criteria as applicants with GED.

2005-2006 Annual costs. Tuition/fees: $3,235; $6,135 out-of-district; $6,135 out-of-state. Per-credit charge: $121 in-state; $242 out-of-state. Tuition discounts available for off-site and off-times courses. Books/supplies: $900. Personal expenses: $900.

2004-2005 Financial aid. All financial aid based on need. 72% of total undergraduate aid awarded as scholarships/grants, 28% as loans/jobs. Need-based aid available for part-time students. Work study available weekends and for part-time students.

Application procedures. Admission: Priority date 8/1; no deadline. $25 fee. Application may be submitted online. Admission notification on a rolling basis. **Financial aid:** Priority date 6/1; no closing date. FAFSA required. Applicants notified on a rolling basis starting 4/1; must reply within 2 week(s) of notification.

Academics. Special study options: Cooperative education, cross-registration, distance learning, double major, dual enrollment of high school students, ESL, exchange student, honors, independent study, internships, liberal arts/career combination, student-designed major, study abroad, teacher certification program, weekend college. Dual admissions with 4-year institutions. License preparation in nursing, paramedic, radiology. **Credit/placement by examination:** AP, CLEP, institutional tests. **Support services:** GED preparation and test center, learning center, pre-admission summer program, reduced course load, remedial instruction, study skills assistance, tutoring, writing center.

Majors. Business: Administrative services, business admin, office management. **Computer sciences:** Information systems. **Construction:** Maintenance. **Education:** Physical. **Family/consumer sciences:** Child care. **Health:** Community health services, medical radiologic technology/radiation therapy, nursing (RN), substance abuse counseling. **Legal studies:** Paralegal. **Liberal arts:** Arts/sciences, humanities. **Personal/culinary services:** Chef training. **Protective services:** Law enforcement admin, police science.

Most popular majors. Business/marketing 11%, health sciences 16%, legal studies 8%, liberal arts 38%, personal/culinary services 7%, security/protective services 7%.

Computing on campus. 386 workstations in library, computer center. Commuter students can connect to campus network. Online course registration, online library, helpline, repair service, student web hosting, wireless network available.

Student life. Freshman orientation: Mandatory, $15 fee. Preregistration for classes offered. **Policies:** Freshmen permitted cars on campus. **Activities:** Bands, choral groups, dance, drama, literary magazine, music ensembles, musical theater, radio station, student government, student newspaper, Black student union, Latino student association, international students club, honors association, environmental awareness organization, campus ministry, Habitat for Humanity, Newman Center, Phi Theta Kappa, bilingual club.

Athletics. NJCAA. **Intercollegiate:** Baseball M, basketball, bowling, cheerleading M, cross-country, diving, football (tackle) M, golf, ice hockey M, soccer, softball W, swimming, track and field, volleyball W. **Team name:** Kats.

Student services. Adult student services, campus ministries, career counseling, services for economically disadvantaged, student employment services, financial aid counseling, health services, minority student services, on-campus daycare, personal counseling, placement for graduates, veterans' counselor, women's services. **Physically disabled:** Services for visually, speech, hearing impaired. **Transfer:** Special adviser, orientation, pre-admission transcript evaluation for new students. Transfer adviser, college fairs on campus for students transferring to 4-year colleges.

Contact. E-mail: cheatom@ecc.edu
Phone: (716) 851-1155 Fax: (716) 851-1129
Petrina Hill-Cheatom, Director of Admissions, Erie Community College: City Campus, 121 Ellicott Street, Buffalo, NY 14203-2698

Erie Community College: North Campus

Williamsville, New York
www.ecc.edu — **CB code: 2228**

- Public 2-year community college
- Commuter campus in large town

General. Founded in 1946. Regionally accredited. SUNY institution. Main campus located in Buffalo; additional campus in Orchard Park. **Enrollment:** 5,101 degree-seeking undergraduates; 540 non-degree-seeking students. **Degrees:** 909 associate awarded. **ROTC:** Army. **Location:** 10 miles from Buffalo. **Calendar:** Semester, limited summer session. **Full-time faculty:** 345 total; 11% minority, 50% women. **Part-time faculty:** 938 total; 6% minority, 43% women. **Special facilities:** Child care centers, athletic fields (North & South campuses), vehicle training technology center, corporate training facility. **Partnerships:** Formal partnerships with Ford Motor Company, DaimlerChrysler, Verizon.

Student profile. Among degree-seeking undergraduates, 41% enrolled in a transfer program, 59% enrolled in a vocational program, 1% already have a bachelor's degree or higher, 1,150 enrolled as first-time, first-year students, 301 transferred in from other institutions.

Part-time:	26%	**Hispanic American:**	2%
Women:	51%	**Native American:**	1%
African American:	12%	**International:**	1%
Asian American:	2%	**25 or older:**	30%

Transfer out. Colleges most students transferred to 2005: SUNY College at Buffalo, SUNY College at Fredonia, SUNY College at Brockport.

Basis for selection. Open admission, but selective for some programs. Selective admission for nursing and occupational therapy programs; interview required. International students must be at least 17 years of age. Students who receive 500 or higher on SAT verbal and/or math waived from placement test. **Adult students:** Entrance exam policies same as for first-time freshmen. **Homeschooled:** Applicants follow same criteria as applicants with GED.

2005-2006 Annual costs. Tuition/fees: $3,235; $6,135 out-of-district; $6,135 out-of-state. Per-credit charge: $121 in-state; $242 out-of-state. Tuition discounts available for off-site and off-times courses. Books/supplies: $900. Personal expenses: $900.

2004-2005 Financial aid. All financial aid based on need. 72% of total undergraduate aid awarded as scholarships/grants, 28% as loans/jobs. Need-based aid available for part-time students. Work study available weekends and for part-time students.

Two-Year Colleges

Application procedures. Admission: Priority date 8/1; no deadline. $25 fee. Application may be submitted online. Admission notification on a rolling basis. **Financial aid:** Priority date 6/1; no closing date. FAFSA required. Applicants notified on a rolling basis starting 4/1; must reply within 2 week(s) of notification.

Academics. Special study options: Cooperative education, cross-registration, distance learning, double major, dual enrollment of high school students, ESL, exchange student, honors, independent study, internships, liberal arts/career combination, student-designed major, study abroad, teacher certification program, weekend college. Dual admissions with 4-year institutions. License preparation in dental hygiene, nursing, paramedic. **Credit/placement by examination:** AP, CLEP, institutional tests. **Support services:** GED preparation and test center, learning center, pre-admission summer program, reduced course load, remedial instruction, study skills assistance, tutoring, writing center.

Majors. Business: Business admin, construction management, office management. **Computer sciences:** General, information systems. **Education:** Physical. **Engineering:** General. **Engineering technology:** Civil, electrical, mechanical. **Health:** Clinical lab technology, dental hygiene, dietician assistant, medical records technology, nursing (RN), occupational therapy assistant, office admin, optician, respiratory therapy technology. **Liberal arts:** Arts/sciences, humanities. **Personal/culinary services:** Chef training, restaurant/catering. **Protective services:** Law enforcement admin, police science.

Most popular majors. Business/marketing 14%, health sciences 25%, liberal arts 35%, security/protective services 12%.

Computing on campus. 436 workstations in library, computer center. Commuter students can connect to campus network. Online course registration, online library, helpline, repair service, student web hosting, wireless network available.

Student life. Freshman orientation: Mandatory, $15 fee. Preregistration for classes offered. Overview headed by dean of students and assistant academic dean. **Policies:** Freshmen permitted cars on campus. **Activities:** Bands, choral groups, dance, drama, literary magazine, music ensembles, musical theater, radio station, student government, student newspaper, black student union, Latino student association, international students club, honors association, environmental awareness organization, campus ministry, Habitat for Humanity, Newman Center, Phi Theta Kappa, bilingual club.

Athletics. NJCAA. **Intercollegiate:** Baseball M, basketball, bowling, cheerleading M, cross-country, diving, football (tackle) M, golf, ice hockey M, soccer, softball W, swimming, track and field, volleyball W. **Team name:** Kats.

Student services. Adult student services, campus ministries, career counseling, services for economically disadvantaged, student employment services, financial aid counseling, health services, minority student services, on-campus daycare, personal counseling, placement for graduates, veterans' counselor, women's services. **Physically disabled:** Services for visually, speech, hearing impaired. **Transfer:** Special adviser, orientation, pre-admission transcript evaluation for new students. Transfer adviser, college fairs on campus for students transferring to 4-year colleges.

Contact. E-mail: cheatom@ecc.edu
Phone: (716) 851-1455 Fax: (716) 851-1429
Petrina Hill-Cheatom, Director of Admissions, Erie Community College: North Campus, 6205 Main Street, Williamsville, NY 14221-7095

Erie Community College: South Campus

Orchard Park, New York
www.ecc.edu **CB code: 2211**

- Public 2-year community college
- Commuter campus in large town

General. Founded in 1974. Regionally accredited. SUNY institution. Main campus located in Buffalo; additional campus in Williamsville. **Enrollment:** 3,253 degree-seeking undergraduates; 814 non-degree-seeking students. **Degrees:** 562 associate awarded. **ROTC:** Army. **Location:** 10 miles from Buffalo. **Calendar:** Semester, limited summer session. **Full-time faculty:** 345 total; 11% minority, 50% women. **Part-time faculty:** 938 total; 6% minority, 43% women. **Special facilities:** Child care centers, athletic fields (North & South campuses), vehicle training technology center, corporate training facility. **Partnerships:** Formal partnerships with Ford Motor Company, DaimlerChrysler, Verizon.

Student profile. Among degree-seeking undergraduates, 56% enrolled in a transfer program, 44% enrolled in a vocational program, 1% already have a bachelor's degree or higher, 898 enrolled as first-time, first-year students, 154 transferred in from other institutions.

Part-time:	23%	**Asian American:**	1%
Out-of-state:	1%	**Hispanic American:**	3%
Women:	41%	**Native American:**	1%
African American:	5%	**25 or older:**	20%

Transfer out. Colleges most students transferred to 2005: SUNY at Buffalo, SUNY College at Fredonia, SUNY College at Brockport.

Basis for selection. Open admission, but selective for some programs. Selective admission for dental laboratory technician program; interview required. Minimum age is 17 for international students. Students who receive 500 or higher on SAT verbal and/or math are waived from placement test. **Adult students:** Entrance exam policies same as for first-time freshmen. **Homeschooled:** Applicants follow same criteria as applicants with GED.

2005-2006 Annual costs. Tuition/fees: $3,235; $6,135 out-of-district; $6,135 out-of-state. Per-credit charge: $121 in-state; $242 out-of-state. Tuition discounts available for off-site and off-times courses. Books/supplies: $900. Personal expenses: $900.

2004-2005 Financial aid. All financial aid based on need. 72% of total undergraduate aid awarded as scholarships/grants, 28% as loans/jobs. Need-based aid available for part-time students. Work study available weekends and for part-time students.

Application procedures. Admission: Priority date 8/1; no deadline. $25 fee. Application may be submitted online. Admission notification on a rolling basis. **Financial aid:** Priority date 6/1; no closing date. FAFSA required. Applicants notified on a rolling basis starting 4/1; must reply within 2 week(s) of notification.

Academics. Special study options: Cooperative education, cross-registration, distance learning, double major, dual enrollment of high school students, ESL, exchange student, honors, independent study, internships, liberal arts/career combination, student-designed major, study abroad, teacher certification program, weekend college. Dual admissions with 4-year institutions, cooperative education. License preparation in paramedic. **Credit/placement by examination:** AP, CLEP, institutional tests. **Support services:** GED preparation and test center, learning center, pre-admission summer program, reduced course load, remedial instruction, study skills assistance, tutoring, writing center.

Majors. Business: Business admin, office management. **Communications:** General. **Communications technology:** Graphic/printing. **Computer sciences:** Information systems. **Education:** Physical. **Engineering technology:** Architectural, computer systems, industrial, mechanical drafting. **Health:** Dental lab technology. **Liberal arts:** Arts/sciences, humanities. **Mechanic/repair:** Auto body, automotive, communications systems. **Parks/recreation:** Facilities management. **Protective services:** Fire services admin.

Most popular majors. Business/marketing 13%, communications/journalism 8%, liberal arts 55%, trade and industry 10%.

Computing on campus. 438 workstations in library, computer center. Commuter students can connect to campus network. Online course registration, online library, helpline, repair service, student web hosting, wireless network available.

Student life. Freshman orientation: Mandatory, $15 fee. Preregistration for classes offered. **Policies:** Freshmen permitted cars on campus. **Activities:** Bands, choral groups, dance, drama, literary magazine, music ensembles, musical theater, radio station, student government, student newspaper, black student union, Latino student association, international students club, honors association, environmental awareness organization, campus ministry, Habitat for Humanity, Newman Center, Phi Theta Kappa, bilingual club.

Athletics. NJCAA. **Intercollegiate:** Baseball M, basketball, bowling, cheerleading M, cross-country, diving, football (tackle) M, golf, ice hockey M, soccer, softball W, swimming, track and field, volleyball W. **Team name:** Kats.

Student services. Adult student services, campus ministries, career counseling, services for economically disadvantaged, student employment services, financial aid counseling, health services, minority student services, on-campus daycare, personal counseling, placement for graduates, veterans' counselor, women's services. **Physically disabled:** Services for visually, speech, hearing impaired. **Transfer:** Special adviser, orientation, pre-admission transcript evaluation for new students. Transfer adviser, college fairs on campus for students transferring to 4-year colleges.

Contact. E-mail: cheatom@ecc.edu
Phone: (716) 851-1655 Fax: (716) 851-1629
Petrina Hill Cheatom, Director of Admissions, Erie Community College: South Campus, 4041 Southwestern Boulevard, Orchard Park, NY 14127-2199

Finger Lakes Community College

Canandaigua, New York
www.flcc.edu **CB code: 2134**

- Public 2-year community college
- Commuter campus in small town

General. Founded in 1965. Regionally accredited. SUNY institution. **Enrollment:** 3,368 degree-seeking undergraduates; 1,542 non-degree-seeking students. **Degrees:** 716 associate awarded. **ROTC:** Army. **Location:** 25 miles from Rochester. **Calendar:** Semester, extensive summer session. **Full-time faculty:** 109 total; 2% minority, 43% women. **Part-time faculty:** 171 total; 53% women. **Class size:** 64% < 20, 36% 20-39, less than 1% 40-49, less than 1% 50-99. **Special facilities:** Outdoor classrooms, nature trails, music recording studio, performing arts center. **Partnerships:** Formal partnerships with local hospitals for nursing clinicals, more informally for co-operative studies and placement of interns.

Student profile. Among degree-seeking undergraduates, 64% enrolled in a transfer program, 36% enrolled in a vocational program, 991 enrolled as first-time, first-year students, 256 transferred in from other institutions.

Part-time:	23%	**Asian American:**	1%
Out-of-state:	1%	**Hispanic American:**	2%
Women:	56%	**Native American:**	1%
African American:	4%	**25 or older:**	32%

Transfer out. Colleges most students transferred to 2005: SUNY at Brockport, SUNY at Geneseo, St. John Fisher College, Nazareth College of Rochester, Rochester Institute of Technology.

Basis for selection. Open admission, but selective for some programs. Admission to nursing program based on high school curriculum and GPA. Selective admission to therapeutic massage/integrated health care program. Interview recommended for all; portfolio recommended for graphic arts program. **Adult students:** Entrance exam policies same as for first-time freshmen. **Homeschooled:** Student must submit certification of high school equivalent program provided by superintendent of school district in which student resides.

High school preparation. One unit each biology, chemistry, and mathematics required of nursing applicants. Students without high school diploma or GED must pass federally approved Ability to Benefit test prior to acceptance. One unit of biology required for therapeutic massage/integrated health care applicants.

2005-2006 Annual costs. Tuition/fees: $3,150; $6,050 out-of-state. Per-credit charge: $117 in-state; $241 out-of-state. Books/supplies: $800. Personal expenses: $1,645.

2004-2005 Financial aid. All financial aid based on need. 66% of total undergraduate aid awarded as scholarships/grants, 34% as loans/jobs. Need-based aid available for part-time students. Work study available nights, weekends and for part-time students.

Application procedures. Admission: No deadline. No application fee. Application may be submitted online. Admission notification on a rolling basis beginning on or about 12/15. Application closing date for nursing program is February 1. **Financial aid:** Priority date 4/1; no closing date. FAFSA, institutional form required. Applicants notified on a rolling basis starting 3/1.

Academics. Special study options: Cooperative education, cross-registration, distance learning, double major, dual enrollment of high school students, ESL, honors, independent study, internships. Credit-bearing travel opportunities. License preparation in nursing, paramedic. **Credit/placement by examination:** AP, CLEP, IB, institutional tests. 32 credit hours maximum toward associate degree. **Support services:** GED preparation, learning center, pre-admission summer program, reduced course load, remedial instruction, study skills assistance, tutoring, writing center.

Majors. Agriculture: Landscaping, ornamental horticulture. **Biology:** Biotechnology. **Business:** General, accounting, administrative services, banking/financial services, business admin, hospitality/recreation, sales/distribution, tourism promotion, tourism/travel. **Communications:** General, broadcast journalism. **Communications technology:** Recording arts. **Computer sciences:** General, computer science, information systems, programming. **Conservation:** General, environmental studies, management/policy. **Engineering:** General, chemical, electrical, science. **Engineering technology:** Architectural. **Health:** Athletic training, massage therapy, nursing (RN), substance abuse counseling. **Legal studies:** Paralegal. **Liberal arts:** Arts/sciences. **Parks/recreation:** Health/fitness, sports admin. **Physical sciences:** Chemistry. **Protective services:** Criminal justice. **Public administration:** Human services. **Science technology:** Biological. **Social sciences:** General. **Visual/performing arts:** Commercial/advertising art, dramatic, studio arts.

Most popular majors. Business/marketing 12%, health sciences 13%, liberal arts 31%, natural resources/environmental science 12%, visual/performing arts 11%.

Computing on campus. 460 workstations in library, computer center, student center. Commuter students can connect to campus network. Online course registration, online library, helpline, repair service, student web hosting, wireless network available.

Student life. Freshman orientation: Available. Preregistration for classes offered. One day program with faculty and student leaders. **Policies:** Student code of conduct policy, grievance procedures, procedures for services for students with disabilities. Freshmen permitted cars on campus. **Activities:** Bands, choral groups, drama, music ensembles, musical theater, radio station, student government, student newspaper, TV station, Phi Theta Kappa International Honor Society, nursing club, social science/human services club, legal society, chemical dependency club, Students for Tolerance and Respect, College Democrats, Finger Lakes Environmental Action, Healthy Living for Students, radio club.

Athletics. NJCAA. **Intercollegiate:** Baseball M, basketball, cross-country, lacrosse, soccer, softball W. **Intramural:** Badminton, basketball, bowling, football (non-tackle) M, soccer, softball, tennis, volleyball.

Student services. Adult student services, alcohol/substance abuse counseling, career counseling, services for economically disadvantaged, student employment services, financial aid counseling, health services, legal services, on-campus daycare, personal counseling, placement for graduates, veterans' counselor. **Physically disabled:** Services for visually, speech, hearing impaired. **Transfer:** Special adviser, orientation, pre-admission transcript evaluation for new students. Transfer center, transfer adviser, college fairs on campus for students transferring to 4-year colleges.

Contact. E-mail: admissions@flcc.edu
Phone: (585) 394-3500 ext. 7278 Fax: (585) 394-5005
Bonnie Ritts, Admissions Office, Finger Lakes Community College, 4355 Lake Shore Drive, Canandaigua, NY 14424-8395

Fulton-Montgomery Community College

Johnstown, New York
www.fmcc.suny.edu **CB code: 2254**

- Public 2-year community college
- Commuter campus in large town

General. Founded in 1963. Regionally accredited. SUNY institution. Cisco certified network associate courses available. **Enrollment:** 1,749 degree-seeking undergraduates. **Degrees:** 345 associate awarded. **Location:** 40 miles from Albany. **Calendar:** Semester, extensive summer session. **Full-time faculty:** 52 total. **Part-time faculty:** 47 total. **Class size:** 49% < 20, 41% 20-39, 5% 40-49, 4% 50-99. **Special facilities:** Spatial information technology center.

Transfer out. Colleges most students transferred to 2005: State University of New York at Plattsburgh, College of Saint Rose, SUNY College at Oneonta, University at Albany.

Basis for selection. Open admission, but selective for some programs. Admission for nursing and radiologic technology programs based on high school GPA, class rank, and any college experience. Must meet program prerequisites. Focal Skills Test for ESL Placement and COMPASS used for placement. Interview recommended. **Homeschooled:** Applicants applying for financial aid may be required to complete Ability to Benefit Test. Applicants from accredited home school who have received or will receive diploma may not be required to take test.

2005-2006 Annual costs. Tuition/fees: $3,215; $6,140 out-of-state. Per-credit charge: $122 in-state; $244 out-of-state. Books/supplies: $500.

2004-2005 Financial aid. Need-based: 64% of total undergraduate aid awarded as scholarships/grants, 36% as loans/jobs. Need-based aid available for part-time students. Work study available nights, weekends and for part-time students. **Non-need-based:** Scholarships awarded for academics.

Application procedures. Admission: No deadline. No application fee. Application must be submitted on paper. Admission notification on a rolling basis. **Financial aid:** Priority date 6/1; no closing date. FAFSA required.

Applicants notified on a rolling basis starting 6/15; must reply within 2 week(s) of notification.

Academics. Career-oriented individual studies program offered. **Special study options:** Accelerated study, cooperative education, cross-registration, distance learning, double major, dual enrollment of high school students, ESL, external degree, honors, independent study, internships, student-designed major, study abroad. 1+1 agreements with SUNY Agricultural and Technical Colleges at Canton and Cobleskill, automotive program at the Career Education Center (HFM Boces), Johnstown, EMT-Paramedic with SUNY Herkimer County Community College. License preparation in nursing, radiology. **Credit/placement by examination:** AP, CLEP, institutional tests. 30 credit hours maximum toward associate degree. **Support services:** Learning center, reduced course load, remedial instruction, study skills assistance, tutoring, writing center.

Majors. Business: General, accounting technology, administrative services, business admin. **Communications:** General, journalism. **Communications technology:** Graphic/printing. **Computer sciences:** General, information systems. **Construction:** General. **Engineering:** General. **Engineering technology:** Computer, electrical. **Family/consumer sciences:** Child care. **Health:** Medical radiologic technology/radiation therapy, nursing (RN), office admin. **Liberal arts:** Arts/sciences, humanities. **Mechanic/repair:** Automotive. **Parks/recreation:** Health/fitness. **Personal/culinary services:** Restaurant/catering. **Protective services:** Criminal justice. **Public administration:** Community org/advocacy. **Visual/performing arts:** Art, commercial/advertising art.

Computing on campus. 400 workstations in library, computer center, student center. Commuter students can connect to campus network. Helpline available.

Student life. Freshman orientation: Available. Preregistration for classes offered. One-day orientation held one or two days before classes begin. **Activities:** Choral groups, drama, musical theater, student government, student newspaper, Phi Theta Kappa, Alpha Omega, international student union, business club, fencing club.

Athletics. NJCAA. **Intercollegiate:** Baseball M, basketball, soccer, softball W, volleyball W. **Intramural:** Basketball M, volleyball. **Team name:** Raiders.

Student services. Adult student services, student employment services, on-campus daycare, personal counseling, veterans' counselor. **Physically disabled:** Services for visually, speech, hearing impaired. **Transfer:** Special adviser, orientation, pre-admission transcript evaluation for new students. Transfer center, college fairs on campus for students transferring to 4-year colleges.

Contact. E-mail: geninfo@fmcc.suny.edu
Phone: (518) 762-4651 ext. 8301 Fax: (518) 762-4334
Jane Kelley, Associate Dean for Enrollment Management,
Fulton-Montgomery Community College, 2805 State Highway 67,
Johnstown, NY 12095

Genesee Community College

Batavia, New York
www.genesee.edu **CB code: 2272**

- Public 2-year community college
- Commuter campus in large town

General. Founded in 1966. Regionally accredited. SUNY institution. Mall-type campus, suited to disabled. Off-campus sites in Orleans, Wyoming, and Livingston counties. **Enrollment:** 3,951 degree-seeking undergraduates; 2,539 non-degree-seeking students. **Degrees:** 649 associate awarded. **Location:** 35 miles from Buffalo, 35 miles from Rochester. **Calendar:** Semester, limited summer session. **Full-time faculty:** 74 total. **Part-time faculty:** 238 total. **Special facilities:** Nature preserve, arts center, new technology building.

Student profile. Among degree-seeking undergraduates, 55% enrolled in a transfer program, 45% enrolled in a vocational program, 1,139 enrolled as first-time, first-year students.

Part-time:	25%	**Women:**	67%

Transfer out. 56% of students enrolled in the transfer program go on to 4-year colleges. **Colleges most students transferred to 2005:** SUNY Brockport, SUNY Buffalo, SUNY Geneseo, SUNY Fredonia.

Basis for selection. Open admission, but selective for some programs. Admission to nursing, physical therapist assistant, paralegal, occupational therapy assistant, and respiratory care programs based on academic achievement, test scores, interview, and school and community activities. ACT and COMPASS used for placement. Although SAT not used as placement test, students above 500 on each part are exempted from remedial courses. Portfolio recommended for digital art program.

High school preparation. Recommended units include English 4, mathematics 2, social studies 4, science 2 and foreign language 2. Additional units of mathematics and science recommended for students planning to transfer to 4-year programs. 18 units, including biology and chemistry, required for nursing applicants. 18 units, including biology and physics, required for physical therapist assistant applicants. Biology and chemistry required for occupational therapy applicants.

2005-2006 Annual costs. Tuition/fees: $3,390; $3,790 out-of-state. Per-credit charge: $120 in-state; $130 out-of-state.

Financial aid. Need-based: Need-based aid available for part-time students. Work study available nights, weekends and for part-time students. **Non-need-based:** Scholarships awarded for athletics, music/drama.

Application procedures. Admission: No deadline. No application fee. Admission notification on a rolling basis beginning on or about 11/15. **Financial aid:** Priority date 3/1, closing date 5/1. FAFSA required. Applicants notified on a rolling basis starting 4/15; must reply within 2 week(s) of notification.

Academics. Special study options: Cooperative education, cross-registration, distance learning, double major, dual enrollment of high school students, ESL, honors, independent study, internships, liberal arts/career combination. License preparation in nursing, physical therapy. **Credit/placement by examination:** AP, CLEP, IB, institutional tests. 31 credit hours maximum toward associate degree. **Support services:** GED preparation, learning center, reduced course load, remedial instruction, study skills assistance, tutoring, writing center.

Honors college/program. Honors program provides academic work of greater depth, scope, originality, and quality. 4 components: honors seminar, interdisciplinary honors courses, mentoring, and enriched course projects.

Majors. Business: Accounting technology, administrative services, business admin, executive assistant, fashion, hotel/motel admin, retailing, travel services. **Communications:** General. **Communications technology:** Radio/tv. **Computer sciences:** General, information systems, networking. **Conservation:** Environmental studies. **Engineering:** General. **Engineering technology:** Computer systems, drafting, electrical, quality control. **Health:** Dietician assistant, nursing (RN), occupational therapy assistant, physical therapy assistant, recreational therapy, respiratory therapy technology, substance abuse counseling. **Legal studies:** Paralegal. **Liberal arts:** Arts/sciences, humanities. **Protective services:** Law enforcement admin. **Public administration:** Community org/advocacy. **Visual/performing arts:** Art, commercial/advertising art, theater design.

Computing on campus. 350 workstations in library, computer center. Commuter students can connect to campus network. Online course registration, online library, helpline available.

Student life. Freshman orientation: Mandatory. Preregistration for classes offered. Day-long orientation before classes begin. **Activities:** Choral groups, drama, film society, literary magazine, musical theater, radio station, student government, student newspaper, Intervarsity Christian Fellowship, Native American student organization, African American interest group, international student organization, student parents, Enjoying Children Through Recreation and Education, Phi Theta Kappa, Distribution Education Clubs of America, adult student group, Habitat for Humanity.

Athletics. NJCAA. **Intercollegiate:** Baseball M, basketball, cross-country, diving, soccer, softball W, swimming, volleyball. **Intramural:** Archery, badminton, baseball M, basketball, golf, skiing, soccer, softball, table tennis, tennis, volleyball. **Team name:** Cougars.

Student services. Adult student services, career counseling, student employment services, financial aid counseling, health services, on-campus daycare, personal counseling, placement for graduates, veterans' counselor. **Physically disabled:** Services for visually, speech, hearing impaired. **Transfer:** Special adviser, orientation, re-entry adviser, pre-admission transcript evaluation for new students. Transfer center, transfer adviser, college fairs on campus for students transferring to 4-year colleges.

Contact. E-mail: tmlanemartin@genesee.suny.edu
Phone: (585) 345-6800 Toll-free number: (866) 225-5422
Fax: (585) 345-6810
Tanya Lane-Martin, Director of Admissions, Genesee Community College,
One College Road, Batavia, NY 14020-9704

Helene Fuld College of Nursing

New York, New York
www.helenefuld.edu **CB code: 2327**

- Private 2-year nursing and junior college
- Commuter campus in very large city
- Interview required

General. Founded in 1945. Regionally accredited. One-year, full-time associate degree program accredited by National League for Nursing Accrediting Commission and Middle States Association of Colleges and Schools. Career ladder for LPNs. Part-time accredited study also offered. All applicants must be licensed practical nurses. **Enrollment:** 350 degree-seeking undergraduates. **Degrees:** 239 associate awarded. **Location:** Uptown. **Calendar:** Quarter, limited summer session. **Full-time faculty:** 17 total. **Part-time faculty:** 23 total. **Class size:** 6% < 20, 47% 20-39, 29% 40-49, 18% 50-99.

Basis for selection. Must be licensed practical nurse with 1 year work experience, PN licensure required. Require satisfactory performance on pre-entrance exams on practical nursing equivalent, mathematics, and English and completion of a prerequisite chemistry and mathematics course. After all entrance requirements fulfilled, including successful completion of testing, 18 credits granted for practical nursing.

2006-2007 Annual costs. Tuition/fees: $13,337. Per-credit charge: $238. Books/supplies: $1,100. Personal expenses: $1,665.

Financial aid. All financial aid based on need. Need-based aid available for part-time students.

Application procedures. Admission: No deadline. $50 fee. Admission notification on a rolling basis. **Financial aid:** No deadline. FAFSA required. Applicants notified on a rolling basis.

Academics. Special study options: Accelerated study, internships, liberal arts/career combination. License preparation in nursing. **Credit/placement by examination:** CLEP, institutional tests. **Support services:** Learning center, reduced course load, study skills assistance, tutoring.

Majors. Health: Nursing (RN).

Computing on campus. 24 workstations in library, computer center. Commuter students can connect to campus network.

Student life. Freshman orientation: Mandatory. Preregistration for classes offered. 2 weeks before term starts. **Activities:** Student government.

Student services. Adult student services, career counseling, financial aid counseling, personal counseling. **Transfer:** Special adviser, orientation, pre-admission transcript evaluation for new students. College fairs on campus for students transferring to 4-year colleges.

Contact. Phone: (212) 423-2768 Fax: (212) 427-2453
Gladys Pineda, Assistant Director of Student Services, Helene Fuld College of Nursing, 1879 Madison Avenue, New York, NY 10035

Herkimer County Community College

Herkimer, New York
www.hccc.ntcnet.com **CB code: 2316**

- Public 2-year community college
- Commuter campus in small town

General. Founded in 1966. Regionally accredited. **Enrollment:** 3,531 degree-seeking undergraduates. **Degrees:** 554 associate awarded. **ROTC:** Army. **Location:** 10 miles from Utica, 55 miles from Syracuse. **Calendar:** Semester, limited summer session. **Full-time faculty:** 117 total. **Part-time faculty:** 26 total. **Class size:** 43% < 20, 55% 20-39, less than 1% 40-49, less than 1% 50-99. **Special facilities:** 500-acre nature center, natural history museum, archeology museum.

Student profile.

Out-of-state:	1%	**Live on campus:**	25%
25 or older:	23%		

Transfer out. Colleges most students transferred to 2005: SUNY Institute of Technology, SUNY Oneonta, SUNY Brockport, SUNY Oswego, SUNY Cortland.

Basis for selection. Open admission, but selective for some programs. ASSET scores used to help determine placement into developmental courses. SAT and ACT scores may be used to waive required college placement test. Interview recommended for emergency medical technician, occupational/physical therapy assistant programs. **Adult students:** Entrance exam policies same as for first-time freshmen.

High school preparation. Physical/occupational therapist assistant applicants should contact admissions office to review high school course requirements.

2005-2006 Annual costs. Tuition/fees: $3,130; $5,330 out-of-state. Per-credit charge: $117 in-state; $208 out-of-state. Books/supplies: $750. Personal expenses: $670.

Financial aid. Need-based: Need-based aid available for part-time students. Work study available nights, weekends and for part-time students.

Application procedures. Admission: Priority date 7/1; no deadline. No application fee. Application may be submitted online. Admission notification on a rolling basis. **Financial aid:** Priority date 5/1; no closing date. FAFSA required. Applicants notified on a rolling basis starting 4/1; must reply within 2 week(s) of notification.

Academics. Special study options: Distance learning, dual enrollment of high school students, ESL, honors, independent study, internships, liberal arts/career combination. License preparation in paramedic. **Credit/placement by examination:** AP, CLEP, institutional tests. 32 credit hours maximum toward associate degree. **Support services:** GED preparation, learning center, reduced course load, remedial instruction, study skills assistance, tutoring.

Honors college/program. Applicants need high school average of 88. Students must maintain GPA of 3.5.

Majors. Biology: General. **Business:** General, accounting, administrative services, business admin, entrepreneurial studies, fashion, human resources, international, logistics, marketing, office management, office technology, office/clerical, tourism/travel. **Communications:** Broadcast journalism. **Communications technology:** General. **Computer sciences:** General, computer science, data processing, networking. **Education:** Early childhood, physical, teacher assistance. **Engineering technology:** Construction. **Health:** Art therapy, EMT paramedic, health care admin, medical secretary, occupational therapy assistant, physical therapy assistant. **Legal studies:** Legal secretary, paralegal. **Liberal arts:** Arts/sciences. **Math:** General. **Parks/recreation:** Health/fitness, sports admin. **Protective services:** Criminal justice, forensics, law enforcement admin. **Public administration:** Human services. **Social sciences:** General. **Visual/performing arts:** Art, arts management, photography, studio arts.

Computing on campus. 239 workstations in library, computer center. Commuter students can connect to campus network. Online library, helpline available.

Student life. Freshman orientation: Mandatory. Preregistration for classes offered. **Policies:** Freshmen permitted cars on campus. **Housing:** Coed dorms, apartments available. **Activities:** Dance, drama, literary magazine, musical theater, radio station, student government, student newspaper, TV station, Students for a Better World, social issues club, Students Against Drunk Driving, Campus Christian Fellowship, cultural exchange club, black student union, Phi Theta Kappa.

Athletics. NJCAA. **Intercollegiate:** Baseball M, basketball, cross-country, diving, field hockey W, lacrosse, soccer, softball W, swimming, tennis, track and field, volleyball W. **Intramural:** Badminton, baseball M, basketball, bowling, lacrosse M, soccer, softball, swimming, tennis, volleyball. **Team name:** Generals.

Student services. Adult student services, alcohol/substance abuse counseling, career counseling, student employment services, financial aid counseling, health services, on-campus daycare, personal counseling, placement for graduates, veterans' counselor. **Physically disabled:** Services for visually, hearing impaired. **Transfer:** Special adviser, orientation, re-entry adviser, pre-admission transcript evaluation for new students. Transfer adviser, college fairs on campus for students transferring to 4-year colleges.

Contact. Phone: (315) 866-0300 Toll-free number: (888) 464-4222
Fax: (315) 866-7253
Scott Hughes, Associate Dean for Enrollment, Herkimer County Community College, 100 Reservoir Road, Herkimer, NY 13350

Hudson Valley Community College

Troy, New York **CB member**
www.hvcc.edu **CB code: 2300**

- Public 2-year community college
- Commuter campus in small city

Two-Year Colleges

General. Founded in 1953. Regionally accredited. SUNY institution. **Enrollment:** 8,879 degree-seeking undergraduates. **Degrees:** 1,532 associate awarded. **ROTC:** Army, Air Force. **Location:** 10 miles from Albany. **Calendar:** Semester, limited summer session. **Full-time faculty:** 274 total. **Part-time faculty:** 371 total. **Special facilities:** Language laboratory, computer laboratories.

Basis for selection. Open admission, but selective for some programs. Admission to some programs, based on school achievement record and test scores. Interview also considered for some programs.

High school preparation. Requirements vary for selective programs.

2005-2006 Annual costs. Tuition/fees: $3,355; $8,755 out-of-state. Per-credit charge: $112 in-state; $336 out-of-state. Books/supplies: $550. Personal expenses: $800.

2005-2006 Financial aid. Need-based: 66% of total undergraduate aid awarded as scholarships/grants, 34% as loans/jobs.

Application procedures. Admission: No deadline. $30 fee, may be waived for applicants with need. Admission notification on a rolling basis. **Financial aid:** Priority date 5/30; no closing date. FAFSA required. Applicants notified on a rolling basis starting 5/1; must reply within 2 week(s) of notification.

Academics. Special study options: Accelerated study, cooperative education, cross-registration, distance learning, double major, internships, student-designed major. License preparation in dental hygiene, nursing, paramedic, radiology. **Credit/placement by examination:** CLEP. 30 credit hours maximum toward associate degree. **Support services:** GED preparation, learning center, pre-admission summer program, reduced course load, remedial instruction, tutoring.

Majors. Business: General, accounting, administrative services, business admin, finance, insurance, international, office technology, real estate. **Computer sciences:** Data processing, networking. **Conservation:** Environmental studies. **Construction:** Carpentry, maintenance. **Education:** Physical. **Engineering:** General, science. **Engineering technology:** Civil, drafting, electrical. **Family/consumer sciences:** Child care. **Health:** Clinical lab science, clinical lab technology, dental hygiene, medical radiologic technology/radiation therapy, medical secretary, nursing (RN), physician assistant, respiratory therapy technology, substance abuse counseling. **Mechanic/repair:** Electronics/electrical, heating/ac/refrig. **Personal/culinary services:** Mortuary science. **Physical sciences:** Chemistry. **Protective services:** Forensics. **Public administration:** Community org/advocacy, social work. **Social sciences:** General.

Computing on campus. 1,000 workstations in library, computer center.

Student life. Activities: Drama, radio station, student government, student newspaper, TV station.

Athletics. NJCAA. **Intercollegiate:** Baseball M, basketball, bowling, cross-country, football (tackle) M, golf, ice hockey M, lacrosse M, soccer, softball W, tennis, track and field, volleyball W. **Intramural:** Baseball M, basketball, bowling, cross-country, field hockey W, golf, ice hockey, lacrosse, racquetball, skiing, soccer, softball, table tennis, tennis, track and field, volleyball, wrestling M.

Student services. Adult student services, career counseling, student employment services, health services, on-campus daycare, personal counseling, placement for graduates, veterans' counselor. **Physically disabled:** Services for visually, speech, hearing impaired.

Contact. E-mail: admissions@hvcc.edu
Phone: (518) 629-7309 Toll-free number: (877) 325-4822
Fax: (518) 629-4576
Mary Bauer, Director of Admissions, Hudson Valley Community College, 80 Vandenburgh Avenue, Troy, NY 12180

Institute of Design and Construction

Brooklyn, New York
www.idc.edu **CB code: 0677**

- Private 2-year junior and technical college
- Commuter campus in very large city

General. Founded in 1947. Regionally accredited. Classes and seminars available for candidates preparing for Architects Registration Exam. **Enrollment:** 200 degree-seeking undergraduates. **Degrees:** 14 associate awarded. **Calendar:** Semester. **Part-time faculty:** 35 total.

Basis for selection. Open admission. Interview recommended.

High school preparation. Recommended units include English 4, mathematics 3 and science 1. One unit of drafting or architecture recommended.

2006-2007 Annual costs. Tuition/fees (projected): $7,250. Per-credit charge: $240. Books/supplies: $800. Personal expenses: $400.

Application procedures. Admission: No deadline. $40 fee, may be waived for applicants with need. Admission notification on a rolling basis. **Financial aid:** No deadline. FAFSA, institutional form required. Applicants notified on a rolling basis starting 3/1; must reply within 4 week(s) of notification.

Academics. Work and study plan available. Students can spend 2 full-time semesters in accelerated study, then complete degree through part-time evening study while working during day as junior drafters. Credits transferable to Pratt Institute and New York Institute of Technology. **Special study options:** Double major. Work and study program. **Credit/placement by examination:** CLEP, institutional tests. 12 credit hours maximum toward associate degree. **Support services:** Learning center, reduced course load, remedial instruction, tutoring.

Majors. Construction: Maintenance. **Engineering technology:** Architectural, drafting. **Visual/performing arts:** Interior design.

Computing on campus. 17 workstations in library, computer center.

Student services. Career counseling, student employment services, personal counseling, placement for graduates, veterans' counselor. **Transfer:** Special adviser, orientation for new students. Transfer adviser for students transferring to 4-year colleges.

Contact. Phone: (718) 855-3661 ext. 16 Fax: (718) 852-5889
Kevin Giannetti, Director of Admissions, Institute of Design and Construction, 141 Willoughby Street, Brooklyn, NY 11201-5380

Interboro Institute

New York, New York
www.interboro.edu **CB code: 1675**

- For-profit 2-year business and junior college
- Commuter campus in very large city
- Interview required

General. Founded in 1888. Regionally accredited. Campuses in Manhattan, Washington Heights, Flushing, and Yonkers. **Enrollment:** 4,319 degree-seeking undergraduates. **Degrees:** 480 associate awarded. **Calendar:** Trimester, extensive summer session. **Full-time faculty:** 69 total. **Part-time faculty:** 225 total. **Special facilities:** Optical shop.

Transfer out. Colleges most students transferred to 2005: Medgar Evers College, Monroe College, St John's University, Pace University.

Basis for selection. Open admission. CPAT required for non-high school graduates.

2005-2006 Annual costs. Tuition/fees: $8,600. Books/supplies: $450. Personal expenses: $1,000.

Financial aid. All financial aid based on need.

Application procedures. Admission: No deadline. No application fee. Admission notification on a rolling basis. **Financial aid:** No deadline. FAFSA, institutional form required. Applicants notified on a rolling basis.

Academics. Terminal degree in ophthalmic dispensing. **Special study options:** Independent study, internships, liberal arts/career combination. **Credit/placement by examination:** CLEP, IB, institutional tests. 15 credit hours maximum toward associate degree. **Support services:** Learning center, reduced course load, remedial instruction, study skills assistance, tutoring.

Majors. Business: General, administrative services. **Health:** Medical secretary, optician. **Legal studies:** Legal secretary, paralegal. **Protective services:** Security services.

Most popular majors. Business/marketing 64%, health sciences 7%, legal studies 21%, security/protective services 8%.

Computing on campus. 619 workstations in library, computer center. Commuter students can connect to campus network. Online library available.

Student life. Freshman orientation: Mandatory. **Activities:** Dance, student government, student newspaper.

Athletics. Intramural: Baseball M.

Student services. Alcohol/substance abuse counseling, career counseling, student employment services, personal counseling, placement for graduates. **Transfer:** Special adviser, orientation, pre-admission transcript evaluation for new students. Transfer adviser for students transferring to 4-year colleges.

Contact. Phone: (212) 399-0091 Fax: (212) 765-5772
Maritza Bedoya, Director of Admissions, Interboro Institute, 450 West 56th Street, New York, NY 10019

Island Drafting and Technical Institute

Amityville, New York
www.idti.edu **CB code: 3048**

- For-profit 2-year technical college
- Commuter campus in large town
- Interview required

General. Accredited by ACCSCT. **Enrollment:** 185 degree-seeking undergraduates. **Degrees:** 90 associate awarded. **Location:** 25 miles from New York City. **Calendar:** Semester, extensive summer session. **Full-time faculty:** 5 total. **Part-time faculty:** 10 total.

Basis for selection. Open admission. School administered test for CADD/ Architecture students.

High school preparation. Recommended units include English 2 and mathematics 2.

2005-2006 Annual costs. Tuition/fees: $12,200. Per-credit charge: $395. Books/supplies: $600.

Financial aid. All financial aid based on need.

Application procedures. Admission: No deadline. $25 fee. Application must be submitted on paper. Admission notification on a rolling basis. **Financial aid:** No deadline. Applicants notified on a rolling basis.

Academics. Special study options: Liberal arts/career combination. **Credit/ placement by examination:** CLEP. **Support services:** Study skills assistance.

Majors. Computer sciences: Computer graphics. **Engineering:** Electrical. **Engineering technology:** Drafting, electrical. **Mechanic/repair:** Electronics/ electrical.

Computing on campus. 100 workstations in library, computer center.

Student life. Freshman orientation: Mandatory.

Student services. Alcohol/substance abuse counseling, career counseling, student employment services, financial aid counseling, personal counseling, placement for graduates, veterans' counselor.

Contact. E-mail: admissions@idti.edu
Phone: (631) 691-8733 Fax: (631) 691-8738
Bob Sinclair, Admissions, Island Drafting and Technical Institute, 128 Broadway, Amityville, NY 11701-2704

ITT Technical Institute: Albany

Albany, New York
www.itt-tech.edu **CB code: 2689**

- For-profit 2-year technical college
- Commuter campus in large city

General. Accredited by ACICS. **Calendar:** Quarter.

Annual costs/financial aid. Tuition varies by program, $260-$368 per credit hour. Books/supplies: $3,300.

Contact. Phone: (518) 452-9300
Director of Recruitment, 13 Airline Drive, Albany, NY 12205

ITT Technical Institute: Getzville

Getzville, New York
www.itt-tech.edu **CB code: 2704**

- For-profit 2-year technical college
- Commuter campus in rural community

General. Accredited by ACICS. **Calendar:** Quarter.

Annual costs/financial aid. Tuition varies by program, $260-$368 per credit hour.

Contact. Phone: (716) 689-2200
Director of Recruitment, 2295 Millersport Highway, Getzville, NY 14068

ITT Technical Institute: Liverpool

Liverpool, New York
www.itt-tech.edu **CB code: 2725**

- For-profit 2-year technical college
- Commuter campus in small town

General. Accredited by ACICS. **Calendar:** Quarter.

Annual costs/financial aid. Tuition varies by program, $260-$368 per credit hour. Books/supplies: $3,300.

Contact. Phone: (315) 461-8000
Director of Recruitment, 235 Greenfield Parkway, Liverpool, NY 13088

Jamestown Business College

Jamestown, New York
www.jbcny.org **CB code: 2346**

- For-profit 2-year business and junior college
- Commuter campus in large town

General. Founded in 1886. Regionally accredited. **Enrollment:** 299 degree-seeking undergraduates. **Degrees:** 116 associate awarded. **Location:** 80 miles from Buffalo, 60 miles from Erie, Pennsylvania. **Calendar:** Quarter, limited summer session. **Full-time faculty:** 8 total; 12% have terminal degrees, 12% minority, 62% women. **Part-time faculty:** 16 total; 12% have terminal degrees, 6% minority, 69% women. **Class size:** 37% < 20, 63% 20-39.

Student profile. Among degree-seeking undergraduates, 86 enrolled as first-time, first-year students, 50 transferred in from other institutions.

Part-time:	4%	**Asian American:**	1%
Out-of-state:	16%	**Hispanic American:**	2%
Women:	78%	**Native American:**	1%
African American:	2%	**25 or older:**	47%

Basis for selection. Class rank and academic record important. School and community activities considered. College uses the Comparative Guidance and Placement program in the admission process. Interview recommended.

2005-2006 Annual costs. Tuition/fees: $8,850. Per-credit charge: $233. Books/supplies: $800. Personal expenses: $1,756.

2004-2005 Financial aid. Need-based: 70% of total undergraduate aid awarded as scholarships/grants, 30% as loans/jobs. Need-based aid available for part-time students. **Non-need-based:** Scholarships awarded for academics.

Application procedures. Admission: No deadline. $25 fee. Admission notification on a rolling basis. **Financial aid:** No deadline. FAFSA required. Applicants notified on a rolling basis starting 2/15.

Academics. Credit/placement by examination: CLEP, institutional tests. **Support services:** Reduced course load, study skills assistance, tutoring.

Majors. Business: Accounting, administrative services, business admin, marketing. **Computer sciences:** General, data processing. **Health:** Medical secretary. **Legal studies:** Legal secretary.

Computing on campus. 100 workstations in library, computer center. Commuter students can connect to campus network. Online library, wireless network available.

Student life. Freshman orientation: Mandatory.

Athletics. Intramural: Baseball, basketball, bowling, softball, volleyball.

Student services. Adult student services, career counseling, student employment services, personal counseling, placement for graduates, veterans' counselor. **Transfer:** Special adviser, orientation, pre-admission transcript evaluation for new students. Transfer adviser for students transferring to 4-year colleges.

Contact. E-mail: admissions@jbcny.org
Phone: (716) 664-5100 Fax: (716) 664-3144
Brenda Salenne, Director of Admissions, Jamestown Business College, 7 Fairmount Avenue, Jamestown, NY 14702-0429

Jamestown Community College

Jamestown, New York
www.sunyjcc.edu **CB code: 2335**

- Public 2-year community college
- Commuter campus in large town

General. Founded in 1950. Regionally accredited. SUNY institution. Branch campus at Olean for Cattaraugus County. Extensions in Dunkirk, NY, Allegany NY, Warren, PA. Bachelor's degree program through Franklin University. **Enrollment:** 3,592 degree-seeking undergraduates; 80 non-degree-seeking students. **Degrees:** 726 associate awarded. **Location:** 70 miles from Erie, Pennsylvania and Buffalo. **Calendar:** Semester, extensive summer session. **Full-time faculty:** 83 total; 13% have terminal degrees, 1% minority, 66% women. **Part-time faculty:** 262 total; 5% have terminal degrees, 2% minority, 51% women. **Class size:** 35% < 20, 39% 20-39, less than 1% 40-49, less than 1% 50-99. **Special facilities:** Natural history institute.

Student profile. Among degree-seeking undergraduates, 62% enrolled in a transfer program, 26% enrolled in a vocational program, 1,129 enrolled as first-time, first-year students, 201 transferred in from other institutions.

Part-time:	32%	**Asian American:**	1%
Out-of-state:	9%	**Hispanic American:**	2%
Women:	59%	**Native American:**	1%
African American:	3%	**25 or older:**	31%

Transfer out. Colleges most students transferred to 2005: SUNY Fredonia, St. Bonaventure University, SUNY College at Buffalo, Houghton College.

Basis for selection. Open admission, but selective for some programs. Preference given to area students in highly subscribed programs. Selective admission to nursing, occupational therapy assistant, with school achievement record very important. ACT and ASSET scores used for placement.

2005-2006 Annual costs. Tuition/fees: $3,676; $6,826 out-of-state. Per-credit charge: $132 in-state; $238 out-of-state. Books/supplies: $820. Personal expenses: $600.

Financial aid. Need-based: Need-based aid available for part-time students. Work study available nights, weekends and for part-time students. **Non-need-based:** Scholarships awarded for academics, alumni affiliation, athletics, music/drama, state residency. **Additional information:** 100% resident tuition scholarship (less federal and state grants) for students in top 20% of high school graduating class with Regents diploma if residents of Chautauqua, Cattaraugus, or Allegany counties. Guaranteed in-state tuition rate for students in Warren, Potter, McKean and Forest counties in Pennsylvania, in top 20% of graduating class with an academic diploma.

Application procedures. Admission: No deadline. $40 fee, may be waived for applicants with need. Application may be submitted online. Admission notification on a rolling basis. Must reply by May 1 or within 2 week(s) if notified thereafter. **Financial aid:** Priority date 3/1; no closing date. FAFSA required. Applicants notified on a rolling basis starting 4/15.

Academics. Strong liberal arts tradition, with a balance between transfer and career-oriented programs. **Special study options:** Cooperative education, cross-registration, distance learning, double major, honors, internships, study abroad, Washington semester, weekend college. License preparation in nursing. **Credit/placement by examination:** AP, CLEP, institutional tests. 36 credit hours maximum toward associate degree. **Support services:** Learning center, pre-admission summer program, reduced course load, remedial instruction, study skills assistance, tutoring.

Majors. Business: Accounting technology, banking/financial services, business admin, marketing, office management. **Computer sciences:** Data processing, programming. **Conservation:** Forestry. **Engineering:** General. **Engineering technology:** Electrical, mechanical. **Health:** Clinical lab technology, nursing (RN), occupational therapy assistant. **Liberal arts:** Arts/sciences, humanities. **Mechanic/repair:** Small engine. **Protective services:** Criminal justice, police science. **Public administration:** Human services. **Social sciences:** General. **Transportation:** Airline/commercial pilot. **Visual/performing arts:** Studio arts.

Most popular majors. Business/marketing 14%, computer/information sciences 7%, health sciences 12%, liberal arts 33%, mathematics 6%, security/protective services 8%, social sciences 16%.

Computing on campus. 800 workstations in library, computer center, student center. Commuter students can connect to campus network. Online course registration, online library available.

Student life. Freshman orientation: Mandatory. **Policies:** Freshmen permitted cars on campus. **Activities:** Bands, choral groups, drama, music ensembles, musical theater, radio station, student government, Earth Awareness, InterVarsity Christian Fellowship, Early Childhood Educators, Political Awareness, nursing club, humanities club, criminal justice club.

Athletics. NJCAA. **Intercollegiate:** Baseball M, basketball, cross-country, diving, golf, soccer, softball W, swimming, volleyball W, wrestling M. **Intramural:** Basketball, bowling, softball, table tennis, tennis, volleyball. **Team name:** Jayhawks.

Student services. Adult student services, alcohol/substance abuse counseling, career counseling, services for economically disadvantaged, student employment services, financial aid counseling, health services, on-campus daycare, personal counseling, placement for graduates, veterans' counselor. **Physically disabled:** Services for visually, speech, hearing impaired. **Transfer:** Special adviser, orientation for new students. Transfer adviser, college fairs on campus for students transferring to 4-year colleges.

Contact. E-mail: admissions@mail.sunyjcc.edu
Phone: (716) 665-5220 Toll-free number: (800) 388-8557
Fax: (716) 338-1450
Wendy Present, Director, Admissions and Recruitment, Jamestown Community College, 525 Falconer Street, Jamestown, NY 14702-0020

Jefferson Community College

Watertown, New York
www.sunyjefferson.edu **CB code: 2345**

- Public 2-year community college
- Commuter campus in large town

General. Founded in 1961. Regionally accredited. **Enrollment:** 3,590 degree-seeking undergraduates. **Degrees:** 560 associate awarded. **Location:** 70 miles from Syracuse. **Calendar:** Semester, limited summer session. **Full-time faculty:** 75 total. **Part-time faculty:** 105 total.

Student profile.

Out-of-state:	1%	**25 or older:**	37%

Transfer out. Colleges most students transferred to 2005: SUNY Empire State College, SUNY Oswego, SUNY Potsdam.

Basis for selection. Open admission, but selective for some programs. Admission to some programs based on grades, class rank, test scores, school recommendation, and personal interview. Waiting list available for nursing program. Interview recommended for engineering science, nursing programs.

High school preparation. Strong background in mathematics and science required for engineering science, computer science, nursing, and science laboratory technologies programs.

2005-2006 Annual costs. Tuition/fees: $3,280; $4,710 out-of-state. Per-credit charge: $122 in-state; $182 out-of-state. Books/supplies: $800. Personal expenses: $600.

2005-2006 Financial aid. All financial aid based on need. Need-based aid available for part-time students. Work study available for part-time students.

Application procedures. Admission: No deadline. No application fee. Admission notification on a rolling basis. **Financial aid:** Priority date 4/1, closing date 8/15. FAFSA, institutional form required. Applicants notified on a rolling basis starting 4/15; must reply within 2 week(s) of notification.

Academics. Students in engineering science, computer science, and computer information systems programs required to purchase or lease microcomputers. **Special study options:** Cooperative education, distance learning, double major, dual enrollment of high school students, honors, independent study, internships, student-designed major, weekend college. Bachelor's degree programs available on campus. **Credit/placement by examination:** AP, CLEP, IB, institutional tests. 30 credit hours maximum toward associate degree. **Support services:** Learning center, reduced course load, remedial instruction, study skills assistance, tutoring.

Majors. Business: Accounting, business admin, office management, office technology, sales/distribution, tourism promotion, tourism/travel. **Computer sciences:** General, computer science, information systems. **Education:** Early childhood, elementary. **Engineering:** Science. **Health:** EMT paramedic, nursing (RN). **Legal studies:** Paralegal. **Liberal arts:** Arts/sciences. **Math:** General. **Protective services:** Law enforcement admin. **Public administration:** Human services.

Computing on campus. 354 workstations in library, computer center, student center. Online library available.

Student life. Freshman orientation: Available. Half-day program held in August and January. **Policies:** Freshmen permitted cars on campus. **Housing:** Privately owned apartments available. **Activities:** Bands, choral groups, drama, literary magazine, music ensembles, student government, student newspaper, veterans club, multicultural club, human services club, environmental club, European excursion club, business club, office technology association, political clubs, Brothers and Sisters in Christ.

Athletics. NJCAA. **Intercollegiate:** Baseball M, basketball, golf, lacrosse, soccer, softball W, tennis W, volleyball W. **Intramural:** Badminton, basketball, soccer, softball, volleyball. **Team name:** Cannoneers.

Student services. Adult student services, campus ministries, career counseling, student employment services, financial aid counseling, health services, on-campus daycare, personal counseling, placement for graduates, veterans' counselor. **Physically disabled:** Services for visually, speech, hearing impaired. **Transfer:** Special adviser, orientation for new students. Transfer adviser, college fairs on campus for students transferring to 4-year colleges.

Contact. E-mail: admissions@sunyjefferson.edu
Phone: (315) 786-2277 Fax: (315) 786-2459
Rosanne Weir, Director of Admissions, Jefferson Community College, 1220 Coffeen Street, Watertown, NY 13601

Katharine Gibbs School: Melville
Melville, New York
www.gibbslongisland.com **CB code: 1039**

- For-profit 2-year junior college
- Small town

General. Founded in 1911. Accredited by ACICS. **Location:** 40 miles from New York City. **Calendar:** Quarter.

Annual costs/financial aid. Certificate and associate programs range from $5,000 to $32,000 for duration of program. Additional charges for laptop and computing-related fees in some programs. Books/supplies: $700.

Contact. Phone: (631) 370-3300
Director of Admissions, 320 South Service Road, Melville, NY 11747

Katharine Gibbs School: New York
New York, New York
www.gibbsny.com **CB code: 2355**

- For-profit 2-year business college
- Very large city
- Interview required

General. Founded in 1918. Accredited by ACICS. **Enrollment:** 2,047 degree-seeking undergraduates. **Degrees:** 600 associate awarded. **ROTC:** Navy. **Calendar:** Quarter, limited summer session. **Full-time faculty:** 26 total. **Part-time faculty:** 250 total.

Basis for selection. School achievement record, test scores, interview, essay or personal statement important. CPAT scores required. Essay required for paralegal program. **Adult students:** Entrance exam policies same as for first-time freshmen.

2005-2006 Annual costs. Tuition for associate degree programs ranges from $22,050 to $24,850. Fees $30 per term, $180 for 18-month program. Books/supplies: $1,275. Personal expenses: $1,900.

Financial aid. Need-based: Need-based aid available for part-time students.

Application procedures. Admission: Priority date 9/30; no deadline. $50 fee. **Financial aid:** No deadline. Applicants notified on a rolling basis; must reply within 3 week(s) of notification.

Academics. Special study options: Accelerated study, cooperative education, internships. **Credit/placement by examination:** CLEP. **Support services:** Remedial instruction.

Majors. Business: Administrative services, business admin.

Student life. Activities: Choral groups, TV station.

Student services. Career counseling, student employment services, personal counseling, placement for graduates.

Contact. Phone: (212) 867-9300 Toll-free number: (800) 378-5677
Fax: (212) 338-9606
Maryann Grillo, Director of Admissions, Katharine Gibbs School: New York, 50 West 40th Street, 1st Floor, New York, NY 10138

Long Island Business Institute
Commack, New York
www.libi.edu **CB code: 3334**

- For-profit 2-year business college
- Commuter campus in large town
- Application essay, interview required

General. Accredited by ACICS. Branch campus in Flushing. **Enrollment:** 888 degree-seeking undergraduates; 2 non-degree-seeking students. **Degrees:** 133 associate awarded. **Calendar:** Semester, extensive summer session. **Full-time faculty:** 14 total; 7% have terminal degrees, 57% minority. **Part-time faculty:** 76 total; 18% minority, 70% women.

Student profile. Among degree-seeking undergraduates, 100% enrolled in a vocational program, 325 enrolled as first-time, first-year students, 40 transferred in from other institutions.

Part-time:	24%	**Hispanic American:**	20%
Women:	77%	**International:**	5%
African American:	3%	**25 or older:**	71%
Asian American:	44%		

Transfer out. Colleges most students transferred to 2005: Suffolk County Community College, Nassau County Community College.

Basis for selection. Open admission, but selective for some programs. Admission to court reporting programs require minimum score of 140 on CPAT. **Adult students:** Entrance exam policies same as for first-time freshmen. SAT/ACT scores not required.

2006-2007 Annual costs. Tuition/fees: $10,125. Per-credit charge: $325. Tuition varies by program. Books/supplies: $700. Personal expenses: $1,750.

2005-2006 Financial aid. Need-based: 290 full-time freshmen applied for aid; 290 were judged to have need; 290 of these received aid. Average need met was 80%. Average scholarship/grant was $3,000; average loan $2,600. 81% of total undergraduate aid awarded as scholarships/grants, 19% as loans/jobs. Need-based aid available for part-time students. Work study available nights and for part-time students. **Non-need-based:** Scholarships awarded for academics.

Application procedures. Admission: No deadline. $50 fee. Admission notification on a rolling basis. **Financial aid:** No deadline. FAFSA required. Applicants notified on a rolling basis starting 9/1; must reply within 2 week(s) of notification.

Academics. Special study options: ESL, independent study, internships. **Credit/placement by examination:** AP, CLEP, institutional tests. Limited to 50% of specific curriculum total credit hours. **Support services:** Remedial instruction, tutoring.

Majors. Business: Accounting, administrative services, business admin, office management. **Computer sciences:** General. **Legal studies:** Court reporting.

Most popular majors. Business/marketing 74%, health sciences 12%, legal studies 14%.

Computing on campus. 50 workstations in library.

Student life. Freshman orientation: Mandatory. Students receive and review the student handbook so that they understand college policies.

Student services. Career counseling, student employment services, financial aid counseling, placement for graduates. **Transfer:** Special adviser, orientation, pre-admission transcript evaluation for new students.

Contact. E-mail: admissions@libi.edu
Phone: (631) 499-7100 Fax: (631) 499-7114
Robert Nazar, Director of Admissions, Long Island Business Institute, 6500 Jericho Turnpike, Commack, NY 11725

Long Island Business Institute: Flushing
Flushing, New York
www.libi.edu

- For-profit 2-year business college
- Commuter campus in very large city

General. Accredited by ACICS. **Calendar:** Semester.

Annual costs/financial aid. Tuition/fees (2005-2006): $8,475. Books/supplies: $400. Need-based financial aid available to full-time and part-time students.

Contact. Phone: (718) 939-5100
Director of Admissions, 37-12 Prince Street, Flushing, NY 11354

Long Island College Hospital School of Nursing
Brooklyn, New York
CB code: 2377

- Private 2-year nursing college
- Commuter campus in very large city
- Application essay, interview required

General. Founded in 1883. Liberal arts courses taken at St. Francis College. **Enrollment:** 147 degree-seeking undergraduates. **Degrees:** 38 associate awarded. **Calendar:** Semester, limited summer session. **Full-time faculty:** 6 total; 100% have terminal degrees, 33% minority, 100% women. **Part-time faculty:** 9 total; 100% have terminal degrees, 100% women. **Class size:** 100% 50-99. **Special facilities:** Computer-assisted learning laboratory featuring interactive videodisc technology, clinical on hospital basis.

Student profile. Among degree-seeking undergraduates, 98% enrolled in a transfer program, 15% already have a bachelor's degree or higher, 2 enrolled as first-time, first-year students, 71 transferred in from other institutions.

Part-time:	50%	**Asian American:**	14%
Women:	80%	**Hispanic American:**	7%
African American:	45%		

Transfer out. 70% of students enrolled in the transfer program go on to 4-year colleges.

Basis for selection. National League for Nursing RN pre-entrance exam score, high school achievement record, college GPA, 2 references, essay considered together. Selected students interviewed. Final decision made by Academic Standing Committee. **Adult students:** Entrance exam policies same as for first-time freshmen. **Homeschooled:** Statement describing homeschool structure and mission, transcript of courses and grades, state high school equivalency certificate, interview, letter of recommendation (nonparent) required.

High school preparation. 19 units recommended. Recommended units include English 4, mathematics 3, social studies 3, history 2, science 2, foreign language 3 and academic electives 2.

2006-2007 Annual costs. Tuition/fees (projected): $24,170. Freshmen typically take a combination of nursing courses at $300 per credit hour and liberal arts and sciences courses at $320 per credit hour. Books/supplies: $1,100. Personal expenses: $1,863.

Application procedures. Admission: Priority date 4/6; deadline 5/6 (receipt date). $50 fee. Application must be submitted on paper. Admission notification on a rolling basis beginning on or about 6/6. Must reply by 8/6. **Financial aid:** Priority date 6/1; no closing date. FAFSA required. Must reply within 2 week(s) of notification.

Academics. Special study options: Combined bachelor's/graduate degree, cooperative education, internships. License preparation in nursing. **Credit/placement by examination:** AP, CLEP. **Support services:** Learning center, remedial instruction, tutoring.

Majors. Health: Nursing (RN).

Computing on campus. 15 workstations in library, computer center, student center.

Student life. Freshman orientation: Mandatory. 2 orientations: general orientation and clinical orientation held beginning of first semester. **Policies:** Freshmen permitted cars on campus. **Housing:** Substance-free housing available. **Activities:** Student government, student newspaper.

Student services. Financial aid counseling, health services. **Transfer:** Special adviser, orientation, pre-admission transcript evaluation for new students.

Contact. E-mail: bevans@chpnet.org
Phone: (718) 780-1071 Fax: (718) 780-1936
Marina Karpovitch, Registrar, Long Island College Hospital School of Nursing, 340 Court Street, Brooklyn, NY 11231

Maria College
Albany, New York **CB member**
www.mariacollege.edu **CB code: 2434**

- Private 2-year junior college
- Commuter campus in small city
- SAT or ACT (ACT writing optional), application essay, interview required

General. Founded in 1958. Regionally accredited. **Enrollment:** 719 degree-seeking undergraduates; 46 non-degree-seeking students. **Degrees:** 142 associate awarded. **ROTC:** Army, Navy, Air Force. **Location:** 150 miles from New York City and Boston. **Calendar:** Semester, limited summer session. **Full-time faculty:** 28 total; 18% have terminal degrees, 4% minority, 89% women. **Part-time faculty:** 41 total; 17% have terminal degrees, 5% minority. **Class size:** 76% < 20, 18% 20-39, 1% 40-49, 4% 50-99.

Student profile. Among degree-seeking undergraduates, 44% enrolled in a transfer program, 56% enrolled in a vocational program, 9% already have a bachelor's degree or higher, 117 enrolled as first-time, first-year students, 234 transferred in from other institutions.

Part-time:	70%	**Hispanic American:**	3%
Out-of-state:	3%	**Native American:**	1%
Women:	88%	**International:**	1%
African American:	19%	**25 or older:**	79%
Asian American:	2%		

Transfer out. Colleges most students transferred to 2005: College of Saint Rose, State University at Albany, Hudson Valley Community College, The Sage Colleges, Schenectady County Community College.

Basis for selection. School achievement record, test scores, interviews, recommendations important. Dual interview required for Nursing (ADN) and Occupational Therapy Assistant. **Adult students:** SAT/ACT scores not required. Applicants who did not take SAT or ACT may be required to take an admissions test, which may be waived on the basis of prior college credit. **Learning Disabled:** Must provide documentation regarding specific diagnosis and services/accommodations being requested. Documentation must be within 3 years of acceptance. Must meet with the Dean of Student Services for coordination of support services.

High school preparation. 21 units required. Required and recommended units include English 4, mathematics 2-3, social studies 4, science 2-3 (laboratory 3). Requirements vary with program.

2005-2006 Annual costs. Tuition/fees: $7,600. Per-credit charge: $270. Books/supplies: $600. Personal expenses: $500.

2005-2006 Financial aid. All financial aid based on need. 59 full-time freshmen applied for aid; 56 were judged to have need; 56 of these received aid. Average need met was 87%. Average scholarship/grant was $4,064; average loan $2,128. 51% of total undergraduate aid awarded as scholarships/grants, 49% as loans/jobs. Need-based aid available for part-time students. Work study available nights, weekends and for part-time students.

Application procedures. Admission: Priority date 8/12; deadline 8/26 (receipt date). $35 fee, may be waived for applicants with need. Application must be submitted on paper. Admission notification on a rolling basis. Must reply by May 1 or within 4 week(s) if notified thereafter. **Financial aid:** No deadline. FAFSA required. Applicants notified on a rolling basis starting 2/1; must reply within 2 week(s) of notification.

Academics. Special study options: Accelerated study, cross-registration, dual enrollment of high school students, independent study, internships, liberal arts/career combination, weekend college. Advanced placement program in nursing for licensed practical nurse and New York State LPN to ADN Nursing Bridge Course. License preparation in nursing, occupational therapy. **Credit/placement by examination:** AP, CLEP, IB, SAT, ACT, institutional tests. 16 credit hours maximum toward associate degree. **Support services:** Learning center, pre-admission summer program, reduced course load, remedial instruction, study skills assistance, tutoring.

Majors. Business: General, accounting, business admin. **Computer sciences:** General. **Education:** Early childhood, teacher assistance. **Health:**

Nursing (RN), occupational therapy assistant. **Legal studies:** Paralegal. **Liberal arts:** Arts/sciences. **Science technology:** Biological.

Most popular majors. Education 11%, health sciences 70%, liberal arts 13%.

Computing on campus. 72 workstations in library, computer center. Commuter students can connect to campus network. Online course registration available.

Student life. Freshman orientation: Mandatory. Preregistration for classes offered. Held one day at beginning of semester. **Policies:** Freshmen permitted cars on campus.

Student services. Adult student services, alcohol/substance abuse counseling, campus ministries, career counseling, student employment services, financial aid counseling, personal counseling, placement for graduates. **Physically disabled:** Services for visually impaired. **Transfer:** Special adviser, orientation, re-entry adviser, pre-admission transcript evaluation for new students. Transfer adviser, college fairs on campus for students transferring to 4-year colleges.

Contact. E-mail: laurieg@mariacollege.edu
Phone: (518) 438-3111 ext. 217 Fax: (518) 453-1366
Laurie Gilmore, Director of Admissions, Maria College, 700 New Scotland Avenue, Albany, NY 12208

Mildred Elley

Latham, New York
www.mildred-elley.edu **CB code: 3335**

- For-profit 2-year business college
- Commuter campus in very large city

General. Accredited by ACICS. **Enrollment:** 400 degree-seeking undergraduates. **Degrees:** 77 associate awarded. **Location:** 10 miles from Albany. **Calendar:** Semester, extensive summer session. **Full-time faculty:** 40 total. **Class size:** 92% < 20, 8% 20-39.

Basis for selection. Open admission. **Adult students:** Entrance exam policies same as for first-time freshmen.

2005-2006 Annual costs. $4,500 per trimester for tuition, fees, books and supplies.

Financial aid. All financial aid based on need. Need-based aid available for part-time students. Work study available nights and for part-time students.

Application procedures. Admission: No deadline. $25 fee, may be waived for applicants with need. Admission notification on a rolling basis. **Financial aid:** FAFSA required.

Academics. Special study options: Cooperative education, double major, independent study, internships. **Credit/placement by examination:** CLEP, institutional tests. **Support services:** GED preparation and test center, learning center, remedial instruction, study skills assistance, tutoring, writing center.

Majors. Business: Business admin. **Computer sciences:** General, information systems. **Health:** Massage therapy, medical assistant. **Legal studies:** General, paralegal.

Most popular majors. Business/marketing 38%, computer/information sciences 22%, health sciences 21%, legal studies 20%.

Computing on campus. Repair service available.

Student life. Freshman orientation: Mandatory. Preregistration for classes offered. **Activities:** Drama, student government.

Student services. Adult student services, alcohol/substance abuse counseling, career counseling, financial aid counseling, legal services, personal counseling, placement for graduates, veterans' counselor, women's services. **Transfer:** Special adviser, orientation for new students. College fairs on campus for students transferring to 4-year colleges.

Contact. E-mail: admissions@mildred-elley.edu
Phone: (518) 786-3171 Toll-free number: (800) 622-6327
Fax: (518) 786-0011
Jim Frederick, Registrar, Mildred Elley, 800 New Loudon Road, Suite 5120, Latham, NY 12110

Mohawk Valley Community College

Utica, New York
www.mvcc.edu **CB code: 2414**

- Public 2-year community college
- Commuter campus in small city

General. Founded in 1946. Regionally accredited. SUNY institution. Branch campus in Rome, New York. **Enrollment:** 4,642 degree-seeking undergraduates; 1,342 non-degree-seeking students. **Degrees:** 776 associate awarded. **ROTC:** Army. **Location:** 50 miles from Syracuse, 96 miles from Albany. **Calendar:** Semester, limited summer session. **Full-time faculty:** 139 total; 18% have terminal degrees, 6% minority, 38% women. **Part-time faculty:** 132 total; 3% minority, 52% women. **Class size:** 49% < 20, 46% 20-39, 4% 40-49, 2% 50-99. **Special facilities:** Distance learning studios, gourmet dining room, human cadaver lab. **Partnerships:** Formal partnership with Verizon for NEXT STEP, a virtual university program for Verizon employees to earn an associate in telecommunications.

Student profile. Among degree-seeking undergraduates, 42% enrolled in a transfer program, 58% enrolled in a vocational program, 1,434 enrolled as first-time, first-year students, 269 transferred in from other institutions.

Part-time:	20%	**Hispanic American:**	3%
Women:	54%	**25 or older:**	26%
African American:	6%	**Live on campus:**	11%
Asian American:	2%		

Transfer out. Colleges most students transferred to 2005: SUNY College at Oneonta, SUNY Institute of Technology (Utica/Rome), Utica College of Syracuse University, SUNY College at Potsdam.

Basis for selection. Open admission, but selective for some programs. Applicants' records reviewed for completion of program-specific prerequisites to determine regular or underprepared acceptance to program. Interview recommended for all, required of respiratory care applicants. **Adult students:** Entrance exam policies same as for first-time freshmen. **Homeschooled:** Must pass ability-to-benefit test (ASSET) prior to acceptance. **Learning Disabled:** Learning-disabled applicants should forward a copy of their IEP to Coordinator for Services to Students with Disabilities.

High school preparation. Recommended units include English 4, mathematics 2, social studies 1 and science 2. Requirements vary for admission to nursing and certain other programs.

2005-2006 Annual costs. Tuition/fees: $3,294; $6,244 out-of-state. Per-credit charge: $115 in-state; $230 out-of-state. Room/board: $6,670. Books/supplies: $1,250. Personal expenses: $975.

2005-2006 Financial aid. Need-based: 1,183 full-time freshmen applied for aid; 757 were judged to have need; 688 of these received aid. Average need met was 92%. Average scholarship/grant was $2,610; average loan $1,940. 67% of total undergraduate aid awarded as scholarships/grants, 33% as loans/jobs. Need-based aid available for part-time students. Work study available nights, weekends and for part-time students.

Application procedures. Admission: No deadline. No application fee. Application must be submitted on paper. Admission notification on a rolling basis beginning on or about 12/1. Within 30 days of date of acceptance due to limited housing availability on campus. **Financial aid:** Priority date 4/15; no closing date. FAFSA, institutional form required. Applicants notified on a rolling basis starting 3/1; must reply within 2 week(s) of notification.

Academics. Special study options: Cross-registration, distance learning, double major, dual enrollment of high school students, ESL, honors, independent study, internships, student-designed major, study abroad, teacher certification program. Bachelor's degree programs available on campus. License preparation in nursing. **Credit/placement by examination:** AP, CLEP, institutional tests. 45 credit hours maximum toward associate degree. Each department has its own policy. **Support services:** Learning center, reduced course load, remedial instruction, study skills assistance, tutoring, writing center.

Majors. Business: Accounting technology, administrative services, banking/financial services, business admin, entrepreneurial studies, hotel/motel admin, management information systems. **Communications:** Advertising. **Computer sciences:** General, programming, webmaster. **Construction:** Maintenance. **Education:** Elementary, secondary. **Engineering:** General. **Engineering technology:** Civil, drafting, electrical, heat/ac/refrig, manufacturing, mechanical, surveying. **Family/consumer sciences:** Institutional food production. **Health:** EMT paramedic, medical assistant, medical radiologic technology/radiation therapy, medical records technology, nursing (RN), respiratory therapy technology, substance abuse counseling. **Interdisciplinary:** Nutrition sciences. **Liberal arts:** Arts/sciences, humanities. **Mechanic/repair:** Aircraft, communications systems, electronics/electrical. **Parks/recreation:** Facilities management. **Personal/culinary services:** Restaurant/catering. **Production:** Welding. **Protective services:** Law enforcement admin. **Public administration:** General, community org/advocacy. **Science technology:** Chemical. **Visual/performing arts:** Art, commercial photography, commercial/advertising art, design, dramatic.

Most popular majors. Business/marketing 13%, engineering/engineering technologies 7%, health sciences 14%, liberal arts 33%, public administration/social services 8%, security/protective services 6%, visual/performing arts 12%.

Computing on campus. 94 workstations in library, computer center. Dormitories wired for high-speed internet access. Commuter students can connect to campus network. Online course registration, online library, helpline, wireless network available.

Student life. **Freshman orientation:** Mandatory. Preregistration for classes offered. Mandatory for resident students at cost of $40 per semester. **Policies:** Freshmen permitted cars on campus. **Housing:** Coed dorms, special housing for disabled, cooperative housing, substance-free housing available. $100 nonrefundable deposit. All halls nonsmoking; 1 residence hall has extended quiet hours. Limited visitation suites available. On-campus housing is on first-come, first-served basis. **Activities:** Bands, choral groups, drama, film society, music ensembles, musical theater, radio station, student government, student newspaper, Black student union, international club, Latino student union, Catch the Spirit Bible Club, student nurses association, Kidz-N-Coaches, women's association, Phi Theta Kappa, returning adult student association.

Athletics. NJCAA. **Intercollegiate:** Baseball M, basketball, bowling, cross-country, golf, ice hockey M, lacrosse M, soccer, softball W, tennis, track and field, volleyball W. **Intramural:** Basketball, cheerleading W, football (non-tackle) M, racquetball, softball, table tennis, tennis, volleyball, weight lifting M. **Team name:** Hawks.

Student services. Adult student services, alcohol/substance abuse counseling, campus ministries, career counseling, student employment services, financial aid counseling, health services, on-campus daycare, personal counseling, placement for graduates, veterans' counselor. **Physically disabled:** Services for visually, speech, hearing impaired. **Transfer:** Special adviser, pre-admission transcript evaluation for new students. Transfer center, transfer adviser, college fairs on campus for students transferring to 4-year colleges.

Contact. E-mail: admissions@mvcc.edu
Phone: (315) 792-5354 Toll-free number: (800) 733-6822
Fax: (315) 792-5527
Denis Kennelty, Assistant Dean for Enrollment Management, Mohawk Valley Community College, 1101 Sherman Drive, Utica, NY 13501-5394

Monroe Community College

Rochester, New York
www.monroecc.edu
CB member
CB code: 2429

- Public 2-year community college
- Commuter campus in large city

General. Founded in 1961. Regionally accredited. SUNY institution. Off-campus extension centers in 2 area high schools, branch campus in downtown Rochester. Applied technology center. **Enrollment:** 15,652 degree-seeking undergraduates. **Degrees:** 2,495 associate awarded. **ROTC:** Army, Navy, Air Force. **Location:** 4 miles from downtown. **Calendar:** Semester, limited summer session. **Full-time faculty:** 311 total. **Part-time faculty:** 597 total. **Class size:** 35% < 20, 59% 20-39, 4% 40-49, 2% 50-99, less than 1% >100. **Special facilities:** Human ecology habitat, human performance laboratory, electronic learning center. **Partnerships:** Design specific programs and offer courses for Xerox, Kodak, Frontier, Wegman's.

Student profile.

Out-of-state:	1%	**Live on campus:**	2%
25 or older:	34%		

Basis for selection. Open admission, but selective for some programs. Admissions to certain programs based on high school records, with preference given to county residents. Applicants to engineering and computer science must have precalculus, chemistry and physics. **Homeschooled:** Must meet Federal Ability to Benefit guidelines on placement exam if not issued a regular high school diploma.

High school preparation. Recommended units include English 4, mathematics 4, social studies 4 and science 4. Individual programs have specific mathematics and science requirements.

2005-2006 Annual costs. Tuition/fees: $2,855; $5,455 out-of-state. Per-credit charge: $109 in-state; $218 out-of-state. Books/supplies: $880. Personal expenses: $1,125.

2004-2005 Financial aid. All financial aid based on need. 71% of total undergraduate aid awarded as scholarships/grants, 29% as loans/jobs. Need-based aid available for part-time students. Work study available nights.

Application procedures. **Admission:** Priority date 3/1; no deadline. $20 fee, may be waived for applicants with need. Application may be submitted online. Admission notification on a rolling basis. Applicants to nursing program are encouraged to apply 1 year prior to registration. **Financial aid:** Priority date 5/1; no closing date. FAFSA required. Applicants notified on a rolling basis; must reply within 2 week(s) of notification.

Academics. **Special study options:** Accelerated study, cooperative education, cross-registration, distance learning, dual enrollment of high school students, ESL, exchange student, honors, independent study, internships, liberal arts/career combination, weekend college. License preparation in aviation, dental hygiene, nursing, paramedic, radiology. **Credit/placement by examination:** AP, CLEP, institutional tests. 30 credit hours maximum toward associate degree. **Support services:** Learning center, pre-admission summer program, reduced course load, remedial instruction, study skills assistance, tutoring, writing center.

Majors. **Architecture:** Landscape. **Biology:** General. **Business:** General, accounting, administrative services, international, marketing, sales/distribution, tourism promotion, tourism/travel. **Communications:** General, advertising. **Communications technology:** General. **Computer sciences:** General, computer science. **Construction:** General. **Education:** Music. **Engineering:** Science. **Engineering technology:** Civil, construction, electrical, manufacturing. **Health:** Dental hygiene, medical records technology, nursing (RN), physics/radiologic health. **History:** General. **Liberal arts:** Arts/sciences. **Math:** General. **Mechanic/repair:** Automotive, heating/ac/refrig. **Parks/recreation:** Health/fitness. **Personal/culinary services:** Culinary arts. **Physical sciences:** Chemistry, optics, physics. **Protective services:** Corrections, criminal justice, fire safety technology, police science. **Public administration:** Human services. **Science technology:** Biological. **Social sciences:** General, political science. **Visual/performing arts:** Commercial/advertising art, interior design, music performance, photography, studio arts.

Computing on campus. 150 workstations in library, computer center, student center. Dormitories wired for high-speed internet access and linked to campus network. Commuter students can connect to campus network. Helpline available.

Student life. **Freshman orientation:** Mandatory. Orientation held 1 week prior to beginning of semester. **Housing:** Coed dorms available. **Activities:** Bands, choral groups, drama, literary magazine, musical theater, radio station, student government, student newspaper, symphony orchestra, Christian, Jewish, and Christian Science groups, Latin American, Italian-American, Black, and international student organizations, veterans and handicapped student clubs, honor society.

Athletics. NJCAA. **Intercollegiate:** Baseball M, basketball, diving, golf M, ice hockey M, lacrosse M, soccer, softball W, swimming, tennis, volleyball W. **Intramural:** Archery, basketball, bowling, cheerleading W, cross-country, diving, lacrosse, racquetball, rugby M, skiing, soccer, softball, swimming, tennis, volleyball, water polo M. **Team name:** Tribunes.

Student services. Adult student services, career counseling, student employment services, financial aid counseling, health services, on-campus daycare, personal counseling, placement for graduates, veterans' counselor. **Physically disabled:** Services for visually, hearing impaired. **Transfer:** Special adviser, orientation for new students. Transfer center, transfer adviser, college fairs on campus for students transferring to 4-year colleges.

Contact. Phone: (585) 292-2200 Fax: (585) 292-3680
Andrew Freeman, Director of Admissions, Monroe Community College, Office of Admissions-Monroe Community College, Rochester, NY 14692-8908

Nassau Community College

Garden City, New York
www.ncc.edu
CB member
CB code: 2563

- Public 2-year community college
- Commuter campus in very large city

General. Founded in 1959. Regionally accredited. Part of SUNY system. Adult students may attend part time at off-campus locations. **Enrollment:** 19,316 degree-seeking undergraduates; 1,663 non-degree-seeking students. **Degrees:** 2,901 associate awarded. **ROTC:** Army. **Location:** 20 miles from New York City. **Calendar:** Semester, extensive summer session. **Full-time**

faculty: 557 total; 38% have terminal degrees, 12% minority, 54% women. **Part-time faculty:** 1,120 total; 23% have terminal degrees, 12% minority. **Class size:** 100% 20-39.

Student profile. Among degree-seeking undergraduates, 5,094 enrolled as first-time, first-year students, 2,285 transferred in from other institutions.

Part-time:	32%	**Women:**	53%

Transfer out. **Colleges most students transferred to 2005:** Hofstra University, Adelphi University, SUNY Old Westbury, SUNY Stony Brook, Dowling College.

Basis for selection. Open admission, but selective for some programs. Class rank and fulfillment of mathematics and science requirements important for admission to accounting, business, engineering, nursing, allied health, mortuary science, civil technology, computer information systems, computer science, electrical technology, paralegal, and telecommunications technology programs. Students without high school diploma or equivalent may apply for GED after successful completion of 24 college credits. SAT scores may result in exemption from placement testing. Interview required for allied health programs; audition required for music program; portfolio review required for fashion apparel design program. **Adult students:** Placement test in reading, English, and math required unless applicant has prior associate's or bachelor's degree or prior college credit for English composition and college-level math.

High school preparation. Recommended units include English 4, mathematics 4, social studies 4, science 4 (laboratory 4), foreign language 3 and academic electives 4.

2005-2006 Annual costs. Tuition/fees: $3,364; $6,504 out-of-state. Per-credit charge: $131 in-state; $262 out-of-state. Books/supplies: $1,040. Personal expenses: $1,440.

2005-2006 Financial aid. **Need-based:** 3,747 full-time freshmen applied for aid; 2,598 were judged to have need; 2,295 of these received aid. Average need met was 80%. Average scholarship/grant was $950; average loan $1,843. Need-based aid available for part-time students. Work study available nights, weekends and for part-time students. **Non-need-based:** Awarded to 3,833 full-time undergraduates, including 2,048 freshmen. Scholarships awarded for academics.

Application procedures. **Admission:** Closing date 8/11 (receipt date). $30 fee. Application must be submitted on paper. Admission notification on a rolling basis beginning on or about 11/15. **Financial aid:** Priority date 6/1; no closing date. FAFSA required. Applicants notified on a rolling basis; must reply within 1 week(s) of notification.

Academics. **Special study options:** Cooperative education, cross-registration, distance learning, ESL, honors, internships, liberal arts/career combination, study abroad, weekend college. Cooperative programs with SUNY College of Technology at Utica-Rome and SUNY at New Paltz, New York State Chiropractic College, Fashion Institute of Technology, Adelphi University; joint admissions with SUNY at Stony Brook and SUNY College at Old Westbury. License preparation in nursing, physical therapy, radiology. **Credit/placement by examination:** AP, CLEP, IB, institutional tests. 33 credit hours maximum toward associate degree. **Support services:** GED preparation and test center, learning center, reduced course load, remedial instruction, study skills assistance, tutoring, writing center.

Majors. **Area/ethnic studies:** African. **Business:** Accounting, administrative services, business admin, fashion, management information systems, sales/distribution. **Communications:** General, broadcast journalism. **Computer sciences:** General, computer science, programming. **Education:** Early childhood. **Engineering:** General. **Engineering technology:** Civil, electrical. **Family/consumer sciences:** Child care. **Health:** Clinical lab science, medical radiologic technology/radiation therapy, medical secretary, nursing (RN), physical therapy assistant, respiratory therapy technology, surgical technology. **Legal studies:** Legal secretary, paralegal. **Liberal arts:** Arts/sciences. **Math:** General. **Parks/recreation:** Health/fitness. **Personal/culinary services:** Mortuary science, restaurant/catering. **Protective services:** Law enforcement admin, security services. **Transportation:** General. **Visual/performing arts:** Commercial/advertising art, interior design, music performance, photography, studio arts.

Most popular majors. Business/marketing 9%, health sciences 8%, liberal arts 58%.

Computing on campus. 1,300 workstations in library, computer center. Commuter students can connect to campus network. Online library available.

Student life. **Freshman orientation:** Available. Full-day program. **Activities:** Bands, choral groups, dance, drama, literary magazine, music ensembles, musical theater, radio station, student government, student newspaper, symphony orchestra, TV station, Haraya Caribbean students organizations, Asian American society, Irish American club, NYPIRG, women center, Association Catholic Community, Jewish students organization, organization of Latinos, multicultural club, Intervarsity Christian Fellowship.

Athletics. NJCAA. **Intercollegiate:** Baseball M, basketball, bowling, cross-country, football (tackle) M, golf, ice hockey M, lacrosse, soccer, softball W, tennis, track and field, volleyball W, wrestling M. **Intramural:** Badminton, baseball M, basketball, football (non-tackle) M, handball, judo, racquetball, soccer, softball, swimming, table tennis, tennis, volleyball. **Team name:** Lions.

Student services. Adult student services, career counseling, student employment services, financial aid counseling, health services, minority student services, on-campus daycare, personal counseling, placement for graduates. **Physically disabled:** Services for visually, speech, hearing impaired. **Transfer:** Special adviser, orientation, pre-admission transcript evaluation for new students. Transfer center, transfer adviser, college fairs on campus for students transferring to 4-year colleges.

Contact. E-mail: admissions@ncc.edu
Phone: (516) 572-7345 Fax: (516) 572-9743
Craig Wright, Vice President Student Academic Affairs, Nassau Community College, Office of Admissions, Garden City, NY 11530

New York Career Institute

New York, New York
www.nyci.com **CB code: 5324**

- For-profit 2-year junior and technical college
- Commuter campus in very large city

General. **Enrollment:** 585 degree-seeking undergraduates. **Degrees:** 71 associate awarded. **Calendar:** Trimester, extensive summer session. **Full-time faculty:** 20 total. **Part-time faculty:** 15 total.

Basis for selection. Open admission. All applicants take English and typing examinations. Paralegal applicants must also submit letter of recommendation. Essay required for paralegal program.

2005-2006 Annual costs. Full-time tuition for court reporting night program $7,650, part-time $5,400. Tuition for paralegal program $250 per-credit-hour. Books/supplies: $800. Personal expenses: $4,000.

Application procedures. **Admission:** No deadline. $25 fee. Admission notification on a rolling basis. **Financial aid:** No deadline. Applicants notified on a rolling basis.

Academics. **Special study options:** Internships. **Credit/placement by examination:** AP, CLEP, institutional tests.

Majors. **Health:** Medical records admin, medical secretary. **Legal studies:** Court reporting, legal secretary, paralegal.

Most popular majors. Health sciences 15%, legal studies 85%.

Student life. **Freshman orientation:** Mandatory.

Student services. Career counseling, student employment services, financial aid counseling, placement for graduates. **Transfer:** Pre-admission transcript evaluation for new students.

Contact. Phone: (212) 962-0002 Fax: (212) 385-7574
Cindy McMahon, Director of Admissions, New York Career Institute, 11 Park Place, New York, NY 10007

Niagara County Community College

Sanborn, New York
www.niagaracc.suny.edu **CB code: 2568**

- Public 2-year community college
- Commuter campus in rural community

General. Founded in 1962. Regionally accredited. SUNY institution. **Enrollment:** 4,062 degree-seeking undergraduates; 1,510 non-degree-seeking students. **Degrees:** 802 associate awarded. **ROTC:** Army. **Location:** 10 miles from Niagara Falls. **Calendar:** Semester, limited summer session. **Full-time faculty:** 126 total; 24% have terminal degrees, 5% minority, 50% women. **Part-time faculty:** 162 total; 2% have terminal degrees, 4% minority, 55% women. **Special facilities:** Biofeedback laboratory.

Student profile. Among degree-seeking undergraduates, 65% enrolled in a transfer program, 35% enrolled in a vocational program, 1,159 enrolled as first-time, first-year students, 227 transferred in from other institutions.

Part-time:	22%	**Hispanic American:**	1%
Out-of-state:	1%	**Native American:**	2%
Women:	60%	**International:**	1%
African American:	6%	**25 or older:**	27%
Asian American:	2%		

Transfer out. **Colleges most students transferred to 2005:** Buffalo State College, Niagara University, SUNY Buffalo, Brockport, Fredonia.

Basis for selection. Open admission, but selective for some programs. Admission to nursing, physical therapist assistant, radiologic technology, and surgical technology programs based on school achievement record and test scores. Admission to programs on space-available basis. SAT/ACT reviewed for placement if submitted. Interview recommended.

High school preparation. 1 drafting required for drafting applicants, 1 biology or chemistry required for nursing applicants, 3 mathematics for engineering technology, 1 biology, 1 chemistry and 2 mathematics for physical therapist assistant, 1 chemistry, 1 biology, 2 mathematics for radiologic technology, 1 biology for surgical technician, 2 mathematics for business administration.

2005-2006 Annual costs. Tuition/fees: $3,396; $4,944 out-of-state. Per-credit charge: $129 in-state; $194 out-of-state. Books/supplies: $700. Personal expenses: $650.

2004-2005 Financial aid. All financial aid based on need. 58% of total undergraduate aid awarded as scholarships/grants, 42% as loans/jobs. Need-based aid available for part-time students. Work study available nights and for part-time students. **Additional information:** Assistance offered placing students in part-time employment. Students can charge books, food coupons, or $100 advance against anticipated financial aid.

Application procedures. **Admission:** Closing date 8/31. No application fee. Application may be submitted online. Admission notification on a rolling basis beginning on or about 8/1. Must reply by May 1 or within 4 week(s) if notified thereafter. **Financial aid:** Priority date 4/1; no closing date. FAFSA required. Applicants notified on a rolling basis starting 5/1; must reply within 2 week(s) of notification.

Academics. Orientation program for Distance Learning students. **Special study options:** Cooperative education, cross-registration, distance learning, double major, dual enrollment of high school students, honors, independent study, internships, study abroad. License preparation in nursing. **Credit/placement by examination:** AP, CLEP, IB, institutional tests. 30 credit hours maximum toward associate degree. **Support services:** Learning center, pre-admission summer program, reduced course load, remedial instruction, study skills assistance, tutoring, writing center.

Majors. **Agriculture:** Animal husbandry. **Business:** Accounting, administrative services, business admin, hospitality admin, retailing. **Communications:** General, digital media. **Computer sciences:** Computer science, data processing, information systems. **Conservation:** Environmental studies. **Education:** Elementary, health. **Engineering technology:** CAD/CADD, electrical, mechanical. **Health:** Medical assistant, medical radiologic technology/radiation therapy, nursing (RN), physical therapy assistant, surgical technology. **Liberal arts:** Arts/sciences, humanities. **Personal/culinary services:** Chef training. **Protective services:** Criminalistics, law enforcement admin. **Public administration:** Human services. **Visual/performing arts:** Dramatic, studio arts.

Most popular majors. Business/marketing 15%, health sciences 11%, liberal arts 36%, security/protective services 12%.

Computing on campus. 415 workstations in library, computer center. Online library, helpline available.

Student life. **Freshman orientation:** Available. One day orientation in August. **Activities:** Jazz band, choral groups, dance, drama, music ensembles, musical theater, radio station, student government, student newspaper, disabled student association, comeback club, African American student association, Native American club, nursing club, human services club, international club, women's studies club.

Athletics. NJCAA. **Intercollegiate:** Baseball M, basketball, golf, soccer, softball W, volleyball W, wrestling M. **Intramural:** Basketball. **Team name:** Trailblazers.

Student services. Adult student services, alcohol/substance abuse counseling, career counseling, student employment services, financial aid counseling, health services, on-campus daycare, personal counseling, placement for graduates, veterans' counselor. **Physically disabled:** Services for visually, speech, hearing impaired. **Transfer:** Special adviser, orientation, pre-admission transcript evaluation for new students. Transfer adviser, college fairs on campus for students transferring to 4-year colleges.

Contact. E-mail: admissions@niagaracc.suny.edu
Phone: (716) 614-6200 Fax: (716) 614-6820
Kathy Saunders, Director of Admissions, Niagara County Community College, 3111 Saunders Settlement Road, Sanborn, NY 14132-9460

North Country Community College

Saranac Lake, New York
www.nccc.edu **CB code: 2571**

- Public 2-year community college
- Commuter campus in small town

General. Founded in 1967. Regionally accredited. Unit of State University of New York. Campuses in Saranac Lake, Malone, and Ticonderoga. **Enrollment:** 1,181 degree-seeking undergraduates; 424 non-degree-seeking students. **Degrees:** 224 associate awarded. **Location:** 150 miles from Albany, 50 miles from Plattsburgh. **Calendar:** Semester, limited summer session. **Full-time faculty:** 41 total; 20% have terminal degrees, 2% minority, 51% women. **Part-time faculty:** 109 total; 6% have terminal degrees, 2% minority, 56% women. **Class size:** 60% < 20, 38% 20-39, less than 1% 40-49, 1% 50-99. **Partnerships:** Formal partnerships with local high schools through College Bridge Program.

Student profile. Among degree-seeking undergraduates, 37% enrolled in a transfer program, 32% enrolled in a vocational program, 1% already have a bachelor's degree or higher, 339 enrolled as first-time, first-year students, 130 transferred in from other institutions.

Part-time:	17%	**Hispanic American:**	1%
Out-of-state:	4%	**Native American:**	3%
Women:	64%	**International:**	2%
African American:	2%	**25 or older:**	38%
Asian American:	1%	**Live on campus:**	4%

Transfer out. 45% of students enrolled in the transfer program go on to 4-year colleges. **Colleges most students transferred to 2005:** SUNY Colleges at Plattsburgh, Potsdam, Cobleskill, Geneseo; SUNY at Buffalo.

Basis for selection. Open admission, but selective for some programs. Special requirements for nursing, radiologic technology, and massage therapy. SAT or ACT and placement tests recommended for competitive programs. **Homeschooled:** Must complete and score in appropriate ranges on College Board Descriptive Tests System in mathematics, English, and reading.

High school preparation. 16 units recommended. Recommended units include English 4, mathematics 3, social studies 4, science 3 (laboratory 1) and foreign language 3. 5 units of math and science recommended (3 math and 2 science or 2 math and 3 science).

2005-2006 Annual costs. Tuition/fees: $3,640; $8,590 out-of-state. Per-credit charge: $130 in-state; $340 out-of-state. Books/supplies: $800. Personal expenses: $800.

2004-2005 Financial aid. All financial aid based on need. 336 full-time freshmen applied for aid; 277 were judged to have need; 277 of these received aid. Average need met was 54%. Average scholarship/grant was $3,785; average loan $1,344. 67% of total undergraduate aid awarded as scholarships/grants, 33% as loans/jobs. Need-based aid available for part-time students. Work study available nights, weekends and for part-time students.

Application procedures. **Admission:** Priority date 2/1; deadline 9/1 (receipt date). No application fee. Application may be submitted online. Admission notification on a rolling basis. Must reply by May 1 or within 4 week(s) if notified thereafter. **Financial aid:** Priority date 4/1; no closing date. FAFSA required. Applicants notified on a rolling basis starting 4/1; must reply within 3 week(s) of notification.

Academics. 23-42 credit hours required in major, 62-70 required for graduation depending on field of study. **Special study options:** Distance learning, double major, dual enrollment of high school students, internships, liberal arts/career combination, student-designed major. License preparation in nursing. **Credit/placement by examination:** AP, CLEP, institutional tests. 31 credit hours maximum toward associate degree. **Support services:** Learning center, reduced course load, remedial instruction, study skills assistance, tutoring.

Majors. **Business:** General, business admin, office/clerical. **Computer sciences:** Computer graphics. **Health:** Health services, massage therapy, medical radiologic technology/radiation therapy, nursing (RN). **Interdisciplinary:** Biological/physical sciences. **Liberal arts:** Arts/sciences. **Parks/recreation:** Facilities management. **Protective services:** Criminal justice.

Most popular majors. Business/marketing 14%, health sciences 27%, interdisciplinary studies 8%, liberal arts 28%, security/protective services 12%.

Computing on campus. 200 workstations in dormitories, library, computer center, student center. Dormitories linked to campus network. Online library, helpline, wireless network available.

Student life. Freshman orientation: Mandatory. Preregistration for classes offered. Day-long session held 1 day prior to start of classes. **Policies:** Freshmen permitted cars on campus. **Housing:** Coed dorms available. $250 deposit. **Activities:** Drama, literary magazine, music ensembles, student government, student newspaper.

Athletics. NJCAA. **Intercollegiate:** Basketball M, ice hockey M, soccer, softball W. **Intramural:** Archery, badminton, basketball, bowling, golf, soccer, softball, swimming, tennis, volleyball, weight lifting. **Team name:** Saints.

Student services. Alcohol/substance abuse counseling, career counseling, student employment services, financial aid counseling, personal counseling, placement for graduates. **Physically disabled:** Services for visually, speech, hearing impaired. **Learning disabled:** Comprehensive services available. **Transfer:** Special adviser, orientation, pre-admission transcript evaluation for new students. Transfer adviser, college fairs on campus for students transferring to 4-year colleges.

Contact. E-mail: info@nccc.edu
Phone: (518) 891-2915 ext. 233 Toll-free number: (888) 879-6222
Fax: (518) 891-0898
Edwin Trathen, Assistant to the President for Enrollment Management, North Country Community College, 23 Santanoni Avenue, Saranac Lake, NY 12983

Olean Business Institute

Olean, New York
www.obi.edu **CB code: 0630**

- For-profit 2-year business college
- Commuter campus in large town

General. Founded in 1961. Accredited by ACICS. **Enrollment:** 87 degree-seeking undergraduates. **Degrees:** 39 associate awarded. **Location:** 90 miles from Buffalo, 90 miles from Erie, Pennsylvania. **Calendar:** Semester, limited summer session. **Full-time faculty:** 8 total. **Part-time faculty:** 4 total.

Student profile.

25 or older:	53%	**Live on campus:**	2%

Basis for selection. Open admission. School achievement record most important. Interview recommended.

2005-2006 Annual costs. Tuition/fees: $9,000. Books/supplies: $700.

Application procedures. Admission: No deadline. $25 fee, may be waived for applicants with need. Admission notification on a rolling basis. **Financial aid:** Priority date 5/1; no closing date. FAFSA required. Applicants notified on a rolling basis.

Academics. Academic offerings intended to provide student with as much work-field knowledge and experience as possible. **Special study options:** Internships. **Credit/placement by examination:** CLEP, institutional tests. **Support services:** Learning center, reduced course load, remedial instruction, tutoring.

Majors. Business: General, accounting, accounting/business management, administrative services, business admin, management science, office management, office technology. **Computer sciences:** General, data entry, data processing, information technology, word processing. **Health:** Medical records admin, medical secretary, office admin. **Legal studies:** Paralegal.

Computing on campus. 75 workstations in dormitories, library, computer center.

Student life. Housing: Single-sex dorms available. Student housing available near campus. **Activities:** Student government.

Student services. Adult student services, career counseling, student employment services, personal counseling, placement for graduates. **Transfer:** Special adviser for new students. Transfer adviser for students transferring to 4-year colleges.

Contact. E-mail: lkincaid@obi.edu
Phone: (716) 372-7978 Fax: (716) 372-2120
Lori Kincaid, Director of Admissions, Olean Business Institute, 301 North Union Street, Olean, NY 14760

Onondaga Community College

Syracuse, New York **CB member**
www.sunyocc.edu **CB code: 2627**

- Public 2-year community college
- Commuter campus in small city

General. Founded in 1962. Regionally accredited. SUNY institution. **Enrollment:** 8,263 degree-seeking undergraduates. **Degrees:** 823 associate awarded. **ROTC:** Army, Air Force. **Location:** 4 miles from downtown. **Calendar:** Semester, extensive summer session. **Full-time faculty:** 160 total. **Part-time faculty:** 339 total. **Special facilities:** Children's learning center, county library branch, dental hygiene clinic, applied technology center. **Partnerships:** Formal partnerships with Syracuse City Schools, Manufacturers Association of Central New York.

Student profile.

Out-of-state:	5%	**25 or older:**	44%

Transfer out. Colleges most students transferred to 2005: SUNY Oswego, SUNY Cortland, Le Moyne College, Syracuse University.

Basis for selection. Open admission, but selective for some programs. Admission to some programs based on high school GPA, test scores, and specific program prerequisites. Mandatory developmental skills courses required as condition of acceptance for students lacking adequate academic background. School achievement record, test scores, special talents considered for placement only. Interview, recommendations required for some programs. Interview required for dental hygiene, graphic arts, radio-television; recommended for nursing, physical therapist assistant. Audition required for music; portfolio required for art, recommended for photography. **Homeschooled:** Submit diplomas from school districts of record, transcripts if available.

High school preparation. 15 units recommended. Recommended units include English 4, mathematics 3, science 3 and foreign language 2. Algebra, biology, chemistry required of dental hygiene, respiratory care, surgical technology, nursing applicants. 4 mathematics required for engineering, science, computer science and physical therapy assistant applicants. Language required for humanities.

2005-2006 Annual costs. Tuition/fees: $3,490; $6,670 out-of-district; $9,850 out-of-state. Per-credit charge: $125 in-district; $250 out-of-district; $375 out-of-state. Books/supplies: $730. Personal expenses: $450.

2004-2005 Financial aid. All financial aid based on need. Need-based aid available for part-time students. Work study available for part-time students.

Application procedures. Admission: Closing date 8/31. $40 fee, may be waived for applicants with need. Admission notification on a rolling basis. **Financial aid:** Priority date 2/15; no closing date. FAFSA required. Applicants notified on a rolling basis starting 4/15; must reply within 4 week(s) of notification.

Academics. Special study options: Cooperative education, cross-registration, distance learning, double major, dual enrollment of high school students, ESL, independent study, internships, liberal arts/career combination, New York semester, study abroad. License preparation in nursing. **Credit/placement by examination:** AP, CLEP, institutional tests. 30 credit hours maximum toward associate degree. **Support services:** GED preparation, learning center, pre-admission summer program, reduced course load, remedial instruction, study skills assistance, tutoring, writing center.

Majors. Architecture: Interior. **Business:** General, accounting, administrative services, banking/financial services, hotel/motel admin, insurance, labor relations, office/clerical, sales/distribution. **Communications:** Advertising, broadcast journalism. **Computer sciences:** General, computer science, networking. **Engineering:** Computer, electrical, science. **Engineering technology:** Construction, electrical. **Health:** Dental hygiene, medical records technology, physical therapy assistant, recreational therapy, respiratory therapy technology. **Interdisciplinary:** Math/computer science. **Liberal arts:** Arts/sciences. **Mechanic/repair:** Automotive. **Parks/recreation:** Facilities management. **Personal/culinary services:** Culinary arts. **Protective services:** Criminal justice, fire safety technology. **Public administration:** Human services. **Visual/performing arts:** Art, commercial/advertising art, interior design, photography.

Computing on campus. 400 workstations in library, computer center. Commuter students can connect to campus network. Helpline, repair service available.

Student life. Freshman orientation: Available. Preregistration for classes offered. Programs held for half day in fall and spring prior to start of classes.

Activities: Bands, choral groups, film society, music ensembles, musical theater, radio station, student government, student newspaper, international students, minority, veterans, interreligious, and older/returning student clubs available.

Athletics. NJCAA. **Intercollegiate:** Baseball M, basketball, cross-country, lacrosse M, softball W, tennis, volleyball W. **Intramural:** Basketball, bowling, fencing, golf, lacrosse M, skiing, skin diving, softball W, swimming, tennis, volleyball. **Team name:** Lazers.

Student services. Campus ministries, career counseling, student employment services, financial aid counseling, health services, on-campus daycare, personal counseling, placement for graduates, veterans' counselor. **Physically disabled:** Services for visually, speech, hearing impaired. **Transfer:** Special adviser, orientation, pre-admission transcript evaluation for new students. Transfer adviser, college fairs on campus for students transferring to 4-year colleges.

Contact. E-mail: admissions@sunyocc.edu
Phone: (315) 498-2201 Fax: (315) 498-2201
Shari Piotrowski, Director of Admissions, Onondaga Community College, 4941 Onondaga Road, Syracuse, NY 13215

Orange County Community College

Middletown, New York — **CB member**
orange.cc.ny.us — **CB code: 2625**

- Public 2-year community college
- Commuter campus in large town

General. Founded in 1950. Regionally accredited. First community college founded as part of SUNY. **Enrollment:** 6,441 degree-seeking undergraduates. **Degrees:** 668 associate awarded. **ROTC:** Army. **Location:** 25 miles from Newburgh, 60 miles from New York City. **Calendar:** Semester, limited summer session. **Full-time faculty:** 140 total. **Part-time faculty:** 250 total.

Student profile. Among degree-seeking undergraduates, 67% enrolled in a transfer program, 33% enrolled in a vocational program, 1,654 enrolled as first-time, first-year students.

Part-time:	48%	**Asian American:**	2%
Out-of-state:	1%	**Hispanic American:**	13%
Women:	61%	**25 or older:**	38%
African American:	10%		

Transfer out. Colleges most students transferred to 2005: SUNY at New Paltz, Mount St. Mary's College, Marist College, Dominican College of Blauvelt.

Basis for selection. Open admission, but selective for some programs. Admission to allied health and nursing programs based on academic record, assessment scores and, to some extent, residency.

High school preparation. 14 units recommended. Recommended units include English 4, mathematics 2, social studies 4, science 2 and foreign language 2. Regents biology required for physical therapist assistant, occupational therapy assistant, radiologic technologist and dental hygienist. Regents chemistry required for dental hygiene.

2005-2006 Annual costs. Tuition/fees: $3,218; $6,118 out-of-state. Per-credit charge: $120 in-state; $240 out-of-state. Books/supplies: $850. Personal expenses: $925.

Financial aid. Need-based: Need-based aid available for part-time students.

Application procedures. Admission: Priority date 2/1; no deadline. $25 fee, may be waived for applicants with need. Admission notification on a rolling basis. February 1 application closing date for allied health/nursing program. Notification by March 15, must reply within 2 weeks. **Financial aid:** Priority date 5/1; no closing date. FAFSA, institutional form required. Applicants notified on a rolling basis starting 5/1; must reply within 4 week(s) of notification.

Academics. Special study options: Cooperative education, distance learning, dual enrollment of high school students, ESL, honors, independent study, internships, weekend college. License preparation in dental hygiene, nursing, real estate. **Credit/placement by examination:** AP, CLEP, institutional tests. 30 credit hours maximum toward associate degree. **Support services:** GED preparation and test center, learning center, reduced course load, remedial instruction, study skills assistance, tutoring, writing center.

Majors. Business: General, accounting, administrative services, business admin, finance, office technology, real estate, sales/distribution. **Communications:** General. **Computer sciences:** General, data processing. **Education:** General, elementary. **Engineering:** General. **Engineering technology:** Architectural, electrical. **Family/consumer sciences:** Child care. **Foreign languages:** General, French, German, Spanish. **Health:** Clinical lab science, clinical lab technology, dental hygiene, health services, medical radiologic technology/radiation therapy, occupational therapy assistant, physical therapy assistant. **Liberal arts:** Arts/sciences. **Math:** General. **Parks/recreation:** Exercise sciences, facilities management. **Protective services:** Criminal justice, police science.

Most popular majors. Business/marketing 18%, health sciences 25%, liberal arts 33%, mathematics 8%.

Computing on campus. 300 workstations in library, computer center, student center. Online library available.

Student life. Freshman orientation: Available. Preregistration for classes offered. **Activities:** Bands, choral groups, dance, drama, literary magazine, music ensembles, musical theater, radio station, student government, student newspaper, TV station, Black and Latino organization, Helping Hands, Patchwork Orange (social service organization).

Athletics. NJCAA. **Intercollegiate:** Baseball M, basketball, golf, soccer, softball W, swimming, tennis, volleyball W. **Intramural:** Football (non-tackle), racquetball, soccer M, softball, tennis, volleyball. **Team name:** Colts.

Student services. Adult student services, alcohol/substance abuse counseling, career counseling, services for economically disadvantaged, student employment services, financial aid counseling, health services, on-campus daycare, personal counseling, placement for graduates, veterans' counselor. **Physically disabled:** Services for visually, speech, hearing impaired. **Transfer:** Special adviser, orientation for new students. Transfer adviser, college fairs on campus for students transferring to 4-year colleges.

Contact. Phone: (845) 341-4030 Fax: (845) 342-8662
Margot St. Lawrence, Director of Admissions, Orange County Community College, 115 South Street, Middletown, NY 10940-0115

Phillips Beth Israel School of Nursing

New York, New York
www.futurenursebi.org — **CB code: 2031**

- Private 2-year nursing college
- Commuter campus in very large city
- Application essay, interview required

General. Founded in 1904. **Enrollment:** 195 degree-seeking undergraduates. **Degrees:** 71 associate awarded. **Calendar:** Semester, limited summer session. **Full-time faculty:** 8 total; 25% have terminal degrees, 12% minority, 100% women. **Part-time faculty:** 8 total; 75% have terminal degrees, 12% minority, 100% women. **Class size:** 56% < 20, 33% 20-39, 11% 40-49.

Student profile. Among degree-seeking undergraduates, 8 enrolled as first-time, first-year students, 101 transferred in from other institutions.

Part-time:	80%	**Women:**	71%
Out-of-state:	5%	**25 or older:**	56%

Transfer out. Colleges most students transferred to 2005: Pace University, New York University.

Basis for selection. Academic achievement, aptitude test scores, personal interview, recommendations, and prior experience of primary consideration. 55th percentile score on National League for Nursing's Preadmission Examination-RN mandatory (65th percentile score recommended). Standing in top half of high school class recommended. High school GPA of 75 or better, college GPA of 2.5 or better, GED minimum score of 250. **Adult students:** Entrance exam policies same as for first-time freshmen.

High school preparation. 16 units required. Required and recommended units include English 4, mathematics 2, social studies 2, history 2, science 2 and academic electives 4. Chemistry and biology required.

2006-2007 Annual costs. Tuition/fees: $16,560. Per-credit charge: $300. Books/supplies: $1,175. Personal expenses: $1,560.

2005-2006 Financial aid. Need-based: Average need met was 34%. Average scholarship/grant was $4,600; average loan $5,125. 54% of total undergraduate aid awarded as scholarships/grants, 46% as loans/jobs. Need-based aid available for part-time students. **Non-need-based:** Scholarships awarded for academics.

Application procedures. Admission: Closing date 5/1 (postmark date). $50 fee, may be waived for applicants with need. Application must be submitted on paper. Admission notification on a rolling basis. Must reply by 6/1. **Financial aid:** Closing date 6/1. FAFSA, institutional form required. Applicants notified by 7/1; must reply within 2 week(s) of notification.

Academics. Special study options: Internships, liberal arts/career combination. License preparation in nursing. **Credit/placement by examination:** AP, CLEP, institutional tests. 33 credit hours maximum toward associate degree. **Support services:** Learning center, pre-admission summer program, reduced course load, remedial instruction, study skills assistance, tutoring.

Majors. Health: Nursing (RN).

Computing on campus. 15 workstations in library, computer center.

Student life. Freshman orientation: Mandatory. 4 full days the week before classes start. **Activities:** Choral groups, student government, student newspaper, National Student Nurses Association Chapter.

Student services. Alcohol/substance abuse counseling, career counseling, financial aid counseling, health services, personal counseling. **Physically disabled:** Services for visually, speech, hearing impaired. **Transfer:** Special adviser, orientation, pre-admission transcript evaluation for new students. Transfer adviser, college fairs on campus for students transferring to 4-year colleges.

Contact. E-mail: bstern@bethisraelny.org
Phone: (212) 614-6108 Fax: (212) 614-6109
Bernice Pass-Stern, Assistant Dean, Phillips Beth Israel School of Nursing, 776 Sixth Avenue, Fourth Floor, New York, NY 10001

Plaza College

Jackson Heights, New York
www.plazacollege.edu **CB code: 0545**

- For-profit 2-year business and junior college
- Commuter campus in very large city
- Application essay, interview required

General. Founded in 1916. Regionally accredited. **Enrollment:** 736 degree-seeking undergraduates. **Degrees:** 236 associate awarded. **Calendar:** Semester, extensive summer session. **Full-time faculty:** 30 total. **Part-time faculty:** 19 total.

Basis for selection. Essay, interview, and test scores most important. Student must pass entrance examination. CPAT and college-administered writing test required of all students. **Adult students:** Entrance exam policies same as for first-time freshmen.

2005-2006 Annual costs. Books/supplies: $600. Personal expenses: $1,800.

Application procedures. Admission: No deadline. $25 fee, may be waived for applicants with need. Application may be submitted online. Admission notification on a rolling basis. **Financial aid:** No deadline. FAFSA, institutional form required. Applicants notified on a rolling basis.

Academics. Special study options: Accelerated study, internships. Bachelor's degree programs available on campus. **Credit/placement by examination:** CLEP, institutional tests. 30 credit hours maximum toward associate degree. **Support services:** Learning center, reduced course load, remedial instruction, study skills assistance, tutoring, writing center.

Majors. Business: Accounting, business admin. **Computer sciences:** Information systems. **Health:** Medical assistant.

Computing on campus. 250 workstations in library, computer center, student center. Wireless network available.

Student life. Freshman orientation: Mandatory. Preregistration for classes offered.

Student services. Career counseling, financial aid counseling, personal counseling, placement for graduates. **Physically disabled:** Services for visually, speech, hearing impaired. **Transfer:** Special adviser, orientation for new students. Transfer adviser for students transferring to 4-year colleges.

Contact. E-mail: plazainfo@plazacollege.edu
Phone: (718) 779-1430 Fax: (718) 779-7423
Rose Ann Black, Associate Dean, Plaza College, 74-09 37th Avenue, Jackson Heights, NY 11372

Rochester Business Institute

Rochester, New York
www.rochester-institute.com **CB code: 2770**

- For-profit 2-year business college
- Commuter campus in large city
- Interview required

General. Founded in 1863. Accredited by ACICS. **Enrollment:** 1,103 degree-seeking undergraduates. **Degrees:** 346 associate awarded. **Calendar:** Quarter, extensive summer session. **Full-time faculty:** 15 total; 7% have terminal degrees, 7% minority, 73% women. **Part-time faculty:** 54 total; 13% have terminal degrees, 17% minority, 65% women. **Class size:** 83% < 20, 17% 20-39.

Student profile. Among degree-seeking undergraduates, 254 transferred in from other institutions.

African American:	47%	**Native American:**	1%
Asian American:	1%	**25 or older:**	60%
Hispanic American:	10%		

Transfer out. Colleges most students transferred to 2005: Roberts Wesleyan.

Basis for selection. Interview, CPAT entrance exam required. **Adult students:** Entrance exam policies same as for first-time freshmen. **Home-schooled:** Transcript of courses and grades, state high school equivalency certificate required.

2005-2006 Annual costs. Tuition/fees: $11,750. Per-credit charge: $250. Books/supplies: $1,200.

Financial aid. All financial aid based on need. Need-based aid available for part-time students. Work study available nights, weekends and for part-time students.

Application procedures. Admission: No deadline. No application fee. Application must be submitted on paper. Admission notification on a rolling basis. **Financial aid:** No deadline. FAFSA, institutional form required. Applicants notified on a rolling basis starting 3/15; must reply within 4 week(s) of notification.

Academics. Special study options: Distance learning, independent study, weekend college. **Credit/placement by examination:** CLEP. 40 credit hours maximum toward associate degree. Maximum of a total of 40 combined transfer and proficiency credits. **Support services:** Reduced course load, study skills assistance, tutoring.

Majors. Business: Accounting, administrative services, business admin, executive assistant, office management, office technology, office/clerical, receptionist. **Computer sciences:** Data entry, data processing, programming, word processing. **Health:** Insurance coding, insurance specialist, medical assistant, medical secretary, office computer specialist. **Interdisciplinary:** Accounting/computer science. **Legal studies:** Legal secretary, paralegal. **Protective services:** Police science.

Most popular majors. Business/marketing 20%, computer/information sciences 15%, health sciences 15%, legal studies 25%.

Computing on campus. 223 workstations in library, computer center. Online library available.

Student life. Freshman orientation: Mandatory. Preregistration for classes offered. **Policies:** Freshmen permitted cars on campus.

Student services. Adult student services, career counseling, services for economically disadvantaged, student employment services, financial aid counseling, personal counseling, placement for graduates, veterans' counselor. **Transfer:** Orientation, re-entry adviser, pre-admission transcript evaluation for new students.

Contact. E-mail: dpfluke@cci.edu
Phone: (585) 266-0430 ext. 101 Fax: (585) 266-8243
Deanna Pfluke, Director of Admissions, Rochester Business Institute, 1630 Portland Avenue, Rochester, NY 14621-3007

Rockland Community College

Suffern, New York **CB member**
www.sunyrockland.edu **CB code: 2767**

- Public 2-year community college
- Commuter campus in large town

General. Founded in 1959. Regionally accredited. SUNY institution. Extension sites/centers located throughout county. **Enrollment:** 6,325 degree-seeking undergraduates. **Degrees:** 801 associate awarded. **Location:** 35 miles from New York City. **Calendar:** Semester, extensive summer session. **Full-time faculty:** 130 total. **Part-time faculty:** 250 total.

Student profile.

Out-of-state:	2%	**25 or older:**	35%

Transfer out. Colleges most students transferred to 2005: SUNY New Paltz, Ramapo College, Dominican College.

Basis for selection. Open admission. Students required to take assessment examination before enrolling full-time.

High school preparation. 18 units recommended. Recommended units include English 4, mathematics 2, social studies 4, history 4, science 2, foreign language 1 and academic electives 4.

2005-2006 Annual costs. Tuition/fees: $3,065; $5,865 out-of-state. Per-credit charge: $116 in-state; $232 out-of-state. Books/supplies: $600. Personal expenses: $600.

2005-2006 Financial aid. Need-based: Need-based aid available for part-time students. Work study available nights and weekends.

Application procedures. Admission: Priority date 8/1; no deadline. $25 fee, may be waived for applicants with need. Application may be submitted online. Admission notification on a rolling basis. **Financial aid:** Priority date 6/15; no closing date. FAFSA, institutional form required. Applicants notified on a rolling basis starting 6/1; must reply within 3 week(s) of notification.

Academics. Special study options: Cross-registration, distance learning, double major, dual enrollment of high school students, ESL, honors, independent study, internships, liberal arts/career combination, student-designed major, study abroad, weekend college. **Credit/placement by examination:** AP, CLEP, IB. 45 credit hours maximum toward associate degree. **Support services:** Learning center, remedial instruction, study skills assistance, tutoring, writing center.

Honors college/program. Mentor/Talented honors program. Business honors degree requires minimum combined SAT score of 1100 (exclusive of Writing) and at least 90 average; interviews, auditions and portfolios recommended.

Majors. Business: General, accounting, accounting technology, administrative services, business admin, hospitality admin, tourism/travel. **Communications:** General. **Computer sciences:** Computer graphics, data processing, programming. **Education:** Elementary. **Engineering technology:** Electrical. **Family/consumer sciences:** Food/nutrition, institutional food production. **Health:** EMT paramedic, medical assistant, medical records technology, nursing (RN), occupational therapy assistant, respiratory therapy technology. **Legal studies:** Paralegal. **Liberal arts:** Arts/sciences. **Mechanic/repair:** Automotive. **Protective services:** Criminal justice, fire safety technology. **Public administration:** Human services. **Social sciences:** General. **Visual/performing arts:** Commercial photography, commercial/advertising art, dramatic, photography, studio arts.

Most popular majors. Business/marketing 15%, computer/information sciences 9%, health sciences 18%, liberal arts 48%.

Computing on campus. 177 workstations in computer center.

Student life. Freshman orientation: Available. Preregistration for classes offered. **Policies:** Freshmen permitted cars on campus. **Activities:** Jazz band, choral groups, dance, drama, literary magazine, musical theater, radio station, student government, student newspaper, symphony orchestra, TV station, special interest clubs.

Athletics. NJCAA. **Intercollegiate:** Baseball M, basketball, bowling, golf M, soccer, softball W, table tennis, tennis, volleyball W. **Intramural:** Basketball, bowling, racquetball, soccer, softball, table tennis, track and field, volleyball. **Team name:** Hawks.

Student services. Adult student services, alcohol/substance abuse counseling, campus ministries, career counseling, services for economically disadvantaged, student employment services, financial aid counseling, health services, minority student services, on-campus daycare, personal counseling, placement for graduates, veterans' counselor. **Physically disabled:** Services for visually, speech, hearing impaired. **Transfer:** Special adviser, orientation, pre-admission transcript evaluation for new students. Transfer adviser, college fairs on campus for students transferring to 4-year colleges.

Contact. E-mail: info@sunyrockland.edu
Phone: (845) 574-4462 Toll-free number: (800) 722-7666
Fax: (845) 574-4433
Lorraine Glynn, Director of Admissions, Rockland Community College, 145 College Road, Suffern, NY 10901

St. Elizabeth College of Nursing

Utica, New York
www.secon.edu **CB code: 2847**

- Private 2-year nursing college affiliated with Roman Catholic Church
- Commuter campus in small city
- SAT or ACT (ACT writing optional), application essay, interview required

General. Regionally accredited. **Enrollment:** 210 degree-seeking undergraduates. **Degrees:** 70 associate awarded. **Location:** 40 miles from Albany, 50 miles from Syracuse. **Calendar:** Semester. One 6-week summer session at the end of first year. **Full-time faculty:** 16 total.

Student profile. Among degree-seeking undergraduates, 9% already have a bachelor's degree or higher, 28 enrolled as first-time, first-year students, 4 transferred in from other institutions.

Part-time:	34%	**Asian American:**	2%
Out-of-state:	1%	**Hispanic American:**	2%
Women:	85%	**International:**	2%
African American:	1%	**25 or older:**	52%

Basis for selection. SAT Subject Tests recommended. **Adult students:** Entrance exam policies same as for first-time freshmen. **Homeschooled:** Strong math and science background required, including coursework in chemistry, biology and equivalent of Math Level 1 and 2. **Learning Disabled:** Written documentation of disability is required in order to set up special testing.

High school preparation. Required and recommended units include English 4, mathematics 2-3, social studies 4, history 4, science 2 (laboratory 2) and foreign language 1.

2006-2007 Annual costs. Tuition/fees (projected): $11,286. Per-credit charge: $230. Books/supplies: $2,100. Personal expenses: $1,300.

2005-2006 Financial aid. Need-based: 55% of total undergraduate aid awarded as scholarships/grants, 45% as loans/jobs. Need-based aid available for part-time students.

Application procedures. Admission: Priority date 5/30; deadline 6/30 (receipt date). $35 fee, may be waived for applicants with need. Application may be submitted online. Admission notification on a rolling basis. Must reply by May 1 or within 2 week(s) if notified thereafter. **Financial aid:** No deadline. FAFSA required. Applicants notified on a rolling basis starting 1/1; must reply within 2 week(s) of notification.

Academics. Special study options: Combined bachelor's/graduate degree, distance learning, liberal arts/career combination, weekend college. Articulation agreements with upper division BSN colleges. License preparation in nursing. **Credit/placement by examination:** CLEP. **Support services:** Remedial instruction, study skills assistance, tutoring.

Majors. Health: Nursing (RN).

Computing on campus. 20 workstations in library, computer center. Commuter students can connect to campus network. Online library, repair service available.

Student life. Freshman orientation: Mandatory. Preregistration for classes offered. Held week prior to classes. **Policies:** Freshmen permitted cars on campus. **Housing:** Option of staying on campus at affiliated college available. **Activities:** Student government.

Student services. Alcohol/substance abuse counseling, campus ministries, financial aid counseling, health services, on-campus daycare. **Transfer:** Special adviser, orientation, pre-admission transcript evaluation for new students. Transfer adviser for students transferring to 4-year colleges.

Contact. E-mail: conadmis@stemc.org
Phone: (315) 798-88189 Fax: (315) 798-8271
Donna Ernst, Recruitment Director, St. Elizabeth College of Nursing, 2215 Genesee Street, Utica, NY 13501

St. Joseph's College of Nursing

Syracuse, New York
www.sjhsyr.org/nursing **CB code: 2825**

- Private 2-year nursing college affiliated with Roman Catholic Church
- Commuter campus in small city
- SAT or ACT (ACT writing optional), application essay, interview required

General. Founded in 1898. Practice in a variety of settings including medical/surgical, maternity, pediatrics, oncology, psychiatry, ambulatory care clinics, and home care and outpatient experiences. **Enrollment:** 271 degree-seeking undergraduates. **Degrees:** 104 associate awarded. **Calendar:** Semester, limited summer session. **Full-time faculty:** 30 total. **Part-time faculty:** 15 total. **Special facilities:** Cardiovascular lab, electro-physiology lab, home care, outpatient services, 462-bed teaching hospital.

Student profile. Among degree-seeking undergraduates, 23 enrolled as first-time, first-year students, 107 transferred in from other institutions.

African American:	5%	**Native American:**	1%
Asian American:	2%	**25 or older:**	49%
Hispanic American:	1%	**Live on campus:**	30%

Transfer out. Colleges most students transferred to 2005: SUNY Health Science Center, SUNY Utica/Rome.

Basis for selection. High school record, SAT/ACT test scores or pre-entrance examination, and personal interview very important. **Adult students:** SAT/ACT scores not required.

High school preparation. 13 units required. Required and recommended units include English 4, mathematics 2-3, social studies 4 and science 3-4. Science units must be in biology and chemistry; advanced biology and/or physics recommended.

2005-2006 Annual costs. Tuition/fees: $8,516. Per-credit charge: $275. Room only: $3,200. Books/supplies: $1,000. Personal expenses: $1,272.

Financial aid. All financial aid based on need. Need-based aid available for part-time students.

Application procedures. Admission: No deadline. $35 fee, may be waived for applicants with need. Application must be submitted on paper. Admission notification on a rolling basis. **Financial aid:** Priority date 4/15; no closing date. FAFSA required. Applicants notified on a rolling basis starting 6/15.

Academics. Weekend program meets every other Friday, Saturday and Sunday year round for 2 years. **Special study options:** Liberal arts/career combination, weekend college. License preparation in nursing. **Credit/placement by examination:** AP, CLEP. **Support services:** Reduced course load, study skills assistance, tutoring.

Majors. Health: Nursing (RN).

Computing on campus. 31 workstations in dormitories, library, computer center. Online library, helpline available.

Student life. Freshman orientation: Mandatory. Preregistration for classes offered. 5 days one week prior to opening day. **Policies:** Freshmen permitted cars on campus. **Housing:** Guaranteed on-campus for all undergraduates. Coed dorms, substance-free housing available. **Activities:** Student government.

Student services. Adult student services, alcohol/substance abuse counseling, campus ministries, career counseling, student employment services, health services, personal counseling, placement for graduates. **Physically disabled:** Services for visually, speech, hearing impaired. **Transfer:** Special adviser, orientation, pre-admission transcript evaluation for new students. Transfer adviser, college fairs on campus for students transferring to 4-year colleges.

Contact. E-mail: joanne.kiggins@sjhsyr.org
Phone: (315) 448-5040 Fax: (315) 448-5745
JoAnne Kiggins, Coordinator, Admissions/Recruitment, St. Joseph's College of Nursing, 206 Prospect Avenue, Syracuse, NY 13203

St. Vincent Catholic Medical Centers

Fresh Meadows, New York
CB code: 3400

- Private 2-year nursing college affiliated with Roman Catholic Church
- Commuter campus in very large city
- Application essay, interview required

General. Founded in 1969. **Enrollment:** 100 degree-seeking undergraduates. **Degrees:** 54 associate awarded. **Location:** 10 miles from Manhattan. **Calendar:** Semester. **Full-time faculty:** 10 total.

Basis for selection. Test scores, high school achievement, interview, and personal essay considered. National League for Nursing test required.

High school preparation. 11 units required. Required units include English 4, mathematics 2, social studies 3 and science 2.

2005-2006 Annual costs. Tuition/fees: $5,892. Per-credit charge: $220. Second year cost: $5862. Books/supplies: $900. Personal expenses: $2,400.

Application procedures. Admission: Closing date 2/15. $35 fee. Admission notification on a rolling basis. Must reply by May 1 or within 3 week(s) if notified thereafter. **Financial aid:** No deadline. FAFSA required. Applicants notified on a rolling basis; must reply within 2 week(s) of notification.

Academics. Special study options: License preparation in nursing. **Credit/placement by examination:** CLEP.

Majors. Health: Nursing (RN).

Student services. Health services, personal counseling.

Contact. Phone: (718) 357-0500 ext. 131 Fax: (718) 357-4683
Nancy Wolinski, Director, Office of Enrollment Management, St. Vincent Catholic Medical Centers, 175-05 Horace Harding Expressway, Fresh Meadows, NY 11356

Schenectady County Community College

Schenectady, New York
www.sunysccc.edu **CB code: 2879**

- Public 2-year community college
- Commuter campus in small city

General. Founded in 1968. Regionally accredited. SUNY institution. **Enrollment:** 3,046 degree-seeking undergraduates. **Degrees:** 47 associate awarded. **ROTC:** Air Force. **Location:** 150 miles from New York City, 20 miles from Albany. **Calendar:** Semester, limited summer session. **Full-time faculty:** 69 total. **Part-time faculty:** 150 total. **Special facilities:** Child care center.

Student profile.

Out-of-state:	1%	**25 or older:**	43%

Transfer out. Colleges most students transferred to 2005: SUNY Albany, College of Saint Rose, Siena College, Sage College of Albany.

Basis for selection. Open admission, but selective for some programs. Special requirements for music program. Interview recommended for all; audition required for music, music merchandising programs. **Home-schooled:** Letter from school district superintendent where they reside attesting to home school equivalency of public system.

High school preparation. Certain programs have specific mathematics and science prerequisites.

2005-2006 Annual costs. Tuition/fees: $2,868; $5,618 out-of-state. Per-credit charge: $108 in-state; $216 out-of-state. Books/supplies: $800. Personal expenses: $900.

2004-2005 Financial aid. All financial aid based on need. 56% of total undergraduate aid awarded as scholarships/grants, 44% as loans/jobs. Need-based aid available for part-time students. Work study available for part-time students.

Application procedures. Admission: No deadline. No application fee. Application may be submitted online. Admission notification on a rolling basis. **Financial aid:** Priority date 5/1; no closing date. FAFSA required. Applicants notified on a rolling basis starting 4/15; must reply by 8/31.

Academics. 25-32 Credit hours required in major depending on program. 60-66 Credit hours required for graduation depending on program. **Special study options:** Cooperative education, cross-registration, distance learning, dual enrollment of high school students, ESL, honors, independent study, internships, liberal arts/career combination, teacher certification program. License preparation in aviation. **Credit/placement by examination:** AP, CLEP, institutional tests. 30 credit hours maximum toward associate degree. **Support services:** GED preparation and test center, learning center, reduced course load, remedial instruction, tutoring.

Majors. **Business:** General, tourism promotion, travel services. **Computer sciences:** General, computer science, programming. **Education:** Early childhood, multi-level teacher. **Engineering technology:** Telecommunications. **Interdisciplinary:** Accounting/computer science, math/computer science. **Liberal arts:** Arts/sciences. **Personal/culinary services:** Food service, restaurant/catering. **Physical sciences:** General. **Protective services:** Criminal justice, security services. **Social sciences:** General. **Transportation:** Aviation, aviation management.

Computing on campus. 400 workstations in library, computer center, student center.

Student life. **Freshman orientation:** Available. Preregistration for classes offered. **Policies:** Freshmen permitted cars on campus. **Activities:** Bands, choral groups, drama, literary magazine, music ensembles, student government, Black and Latino Student Alliance, Christian Fellowship, human services club, Disabled Student Awareness Committee, culinary club.

Athletics. NJCAA. **Intercollegiate:** Baseball M, basketball, bowling, softball W. **Team name:** The Royals.

Student services. Adult student services, alcohol/substance abuse counseling, career counseling, services for economically disadvantaged, student employment services, financial aid counseling, minority student services, on-campus daycare, personal counseling, placement for graduates, veterans' counselor. **Physically disabled:** Services for visually, speech, hearing impaired. **Transfer:** Special adviser, orientation for new students. Transfer adviser, college fairs on campus for students transferring to 4-year colleges.

Contact. E-mail: sampsondg@gw.sunysccc.edu
Phone: (518) 381-1366 Fax: (518) 346-0379
David Sampson, Director of Admissions, Schenectady County Community College, 78 Washington Avenue, Schenectady, NY 12305

State University of New York College of Agriculture and Technology at Cobleskill

Cobleskill, New York
www.cobleskill.edu **CB code: 2524**

- Public 2-year agricultural and technical college
- Residential campus in small town
- SAT or ACT (ACT writing recommended) required

General. Founded in 1911. Regionally accredited. 4-year Bachelor of Technology degrees in agriculture and information technology, Bachelor of Business administration offered in Technology Management and Bachelor of Science degree in early childhood also offered. **Enrollment:** 2,511 degree-seeking undergraduates. **Degrees:** 153 bachelor's, 292 associate awarded. **Location:** 35 miles from Albany, 39 miles from Oneonta. **Calendar:** Semester, limited summer session. **Full-time faculty:** 113 total; 18% have terminal degrees, 35% women. **Part-time faculty:** 36 total; 39% women. **Class size:** 53% < 20, 39% 20-39, 3% 40-49, 5% 50-99, less than 1% >100. **Special facilities:** Arboretum, 14 greenhouses, livestock pavilion, 350-acre farm, modern chemical and biological technology laboratories, student-operated restaurant, fish hatchery, ski area. **Partnerships:** Formal partnership with John Deere Company for agricultural engineering.

Student profile. Among degree-seeking undergraduates, 884 enrolled as first-time, first-year students, 1,179 transferred in from other institutions.

Part-time:	3%	**25 or older:**	11%
Out-of-state:	12%	**Live on campus:**	64%
Women:	46%		

Transfer out. **Colleges most students transferred to 2005:** Cornell University, College of St. Rose, SUNY Albany, SUNY Oneonta, SUNY Plattsburgh.

Basis for selection. Strength of high school curriculum most important. GPA, SAT/ACT scores considered. Letters of recommendation, interview recommended. SAT or ACT scores optional for associates degree students. **Homeschooled:** Transcript of courses and grades required. Acceptable GED score required.

High school preparation. Required and recommended units include English 4, mathematics 1-3, social studies 3, science 1-3 (laboratory 2) and academic electives 12. Additional recommendations for some programs.

2005-2006 Annual costs. Tuition/fees: $5,370; $11,630 out-of-state. Per-credit charge: $181 in-state; $442 out-of-state. Room/board: $7,670. Books/supplies: $1,000. Personal expenses: $900.

2004-2005 Financial aid. **Need-based:** 914 full-time freshmen applied for aid; 734 were judged to have need; 723 of these received aid. Average need met was 59%. Average scholarship/grant was $4,515; average loan $2,794. 43% of total undergraduate aid awarded as scholarships/grants, 57% as loans/jobs. Work study available nights and weekends. **Non-need-based:** Awarded to 125 full-time undergraduates, including 80 freshmen. Scholarships awarded for academics, alumni affiliation, leadership, state residency.

Application procedures. **Admission:** Priority date 5/1; no deadline. $40 fee, may be waived for applicants with need. Application must be submitted on paper. Admission notification on a rolling basis beginning on or about 11/1. Must reply by May 1 or within 4 week(s) if notified thereafter. **Financial aid:** Closing date 3/15. FAFSA, CSS PROFILE required. Applicants notified by 4/15; must reply within 2 week(s) of notification.

Academics. Personal or laptop computer required of students in some programs. Adult Study Center offered. **Special study options:** Cooperative education, distance learning, ESL, honors, independent study, internships, liberal arts/career combination, study abroad, weekend college. **Credit/placement by examination:** AP, CLEP, institutional tests. 33 credit hours maximum toward associate degree, 60 toward bachelor's. **Support services:** Learning center, pre-admission summer program, reduced course load, remedial instruction, study skills assistance, tutoring, writing center.

Majors. **Agriculture:** General, agronomy, animal sciences, business, crop production, dairy, dairy husbandry, equestrian studies, greenhouse operations, horticultural science, horticulture, landscaping, nursery operations, ornamental horticulture, plant sciences, power machinery, products processing, soil science, turf management. **Business:** General, accounting, business admin, finance, hospitality admin, hospitality/recreation, office management, tourism promotion, tourism/travel. **Computer sciences:** General, applications programming, computer science, data processing, information systems, networking, programming, systems analysis. **Conservation:** General, environmental studies, fisheries, wildlife. **Education:** Early childhood. **Engineering:** Agricultural. **Family/consumer sciences:** Child care. **Health:** Clinical lab assistant. **Interdisciplinary:** Biological/physical sciences, natural sciences. **Liberal arts:** Arts/sciences. **Math:** General. **Mechanic/repair:** Diesel. **Parks/recreation:** Facilities management. **Personal/culinary services:** Chef training, culinary arts, institutional food service, restaurant/catering. **Psychology:** General. **Science technology:** Biological. **Social sciences:** General. **Visual/performing arts:** Commercial/advertising art.

Most popular majors. Agriculture 18%, business/marketing 16%, computer/information sciences 6%, family/consumer sciences 17%, liberal arts 22%.

Computing on campus. 260 workstations in dormitories, library, computer center, student center. Dormitories wired for high-speed internet access and linked to campus network. Commuter students can connect to campus network. Online course registration, online library, helpline, repair service, student web hosting, wireless network available.

Student life. **Freshman orientation:** Mandatory. Preregistration for classes offered. Two-day academic and social program held first week of classes. **Policies:** Freshmen permitted cars on campus. **Housing:** Guaranteed on-campus for freshmen. Coed dorms, single-sex dorms, substance-free housing available. $55 fully refundable deposit. **Activities:** Jazz band, choral groups, drama, student government, student newspaper, Phi Theta Kappa, activities team, community club, Student Christian Fellowship, student medical response team, X-Pressions of Kolor, black and Latino alliance.

Athletics. NJCAA. **Intercollegiate:** Baseball M, basketball, cross-country, diving, equestrian, golf, lacrosse M, soccer, softball W, swimming, tennis, track and field, volleyball W, wrestling M. **Intramural:** Basketball, bowling, cheerleading, football (non-tackle), skiing, soccer, softball, swimming, tennis, volleyball. **Team name:** Tigers.

Student services. Adult student services, alcohol/substance abuse counseling, campus ministries, career counseling, services for economically disadvantaged, student employment services, financial aid counseling, health services, minority student services, on-campus daycare, personal counseling, placement for graduates, veterans' counselor. **Physically disabled:** Services for visually, speech, hearing impaired. **Learning disabled:** Comprehensive services available. **Transfer:** Special adviser, orientation for new students. Transfer adviser, college fairs on campus for students transferring to 4-year colleges.

Contact. E-mail: admissions@cobleskill.edu
Phone: (518) 255-5525 Toll-free number: (800) 295-8988
Fax: (518) 255-6769
Christopher Tacea, Director of Admissions and Marketing, State University of New York College of Agriculture and Technology at Cobleskill, Cobleskill, NY 12043

State University of New York College of Agriculture and Technology at Morrisville

Morrisville, New York
www.morrisville.edu **CB code: 2527**

- Public 2-year junior and technical college
- Residential campus in small town

General. Founded in 1908. Regionally accredited. Norwich and Oneida evening extension centers offer liberal arts and some technical courses. **Enrollment:** 3,009 degree-seeking undergraduates; 289 non-degree-seeking students. **Degrees:** 59 bachelor's, 577 associate awarded. **ROTC:** Army. **Location:** 30 miles from Syracuse and Utica. **Calendar:** Semester, limited summer session. **Full-time faculty:** 127 total; 20% have terminal degrees, 9% minority, 42% women. **Part-time faculty:** 82 total; 12% have terminal degrees, 2% minority, 45% women. **Special facilities:** Horse arena, race track, dairy farm, aquaculture (fish rearing) ponds, observatory, wildlife museum, ice arena, student-operated flower shop.

Student profile. Among degree-seeking undergraduates, 50% enrolled in a transfer program, 1,116 enrolled as first-time, first-year students, 188 transferred in from other institutions.

Part-time:	13%	**25 or older:**	22%
Out-of-state:	7%	**Live on campus:**	55%
Women:	43%		

Transfer out. Colleges most students transferred to 2005: Cornell, Rochester Institute of Technology, Clarkson, State University of New York.

Basis for selection. High school record most important. SAT required for bachelor's degree applicants, SAT or ACT required for students seeking academic scholarship. Essays or interviews not required, but students welcome to submit essay or visit for interview. **Adult students:** Entrance exam policies same as for first-time freshmen. **Homeschooled:** State high school equivalency certificate required. GED required for students without supporting documentation.

High school preparation. Recommended units include English 4, mathematics 3, social studies 4 and science 4. Requirements depend on program. Mathematics and science preparation important for technical majors.

2005-2006 Annual costs. Tuition/fees: $5,215; $11,475 out-of-state. Per-credit charge: $181 in-state; $442 out-of-state. Out-of-state associate degree students pay $7,210 tuition. Room/board: $7,070. Books/supplies: $800. Personal expenses: $800.

2005-2006 Financial aid. Need-based: 989 full-time freshmen applied for aid; 872 were judged to have need; 867 of these received aid. Average need met was 15%. Average scholarship/grant was $4,439; average loan $2,510. 28% of total undergraduate aid awarded as scholarships/grants, 72% as loans/jobs. Need-based aid available for part-time students. Work study available nights, weekends and for part-time students. **Non-need-based:** Awarded to 366 full-time undergraduates, including 181 freshmen. Scholarships awarded for academics.

Application procedures. Admission: Priority date 11/1; no deadline. $40 fee, may be waived for applicants with need. Application may be submitted online. Admission notification on a rolling basis beginning on or about 11/1. Housing deposit refundable only through June 1. **Financial aid:** Priority date 2/1; no closing date. FAFSA required. Applicants notified on a rolling basis starting 3/1.

Academics. Think-Pad university in partnership with IBM. **Special study options:** Distance learning, dual enrollment of high school students, ESL, honors, internships, liberal arts/career combination, student-designed major, weekend college. Joint program with SUNY Forest Technology School at Wanakena, 2-2 transfer program with SUNY College of Environmental Science and Forestry. Bachelor's degree programs available on campus. License preparation in nursing. **Credit/placement by examination:** AP, CLEP, institutional tests. 21 credit hours maximum toward associate degree. **Support services:** Learning center, pre-admission summer program, reduced course load, remedial instruction, study skills assistance, tutoring.

Majors. Agriculture: General, agribusiness operations, animal husbandry, animal sciences, aquaculture, business, business technology, dairy, dairy husbandry, equestrian studies, equine science, equipment technology, farm/ranch, floriculture, greenhouse operations, horticultural science, horticulture, landscaping, livestock, mechanization, nursery operations, ornamental horticulture, power machinery. **Architecture:** Landscape, technology. **Biology:** General, conservation, marine. **Business:** General, accounting, accounting technology, accounting/business management, accounting/finance, administrative services, business admin, office management, office technology, restaurant/food services, tourism promotion, tourism/travel, travel services. **Communications:** Journalism. **Computer sciences:** General, applications programming, computer science, information technology, programming. **Conservation:** General, environmental science, environmental studies, fisheries, forest management, forest sciences, forest technology, forestry, management/policy, wood science. **Construction:** General, building inspection, carpentry, maintenance. **Engineering:** General, architectural, computer, computer hardware, construction, electrical, mechanics, polymer, science, software. **Engineering technology:** General, architectural, architectural drafting, automotive, CAD/CADD, computer hardware, computer systems, construction, electrical, manufacturing, mechanical, plastics. **English:** English lit, technical writing. **Family/consumer sciences:** Food/nutrition. **Health:** Clinical lab technology, massage therapy, nursing (RN), prenursing. **Interdisciplinary:** Nutrition sciences. **Liberal arts:** Arts/sciences, humanities. **Math:** General. **Mechanic/repair:** Auto body, automotive, diesel, electronics/electrical, heavy equipment. **Parks/recreation:** Exercise sciences, facilities management, health/fitness, sports admin. **Personal/culinary services:** Food service. **Physical sciences:** Chemistry, physics. **Production:** Furniture, woodworking. **Social sciences:** General.

Computing on campus. 120 workstations in dormitories, library, computer center, student center. Dormitories linked to campus network. Commuter students can connect to campus network. Helpline, repair service, wireless network available.

Student life. Freshman orientation: Mandatory. **Policies:** Freshmen permitted cars on campus. **Housing:** Guaranteed on-campus for all undergraduates. Coed dorms, substance-free housing available. $50 deposit, deadline 5/1. Special interest housing available. **Activities:** Bands, choral groups, drama, literary magazine, music ensembles, musical theater, radio station, student government, student newspaper, Newman Society, Latin American student organization, African student union/Black alliance.

Athletics. NCAA. **Intercollegiate:** Basketball, diving, equestrian, field hockey W, football (tackle) M, ice hockey M, lacrosse, rifle, skiing, soccer, softball W, swimming, volleyball W, wrestling M. **Intramural:** Archery, badminton, basketball, diving, equestrian, golf, handball, racquetball, soccer, swimming, table tennis, tennis, volleyball, wrestling M. **Team name:** Mustangs.

Student services. Adult student services, alcohol/substance abuse counseling, campus ministries, career counseling, services for economically disadvantaged, student employment services, financial aid counseling, health services, minority student services, on-campus daycare, personal counseling, placement for graduates, veterans' counselor. **Physically disabled:** Services for visually, speech, hearing impaired. **Transfer:** Special adviser, orientation, pre-admission transcript evaluation for new students. Transfer center, transfer adviser, college fairs on campus for students transferring to 4-year colleges.

Contact. E-mail: admissions@morrisville.edu
Phone: (315) 684-6046 Toll-free number: (800) 258-0111
Fax: (315) 684-6427
Tim Williams, Dean of Enrollment Management, State University of New York College of Agriculture and Technology at Morrisville, PO Box 901, Morrisville, NY 13408-0901

State University of New York College of Technology at Alfred

Alfred, New York
www.alfredstate.edu **CB code: 2522**

- Public 2-year agricultural, liberal arts and technical college
- Residential campus in rural community

General. Founded in 1908. Regionally accredited. 4-year bachelor programs in business and engineering-related technologies available. Vocational campus located in Wellsville. **Enrollment:** 3,184 degree-seeking undergraduates. **Degrees:** 155 bachelor's, 748 associate awarded. **ROTC:** Army. **Location:** 75 miles from Rochester, 90 miles from Buffalo. **Calendar:** Semester, limited summer session. **Full-time faculty:** 148 total. **Part-time faculty:** 43 total. **Class size:** 42% < 20, 52% 20-39, 4% 40-49, 2% 50-99, less than 1% >100. **Special facilities:** 750-acre dairy farm.

Student profile. Among degree-seeking undergraduates, 24% enrolled in a vocational program, 1,118 enrolled as first-time, first-year students.

Part-time:	5%	**25 or older:**	23%
Out-of-state:	7%	**Live on campus:**	80%
Women:	33%		

Transfer out. 93% of students enrolled in the transfer program go on to 4-year colleges.

Basis for selection. School achievement record most important, test scores, class rank, school and community service considered. Portfolio required for computer art and design program. Letters of recommendation and personal essay recommended but not required. SAT or ACT recommended. SAT or ACT required for students applying for bechelor's degree programs. Essay, interview recommended.

High school preparation. Recommended units include English 4, mathematics 4, social studies 4 and science 4. Course requirements vary depending on program.

2005-2006 Annual costs. Tuition/fees: $5,343; $8,203 out-of-state. Per-credit charge: $181 in-state; $300 out-of-state. Tuition for bachelor's degree: full-time out-of-state tuition $10,610; per-credit-hour $442 out-of-state. Room/board: $7,230. Books/supplies: $1,000. Personal expenses: $700.

2004-2005 Financial aid. Need-based: 59% of total undergraduate aid awarded as scholarships/grants, 41% as loans/jobs. Need-based aid available for part-time students. Work study available nights, weekends and for part-time students. **Non-need-based:** Scholarships awarded for academics, alumni affiliation, job skills, minority status.

Application procedures. Admission: Priority date 11/1; no deadline. $40 fee, may be waived for applicants with need. Application may be submitted online. Admission notification on a rolling basis beginning on or about 11/1. Must reply by May 1 or within 4 week(s) if notified thereafter. Early application recommended for vocational studies. **Financial aid:** Priority date 3/1; no closing date. FAFSA required. Applicants notified on a rolling basis starting 3/1; must reply within 3 week(s) of notification.

Academics. Bachelor of science degree offered in several engineering technology and business majors. **Special study options:** Cooperative education, cross-registration, distance learning, honors, independent study, internships, liberal arts/career combination, student-designed major, study abroad. Bachelor's degree programs available on campus. License preparation in nursing, real estate. **Credit/placement by examination:** AP, CLEP, institutional tests. 30 credit hours maximum toward associate degree. **Support services:** Learning center, reduced course load, remedial instruction, study skills assistance, tutoring, writing center.

Majors. Agriculture: Agronomy, animal sciences, business, dairy, landscaping. **Architecture:** Landscape. **Biology:** General. **Business:** Accounting, administrative services, business admin, entrepreneurial studies, finance, financial planning, management information systems, marketing, office technology. **Communications technology:** Graphics. **Computer sciences:** General, computer graphics, computer science, data processing. **Conservation:** General. **Construction:** Carpentry, maintenance, masonry, pipefitting. **Engineering:** General, computer, electrical, manufacturing, mechanical, science, surveying. **Engineering technology:** Architectural, civil, construction, drafting, electrical, robotics, surveying. **Health:** Clinical lab technology, medical assistant, medical records technology, medical transcription, nursing (RN), veterinary technology/assistant. **Interdisciplinary:** Biological/physical sciences. **Legal studies:** Court reporting. **Liberal arts:** Arts/sciences. **Math:** General. **Mechanic/repair:** General, auto body, automotive, diesel, electronics/electrical, heating/ac/refrig. **Parks/recreation:** Sports admin. **Personal/culinary services:** Culinary arts. **Physical sciences:** Chemistry. **Production:** Welding. **Public administration:** Human services. **Science technology:** Biological. **Social sciences:** General. **Visual/performing arts:** Graphic design, interior design.

Most popular majors. Agriculture 7%, architecture 6%, biological/life sciences 6%, business/marketing 10%, computer/information sciences 13%, engineering/engineering technologies 6%, social sciences 7%, trade and industry 30%.

Computing on campus. 1,600 workstations in dormitories, library, computer center. Dormitories wired for high-speed internet access and linked to campus network. Commuter students can connect to campus network. Online course registration, online library, helpline, repair service, student web hosting, wireless network available.

Student life. Freshman orientation: Mandatory, $60 fee. Preregistration for classes offered. **Policies:** Freshmen permitted cars on campus. **Housing:** Guaranteed on-campus for all undergraduates. Coed dorms, fraternity/sorority housing, substance-free housing available. $50 deposit. Smoking, nonsmoking, freshman, computerized, quiet study, wellness, over 21, over 24, single-room options. **Activities:** Bands, choral groups, drama, literary magazine, music ensembles, musical theater, radio station, student government, student newspaper, symphony orchestra, environmental club, community action group, Alfred/Wellsville activities council, Black student union, international club, women in nontraditional studies, rescue and response team, peer education network, outdoor recreation club.

Athletics. NJCAA. **Intercollegiate:** Baseball M, basketball, cheerleading, cross-country, football (tackle) M, lacrosse M, soccer, softball W, swimming, track and field, volleyball W, wrestling M. **Intramural:** Baseball M, basketball, bowling, golf, lacrosse, rifle, soccer, softball, table tennis, tennis, volleyball. **Team name:** Pioneers.

Student services. Adult student services, alcohol/substance abuse counseling, campus ministries, career counseling, student employment services, financial aid counseling, health services, minority student services, personal counseling, placement for graduates, veterans' counselor. **Physically disabled:** Services for visually, hearing impaired. **Transfer:** Special adviser, orientation for new students. Transfer center, transfer adviser, college fairs on campus for students transferring to 4-year colleges.

Contact. E-mail: admissions@alfredstate.edu
Phone: (607) 587-4215 Toll-free number: (800) 425-3733
Fax: (607) 587-4299
Deborah Goodrich, Director of Admissions, State University of New York College of Technology at Alfred, Huntington Administration Building, Alfred, NY 14802-1196

State University of New York College of Technology at Canton

Canton, New York
www.canton.edu **CB code: 2523**

- Public 2-year technical college
- Residential campus in small town

General. Founded in 1906. Regionally accredited. **Enrollment:** 2,246 degree-seeking undergraduates; 235 non-degree-seeking students. **Degrees:** 38 bachelor's, 487 associate awarded. **ROTC:** Army, Air Force. **Location:** 135 miles from Syracuse, 120 miles from Montreal, Canada. **Calendar:** Semester, limited summer session. **Full-time faculty:** 86 total; 27% have terminal degrees, 7% minority, 45% women. **Part-time faculty:** 55 total; 9% minority, 42% women. **Class size:** 36% < 20, 45% 20-39, 14% 40-49, 4% 50-99, less than 1% >100. **Special facilities:** Cross-country trails.

Student profile. Among degree-seeking undergraduates, 816 enrolled as first-time, first-year students.

Part-time:	7%	**Hispanic American:**	3%
Out-of-state:	3%	**Native American:**	2%
Women:	51%	**International:**	1%
African American:	8%	**25 or older:**	22%
Asian American:	1%	**Live on campus:**	43%

Transfer out. Colleges most students transferred to 2005: SUNY College at Potsdam, Clarkson University, SUNY Institute of Technology at Utica/Rome, Rochester Institute of Technology, SUNY College at Plattsburgh.

Basis for selection. High school record most important. Admission requirements vary according to program of study. COMPASS required for some. SAT or ACT recommended. SAT or ACT required of bachelor degree program applicants. Interview recommended. **Adult students:** Entrance exam policies same as for first-time freshmen. **Homeschooled:** Applicants must have diploma from accredited high school or have taken the GED. **Learning Disabled:** Students with documented needs should request accommodations through coordinator of Accommodative Services.

High school preparation. 12 units recommended. Recommended units include English 4, mathematics 2, social studies 4 and science 2. Required high school courses vary with major. Engineering science technologies, allied health, and life sciences stress mathematics and science; business technologies stress algebra.

2005-2006 Annual costs. Tuition/fees: $5,370; $8,230 out-of-state. Per-credit charge: $181 in-state; $300 out-of-state. Out-of-state tuition for bachelor's degree program: $10,610; $442 per-credit-hour. Room/board: $7,760. Books/supplies: $800. Personal expenses: $800.

Financial aid. Need-based: Need-based aid available for part-time students.

Application procedures. Admission: Priority date 3/1; no deadline. $40 fee, may be waived for applicants with need. Application may be submitted online. Admission notification on a rolling basis beginning on or about 12/1. Some enrolled freshmen must complete COMPASS placement test on campus before classes begin. Students notified of testing dates and whether they need COMPASS. **Financial aid:** Priority date 3/15; no closing date. FAFSA required. Applicants notified on a rolling basis starting 2/1; must reply within 4 week(s) of notification.

Academics. Special study options: Cross-registration, distance learning, dual enrollment of high school students, independent study, internships, liberal arts/career combination, student-designed major. Criminal justice students can complete Police Academy during spring semester of senior year. Bachelor's degree programs available on campus. License preparation in nursing, physical therapy. **Credit/placement by examination:** AP, CLEP, institutional tests. 45 credit hours maximum toward associate degree. **Support services:** Learning center, reduced course load, remedial instruction, study skills assistance, tutoring, writing center.

Majors. Biology: General. **Business:** Accounting, administrative services, business admin. **Computer sciences:** General. **Education:** Early childhood. **Engineering:** Science. **Engineering technology:** Automotive, civil, construction, electrical, environmental, heat/ac/refrig, industrial, manufacturing, mechanical. **Health:** Nursing (RN), occupational therapy assistant, physical therapy assistant, veterinary technology/assistant. **Liberal arts:** Arts/sciences. **Mechanic/repair:** Automotive. **Personal/culinary services:** Embalming, mortuary science. **Protective services:** Criminal justice. **Psychology:** General. **Social sciences:** General.

Most popular majors. Business/marketing 16%, engineering/engineering technologies 13%, health sciences 23%, liberal arts 20%, security/protective services 15%.

Computing on campus. 300 workstations in dormitories, library, computer center, student center. Dormitories linked to campus network. Commuter students can connect to campus network. Helpline, wireless network available.

Student life. Freshman orientation: Mandatory, $60 fee. Preregistration for classes offered. 2-day orientation for resident students and 1-day for commuters. **Policies:** Freshmen permitted cars on campus. **Housing:** Guaranteed on-campus for freshmen. Coed dorms, special housing for disabled, fraternity/sorority housing available. $55 deposit. Pets allowed in dorm rooms. All full-time students must live in college housing unless requirement waived by Residence Life office. **Activities:** Choral groups, dance, drama, radio station, student government, student newspaper, Afro-Latin Society, Native American Society, Inter-Varsity Christian Fellowship.

Athletics. NJCAA. **Intercollegiate:** Basketball, football (tackle) M, ice hockey M, lacrosse M, soccer, softball W, volleyball W. **Intramural:** Basketball, golf, soccer, softball, tennis, volleyball. **Team name:** Northstars.

Student services. Adult student services, alcohol/substance abuse counseling, campus ministries, career counseling, services for economically disadvantaged, student employment services, financial aid counseling, health services, minority student services, personal counseling, placement for graduates, veterans' counselor. **Physically disabled:** Services for visually, speech, hearing impaired. **Learning disabled:** Comprehensive services available. **Transfer:** Special adviser, orientation for new students. Transfer adviser, college fairs on campus for students transferring to 4-year colleges.

Contact. E-mail: admissions@canton.edu
Phone: (315) 386-7123 Toll-free number: (800) 388-7123
Fax: (315) 386-7929
Jodi Revill, Director of Admissions, State University of New York College of Technology at Canton, 34 Cornell Drive, Canton, NY 13617-1098

State University of New York College of Technology at Delhi

Delhi, New York
www.delhi.edu **CB code: 2525**

- Public 2-year technical college
- Residential campus in small town

General. Founded in 1913. Regionally accredited. **Enrollment:** 2,483 degree-seeking undergraduates; 224 non-degree-seeking students. **Degrees:** 66 bachelor's, 476 associate awarded. **Location:** 70 miles from Albany and Binghamton. **Calendar:** Semester, limited summer session. **Full-time faculty:** 103 total; 28% have terminal degrees, 6% minority, 44% women. **Part-time faculty:** 54 total; 7% have terminal degrees, 4% minority, 56% women. **Special facilities:** Demonstration forest and arboretum, student-operated restaurant, veterinary science laboratory, golf course.

Student profile. Among degree-seeking undergraduates, 1,152 enrolled as first-time, first-year students, 221 transferred in from other institutions.

Part-time:	12%	**Hispanic American:**	6%
Out-of-state:	2%	**International:**	2%
Women:	44%	**25 or older:**	16%
African American:	11%	**Live on campus:**	66%
Asian American:	2%		

Basis for selection. Open admission, but selective for some programs. SAT or ACT recommended. Interview recommended. **Adult students:** Entrance exam policies same as for first-time freshmen. **Homeschooled:** Transcript of courses and grades, state high school equivalency certificate required.

High school preparation. 18 units recommended. Recommended units include English 4, mathematics 2, social studies 4, science 2 and foreign language 2. Requirements vary by program.

2005-2006 Annual costs. Tuition/fees: $5,319; $8,179 out-of-state. Per-credit charge: $181 in-state; $300 out-of-state. Out-of-state tuition for bachelor's program: $10,610; per-credit-hour $442. Room/board: $7,380. Books/supplies: $1,200. Personal expenses: $1,410.

2004-2005 Financial aid. Need-based: 64% of total undergraduate aid awarded as scholarships/grants, 36% as loans/jobs. Need-based aid available for part-time students.

Application procedures. Admission: No deadline. $40 fee, may be waived for applicants with need. Admission notification on a rolling basis beginning on or about 11/1. **Financial aid:** Priority date 2/15; no closing date. FAFSA required. Applicants notified on a rolling basis starting 3/1; must reply within 2 week(s) of notification.

Academics. Special study options: Distance learning, double major, dual enrollment of high school students, honors, independent study, internships, student-designed major, weekend college. Bachelor's degree programs available on campus. License preparation in nursing. **Credit/placement by examination:** CLEP, institutional tests. 30 credit hours maximum toward associate degree. **Support services:** Learning center, reduced course load, remedial instruction, study skills assistance, tutoring.

Majors. Agriculture: Animal sciences, horticultural science, horticulture, landscaping, ornamental horticulture, turf management. **Architecture:** Landscape, technology. **Business:** Accounting, administrative services, business admin, management information systems, tourism promotion, tourism/travel. **Construction:** Carpentry, electrician, masonry. **Education:** Physical. **Engineering:** Science. **Engineering technology:** Architectural, construction, drafting. **Family/consumer sciences:** Institutional food production. **Health:** Nursing (RN), veterinary technology/assistant. **Legal studies:** Legal secretary. **Liberal arts:** Arts/sciences. **Mechanic/repair:** Automotive, heating/ac/refrig. **Parks/recreation:** Facilities management. **Social sciences:** General.

Computing on campus. 230 workstations in library, computer center. Dormitories wired for high-speed internet access and linked to campus network. Commuter students can connect to campus network. Online course registration, helpline, student web hosting, wireless network available.

Student life. Freshman orientation: Available, $75 fee. **Policies:** Freshmen permitted cars on campus. **Housing:** Guaranteed on-campus for freshmen. Coed dorms, apartments, substance-free housing available. $100 fully refundable deposit. **Activities:** Drama, literary magazine, musical theater, radio station, student government, student newspaper, TV station, University Christian Movement, Third World Caucus-Students Caring for Students.

Athletics. NAIA, NJCAA. **Intercollegiate:** Basketball, cross-country, golf, lacrosse M, soccer, softball W, swimming, tennis, track and field, volleyball W, wrestling M. **Intramural:** Badminton, baseball M, basketball, bowling, cross-country, equestrian, golf, handball, racquetball, skiing, soccer, softball, swimming, table tennis, tennis, volleyball, wrestling M. **Team name:** Broncos.

Student services. Adult student services, career counseling, student employment services, health services, on-campus daycare, personal counseling, placement for graduates, veterans' counselor. **Physically disabled:** Services for visually, hearing impaired. **Transfer:** Special adviser, orientation for new students. Transfer adviser, college fairs on campus for students transferring to 4-year colleges.

Contact. E-mail: enroll@delhi.edu
Phone: (607) 746-4550 Toll-free number: (800) 963-3544
Fax: (607) 746-4104
Robert Mazzei, Director of Admissions, State University of New York College of Technology at Delhi, 2 Main Street, Delhi, NY 13753-1190

Suffolk County Community College

Selden, New York **CB member**
www.sunysuffolk.edu **CB code: 2827**

- Public 2-year community college
- Commuter campus in large town

General. Founded in 1959. Regionally accredited. 3 campuses in Suffolk County: Brentwood, Selden, Riverhead. **Enrollment:** 21,180 degree-seeking undergraduates. **Degrees:** 2,576 associate awarded. **Location:** 60 miles from New York City. **Calendar:** Semester, extensive summer session.

Full-time faculty: 308 total. **Part-time faculty:** 854 total. **Special facilities:** Planetarium. **Partnerships:** Formal partnership with Computer Associates.

Student profile.

Out-of-state:	2%	**25 or older:**	51%

Transfer out. Colleges most students transferred to 2005: SUNY Stony Brook, Hofstra University, St. Joseph's College, C.W. Post, Dowling College.

Basis for selection. Open admission, but selective for some programs. Admission to some programs based on high school record. Admission tests may be used for admission or placement in certain programs in conjunction with high school record. Portfolio required for visual arts program; interview recommended for broadcast telecommunications, fine arts, health career, and paralegal assistant programs. Audition recommended for performing arts programs. **Homeschooled:** Must be certified by State Education Department.

High school preparation. Special course requirements vary by program.

2005-2006 Annual costs. Tuition/fees: $3,326; $6,416 out-of-state. Per-credit charge: $129 in-state; $258 out-of-state. Books/supplies: $550. Personal expenses: $1,048.

2004-2005 Financial aid. Need-based: 83% of total undergraduate aid awarded as scholarships/grants, 17% as loans/jobs. Need-based aid available for part-time students. **Non-need-based:** Scholarships awarded for academics, minority status, state residency.

Application procedures. Admission: No deadline. $35 fee, may be waived for applicants with need. Application may be submitted online. Admission notification on a rolling basis. Must reply by May 1 or within 2 week(s) if notified thereafter. **Financial aid:** Priority date 4/15, closing date 6/1. FAFSA required. Applicants notified on a rolling basis starting 5/15; must reply within 2 week(s) of notification.

Academics. Special study options: Cooperative education, distance learning, dual enrollment of high school students, ESL, honors, independent study, internships. Joint admissions with other SUNY units and private institutions. License preparation in nursing, real estate. **Credit/placement by examination:** AP, CLEP, IB, institutional tests. 30 credit hours maximum toward associate degree. **Support services:** GED preparation, learning center, reduced course load, remedial instruction, tutoring, writing center.

Majors. Agriculture: Horticulture, landscaping, ornamental horticulture. **Architecture:** Environmental design, interior. **Area/ethnic studies:** Women's. **Biology:** General, biotechnology. **Business:** General, accounting, administrative services, business admin, finance, human resources, insurance, management science, marketing, office management, office technology, real estate, sales/distribution. **Communications:** General, broadcast journalism. **Communications technology:** General. **Computer sciences:** General, computer graphics, computer science, information systems, information technology, webmaster. **Conservation:** Environmental science, environmental studies. **Construction:** Maintenance. **Education:** Early childhood, secondary. **Engineering:** Electrical, science. **Engineering technology:** Architectural, construction, drafting, electrical, heat/ac/refrig. **Family/consumer sciences:** Food/nutrition. **Foreign languages:** Sign language interpretation. **Health:** Medical assistant, nursing (RN), occupational therapy assistant, optician, physical therapy assistant, substance abuse counseling, veterinary technology/assistant. **History:** General. **Legal studies:** Paralegal. **Liberal arts:** Arts/sciences. **Math:** General. **Mechanic/repair:** Automotive. **Parks/recreation:** General, health/fitness. **Personal/culinary services:** Culinary arts. **Physical sciences:** Astronomy, chemistry, geology, meteorology, physics, planetary. **Protective services:** Firefighting. **Psychology:** General. **Public administration:** Community org/advocacy, human services. **Social sciences:** General, economics, political science. **Visual/performing arts:** Commercial/advertising art, dramatic, interior design, studio arts, theater design.

Computing on campus. 1,785 workstations in library, computer center, student center. Commuter students can connect to campus network. Online course registration, helpline available.

Student life. Freshman orientation: Mandatory. Preregistration for classes offered. **Activities:** Bands, choral groups, drama, literary magazine, music ensembles, musical theater, radio station, student government, student newspaper, over 60 clubs available.

Athletics. NJCAA. **Intercollegiate:** Baseball M, basketball, bowling M, cross-country, golf M, lacrosse M, soccer M, softball, tennis, track and field, triathlon W. **Intramural:** Basketball, bowling, softball.

Student services. Adult student services, career counseling, services for economically disadvantaged, student employment services, financial aid counseling, health services, minority student services, on-campus daycare, personal counseling, placement for graduates, veterans' counselor. **Physically disabled:** Services for visually, speech, hearing impaired. **Transfer:** Special adviser, orientation, pre-admission transcript evaluation for new students. Transfer adviser, college fairs on campus for students transferring to 4-year colleges.

Contact. E-mail: admissions@sunysuffolk.edu
Phone: (631) 451-4000 Fax: (631) 451-4415
Kate Rowe, College Dean of Enrollment Management, Suffolk County Community College, 533 College Road, Selden, NY 11784

Sullivan County Community College

Loch Sheldrake, New York
www.sullivan.suny.edu **CB code: 2855**

- Public 2-year community college
- Commuter campus in small town

General. Founded in 1962. Regionally accredited. **Enrollment:** 1,428 degree-seeking undergraduates; 256 non-degree-seeking students. **Degrees:** 202 associate awarded. **Location:** 100 miles from New York City, 90 miles from Binghamton. **Calendar:** 4-1-4, limited summer session. **Full-time faculty:** 49 total; 45% women. **Part-time faculty:** 85 total; 55% women. **Special facilities:** Complete kitchen, dining room for hospitality programs, mini-travel agency for travel and tourism program, color and black and white darkrooms, computer graphics labs, child development center.

Student profile. Among degree-seeking undergraduates, 505 enrolled as first-time, first-year students.

Part-time:	26%	**Asian American:**	1%
Out-of-state:	5%	**Hispanic American:**	11%
Women:	60%	**International:**	1%
African American:	20%	**25 or older:**	43%

Basis for selection. Open admission, but selective for some programs. Special requirements for nursing program and university parallel business administration program. SAT or ACT recommended for placement and counseling. Interview recommended.

High school preparation. Liberal arts applicants entering science programs should have 3 units each in mathematics and sciences. Computer science applicants, 3 units mathematics and 1 chemistry or physics. Nursing applicants, 1 mathematics and 1 laboratory biology. Engineering science, 3.5 units mathematics and 1 unit chemistry or physics.

2005-2006 Annual costs. Tuition/fees: $3,276; $6,276 out-of-state. Per-credit charge: $112 in-state; $149 out-of-state. Books/supplies: $600. Personal expenses: $700.

Financial aid. Need-based: Need-based aid available for part-time students. **Additional information:** 60% of students hold part-time jobs locally.

Application procedures. Admission: No deadline. No application fee. Admission notification on a rolling basis. Recommended priority application date for nursing department is December 1. **Financial aid:** Priority date 4/15; no closing date. FAFSA required. Applicants notified on a rolling basis starting 5/15; must reply within 2 week(s) of notification.

Academics. Practical experience in class laboratory situations emphasized in technical programs. **Special study options:** Dual enrollment of high school students, exchange student, honors, independent study, internships, study abroad. Joint admissions with SUNY New Paltz in elementary education. **Credit/placement by examination:** AP, CLEP, institutional tests. 31 credit hours maximum toward associate degree. **Support services:** Learning center, reduced course load, remedial instruction, tutoring.

Majors. Business: General, accounting, business admin, insurance, management information systems, office management, office technology, sales/distribution. **Communications:** General, broadcast journalism. **Computer sciences:** General, data processing. **Conservation:** General, forestry. **Education:** Early childhood, elementary. **Engineering:** General, science. **Engineering technology:** Surveying. **Family/consumer sciences:** Child care, institutional food production. **Health:** Nursing (RN), predentistry, premedicine, prepharmacy, preveterinary, substance abuse counseling. **History:** General. **Legal studies:** Paralegal, prelaw. **Liberal arts:** Arts/sciences. **Math:** General. **Parks/recreation:** Facilities management. **Personal/culinary services:** Cosmetic. **Philosophy/religion:** Philosophy. **Protective services:** Criminal justice, police science. **Psychology:** General. **Public administration:** Human services. **Social sciences:** General, sociology. **Visual/performing arts:** Commercial photography, commercial/advertising art.

Computing on campus. 80 workstations in library, computer center.

Student life. Policies: 45 percent of students are county residents. **Housing:** College-approved housing adjacent to campus. **Activities:** Drama, radio station, student government, Black student union, Latin student union.

Athletics. NJCAA. **Intercollegiate:** Basketball M, golf, softball W, volleyball W. **Intramural:** Archery, badminton, basketball, bowling, equestrian, golf, handball, racquetball, skiing, soccer, softball, swimming, table tennis, tennis, volleyball. **Team name:** Generals.

Student services. Adult student services, career counseling, student employment services, health services, on-campus daycare, personal counseling, placement for graduates, veterans' counselor. **Transfer:** Special adviser for new students. Transfer adviser, college fairs on campus for students transferring to 4-year colleges.

Contact. Phone: (845) 434-5750 ext. 4287 Toll-free number: (800) 577-5243 Fax: (845) 434-0923
Ray Sheenan, Director of Admissions and Registration Services, Sullivan County Community College, 112 College Road, Loch Sheldrake, NY 12759-5151

Swedish Institute

New York, New York
www.swedishinstitute.com

- For-profit 2-year health science college
- Very large city
- Interview required

General. Accredited by ACCSCT. **Enrollment:** 400 undergraduates. **Degrees:** 295 associate awarded; master's offered. **Calendar:** Trimester. **Full-time faculty:** 10 total. **Part-time faculty:** 40 total.

2005-2006 Annual costs. Tuition/fees: $8,388. Per-credit charge: $275. Personal expenses: $199.

Financial aid. All financial aid based on need. Need-based aid available for part-time students.

Application procedures. Admission: No deadline. $45 fee. **Financial aid:** No deadline. FAFSA, institutional form required.

Academics. Credit/placement by examination: CLEP, institutional tests. **Support services:** Reduced course load, study skills assistance, tutoring.

Majors. Health: Asian bodywork therapy, massage therapy.

Computing on campus. 7 workstations in library, computer center.

Contact. E-mail: admissions@swedishinstitute.edu
Phone: (212) 924-5900 Fax: (212) 924-7600
Swedish Institute, 226 West 26th Street, 5th Floor, New York, NY 10001-6700

Taylor Business Institute

New York, New York
www.tbiglobal.com **CB code: 0434**

- For-profit 2-year business and technical college
- Very large city
- Interview required

General. Founded in 1961. Accredited by ACICS. **Enrollment:** 900 full-time, degree-seeking students. **Degrees:** 325 associate awarded. **Calendar:** Quarter, extensive summer session. **Full-time faculty:** 15 total. **Part-time faculty:** 18 total.

Basis for selection. Open admission.

2005-2006 Annual costs. Tuition/fees: $10,500.

Application procedures. Admission: No deadline. No application fee. Admission notification on a rolling basis. **Financial aid:** No deadline. FAFSA, institutional form required. Applicants notified on a rolling basis.

Academics. Credit/placement by examination: CLEP, institutional tests. **Support services:** Remedial instruction.

Majors. Business: Accounting technology, administrative services, business admin, tourism/travel.

Student life. Activities: Dance, literary magazine, student newspaper.

Student services. Career counseling, student employment services, personal counseling, placement for graduates. **Transfer:** Special adviser, orientation for new students. Transfer adviser, college fairs on campus for students transferring to 4-year colleges.

Contact. E-mail: admissions@TBIglobal.com
Phone: (212) 229-1963 Toll-free number: (800) 959-9999
Fax: (212) 229-2187
Chris Carbonella, Director of Admissions, Taylor Business Institute, 23 West 17th Street, 7th Floor, New York, NY 10011-5501

Technical Career Institutes

New York, New York
www.tcicollege.net **CB code: 2755**

- For-profit 2-year junior and technical college
- Commuter campus in very large city
- Interview required

General. Founded in 1909. Regionally accredited. **Enrollment:** 2,800 degree-seeking undergraduates. **Degrees:** 804 associate awarded. **Location:** Downtown. **Calendar:** Semester, extensive summer session. **Full-time faculty:** 80 total. **Part-time faculty:** 90 total.

Basis for selection. Open admission. School record most important, interview important. Students without GED/high school diploma must pass CPAT to be admitted.

High school preparation. High school algebra 1 unit, general science 1 required for engineering technology program. Geometry, trigonometry, physics preferred for engineering program.

2005-2006 Annual costs. Tuition/fees: $9,565. Per-credit charge: $380. Required fees $250/year for second-year students. Books/supplies: $800. Personal expenses: $1,280.

Application procedures. Admission: Closing date 9/4. No application fee. Admission notification on a rolling basis beginning on or about 3/1. **Financial aid:** Priority date 6/20; no closing date. FAFSA, institutional form required. Applicants notified on a rolling basis.

Academics. Special study options: Cooperative education, distance learning, ESL, honors, independent study, internships. **Credit/placement by examination:** CLEP, institutional tests. **Support services:** Learning center, reduced course load, remedial instruction, tutoring.

Majors. Business: Accounting, administrative services, office technology. **Computer sciences:** General, LAN/WAN management. **Engineering technology:** Construction, electrical. **Mechanic/repair:** Electronics/electrical, heating/ac/refrig.

Computing on campus. 350 workstations in library, computer center, student center.

Student life. Activities: Choral groups, music ensembles, student government, student newspaper, student chapter of Institute of Electrical and Electronics Engineering, Tau Alpha Pi honor fraternity, American Society of Heating, Refrigeration, and Air Conditioning Engineers, chess club, Future Business Leaders, photography club, Society of Women Engineers, Dare to Dream Volunteer Project.

Athletics. NJCAA. **Intercollegiate:** Basketball M.

Student services. Career counseling, student employment services, personal counseling, placement for graduates, veterans' counselor. **Transfer:** Special adviser, orientation for new students. Transfer adviser for students transferring to 4-year colleges.

Contact. E-mail: admissions@tcicollege.net
Phone: (212) 594-4001 Toll-free number: (800) 878-8246
Fax: (212) 629-3937
Bernard Price, Vice President for Admissions, Technical Career Institutes, 320 West 31st Street, New York, NY 10001

Tompkins-Cortland Community College

Dryden, New York
www.tc3.edu **CB code: 2904**

- Public 2-year community college
- Commuter campus in small town

General. Founded in 1968. Regionally accredited. State University of New York institution. **Enrollment:** 2,812 degree-seeking undergraduates; 362 non-degree-seeking students. **Degrees:** 499 associate awarded. **Location:** 45 miles from Syracuse. **Calendar:** Semester, extensive summer session. **Full-time faculty:** 69 total; 25% have terminal degrees, 4% minority, 54% women. **Part-time faculty:** 208 total; 16% have terminal degrees, 4% minority, 54% women. **Class size:** 63% < 20, 37% 20-39, less than 1% 40-49, less than 1% 50-99.

Student profile. Among degree-seeking undergraduates, 758 enrolled as first-time, first-year students, 318 transferred in from other institutions.

Part-time:	25%	**Hispanic American:**	3%
Out-of-state:	2%	**International:**	3%
Women:	59%	**25 or older:**	33%
African American:	6%	**Live on campus:**	7%
Asian American:	2%		

Transfer out. Colleges most students transferred to 2005: SUNY Cortland, Ithaca College, Cornell University, Binghamton University, Oswego State University.

Basis for selection. Open admission, but selective for some programs. Special requirements for nursing students. Nursing requires high school average of B or better, plus math and science prerequisites. ACT required for nursing program. Interview required for aviation science, recommended for nursing. **Adult students:** Entrance exam policies same as for first-time freshmen. **Homeschooled:** Completion of an IHIP pursuant to section 100.10 of the Regulations of the Commissions of Education required.

2005-2006 Annual costs. Tuition/fees: $3,653; $7,053 out-of-state. Per-credit charge: $120 in-state; $250 out-of-state. Books/supplies: $1,000. Personal expenses: $1,000.

2004-2005 Financial aid. Need-based: 45% of total undergraduate aid awarded as scholarships/grants, 55% as loans/jobs. Need-based aid available for part-time students. Work study available nights, weekends and for part-time students. **Non-need-based:** Scholarships awarded for academics.

Application procedures. Admission: No deadline. $15 fee, may be waived for applicants with need. Application may be submitted online. Admission notification on a rolling basis. **Financial aid:** Priority date 4/15; no closing date. FAFSA, institutional form required. Applicants notified on a rolling basis starting 3/15; must reply within 4 week(s) of notification.

Academics. Special study options: Cooperative education, cross-registration, distance learning, dual enrollment of high school students, ESL, honors, independent study, internships, liberal arts/career combination, study abroad, weekend college. License preparation in aviation, nursing. **Credit/placement by examination:** AP, CLEP. 47 credit hours maximum toward associate degree. **Support services:** GED preparation, learning center, reduced course load, remedial instruction, study skills assistance, tutoring, writing center.

Majors. Biology: Biotechnology. **Business:** Accounting technology, administrative services, business admin, hotel/motel admin, international, labor relations, retailing, travel services. **Communications:** General, advertising, broadcast journalism. **Communications technology:** Radio/tv. **Computer sciences:** General, information systems, webmaster. **Conservation:** General. **Construction:** General. **Education:** Kindergarten/preschool, secondary. **Engineering:** General. **Engineering technology:** Electrical, mechanical. **Family/consumer sciences:** Child care. **Health:** Nursing (RN), substance abuse counseling. **Legal studies:** Paralegal. **Liberal arts:** Arts/sciences, humanities. **Mechanic/repair:** Avionics. **Parks/recreation:** Facilities management, sports admin. **Personal/culinary services:** Restaurant/catering. **Protective services:** Forensics, police science. **Public administration:** Community org/advocacy. **Visual/performing arts:** Commercial/advertising art, photography.

Most popular majors. Business/marketing 26%, health sciences 10%, liberal arts 31%, security/protective services 8%.

Computing on campus. 400 workstations in library, computer center. Dormitories wired for high-speed internet access and linked to campus network. Commuter students can connect to campus network. Online course registration, online library, helpline, wireless network available.

Student life. Freshman orientation: Available. Preregistration for classes offered. Held prior to each semester. Multiple sessions offered: new students, international students, and adult students. **Policies:** All campus organizations must apply for recognition, must have a staff adviser, and are funded by the activity fee through faculty-student association and student government. Freshmen permitted cars on campus. **Housing:** Apartments available. $400 fully refundable deposit, deadline 5/15. **Activities:** Choral groups, dance, drama, film society, literary magazine, radio station, student government, Chi Alpha Christian group, black student union; organizations for African students, Asian students.

Athletics. NJCAA. **Intercollegiate:** Baseball M, basketball, cheerleading, golf, soccer, softball W, volleyball W. **Intramural:** Badminton, basketball, bowling, football (tackle), golf, lacrosse, racquetball, skiing, soccer, softball, squash, swimming, table tennis, tennis, volleyball, water polo. **Team name:** Panthers.

Student services. Adult student services, career counseling, student employment services, financial aid counseling, minority student services, on-campus daycare, personal counseling, placement for graduates, veterans' counselor. **Physically disabled:** Services for visually, speech, hearing impaired. **Transfer:** Special adviser, orientation, pre-admission transcript evaluation for new students. Transfer adviser, college fairs on campus for students transferring to 4-year colleges.

Contact. E-mail: admissions@tc3.edu
Phone: (607) 844-6580 Toll-free number: (888) 567-8211
Fax: (607) 844-6541
Sandy Drumluk, Director of Admissions, Tompkins-Cortland Community College, 170 North Street, Dryden, NY 13053-0139

Trocaire College

Buffalo, New York
www.trocaire.edu **CB code: 2856**

- Private 2-year junior college affiliated with Roman Catholic Church
- Commuter campus in large city

General. Founded in 1958. Regionally accredited. Affiliated with Sisters of Mercy, Buffalo Diocese. **Enrollment:** 1,109 degree-seeking undergraduates. **Degrees:** 152 associate awarded. **Calendar:** Semester, limited summer session. **Full-time faculty:** 34 total. **Part-time faculty:** 52 total. **Class size:** 79% < 20, 21% 20-39.

Basis for selection. Open admission, but selective for some programs. Selective admissions to health-related fields.

High school preparation. 16 units required. Laboratory science and mathematics required for some programs.

2006-2007 Annual costs. Tuition/fees: $10,771. Per-credit charge: $410. Books/supplies: $1,000. Personal expenses: $700.

Financial aid. Need-based: Need-based aid available for part-time students. **Non-need-based:** Scholarships awarded for academics, alumni affiliation.

Application procedures. Admission: No deadline. $25 fee, may be waived for applicants with need. Admission notification on a rolling basis. Must reply by May 1 or within 4 week(s) if notified thereafter. **Financial aid:** Priority date 3/31; no closing date. FAFSA required. Applicants notified on a rolling basis starting 3/1; must reply within 2 week(s) of notification.

Academics. Special study options: Cross-registration, dual enrollment of high school students, independent study, internships. **Credit/placement by examination:** CLEP, institutional tests. 30 credit hours maximum toward associate degree. **Support services:** Learning center, reduced course load, remedial instruction, study skills assistance, tutoring.

Majors. Business: Administrative services, business admin, office management, sales/distribution. **Computer sciences:** General, LAN/WAN management. **Conservation:** General. **Education:** Early childhood. **Health:** Massage therapy, medical assistant, medical radiologic technology/radiation therapy, medical records technology, nursing (RN), surgical technology. **Legal studies:** Legal secretary. **Liberal arts:** Arts/sciences.

Most popular majors. Business/marketing 16%, education 7%, health sciences 71%.

Computing on campus. 114 workstations in library, computer center, student center. Helpline available.

Student life. Freshman orientation: Mandatory. **Activities:** Student government.

Student services. Adult student services, career counseling, student employment services, health services, personal counseling, placement for graduates, veterans' counselor. **Physically disabled:** Services for visually, hearing impaired. **Transfer:** Special adviser, orientation, pre-admission transcript evaluation for new students. Transfer center, transfer adviser, college fairs on campus for students transferring to 4-year colleges.

Contact. E-mail: info@trocaire.edu
Phone: (716) 826-1200 Fax: (716) 828-6107
Claudia Lesinski, Director of Enrollment Management/Admissions, Trocaire College, 360 Choate Avenue, Buffalo, NY 14220

Ulster County Community College

Stone Ridge, New York
www.sunyulster.edu **CB code: 2938**

- Public 2-year community college
- Commuter campus in small town

General. Founded in 1963. Regionally accredited. SUNY institution. **Enrollment:** 2,238 degree-seeking undergraduates. **Degrees:** 347 associate awarded. **Location:** 8 miles from Kingston. **Calendar:** Semester, extensive summer session. **Full-time faculty:** 65 total. **Part-time faculty:** 133 total. **Special facilities:** Word processing laboratories, computer art graphic laboratory, geological information systems.

Basis for selection. Open admission, but selective for some programs. Special requirements for nursing and honors programs, with school achievement record very important. SAT or ACT recommended for all applicants. Interview required for nursing, honors program, early admissions applicants; recommended for others. Portfolio recommended for graphic arts.

High school preparation. 18 units recommended. Recommended units include English 4 and social studies 4. 3 mathematics and 3 science, including chemistry and physics, required of engineering applicants. 4 English, 3 mathematics, 3 language required of honors program applicants.

2005-2006 Annual costs. Tuition/fees: $3,596; $6,796 out-of-state. Per-credit charge: $107 in-state; $214 out-of-state. Books/supplies: $650. Personal expenses: $480.

2005-2006 Financial aid. Need-based: Need-based aid available for part-time students.

Application procedures. Admission: No deadline. No application fee. Admission notification on a rolling basis. **Financial aid:** Priority date 6/1; no closing date. FAFSA required. Applicants notified on a rolling basis starting 6/1; must reply within 2 week(s) of notification.

Academics. Special study options: Cooperative education, cross-registration, distance learning, double major, dual enrollment of high school students, honors, independent study, internships, student-designed major. **Credit/placement by examination:** AP, CLEP, institutional tests. 30 credit hours maximum toward associate degree. **Support services:** Learning center, pre-admission summer program, reduced course load, remedial instruction, study skills assistance, tutoring, writing center.

Majors. Business: General, accounting, business admin, finance, office technology. **Communications:** General. **Computer sciences:** General. **Education:** Elementary. **Engineering:** General. **Engineering technology:** Drafting. **Health:** Nursing (RN), substance abuse counseling. **Legal studies:** Legal secretary. **Liberal arts:** Arts/sciences. **Math:** General. **Parks/recreation:** General. **Public administration:** Community org/advocacy, social work. **Social sciences:** General. **Visual/performing arts:** Commercial/advertising art.

Computing on campus. 243 workstations in computer center.

Student life. Activities: Concert band, choral groups, drama, literary magazine, music ensembles, musical theater, radio station, student government, student newspaper, TV station, Children's center club, environmental awareness club, international students club, multicultural club, Phi Theta Kappa, earth science/geology club, Brothers and Sisters in Christ.

Athletics. NJCAA. **Intercollegiate:** Baseball M, basketball, bowling M, cross-country, golf, skiing, soccer M, softball W, tennis, track and field, volleyball W, wrestling M. **Intramural:** Badminton, basketball M, soccer M, softball, volleyball.

Student services. Adult student services, career counseling, student employment services, health services, on-campus daycare, personal counseling, placement for graduates, veterans' counselor. **Transfer:** Special adviser, orientation for new students. Transfer adviser, college fairs on campus for students transferring to 4-year colleges.

Contact. Phone: (845) 687-5022 Toll-free number: (800) 724-5022
Fax: (845) 687-5083
Susan Weatherly, Director of Admissions, Ulster County Community College, Cottekill Road, Stone Ridge, NY 12484

Utica School of Commerce

Utica, New York
www.uscny.edu **CB code: 0343**

- For-profit 2-year business college
- Commuter campus in small city
- Interview required

General. Founded in 1896. Regionally accredited; also accredited by ACICS. Branch campuses in Oneonta and Canastota. **Enrollment:** 400 degree-seeking undergraduates. **Degrees:** 82 associate awarded. **Location:** 50 miles from Syracuse. **Calendar:** Semester, extensive summer session. **Full-time faculty:** 47 total. **Part-time faculty:** 64 total. **Special facilities:** Museum of business education.

Student profile.

Out-of-state:	1%	**25 or older:**	30%

Transfer out. Colleges most students transferred to 2005: SUNY College of Technology, St. Rose College, SUNY at Oneonta.

Basis for selection. Open admission. Admissions interview required. High School diploma or GED required.

2006-2007 Annual costs. Tuition/fees (projected): $10,140. Books/supplies: $1,185.

Financial aid. All financial aid based on need.

Application procedures. Admission: No deadline. No application fee. Application may be submitted online. Admission notification on a rolling basis. Must reply by May 1 or within 3 week(s) if notified thereafter. **Financial aid:** No deadline. FAFSA, institutional form required. Applicants notified on a rolling basis.

Academics. Special study options: Accelerated study, dual enrollment of high school students, liberal arts/career combination. Joint admissions with SUNY Institute of Technology. **Credit/placement by examination:** CLEP, institutional tests. 30 credit hours maximum toward associate degree. **Support services:** Learning center, reduced course load, remedial instruction, tutoring.

Majors. Business: General, accounting, administrative services, business admin, executive assistant, management information systems, nonprofit/public, retailing, sales/distribution. **Computer sciences:** General, data processing, programming, word processing. **Health:** Health care admin, medical records technology, medical secretary. **Legal studies:** Legal secretary.

Most popular majors. Business/marketing 81%, computer/information sciences 19%.

Computing on campus. 168 workstations in library, computer center.

Student life. Freshman orientation: Mandatory. **Activities:** Student government, student newspaper, future secretaries association, accounting association.

Student services. Career counseling, student employment services, personal counseling, placement for graduates, veterans' counselor. **Physically disabled:** Services for visually, hearing impaired. **Transfer:** Special adviser, orientation for new students. Transfer adviser, college fairs on campus for students transferring to 4-year colleges.

Contact. E-mail: admissions@uscny.edu
Phone: (315) 733-2307 Toll-free number: (800) 321-4872
Fax: (315) 733-9281
Cindy DeLaney, Director of Admissions, Utica School of Commerce, 201 Bleecker Street, Utica, NY 13501

Utica School of Commerce: Canastota

Canastota, New York
www.uscny.edu **CB code: 3340**

- For-profit 2-year business college
- Commuter campus in small town

General. Regionally accredited. **Calendar:** Semester.

Annual costs/financial aid. Tuition/fees (2005-2006): $10,140.

Contact. Phone: (315) 697-8200
P.O. Box 462, Canastota, NY 13032

Utica School of Commerce: Oneonta

Oneonta, New York
www.uscny.edu **CB code: 3341**

- For-profit 2-year branch campus and business college
- Small city

General. Regionally accredited. **Location:** 70 miles from Albany. **Calendar:** Quarter.

Annual costs/financial aid. Tuition/fees (2005-2006): $10,140.

Contact. Phone: (607) 732-7003
17 Elm Street, Oneonta, NY 13820

Villa Maria College of Buffalo

Buffalo, New York
www.villa.edu **CB code: 2962**

- Private 2-year liberal arts college affiliated with Roman Catholic Church
- Commuter campus in large city
- Interview required

General. Founded in 1960. Regionally accredited. **Enrollment:** 489 degree-seeking undergraduates; 13 non-degree-seeking students. **Degrees:** 104 associate awarded. **Location:** 2 miles from downtown. **Calendar:** Semester, limited summer session. **Full-time faculty:** 26 total; 27% have terminal degrees, 4% minority, 50% women. **Part-time faculty:** 46 total; 28% have terminal degrees, 6% minority, 39% women. **Class size:** 87% < 20, 13% 20-39. **Special facilities:** Interior design resource center, education resource center, music building, recording studio, digital photography lab. **Partnerships:** Formal partnerships with American Institute of Banking to transfer business courses, and with BOCES centers for advanced placement credits.

Student profile. Among degree-seeking undergraduates, 85% enrolled in a transfer program, 15% enrolled in a vocational program, 5% already have a bachelor's degree or higher, 132 enrolled as first-time, first-year students.

Part-time:	19%	**Hispanic American:**	1%
Women:	74%	**Native American:**	1%
African American:	30%	**25 or older:**	39%
Asian American:	1%		

Transfer out. 61% of students enrolled in the transfer program go on to 4-year colleges. **Colleges most students transferred to 2005:** SUNY at Buffalo, Buffalo State College, Medaille College, D'Youville College, Canisius College.

Basis for selection. Open admission, but selective for some programs. Audition required for music programs; portfolio recommended for fine arts, interior design, photography programs. **Adult students:** Entrance exam policies same as for first-time freshmen. **Homeschooled:** Statement describing homeschool structure and mission, transcript of courses and grades, interview required. Letter verifying completion from school district in which home-schooled individual resides required. **Learning Disabled:** Must submit all documentation to Coordinator for Students with Disabilities prior to admission and must take VMCAPP.

High school preparation. Recommended units include English 4, mathematics 2, social studies 4 and science 2. General physics with lab required for physical therapy assistant applicants.

2006-2007 Annual costs. Tuition/fees: $11,705. Per-credit charge: $380. Costs quoted for 2-year programs. Bachelor's degree program costs as of Fall 2006: $13,300 tuition, $495 required fees, $445/credit hour. Books/supplies: $1,200. Personal expenses: $700.

2004-2005 Financial aid. Need-based: 133 full-time freshmen applied for aid; 109 were judged to have need; 109 of these received aid. Average need met was 1%. Average scholarship/grant was $1; average loan $1. 59% of total undergraduate aid awarded as scholarships/grants, 41% as loans/jobs. Need-based aid available for part-time students. Work study available nights. **Non-need-based:** Awarded to 47 full-time undergraduates, including 21 freshmen. Scholarships awarded for academics, alumni affiliation, art, leadership, minority status, music/drama, religious affiliation, state residency.

Application procedures. Admission: No deadline. No application fee. Application may be submitted online. Admission notification on a rolling basis. **Financial aid:** Priority date 4/1; no closing date. FAFSA required. Applicants notified by 5/1; must reply within 3 week(s) of notification.

Academics. Implemented Adviser/Advisee Action Plan provides early identification of students encountering difficulty with scheduling, finances, academic skills, personal problems, and employment. **Special study options:** Cooperative education, cross-registration, double major, dual enrollment of high school students, internships, liberal arts/career combination, study abroad. Evening modules for adult students, member Western New York Consortium of Institutions of Higher Education. Bachelor's degree programs available on campus. **Credit/placement by examination:** AP, CLEP, institutional tests. 30 credit hours maximum toward associate degree. **Support services:** Learning center, pre-admission summer program, reduced course load, remedial instruction, study skills assistance, tutoring.

Majors. Business: Business admin. **Computer sciences:** General. **Education:** General, early childhood. **Health:** Physical therapy assistant. **Liberal arts:** Arts/sciences, humanities. **Visual/performing arts:** Commercial/advertising art, interior design, jazz, music management, music performance, photography, studio arts.

Most popular majors. Business/marketing 15%, education 18%, liberal arts 9%, visual/performing arts 54%.

Computing on campus. 100 workstations in library, computer center. Commuter students can connect to campus network. Online library available.

Student life. Freshman orientation: Mandatory, $50 fee. Preregistration for classes offered. 2 days for students and 1 day for parents/spouses in August. **Policies:** Freshmen permitted cars on campus. **Activities:** Jazz band, choral groups, literary magazine, music ensembles, student government, student newspaper, Helping Adults' New Dreams Succeed, Students Actively Striving for Success, Students Against Destructive Decision Making, multicultural club.

Student services. Adult student services, alcohol/substance abuse counseling, campus ministries, career counseling, services for economically disadvantaged, student employment services, financial aid counseling, health services, minority student services, personal counseling, placement for graduates, veterans' counselor. **Transfer:** Special adviser, orientation, re-entry adviser, pre-admission transcript evaluation for new students. Transfer center, transfer adviser, college fairs on campus for students transferring to 4-year colleges.

Contact. E-mail: admissions@villa.edu
Phone: (716) 896-0700 ext. 1805 Fax: (716) 896-0705
Kevin Donovan, Director of Admissions, Villa Maria College of Buffalo, 240 Pine Ridge Road, Buffalo, NY 14225

Westchester Community College

Valhalla, New York **CB member**
www.sunywcc.edu **CB code: 2972**

- Public 2-year community college
- Commuter campus in large town

General. Founded in 1946. Regionally accredited. SUNY institution. **Enrollment:** 9,470 degree-seeking undergraduates. **Degrees:** 1,065 associate awarded. **Location:** 30 miles from New York City, 6 miles from White Plains. **Calendar:** Semester, extensive summer session. **Full-time faculty:** 156 total; 28% have terminal degrees, 12% minority, 49% women. **Part-time faculty:** 757 total; 9% minority, 49% women. **Special facilities:** On-campus child care center.

Student profile. Among degree-seeking undergraduates, 49% enrolled in a transfer program, 51% enrolled in a vocational program, 4% already have a bachelor's degree or higher, 2,137 enrolled as first-time, first-year students, 868 transferred in from other institutions.

Out-of-state:	1%	**25 or older:**	37%

Transfer out. Colleges most students transferred to 2005: SUNY Purchase, Pace University, Mercy College, Iona College, Manhattanville College.

Basis for selection. Open admission, but selective for some programs. Competitive programs in allied health curricula. High school diploma or GED required of applicants 18 years of age or younger. Interview recommended. **Adult students:** Entrance exam policies same as for first-time freshmen. **Homeschooled:** Statement describing homeschool structure and mission required. Students must submit letter from superintendent of district in which they reside certifying that home instruction program is equivalent of high school program.

2005-2006 Annual costs. Tuition/fees: $3,493; $8,219 out-of-state. Per-credit charge: $132 in-state; $330 out-of-state. Books/supplies: $800. Personal expenses: $500.

2004-2005 Financial aid. Need-based: 91% of total undergraduate aid awarded as scholarships/grants, 9% as loans/jobs. Need-based aid available for part-time students. Work study available nights, weekends and for part-time students. **Non-need-based:** Scholarships awarded for academics.

Application procedures. Admission: No deadline. $25 fee, may be waived for applicants with need. Application must be submitted on paper.

Admission notification on a rolling basis beginning on or about 2/1. **Financial aid:** No deadline. FAFSA, institutional form required. Applicants notified on a rolling basis; must reply within 4 week(s) of notification.

Academics. Extensive ESL program. **Special study options:** Accelerated study, cooperative education, cross-registration, distance learning, double major, ESL, honors, independent study, internships, liberal arts/career combination, student-designed major, study abroad. Cambridge University summer program; Italian language study program in Italy. License preparation in nursing, paramedic, radiology, real estate. **Credit/placement by examination:** AP, CLEP, IB, institutional tests. 32 credit hours maximum toward associate degree. **Support services:** Learning center, reduced course load, remedial instruction, study skills assistance, tutoring, writing center.

Majors. Business: Accounting, administrative services, business admin, international, marketing, merchandising, office/clerical, sales/distribution. **Communications:** General. **Computer sciences:** General, computer science, information systems, LAN/WAN management. **Education:** Early childhood. **Engineering:** General, science. **Engineering technology:** Civil, electrical. **Family/consumer sciences:** Child care, food/nutrition, institutional food production. **Health:** EMT paramedic, medical radiologic technology/radiation therapy, nursing (RN), nursing assistant, respiratory therapy technology, substance abuse counseling. **Legal studies:** Paralegal. **Liberal arts:** Arts/sciences. **Mechanic/repair:** Automotive. **Personal/culinary services:** Culinary arts, restaurant/catering. **Physical sciences:** General. **Protective services:** Corrections, police science. **Public administration:** Social work. **Social sciences:** General. **Visual/performing arts:** General, dramatic, music performance.

Computing on campus. 826 workstations in library, computer center, student center. Online library, helpline, wireless network available.

Student life. Freshman orientation: Available. **Policies:** Freshmen permitted cars on campus. **Activities:** Choral groups, dance, drama, literary magazine, musical theater, radio station, student government, student newspaper, TV station, international friendship club, Black student union, Brazilian club, Haitian club, El Club Hispano Americano, Irish Society, Jamaican club, Il Club Italiano, French club, Amnesty International.

Athletics. NJCAA. **Intercollegiate:** Baseball M, basketball, bowling, golf M, soccer M, softball W, volleyball W. **Intramural:** Basketball M, soccer M, softball, volleyball. **Team name:** Westcos.

Student services. Adult student services, alcohol/substance abuse counseling, career counseling, student employment services, financial aid counseling, health services, minority student services, on-campus daycare, personal counseling, placement for graduates, veterans' counselor, women's services. **Physically disabled:** Services for visually, speech, hearing impaired. **Transfer:** Pre-admission transcript evaluation for new students. Transfer center, transfer adviser, college fairs on campus for students transferring to 4-year colleges.

Contact. E-mail: admissions@sunywcc.edu
Phone: (914) 606-6735 Fax: (914) 606-6540
Teresita Wisell, Director of Admissions, Westchester Community College, 75 Grasslands Road, Valhalla, NY 10595

Wood Tobe-Coburn School

New York, New York
www.woodtobecoburn.com **CB code: 2913**

- For-profit 2-year professional college
- Commuter campus in very large city
- Interview required

General. Founded in 1879. Regionally accredited. **Enrollment:** 257 degree-seeking undergraduates. **Degrees:** 139 associate awarded. **Calendar:** Semester, extensive summer session. **Full-time faculty:** 5 total. **Part-time faculty:** 15 total.

Student profile.

Out-of-state:	5%	**25 or older:**	2%

Basis for selection. High school record and personal interview most important. Portfolio recommended.

2005-2006 Annual costs. Tuition/fees: $13,800. Graphic design, fashion design and fashion merchandising programs cost $15,200 per year. Fees vary by program. Books/supplies: $1,165. Personal expenses: $2,110.

Application procedures. Admission: No deadline. $50 fee, may be waived for applicants with need. Admission notification on a rolling basis. **Financial aid:** No deadline. Applicants notified on a rolling basis.

Academics. 16-month accelerated program available for fashion students, and 8 weeks of supervised on-the-job training each year. **Special study options:** Internships. Externships. **Credit/placement by examination:** CLEP.

Majors. Business: Accounting, administrative services, fashion. **Computer sciences:** Networking, programming. **Engineering:** Software. **Health:** Medical assistant. **Visual/performing arts:** Fashion design.

Most popular majors. Business/marketing 59%, visual/performing arts 41%.

Computing on campus. 116 workstations in computer center.

Student services. Career counseling, student employment services, placement for graduates.

Contact. Phone: (212) 686-9040 Fax: (212) 686-9171
Sandra Andujar-Wendland, Director of Admissions, Wood Tobe-Coburn School, 8 East 40th Street, New York, NY 10016-0190

North Carolina

Alamance Community College

Graham, North Carolina
www.alamancecc.edu **CB code: 5790**

- Public 2-year community college
- Commuter campus in large town

General. Founded in 1958. Regionally accredited. **Enrollment:** 3,428 degree-seeking undergraduates; 857 non-degree-seeking students. **Degrees:** 330 associate awarded. **Location:** 4 miles from Burlington, 30 miles from Greensboro. **Calendar:** Semester, extensive summer session. **Full-time faculty:** 99 total; 6% have terminal degrees, 7% minority, 58% women. **Part-time faculty:** 139 total; 6% have terminal degrees, 10% minority, 40% women. **Class size:** 67% < 20, 32% 20-39, less than 1% 40-49.

Student profile. Among degree-seeking undergraduates, 25% enrolled in a transfer program, 75% enrolled in a vocational program, 4% already have a bachelor's degree or higher, 599 enrolled as first-time, first-year students, 1,158 transferred in from other institutions.

Part-time:	53%	**Women:**	67%
Out-of-state:	1%	**25 or older:**	52%

Transfer out. Colleges most students transferred to 2005: University of North Carolina System.

Basis for selection. Open admission, but selective for some programs. Special requirements for allied health programs, interview required. SAT or ACT score may waive required testing for placement. Portfolio recommended for advertising design, commercial art majors. **Adult students:** Entrance exam policies same as for first-time freshmen. **Learning Disabled:** Disabilities must be documented with special needs counselor. Contact Student Development Office.

High school preparation. 21 units recommended. Recommended units include English 4, mathematics 3, social studies 2, history 1, science 3 (laboratory 1), foreign language 2 and academic electives 6. Biology, chemistry required for nursing.

2005-2006 Annual costs. Tuition/fees: $1,215; $6,615 out-of-state. Per-credit charge: $40 in-state; $220 out-of-state. Books/supplies: $800. Personal expenses: $800.

2004-2005 Financial aid. Need-based: 263 full-time freshmen applied for aid; 260 were judged to have need; 250 of these received aid. Average need met was 40%. Average scholarship/grant was $3,000. 95% of total undergraduate aid awarded as scholarships/grants, 5% as loans/jobs. Need-based aid available for part-time students. Work study available nights and for part-time students. **Non-need-based:** Awarded to 100 full-time undergraduates, including 150 freshmen. Scholarships awarded for academics, state residency.

Application procedures. Admission: No deadline. No application fee. Admission notification on a rolling basis. **Financial aid:** Priority date 5/15; no closing date. FAFSA required. Applicants notified on a rolling basis starting 3/15; must reply within 2 week(s) of notification.

Academics. Special study options: Cooperative education, distance learning, double major, dual enrollment of high school students, ESL, independent study, internships, weekend college. License preparation in nursing, real estate. **Credit/placement by examination:** AP, CLEP, IB, institutional tests. 18 credit hours maximum toward associate degree. Maximum 25% of hours for degree by examination. **Support services:** GED preparation and test center, learning center, reduced course load, remedial instruction, study skills assistance, tutoring.

Majors. Agriculture: Horticultural science, horticulture. **Biology:** Biotechnology. **Business:** General, accounting, administrative services, banking/financial services, business admin, management science, office management, real estate, sales/distribution. **Computer sciences:** Applications programming, information systems, programming. **Education:** Early childhood. **Engineering:** Electrical. **Engineering technology:** Drafting. **Health:** Clinical lab assistant, clinical lab technology, medical records admin, medical secretary, nursing (RN). **Legal studies:** Legal secretary. **Liberal arts:** Arts/sciences. **Mechanic/repair:** Electronics/electrical, heating/ac/refrig, industrial. **Personal/culinary services:** Culinary arts. **Protective services:** Criminal justice, firefighting, law enforcement admin.

Most popular majors. Business/marketing 21%, computer/information sciences 6%, health sciences 26%, liberal arts 16%, security/protective services 6%, trade and industry 21%.

Computing on campus. 140 workstations in library, computer center.

Student life. Freshman orientation: Available. Preregistration for classes offered. General orientation available; some programs have additional orientations. **Activities:** Choral groups, student government, ethnic student association, marketing club, Phi Beta Lambda (service organization), criminal justice club, early childhood education club, Phi Theta Kappa, nursing club, medical assisting club, Sigma Psi, animal care club, biotechnology, college transfer student club.

Student services. Career counseling, student employment services, financial aid counseling, health services, on-campus daycare, personal counseling, placement for graduates, veterans' counselor. **Physically disabled:** Services for visually, speech, hearing impaired. **Transfer:** Special adviser, orientation, pre-admission transcript evaluation for new students. Transfer adviser, college fairs on campus for students transferring to 4-year colleges.

Contact. E-mail: accadmissions@alamancecc.edu
Phone: (336) 506-4405 Fax: (336) 578-1987
Suzanne Lucier, Director of Enrollment, Alamance Community College, Box 8000, Graham, NC 27253

Asheville-Buncombe Technical Community College

Asheville, North Carolina **CB member**
www.abtech.edu **CB code: 5033**

- Public 2-year community and technical college
- Commuter campus in small city

General. Founded in 1959. Regionally accredited. Certain credit courses offered at the Madison Campus during evening hours. **Enrollment:** 6,048 undergraduates. **Degrees:** 453 associate awarded. **Location:** 115 miles from Charlotte. **Calendar:** Semester. **Full-time faculty:** 341 total. **Part-time faculty:** 498 total.

Student profile.

Out-of-state:	1%	**25 or older:**	48%

Basis for selection. Open admission, but selective for some programs. Admission to allied health programs based on academic record and state residency. Computerized Placement Test (CPT) administered by college. SAT and/or ACT scores may be used in lieu of CPT for English and math placement. For allied health programs, tests used to earn admission through point system. Provisional or unconditional admission to individual programs will be determined by scores on the test requirements. Placement interview required of all entering students; interview required for all medical programs.

High school preparation. 8 units recommended. Recommended units include English 4, mathematics 2 and science 2. Algebra I and algebra II or geometry for engineering; algebra I, chemistry and biology for nursing, medical laboratory and dental programs; algebra I for radiologic technology; biology and 1 mathematics for practical nursing.

2005-2006 Annual costs. Tuition/fees: $1,219; $6,619 out-of-state. Per-credit charge: $40 in-state; $220 out-of-state. Books/supplies: $550.

Financial aid. Non-need-based: Scholarships awarded for academics, leadership.

Application procedures. Admission: No deadline. No application fee. Application may be submitted online. On a rolling basis except for allied health applicants notified in mid-April. **Financial aid:** Priority date 3/15, closing date 3/31. FAFSA required. Applicants notified on a rolling basis starting 5/1; must reply within 2 week(s) of notification.

Academics. Special study options: Cooperative education, distance learning, double major, dual enrollment of high school students, ESL, independent study, internships, liberal arts/career combination. License preparation in real estate. **Credit/placement by examination:** CLEP, institutional tests. **Support services:** GED preparation and test center, learning center, preadmission summer program, reduced course load, remedial instruction, tutoring.

Majors. Business: Accounting, administrative services, business admin, management information systems, office technology, office/clerical, operations, sales/distribution. **Computer sciences:** Applications programming. **Engineering technology:** Civil, drafting, electrical, surveying. **Family/consumer sciences:** Child care, institutional food production. **Health:** Clinical lab technology, dental hygiene, EMT paramedic, medical radiologic technology/radiation therapy, nursing (RN). **Liberal arts:** Arts/sciences. **Mechanic/repair:** Automotive, heating/ac/refrig. **Protective services:** Police science. **Public administration:** Social work. **Transportation:** Flight attendant.

Most popular majors. Business/marketing 15%, engineering/engineering technologies 11%, health sciences 34%, liberal arts 23%.

Computing on campus. 300 workstations in library, computer center.

Student life. Activities: Literary magazine, student government, student newspaper.

Student services. Career counseling, student employment services, on-campus daycare, personal counseling, placement for graduates, veterans' counselor. **Physically disabled:** Services for visually, speech, hearing impaired. **Transfer:** Special adviser for new students. Transfer adviser, college fairs on campus for students transferring to 4-year colleges.

Contact. E-mail: admissions@abtech.edu
Phone: (828) 254-1921 ext. 144 Fax: (828) 251-6718
Scott Douglas, Director, Enrollment Management, Asheville-Buncombe Technical Community College, 340 Victoria Road, Asheville, NC 28801-4897

Beaufort County Community College

Washington, North Carolina
www.beaufortccc.edu **CB code: 7307**

- Public 2-year community college
- Commuter campus in small town

General. Founded in 1967. Regionally accredited. **Enrollment:** 733 degree-seeking undergraduates. **Degrees:** 148 associate awarded. **Location:** 23 miles from Greenville. **Calendar:** Semester, limited summer session. **Full-time faculty:** 66 total. **Part-time faculty:** 17 total.

Transfer out. Colleges most students transferred to 2005: East Carolina University.

Basis for selection. Open admission, but selective for some programs. Special requirements for allied health programs. **Homeschooled:** Must provide proof that the home-school is registered with the appropriate state agencies.

High school preparation. One unit chemistry required for nursing and medical technology applicants.

2005-2006 Annual costs. Tuition/fees: $1,245; $6,645 out-of-state. Per-credit charge: $40 in-state; $220 out-of-state. Books/supplies: $700.

Financial aid. Need-based: Need-based aid available for part-time students. **Non-need-based:** Scholarships awarded for academics, leadership.

Application procedures. Admission: Priority date 7/15; no deadline. No application fee. Application may be submitted online. **Financial aid:** Priority date 6/1; no closing date. FAFSA required. Applicants notified on a rolling basis starting 5/1; must reply within 2 week(s) of notification.

Academics. Special study options: Cooperative education, distance learning, dual enrollment of high school students, ESL, internships, liberal arts/career combination. License preparation in aviation, nursing, real estate. **Credit/placement by examination:** AP, CLEP, institutional tests. **Support services:** GED preparation and test center, learning center, remedial instruction, study skills assistance, tutoring.

Majors. Agriculture: Mechanization. **Business:** Accounting, administrative services, business admin. **Computer sciences:** Applications programming, information systems, networking, programming, vendor certification. **Construction:** Electrician. **Education:** General, early childhood. **Engineering technology:** Drafting, electrical. **Family/consumer sciences:** Child care, child development. **Health:** Clinical lab technology, medical secretary, nursing (RN), office admin. **Liberal arts:** Arts/sciences. **Mechanic/repair:** Automotive. **Production:** Welding. **Protective services:** Criminal justice. **Public administration:** Human services. **Science technology:** Biological.

Computing on campus. Commuter students can connect to campus network. Online library available.

Student life. Activities: Student government.

Student services. Career counseling, services for economically disadvantaged, student employment services, financial aid counseling, personal counseling, placement for graduates, veterans' counselor. **Transfer:** Special adviser, pre-admission transcript evaluation for new students. Transfer adviser, college fairs on campus for students transferring to 4-year colleges.

Contact. E-mail: garyb@email.beaufort.cc.nc.us
Phone: (252) 940-6237 Fax: (252) 940-6393
Gary Burbage, Director of Admissions and Recruitment, Beaufort County Community College, Box 1069, Washington, NC 27889

Bladen Community College

Dublin, North Carolina
www.bladen.cc.nc.us **CB code: 3082**

- Public 2-year community college
- Commuter campus in rural community

General. Founded in 1967. Regionally accredited. **Enrollment:** 1,340 degree-seeking undergraduates. **Degrees:** 111 associate awarded. **Location:** 35 miles from Fayetteville. **Calendar:** Semester, limited summer session. **Full-time faculty:** 50 total; 6% have terminal degrees, 22% minority, 64% women. **Part-time faculty:** 60 total; 7% have terminal degrees, 27% minority, 48% women. **Class size:** 82% < 20, 18% 20-39.

Student profile. Among degree-seeking undergraduates, 33% enrolled in a transfer program, 67% enrolled in a vocational program.

Transfer out. Colleges most students transferred to 2005: University of North Carolina-Wilmington, University of North Carolina-Pembroke, Fayetteville State University, East Carolina University, North Carolina State University.

Basis for selection. Open admission, but selective for some programs. Practical nursing program requires submission of appropriate test results and completion of high school biology and algebra courses with grade of C or better. ADN program requires biology and algebra, plus general chemistry. Biology and chemistry must be within last 5 years for ADN.

High school preparation. 24 units recommended. Recommended units include English 4, mathematics 3, social studies 1, history 1, science 3 (laboratory 1), foreign language 2 and academic electives 10.

2005-2006 Annual costs. Tuition/fees: $1,245; $6,645 out-of-state. Per-credit charge: $40 in-state; $220 out-of-state. Books/supplies: $800. Personal expenses: $725.

Financial aid. Need-based: Need-based aid available for part-time students. Work study available nights and for part-time students.

Application procedures. Admission: Priority date 8/15; no deadline. No application fee. Application may be submitted online. Admission notification on a rolling basis beginning on or about 6/15. **Financial aid:** Priority date 6/1; no closing date. FAFSA required. Applicants notified on a rolling basis starting 8/1; must reply within 2 week(s) of notification.

Academics. Special study options: Cooperative education, distance learning, double major, dual enrollment of high school students, ESL, independent study, internships, liberal arts/career combination, weekend college. Bachelor's degree programs available on campus. **Credit/placement by examination:** CLEP, institutional tests. 10 credit hours maximum toward associate degree. **Support services:** GED preparation and test center, learning center, reduced course load, remedial instruction, study skills assistance, tutoring, writing center.

Majors. Biology: Biotechnology. **Business:** Business admin, office technology, office/clerical. **Computer sciences:** General, applications programming, programming. **Education:** General. **Engineering technology:** Electrical, industrial. **Health:** Nursing (RN). **Liberal arts:** Arts/sciences. **Mechanic/repair:** Electronics/electrical. **Personal/culinary services:** Cosmetic. **Production:** Welding. **Protective services:** Law enforcement admin.

Computing on campus. 100 workstations in library, computer center.

Student life. Freshman orientation: Mandatory. Preregistration for classes offered. **Policies:** Freshmen permitted cars on campus. **Activities:** Drama, literary magazine, student government, student newspaper.

Athletics. Team name: Eagles.

Student services. Adult student services, alcohol/substance abuse counseling, career counseling, services for economically disadvantaged, student employment services, financial aid counseling, minority student services, personal counseling, placement for graduates, veterans' counselor. **Physically disabled:** Services for visually, speech, hearing impaired. **Transfer:** Special adviser, orientation, pre-admission transcript evaluation for new students. Transfer center, transfer adviser, college fairs on campus for students transferring to 4-year colleges.

Contact. E-mail: ywilloughby@bladen.cc.nc.us
Phone: (910) 879-5593 Fax: (910) 879-5564
Jeffrey Kornegay, Vice President of Student Services, Bladen Community College, Box 266, Dublin, NC 28332

Blue Ridge Community College
Flat Rock, North Carolina
www.blueridge.edu **CB code: 5644**

- Public 2-year community college
- Commuter campus in small town

General. Founded in 1969. Regionally accredited. **Enrollment:** 2,075 undergraduates. **Degrees:** 148 associate awarded. **Location:** 25 miles from Asheville. **Calendar:** Semester, limited summer session. **Full-time faculty:** 75 total. **Part-time faculty:** 230 total. **Class size:** 81% < 20, 19% 20-39, less than 1% 40-49.

Student profile.

Out-of-state:	2%	**25 or older:**	29%

Basis for selection. Open admission, but selective for some programs. Mathematics and science requirements for allied health programs in surgical technology, pharmacy technology, nursing.

High school preparation. 3 units of science, one of which must be lab, required for allied health programs only.

2005-2006 Annual costs. Tuition/fees: $1,255; $6,655 out-of-state. Per-credit charge: $40 in-state; $220 out-of-state. Books/supplies: $750.

2004-2005 Financial aid. Need-based: 98% of total undergraduate aid awarded as scholarships/grants, 2% as loans/jobs. Need-based aid available for part-time students. Work study available nights and for part-time students. **Non-need-based:** Scholarships awarded for academics, athletics, leadership, minority status, state residency.

Application procedures. Admission: No deadline. No application fee. Application may be submitted online. Admission notification on a rolling basis. **Financial aid:** Priority date 6/30; no closing date. FAFSA, institutional form required. Applicants notified on a rolling basis starting 2/1; must reply within 4 week(s) of notification.

Academics. Special study options: Cooperative education, distance learning, double major, dual enrollment of high school students, ESL. Bachelor's degree programs available on campus. License preparation in nursing, paramedic, physical therapy, real estate. **Credit/placement by examination:** CLEP, institutional tests. Maximum of 50% of credit hours by examination may be counted toward degree. **Support services:** GED preparation and test center, learning center, reduced course load, remedial instruction, study skills assistance, tutoring.

Majors. Agriculture: Horticulture. **Business:** General, administrative services, sales/distribution, tourism promotion, tourism/travel. **Computer sciences:** Information systems, programming. **Conservation:** General. **Engineering:** Electrical. **Engineering technology:** Drafting, electrical. **Family/consumer sciences:** Child care. **Foreign languages:** Sign language interpretation. **Health:** Nursing (RN), surgical technology. **Liberal arts:** Arts/sciences.

Most popular majors. Business/marketing 14%, computer/information sciences 26%, health sciences 12%, liberal arts 23%.

Computing on campus. 200 workstations in library, computer center.

Student life. Freshman orientation: Mandatory. Preregistration for classes offered. **Policies:** Freshmen permitted cars on campus. **Activities:** Drama, literary magazine, student government, Circle-K, Rotaract, Phi Theta Kappa, National Vocational-Technical Honor Society.

Athletics. NJCAA. **Intercollegiate:** Bowling M, volleyball W.

Student services. Adult student services, career counseling, student employment services, financial aid counseling, on-campus daycare, personal counseling, placement for graduates, veterans' counselor. **Physically disabled:** Services for visually, speech, hearing impaired. **Transfer:** Special adviser, orientation, pre-admission transcript evaluation for new students. Transfer adviser, college fairs on campus for students transferring to 4-year colleges.

Contact. E-mail: kirstenb@blueridge.edu
Phone: (828) 694-1800 Fax: (828) 694-1693
Frank Byrd, Dean for Student Services, Blue Ridge Community College, 180 West Campus Drive, Flat Rock, NC 28731-9624

Brunswick Community College
Supply, North Carolina
www.brunswickcc.edu **CB code: 7314**

- Public 2-year community college
- Commuter campus in small town

General. Founded in 1979. Regionally accredited. **Enrollment:** 993 degree-seeking undergraduates; 40 non-degree-seeking students. **Degrees:** 97 associate awarded. **Location:** 25 miles from Wilmington, 30 miles from Myrtle Beach, South Carolina. **Calendar:** Semester, limited summer session. **Full-time faculty:** 32 total; 16% have terminal degrees, 3% minority, 53% women. **Part-time faculty:** 72 total; 7% have terminal degrees, 7% minority, 65% women. **Class size:** 79% < 20, 21% 20-39.

Student profile. Among degree-seeking undergraduates, 31% enrolled in a transfer program, 45% enrolled in a vocational program, 2% already have a bachelor's degree or higher, 226 enrolled as first-time, first-year students.

Part-time:	49%	**Asian American:**	1%
Out-of-state:	3%	**Hispanic American:**	2%
Women:	73%	**Native American:**	1%
African American:	21%	**25 or older:**	50%

Transfer out. Colleges most students transferred to 2005: University of North Carolina at Wilmington.

Basis for selection. Open admission, but selective for some programs. Phlebotomy, basic law enforcement technology, practical nursing, associate degree nursing, and health information technology program applicants must have completed specific course work before they are considered. Limited slots. May also enter based on test scores. SAT accepted in lieu of ASSET Placement Test. Interview is required to review admission procedures and file; does not determine acceptance. **Adult students:** Entrance exam policies same as for first-time freshmen. **Learning Disabled:** Requests for any accommodations should be made at least 2 weeks prior to beginning of applicant's first semester.

2005-2006 Annual costs. Tuition/fees: $1,258; $6,658 out-of-state. Per-credit charge: $40 in-state; $220 out-of-state. Books/supplies: $600. Personal expenses: $800.

Financial aid. Need-based: Need-based aid available for part-time students. **Non-need-based:** Scholarships awarded for academics, state residency. **Additional information:** Attendance required at financial aid orientation session for those receiving federal student aid.

Application procedures. Admission: No deadline. No application fee. Application may be submitted online. Admission notification on a rolling basis. **Financial aid:** Priority date 6/1, closing date 6/15. FAFSA, institutional form required. Applicants notified on a rolling basis starting 3/1; must reply by 6/30 or within 2 week(s) of notification.

Academics. Special study options: Distance learning, dual enrollment of high school students, ESL, internships. License preparation in aviation, nursing, paramedic, real estate. **Credit/placement by examination:** AP, CLEP, institutional tests. No limits on credit by examination hours that may be applied toward an associate degree. **Support services:** GED preparation and test center, learning center, reduced course load, remedial instruction, study skills assistance, tutoring.

Majors. Agriculture: Aquaculture, horticultural science, turf management. **Business:** Administrative services, business admin. **Computer sciences:** Information systems, programming. **Education:** Early childhood. **Engineering technology:** Electrical. **Health:** Medical records technology, nursing (RN). **Liberal arts:** Arts/sciences. **Mechanic/repair:** Industrial. **Personal/culinary services:** Cosmetic.

Computing on campus. 146 workstations in library, computer center.

Student life. Freshman orientation: Available. Preregistration for classes offered. **Policies:** All facilities are nonsmoking. Smoking allowed in designated outdoor areas only. Freshmen permitted cars on campus. **Activities:** Student government, student newspaper, National Technical Honor Society, Phi Theta Kappa, science club, journalism club, Loaves and Fishes.

Athletics. NJCAA. **Intercollegiate:** Basketball, softball W. **Team name:** Dolphins.

Student services. Career counseling, student employment services, financial aid counseling, personal counseling, placement for graduates, veterans' counselor. **Physically disabled:** Services for visually, hearing impaired. **Transfer:** Special adviser, orientation, pre-admission transcript evaluation for new students. Transfer adviser, college fairs on campus for students transferring to 4-year colleges.

Contact. E-mail: olsenj@brunswick.cc.nc.us
Phone: (910) 755-7324 Toll-free number: (800) 754-1050 ext. 324
Fax: (910) 754-9609
Julie Olsen, Admissions Counselor, Brunswick Community College, Box 30, Supply, NC 28462

Caldwell Community College and Technical Institute

Hudson, North Carolina
www.cccti.edu **CB code: 5146**

- Public 2-year community and technical college
- Commuter campus in small town

General. Founded in 1964. Regionally accredited. **Enrollment:** 3,108 degree-seeking undergraduates; 636 non-degree-seeking students. **Degrees:** 319 associate awarded. **Location:** 70 miles from Charlotte. **Calendar:** Semester, limited summer session. **Full-time faculty:** 135 total. **Part-time faculty:** 434 total. **Class size:** 68% < 20, 31% 20-39, 1% 40-49, less than 1% 50-99, less than 1% >100.

Student profile. Among degree-seeking undergraduates, 763 enrolled as first-time, first-year students.

Part-time:	60%	**Women:**	60%
Out-of-state:	2%	**25 or older:**	43%

Basis for selection. Open admission, but selective for some programs. Limited number of applicants admitted to health science programs, interview required. College-administered examination used for placement.

2005-2006 Annual costs. Tuition/fees: $1,225; $6,625 out-of-state. Per-credit charge: $40 in-state; $220 out-of-state. Books/supplies: $925. Personal expenses: $1,350.

Financial aid. All financial aid based on need. Need-based aid available for part-time students. Work study available for part-time students.

Application procedures. Admission: No deadline. No application fee. Admission notification on a rolling basis. **Financial aid:** Priority date 4/1; no closing date. FAFSA required. Applicants notified on a rolling basis starting 6/30.

Academics. Special study options: Cooperative education, distance learning, dual enrollment of high school students, independent study. License preparation in aviation, nursing, occupational therapy, physical therapy, real estate. **Credit/placement by examination:** CLEP, institutional tests. 16 credit hours maximum toward associate degree. **Support services:** GED preparation and test center, learning center, reduced course load, remedial instruction, tutoring.

Majors. Business: Accounting, administrative services, business admin. **Computer sciences:** Applications programming, data processing, programming. **Education:** Early childhood. **Engineering technology:** Drafting, electrical. **Health:** Cardiovascular technology, medical radiologic technology/radiation therapy, medical secretary, nuclear medical technology, nursing (RN), physical therapy assistant, sonography. **Legal studies:** Paralegal. **Liberal arts:** Arts/sciences. **Math:** General. **Mechanic/repair:** Industrial. **Transportation:** Aviation management. **Visual/performing arts:** Art.

Most popular majors. Business/marketing 22%, computer/information sciences 12%, health sciences 37%, liberal arts 16%.

Computing on campus. 750 workstations in library, computer center.

Student life. Freshman orientation: Available. Preregistration for classes offered. 2-day session held prior to beginning of fall semester. **Policies:** Freshmen permitted cars on campus. **Activities:** Choral groups, drama, student government, TV station, Ebony Kinship, special interest clubs, Phi Theta Kappa, Alpha Omega (non-denominational religious organization).

Athletics. NJCAA. **Intercollegiate:** Basketball M, volleyball W. **Intramural:** Basketball, tennis. **Team name:** Cobras.

Student services. Career counseling, student employment services, financial aid counseling, personal counseling, placement for graduates, veterans' counselor. **Physically disabled:** Services for visually, hearing impaired. **Transfer:** Special adviser, orientation for new students. Transfer adviser, college fairs on campus for students transferring to 4-year colleges.

Contact. Phone: (828) 726-2700 Fax: (828) 726-2709
Carolyan Woodard, Director of Admissions, Caldwell Community College and Technical Institute, 2855 Hickory Boulevard, Hudson, NC 28638-2672

Cape Fear Community College

Wilmington, North Carolina
www.cfcc.edu **CB code: 5094**

- Public 2-year community college
- Commuter campus in small city

General. Founded in 1959. Regionally accredited. Campuses at Burgaw, Hampstead, and North Campus, 7 miles from downtown Wilmington. **Enrollment:** 6,156 degree-seeking undergraduates. **Degrees:** 312 associate awarded. **Location:** 125 miles from Raleigh. **Calendar:** Semester, limited summer session. **Full-time faculty:** 223 total. **Part-time faculty:** 409 total. **Class size:** 56% < 20, 44% 20-39.

Student profile. Among degree-seeking undergraduates, 50% enrolled in a transfer program, 50% enrolled in a vocational program.

Out-of-state:	8%	**25 or older:**	38%

Transfer out. Colleges most students transferred to 2005: University of North Carolina at Wilmington.

Basis for selection. Open admission, but selective for some programs. Special requirements for nursing and allied health programs: Psychological Corporation Pre-Nursing Examination and interview required. **Adult students:** Entrance exam policies same as for first-time freshmen. **Homeschooled:** A copy of approval from North Carolina Department of Non-Public Instruction required. **Learning Disabled:** Students must register with Disability Services.

2005-2006 Annual costs. Tuition/fees: $1,253; $6,653 out-of-state. Per-credit charge: $40 in-state; $220 out-of-state. Books/supplies: $900. Personal expenses: $900.

2004-2005 Financial aid. Need-based: Need-based aid available for part-time students. Work study available nights. **Non-need-based:** Scholarships awarded for academics, job skills.

Application procedures. Admission: No deadline. No application fee. Application may be submitted online. Admission notification on a rolling basis. **Financial aid:** Priority date 6/1; no closing date. FAFSA required. Applicants notified on a rolling basis starting 4/1; must reply within 2 week(s) of notification.

Academics. Special study options: Cooperative education, distance learning, dual enrollment of high school students, internships. License preparation in dental hygiene, nursing, paramedic, real estate. **Credit/placement by examination:** AP, CLEP, institutional tests. **Support services:** GED preparation and test center, learning center, remedial instruction, study skills assistance, tutoring.

Majors. Agriculture: Landscaping. **Business:** Accounting technology, administrative services, business admin, executive assistant, hospitality admin, hotel/motel admin, restaurant/food services. **Computer sciences:** Information technology. **Conservation:** General. **Construction:** Electrician. **Engineering:** Chemical. **Engineering technology:** Architectural, computer systems, electrical, instrumentation, mechanical. **Family/consumer sciences:** Child care, institutional food production. **Health:** Dental hygiene, medical radiologic technology/radiation therapy, nursing (RN), occupational therapy assistant, sonography. **Legal studies:** Paralegal. **Liberal arts:** Arts/sciences. **Mechanic/repair:** Automotive. **Personal/culinary services:** Cosmetic, culinary arts. **Physical sciences:** Oceanography. **Production:** Machine shop technology, welding. **Protective services:** Police science. **Visual/performing arts:** Cinematography, interior design.

Most popular majors. Business/marketing 16%, engineering/engineering technologies 13%, health sciences 11%, liberal arts 44%.

Computing on campus. 80 workstations in library, computer center.

Student life. Freshman orientation: Available. Preregistration for classes offered. **Policies:** Freshmen permitted cars on campus. **Activities:** Choral groups, student government, student newspaper, Phi Theta Kappa Honor Society.

Athletics. NJCAA. **Intercollegiate:** Basketball M, golf, volleyball W. **Intramural:** Cheerleading, soccer. **Team name:** Sea Devils.

Student services. Alcohol/substance abuse counseling, career counseling, student employment services, financial aid counseling, on-campus daycare, personal counseling, placement for graduates, veterans' counselor. **Physically disabled:** Services for visually, speech, hearing impaired. **Transfer:** Special adviser, orientation, pre-admission transcript evaluation for new students. Transfer adviser, college fairs on campus for students transferring to 4-year colleges.

Contact. Phone: (910) 362-7557 Fax: (910) 362-7080
Linda Kasyan, Director of Enrollment Management, Cape Fear Community College, 411 North Front Street, Wilmington, NC 28401-3910

Carolinas College of Health Sciences

Charlotte, North Carolina
www.carolinascollege.edu **CB code: 6211**

- Public 2-year health science and junior college
- Commuter campus in very large city
- SAT or ACT required

General. Regionally accredited. Institution supported by public hospital system. **Enrollment:** 401 degree-seeking undergraduates. **Degrees:** 71 associate awarded. **Calendar:** Semester, limited summer session. **Full-time faculty:** 45 total. **Part-time faculty:** 20 total. **Class size:** 40% < 20, 57% 20-39, 3% 40-49.

Transfer out. Colleges most students transferred to 2005: Queens College, University of North Carolina at Charlotte, Winston-Salem State University, Central Piedmont Community College, Mercy School of Nursing.

Basis for selection. Selection based on SAT/ACT test scores and high school GPA. Only students with permanent resident status will be considered for enrollment.

High school preparation. Required units include mathematics 1, science 2 (laboratory 2). Algebra, biology, chemistry required.

2006-2007 Annual costs. Tuition/fees: $5,750. Per-credit charge: $185. Tuition varies by program. Books/supplies: $500.

2004-2005 Financial aid. Need-based: 37% of total undergraduate aid awarded as scholarships/grants, 63% as loans/jobs. Need-based aid available for part-time students. Work study available for part-time students. **Non-need-based:** Scholarships awarded for academics.

Application procedures. Admission: Priority date 2/1; no deadline. $50 fee. Must reply by May 1 or within 6 week(s) if notified thereafter. Application deadlines vary by program. **Financial aid:** Priority date 5/1; no closing date. FAFSA, institutional form required. Applicants notified on a rolling basis starting 5/1.

Academics. Special study options: Distance learning, independent study, liberal arts/career combination. License preparation in nursing. **Credit/placement by examination:** CLEP, institutional tests. 15 credit hours maximum toward associate degree. **Support services:** Learning center, tutoring.

Majors. Health: Medical radiologic technology/radiation therapy.

Computing on campus. 25 workstations in computer center. Online library available.

Student life. Freshman orientation: Mandatory. **Policies:** Freshmen permitted cars on campus. **Housing:** Apartments owned by health care system available. **Activities:** Student government.

Student services. Alcohol/substance abuse counseling, campus ministries, career counseling, student employment services, financial aid counseling, health services, personal counseling, placement for graduates. **Transfer:** Special adviser, orientation, pre-admission transcript evaluation for new students. College fairs on campus for students transferring to 4-year colleges.

Contact. E-mail: cchsinformation@carolinas.org
Phone: (704) 355-5583 Fax: (704) 355-9336
Elizabeth West, Admissions Officer, Carolinas College of Health Sciences, PO Box 32861, Charlotte, NC 28232

Carteret Community College

Morehead City, North Carolina
www.carteret.cc.nc.us **CB code: 5092**

- Public 2-year community college
- Commuter campus in small town

General. Founded in 1963. Regionally accredited. Health science programs and library learning resources center on Bogue Sound. **Enrollment:** 1,700 degree-seeking undergraduates. **Degrees:** 112 associate awarded. **Location:** 150 miles from Raleigh, 87 miles from Wilmington. **Calendar:** Semester, limited summer session. **Full-time faculty:** 59 total. **Part-time faculty:** 82 total. **Special facilities:** Civic center, county historical research headquarters, center for marine and science technology.

Student profile. Among degree-seeking undergraduates, 43% enrolled in a transfer program, 57% enrolled in a vocational program, 1% already have a bachelor's degree or higher, 400 enrolled as first-time, first-year students.

Part-time:	55%	**Women:**	67%
Out-of-state:	2%	**25 or older:**	48%

Transfer out. Colleges most students transferred to 2005: University of North Carolina at Wilmington, East Carolina University.

Basis for selection. Open admission, but selective for some programs. Admission to allied health programs based uponcourse work, grades and test scores; interview required. SAT required of radiologic technology and respiratory therapy applicants; score report due by January 1. **Learning Disabled:** Students requesting academic accomadations must present proper documentation.

High school preparation. Extensive science and mathematics recommended for allied health programs, particularly respiratory therapy, radiologic technology, and nursing.

2005-2006 Annual costs. Tuition/fees: $1,236; $6,636 out-of-state. Per-credit charge: $40 in-state; $220 out-of-state. Books/supplies: $500. Personal expenses: $1,665.

Financial aid. Need-based: Need-based aid available for part-time students. **Non-need-based:** Scholarships awarded for academics, leadership, minority status, state residency. **Additional information:** Institutional student loan program administered by college. Student may charge up to $600 for books, supplies and tuition per quarter. Repayment due by 11th week of semester.

Application procedures. Admission: No deadline. No application fee. Application may be submitted online. Admission notification on a rolling basis. **Financial aid:** No deadline. FAFSA, institutional form required. Applicants notified on a rolling basis; must reply within 2 week(s) of notification.

Academics. Special study options: Cross-registration, distance learning, double major, dual enrollment of high school students, ESL, internships, liberal arts/career combination, teacher certification program. License preparation in nursing, paramedic, radiology, real estate. **Credit/placement by examination:** CLEP, institutional tests. **Support services:** GED preparation and test center, learning center, pre-admission summer program, reduced course load, remedial instruction, study skills assistance, tutoring, writing center.

Majors. Agriculture: Greenhouse operations, horticultural science, horticulture. **Business:** General, administrative services, e-commerce, hotel/motel admin, office/clerical. **Communications:** Photojournalism. **Communications technology:** Photo/film/video. **Computer sciences:** General, information technology, LAN/WAN management, web page design, webmaster. **Education:** General, teacher assistance. **Family/consumer sciences:** Child development. **Health:** EMT ambulance attendant, massage therapy, medical radiologic technology/radiation therapy, office admin, predentistry, premedicine, prenursing, prepharmacy, preveterinary, radiologic technology/medical imaging, recreational therapy, respiratory therapy technology. **Legal studies:** Legal secretary, paralegal. **Liberal arts:** Arts/sciences. **Mechanic/repair:** Marine. **Parks/recreation:** General. **Personal/culinary services:** Restaurant/catering. **Protective services:** Criminal justice, police science. **Visual/performing arts:** General, interior design, photography.

Most popular majors. Business/marketing 70%, health sciences 25%.

Computing on campus. 100 workstations in library, computer center, student center. Helpline available.

Student life. Freshman orientation: Available. Preregistration for classes offered. **Activities:** Choral groups, literary magazine, student government, student newspaper, Psi Beta (honorary society for psychology majors), Phi Beta Lambda (business organization).

Student services. Adult student services, alcohol/substance abuse counseling, career counseling, services for economically disadvantaged, student employment services, financial aid counseling, personal counseling, placement for graduates, veterans' counselor. **Transfer:** Special adviser, orientation, pre-admission transcript evaluation for new students. Transfer adviser, college fairs on campus for students transferring to 4-year colleges.

Contact. E-mail: mhw@carteret.cc.nc.us
Phone: (252) 222-6154 Fax: (252) 222-6265
Margie Ward, Admissions Officer, Carteret Community College, 3505 Arendell Street, Morehead City, NC 28557-2989

Catawba Valley Community College

Hickory, North Carolina
www.cvcc.edu **CB code: 5098**

- Public 2-year community college
- Commuter campus in large town

General. Founded in 1960. Regionally accredited. **Enrollment:** 4,200 degree-seeking undergraduates; 730 non-degree-seeking students. **Degrees:** 469 associate awarded. **Location:** 50 miles from Charlotte. **Calendar:** Semester, limited summer session. **Full-time faculty:** 144 total; 3% minority, 49% women. **Part-time faculty:** 339 total; 8% minority, 61% women. **Class size:** 49% < 20, 39% 20-39, less than 1% 40-49.

Student profile. Among degree-seeking undergraduates, 29% enrolled in a transfer program, 71% enrolled in a vocational program, 1% already have a bachelor's degree or higher, 898 enrolled as first-time, first-year students, 480 transferred in from other institutions.

Part-time:	50%	**25 or older:**	52%
Women:	61%		

Basis for selection. Open admission, but selective for some programs. Special requirements for nursing, emergency medical science, surgical technology, respiratory care, health information technology, dental hygiene, speech-language pathology assistant, advertising and graphic design, photography. Interview required for health program applicants, advertising and graphic design applicants, and photography applicants; recommended for all others. **Homeschooled:** Transcript of courses and grades, state high school equivalency certificate required.

2005-2006 Annual costs. Tuition/fees: $1,209; $6,609 out-of-state. Per-credit charge: $40 in-state; $220 out-of-state. Books/supplies: $700. Personal expenses: $1,386.

2004-2005 Financial aid. Need-based: 507 full-time freshmen applied for aid; 285 were judged to have need; 239 of these received aid. 99% of total undergraduate aid awarded as scholarships/grants, 1% as loans/jobs. Need-based aid available for part-time students. **Non-need-based:** Awarded to 76 full-time undergraduates, including 31 freshmen. Scholarships awarded for academics, athletics, leadership, music/drama.

Application procedures. Admission: No deadline. No application fee. Application may be submitted online. Admission notification on a rolling basis. **Financial aid:** Closing date 3/15. FAFSA required. Applicants notified on a rolling basis starting 5/15.

Academics. Special study options: Cooperative education, distance learning, double major, dual enrollment of high school students, independent study, student-designed major, teacher certification program. License preparation in dental hygiene, nursing, paramedic, real estate. **Credit/placement by examination:** AP, CLEP, IB, institutional tests. Maximum of 65% of total credit hours required for degree may be obtained by examination. **Support services:** GED preparation and test center, learning center, reduced course load, remedial instruction, study skills assistance, tutoring.

Majors. Agriculture: Horticultural science, turf management. **Architecture:** Technology. **Business:** Accounting, administrative services, business admin, finance, management information systems. **Communications technology:** Photo/film/video. **Computer sciences:** Information systems, information technology, LAN/WAN management, programming. **Education:** Early childhood. **Engineering technology:** Architectural, computer, electrical, electromechanical, mechanical. **Health:** Dental hygiene, EMT paramedic, medical radiologic technology/radiation therapy, medical records technology, nursing (RN), respiratory therapy assistant, respiratory therapy technology. **Liberal arts:** Arts/sciences. **Mechanic/repair:** Automotive. **Production:** Furniture. **Protective services:** Criminal justice. **Visual/performing arts:** Commercial/advertising art.

Most popular majors. Business/marketing 18%, computer/information sciences 7%, engineering/engineering technologies 7%, health sciences 27%, liberal arts 25%.

Computing on campus. 1,300 workstations in library, computer center. Commuter students can connect to campus network. Repair service, wireless network available.

Student life. Freshman orientation: Available. Available for degree-seeking students. **Policies:** Freshmen permitted cars on campus. **Activities:** Choral groups, music ensembles, student government, student newspaper, Phi Theta Kappa International Honor Society, student government association, Association of Nursing Students, Certifiable Club, Rotaract Club, Student American Dental Hygiene Association, Students in Free Enterprise.

Athletics. NJCAA. **Intercollegiate:** Basketball M, volleyball W. **Team name:** Buccaneers.

Student services. Career counseling, student employment services, personal counseling, placement for graduates, veterans' counselor. **Physically disabled:** Services for visually, hearing impaired. **Transfer:** Special adviser, orientation, pre-admission transcript evaluation for new students. Transfer adviser, college fairs on campus for students transferring to 4-year colleges.

Contact. Phone: (828) 327-7000 Fax: (828) 327-7276
LaDonna Goodson, Director of Admissions and Counseling Services, Catawba Valley Community College, 2550 Highway 70 Southeast, Hickory, NC 28602

Central Carolina Community College

Sanford, North Carolina
www.cccc.edu **CB code: 5147**

- Public 2-year community college
- Commuter campus in large town

General. Founded in 1958. Regionally accredited. **Enrollment:** 3,366 degree-seeking undergraduates. **Degrees:** 278 associate awarded. **Location:** 45 miles from Raleigh. **Calendar:** Semester, limited summer session. **Full-time faculty:** 145 total. **Part-time faculty:** 280 total. **Class size:** 73% < 20, 25% 20-39, less than 1% 40-49, less than 1% 50-99.

Student profile.

Out-of-state:	2%	**25 or older:**	49%

Transfer out. Colleges most students transferred to 2005: ECU, NCSU, UNC-G, UNC-W, ASU.

Basis for selection. Open admission, but selective for some programs. Special requirements for veterinary technician, nursing education, radio-television broadcasting, laser electro-optic, electronics and instrumentation technology, cosmetology, medical assisting programs. ACT/SAT scores may exempt student from placement tests. **Adult students:** Entrance exam policies same as for first-time freshmen. **Homeschooled:** Must be registered with local county Board of Education and NC Non-public Education office; must submit documentation of successful completion of NC Competency Exam, copies of transcript and high school diploma. **Learning Disabled:** Students must sign up with special populations office and request accommodations and services.

High school preparation. Strong background in mathematics, biology, and chemistry required for veterinary technician and nursing education option programs.

2005-2006 Annual costs. Tuition/fees: $1,223; $6,623 out-of-state. Per-credit charge: $40 in-state; $220 out-of-state. Books/supplies: $666.

Financial aid. Need-based: Need-based aid available for part-time students. Work study available nights and for part-time students. **Non-need-based:** Scholarships awarded for academics.

Application procedures. Admission: No deadline. No application fee. Application may be submitted online. Admission notification on a rolling basis. **Financial aid:** Priority date 3/15, closing date 5/1. FAFSA, institutional form required. Applicants notified on a rolling basis starting 7/1; must reply within 2 week(s) of notification.

Academics. Special study options: Distance learning, dual enrollment of high school students, honors, independent study, internships, liberal arts/career combination, weekend college. License preparation in nursing, real estate. **Credit/placement by examination:** CLEP, institutional tests. Placement interview required. **Support services:** GED preparation, learning center, reduced course load, remedial instruction, study skills assistance, tutoring, writing center.

Majors. Business: Accounting, administrative services, business admin, office/clerical. **Communications:** Broadcast journalism. **Computer sciences:** Applications programming, information systems, networking, programming. **Education:** General, early childhood. **Engineering:** Civil, computer. **Engineering technology:** Architectural, civil, drafting, electrical, manufacturing, robotics, surveying. **Family/consumer sciences:** Child care. **Health:** Licensed practical nurse, medical assistant, medical secretary, nursing (RN), veterinary technology/assistant. **Legal studies:** Legal secretary, paralegal. **Liberal arts:** Arts/sciences. **Mechanic/repair:** Automotive, industrial. **Personal/culinary services:** General, cosmetic. **Protective services:** Criminal justice. **Public administration:** Human services. **Science technology:** Biological.

Most popular majors. Business/marketing 35%, engineering/engineering technologies 8%, health sciences 43%, liberal arts 12%.

Computing on campus. Online library, helpline, repair service available.

Student life. Freshman orientation: Mandatory. **Policies:** Freshmen permitted cars on campus. **Activities:** Radio station, student government, Student Nurses Association, Student Ambassador Program, Veterinary Medical Technician Student Organization.

Athletics. NJCAA. **Intercollegiate:** Basketball M, golf, softball, volleyball. **Intramural:** Basketball M, bowling, golf, softball, tennis M, volleyball.

Student services. Career counseling, student employment services, financial aid counseling, personal counseling, placement for graduates, veterans' counselor. **Physically disabled:** Services for visually, speech, hearing impaired. **Transfer:** Special adviser for new students. Transfer adviser for students transferring to 4-year colleges.

Contact. E-mail: khoyle@cccc.edu
Phone: (919) 775-5401 Toll-free number: (800) 682-8353
Fax: (919) 718-7379
Ken Hoyle, Dean of Student Support Services, Central Carolina Community College, 1105 Kelly Drive, Sanford, NC 27330

Two-Year Colleges

Central Piedmont Community College

Charlotte, North Carolina **CB member**
www.cpcc.edu **CB code: 5102**

- Public 2-year community college
- Commuter campus in very large city

General. Founded in 1963. Regionally accredited. **Enrollment:** 10,535 degree-seeking undergraduates; 6,101 non-degree-seeking students. **Degrees:** 896 associate awarded. **Location:** 247 miles from Atlanta. **Calendar:** Semester, extensive summer session. **Full-time faculty:** 309 total. **Part-time faculty:** 1,726 total.

Student profile. Among degree-seeking undergraduates, 54% enrolled in a transfer program, 46% enrolled in a vocational program, 5% already have a bachelor's degree or higher, 1,377 enrolled as first-time, first-year students.

Part-time:	57%	**Hispanic American:**	3%
Out-of-state:	2%	**Native American:**	1%
Women:	60%	**International:**	9%
African American:	32%	**25 or older:**	48%
Asian American:	3%		

Basis for selection. Open admission, but selective for some programs. Placement test scores used for admission to some programs with specific requirements. **Adult students:** Entrance exam policies same as for first-time freshmen.

High school preparation. Recommended units include English 4, mathematics 3, social studies 3 and science 3.

2005-2006 Annual costs. Tuition/fees: $1,255; $6,655 out-of-state. Per-credit charge: $40 in-state; $220 out-of-state. Books/supplies: $1,100. Personal expenses: $596.

Financial aid. Need-based: Need-based aid available for part-time students. **Non-need-based:** Scholarships awarded for academics, minority status.

Application procedures. Admission: No deadline. No application fee. Application may be submitted online. Admission notification on a rolling basis. **Financial aid:** Priority date 4/3, closing date 6/3. FAFSA required. Applicants notified on a rolling basis.

Academics. Special study options: Cooperative education, cross-registration, distance learning, double major, dual enrollment of high school students, ESL, honors, independent study, internships, weekend college. **Credit/placement by examination:** AP, CLEP, institutional tests. **Support services:** GED preparation and test center, learning center, reduced course load, remedial instruction, study skills assistance, tutoring, writing center.

Majors. Agriculture: Horticulture, turf management. **Business:** Accounting technology, administrative services, business admin, hospitality admin, international, management information systems, real estate, retailing, tourism/travel. **Communications technology:** Graphic/printing. **Computer sciences:** Database management, information technology, LAN/WAN management, programming, webmaster. **Construction:** Electrician. **Education:** Early childhood. **Engineering technology:** Architectural, civil, electrical, industrial management, mechanical, occupational safety, surveying. **Family/consumer sciences:** Child care. **Foreign languages:** Sign language interpretation. **Health:** Cardiovascular technology, clinical lab assistant, cytotechnology, dental hygiene, medical assistant, medical records technology, mental health services, nursing (RN), physical therapy assistant, respiratory therapy technology, substance abuse counseling. **Legal studies:** Legal secretary, paralegal. **Liberal arts:** Arts/sciences. **Mechanic/repair:** Automotive, diesel, heating/ac/refrig. **Parks/recreation:** Facilities management. **Personal/culinary services:** Chef training. **Production:** Machine shop technology, welding. **Protective services:** Corrections, fire safety technology. **Visual/performing arts:** Commercial/advertising art, interior design.

Most popular majors. Business/marketing 8%, health sciences 14%, liberal arts 49%.

Computing on campus. 2,591 workstations in library, computer center, student center. Online course registration, helpline, wireless network available.

Student life. Freshman orientation: Available. **Policies:** Freshmen permitted cars on campus. **Activities:** Bands, choral groups, dance, drama, film society, literary magazine, music ensembles, musical theater, opera, radio station, student government, student newspaper, symphony orchestra, TV station, Afro-American cultural club, Baptist student union, international students club, chess club, Phi Theta Kappa.

Athletics. NJCAA. **Intramural:** Soccer.

Student services. Adult student services, campus ministries, career counseling, student employment services, financial aid counseling, personal counseling, placement for graduates, veterans' counselor, women's services. **Physically disabled:** Services for visually, speech, hearing impaired. **Transfer:** Special adviser, orientation, re-entry adviser, pre-admission transcript evaluation for new students. Transfer adviser, college fairs on campus for students transferring to 4-year colleges.

Contact. Phone: (704) 330-2722 Fax: (704) 330-6007
Linda McComb, Associate Dean of Admissions/Registration/Records, Central Piedmont Community College, Box 35009, Charlotte, NC 28235-5009

Cleveland Community College

Shelby, North Carolina **CB member**
www.clevelandcommunitycollege.edu **CB code: 5140**

- Public 2-year community college
- Commuter campus in large town

General. Founded in 1965. Regionally accredited. **Enrollment:** 1,749 degree-seeking undergraduates; 1,298 non-degree-seeking students. **Degrees:** 220 associate awarded. **Location:** 45 miles from Charlotte. **Calendar:** Semester, limited summer session. **Full-time faculty:** 75 total. **Part-time faculty:** 140 total. **Class size:** 71% < 20, 28% 20-39, less than 1% 40-49. **Special facilities:** Nature trail. **Partnerships:** Tech Prep, Huskins Classes.

Student profile. Among degree-seeking undergraduates, 30% enrolled in a transfer program, 70% enrolled in a vocational program, 10% already have a bachelor's degree or higher, 279 enrolled as first-time, first-year students.

Part-time:	53%	**Asian American:**	1%
Out-of-state:	1%	**Hispanic American:**	1%
Women:	69%	**25 or older:**	68%
African American:	23%		

Transfer out. Colleges most students transferred to 2005: Gardner-Webb University, University of North Carolina-Charlotte, Appalachian State University, Western Carolina University, North Carolina State University.

Basis for selection. Open admission, but selective for some programs. Special requirements for allied health programs. Satisfactory SAT or ACT scores may be used in lieu of academic placement testing for all programs except allied health. Interview required for nursing, radiography, and phlebotomy programs. **Learning Disabled:** Contact Director of Admissions for assistance.

2005-2006 Annual costs. Tuition/fees: $1,223; $6,623 out-of-state. Per-credit charge: $40 in-state; $220 out-of-state. Books/supplies: $800.

2004-2005 Financial aid. Need-based: 98% of total undergraduate aid awarded as scholarships/grants, 2% as loans/jobs. Need-based aid available for part-time students. Work study available for part-time students.

Application procedures. Admission: No deadline. No application fee. Application may be submitted online. Applicants notified immediately except for allied health applicants. **Financial aid:** Priority date 7/1; no closing date. FAFSA required. Applicants notified on a rolling basis.

Academics. Special study options: Accelerated study, cooperative education, cross-registration, distance learning, double major, dual enrollment of high school students, ESL, honors, independent study, internships, liberal arts/career combination. Bachelor's degree programs available on campus. License preparation in nursing, paramedic, real estate. **Credit/placement by examination:** AP, CLEP, IB, institutional tests. 28 credit hours maximum toward associate degree. Credit determined on individual basis. **Support services:** GED preparation and test center, learning center, reduced course load, remedial instruction, study skills assistance, tutoring.

Majors. Business: Accounting, administrative services, business admin, e-commerce, operations. **Communications technology:** General. **Computer sciences:** Applications programming, information systems, networking, programming. **Engineering:** General. **Engineering technology:** General, electrical. **Family/consumer sciences:** Child care. **Health:** Medical radiologic technology/radiation therapy, medical secretary, nursing (RN). **Legal studies:** Legal secretary. **Liberal arts:** Arts/sciences. **Protective services:** Criminal justice, fire safety technology.

Computing on campus. 372 workstations in library, computer center. Online library available.

Student life. Freshman orientation: Available. Preregistration for classes offered. **Policies:** Freshmen permitted cars on campus. **Activities:** Choral groups, drama, musical theater, student government, student newspaper, TV station, black awareness club, communications club, criminal justice club, radiologic technology club, nursing club, Students in Free Enterprise, Mu Epsilon Delta, Baptist Union.

Athletics. Intramural: Basketball, golf, softball, tennis.

Student services. Adult student services, career counseling, student employment services, financial aid counseling, personal counseling, placement for graduates, veterans' counselor. **Physically disabled:** Services for visually, speech, hearing impaired. **Transfer:** Special adviser, orientation, preadmission transcript evaluation for new students. Transfer adviser, college fairs on campus for students transferring to 4-year colleges.

Contact. E-mail: maddox@cleveland.cc.nc.us
Phone: (704) 484-4103 Fax: (704) 484-5305
Alan Price, Dean of Enrollment Management, Cleveland Community College, 137 South Post Road, Shelby, NC 28152

Coastal Carolina Community College

Jacksonville, North Carolina
www.coastal.cc.nc.us **CB code: 5134**

- Public 2-year community college
- Commuter campus in large town

General. Founded in 1964. Regionally accredited. Off-campus classes available at Camp Lejeune Marine Corps Base and New River Marine Corps Air Station. **Enrollment:** 3,801 degree-seeking undergraduates; 316 non-degree-seeking students. **Degrees:** 444 associate awarded. **Location:** 100 miles from Raleigh. **Calendar:** Semester, limited summer session. **Full-time faculty:** 123 total; 10% have terminal degrees, 6% minority, 58% women. **Part-time faculty:** 156 total; 12% have terminal degrees, 13% minority, 53% women. **Class size:** 58% < 20, 42% 20-39.

Student profile. Among degree-seeking undergraduates, 58% enrolled in a transfer program, 33% enrolled in a vocational program, 2% already have a bachelor's degree or higher, 836 enrolled as first-time, first-year students, 645 transferred in from other institutions.

Part-time:	49%	**Hispanic American:**	9%
Out-of-state:	29%	**Native American:**	1%
Women:	65%	**International:**	1%
African American:	19%	**25 or older:**	45%
Asian American:	3%		

Transfer out. Colleges most students transferred to 2005: University of North Carolina - Wilmington, East Carolina University, North Carolina State University.

Basis for selection. Open admission, but selective for some programs. Admission to limited enrollment programs based on examination. **Adult students:** SAT/ACT scores not required.

High school preparation. Recommended units include English 4, mathematics 3, social studies 2, history 1, science 3 (laboratory 1) and academic electives 6.

2005-2006 Annual costs. Tuition/fees: $1,215; $6,615 out-of-state. Per-credit charge: $40 in-state; $220 out-of-state. Books/supplies: $1,000. Personal expenses: $1,934.

Financial aid. Need-based: Need-based aid available for part-time students. Work study available nights, weekends and for part-time students. **Non-need-based:** Scholarships awarded for academics, state residency.

Application procedures. Admission: No deadline. No application fee. Admission notification on a rolling basis beginning on or about 2/15. **Financial aid:** Priority date 5/15; no closing date. FAFSA, institutional form required. Applicants notified on a rolling basis starting 5/15; must reply within 2 week(s) of notification.

Academics. Special study options: Cooperative education, distance learning, dual enrollment of high school students, independent study, internships, liberal arts/career combination. License preparation in dental hygiene, nursing, paramedic. **Credit/placement by examination:** AP, CLEP, IB, institutional tests. 30 credit hours maximum toward associate degree. **Support services:** GED preparation and test center, learning center, reduced course load, remedial instruction, tutoring.

Majors. Business: Accounting technology, administrative services, business admin, information resources management. **Computer sciences:** Information systems. **Education:** Early childhood. **Engineering technology:** Architectural. **Health:** Clinical lab technology, dental hygiene, EMT paramedic, nursing (RN), surgical technology. **Legal studies:** Paralegal. **Liberal arts:** Arts/sciences. **Mechanic/repair:** Electronics/electrical. **Protective services:** Fire safety technology, police science.

Most popular majors. Business/marketing 8%, computer/information sciences 8%, health sciences 18%, liberal arts 52%.

Computing on campus. 646 workstations in library, computer center, student center. Online library, helpline available.

Student life. Freshman orientation: Available. Preregistration for classes offered. **Activities:** Choral groups, drama, student government, Phi Theta Kappa, Shell (environmental group), Star of Life, SPYS (social science group), Association of Nursing Students.

Athletics. NCAA. **Intercollegiate:** Soccer W.

Student services. Career counseling, student employment services, financial aid counseling, personal counseling, placement for graduates, veterans' counselor. **Physically disabled:** Services for visually, speech, hearing impaired. **Transfer:** Special adviser for new students. Transfer adviser, college fairs on campus for students transferring to 4-year colleges.

Contact. E-mail: herringd@coastal.cc.nc.us
Phone: (910) 938-6250 Fax: (910) 455-2767
Don Herring, Director of Admissions, Coastal Carolina Community College, 444 Western Boulevard, Jacksonville, NC 28546-6877

College of the Albemarle

Elizabeth City, North Carolina
www.albemarle.cc.nc.us **CB code: 5133**

- Public 2-year branch campus and community college
- Commuter campus in large town

General. Founded in 1960. Regionally accredited. Multi-campus institution with campuses in: Elizabeth City, Dare County, and Edenton-Chowan. **Enrollment:** 1,200 degree-seeking undergraduates. **Degrees:** 135 associate awarded. **ROTC:** Army. **Location:** 45 miles from Norfolk, Virginia. **Calendar:** Semester, limited summer session. **Full-time faculty:** 91 total; 7% have terminal degrees, 10% minority, 55% women. **Part-time faculty:** 210 total; 3% have terminal degrees, 13% minority, 49% women. **Special facilities:** Community theater, civic auditorium.

Transfer out. Colleges most students transferred to 2005: Elizabeth City State University, East Carolina University, North Carolina State University, UNC-Chapel Hill, UNC-Wilmington.

Basis for selection. Open admission, but selective for some programs. Limited enrollment programs have additional admissions criteria. Admission limited to fall semester for associate degree in nursing, practical nursing, associate degree nursing, electrical/electronics technology, AC/HR, machining technology, surgical technology and medical assisting. New students admitted to cosmetology program as spaces become available. All degree-seeking students required to take placement test. Students may waive placement test if scores for SAT or ACT are acceptable. Interview required for allied health programs. **Adult students:** Entrance exam policies same as for first-time freshmen.

High school preparation. Recommended units include English 4, mathematics 3, social studies 3, history 3, science 3 and academic electives 6.

2005-2006 Annual costs. Tuition/fees: $1,255; $6,655 out-of-state. Per-credit charge: $40 in-state; $220 out-of-state. Books/supplies: $1,000.

Financial aid. Need-based: Need-based aid available for part-time students. **Non-need-based:** Scholarships awarded for academics, art, leadership, minority status, music/drama, state residency. **Additional information:** Separate application must be submitted for COA Private Scholarships.

Application procedures. Admission: No deadline. No application fee. Application must be submitted on paper. Admission notification on a rolling basis. Applicants to nursing program must complete admission requirements by January 15 prior to fall semester of year they enroll. **Financial aid:** Priority date 3/15; no closing date. FAFSA required. Applicants notified on a rolling basis starting 5/1; must reply within 2 week(s) of notification.

Academics. Special study options: Cooperative education, distance learning, double major, dual enrollment of high school students, ESL, honors, independent study, internships, liberal arts/career combination. Agreement with Elizabeth City State University to offer the first 2 years of Elementary Education. License preparation in nursing, real estate. **Credit/placement by examination:** AP, CLEP, institutional tests. 30 credit hours maximum toward associate degree. Credit by examination not granted until examinee has enrolled at COA and passed 12 credit hours with 2.0 or better grade point average. **Support services:** GED preparation and test center, learning center, reduced course load, remedial instruction, study skills assistance, tutoring, writing center.

Majors. Architecture: Technology. **Business:** Administrative services, business admin, office/clerical. **Computer sciences:** General, applications programming, information systems, networking, programming. **Conservation:** Fisheries. **Education:** General, early childhood. **Engineering:** Computer. **Engineering technology:** Electrical, heat/ac/refrig. **Health:** Medical assistant, medical secretary, nursing (RN), office admin. **Legal studies:** Prelaw. **Liberal arts:** Arts/sciences. **Production:** Machine shop technology. **Protective services:** Law enforcement admin. **Visual/performing arts:** Art, dramatic.

Computing on campus. 475 workstations in library, computer center. Online library available.

Student life. Freshman orientation: Available. Preregistration for classes offered. Monthly information sessions held for all COA programs. **Policies:** Freshmen permitted cars on campus. **Activities:** Bands, drama, literary magazine, musical theater, student government, student newspaper, Phi Theta Kappa, Environmental club, Literacy Round Table, Nursing club, SADD.

Athletics. Intramural: Archery, badminton, baseball, basketball, bowling, football (non-tackle), golf, racquetball, sailing, soccer, softball, swimming, tennis, volleyball.

Student services. Adult student services, career counseling, services for economically disadvantaged, student employment services, financial aid counseling, personal counseling, placement for graduates, veterans' counselor. **Physically disabled:** Services for visually, speech, hearing impaired. **Transfer:** Special adviser, orientation, pre-admission transcript evaluation for new students. College fairs on campus for students transferring to 4-year colleges.

Contact. Phone: (252) 335-0821 ext. 2290 Fax: (252) 335-2011
Kenneth Krentz, Assistant Dean for Admissions and Testing, College of the Albemarle, 1208 North Road Street, Elizabeth City, NC 27906-2327

Craven Community College
New Bern, North Carolina
www.cravencc.edu **CB code: 5148**

- Public 2-year community college
- Commuter campus in large town
- Interview required

General. Founded in 1965. Regionally accredited. Campuses in New Bern and Havelock. **Enrollment:** 2,988 degree-seeking undergraduates. **Degrees:** 283 associate awarded. **Location:** 100 miles from Raleigh, 45 miles from Greenville. **Calendar:** Semester, limited summer session. **Full-time faculty:** 72 total. **Part-time faculty:** 111 total. **Class size:** 69% < 20, 31% 20-39, less than 1% 40-49.

Student profile.

Out-of-state:	17%	**25 or older:**	50%

Transfer out. Colleges most students transferred to 2005: East Carolina University, University of North Carolina at Wilmington, North Carolina State University, Mount Olive College.

Basis for selection. Open admission, but selective for some programs. Admission to nursing program based on school achievement record and test scores. Tests in math, English and reading required for placement for degree-seeking students. **Adult students:** Entrance exam policies same as for first-time freshmen.

High school preparation. 20 units recommended. Recommended units include English 4, mathematics 3, social studies 1, history 1, science 3 (laboratory 1), foreign language 2 and academic electives 6.

2005-2006 Annual costs. Tuition/fees: $1,255; $6,655 out-of-state. Per-credit charge: $40 in-state; $220 out-of-state. Books/supplies: $700. Personal expenses: $1,056.

2004-2005 Financial aid. All financial aid based on need. 86% of total undergraduate aid awarded as scholarships/grants, 14% as loans/jobs.

Application procedures. Admission: No deadline. No application fee. Application may be submitted online. Admission notification on a rolling basis. **Financial aid:** Priority date 3/31; no closing date. FAFSA required. Applicants notified on a rolling basis starting 6/1.

Academics. Level 2 CRLA tutoring center. **Special study options:** Accelerated study, cooperative education, distance learning, double major, dual enrollment of high school students, independent study, internships, liberal arts/career combination, student-designed major, study abroad. Bachelor's degree programs available on campus. License preparation in aviation, nursing. **Credit/placement by examination:** AP, CLEP, institutional tests. 20 credit hours maximum toward associate degree. **Support services:** GED preparation and test center, learning center, reduced course load, remedial instruction, study skills assistance, tutoring, writing center.

Majors. Business: Accounting, business admin, management information systems, sales/distribution. **Computer sciences:** Applications programming, networking. **Education:** Teacher assistance. **Engineering technology:** Electrical, manufacturing. **Family/consumer sciences:** Child care. **Health:** Medical secretary, nursing (RN). **Legal studies:** Legal secretary. **Liberal arts:** Arts/sciences. **Mechanic/repair:** Automotive, heating/ac/refrig, industrial. **Protective services:** Law enforcement admin.

Computing on campus. 500 workstations in library, computer center.

Student life. Freshman orientation: Available. Preregistration for classes offered. **Policies:** Freshmen permitted cars on campus. **Activities:** Concert band, choral groups, drama, film society, literary magazine, music ensembles, student government, student newspaper, Phi Beta Lambda (business), cosmetology club, nursing club, accounting club, banking and marketing club, Spanish club, bible club, criminal justice club, electronics club, learning community club.

Athletics. Intramural: Baseball M, basketball, bowling, football (non-tackle) M, golf, soccer, tennis, volleyball. **Team name:** Panthers.

Student services. Career counseling, student employment services, financial aid counseling, personal counseling, placement for graduates, veterans' counselor. **Physically disabled:** Services for visually, speech, hearing impaired. **Transfer:** Special adviser, orientation, pre-admission transcript evaluation for new students. Transfer center, transfer adviser, college fairs on campus for students transferring to 4-year colleges.

Contact. Phone: (252) 638-7227 Fax: (252) 638-4649
Wanda Thomas, Director of Admissions and Counseling Services, Craven Community College, 800 College Court, New Bern, NC 28562

Davidson County Community College
Lexington, North Carolina
www.davidson.cc.nc.us **CB code: 5170**

- Public 2-year community college
- Commuter campus in large town

General. Founded in 1958. Regionally accredited. Davie Campus in Mocksville has 3 buildings and an emergency services training facility on 45 acres. **Enrollment:** 2,685 degree-seeking undergraduates. **Degrees:** 270 associate awarded. **Location:** 30 miles from Greensboro. **Calendar:** Semester, limited summer session. **Full-time faculty:** 95 total. **Part-time faculty:** 115 total. **Class size:** 59% < 20, 39% 20-39, less than 1% 40-49, less than 1% 50-99.

Student profile.

Out-of-state:	1%	**25 or older:**	46%

Transfer out. Colleges most students transferred to 2005: University of North Carolina-Greensboro, University of North Carolina-Charlotte, High Point University, Winston-Salem State University, Catawba College.

Basis for selection. Open admission, but selective for some programs. Admissions to nursing program under points system; based on test scores and grades. ASSET required unless acceptable test scores submitted. **Adult students:** Entrance exam policies same as for first-time freshmen.

High school preparation. Recommended units include English 4, mathematics 3, social studies 2, history 2, science 3 and foreign language 2.

2005-2006 Annual costs. Tuition/fees: $1,255; $6,655 out-of-state. Per-credit charge: $40 in-state; $220 out-of-state. Books/supplies: $1,000. Personal expenses: $600.

2004-2005 Financial aid. Need-based: 98% of total undergraduate aid awarded as scholarships/grants, 2% as loans/jobs. Need-based aid available for part-time students. **Non-need-based:** Scholarships awarded for academics, leadership.

Application procedures. Admission: No deadline. No application fee. Application may be submitted online. Admission notification on a rolling basis. Nursing program deadline 01/31, Allied Health program deadline 03/15 and 05/15. **Financial aid:** Priority date 7/1; no closing date. FAFSA, institutional form required. Applicants notified on a rolling basis starting 7/1; must reply within 2 week(s) of notification.

Academics. Special study options: Distance learning, dual enrollment of high school students, ESL, independent study. License preparation in nursing, paramedic, real estate. **Credit/placement by examination:** AP, CLEP, institutional tests. Students must complete 25% of hours required for graduation in residence. **Support services:** GED preparation and test center, learning center, pre-admission summer program, reduced course load, remedial instruction, study skills assistance, tutoring, writing center.

Majors. Business: Accounting, business admin, e-commerce, human resources. **Computer sciences:** Information technology, networking, programming. **Education:** Early childhood. **Engineering technology:** Computer, electrical, plastics. **Health:** Clinical lab technology, EMT paramedic, medical assistant, medical records technology, nursing (RN). **Legal studies:** Paralegal. **Liberal arts:** Arts/sciences. **Mechanic/repair:** Automotive. **Production:** Tool and die. **Protective services:** Criminal justice, fire safety technology.

Most popular majors. Business/marketing 14%, computer/information sciences 7%, education 6%, health sciences 33%, liberal arts 22%, security/protective services 8%.

Computing on campus. 450 workstations in library, computer center. Commuter students can connect to campus network. Helpline available.

Student life. Freshman orientation: Available. Preregistration for classes offered. **Policies:** Freshmen permitted cars on campus. **Activities:** Literary magazine, student government, criminal justice club, DCCC Association of Nursing Students, Phi Theta Kappa, Rotaract, spanish club, cosmetology club, Christian organization, computer system technology association, Future Educators club, electronics club.

Athletics. Intramural: Basketball, golf.

Student services. Career counseling, student employment services, financial aid counseling, on-campus daycare, personal counseling, placement for graduates, veterans' counselor. **Physically disabled:** Services for visually, speech, hearing impaired. **Transfer:** Special adviser, orientation, pre-admission transcript evaluation for new students. Transfer adviser, college fairs on campus for students transferring to 4-year colleges.

Contact. E-mail: admissions@davidsonccc.edu
Phone: (336) 249-8186 ext. 6731 Fax: (336) 224-0240
Kim Sepich, Director, Admissions and Retention, Davidson County Community College, PO Box 1287, Lexington, NC 27293-1287

Durham Technical Community College

Durham, North Carolina
www.durhamtech.edu **CB code: 5172**

- Public 2-year community and technical college
- Commuter campus in small city

General. Founded in 1958. Regionally accredited. Most programs structured to begin in fall and continue for 5 or 6 consecutive semesters. Off-campus sites in northern Durham and Orange Counties. **Enrollment:** 5,698 undergraduates. **Degrees:** 278 associate awarded. **Location:** 25 miles from Raleigh, 50 miles from Greensboro. **Calendar:** Semester, limited summer session. **Full-time faculty:** 131 total. **Part-time faculty:** 387 total. **Class size:** 57% < 20, 43% 20-39.

Transfer out. Colleges most students transferred to 2005: University of North Carolina - Chapel Hill, North Carolina Central University, North Carolina State University.

Basis for selection. Open admission, but selective for some programs. Admission to some programs, including nursing and allied health, based on placement test scores and completion of prerequisite courses. Placement testing required for all first-time students and for all applicants to certain programs. ASSET and COMPASS used. **Adult students:** Entrance exam policies same as for first-time freshmen. **Homeschooled:** High school transcript, documentation of state recognition of home school required.

High school preparation. Algebra, chemistry, and biology required for allied health programs. Algebra and science courses recommended for most associate degree programs.

2005-2006 Annual costs. Tuition/fees: $1,230; $6,630 out-of-state. Per-credit charge: $40 in-state; $220 out-of-state. Personal expenses: $562.

Financial aid. Need-based: Need-based aid available for part-time students. Work study available nights and for part-time students. **Non-need-based:** Scholarships awarded for academics, state residency. **Additional information:** Special funds available to single parents or displaced homemakers for tuition, fees, books, supplies and child care expenses.

Application procedures. Admission: No deadline. No application fee. Admission notification on a rolling basis. **Financial aid:** FAFSA required. Applicants notified on a rolling basis; must reply within 3 week(s) of notification.

Academics. Special study options: Distance learning, dual enrollment of high school students, ESL, weekend college. License preparation in nursing, occupational therapy, real estate. **Credit/placement by examination:** AP, CLEP, institutional tests. Maximum of 10% of total curriculum hours of credit by examination may be counted toward degree. **Support services:** GED preparation and test center, learning center, remedial instruction, study skills assistance, tutoring.

Majors. Business: Accounting, administrative services, business admin, operations. **Computer sciences:** Applications programming, information systems, programming, systems analysis. **Education:** Early childhood, teacher assistance. **Engineering:** Electrical. **Engineering technology:** Architectural, drafting, electrical. **Health:** Clinical lab science, dental lab technology, environmental health, medical records admin, medical secretary, nursing (RN), occupational health, occupational therapy assistant, optician, respiratory therapy technology. **Legal studies:** Paralegal. **Liberal arts:** Arts/sciences. **Mechanic/repair:** Automotive, electronics/electrical.

Most popular majors. Architecture 9%, business/marketing 15%, computer/information sciences 15%, health sciences 17%, liberal arts 30%.

Student life. Freshman orientation: Available. **Policies:** Freshmen permitted cars on campus. **Activities:** Drama, literary magazine, student government.

Student services. Career counseling, services for economically disadvantaged, financial aid counseling, personal counseling, veterans' counselor. **Physically disabled:** Services for visually, speech, hearing impaired. **Transfer:** Special adviser, orientation for new students. College fairs on campus for students transferring to 4-year colleges.

Contact. E-mail: admissions@durhamtech.edu
Phone: (919) 686-3333 Fax: (919) 686-3669
Penny Augustine, Director of Admissions, Durham Technical Community College, 1637 Lawson Street, Durham, NC 27703

ECPI Technical College

Raleigh, North Carolina
www.ecpi.edu/campus/ral

- For-profit 2-year technical college
- Commuter campus in large town

General. Accredited by ACCSCT. **Calendar:** Semester.

Annual costs/financial aid. Need-based financial aid available to full-time and part-time students.

Two-Year Colleges

Contact. Phone: (919) 571-0057
Campus President, 4101 Doie Cope Road, Raleigh, NC 27613

Edgecombe Community College

Tarboro, North Carolina — **CB member**
www.edgecombe.edu — **CB code: 5199**

- Public 2-year community college
- Commuter campus in large town

General. Founded in 1967. Regionally accredited. Branch campus in Rocky Mount. **Enrollment:** 1,727 degree-seeking undergraduates; 699 non-degree-seeking students. **Degrees:** 165 associate awarded. **Location:** 75 miles from Raleigh. **Calendar:** Semester, limited summer session. **Full-time faculty:** 93 total; 10% have terminal degrees, 40% minority, 62% women. **Part-time faculty:** 109 total; 7% have terminal degrees, 33% minority, 66% women. **Class size:** 77% < 20, 20% 20-39, 2% 40-49, less than 1% 50-99. **Special facilities:** Wildlife preserve.

Student profile. Among degree-seeking undergraduates, 16% enrolled in a transfer program, 84% enrolled in a vocational program, 4% already have a bachelor's degree or higher, 188 enrolled as first-time, first-year students, 69 transferred in from other institutions.

Part-time:	56%	**African American:**	61%
Out-of-state:	1%	**Native American:**	1%
Women:	79%	**25 or older:**	46%

Transfer out. Colleges most students transferred to 2005: East Carolina University, Pitt Community College, NC Wesleyan College, North Carolina Agricultural and Technical State University.

Basis for selection. Open admission, but selective for some programs. Special requirements for allied health programs and networking technology. Criteria include admission tests and personal interview. TEAS Nursing Test required for nursing applicants. Interview considered for some Allied Health programs. **Adult students:** Entrance exam policies same as for first-time freshmen.

2005-2006 Annual costs. Tuition/fees: $1,209; $6,609 out-of-state. Per-credit charge: $40 in-state; $220 out-of-state. Books/supplies: $750. Personal expenses: $1,800.

2004-2005 Financial aid. All financial aid based on need. 102 full-time freshmen applied for aid; 91 were judged to have need; 91 of these received aid. Average need met was 90%. Average scholarship/grant was $2,050; average loan $3,600. 97% of total undergraduate aid awarded as scholarships/grants, 3% as loans/jobs. Need-based aid available for part-time students.

Application procedures. Admission: No deadline. No application fee. Application may be submitted online. Admission notification on a rolling basis. **Financial aid:** Closing date 6/30. FAFSA, institutional form required. Applicants notified on a rolling basis starting 8/15; must reply within 3 week(s) of notification.

Academics. Special study options: Combined bachelor's/graduate degree, cooperative education, distance learning, double major, dual enrollment of high school students, ESL, independent study, weekend college. Bachelor's degree programs available on campus. License preparation in nursing, radiology. **Credit/placement by examination:** AP, CLEP, institutional tests. 24 credit hours maximum toward associate degree. **Support services:** GED preparation and test center, learning center, reduced course load, remedial instruction, study skills assistance, tutoring.

Majors. Business: Accounting, administrative services, business admin. **Computer sciences:** General, information systems, networking. **Education:** Early childhood, teacher assistance. **Engineering:** Manufacturing. **Engineering technology:** Electrical, manufacturing, plastics. **Family/consumer sciences:** Child care. **Health:** Medical assistant, medical radiologic technology/radiation therapy, medical records technology, nursing (RN), respiratory therapy technology. **Liberal arts:** Arts/sciences. **Personal/culinary services:** Mortuary science. **Protective services:** Criminal justice.

Most popular majors. Business/marketing 13%, computer/information sciences 6%, education 14%, health sciences 48%, liberal arts 13%.

Computing on campus. 120 workstations in library, computer center. Online library, helpline available.

Student life. Policies: Freshmen permitted cars on campus. **Activities:** Drama, student government.

Athletics. Team name: Eagles.

Student services. Alcohol/substance abuse counseling, career counseling, student employment services, financial aid counseling, minority student services, personal counseling, placement for graduates, veterans' counselor. **Physically disabled:** Services for visually, hearing impaired. **Transfer:** Special adviser, orientation, pre-admission transcript evaluation for new students. Transfer adviser, college fairs on campus for students transferring to 4-year colleges.

Contact. Phone: (252) 823-5166 ext. 254 Fax: (252) 823-6817
Ginny McLendon, Dean of Enrollment Management, Edgecombe Community College, 2009 West Wilson Street, Tarboro, NC 27886

Fayetteville Technical Community College

Fayetteville, North Carolina
www.faytechcc.edu — **CB code: 5208**

- Public 2-year community and technical college
- Commuter campus in large city

General. Founded in 1961. Regionally accredited. Offers only funeral services curriculum in North Carolina community college system. **Enrollment:** 9,403 degree-seeking undergraduates; 548 non-degree-seeking students. **Degrees:** 849 associate awarded. **Location:** 60 miles from Raleigh. **Calendar:** Semester, limited summer session. **Full-time faculty:** 300 total; 23% minority, 53% women. **Part-time faculty:** 545 total; 34% minority, 59% women. **Class size:** 63% < 20, 36% 20-39, 1% 40-49, less than 1% 50-99. **Special facilities:** Center for applied technology. **Partnerships:** Formal partnership with Cumberland and County High School system.

Student profile. Among degree-seeking undergraduates, 16% enrolled in a transfer program, 54% enrolled in a vocational program, 3% already have a bachelor's degree or higher, 2,211 enrolled as first-time, first-year students, 799 transferred in from other institutions.

Part-time:	55%	**Women:**	67%
Out-of-state:	18%	**25 or older:**	59%

Transfer out. Colleges most students transferred to 2005: Forsyth Technical Community College, Central Piedmont Community College, Wilson Technical Community College, Pitt Community College, Catawba Community College.

Basis for selection. Open admission, but selective for some programs. Admission of health applicants based on transcripts, academic average, interview, and institutional assessment evaluation of reading, writing, and math. Interview required for health and paralegal programs. **Adult students:** Entrance exam policies same as for first-time freshmen. **Learning Disabled:** Documentation of disability is required if applicant desires any academic accommodations.

High school preparation. Engineering programs require 2 algebra units. Health programs require up to 2 algebra, 1 biology, and 1 chemistry.

2005-2006 Annual costs. Tuition/fees: $1,245; $6,645 out-of-state. Per-credit charge: $40 in-state; $220 out-of-state. Books/supplies: $950. Personal expenses: $2,900.

2004-2005 Financial aid. Need-based: 72% of total undergraduate aid awarded as scholarships/grants, 28% as loans/jobs. Need-based aid available for part-time students. Work study available for part-time students.

Application procedures. Admission: No deadline. No application fee. Application may be submitted online. Admission notification on a rolling basis. Deadline for health program applicants is January 30. Applicants admitted to these programs must reply immediately upon notification. **Financial aid:** Priority date 6/1, closing date 7/15. FAFSA required. Applicants notified on a rolling basis starting 5/1; must reply by 8/8 or within 2 week(s) of notification.

Academics. Special study options: Cooperative education, distance learning, dual enrollment of high school students, ESL, liberal arts/career combination, weekend college. License preparation in dental hygiene, nursing, paramedic, radiology. **Credit/placement by examination:** AP, CLEP, institutional tests. Transfer students must complete a minimum of 25% of resident credit in residence to be eligible to receive an associates degree. **Support services:** GED preparation and test center, learning center, pre-admission summer program, reduced course load, remedial instruction, study skills assistance, tutoring.

Majors. Agriculture: Horticulture. **Business:** Accounting, accounting technology, administrative services, banking/financial services, business admin, e-commerce, executive assistant, hotel/motel admin, human resources, information resources management, management information systems, marketing, office management, operations. **Computer sciences:** Information systems, information technology, LAN/WAN management, programming, security.

Construction: Electrician, plumbing. **Education:** General, early childhood, elementary, special. **Engineering technology:** Architectural, civil, electrical, surveying. **Family/consumer sciences:** Child care. **Foreign languages:** Translation. **Health:** Dental hygiene, EMT paramedic, management/clinical assistant, medical radiologic technology/radiation therapy, medical records technology, nuclear medical technology, nursing (RN), office admin, physical therapy assistant, radiologic technology/medical imaging, respiratory therapy technology, surgical technology. **Legal studies:** Paralegal. **Liberal arts:** Arts/sciences. **Mechanic/repair:** Automotive, heating/ac/refrig. **Personal/culinary services:** Chef training, mortuary science. **Production:** Machine shop technology. **Protective services:** Criminal justice, fire safety technology, forensics. **Public administration:** General. **Science technology:** Biological. **Visual/performing arts:** Commercial/advertising art.

Computing on campus. 200 workstations in library, computer center.

Student life. **Freshman orientation:** Mandatory. Preregistration for classes offered. Two hours, held the first day of new student registration. **Policies:** Freshmen permitted cars on campus. **Activities:** Choral groups, student government, student newspaper, African-American heritage club, Democratic club, international club, Nos Otros: Latino cultural organization, Parents for Higher Education, Students Against Destructive Decisions.

Athletics. **Intramural:** Basketball, bowling, golf, softball, tennis, volleyball.

Student services. Career counseling, student employment services, financial aid counseling, health services, on-campus daycare, personal counseling, placement for graduates, veterans' counselor. **Physically disabled:** Services for visually, speech, hearing impaired. **Transfer:** Special adviser, orientation for new students. Transfer adviser, college fairs on campus for students transferring to 4-year colleges.

Contact. E-mail: kelleyj@faytechcc.edu
Phone: (910) 678-8274 Fax: (910) 678-8407
James Kelley, Director of Admissions, Fayetteville Technical Community College, PO Box 35236, Fayetteville, NC 28303-0236

Forsyth Technical Community College

Winston-Salem, North Carolina — **CB member**
www.forsyth.tec.nc.us — **CB code: 5234**

- Public 2-year community and technical college
- Commuter campus in small city

General. Founded in 1964. Regionally accredited. **Enrollment:** 6,996 degree-seeking undergraduates. **Degrees:** 970 associate awarded. **Location:** 32 miles from Greensboro, 85 miles from Charlotte. **Calendar:** Semester, extensive summer session. **Full-time faculty:** 176 total. **Part-time faculty:** 536 total.

Transfer out. **Colleges most students transferred to 2005:** Winston-Salem State University, Gardner-Webb University, High Point University, Appalachian State University, North Carolina A&T State University.

Basis for selection. Open admission, but selective for some programs. Admission to health program based on school record and test scores. Health information session attendance required. SAT or ACT used for admission to health and developmental programs and for placement in other programs. **Adult students:** Entrance exam policies same as for first-time freshmen. **Homeschooled:** NCDPI registration information or similar information from the respective state's department of education authorizing the home school to provide instruction.

High school preparation. Algebra I required for allied health and engineering programs. Biology and chemistry required for allied health programs.

2005-2006 Annual costs. Tuition/fees: $1,235; $6,635 out-of-state. Per-credit charge: $40 in-state; $220 out-of-state. Books/supplies: $650. Personal expenses: $750.

2004-2005 Financial aid. All financial aid based on need. 99% of total undergraduate aid awarded as scholarships/grants, 1% as loans/jobs. Need-based aid available for part-time students. Work study available nights and for part-time students. **Additional information:** Apply for aid as close to January 1 as possible for best consideration.

Application procedures. **Admission:** Priority date 5/1; no deadline. No application fee. Application may be submitted online. Admission notification on a rolling basis. **Financial aid:** Priority date 6/1; no closing date. FAFSA, institutional form required. Applicants notified on a rolling basis starting 7/1; must reply within 2 week(s) of notification.

Academics. **Special study options:** Cooperative education, cross-registration, distance learning, double major, dual enrollment of high school students, ESL, exchange student, external degree, honors, independent study, internships, liberal arts/career combination, student-designed major. License preparation in dental hygiene, nursing, radiology, real estate. **Credit/placement by examination:** CLEP, institutional tests. **Support services:** GED preparation and test center, learning center, pre-admission summer program, reduced course load, remedial instruction, study skills assistance, tutoring, writing center.

Majors. **Agriculture:** Horticulture. **Business:** Accounting, business admin, finance, office/clerical. **Computer sciences:** Applications programming, data entry. **Education:** Early childhood, science. **Engineering technology:** Architectural, drafting, electrical, robotics. **Health:** Licensed practical nurse, medical assistant, medical radiologic technology/radiation therapy, nuclear medical technology, nursing (RN), respiratory therapy technology, sonography. **Legal studies:** Paralegal. **Liberal arts:** Arts/sciences. **Protective services:** Law enforcement admin.

Computing on campus. 400 workstations in library, computer center. Student web hosting available.

Student life. **Freshman orientation:** Mandatory. Preregistration for classes offered. **Policies:** Freshmen permitted cars on campus. **Activities:** Drama, literary magazine, student government, student newspaper, Circle-K, Afro-American Society, minority male mentoring program, women's center.

Athletics. NJCAA. **Intercollegiate:** Basketball M, softball. **Intramural:** Basketball, bowling, golf, softball, volleyball. **Team name:** Tech Tigers.

Student services. Adult student services, alcohol/substance abuse counseling, career counseling, services for economically disadvantaged, student employment services, financial aid counseling, health services, minority student services, personal counseling, placement for graduates, veterans' counselor, women's services. **Physically disabled:** Services for visually, speech, hearing impaired. **Transfer:** Special adviser, orientation for new students. Transfer adviser, college fairs on campus for students transferring to 4-year colleges.

Contact. Phone: (336) 734-7253 Fax: (336) 734-7291
Patrice Mitchell, Dean of Enrollment Management, Forsyth Technical Community College, 2100 Silas Creek Parkway, Winston-Salem, NC 27103

Gaston College

Dallas, North Carolina
www.gaston.cc.nc.us — **CB code: 5262**

- Public 2-year community college
- Commuter campus in small town

General. Founded in 1963. Regionally accredited. Branch campus at Lincolnton. **Enrollment:** 2,000 full-time, degree-seeking students. **Degrees:** 480 associate awarded. **Location:** 25 miles from Charlotte. **Calendar:** Semester, limited summer session. **Full-time faculty:** 116 total. **Part-time faculty:** 430 total.

Student profile.

Out-of-state:	1%	**25 or older:**	54%

Basis for selection. Open admission, but selective for some programs. Admission to health services programs, including nursing, based on ACT scores and interview. Basic literacy must be demonstrated, after admission, in order to take certain courses. ACT required for health services programs. Interview recommended for emergency medical technician, medical assistant, nursing programs; audition recommended for music programs; portfolio recommended for art programs. **Adult students:** Entrance exam policies same as for first-time freshmen.

2005-2006 Annual costs. Tuition/fees: $1,211; $6,611 out-of-state. Per-credit charge: $40 in-state; $220 out-of-state. Books/supplies: $1,000. Personal expenses: $1,000.

2004-2005 Financial aid. **Need-based:** 90% of total undergraduate aid awarded as scholarships/grants, 10% as loans/jobs. Work study available for part-time students. **Non-need-based:** Scholarships awarded for academics, state residency. **Additional information:** Grants/scholarships available for women pursuing nontraditional roles.

Application procedures. **Admission:** No deadline. No application fee. Application may be submitted online. Admission notification on a rolling basis. **Financial aid:** Priority date 3/15; no closing date. FAFSA, institutional form required. Applicants notified on a rolling basis.

Academics. **Special study options:** Cooperative education, cross-registration, distance learning, double major, dual enrollment of high school students, ESL, independent study, internships, weekend college. **Credit/**

placement by examination: CLEP, institutional tests. 18 credit hours maximum toward associate degree. **Support services:** GED preparation and test center, learning center, reduced course load, remedial instruction, study skills assistance, tutoring, writing center.

Majors. Architecture: Technology. **Business:** Accounting, administrative services, business admin. **Communications:** Broadcast journalism. **Computer sciences:** Applications programming, information technology, programming. **Education:** Early childhood. **Engineering technology:** Architectural, biomedical, civil, computer, electrical, industrial. **Health:** Dietetic technician, EMT paramedic, massage therapy, medical assistant, medical secretary, nursing (RN), office admin, veterinary technology/assistant. **Legal studies:** Legal secretary, paralegal. **Liberal arts:** Arts/sciences. **Protective services:** Fire safety technology. **Public administration:** Social work.

Computing on campus. 233 workstations in library, computer center.

Student life. Freshman orientation: Available. **Policies:** Freshmen permitted cars on campus. **Activities:** Literary magazine, music ensembles, radio station, student government.

Student services. Adult student services, career counseling, student employment services, financial aid counseling, on-campus daycare, placement for graduates, veterans' counselor. **Physically disabled:** Services for visually, speech, hearing impaired. **Transfer:** Special adviser, orientation for new students. Transfer adviser, college fairs on campus for students transferring to 4-year colleges.

Contact. E-mail: wray.michelle@gaston.edu
Phone: (704) 922-6214 Fax: (704) 922-2344
Michelle Wray, Director of Admissions/Enrollment Management, Gaston College, 201 Highway 321 South, Dallas, NC 28034-1499

Guilford Technical Community College

Jamestown, North Carolina
www.gtcc.edu **CB code: 5275**

- Public 2-year community college
- Commuter campus in large city

General. Founded in 1958. Regionally accredited. Campuses in Greensboro and High Point. **Enrollment:** 9,448 degree-seeking undergraduates. **Degrees:** 634 associate awarded. **ROTC:** Army, Navy, Air Force. **Location:** 2 miles from Greensboro, 5 miles from High Point. **Calendar:** Semester, limited summer session. **Full-time faculty:** 237 total. **Part-time faculty:** 571 total. **Special facilities:** Observatory.

Student profile.

Out-of-state:	2%	25 or older:	45%

Transfer out. Colleges most students transferred to 2005: University of North Carolina-Greensboro, University of North Carolina-Charlotte, North Carolina A&T, University of North Carolina-Chapel Hill, North Carolina State University.

Basis for selection. Open admission, but selective for some programs. Admission to allied health programs based on specific course grades. Some programs require students to take standardized test administered by college. **Learning Disabled:** Contact Disability Access Services office.

High school preparation. Allied health programs have specific course requirements that vary according to program.

2005-2006 Annual costs. Tuition/fees: $1,260; $6,660 out-of-state. Per-credit charge: $40 in-state; $220 out-of-state. Books/supplies: $900. Personal expenses: $1,151.

Financial aid. Need-based: Need-based aid available for part-time students. Work study available for part-time students.

Application procedures. Admission: No deadline. No application fee. Admission notification on a rolling basis. Applicants for limited enrollment programs (nursing, aviation maintenance/mechanic, dental hygiene, dental assistant, medical assistant, surgical technology cosmetology, emergency medical science) advised to apply before December 31. **Financial aid:** Priority date 3/15; no closing date. FAFSA required. Applicants notified on a rolling basis starting 7/1; must reply within 2 week(s) of notification.

Academics. Special study options: Cooperative education, cross-registration, distance learning, dual enrollment of high school students, ESL, independent study, internships. License preparation in aviation, dental hygiene, nursing, paramedic, physical therapy, real estate. **Credit/placement by examination:** AP, CLEP, IB, institutional tests. 60 credit hours maximum toward associate degree. **Support services:** GED preparation and test center, learning center, reduced course load, remedial instruction, study skills assistance, tutoring, writing center.

Majors. Agriculture: Turf management. **Business:** Accounting technology, business admin, executive assistant, human resources, management information systems. **Communications technology:** Recording arts. **Computer sciences:** Information systems. **Construction:** Electrician, maintenance. **Education:** General, early childhood, family/consumer sciences. **Engineering technology:** Architectural, civil, electrical, mechanical, plastics, surveying. **Health:** Clinical lab technology, dental hygiene, EMT paramedic, medical assistant, mental health services, nursing (RN), physical therapy assistant, substance abuse counseling, surgical technology. **Legal studies:** Paralegal. **Liberal arts:** Arts/sciences. **Mechanic/repair:** Automotive, avionics, heating/ac/refrig. **Personal/culinary services:** Cosmetic. **Production:** Machine shop technology. **Protective services:** Criminal justice, fire safety technology. **Science technology:** Chemical. **Transportation:** Airline/commercial pilot. **Visual/performing arts:** Commercial/advertising art, music management.

Computing on campus. 130 workstations in library, computer center. Online library, helpline, repair service available.

Student life. Freshman orientation: Available. **Policies:** Freshmen permitted cars on campus. **Activities:** Drama, student government, student newspaper, American Muslim student association, Ambassadors for Christ, international student association, market place of ideas (political), Nurses Christian Fellowship, veterans and students organization, Black student union, single parent club, students in free enterprise.

Student services. Career counseling, student employment services, financial aid counseling, on-campus daycare, personal counseling, placement for graduates, veterans' counselor, women's services. **Physically disabled:** Services for visually, speech, hearing impaired. **Transfer:** Special adviser, orientation for new students. Transfer adviser, college fairs on campus for students transferring to 4-year colleges.

Contact. E-mail: groomej@gtcc.cc.nc.us
Phone: (336) 344-4822 Fax: (336) 819-2022
Jean Groome, Assistant Director of Admissions, Guilford Technical Community College, PO Box 309, Jamestown, NC 27282

Halifax Community College

Weldon, North Carolina
www.halfaxcc.edu **CB code: 0621**

- Public 2-year community college
- Small town

General. Founded in 1967. Regionally accredited. **Enrollment:** 1,500 degree-seeking undergraduates. **Degrees:** 143 associate awarded. **Location:** 83 miles from Raleigh. **Calendar:** Semester, limited summer session. **Full-time faculty:** 67 total. **Part-time faculty:** 96 total.

Basis for selection. Open admission, but selective for some programs. Selective admission for nursing and allied health programs.

High school preparation. High school chemistry or equivalent and developmental mathematics required for nursing applicants.

2005-2006 Annual costs. Tuition/fees: $1,245; $6,645 out-of-state. Per-credit charge: $40 in-state; $220 out-of-state. Books/supplies: $500. Personal expenses: $896.

Application procedures. Admission: No deadline. No application fee. Admission notification on a rolling basis. **Financial aid:** Priority date 7/1; no closing date. Applicants notified on a rolling basis starting 8/1; must reply within 2 week(s) of notification.

Academics. Special study options: Dual enrollment of high school students, independent study, internships. **Credit/placement by examination:** CLEP, institutional tests. **Support services:** Learning center, reduced course load, remedial instruction, tutoring.

Majors. Business: Accounting, business admin, office management, office technology, office/clerical. **Communications:** Advertising. **Computer sciences:** General. **Conservation:** Wood science. **Education:** Early childhood, multi-level teacher, teacher assistance. **Engineering technology:** Electrical. **Health:** Clinical lab technology, medical secretary, nursing (RN), phlebotomy. **Liberal arts:** Arts/sciences. **Mechanic/repair:** Industrial. **Production:** Welding. **Public administration:** Human services, social work. **Visual/performing arts:** Commercial/advertising art, interior design.

Most popular majors. Business/marketing 11%, engineering/engineering technologies 18%, health sciences 29%, liberal arts 15%, security/protective services 14%, visual/performing arts 8%.

Computing on campus. 100 workstations in computer center.

Student life. Freshman orientation: Available. Preregistration for classes offered. **Activities:** Student government, student newspaper.

Student services. Career counseling, student employment services, personal counseling, placement for graduates, veterans' counselor. **Transfer:** Transfer adviser, college fairs on campus for students transferring to 4-year colleges.

Contact. E-mail: dickenss@halifax.hcc.cc.nc.us
Phone: (252) 536-7220 Fax: (252) 538-4311
Scottie Dickens, Director of Admissions, Halifax Community College, Drawer 809, Weldon, NC 27890

Haywood Community College

Clyde, North Carolina
www.haywood.edu **CB code: 5289**

- Public 2-year community and technical college
- Commuter campus in rural community

General. Founded in 1965. Regionally accredited. **Enrollment:** 1,411 degree-seeking undergraduates. **Degrees:** 232 associate awarded. **Location:** 25 miles from Asheville. **Calendar:** Semester, extensive summer session. **Full-time faculty:** 67 total. **Part-time faculty:** 128 total. **Class size:** 85% < 20, 14% 20-39, less than 1% 40-49.

Student profile.

Out-of-state:	14%	**25 or older:**	39%

Transfer out. Colleges most students transferred to 2005: Western Carolina University, Appalachian State University, University of North Carolina - Asheville.

Basis for selection. Open admission, but selective for some programs. Admission to nursing program based on admission test scores, high school record, GPA, prerequisite courses, and health occupations aptitude examination. Completion of Accuplacer, SAT score of 500 or higher on each section, ACT composite score of 21 or higher, or official transcript with "C" or better in college-level English and algebra required. Informational interview required for electrical engineering technology, manufacturing engineering technology, cosmetology, and professional crafts programs. **Adult students:** Entrance exam policies same as for first-time freshmen. **Learning Disabled:** Accommodations made upon request.

High school preparation. Algebra, biology and chemistry required for nursing. Algebra recommended for electrical and manufacturing engineering, microcomputer systems and college transfer.

2005-2006 Annual costs. Tuition/fees: $1,234; $6,634 out-of-state. Per-credit charge: $40 in-state; $220 out-of-state. Books/supplies: $1,000. Personal expenses: $1,656.

2004-2005 Financial aid. Need-based: Need-based aid available for part-time students. Work study available for part-time students. **Non-need-based:** Scholarships awarded for academics. **Additional information:** Complete FAFSA by priority filing date for consideration for institutional scholarships.

Application procedures. Admission: No deadline. No application fee. Application may be submitted online. Admission notification on a rolling basis. **Financial aid:** Priority date 4/1; no closing date. FAFSA, institutional form required. Applicants notified on a rolling basis starting 4/15; must reply within 2 week(s) of notification.

Academics. Special study options: Cooperative education, distance learning, dual enrollment of high school students, independent study, internships. **Credit/placement by examination:** CLEP, institutional tests. 18 credit hours maximum toward associate degree. **Support services:** GED preparation and test center, learning center, reduced course load, remedial instruction, tutoring.

Majors. Agriculture: Horticulture. **Business:** Accounting, administrative services, business admin. **Computer sciences:** Applications programming, networking. **Conservation:** Fisheries, forest resources, forestry, wildlife, wood science. **Construction:** Electrician, maintenance. **Engineering:** Computer. **Engineering technology:** Electrical, industrial management. **Family/consumer sciences:** Child care. **Health:** Medical assistant, nursing (RN). **Liberal arts:** Arts/sciences. **Mechanic/repair:** Automotive. **Personal/culinary services:** Cosmetic. **Production:** Woodworking. **Protective services:** Criminal justice. **Visual/performing arts:** Ceramics, fiber arts, metal/jewelry.

Most popular majors. Agriculture 6%, business/marketing 10%, engineering/engineering technologies 7%, family/consumer sciences 6%, health sciences 10%, liberal arts 15%, natural resources/environmental science 19%, trade and industry 8%, visual/performing arts 8%.

Computing on campus. 10 workstations in library.

Student life. Freshman orientation: Available. Preregistration for classes offered. **Activities:** Student government, Phi Theta Kappa, Phi Beta Lambda.

Athletics. Intramural: Basketball, bowling, football (non-tackle), softball, volleyball.

Student services. Career counseling, student employment services, financial aid counseling, on-campus daycare, personal counseling, placement for graduates, veterans' counselor. **Physically disabled:** Services for visually, speech, hearing impaired. **Transfer:** Special adviser, orientation for new students. Transfer adviser for students transferring to 4-year colleges.

Contact. E-mail: drowland@haywood.cc.nc.us
Phone: (828) 627-4505 Toll-free number: (866) 468-6422
Fax: (828) 627-4513
Debbie Rowland, Coordinator Admissions, Haywood Community College, 185 Freelander Drive, Clyde, NC 28721-9454

Isothermal Community College

Spindale, North Carolina
www.isothermal.edu **CB code: 5319**

- Public 2-year community college
- Commuter campus in small town

General. Founded in 1964. Regionally accredited. **Enrollment:** 1,743 degree-seeking undergraduates. **Degrees:** 183 associate awarded. **Location:** 65 miles from Charlotte, 48 miles from Asheville. **Calendar:** Semester, extensive summer session. **Full-time faculty:** 60 total. **Part-time faculty:** 55 total. **Class size:** 79% < 20, 20% 20-39, less than 1% 40-49, less than 1% 50-99.

Student profile.

Out-of-state:	1%	**25 or older:**	54%

Basis for selection. Open admission.

2005-2006 Annual costs. Tuition/fees: $1,213; $6,613 out-of-state. Per-credit charge: $40 in-state; $220 out-of-state. Books/supplies: $500. Personal expenses: $760.

Financial aid. Need-based: Need-based aid available for part-time students. Work study available nights and for part-time students. **Non-need-based:** Scholarships awarded for academics, job skills, leadership, minority status, music/drama, state residency.

Application procedures. Admission: No deadline. No application fee. Application may be submitted online. Admission notification on a rolling basis. **Financial aid:** Priority date 5/31; no closing date. FAFSA, institutional form required. Applicants notified on a rolling basis starting 4/30; must reply within 4 week(s) of notification.

Academics. Special study options: Cooperative education, distance learning, dual enrollment of high school students, honors, independent study. Bachelor's degree programs available on campus. License preparation in nursing, real estate. **Credit/placement by examination:** CLEP, institutional tests. 12 credit hours maximum toward associate degree. **Support services:** GED preparation and test center, learning center, pre-admission summer program, reduced course load, remedial instruction.

Majors. Business: Banking/financial services, business admin, e-commerce, marketing, office management, operations. **Communications technology:** Radio/tv. **Computer sciences:** Applications programming, information technology, networking. **Construction:** Electrician. **Education:** General, early childhood, elementary. **Engineering technology:** Computer, electrical, mechanical, mechanical drafting, plastics. **Health:** Nursing (RN), office admin. **Legal studies:** Paralegal. **Liberal arts:** Arts/sciences. **Mechanic/repair:** Auto body. **Personal/culinary services:** Cosmetic. **Production:** Machine shop technology, welding. **Protective services:** Criminal justice. **Visual/performing arts:** Commercial/advertising art.

Most popular majors. Business/marketing 10%, liberal arts 13%.

Computing on campus. 25 workstations in library, computer center.

Student life. Freshman orientation: Available. Preregistration for classes offered. **Policies:** Freshmen permitted cars on campus. **Activities:** Choral groups, drama, literary magazine, radio station, student government, student newspaper, TV station, Afro-American club, Phi Theta Kappa, Phi Beta Lambda.

Athletics. Intramural: Basketball, football (non-tackle), volleyball.

Student services. Career counseling, health services, placement for graduates, veterans' counselor. **Transfer:** Special adviser, orientation for new students. College fairs on campus for students transferring to 4-year colleges.

Contact. Phone: (828) 286-3636 ext. 288 Fax: (828) 286-8109
Maggie Killoran, Director, Enrollment Management, Isothermal Community College, PO Box 804, Spindale, NC 28160

James Sprunt Community College

Kenansville, North Carolina
www.sprunt.com **CB code: 6256**

- Public 2-year community college
- Commuter campus in rural community

General. Founded in 1964. Regionally accredited. **Enrollment:** 936 degree-seeking undergraduates; 434 non-degree-seeking students. **Degrees:** 184 associate awarded. **Location:** 75 miles from Raleigh, 45 miles from Wilmington. **Calendar:** Semester, limited summer session. **Full-time faculty:** 60 total; 2% have terminal degrees, 55% women. **Part-time faculty:** 69 total; 1% have terminal degrees, 58% women. **Class size:** 86% < 20, 14% 20-39.

Student profile. Among degree-seeking undergraduates, 21% enrolled in a transfer program, 59% enrolled in a vocational program, 1% already have a bachelor's degree or higher, 151 enrolled as first-time, first-year students, 243 transferred in from other institutions.

Part-time:	40%	**Hispanic American:**	2%
Out-of-state:	1%	**Native American:**	1%
Women:	74%	**International:**	1%
African American:	44%	**25 or older:**	51%

Transfer out. 75% of students enrolled in the transfer program go on to 4-year colleges. **Colleges most students transferred to 2005:** University of North Carolina at Wilmington, East Carolina University, Mount Olive College.

Basis for selection. Open admission, but selective for some programs. Admission to nursing programs based on test scores and high school courses. 2.0 GPA in biology, chemistry, and algebra required. SAT or ACT accepted in lieu of academic placement tests. Nursing Entrance Test (NET) required for nursing applicants. Credit may be awarded for graphic arts classes based on portfolio. **Adult students:** Entrance exam policies same as for first-time freshmen.

2005-2006 Annual costs. Tuition/fees: $1,255; $6,655 out-of-state. Per-credit charge: $40 in-state; $220 out-of-state. Books/supplies: $1,200. Personal expenses: $600.

2004-2005 Financial aid. All financial aid based on need. 46 full-time freshmen applied for aid; 46 were judged to have need; 46 of these received aid. Average need met was 60%. Average scholarship/grant was $600; average loan $2,500. 95% of total undergraduate aid awarded as scholarships/grants, 5% as loans/jobs. Need-based aid available for part-time students. Work study available nights and for part-time students.

Application procedures. Admission: No deadline. No application fee. Application may be submitted online. Admission notification on a rolling basis. **Financial aid:** Priority date 6/1; no closing date. FAFSA, institutional form required. Applicants notified on a rolling basis starting 7/15; must reply within 2 week(s) of notification.

Academics. Special study options: Cooperative education, distance learning, double major, dual enrollment of high school students, ESL, internships, liberal arts/career combination. License preparation in nursing. **Credit/placement by examination:** AP, CLEP, institutional tests. 48 credit hours maximum toward associate degree. **Support services:** GED preparation and test center, learning center, pre-admission summer program, reduced course load, remedial instruction, study skills assistance, tutoring.

Majors. Agriculture: Animal husbandry, animal sciences, business, poultry. **Business:** Accounting, administrative services, business admin. **Computer sciences:** Applications programming. **Education:** General, elementary, secondary. **Family/consumer sciences:** Child care. **Health:** Medical assistant, nursing (RN). **Liberal arts:** Arts/sciences. **Personal/culinary services:** Cosmetic. **Protective services:** Police science. **Visual/performing arts:** Commercial/advertising art.

Computing on campus. 257 workstations in library, computer center.

Student life. Freshman orientation: Available. Preregistration for classes offered. **Activities:** Student government, student newspaper, Phi Theta Kappa, Student Nurses' Association, National Vocational-Technical Honor Society, Ambassador Program, Criminal Justice Club.

Athletics. Intercollegiate: Softball, tennis, volleyball.

Student services. Career counseling, services for economically disadvantaged, student employment services, financial aid counseling, personal counseling, placement for graduates, veterans' counselor. **Physically disabled:** Services for visually, hearing impaired. **Transfer:** Special adviser, orientation, pre-admission transcript evaluation for new students. Transfer adviser, college fairs on campus for students transferring to 4-year colleges.

Contact. E-mail: lgrady@jscc.cc.nc.us
Phone: (910) 296-2500 Fax: (910) 296-1222
Rita Brown, Director of Admissions, James Sprunt Community College, Box 398, Kenansville, NC 28349-0398

Johnston Community College

Smithfield, North Carolina **CB member**
www.johnston.cc.nc.us **CB code: 0727**

- Public 2-year community and technical college
- Commuter campus in large town

General. Founded in 1969. Regionally accredited. **Enrollment:** 4,088 degree-seeking undergraduates; 7 non-degree-seeking students. **Degrees:** 289 associate awarded. **Location:** 30 miles from Raleigh. **Calendar:** Semester, limited summer session. **Full-time faculty:** 115 total. **Part-time faculty:** 190 total. **Class size:** 63% < 20, 36% 20-39, less than 1% 50-99, less than 1% >100.

Student profile. Among degree-seeking undergraduates, 53% enrolled in a transfer program, 47% enrolled in a vocational program, 3% already have a bachelor's degree or higher, 1,565 enrolled as first-time, first-year students.

Part-time:	60%	**African American:**	20%
Out-of-state:	1%	**Hispanic American:**	4%
Women:	64%		

Transfer out. Colleges most students transferred to 2005: East Carolina University, University of North Carolina at Wilmington, North Carolina State University.

Basis for selection. Open admission, but selective for some programs. Admission to health programs based on test scores, high school record and related completed courses. PSB required for admission to nursing and radiologic technology programs. Placement interview required for all applicants; interview required for health programs. **Adult students:** Entrance exam policies same as for first-time freshmen.

2005-2006 Annual costs. Tuition/fees: $1,253; $6,653 out-of-state. Per-credit charge: $40 in-state; $220 out-of-state. Books/supplies: $450. Personal expenses: $900.

2004-2005 Financial aid. All financial aid based on need. 85% of total undergraduate aid awarded as scholarships/grants, 15% as loans/jobs. Need-based aid available for part-time students. Work study available for part-time students.

Application procedures. Admission: Priority date 8/1; no deadline. No application fee. Application may be submitted online. Admission notification on a rolling basis. **Financial aid:** Priority date 5/31; no closing date. FAFSA, institutional form required. Applicants notified on a rolling basis starting 6/1; must reply within 2 week(s) of notification.

Academics. Special study options: Cross-registration, distance learning, double major, dual enrollment of high school students, internships. Bachelor's degree programs available on campus. **Credit/placement by examination:** AP, CLEP, institutional tests. **Support services:** GED preparation and test center, learning center, pre-admission summer program, reduced course load, remedial instruction, tutoring.

Majors. Business: Accounting, administrative services, business admin, office/clerical, operations. **Computer sciences:** Programming. **Engineering:** Civil. **Family/consumer sciences:** Child care. **Health:** Cardiopulmonary technology, medical assistant, medical radiologic technology/radiation therapy, medical secretary, radiologic technology/medical imaging. **Legal studies:** Paralegal. **Liberal arts:** Arts/sciences. **Mechanic/repair:** Diesel, heating/ac/refrig. **Protective services:** Law enforcement admin, police science. **Visual/performing arts:** Commercial/advertising art.

Most popular majors. Business/marketing 17%, computer/information sciences 8%, education 8%, health sciences 22%, liberal arts 25%, visual/performing arts 8%.

Computing on campus. 29 workstations in library, computer center. Commuter students can connect to campus network.

Student life. **Freshman orientation:** Mandatory, $40 fee. Preregistration for classes offered. **Activities:** Jazz band, choral groups, student government.

Athletics. NJCAA. **Intercollegiate:** Golf M, softball W. **Team name:** Jaguars.

Student services. Campus ministries, career counseling, student employment services, financial aid counseling, minority student services, on-campus daycare, personal counseling, placement for graduates, veterans' counselor. **Physically disabled:** Services for visually, speech, hearing impaired. **Transfer:** Special adviser, pre-admission transcript evaluation for new students. College fairs on campus for students transferring to 4-year colleges.

Contact. Phone: (919) 209-2128 Fax: (919) 989-7862
Joan McLendon, Director of Admissions and Counseling, Johnston Community College, Box 2350, Smithfield, NC 27577

King's College
Charlotte, North Carolina
www.kingscollegecharlotte.edu **CB code: 5361**

- For-profit 2-year community and technical college
- Large city
- Interview required

General. Accredited by ACICS. **Enrollment:** 537 degree-seeking undergraduates. **Degrees:** 296 associate awarded. **Calendar:** Semester. **Full-time faculty:** 18 total. **Part-time faculty:** 7 total.

Student profile.

Out-of-state:	10%	**Live on campus:**	35%
25 or older:	10%		

Basis for selection. Scholastic level exam required for admission. **Adult students:** Entrance exam policies same as for first-time freshmen.

2006-2007 Annual costs. Tuition/fees: $11,960. Room/board: $5,960.

Financial aid. All financial aid based on need.

Application procedures. **Admission:** No deadline. $50 fee. Admission notification on a rolling basis. **Financial aid:** FAFSA required. Applicants notified on a rolling basis.

Academics. **Credit/placement by examination:** CLEP.

Majors. **Business:** Accounting, administrative services, tourism/travel. **Computer sciences:** Applications programming. **Health:** Medical secretary. **Legal studies:** Legal secretary, paralegal. **Visual/performing arts:** Commercial/advertising art.

Student life. **Freshman orientation:** Mandatory. Held on the day prior to the start of classes. **Policies:** Dress code observed; no alcoholic beverages or drugs on campus. Freshmen permitted cars on campus. **Housing:** Single-sex dorms available. $100 deposit, deadline 7/1. **Activities:** Student government, Sigma Chi Kappa, Lambda Epsilon Chi.

Student services. Career counseling, financial aid counseling, placement for graduates. **Transfer:** Special adviser for new students.

Contact. Phone: (704) 372-0266 Toll-free number: (800) 768-2255
Fax: (704) 348-2029
Diane Ryon, Director, King's College , 322 Lamar Avenue, Charlotte, NC 28204

Lenoir Community College
Kinston, North Carolina
www.lenoir.cc.nc.us **CB code: 5378**

- Public 2-year community college
- Commuter campus in large town

General. Founded in 1958. Regionally accredited. Extension campuses in Jones and Greene Counties. **Enrollment:** 2,016 degree-seeking undergraduates; 563 non-degree-seeking students. **Degrees:** 234 associate awarded. **Location:** 75 miles from Raleigh, 25 miles from Greenville. **Calendar:** Semester, extensive summer session. **Full-time faculty:** 88 total. **Part-time faculty:** 350 total. **Class size:** 73% < 20, 26% 20-39, 1% 40-49, less than 1% 50-99. **Special facilities:** Facility for local history, genealogy collection.

Student profile. Among degree-seeking undergraduates, 57% enrolled in a transfer program, 43% enrolled in a vocational program, 1% already have a bachelor's degree or higher, 400 enrolled as first-time, first-year students.

Part-time:	40%	**Women:**	69%
Out-of-state:	2%		

Transfer out. **Colleges most students transferred to 2005:** East Carolina University.

Basis for selection. Open admission, but selective for some programs. Special requirements for allied health programs. Interview required for surgical technology program. **Adult students:** Entrance exam policies same as for first-time freshmen.

High school preparation. Recommended units include English 4, mathematics 2, social studies 2, history 1, science 2 (laboratory 1). One biology, 1 chemistry required for registered nursing program.

2005-2006 Annual costs. Tuition/fees: $1,260; $6,660 out-of-state. Per-credit charge: $40 in-state; $220 out-of-state. Books/supplies: $800. Personal expenses: $540.

Financial aid. **Need-based:** Need-based aid available for part-time students. Work study available nights and for part-time students. **Non-need-based:** Scholarships awarded for academics, athletics, leadership, state residency.

Application procedures. **Admission:** No deadline. No application fee. Application may be submitted online. Admission notification on a rolling basis. Separate application required for allied health programs. January 31 deadline for nursing and April 30 for surgical technology. **Financial aid:** Priority date 6/1, closing date 7/15. Institutional form required. Applicants notified on a rolling basis starting 7/1; must reply within 2 week(s) of notification.

Academics. **Special study options:** Cooperative education, distance learning, dual enrollment of high school students, honors, liberal arts/career combination, study abroad, weekend college. License preparation in aviation, nursing, paramedic, real estate. **Credit/placement by examination:** CLEP, IB, institutional tests. **Support services:** GED preparation and test center, learning center, pre-admission summer program, reduced course load, remedial instruction, tutoring.

Majors. **Agriculture:** Horticulture. **Business:** Accounting, administrative services, business admin, e-commerce, executive assistant, management information systems. **Computer sciences:** Data processing, programming. **Conservation:** Water/wetlands/marine. **Education:** General, art, biology, chemistry, early childhood, elementary, English, health, history, physical, social science, teacher assistance. **Engineering:** General. **Engineering technology:** Electrical, mechanical. **Family/consumer sciences:** Child care. **Health:** Massage therapy, medical assistant, medical secretary, nursing (RN), radiologic technology/medical imaging. **Legal studies:** Court reporting. **Liberal arts:** Arts/sciences. **Math:** General. **Mechanic/repair:** Automotive, electronics/electrical. **Personal/culinary services:** Culinary arts. **Production:** Machine shop technology, welding. **Psychology:** General. **Public administration:** Social work. **Transportation:** Airline/commercial pilot, aviation management. **Visual/performing arts:** Commercial/advertising art, studio arts.

Computing on campus. 100 workstations in library, computer center, student center. Commuter students can connect to campus network. Online course registration available.

Student life. **Freshman orientation:** Available. Preregistration for classes offered. **Activities:** Choral groups, radio station, student government, student newspaper, Phi Theta Kappa, various clubs related to major fields of study.

Athletics. NJCAA. **Intercollegiate:** Baseball M, basketball M, volleyball W. **Intramural:** Basketball M. **Team name:** Lancers.

Student services. Adult student services, career counseling, student employment services, financial aid counseling, health services, personal counseling, placement for graduates, veterans' counselor. **Transfer:** Special adviser, orientation, pre-admission transcript evaluation for new students. Transfer adviser, college fairs on campus for students transferring to 4-year colleges.

Contact. Phone: (252) 527-6223 Fax: (252) 527-6223 ext. 323
Tammy Buck, Director of Enrollment Management, Lenoir Community College, Box 188, Kinston, NC 28502-0188

Louisburg College

Louisburg, North Carolina **CB member**
www.louisburg.edu **CB code: 5369**

- Private 2-year junior college affiliated with United Methodist Church
- Residential campus in small town
- SAT or ACT (ACT writing optional) required

General. Founded in 1787. Regionally accredited. **Enrollment:** 771 degree-seeking undergraduates. **Degrees:** 64 associate awarded. **Location:** 30 miles from Raleigh. **Calendar:** Semester, limited summer session. **Full-time faculty:** 35 total. **Part-time faculty:** 15 total.

Student profile.

Out-of-state:	20%	**Live on campus:**	80%
25 or older:	3%		

Transfer out. Colleges most students transferred to 2005: North Carolina State University, East Carolina University, Appalachian State University, University of North Carolina at Wilmington, University of North Carolina at Greensboro, University of North Carolina at Chapel Hill.

Basis for selection. School achievement most important, followed by test scores and recommendations. Interview recommended for some applicants. Students more than one year out of high school not required to submit test scores. **Learning Disabled:** Comprehensive tutorial program available for learning-disabled students.

High school preparation. 20 units recommended. Recommended units include English 4, mathematics 3, social studies 3, science 2 and foreign language 2.

2006-2007 Annual costs. Tuition/fees: $11,690. Room/board: $6,890. Books/supplies: $900. Personal expenses: $1,125.

2005-2006 Financial aid. Need-based: Work study available nights and weekends. **Additional information:** Job location and development program helps students obtain work in the community.

Application procedures. Admission: No deadline. $50 fee, may be waived for applicants with need. Admission notification on a rolling basis. Must reply by May 1 or within 2 week(s) if notified thereafter. **Financial aid:** Priority date 3/15; no closing date. FAFSA, institutional form required. Applicants notified on a rolling basis starting 3/15.

Academics. Special study options: Cooperative education, dual enrollment of high school students, independent study. Louisburg Learning Partners for Students with Learning Differences. **Credit/placement by examination:** AP, CLEP, IB, institutional tests. 30 credit hours maximum toward associate degree. **Support services:** Learning center, pre-admission summer program, reduced course load, remedial instruction, study skills assistance, tutoring, writing center.

Majors. Biology: General. **Business:** General, business admin. **Communications:** General. **Computer sciences:** General. **Education:** General, biology, chemistry, early childhood, elementary, English, history, mathematics, physical, science, secondary. **Engineering:** General. **Health:** Athletic training, premedicine, prepharmacy. **History:** General. **Liberal arts:** Arts/sciences. **Math:** General. **Parks/recreation:** General, exercise sciences, facilities management. **Physical sciences:** Chemistry. **Psychology:** General. **Public administration:** Social work. **Social sciences:** General, sociology. **Visual/performing arts:** Art, dance, dramatic.

Most popular majors. Liberal arts 92%.

Computing on campus. 75 workstations in library, computer center. Dormitories linked to campus network. Online library available.

Student life. Freshman orientation: Mandatory. Preregistration for classes offered. **Policies:** Non-resident undergraduates under 21 must live at home. **Housing:** Guaranteed on-campus for all undergraduates. Single-sex dorms available. $200 deposit. **Activities:** Choral groups, dance, drama, literary magazine, music ensembles, musical theater, radio station, student government, student newspaper, Christian Life Council, Young Democrats, Young Republicans, Spanish club, Workers Actively Volunteering Energetic Services, peace group, French club, Phi Theta Kappa, Appalachian Trail White Water Club, ecological concerns club.

Athletics. NJCAA. **Intercollegiate:** Baseball M, basketball, cheerleading, golf, soccer, softball W, volleyball W. **Intramural:** Basketball, football (tackle), soccer, softball, table tennis, tennis, volleyball. **Team name:** Hurricanes.

Student services. Adult student services, alcohol/substance abuse counseling, campus ministries, career counseling, student employment services, financial aid counseling, health services, personal counseling, veterans' counselor. **Learning disabled:** Comprehensive services available. **Transfer:** Special adviser, orientation for new students. Transfer adviser, college fairs on campus for students transferring to 4-year colleges.

Contact. E-mail: admissions@louisburg.edu
Phone: (919) 497-3222 Toll-free number: (800) 775-0208
Fax: (919) 496-1788
Stephanie Buchanan, Vice President of Enrollment Management, Louisburg College, 501 North Main Street, Louisburg, NC 27549

Martin Community College

Williamston, North Carolina
www.martincc.edu **CB code: 5445**

- Public 2-year community and technical college
- Commuter campus in small town

General. Founded in 1967. Regionally accredited. **Enrollment:** 658 degree-seeking undergraduates; 306 non-degree-seeking students. **Degrees:** 73 associate awarded. **Location:** 30 miles from Greenville, 100 miles from Raleigh. **Calendar:** Semester, limited summer session. **Full-time faculty:** 30 total. **Part-time faculty:** 60 total. **Special facilities:** Equine arena, bull riding, rodeos.

Student profile. Among degree-seeking undergraduates, 10% enrolled in a transfer program, 59% enrolled in a vocational program, 110 enrolled as first-time, first-year students, 116 transferred in from other institutions.

Part-time:	36%	**Women:**	81%
Out-of-state:	1%	**25 or older:**	58%

Transfer out. Colleges most students transferred to 2005: East Carolina University.

Basis for selection. Open admission, but selective for some programs. Limited enrollment in physical therapy assistant program. Selection based on high school record, placement test results, completion of required courses and interview. Selection of Dental Assisting applications includes high school record, completion of required courses, and an interview. COMPASS required of some students. Interview required for physical therapist assistant applicants and dental assisting applicants. **Adult students:** Entrance exam policies same as for first-time freshmen. **Homeschooled:** Statement describing homeschool structure and mission, transcript of courses and grades required.

High school preparation. 22 units recommended. Recommended units include English 4, mathematics 3, social studies 2, history 1, science 3 (laboratory 1) and academic electives 9.

2005-2006 Annual costs. Tuition/fees: $1,223; $6,623 out-of-state. Per-credit charge: $40 in-state; $220 out-of-state. Books/supplies: $600. Personal expenses: $400.

2004-2005 Financial aid. Need-based: 68% of total undergraduate aid awarded as scholarships/grants, 32% as loans/jobs. Need-based aid available for part-time students. Work study available nights and for part-time students. **Non-need-based:** Scholarships awarded for academics.

Application procedures. Admission: No deadline. No application fee. Application may be submitted online. Admission notification on a rolling basis. Closing date for physical therapist assistant program applicants May 15. **Financial aid:** Priority date 5/1; no closing date. FAFSA required. Applicants notified on a rolling basis starting 5/1.

Academics. Special study options: Cooperative education, distance learning, double major, dual enrollment of high school students, ESL, independent study, internships, liberal arts/career combination. License preparation in real estate. **Credit/placement by examination:** AP, CLEP, institutional tests. No more than half of credits required in program of study may be earned through credit by exam (including CLEP). **Support services:** GED preparation and test center, learning center, reduced course load, remedial instruction, study skills assistance, tutoring.

Majors. Agriculture: Equestrian studies. **Business:** Accounting technology, business admin, executive assistant, management information systems. **Computer sciences:** Information systems. **Construction:** Electrician. **Education:** General, early childhood, elementary, secondary. **Health:** Medical assistant, medical secretary, physical therapy assistant. **Liberal arts:** Arts/

sciences. **Mechanic/repair:** Automotive, heating/ac/refrig. **Personal/culinary services:** Cosmetic.

Most popular majors. Agriculture 6%, business/marketing 43%, education 15%, health sciences 27%.

Computing on campus. 31 workstations in library, computer center. Commuter students can connect to campus network.

Student life. Freshman orientation: Available. Offered on registration day. **Policies:** Freshmen permitted cars on campus. **Activities:** Student government, physical therapist assistant club, Phi Theta Kappa, equine club, medical assisting club, Alpha Beta Gamma.

Athletics. Team name: Screaming Eagles.

Student services. Career counseling, services for economically disadvantaged, student employment services, financial aid counseling, on-campus daycare, personal counseling, placement for graduates, veterans' counselor. **Transfer:** Special adviser, orientation, pre-admission transcript evaluation for new students. Transfer adviser, college fairs on campus for students transferring to 4-year colleges.

Contact. E-mail: jbussell@martincc.edu
Phone: (252) 792-1521 ext. 268 Fax: (252) 792-0826
Jim Bussell, Admissions Officer, Martin Community College, 1161 Kehukee Park Road, Williamston, NC 27892-9988

Mayland Community College

Spruce Pine, North Carolina — **CB member**
www.mayland.edu — **CB code: 0795**

- Public 2-year community college
- Commuter campus in small town

General. Founded in 1971. Regionally accredited. **Enrollment:** 1,500 degree-seeking undergraduates. **Degrees:** 78 associate awarded. **Location:** 50 miles from Asheville. **Calendar:** Semester, extensive summer session. **Full-time faculty:** 45 total. **Part-time faculty:** 50 total. **Class size:** 71% < 20, 29% 20-39. **Special facilities:** Child development center.

Student profile.

Out-of-state:	3%	**25 or older:**	60%

Transfer out. Colleges most students transferred to 2005: Appalachian State University, University of North Carolina-Asheville, Western Carolina University, Mars Hill College.

Basis for selection. Open admission, but selective for some programs. Associate degree nursing program admission based on competitive ranking system. Placement assessment required of all degree-seeking students.

2005-2006 Annual costs. Tuition/fees: $1,245; $6,645 out-of-state. Per-credit charge: $40 in-state; $220 out-of-state. Books/supplies: $750. Personal expenses: $1,087.

Financial aid. Need-based: Need-based aid available for part-time students.

Application procedures. Admission: No deadline. No application fee. Admission notification on a rolling basis beginning on or about 3/1. Application by April 1 recommended for nursing program. **Financial aid:** Priority date 3/15; no closing date. FAFSA, institutional form required. Applicants notified on a rolling basis starting 6/15.

Academics. Special study options: Cooperative education, cross-registration, distance learning, double major, dual enrollment of high school students, independent study, internships, liberal arts/career combination. Bachelor's degree programs available on campus. License preparation in nursing. **Credit/placement by examination:** CLEP, institutional tests. Maximum 25% of program hours can be earned via credit by examination. **Support services:** GED preparation and test center, learning center, pre-admission summer program, reduced course load, remedial instruction, tutoring.

Majors. Agriculture: Horticulture. **Business:** Accounting, administrative services, business admin. **Computer sciences:** Systems analysis. **Education:** General, early childhood. **Engineering:** Electrical. **Health:** Medical secretary, nursing (RN). **Liberal arts:** Arts/sciences. **Personal/culinary services:** Cosmetic.

Most popular majors. Business/marketing 28%, education 7%, engineering/engineering technologies 7%, health sciences 31%, liberal arts 19%.

Computing on campus. 150 workstations in library, computer center. Online library available.

Student life. Freshman orientation: Available. Preregistration for classes offered. One-hour class each semester. **Activities:** Literary magazine, student government, Phi Theta Kappa, National Nursing Association, early childhood students' association.

Student services. Career counseling, services for economically disadvantaged, student employment services, financial aid counseling, on-campus daycare, personal counseling, placement for graduates, veterans' counselor. **Physically disabled:** Services for visually, speech, hearing impaired. **Transfer:** Special adviser, orientation for new students. Transfer adviser, college fairs on campus for students transferring to 4-year colleges.

Contact. Phone: (828) 765-7351 Toll-free number: (800) 462-9526
Fax: (828) 765-0728
Cathy Morrison, Vice President, Student Services, Mayland Community College, Box 547, Spruce Pine, NC 28777

McDowell Technical Community College

Marion, North Carolina
www.mcdowelltech.cc.nc.us — **CB code: 0789**

- Public 2-year community and technical college
- Commuter campus in small town

General. Founded in 1964. Regionally accredited. **Enrollment:** 755 degree-seeking undergraduates. **Degrees:** 97 associate awarded. **Location:** 35 miles from Asheville. **Calendar:** Semester, limited summer session. **Full-time faculty:** 48 total. **Part-time faculty:** 102 total. **Special facilities:** Color and black/white photography laboratories.

Student profile.

Out-of-state:	1%	**25 or older:**	37%

Basis for selection. Open admission, but selective for some programs. Selective admission to nursing programs. Interview required for nursing applicants, recommended for all others.

2005-2006 Annual costs. Tuition/fees: $1,203; $6,603 out-of-state. Per-credit charge: $40 in-state; $220 out-of-state. Books/supplies: $700. Personal expenses: $1,548.

2004-2005 Financial aid. All financial aid based on need. 99% of total undergraduate aid awarded as scholarships/grants, 1% as loans/jobs. Work study available nights and for part-time students.

Application procedures. Admission: No deadline. No application fee. Admission notification on a rolling basis. **Financial aid:** Priority date 3/15; no closing date. FAFSA, institutional form required. Applicants notified on a rolling basis starting 7/1.

Academics. Special study options: Cooperative education, distance learning, double major, dual enrollment of high school students, independent study, internships, liberal arts/career combination. Bachelor's degree programs available on campus. License preparation in nursing. **Credit/placement by examination:** CLEP, institutional tests. 20 credit hours maximum toward associate degree. **Support services:** GED preparation and test center, learning center, reduced course load, remedial instruction, tutoring.

Majors. Business: General, accounting, office/clerical. **Communications technology:** Graphic/printing. **Computer sciences:** Applications programming, programming. **Education:** General. **Health:** Nursing (RN). **Liberal arts:** Arts/sciences. **Mechanic/repair:** Electronics/electrical, industrial. **Visual/performing arts:** Commercial photography, commercial/advertising art.

Most popular majors. Business/marketing 27%, computer/information sciences 12%, health sciences 26%, liberal arts 18%, visual/performing arts 17%.

Computing on campus. 80 workstations in library, computer center.

Student life. Freshman orientation: Mandatory. **Activities:** Student government, student newspaper.

Athletics. Intercollegiate: Tennis M. **Intramural:** Basketball, golf, skiing, tennis, volleyball. **Team name:** Jays.

Student services. Adult student services, career counseling, student employment services, on-campus daycare, personal counseling, placement for graduates, veterans' counselor. **Physically disabled:** Services for visually, speech, hearing impaired. **Transfer:** Special adviser for new students. Transfer adviser for students transferring to 4-year colleges.

Contact. E-mail: shirleyb@mail.mcdowell.cc.nc.us
Phone: (828) 652-0676 Fax: (828) 652-1014
Rick Wilson, Registrar, McDowell Technical Community College, 54 College Drive, Marion, NC 28752

Mitchell Community College

Statesville, North Carolina **CB member**
www.mitchell.cc.nc.us **CB code: 5412**

- Public 2-year community college
- Commuter campus in large town

General. Founded in 1852. Regionally accredited. **Enrollment:** 986 full-time, degree-seeking students. **Degrees:** 210 associate awarded. **Location:** 40 miles from Charlotte, 40 miles from Winston-Salem. **Calendar:** Semester, limited summer session. **Full-time faculty:** 57 total. **Part-time faculty:** 71 total.

Student profile.

Out-of-state:	70%	**25 or older:**	49%

Transfer out. Colleges most students transferred to 2005: University of North Carolina-Charlotte, Appalachian State University, Gardner-Webb University, Lenoir-Rhyne University.

Basis for selection. Open admission, but selective for some programs. Nursing program applicants must meet minimum admissions requirements; interview and essay required. All applicants must take College Placement Tests to determine readiness for college-level studies. **Adult students:** Entrance exam policies same as for first-time freshmen.

2005-2006 Annual costs. Tuition/fees: $1,245; $6,645 out-of-state. Per-credit charge: $40 in-state; $220 out-of-state. Books/supplies: $900. Personal expenses: $1,448.

Financial aid. Need-based: Need-based aid available for part-time students. Work study available for part-time students.

Application procedures. Admission: No deadline. No application fee. Admission notification on a rolling basis. **Financial aid:** No deadline. FAFSA, institutional form required. Applicants notified on a rolling basis starting 3/1; must reply within 2 week(s) of notification.

Academics. Special study options: Cooperative education, distance learning, dual enrollment of high school students, independent study. License preparation in nursing, paramedic, real estate. **Credit/placement by examination:** AP, CLEP, institutional tests. 20 credit hours maximum toward associate degree. **Support services:** GED preparation and test center, learning center, reduced course load, remedial instruction, tutoring.

Majors. Business: Accounting, administrative services, business admin, operations. **Computer sciences:** Information systems, programming. **Education:** Early childhood, teacher assistance. **Engineering:** Electrical. **Engineering technology:** Construction, drafting, electrical, industrial management, manufacturing. **Health:** Nursing (RN), predentistry, premedicine, prepharmacy, preveterinary. **Legal studies:** Prelaw. **Liberal arts:** Arts/sciences. **Mechanic/repair:** Industrial. **Production:** Machine shop technology. **Protective services:** Police science. **Public administration:** Human services. **Visual/performing arts:** Studio arts.

Most popular majors. Business/marketing 15%, computer/information sciences 13%, engineering/engineering technologies 6%, health sciences 26%, liberal arts 18%, personal/culinary services 8%.

Computing on campus. 45 workstations in library, computer center.

Student life. Freshman orientation: Available. Usually held immediately prior to fall semester for approximately 2.5 hours. **Activities:** Concert band, choral groups, literary magazine, student government, Circle-K, Christian Student Fellowship, Ebony Kinship.

Student services. Campus ministries, career counseling, student employment services, financial aid counseling, personal counseling, placement for graduates, veterans' counselor. **Physically disabled:** Services for visually, hearing impaired. **Transfer:** Special adviser, orientation for new students. College fairs on campus for students transferring to 4-year colleges.

Contact. E-mail: gstanley@mitchell.cc.nc.us
Phone: (704) 878-3243 Fax: (704) 878-0872
Gregory Stanley, Director of Admissions and Records, Mitchell Community College, 500 West Broad Street, Statesville, NC 28677

Montgomery Community College

Troy, North Carolina
www.montgomery.edu **CB code: 0785**

- Public 2-year community college
- Commuter campus in small town

General. Founded in 1967. Regionally accredited. **Enrollment:** 631 degree-seeking undergraduates; 220 non-degree-seeking students. **Degrees:** 85 associate awarded. **Location:** 50 miles from Greensboro, 62 miles from Charlotte. **Calendar:** Semester, limited summer session. **Full-time faculty:** 33 total. **Part-time faculty:** 40 total. **Class size:** 91% <20, 7% 20-39, 2% 40-49, less than 1% 50-99. **Special facilities:** Rifle/pistol firing range.

Student profile. Among degree-seeking undergraduates, 15% enrolled in a transfer program, 51% enrolled in a vocational program, 2% already have a bachelor's degree or higher, 153 enrolled as first-time, first-year students, 125 transferred in from other institutions.

Part-time:	49%	**Asian American:**	3%
Out-of-state:	1%	**Hispanic American:**	4%
Women:	71%	**Native American:**	1%
African American:	25%	**25 or older:**	57%

Transfer out. Colleges most students transferred to 2005: Pfeiffer University, Gardner-Webb University, University of North Carolina at Greensboro.

Basis for selection. Open admission, but selective for some programs. Special requirements for nursing program. Secondary school record and test scores considered. **Adult students:** Entrance exam policies same as for first-time freshmen. **Homeschooled:** Home school must provide copy of "Notification of intent to operate" card from NC Department of Non-Public Education.

High school preparation. 28 units recommended. Recommended units include English 4, mathematics 3, social studies 3, science 3 (laboratory 1) and academic electives 15.

2005-2006 Annual costs. Tuition/fees: $1,245; $6,645 out-of-state. Per-credit charge: $40 in-state; $220 out-of-state. Books/supplies: $1,050.

Financial aid. Need-based: Need-based aid available for part-time students. Work study available nights and for part-time students. **Non-need-based:** Scholarships awarded for academics, minority status, state residency.

Application procedures. Admission: No deadline. No application fee. Application must be submitted on paper. Admission notification on a rolling basis. Practical Nursing Program applicants must apply by October 15 for following fall program. **Financial aid:** Priority date 7/15; no closing date. FAFSA, institutional form required. Applicants notified on a rolling basis starting 6/1.

Academics. Special study options: Distance learning, double major, dual enrollment of high school students. License preparation in nursing, paramedic. **Credit/placement by examination:** AP, CLEP, institutional tests. 16 credit hours maximum toward associate degree. **Support services:** GED preparation and test center, learning center, reduced course load, remedial instruction, tutoring.

Majors. Business: Accounting, business admin, office management. **Computer sciences:** Information systems, information technology. **Conservation:** Forest technology. **Construction:** Electrician. **Education:** Early childhood. **Health:** EMT paramedic, medical assistant. **Liberal arts:** Arts/sciences. **Mechanic/repair:** Gunsmithing. **Protective services:** Criminal justice. **Visual/performing arts:** Crafts.

Most popular majors. Business/marketing 18%, computer/information sciences 7%, education 13%, health sciences 25%, liberal arts 12%, natural resources/environmental science 9%, security/protective services 7%, trade and industry 9%.

Computing on campus. 80 workstations in library, computer center. Commuter students can connect to campus network.

Student life. Freshman orientation: Available. **Policies:** Freshmen permitted cars on campus. **Activities:** Student government, gunsmithing society, forestry club, business technologies club, practical nursing club, medical assisting club.

Student services. Career counseling, student employment services, financial aid counseling, on-campus daycare, personal counseling, veterans' counselor. **Physically disabled:** Services for visually, speech, hearing impaired. **Transfer:** Special adviser, orientation for new students. Transfer adviser, college fairs on campus for students transferring to 4-year colleges.

Two-Year Colleges

Contact. E-mail: fryek@montgomery.edu
Phone: (910) 576-6222 ext. 240 Fax: (910) 576-2176
Karen Frye, Admissions Officer, Montgomery Community College, 1011 Page Street, Troy, NC 27371-0787

Nash Community College
Rocky Mount, North Carolina **CB member**
www.nash.cc.nc.us **CB code: 5881**

- Public 2-year community college
- Commuter campus in small city

General. Founded in 1967. Regionally accredited. **Enrollment:** 1,948 degree-seeking undergraduates. **Degrees:** 157 associate awarded. **Location:** 55 miles from Raleigh. **Calendar:** Semester, limited summer session. **Full-time faculty:** 70 total. **Part-time faculty:** 180 total. **Class size:** 54% < 20, 46% 20-39. **Partnerships:** Formal partnership with high schools to provide students opportunity to earn college credit.

Student profile.

Out-of-state:	1%	**25 or older:**	52%

Transfer out. Colleges most students transferred to 2005: University of North Carolina system universities.

Basis for selection. Open admission, but selective for some programs. Special requirements for nursing, physical therapy assistant, phlebotomy, cosmetology programs. Students may use ACT or SAT scores for placement, or take ASSET or COMPASS. **Adult students:** College recommends ASSET or COMPASS placement test if student does not have SAT scores.

High school preparation. Appropriate biology courses required for nursing and physical therapist assistant programs.

2005-2006 Annual costs. Tuition/fees: $1,245; $6,645 out-of-state. Per-credit charge: $40 in-state; $220 out-of-state. Books/supplies: $900. Personal expenses: $2,000.

Financial aid. Need-based: Need-based aid available for part-time students. **Non-need-based:** Scholarships awarded for academics.

Application procedures. Admission: No deadline. No application fee. Admission notification on a rolling basis. **Financial aid:** Priority date 6/30; no closing date. FAFSA, institutional form required. Applicants notified on a rolling basis starting 7/15.

Academics. Special study options: Accelerated study, distance learning, dual enrollment of high school students, ESL, liberal arts/career combination. License preparation in nursing, paramedic, physical therapy, real estate. **Credit/placement by examination:** CLEP, IB, institutional tests. **Support services:** GED preparation and test center, learning center, reduced course load, remedial instruction, study skills assistance, tutoring.

Majors. Architecture: Technology. **Business:** Accounting, administrative services, business admin, hotel/motel admin, management information systems. **Computer sciences:** Information systems. **Construction:** Lineworker. **Education:** General, early childhood, teacher assistance. **Engineering:** Electrical. **Engineering technology:** Architectural, computer, electrical, industrial safety. **Family/consumer sciences:** Child care. **Health:** Licensed practical nurse, medical secretary, nursing (RN). **Legal studies:** Legal secretary. **Liberal arts:** Arts/sciences. **Personal/culinary services:** Culinary arts. **Protective services:** Police science.

Most popular majors. Business/marketing 18%, computer/information sciences 8%, engineering/engineering technologies 16%, health sciences 21%, liberal arts 21%, social sciences 7%.

Computing on campus. 110 workstations in library, computer center. Online library available.

Student life. Freshman orientation: Available. Preregistration for classes offered. **Activities:** Student government.

Student services. Career counseling, services for economically disadvantaged, student employment services, financial aid counseling, placement for graduates, veterans' counselor. **Physically disabled:** Services for visually, speech, hearing impaired. **Transfer:** Special adviser, orientation, preadmission transcript evaluation for new students. Transfer adviser, college fairs on campus for students transferring to 4-year colleges.

Contact. Phone: (252) 443-4011 ext. 300 Fax: (252) 443-0828
Dot Gardner, Admissions Officer, Nash Community College, Box 7488, Rocky Mount, NC 27804-0488

Pamlico Community College
Grantsboro, North Carolina
www.pamlico.cc.nc.us **CB code: 0864**

- Public 2-year community college
- Commuter campus in rural community

General. Founded in 1962. Regionally accredited. **Enrollment:** 400 degree-seeking undergraduates. **Degrees:** 39 associate awarded. **Location:** 20 miles from New Bern. **Calendar:** Semester, limited summer session. **Full-time faculty:** 21 total. **Part-time faculty:** 12 total.

Basis for selection. Open admission.

2005-2006 Annual costs. Tuition/fees: $1,200; $6,600 out-of-state. Per-credit charge: $40 in-state; $220 out-of-state. Books/supplies: $380. Personal expenses: $1,630.

2005-2006 Financial aid. Need-based: 93% of total undergraduate aid awarded as scholarships/grants, 7% as loans/jobs. **Additional information:** Jobs Training Partner Act and Displaced Homemaker Programs cover tuition, books, fees.

Application procedures. Admission: No deadline. No application fee. Admission notification on a rolling basis. **Financial aid:** No deadline. FAFSA required. Applicants notified on a rolling basis.

Academics. Special study options: Dual enrollment of high school students, independent study, internships. **Credit/placement by examination:** CLEP, institutional tests. **Support services:** Learning center, reduced course load, remedial instruction, tutoring.

Majors. Business: Accounting, business admin, office/clerical. **Conservation:** General. **Education:** General, early childhood. **Engineering:** Electrical. **Engineering technology:** Electrical.

Computing on campus. 40 workstations in library.

Student life. Freshman orientation: Available. **Activities:** Student government, student newspaper.

Athletics. Intramural: Basketball, softball, table tennis, tennis, volleyball.

Student services. Career counseling, student employment services, health services, personal counseling, placement for graduates, veterans' counselor.

Contact. E-mail: jjones@pamlico.cc.nc.us
Phone: (252) 249-1851 Fax: (252) 249-2377
John Jones, Dean of Student Enrollment Services, Pamlico Community College, PO Box 185, Grantsboro, NC 28529

Piedmont Community College
Roxboro, North Carolina
www.piedmont.cc.nc.us **CB code: 5518**

- Public 2-year community college
- Small town

General. Founded in 1970. Regionally accredited. Branch campus in Caswell County. Correctional education offered at Hillsborough, Yanceyville, and Roxboro. **Enrollment:** 2,610 degree-seeking undergraduates. **Degrees:** 187 associate awarded. **Location:** 30 miles from Durham, 45 miles from Chapel Hill. **Calendar:** Semester, limited summer session. **Full-time faculty:** 74 total. **Part-time faculty:** 67 total. **Special facilities:** 4-mile nature trail.

Student profile.

Out-of-state:	5%	**25 or older:**	51%

Basis for selection. Open admission, but selective for some programs. Admission for nursing based on test scores, interview and recommendations. Nursing applicants must provide health data.

2005-2006 Annual costs. Tuition/fees: $1,215; $6,615 out-of-state. Per-credit charge: $40 in-state; $220 out-of-state. Books/supplies: $800. Personal expenses: $750.

Application procedures. Admission: No deadline. No application fee. Admission notification on a rolling basis. Certain certificate programs do not require high school diploma. **Financial aid:** Priority date 4/15; no closing date. FAFSA required. Applicants notified on a rolling basis; must reply within 2 week(s) of notification.

Academics. **Special study options:** Cooperative education, cross-registration, distance learning, double major, dual enrollment of high school students, independent study, internships, weekend college. License preparation in nursing. **Credit/placement by examination:** CLEP, institutional tests. Maximum of 50% of coursework may be completed through credit by examination. **Support services:** GED preparation and test center, learning center, reduced course load, remedial instruction, study skills assistance, tutoring.

Majors. **Business:** General, accounting, administrative services, business admin, office technology. **Computer sciences:** Applications programming, programming. **Health:** Medical secretary, nursing (RN). **Legal studies:** Legal secretary. **Liberal arts:** Arts/sciences. **Mechanic/repair:** Electronics/electrical, gunsmithing. **Personal/culinary services:** General, cosmetic. **Protective services:** Criminal justice. **Public administration:** Social work.

Computing on campus. 140 workstations in library, computer center.

Student life. **Freshman orientation:** Available. **Activities:** Student government, student newspaper, Phi Theta Kappa, Student Nursing Association, gunsmithing club, taxidermy club, cosmetology club, criminal justice club, CARE.

Athletics. **Team name:** Pacers.

Student services. Career counseling, services for economically disadvantaged, student employment services, financial aid counseling, on-campus daycare, personal counseling, placement for graduates, veterans' counselor. **Physically disabled:** Services for visually, hearing impaired. **Transfer:** Orientation for new students. Transfer adviser for students transferring to 4-year colleges.

Contact. Phone: (336) 599-1181 Fax: (336) 597-3817
Shelia Williamson, Coordinator of Admissions, Piedmont Community College, 1715 College Drive, Roxboro, NC 27573-1197

Pitt Community College

Greenville, North Carolina
www.pitt.cc.nc.us **CB code: 5556**

- Public 2-year community and technical college
- Commuter campus in small city

General. Founded in 1961. Regionally accredited. **Enrollment:** 5,100 degree-seeking undergraduates. **Degrees:** 513 associate awarded. **ROTC:** Army. **Location:** 85 miles from Raleigh. **Calendar:** Semester, limited summer session. **Full-time faculty:** 151 total. **Part-time faculty:** 303 total. **Class size:** 66% < 20, 34% 20-39, less than 1% 40-49, less than 1% 50-99.

Student profile.

Out-of-state:	2%	**25 or older:**	39%

Transfer out. **Colleges most students transferred to 2005:** East Carolina University, University of North Carolina at Wilmington, Barton College.

Basis for selection. Open admission, but selective for some programs. Special admission requirements for some allied health programs. SAT and/or ACT may be used in lieu of the college's placement test for placement into English and math courses. **Adult students:** Entrance exam policies same as for first-time freshmen.

2005-2006 Annual costs. Tuition/fees: $1,255; $6,655 out-of-state. Per-credit charge: $40 in-state; $220 out-of-state. Books/supplies: $600.

Financial aid. **Need-based:** Need-based aid available for part-time students. Work study available nights and for part-time students. **Non-need-based:** Scholarships awarded for academics, athletics, ROTC.

Application procedures. **Admission:** No deadline. No application fee. Application may be submitted online. Admission notification on a rolling basis. **Financial aid:** Priority date 3/15; no closing date. FAFSA required. Applicants notified on a rolling basis starting 2/1.

Academics. **Special study options:** Cooperative education, distance learning, double major, dual enrollment of high school students, ESL, internships. License preparation in nursing, occupational therapy, paramedic, radiology, real estate. **Credit/placement by examination:** CLEP, institutional tests. 40 credit hours maximum toward associate degree. Credit by examination can not be included in the 25% residency requirement. **Support services:** GED preparation and test center, learning center, remedial instruction, tutoring.

Majors. **Business:** Accounting, business admin, e-commerce, human resources, marketing, office management, operations, sales/distribution, training/development. **Computer sciences:** Applications programming, information systems, vendor certification. **Construction:** Electrician. **Education:** Early childhood. **Engineering technology:** Architectural, electrical, industrial management, manufacturing. **Health:** Health services, medical assistant, medical radiologic technology/radiation therapy, medical records technology, medical secretary, mental health services, nuclear medical technology, nursing (RN), occupational therapy assistant, office admin, respiratory therapy assistant, respiratory therapy technology, sonography. **Legal studies:** Paralegal. **Liberal arts:** Arts/sciences. **Mechanic/repair:** Automotive, electronics/electrical, heating/ac/refrig. **Personal/culinary services:** Cosmetic, mortuary science. **Production:** Machine shop technology, welding. **Protective services:** Criminal justice, police science. **Science technology:** Biological. **Visual/performing arts:** Commercial/advertising art.

Most popular majors. Business/marketing 10%, computer/information sciences 10%, engineering/engineering technologies 10%, health sciences 33%, liberal arts 20%.

Computing on campus. 50 workstations in library, computer center. Helpline available.

Student life. **Freshman orientation:** Available. Preregistration for classes offered. **Policies:** Freshmen permitted cars on campus. **Activities:** Student government, Gamma Beta Phi, student government association, Southern Organization of Human Services Organization, Society of Advancement of Management, Delta Epsilon Chi, multicultural/international Club, Students Monitoring Students.

Athletics. NJCAA. **Intercollegiate:** Baseball M, golf M, softball W, volleyball W. **Intramural:** Basketball, football (non-tackle), volleyball. **Team name:** Bulldogs.

Student services. Adult student services, alcohol/substance abuse counseling, career counseling, services for economically disadvantaged, student employment services, financial aid counseling, on-campus daycare, personal counseling, veterans' counselor. **Physically disabled:** Services for visually, speech, hearing impaired. **Transfer:** Transfer adviser, college fairs on campus for students transferring to 4-year colleges.

Contact. E-mail: pittadm@pcc.pitt.cc.nc.us
Phone: (252) 321-4245 Fax: (252) 321-4612
Joanne Ceres, Director of Admissions, Pitt Community College, PO Drawer 7007, Greenville, NC 27835-7007

Randolph Community College

Asheboro, North Carolina
www.randolph.edu **CB code: 5585**

- Public 2-year community and technical college
- Commuter campus in large town

General. Founded in 1962. Regionally accredited. **Enrollment:** 2,291 degree-seeking undergraduates. **Degrees:** 214 associate awarded. **Location:** 65 miles from Charlotte, 26 miles from Greensboro. **Calendar:** Semester, limited summer session. **Full-time faculty:** 50 total. **Part-time faculty:** 100 total.

Transfer out. **Colleges most students transferred to 2005:** University of North Carolina-Greensboro, High Point University, Guilford College, University of North Carolina-Charlotte.

Basis for selection. Open admission, but selective for some programs. Admission to nursing program based primarily on test scores. ASSET/COMPASS used for placement for all associate-level admission. Appropriate test scores are prerequisites for certain English and math courses.

2005-2006 Annual costs. Tuition/fees: $1,245; $6,645 out-of-state. Per-credit charge: $40 in-state; $220 out-of-state. Personal expenses: $832.

Financial aid. **Need-based:** Work study available nights and for part-time students. **Non-need-based:** Scholarships awarded for academics, leadership, minority status, state residency.

Application procedures. **Admission:** No deadline. No application fee. Admission notification on a rolling basis. **Financial aid:** Priority date 5/1; no closing date. FAFSA required. Applicants notified on a rolling basis; must reply within 4 week(s) of notification.

Academics. **Special study options:** Cooperative education, distance learning, double major, dual enrollment of high school students, ESL, internships, liberal arts/career combination, weekend college. **Credit/placement by examination:** CLEP, IB, institutional tests. 16 credit hours maximum toward associate degree. **Support services:** GED preparation and test center, learning center, remedial instruction, tutoring.

Majors. **Business:** Accounting, administrative services, business admin, management information systems. **Communications technology:** Photo/film/video. **Computer sciences:** Networking. **Construction:** Electrician. **Engineering technology:** Electrical, manufacturing. **Family/consumer sciences:** Child care. **Foreign languages:** Sign language interpretation. **Health:** EMT paramedic, nursing (RN). **Interdisciplinary:** Historic preservation. **Liberal arts:** Arts/sciences. **Mechanic/repair:** Automotive. **Protective services:** Police science. **Visual/performing arts:** Commercial photography, commercial/advertising art, interior design, photography, studio arts.

Most popular majors. Business/marketing 44%, health sciences 11%, liberal arts 12%, security/protective services 6%, visual/performing arts 22%.

Student life. **Freshman orientation:** Mandatory. 30 minute overview of policies and procedures. **Activities:** Student government, student newspaper.

Athletics. **Team name:** Armadillos.

Student services. Adult student services, career counseling, student employment services, personal counseling, placement for graduates, veterans' counselor. **Physically disabled:** Services for visually, speech, hearing impaired. **Transfer:** Special adviser, orientation, pre-admission transcript evaluation for new students. Transfer adviser, college fairs on campus for students transferring to 4-year colleges.

Contact. E-mail: bbhall@randolph.edu
Phone: (336) 633-0224 Fax: (336) 629-9547
Carol Elmore, Director of Admissions/Registrar, Randolph Community College, PO Box 1009, Asheboro, NC 27204-1009

Richmond Community College

Hamlet, North Carolina **CB member**
www.richmondcc.edu **CB code: 5588**

- Public 2-year community college
- Commuter campus in small town

General. Founded in 1964. Regionally accredited. **Enrollment:** 1,500 degree-seeking undergraduates. **Degrees:** 260 associate awarded. **Location:** 75 miles from Charlotte. **Calendar:** Semester, limited summer session. **Full-time faculty:** 57 total. **Part-time faculty:** 140 total.

Student profile.

Out-of-state:	2%	**25 or older:**	45%

Transfer out. **Colleges most students transferred to 2005:** UNC-Pembroke, Gardner-Webb University, UNC-Charlotte.

Basis for selection. Open admission, but selective for some programs. Admission to nursing program based on academic record and completion of admission requirements, interview required. **Homeschooled:** Transcript of courses and grades required.

2005-2006 Annual costs. Tuition/fees: $1,223; $6,623 out-of-state. Per-credit charge: $40 in-state; $220 out-of-state. Books/supplies: $600. Personal expenses: $900.

Financial aid. **Need-based:** Need-based aid available for part-time students. Work study available nights and for part-time students. **Non-need-based:** Scholarships awarded for academics, leadership.

Application procedures. **Admission:** No deadline. No application fee. Application may be submitted online. Admission notification on a rolling basis. **Financial aid:** Priority date 5/1; no closing date. FAFSA, institutional form required. Applicants notified on a rolling basis starting 6/1; must reply within 2 week(s) of notification.

Academics. **Special study options:** Cooperative education, cross-registration, distance learning, double major, dual enrollment of high school students, ESL, independent study, internships, student-designed major, teacher certification program. License preparation in nursing. **Credit/placement by examination:** AP, CLEP, institutional tests. 15 credit hours maximum toward associate degree. Interview required for placement and counseling. **Support services:** GED preparation and test center, learning center, reduced course load, remedial instruction, study skills assistance, tutoring.

Majors. **Business:** Accounting, administrative services, business admin, management information systems. **Computer sciences:** Information systems, networking. **Engineering:** Electrical. **Engineering technology:** Electrical, manufacturing. **Family/consumer sciences:** Child care. **Health:** Medical assistant, mental health services, nursing (RN). **Liberal arts:** Arts/sciences. **Public administration:** Social work.

Computing on campus. 185 workstations in library, computer center.

Student life. **Freshman orientation:** Mandatory. **Activities:** Student government, student newspaper.

Student services. Career counseling, student employment services, health services, personal counseling, placement for graduates, veterans' counselor. **Physically disabled:** Services for visually, hearing impaired. **Transfer:** Special adviser, orientation for new students. Transfer adviser, college fairs on campus for students transferring to 4-year colleges.

Contact. Phone: (910) 582-7120 Fax: (910) 582-7102
Wanda Watts, Director of Admissions and Registrar, Richmond Community College, Box 1189, Hamlet, NC 28345

Roanoke-Chowan Community College

Ahoskie, North Carolina
www.roanokechowan.edu **CB code: 5564**

- Public 2-year community college
- Commuter campus in small town

General. Founded in 1967. Regionally accredited. **Enrollment:** 950 degree-seeking undergraduates. **Degrees:** 101 associate awarded. **Location:** 60 miles from Greenville, 65 miles from Norfolk, Virginia. **Calendar:** Semester, limited summer session. **Full-time faculty:** 40 total. **Part-time faculty:** 79 total. **Class size:** 70% < 20, 29% 20-39, 2% 40-49. **Special facilities:** Arboretum/environmental science outdoor laboratory.

Basis for selection. Open admission, but selective for some programs. Selective admission to nursing program based on interview and test scores.

2005-2006 Annual costs. Tuition/fees: $1,255; $6,655 out-of-state. Per-credit charge: $40 in-state; $220 out-of-state. Books/supplies: $680. Personal expenses: $1,555.

Financial aid. **Need-based:** Need-based aid available for part-time students. **Non-need-based:** Scholarships awarded for academics.

Application procedures. **Admission:** No deadline. No application fee. Admission notification on a rolling basis. **Financial aid:** No deadline. FAFSA required. Applicants notified on a rolling basis starting 7/1.

Academics. **Special study options:** Cooperative education, distance learning, dual enrollment of high school students, independent study, internships, liberal arts/career combination. License preparation in nursing, real estate. **Credit/placement by examination:** CLEP, institutional tests. **Support services:** GED preparation and test center, learning center, reduced course load, remedial instruction, study skills assistance, tutoring.

Majors. **Architecture:** Technology. **Business:** Administrative services, business admin, management information systems. **Computer sciences:** Information systems. **Conservation:** Environmental science. **Education:** Early childhood, teacher assistance. **Engineering technology:** Industrial. **Family/consumer sciences:** Child care. **Health:** Mental health services, nursing (RN), substance abuse counseling. **Interdisciplinary:** Global studies. **Liberal arts:** Arts/sciences. **Protective services:** Criminal justice.

Most popular majors. Business/marketing 56%, education 8%, health sciences 22%, liberal arts 6%, security/protective services 6%.

Computing on campus. 200 workstations in library, computer center. Online library available.

Student life. **Freshman orientation:** Available. Preregistration for classes offered. Held week before fall semester registration. **Policies:** Freshmen permitted cars on campus. **Activities:** Student government.

Athletics. **Intercollegiate:** Basketball M. **Intramural:** Basketball, softball, volleyball.

Student services. Career counseling, services for economically disadvantaged, student employment services, financial aid counseling, personal counseling, placement for graduates, veterans' counselor. **Physically disabled:** Services for visually, speech, hearing impaired. **Transfer:** Special adviser, orientation for new students. Transfer adviser for students transferring to 4-year colleges.

Contact. Phone: (252) 862-1200 Fax: (252) 862-1355
Sandra Copeland, Director of Admissions/Counseling, Roanoke-Chowan Community College, 109 Community College Road, Ahoskie, NC 27910-9522

Robeson Community College
Lumberton, North Carolina
www.robeson.cc.nc.us **CB code: 5594**

- Public 2-year community and technical college
- Commuter campus in large town

General. Founded in 1965. Regionally accredited. **Enrollment:** 2,365 undergraduates. **Degrees:** 240 associate awarded. **Location:** 30 miles from Fayetteville. **Calendar:** Semester, limited summer session. **Full-time faculty:** 60 total. **Part-time faculty:** 65 total.

Basis for selection. Open admission, but selective for some programs. Special requirements for allied health programs. Interview recommended.

2005-2006 Annual costs. Tuition/fees: $1,245; $6,645 out-of-state. Per-credit charge: $40 in-state; $220 out-of-state. Books/supplies: $600. Personal expenses: $75.

Financial aid. Need-based: Need-based aid available for part-time students.

Application procedures. Admission: Closing date 7/1. No application fee. Admission notification on a rolling basis. **Financial aid:** Priority date 5/15; no closing date. FAFSA required. Applicants notified on a rolling basis starting 7/31.

Academics. Special study options: Distance learning, double major, dual enrollment of high school students. **Credit/placement by examination:** CLEP, institutional tests. 40 credit hours maximum toward associate degree. **Support services:** Learning center, reduced course load, remedial instruction, tutoring.

Majors. Business: Business admin. **Computer sciences:** Information technology. **Engineering technology:** Electrical. **Health:** EMT paramedic, nursing (RN), radiologic technology/medical imaging, respiratory therapy technology. **Personal/culinary services:** Culinary arts. **Protective services:** Criminal justice.

Student life. Activities: Choral groups, literary magazine, student government, student newspaper.

Student services. Adult student services, career counseling, student employment services, health services, personal counseling, placement for graduates, veterans' counselor. **Physically disabled:** Services for hearing impaired. **Transfer:** Special adviser, orientation for new students. Transfer adviser, college fairs on campus for students transferring to 4-year colleges.

Contact. E-mail: jrevels@robeson.cc.nc.us
Phone: (910) 272-3700 ext. 3347 Fax: (910) 618-5686
Judith Revels, Director of Admissions, Robeson Community College, PO Box 1420, Lumberton, NC 28359

Rockingham Community College
Wentworth, North Carolina
www.rcc.cc.nc.us **CB code: 5582**

- Public 2-year community college
- Commuter campus in rural community

General. Founded in 1963. Regionally accredited. **Enrollment:** 1,762 degree-seeking undergraduates. **Degrees:** 142 associate awarded. **Location:** 26 miles from Greensboro. **Calendar:** Semester, extensive summer session. **Full-time faculty:** 62 total. **Part-time faculty:** 45 total.

Transfer out. Colleges most students transferred to 2005: University of North Carolina at Greensboro, North Carolina A&T University.

Basis for selection. Open admission, but selective for some programs. All allied health programs and some other programs require all or some of the following: qualifying high school and college GPA, placement testing, specific high school courses, professional certification, other exams. Interview required for nursing and occupational therapy assistant programs. **Homeschooled:** Need complete record of all courses taken in grades 9-12.

High school preparation. Recommended units include English 4, mathematics 3, social studies 2, history 1, science 3 (laboratory 1) and foreign language 2.

2005-2006 Annual costs. Tuition/fees: $1,259; $6,659 out-of-state. Per-credit charge: $40 in-state; $220 out-of-state. Books/supplies: $450. Personal expenses: $1,000.

2004-2005 Financial aid. Need-based: 57% of total undergraduate aid awarded as scholarships/grants, 43% as loans/jobs. Need-based aid available for part-time students. **Non-need-based:** Scholarships awarded for academics, art, job skills, leadership, minority status, state residency.

Application procedures. Admission: No deadline. No application fee. Admission notification on a rolling basis. **Financial aid:** Priority date 3/15; no closing date. FAFSA, institutional form required. Applicants notified on a rolling basis starting 5/30; must reply within 2 week(s) of notification.

Academics. Special study options: Cooperative education, distance learning, dual enrollment of high school students, independent study, student-designed major. Preengineering program leading to transfer to North Carolina State University, North Carolina Agricultural and Technical State University, or University of North Carolina at Charlotte. License preparation in nursing. **Credit/placement by examination:** AP, CLEP, institutional tests. **Support services:** GED preparation and test center, learning center, reduced course load, remedial instruction, study skills assistance, tutoring.

Majors. Agriculture: Horticultural science. **Business:** Accounting, business admin, office technology, office/clerical. **Computer sciences:** Information systems. **Education:** Early childhood. **Engineering:** Electrical. **Health:** EMT paramedic, medical secretary, nursing (RN), occupational therapy assistant, respiratory therapy technology. **Legal studies:** Legal secretary, paralegal. **Liberal arts:** Arts/sciences. **Mechanic/repair:** General, electronics/electrical. **Production:** Woodworking. **Protective services:** Fire safety technology, law enforcement admin. **Visual/performing arts:** Studio arts.

Most popular majors. Business/marketing 18%, computer/information sciences 10%, health sciences 25%, liberal arts 32%, personal/culinary services 7%.

Computing on campus. 200 workstations in library, computer center.

Student life. Freshman orientation: Mandatory. **Activities:** Student government, student newspaper, Phi Theta Kappa, nature study club, astronomy club, science fiction club, trips and outings clubs, cultural diversity awareness club.

Athletics. NJCAA. **Intercollegiate:** Baseball M, basketball, volleyball W. **Intramural:** Basketball, golf, table tennis, tennis, volleyball. **Team name:** Eagles.

Student services. Career counseling, student employment services, on-campus daycare, personal counseling, placement for graduates. **Physically disabled:** Services for visually, hearing impaired. **Transfer:** Special adviser, orientation for new students. Transfer adviser, college fairs on campus for students transferring to 4-year colleges.

Contact. E-mail: dunnm@rockinghamcc.edu
Phone: (336) 342-4261 ext. 2114 Fax: (336) 342-1809
Leigh Hawkins, Admissions Director, Rockingham Community College, Box 38, Wentworth, NC 27375-0038

Rowan-Cabarrus Community College
Salisbury, North Carolina
www.rccc.cc.nc.us **CB code: 5589**

- Public 2-year community and technical college
- Commuter campus in large town

General. Founded in 1961. Regionally accredited. **Enrollment:** 5,431 degree-seeking undergraduates. **Degrees:** 409 associate awarded. **Location:** 40 miles from Charlotte. **Calendar:** Semester, extensive summer session. **Full-time faculty:** 140 total. **Part-time faculty:** 200 total. **Class size:** 58% < 20, 39% 20-39, 2% 40-49, less than 1% 50-99.

Transfer out. Colleges most students transferred to 2005: University of North Carolina-Charlotte, Pfeiffer University, Catawba College.

Basis for selection. Open admission, but selective for some programs. Selective admission, interview required for allied health programs. Placement test required for all allied health applicants and candidates for diplomas, AAS degrees, or AA degrees.

2005-2006 Annual costs. Tuition/fees: $1,249; $6,649 out-of-state. Per-credit charge: $40 in-state; $220 out-of-state.

Financial aid. Need-based: Need-based aid available for part-time students. Work study available nights and for part-time students. **Non-need-based:** Scholarships awarded for academics, job skills, state residency.

Application procedures. Admission: No deadline. No application fee. Admission notification on a rolling basis. **Financial aid:** Priority date 3/15, closing date 5/1. FAFSA required. Applicants notified on a rolling basis starting 5/1; must reply within 3 week(s) of notification.

Academics. Special study options: Cooperative education, distance learning, dual enrollment of high school students, ESL, liberal arts/career combination, teacher certification program. License preparation in nursing, radiology, real estate. **Credit/placement by examination:** CLEP, institutional tests. 75 credit hours maximum toward associate degree. Student must complete 25% of credits required for graduation in resident classes. **Support services:** GED preparation and test center, learning center, reduced course load, remedial instruction, tutoring, writing center.

Majors. Business: Accounting, business admin, office technology. **Computer sciences:** Information systems, programming. **Education:** Early childhood. **Engineering technology:** Biomedical, drafting, electrical, industrial. **Health:** Nursing (RN), radiologic technology/medical imaging. **Legal studies:** Paralegal. **Mechanic/repair:** Industrial. **Protective services:** Criminal justice, fire safety technology.

Student life. Freshman orientation: Available. Fall and spring orientation. **Activities:** Student government.

Student services. Career counseling, student employment services, on-campus daycare, personal counseling, placement for graduates, veterans' counselor. **Physically disabled:** Services for visually, speech, hearing impaired. **Learning disabled:** Comprehensive services available. **Transfer:** Special adviser, orientation, pre-admission transcript evaluation for new students. College fairs on campus for students transferring to 4-year colleges.

Contact. Phone: (704) 637-0760 Fax: (704) 633-6804
Kenneth Hayes, Director, Admissions and Recruitment, Rowan-Cabarrus Community College, Box 1595, Salisbury, NC 28145

Sampson Community College

Clinton, North Carolina
www.sampson.cc.nc.us **CB code: 0505**

- Public 2-year community college
- Commuter campus in small town

General. Founded in 1965. Regionally accredited. **Enrollment:** 1,467 undergraduates. **Degrees:** 113 associate awarded. **Location:** 30 miles from Fayetteville. **Calendar:** Semester, limited summer session. **Full-time faculty:** 55 total. **Part-time faculty:** 57 total.

Student profile.

Out-of-state:	1%	**25 or older:**	47%

Transfer out. Colleges most students transferred to 2005: Fayetteville State University, UNC-Wilmington, Campbell University, Mt. Olive College.

Basis for selection. Open admission, but selective for some programs. Special requirements for nursing and practical nursing; secondary school record and test scores important. Interview required for nursing programs.

High school preparation. 15 units recommended. Recommended units include English 4, mathematics 3, social studies 3, science 4 and foreign language 2. Algebra, chemistry and biology required for nursing programs.

2005-2006 Annual costs. Tuition/fees: $1,241; $6,641 out-of-state. Per-credit charge: $40 in-state; $220 out-of-state. Books/supplies: $600. Personal expenses: $900.

Financial aid. Need-based: Need-based aid available for part-time students. **Non-need-based:** Scholarships awarded for academics, state residency. **Additional information:** Short-term loans available to students waiting for federal aid to be approved. Covers tuition, fees and books only.

Application procedures. Admission: No deadline. No application fee. Admission notification on a rolling basis. **Financial aid:** Priority date 7/1; no closing date. FAFSA required. Applicants notified on a rolling basis starting 7/15; must reply within 2 week(s) of notification.

Academics. Special study options: Cooperative education, distance learning, dual enrollment of high school students, independent study, internships, liberal arts/career combination, weekend college. License preparation in nursing, real estate. **Credit/placement by examination:** CLEP, institutional tests. 15 credit hours maximum toward associate degree. **Support services:** GED preparation and test center, learning center, pre-admission summer program, reduced course load, remedial instruction, study skills assistance, tutoring.

Majors. Agriculture: Horticulture, ornamental horticulture. **Business:** Accounting, administrative services, business admin, office/clerical. **Computer sciences:** General, applications programming, information systems. **Education:** General, early childhood. **Health:** Licensed practical nurse, nursing (RN). **Mechanic/repair:** Industrial. **Personal/culinary services:** Cosmetic.

Most popular majors. Business/marketing 27%, computer/information sciences 14%, education 21%, health sciences 35%.

Computing on campus. 110 workstations in library, computer center.

Student life. Freshman orientation: Mandatory. Preregistration for classes offered. **Activities:** Student government, student newspaper.

Athletics. Intramural: Basketball M.

Student services. Adult student services, career counseling, student employment services, financial aid counseling, personal counseling, placement for graduates, veterans' counselor. **Physically disabled:** Services for visually, speech, hearing impaired. **Transfer:** Special adviser, orientation, pre-admission transcript evaluation for new students. Transfer adviser, college fairs on campus for students transferring to 4-year colleges.

Contact. Phone: (910) 592-8084 Fax: (910) 592-8048
William Jordan, Director of Admissions, Sampson Community College, PO Box 318, Clinton, NC 28329

Sandhills Community College

Pinehurst, North Carolina
www.sandhills.edu **CB code: 5649**

- Public 2-year community college
- Commuter campus in small town

General. Founded in 1963. Regionally accredited. **Enrollment:** 1,300 degree-seeking undergraduates. **Degrees:** 403 associate awarded. **Location:** 41 miles from Fayetteville, 71 miles from Raleigh. **Calendar:** Semester, limited summer session. **Full-time faculty:** 110 total; 9% have terminal degrees, 8% minority, 54% women. **Part-time faculty:** 118 total; 50% women. **Class size:** 51% < 20, 46% 20-39, 1% 40-49, 2% 50-99. **Special facilities:** Student maintained 30-acre garden.

Student profile.

Out-of-state:	1%	**25 or older:**	41%

Transfer out. Colleges most students transferred to 2005: University of North Carolina-Chapel Hill, University of North Carolina-Charlotte, University of North Carolina-Pembroke, North Carolina State University, Appalachian State University.

Basis for selection. Open admission, but selective for some programs. Specific scores on Accuplacer required for admission to landscape gardening, golf course turf management and health sciences programs. Students not achieving minimum scores may enroll in general college, take developmental courses and reapply for programs later. Chemistry, algebra, and NA registry required for entrance into associate nursing program. Students with minimum SAT score of 500 verbal and 500 math or ACT scores of 21 English, 21 math, and 21 reading may be placed in college-level English and math without taking ASSET or COMPASS. All students applying to restricted enrollment programs must have taken ASSET or COMPASS within past 5 years. Nursing program accepts SAT and ACT scores for exemption, however the HOBET must be taken. **Adult students:** Entrance exam policies same as for first-time freshmen. **Homeschooled:** Copy of state registration required. **Learning Disabled:** Students with learning disabilities recommended to take classes in Continuing Education Program first.

2005-2006 Annual costs. Tuition/fees: $1,255; $6,655 out-of-state. Per-credit charge: $40 in-state; $220 out-of-state. Books/supplies: $547. Personal expenses: $1,080.

Financial aid. Need-based: Need-based aid available for part-time students. **Non-need-based:** Scholarships awarded for academics. **Additional information:** Scholarships available, limited loan capability.

Application procedures. Admission: No deadline. No application fee. Application may be submitted online. Admission notification on a rolling basis. **Financial aid:** Priority date 6/1; no closing date. FAFSA required. Applicants notified on a rolling basis starting 2/1; must reply by 8/1 or within 4 week(s) of notification.

Academics. Weekend support services held at satellite campus. **Special study options:** Cooperative education, distance learning, double major, dual enrollment of high school students, ESL, honors, independent study, internships, liberal arts/career combination, teacher certification program. Third and fourth year courses offered on campus evenings by St. Andrews Presbyterian College and UNC Pembroke, distance learning classes through Franklin University. Bachelor's degree programs available on campus. License preparation in nursing, paramedic, radiology, real estate. **Credit/placement by examination:** AP, CLEP, institutional tests. **Support services:** GED preparation and test center, learning center, reduced course load, remedial instruction, study skills assistance, tutoring.

Majors. Agriculture: Landscaping, turf management. **Architecture:** Technology. **Biology:** General. **Business:** Accounting, administrative services, business admin, e-commerce, hotel/motel admin, restaurant/food services. **Computer sciences:** General, applications programming, computer science, information systems, programming, webmaster. **Education:** Biology, chemistry, early childhood, elementary, history, science, secondary, social science, social studies, teacher assistance. **Engineering technology:** Architectural, civil, computer, drafting, surveying. **Family/consumer sciences:** Child care. **Health:** Clinical lab technology, EMT ambulance attendant, EMT paramedic, massage therapy, medical radiologic technology/radiation therapy, medical records admin, nursing (RN), predentistry, premedicine, prenursing, prepharmacy, preveterinary, respiratory therapy technology, substance abuse counseling, surgical technology. **Legal studies:** Prelaw. **Liberal arts:** Arts/sciences. **Math:** General. **Mechanic/repair:** Automotive. **Personal/culinary services:** Cosmetic, culinary arts. **Protective services:** Criminal justice. **Psychology:** General. **Public administration:** Social work. **Social sciences:** General. **Visual/performing arts:** Art.

Most popular majors. Business/marketing 8%, computer/information sciences 6%, health sciences 42%, liberal arts 11%, trade and industry 11%.

Computing on campus. 400 workstations in library, computer center. Commuter students can connect to campus network.

Student life. Freshman orientation: Mandatory. Preregistration for classes offered. 2-hour information session, course planning, and registration. **Activities:** Bands, choral groups, music ensembles, student government, student newspaper, symphony orchestra, Minority Students for Academic and Cultural Enrichment, Circle-K, Young Democrats, Young Republicans, Phi Theta Kappa, Student Government Association.

Student services. Alcohol/substance abuse counseling, career counseling, student employment services, financial aid counseling, personal counseling, placement for graduates, veterans' counselor. **Physically disabled:** Services for visually, hearing impaired. **Transfer:** Special adviser, orientation, pre-admission transcript evaluation for new students. Transfer adviser, college fairs on campus for students transferring to 4-year colleges.

Contact. E-mail: mcallisterr@sandhills.edu
Phone: (910) 692-6185 Toll-free number: (800) 338-3944
Fax: (910) 695-3981
Rosa McAllister-McRae, Admissions Coordinator, Sandhills Community College, 3395 Airport Road, Pinehurst, NC 28374

South College
Asheville, North Carolina

CB code: 0508

- For-profit 2-year health science and technical college
- Commuter campus in small city
- Interview required

General. Founded in 1905. Candidate for regional accreditation; also accredited by ACICS. **Enrollment:** 120 degree-seeking undergraduates. **Degrees:** 29 associate awarded. **Location:** 4 miles from downtown. **Calendar:** Quarter, extensive summer session. **Full-time faculty:** 10 total; 10% have terminal degrees, 70% women. **Part-time faculty:** 45 total; 9% have terminal degrees, 71% women. **Class size:** 91% < 20, 9% 20-39.

Transfer out. Colleges most students transferred to 2005: Asheville-Buncombe Technical Community College, Blue Ridge Community College, Mars Hill College, Montreat College.

Basis for selection. Open admission, but selective for some programs. College-administered exam required of all applicants. Scores used for admission and program placement. **Adult students:** Entrance exam policies same as for first-time freshmen. **Homeschooled:** Copy of home-school diploma required.

2005-2006 Annual costs. Books/supplies: $1,050. Personal expenses: $1,080.

Financial aid. Need-based: Need-based aid available for part-time students. Work study available for part-time students.

Application procedures. Admission: No deadline. $40 fee, may be waived for applicants with need. Admission notification on a rolling basis. **Financial aid:** No deadline. FAFSA required. Applicants notified on a rolling basis.

Academics. Special study options: Accelerated study, cooperative education, double major, internships, liberal arts/career combination. Bachelor's degree programs available on campus. License preparation in physical therapy, radiology. **Credit/placement by examination:** CLEP, institutional tests. Varies with program, but no more than 60% of any program. **Support services:** Reduced course load, study skills assistance, tutoring.

Majors. Business: Accounting, administrative services, business admin. **Computer sciences:** General. **Health:** Medical assistant. **Legal studies:** Paralegal. **Protective services:** Law enforcement admin.

Computing on campus. 28 workstations in library, computer center.

Student life. Freshman orientation: Mandatory. Orientation is held prior to each quarter.

Student services. Career counseling, student employment services, financial aid counseling, personal counseling, placement for graduates, veterans' counselor. **Transfer:** Special adviser, orientation, pre-admission transcript evaluation for new students.

Contact. Phone: (828) 277-5521 Fax: (828) 252-8558
Robert Haden, Director of Admissions, South College, 29 Turtle Creek Drive, Asheville, NC 28803

South Piedmont Community College
Polkton, North Carolina

www.spcc.edu **CB code: 0457**

- Public 2-year community college
- Commuter campus in small city

General. Founded in 1962. Regionally accredited. Multiple campus locations near Charlotte. **Enrollment:** 1,928 degree-seeking undergraduates. **Degrees:** 97 associate awarded. **Location:** 55 miles from Charlotte. **Calendar:** Semester, limited summer session. **Full-time faculty:** 65 total. **Part-time faculty:** 210 total. **Partnerships:** Formal partnership with local high schools.

Student profile. Among degree-seeking undergraduates, 1,928 enrolled as first-time, first-year students.

Out-of-state:	1%	**25 or older:**	66%

Basis for selection. Open admission, but selective for some programs. Special requirements for practical nursing program and medical assisting program. Interview required for practical nursing students. **Homeschooled:** Students should have state certification number, successful completion of competency exam, registered with local board of education, copy of transcript and diploma.

2005-2006 Annual costs. Tuition/fees: $1,263; $6,663 out-of-state. Per-credit charge: $40 in-state; $220 out-of-state. Books/supplies: $650. Personal expenses: $900.

Financial aid. Need-based: Need-based aid available for part-time students. Work study available nights and weekends. **Additional information:** Small amount of nonfederal scholarship aid available.

Application procedures. Admission: No deadline. No application fee. Application may be submitted online. Admission notification on a rolling basis. **Financial aid:** No deadline. FAFSA required. Applicants notified on a rolling basis.

Academics. Special study options: Cooperative education, cross-registration, distance learning, dual enrollment of high school students, independent study, internships. **Credit/placement by examination:** CLEP, institutional tests. **Support services:** GED preparation and test center, learning center, reduced course load, remedial instruction, tutoring.

Majors. Business: Accounting, administrative services, business admin, logistics, office/clerical. **Computer sciences:** General, applications programming, information systems, networking, programming. **Education:** General. **Engineering technology:** Drafting, electrical, manufacturing. **Family/consumer sciences:** Child care. **Health:** Health services, medical assistant, medical records technology, medical secretary. **Legal studies:** Legal secretary, paralegal. **Liberal arts:** Arts/sciences. **Mechanic/repair:** Heating/ac/refrig. **Protective services:** Criminal justice. **Public administration:** Human services. **Visual/performing arts:** Commercial/advertising art.

Computing on campus. 200 workstations in library, computer center.

Student life. Freshman orientation: Available. Preregistration for classes offered. **Activities:** Student government, student newspaper, Phi Beta Lambda business organization, criminal justice student association, social services club, Phi Theta Kappa.

Athletics. Intramural: Softball. **Team name:** Patriots.

Student services. Alcohol/substance abuse counseling, career counseling, student employment services, financial aid counseling, personal counseling, placement for graduates, veterans' counselor. **Physically disabled:** Services for visually, hearing impaired. **Transfer:** Special adviser, orientation for new students. Transfer adviser for students transferring to 4-year colleges.

Contact. E-mail: jcurtis@spcc.edu
Phone: (704) 272-5324 Toll-free number: (800) 766-0319
Fax: (704) 272-5350
John Curtis, Director of Admissions and Enrollment Services, South Piedmont Community College, PO Box 126, Polkton, NC 28135

Southeastern Community College

Whiteville, North Carolina
www.sccnc.edu **CB code: 5651**

- Public 2-year community college
- Commuter campus in small town

General. Founded in 1964. Regionally accredited. **Enrollment:** 1,593 degree-seeking undergraduates; 279 non-degree-seeking students. **Degrees:** 102 associate awarded. **Location:** 45 miles from Wilmington, 105 miles from Raleigh. **Calendar:** Semester, limited summer session. **Full-time faculty:** 82 total; 2% have terminal degrees, 11% minority, 63% women. **Part-time faculty:** 104 total; 4% have terminal degrees, 14% minority, 59% women. **Class size:** 68% < 20, 30% 20-39, less than 1% 40-49, 2% 50-99.

Student profile. Among degree-seeking undergraduates, 56% enrolled in a transfer program, 39% enrolled in a vocational program, 2% already have a bachelor's degree or higher, 352 enrolled as first-time, first-year students, 74 transferred in from other institutions.

Part-time:	42%	**Women:**	66%
Out-of-state:	1%	**25 or older:**	42%

Transfer out. Colleges most students transferred to 2005: University of North Carolina at Wilmington, University of North Carolina at Pembroke, Fayetteville State University, East Carolina University.

Basis for selection. Open admission, but selective for some programs. Special requirements for allied health programs and Basic Law Enforcement Training. SAT may be substituted for placement test. **Adult students:** Entrance exam policies same as for first-time freshmen. **Learning Disabled:** Applicant must provide proof of disability and list of desired accommodations.

High school preparation. Recommended units include English 4, mathematics 3, social studies 2 and science 3.

2005-2006 Annual costs. Tuition/fees: $1,246; $6,646 out-of-state. Per-credit charge: $40 in-state; $220 out-of-state. Books/supplies: $482. Personal expenses: $1,050.

2005-2006 Financial aid. Need-based: 93% of total undergraduate aid awarded as scholarships/grants, 7% as loans/jobs. Need-based aid available for part-time students. Work study available for part-time students. **Non-need-based:** Scholarships awarded for academics, athletics, leadership, music/drama, state residency.

Application procedures. Admission: No deadline. No application fee. Application may be submitted online. Admission notification on a rolling basis. **Financial aid:** Priority date 4/1; no closing date. FAFSA required. Applicants notified on a rolling basis starting 6/1; must reply within 2 week(s) of notification.

Academics. Special study options: Cooperative education, distance learning, double major, dual enrollment of high school students, honors, independent study, internships, liberal arts/career combination. License preparation in nursing, real estate. **Credit/placement by examination:** AP, CLEP, institutional tests. **Support services:** GED preparation and test center, learning center, reduced course load, remedial instruction, study skills assistance, tutoring, writing center.

Majors. Business: Banking/financial services, business admin, office/clerical. **Computer sciences:** Information technology. **Conservation:** Environmental science, forest management. **Education:** Early childhood, elementary, secondary. **Engineering technology:** Electrical. **Family/consumer sciences:** Child care. **Health:** Clinical lab technology, nursing (RN). **Interdisciplinary:** Biological/physical sciences. **Liberal arts:** Arts/sciences. **Mechanic/repair:** Industrial. **Parks/recreation:** Facilities management. **Visual/performing arts:** Art.

Computing on campus. 115 workstations in library, computer center.

Student life. Freshman orientation: Available. Preregistration for classes offered. **Policies:** Freshmen permitted cars on campus. **Activities:** Concert band, choral groups, drama, literary magazine, student government, student newspaper, Student Ambassadors.

Athletics. NJCAA. **Intercollegiate:** Baseball M, volleyball W. **Intramural:** Basketball. **Team name:** Rams.

Student services. Adult student services, career counseling, services for economically disadvantaged, student employment services, financial aid counseling, on-campus daycare, personal counseling, placement for graduates, veterans' counselor. **Physically disabled:** Services for visually, speech, hearing impaired. **Transfer:** Special adviser, orientation, pre-admission transcript evaluation for new students. Transfer adviser, college fairs on campus for students transferring to 4-year colleges.

Contact. E-mail: start@sccnc.edu
Phone: (910) 642-7141 ext. 249 Fax: (910) 642-1267
Sylvia Tart, Director of Student Records/Registrar, Southeastern Community College, 4564 Chadbourn Highway, Whiteville, NC 28472-0151

Southwestern Community College

Sylva, North Carolina
www.southwest.cc.nc.us **CB code: 5667**

- Public 2-year community college
- Commuter campus in rural community

General. Founded in 1964. Regionally accredited. Five off-campus sites serve two adjoining counties. **Enrollment:** 1,540 degree-seeking undergraduates. **Degrees:** 239 associate awarded. **Location:** 48 miles from Asheville. **Calendar:** Semester, limited summer session. **Full-time faculty:** 69 total; 9% have terminal degrees, 3% minority, 46% women. **Part-time faculty:** 175 total; 3% have terminal degrees, 1% minority, 47% women. **Class size:** 80% < 20, 20% 20-39.

Student profile.

Out-of-state:	1%	**25 or older:**	46%

Transfer out. Colleges most students transferred to 2005: Western Carolina University.

Basis for selection. Open admission, but selective for some programs. Admission to allied health programs based on test scores, academic record, interview, and recommendations. Interview required for allied health applicants; recommended for all others.

High school preparation. Algebra, biology, and chemistry required for allied health program applicants.

2005-2006 Annual costs. Tuition/fees: $1,247; $6,647 out-of-state. Per-credit charge: $40 in-state; $220 out-of-state. Books/supplies: $750. Personal expenses: $1,238.

2004-2005 Financial aid. Need-based: 91% of total undergraduate aid awarded as scholarships/grants, 9% as loans/jobs. Need-based aid available for part-time students. Work study available for part-time students.

Application procedures. Admission: No deadline. No application fee. Admission notification on a rolling basis. **Financial aid:** Priority date 4/30; no closing date. FAFSA required. Applicants notified on a rolling basis starting 5/1; must reply within 2 week(s) of notification.

Academics. Special study options: Cooperative education, double major, dual enrollment of high school students, ESL, independent study, internships, liberal arts/career combination. License preparation in nursing, paramedic, physical therapy, radiology, real estate. **Credit/placement by examination:** CLEP, institutional tests. **Support services:** GED preparation and test center, learning center, reduced course load, remedial instruction, tutoring.

Majors. Business: Accounting, administrative services, business admin, marketing. **Computer sciences:** General, networking, programming. **Education:** General, early childhood, trade/industrial. **Engineering:** Computer, electrical, surveying. **Engineering technology:** Electrical. **Family/consumer sciences:** Child care. **Health:** Clinical lab science, clinical lab technology, EMT paramedic, medical radiologic technology/radiation therapy, medical records technology, mental health services, nursing (RN), physical therapy assistant, respiratory therapy assistant, respiratory therapy technology, sonography, substance abuse counseling. **Legal studies:** Paralegal. **Liberal arts:** Arts/sciences. **Mechanic/repair:** Automotive. **Parks/recreation:** General. **Personal/culinary services:** Cosmetic, culinary arts. **Protective services:** Criminal justice. **Visual/performing arts:** Commercial/advertising art.

Most popular majors. Business/marketing 7%, health sciences 35%, liberal arts 22%, security/protective services 10%.

Computing on campus. 200 workstations in computer center. Commuter students can connect to campus network.

Student life. Freshman orientation: Mandatory. Preregistration for classes offered. One-day live orientation held on Jackson Campus at beginning of Fall Semester for all students enrolling for first time. New students enrolling in Spring or Summer semesters take on-line orientation program. **Activities:** Literary magazine, student government, Phi Theta Kappa, Native American Society, Spanish Club.

Student services. Career counseling, services for economically disadvantaged, student employment services, financial aid counseling, on-campus daycare, personal counseling, placement for graduates, veterans' counselor. **Physically disabled:** Services for visually, speech, hearing impaired. **Transfer:** Special adviser, orientation, pre-admission transcript evaluation for new students. Transfer adviser for students transferring to 4-year colleges.

Contact. Phone: (828) 586-4091 ext. 352 Toll-free number: (800) 447-4091 Fax: (828) 586-3129
Phil Weast, Dean of Student Services, Southwestern Community College, 447 College Drive, Sylva, NC 28779

Stanly Community College

Albemarle, North Carolina
www.stanly.edu **CB code: 0496**

- Public 2-year community college
- Commuter campus in large town

General. Founded in 1971. Regionally accredited. **Enrollment:** 1,500 degree-seeking undergraduates. **Degrees:** 249 associate awarded. **Location:** 30 miles from Charlotte. **Calendar:** Semester, limited summer session. **Full-time faculty:** 65 total. **Part-time faculty:** 50 total.

Student profile.

Out-of-state:	6%	25 or older:	41%

Transfer out. Colleges most students transferred to 2005: University of North Carolina at Charlotte, Pfeiffer University.

Basis for selection. Open admission, but selective for some programs. Special requirements for nursing and radiography majors. **Learning Disabled:** Written verification of disability required at least 60 days prior to enrollment.

2005-2006 Annual costs. Tuition/fees: $1,255; $6,655 out-of-state. Per-credit charge: $40 in-state; $220 out-of-state. Books/supplies: $900. Personal expenses: $1,050.

Financial aid. All financial aid based on need. Need-based aid available for part-time students. Work study available for part-time students.

Application procedures. Admission: No deadline. No application fee. Application may be submitted online. Admission notification on a rolling basis. **Financial aid:** Priority date 4/15; no closing date. FAFSA, institutional form required. Applicants notified on a rolling basis starting 6/5; must reply within 2 week(s) of notification.

Academics. Special study options: Distance learning, dual enrollment of high school students, ESL, weekend college. **Credit/placement by examination:** AP, CLEP, institutional tests. **Support services:** GED preparation and test center, remedial instruction, study skills assistance, tutoring.

Majors. Business: Accounting, business admin, human resources. **Computer sciences:** Information systems, information technology, LAN/WAN management, programming. **Education:** Early childhood, elementary, special. **Engineering technology:** Biomedical, computer, electrical. **Health:** EMT paramedic, medical assistant, nursing (RN), radiologic technology/medical imaging, respiratory therapy technology. **Liberal arts:** Arts/sciences. **Personal/culinary services:** Cosmetic. **Protective services:** Criminal justice.

Most popular majors. Business/marketing 9%, computer/information sciences 13%, education 10%, health sciences 34%, liberal arts 11%, security/protective services 7%.

Computing on campus. 100 workstations in library, computer center, student center.

Student life. Freshman orientation: Available. Preregistration for classes offered. **Activities:** Student government.

Student services. Career counseling, student employment services, financial aid counseling, personal counseling, placement for graduates, veterans' counselor. **Transfer:** Pre-admission transcript evaluation for new students. Transfer adviser, college fairs on campus for students transferring to 4-year colleges.

Contact. E-mail: pardsdf@stanly.edu
Phone: (704) 991-0226 Fax: (704) 991-0255
Ronnie Hinson, Associate Dean of Admissions, Stanly Community College, 141 College Drive, Albemarle, NC 28001

Surry Community College

Dobson, North Carolina
www.surry.edu **CB code: 5656**

- Public 2-year community college
- Commuter campus in rural community

General. Founded in 1964. Regionally accredited. **Enrollment:** 3,273 undergraduates. **Degrees:** 376 associate awarded. **Location:** 40 miles from Winston-Salem. **Calendar:** Semester, extensive summer session. **Full-time faculty:** 94 total. **Part-time faculty:** 217 total. **Special facilities:** Working vineyard and wine-making facilities.

Student profile. 25% enrolled in a transfer program, 74% enrolled in a vocational program, 3% already have a bachelor's degree or higher.

Out-of-state:	3%	25 or older:	44%

Transfer out. 85% of students enrolled in the transfer program go on to 4-year colleges. **Colleges most students transferred to 2005:** Appalachian State University, Gardner-Webb University, Lees-McRae University, University of North Carolina-Greensboro, Winston-Salem State University.

Basis for selection. Open admission, but selective for some programs. Competitive admission to associate degree nursing program (RN) and practical nursing program (LPN) based primarily on academic standing; test scores considered. Portfolio required for admission to advertising and graphic design programs. **Adult students:** Entrance exam policies same as for first-time freshmen.

2005-2006 Annual costs. Tuition/fees: $1,243; $6,643 out-of-state. Per-credit charge: $40 in-state; $220 out-of-state. Books/supplies: $800. Personal expenses: $900.

2004-2005 Financial aid. Need-based: 96% of total undergraduate aid awarded as scholarships/grants, 4% as loans/jobs. Need-based aid available for part-time students. Work study available nights and for part-time students. **Non-need-based:** Scholarships awarded for academics.

Application procedures. Admission: No deadline. No application fee. Application may be submitted online. Admission notification on a rolling basis. **Financial aid:** Priority date 5/1; no closing date. FAFSA, institutional form required. Applicants notified on a rolling basis starting 6/1; must reply within 2 week(s) of notification.

Academics. Special study options: Accelerated study, cooperative education, distance learning, double major, dual enrollment of high school students, ESL, independent study, internships, weekend college. Bachelor's degree programs available on campus. License preparation in nursing, paramedic, real estate. **Credit/placement by examination:** AP, CLEP, institutional tests. **Support services:** GED preparation and test center, learning center, reduced course load, remedial instruction, study skills assistance, tutoring.

Majors. Agriculture: Business, horticulture, poultry. **Business:** Accounting, business admin, e-commerce, office/clerical. **Computer sciences:** Applications programming, information systems, LAN/WAN management. **Construction:** General. **Education:** Early childhood. **Engineering:** Computer, electrical. **Engineering technology:** Drafting. **Health:** Medical assistant, nursing (RN), office admin. **Legal studies:** Paralegal. **Liberal arts:** Arts/sciences. **Mechanic/repair:** Automotive, heating/ac/refrig, industrial, industrial electronics. **Personal/culinary services:** Cosmetic. **Production:** Machine tool. **Protective services:** Law enforcement admin. **Visual/performing arts:** Commercial/advertising art.

Computing on campus. 500 workstations in library, computer center. Online library, helpline, wireless network available.

Student life. Freshman orientation: Available. Preregistration for classes offered. **Policies:** Freshmen permitted cars on campus. **Activities:** Choral groups, literary magazine, radio station, student government.

Athletics. NJCAA. **Intercollegiate:** Baseball M, basketball M, volleyball W. **Team name:** Knights.

Student services. Adult student services, career counseling, services for economically disadvantaged, student employment services, financial aid counseling, personal counseling, placement for graduates, veterans' counselor. **Physically disabled:** Services for visually, hearing impaired. **Transfer:** Special adviser, orientation for new students. Transfer adviser, college fairs on campus for students transferring to 4-year colleges.

Contact. E-mail: childressj@surry.edu
Phone: (336) 386-3238 Fax: (336) 386-8951
Jamie Childress, Vice President for Student Services, Surry Community College, 630 South Main Street, Dobson, NC 27017

Tri-County Community College

Murphy, North Carolina
www.tricountycc.edu **CB code: 5785**

- Public 2-year community college
- Commuter campus in rural community
- Interview required

General. Founded in 1964. Regionally accredited. **Enrollment:** 741 degree-seeking undergraduates. **Degrees:** 143 associate awarded. **Location:** 110 miles from Asheville, 96 miles from Chattanooga, Tennessee. **Calendar:** Semester, extensive summer session. **Full-time faculty:** 36 total. **Part-time faculty:** 40 total. **Class size:** 22% < 20, 57% 20-39, 20% 40-49, 1% 50-99.

Student profile.

Out-of-state:	9%	**25 or older:**	54%

Transfer out. Colleges most students transferred to 2005: Western Carolina University, South Western Community College.

Basis for selection. Open admission. Interview required for placement and counseling. **Learning Disabled:** Tutoring is available.

2005-2006 Annual costs. Tuition/fees: $1,241; $6,641 out-of-state. Per-credit charge: $40 in-state; $220 out-of-state. Books/supplies: $300. Personal expenses: $450.

2004-2005 Financial aid. All financial aid based on need. 98% of total undergraduate aid awarded as scholarships/grants, 2% as loans/jobs. Need-based aid available for part-time students.

Application procedures. Admission: No deadline. No application fee. Admission notification on a rolling basis. **Financial aid:** Priority date 6/30; no closing date. FAFSA required. Applicants notified on a rolling basis starting 6/1; must reply within 4 week(s) of notification.

Academics. Special study options: Double major, dual enrollment of high school students, independent study, internships. License preparation in real estate. **Credit/placement by examination:** CLEP, institutional tests. 6 credit hours maximum toward associate degree. **Support services:** GED preparation and test center, learning center, reduced course load, remedial instruction, study skills assistance, tutoring.

Majors. Business: Accounting, administrative services, business admin. **Computer sciences:** Information systems. **Construction:** Electrician. **Engineering technology:** Surveying. **Health:** EMT paramedic, medical assistant, nursing (RN). **Liberal arts:** Arts/sciences. **Mechanic/repair:** Automotive, electronics/electrical.

Most popular majors. Business/marketing 24%, liberal arts 43%, trade and industry 35%.

Computing on campus. 42 workstations in library, computer center. Online library available.

Student life. Freshman orientation: Mandatory. Preregistration for classes offered. **Policies:** Freshmen permitted cars on campus. **Activities:** Student government, student newspaper, honor society.

Student services. Career counseling, services for economically disadvantaged, student employment services, financial aid counseling, on-campus daycare, personal counseling, placement for graduates, veterans' counselor. **Physically disabled:** Services for visually, hearing impaired. **Transfer:** Special adviser, orientation, pre-admission transcript evaluation for new students. College fairs on campus for students transferring to 4-year colleges.

Contact. E-mail: jchambers@tricountycc.edu
Phone: (828) 837-6810 Toll-free number: (828) 835-4225
Fax: (828) 837-3266
Jason Chambers, Director of Admissions, Tri-County Community College, 4600 Highway 64 East, Murphy, NC 28906

Vance-Granville Community College

Henderson, North Carolina **CB member**
www.vgcc.edu **CB code: 0617**

- Public 2-year community college
- Commuter campus in large town

General. Founded in 1969. Regionally accredited. 4 rural counties served with satellite campuses in Warrenton, Butner and Louisburg. **Enrollment:** 3,500 degree-seeking undergraduates. **Degrees:** 345 associate awarded. **Location:** 42 miles from Raleigh. **Calendar:** Semester, limited summer session. **Full-time faculty:** 141 total. **Part-time faculty:** 135 total.

Basis for selection. Open admission, but selective for some programs. Admission to nursing, radiologic technology, and medical assisting is based on academic record, health education aptitude test, and other criteria. Test scores neither required nor recommended. Used for placement if available. Interview recommended for nursing, radiologic technology programs.

2005-2006 Annual costs. Tuition/fees: $1,223; $6,623 out-of-state. Per-credit charge: $40 in-state; $220 out-of-state. Books/supplies: $800. Personal expenses: $400.

2005-2006 Financial aid. Need-based: 2% of total undergraduate aid awarded as scholarships/grants, 98% as loans/jobs. Need-based aid available for part-time students. **Non-need-based:** Scholarships awarded for academics.

Application procedures. Admission: No deadline. No application fee. Admission notification on a rolling basis. College placement examinations required of all students, unless acceptable scores on SAT/ACT or special students. **Financial aid:** Priority date 7/15; no closing date. FAFSA required. Applicants notified on a rolling basis starting 5/1; must reply within 2 week(s) of notification.

Academics. Special study options: Cooperative education, distance learning, double major, dual enrollment of high school students, independent study, internships. License preparation in real estate. **Credit/placement by examination:** CLEP, institutional tests. **Support services:** GED preparation and test center, learning center, pre-admission summer program, reduced course load, remedial instruction, study skills assistance, tutoring.

Majors. Business: Accounting, administrative services, business admin, office technology. **Computer sciences:** Information systems. **Education:** General, early childhood, teacher assistance. **Engineering:** Electrical. **Engineering technology:** Electrical. **Family/consumer sciences:** Child care. **Health:** Medical assistant, medical radiologic technology/radiation therapy, nursing (RN), recreational therapy. **Liberal arts:** Arts/sciences. **Mechanic/repair:** Electronics/electrical. **Parks/recreation:** General.

Most popular majors. Business/marketing 34%, computer/information sciences 10%, liberal arts 12%, parks/recreation 7%, trade and industry 24%.

Computing on campus. 48 workstations in library, computer center.

Student life. Freshman orientation: Available. **Activities:** Drama, student government, departmental clubs.

Student services. Adult student services, career counseling, student employment services, financial aid counseling, on-campus daycare, personal counseling, placement for graduates, veterans' counselor. **Physically disabled:** Services for visually, hearing impaired. **Transfer:** Special adviser, orientation for new students. Transfer adviser for students transferring to 4-year colleges.

Contact. Phone: (252) 492-2061 Fax: (252) 430-0460
Brenda Beck, Admissions Officer, Vance-Granville Community College, Box 917, Henderson, NC 27536

Wake Technical Community College

Raleigh, North Carolina
www.wake.tec.nc.us **CB code: 5928**

- Public 2-year community and technical college
- Commuter campus in small city

General. Founded in 1958. Regionally accredited. **Enrollment:** 10,500 degree-seeking undergraduates. **Degrees:** 999 associate awarded. **Location:** 10 miles from Raleigh. **Calendar:** Semester, extensive summer session. **Full-time faculty:** 307 total. **Part-time faculty:** 630 total. **Partnerships:** Formal partnership with NORTEL.

Student profile. Among degree-seeking undergraduates, 40% enrolled in a transfer program, 60% enrolled in a vocational program.

Transfer out. Colleges most students transferred to 2005: North Carolina State University, University of North Carolina at Chapel Hill, East Carolina University, University of North Carolina at Greensboro, Appalchian State University.

Basis for selection. Open admission, but selective for some programs. Admission to health programs based on standardized test scores, post-secondary coursework. Placement tests required of all degree and diploma students with SAT scores below 480 verbal or math, or below ACT math 20, reading 19, and writing 19. Interview recommended. **Adult students:** Entrance exam policies same as for first-time freshmen. **Homeschooled:** Must include home-school transcript and test scores.

High school preparation. Recommended units include English 4 and mathematics 4. One chemistry required for health sciences associate degree programs.

2005-2006 Annual costs. Tuition/fees: $1,235; $6,635 out-of-state. Per-credit charge: $40 in-state; $220 out-of-state. Books/supplies: $1,000. Personal expenses: $1,350.

Financial aid. Need-based: Need-based aid available for part-time students. Work study available for part-time students. **Non-need-based:** Scholarships awarded for academics, job skills, leadership, state residency.

Application procedures. Admission: No deadline. No application fee. Admission notification on a rolling basis. **Financial aid:** Priority date 3/15; no closing date. FAFSA, institutional form required. Applicants notified on a rolling basis starting 4/1; must reply within 2 week(s) of notification.

Academics. Special study options: Cooperative education, distance learning, double major, dual enrollment of high school students, ESL, liberal arts/career combination. License preparation in dental hygiene, nursing, paramedic, radiology, real estate. **Credit/placement by examination:** AP, CLEP, institutional tests. 25% of degree requirement must be taken as classwork at Wake Tech. **Support services:** GED preparation and test center, learning center, pre-admission summer program, reduced course load, remedial instruction, tutoring.

Majors. Architecture: Landscape. **Business:** General, accounting, administrative services, hospitality/recreation. **Computer sciences:** General, applications programming, computer graphics, programming. **Conservation:** General. **Construction:** Power transmission. **Education:** Early childhood. **Engineering technology:** Architectural, civil, drafting, electrical, manufacturing, robotics, surveying. **Health:** Clinical lab technology, dental hygiene, EMT paramedic, medical assistant, medical radiologic technology/radiation therapy, medical records technology, medical secretary, nursing (RN), surgical technology. **Interdisciplinary:** Global studies. **Legal studies:** Legal secretary. **Liberal arts:** Arts/sciences. **Mechanic/repair:** Electronics/electrical, industrial. **Personal/culinary services:** Culinary arts. **Protective services:** Police science. **Public administration:** Human services.

Most popular majors. Business/marketing 23%, computer/information sciences 15%, engineering/engineering technologies 17%, health sciences 15%, liberal arts 25%.

Computing on campus. 62 workstations in library, computer center.

Student life. Freshman orientation: Available. Held on first day of class. **Policies:** Freshmen permitted cars on campus. **Activities:** Choral groups, radio station, student government, student newspaper.

Student services. Career counseling, student employment services, health services, on-campus daycare, personal counseling, placement for graduates, veterans' counselor. **Physically disabled:** Services for visually, speech, hearing impaired. **Transfer:** Special adviser, orientation for new students. Transfer adviser, college fairs on campus for students transferring to 4-year colleges.

Contact. Phone: (919) 662-3500 Fax: (919) 661-0117
Susan Bloomfield, Director of Admissions, Wake Technical Community College, 9101 Fayetteville Road, Raleigh, NC 27603

Wayne Community College
Goldsboro, North Carolina
www.wayne.cc.nc.us **CB code: 5926**

- Public 2-year community college
- Commuter campus in large town

General. Founded in 1957. Regionally accredited. **Enrollment:** 2,919 degree-seeking undergraduates. **Degrees:** 302 associate awarded. **Location:** 55 miles from Raleigh. **Calendar:** Semester, limited summer session. **Full-time faculty:** 91 total. **Part-time faculty:** 122 total.

Student profile.

Out-of-state:	16%	**25 or older:**	45%

Transfer out. Colleges most students transferred to 2005: East Carolina University, Mount Olive College, Bonton College, Campbell University, North Carolina State.

Basis for selection. Open admission, but selective for some programs. Admission to allied health programs based on placement test, academic record, interview. Interviews required for allied health programs. Placement interview required of all applicants.

High school preparation. 14 units recommended. Recommended units include English 4, mathematics 3, social studies 1, history 1, science 3 (laboratory 1) and foreign language 2.

2005-2006 Annual costs. Tuition/fees: $1,217; $6,617 out-of-state. Per-credit charge: $40 in-state; $220 out-of-state. Books/supplies: $800. Personal expenses: $400.

Financial aid. Need-based: Need-based aid available for part-time students. Work study available nights and for part-time students. **Non-need-based:** Scholarships awarded for academics, job skills.

Application procedures. Admission: No deadline. No application fee. Admission notification on a rolling basis. **Financial aid:** Priority date 3/15; no closing date. FAFSA, institutional form required. Applicants notified on a rolling basis starting 6/1; must reply within 2 week(s) of notification.

Academics. Special study options: Accelerated study, cooperative education, distance learning, double major, dual enrollment of high school students, internships, weekend college. License preparation in aviation, nursing. **Credit/placement by examination:** CLEP, institutional tests. **Support services:** GED preparation and test center, learning center, reduced course load, remedial instruction, study skills assistance, tutoring, writing center.

Majors. Agriculture: Agribusiness operations, poultry, turf management. **Business:** General, accounting, administrative services, business admin, sales/distribution. **Conservation:** Forest resources. **Family/consumer sciences:** Child care. **Health:** Dental hygiene, licensed practical nurse, medical assistant, medical secretary, mental health services, nursing (RN). **Interdisciplinary:** Biological/physical sciences. **Legal studies:** Legal secretary. **Liberal arts:** Arts/sciences. **Mechanic/repair:** Aircraft. **Parks/recreation:** Facilities management. **Protective services:** Police science. **Public administration:** Human services.

Computing on campus. 400 workstations in library, computer center.

Student life. Freshman orientation: Mandatory. Preregistration for classes offered. **Policies:** Student government organizes sports program. **Activities:** Concert band, choral groups, student government, student newspaper.

Athletics. Intramural: Basketball, bowling, golf, softball, table tennis, tennis, volleyball.

Student services. Adult student services, career counseling, student employment services, financial aid counseling, health services, minority student services, on-campus daycare, personal counseling, placement for graduates, veterans' counselor, women's services. **Physically disabled:** Services for visually, speech, hearing impaired. **Transfer:** Special adviser, orientation for new students. Transfer adviser, college fairs on campus for students transferring to 4-year colleges.

Contact. E-mail: msm@waynecc.edu
Phone: (919) 735-5151 ext. 238 Fax: (919) 736-9425
Susan Sasser, Director of Admissions and Records, Wayne Community College, PO Box 8002, Goldsboro, NC 27533-8002

Western Piedmont Community College
Morganton, North Carolina
www.wpcc.edu **CB code: 5922**

- Public 2-year community college
- Commuter campus in large town

General. Founded in 1964. Regionally accredited. **Enrollment:** 2,223 degree-seeking undergraduates. **Degrees:** 315 associate awarded. **Location:** 50 miles from Asheville. **Calendar:** Semester, extensive summer session. **Full-time faculty:** 72 total; 6% have terminal degrees, 6% minority, 53% women.

Part-time faculty: 337 total. **Special facilities:** Greenhouse, fitness and nature trails, alpine climbing tower.

Student profile.

Out-of-state:	1%	**25 or older:**	50%

Transfer out. Colleges most students transferred to 2005: Appalachian State University, Gardner-Webb University, Western Carolina University, Lenoir-Rhyne College, and University of North Carolina-Greensboro.

Basis for selection. Open admission, but selective for some programs. Special requirements for health programs. Interview recommended for some programs; portfolio recommended for fine arts program. **Adult students:** Entrance exam policies same as for first-time freshmen.

2005-2006 Annual costs. Tuition/fees: $1,212; $6,612 out-of-state. Per-credit charge: $40 in-state; $220 out-of-state. Books/supplies: $868. Personal expenses: $3,568.

2005-2006 Financial aid. Need-based: 93% of total undergraduate aid awarded as scholarships/grants, 7% as loans/jobs. Need-based aid available for part-time students. Work study available for part-time students. **Non-need-based:** Scholarships awarded for academics.

Application procedures. Admission: No deadline. No application fee. Application may be submitted online. Admission notification on a rolling basis. Application closing date for nursing, medical laboratory applicants is January 1 for fall admission. **Financial aid:** Priority date 6/1; no closing date. FAFSA required. Applicants notified on a rolling basis starting 6/15; must reply within 2 week(s) of notification.

Academics. Special study options: Cooperative education, distance learning, dual enrollment of high school students. Bachelor's degree programs available on campus. License preparation in nursing. **Credit/placement by examination:** AP, CLEP, IB, institutional tests. 15 credit hours maximum toward associate degree. **Support services:** GED preparation and test center, learning center, reduced course load, remedial instruction, tutoring.

Majors. Agriculture: Horticulture. **Business:** Accounting, administrative services, business admin, office technology, office/clerical, operations, sales/distribution. **Computer sciences:** Computer science, data processing, information systems, systems analysis. **Conservation:** General. **Construction:** Maintenance. **Education:** Early childhood. **Engineering:** General, civil, electrical, mechanical. **Engineering technology:** Construction. **Family/consumer sciences:** Child care. **Health:** Clinical lab assistant, medical assistant, nursing (RN), office admin, recreational therapy. **Interdisciplinary:** Natural sciences. **Legal studies:** Legal secretary, paralegal. **Liberal arts:** Arts/sciences. **Protective services:** Criminal justice. **Visual/performing arts:** Interior design, studio arts.

Most popular majors. Business/marketing 21%, health sciences 24%, liberal arts 25%, security/protective services 9%.

Computing on campus. 280 workstations in library, computer center. Commuter students can connect to campus network. Online library available.

Student life. Freshman orientation: Available. Preregistration for classes offered. **Policies:** Freshmen permitted cars on campus. **Activities:** Drama, student government, Phi Beta Lambda, Phi Theta Kappa, African American Students Association, Students for Christ.

Athletics. Team name: Pioneers.

Student services. Adult student services, career counseling, services for economically disadvantaged, student employment services, financial aid counseling, personal counseling, placement for graduates, veterans' counselor. **Physically disabled:** Services for visually, speech, hearing impaired. **Transfer:** Special adviser, orientation for new students. Transfer adviser, college fairs on campus for students transferring to 4-year colleges.

Contact. E-mail: swilliams@wpcc.edu
Phone: (828) 438-6051 Fax: (828) 438-6065
Susan Williams, Director of Admissions, Western Piedmont Community College, 1001 Burkemont Avenue, Morganton, NC 28655-4511

Wilkes Community College

Wilkesboro, North Carolina
www.wilkescc.edu **CB code: 5921**

- Public 2-year community college
- Commuter campus in small town

General. Founded in 1965. Regionally accredited. **Enrollment:** 2,414 degree-seeking undergraduates; 203 non-degree-seeking students. **Degrees:** 359 associate awarded. **Location:** 50 miles from Winston-Salem. **Calendar:** Semester, limited summer session. **Full-time faculty:** 73 total; 6% have terminal degrees, 1% minority, 47% women. **Part-time faculty:** 289 total; 6% have terminal degrees, 2% minority, 50% women. **Class size:** 80% < 20, 19% 20-39, 1% 40-49, less than 1% 50-99. **Special facilities:** Community center.

Student profile. Among degree-seeking undergraduates, 33% enrolled in a transfer program, 67% enrolled in a vocational program, 2% already have a bachelor's degree or higher, 707 enrolled as first-time, first-year students, 118 transferred in from other institutions.

Part-time:	47%	**Asian American:**	1%
Out-of-state:	1%	**Hispanic American:**	2%
Women:	63%	**25 or older:**	39%
African American:	5%		

Transfer out. 65% of students enrolled in the transfer program go on to 4-year colleges. **Colleges most students transferred to 2005:** Appalachian State University, Gardner-Webb University, Winston-Salem State University.

Basis for selection. Open admission, but selective for some programs. Special requirements for nursing program. **Adult students:** Entrance exam policies same as for first-time freshmen.

High school preparation. 20 units recommended. Recommended units include English 4, mathematics 4, social studies 3, history 2, science 3 (laboratory 1), foreign language 2 and academic electives 2.

2005-2006 Annual costs. Tuition/fees: $1,248; $6,648 out-of-state. Per-credit charge: $40 in-state; $220 out-of-state. Books/supplies: $1,000. Personal expenses: $500.

2004-2005 Financial aid. Need-based: 198 full-time freshmen applied for aid; 164 were judged to have need; 126 of these received aid. Average need met was 63%. Average scholarship/grant was $400; average loan $1,800. 94% of total undergraduate aid awarded as scholarships/grants, 6% as loans/jobs. Need-based aid available for part-time students. Work study available nights and for part-time students. **Non-need-based:** Awarded to 33 full-time undergraduates, including 60 freshmen. Scholarships awarded for academics, art, job skills, leadership, minority status, music/drama, state residency.

Application procedures. Admission: No deadline. No application fee. Application may be submitted online. Admission notification on a rolling basis. **Financial aid:** Priority date 5/1, closing date 6/1. FAFSA required. Applicants notified on a rolling basis starting 4/1; must reply by 8/1.

Academics. Special study options: Cooperative education, distance learning, double major, dual enrollment of high school students, ESL, independent study, internships. Bachelor's degree programs available on campus. License preparation in nursing, paramedic, real estate. **Credit/placement by examination:** AP, CLEP, IB, institutional tests. 16 credit hours maximum toward associate degree. **Support services:** GED preparation and test center, learning center, pre-admission summer program, reduced course load, remedial instruction, study skills assistance, tutoring, writing center.

Majors. Agriculture: Horticulture. **Business:** Accounting, business admin, marketing, office management. **Communications technology:** Radio/tv. **Computer sciences:** Computer graphics, information systems, information technology, LAN/WAN management, programming. **Construction:** General, electrician. **Education:** Early childhood, elementary. **Engineering technology:** Architectural, computer, electrical, industrial. **Health:** Health services, medical assistant, nursing (RN). **Liberal arts:** Arts/sciences. **Mechanic/repair:** Automotive, diesel. **Personal/culinary services:** Baking, chef training. **Protective services:** Criminal justice.

Most popular majors. Business/marketing 18%, education 7%, engineering/engineering technologies 11%, health sciences 16%, liberal arts 26%, trade and industry 9%.

Computing on campus. 150 workstations in library, computer center, student center.

Student life. Freshman orientation: Mandatory. Preregistration for classes offered. **Policies:** Freshmen permitted cars on campus. **Activities:** Choral groups, drama, literary magazine, music ensembles, musical theater, radio station, student government, student newspaper, Baptist student union, Ye Hosts food service club, camera club, Phi Theta Kappa, Association of Information Technology Professionals, Rotaract, human services club, medical assisting club, student government association, Student Ambassadors.

Athletics. NJCAA. **Intercollegiate:** Baseball M, basketball, volleyball W. **Intramural:** Basketball, table tennis, tennis, volleyball. **Team name:** Cougars.

Student services. Adult student services, career counseling, services for economically disadvantaged, student employment services, financial aid counseling, minority student services, personal counseling, placement for graduates, veterans' counselor. **Physically disabled:** Services for visually, speech, hearing impaired. **Transfer:** Special adviser, orientation, pre-admission transcript evaluation for new students. Transfer adviser, college fairs on campus for students transferring to 4-year colleges.

Contact. E-mail: mac.warren@wilkescc.edu
Phone: (336) 838-6135 Fax: (336) 838-6547
C. Warren, Director of Admissions, Wilkes Community College, 1328 South Collegiate Drive, Wilkesboro, NC 28697-0120

Wilson Technical Community College

Wilson, North Carolina
www.wilsontech.edu **CB code: 5930**

- Public 2-year community and technical college
- Commuter campus in large town

General. Founded in 1958. Regionally accredited. **Enrollment:** 1,686 degree-seeking undergraduates; 239 non-degree-seeking students. **Degrees:** 159 associate awarded. **Location:** 50 miles from Raleigh. **Calendar:** Semester, limited summer session. **Full-time faculty:** 54 total; 7% have terminal degrees, 13% minority, 65% women. **Part-time faculty:** 49 total; 6% have terminal degrees, 8% minority, 61% women. **Class size:** 64% < 20, 33% 20-39, 2% 40-49, less than 1% 50-99.

Student profile. Among degree-seeking undergraduates, 17% enrolled in a transfer program, 83% enrolled in a vocational program, 3% already have a bachelor's degree or higher, 149 enrolled as first-time, first-year students.

Part-time:	49%	**African American:**	48%
Out-of-state:	1%	**Hispanic American:**	2%
Women:	75%	**25 or older:**	57%

Transfer out. 80% of students enrolled in the transfer program go on to 4-year colleges.

Basis for selection. Open admission, but selective for some programs. Admission for nursing based on test scores, high school record, skills, and experience. Health requirement for emergency medical technology. Interview recommended.

High school preparation. High school diploma not required for certificate programs.

2005-2006 Annual costs. Tuition/fees: $1,302; $7,062 out-of-state. Per-credit charge: $40 in-state; $220 out-of-state. Books/supplies: $800. Personal expenses: $4,200.

2004-2005 Financial aid. Need-based: Average need met was 65%. Average scholarship/grant was $3,900. Need-based aid available for part-time students. **Non-need-based:** Scholarships awarded for academics.

Application procedures. Admission: No deadline. No application fee. Admission notification on a rolling basis beginning on or about 1/1. Applicants accepted to nursing program must reply by May 1. **Financial aid:** Priority date 3/15; no closing date. FAFSA, institutional form required. Applicants notified on a rolling basis.

Academics. Special program assistance for hearing-impaired students. **Special study options:** Cooperative education, distance learning, double major, dual enrollment of high school students, ESL, liberal arts/career combination. License preparation in nursing. **Credit/placement by examination:** AP, CLEP, institutional tests. 50 credit hours maximum toward associate degree. **Support services:** GED preparation and test center, learning center, pre-admission summer program, reduced course load, remedial instruction, tutoring.

Majors. Business: Accounting, business admin, executive assistant, operations. **Computer sciences:** General, applications programming, programming, systems analysis. **Conservation:** General. **Education:** Early childhood. **Engineering:** Polymer. **Engineering technology:** Drafting, electrical, mechanical. **Family/consumer sciences:** Child care. **Foreign languages:** Sign language interpretation, translation. **Health:** Licensed practical nurse, nursing (RN). **Legal studies:** Paralegal. **Liberal arts:** Arts/sciences. **Mechanic/repair:** Electronics/electrical. **Protective services:** Criminal justice, fire safety technology.

Most popular majors. Business/marketing 12%, computer/information sciences 8%, education 18%, foreign language 6%, health sciences 13%, legal studies 6%, liberal arts 15%, security/protective services 16%.

Computing on campus. 33 workstations in library, computer center.

Student life. Freshman orientation: Available. Preregistration for classes offered. **Policies:** Freshmen permitted cars on campus. **Activities:** Choral groups, student government.

Student services. Career counseling, services for economically disadvantaged, student employment services, placement for graduates, veterans' counselor. **Physically disabled:** Services for hearing impaired. **Transfer:** Special adviser, orientation for new students. Transfer adviser, college fairs on campus for students transferring to 4-year colleges.

Contact. E-mail: lmansfield@email.wilsontech.edu
Phone: (252) 246-1285 Fax: (252) 246-1384
Leonard Mansfield, Director of Admissions and Records, Wilson Technical Community College, Box 4305, Wilson, NC 27893-0305

North Dakota

Aakers College: Bismarck

Bismarck, North Dakota
www.aakers.edu

- For-profit 2-year business college
- Commuter campus

General. Accredited by ACICS.

Contact. Phone: (701) 530-9600
Director of Admissions, 1701 East Century Avenue, Bismarck, ND 58503

Aakers College: Fargo

Fargo, North Dakota
www.aakers.edu **CB code: 3343**

- For-profit 2-year business college
- Commuter campus in small city
- Interview required

General. Accredited by ACICS. **Enrollment:** 577 degree-seeking undergraduates; 7 non-degree-seeking students. **Degrees:** 118 associate awarded. **Calendar:** Quarter, extensive summer session. **Full-time faculty:** 8 total. **Part-time faculty:** 31 total. **Class size:** 78% < 20, 22% 20-39.

Student profile. Among degree-seeking undergraduates, 100% enrolled in a vocational program, 1% already have a bachelor's degree or higher, 253 enrolled as first-time, first-year students, 92 transferred in from other institutions.

Part-time:	37%	**Hispanic American:**	1%
Out-of-state:	23%	**Native American:**	1%
Women:	79%	**25 or older:**	48%
Asian American:	1%		

Transfer out. Colleges most students transferred to 2005: University of Mary - Fargo.

Basis for selection. Open admission. Applicants must have high school diploma or GED and pass entrance assessments (COMPASS exam). **Adult students:** Entrance exam policies same as for first-time freshmen.

2006-2007 Annual costs. Tuition/fees (projected): $10,048. Per course tuition is $785 for general courses and $1000 for network support courses. Books/supplies: $900.

2004-2005 Financial aid. All financial aid based on need. 16% of total undergraduate aid awarded as scholarships/grants, 84% as loans/jobs. Need-based aid available for part-time students. Work study available nights and for part-time students.

Application procedures. Admission: No deadline. $60 fee. Application may be submitted online. Admission notification on a rolling basis. **Financial aid:** No deadline. FAFSA, institutional form required. Applicants notified on a rolling basis starting 1/1.

Academics. Special study options: Distance learning, liberal arts/career combination. **Credit/placement by examination:** CLEP. **Support services:** Reduced course load, remedial instruction, tutoring.

Majors. Business: Accounting, business admin, tourism/travel. **Computer sciences:** Programming. **Health:** Insurance coding, medical secretary, medical transcription. **Legal studies:** Legal secretary. **Social sciences:** Criminology.

Most popular majors. Business/marketing 66%, computer/information sciences 13%, health sciences 13%, legal studies 10%.

Computing on campus. 95 workstations in library, computer center. Online library, helpline available.

Student life. Freshman orientation: Mandatory. Preregistration for classes offered. 2-hour session held 3 weeks before classes begin. **Policies:** Freshmen permitted cars on campus. **Activities:** Student government.

Student services. Career counseling, student employment services, financial aid counseling, placement for graduates. **Transfer:** Orientation, pre-admission transcript evaluation for new students.

Contact. E-mail: fargoadmissions@aakers.edu
Phone: (701) 277-3889 Toll-free number: (800) 817-0009
Fax: (701) 277-5604
John Wilson, Director of Admissions, Aakers College: Fargo, 4012 19th Avenue Southwest, Fargo, ND 58103

Bismarck State College

Bismarck, North Dakota
www.bismarckstate.edu **CB code: 6041**

- Public 2-year community college
- Commuter campus in small city

General. Founded in 1939. Regionally accredited. **Enrollment:** 3,370 degree-seeking undergraduates. **Degrees:** 637 associate awarded. **Location:** 200 miles from Fargo. **Calendar:** Semester, limited summer session. **Full-time faculty:** 112 total. **Part-time faculty:** 166 total.

Student profile.

Out-of-state:	11%	**Live on campus:**	11%
25 or older:	30%		

Basis for selection. Open admission, but selective for some programs. Test scores required for selective admission programs in air conditioning, heating and refrigeration, automotive technology, automotive collision technology, carpentry, electronics technology, line worker (electrical), power plant technology, process plant technology, welding, hotel restaurant management, commercial art. Interview recommended for some programs; portfolio recommended for graphic arts program. **Adult students:** Entrance exam policies same as for first-time freshmen. Students aged 25 or older must submit COMPASS assessment scores in the areas of English, math, and reading.

High school preparation. Recommended units include English 4, mathematics 3, social studies 3, science 3 and foreign language 2.

2005-2006 Annual costs. Tuition/fees: $3,369; $8,022 out-of-state. Per-credit charge: $93 in-state; $248 out-of-state. Full-time annual tuition for residents of Minnesota: $3,600. Full-time annual tuition for residents of South Dakota, Montana, Manitoba, Saskatchewan: $3,483. Full-time annual tuition for residents of Alaska, Arizona, California, Colorado, Hawaii, Idaho, New Mexico, Nevada, Oregon, Utah, Washington, and Wyoming: $3,944. Tuition for Internet courses $140 per credit hour. Room/board: $3,628. Books/supplies: $750. Personal expenses: $1,900.

Financial aid. All financial aid based on need. Need-based aid available for part-time students. Work study available nights, weekends and for part-time students.

Application procedures. Admission: No deadline. $35 fee. Application may be submitted online. Admission notification on a rolling basis beginning on or about 1/1. **Financial aid:** Priority date 3/15; no closing date. FAFSA required. Applicants notified on a rolling basis starting 6/1; must reply within 3 week(s) of notification.

Academics. Special study options: Cooperative education, distance learning, dual enrollment of high school students, internships. Bachelor's degree programs available on campus. License preparation in nursing, paramedic. **Credit/placement by examination:** CLEP, institutional tests. 30 credit hours maximum toward associate degree. **Support services:** Learning center, remedial instruction, study skills assistance, tutoring, writing center.

Majors. Agriculture: Agribusiness operations. **Business:** General, administrative services, hospitality admin, office technology, sales/distribution, transportation. **Communications:** Media studies. **Computer sciences:** Networking. **Construction:** Carpentry, lineworker. **Engineering technology:** Civil, electrical, instrumentation. **Health:** Clinical lab technology, EMT paramedic, licensed practical nurse, massage therapy, surgical technology. **Legal studies:** Legal secretary. **Liberal arts:** Arts/sciences. **Mechanic/repair:** Auto body, automotive, electronics/electrical, heating/ac/refrig. **Production:** Welding. **Protective services:** Criminal justice. **Visual/performing arts:** Commercial/advertising art.

Most popular majors. Business/marketing 7%, engineering/engineering technologies 19%, health sciences 6%, liberal arts 55%.

Computing on campus. 450 workstations in library, computer center, student center. Commuter students can connect to campus network. Online course registration, online library, helpline available.

Student life. **Freshman orientation:** Available. Preregistration for classes offered. **Policies:** Freshmen permitted cars on campus. **Housing:** Single-sex dorms, substance-free housing available. $100 deposit. **Activities:** Bands, choral groups, dance, drama, literary magazine, music ensembles, musical theater, student government, student newspaper.

Athletics. NJCAA. **Intercollegiate:** Baseball M, basketball, golf, tennis, volleyball W. **Intramural:** Basketball, bowling, golf, soccer, softball, table tennis, volleyball. **Team name:** Mystics.

Student services. Career counseling, student employment services, financial aid counseling, personal counseling, placement for graduates, veterans' counselor. **Physically disabled:** Services for visually, speech, hearing impaired. **Transfer:** Special adviser, orientation, pre-admission transcript evaluation for new students. Transfer adviser, college fairs on campus for students transferring to 4-year colleges.

Contact. E-mail: karla.gabriel@bsc.nodak.edu
Phone: (701) 224-5429 Toll-free number: (800) 445-5073
Fax: (701) 224-5643
Karla Gabriel, Dean of Admissions and Enrollment Services, Bismarck State College, PO Box 5587, Bismarck, ND 58506-5587

Cankdeska Cikana Community College

Fort Totten, North Dakota
www.littlehoop.edu **CB code: 1306**

- Public 2-year community college
- Residential campus in rural community

General. Founded in 1974. Regionally accredited. **Enrollment:** 167 degree-seeking undergraduates. **Degrees:** 35 associate awarded. **Location:** 13 miles from Devils Lake. **Calendar:** Semester, limited summer session. **Full-time faculty:** 8 total. **Part-time faculty:** 5 total.

Basis for selection. Open admission.

2006-2007 Annual costs. Tuition/fees: $2,190. Per-credit charge: $85. Books/supplies: $600. Personal expenses: $1,000.

2004-2005 Financial aid. All financial aid based on need. 78% of total undergraduate aid awarded as scholarships/grants, 22% as loans/jobs. Need-based aid available for part-time students.

Application procedures. **Admission:** Closing date 8/20. , may be waived for applicants with need. No application fee. Admission notification on a rolling basis. **Financial aid:** Closing date 8/20. FAFSA, institutional form required. Applicants notified on a rolling basis.

Academics. **Special study options:** Cooperative education, independent study. **Credit/placement by examination:** CLEP. **Support services:** Learning center, remedial instruction, tutoring.

Majors. **Agriculture:** General. **Business:** General, office technology. **Computer sciences:** General, applications programming. **Education:** Early childhood. **Health:** Prenursing. **Mechanic/repair:** Automotive.

Computing on campus. 30 workstations in computer center.

Student life. **Activities:** Drama, student government, Indian organization.

Athletics. **Intercollegiate:** Basketball, bowling, volleyball.

Student services. Career counseling, on-campus daycare, personal counseling. **Transfer:** Special adviser, orientation for new students. College fairs on campus for students transferring to 4-year colleges.

Contact. Phone: (701) 766-1342 Fax: (701) 766-4077
Ermen Brown, Registrar, Cankdeska Cikana Community College, Box 269, Fort Totten, ND 58335

Fort Berthold Community College

New Town, North Dakota
CB code: 7304

- Public 2-year community college
- Small town

General. Founded in 1973. Regionally accredited. Affiliated with American Indian Higher Education Consortium. **Enrollment:** 285 degree-seeking undergraduates. **Degrees:** 30 associate awarded. **Calendar:** Semester. **Full-time faculty:** 18 total. **Part-time faculty:** 40 total.

Basis for selection. Open admission.

2005-2006 Annual costs. Tuition/fees: $3,340. Per-credit charge: $110. Books/supplies: $400. Personal expenses: $800.

Application procedures. **Admission:** No deadline. No application fee.

Academics. **Special study options:** Double major, independent study. **Credit/placement by examination:** CLEP. **Support services:** Remedial instruction, tutoring.

Student life. **Activities:** Drama, student government.

Athletics. **Intercollegiate:** Basketball, cross-country.

Student services. Adult student services, personal counseling, veterans' counselor. **Transfer:** Special adviser, orientation for new students. Transfer adviser for students transferring to 4-year colleges.

Contact. Phone: (701) 627-3665 Fax: (701) 627-3609
Twila Aulaumea, Admissions Director, Fort Berthold Community College, Box 490, New Town, ND 58763

Lake Region State College

Devils Lake, North Dakota
www.lrsc.nodak.edu **CB code: 6163**

- Public 2-year community college
- Commuter campus in small town

General. Founded in 1941. Regionally accredited. Satellite center at Grand Forks Air Force Base. **Enrollment:** 640 degree-seeking undergraduates; 831 non-degree-seeking students. **Degrees:** 152 associate awarded. **Location:** 90 miles from Grand Forks. **Calendar:** Semester, limited summer session. **Full-time faculty:** 30 total; 7% have terminal degrees, 3% minority, 47% women. **Part-time faculty:** 76 total; 14% have terminal degrees, 5% minority, 58% women. **Partnerships:** Formal partnership with CISCO.

Student profile. Among degree-seeking undergraduates, 55% enrolled in a transfer program, 45% enrolled in a vocational program, 1% already have a bachelor's degree or higher, 164 enrolled as first-time, first-year students, 37 transferred in from other institutions.

Part-time:	42%	**25 or older:**	28%
Out-of-state:	10%	**Live on campus:**	20%
Women:	56%		

Transfer out. **Colleges most students transferred to 2005:** Mayville State University, Minot State University, University of North Dakota, North Dakota State University, Valley City State University.

Basis for selection. Open admission, but selective for some programs. Special requirements for peace officer training program, nursing, sign language, and interpretive studies. **Adult students:** Entrance exam policies same as for first-time freshmen.

High school preparation. Recommended units include English 4, mathematics 3, social studies 3, science 3 (laboratory 2) and foreign language 2.

2005-2006 Annual costs. Tuition/fees: $3,339; $3,339 out-of-state. Per-credit charge: $106 in-state; $106 out-of-state. Tuition for Minnesota residents must follow reciprocity procedures, but tuition will be waived to the ND rate. Room/board: $3,790. Books/supplies: $750. Personal expenses: $2,850.

2005-2006 Financial aid. **Need-based:** 42% of total undergraduate aid awarded as scholarships/grants, 58% as loans/jobs. Need-based aid available for part-time students. Work study available nights, weekends and for part-time students. **Non-need-based:** Scholarships awarded for academics, athletics, leadership, music/drama, state residency.

Application procedures. **Admission:** No deadline. $35 fee. Application may be submitted online. Admission notification on a rolling basis. **Financial aid:** Priority date 3/15; no closing date. FAFSA required. Applicants notified on a rolling basis starting 5/15; must reply within 2 week(s) of notification.

Academics. **Special study options:** Combined bachelor's/graduate degree, cooperative education, distance learning, dual enrollment of high school students, ESL, internships, liberal arts/career combination. License preparation in nursing. **Credit/placement by examination:** AP, CLEP, institutional tests. **Support services:** GED preparation and test center, learning center, reduced course load, remedial instruction, study skills assistance, tutoring, writing center.

Majors. **Agriculture:** Business. **Business:** Accounting, accounting technology, administrative services, business admin, executive assistant, fashion, management information systems, market research, office management, office/clerical, sales/distribution, small business admin. **Computer sciences:** General, computer science, data processing, networking, vendor certification. **Education:** Voc/tech. **Engineering:** Electrical. **Family/consumer sciences:** Child care. **Health:** Licensed practical nurse, medical secretary. **Legal studies:** Legal secretary, paralegal. **Liberal arts:** Arts/sciences. **Mechanic/repair:** Automotive, avionics, diesel, electronics/electrical. **Protective services:** Police science. **Transportation:** General.

Most popular majors. Business/marketing 21%, health sciences 10%, liberal arts 57%.

Computing on campus. 285 workstations in dormitories, library, computer center, student center. Dormitories wired for high-speed internet access and linked to campus network. Commuter students can connect to campus network. Online course registration, online library, helpline available.

Student life. **Freshman orientation:** Mandatory, $10 fee. Preregistration for classes offered. Freshmen encouraged to attend a summer orientation and required to attend orientation the day before classes start. **Policies:** Alcohol not allowed on campus. Freshmen permitted cars on campus. **Housing:** Single-sex dorms, special housing for disabled, apartments, substance-free housing available. $50 nonrefundable deposit, deadline 9/1. **Activities:** Drama, literary magazine, student government, symphony orchestra, Distributive Education Clubs of America, Vocational Industrial Clubs of America, Students Other than Average, residents' housing association, business club, legal assistant club, simulator maintenance technician club, drama club, Campus Crusade for Christ, agriculture club, international club.

Athletics. NJCAA. **Intercollegiate:** Basketball. **Intramural:** Basketball, bowling, football (non-tackle), golf, ice hockey, softball, table tennis, volleyball. **Team name:** Royals.

Student services. Adult student services, career counseling, services for economically disadvantaged, student employment services, financial aid counseling, on-campus daycare, personal counseling, placement for graduates, veterans' counselor, women's services. **Physically disabled:** Services for speech, hearing impaired. **Learning disabled:** Comprehensive services available. **Transfer:** Special adviser, orientation for new students. Transfer adviser, college fairs on campus for students transferring to 4-year colleges.

Contact. E-mail: diane.knodel@lrsc.nodak.edu
Phone: (701) 662-1514 Toll-free number: (800) 443-1313
Fax: (701) 662-1581
Laurel Goulding, Vice President for Student Services, Lake Region State College, 1801 North College Drive, Devils Lake, ND 58301-1598

Minot State University: Bottineau Campus

Bottineau, North Dakota
www.misu-b.nodak.edu **CB code: 1540**

- Public 2-year branch campus and junior college
- Residential campus in small town

General. Founded in 1907. Regionally accredited. **Enrollment:** 300 full-time, degree-seeking students. **Degrees:** 113 associate awarded. **Location:** 80 miles from Minot. **Calendar:** Semester, limited summer session. **Full-time faculty:** 25 total; 8% have terminal degrees, 24% women. **Part-time faculty:** 12 total; 8% have terminal degrees, 58% women. **Special facilities:** Headquarters for North Dakota Forest Service, outdoor laboratories on state and federally owned refuges, forests, and parklands. **Partnerships:** Formal parterships with high schools where students have taken CISCO and A+ modules for certification to transfer into information technology - network engineering program.

Student profile.

Out-of-state:	20%	**Live on campus:**	44%
25 or older:	28%		

Basis for selection. Open admission. ACT examination offered on campus first weekend. **Adult students:** SAT/ACT scores not required if applicant over 25.

2005-2006 Annual costs. Tuition/fees: $3,202; $7,502 out-of-state. Per-credit charge: $107 in-state; $286 out-of-state. Tuition for Minnesota residents: $3,600. Tuition for South Dakota, Montana residents: $3,219. Tuition for Canadian provinces: $2,575. Room/board: $3,511. Books/supplies: $600. Personal expenses: $1,200.

Financial aid. **Need-based:** Need-based aid available for part-time students. Work study available nights, weekends and for part-time students. **Non-need-based:** Scholarships awarded for academics, alumni affiliation, athletics, music/drama.

Application procedures. **Admission:** No deadline. $35 fee. Application may be submitted online. Admission notification on a rolling basis. **Financial aid:** Priority date 4/15; no closing date. FAFSA required. Applicants notified on a rolling basis starting 6/1; must reply within 2 week(s) of notification.

Academics. **Special study options:** Cooperative education, distance learning, double major, dual enrollment of high school students, independent study, internships, liberal arts/career combination. **Credit/placement by examination:** CLEP, institutional tests. **Support services:** Learning center, reduced course load, remedial instruction, study skills assistance, tutoring.

Majors. **Agriculture:** Greenhouse operations, landscaping, turf management. **Biology:** General. **Business:** Accounting technology, administrative services. **Communications:** Advertising. **Computer sciences:** Webmaster. **Conservation:** General, urban forestry, wildlife. **Education:** Teacher assistance. **Engineering technology:** Environmental, water quality. **Health:** Medical assistant, medical secretary. **History:** General. **Liberal arts:** Arts/sciences.

Most popular majors. Agriculture 18%, health sciences 23%, liberal arts 56%.

Computing on campus. 80 workstations in library, computer center, student center. Dormitories wired for high-speed internet access. Online library, repair service, wireless network available.

Student life. **Freshman orientation:** Mandatory. Preregistration for classes offered. 2 official orientation summer sessions and 2-week freshman seminar class offered. **Policies:** Freshmen permitted cars on campus. **Housing:** Coed dorms, single-sex dorms, substance-free housing available. $75 deposit. **Activities:** Bands, choral groups, drama, music ensembles, student government, student newspaper.

Athletics. NJCAA. **Intercollegiate:** Baseball M, basketball, ice hockey M, volleyball W. **Intramural:** Badminton, basketball, bowling, football (non-tackle), skiing, soccer, softball, volleyball. **Team name:** Lumberjacks and Ladyjacks.

Student services. Adult student services, alcohol/substance abuse counseling, career counseling, student employment services, financial aid counseling, health services, personal counseling, veterans' counselor. **Learning disabled:** Comprehensive services available. **Transfer:** Special adviser for new students. Transfer adviser, college fairs on campus for students transferring to 4-year colleges.

Contact. E-mail: klierj@misu.nodak.edu
Phone: (701) 228-5426 Toll-free number: (800) 542-6866
Fax: (701) 228-5499
Paula Berg, Associate Dean, Minot State University: Bottineau Campus, 105 Simrall Boulevard, Bottineau, ND 58318-1198

North Dakota State College of Science

Wahpeton, North Dakota
www.ndscs.nodak.edu **CB code: 6476**

- Public 2-year junior and technical college
- Residential campus in small town

General. Founded in 1903. Regionally accredited. **Enrollment:** 2,457 degree-seeking undergraduates. **Degrees:** 627 associate awarded. **Location:** 50 miles from Fargo, 200 miles from Sioux Falls, South Dakota. **Calendar:** Semester, limited summer session. **Full-time faculty:** 130 total. **Part-time faculty:** 40 total. **Class size:** 57% < 20, 36% 20-39, 5% 40-49, 2% 50-99. **Partnerships:** Formal partnerships with Caterpillar Corporation and John Deere.

Student profile.

Out-of-state:	28%	**Live on campus:**	52%
25 or older:	20%		

Transfer out. **Colleges most students transferred to 2005:** Minnesota State University Moorhead, North Dakota State University, University of North Dakota, Northwest Technical College-Moorhead.

Basis for selection. Open admission, but selective for some programs. Special requirements for allied health programs. **Adult students:** SAT/ACT scores not required if applicant over 25.

High school preparation. Chemistry, English and anatomy & physiology required for dental hygiene.

2005-2006 Annual costs. Tuition/fees: $3,268; $7,990 out-of-state. Per-credit charge: $94 in-state; $252 out-of-state. Full-time tuition for Minnesota residents $3,600. Full-time tuition for South Dakota, Montana, Saskatchewan, Manitoba residents $3,533. Room/board: $3,898. Books/supplies: $700. Personal expenses: $1,850.

Financial aid. Need-based: Need-based aid available for part-time students. Work study available nights, weekends and for part-time students. **Non-need-based:** Scholarships awarded for academics, athletics, job skills, music/drama, state residency.

Application procedures. Admission: No deadline. $35 fee, may be waived for applicants with need. Application may be submitted online. Admission notification on a rolling basis. **Financial aid:** Priority date 4/15; no closing date. FAFSA, institutional form required. Applicants notified on a rolling basis starting 6/1; must reply within 2 week(s) of notification.

Academics. Special study options: Cooperative education, distance learning, dual enrollment of high school students, ESL, internships, liberal arts/career combination, student-designed major. License preparation in dental hygiene, nursing, occupational therapy. **Credit/placement by examination:** CLEP, institutional tests. **Support services:** Learning center, pre-admission summer program, reduced course load, remedial instruction, study skills assistance, tutoring, writing center.

Majors. Agriculture: Agribusiness operations, business, power machinery, supplies. **Architecture:** Technology. **Business:** General, administrative services, banking/financial services, business admin, executive assistant, finance, office management, office/clerical, restaurant/food services. **Computer sciences:** Applications programming, data entry, information systems, LAN/WAN management, web page design. **Construction:** General, carpentry, electrician, maintenance. **Engineering technology:** Architectural, architectural drafting, automotive, civil, civil drafting, computer hardware, construction, electrical, heat/ac/refrig, mechanical drafting, software. **Family/consumer sciences:** Institutional food production. **Health:** Dental hygiene, insurance coding, licensed practical nurse, medical records technology, medical transcription, mental health services, occupational therapy assistant, office admin, office assistant, pharmacy assistant. **Liberal arts:** Arts/sciences. **Mechanic/repair:** Auto body, automotive, diesel, electronics/electrical, heating/ac/refrig, small engine. **Personal/culinary services:** Baking, culinary arts, restaurant/catering. **Production:** Machine tool, welding.

Most popular majors. Agriculture 7%, business/marketing 14%, engineering/engineering technologies 21%, health sciences 18%, liberal arts 20%, trade and industry 19%.

Computing on campus. 550 workstations in dormitories, library, computer center, student center. Dormitories linked to campus network. Online course registration, helpline, wireless network available.

Student life. Freshman orientation: Mandatory, $25 fee. Preregistration for classes offered. Orientation is held the day before classes start. **Policies:** Freshmen permitted cars on campus. **Housing:** Guaranteed on-campus for freshmen. Coed dorms, single-sex dorms, special housing for disabled, apartments available. $40 deposit. **Activities:** Bands, choral groups, drama, music ensembles, student government, Intervarsity Christian Fellowship.

Athletics. NJCAA. **Intercollegiate:** Basketball, football (tackle) M, volleyball W. **Intramural:** Basketball, racquetball, softball, volleyball. **Team name:** Wildcats.

Student services. Alcohol/substance abuse counseling, career counseling, student employment services, financial aid counseling, health services, on-campus daycare, personal counseling, placement for graduates, veterans' counselor. **Physically disabled:** Services for visually, hearing impaired. **Transfer:** Special adviser, orientation, pre-admission transcript evaluation for new students. Transfer adviser, college fairs on campus for students transferring to 4-year colleges.

Contact. E-mail: admissions@kitten.ndscs.nodak.edu
Phone: (701) 671-2202 Toll-free number: (800) 342-4325 ext. 32202
Fax: (701) 671-2201
Karen Reilly, Director of Enrollment Services and Records, North Dakota State College of Science, 800 North 6th Street, Wahpeton, ND 58076

Sitting Bull College
Fort Yates, North Dakota
www.sittingbull.edu **CB code: 0310**

- Public 2-year community college
- Residential campus in small town

General. Founded in 1971. Regionally accredited. **Enrollment:** 289 degree-seeking undergraduates. **Degrees:** 34 associate awarded. **Location:** 75 miles from Bismarck, 60 miles from Mobridge, South Dakota. **Calendar:** Semester, limited summer session. **Full-time faculty:** 21 total. **Part-time faculty:** 22 total.

Transfer out. Colleges most students transferred to 2005: Northern State College, Black Hills State College, Minot State University, United Tribes Technical College.

Basis for selection. Open admission. High school students may enroll with approval of Vice President of academic affairs and parents. Letters of recommendation from high school counselor or principal required. TABE (Test of Adult Basic Education) required of students without 2-year college degree. **Adult students:** Entrance exam policies same as for first-time freshmen. Compass Test required for placement in Math and English.

2005-2006 Annual costs. Tuition/fees: $3,140. Per-credit charge: $80. Books/supplies: $800. Personal expenses: $1,170.

Financial aid. Need-based: Need-based aid available for part-time students.

Application procedures. Admission: No deadline. $10 fee. Admission notification on a rolling basis. **Financial aid:** Priority date 5/1; no closing date. FAFSA, institutional form required. Applicants notified on a rolling basis starting 7/15; must reply within 6 week(s) of notification.

Academics. Special study options: Cooperative education, dual enrollment of high school students, independent study. Bachelor's degree programs available on campus. **Credit/placement by examination:** CLEP. **Support services:** GED preparation and test center, learning center, remedial instruction, study skills assistance, tutoring.

Majors. Agriculture: Agribusiness operations. **Area/ethnic studies:** Native American. **Business:** Business admin, entrepreneurial studies, office technology, small business admin. **Computer sciences:** Applications programming. **Conservation:** Environmental science, wildlife. **Construction:** Carpentry. **Education:** Early childhood, elementary, multi-level teacher. **Health:** Licensed practical nurse. **Public administration:** Human services.

Computing on campus. Online course registration, wireless network available.

Student life. Housing: Very limited housing available for single parents or married students. **Activities:** Student government, cultural club, Phi Beta Lambda, Rodeo Club.

Athletics. Team name: Suns.

Student services. Career counseling, student employment services, personal counseling, placement for graduates, veterans' counselor. **Transfer:** Special adviser, orientation for new students. Transfer adviser for students transferring to 4-year colleges.

Contact. E-mail: melodya@sbci.edu
Phone: (701) 854-3861 ext. 8020 Fax: (701) 854-3403
Melody Azure, Director of Admissions/Registrar, Sitting Bull College, 1341 92nd Street, Fort Yates, ND 58538

Turtle Mountain Community College
Belcourt, North Dakota
www.tm.edu **CB code: 0352**

- Public 2-year community college
- Commuter campus in rural community

General. Regionally accredited. **Enrollment:** 1,000 degree-seeking undergraduates. **Degrees:** 1 bachelor's, 50 associate awarded. **Calendar:** Semester. **Full-time faculty:** 40 total. **Part-time faculty:** 21 total.

Basis for selection. Open admission, but selective for some programs. Special requirements for Bachelor of Science Elementary Education program.

2005-2006 Annual costs. Tuition/fees: $1,776. Per-credit charge: $74. Books/supplies: $400.

Application procedures. Admission: No deadline. No application fee. Admission notification on a rolling basis. **Financial aid:** Priority date 4/15, closing date 5/1. FAFSA required.

Academics. Special study options: Bachelor's degree programs available on campus. **Credit/placement by examination:** CLEP.

Majors. Business: Business admin. **Computer sciences:** Computer science. **Construction:** General. **Education:** Early childhood. **Health:** Insurance coding.

Student life. Activities: Student government.

Contact. E-mail: jlafontaine@tm.edu
Phone: (701) 477-7862 Fax: (701) 477-7892
Joni LaFontaine, Admissions/Records Officer, Turtle Mountain Community College, PO Box 340, Belcourt, ND 58316

United Tribes Technical College
Bismarck, North Dakota
www.uttc.edu **CB code: 4915**

- Private 2-year technical college
- Small city

General. Regionally accredited. **Calendar:** Semester.

Annual costs/financial aid. Tuition/fees (2005-2006): $3,255. One-time $100 records fee. Room/board: $3,000. Books/supplies: $600. Personal expenses: $2,060. Need-based financial aid available to full-time and part-time students.

Contact. Phone: (701) 255-3285
President, 3315 University Drive, Bismarck, ND 58504

Williston State College
Williston, North Dakota
www.wsc.nodak.edu **CB code: 6905**

- Public 2-year community college
- Commuter campus in large town

General. Founded in 1957. Regionally accredited. Baccalaureate, post-baccalaureate programs from other campuses available on-campus, all via interactive video network. **Enrollment:** 947 degree-seeking undergraduates. **Degrees:** 224 associate awarded. **Location:** 250 miles from Bismarck, 130 miles from Minot. **Calendar:** Semester, limited summer session. **Full-time faculty:** 26 total. **Part-time faculty:** 67 total.

Student profile. Among degree-seeking undergraduates, 187 enrolled as first-time, first-year students.

Part-time:	41%	**25 or older:**	28%
Out-of-state:	12%	**Live on campus:**	20%
Women:	73%		

Transfer out. 90% of students enrolled in the transfer program go on to 4-year colleges. **Colleges most students transferred to 2005:** University of North Dakota, Minot State University, Dickinson State University, North Dakota State University, Montana State University.

Basis for selection. Open admission, but selective for some programs. Special requirements for practical nursing and physical therapist assistant programs. Immunization records required for applicants born after 1956. **Adult students:** Entrance exam policies same as for first-time freshmen.

High school preparation. 15 units recommended. Recommended units include English 4, mathematics 3, social studies 3, science 3 (laboratory 1) and foreign language 1.

2005-2006 Annual costs. Tuition/fees: $2,850; $3,950 out-of-state. Per-credit charge: $85 in-state; $127 out-of-state. Tuition for Minnesota residents: $3,600. Room/board: $2,800. Books/supplies: $600. Personal expenses: $500.

Financial aid. Need-based: Need-based aid available for part-time students. Work study available nights, weekends and for part-time students. **Non-need-based:** Scholarships awarded for academics, athletics.

Application procedures. Admission: No deadline. $35 fee. Application may be submitted online. Admission notification on a rolling basis. **Financial aid:** Priority date 3/15; no closing date. FAFSA required. Applicants notified on a rolling basis starting 5/15.

Academics. Special study options: Cooperative education, cross-registration, distance learning, double major, dual enrollment of high school students, ESL, internships, liberal arts/career combination, student-designed major. Bachelor's degree programs available on campus. License preparation in aviation, nursing, physical therapy. **Credit/placement by examination:** AP, CLEP, institutional tests. 15 credit hours maximum toward associate degree. **Support services:** GED preparation and test center, learning center, reduced course load, remedial instruction, study skills assistance, tutoring, writing center.

Majors. Business: Accounting technology, administrative services, entrepreneurial studies, marketing. **Computer sciences:** Data processing, system admin, systems analysis, vendor certification, web page design. **Education:** Teacher assistance. **Health:** Licensed practical nurse, massage therapy, medical records technology, medical transcription, nursing (RN), physical therapy assistant. **Liberal arts:** Arts/sciences. **Mechanic/repair:** Automotive, diesel. **Transportation:** Airline/commercial pilot.

Most popular majors. Health sciences 31%, liberal arts 47%.

Computing on campus. 70 workstations in library, computer center. Dormitories linked to campus network. Online library available.

Student life. Freshman orientation: Available. Preregistration for classes offered. Activities take place on the day prior to first day of fall semester. **Policies:** Freshmen permitted cars on campus. **Housing:** Coed dorms, single-sex dorms, apartments available. $100 fully refundable deposit. Separate housing for athletes. **Activities:** Choral groups, drama, literary magazine, music ensembles, student government, Campus Crusade.

Athletics. NJCAA. **Intercollegiate:** Baseball M, basketball, volleyball W. **Intramural:** Basketball, softball, volleyball. **Team name:** Tetons.

Student services. Alcohol/substance abuse counseling, career counseling, student employment services, financial aid counseling, minority student services, personal counseling, placement for graduates, veterans' counselor. **Physically disabled:** Services for visually, speech, hearing impaired. **Transfer:** Special adviser, orientation, pre-admission transcript evaluation for new students. Transfer adviser, college fairs on campus for students transferring to 4-year colleges.

Contact. E-mail: wsc.admission@wsc.nodak.edu
Phone: (701) 774-4210 Toll-free number: (888) 863-9455
Fax: (701) 774-4211
Jan Solem, Director for Admission & Records, Williston State College, 1410 University Avenue, Williston, ND 58802-1326

Ohio

Academy of Court Reporting
Cleveland, Ohio
CB code: 2173

- For-profit 2-year technical college
- Commuter campus in very large city

General. Accredited by ACICS. **Calendar:** Quarter.

Annual costs/financial aid. Tuition/fees (2005-2006): $8,985. Books/supplies: $1,500. Need-based financial aid available to full-time and part-time students.

Contact. Phone: (216) 861-3222
Director of Admissions, 614 Superior Avenue NW, Cleveland, OH 44113

Academy of Court Reporting: Akron
Akron, Ohio
CB code: 3250

- For-profit 2-year college of court reporting
- Commuter campus in small city

General. Accredited by ACICS. **Location:** 30 miles from Cleveland. **Calendar:** Continuous.

Annual costs/financial aid. Tuition/fees (2005-2006): $8,985. Books/supplies: $1,500. Personal expenses: $1,000.

Contact. Phone: (330) 867-4030
Director of Admissions, 2930 West Market Street, Akron, OH 44333

Academy of Court Reporting: Cincinnati
Cincinnati, Ohio

- For-profit 2-year business college
- Large city

General. Accredited by ACICS. **Calendar:** Quarter.

Contact. Phone: (513) 723-0520
830 Main Street, Suite 1000, Cincinnati, OH 45202

Academy of Court Reporting: Columbus
Columbus, Ohio
CB code: 3344

- For-profit 2-year junior college
- Commuter campus in very large city

General. Accredited by ACICS. **Calendar:** Continuous.

Annual costs/financial aid. Tuition/fees (2005-2006): $8,985. Books/supplies: $1,500.

Contact. Phone: (614) 221-7770
Director of Admissions, 630 East Broad Street, Columbus, OH 43215

Antonelli College
Cincinnati, Ohio
www.antonellic.com
CB code: 0611

- For-profit 2-year art and technical college
- Commuter campus in large city

General. Founded in 1947. Accredited by ACCSCT. **Location:** 55 miles from Dayton, 90 miles from Lexington, Kentucky. **Calendar:** Quarter.

Annual costs/financial aid. Tuition/fees (2005-2006): $11,585. Tuition and fees vary by program. Quoted tuition is an average.

Contact. Phone: (513) 241-4338
Registrar, 124 East Seventh Street, Cincinnati, OH 45202

Art Institute of Cincinnati
Cincinnati, Ohio
www.theartinstituteofcincinnati.com
CB code: 3181

- For-profit 2-year visual arts college
- Commuter campus in large city
- Interview required

General. Accredited by ACCSCT. **Enrollment:** 121 degree-seeking undergraduates. **Degrees:** 31 associate awarded. **Location:** 12 miles from downtown. **Calendar:** Quarter. **Full-time faculty:** 8 total; 50% have terminal degrees, 25% women. **Part-time faculty:** 5 total; 100% have terminal degrees. **Class size:** 100% 20-39.

Student profile. Among degree-seeking undergraduates, 31 enrolled as first-time, first-year students.

Basis for selection. Admission determined by applicant's artistic ability. Portfolio, letter of recommendation from art teacher required. **Homeschooled:** Portfolio presentation of at least 10 pieces of art with variety of media and subject matter.

High school preparation. Required and recommended units include English 2-3, mathematics 1, social studies 1, history 1, science 1 and foreign language 1.

2005-2006 Annual costs. Tuition/fees: $15,304. Books/supplies: $3,029.

2004-2005 Financial aid. Non-need-based: Scholarships awarded for academics, art.

Application procedures. Admission: Closing date 8/30 (receipt date). $25 fee. Application must be submitted on paper. Admission notification on a rolling basis. Must reply by 8/30. **Financial aid:** No deadline. FAFSA required. Applicants notified on a rolling basis starting 9/1; must reply within 1 week(s) of notification.

Academics. Credit/placement by examination: CLEP.

Majors. Computer sciences: Computer graphics. **Visual/performing arts:** Design.

Computing on campus. Online library available.

Student life. Freshman orientation: Mandatory. **Policies:** Freshmen permitted cars on campus.

Student services. Financial aid counseling, placement for graduates. **Transfer:** Orientation, pre-admission transcript evaluation for new students.

Contact. E-mail: aic@theartinstituteofcincinnati.com
Phone: (513) 751-1206 Fax: (513) 751-1209
Cyndi Mendell, Vice President, Admissions, Art Institute of Cincinnati, 1171 East Kemper Road, Cincinnati, OH 45246

ATS Institute of Technology
Highland Heights, Ohio
www.atsinstitute.com

- For-profit 2-year technical college

General. Accredited by ACICS. **Calendar:** Quarter.

Annual costs/financial aid. Tuition and fees vary by program. Practical nursing program: $8,920 per year; $280 testing fee; $20 malpractice insurance fee; additional fees for uniforms, books and supplies.

Contact. Phone: (440) 449-1700
Academic Director, 230 Alpha Park, Highland Heights, OH 44143

Belmont Technical College
St. Clairsville, Ohio
www.btc.edu
CB code: 1072

- Public 2-year community and technical college
- Commuter campus in small town

General. Founded in 1969. Regionally accredited. **Enrollment:** 1,630 undergraduates. **Degrees:** 219 associate awarded. **Location:** 15 miles from Wheeling, West Virginia. **Calendar:** Quarter, limited summer session. **Full-time faculty:** 40 total. **Part-time faculty:** 115 total. **Class size:** 79% < 20, 20% 20-39, less than 1% 40-49, less than 1% 50-99.

Student profile.

Out-of-state:	15%	25 or older:	52%

Transfer out. Colleges most students transferred to 2005: Wheeling Jesuit University, Ohio University Eastern Campus, West Liberty State College.

Basis for selection. Open admission, but selective for some programs. Admission to registered nursing and LPN programs predicated on completion of remediation with grade of C or better and completion of selected general courses with C or better, based on COMPASS placement test scores. Applicants for paramedic program must take admissions test on campus. ACT scores accepted for placement if provided. Interview required for nursing and paramedic applicants, recommended for all others. **Adult students:** Entrance exam policies same as for first-time freshmen.

2005-2006 Annual costs. Tuition/fees: $3,555; $6,255 out-of-state. Per-credit charge: $79 in-state; $139 out-of-state. Books/supplies: $600.

Financial aid. Need-based: Need-based aid available for part-time students. **Non-need-based:** Scholarships awarded for state residency.

Application procedures. Admission: No deadline. No application fee. Admission notification on a rolling basis. **Financial aid:** No deadline. FAFSA required. Applicants notified on a rolling basis starting 6/1; must reply within 2 week(s) of notification.

Academics. Special study options: Cross-registration, distance learning, double major, dual enrollment of high school students, internships, student-designed major, weekend college. **Credit/placement by examination:** CLEP, institutional tests. **Support services:** GED test center, learning center, reduced course load, remedial instruction, tutoring.

Majors. Business: General, accounting, office/clerical. **Computer sciences:** General, computer graphics, programming. **Education:** Early childhood. **Engineering:** Civil, electrical. **Health:** EMT paramedic, health services, medical assistant, nursing (RN). **Interdisciplinary:** Historic preservation. **Mechanic/repair:** Heating/ac/refrig.

Most popular majors. Business/marketing 16%, computer/information sciences 13%, engineering/engineering technologies 22%, health sciences 38%, legal studies 8%.

Computing on campus. 250 workstations in library, computer center, student center. Wireless network available.

Student life. Freshman orientation: Available. Preregistration for classes offered. **Policies:** Freshmen permitted cars on campus. **Activities:** Phi Theta Kappa.

Student services. Adult student services, career counseling, student employment services, on-campus daycare, personal counseling, placement for graduates, veterans' counselor. **Physically disabled:** Services for visually, hearing impaired. **Transfer:** Special adviser, orientation, pre-admission transcript evaluation for new students. Transfer adviser, college fairs on campus for students transferring to 4-year colleges.

Contact. E-mail: info@btc.edu
Phone: (740) 695-9500 ext. 1158 Fax: (740) 699-3049
Timothy Houston, Dean of Student Services, Belmont Technical College, 120 Fox Shannon Place, St. Clairsville, OH 43950

Bohecker College

Ravenna, Ohio
www.boheckers.com **CB code: 2195**

- For-profit 2-year business college
- Large town

General. Accredited by ACICS. **Calendar:** Five 10-week sessions per calendar year.

Annual costs/financial aid. Tuition/fees (2005-2006): $9,120. Need-based financial aid available to full-time and part-time students.

Contact. Phone: (330) 297-7319
Director of Admissions, 326 East Main Street, Ravenna, OH 44266

Bowling Green State University: Firelands College

Huron, Ohio
www.firelands.bgsu.edu **CB code: 0749**

- Public 2-year branch campus college
- Commuter campus in small town

General. Founded in 1967. Regionally accredited. Some graduate courses (primarily in education) and some upper-division courses offered. Upper-division program in nursing available for registered nurses who hold associate degree or have completed 3-year diploma program. Satellite associate degree registered nursing program from Lorain County Community College. Upper division programs available in liberal studies, general studies in business, applied health science, early childhood studies, criminal justice, manufacturing technology, visual communication technology. **Enrollment:** 2,055 degree-seeking undergraduates. **Degrees:** 113 associate awarded. **Location:** 50 miles from Cleveland, 60 miles from Toledo. **Calendar:** Semester, limited summer session. **Full-time faculty:** 43 total; 56% have terminal degrees, 12% minority, 49% women. **Part-time faculty:** 65 total; 15% have terminal degrees, 3% minority, 54% women. **Class size:** 52% < 20, 47% 20-39, less than 1% 40-49, less than 1% 50-99. **Special facilities:** Arboretum.

Basis for selection. Open admission. ACT or SAT scores recommended of students who graduated from high school within the last 3 years. However, no minimum score required. If ACT or SAT not available, COMPASS test administered to determine placement.

High school preparation. 16 units recommended. Recommended units include English 4, mathematics 3, social studies 3, science 3 (laboratory 2) and foreign language 2. One visual or performing arts recommended.

2005-2006 Annual costs. Tuition/fees: $4,098; $11,406 out-of-state. Per-credit charge: $201 in-state; $550 out-of-state. Books/supplies: $728. Personal expenses: $2,026.

2005-2006 Financial aid. All financial aid based on need. 28% of total undergraduate aid awarded as scholarships/grants, 72% as loans/jobs. Need-based aid available for part-time students. Work study available for part-time students. **Additional information:** Scholarship application deadline May 1. Technology computer loan program available. Based on need, students may receive computer on semester by semester loan basis.

Application procedures. Admission: Priority date 2/1; deadline 7/15 (receipt date). $40 fee, may be waived for applicants with need. Application may be submitted online. Admission notification on a rolling basis. **Financial aid:** Priority date 3/1; no closing date. FAFSA required. Applicants notified on a rolling basis starting 4/15; must reply within 2 week(s) of notification.

Academics. Special study options: Cross-registration, distance learning, dual enrollment of high school students, independent study, internships, liberal arts/career combination, student-designed major, teacher certification program. Satellite associate degree registered nurse program from Lorain County Community College. Bachelor's degree programs available on campus. License preparation in nursing. **Credit/placement by examination:** AP, CLEP, SAT, ACT, institutional tests. 15 credit hours maximum toward associate degree. **Support services:** Learning center, reduced course load, remedial instruction, tutoring.

Majors. Business: General, accounting, administrative services, business admin, operations. **Communications technology:** General. **Computer sciences:** Programming. **Engineering:** Electrical. **Engineering technology:** General, computer, electrical, manufacturing. **Health:** Medical radiologic technology/radiation therapy, medical records technology, nursing (RN), respiratory therapy technology. **Interdisciplinary:** Biological/physical sciences. **Liberal arts:** Arts/sciences. **Protective services:** Criminal justice. **Public administration:** Human services. **Social sciences:** General.

Most popular majors. Business/marketing 6%, engineering/engineering technologies 7%, health sciences 16%, liberal arts 61%, security/protective services 6%.

Computing on campus. 300 workstations in library, computer center. Commuter students can connect to campus network. Online library, helpline, wireless network available.

Student life. Freshman orientation: Available. **Activities:** Drama, student government, allied health club, Campus Fellowship, theater group, writing center, Model United Nations, Peace and Justice club, virtual communication technology organization, women's resource group.

Athletics. Intramural: Basketball, football (non-tackle) M, table tennis, volleyball.

Student services. Adult student services, career counseling, student employment services, financial aid counseling, personal counseling, placement for graduates. **Physically disabled:** Services for visually, hearing impaired. **Transfer:** Special adviser, orientation for new students. Transfer adviser, college fairs on campus for students transferring to 4-year colleges.

Contact. E-mail: fireadm@bgsu.edu
Phone: (419) 433-5560 ext. 20607 Fax: (419) 372-0604
Debralee Divers, Director of Admissions and Financial Aid, Bowling Green State University: Firelands College, One University Drive, Huron, OH 44839

Bradford School
Columbus, Ohio
www.bradfordschoolcolumbus.edu **CB code: 3952**

- For-profit 2-year business and technical college
- Commuter campus in very large city
- Interview required

General. Founded in 1911. Accredited by ACICS. **Enrollment:** 429 degree-seeking undergraduates. **Degrees:** 80 associate awarded. **Location:** 10 minutes from downtown. **Calendar:** Semester, extensive summer session. **Full-time faculty:** 9 total; 67% have terminal degrees, 11% minority, 67% women. **Part-time faculty:** 5 total; 100% have terminal degrees, 20% minority, 80% women.

Student profile. Among degree-seeking undergraduates, 100% enrolled in a vocational program, 429 enrolled as first-time, first-year students.

Women:	78%	**Asian American:**	1%
African American:	29%	**Live on campus:**	51%

Basis for selection. Interview required to ensure interest in business or health care education. Student conditionally accepted based on high school transcript. Final transcript requested upon graduation.

2006-2007 Annual costs. Tuition/fees (projected): $12,180. Room only: $5,600.

Financial aid. All financial aid based on need.

Application procedures. Admission: No deadline. $50 fee. Application may be submitted online. Admission notification on a rolling basis. **Financial aid:** No deadline. FAFSA required. Applicants notified on a rolling basis.

Academics. Special study options: Internships. **Credit/placement by examination:** CLEP.

Majors. Business: Accounting, office management. **Computer sciences:** LAN/WAN management, programming. **Health:** Veterinary technology/assistant. **Legal studies:** Legal secretary, paralegal.

Computing on campus. 110 workstations in library, computer center. Dormitories wired for high-speed internet access.

Student life. Freshman orientation: Mandatory. **Policies:** Freshmen permitted cars on campus. **Housing:** Single-sex dorms available. $100 nonrefundable deposit, deadline 3/1. **Activities:** Student government.

Student services. Career counseling, financial aid counseling, personal counseling, placement for graduates.

Contact. E-mail: bradfordcols@bradfordschoolcolumbus.edu
Phone: (614) 416-6200 Toll-free number: (800) 678-7981
Fax: (614) 416-6210
Raeann Lee, Director of Admissions, Bradford School, 2469 Stelzer Road, Columbus, OH 43219

Brown Mackie College: Akron
Akron, Ohio
www.brownmackie.edu **CB code: 3266**

- For-profit 2-year business college
- Commuter campus in small city

General. Accredited by ACICS. **Enrollment:** 521 degree-seeking undergraduates. **Degrees:** 128 associate awarded. **Calendar:** Quarter. **Full-time faculty:** 8 total. **Part-time faculty:** 17 total.

Student profile. Among degree-seeking undergraduates, 318 enrolled as first-time, first-year students.

Women:	83%	**Hispanic American:**	1%
African American:	44%	**Native American:**	1%

Basis for selection. Open admission.

2005-2006 Annual costs. Tuition/fees: $8,535. Per-credit charge: $179. Books/supplies: $1,000. Personal expenses: $2,664.

Application procedures. Admission: No deadline. No application fee. **Financial aid:** No deadline.

Academics. Credit/placement by examination: CLEP. **Support services:** Tutoring.

Majors. Business: Accounting, business admin, office technology. **Computer sciences:** Networking, programming. **Engineering:** Electrical. **Engineering technology:** Drafting. **Health:** Medical assistant, pharmacy assistant. **Legal studies:** Paralegal. **Protective services:** Law enforcement admin.

Computing on campus. 101 workstations in library, computer center.

Student services. Career counseling, financial aid counseling, personal counseling, placement for graduates.

Contact. Phone: (330) 733-8766 Fax: (330) 733-5853
Tanya Foose, Director of Admissions, Brown Mackie College: Akron, 2791 Mogadore Road, Akron, OH 44312

Brown Mackie College: Cincinnati
Cincinnati, Ohio
www.brownmackie.edu **CB code: 0297**

- For-profit 2-year business and nursing college
- Commuter campus in large city

General. Founded in 1927. Accredited by ACICS. **Location:** 10 miles from downtown. **Calendar:** Quarter.

Annual costs/financial aid. Tuition/fees (2005-2006): $8,035. Books/supplies: $675. Need-based financial aid available to full-time and part-time students.

Contact. Phone: (513) 771-2424
Director of Admissions, 1011 Glendale-Milford Road, Cincinnati, OH 45215

Brown Mackie College: Findlay
Findlay, Ohio
www.socaec.com

- For-profit 2-year community college
- Commuter campus

General. Accredited by ACICS. **Calendar:** Continuous.

Annual costs/financial aid. Tuition/fees (2005-2006): $8,035.

Contact. Phone: (419) 423-2211
Admissions Director, 1700 Fostoria Avenue, Suite 100, Findlay, OH 45840

Brown Mackie College: North Canton
North Canton, Ohio

- For-profit 2-year business college
- Commuter campus

General. Accredited by ACICS. **Calendar:** Continuous.

Annual costs/financial aid. Tuition is $156 per credit hour and fees are $10 per credit hour.

Contact. Phone: (888) 300-9277
Director of Admissions, 1320 West Maple Street, North Canton, OH 44720

Bryant & Stratton College: Cleveland
Cleveland, Ohio
www.bryantstratton.edu **CB code: 0814**

- For-profit 2-year technical college
- Commuter campus in very large city
- Interview required

General. Founded in 1929. Candidate for regional accreditation; also accredited by ACCSCT. **Enrollment:** 254 degree-seeking undergraduates. **Degrees:** 9 bachelor's, 36 associate awarded. **Location:** Downtown. **Calendar:** Trimester, extensive summer session. **Full-time faculty:** 8 total. **Part-time faculty:** 26 total. **Class size:** 79% < 20, 21% 20-39.

Transfer out. Colleges most students transferred to 2005: ITT Technical Institute, Cuyahoga Community College, Myer University, Cleveland State University.

Basis for selection. Institutional test scores and interview most important. Passing scores on entrance exams required. CPAT entrance exam required. If ACT or SAT scores are high enough, they may be submitted in lieu of CPAT. **Adult students:** Entrance exam policies same as for first-time freshmen.

2005-2006 Annual costs. Tuition/fees: $11,820. Per-credit charge: $394. Books/supplies: $600. Personal expenses: $1,530.

2004-2005 Financial aid. Need-based: 65% of total undergraduate aid awarded as scholarships/grants, 35% as loans/jobs. Need-based aid available for part-time students. Work study available nights. **Non-need-based:** Scholarships awarded for academics.

Application procedures. Admission: No deadline. $25 fee. Application may be submitted online. Admission notification on a rolling basis. **Financial aid:** Priority date 9/1, closing date 10/31. FAFSA, institutional form required. Applicants notified on a rolling basis starting 5/1; must reply within 2 week(s) of notification.

Academics. Special study options: Distance learning, double major, independent study, internships, liberal arts/career combination. Bachelor's degree programs available on campus. **Credit/placement by examination:** AP, CLEP, institutional tests. 26 credit hours maximum toward associate degree. **Support services:** Learning center, reduced course load, remedial instruction, study skills assistance, tutoring, writing center.

Majors. Business: General, administrative services. **Computer sciences:** Information technology. **Engineering technology:** CAD/CADD, electrical.

Most popular majors. Architecture 38%, computer/information sciences 38%, engineering/engineering technologies 25%.

Computing on campus. 106 workstations in library, computer center. Online library available.

Student life. Freshman orientation: Available. Preregistration for classes offered. 3-hour session 1 week prior to start of semester. **Policies:** Freshmen permitted cars on campus. **Activities:** Literary magazine, student government, student newspaper.

Athletics. Intramural: Softball. **Team name:** Bobcats.

Student services. Adult student services, alcohol/substance abuse counseling, career counseling, student employment services, financial aid counseling, personal counseling, placement for graduates. **Transfer:** Special adviser, orientation, pre-admission transcript evaluation for new students. Transfer adviser, college fairs on campus for students transferring to 4-year colleges.

Contact. E-mail: stkampa@bryantstratton.edu
Phone: (216) 771-1700 Fax: (216) 771-7787
Shawn Kampa, Director of Admissions, Bryant & Stratton College: Cleveland, 1700 East 13th Street, Cleveland, OH 44114-3203

Bryant & Stratton College: Parma
Parma, Ohio
www.bryantstratton.edu **CB code: 0577**

- For-profit 2-year business and junior college
- Commuter campus in small city
- Interview required

General. Founded in 1854. Regionally accredited; also accredited by ACICS. On-line classes available. **Enrollment:** 329 degree-seeking undergraduates. **Degrees:** 6 bachelor's, 54 associate awarded. **Location:** 10 miles from Cleveland. **Calendar:** Semester, extensive summer session. **Full-time faculty:** 8 total; 100% have terminal degrees, 12% minority, 38% women. **Part-time faculty:** 26 total. **Class size:** 79% < 20, 21% 20-39. **Partnerships:** Formal partnerships with area businesses to offer apprenticeships, internships, industry-specific training.

Student profile. Among degree-seeking undergraduates, 135 enrolled as first-time, first-year students.

Part-time:	44%	**Hispanic American:**	13%
Women:	74%	**25 or older:**	50%
African American:	25%		

Transfer out. Colleges most students transferred to 2005: David N. Myers College.

Basis for selection. Interview and entrance test important; high school transcript preferred. Test of Adult Basic Education required for admission. Applicants with high school diploma or GED must take reading portion; others must take full test. Portfolio recommended. **Adult students:** Entrance exam policies same as for first-time freshmen.

2006-2007 Annual costs. Tuition/fees (projected): $11,820. Per-credit charge: $394. Books/supplies: $1,200. Personal expenses: $2,725.

2005-2006 Financial aid. All financial aid based on need. 35% of total undergraduate aid awarded as scholarships/grants, 65% as loans/jobs. Need-based aid available for part-time students. Work study available nights and for part-time students. **Additional information:** Competitive and matching scholarships offered to high school seniors.

Application procedures. Admission: No deadline. $25 fee. Application may be submitted online. Admission notification on a rolling basis. **Financial aid:** No deadline. FAFSA required. Applicants notified on a rolling basis starting 6/1.

Academics. Special study options: Cooperative education, distance learning, double major, dual enrollment of high school students, independent study, internships. Bachelor's degree programs available on campus. **Credit/placement by examination:** AP, CLEP. 30 credit hours maximum toward associate degree, 60 toward bachelor's. **Support services:** GED test center, learning center, remedial instruction, study skills assistance, tutoring.

Majors. Business: General, accounting, administrative services, sales/distribution. **Computer sciences:** Information systems. **Health:** Medical assistant, medical secretary. **Legal studies:** Legal secretary.

Most popular majors. Business/marketing 57%, computer/information sciences 29%, health sciences 14%.

Computing on campus. 71 workstations in library, computer center. Online library available.

Student life. Freshman orientation: Mandatory. Preregistration for classes offered. **Policies:** Freshmen permitted cars on campus. **Activities:** Student government, student newspaper.

Student services. Adult student services, career counseling, student employment services, personal counseling, placement for graduates. **Transfer:** Special adviser, pre-admission transcript evaluation for new students. College fairs on campus for students transferring to 4-year colleges.

Contact. E-mail: flnelly@bryantstratton.edu
Phone: (216) 265-3151 ext. 229 Fax: (216) 265-0325
F Nelly, Director of Admissions, Bryant & Stratton College: Parma, 12955 Snow Road, Parma, OH 44130-1013

Bryant & Stratton College: Willoughby Hills
Willoughby Hills, Ohio
www.bryantstratton.edu **CB code: 3251**

- For-profit 2-year business college
- Commuter campus in small town
- Interview required

General. Accredited by ACICS. **Enrollment:** 271 degree-seeking undergraduates. **Degrees:** 39 associate awarded. **Location:** 15 miles from downtown Cleveland. **Calendar:** Continuous, limited summer session. **Full-time faculty:** 7 total. **Part-time faculty:** 12 total. **Class size:** 98% < 20, 2% 20-39.

Transfer out. Colleges most students transferred to 2005: Cleveland State University, University of Phoenix, Myers University.

Basis for selection. Open admission. Student's evaluation and diagnostic tests must show qualification for at least pre-college, preparatory math and English courses. Applicants must complete institutional entrance evaluation, math, writing and computer diagnostic tests for placement. **Adult students:** Entrance exam policies same as for first-time freshmen. **Learning Disabled:** Students with learning disability must provide instructional effectiveness plan from high school counselor.

2005-2006 Annual costs. Tuition/fees: $11,820. Per-credit charge: $394. Books/supplies: $1,000. Personal expenses: $300.

2004-2005 Financial aid. Need-based: Need-based aid available for part-time students. Work study available for part-time students. **Non-need-based:** Scholarships awarded for academics.

Application procedures. Admission: Closing date 9/15 (receipt date). $25 fee. Application may be submitted online. Admission notification on a rolling basis. **Financial aid:** No deadline. FAFSA required. Applicants notified on a rolling basis.

Academics. ACTIVUM learning system facilitates students in developing technical and career-based skills through field trips, portfolio presentations, computer simulations and internship opportunities. **Special study options:** Distance learning, double major, dual enrollment of high school students, independent study, internships. Professional skills center offers medical coding courses and computer certification. **Credit/placement by examination:** AP, CLEP, institutional tests. 12 credit hours maximum toward associate degree. **Support services:** Remedial instruction, study skills assistance, tutoring.

Majors. Business: General, accounting, administrative services. **Computer sciences:** General.

Most popular majors. Business/marketing 28%, computer/information sciences 23%.

Computing on campus. 89 workstations in library, computer center. Commuter students can connect to campus network. Helpline, repair service available.

Student life. Freshman orientation: Mandatory. Preregistration for classes offered. Various 4-hour sessions over 1-2 days prior to start of each term. **Policies:** Freshmen permitted cars on campus. **Activities:** Student government, student newspaper, student council, Institute of Management Accountants, PC users group, campus ambassador society.

Athletics. NJCAA. **Intercollegiate:** Soccer M. **Team name:** Bobcats.

Student services. Adult student services, student employment services, financial aid counseling, placement for graduates. **Physically disabled:** Services for visually, speech, hearing impaired. **Transfer:** Special adviser, orientation, pre-admission transcript evaluation for new students. Transfer adviser for students transferring to 4-year colleges.

Contact. E-mail: stkampa@bryantstratton.edu
Phone: (440) 944-6800 Toll-free number: (800) 327-3151
Fax: (440) 944-9260
Melanie Johnson, Bryant & Stratton College: Willoughby Hills, 27557 Chardon Road, Willoughby Hills, OH 44092

Central Ohio Technical College

Newark, Ohio
www.cotc.edu **CB code: 7331**

- Public 2-year technical college
- Commuter campus in large town

General. Founded in 1971. Regionally accredited. Campus shared with Ohio State University: Newark campus. Off-campus evening classes are taught in Mount Vernon and Coshocton. Students can take classes at Ohio State Newark. **Enrollment:** 2,884 degree-seeking undergraduates; 167 non-degree-seeking students. **Degrees:** 314 associate awarded. **Location:** 45 miles from Columbus. **Calendar:** Quarter, limited summer session. **Full-time faculty:** 57 total; 4% minority, 63% women. **Part-time faculty:** 146 total; 6% minority, 57% women. **Class size:** 57% < 20, 42% 20-39, 2% 40-49, less than 1% 50-99.

Student profile. Among degree-seeking undergraduates, 427 enrolled as first-time, first-year students, 288 transferred in from other institutions.

Part-time:	52%	**Asian American:**	1%
Out-of-state:	1%	**Hispanic American:**	1%
Women:	73%	**25 or older:**	52%
African American:	7%	**Live on campus:**	1%

Transfer out. 19% of students enrolled in the transfer program go on to 4-year colleges. **Colleges most students transferred to 2005:** Franklin University, Mount Vernon Nazarene, Ohio State University.

Basis for selection. Open admission, but selective for some programs. High ACT scores may replace COMPASS placement tests. **Adult students:** Entrance exam policies same as for first-time freshmen. **Homeschooled:** Degree-seeking applicants must be 18 years or older and meet minimum scores on the COTC Compass test or ACT or meet COTC waiver eligibility of all 3 Compass tests due to applicant transferring from another college. Compass scores must be at least 32 on writing, 62 on reading and 25 on pre-algebra test. ACT of at least 14 in english and 15 in math.

High school preparation. 1 chemistry, 1 algebra and 1 biology required for medical sonography, nursing and surgical technology; 1 chemistry, 1 algebra, 1 math beyond algebra I, 1 biology required for radiographic.

2005-2006 Annual costs. Tuition/fees: $3,384; $5,634 out-of-state. Per-credit charge: $94 in-state; $169 out-of-state. Books/supplies: $1,179. Personal expenses: $2,115.

2004-2005 Financial aid. Need-based: 41% of total undergraduate aid awarded as scholarships/grants, 59% as loans/jobs. Need-based aid available for part-time students. **Non-need-based:** Scholarships awarded for academics.

Application procedures. Admission: Priority date 6/15; no deadline. $20 fee, may be waived for applicants with need. Application may be submitted online. Admission notification on a rolling basis. **Financial aid:** Priority date 3/1; no closing date. FAFSA required. Applicants notified on a rolling basis starting 5/1; must reply within 3 week(s) of notification.

Academics. Special study options: Cooperative education, double major, dual enrollment of high school students, ESL, internships, weekend college. License preparation in nursing, paramedic, radiology. **Credit/placement by examination:** CLEP, IB, institutional tests. 55 credit hours maximum toward associate degree. **Support services:** Learning center, reduced course load, remedial instruction, study skills assistance, tutoring.

Majors. Business: Accounting, administrative services, business admin, human resources. **Communications technology:** Desktop publishing. **Computer sciences:** Applications programming, data entry, web page design. **Education:** Early childhood. **Engineering technology:** Architectural drafting, CAD/CADD, civil drafting, electrical, electromechanical. **Health:** EMT paramedic, medical radiologic technology/radiation therapy, nursing (RN), sonography, surgical technology. **Protective services:** Criminal justice, forensics, law enforcement admin. **Public administration:** Human services, social work.

Most popular majors. Business/marketing 16%, computer/information sciences 6%, engineering/engineering technologies 8%, health sciences 52%, security/protective services 6%.

Computing on campus. 40 workstations in library, computer center. Commuter students can connect to campus network. Online course registration, helpline, wireless network available.

Student life. Freshman orientation: Mandatory. 3-hour program. **Policies:** Freshmen permitted cars on campus. **Housing:** Apartments available. **Activities:** Choral groups, drama, music ensembles, student government, student newspaper, Phi Theta Kappa, theatre arts association, student nurses organization, criminal justice club, rad tech club, Habitat for Humanity College Chapter, ski club, students in free enterpise.

Athletics. NJCAA. **Intercollegiate:** Baseball M, basketball, cross-country, golf, soccer M, softball W, volleyball. **Intramural:** Badminton, basketball, bowling, football (non-tackle), softball, table tennis, tennis, volleyball.

Student services. Career counseling, student employment services, financial aid counseling, on-campus daycare, personal counseling, placement for graduates, veterans' counselor. **Physically disabled:** Services for visually, speech, hearing impaired. **Transfer:** Special adviser, orientation for new students. Transfer adviser, college fairs on campus for students transferring to 4-year colleges.

Contact. E-mail: kquick@cotc.tec.oh.us
Phone: (740) 366-9222 Fax: (740) 366-5047
John Merrin, Coordinator of Admissions, Central Ohio Technical College, 1179 University Drive, Newark, OH 43055

Chatfield College

St. Martin, Ohio
www.chatfield.edu **CB code: 1143**

- Private 2-year community and liberal arts college affiliated with Roman Catholic Church
- Commuter campus in rural community

General. Founded in 1970. Regionally accredited. Third-year option: student can complete junior year at school through arrangements with several regional 4-year colleges. **Enrollment:** 280 degree-seeking undergraduates. **Degrees:** 33 associate awarded. **Location:** 40 miles from Cincinnati. **Calendar:** Semester, limited summer session. **Full-time faculty:** 5 total. **Part-time faculty:** 40 total. **Class size:** 95% < 20, 5% 20-39.

Transfer out. Colleges most students transferred to 2005: Wilmington College, Xavier University, Mount St. Joseph, Northern Kentucky University.

Basis for selection. Open admission. Interview recommended. **Adult students:** Entrance exam policies same as for first-time freshmen. **Home-schooled:** Official documentation of home school program required.

High school preparation. 16 units recommended. Recommended units include English 4, mathematics 3, social studies 3, science 3 and foreign language 2. Computer science recommended.

2005-2006 Annual costs. Tuition/fees: $8,740. Per-credit charge: $280. Books/supplies: $650. Personal expenses: $1,922.

Financial aid. Need-based: Need-based aid available for part-time students. Work study available for part-time students. **Non-need-based:** Scholarships awarded for academics, leadership. **Additional information:** Institutional grants/scholarships given primarily to first-year students to reduce debt load during initial year.

Application procedures. Admission: No deadline. $10 fee. Application may be submitted online. Admission notification on a rolling basis. **Financial aid:** Priority date 4/25, closing date 8/7. FAFSA, institutional form required. Applicants notified on a rolling basis starting 4/1; must reply within 2 week(s) of notification.

Academics. Special study options: Cooperative education, cross-registration, dual enrollment of high school students, independent study, internships, liberal arts/career combination. Cooperative programs leading to bachelor's in business and liberal studies with 2 local institutions. **Credit/placement by examination:** CLEP, institutional tests. **Support services:** Learning center, remedial instruction, study skills assistance, tutoring, writing center.

Majors. Business: Business admin. **Education:** Early childhood. **Liberal arts:** Arts/sciences. **Public administration:** Human services.

Computing on campus. 26 workstations in library, computer center.

Student life. Freshman orientation: Available. **Activities:** Student newspaper.

Student services. Adult student services, career counseling, financial aid counseling, personal counseling. **Transfer:** Special adviser, orientation for new students. Transfer adviser, college fairs on campus for students transferring to 4-year colleges.

Contact. E-mail: danac@chatfield.edu
Phone: (513) 875-3344 Fax: (513) 875-3912
Bill Balzano, Director of Advancement, Chatfield College, 20918 State Route 251, St. Martin, OH 45118

Cincinnati State Technical and Community College

Cincinnati, Ohio
www.cincinnatistate.edu **CB code: 1984**

- Public 2-year community and technical college
- Commuter campus in large city

General. Founded in 1966. Regionally accredited. **Enrollment:** 7,489 degree-seeking undergraduates; 981 non-degree-seeking students. **Degrees:** 896 associate awarded. **ROTC:** Army. **Location:** 5 miles from downtown. **Calendar:** Five 10-week terms. Extensive summer session. **Full-time faculty:** 187 total; 9% have terminal degrees, 13% minority, 54% women. **Part-time faculty:** 462 total. **Class size:** 37% < 20, 63% 20-39, less than 1% 50-99. **Special facilities:** Airport.

Student profile. Among degree-seeking undergraduates, 15% enrolled in a transfer program, 85% enrolled in a vocational program, 3% already have a bachelor's degree or higher, 1,947 enrolled as first-time, first-year students.

Part-time:	55%	**Asian American:**	1%
Out-of-state:	11%	**Hispanic American:**	1%
Women:	59%	**International:**	1%
African American:	26%	**25 or older:**	40%

Transfer out. Colleges most students transferred to 2005: University of Cincinnati, Northern Kentucky University, College of Mount St. Joseph, Xavier University.

Basis for selection. Open admission, but selective for some programs. Health technology programs require biology and chemistry courses to have been taken in last 7 years. COMPASS test required for placement. **Adult students:** Entrance exam policies same as for first-time freshmen. **Home-schooled:** Statement describing homeschool structure and mission, transcript of courses and grades required.

High school preparation. Specific course prerequisites for some programs.

2005-2006 Annual costs. Tuition/fees: $3,507; $6,912 out-of-state. Per-credit charge: $76 in-state; $151 out-of-state. Books/supplies: $1,500. Personal expenses: $1,200.

Financial aid. Need-based: Need-based aid available for part-time students. Work study available nights, weekends and for part-time students. **Non-need-based:** Scholarships awarded for academics, athletics, state residency.

Application procedures. Admission: No deadline. No application fee. Application may be submitted online. Admission notification on a rolling basis. **Financial aid:** Priority date 2/15; no closing date. FAFSA required. Applicants notified on a rolling basis starting 3/15; must reply within 4 week(s) of notification.

Academics. Special study options: Cooperative education, cross-registration, distance learning, double major, dual enrollment of high school students, ESL, honors, independent study, internships, student-designed major. License preparation in aviation, nursing, occupational therapy, paramedic, real estate. **Credit/placement by examination:** AP, CLEP, IB, institutional tests. 55 credit hours maximum toward associate degree. **Support services:** GED preparation and test center, reduced course load, remedial instruction, study skills assistance, tutoring, writing center.

Majors. Agriculture: Landscaping, turf management. **Business:** Accounting, administrative services, business admin, finance, hospitality admin, hotel/motel admin, international, marketing, office management, office/clerical, purchasing, real estate, restaurant/food services. **Communications technology:** Desktop publishing. **Computer sciences:** General, applications programming, networking. **Education:** Deaf/hearing impaired, early childhood. **Engineering technology:** Aerospace, architectural, automotive, biomedical, civil, computer, computer systems, construction, electrical, electromechanical, environmental, industrial, laser/optical, manufacturing, mechanical, plastics, surveying. **English:** Technical writing. **Family/consumer sciences:** Child care, institutional food production. **Foreign languages:** Sign language interpretation. **Health:** Clinical lab assistant, clinical lab technology, dietetic technician, EMT paramedic, massage therapy, medical assistant, medical records technology, nursing (RN), occupational therapy assistant, respiratory therapy technology, sonography, surgical technology, ward clerk. **Legal studies:** Legal secretary. **Liberal arts:** Arts/sciences. **Mechanic/repair:** Aircraft, automotive, computer. **Personal/culinary services:** Chef training, culinary arts, food prep, restaurant/catering. **Production:** Machine tool. **Protective services:** Firefighting. **Visual/performing arts:** Cinematography, commercial/advertising art.

Most popular majors. Business/marketing 20%, engineering/engineering technologies 21%, health sciences 22%, liberal arts 12%.

Computing on campus. 150 workstations in library, computer center, student center. Commuter students can connect to campus network. Online course registration, online library, helpline, wireless network available.

Student life. Freshman orientation: Available. 3-4 hour programs held during the day and in the evening before start of classes. **Activities:** Drama, student government, United African American Association, international students, Phi Theta Kappa, adult learners on campus, environmental club, students in free enterprise.

Athletics. NJCAA. **Intercollegiate:** Basketball, golf, soccer. **Team name:** Surge.

Student services. Adult student services, alcohol/substance abuse counseling, career counseling, services for economically disadvantaged, student employment services, financial aid counseling, on-campus daycare, personal counseling, veterans' counselor. **Physically disabled:** Services for visually, speech, hearing impaired. **Transfer:** Special adviser, orientation for new students. College fairs on campus for students transferring to 4-year colleges.

Contact. E-mail: adm@cincinnatistate.edu
Phone: (513) 861-7700 Fax: (513) 569-1562
Gabriele Boeckermann, Director of Admission, Cincinnati State Technical and Community College, 3520 Central Parkway, Cincinnati, OH 45223-2690

Clark State Community College
Springfield, Ohio
www.clark.cc.oh.us **CB code: 0777**

- Public 2-year community college
- Commuter campus in small city

General. Founded in 1966. Regionally accredited. **Enrollment:** 3,472 degree-seeking undergraduates. **Degrees:** 286 associate awarded. **Location:** 30 miles from Dayton, 45 miles from Columbus. **Calendar:** Quarter, limited summer session. **Full-time faculty:** 66 total; 24% have terminal degrees, 30% minority, 59% women. **Part-time faculty:** 443 total; 6% have terminal degrees, 5% minority, 47% women. **Special facilities:** Performing arts center.

Transfer out. Colleges most students transferred to 2005: Wright State University.

Basis for selection. Open admission, but selective for some programs. Nursing and allied health applicants must have high school chemistry; allied health must also have algebra or equivalent with grade of 2.0 or better. Mathematics placement test with score of 12 or better required for nursing.

High school preparation. 15 units recommended. Recommended units include English 4, mathematics 3, social studies 3, science 3 and foreign language 2. Chemistry required for nursing and medical technology. Algebra required for medical technology. 2 units mathematics required for engineering programs.

2005-2006 Annual costs. Tuition/fees: $3,308; $6,120 out-of-state. Per-credit charge: $74 in-state; $136 out-of-state. Books/supplies: $800. Personal expenses: $550.

Application procedures. Admission: No deadline. $15 fee. Application may be submitted online. Admission notification on a rolling basis. Early admission open to high school juniors and seniors. Placement test and high school approval required. High school GPA must be 3.0 or higher. **Financial aid:** Priority date 6/15; no closing date. FAFSA required. Applicants notified on a rolling basis.

Academics. Special study options: Accelerated study, cooperative education, cross-registration, distance learning, double major, dual enrollment of high school students, honors, independent study, internships, liberal arts/career combination, student-designed major, study abroad, weekend college. Bachelor's degree programs available on campus. License preparation in paramedic, physical therapy. **Credit/placement by examination:** AP, CLEP, institutional tests. 24 credit hours maximum toward associate degree. **Support services:** Learning center, pre-admission summer program, reduced course load, remedial instruction, tutoring.

Majors. Agriculture: Agribusiness operations, horticulture, landscaping, turf management. **Business:** General, accounting, administrative services. **Computer sciences:** LAN/WAN management. **Education:** Early childhood. **Engineering technology:** Civil, construction, drafting, manufacturing. **Health:** Clinical lab technology, EMT paramedic, nursing (RN), physical therapy assistant. **Interdisciplinary:** Biological/physical sciences. **Legal studies:** Court reporting, legal secretary. **Liberal arts:** Arts/sciences. **Protective services:** Corrections, law enforcement admin. **Public administration:** Social work. **Visual/performing arts:** Commercial/advertising art, theater design.

Computing on campus. Commuter students can connect to campus network. Online course registration, online library, helpline available.

Student life. Freshman orientation: Available. Preregistration for classes offered. **Activities:** Choral groups, dance, drama, student government, student newspaper, professional and technological fraternities and sororities, interfaith campus ministry, minority student forum, Phi Theta Kappa, social work club.

Athletics. NJCAA. **Intercollegiate:** Baseball M, basketball, softball W, volleyball W. **Intramural:** Basketball, tennis, volleyball. **Team name:** Eagles.

Student services. Campus ministries, career counseling, student employment services, health services, minority student services, on-campus daycare, personal counseling, placement for graduates, veterans' counselor. **Physically disabled:** Services for visually, hearing impaired. **Transfer:** Special adviser, orientation for new students. Transfer adviser, college fairs on campus for students transferring to 4-year colleges.

Contact. Phone: (937) 328-6028 Fax: (937) 328-3853
Director of Admissions, Clark State Community College, Box 570, Springfield, OH 45501

Cleveland Institute of Electronics
Cleveland, Ohio
www.cie-wc.edu **CB code: 0802**

- For-profit 2-year technical college
- Very large city

General. Founded in 1934. Accredited by DETC. Curriculum completed entirely through home study with no classroom attendance. **Enrollment:** 2,401 undergraduates. **Degrees:** 39 associate awarded. **Calendar:** Continuous. **Full-time faculty:** 3 total. **Part-time faculty:** 75 total.

Basis for selection. Open admission.

2006-2007 Annual costs. Tuition/fees (projected): $3,540. Tuition listed is for the Bachelor's program. The associate degree tuition is $1770 per 6 month term.

Application procedures. Admission: No deadline. No application fee. Application may be submitted online. Admission notification on a rolling basis. High school students permitted to enroll with signed approval of parents and guidance counselors (if students are minors). **Financial aid:** No deadline.

Academics. Special study options: Independent study. **Credit/placement by examination:** CLEP.

Majors. Engineering technology: Electrical. **Mechanic/repair:** Electronics/electrical.

Computing on campus. Online course registration available.

Student life. Activities: Student newspaper.

Student services. Student employment services, veterans' counselor.

Contact. E-mail: instruct@cie-wc.edu
Phone: (216) 781-9400 Fax: (216) 781-0331
Keith Conn, Admissions Director, Cleveland Institute of Electronics, 1776 East 17th Street, Cleveland, OH 44114-3679

College of Art Advertising
Cincinnati, Ohio
CB code: 3210

- For-profit 2-year visual arts college
- Commuter campus in large city
- Application essay, interview required

General. Accredited by ACCSCT. **Enrollment:** 20 degree-seeking undergraduates. **Degrees:** 5 associate awarded. **Calendar:** Quarter. **Part-time faculty:** 5 total; 20% have terminal degrees, 40% women.

Student profile. Among degree-seeking undergraduates, 2% enrolled in a transfer program, 2 enrolled as first-time, first-year students.

Out-of-state:	5%	**25 or older:**	30%
Women:	70%		

Basis for selection. Open admission. Admission decisions based on applicant's artistic ability, demonstrated by portfolio. Portfolio required. **Adult students:** Entrance exam policies same as for first-time freshmen. **Homeschooled:** Transcript of courses and grades, state high school equivalency certificate required.

2005-2006 Annual costs. Tuition/fees: $8,265. Books/supplies: $800.

Financial aid. Need-based: Need-based aid available for part-time students.

Application procedures. Admission: No deadline. $105 fee, may be waived for applicants with need. Admission notification on a rolling basis. **Financial aid:** No deadline. FAFSA required.

Academics. **Special study options:** Independent study. **Credit/placement by examination:** CLEP. **Support services:** Study skills assistance.

Majors. **Visual/performing arts:** Commercial/advertising art.

Computing on campus. 10 workstations in computer center. Online library available.

Student life. **Freshman orientation:** Mandatory. **Policies:** Freshmen permitted cars on campus.

Student services. Career counseling, services for economically disadvantaged, financial aid counseling, placement for graduates. **Transfer:** Special adviser, orientation, pre-admission transcript evaluation for new students. Transfer adviser for students transferring to 4-year colleges.

Contact. E-mail: neff@fuse.net
Phone: (513) 574-1010
Mark Henry, Campus Director, College of Art Advertising, 4343 Bridgetown Road, Cincinnati, OH 45211-4427

Columbus State Community College

Columbus, Ohio
www.cscc.edu **CB code: 1148**

- Public 2-year community and technical college
- Commuter campus in very large city

General. Founded in 1967. Regionally accredited. Courses offered at 10 off-campus centers. **Enrollment:** 15,268 degree-seeking undergraduates. **Degrees:** 1,450 associate awarded. **ROTC:** Army, Air Force. **Location:** 2 miles from downtown. **Calendar:** Quarter, extensive summer session. **Full-time faculty:** 269 total. **Part-time faculty:** 1,120 total. **Special facilities:** College-owned building for aviation maintenance program at Bolton Field Airport. **Partnerships:** Formal partnerships with local high schools.

Basis for selection. Open admission, but selective for some programs. Select applicant populations such as underage, international, felon, and dismissed transfer students may be required to submit documentation to determine admission status. Some technology programs have special admission requirements. English as a Second Language applicants required to complete ESL placement test. Placement testing required for all students who plan to take courses that have an English, math, and/or reading prerequisite. COMPASS required for placement. Interview required for chef apprenticeship and most health and human service techology programs. **Home-schooled:** Some academic programs may require completion of GED. Recommend completing COMPASS Ability to Benefit Placement Test if applying for financial aid. **Learning Disabled:** Students must provide documentation and register with Disability Services to receive services.

High school preparation. Algebra required for transfer programs and engineering, health, and business technology programs. Chemistry and biology required for health programs.

2005-2006 Annual costs. Tuition/fees: $3,420; $7,560 out-of-state. Per-credit charge: $76 in-state; $168 out-of-state. Books/supplies: $1,050. Personal expenses: $168.

2004-2005 Financial aid. **Need-based:** 62% of total undergraduate aid awarded as scholarships/grants, 38% as loans/jobs. Need-based aid available for part-time students. Work study available nights, weekends and for part-time students. **Non-need-based:** Scholarships awarded for athletics, state residency.

Application procedures. **Admission:** No deadline. $10 fee. Application may be submitted online. Admission notification on a rolling basis. Most health programs admit qualified students on space-available basis; students advised to apply early. **Financial aid:** Priority date 7/24; no closing date. FAFSA required. Applicants notified on a rolling basis starting 4/1.

Academics. **Special study options:** Cooperative education, cross-registration, distance learning, double major, dual enrollment of high school students, ESL, honors, independent study, internships, liberal arts/career combination, student-designed major, study abroad, teacher certification program, weekend college. License preparation in dental hygiene, nursing, paramedic, real estate. **Credit/placement by examination:** AP, CLEP, IB, institutional tests. **Support services:** GED preparation and test center, learning center, pre-admission summer program, reduced course load, remedial instruction, study skills assistance, tutoring, writing center.

Majors. **Architecture:** Landscape. **Business:** Accounting, administrative services, business admin, hospitality admin, hospitality/recreation, human resources, logistics, office management, office technology, office/clerical, purchasing, real estate, sales/distribution, tourism promotion, tourism/travel. **Communications technology:** General, graphic/printing. **Computer sciences:** Computer graphics, information systems, programming. **Conservation:** Environmental studies. **Construction:** Maintenance. **Education:** Early childhood. **Engineering technology:** Architectural, civil, construction, electrical. **Foreign languages:** Sign language interpretation. **Health:** Clinical lab assistant, clinical lab technology, dental hygiene, dental lab technology, EMT paramedic, health services, medical radiologic technology/radiation therapy, medical records technology, medical secretary, mental health services, nursing (RN), respiratory therapy technology, substance abuse counseling, surgical technology, veterinary technology/assistant. **Legal studies:** Legal secretary, paralegal. **Liberal arts:** Arts/sciences. **Mechanic/repair:** Aircraft, automotive, electronics/electrical, heating/ac/refrig. **Parks/recreation:** Facilities management, sports admin. **Personal/culinary services:** Culinary arts. **Protective services:** Corrections, firefighting, law enforcement admin, police science. **Transportation:** General.

Computing on campus. Commuter students can connect to campus network. Online course registration, online library, helpline available.

Student life. **Freshman orientation:** Available. **Policies:** Freshmen permitted cars on campus. **Housing:** Students may live in residence halls of other local colleges if space is available. **Activities:** Concert band, choral groups, dance, drama, literary magazine, music ensembles, musical theater, student government, student newspaper.

Athletics. NJCAA. **Intercollegiate:** Baseball M, basketball, cross-country, golf M, soccer M, softball W, volleyball W. **Intramural:** Basketball, bowling, football (non-tackle), soccer, softball, volleyball. **Team name:** Cougars.

Student services. Adult student services, alcohol/substance abuse counseling, career counseling, services for economically disadvantaged, student employment services, financial aid counseling, minority student services, on-campus daycare, personal counseling, placement for graduates, veterans' counselor. **Physically disabled:** Services for visually, speech, hearing impaired. **Learning disabled:** Comprehensive services available. **Transfer:** Special adviser, orientation for new students. Transfer adviser, college fairs on campus for students transferring to 4-year colleges.

Contact. Phone: (614) 287-2669 Toll-free number: (800) 621-6407 ext. 2669 Fax: (614) 287-6019
Tari Blaney, Director of Admissions, Columbus State Community College, 550 East Spring Street, Columbus, OH 43216-1609

Cuyahoga Community College: Eastern Campus

Highland Hills, Ohio
www.tri-c.cc.oh.us **CB code: 1978**

- Public 2-year branch campus and community college
- Commuter campus in large city

General. Founded in 1971. Regionally accredited. **Location:** 3 miles from Cleveland. **Calendar:** Semester.

Annual costs/financial aid. Tuition/fees (2005-2006): $2,300; $3,044 out-of-district; $6,230 out-of-state. Books/supplies: $900. Personal expenses: $1,504. Need-based financial aid available to full-time and part-time students.

Contact. Phone: (216) 987-2024
Interim Director of Admissions, 4250 Richmond Road, Highland Hills, OH 44122

Cuyahoga Community College: Metropolitan Campus

Cleveland, Ohio **CB member**
www.tri-c.edu **CB code: 1159**

- Public 2-year community college
- Commuter campus in very large city

General. Founded in 1963. Regionally accredited. Additional campuses in Highland Hills and Parma. **Enrollment:** 11,416 degree-seeking undergraduates; 13,942 non-degree-seeking students. **Degrees:** 1,561 associate awarded. **ROTC:** Navy, Air Force. **Location:** Downtown. **Calendar:** Semester, limited summer session. **Full-time faculty:** 294 total; 4% have terminal degrees, 20% minority, 52% women. **Part-time faculty:** 1,210 total; 6% have terminal degrees, 18% minority, 49% women. **Class size:** 58% < 20, 38% 20-39, 2% 40-49, 2% 50-99, less than 1% >100. **Special facilities:** Unified technology center to provide business training.

Student profile. Among degree-seeking undergraduates, 29% enrolled in a transfer program, 71% enrolled in a vocational program, 2,251 enrolled as first-time, first-year students, 1,653 transferred in from other institutions.

Part-time:	52%	**Hispanic American:**	4%
Women:	61%	**Native American:**	1%
African American:	30%	**International:**	2%
Asian American:	2%	**25 or older:**	52%

Transfer out. 49% of students enrolled in the transfer program go on to 4-year colleges. **Colleges most students transferred to 2005:** Cleveland State University, Baldwin-Wallace College, Kent State University, University of Akron.

Basis for selection. Open admission, but selective for some programs. Special requirements for some health technology programs (SAT or ACT required). English placement test required. **Adult students:** Entrance exam policies same as for first-time freshmen.

2005-2006 Annual costs. Tuition/fees: $2,300; $3,044 out-of-district; $6,230 out-of-state. Per-credit charge: $77 in-district; $101 out-of-district; $208 out-of-state. Books/supplies: $950. Personal expenses: $1,190.

2005-2006 Financial aid. Need-based: Average need met was 100%. Average scholarship/grant was $4,683; average loan $2,697. 79% of total undergraduate aid awarded as scholarships/grants, 21% as loans/jobs. Need-based aid available for part-time students. Work study available nights, weekends and for part-time students. **Non-need-based:** Scholarships awarded for academics, art, athletics, leadership, minority status, music/drama.

Application procedures. Admission: No deadline. No application fee. Admission notification on a rolling basis. **Financial aid:** No deadline. FAFSA, institutional form required. Applicants notified on a rolling basis starting 5/6.

Academics. Special study options: Cooperative education, cross-registration, distance learning, dual enrollment of high school students, ESL, honors, independent study. **Credit/placement by examination:** AP, CLEP, institutional tests. 30 credit hours maximum toward associate degree. **Support services:** GED preparation and test center, learning center, reduced course load, remedial instruction, study skills assistance, tutoring, writing center.

Majors. Agriculture: Horticulture. **Business:** General, accounting, administrative services, business admin, entrepreneurial studies, hospitality admin, management information systems, real estate. **Communications technology:** General. **Computer sciences:** General. **Education:** Early childhood. **Engineering technology:** Architectural, drafting, electrical. **Family/consumer sciences:** Child care. **Foreign languages:** Sign language interpretation. **Health:** Clinical lab technology, dental assistant, dental hygiene, dental lab technology, EMT paramedic, health services, medical assistant, medical records admin, medical records technology, nursing (RN), occupational therapy assistant, optician, pharmacy assistant, physical therapy assistant, surgical technology. **Legal studies:** Court reporting, paralegal. **Liberal arts:** Arts/sciences. **Mechanic/repair:** Automotive. **Personal/culinary services:** Culinary arts. **Protective services:** Corrections, fire safety technology, police science. **Visual/performing arts:** Commercial/advertising art, photography.

Most popular majors. Business/marketing 14%, health sciences 28%, liberal arts 40%.

Computing on campus. 750 workstations in library, computer center, student center. Online course registration, online library, helpline available.

Student life. Freshman orientation: Available. **Activities:** Bands, choral groups, dance, drama, musical theater, student government, student newspaper, Hillel, Afro-American Society, veterans service fraternity, Young Socialist Alliance, Student Coalition Against Racism, National Education Association, Hispanic club, Phi Theta Kappa.

Athletics. NJCAA. **Intercollegiate:** Baseball M, basketball, cross-country, soccer, softball W, track and field, volleyball W, wrestling M. **Intramural:** Baseball M, basketball, bowling, gymnastics, handball, racquetball, softball, tennis, volleyball, weight lifting. **Team name:** Challengers.

Student services. Adult student services, alcohol/substance abuse counseling, career counseling, student employment services, financial aid counseling, health services, minority student services, on-campus daycare, personal counseling, placement for graduates, veterans' counselor, women's services. **Physically disabled:** Services for visually, speech, hearing impaired. **Learning disabled:** Comprehensive services available. **Transfer:** Special adviser for new students. Transfer adviser, college fairs on campus for students transferring to 4-year colleges.

Contact. Phone: (216) 987-4200 Fax: (216) 696-2567
Kevin McDaniel, Director of Admissions, Cuyahoga Community College: Metropolitan Campus, 2900 Community College Avenue, Cleveland, OH 44115-2878

Cuyahoga Community College: Western Campus

Parma, Ohio
www.tri-c.edu **CB code: 1985**

- Public 2-year community college
- Commuter campus in small city

General. Founded in 1966. Regionally accredited. **Location:** 15 miles from Cleveland. **Calendar:** Semester.

Annual costs/financial aid. Tuition/fees (2005-2006): $2,300; $3,044 out-of-district; $6,230 out-of-state. Books/supplies: $900. Personal expenses: $1,504. Need-based financial aid available to full-time and part-time students.

Contact. Phone: (216) 987-5150
Director of Admissions and Records, 11000 Pleasant Valley Road, Parma, OH 44130

Davis College

Toledo, Ohio
www.daviscollege.edu **CB code: 2155**

- For-profit 2-year junior college
- Commuter campus in large city
- Interview required

General. Founded in 1858. Regionally accredited. **Enrollment:** 440 degree-seeking undergraduates; 11 non-degree-seeking students. **Degrees:** 70 associate awarded. **Location:** 6 miles from downtown, 45 miles from Detroit. **Calendar:** Quarter, limited summer session. **Full-time faculty:** 14 total; 86% women. **Part-time faculty:** 9 total; 11% have terminal degrees, 78% women. **Class size:** 76% < 20, 24% 20-39.

Student profile. Among degree-seeking undergraduates, 72 enrolled as first-time, first-year students, 155 transferred in from other institutions.

Part-time:	51%	**Women:**	85%

Transfer out. Colleges most students transferred to 2005: Lourdes College, Spring Arbor University, University of Toledo, Owens Community College, Monroe Community College.

Basis for selection. Character and personal qualities very important; CPAT test score, interview, talent and ability important. School and College Ability Tests (CPAT) required. Portfolio required for some graphic design degree programs. **Adult students:** Entrance exam policies same as for first-time freshmen. **Homeschooled:** State high school equivalency certificate required.

2006-2007 Annual costs. Tuition/fees (projected): $8,580. Per-credit charge: $225. Books/supplies: $1,275. Personal expenses: $1,840.

2004-2005 Financial aid. All financial aid based on need. 88 full-time freshmen applied for aid; 88 were judged to have need; 88 of these received aid. Average need met was 12%. Average scholarship/grant was $6,461; average loan $2,203. 46% of total undergraduate aid awarded as scholarships/grants, 54% as loans/jobs. Need-based aid available for part-time students. Work study available nights and weekends.

Application procedures. Admission: Closing date 9/1 (receipt date). $30 fee. Application may be submitted online. Admission notification on a rolling basis. **Financial aid:** No deadline. FAFSA required. Applicants notified on a rolling basis.

Academics. Special study options: Distance learning, internships, liberal arts/career combination. **Credit/placement by examination:** CLEP, institutional tests. 16 credit hours maximum toward associate degree. **Support services:** Reduced course load, remedial instruction, tutoring.

Majors. Business: General, accounting, accounting technology, administrative services, business admin, fashion, marketing, tourism/travel. **Computer sciences:** Database management, LAN/WAN management, web page design. **Health:** Insurance coding, medical assistant, medical secretary, medical transcription. **Legal studies:** Legal secretary. **Visual/performing arts:** Commercial/advertising art, interior design.

Most popular majors. Business/marketing 64%, computer/information sciences 7%, health sciences 14%, visual/performing arts 15%.

Computing on campus. 78 workstations in library, computer center.

Student life. **Freshman orientation:** Mandatory. **Activities:** Student newspaper.

Student services. Career counseling, student employment services, financial aid counseling, personal counseling, placement for graduates, veterans' counselor. **Transfer:** Special adviser, orientation, pre-admission transcript evaluation for new students.

Contact. E-mail: dstern@daviscollege.edu
Phone: (419) 473-2700 Toll-free number: (800) 477-7021
Fax: (419) 473-2472
Dana Stern, Senior Career Coordinator, Davis College, 4747 Monroe Street, Toledo, OH 43623

Edison State Community College

Piqua, Ohio
www.edisonohio.edu **CB code: 1191**

- Public 2-year community college
- Commuter campus in large town

General. Founded in 1973. Regionally accredited. **Enrollment:** 3,095 degree-seeking undergraduates. **Degrees:** 317 associate awarded. **Location:** 30 miles from Dayton. **Calendar:** Semester, extensive summer session. **Full-time faculty:** 39 total; 23% have terminal degrees, 3% minority, 44% women. **Part-time faculty:** 166 total; 8% have terminal degrees, 5% minority, 51% women. **Class size:** 62% < 20, 37% 20-39, less than 1% 40-49, less than 1% 50-99. **Partnerships:** Formal partnership with Tech Prep.

Student profile. Among degree-seeking undergraduates, 44% enrolled in a transfer program, 56% enrolled in a vocational program, 1% already have a bachelor's degree or higher, 321 enrolled as first-time, first-year students, 40 transferred in from other institutions.

Part-time:	64%	**Asian American:**	1%
Out-of-state:	1%	**Hispanic American:**	1%
Women:	64%	**25 or older:**	42%
African American:	2%		

Transfer out. **Colleges most students transferred to 2005:** Wright State University,Sinclair Community College.

Basis for selection. Open admission, but selective for some programs. Special admissions requirements for nursing and early childhood development programs. Degree-seeking students without recent ACT or SAT scores must complete COMPASS or ASSET for placement. **Adult students:** SAT/ACT scores not required. **Homeschooled:** State high school equivalency certificate required.

High school preparation. College-preparatory program recommended. Recommended units include English 4, mathematics 3, social studies 3, science 3 and foreign language 2.

2005-2006 Annual costs. Tuition/fees: $3,270; $6,060 out-of-state. Per-credit charge: $93 in-state; $186 out-of-state. Books/supplies: $1,300. Personal expenses: $756.

Financial aid. **Need-based:** Need-based aid available for part-time students. Work study available nights and weekends. **Non-need-based:** Scholarships awarded for academics, athletics.

Application procedures. **Admission:** No deadline. $20 fee, may be waived for applicants with need. Application may be submitted online. Admission notification on a rolling basis. **Financial aid:** Priority date 5/2; no closing date. FAFSA, institutional form required. Applicants notified on a rolling basis starting 5/15.

Academics. **Special study options:** Combined bachelor's/graduate degree, cross-registration, distance learning, double major, dual enrollment of high school students, independent study, internships, student-designed major, weekend college. Bachelor's degree programs available on campus. License preparation in nursing, real estate. **Credit/placement by examination:** AP, CLEP, institutional tests. 30 credit hours maximum toward associate degree. DANTES DSST and professional exams recommended by the American Council on Education are accepted. **Support services:** Learning center, pre-admission summer program, reduced course load, remedial instruction, study skills assistance, tutoring, writing center.

Majors. **Business:** General, accounting, administrative services, business admin, communications, executive assistant, finance, human resources, labor relations, logistics, marketing, office management, operations, real estate, sales/distribution. **Computer sciences:** General, computer graphics, information technology, networking, programming, web page design. **Education:** General, early childhood. **Engineering:** General, electrical, systems. **Engineering technology:** Computer, electrical, industrial, manufacturing, mechanical, mechanical drafting, plastics, quality control. **English:** Technical writing. **Family/consumer sciences:** Child care, child development. **Health:** Medical assistant, medical secretary, nursing (RN), prenursing. **Legal studies:** Legal secretary, paralegal. **Liberal arts:** Arts/sciences. **Mechanic/repair:** Electronics/electrical. **Production:** Welding. **Protective services:** Police science. **Public administration:** Human services. **Visual/performing arts:** Art, commercial/advertising art, design, dramatic.

Most popular majors. Business/marketing 20%, computer/information sciences 8%, engineering/engineering technologies 12%, health sciences 17%, liberal arts 28%, public administration/social services 6%.

Computing on campus. 300 workstations in library, computer center, student center. Commuter students can connect to campus network. Online course registration, online library, helpline, wireless network available.

Student life. **Freshman orientation:** Available. **Activities:** Drama, student government, Phi Theta Kappa, photo society, writers club, student ambassadors, theater group, international club, digital media club, arts league, society of human resource management, campus crusade for christ.

Athletics. NJCAA. **Intercollegiate:** Basketball, golf. **Team name:** Chargers.

Student services. Adult student services, career counseling, student employment services, financial aid counseling, health services, on-campus daycare, personal counseling, placement for graduates, veterans' counselor. **Physically disabled:** Services for visually, speech, hearing impaired. **Transfer:** Special adviser, orientation, pre-admission transcript evaluation for new students. Transfer adviser, college fairs on campus for students transferring to 4-year colleges.

Contact. E-mail: info@edisonohio.edu
Phone: (937) 778-7868 Toll-free number: (800) 922-3722
Fax: (937) 778-1920
Velina Bogart, Coordinator of Admissions, Edison State Community College, 1973 Edison Drive, Piqua, OH 45356-9253

EduTek College

Stow, Ohio
www.edutekcollege.com

- Private 2-year health science college
- Commuter campus

General. Accredited by ACICS.

Contact. Phone: (330) 677-4667
3855 Fishcreek Road, Stow, OH 44224

ETI Technical College of Niles

Niles, Ohio
www.eticollege.edu **CB code: 3149**

- For-profit 2-year technical college
- Commuter campus in large city
- Interview required

General. Accredited by ACCSCT. **Enrollment:** 323 degree-seeking undergraduates. **Degrees:** 76 associate awarded. **Location:** 50 miles from Cleveland and Pittsburgh. **Calendar:** Semester. **Full-time faculty:** 10 total. **Part-time faculty:** 10 total.

Basis for selection. Open admission, but selective for some programs.

2005-2006 Financial aid. **Need-based:** 69% of total undergraduate aid awarded as scholarships/grants, 31% as loans/jobs.

Application procedures. **Admission:** No deadline. $50 fee. Admission notification on a rolling basis.

Academics. **Special study options:** Internships. License preparation in real estate. **Credit/placement by examination:** CLEP. **Support services:** GED preparation, tutoring.

Majors. **Computer sciences:** Data entry, information technology, web page design, word processing. **Engineering technology:** Electrical. **Health:** Insurance coding, medical assistant, medical secretary, medical transcription. **Legal studies:** Legal secretary, paralegal.

Most popular majors. Computer/information sciences 24%, engineering/engineering technologies 11%, health sciences 46%, legal studies 20%.

Student life. Freshman orientation: Available. **Policies:** Freshmen permitted cars on campus. **Activities:** Student government, student newspaper.

Student services. Career counseling, financial aid counseling, placement for graduates.

Contact. E-mail: etiadmissionsdir@hotmail.com
Phone: (330) 652-9919 Fax: (330) 652-4399
Diane Marsteller, Director of Admissions, ETI Technical College of Niles, 2076 Youngstown Warren Road, Niles, OH 44446-4398

Gallipolis Career College

Gallipolis, Ohio
www.gallipoliscareercollege.com **CB code: 2469**

- For-profit 2-year business and technical college
- Commuter campus in small town
- Interview required

General. Accredited by ACICS. **Enrollment:** 157 degree-seeking undergraduates; 2 non-degree-seeking students. **Degrees:** 57 associate awarded. **Location:** 45 miles from Huntington, West Virginia, 45 miles from Charleston, West Virginia. **Calendar:** Quarter, extensive summer session. **Full-time faculty:** 2 total; 50% women. **Part-time faculty:** 13 total; 38% women. **Class size:** 88% < 20, 12% 20-39.

Student profile. Among degree-seeking undergraduates, 29 enrolled as first-time, first-year students.

Part-time:	5%	**Women:**	83%
Out-of-state:	20%	**25 or older:**	55%

Transfer out. Colleges most students transferred to 2005: University of Rio Grande.

Basis for selection. Open admission. Testing for counseling/placement purposes only. **Adult students:** Entrance exam policies same as for first-time freshmen.

2005-2006 Annual costs. Tuition/fees: $8,100. Per-credit charge: $180. One-time registration fee $50; fee for one hour lab $60 per quarter; fee for two hour lab $70 per quarter. Books/supplies: $1,400. Personal expenses: $4,000.

Financial aid. All financial aid based on need. Need-based aid available for part-time students.

Application procedures. Admission: No deadline. $50 fee. Application must be submitted on paper. Admission notification on a rolling basis. **Financial aid:** No deadline. FAFSA, institutional form required.

Academics. Special study options: Double major, independent study, internships. License preparation in real estate. **Credit/placement by examination:** CLEP, institutional tests. 16 credit hours maximum toward associate degree. **Support services:** Remedial instruction, tutoring.

Majors. Business: Accounting, administrative services, business admin. **Computer sciences:** General. **Health:** Medical secretary.

Most popular majors. Business/marketing 25%, computer/information sciences 38%.

Computing on campus. 32 workstations in computer center.

Student life. Freshman orientation: Available. Preregistration for classes offered. Held quarterly at 6:00 pm on the preceding Monday of the quarter start, lasts approximately one hour.

Student services. Career counseling, student employment services, financial aid counseling, placement for graduates. **Transfer:** Special adviser, orientation, pre-admission transcript evaluation for new students.

Contact. Phone: (740) 446-4367 ext. 12 Toll-free number: (800) 214-0452 Fax: (740) 446-4124
Jack Henson, Director of Admissions, Gallipolis Career College, 1176 Jackson Pike, Suite 312, Gallipolis, OH 45631

Good Samaritan College of Nursing and Health Science

Cincinnati, Ohio
www.goodsamaritancollege.com **CB code: 1259**

- Private 2-year nursing college
- Very large city
- SAT or ACT (ACT writing optional) required

General. Enrollment: 340 degree-seeking undergraduates. **Degrees:** 93 associate awarded. **Calendar:** Semester. **Full-time faculty:** 22 total. **Part-time faculty:** 7 total.

Basis for selection. Test scores very important. COMPASS and ATI-critical thinking used for advising only. **Adult students:** SAT/ACT scores not required if out of high school 5 year(s) or more.

2005-2006 Annual costs. Tuition/fees: $9,766. Per-credit charge: $315.

Application procedures. Admission: No deadline. $40 fee. Admission notification on a rolling basis.

Academics. Credit/placement by examination: CLEP.

Majors. Health: Nursing (RN).

Contact. E-mail: joan_dornette@trihealth.com
Phone: (513) 872-2743
Joan Dornette, Admissions Director, Good Samaritan College of Nursing and Health Science, 375 Dixmyth Avenue, Cincinnati, OH 45220

Hocking Technical College

Nelsonville, Ohio
www.hocking.edu **CB code: 1822**

- Public 2-year technical college
- Commuter campus in small town

General. Founded in 1968. Regionally accredited. Courses available at Perry Campus, New Lexington High School, Sauber Center, 5 prisons (classes available for inmates and employees). Courses also available online. Apprenticeship program with Ohio University and Great Oaks Career Center. Co-ops with several trade associations. **Enrollment:** 3,362 degree-seeking undergraduates; 1,082 non-degree-seeking students. **Degrees:** 703 associate awarded. **ROTC:** Army, Air Force. **Location:** 15 miles from Athens, 55 miles from Columbus. **Calendar:** Quarter, limited summer session. **Full-time faculty:** 192 total; 6% have terminal degrees, 2% minority, 51% women. **Part-time faculty:** 261 total; 3% have terminal degrees, less than 1% minority, 40% women. **Class size:** 59% < 20, 35% 20-39, 4% 40-49, 2% 50-99, 1% >100. **Special facilities:** Nature center, living history village, college-operated inn, land lab, firing range, burn building, college operated travel agency, early learning center, fish hatchery. **Partnerships:** Formal partnerships with local career centers.

Student profile. Among degree-seeking undergraduates, 1,165 enrolled as first-time, first-year students, 801 transferred in from other institutions.

Part-time:	25%	**25 or older:**	35%
Out-of-state:	3%	**Live on campus:**	12%
Women:	50%		

Transfer out. Colleges most students transferred to 2005: Ohio University, Rio Grande University.

Basis for selection. Open admission, but selective for some programs. Selective admissions to nursing program (based on test scores), physical therapist assistant program (based on grades), and radiologic and surgical/operating room technology (based on test scores and grades). Some programs have additional admission requirements. Interview recommended. **Adult students:** Entrance exam policies same as for first-time freshmen. **Home-schooled:** Applicants to health and public safety technology must have GED before classes begin. **Learning Disabled:** Documentation required for admission into Access Center - Office of Disability Services.

High school preparation. College-preparatory program recommended. Recommended units include English 4, mathematics 3 and science 3. 1 algebra, 1 biology highly recommended for recreation/wildlife and forestry applicants.

2005-2006 Annual costs. Tuition/fees: $3,348; $6,696 out-of-state. Per-credit charge: $93 in-state; $186 out-of-state. Books/supplies: $1,200. Personal expenses: $550.

2004-2005 Financial aid. Need-based: 955 full-time freshmen applied for aid; 754 were judged to have need; 754 of these received aid. 61% of total undergraduate aid awarded as scholarships/grants, 39% as loans/jobs. Need-based aid available for part-time students. Work study available nights, weekends and for part-time students. **Non-need-based:** Awarded to 623 full-time undergraduates, including 218 freshmen. Scholarships awarded for academics, minority status, state residency.

Application procedures. Admission: No deadline. $15 fee. Application may be submitted online. Admission notification on a rolling basis. **Financial aid:** Priority date 2/28; no closing date. FAFSA, institutional form required. Applicants notified on a rolling basis starting 4/15.

Academics. Alternative education programs available. Enrollment possible any day the college is in session. **Special study options:** Accelerated study, cooperative education, cross-registration, distance learning, double major, dual enrollment of high school students, ESL, independent study, internships, student-designed major, study abroad, weekend college. Bachelor's degree programs available on campus. License preparation in nursing, paramedic, physical therapy, radiology, real estate. **Credit/placement by examination:** AP, CLEP, institutional tests. 60 credit hours maximum toward associate degree. **Support services:** GED test center, learning center, pre-admission summer program, reduced course load, remedial instruction, study skills assistance, tutoring, writing center.

Majors. Agriculture: Equestrian studies. **Business:** General, accounting technology, administrative services, hotel/motel admin. **Computer sciences:** Networking, programming. **Conservation:** General, fisheries, forest management, management/policy, wildlife. **Education:** Teacher assistance. **Engineering:** Materials science. **Engineering technology:** Construction, drafting, electrical, energy systems, heat/ac/refrig. **Health:** Dietetics, EMT paramedic, massage therapy, medical assistant, medical records technology, nursing (RN), optician, physical therapy assistant. **Parks/recreation:** Sports admin. **Personal/culinary services:** Chef training. **Protective services:** Corrections, firefighting, police science. **Visual/performing arts:** Art, theater design.

Most popular majors. Business/marketing 15%, health sciences 27%, natural resources/environmental science 22%, security/protective services 15%.

Computing on campus. 863 workstations in dormitories, library, computer center, student center. Dormitories wired for high-speed internet access and linked to campus network. Commuter students can connect to campus network. Online course registration, online library, repair service available.

Student life. Freshman orientation: Mandatory, $10 fee. Preregistration for classes offered. Optional orientation week before fall classes begin; a half-day registration held in May to September. **Policies:** All students have full use of student center. Clubs must be sanctioned by college. Freshmen permitted cars on campus. **Housing:** Coed dorms, substance-free housing available. $100 deposit. **Activities:** Dance, drama, literary magazine, radio station, student government, student newspaper, Phi Theta Kappa, Kappa Beta Delta, SIFE, Unity Board, technology based clubs, Hocking Heights hall council, Campus Ministry.

Athletics. Intramural: Baseball, basketball, fencing, football (non-tackle), golf, soccer, softball, swimming, table tennis, tennis, volleyball, wrestling.

Student services. Adult student services, alcohol/substance abuse counseling, campus ministries, career counseling, student employment services, financial aid counseling, health services, legal services, on-campus daycare, personal counseling, placement for graduates, veterans' counselor, women's services. **Physically disabled:** Services for visually, speech, hearing impaired. **Transfer:** Special adviser, pre-admission transcript evaluation for new students. Transfer center, transfer adviser, college fairs on campus for students transferring to 4-year colleges.

Contact. E-mail: admissions@hocking.edu
Phone: (740) 753-7049 Toll-free number: (800) 282-4163
Fax: (740) 753-7065
Lynn Hull, Dean of Enrollment Services, Hocking Technical College, 3301 Hocking Parkway, Nelsonville, OH 45764-9704

Hondros College

Westerville, Ohio
www.hondros.edu **CB code: 3255**

- For-profit 2-year business and technical college
- Commuter campus in very large city

General. Accredited by ACICS. **Location:** 10 miles from Columbus. **Calendar:** Quarter.

Annual costs/financial aid. Tuition/fees (projected): $6,009. Per-credit-hour charges vary by program. Books/supplies: $850.

Contact. Phone: (614) 508-6252
Manager, Degree Admissions & Advising, 4140 Executive Parkway, Westerville, OH 43081-3855

International College of Broadcasting

Dayton, Ohio
www.icbcollege.com **CB code: 3047**

- For-profit 2-year technical college
- Commuter campus in small city

General. Accredited by ACCSCT. **Enrollment:** 120 degree-seeking undergraduates. **Degrees:** 37 associate awarded. **Location:** 50 miles from Cincinnati, 70 miles from Columbus. **Calendar:** Semester, limited summer session. **Full-time faculty:** 10 total. **Part-time faculty:** 4 total.

Student profile. Among degree-seeking undergraduates, 97 transferred in from other institutions.

Out-of-state:	3%	**25 or older:**	20%

Basis for selection. Tour of the campus and interview required before admission.

2006-2007 Annual costs. Tuition/fees (projected): $8,235. Per-credit charge: $268. Personal expenses: $2,862.

Financial aid. Need-based: Need-based aid available for part-time students.

Application procedures. Admission: No deadline. No application fee. **Financial aid:** No deadline. FAFSA required. Applicants notified on a rolling basis starting 11/1.

Academics. Credit/placement by examination: CLEP. **Support services:** Reduced course load.

Majors. Communications: General. **Visual/performing arts:** General.

Computing on campus. Wireless network available.

Student life. Policies: Freshmen permitted cars on campus.

Contact. E-mail: zenaicb@aol.com
Phone: (937) 258-8251 ext. 202 Fax: (937) 258-8714
Aan McIntosh, Director of Admissions, International College of Broadcasting, 6 South Smithville Road, Dayton, OH 45431

ITT Technical Institute: Dayton

Dayton, Ohio
www.itt-tech.edu **CB code: 7312**

- For-profit 2-year technical college
- Commuter campus in small city

General. Founded in 1935. Accredited by ACICS. **Location:** 5 miles from downtown. **Calendar:** Quarter.

Annual costs/financial aid. Tuition varies by program, $260-$368 per credit hour.

Contact. Phone: (937) 454-2267
Director of Recruitment, 3325 Stop Eight Road, Dayton, OH 45414

ITT Technical Institute: Norwood

Norwood, Ohio
www.itt-tech.edu **CB code: 2739**

- For-profit 2-year technical college
- Commuter campus in large town

General. Accredited by ACICS. **Calendar:** Quarter.

Annual costs/financial aid. Tuition varies by program, $260-$368 per credit hour.

Contact. Phone: (513) 531-8300
Director of Recruitment, 4750 Wesley Avenue, Norwood, OH 45212

ITT Technical Institute: Strongsville

Strongsville, Ohio
www.itt-tech.edu **CB code: 2773**

- For-profit 2-year technical college
- Commuter campus in large town

General. Accredited by ACICS. **Calendar:** Quarter.

Annual costs/financial aid. Tuition varies by program, $260-$368 per credit hour.

Contact. Phone: (440) 234-9091
Director of Recruitment, 14955 Sprague Road, Strongsville, OH 44136

ITT Technical Institute: Youngstown

Youngstown, Ohio
www.itt-tech.edu **CB code: 0418**

- For-profit 2-year technical college
- Commuter campus in small city

General. Founded in 1967. Accredited by ACICS. **Location:** 60 miles from Cleveland, 60 miles from Pittsburgh. **Calendar:** Quarter.

Annual costs/financial aid. Tuition varies by program, $260-$368 per credit hour.

Contact. Phone: (330) 270-1600
Director of Recruitment, 1030 North Meridian Road, Youngstown, OH 44509

James A. Rhodes State College

Lima, Ohio
www.rhodesstate.edu **CB code: 0754**

- Public 2-year technical college
- Commuter campus in large town

General. Founded in 1971. Regionally accredited. **Enrollment:** 2,558 degree-seeking undergraduates. **Degrees:** 431 associate awarded. **Location:** 75 miles from Dayton, 75 miles from Toledo. **Calendar:** Quarter, limited summer session. **Full-time faculty:** 60 total; 12% have terminal degrees, 3% minority, 72% women. **Part-time faculty:** 160 total; 2% minority, 61% women. **Class size:** 66% < 20, 29% 20-39, 4% 40-49, 1% 50-99. **Special facilities:** Ford training center, child care center. **Partnerships:** Formal partnerships with Tech Prep/PSEOP, Ford Training Center, Lima City High School, Allen County Health Partners, Agile Manufacturing, and West Ohio Manufacturing Consortium.

Student profile. Among degree-seeking undergraduates, 201 transferred in from other institutions.

African American:	7%	**Native American:**	1%
Hispanic American:	1%	**25 or older:**	43%

Transfer out. Colleges most students transferred to 2005: Bowling Green State University, University of Toledo, Ohio State University, Wright State University, University of Miami.

Basis for selection. Open admission, but selective for some programs. Special requirements for health programs (ACT required); interview recommended. **Adult students:** SAT/ACT scores not required. **Homeschooled:** Transcript of courses and grades required. **Learning Disabled:** Students must self-disclose; accomodations are available.

High school preparation. Recommended units include English 4, mathematics 3, social studies 3 and science 3.

2005-2006 Annual costs. Tuition/fees: $3,951; $7,902 out-of-state. Per-credit charge: $88 in-state; $176 out-of-state. Books/supplies: $945. Personal expenses: $473.

Financial aid. Need-based: Need-based aid available for part-time students. Work study available nights, weekends and for part-time students. **Non-need-based:** Scholarships awarded for academics.

Application procedures. Admission: No deadline. $25 fee ($25 out-of-state). Application may be submitted online. Admission notification on a rolling basis. **Financial aid:** Priority date 4/1; no closing date. FAFSA required. Applicants notified on a rolling basis starting 5/1; must reply within 2 week(s) of notification.

Academics. Associate of technical studies degree program offered, integrating technology and business. **Special study options:** Cooperative education, cross-registration, distance learning, double major, dual enrollment of high school students, independent study, internships, liberal arts/career combination, student-designed major. License preparation in dental hygiene, nursing, occupational therapy, paramedic, physical therapy, radiology, real estate. **Credit/placement by examination:** AP, CLEP, institutional tests. 15 credit hours maximum toward associate degree. ASSET required for placement for all new students. Maximum 45 credit hours, 15 each from life experiences (non-academic learning); knowledge (by exam) and work training/experience. **Support services:** Learning center, pre-admission summer program, reduced course load, remedial instruction, study skills assistance, tutoring.

Majors. Business: General, accounting, administrative services, business admin, finance, management information systems, marketing, office management. **Computer sciences:** General, LAN/WAN management, networking, programming, security, web page design. **Education:** Early childhood. **Engineering technology:** General, civil, electrical, environmental, industrial, industrial safety, manufacturing, mechanical, quality control. **Family/consumer sciences:** Family/community services. **Health:** Dental assistant, EMT paramedic, medical assistant, medical radiologic technology/radiation therapy, medical secretary, nursing (RN), occupational therapy assistant, office assistant, phlebotomy, physical therapy assistant, radiologic technology/medical imaging, respiratory therapy assistant. **Legal studies:** Legal secretary, paralegal. **Protective services:** Corrections, law enforcement admin, police science. **Public administration:** Human services.

Most popular majors. Business/marketing 19%, computer/information sciences 15%, engineering/engineering technologies 12%, health sciences 30%, public administration/social services 7%, security/protective services 7%.

Computing on campus. 332 workstations in library, computer center. Commuter students can connect to campus network. Online course registration, helpline, repair service, student web hosting available.

Student life. Freshman orientation: Mandatory. Preregistration for classes offered. Orientation programs are held before each quarter begins; specific dates and times are mailed after application is made. **Policies:** Freshmen permitted cars on campus. **Activities:** Choral groups, drama, music ensembles, student government, academic area organizations, political party clubs, special interest clubs, campus ministry, fellowship and bible study.

Athletics. Intercollegiate: Golf M. **Intramural:** Baseball M, basketball, bowling, football (non-tackle), softball, volleyball. **Team name:** Barons.

Student services. Career counseling, student employment services, financial aid counseling, on-campus daycare, placement for graduates, veterans' counselor. **Physically disabled:** Services for visually, speech, hearing impaired. **Transfer:** Special adviser, orientation, pre-admission transcript evaluation for new students. College fairs on campus for students transferring to 4-year colleges.

Contact. Phone: (419) 995-8000 ext. 8311 Fax: (419) 995-8098
Traci Cox, Director of Admissions, Student Advising and Development, James A. Rhodes State College, 4240 Campus Drive, Lima, OH 45804-3597

Jefferson Community College

Steubenville, Ohio
www.jcc.edu **CB code: 2264**

- Public 2-year community and technical college
- Commuter campus in large town

General. Founded in 1966. Regionally accredited. **Enrollment:** 1,697 degree-seeking undergraduates. **Degrees:** 176 associate awarded. **Location:** 30 miles from Pittsburgh, Pennsylvania. **Calendar:** Semester, limited summer session. **Full-time faculty:** 33 total; 6% have terminal degrees, 3% minority, 70% women. **Part-time faculty:** 142 total; 1% have terminal degrees, 4% minority, 51% women. **Class size:** 78% < 20, 21% 20-39, less than 1% 40-49.

Student profile. Among degree-seeking undergraduates, 35% enrolled in a transfer program, 65% enrolled in a vocational program, 450 enrolled as first-time, first-year students.

Part-time:	46%	**Women:**	62%
Out-of-state:	17%		

Transfer out. Colleges most students transferred to 2005: Fransiscan University of Steubenville, Franklin University, West Liberty State College, Kent State University.

Basis for selection. Open admission, but selective for some programs. Special requirements for all allied health technologies programs. ACT required for admission to radiology, medical laboratory, medical assisting, and dental assisting technologies. **Homeschooled:** Final transcript showing successful home-school completion signed and dated by home-school principal required.

2005-2006 Annual costs. Tuition/fees: $2,550; $2,730 out-of-district; $3,450 out-of-state. Per-credit charge: $85 in-district; $91 out-of-district; $115 out-of-state. Residents of 5 neighboring West Virginia counties eligible for in-state, out-of-district tuition rates. Books/supplies: $700. Personal expenses: $400.

2004-2005 Financial aid. All financial aid based on need. 292 full-time freshmen applied for aid; 188 were judged to have need; 186 of these received aid. Average need met was 75%. Average scholarship/grant was $3,576. 99% of total undergraduate aid awarded as scholarships/grants, 1% as loans/jobs. Need-based aid available for part-time students. Work study available nights, weekends and for part-time students.

Application procedures. Admission: No deadline. $20 fee. Admission notification on a rolling basis. **Financial aid:** Priority date 7/1; no closing date. FAFSA, institutional form required. Applicants notified on a rolling basis starting 6/15.

Academics. Special study options: Distance learning, double major, dual enrollment of high school students, external degree, honors, independent study, internships, weekend college. License preparation in paramedic, radiology, real estate. **Credit/placement by examination:** CLEP, institutional tests. 42 credit hours maximum toward associate degree. **Support services:** GED preparation and test center, learning center, pre-admission summer program, remedial instruction, study skills assistance, tutoring.

Majors. Biology: General. **Business:** General, accounting, administrative services, banking/financial services, business admin, management information systems, office management. **Computer sciences:** General, applications programming, computer science, data processing, information systems, systems analysis. **Construction:** Maintenance, power transmission. **Education:** Early childhood. **Engineering:** General, science, systems. **Engineering technology:** Construction, drafting, electrical, manufacturing, robotics. **English:** English lit. **Family/consumer sciences:** Child care. **Health:** Clinical lab assistant, clinical lab technology, dental assistant, EMT paramedic, medical assistant, medical radiologic technology/radiation therapy, medical secretary, respiratory therapy technology. **Interdisciplinary:** Biological/physical sciences, math/computer science. **Legal studies:** Legal secretary. **Liberal arts:** Arts/sciences. **Mechanic/repair:** Electronics/electrical, industrial. **Physical sciences:** Chemistry, physics. **Protective services:** Police science. **Psychology:** General.

Most popular majors. Business/marketing 34%, engineering/engineering technologies 13%, family/consumer sciences 8%, health sciences 10%, liberal arts 27%, security/protective services 8%.

Computing on campus. 200 workstations in library, computer center.

Student life. Freshman orientation: Mandatory. **Housing:** Students may live in dormitory of local university on space-available basis. **Activities:** Drama, student government, student newspaper.

Athletics. Intramural: Baseball M, basketball, bowling, football (non-tackle), softball, table tennis, tennis, volleyball.

Student services. Adult student services, career counseling, student employment services, financial aid counseling, health services, on-campus daycare, personal counseling, placement for graduates, veterans' counselor. **Physically disabled:** Services for visually, hearing impaired. **Transfer:** Special adviser, orientation, re-entry adviser, pre-admission transcript evaluation for new students. Transfer center, transfer adviser, college fairs on campus for students transferring to 4-year colleges.

Contact. E-mail: cmascellino@jcc.edu
Phone: (740) 264-5591 ext. 106 Toll-free number: (800) 682-6553 ext. 106
Fax: (740) 266-2944
Chuck Mascellino, Director of Admissions, Jefferson Community College, 4000 Sunset Boulevard, Steubenville, OH 43952

Kent State University: Ashtabula Regional Campus

Ashtabula, Ohio
www.ashtabula.kent.edu **CB code: 1485**

- Public 2-year branch campus college
- Commuter campus in large town

General. Founded in 1958. Regionally accredited. Off-site courses available. **Enrollment:** 1,313 degree-seeking undergraduates; 204 non-degree-seeking students. **Degrees:** 114 associate awarded. **ROTC:** Army, Air Force. **Location:** 50 miles from Cleveland. **Calendar:** Semester, limited summer session. **Full-time faculty:** 44 total; 25% have terminal degrees, 9% minority, 52% women. **Part-time faculty:** 67 total; 8% have terminal degrees, 4% minority, 55% women. **Class size:** 61% < 20, 32% 20-39, 4% 40-49, 3% 50-99. **Special facilities:** Interactive television link with all county high schools.

Student profile. Among degree-seeking undergraduates, 267 enrolled as first-time, first-year students, 109 transferred in from other institutions.

Part-time:	49%	**Asian American:**	1%
Out-of-state:	1%	**Hispanic American:**	2%
Women:	70%	**Native American:**	1%
African American:	4%	**25 or older:**	49%

Transfer out. Colleges most students transferred to 2005: Lakeland Community College, Mount Union College, University of Akron, Edinboro University.

Basis for selection. Open admission, but selective for some programs. Special requirements for nursing, human services, physical therapy assisting progams. **Adult students:** Entrance exam policies same as for first-time freshmen.

High school preparation. 16 units recommended. Recommended units include English 4, mathematics 3, social studies 3, science 3 (laboratory 2) and foreign language 2. One art unit recommended.

2005-2006 Annual costs. Tuition/fees: $4,586; $12,018 out-of-state. Per-credit charge: $209 in-state; $547 out-of-state. Per-credit-hour charges for upper division classes are $227 in-state and $547 out-of-state. Books/supplies: $990. Personal expenses: $1,900.

2005-2006 Financial aid. Need-based: Average need met was 55%. Average scholarship/grant was $4,365; average loan $2,632. 41% of total undergraduate aid awarded as scholarships/grants, 59% as loans/jobs. Need-based aid available for part-time students. **Non-need-based:** Scholarships awarded for academics, alumni affiliation, art, athletics, job skills, leadership, minority status, music/drama, ROTC, state residency.

Application procedures. Admission: No deadline. $30 fee, may be waived for applicants with need. Application may be submitted online. Admission notification on a rolling basis beginning on or about 10/1. **Financial aid:** Priority date 3/1; no closing date. FAFSA required. Applicants notified on a rolling basis starting 3/15; must reply within 2 week(s) of notification.

Academics. Special study options: Accelerated study, distance learning, double major, dual enrollment of high school students, independent study, internships, liberal arts/career combination, student-designed major. Bachelor's degree programs available on campus. License preparation in nursing. **Credit/placement by examination:** AP, CLEP, institutional tests. 12 credit hours maximum toward associate degree. **Support services:** Learning center, remedial instruction, tutoring.

Majors. Business: General, accounting technology, administrative services. **Computer sciences:** Applications programming. **Education:** Early childhood. **Engineering technology:** Electrical, mechanical. **Health:** Health care admin, nursing (RN), physical therapy assistant, preop/surgical nursing. **Liberal arts:** Arts/sciences. **Protective services:** Criminal justice.

Most popular majors. Business/marketing 11%, computer/information sciences 9%, health sciences 50%, liberal arts 18%.

Computing on campus. 82 workstations in library, computer center. Online course registration, online library, helpline, student web hosting available.

Student life. Freshman orientation: Available. Preregistration for classes offered. **Policies:** Freshmen permitted cars on campus. **Activities:** Dance, drama, radio station, student government, student newspaper, world affairs club, social issues club.

Athletics. Intramural: Basketball, football (non-tackle), softball W, volleyball, weight lifting. **Team name:** Golden Flashes.

Student services. Adult student services, career counseling, student employment services, on-campus daycare, personal counseling, placement for graduates, veterans' counselor. **Physically disabled:** Services for visually impaired. **Transfer:** Special adviser, orientation for new students. Transfer adviser for students transferring to 4-year colleges.

Contact. E-mail: sanford@ashtabula.kent.edu
Phone: (440) 964-4217 Fax: (440) 964-4217
Kelly Sanford, Admissions Counselor, Kent State University: Ashtabula Regional Campus, 3325 West 13th Street, Ashtabula, OH 44004

Kent State University: East Liverpool Regional Campus

East Liverpool, Ohio
www.kenteliv.kent.edu **CB code: 0328**

- Public 2-year branch campus college
- Commuter campus in large town

General. Founded in 1965. Regionally accredited. **Enrollment:** 765 degree-seeking undergraduates; 53 non-degree-seeking students. **Degrees:** 83 associate awarded. **ROTC:** Army, Air Force. **Location:** 45 miles from Youngstown, 40 miles from Pittsburgh. **Calendar:** Semester, extensive summer session. **Full-time faculty:** 24 total; 29% have terminal degrees, 17% minority, 58% women. **Part-time faculty:** 46 total; 4% have terminal degrees, 6% minority, 54% women. **Class size:** 73% < 20, 26% 20-39, 2% 40-49.

Student profile. Among degree-seeking undergraduates, 121 enrolled as first-time, first-year students, 44 transferred in from other institutions.

Part-time:	56%	**Asian American:**	1%
Out-of-state:	2%	**Hispanic American:**	1%
Women:	75%	**25 or older:**	51%
African American:	4%		

Transfer out. Colleges most students transferred to 2005: Youngstown State University, Jefferson Community College, West Virginia Northern Community College, Hannah Mullins School of Nursing.

Basis for selection. Open admission, but selective for some programs. Special requirements for nursing, occupational therapy, and physical therapy applicants. ACT recommended for students under 21. Interview recommended. **Adult students:** SAT/ACT scores not required if applicant over 21.

High school preparation. 16 units recommended. Recommended units include English 4, mathematics 3, social studies 3, science 3 (laboratory 2) and foreign language 2. One unit algebra, 1 unit chemistry, 1 unit biology required for nursing applicants. One unit algebra, 1 unit biology required for physical therapy and occupational therapy. One art unit recommended for all.

2005-2006 Annual costs. Tuition/fees: $4,586; $12,018 out-of-state. Per-credit charge: $209 in-state; $547 out-of-state. Books/supplies: $550. Personal expenses: $1,315.

2005-2006 Financial aid. Need-based: Average need met was 52%. Average scholarship/grant was $4,173; average loan $2,632. 42% of total undergraduate aid awarded as scholarships/grants, 58% as loans/jobs. Need-based aid available for part-time students. Work study available for part-time students. **Non-need-based:** Scholarships awarded for academics, alumni affiliation, art, athletics, leadership, minority status, music/drama, ROTC, state residency.

Application procedures. Admission: Priority date 8/1; no deadline. $30 fee, may be waived for applicants with need. Application may be submitted online. Admission notification on a rolling basis beginning on or about 10/1. All new applicants must complete basic skills assessment tests. **Financial aid:** Priority date 3/1; no closing date. FAFSA required. Applicants notified on a rolling basis starting 3/15; must reply within 2 week(s) of notification.

Academics. Special study options: Accelerated study, distance learning, double major, dual enrollment of high school students, independent study, internships, student-designed major. License preparation in nursing. **Credit/placement by examination:** AP, CLEP, institutional tests. 14 credit hours maximum toward associate degree. **Support services:** Learning center, pre-admission summer program, reduced course load, remedial instruction, study skills assistance, tutoring, writing center.

Honors college/program. 3.5 GPA, 24 ACT, recommendation, interview, placement exam required. Various course offerings plus Freshman Year Colloquium to replace university composition requirement.

Majors. Business: General, accounting technology. **Computer sciences:** Applications programming. **Health:** Nursing (RN), occupational therapy assistant, physical therapy assistant. **Legal studies:** Paralegal. **Liberal arts:** Arts/sciences. **Protective services:** Criminal justice.

Most popular majors. Business/marketing 6%, health sciences 78%, legal studies 6%, liberal arts 6%.

Computing on campus. 114 workstations in library, computer center. Online course registration, online library, helpline, student web hosting available.

Student life. Freshman orientation: Available. Preregistration for classes offered. **Policies:** Freshmen permitted cars on campus. **Activities:** Literary magazine, student government, student newspaper.

Athletics. Team name: Golden Flashes.

Student services. Career counseling, student employment services, placement for graduates, veterans' counselor. **Learning disabled:** Comprehensive services available. **Transfer:** Special adviser, orientation for new students. Transfer adviser, college fairs on campus for students transferring to 4-year colleges.

Contact. E-mail: admissions@eliv.kent.edu
Phone: (330) 385-3805 Fax: (330) 382-7562
Nancy Dellavecchia, Director, Kent State University: East Liverpool Regional Campus, 400 East Fourth Street, East Liverpool, OH 43920

Kent State University: Salem Regional Campus

Salem, Ohio
www.salem.kent.edu **CB code: 0683**

- Public 2-year branch campus college
- Commuter campus in large town

General. Founded in 1962. Regionally accredited. **Enrollment:** 1,174 degree-seeking undergraduates; 76 non-degree-seeking students. **Degrees:** 15 bachelor's, 100 associate awarded. **ROTC:** Army, Air Force. **Location:** 25 miles from Youngstown, 40 miles from Canton. **Calendar:** Semester, limited summer session. **Full-time faculty:** 39 total; 38% have terminal degrees, 13% minority, 59% women. **Part-time faculty:** 49 total; 6% have terminal degrees, 4% minority, 63% women. **Class size:** 69% < 20, 29% 20-39, 1% 40-49, less than 1% 50-99. **Special facilities:** Writers' workshop, career planning center, science and mathematics lab, academic center.

Student profile. Among degree-seeking undergraduates, 204 enrolled as first-time, first-year students, 77 transferred in from other institutions.

Part-time:	47%	**African American:**	1%
Out-of-state:	1%	**Asian American:**	1%
Women:	72%	**25 or older:**	40%

Transfer out. Colleges most students transferred to 2005: Youngstown State University, Stark State College of Technology, University of Akron, Ohio State University, ITT Technical Institute.

Basis for selection. Open admission, but selective for some programs. Radiologic technology program requires 2.5 minimum GPA, completion of certain courses. Nursing program requires 2.5 minimum GPA. SAT or ACT required for admission to nursing, radiologic technology programs. **Adult students:** Entrance exam policies same as for first-time freshmen.

High school preparation. College-preparatory program recommended. 16 units recommended. Recommended units include English 4, mathematics 3, social studies 3, science 3 (laboratory 2) and foreign language 2. One visual or performing arts may be substituted for 1 foreign language.

2005-2006 Annual costs. Tuition/fees: $4,586; $12,018 out-of-state. Per-credit charge: $209 in-state; $547 out-of-state. Books/supplies: $700. Personal expenses: $1,500.

2005-2006 Financial aid. Need-based: Average need met was 52%. Average scholarship/grant was $3,285; average loan $2,557. 40% of total undergraduate aid awarded as scholarships/grants, 60% as loans/jobs. Need-based aid available for part-time students. **Non-need-based:** Scholarships awarded for academics, alumni affiliation, art, athletics, leadership, minority status, music/drama, ROTC.

Application procedures. Admission: Priority date 8/1; no deadline. $30 fee, may be waived for applicants with need. Application may be submitted online. Admission notification on a rolling basis beginning on or about 10/1. **Financial aid:** Priority date 3/1; no closing date. FAFSA required. Applicants notified by 3/15; must reply within 2 week(s) of notification.

Academics. Special study options: Accelerated study, distance learning, double major, dual enrollment of high school students, independent study, internships, liberal arts/career combination, student-designed major. Bachelor's degree programs available on campus. **Credit/placement by examination:** AP, CLEP, institutional tests. 24 credit hours maximum toward associate degree. **Support services:** Learning center, remedial instruction, study skills assistance, tutoring, writing center.

Honors college/program. 17 students admitted each year. Minimum 3.3 GPA and 23 ACT score required. Full tuition scholarships awarded renewable for 1 additional year.

Majors. Agriculture: Horticulture. **Business:** General, administrative services. **Computer sciences:** Applications programming. **Education:** Elementary. **Engineering technology:** Industrial. **Health:** Health care admin, medical radiologic technology/radiation therapy, nuclear medical technology. **Liberal arts:** Arts/sciences. **Protective services:** Criminal justice.

Most popular majors. Business/marketing 12%, computer/information sciences 11%, education 20%, engineering/engineering technologies 8%, health sciences 39%, liberal arts 8%.

Computing on campus. 118 workstations in library, computer center. Commuter students can connect to campus network. Online course registration, student web hosting available.

Student life. Freshman orientation: Available. Preregistration for classes offered. **Policies:** Freshmen permitted cars on campus. **Activities:** Choral groups, drama, music ensembles, student government, student newspaper, professional business and engineering clubs, art club, nontraditional student club, ski club, Women of Wonder, horticulture, criminal justice club, psychology club.

Athletics. Intramural: Basketball, racquetball, skiing, table tennis, tennis, volleyball. **Team name:** Golden Flashes.

Student services. Adult student services, career counseling, financial aid counseling, personal counseling, placement for graduates, veterans' counselor. **Physically disabled:** Services for visually, hearing impaired. **Learning disabled:** Comprehensive services available. **Transfer:** Special adviser, orientation for new students. Transfer adviser for students transferring to 4-year colleges.

Contact. E-mail: ask-us@salem.kent.edu
Phone: (330) 332-0361 Fax: (330) 332-9256
Michelle Schuster, Director, Enrollment Management and Student Services, Kent State University: Salem Regional Campus, 2491 State Route 45 South, Salem, OH 44460

Kent State University: Stark Campus

Canton, Ohio
www.stark.kent.edu **CB code: 0585**

- Public 2-year branch campus college
- Commuter campus in small city

General. Founded in 1946. Regionally accredited. **Enrollment:** 3,418 degree-seeking undergraduates; 266 non-degree-seeking students. **Degrees:** 124 associate awarded. **ROTC:** Army, Air Force. **Location:** 14 miles from Akron, 60 miles from Cleveland. **Calendar:** Semester, limited summer session. **Full-time faculty:** 88 total; 62% have terminal degrees, 9% minority, 49% women. **Part-time faculty:** 109 total; 11% have terminal degrees, 6% minority, 41% women. **Class size:** 41% < 20, 49% 20-39, 8% 40-49, 3% 50-99.

Student profile. Among degree-seeking undergraduates, 686 enrolled as first-time, first-year students, 245 transferred in from other institutions.

Part-time:	39%	**Asian American:**	1%
Women:	61%	**Hispanic American:**	1%
African American:	5%	**25 or older:**	29%

Basis for selection. Open admission, but selective for some programs. Special requirements for honors college, art, music, education, nursing, business. COMPASS test required for placement. Essay required for honors college, early admission; audition required for music programs; portfolio required for art programs. **Adult students:** Entrance exam policies same as for first-time freshmen.

High school preparation. 16 units recommended. Recommended units include English 4, mathematics 3, social studies 3, science 3 (laboratory 2) and foreign language 2. One unit of fine arts may be substituted for 1 unit of foreign language; math units should be in algebra I & II and geometry.

2005-2006 Annual costs. Tuition/fees: $4,586; $12,018 out-of-state. Per-credit charge: $209 in-state; $547 out-of-state. Books/supplies: $900. Personal expenses: $1,826.

2005-2006 Financial aid. Need-based: 458 full-time freshmen applied for aid; 379 were judged to have need; 379 of these received aid. Average need met was 52%. Average scholarship/grant was $3,076; average loan $2,668. 39% of total undergraduate aid awarded as scholarships/grants, 61% as loans/jobs. Need-based aid available for part-time students. Work study available for part-time students. **Non-need-based:** Awarded to 73 full-time undergraduates, including 26 freshmen. Scholarships awarded for academics, alumni affiliation, art, athletics, leadership, minority status, music/drama, ROTC, state residency.

Application procedures. Admission: No deadline. $30 fee, may be waived for applicants with need. Application may be submitted online. Admission notification on a rolling basis beginning on or about 10/1. Early admission available to high school juniors or seniors in top 15 percent of class with ACT of 24 or above and GPA of 3.4 or higher through Ohio PSEO Program. **Financial aid:** Priority date 3/1; no closing date. FAFSA required. Applicants notified on a rolling basis starting 3/15; must reply within 2 week(s) of notification.

Academics. Special study options: Accelerated study, distance learning, double major, dual enrollment of high school students, honors, independent study, internships, student-designed major. Access program for senior citizens, video conference advising. Bachelor's degree programs available on campus. **Credit/placement by examination:** AP, CLEP, institutional tests. 24 credit hours maximum toward associate degree. **Support services:** Learning center, reduced course load, remedial instruction, study skills assistance, tutoring, writing center.

Honors college/program. 3.2 cumulative high school GPA, essay, ACT Composite score of 24 required.

Majors. Liberal arts: Arts/sciences. **Protective services:** Criminal justice.

Most popular majors. Liberal arts 93%, security/protective services 7%.

Computing on campus. 145 workstations in library, computer center, student center. Commuter students can connect to campus network. Online course registration, online library, helpline, student web hosting available.

Student life. Freshman orientation: Mandatory. **Policies:** Freshmen permitted cars on campus. **Activities:** Bands, choral groups, dance, drama, literary magazine, music ensembles, musical theater, student government, political science forum, Interfaith Campus Ministry, Academy of Life Sciences, student education association, Pan African Student Alliance.

Athletics. Team name: Golden Flashes.

Student services. Campus ministries, career counseling, student employment services, financial aid counseling, personal counseling, veterans' counselor. **Physically disabled:** Services for visually, speech, hearing impaired. **Transfer:** Special adviser, orientation for new students. Transfer adviser for students transferring to 4-year colleges.

Contact. E-mail: admit@stark.kent.edu
Phone: (330) 499-9600 Fax: (330) 494-0301
Deborah Speck, Director of Admissions, Kent State University: Stark Campus, 6000 Frank Avenue NW, Canton, OH 44720-7599

Kent State University: Trumbull Campus

Warren, Ohio
www.trumbull.kent.edu **CB code: 0593**

- Public 2-year branch campus college
- Commuter campus in small city

General. Founded in 1954. Regionally accredited. **Enrollment:** 1,897 degree-seeking undergraduates; 139 non-degree-seeking students. **Degrees:** 101 associate awarded. **ROTC:** Army, Air Force. **Location:** 2 miles from downtown. **Calendar:** Semester, limited summer session. **Full-time faculty:** 58 total; 57% have terminal degrees, 17% minority, 34% women. **Part-time faculty:** 66 total; 15% have terminal degrees, 3% minority, 47% women. **Class size:** 57% < 20, 40% 20-39, 2% 40-49, 1% 50-99. **Special facilities:** One-mile fitness trail.

Student profile. Among degree-seeking undergraduates, 315 enrolled as first-time, first-year students, 102 transferred in from other institutions.

Part-time:	54%	**African American:**	12%
Out-of-state:	1%	**Hispanic American:**	1%
Women:	63%	**25 or older:**	46%

Basis for selection. Open admission. Current high school students eligible for part-time early admission with a 3.5 GPA, 26 ACT, and letter of recommendation. COMPASS may be used for placement only. Interview recommended. **Adult students:** Entrance exam policies same as for first-time freshmen.

High school preparation. College-preparatory program recommended. 16 units recommended. Recommended units include English 4, mathematics 3, social studies 3, science 3 (laboratory 2) and foreign language 2. 1 art recommended.

2005-2006 Annual costs. Tuition/fees: $4,586; $12,018 out-of-state. Per-credit charge: $209 in-state; $547 out-of-state. Books/supplies: $990. Personal expenses: $1,900.

2005-2006 Financial aid. Need-based: 198 full-time freshmen applied for aid; 166 were judged to have need; 166 of these received aid. Average need met was 52%. Average scholarship/grant was $3,876; average loan $2,669. 42% of total undergraduate aid awarded as scholarships/grants, 58% as loans/jobs. Need-based aid available for part-time students. **Non-need-based:** Scholarships awarded for academics, alumni affiliation, art, athletics, leadership, minority status, music/drama, ROTC, state residency.

Application procedures. Admission: No deadline. $30 fee, may be waived for applicants with need. Application may be submitted online. Admission notification on a rolling basis beginning on or about 10/1. International students must apply through main campus at Kent. **Financial aid:** Priority date 3/1; no closing date. FAFSA required. Applicants notified on a rolling basis starting 3/15; must reply within 2 week(s) of notification.

Academics. Special study options: Accelerated study, distance learning, double major, dual enrollment of high school students, honors, independent study, internships, student-designed major, weekend college. **Credit/placement by examination:** AP, CLEP, IB, institutional tests. 6 credit hours maximum toward associate degree. **Support services:** Learning center, pre-admission summer program, reduced course load, remedial instruction, tutoring.

Majors. Biology: General. **Business:** General, accounting technology, administrative services, office technology, office/clerical. **Computer sciences:** Applications programming. **Engineering technology:** Electrical, industrial, mechanical, plastics. **Legal studies:** Paralegal. **Liberal arts:** Arts/sciences. **Protective services:** Criminal justice.

Most popular majors. Business/marketing 24%, computer/information sciences 29%, engineering/engineering technologies 18%, liberal arts 20%.

Computing on campus. 265 workstations in library, computer center. Online course registration, online library, helpline, student web hosting available.

Student life. Freshman orientation: Available. Preregistration for classes offered. **Policies:** Freshmen permitted cars on campus. **Activities:** Drama, student government, student newspaper, nontraditional student and minority student organizations; independent black/minority coalition; Christian Fellowship; Environmental Council; alcohol, drugs and AIDS awareness programs.

Athletics. NJCAA. **Team name:** Golden Flashes.

Student services. Adult student services, career counseling, student employment services, health services, personal counseling, placement for graduates, veterans' counselor. **Physically disabled:** Services for visually, speech, hearing impaired. **Transfer:** Special adviser, orientation for new students. Transfer adviser, college fairs on campus for students transferring to 4-year colleges.

Contact. E-mail: info@trumbull.kent.edu
Phone: (330) 847-0571 Fax: (330) 847-6571
Randi Schneider, Director of Enrollment Management, Kent State University: Trumbull Campus, 4314 Mahoning Avenue, NW, Warren, OH 44483-1998

Kent State University: Tuscarawas Campus

New Philadelphia, Ohio
www.tusc.kent.edu **CB code: 1434**

- Public 2-year branch campus college
- Commuter campus in large town

General. Founded in 1962. Regionally accredited. **Enrollment:** 1,682 degree-seeking undergraduates; 223 non-degree-seeking students. **Degrees:** 211 associate awarded. **ROTC:** Army, Air Force. **Location:** 80 miles from Cleveland. **Calendar:** Semester, limited summer session. **Full-time faculty:** 48 total; 46% have terminal degrees, 12% minority, 48% women. **Part-time faculty:** 74 total; 12% have terminal degrees, 3% minority, 53% women. **Class size:** 56% < 20, 36% 20-39, 4% 40-49, 3% 50-99. **Partnerships:** Formal partnership with Buckeye Career Center engaged in Tech Prep program.

Student profile. Among degree-seeking undergraduates, 330 enrolled as first-time, first-year students, 108 transferred in from other institutions.

Part-time:	49%	**Hispanic American:**	1%
Women:	62%	**25 or older:**	38%
African American:	1%		

Basis for selection. Open admission, but selective for some programs and for out-of-state students. Special requirements for nursing program. **Adult students:** Test scores not required for placement if applicant is over 21 years of age.

High school preparation. 16 units recommended. Recommended units include English 4, mathematics 3, social studies 3, science 3 (laboratory 2) and foreign language 2. One arts unit recommended.

2005-2006 Annual costs. Tuition/fees: $4,586; $12,018 out-of-state. Per-credit charge: $209 in-state; $547 out-of-state.

2005-2006 Financial aid. Need-based: Average need met was 53%. Average scholarship/grant was $3,588; average loan $2,683. 41% of total undergraduate aid awarded as scholarships/grants, 59% as loans/jobs. Need-based aid available for part-time students. Work study available nights, weekends and for part-time students. **Non-need-based:** Scholarships awarded for academics, alumni affiliation, art, athletics, leadership, minority status, music/drama, ROTC.

Application procedures. Admission: No deadline. $30 fee, may be waived for applicants with need. Application may be submitted online. Admission notification on a rolling basis beginning on or about 5/31. **Financial aid:** Closing date 3/1. FAFSA required. Applicants notified on a rolling basis starting 3/15; must reply within 2 week(s) of notification.

Academics. Special study options: Accelerated study, distance learning, double major, dual enrollment of high school students, honors, independent study, internships, student-designed major. License preparation in nursing. **Credit/placement by examination:** AP, CLEP, institutional tests. 15 credit hours maximum toward associate degree. **Support services:** Learning center, reduced course load, remedial instruction, study skills assistance, tutoring, writing center.

Majors. Business: General, accounting technology, administrative services. **Computer sciences:** Applications programming. **Education:** Early childhood. **Engineering technology:** Industrial, mechanical, plastics. **Health:** Nursing (RN). **Liberal arts:** Arts/sciences. **Protective services:** Criminal justice.

Most popular majors. Business/marketing 10%, computer/information sciences 9%, engineering/engineering technologies 16%, health sciences 24%, liberal arts 30%, security/protective services 7%.

Computing on campus. 300 workstations in library, computer center. Online course registration, online library, helpline, student web hosting available.

Student life. Freshman orientation: Mandatory. Preregistration for classes offered. **Policies:** Freshmen permitted cars on campus. **Activities:** Choral groups.

Athletics. Intramural: Basketball M, volleyball. **Team name:** Golden Flashes.

Student services. Career counseling, student employment services, on-campus daycare. **Physically disabled:** Services for visually, hearing impaired. **Transfer:** Special adviser for new students. Transfer adviser for students transferring to 4-year colleges.

Contact. E-mail: info@tusc.kent.edu
Phone: (330) 339-3391 ext. 47425 Fax: (330) 339-3321
Denise Testa, Director of Enrollment Management, Kent State University: Tuscarawas Campus, 330 University Drive Northeast, New Philadelphia, OH 44663-9403

Kettering College of Medical Arts

Kettering, Ohio
www.kcma.edu **CB code: 0602**

- Private 2-year health science and nursing college affiliated with Seventh-day Adventists
- Commuter campus in small city

General. Founded in 1967. Regionally accredited. Institution is educational division of Kettering Medical Center. **Enrollment:** 738 degree-seeking undergraduates; 30 non-degree-seeking students. **Degrees:** 34 bachelor's, 117 associate awarded; master's offered. **Location:** 5 miles from Dayton. **Calendar:** Semester, limited summer session. **Full-time faculty:** 50 total. **Part-time faculty:** 56 total. **Special facilities:** Medical center.

Student profile. Among degree-seeking undergraduates, 72 enrolled as first-time, first-year students.

Part-time:	42%	**Asian American:**	1%
Out-of-state:	13%	**Hispanic American:**	2%
Women:	81%	**25 or older:**	48%
African American:	7%		

Basis for selection. High school GPA, test scores, personal references most important. Essay recommended for all applicants; interview required for physician assistant applicants.

High school preparation. 14 units recommended. Recommended units include English 4, mathematics 2 and science 3. Strong mathematics and science background recommended.

2005-2006 Annual costs. Tuition/fees: $8,020. Per-credit charge: $260. Tuition and fees may vary by program. Books/supplies: $973. Personal expenses: $2,820.

Financial aid. Need-based: Need-based aid available for part-time students. **Non-need-based:** Scholarships awarded for academics.

Application procedures. Admission: No deadline. $25 fee, may be waived for applicants with need. Admission notification on a rolling basis. **Financial aid:** Priority date 3/31; no closing date. FAFSA, institutional form required. Applicants notified on a rolling basis starting 5/15; must reply within 3 week(s) of notification.

Academics. Special study options: Accelerated study, cross-registration, dual enrollment of high school students. Bachelor's degree programs available on campus. **Credit/placement by examination:** CLEP, SAT, ACT, institutional tests. **Support services:** Learning center, reduced course load, study skills assistance, tutoring, writing center.

Majors. Education: General. **Engineering technology:** Biomedical. **Health:** Medical radiologic technology/radiation therapy, nuclear medical technology, nursing (RN), physician assistant, predentistry, premedicine, respiratory therapy technology, sonography.

Computing on campus. 25 workstations in library, computer center.

Student life. Housing: Single-sex dorms available. $75 deposit. **Activities:** Drama, music ensembles, religious life organizations.

Student services. Career counseling, student employment services, health services, personal counseling, placement for graduates, veterans' counselor. **Transfer:** Special adviser, orientation, pre-admission transcript evaluation for new students. Transfer adviser for students transferring to 4-year colleges.

Contact. E-mail: becky.edler@kcma.edu
Phone: (937) 395-8628 Toll-free number: (800) 433-5262
Fax: (937) 395-8338
Becky Edler, Associate Director of Enrollment Services, Kettering College of Medical Arts, 3737 Southern Boulevard, Kettering, OH 45429-1299

Lakeland Community College

Kirtland, Ohio — **CB member**
www.lakelandcc.edu — **CB code: 1422**

- Public 2-year community college
- Commuter campus in large town

General. Founded in 1967. Regionally accredited. **Enrollment:** 8,600 undergraduates. **Degrees:** 830 associate awarded. **Location:** 15 miles from Cleveland. **Calendar:** Semester, extensive summer session. **Full-time faculty:** 125 total. **Part-time faculty:** 500 total. **Special facilities:** Planetarium, observatory, licensed preschool program laboratory.

Student profile.

Out-of-state:	1%	**25 or older:**	46%

Transfer out. Colleges most students transferred to 2005: Cleveland State University, University of Akron, Kent State University, Ohio State University, John Carroll University.

Basis for selection. Open admission, but selective for some programs. Admissions to health technology programs based on test scores and school achievement record.

High school preparation. Recommended units include English 4, mathematics 3, social studies 3, science 3 and foreign language 2. Health technology programs require algebra, biology, chemistry.

2005-2006 Annual costs. Tuition/fees: $2,546; $3,119 out-of-district; $6,670 out-of-state. Per-credit charge: $74 in-district; $94 out-of-district; $212 out-of-state. Books/supplies: $775. Personal expenses: $1,350.

Financial aid. Need-based: Need-based aid available for part-time students. Work study available nights, weekends and for part-time students. **Non-need-based:** Scholarships awarded for academics, art, athletics, job skills, leadership, minority status, music/drama, state residency. **Additional information:** Loans available for tuition and books.

Application procedures. Admission: No deadline. $15 fee, may be waived for applicants with need. Application may be submitted online. Admission notification on a rolling basis beginning on or about 12/1. **Financial aid:** Priority date 3/1; no closing date. FAFSA, institutional form required. Applicants notified on a rolling basis starting 5/1.

Academics. Special study options: Cooperative education, cross-registration, distance learning, dual enrollment of high school students, independent study, liberal arts/career combination, weekend college. Bachelor's degree programs available on campus. License preparation in nursing, real estate. **Credit/placement by examination:** AP, CLEP, institutional tests. 44 credit hours maximum toward associate degree. **Support services:** Learning center, reduced course load, remedial instruction, study skills assistance, tutoring.

Majors. Biology: Biotechnology. **Business:** Accounting, administrative services, business admin, e-commerce, hospitality admin, management information systems, small business admin, tourism promotion, tourism/travel. **Computer sciences:** Information systems, LAN/WAN management, programming, web page design. **Education:** Early childhood. **Engineering technology:** Civil, electrical, electrical drafting, manufacturing, mechanical, nuclear. **Family/consumer sciences:** Child care. **Health:** Clinical lab technology, dental hygiene, histologic technology, medical radiologic technology/radiation therapy, nursing (RN), ophthalmic lab technology, optician, respiratory therapy technology, surgical technology. **Legal studies:** Paralegal. **Liberal arts:** Arts/sciences. **Protective services:** Corrections, firefighting, police science, security services. **Public administration:** Human services. **Science technology:** Biological, nuclear power. **Visual/performing arts:** Commercial/advertising art.

Computing on campus. 500 workstations in library, computer center, student center. Online course registration available.

Student life. Freshman orientation: Available. **Activities:** Bands, choral groups, drama, music ensembles, radio station, student government, student newspaper, TV station, Access Unlimited, Minority Student Union, Newman Catholic Student Association, La Tertulia.

Athletics. NJCAA. **Intercollegiate:** Baseball M, basketball, golf, soccer M, softball W, volleyball W. **Intramural:** Basketball, racquetball, skiing, softball, tennis, volleyball. **Team name:** Lakers.

Student services. Adult student services, career counseling, student employment services, financial aid counseling, health services, on-campus daycare, personal counseling, placement for graduates, veterans' counselor, women's services. **Physically disabled:** Services for visually, speech, hearing impaired. **Transfer:** Special adviser, orientation for new students. Transfer center, transfer adviser, college fairs on campus for students transferring to 4-year colleges.

Contact. E-mail: tcooper@lakelandcc.edu
Phone: (440) 953-7100 Toll-free number: (800) 589-8520
Fax: (440) 975-4330
Tracey Cooper, Director of Admissions/Registrar, Lakeland Community College, 7700 Clocktower Drive, Kirtland, OH 44094

Lorain County Community College

Elyria, Ohio
www.lorainccc.edu — **CB code: 1417**

- Public 2-year community college
- Commuter campus in small city

General. Founded in 1963. Regionally accredited. **Location:** 26 miles south of Cleveland. **Calendar:** Semester.

Two-Year Colleges

Annual costs/financial aid. Tuition/fees (2005-2006): $2,308; $2,779 out-of-district; $5,616 out-of-state. Books/supplies: $955. Need-based financial aid available to full-time and part-time students.

Contact. Phone: (440) 366-4032
Director of Enrollment Services, 1005 Abbe Road North, Elyria, OH 44035-1691

Marion Technical College

Marion, Ohio
www.mtc.edu **CB code: 0699**

- Public 2-year technical college
- Commuter campus in large town

General. Founded in 1971. Regionally accredited. Common campus and some shared facilities with Ohio State University: Marion. **Enrollment:** 1,425 degree-seeking undergraduates. **Degrees:** 201 associate awarded. **Location:** 45 miles from Columbus. **Calendar:** Quarter, limited summer session. **Full-time faculty:** 37 total. **Part-time faculty:** 104 total.

Student profile.

Out-of-state:	1%	**25 or older:**	52%

Basis for selection. Open admission, but selective for some programs. Selective programs include Medical Assisting, Phlebotomy, Human and Social Services, Medical Administrative Assistant, Medical Lab Technician, Nursing, PTA, Radiology. Application to the program is additional to application to the college. Programs accept on a rolling basis once minimum criteria are met. ACT scores required of Nursing, Human and Social Services applicants and recommended for PTA and Med Lab Technician applicants for admissions, placement and counseling; recommended for other applicants for counseling. ACT scores required of health technology, public/social service technology applicants for admissions, placement, and counseling; recommended for all other applicants for counseling. Interview required for health technologies, human and social services, law enforcement academy. **Adult students:** Entrance exam policies same as for first-time freshmen. ACT may be reqired for limited enrollment programs. **Homeschooled:** Transcript of courses and grades, interview required. Appropriate standardized test or other documentation as defined by policy. **Learning Disabled:** Students must meet with Student Resource Center for assessment of special accommodations.

High school preparation. College-preparatory program recommended. Recommended units include English 4, mathematics 2, social studies 1, science 2 and foreign language 2. Algebra, biology, and chemistry required for health technology applicants. Algebra and physics recommended for engineering applicants.

2005-2006 Annual costs. Tuition/fees: $3,456; $5,364 out-of-state. Per-credit charge: $96 in-state; $149 out-of-state. Books/supplies: $800. Personal expenses: $900.

2005-2006 Financial aid. Need-based: 97% of total undergraduate aid awarded as scholarships/grants, 3% as loans/jobs. Need-based aid available for part-time students. Work study available for part-time students. **Non-need-based:** Scholarships awarded for academics, leadership, minority status.

Application procedures. Admission: Priority date 6/1; no deadline. $20 fee, may be waived for applicants with need. Application may be submitted online. Admission notification on a rolling basis. **Financial aid:** Closing date 6/1. FAFSA, institutional form required. Applicants notified on a rolling basis.

Academics. Special study options: Cooperative education, cross-registration, distance learning, double major, dual enrollment of high school students, independent study, internships, liberal arts/career combination, student-designed major. License preparation in nursing, physical therapy, radiology, real estate. **Credit/placement by examination:** AP, CLEP, institutional tests. Maximum of 48 quarter hours of credit may be earned through exam, life experience or combination. **Support services:** Learning center, reduced course load, remedial instruction, tutoring.

Majors. Business: General, accounting, accounting technology, administrative services, business admin, e-commerce, executive assistant, human resources, marketing, office management, office technology, real estate. **Computer sciences:** General, applications programming, data entry, information technology, LAN/WAN management, networking, programming, vendor certification, web page design, webmaster, word processing. **Engineering technology:** Electrical, electromechanical, manufacturing, mechanical, quality control, telecommunications. **Health:** Clinical lab technology, medical radiologic technology/radiation therapy, medical secretary, nursing (RN), physical therapy assistant. **Legal studies:** Paralegal. **Protective services:** Law enforcement admin. **Public administration:** Human services.

Computing on campus. 229 workstations in computer center.

Student life. Freshman orientation: Available. Held a week or two before classes begin. **Policies:** Freshmen permitted cars on campus. **Activities:** Choral groups, drama, literary magazine, student government, joint activities committee, Campus Christian Fellowship, program of outdoor pursuits club, cultural arts program, student organized clubs/organizations, indoor rock climbing, wellness and conditioning, aerobics center, Beta Nu Pi honorary society (Phi Theta Kappa local chapter).

Athletics. Intercollegiate: Cheerleading M, golf, soccer, volleyball W. **Intramural:** Badminton, basketball, cross-country, football (non-tackle), racquetball, skiing, volleyball.

Student services. Adult student services, career counseling, student employment services, financial aid counseling, personal counseling, placement for graduates, veterans' counselor. **Physically disabled:** Services for visually, speech, hearing impaired. **Transfer:** College fairs on campus for students transferring to 4-year colleges.

Contact. E-mail: enroll@mtc.edu
Phone: (740) 389-4636 ext. 260 Fax: (740) 389-6136
Joel Liles, Director of Admission and Career Services, Marion Technical College, 1467 Mount Vernon Avenue, Marion, OH 43302-5694

Miami University: Hamilton Campus

Hamilton, Ohio
www.ham.muohio.edu **CB code: 1526**

- Public 2-year branch campus college
- Commuter campus in small city

General. Founded in 1968. Regionally accredited. Degrees earned on Hamilton campus conferred by main (Oxford) campus. **Enrollment:** 3,223 degree-seeking undergraduates. **Degrees:** 34 bachelor's, 122 associate awarded. **ROTC:** Navy, Air Force. **Location:** 25 miles from Cincinnati. **Calendar:** Semester, limited summer session. **Full-time faculty:** 91 total. **Part-time faculty:** 138 total. **Class size:** 54% < 20, 40% 20-39, 5% 40-49, 1% 50-99, less than 1% >100.

Student profile.

African American:	6%	**Native American:**	1%
Asian American:	2%	**25 or older:**	24%
Hispanic American:	1%		

Basis for selection. Open admission, but selective for some programs. Test scores required for consideration in nursing and teacher education programs. Interviews recommended. **Adult students:** SAT/ACT scores not required if out of high school 2 year(s) or more. **Homeschooled:** Applicants must present GED scores or credentials that demonstrate equivalent levels of academic achievement, ability and performance to that of state-chartered diploma at least 8 weeks before classes begin.

High school preparation. 16 units recommended. Recommended units include English 4, mathematics 3, social studies 2, history 1, science 3 and foreign language 2. One fine arts also recommended.

2005-2006 Annual costs. Tuition/fees: $4,068; $15,600 out-of-state. Per-credit charge: $170 in-state; $650 out-of-state. Books/supplies: $580. Personal expenses: $1,732.

Financial aid. Need-based: Need-based aid available for part-time students. Work study available nights, weekends and for part-time students. **Non-need-based:** Scholarships awarded for academics, athletics, leadership, minority status, state residency. **Additional information:** Special gift funds for needy, multicultural students who enter with appropriate academic record. Separate application required for scholarships; closing date January 31.

Application procedures. Admission: No deadline. $35 fee. Application may be submitted online. Admission notification on a rolling basis. ADN application deadline for Fall admission is Feb. 01. **Financial aid:** Priority date 2/15; no closing date. FAFSA required. Applicants notified on a rolling basis starting 4/1.

Academics. Some upper division and graduate course work available, including part-time MBA and several M.Ed programs. **Special study options:** Cooperative education, cross-registration, distance learning, double major, dual enrollment of high school students, ESL, honors, independent study, internships, liberal arts/career combination, student-designed major, study abroad, teacher certification program. Bachelor's degree programs available on campus. License preparation in nursing, real estate. **Credit/placement by examination:** AP, CLEP, IB, institutional tests. 32 credit hours maximum toward associate degree, 32 toward bachelor's. **Support services:** Learning center, reduced course load, remedial instruction, study skills assistance, tutoring.

Majors. Business: Accounting, business admin, management information systems, marketing, office management, office/clerical, real estate. **Computer sciences:** General. **Education:** Kindergarten/preschool. **Engineering technology:** Computer systems, electrical, industrial management, mechanical. **Health:** Nursing (RN).

Computing on campus. 300 workstations in library, computer center, student center. Commuter students can connect to campus network. Online course registration, helpline, wireless network available.

Student life. Freshman orientation: Available. **Policies:** Freshmen permitted cars on campus. **Activities:** Choral groups, drama, musical theater, student government, student newspaper, campus activities committee, ski club, student nursing association, minority action committee, Campus Crusade for Christ, athletic club, Organization for Wiser and Worldwide Learners, fitness and weightlifting club, soccer club.

Athletics. Intramural: Basketball, bowling, skiing, soccer, softball, table tennis, tennis, volleyball, weight lifting. **Team name:** Harriers.

Student services. Career counseling, student employment services, financial aid counseling, minority student services, on-campus daycare, personal counseling, placement for graduates, veterans' counselor. **Physically disabled:** Services for visually, speech, hearing impaired. **Transfer:** Special adviser, orientation, pre-admission transcript evaluation for new students.

Contact. Phone: (513) 785-3111 Fax: (513) 785-3148
Archie Nelson, Director of Admission and Financial Aid, Miami University: Hamilton Campus, 1601 University Boulevard, Hamilton, OH 45011-3399

Miami University: Middletown Campus

Middletown, Ohio
www.mid.muohio.edu **CB code: 1509**

- Public 2-year branch campus and community college
- Commuter campus in large town

General. Founded in 1963. Regionally accredited. **Location:** 30 miles from Cincinnati, 20 miles from Dayton. **Calendar:** Semester.

Annual costs/financial aid. Tuition/fees (2005-2006): $4,068; $15,600 out-of-state. Students paying by the credit hour pay $15 general fee per credit hour. Books/supplies: $600. Personal expenses: $1,912. Need-based financial aid available to full-time and part-time students.

Contact. Phone: (513) 727-3216
Director of Enrollment Services, 4200 East University Boulevard, Middletown, OH 45042

Miami-Jacobs Career College

Dayton, Ohio
www.miamijacobs.edu **CB code: 1528**

- For-profit 2-year junior college
- Commuter campus in small city

General. Founded in 1860. Accredited by ACICS. **Location:** Downtown. **Calendar:** Quarter.

Annual costs/financial aid. Tuition/fees (2005-2006): $9,450. Personal expenses: $2,500. Need-based financial aid available to full-time and part-time students.

Contact. Phone: (937) 222-7337
Director of Admissions, 110 North Patterson Boulevard, Dayton, OH 45402

National College of Business & Technology: Dayton

Kettering, Ohio

- For-profit 2-year business and technical college
- Large city

General. Accredited by ACICS. **Enrollment:** 331 degree-seeking undergraduates. **Calendar:** Quarter. **Full-time faculty:** 1 total. **Part-time faculty:** 29 total.

Basis for selection. Open admission.

2006-2007 Annual costs. Tuition/fees: $8,976. Per-credit charge: $187.

Application procedures. Admission: No deadline. $30 fee.

Academics. Credit/placement by examination: CLEP.

Contact. Phone: (937) 299-9450
Larry Steele, Director of Admissions, National College of Business & Technology: Dayton, 1837 Woodman Center Drive, Kettering, OH 45420

National Institute of Technology

Cuyahoga Falls, Ohio
www.nationalinstituteoftechnology.edu

- For-profit 2-year health science and technical college
- Commuter campus

General. Accredited by ACCSCT.

Contact. Phone: (330) 923-9959
Director of Admissions, 2545 Bailey Road, Cuyahoga Falls, OH 44221

North Central State College

Mansfield, Ohio
www.ncstatecollege.edu **CB code: 0721**

- Public 2-year technical college
- Commuter campus in small city

General. Founded in 1961. Regionally accredited. **Location:** 70 miles from Cleveland and Columbus. **Calendar:** Quarter.

Annual costs/financial aid. Tuition/fees (2005-2006): $3,431; $6,863 out-of-state. Books/supplies: $705. Personal expenses: $726. Need-based financial aid available to full-time and part-time students.

Contact. Phone: (419) 755-4888
Director of Student Development/Admissions, Box 698, Mansfield, OH 44901

Northwest State Community College

Archbold, Ohio
www.nscc.cc.oh.us **CB code: 1235**

- Public 2-year community and technical college
- Commuter campus in small town

General. Founded in 1968. Regionally accredited. **Location:** 45 miles from Toledo. **Calendar:** Semester.

Annual costs/financial aid. Tuition/fees (2005-2006): $3,720; $6,810 out-of-state. Personal expenses: $750. Need-based financial aid available to full-time and part-time students.

Contact. Phone: (419) 267-5511 ext. 320
Director of Admissions, 22600 State Route 34, Archbold, OH 43502

Ohio Business College

Lorain, Ohio
www.ohiobusinesscollege.edu **CB code: 2470**

- For-profit 2-year branch campus and business college
- Commuter campus in small city

General. Founded in 1903. Accredited by ACICS. **Location:** 35 miles from Cleveland. **Calendar:** Quarter.

Annual costs/financial aid. Tuition/fees (2005-2006): $8,685. $260 per-credit-hour for PC Support students. Books/supplies: $1,080. Need-based financial aid available to full-time and part-time students.

Contact. Phone: (440) 277-0021
Admissions Manager, 1907 North Ridge Road, Lorain, OH 44055

Ohio Business College: Sandusky

Sandusky, Ohio
www.ohiobusinesscollege.edu **CB code: 3260**

- For-profit 2-year business college
- Commuter campus in small city
- Interview required

General. Accredited by ACICS. **Enrollment:** 260 degree-seeking undergraduates. **Degrees:** 39 associate awarded. **Location:** 60 miles from Cleveland and Toledo. **Calendar:** Quarter, limited summer session. **Full-time faculty:** 5 total. **Part-time faculty:** 15 total.

Transfer out. Colleges most students transferred to 2005: Ashland University.

Basis for selection. Open admission. CPAT required for placement.

2005-2006 Annual costs. Tuition/fees: $8,685. Per-credit charge: $183. Books/supplies: $1,200.

Financial aid. Need-based: Need-based aid available for part-time students.

Application procedures. Admission: No deadline. $25 fee. Application must be submitted on paper. Admission notification on a rolling basis. **Financial aid:** No deadline. FAFSA required.

Academics. Special study options: Double major, independent study, liberal arts/career combination. Externships. License preparation in real estate. **Credit/placement by examination:** CLEP. **Support services:** Tutoring.

Majors. Business: Accounting, administrative services, business admin. **Computer sciences:** Data entry, programming. **Engineering:** Software. **Health:** Medical records admin, medical secretary. **Legal studies:** Legal secretary, paralegal.

Most popular majors. Business/marketing 55%, computer/information sciences 12%, health sciences 25%, legal studies 8%.

Student life. Freshman orientation: Available.

Student services. Transfer: Special adviser for new students.

Contact. E-mail: sandusky@ohiobusinesscollege.edu
Phone: (419) 627-8345 Toll-free number: (888) 627-8345
Fax: (419) 627-1958
Ohio Business College: Sandusky, 4020 Milan Road, Sandusky, OH 44870

Ohio College of Massotherapy

Akron, Ohio
www.ocm.edu **CB code: 2985**

- For-profit 2-year health science college
- Commuter campus in very large city

General. Accredited by ACCSCT. **Enrollment:** 284 undergraduates. **Degrees:** 64 associate awarded. **Calendar:** Continuous. **Part-time faculty:** 24 total. **Special facilities:** Massage and spa clinic.

Basis for selection. Open admission. **Homeschooled:** State high school equivalency certificate required.

2005-2006 Annual costs. Tuition/fees: $9,675. Per-credit charge: $215.

Application procedures. Admission: No deadline. $25 fee.

Academics. Special study options: Distance learning. **Credit/placement by examination:** CLEP. **Support services:** Reduced course load, tutoring.

Majors. Health: Massage therapy.

Computing on campus. 4 workstations in computer center.

Student life. Freshman orientation: Mandatory.

Contact. E-mail: admissions@ocm.edu
Phone: (330) 665-1084 Fax: (330) 665-5021
John Adkins, Admissions/Marketing Manager, Ohio College of Massotherapy, 225 Heritage Woods Drive, Akron, OH 44321

Ohio Institute of Photography and Technology

Dayton, Ohio
www.oipt.com **CB code: 3380**

- For-profit 2-year technical college
- Commuter campus in small city
- Interview required

General. Founded in 1971. Accredited by ACCSCT. **Enrollment:** 658 degree-seeking undergraduates; 76 non-degree-seeking students. **Degrees:** 165 associate awarded. **Location:** 55 miles from Cincinnati, 80 miles from Columbus. **Calendar:** Quarter, extensive summer session. **Full-time faculty:** 20 total. **Part-time faculty:** 33 total. **Special facilities:** Photographic laboratories, computer laboratory for electronic imaging and desktop media.

Student profile. Among degree-seeking undergraduates, 100% enrolled in a vocational program, 138 enrolled as first-time, first-year students.

Out-of-state:	19%	**25 or older:**	33%
Women:	79%		

Basis for selection. Open admission, but selective for some programs. CPAT test and interview required. Minimum CPAT score of 150 required for pharmacy technician students. Essay and portfolio recommended. **Adult students:** Entrance exam policies same as for first-time freshmen.

2005-2006 Annual costs. Tuition/fees: $18,732. Per-credit charge: $333. Tuition listed reflects the Photographic Techonology program. Tuition varies by program. Books/supplies: $1,350. Personal expenses: $1,701.

Financial aid. Need-based: Need-based aid available for part-time students.

Application procedures. Admission: No deadline. No application fee. Application may be submitted online. Admission notification on a rolling basis. **Financial aid:** No deadline. FAFSA, institutional form required. Applicants notified on a rolling basis starting 3/1.

Academics. Training directed toward technical and professional aspects of photography. **Special study options:** Double major, independent study, internships. **Credit/placement by examination:** AP, CLEP, institutional tests. **Support services:** GED preparation, reduced course load, tutoring.

Majors. Health: Office admin. **Protective services:** Law enforcement admin. **Visual/performing arts:** Commercial photography, graphic design, photography.

Most popular majors. Health sciences 42%, visual/performing arts 55%.

Computing on campus. 36 workstations in library.

Student life. Freshman orientation: Available. Preregistration for classes offered. 3 hours, prior to first day of classes. **Policies:** Freshmen permitted cars on campus. **Activities:** Student newspaper.

Student services. Career counseling, student employment services, financial aid counseling, placement for graduates, veterans' counselor. **Transfer:** Special adviser, orientation, pre-admission transcript evaluation for new students. Transfer adviser for students transferring to 4-year colleges.

Contact. E-mail: info@oipt.com
Phone: (937) 294-6155 Toll-free number: (800) 932-9698
Fax: (937) 294-2259
Norman Dorn, Director of Admissions, Ohio Institute of Photography and Technology, 2029 Edgefield Road, Dayton, OH 45439

Ohio State University Agricultural Technical Institute

Wooster, Ohio
www.ati.osu.edu **CB code: 1009**

- Public 2-year agricultural college
- Residential campus in large town

General. Founded in 1971. Regionally accredited. **Enrollment:** 821 degree-seeking undergraduates. **Degrees:** 96 associate awarded. **Location:** 30 miles from Akron, 60 miles from Cleveland. **Calendar:** Quarter, limited summer session. **Full-time faculty:** 33 total. **Part-time faculty:** 43 total. **Class size:** 59% < 20, 35% 20-39, 5% 40-49, 2% 50-99. **Special facilities:** 1800-acre farm operation/enterprise laboratory, horticulture complex including greenhouses and polyhouses, conservatory and display gardens.

Student profile. Among degree-seeking undergraduates, 337 enrolled as first-time, first-year students, 44 transferred in from other institutions.

Part-time:	12%	**Women:**	33%
Out-of-state:	3%	**Live on campus:**	54%

Basis for selection. Open admission, but selective for out-of-state students. Out-of-state applicants evaluated on basis of GPA, class rank, curriculum, principal/counselor recommendations, and SAT or ACT scores. **Home-schooled:** SAT or ACT required.

High school preparation. College-preparatory program recommended. 15 units recommended. Recommended units include English 4, mathematics 3, social studies 2, science 2, foreign language 2 and academic electives 1. Science units should include biology and chemistry. Physics recommended for engineering technology majors. One unit of visual or performing arts recommended.

2005-2006 Annual costs. Tuition/fees: $5,478; $16,701 out-of-state. $900 optional meal plan. Books/supplies: $1,080.

2005-2006 Financial aid. All financial aid based on need. 317 full-time freshmen applied for aid; 266 were judged to have need; 227 of these received aid. Average need met was 55%. Average scholarship/grant was $1,884. 36% of total undergraduate aid awarded as scholarships/grants, 64% as loans/jobs. Need-based aid available for part-time students. Work study available nights, weekends and for part-time students.

Application procedures. Admission: Closing date 7/1 (postmark date). $40 fee, may be waived for applicants with need. Application may be submitted online. Admission notification on a rolling basis beginning on or about 10/1. **Financial aid:** Priority date 3/1; no closing date. FAFSA required. Applicants notified on a rolling basis starting 5/1; must reply within 4 week(s) of notification.

Academics. One quarter of occupational internship required. **Special study options:** Cross-registration, double major, dual enrollment of high school students, independent study, internships, student-designed major, study abroad. **Credit/placement by examination:** AP, CLEP, institutional tests. 45 credit hours maximum toward associate degree. **Support services:** Learning center, reduced course load, remedial instruction, study skills assistance, tutoring, writing center.

Majors. Agriculture: General, agronomy, animal husbandry, business, communications, crop production, dairy, equine science, equipment technology, floriculture, greenhouse operations, horticultural science, horticulture, landscaping, nursery operations, ornamental horticulture, plant sciences, power machinery, soil science, turf management. **Business:** Business admin, restaurant/food services. **Conservation:** General, environmental studies. **Construction:** Power transmission. **Education:** Agricultural. **Engineering technology:** Construction, hydraulics. **Personal/culinary services:** Restaurant/catering.

Most popular majors. Agriculture 76%, education 6%, engineering/engineering technologies 9%.

Computing on campus. 85 workstations in dormitories, library, computer center. Dormitories wired for high-speed internet access. Commuter students can connect to campus network. Online course registration, online library, helpline, repair service available.

Student life. Freshman orientation: Mandatory, $75 fee. **Policies:** Resident freshmen under 21 required to live on campus. Freshmen permitted cars on campus. **Housing:** Coed dorms, apartments, substance-free housing available. **Activities:** Student government, Phi Theta Kappa.

Athletics. Intramural: Basketball, football (tackle), racquetball, softball, volleyball. **Team name:** Buckeyes.

Student services. Adult student services, career counseling, student employment services, health services, minority student services, personal counseling, placement for graduates. **Physically disabled:** Services for visually, speech, hearing impaired. **Transfer:** Special adviser, orientation for new students.

Contact. E-mail: ati@osu.edu
Phone: (330) 287-1327 Toll-free number: (800) 647-8283
Fax: (330) 287-1333
Jill Byers, Coordinator of Admissions, Ohio State University Agricultural Technical Institute, 1328 Dover Road, Wooster, OH 44691

Ohio Technical College
Cleveland, Ohio
www.ohiotechnicalcollege.com **CB code: 2999**

- For-profit 2-year technical college
- Very large city

General. Accredited by ACCSCT. **Calendar:** Continuous.

Annual costs/financial aid. Tuition for full associate program $22,300 or $22,800 depending on program; full diploma programs range from $16,900 to $26,900; full certificate programs range from $1,974 to $4,927. Fees are $100. Books/supplies: $850. Personal expenses: $1,837.

Contact. Phone: (216) 881-1700
President, 1374 East 51st Street, Cleveland, OH 44103-1269

Ohio Valley College of Technology
East Liverpool, Ohio
www.ovct.edu **CB code: 5852**

- For-profit 2-year business and technical college
- Commuter campus in large town
- Interview required

General. Founded in 1886. Accredited by ACICS. **Enrollment:** 174 undergraduates. **Degrees:** 67 associate awarded. **Location:** 30 miles from Youngstown, 35 miles from Pittsburgh. **Calendar:** Semester, extensive summer session. **Full-time faculty:** 4 total. **Part-time faculty:** 7 total.

Student profile.

Out-of-state:	13%	**25 or older:**	75%

Basis for selection. CPAT scores most important.

2006-2007 Annual costs. Tuition/fees (projected): $7,490.

Financial aid. All financial aid based on need. Need-based aid available for part-time students.

Application procedures. Admission: No deadline. $75 fee. Admission notification on a rolling basis. **Financial aid:** No deadline. FAFSA required. Applicants notified on a rolling basis; must reply within 6 week(s) of notification.

Academics. Special study options: Double major, internships, liberal arts/career combination. **Credit/placement by examination:** CLEP, institutional tests. **Support services:** Reduced course load, remedial instruction.

Majors. Business: General, accounting, administrative services, office/clerical. **Computer sciences:** General, data processing. **Health:** Dental assistant, medical assistant, medical secretary.

Computing on campus. 20 workstations in computer center.

Student life. Activities: Student government.

Student services. Student employment services, personal counseling, placement for graduates. **Transfer:** Special adviser, orientation for new students. Transfer adviser for students transferring to 4-year colleges.

Contact. E-mail: info@ovct.edu
Phone: (330) 385-1070 Fax: (330) 385-4606
Jessica Ewing, Director of Admissions, Ohio Valley College of Technology, 16808 St. Clair Avenue, PO Box 7000, East Liverpool, OH 43920

Owens Community College: Findlay Campus
Findlay, Ohio
www.owens.edu **CB code: 5487**

- Public 2-year branch campus and community college
- Commuter campus in large town

General. Founded in 1983. Regionally accredited. **Location:** 45 miles from Toledo. **Calendar:** Semester.

Annual costs/financial aid. Tuition/fees (2005-2006): $2,784; $5,208 out-of-state. Books/supplies: $525.

Contact. Phone: (567) 429-3509
Vice President of Student Services, 300 Davis Street, Findlay, OH 45840-3600

Owens Community College: Toledo

Toledo, Ohio
www.owens.edu **CB code: 1643**

- Public 2-year community college
- Commuter campus in large city

General. Founded in 1966. Regionally accredited. Branch campus in Findlay 45 miles frotm Toledo campus. **Enrollment:** 8,485 degree-seeking undergraduates; 11,759 non-degree-seeking students. **Degrees:** 1,083 associate awarded. **ROTC:** Army, Air Force. **Location:** 6 miles from downtown. **Calendar:** Semester, limited summer session. **Full-time faculty:** 187 total. **Part-time faculty:** 1,031 total.

Student profile. Among degree-seeking undergraduates, 7% enrolled in a transfer program, 93% enrolled in a vocational program, 1,705 enrolled as first-time, first-year students.

Part-time:	51%	**Asian American:**	1%
Women:	64%	**Hispanic American:**	4%
African American:	13%	**International:**	1%

Transfer out. Colleges most students transferred to 2005: Bowling Green State University, Lourdes College, University of Findlay, University of Toledo.

Basis for selection. Open admission, but selective for some programs. Admission to health technologies, Peace Officer Academy, and early childhood education requires high school transcripts and test scores. ACT required for select health technology programs. ACT or SAT required for other health technology programs. **Adult students:** Entrance exam policies same as for first-time freshmen.

High school preparation. 19 units recommended. Recommended units include English 4, science 3 (laboratory 3).

2005-2006 Annual costs. Tuition/fees: $2,784; $5,208 out-of-state. Per-credit charge: $116 in-state; $217 out-of-state. Books/supplies: $525.

2004-2005 Financial aid. Need-based: 1,361 full-time freshmen applied for aid; 1,058 were judged to have need; 1,049 of these received aid. Average need met was 51%. Average scholarship/grant was $1,869; average loan $2,218. 61% of total undergraduate aid awarded as scholarships/grants, 39% as loans/jobs. Need-based aid available for part-time students. Work study available nights, weekends and for part-time students. **Non-need-based:** Awarded to 125 full-time undergraduates, including 46 freshmen. Scholarships awarded for academics, alumni affiliation, athletics, leadership, state residency. **Additional information:** Other types of financial aid available: federal family education loan program, private foundation loan (SCHELL).

Application procedures. Admission: No deadline. No application fee. Application must be submitted on paper. Admission notification on a rolling basis. February 1 application deadline for dental hygiene and physical therapist assistant programs. **Financial aid:** Priority date 3/31; no closing date. FAFSA required. Applicants notified by 2/7.

Academics. Special study options: Cooperative education, distance learning, double major, dual enrollment of high school students, honors, independent study, internships, student-designed major, weekend college. License preparation in dental hygiene, nursing, paramedic, radiology, real estate. **Credit/placement by examination:** AP, CLEP, institutional tests. No limit placed upon the number of credit hours a student may obtain via proficiency exams as long as the student has met the graduation residency requirement. **Support services:** GED preparation, learning center, pre-admission summer program, reduced course load, remedial instruction, study skills assistance, tutoring, writing center.

Majors. Agriculture: Business, landscaping, mechanization. **Area/ethnic studies:** African-American, Canadian, women's. **Biology:** General, biotechnology. **Business:** General, accounting technology, business admin, executive assistant, office management, operations, restaurant/food services. **Communications:** General. **Communications technology:** General. **Computer sciences:** Applications programming, information technology. **Education:** General, early childhood, multi-level teacher. **Engineering:** General. **Engineering technology:** Architectural, architectural drafting, automotive, biomedical, computer, construction, electrical, electromechanical, environmental, hydraulics, industrial, manufacturing, mechanical, quality control, surveying. **English:** Creative writing, English lit. **Foreign languages:** General. **Health:** Dental hygiene, dietetics, health care admin, management/clinical assistant, medical radiologic technology/radiation therapy, medical records technology, medical secretary, nuclear medical technology, nursing (RN), occupational therapy assistant, physical therapy assistant, sonography, surgical technology. **History:** General. **Math:** General. **Military:** General. **Physical sciences:** Chemistry. **Production:** Tool and die, welding. **Protective services:** Corrections, fire safety technology, firefighting, law enforcement admin, police science, security services. **Psychology:** General. **Public administration:** General, social work. **Social sciences:** Sociology. **Visual/performing arts:** Arts management, commercial photography, commercial/advertising art, dance, dramatic, interior design, music history, music management, music performance, theater design.

Most popular majors. Business/marketing 25%, education 7%, engineering/engineering technologies 11%, health sciences 33%, liberal arts 7%, security/protective services 9%.

Computing on campus. 1,345 workstations in library, computer center. Commuter students can connect to campus network. Online course registration, online library, helpline available.

Student life. Activities: Jazz band, choral groups, drama, student government, student newspaper, Bible study club, College Republicans, environmental club, Japanese club, ski club, students in free enterprise.

Athletics. NJCAA. **Intercollegiate:** Baseball M, basketball, soccer, softball W, volleyball W. **Intramural:** Basketball, bowling, football (non-tackle), golf, skiing, softball, table tennis, tennis, volleyball, weight lifting. **Team name:** Express.

Student services. Adult student services, career counseling, services for economically disadvantaged, student employment services, financial aid counseling, on-campus daycare, personal counseling, placement for graduates, veterans' counselor. **Physically disabled:** Services for visually, hearing impaired. **Transfer:** Special adviser, orientation for new students. Transfer adviser, college fairs on campus for students transferring to 4-year colleges.

Contact. Phone: (567) 661-7225 Toll-free number: (800) 466-9367 ext. 7777 Fax: (567) 661-7734
Donna Gruber, Director Enrollment Services, Owens Community College: Toledo, PO Box 10000, Toledo, OH 43699-1947

Remington College: Cleveland

Cleveland, Ohio
www.remingtoncollege.edu **CB code: 3154**

- For-profit 2-year technical college
- Commuter campus in very large city
- Interview required

General. Accredited by ACCSCT. **Enrollment:** 682 degree-seeking undergraduates. **Degrees:** 165 associate awarded. **Location:** 8 miles from Cleveland. **Calendar:** Continuous. **Full-time faculty:** 40 total. **Part-time faculty:** 15 total. **Class size:** 100% 20-39.

Basis for selection. Entrance examination required.

2006-2007 Annual costs. Costs for full 24-month Associate Degree program $31,490; includes tuition, fees, books and supplies, laptop computer. Cost of 8-month Diploma program $11,730.

Financial aid. All financial aid based on need. Work study available nights.

Application procedures. Admission: No deadline. $50 fee. **Financial aid:** No deadline. FAFSA required.

Academics. Special study options: Cooperative education, independent study, internships. **Credit/placement by examination:** CLEP, IB. **Support services:** GED preparation, learning center, study skills assistance, tutoring.

Majors. Business: General, office technology. **Computer sciences:** General, networking. **Protective services:** Law enforcement admin, police science.

Most popular majors. Business/marketing 50%, computer/information sciences 50%.

Computing on campus. 120 workstations in library, computer center. Online library, repair service available.

Student life. Freshman orientation: Mandatory. **Policies:** Freshmen permitted cars on campus.

Student services. Adult student services, career counseling, student employment services, financial aid counseling, placement for graduates. **Transfer:** Orientation for new students.

Contact. E-mail: william.cassidy@remingtoncollege.edu
Phone: (216) 475-7520 Toll-free number: (800) 229-0185
Fax: (216) 475-6055
William Cassidy, Director of Recruitment, Remington College: Cleveland, 14445 Broadway Avenue, Cleveland, OH 44125

Remington College: Cleveland West

North Olmsted, Ohio
www.remingtoncollege.edu/clevelandwest/

- Private 2-year technical college
- Large town

General. Accredited by ACCSCT. **Calendar:** Quarter.

Contact. Phone: (440) 777-2560
26350 Brookpark Road, North Olmsted, OH 44070

RETS Tech Center

Centerville, Ohio
www.retstechcenter.com **CB code: 1610**

- For-profit 2-year junior and technical college
- Commuter campus in large town

General. Founded in 1953. Accredited by ACCSCT. **Location:** 15 miles from Dayton. **Calendar:** Semester.

Annual costs/financial aid. Costs are charged per entire associate degree or diploma program and vary with specific program. Associate programs range from $17,015 to $24,785. Diploma programs range from $8,400 to $17,085. Books/supplies: $950. Personal expenses: $945. Need-based financial aid available to full-time and part-time students.

Contact. Phone: (937) 433-3410
Director, 555 East Alex Bell Road, Centerville, OH 45459-9627

Rosedale Bible College

Irwin, Ohio
www.rosedale.edu **CB code: 3936**

- Private 2-year Bible and junior college affiliated with Mennonite Church
- Residential campus in rural community

General. Accredited by ABHE. **Enrollment:** 81 degree-seeking undergraduates. **Degrees:** 12 associate awarded. **Location:** 20 miles from Columbus. **Calendar:** Five 6-week terms. **Part-time faculty:** 14 total; 7% have terminal degrees, 14% women. **Class size:** 38% < 20, 50% 20-39, 12% 40-49.

Student profile. Among degree-seeking undergraduates, 1 transferred in from other institutions.

Hispanic American:	3%	**Live on campus:**	96%
International:	1%		

Basis for selection. Loyal devotion to Christ most important. **Adult students:** SAT/ACT scores not required.

2005-2006 Annual costs. Tuition/fees: $4,540. Per-credit charge: $148. Room/board: $4,010.

Application procedures. Admission: No deadline. $30 fee. Application may be submitted online. Admission notification on a rolling basis. **Financial aid:** FAFSA, institutional form required. Applicants notified on a rolling basis.

Academics. Special study options: Dual enrollment of high school students. **Credit/placement by examination:** AP, CLEP. **Support services:** Reduced course load.

Majors. Theology: Bible.

Computing on campus. 12 workstations in dormitories, library, computer center.

Student life. Freshman orientation: Mandatory. Preregistration for classes offered. **Policies:** Religious observance required. Freshmen permitted cars on campus. **Housing:** Guaranteed on-campus for all undergraduates. Single-sex dorms, apartments, substance-free housing available. **Activities:** Choral groups, drama, student government, student newspaper.

Athletics. Intramural: Basketball, soccer, table tennis, volleyball.

Student services. Campus ministries, financial aid counseling, health services. **Transfer:** Orientation, pre-admission transcript evaluation for new students.

Contact. E-mail: admissions@rosedale.edu
Phone: (740) 857-1311 Fax: (877) 857-1312
Kevin Mayer, Director of Enrollment Services, Rosedale Bible College, 2270 Rosedale Road, Irwin, OH 43029

School of Advertising Art

Kettering, Ohio
www.saacollege.com

- For-profit 2-year visual arts and technical college
- Commuter campus in small city
- Interview required

General. Accredited by ACCSCT. **Enrollment:** 143 degree-seeking undergraduates. **Degrees:** 39 associate awarded. **Location:** 5 miles from downtown. **Calendar:** Quarter. **Full-time faculty:** 11 total; 27% minority, 27% women. **Part-time faculty:** 5 total; 20% minority, 60% women. **Class size:** 100% < 20.

Student profile. Among degree-seeking undergraduates, 100% enrolled in a vocational program, 1% already have a bachelor's degree or higher, 86 enrolled as first-time, first-year students, 10 transferred in from other institutions.

Out-of-state:	8%	**Hispanic American:**	1%
Women:	50%	**International:**	1%
African American:	4%	**25 or older:**	1%
Asian American:	1%		

Transfer out. Colleges most students transferred to 2005: Art Institute of Pittsburgh, Art Institute of Atlanta, Columbus College of Art and Design, American Inter-Continental University of London, England.

Basis for selection. Portfolio and creative potential most important. Portfolio of 8 to 12 pieces of own artwork required. Depending on your GPA and attendance, a personal essay and letter of recommendation may be required. **Adult students:** Entrance exam policies same as for first-time freshmen. **Homeschooled:** Proof of completion of high school requirements is required.

High school preparation. Recommended units include English 4. 3 art units recommended.

2006-2007 Annual costs. Tuition/fees (projected): $20,130. First year tuition for diploma program $15,660, required fees $2,085.

2005-2006 Financial aid. All financial aid based on need. Average scholarship/grant was $5,000; average loan $2,625. 49% of total undergraduate aid awarded as scholarships/grants, 51% as loans/jobs.

Application procedures. Admission: No deadline. $90 fee. Application must be submitted on paper. Admission notification on a rolling basis. Students find out if they are accepted at the time of his or her portfolio review. Acceptance is conditional pending the receipt of a final high school transcript. Upon acceptance, student will receive enrollment agreement. To reserve a seat in the class, student must submit completed enrollment agreement and enrollment fee. **Financial aid:** Priority date 7/15, closing date 8/1. FAFSA, institutional form required. Applicants notified by 8/1; must reply by 8/1 or within 1 week(s) of notification.

Academics. Credit/placement by examination: CLEP, institutional tests. **Support services:** Remedial instruction, tutoring.

Majors. Communications: Advertising. **Computer sciences:** Computer graphics, webmaster. **Visual/performing arts:** Commercial/advertising art.

Computing on campus. PC or laptop required. 65 workstations in computer center. Wireless network available.

Student life. Freshman orientation: Mandatory. Three-hour session held on a Saturday in the spring. **Policies:** Freshmen permitted cars on campus. **Activities:** Student government.

Student services. Career counseling, financial aid counseling, personal counseling, placement for graduates. **Transfer:** Orientation, re-entry adviser, pre-admission transcript evaluation for new students. Transfer adviser for students transferring to 4-year colleges.

Contact. E-mail: jayne@saacollege.com
Phone: (937) 294-0592 ext. 102 Toll-free number: (877) 300-9326 ext. 102
Fax: (937) 294-5869
Jayne Fahncke, Director of Admissions, School of Advertising Art, 1725 East David Road, Kettering, OH 45440-1612

Sinclair Community College

Dayton, Ohio **CB member**
www.sinclair.edu **CB code: 1720**

- Public 2-year community college
- Commuter campus in small city

General. Founded in 1887. Regionally accredited. Member of the League for Innovation. College offers both transfer and technical academic programs. **Enrollment:** 15,215 degree-seeking undergraduates; 3,722 non-degree-seeking students. **Degrees:** 1,240 associate awarded. **ROTC:** Army, Air Force. **Location:** 50 miles from Cincinnati, 80 miles from Columbus. **Calendar:** Quarter, extensive summer session. **Full-time faculty:** 480 total; 100% have terminal degrees, 16% minority, 52% women. **Part-time faculty:** 694 total; 50% have terminal degrees, 14% minority, 42% women. **Class size:** 54% < 20, 45% 20-39, less than 1% 40-49, less than 1% 50-99, less than 1% >100. **Special facilities:** Art galleries, theater, center for corporate and community events. **Partnerships:** Formal partnerships with eight area high schools.

Student profile. Among degree-seeking undergraduates, 2,124 enrolled as first-time, first-year students, 1,061 transferred in from other institutions.

Part-time:	55%	**Women:**	58%
Out-of-state:	2%	**25 or older:**	47%

Transfer out. Colleges most students transferred to 2005: Wright State University, University of Cincinnati, University of Dayton, Capital University, Park College, Ohio State University.

Basis for selection. Open admission, but selective for some programs. Admission to allied health programs, paralegal program, tool and machining program, early childhood education all based on placement test scores and/or high school grades and specific program criteria. Allied Health Aptitude Test required for some selective programs. PAX required for nursing program. Interview required for some allied health programs.

2005-2006 Annual costs. Tuition/fees: $1,910; $3,121 out-of-district; $5,940 out-of-state. Per-credit charge: $42 in-district; $69 out-of-district; $132 out-of-state. Books/supplies: $810. Personal expenses: $2,000.

2005-2006 Financial aid. Need-based: Average scholarship/grant was $1,638; average loan $911. 77% of total undergraduate aid awarded as scholarships/grants, 23% as loans/jobs. Need-based aid available for part-time students. Work study available nights, weekends and for part-time students. **Non-need-based:** Scholarships awarded for academics, athletics, state residency.

Application procedures. Admission: No deadline. $20 fee. Application may be submitted online. Admission notification on a rolling basis. Closing dates for allied health programs vary by program. **Financial aid:** Priority date 5/1, closing date 8/1. FAFSA, institutional form required. Applicants notified on a rolling basis.

Academics. Special study options: Cooperative education, cross-registration, distance learning, dual enrollment of high school students, ESL, honors, independent study, internships, liberal arts/career combination, student-designed major. License preparation in aviation, dental hygiene, nursing, occupational therapy, paramedic, physical therapy, radiology, real estate. **Credit/placement by examination:** AP, CLEP, IB, institutional tests. 45 credit hours maximum toward associate degree. **Support services:** Learning center, pre-admission summer program, reduced course load, remedial instruction, study skills assistance, tutoring, writing center.

Majors. Architecture: Technology. **Area/ethnic studies:** African-American. **Biology:** General, biotechnology. **Business:** General, accounting, administrative services, banking/financial services, business admin, hospitality admin, labor relations, labor studies, logistics, purchasing, real estate, retailing, sales/distribution, tourism promotion, tourism/travel. **Communications:** General. **Computer sciences:** General, applications programming, webmaster. **Education:** Elementary, multiple handicapped, music, physical, secondary, special. **Engineering:** General. **Engineering technology:** Architectural, automotive, CAD/CADD, civil, drafting, electrical, electromechanical, environmental, manufacturing, mechanical, plastics, robotics, surveying. **Family/consumer sciences:** Child care, food/nutrition, institutional food production. **Foreign languages:** Sign language interpretation. **Health:** Dental hygiene, dietetic technician, EMT paramedic, health services, licensed practical nurse, massage therapy, medical radiologic technology/radiation therapy, medical records technology, mental health services, occupational therapy assistant, physical therapy assistant, radiologic technology/medical imaging, respiratory therapy assistant, respiratory therapy technology, surgical technology. **History:** General. **Legal studies:** Legal secretary, paralegal. **Liberal arts:** Arts/sciences. **Math:** General. **Mechanic/repair:** Automotive, heating/ac/refrig. **Parks/recreation:** Health/fitness. **Personal/culinary services:** Culinary arts. **Physical sciences:** Chemistry, geology, physics. **Production:** Tool and die. **Protective services:** Corrections, criminal justice, fire safety technology, police science. **Psychology:** General. **Public administration:** General, human services, social work. **Social sciences:** Geography, sociology, urban studies. **Transportation:** Aviation management. **Visual/performing arts:** General, commercial/advertising art, dance, dramatic, interior design, music history, music performance, studio arts, theater design.

Most popular majors. Business/marketing 17%, computer/information sciences 6%, engineering/engineering technologies 12%, health sciences 27%, liberal arts 12%, visual/performing arts 6%.

Computing on campus. 1,000 workstations in library, computer center, student center. Commuter students can connect to campus network. Online course registration, helpline available.

Student life. Freshman orientation: Mandatory. Required for degree and certificate-seeking students. **Policies:** Freshmen permitted cars on campus. **Activities:** Bands, choral groups, dance, drama, music ensembles, musical theater, opera, student government, student newspaper, African American cultural club, Native American cultural club, Latinos Unidos en Sinclair club, Phi Theta Kappa honorary club, Rowdy Tartan pep club, social issues club, Appalachian club, College Republican's club, international students' club, think tank.

Athletics. NJCAA. **Intercollegiate:** Baseball M, basketball, golf, tennis, volleyball W. **Team name:** Tartans.

Student services. Adult student services, alcohol/substance abuse counseling, campus ministries, career counseling, services for economically disadvantaged, student employment services, financial aid counseling, personal counseling, placement for graduates, veterans' counselor, women's services. **Physically disabled:** Services for visually, speech, hearing impaired. **Transfer:** Special adviser, orientation, pre-admission transcript evaluation for new students. Transfer adviser for students transferring to 4-year colleges.

Contact. E-mail: admit@sinclair.edu
Phone: (937) 512-3000 Toll-free number: (800) 315-3000
Fax: (937) 512-2393
Sara Smith, Director and Systems Manager for Outreach Services, Sinclair Community College, 444 West Third Street, Dayton, OH 45402-1460

Southeastern Business College

Chillicothe, Ohio
www.careersohio.com **CB code: 2468**

- For-profit 2-year business college
- Commuter campus in large town
- Interview required

General. Founded in 1962. Accredited by ACICS. **Enrollment:** 96 degree-seeking undergraduates. **Degrees:** 19 associate awarded. **Location:** 45 miles from Columbus, 90 miles from Cincinnati. **Calendar:** Quarter, extensive summer session. **Full-time faculty:** 2 total. **Part-time faculty:** 8 total.

Student profile. Among degree-seeking undergraduates, 20 enrolled as first-time, first-year students.

Part-time:	25%	**25 or older:**	75%
Women:	78%		

Basis for selection. Open admission. Placement tests in English and math required.

2005-2006 Annual costs. Per-credit charge: $185. Per-credit-hour cost is $185, plus $300 annual technology fee.

Financial aid. All financial aid based on need. Need-based aid available for part-time students.

Application procedures. Admission: $50 fee. Admission notification on a rolling basis. **Financial aid:** FAFSA, institutional form required.

Academics. Credit/placement by examination: CLEP. **Support services:** Remedial instruction, tutoring.

Majors. Business: Accounting, administrative services, business admin. **Computer sciences:** System admin. **Health:** Medical secretary.

Computing on campus. 28 workstations in computer center.

Student life. Freshman orientation: Mandatory.

Student services. Career counseling, financial aid counseling, placement for graduates. **Transfer:** Orientation for new students.

Contact. Phone: (740) 774-6300 Fax: (740) 774-6317
Liz Scott, Admissions Representative, Southeastern Business College, 1855 Western Avenue, Chillicothe, OH 45601-1038

Southeastern Business College: Jackson

Jackson, Ohio
www.southeasternbusinesscollege.com **CB code: 3264**

- For-profit 2-year business college
- Commuter campus in large town
- Interview required

General. Accredited by ACICS. **Enrollment:** 72 degree-seeking undergraduates. **Degrees:** 15 associate awarded. **Calendar:** Quarter. **Full-time faculty:** 2 total; 100% women. **Part-time faculty:** 9 total; 11% have terminal degrees, 56% women.

Student profile. Among degree-seeking undergraduates, 100% enrolled in a vocational program, 56 enrolled as first-time, first-year students.

Part-time:	24%	**25 or older:**	85%
Women:	81%		

Basis for selection. Open admission.

2005-2006 Annual costs. Per-credit charge: $185. Per-credit-hour cost is $185 plus $300 annual technology fee.

Financial aid. All financial aid based on need. Need-based aid available for part-time students. Work study available nights.

Application procedures. Admission: Closing date 9/10. No application fee. Application must be submitted on paper. Application closing dates vary by term and year. Applications must be received prior to start of classes. Students admitted year-round. **Financial aid:** No deadline. FAFSA, institutional form required. Applicants notified on a rolling basis.

Academics. Credit/placement by examination: CLEP. **Support services:** Tutoring.

Majors. Computer sciences: System admin.

Computing on campus. 35 workstations in library, computer center.

Student life. Freshman orientation: Mandatory. Preregistration for classes offered.

Contact. Phone: (740) 286-1554
Karen Osborne, Director/Registrar, Southeastern Business College: Jackson, 504 McCarty Lane, Jackson, OH 45640

Southeastern Business College: Lancaster

Lancaster, Ohio
www.careersohio.com **CB code: 3263**

- For-profit 2-year business and technical college
- Residential campus in large town

General. Accredited by ACICS. **Enrollment:** 71 degree-seeking undergraduates. **Degrees:** 5 associate awarded. **Location:** 25 miles from Columbus. **Calendar:** Quarter, extensive summer session. **Full-time faculty:** 1 total. **Part-time faculty:** 14 total.

Transfer out. 2% of students enrolled in the transfer program go on to 4-year colleges.

Basis for selection. Open admission.

2006-2007 Annual costs. Tuition/fees (projected): $9,380. Per-credit charge: $185. Books/supplies: $1,380. Personal expenses: $2,460.

Financial aid. All financial aid based on need. Need-based aid available for part-time students. Work study available nights and for part-time students.

Application procedures. Admission: $50 fee. Application may be submitted online. Admission notification on a rolling basis. **Financial aid:** Closing date 4/30. FAFSA, institutional form required. Applicants notified by 6/1; must reply within 2 week(s) of notification.

Academics. Credit/placement by examination: CLEP. **Support services:** Tutoring.

Majors. Business: Accounting, business admin. **Computer sciences:** General. **Health:** Medical secretary.

Computing on campus. 35 workstations in library, computer center. Online library, wireless network available.

Student life. Freshman orientation: Mandatory. Preregistration for classes offered.

Student services. Transfer: Special adviser, orientation, re-entry adviser for new students. College fairs on campus for students transferring to 4-year colleges.

Contact. E-mail: dir_lanc@yahoo.com
Phone: (740) 687-6126 Fax: (740) 687-0431
Jamie Fauble, Admissions, Southeastern Business College: Lancaster, 1522 Sheridan Drive, Lancaster, OH 43130-1303

Southeastern Business College: New Boston

New Boston, Ohio
www.southeasternbusinesscollege.com

- For-profit 2-year branch campus and business college
- Commuter campus in rural community

General. Accredited by ACICS. **Enrollment:** 80 degree-seeking undergraduates; 1 non-degree-seeking students. **Degrees:** 12 associate awarded. **Calendar:** Quarter. **Full-time faculty:** 1 total. **Part-time faculty:** 13 total; 62% women.

Student profile. Among degree-seeking undergraduates, 14 enrolled as first-time, first-year students.

Part-time:	15%	**Women:**	80%
Out-of-state:	3%		

Basis for selection. Open admission. **Adult students:** Entrance exam policies same as for first-time freshmen.

Financial aid. Need-based: Need-based aid available for part-time students.

Application procedures. Admission: No deadline. $50 fee. Application must be submitted on paper. **Financial aid:** No deadline. FAFSA required.

Academics. Special study options: Cooperative education. **Credit/placement by examination:** AP, CLEP. 16 credit hours maximum toward associate degree. **Support services:** Tutoring.

Majors. Business: Accounting, administrative services, business admin. **Computer sciences:** General. **Health:** Office admin.

Computing on campus. 30 workstations in library, computer center.

Student life. Freshman orientation: Mandatory.

Student services. Career counseling, financial aid counseling.

Contact. E-mail: admit_nb@yahoo.com
Phone: (740) 456-4124 Fax: (740) 456-5163
Rebecca Mowery, Admissions Representative, Southeastern Business College: New Boston, 3879 Rhodes Avenue, New Boston, OH 45662

Southern State Community College

Hillsboro, Ohio
www.sscc.edu **CB code: 1752**

- Public 2-year community college
- Commuter campus in small town

General. Founded in 1975. Regionally accredited. **Enrollment:** 2,311 degree-seeking undergraduates. **Degrees:** 259 associate awarded. **Location:** 60 miles

from Cincinnati, 55 miles from Columbus. **Calendar:** Quarter, limited summer session. **Full-time faculty:** 52 total; 15% have terminal degrees, 52% women. **Part-time faculty:** 82 total; 1% have terminal degrees, 52% women. **Class size:** 67% < 20, 32% 20-39, less than 1% 40-49, less than 1% 50-99.

Student profile. Among degree-seeking undergraduates, 67% enrolled in a transfer program, 33% enrolled in a vocational program, 590 enrolled as first-time, first-year students.

Part-time:	44%	**African American:**	1%
Out-of-state:	1%	**25 or older:**	45%
Women:	74%		

Basis for selection. Open admission, but selective for some programs. Special requirements for nursing and EMT programs. Interview required for nursing program. **Adult students:** Entrance exam policies same as for first-time freshmen. **Learning Disabled:** If modifications are requested, an appointment with Disabilities Service Coordinator is required.

2005-2006 Annual costs. Tuition/fees: $3,213; $6,189 out-of-state. Per-credit charge: $82 in-state; $159 out-of-state. Books/supplies: $1,500.

2004-2005 Financial aid. Need-based: 59% of total undergraduate aid awarded as scholarships/grants, 41% as loans/jobs. Need-based aid available for part-time students. Work study available for part-time students. **Non-need-based:** Scholarships awarded for academics, art, athletics, music/drama.

Application procedures. Admission: No deadline. No application fee. Admission notification on a rolling basis. **Financial aid:** Priority date 7/1, closing date 9/1. FAFSA, institutional form required. Applicants notified by 4/15; must reply within 2 week(s) of notification.

Academics. Special study options: Cross-registration, distance learning, dual enrollment of high school students, liberal arts/career combination, student-designed major. Bachelor's degree programs available on campus. License preparation in nursing, paramedic, real estate. **Credit/placement by examination:** AP, CLEP, institutional tests. 45 credit hours maximum toward associate degree. **Support services:** GED preparation and test center, learning center, remedial instruction, tutoring.

Majors. Agriculture: General. **Business:** General, accounting technology, administrative services, business admin, real estate. **Computer sciences:** Applications programming, programming, systems analysis. **Education:** Early childhood, teacher assistance. **Engineering technology:** Drafting, electrical. **Health:** EMT paramedic, medical assistant, nursing (RN), substance abuse counseling. **Liberal arts:** Arts/sciences. **Protective services:** Corrections, police science. **Public administration:** Human services.

Most popular majors. Business/marketing 17%, computer/information sciences 7%, health sciences 20%, liberal arts 44%.

Computing on campus. 300 workstations in library, computer center. Commuter students can connect to campus network. Online library, helpline available.

Student life. Freshman orientation: Available. **Activities:** Bands, choral groups, drama.

Athletics. NJCAA. **Intercollegiate:** Basketball, soccer M, softball W, volleyball W. **Team name:** Patriots.

Student services. Career counseling, student employment services, financial aid counseling, on-campus daycare, personal counseling, placement for graduates. **Physically disabled:** Services for visually, speech, hearing impaired. **Transfer:** Special adviser for new students. Transfer adviser, college fairs on campus for students transferring to 4-year colleges.

Contact. E-mail: info@sscc.edu
Phone: (937) 393-3431 Fax: (937) 393-6682
Wendy Johnson, Director of Admissions, Southern State Community College, 100 Hobart Drive, Hillsboro, OH 45133

Southwestern College: Dayton
Dayton, Ohio
www.swcollege.net **CB code: 2483**

- For-profit 2-year business college
- Commuter campus in small city

General. Accredited by ACICS. **Calendar:** Quarter.

Annual costs/financial aid. Tuition/fees (2005-2006): $8,370. Books/supplies: $600. Need-based financial aid available to full-time and part-time students.

Contact. Phone: (937) 224-0061
Director, 111 West 1st Street, Dayton, OH 45402

Southwestern College: Franklin
Franklin, Ohio
www.swcollege.net **CB code: 3268**

- For-profit 2-year health science and technical college
- Large town

General. Accredited by ACICS. **Enrollment:** 183 degree-seeking undergraduates. **Degrees:** 10 associate awarded. **Location:** 7 miles from Middletown. **Calendar:** Quarter, extensive summer session. **Full-time faculty:** 3 total. **Part-time faculty:** 15 total.

Student profile. Among degree-seeking undergraduates, 3% enrolled in a transfer program, 10% enrolled in a vocational program.

Basis for selection. Open admission. **Adult students:** Entrance exam policies same as for first-time freshmen.

2005-2006 Annual costs. Tuition/fees: $8,370.

Application procedures. Admission: No deadline. $20 fee. Application must be submitted on paper. Admission notification on a rolling basis.

Academics. Credit/placement by examination: CLEP.

Majors. Business: Business admin, office technology. **Health:** Medical secretary.

Student life. Activities: Student government, student newspaper.

Student services. Transfer: Special adviser, orientation, re-entry adviser, pre-admission transcript evaluation for new students. Transfer adviser for students transferring to 4-year colleges.

Contact. E-mail: lreilly@swcollege.net
Phone: (937) 746-6633 ext. 45103 Fax: (937) 746-6754
Lynne Riley, Director of Admissions, Southwestern College: Franklin, 201 East Second Street, Franklin, OH 45005

Southwestern College: Tri-County
Cincinnati, Ohio
www.swcollege.net **CB code: 2478**

- For-profit 2-year business and nursing college
- Small city

General. Accredited by ACICS. **Enrollment:** 220 undergraduates. **Degrees:** 11 associate awarded. **Calendar:** Quarter, extensive summer session. **Full-time faculty:** 5 total. **Part-time faculty:** 15 total.

Student profile. 100% enrolled in a vocational program, 1% already have a bachelor's degree or higher.

Basis for selection. Open admission.

2005-2006 Annual costs. Tuition/fees: $8,670. One time $100 registration fee for the first quarter.

Financial aid. All financial aid based on need.

Application procedures. Admission: No deadline. $100 fee. Admission notification on a rolling basis. **Financial aid:** FAFSA required.

Academics. Credit/placement by examination: CLEP.

Student life. Freshman orientation: Available.

Contact. E-mail: rkimble@swcollege.net
Phone: (513) 874-0432
Southwestern College: Tri-County, 149 Northland Boulevard, Cincinnati, OH 45246

Southwestern College: Vine Street Campus
Cincinnati, Ohio
www.swcollege.net **CB code: 3267**

- For-profit 2-year business and health science college
- Large city

General. Accredited by ACICS. **Enrollment:** 87 degree-seeking undergraduates; 194 non-degree-seeking students. **Degrees:** 11 associate awarded. **Calendar:** Quarter, extensive summer session. **Part-time faculty:** 12 total.

Student profile. Among degree-seeking undergraduates, 36 enrolled as first-time, first-year students.

Basis for selection. Open admission.

2005-2006 Annual costs. Tuition/fees: $8,370. Personal expenses: $2,500.

Application procedures. Admission: No deadline. $20 fee. **Financial aid:** FAFSA required.

Academics. Credit/placement by examination: CLEP.

Majors. Business: General.

Student life. Freshman orientation: Mandatory.

Contact. Phone: (513) 421-3212 Fax: (513) 421-8325
Betty Streber, Admissions Director, Southwestern College: Vine Street Campus, 632 Vine Street, Cincinnati, OH 45202

Stark State College of Technology

North Canton, Ohio
www.starkstate.edu **CB code: 1688**

- Public 2-year technical college
- Commuter campus in small city

General. Founded in 1970. Regionally accredited. **Enrollment:** 4,235 degree-seeking undergraduates; 2,605 non-degree-seeking students. **Degrees:** 656 associate awarded. **Location:** 50 miles from Cleveland. **Calendar:** Semester, limited summer session. **Full-time faculty:** 123 total; 69% have terminal degrees, 9% minority, 49% women. **Part-time faculty:** 301 total; 10% minority, 50% women.

Student profile. Among degree-seeking undergraduates, 1,531 enrolled as first-time, first-year students.

Part-time:	64%	**Women:**	55%
Out-of-state:	1%	**25 or older:**	50%

Basis for selection. Open admission, but selective for some programs. Selective admission to allied health programs. **Learning Disabled:** All students should meet with disability services coordinator.

High school preparation. Recommended units include English 4, mathematics 3 and science 3.

2005-2006 Annual costs. Tuition/fees: $3,600; $5,100 out-of-state. Per-credit charge: $100 in-state; $150 out-of-state. Books/supplies: $900.

2005-2006 Financial aid. All financial aid based on need. 569 full-time freshmen applied for aid; 480 were judged to have need; 457 of these received aid. Average need met was 65%. Average scholarship/grant was $1,055; average loan $1,151. 54% of total undergraduate aid awarded as scholarships/grants, 46% as loans/jobs. Need-based aid available for part-time students. Work study available nights, weekends and for part-time students.

Application procedures. Admission: Priority date 6/1; no deadline. No application fee. Application may be submitted online. Admission notification on a rolling basis. **Financial aid:** Priority date 5/1; no closing date. FAFSA, institutional form required. Applicants notified on a rolling basis starting 4/1; must reply within 4 week(s) of notification.

Academics. Special study options: Accelerated study, cooperative education, cross-registration, distance learning, double major, dual enrollment of high school students, independent study, internships, liberal arts/career combination, student-designed major, weekend college. License preparation in dental hygiene, nursing, paramedic. **Credit/placement by examination:** CLEP, institutional tests. 12 credit hours maximum toward associate degree. **Support services:** Learning center, pre-admission summer program, reduced course load, remedial instruction, study skills assistance, tutoring, writing center.

Majors. Architecture: Environmental design, urban/community planning. **Business:** General, accounting, accounting technology, accounting/business management, accounting/finance, administrative services, business admin, communications, construction management, e-commerce, executive assistant, hospitality admin, international, logistics, management information systems, market research, marketing, office management, office technology, operations, sales/distribution, taxation. **Computer sciences:** General, applications programming, computer graphics, computer science, data entry, data processing, database management, information systems, information technology, networking, programming, security, systems analysis, web page design, webmaster, word processing. **Conservation:** Environmental studies. **Education:** Early childhood. **Engineering:** Architectural, civil, electrical, environmental, software. **Engineering technology:** Architectural, civil, construction, electrical, manufacturing, surveying. **Family/consumer sciences:** Aging. **Health:** Clinical lab assistant, clinical lab technology, dental hygiene, massage therapy, medical assistant, medical records technology, nursing (RN), occupational therapy assistant, office assistant, physical therapy assistant, respiratory therapy assistant, respiratory therapy technology. **Legal studies:** Court reporting, legal secretary. **Liberal arts:** Arts/sciences. **Math:** General. **Mechanic/repair:** Automotive, electronics/electrical, heating/ac/refrig, industrial. **Protective services:** Firefighting. **Public administration:** Human services. **Social sciences:** General.

Computing on campus. 500 workstations in computer center, student center. Helpline, wireless network available.

Student life. Freshman orientation: Available. Preregistration for classes offered. Half-day prior to all semesters. Evening sessions are 2 hours. **Activities:** Literary magazine, student newspaper, Bible study group, Minority Awareness Association, Phi Theta Kappa.

Student services. Adult student services, campus ministries, career counseling, services for economically disadvantaged, student employment services, financial aid counseling, minority student services, on-campus daycare, personal counseling, placement for graduates, veterans' counselor. **Physically disabled:** Services for visually, speech, hearing impaired. **Learning disabled:** Comprehensive services available. **Transfer:** Special adviser, orientation, pre-admission transcript evaluation for new students. Transfer adviser, college fairs on campus for students transferring to 4-year colleges.

Contact. E-mail: info@starkstate.edu
Phone: (330) 494-6170 ext. 4228 Toll-free number: (800) 797-8275
Fax: (330) 497-6313
Wallace Hoffer, Dean Student Services, Stark State College of Technology, 6200 Frank Avenue NW, North Canton, OH 44720

Stautzenberger College

Toledo, Ohio
www.sctoday.edu **CB code: 2487**

- For-profit 2-year business and technical college
- Commuter campus in large city
- Interview required

General. Founded in 1928. Accredited by ACICS. **Enrollment:** 750 degree-seeking undergraduates. **Degrees:** 97 associate awarded. **Location:** 50 miles from Detroit, 120 miles from Cleveland. **Calendar:** Quarter, extensive summer session. **Full-time faculty:** 10 total; 60% have terminal degrees, 10% minority, 60% women. **Part-time faculty:** 40 total; 62% have terminal degrees, 8% minority, 68% women. **Class size:** 81% < 20, 19% 20-39. **Special facilities:** Veterinary technician labs, medical assisting labs, computer labs. **Partnerships:** Formal partnerships with Microsoft IT Academy, Novell Training Partner.

Basis for selection. Open admission. Campus visit and completion of Program Questionaire required. **Learning Disabled:** Any special accommodations must be requested in writing. Dean of Students will review in conjunction with school ADA counselor. Approval needed before acceptance.

2006-2007 Annual costs. Tuition/fees (projected): $4,795. Per-credit charge: $155. Tuition ranges from $155 to $330 per-credit-hour depending on program. Books/supplies: $1,050. Personal expenses: $2,619.

Financial aid. All financial aid based on need. Need-based aid available for part-time students.

Application procedures. Admission: No deadline. $25 fee. Application must be submitted on paper. Admission notification on a rolling basis. **Financial aid:** No deadline. FAFSA required. Applicants notified on a rolling basis.

Academics. Special study options: License preparation in real estate. **Credit/placement by examination:** CLEP. **Support services:** Learning center, study skills assistance, tutoring.

Majors. Business: Accounting technology, entrepreneurial studies, office technology. **Computer sciences:** Data entry, LAN/WAN management, web page design. **Health:** Insurance coding, massage therapy, medical assistant, medical secretary, medical transcription, receptionist, veterinary technology/assistant. **Legal studies:** Paralegal.

Computing on campus. 200 workstations in library, computer center.

Student life. **Freshman orientation:** Available.

Student services. Financial aid counseling, placement for graduates, veterans' counselor. **Transfer:** Special adviser, orientation, pre-admission transcript evaluation for new students.

Contact. E-mail: admissions@stautzenberger.com
Phone: (419) 866-0261 Toll-free number: (800) 552-5099
Fax: (419) 867-9821
Karen Fitzgerald, Director of Admission, Stautzenberger College, 5355 Southwyck Boulevard, Toledo, OH 43614

Stautzenberger College: Strongsville

Strongsville, Ohio
www.sctoday.edu/strongsville

- For-profit 2-year business and health science college
- Large town

General. Accredited by ACICS. **Calendar:** Quarter.

Annual costs/financial aid. Tuition/fees (projected): $7,810.

Contact. Phone: (440) 846-1999
12925 Pearl Road, Strongsville, OH 44136

Technology Education College

Columbus, Ohio
www.teceducation.com **CB code: 3035**

- For-profit 2-year technical college
- Commuter campus in very large city
- Interview required

General. Accredited by ACCSCT. **Enrollment:** 500 undergraduates. **Degrees:** 121 associate awarded. **Calendar:** Quarter, extensive summer session. **Full-time faculty:** 25 total. **Part-time faculty:** 8 total.

Basis for selection. Open admission. Entrance test scores, interview important. Applicants with ACT score of 18 or SAT score of 840 (exclusive of Writing) not required to take entrance examination.

2005-2006 Annual costs. Tuition varies per program, but averages $9,300 per academic year. Books/supplies: $578. Personal expenses: $2,600.

Financial aid. All financial aid based on need. Need-based aid available for part-time students.

Application procedures. **Admission:** No deadline. $35 fee, may be waived for applicants with need. Admission notification on a rolling basis. **Financial aid:** No deadline. FAFSA required. Applicants notified on a rolling basis.

Academics. **Credit/placement by examination:** CLEP. **Support services:** Tutoring.

Majors. **Computer sciences:** General, applications programming, programming. **Health:** Medical assistant, office assistant, pharmacy assistant. **Protective services:** Police science.

Computing on campus. 100 workstations in computer center.

Student life. **Freshman orientation:** Mandatory. **Policies:** Freshmen permitted cars on campus. **Housing:** Single-sex dorms available.

Student services. Career counseling, student employment services, financial aid counseling, personal counseling, placement for graduates.

Contact. Phone: (614) 456-4600 Toll-free number: (800) 838-3233
Fax: (614) 456-4640
Rhonda Fraizer, Director of Admissions, Technology Education College, 2745 Winchester Pike, Columbus, OH 43232

Terra State Community College

Fremont, Ohio
www.terra.edu **CB code: 0365**

- Public 2-year community and technical college
- Commuter campus in large town

General. Founded in 1968. Regionally accredited. **Location:** 33 miles from Toledo, 86 miles from Columbus. **Calendar:** Quarter.

Annual costs/financial aid. Tuition/fees (2005-2006): $3,386; $6,938 out-of-state. Books/supplies: $675. Personal expenses: $400. Need-based financial aid available to full-time and part-time students.

Contact. Phone: (419) 334-8400 ext. 349
Assistant Dean of Student Support Services, 2830 Napoleon Road, Fremont, OH 43420-9600

Trumbull Business College

Warren, Ohio
www.tbc-trumbullbusiness.com **CB code: 3270**

- For-profit 2-year business college
- Commuter campus in small town

General. Accredited by ACICS. **Enrollment:** 415 degree-seeking undergraduates. **Degrees:** 86 associate awarded. **Calendar:** Quarter. **Full-time faculty:** 10 total. **Part-time faculty:** 6 total.

Basis for selection. Open admission.

2005-2006 Annual costs. Tuition/fees: $9,525. Per-credit charge: $210. Books/supplies: $936. Personal expenses: $1,485.

Financial aid. **Need-based:** Need-based aid available for part-time students.

Application procedures. **Admission:** No deadline. $75 fee. Admission notification on a rolling basis. **Financial aid:** FAFSA required.

Academics. **Credit/placement by examination:** AP, CLEP.

Majors. **Business:** Accounting, business admin, office technology. **Computer sciences:** General, applications programming. **Health:** Medical secretary. **Legal studies:** Legal secretary.

Student life. **Freshman orientation:** Available.

Contact. E-mail: admissions@tbc-trumbullbusiness.com
Phone: (330) 369-3200 ext. 26
Trumbull Business College, 3200 Ridge Road, Warren, OH 44484

University of Akron: Wayne College

Orrville, Ohio
www.wayne.uakron.edu **CB code: 1892**

- Public 2-year branch campus and junior college
- Commuter campus in small town

General. Founded in 1972. Regionally accredited. **Enrollment:** 1,540 degree-seeking undergraduates; 197 non-degree-seeking students. **Degrees:** 94 associate awarded. **ROTC:** Army, Air Force. **Location:** 35 miles from Akron. **Calendar:** Semester, limited summer session. **Full-time faculty:** 29 total. **Part-time faculty:** 104 total. **Class size:** 65% < 20, 31% 20-39, 3% 40-49, less than 1% 50-99. **Special facilities:** Nature trail, arboretum, wetlands, mock hazardous spill facility, distance learning room.

Student profile. Among degree-seeking undergraduates, 232 enrolled as first-time, first-year students.

Part-time:	41%	**Asian American:**	1%
Women:	63%	**Hispanic American:**	1%
African American:	3%	**25 or older:**	40%

Transfer out. **Colleges most students transferred to 2005:** Ashland University, Kent State, Cleveland State, Ohio State, Ohio University.

Basis for selection. Open admission. **Adult students:** SAT/ACT scores not required if applicant over 21. **Homeschooled:** Recommend completion of GED.

High school preparation. Recommended units include English 4, mathematics 3, social studies 3, science 3 and foreign language 2.

2005-2006 Annual costs. Tuition/fees: $5,029; $12,837 out-of-state. Books/supplies: $600. Personal expenses: $1,465.

Financial aid. **Need-based:** Need-based aid available for part-time students. Work study available nights and weekends. **Non-need-based:** Scholarships awarded for academics, art, athletics, leadership, minority status, music/drama, state residency. **Additional information:** All financial aid processed through University of Akron.

Application procedures. **Admission:** No deadline. $30 fee, may be waived for applicants with need. Application may be submitted online. Admission notification on a rolling basis. **Financial aid:** Closing date 3/15. FAFSA, institutional form required. Applicants notified on a rolling basis starting 4/15.

Academics. First 2 years of general bachelor's degree classes available for students who plan to continue at University of Akron or other colleges and universities. Paraprofessional and technical programs (associates and certificates) available in business, industry, public services occupation areas. **Special study options:** Cooperative education, cross-registration, distance learning, dual enrollment of high school students, honors, independent study, internships, liberal arts/career combination, student-designed major, weekend college. **Credit/placement by examination:** AP, CLEP, institutional tests. **Support services:** Learning center, remedial instruction, study skills assistance, tutoring, writing center.

Majors. **Business:** General, accounting, administrative services, business admin, management information systems, marketing, office management, office technology. **Computer sciences:** Applications programming, data processing, networking. **Health:** Environmental health, health care admin, medical assistant, medical radiologic technology/radiation therapy, medical secretary, respiratory therapy technology, surgical technology. **Legal studies:** Legal secretary. **Liberal arts:** Arts/sciences. **Public administration:** Social work.

Most popular majors. Business/marketing 57%, health sciences 6%, liberal arts 20%, security/protective services 13%.

Computing on campus. 140 workstations in library, computer center, student center. Commuter students can connect to campus network. Online course registration, helpline available.

Student life. **Freshman orientation:** Mandatory. **Activities:** Literary magazine, student government, student newspaper.

Athletics. NJCAA. **Intercollegiate:** Basketball, cheerleading M, golf M, volleyball W. **Intramural:** Basketball, racquetball, volleyball W. **Team name:** Warriors.

Student services. Adult student services, career counseling, student employment services, financial aid counseling, personal counseling, placement for graduates, veterans' counselor. **Physically disabled:** Services for visually, speech, hearing impaired. **Learning disabled:** Comprehensive services available. **Transfer:** Special adviser, orientation, pre-admission transcript evaluation for new students. Transfer adviser, college fairs on campus for students transferring to 4-year colleges.

Contact. E-mail: wayneadmissions@uakron.edu
Phone: (330) 683-2010 Toll-free number: (800) 221-8308 ext. 8900
Fax: (330) 684-8989
Alicia Broadus, Enrollment Specialist, University of Akron: Wayne College, 1901 Smucker Road, Orrville, OH 44667-9758

University of Cincinnati: Clermont College

Batavia, Ohio
www.ucclermont.edu **CB code: 3073**

- Public 2-year branch campus college
- Commuter campus in small town

General. Founded in 1972. Regionally accredited. College serves Clermont, Brown, and eastern Hamilton counties. One of 2 open-access regional campuses of the University of Cincinnati. **Enrollment:** 2,452 degree-seeking undergraduates; 363 non-degree-seeking students. **Degrees:** 306 associate awarded. **ROTC:** Army. **Location:** 17 miles from Cincinnati. **Calendar:** Quarter, limited summer session. **Full-time faculty:** 49 total; 47% have terminal degrees, 6% minority, 57% women. **Partnerships:** Formal partnerships with Barnes Aerospace and the Tech Prep Consortium.

Student profile. Among degree-seeking undergraduates, 57% enrolled in a transfer program, 43% enrolled in a vocational program, 595 enrolled as first-time, first-year students, 162 transferred in from other institutions.

Part-time:	36%	**Asian American:**	1%
Out-of-state:	3%	**Hispanic American:**	1%
Women:	63%	**25 or older:**	34%
African American:	2%		

Transfer out. **Colleges most students transferred to 2005:** Northern Kentucky University, University of Cincinnati, Wilmington College.

Basis for selection. Open admission, but selective for some programs. Admissions to surgical technology and respiratory programs requires satisfactory completion of biology and chemistry within past 5 years. **Adult students:** Entrance exam policies same as for first-time freshmen. **Home-schooled:** All existing school records and formal documentation of high school curriculum required. Course content descriptions, copy of the superintendent release form, notarized statement from parent, and precollege curriculum form completed and signed by parent may also be required. Appointment involving student, teacher, and admissions representative may be encouraged.

High school preparation. 16 units recommended. Recommended units include English 4, mathematics 3, social studies 2, science 2, foreign language 2 and academic electives 2. 1 fine arts recommended.

2005-2006 Annual costs. Tuition/fees: $4,299; $10,785 out-of-state. Per-credit charge: $120 in-state; $300 out-of-state.

2005-2006 Financial aid. **Need-based:** 21 full-time freshmen applied for aid; 19 were judged to have need; 17 of these received aid. Average need met was 37%. Average scholarship/grant was $1,135; average loan $1,759. 56% of total undergraduate aid awarded as scholarships/grants, 44% as loans/jobs. Need-based aid available for part-time students. Work study available nights, weekends and for part-time students. **Non-need-based:** Awarded to 81 full-time undergraduates, including 3 freshmen. Scholarships awarded for academics, state residency. **Additional information:** All financial aid applications and awards administered through Uptown campus except in-house loans and scholarships.

Application procedures. **Admission:** No deadline. $35 fee, may be waived for applicants with need. Application may be submitted online. Admission notification on a rolling basis. **Financial aid:** No deadline. FAFSA required. Applicants notified on a rolling basis.

Academics. **Special study options:** Cooperative education, cross-registration, distance learning, double major, dual enrollment of high school students, independent study, internships, student-designed major, study abroad, weekend college. Bachelor's degree programs available on campus. License preparation in aviation, nursing, paramedic. **Credit/placement by examination:** AP, CLEP, IB, institutional tests. 50% of hours needed for degree may be earned by examination. **Support services:** GED test center, learning center, reduced course load, remedial instruction, study skills assistance, tutoring.

Majors. **Architecture:** Urban/community planning. **Biology:** General. **Business:** General, accounting technology, administrative services, business admin, office management, office technology. **Communications:** Digital media. **Computer sciences:** General, applications programming, computer graphics, data entry, data processing, information technology, networking, programming, vendor certification, web page design. **Education:** Early childhood, elementary, kindergarten/preschool, middle, secondary. **Engineering technology:** CAD/CADD, computer systems. **Health:** EMT ambulance attendant, EMT paramedic, nursing (RN), predentistry, premedicine, prenursing, prepharmacy, preveterinary, respiratory therapy technology, surgical technology. **Legal studies:** Legal secretary, paralegal, prelaw. **Liberal arts:** Arts/sciences. **Physical sciences:** Chemistry. **Protective services:** Corrections, criminal justice, forensics, law enforcement admin, security services. **Public administration:** Social work. **Social sciences:** Urban studies. **Transportation:** Aviation, flight instructor.

Computing on campus. 77 workstations in library, computer center, student center. Commuter students can connect to campus network. Online course registration, online library, helpline, wireless network available.

Student life. **Freshman orientation:** Available. Preregistration for classes offered. Programs held each quarter for 2-3 hours. **Policies:** Freshmen permitted cars on campus. **Activities:** Student government, student newspaper, student tribunal, Christian Fellowship, foreign language club, campus ministry, Young Democrats, Circle K Club (Kiwanis).

Athletics. USCAA. **Intercollegiate:** Basketball, cheerleading M, golf M, softball W, tennis, volleyball W. **Intramural:** Golf, table tennis, volleyball. **Team name:** Cougars.

Student services. Career counseling, services for economically disadvantaged, student employment services, financial aid counseling, placement for graduates, veterans' counselor, women's services. **Physically disabled:** Services for visually, speech, hearing impaired. **Transfer:** Special adviser, orientation for new students. Transfer adviser, college fairs on campus for students transferring to 4-year colleges.

Contact. E-mail: clc.admissions@uc.edu
Phone: (513) 732-5202 Toll-free number: (866) 446-2822
Fax: (513) 732-5303
Blaine Kelley, Director of Enrollment Services, University of Cincinnati: Clermont College, 4200 Clermont College Drive, Batavia, OH 45103

University of Cincinnati: Raymond Walters College

Cincinnati, Ohio
www.rwc.uc.edu **CB code: 0354**

- Public 2-year branch campus college
- Commuter campus in large city

General. Founded in 1967. Regionally accredited. **Enrollment:** 3,942 degree-seeking undergraduates. **Degrees:** 2 bachelor's, 438 associate awarded. **ROTC:** Army, Navy, Air Force. **Location:** 15 miles from downtown. **Calendar:** Quarter, limited summer session. **Full-time faculty:** 150 total. **Part-time faculty:** 150 total. **Class size:** 41% < 20, 58% 20-39, less than 1% 40-49, less than 1% 50-99. **Partnerships:** Formal partnerships with GEAE Sharonville, Ford, GM, Ethicon Blue Ash, Soft Skills & IT Training, Ford, Sara Lee, 30 small companies.

Transfer out. Colleges most students transferred to 2005: University of Cincinnati, Xavier University, Northern Kentucky University, College of Mount St. Joseph.

Basis for selection. Open admission, but selective for some programs. Most health programs require lab science in biology and chemistry with grade of C or higher within the last 6 years. TOEFL or ability to benefit test required of non-native English speakers for placement. SAT/ACT required for high school seniors applying to nursing and dental hygiene. **Adult students:** Entrance exam policies same as for first-time freshmen. **Homeschooled:** Students should have 17 ACT or 870 SAT (exclusive of Writing), copy of curriculum, and high school transcript.

High school preparation. Recommended units include English 4, mathematics 3, social studies 2, history 2, science 2 and foreign language 2.

2005-2006 Annual costs. Tuition/fees: $4,938; $12,801 out-of-state. Per-credit charge: $138 in-state; $356 out-of-state. Books/supplies: $700.

Financial aid. All financial aid based on need. Need-based aid available for part-time students. Work study available for part-time students. **Additional information:** All financial aid applications and awards administered through main campus.

Application procedures. Admission: No deadline. $35 fee, may be waived for applicants with need. Application may be submitted online. Admission notification on a rolling basis. **Financial aid:** Priority date 3/15; no closing date. FAFSA required. Applicants notified on a rolling basis starting 3/15; must reply within 2 week(s) of notification.

Academics. Special study options: Accelerated study, cooperative education, cross-registration, distance learning, double major, dual enrollment of high school students, independent study, internships, liberal arts/career combination, student-designed major, study abroad, teacher certification program, weekend college. Bachelor's degree programs available on campus. License preparation in dental hygiene, nursing, paramedic, radiology, real estate. **Credit/placement by examination:** AP, CLEP, IB, institutional tests. Students must complete at least 45 credits at school to receive degree. CLEP credit by evaluation and credit by portfolio may be available. **Support services:** Learning center, pre-admission summer program, reduced course load, remedial instruction, study skills assistance, tutoring, writing center.

Majors. Biology: General. **Business:** General, accounting technology, administrative services, business admin, executive assistant, financial planning, office/clerical, real estate, sales/distribution. **Communications:** General, digital media. **Communications technology:** Graphics. **Computer sciences:** General, computer graphics, information technology, web page design, webmaster. **Education:** General, early childhood, elementary, middle, secondary. **Family/consumer sciences:** Food/nutrition. **Health:** Clinical nutrition, community health, dental hygiene, dietetics, EMT paramedic, health services, insurance specialist, medical radiologic technology/radiation therapy, medical secretary, medical transcription, nuclear medical technology, nursing (RN), office assistant, predentistry, premedicine, prepharmacy, preveterinary, radiation protection, radiologic technology/medical imaging, veterinary technology/assistant, vocational rehab counseling. **Interdisciplinary:** Nutrition sciences. **Legal studies:** Legal secretary, prelaw. **Liberal arts:** Arts/sciences. **Mechanic/repair:** Automotive, computer. **Personal/culinary services:** Mortuary science. **Physical sciences:** Chemistry. **Protective services:** Criminal justice. **Public administration:** Social work. **Science technology:** Biological, chemical. **Social sciences:** Economics, urban studies. **Visual/performing arts:** Design, graphic design.

Most popular majors. Business/marketing 18%, communications/journalism 8%, computer/information sciences 16%, education 6%, health sciences 39%.

Computing on campus. 275 workstations in computer center. Commuter students can connect to campus network. Online course registration, online library, helpline available.

Student life. Freshman orientation: Available, $30 fee. Preregistration for classes offered. One-day program. **Policies:** Student organization members must be in good academic standing. Freshmen permitted cars on campus. **Activities:** Student government, student newspaper, Campus Ministry, international student club.

Athletics. Intramural: Golf.

Student services. Adult student services, career counseling, student employment services, financial aid counseling, minority student services, on-campus daycare, placement for graduates. **Physically disabled:** Services for visually, hearing impaired. **Transfer:** Special adviser, pre-admission transcript evaluation for new students. College fairs on campus for students transferring to 4-year colleges.

Contact. Phone: (513) 745-5700 Fax: (513) 745-5768
Chris Powers, Director, Enrollment Services, University of Cincinnati: Raymond Walters College, 9555 Plainfield Road, Cincinnati, OH 45236-1096

University of Northwestern Ohio

Lima, Ohio
www.unoh.edu **CB code: 0816**

- Private 2-year business and technical college
- Residential campus in large town

General. Founded in 1920. Regionally accredited. **Enrollment:** 2,087 degree-seeking undergraduates; 828 non-degree-seeking students. **Degrees:** 102 bachelor's, 403 associate awarded. **Location:** 75 miles from Toledo, 90 miles from Columbus. **Calendar:** Differs by program. Quarter and 6-week session. Extensive summer session. **Full-time faculty:** 80 total; 2% have terminal degrees, 21% women. **Part-time faculty:** 27 total; 52% women.

Student profile. Among degree-seeking undergraduates, 42% enrolled in a vocational program, 630 enrolled as first-time, first-year students.

Part-time:	11%	**African American:**	1%
Out-of-state:	21%	**25 or older:**	18%
Women:	27%	**Live on campus:**	65%

Transfer out. Colleges most students transferred to 2005: Lima Technical College, Ohio State University, Wright State University, Bowling Green State University.

Basis for selection. Students with high school GPA of 1.5 or lower admitted conditionally. **Adult students:** Entrance exam policies same as for first-time freshmen. **Homeschooled:** Statement describing homeschool structure and mission required. **Learning Disabled:** Students must self-disclose personal needs and provide an IEP.

2005-2006 Annual costs. Tuition/fees: $8,730. Per-credit charge: $190. $235 per credit hour charge for virtual classes. Room/board: $6,020. Books/supplies: $1,798. Personal expenses: $1,818.

2004-2005 Financial aid. Need-based: 588 full-time freshmen applied for aid; 242 were judged to have need; 242 of these received aid. Average need met was 83%. Average scholarship/grant was $4,211. 33% of total undergraduate aid awarded as scholarships/grants, 67% as loans/jobs. Need-based aid available for part-time students. Work study available nights and for part-time students. **Non-need-based:** Awarded to 1,045 full-time undergraduates, including 255 freshmen. Scholarships awarded for academics, job skills, minority status.

Application procedures. Admission: No deadline. $50 fee. Application may be submitted online. Admission notification on a rolling basis. **Financial aid:** Priority date 4/1; no closing date. FAFSA required. Applicants notified on a rolling basis starting 4/30; must reply within 2 week(s) of notification.

Academics. Students wanting credit for life experience must register for 1-hour course in portfolio development. **Special study options:** Accelerated study, cooperative education, distance learning, double major, weekend college. Bachelor's degree programs available on campus. **Credit/placement by examination:** AP, CLEP, institutional tests. 25 credit hours maximum toward associate degree. **Support services:** Learning center, remedial instruction, tutoring.

Majors. Agriculture: Business. **Business:** Accounting, administrative services, business admin, marketing, office technology, tourism/travel. **Computer sciences:** General, applications programming. **Health:** Medical assistant, medical secretary, pharmacy assistant. **Legal studies:** Legal secretary, paralegal. **Mechanic/repair:** Automotive, diesel, heating/ac/refrig.

Most popular majors. Business/marketing 6%, trade and industry 73%.

Computing on campus. 212 workstations in library, computer center, student center. Commuter students can connect to campus network. Online course registration available.

Student life. Freshman orientation: Available. Held 4 to 6 weeks before quarter or session begins. **Policies:** Freshmen permitted cars on campus. **Housing:** Guaranteed on-campus for all undergraduates. Single-sex dorms, special housing for disabled, apartments, substance-free housing available. $100 deposit. **Activities:** Student government, student newspaper, TV station.

Athletics. Intramural: Bowling, volleyball.

Student services. Adult student services, career counseling, student employment services, financial aid counseling, minority student services, personal counseling, placement for graduates, veterans' counselor. **Physically disabled:** Services for visually, hearing impaired. **Transfer:** Special adviser, pre-admission transcript evaluation for new students.

Contact. E-mail: info@unoh.edu
Phone: (419) 998-3120 Fax: (419) 229-6926
Rick Morrison, Director of Admissions, University of Northwestern Ohio, 1441 North Cable Road, Lima, OH 45805

Vatterott College: Cleveland

Broadview Heights, Ohio
www.vatterott-college.edu

- For-profit 2-year technical college
- Commuter campus

General. Accredited by ACCSCT. **Calendar:** Semester.

Contact. Phone: (440) 526-1660
Director of Admissions, 5025 East Royalton Road, Broadview Heights, OH 44147

Virginia Marti College of Art and Design

Lakewood, Ohio
www.vmcad.edu **CB code: 0396**

- For-profit 2-year art and business college
- Commuter campus in small city

General. Founded in 1966. Accredited by ACCSCT. **Location:** 7 miles from Cleveland. **Calendar:** Continuous.

Annual costs/financial aid. Tuition/fees (2005-2006): $14,175. Books/supplies: $1,200. Personal expenses: $1,746. Need-based financial aid available for full-time students.

Contact. Phone: (216) 221-8584
Assistant Director, 11724 Detroit Avenue, Lakewood, OH 44107

Washington State Community College

Marietta, Ohio
www.wscc.edu **CB code: 0381**

- Public 2-year community college
- Commuter campus in large town

General. Founded in 1971. Regionally accredited. **Enrollment:** 2,300 undergraduates. **Degrees:** 295 associate awarded. **Location:** 112 miles from Columbus. **Calendar:** Quarter, limited summer session. **Full-time faculty:** 59 total. **Part-time faculty:** 100 total.

Student profile.

Out-of-state:	12%	**25 or older:**	46%

Basis for selection. Open admission, but selective for some programs. Special requirements for medical laboratory technology, nursing, physical therapist assistant, radiology, respiratory therapy programs. ACT required for nursing, radiologic technology programs. 3/28 scores submission deadline for nursing program. Interview required for programs with selective admission. **Adult students:** Entrance exam policies same as for first-time freshmen.

2005-2006 Annual costs. Tuition/fees: $3,510; $6,885 out-of-state. Per-credit charge: $75 in-state; $150 out-of-state. Books/supplies: $705. Personal expenses: $4,145.

Application procedures. Admission: No deadline. No application fee. Application may be submitted online. Admission notification on a rolling basis. **Financial aid:** No deadline. FAFSA, institutional form required. Applicants notified on a rolling basis starting 5/15; must reply within 2 week(s) of notification.

Academics. Special study options: Distance learning, double major, dual enrollment of high school students, independent study, internships, student-designed major. License preparation in nursing, radiology. **Credit/placement by examination:** CLEP, institutional tests. 60 credit hours maximum toward associate degree. **Support services:** Learning center, pre-admission summer program, reduced course load, remedial instruction, tutoring.

Majors. Business: General, accounting, business admin, e-commerce, marketing. **Communications:** Broadcast journalism, media studies. **Communications technology:** Animation/special effects. **Computer sciences:** Computer graphics, data processing, programming. **Education:** General, elementary, multi-level teacher, secondary. **Engineering:** General, electrical. **Engineering technology:** Drafting, electrical. **Health:** Clinical lab assistant, medical radiologic technology/radiation therapy, medical transcription, nursing (RN), physical therapy assistant, respiratory therapy technology. **Interdisciplinary:** Natural sciences. **Liberal arts:** Arts/sciences. **Math:** General. **Mechanic/repair:** Automotive, diesel, heating/ac/refrig. **Protective services:** Corrections, law enforcement admin. **Public administration:** Human services. **Science technology:** Biological.

Student life. Freshman orientation: Available. Preregistration for classes offered. **Activities:** Choral groups, music ensembles, student government, student newspaper, Veterans Club, Phi Theta Kappa honor fraternity.

Student services. Adult student services, career counseling, student employment services, financial aid counseling, personal counseling, placement for graduates, veterans' counselor. **Physically disabled:** Services for visually, hearing impaired. **Transfer:** Special adviser for new students. Transfer adviser, college fairs on campus for students transferring to 4-year colleges.

Contact. E-mail: admissions@wscc.edu
Phone: (740) 568-1900 Fax: (740) 373-7496
Rebecca Peroni, Director of Admissions, Washington State Community College, 710 Colegate Drive, Marietta, OH 45750

Wright State University: Lake Campus

Celina, Ohio
www.wright.edu/lake **CB code: 1947**

- Public 2-year branch campus college
- Commuter campus in small town

General. Founded in 1969. Regionally accredited. **Enrollment:** 665 degree-seeking undergraduates; 163 non-degree-seeking students. **Degrees:** 79 associate awarded. **Location:** 70 miles from Dayton. **Calendar:** Quarter, limited summer session. **Full-time faculty:** 20 total. **Part-time faculty:** 50 total. **Class size:** 83% < 20, 17% 20-39.

Student profile. Among degree-seeking undergraduates, 3% enrolled in a transfer program, 2% already have a bachelor's degree or higher, 150 enrolled as first-time, first-year students, 36 transferred in from other institutions.

Part-time:	21%	**Asian American:**	1%
Women:	68%	**Hispanic American:**	1%

Basis for selection. Open admission, but selective for some programs. Special requirements for engineering and education programs. SAT/ACT required for all students but only used for placement in selective programs.

High school preparation. 16 units recommended. Recommended units include English 4, mathematics 3, social studies 3, science 3 (laboratory 3) and foreign language 2. One unit of art recommended.

2005-2006 Annual costs. Tuition/fees: $4,617; $10,992 out-of-state. Per-credit charge: $142 in-state; $337 out-of-state.

Financial aid. Need-based: Need-based aid available for part-time students. **Non-need-based:** Scholarships awarded for academics, athletics, state residency. **Additional information:** Academic scholarship application deadline February 1. All financial aid applications and awards administered by Dayton campus.

Application procedures. Admission: No deadline. $30 fee. Application may be submitted online. Admission notification on a rolling basis. **Financial aid:** Priority date 2/15; no closing date. FAFSA, institutional form required. Applicants notified on a rolling basis; must reply within 2 week(s) of notification.

Academics. Bachelor's degrees awarded through main campus. **Special study options:** Cooperative education, cross-registration, distance learning, double major, dual enrollment of high school students, honors, independent study, internships, student-designed major. Bachelor's degree programs available on campus. **Credit/placement by examination:** CLEP, IB, institutional tests. **Support services:** Learning center, pre-admission summer program, reduced course load, remedial instruction, tutoring.

Majors. Biology: General. **Business:** General, business admin, management information systems. **Communications:** General. **Computer sciences:** Information systems. **Engineering technology:** General, drafting, manufacturing. **History:** General. **Liberal arts:** Arts/sciences. **Physical sciences:** Chemistry. **Psychology:** General. **Public administration:** Social work. **Social sciences:** Sociology.

Most popular majors. Business/marketing 56%, engineering/engineering technologies 24%.

Computing on campus. 105 workstations in computer center. Commuter students can connect to campus network. Online library available.

Student life. Freshman orientation: Available. **Policies:** Freshmen permitted cars on campus. **Activities:** Drama, student government, student newspaper, Business Professionals of America, Student Manufacturing Engineers.

Athletics. NCAA. **Intercollegiate:** Basketball, golf M, volleyball W. **Team name:** Raiders.

Student services. Adult student services, career counseling, financial aid counseling, on-campus daycare, personal counseling, placement for graduates, veterans' counselor. **Physically disabled:** Services for visually, hearing impaired. **Transfer:** Special adviser, orientation for new students.

Contact. Phone: (419) 586-0324 Toll-free number: (800) 237-1477
Fax: (419) 586-0358
Stanford Baddley, Director of Student Services, Wright State University: Lake Campus, 7600 State Route 703, Celina, OH 45822-2952

Youngstown College of Massotherapy

Struthers, Ohio
www.yocm.com/

- For-profit 2-year health science and technical college
- Small city

General. Accredited by ACCSCT. **Calendar:** Semester.

Contact. Phone: (330) 755-1406
14 Highland Avenue, Struthers, OH 44471

Zane State College

Zanesville, Ohio
www.zanestate.edu **CB code: 1535**

- Public 2-year technical college
- Commuter campus in large town

General. Founded in 1969. Regionally accredited. **Enrollment:** 1,537 degree-seeking undergraduates; 269 non-degree-seeking students. **Degrees:** 311 associate awarded. **Location:** 60 miles from Columbus. **Calendar:** Quarter, limited summer session. **Full-time faculty:** 46 total. **Part-time faculty:** 101 total.

Student profile. Among degree-seeking undergraduates, 4% enrolled in a transfer program, 350 enrolled as first-time, first-year students.

Part-time:	33%	**Native American:**	1%
Women:	65%	**25 or older:**	60%
African American:	3%		

Transfer out. Colleges most students transferred to 2005: Ohio University, Ohio State University, Muskingum College, Franklin University.

Basis for selection. Open admission, but selective for some programs. Special requirements for allied health programs.

High school preparation. 15 units recommended. Recommended units include English 4, mathematics 3, social studies 4 and science 4.

2005-2006 Annual costs. Tuition/fees: $3,623; $7,245 out-of-state. Per-credit charge: $81 in-state; $161 out-of-state. Books/supplies: $675.

Financial aid. Need-based: Need-based aid available for part-time students.

Application procedures. Admission: No deadline. $20 fee. Application must be submitted on paper. Admission notification on a rolling basis. **Financial aid:** Priority date 5/1, closing date 7/15. FAFSA required. Must reply by 9/1.

Academics. Special study options: Cross-registration, distance learning, dual enrollment of high school students, internships, student-designed major. **Credit/placement by examination:** AP, CLEP, institutional tests. All new freshmen must take assessment tests for English and mathematics. **Support services:** Learning center, reduced course load, remedial instruction, study skills assistance, tutoring, writing center.

Majors. Business: Accounting, administrative services, business admin, marketing, sales/distribution. **Computer sciences:** General, computer science, information systems. **Conservation:** Management/policy. **Engineering technology:** Drafting, electrical. **Family/consumer sciences:** Child care. **Health:** Clinical lab technology, health services, medical assistant, medical radiologic technology/radiation therapy, occupational therapy assistant, physical therapy assistant. **Legal studies:** Paralegal. **Mechanic/repair:** Automotive. **Personal/culinary services:** Culinary arts. **Production:** Tool and die. **Public administration:** Social work.

Most popular majors. Business/marketing 25%, computer/information sciences 13%, engineering/engineering technologies 15%, health sciences 24%, security/protective services 8%.

Student life. Freshman orientation: Available. **Activities:** Student government, student newspaper.

Athletics. Intercollegiate: Baseball M, basketball, cheerleading, volleyball W. **Intramural:** Basketball M, bowling, golf M, softball, tennis, volleyball.

Student services. Adult student services, career counseling, student employment services, financial aid counseling, personal counseling, placement for graduates, veterans' counselor. **Transfer:** Special adviser, pre-admission transcript evaluation for new students. Transfer adviser for students transferring to 4-year colleges.

Contact. E-mail: pyoung@zanestate.edu
Phone: (740) 454-2501 ext. 1225 Toll-free number: (800) 686-8324 ext. 1226 Fax: (740) 454-0035
Paul Young, Director of Admissions, Zane State College, 1555 Newark Road, Zanesville, OH 43701-2626

Oklahoma

Carl Albert State College

Poteau, Oklahoma
www.carlalbert.edu **CB code: 1474**

- Public 2-year community and junior college
- Commuter campus in large town

General. Founded in 1932. Regionally accredited. **Enrollment:** 2,535 degree-seeking undergraduates; 190 non-degree-seeking students. **Degrees:** 383 associate awarded. **Location:** 35 miles from Fort Smith, Arkansas. **Calendar:** Semester, limited summer session. **Full-time faculty:** 40 total. **Part-time faculty:** 8 total.

Student profile. Among degree-seeking undergraduates, 80% enrolled in a transfer program, 1% already have a bachelor's degree or higher, 685 enrolled as first-time, first-year students.

Part-time:	36%	**Hispanic American:**	5%
Women:	68%	**Native American:**	31%
African American:	7%	**Live on campus:**	2%

Transfer out. Colleges most students transferred to 2005: Northeastern State University, University of Arkansas, Southeastern State University, University of Central Oklahoma.

Basis for selection. Open admission, but selective for some programs. Nursing, radiographic technology, and physical therapy assistant programs employ selective enrollment. ACT required for all students under 21 and all international students. SAT considered if submitted. **Adult students:** SAT/ACT scores not required if applicant over 21. Admissions testing is required, but adult students may test with COMPASS in lieu of ACT.

High school preparation. 15 units recommended. Recommended units include English 4, mathematics 3, social studies 1, history 2, science 2 (laboratory 2) and academic electives 1. One social science unit should be in American history.

2005-2006 Annual costs. Tuition/fees: $2,042; $5,012 out-of-state. Per-credit charge: $45 in-state; $144 out-of-state. Room/board: $2,924. Books/supplies: $750. Personal expenses: $1,678.

Financial aid. All financial aid based on need. Need-based aid available for part-time students. Work study available nights and for part-time students.

Application procedures. Admission: No deadline. No application fee. Admission notification on a rolling basis. **Financial aid:** No deadline. FAFSA, institutional form required. Applicants notified on a rolling basis.

Academics. Special study options: Distance learning, dual enrollment of high school students, honors, independent study, liberal arts/career combination. Bachelor's degree programs available on campus. License preparation in nursing, physical therapy, radiology. **Credit/placement by examination:** AP, CLEP, institutional tests. 18 credit hours maximum toward associate degree. **Support services:** GED test center, learning center, remedial instruction, study skills assistance, tutoring.

Majors. Biology: General, zoology. **Business:** General, accounting, administrative services, business admin. **Communications:** Journalism. **Computer sciences:** Computer science. **Education:** Elementary, secondary. **English:** Speech/rhetoric. **Health:** Nursing (RN), physical therapy assistant, premedicine, prepharmacy, preveterinary. **Legal studies:** Prelaw. **Math:** General. **Parks/recreation:** Health/fitness. **Protective services:** Criminal justice. **Psychology:** General. **Social sciences:** General, sociology. **Visual/performing arts:** Art, dramatic.

Most popular majors. Business/marketing 16%, education 25%, family/consumer sciences 14%, health sciences 22%, psychology 10%.

Computing on campus. 50 workstations in library, computer center. Dormitories wired for high-speed internet access. Commuter students can connect to campus network. Online library available.

Student life. Freshman orientation: Mandatory. Preregistration for classes offered. 1 day session held at beginning of semester. **Policies:** Freshmen permitted cars on campus. **Housing:** Single-sex dorms available. Scholar's housing available. **Activities:** Choral groups, dance, drama, music ensembles, musical theater, radio station, student government, student newspaper, African-American Awareness, American Indian Student Association, Young Democrats, Young Republicans.

Athletics. NJCAA. **Intercollegiate:** Baseball M, basketball M, cheerleading M. **Team name:** Vikings.

Student services. Campus ministries, career counseling, services for economically disadvantaged, financial aid counseling, on-campus daycare, veterans' counselor. **Physically disabled:** Services for hearing impaired. **Transfer:** Special adviser, orientation, pre-admission transcript evaluation for new students. Transfer adviser, college fairs on campus for students transferring to 4-year colleges.

Contact. E-mail: ddickerson@carlalbert.edu
Phone: (918) 647-1300 Fax: (918) 647-1306
Dee Ann Dickerson, Registrar, Carl Albert State College, 1507 South McKenna, Poteau, OK 74953-5208

Connors State College

Warner, Oklahoma
www.connorsstate.edu **CB code: 6117**

- Public 2-year community and junior college
- Commuter campus in rural community

General. Founded in 1908. Regionally accredited. Main campus in Warner. Branch campus in Muskogee. **Enrollment:** 1,984 degree-seeking undergraduates; 217 non-degree-seeking students. **Degrees:** 308 associate awarded. **Location:** 20 miles from Muskogee, 65 miles from Tulsa. **Calendar:** Semester, limited summer session. **Full-time faculty:** 50 total; 10% have terminal degrees, 20% minority, 60% women. **Part-time faculty:** 60 total; 7% have terminal degrees, 20% minority, 60% women. **Class size:** 64% < 20, 32% 20-39, 3% 40-49, 1% 50-99. **Special facilities:** 1300 acre wetlands and nature preserve.

Student profile. Among degree-seeking undergraduates, 666 enrolled as first-time, first-year students, 134 transferred in from other institutions.

Part-time:	34%	**Hispanic American:**	2%
Out-of-state:	4%	**Native American:**	26%
Women:	68%	**25 or older:**	40%
African American:	11%	**Live on campus:**	13%
Asian American:	1%		

Transfer out. Colleges most students transferred to 2005: Northeastern State University, Oklahoma State University.

Basis for selection. Open admission, but selective for some programs. Special requirements for nursing and equine programs; interview required. **Adult students:** SAT/ACT scores not required if applicant over 21. Must complete secondary assessment. **Learning Disabled:** Students with documented disabilities must complete designated paperwork in the office of the Dean of Students.

High school preparation. Recommended units include English 4, mathematics 3, social studies 1, history 2, science 2 (laboratory 1) and academic electives 3.

2005-2006 Annual costs. Tuition/fees: $2,190; $5,245 out-of-state. Per-credit charge: $56 in-state; $158 out-of-state. Room/board: $5,804. Books/supplies: $900. Personal expenses: $1,576.

2005-2006 Financial aid. Need-based: 74% of total undergraduate aid awarded as scholarships/grants, 26% as loans/jobs. Need-based aid available for part-time students. **Non-need-based:** Scholarships awarded for academics, alumni affiliation, athletics, leadership, state residency.

Application procedures. Admission: No deadline. No application fee. Admission notification on a rolling basis. Admission available to all students 18 years or over or younger than 18 years with a high school diploma. **Financial aid:** Priority date 2/28, closing date 5/1. FAFSA, institutional form required. Applicants notified on a rolling basis starting 4/1; must reply within 2 week(s) of notification.

Academics. Special study options: Distance learning, dual enrollment of high school students, internships, liberal arts/career combination. License preparation in nursing. **Credit/placement by examination:** CLEP, institutional tests. 18 credit hours maximum toward associate degree. **Support services:** Learning center, remedial instruction, tutoring.

Majors. Agriculture: Equestrian studies. **Biology:** General. **Business:** General, accounting, business admin. **Communications:** General, journalism.

Computer sciences: General, data processing. **Education:** General, early childhood, elementary, physical, secondary. **Engineering:** General. **English:** Speech/rhetoric. **Family/consumer sciences:** General, business, child care. **Health:** Nursing (RN), predentistry, premedicine, prepharmacy, preveterinary. **History:** General. **Interdisciplinary:** Math/computer science. **Legal studies:** Prelaw. **Liberal arts:** Arts/sciences. **Math:** General. **Physical sciences:** Chemistry, physics. **Protective services:** Police science. **Psychology:** General. **Public administration:** Social work. **Social sciences:** General, sociology. **Visual/performing arts:** Art, music history.

Most popular majors. Agriculture 7%, biological/life sciences 7%, business/marketing 13%, education 33%, health sciences 27%.

Computing on campus. 217 workstations in library, computer center. Dormitories linked to campus network. Wireless network available.

Student life. Freshman orientation: Mandatory. Preregistration for classes offered. **Policies:** Freshmen permitted cars on campus. **Housing:** Single-sex dorms, apartments, substance-free housing available. $55 deposit. **Activities:** Drama, student government, student newspaper, Phi Theta Kappa, Mu Alpha Theta, Aggie Club, Black Student Society, Indian club, business club, English club, psychology club.

Athletics. NJCAA. **Intercollegiate:** Baseball M, basketball, rodeo, softball W. **Intramural:** Basketball, softball, tennis. **Team name:** Cowboys.

Student services. Career counseling, health services, on-campus daycare, personal counseling, veterans' counselor. **Transfer:** Special adviser, pre-admission transcript evaluation for new students. College fairs on campus for students transferring to 4-year colleges.

Contact. Phone: (918) 463-2931 Fax: (918) 463-6336
Ron Ramming, Director of Admissions, Connors State College, RR 1, Box 1000, Warner, OK 74469-9700

Eastern Oklahoma State College

Wilburton, Oklahoma
www.eosc.edu **CB code: 6189**

- Public 2-year community college
- Commuter campus in small town

General. Founded in 1908. Regionally accredited. **Enrollment:** 2,976 degree-seeking undergraduates. **Degrees:** 357 associate awarded. **Location:** 90 miles from Tulsa. **Calendar:** Semester, limited summer session. **Full-time faculty:** 48 total. **Part-time faculty:** 33 total. **Class size:** 22% < 20, 61% 20-39, 16% 40-49, less than 1% 50-99, less than 1% >100. **Special facilities:** Oklahoma Miner Training Institute, Center for Correction Officer Studies.

Student profile.

Out-of-state:	2%	**Live on campus:**	20%
25 or older:	65%		

Transfer out. Colleges most students transferred to 2005: East Central State University, Northeastern State University, Southeastern Oklahoma State University.

Basis for selection. Open admission, but selective for some programs. Special requirements for nursing program; interview required. **Adult students:** Entrance exam policies same as for first-time freshmen.

High school preparation. 12 units recommended. Recommended units include English 4, mathematics 3, social studies 2 and science 2. 1 citizenship or government.

2005-2006 Annual costs. Tuition/fees: $2,278; $5,559 out-of-state. Per-credit charge: $62 in-state; $171 out-of-state. Room/board: $3,494. Books/supplies: $578. Personal expenses: $500.

Financial aid. All financial aid based on need. Need-based aid available for part-time students.

Application procedures. Admission: No deadline. $10 fee. Application may be submitted online. Admission notification on a rolling basis. **Financial aid:** Priority date 3/1; no closing date. FAFSA, institutional form required. Applicants notified on a rolling basis starting 5/1; must reply within 2 week(s) of notification.

Academics. Special study options: Cooperative education, distance learning, dual enrollment of high school students, honors, internships. License preparation in nursing. **Credit/placement by examination:** AP, CLEP, institutional tests. 30 credit hours maximum toward associate degree. **Support services:** Learning center, remedial instruction, tutoring.

Majors. Agriculture: General, agronomy, animal sciences, business, economics, farm/ranch, food science, horticultural science, horticulture, ornamental horticulture, products processing, soil science. **Biology:** General, bacteriology, entomology. **Business:** General, accounting, administrative services, business admin, management information systems, office/clerical. **Communications:** Journalism. **Computer sciences:** General, computer science, programming, systems analysis. **Conservation:** General, environmental studies, forestry, wildlife. **Education:** Agricultural, art, biology, business, chemistry, computer, drama/dance, elementary, English, health, history, mathematics, music, physical, physics, science, secondary, social science, social studies, speech. **Engineering:** General. **Family/consumer sciences:** Child care. **Health:** Medical secretary, nursing (RN), predentistry, premedicine, prenursing, prepharmacy, preveterinary. **History:** General. **Interdisciplinary:** Biological/physical sciences. **Legal studies:** Legal secretary, prelaw. **Math:** General. **Parks/recreation:** Facilities management, health/fitness. **Physical sciences:** Chemistry, physics. **Protective services:** Criminal justice, law enforcement admin. **Psychology:** General. **Social sciences:** General, sociology. **Visual/performing arts:** Dramatic.

Most popular majors. Agriculture 18%, business/marketing 20%, education 6%, legal studies 8%, liberal arts 16%, psychology 16%.

Computing on campus. 250 workstations in dormitories, library, computer center. Dormitories linked to campus network. Commuter students can connect to campus network. Online library, helpline, wireless network available.

Student life. Freshman orientation: Mandatory, $12 fee. Preregistration for classes offered. **Policies:** Freshmen permitted cars on campus. **Housing:** Coed dorms, single-sex dorms, special housing for disabled, apartments available. $50 deposit, deadline 8/15. **Activities:** Choral groups, drama, music ensembles, musical theater, radio station, student government, student newspaper, campus religious organizations, Afro-American and Native American clubs, professional clubs.

Athletics. NJCAA. **Intercollegiate:** Baseball M, basketball, cheerleading, rodeo, softball W. **Intramural:** Basketball, handball, racquetball, softball, swimming, table tennis, tennis, volleyball. **Team name:** Mountaineers.

Student services. Adult student services, campus ministries, career counseling, student employment services, financial aid counseling, personal counseling, placement for graduates, veterans' counselor. **Physically disabled:** Services for visually, speech, hearing impaired. **Transfer:** Special adviser, orientation, pre-admission transcript evaluation for new students. Transfer adviser, college fairs on campus for students transferring to 4-year colleges.

Contact. Phone: (918) 465-2361 Fax: (918) 465-2431
Leah Miller, Director of Enrollment Management, Eastern Oklahoma State College, 1301 West Main Street, Wilburton, OK 74578-4999

Heritage College Hair Design

Oklahoma City, Oklahoma
www.heritage-education.com

- For-profit 2-year community college

General. Accredited by ACCSCT. **Enrollment:** 521 degree-seeking undergraduates. **Degrees:** 281 associate awarded. **Calendar:** Continuous. **Full-time faculty:** 14 total. **Part-time faculty:** 8 total.

Basis for selection. Open admission, but selective for some programs. Special requirements for the surgical technician program.

2005-2006 Annual costs. Costs vary by program from $8,031 to $19,850 including tuition, fees, books, and supplies.

Application procedures. Admission: No deadline. No application fee. Admission notification on a rolling basis.

Academics. Credit/placement by examination: CLEP.

Majors. Health: Massage therapy, radiologic technology/medical imaging. **Personal/culinary services:** Barbering.

Student life. Freshman orientation: Available.

Contact. Phone: (405) 631-3399
Desiree Archer, Director of Admissions, Heritage College Hair Design, 7100 I-35 Services Road, Suite 7118, Oklahoma City, OK 73149

Murray State College

Tishomingo, Oklahoma
www.msc.cc.ok.us **CB code: 6421**

- Public 2-year junior college
- Commuter campus in small town

General. Founded in 1908. Regionally accredited. **Enrollment:** 1,864 degree-seeking undergraduates. **Degrees:** 293 associate awarded. **Location:** 32 miles from Ardmore. **Calendar:** Semester, limited summer session. **Full-time faculty:** 50 total. **Part-time faculty:** 25 total.

Student profile.

Out-of-state:	3%	**Live on campus:**	6%

Basis for selection. Open admission, but selective for some programs. Special requirements for nursing and vet tech programs.

High school preparation. 15 units recommended. Recommended units include English 4, mathematics 3, social studies 1, history 2, science 2 (laboratory 2) and academic electives 3. Recommend 1 unit in citizenship.

2005-2006 Annual costs. Tuition/fees: $2,270; $5,270 out-of-state. Per-credit charge: $64 in-state; $164 out-of-state. Room/board: $4,450. Books/supplies: $600. Personal expenses: $1,984.

Application procedures. Admission: No deadline. No application fee. Admission notification on a rolling basis beginning on or about 4/15. **Financial aid:** Priority date 4/15; no closing date. Applicants notified on a rolling basis starting 5/1.

Academics. Special study options: Honors. License preparation in nursing. **Credit/placement by examination:** CLEP. **Support services:** Learning center, remedial instruction, tutoring.

Majors. Business: Administrative services, business admin. **Computer sciences:** General, computer science. **Education:** Elementary. **Family/consumer sciences:** Child care. **Health:** Preveterinary. **History:** General. **Interdisciplinary:** Behavioral sciences. **Liberal arts:** Arts/sciences. **Math:** General. **Visual/performing arts:** General.

Most popular majors. Business/marketing 18%, health sciences 30%, liberal arts 39%.

Computing on campus. Commuter students can connect to campus network. Helpline available.

Student life. Freshman orientation: Mandatory. **Housing:** Coed dorms available. $50 deposit. **Activities:** Drama, music ensembles, student government.

Athletics. NJCAA. **Intercollegiate:** Baseball M, basketball. **Intramural:** Baseball M, basketball.

Student services. Career counseling, veterans' counselor. **Transfer:** Special adviser for new students. College fairs on campus for students transferring to 4-year colleges.

Contact. Phone: (580) 371-2371 ext. 108 Fax: (580) 371-9844
Ann Beck, Registrar and Director of Admissions, Murray State College, One Murray Campus, Tishomingo, OK 73460

Northeastern Oklahoma Agricultural and Mechanical College

Miami, Oklahoma — **CB member**
www.neoam.edu — **CB code: 6484**

- Public 2-year community and junior college
- Commuter campus in large town

General. Founded in 1919. Regionally accredited. Extension courses offered in neighboring towns and on the Internet. **Enrollment:** 1,812 degree-seeking undergraduates; 226 non-degree-seeking students. **Degrees:** 294 associate awarded. **ROTC:** Air Force. **Location:** 76 miles from Tulsa. **Calendar:** Semester, limited summer session. **Full-time faculty:** 77 total; 9% have terminal degrees, 14% minority, 48% women. **Part-time faculty:** 33 total; 12% minority, 70% women. **Class size:** 58% < 20, 42% 20-39, less than 1% 40-49, less than 1% 50-99. **Special facilities:** College farm, equine center.

Student profile. Among degree-seeking undergraduates, 74% enrolled in a transfer program, 26% enrolled in a vocational program, 1% already have a bachelor's degree or higher, 46 enrolled as first-time, first-year students.

Part-time:	21%	**Asian American:**	1%
Out-of-state:	16%	**Hispanic American:**	2%
Women:	58%	**Native American:**	25%
African American:	10%		

Transfer out. Colleges most students transferred to 2005: Oklahoma State University, Missouri Southern State College, Pittsburg State University, Northeastern State University, Rogers State University.

Basis for selection. Open admission. **Adult students:** SAT/ACT scores not required if applicant over 21. Students over the age of 21 must complete placement testing (CPT) before enrolling in classes.

High school preparation. 15 units recommended. Recommended units include English 4, mathematics 3, social studies 1, history 2, science 2 (laboratory 2) and academic electives 3.

2005-2006 Annual costs. Tuition/fees: $2,067; $5,190 out-of-state. Per-credit charge: $47 in-state; $151 out-of-state. Room/board: $3,628. Books/supplies: $800. Personal expenses: $1,000.

2004-2005 Financial aid. Need-based: 578 full-time freshmen applied for aid; 430 were judged to have need; 430 of these received aid. Average need met was 74%. Average scholarship/grant was $3,884; average loan $1,613. 74% of total undergraduate aid awarded as scholarships/grants, 26% as loans/jobs. Need-based aid available for part-time students. Work study available nights, weekends and for part-time students. **Non-need-based:** Awarded to 668 full-time undergraduates, including 300 freshmen. Scholarships awarded for academics, art, athletics, leadership, music/drama, state residency.

Application procedures. Admission: No deadline. No application fee. Application may be submitted online. Admission notification on a rolling basis. **Financial aid:** Priority date 4/1; no closing date. FAFSA, institutional form required. Applicants notified on a rolling basis starting 4/1; must reply by 8/30 or within 2 week(s) of notification.

Academics. Special study options: Distance learning, dual enrollment of high school students, honors, internships. Bachelor's degree programs available on campus. License preparation in nursing, physical therapy. **Credit/placement by examination:** AP, CLEP, institutional tests. 36 credit hours maximum toward associate degree. **Support services:** GED preparation and test center, learning center, reduced course load, remedial instruction, study skills assistance, tutoring, writing center.

Majors. Agriculture: General, equestrian studies, farm/ranch. **Area/ethnic studies:** Native American. **Biology:** General. **Business:** General, accounting, administrative services, business admin, marketing. **Communications:** General, broadcast journalism, journalism, media studies, radio/tv. **Computer sciences:** General, applications programming, information technology, programming. **Conservation:** Forestry, wildlife. **Education:** Early childhood. **Engineering technology:** CAD/CADD. **English:** Speech/rhetoric. **Health:** Athletic training, clinical lab technology, medical secretary, nursing (RN), physical therapy assistant, predentistry, premedicine, prenursing, prepharmacy, preveterinary. **History:** General. **Interdisciplinary:** Biological/physical sciences. **Legal studies:** Legal secretary. **Math:** General. **Parks/recreation:** Health/fitness. **Physical sciences:** General. **Protective services:** Criminal justice. **Psychology:** General. **Public administration:** Social work. **Social sciences:** General, sociology. **Visual/performing arts:** Art, dramatic.

Most popular majors. Agriculture 10%, business/marketing 8%, computer/information sciences 11%, education 8%, engineering/engineering technologies 17%, health sciences 6%, liberal arts 8%, psychology 6%, social sciences 8%, visual/performing arts 6%.

Computing on campus. 85 workstations in dormitories, library, computer center. Dormitories linked to campus network. Commuter students can connect to campus network. Online library, helpline, wireless network available.

Student life. Freshman orientation: Mandatory, $69 fee. Preregistration for classes offered. One day, on Saturday before the beginning of fall classes. **Policies:** Single students under the age of 21 who reside more than 50 miles from campus are required to live on campus. Freshmen permitted cars on campus. **Housing:** Guaranteed on-campus for all undergraduates. Single-sex dorms, special housing for disabled, apartments, substance-free housing available. $75 fully refundable deposit. **Activities:** Bands, choral groups, drama, music ensembles, musical theater, student government, student newspaper, TV station, Ministerial Alliance, Baptist student union, Aggie Society, Collegiates for Christ, Young Democrats, Young Republicans, Phi Theta Kappa, Afro-American Society, Native American student association, Masquers.

Athletics. NJCAA. **Intercollegiate:** Baseball M, basketball, football (tackle) M, rodeo, softball W, volleyball W. **Intramural:** Baseball, basketball, bowling, football (tackle) M, soccer, softball, swimming, volleyball, weight lifting. **Team name:** Norsemen.

Student services. Alcohol/substance abuse counseling, career counseling, services for economically disadvantaged, financial aid counseling, health services, personal counseling, veterans' counselor. **Physically disabled:** Services for visually, hearing impaired. **Transfer:** Special adviser, orientation for new students. Transfer adviser, college fairs on campus for students transferring to 4-year colleges.

Contact. E-mail: neoadmission@neoam.edu
Phone: (918) 540-6210 Toll-free number: (888) 464-6636
Fax: (918) 540-6946
Amy Ishmael, Dean of Enrollment Management and Student Records, Northeastern Oklahoma Agricultural and Mechanical College, 200 I Street NE, Miami, OK 74354-6497

Northern Oklahoma College

Tonkawa, Oklahoma — **CB member**
www.north-ok.edu — **CB code: 6486**

- Public 2-year community college
- Commuter campus in small town

General. Founded in 1901. Regionally accredited. **Location:** 90 miles from Oklahoma City, 70 miles from Wichita, Kansas. **Calendar:** Semester.

Annual costs/financial aid. Tuition/fees (2005-2006): $1,992; $4,954 out-of-state. Room/board: $2,950. Books/supplies: $600. Personal expenses: $1,200. Need-based financial aid available to full-time and part-time students.

Contact. Phone: (580) 628-6221
Registrar, Box 310, Tonkawa, OK 74653

Oklahoma City Community College

Oklahoma City, Oklahoma — **CB member**
www.okccc.edu — **CB code: 0270**

- Public 2-year community college
- Commuter campus in large city

General. Founded in 1969. Regionally accredited. **Enrollment:** 12,589 undergraduates. **Degrees:** 1,033 associate awarded. **Calendar:** Semester, extensive summer session. **Full-time faculty:** 120 total. **Part-time faculty:** 408 total. **Class size:** 33% < 20, 59% 20-39, 7% 40-49, less than 1% 50-99. **Special facilities:** Olympic size swimming pool, diving well. **Partnerships:** Cooperative agreements with 4 area technical centers.

Student profile.

Out-of-state:	1%	**25 or older:**	39%

Transfer out. Colleges most students transferred to 2005: University of Central Oklahoma, University of Oklahoma-OU Health Science Center, Oklahoma State University, University of Oklahoma.

Basis for selection. Open admission, but selective for some programs. Special requirements for nursing, occupational therapy and physical therapy programs; reading test required. **Adult students:** Entrance exam policies same as for first-time freshmen.

High school preparation. 15 units recommended. Recommended units include English 4, mathematics 3, history 2, science 2 (laboratory 2), foreign language 3 and academic electives 1. Academic electives include citizenship skills.

2005-2006 Annual costs. Tuition/fees: $2,071; $5,413 out-of-state. Per-credit charge: $48 in-state; $160 out-of-state. Books/supplies: $675. Personal expenses: $600.

Financial aid. Need-based: Need-based aid available for part-time students. Work study available nights, weekends and for part-time students. **Non-need-based:** Scholarships awarded for academics, state residency.

Application procedures. Admission: No deadline. $25 fee, may be waived for applicants with need. Application may be submitted online. Admission notification on a rolling basis. **Financial aid:** Priority date 7/1; no closing date. FAFSA, institutional form required. Applicants notified on a rolling basis starting 5/1.

Academics. Special study options: Accelerated study, distance learning, double major, dual enrollment of high school students, ESL, honors, independent study, internships, liberal arts/career combination, student-designed major, weekend college. License preparation in nursing, occupational therapy, paramedic, physical therapy, real estate. **Credit/placement by examination:** AP, CLEP, IB, institutional tests. 45 credit hours maximum toward associate degree. **Support services:** GED preparation and test center, learning center, reduced course load, remedial instruction, study skills assistance, tutoring, writing center.

Majors. Biology: General, biotechnology. **Business:** General, finance, office/clerical, real estate, tourism promotion, tourism/travel. **Communications:** Broadcast journalism, journalism. **Computer sciences:** General, computer science, data processing, programming, security, systems analysis, web page design. **Education:** General, multi-level teacher, secondary. **Engineering:** General. **Engineering technology:** Drafting, electrical, manufacturing. **Family/consumer sciences:** Child care. **Foreign languages:** French, Spanish, translation. **Health:** EMT paramedic, nursing (RN), occupational therapy assistant, physical therapy assistant. **History:** General. **Legal studies:** Prelaw. **Liberal arts:** Arts/sciences. **Math:** General. **Mechanic/repair:** General. **Physical sciences:** Chemistry, physics. **Psychology:** General. **Social sciences:** Sociology. **Transportation:** Aviation. **Visual/performing arts:** Commercial/advertising art, studio arts, theater design.

Most popular majors. Business/marketing 15%, computer/information sciences 6%, health sciences 26%, liberal arts 23%, psychology 7%.

Computing on campus. 150 workstations in library, computer center, student center. Commuter students can connect to campus network. Online course registration, online library, helpline, wireless network available.

Student life. Freshman orientation: Available. Preregistration for classes offered. Held the week prior to classes for 3 hours on days, evenings and weekends. **Policies:** Freshmen permitted cars on campus. **Activities:** Choral groups, drama, literary magazine, music ensembles, student government, student newspaper, Phi Theta Kappa, Baptist Campus Ministries, Chi Alpha, Christians on Campus, African-American Student Association, Asian Cultural Exchange, Native American Cultural Awareness Organization, Young Democrats, Deaf Student Association.

Athletics. Intramural: Baseball M, basketball, golf, soccer, softball, volleyball.

Student services. Career counseling, student employment services, financial aid counseling, on-campus daycare, personal counseling, placement for graduates, veterans' counselor. **Physically disabled:** Services for visually, speech, hearing impaired. **Transfer:** Special adviser, orientation for new students. Transfer adviser, college fairs on campus for students transferring to 4-year colleges.

Contact. E-mail: AdmissionsandRecords@occc.edu
Phone: (405) 682-7512 Fax: (405) 682-7521
Gloria Barton, Dean of Admissions/Registrar, Oklahoma City Community College, 7777 South May Avenue, Oklahoma City, OK 73159

Oklahoma State University: Oklahoma City

Oklahoma City, Oklahoma — **CB member**
www.osuokc.edu — **CB code: 1436**

- Public 2-year community and technical college
- Commuter campus in very large city

General. Founded in 1961. Regionally accredited. **Enrollment:** 5,879 degree-seeking undergraduates. **Degrees:** 462 associate awarded. **Location:** 5 miles from downtown. **Calendar:** Semester, extensive summer session. **Full-time faculty:** 71 total. **Part-time faculty:** 226 total. **Special facilities:** Fire/police/EMS training, horticulture center, precision driving training center, child development center, golf maintenance training facility, learning resource center, power transmission distribution pole yard.

Student profile.

Out-of-state:	5%	**25 or older:**	49%

Transfer out. Colleges most students transferred to 2005: University of Central Oklahoma, Oklahoma State University - Stillwater, University of Oklahoma.

Basis for selection. Open admission, but selective for some programs. Special requirements for nursing program; interview required. All students required to take COMPASS Test. Veternarian Tech students required to take ACT test. Essay, audition recommended for all. **Adult students:** ACT/SAT not required for placement if applicant is over 21 years of age.

High school preparation. 15 units recommended. Recommended units include English 4, mathematics 3, social studies 1, history 2, (laboratory 2) and academic electives 3. Other: from any of the subjects listed above or selected from the following: Computer Science, Foreign Language.

2005-2006 Annual costs. Tuition/fees: $2,450; $6,290 out-of-state. Per-credit charge: $63 in-state; $191 out-of-state. Books/supplies: $1,080.

Financial aid. All financial aid based on need.

Application procedures. Admission: No deadline. No application fee in-state; $15 out-of-state. Application may be submitted online. Admission notification on a rolling basis. **Financial aid:** Priority date 7/15; no closing date. FAFSA required. Applicants notified on a rolling basis starting 8/1; must reply within 2 week(s) of notification.

Academics. Special study options: Cooperative education, distance learning, double major, dual enrollment of high school students, honors, independent study, liberal arts/career combination, weekend college. License preparation in nursing. **Credit/placement by examination:** CLEP, institutional tests. 30 credit hours maximum toward associate degree. Credit for: Fundamentals of Nursing (6 hrs.), Adult Nursing (8 hrs.). **Support services:** GED preparation and test center, learning center, remedial instruction, study skills assistance, tutoring, writing center.

Majors. Agriculture: Horticulture, turf management. **Architecture:** Technology. **Business:** Accounting, accounting/finance, business admin, construction management, management science. **Communications technology:** General. **Computer sciences:** General, applications programming, LAN/WAN management. **Education:** General, early childhood. **Engineering:** General, architectural, civil, computer, electrical, surveying. **Engineering technology:** General, architectural, civil, construction, drafting, manufacturing, occupational safety, surveying. **Family/consumer sciences:** Child care. **Foreign languages:** Sign language interpretation. **Health:** Health care admin, health services, nursing (RN), substance abuse counseling, veterinary technology/assistant. **Protective services:** Firefighting, police science. **Public administration:** Human services. **Visual/performing arts:** Commercial/advertising art.

Computing on campus. 372 workstations in library, computer center. Commuter students can connect to campus network. Online course registration, repair service, wireless network available.

Student life. Freshman orientation: Mandatory. Preregistration for classes offered. **Policies:** Freshmen permitted cars on campus. **Activities:** Student government, Students Offering Support, Phi Theta Kappa, Project Second Chance, Native American Students, student government association, Hispanic student association, College Republicans, Young Democrats, Deaf/Hearing student association, student nursing association.

Student services. Adult student services, career counseling, student employment services, financial aid counseling, on-campus daycare, personal counseling, placement for graduates, veterans' counselor. **Physically disabled:** Services for visually, speech, hearing impaired. **Transfer:** Special adviser, orientation for new students. Transfer center, transfer adviser, college fairs on campus for students transferring to 4-year colleges.

Contact. E-mail: jkubier@osuokc.edu
Phone: (405) 945-3224 Fax: (405) 945-3277
Jeanne Kubier, Director of Admissions and Registrar, Oklahoma State University: Oklahoma City, 900 North Portland, Oklahoma City, OK 73107-6195

Oklahoma State University: Okmulgee

Okmulgee, Oklahoma — **CB member**
www.osu-okmulgee.edu — **CB code: 3382**

- Public 2-year branch campus and technical college
- Commuter campus in large town

General. Founded in 1946. Regionally accredited. **Enrollment:** 2,240 degree-seeking undergraduates. **Degrees:** 459 associate awarded. **Location:** 35 miles from Tulsa. **Calendar:** Trimester, extensive summer session. **Full-time faculty:** 130 total. **Part-time faculty:** 25 total.

Student profile.

Out-of-state:	9%	**Live on campus:**	35%
25 or older:	33%		

Basis for selection. Open admission, but selective for some programs. Special requirements for multimedia and engineering technologies programs.

High school preparation. Recommended units include English 4, mathematics 3, social studies 2, science 2, foreign language 3 and academic electives 1.

2005-2006 Annual costs. Tuition/fees: $3,150; $7,500 out-of-state. Per-credit charge: $75 in-state; $220 out-of-state. Room/board: $4,851. Books/supplies: $640.

Financial aid. Need-based: Need-based aid available for part-time students. Work study available nights, weekends and for part-time students.

Application procedures. Admission: No deadline. $15 fee. Application may be submitted online. Admission notification on a rolling basis. **Financial aid:** Priority date 4/1; no closing date. FAFSA, institutional form required. Applicants notified on a rolling basis.

Academics. Special study options: Cooperative education, distance learning, double major, dual enrollment of high school students, internships, liberal arts/career combination. License preparation in nursing. **Credit/placement by examination:** AP, CLEP, institutional tests. **Support services:** Learning center, remedial instruction, tutoring.

Majors. Business: General, accounting, administrative services, business admin, hospitality/recreation, management information systems. **Communications technology:** Graphic/printing. **Computer sciences:** General, applications programming, computer graphics, networking, programming. **Construction:** Electrician, maintenance, pipefitting, power transmission. **Education:** General. **Engineering:** Civil, electrical. **Engineering technology:** Civil, construction, drafting, electrical, manufacturing. **Health:** Medical secretary, medical transcription, orthotics/prosthetics. **Legal studies:** Legal secretary. **Mechanic/repair:** Auto body, automotive, diesel, heating/ac/refrig, watch/jewelry. **Personal/culinary services:** Culinary arts. **Visual/performing arts:** Commercial/advertising art, photography.

Computing on campus. 50 workstations in dormitories, library, computer center. Dormitories wired for high-speed internet access and linked to campus network. Online library, helpline, repair service available.

Student life. Freshman orientation: Available. **Policies:** Freshmen permitted cars on campus. **Housing:** Guaranteed on-campus for all undergraduates. Coed dorms, single-sex dorms, apartments available. $100 deposit. Housing for parents with dependent children. **Activities:** Film society, radio station, student government, student newspaper, Baptist Student Union, Black Student Society, Native American student association, Junior Ambassadors.

Athletics. NAIA. **Intercollegiate:** Rodeo. **Intramural:** Basketball, bowling, football (non-tackle), handball, racquetball, soccer, softball, table tennis, volleyball. **Team name:** Cowboys.

Student services. Alcohol/substance abuse counseling, career counseling, student employment services, financial aid counseling, health services, on-campus daycare, personal counseling, placement for graduates, veterans' counselor. **Physically disabled:** Services for visually, speech, hearing impaired. **Transfer:** Orientation, pre-admission transcript evaluation for new students. College fairs on campus for students transferring to 4-year colleges.

Contact. Phone: (918) 293-4680 Toll-free number: (800) 722-4471 ext. 4680 Fax: (918) 293-4643
Mary Graves, Director of Admissions, Oklahoma State University: Okmulgee, 1801 East Fourth Street, Okmulgee, OK 74447-3901

Platt College: Tulsa

Tulsa, Oklahoma
www.plattcollege.org

- For-profit 1-year health science college
- Commuter campus

General. Accredited by ACCSCT. **Enrollment:** 52 degree-seeking undergraduates. **Calendar:** Continuous. **Full-time faculty:** 35 total. **Part-time faculty:** 20 total. **Class size:** 17% < 20, 25% 20-39, 58% 40-49.

Basis for selection. Open admission. High school diploma or GED are required for some programs. Others require successful completion of entrance exams. **Homeschooled:** Applicants must pass an entrance exam.

2005-2006 Annual costs. Tuition varies by program.

Financial aid. All financial aid based on need. Need-based aid available for part-time students.

Application procedures. Admission: No deadline. $100 fee. **Financial aid:** No deadline. FAFSA required.

Academics. Special study options: Liberal arts/career combination. License preparation in nursing. **Credit/placement by examination:** CLEP. **Support services:** Remedial instruction, tutoring.

Majors. Health: Licensed practical nurse.

Computing on campus. 5 workstations in library. Online library available.

Two-Year Colleges

Student life. Freshman orientation: Mandatory. Preregistration for classes offered. Held for 5 hours on the first day of classes.

Student services. Career counseling, student employment services, financial aid counseling, placement for graduates.

Contact. E-mail: angies@plattcollege.org
Phone: (918) 663-9000 Fax: (918) 622-1240
Renee Jackson, Admission Director, Platt College: Tulsa, 3801 South Sheridan, Tulsa, OK 74145-1132

Redlands Community College
El Reno, Oklahoma
www.redlandscc.edu **CB code: 7324**

- Public 2-year community college
- Commuter campus in large town

General. Founded in 1938. Regionally accredited. **Enrollment:** 1,986 degree-seeking undergraduates; 483 non-degree-seeking students. **Degrees:** 234 associate awarded. **Location:** 25 miles from Oklahoma City. **Calendar:** Semester, limited summer session. **Full-time faculty:** 35 total. **Part-time faculty:** 76 total. **Class size:** 69% < 20, 28% 20-39, 2% 40-49, less than 1% 50-99. **Special facilities:** Equine center, bovine center, working farm.

Student profile. Among degree-seeking undergraduates, 53% enrolled in a transfer program, 47% enrolled in a vocational program, 455 enrolled as first-time, first-year students, 595 transferred in from other institutions.

Part-time:	56%	**25 or older:**	40%
Women:	69%		

Basis for selection. Open admission, but selective for some programs. Nursing and paramedic programs selective. Assessment test administered for students not submitting ACT scores. Interview required for nursing program.

High school preparation. Recommended units include English 4, mathematics 3, social studies 2, science 2 and foreign language 1.

2005-2006 Annual costs. Tuition/fees: $2,310; $4,560 out-of-state. Per-credit charge: $46 in-state; $121 out-of-state. Books/supplies: $960. Personal expenses: $1,305.

2004-2005 Financial aid. Need-based: 82% of total undergraduate aid awarded as scholarships/grants, 18% as loans/jobs. Need-based aid available for part-time students. Work study available nights, weekends and for part-time students. **Non-need-based:** Scholarships awarded for academics, athletics, leadership.

Application procedures. Admission: No deadline. $25 fee, may be waived for applicants with need. Application may be submitted online. Admission notification on a rolling basis. **Financial aid:** Priority date 3/30; no closing date. FAFSA required. Applicants notified on a rolling basis starting 6/1; must reply within 2 week(s) of notification.

Academics. Special study options: Accelerated study, cooperative education, cross-registration, distance learning, dual enrollment of high school students, honors, independent study, internships, liberal arts/career combination. License preparation in nursing. **Credit/placement by examination:** AP, CLEP, ACT, institutional tests. 32 credit hours maximum toward associate degree. **Support services:** Learning center, pre-admission summer program, reduced course load, remedial instruction, study skills assistance, tutoring.

Majors. Agriculture: General, equestrian studies. **Business:** Business admin. **Computer sciences:** General. **Education:** General. **English:** English lit, speech/rhetoric. **Family/consumer sciences:** Child care. **Health:** EMT paramedic, health services, nursing (RN), veterinary technology/assistant. **Math:** General. **Parks/recreation:** Exercise sciences, health/fitness. **Physical sciences:** General. **Protective services:** Police science. **Psychology:** General. **Social sciences:** General. **Visual/performing arts:** Art.

Computing on campus. 180 workstations in library, computer center. Commuter students can connect to campus network.

Student life. Freshman orientation: Available. Preregistration for classes offered. Orientation for students testing into developmental courses. **Policies:** Freshmen permitted cars on campus. **Activities:** Choral groups, student government, Baptist Student Union, nursing club, Aggie club, Phi Theta Kappa, Young Democrats, Young Republicans, environmental club, RCC Student Ambassadors, Native American club, ACES (adult students), Phi Beta Lambda.

Athletics. NJCAA. **Intercollegiate:** Baseball M, basketball, golf W, volleyball W. **Team name:** Cougars.

Student services. Adult student services, career counseling, services for economically disadvantaged, student employment services, financial aid counseling, personal counseling, placement for graduates, veterans' counselor. **Transfer:** Special adviser for new students. Transfer adviser, college fairs on campus for students transferring to 4-year colleges.

Contact. E-mail: studentservices@redlandscc.edu
Phone: (405) 262-2552 ext. 1417 Toll-free number: (866) 415-6367
Fax: (405) 422-1200
Tricia Hobson, Director of Enrollment Management, Redlands Community College, 1300 South Country Club Road, El Reno, OK 73036

Rose State College
Midwest City, Oklahoma
www.rose.edu **CB code: 1462**

- Public 2-year community college
- Commuter campus in small city

General. Founded in 1968. Regionally accredited. **Enrollment:** 8,125 degree-seeking undergraduates. **Degrees:** 734 associate awarded. **ROTC:** Army, Air Force. **Location:** 5 miles from Oklahoma City. **Calendar:** Semester, extensive summer session. **Full-time faculty:** 120 total; 14% have terminal degrees, 11% minority, 60% women. **Part-time faculty:** 271 total. **Special facilities:** Regional history center, 1400-seat performing arts theater, wetlands project.

Student profile. Among degree-seeking undergraduates, 49% enrolled in a transfer program, 51% enrolled in a vocational program, 1,329 enrolled as first-time, first-year students, 1,024 transferred in from other institutions.

Part-time:	63%	**Asian American:**	3%
Out-of-state:	1%	**Hispanic American:**	4%
Women:	62%	**Native American:**	10%
African American:	18%	**25 or older:**	49%

Transfer out. Colleges most students transferred to 2005: Oklahoma State University, Southwestern Oklahoma State University, University of Oklahoma, University of Central Oklahoma.

Basis for selection. Open admission, but selective for some programs. Interview required for health science programs.

High school preparation. Recommended units include English 4, mathematics 3, social studies 2, history 1, science 2 and academic electives 3.

2005-2006 Annual costs. Tuition/fees: $1,963; $5,252 out-of-state. Per-credit charge: $47 in-state; $157 out-of-state. Books/supplies: $1,247.

2004-2005 Financial aid. Need-based: 48% of total undergraduate aid awarded as scholarships/grants, 52% as loans/jobs. Need-based aid available for part-time students. Work study available nights, weekends and for part-time students. **Non-need-based:** Scholarships awarded for academics, athletics.

Application procedures. Admission: Closing date 8/28 (receipt date). $15 fee. Application must be submitted on paper. Admission notification on a rolling basis. **Financial aid:** Priority date 6/1; no closing date. FAFSA required. Applicants notified on a rolling basis starting 3/1; must reply within 4 week(s) of notification.

Academics. Special study options: Accelerated study, distance learning, double major, dual enrollment of high school students, honors, independent study, internships. License preparation in dental hygiene, nursing, radiology. **Credit/placement by examination:** AP, CLEP, institutional tests. 50 credit hours maximum toward associate degree. **Support services:** GED preparation and test center, learning center, reduced course load, remedial instruction, study skills assistance, tutoring, writing center.

Majors. Biology: General. **Business:** General, accounting technology, business admin, e-commerce, human resources, small business admin. **Communications:** Broadcast journalism, digital media, journalism. **Computer sciences:** General, LAN/WAN management, networking, web page design, webmaster. **Conservation:** Environmental science. **Construction:** Carpentry, masonry, plumbing. **Education:** Early childhood, multi-level teacher. **Engineering:** General. **Engineering technology:** Drafting, electrical, heat/ac/refrig, telecommunications, water quality. **Family/consumer sciences:** General, child care, child development. **Foreign languages:** General. **Health:** Athletic training, clinical lab assistant, clinical lab technology, dental assistant, dental hygiene, EMT paramedic, medical records technology, nursing (RN), predentistry, premedicine, prenursing, prepharmacy, radiologic technology/

medical imaging, respiratory therapy assistant, respiratory therapy technology. **History:** General. **Legal studies:** Court reporting, paralegal. **Liberal arts:** Arts/sciences, library assistant. **Math:** General. **Mechanic/repair:** Auto body, automotive, heating/ac/refrig. **Parks/recreation:** Health/fitness. **Physical sciences:** Chemistry, geology, physics. **Protective services:** Police science. **Psychology:** General. **Public administration:** Social work. **Social sciences:** General, international relations, political science, sociology. **Transportation:** Aviation. **Visual/performing arts:** General, art, dramatic.

Computing on campus. 150 workstations in library, computer center, student center. Commuter students can connect to campus network. Online course registration, online library, helpline, student web hosting available.

Student life. Freshman orientation: Mandatory. Preregistration for classes offered. **Activities:** Jazz band, choral groups, dance, drama, music ensembles, student government, student newspaper, Phi Theta Kappa, Future Criminal Justice Club, Black Student Association, broadcasting club, drama club, Oklahoma Intercollegiate Legislature, American Indian Association.

Athletics. NJCAA. **Intercollegiate:** Baseball M, basketball, cheerleading, softball W. **Intramural:** Basketball, bowling, soccer, softball M, swimming, table tennis, tennis, volleyball, water polo. **Team name:** Raiders.

Student services. Adult student services, alcohol/substance abuse counseling, career counseling, student employment services, financial aid counseling, on-campus daycare, personal counseling, placement for graduates, veterans' counselor. **Physically disabled:** Services for visually, speech, hearing impaired. **Learning disabled:** Comprehensive services available. **Transfer:** Special adviser, orientation, pre-admission transcript evaluation for new students. Transfer center, transfer adviser, college fairs on campus for students transferring to 4-year colleges.

Contact. Phone: (405) 733-7312 Toll-free number: (866) 621-0987
Fax: (405) 736-0309
Evelyn Hutchings, Registrar/Director of Admissions, Rose State College, 6420 Southeast 15th Street, Midwest City, OK 73110

Seminole State College

Seminole, Oklahoma
www.ssc.cc.ok.us **CB code: 0316**

- Public 2-year community college
- Commuter campus in small town

General. Founded in 1931. Regionally accredited. **Enrollment:** 1,806 degree-seeking undergraduates. **Degrees:** 320 associate awarded. **Location:** 55 miles from Oklahoma City. **Calendar:** Semester, extensive summer session. **Full-time faculty:** 44 total. **Part-time faculty:** 43 total.

Student profile.

Out-of-state:	3%	Live on campus:	3%

Basis for selection. Open admission, but selective for some programs. Additional requirements for admission to A.D. Nursing Program and MLT Program include minimum ACT composite score of 19 and minimum score of 15 on Nelson Denny Reading Test.

High school preparation. 15 units recommended. Recommended units include English 4, mathematics 3, social studies 2, history 2, science 2 and academic electives 2.

2005-2006 Annual costs. Tuition/fees: $2,293; $5,384 out-of-state. Per-credit charge: $46 in-state; $150 out-of-state. Room/board: $4,464. Books/supplies: $350. Personal expenses: $920.

2004-2005 Financial aid. Need-based: 75% of total undergraduate aid awarded as scholarships/grants, 25% as loans/jobs. **Non-need-based:** Scholarships awarded for academics, athletics, state residency.

Application procedures. Admission: No deadline. $15 fee. Admission notification on a rolling basis. **Financial aid:** Priority date 7/15; no closing date. FAFSA, institutional form required. Applicants notified on a rolling basis starting 3/1; must reply within 4 week(s) of notification.

Academics. Special study options: Dual enrollment of high school students, honors. Bachelor's degree programs available on campus. **Credit/placement by examination:** CLEP, institutional tests. 30 credit hours maximum toward associate degree. **Support services:** Learning center, remedial instruction, tutoring, writing center.

Majors. Business: Business admin, office management, office/clerical. **Computer sciences:** Computer science. **Education:** General, elementary. **Health:** Clinical lab technology, nursing (RN). **Interdisciplinary:** Behavioral sciences. **Liberal arts:** Arts/sciences. **Math:** General. **Parks/recreation:** Health/fitness. **Social sciences:** General. **Visual/performing arts:** Art.

Most popular majors. Business/marketing 20%, computer/information sciences 10%, health sciences 10%, liberal arts 60%.

Computing on campus. 310 workstations in dormitories, library, computer center, student center. Dormitories wired for high-speed internet access and linked to campus network. Commuter students can connect to campus network. Helpline, repair service available.

Student life. Freshman orientation: Mandatory. Preregistration for classes offered. **Policies:** Freshmen permitted cars on campus. **Housing:** Coed dorms, single-sex dorms available. $50 deposit. **Activities:** Concert band, student government, student newspaper, student government, Native American student association, Baptist student union.

Athletics. NJCAA. **Intercollegiate:** Baseball M, basketball, golf, softball W, tennis, volleyball. **Intramural:** Baseball M, basketball. **Team name:** Trojans.

Student services. Career counseling, services for economically disadvantaged, financial aid counseling, personal counseling, veterans' counselor. **Physically disabled:** Services for visually, speech, hearing impaired. **Transfer:** Special adviser for new students. Transfer adviser, college fairs on campus for students transferring to 4-year colleges.

Contact. E-mail: benton-k@scc.cc.ok.us
Phone: (405) 382-9950 ext. 230 Fax: (405) 382-9524
Chris Lindley, Director of Enrollment Management, Seminole State College, 2701 Boren Boulevard, Seminole, OK 74868

Tulsa Community College

Tulsa, Oklahoma **CB member**
www.tulsacc.edu **CB code: 6839**

- Public 2-year community college
- Commuter campus in large city

General. Founded in 1968. Regionally accredited. 4 branch campuses located in Tulsa. **Enrollment:** 13,274 degree-seeking undergraduates. **Degrees:** 1,765 associate awarded. **Calendar:** Semester, extensive summer session. **Full-time faculty:** 278 total. **Part-time faculty:** 678 total.

Student profile. Among degree-seeking undergraduates, 71% enrolled in a transfer program, 29% enrolled in a vocational program.

Out-of-state:	2%	25 or older:	59%

Transfer out. Colleges most students transferred to 2005: University of Oklahoma, Oklahoma State University, Northeastern Oklahoma State University, Tulsa University, University of Central Oklahoma.

Basis for selection. Open admission, but selective for some programs. Special requirements for health-related, legal assistant, and management programs. Interview required for health, legal assistant, and nursing programs.

High school preparation. 15 units recommended. Recommended units include English 4, mathematics 3, social studies 1, history 2, science 2 (laboratory 2) and academic electives 3.

2005-2006 Annual costs. Tuition/fees: $2,276; $6,008 out-of-state. Per-credit charge: $48 in-state; $172 out-of-state. Books/supplies: $600. Personal expenses: $900.

Financial aid. Need-based: Need-based aid available for part-time students. Work study available nights, weekends and for part-time students. **Non-need-based:** Scholarships awarded for academics, art, leadership, music/drama, state residency.

Application procedures. Admission: No deadline. $20 fee. Admission notification on a rolling basis. **Financial aid:** Priority date 8/1; no closing date. FAFSA, institutional form required. Applicants notified on a rolling basis starting 4/1; must reply within 2 week(s) of notification.

Academics. Many short-period intensive courses within conventional semesters. **Special study options:** Cross-registration, distance learning, dual enrollment of high school students, ESL, honors, independent study, internships, weekend college. **Credit/placement by examination:** CLEP, institutional tests. 30 credit hours maximum toward associate degree. **Support services:** Learning center, remedial instruction, study skills assistance, tutoring, writing center.

Majors. Agriculture: Horticultural science. **Business:** General, accounting, administrative services, business admin, fashion, finance, hospitality admin, hospitality/recreation, human resources, insurance, management information systems, managerial economics, office technology, real estate, tourism/

travel. **Communications:** Journalism. **Communications technology:** General. **Computer sciences:** General, applications programming, programming. **Education:** General, physical. **Engineering:** General. **Engineering technology:** Civil, drafting, electrical. **English:** Speech/rhetoric. **Family/consumer sciences:** Child care. **Foreign languages:** French, German, Italian, Japanese, Russian, sign language interpretation, Spanish. **Health:** Clinical lab assistant, clinical lab technology, dental hygiene, medical assistant, medical radiologic technology/radiation therapy, medical secretary, occupational therapy assistant, physical therapy assistant, respiratory therapy technology. **History:** General. **Legal studies:** Legal secretary, paralegal. **Liberal arts:** Library science. **Math:** General. **Mechanic/repair:** Avionics, electronics/electrical, heating/ac/refrig. **Philosophy/religion:** Philosophy. **Physical sciences:** Astronomy, chemistry, geology, physics. **Protective services:** Criminal justice, fire safety technology, police science. **Psychology:** General. **Social sciences:** General, economics, geography, political science, sociology. **Transportation:** Aviation management. **Visual/performing arts:** Dramatic, interior design.

Computing on campus. 2,306 workstations in library, computer center. Online course registration, online library available.

Student life. Freshman orientation: Available. **Policies:** Freshmen permitted cars on campus. **Activities:** Bands, choral groups, drama, music ensembles, student government, student newspaper.

Athletics. Intramural: Basketball, soccer, softball, table tennis, tennis, volleyball.

Student services. Career counseling, student employment services, health services, on-campus daycare, personal counseling, placement for graduates, veterans' counselor. **Physically disabled:** Services for visually, hearing impaired. **Transfer:** Orientation for new students. College fairs on campus for students transferring to 4-year colleges.

Contact. E-mail: lbrewer@tulsacc.edu
Phone: (918) 595-7811 Fax: (918) 595-7987
Leanne Brewer, Director of Admissions and Records, Tulsa Community College, 6111 East Skelly Drive, Tulsa, OK 74135

Tulsa Welding School

Tulsa, Oklahoma
www.weldingschool.com **CB code: 2958**

- For-profit 2-year technical college
- Commuter campus in very large city
- Interview required

General. Accredited by ACCSCT. **Enrollment:** 515 degree-seeking undergraduates. **Degrees:** 26 associate awarded. **Calendar:** Continuous. **Full-time faculty:** 15 total. **Part-time faculty:** 1 total.

Student profile. Among degree-seeking undergraduates, 100% enrolled in a vocational program.

Out-of-state:	41%	**25 or older:**	36%

Basis for selection. Open admission. Must have high school diploma or GED. **Homeschooled:** Applicants must pass ATB test.

2005-2006 Annual costs. Tuition and fees vary by program from $7,110 to $12,490. Books/supplies: $490.

Financial aid. All financial aid based on need.

Application procedures. Admission: No deadline. $25 fee. Admission notification on a rolling basis. **Financial aid:** FAFSA required.

Academics. Credit/placement by examination: CLEP.

Majors. Production: Welding.

Computing on campus. 2 workstations in computer center.

Student life. Freshman orientation: Mandatory. **Policies:** Freshmen permitted cars on campus.

Student services. Career counseling, student employment services, financial aid counseling, personal counseling, placement for graduates. **Physically disabled:** Services for hearing impaired.

Contact. E-mail: tws@ionet.net
Phone: (918) 587-6789 ext. 240 Toll-free number: (800) 331-2934 ext. 221
Fax: (918) 587-8170
Mike Thurber, Director of Admissions, Tulsa Welding School, 2545 East 11th Street, Tulsa, OK 74104-3909

Vatterott College

Oklahoma City, Oklahoma
www.vatterott-college.com **CB code: 2899**

- For-profit 1-year branch campus and technical college
- Very large city

General. Accredited by ACCSCT. **Enrollment:** 375 degree-seeking undergraduates. **Degrees:** 53 associate awarded. **Calendar:** Continuous. 10-week sessions. **Full-time faculty:** 18 total. **Part-time faculty:** 4 total. **Class size:** 75% < 20, 25% 20-39.

Basis for selection. Open admission. Program-specific institutional entrance exams are administered.

2005-2006 Annual costs. Diploma programs $20,000. Associate programs $30,000. Bachelor's program in heating, air conditioning, refrigeration, and ventilation is $52,000. Cost includes tuition, fees, books, supplies, and labs.

Financial aid. All financial aid based on need.

Application procedures. Admission: No deadline. No application fee. **Financial aid:** No deadline. FAFSA required.

Academics. Credit/placement by examination: CLEP. **Support services:** GED preparation.

Majors. Computer sciences: General, information technology, LAN/WAN management, programming. **Mechanic/repair:** Heating/ac/refrig.

Most popular majors. Computer/information sciences 45%, engineering/engineering technologies 39%, trade and industry 16%.

Student life. Freshman orientation: Mandatory.

Contact. Phone: (405) 945-0088
Mark Hybers, Director of Admissions, Vatterott College, 4629 Northwest 23rd Street, Oklahoma City, OK 73127

Vatterott College: Tulsa

Tulsa, Oklahoma
www.vatterott-college.edu **CB code: 3637**

- For-profit 2-year branch campus and technical college
- Commuter campus in large city
- Interview required

General. Accredited by ACCSCT. **Enrollment:** 535 full-time, degree-seeking students. **Degrees:** 77 associate awarded. **Calendar:** Continuous. **Full-time faculty:** 16 total; 19% women. **Part-time faculty:** 1 total; 100% women. **Special facilities:** Extensive HVAC lab.

Student profile. Among full-time, degree-seeking students, 100% enrolled in a vocational program.

Basis for selection. High school diploma or GED and interview required. **Adult students:** Entrance exam policies same as for first-time freshmen.

2005-2006 Annual costs. Tuition varies by program. Diploma programs range from $17,500 to $21,400. Associate degrees range from $26,800 to $32,400. Costs are for total programs and include books.

Application procedures. Admission: No deadline. No application fee.

Academics. Credit/placement by examination: CLEP. **Support services:** Study skills assistance, tutoring.

Majors. Computer sciences: LAN/WAN management, web page design. **Health:** Office assistant. **Mechanic/repair:** Computer, electronics/electrical, heating/ac/refrig.

Computing on campus. 20 workstations in library, computer center.

Student life. Freshman orientation: Available. **Activities:** Student newspaper.

Student services. Transfer: Orientation, pre-admission transcript evaluation for new students. College fairs on campus for students transferring to 4-year colleges.

Contact. E-mail: tulsa@vatterott-college.edu
Phone: (918) 835-8288 Toll-free number: (888) 857-4016
Fax: (918) 835-9698
Gerald Parr, Director of Admissions, Vatterott College: Tulsa, 4343 South 118th East Avenue, Tulsa, OK 74146

Western College of Southern California

Oklahoma City, Oklahoma
www.platt.org

- For-profit 1-year branch campus and health science college
- Small city
- Interview required

General. Accredited by ACCSCT. **Enrollment:** 220 degree-seeking undergraduates. **Calendar:** Continuous. **Full-time faculty:** 40 total. **Part-time faculty:** 2 total.

Basis for selection. Open admission, but selective for some programs. Students admitted based on interview, High School Diploma, GED or ATB. Entrance exam required for Practical Nursing and Surgical Technologist Programs.

2005-2006 Annual costs. Tuition varies by program. Full-time tuition ranges from $7,295 to $13,345. Required fees $100.

Application procedures. Admission: No deadline. $100 fee. Admission notification on a rolling basis. **Financial aid:** FAFSA required.

Academics. Credit/placement by examination: CLEP.

Majors. Health: Licensed practical nurse.

Student life. Freshman orientation: Mandatory.

Student services. Adult student services, alcohol/substance abuse counseling, career counseling, financial aid counseling, personal counseling, placement for graduates.

Contact. E-mail: angiem@plattcollege.org
Phone: (405) 946-7799 Fax: (405) 943-2150
R. Jackson, Director of Admissions, Western College of Southern California, 309 South Ann Arbor, Oklahoma City, OK 73128

Western Oklahoma State College

Altus, Oklahoma **CB member**
www.wosc.edu **CB code: 6020**

- Public 2-year community college
- Commuter campus in large town

General. Founded in 1926. Regionally accredited. **Enrollment:** 1,919 undergraduates. **Degrees:** 262 associate awarded. **Location:** 60 miles from Lawton, 140 miles from Oklahoma City. **Calendar:** Semester, limited summer session. **Full-time faculty:** 32 total. **Part-time faculty:** 50 total. **Special facilities:** Learning resource center.

Student profile. 50% enrolled in a transfer program, 50% enrolled in a vocational program, 5% already have a bachelor's degree or higher.

Basis for selection. Open admission. SAT or ACT required for applicants under 21 for placement; no minimum score required. **Adult students:** ACT required for adults who don't have high school diploma or GED. Must demonstrate proficiency in English, math, science, and reading through COMPASS or ACT subtest scores. **Homeschooled:** Must have ACT or SAT. High school class must have graduated and must satisfy curricular requirements.

High school preparation. 15 units recommended. Recommended units include English 4, mathematics 3, history 3, science 2 and academic electives 3. Recommend 2 units fine arts.

2005-2006 Annual costs. Tuition/fees: $2,230; $5,365 out-of-state. Per-credit charge: $47 in-state; $151 out-of-state. Room/board: $3,600. Books/supplies: $1,000. Personal expenses: $1,200.

2004-2005 Financial aid. Need-based: 69% of total undergraduate aid awarded as scholarships/grants, 31% as loans/jobs. Need-based aid available for part-time students. Work study available nights, weekends and for part-time students. **Non-need-based:** Scholarships awarded for academics, alumni affiliation, art, athletics, leadership, music/drama, state residency.

Application procedures. Admission: No deadline. $15 fee. Application may be submitted online. Admission notification on a rolling basis. **Financial aid:** Priority date 3/1; no closing date. FAFSA, institutional form required. Applicants notified on a rolling basis; must reply within 3 week(s) of notification.

Academics. Special study options: Distance learning, dual enrollment of high school students, honors, liberal arts/career combination. Cooperative agreements with local technology centers. Students may co-enroll and earn college credits for votech courses. License preparation in aviation, nursing, radiology. **Credit/placement by examination:** AP, CLEP, institutional tests. 30 credit hours maximum toward associate degree. **Support services:** Learning center, remedial instruction, study skills assistance, tutoring.

Majors. Biology: General. **Business:** General, administrative services, business admin, management science, office technology, office/clerical. **Computer sciences:** General, computer science, information systems, programming. **Conservation:** Wildlife. **Education:** General, physical, social studies. **Engineering:** General. **Engineering technology:** Construction, drafting, manufacturing. **Family/consumer sciences:** Child care. **Foreign languages:** Spanish. **Health:** EMT paramedic, medical radiologic technology/radiation therapy, medical records admin, medical secretary, nursing (RN). **History:** General. **Liberal arts:** Arts/sciences. **Math:** General. **Mechanic/repair:** Auto body, automotive, diesel, electronics/electrical. **Parks/recreation:** Health/fitness. **Protective services:** Corrections, firefighting, police science. **Psychology:** General. **Social sciences:** General, political science, sociology. **Transportation:** Aviation, aviation management. **Visual/performing arts:** Art.

Most popular majors. Business/marketing 13%, family/consumer sciences 6%, health sciences 21%, liberal arts 24%, security/protective services 8%.

Computing on campus. 50 workstations in library. Dormitories linked to campus network.

Student life. Freshman orientation: Mandatory. Preregistration for classes offered. **Policies:** Freshmen permitted cars on campus. **Housing:** Coed dorms, substance-free housing available. $50 deposit. **Activities:** Bands, choral groups, drama, music ensembles, musical theater, radio station, student government, student newspaper, Baptist Student Union, Wesley Foundation, tutoring club, College Democrats, College Republicans, Fellowship of Christians.

Athletics. NJCAA. **Intercollegiate:** Baseball M, basketball, softball W. **Intramural:** Basketball, volleyball. **Team name:** Pioneers.

Student services. Career counseling, financial aid counseling, health services, personal counseling, veterans' counselor. **Transfer:** Special adviser, orientation for new students. Transfer adviser, college fairs on campus for students transferring to 4-year colleges.

Contact. E-mail: tanya.wingate@wosc.edu
Phone: (580) 477-2000 Fax: (580) 477-7723
Larry Paxton, Director of Academic Services, Western Oklahoma State College, 2801 North Main Street, Altus, OK 73521

Oregon

Blue Mountain Community College
Pendleton, Oregon
www.bluecc.edu **CB code: 4025**

- Public 2-year community college
- Commuter campus in large town

General. Founded in 1962. Regionally accredited. Located in agricultural area. **Enrollment:** 1,252 degree-seeking undergraduates; 898 non-degree-seeking students. **Degrees:** 184 associate awarded. **Location:** 200 miles from Portland. **Calendar:** Quarter, limited summer session. **Full-time faculty:** 60 total. **Part-time faculty:** 155 total. **Class size:** 74% < 20, 25% 20-39, less than 1% 40-49, less than 1% 50-99.

Student profile. Among degree-seeking undergraduates, 1% already have a bachelor's degree or higher, 349 enrolled as first-time, first-year students.

Part-time:	58%	**Asian American:**	2%
Out-of-state:	6%	**Hispanic American:**	11%
Women:	45%	**Native American:**	5%
African American:	1%	**25 or older:**	55%

Transfer out. Colleges most students transferred to 2005: Eastern Oregon University, Oregon State University, University of Oregon.

Basis for selection. Open admission, but selective for some programs. Admission to nursing program based on prerequisite course work, GPA, security check, point system. Dental Assisting students admitted based on prerequisites and GPA. **Adult students:** SAT/ACT scores not required.

2006-2007 Annual costs. Tuition/fees (projected): $2,796; $5,496 out-of-state. Per-credit charge: $60 in-state; $120 out-of-state. Washington, Idaho, Nevada, and California state residents pay in-state tuition. Books/supplies: $1,000. Personal expenses: $390.

Financial aid. Need-based: Need-based aid available for part-time students. Work study available nights, weekends and for part-time students. **Non-need-based:** Scholarships awarded for athletics, music/drama.

Application procedures. Admission: No deadline. No application fee. Application may be submitted online. Admission notification on a rolling basis. **Financial aid:** Priority date 3/30; no closing date. FAFSA required. Applicants notified on a rolling basis starting 4/1; must reply within 2 week(s) of notification.

Academics. Learning Disabilities Diagnostician. **Special study options:** Cooperative education, cross-registration, distance learning, double major, dual enrollment of high school students, ESL, liberal arts/career combination. Bachelor's degree programs available on campus. License preparation in nursing. **Credit/placement by examination:** AP, CLEP, institutional tests. 15 credit hours maximum toward associate degree. **Support services:** GED preparation and test center, learning center, reduced course load, remedial instruction, study skills assistance, tutoring.

Majors. Agriculture: Animal husbandry, business, crop production, farm/ranch, production. **Business:** Accounting technology, administrative services, business admin, marketing. **Education:** Early childhood, teacher assistance. **Engineering technology:** Civil, drafting, electrical. **Family/consumer sciences:** Family/community services. **Health:** Medical secretary, nursing (RN). **Liberal arts:** Arts/sciences. **Mechanic/repair:** Industrial. **Parks/recreation:** Health/fitness. **Public administration:** Human services.

Computing on campus. 200 workstations in library, computer center. Online course registration, online library, helpline, wireless network available.

Student life. Freshman orientation: Available. Preregistration for classes offered. 1/2 day in fall prior to classes. **Policies:** Freshmen permitted cars on campus. **Activities:** Jazz band, choral groups, drama, music ensembles, musical theater, student government, multicultural club, MECHA, Native American club.

Athletics. Intercollegiate: Baseball M, basketball, rodeo, softball W, volleyball W. **Team name:** Timberwolves.

Student services. Alcohol/substance abuse counseling, career counseling, services for economically disadvantaged, student employment services, financial aid counseling, personal counseling, placement for graduates, veterans' counselor. **Physically disabled:** Services for visually, speech, hearing impaired. **Learning disabled:** Comprehensive services available. **Transfer:** Special adviser, orientation, pre-admission transcript evaluation for new students. Transfer center, transfer adviser, college fairs on campus for students transferring to 4-year colleges.

Contact. E-mail: onlineinquiry@bluecc.edu
Phone: (541) 278-5759 Fax: (541) 278-5871
Valerie Fouquette, Senior Director, Student and Enrollment Services, Blue Mountain Community College, PO Box 100, Pendleton, OR 97801

Central Oregon Community College
Bend, Oregon
www.cocc.edu **CB code: 4090**

- Public 2-year community college
- Commuter campus in small city

General. Founded in 1949. Regionally accredited. **Enrollment:** 3,233 degree-seeking undergraduates; 987 non-degree-seeking students. **Degrees:** 417 associate awarded. **Location:** 150 miles from Portland, 120 miles from Salem. **Calendar:** Quarter, limited summer session. **Full-time faculty:** 96 total; 41% have terminal degrees, 6% minority, 56% women. **Part-time faculty:** 177 total. **Class size:** 47% < 20, 50% 20-39, 2% 40-49, less than 1% 50-99, less than 1% >100. **Special facilities:** Exercise physiology laboratory, dental clinic.

Student profile. Among degree-seeking undergraduates, 66% enrolled in a transfer program, 34% enrolled in a vocational program, 10% already have a bachelor's degree or higher, 744 enrolled as first-time, first-year students, 336 transferred in from other institutions.

Part-time:	55%	**25 or older:**	46%
Out-of-state:	2%	**Live on campus:**	2%
Women:	59%		

Transfer out. Colleges most students transferred to 2005: Oregon State University, University of Oregon, Southern Oregon University, Portland State University.

Basis for selection. Open admission, but selective for some programs. Selective admissions for nursing, emergency medical services. Limited enrollment (first-come first-served basis, with fall term only start date) for medical assistant, dental assistant, and massage therapy. **Adult students:** Entrance exam policies same as for first-time freshmen. **Homeschooled:** High school diploma or GED is not required if student is 18 or older.

2005-2006 Annual costs. Tuition/fees: $2,903; $3,893 out-of-district; $7,898 out-of-state. Per-credit charge: $61 in-district; $83 out-of-district. Room/board: $6,380. Books/supplies: $900. Personal expenses: $1,100.

Financial aid. Need-based: Need-based aid available for part-time students. Work study available for part-time students. **Non-need-based:** Scholarships awarded for academics, leadership. **Additional information:** Institution-sponsored short-term loans. Extensive part-time student employment.

Application procedures. Admission: Priority date 6/15; no deadline. $25 fee, may be waived for applicants with need. Application may be submitted online. Admission notification on a rolling basis. **Financial aid:** Priority date 3/31; no closing date. FAFSA, institutional form required. Applicants notified on a rolling basis starting 5/1; must reply within 4 week(s) of notification.

Academics. Special study options: Cooperative education, distance learning, double major, dual enrollment of high school students, honors, independent study, internships, student-designed major, study abroad. Bachelor's degree programs available on campus. License preparation in aviation, nursing, paramedic, physical therapy. **Credit/placement by examination:** AP, CLEP, IB, institutional tests. Credit for prior training or certification varies by program. **Support services:** GED preparation, learning center, pre-admission summer program, reduced course load, remedial instruction, study skills assistance, tutoring, writing center.

Majors. Agriculture: Horticultural science, landscaping, turf management. **Architecture:** Landscape. **Biology:** General. **Business:** Accounting, administrative services, business admin, hospitality admin, hospitality/recreation, hotel/motel admin, management information systems, office management, resort management, tourism/travel. **Communications:** General. **Computer sciences:** General, computer science. **Conservation:** Fisheries, forestry, wildlife. **Education:** General, early childhood. **Engineering:** General. **Engineering technology:** Manufacturing. **English:** British lit. **Family/consumer sciences:** Human nutrition. **Foreign languages:** General. **Health:** EMT paramedic, medical records technology, nursing (RN), predentistry,

Two-Year Colleges

premedicine, prepharmacy. **History:** General. **Legal studies:** Prelaw. **Liberal arts:** Arts/sciences. **Math:** General. **Mechanic/repair:** Electronics/electrical. **Parks/recreation:** Exercise sciences, facilities management, health/fitness. **Personal/culinary services:** General. **Physical sciences:** Chemistry, geology, physics. **Production:** Machine tool, welding. **Protective services:** Firefighting, law enforcement admin. **Psychology:** General. **Social sciences:** General, anthropology, cartography, economics, geography, sociology. **Transportation:** Airline/commercial pilot. **Visual/performing arts:** General, studio arts.

Computing on campus. 350 workstations in dormitories, library, computer center. Dormitories wired for high-speed internet access and linked to campus network. Commuter students can connect to campus network. Online course registration, online library, helpline, wireless network available.

Student life. **Freshman orientation:** Available, $25 fee. Preregistration for classes offered. **Policies:** Freshmen permitted cars on campus. **Housing:** Coed dorms available. $500 nonrefundable deposit, deadline 8/15. **Activities:** Bands, choral groups, opera, student government, student newspaper, symphony orchestra, AmeriCorp, student Bible group.

Athletics. **Intramural:** Badminton, basketball, cross-country, football (non-tackle) M, golf, skiing, soccer, softball, table tennis, tennis, track and field, volleyball, water polo, weight lifting. **Team name:** Bobcats.

Student services. Adult student services, alcohol/substance abuse counseling, career counseling, services for economically disadvantaged, student employment services, financial aid counseling, health services, minority student services, personal counseling, placement for graduates, veterans' counselor, women's services. **Physically disabled:** Services for visually, speech, hearing impaired. **Transfer:** Special adviser, orientation, pre-admission transcript evaluation for new students. Transfer adviser, college fairs on campus for students transferring to 4-year colleges.

Contact. E-mail: welcome@cocc.edu
Phone: (541) 383-7500 Fax: (541) 383-7506
Alicia Moore, Director, Admissions and Records, Central Oregon Community College, 2600 Northwest College Way, Bend, OR 97701-5998

Chemeketa Community College

Salem, Oregon
www.chemeketa.edu — **CB code: 4745**

- Public 2-year community and junior college
- Commuter campus in small city

General. Founded in 1962. Regionally accredited. **Enrollment:** 9,838 undergraduates. **Degrees:** 923 associate awarded. **Location:** 45 miles from Portland. **Calendar:** Quarter, extensive summer session. **Full-time faculty:** 210 total; 86% have terminal degrees, 7% minority, 52% women. **Part-time faculty:** 485 total; 7% minority, 59% women. **Class size:** 43% < 20, 52% 20-39, 4% 40-49, less than 1% 50-99, less than 1% >100. **Special facilities:** Planetarium, vineyard and winemaking facility. **Partnerships:** Formal partnerships with local high schools.

Student profile. 80% enrolled in a transfer program, 20% enrolled in a vocational program, 10% already have a bachelor's degree or higher.

Out-of-state:	5%	**25 or older:**	60%

Transfer out. **Colleges most students transferred to 2005:** University of Oregon, Oregon State University, Western Oregon University, Eastern Oregon University, Portland State University.

Basis for selection. Open admission, but selective for some programs. Interview required for limited enrollment programs; preparatory courses may be required. Placement tests required for degree-seeking students, available to all students. **Adult students:** Entrance exam policies same as for first-time freshmen.

2005-2006 Annual costs. Tuition/fees: $2,790; $9,135 out-of-state. Per-credit charge: $58 in-state; $199 out-of-state. Domestic out-of-state students pay in-state rate after first quarter; international students have additional required fees. Books/supplies: $1,125. Personal expenses: $300.

2004-2005 Financial aid. All financial aid based on need. 51% of total undergraduate aid awarded as scholarships/grants, 49% as loans/jobs. Need-based aid available for part-time students. Work study available nights, weekends and for part-time students.

Application procedures. **Admission:** No deadline. No application fee. Application must be submitted on paper. Admission notification on a rolling basis. **Financial aid:** Priority date 4/1; no closing date. FAFSA required. Applicants notified on a rolling basis starting 6/30; must reply within 2 week(s) of notification.

Academics. **Special study options:** Accelerated study, cooperative education, distance learning, double major, dual enrollment of high school students, ESL, independent study, internships, study abroad, teacher certification program, weekend college. Bachelor's degree programs available on campus. License preparation in dental hygiene, nursing, paramedic. **Credit/placement by examination:** AP, CLEP, IB, institutional tests. 12 credit hours maximum toward associate degree. **Support services:** GED preparation and test center, learning center, pre-admission summer program, reduced course load, remedial instruction, study skills assistance, tutoring, writing center.

Majors. **Agriculture:** Agribusiness operations, horticultural science. **Biology:** General, entomology, zoology. **Business:** Accounting, administrative services, business admin, hospitality admin, management information systems, management science, office management, office technology, operations, real estate, tourism/travel. **Communications:** Journalism. **Communications technology:** Graphic/printing. **Computer sciences:** General, applications programming, programming. **Conservation:** Forestry. **Construction:** Building inspection, maintenance. **Education:** Bilingual, early childhood, elementary, health, physical, secondary, teacher assistance, technology/industrial arts. **Engineering:** General, electrical. **Engineering technology:** Civil, construction, drafting, electrical. **English:** Speech/rhetoric. **Family/consumer sciences:** General, child care, family studies. **Foreign languages:** General, comparative lit. **Health:** Dental assistant, EMT paramedic, health care admin, medical records admin, medical secretary, medical transcription, nursing (RN), predentistry, premedicine, prenursing, prepharmacy, substance abuse counseling. **History:** General. **Interdisciplinary:** Gerontology. **Legal studies:** Legal secretary, prelaw. **Liberal arts:** Arts/sciences. **Math:** General. **Mechanic/repair:** Automotive, industrial. **Parks/recreation:** General. **Philosophy/religion:** Philosophy. **Physical sciences:** Chemistry, geology, physics. **Protective services:** Criminal justice, fire safety technology, firefighting, law enforcement admin, police science. **Psychology:** General. **Public administration:** Community org/advocacy, human services, social work. **Social sciences:** Anthropology, economics, geography, political science, sociology. **Visual/performing arts:** Art, design, theater design.

Computing on campus. 1,000 workstations in library, computer center. Commuter students can connect to campus network. Online course registration, online library, helpline, wireless network available.

Student life. **Freshman orientation:** Available. Preregistration for classes offered. **Policies:** Freshmen permitted cars on campus. **Activities:** Choral groups, dance, drama, literary magazine, musical theater, student government, student newspaper, TV station, Multicultural Center, Triangle Society (sexual minority students), Christian Student Organization, LDS Club, College Republicians, Democratic Students, Phi Theta Kappa, Latino Development Network.

Athletics. NJCAA. **Intercollegiate:** Baseball M, basketball, softball W, volleyball W. **Intramural:** Softball W, tennis. **Team name:** Storm.

Student services. Adult student services, alcohol/substance abuse counseling, career counseling, services for economically disadvantaged, student employment services, financial aid counseling, minority student services, placement for graduates. **Physically disabled:** Services for visually, hearing impaired. **Transfer:** Special adviser, orientation, pre-admission transcript evaluation for new students. Transfer adviser, college fairs on campus for students transferring to 4-year colleges.

Contact. E-mail: admissions@chemeketa.edu
Phone: (503) 399-5006 Fax: (503) 399-3918
Melissa Frey, Admissions Coordinator, Chemeketa Community College, Attention: Admissions, Salem, OR 97309-7070

Clackamas Community College

Oregon City, Oregon
www.clackamas.cc.or.us — **CB code: 4111**

- Public 2-year community college
- Commuter campus in small city

General. Founded in 1966. Regionally accredited. **Enrollment:** 7,727 undergraduates. **Degrees:** 539 associate awarded. **ROTC:** Air Force. **Location:** 15 miles from Portland. **Calendar:** Quarter, limited summer session. **Full-time faculty:** 163 total. **Part-time faculty:** 382 total. **Class size:** 57% < 20, 39% 20-39, 3% 40-49, less than 1% 50-99. **Special facilities:** Environmental learning center, observatory. **Partnerships:** Intel Microelectronics program, Portland General Electric/Pacificorps, ACC District High Schools.

Student profile.

Out-of-state:	2%	**25 or older:**	47%

Two-Year Colleges

Transfer out. **Colleges most students transferred to 2005:** Portland State University, Oregon State University, University of Oregon.

Basis for selection. Open admission, but selective for some programs. Special prerequisite requirements for nursing, medical assistant, medical technician and water quality programs. Special admission process for accelerated degree and CCC/PSU co-admittance programs. **Adult students:** Entrance exam policies same as for first-time freshmen.

2005-2006 Annual costs. Tuition/fees: $2,700; $8,910 out-of-state. Per-credit charge: $56 in-state; $194 out-of-state. In-state tuition applies to residents of Oregon, Washington, Idaho, Nevada and California. Books/supplies: $975. Personal expenses: $2,250.

Financial aid. **Need-based:** Need-based aid available for part-time students. Work study available nights, weekends and for part-time students. **Non-need-based:** Scholarships awarded for academics, art, athletics, leadership, music/drama. **Additional information:** Institutional tuition rebate guarantee. Frozen tuition rates for new fall students who graduate within 3 years. Any tuition increase levied by college during those 3 years will be refunded to student upon graduation.

Application procedures. **Admission:** No deadline. No application fee. Application may be submitted online. Admission notification on a rolling basis. **Financial aid:** Priority date 4/10; no closing date. FAFSA required. Applicants notified on a rolling basis starting 3/15; must reply within 3 week(s) of notification.

Academics. Some occupational technologies offered as self-paced programs. **Special study options:** Accelerated study, cooperative education, cross-registration, distance learning, double major, dual enrollment of high school students, ESL, honors, independent study, internships, liberal arts/career combination, study abroad. License preparation in nursing, paramedic, real estate. **Credit/placement by examination:** CLEP, institutional tests. 12 credit hours maximum toward associate degree. **Support services:** GED preparation and test center, learning center, reduced course load, remedial instruction, study skills assistance, tutoring.

Majors. **Agriculture:** Ornamental horticulture. **Business:** Accounting, office management, sales/distribution. **Engineering technology:** Construction, drafting, electrical, water quality. **Health:** Nursing (RN). **Liberal arts:** Arts/sciences. **Mechanic/repair:** Auto body, automotive, electronics/electrical. **Protective services:** Corrections, firefighting, police science. **Public administration:** Community org/advocacy.

Most popular majors. Health sciences 8%, liberal arts 64%, trade and industry 14%.

Computing on campus. 500 workstations in library, computer center. Online course registration, helpline available.

Student life. **Freshman orientation:** Available. One-day program during the week before classes begin. **Policies:** Freshmen permitted cars on campus. **Activities:** Jazz band, choral groups, drama, literary magazine, music ensembles, student government, student newspaper, environmental group, Baptist Student Ministries, foreign language clubs, Campus Crusade for Christ, nursing organization, Chatino Club, service club, computer club, Rainbow Club, speech/forensics club.

Athletics. NJCAA. **Intercollegiate:** Baseball M, basketball, cross-country, soccer W, softball W, track and field, volleyball W, wrestling M. **Intramural:** Basketball, racquetball, soccer, tennis, volleyball. **Team name:** Cougars.

Student services. Adult student services, alcohol/substance abuse counseling, career counseling, student employment services, financial aid counseling, minority student services, on-campus daycare, personal counseling, placement for graduates, veterans' counselor, women's services. **Physically disabled:** Services for visually, speech, hearing impaired. **Transfer:** Special adviser, orientation for new students. Transfer adviser, college fairs on campus for students transferring to 4-year colleges.

Contact. E-mail: pattyw@clackamas.cc.or.us
Phone: (503) 657-6958 ext. 2263 Fax: (503) 722-5864
Tara Sprehe, Registrar, Clackamas Community College, 19600 South Molalla Avenue, Oregon City, OR 97045

Clatsop Community College

Astoria, Oregon
www.clatsop.cc.or.us **CB code: 4089**

- Public 2-year community college
- Commuter campus in large town

General. Founded in 1958. Regionally accredited. **Enrollment:** 1,610 undergraduates. **Degrees:** 68 associate awarded. **Location:** 100 miles from Portland. **Calendar:** Quarter, limited summer session. **Full-time faculty:** 42 total; 2% minority, 52% women. **Part-time faculty:** 76 total; 3% minority, 54% women. **Class size:** 83% < 20, 15% 20-39, less than 1% 40-49, 1% 50-99, less than 1% >100. **Special facilities:** 51-foot commercial fishing vessel; vessel fire fighting training.

Student profile.

Out-of-state:	13%	**25 or older:**	42%

Basis for selection. Open admission, but selective for some programs. Special admissions requirements for nursing program applicants and international students. **Adult students:** Entrance exam policies same as for first-time freshmen.

2005-2006 Annual costs. Tuition/fees: $2,835; $5,400 out-of-state. Per-credit charge: $57 in-state; $114 out-of-state. Books/supplies: $1,050. Personal expenses: $642.

Financial aid. **Need-based:** Need-based aid available for part-time students. Work study available for part-time students. **Non-need-based:** Scholarships awarded for academics.

Application procedures. **Admission:** No deadline. No application fee. Admission notification on a rolling basis. **Financial aid:** Priority date 5/1; no closing date. FAFSA, institutional form required. Applicants notified on a rolling basis starting 2/1.

Academics. **Special study options:** Cooperative education, distance learning, double major, dual enrollment of high school students, student-designed major, teacher certification program. License preparation in nursing. **Credit/placement by examination:** CLEP, institutional tests. 24 credit hours maximum toward associate degree. **Support services:** GED preparation and test center, learning center, reduced course load, remedial instruction, study skills assistance, tutoring, writing center.

Majors. **Business:** Accounting, business admin, management information systems, office management, office technology. **Computer sciences:** Applications programming, networking. **Health:** Medical assistant, medical secretary, nursing (RN). **Legal studies:** Legal secretary. **Liberal arts:** Arts/sciences. **Protective services:** Criminal justice, firefighting.

Most popular majors. Business/marketing 7%, health sciences 23%, liberal arts 64%.

Computing on campus. 80 workstations in library, computer center, student center.

Student life. **Freshman orientation:** Mandatory. Preregistration for classes offered. **Activities:** Concert band, dance, drama, student government.

Athletics. **Intramural:** Volleyball M.

Student services. Career counseling, services for economically disadvantaged, student employment services, financial aid counseling, personal counseling, veterans' counselor. **Physically disabled:** Services for visually, speech, hearing impaired. **Transfer:** Special adviser, orientation, pre-admission transcript evaluation for new students. Transfer center, transfer adviser, college fairs on campus for students transferring to 4-year colleges.

Contact. Phone: (503) 338-2411 Toll-free number: (866) 252-8768
Fax: (503) 325-5738
Joanne Swenson, Coordinator of Admissions, Clatsop Community College, 1653 Jerome Avenue, Astoria, OR 97103

Everest College: Portland

Portland, Oregon
www.everest-college.com **CB code: 2152**

- Private 2-year branch campus and business college
- Very large city

General. Accredited by ACICS. **Enrollment:** 659 degree-seeking undergraduates. **Degrees:** 147 associate awarded. **Calendar:** Quarter. **Full-time faculty:** 22 total. **Part-time faculty:** 17 total.

Basis for selection. Applicants must complete an entrance examination before admission. CPAT test required for admission.

2005-2006 Annual costs. Tuition/fees: $11,875. Per-credit charge: $246. $100 per-course online fee for distance learning. Books/supplies: $750. Personal expenses: $1,476.

Application procedures. **Admission:** No deadline. $25 fee. **Financial aid:** No deadline. FAFSA required. Applicants notified on a rolling basis.

Academics. **Credit/placement by examination:** CLEP.

Majors. **Business:** Accounting, business admin, office management, tourism/travel. **Computer sciences:** General. **Health:** Medical secretary, pharmacy assistant. **Legal studies:** General, paralegal. **Protective services:** Police science.

Contact. Phone: (503) 222-3225 ext. 102 Fax: (503) 228-6926
Everest College: Portland, 425 SW Washington Street, Portland, OR 97204

Klamath Community College

Klamath Falls, Oregon
www.kcc.cc.or.us **CB code: 4127**

- Public 2-year community college
- Small city

General. Regionally accredited. **Enrollment:** 900 undergraduates. **Degrees:** 54 associate awarded. **Calendar:** Semester.

Basis for selection. Open admission.

2005-2006 Annual costs. Tuition/fees: $2,805; $6,315 out-of-state. Per-credit charge: $60 in-state; $138 out-of-state.

Application procedures. **Admission:** No deadline. No application fee. **Financial aid:** FAFSA required.

Academics. **Credit/placement by examination:** CLEP.

Contact. Phone: (541) 882-3521
Student Services Offices, Klamath Community College, 7390 South 6th Street, Klamath Falls, OR 97603

Lane Community College

Eugene, Oregon **CB member**
www.lanecc.edu **CB code: 4407**

- Public 2-year community college
- Commuter campus in small city

General. Founded in 1964. Regionally accredited. Outreach centers in downtown Eugene, Cottage Grove and Florence. **Enrollment:** 5,266 degree-seeking undergraduates. **Degrees:** 771 associate awarded. **Location:** 110 miles from Portland. **Calendar:** Quarter, extensive summer session. **Full-time faculty:** 269 total. **Part-time faculty:** 332 total. **Partnerships:** Professional technical advisory groups, learning community centers in local high school facilities.

Student profile.

Out-of-state:	2%	**25 or older:**	40%

Transfer out. **Colleges most students transferred to 2005:** University of Oregon, Oregon State University.

Basis for selection. Open admission, but selective for some programs. Special requirements for allied health and flight technology programs. Sequential Tests of Educational Progress required for dental applicants, School and College Ability Tests for nursing applicants, Nelson-Denny Reading Test for dental and medical assistant applicants.

2005-2006 Annual costs. Tuition/fees: $3,323; $10,838 out-of-state. Per-credit charge: $67 in-state; $234 out-of-state. Books/supplies: $795. Personal expenses: $1,800.

2004-2005 Financial aid. **Need-based:** 52% of total undergraduate aid awarded as scholarships/grants, 48% as loans/jobs. Need-based aid available for part-time students. Work study available nights and weekends. **Non-need-based:** Scholarships awarded for art, athletics, minority status, music/drama.

Application procedures. **Admission:** No deadline. No application fee. Admission notification on a rolling basis. **Financial aid:** Priority date 2/15; no closing date. FAFSA required. Applicants notified on a rolling basis starting 6/1; must reply within 2 week(s) of notification.

Academics. **Special study options:** Accelerated study, cooperative education, cross-registration, distance learning, double major, dual enrollment of high school students, ESL, independent study, internships, liberal arts/career combination, study abroad, weekend college. License preparation in aviation, nursing. **Credit/placement by examination:** CLEP, institutional tests. **Support services:** GED preparation and test center, learning center, pre-admission summer program, reduced course load, remedial instruction, study skills assistance, tutoring, writing center.

Majors. **Business:** Accounting, administrative services, office management, real estate. **Communications:** Broadcast journalism, journalism. **Communications technology:** General. **Computer sciences:** Data processing, programming, systems analysis, web page design. **Construction:** Electrician, maintenance. **Engineering technology:** Construction, drafting, electrical. **Family/consumer sciences:** Child care. **Health:** Dental hygiene, EMT paramedic, nursing (RN), respiratory therapy technology, substance abuse counseling. **Legal studies:** Legal secretary. **Liberal arts:** Arts/sciences. **Mechanic/repair:** Aircraft, auto body, automotive, diesel, electronics/electrical, heating/ac/refrig. **Parks/recreation:** Health/fitness. **Personal/culinary services:** Culinary arts. **Production:** Machine tool. **Protective services:** Criminal justice. **Public administration:** Community org/advocacy. **Transportation:** Aviation. **Visual/performing arts:** Commercial/advertising art.

Most popular majors. Business/marketing 7%, computer/information sciences 7%, health sciences 17%, liberal arts 51%, trade and industry 9%.

Computing on campus. 800 workstations in library, computer center. Commuter students can connect to campus network. Helpline available.

Student life. **Freshman orientation:** Available. Preregistration for classes offered. Each field of study has its own orientation program. Program also available for undecided majors. **Activities:** Bands, choral groups, dance, drama, literary magazine, music ensembles, musical theater, radio station, student government, student newspaper, OSPIRG, campus ministry, women's center, Associate Students of Lane Community College.

Athletics. **Intercollegiate:** Baseball M, basketball, cross-country, track and field, volleyball W. **Intramural:** Badminton, basketball, golf, skiing, soccer, volleyball.

Student services. Adult student services, campus ministries, career counseling, student employment services, financial aid counseling, health services, minority student services, on-campus daycare, personal counseling, placement for graduates, veterans' counselor, women's services. **Physically disabled:** Services for visually, speech, hearing impaired. **Transfer:** Special adviser, orientation, pre-admission transcript evaluation for new students. Transfer adviser, college fairs on campus for students transferring to 4-year colleges.

Contact. E-mail: garretth@lanecc.edu
Phone: (541) 463-3100 Fax: (541) 463-3995
Helen Garrett, Director of Admissions, Lane Community College, 4000 East 30th Avenue, Eugene, OR 97405

Linn-Benton Community College

Albany, Oregon
www.linnbenton.edu **CB code: 4413**

- Public 2-year community college
- Commuter campus in large town

General. Founded in 1966. Regionally accredited. Courses available at off-campus centers in Corvallis, Lebanon, and Sweet Home. **Enrollment:** 5,049 degree-seeking undergraduates; 200 non-degree-seeking students. **Degrees:** 586 associate awarded. **ROTC:** Army, Air Force. **Location:** 70 miles from Portland, 45 miles from Eugene. **Calendar:** Quarter, limited summer session. **Full-time faculty:** 157 total; 5% minority, 57% women. **Part-time faculty:** 327 total; 4% minority, 64% women. **Special facilities:** Stables, riding arena.

Student profile. Among degree-seeking undergraduates, 60% enrolled in a transfer program, 40% enrolled in a vocational program, 1,406 enrolled as first-time, first-year students.

Part-time:	46%	**Women:**	54%

Transfer out. 16% of students enrolled in the transfer program go on to 4-year colleges. **Colleges most students transferred to 2005:** Oregon State University, Western Oregon University, University of Oregon, Portland State University, Southern Oregon University.

Basis for selection. Open admission, but selective for some programs. Special requirements for nursing, dental assistant, veterinary technology, pharmacy technology, phlebotomy, public safety dispatcher and radiologic technology programs. High school diploma or GED required of applicants under 18. **Adult students:** Entrance exam policies same as for first-time freshmen.

2006-2007 Annual costs. Tuition/fees (projected): $3,109; $7,654 out-of-state. Per-credit charge: $65 in-state; $166 out-of-state. Books/supplies: $900. Personal expenses: $1,080.

2004-2005 Financial aid. Need-based: 64% of total undergraduate aid awarded as scholarships/grants, 36% as loans/jobs. Need-based aid available for part-time students. Work study available nights, weekends and for part-time students. **Non-need-based:** Scholarships awarded for academics, art, job skills, leadership, music/drama, state residency.

Application procedures. Admission: Priority date 7/14; deadline 10/4 (receipt date). $25 fee. Admission notification on a rolling basis beginning on or about 7/1. **Financial aid:** Priority date 4/1; no closing date. FAFSA required. Applicants notified on a rolling basis starting 4/15; must reply within 2 week(s) of notification.

Academics. Special study options: Cooperative education, cross-registration, distance learning, dual enrollment of high school students, ESL, independent study, internships, student-designed major, study abroad. Evening degree program. License preparation in nursing, paramedic, radiology, real estate. **Credit/placement by examination:** AP, CLEP, institutional tests. 24 credit hours maximum toward associate degree. **Support services:** GED preparation and test center, learning center, remedial instruction, study skills assistance, tutoring, writing center.

Majors. Agriculture: General, animal sciences, business, dairy, equestrian studies, equine science, horticultural science. **Biology:** General. **Business:** Accounting technology, administrative services, business admin, office management. **Communications:** Journalism. **Computer sciences:** General, applications programming, system admin. **Construction:** Carpentry, electrician, painting, pipefitting. **Education:** General, elementary, physical, secondary, teacher assistance. **Engineering:** General. **Engineering technology:** Drafting, electrical, water quality. **English:** Speech/rhetoric, technical writing. **Family/consumer sciences:** General, child care. **Foreign languages:** Spanish. **Health:** Medical assistant, medical records admin, medical secretary, nursing (RN), office assistant, predentistry, premedicine, prenursing, prepharmacy, preveterinary. **History:** General. **Interdisciplinary:** Biological/physical sciences. **Legal studies:** Legal secretary, paralegal, prelaw. **Liberal arts:** Arts/sciences. **Math:** General. **Mechanic/repair:** General, automotive, diesel, electronics/electrical, heavy equipment, industrial. **Personal/culinary services:** Chef training, restaurant/catering. **Physical sciences:** Chemistry, physics. **Protective services:** Criminal justice, police science. **Psychology:** General. **Social sciences:** General, anthropology, economics, geography, political science, sociology. **Visual/performing arts:** Art, commercial/advertising art, dramatic, photography.

Most popular majors. Business/marketing 12%, engineering/engineering technologies 9%, health sciences 14%, liberal arts 40%.

Computing on campus. 500 workstations in library, computer center, student center. Commuter students can connect to campus network. Online course registration, online library, helpline, wireless network available.

Student life. Freshman orientation: Mandatory. 2-hour program. Orientation also available on-line. **Policies:** Freshmen permitted cars on campus. **Activities:** Concert band, choral groups, dance, drama, student government, student newspaper, Pacific party, Campus Crusade for Christ, Baha'i, Christians on Campus, Chi Alpha Radical Reality, Phi Theta Kappa, campus family co-op, student ambassadors, livestock judging.

Athletics. Intercollegiate: Baseball M, basketball, equestrian, volleyball W. **Intramural:** Basketball, bowling, tennis. **Team name:** Roadrunners.

Student services. Adult student services, career counseling, services for economically disadvantaged, student employment services, financial aid counseling, minority student services, on-campus daycare, personal counseling, placement for graduates, veterans' counselor. **Physically disabled:** Services for visually, speech, hearing impaired. **Transfer:** Special adviser, orientation for new students. Transfer center, transfer adviser, college fairs on campus for students transferring to 4-year colleges.

Contact. E-mail: admissions@linnbenton.edu
Phone: (541) 917-4811 Fax: (541) 917-4868
Christine Baker, Admissions Outreach Coordinator, Linn-Benton Community College, 6500 Southwest Pacific Boulevard, Albany, OR 97321-3779

Mount Hood Community College

Gresham, Oregon
www.mhcc.cc.or.us/ **CB code: 4508**

- Public 2-year community college
- Commuter campus in small city

General. Founded in 1965. Regionally accredited. **Enrollment:** 7,356 degree-seeking undergraduates. **Degrees:** 785 associate awarded. **Location:** 12 miles from Portland. **Calendar:** Quarter, limited summer session. **Full-time faculty:** 153 total. **Part-time faculty:** 423 total. **Special facilities:** Planetarium, solar observatory.

Student profile.

Out-of-state:	5%	**25 or older:**	54%

Basis for selection. Open admission, but selective for some programs. Allied health programs require minimum high school GPA of 2.5. SAT scores may be used in place of in-house placement test. Interview required for cosmetology and most health services.

High school preparation. Requirements for health programs include 1 algebra, 1 biology, and 1 chemistry.

2005-2006 Annual costs. Tuition/fees: $3,038; $9,608 out-of-state. Per-credit charge: $63 in-state; $209 out-of-state. Washington State residents pay in-state tuition, plus $11 per-credit additional required fees. Books/supplies: $620. Personal expenses: $540.

Financial aid. Non-need-based: Scholarships awarded for academics.

Application procedures. Admission: No deadline. $25 fee. Admission notification on a rolling basis. Most health services majors must apply between November 1 and March 30 for fall admission. Application fee for these programs $15. Application deadlines and priority dates vary by program. **Financial aid:** No deadline. FAFSA, institutional form required. Applicants notified on a rolling basis starting 2/15; must reply within 4 week(s) of notification.

Academics. Special study options: Accelerated study, cooperative education, distance learning, double major, dual enrollment of high school students, exchange student, honors, independent study, internships, study abroad, weekend college. **Credit/placement by examination:** CLEP, institutional tests. 45 credit hours maximum toward associate degree. College placement test required for chemistry, mathematics, writing, or reading courses. **Support services:** Learning center, pre-admission summer program, reduced course load, remedial instruction, tutoring.

Majors. Agriculture: Horticulture. **Business:** General, accounting, administrative services, hospitality admin, tourism/travel. **Communications:** Broadcast journalism, journalism. **Communications technology:** Graphic/printing. **Computer sciences:** General. **Conservation:** Fisheries, forestry, management/policy. **Education:** Early childhood. **Engineering technology:** Architectural, civil. **Health:** Dental hygiene, health services, medical assistant, medical records admin, occupational therapy assistant, physical therapy assistant, respiratory therapy technology, surgical technology. **Legal studies:** Legal secretary. **Mechanic/repair:** Automotive, electronics/electrical. **Personal/culinary services:** Cosmetic, mortuary science. **Protective services:** Firefighting. **Transportation:** Aviation. **Visual/performing arts:** Commercial/advertising art, dramatic.

Most popular majors. Business/marketing 7%, health sciences 20%, liberal arts 55%, personal/culinary services 6%, trade and industry 7%.

Student life. Activities: Bands, choral groups, dance, drama, music ensembles, musical theater, radio station, student government, student newspaper, symphony orchestra, TV station.

Athletics. NCAA. **Intercollegiate:** Baseball M, basketball, cross-country, golf M, tennis, track and field, volleyball W. **Intramural:** Archery, badminton M, basketball, bowling, cross-country, golf, racquetball, skiing, soccer, softball, swimming, tennis, track and field, volleyball, wrestling M.

Student services. Career counseling, student employment services, health services, on-campus daycare, personal counseling, placement for graduates, veterans' counselor. **Physically disabled:** Services for visually, speech, hearing impaired. **Transfer:** Special adviser, orientation for new students. Transfer adviser, college fairs on campus for students transferring to 4-year colleges.

Contact. Phone: (503) 491-7391 Fax: (503) 491-6006
Patricia Martin, Associate Dean, Enrollment Services, Mount Hood Community College, 26000 Southeast Stark Street, Gresham, OR 97030

Pioneer Pacific College: Springfield

Springfield, Oregon
www.pioneerpacific.edu

- For-profit 2-year branch campus and technical college
- Commuter campus in small city
- Interview required

General. Accredited by ACICS. Main campus - Wilsonville; health career institute - Wilsonville; learning site - Clackamas; and branch campus - Springfield. **Enrollment:** 264 degree-seeking undergraduates; 156 non-degree-seeking students. **Degrees:** 155 associate awarded. **Location:** 10 miles from Eugene. **Calendar:** Quarter, extensive summer session. **Full-time faculty:** 12 total; 33% have terminal degrees, 17% minority, 50% women. **Part-time faculty:** 25 total; 20% have terminal degrees, 28% minority, 60% women. **Class size:** 79% < 20, 21% 20-39.

Student profile. Among degree-seeking undergraduates, 83 enrolled as first-time, first-year students.

Women:	70%	**Hispanic American:**	1%
Asian American:	1%	**25 or older:**	67%

Transfer out. Colleges most students transferred to 2005: Clackamas Community College, Chemeketa Community College, University of Phoenix.

Basis for selection. Open admission, but selective for some programs. **Adult students:** Entrance exam policies same as for first-time freshmen.

2006-2007 Annual costs. Tuition/fees (projected): $9,560. Costs vary by program from $9,358 to $22,053. Quoted annual tuition is for criminal justice. Certain programs have additional lab fees. Personal expenses: $1,169.

Application procedures. Admission: No deadline. $50 fee. Application must be submitted on paper. Admission notification on a rolling basis. **Financial aid:** No deadline. FAFSA required. Applicants notified on a rolling basis starting 3/15.

Academics. Special study options: Accelerated study, honors, liberal arts/career combination, weekend college. **Credit/placement by examination:** CLEP. **Support services:** Study skills assistance, tutoring.

Majors. Business: Accounting, business admin, sales/distribution. **Computer sciences:** Information systems. **Health:** Health care admin, medical assistant. **Protective services:** Criminal justice.

Most popular majors. Business/marketing 35%, computer/information sciences 20%, health sciences 23%, security/protective services 21%.

Computing on campus. 90 workstations in computer center. Online library available.

Student life. Freshman orientation: Mandatory. **Policies:** Freshmen permitted cars on campus.

Student services. Career counseling, student employment services, financial aid counseling, placement for graduates. **Transfer:** Special adviser, orientation for new students.

Contact. E-mail: inquiries@pioneerpacific.edu
Phone: (541) 684-4644 Toll-free number: (800) 772-4636
Debra Marcus, Executive Director, Pioneer Pacific College: Springfield, 3800 Sports Way, Springfield, OR 97477

Portland Community College

Portland, Oregon — **CB member**
www.pcc.edu — **CB code: 4617**

- Public 2-year community college
- Commuter campus in very large city

General. Founded in 1961. Regionally accredited. 3 comprehensive campuses; classes offered at several centers throughout district. **Enrollment:** 22,142 degree-seeking undergraduates. **Degrees:** 1,719 associate awarded. **Location:** 5 miles from downtown. **Calendar:** Quarter, extensive summer session. **Full-time faculty:** 387 total. **Part-time faculty:** 837 total.

Student profile.

Out-of-state:	4%	**25 or older:**	50%

Transfer out. Colleges most students transferred to 2005: Portland State University, University of Oregon, Oregon State University.

Basis for selection. Open admission, but selective for some programs. Enrollment in certain programs or courses may require prerequisite course work or permission by a department representative.

High school preparation. High school diploma required for some allied health programs.

2005-2006 Annual costs. Tuition/fees: $2,970; $8,730 out-of-state. Per-credit charge: $62 in-state; $190 out-of-state. Books/supplies: $1,320. Personal expenses: $1,140.

Financial aid. All financial aid based on need. Need-based aid available for part-time students. Work study available nights, weekends and for part-time students.

Application procedures. Admission: No deadline. $25 fee. Application may be submitted online. **Financial aid:** Priority date 3/1; no closing date. FAFSA required. Applicants notified on a rolling basis starting 6/1; must reply within 3 week(s) of notification.

Academics. Special study options: Distance learning, double major, dual enrollment of high school students, ESL, internships, study abroad, weekend college. License preparation in aviation, dental hygiene, nursing, paramedic, radiology, real estate. **Credit/placement by examination:** AP, CLEP, institutional tests. 45 credit hours maximum toward associate degree. **Support services:** GED preparation and test center, learning center, reduced course load, remedial instruction, study skills assistance, tutoring, writing center.

Majors. Agriculture: Landscaping. **Business:** General, accounting, administrative services, business admin, office management, office technology, real estate. **Construction:** Building inspection. **Education:** Early childhood. **Engineering technology:** Civil, computer systems, construction, drafting, electrical, manufacturing. **Family/consumer sciences:** Child care. **Foreign languages:** Sign language interpretation. **Health:** Clinical lab technology, dental hygiene, dental lab technology, EMT paramedic, medical radiologic technology/radiation therapy, medical records admin, substance abuse counseling, veterinary technology/assistant. **Interdisciplinary:** Gerontology. **Legal studies:** Legal secretary, paralegal. **Liberal arts:** Arts/sciences. **Mechanic/repair:** Aircraft, aircraft powerplant, auto body, automotive, diesel, heating/ac/refrig. **Parks/recreation:** Health/fitness. **Protective services:** Criminal justice, fire safety technology. **Visual/performing arts:** Commercial/advertising art, interior design, music performance.

Computing on campus. 3,100 workstations in library, computer center, student center. Commuter students can connect to campus network. Online course registration, helpline available.

Student life. Freshman orientation: Available. **Policies:** Freshmen permitted cars on campus. **Activities:** Bands, choral groups, dance, drama, literary magazine, music ensembles, student government, student newspaper.

Athletics. Intercollegiate: Basketball. **Intramural:** Basketball, bowling, cross-country, golf, racquetball, softball, swimming, tennis, volleyball. **Team name:** Panthers.

Student services. Career counseling, services for economically disadvantaged, student employment services, financial aid counseling, minority student services, on-campus daycare, personal counseling, placement for graduates, veterans' counselor, women's services. **Physically disabled:** Services for visually, speech, hearing impaired. **Learning disabled:** Comprehensive services available. **Transfer:** Special adviser, orientation, preadmission transcript evaluation for new students. Transfer adviser, college fairs on campus for students transferring to 4-year colleges.

Contact. Phone: (503) 977-4519 Fax: (503) 977-4740
Craig Kolins, Director of Admissions, Portland Community College, Box 19000, Portland, OR 97280-0990

Rogue Community College

Grants Pass, Oregon
www.roguecc.edu — **CB code: 4653**

- Public 2-year community college
- Commuter campus in large town

General. Founded in 1970. Regionally accredited. Branch campuses in Medford and White City, learning centers in Medford and Cave Junction. **Enrollment:** 3,349 degree-seeking undergraduates; 1,089 non-degree-seeking students. **Degrees:** 241 associate awarded. **Location:** 30 miles from Medford, 240 miles from Portland. **Calendar:** Quarter, limited summer session. **Full-time faculty:** 102 total; 1% minority, 61% women. **Part-time faculty:** 414 total; 4% minority, 50% women. **Class size:** 63% < 20, 34% 20-39, 2% 40-49, less than 1% 50-99, less than 1% >100. **Special facilities:** Outdoor concert bowl.

Student profile. Among degree-seeking undergraduates, 52% enrolled in a transfer program, 38% enrolled in a vocational program, 651 enrolled as first-time, first-year students.

Part-time:	58%	**Hispanic American:**	6%
Women:	62%	**Native American:**	3%
African American:	1%	**25 or older:**	55%
Asian American:	2%		

Basis for selection. Open admission, but selective for some programs. Special admissions for nursing, respiratory therapy, emergency medical technology, human services, mental health technician. Interview recommended for allied health, nursing programs. **Adult students:** SAT/ACT scores not required.

2005-2006 Annual costs. Tuition/fees: $2,985; $3,525 out-of-state. Per-credit charge: $59 in-state; $71 out-of-state. Washington, Idaho, Nevada and California residents pay in-state tuition. Books/supplies: $1,200. Personal expenses: $825.

Financial aid. Need-based: Need-based aid available for part-time students.

Application procedures. Admission: No deadline. No application fee. Admission notification on a rolling basis. **Financial aid:** Priority date 5/1; no closing date. FAFSA, institutional form required. Applicants notified on a rolling basis; must reply within 2 week(s) of notification.

Academics. Special study options: Cooperative education, distance learning, double major, dual enrollment of high school students, ESL, independent study, study abroad. License preparation in nursing, paramedic. **Credit/placement by examination:** AP, CLEP, institutional tests. Students required to take ASSET or COMPASS test prior to registration. **Support services:** GED preparation and test center, learning center, remedial instruction, study skills assistance, tutoring, writing center.

Majors. Business: General, business admin. **Construction:** General. **Education:** General, early childhood. **Engineering technology:** Construction, electrical, manufacturing. **Family/consumer sciences:** Child care. **Health:** EMT paramedic, nursing (RN), substance abuse counseling. **Liberal arts:** Arts/sciences. **Mechanic/repair:** Automotive, diesel, electronics/electrical, industrial. **Production:** Welding. **Protective services:** Fire safety technology, police science. **Public administration:** Social work. **Social sciences:** General.

Most popular majors. Business/marketing 8%, health sciences 16%, liberal arts 56%.

Computing on campus. 115 workstations in library, computer center. Online course registration available.

Student life. Freshman orientation: Available. Preregistration for classes offered. **Policies:** Freshmen permitted cars on campus. **Activities:** Concert band, choral groups, drama, literary magazine, musical theater, student government, student newspaper, Club Latino.

Athletics. Intramural: Badminton, basketball, skiing, softball, tennis, volleyball.

Student services. Career counseling, services for economically disadvantaged, student employment services, financial aid counseling, on-campus daycare, personal counseling, placement for graduates, veterans' counselor. **Physically disabled:** Services for visually, speech, hearing impaired. **Transfer:** Special adviser, orientation, pre-admission transcript evaluation for new students. Transfer adviser, college fairs on campus for students transferring to 4-year colleges.

Contact. E-mail: Csullivan@roguecc.edu
Phone: (541) 956-7501
Claudia Sullivan, Director of Enrollment Services, Rogue Community College, 3345 Redwood Highway, Grants Pass, OR 97527

Southwestern Oregon Community College

Coos Bay, Oregon
www.socc.edu **CB code: 4729**

- Public 2-year culinary school and community college
- Commuter campus in large town

General. Founded in 1961. Regionally accredited. **Enrollment:** 1,923 degree-seeking undergraduates; 590 non-degree-seeking students. **Degrees:** 173 associate awarded. **Location:** 125 miles from Eugene. **Calendar:** Quarter, limited summer session. **Full-time faculty:** 72 total. **Part-time faculty:** 196 total. **Special facilities:** Business development center, culinary institute.

Student profile. Among degree-seeking undergraduates, 399 enrolled as first-time, first-year students.

Part-time:	49%	**Women:**	58%
Out-of-state:	1%		

Transfer out. Colleges most students transferred to 2005: Oregon State University, Southern Oregon University, University of Oregon, Linfield College, Eastern Oregon University.

Basis for selection. Open admission, but selective for some programs. Placement test, interview, high school chemistry and algebra required for nursing. Background check required for emergency response and EMTs. **Adult students:** Entrance exam policies same as for first-time freshmen.

High school preparation. 1 chemistry and 1 algebra required of nursing majors.

2005-2006 Annual costs. Tuition/fees: $3,105. Per-credit charge: $60. Room/board: $5,155. Books/supplies: $840. Personal expenses: $540.

2004-2005 Financial aid. Need-based: 56% of total undergraduate aid awarded as scholarships/grants, 44% as loans/jobs. Need-based aid available for part-time students.

Application procedures. Admission: No deadline. $30 fee, may be waived for applicants with need. Application may be submitted online. Admission notification on a rolling basis. **Financial aid:** Priority date 2/28, closing date 6/30. FAFSA required. Applicants notified on a rolling basis starting 5/1; must reply within 3 week(s) of notification.

Academics. Oregon transfer (AAOT) degree accepted at Oregon 4-year institutions where students enter as juniors. **Special study options:** Cooperative education, distance learning, double major, dual enrollment of high school students, ESL, honors, independent study, internships, liberal arts/career combination. Bachelor's degree programs available on campus. License preparation in nursing. **Credit/placement by examination:** AP, CLEP, institutional tests. **Support services:** GED preparation and test center, learning center, remedial instruction, tutoring, writing center.

Majors. Business: Accounting, administrative services, banking/financial services, business admin, entrepreneurial studies, management information systems, office management, sales/distribution. **Computer sciences:** Applications programming, computer science, information systems, webmaster. **Conservation:** Environmental studies. **Engineering:** General. **Family/consumer sciences:** Child care, family studies. **Health:** Licensed practical nurse, medical assistant, substance abuse counseling. **Liberal arts:** Arts/sciences. **Personal/culinary services:** Culinary arts. **Protective services:** Criminal justice, firefighting. **Public administration:** Social work.

Most popular majors. Business/marketing 15%, health sciences 45%, liberal arts 25%, security/protective services 8%.

Computing on campus. 60 workstations in dormitories, library, computer center. Dormitories wired for high-speed internet access and linked to campus network. Commuter students can connect to campus network. Online course registration, helpline, repair service, wireless network available.

Student life. Freshman orientation: Available. **Policies:** Freshmen permitted cars on campus. **Housing:** Guaranteed on-campus for freshmen. Single-sex dorms, special housing for disabled, apartments, substance-free housing available. $250 deposit. **Activities:** Bands, choral groups, drama, literary magazine, music ensembles, student government, student newspaper, Rotaract, Phi Theta Kappa.

Athletics. NJCAA. **Intercollegiate:** Baseball M, basketball, cross-country, golf, soccer, softball W, track and field, volleyball W, wrestling M. **Intramural:** Basketball. **Team name:** Lakers.

Student services. Adult student services, alcohol/substance abuse counseling, career counseling, services for economically disadvantaged, student employment services, financial aid counseling, health services, on-campus daycare, personal counseling, placement for graduates, veterans' counselor. **Physically disabled:** Services for visually, speech, hearing impaired. **Learning disabled:** Comprehensive services available. **Transfer:** Special adviser, orientation for new students. Transfer center, college fairs on campus for students transferring to 4-year colleges.

Contact. E-mail: admissions@socc.edu
Phone: (541) 888-7352 Toll-free number: (800) 962-2838 ext. 7352
Fax: (541) 888-7285
Tom Nicholls, Director of Enrollment Management, Southwestern Oregon Community College, 1988 Newmark Avenue, Coos Bay, OR 97420-2956

Treasure Valley Community College

Ontario, Oregon
www.tvcc.cc **CB code: 4825**

- Public 2-year community college
- Commuter campus in small town

General. Founded in 1961. Regionally accredited. **Enrollment:** 1,762 degree-seeking undergraduates; 184 non-degree-seeking students. **Degrees:** 208 associate awarded. **Location:** 60 miles from Boise, Idaho. **Calendar:** Quarter, limited summer session. **Full-time faculty:** 45 total. **Part-time faculty:** 30 total.

Student profile. Among degree-seeking undergraduates, 78% enrolled in a transfer program, 22% enrolled in a vocational program, 622 enrolled as first-time, first-year students, 90 transferred in from other institutions.

Part-time:	41%	**Hispanic American:**	17%
Out-of-state:	64%	**Native American:**	1%
Women:	62%	**25 or older:**	41%
African American:	1%	**Live on campus:**	12%
Asian American:	2%		

Basis for selection. Open admission.

2006-2007 Annual costs. Tuition/fees (projected): $3,420; $3,870 out-of-state. Per-credit charge: $67 in-state; $77 out-of-state. Room/board: $4,845. Books/supplies: $1,050. Personal expenses: $1,500.

2005-2006 Financial aid. Need-based: Average need met was 33%. Average scholarship/grant was $3,364; average loan $2,109. 58% of total undergraduate aid awarded as scholarships/grants, 42% as loans/jobs. Need-based aid available for part-time students. Work study available for part-time students. **Non-need-based:** Scholarships awarded for academics, athletics, leadership, music/drama, state residency.

Application procedures. Admission: No deadline. No application fee. Application must be submitted on paper. Admission notification on a rolling basis. **Financial aid:** Priority date 4/1; no closing date. FAFSA required. Applicants notified on a rolling basis starting 5/1.

Academics. Special study options: Cooperative education, distance learning, double major, dual enrollment of high school students, ESL, independent study, internships. Elementary education program with Eastern Oregon State College and satellite program with Boise State University. License preparation in nursing. **Credit/placement by examination:** AP, CLEP, institutional tests. 45 credit hours maximum toward associate degree. **Support services:** GED preparation and test center, learning center, reduced course load, remedial instruction, tutoring.

Majors. Agriculture: Agronomy, animal sciences, business, economics, farm/ranch. **Biology:** General. **Business:** General, business admin, management information systems, office management, office/clerical. **Communications:** General. **Computer sciences:** General, computer science. **Conservation:** Management/policy, wildlife. **Education:** Bilingual, elementary, secondary. **Engineering:** General. **Engineering technology:** Computer, drafting. **Foreign languages:** General. **Health:** Athletic training, medical secretary, medical transcription, nursing (RN), predentistry, premedicine, preveterinary. **History:** General. **Legal studies:** Legal secretary, paralegal, prelaw. **Liberal arts:** Arts/sciences. **Math:** General. **Physical sciences:** Chemistry, geology, physics. **Production:** Welding. **Protective services:** Criminal justice, fire safety technology, firefighting, law enforcement admin, police science. **Psychology:** General. **Public administration:** Social work. **Social sciences:** General, political science. **Visual/performing arts:** General, art.

Most popular majors. Business/marketing 12%, education 16%, health sciences 13%, liberal arts 31%, security/protective services 6%.

Computing on campus. 50 workstations in library, computer center. Dormitories wired for high-speed internet access and linked to campus network. Online course registration, helpline, repair service, wireless network available.

Student life. Freshman orientation: Available. Preregistration for classes offered. First five weeks of each quarter. **Policies:** Freshmen permitted cars on campus. **Housing:** Single-sex dorms, substance-free housing available. **Activities:** Bands, choral groups, drama, music ensembles, musical theater, student government.

Athletics. Intercollegiate: Baseball M, basketball, cross-country, golf, rodeo, soccer, tennis, track and field, volleyball. **Intramural:** Basketball, softball, volleyball. **Team name:** Chukars.

Student services. Career counseling, student employment services, health services, on-campus daycare, personal counseling, placement for graduates, veterans' counselor, women's services. **Physically disabled:** Services for visually impaired. **Transfer:** Special adviser, pre-admission transcript evaluation for new students. College fairs on campus for students transferring to 4-year colleges.

Contact. E-mail: clbell@tvcc.cc
Phone: (541) 881-8822 Fax: (541) 881-2721
Cathy Yasuda, Director of Outreach & Support Services, Treasure Valley Community College, 650 College Boulevard, Ontario, OR 97914

Umpqua Community College

Roseburg, Oregon
www.umpqua.edu **CB code: 4862**

- Public 2-year community college
- Commuter campus in large town

General. Founded in 1964. Regionally accredited. **Enrollment:** 2,133 undergraduates. **Degrees:** 152 associate awarded. **Location:** 60 miles from Eugene. **Calendar:** Quarter, limited summer session. **Full-time faculty:** 60 total. **Part-time faculty:** 120 total. **Class size:** 69% < 20, 28% 20-39, 2% 40-49, less than 1% 50-99, less than 1% >100.

Student profile. 40% enrolled in a transfer program, 50% enrolled in a vocational program, 10% already have a bachelor's degree or higher, 40 transferred in from other institutions.

Out-of-state:	2%	**Hispanic American:**	3%
African American:	1%	**Native American:**	1%
Asian American:	2%	**25 or older:**	41%

Transfer out. Colleges most students transferred to 2005: Oregon State University, University of Oregon, Northwest Christian College, Western Oregon University, Southern Oregon University.

Basis for selection. Open admission. Special requirements for nursing program. **Adult students:** Entrance exam policies same as for first-time freshmen.

2005-2006 Annual costs. Tuition/fees: $2,880; $8,100 out-of-state. Per-credit charge: $59 in-state; $175 out-of-state. Books/supplies: $900. Personal expenses: $1,200.

Financial aid. All financial aid based on need. Need-based aid available for part-time students.

Application procedures. Admission: No deadline. $25 fee. Application must be submitted on paper. Admission notification on a rolling basis. **Financial aid:** Priority date 3/1; no closing date. FAFSA required. Applicants notified on a rolling basis starting 5/1; must reply within 2 week(s) of notification.

Academics. Special study options: Cooperative education, distance learning, double major, ESL, independent study, internships, student-designed major. Bachelor's degree programs available on campus. License preparation in nursing, paramedic. **Credit/placement by examination:** AP, CLEP, institutional tests. 45 credit hours maximum toward associate degree. 24 hours of credit by exam may be counted toward 1-year certificate program. **Support services:** GED preparation and test center, learning center, remedial instruction, study skills assistance, tutoring.

Majors. Business: General, accounting, administrative services. **Computer sciences:** Information systems. **Education:** General, early childhood. **Engineering technology:** Civil. **Health:** EMT paramedic, medical secretary, nursing (RN). **Legal studies:** Legal secretary. **Liberal arts:** Arts/sciences. **Mechanic/repair:** Automotive, electronics/electrical. **Personal/culinary services:** Cosmetic. **Protective services:** Firefighting.

Most popular majors. Business/marketing 6%, engineering/engineering technologies 8%, health sciences 25%, liberal arts 36%, trade and industry 8%.

Computing on campus. 200 workstations in library, computer center, student center. Wireless network available.

Student life. Freshman orientation: Mandatory. Preregistration for classes offered. Orientation held the Thursday or Friday prior to the beginning of each term, except summer term. **Policies:** Freshmen permitted cars on campus. **Activities:** Bands, choral groups, drama, music ensembles, musical theater, student government, student newspaper.

Athletics. Intercollegiate: Basketball. **Team name:** Timbermen/Timberwomen.

Student services. Career counseling, student employment services, on-campus daycare, personal counseling, placement for graduates, veterans' counselor. **Physically disabled:** Services for visually, hearing impaired. **Transfer:** Special adviser, orientation, pre-admission transcript evaluation for new students. Transfer center, transfer adviser, college fairs on campus for students transferring to 4-year colleges.

Contact. E-mail: nordlil@umpqua.edu
Phone: (541) 957-4519 Toll-free number: (800) 820-5161
Fax: (541) 440-4612
David Farrington, Director of Enrollment Services, Umpqua Community College, 1140 College Road, Roseburg, OR 97470-0226

Western Culinary Institute

Portland, Oregon
www.wci.edu

- For-profit 2-year culinary school
- Commuter campus

General. Accredited by ACCSCT. **Calendar:** Semester.

Contact. Phone: (503) 223-2245
Manager of Admissions Services, 921 SW Morrison Street, Suite 400, Portland, OR 97205

Pennsylvania

Academy of Medical Arts and Business

Harrisburg, Pennsylvania
www.acadcampus.com **CB code: 3188**

- For-profit 2-year business and health science college
- Commuter campus in small city
- Interview required

General. Accredited by ACCSCT. **Enrollment:** 230 degree-seeking undergraduates. **Degrees:** 110 associate awarded. **Location:** 206 miles from Philadelphia, 200 miles from Washington, DC. **Calendar:** Continuous. **Full-time faculty:** 10 total. **Part-time faculty:** 9 total.

Transfer out. Colleges most students transferred to 2005: Penn College of Technology, Shippensburg University, Harrisburg Area Community College.

Basis for selection. All applicants must tour Academy and have personal interview with representative. **Adult students:** Entrance exam policies same as for first-time freshmen. **Homeschooled:** For state grants, applicants must submit either accredited diploma or certification from local superintendent of compliance with Home Education Act. **Learning Disabled:** Provide copy of independent educational program.

2005-2006 Annual costs. Tuition/fees: $10,440. Books/supplies: $1,430. Personal expenses: $1,000.

Financial aid. All financial aid based on need. Need-based aid available for part-time students. Work study available nights.

Application procedures. Admission: No deadline. $150 fee, may be waived for applicants with need. Admission notification on a rolling basis. **Financial aid:** No deadline. FAFSA required. Applicants notified on a rolling basis.

Academics. Special study options: Honors, internships, liberal arts/career combination. License preparation in radiology. **Credit/placement by examination:** AP, CLEP. **Support services:** Study skills assistance, tutoring.

Majors. Business: General, accounting, administrative services, business admin, office technology. **Computer sciences:** General, data entry, data processing, information systems, programming, systems analysis. **Family/consumer sciences:** Child care. **Health:** Asian bodywork therapy, Chinese medicine/herbology, dental assistant, hematology, massage therapy, medical assistant, medical records admin, medical records technology, medical secretary, medical transcription, movement therapy, physical therapy assistant. **Legal studies:** Paralegal. **Personal/culinary services:** Culinary arts.

Most popular majors. Business/marketing 6%, computer/information sciences 11%, health sciences 39%, legal studies 11%, personal/culinary services 33%.

Computing on campus. 65 workstations in computer center. Online library, helpline, repair service available.

Student life. Freshman orientation: Mandatory. Preregistration for classes offered. Held first day of class for all new students.

Student services. Adult student services, alcohol/substance abuse counseling, career counseling, services for economically disadvantaged, student employment services, financial aid counseling, on-campus daycare, placement for graduates. **Transfer:** Special adviser, orientation, re-entry adviser, pre-admission transcript evaluation for new students. Transfer adviser for students transferring to 4-year colleges.

Contact. E-mail: info@acadcampus.com
Phone: (717) 545-4747
Gary Kay, President, Academy of Medical Arts and Business, 2301 Academy Drive, Harrisburg, PA 17112-1012

Allied Medical and Technical Institute

Forty Fort, Pennsylvania
www.alliedteched.edu **CB code: 3190**

- For-profit 2-year technical college
- Small town

General. Accredited by ACCSCT. **Enrollment:** 210 undergraduates. **Degrees:** 13 associate awarded. **Calendar:** Continuous. **Part-time faculty:** 10 total.

Basis for selection. Must be a high school graduate.

2005-2006 Annual costs. Cost of full programs ranges from $9,474 to $19,470 depending on program.

Application procedures. Admission: No deadline.

Academics. Credit/placement by examination: CLEP.

Majors. Business: General. **Personal/culinary services:** General.

Contact. Phone: (570) 288-8400
Candice Sheilek, Admissions Director, Allied Medical and Technical Institute, 166 Slocum Avenue, Forty Fort, PA 18704-2936

Antonelli Institute of Art and Photography

Erdenheim, Pennsylvania
www.antonelli.edu **CB code: 0971**

- For-profit 2-year visual arts and junior college
- Commuter campus in large town
- Interview required

General. Founded in 1938. Accredited by ACCSCT. **Enrollment:** 187 degree-seeking undergraduates; 2 non-degree-seeking students. **Degrees:** 63 associate awarded. **Location:** 1 mile from Philadelphia. **Calendar:** Semester, limited summer session. **Full-time faculty:** 11 total. **Part-time faculty:** 5 total; 20% have terminal degrees, 40% women. **Class size:** 100% < 20. **Special facilities:** Color photography processor, black and white and color darkrooms, computer graphics labs, digital photo darkroom.

Student profile. Among degree-seeking undergraduates, 100% enrolled in a vocational program, 1% already have a bachelor's degree or higher, 119 enrolled as first-time, first-year students, 4 transferred in from other institutions.

Part-time:	2%	**Hispanic American:**	3%
Out-of-state:	20%	**25 or older:**	7%
Women:	65%	**Live on campus:**	51%
African American:	5%		

Transfer out. 9% of students enrolled in the transfer program go on to 4-year colleges. **Colleges most students transferred to 2005:** Brooks Institute, University of the Arts, Arcadia University, Point Park Colllege.

Basis for selection. Emphasis placed on interview, recommendations, and samples of art and photography or portfolio. Although not required, student portfolios will be evaluated. **Homeschooled:** Documentation of high school graduation/equivalency from local school district, state department of education or recognized home school organization required.

2006-2007 Annual costs. Annual Tuition for graphic design/commercial art students is $15,450; for photography students $17,150. Required fees $125. Books/supplies: $1,600. Personal expenses: $1,500.

2005-2006 Financial aid. All financial aid based on need. Average need met was 35%. 18% of total undergraduate aid awarded as scholarships/grants, 82% as loans/jobs. Need-based aid available for part-time students. Work study available nights.

Application procedures. Admission: No deadline. $25 fee, may be waived for applicants with need. Application may be submitted online. Admission notification on a rolling basis. **Financial aid:** No deadline. FAFSA required. Applicants notified on a rolling basis; must reply within 2 week(s) of notification.

Academics. Credit/placement by examination: CLEP.

Majors. Visual/performing arts: Commercial photography, commercial/advertising art, design, photography.

Two-Year Colleges

Computing on campus. 53 workstations in library, computer center.

Student life. **Freshman orientation:** Mandatory. **Policies:** Freshmen permitted cars on campus. **Housing:** Coed dorms, apartments, substance-free housing available. $375 partly refundable deposit. Dormitory facilities available from local apartments.

Athletics. **Intramural:** Volleyball.

Student services. Career counseling, student employment services, financial aid counseling, personal counseling, placement for graduates. **Transfer:** Special adviser, pre-admission transcript evaluation for new students. Transfer adviser for students transferring to 4-year colleges.

Contact. E-mail: admissions@antonelli.edu
Phone: (800) 722-7871 Toll-free number: (800) 722-7871
Fax: (215) 836-2794
Anthony DeTore, Director of Admissions, Antonelli Institute of Art and Photography, 300 Montgomery Avenue, Erdenheim, PA 19038-8242

Berean Institute
Philadelphia, Pennsylvania
www.bereaninstitute.org **CB code: 1045**

- Private 2-year business and technical college
- Very large city

General. Founded in 1899. Accredited by ACCSCT. **Enrollment:** 290 undergraduates. **Degrees:** 18 associate awarded. **Location:** Downtown. **Calendar:** Trimester, limited summer session. **Full-time faculty:** 17 total.

Basis for selection. Open admission.

2005-2006 Annual costs. Tuition ranges from $2,500 to $6,500, depending on program. Books/supplies: $400. Personal expenses: $500.

Application procedures. **Admission:** No deadline. $25 fee, may be waived for applicants with need. Application may be submitted online. Admission notification on a rolling basis. Interview required.

Academics. **Special study options:** Independent study, internships, liberal arts/career combination. **Credit/placement by examination:** CLEP, institutional tests. 30 credit hours maximum toward associate degree. **Support services:** Learning center, pre-admission summer program, tutoring.

Majors. **Business:** Accounting, business admin. **Computer sciences:** General. **Engineering technology:** Electrical.

Student life. **Activities:** Drama, student government, student newspaper.

Athletics. **Intercollegiate:** Basketball M. **Intramural:** Basketball M.

Student services. Adult student services, career counseling, personal counseling, placement for graduates, veterans' counselor.

Contact. Phone: (215) 763-4833 Fax: (215) 236-6011
John Spruill, Director of Student Services, Berean Institute, 1901 West Girard Avenue, Philadelphia, PA 19130

Berks Technical Institute
Wyomissing, Pennsylvania
www.berks.edu **CB code: 3198**

- For-profit 2-year business and technical college
- Commuter campus in small city

General. Accredited by ACCSCT. **Enrollment:** 585 undergraduates. **Degrees:** 108 associate awarded. **Location:** 64 miles from Philadelphia. **Calendar:** Quarter. **Full-time faculty:** 41 total. **Part-time faculty:** 10 total.

Basis for selection. Open admission. **Learning Disabled:** Meeting with dean of education and department head if deemed necessary by dean of education.

2005-2006 Annual costs. Tuition for diploma program ranges from $9,600 to $17,000; tuition for degree program ranges from $21,000 to $30,000. Books/supplies: $992.

Financial aid. All financial aid based on need. Need-based aid available for part-time students.

Application procedures. **Admission:** No deadline. $50 fee. Admission notification on a rolling basis. **Financial aid:** No deadline. FAFSA required. Applicants notified on a rolling basis; must reply within 2 week(s) of notification.

Academics. **Special study options:** Internships. **Credit/placement by examination:** CLEP. **Support services:** Learning center, reduced course load, remedial instruction, study skills assistance, tutoring, writing center.

Majors. **Business:** Accounting, business admin. **Computer sciences:** General, computer graphics, computer science, networking, programming. **Engineering technology:** Drafting. **Health:** Medical assistant, medical secretary. **Legal studies:** Paralegal. **Protective services:** Law enforcement admin. **Visual/performing arts:** Commercial/advertising art.

Computing on campus. 200 workstations in library, computer center. Repair service available.

Student life. **Freshman orientation:** Mandatory.

Student services. Financial aid counseling, placement for graduates. **Transfer:** Special adviser, orientation, pre-admission transcript evaluation for new students. Transfer adviser for students transferring to 4-year colleges.

Contact. E-mail: platham@berks.edu
Phone: (610) 372-1722 Toll-free number: (800) 490-6992
Pat Latham, Registrar, Berks Technical Institute, 2205 Ridgewood Road, Wyomissing, PA 19610

Bidwell Training Center
Pittsburgh, Pennsylvania
www.bidwell-training.org **CB code: 3199**

- For-profit 1-year business and health science college
- Commuter campus in large city
- Interview required

General. Accredited by ACCSCT. **Enrollment:** 130 undergraduates. **Degrees:** 16 associate awarded. **Calendar:** Continuous. **Full-time faculty:** 19 total; 5% have terminal degrees, 21% minority, 79% women. **Part-time faculty:** 1 total; 100% women.

Basis for selection. Interview and test scores very important. **Adult students:** Entrance exam policies same as for first-time freshmen. **Learning Disabled:** Academic support available.

2005-2006 Annual costs. Tuition per year ranges from $6,000 to $10,000, includes all fees. Programs offered at no cost to Pennsylvania residents.

Financial aid. All financial aid based on need.

Application procedures. **Admission:** No deadline. No application fee. Admission notification on a rolling basis. **Financial aid:** No deadline. FAFSA required. Applicants notified on a rolling basis.

Academics. **Special study options:** Internships. **Credit/placement by examination:** CLEP, institutional tests. **Support services:** GED preparation, remedial instruction, study skills assistance, tutoring.

Majors. **Science technology:** Chemical.

Computing on campus. 85 workstations in library, computer center.

Student life. **Freshman orientation:** Mandatory. Preregistration for classes offered.

Student services. Adult student services, career counseling, student employment services, financial aid counseling, personal counseling, placement for graduates.

Contact. E-mail: dfarah@mcg-btc.org
Phone: (412) 323-4000 ext. 156 Toll-free number: (800) 516-1800 ext. 155
Fax: (412) 321-2120
Ken Huselton, Director of Student Services, Bidwell Training Center, 1815 Metropolitan Street, Pittsburgh, PA 15233

Bradford School: Pittsburgh
Pittsburgh, Pennsylvania
www.bradfordpittsburgh.edu **CB code: 2206**

- For-profit 2-year junior college
- Commuter campus in very large city

General. Accredited by ACICS. **Calendar:** Semester.

Annual costs/financial aid. Tuition/fees (2005-2006): $12,600. Room/board: $6,040. Need-based financial aid available for full-time students.

Contact. Phone: (412) 391-6710
Director of Admissions, 125 West Station Square Drive, Pittsburgh, PA 15219

Bradley Academy for the Visual Arts

York, Pennsylvania
www.aiba.artinstitutes.edu **CB code: 1548**

- For-profit 2-year visual arts and technical college
- Commuter campus in large town
- Application essay, interview required

General. Founded in 1952. Accredited by ACCSCT. **Enrollment:** 613 degree-seeking undergraduates. **Degrees:** 152 associate awarded. **Location:** 20 miles from Harrisburg, 90 miles from Philadelphia. **Calendar:** Quarter, extensive summer session. **Full-time faculty:** 14 total; 29% have terminal degrees, 29% women. **Part-time faculty:** 44 total; 16% have terminal degrees, 7% minority, 54% women. **Class size:** 86% < 20, 14% 20-39.

Student profile. Among degree-seeking undergraduates, 195 enrolled as first-time, first-year students.

Part-time:	13%	**25 or older:**	10%
Women:	64%		

Basis for selection. Open admission, but selective for some programs. High school record and attendance, recommendations, and admissions interview most important. Portfolio review also important where required. Portfolio required for animation program. **Adult students:** Entrance exam policies same as for first-time freshmen. **Homeschooled:** Transcript of courses and grades, state high school equivalency certificate, interview required. 150-word essay required.

2006-2007 Annual costs. Tuition/fees (projected): $15,140. Books/supplies: $1,250. Personal expenses: $2,610.

Financial aid. All financial aid based on need.

Application procedures. Admission: No deadline. $50 fee. Application may be submitted online. Admission notification on a rolling basis. Admitted applicants must reply within 10 days of personal interview. **Financial aid:** Priority date 8/1; no closing date. FAFSA required. Applicants notified on a rolling basis starting 6/1.

Academics. All students in degree programs (except Fashion Marketing) required to own laptop computer. Laptop specifications for each program available through Information Technology Department. **Special study options:** Internships. **Credit/placement by examination:** CLEP, SAT, ACT. **Support services:** Learning center, pre-admission summer program, reduced course load, remedial instruction, study skills assistance, tutoring, writing center.

Majors. Business: Fashion. **Communications technology:** Animation/special effects. **Computer sciences:** Web page design. **Visual/performing arts:** Commercial/advertising art, interior design.

Most popular majors. Business/marketing 15%, visual/performing arts 85%.

Computing on campus. PC or laptop required. 175 workstations in library, computer center, student center. Repair service, wireless network available.

Student life. Freshman orientation: Mandatory. Half-day program, 3-6 days before school starts. **Policies:** Freshmen permitted cars on campus. **Activities:** Student government, student newspaper.

Student services. Career counseling, student employment services, financial aid counseling, personal counseling, placement for graduates. **Transfer:** Special adviser, orientation, pre-admission transcript evaluation for new students.

Contact. E-mail: info@bradlyacademy.edu
Phone: (800) 864-7725 Fax: (717) 840-1951
James Hannigan, Director of Admissions, Bradley Academy for the Visual Arts, 1409 Williams Road, York, PA 17402

Bucks County Community College

Newtown, Pennsylvania **CB member**
www.bucks.edu **CB code: 2066**

- Public 2-year community college
- Commuter campus in large town

General. Founded in 1964. Regionally accredited. Credit courses available at several off-campus locations. **Enrollment:** 9,596 degree-seeking undergraduates. **Degrees:** 771 associate awarded. **Location:** 35 miles from Philadelphia. **Calendar:** Semester, limited summer session. **Full-time faculty:** 143 total; 26% have terminal degrees, 5% minority, 48% women. **Part-time faculty:** 430 total; 5% minority, 50% women. **Special facilities:** Art gallery. **Partnerships:** Formal partnerships with Bucks County Technical High School, Eastern Center for Arts & Technology, Middle Bucks Institute of Technology, Northern Montgomery County Technical Career Center, Upper Bucks County Area Vocational Technical High School, Western Center for Technical Studies.

Student profile. Among degree-seeking undergraduates, 75% enrolled in a transfer program, 25% enrolled in a vocational program, 7% already have a bachelor's degree or higher, 2,672 enrolled as first-time, first-year students, 325 transferred in from other institutions.

Part-time:	58%	**Women:**	58%
Out-of-state:	1%	**25 or older:**	39%

Transfer out. Colleges most students transferred to 2005: Temple University, Holy Family University, Pennsylvania State University, Drexel University.

Basis for selection. Open admission, but selective for some programs. Admissions to nursing, fine arts, chef apprenticeship and fine woodworking programs based on GPA and satisfaction of prerequisites. Admission to music program based on above, plus audition. Admission to art program based on above, plus portfolio. College's own test administered for placement purposes, after admission. Interview required for chef apprentice, fine arts, fine woodworking, and nursing programs. Audition required for music program; portfolio required for art, fine woodworking programs; essay required for chef apprentice program. **Adult students:** Entrance exam policies same as for first-time freshmen. Students over 65 exempt from placement tests. **Homeschooled:** Final official transcript certified by state required. **Learning Disabled:** Special testing accommodations can be provided for the entrance assessment test for students with learning disabilities.

2005-2006 Annual costs. Tuition/fees: $3,157; $5,827 out-of-district; $8,497 out-of-state. Per-credit charge: $89 in-district; $178 out-of-district; $267 out-of-state. In-state out-of-district required fees $787; out-of-state required fees $1087. Books/supplies: $700.

2004-2005 Financial aid. Need-based: 66% of total undergraduate aid awarded as scholarships/grants, 34% as loans/jobs. Need-based aid available for part-time students. Work study available nights, weekends and for part-time students. **Non-need-based:** Scholarships awarded for academics.

Application procedures. Admission: Closing date 5/1 (postmark date). $30 fee. Application must be submitted on paper. Admission notification on a rolling basis. **Financial aid:** Priority date 5/1; no closing date. FAFSA, institutional form required. Applicants notified on a rolling basis starting 6/1; must reply within 2 week(s) of notification.

Academics. Special study options: Cooperative education, distance learning, dual enrollment of high school students, ESL, external degree, honors, independent study, internships, student-designed major, weekend college. Bachelor's degree programs available on campus. License preparation in nursing, occupational therapy, physical therapy, radiology, real estate. **Credit/placement by examination:** AP, CLEP, institutional tests. 30 credit hours maximum toward associate degree. Portfolio development, foreign language exams, CLEP, DANTES, etc. **Support services:** GED preparation and test center, learning center, reduced course load, remedial instruction, study skills assistance, tutoring, writing center.

Majors. Area/ethnic studies: American. **Biology:** General. **Business:** General, accounting, administrative services, banking/financial services, business admin, hospitality admin, hotel/motel admin, marketing, office management, office/clerical, operations, restaurant/food services, retailing, small business admin, tourism/travel. **Communications:** General, journalism. **Communications technology:** Animation/special effects, graphic/printing. **Computer sciences:** General, computer graphics, computer science, data processing, information systems, networking, programming. **Conservation:** Environmental science. **Education:** General, early childhood, health, physical, teacher assistance. **Engineering:** General. **Family/consumer sciences:** Institutional food production. **Health:** Health services, management/clinical assistant, medical assistant, nursing (RN), office assistant. **Legal studies:** Legal secretary, paralegal. **Liberal arts:** Arts/sciences, humanities. **Math:** General.

Parks/recreation: Health/fitness, sports admin. **Personal/culinary services:** Baking, culinary arts, restaurant/catering. **Physical sciences:** Chemistry. **Production:** Woodworking. **Protective services:** Correctional facilities, corrections, criminal justice, firefighting, police science. **Psychology:** General. **Public administration:** Social work. **Social sciences:** General. **Visual/performing arts:** General, cinematography, commercial/advertising art, dramatic, graphic design, studio arts.

Most popular majors. Business/marketing 23%, education 15%, health sciences 15%, liberal arts 12%, security/protective services 6%.

Computing on campus. 450 workstations in library, computer center. Commuter students can connect to campus network. Online course registration, online library, helpline, wireless network available.

Student life. Freshman orientation: Available. **Policies:** Freshmen permitted cars on campus. **Activities:** Bands, choral groups, dance, drama, film society, literary magazine, music ensembles, student government, student newspaper, TV station, wide variety of service, social, and recreational programs.

Athletics. NJCAA. **Intercollegiate:** Baseball M, basketball M, equestrian, golf, soccer, tennis, volleyball W. **Intramural:** Baseball M, basketball M, bowling W, equestrian, skiing, softball, volleyball. **Team name:** Centurions.

Student services. Adult student services, alcohol/substance abuse counseling, career counseling, services for economically disadvantaged, student employment services, financial aid counseling, minority student services, on-campus daycare, personal counseling, veterans' counselor, women's services. **Physically disabled:** Services for visually, speech, hearing impaired. **Learning disabled:** Comprehensive services available. **Transfer:** Special adviser, orientation, pre-admission transcript evaluation for new students. Transfer center, transfer adviser, college fairs on campus for students transferring to 4-year colleges.

Contact. E-mail: admissions@bucks.edu
Phone: (215) 968-8100 Fax: (215) 968-8110
Amy Wilson, Director of Admissions, Bucks County Community College, 275 Swamp Road, Newtown, PA 18940

Business Institute of Pennsylvania

Sharon, Pennsylvania
www.biop.com **CB code: 2466**

- For-profit 2-year business and technical college
- Commuter campus in large town
- Interview required

General. Accredited by ACICS. Branch campus located in Meadville. **Enrollment:** 94 degree-seeking undergraduates; 1 non-degree-seeking students. **Degrees:** 42 associate awarded. **Location:** 50 miles from Pittsburgh, 15 miles from Youngstown, Ohio. **Calendar:** Quarter, extensive summer session. **Full-time faculty:** 2 total; 100% have terminal degrees, 100% women. **Part-time faculty:** 8 total; 100% have terminal degrees, 100% women. **Class size:** 76% < 20, 24% 20-39.

Student profile. Among degree-seeking undergraduates, 100% enrolled in a vocational program, 53 enrolled as first-time, first-year students, 5 transferred in from other institutions.

Out-of-state:	7%	**African American:**	17%
Women:	90%	**25 or older:**	45%

Basis for selection. Applicants must have achieved High School Diploma or State Issued GED and pass cPAT admission test. If applicant has taken SAT or ACT, with satisfactory results, the cPAT admission test is waived. **Adult students:** Entrance exam policies same as for first-time freshmen.

High school preparation. Recommended units include English 3, mathematics 3 and science 2. Accounting, business, computer and English preferred.

2006-2007 Annual costs. Tuition/fees (projected): $8,050. Per-credit charge: $250. Books/supplies: $1,200.

Financial aid. Non-need-based: Scholarships awarded for academics.

Application procedures. Admission: No deadline. $50 fee. Admission notification on a rolling basis. **Financial aid:** Institutional form required.

Academics. Special study options: Internships. **Credit/placement by examination:** CLEP, institutional tests. 15 credit hours maximum toward associate degree. **Support services:** Study skills assistance.

Majors. Business: Accounting, accounting technology, accounting/business management, administrative services, business admin, executive assistant, marketing, office technology. **Computer sciences:** General, data entry, data processing, information technology, word processing. **Health:** Insurance coding, insurance specialist, medical records admin, medical records technology, medical secretary, office admin, office assistant, office computer specialist, receptionist. **Legal studies:** Legal secretary.

Most popular majors. Business/marketing 15%, computer/information sciences 15%.

Computing on campus. 35 workstations in computer center.

Student life. Freshman orientation: Mandatory. Orientation takes place the first day of each quarter. **Policies:** Freshmen permitted cars on campus. **Activities:** Student government, student newspaper.

Student services. Career counseling, financial aid counseling, placement for graduates. **Transfer:** Special adviser, orientation, pre-admission transcript evaluation for new students.

Contact. E-mail: info@biop.edu
Phone: (724) 983-0700 Fax: (724) 983-8355
Shannon McNamara, Admissions Officer, Business Institute of Pennsylvania, 335 Boyd Drive, Sharon, PA 16146

Business Institute of Pennsylvania: Meadville

Meadville, Pennsylvania
www.biop.edu **CB code: 3273**

- For-profit 2-year business college
- Commuter campus in large town
- Interview required

General. Accredited by ACICS. Hands-on training for business, office and medical careers. **Enrollment:** 69 degree-seeking undergraduates. **Degrees:** 27 associate awarded. **Location:** 40 from Erie, 70 miles from Pittsburgh. **Calendar:** Quarter, extensive summer session. **Full-time faculty:** 2 total; 100% have terminal degrees. **Part-time faculty:** 3 total; 100% have terminal degrees, 100% women. **Class size:** 67% < 20, 33% 20-39.

Student profile. Among degree-seeking undergraduates, 100% enrolled in a vocational program, 44 enrolled as first-time, first-year students.

Women:	88%	**Native American:**	1%
African American:	3%	**25 or older:**	45%

Basis for selection. Applicants must have achieved high school diploma or state issued GED and pass cPAT admission test. If applicant has taken SAT or ACT with satisfactory results, the cPAT admission test is waived. **Adult students:** Entrance exam policies same as for first-time freshmen. **Homeschooled:** Transcript of courses and grades required. Must have State issued diploma.

High school preparation. Recommended units include English 3, mathematics 3 and science 2. Accounting, computers, business subjects and English recommended.

2006-2007 Annual costs. Tuition/fees (projected): $8,050. Per-credit charge: $250. Books/supplies: $1,200.

Financial aid. Need-based: Need-based aid available for part-time students. **Non-need-based:** Scholarships awarded for academics.

Application procedures. Admission: No deadline. $50 fee. Admission notification on a rolling basis. **Financial aid:** FAFSA required.

Academics. Special study options: Internships. **Credit/placement by examination:** CLEP, institutional tests. **Support services:** Study skills assistance.

Majors. Business: Accounting, accounting technology, accounting/business management, administrative services, business admin, executive assistant, marketing, office technology. **Computer sciences:** General, data entry, data processing, information technology, word processing. **Health:** Insurance coding, insurance specialist, medical assistant, medical records admin, medical records technology, medical secretary, office admin, office assistant, office computer specialist, receptionist. **Legal studies:** Legal secretary.

Most popular majors. Business/marketing 35%, computer/information sciences 30%, health sciences 25%.

Computing on campus. 20 workstations in computer center.

Student life. **Freshman orientation:** Mandatory. Orientation takes place the first day of each quarter. **Policies:** Freshmen permitted cars on campus. **Activities:** Student government, student newspaper.

Student services. Career counseling, financial aid counseling, placement for graduates. **Transfer:** Special adviser, orientation, pre-admission transcript evaluation for new students.

Contact. E-mail: info@biop.edu
Phone: (814) 724-0700 Fax: (814) 724-2777
Anne Berger, Director of Admissions, Business Institute of Pennsylvania: Meadville, 628 Arch Street, Suite B105, Meadville, PA 16335

Butler County Community College
Butler, Pennsylvania
www.bc3.edu **CB code: 2069**

- Public 2-year community college
- Commuter campus in large town

General. Founded in 1965. Regionally accredited. Classes also offered in Cranberry township, Mercer, and Lawrence counties. Distance learning courses via Internet and videotape available. **Enrollment:** 3,809 degree-seeking undergraduates. **Degrees:** 407 associate awarded. **Location:** 35 miles from Pittsburgh. **Calendar:** Semester, limited summer session. **Full-time faculty:** 64 total; 19% have terminal degrees, 52% women. **Part-time faculty:** 241 total; 2% have terminal degrees, 47% women. **Special facilities:** Environmental education center, cultural center/theater, art gallery, metrology lab, computer forensics lab. **Partnerships:** Formal partnerships with American Management Association, Workforce & Economic Development Network of PA, Backflow Management, Inc., Carnegie Mellon University, 13 regional fire schools, 12 local high schools.

Student profile. Among degree-seeking undergraduates, 63% enrolled in a transfer program, 37% enrolled in a vocational program, 1% already have a bachelor's degree or higher, 633 enrolled as first-time, first-year students, 341 transferred in from other institutions.

Part-time:	48%	**Women:**	60%
Out-of-state:	1%	**25 or older:**	37%

Transfer out. 75% of students enrolled in the transfer program go on to 4-year colleges. **Colleges most students transferred to 2005:** Slippery Rock University of Pennsylvania, Clarion University of Pennsylvania, Indiana University of Pennsylvania.

Basis for selection. Open admission, but selective for some programs. Admission to nursing, medical assistant, physical therapist assistant, massage therapy, and metrology programs based on high school record.

2005-2006 Annual costs. Tuition/fees: $2,640; $4,770 out-of-district; $6,900 out-of-state. Per-credit charge: $71 in-district; $142 out-of-district; $213 out-of-state. Books/supplies: $850. Personal expenses: $900.

2004-2005 Financial aid. **Need-based:** 51% of total undergraduate aid awarded as scholarships/grants, 49% as loans/jobs. Need-based aid available for part-time students. Work study available for part-time students. **Non-need-based:** Scholarships awarded for academics, state residency.

Application procedures. **Admission:** No deadline. $25 fee, may be waived for applicants with need. Application must be submitted on paper. Admission notification on a rolling basis. **Financial aid:** Priority date 4/15; no closing date. FAFSA required. Applicants notified on a rolling basis starting 5/1; must reply within 2 week(s) of notification.

Academics. **Special study options:** Cooperative education, distance learning, independent study, internships. License preparation in nursing, physical therapy. **Credit/placement by examination:** AP, CLEP, institutional tests. 45 credit hours maximum toward associate degree. **Support services:** GED preparation, learning center, pre-admission summer program, reduced course load, remedial instruction, study skills assistance, tutoring, writing center.

Majors. **Biology:** General. **Business:** Accounting technology, administrative services, business admin, human resources, marketing, tourism promotion. **Communications:** Organizational. **Computer sciences:** Programming, security, web page design. **Education:** Elementary, kindergarten/preschool, secondary. **Engineering:** General. **Engineering technology:** Architectural drafting, civil, computer systems, electrical, industrial management, instrumentation, manufacturing, mechanical drafting. **English:** English lit. **Family/consumer sciences:** Institutional food production. **Health:** Health care admin, medical assistant, nursing (RN), physical therapy assistant. **Legal studies:** Legal secretary. **Math:** General. **Parks/recreation:** General, sports admin. **Physical sciences:** General. **Production:** Machine shop technology. **Protective services:** Law enforcement admin, police science. **Psychology:** General. **Visual/performing arts:** Graphic design.

Most popular majors. Business/marketing 22%, computer/information sciences 14%, education 7%, engineering/engineering technologies 7%, health sciences 20%, liberal arts 9%.

Computing on campus. 108 workstations in library, computer center. Online course registration available.

Student life. **Freshman orientation:** Available. **Activities:** Drama, literary magazine, student government, student newspaper, Christian outreach organization.

Athletics. NJCAA. **Intercollegiate:** Baseball M, basketball, cheerleading, golf M, softball W, volleyball W. **Intramural:** Basketball, golf, table tennis, volleyball, weight lifting. **Team name:** Pioneers.

Student services. Adult student services, career counseling, services for economically disadvantaged, student employment services, financial aid counseling, on-campus daycare, personal counseling, placement for graduates, veterans' counselor. **Physically disabled:** Services for visually, hearing impaired. **Transfer:** Special adviser, orientation, pre-admission transcript evaluation for new students. Transfer adviser, college fairs on campus for students transferring to 4-year colleges.

Contact. E-mail: pattie.bajuszik@bc3.edu
Phone: (724) 287-8711 ext. 8346 Toll-free number: (888) 826-2829
Fax: (724) 287-3460
Pattie Bajuszik, Director of Admissions, Butler County Community College, PO Box 1203, Butler, PA 16003-1203

Cambria-Rowe Business College
Johnstown, Pennsylvania
www.crbc.net **CB code: 2210**

- For-profit 2-year business college
- Commuter campus in small city

General. Founded in 1891. Accredited by ACICS. **Enrollment:** 232 undergraduates. **Degrees:** 108 associate awarded. **Location:** 60 miles from Pittsburgh. **Calendar:** Quarter, extensive summer session. **Full-time faculty:** 10 total.

Student profile. 85 transferred in from other institutions.

Transfer out. **Colleges most students transferred to 2005:** St. Francis University, Mt. Aloysius College.

Basis for selection. Students must pass entrance exam. High school transcipt, GED scores reviewed. Interview recommended.

2005-2006 Annual costs. Tuition/fees: $8,325. Depending on choice of laptop, fees could be as much as $990. Books/supplies: $1,000.

Financial aid. **Need-based:** Need-based aid available for part-time students. **Non-need-based:** Scholarships awarded for academics, leadership.

Application procedures. **Admission:** No deadline. $15 fee. Application may be submitted online. Students notified within 2 weeks of receipt of application. **Financial aid:** Closing date 8/1. FAFSA required. Applicants notified on a rolling basis.

Academics. **Special study options:** Accelerated study, liberal arts/career combination. **Credit/placement by examination:** CLEP, institutional tests. **Support services:** Pre-admission summer program, reduced course load, tutoring.

Majors. **Business:** General, accounting, administrative services, business admin. **Health:** Medical secretary, medical transcription. **Legal studies:** Legal secretary.

Computing on campus. Wireless network available.

Student life. **Freshman orientation:** Mandatory. Preregistration for classes offered. Usually held 3 weeks prior to start date.

Student services. Adult student services, career counseling, student employment services, financial aid counseling, personal counseling, placement for graduates. **Transfer:** Special adviser, orientation for new students. Transfer adviser for students transferring to 4-year colleges.

Contact. Phone: (814) 536-5168 Fax: (814) 536-5160
Amanda Artim, Director of Admissions, Cambria-Rowe Business College, 221 Central Avenue, Johnstown, PA 15902

Cambria-Rowe Business College: Indiana

Indiana, Pennsylvania
www.crbc.net **CB code: 3274**

- For-profit 2-year business and technical college
- Large town

General. Accredited by ACICS. **Enrollment:** 130 degree-seeking undergraduates. **Degrees:** 55 associate awarded. **Calendar:** Quarter. **Full-time faculty:** 8 total; 88% women. **Part-time faculty:** 1 total.

Basis for selection. Open admission.

2005-2006 Annual costs. Tuition/fees: $8,325. Depending on choice of laptop, fees could be as much as $990.

Financial aid. Need-based: Need-based aid available for part-time students.

Application procedures. Admission: No deadline. $15 fee. Admission notification on a rolling basis. **Financial aid:** No deadline. FAFSA required. Applicants notified on a rolling basis.

Academics. Credit/placement by examination: CLEP.

Majors. Business: Accounting, administrative services, management information systems. **Health:** Medical secretary.

Contact. E-mail: rgresh@crbc.net
Phone: (724) 463-0222
Laurie Price, Admissions Representative, Cambria-Rowe Business College: Indiana, 422 South 13th Street, Indiana, PA 15701

Career Training Academy

New Kensington, Pennsylvania
www.careerta.com **CB code: 3205**

- For-profit 2-year career school
- Commuter campus in small town
- Application essay required

General. Accredited by ACCSCT. **Enrollment:** 191 degree-seeking undergraduates. **Degrees:** 23 associate awarded. **Location:** 18 miles from Pittsburgh. **Calendar:** Quarter, extensive summer session. **Full-time faculty:** 15 total. **Part-time faculty:** 3 total. **Special facilities:** Day care center. **Partnerships:** Training partnership with Children's Community Pediatrics, a subsidiary of Children's Hospital of Pittsburgh, PA for the Medical Assistant Comprehensive and Advanced Medical Coder/Biller programs.

Basis for selection. Open admission, but selective for some programs. Health programs require interview, essay, 1.5+ GPA or 235+ GED, and health form. Paralegal program requires 45 collegiate credits.

2005-2006 Annual costs. Total cost of 15-month associate degree program in massage therapy: $18,366 (includes tuition, books, portable massage table, uniforms, lab fees, insurance, graduation fees). Total cost of 15-month associate degree program in medical assistance: $14,572 (includes tuition, books, uniforms, lab fees, insurance, graduation fees). Other diploma programs will vary in cost and required length of study.

Financial aid. All financial aid based on need. **Additional information:** Work study available after class day.

Application procedures. Admission: No deadline. $30 fee. Application must be submitted on paper. Admission notification on a rolling basis. **Financial aid:** No deadline. FAFSA, institutional form required.

Academics. Mentor program available to all students. **Special study options:** Distance learning, internships. Externships. **Credit/placement by examination:** CLEP, IB.

Majors. Health: Massage therapy, medical assistant, medical secretary.

Student life. Freshman orientation: Mandatory. Preregistration for classes offered. **Policies:** Freshmen permitted cars on campus.

Student services. Adult student services, alcohol/substance abuse counseling, career counseling, services for economically disadvantaged, student employment services, financial aid counseling, on-campus daycare, personal counseling, placement for graduates, veterans' counselor, women's services. **Transfer:** Pre-admission transcript evaluation for new students.

Contact. Phone: (724) 337-1000 Fax: (724) 335-7140
Tyna Putignano, Director of Admissions, Career Training Academy, 950 Fifth Avenue, New Kensington, PA 15068

Career Training Academy: Monroeville

Monroeville, Pennsylvania
www.careerta.edu **CB code: 3207**

- For-profit 2-year branch campus college
- Commuter campus in small city
- Application essay required

General. Accredited by ACCSCT. **Enrollment:** 86 degree-seeking undergraduates. **Degrees:** 11 associate awarded. **Location:** 10 miles from Pittsburgh. **Calendar:** Continuous. **Full-time faculty:** 10 total. **Part-time faculty:** 5 total.

Student profile. Among degree-seeking undergraduates, 13 enrolled as first-time, first-year students.

Basis for selection. Open admission.

2005-2006 Annual costs. Tuition ranges from $3,300 to $16,500 depending on program; required fees range from $180 to $1,100 depending on program. Books/supplies: $750. Personal expenses: $2,889.

Financial aid. All financial aid based on need. Need-based aid available for part-time students.

Application procedures. Admission: No deadline. $25 fee. **Financial aid:** FAFSA, institutional form required.

Academics. Special study options: Internships. **Credit/placement by examination:** CLEP. **Support services:** Remedial instruction, study skills assistance, tutoring.

Majors. Health: Medical assistant, ward clerk.

Student life. Freshman orientation: Mandatory.

Student services. Career counseling, student employment services, financial aid counseling, placement for graduates.

Contact. E-mail: Admissions2@careerta.edu
Phone: (412) 372-3900
Tyna Putignano, Director of Admissions, Career Training Academy: Monroeville, 4314 Old William Penn Highway #103, Monroeville, PA 15146

CHI Institute: Broomall

Broomall, Pennsylvania
www.chitraining.com **CB code: 3398**

- For-profit 2-year technical college
- Large town

General. Accredited by ACCSCT. **Enrollment:** 865 undergraduates. **Degrees:** 38 associate awarded. **Location:** 7 miles from Philadelphia. **Calendar:** Quarter. **Full-time faculty:** 40 total. **Part-time faculty:** 10 total.

Basis for selection. Institutional examination most important. Interview and recommendations also important.

2005-2006 Annual costs. Tuition ranges from $9,000 - $21,000 per 18-month program. Required fees $400.

Financial aid. Need-based: Need-based aid available for part-time students.

Application procedures. Admission: No deadline. $100 fee. Admission notification on a rolling basis. **Financial aid:** No deadline. FAFSA required. Applicants notified on a rolling basis.

Academics. Credit/placement by examination: CLEP.

Majors. Engineering technology: Electrical.

Student services. Adult student services, career counseling, student employment services, personal counseling, placement for graduates, veterans' counselor.

Contact. Phone: (610) 353-7630
Paul Richardson, Director of Admissions, CHI Institute: Broomall, 1991 Sproul Road, Suite 42, Broomall, PA 19008

CHI Institute: Southampton
Southampton, Pennsylvania
www.chitraining.com **CB code: 3386**

- For-profit 2-year technical college
- Commuter campus in large town
- Interview required

General. Founded in 1981. Accredited by ACCSCT. **Enrollment:** 700 undergraduates. **Degrees:** 98 associate awarded. **Location:** 5 miles from Philadelphia. **Calendar:** Continuous, extensive summer session. **Full-time faculty:** 30 total. **Part-time faculty:** 15 total.

Basis for selection. Institutional aptitude evaluation test most important. Interview also important.

2005-2006 Annual costs. Reported costs are for associate degree program in computer programming. Costs of other programs will vary. Books/supplies: $765.

Financial aid. Additional information: Scholarships for graduating seniors. Awards based on institutional scholarship aptitude test and interview with independent committee. Parental income not considered.

Application procedures. Admission: No deadline. No application fee. Admission notification on a rolling basis. **Financial aid:** Closing date 9/20. Applicants notified on a rolling basis.

Academics. Special study options: Internships. **Credit/placement by examination:** CLEP.

Majors. Computer sciences: Computer graphics, computer science, programming, systems analysis. **Engineering technology:** Electrical. **Protective services:** Criminal justice.

Student services. Career counseling, student employment services, placement for graduates.

Contact. Phone: (215) 357-5100
Eric Heller, Admissions Director, CHI Institute: Southampton, 520 Street Road, Southampton, PA 18966

Commonwealth Technical Institute
Johnstown, Pennsylvania
www.hgac.org **CB code: 3125**

- Private 2-year technical college
- Residential campus in small city

General. Accredited by ACCSCT. Specially geared toward students with disabilities. **Enrollment:** 101 degree-seeking undergraduates. **Degrees:** 41 associate awarded. **Calendar:** Semester. **Full-time faculty:** 35 total.

Student profile. Among degree-seeking undergraduates, 101 enrolled as first-time, first-year students.

Women:	37%	**Hispanic American:**	1%
African American:	11%	**Native American:**	1%
Asian American:	1%		

Transfer out. Colleges most students transferred to 2005: Cambria County Area Community College.

Basis for selection. Open admission.

2005-2006 Annual costs. Tuition/fees: $11,224. Room/board: $9,516.

Financial aid. Need-based: Work study available nights and weekends.

Application procedures. Admission: No deadline. No application fee. Admission notification on a rolling basis. **Financial aid:** Closing date 5/1. FAFSA required. Applicants notified on a rolling basis.

Academics. Credit/placement by examination: AP, CLEP. **Support services:** GED preparation and test center, remedial instruction, tutoring.

Majors. Business: Accounting. **Computer sciences:** General. **Engineering technology:** Drafting. **Health:** Dental lab technology, medical secretary. **Personal/culinary services:** Culinary arts.

Student life. Policies: Freshmen permitted cars on campus. **Housing:** Single-sex dorms, special housing for disabled available. **Activities:** Choral groups, student government.

Student services. Alcohol/substance abuse counseling, financial aid counseling, health services, personal counseling, veterans' counselor. **Physically disabled:** Services for visually, speech, hearing impaired.

Contact. Phone: (814) 255-8237
Rebecca Halza, Director of Admissions, Commonwealth Technical Institute, 727 Goucher Street, Johnstown, PA 15905-3902

Community College of Allegheny County
Pittsburgh, Pennsylvania **CB member**
www.ccac.edu **CB code: 2122**

- Public 2-year community college
- Commuter campus in very large city

General. Founded in 1966. Regionally accredited. Campuses located in and around Pittsburgh. **Enrollment:** 9,918 degree-seeking undergraduates. **Degrees:** 1,754 associate awarded. **Calendar:** Semester, extensive summer session. **Full-time faculty:** 268 total. **Part-time faculty:** 1,362 total.

Student profile.

Out-of-state:	2%	**25 or older:**	64%

Transfer out. Colleges most students transferred to 2005: University of Pittsburgh, Robert Morris University, Duquesne University, Point Park University, Carlow College.

Basis for selection. Open admission, but selective for some programs. Special requirements for some health-related, culinary arts, and automotive programs. COMPASS used for placement. Audition recommended for music program. **Adult students:** SAT/ACT scores not required.

2005-2006 Annual costs. Tuition/fees: $2,669; $5,069 out-of-district; $7,469 out-of-state. Per-credit charge: $80 in-district; $160 out-of-district; $240 out-of-state. Required fees vary for out-of-district and out-of-state students; out-of-district tuition varies based on county. If county has own community college, tuition is $4800 per year (fees $374). If county does not have community college, tuition is $2820 per year (fees $374). Nursing and allied health courses subject to $16 per-credit fee. Books/supplies: $600. Personal expenses: $950.

2004-2005 Financial aid. Need-based: 74% of total undergraduate aid awarded as scholarships/grants, 26% as loans/jobs. Need-based aid available for part-time students. Work study available nights, weekends and for part-time students. **Non-need-based:** Scholarships awarded for academics, athletics, minority status.

Application procedures. Admission: No deadline. No application fee. Admission notification on a rolling basis. **Financial aid:** Priority date 5/1; no closing date. FAFSA required. Applicants notified by 5/20.

Academics. Special study options: Cross-registration, distance learning, dual enrollment of high school students, ESL, external degree, honors, independent study, liberal arts/career combination, study abroad. License preparation in nursing. **Credit/placement by examination:** AP, CLEP, institutional tests. 30 credit hours maximum toward associate degree. **Support services:** GED preparation and test center, learning center, reduced course load, remedial instruction, study skills assistance, tutoring, writing center.

Majors. Agriculture: Horticulture, landscaping, turf management. **Biology:** General. **Business:** Accounting technology, administrative services, banking/financial services, business admin, entrepreneurial studies, human resources, management information systems, marketing. **Communications:** Journalism. **Construction:** General, electrician, maintenance, painting, power transmission. **Education:** Elementary, teacher assistance. **Engineering technology:** Automotive, civil, electrical, environmental, hydraulics, robotics. **Family/consumer sciences:** Child development. **Foreign languages:** General. **Health:** Cardiovascular technology, clinical lab technology, medical assistant, medical radiologic technology/radiation therapy, medical records technology, mental health services, nuclear medical technology, nursing (RN), occupational therapy assistant, pharmacy assistant, physical therapy assistant, respiratory therapy technology, sonography, surgical technology. **Liberal arts:** Arts/sciences, humanities. **Math:** General. **Mechanic/repair:** Business machine, heating/ac/refrig. **Parks/recreation:** Health/fitness. **Personal/culinary services:** Chef training, restaurant/catering. **Physical sciences:**

Chemistry, physics. **Production:** Welding. **Protective services:** Corrections, fire safety technology, police science. **Psychology:** General. **Public administration:** Social work. **Science technology:** Chemical. **Social sciences:** General, sociology. **Transportation:** Airline/commercial pilot, aviation management. **Visual/performing arts:** Art, commercial/advertising art.

Computing on campus. 3,700 workstations in library, computer center. Commuter students can connect to campus network. Helpline available.

Student life. **Freshman orientation:** Available. **Activities:** Jazz band, choral groups, drama, music ensembles, student government, student newspaper.

Athletics. NJCAA. **Intercollegiate:** Baseball M, basketball, bowling, golf, ice hockey M, softball W, tennis, volleyball W.

Student services. Adult student services, career counseling, student employment services, health services, on-campus daycare, personal counseling, placement for graduates, veterans' counselor. **Physically disabled:** Services for visually, speech, hearing impaired. **Transfer:** Special adviser for new students. Transfer adviser for students transferring to 4-year colleges.

Contact. Phone: (412) 323-2323
Community College of Allegheny County, 800 Allegheny Avenue, Pittsburgh, PA 15233

Community College of Beaver County

Monaca, Pennsylvania — **CB member**
www.ccbc.edu — **CB code: 2126**

- Public 2-year community college
- Commuter campus in small town

General. Founded in 1966. Regionally accredited. Aviation sciences facility approximately 15 miles from campus at Beaver County Airport. **Enrollment:** 2,535 degree-seeking undergraduates. **Degrees:** 391 associate awarded. **Location:** 30 miles from Pittsburgh. **Calendar:** Semester, limited summer session. **Full-time faculty:** 47 total. **Part-time faculty:** 104 total. **Special facilities:** Student-monitored control tower for aviation, computerized mannequins for nursing and allied health programs.

Student profile.

Out-of-state:	1%	**25 or older:**	50%

Transfer out. **Colleges most students transferred to 2005:** Slippery Rock State University, Geneva College, Robert Morris College, Edinboro State University.

Basis for selection. Open admission, but selective for some programs. NLN Pre-Admission PN test given for admission into nursing program. Interview recommended for all others. **Adult students:** Entrance exam policies same as for first-time freshmen.

2005-2006 Annual costs. Tuition/fees: $2,925; $6,825 out-of-district; $10,200 out-of-state. Per-credit charge: $80 in-district; $195 out-of-district; $293 out-of-state. Out-of-district students pay additional $450 fee; out-of-state students pay additional $900 fee. Books/supplies: $700. Personal expenses: $1,100.

2004-2005 Financial aid. **Need-based:** 67% of total undergraduate aid awarded as scholarships/grants, 33% as loans/jobs. Need-based aid available for part-time students. Work study available nights, weekends and for part-time students. **Non-need-based:** Scholarships awarded for academics, athletics, state residency.

Application procedures. **Admission:** Priority date 6/1; no deadline. No application fee. Application must be submitted on paper. Admission notification on a rolling basis. Application deadline January 20 for nursing, must reply within 3 weeks of notification. **Financial aid:** Priority date 5/1, closing date 7/1. FAFSA, institutional form required. Applicants notified on a rolling basis starting 8/5; must reply within 2 week(s) of notification.

Academics. **Special study options:** Cross-registration, distance learning, double major, dual enrollment of high school students, independent study, internships, liberal arts/career combination. License preparation in aviation, nursing, radiology. **Credit/placement by examination:** AP, CLEP, institutional tests. 45 credit hours maximum toward associate degree. **Support services:** GED preparation and test center, learning center, reduced course load, remedial instruction, study skills assistance, tutoring, writing center.

Majors. **Business:** Accounting technology, business admin, human resources, management information systems, marketing. **Communications technology:** General. **Computer sciences:** Applications programming, networking. **Education:** Teacher assistance. **Engineering technology:** Aerospace. **Health:** Health aide, medical secretary, nursing (RN). **Interdisciplinary:** Biological/physical sciences. **Liberal arts:** Arts/sciences, humanities. **Personal/culinary services:** Chef training. **Social sciences:** General. **Transportation:** Air traffic control, aviation management. **Visual/performing arts:** Studio arts.

Computing on campus. 220 workstations in library, computer center, student center. Online library available.

Student life. **Freshman orientation:** Available. Preregistration for classes offered. **Policies:** Freshmen permitted cars on campus. **Activities:** Drama, literary magazine, student government.

Athletics. NJCAA. **Intercollegiate:** Basketball M, softball W, volleyball W. **Intramural:** Basketball M, football (non-tackle), softball, table tennis, volleyball. **Team name:** Titans.

Student services. Adult student services, career counseling, services for economically disadvantaged, financial aid counseling, on-campus daycare, personal counseling, veterans' counselor. **Physically disabled:** Services for visually, speech, hearing impaired. **Transfer:** Special adviser, orientation for new students. Transfer adviser, college fairs on campus for students transferring to 4-year colleges.

Contact. E-mail: dan.slater@ccbc.edu
Phone: (724) 775-8561 ext. 330 Toll-free number: (800) 335-0222 ext. 330
Fax: (724) 728-7599
Daniel Slater, Registrar, Community College of Beaver County, One Campus Drive, Monaca, PA 15061-2588

Community College of Philadelphia

Philadelphia, Pennsylvania — **CB member**
www.ccp.edu — **CB code: 2682**

- Public 2-year community college
- Commuter campus in very large city

General. Founded in 1965. Regionally accredited. Regional centers located in northeast, northwest, and west Philadelphia. Many additional temporary facilities located throughout city. **Enrollment:** 16,670 degree-seeking undergraduates. **Degrees:** 1,446 associate awarded. **ROTC:** Army. **Calendar:** Semester, extensive summer session. **Full-time faculty:** 399 total. **Part-time faculty:** 787 total.

Student profile. Among degree-seeking undergraduates, 4,550 enrolled as first-time, first-year students.

Part-time:	71%	**Women:**	67%
Out-of-state:	1%	**25 or older:**	50%

Transfer out. **Colleges most students transferred to 2005:** Temple University, Drexel University, St. Joseph's University, Holy Family College, Chestnut Hill College.

Basis for selection. Open admission, but selective for some programs. Special requirements for health, music, art and some technical programs. Audition required for music program; portfolio required for art program. **Adult students:** Entrance exam policies same as for first-time freshmen.

High school preparation. One chemistry, 2 mathematics required of health program applicants.

2005-2006 Annual costs. Tuition/fees: $3,900; $7,200 out-of-district; $10,140 out-of-state. Per-credit charge: $104 in-district; $208 out-of-district; $312 out-of-state. Non-Philadelphia residents pay additional fee of $10 per credit hour; out-of-state residents pay additional $20 per credit hour. Books/supplies: $545. Personal expenses: $856.

Financial aid. All financial aid based on need. Need-based aid available for part-time students. Work study available nights, weekends and for part-time students.

Application procedures. **Admission:** No deadline. $20 fee. Application may be submitted online. Admission notification on a rolling basis. **Financial aid:** Closing date 5/1. FAFSA, institutional form required. Applicants notified on a rolling basis.

Academics. **Special study options:** Accelerated study, distance learning, dual enrollment of high school students, ESL, honors, internships, study abroad, weekend college. License preparation in dental hygiene, nursing, radiology, real estate. **Credit/placement by examination:** AP, CLEP, institutional tests. 30 credit hours maximum toward associate degree. **Support services:** GED preparation and test center, learning center, pre-admission summer program, reduced course load, remedial instruction, tutoring.

Majors. **Area/ethnic studies:** Women's. **Business:** General, accounting, administrative services, business admin, fashion, international marketing, office/clerical, operations, real estate, sales/distribution. **Computer sciences:** General, applications programming, networking. **Education:** General, business. **Engineering:** General. **Engineering technology:** Architectural, construction, drafting, electrical. **English:** Speech/rhetoric. **Family/consumer sciences:** Child care, institutional food production. **Foreign languages:** Sign language interpretation. **Health:** Clinical lab technology, dental hygiene, medical assistant, medical radiologic technology/radiation therapy, medical records technology, mental health services, nursing (RN), respiratory therapy technology. **Legal studies:** Paralegal. **Liberal arts:** Arts/sciences. **Math:** General. **Personal/culinary services:** Culinary arts. **Physical sciences:** General. **Protective services:** Fire safety technology, forensics, police science. **Visual/performing arts:** Art, commercial photography, commercial/advertising art, dramatic, music performance.

Most popular majors. Business/marketing 18%, health sciences 19%, liberal arts 36%.

Computing on campus. 994 workstations in library, student center. Commuter students can connect to campus network. Helpline available.

Student life. **Freshman orientation:** Available. Preregistration for classes offered. **Policies:** Freshmen permitted cars on campus. **Activities:** Jazz band, choral groups, dance, drama, music ensembles, radio station, student government, student newspaper, TV station, Christian Coalition, Newman Club, Black Student Congress, Latin American Student Organization, Phi Theta Kappa, Muslim Student Association, Vietnamese Student Organization, Asian-American Association.

Athletics. **Intercollegiate:** Baseball M, basketball, cross-country, soccer M, softball W, volleyball W. **Intramural:** Basketball, soccer, softball, tennis, track and field, volleyball. **Team name:** Colonials.

Student services. Adult student services, career counseling, student employment services, financial aid counseling, health services, on-campus daycare, personal counseling, placement for graduates, women's services. **Physically disabled:** Services for visually, speech, hearing impaired. **Transfer:** Orientation for new students. Transfer adviser, college fairs on campus for students transferring to 4-year colleges.

Contact. Phone: (215) 751-8010
Elizabeth Bahm, Director of Recruitment and Admissions, Community College of Philadelphia, 1700 Spring Garden Street, Philadelphia, PA 19130-3991

Consolidated School of Business: Lancaster

Lancaster, Pennsylvania
www.csb.edu **CB code: 2240**

- For-profit 2-year business college
- Commuter campus in small city
- Interview required

General. Founded in 1986. Accredited by ACICS. Lifelong placement assistance. 92 percent placement of graduates. Additional campus in York. **Enrollment:** 143 undergraduates. **Degrees:** 63 associate awarded. **Location:** 85 miles from Philadelphia, 35 miles from Harrisburg. **Calendar:** Continuous. **Full-time faculty:** 17 total. **Part-time faculty:** 3 total.

Basis for selection. Open admission. Interview and tour must be completed before acceptance issued. All financial aid matters must be satisfied before classes begin.

High school preparation. Recommended computer application coursework for accelerated or advanced placement.

2005-2006 Annual costs. Pre-evaluation placement testing fee $50. Books/supplies: $1,500.

Financial aid. **Need-based:** Need-based aid available for part-time students.

Application procedures. **Admission:** No deadline. $25 fee. Admission notification on a rolling basis. **Financial aid:** No deadline. FAFSA required. Applicants notified on a rolling basis.

Academics. Programs consist of 3 core elements: business English, computer applications and approximately 34 credit hours of specialty courses. Curriculum developed with area employer's input to maximize job placement. **Special study options:** Accelerated study, internships. **Credit/placement by examination:** CLEP. **Support services:** Study skills assistance, tutoring.

Majors. **Business:** Accounting, accounting technology, administrative services, business admin, executive assistant, office technology. **Computer sciences:** Data entry, data processing, web page design, webmaster, word processing. **Health:** Insurance coding, insurance specialist, management/clinical assistant, medical records admin, medical secretary, medical transcription, office admin, office assistant, office computer specialist, receptionist, ward clerk. **Legal studies:** Legal secretary.

Computing on campus. 125 workstations in library.

Student life. **Freshman orientation:** Mandatory. **Policies:** Freshmen permitted cars on campus.

Student services. Adult student services, career counseling, student employment services, financial aid counseling, placement for graduates. **Physically disabled:** Services for speech, hearing impaired. **Transfer:** Pre-admission transcript evaluation for new students.

Contact. E-mail: admissions@csb.edu
Phone: (717) 394-6211 Toll-free number: (800) 541-8298
Fax: (717) 394-6213
Consolidated School of Business: Lancaster, 2124 Ambassador Circle, Lancaster, PA 17603

Consolidated School of Business: York

York, Pennsylvania
www.csb.edu **CB code: 2242**

- For-profit 2-year business college
- Commuter campus in small city
- Interview required

General. Founded in 1986. Accredited by ACICS. Lifelong placement assistance. 95% placement of graduates. Additional campus in Lancaster. **Enrollment:** 160 undergraduates. **Degrees:** 80 associate awarded. **Location:** 28 miles from Harrisburg, 33 miles from Baltimore. **Calendar:** Continuous. **Full-time faculty:** 26 total; 8% have terminal degrees, 4% minority, 81% women. **Part-time faculty:** 6 total; 17% have terminal degrees, 83% women.

Basis for selection. Open admission. Interview and tour must be completed before acceptance issued. All financial aid matters must be satisfied before classes begin.

2005-2006 Annual costs. Pre-evaluation/placement testing fee $50. Books/supplies: $900.

Financial aid. **Need-based:** Need-based aid available for part-time students.

Application procedures. **Admission:** No deadline. $25 fee. Admission notification on a rolling basis. **Financial aid:** No deadline. FAFSA required. Applicants notified on a rolling basis.

Academics. Programs consist of 3 core elements: business English, computer applications and approximately 34 credit hours of specialty courses. Curriculum developed with area employers' input to maximize job placement. **Special study options:** Accelerated study, internships. **Credit/placement by examination:** CLEP. **Support services:** Study skills assistance, tutoring.

Majors. **Business:** Accounting, accounting technology, administrative services, business admin, executive assistant, office technology, tourism promotion, tourism/travel, travel services. **Computer sciences:** Data processing, LAN/WAN management, web page design, webmaster, word processing. **Health:** Insurance coding, insurance specialist, management/clinical assistant, medical secretary, medical transcription, office computer specialist, receptionist, ward clerk. **Legal studies:** Legal secretary, paralegal.

Student life. **Freshman orientation:** Mandatory.

Student services. Adult student services, career counseling, student employment services, placement for graduates. **Transfer:** Pre-admission transcript evaluation for new students.

Contact. E-mail: admissions@csb.edu
Phone: (717) 764-9550 Toll-free number: (800) 520-0691
Robert Safran, V.P. of Administration, Director of Admissions, Consolidated School of Business: York, York City Business and Industry Park, York, PA 17404

Dean Institute of Technology
Pittsburgh, Pennsylvania
www.deantech.edu **CB code: 2199**

- For-profit 2-year technical college
- Commuter campus in large city
- Interview required

General. Founded in 1948. Accredited by ACCSCT. **Enrollment:** 221 degree-seeking undergraduates. **Degrees:** 50 associate awarded. **Location:** 2 miles from downtown. **Calendar:** Quarter, extensive summer session. **Full-time faculty:** 10 total. **Part-time faculty:** 10 total.

Student profile. Among degree-seeking undergraduates, 68 enrolled as first-time, first-year students.

Part-time:	39%	**Women:**	5%
Out-of-state:	2%		

Transfer out. 4% of students enrolled in the transfer program go on to 4-year colleges. **Colleges most students transferred to 2005:** Point Park College.

Basis for selection. Open admission.

2005-2006 Annual costs. Air-conditioning/refrigeration: 15-month day course $16,400, night course $7,800. 7-month courses in welding or building maintenance $6,600. Electrical technician: 15-month day course or 30-month night course, $16,400. Tools/materials fees not included in tuition. Books/supplies: $709. Personal expenses: $1,440.

Financial aid. Need-based: Need-based aid available for part-time students.

Application procedures. Admission: No deadline. $50 fee. Admission notification on a rolling basis. Must reply by May 1 or within 3 week(s) if notified thereafter. **Financial aid:** Closing date 8/1. FAFSA required. Applicants notified on a rolling basis; must reply within 8 week(s) of notification.

Academics. Special study options: Cooperative education. **Credit/placement by examination:** CLEP, institutional tests. 12 credit hours maximum toward associate degree. **Support services:** Tutoring.

Majors. Construction: Power transmission. **Mechanic/repair:** Heating/ac/refrig.

Student life. Policies: Freshmen permitted cars on campus.

Student services. Career counseling, personal counseling, placement for graduates, veterans' counselor. **Transfer:** Special adviser, orientation for new students. Transfer adviser for students transferring to 4-year colleges.

Contact. E-mail: info@deantech.edu
Phone: (412) 531-4433 Fax: (412) 531-4435
Richard Ali, Admissions Director, Dean Institute of Technology, 1501 West Liberty Avenue, Pittsburgh, PA 15226

Delaware County Community College
Media, Pennsylvania
www.dccc.edu **CB member** **CB code: 2125**

- Public 2-year community college
- Commuter campus in large town

General. Founded in 1967. Regionally accredited. **Enrollment:** 10,627 degree-seeking undergraduates. **Degrees:** 867 associate awarded. **Location:** 20 miles from Philadelphia. **Calendar:** Semester, limited summer session. **Full-time faculty:** 142 total; 11% minority, 58% women. **Part-time faculty:** 519 total; 7% minority, 46% women. **Special facilities:** CAD laboratory, solar laboratory.

Student profile. Among degree-seeking undergraduates, 63% enrolled in a transfer program, 35% enrolled in a vocational program, 2,541 enrolled as first-time, first-year students.

Part-time:	58%	**Asian American:**	4%
Out-of-state:	1%	**Hispanic American:**	2%
Women:	57%	**International:**	2%
African American:	17%	**25 or older:**	44%

Transfer out. 67% of students enrolled in the transfer program go on to 4-year colleges. **Colleges most students transferred to 2005:** Temple University, West Chester University of Pennsylvania, Widener University, Drexel University, Penn State University.

Basis for selection. Open admission, but selective for some programs. Special requirements for nursing, respiratory therapy, surgical technology, municipal police training, paramedic, and plumbing programs, and for international students. **Adult students:** Entrance exam policies same as for first-time freshmen.

2005-2006 Annual costs. Tuition/fees: $2,560; $5,020 out-of-district; $7,480 out-of-state. Per-credit charge: $82 in-district; $164 out-of-district; $246 out-of-state. Additional instructional support fee of $570-$870 based on courses taken. Books/supplies: $1,350. Personal expenses: $1,200.

2005-2006 Financial aid. Need-based: 68% of total undergraduate aid awarded as scholarships/grants, 32% as loans/jobs. Need-based aid available for part-time students. Work study available nights, weekends and for part-time students. **Additional information:** COPE grants offered to educationally and economically disadvantaged students.

Application procedures. Admission: No deadline. $20 fee, may be waived for applicants with need. Application must be submitted on paper. Admission notification on a rolling basis. Limited-admission programs have differing closing dates for applications. **Financial aid:** Priority date 5/1; no closing date. FAFSA required. Applicants notified on a rolling basis starting 5/30; must reply within 4 week(s) of notification.

Academics. Special study options: Accelerated study, cooperative education, distance learning, double major, dual enrollment of high school students, ESL, independent study, internships, student-designed major, study abroad. **Credit/placement by examination:** AP, CLEP, institutional tests. 45 credit hours maximum toward associate degree. If any of the credits are awarded as "T" (transfer) grades, only 36 can be transferred. Of these 36, only 15 can be from AP exams. **Support services:** GED preparation and test center, learning center, pre-admission summer program, reduced course load, remedial instruction, study skills assistance, tutoring, writing center.

Majors. Biology: Biomedical sciences. **Business:** Accounting technology, banking/financial services, business admin, entrepreneurial studies, management information systems, office management, operations, sales/distribution. **Communications:** General, journalism. **Communications technology:** General. **Computer sciences:** General, applications programming, data entry, information systems, networking. **Construction:** Maintenance. **Education:** Multi-level teacher, teacher assistance. **Engineering:** General. **Engineering technology:** Architectural, architectural drafting, CAD/CADD, construction, electrical, mechanical, robotics. **Health:** Medical assistant, nursing (RN), respiratory therapy technology, surgical technology. **Interdisciplinary:** Biological/physical sciences. **Legal studies:** Paralegal. **Liberal arts:** Arts/sciences. **Production:** Machine tool. **Protective services:** Fire safety technology, police science. **Psychology:** General. **Social sciences:** Anthropology, sociology. **Visual/performing arts:** Commercial/advertising art, dramatic.

Computing on campus. 1,300 workstations in computer center.

Student life. Freshman orientation: Available. Preregistration for classes offered. **Activities:** Drama, literary magazine, radio station, student government, student newspaper, Black Student Union, Christian Fellowship, international club, Newman club, Phi Theta Kappa, Gay Straight Alliance, political science club.

Athletics. Intercollegiate: Baseball M, basketball, golf, soccer M, softball W, tennis, volleyball W. **Intramural:** Basketball, bowling, cheerleading, cross-country, lacrosse M, volleyball.

Student services. Alcohol/substance abuse counseling, career counseling, services for economically disadvantaged, student employment services, health services, minority student services, personal counseling, placement for graduates, veterans' counselor, women's services. **Physically disabled:** Services for visually, speech, hearing impaired. **Transfer:** Special adviser, orientation for new students. Transfer center, transfer adviser, college fairs on campus for students transferring to 4-year colleges.

Contact. E-mail: admiss@dccc.edu
Phone: (610) 359-5050 Fax: (610) 359-7379
Hope Lentine, Director of Admissions and Enrollment Services, Delaware County Community College, 901 South Media Line Road, Media, PA 19063

Douglas Education Center
Monessen, Pennsylvania
www.douglas-school.com **CB code: 3288**

- For-profit 2-year visual arts and business college
- Small town
- Interview required

General. Accredited by ACICS. **Enrollment:** 233 undergraduates. **Degrees:** 72 associate awarded. **Location:** 25 miles from Pittsburgh. **Calendar:** Semester, extensive summer session. **Full-time faculty:** 7 total. **Part-time faculty:** 8 total.

Basis for selection. Applicants must pass the Wonderlic entrance exam. Portfolios recommended.

2005-2006 Annual costs. Books/supplies: $2,000.

Financial aid. All financial aid based on need. Need-based aid available for part-time students. Work study available nights, weekends and for part-time students.

Application procedures. Admission: $50 fee. Application may be submitted online. Admission notification on a rolling basis. **Financial aid:** No deadline. Applicants notified on a rolling basis.

Academics. Special study options: Accelerated study, double major, internships, liberal arts/career combination. **Credit/placement by examination:** CLEP. **Support services:** GED preparation, learning center, reduced course load, remedial instruction, study skills assistance, tutoring.

Majors. Business: Business admin, executive assistant. **Communications technology:** Animation/special effects. **Computer sciences:** Computer graphics, webmaster. **Health:** Medical assistant, medical secretary, office admin, office assistant. **Visual/performing arts:** General, commercial/advertising art.

Student life. Freshman orientation: Available. **Policies:** Freshmen permitted cars on campus. **Activities:** Student government.

Student services. Adult student services, alcohol/substance abuse counseling, career counseling, services for economically disadvantaged, student employment services, financial aid counseling, placement for graduates. **Transfer:** Orientation, pre-admission transcript evaluation for new students. Transfer center for students transferring to 4-year colleges.

Contact. E-mail: dec@douglas-school.com
Phone: (724) 684-3684 ext. 100 Toll-free number: (800) 416-6013 ext. 100
Sherry Walters, Douglas Education Center, 130 Seventh Street, Monessen, PA 15062

DuBois Business College

DuBois, Pennsylvania
www.dbcollege.com **CB code: 3886**

- For-profit 2-year business and technical college
- Commuter campus in large town
- Interview required

General. Founded in 1885. Accredited by ACICS. **Enrollment:** 250 degree-seeking undergraduates. **Degrees:** 126 associate awarded. **Location:** 100 miles from Pittsburgh. **Calendar:** Quarter, extensive summer session. **Full-time faculty:** 15 total. **Part-time faculty:** 2 total. **Partnerships:** Formal articulation agreements with 32 Tech Prep high schools.

Student profile.

Out-of-state:	1%	**Live on campus:**	40%
25 or older:	40%		

Basis for selection. Open admission.

High school preparation. Courses in shorthand, accounting, computer, typing, law, psychology, and speech recommended.

2005-2006 Annual costs. Books/supplies: $1,000.

Application procedures. Admission: No deadline. $25 fee, may be waived for applicants with need. Application may be submitted online. Admission notification on a rolling basis. Must reply by May 1 or within 5 week(s) if notified thereafter. **Financial aid:** Closing date 8/1. FAFSA required. Applicants notified on a rolling basis.

Academics. Special study options: Cooperative education, double major, internships, liberal arts/career combination, study abroad. **Credit/placement by examination:** AP, CLEP, institutional tests. **Support services:** Reduced course load, remedial instruction, tutoring.

Majors. Business: General, accounting, administrative services, business admin. **Health:** Medical secretary. **Legal studies:** Legal secretary.

Computing on campus. 100 workstations in library, computer center.

Student life. Freshman orientation: Mandatory. **Housing:** Single-sex dorms available. $225 deposit. **Activities:** Student government, student newspaper, DBC Student Association.

Athletics. Intercollegiate: Volleyball. **Intramural:** Volleyball.

Student services. Adult student services, career counseling, student employment services, financial aid counseling, personal counseling, placement for graduates, veterans' counselor. **Physically disabled:** Services for visually, speech, hearing impaired. **Transfer:** Special adviser, orientation for new students. Transfer adviser for students transferring to 4-year colleges.

Contact. E-mail: admissions@dbcollege.com
Phone: (814) 371-6920 Toll-free number: (800) 692-6213
Fax: (814) 371-3974
Lisa Doty, Director of Admissions, DuBois Business College, One Beaver Drive, DuBois, PA 15801

DuBois Business College: Huntingdon

Huntingdon, Pennsylvania
dbcollege.com **CB code: 3290**

- For-profit 2-year business college
- Small town

General. Accredited by ACICS. **Enrollment:** 68 degree-seeking undergraduates. **Degrees:** 14 associate awarded. **Calendar:** Continuous. **Full-time faculty:** 4 total. **Part-time faculty:** 2 total.

Basis for selection. Open admission.

2006-2007 Annual costs. Tuition/fees (projected): $8,275. Per-credit charge: $160.

Application procedures. Admission: No deadline. $25 fee. Admission notification on a rolling basis. **Financial aid:** Closing date 8/1.

Academics. Credit/placement by examination: CLEP.

Majors. Business: General, accounting. **Health:** Medical secretary. **Legal studies:** Legal secretary.

Contact. Phone: (814) 371-6920
Lisa Doty, Admissions Director, DuBois Business College: Huntingdon, 1001 Moore Street, Huntingdon, PA 16652

DuBois Business College: Oil City

Oil City, Pennsylvania
www.dbcollege.com **CB code: 3292**

- For-profit 2-year branch campus and business college
- Large town

General. Accredited by ACICS. **Enrollment:** 90 degree-seeking undergraduates. **Degrees:** 45 associate awarded. **Location:** 90 miles from Pittsburgh. **Calendar:** Quarter. **Full-time faculty:** 5 total. **Part-time faculty:** 5 total.

Basis for selection. Open admission.

2005-2006 Annual costs. Books/supplies: $2,500.

Application procedures. Admission: No deadline. $25 fee. Admission notification on a rolling basis. **Financial aid:** FAFSA required.

Academics. Credit/placement by examination: CLEP.

Majors. Business: Accounting, administrative services. **Computer sciences:** Information systems. **Health:** Medical secretary. **Legal studies:** Legal secretary.

Contact. E-mail: dbcollege@usachoice.net
Phone: (814) 677-1322
Lisa Doty, Director of Admissions, DuBois Business College: Oil City, 701 East Third Street, Oil City, PA 16301

Duff's Business Institute

Pittsburgh, Pennsylvania
www.duffsinstitute.com **CB code: 2201**

- For-profit 2-year business college
- Large city

General. Accredited by ACICS. **Enrollment:** 675 degree-seeking undergraduates. **Degrees:** 87 associate awarded. **Calendar:** Semester. **Full-time faculty:** 13 total. **Part-time faculty:** 36 total.

Basis for selection. Proof of high school graduation or GED. CPAT important. Students with ACT score of 15 or SAT 700 (exclusive of writing) accepted in lieu of the CPAT.

2005-2006 Annual costs. Tuition/fees: $13,206. Per-credit charge: $259. Books/supplies: $400. Personal expenses: $1,944.

Application procedures. Admission: No deadline. Admission notification on a rolling basis. **Financial aid:** Institutional form required.

Academics. Credit/placement by examination: CLEP.

Contact. Phone: (412) 261-4520 Fax: (412) 261-4546
Lynn Fisher, Director of Admissions, Duff's Business Institute, 100 Forbes Avenue, Suite 1200, Pittsburgh, PA 15222

Erie Business Center

Erie, Pennsylvania
www.eriebc.edu **CB code: 2215**

- For-profit 2-year business college
- Commuter campus in small city

General. Founded in 1884. Accredited by ACICS. **Enrollment:** 455 degree-seeking undergraduates. **Degrees:** 96 associate awarded. **Location:** 95 miles from Cleveland. **Calendar:** Semester, extensive summer session. **Full-time faculty:** 13 total. **Part-time faculty:** 26 total.

Basis for selection. Open admission. **Adult students:** Entrance exam policies same as for first-time freshmen.

2005-2006 Annual costs. Tuition/fees: $7,870. Per-credit charge: $234. Room only: $2,560. Books/supplies: $800.

Financial aid. Need-based: Need-based aid available for part-time students.

Application procedures. Admission: No deadline. $25 fee, may be waived for applicants with need. Application may be submitted online. Admission notification on a rolling basis. **Financial aid:** No deadline. FAFSA required.

Academics. Special study options: Independent study, internships, weekend college. **Credit/placement by examination:** CLEP. **Support services:** Reduced course load, study skills assistance, tutoring.

Majors. Business: Accounting, administrative services, marketing, tourism/travel. **Computer sciences:** Computer graphics, networking, programming. **Health:** Medical assistant, medical secretary, medical transcription. **Legal studies:** Legal secretary, paralegal.

Computing on campus. Online library available.

Student life. Freshman orientation: Mandatory, $25 fee. Preregistration for classes offered. **Policies:** Freshmen permitted cars on campus. **Housing:** Apartments available. **Activities:** Drama, musical theater.

Student services. Student employment services, financial aid counseling, placement for graduates. **Transfer:** Orientation for new students.

Contact. E-mail: admissions@eriebc.edu
Phone: (814) 456-7504 ext. 32 Toll-free number: (800) 352-3743 ext. 32
Fax: (814) 456-4882
Donna Perino, Director of Admissions, Erie Business Center, 246 West Ninth Street, Erie, PA 16501

Erie Business Center South

New Castle, Pennsylvania
www.eriebc.edu/newcastle **CB code: 2577**

- For-profit 2-year branch campus college
- Large town

General. Accredited by ACICS. **Enrollment:** 105 undergraduates. **Degrees:** 25 associate awarded. **Calendar:** Trimester. **Full-time faculty:** 4 total. **Part-time faculty:** 3 total.

Basis for selection. Open admission.

2005-2006 Annual costs. $11,400 tuition for full program of two-year associate degree. Books/supplies: $900. Personal expenses: $1,107.

Application procedures. Admission: $25 fee.

Academics. Credit/placement by examination: CLEP.

Majors. Business: Accounting, business admin, marketing, tourism/travel. **Computer sciences:** General. **Health:** Medical records admin, medical transcription.

Contact. E-mail: hallr@eriebcs.com
Phone: (724) 658-9066 Toll-free number: (800) 722-6227
Fax: (724) 658-3083
Rose Hall, Admissions Representative, Erie Business Center South, 170 Cascade Galleria, New Castle, PA 16101

Erie Institute of Technology

Erie, Pennsylvania
www.erieit.org **CB code: 2284**

- For-profit 2-year technical college
- Small city

General. Accredited by ACCSCT. **Enrollment:** 150 degree-seeking undergraduates. **Degrees:** 12 associate awarded. **Calendar:** Semester. **Full-time faculty:** 11 total. **Part-time faculty:** 11 total.

Basis for selection. Open admission, but selective for some programs. Math requirement.

Application procedures. Admission: No deadline. $25 fee.

Academics. Credit/placement by examination: CLEP.

Contact. Phone: (814) 868-9900 Toll-free number: (866) 868-3743
Fax: (814) 868-9977
Lisa Preszel, Director of Admissions, Erie Institute of Technology, 5539 Peach Street, Erie, PA 16509-2954

Harcum College

Bryn Mawr, Pennsylvania **CB member**
www.harcum.edu **CB code: 2287**

- Private 2-year junior college
- Commuter campus in large town
- Application essay required

General. Founded in 1915. Regionally accredited. **Enrollment:** 734 degree-seeking undergraduates; 84 non-degree-seeking students. **Degrees:** 153 associate awarded. **Location:** 10 miles from Philadelphia. **Calendar:** Semester, limited summer session. **Full-time faculty:** 25 total. **Part-time faculty:** 70 total. **Class size:** 87% < 20, 12% 20-39, less than 1% 40-49. **Special facilities:** Veterinary services building, physical therapist assistant lab, dental clinic, nursing lab, radiology lab.

Student profile. Among degree-seeking undergraduates, 100% enrolled in a vocational program, 154 enrolled as first-time, first-year students.

Part-time:	31%	**Hispanic American:**	2%
Out-of-state:	10%	**International:**	2%
Women:	85%	**25 or older:**	40%
African American:	25%	**Live on campus:**	17%
Asian American:	2%		

Transfer out. Colleges most students transferred to 2005: Cabrini College, West Chester University, Temple University, Rosemont College, Widener University.

Basis for selection. School record of primary importance. Writing sample required. 750 SAT (exclusive of Writing) and/or 2.0 GPA required. Nursing, dental hygiene, physical therapy assistant, veterinary technology require 900 SAT (exclusive of Writing) and 2.5 GPA. Interview recommended. TOEFL required for students whose first language is not English. SAT or ACT recommended. Students with 12 or more college credits not required to submit SAT scores. Score of 900 (exclusive of Writing) required for health science programs, 750 for all others. Interview required of borderline applicants, recommended for all others. **Adult students:** SAT/ACT scores not required if out of high school 3 year(s) or more. **Learning Disabled:** Must provide documentation of disability to ensure proper accommodations are made.

High school preparation. Recommended units include English 4, mathematics 2, social studies 2, history 2, science 2 and academic electives 2. Required units for veterinary technology, dental hygiene, and physical therapy assistant programs include 2 algebra, geometry, biology, chemistry. 1 unit biology and algebra required for dental assisting program. 2 algebra, biology, and chemistry required for medical laboratory technology.

2005-2006 Annual costs. Tuition/fees: $14,522. Per-credit charge: $478. Room/board: $6,900. Books/supplies: $910. Personal expenses: $1,530.

Financial aid. Need-based: Need-based aid available for part-time students. Work study available nights, weekends and for part-time students. **Non-need-based:** Scholarships awarded for academics, leadership.

Application procedures. Admission: Priority date 5/1; no deadline. $25 fee, may be waived for applicants with need. Application may be submitted online. Admission notification on a rolling basis. **Financial aid:** Priority date 4/15; no closing date. FAFSA, institutional form required. Applicants notified on a rolling basis starting 3/1; must reply within 3 week(s) of notification.

Academics. 86% of academic programs offered have internship/practicum component. **Special study options:** Accelerated study, cooperative education, distance learning, double major, dual enrollment of high school students, ESL, independent study, internships, liberal arts/career combination, study abroad. **Credit/placement by examination:** AP, CLEP, institutional tests. 20 credit hours maximum toward associate degree. Maximum of 30 credits total for transfer credits, life experience, challenge examination, and CLEP. **Support services:** Learning center, pre-admission summer program, reduced course load, remedial instruction, study skills assistance, tutoring.

Majors. Agriculture: Animal sciences. **Business:** General, business admin, fashion, sales/distribution. **Education:** Early childhood. **Health:** Clinical lab technology, dental assistant, dental hygiene, health services, physical therapy assistant, radiologic technology/medical imaging, veterinary technology/assistant. **Liberal arts:** Arts/sciences. **Protective services:** Law enforcement admin. **Psychology:** General. **Visual/performing arts:** Fashion design, interior design.

Most popular majors. Business/marketing 8%, education 9%, health sciences 63%, visual/performing arts 14%.

Computing on campus. 86 workstations in dormitories, library, computer center, student center. Online library available.

Student life. Freshman orientation: Available. Preregistration for classes offered. One-day introduction to campus services, separate evening orientation for Lifelong Learners. **Policies:** Freshmen permitted cars on campus. **Housing:** Guaranteed on-campus for all undergraduates. Coed dorms, special housing for disabled available. $200 deposit. **Activities:** Drama, literary magazine, student government, student newspaper, Ebony club, Campus Ambassadors, Organization of Animal Technician Students (OATS), Phi Theta Kappa, international club, AIM Peer Mentors, community service club, dental assisting club, Harcum Association for the Education of Young Children, physical therapy assistant club.

Athletics. NJCAA. **Intercollegiate:** Basketball, volleyball W. **Team name:** Bears.

Student services. Adult student services, alcohol/substance abuse counseling, career counseling, services for economically disadvantaged, student employment services, financial aid counseling, health services, minority student services, on-campus daycare, personal counseling, placement for graduates, veterans' counselor, women's services. **Physically disabled:** Services for visually, speech, hearing impaired. **Transfer:** Special adviser, orientation, re-entry adviser, pre-admission transcript evaluation for new students. Transfer center, transfer adviser, college fairs on campus for students transferring to 4-year colleges.

Contact. E-mail: journey@harcum.edu
Phone: (610) 526-6050 Toll-free number: (800) 345-2600
Fax: (610) 526-6147
Nicola DiFronzo, Dean of Admissions, Harcum College, 750 Montgomery Avenue, Bryn Mawr, PA 19010-3476

Harrisburg Area Community College

Harrisburg, Pennsylvania — **CB member**
www.hacc.edu — **CB code: 2309**

- Public 2-year community college
- Commuter campus in small city

General. Founded in 1964. Regionally accredited. 8 county high schools utilized for credit-course offerings. Availability varies by semester. **Enrollment:** 9,507 degree-seeking undergraduates; 7,392 non-degree-seeking students. **Degrees:** 1,226 associate awarded. **ROTC:** Army. **Location:** 90 miles from Philadelphia, 180 miles from New York City. **Calendar:** Semester, limited summer session. **Full-time faculty:** 261 total; 16% have terminal degrees, 14% minority, 59% women. **Part-time faculty:** 716 total; 6% minority, 56% women. **Class size:** 45% < 20, 52% 20-39, 2% 40-49, less than 1% 50-99, less than 1% >100. **Partnerships:** Tech Prep program for selected career programs.

Student profile. Among degree-seeking undergraduates, 29% enrolled in a transfer program, 71% enrolled in a vocational program, 1,756 enrolled as first-time, first-year students, 1,187 transferred in from other institutions.

Part-time:	67%	**Asian American:**	2%
Out-of-state:	1%	**Hispanic American:**	6%
Women:	71%	**International:**	1%
African American:	10%	**25 or older:**	48%

Transfer out. 68% of students enrolled in the transfer program go on to 4-year colleges. **Colleges most students transferred to 2005:** Penn State University, Shippensburg University, Millersville University, Elizabethtown College, York College.

Basis for selection. Open admission, but selective for some programs. Special requirements for allied health programs and chef's apprenticeship. Non-native speakers of English must complete in-house English placement testing if ELPT scores are not submitted. ACT required for allied health programs, score report by February 1. Interview required for allied health, and chef apprenticeship programs; essay required for chef apprenticeship program.

2005-2006 Annual costs. Tuition/fees: $3,360; $5,760 out-of-district; $8,160 out-of-state. Per-credit charge: $95 in-district; $175 out-of-district; $255 out-of-state. Out-of-district students pay $570 in yearly fees; out-of-state, $630. Books/supplies: $1,200. Personal expenses: $1,600.

2004-2005 Financial aid. Need-based: 31% of total undergraduate aid awarded as scholarships/grants, 69% as loans/jobs. Need-based aid available for part-time students. Work study available for part-time students. **Non-need-based:** Scholarships awarded for academics. **Additional information:** Federal work study community service positions available.

Application procedures. Admission: No deadline. $30 fee, may be waived for applicants with need. Application may be submitted online. Admission notification on a rolling basis. Must reply by May 1 or within 5 week(s) if notified thereafter. **Financial aid:** Priority date 4/1; no closing date. FAFSA, institutional form required. Applicants notified on a rolling basis starting 6/1.

Academics. Special study options: Distance learning, double major, dual enrollment of high school students, ESL, honors, independent study, internships, student-designed major, study abroad, weekend college. Dual admissions with 6 United Negro College Fund institutions, with Penn State Harrisburg Capital College, and with Cheney University of Pennsylvania. License preparation in dental hygiene, nursing, paramedic, radiology, real estate. **Credit/placement by examination:** AP, CLEP, IB, institutional tests. 30 credit hours maximum toward associate degree. **Support services:** GED preparation and test center, learning center, pre-admission summer program, reduced course load, remedial instruction, study skills assistance, tutoring, writing center.

Majors. Agriculture: Agribusiness operations. **Biology:** General. **Business:** General, accounting technology, accounting/business management, administrative services, banking/financial services, business admin, hospitality admin, hotel/motel admin, real estate, restaurant/food services, retailing, sales/distribution, small business admin, tourism/travel. **Communications:** Media studies. **Computer sciences:** General, computer science, information technology, networking, web page design. **Conservation:** Environmental science, environmental studies. **Construction:** General, electrician. **Education:** Early childhood, elementary, secondary. **Engineering:** General. **Engineering technology:** Architectural, civil, construction, electrical, mechanical. **Family/consumer sciences:** Institutional food production. **Health:** Cardiovascular technology, clinical lab technology, dental hygiene, dietetics, EMT paramedic, health care admin, health services admin, medical assistant, medical records admin, nuclear medical technology, nursing (RN), radiologic technology/medical imaging, respiratory therapy technology, sonography, surgical technology. **Legal studies:** Paralegal. **Math:** General. **Mechanic/repair:** Automotive, computer, heating/ac/refrig, industrial. **Personal/culinary services:** Chef training. **Physical sciences:** General, chemistry. **Protective services:** Criminalistics, firefighting, law enforcement admin, police science. **Psychology:** General. **Public administration:** Human services, social work. **Social sciences:** General, international relations. **Visual/performing arts:** General, art, crafts, design, dramatic, graphic design, music management, photography.

Most popular majors. Business/marketing 21%, computer/information sciences 9%, education 10%, health sciences 19%, security/protective services 8%, visual/performing arts 8%.

Computing on campus. 260 workstations in library, computer center, student center. Commuter students can connect to campus network. Online course registration, online library, helpline, wireless network available.

Student life. Freshman orientation: Mandatory. Preregistration for classes offered. **Activities:** Jazz band, choral groups, drama, film society, music ensembles, musical theater, radio station, student government, student newspaper, black student union, Volunteers Interested in People, Asian-American club, latino club, international student club.

Athletics. Intercollegiate: Basketball, soccer M, tennis, volleyball W. **Intramural:** Basketball, soccer, swimming, tennis, volleyball.

Student services. Career counseling, student employment services, financial aid counseling, minority student services, on-campus daycare, personal counseling, placement for graduates, veterans' counselor. **Physically disabled:** Services for visually, hearing impaired. **Transfer:** Special adviser, orientation for new students. Transfer adviser, college fairs on campus for students transferring to 4-year colleges.

Contact. E-mail: admit@hacc.edu
Phone: (717) 780-2400 Toll-free number: (800) 222-4222
Fax: (717) 236-7674
Jennifer Baker, Director, Harrisburg Area Community College, One HACC Drive, Cooper 206, Harrisburg, PA 17110-2999

Hussian School of Art

Philadelphia, Pennsylvania
www.hussianart.edu **CB code: 7309**

- For-profit 2-year visual arts and technical college
- Commuter campus in very large city
- Interview required

General. Founded in 1946. Accredited by ACCSCT. **Enrollment:** 155 degree-seeking undergraduates. **Degrees:** 33 associate awarded. **Calendar:** Semester. **Full-time faculty:** 3 total; 33% women. **Part-time faculty:** 23 total; 13% have terminal degrees, 4% minority, 26% women. **Class size:** 31% < 20, 69% 20-39. **Special facilities:** Air-brush and computer graphics facilities.

Student profile. Among degree-seeking undergraduates, 100% enrolled in a vocational program, 43 enrolled as first-time, first-year students.

Out-of-state:	10%	**Asian American:**	2%
Women:	36%	**Hispanic American:**	3%
African American:	12%	**25 or older:**	2%

Basis for selection. Interview, portfolio, and talent/ability more important. Portfolio required. **Adult students:** Entrance exam policies same as for first-time freshmen.

High school preparation. High school art or other art training recommended.

2006-2007 Annual costs. Tuition/fees: $10,465. Per-credit charge: $300. Books/supplies: $725. Personal expenses: $2,196.

2004-2005 Financial aid. All financial aid based on need. 39% of total undergraduate aid awarded as scholarships/grants, 61% as loans/jobs. Need-based aid available for part-time students.

Application procedures. Admission: No deadline. $25 fee, may be waived for applicants with need. Admission notification on a rolling basis. **Financial aid:** No deadline. FAFSA, institutional form required. Applicants notified on a rolling basis starting 2/15; must reply within 3 week(s) of notification.

Academics. Second-semester freshmen must earn GPA of 2.0 or above to continue in good standing. **Special study options:** Internships. **Credit/placement by examination:** CLEP. **Support services:** Pre-admission summer program, tutoring.

Majors. Visual/performing arts: Commercial/advertising art, graphic design.

Computing on campus. PC or laptop required. 60 workstations in computer center.

Student life. Freshman orientation: Available. Preregistration for classes offered. Morning program held 2 weeks prior to official start of classes. **Activities:** Student newspaper.

Student services. Career counseling, financial aid counseling, placement for graduates. **Transfer:** Special adviser, orientation, pre-admission transcript evaluation for new students.

Contact. E-mail: hussian@pond.com
Phone: (215) 981-0900 Fax: (215) 864-9115
Lynne Wartman, Admissions Director, Hussian School of Art, 1118 Market Street, Philadelphia, PA 19107

ICM School of Business & Medical Careers

Pittsburgh, Pennsylvania
www.icmschool.com **CB code: 3823**

- For-profit 2-year business and health science college
- Commuter campus in large city
- Application essay, interview required

General. Accredited by ACICS. **Enrollment:** 1,189 degree-seeking undergraduates. **Degrees:** 314 associate awarded. **Calendar:** Quarter, extensive summer session. **Full-time faculty:** 32 total. **Part-time faculty:** 31 total.

Student profile. Among degree-seeking undergraduates, 312 enrolled as first-time, first-year students.

Part-time:	5%	**Women:**	72%

Basis for selection. Wonderlic required.

2005-2006 Annual costs. Tuition/fees: $14,848. Tuition costs include books and supplies.

2004-2005 Financial aid. Need-based: 74% of total undergraduate aid awarded as scholarships/grants, 26% as loans/jobs.

Application procedures. Admission: No deadline. $30 fee, may be waived for applicants with need. Admission notification on a rolling basis. **Financial aid:** Closing date 4/30.

Academics. Special study options: Double major, internships. Bachelor's degree programs available on campus. License preparation in occupational therapy. **Credit/placement by examination:** CLEP. **Support services:** Reduced course load, study skills assistance, tutoring.

Majors. Business: Accounting, administrative services, business admin, fashion, tourism/travel. **Computer sciences:** General, applications programming, information technology, LAN/WAN management, programming, security, systems analysis, webmaster. **Engineering:** Computer. **Health:** Medical assistant, medical secretary, occupational therapy assistant. **Legal studies:** Legal secretary. **Protective services:** Corrections, criminal justice, law enforcement admin, police science, security services.

Computing on campus. 225 workstations in library, computer center. Online library, helpline, repair service available.

Student life. Freshman orientation: Mandatory. Preregistration for classes offered. **Policies:** Freshmen permitted cars on campus.

Student services. Career counseling, student employment services, financial aid counseling, personal counseling, placement for graduates.

Contact. E-mail: cmoore@icmschool.com
Phone: (412) 261-2647 Toll-free number: (800) 441-5222
Fax: (412) 261-0998
Chris Moore, Director of Admissions, ICM School of Business & Medical Careers, 10 Wood Street, Pittsburgh, PA 15222

International Academy of Design and Technology: Pittsburgh

Pittsburgh, Pennsylvania
www.iadtpitt.edu **CB code: 2236**

- For-profit 2-year business and technical college
- Commuter campus in large city
- Application essay, interview required

General. Founded in 1967. Accredited by ACICS. **Enrollment:** 600 undergraduates. **Degrees:** 125 associate awarded. **Location:** 450 miles from Philadelphia, 140 miles from Cleveland. **Calendar:** Semester. **Full-time faculty:** 18 total. **Part-time faculty:** 30 total.

Basis for selection. Test scores on IBM Programmers Aptitude Test, Wonderlic Test, Gordons Personal Profile Inventory, interview, essay most important.

2005-2006 Annual costs. Tuition for 18-month associate program in computer information management $19,250; books and supplies for entire program $1,891.

Application procedures. Admission: No deadline. $50 fee. Admission notification on a rolling basis beginning on or about 8/1. **Financial aid:** No deadline. FAFSA required.

Academics. Credit/placement by examination: CLEP. **Support services:** Tutoring.

Majors. Computer sciences: General, applications programming. **Family/consumer sciences:** Institutional food production. **Health:** Surgical technology. **Personal/culinary services:** Culinary arts.

Most popular majors. Computer/information sciences 40%, health sciences 20%, trade and industry 40%.

Computing on campus. 110 workstations in library, computer center.

Student services. Career counseling, student employment services, personal counseling, placement for graduates, veterans' counselor. **Physically disabled:** Services for hearing impaired.

Contact. E-mail: clang@iadtpitt.edu
Phone: (412) 391-4197 Toll-free number: (800) 447-8324
Christopher Lang, Director of Admissions, International Academy of Design and Technology: Pittsburgh, 555 Grant Street, Pittsburgh, PA 15219

ITT Technical Institute: Bensalem

Bensalem, Pennsylvania
www.itt-tech.edu

- For-profit 2-year technical college
- Small city

General. Accredited by ACICS. **Calendar:** Quarter.

Annual costs/financial aid. Tuition varies by program, $260-$368 per credit hour.

Contact. Phone: (215) 244-8871
Director of Recruitment, 3330 Tillman Drive, Bensalem, PA 19020

ITT Technical Institute: Mechanicsburg

Mechanicsburg, Pennsylvania
www.itt-tech.edu **CB code: 2730**

- For-profit 2-year technical college
- Commuter campus in small town

General. Accredited by ACICS. **Calendar:** Quarter.

Annual costs/financial aid. Tuition varies by program, $260-$368 per credit hour.

Contact. Phone: (717) 691-9263
Director of Recruitment, 5020 Louise Drive, Mechanicsburg, PA 17055

ITT Technical Institute: Monroeville

Monroeville, Pennsylvania
www.itt-tech.edu **CB code: 2735**

- For-profit 2-year technical college
- Commuter campus in large town

General. Accredited by ACICS. **Calendar:** Quarter.

Annual costs/financial aid. Tuition varies by program, $260-$368 per credit hour.

Contact. Phone: (412) 856-5920
Director of Recruitment, 105 Mall Boulevard, Suite 200E, Monroeville, PA 15146

ITT Technical Institute: Pittsburgh

Pittsburgh, Pennsylvania
www.itt-tech.edu **CB code: 2745**

- For-profit 2-year technical college
- Commuter campus in large city

General. Accredited by ACICS. **Calendar:** Quarter.

Annual costs/financial aid. Tuition varies by program, $260-$368 per credit hour.

Contact. Phone: (412) 937-9150
Director of Recruitment, 10 Parkway Center, Pittsburgh, PA 15220

JNA Institute of Culinary Arts

Philadelphia, Pennsylvania
www.culinaryarts.com **CB code: 3049**

- For-profit 2-year technical college
- Commuter campus in very large city

General. Accredited by ACCSCT. **Enrollment:** 64 degree-seeking undergraduates. **Degrees:** 17 associate awarded. **Calendar:** Continuous, extensive summer session. **Full-time faculty:** 5 total. **Part-time faculty:** 7 total.

Student profile.

Out-of-state:	10%	**25 or older:**	45%

Basis for selection. Open admission.

2006-2007 Annual costs. Tuition for 15-month associate program, $14,000; 6-month professional cooking diploma program, $7,000. Required fees $75 for both programs. Books and supplies are $225 for the diploma program and $1,065 for the associate program.

Application procedures. Admission: No deadline. No application fee. **Financial aid:** FAFSA required.

Academics. Special study options: Distance learning. **Credit/placement by examination:** AP, CLEP.

Majors. Personal/culinary services: Culinary arts.

Student life. Freshman orientation: Mandatory.

Student services. Alcohol/substance abuse counseling, career counseling, student employment services, financial aid counseling, legal services, placement for graduates.

Contact. E-mail: admissions@culinaryarts.com
Phone: (215) 468-8800 Toll-free number: (877) 872-3197
Richard Blumberg, Director of Admissions, JNA Institute of Culinary Arts, 1212 South Broad Street, Philadelphia, PA 19146

Johnson College

Scranton, Pennsylvania **CB member**
www.johnson.edu **CB code: 1542**

- Private 2-year technical college
- Commuter campus in small city
- SAT or ACT (ACT writing optional) required

General. Founded in 1912. Accredited by ACCSCT. **Enrollment:** 376 degree-seeking undergraduates. **Degrees:** 150 associate awarded. **Location:** 117 miles from Philadelphia, 125 miles from New York City. **Calendar:** Semester, limited summer session. **Full-time faculty:** 25 total. **Part-time faculty:** 5 total. **Class size:** 44% < 20, 56% 20-39. **Special facilities:** Materials test laboratory, veterinary hospital. **Partnerships:** Tech prep agreements.

Student profile.

Out-of-state:	6%	**Live on campus:**	10%
25 or older:	53%		

Transfer out. Colleges most students transferred to 2005: State University of New York Utica/Rome.

Basis for selection. Open admission, but selective for some programs. For selective programs, high school record, test scores, recommendations,

Two-Year Colleges

interview important. ACT (Writing optional) or SAT (old or new) accepted for selective programs. Institutional entrance examination required for applicants who have not taken SAT or ACT. Standardized test scores required for associate in science degree programs only. All test scores due at time of application.

High school preparation. 1 units required. Required and recommended units include English 2 and mathematics 1. One chemistry or biology required for veterinary science technology majors.

2005-2006 Annual costs. Tuition/fees: $12,763. Per-credit charge: $300. Room only: $2,975. Books/supplies: $1,500. Personal expenses: $1,100.

2005-2006 Financial aid. Need-based: Need-based aid available for part-time students. Work study available nights, weekends and for part-time students. **Non-need-based:** Scholarships awarded for academics.

Application procedures. Admission: No deadline. $30 fee, may be waived for applicants with need. Application may be submitted online. Admission notification on a rolling basis. Within 30 days. **Financial aid:** Priority date 4/28; no closing date. FAFSA, institutional form required. Applicants notified on a rolling basis starting 4/15; must reply within 2 week(s) of notification.

Academics. Extensive shop and laboratory facilities. **Special study options:** Internships. **Credit/placement by examination:** CLEP, institutional tests. 9 credit hours maximum toward associate degree. **Support services:** Learning center, pre-admission summer program, reduced course load, remedial instruction, study skills assistance, tutoring.

Majors. Computer sciences: General. **Construction:** Carpentry, maintenance. **Engineering technology:** Drafting, manufacturing. **Health:** Pharmacy assistant, veterinary technology/assistant. **Mechanic/repair:** General, automotive, diesel, electronics/electrical, industrial. **Production:** Woodworking.

Most popular majors. Health sciences 23%, trade and industry 77%.

Computing on campus. 52 workstations in library, computer center. Repair service available.

Student life. Freshman orientation: Mandatory, $100 fee. **Policies:** Freshmen permitted cars on campus. **Housing:** Apartments available. $300 deposit. **Activities:** Student government, Social Force.

Athletics. Intercollegiate: Basketball, bowling, cross-country, golf. **Intramural:** Basketball, football (non-tackle) M, skiing, soccer, softball, table tennis, volleyball. **Team name:** Jaguars.

Student services. Career counseling, student employment services, financial aid counseling, personal counseling, placement for graduates, veterans' counselor. **Physically disabled:** Services for visually, hearing impaired. **Transfer:** Special adviser, orientation, pre-admission transcript evaluation for new students. Transfer adviser, college fairs on campus for students transferring to 4-year colleges.

Contact. E-mail: admit@johnson.edu
Phone: (570) 342-6404 ext. 125 Toll-free number: (800) 293-9675
Fax: (570) 348-2181
Melissa Ide, Acting Director of Admissions, Johnson College, 3427 North Main Avenue, Scranton, PA 18508

Katharine Gibbs School: Norristown
Norristown, Pennsylvania
www.gibbspa.com

- For-profit 2-year junior college
- Commuter campus

General. Accredited by ACICS. **Calendar:** Quarter.

Contact. Phone: (610) 676-0500
Director of Admissions, 2501 Monroe Boulevard, Norristown, PA 19403

Lackawanna College
Scranton, Pennsylvania
www.lackawanna.edu **CB code: 2373**

- Private 2-year junior college
- Commuter campus in small city
- Interview required

General. Founded in 1894. Regionally accredited. **Enrollment:** 1,195 degree-seeking undergraduates; 74 non-degree-seeking students. **Degrees:** 215 associate awarded. **ROTC:** Army, Air Force. **Location:** 150 miles from New York City, 120 miles from Philadelphia. **Calendar:** Semester, limited summer session. **Full-time faculty:** 20 total. **Part-time faculty:** 120 total. **Class size:** 80% < 20, 20% 20-39.

Student profile. Among degree-seeking undergraduates, 414 enrolled as first-time, first-year students.

Part-time:	33%	**Asian American:**	1%
Out-of-state:	9%	**Hispanic American:**	3%
Women:	54%	**25 or older:**	33%
African American:	11%	**Live on campus:**	12%

Transfer out. Colleges most students transferred to 2005: Marywood University, Keystone College, College Misericordia, East Stroudsburg University, Bloomsburg University.

Basis for selection. Open admission. TOEFL exam is required for all non-native English speaking students. Students who do not submit recent SAT or ACT scores required to take college-administered placement tests. **Adult students:** Entrance exam policies same as for first-time freshmen. **Learning Disabled:** Current documentation of disability (for arrangement of accommodations).

High school preparation. 11 units recommended. Recommended units include English 4, mathematics 3, social studies 1 and science 3.

2005-2006 Annual costs. Tuition/fees: $9,470. Per-credit charge: $310. Room/board: $6,300. Books/supplies: $1,200. Personal expenses: $1,450.

2004-2005 Financial aid. Need-based: 288 full-time freshmen applied for aid; 267 were judged to have need; 262 of these received aid. Average need met was 65%. Average scholarship/grant was $6,450; average loan $2,625. 44% of total undergraduate aid awarded as scholarships/grants, 56% as loans/jobs. Need-based aid available for part-time students. Work study available nights, weekends and for part-time students. **Non-need-based:** Awarded to 178 full-time undergraduates, including 70 freshmen. Scholarships awarded for academics, athletics, leadership. **Additional information:** To receive institutional funds, all students, including athletes, must apply for financial aid.

Application procedures. Admission: Priority date 8/15; no deadline. $30 fee, may be waived for applicants with need. Application may be submitted online. Admission notification on a rolling basis. **Financial aid:** Priority date 5/1; no closing date. FAFSA, institutional form required. Applicants notified on a rolling basis starting 5/1.

Academics. Special study options: Cooperative education, distance learning, double major, dual enrollment of high school students, ESL, honors, independent study, internships. License preparation in paramedic. **Credit/placement by examination:** AP, CLEP, IB, institutional tests. 31 credit hours maximum toward associate degree. **Support services:** GED preparation and test center, learning center, pre-admission summer program, reduced course load, remedial instruction, study skills assistance, tutoring, writing center.

Majors. Biology: Biotechnology. **Business:** General, accounting, administrative services, banking/financial services, business admin, management information systems. **Communications:** Media studies. **Computer sciences:** General. **Conservation:** Environmental studies. **Education:** General, early childhood. **Health:** Cardiovascular technology, EMT paramedic, medical secretary. **Legal studies:** Paralegal. **Liberal arts:** Arts/sciences, humanities. **Mechanic/repair:** Industrial electronics. **Protective services:** Criminal justice, police science. **Public administration:** Human services. **Visual/performing arts:** Dramatic.

Most popular majors. Business/marketing 41%, education 9%, health sciences 19%, security/protective services 24%.

Computing on campus. 300 workstations in dormitories, library, computer center. Dormitories wired for high-speed internet access. Online library, helpline available.

Student life. Freshman orientation: Mandatory. One-day program to introduce students to key college personnel, facilitate social interaction, and review policies and procedures. **Policies:** Freshmen permitted cars on campus. **Housing:** Single-sex dorms, substance-free housing available. $250 deposit, deadline 8/15. **Activities:** Choral groups, drama, literary magazine, student government, student newspaper, diversity club and social justice center.

Athletics. NJCAA. **Intercollegiate:** Baseball M, basketball, cheerleading M, cross-country, football (tackle) M, golf, softball W, volleyball W. **Team name:** FIghting Falcons.

Student services. Adult student services, career counseling, services for economically disadvantaged, student employment services, financial aid counseling, minority student services, personal counseling, placement for graduates, veterans' counselor. **Transfer:** Special adviser, orientation, pre-admission transcript evaluation for new students. Transfer adviser, college fairs on campus for students transferring to 4-year colleges.

Contact. E-mail: adminfo@lackawanna.edu
Phone: (570) 961-7814 Toll-free number: (877) 346-3552
Fax: (570) 961-7843
Mark Duda, Director of Admissions, Lackawanna College, 501 Vine Street, Scranton, PA 18509

Lansdale School of Business

North Wales, Pennsylvania
www.lsb.edu **CB code: 5853**

- For-profit 2-year business college
- Commuter campus in small town
- Interview required

General. Accredited by ACICS. **Enrollment:** 370 undergraduates. **Degrees:** 89 associate awarded. **Location:** 25 miles north of Philadelphia. **Calendar:** Semester, extensive summer session. **Full-time faculty:** 12 total. **Part-time faculty:** 30 total.

Transfer out. Colleges most students transferred to 2005: Eastern College, Delaware Valley College.

Basis for selection. Open admission.

2005-2006 Annual costs. 17-month associate degree program: $10,500 tuition; $300 required fees; $188 per-credit-hour charge for day, $158 for evening; $1700 books and supplies estimate. Computer lab fees vary by program.

Application procedures. Admission: No deadline. $20 fee, may be waived for applicants with need. Admission notification on a rolling basis. **Financial aid:** Priority date 7/1, closing date 8/16. FAFSA required.

Academics. Special study options: Double major, internships. **Credit/placement by examination:** CLEP, institutional tests. 30 credit hours maximum toward associate degree. **Support services:** Reduced course load.

Majors. Business: Accounting, office management. **Health:** Medical assistant.

Most popular majors. Business/marketing 40%, computer/information sciences 40%, health sciences 20%.

Computing on campus. 64 workstations in library, computer center.

Student life. Activities: Student government.

Student services. Transfer: Orientation for new students.

Contact. E-mail: mjohnson@lsb.edu
Phone: (215) 699-5700 Fax: (215) 699-8770
Marianne Johnson, Director of Admissions, Lansdale School of Business, 201 Church Road, North Wales, PA 19454

Laurel Business Institute

Uniontown, Pennsylvania
www.laurelbusiness.edu **CB code: 2329**

- For-profit 2-year business and technical college
- Commuter campus in large town
- Interview required

General. Founded in 1985. Accredited by ACICS. **Enrollment:** 300 degree-seeking undergraduates. **Degrees:** 76 associate awarded. **Location:** 50 miles from Pittsburgh. **Calendar:** Semester, extensive summer session. **Full-time faculty:** 23 total. **Part-time faculty:** 17 total. **Class size:** 95% < 20, 5% 20-39. **Special facilities:** Microsoft testing center, Prometric Testing Site.

Student profile.

Out-of-state:	1%	**25 or older:**	85%

Transfer out. Colleges most students transferred to 2005: Robert Morris College, Point Park College, California University.

Basis for selection. Test scores, high school grades or GED, and personal interview most important.

2005-2006 Annual costs. Books/supplies: $750.

Financial aid. All financial aid based on need. Work study available nights, weekends and for part-time students.

Application procedures. Admission: No deadline. $55 fee, may be waived for applicants with need. Admission notification on a rolling basis. **Financial aid:** Closing date 8/1. FAFSA, institutional form required. Applicants notified on a rolling basis; must reply within 4 week(s) of notification.

Academics. Special study options: Cooperative education, double major, internships. **Credit/placement by examination:** CLEP. **Support services:** GED preparation, reduced course load, remedial instruction, tutoring.

Majors. Business: Accounting, administrative services, office/clerical. **Computer sciences:** Data processing, programming, systems analysis. **Education:** Teacher assistance. **Family/consumer sciences:** Child care. **Health:** Medical assistant, medical records admin, medical secretary, medical transcription, nursing assistant. **Legal studies:** Legal secretary.

Computing on campus. 120 workstations in computer center.

Student life. Freshman orientation: Mandatory. **Activities:** Student government, student newspaper, health care careers club, Success club, student government.

Student services. Student employment services, personal counseling, placement for graduates. **Physically disabled:** Services for visually, speech, hearing impaired. **Transfer:** Special adviser, orientation, pre-admission transcript evaluation for new students.

Contact. E-mail: lbi@laurelbusiness.net
Phone: (724) 439-4900 Fax: (724) 439-3607
Douglas Decker, Laurel Business Institute, 11 North Penn Street, Uniontown, PA 15401

Lehigh Carbon Community College

Schnecksville, Pennsylvania
www.lccc.edu **CB code: 2381**

- Public 2-year community college
- Commuter campus in small town

General. Founded in 1966. Regionally accredited. A total of 3 campuses enables students from northern rural areas as well as city dwellers residing south of main campus to take classes close to home. **Enrollment:** 6,564 degree-seeking undergraduates. **Degrees:** 527 associate awarded. **ROTC:** Army. **Location:** 8 miles from Allentown, 50 miles from Philadelphia. **Calendar:** Semester, limited summer session. **Full-time faculty:** 106 total; 12% have terminal degrees, 4% minority, 65% women. **Part-time faculty:** 395 total; 4% minority, 43% women. **Class size:** 62% < 20, 38% 20-39, less than 1% 40-49. **Partnerships:** Non-credit adult education programs with district high schools; job training programs with local small businesses.

Student profile. Among degree-seeking undergraduates, 55% enrolled in a transfer program, 45% enrolled in a vocational program, 2% already have a bachelor's degree or higher, 1,655 enrolled as first-time, first-year students, 217 transferred in from other institutions.

Part-time:	61%	**Asian American:**	2%
Out-of-state:	1%	**Hispanic American:**	8%
Women:	62%	**International:**	1%
African American:	5%	**25 or older:**	39%

Transfer out. 46% of students enrolled in the transfer program go on to 4-year colleges. **Colleges most students transferred to 2005:** Kutztown University, DeSales University, Cedar Crest College, Albright College, Penn State University.

Basis for selection. Open admission, but selective for some programs. Special requirements for aviation, allied health, nursing and veterinary technician programs. High school diploma or GED required of applicants to allied health and professional pilot programs, and applicants under the age of 18. COMPASS used for course placement. Interview required for allied health, aviation, medical assistant, veterinary technician programs. **Adult students:** Entrance exam policies same as for first-time freshmen. **Home-schooled:** Personal interview encouraged.

High school preparation. Special requirements for allied health programs and nursing.

2006-2007 Annual costs. Tuition/fees (projected): $2,715; $5,010 out-of-district; $7,305 out-of-state. Per-credit charge: $77 in-district; $154 out-of-district; $231 out-of-state. Out-of-district students pay $690 in fees; out-of-state students pay $960 in fees. Books/supplies: $1,200. Personal expenses: $1,000.

2004-2005 Financial aid. Need-based: 502 full-time freshmen applied for aid; 361 were judged to have need; 345 of these received aid. Average need met was 60%. Average scholarship/grant was $3,093; average loan $2,309. 54% of total undergraduate aid awarded as scholarships/grants, 46% as loans/jobs. Need-based aid available for part-time students. Work study available nights and for part-time students. **Non-need-based:** Awarded to 37 full-time undergraduates, including 27 freshmen. Scholarships awarded for academics, state residency.

Application procedures. Admission: No deadline. $30 fee. Application may be submitted online. Admission notification on a rolling basis. **Financial aid:** No deadline. FAFSA required. Applicants notified on a rolling basis starting 5/5; must reply within 2 week(s) of notification.

Academics. Special study options: Cooperative education, cross-registration, distance learning, dual enrollment of high school students, ESL, honors, independent study, internships, study abroad. Bachelor's degree programs available on campus. License preparation in aviation, nursing, occupational therapy, paramedic, physical therapy, real estate. **Credit/placement by examination:** AP, CLEP, institutional tests. 18 credit hours maximum toward associate degree. **Support services:** GED preparation and test center, learning center, pre-admission summer program, reduced course load, remedial instruction, study skills assistance, tutoring, writing center.

Majors. Agriculture: Horticultural science. **Architecture:** Interior. **Biology:** General, biotechnology. **Business:** Accounting technology, administrative services, business admin, executive assistant, hotel/motel admin, human resources, logistics, operations, real estate, restaurant/food services, travel services. **Communications:** General, digital media. **Computer sciences:** Information systems. **Construction:** Lineworker. **Education:** General, special. **Engineering:** General, mechanical. **Engineering technology:** Biomedical, computer, construction, drafting, electrical, industrial, manufacturing, mechanical. **Family/consumer sciences:** Aging. **Health:** Medical assistant, medical records technology, nursing (RN), occupational therapy assistant, physical therapy assistant, respiratory therapy technology, veterinary technology/assistant. **Legal studies:** Legal secretary, paralegal. **Liberal arts:** Arts/sciences, humanities. **Math:** General. **Mechanic/repair:** Avionics, heating/ac/refrig. **Parks/recreation:** Sports admin. **Personal/culinary services:** Chef training. **Physical sciences:** General. **Production:** Welding. **Protective services:** Forensics, law enforcement admin, police science. **Psychology:** General. **Public administration:** Social work. **Social sciences:** General. **Transportation:** Airline/commercial pilot, aviation management. **Visual/performing arts:** Art, commercial/advertising art, fashion design.

Most popular majors. Business/marketing 17%, computer/information sciences 7%, education 12%, engineering/engineering technologies 12%, health sciences 18%, liberal arts 16%, security/protective services 7%.

Computing on campus. 894 workstations in library, computer center. Commuter students can connect to campus network. Online course registration, online library, wireless network available.

Student life. Freshman orientation: Available. Morning or afternoon sessions at 3 separate campuses 1 week before classes. Lasts about 2 hours. **Policies:** Must follow student bill of rights and responsibilities. Freshmen permitted cars on campus. **Activities:** Choral groups, drama, literary magazine, radio station, student government, Campus Christian Fellowship, multicultural student association, political society, justice society, returning adult program, entertainment club.

Athletics. NJCAA. **Intercollegiate:** Baseball, basketball, cheerleading, golf, soccer M, softball W, volleyball W. **Intramural:** Baseball, basketball, bowling, field hockey W, football (non-tackle), golf, racquetball, soccer, softball, table tennis, tennis, track and field M, volleyball, weight lifting. **Team name:** Cougars.

Student services. Adult student services, career counseling, services for economically disadvantaged, student employment services, financial aid counseling, minority student services, on-campus daycare, personal counseling, placement for graduates, veterans' counselor. **Physically disabled:** Services for visually, speech, hearing impaired. **Transfer:** Pre-admission transcript evaluation for new students. Transfer adviser, college fairs on campus for students transferring to 4-year colleges.

Contact. E-mail: admissions@lccc.edu
Phone: (610) 799-1171 Toll-free number: (800) 414-3975
Fax: (610) 799-1629
Jay Wilt, Associate Dean of Enrollment, Lehigh Carbon Community College, 4525 Education Park Drive, Schnecksville, PA 18078

Lehigh Valley College

Center Valley, Pennsylvania
www.lehighvalley.edu **CB code: 3271**

- For-profit 2-year business and technical college
- Commuter campus in small city
- Interview required

General. Accredited by ACICS. **Enrollment:** 1,236 degree-seeking undergraduates. **Degrees:** 414 associate awarded. **Location:** 60 miles from Philadelphia, 80 miles from New York City. **Calendar:** Quarter. **Full-time faculty:** 42 total. **Part-time faculty:** 46 total. **Special facilities:** All classes taught utilizing wireless network.

Student profile.

Out-of-state:	1%	25 or older:	45%

Transfer out. Colleges most students transferred to 2005: DeSale University, Collins College, Pierce College, Deleware Valley College.

Basis for selection. Open admission. Foreign students with TOEFL score under 450 must take entrance exam. ACT is accepted for placement out of the school placement exam. **Homeschooled:** Applicants must have received diploma from PA approved agency. **Learning Disabled:** Students with learning disabilities should meet with a student service coordinator prior to enrollment, to ensure that their requirements can be met.

2005-2006 Annual costs. Tuition varies from $26,280 to $29,520 depending on program. Fees vary by program. Books/supplies: $3,600. Personal expenses: $1,596.

Financial aid. Need-based: Need-based aid available for part-time students. Work study available nights, weekends and for part-time students.

Application procedures. Admission: No deadline. $20 fee. Application may be submitted online. **Financial aid:** No deadline. FAFSA, institutional form required. Applicants notified on a rolling basis.

Academics. Special study options: Distance learning, internships, liberal arts/career combination, study abroad. **Credit/placement by examination:** CLEP, institutional tests. 45 credit hours maximum toward associate degree. **Support services:** Reduced course load, study skills assistance, tutoring, writing center.

Majors. Business: Accounting, administrative services, business admin, hospitality/recreation, hotel/motel admin, tourism promotion, tourism/travel, travel services. **Computer sciences:** Applications programming, LAN/WAN management, networking, web page design, webmaster. **Education:** Early childhood. **Health:** Medical secretary. **Legal studies:** Paralegal. **Protective services:** Criminal justice. **Visual/performing arts:** Design, photography.

Most popular majors. Business/marketing 30%, computer/information sciences 15%, health sciences 12%, legal studies 30%, visual/performing arts 12%.

Computing on campus. PC or laptop required. 50 workstations in library, computer center. Commuter students can connect to campus network. Online library, repair service, wireless network available.

Student life. Freshman orientation: Mandatory. Preregistration for classes offered. Half-day session week before classes start, to pick up schedules and books, complete required paperwork, and prepare for class. **Policies:** Freshmen permitted cars on campus. **Housing:** Housing is available through outside service.

Student services. Adult student services, career counseling, student employment services, financial aid counseling, placement for graduates. **Transfer:** Pre-admission transcript evaluation for new students.

Contact. Phone: (610) 791-5100
Michael Venier, Vice President of Marketing & Admissions, Lehigh Valley College, 2809 East Saucon Valley Road, Center Valley, PA 18034

Lincoln Technical Institute

Allentown, Pennsylvania
www.lincolntech.com **CB code: 2741**

- Public 2-year technical college
- Commuter campus in small city
- Interview required

General. Founded in 1946. Accredited by ACCSCT. **Enrollment:** 504 undergraduates. **Degrees:** 96 associate awarded. **Location:** 60 miles from Philadelphia. **Calendar:** Semester.

Basis for selection. Open admission.

2005-2006 Annual costs. Total program costs range from $11,025 to $26,650. Cost of books is included in tuition.

Application procedures. **Admission:** No deadline. $25 fee, may be waived for applicants with need. **Financial aid:** No deadline.

Academics. **Credit/placement by examination:** AP, CLEP.

Majors. **Engineering technology:** Drafting, electrical.

Student life. **Freshman orientation:** Mandatory. **Policies:** Freshmen permitted cars on campus. **Housing:** Substance-free housing available. **Activities:** TV station.

Contact. Phone: (610) 398-5300 Fax: (610) 395-2706
Craig Avery, Director of Admissions, Lincoln Technical Institute , 5151 Tilghman Street, Allentown, PA 18104

Lincoln Technical Institute: Philadelphia
Philadelphia, Pennsylvania
www.lincolntech.com **CB code: 9010**

- For-profit 2-year technical college
- Very large city

General. Accredited by ACCSCT. **Enrollment:** 650 undergraduates. **Degrees:** 238 associate awarded. **Calendar:** Quarter. **Full-time faculty:** 20 total.

Basis for selection. Open admission.

2005-2006 Annual costs. Tuition ranges from $9,555 to $23,714 for full programs. Cost of books and tools included in tuition.

Academics. **Credit/placement by examination:** CLEP.

Majors. **Mechanic/repair:** General.

Contact. E-mail: dcunningham@lincolntech.com
Phone: (215) 335-0800
Donald Cunningham, Director of Admissions, Lincoln Technical Institute: Philadelphia, 9191 Torresdale Avenue, Philadelphia, PA 19136

Luzerne County Community College
Nanticoke, Pennsylvania
www.luzerne.edu **CB code: 2382**

- Public 2-year community college
- Commuter campus in large town

General. Founded in 1966. Regionally accredited. **Enrollment:** 6,144 degree-seeking undergraduates. **Degrees:** 754 associate awarded. **ROTC:** Air Force. **Location:** 8 miles from Wilkes-Barre. **Calendar:** Semester, extensive summer session. **Full-time faculty:** 130 total. **Part-time faculty:** 390 total.

Student profile. Among degree-seeking undergraduates, 53% enrolled in a transfer program, 47% enrolled in a vocational program, 4% already have a bachelor's degree or higher.

African American:	2%	Hispanic American:	2%
Asian American:	1%	25 or older:	39%

Transfer out. **Colleges most students transferred to 2005:** Bloomsburg University, Wilkes University, King's College, College Misericordia.

Basis for selection. Open admission, but selective for some programs. High school record and test scores considered for admission to health sciences programs. Nurse Entrance Test required of nursing applicants. Interview recommended for health sciences program. **Learning Disabled:** Comprehensive services for special needs students at no cost providing the students present the required documentation.

High school preparation. One algebra, 1 chemistry, 1 biology required of nursing, respiratory therapy, and dental hygiene applicants.

2005-2006 Annual costs. Tuition/fees: $2,760; $5,340 out-of-district; $7,920 out-of-state. Per-credit charge: $76 in-district; $152 out-of-district; $228 out-of-state. Books/supplies: $800.

Financial aid. **Need-based:** Need-based aid available for part-time students.

Application procedures. **Admission:** No deadline. $40 fee. Admission notification on a rolling basis. **Financial aid:** Priority date 4/15; no closing date. FAFSA, institutional form required. Applicants notified on a rolling basis starting 7/1.

Academics. **Special study options:** Cooperative education, distance learning, ESL, external degree, honors, independent study, internships, liberal arts/career combination, weekend college. **Credit/placement by examination:** AP, CLEP, institutional tests. 30 credit hours maximum toward associate degree. **Support services:** GED preparation, learning center, preadmission summer program, reduced course load, remedial instruction, study skills assistance, tutoring, writing center.

Majors. **Agriculture:** Horticulture, landscaping. **Business:** Accounting, accounting technology, administrative services, banking/financial services, business admin, international, management information systems, real estate, tourism promotion. **Communications:** Journalism. **Communications technology:** Computer typography, radio/tv, recording arts. **Computer sciences:** General. **Construction:** Electrician, maintenance. **Education:** General. **Engineering technology:** Architectural drafting, automotive, computer systems, drafting, electrical, mechanical. **Health:** Dental hygiene, EMT paramedic, mental health services, nursing (RN), office admin, prepharmacy, respiratory therapy technology, surgical technology. **Interdisciplinary:** Biological/physical sciences. **Legal studies:** Court reporting, paralegal. **Liberal arts:** Arts/sciences, humanities. **Math:** General. **Mechanic/repair:** Automotive, heating/ac/refrig. **Personal/culinary services:** Institutional food service, mortuary science. **Protective services:** Fire safety technology, police science. **Social sciences:** General. **Transportation:** Airline/commercial pilot, aviation management. **Visual/performing arts:** Commercial/advertising art.

Most popular majors. Business/marketing 15%, engineering/engineering technologies 6%, health sciences 29%, liberal arts 11%, security/protective services 7%, visual/performing arts 6%.

Computing on campus. 150 workstations in library, computer center, student center. Online course registration, online library, helpline, repair service, wireless network available.

Student life. **Freshman orientation:** Mandatory. Preregistration for classes offered. **Activities:** Drama, literary magazine, radio station, student government, student newspaper, TV station, Circle K, Brothers and Sisters in Christ.

Athletics. NJCAA. **Intercollegiate:** Baseball M, basketball, cross-country, golf, softball W, volleyball W. **Intramural:** Badminton, basketball, fencing, football (non-tackle), volleyball. **Team name:** Trailblazers.

Student services. Adult student services, career counseling, student employment services, health services, personal counseling, placement for graduates, veterans' counselor. **Transfer:** Special adviser, orientation for new students. Transfer adviser, college fairs on campus for students transferring to 4-year colleges.

Contact. E-mail: admissions@luzerne.edu
Phone: (570) 740-0337 Fax: (570) 740-0238
Francis Curry, Director of Admissions, Luzerne County Community College, 1333 South Prospect Street, Nanticoke, PA 18634-9804

Manor College
Jenkintown, Pennsylvania
www.manor.edu **CB code: 2260**

- Private 2-year junior college affiliated with Ukrainian Catholic Church
- Commuter campus in small town
- SAT or ACT (ACT writing recommended), interview required

General. Founded in 1947. Regionally accredited. **Enrollment:** 738 degree-seeking undergraduates; 64 non-degree-seeking students. **Degrees:** 129 associate awarded. **Location:** 15 miles from downtown Philadelphia. **Calendar:** Semester, limited summer session. **Full-time faculty:** 23 total; 17% have terminal degrees, 78% women. **Part-time faculty:** 98 total; 36% have terminal degrees, 3% minority, 57% women. **Class size:** 73% < 20, 27% 20-39. **Special facilities:** Ukrainian Heritage Studies Center and Museum, dental health center, law library, veterinary technology radiology lab, surgical suite.

Student profile. Among degree-seeking undergraduates, 63% enrolled in a transfer program, 37% enrolled in a vocational program, 2% already have

Two-Year Colleges

a bachelor's degree or higher, 183 enrolled as first-time, first-year students, 106 transferred in from other institutions.

Part-time:	39%	**Asian American:**	1%
Out-of-state:	3%	**Hispanic American:**	5%
Women:	83%	**International:**	1%
African American:	15%	**Live on campus:**	8%

Transfer out. 97% of students enrolled in the transfer program go on to 4-year colleges. **Colleges most students transferred to 2005:** Holy Family University, LaSalle University, Temple University, Drexel University, Thomas Jefferson University.

Basis for selection. Class rank, high school GPA, high school course selection, recommendation of counselor or teacher, SAT or ACT scores, interview with admissions counselor. Institutional entrance test required of all applicants except those holding bachelor's degree. **Adult students:** Entrance exam policies same as for first-time freshmen. SAT/ACT scores not required if applicant over 21. **Homeschooled:** Statement describing homeschool structure and mission, state high school equivalency certificate required. **Learning Disabled:** No learning disabilities-specific courses or programs; IEP required for all, with diagnosed disability.

High school preparation. 16 units required. Required and recommended units include English 4, mathematics 2, social studies 2, science 1-2 (laboratory 1-2) and academic electives 6. Biology with laboratory, chemistry with laboratory, 3 mathematics courses required of all allied health science applicants.

2005-2006 Annual costs. Tuition/fees: $10,900. Per-credit charge: $229. Tuition for allied health program $10,960 per year, $325 per credit hour. Room/board: $5,096. Books/supplies: $564. Personal expenses: $787.

2005-2006 Financial aid. All financial aid based on need. 145 full-time freshmen applied for aid; 121 were judged to have need; 121 of these received aid. Average need met was 40%. Average scholarship/grant was $4,751; average loan $2,625. 57% of total undergraduate aid awarded as scholarships/grants, 43% as loans/jobs. Need-based aid available for part-time students. Work study available nights, weekends and for part-time students.

Application procedures. Admission: Closing date 9/1 (postmark date). $25 fee, may be waived for applicants with need. Application may be submitted online. Admission notification on a rolling basis beginning on or about 10/15. Must reply by May 1 or within 2 week(s) if notified thereafter. **Financial aid:** Priority date 5/1; no closing date. FAFSA, institutional form required. Applicants notified on a rolling basis starting 3/1; must reply within 2 week(s) of notification.

Academics. Special study options: Accelerated study, cross-registration, distance learning, double major, dual enrollment of high school students, ESL, honors, independent study, internships. License preparation in real estate. **Credit/placement by examination:** AP, CLEP, institutional tests. 30 credit hours maximum toward associate degree. **Support services:** GED preparation, learning center, pre-admission summer program, reduced course load, remedial instruction, study skills assistance, tutoring, writing center.

Majors. Business: General, accounting, business admin, human resources, international, marketing. **Communications:** General. **Computer sciences:** Applications programming. **Education:** Early childhood, elementary. **Health:** Dental assistant, dental hygiene, health services, prenursing, preveterinary, veterinary technology/assistant. **Legal studies:** Paralegal. **Liberal arts:** Arts/sciences. **Psychology:** General. **Theology:** Religious ed.

Most popular majors. Business/marketing 16%, education 6%, health sciences 42%, legal studies 10%, liberal arts 14%, psychology 6%.

Computing on campus. 111 workstations in dormitories, library, computer center. Dormitories wired for high-speed internet access and linked to campus network. Commuter students can connect to campus network. Online library, wireless network available.

Student life. Freshman orientation: Mandatory, $25 fee. Four 1-day orientations held annually in January, June, and August; includes testing. **Policies:** Alcohol and drug policy reinforced. Freshmen permitted cars on campus. **Housing:** Guaranteed on-campus for all undergraduates. Coed dorms, substance-free housing available. $100 fully refundable deposit. Housing arranged within local community for foreign and out-of-state students when necessary. **Activities:** Dance, drama, film society, literary magazine, music ensembles, student government, international students club, students united for nature, campus ministry, black student club, community outreach program, Ukrainian club, ROTARACT, French language club, music ministry, student senate.

Athletics. Intercollegiate: Basketball, soccer. **Team name:** Blue Jays.

Student services. Adult student services, alcohol/substance abuse counseling, campus ministries, career counseling, student employment services, financial aid counseling, health services, personal counseling, placement for graduates, women's services. **Transfer:** Special adviser, orientation, pre-admission transcript evaluation for new students. Transfer center, transfer adviser, college fairs on campus for students transferring to 4-year colleges.

Contact. E-mail: ftadmiss@manor.edu
Phone: (215) 884-2216 Fax: (215) 576-6564
I. Czenstuch, Vice President for Enrollment Management, Manor College, 700 Fox Chase Road, Jenkintown, PA 19046-3319

McCann School of Business: Hazleton

Hazleton, Pennsylvania
www.mccannschool.com **CB code: 3887**

- For-profit 2-year business college
- Commuter campus in small town

General. Founded in 1897. Accredited by ACICS. **Location:** 20 miles from Hazleton. **Calendar:** Quarter.

Annual costs/financial aid. Tuition/fees (2005-2006): $8,485. Books/supplies: $900. Personal expenses: $1,600.

Contact. Phone: (570) 454-6172
Director of Admissions, 14 Maplewood Drive, Hazleton, PA 18202

McCann School of Business: Pottsville

Pottsville, Pennsylvania
www.mccannschool.edu **CB code: 3296**

- For-profit 2-year branch campus and technical college
- Small town

General. Accredited by ACICS. **Enrollment:** 400 undergraduates. **Degrees:** 190 associate awarded. **Calendar:** Quarter. **Full-time faculty:** 8 total. **Part-time faculty:** 25 total.

Basis for selection. Open admission.

2005-2006 Annual costs. Tuition/fees: $8,485. Per-credit charge: $186.

Application procedures. Admission: No deadline. $40 fee.

Academics. Credit/placement by examination: CLEP.

Majors. Business: Accounting, administrative services, business admin. **Computer sciences:** General. **Legal studies:** Paralegal.

Contact. E-mail: lmw@mccannschool.edu
Phone: (570) 622-7622 Fax: (570) 622-7770
Linda Walinsky, Interim Director, McCann School of Business: Pottsville, 2650 Woodglen Road, Pottsville, PA 17901

McCann School of Business: Sunbury

Sunbury, Pennsylvania
www.mccannschool.com **CB code: 3298**

- For-profit 2-year branch campus and technical college
- Small town

General. Accredited by ACICS. **Calendar:** Quarter.

Annual costs/financial aid. Tuition/fees (2005-2006): $8,485.

Contact. Phone: (570) 286-3058
Lead Admissions Representative, 1147 North 4th Street, Sunbury, PA 17801

Metropolitan Career Center

Philadelphia, Pennsylvania
www.mccweb-gt.org **CB code: 3065**

- Private 2-year technical college
- Commuter campus in very large city
- Interview required

General. Accredited by ACCSCT. **Enrollment:** 135 undergraduates. **Calendar:** Semester. **Full-time faculty:** 7 total. **Part-time faculty:** 6 total.

Transfer out. **Colleges most students transferred to 2005:** University of Phoenix.

Basis for selection. Open admission. Applicants 18 years or older (or with an official dropout slip from high school) must have high school diploma or GED, score at least 9.0 in both verbal and quantitative on standardized achievement test. ELPT not required.

High school preparation. Students must have a high school diploma or GED.

2005-2006 Annual costs. Tuition/fees: $8,494. Per-credit charge: $274. Books and supplies included in cost of tuition. Personal expenses: $1,890.

Financial aid. Need-based: Need-based aid available for part-time students.

Application procedures. Admission: No deadline. No application fee. Application may be submitted online. Admission notification on a rolling basis. **Financial aid:** FAFSA required.

Academics. Credit/placement by examination: CLEP. **Support services:** GED preparation, study skills assistance, tutoring.

Majors. Business: Business admin.

Student services. Career counseling, services for economically disadvantaged, student employment services. **Transfer:** Special adviser, orientation for new students.

Contact. E-mail: admissions@mcc2000.org
Phone: (215) 568-9218 Fax: (215) 568-3511
Don Cave, Director of Admission, Metropolitan Career Center, 100 South Broad Street, Suite 830, Philadelphia, PA 19110

Metropolitan Career Center Computer Technology Institute

Philadelphia, Pennsylvania
www.mccweb-gt.org

- Private 2-year technical college
- Very large city

General. Accredited by ACCSCT. **Enrollment:** 150 degree-seeking undergraduates. **Degrees:** 60 associate awarded. **Calendar:** Continuous. **Full-time faculty:** 4 total. **Part-time faculty:** 2 total.

Basis for selection. Applicants 18 years or older (or with an official dropout slip from high school) must have high school diploma or GED, score at least 9.0 in both verbal and quantitative on standardized achievement test.

2005-2006 Annual costs. Per-credit charge: $274. Full program cost is $16,988, and includes all fees, books and supplies.

Academics. Credit/placement by examination: CLEP.

Majors. Computer sciences: Programming.

Contact. Phone: (215) 568-9215 Fax: (215) 568-3511
Mario Verden, Admissions Director, Metropolitan Career Center Computer Technology Institute, 100 South Broad Street, Suite 830, Philadelphia, PA 19110

Montgomery County Community College

Blue Bell, Pennsylvania **CB member**
www.mc3.edu **CB code: 2445**

- Public 2-year community college
- Commuter campus in large town

General. Founded in 1964. Regionally accredited. Campus in Pottstown serves students in western part of the county. Several off-campus sites: Lansdale, Willow Grove Naval Air Station. **Enrollment:** 10,874 degree-seeking undergraduates. **Degrees:** 965 associate awarded. **Location:** 20 miles from Philadelphia. **Calendar:** Semester, extensive summer session. **Full-time faculty:** 167 total; 6% minority, 54% women. **Part-time faculty:** 497 total; 8% minority, 51% women. **Class size:** 65% < 20, 35% 20-39. **Special facilities:** Dental hygiene clinic.

Student profile. Among degree-seeking undergraduates, 62% enrolled in a transfer program, 38% enrolled in a vocational program, 3,676 enrolled as first-time, first-year students, 297 transferred in from other institutions.

Part-time:	56%	**Asian American:**	6%
Out-of-state:	1%	**Hispanic American:**	3%
Women:	59%	**International:**	1%
African American:	9%	**25 or older:**	38%

Transfer out. 68% of students enrolled in the transfer program go on to 4-year colleges. **Colleges most students transferred to 2005:** Temple University, Gwynedd Mercy College, West Chester University, Penn State.

Basis for selection. Open admission, but selective for some programs. Special requirements for allied health and automotive technology programs. County residents given priority. High school transcript required for students less than 5 years out of high school. Exemption from placement testing: SAT Math score 550 or above, exempt from math placement test; SAT Verbal score 500 or above, exempt from reading placement test. ACT or SAT required for allied health applicants; report score by August 1. **Adult students:** Entrance exam policies same as for first-time freshmen. SAT/ACT scores not required. **Homeschooled:** Transcript of courses and grades required. Must provide approved curriculum and portfolio. **Learning Disabled:** Recommend meeting with Director of Services for Students with Disabilities. Require current documentation from students of accommodations needed.

High school preparation. Biology, chemistry, and algebra required of nursing and medical laboratory technician applicants, chemistry of dental hygiene applicants.

2006-2007 Annual costs. Tuition/fees (projected): $2,910; $5,430 out-of-district; $7,950 out-of-state. Per-credit charge: $84 in-district; $168 out-of-district; $252 out-of-state. Required fees for out-of-county students $690; for out-of-state $990. Books/supplies: $980. Personal expenses: $1,040.

2004-2005 Financial aid. Need-based: 837 full-time freshmen applied for aid; 551 were judged to have need; 431 of these received aid. Average need met was 18%. Average scholarship/grant was $1,747; average loan $1,257. 64% of total undergraduate aid awarded as scholarships/grants, 36% as loans/jobs. Need-based aid available for part-time students. Work study available nights, weekends and for part-time students. **Non-need-based:** Awarded to 477 full-time undergraduates, including 191 freshmen. Scholarships awarded for academics.

Application procedures. Admission: No deadline. $25 fee, may be waived for applicants with need. Application may be submitted online. Admission notification on a rolling basis. **Financial aid:** Closing date 5/1. FAFSA required. Applicants notified on a rolling basis starting 2/1.

Academics. Special study options: Accelerated study, cooperative education, distance learning, dual enrollment of high school students, ESL, honors, independent study, internships, student-designed major, study abroad, teacher certification program, weekend college. Chef apprenticeship with food and pastry options. License preparation in dental hygiene, nursing, radiology, real estate. **Credit/placement by examination:** AP, CLEP, institutional tests. 30 credit hours maximum toward associate degree. **Support services:** Learning center, reduced course load, remedial instruction, study skills assistance, tutoring.

Majors. Biology: General, biotechnology. **Business:** General, accounting, accounting technology, administrative services, business admin, communications, hospitality/recreation, management information systems, real estate, sales/distribution, travel services. **Communications:** General. **Computer sciences:** General, information systems, programming. **Education:** Elementary, physical, secondary, teacher assistance. **Engineering:** Science. **Engineering technology:** General, automotive, drafting. **Family/consumer sciences:** Child care. **Health:** Clinical lab technology, dental hygiene, medical radiologic technology/radiation therapy, mental health services, nursing (RN), surgical technology. **Liberal arts:** Arts/sciences, humanities. **Math:** General. **Personal/culinary services:** Baking, chef training. **Physical sciences:** General. **Protective services:** Fire safety technology, police science, security services. **Social sciences:** General. **Visual/performing arts:** Art, commercial/advertising art.

Most popular majors. Business/marketing 16%, education 6%, health sciences 18%, liberal arts 40%.

Computing on campus. PC or laptop required. 758 workstations in library, student center. Commuter students can connect to campus network. Online course registration, online library, helpline, wireless network available.

Student life. Freshman orientation: Available. Preregistration for classes offered. One-day, a week before semester starts. **Policies:** Freshmen permitted cars on campus. **Activities:** Jazz band, choral groups, dance, drama, film society, literary magazine, music ensembles, radio station, student government, student newspaper, TV station, African-American club, Asian club, environmental club, writers' club, Meridian club, animal rights club, Christian fellowship club, diversity club, Latino club, Pride club.

Athletics. Intramural: Badminton, baseball M, basketball, bowling, cross-country, football (non-tackle) M, judo, racquetball, soccer, softball, table tennis, tennis, volleyball, weight lifting. **Team name:** Mustangs.

Student services. Career counseling, student employment services, financial aid counseling, health services, minority student services, on-campus daycare, personal counseling, placement for graduates, veterans' counselor. **Physically disabled:** Services for visually, speech, hearing impaired. **Transfer:** Special adviser, orientation, pre-admission transcript evaluation for new students. Transfer center, transfer adviser, college fairs on campus for students transferring to 4-year colleges.

Contact. E-mail: admissionsregistration@mc3.edu
Phone: (215) 641-6551 Fax: (215) 641-6681
Erick Hyde, Assistant Director of Admissions, Montgomery County Community College, 340 DeKalb Pike, Blue Bell, PA 19422

New Castle School of Trades

Pulaski, Pennsylvania
www.ncstrades.com **CB code: 2404**

- For-profit 2-year technical college
- Commuter campus in rural community
- Interview required

General. Accredited by ACCSCT. **Enrollment:** 364 degree-seeking undergraduates. **Degrees:** 246 associate awarded. **Calendar:** Differs by program. **Full-time faculty:** 20 total. **Part-time faculty:** 15 total.

2006-2007 Annual costs. Tuition/fees (projected): $14,280. Figure given, which is an average cost of all programs, is for school's entire 15-month course of study. Books/supplies: $1,000.

2004-2005 Financial aid. Need-based: 43% of total undergraduate aid awarded as scholarships/grants, 57% as loans/jobs. Need-based aid available for part-time students.

Application procedures. Admission: No deadline. $25 fee. Admission notification on a rolling basis.

Academics. Credit/placement by examination: CLEP. **Support services:** Study skills assistance, tutoring.

Majors. Engineering technology: Construction, electrical. **Mechanic/repair:** Automotive.

Student life. Freshman orientation: Available. Preregistration for classes offered.

Student services. Career counseling, financial aid counseling, personal counseling, placement for graduates.

Contact. E-mail: ncstrades@aol.com
Phone: (724) 964-8811 Toll-free number: (800) 837-8299
Fax: (724) 964-8177
Jim Catheline, Director of Admissions, New Castle School of Trades, 4164 US 422, Pulaski, PA 16143-9721

Newport Business Institute

Lower Burrell, Pennsylvania
www.newportbusiness.com **CB code: 2413**

- Private 2-year business college
- Commuter campus in small town
- Interview required

General. Accredited by ACICS. **Enrollment:** 90 undergraduates. **Degrees:** 50 associate awarded. **Location:** 15 miles from Pittsburgh. **Calendar:** Quarter. **Full-time faculty:** 8 total. **Special facilities:** All students receive a laptop to use while enrolled. **Partnerships:** Formal partnerships with Microsoft Testing Center, Prometrics Testing Center.

Basis for selection. Open admission.

2005-2006 Annual costs. Tuition/fees: $8,700. Books/supplies: $825.

Financial aid. Need-based: Need-based aid available for part-time students. **Non-need-based:** Scholarships awarded for academics, leadership.

Application procedures. Admission: No deadline. $25 fee. Admission notification on a rolling basis. **Financial aid:** Closing date 5/1. FAFSA required. Applicants notified on a rolling basis starting 5/1.

Academics. Special study options: Liberal arts/career combination. Bachelor's degree programs available on campus. **Credit/placement by examination:** CLEP. **Support services:** Tutoring.

Majors. Business: Accounting, accounting technology, accounting/business management, administrative services, business admin, customer service, executive assistant, hospitality admin, hospitality/recreation, hotel/motel admin, office technology, office/clerical, receptionist, resort management, retailing, small business admin, tourism/travel, travel services. **Computer sciences:** Data entry, data processing, database management, web page design, word processing. **Health:** Insurance coding, insurance specialist, medical records admin, medical secretary, medical transcription, office admin, office assistant, office computer specialist, receptionist. **Visual/performing arts:** Music.

Most popular majors. Business/marketing 60%, computer/information sciences 34%, health sciences 16%.

Computing on campus. PC or laptop required. 2 workstations in computer center. Helpline, repair service, wireless network available.

Student life. Freshman orientation: Mandatory. Preregistration for classes offered.

Student services. Adult student services, career counseling, student employment services, financial aid counseling, placement for graduates. **Transfer:** Special adviser, orientation, pre-admission transcript evaluation for new students.

Contact. E-mail: admissions1@newportbusiness.com
Phone: (724) 339-7542 Toll-free number: (800) 752-7695
Fax: (724) 339-2950
Tara Pomatto, Director of Admissions, Newport Business Institute, 945 Greensburg Road, Lower Burrell, PA 15068

Newport Business Institute

Williamsport, Pennsylvania
www.newportbusiness.com **CB code: 2551**

- For-profit 2-year business college
- Commuter campus in small city
- Interview required

General. Accredited by ACICS. **Enrollment:** 103 degree-seeking undergraduates. **Degrees:** 54 associate awarded. **Calendar:** Quarter. **Full-time faculty:** 6 total; 67% women. **Part-time faculty:** 1 total; 100% women.

Student profile. Among degree-seeking undergraduates, 36 enrolled as first-time, first-year students, 8 transferred in from other institutions.

Women:	85%	**Asian American:**	1%
African American:	7%		

Basis for selection. Open admission. Interview important.

2006-2007 Annual costs. Tuition/fees: $9,300. Per-credit charge: $197. Books/supplies: $900.

Application procedures. Admission: No deadline. $25 fee. Application may be submitted online. Admission notification on a rolling basis. **Financial aid:** No deadline. FAFSA required.

Academics. Special study options: Internships. **Credit/placement by examination:** CLEP.

Majors. Business: Business admin, executive assistant. **Health:** Medical secretary. **Legal studies:** Legal secretary.

Most popular majors. Business/marketing 46%, health sciences 30%, legal studies 15%.

Student life. Freshman orientation: Mandatory.

Student services. Financial aid counseling, personal counseling, placement for graduates. **Transfer:** Special adviser, orientation, pre-admission transcript evaluation for new students.

Contact. E-mail: admissions_nbi@suscom.net
Phone: (570) 326-2869 Fax: (570) 326-2136
Mary Weaver, Director, Newport Business Institute, 941 West Third Street, Williamsport, PA 17701

North Central Industrial Technical Education Center

Ridgway, Pennsylvania
www.ncitec.edu

- For-profit 2-year technical college
- Small town

General. Accredited by ACCSCT. **Enrollment:** 22 undergraduates. **Degrees:** 4 associate awarded. **Calendar:** Continuous. **Full-time faculty:** 6 total. **Part-time faculty:** 4 total.

Basis for selection. Student must pass institutional entrance exam.

Application procedures. Admission: No deadline. $50 fee. Admission notification on a rolling basis. **Financial aid:** No deadline.

Academics. Credit/placement by examination: CLEP.

Contact. E-mail: jnelson@ncentral.com
Phone: (814) 772-1012
Jim Nelson, Director, North Central Industrial Technical Education Center, 653 Montmorenci Avenue, Ridgway, PA 15853-1554

Northampton County Area Community College

Bethlehem, Pennsylvania **CB member**
www.northampton.edu **CB code: 2573**

- Public 2-year community college
- Commuter campus in small city

General. Founded in 1966. Regionally accredited. Distance education for students who cannot attend classes regularly. Branch campus at Monroe County. Off-campus sites downtown at Lehigh Valley Industrial Park IV and in Pike County. Individualized transfer study program. **Enrollment:** 8,563 degree-seeking undergraduates; 191 non-degree-seeking students. **Degrees:** 792 associate awarded. **Location:** 60 miles from Philadelphia, 90 miles from New York City. **Calendar:** Semester, limited summer session. **Full-time faculty:** 106 total; 38% have terminal degrees, 13% minority, 54% women. **Part-time faculty:** 436 total; 18% have terminal degrees, 5% minority, 52% women. **Special facilities:** Electrotechnology applications center. **Partnerships:** Tech Prep; partnerships with General Motors, and Daimler Chrysler.

Student profile. Among degree-seeking undergraduates, 63% enrolled in a transfer program, 37% enrolled in a vocational program, 2% already have a bachelor's degree or higher, 2,714 enrolled as first-time, first-year students, 841 transferred in from other institutions.

Part-time:	57%	**Hispanic American:**	10%
Out-of-state:	3%	**International:**	1%
Women:	63%	**25 or older:**	41%
African American:	7%	**Live on campus:**	3%
Asian American:	2%		

Transfer out. 72% of students enrolled in the transfer program go on to 4-year colleges. **Colleges most students transferred to 2005:** DeSales University, East Stroudsburg University, Kutztown University, Moravian College, Cedar Crest College.

Basis for selection. Open admission, but selective for some programs. Special requirements for allied health, veterinary technician, and culinary arts programs. Non-native speakers of English take additional placement test. All students applying for admission into certificate or degree programs must take placement tests in reading and writing before they register; must take placement test in mathematics before registering for 18th credit applicable to degree or certificate. Interview required for radiography, veterinary technology, and diagnostic medical sonography programs; portfolio required for communication design, fine arts programs; audition required for theater program. **Adult students:** Entrance exam policies same as for first-time freshmen.

High school preparation. Biology, chemistry, and algebra requirements for allied health, veterinary technician, and culinary arts programs.

2005-2006 Annual costs. Tuition/fees: $2,820; $4,920 out-of-district; $7,020 out-of-state. Per-credit charge: $70 in-district; $140 out-of-district; $210 out-of-state. Out-of-district students pay $60 fee per credit hour; out-of-state students pay $87 fee per credit hour. Room/board: $5,944. Books/supplies: $1,000. Personal expenses: $2,100.

2005-2006 Financial aid. Need-based: 69% of total undergraduate aid awarded as scholarships/grants, 31% as loans/jobs. Need-based aid available for part-time students. Work study available nights, weekends and for part-time students. **Non-need-based:** Scholarships awarded for academics, alumni affiliation, art, leadership, minority status, music/drama.

Application procedures. Admission: No deadline. $25 fee, may be waived for applicants with need. Application may be submitted online. Admission notification on a rolling basis. **Financial aid:** Closing date 3/31. FAFSA, institutional form required. Applicants notified on a rolling basis starting 6/1; must reply within 2 week(s) of notification.

Academics. Special study options: Accelerated study, combined bachelor's/graduate degree, cooperative education, distance learning, double major, dual enrollment of high school students, ESL, honors, internships, student-designed major, study abroad, teacher certification program. Bachelor's degree programs available on campus. License preparation in dental hygiene, nursing, radiology, real estate. **Credit/placement by examination:** AP, CLEP, institutional tests. 30 credit hours maximum toward associate degree. **Support services:** GED preparation, learning center, reduced course load, remedial instruction, study skills assistance, tutoring, writing center.

Majors. Biology: General, biotechnology. **Business:** General, accounting technology, administrative services, business admin, hotel/motel admin, restaurant/food services. **Communications:** General, journalism. **Communications technology:** Radio/tv. **Computer sciences:** Computer science, networking, programming, security. **Construction:** Electrician. **Education:** General, teacher assistance. **Engineering:** General. **Engineering technology:** Architectural, CAD/CADD, electrical, electromechanical, quality control. **Health:** Dental hygiene, medical secretary, nursing (RN), radiologic technology/medical imaging, sonography, surgical technology, veterinary technology/assistant. **Legal studies:** Legal secretary, paralegal. **Liberal arts:** Arts/sciences. **Math:** General. **Mechanic/repair:** Automotive, computer, heating/ac/refrig, industrial electronics. **Parks/recreation:** Sports admin. **Personal/culinary services:** Food prep, mortuary science. **Physical sciences:** Chemistry, physics. **Protective services:** Criminal justice, fire services admin. **Public administration:** Social work. **Science technology:** Chemical. **Visual/performing arts:** Acting, graphic design, interior design, studio arts.

Most popular majors. Business/marketing 14%, education 8%, family/consumer sciences 6%, health sciences 18%, liberal arts 14%, security/protective services 6%, visual/performing arts 6%.

Computing on campus. 1,400 workstations in dormitories, library, computer center, student center. Dormitories wired for high-speed internet access and linked to campus network. Commuter students can connect to campus network. Online course registration, online library, helpline, student web hosting, wireless network available.

Student life. Freshman orientation: Available. Preregistration for classes offered. Held over 2 weeks during the summer. **Policies:** Freshmen permitted cars on campus. **Housing:** Coed dorms, apartments available. $150 fully refundable deposit. **Activities:** Choral groups, drama, literary magazine, music ensembles, radio station, student government, student newspaper.

Athletics. Intercollegiate: Baseball M, basketball, bowling, golf, ice hockey, soccer, softball W, tennis, volleyball, wrestling M. **Intramural:** Basketball, bowling, football (non-tackle), golf, racquetball, soccer, volleyball. **Team name:** Spartans.

Student services. Adult student services, alcohol/substance abuse counseling, career counseling, services for economically disadvantaged, student employment services, financial aid counseling, health services, minority student services, on-campus daycare, personal counseling, placement for graduates, veterans' counselor, women's services. **Physically disabled:** Services for visually, speech, hearing impaired. **Learning disabled:** Comprehensive services available. **Transfer:** Special adviser, orientation, pre-admission transcript evaluation for new students. Transfer center, transfer adviser, college fairs on campus for students transferring to 4-year colleges.

Contact. E-mail: adminfo@northampton.edu
Phone: (610) 861-5500 Fax: (610) 861-4560
James McCarthy, Director of Admissions, Northampton County Area Community College, 3835 Green Pond Road, Bethlehem, PA 18020

Oakbridge Academy of Arts

Lower Burrell, Pennsylvania
www.oakbridgeacademy.com **CB code: 2984**

- Private 2-year visual arts college
- Commuter campus in large town
- Interview required

General. Accredited by ACCSCT. **Enrollment:** 90 undergraduates. **Degrees:** 17 associate awarded. **Location:** 21 miles from Pittsburgh. **Calendar:** Quarter, extensive summer session. **Full-time faculty:** 4 total. **Part-time faculty:** 4 total. **Class size:** 100% < 20.

Basis for selection. Good attendance record required for admission. Portfolio review required for commercial arts program and recommended for photography program.

2005-2006 Annual costs. Tuition/fees: $9,150. Books/supplies: $1,000. Personal expenses: $4,123.

Financial aid. All financial aid based on need. Need-based aid available for part-time students.

Application procedures. Admission: No deadline. $50 fee. Application may be submitted online. Admission notification on a rolling basis. **Financial aid:** Closing date 5/1. FAFSA required. Applicants notified on a rolling basis.

Academics. Special study options: Internships. **Credit/placement by examination:** CLEP.

Majors. Communications: Advertising. **Visual/performing arts:** General, commercial photography, commercial/advertising art, design, drawing, graphic design, painting, photography.

Computing on campus. 40 workstations in computer center.

Student life. Freshman orientation: Mandatory. Preregistration for classes offered. **Policies:** Freshmen permitted cars on campus. **Activities:** Student government.

Student services. Placement for graduates. **Transfer:** Special adviser, orientation for new students.

Contact. E-mail: admissions@oakbridgeacademy.com
Phone: (724) 335-5336 Toll-free number: (800) 734-5601
Fax: (724) 339-2950
Tara Pomatto, Director of Admissions, Oakbridge Academy of Arts, 1250 Greensburg Road, Lower Burrell, PA 15068

Orleans Technical Institute - Center City Campus

Philadelphia, Pennsylvania
www.orleanstech.org **CB code: 3127**

- Private 2-year technical college
- Commuter campus in very large city
- Interview required

General. Accredited by ACCSCT. **Enrollment:** 135 undergraduates. **Degrees:** 11 associate awarded. **Calendar:** Continuous, extensive summer session. **Full-time faculty:** 6 total. **Part-time faculty:** 15 total.

Transfer out. Colleges most students transferred to 2005: Community College of Philadelphia.

Basis for selection. Successful applicants must meet minimum score on admission test administered by school.

2005-2006 Annual costs. Tuition/fees: $7,575. Tuition for full associate program (28 months) $25,750. Books/supplies: $2,000.

Financial aid. Need-based: Need-based aid available for part-time students.

Application procedures. Admission: No deadline. $125 fee. Admission notification on a rolling basis. **Financial aid:** No deadline. FAFSA, institutional form required. Applicants notified on a rolling basis.

Academics. Credit/placement by examination: CLEP, institutional tests.

Majors. Business: Business admin.

Student life. Freshman orientation: Mandatory. **Policies:** Freshmen permitted cars on campus.

Student services. Adult student services, career counseling, financial aid counseling, personal counseling, placement for graduates. **Physically disabled:** Services for visually impaired. **Transfer:** Special adviser, orientation, re-entry adviser, pre-admission transcript evaluation for new students.

Contact. Phone: (215) 854-1842 Fax: (215) 854-1880
Gary Bello, Director, Orleans Technical Institute - Center City Campus, 1845 Walnut Street, 7th Floor, Philadelphia, PA 19103-4707

Pace Institute

Reading, Pennsylvania
www.paceinstitute.com **CB code: 2438**

- For-profit 2-year junior college
- Large city

General. Accredited by ACICS. **Enrollment:** 280 undergraduates. **Degrees:** 48 associate awarded. **Calendar:** Continuous. **Full-time faculty:** 18 total. **Part-time faculty:** 16 total.

Basis for selection. Open admission.

2005-2006 Annual costs. Tuition varies by program from $7,118 to $21,326 annually.

Application procedures. Admission: No deadline. $10 fee, may be waived for applicants with need.

Academics. Credit/placement by examination: CLEP.

Contact. E-mail: pace4u2@aol.com
Phone: (610) 375-1212
Amy Hafer, Admissions Director, Pace Institute, 606 Court Street, Reading, PA 19601

Penn Commercial Business and Technical School

Washington, Pennsylvania
www.penncommercial.net **CB code: 3300**

- For-profit 2-year business and technical college
- Small city

General. Accredited by ACICS. **Enrollment:** 425 undergraduates. **Degrees:** 131 associate awarded. **Calendar:** Continuous. **Full-time faculty:** 20 total. **Part-time faculty:** 15 total.

Basis for selection. Open admission, but selective for some programs.

2005-2006 Annual costs. Quoted costs are for computer management program. Tuition and fees range from $8,390 to $9,150 per academic year depending on program. Books/supplies: $945. Personal expenses: $2,438.

Academics. Credit/placement by examination: CLEP.

Majors. Business: General. **Mechanic/repair:** General.

Contact. E-mail: pcadmissions@penncommercial.net
Phone: (724) 222-5330
Attn: Admissions, Penn Commercial Business and Technical School, 242 Oak Spring Road, Washington, PA 15301

Penn Foster Career School

Scranton, Pennsylvania
www.educationdirect.com **CB code: 7313**

- For-profit 2-year virtual college
- Commuter campus in small city

General. Founded in 1975. Accredited by DETC. **Location:** 175 miles from Philadelphia. **Calendar:** Continuous.

Annual costs/financial aid. Tuition/fees: $3,840. Cost of degree programs range from $3,840 to $4,790 depending on program. Additional costs to fulfill resident laboratory requirement in technology programs.

Contact. Phone: (570) 342-7701
Manager, DP Services, 925 Oak Street, Scranton, PA 18515

Penn State Beaver
Monaca, Pennsylvania
www.br.psu.edu **CB code: 2660**

- Public 2-year branch campus college
- Residential campus in small town
- SAT or ACT (ACT writing optional) required

General. Founded in 1964. Regionally accredited. **Enrollment:** 574 degree-seeking undergraduates; 58 non-degree-seeking students. **Degrees:** 59 bachelor's, 6 associate awarded. **Location:** 30 miles from Pittsburgh. **Calendar:** Semester, limited summer session. **Full-time faculty:** 32 total; 59% have terminal degrees, 19% minority, 50% women. **Part-time faculty:** 23 total; 9% have terminal degrees, 35% women. **Class size:** 57% < 20, 39% 20-39, 3% 40-49, 1% 50-99.

Student profile. Among degree-seeking undergraduates, 203 enrolled as first-time, first-year students, 28 transferred in from other institutions.

Part-time:	10%	**Asian American:**	2%
Out-of-state:	4%	**Hispanic American:**	1%
Women:	43%	**25 or older:**	12%
African American:	4%	**Live on campus:**	25%

Transfer out. Colleges most students transferred to 2005: University of Pittsburgh, Robert Morris University, Slippery Rock University, Geneva College.

Basis for selection. Admission decisions based upon high school GPA as well as other factors, including standardized verbal and math test scores, class rank, personal statements, activities lists. Essay considered if submitted; portfolios required for select majors. **Adult students:** SAT/ACT scores not required if out of high school 5 year(s) or more. SAT/ACT test scores not required for veterans with 4 or more years service with an honorable discharge. **Homeschooled:** Helpful if applicants provide complete documentation showing courses studied and all evaluations from home school evaluator or supervisor assigned to student in cooperation with local school district or evaluator approved through program.

High school preparation. College-preparatory program recommended. Required units include English 4, mathematics 3, social studies 3, science 3 and foreign language 2.

2005-2006 Annual costs. Tuition/fees: $10,200; $15,332 out-of-state. Per-credit charge: $393 in-state; $619 out-of-state. Room/board: $7,060. Books/supplies: $816. Personal expenses: $2,016.

2004-2005 Financial aid. Need-based: 180 full-time freshmen applied for aid; 149 were judged to have need; 148 of these received aid. Average need met was 64%. Average scholarship/grant was $4,526; average loan $2,587. 53% of total undergraduate aid awarded as scholarships/grants, 47% as loans/jobs. Need-based aid available for part-time students. Work study available nights and weekends. **Non-need-based:** Awarded to 129 full-time undergraduates, including 59 freshmen. Scholarships awarded for academics, athletics, minority status, ROTC.

Application procedures. Admission: Priority date 11/30; no deadline. $50 fee, may be waived for applicants with need. Application may be submitted online. Admission notification on a rolling basis beginning on or about 11/1. Must reply by 5/1. All freshmen applications processed at University Park Campus. **Financial aid:** Priority date 2/15; no closing date. FAFSA required. Applicants notified on a rolling basis starting 2/15.

Academics. Special study options: Accelerated study, cross-registration, distance learning, double major, dual enrollment of high school students, ESL, honors, independent study, internships, semester at sea, study abroad. Bachelor's degree programs available on campus. License preparation in real estate. **Credit/placement by examination:** AP, CLEP, IB, SAT. 60 credit hours maximum toward bachelor's degree. **Support services:** Learning center, reduced course load, remedial instruction, study skills assistance, tutoring, writing center.

Majors. Agriculture: Business. **Business:** General, hospitality admin. **Computer sciences:** Information systems. **Engineering technology:** Biomedical, electrical, telecommunications. **Interdisciplinary:** Biological/physical sciences. **Liberal arts:** Arts/sciences. **Parks/recreation:** Exercise sciences.

Most popular majors. Business/marketing 67%, liberal arts 33%.

Computing on campus. 149 workstations in library, computer center, student center. Dormitories wired for high-speed internet access and linked to campus network. Commuter students can connect to campus network. Online course registration, online library, helpline, repair service, student web hosting available.

Student life. Freshman orientation: Mandatory, $20 fee. Preregistration for classes offered. **Policies:** Acts of intolerance and high-risk drinking discouraged at all locations. All facilities designated as smoke-free. Freshmen permitted cars on campus. **Housing:** Coed dorms available. $100 partly refundable deposit, deadline 5/1. Townhouses available. **Activities:** Drama, literary magazine, radio station, student government, student newspaper, Common Ground Christian club, Big Brothers/Big Sisters mentoring program, campus ministry.

Athletics. NJCAA. **Intercollegiate:** Baseball M, basketball M, softball, volleyball W. **Intramural:** Basketball, bowling, football (non-tackle), golf, soccer, softball, table tennis, volleyball W. **Team name:** Nittany Lions.

Student services. Adult student services, alcohol/substance abuse counseling, campus ministries, career counseling, services for economically disadvantaged, student employment services, financial aid counseling, health services, personal counseling, placement for graduates, veterans' counselor. **Physically disabled:** Services for visually, speech, hearing impaired. **Transfer:** Special adviser, orientation, pre-admission transcript evaluation for new students. College fairs on campus for students transferring to 4-year colleges.

Contact. E-mail: br-admissions@psu.edu
Phone: (724) 773-3800 Fax: (724) 773-3658
Randall Deike, Assistant Vice Provost for Enrollment Management and Director of Admissions, Penn State Beaver, 100 University Drive, Monaca, PA 15061-2799

Two-Year Colleges

Penn State Delaware County
Media, Pennsylvania
www.de.psu.edu **CB code: 2660**

- Public 2-year branch campus college
- Commuter campus in small town
- SAT or ACT (ACT writing optional) required

General. Founded in 1966. Regionally accredited. **Enrollment:** 1,388 degree-seeking undergraduates; 201 non-degree-seeking students. **Degrees:** 167 bachelor's, 8 associate awarded. **ROTC:** Army, Air Force. **Location:** 20 miles from Philadelphia. **Calendar:** Semester, limited summer session. **Full-time faculty:** 70 total; 56% have terminal degrees, 16% minority, 56% women. **Part-time faculty:** 55 total; 18% have terminal degrees, 7% minority, 47% women. **Class size:** 42% < 20, 46% 20-39, 7% 40-49, 4% 50-99, less than 1% >100.

Student profile. Among degree-seeking undergraduates, 394 enrolled as first-time, first-year students, 67 transferred in from other institutions.

Part-time:	11%	**Asian American:**	7%
Out-of-state:	3%	**Hispanic American:**	2%
Women:	45%	**25 or older:**	10%
African American:	15%		

Basis for selection. Admission decisions based on high school GPA, as well as other factors, which may include standardized verbal and math test scores, class rank, personal statements, and list of activities. Essay considered if submitted; portfolios required for select majors. **Adult students:** SAT/ACT scores not required if out of high school 5 year(s) or more. SAT/ACT test scores not required for veterans with 4 or more years service with an honorable discharge. **Homeschooled:** Applicants should provide complete documentation showing courses studied and all evaluations presented from evaluator or supervisor assigned to student in cooperation with local school district or evaluator approved through program.

High school preparation. Required units include English 4, mathematics 3, social studies 3, science 3 and foreign language 2.

2005-2006 Annual costs. Tuition/fees: $10,200; $15,332 out-of-state. Per-credit charge: $393 in-state; $619 out-of-state. Books/supplies: $1,040. Personal expenses: $1,854.

2004-2005 Financial aid. Need-based: 322 full-time freshmen applied for aid; 232 were judged to have need; 229 of these received aid. Average need met was 62%. Average scholarship/grant was $4,950; average loan $2,382. 58% of total undergraduate aid awarded as scholarships/grants, 42% as loans/jobs. Need-based aid available for part-time students. Work study available nights. **Non-need-based:** Awarded to 305 full-time undergraduates, including 126 freshmen. Scholarships awarded for academics, athletics, minority status, ROTC.

Application procedures. Admission: Priority date 11/30; no deadline. $50 fee, may be waived for applicants with need. Application may be submitted online. Admission notification on a rolling basis beginning on or

about 11/1. Must reply by 5/1. All freshmen applications processed at University Park Campus. **Financial aid:** Priority date 2/15; no closing date. FAFSA required. Applicants notified on a rolling basis starting 2/15.

Academics. Special study options: Combined bachelor's/graduate degree, distance learning, double major, dual enrollment of high school students, ESL, honors, independent study, internships, study abroad, teacher certification program. Bachelor's degree programs available on campus. **Credit/placement by examination:** CLEP, IB, SAT. 60 credit hours maximum toward bachelor's degree. **Support services:** Learning center, pre-admission summer program, reduced course load, remedial instruction, study skills assistance, tutoring, writing center.

Majors. Agriculture: Business. **Business:** General. **Family/consumer sciences:** Family studies. **Liberal arts:** Arts/sciences.

Most popular majors. Business/marketing 63%, liberal arts 38%.

Computing on campus. 206 workstations in library, computer center, student center. Commuter students can connect to campus network. Online course registration, online library, helpline, repair service, student web hosting, wireless network available.

Student life. Freshman orientation: Available. Preregistration for classes offered. Held in summer, prior to fall semester. **Policies:** Acts of intolerance and high-risk drinking discouraged at all locations. All facilities designated smoke-free. Freshmen permitted cars on campus. **Activities:** Choral groups, dance, drama, film society, literary magazine, student government, student newspaper, Asian American Association, Black Student League, Nittany Christian Fellowship, Caribbean Student Association, Gay-Straight Alliance, Muslim Student Association, International Awareness Club, African Awareness Club, Gospel Ensemble, Jewish Student League.

Athletics. Intercollegiate: Baseball M, basketball, soccer, tennis, volleyball W. **Intramural:** Basketball, soccer. **Team name:** Nittany Lions.

Student services. Adult student services, alcohol/substance abuse counseling, career counseling, services for economically disadvantaged, student employment services, financial aid counseling, health services, minority student services, personal counseling, placement for graduates, veterans' counselor, women's services. **Physically disabled:** Services for visually, speech, hearing impaired. **Transfer:** Special adviser, orientation, re-entry adviser, pre-admission transcript evaluation for new students. College fairs on campus for students transferring to 4-year colleges.

Contact. E-mail: admissions-delco@psu.edu
Phone: (610) 892-1200 Fax: (610) 892-1320
Randall Deike, Asst. Vice Provost for Enrollment Management and Director of Admissions, Penn State Delaware County, 25 Yearsley Mill Road, Media, PA 19063-5596

Penn State Dubois

DuBois, Pennsylvania
www.ds.psu.edu **CB code: 2660**

- Public 2-year branch campus college
- Commuter campus in small town
- SAT or ACT (ACT writing optional) required

General. Founded in 1935. Regionally accredited. **Enrollment:** 658 degree-seeking undergraduates; 146 non-degree-seeking students. **Degrees:** 48 bachelor's, 95 associate awarded. **Location:** 120 miles from Pittsburgh. **Calendar:** Semester, limited summer session. **Full-time faculty:** 45 total; 60% have terminal degrees, 4% minority, 40% women. **Part-time faculty:** 37 total; 30% have terminal degrees, 40% women. **Class size:** 63% < 20, 31% 20-39, 3% 40-49, 3% 50-99.

Student profile. Among degree-seeking undergraduates, 174 enrolled as first-time, first-year students, 23 transferred in from other institutions.

Part-time:	17%	**African American:**	1%
Out-of-state:	1%	**25 or older:**	32%
Women:	51%		

Basis for selection. Admission decisions based upon high school GPA, as well as other factors, which may include standardized verbal and math test scores, class rank, personal statements, and list of activities. Essay considered if submitted; portfolios required for select majors. **Adult students:** SAT/ACT scores not required if out of high school 5 year(s) or more. SAT/ACT test scores not required for veterans with 4 or more years service with an honorable discharge. **Homeschooled:** Applicants should provide complete documentation showing the courses studied and all evaluations presented from evaluator or supervisor assigned to student in cooperation with local school district or evaluator who is approved through the program.

High school preparation. Required units include English 4, mathematics 3, social studies 3, science 3 and foreign language 2.

2005-2006 Annual costs. Tuition/fees: $10,190; $15,322 out-of-state. Per-credit charge: $393 in-state; $619 out-of-state. Books/supplies: $1,040. Personal expenses: $1,854.

2004-2005 Financial aid. Need-based: 200 full-time freshmen applied for aid; 178 were judged to have need; 178 of these received aid. Average need met was 72%. Average scholarship/grant was $4,480; average loan $2,609. 58% of total undergraduate aid awarded as scholarships/grants, 42% as loans/jobs. Need-based aid available for part-time students. Work study available nights, weekends and for part-time students. **Non-need-based:** Awarded to 278 full-time undergraduates, including 99 freshmen. Scholarships awarded for academics, athletics, minority status, ROTC.

Application procedures. Admission: Priority date 11/30; no deadline. $50 fee, may be waived for applicants with need. Application may be submitted online. Admission notification on a rolling basis beginning on or about 11/1. Must reply by 5/1. All freshmen applications processed at University Park Campus. **Financial aid:** No deadline. FAFSA required. Applicants notified on a rolling basis starting 2/15.

Academics. Special study options: Accelerated study, cross-registration, distance learning, double major, dual enrollment of high school students, honors, independent study, internships, student-designed major, study abroad. Bachelor's degree programs available on campus. License preparation in occupational therapy, physical therapy. **Credit/placement by examination:** CLEP, IB, SAT. 60 credit hours maximum toward bachelor's degree. **Support services:** Learning center, study skills assistance, tutoring, writing center.

Majors. Agriculture: Business. **Business:** General. **Computer sciences:** Information systems. **Conservation:** Wildlife. **Engineering technology:** Biomedical, electrical, industrial, mechanical, telecommunications. **Family/consumer sciences:** Family studies. **Health:** Clinical lab technology, occupational therapy assistant, physical therapy assistant. **Interdisciplinary:** Biological/physical sciences. **Liberal arts:** Arts/sciences.

Most popular majors. Business/marketing 8%, computer/information sciences 6%, engineering/engineering technologies 20%, family/consumer sciences 11%, health sciences 24%, natural resources/environmental science 27%.

Computing on campus. 130 workstations in computer center, student center. Commuter students can connect to campus network. Online course registration, online library, helpline, repair service, student web hosting available.

Student life. Freshman orientation: Available. Preregistration for classes offered. 3-day program before Fall semester; 1-day program before Spring semester. **Policies:** Acts of intolerance and high risk drinking discouraged at all locations. All facilities designated smoke free. Students expected to abide by The Penn State Principles. Freshmen permitted cars on campus. **Activities:** Choral groups, drama, film society, literary magazine, student government, student newspaper, Diversity Club, Women's Liaison Committee, Veterans' Club, Adult Learner Student Organization, Environmental Conservation and Outing Club, Campus Crusade for Christ, World Cultures Club.

Athletics. Intercollegiate: Basketball M, cross-country, golf, volleyball W. **Intramural:** Basketball, bowling, golf, soccer, table tennis, volleyball. **Team name:** Nittany Lions.

Student services. Adult student services, alcohol/substance abuse counseling, career counseling, services for economically disadvantaged, student employment services, financial aid counseling, health services, personal counseling, placement for graduates, veterans' counselor, women's services. **Physically disabled:** Services for visually, speech, hearing impaired. **Transfer:** Special adviser, pre-admission transcript evaluation for new students.

Contact. E-mail: ds-admissions@psu.edu
Phone: (814) 375-4720 Toll-free number: (800) 346-7627
Fax: (814) 375-4784
Randall Deike, Asst. Vice Provost for Enrollment Management and Director of Admissions, Penn State Dubois, 101 Hiller, DuBois, PA 15801

Penn State Fayette

Uniontown, Pennsylvania
www.fe.psu.edu **CB code: 2660**

- Public 2-year branch campus college
- Commuter campus in large town
- SAT or ACT (ACT writing optional) required

General. Founded in 1934. Regionally accredited. **Enrollment:** 839 degree-seeking undergraduates; 156 non-degree-seeking students. **Degrees:** 87 bachelor's, 86 associate awarded. **Location:** 40 miles from Pittsburgh. **Calendar:** Semester, limited summer session. **Full-time faculty:** 50 total; 48% have terminal degrees, 4% minority, 36% women. **Part-time faculty:** 35 total; 20% have terminal degrees, 3% minority, 54% women. **Class size:** 64% < 20, 30% 20-39, 5% 40-49, less than 1% 50-99. **Partnerships:** Formal partnership with UPS.

Student profile. Among degree-seeking undergraduates, 177 enrolled as first-time, first-year students, 34 transferred in from other institutions.

Part-time:	22%	**African American:**	7%
Out-of-state:	1%	**Asian American:**	1%
Women:	63%	**25 or older:**	40%

Basis for selection. Admission decisions based on high school GPA, as well as other factors, which may include standardized verbal and math test scores, class rank, personal statements, and activities lists. Essay considered if submitted; portfolios required for select majors. **Adult students:** SAT/ACT scores not required if out of high school 5 year(s) or more. SAT/ACT test scores not required for veterans with 4 or more years service with an honorable discharge. **Homeschooled:** Complete documentation helpful, showing courses studied and all evaluations presented from home school evaluator, supervisor assigned to student in cooperation with local school district, or evaluator approved through program. **Learning Disabled:** Prospective students with disabilities are encouraged to contact or visit the Office for Disability Services in their junior or senior years in high school in order to find out more about disability services at the college level.

High school preparation. College-preparatory program recommended. Required units include English 4, mathematics 3, social studies 3, science 3 and foreign language 2.

2005-2006 Annual costs. Tuition/fees: $10,190; $15,322 out-of-state. Per-credit charge: $393 in-state; $619 out-of-state. Books/supplies: $1,040. Personal expenses: $1,854.

2004-2005 Financial aid. Need-based: 137 full-time freshmen applied for aid; 125 were judged to have need; 124 of these received aid. Average need met was 68%. Average scholarship/grant was $4,556; average loan $2,667. 57% of total undergraduate aid awarded as scholarships/grants, 43% as loans/jobs. Need-based aid available for part-time students. Work study available nights and weekends. **Non-need-based:** Awarded to 302 full-time undergraduates, including 64 freshmen. Scholarships awarded for academics, athletics, minority status, ROTC.

Application procedures. Admission: Priority date 11/30; no deadline. $50 fee, may be waived for applicants with need. Application may be submitted online. Admission notification on a rolling basis beginning on or about 11/1. Must reply by 5/1. All freshmen applications processed at University Park Campus. **Financial aid:** Priority date 2/15; no closing date. FAFSA required. Applicants notified on a rolling basis starting 2/15.

Academics. Special study options: Accelerated study, cross-registration, distance learning, double major, dual enrollment of high school students, honors, independent study, internships, student-designed major, study abroad, weekend college. Bachelor's degree programs available on campus. License preparation in nursing, real estate. **Credit/placement by examination:** AP, CLEP, IB, SAT. 60 credit hours maximum toward bachelor's degree. **Support services:** Learning center, study skills assistance, tutoring, writing center.

Majors. Agriculture: Business. **Business:** General. **Computer sciences:** Information systems. **Engineering technology:** Architectural, biomedical, electrical, manufacturing, mechanical, telecommunications. **Family/consumer sciences:** Family studies. **Health:** Nursing (RN). **Liberal arts:** Arts/sciences.

Most popular majors. Business/marketing 8%, computer/information sciences 8%, engineering/engineering technologies 21%, family/consumer sciences 7%, health sciences 37%, liberal arts 17%.

Computing on campus. 201 workstations in library, computer center, student center. Commuter students can connect to campus network. Online course registration, online library, helpline, repair service, student web hosting available.

Student life. Freshman orientation: Available. Preregistration for classes offered. **Policies:** Acts of intolerance and high-risk drinking discouraged at all locations. All facilities designated smoke-free. Freshmen permitted cars on campus. **Activities:** Choral groups, drama, student government, student newspaper, adult student organization, Humanities Society, In the Light Christian Club, minority students association, Women in Science Engineering & Technology, Students Against Destructive Decisions.

Athletics. Intercollegiate: Baseball M, basketball M, softball W, volleyball W. **Intramural:** Basketball, football (non-tackle), racquetball, softball, tennis. **Team name:** Nittany Lions.

Student services. Adult student services, alcohol/substance abuse counseling, career counseling, services for economically disadvantaged, student employment services, financial aid counseling, health services, on-campus daycare, personal counseling, placement for graduates, veterans' counselor. **Physically disabled:** Services for visually, speech, hearing impaired. **Transfer:** Special adviser, pre-admission transcript evaluation for new students. Transfer adviser, college fairs on campus for students transferring to 4-year colleges.

Contact. E-mail: feadm@psu.edu
Phone: (724) 430-4130 Toll-free number: (877) 568-4130
Fax: (724) 430-4175
Randall Deike, Assistant Vice Provost for Enrollment Management and Director of Admissions, Penn State Fayette, 108 Williams Building, Uniontown, PA 15401-0519

Two-Year Colleges

Penn State Hazleton

Hazleton, Pennsylvania
www.hn.psu.edu **CB code: 2660**

- Public 2-year branch campus college
- Residential campus in large town
- SAT or ACT (ACT writing optional) required

General. Founded in 1934. Regionally accredited. **Enrollment:** 1,015 degree-seeking undergraduates; 50 non-degree-seeking students. **Degrees:** 58 bachelor's, 37 associate awarded. **ROTC:** Army, Air Force. **Location:** 4 miles from Hazleton. **Calendar:** Semester, limited summer session. **Full-time faculty:** 53 total; 57% have terminal degrees, 17% minority, 43% women. **Part-time faculty:** 29 total; 21% have terminal degrees, 3% minority, 34% women. **Class size:** 48% < 20, 41% 20-39, 6% 40-49, 6% 50-99. **Special facilities:** Weather station.

Student profile. Among degree-seeking undergraduates, 454 enrolled as first-time, first-year students, 29 transferred in from other institutions.

Part-time:	3%	**Asian American:**	6%
Out-of-state:	25%	**Hispanic American:**	7%
Women:	40%	**25 or older:**	5%
African American:	7%	**Live on campus:**	45%

Basis for selection. Admission decisions based on high school GPA, as well as other factors, which may include standardized verbal and math test scores, class rank, personal statements, and activities lists. Essay considered if submitted; portfolios required for select majors. **Adult students:** SAT/ACT scores not required if out of high school 5 year(s) or more. SAT/ACT test scores not required for veterans with 4 or more years service with an honorable discharge. **Homeschooled:** Complete documentation helpful, showing courses studied and all evaluations presented from home school evaluator, supervisor assigned to student in cooperation with local school district, or evaluator approved through program.

High school preparation. College-preparatory program recommended. Required units include English 4, mathematics 3, social studies 3, science 3 and foreign language 2.

2005-2006 Annual costs. Tuition/fees: $10,190; $15,322 out-of-state. Per-credit charge: $393 in-state; $619 out-of-state. Room/board: $7,060. Books/supplies: $1,040. Personal expenses: $2,016.

2004-2005 Financial aid. Need-based: 403 full-time freshmen applied for aid; 318 were judged to have need; 313 of these received aid. Average need met was 65%. Average scholarship/grant was $4,479; average loan $2,625. 55% of total undergraduate aid awarded as scholarships/grants, 45% as loans/jobs. Need-based aid available for part-time students. Work study available nights and weekends. **Non-need-based:** Awarded to 300 full-time undergraduates, including 135 freshmen. Scholarships awarded for academics, athletics, minority status, ROTC.

Application procedures. Admission: Priority date 11/30; no deadline. $50 fee, may be waived for applicants with need. Application may be submitted online. Admission notification on a rolling basis beginning on or about 11/1. Must reply by 5/1. All freshman applications processed at University Park Campus. **Financial aid:** Priority date 2/15; no closing date. FAFSA required. Applicants notified on a rolling basis starting 2/15.

Academics. Special study options: Accelerated study, cross-registration, distance learning, double major, dual enrollment of high school students, ESL, honors, independent study, internships, student-designed major, study abroad. Bachelor's degree programs available on campus. License preparation in physical therapy. **Credit/placement by examination:** AP, CLEP, IB,

SAT. 60 credit hours maximum toward bachelor's degree. **Support services:** Learning center, remedial instruction, study skills assistance, tutoring, writing center.

Honors college/program. 300 admitted university-wide each year in Schreyer Honors College.

Majors. Agriculture: Business. **Business:** General. **Computer sciences:** Information systems. **Engineering technology:** Biomedical, electrical, mechanical, telecommunications. **Health:** Clinical lab technology, physical therapy assistant. **Liberal arts:** Arts/sciences.

Most popular majors. Computer/information sciences 16%, engineering/engineering technologies 44%, health sciences 32%.

Computing on campus. 229 workstations in library, student center. Dormitories wired for high-speed internet access and linked to campus network. Commuter students can connect to campus network. Online course registration, online library, helpline, repair service, student web hosting available.

Student life. Freshman orientation: Available. Preregistration for classes offered. **Policies:** Acts of intolerance and high-risk drinking discouraged at all locations. All facilities designated as smoke-free. Students expected to abide by The Penn State Principles. Freshmen permitted cars on campus. **Housing:** Coed dorms, substance-free housing available. $100 partly refundable deposit, deadline 5/1. Townhouses. **Activities:** Choral groups, dance, drama, literary magazine, radio station, student government, student newspaper, multicultural club, Circle K, Allies, Fellowship of Christian Athletes, Helping Hands.

Athletics. Intercollegiate: Baseball M, basketball, cheerleading, soccer M, softball W, tennis, volleyball. **Intramural:** Basketball, fencing, soccer, volleyball. **Team name:** Nittany Lions.

Student services. Adult student services, alcohol/substance abuse counseling, campus ministries, career counseling, services for economically disadvantaged, student employment services, financial aid counseling, health services, legal services, minority student services, personal counseling, placement for graduates, veterans' counselor, women's services. **Physically disabled:** Services for visually, speech, hearing impaired. **Transfer:** Special adviser, orientation, pre-admission transcript evaluation for new students. Transfer center, transfer adviser, college fairs on campus for students transferring to 4-year colleges.

Contact. E-mail: admissions-hn@psu.edu
Phone: (570) 450-3142 Toll-free number: (800) 279-8495
Fax: (570) 450-3182
Randall Deike, Asst. Vice Provost for Enrollment Management and Director of Admissions, Penn State Hazleton, 110 Admin. Building, 76 University Drive, Hazleton, PA 18202

Penn State McKeesport

McKeesport, Pennsylvania
www.mk.psu.edu **CB code: 2660**

- Public 2-year branch campus college
- Residential campus in large town
- SAT or ACT (ACT writing optional) required

General. Founded in 1947. Regionally accredited. **Enrollment:** 611 degree-seeking undergraduates; 71 non-degree-seeking students. **Degrees:** 93 bachelor's, 4 associate awarded. **Location:** 15 miles from Pittsburgh. **Calendar:** Semester, limited summer session. **Full-time faculty:** 38 total; 71% have terminal degrees, 18% minority, 47% women. **Part-time faculty:** 34 total; 6% have terminal degrees, 3% minority, 47% women. **Class size:** 51% < 20, 44% 20-39, 4% 40-49, 1% 50-99. **Special facilities:** Computer-based lab science equipment; special computer labs: systems integration, networking.

Student profile. Among degree-seeking undergraduates, 170 enrolled as first-time, first-year students, 21 transferred in from other institutions.

Part-time:	9%	**Asian American:**	3%
Out-of-state:	6%	**Hispanic American:**	1%
Women:	38%	**25 or older:**	11%
African American:	14%	**Live on campus:**	15%

Basis for selection. Admission decisions based upon high school GPA, as well as other factors, which may include standardized verbal and math test scores, class rank, personal statements, and list of activities. Essay considered if submitted; portfolios required for select majors. **Adult students:** SAT/ACT scores not required if out of high school 5 year(s) or more. SAT/ACT test scores not required for veterans with 4 or more years service with an honorable discharge. **Homeschooled:** Applicants should provide complete documentation showing the courses studied and all evaluations presented from evaluator or supervisor assigned to student in cooperation with local school district or evaluator who is approved through the program.

High school preparation. College-preparatory program recommended. Required units include English 4, mathematics 3, social studies 3, science 3 and foreign language 2.

2005-2006 Annual costs. Tuition/fees: $10,180; $15,312 out-of-state. Per-credit charge: $393 in-state; $619 out-of-state. Room/board: $7,060. Books/supplies: $1,040. Personal expenses: $2,016.

2004-2005 Financial aid. Need-based: 202 full-time freshmen applied for aid; 172 were judged to have need; 168 of these received aid. Average need met was 68%. Average scholarship/grant was $4,393; average loan $2,609. 54% of total undergraduate aid awarded as scholarships/grants, 46% as loans/jobs. Need-based aid available for part-time students. Work study available nights and weekends. **Non-need-based:** Awarded to 224 full-time undergraduates, including 100 freshmen. Scholarships awarded for academics, athletics, minority status, ROTC.

Application procedures. Admission: Priority date 11/30; no deadline. $50 fee, may be waived for applicants with need. Application may be submitted online. Admission notification on a rolling basis beginning on or about 11/1. Must reply by 5/1. **Financial aid:** Priority date 2/15; no closing date. FAFSA required. Applicants notified on a rolling basis starting 2/15.

Academics. Special study options: Accelerated study, cross-registration, distance learning, double major, dual enrollment of high school students, honors, independent study, internships, study abroad. Bachelor's degree programs available on campus. **Credit/placement by examination:** AP, CLEP, IB, SAT. 60 credit hours maximum toward bachelor's degree. **Support services:** Learning center, pre-admission summer program, remedial instruction, study skills assistance, tutoring, writing center.

Majors. Agriculture: Business. **Business:** General. **Interdisciplinary:** Biological/physical sciences. **Liberal arts:** Arts/sciences.

Computing on campus. 231 workstations in dormitories, library, computer center, student center. Dormitories wired for high-speed internet access and linked to campus network. Commuter students can connect to campus network. Online course registration, online library, helpline, student web hosting, wireless network available.

Student life. Freshman orientation: Mandatory. Preregistration for classes offered. Orientation is academically based with student life components and is held prior to the opening of the semester. **Policies:** Acts of intolerance and high-risk drinking discouraged at all locations. All facilities designated as smoke-free. Students expected to abide by The Penn State Principles. Freshmen permitted cars on campus. **Housing:** Coed dorms, substance-free housing available. $100 partly refundable deposit, deadline 5/1. **Activities:** Jazz band, choral groups, dance, drama, literary magazine, radio station, student government, student newspaper, Black Student Union, Christian Fellowship, Gospel Choir, Spanish Club, Multicultural Organization for Students.

Athletics. Intercollegiate: Baseball M, basketball M, softball W, volleyball W. **Intramural:** Basketball, football (non-tackle), racquetball, softball, volleyball.

Student services. Adult student services, alcohol/substance abuse counseling, campus ministries, career counseling, services for economically disadvantaged, student employment services, financial aid counseling, health services, minority student services, personal counseling, placement for graduates, veterans' counselor, women's services. **Physically disabled:** Services for visually, speech, hearing impaired. **Transfer:** Special adviser, orientation, pre-admission transcript evaluation for new students.

Contact. E-mail: psumk@psu.edu
Phone: (412) 675-9010 Fax: (412) 675-9046
Randall Deike, Asst. Vice Provost for Enrollment Management and Director of Admissions, Penn State McKeesport, 101 Frable Building, 4000 University Drive, McKeesport, PA 15132

Penn State Mont Alto

Mont Alto, Pennsylvania
www.ma.psu.edu **CB code: 2660**

- Public 2-year branch campus college
- Residential campus in rural community
- SAT or ACT (ACT writing optional) required

General. Founded in 1929. Regionally accredited. **Enrollment:** 847 degree-seeking undergraduates; 85 non-degree-seeking students. **Degrees:** 49 bachelor's, 100 associate awarded. **ROTC:** Army. **Location:** 12 miles from Chambersburg. **Calendar:** Semester, limited summer session. **Full-time faculty:** 52 total; 48% have terminal degrees, 6% minority, 58% women. **Part-time faculty:** 39 total; 10% have terminal degrees, 46% women. **Class size:** 60% < 20, 34% 20-39, 6% 40-49, less than 1% 50-99.

Student profile. Among degree-seeking undergraduates, 274 enrolled as first-time, first-year students, 27 transferred in from other institutions.

Part-time:	24%	**Asian American:**	2%
Out-of-state:	12%	**Hispanic American:**	3%
Women:	58%	**25 or older:**	24%
African American:	9%	**Live on campus:**	36%

Basis for selection. Admission decisions based upon high school GPA, as well as other factors, which may include standardized verbal and math test scores, class rank, personal statements, and list of activities. Essay considered if submitted; portfolios required for select majors. **Adult students:** SAT/ACT scores not required if out of high school 5 year(s) or more. SAT/ACT test scores not required for veterans with 4 or more years of service with an honorable discharge. **Homeschooled:** Applicants should provide complete documentation showing the courses studied and all evaluations presented from evaluator or supervisor assigned to student in cooperation with local school district or evaluator who is approved through the program.

High school preparation. Required units include English 4, mathematics 3, social studies 3, science 3 and foreign language 2.

2005-2006 Annual costs. Tuition/fees: $10,200; $15,332 out-of-state. Per-credit charge: $393 in-state; $619 out-of-state. Room/board: $7,060. Books/supplies: $1,040. Personal expenses: $2,016.

2004-2005 Financial aid. Need-based: 229 full-time freshmen applied for aid; 189 were judged to have need; 187 of these received aid. Average need met was 69%. Average scholarship/grant was $4,827; average loan $2,824. 56% of total undergraduate aid awarded as scholarships/grants, 44% as loans/jobs. Need-based aid available for part-time students. Work study available nights, weekends and for part-time students. **Non-need-based:** Awarded to 252 full-time undergraduates, including 114 freshmen. Scholarships awarded for academics, athletics, minority status, ROTC.

Application procedures. Admission: Priority date 11/30; no deadline. $50 fee, may be waived for applicants with need. Application may be submitted online. Admission notification on a rolling basis beginning on or about 11/1. Must reply by 5/1. All freshmen applications processed at University Park Campus. **Financial aid:** Priority date 2/15; no closing date. FAFSA required. Applicants notified on a rolling basis starting 2/15.

Academics. Special study options: Accelerated study, cross-registration, distance learning, double major, dual enrollment of high school students, honors, independent study, internships, study abroad. Bachelor's degree programs available on campus. License preparation in nursing, occupational therapy, physical therapy, real estate. **Credit/placement by examination:** AP, CLEP, IB, SAT. 60 credit hours maximum toward bachelor's degree. **Support services:** Learning center, remedial instruction, study skills assistance, tutoring, writing center.

Majors. Agriculture: Business. **Business:** General. **Computer sciences:** Information systems. **Conservation:** Forest resources. **Family/consumer sciences:** Family studies. **Health:** Nursing (RN), occupational therapy assistant, physical therapy assistant. **Liberal arts:** Arts/sciences.

Most popular majors. Business/marketing 8%, family/consumer sciences 6%, health sciences 60%, natural resources/environmental science 19%.

Computing on campus. 204 workstations in computer center, student center. Dormitories wired for high-speed internet access and linked to campus network. Commuter students can connect to campus network. Online course registration, online library, helpline, repair service, student web hosting available.

Student life. Freshman orientation: Available. Preregistration for classes offered. **Policies:** Acts of intolerance and high-risk drinking discouraged at all locations. All facilities designated as smoke-free. Freshmen permitted cars on campus. **Housing:** Coed dorms, special housing for disabled, substance-free housing available. $100 partly refundable deposit, deadline 5/1. Suites, special interest housing, townhouses. **Activities:** Jazz band, dance, drama, radio station, student government, student newspaper, Christian Fellowship, language club, multicultural club, volunteer club, Black Student Union, Asian student association.

Athletics. Intercollegiate: Basketball, cheerleading, cross-country, golf, soccer, softball W, tennis, volleyball W. **Intramural:** Badminton, basketball, racquetball, soccer, softball W, volleyball. **Team name:** Nittany Lions.

Student services. Adult student services, alcohol/substance abuse counseling, campus ministries, career counseling, services for economically disadvantaged, student employment services, financial aid counseling, health services, minority student services, placement for graduates, veterans' counselor, women's services. **Physically disabled:** Services for visually, speech, hearing impaired. **Transfer:** Special adviser, orientation, pre-admission transcript evaluation for new students.

Contact. E-mail: psuma@psu.edu
Phone: (717) 749-6130 Toll-free number: (800) 392-6173
Fax: (717) 749-6132
Randall Deike, Asst. Vice Provost for Enrollment Management and Director of Admissions, Penn State Mont Alto, 1 Campus Drive, Mont Alto, PA 17237-9703

Two-Year Colleges

Penn State New Kensington
New Kensington, Pennsylvania
www.nk.psu.edu **CB code: 2660**

- Public 2-year branch campus college
- Commuter campus in large town
- SAT or ACT (ACT writing optional) required

General. Founded in 1958. Regionally accredited. **Enrollment:** 733 degree-seeking undergraduates; 147 non-degree-seeking students. **Degrees:** 76 bachelor's, 84 associate awarded. **Location:** 22 miles from Pittsburgh. **Calendar:** Semester, limited summer session. **Full-time faculty:** 44 total; 57% have terminal degrees, 9% minority, 36% women. **Part-time faculty:** 44 total; 23% have terminal degrees, 7% minority, 36% women. **Class size:** 70% < 20, 26% 20-39, 3% 40-49, less than 1% 50-99.

Student profile. Among degree-seeking undergraduates, 198 enrolled as first-time, first-year students, 46 transferred in from other institutions.

Part-time:	20%	**Asian American:**	1%
Out-of-state:	2%	**Hispanic American:**	1%
Women:	41%	**25 or older:**	22%
African American:	2%		

Basis for selection. Admission decisions based upon high school GPA, as well as other factors, which may include standardized verbal and math test scores, class rank, personal statements, and list of activities. Essay considered if submitted; portfolios required for select majors. **Adult students:** SAT/ACT scores not required if out of high school 5 year(s) or more. SAT/ACT test scores not required for veterans with 4 or more years service with an honorable discharge. **Homeschooled:** Applicants should provide complete documentation showing the courses studied and all evaluations presented from evaluator or supervisor assigned to student in cooperation with local school district or evaluator who is approved through the program.

High school preparation. College-preparatory program recommended. Required units include English 4, mathematics 3, social studies 3, science 3 and foreign language 2.

2005-2006 Annual costs. Tuition/fees: $10,200; $15,332 out-of-state. Per-credit charge: $393 in-state; $619 out-of-state. Books/supplies: $1,040. Personal expenses: $1,854.

2004-2005 Financial aid. Need-based: 155 full-time freshmen applied for aid; 123 were judged to have need; 122 of these received aid. Average need met was 63%. Average scholarship/grant was $3,694; average loan $2,576. 52% of total undergraduate aid awarded as scholarships/grants, 48% as loans/jobs. Need-based aid available for part-time students. Work study available nights, weekends and for part-time students. **Non-need-based:** Awarded to 176 full-time undergraduates, including 62 freshmen. Scholarships awarded for academics, athletics, minority status, ROTC.

Application procedures. Admission: Priority date 11/30; no deadline. $50 fee, may be waived for applicants with need. Application may be submitted online. Admission notification on a rolling basis beginning on or about 11/1. Must reply by 5/1. All freshmen applications processed at University Park Campus. **Financial aid:** Priority date 2/15; no closing date. FAFSA required. Applicants notified on a rolling basis starting 2/15.

Academics. Special study options: Cross-registration, distance learning, double major, dual enrollment of high school students, external degree, honors, independent study, internships, study abroad. Bachelor's degree programs available on campus. License preparation in radiology. **Credit/placement by examination:** AP, CLEP, IB, SAT. 60 credit hours maximum toward bachelor's degree. **Support services:** Learning center, study skills assistance, tutoring, writing center.

Majors. Agriculture: Business. **Business:** Business admin. **Computer sciences:** Information systems. **Engineering:** Materials. **Engineering technology:** Biomedical, computer, electrical, mechanical, telecommunications. **Family/**

consumer sciences: Family studies. **Health:** Clinical lab technology. **Interdisciplinary:** Biological/physical sciences. **Liberal arts:** Arts/sciences.

Most popular majors. Business/marketing 9%, computer/information sciences 6%, engineering/engineering technologies 55%, health sciences 21%.

Computing on campus. 328 workstations in computer center. Commuter students can connect to campus network. Online course registration, online library, helpline, repair service, student web hosting available.

Student life. **Freshman orientation:** Mandatory, $25 fee. Preregistration for classes offered. 2 day program, prior to beginning of classes. **Policies:** Acts of intolerance and high-risk drinking discouraged at all locations. All facilities designated as smoke-free. Students expected to abide by The Penn State Principles. Freshmen permitted cars on campus. **Activities:** Bands, choral groups, dance, drama, literary magazine, student government, student newspaper, Multicultural Club, Society of Women Engineers, Spanish Culture Club.

Athletics. **Intercollegiate:** Baseball M, basketball, cheerleading, golf, softball W, volleyball W. **Intramural:** Badminton, basketball, bowling, football (non-tackle), racquetball, soccer, softball W, volleyball. **Team name:** Nittany Lions.

Student services. Adult student services, alcohol/substance abuse counseling, campus ministries, career counseling, services for economically disadvantaged, student employment services, financial aid counseling, health services, minority student services, placement for graduates, veterans' counselor, women's services. **Physically disabled:** Services for visually, speech, hearing impaired. **Transfer:** Special adviser, orientation, pre-admission transcript evaluation for new students.

Contact. E-mail: nkadmissions@psu.edu
Phone: (724) 334-5466 Toll-free number: (888) 968-7297
Fax: (724) 334-6111
Randall Deike, Asst. Vice Provost for Enrollment Management and Director of Admissions, Penn State New Kensington, 3550 Seventh Street Road, Route 780, New Kensington, PA 15068-1765

Penn State Shenango

Sharon, Pennsylvania
www.shenango.psu.edu **CB code: 2660**

- Public 2-year branch campus college
- Commuter campus in large town
- SAT or ACT (ACT writing optional) required

General. Founded in 1965. Regionally accredited. **Enrollment:** 665 degree-seeking undergraduates; 190 non-degree-seeking students. **Degrees:** 47 bachelor's, 65 associate awarded. **Location:** 17 miles from Youngstown, Ohio. **Calendar:** Semester, limited summer session. **Full-time faculty:** 29 total; 48% have terminal degrees, 10% minority, 41% women. **Part-time faculty:** 42 total; 14% have terminal degrees, 43% women. **Class size:** 66% < 20, 30% 20-39, 3% 40-49, less than 1% 50-99, less than 1% >100. **Special facilities:** Scanning electron microscope.

Student profile. Among degree-seeking undergraduates, 126 enrolled as first-time, first-year students, 30 transferred in from other institutions.

Part-time:	34%	**African American:**	8%
Out-of-state:	11%	**Hispanic American:**	1%
Women:	65%	**25 or older:**	48%

Basis for selection. Admission decisions are based upon the high school grade-point average, as well as other factors, which may include standardized verbal and math test scores, class rank, personal statements, and activities lists. Essay considered if submitted; portfolios required for select majors. **Adult students:** SAT/ACT scores not required if out of high school 5 year(s) or more. SAT/ACT test scores not required for veterans with 4 or more years service with an honorable discharge. **Homeschooled:** It is helpful if applicants provide complete documentation showing the courses studied and all the evaluations presented from a home school evaluator or supervisor assigned to the student in cooperation with the local school district or an evaluator who is approved through the program.

High school preparation. College-preparatory program recommended. Required units include English 4, mathematics 3, social studies 3, science 3 and foreign language 2.

2005-2006 Annual costs. Tuition/fees: $10,200; $15,332 out-of-state. Per-credit charge: $393 in-state; $619 out-of-state. Books/supplies: $1,040. Personal expenses: $1,854.

2004-2005 Financial aid. **Need-based:** 129 full-time freshmen applied for aid; 107 were judged to have need; 106 of these received aid. Average need met was 66%. Average scholarship/grant was $4,908; average loan $2,705. 55% of total undergraduate aid awarded as scholarships/grants, 45% as loans/jobs. Need-based aid available for part-time students. Work study available nights, weekends and for part-time students. **Non-need-based:** Awarded to 215 full-time undergraduates, including 71 freshmen. Scholarships awarded for academics, athletics, minority status, ROTC.

Application procedures. **Admission:** Priority date 11/30; no deadline. $50 fee, may be waived for applicants with need. Application may be submitted online. Admission notification on a rolling basis beginning on or about 11/1. Must reply by 5/1. All freshmen applications processed at University Park Campus. **Financial aid:** Priority date 2/15; no closing date. FAFSA required. Applicants notified on a rolling basis starting 2/15.

Academics. **Special study options:** Accelerated study, cross-registration, distance learning, double major, dual enrollment of high school students, honors, independent study, internships, student-designed major, study abroad. Bachelor's degree programs available on campus. License preparation in physical therapy, real estate. **Credit/placement by examination:** AP, CLEP, IB, SAT. 60 credit hours maximum toward bachelor's degree. **Support services:** Learning center, remedial instruction, study skills assistance, tutoring, writing center.

Majors. **Agriculture:** Business. **Business:** General. **Computer sciences:** Information systems. **Engineering technology:** Biomedical, mechanical, telecommunications. **Family/consumer sciences:** Family studies. **Health:** Physical therapy assistant. **Interdisciplinary:** Biological/physical sciences. **Liberal arts:** Arts/sciences.

Most popular majors. Business/marketing 31%, computer/information sciences 22%, family/consumer sciences 14%, health sciences 11%, liberal arts 18%.

Computing on campus. 161 workstations in library, computer center, student center. Commuter students can connect to campus network. Online course registration, online library, helpline, repair service, student web hosting available.

Student life. **Freshman orientation:** Mandatory. Preregistration for classes offered. One day, prior to the start of each semester. **Policies:** Acts of intolerance and high risk drinking discouraged at all locations. All facilities designated as smoke-free. Students expected to abide by The Penn State Principles. Freshmen permitted cars on campus. **Activities:** Drama, literary magazine, student government, environmental club, Students for Cultural Diversity, Women in Transition, Word of God Bible Study Club, Adults Seeking Knowledge.

Athletics. **Intramural:** Basketball, golf, softball, volleyball. **Team name:** Nittany Lions.

Student services. Adult student services, alcohol/substance abuse counseling, career counseling, student employment services, financial aid counseling, health services, minority student services, placement for graduates, veterans' counselor, women's services. **Physically disabled:** Services for visually, speech, hearing impaired. **Transfer:** Special adviser, pre-admission transcript evaluation for new students. Transfer adviser, college fairs on campus for students transferring to 4-year colleges.

Contact. E-mail: psushenango@psu.edu
Phone: (724) 983-2800 Fax: (724) 983-2820
Randall Deike, Assistant Vice Provost for Enrollment Management and Director of Admissions, Penn State Shenango, 147 Shenango Avenue, Room 206, Sharon Hall, Sharon, PA 16146-1597

Penn State Worthington Scranton

Dunmore, Pennsylvania
www.sn.psu.edu **CB code: 2660**

- Public 2-year branch campus college
- Commuter campus in large town
- SAT or ACT (ACT writing optional) required

General. Founded in 1923. Regionally accredited. **Enrollment:** 1,077 degree-seeking undergraduates; 164 non-degree-seeking students. **Degrees:** 113 bachelor's, 66 associate awarded. **ROTC:** Air Force. **Location:** 1 mile from Scranton. **Calendar:** Semester, limited summer session. **Full-time faculty:** 61 total; 56% have terminal degrees, 13% minority, 52% women. **Part-time faculty:** 43 total; 12% have terminal degrees, 46% women. **Class size:** 48% < 20, 46% 20-39, 3% 40-49, 2% 50-99.

Student profile. Among degree-seeking undergraduates, 253 enrolled as first-time, first-year students, 67 transferred in from other institutions.

Part-time:	21%	**Asian American:**	1%
Out-of-state:	1%	**Hispanic American:**	2%
Women:	51%	**25 or older:**	27%
African American:	2%		

Basis for selection. Admission decisions based upon high school GPA, as well as other factors, which may include standardized verbal and math test scores, class rank, personal statements, and list of activities. Essay considered if submitted; portfolios required for select majors. **Adult students:** SAT/ACT scores not required if out of high school 5 year(s) or more. SAT/ACT test scores not required for veterans with 4 or more years service with an honorable discharge. **Homeschooled:** Applicants should provide complete documentation showing the courses studied and all evaluations presented from evaluator or supervisor assigned to student in cooperation with local school district or evaluator who is approved through the program.

High school preparation. College-preparatory program recommended. Required units include English 4, mathematics 3, social studies 3, science 3 and foreign language 2.

2005-2006 Annual costs. Tuition/fees: $10,180; $15,312 out-of-state. Per-credit charge: $393 in-state; $619 out-of-state. Books/supplies: $1,040. Personal expenses: $1,854.

2004-2005 Financial aid. Need-based: 219 full-time freshmen applied for aid; 184 were judged to have need; 181 of these received aid. Average need met was 62%. Average scholarship/grant was $3,987; average loan $2,517. 54% of total undergraduate aid awarded as scholarships/grants, 46% as loans/jobs. Need-based aid available for part-time students. Work study available nights, weekends and for part-time students. **Non-need-based:** Awarded to 217 full-time undergraduates, including 73 freshmen. Scholarships awarded for academics, athletics, minority status, ROTC.

Application procedures. Admission: Priority date 11/30; no deadline. $50 fee, may be waived for applicants with need. Application may be submitted online. Admission notification on a rolling basis beginning on or about 11/1. Must reply by 5/1. All freshmen applications processed at University Park Campus. **Financial aid:** Priority date 2/15; no closing date. FAFSA required. Applicants notified on a rolling basis starting 2/15.

Academics. Special study options: Accelerated study, cooperative education, cross-registration, distance learning, double major, dual enrollment of high school students, honors, independent study, internships, study abroad. Bachelor's degree programs available on campus. License preparation in nursing, real estate. **Credit/placement by examination:** AP, CLEP, IB, SAT. 60 credit hours maximum toward bachelor's degree. **Support services:** Learning center, remedial instruction, study skills assistance, tutoring, writing center.

Majors. Agriculture: Business. **Business:** General. **Computer sciences:** Information systems. **Engineering technology:** Architectural. **Family/consumer sciences:** Family studies. **Health:** Nursing (RN), occupational therapy assistant. **Liberal arts:** Arts/sciences.

Most popular majors. Computer/information sciences 9%, engineering/engineering technologies 12%, health sciences 65%, liberal arts 8%.

Computing on campus. 153 workstations in library, computer center, student center. Commuter students can connect to campus network. Online course registration, online library, helpline, repair service, student web hosting, wireless network available.

Student life. Freshman orientation: Available. Preregistration for classes offered. **Policies:** Acts of intolerance and high-risk drinking discouraged at all locations. All facilities designated as smoke-free. Students expected to abide by The Penn State Principles. Freshmen permitted cars on campus. **Activities:** Jazz band, choral groups, drama, literary magazine, music ensembles, student government, student newspaper, Community Human Service Organization, Faith and Values, German club, Lighthouse club, multicultural club, veterans club, public affairs club.

Athletics. Intercollegiate: Baseball M, basketball, cross-country, soccer M, softball W, volleyball W. **Intramural:** Basketball, soccer, softball, volleyball, weight lifting. **Team name:** Nittany Lions.

Student services. Adult student services, alcohol/substance abuse counseling, career counseling, services for economically disadvantaged, student employment services, financial aid counseling, health services, personal counseling, placement for graduates, veterans' counselor, women's services. **Physically disabled:** Services for visually, speech, hearing impaired. **Transfer:** Special adviser, orientation, pre-admission transcript evaluation for new students. Transfer adviser, college fairs on campus for students transferring to 4-year colleges.

Contact. E-mail: wsadmissions@psu.edu
Phone: (570) 963-2500 Fax: (570) 963-2524
Randall Deike, Asst. Vice Provost for Enrollment Management and Director of Admissions, Penn State Worthington Scranton, 120 Ridge View Drive, Dunmore, PA 18512-1602

Penn State York

York, Pennsylvania
www.yk.psu.edu **CB code: 2660**

- Public 2-year branch campus college
- Commuter campus in large town
- SAT or ACT (ACT writing optional) required

General. Founded in 1926. Regionally accredited. **Enrollment:** 1,053 degree-seeking undergraduates; 362 non-degree-seeking students. **Degrees:** 95 bachelor's, 101 associate awarded. **Calendar:** Semester, limited summer session. **Full-time faculty:** 59 total; 64% have terminal degrees, 14% minority, 34% women. **Part-time faculty:** 64 total; 17% have terminal degrees, 3% minority, 47% women. **Class size:** 54% < 20, 40% 20-39, 4% 40-49, 2% 50-99. **Partnerships:** Project Talent Connections with York City Schools offers enrichment for at-risk middle and high school students.

Student profile. Among degree-seeking undergraduates, 269 enrolled as first-time, first-year students, 40 transferred in from other institutions.

Part-time:	29%	**Asian American:**	6%
Out-of-state:	2%	**Hispanic American:**	4%
Women:	44%	**25 or older:**	32%
African American:	4%		

Transfer out. Colleges most students transferred to 2005: York College, Shippensburg University, Millersville University.

Basis for selection. Admission decisions based upon high school GPA and other factors, which may include standardized verbal and math test scores, class rank, personal statements, activities lists. Essay considered if submitted; portfolios required for select majors. **Adult students:** SAT/ACT scores not required if out of high school 5 year(s) or more. SAT/ACT test scores not required for veterans with 4 or more years service and honorable discharge. **Homeschooled:** Complete documentation showing courses studied and all evaluations from home school evaluator or supervisor assigned to student in cooperation with local school district or evaluator approved through program.

High school preparation. Required units include English 4, mathematics 3, social studies 3, science 3 and foreign language 2.

2005-2006 Annual costs. Tuition/fees: $10,180; $15,312 out-of-state. Per-credit charge: $393 in-state; $619 out-of-state. Books/supplies: $1,040. Personal expenses: $1,854.

2004-2005 Financial aid. Need-based: 227 full-time freshmen applied for aid; 170 were judged to have need; 169 of these received aid. Average need met was 64%. Average scholarship/grant was $3,285; average loan $2,337. 58% of total undergraduate aid awarded as scholarships/grants, 42% as loans/jobs. Need-based aid available for part-time students. Work study available nights, weekends and for part-time students. **Non-need-based:** Awarded to 281 full-time undergraduates, including 103 freshmen. Scholarships awarded for academics, athletics, minority status, ROTC.

Application procedures. Admission: Priority date 11/30; no deadline. $50 fee, may be waived for applicants with need. Application may be submitted online. Admission notification on a rolling basis beginning on or about 11/1. Must reply by 5/1. All freshmen applications processed at University Park Campus. **Financial aid:** Priority date 2/15; no closing date. FAFSA required. Applicants notified on a rolling basis starting 2/15.

Academics. Special study options: Accelerated study, cross-registration, distance learning, double major, ESL, honors, independent study, internships, student-designed major, study abroad. Bachelor's degree programs available on campus. **Credit/placement by examination:** AP, CLEP, IB, SAT. 60 credit hours maximum toward bachelor's degree. **Support services:** Learning center, pre-admission summer program, reduced course load, remedial instruction, study skills assistance, tutoring, writing center.

Majors. Agriculture: Business. **Business:** General. **Computer sciences:** Information systems. **Engineering technology:** Biomedical, electrical, manufacturing, mechanical, telecommunications. **Family/consumer sciences:** Family studies. **Liberal arts:** Arts/sciences.

Most popular majors. Business/marketing 30%, computer/information sciences 24%, engineering/engineering technologies 15%, family/consumer sciences 14%, liberal arts 18%.

Computing on campus. 183 workstations in computer center. Commuter students can connect to campus network. Online course registration, online library, helpline, repair service, student web hosting available.

Student life. Freshman orientation: Mandatory. Preregistration for classes offered. **Policies:** Acts of intolerance and high-risk drinking discouraged at all locations. All facilities designated as smoke-free. Students expected to abide by The Penn State Principles. Freshmen permitted cars on campus. **Activities:** Dance, student government, student newspaper, Black Student Union, Christian Fellowship, Hispanic Students Association, Rainbow Alliance, veterans club, Asian culture club, foreign policy and debate club.

Athletics. Intercollegiate: Baseball M, basketball, cross-country, soccer, softball W, tennis, volleyball. **Intramural:** Badminton, basketball, football (non-tackle) M, handball, soccer, softball, table tennis, tennis, volleyball. **Team name:** Nittany Lions.

Student services. Adult student services, alcohol/substance abuse counseling, campus ministries, career counseling, services for economically disadvantaged, student employment services, financial aid counseling, health services, minority student services, personal counseling, placement for graduates, veterans' counselor, women's services. **Physically disabled:** Services for visually, speech, hearing impaired. **Learning disabled:** Comprehensive services available. **Transfer:** Special adviser, orientation, pre-admission transcript evaluation for new students.

Contact. E-mail: ykadmission@psu.edu
Phone: (717) 771-4040 Toll-free number: (800) 778-6227
Fax: (717) 771-4062
Randall Deike, Assistant Vice Provost for Enrollment Management and Director of Admissions, Penn State York, 1031 Edgecomb Avenue, York, PA 17403-3398

Pennco Tech
Bristol, Pennsylvania
www.penncotech.com **CB code: 0380**

- For-profit 2-year technical college
- Large town
- Interview required

General. Founded in 1973. Accredited by ACCSCT. Branch campus in Blackwood, New Jersey. **Enrollment:** 700 undergraduates. **Degrees:** 71 associate awarded. **Location:** 18 miles from Philadelphia. **Calendar:** Modular, year-round calendar. Limited summer session. **Full-time faculty:** 70 total. **Part-time faculty:** 10 total.

Basis for selection. Institution's entrance examination and campus interview most important.

2005-2006 Annual costs. Tuition ranges from $6,000 to $25,000 depending on program. Room only: $2,100. Books/supplies: $850.

Application procedures. Admission: No deadline. $100 fee. Admission notification on a rolling basis. **Financial aid:** No deadline. Applicants notified on a rolling basis.

Academics. Credit/placement by examination: CLEP, institutional tests. 30 credit hours maximum toward associate degree. **Support services:** Tutoring.

Majors. Business: Hospitality admin. **Computer sciences:** Programming. **Engineering:** Electrical. **Mechanic/repair:** Auto body, automotive.

Student life. Housing: Single-sex dorms available. **Activities:** Choral groups, TV station.

Student services. Career counseling, student employment services, on-campus daycare, personal counseling, placement for graduates.

Contact. E-mail: admissions@penncotech.com
Phone: (215) 824-3200 Toll-free number: (800) 575-9399
Glenn Slater, Director of Admissions, Pennco Tech, 3815 Otter Street, Bristol, PA 19007

Pennsylvania Highlands Community College
Johnstown, Pennsylvania
www.pennhighlands.edu **CB code: 2484**

- Public 2-year community college
- Commuter campus in large town

General. Regionally accredited. **Enrollment:** 1,300 undergraduates. **Degrees:** 146 associate awarded. **Calendar:** Continuous, extensive summer session. **Full-time faculty:** 25 total. **Part-time faculty:** 80 total. **Class size:** 84% < 20, 16% 20-39. **Partnerships:** Internships, placement opportunities, and articulation programs.

Transfer out. Colleges most students transferred to 2005: University of Pittsburgh at Johnstown, Saint Francis College, Indiana University of Pennsylvania, Geneva College, Mount Aloysius College.

Basis for selection. Open admission.

2005-2006 Annual costs. Tuition/fees: $2,610; $4,710 out-of-district; $6,810 out-of-state. Per-credit charge: $70 in-district; $140 out-of-district; $210 out-of-state. Books/supplies: $500. Personal expenses: $500.

Financial aid. Need-based: Need-based aid available for part-time students. Work study available nights and for part-time students. **Non-need-based:** Scholarships awarded for academics, state residency.

Application procedures. Admission: No deadline. $20 fee, may be waived for applicants with need. Notification within one week of application. **Financial aid:** Closing date 5/1. FAFSA required. Applicants notified on a rolling basis starting 1/1; must reply within 1 week(s) of notification.

Academics. Special study options: Cooperative education, distance learning, honors, independent study, internships. **Credit/placement by examination:** CLEP, institutional tests. **Support services:** Reduced course load, remedial instruction, study skills assistance, tutoring.

Majors. Business: Accounting, administrative services, business admin, logistics. **Computer sciences:** General, programming. **Education:** Early childhood, multi-level teacher. **Engineering technology:** Architectural, environmental. **Family/consumer sciences:** Institutional food production. **Health:** Health care admin. **Legal studies:** Court reporting. **Liberal arts:** Arts/sciences. **Mechanic/repair:** Heating/ac/refrig. **Social sciences:** General, demography.

Most popular majors. Business/marketing 16%, computer/information sciences 21%, engineering/engineering technologies 8%, health sciences 26%, liberal arts 10%, social sciences 12%.

Computing on campus. 75 workstations in library, computer center. Online library available.

Student life. Freshman orientation: Available. Preregistration for classes offered. **Policies:** Freshmen permitted cars on campus. **Activities:** Literary magazine.

Athletics. Team name: Cardinals.

Student services. Career counseling, services for economically disadvantaged, student employment services, financial aid counseling, placement for graduates. **Transfer:** Special adviser, orientation, pre-admission transcript evaluation for new students. Transfer center, transfer adviser, college fairs on campus for students transferring to 4-year colleges.

Contact. E-mail: jmaul@pennhighlands.edu
Phone: (814) 532-5327 Fax: (814) 532-5320
Jeff Maul, Director of Admissions, Pennsylvania Highlands Community College, PO Box 68, Johnstown, PA 15907-0068

Pennsylvania Institute of Culinary Arts
Pittsburgh, Pennsylvania
www.paculinary.com **CB code: 2440**

- For-profit 2-year culinary school and technical college
- Residential campus in large city
- Interview required

General. Founded in 1986. Accredited by ACCSCT. **Enrollment:** 970 degree-seeking undergraduates. **Degrees:** 762 associate awarded. **Location:** 300 miles from Philadelphia. **Calendar:** Semester, extensive summer session. **Full-time faculty:** 40 total.

Student profile. Among degree-seeking undergraduates, 100% enrolled in a vocational program.

Out-of-state:	49%	**Live on campus:**	25%
25 or older:	21%		

Basis for selection. Interview, high school diploma or GED, Wonderlic reading assessment important. SAT or ACT recommended. Wonderlic assessment is required of all students who do not provide qualified SAT or

ACT scores. **Adult students:** Entrance exam policies same as for first-time freshmen. **Homeschooled:** State high school equivalency certificate required.

2005-2006 Annual costs. Total costs vary by program. Books/supplies: $1,671.

2005-2006 Financial aid. All financial aid based on need.

Application procedures. Admission: No deadline. $100 fee. Application may be submitted online. Admission notification on a rolling basis. **Financial aid:** No deadline. FAFSA, institutional form required. Applicants notified on a rolling basis.

Academics. Special study options: Internships. **Credit/placement by examination:** AP, CLEP, institutional tests. **Support services:** Learning center, remedial instruction, study skills assistance, tutoring.

Majors. Personal/culinary services: Culinary arts.

Computing on campus. 80 workstations in library, computer center. Online library available.

Student life. Freshman orientation: Mandatory. Approximately 2 hours, held day before classes start. **Policies:** Freshmen permitted cars on campus. **Housing:** Guaranteed on-campus for all undergraduates. Coed dorms available. $200 fully refundable deposit. **Activities:** Student government, student newspaper.

Student services. Alcohol/substance abuse counseling, career counseling, student employment services, financial aid counseling, personal counseling, placement for graduates. **Transfer:** Special adviser, orientation, preadmission transcript evaluation for new students.

Contact. E-mail: info@paculinary.com
Phone: (412) 566-2433 Toll-free number: (800) 432-2433
Fax: (412) 566-2434
Chris O'Dell, Vice President of Admissions and Marketing, Pennsylvania Institute of Culinary Arts, 717 Liberty Avenue, Pittsburgh, PA 15222

Pennsylvania Institute of Technology

Media, Pennsylvania
www.pit.edu **CB code: 2675**

- Private 2-year technical college
- Commuter campus in small town
- Application essay, interview required

General. Founded in 1953. Regionally accredited. **Enrollment:** 257 degree-seeking undergraduates. **Degrees:** 62 associate awarded. **Location:** 13 miles from Philadelphia, 15 miles from Wilmington, Delaware. **Calendar:** Semester, extensive summer session. **Full-time faculty:** 21 total. **Part-time faculty:** 26 total. **Class size:** 99% < 20, less than 1% 20-39. **Partnerships:** Tech Prep in high schools.

Basis for selection. Open admission. Interview and essay used for placement purposes only.

2005-2006 Annual costs. Tuition/fees: $9,000. Per-credit charge: $300. Part time students pay a technology fee of $11 per credit hour. Books/supplies: $900.

2005-2006 Financial aid. Need-based: 31% of total undergraduate aid awarded as scholarships/grants, 69% as loans/jobs. Need-based aid available for part-time students. Work study available nights, weekends and for part-time students. **Non-need-based:** Scholarships awarded for academics, leadership.

Application procedures. Admission: No deadline. $25 fee, may be waived for applicants with need. Application may be submitted online. Admission notification on a rolling basis. **Financial aid:** Closing date 8/1. FAFSA, institutional form required. Applicants notified on a rolling basis starting 7/1.

Academics. Curricula designed to prepare students for positions in industry through combination of general education and job specific courses. **Special study options:** Accelerated study, cooperative education, double major, independent study, internships. **Credit/placement by examination:** AP, CLEP, institutional tests. 60 credit hours maximum toward associate degree. **Support services:** Learning center, reduced course load, remedial instruction, tutoring.

Majors. Business: Administrative services, business admin. **Computer sciences:** Computer science. **Engineering technology:** Architectural, civil, electrical. **Health:** Medical secretary.

Most popular majors. Business/marketing 16%, engineering/engineering technologies 84%.

Computing on campus. 80 workstations in library, computer center. Commuter students can connect to campus network.

Student life. Freshman orientation: Mandatory. Orientation lasts several days, held 1 week before start of classes. **Activities:** Radio station, student government, student newspaper, amateur radio club.

Athletics. Intramural: Basketball M, softball M, volleyball.

Student services. Adult student services, career counseling, student employment services, personal counseling, placement for graduates, veterans' counselor. **Physically disabled:** Services for speech, hearing impaired. **Transfer:** Special adviser, orientation for new students. Transfer adviser, college fairs on campus for students transferring to 4-year colleges.

Contact. E-mail: info@pit.edu
Phone: (610) 565-7900 Fax: (610) 892-1510
Angela Cassetta, Director of Admissions, Pennsylvania Institute of Technology, 800 Manchester Avenue, Media, PA 19063-4098

Pennsylvania School of Business

Allentown, Pennsylvania
www.pennschoolofbusiness.edu **CB code: 3044**

- For-profit 2-year technical college
- Small city

General. Accredited by ACCSCT. **Enrollment:** 200 degree-seeking undergraduates. **Degrees:** 9 associate awarded. **Calendar:** Continuous. **Full-time faculty:** 20 total. **Part-time faculty:** 8 total.

Basis for selection. Open admission.

2005-2006 Annual costs. Tuition for associate-degree program (15 months): $16,202. Books/supplies: $800.

Financial aid. Need-based: Need-based aid available for part-time students.

Application procedures. Admission: No deadline. $50 fee. Admission notification on a rolling basis. **Financial aid:** No deadline. FAFSA required. Applicants notified on a rolling basis.

Academics. Credit/placement by examination: CLEP.

Majors. Business: Business admin. **Computer sciences:** General.

Contact. Phone: (610) 841-3333
Bill Barber, Director, Pennsylvania School of Business, 2201 Hangar Place, Allentown, PA 18103

Pittsburgh Institute of Aeronautics

Pittsburgh, Pennsylvania
www.pia.edu **CB code: 0652**

- Private 2-year technical college
- Commuter campus in large city

General. Founded in 1929. Accredited by ACCSCT. Located in an active county airport. **Enrollment:** 200 degree-seeking undergraduates. **Degrees:** 115 associate awarded. **Calendar:** Quarter, extensive summer session. **Full-time faculty:** 25 total. **Part-time faculty:** 1 total. **Special facilities:** Modern aeronautics and aviation electronics laboratories.

Student profile.

Out-of-state:	35%	**25 or older:**	25%

Basis for selection. Entrance examination score very important.

2005-2006 Annual costs. Tuition/fees: $10,335. Books/supplies: $900. Personal expenses: $400.

Application procedures. Admission: No deadline. $150 fee. Admission notification on a rolling basis. **Financial aid:** Priority date 5/1; no closing date. FAFSA required. Applicants notified on a rolling basis.

Academics. Special study options: License preparation in aviation. **Credit/placement by examination:** CLEP, institutional tests. **Support services:** Remedial instruction, tutoring.

Majors. **Education:** Technology/industrial arts, voc/tech. **Engineering:** General, electrical. **Engineering technology:** Electrical. **Mechanic/repair:** Aircraft, electronics/electrical.

Computing on campus. 30 workstations in computer center.

Student life. **Housing:** Referral housing available. **Activities:** Student government.

Student services. Adult student services, career counseling, student employment services, personal counseling, placement for graduates, veterans' counselor. **Transfer:** Pre-admission transcript evaluation for new students.

Contact. E-mail: admissions@pia.edu
Phone: (412) 346-2100 Toll-free number: (800) 444-1440
Fax: (412) 466-0513
Vincent Mezza, Director of Admissions, Pittsburgh Institute of Aeronautics, Box 10897, Pittsburgh, PA 15236-0897

Pittsburgh Institute of Mortuary Science

Pittsburgh, Pennsylvania
www.p-i-m-s.com **CB code: 7030**

- Private 2-year technical college
- Commuter campus in large city

General. Founded in 1939. Accredited by American Board of Funeral Services Education, Inc. **Enrollment:** 150 undergraduates. **Degrees:** 51 associate awarded. **Calendar:** Trimester, extensive summer session. **Full-time faculty:** 4 total; 25% women. **Part-time faculty:** 21 total; 14% have terminal degrees, 5% minority, 24% women. **Special facilities:** Embalming facility, specialized library.

Transfer out. **Colleges most students transferred to 2005:** Point Park College.

Basis for selection. Open admission. **Learning Disabled:** Diagnosis documentation within 3 years of enrollment required.

2005-2006 Annual costs. Tuition/fees: $12,800. Per-credit charge: $240. Books/supplies: $700.

Financial aid. **Need-based:** Need-based aid available for part-time students.

Application procedures. **Admission:** Priority date 9/1; no deadline. $40 fee. Application may be submitted online. Admission notification on a rolling basis. **Financial aid:** No deadline. FAFSA required. Applicants notified on a rolling basis.

Academics. Four-pronged approach to funeral service management via natural sciences, social sciences, mortuary sciences, and humanities. Students with previous associate degrees will earn diploma or another associate degree in embalming and funeral directing. **Special study options:** Distance learning. **Credit/placement by examination:** CLEP, institutional tests. 48 credit hours maximum toward associate degree. **Support services:** Reduced course load, tutoring.

Majors. **Personal/culinary services:** Mortuary science.

Computing on campus. 10 workstations in library, computer center.

Student life. **Freshman orientation:** Mandatory. Preregistration for classes offered. Generally held week before start of classes. **Policies:** Freshmen permitted cars on campus. **Housing:** Housing available at local funeral homes. **Activities:** Student government.

Student services. Career counseling, student employment services, financial aid counseling, personal counseling, placement for graduates, veterans' counselor. **Transfer:** Special adviser, orientation, pre-admission transcript evaluation for new students. Transfer adviser for students transferring to 4-year colleges.

Contact. E-mail: pims5808@aol.com
Phone: (412) 362-8500 Toll-free number: (800) 933-5808
Fax: (412) 362-1684
Karen Rocco, Registrar, Pittsburgh Institute of Mortuary Science, 5808 Baum Boulevard, Pittsburgh, PA 15206-3706

Pittsburgh Technical Institute

Oakdale, Pennsylvania **CB member**
www.pti.edu **CB code: 0382**

- For-profit 2-year technical college
- Commuter campus in large town
- Interview required

General. Founded in 1946. Accredited by ACICS. Three locations in the Pittsburgh area. Evening certificate and on-line/on-site degrees for adult students ages 22+. Boyd School division offers travel and hospitality career preparation. **Enrollment:** 1,860 degree-seeking undergraduates; 5 non-degree-seeking students. **Degrees:** 604 associate awarded. **Location:** 12 miles from Pittsburgh. **Calendar:** Quarter, extensive summer session. **Full-time faculty:** 70 total; 19% have terminal degrees, 4% minority, 29% women. **Part-time faculty:** 34 total; 9% have terminal degrees, 41% women.

Student profile. Among degree-seeking undergraduates, 1,041 enrolled as first-time, first-year students.

Out-of-state:	19%	**Asian American:**	1%
Women:	34%	**Live on campus:**	28%
African American:	4%		

Transfer out. **Colleges most students transferred to 2005:** Point Park, Robert Morris, California University of Pennsylvania.

Basis for selection. Open admission, but selective for some programs. Computer Programming: upper 50% of graduating class or passing score on CPAT. BA-Safety and Security Administration: pass criminal background check. Graphic Design and Multimedia Technologies: upper 80% of graduating class or passing score on CPAT and portfolio review. Surgical Technology: pass criminal background check and dexterity test. Foreign students must complete application in English, show official certification of fund sources and amounts, and submit letter certifying sponsorship. **Adult students:** Entrance exam policies same as for first-time freshmen.

2005-2006 Annual costs. Tuition and supply costs vary by program and student use.

2004-2005 Financial aid. **Need-based:** 57% of total undergraduate aid awarded as scholarships/grants, 43% as loans/jobs. Need-based aid available for part-time students.

Application procedures. **Admission:** No deadline. No application fee. Application may be submitted online. Admission notification on a rolling basis. **Financial aid:** Priority date 3/15; no closing date. FAFSA, institutional form required. Applicants notified on a rolling basis.

Academics. All associate degree programs and selected certificate programs include industry-based internship. **Special study options:** Distance learning, internships. **Credit/placement by examination:** CLEP, institutional tests. **Support services:** Learning center, remedial instruction, study skills assistance, tutoring, writing center.

Majors. **Business:** Accounting, business admin, hotel/motel admin, sales/distribution, tourism promotion. **Computer sciences:** Programming, web page design. **Engineering technology:** Computer systems, drafting, electrical. **Health:** Management/clinical assistant, office assistant, surgical technology. **Visual/performing arts:** Commercial/advertising art.

Most popular majors. Business/marketing 15%, computer/information sciences 13%, engineering/engineering technologies 52%, visual/performing arts 10%.

Computing on campus. 1,000 workstations in library, computer center, student center. Online library, helpline, student web hosting, wireless network available.

Student life. **Freshman orientation:** Mandatory. Held every June and September, 1 month before July and October classes start; also every January, 1 week before classes start. **Housing:** Apartments available. $350 deposit.

Athletics. **Intramural:** Softball.

Student services. Adult student services, alcohol/substance abuse counseling, career counseling, student employment services, financial aid counseling, personal counseling, placement for graduates. **Transfer:** Special adviser, orientation, re-entry adviser, pre-admission transcript evaluation for new students. Transfer adviser, college fairs on campus for students transferring to 4-year colleges.

Contact. E-mail: james@pti.edu
Phone: (412) 809-5100 Toll-free number: (800) 784-9675
Fax: (412) 809-5388
Marylu Zuk, Vice President of Admissions, Pittsburgh Technical Institute, 1111 McKee Road, Oakdale, PA 15071-3205

PJA School

Upper Darby, Pennsylvania
www.pjaschool.com **CB code: 2887**

- For-profit 2-year business and junior college
- Commuter campus in very large city
- Application essay, interview required

General. Accredited by ACCSCT. **Enrollment:** 245 degree-seeking undergraduates. **Degrees:** 70 associate awarded. **Location:** 4 miles from downtown Philadelphia. **Calendar:** Semester, extensive summer session. **Full-time faculty:** 5 total. **Part-time faculty:** 25 total. **Class size:** 25% < 20, 75% 20-39. **Special facilities:** Law library.

Student profile.

Out-of-state:	6%	**25 or older:**	58%

Basis for selection. Applicants considered based on total background, including education, employment experience, communication skills, speech, appearance and maturity. Reference letters and entrance exam required. **Adult students:** SAT/ACT scores not required.

2005-2006 Annual costs. Tuition/fees: $9,930. Books and materials included in cost of tuition. Personal expenses: $2,067.

Financial aid. All financial aid based on need. Need-based aid available for part-time students. **Additional information:** PJA works with various funding agencies, including the Office of Vocational Rehabilitation, Delaware County Office of Employment and Training, Chester County Office of Employment and Training, Philadelphia Workforce Development Corporation, and Veteran's Administration. PJA also offers an interest-free payment plan.

Application procedures. Admission: No deadline. No application fee. Admission notification on a rolling basis. **Financial aid:** No deadline. FAFSA, institutional form required. Applicants notified on a rolling basis.

Academics. Special study options: Accelerated study, double major, independent study, internships, liberal arts/career combination. Bachelor's degree programs available on campus. **Credit/placement by examination:** CLEP, institutional tests. No more than 20% of credits required for degree may be awarded for prior work or life experience. **Support services:** Learning center, reduced course load, remedial instruction, study skills assistance, tutoring.

Majors. Business: General, accounting. **Legal studies:** Paralegal.

Most popular majors. Business/marketing 11%, interdisciplinary studies 42%, legal studies 47%.

Computing on campus. 120 workstations in library, computer center, student center.

Student life. Freshman orientation: Mandatory. Preregistration for classes offered. **Policies:** Freshmen permitted cars on campus.

Athletics. Team name: Scales of Justice.

Student services. Adult student services, career counseling, student employment services, financial aid counseling, personal counseling, placement for graduates, veterans' counselor.

Contact. E-mail: pjaschool@dvol.com
Phone: (610) 789-6700 Toll-free number: (800) 746-4752
Fax: (610) 789-5208
Daniel Alpert, Director of Institutional Development, PJA School, 7900 West Chester Pike, Upper Darby, PA 19082

Reading Area Community College

Reading, Pennsylvania
www.racc.cc.pa.us **CB code: 2743**

- Public 2-year community college
- Commuter campus in small city

General. Founded in 1971. Regionally accredited. **Enrollment:** 4,300 undergraduates. **Degrees:** 369 associate awarded. **Location:** 55 miles from Philadelphia. **Calendar:** 3 ten week terms per year. Limited summer session. **Full-time faculty:** 75 total. **Part-time faculty:** 176 total.

Basis for selection. Open admission, but selective for some programs. Special requirements for nursing, radiology, respiratory therapy and clinical portion of medical laboratory technician program. Interview, science background considered. Interview recommended.

High school preparation. 16 units required for nursing program, including 4 English, 3 social studies, 2 mathematics (1 must be algebra), and 2 science with related laboratory or equivalent.

2005-2006 Annual costs. Books/supplies: $500. Personal expenses: $1,200.

Application procedures. Admission: No deadline. $20 fee, may be waived for applicants with need. Admission notification on a rolling basis. **Financial aid:** Priority date 7/1; no closing date. FAFSA, institutional form required. Applicants notified on a rolling basis starting 4/15; must reply within 2 week(s) of notification.

Academics. Special study options: Cooperative education, distance learning, dual enrollment of high school students, independent study, internships, student-designed major, weekend college. **Credit/placement by examination:** AP, CLEP, institutional tests. 45 credit hours maximum toward associate degree. **Support services:** Learning center, pre-admission summer program, reduced course load, remedial instruction, tutoring.

Majors. Biology: General. **Business:** General, accounting, administrative services, banking/financial services, business admin, entrepreneurial studies, human resources, management information systems, office management, office technology, office/clerical, operations, tourism promotion. **Computer sciences:** Data processing, networking, programming. **Education:** General, business, early childhood, elementary, middle, secondary. **Engineering:** General, electrical. **Engineering technology:** Electrical. **Family/consumer sciences:** Child care. **Health:** Clinical lab science, health services, licensed practical nurse, medical radiologic technology/radiation therapy, medical secretary, nursing (RN), predentistry, premedicine, prepharmacy, respiratory therapy technology. **Interdisciplinary:** Gerontology. **Legal studies:** Legal secretary, prelaw. **Liberal arts:** Arts/sciences. **Mechanic/repair:** Industrial. **Personal/culinary services:** Culinary arts. **Physical sciences:** Chemistry. **Protective services:** Law enforcement admin, police science. **Psychology:** General. **Public administration:** General, social work. **Social sciences:** General, criminology.

Computing on campus. 90 workstations in library, computer center.

Student life. Freshman orientation: Mandatory. Preregistration for classes offered. **Activities:** Radio station, student government, student newspaper, TV station.

Athletics. Intercollegiate: Basketball M, cross-country, soccer M, volleyball W. **Intramural:** Basketball M. **Team name:** Rockets.

Student services. Career counseling, student employment services, on-campus daycare, personal counseling, placement for graduates, veterans' counselor. **Physically disabled:** Services for visually, hearing impaired. **Transfer:** Special adviser, orientation for new students. Transfer adviser, college fairs on campus for students transferring to 4-year colleges.

Contact. E-mail: nw4964@email.racc.cc.pa.us
Phone: (800) 626-1665 Fax: (610) 607-6290
David Adams, Director of Admissions, Reading Area Community College, 10 South Second Street, Reading, PA 19603-1706

Rosedale Technical Institute

Pittsburgh, Pennsylvania
www.rosedaletech.org **CB code: 3025**

- Private 2-year technical college
- Large city

General. Accredited by ACCSCT. **Enrollment:** 240 degree-seeking undergraduates. **Degrees:** 100 associate awarded. **Calendar:** Continuous. **Full-time faculty:** 19 total. **Part-time faculty:** 1 total.

Basis for selection. Open admission. Wonderlic exam required.

2005-2006 Annual costs. Tuition/fees: $9,060.

Application procedures. Admission: No deadline. $10 fee. Admission notification on a rolling basis. **Financial aid:** Closing date 8/1. FAFSA required.

Academics. Credit/placement by examination: CLEP.

Majors. Mechanic/repair: General.

Student life. Freshman orientation: Available. Generally held 2 weeks prior to the start of classes.

Contact. Phone: (412) 521-6200 Toll-free number: (800) 521-6262
Kevin Auld, Director of Admissions, Rosedale Technical Institute, 4634 Browns Hill Road, Pittsburgh, PA 15217

Schuylkill Institute of Business & Technology

Pottsville, Pennsylvania
www.sibt.edu **CB code: 2465**

- For-profit 2-year technical college
- Commuter campus in small town
- Interview required

General. Accredited by ACICS. **Enrollment:** 135 degree-seeking undergraduates. **Degrees:** 55 associate awarded. **Calendar:** Semester. **Full-time faculty:** 15 total. **Part-time faculty:** 1 total. **Class size:** 100% < 20. **Special facilities:** Massage clinic, medical clinic.

Student profile. Among degree-seeking undergraduates, 36 enrolled as first-time, first-year students.

Women:	64%	**Native American:**	1%
African American:	1%		

Basis for selection. Open admission. **Adult students:** Entrance exam policies same as for first-time freshmen.

2005-2006 Annual costs. Tuition/fees: $10,500. Per-credit charge: $271. Programs cost between $7,100 and $25,000 and last between 9 and 24 months.

2005-2006 Financial aid. All financial aid based on need. Need-based aid available for part-time students.

Application procedures. Admission: No deadline. $50 fee, may be waived for applicants with need. Admission notification on a rolling basis. **Financial aid:** Priority date 4/25, closing date 5/1. FAFSA required. Applicants notified by 10/1; must reply by 10/15.

Academics. Special study options: Internships. **Credit/placement by examination:** CLEP. **Support services:** Tutoring.

Majors. Business: Accounting, administrative services. **Computer sciences:** General. **Health:** Medical assistant, medical secretary. **Legal studies:** Paralegal.

Most popular majors. Business/marketing 10%, computer/information sciences 25%, health sciences 50%, legal studies 15%.

Computing on campus. 40 workstations in library, computer center, student center. Repair service available.

Student life. Freshman orientation: Available. Two-hour introduction to staff and faculty, plus program overviews and book distribution. **Activities:** Student newspaper.

Student services. Career counseling, student employment services, financial aid counseling, placement for graduates. **Transfer:** Orientation for new students.

Contact. E-mail: admissions@sibt.edu
Phone: (800) 829-5666 Fax: (570) 622-6563
Gayle Holden, Admissions Representative, Schuylkill Institute of Business & Technology, 118 South Centre Street, Pottsville, PA 17901

South Hills School of Business & Technology

State College, Pennsylvania
www.southhills.edu **CB code: 2467**

- For-profit 2-year business and technical college
- Commuter campus in large town
- Interview required

General. Founded in 1970. Regionally accredited; also accredited by ACICS. Free brush-up classes for graduates. Branch campuses in Altoona, Lewistown, and Philipsburg. Career services assistance to all graduates. **Enrollment:** 646 degree-seeking undergraduates; 18 non-degree-seeking students. **Degrees:** 231 associate awarded. **Location:** 125 miles from Pittsburgh, 200 miles from Philadelphia. **Calendar:** Quarter, limited summer session. **Full-time faculty:** 42 total; 2% have terminal degrees, 64% women. **Part-time faculty:** 21 total; 5% have terminal degrees, 48% women.

Student profile. Among degree-seeking undergraduates, 100% enrolled in a vocational program, 2% already have a bachelor's degree or higher, 343 enrolled as first-time, first-year students.

Part-time:	6%	**Women:**	68%
Out-of-state:	1%	**25 or older:**	40%

Transfer out. Colleges most students transferred to 2005: St. Francis University, Lock Haven University, Mount Aloysius, Pennsylvania State University.

Basis for selection. Open admission, but selective for some programs. In addition to providing a high school transcript and/or GED transcript that shows completion, all students are required to pass entrance examination and to complete interview. Applicants for diagnostic medical sonography program required to submit 2 letters of recommendation. **Adult students:** Entrance exam policies same as for first-time freshmen. **Homeschooled:** Transcript of courses and grades required. **Learning Disabled:** With documented learning disabilities, applicant may have extended time for entrance exam.

High school preparation. Recommended units include English 4, mathematics 3, social studies 4 and science 3.

2006-2007 Annual costs. Tuition/fees (projected): $11,737. Per-credit charge: $323. Books/supplies: $1,500.

2004-2005 Financial aid. All financial aid based on need. 366 full-time freshmen applied for aid; 366 were judged to have need; 366 of these received aid. Average need met was 73%. Average scholarship/grant was $73; average loan $2,625. 67% of total undergraduate aid awarded as scholarships/grants, 33% as loans/jobs. Need-based aid available for part-time students.

Application procedures. Admission: No deadline. $25 fee. Application may be submitted online. Admission notification on a rolling basis. **Financial aid:** Closing date 6/30. FAFSA required. Applicants notified on a rolling basis starting 7/5.

Academics. Special study options: Double major, internships. Technical preparatory program. **Credit/placement by examination:** AP, CLEP. 51 credit hours maximum toward associate degree. **Support services:** Preadmission summer program, study skills assistance, tutoring.

Majors. Business: Accounting, accounting/business management, administrative services, business admin, marketing, office management, office/clerical. **Computer sciences:** General, applications programming, computer science, data entry, data processing, information technology, LAN/WAN management, networking, programming, system admin, systems analysis, web page design. **Engineering:** General. **Engineering technology:** General, computer, computer hardware, computer systems, software. **Health:** Insurance coding, insurance specialist, medical records admin, medical records technology, medical secretary, medical transcription, office admin, office assistant, office computer specialist, receptionist, sonography. **Legal studies:** Legal secretary. **Production:** Machine tool.

Most popular majors. Business/marketing 23%, computer/information sciences 50%, health sciences 20%.

Computing on campus. 380 workstations in library, computer center, student center. Commuter students can connect to campus network. Online library, wireless network available.

Student life. Freshman orientation: Mandatory. One-day program. **Policies:** Freshmen permitted cars on campus. **Activities:** Student government, student newspaper.

Athletics. Intramural: Basketball M, volleyball.

Student services. Career counseling, student employment services, placement for graduates. **Transfer:** Special adviser, orientation, pre-admission transcript evaluation for new students. Transfer adviser, college fairs on campus for students transferring to 4-year colleges.

Contact. E-mail: admissions@southhills.edu
Phone: (814) 234-7755 Toll-free number: (888) 282-7427
Fax: (814) 234-0926
Diane Brown, Director of Admissions, South Hills School of Business & Technology, 480 Waupelani Drive, State College, PA 16801-4516

South Hills School of Business & Technology

Altoona, Pennsylvania
www.southhills.edu **CB code: 2176**

- For-profit 2-year technical college
- Small city

General. Accredited by ACICS. **Calendar:** Semester.

Annual costs/financial aid. Tuition $3,900 per term; fees $25 per term. Books/supplies: $600.

Contact. Phone: (814) 944-6134
Registrar, 508 58th Street, Altoona, PA 16602

Thaddeus Stevens College of Technology

Lancaster, Pennsylvania
www.stevenstech.org **CB code: 0560**

- Public 2-year technical college
- Residential campus in small city

General. Founded in 1905. Regionally accredited. **Enrollment:** 660 undergraduates. **Degrees:** 212 associate awarded. **Location:** 60 miles from Philadelphia, 30 miles from Harrisburg. **Calendar:** Semester, limited summer session. **Full-time faculty:** 40 total. **Part-time faculty:** 10 total.

Basis for selection. Priority given to orphans and financially needy students. Admission based on school achievement record and institutional placement examination (ASSET). Interview recommended for associate of specialized technology program.

High school preparation. 14 units required. Required and recommended units include English 4, mathematics 4 and science 2-6. Algebra required for entry to some associate degree programs.

2005-2006 Annual costs. Tuition/fees: $5,170. Room/board: $4,872. Books/supplies: $275. Personal expenses: $300.

Financial aid. Additional information: Tuition and room and board costs waived for students with adjusted family income of $18,500 or less. Tuition and other costs also waived for orphans.

Application procedures. Admission: Priority date 1/1; deadline 7/30. $25 fee, may be waived for applicants with need. Application may be submitted online. Admission notification on a rolling basis beginning on or about 10/15. Applicant must reply within 30 days of receiving notification of decision. **Financial aid:** Priority date 3/15; no closing date. Applicants notified on a rolling basis starting 7/15.

Academics. Modern technological equipment kept current with industry standards. **Credit/placement by examination:** CLEP, institutional tests. **Support services:** Learning center, pre-admission summer program, reduced course load, remedial instruction, tutoring.

Majors. Business: Office/clerical. **Communications technology:** Graphic/printing. **Construction:** Power transmission. **Engineering technology:** Drafting. **Mechanic/repair:** Electronics/electrical, heating/ac/refrig.

Computing on campus. 32 workstations in library, computer center.

Student life. Freshman orientation: Mandatory. **Policies:** Freshmen permitted cars on campus. **Housing:** Coed dorms, single-sex dorms available. **Activities:** Student government, student newspaper, Bible study group, dormitory council, outdoor club.

Athletics. NJCAA. **Intercollegiate:** Basketball M, cross-country, football (tackle) M, track and field M, wrestling M. **Intramural:** Archery, badminton, basketball, bowling, fencing, golf, soccer, softball, table tennis, tennis, track and field, volleyball, wrestling M.

Student services. Adult student services, career counseling, student employment services, health services, personal counseling, placement for graduates. **Transfer:** Special adviser, orientation for new students. Transfer adviser for students transferring to 4-year colleges.

Contact. Phone: (717) 299-7701 Toll-free number: (800) 842-3832
Fax: (717) 391-6929
Erin Nelson, Director of Enrollment Services, Thaddeus Stevens College of Technology, 750 East King Street, Lancaster, PA 17602

Thompson Institute

Harrisburg, Pennsylvania
www.thompson.edu **CB code: 3212**

- For-profit 2-year health science and technical college
- Small city

General. Accredited by ACICS. **Enrollment:** 550 undergraduates. **Degrees:** 99 associate awarded. **Calendar:** Continuous. **Full-time faculty:** 23 total. **Part-time faculty:** 7 total.

Basis for selection. Open admission.

2005-2006 Annual costs. Tuition/fees: $12,231. Figures provided represent average costs of tuition and fees based on three quarters. Books/supplies: $2,040. Personal expenses: $2,862.

Academics. Credit/placement by examination: CLEP.

Majors. Business: Business admin. **Engineering:** General.

Contact. E-mail: jdunn@thompson.edu
Phone: (717) 564-4112 Toll-free number: (888) 532-7645
Fax: (717) 564-3779
James Dunn, Admissions Director, Thompson Institute, 5650 Derry Street, Harrisburg, PA 17111-4112

Thompson Institute: Philadelphia

Philadelphia, Pennsylvania
www.thompson.edu **CB code: 3213**

- For-profit 1-year health science and technical college
- Residential campus in very large city

General. Accredited by ACICS. **Enrollment:** 581 degree-seeking undergraduates. **Calendar:** Continuous. **Full-time faculty:** 28 total; 86% minority, 82% women. **Part-time faculty:** 5 total; 20% women.

Student profile. Among degree-seeking undergraduates, 5 transferred in from other institutions.

Basis for selection. Open admission. Students must either supply a copy of a High school diploma, an official transcripts, a copy of a GED or take our standard Ability to Benefit (ATB) test. **Homeschooled:** Transcript of courses and grades required.

Application procedures. Admission: No deadline. $25 fee. Admission notification on a rolling basis. **Financial aid:** No deadline.

Academics. Special study options: Cooperative education. License preparation in radiology. **Credit/placement by examination:** CLEP. **Support services:** GED preparation, tutoring.

Computing on campus. 129 workstations in computer center. Online library, repair service, wireless network available.

Student life. Freshman orientation: Mandatory. Preregistration for classes offered.

Student services. Adult student services, career counseling, student employment services, financial aid counseling, personal counseling, placement for graduates. **Physically disabled:** Services for visually, hearing impaired. **Transfer:** Special adviser, orientation, re-entry adviser for new students.

Contact. Phone: (215) 594-4013 Fax: (215) 594-4089
Scott Dams, Director of Admissions, Thompson Institute: Philadelphia, 3010 Market Street, Philadelphia, PA 19104

Tri-State Business Institute

Erie, Pennsylvania
www.tsbi.edu **CB code: 2502**

- For-profit 2-year business college
- Small city

General. Accredited by ACICS. **Enrollment:** 950 undergraduates. **Degrees:** 162 associate awarded. **Calendar:** Quarter, extensive summer session. **Full-time faculty:** 15 total. **Part-time faculty:** 20 total.

Basis for selection. Open admission.

2005-2006 Annual costs. Tuition ranges from $9,900 to $12,100 and required fees from $1,680 to $1,830 per academic year, depending on program.

Application procedures. Admission: No deadline. $50 fee. Admission notification on a rolling basis.

Academics. Special study options: Internships, liberal arts/career combination. **Credit/placement by examination:** CLEP.

Two-Year Colleges

Majors. Business: Accounting, business admin. **Computer sciences:** General, computer science, information systems, programming. **Health:** Medical records technology, medical transcription. **Legal studies:** Paralegal.

Most popular majors. Business/marketing 17%, computer/information sciences 60%, health sciences 14%, legal studies 9%.

Student life. Freshman orientation: Mandatory.

Student services. Career counseling, student employment services, personal counseling, placement for graduates, veterans' counselor. **Transfer:** Special adviser for new students. Transfer adviser for students transferring to 4-year colleges.

Contact. E-mail: webadmissions@tsbi.edu
Phone: (814) 838-7673 Fax: (814) 838-8642
Karen LaPaglia, Enrollment Coordinator, Tri-State Business Institute, 5757 West Twenty-Sixth Street, Erie, PA 16506

Triangle Tech: DuBois
DuBois, Pennsylvania
www.triangle-tech.edu **CB code: 7133**

- For-profit 2-year technical college
- Commuter campus in small city

General. Accredited by ACCSCT. **Enrollment:** 243 degree-seeking undergraduates. **Degrees:** 149 associate awarded. **Location:** 135 miles from Pittsburgh. **Calendar:** Semester, extensive summer session. **Full-time faculty:** 22 total; 27% women. **Class size:** 95% < 20, 5% 20-39.

Student profile. Among degree-seeking undergraduates, 100% enrolled in a vocational program, 139 enrolled as first-time, first-year students, 2 transferred in from other institutions.

Basis for selection. Open admission. **Adult students:** Entrance exam policies same as for first-time freshmen.

2006-2007 Annual costs. Tuition/fees (projected): $11,866. Books/supplies: $990. Personal expenses: $1,608.

2004-2005 Financial aid. All financial aid based on need. 47% of total undergraduate aid awarded as scholarships/grants, 53% as loans/jobs. Need-based aid available for part-time students.

Application procedures. Admission: No deadline. No application fee. Admission notification on a rolling basis. Interview and TABE test required. Some students may be recommended for remediation. **Financial aid:** No deadline. FAFSA, institutional form required. Applicants notified on a rolling basis.

Academics. Special study options: Cooperative education, dual enrollment of high school students. **Credit/placement by examination:** CLEP. **Support services:** Learning center, remedial instruction, study skills assistance, tutoring.

Majors. Construction: Carpentry, electrician. **Engineering technology:** Architectural drafting, mechanical drafting. **Production:** Welding.

Most popular majors. Engineering/engineering technologies 14%, trade and industry 86%.

Computing on campus. 53 workstations in library, computer center.

Student life. Freshman orientation: Mandatory. Orientation held Thursday before classes begin, approximately 1-1/2 hours in length. **Policies:** Freshmen permitted cars on campus. **Activities:** Student government.

Student services. Alcohol/substance abuse counseling, career counseling, student employment services, financial aid counseling, legal services, personal counseling, placement for graduates. **Transfer:** Orientation, pre-admission transcript evaluation for new students.

Contact. Phone: (814) 371-2090 Toll-free number: (800) 874-8324
Fax: (814) 371-9227
Jason Vallozzi, Director of Admissions, Triangle Tech: DuBois, PO Box 551, DuBois, PA 15801-0551

Triangle Tech: Erie
Erie, Pennsylvania
www.triangle-tech.edu **CB code: 1572**

- For-profit 2-year technical college
- Commuter campus in small city
- Interview required

General. Founded in 1976. Accredited by ACCSCT. **Enrollment:** 137 degree-seeking undergraduates; 4 non-degree-seeking students. **Degrees:** 83 associate awarded. **Location:** 100 miles from Pittsburgh and Cleveland. **Calendar:** Semester, extensive summer session. **Full-time faculty:** 14 total; 21% women. **Part-time faculty:** 1 total.

Student profile. Among degree-seeking undergraduates, 100% enrolled in a vocational program, 53 enrolled as first-time, first-year students.

Out-of-state:	5%	**Asian American:**	1%
Women:	5%	**Hispanic American:**	1%
African American:	4%		

Basis for selection. Open admission. **Adult students:** Entrance exam policies same as for first-time freshmen.

2005-2006 Annual costs. Books/supplies: $900. Personal expenses: $1,656.

2004-2005 Financial aid. Need-based: 39% of total undergraduate aid awarded as scholarships/grants, 61% as loans/jobs. Need-based aid available for part-time students.

Application procedures. Admission: No deadline. $75 fee. Admission notification on a rolling basis. **Financial aid:** FAFSA required. Applicants notified on a rolling basis.

Academics. Credit/placement by examination: AP, CLEP, institutional tests. **Support services:** Remedial instruction, study skills assistance, tutoring.

Majors. Construction: Carpentry, electrician. **Engineering technology:** Architectural drafting, mechanical drafting.

Most popular majors. Engineering/engineering technologies 31%, trade and industry 69%.

Computing on campus. 50 workstations in computer center.

Student life. Freshman orientation: Mandatory. Preregistration for classes offered. **Policies:** Freshmen permitted cars on campus. **Activities:** Student government, student newspaper.

Student services. Career counseling, student employment services, financial aid counseling, personal counseling, placement for graduates. **Transfer:** Special adviser, orientation, re-entry adviser, pre-admission transcript evaluation for new students. Transfer center, transfer adviser for students transferring to 4-year colleges.

Contact. Phone: (814) 453-6016 Fax: (814) 454-2818
Jason Vallozzi, Director of Admissions, Triangle Tech: Erie, 2000 Liberty Street, Erie, PA 16502-2594

Triangle Tech: Greensburg
Greensburg, Pennsylvania
www.triangle-tech.edu **CB code: 0658**

- For-profit 2-year technical college
- Commuter campus in large town
- Interview required

General. Founded in 1944. Accredited by ACCSCT. **Enrollment:** 243 degree-seeking undergraduates; 24 non-degree-seeking students. **Degrees:** 144 associate awarded. **Location:** 40 miles from Pittsburgh. **Calendar:** Semester, extensive summer session. **Full-time faculty:** 21 total; 14% women. **Part-time faculty:** 5 total; 20% women.

Student profile. Among degree-seeking undergraduates, 100% enrolled in a vocational program, 1% already have a bachelor's degree or higher, 104 enrolled as first-time, first-year students.

Out-of-state:	1%	**Women:**	1%

Transfer out. 1% of students enrolled in the transfer program go on to 4-year colleges.

Basis for selection. Open admission. **Adult students:** Entrance exam policies same as for first-time freshmen.

2005-2006 Annual costs. Tuition/fees: $11,712. Per-credit charge: $317. Books/supplies: $990. Personal expenses: $1,608.

2004-2005 Financial aid. Need-based: 46% of total undergraduate aid awarded as scholarships/grants, 54% as loans/jobs. Need-based aid available for part-time students.

Application procedures. Admission: No deadline. $75 fee. Admission notification on a rolling basis. **Financial aid:** No deadline. FAFSA required. Applicants notified on a rolling basis.

Academics. Credit/placement by examination: AP, CLEP, institutional tests. **Support services:** Learning center, remedial instruction, study skills assistance, tutoring.

Majors. Construction: Carpentry, electrician. **Engineering technology:** Architectural drafting, heat/ac/refrig, mechanical drafting.

Most popular majors. Engineering/engineering technologies 47%, trade and industry 53%.

Computing on campus. 100 workstations in library, computer center.

Student life. Freshman orientation: Mandatory. Preregistration for classes offered. **Policies:** Freshmen permitted cars on campus. **Activities:** Student government, student newspaper.

Student services. Career counseling, student employment services, personal counseling, placement for graduates, veterans' counselor. **Transfer:** Special adviser, orientation, re-entry adviser, pre-admission transcript evaluation for new students. Transfer center, transfer adviser, college fairs on campus for students transferring to 4-year colleges.

Contact. Phone: (724) 832-1050 Fax: (724) 834-0325
Jason Vallozzi, Director of Admissions, Triangle Tech: Greensburg, 222 East Pittsburgh Street, Suite A, Greensburg, PA 15601-3304

Triangle Tech: Pittsburgh

Pittsburgh, Pennsylvania
www.triangle-tech.edu **CB code: 0734**

- For-profit 2-year technical college
- Commuter campus in very large city

General. Founded in 1944. Accredited by ACCSCT. **Enrollment:** 309 degree-seeking undergraduates. **Degrees:** 217 associate awarded. **Location:** 5 miles from downtown. **Calendar:** Semester, extensive summer session. **Full-time faculty:** 25 total. **Part-time faculty:** 5 total.

Student profile. Among degree-seeking undergraduates, 3% already have a bachelor's degree or higher, 95 enrolled as first-time, first-year students.

Out-of-state:	15%	**25 or older:**	46%
Women:	2%		

Transfer out. Colleges most students transferred to 2005: Point Park College, Robert Morris College, Youngstown State University, Slippery Rock University.

Basis for selection. Open admission. Must have high school diploma or GED. Applicants must take TABE test for placement. **Adult students:** Entrance exam policies same as for first-time freshmen. **Homeschooled:** Transcript of courses and grades, state high school equivalency certificate required.

2005-2006 Annual costs. Tuition/fees: $11,712. Per-credit charge: $317. Books/supplies: $1,010. Personal expenses: $1,608.

2004-2005 Financial aid. All financial aid based on need. Work study available nights.

Application procedures. Admission: No deadline. $75 fee. Admission notification on a rolling basis. **Financial aid:** No deadline. Institutional form required. Applicants notified on a rolling basis.

Academics. Credit/placement by examination: CLEP. 36 credit hours maximum toward associate degree. **Support services:** Learning center, tutoring.

Majors. Construction: Carpentry, electrician, maintenance, power transmission. **Engineering technology:** Drafting. **Mechanic/repair:** Heating/ac/refrig.

Computing on campus. 46 workstations in library, computer center. Online library available.

Student life. Freshman orientation: Mandatory. Held approximately 5 days prior to start; approximately 2-and-one-half hours long. **Policies:** Freshmen permitted cars on campus.

Student services. Career counseling, student employment services, financial aid counseling, personal counseling, placement for graduates. **Transfer:** Special adviser, orientation, pre-admission transcript evaluation for new students. College fairs on campus for students transferring to 4-year colleges.

Contact. E-mail: info@triangle-tech.edu
Phone: (412) 359-1000 Toll-free number: (800) 874-8324
Fax: (412) 359-1012
John Mazzarese, Vice President of Admissions, Triangle Tech: Pittsburgh, 1940 Perrysville Avenue, Pittsburgh, PA 15214-3897

Triangle Tech: Sunbury

Sunbury, Pennsylvania
www.triangle-tech.com/mainloc_sunbury

- Private 2-year technical college
- Small city

General. Accredited by ACCSCT. **Calendar:** Semester.

Contact. Phone: (570) 988-0700
RR 1 Box 51, Sunbury, PA 17801

University of Pittsburgh at Titusville

Titusville, Pennsylvania
www.upt.pitt.edu **CB code: 2937**

- Public 2-year branch campus and liberal arts college
- Residential campus in small town

General. Founded in 1963. Regionally accredited. **Enrollment:** 523 degree-seeking undergraduates; 24 non-degree-seeking students. **Degrees:** 33 associate awarded. **Location:** 100 miles from Pittsburgh, 50 miles from Erie. **Calendar:** Semester, limited summer session. **Full-time faculty:** 20 total. **Part-time faculty:** 40 total. **Class size:** 78% < 20, 20% 20-39, 2% 40-49.

Student profile. Among degree-seeking undergraduates, 165 enrolled as first-time, first-year students, 51 transferred in from other institutions.

Part-time:	22%	**Asian American:**	2%
Out-of-state:	6%	**Hispanic American:**	1%
Women:	64%	**Live on campus:**	44%
African American:	16%		

Transfer out. 30% of students enrolled in the transfer program go on to 4-year colleges. **Colleges most students transferred to 2005:** Clarion University of Pennsylvania, Community College of Allegheny County, Carlow College, Edinboro University of Pennsylvania, Indiana University of Pennsylvania.

Basis for selection. Decisions based on academic performance. Applicants deserving additional consideration referred to Admissions Committee. Essay, interview recommended. **Adult students:** Entrance exam policies same as for first-time freshmen. SAT/ACT scores not required if out of high school 1 year(s) or more. **Homeschooled:** Transcript of courses and grades required. SAT/ACT recommended. Math/English placement tests required. **Learning Disabled:** Students with disabilities asked to provide comprehensive documentation to Disability Resources and Services representative to establish eligibility for accommodations.

High school preparation. College-preparatory program recommended. 15 units required. Required and recommended units include English 4, mathematics 2, history 1, science 1 (laboratory 1), foreign language 3 and academic electives 7. One unit lab science required.

2005-2006 Annual costs. Tuition/fees: $9,400; $18,300 out-of-state. Per-credit charge: $335 in-state; $677 out-of-state. Room/board: $7,334. Books/supplies: $800. Personal expenses: $1,600.

2005-2006 Financial aid. Need-based: Average need met was 85%. Average scholarship/grant was $7,443; average loan $2,625. 48% of total undergraduate aid awarded as scholarships/grants, 52% as loans/jobs. Need-based aid available for part-time students. Work study available nights and weekends. **Non-need-based:** Scholarships awarded for academics, athletics, state residency.

Application procedures. Admission: No deadline. $35 fee, may be waived for applicants with need. Application may be submitted online. Admission notification on a rolling basis beginning on or about 11/1. **Financial aid:** No deadline. FAFSA, institutional form required. Applicants notified on a rolling basis; must reply within 2 week(s) of notification.

Academics. Fresh Start program provides intensive academic advising. **Special study options:** Cross-registration, distance learning, independent study, internships, liberal arts/career combination, study abroad. Bachelor's degree programs available on campus. License preparation in real estate. **Credit/placement by examination:** AP, CLEP, SAT, ACT, institutional tests. 6 credit hours maximum toward associate degree. **Support services:** Learning center, reduced course load, remedial instruction, study skills assistance, tutoring.

Majors. Business: General, accounting, management information systems. **Family/consumer sciences:** General. **Health:** Nursing (RN), physical therapy assistant. **Interdisciplinary:** Natural sciences. **Liberal arts:** Arts/sciences.

Most popular majors. Biological/life sciences 8%, business/marketing 36%, computer/information sciences 11%, health sciences 28%, liberal arts 8%, social sciences 8%.

Computing on campus. 62 workstations in dormitories, library, computer center, student center. Dormitories wired for high-speed internet access and linked to campus network. Commuter students can connect to campus network. Online library, helpline, repair service, student web hosting, wireless network available.

Student life. Freshman orientation: Mandatory, $45 fee. Preregistration for classes offered. Students learn policies and services, take placement tests, engage in social activities. **Policies:** Organizations must complete 1 community service and fundraising activity per year to receive student activity funding. Freshmen permitted cars on campus. **Housing:** Guaranteed on-campus for all undergraduates. Coed dorms, special housing for disabled, substance-free housing available. $100 fully refundable deposit. Townhouse apartments without cooking facilities available. **Activities:** Dance, drama, student government, drama club, accounting and business club, commuter student association, Alpha Omega Christian fellowship, Phi Theta Kappa, student activities board, chemistry club, travel club, student government association, student physical therapy association.

Athletics. NJCAA. **Intercollegiate:** Basketball, golf M, volleyball W. **Intramural:** Basketball, bowling, football (non-tackle), racquetball, skiing, soccer, softball, swimming, table tennis, tennis, volleyball. **Team name:** Panthers.

Student services. Adult student services, alcohol/substance abuse counseling, campus ministries, career counseling, student employment services, financial aid counseling, health services, minority student services, personal counseling, placement for graduates. **Physically disabled:** Services for visually impaired. **Transfer:** Special adviser, orientation, pre-admission transcript evaluation for new students. Transfer adviser, college fairs on campus for students transferring to 4-year colleges.

Contact. E-mail: uptadm@pitt.edu
Phone: (814) 827-4427 Toll-free number: (888) 878-0462
Fax: (814) 827-4519
John Mumford, Executive Director of Enrollment Management, University of Pittsburgh at Titusville, UPT Admissions Office, Titusville, PA 16354

Valley Forge Military College

Wayne, Pennsylvania — **CB member**
www.vfmac.edu — **CB code: 2955**

- Private 2-year junior and military college
- Residential campus in small city
- SAT or ACT (ACT writing optional) required

General. Founded in 1928. Regionally accredited. One of only 5 military junior colleges in nation offering Army ROTC early commissioning program leading to commission as second lieutenant in U.S. Army Reserve at end of second year. Regimental marching band, drum and bugle corps, regimental choir. **Enrollment:** 188 degree-seeking undergraduates. **Degrees:** 72 associate awarded. **ROTC:** Army, Air Force. **Location:** 15 miles from Philadelphia. **Calendar:** Semester. **Full-time faculty:** 16 total. **Part-time faculty:** 25 total. **Special facilities:** Motorized artillery unit, mounted cavalry troop.

Student profile.

Out-of-state:	78%	**Live on campus:**	100%

Transfer out. Colleges most students transferred to 2005: Lehigh University, Villanova University, Drexel University, The Citadel, George Mason University.

Basis for selection. School achievement record, test scores, and personal character most important. TOEFL score accepted in lieu of SAT or ACT scores for international students. Interview recommended. **Adult students:** Entrance exam policies same as for first-time freshmen.

High school preparation. Required and recommended units include English 4, mathematics 3, science 3 and foreign language 2.

2005-2006 Annual costs. Tuition/fees: $22,070. Room/board: $6,480. Books/supplies: $1,000.

Financial aid. Non-need-based: Scholarships awarded for academics, alumni affiliation, athletics, music/drama, ROTC, state residency. **Additional information:** Students enrolled in advanced military science program can receive up to $5,000 from the Army. In addition, competitively awarded ROTC scholarships pay average of another $14,100 per school year for direct educational expenses.

Application procedures. Admission: Closing date 8/1 (receipt date). $25 fee. Application may be submitted online. Admission notification on a rolling basis. Must reply by May 1 or within 2 week(s) if notified thereafter. **Financial aid:** Closing date 5/1. FAFSA, institutional form required. Applicants notified on a rolling basis starting 5/15; must reply within 2 week(s) of notification.

Academics. Special study options: Double major, dual enrollment of high school students, ESL, honors, study abroad. **Credit/placement by examination:** AP, CLEP, SAT, ACT, institutional tests. 30 credit hours maximum toward associate degree. **Support services:** Reduced course load, remedial instruction, tutoring, writing center.

Majors. Business: General. **Engineering:** General, science. **Liberal arts:** Arts/sciences. **Protective services:** Criminal justice.

Computing on campus. PC or laptop required. 44 workstations in library, computer center. Dormitories linked to campus network. Helpline, repair service available.

Student life. Freshman orientation: Mandatory. Preregistration for classes offered. 3-day orientation with placement testing. **Policies:** Religious observance required. **Housing:** Guaranteed on-campus for all undergraduates. Coed dorms available. $1,000 partly refundable deposit, deadline 5/1. **Activities:** Bands, choral groups, drama, music ensembles, radio station, student government, student newspaper, Catholic Fellowship, Jewish Fellowship, Christian Fellowship, Muslim Fellowship, Young Republicans.

Athletics. Intercollegiate: Basketball M, cross-country M, equestrian M, football (tackle) M, lacrosse M, rifle M, soccer M, tennis M, wrestling M. **Intramural:** Baseball M, basketball M, fencing M, football (tackle) M, golf M, judo M, rugby M, soccer M, softball M, volleyball M, water polo M, weight lifting M. **Team name:** Trojans.

Student services. Career counseling, health services, personal counseling, placement for graduates. **Transfer:** Special adviser for new students. Transfer adviser for students transferring to 4-year colleges.

Contact. E-mail: admission@vfmac.edu
Phone: (610) 989-1300 Toll-free number: (800) 234-8362
Fax: (610) 688-1545
Gregg Potts, Director of Admissions and Financial Aid, Valley Forge Military College, 1001 Eagle Road, Wayne, PA 19087

Vet Tech Institute

Pittsburgh, Pennsylvania
www.vettechinstitute.com — **CB code: 7134**

- For-profit 2-year health science and technical college
- Commuter campus in large city

General. Accredited by ACCSCT. Veterinary technician AVMA accredited. **Enrollment:** 296 degree-seeking undergraduates. **Degrees:** 124 associate awarded. **Calendar:** Semester. **Full-time faculty:** 9 total. **Part-time faculty:** 2 total. **Special facilities:** Animal tech rooms, on-site kennel.

Transfer out. Colleges most students transferred to 2005: Point Park College.

Basis for selection. Satisfactory performance on school admission test required. Essay, interview recommended.

2005-2006 Annual costs. Tuition/fees: $23,700.

Financial aid. Need-based: Work study available nights. **Non-need-based:** Scholarships awarded for academics.

Application procedures. Admission: No deadline. $50 fee. Application may be submitted online. Admission notification on a rolling basis. **Financial aid:** No deadline. FAFSA required. Applicants notified on a rolling basis.

Academics. Special study options: Internships. **Credit/placement by examination:** AP, CLEP. **Support services:** Tutoring.

Majors. Health: Veterinary technology/assistant.

Computing on campus. 38 workstations in library, computer center.

Student life. Freshman orientation: Mandatory.

Student services. Career counseling, placement for graduates. **Transfer:** Orientation for new students.

Contact. E-mail: admissions@vettechinstitute.com
Phone: (412) 391-7021 Toll-free number: (800) 570-0693
Fax: (412) 232-4348
Terry Taylor, Senior Admissions Coordinator, Vet Tech Institute, 125 Seventh Street, Pittsburgh, PA 15222-3400

West Virginia Career Institute

Mount Braddock, Pennsylvania
www.wvci.edu **CB code: 3214**

- For-profit 2-year business college
- Small town
- Interview required

General. Accredited by ACICS. **Enrollment:** 188 undergraduates. **Degrees:** 84 associate awarded. **Calendar:** Continuous. **Full-time faculty:** 4 total. **Part-time faculty:** 4 total.

Basis for selection. Open admission.

2005-2006 Annual costs. Tuition/fees: $9,000. Quoted tuition is for associate programs. Tuition for diploma programs $8,550 with no required fees.

Application procedures. Admission: No deadline. $25 fee.

Academics. Credit/placement by examination: CLEP.

Majors. Business: General, administrative services. **Health:** Medical secretary.

Contact. Phone: (724) 437-4600 Fax: (724) 437-6053
Amanda Rugg, Admissions Director, West Virginia Career Institute, Rt 119 North and Mount Braddock Road, Mount Braddock, PA 15465

Western School of Health and Business Careers

Pittsburgh, Pennsylvania
www.westernschoolpitt.com **CB code: 2933**

- For-profit 2-year technical college
- Very large city
- Interview required

General. Accredited by ACCSCT. **Enrollment:** 550 undergraduates. **Degrees:** 133 associate awarded. **Location:** Downtown. **Calendar:** Continuous. **Full-time faculty:** 100 total. **Part-time faculty:** 15 total.

Student profile. 100% enrolled in a vocational program.

Basis for selection. Open admission, but selective for some programs. Interview with director of chosen program very important. Standardized test scores considered.

2005-2006 Annual costs. Depending on program, cost ranges from $8,000 to $28,800, includes lab fees, books, and registration fee.

Application procedures. Admission: No deadline. No application fee. Application may be submitted online. Admission notification on a rolling basis. **Financial aid:** No deadline. FAFSA required. Applicants notified on a rolling basis.

Academics. Credit/placement by examination: CLEP.

Majors. Business: Business admin. **Family/consumer sciences:** Child care. **Health:** Clinical lab assistant, clinical lab technology, medical records technology, optician, respiratory therapy technology, sonography, surgical technology. **Legal studies:** General, paralegal.

Contact. E-mail: admissions@western-school.com
Phone: (800) 333-6607
Michael Joyce, Director of Admissions, Western School of Health and Business Careers, 421 Seventh Avenue, Pittsburgh, PA 15219

Western School of Health and Business Careers: Monroeville

Monroeville, Pennsylvania
www.wshb-monroeville.com **CB code: 2939**

- For-profit 2-year business and health science college
- Large town

General. Accredited by ACCSCT. **Enrollment:** 525 undergraduates. **Degrees:** 98 associate awarded. **Calendar:** Courses begin every 3 months. **Full-time faculty:** 35 total. **Part-time faculty:** 4 total.

Basis for selection. Assessment test and meeting with admission representatives very important.

2005-2006 Annual costs. Tuition ranges from $8,825 for dental assistant diploma program to $17,925 for 15-month associate degree surgical technician program. Tuition includes books, registration and lab fees.

Financial aid. Need-based: Need-based aid available for part-time students.

Application procedures. Admission: No deadline. No application fee. Admission notification on a rolling basis. **Financial aid:** No deadline. Applicants notified on a rolling basis.

Academics. Credit/placement by examination: CLEP.

Majors. Business: Business admin. **Health:** Pharmacy assistant, surgical technology. **Legal studies:** General, paralegal.

Contact. Phone: (412) 373-6400 Fax: (412) 373-2544
Timothy Babyok, Director of Admission, Western School of Health and Business Careers: Monroeville, One Monroeville Center, Suite 125, Monroeville, PA 15146

Westmoreland County Community College

Youngwood, Pennsylvania
www.wccc-pa.edu **CB code: 2968**

- Public 2-year community college
- Commuter campus in small town

General. Founded in 1970. Regionally accredited. **Enrollment:** 5,146 degree-seeking undergraduates; 995 non-degree-seeking students. **Degrees:** 408 associate awarded. **Location:** 30 miles from Pittsburgh. **Calendar:** Semester, limited summer session. **Full-time faculty:** 76 total; 3% minority, 47% women. **Part-time faculty:** 383 total; 16% minority, 53% women. **Class size:** 75% < 20, 25% 20-39. **Special facilities:** Culinary arts kitchens, greenhouse, student lounges, art gallery, theater.

Student profile. Among degree-seeking undergraduates, 44% enrolled in a transfer program, 56% enrolled in a vocational program, 1,115 enrolled as first-time, first-year students, 623 transferred in from other institutions.

Part-time:	52%	**25 or older:**	55%
Women:	64%		

Transfer out. Colleges most students transferred to 2005: University of Pittsburgh, Indiana University of Pennsylvania, California University of Pennsylvania, Seton Hill University, St. Vincent College.

Basis for selection. Open admission, but selective for some programs. Nursing applicants required to take Comparative Guidance and Placement test, submit application by November 30 of year prior to enrollment in fall semester, and submit satisfactory results from pre-entrance physicals. Interview recommended. **Adult students:** SAT/ACT scores not required. WCCC Placement Test Required.

2005-2006 Annual costs. Tuition/fees: $2,100; $4,050 out-of-district; $6,000 out-of-state. Per-credit charge: $65 in-district; $130 out-of-district; $195 out-of-state. Out of district and out of state students pay an addition $150 in fees. Books/supplies: $600.

Financial aid. Need-based: Need-based aid available for part-time students. Work study available nights and for part-time students. **Non-need-based:** Scholarships awarded for academics.

Application procedures. Admission: No deadline. $10 fee, may be waived for applicants with need. Application may be submitted online. Admission notification on a rolling basis. **Financial aid:** No deadline. FAFSA, institutional form required. Applicants notified on a rolling basis starting 5/1.

Academics. Special study options: Cooperative education, cross-registration, distance learning, double major, honors, independent study, internships, student-designed major, study abroad. Bachelor's degree programs available on campus. License preparation in dental hygiene, nursing, real estate. **Credit/placement by examination:** AP, CLEP, institutional tests. 30 credit hours maximum toward associate degree. **Support services:** GED preparation and test center, learning center, remedial instruction, study skills assistance, tutoring.

Majors. Agriculture: Greenhouse operations, horticultural science, horticulture, turf management. **Business:** Accounting, administrative services, banking/financial services, business admin, fashion, sales/distribution, tourism promotion, tourism/travel. **Communications technology:** General, graphic/printing. **Computer sciences:** Computer science, data processing, programming. **Engineering technology:** Drafting, electrical. **Family/consumer sciences:** Child care, institutional food production. **Health:** Dental hygiene, medical secretary, medical transcription, mental health services, nursing (RN), optician. **Legal studies:** Legal secretary, paralegal. **Liberal arts:** Arts/sciences. **Mechanic/repair:** Heating/ac/refrig, industrial. **Personal/culinary services:** Culinary arts. **Protective services:** Fire safety technology, police science. **Public administration:** Human services. **Visual/performing arts:** Commercial/advertising art, photography.

Most popular majors. Business/marketing 15%, computer/information sciences 11%, family/consumer sciences 8%, health sciences 29%, liberal arts 10%, personal/culinary services 7%, security/protective services 7%, trade and industry 12%.

Computing on campus. 450 workstations in library, computer center. Online course registration, helpline available.

Student life. Freshman orientation: Available. Program designed to increase student awareness of campus services, help students develop positive identification with school, and increase student involvement in campus life. **Activities:** Student government, student newspaper, Aware Student Coalition, Human Services club, Reach Out club.

Athletics. NJCAA. **Intercollegiate:** Baseball M, golf, softball W, tennis, volleyball W. **Intramural:** Baseball M, basketball, bowling, golf, racquetball, skiing, soccer, softball, table tennis, volleyball. **Team name:** Wolfpack.

Student services. Career counseling, services for economically disadvantaged, student employment services, financial aid counseling, on-campus daycare, personal counseling, placement for graduates, veterans' counselor. **Physically disabled:** Services for visually, speech, hearing impaired. **Transfer:** Special adviser, orientation, pre-admission transcript evaluation for new students. Transfer adviser, college fairs on campus for students transferring to 4-year colleges.

Contact. E-mail: tatarj@wccc-pa.edu
Phone: (724) 925-4062 Toll-free number: (800) 262-2103 ext. 4062
Fax: (724) 925-5802
Randal Finfrock, Director of Enrollment Management, Westmoreland County Community College, 400 Armbrust Road, Youngwood, PA 15697-1895

York Technical Institute

York, Pennsylvania
www.yti.edu **CB code: 2943**

- For-profit 2-year junior and technical college
- Commuter campus in large city

General. Candidate for regional accreditation; also accredited by ACCSCT. **Enrollment:** 1,500 degree-seeking undergraduates. **Degrees:** 445 associate awarded. **Calendar:** Quarter, extensive summer session. **Full-time faculty:** 60 total. **Part-time faculty:** 20 total.

Student profile.

Out-of-state:	8%	**25 or older:**	15%

Basis for selection. Open admission. For Public Safety and Security Administration program, requirements also include a minimum age of 18 years old, plus passing a criminal background check. **Adult students:** Entrance exam policies same as for first-time freshmen.

2005-2006 Annual costs. Tuition/fees: $16,020. Quoted tuition is for computer systems specialist program. Academic-year costs for other programs range from $10,170 to $14,940. Books/supplies: $1,500.

Application procedures. Admission: No deadline. $40 fee, may be waived for applicants with need. Admission notification on a rolling basis.

Academics. Special study options: Cooperative education, internships. **Credit/placement by examination:** CLEP, institutional tests. **Support services:** Pre-admission summer program, remedial instruction, study skills assistance, tutoring.

Majors. Business: Accounting, business admin. **Computer sciences:** General, a.i./robotics, security. **Health:** Medical assistant. **Personal/culinary services:** Culinary arts. **Protective services:** Law enforcement admin, police science, security services.

Computing on campus. 250 workstations in library, computer center. Commuter students can connect to campus network. Helpline, repair service, wireless network available.

Student life. Freshman orientation: Mandatory. Preregistration for classes offered. **Housing:** Apartments available.

Student services. Adult student services, career counseling, student employment services, financial aid counseling, placement for graduates. **Transfer:** Orientation, re-entry adviser, pre-admission transcript evaluation for new students. Transfer adviser for students transferring to 4-year colleges.

Contact. Phone: (717) 757-1100 Toll-free number: (800) 227-9675
Fax: (717) 757-4964
. Diane Merino, Director of Admissions, York Technical Institute, 1405 Williams Road, York, PA 17402

Yorktowne Business Institute

York, Pennsylvania
www.ybi.edu **CB code: 2553**

- For-profit 2-year business and health science college
- Commuter campus in small city
- Application essay, interview required

General. Founded in 1976. Accredited by ACICS. **Enrollment:** 315 undergraduates. **Degrees:** 98 associate awarded. **Location:** 100 miles from Philadelphia, 50 miles from Baltimore. **Calendar:** Trimester, extensive summer session. **Part-time faculty:** 32 total. **Special facilities:** Culinary arts center with teaching kitchens and student-run restaurant.

Basis for selection. Open admission, but selective for some programs.

2005-2006 Annual costs. Tuition $17,625 for business and medical programs with $55 student fee, $27,225 for culinary program with $130 student fee. Books/supplies: $2,900. Personal expenses: $1,128.

Financial aid. Need-based: Need-based aid available for part-time students.

Application procedures. Admission: No deadline. No application fee. Admission notification on a rolling basis. **Financial aid:** Priority date 5/1; no closing date. FAFSA required.

Academics. Special study options: Double major. Bachelor's degree programs available on campus. **Credit/placement by examination:** CLEP. **Support services:** Reduced course load, tutoring.

Majors. Business: Accounting, administrative services, business admin, hospitality admin, hospitality/recreation, tourism promotion. **Computer sciences:** General, data processing. **Health:** Dental assistant, medical assistant, medical records technology, medical secretary. **Legal studies:** Legal secretary, paralegal. **Personal/culinary services:** Culinary arts.

Computing on campus. 100 workstations in library, computer center.

Student services. Career counseling, student employment services, personal counseling, placement for graduates, veterans' counselor. **Transfer:** Special adviser, orientation, pre-admission transcript evaluation for new students.

Contact. E-mail: admissions@ybi.edu
Phone: (717) 846-5000 Toll-free number: (800) 840-1004
Fax: (717) 848-4584
Jane Regan, Director of Admissions, Yorktowne Business Institute, West 7th Avenue, York, PA 17404-2034

Puerto Rico

Centro de Estudios Multidisciplinarios
San Juan, Puerto Rico

- Private 2-year health science college

General. Accredited by ACCSCT.

Contact. Phone: (787) 765-4210
1206 13th Street, Ext. San Augustin, San Juan, PR 00926-1931

Colegio de las Ciencias Artes y Television
Bayamon, Puerto Rico
www.ccat.edu

- Private 2-year liberal arts and technical college
- Small city

General. Accredited by ACCSCT. **Calendar:** Semester.

Contact. Phone: (787) 779-2500
P.O. Box 10774, San Juan, PR 00922

Columbia Centro Universitario
Yauco, Puerto Rico
www.columbiaco.edu **CB code: 3215**

- For-profit 2-year business college
- Large town

General. Accredited by ACICS. **Calendar:** Continuous.

Contact. Phone: (787) 743-4041
Director, Box 3062, Yauco, PR 00698

Huertas Junior College
Caguas, Puerto Rico **CB member**
www.huertas.edu **CB code: 3406**

- For-profit 2-year junior and technical college
- Commuter campus in small city

General. Founded in 1945. Accredited by ACICS. **Location:** 25 miles from San Juan, 32 miles from Navanjito. **Calendar:** Trimester.

Annual costs/financial aid. Tuition/fees (2005-2006): $5,217. Books/supplies: $800. Personal expenses: $800. Need-based financial aid available to full-time and part-time students.

Contact. Phone: (787) 743-1242
Director of Admissions, P.O. Box 8429, Caguas, PR 00726

Humacao Community College
Humacao, Puerto Rico
www.humacaocommunitycollege.com **CB code: 2313**

- Private 2-year business and community college
- Commuter campus in large city
- Interview required

General. Founded in 1956. Accredited by ACICS. **Enrollment:** 501 degree-seeking undergraduates; 11 non-degree-seeking students. **Degrees:** 109 associate awarded. **Location:** 42 miles from San Juan. **Calendar:** Trimester. **Full-time faculty:** 12 total; 100% minority. **Part-time faculty:** 11 total; 100% minority. **Class size:** 61% < 20, 37% 20-39, 2% 40-49, less than 1% 50-99.

Student profile. Among degree-seeking undergraduates, 1% already have a bachelor's degree or higher, 182 enrolled as first-time, first-year students, 27 transferred in from other institutions.

Part-time:	30%	**25 or older:**	38%
Women:	58%		

Transfer out. 17% of students enrolled in the transfer program go on to 4-year colleges. **Colleges most students transferred to 2005:** Turabo University, University of Puerto Rico (all campuses), Inter American University of Puerto Rico (all campuses), Huertas Junior College.

Basis for selection. Open admission.

High school preparation. 18 units recommended. Recommended units include English 3, mathematics 3, social studies 3, science 3, foreign language 3 and academic electives 3.

2005-2006 Annual costs. Tuition/fees: $4,275. Per-credit charge: $100. Books/supplies: $937. Personal expenses: $1,530.

Financial aid. All financial aid based on need. Need-based aid available for part-time students. Work study available nights and for part-time students.

Application procedures. Admission: No deadline. $15 fee. Application must be submitted on paper. Admission notification on a rolling basis. **Financial aid:** Priority date 1/1, closing date 6/30. FAFSA, institutional form required. Applicants notified on a rolling basis starting 3/4.

Academics. Special study options: Internships. **Credit/placement by examination:** AP, CLEP. 9 credit hours maximum toward associate degree. **Support services:** Learning center, remedial instruction, tutoring.

Majors. Business: Administrative services, business admin. **Computer sciences:** Information systems. **Engineering technology:** Electrical, heat/ac/refrig. **Health:** Medical secretary, pharmacy assistant.

Most popular majors. Business/marketing 27%, computer/information sciences 26%, engineering/engineering technologies 17%, health sciences 39%.

Computing on campus. 104 workstations in library, computer center, student center. Online library available.

Student life. Freshman orientation: Mandatory. Preregistration for classes offered. Counseling and Orientation department holds group meetings (75 participants per session) for all freshmen. Usually held during the first four weeks of each term, these meetings have a duration of approximately 90 minutes. **Policies:** Freshmen permitted cars on campus. **Activities:** Student government.

Student services. Adult student services, alcohol/substance abuse counseling, career counseling, student employment services, financial aid counseling, personal counseling, placement for graduates. **Transfer:** Special adviser, orientation, pre-admission transcript evaluation for new students. Transfer adviser for students transferring to 4-year colleges.

Contact. E-mail: admisiones@humacaocommunitycollege.com
Phone: (787) 852-1430 ext. 58 Fax: (787) 850-1577
Xiomara Sanchez, Admissions Director, Humacao Community College, PO Box 9139, Humacao, PR 00792

ICPR Junior College
San Juan, Puerto Rico **CB member**
www.icprjc.edu **CB code: 7315**

- For-profit 2-year business and junior college
- Commuter campus in large city

General. Founded in 1946. Regionally accredited. **Calendar:** Trimester.

Annual costs/financial aid. Tuition/fees (2005-2006): $5,625. Books/supplies: $954. Personal expenses: $2,556.

Contact. Phone: (787) 763-1010
Director of Admissions, PO Box 190304, San Juan, PR 00919-0304

International Junior College of Business and Technology
Santurce, Puerto Rico
www.internationaljuniorcollege.com **CB code: 3220**

- For-profit 2-year business and technical college
- Commuter campus

Two-Year Colleges

General. Accredited by ACICS.

Contact. Phone: (787) 722-2293
Admissions Director, 1254 Avenue Ponce de Leon, pda. 18 1/2, Santurce, PR 00908

National College of Business & Technology: Arecibo

Arecibo, Puerto Rico
www.nationalcollegepr.edu **CB code: 3222**

- For-profit 2-year business college
- Commuter campus in small city

General. Accredited by ACICS. **Enrollment:** 1,439 degree-seeking undergraduates. **Degrees:** 81 bachelor's, 204 associate awarded. **Calendar:** Trimester. **Full-time faculty:** 21 total; 19% have terminal degrees. **Part-time faculty:** 47 total. **Class size:** 41% < 20, 46% 20-39, 10% 40-49, 3% 50-99.

Basis for selection. Admissions based on high school record and test scores. College Entrance Examination Board test or institutional tests required for admissions.

Financial aid. Need-based: Need-based aid available for part-time students. Work study available nights, weekends and for part-time students.

Application procedures. Admission: No deadline. $25 fee. Application must be submitted on paper. Admission notification on a rolling basis. **Financial aid:** Priority date 12/31, closing date 4/29. Applicants notified on a rolling basis starting 5/2; must reply by 5/15 or within 2 week(s) of notification.

Academics. Special study options: ESL, independent study, internships, teacher certification program. **Credit/placement by examination:** CLEP. **Support services:** Tutoring.

Majors. Business: Administrative services, business admin, office/clerical. **Computer sciences:** General. **Engineering technology:** Electrical. **Health:** Dental assistant, medical secretary, nursing (RN), pharmacy assistant. **Legal studies:** Legal secretary.

Computing on campus. Online library, helpline, repair service, student web hosting available.

Student life. Freshman orientation: Available. Preregistration for classes offered. **Activities:** Student newspaper.

Athletics. Intramural: Basketball M, table tennis, volleyball M.

Student services. Career counseling, financial aid counseling, personal counseling, placement for graduates, veterans' counselor. **Transfer:** Special adviser, orientation for new students.

Contact. E-mail: aaviles@nationalcollegepr.edu
Phone: (787) 879-5044 ext. 2504 Toll-free number: (800) 780-5134
Fax: (787) 879-5047
Mercedes Pagan, Admissions Directors, National College of Business & Technology: Arecibo, Arecibo Centro Plaza, Arecibo, PR 00614

National College of Business & Technology: Bayamon

Bayamon, Puerto Rico
www.nationalcollegepr.edu **CB code: 7135**

- For-profit 2-year business and technical college
- Commuter campus in small city

General. Accredited by ACICS. **Enrollment:** 2,102 degree-seeking undergraduates. **Degrees:** 35 bachelor's, 442 associate awarded. **Location:** 25 miles from San Juan. **Calendar:** Trimester. **Full-time faculty:** 36 total; 67% women. **Part-time faculty:** 56 total; 5% have terminal degrees, 55% women. **Class size:** 35% < 20, 52% 20-39, 11% 40-49, 3% 50-99.

Transfer out. Colleges most students transferred to 2005: Inter-American University, UCB-Central University of Bayamon, Caribbean University.

Basis for selection. Open admission, but selective for some programs.

High school preparation. Required units include English 3, mathematics 2, history 2, science 2, foreign language 3 and academic electives 3.

2004-2005 Financial aid. All financial aid based on need. 662 full-time freshmen applied for aid; 649 were judged to have need; 649 of these received aid. Average need met was 60%. Average scholarship/grant was $4,650; average loan $2,000. 97% of total undergraduate aid awarded as scholarships/grants, 3% as loans/jobs. Need-based aid available for part-time students. Work study available nights, weekends and for part-time students.

Application procedures. Admission: No deadline. $25 fee. Application must be submitted on paper. Admission notification on a rolling basis. **Financial aid:** Priority date 12/31, closing date 4/29. FAFSA required. Applicants notified on a rolling basis starting 5/2; must reply by 5/15 or within 2 week(s) of notification.

Academics. Special study options: ESL, independent study, internships, teacher certification program. **Credit/placement by examination:** AP, CLEP. **Support services:** Tutoring.

Majors. Business: Accounting, administrative services, entrepreneurial studies, office technology, tourism/travel. **Computer sciences:** Information systems, programming. **Education:** ESL. **Engineering technology:** Electrical. **Health:** Dental assistant, nursing (RN), pharmacy assistant. **Legal studies:** Court reporting, legal secretary.

Most popular majors. Business/marketing 20%, computer/information sciences 13%, health sciences 51%, legal studies 12%.

Computing on campus. 190 workstations in library, computer center. Online library, helpline, repair service, student web hosting available.

Student life. Freshman orientation: Available. Preregistration for classes offered. **Activities:** Student newspaper.

Athletics. Intramural: Basketball M, softball M, table tennis, volleyball W.

Student services. Career counseling, financial aid counseling, personal counseling, placement for graduates, veterans' counselor. **Transfer:** Special adviser, orientation, re-entry adviser for new students. Transfer adviser for students transferring to 4-year colleges.

Contact. E-mail: rnieves@nationalcollegepr.edu
Phone: (787) 780-5134 ext. 4000 Toll-free number: (800) 780-5134
Fax: (787) 740-7360
Ricardo Nieves, Admissions and Marketing Director, National College of Business & Technology: Bayamon, PO Box 2036, Highway 2, Bayamon, PR 00960

National College of Business & Technology: Rio Grande

Rio Grande, Puerto Rico
www.nationalcollegepr.edu

- For-profit 2-year business and health science college
- Small town

General. Accredited by ACICS. **Calendar:** Trimester.

Annual costs/financial aid. Tuition/fees (projected): $4,485.

Contact. Phone: (800) 981-0812
State Road #3, km 22.1 Bo. Cienaga Baja, Rio Grande, PR 00745

Ponce Paramedical College

Ponce, Puerto Rico
www.popac.edu

- For-profit 2-year health science and junior college

General. Accredited by ACCSCT.

Contact. Phone: (787) 848-1589
Director of Admissions, Calle Acacia L-15, Urb. Villa Flores, Ponce, PR 00731

Puerto Rico Tech Junior College

Hato Rey, Puerto Rico
www.puertoricotechjuniorcollege.com **CB code: 3022**

- For-profit 2-year technical college
- Large city

General. Accredited by ACCSCT. **Calendar:** Continuous.

Annual costs/financial aid. Tuition $8,175 for 20 month associate's program.

Contact. Phone: (787) 751-0628
Director of Admissions, Avenue Ponce de Leon #703, Esq. Calle Ponce, Hato Rey, PR 00917

Ramirez College of Business and Technology
San Juan, Puerto Rico
CB code: 0386

- Private 2-year business and technical college
- Large city

General. Accredited by ACICS. **Calendar:** Quarter.

Annual costs/financial aid. Books/supplies: $325. Personal expenses: $1,300. Need-based financial aid available to full-time and part-time students.

Contact. Phone: (787) 763-3120
P.O. Box 1954611, San Juan, PR 00909-5411

Universal Technology College of Puerto Rico
Aguadilla, Puerto Rico
www.unitecpr.edu/

- Private 2-year business and health science college

General. Accredited by ACCSCT.

Contact. Phone: (787) 882-2065
Apartado 1955, Victoria Station, Aguadilla, PR 00605

University College of San Juan
San Juan, Puerto Rico
www.cunisanjuan.edu
CB member
CB code: 0391

- Public 2-year community and technical college
- Commuter campus in very large city

General. Founded in 1972. Regionally accredited. **Enrollment:** 961 degree-seeking undergraduates. **Degrees:** 30 bachelor's, 139 associate awarded. **Calendar:** Semester, limited summer session. **Full-time faculty:** 40 total; 8% have terminal degrees, 100% minority, 68% women. **Part-time faculty:** 46 total; 100% minority, 56% women. **Class size:** 63% < 20, 37% 20-39, less than 1% 40-49. **Special facilities:** Language laboratory, learning resource center, amphitheater.

Student profile. Among degree-seeking undergraduates, 225 enrolled as first-time, first-year students, 52 transferred in from other institutions.

Part-time:	16%	**25 or older:**	48%
Women:	45%		

Transfer out. Colleges most students transferred to 2005: University of Puerto Rico, Inter-American University of Puerto Rico, Caribbean University, Sacred Heart University.

Basis for selection. Combined College Board PAA test scores of 2000 and 2.0 high school GPA required for regular students. Special consideration and priority to applicants from low-income families. SAT/ACT accepted from US applicants. Interview required for nursing program. **Adult students:** CEEB not required if applicant is over 24.

High school preparation. 16 units required. Required units include English 3, mathematics 2, social studies 2, history 2, science 1 and academic electives 2. 3 Spanish courses required.

2006-2007 Annual costs. Tuition/fees (projected): $2,380. Per-credit charge: $85. Books/supplies: $800. Personal expenses: $920.

Financial aid. All financial aid based on need. Need-based aid available for part-time students.

Application procedures. Admission: Priority date 7/31; deadline 5/1. $15 fee. Application may be submitted online. Admission notification 6/1. Admission after July 31 depends on space. **Financial aid:** Closing date 9/30. FAFSA, institutional form required. Applicants notified by 10/30.

Academics. Special study options: Cooperative education, double major, exchange student, honors, study abroad. Bachelor's degree programs available on campus. License preparation in nursing. **Credit/placement by examination:** AP, CLEP. **Support services:** GED preparation, remedial instruction, tutoring.

Majors. Business: Accounting, administrative services. **Computer sciences:** General. **Engineering technology:** Electrical, instrumentation. **Health:** Nursing (RN). **Protective services:** Police science.

Most popular majors. Computer/information sciences 15%, engineering/engineering technologies 33%, health sciences 37%.

Computing on campus. 135 workstations in library, computer center. Online library, wireless network available.

Student life. Freshman orientation: Mandatory. One-day program in summer that offers opportunity to meet faculty and staff. **Activities:** Drama, student government.

Athletics. Intercollegiate: Basketball M, cross-country, softball, table tennis, tennis, track and field, volleyball, weight lifting. **Intramural:** Basketball, bowling, cross-country, handball, racquetball, softball M, table tennis, tennis, track and field, volleyball. **Team name:** Falcons.

Student services. Career counseling, student employment services, health services, personal counseling, placement for graduates, veterans' counselor. **Physically disabled:** Services for visually, speech, hearing impaired. **Transfer:** Special adviser, orientation, pre-admission transcript evaluation for new students. Transfer adviser for students transferring to 4-year colleges.

Contact. E-mail: admisiones@cts.sanjuancapital.com
Phone: (787) 250-7375 Fax: (787) 250-7395
Ruth Vicens, Admissions Officer, University College of San Juan, 180 Jose R. Oliver Avenue, San Juan, PR 00918

Rhode Island

Community College of Rhode Island

Warwick, Rhode Island **CB member**
www.ccri.edu **CB code: 3733**

- Public 2-year community college
- Commuter campus in small city

General. Founded in 1964. Regionally accredited. Additional campuses in Lincoln, Providence and Newport. **Enrollment:** 13,086 degree-seeking undergraduates; 2,956 non-degree-seeking students. **Degrees:** 1,107 associate awarded. **ROTC:** Army. **Location:** 10 miles from Providence. **Calendar:** Semester, extensive summer session. **Full-time faculty:** 321 total; 60% women. **Part-time faculty:** 426 total; 48% women. **Class size:** 23% < 20, 77% 20-39, less than 1% 40-49. **Special facilities:** Observatory.

Student profile. Among degree-seeking undergraduates, 2,946 enrolled as first-time, first-year students.

Part-time:	60%	**Asian American:**	3%
Out-of-state:	6%	**Hispanic American:**	11%
Women:	65%	**Native American:**	1%
African American:	8%	**25 or older:**	42%

Transfer out. Colleges most students transferred to 2005: Rhode Island College, University of Rhode Island, New England Institute of Technology, Johnson and Wales University, Roger Williams University.

Basis for selection. Open admission, but selective for some programs. Placement testing in mathematics and English is required and chemistry may be required for programs with limited enrollment.

High school preparation. Some programs may require mathematics and science background. Special considerations for nursing and allied health applicants.

2005-2006 Annual costs. Tuition/fees: $2,470; $6,700 out-of-state. Per-credit charge: $102 in-state; $307 out-of-state.

Financial aid. Need-based: Need-based aid available for part-time students. Work study available nights, weekends and for part-time students. **Non-need-based:** Scholarships awarded for athletics.

Application procedures. Admission: No deadline. $20 fee, may be waived for applicants with need. Application may be submitted online. Admission notification on a rolling basis beginning on or about 1/1. Application closing date and admitted student reply deadline is the first week of fall semester in September and first week of spring semester in January. After the first week of each semester, applicants are processed for the following semester. **Financial aid:** Priority date 3/1; no closing date. FAFSA, institutional form required. Applicants notified on a rolling basis starting 5/1; must reply within 2 week(s) of notification.

Academics. Special study options: Cooperative education, cross-registration, distance learning, double major, dual enrollment of high school students, ESL, honors, internships, study abroad, weekend college. License preparation in dental hygiene, nursing, occupational therapy, physical therapy, radiology, real estate. **Credit/placement by examination:** AP, CLEP. 30 credit hours maximum toward associate degree. **Support services:** GED preparation and test center, learning center, reduced course load, remedial instruction, study skills assistance, tutoring, writing center.

Majors. Business: General, accounting, administrative services, banking/financial services, business admin, fashion, marketing, real estate, retailing. **Computer sciences:** Applications programming, networking. **Education:** General, kindergarten/preschool, special. **Engineering:** General, manufacturing. **Engineering technology:** Computer, computer hardware, electrical, instrumentation, manufacturing, mechanical, telecommunications. **Family/consumer sciences:** Aging. **Health:** Clinical lab technology, dental hygiene, health services, massage therapy, medical secretary, nursing (RN), occupational therapy assistant, physical therapy assistant, radiologic technology/medical imaging, respiratory therapy technology, substance abuse counseling. **Interdisciplinary:** Biological/physical sciences. **Legal studies:** Legal secretary, paralegal. **Liberal arts:** Arts/sciences. **Protective services:** Firefighting, police science. **Public administration:** Social work. **Science technology:** Chemical. **Social sciences:** Urban studies. **Visual/performing arts:** Art, dramatic, jazz, theater design.

Most popular majors. Business/marketing 13%, education 7%, health sciences 25%, liberal arts 34%, security/protective services 7%.

Computing on campus. 1,200 workstations in library, computer center, student center. Commuter students can connect to campus network. Online course registration, online library, helpline available.

Student life. Freshman orientation: Mandatory. Preregistration for classes offered. **Activities:** Bands, choral groups, dance, drama, music ensembles, student government, student newspaper, Black American Student Association, Latin American Student Organization, Spanish club, German club, Portuguese club, French club, South East Asian club, ABLE (organization for students with disabilities), minority mentoring program, Distributive Education Club of America.

Athletics. NJCAA. **Intercollegiate:** Baseball M, basketball, cross-country, golf, soccer, softball W, tennis, track and field, volleyball W. **Intramural:** Basketball, cross-country, volleyball, water polo. **Team name:** Knights.

Student services. Adult student services, alcohol/substance abuse counseling, campus ministries, career counseling, services for economically disadvantaged, student employment services, financial aid counseling, health services, minority student services, on-campus daycare, personal counseling, placement for graduates, veterans' counselor, women's services. **Physically disabled:** Services for visually, speech, hearing impaired. **Transfer:** Special adviser, orientation, re-entry adviser, pre-admission transcript evaluation for new students. Transfer adviser, college fairs on campus for students transferring to 4-year colleges.

Contact. Phone: (401) 825-2003 Fax: (401) 825-2394
John Panzica, Dean of Enrollment Services, Community College of Rhode Island, 400 East Avenue, Warwick, RI 02886-1807

South Carolina

Aiken Technical College
Graniteville, South Carolina
www.atc.edu **CB code: 5037**

- Public 2-year community and technical college
- Commuter campus in small city

General. Founded in 1972. Regionally accredited. **Enrollment:** 2,432 degree-seeking undergraduates; 84 non-degree-seeking students. **Degrees:** 213 associate awarded. **Location:** 8 miles from Aiken, 10 miles from Augusta, Georgia. **Calendar:** Semester, extensive summer session. **Full-time faculty:** 55 total; 16% minority, 42% women. **Part-time faculty:** 109 total; 19% minority, 56% women. **Class size:** 67% < 20, 33% 20-39.

Student profile. Among degree-seeking undergraduates, 9% enrolled in a transfer program, 87% enrolled in a vocational program, 586 enrolled as first-time, first-year students, 180 transferred in from other institutions.

Part-time:	43%	**Women:**	65%
Out-of-state:	13%	**25 or older:**	40%

Transfer out. Colleges most students transferred to 2005: Augusta State University, Lander University, University of South Carolina.

Basis for selection. Open admission, but selective for some programs. Special requirements for nursing, dental assisting, predental hygiene, pre-physical therapy, and prepharmacy technician. Test scores considered if submitted. Interview recommended. **Adult students:** SAT/ACT scores not required.

High school preparation. 18 units recommended. Recommended units include English 4, mathematics 4, social studies 2, history 2, science 2, foreign language 2 and academic electives 2.

2005-2006 Annual costs. Tuition/fees: $3,036; $3,396 out-of-district; $8,330 out-of-state. Out of state students pay an additional $188 in fees. Books/supplies: $450. Personal expenses: $900.

2004-2005 Financial aid. Need-based: Average scholarship/grant was $1,622. 95% of total undergraduate aid awarded as scholarships/grants, 5% as loans/jobs. Need-based aid available for part-time students. Work study available nights, weekends and for part-time students. **Non-need-based:** Scholarships awarded for academics, athletics, leadership, minority status, state residency.

Application procedures. Admission: Priority date 7/1; no deadline. No application fee. Application must be submitted on paper. Admission notification on a rolling basis. **Financial aid:** Priority date 5/1, closing date 6/30. FAFSA required. Applicants notified on a rolling basis starting 4/1; must reply within 2 week(s) of notification.

Academics. Special study options: Combined bachelor's/graduate degree, cooperative education, cross-registration, distance learning, double major, dual enrollment of high school students, ESL, independent study, internships, liberal arts/career combination. License preparation in aviation, nursing, real estate. **Credit/placement by examination:** AP, CLEP, institutional tests. **Support services:** Learning center, reduced course load, remedial instruction, study skills assistance, tutoring, writing center.

Majors. Business: Accounting, administrative services, business admin, sales/distribution. **Computer sciences:** Data processing. **Education:** Voc/tech. **Engineering:** Computer, electrical, mechanical, nuclear. **Engineering technology:** Computer, electrical, electromechanical, mechanical drafting. **Health:** Medical radiologic technology/radiation therapy, nursing (RN). **Liberal arts:** Arts/sciences. **Mechanic/repair:** Industrial. **Production:** Machine tool. **Protective services:** Criminal justice. **Public administration:** Human services, social work. **Science technology:** Nuclear power.

Most popular majors. Business/marketing 20%, computer/information sciences 6%, engineering/engineering technologies 6%, family/consumer sciences 11%, interdisciplinary studies 21%, liberal arts 17%, public administration/social services 7%.

Computing on campus. 1,000 workstations in library, computer center, student center. Online library, helpline, repair service available.

Student life. Freshman orientation: Available. Preregistration for classes offered. **Policies:** Freshmen permitted cars on campus. **Activities:** Drama, student government, student newspaper, Phi Theta Kappa Honor Society.

Athletics. NJCAA. **Intercollegiate:** Basketball M, golf M, softball W. **Intramural:** Basketball, softball, volleyball. **Team name:** Knights.

Student services. Adult student services, career counseling, student employment services, financial aid counseling, on-campus daycare, personal counseling, placement for graduates, veterans' counselor. **Physically disabled:** Services for visually, speech, hearing impaired. **Transfer:** Special adviser, orientation, pre-admission transcript evaluation for new students. Transfer adviser, college fairs on campus for students transferring to 4-year colleges.

Contact. E-mail: admiss2@atc.edu
Phone: (803) 593-9954 ext. 1223 Fax: (803) 593-6526
Evelynn Pride-Patterson, Director of Admissions and Records, Aiken Technical College, PO Box 400, Graniteville, SC 29829

Central Carolina Technical College
Sumter, South Carolina
www.cctech.edu **CB code: 5665**

- Public 2-year community and technical college
- Commuter campus in large town

General. Founded in 1963. Regionally accredited. Additional campuses in Manning, Shaw Air Force Base, Camden and Lee County. **Enrollment:** 3,244 degree-seeking undergraduates. **Degrees:** 239 associate awarded. **Location:** 45 miles from Columbia. **Calendar:** Semester, limited summer session. **Full-time faculty:** 85 total. **Part-time faculty:** 150 total. **Special facilities:** South Carolina Environmental Training Center.

Student profile. Among degree-seeking undergraduates, 6% enrolled in a transfer program, 94% enrolled in a vocational program, 567 enrolled as first-time, first-year students.

Part-time:	71%	**25 or older:**	30%
Women:	70%		

Transfer out. Colleges most students transferred to 2005: Unversity of South Carolina, Clemson University, Coker College, Lander University, St Leo University.

Basis for selection. Open admission, but selective for some programs. Minimum SAT Verbal 510 and Mathematical 510 or minimum ACT 22 composite required of nursing applicants. Test scores required for placement. Interview required for nursing program.

2005-2006 Annual costs. Tuition/fees: $2,700; $3,168 out-of-district; $4,800 out-of-state. Books/supplies: $600.

Financial aid. All financial aid based on need. Need-based aid available for part-time students. Work study available nights and for part-time students.

Application procedures. Admission: No deadline. $25 fee. Admission notification on a rolling basis. **Financial aid:** Priority date 6/15; no closing date. FAFSA required. Applicants notified on a rolling basis; must reply within 2 week(s) of notification.

Academics. Special study options: Cooperative education, distance learning, dual enrollment of high school students, independent study, internships. License preparation in nursing. **Credit/placement by examination:** AP, CLEP, institutional tests. 15 credit hours maximum toward associate degree. **Support services:** GED preparation and test center, learning center, reduced course load, remedial instruction, study skills assistance, tutoring.

Majors. Business: Accounting, administrative services, management science, marketing. **Computer sciences:** Programming. **Conservation:** Management/policy. **Engineering technology:** Civil, drafting. **Health:** Nursing (RN), surgical technology. **Legal studies:** Paralegal. **Liberal arts:** Arts/sciences.

Computing on campus. 75 workstations in library, computer center.

Student life. Freshman orientation: Available. Preregistration for classes offered. **Activities:** Phi Theta Kappa, Earth club, computer club.

Student services. Career counseling, student employment services, financial aid counseling, personal counseling, placement for graduates, veterans' counselor. **Physically disabled:** Services for visually, speech, hearing impaired. **Transfer:** Special adviser, orientation, pre-admission transcript evaluation for new students. Transfer adviser, college fairs on campus for students transferring to 4-year colleges.

Contact. E-mail: admissions@sumtec.sc.us
Phone: (803) 778-6605 Toll-free number: (800) 221-8711 ext. 205
Fax: (803) 778-6696
Juanita Colman, Director, Admissions and Counseling Services, Central Carolina Technical College, 506 North Guignard Drive, Sumter, SC 29150

Denmark Technical College

Denmark, South Carolina
www.denmarktech.edu **CB code: 5744**

- Public 2-year technical college
- Residential campus in small town

General. Founded in 1948. Regionally accredited. **Enrollment:** 1,232 degree-seeking undergraduates. **Degrees:** 142 associate awarded. **ROTC:** Army. **Location:** 55 miles from Columbia. **Calendar:** Semester, extensive summer session. **Full-time faculty:** 40 total. **Part-time faculty:** 15 total.

Student profile.

Out-of-state:	3%	**Live on campus:**	50%

Basis for selection. Open admission. Interview recommended.

High school preparation. Recommended units include English 4, mathematics 4, social studies 2, science 2 and foreign language 2. College preparatory program required for AA and AS transfer college programs.

2005-2006 Annual costs. Tuition/fees: $2,278; $4,366 out-of-state. Room/board: $3,096. Books/supplies: $1,100. Personal expenses: $2,000.

Financial aid. Need-based: Need-based aid available for part-time students.

Application procedures. Admission: No deadline. $10 fee, may be waived for applicants with need. Admission notification on a rolling basis. **Financial aid:** No deadline. FAFSA required. Applicants notified on a rolling basis starting 6/1; must reply within 2 week(s) of notification.

Academics. Special study options: Cooperative education, cross-registration, independent study, internships. **Credit/placement by examination:** AP, CLEP, institutional tests. **Support services:** Learning center, reduced course load, remedial instruction, tutoring.

Majors. Business: General. **Liberal arts:** Arts/sciences. **Mechanic/repair:** Electronics/electrical. **Public administration:** Human services.

Computing on campus. 75 workstations in library.

Student life. Freshman orientation: Available. **Housing:** Single-sex dorms available. **Activities:** Choral groups, student government, student newspaper, Student Christian Association.

Athletics. Intercollegiate: Basketball. **Intramural:** Basketball.

Student services. Career counseling, student employment services, health services, personal counseling, placement for graduates, veterans' counselor. **Transfer:** Special adviser, orientation for new students. College fairs on campus for students transferring to 4-year colleges.

Contact. E-mail: cokleys@den.tec.sc.us
Phone: (803) 793-5176 Fax: (803) 793-5942
Teresa Mack, Admissions Director, Denmark Technical College, Solomon Blatt Boulevard, Denmark, SC 29042

Florence-Darlington Technical College

Florence, South Carolina **CB member**
www.fdtc.edu **CB code: 5207**

- Public 2-year community and technical college
- Commuter campus in small city

General. Founded in 1964. Regionally accredited. **Enrollment:** 3,994 degree-seeking undergraduates; 247 non-degree-seeking students. **Degrees:** 404 associate awarded. **Location:** 80 miles from Columbia, 50 miles from Myrtle Beach. **Calendar:** Semester, limited summer session. **Full-time faculty:** 105 total. **Part-time faculty:** 115 total. **Partnerships:** Formal partnerships with local, regional, and national corporations which enhance student opportunities for training.

Student profile. Among degree-seeking undergraduates, 932 enrolled as first-time, first-year students.

Part-time:	45%	**25 or older:**	34%
Women:	70%		

Transfer out. Colleges most students transferred to 2005: Francis Marion University, Clemson University, University of South Carolina.

Basis for selection. Open admission, but selective for some programs. Special requirements for allied health and nursing programs. Computerized Placement Test administered as alternative to SAT or ACT for placement for most programs. RSAT, NLN, HOAE or HOBET required for some allied health programs. Interview required for allied health, nursing programs. **Homeschooled:** GED may be required.

High school preparation. Recommended units include English 4, mathematics 3, social studies 2, history 1, science 2 (laboratory 2), foreign language 2 and academic electives 2. Algebra I, algebra II, biology, and chemistry required for most health programs.

2005-2006 Annual costs. Tuition/fees: $2,986; $3,248 out-of-district; $5,082 out-of-state. Books/supplies: $900. Personal expenses: $2,338.

Financial aid. Need-based: Need-based aid available for part-time students. Work study available for part-time students. **Non-need-based:** Scholarships awarded for academics.

Application procedures. Admission: Priority date 7/15; deadline 8/10. $20 fee, may be waived for applicants with need. Application may be submitted online. Admission notification on a rolling basis beginning on or about 1/1. **Financial aid:** Priority date 5/1; no closing date. FAFSA required. Applicants notified on a rolling basis starting 7/1; must reply within 2 week(s) of notification.

Academics. Special study options: Cooperative education, cross-registration, distance learning, dual enrollment of high school students, independent study, internships, liberal arts/career combination. Cooperative program with Greenville Technical College for physical therapy, Fayetteville Technical College for funeral services. License preparation in dental hygiene, nursing, physical therapy. **Credit/placement by examination:** AP, CLEP, IB, institutional tests. Student may receive credit for up to 50% of the course work required by his or her major. **Support services:** GED preparation, learning center, reduced course load, remedial instruction, tutoring.

Majors. Business: Accounting, administrative services, entrepreneurial studies, sales/distribution. **Computer sciences:** Data processing. **Education:** Voc/tech. **Engineering technology:** Civil, drafting, electrical. **Health:** Clinical lab technology, dental hygiene, medical radiologic technology/radiation therapy, medical records technology, nursing (RN), physical therapy assistant, respiratory therapy technology. **Legal studies:** Paralegal. **Liberal arts:** Arts/sciences. **Mechanic/repair:** Automotive, heating/ac/refrig. **Personal/culinary services:** Mortuary science. **Physical sciences:** General. **Protective services:** Criminal justice. **Public administration:** Social work.

Computing on campus. 128 workstations in library, computer center. Commuter students can connect to campus network.

Student life. Freshman orientation: Mandatory. Preregistration for classes offered. **Activities:** Music ensembles, student government, student newspaper.

Athletics. NJCAA. **Intercollegiate:** Baseball M, softball W. **Team name:** Stingers.

Student services. Career counseling, services for economically disadvantaged, student employment services, financial aid counseling, on-campus daycare, personal counseling, placement for graduates, veterans' counselor. **Physically disabled:** Services for hearing impaired. **Transfer:** Special adviser, orientation for new students. Transfer adviser for students transferring to 4-year colleges.

Contact. E-mail: admissions@fdtc.edu
Phone: (843) 661-8324 Toll-free number: (800) 228-5745
Fax: (843) 661-8041
Vivian Gallman, Director of Admissions, Florence-Darlington Technical College, PO Box 100548, Florence, SC 29501-0548

Forrest Junior College

Anderson, South Carolina
www.forrestcollege.edu **CB code: 7138**

- For-profit 2-year community and junior college
- Commuter campus in large town
- Application essay, interview required

General. Accredited by ACICS. Majority of students are working adults with children. Free child care for toilet-trained children provided while parent attends class. **Enrollment:** 126 degree-seeking undergraduates. **Degrees:** 34 associate awarded. **Location:** 30 miles from Greenville. **Calendar:** Quarter, extensive summer session. **Full-time faculty:** 3 total; 33% have terminal degrees, 100% women. **Part-time faculty:** 20 total; 75% have terminal degrees, 35% minority, 90% women.

Student profile. Among degree-seeking undergraduates, 3 enrolled as first-time, first-year students, 20 transferred in from other institutions.

Part-time:	10%	**25 or older:**	75%
Women:	92%		

Transfer out. Colleges most students transferred to 2005: Greenville Technical College, Piedmont Technical College, Lander University, Strayer University.

Basis for selection. Open admission, but selective for some programs. Audition, portfolio recommended.

2006-2007 Annual costs. Tuition/fees: $5,350. Per-credit charge: $110.

Financial aid. All financial aid based on need. Need-based aid available for part-time students. Work study available nights, weekends and for part-time students.

Application procedures. Admission: No deadline. $25 fee. Admission notification on a rolling basis. **Financial aid:** No deadline. FAFSA required. Applicants notified on a rolling basis starting 4/30; must reply by 5/31 or within 4 week(s) of notification.

Academics. Special study options: Cooperative education, double major, ESL, independent study, internships, liberal arts/career combination, weekend college. **Credit/placement by examination:** AP, CLEP, institutional tests. **Support services:** Reduced course load, tutoring.

Majors. Business: General, accounting, administrative services, business admin, communications, human resources, managerial economics, marketing, office management, office technology, office/clerical. **Computer sciences:** General, information systems. **Education:** Early childhood, sales/marketing, teacher assistance. **Family/consumer sciences:** Child care. **Health:** Clinical lab assistant, clinical lab technology, medical assistant, medical records admin, medical records technology, medical secretary, medical transcription. **Legal studies:** Legal secretary, paralegal. **Personal/culinary services:** General.

Computing on campus. 52 workstations in library, computer center. Repair service available.

Student life. Freshman orientation: Mandatory. Preregistration for classes offered. **Policies:** Freshmen permitted cars on campus. **Activities:** Literary magazine, student government, student newspaper.

Student services. Adult student services, career counseling, student employment services, financial aid counseling, on-campus daycare, placement for graduates. **Transfer:** Pre-admission transcript evaluation for new students.

Contact. E-mail: debbiewilliams@forrestcollege.com
Phone: (864) 225-7653 ext. 208 Fax: (864) 261-7471
Debbie Williams, Admissions Officer, Forrest Junior College, 601 East River Street, Anderson, SC 29624

Golf Academy of the Carolinas

Scottsdale, Arizona
www.sdgagolf.com **CB code: 3223**

- For-profit 2-year golf academy
- Large town

General. Accredited by ACICS. **Calendar:** Continuous.

Annual costs/financial aid. Books/supplies: $700. Personal expenses: $1,552.

Contact. Phone: (480) 905-9288
Admissions Director, 7373 North Scottsdale Road, Suite B-100, Scottsdale, AZ 82253

Greenville Technical College

Greenville, South Carolina
www.greenvilletech.com **CB code: 5278**

- Public 2-year community and technical college
- Commuter campus in large city

General. Founded in 1962. Regionally accredited. Classes and some programs offered at satellite campuses in Greenville County. **Enrollment:** 11,619 degree-seeking undergraduates; 1,738 non-degree-seeking students. **Degrees:** 939 associate awarded. **Location:** 100 miles from Columbia, 100 miles from Charlotte, North Carolina. **Calendar:** Semester, extensive summer session. **Full-time faculty:** 334 total; 10% have terminal degrees, 10% minority, 57% women. **Part-time faculty:** 403 total; 8% have terminal degrees, 11% minority, 63% women.

Student profile. Among degree-seeking undergraduates, 23% enrolled in a transfer program, 64% enrolled in a vocational program, 2,365 enrolled as first-time, first-year students.

Part-time:	54%	**Asian American:**	2%
Out-of-state:	.3%	**Hispanic American:**	2%
Women:	62%	**25 or older:**	49%
African American:	22%		

Transfer out. 85% of students enrolled in the transfer program go on to 4-year colleges.

Basis for selection. Open admission, but selective for some programs. Weighted admissions requirements for registered nursing, licensed practical nursing, certain allied health programs. ASSET/COMPASS scores may be submitted for placement in place of SAT or ACT scores. Minimum SAT, ACT, or ASSET scores required for allied health and nursing applicants. Interview required for allied health sciences, nursing, arts, and aircraft mechanic applicants; recommended for all others. Portfolio required for visual arts program. **Adult students:** Entrance exam policies same as for first-time freshmen.

High school preparation. Algebra, biology, and chemistry required for most health care program applicants.

2005-2006 Annual costs. Tuition/fees: $3,000; $3,250 out-of-district; $6,110 out-of-state. Books/supplies: $976. Personal expenses: $656.

2004-2005 Financial aid. Need-based: 53% of total undergraduate aid awarded as scholarships/grants, 47% as loans/jobs. Need-based aid available for part-time students. Work study available nights and for part-time students. **Non-need-based:** Scholarships awarded for academics, state residency.

Application procedures. Admission: No deadline. $35 fee. Application may be submitted online. Admission notification on a rolling basis. **Financial aid:** Priority date 5/1; no closing date. FAFSA required. Applicants notified on a rolling basis starting 6/15; must reply within 2 week(s) of notification.

Academics. Special study options: Accelerated study, cooperative education, distance learning, dual enrollment of high school students, ESL, honors, independent study, internships, liberal arts/career combination, teacher certification program, weekend college. License preparation in aviation, dental hygiene, nursing, occupational therapy, paramedic, physical therapy, radiology, real estate. **Credit/placement by examination:** AP, CLEP, IB, institutional tests. Credits for work experience evaluated and awarded by program department head. Courses requiring research cannot be completed by exam. **Support services:** GED preparation, learning center, reduced course load, remedial instruction, study skills assistance, tutoring, writing center.

Honors college/program. Require 3.5 GPA and interview with head of department.

Majors. Business: Accounting, administrative services, business admin, purchasing, sales/distribution. **Computer sciences:** Data processing. **Engineering technology:** Architectural, construction, electrical, mechanical, mechanical drafting. **Family/consumer sciences:** Child care. **Health:** Clinical lab technology, dental hygiene, EMT paramedic, medical radiologic technology/radiation therapy, medical records technology, nursing (RN), occupational therapy assistant, physical therapy assistant, respiratory therapy technology. **Legal studies:** Paralegal. **Liberal arts:** Arts/sciences. **Mechanic/repair:** General, automotive, industrial. **Personal/culinary services:** Institutional food service. **Production:** Machine tool. **Protective services:** Criminal justice. **Public administration:** Social work. **Social sciences:** Cartography.

Computing on campus. 866 workstations in library, computer center. Commuter students can connect to campus network. Online library available.

Student life. Freshman orientation: Available. Preregistration for classes offered. Online orientation. **Policies:** Freshmen permitted cars on campus. **Activities:** Drama, student government, American Criminal Justice Association, Baptist collegiate ministry, Campus Crusade for Christ, international student organization, human services organization, Spanish club, national technical honor society, Phi Theta Kappa, critics choice club.

Student services. Adult student services, alcohol/substance abuse counseling, campus ministries, career counseling, services for economically disadvantaged, student employment services, financial aid counseling, on-campus daycare, personal counseling, placement for graduates, veterans' counselor. **Physically disabled:** Services for visually, speech, hearing impaired. **Transfer:** Special adviser, orientation, pre-admission transcript evaluation for new students. Transfer adviser for students transferring to 4-year colleges.

Contact. E-mail: carolyn.watkins@gvltec.edu
Phone: (864) 250-8109 Toll-free number: (800) 922-1183
Fax: (864) 250-8534
Martha White, Director of Admissions, Greenville Technical College, P. O. Box 5616, Greenville, SC 29606-5616

Horry-Georgetown Technical College

Conway, South Carolina
www.hgtc.edu **CB code: 5305**

- Public 2-year community and technical college
- Commuter campus in large town

General. Founded in 1965. Regionally accredited. **Enrollment:** 5,348 degree-seeking undergraduates. **Degrees:** 507 associate awarded. **Location:** 4 miles from Conway, 8 miles from Myrtle Beach. **Calendar:** Semester, extensive summer session. **Full-time faculty:** 125 total. **Part-time faculty:** 150 total. **Special facilities:** Art gallery, golf club.

Student profile. Among degree-seeking undergraduates, 26% enrolled in a transfer program.

Transfer out. Colleges most students transferred to 2005: Coastal Carolina University.

Basis for selection. Open admission, but selective for some programs. Special requirements for engineering, technology, allied health, science programs.

2005-2006 Annual costs. Tuition/fees: $2,864; $3,448 out-of-district; $4,472 out-of-state. Books/supplies: $1,000. Personal expenses: $1,615.

2005-2006 Financial aid. Need-based: 91% of total undergraduate aid awarded as scholarships/grants, 9% as loans/jobs. Need-based aid available for part-time students. **Additional information:** Participates in South Carolina lottery tuition assistance program. Full-time technical college students who are state residents receive assistance for tuition not covered by federal or need-based grants.

Application procedures. Admission: No deadline. $25 fee, may be waived for applicants with need. Application may be submitted online. Admission notification on a rolling basis. **Financial aid:** Priority date 4/1, closing date 6/30. FAFSA required. Applicants notified on a rolling basis starting 4/1.

Academics. Special study options: Distance learning, double major, dual enrollment of high school students, exchange student, independent study, internships. License preparation in dental hygiene, nursing, radiology, real estate. **Credit/placement by examination:** CLEP, institutional tests. **Support services:** Learning center, reduced course load, remedial instruction, tutoring.

Majors. Agriculture: Horticulture, turf management. **Business:** General, accounting, administrative services, hotel/motel admin. **Computer sciences:** Data processing. **Conservation:** Forest technology. **Education:** Voc/tech. **Engineering:** Electrical. **Engineering technology:** Civil, construction, electrical. **Family/consumer sciences:** Child care. **Health:** Dental hygiene, EMT paramedic, medical radiologic technology/radiation therapy, nursing (RN), pharmacy assistant. **Legal studies:** Paralegal. **Liberal arts:** Arts/sciences. **Mechanic/repair:** Heating/ac/refrig, industrial electronics. **Parks/recreation:** General, facilities management. **Personal/culinary services:** Chef training. **Production:** Machine tool. **Protective services:** Criminal justice. **Public administration:** Social work. **Visual/performing arts:** Design.

Most popular majors. Agriculture 6%, business/marketing 22%, health sciences 25%, liberal arts 14%, security/protective services 8%.

Computing on campus. 900 workstations in library, computer center, student center. Commuter students can connect to campus network. Online library, helpline available.

Student life. Freshman orientation: Available. Preregistration for classes offered. **Activities:** Choral groups.

Student services. Career counseling, financial aid counseling, on-campus daycare, personal counseling, placement for graduates, veterans' counselor. **Transfer:** Special adviser, orientation for new students. Transfer adviser for students transferring to 4-year colleges.

Contact. E-mail: Admissions@hgtc.edu
Phone: (843) 349-5277 Fax: (843) 349-7501
Teresa Hilburn, Enrollment Development, Horry-Georgetown Technical College, PO Box 261966, Conway, SC 29528

Midlands Technical College

Columbia, South Carolina **CB member**
www.midlandstech.edu **CB code: 5584**

- Public 2-year technical college
- Commuter campus in small city

General. Founded in 1974. Regionally accredited. Additional campuses include Airport Campus, Beltline Campus, Enterprise Campus/Center and Harbison Center. **Enrollment:** 10,243 degree-seeking undergraduates; 536 non-degree-seeking students. **Degrees:** 844 associate awarded. **ROTC:** Army, Navy, Air Force. **Location:** 10 miles from Columbia. **Calendar:** Semester, limited summer session. **Full-time faculty:** 220 total. **Part-time faculty:** 435 total. **Partnerships:** Formal partnerships with middle schools.

Student profile. Among degree-seeking undergraduates, 1,308 transferred in from other institutions.

Part-time:	54%	**Asian American:**	2%
Out-of-state:	3%	**Hispanic American:**	2%
Women:	63%	**Native American:**	1%
African American:	37%	**25 or older:**	41%

Transfer out. Colleges most students transferred to 2005: University of South Carolina.

Basis for selection. Open admission, but selective for some programs. High school record, SAT/ACT or college placement test scores, and interviews considered for nursing/health science applicants. Admission cut-off scores established for full admission into each program. Students falling below cut-off scores may enter in developmental studies. National League for Nursing Test required of nursing applicants in place of SAT or ACT. Interview, orientation required for health science and nursing programs. **Adult students:** Entrance exam policies same as for first-time freshmen. **Home-schooled:** Must be an approved Home School Association in South Carolina. If home schooler is applying for concurrent admission they must have a letter of permission from the home school association and a letter of permission from their parent/guardian.

2005-2006 Annual costs. Tuition/fees: $3,004; $3,876 out-of-district; $8,812 out-of-state. Books/supplies: $1,240. Personal expenses: $1,200.

Financial aid. Need-based: Need-based aid available for part-time students.

Application procedures. Admission: Priority date 7/20; no deadline. No application fee. Application may be submitted online. Admission notification on a rolling basis. **Financial aid:** Priority date 4/15; no closing date. FAFSA required. Applicants notified on a rolling basis; must reply within 2 week(s) of notification.

Academics. Special study options: Cooperative education, distance learning, dual enrollment of high school students, ESL, liberal arts/career combination. License preparation in nursing, physical therapy, radiology. **Credit/placement by examination:** AP, CLEP, institutional tests. **Support services:** GED preparation, learning center, remedial instruction, study skills assistance, tutoring, writing center.

Majors. Business: Accounting, administrative services, business admin. **Computer sciences:** Data processing. **Engineering technology:** Architectural, civil, drafting, electrical. **Health:** Clinical lab technology, dental assistant, dental hygiene, medical radiologic technology/radiation therapy, medical records technology, nuclear medical technology, nursing (RN), pharmacy assistant, physical therapy assistant, respiratory therapy technology. **Legal studies:** Court reporting, paralegal. **Liberal arts:** Arts/sciences. **Mechanic/repair:** Automotive, heating/ac/refrig. **Protective services:** Criminal justice. **Public administration:** Social work. **Visual/performing arts:** Commercial/advertising art.

Most popular majors. Business/marketing 19%, computer/information sciences 6%, health sciences 21%, liberal arts 30%, security/protective services 6%, trade and industry 9%.

Computing on campus. 125 workstations in library, computer center, student center. Commuter students can connect to campus network. Online course registration, online library, helpline available.

Student life. Freshman orientation: Available. Preregistration for classes offered. **Policies:** Freshmen permitted cars on campus. **Activities:** Drama, literary magazine, student government, student newspaper, Campus Crusade for Christ, student human services organization, Baptist collegiate ministry.

Student services. Adult student services, career counseling, services for economically disadvantaged, student employment services, financial aid counseling, placement for graduates, veterans' counselor. **Physically disabled:** Services for visually, speech, hearing impaired. **Learning disabled:** Comprehensive services available. **Transfer:** Special adviser, re-entry adviser, pre-admission transcript evaluation for new students. Transfer adviser, college fairs on campus for students transferring to 4-year colleges.

Contact. E-mail: mtcinfo@midlandstech.edu
Phone: (803) 738-8324 Toll-free number: (800) 922-8038
Fax: (803) 738-7784
Sylvia Littlejohn, Vice President of Admissions, Midlands Technical College, PO Box 2408, Columbia, SC 29202

Miller-Motte Technical College

North Charleston, South Carolina
www.miller-motte.net

- For-profit 2-year branch campus and technical college
- Small city

General. Accredited by ACICS. **Enrollment:** 500 degree-seeking undergraduates. **Degrees:** 163 associate awarded. **Calendar:** Quarter. **Full-time faculty:** 15 total. **Part-time faculty:** 40 total.

Application procedures. Admission: No deadline. $25 fee. **Financial aid:** FAFSA, institutional form required. Applicants notified on a rolling basis.

Academics. Credit/placement by examination: CLEP.

Majors. Business: Accounting/business management, business admin. **Health:** Massage therapy, medical assistant, surgical technology. **Legal studies:** Paralegal. **Social sciences:** Demography.

Contact. Phone: (843) 574-0101 Toll-free number: (877) 617-4740
Fax: (843) 266-3424
Kerrie Tobias, Admissions Director, Miller-Motte Technical College, 8085 Rivers Avenue, Suite E, North Charleston, SC 29406

Northeastern Technical College

Cheraw, South Carolina
www.netc.edu **CB code: 5095**

- Public 2-year community and technical college
- Commuter campus in small town

General. Founded in 1969. Regionally accredited. High percentage of nontraditional students. **Enrollment:** 999 degree-seeking undergraduates; 44 non-degree-seeking students. **Degrees:** 128 associate awarded. **Location:** 89 miles from Columbia. **Calendar:** Semester, extensive summer session. **Full-time faculty:** 30 total; 3% have terminal degrees, 3% minority, 57% women. **Part-time faculty:** 84 total; 4% have terminal degrees, 20% minority, 63% women.

Student profile. Among degree-seeking undergraduates, 35% enrolled in a transfer program, 65% enrolled in a vocational program, 266 enrolled as first-time, first-year students.

Part-time:	47%	**Women:**	72%
Out-of-state:	1%	**25 or older:**	36%

Transfer out. Colleges most students transferred to 2005: Francis Marion University, Clemson University, Coastal Carolina University, Florence-Darlington Technical College, University of South Carolina.

Basis for selection. Open admission, but selective for some programs. Special requirements for nursing program, including high school math and science courses and SAT (exclusive of writing) combined score of 960. Interview recommended.

High school preparation. Algebra I and II, chemistry with laboratory required for nursing applicants.

2005-2006 Annual costs. Tuition/fees: $2,526; $2,718 out-of-district; $4,110 out-of-state. Books/supplies: $1,200. Personal expenses: $1,800.

2005-2006 Financial aid. Need-based: 97% of total undergraduate aid awarded as scholarships/grants, 3% as loans/jobs.

Application procedures. Admission: Closing date 8/14. $13 fee, may be waived for applicants with need. Admission notification on a rolling basis. **Financial aid:** No deadline. FAFSA required. Applicants notified on a rolling basis; must reply within 8 week(s) of notification.

Academics. Special study options: Cross-registration, distance learning, independent study, liberal arts/career combination. **Credit/placement by examination:** AP, CLEP, institutional tests. Credit by examination limited to 50% of semester hours required for degree. ASSET and English language proficiency required for placement. **Support services:** Remedial instruction, tutoring.

Majors. Business: Accounting, administrative services, business admin, office technology, office/clerical. **Computer sciences:** Data processing. **Education:** General. **Engineering technology:** Electrical. **Liberal arts:** Arts/sciences.

Computing on campus. 125 workstations in library, computer center.

Student life. Freshman orientation: Available. Preregistration for classes offered. Four early orientations held in the summer. **Activities:** Student government, service-leadership organization.

Student services. Career counseling, student employment services, personal counseling, placement for graduates, veterans' counselor. **Transfer:** Special adviser, orientation for new students. Transfer adviser for students transferring to 4-year colleges.

Contact. E-mail: mnewton@netc.edu
Phone: (843) 921-6900 Fax: (843) 537-6148
Mary Newton, Dean of Students, Northeastern Technical College, Drawer 1007, Cheraw, SC 29520

Orangeburg-Calhoun Technical College

Orangeburg, South Carolina
www.octech.edu **CB code: 5527**

- Public 2-year community and technical college
- Commuter campus in large town

General. Founded in 1968. Regionally accredited. **Enrollment:** 2,453 degree-seeking undergraduates. **Degrees:** 239 associate awarded. **ROTC:** Army. **Location:** 75 miles from Charleston, 45 miles from Columbia. **Calendar:** Semester, extensive summer session. **Full-time faculty:** 83 total. **Part-time faculty:** 74 total.

Basis for selection. Open admission, but selective for some programs. Admission to nursing and allied health programs based on school achievement record and test scores. ASSET used for placement. SAT or ACT may be submitted in place of ASSET. **Adult students:** Entrance exam policies same as for first-time freshmen.

High school preparation. 24 units recommended. Recommended units include English 4, mathematics 3, social studies 3, history 2, science 2, foreign language 3 and academic electives 7.

2005-2006 Annual costs. Tuition/fees: $2,640; $3,288 out-of-district; $4,734 out-of-state. Books/supplies: $400. Personal expenses: $500.

Financial aid. All financial aid based on need. Need-based aid available for part-time students.

Application procedures. Admission: No deadline. $15 fee, may be waived for applicants with need. Application may be submitted online. Admission notification on a rolling basis beginning on or about 1/1. $15 application processing fee due upon notification of acceptance. **Financial aid:** Priority date 6/4; no closing date. FAFSA, institutional form required. Applicants notified on a rolling basis starting 5/1; must reply within 2 week(s) of notification.

Academics. Special study options: Cooperative education, cross-registration, distance learning, double major, dual enrollment of high school students, independent study, liberal arts/career combination. License preparation in nursing, real estate. **Credit/placement by examination:** CLEP, institutional tests. 60% of hours needed for degree may be earned by examination. **Support services:** Learning center, pre-admission summer program, reduced course load, remedial instruction, study skills assistance, tutoring, writing center.

Majors. **Business:** General, accounting, administrative services. **Computer sciences:** Data processing, programming. **Conservation:** Forest resources. **Engineering technology:** Drafting, electrical. **Health:** Clinical lab assistant, clinical lab technology, medical radiologic technology/radiation therapy, nursing (RN). **Legal studies:** Paralegal. **Liberal arts:** Arts/sciences. **Mechanic/repair:** Automotive, electronics/electrical. **Protective services:** Criminal justice.

Computing on campus. 100 workstations in library, computer center, student center. Commuter students can connect to campus network. Online course registration, online library, repair service, wireless network available.

Student life. **Freshman orientation:** Available. Preregistration for classes offered. **Activities:** Student government, honor fraternities, curriculum clubs.

Athletics. **Intramural:** Basketball, volleyball.

Student services. Adult student services, career counseling, services for economically disadvantaged, student employment services, financial aid counseling, minority student services, personal counseling, placement for graduates, veterans' counselor. **Physically disabled:** Services for visually, speech, hearing impaired. **Transfer:** Special adviser, orientation, pre-admission transcript evaluation for new students. Transfer adviser, college fairs on campus for students transferring to 4-year colleges.

Contact. E-mail: felderb@octech.edu
Phone: (803) 535-1218 Fax: (803) 535-1388
Bobbie Felder, Dean of Students, Orangeburg-Calhoun Technical College, 3250 St. Matthews Road, Orangeburg, SC 29118-8222

Piedmont Technical College

Greenwood, South Carolina
www.ptc.edu **CB code: 5550**

- Public 2-year community and technical college
- Commuter campus in small city

General. Founded in 1966. Regionally accredited. Serves a 7-county region of the state (satellite campus in each county offering internet classes, traditional classes and interactive televised classes with main campus). **Enrollment:** 4,680 degree-seeking undergraduates. **Degrees:** 491 associate awarded. **Location:** 75 miles from Columbia, 50 miles from Greenville. **Calendar:** Semester, extensive summer session. **Full-time faculty:** 100 total. **Part-time faculty:** 145 total. **Class size:** 72% < 20, 28% 20-39, less than 1% 40-49, less than 1% 50-99. **Special facilities:** Computer graphics center, distance learning network.

Student profile.

Out-of-state:	1%	**25 or older:**	45%

Transfer out. **Colleges most students transferred to 2005:** Lander University, Clemson University, University of South Carolina, South Carolina State University.

Basis for selection. Open admission, but selective for some programs. Special requirements for health science programs. Specific ASSET/COMPASS test scores and high school courses required for placement on wait list for program entry. Students not meeting requirements are remediated. Students with SAT verbal of at least 480 and SAT math of at least 440 or ACT composite of at least 20 do not need to take institutional placement tests. Interview recommended. **Adult students:** Adult students may take COMPASS or ASSET.

High school preparation. Biology required for health sciences and nursing applicants.

2005-2006 Annual costs. Tuition/fees: $2,740; $3,172 out-of-district; $4,372 out-of-state. The full-time in-district rates for two semesters are $2496 or $2784, determined by county of residence. The per-credit-hour in-district rates are $104 or $116. Books/supplies: $850. Personal expenses: $200.

Financial aid. All financial aid based on need. Need-based aid available for part-time students. Work study available nights, weekends and for part-time students.

Application procedures. **Admission:** No deadline. No application fee. Application may be submitted online. Admission notification on a rolling basis. **Financial aid:** Priority date 5/1; no closing date. FAFSA required. Applicants notified on a rolling basis starting 6/1; must reply within 2 week(s) of notification.

Academics. **Special study options:** Cooperative education, distance learning, double major, dual enrollment of high school students, independent study, internships, liberal arts/career combination, weekend college. Bachelor's degree programs available on campus. License preparation in nursing, real estate. **Credit/placement by examination:** CLEP, IB, institutional tests. 24 credit hours maximum toward associate degree. **Support services:** GED preparation, learning center, pre-admission summer program, reduced course load, remedial instruction, study skills assistance, tutoring, writing center.

Majors. **Business:** General, administrative services. **Computer sciences:** Data processing. **Education:** Voc/tech. **Engineering technology:** Construction, drafting, electrical, surveying. **Health:** Medical radiologic technology/radiation therapy, nursing (RN), respiratory therapy technology. **Interdisciplinary:** Global studies. **Liberal arts:** Arts/sciences. **Mechanic/repair:** Automotive, electronics/electrical, heating/ac/refrig, industrial electronics. **Personal/culinary services:** Mortuary science. **Production:** Machine tool, welding. **Protective services:** Criminal justice. **Public administration:** Social work.

Most popular majors. Business/marketing 25%, engineering/engineering technologies 9%, health sciences 13%, liberal arts 13%, security/protective services 10%, trade and industry 26%.

Computing on campus. 250 workstations in computer center, student center. Commuter students can connect to campus network. Online library, helpline, repair service available.

Student life. **Freshman orientation:** Available. Preregistration for classes offered. Online orientation on college website. **Activities:** Choral groups, student government, Human Services club, Psychology club, Inter-club council, Psi Beta, international club.

Athletics. **Intramural:** Basketball, football (non-tackle), softball.

Student services. Adult student services, career counseling, services for economically disadvantaged, student employment services, financial aid counseling, minority student services, personal counseling, placement for graduates, veterans' counselor, women's services. **Learning disabled:** Comprehensive services available. **Transfer:** Special adviser, orientation, pre-admission transcript evaluation for new students. Transfer adviser, college fairs on campus for students transferring to 4-year colleges.

Contact. E-mail: barnette.m@ptc.edu
Phone: (864) 941-8369 Toll-free number: (800) 868-5528
Fax: (864) 941-8555
Martha Barnette, Associate Dean of Enrollment Services, Piedmont Technical College, Box 1467, Greenwood, SC 29648

Spartanburg Methodist College

Spartanburg, South Carolina **CB member**
www.smcsc.edu **CB code: 5627**

- Private 2-year junior and liberal arts college affiliated with United Methodist Church
- Residential campus in small city
- SAT or ACT with writing required

General. Founded in 1911. Regionally accredited. Offers religious life program devoted to fostering development of faith in all students. Very strong community service programs. **Enrollment:** 716 degree-seeking undergraduates. **Degrees:** 147 associate awarded. **ROTC:** Army. **Location:** 30 miles from Greenville, 60 miles from Charlotte, North Carolina. **Calendar:** Semester, limited summer session. **Full-time faculty:** 25 total. **Part-time faculty:** 20 total. **Class size:** 27% < 20, 71% 20-39, 1% 40-49, less than 1% >100.

Student profile. Among degree-seeking undergraduates, 100% enrolled in a transfer program, 401 enrolled as first-time, first-year students, 29 transferred in from other institutions.

Part-time:	3%	**Asian American:**	1%
Out-of-state:	7%	**Hispanic American:**	2%
Women:	50%	**International:**	2%
African American:	32%	**Live on campus:**	72%

Transfer out. 90% of students enrolled in the transfer program go on to 4-year colleges. **Colleges most students transferred to 2005:** University of South Carolina-Spartanburg, Clemson University, University of South Carolina, Lander University, College of Charleston.

Basis for selection. High school GPA, SAT/ACT scores, and class rank very important. Audition, essay, interview recommended. **Adult students:** SAT/ACT scores not required if applicant over 21. **Homeschooled:** Applicants need a complete high school academic transcript. Recommend that students be supervised through an accredited home school association to provide curriculum and academic oversight throughout the high school program.

High school preparation. Recommended units include English 4, mathematics 4, social studies 2, history 1, science 3, foreign language 1 and academic electives 7. One computer science recommended.

2005-2006 Annual costs. Tuition/fees: $9,966. Per-credit charge: $260. $150 enrollment fee for first-time enrollees. Room/board: $5,510.

2005-2006 Financial aid. Need-based: 400 full-time freshmen applied for aid; 393 were judged to have need; 393 of these received aid. Average need met was 80%. Average scholarship/grant was $2,500; average loan $2,400. 83% of total undergraduate aid awarded as scholarships/grants, 17% as loans/jobs. Need-based aid available for part-time students. Work study available nights, weekends and for part-time students. **Non-need-based:** Awarded to 854 full-time undergraduates, including 488 freshmen. Scholarships awarded for academics, athletics, job skills, leadership, music/drama, religious affiliation, state residency. **Additional information:** College strives to meet 100% of established financial need of all students.

Application procedures. Admission: No deadline. $20 fee, may be waived for applicants with need. Application may be submitted online. Admission notification on a rolling basis beginning on or about 9/1. Applicant notified of decision within a week. **Financial aid:** Priority date 6/30, closing date 8/22. FAFSA required. Applicants notified on a rolling basis starting 3/1; must reply within 2 week(s) of notification.

Academics. Special study options: Dual enrollment of high school students, ESL, independent study, liberal arts/career combination, study abroad. **Credit/placement by examination:** AP, CLEP, institutional tests. 15 credit hours maximum toward associate degree. **Support services:** Learning center, pre-admission summer program, reduced course load, remedial instruction, study skills assistance, tutoring, writing center.

Majors. Computer sciences: Information systems. **Liberal arts:** Arts/sciences. **Protective services:** Police science.

Computing on campus. 45 workstations in library, computer center, student center. Dormitories wired for high-speed internet access and linked to campus network. Commuter students can connect to campus network. Online library, helpline, repair service available.

Student life. Freshman orientation: Mandatory, $25 fee. Preregistration for classes offered. 3 sessions in mid-July and late August; 1 session during move-in weekend. **Policies:** No alcohol, drugs, or firearms allowed on campus. All campus buildings are smoke free. Freshmen permitted cars on campus. **Housing:** Guaranteed on-campus for all undergraduates. Coed dorms, single-sex dorms, special housing for disabled, substance-free housing available. $100 deposit, deadline 9/1. **Activities:** Choral groups, dance, drama, literary magazine, music ensembles, student government, student newspaper, Fellowship of Christian Athletes, African American Association, criminal justice club, campus union, Alpha Phi Omega, business club, student ambassadors, gospel choir, international club.

Athletics. NJCAA. **Intercollegiate:** Baseball M, basketball, cheerleading, cross-country, golf M, soccer, softball W, tennis, volleyball W, wrestling M. **Intramural:** Basketball, bowling, football (non-tackle) M, softball, table tennis, tennis, volleyball. **Team name:** Pioneers.

Student services. Adult student services, alcohol/substance abuse counseling, campus ministries, career counseling, services for economically disadvantaged, student employment services, financial aid counseling, health services, personal counseling, placement for graduates, veterans' counselor. **Physically disabled:** Services for visually, speech, hearing impaired. **Transfer:** Special adviser, orientation, pre-admission transcript evaluation for new students. Transfer center, transfer adviser, college fairs on campus for students transferring to 4-year colleges.

Contact. E-mail: admiss@smcsc.edu
Phone: (864) 587-4213 Toll-free number: (800) 772-7286
Fax: (864) 587-4355
Daniel Philbeck, Vice President for Enrollment Management, Spartanburg Methodist College, 1000 Powell Mill Road, Spartanburg, SC 29301-5899

Spartanburg Technical College

Spartanburg, South Carolina — **CB member**
www.stcsc.edu — **CB code: 5668**

- Public 2-year community and technical college
- Commuter campus in large town
- Interview required

General. Founded in 1961. Regionally accredited. Satellite campuses located in Greer and Gaffney. **Enrollment:** 4,409 undergraduates. **Degrees:** 370 associate awarded. **Location:** 4 miles from downtown. **Calendar:** Semester, limited summer session. **Full-time faculty:** 110 total. **Part-time faculty:** 170 total. **Special facilities:** Horticultural arboretum. **Partnerships:** Formal partnership with Ford Asset Program (mechanic training program).

Student profile. 50% enrolled in a transfer program, 50% enrolled in a vocational program, 10% already have a bachelor's degree or higher.

Out-of-state:	2%	**25 or older:**	43%

Transfer out. 88% of students enrolled in the transfer program go on to 4-year colleges. **Colleges most students transferred to 2005:** Clemson University, University of South Carolina Upstate, University of South Carolina at Columbia, Wofford University, Spartanburg Methodist College.

Basis for selection. Open admission, but selective for some programs. Admission to some health science programs usually based on size of class. Score of 450 or better (paper-based) or 133 (computer-based) on TOEFL required of non-native English speakers. Test of Adult Basic Education required for admissions. Programmer's Aptitude Test required for computer programming and data processing. Essay recommended. **Adult students:** Entrance exam policies same as for first-time freshmen.

High school preparation. 21 units required. Required units include English 4, mathematics 2, social studies 2, history 2, science 2 (laboratory 2), foreign language 1 and academic electives 6. One biology and/or chemistry and 1 algebra required for most health programs. Algebra required for all engineering and computer programs.

2005-2006 Annual costs. Tuition/fees: $2,902; $3,618 out-of-district; $5,490 out-of-state. Books/supplies: $900. Personal expenses: $2,484.

2004-2005 Financial aid. Need-based: 97% of total undergraduate aid awarded as scholarships/grants, 3% as loans/jobs. Need-based aid available for part-time students. Work study available for part-time students. **Additional information:** Participates in South Carolina lottery tuition assistance program. Full-time technical college students who are state residents receive assistance for tuition not covered by federal or need-based grants.

Application procedures. Admission: No deadline. No application fee. Application may be submitted online. Admission notification on a rolling basis. **Financial aid:** Priority date 2/28, closing date 5/1. FAFSA required. Applicants notified on a rolling basis starting 5/1.

Academics. Special study options: Cooperative education, distance learning, double major, dual enrollment of high school students, ESL, independent study, weekend college. License preparation in dental hygiene, nursing, occupational therapy, physical therapy, radiology. **Credit/placement by examination:** AP, CLEP, institutional tests. **Support services:** GED preparation and test center, learning center, remedial instruction, tutoring.

Majors. Agriculture: Horticulture. **Business:** Accounting, administrative services, business admin, hospitality admin, hotel/motel admin, marketing, restaurant/food services. **Computer sciences:** General. **Education:** Voc/tech. **Engineering technology:** General, civil, electrical, mechanical. **Health:** Clinical lab technology, medical radiologic technology/radiation therapy, nursing (RN), predentistry, respiratory therapy technology. **Liberal arts:** Arts/sciences. **Mechanic/repair:** Automotive, industrial electronics. **Production:** Machine tool.

Most popular majors. Business/marketing 16%, computer/information sciences 8%, engineering/engineering technologies 13%, health sciences 23%, liberal arts 21%, trade and industry 15%.

Computing on campus. 500 workstations in library, computer center, student center. Commuter students can connect to campus network. Online course registration, helpline, repair service, wireless network available.

Student life. Freshman orientation: Available. Preregistration for classes offered. **Activities:** Drama, student government, student newspaper.

Student services. Adult student services, career counseling, student employment services, financial aid counseling, personal counseling, placement for graduates, veterans' counselor, women's services. **Physically disabled:** Services for visually, speech, hearing impaired. **Transfer:** Special adviser, orientation for new students. Transfer adviser, college fairs on campus for students transferring to 4-year colleges.

Contact. Phone: (864) 592-4800 Toll-free number: (866) 592-4700
Fax: (864) 592-4642
Nancy Garmroth, Dean of Admissions and Financial Aid, Spartanburg Technical College, Box 4386, Spartanburg, SC 29305

Two-Year Colleges

Technical College of the Lowcountry

Beaufort, South Carolina
www.tcl.edu **CB code: 5047**

- Public 2-year community and technical college
- Commuter campus in small town

General. Founded in 1972. Regionally accredited. Several off-campus extension locations, including Hampton, Hilton Head, Parris Island, Marine Corps Air Station. **Enrollment:** 1,689 degree-seeking undergraduates. **Degrees:** 157 associate awarded. **Location:** 45 miles from Hilton Head, 45 miles from Savannah, Georgia. **Calendar:** Semester, extensive summer session. **Full-time faculty:** 50 total. **Part-time faculty:** 60 total.

Student profile.

Out-of-state:	3%	25 or older:	95%

Basis for selection. Open admission, but selective for some programs. Nursing students are encouraged to have a personal interview and must submit NET test results. SAT or ACT required for placement and counseling. Interview recommended for nursing program.

2005-2006 Annual costs. Tuition/fees: $3,050; $5,932 out-of-state. Books/supplies: $425. Personal expenses: $1,600.

Financial aid. All financial aid based on need. Need-based aid available for part-time students. **Additional information:** State lottery aid may be available to South Carolina residents who take 6 credit hours or more.

Application procedures. Admission: No deadline. $20 fee. Admission notification on a rolling basis beginning on or about 5/1. **Financial aid:** No deadline. FAFSA required. Applicants notified on a rolling basis starting 7/1.

Academics. Special study options: Cooperative education, cross-registration, distance learning, double major, dual enrollment of high school students, ESL, independent study, internships. License preparation in nursing, radiology, real estate. **Credit/placement by examination:** AP, CLEP, institutional tests. **Support services:** GED preparation and test center, learning center, pre-admission summer program, reduced course load, remedial instruction, study skills assistance, tutoring.

Majors. Agriculture: Horticulture. **Business:** General, accounting, administrative services, hospitality/recreation, office management. **Computer sciences:** General, data processing, programming. **Engineering:** Electrical. **Engineering technology:** Construction. **Family/consumer sciences:** Child care. **Health:** Nursing (RN). **Liberal arts:** Arts/sciences. **Mechanic/repair:** Heating/ac/refrig. **Personal/culinary services:** Cosmetic. **Protective services:** Criminal justice, law enforcement admin.

Most popular majors. Business/marketing 6%, health sciences 35%, legal studies 14%, trade and industry 38%.

Computing on campus. 400 workstations in library, computer center, student center. Online library, helpline available.

Student life. Freshman orientation: Available. Preregistration for classes offered. 1-day on-campus orientation at start of fall semester. **Activities:** Student government, Phi Theta Kappa, Rotaract Club, professional societies.

Student services. Career counseling, student employment services, personal counseling, placement for graduates, veterans' counselor. **Transfer:** Special adviser, orientation for new students. Transfer adviser for students transferring to 4-year colleges.

Contact. E-mail: mgallion@tcl.edu
Phone: (843) 525-8208 Toll-free number: (800) 768-8252
Fax: (843) 525-8285
Melanie Gallion, Director of Admissions, Technical College of the Lowcountry, 921 South Ribaut Road, Beaufort, SC 29901-1288

Tri-County Technical College

Pendleton, South Carolina
www.tctc.edu **CB code: 5789**

- Public 2-year technical college
- Commuter campus in small town

General. Founded in 1962. Regionally accredited. **Enrollment:** 3,800 degree-seeking undergraduates. **Degrees:** 470 associate awarded. **ROTC:** Army, Air Force. **Location:** 5 miles from Clemson. **Calendar:** Semester, limited summer session. **Full-time faculty:** 115 total. **Part-time faculty:** 160 total. **Special facilities:** Amphitheater. **Partnerships:** Formal partnerships with 7 area school districts, local businesses and industries, National Drop-out Prevention Center at Clemson, the Anderson and Oconee County Business and Education Partnerships, the Career Center and Technology Center, and Tri-County Tech in a Partnership for Academic and Career Education (business and education consortium to initiate Tech Prep/School-to-Work programs).

Student profile.

Out-of-state:	2%	25 or older:	85%

Transfer out. Colleges most students transferred to 2005: Clemson University.

Basis for selection. Open admission, but selective for some programs. SAT used only for admission to nursing: 450 verbal and 420 math score required.

High school preparation. High school unit or college course in chemistry, biology, and algebra taken within past 5 years required for nursing, medical laboratory, practical nursing, surgical technology, dental assisting, and veterinary technology.

2005-2006 Annual costs. Tuition/fees: $2,738; $3,024 out-of-district; $6,084 out-of-state. Books/supplies: $650.

Financial aid. Need-based: Need-based aid available for part-time students. Work study available nights and for part-time students. **Non-need-based:** Scholarships awarded for academics, state residency. **Additional information:** Deadline for application to institutional scholarships April 2.

Application procedures. Admission: No deadline. $20 fee. Application must be submitted on paper. Admission notification on a rolling basis. **Financial aid:** Priority date 6/30; no closing date. FAFSA required. Applicants notified on a rolling basis starting 6/15; must reply within 2 week(s) of notification.

Academics. Electronic engineering majors may transfer to any 4-year college accredited by the Technology Accreditation Commission of the Accreditation Board for Engineering and Technology. **Special study options:** Cooperative education, distance learning, dual enrollment of high school students, ESL, internships, liberal arts/career combination, student-designed major. License preparation in dental hygiene, nursing, real estate. **Credit/placement by examination:** AP, CLEP, institutional tests. Credit available from documented work experience, course waiver, noncollective organization training programs, technical advanced placement. **Support services:** GED preparation, learning center, reduced course load, remedial instruction, study skills assistance, tutoring, writing center.

Majors. Business: Accounting, administrative services, business admin. **Communications:** Broadcast journalism. **Computer sciences:** General, data processing, programming. **Engineering technology:** Drafting, electrical. **Family/consumer sciences:** Clothing/textiles. **Health:** Clinical lab technology, nursing (RN), veterinary technology/assistant. **Liberal arts:** Arts/sciences. **Mechanic/repair:** Heating/ac/refrig, industrial.

Computing on campus. 700 workstations in library, computer center. Helpline available.

Student life. Freshman orientation: Available. Preregistration for classes offered. **Activities:** Student government, student newspaper, minority student association, international student association, criminal justice club, gospel choir, North American Veterinary Technician Association, student nurses association, forensics team, South Carolina Society of Clinical Laboratory Science.

Athletics. Team name: Lynx.

Student services. Alcohol/substance abuse counseling, career counseling, services for economically disadvantaged, student employment services, financial aid counseling, minority student services, placement for graduates, veterans' counselor. **Transfer:** Special adviser, orientation for new students. Transfer adviser, college fairs on campus for students transferring to 4-year colleges.

Contact. E-mail: infocent@tctc.edu
Phone: (864) 646-1550 Fax: (864) 646-1890
Becki James, Coordinator of Admissions, Tri-County Technical College, Box 587, Pendleton, SC 29670

Trident Technical College

Charleston, South Carolina
www.tridenttech.edu **CB code: 5049**

- Public 2-year community and technical college
- Commuter campus in large city

General. Founded in 1964. Regionally accredited. 3 campuses: Palmer Campus in downtown Charleston, Main Campus in North Charleston and Berkeley Campus in Moncks Corner. Many courses offered online. **Enrollment:** 10,128 degree-seeking undergraduates. **Degrees:** 920 associate awarded. **Location:** 15 miles from downtown. **Calendar:** Semester, extensive summer session.

Basis for selection. Open admission, but selective for some programs.

2005-2006 Annual costs. Tuition/fees: $2,950; $3,276 out-of-district; $5,586 out-of-state.

Financial aid. Need-based: Need-based aid available for part-time students.

Application procedures. Admission: Closing date 8/4 (postmark date). $25 fee. Application may be submitted online. Admission notification on a rolling basis. Applicants to early admissions program must rank in upper half of high school class and must have combined SAT score (exclusive of writing) of 800 or ACT composite score of 17. **Financial aid:** No deadline. FAFSA required. Applicants notified on a rolling basis; must reply within 6 week(s) of notification.

Academics. Special study options: Accelerated study, cooperative education, cross-registration, distance learning, double major, dual enrollment of high school students, ESL, independent study, internships. **Credit/placement by examination:** CLEP, institutional tests. **Support services:** Learning center, reduced course load, remedial instruction, study skills assistance, tutoring.

Majors. Agriculture: Horticultural science, horticulture. **Business:** General, accounting, administrative services, business admin, customer service, e-commerce, entrepreneurial studies, hospitality admin, hotel/motel admin, logistics, marketing, office management, restaurant/food services, tourism/travel, transportation. **Communications:** Broadcast journalism. **Communications technology:** General. **Computer sciences:** Data processing, information systems, programming. **Construction:** Electrician. **Education:** Voc/tech. **Engineering technology:** Architectural, civil, electrical, manufacturing, robotics. **Family/consumer sciences:** Child care. **Health:** Clinical lab technology, dental hygiene, medical radiologic technology/radiation therapy, nursing (RN), occupational therapy assistant, physical therapy assistant, respiratory therapy technology. **Legal studies:** Paralegal. **Liberal arts:** Arts/sciences. **Mechanic/repair:** General, aircraft, automotive, industrial. **Personal/culinary services:** Culinary arts. **Physical sciences:** General. **Protective services:** Fire services admin, law enforcement admin. **Public administration:** Human services. **Transportation:** General. **Visual/performing arts:** Commercial/advertising art, graphic design.

Student life. Freshman orientation: Available. **Activities:** Student government, student newspaper, Phi Theta Kappa international honor society, Alpha Mu Gamma, Asian Studies, Black student association, Campus Crusade for Christ, La Sociedad Hispanoamericana, international club, society of student leaders.

Student services. Adult student services, alcohol/substance abuse counseling, career counseling, services for economically disadvantaged, student employment services, financial aid counseling, personal counseling, placement for graduates, veterans' counselor. **Physically disabled:** Services for visually, hearing impaired. **Transfer:** Special adviser, orientation, preadmission transcript evaluation for new students. Transfer adviser, college fairs on campus for students transferring to 4-year colleges.

Contact. E-mail: admissions@tridenttech.edu
Phone: (843) 574-6125 Toll-free number: (877) 349-7184
Fax: (843) 574-6483
Clara Martin, Director of Admissions, Trident Technical College, Box 118067, AM-M, Charleston, SC 29423-8067

University of South Carolina at Lancaster

Lancaster, South Carolina
www.usclancaster.sc.edu **CB code: 5849**

- Public 2-year branch campus and junior college
- Commuter campus in large town

General. Founded in 1959. Regionally accredited. **Enrollment:** 768 degree-seeking undergraduates. **Degrees:** 121 associate awarded. **ROTC:** Army. **Location:** 50 miles from Columbia, 40 miles from Charlotte, North Carolina. **Calendar:** Semester, limited summer session. **Full-time faculty:** 34 total. **Part-time faculty:** 23 total. **Special facilities:** Health sciences facilities; diabetic education center.

Student profile.

Out-of-state:	1%	**25 or older:**	20%

Transfer out. Colleges most students transferred to 2005: University of South Carolina-Columbia, Winthrop University, Clemson University, York Technical College.

Basis for selection. Open admission. SAT or ACT required in admissions process but applicants with scores below required levels will be admitted provisionally. **Adult students:** SAT/ACT scores not required if applicant over 25.

High school preparation. 20 units recommended. Recommended units include English 4, mathematics 3, social studies 3, science 3 (laboratory 3), foreign language 2 and academic electives 4. One unit physical education/ROTC required.

2005-2006 Annual costs. Tuition/fees: $4,344; $10,404 out-of-state. Per-credit charge: $169 in-state; $422 out-of-state. Books/supplies: $500. Personal expenses: $938.

Application procedures. Admission: Priority date 8/30; no deadline. $40 fee, may be waived for applicants with need. Application may be submitted online. Admission notification on a rolling basis. **Financial aid:** Priority date 4/15; no closing date. FAFSA required. Applicants notified on a rolling basis starting 6/1; must reply within 2 week(s) of notification.

Academics. Special study options: Accelerated study, combined bachelor's/graduate degree, cross-registration, distance learning, dual enrollment of high school students, honors, independent study, internships, liberal arts/career combination. License preparation in nursing. **Credit/placement by examination:** AP, CLEP, IB, institutional tests. 30 credit hours maximum toward associate degree. **Support services:** Learning center, remedial instruction, study skills assistance, tutoring.

Majors. Business: Administrative services, business admin. **Health:** Nursing (RN). **Liberal arts:** Arts/sciences. **Protective services:** Criminal justice. **Visual/performing arts:** Art.

Computing on campus. 110 workstations in library, computer center. Commuter students can connect to campus network. Online course registration, repair service, wireless network available.

Student life. Freshman orientation: Mandatory, $25 fee. Preregistration for classes offered. 2-day program. **Activities:** Drama, literary magazine, student government, student newspaper, Black Awareness Group, Baptist Student Ministry, Adult Group for Education, Campus Crusade for Christ.

Athletics. Intramural: Basketball, table tennis, volleyball.

Student services. Adult student services, career counseling, student employment services, financial aid counseling, health services, personal counseling, veterans' counselor. **Transfer:** Special adviser, orientation, preadmission transcript evaluation for new students.

Contact. Phone: (803) 313-7073 Fax: (803) 313-7116
Rebecca Parker, Director of Enrollment Management, University of South Carolina at Lancaster, Box 889, Lancaster, SC 29721

University of South Carolina at Sumter

Sumter, South Carolina
www.uscsumter.edu **CB code: 5821**

- Public 2-year branch campus college
- Commuter campus in small city
- SAT or ACT (ACT writing recommended) required

General. Founded in 1966. Regionally accredited. **Enrollment:** 823 degree-seeking undergraduates; 197 non-degree-seeking students. **Degrees:** 126 bachelor's, 84 associate awarded. **ROTC:** Army. **Location:** 40 miles from Columbia, 98 miles from Charleston. **Calendar:** Semester, limited summer session. **Full-time faculty:** 40 total; 82% have terminal degrees, 12% minority, 25% women. **Part-time faculty:** 35 total; 29% have terminal degrees, 11% minority, 43% women. **Class size:** 70% < 20, 29% 20-39, less than 1% 40-49. **Partnerships:** College-level courses for eligible high school students.

Student profile. Among degree-seeking undergraduates, 197 enrolled as first-time, first-year students, 510 transferred in from other institutions.

Part-time:	31%	**Women:**	61%
Out-of-state:	1%	**25 or older:**	28%

Transfer out. 48% of students enrolled in the transfer program go on to 4-year colleges. **Colleges most students transferred to 2005:** Central Carolina Technical College, College of Charleston, Midlands Technical College.

Basis for selection. Entering freshmen must have 2.25 GPA. Class rank and test scores also important. All freshmen required to take foreign language tests. Placement in mathematics may require additional testing. Interview required for academically marginal. **Adult students:** SAT/ACT scores not required if applicant over 23. **Homeschooled:** Official transcripts, SAT/ACT and a GPR converted to the South Carolina Uniform grading scale if home schooled in South Carolina. **Learning Disabled:** Must submit recent documentation.

High school preparation. College-preparatory program required. 20 units required. Required and recommended units include English 4, mathematics 3-4, social studies 3, history 2, science 3 (laboratory 3), foreign language 2-3 and academic electives 4. 1 physical education required, 1 computer science recommended.

2005-2006 Annual costs. Tuition/fees: $4,344; $10,404 out-of-state. Per-credit charge: $169 in-state; $422 out-of-state. Books/supplies: $932. Personal expenses: $2,053.

2005-2006 Financial aid. All financial aid based on need. 68% of total undergraduate aid awarded as scholarships/grants, 32% as loans/jobs. Need-based aid available for part-time students. Work study available nights, weekends and for part-time students.

Application procedures. Admission: Priority date 8/1; no deadline. $40 fee, may be waived for applicants with need. Application may be submitted online. Admission notification on a rolling basis. **Financial aid:** Priority date 4/15; no closing date. FAFSA required. Applicants notified on a rolling basis starting 4/16; must reply within 2 week(s) of notification.

Academics. Special study options: Combined bachelor's/graduate degree, cross-registration, distance learning, dual enrollment of high school students, independent study, liberal arts/career combination, student-designed major, teacher certification program. Bachelor's degree programs available on campus. **Credit/placement by examination:** AP, CLEP, institutional tests. 30 credit hours maximum toward associate degree. **Support services:** Learning center, remedial instruction, study skills assistance, tutoring, writing center.

Majors. Liberal arts: Arts/sciences.

Computing on campus. 132 workstations in library, computer center, student center. Commuter students can connect to campus network. Online course registration, online library, student web hosting available.

Student life. Freshman orientation: Mandatory. Preregistration for classes offered. **Policies:** Freshmen permitted cars on campus. **Activities:** Choral groups, drama, literary magazine, music ensembles, student government, student newspaper, African-American club, Baptist Student clubs, campus activities board, Circle K, student art guild, student education association, student nursing organization.

Athletics. NAIA. **Intramural:** Baseball M, basketball, bowling, football (non-tackle), golf, handball, racquetball, soccer M, softball, table tennis, tennis, volleyball, weight lifting.

Student services. Adult student services, campus ministries, career counseling, services for economically disadvantaged, student employment services, financial aid counseling, personal counseling, veterans' counselor. **Physically disabled:** Services for visually, speech, hearing impaired. **Transfer:** Special adviser, orientation for new students.

Contact. E-mail: bobf@uscsumter.edu
Phone: (803) 938-3762 Fax: (803) 938-3901
Keith Britton, Director of Admissions, University of South Carolina at Sumter, 200 Miller Road, Sumter, SC 29150-2498

University of South Carolina at Union

Union, South Carolina
http://uscunion.sc.edu **CB code: 5846**

- Public 2-year branch campus college
- Commuter campus in small town
- SAT or ACT required

General. Founded in 1965. Regionally accredited. Off-campus site at Laurens offers full range of courses. **Enrollment:** 300 degree-seeking undergraduates. **Degrees:** 50 associate awarded. **Location:** 30 miles from Spartanburg, 60 miles from Columbia. **Calendar:** Semester, limited summer session. **Full-time faculty:** 10 total. **Part-time faculty:** 15 total.

Student profile.

Out-of-state:	1%	25 or older:	40%

Basis for selection. Secondary school record most important. Standardized test scores and class rank also important. Students with high school diploma or GED but without required high school curriculum units may be admitted into Opportunity Program based on school achievement record and SAT or ACT scores. Institutional placement tests in mathematics and writing required of all freshmen. **Adult students:** SAT/ACT scores not required.

High school preparation. 20 units required. Required units include English 4, mathematics 3, social studies 3, science 3 (laboratory 3), foreign language 2 and academic electives 4.

2005-2006 Annual costs. Tuition/fees: $4,344; $10,404 out-of-state. Per-credit charge: $169 in-state; $422 out-of-state. Books/supplies: $744. Personal expenses: $1,307.

Financial aid. All financial aid based on need. Work study available nights, weekends and for part-time students.

Application procedures. Admission: No deadline. $40 fee, may be waived for applicants with need. Admission notification on a rolling basis beginning on or about 6/1. **Financial aid:** Priority date 4/15; no closing date. FAFSA required. Applicants notified on a rolling basis starting 7/15; must reply within 2 week(s) of notification.

Academics. Upper division courses leading to bachelor's degree in interdisciplinary studies available. Degree awarded by Columbia campus. **Special study options:** Cross-registration, distance learning, dual enrollment of high school students, independent study, internships, student-designed major. **Credit/placement by examination:** AP, CLEP, institutional tests. **Support services:** Pre-admission summer program, reduced course load, remedial instruction, tutoring.

Majors. Liberal arts: Arts/sciences.

Student life. Freshman orientation: Mandatory. Preregistration for classes offered. **Activities:** Drama, literary magazine, student government, student newspaper, Afro-American and political groups, student media association, computer club, history club, art club, travel club, music club, biology club.

Athletics. Intercollegiate: Basketball M, softball W. **Intramural:** Baseball M, basketball, bowling, gymnastics, racquetball, skiing, softball, table tennis, tennis, volleyball.

Student services. Adult student services, career counseling, student employment services, on-campus daycare, personal counseling. **Transfer:** Special adviser, orientation for new students. College fairs on campus for students transferring to 4-year colleges.

Contact. Phone: (864) 429-8728 Fax: (864) 427-3682
Terry Young, Director of Enrollment Services, University of South Carolina at Union, PO Drawer 729, Union, SC 29379

University of South Carolina: Salkehatchie Regional Campus

Allendale, South Carolina
www.uscsalkehatchie.sc.edu **CB code: 5847**

- Public 2-year branch campus college
- Commuter campus in small town
- SAT or ACT required

General. Founded in 1965. Regionally accredited. **Enrollment:** 547 degree-seeking undergraduates. **Degrees:** 115 associate awarded. **ROTC:** Army, Navy, Air Force. **Location:** 75 miles from Columbia, 75 miles from Charleston. **Calendar:** Semester, limited summer session. **Full-time faculty:** 25 total. **Part-time faculty:** 40 total. **Special facilities:** Civic arts center.

Student profile.

Out-of-state:	1%	25 or older:	26%

Transfer out. Colleges most students transferred to 2005: University of South Carolina - Columbia, University of South Carolina - Aiken.

Basis for selection. Secondary schoool record and class rank most important. Standardized test scores also important. **Adult students:** SAT/ACT scores not required if applicant over 25.

High school preparation. Required units include English 4, mathematics 3, social studies 3, history 1, science 2 (laboratory 2), foreign language 2 and academic electives 2.

2005-2006 Annual costs. Tuition/fees: $4,344; $10,404 out-of-state. Per-credit charge: $169 in-state; $422 out-of-state. Books/supplies: $744. Personal expenses: $1,159.

2004-2005 Financial aid. Need-based: Need-based aid available for part-time students. Work study available nights, weekends and for part-time students. **Non-need-based:** Scholarships awarded for academics.

Application procedures. Admission: Priority date 8/19; no deadline. $40 fee, may be waived for applicants with need. Admission notification on a rolling basis. **Financial aid:** Priority date 4/30; no closing date. FAFSA required. Applicants notified on a rolling basis starting 6/1.

Academics. Special study options: Cross-registration, dual enrollment of high school students, independent study, student-designed major, study abroad. **Credit/placement by examination:** CLEP, IB, institutional tests. 15 credit hours maximum toward associate degree. **Support services:** Learning center, pre-admission summer program, reduced course load, remedial instruction, tutoring.

Majors. Liberal arts: Arts/sciences.

Computing on campus. 102 workstations in library, computer center.

Student life. Freshman orientation: Mandatory. **Activities:** Choral groups, drama, student government, student newspaper, minority student organization.

Athletics. NJCAA. **Intercollegiate:** Baseball M. **Intramural:** Basketball, soccer, softball W, table tennis, tennis, volleyball.

Student services. Career counseling, personal counseling, veterans' counselor. **Physically disabled:** Services for visually, hearing impaired. **Transfer:** Special adviser for new students.

Contact. Phone: (803) 584-3446 Toll-free number: (800) 922-5500
Fax: (803) 584-5038
Jane Brewer, Dean for Student Services, University of South Carolina: Salkehatchie Regional Campus, PO Box 617, Allendale, SC 29810

Williamsburg Technical College

Kingstree, South Carolina
www.wiltech.edu **CB code: 5892**

- Public 2-year community and technical college
- Commuter campus in small town

General. Founded in 1969. Regionally accredited. **Enrollment:** 300 degree-seeking undergraduates. **Degrees:** 42 associate awarded. **Location:** 75 miles from Charleston, 40 miles from Florence. **Calendar:** Semester, extensive summer session. **Full-time faculty:** 15 total. **Part-time faculty:** 35 total. **Class size:** 90% < 20, 10% 20-39. **Partnerships:** Formal partnerships with Tupperware, Firestone and Williamsburg County school district.

Transfer out. Colleges most students transferred to 2005: Francis Marion University, Coker College, Limestone College, University of South Carolina, Coastal Carolina University.

Basis for selection. Open admission. Academically weak students must enroll in Applied Studies Program.

High school preparation. 25 units recommended. Recommended units include English 4, mathematics 4, social studies 3, history 1, science 3, foreign language 1 and academic electives 7. Recommend one unit physical education/JROTC. 1 unit computer technology, 6 or more units in occupational area will substitute for one science.

2005-2006 Annual costs. Tuition/fees: $2,692; $4,990 out-of-state.

Financial aid. Need-based: Need-based aid available for part-time students. Work study available nights, weekends and for part-time students. **Non-need-based:** Scholarships awarded for academics, leadership, minority status, state residency. **Additional information:** Tuition waivers for children of war veterans.

Application procedures. Admission: No deadline. $10 fee, may be waived for applicants with need. Admission notification on a rolling basis. **Financial aid:** Priority date 4/15; no closing date. FAFSA required. Applicants notified on a rolling basis starting 7/1; must reply within 4 week(s) of notification.

Academics. Special study options: Distance learning, dual enrollment of high school students, honors, independent study, internships, liberal arts/career combination, student-designed major. **Credit/placement by examination:** CLEP, institutional tests. 18 credit hours maximum toward associate degree. **Support services:** GED preparation, learning center, pre-admission summer program, remedial instruction, study skills assistance, tutoring.

Majors. Business: General, administrative services, information resources management, office management. **Computer sciences:** General. **Education:** Early childhood, teacher assistance. **Engineering:** Electrical. **Engineering technology:** Drafting. **Liberal arts:** Arts/sciences. **Mechanic/repair:** General, heating/ac/refrig. **Production:** Machine tool.

Most popular majors. Business/marketing 52%, interdisciplinary studies 19%, liberal arts 30%.

Computing on campus. 60 workstations in library, computer center. Online library, wireless network available.

Student life. Freshman orientation: Available. **Policies:** Freshmen permitted cars on campus. **Activities:** Student government.

Student services. Career counseling, services for economically disadvantaged, financial aid counseling, personal counseling, placement for graduates, veterans' counselor. **Physically disabled:** Services for hearing impaired. **Transfer:** Special adviser, orientation, pre-admission transcript evaluation for new students. College fairs on campus for students transferring to 4-year colleges.

Contact. E-mail: hannas@wiltech.edu
Phone: (843) 355-4162 Toll-free number: (800) 768-2021 ext. 4162
Fax: (843) 355-4289
Sharon Hanna, Admissions Director, Williamsburg Technical College, 601 Martin Luther King Jr. Avenue, Kingstree, SC 29556-4197

York Technical College

Rock Hill, South Carolina
www.yorktech.com **CB code: 5989**

- Public 2-year technical college
- Commuter campus in large town

General. Founded in 1962. Regionally accredited. Member of Charlotte Area Consortium of Colleges and Universities. **Enrollment:** 3,583 degree-seeking undergraduates; 570 non-degree-seeking students. **Degrees:** 266 associate awarded. **Location:** 70 miles from Columbia, 14 miles from Charlotte, North Carolina. **Calendar:** Semester, extensive summer session. **Full-time faculty:** 128 total. **Part-time faculty:** 139 total. **Partnerships:** Formal partnership with Okuma America Corporation.

Student profile. Among degree-seeking undergraduates, 24% enrolled in a transfer program, 61% enrolled in a vocational program, 10% already have a bachelor's degree or higher, 786 enrolled as first-time, first-year students.

Part-time:	43%	**Asian American:**	1%
Women:	64%	**Hispanic American:**	1%
African American:	26%	**Native American:**	2%

Transfer out. Colleges most students transferred to 2005: Winthrop University, Clemson University, University of South Carolina.

Basis for selection. Open admission, but selective for some programs. Specific testing and/or courses required for admission to Health Science programs. COMPASS, SAT, or ACT scores may be used for placement. **Adult students:** Entrance exam policies same as for first-time freshmen. **Homeschooled:** Applicants must have graduated from an approved South Carolina Home School Association to be classified as a high school graduate. **Learning Disabled:** Students with disabilities who wish to receive special testing accommodations should contact the Special Resources Office in Student Services.

High school preparation. One unit of chemistry required for dental hygiene and nursing program.

2005-2006 Annual costs. Tuition/fees: $3,036; $3,400 out-of-district; $6,664 out-of-state. Books/supplies: $900.

2005-2006 Financial aid. Need-based: Average scholarship/grant was $1,250. 97% of total undergraduate aid awarded as scholarships/grants, 3% as loans/jobs. Need-based aid available for part-time students. Work study available nights and for part-time students.

Application procedures. Admission: No deadline. No application fee. Application may be submitted online. Admission notification on a rolling

basis. **Financial aid:** Priority date 6/1; no closing date. FAFSA required. Applicants notified on a rolling basis starting 7/1.

Academics. Special study options: Cooperative education, distance learning, dual enrollment of high school students, ESL, liberal arts/career combination. License preparation in dental hygiene, nursing, paramedic, real estate. **Credit/placement by examination:** AP, CLEP, institutional tests. **Support services:** GED preparation, learning center, pre-admission summer program, reduced course load, remedial instruction, study skills assistance, tutoring, writing center.

Majors. Business: General, accounting, administrative services, business admin. **Computer sciences:** Applications programming, LAN/WAN management, programming. **Education:** Early childhood. **Engineering technology:** CAD/CADD, computer, computer systems, drafting, electrical, heat/ac/refrig, mechanical, mechanical drafting. **Health:** Clinical lab technology, dental hygiene, medical radiologic technology/radiation therapy, nursing (RN), radiologic technology/medical imaging. **Legal studies:** Paralegal. **Liberal arts:** Arts/sciences. **Mechanic/repair:** General, automotive, electronics/electrical, heating/ac/refrig, industrial. **Production:** Machine tool, tool and die, welding.

Most popular majors. Business/marketing 27%, engineering/engineering technologies 11%, family/consumer sciences 8%, health sciences 19%, interdisciplinary studies 12%, liberal arts 14%.

Computing on campus. 180 workstations in library, computer center. Commuter students can connect to campus network. Online course registration, online library, wireless network available.

Student life. Freshman orientation: Mandatory. Preregistration for classes offered. The START Center provides first-time freshmen students with orientation and first-semester advising and registration. **Activities:** Student government, student newspaper, Jacobin Society, Phi Theta Kappa, Christian Fellowship, Students With Vision.

Student services. Career counseling, student employment services, financial aid counseling, on-campus daycare, personal counseling, placement for graduates, veterans' counselor, women's services. **Physically disabled:** Services for visually, hearing impaired. **Transfer:** Special adviser, orientation for new students. Transfer adviser, college fairs on campus for students transferring to 4-year colleges.

Contact. E-mail: kaldridge@yorktech.com
Phone: (803) 327-8008 Toll-free number: (800) 922-8324
Fax: (803) 327-7237
Kenny Aldridge, Admissions Department Manager, York Technical College, 452 South Anderson Road, Rock Hill, SC 29730

South Dakota

Kilian Community College
Sioux Falls, South Dakota
www.kilian.edu **CB code: 6149**

- Private 2-year community college
- Commuter campus in small city

General. Founded in 1976. Regionally accredited. **Enrollment:** 506 degree-seeking undergraduates; 32 non-degree-seeking students. **Degrees:** 60 associate awarded. **Location:** 180 miles from Omaha, Nebraska, 240 miles from Minneapolis-St. Paul. **Calendar:** Trimester, extensive summer session. **Full-time faculty:** 7 total; 14% have terminal degrees, 86% women. **Part-time faculty:** 75 total; 7% have terminal degrees, 8% minority, 61% women. **Class size:** 100% < 20.

Student profile. Among degree-seeking undergraduates, 44% enrolled in a transfer program, 56% enrolled in a vocational program, 2% already have a bachelor's degree or higher, 75 enrolled as first-time, first-year students, 62 transferred in from other institutions.

Part-time:	80%	**Women:**	77%
Out-of-state:	20%	**25 or older:**	33%

Transfer out. Colleges most students transferred to 2005: University of Sioux Falls, Colorado Technical University, University of South Dakota.

Basis for selection. Open admission. Students graduating from non-US high schools must have a 12-year, translated high school diploma and a minimum score of 3 on the Compass ESL assessment. **Adult students:** SAT/ACT scores not required. **Learning Disabled:** Must provide documentation to the academic director prior to enrolling in classes.

2005-2006 Annual costs. Tuition/fees: $5,950. Per-credit charge: $195. Books/supplies: $100. Personal expenses: $600.

2004-2005 Financial aid. Need-based: 24 full-time freshmen applied for aid; 24 were judged to have need; 24 of these received aid. Average need met was 60%. Average scholarship/grant was $2,000; average loan $2,625. 25% of total undergraduate aid awarded as scholarships/grants, 75% as loans/jobs. Need-based aid available for part-time students. Work study available nights and for part-time students. **Non-need-based:** Awarded to 11 full-time undergraduates, including 4 freshmen. Scholarships awarded for academics, leadership.

Application procedures. Admission: No deadline. $25 fee. Application must be submitted on paper. Admission notification on a rolling basis. **Financial aid:** No deadline. FAFSA, institutional form required. Applicants notified on a rolling basis starting 7/1; must reply within 2 week(s) of notification.

Academics. Special study options: Cross-registration, distance learning, double major, dual enrollment of high school students, ESL, honors, independent study, internships. Bachelor's degree programs available on campus. **Credit/placement by examination:** AP, CLEP, institutional tests. 18 credit hours maximum toward associate degree. **Support services:** GED test center, learning center, remedial instruction, study skills assistance, tutoring, writing center.

Majors. Business: Accounting, administrative services, business admin. **Computer sciences:** Information systems. **Health:** Insurance coding, medical secretary, medical transcription, substance abuse counseling. **Liberal arts:** Arts/sciences. **Protective services:** Law enforcement admin. **Public administration:** Social work.

Most popular majors. Business/marketing 27%, health sciences 35%, liberal arts 18%, security/protective services 10%, social sciences 10%.

Computing on campus. 47 workstations in computer center. Helpline available.

Student life. Policies: Freshmen permitted cars on campus. **Activities:** Student government, student newspaper.

Student services. Adult student services, career counseling, student employment services, financial aid counseling, personal counseling, placement for graduates, veterans' counselor. **Transfer:** Special adviser, pre-admission transcript evaluation for new students. Transfer adviser, college fairs on campus for students transferring to 4-year colleges.

Contact. E-mail: jdanielson@kilian.edu
Phone: (605) 221-3100 Toll-free number: (800) 888-1147
Fax: (605) 336-2606
Amy Modrell, Director of Admissions, Kilian Community College, 300 East 6th Street, Sioux Falls, SD 57103-7020

Lake Area Technical Institute
Watertown, South Dakota
www.lati.tec.sd.us **CB code: 0717**

- Public 2-year technical college
- Commuter campus in large town

General. Founded in 1965. Regionally accredited. **Enrollment:** 1,170 degree-seeking undergraduates. **Degrees:** 239 associate awarded. **Location:** 90 miles from Sioux Falls, 140 miles from Fargo, North Dakota. **Calendar:** Semester, limited summer session. **Full-time faculty:** 70 total. **Part-time faculty:** 6 total.

Basis for selection. Test scores most important; school record important. ACT recommended. Testing requirements vary by program. Interview required for medical laboratory technician, physical therapy assistant, practical nursing, occupational therapy assistant programs.

High school preparation. 3 units mathematics/science required. 1 Latin and typing recommended.

2005-2006 Annual costs. Tuition/fees: $3,350. Per-credit charge: $64. Books/supplies: $550. Personal expenses: $750.

Financial aid. All financial aid based on need. Need-based aid available for part-time students.

Application procedures. Admission: No deadline. $15 fee. Application may be submitted online. Admission notification on a rolling basis. **Financial aid:** Priority date 4/15; no closing date. FAFSA required. Applicants notified on a rolling basis starting 5/1.

Academics. Special study options: Internships. **Credit/placement by examination:** CLEP, institutional tests. **Support services:** Learning center, pre-admission summer program, reduced course load, tutoring.

Majors. Agriculture: General, agribusiness operations. **Business:** Accounting, banking/financial services, business admin, finance. **Computer sciences:** General, data processing, programming. **Engineering:** Civil, mechanical. **Engineering technology:** Drafting. **Health:** Clinical lab technology, nursing (RN), occupational therapy assistant, physical therapy assistant. **Mechanic/repair:** General, aircraft, aircraft powerplant, automotive, diesel, electronics/electrical. **Production:** Tool and die, welding.

Most popular majors. Agriculture 27%, business/marketing 43%, computer/information sciences 25%.

Computing on campus. 70 workstations in library, computer center.

Student life. Activities: Student government, student newspaper.

Athletics. Intercollegiate: Rodeo. **Intramural:** Basketball, bowling, softball, volleyball.

Student services. Career counseling, student employment services, health services, on-campus daycare, personal counseling, placement for graduates, veterans' counselor. **Transfer:** Special adviser, orientation for new students. Transfer adviser for students transferring to 4-year colleges.

Contact. Phone: (605) 882-5284 Toll-free number: (800) 657-4344
Fax: (605) 882-6299
Dale Dobberpuhl, Curriculum Coordinator, Lake Area Technical Institute, PO Box 730, Watertown, SD 57201

Mitchell Technical Institute
Mitchell, South Dakota
www.mitchelltech.com **CB code: 7038**

- Public 2-year culinary school and technical college
- Residential campus in large town

General. Founded in 1968. Regionally accredited. **Enrollment:** 807 degree-seeking undergraduates. **Degrees:** 335 associate awarded. **Location:** 70 miles from Sioux Falls. **Calendar:** Semester, limited summer session. **Full-time**

faculty: 50 total. **Part-time faculty:** 5 total. **Special facilities:** Satellite communications earth station.

Student profile. Among degree-seeking undergraduates, 100% enrolled in a vocational program, 1% already have a bachelor's degree or higher, 549 enrolled as first-time, first-year students.

Part-time:	16%	**Women:**	30%
Out-of-state:	7%		

Transfer out. 15% of students enrolled in the transfer program go on to 4-year colleges.

Basis for selection. Open admission. TABE test used for placement. Interview recommended.

High school preparation. 16 units recommended. Recommended units include English 4, mathematics 2, social studies 2 and science 2.

2005-2006 Annual costs. Tuition/fees: $3,000. Per-credit charge: $60. Books/supplies: $800. Personal expenses: $750.

2005-2006 Financial aid. **Need-based:** Average need met was 62%. Average scholarship/grant was $2,951; average loan $2,550. 24% of total undergraduate aid awarded as scholarships/grants, 76% as loans/jobs. Need-based aid available for part-time students.

Application procedures. **Admission:** No deadline. $35 fee. Application may be submitted online. Admission notification on a rolling basis. **Financial aid:** No deadline. FAFSA required. Applicants notified on a rolling basis; must reply within 3 week(s) of notification.

Academics. **Special study options:** Cooperative education, dual enrollment of high school students, independent study, internships. **Credit/placement by examination:** AP, CLEP, institutional tests. **Support services:** Learning center, pre-admission summer program, reduced course load, remedial instruction, study skills assistance, tutoring.

Majors. **Architecture:** Technology. **Computer sciences:** General. **Health:** Clinical lab technology, medical radiologic technology/radiation therapy, medical transcription, office assistant. **Mechanic/repair:** Electronics/electrical, heating/ac/refrig.

Computing on campus. 40 workstations in library, computer center. Commuter students can connect to campus network. Repair service, wireless network available.

Student life. **Freshman orientation:** Mandatory. Preregistration for classes offered. **Activities:** Student government, student newspaper.

Athletics. **Intercollegiate:** Rodeo. **Intramural:** Basketball, bowling, softball, volleyball.

Student services. Adult student services, career counseling, services for economically disadvantaged, student employment services, financial aid counseling, on-campus daycare, personal counseling, placement for graduates, women's services. **Physically disabled:** Services for visually, speech, hearing impaired. **Transfer:** Special adviser, orientation for new students.

Contact. E-mail: questions@mti.tec.sd.us
Phone: (605) 995-3025 Toll-free number: (800) 684-1969
Fax: (605) 996-3299
Tim Edwards, Director of Student Services, Mitchell Technical Institute, 821 North Capital, Mitchell, SD 57301

Sisseton Wahpeton College

Sisseton, South Dakota
www.swc.tc **CB code: 3403**

- Public 2-year community and technical college
- Commuter campus in rural community

General. Founded in 1979. Regionally accredited. Member of the American Indian Higher Education Consortium. Dakota language and culture resource. **Enrollment:** 290 degree-seeking undergraduates. **Degrees:** 25 associate awarded. **Location:** 48 miles from Watertown, 85 miles from Fargo, North Dakota. **Calendar:** Semester, limited summer session. **Full-time faculty:** 10 total. **Part-time faculty:** 15 total. **Special facilities:** Indians in North America book collection, Song to the Great Spirit Building, Institute for Excellence in Dakota Language.

Basis for selection. Open admission. If a student is a member of a recognized Native American tribe, they must submit certification of tribal membership. Students entering vocational program may complete GED certificate while enrolled in classes. **Homeschooled:** State high school equivalency certificate required.

High school preparation. 16 units recommended. Recommended units include English 4, mathematics 4 and science 8.

2005-2006 Annual costs. Tuition/fees: $3,370. Per-credit charge: $96. Books/supplies: $440. Personal expenses: $1,680.

Application procedures. **Admission:** Closing date 7/1. No application fee. Admission notification on a rolling basis. **Financial aid:** No deadline. FAFSA required. Applicants notified on a rolling basis.

Academics. **Special study options:** Distance learning, double major, dual enrollment of high school students, independent study, internships, liberal arts/career combination. Bachelor's degree programs available on campus. **Credit/placement by examination:** CLEP, institutional tests. **Support services:** GED preparation and test center, learning center, remedial instruction, tutoring.

Majors. **Area/ethnic studies:** Native American. **Business:** Accounting, business admin, hospitality admin. **Computer sciences:** General. **Education:** Early childhood. **Family/consumer sciences:** Food/nutrition. **Health:** Nursing (RN), substance abuse counseling. **Interdisciplinary:** Natural sciences. **Liberal arts:** Arts/sciences. **Physical sciences:** Planetary.

Computing on campus. 26 workstations in library, computer center, student center.

Student life. **Freshman orientation:** Mandatory. 2-day program. **Activities:** Student government.

Student services. Career counseling, personal counseling. **Transfer:** Special adviser, orientation for new students. Transfer adviser for students transferring to 4-year colleges.

Contact. E-mail: dredday@swc.tc
Phone: (605) 698-3966 Fax: (605) 698-3132
Darlene Redday, Admissions Officer/Registrar, Sisseton Wahpeton College, BIA 700, Box 689, Agency Village, SD 57262-0689

Southeast Technical Institute

Sioux Falls, South Dakota
www.southeasttech.com **CB code: 7054**

- Public 2-year technical college
- Commuter campus in small city

General. Founded in 1969. Regionally accredited. **Enrollment:** 2,320 degree-seeking undergraduates; 43 non-degree-seeking students. **Degrees:** 711 associate awarded. **Location:** 220 miles from Minneapolis-St. Paul, 200 miles from Omaha, Nebraska. **Calendar:** Semester, limited summer session. **Full-time faculty:** 79 total; 5% have terminal degrees, 42% women. **Part-time faculty:** 64 total; 38% women.

Student profile. Among degree-seeking undergraduates, 100% enrolled in a vocational program, 6% already have a bachelor's degree or higher, 621 enrolled as first-time, first-year students.

Part-time:	18%	**25 or older:**	16%
Out-of-state:	9%	**Live on campus:**	1%
Women:	47%		

Basis for selection. Open admission, but selective for some programs. Additional testing and background checks required for all health and criminal justice programs. ACT recommended for those programs that are not open admissions. **Adult students:** Entrance exam policies same as for first-time freshmen. **Homeschooled:** Statement describing homeschool structure and mission, transcript of courses and grades, interview required. ACT and institutional entrance exam required.

High school preparation. 18 units recommended. Recommended units include English 4, mathematics 2, social studies 2, science 2 and academic electives 8.

2005-2006 Annual costs. Tuition/fees: $3,160. Per-credit charge: $64. $450 per semester laptop fee required for some students. Students able to keep laptop after paying for 4 semesters of the lease. Books/supplies: $700. Personal expenses: $1,350.

Financial aid. All financial aid based on need. Need-based aid available for part-time students.

Application procedures. **Admission:** No deadline. No application fee. Application may be submitted online. Admission notification on a rolling basis. Must reply by May 1 or within 4 week(s) if notified thereafter. **Financial aid:** Priority date 5/1; no closing date. FAFSA required. Applicants notified on a rolling basis starting 5/1; must reply within 3 week(s) of notification.

Academics. **Special study options:** Accelerated study, double major. License preparation in nursing, real estate. **Credit/placement by examination:** AP, CLEP, IB, institutional tests. 30 credit hours maximum toward associate degree. **Support services:** GED preparation and test center, learning center, reduced course load, remedial instruction, study skills assistance, tutoring.

Majors. **Agriculture:** Greenhouse operations, horticulture, landscaping, nursery operations, turf management. **Biology:** Biomedical sciences. **Business:** Accounting, banking/financial services, business admin, marketing. **Communications:** Advertising. **Communications technology:** Graphic/printing. **Computer sciences:** General, applications programming, LAN/WAN management, networking, programming. **Engineering technology:** Architectural, biomedical, civil, computer hardware, drafting, electrical, heat/ac/refrig, laser/optical, mechanical, mechanical drafting, surveying. **Health:** Cardiovascular technology, medical transcription, nuclear medical technology, sonography. **Mechanic/repair:** General, auto body, automotive, diesel, electronics/electrical, heating/ac/refrig. **Production:** Machine shop technology, machine tool. **Protective services:** Corrections, law enforcement admin. **Visual/performing arts:** Commercial/advertising art.

Computing on campus. PC or laptop required. 101 workstations in library, computer center. Commuter students can connect to campus network. Online library, helpline, student web hosting, wireless network available.

Student life. **Freshman orientation:** Available. Preregistration for classes offered. **Policies:** Freshmen permitted cars on campus. **Housing:** Apartments available. **Activities:** Student government.

Athletics. **Intramural:** Basketball, volleyball.

Student services. Career counseling, student employment services, financial aid counseling, on-campus daycare, personal counseling, placement for graduates. **Physically disabled:** Services for visually, speech, hearing impaired. **Transfer:** Special adviser, orientation, pre-admission transcript evaluation for new students. College fairs on campus for students transferring to 4-year colleges.

Contact. E-mail: darrell.borgen@southeasttech.com
Phone: (605) 367-7624 Toll-free number: (800) 247-0789
Fax: (605) 367-4372
Jim Rokusek, Director of Student Services, Southeast Technical Institute, 2320 North Career Avenue, Sioux Falls, SD 57107

Western Dakota Technical Institute

Rapid City, South Dakota
www.westerndakotatech.org **CB code: 6393**

- Public 2-year technical college
- Commuter campus in small city

General. Founded in 1978. Regionally accredited. **Enrollment:** 817 full-time, degree-seeking students. **Degrees:** 171 associate awarded. **Location:** 3 miles from downtown. **Calendar:** Semester, limited summer session. **Full-time faculty:** 60 total. **Part-time faculty:** 20 total. **Special facilities:** 500-acre operating ranch for agricultural production students. **Partnerships:** Formal partnership with Boeing.

Student profile.

Out-of-state:	8%	**25 or older:**	41%

Transfer out. **Colleges most students transferred to 2005:** Black Hills State University.

Basis for selection. Open admission, but selective for some programs. Selective admissions to nursing, law enforcement, surgical technology, phlebotomy and paralegal programs. Applicants may be placed on waiting lists for programs reaching capacity. Institution requires Test of Adult Basic Education or equivalent unless other recent test results indicate ability to benefit from instruction. Interview, recommendations required for law enforcement, practical nursing, surgical technology and phlebotomy programs. **Adult students:** Entrance exam policies same as for first-time freshmen.

High school preparation. Recommended units include English 4 and mathematics 2.

2005-2006 Annual costs. Tuition/fees: $3,453. Per-credit charge: $64. Total program cost ranges from $4,500- $12,700 depending on course of study. Books/supplies: $816. Personal expenses: $1,353.

Financial aid. **Need-based:** Need-based aid available for part-time students. Work study available nights, weekends and for part-time students.

Application procedures. **Admission:** Closing date 8/1 (postmark date). $20 fee. Application may be submitted online. Admission notification on a rolling basis. **Financial aid:** Priority date 4/20; no closing date. FAFSA required. Applicants notified on a rolling basis starting 6/30; must reply within 2 week(s) of notification.

Academics. **Special study options:** Dual enrollment of high school students, internships. License preparation in nursing. **Credit/placement by examination:** CLEP, institutional tests. 35 credit hours maximum toward associate degree. **Support services:** Learning center, pre-admission summer program, reduced course load, remedial instruction, study skills assistance, tutoring.

Majors. **Agriculture:** General, agribusiness operations, business, farm/ranch. **Business:** Accounting, marketing. **Construction:** Electrician, power transmission. **Engineering technology:** Drafting. **Health:** Medical transcription. **Legal studies:** Paralegal. **Mechanic/repair:** Automotive, electronics/electrical, industrial. **Protective services:** Police science.

Most popular majors. Agriculture 13%, business/marketing 23%, legal studies 12%, security/protective services 9%, trade and industry 43%.

Computing on campus. 210 workstations in library, computer center. Commuter students can connect to campus network. Repair service, wireless network available.

Student life. **Freshman orientation:** Mandatory. Preregistration for classes offered. 1-day session held prior to start of classes. **Policies:** Regular attendance required. Must make commitment to attend classes/labs 5 days a week from 8 a.m. to 3 p.m. Freshmen permitted cars on campus. **Activities:** Student government, minority club, single-parent club.

Athletics. **Intercollegiate:** Rodeo.

Student services. Adult student services, alcohol/substance abuse counseling, career counseling, services for economically disadvantaged, student employment services, financial aid counseling, minority student services, on-campus daycare, personal counseling, placement for graduates, veterans' counselor, women's services. **Physically disabled:** Services for visually, speech, hearing impaired. **Transfer:** Special adviser, orientation, pre-admission transcript evaluation for new students. Transfer adviser for students transferring to 4-year colleges.

Contact. E-mail: admissions@wdti.tec.sd.us
Phone: (605) 394-4034 ext. 113 Toll-free number: (800) 544-8765
Fax: (605) 394-2204
Jill Tolsma, Admissions Specialist, Western Dakota Technical Institute, 800 Mickelson Drive, Rapid City, SD 57703

Tennessee

Chattanooga State Technical Community College
Chattanooga, Tennessee
www.chattanoogastate.edu **CB code: 1084**

- Public 2-year community and technical college
- Commuter campus in small city

General. Founded in 1963. Regionally accredited. Credit-bearing courses offered at various off-campus locations. **Enrollment:** 6,542 degree-seeking undergraduates; 1,294 non-degree-seeking students. **Degrees:** 635 associate awarded. **Location:** 129 miles from Nashville. **Calendar:** Semester, limited summer session. **Full-time faculty:** 203 total. **Part-time faculty:** 1 total.

Student profile. Among degree-seeking undergraduates, 33% enrolled in a transfer program, 1,269 enrolled as first-time, first-year students.

Part-time:	50%	**Asian American:**	2%
Out-of-state:	7%	**Hispanic American:**	2%
Women:	63%	**25 or older:**	44%
African American:	19%		

Basis for selection. Open admission, but selective for some programs. Special requirements for allied health program. National standardized dental assisting and dental hygiene tests required of applicants to these programs. Interview required for allied health, nursing programs. **Adult students:** SAT/ACT scores not required if applicant over 21. Placement Test. **Homeschooled:** Transcript of courses and grades required. Students are required to register with their local department/board of education or present affiliation with accredited home school agency.

High school preparation. 19 units recommended. Recommended units include English 4, mathematics 4, social studies 4, history 2, science 2 and foreign language 2. Visual/performing arts 1. College preparatory program required for students choosing transfer majors.

2005-2006 Annual costs. Tuition/fees: $2,413; $8,827 out-of-state. Per-credit charge: $91 in-state; $369 out-of-state. Books/supplies: $650. Personal expenses: $2,150.

2005-2006 Financial aid. Need-based: 845 full-time freshmen applied for aid; 659 were judged to have need; 642 of these received aid. Average need met was 73%. Average scholarship/grant was $3,230; average loan $1,975. 61% of total undergraduate aid awarded as scholarships/grants, 39% as loans/jobs. Need-based aid available for part-time students. Work study available nights, weekends and for part-time students. **Non-need-based:** Awarded to 598 full-time undergraduates, including 311 freshmen. Scholarships awarded for state residency.

Application procedures. Admission: Priority date 8/15; no deadline. $15 fee. Application may be submitted online. Admission notification on a rolling basis. **Financial aid:** Priority date 4/1; no closing date. FAFSA required. Applicants notified on a rolling basis starting 4/1; must reply within 2 week(s) of notification.

Academics. Special study options: Accelerated study, cooperative education, cross-registration, distance learning, double major, dual enrollment of high school students, honors, independent study, internships, student-designed major, weekend college. Bachelor's degree programs available on campus. License preparation in dental hygiene, nursing, paramedic, radiology, real estate. **Credit/placement by examination:** AP, CLEP, IB, institutional tests. Final 20 hours must be taken in residency; maximun of 40 hours may be awarded by combination of credit by exam and credit for experience. **Support services:** GED preparation and test center, learning center, pre-admission summer program, reduced course load, remedial instruction, tutoring, writing center.

Majors. Business: Accounting, management science, office/clerical. **Communications:** Advertising. **Computer sciences:** Information systems, programming. **Education:** Early childhood. **Engineering:** Civil, mechanical. **English:** Technical writing. **Health:** Dental hygiene, medical radiologic technology/radiation therapy, medical records admin, physical therapy assistant, respiratory therapy technology. **Legal studies:** Court reporting, paralegal. **Liberal arts:** Arts/sciences. **Visual/performing arts:** Commercial/advertising art.

Computing on campus. 1,200 workstations in library, computer center, student center. Commuter students can connect to campus network. Online course registration, online library, helpline, wireless network available.

Student life. Freshman orientation: Mandatory. Preregistration for classes offered. Sessions begin in June and end in August for the fall term. Sessions are 9:00 am - 2:00 pm. **Activities:** Jazz band, choral groups, drama, music ensembles, radio station, student government, student newspaper, TV station, Baptist student union.

Athletics. NJCAA. **Intercollegiate:** Baseball M, basketball. **Intramural:** Racquetball, soccer, softball, table tennis, tennis. **Team name:** Tigers.

Student services. Adult student services, alcohol/substance abuse counseling, career counseling, services for economically disadvantaged, student employment services, financial aid counseling, minority student services, on-campus daycare, personal counseling, placement for graduates, veterans' counselor. **Physically disabled:** Services for visually, speech, hearing impaired. **Learning disabled:** Comprehensive services available. **Transfer:** Special adviser, orientation for new students. Transfer adviser, college fairs on campus for students transferring to 4-year colleges.

Contact. E-mail: admissions@chattanoogastate.edu
Phone: (423) 697-4401 Fax: (423) 697-4709
Diane Norris, Director, Chattanooga State Technical Community College, 4501 Amnicola Highway, Chattanooga, TN 37406

Cleveland State Community College
Cleveland, Tennessee
www.clevelandstatecc.edu **CB code: 2848**

- Public 2-year community college
- Commuter campus in small city

General. Founded in 1967. Regionally accredited. **Enrollment:** 2,367 degree-seeking undergraduates; 660 non-degree-seeking students. **Degrees:** 291 associate awarded. **Location:** 30 miles from Chattanooga, 80 miles from Knoxville. **Calendar:** Semester, extensive summer session. **Full-time faculty:** 72 total; 15% have terminal degrees, 8% minority, 50% women. **Part-time faculty:** 118 total; 17% have terminal degrees, 3% minority, 53% women. **Class size:** 59% < 20, 37% 20-39, 3% 40-49, less than 1% 50-99, less than 1% >100. **Special facilities:** Observatory.

Student profile. Among degree-seeking undergraduates, 48% enrolled in a transfer program, 32% enrolled in a vocational program, 5% already have a bachelor's degree or higher, 557 enrolled as first-time, first-year students, 193 transferred in from other institutions.

Part-time:	39%	**Asian American:**	1%
Out-of-state:	1%	**Hispanic American:**	2%
Women:	64%	**Native American:**	1%
African American:	5%	**25 or older:**	44%

Transfer out. Colleges most students transferred to 2005: University of Tennessee-Chattanooga, University of Tennessee-Knoxville, Tennessee Technological University, Lee University.

Basis for selection. Open admission, but selective for some programs. Program admission required for nursing and medical office assistant. **Adult students:** SAT/ACT scores not required if applicant over 21. COMPASS used.

High school preparation. 14 units required. Required units include English 4, mathematics 3, social studies 1, history 1, science 2 (laboratory 1), foreign language 2 and academic electives 1. College-preparatory program required for transfer programs: 14 total academic units, 4 English, 2 foreign language, 3 mathematics, 1 social science, 2 science, 1 US history, 1 visual or performing arts. Same units recommended for career/technical programs.

2005-2006 Annual costs. Tuition/fees: $2,385; $8,799 out-of-state. Per-credit charge: $91 in-state; $369 out-of-state. Books/supplies: $800. Personal expenses: $900.

2005-2006 Financial aid. Need-based: Average need met was 73%. Average scholarship/grant was $4,034; average loan $2,314. 78% of total undergraduate aid awarded as scholarships/grants, 22% as loans/jobs. Need-based aid available for part-time students. **Non-need-based:** Scholarships awarded for athletics, minority status.

Application procedures. Admission: No deadline. $10 fee. Application must be submitted on paper. Admission notification on a rolling basis. **Financial aid:** Priority date 6/15; no closing date. FAFSA, institutional form required. Applicants notified on a rolling basis starting 7/1; must reply within 2 week(s) of notification.

Academics. **Special study options:** Cooperative education, cross-registration, distance learning, double major, dual enrollment of high school students, ESL, honors, independent study, internships. License preparation in nursing. **Credit/placement by examination:** AP, CLEP, institutional tests. 15 credit hours maximum toward associate degree. Students scoring above 32 on the English portion of the enhanced ACT receive 6 credits of English composition. AP credit awarded is determined on an individual basis by the relevant department for grades of 3 or higher. **Support services:** GED test center, learning center, reduced course load, remedial instruction, study skills assistance, tutoring.

Majors. **Business:** Administrative services, business admin. **Engineering technology:** Industrial. **Family/consumer sciences:** Child development. **Health:** Nursing (RN). **Liberal arts:** Arts/sciences.

Most popular majors. Business/marketing 12%, engineering/engineering technologies 6%, health sciences 16%, liberal arts 46%, science technologies 13%.

Computing on campus. 500 workstations in library, computer center, student center. Commuter students can connect to campus network. Online course registration, online library, helpline, wireless network available.

Student life. **Freshman orientation:** Available. Preregistration for classes offered. Half-day program includes campus tour, career and academic counseling, placement assessment, and registration. **Policies:** Freshmen permitted cars on campus. **Activities:** Choral groups, literary magazine, student government, student newspaper, Baptist Student Union, Methodist Campus Ministry, Circle-K, Phi Theta Kappa, Professional Secretaries International, Adult Student League.

Athletics. NJCAA. **Intercollegiate:** Baseball M, basketball, cheerleading, softball W. **Intramural:** Badminton, basketball, golf, softball, table tennis, tennis, volleyball. **Team name:** Cougars.

Student services. Adult student services, career counseling, student employment services, financial aid counseling, minority student services, personal counseling, placement for graduates, veterans' counselor. **Physically disabled:** Services for visually, speech, hearing impaired. **Transfer:** Special adviser, orientation, re-entry adviser, pre-admission transcript evaluation for new students. Transfer adviser, college fairs on campus for students transferring to 4-year colleges.

Contact. E-mail: mburnette@clevelandstatecc.edu
Phone: (423) 478-6212 Toll-free number: (800) 604-2722
Fax: (423) 478-6255
Midge Burnette, Director of Admissions and Records, Cleveland State Community College, 3535 Adkisson Drive, Cleveland, TN 37320-3570

Columbia State Community College
Columbia, Tennessee
www.columbiastate.edu **CB code: 1081**

- Public 2-year community college
- Commuter campus in large town

General. Founded in 1966. Regionally accredited. **Enrollment:** 4,056 degree-seeking undergraduates; 691 non-degree-seeking students. **Degrees:** 534 associate awarded. **Location:** 40 miles from Nashville. **Calendar:** Semester, limited summer session. **Full-time faculty:** 100 total. **Part-time faculty:** 140 total. **Class size:** 34% < 20, 21% 20-39, 9% 40-49, 16% 50-99, 20% >100.

Student profile. Among degree-seeking undergraduates, 52% enrolled in a transfer program, 48% enrolled in a vocational program, 821 enrolled as first-time, first-year students.

Part-time:	46%	**Asian American:**	1%
Women:	66%	**Hispanic American:**	2%
African American:	8%	**25 or older:**	28%

Basis for selection. Open admission, but selective for some programs. Special requirements for allied health sciences.

High school preparation. Recommended units include English 4, mathematics 3, social studies 1, history 1, science 2 (laboratory 1) and foreign language 2. One visual and performing arts recommended.

2005-2006 Annual costs. Tuition/fees: $2,373; $8,787 out-of-state. Per-credit charge: $91 in-state; $369 out-of-state. Personal expenses: $625.

Financial aid. **Need-based:** Need-based aid available for part-time students. **Non-need-based:** Scholarships awarded for academics, athletics, state residency.

Application procedures. **Admission:** No deadline. $10 fee. Admission notification on a rolling basis. **Financial aid:** Closing date 3/15. FAFSA, institutional form required. Applicants notified on a rolling basis starting 5/15; must reply within 2 week(s) of notification.

Academics. **Special study options:** Cooperative education, distance learning, dual enrollment of high school students. **Credit/placement by examination:** AP, CLEP. 30 credit hours maximum toward associate degree. **Support services:** Learning center, remedial instruction, study skills assistance, tutoring.

Majors. **Agriculture:** Business. **Biology:** General. **Business:** General, accounting, administrative services. **Communications:** Journalism. **Computer sciences:** General. **Education:** Early childhood, elementary. **Engineering:** General. **Engineering technology:** Electrical. **Health:** Clinical lab technology, dental hygiene, medical radiologic technology/radiation therapy, predentistry, premedicine, prepharmacy, respiratory therapy technology, veterinary technology/assistant. **History:** General. **Legal studies:** Prelaw. **Liberal arts:** Arts/sciences. **Math:** General. **Parks/recreation:** Health/fitness. **Physical sciences:** Chemistry, physics. **Psychology:** General. **Social sciences:** Economics, geography, sociology. **Visual/performing arts:** Art.

Most popular majors. Business/marketing 6%, health sciences 29%, liberal arts 58%.

Computing on campus. 60 workstations in library, computer center.

Student life. **Activities:** Choral groups, drama, student government, Baptist Student Union, Students in Free Enterprise, Circle K Club, Collegiate Secretaries International, computer club, Geste, Gamma Beta Phi, returning adults organization.

Athletics. NJCAA. **Intercollegiate:** Baseball M, basketball, softball W. **Intramural:** Basketball, softball M, table tennis, volleyball. **Team name:** Chargers, Lady Chargers.

Student services. Career counseling, health services, personal counseling, placement for graduates, veterans' counselor. **Physically disabled:** Services for visually, hearing impaired. **Transfer:** Special adviser, orientation for new students. College fairs on campus for students transferring to 4-year colleges.

Contact. E-mail: scruggs@columbiastate.edu
Phone: (931) 540-2545 Fax: (931) 540-2535
Sharon Bowen, Director of Admissions/Registrar, Columbia State Community College, 1665 Hampshire Pike, Columbia, TN 38401

Draughons Junior College: Clarksville
Clarksville, Tennessee
www.draughons.edu **CB code: 3225**

- For-profit 2-year business college
- Small city

General. Accredited by ACICS. **Calendar:** Continuous.

Annual costs/financial aid. Books/supplies: $700.

Contact. Phone: (931) 552-7600
Campus Director, 1860 Wilma Rudolph Boulevard, Clarksville, TN 37040

Draughons Junior College: Murfreesboro
Murfreesboro, Tennessee
www.draughons.edu

- For-profit 2-year junior college
- Commuter campus

General. Accredited by ACICS. **Calendar:** Semester.

Contact. Phone: (615) 217-9347
Campus Director, 415 Golden Bear Court, Murfreesboro, TN 37128

Draughons Junior College: Nashville
Nashville, Tennessee
www.draughons.edu **CB code: 7325**

- For-profit 2-year business and junior college
- Commuter campus in very large city

General. Founded in 1884. Accredited by ACICS. **Location:** 2 miles from downtown. **Calendar:** Semester.

Annual costs/financial aid. Books/supplies: $500. Need-based financial aid available to full-time and part-time students.

Contact. Phone: (615) 361-7555
Campus Director, 340 Plus Park at Pavilion Boulevard, Nashville, TN 37217

Dyersburg State Community College
Dyersburg, Tennessee
www.dscc.edu **CB code: 7323**

- Public 2-year community college
- Commuter campus in large town

General. Founded in 1967. Regionally accredited. **Enrollment:** 2,213 degree-seeking undergraduates. **Degrees:** 235 associate awarded. **Location:** 78 miles from Memphis. **Calendar:** Semester, limited summer session. **Full-time faculty:** 56 total; 25% have terminal degrees, 12% minority, 62% women. **Part-time faculty:** 118 total. **Class size:** 46% < 20, 52% 20-39, 1% 40-49, less than 1% 50-99.

Student profile.

Out-of-state:	1%	25 or older:	55%

Transfer out. Colleges most students transferred to 2005: University of Tennessee-Martin, University of Memphis, Middle Tennessee State University.

Basis for selection. Open admission, but selective for some programs. Acceptance into nursing program is based on point system, taking into consideration National League of Nursing test score, GPA, science courses completed with grade of C or above, and required courses that have been successfully completed. High school students who meet specific admission requirements may enroll as first time freshmen. **Adult students:** Entrance exam policies same as for first-time freshmen. **Learning Disabled:** Students with learning disabilities are encouraged to self-identify with the college's ADA coordinator.

High school preparation. 14 units recommended. Recommended units include English 4, mathematics 3, social studies 2, history 1, science 2 and foreign language 2.

2005-2006 Annual costs. Tuition/fees: $2,393; $8,807 out-of-state. Per-credit charge: $91 in-state; $369 out-of-state. Books/supplies: $950. Personal expenses: $900.

2004-2005 Financial aid. Need-based: 458 full-time freshmen applied for aid; 363 were judged to have need; 336 of these received aid. Average need met was 37%. Average scholarship/grant was $2,868; average loan $2,325. 83% of total undergraduate aid awarded as scholarships/grants, 17% as loans/jobs. Need-based aid available for part-time students. Work study available nights and for part-time students. **Non-need-based:** Awarded to 219 full-time undergraduates, including 99 freshmen. Scholarships awarded for academics, alumni affiliation, athletics, job skills, leadership, minority status, music/drama, state residency.

Application procedures. Admission: Priority date 8/1; no deadline. $10 fee. Admission notification on a rolling basis. **Financial aid:** Priority date 3/1; no closing date. FAFSA required. Applicants notified on a rolling basis starting 3/1; must reply within 2 week(s) of notification.

Academics. Special study options: Cooperative education, distance learning, dual enrollment of high school students, honors, independent study, internships, liberal arts/career combination. **Credit/placement by examination:** AP, CLEP, institutional tests. 24 credit hours maximum toward associate degree. **Support services:** GED preparation and test center, learning center, reduced course load, remedial instruction, study skills assistance, tutoring.

Majors. Biology: General. **Business:** Business admin. **Computer sciences:** Information systems. **Education:** General. **Engineering technology:** Electrical. **Family/consumer sciences:** Child development. **Health:** Medical records technology, nursing (RN). **Liberal arts:** Arts/sciences. **Math:** General. **Protective services:** Police science. **Psychology:** General. **Social sciences:** General.

Most popular majors. Business/marketing 18%, computer/information sciences 11%, health sciences 15%, liberal arts 50%.

Computing on campus. 524 workstations in library, computer center, student center. Commuter students can connect to campus network. Online course registration, online library, helpline available.

Student life. Freshman orientation: Available. Preregistration for classes offered. Half-day programs with pre-registration. **Policies:** Freshmen permitted cars on campus. **Activities:** Choral groups, drama, music ensembles, student government, student newspaper, Baptist collegiate ministries, American Chemical Society Affiliates, business and office systems association, student nurses association, Minority Association for Successful Students, astronomy club, advanced technology association, music club, Phi Theta Kappa, psychology club.

Athletics. NJCAA. **Intercollegiate:** Baseball M, basketball, softball W. **Intramural:** Basketball, volleyball. **Team name:** Eagles.

Student services. Adult student services, alcohol/substance abuse counseling, career counseling, services for economically disadvantaged, student employment services, financial aid counseling, minority student services, personal counseling, placement for graduates, veterans' counselor, women's services. **Physically disabled:** Services for visually, speech, hearing impaired. **Transfer:** Special adviser, orientation, pre-admission transcript evaluation for new students. Transfer adviser, college fairs on campus for students transferring to 4-year colleges.

Contact. E-mail: enroll@dscc.edu
Phone: (731) 286-3330 Fax: (731) 286-3325
J Gullett, Assistant Vice President for Academic Affairs, Dyersburg State Community College, 1510 Lake Road, Dyersburg, TN 38024

Electronic Computer Programming College
Chattanooga, Tennessee
www.ecpconline.com **CB code: 2267**

- For-profit 2-year technical college
- Large city

General. Accredited by ACCSCT. **Calendar:** Quarter.

Contact. Phone: (423) 624-0077
Director of Admissions, 3805 Brainerd Road, Chattanooga, TN 37411

Fountainhead College of Technology
Knoxville, Tennessee
www.fountainheadcollege.edu **CB code: 0446**

- For-profit 2-year technical college
- Commuter campus in small city

General. Founded in 1947. Accredited by ACCSCT. **Location:** 200 miles from Nashville, 200 miles from Atlanta, Georgia. **Calendar:** Quarter.

Annual costs/financial aid. Tuition for full associate programs ranges from $16,000 to $21,000; bachelor's degree additional $12,000. Cost of supplies ranges from $2,000 to $3,000. Books/supplies: $600. Personal expenses: $1,200.

Contact. Phone: (865) 688-9422
Director of Admissions, 3203 Tazewell Pike, Knoxville, TN 37918

High-Tech Institute
Nashville, Tennessee
www.hightechinstitute.edu

- For-profit 2-year technical college
- Very large city

General. Accredited by ACCSCT. **Calendar:** Continuous.

Contact. Phone: (615) 902-9705
Director of Admissions, 560 Royal Parkway, Nashville, TN 37214

Hiwassee College
Madisonville, Tennessee
www.hiwassee.edu **CB code: 1298**

- Private 2-year junior and liberal arts college affiliated with United Methodist Church
- Residential campus in small town
- SAT or ACT (ACT writing optional) required

General. Founded in 1849. Regionally accredited. Christian principles emphasized; involvement in total campus life encouraged. **Enrollment:** 381

degree-seeking undergraduates; 2 non-degree-seeking students. **Degrees:** 83 associate awarded. **Location:** 50 miles from Knoxville, 75 miles from Chattanooga. **Calendar:** Semester, limited summer session. **Full-time faculty:** 20 total; 50% have terminal degrees, 10% minority, 35% women. **Part-time faculty:** 9 total; 44% have terminal degrees, 33% women. **Class size:** 76% < 20, 23% 20-39, less than 1% 50-99, less than 1% >100. **Special facilities:** Nature preserve, equestrian facilities, natatorium.

Student profile. Among degree-seeking undergraduates, 98% enrolled in a transfer program, 2% enrolled in a vocational program, 142 enrolled as first-time, first-year students, 32 transferred in from other institutions.

Part-time:	29%	**Hispanic American:**	3%
Out-of-state:	14%	**Native American:**	1%
Women:	54%	**International:**	4%
African American:	14%	**25 or older:**	15%
Asian American:	1%	**Live on campus:**	44%

Transfer out. Colleges most students transferred to 2005: University of Tennessee, Knoxville; University of Tennessee, Chattanooga; Tennessee Weleyan College; Tennessee Technological University; Lincoln Memorial University.

Basis for selection. Minimum high school GPA of 2.5, class rank in top two-thirds, and test scores important. Students admitted conditionally or provisionally required to take COMPASS placement exam. Interview recommended for academically weak. **Adult students:** Require all adult (nontraditional) students to take the ACT COMPASS reading, writing and mathematics placement exams. **Homeschooled:** Statement describing homeschool structure and mission, transcript of courses and grades required. **Learning Disabled:** Differently abled students who need or desire special accommodations within classes or their overall curriculum are expected to take the initiative in making the Admissions Staff, Academic Dean, and appropriate faculty members aware of such a need.

High school preparation. College-preparatory program recommended. Required and recommended units include English 4, mathematics 3, social studies 3, history 1, science 3 (laboratory 2), foreign language 2 and academic electives 4.

2005-2006 Annual costs. Tuition/fees: $9,780. Per-credit charge: $395. Room/board: $5,500. Books/supplies: $750. Personal expenses: $900.

2004-2005 Financial aid. Need-based: 75% of total undergraduate aid awarded as scholarships/grants, 25% as loans/jobs. Need-based aid available for part-time students. Work study available nights, weekends and for part-time students. **Non-need-based:** Scholarships awarded for academics, alumni affiliation, athletics, job skills, leadership, music/drama, religious affiliation, state residency.

Application procedures. Admission: Priority date 5/1; no deadline. No application fee. Application may be submitted online. Admission notification on a rolling basis beginning on or about 10/1. **Financial aid:** Priority date 5/1; no closing date. FAFSA, institutional form required. Applicants notified on a rolling basis starting 4/1; must reply within 2 week(s) of notification.

Academics. Special study options: Dual enrollment of high school students, ESL, honors, independent study, internships, study abroad. License preparation in nursing. **Credit/placement by examination:** AP, CLEP, institutional tests. 33 credit hours maximum toward associate degree. **Support services:** Learning center, reduced course load, remedial instruction, study skills assistance, tutoring.

Majors. Agriculture: Animal sciences, business, economics, food science, horticultural science, plant sciences, soil science. **Biology:** General. **Business:** General, accounting, business admin, finance, hospitality admin, hospitality/recreation, managerial economics. **Communications:** General. **Computer sciences:** General. **Conservation:** Forest resources, forestry. **Education:** General, college student counseling, early childhood, elementary, music, physical, secondary. **English:** English lit. **Family/consumer sciences:** General, clothing/textiles, food/nutrition. **Foreign languages:** French, Spanish. **Health:** Predentistry, premedicine, prenursing, prepharmacy, preveterinary. **History:** General. **Legal studies:** Prelaw. **Liberal arts:** Arts/sciences. **Math:** General. **Parks/recreation:** Health/fitness. **Philosophy/religion:** Religion. **Physical sciences:** Chemistry, physics. **Protective services:** Criminal justice. **Psychology:** General. **Public administration:** Human services. **Social sciences:** General, criminology, economics, sociology. **Theology:** Bible, preministerial. **Visual/performing arts:** Dramatic, music performance, piano/organ, voice/opera.

Most popular majors. Business/marketing 20%, education 16%, health sciences 16%, liberal arts 29%.

Computing on campus. 61 workstations in library, computer center, student center. Dormitories wired for high-speed internet access and linked to campus network. Commuter students can connect to campus network. Online library, helpline, wireless network available.

Student life. Freshman orientation: Mandatory. Preregistration for classes offered. **Policies:** Religious observance required. Freshmen permitted cars on campus. **Housing:** Guaranteed on-campus for all undergraduates. Single-sex dorms, substance-free housing available. $50 fully refundable deposit, deadline 8/1. **Activities:** Choral groups, dance, drama, literary magazine, music ensembles, musical theater, student government, student newspaper, Christian student movement.

Athletics. NJCAA. **Intercollegiate:** Baseball M, basketball, cheerleading, cross-country, golf, soccer, softball W, volleyball W. **Intramural:** Basketball, football (non-tackle), softball, swimming, table tennis, tennis, volleyball. **Team name:** Tigers.

Student services. Adult student services, alcohol/substance abuse counseling, campus ministries, career counseling, services for economically disadvantaged, financial aid counseling, health services, personal counseling, veterans' counselor. **Transfer:** Special adviser, orientation, pre-admission transcript evaluation for new students. Transfer adviser, college fairs on campus for students transferring to 4-year colleges.

Contact. E-mail: enroll@hiwassee.edu
Phone: (423) 420-1212 Toll-free number: (800) 356-2187
Fax: (423) 442-3520
Lynne Henderson, Director of Admissions, Hiwassee College, 225 Hiwassee College Drive, Madisonville, TN 37354-6099

Huntington College of Health Sciences

Knoxville, Tennessee
www.hchs.edu **CB code: 3945**

- For-profit 2-year health science college
- Very large city

General. Accredited by DETC. **Calendar:** Continuous.

Contact. Phone: (865) 524-8079
Registrar, Director of Student Services, 1204D Kenesaw, Knoxville, TN 37919-7736

Jackson State Community College

Jackson, Tennessee
www.jscc.edu **CB code: 2266**

- Public 2-year community college
- Commuter campus in small city

General. Founded in 1965. Regionally accredited. **Enrollment:** 3,859 degree-seeking undergraduates. **Degrees:** 451 associate awarded. **ROTC:** Army. **Location:** 80 miles from Memphis, 130 miles from Nashville. **Calendar:** Semester, limited summer session. **Full-time faculty:** 118 total; 12% have terminal degrees, 6% minority, 61% women. **Part-time faculty:** 104 total; 6% have terminal degrees, 4% minority, 54% women. **Class size:** 49% < 20, 48% 20-39, 1% 40-49, 2% 50-99, less than 1% >100.

Student profile. Among degree-seeking undergraduates, 49% enrolled in a transfer program, 51% enrolled in a vocational program, 1% already have a bachelor's degree or higher, 732 enrolled as first-time, first-year students, 231 transferred in from other institutions.

Part-time:	47%	**Hispanic American:**	1%
Women:	65%	**25 or older:**	40%
African American:	18%		

Transfer out. 94% of students enrolled in the transfer program go on to 4-year colleges. **Colleges most students transferred to 2005:** Union University, University of Memphis, University of Tennessee at Martin, Middle Tennessee State University, Lambuth University.

Basis for selection. Open admission, but selective for some programs. Special requirements for nursing, medical laboratory technology, radiologic technology, respiratory care, physical therapy assistant programs. ACT for placement must be received by registration for fall-term admission. Interview required for alllied health, nursing programs. **Adult students:** SAT/ACT scores not required if applicant over 21. Compass test if degree-seeking first-time adult students. **Homeschooled:** Transcript of courses and grades required.

High school preparation. 14 units recommended. Recommended units include English 4, mathematics 3, social studies 1, history 1, science 2 (laboratory 1) and foreign language 2. One visual and performing arts credit recommended. College preparatory program required by state for transfer associate degree programs; not required for other programs.

2005-2006 Annual costs. Tuition/fees: $2,395; $8,809 out-of-state. Per-credit charge: $91 in-state; $369 out-of-state. Books/supplies: $800. Personal expenses: $781.

2004-2005 Financial aid. Need-based: 446 full-time freshmen applied for aid; 346 were judged to have need; 331 of these received aid. Average need met was 81%. Average scholarship/grant was $3,008; average loan $6,873. 97% of total undergraduate aid awarded as scholarships/grants, 3% as loans/jobs. Need-based aid available for part-time students. Work study available nights, weekends and for part-time students. **Non-need-based:** Awarded to 578 full-time undergraduates, including 237 freshmen. Scholarships awarded for academics, art, athletics, job skills, leadership, minority status, music/drama.

Application procedures. Admission: Priority date 7/1; no deadline. $10 fee. Application may be submitted online. Admission notification on a rolling basis. Closing date for applications to allied health and nursing programs is April 15. **Financial aid:** Priority date 4/1; no closing date. FAFSA, institutional form required. Applicants notified on a rolling basis starting 6/1; must reply within 2 week(s) of notification.

Academics. Special study options: Cooperative education, distance learning, dual enrollment of high school students, honors, internships, liberal arts/career combination. Bachelor's degree programs available on campus. License preparation in nursing, paramedic, physical therapy, radiology. **Credit/placement by examination:** CLEP, institutional tests. 28 credit hours maximum toward associate degree. Must complete additional 15 college credit hours before credit by examination awarded. **Support services:** GED preparation and test center, learning center, reduced course load, remedial instruction, tutoring.

Honors college/program. Cumulative 3.5 grade point average or 31 on ACT required.

Majors. Agriculture: Business. **Biology:** General. **Business:** Accounting, business admin. **Communications:** General. **Computer sciences:** General. **Education:** General, early childhood. **Engineering:** General. **Engineering technology:** Industrial. **English:** English lit. **Health:** Clinical lab technology, medical radiologic technology/radiation therapy, nursing (RN), physical therapy assistant, premedicine, prenursing, respiratory therapy technology. **History:** General. **Legal studies:** Prelaw. **Liberal arts:** Arts/sciences. **Math:** General. **Parks/recreation:** Health/fitness. **Physical sciences:** General, chemistry. **Protective services:** Police science. **Psychology:** General. **Public administration:** General, social work. **Social sciences:** Political science, sociology. **Visual/performing arts:** Art, commercial/advertising art.

Most popular majors. Business/marketing 10%, engineering/engineering technologies 6%, health sciences 36%, liberal arts 41%.

Computing on campus. 50 workstations in library. Commuter students can connect to campus network. Online course registration, online library available.

Student life. Freshman orientation: Available. **Policies:** Freshmen permitted cars on campus. **Activities:** Bands, choral groups, drama, music ensembles, student government, student newspaper.

Athletics. NJCAA. **Intercollegiate:** Baseball M, basketball, softball W. **Intramural:** Basketball, softball, tennis, volleyball. **Team name:** Generals.

Student services. Career counseling, student employment services, financial aid counseling, health services, personal counseling, placement for graduates, veterans' counselor. **Physically disabled:** Services for visually, speech, hearing impaired. **Transfer:** Special adviser, orientation, pre-admission transcript evaluation for new students. Transfer center, transfer adviser, college fairs on campus for students transferring to 4-year colleges.

Contact. E-mail: mray@jscc.edu
Phone: (731) 425-2644 Fax: (731) 425-9559
Monica Ray, Director of Admissions/Records, Jackson State Community College, 2046 North Parkway, Jackson, TN 38301-3797

John A. Gupton College

Nashville, Tennessee
www.guptoncollege.com **CB code: 0539**

- Private 2-year school of mortuary science
- Commuter campus in large city

General. Founded in 1946. Regionally accredited. **Enrollment:** 98 degree-seeking undergraduates. **Degrees:** 41 associate awarded. **Calendar:** Semester, limited summer session. **Full-time faculty:** 6 total; 17% have terminal degrees. **Part-time faculty:** 11 total; 46% have terminal degrees, 18% minority, 36% women. **Class size:** 8% < 20, 33% 20-39, 58% 50-99.

Student profile. Among degree-seeking undergraduates, 1% already have a bachelor's degree or higher, 43 enrolled as first-time, first-year students, 18 transferred in from other institutions.

Part-time:	11%	**25 or older:**	43%
Out-of-state:	41%	**Live on campus:**	12%
Women:	44%		

Transfer out. Colleges most students transferred to 2005: Middle Tennessee State University, Western Kentucky University, Jackson State Community College.

Basis for selection. Open admission. 2 letters of recommendation are needed, plus completed health form as required by the Tennessee State Board of Health. SAT or ACT required for files and not used in admissions decisions. Interview recommended.

High school preparation. 10 units recommended. Recommended units include English 4, mathematics 3 and science 3.

2005-2006 Annual costs. Tuition/fees: $6,880. Per-credit charge: $215. Room only: $3,600. Books/supplies: $850.

2004-2005 Financial aid. All financial aid based on need. 64% of total undergraduate aid awarded as scholarships/grants, 36% as loans/jobs. Need-based aid available for part-time students.

Application procedures. Admission: No deadline. $20 fee. Application must be submitted on paper. Admission notification on a rolling basis. **Financial aid:** No deadline. FAFSA required. Applicants notified on a rolling basis.

Academics. Credit/placement by examination: AP, CLEP.

Majors. Personal/culinary services: Funeral direction, mortuary science.

Computing on campus. 8 workstations in library, computer center. Helpline available.

Student life. Freshman orientation: Mandatory. Preregistration for classes offered. **Policies:** Freshmen permitted cars on campus. **Housing:** Apartments, substance-free housing available. $450 deposit. **Activities:** Student government.

Student services. Career counseling. **Transfer:** Special adviser, orientation, pre-admission transcript evaluation for new students.

Contact. E-mail: collard@guptoncollege.com
Phone: (615) 327-3927 Fax: (615) 321-4518
Lisa Bolin, Registrar, John A. Gupton College, 1616 Church Street, Nashville, TN 37203-2920

Miller-Motte Technical College

Clarksville, Tennessee
www.miller-motte.com/clarksvillemain.html **CB code: 3228**

- For-profit 2-year business and health science college
- Commuter campus in small city
- Interview required

General. Accredited by ACICS. **Enrollment:** 356 degree-seeking undergraduates. **Degrees:** 81 associate awarded. **Location:** 45 miles from Nashville. **Calendar:** Quarter, extensive summer session. **Full-time faculty:** 18 total. **Part-time faculty:** 38 total. **Special facilities:** Simulated operating rooms, medical laboratories, simulated doctor's exam room.

Student profile.

Out-of-state:	50%	**25 or older:**	60%

Transfer out. Colleges most students transferred to 2005: Austin Peay University, Hopkinsville Community College.

Basis for selection. Open admission, but selective for some programs. 2 years experience or 2-year/4-year degree and interview with department head required for entrance into network engineer certificate program. **Learning Disabled:** Letter of request for any accommodation required.

2005-2006 Annual costs. Books/supplies: $900. Personal expenses: $1,350.

Financial aid. All financial aid based on need. Need-based aid available for part-time students. Work study available nights, weekends and for part-time students.

Application procedures. Admission: No deadline. No application fee. Admission notification on a rolling basis. **Financial aid:** No deadline. FAFSA, institutional form required. Applicants notified on a rolling basis.

Academics. Special study options: Weekend college. **Credit/placement by examination:** CLEP, institutional tests. No more than 50% of required credit hours in a program. **Support services:** Reduced course load, remedial instruction, study skills assistance, tutoring.

Majors. Business: Accounting, business admin. **Computer sciences:** General. **Health:** Massage therapy, medical assistant, phlebotomy, surgical technology. **Legal studies:** Paralegal.

Most popular majors. Business/marketing 7%, computer/information sciences 22%, engineering/engineering technologies 6%, health sciences 46%, legal studies 15%.

Computing on campus. 75 workstations in library, computer center. Online library available.

Student life. Freshman orientation: Mandatory. Preregistration for classes offered. **Policies:** Freshmen permitted cars on campus. **Activities:** Student government, student newspaper.

Student services. Adult student services, alcohol/substance abuse counseling, career counseling, student employment services, financial aid counseling, placement for graduates, veterans' counselor. **Transfer:** Special adviser, orientation, re-entry adviser, pre-admission transcript evaluation for new students.

Contact. E-mail: rgreen@miller-motte.com
Phone: (931) 553-0071 Toll-free number: (800) 558-0071
Lisa Teague, Admissions Director, Miller-Motte Technical College, 1820 Business Park Drive, Clarksville, TN 37040

Miller-Motte Technical College: Chattanooga

Chattanooga, Tennessee
www.miller-motte.com/chattanoogawelcome.html

- For-profit 2-year technical college
- Commuter campus

General. Accredited by ACICS. **Calendar:** Quarter.

Contact. Phone: (423) 510-9675
Director of Admissions, 6020 Shallowford Road, Suite 100, Chattanooga, TN 37421

Motlow State Community College

Lynchburg, Tennessee
www.mscc.cc.tn.us **CB code: 1543**

- Public 2-year community college
- Commuter campus in rural community

General. Founded in 1969. Regionally accredited. **Enrollment:** 3,030 degree-seeking undergraduates; 377 non-degree-seeking students. **Degrees:** 426 associate awarded. **Location:** 65 miles from Nashville. **Calendar:** Semester, limited summer session. **Full-time faculty:** 74 total; 10% minority, 35% women. **Part-time faculty:** 133 total; 6% minority, 61% women.

Student profile. Among degree-seeking undergraduates, 66% enrolled in a transfer program, 34% enrolled in a vocational program, 924 enrolled as first-time, first-year students, 241 transferred in from other institutions.

Part-time:	34%	**Asian American:**	1%
Out-of-state:	2%	**Hispanic American:**	2%
Women:	64%	**25 or older:**	38%
African American:	8%		

Transfer out. 60% of students enrolled in the transfer program go on to 4-year colleges. **Colleges most students transferred to 2005:** Middle Tennessee State University, Tennesee Technological University.

Basis for selection. Open admission. Interview required for nursing program. **Adult students:** SAT/ACT scores not required if applicant over 21. **Homeschooled:** Transcript of courses and grades required.

High school preparation. 16 units recommended. Recommended units include English 4, mathematics 3, social studies 2, history 1, science 2 (laboratory 1) and foreign language 2.

2005-2006 Annual costs. Tuition/fees: $2,389; $8,803 out-of-state. Per-credit charge: $91 in-state; $369 out-of-state. Books/supplies: $600. Personal expenses: $3,200.

Financial aid. Need-based: Need-based aid available for part-time students. Work study available for part-time students. **Non-need-based:** Scholarships awarded for academics, alumni affiliation, art, athletics, leadership, state residency.

Application procedures. Admission: $10 fee. Application may be submitted online. Admission notification on a rolling basis. **Financial aid:** No deadline. FAFSA required. Applicants notified on a rolling basis starting 3/15.

Academics. Special study options: Cooperative education, distance learning, double major, dual enrollment of high school students, honors, independent study. License preparation in nursing. **Credit/placement by examination:** AP, CLEP, institutional tests. Maximum number of credits by examination that may be earned is limited to 25% of total number of credits needed for graduation. **Support services:** Learning center, reduced course load, remedial instruction, study skills assistance, tutoring, writing center.

Majors. Business: Business admin. **Education:** General, elementary, secondary. **Liberal arts:** Arts/sciences.

Most popular majors. Business/marketing 17%, education 17%, engineering/engineering technologies 17%, health sciences 17%, liberal arts 32%.

Computing on campus. 250 workstations in library, computer center. Commuter students can connect to campus network. Online library, helpline, repair service available.

Student life. Freshman orientation: Mandatory. **Policies:** Freshmen permitted cars on campus. **Activities:** Choral groups, drama, literary magazine, student government, student newspaper, Baptist Student Union, African American Student Association, outing club, communications club, law and government club, literary club, Phi Theta Kappa, psychology club, Tennessee Association of Student Nurses.

Athletics. NJCAA. **Intercollegiate:** Baseball M, basketball, softball W. **Intramural:** Baseball M, basketball, bowling, football (tackle) M, softball, table tennis, tennis, volleyball. **Team name:** Bucks.

Student services. Adult student services, career counseling, student employment services, health services, personal counseling, placement for graduates, veterans' counselor. **Physically disabled:** Services for visually impaired. **Transfer:** Special adviser, pre-admission transcript evaluation for new students. College fairs on campus for students transferring to 4-year colleges.

Contact. E-mail: GALSUP@MSCC.EDU
Phone: (931) 393-1529 Toll-free number: (800) 654-4877
Fax: (931) 393-1971
Greer Alsup, Director of Admissions and Records, Motlow State Community College, Box 8500, Lynchburg, TN 37352

Nashville Auto-Diesel College

Nashville, Tennessee
www.nadcedu.com **CB code: 3098**

- For-profit 1-year technical college
- Commuter campus in large city

General. Accredited by ACCSCT. **Calendar:** Continuous.

Annual costs/financial aid. Full program costs range from $17,750 to $23,400 for diploma programs; $22,250 to $26,300 for associate programs. Need-based financial aid available for full-time students.

Contact. Phone: (615) 226-3990
Director of Admissions, 1524 Gallatin Road, Nashville, TN 37206

Nashville State Community College

Nashville, Tennessee
www.nscc.edu **CB code: 0850**

- Public 2-year community and technical college
- Commuter campus in large city

General. Founded in 1969. Regionally accredited. **Enrollment:** 7,198 degree-seeking undergraduates. **Degrees:** 495 associate awarded. **Location:** 6 miles from Nashville, 200 miles from Memphis. **Calendar:** Semester, limited summer session. **Full-time faculty:** 126 total. **Part-time faculty:** 269 total. **Special facilities:** Television production studio.

Student profile.

Out-of-state:	6%	25 or older:	54%

Transfer out. Colleges most students transferred to 2005: Middle Tennessee University, Tennessee State University, Tennessee Technical University.

Basis for selection. Open admission, but selective for some programs. Students may have to take AAPT for placement. Interview required for automotive services technology, occupational therapy assistant, surgical technology programs.

High school preparation. Recommended units include English 4, mathematics 3, social studies 2, science 2 and foreign language 2. One visual/performing art recommended. Business technologies majors: 1 unit bookkeeping or accounting recommended. Engineering technologies majors: additional math and science recommended.

2005-2006 Annual costs. Tuition/fees: $2,377; $8,791 out-of-state. Per-credit charge: $91 in-state; $369 out-of-state. Books/supplies: $800. Personal expenses: $500.

2005-2006 Financial aid. Need-based: 61% of total undergraduate aid awarded as scholarships/grants, 39% as loans/jobs. Need-based aid available for part-time students. Work study available nights, weekends and for part-time students. **Non-need-based:** Scholarships awarded for academics, minority status.

Application procedures. Admission: No deadline. $5 fee. Application may be submitted online. Admission notification on a rolling basis. Automotive services technology applicants must have automobile dealer sponsorship prior to acceptance. **Financial aid:** Priority date 3/1; no closing date. FAFSA, institutional form required. Applicants notified on a rolling basis starting 6/1; must reply within 2 week(s) of notification.

Academics. Special study options: Cooperative education, distance learning, double major, dual enrollment of high school students, ESL, honors, internships, student-designed major. **Credit/placement by examination:** CLEP, institutional tests. 20 credit hours maximum toward associate degree. **Support services:** GED preparation, learning center, reduced course load, remedial instruction, study skills assistance, tutoring, writing center.

Majors. Business: Accounting, business admin. **Communications technology:** General. **Computer sciences:** General. **Education:** Early childhood. **Engineering technology:** Architectural, civil, construction, electrical. **Foreign languages:** Sign language interpretation. **Health:** Medical secretary. **Legal studies:** Legal secretary. **Mechanic/repair:** Automotive. **Personal/culinary services:** Culinary arts. **Protective services:** Police science. **Visual/performing arts:** Commercial/advertising art, photography.

Computing on campus. 518 workstations in library, computer center. Commuter students can connect to campus network. Online course registration, helpline available.

Student life. Freshman orientation: Available. **Policies:** Freshmen permitted cars on campus. **Activities:** Literary magazine, student government, student newspaper, Black student organization, international student organization.

Athletics. Intramural: Softball, table tennis, volleyball.

Student services. Adult student services, career counseling, student employment services, personal counseling, placement for graduates, veterans' counselor. **Physically disabled:** Services for visually, hearing impaired. **Transfer:** Special adviser, orientation, pre-admission transcript evaluation for new students. College fairs on campus for students transferring to 4-year colleges.

Contact. Phone: (615) 353-3333 Toll-free number: (800) 272-7363
Fax: (615) 353-3243
Charles McCorkle, Director of Admissions, Nashville State Community College, 120 White Bridge Road, Nashville, TN 37209-4515

National College of Business & Technology: Knoxville

Knoxville, Tennessee

- For-profit 2-year business and technical college
- Large city

General. Accredited by ACICS. **Enrollment:** 278 degree-seeking undergraduates. **Degrees:** 9 associate awarded. **Calendar:** Quarter. **Full-time faculty:** 7 total. **Part-time faculty:** 30 total.

Basis for selection. Open admission. Interviews recomended.

2006-2007 Annual costs. Tuition/fees: $8,976. Per-credit charge: $187.

Application procedures. Admission: No deadline. $30 fee.

Academics. Credit/placement by examination: CLEP.

Contact. Phone: (865) 539-2011
Larry Steele, Director of Admissions, National College of Business & Technology: Knoxville, 8415 Kingston Pike, Knoxville, TN 37919

National College of Business & Technology: Tennessee

Nashville, Tennessee
www.ncbt.edu **CB code: 3227**

- For-profit 2-year business and technical college
- Commuter campus in large city

General. Accredited by ACICS. **Enrollment:** 382 degree-seeking undergraduates. **Degrees:** 51 associate awarded. **Calendar:** Quarter. **Full-time faculty:** 7 total. **Part-time faculty:** 34 total.

Basis for selection. Open admission. Interview recommended.

2006-2007 Annual costs. Tuition/fees: $8,976. Per-credit charge: $187. Books/supplies: $900. Personal expenses: $3,259.

Financial aid. All financial aid based on need. Need-based aid available for part-time students.

Application procedures. Admission: No deadline. $30 fee. **Financial aid:** No deadline. FAFSA required.

Academics. Special study options: Liberal arts/career combination. **Credit/placement by examination:** CLEP.

Majors. Business: Accounting, administrative services, business admin. **Computer sciences:** General. **Health:** Medical assistant, medical secretary.

Student life. Freshman orientation: Mandatory. Preregistration for classes offered.

Student services. Transfer: Special adviser, orientation for new students.

Contact. E-mail: market@educorp.edu
Phone: (615) 333-3344
Larry Steele, Director of Admission, National College of Business & Technology: Tennessee, PO Box 6400, Roanoke, VA 24017

Northeast State Technical Community College

Blountville, Tennessee
www.NortheastState.edu **CB code: 0453**

- Public 2-year community and technical college
- Commuter campus in small city

General. Founded in 1965. Regionally accredited. **Enrollment:** 4,860 degree-seeking undergraduates. **Degrees:** 500 associate awarded. **Location:** 12 miles from Johnson City, 10 miles from Kingsport. **Calendar:** Semester, limited summer session. **Full-time faculty:** 94 total. **Part-time faculty:** 152 total.

Student profile. Among degree-seeking undergraduates, 921 enrolled as first-time, first-year students.

Part-time:	46%	Women:	53%
Out-of-state:	3%		

Transfer out. Colleges most students transferred to 2005: East Tennessee State University, Milligan College, Tennessee Tech, University of Tennessee.

Basis for selection. Open admission, but selective for some programs. Special requirements for health related professions division. **Adult students:** COMPASS test required for applicants 21 and older without math or English transfer credit.

High school preparation. 20 units recommended. Required and recommended units include English 4, mathematics 3, social studies 1, history 1, science 2 (laboratory 1) and foreign language 2. Visual/performing arts 1 indicated.

2005-2006 Annual costs. Tuition/fees: $2,393; $8,807 out-of-state. Per-credit charge: $91 in-state; $369 out-of-state. Books/supplies: $700. Personal expenses: $2,400.

2005-2006 Financial aid. Need-based: 75% of total undergraduate aid awarded as scholarships/grants, 25% as loans/jobs. Need-based aid available for part-time students. Work study available nights and for part-time students. **Non-need-based:** Scholarships awarded for academics, alumni affiliation, art, job skills, leadership, minority status, music/drama, religious affiliation.

Application procedures. Admission: No deadline. $10 fee. Application may be submitted online. Admission notification on a rolling basis beginning on or about 6/1. **Financial aid:** Priority date 3/31; no closing date. FAFSA required. Applicants notified on a rolling basis starting 3/1; must reply within 3 week(s) of notification.

Academics. Special study options: Accelerated study, cooperative education, distance learning, double major, dual enrollment of high school students, honors, weekend college. License preparation in paramedic. **Credit/placement by examination:** AP, CLEP, institutional tests. 15 credit hours maximum toward associate degree. **Support services:** GED test center, reduced course load, remedial instruction, tutoring.

Majors. Business: Administrative services, business admin. **Computer sciences:** General, webmaster. **Construction:** Electrician, power transmission. **Engineering technology:** Drafting, electrical, mechanical drafting. **Family/consumer sciences:** Child development, family studies. **Health:** Cardiovascular technology, clinical lab assistant, dental lab technology, medical assistant. **Liberal arts:** Arts/sciences. **Mechanic/repair:** General, automotive, industrial. **Social sciences:** General.

Most popular majors. Business/marketing 28%, engineering/engineering technologies 6%, liberal arts 36%, trade and industry 18%.

Computing on campus. 900 workstations in library, computer center. Commuter students can connect to campus network. Online library available.

Student life. Freshman orientation: Mandatory. Preregistration for classes offered. **Activities:** Drama, literary magazine, student government, Campus Christian Fellowship.

Athletics. Intramural: Golf.

Student services. Career counseling, services for economically disadvantaged, student employment services, financial aid counseling, health services, minority student services, personal counseling, placement for graduates, veterans' counselor. **Physically disabled:** Services for visually, speech, hearing impaired. **Transfer:** Special adviser, orientation for new students. Transfer adviser, college fairs on campus for students transferring to 4-year colleges.

Contact. E-mail: jpharr@NortheastState.edu
Phone: (423) 323-3191 Toll-free number: (800) 836-7822
Fax: (423) 323-0215
Jon Harr, Dean of Admissions and Records, Northeast State Technical Community College, Box 246, Blountville, TN 37617-0246

Nossi College of Art

Goodlettsville, Tennessee
www.nossi.com **CB code: 3118**

- Private 2-year visual arts and technical college
- Commuter campus in large town
- Interview required

General. Accredited by ACCSCT. **Enrollment:** 330 degree-seeking undergraduates. **Degrees:** 59 associate awarded. **Location:** 20 miles from Nashville. **Calendar:** Semester, extensive summer session. **Part-time faculty:** 21 total.

Basis for selection. Interview and talent most important. Portfolio required for commercial art program. **Adult students:** SAT/ACT scores not required.

2005-2006 Annual costs. Tuition for first year (3 semesters) $9,535; required fees $240. Books/supplies: $1,800.

Financial aid. Need-based: Need-based aid available for part-time students.

Application procedures. Admission: No deadline. $100 fee.

Academics. Credit/placement by examination: CLEP.

Majors. Visual/performing arts: General, commercial photography, commercial/advertising art.

Computing on campus. 40 workstations in library, computer center.

Student life. Freshman orientation: Mandatory. **Policies:** Freshmen permitted cars on campus.

Student services. Alcohol/substance abuse counseling, career counseling, student employment services, financial aid counseling, personal counseling, placement for graduates. **Transfer:** Orientation for new students.

Contact. E-mail: admissions@nossi.com
Phone: (615) 851-1088 ext. 17 Toll-free number: (887) 860-1601
Fax: (615) 851-1087
Mary Alexander, Director of Admissions, Nossi College of Art, 907 Rivergate Parkway, Building E-6, Goodlettsville, TN 37072

Pellissippi State Technical Community College

Knoxville, Tennessee
www.pstcc.edu **CB code: 0319**

- Public 2-year community and technical college
- Commuter campus in small city

General. Founded in 1974. Regionally accredited. **Enrollment:** 6,430 degree-seeking undergraduates; 1,256 non-degree-seeking students. **Degrees:** 672 associate awarded. **ROTC:** Army. **Location:** 178 miles from Nashville, 388 miles from Memphis. **Calendar:** Semester, extensive summer session. **Full-time faculty:** 184 total. **Part-time faculty:** 245 total. **Class size:** 46% < 20, 52% 20-39, 2% 40-49, less than 1% 50-99, less than 1% >100.

Student profile. Among degree-seeking undergraduates, 76% enrolled in a transfer program, 24% enrolled in a vocational program, 3% already have a bachelor's degree or higher, 1,388 enrolled as first-time, first-year students.

Part-time:	42%	**Hispanic American:**	2%
Out-of-state:	1%	**Native American:**	1%
Women:	53%	**International:**	1%
African American:	8%	**25 or older:**	40%
Asian American:	2%		

Transfer out. Colleges most students transferred to 2005: University of Tennessee in Knoxville, East Tennessee State University, Tennessee Technological University, Maryville College, Middle Tennessee State University.

Basis for selection. Open admission. Credit may be awarded for coursework taken at international colleges or universities. ACT/SAT scores for placement purposes. **Adult students:** SAT/ACT scores not required if applicant over 21. Institutional placement test required of students 21 and older who have not had college-level math or English. **Learning Disabled:** Accommodations for testing/programs are provided on a case-by-case basis with supporting documentation.

High school preparation. 14 units recommended. Recommended units include English 4, mathematics 3, social studies 1, history 1, science 1 (laboratory 1) and foreign language 2. 1 U.S. history and one visual and performing arts required.

2005-2006 Annual costs. Tuition/fees: $2,414; $8,828 out-of-state. Per-credit charge: $91 in-state; $369 out-of-state. Books/supplies: $800. Personal expenses: $1,500.

2005-2006 Financial aid. Need-based: 73% of total undergraduate aid awarded as scholarships/grants, 27% as loans/jobs. Need-based aid available for part-time students. Work study available nights, weekends and for part-time students. **Non-need-based:** Scholarships awarded for academics, art, minority status, music/drama.

Application procedures. Admission: Closing date 8/24 (postmark date). $10 fee, may be waived for applicants with need. Application may be submitted online. Admission notification on a rolling basis beginning on or about 9/1. **Financial aid:** Priority date 5/1; no closing date. FAFSA required. Applicants notified on a rolling basis starting 7/15; must reply within 2 week(s) of notification.

Academics. Special study options: Cooperative education, distance learning, double major, dual enrollment of high school students, ESL, honors, independent study, internships, liberal arts/career combination, weekend college. **Credit/placement by examination:** AP, CLEP, IB, institutional tests. 36 credit hours maximum toward associate degree. **Support services:** GED preparation and test center, learning center, pre-admission summer program, reduced course load, remedial instruction, study skills assistance, tutoring, writing center.

Majors. Business: Accounting technology, administrative services, business admin, e-commerce. **Computer sciences:** Computer science, information systems, web page design. **Engineering technology:** CAD/CADD, civil, electrical, mechanical. **Family/consumer sciences:** Child development. **Legal studies:** Paralegal. **Liberal arts:** Arts/sciences. **Public administration:** Community org/advocacy. **Social sciences:** Cartography. **Visual/performing arts:** Cinematography, commercial/advertising art, interior design.

Most popular majors. Business/marketing 9%, liberal arts 59%, visual/performing arts 9%.

Computing on campus. 1,290 workstations in library, computer center, student center. Commuter students can connect to campus network. Online course registration, online library, helpline, repair service, wireless network available.

Student life. Freshman orientation: Available. Preregistration for classes offered. **Policies:** Freshmen permitted cars on campus. **Activities:** Jazz band, choral groups, drama, literary magazine, music ensembles, musical theater, student government, student newspaper, Association of Information Technology Professionals, Institute of Electrical and Electronics Engineers, paralegal association, Active Black Students Association, international club, Students In Free Enterprise, Muslim student association, Baptist collegiate ministries, Phi Theta Kappa, Catholic campus organization.

Athletics. Intramural: Archery, basketball, football (non-tackle), golf, soccer, softball, tennis, volleyball.

Student services. Career counseling, student employment services, personal counseling, placement for graduates, veterans' counselor. **Physically disabled:** Services for visually, speech, hearing impaired. **Transfer:** Special adviser, orientation for new students. Transfer adviser, college fairs on campus for students transferring to 4-year colleges.

Contact. E-mail: latouzeau@pstcc.edu
Phone: (865) 694-6570 Fax: (865) 539-7217
Leigh Touzeau, Director of Admissions and Records, Pellissippi State Technical Community College, Box 22990, Knoxville, TN 37933-0990

Remington College: Memphis

Memphis, Tennessee
www.remingtoncollege.edu **CB code: 3159**

- For-profit 2-year business and technical college
- Commuter campus in very large city

General. Accredited by ACCSCT. **Calendar:** Quarter.

Annual costs/financial aid. Need-based financial aid available to full-time and part-time students.

Contact. Phone: (901) 345-1000
President, 2731 Nonconnah Boulevard, Memphis, TN 38132

Roane State Community College

Harriman, Tennessee
www.roanestate.edu **CB code: 1656**

- Public 2-year community and junior college
- Commuter campus in small town

General. Founded in 1971. Regionally accredited. **Enrollment:** 4,352 degree-seeking undergraduates; 803 non-degree-seeking students. **Degrees:** 682 associate awarded. **ROTC:** Army, Air Force. **Location:** 40 miles from Knoxville. **Calendar:** Semester, limited summer session. **Full-time faculty:** 128 total. **Part-time faculty:** 205 total. **Special facilities:** Observatory.

Student profile. Among degree-seeking undergraduates, 48% enrolled in a transfer program, 52% enrolled in a vocational program, 978 enrolled as first-time, first-year students, 325 transferred in from other institutions.

Part-time:	39%	**Asian American:**	1%
Out-of-state:	1%	**Hispanic American:**	1%
Women:	69%	**25 or older:**	39%
African American:	2%		

Transfer out. Colleges most students transferred to 2005: University of Tennessee-Knoxville, Tennessee Technological University, Middle Tennessee State University, East Tennessee State University.

Basis for selection. Open admission, but selective for some programs. All health science A.A.S. programs require minimum ACT score of 20 and 2.5 GPA for 8 hours general course work. Additional requirements for nursing program: minimum 2.75 GPA for 12 hours general course work and pre-admissions test. Interview required for some health programs; audition required for music program. **Adult students:** SAT/ACT scores not required if applicant over 21. Those who do not submit SAT/ACT scores must undergo placement assessment.

High school preparation. 20 units recommended. Recommended units include English 4, mathematics 3, social studies 1, history 1, science 2 and foreign language 2.

2005-2006 Annual costs. Tuition/fees: $2,387; $8,801 out-of-state. Per-credit charge: $91 in-state; $369 out-of-state. Books/supplies: $1,000.

Financial aid. Need-based: Need-based aid available for part-time students. Work study available nights, weekends and for part-time students. **Non-need-based:** Scholarships awarded for academics, art, athletics, leadership, music/drama, state residency.

Application procedures. Admission: No deadline. $10 fee. Application may be submitted online. Admission notification on a rolling basis. **Financial aid:** Priority date 4/1; no closing date. FAFSA, institutional form required. Applicants notified on a rolling basis starting 5/1.

Academics. Special study options: Accelerated study, cooperative education, distance learning, double major, dual enrollment of high school students, honors, independent study, internships, liberal arts/career combination, teacher certification program, weekend college. License preparation in dental hygiene, nursing, occupational therapy, paramedic, physical therapy, radiology. **Credit/placement by examination:** CLEP, institutional tests. 18 credit hours maximum toward associate degree. **Support services:** GED test center, learning center, remedial instruction, study skills assistance, tutoring, writing center.

Honors college/program. A student may apply to the honors program if: 1) freshman with 3.5 high school GPA or scored 25 or above on ACT, 2) current student with a minimum of 12 college-level credits and a 3.5 college GPA, 3) transfer student who has attained 3.5 GPA with minimum 12 college-level credits from another accredited institution.

Majors. Agriculture: General. **Biology:** General. **Business:** Business admin, management science. **Communications:** General. **Computer sciences:** Computer graphics, computer science. **Conservation:** Fisheries, forestry, wildlife. **Education:** General. **Engineering:** General. **English:** Technical writing. **Family/consumer sciences:** Child development. **Health:** Dental hygiene, environmental health, medical radiologic technology/radiation therapy, medical records technology, nursing (RN), occupational therapy assistant, optician, physical therapy assistant, predentistry, premedicine, prenursing, prepharmacy, preveterinary, respiratory therapy technology. **Legal studies:** Paralegal, prelaw. **Liberal arts:** Arts/sciences. **Math:** General. **Physical sciences:** Chemistry, physics. **Protective services:** Police science. **Psychology:** General. **Public administration:** Community org/advocacy. **Social sciences:** General, cartography, economics, political science, sociology. **Visual/performing arts:** General, art, dramatic.

Most popular majors. Business/marketing 16%, health sciences 33%, liberal arts 36%, science technologies 9%.

Computing on campus. 600 workstations in library, computer center. Commuter students can connect to campus network. Online course registration, helpline available.

Student life. Freshman orientation: Mandatory. Preregistration for classes offered. Two half-day orientations for all first time freshmen. Students attend orientations at their designated home campus on the second half-day. **Activities:** Jazz band, choral groups, dance, drama, music ensembles, student government, student newspaper, Baptist Student Union, Phi Theta Kappa Honor Society, Student Council, Art Major Club, Southwest Field Trip, PSY/SOC Club, Chess Club.

Athletics. NJCAA. **Intercollegiate:** Baseball M, basketball, softball W. **Intramural:** Basketball, football (non-tackle) M, soccer M, softball, volleyball, weight lifting M. **Team name:** Raiders.

Student services. Career counseling, student employment services, financial aid counseling, health services, minority student services, personal counseling, placement for graduates, veterans' counselor. **Physically disabled:** Services for visually, speech, hearing impaired. **Transfer:** Special adviser, orientation for new students. Transfer adviser, college fairs on campus for students transferring to 4-year colleges.

Contact. E-mail: maringegl@roanestate.edu
Phone: (865) 882-4523 Toll-free number: (866) 462-7722 ext. 4523
Fax: (865) 882-4562
Maria Gonzales, Director of Admissions, Roane State Community College, 276 Patton Lane, Harriman, TN 37748

Southwest Tennessee Community College

Memphis, Tennessee
www.southwest.tn.edu **CB code: 0274**

- Public 2-year community and technical college
- Commuter campus in very large city

General. Founded in 1970. Regionally accredited. Accredited associate degrees available for transfer to state universities or for immediate career entry. **Enrollment:** 9,518 degree-seeking undergraduates. **Degrees:** 724 associate awarded. **ROTC:** Army, Air Force. **Calendar:** Semester, extensive summer session. **Full-time faculty:** 262 total. **Part-time faculty:** 300 total. **Class size:** 100% < 20. **Partnerships:** Middle College High School.

Student profile.

Out-of-state:	3%	**25 or older:**	50%

Transfer out. Colleges most students transferred to 2005: University of Memphis, Christian Brothers University.

Basis for selection. Open admission, but selective for some programs. Special requirements for admission to nursing, dietetic technician, laboratory phlebotomy, medical assistant, medical laboratory technician, physical therapist assistant, radiologic technology, paramedic programs. **Adult students:** SAT/ACT scores not required if applicant over 21. ACT COMPASS exam required. **Learning Disabled:** Require documentation of disability to be shown to disability counselor.

High school preparation. 14 units recommended. Recommended units include English 4, mathematics 3, social studies 1, history 1, science 2 (laboratory 1), foreign language 2 and academic electives 1.

2005-2006 Annual costs. Tuition/fees: $2,377; $8,791 out-of-state. Per-credit charge: $91 in-state; $369 out-of-state. Personal expenses: $1,400.

Financial aid. All financial aid based on need. Need-based aid available for part-time students. **Additional information:** State grants available to eligible students who apply by 4/1.

Application procedures. Admission: Priority date 7/1; no deadline. $5 fee. Admission notification on a rolling basis beginning on or about 3/1. **Financial aid:** Priority date 3/15; no closing date. FAFSA required. Applicants notified on a rolling basis starting 6/1; must reply within 4 week(s) of notification.

Academics. Special study options: Cooperative education, distance learning, double major, dual enrollment of high school students, ESL, honors, independent study, internships, liberal arts/career combination, student-designed major, weekend college. On-site extension courses at business, industry and government installations. License preparation in nursing, paramedic, real estate. **Credit/placement by examination:** CLEP, institutional tests. 24 credit hours maximum toward associate degree. **Support services:** GED preparation and test center, learning center, pre-admission summer program, reduced course load, remedial instruction, study skills assistance, tutoring.

Majors. Agriculture: Horticulture. **Business:** General, accounting, administrative services, business admin, finance, management information systems, office technology. **Computer sciences:** General, computer science. **Construction:** Maintenance. **Education:** General, early childhood. **Engineering technology:** Architectural, civil, electrical. **Family/consumer sciences:** Child care, family studies, food/nutrition, institutional food production. **Health:** Clinical lab technology, EMT paramedic, medical radiologic technology/radiation therapy, medical transcription, nursing (RN), physical therapy assistant. **Legal studies:** Court reporting, paralegal. **Liberal arts:** Arts/sciences. **Mechanic/repair:** General, automotive, electronics/electrical, industrial. **Physical sciences:** General. **Protective services:** Firefighting, police science. **Social sciences:** Geography. **Visual/performing arts:** Commercial/advertising art.

Computing on campus. 350 workstations in library, computer center. Commuter students can connect to campus network. Online course registration, helpline available.

Student life. Freshman orientation: Available. Preregistration for classes offered. Freshmen orientation held for 4 hours during 2 months prior to fall registration and again in November. **Policies:** Freshmen permitted cars on campus. **Activities:** Bands, choral groups, drama, music ensembles, student government, student newspaper, NAACP, Baptist Student Union, Human Key Society, National Student Support Council for Africa, Black Student Association, Phi Theta Kappa Honor Society, Police Science Association, science club, Radiologic Technology Student Association, Collegiate Secretaries.

Athletics. NJCAA. **Intercollegiate:** Baseball M, basketball, softball W. **Team name:** Saluqis.

Student services. Adult student services, campus ministries, career counseling, student employment services, financial aid counseling, on-campus daycare, personal counseling, placement for graduates, veterans' counselor. **Physically disabled:** Services for visually, speech, hearing impaired. **Transfer:** Special adviser, orientation, pre-admission transcript evaluation for new students. Transfer center, transfer adviser, college fairs on campus for students transferring to 4-year colleges.

Contact. Phone: (901) 333-4194 Toll-free number: (877) 717-7822
Fax: (901) 333-4473
Kathryn Johnson, Enrollment Management, Southwest Tennessee Community College, PO Box 780, Memphis, TN 38101-0780

Vatterott College: Memphis

Memphis, Tennessee
www.vatterott-college.edu

- For-profit 2-year technical college
- Commuter campus in large city

General. Accredited by ACCSCT. **Enrollment:** 220 degree-seeking undergraduates. **Degrees:** 31 associate awarded. **Calendar:** Continuous.

Basis for selection. Open admission.

Application procedures. Admission: No deadline. No application fee.

Academics. Credit/placement by examination: CLEP.

Computing on campus. 20 workstations in library.

Contact. E-mail: joe.lockwood@vatterott-college.edu
Phone: (901) 761-5730 Fax: (901) 763-2897
Ray Hughes, Director of Admissions, Vatterott College: Memphis, 6152 Macon, Memphis, TN 38134

Volunteer State Community College

Gallatin, Tennessee
www.volstate.edu **CB code: 1881**

- Public 2-year community and junior college
- Commuter campus in small city

General. Founded in 1970. Regionally accredited. **Enrollment:** 5,643 degree-seeking undergraduates; 1,507 non-degree-seeking students. **Degrees:** 570 associate awarded. **Location:** 25 miles from downtown Nashville. **Calendar:** Semester, limited summer session. **Full-time faculty:** 147 total; 14% minority, 52% women. **Part-time faculty:** 247 total; 7% minority, 56% women. **Class size:** 52% < 20, 42% 20-39, 1% 40-49, less than 1% 50-99. **Partnerships:** Formal partnerships with GAP Inc., Peterbilt Motors, Bosch Braking Systems.

Student profile. Among degree-seeking undergraduates, 55% enrolled in a transfer program, 45% enrolled in a vocational program, 1,241 enrolled as first-time, first-year students, 664 transferred in from other institutions.

Part-time:	43%	**Asian American:**	1%
Out-of-state:	1%	**Hispanic American:**	2%
Women:	64%	**25 or older:**	39%
African American:	10%		

Two-Year Colleges

Transfer out. 18% of students enrolled in the transfer program go on to 4-year colleges. **Colleges most students transferred to 2005:** Middle Tennessee State University, Austin Peay State University, Tennessee State University, Tennessee Technical University.

Basis for selection. Open admission, but selective for some programs. Allied health students screened into programs after completing designated amount of college coursework. Screening based on GPA and interview. Test scores where required in selective programs must be received by August 30. Interview required for allied health program. **Adult students:** SAT/ACT scores not required if applicant over 21. Unless exempt by ACT scores, must take COMPASS or ASSET.

High school preparation. 14 units recommended. Recommended units include English 4, mathematics 3, social studies 1, history 1, science 2 and foreign language 2. 1 visual and/or performing arts also required.

2005-2006 Annual costs. Tuition/fees: $2,383; $8,797 out-of-state. Per-credit charge: $91 in-state; $369 out-of-state. Books/supplies: $900. Personal expenses: $400.

2004-2005 Financial aid. Need-based: 66% of total undergraduate aid awarded as scholarships/grants, 34% as loans/jobs. Need-based aid available for part-time students. Work study available for part-time students. **Non-need-based:** Scholarships awarded for academics, art, athletics, leadership, minority status, music/drama, religious affiliation, state residency.

Application procedures. Admission: Priority date 7/31; deadline 8/28 (receipt date). $10 fee. Application may be submitted online. Admission notification on a rolling basis. **Financial aid:** Priority date 4/15; no closing date. FAFSA, institutional form required. Applicants notified on a rolling basis; must reply within 2 week(s) of notification.

Academics. Special study options: Cooperative education, distance learning, double major, dual enrollment of high school students, ESL, honors, independent study. Bachelor's degree programs available on campus. License preparation in dental hygiene, paramedic, physical therapy, radiology, real estate. **Credit/placement by examination:** AP, CLEP, institutional tests. 36 credit hours maximum toward associate degree. Maximum 12 hours of credit by examination in specific allied health programs. **Support services:** GED test center, learning center, pre-admission summer program, reduced course load, remedial instruction, study skills assistance, tutoring, writing center.

Majors. Business: Business admin. **Family/consumer sciences:** Child development. **Health:** Clinical lab technology, medical radiologic technology/radiation therapy, medical records technology, ophthalmic technology, physical therapy assistant, respiratory therapy technology. **Legal studies:** Paralegal. **Liberal arts:** Arts/sciences. **Protective services:** Firefighting. **Public administration:** Community org/advocacy.

Most popular majors. Business/marketing 14%, health sciences 21%, liberal arts 58%.

Computing on campus. 800 workstations in library, computer center. Commuter students can connect to campus network. Online course registration, online library, helpline, wireless network available.

Student life. Freshman orientation: Available. Preregistration for classes offered. **Policies:** Freshmen permitted cars on campus. **Activities:** Choral groups, drama, literary magazine, radio station, student government, student newspaper, Baptist Student Union, African-American Student Union, Gamma Beta Phi, returning women's organization.

Athletics. NJCAA. **Intercollegiate:** Baseball M, basketball, softball W. **Team name:** Pioneers.

Student services. Career counseling, financial aid counseling, health services, personal counseling, placement for graduates, veterans' counselor. **Physically disabled:** Services for visually, speech, hearing impaired. **Transfer:** Special adviser, orientation, pre-admission transcript evaluation for new students. Transfer adviser, college fairs on campus for students transferring to 4-year colleges.

Contact. E-mail: admissions@volstate.edu
Phone: (615) 452-8600 ext. 3688 Toll-free
number: (888) 335-8722 ext. 3688 Fax: (615) 230-4875
Tim Amyx, Director of Admissions, Volunteer State Community College, 1480 Nashville Pike, Gallatin, TN 37066

Walters State Community College

Morristown, Tennessee — **CB member**
www.ws.edu — **CB code: 1893**

- Public 2-year community college
- Commuter campus in small city

General. Founded in 1970. Regionally accredited. Offers degree programs and a variety of courses at sites throughout 10-county service delivery area with facilities located in Greeneville, Sevierville, and Tazewell. Instructional alternatives include interactive television, web-based, and telecourses. **Enrollment:** 4,325 degree-seeking undergraduates; 1,580 non-degree-seeking students. **Degrees:** 569 associate awarded. **ROTC:** Army. **Location:** 45 miles from Knoxville. **Calendar:** Semester, extensive summer session. **Full-time faculty:** 130 total; 21% have terminal degrees, 50% women. **Part-time faculty:** 208 total; 56% women. **Special facilities:** Observatory, center for educational technology and video including television studio, training restaurant, exposition center, industrial technology manufacturing laboratory with complete computer integrated manufacturing (CIM) and Work Center and Coordinate Measuring Machine (MM), public safety training center, early learning center, greenhouse, production horticulture, turf grass management facility.

Student profile. Among degree-seeking undergraduates, 1,045 enrolled as first-time, first-year students, 266 transferred in from other institutions.

Part-time:	35%	**Asian American:**	1%
Out-of-state:	1%	**Hispanic American:**	1%
Women:	65%	**25 or older:**	37%
African American:	4%		

Transfer out. Colleges most students transferred to 2005: University of Tennessee-Knoxville, East Tennessee State University, Carson Newman College.

Basis for selection. Open admission, but selective for some programs. Special requirements for education programs, allied health, public safety. International students must submit application 60 days prior to start of term. Placement test required for applicants with ACT scores below 18. **Adult students:** SAT/ACT scores not required if applicant over 21. Required to take placement assessment prior to enrollment.

High school preparation. College-preparatory program required for 2-year transfer program: 1 unit biological science, 4 English, 2 foreign language, 3 mathematics, 1 physical science, 2 social science, 1 visual or performing arts. Same preparation recommended for all students.

2005-2006 Annual costs. Tuition/fees: $2,381; $8,795 out-of-state. Per-credit charge: $91 in-state; $369 out-of-state. Books/supplies: $750. Personal expenses: $1,050.

2004-2005 Financial aid. Need-based: 649 full-time freshmen applied for aid; 449 were judged to have need; 427 of these received aid. Average need met was 59%. Average scholarship/grant was $2,802; average loan $1,621. 83% of total undergraduate aid awarded as scholarships/grants, 17% as loans/jobs. Need-based aid available for part-time students. **Non-need-based:** Awarded to 553 full-time undergraduates, including 209 freshmen. Scholarships awarded for academics, athletics, music/drama, state residency.

Application procedures. Admission: No deadline. $10 fee. Application may be submitted online. Admission notification on a rolling basis. **Financial aid:** No deadline. FAFSA required. Applicants notified on a rolling basis.

Academics. Special study options: Distance learning, dual enrollment of high school students, ESL, honors, liberal arts/career combination, weekend college. License preparation in nursing, paramedic, physical therapy. **Credit/placement by examination:** AP, CLEP, ACT, institutional tests. 40 credit hours maximum toward associate degree. **Support services:** GED test center, learning center, reduced course load, remedial instruction, study skills assistance, tutoring, writing center.

Majors. Agriculture: Greenhouse operations, ornamental horticulture, turf management. **Area/ethnic studies:** African. **Biology:** General. **Business:** General, accounting, administrative services, office management. **Computer sciences:** General, information systems. **Construction:** Power transmission. **Education:** General, early childhood. **Engineering:** General. **Engineering technology:** Manufacturing. **Family/consumer sciences:** Child care. **Health:** EMT paramedic, medical records technology, medical transcription, nursing (RN), physical therapy assistant, predentistry, premedicine, prepharmacy, preveterinary, respiratory therapy assistant. **Legal studies:** Paralegal. **Liberal arts:** Arts/sciences. **Math:** General. **Parks/recreation:** Health/fitness. **Personal/culinary services:** Culinary arts. **Philosophy/religion:** Philosophy. **Protective services:** Police science. **Psychology:** General. **Visual/performing arts:** Art, dramatic.

Most popular majors. Business/marketing 11%, health sciences 29%, liberal arts 49%.

Computing on campus. 900 workstations in library, computer center. Commuter students can connect to campus network. Online course registration, online library, helpline, wireless network available.

Student life. Freshman orientation: Mandatory. Preregistration for classes offered. **Activities:** Bands, choral groups, dance, drama, literary magazine, music ensembles, student government, student newspaper.

Athletics. NJCAA. **Intercollegiate:** Baseball M, basketball, golf, softball W. **Intramural:** Basketball, softball. **Team name:** Senators.

Student services. Adult student services, alcohol/substance abuse counseling, campus ministries, career counseling, student employment services, financial aid counseling, health services, minority student services, on-campus daycare, personal counseling, placement for graduates, veterans' counselor. **Physically disabled:** Services for visually, speech, hearing impaired. **Transfer:** Special adviser, orientation, re-entry adviser for new students. Transfer center, transfer adviser, college fairs on campus for students transferring to 4-year colleges.

Contact. E-mail: jim.wilder@ws.edu
Phone: (423) 585-0828 Toll-free number: (800) 225-4770
Fax: (423) 585-2631
Mike Campbell, Dean, Walters State Community College, 500 South Davy Crockett Parkway, Morristown, TN 37813-6899

West Tennessee Business College
Jackson, Tennessee
www.wtbc.com

- For-profit 2-year business and health science college
- Commuter campus

General. Accredited by ACICS. **Calendar:** Quarter.

Contact. Phone: (731) 668-7240
Admissions, 1186 Highway 45 Bypass, Jackson, TN 38301

Texas

Alvin Community College

Alvin, Texas
www.alvincollege.edu **CB code: 6005**

- Public 2-year community and liberal arts college
- Residential campus in large town

General. Founded in 1948. Regionally accredited. **Enrollment:** 2,819 degree-seeking undergraduates. **Degrees:** 394 associate awarded. **Location:** 32 miles from Houston. **Calendar:** Semester, extensive summer session. **Full-time faculty:** 94 total. **Part-time faculty:** 160 total. **Special facilities:** Radio station, recording studio, indoor firing range for law enforcement program, Nolan Ryan exhibit.

Transfer out. Colleges most students transferred to 2005: University of Houston-Clear Lake, University of Houston, Texas A&M, Sam Houston State University, Southwest Texas State University.

Basis for selection. Open admission, but selective for some programs. Special requirements for nursing, respiratory therapy, criminal justice, court reporting, musical theater, EMT, diagnostic cardiovascular sonography programs. Texas Academic Skills Program test required by Texas law. Interview required for court reporting, medical laboratory technology, nursing, respiratory therapy programs; audition required for music, musical theater programs. **Adult students:** Entrance exam policies same as for first-time freshmen.

High school preparation. 25 units recommended. Recommended units include English 4, mathematics 4, social studies 4, science 3, foreign language 3 and academic electives 7.

2005-2006 Annual costs. Tuition/fees: $1,146; $1,926 out-of-district; $3,606 out-of-state. Per-credit charge: $28 in-district; $54 out-of-district; $110 out-of-state. Books/supplies: $1,350. Personal expenses: $2,470.

Financial aid. All financial aid based on need. Need-based aid available for part-time students. Work study available nights, weekends and for part-time students.

Application procedures. Admission: No deadline. No application fee. Admission notification on a rolling basis. **Financial aid:** Priority date 6/30; no closing date. FAFSA required. Applicants notified on a rolling basis; must reply within 2 week(s) of notification.

Academics. Special study options: Cooperative education, cross-registration, distance learning, dual enrollment of high school students, ESL, honors, internships, liberal arts/career combination, study abroad. License preparation in nursing, paramedic. **Credit/placement by examination:** CLEP, institutional tests. **Support services:** GED preparation and test center, learning center, reduced course load, remedial instruction, study skills assistance, tutoring, writing center.

Majors. Biology: General. **Business:** General, business admin, executive assistant. **Communications:** Radio/tv. **Computer sciences:** Programming. **Education:** Early childhood, physical. **Engineering technology:** Electrical. **Family/consumer sciences:** Child development. **Health:** Cardiovascular technology, EMT paramedic, mental health services, nursing (RN), respiratory therapy technology. **Legal studies:** Paralegal. **Liberal arts:** Arts/sciences. **Math:** General. **Parks/recreation:** Health/fitness. **Physical sciences:** General. **Protective services:** Corrections, criminal justice. **Science technology:** Chemical. **Visual/performing arts:** Art, dramatic, music performance.

Most popular majors. Business/marketing 10%, health sciences 23%, liberal arts 37%, science technologies 7%.

Computing on campus. 600 workstations in library, computer center. Online course registration, online library available.

Student life. Freshman orientation: Mandatory. Preregistration for classes offered. **Policies:** Freshmen permitted cars on campus. **Housing:** Housing provided for scholarship athletes. **Activities:** Bands, choral groups, drama, literary magazine, music ensembles, musical theater, radio station, student government, student newspaper, TV station, Newman Association, Phi Theta Kappa, Pan American College Forum, Baptist Student Union.

Athletics. NJCAA. **Intercollegiate:** Baseball M, softball W, volleyball W. **Team name:** Dolphins.

Student services. Career counseling, student employment services, financial aid counseling, on-campus daycare, personal counseling, placement for graduates, veterans' counselor. **Physically disabled:** Services for visually, speech, hearing impaired. **Transfer:** Special adviser, orientation for new students. Transfer adviser, college fairs on campus for students transferring to 4-year colleges.

Contact. E-mail: admiss@alvincollege.edu
Phone: (281) 756-3531 Fax: (281) 756-3843
Stephanie Stockstill, Director of Admissions/Academic Advising, Alvin Community College, 3110 Mustang Road, Alvin, TX 77511-4898

Amarillo College

Amarillo, Texas
www.actx.edu **CB code: 6006**

- Public 2-year community college
- Commuter campus in small city

General. Founded in 1929. Regionally accredited. In addition to traditional population pursuing courses for credit, institution serves 12,000 workforce development and leisure studies students. **Enrollment:** 8,240 degree-seeking undergraduates; 2,333 non-degree-seeking students. **Degrees:** 1,269 associate awarded. **Location:** 300 miles from Dallas, 300 miles from Denver. **Calendar:** Semester, extensive summer session. **Full-time faculty:** 220 total. **Part-time faculty:** 185 total. **Class size:** 53% < 20, 38% 20-39, 4% 40-49, 4% 50-99, less than 1% >100. **Special facilities:** Art museum, natural science museum, children's theatre.

Student profile. Among degree-seeking undergraduates, 1,439 enrolled as first-time, first-year students.

Part-time:	61%	**Hispanic American:**	24%
Out-of-state:	1%	**Native American:**	1%
Women:	63%	**25 or older:**	48%
African American:	4%	**Live on campus:**	1%
Asian American:	2%		

Transfer out. Colleges most students transferred to 2005: West Texas A&M University, Texas Tech University.

Basis for selection. Open admission.

High school preparation. 18 units recommended. Recommended units include English 4, mathematics 2, social studies 2, history 2, science 2, foreign language 3 and academic electives 3.

2005-2006 Annual costs. Tuition/fees: $1,175; $1,625 out-of-district; $2,615 out-of-state. Per-credit charge: $39 in-district; $54 out-of-district; $87 out-of-state. Room only: $1,800. Books/supplies: $800. Personal expenses: $1,084.

Financial aid. Non-need-based: Scholarships awarded for academics, state residency.

Application procedures. Admission: Priority date 8/1; no deadline. No application fee. Admission notification on a rolling basis. **Financial aid:** Priority date 6/15; no closing date. FAFSA, institutional form required. Applicants notified on a rolling basis starting 6/15; must reply within 2 week(s) of notification.

Academics. Special study options: Accelerated study, cooperative education, distance learning, dual enrollment of high school students, ESL, honors, internships, weekend college. License preparation in nursing, real estate. **Credit/placement by examination:** CLEP, institutional tests. 15 credit hours maximum toward associate degree. **Support services:** GED preparation and test center, learning center, remedial instruction, study skills assistance, tutoring, writing center.

Majors. Biology: General. **Business:** General, accounting, administrative services, finance, office/clerical, real estate, tourism promotion. **Communications:** General, advertising, broadcast journalism, journalism. **Communications technology:** General. **Computer sciences:** General, computer graphics, information systems, programming. **Construction:** Power transmission. **Education:** General, elementary, music, physical. **Engineering:** General, computer. **Engineering technology:** Drafting, electrical. **English:** Speech/rhetoric. **Family/consumer sciences:** Child care. **Health:** Clinical lab science, clinical lab technology, dental hygiene, EMT paramedic, medical radiologic technology/radiation therapy, medical records technology, nuclear medical technology, nursing (RN), occupational therapy assistant, physical therapy assistant, predentistry, premedicine, prepharmacy, preveterinary, respiratory therapy technology, substance abuse counseling, surgical technology. **Legal studies:** Court reporting, prelaw. **Liberal arts:** Arts/sciences. **Math:** General. **Mechanic/repair:** Aircraft, automotive, electronics/electrical, industrial. **Parks/recreation:** Health/fitness. **Personal/culinary services:** Mortuary science. **Philosophy/religion:** Religion. **Physical sciences:** General, chemistry, geology, physics. **Protective services:** Corrections, fire safety technology, police science. **Psychology:** General. **Public administration:** Social work. **Social sciences:** General. **Visual/performing arts:** Art, commercial photography, commercial/advertising art, design, dramatic, interior design, photography.

Computing on campus. Online course registration, online library, helpline available.

Student life. **Freshman orientation:** Mandatory. **Housing:** Apartments available. **Activities:** Bands, choral groups, dance, drama, literary magazine, music ensembles, musical theater, opera, radio station, student government, student newspaper, TV station.

Athletics. **Intramural:** Basketball, tennis, volleyball.

Student services. Adult student services, career counseling, student employment services, on-campus daycare, personal counseling, placement for graduates, veterans' counselor. **Physically disabled:** Services for visually, speech, hearing impaired. **Transfer:** Transfer adviser, college fairs on campus for students transferring to 4-year colleges.

Contact. Phone: (806) 371-5030 Fax: (806) 371-5066
Diane Brice, Registrar and Director of Admissions, Amarillo College, Box 447, Amarillo, TX 79178

Angelina College
Lufkin, Texas
www.angelina.edu **CB code: 6025**

- Public 2-year community college
- Commuter campus in large town

General. Founded in 1966. Regionally accredited. Teaching centers located in 5 contiguous counties. Branch campus located in Jasper. **Enrollment:** 4,778 degree-seeking undergraduates; 10 non-degree-seeking students. **Degrees:** 331 associate awarded. **ROTC:** Army. **Location:** 125 miles from Houston. **Calendar:** Semester, extensive summer session. **Full-time faculty:** 87 total; 10% have terminal degrees, 21% minority, 59% women. **Part-time faculty:** 223 total; 12% have terminal degrees, 2% minority, 60% women. **Class size:** 65% < 20, 34% 20-39, 1% 40-49, less than 1% 50-99. **Special facilities:** Computer-aided design laboratory, environmental trail, performing arts center.

Student profile. Among degree-seeking undergraduates, 5% enrolled in a transfer program, 20% enrolled in a vocational program, 1% already have a bachelor's degree or higher, 805 enrolled as first-time, first-year students, 625 transferred in from other institutions.

Part-time:	52%	**Asian American:**	1%
Out-of-state:	1%	**Hispanic American:**	10%
Women:	63%	**25 or older:**	33%
African American:	14%	**Live on campus:**	2%

Transfer out. **Colleges most students transferred to 2005:** Stephen F. Austin State University, Sam Houston State University.

Basis for selection. Open admission, but selective for some programs. Special requirements for nursing, respiratory care, EMS, pharmacy, and radiologic technology programs; interview required. General Aptitude Test Battery required of nursing applicants. All students must take Texas Higher Education Assessment Test or ACCUPLACER before enrolling in 2-year degree program. Physical education requirements waived for veterans, adults 25 and over, and some part-time students. TASP testing used for placement; remediation may be required if applicant score falls below college level standard. **Adult students:** Entrance exam policies same as for first-time freshmen. **Homeschooled:** Transcript of courses and grades required. **Learning Disabled:** May have to take different test based on disability.

2005-2006 Annual costs. Tuition/fees: $1,050; $1,560 out-of-district; $2,160 out-of-state. Per-credit charge: $28 in-district; $45 out-of-district; $65 out-of-state. Students taking 1-3 credits pay higher per-credit-hour charge. Room/board: $4,250. Books/supplies: $1,200. Personal expenses: $1,760.

2004-2005 Financial aid. All financial aid based on need. 749 full-time freshmen applied for aid; 703 were judged to have need; 681 of these received aid. 97% of total undergraduate aid awarded as scholarships/grants, 3% as loans/jobs. Need-based aid available for part-time students. Work study available nights and for part-time students.

Application procedures. **Admission:** Priority date 7/1; no deadline. No application fee. Application may be submitted online. Admission notification on a rolling basis beginning on or about 8/1. **Financial aid:** Priority date 7/15; no closing date. FAFSA, institutional form required. Applicants notified on a rolling basis starting 7/15.

Academics. **Special study options:** Accelerated study, cooperative education, distance learning, dual enrollment of high school students, internships, liberal arts/career combination. **Credit/placement by examination:** AP, CLEP, institutional tests. 15 credit hours maximum toward associate degree. **Support services:** Learning center, reduced course load, remedial instruction, study skills assistance, tutoring.

Majors. **Biology:** General. **Business:** General, accounting, administrative services, business admin. **Communications:** General. **Computer sciences:** General, data processing. **Education:** General, health. **Engineering:** General. **Engineering technology:** Drafting, electrical, electromechanical, environmental. **Family/consumer sciences:** Child development. **Health:** Clinical lab technology, EMT paramedic, nursing (RN), predentistry, premedicine, prepharmacy, preveterinary, radiologic technology/medical imaging, respiratory therapy technology, substance abuse counseling. **Interdisciplinary:** Science/society. **Legal studies:** Paralegal, prelaw. **Math:** General. **Physical sciences:** Physics. **Production:** Machine tool, welding. **Protective services:** Criminal justice. **Public administration:** Human services, social work. **Visual/performing arts:** Art, design, dramatic, music management, piano/organ, voice/opera.

Most popular majors. Business/marketing 10%, engineering/engineering technologies 7%, health sciences 35%, liberal arts 8%, public administration/social services 9%.

Computing on campus. 200 workstations in library, computer center. Online course registration available.

Student life. **Freshman orientation:** Mandatory. Preregistration for classes offered. **Policies:** Freshmen permitted cars on campus. **Housing:** Coed dorms, substance-free housing available. $100 fully refundable deposit, deadline 7/15. Apartments for single mothers. **Activities:** Concert band, choral groups, dance, drama, music ensembles, musical theater, student government, student newspaper, Baptist Student Union.

Athletics. NJCAA. **Intercollegiate:** Baseball M, basketball. **Intramural:** Golf, softball, swimming M, volleyball. **Team name:** Roadrunners.

Student services. Adult student services, career counseling, services for economically disadvantaged, student employment services, financial aid counseling, health services, personal counseling, placement for graduates, veterans' counselor. **Physically disabled:** Services for visually, speech, hearing impaired. **Transfer:** Special adviser, orientation, pre-admission transcript evaluation for new students. Transfer adviser, college fairs on campus for students transferring to 4-year colleges.

Contact. E-mail: registrar@angelina.edu
Phone: (936) 639-5212 Fax: (936) 633-5455
Craig Lee, Director of Enrollment Services, Angelina College, PO Box 1768, Lufkin, TX 75902-1768

ATI Career Training Center
Dallas, Texas
http://ati.edu-search.com/

- For-profit 2-year technical college
- Very large city
- Interview required

General. Accredited by ACCSCT. **Enrollment:** 820 full-time, degree-seeking students. **Degrees:** 49 associate awarded. **Calendar:** Semester, extensive summer session. **Full-time faculty:** 40 total. **Part-time faculty:** 20 total. **Class size:** 100% 20-39.

Basis for selection. Students must score 18 minimum on the Wonderlic Test. **Adult students:** Entrance exam policies same as for first-time freshmen.

2005-2006 Annual costs. One-time comprehensive rate per program ranging from $3,715 for 12-month massage therapy program to $31,243 for 2-year respiratory therapy technician program.

Financial aid. All financial aid based on need. **Additional information:** Limited work-study positions available during school hours.

Application procedures. **Admission:** No deadline. $100 fee. Admission notification on a rolling basis. **Financial aid:** FAFSA, institutional form required.

Academics. **Credit/placement by examination:** CLEP. **Support services:** Tutoring.

Majors. **Health:** Respiratory therapy technology.

Computing on campus. 3 workstations in library.

Student life. **Freshman orientation:** Mandatory.

Student services. Financial aid counseling, personal counseling.

Contact. Phone: (214) 902-8191
Steven Brewster, Director of Admissions, ATI Career Training Center, 10003 Technology Boulevard, West, Dallas, TX 75220

Austin Business College

Austin, Texas
www.abctx.edu
CB code: 3230

- For-profit 2-year business and technical college
- Very large city

General. Accredited by ACICS. **Enrollment:** 345 degree-seeking undergraduates. **Degrees:** 25 associate awarded. **Calendar:** Continuous. **Full-time faculty:** 35 total.

Basis for selection. Admission based on high school diploma or GED plus results of Wonderlic Scholastic Level Exam form TSI3T71 used as entrance exam.

2005-2006 Annual costs. Tuition for certificate programs range from $8,015 - $11,476. Tuition for associate degree programs range from $21,008 - $23,292. Books/supplies: $913.

Application procedures. **Admission:** No deadline. No application fee. Admission notification on a rolling basis.

Academics. **Credit/placement by examination:** CLEP.

Majors. **Business:** Business admin.

Contact. E-mail: admissions@mail.abctx.edu
Phone: (512) 447-9415 Fax: (512) 447-0194
Pam Briggs, Director of Admissions, Austin Business College, 2101 IH 35 South, Third Floor, Austin, TX 78741

Austin Community College

Austin, Texas
www.austincc.edu
CB member
CB code: 6759

- Public 2-year community college
- Commuter campus in very large city

General. Founded in 1972. Regionally accredited. 7 campuses serving greater Austin, 9 instructional centers in surrounding towns. **Enrollment:** 31,908 degree-seeking undergraduates. **Degrees:** 906 associate awarded. **ROTC:** Army, Air Force. **Location:** 85 miles from San Antonio. **Calendar:** Semester, extensive summer session. **Full-time faculty:** 444 total; 21% minority, 55% women. **Part-time faculty:** 1,157 total; 18% minority, 44% women. **Class size:** 45% < 20, 55% 20-39, less than 1% 40-49. **Special facilities:** Water-quality monitoring well. **Partnerships:** Formal partnerships with Sustainability Project, Semiconductor Manufacturing Program, Seton Health.

Student profile. Among degree-seeking undergraduates, 74% enrolled in a transfer program, 26% enrolled in a vocational program, 4,986 enrolled as first-time, first-year students.

Part-time:	72%	**Hispanic American:**	23%
Out-of-state:	3%	**Native American:**	1%
Women:	57%	**International:**	2%
African American:	7%	**25 or older:**	39%
Asian American:	5%		

Transfer out. **Colleges most students transferred to 2005:** University of Texas at Austin, Texas State University.

Basis for selection. Open admission, but selective for some programs. Special requirements for health sciences programs. Students may submit SAT or ACT test scores for exemption from Texas Academic Skills Program (TASP) requirements. **Adult students:** SAT/ACT scores not required. Texas Success Initiative test may be required.

2005-2006 Annual costs. Tuition/fees: $1,590; $3,480 out-of-district; $6,090 out-of-state. Per-credit charge: $39 in-district; $102 out-of-district; $189 out-of-state. Books/supplies: $750. Personal expenses: $1,310.

2004-2005 Financial aid. **Need-based:** 627 full-time freshmen applied for aid; 462 were judged to have need; 392 of these received aid. 68% of total undergraduate aid awarded as scholarships/grants, 32% as loans/jobs. Need-based aid available for part-time students.

Application procedures. **Admission:** No deadline. No application fee. Application may be submitted online. No notification. Applications accepted at all times for any future semester enrollment. **Financial aid:** Closing date 4/1. FAFSA, institutional form required. Applicants notified on a rolling basis starting 6/1; must reply within 2 week(s) of notification.

Academics. **Special study options:** Accelerated study, distance learning, dual enrollment of high school students, ESL, honors, independent study, internships, study abroad, teacher certification program, weekend college. License preparation in dental hygiene, nursing, occupational therapy, paramedic, physical therapy, radiology, real estate. **Credit/placement by examination:** CLEP, institutional tests. 30 credit hours maximum toward associate degree. **Support services:** GED preparation and test center, learning center, reduced course load, remedial instruction, study skills assistance, tutoring.

Majors. **Biology:** General. **Business:** General, accounting, administrative services, business admin, fashion, hospitality admin, marketing, real estate, tourism/travel. **Communications:** Broadcast journalism, journalism. **Computer sciences:** General, computer science, networking, programming. **Education:** Health. **Engineering:** General. **Engineering technology:** Drafting, electrical, environmental, heat/ac/refrig, surveying. **English:** Creative writing, speech/rhetoric, technical writing. **Family/consumer sciences:** Child care. **Foreign languages:** French, German, Japanese, Latin, Russian, sign language interpretation, Spanish. **Health:** Clinical lab assistant, clinical lab technology, EMT paramedic, medical radiologic technology/radiation therapy, medical secretary, occupational therapy assistant, physical therapy assistant, predentistry, premedicine, prepharmacy, preveterinary, recreational therapy, sonography, substance abuse counseling, surgical technology. **History:** General. **Legal studies:** Legal secretary, paralegal. **Liberal arts:** Arts/sciences. **Math:** General. **Mechanic/repair:** Automotive. **Parks/recreation:** Health/fitness. **Personal/culinary services:** Chef training. **Physical sciences:** Astronomy, chemistry, geology, physics. **Protective services:** Firefighting, police science. **Psychology:** General. **Public administration:** Human services, social work. **Science technology:** Biological. **Social sciences:** Anthropology, economics, geography, political science, sociology. **Visual/performing arts:** Art, commercial photography, commercial/advertising art, dance, dramatic, photography.

Most popular majors. Business/marketing 16%, engineering/engineering technologies 8%, health sciences 28%, security/protective services 6%, visual/performing arts 9%.

Computing on campus. 307 workstations in library, computer center. Commuter students can connect to campus network. Online course registration, online library, helpline available.

Student life. **Freshman orientation:** Mandatory. Preregistration for classes offered. **Policies:** No alcohol, no drugs, no hazing. Freshmen permitted cars on campus. **Activities:** Jazz band, dance, drama, literary magazine, music ensembles, student government, student newspaper, Phi Theta Kappa, Hispanic student association, Biomass, Peer Players, Austin Society for Semi-Conductor Electronics Technicians, Campus Crusade for Christ, Toastmasters, American Drafting Design Association, associate degree student nursing association, black student alliance.

Student services. Alcohol/substance abuse counseling, career counseling, services for economically disadvantaged, student employment services, financial aid counseling, minority student services, on-campus daycare, placement for graduates, veterans' counselor. **Physically disabled:** Services for visually, speech, hearing impaired. **Transfer:** Special adviser, orientation for new students. Transfer center, transfer adviser, college fairs on campus for students transferring to 4-year colleges.

Contact. E-mail: admission@austincc.edu
Phone: (512) 223-7001 Fax: (512) 223-7665
Linda Kluck, Director of Admissions and Records, Austin Community College, 5930 Middle Fiskville Road, Austin, TX 78752-4390

Blinn College

Brenham, Texas
www.blinn.edu
CB code: 6043

- Public 2-year junior college
- Commuter campus in large town

General. Founded in 1883. Regionally accredited. **Enrollment:** 7,085 full-time, degree-seeking students. **Degrees:** 692 associate awarded. **Location:** 79 miles from Houston, 90 miles from Austin. **Calendar:** Semester, limited summer session. **Full-time faculty:** 275 total. **Part-time faculty:** 250 total. **Special facilities:** Museum, creameries.

Student profile.

Out-of-state:	1%	**Live on campus:**	10%
25 or older:	20%		

Transfer out. Colleges most students transferred to 2005: Texas A&M -College Station, Sam Houston State University, Southwest Texas State University, University of Texas at Austin, University of Houston.

Basis for selection. Open admission, but selective for some programs. Special requirements for registered nursing program, dental hygiene, physical therapy, various other allied health and some technology-based programs. TASP test required for all as per Texas state law.

2005-2006 Annual costs. Tuition/fees: $1,680; $2,460 out-of-district; $4,890 out-of-state. Per-credit charge: $28 in-district; $54 out-of-district; $135 out-of-state. Room/board: $3,800. Books/supplies: $720. Personal expenses: $1,094.

Financial aid. Need-based: Need-based aid available for part-time students.

Application procedures. Admission: No deadline. No application fee. Admission notification on a rolling basis beginning on or about 5/30. **Financial aid:** Priority date 6/1; no closing date. FAFSA, institutional form required. Applicants notified on a rolling basis starting 7/1.

Academics. Special study options: Cross-registration, distance learning, dual enrollment of high school students, ESL, liberal arts/career combination, teacher certification program. License preparation in dental hygiene, nursing, paramedic, physical therapy, radiology, real estate. **Credit/placement by examination:** CLEP, institutional tests. 12 credit hours maximum toward associate degree. TASP (Texas Academic Skills Placement) test used for placement; students submitting sufficient score on SAT or ACT exempt. (Education students must take TASP). **Support services:** GED test center, learning center, reduced course load, remedial instruction, tutoring.

Majors. Biology: General. **Business:** General, accounting, office/clerical. **Communications:** General. **Computer sciences:** General. **English:** Speech/rhetoric. **Family/consumer sciences:** Child care. **Foreign languages:** General, French, German, sign language interpretation, Spanish. **Health:** Dental hygiene, medical radiologic technology/radiation therapy, mental health services, nursing (RN). **History:** General. **Legal studies:** Paralegal. **Liberal arts:** Arts/sciences. **Math:** General. **Parks/recreation:** Exercise sciences. **Philosophy/religion:** Philosophy. **Physical sciences:** Chemistry, physics. **Protective services:** Criminal justice, firefighting. **Psychology:** General.

Most popular majors. Biological/life sciences 9%, business/marketing 18%, computer/information sciences 8%, English 9%, health sciences 18%, liberal arts 23%.

Computing on campus. 500 workstations in library, computer center. Online course registration available.

Student life. Freshman orientation: Available. Held 3-4 times during summer, parents welcome. **Housing:** Single-sex dorms, special housing for disabled, apartments available. $200 deposit. **Activities:** Bands, choral groups, dance, drama, music ensembles, musical theater, student government, student newspaper, Baptist Student Ministries, Circle K International, Phi Theta Kappa, Fellowship of Christian Athletes, College Republicans, Young Democrats.

Athletics. NJCAA. **Intercollegiate:** Baseball M, basketball, football (tackle) M, softball W, volleyball W. **Intramural:** Basketball, softball, volleyball. **Team name:** Buccaneer.

Student services. Career counseling, personal counseling, veterans' counselor. **Physically disabled:** Services for visually, speech, hearing impaired. **Transfer:** Special adviser, orientation for new students. Transfer adviser, college fairs on campus for students transferring to 4-year colleges.

Contact. E-mail: recruit@blinn.edu
Phone: (979) 830-4140 Fax: (979) 830-4009
Dennis Crowson, Registrar, Blinn College, 902 College Avenue, Brenham, TX 77833

Brazosport College
Lake Jackson, Texas
www.brazosport.edu **CB code: 6054**

- Public 2-year community college
- Commuter campus in large town

General. Founded in 1948. Regionally accredited. **Enrollment:** 3,607 degree-seeking undergraduates. **Degrees:** 172 associate awarded. **Location:** 50 miles from Houston. **Calendar:** Semester, extensive summer session. **Full-time faculty:** 70 total. **Part-time faculty:** 130 total. **Class size:** 49% < 20, 50% 20-39, 1% 40-49. **Special facilities:** Chemical unit operations laboratory, music performance hall.

Student profile.

Out-of-state:	1%	**25 or older:**	32%

Transfer out. 25% of students enrolled in the transfer program go on to 4-year colleges. **Colleges most students transferred to 2005:** University of Houston, Sam Houston State University, Texas A&M University, Stephen F. Austin State University, University of Texas.

Basis for selection. Open admission, but selective for some programs. Special requirements for nursing programs and Bachelor of Applied Technology program. **Adult students:** Entrance exam policies same as for first-time freshmen.

2005-2006 Annual costs. Tuition/fees: $1,140; $1,770 out-of-district; $3,180 out-of-state. Per-credit charge: $28 in-district; $49 out-of-district; $96 out-of-state. Books/supplies: $702. Personal expenses: $1,070.

2004-2005 Financial aid. Need-based: 95% of total undergraduate aid awarded as scholarships/grants, 5% as loans/jobs. Need-based aid available for part-time students. Work study available for part-time students. **Non-need-based:** Scholarships awarded for academics, art, job skills, leadership, music/drama, state residency.

Application procedures. Admission: No deadline. No application fee. Admission notification on a rolling basis. **Financial aid:** Priority date 7/1; no closing date. FAFSA, institutional form required. Applicants notified on a rolling basis starting 5/1.

Academics. Special study options: Cooperative education, distance learning, dual enrollment of high school students, ESL, honors, internships. Bachelor's degree programs available on campus. License preparation in nursing, paramedic. **Credit/placement by examination:** CLEP, institutional tests. 24 credit hours maximum toward associate degree. Minimum of 6 semester credit hours must be earned in residence before credit posted on transcript. **Support services:** GED preparation and test center, learning center, remedial instruction, study skills assistance, tutoring.

Majors. Agriculture: General. **Biology:** General. **Business:** General, accounting, administrative services, business admin, finance, purchasing. **Communications:** General. **Computer sciences:** General, programming. **Construction:** Electrician, pipefitting. **Education:** General, elementary, health, secondary. **Engineering:** General. **Engineering technology:** Construction, drafting, electrical. **English:** Speech/rhetoric. **Family/consumer sciences:** General, child care. **Foreign languages:** General. **Health:** Nursing (RN). **History:** General. **Legal studies:** General, paralegal. **Liberal arts:** Arts/sciences, library science. **Math:** General. **Mechanic/repair:** Automotive, heating/ac/refrig. **Physical sciences:** General, chemistry, physics, planetary. **Protective services:** Police science. **Psychology:** General. **Public administration:** General. **Social sciences:** Economics, political science, sociology. **Theology:** Theology. **Visual/performing arts:** Art, dramatic.

Computing on campus. 40 workstations in library, computer center. Online course registration, wireless network available.

Student life. Freshman orientation: Mandatory. Preregistration for classes offered. Half-hour video presentation. **Activities:** Bands, choral groups, drama, music ensembles, student government, student newspaper, Baptist student ministry, Phi Theta Kappa.

Athletics. Intramural: Archery, basketball, bowling, fencing, football (non-tackle), golf, soccer, softball, table tennis, tennis, volleyball.

Student services. Career counseling, student employment services, financial aid counseling, on-campus daycare, personal counseling, placement for graduates, veterans' counselor. **Physically disabled:** Services for visually impaired. **Transfer:** Special adviser for new students. Transfer adviser, college fairs on campus for students transferring to 4-year colleges.

Contact. E-mail: regist@brazosport.edu
Phone: (979) 230-3216 Fax: (979) 230-3376
Patricia Leyendecker, Director of Admissions and Registrar, Brazosport College, 500 College Drive, Lake Jackson, TX 77566

Brookhaven College

Farmers Branch, Texas **CB member**
www.brookhavencollege.edu **CB code: 6070**

- Public 2-year community college
- Commuter campus in large town

General. Founded in 1965. Regionally accredited. **Enrollment:** 3,135 full-time, degree-seeking students. **Degrees:** 333 associate awarded. **Location:** 12 miles from downtown Dallas. **Calendar:** Semester, limited summer session. **Full-time faculty:** 110 total. **Part-time faculty:** 400 total.

Basis for selection. Open admission. Observes TASP guidelines. **Adult students:** Entrance exam policies same as for first-time freshmen.

2005-2006 Annual costs. Tuition/fees: $990; $1,800 out-of-district; $2,880 out-of-state. Per-credit charge: $33 in-district; $60 out-of-district; $96 out-of-state. Books/supplies: $800. Personal expenses: $920.

Financial aid. Additional information: Some tuition waivers available based upon state residency.

Application procedures. Admission: No deadline. No application fee. Application may be submitted online. Admission notification on a rolling basis. **Financial aid:** Priority date 6/1; no closing date. FAFSA required. Applicants notified on a rolling basis.

Academics. Special study options: Cooperative education, distance learning, dual enrollment of high school students, ESL, honors, internships, study abroad, weekend college. License preparation in nursing, paramedic, radiology, real estate. **Credit/placement by examination:** CLEP. At least 25% of credit hours required for graduation must be taken by instruction and not by credit-by-exam. **Support services:** GED preparation, remedial instruction, study skills assistance, tutoring, writing center.

Majors. Business: Accounting, business admin, entrepreneurial studies, fashion, management information systems, marketing, office management, office technology. **Computer sciences:** Information systems, programming. **Education:** Early childhood. **Engineering technology:** Electrical. **Legal studies:** Legal secretary. **Transportation:** General. **Visual/performing arts:** Commercial/advertising art.

Computing on campus. Helpline available.

Student life. Activities: Choral groups, drama, film society, music ensembles, musical theater, student newspaper.

Athletics. NJCAA. **Intercollegiate:** Baseball M, golf M, soccer M, tennis. **Intramural:** Soccer. **Team name:** Bears.

Student services. Adult student services, career counseling, student employment services, health services, personal counseling, placement for graduates, veterans' counselor. **Physically disabled:** Services for visually, speech impaired. **Transfer:** College fairs on campus for students transferring to 4-year colleges.

Contact. E-mail: bhcAdmissions@dcccd.edu
Phone: (972) 860-4883 Fax: (972) 860-4886
Thoa Vo, Director of Admissions, Brookhaven College, 3939 Valley View Lane, Farmers Branch, TX 75244-4997

Cedar Valley College

Lancaster, Texas
www.cedarvalleycollege.edu **CB code: 6148**

- Public 2-year community college
- Commuter campus in large town

General. Founded in 1974. Regionally accredited. **Enrollment:** 3,331 degree-seeking undergraduates; 959 non-degree-seeking students. **Degrees:** 231 associate awarded. **ROTC:** Army. **Location:** 10 miles from Dallas. **Calendar:** Semester, limited summer session. **Full-time faculty:** 67 total; 24% minority. **Part-time faculty:** 145 total. **Special facilities:** Veterinary technology facilities, commercial music facilities including recording studios. **Partnerships:** Formal partnerships with Vartec, Owens Corning, University of North Texas, Upward Bound.

Student profile. Among degree-seeking undergraduates, 2% already have a bachelor's degree or higher, 547 enrolled as first-time, first-year students.

Part-time:	65%	**Asian American:**	1%
Women:	64%	**Hispanic American:**	12%
African American:	55%	**25 or older:**	45%

Transfer out. 20% of students enrolled in the transfer program go on to 4-year colleges. **Colleges most students transferred to 2005:** University of Texas at Arlington, Texas A&M at Commerce, University of North Texas.

Basis for selection. Open admission. Student must be graduate of accredited high school, or at least 18 years of age, or be admitted by individual approval. **Adult students:** Entrance exam policies same as for first-time freshmen.

2005-2006 Annual costs. Tuition/fees: $990; $1,800 out-of-district; $2,880 out-of-state. Per-credit charge: $33 in-district; $60 out-of-district; $96 out-of-state. Books/supplies: $800. Personal expenses: $1,045.

Application procedures. Admission: No deadline. No application fee. Admission notification on a rolling basis. **Financial aid:** Priority date 5/1; no closing date. FAFSA required. Applicants notified on a rolling basis.

Academics. Special study options: Cooperative education, distance learning, dual enrollment of high school students, liberal arts/career combination, student-designed major, study abroad. License preparation in real estate. **Credit/placement by examination:** CLEP, institutional tests. 45 credit hours maximum toward associate degree. **Support services:** GED preparation, learning center, reduced course load, remedial instruction, study skills assistance, tutoring, writing center.

Majors. Business: Accounting/business management, administrative services, business admin, management information systems, marketing, office management, office technology, real estate. **Communications technology:** Recording arts. **Computer sciences:** Data processing, networking, programming. **Health:** Veterinary technology/assistant. **Mechanic/repair:** Heating/ac/refrig. **Protective services:** Law enforcement admin. **Visual/performing arts:** Design, music performance.

Computing on campus. 400 workstations in library, computer center, student center. Online course registration, helpline, repair service available.

Student life. Freshman orientation: Mandatory. 1-day program includes assessment testing. **Policies:** Freshmen permitted cars on campus. **Activities:** Jazz band, choral groups, drama, music ensembles, musical theater, student government, student newspaper, student government, Sierra club, Christian Student Union, Latin American student organization, Phi Theta Kappa, student ambassadors, preprofessional club, art club, veterinary technology club.

Athletics. NJCAA. **Intercollegiate:** Baseball M, basketball M. **Intramural:** Cheerleading W, football (non-tackle) M, golf, soccer W, volleyball W.

Student services. Career counseling, services for economically disadvantaged, student employment services, financial aid counseling, health services, personal counseling, placement for graduates, veterans' counselor. **Physically disabled:** Services for visually, speech, hearing impaired. **Transfer:** Pre-admission transcript evaluation for new students.

Contact. E-mail: cdw3310@dcccd.edu
Phone: (972) 860-8201 Fax: (972) 860-8001
Carolyn Boswell-Ward, Director of Admissions and Registrar, Cedar Valley College, 3030 North Dallas Avenue, Lancaster, TX 75134

Central Texas College

Killeen, Texas
www.ctcd.edu **CB code: 6130**

- Public 2-year community and technical college
- Commuter campus in small city

General. Founded in 1965. Regionally accredited. **Enrollment:** 12,781 degree-seeking undergraduates; 5,570 non-degree-seeking students. **Degrees:** 772 associate awarded. **ROTC:** Army. **Location:** 5 miles from downtown. **Calendar:** Semester, extensive summer session. **Full-time faculty:** 148 total. **Part-time faculty:** 225 total. **Partnerships:** Formal partnerships with Killeen and Copperas Cove ISDs (school to career facilitator program).

Student profile. Among degree-seeking undergraduates, 3,791 enrolled as first-time, first-year students.

Part-time:	88%	**25 or older:**	50%
Out-of-state:	3%	**Live on campus:**	2%
Women:	38%		

Transfer out. Colleges most students transferred to 2005: Mary-Hardin Baylor University, Tarleton State University, Texas A&M University, Southwest Texas State University, University of Texas.

Basis for selection. Open admission, but selective for some programs. Special requirements for registered nursing, paramedic, EMT programs; entrance test required. Observes TASP requirements. Interview required for medical laboratory technician, nursing programs; audition recommended for music; portfolio recommended for art.

High school preparation. 22 units recommended. Recommended units include English 4, mathematics 3, social studies 3, science 2 and foreign language 1.

2005-2006 Annual costs. Tuition/fees: $1,200; $1,410 out-of-district; $4,140 out-of-state. Per-credit charge: $32 in-district; $39 out-of-district; $130 out-of-state. Room/board: $3,140. Books/supplies: $1,140. Personal expenses: $1,200.

2004-2005 Financial aid. All financial aid based on need. 86% of total undergraduate aid awarded as scholarships/grants, 14% as loans/jobs. Need-based aid available for part-time students. Work study available nights, weekends and for part-time students.

Application procedures. Admission: No deadline. No application fee. Application must be submitted on paper. Admission notification on a rolling basis. $400 deposit required of international students, refundable if student does not enroll. **Financial aid:** Closing date 7/1. FAFSA, institutional form required. Applicants notified on a rolling basis starting 3/1; must reply within 4 week(s) of notification.

Academics. Special study options: Cross-registration, distance learning, dual enrollment of high school students, ESL, independent study, internships, liberal arts/career combination. License preparation in aviation, nursing, paramedic, real estate. **Credit/placement by examination:** AP, CLEP, institutional tests. 45 credit hours maximum toward associate degree. All incoming freshmen must take placement examination. **Support services:** GED preparation and test center, learning center, reduced course load, remedial instruction, study skills assistance, tutoring.

Majors. Agriculture: Farm/ranch. **Biology:** General. **Business:** General, administrative services, business admin, hospitality admin, office management, real estate, tourism promotion. **Communications:** Broadcast journalism. **Communications technology:** Graphic/printing. **Computer sciences:** General, computer science, data processing, information systems, networking, programming. **Education:** General. **Engineering:** General. **Engineering technology:** Drafting. **Family/consumer sciences:** Child care. **Foreign languages:** General. **Health:** Clinical lab assistant, clinical lab technology, nursing (RN), premedicine, substance abuse counseling. **Interdisciplinary:** Biological/physical sciences. **Legal studies:** General, paralegal, prelaw. **Liberal arts:** Arts/sciences. **Math:** General. **Mechanic/repair:** General, auto body, automotive, diesel, electronics/electrical, heating/ac/refrig. **Personal/culinary services:** Culinary arts. **Physical sciences:** Chemistry, geology, physics. **Protective services:** Law enforcement admin. **Social sciences:** General. **Visual/performing arts:** Art.

Computing on campus. 530 workstations in library, computer center. Commuter students can connect to campus network. Online library, helpline available.

Student life. Freshman orientation: Available. Preregistration for classes offered. **Policies:** Freshmen permitted cars on campus. **Housing:** Coed dorms, apartments available. $100 deposit, deadline 8/1. **Activities:** Choral groups, drama, radio station, student government, student newspaper, TV station, Baptist Student Union, ethnic clubs.

Athletics. Intramural: Badminton, baseball M, basketball, bowling, football (non-tackle), golf, soccer, softball, swimming, table tennis, tennis, volleyball.

Student services. Adult student services, alcohol/substance abuse counseling, career counseling, services for economically disadvantaged, student employment services, financial aid counseling, on-campus daycare, personal counseling, placement for graduates, veterans' counselor, women's services. **Physically disabled:** Services for visually, speech, hearing impaired. **Transfer:** Special adviser, orientation for new students. Transfer adviser, college fairs on campus for students transferring to 4-year colleges.

Contact. E-mail: David.McClure@ctcd.edu
Phone: (254) 526-1104 Toll-free number: (800) 792-3348 ext. 1104
Fax: (254) 526-0817
Cindy Kendall, Director of Admissions & Registration, Central Texas College, Box 1800, Killeen, TX 76540

Cisco Junior College

Cisco, Texas
www.cisco.cc.tx.us **CB code: 6096**

- Public 2-year junior college
- Commuter campus in small town

General. Founded in 1940. Regionally accredited. **Enrollment:** 3,575 degree-seeking undergraduates. **Degrees:** 190 associate awarded. **Location:** 100 miles from Fort Worth. **Calendar:** Semester, limited summer session. **Full-time faculty:** 98 total. **Part-time faculty:** 96 total.

Student profile.

Out-of-state:	8%	**Live on campus:**	28%
25 or older:	90%		

Basis for selection. Open admission.

2005-2006 Annual costs. Tuition/fees: $1,930; $2,172 out-of-district; $2,478 out-of-state. Room/board: $2,900. Books/supplies: $800. Personal expenses: $1,986.

Application procedures. Admission: No deadline. No application fee. Admission notification on a rolling basis. **Financial aid:** Priority date 8/15; no closing date. FAFSA required. Applicants notified on a rolling basis starting 8/15.

Academics. Special study options: Dual enrollment of high school students. **Credit/placement by examination:** CLEP. 22 credit hours maximum toward associate degree. **Support services:** GED test center, remedial instruction, tutoring.

Majors. Agriculture: Animal sciences, business. **Biology:** General. **Business:** General, accounting. **Communications:** General. **Computer sciences:** General. **Education:** General. **Engineering:** General. **Engineering technology:** Drafting. **Foreign languages:** Comparative lit, French, Spanish. **Health:** Medical records technology. **History:** General. **Legal studies:** Prelaw. **Math:** General. **Mechanic/repair:** General. **Physical sciences:** Chemistry. **Psychology:** General. **Public administration:** Social work. **Social sciences:** General, economics, sociology. **Visual/performing arts:** Art, dramatic.

Student life. Housing: Single-sex dorms available. **Activities:** Bands, choral groups, drama, music ensembles, student government, student newspaper.

Athletics. Intercollegiate: Baseball W, basketball, football (tackle) M, golf, rodeo, soccer W, volleyball W. **Intramural:** Basketball, track and field. **Team name:** Wranglers.

Student services. Health services, personal counseling.

Contact. Phone: (254) 442-2567 Fax: (254) 442-2546
Olin Odom, Dean of Enrollment Management, Cisco Junior College, 101 College Heights, Cisco, TX 76437

Clarendon College

Clarendon, Texas
www.clarendoncollege.edu **CB code: 6097**

- Public 2-year community college
- Residential campus in rural community

General. Founded in 1898. Regionally accredited. **Enrollment:** 1,051 degree-seeking undergraduates; 72 non-degree-seeking students. **Degrees:** 84 associate awarded. **Location:** 60 miles from Amarillo. **Calendar:** Semester, limited summer session. **Full-time faculty:** 30 total; 7% have terminal degrees, 40% women. **Part-time faculty:** 37 total; 8% have terminal degrees, 49% women. **Class size:** 69% < 20, 29% 20-39, 1% 50-99. **Partnerships:** Formal partnership with Tech Prep.

Student profile. Among degree-seeking undergraduates, 7% enrolled in a vocational program, 536 enrolled as first-time, first-year students, 80 transferred in from other institutions.

Part-time:	51%	**Asian American:**	1%
Out-of-state:	9%	**Hispanic American:**	17%
Women:	46%	**Native American:**	1%
African American:	11%	**Live on campus:**	26%

Transfer out. 87% of students enrolled in the transfer program go on to 4-year colleges. **Colleges most students transferred to 2005:** West Texas A&M University, Texas Tech University, Texas A&M University, Tarleton State University, Midwestern State University.

Basis for selection. Open admission, but selective for some programs. Special requirements for certain technical programs and vocational nursing. SAT/ACT used for counseling; ACT preferred. Institution observes all TASP requirements. Pre-entrance examination required for vocational nursing applicants. Interview before May 1 required for ranch and feedlot operations program. 3 personal references, interview required for vocational nursing program.

High school preparation. 23 units recommended. Recommended units include English 4, mathematics 3, social studies 1.5, history 2, science 3, foreign language 3, academic electives 3.5. .5 health, .5 economics, 1 computer, .5 speech recommended.

2005-2006 Annual costs. Tuition/fees: $1,860; $2,370 out-of-district; $2,820 out-of-state. Per-credit charge: $62 in-district; $79 out-of-district; $94 out-of-state. Room/board: $3,250. Books/supplies: $800. Personal expenses: $2,075.

2004-2005 Financial aid. Need-based: 150 full-time freshmen applied for aid; 150 were judged to have need; 150 of these received aid. Average need met was 60%. Average scholarship/grant was $3,500; average loan $1,750. 61% of total undergraduate aid awarded as scholarships/grants, 39% as loans/jobs. Need-based aid available for part-time students. Work study available nights, weekends and for part-time students. **Non-need-based:** Scholarships awarded for academics, art, athletics, leadership, music/drama, state residency.

Application procedures. Admission: Priority date 8/15; no deadline. No application fee. Admission notification on a rolling basis. **Financial aid:** Priority date 7/1, closing date 9/1. FAFSA, institutional form required. Applicants notified on a rolling basis starting 8/1; must reply by 8/15 or within 2 week(s) of notification.

Academics. Special study options: Cross-registration, distance learning, dual enrollment of high school students, internships, liberal arts/career combination, student-designed major. License preparation in nursing. **Credit/placement by examination:** AP, CLEP. 30 credit hours maximum toward associate degree. **Support services:** GED test center, learning center, remedial instruction, tutoring.

Majors. Agriculture: General, agronomy, animal sciences, business, economics, equestrian studies, farm/ranch. **Biology:** General. **Business:** General, accounting, finance, management science, marketing, office technology. **Communications:** General. **Computer sciences:** General. **Conservation:** Environmental science. **Education:** General, elementary, secondary. **Engineering:** General. **Engineering technology:** Computer systems. **English:** English lit, speech/rhetoric. **Foreign languages:** General. **Health:** EMT paramedic, health services, nursing (RN), predentistry, premedicine, prepharmacy, preveterinary. **History:** General. **Legal studies:** Prelaw. **Liberal arts:** Arts/sciences. **Math:** General. **Parks/recreation:** General, exercise sciences, health/fitness. **Philosophy/religion:** Religion. **Physical sciences:** Chemistry, geology, physics. **Protective services:** Criminal justice. **Psychology:** General. **Public administration:** Social work. **Social sciences:** Economics, political science, sociology. **Visual/performing arts:** Art, commercial/advertising art, dramatic.

Computing on campus. 203 workstations in library, computer center. Dormitories wired for high-speed internet access. Commuter students can connect to campus network. Online course registration, online library, wireless network available.

Student life. Freshman orientation: Mandatory, $79 fee. Preregistration for classes offered. **Policies:** Freshmen permitted cars on campus. **Housing:** Coed dorms, single-sex dorms, special housing for disabled, apartments, substance-free housing available. $100 deposit. **Activities:** Jazz band, choral groups, drama, music ensembles, student government, multicultural club, student ambassadors, Block & Bridle, rodeo club.

Athletics. NJCAA. **Intercollegiate:** Baseball M, basketball, cheerleading, rodeo, softball W, volleyball W. **Intramural:** Basketball, football (non-tackle), golf, rodeo, volleyball. **Team name:** Bulldogs.

Student services. Career counseling, financial aid counseling. **Physically disabled:** Services for visually, speech, hearing impaired. **Transfer:** Special adviser for new students. Transfer adviser, college fairs on campus for students transferring to 4-year colleges.

Contact. Phone: (806) 874-3571 Toll-free number: (800) 687-9737
Fax: (806) 874-3201
Sharon Hannon, Director of Admissions and Registrar, Clarendon College, PO Box 968, Clarendon, TX 79226

Coastal Bend College

Beeville, Texas
www.coastalbend.edu **CB code: 6055**

- Public 2-year community college
- Commuter campus in large town

General. Founded in 1965. Regionally accredited. **Enrollment:** 3,366 degree-seeking undergraduates. **Degrees:** 253 associate awarded. **Location:** 60 miles from Corpus Christi, 90 miles from San Antonio. **Calendar:** Semester, limited summer session. **Full-time faculty:** 96 total. **Part-time faculty:** 71 total. **Class size:** 69% < 20, 29% 20-39, 2% 40-49, less than 1% 50-99. **Partnerships:** Formal partnerships with national corporations to provide truck driver training, with local businesses to provide training for employees, and with high schools and tech prep programs.

Student profile.

25 or older:	60%	**Live on campus:**	5%

Transfer out. Colleges most students transferred to 2005: Texas A&M-Corpus Christi, Texas A&M-Kingsville, Southwest Texas State University, Texas A&M-College Station, University of Texas.

Basis for selection. Open admission, but selective for some programs. Special requirements for dental hygiene and vocational nursing programs. Texas requires that all students satisfy Texas TASP test requirements before being enrolled in college-level courses in public college or university. Scores not used in admission decisions.

2005-2006 Annual costs. Tuition/fees: $1,730; $3,500 out-of-district; $3,950 out-of-state. Meal ticket (a la carte) food service available. Room only: $1,560. Books/supplies: $600. Personal expenses: $1,500.

2004-2005 Financial aid. Need-based: 79% of total undergraduate aid awarded as scholarships/grants, 21% as loans/jobs. Need-based aid available for part-time students. **Non-need-based:** Scholarships awarded for academics, leadership.

Application procedures. Admission: No deadline. No application fee. Application may be submitted online. Admission notification on a rolling basis. **Financial aid:** Priority date 4/1; no closing date. FAFSA, institutional form required. Applicants notified on a rolling basis starting 5/1; must reply within 2 week(s) of notification.

Academics. Special study options: Cooperative education, cross-registration, distance learning, dual enrollment of high school students, internships, liberal arts/career combination. License preparation in dental hygiene, nursing. **Credit/placement by examination:** CLEP, institutional tests. 30 credit hours maximum toward associate degree. ACCUPLACER, ASSET, COMPASS, MAPS tests may be used instead of TASP. **Support services:** GED test center, learning center, remedial instruction, study skills assistance, tutoring.

Majors. Biology: General. **Business:** General, accounting, administrative services, business admin, finance, office technology, office/clerical, real estate. **Communications:** General. **Communications technology:** General. **Computer sciences:** General, computer science, data processing, programming. **Conservation:** General. **Education:** General, elementary, secondary. **Engineering:** General. **Engineering technology:** Drafting. **English:** Speech/rhetoric. **Family/consumer sciences:** General, child care. **Foreign languages:** French, German, Spanish. **Health:** Dental hygiene, medical records technology, medical secretary, nursing (RN), predentistry, premedicine, prepharmacy, preveterinary. **History:** General. **Legal studies:** Prelaw. **Liberal arts:** Arts/sciences. **Math:** General. **Mechanic/repair:** Heating/ac/refrig. **Physical sciences:** Chemistry, geology, physics. **Protective services:** Corrections, criminal justice, police science. **Psychology:** General. **Social sciences:** Political science, sociology. **Visual/performing arts:** General, commercial/advertising art, studio arts.

Computing on campus. 500 workstations in library, computer center. Commuter students can connect to campus network. Online course registration, online library, helpline available.

Student life. Freshman orientation: Mandatory. Preregistration for classes offered. Half-day program, parents welcome. **Policies:** Freshmen permitted cars on campus. **Housing:** Single-sex dorms, apartments available. $100 deposit, deadline 8/15. **Activities:** Student government, Baptist Student Union, Newman Club.

Athletics. Intramural: Archery, badminton, basketball, bowling, cross-country, golf, soccer, softball, swimming, table tennis, tennis, track and field, volleyball, weight lifting. **Team name:** Cougars.

Student services. Career counseling, services for economically disadvantaged, student employment services, financial aid counseling, on-campus daycare, personal counseling, placement for graduates, veterans' counselor. **Physically disabled:** Services for visually, speech, hearing impaired. **Transfer:** Special adviser, orientation, pre-admission transcript evaluation for new students. Transfer adviser, college fairs on campus for students transferring to 4-year colleges.

Contact. E-mail: register@coastalbend.edu
Phone: (361) 354-2254 Toll-free number: (800) 722-2838 ext. 2254
Fax: (361) 354-2554
Alicia Ulloa, Registrar and Director Admissions, Coastal Bend College, 3800 Charco Road, Beeville, TX 78102

College of the Mainland

Texas City, Texas
www.com.edu **CB code: 6133**

- Public 2-year community and technical college
- Commuter campus in large town

General. Founded in 1966. Regionally accredited. **Enrollment:** 4,019 undergraduates. **Degrees:** 257 associate awarded. **Location:** 25 miles from Houston. **Calendar:** Semester, extensive summer session. **Full-time faculty:** 90 total. **Part-time faculty:** 140 total.

Student profile.

Out-of-state:	1%	**25 or older:**	44%

Transfer out. Colleges most students transferred to 2005: University of Houston-Clear Lake.

Basis for selection. Open admission, but selective for some programs. Special requirements for nursing program.

2005-2006 Annual costs. Tuition/fees: $956; $1,946 out-of-district; $2,846 out-of-state. Per-credit charge: $26 in-district; $59 out-of-district; $89 out-of-state. Books/supplies: $800. Personal expenses: $1,087.

Financial aid. All financial aid based on need. Need-based aid available for part-time students. Work study available nights, weekends and for part-time students.

Application procedures. Admission: No deadline. No application fee. Application may be submitted online. Admission notification on a rolling basis. **Financial aid:** No deadline. FAFSA, institutional form required. Applicants notified on a rolling basis.

Academics. Special study options: Cooperative education, cross-registration, distance learning, double major, dual enrollment of high school students, independent study, internships, weekend college. License preparation in nursing, paramedic, real estate. **Credit/placement by examination:** CLEP, institutional tests. 24 credit hours maximum toward associate degree. **Support services:** GED preparation and test center, learning center, remedial instruction, tutoring, writing center.

Majors. Biology: General. **Business:** General, accounting, administrative services, banking/financial services, business admin, labor relations, marketing, office management, office technology, office/clerical, real estate. **Communications:** Journalism. **Computer sciences:** General, programming. **Education:** Elementary, secondary. **Engineering:** General. **Engineering technology:** Drafting, electrical. **Family/consumer sciences:** Child care. **Health:** Licensed practical nurse. **History:** General. **Interdisciplinary:** Biological/physical sciences. **Liberal arts:** Arts/sciences. **Math:** General. **Mechanic/repair:** Diesel, heating/ac/refrig. **Physical sciences:** Chemistry, planetary. **Protective services:** Fire safety technology, police science. **Psychology:** General. **Public administration:** General, social work. **Social sciences:** General, economics, political science, sociology. **Visual/performing arts:** General, dramatic, studio arts.

Computing on campus. 100 workstations in library, computer center.

Student life. Freshman orientation: Mandatory. **Activities:** Bands, choral groups, drama, literary magazine, music ensembles, musical theater, student government, student newspaper, Phi Beta Kappa, Students for Christ, Con Amigos, Organization of African-American Culture.

Athletics. Intramural: Basketball, racquetball, softball, tennis, volleyball. **Team name:** Ducks.

Student services. Career counseling, student employment services, financial aid counseling, on-campus daycare, personal counseling, placement for graduates, veterans' counselor. **Physically disabled:** Services for visually, speech, hearing impaired. **Transfer:** Special adviser, orientation for new students. Transfer adviser, college fairs on campus for students transferring to 4-year colleges.

Contact. Phone: (409) 938-1211 ext. 264 Fax: (409) 938-3126
Kelly Musick, Director of Admissions and Records/Registrar, College of the Mainland, 1200 Amburn Road, Texas City, TX 77591

Collin County Community College District

Plano, Texas **CB member**
www.ccccd.edu **CB code: 1951**

- Public 2-year community college
- Commuter campus in large city

General. Founded in 1985. Regionally accredited. **Enrollment:** 18,039 degree-seeking undergraduates; 418 non-degree-seeking students. **Degrees:** 965 associate awarded. **Location:** 25 miles from Dallas. **Calendar:** Semester, extensive summer session. **Full-time faculty:** 252 total; 12% minority, 55% women. **Part-time faculty:** 822 total; 14% minority, 52% women. **Class size:** 33% < 20, 66% 20-39, 1% 40-49, less than 1% 50-99. **Special facilities:** Regional fire training facility. **Partnerships:** Formal partnership with Cisco to provide Certified Network Professional Certification.

Student profile. Among degree-seeking undergraduates, 3,676 enrolled as first-time, first-year students.

Part-time:	60%	**Hispanic American:**	10%
Out-of-state:	3%	**Native American:**	1%
Women:	56%	**International:**	3%
African American:	8%	**25 or older:**	37%
Asian American:	8%		

Transfer out. Colleges most students transferred to 2005: University of Texas at Dallas, University of North Texas, Texas A&M University, University of Texas at Austin, Texas Tech University.

Basis for selection. Open admission, but selective for some programs. Special requirements for programs in nursing, dental hygiene, emergency medical services, firefighter, respiratory care, interpreter prep, honors institute, center for advanced study in mathematics and natural sciences. For placement only, institution administers local assessments in reading, writing, math to new students. TASP guidelines observed, though TASP testing waived if acceptable scores on ACT, SAT or other accepted substitute tests presented. **Adult students:** Entrance exam policies same as for first-time freshmen. **Homeschooled:** If under 18 years must provide written parental/guardian permission.

High school preparation. 17 units recommended. Recommended units include English 4, mathematics 3, social studies 2, history 2, science 2 (laboratory 2) and foreign language 2.

2005-2006 Annual costs. Tuition/fees: $1,114; $1,294 out-of-district; $2,704 out-of-state. Per-credit charge: $37 in-district; $43 out-of-district; $90 out-of-state. Books/supplies: $602. Personal expenses: $1,332.

2005-2006 Financial aid. Need-based: 899 full-time freshmen applied for aid; 676 were judged to have need; 585 of these received aid. Average need met was 34%. Average scholarship/grant was $3,444; average loan $2,243. 61% of total undergraduate aid awarded as scholarships/grants, 39% as loans/jobs. Need-based aid available for part-time students. Work study available nights, weekends and for part-time students. **Non-need-based:** Awarded to 583 full-time undergraduates, including 300 freshmen. Scholarships awarded for academics, art, athletics, music/drama.

Application procedures. Admission: No deadline. No application fee. Application may be submitted online. Admission notification on a rolling basis. **Financial aid:** Priority date 6/1, closing date 6/30. FAFSA, institutional form required. Applicants notified on a rolling basis starting 5/1; must reply within 2 week(s) of notification.

Academics. Special study options: Cooperative education, distance learning, dual enrollment of high school students, ESL, exchange student, honors, internships, study abroad, teacher certification program. Learning communities. License preparation in dental hygiene, nursing. **Credit/placement by examination:** CLEP, institutional tests. 18 credit hours maximum toward associate degree. 6 hours traditional credit must be completed in residence before examination credit awarded. **Support services:** Learning center, remedial instruction, study skills assistance, tutoring, writing center.

Honors college/program. Students with GPA of 3.5 or over admitted to Honors Institute.

Majors. Business: Business admin, hospitality admin, office technology, real estate, sales/distribution. **Communications technology:** Animation/special effects. **Computer sciences:** General, networking, programming, web page design. **Engineering technology:** Drafting, electrical, electrical drafting, telecommunications. **Family/consumer sciences:** Child development. **Foreign languages:** Sign language interpretation. **Health:** Dental hygiene, EMT paramedic, nursing (RN), respiratory therapy technology. **Legal studies:** Paralegal. **Mechanic/repair:** Electronics/electrical. **Protective services:** Fire safety technology. **Science technology:** Biological. **Visual/performing arts:** Commercial/advertising art, interior design, music management.

Most popular majors. Health sciences 9%, liberal arts 76%.

Computing on campus. 1,980 workstations in library, computer center. Online course registration, helpline, repair service, wireless network available.

Student life. Freshman orientation: Available. One-day program; online section available for distance learning students. **Policies:** Freshmen permitted cars on campus. **Housing:** Apartments available. **Activities:** Jazz band, choral groups, dance, drama, literary magazine, music ensembles, musical theater, student government, American Sign Language club, black student association, nursing student association, hospitality and culinary arts student society, Latter-day Saints student association, Muslim student association, College Republicans, Baptist student ministry.

Athletics. NJCAA. **Intercollegiate:** Basketball, tennis. **Team name:** Cougars.

Student services. Adult student services, alcohol/substance abuse counseling, career counseling, student employment services, financial aid counseling, on-campus daycare, personal counseling, placement for graduates. **Physically disabled:** Services for visually, speech, hearing impaired. **Transfer:** Special adviser, orientation for new students. Transfer adviser, college fairs on campus for students transferring to 4-year colleges.

Contact. E-mail: smeinhardt@ccccd.edu
Phone: (972) 881-5710 Fax: (972) 881-5175
Stephanie Meinhardt, Registrar/ Director of Admissions, Collin County Community College District, 2800 East Spring Creek Parkway, Plano, TX 75074

Commonwealth Institute of Funeral Service

Houston, Texas
www.commonwealthinst.org **CB code: 7031**

- Private 2-year school of mortuary science
- Commuter campus in very large city

General. Founded in 1988. Accredited by American Board of Funeral Service Education, Inc. **Enrollment:** 136 degree-seeking undergraduates. **Degrees:** 57 associate awarded. **Location:** 15 miles from downtown. **Calendar:** Quarter. **Full-time faculty:** 3 total. **Part-time faculty:** 5 total. **Class size:** 50% < 20, 50% 50-99. **Special facilities:** Museum.

Student profile. Among degree-seeking undergraduates, 43 enrolled as first-time, first-year students.

Part-time:	7%	**Women:**	54%
Out-of-state:	20%	**25 or older:**	49%

Basis for selection. Class rank and standardized test scores most important. SAT or ACT recommended. TASP required.

2005-2006 Annual costs. Full five-quarter program costs $9,500, which includes application and graduation fee. Books/supplies: $1,183. Personal expenses: $1,102.

Financial aid. All financial aid based on need. Need-based aid available for part-time students.

Application procedures. Admission: No deadline. $50 fee. Admission notification on a rolling basis beginning on or about 8/28. **Financial aid:** Priority date 7/10; no closing date. FAFSA required. Applicants notified on a rolling basis starting 7/12.

Academics. Credit/placement by examination: CLEP. **Support services:** Tutoring.

Majors. Personal/culinary services: Mortuary science.

Computing on campus. 15 workstations in library, computer center.

Student life. Policies: Freshmen permitted cars on campus. **Housing:** Some local funeral homes provide student employees accommodations while attending college. **Activities:** Student government.

Student services. Career counseling, student employment services, financial aid counseling, personal counseling, placement for graduates, veterans' counselor. **Transfer:** Special adviser, re-entry adviser, pre-admission transcript evaluation for new students. Transfer adviser for students transferring to 4-year colleges.

Contact. Phone: (281) 873-0262 Fax: (281) 873-5232
Patricia Moreno, Registrar, Commonwealth Institute of Funeral Service, 415 Barren Springs Drive, Houston, TX 77090-5913

Court Reporting Institute of Dallas

Dallas, Texas
www.crid.com **CB code: 3231**

- For-profit 2-year technical college
- Very large city

General. Accredited by ACICS. **Enrollment:** 770 full-time, degree-seeking students. **Degrees:** 35 associate awarded. **Calendar:** Quarter. **Full-time faculty:** 15 total. **Part-time faculty:** 10 total.

Basis for selection. Open admission.

2005-2006 Annual costs. Tuition/fees: $7,065. Other fees vary per program. Machine rental available. Books/supplies: $700.

Application procedures. Admission: No deadline. $100 fee.

Academics. Credit/placement by examination: CLEP.

Majors. Legal studies: Court reporting.

Contact. Phone: (214) 350-9722 Toll-free number: (800) 880- ext. 9722
Court Reporting Institute of Dallas, 8585 North Stemmons Freeway, Suite 200, Dallas, TX 75247

Court Reporting Institute of Houston

Houston, Texas
www.crid.com/houston/indexhouston.asp

- For-profit 2-year technical college
- Commuter campus

General. Accredited by ACICS. **Calendar:** Quarter.

Contact. Phone: (713) 996-8300
Admissions Representative, 13101 Northwest Freeway, Suite 100, Houston, TX 77040

Dallas Institute of Funeral Service

Dallas, Texas
www.dallasinstitute.edu **CB code: 7032**

- Private 2-year school of mortuary science
- Commuter campus in very large city

General. Regionally accredited. 15-month AAS in funeral service program and 6-month funeral director's program (Texas, Louisiana, and Missouri students only). **Enrollment:** 206 degree-seeking undergraduates; 41 non-degree-seeking students. **Degrees:** 89 associate awarded. **Calendar:** Quarter, limited summer session. **Full-time faculty:** 5 total. **Part-time faculty:** 6 total. **Special facilities:** On-campus embalming facilities.

Student profile. Among degree-seeking undergraduates, 96 enrolled as first-time, first-year students.

Basis for selection. Open admission. **Adult students:** Entrance exam policies same as for first-time freshmen.

2005-2006 Annual costs. Per-credit charge: $200. Tuition $12,500 for 15-month associate program; $5,000 for 6-month funeral director program. Personal expenses: $1,190.

Application procedures. **Admission:** No deadline. $50 fee. Application may be submitted online. Admission notification on a rolling basis. **Financial aid:** No deadline. Applicants notified on a rolling basis.

Academics. **Special study options:** Distance learning. **Credit/placement by examination:** AP, CLEP, IB. **Support services:** Study skills assistance, tutoring.

Majors. **Personal/culinary services:** Mortuary science.

Computing on campus. 26 workstations in library, computer center.

Student life. **Policies:** Freshmen permitted cars on campus.

Student services. **Physically disabled:** Services for visually, hearing impaired. **Transfer:** Special adviser for new students.

Contact. Phone: (214) 388-5466 Fax: (214) 388-0316
Terry Parrish, Director of Admissions, Dallas Institute of Funeral Service, 3909 South Buckner Boulevard, Dallas, TX 75227

Del Mar College

Corpus Christi, Texas
www.delmar.edu **CB code: 6160**

- Public 2-year community college
- Commuter campus in large city

General. Founded in 1935. Regionally accredited. Courses taught at 7 off-campus sites in the Coastal Bend Region. Center for Early Learning provides day-care on campus. **Enrollment:** 12,006 degree-seeking undergraduates. **Degrees:** 790 associate awarded. **ROTC:** Army. **Location:** 155 miles from San Antonio. **Calendar:** Semester, extensive summer session. **Full-time faculty:** 306 total; 19% have terminal degrees, 31% minority, 49% women. **Part-time faculty:** 389 total.

Student profile. Among degree-seeking undergraduates, 32% enrolled in a transfer program, 47% enrolled in a vocational program, 1,841 enrolled as first-time, first-year students.

Part-time:	69%	**Asian American:**	2%
Out-of-state:	1%	**Hispanic American:**	56%
Women:	61%	**25 or older:**	37%
African American:	3%		

Transfer out. **Colleges most students transferred to 2005:** Texas A&M University (College Station, Corpus Christi, Kingsville); University of Texas (Austin, San Antonio).

Basis for selection. Open admission, but selective for some programs. Admissions criteria for health science programs vary by program. Interview required for health science programs. **Adult students:** Entrance exam policies same as for first-time freshmen. **Homeschooled:** Students admitted under individual approval plan.

High school preparation. 24 units recommended. Recommended units include English 4, mathematics 3, social studies 1, history 2, science 2, foreign language 2 and academic electives 10.

2006-2007 Annual costs. Tuition/fees (projected): $1,910; $4,160 out-of-district; $5,210 out-of-state. Per-credit charge: $35 in-district; $110 out-of-district; $145 out-of-state. Books/supplies: $1,000. Personal expenses: $978.

2004-2005 Financial aid. All financial aid based on need. 73% of total undergraduate aid awarded as scholarships/grants, 27% as loans/jobs. Need-based aid available for part-time students. Work study available nights, weekends and for part-time students.

Application procedures. **Admission:** No deadline. No application fee. Admission notification on a rolling basis. **Financial aid:** Priority date 5/1; no closing date. FAFSA required. Applicants notified on a rolling basis starting 7/1; must reply within 2 week(s) of notification.

Academics. Short semester courses, accelerated associate degree program. **Special study options:** Accelerated study, cooperative education, distance learning, dual enrollment of high school students, ESL, honors, independent study, internships, weekend college. License preparation in dental hygiene, nursing, occupational therapy, paramedic, physical therapy, radiology, real estate. **Credit/placement by examination:** AP, CLEP, institutional tests. 30 credit hours maximum toward associate degree. Credit may not be earned by examination for most performance-oriented courses. **Support services:** GED preparation and test center, learning center, remedial instruction, tutoring, writing center.

Majors. **Agriculture:** Business. **Biology:** General. **Business:** Accounting, administrative services, business admin, fashion, finance, hotel/motel admin, management information systems, operations, restaurant/food services, tourism/travel. **Communications:** Broadcast journalism, digital media, journalism, radio/tv. **Computer sciences:** General, computer science, LAN/WAN management, programming, web page design. **Construction:** Maintenance. **Education:** Art, bilingual, biology, early childhood, English, health, history, mathematics, music, physical, physics, reading, science, social science, special. **Engineering:** General, electrical. **Engineering technology:** Architectural, drafting, electrical. **English:** Speech/rhetoric. **Family/consumer sciences:** Child care, child development. **Foreign languages:** General, sign language interpretation. **Health:** Clinical lab science, clinical lab technology, dental assistant, dental hygiene, EMT paramedic, medical radiologic technology/radiation therapy, medical secretary, mental health services, nursing (RN), occupational therapy assistant, physical therapy assistant, predentistry, premedicine, prenursing, prepharmacy, preveterinary, respiratory therapy assistant, respiratory therapy technology, sonography, surgical technology. **History:** General. **Legal studies:** Court reporting, legal secretary, paralegal. **Liberal arts:** Arts/sciences. **Math:** General. **Mechanic/repair:** Aircraft, aircraft powerplant, appliance, automotive, diesel, electronics/electrical, heating/ac/refrig. **Parks/recreation:** General, health/fitness. **Personal/culinary services:** Culinary arts, restaurant/catering. **Physical sciences:** Chemistry, geology, physics. **Production:** Machine tool, welding. **Protective services:** Criminal justice, fire safety technology, police science. **Psychology:** General. **Public administration:** General, social work. **Science technology:** Chemical. **Social sciences:** Geography, political science, sociology. **Visual/performing arts:** Art, dramatic, music performance, music theory/composition.

Computing on campus. 450 workstations in library, computer center, student center. Online course registration available.

Student life. **Freshman orientation:** Available. Preregistration for classes offered. 2-hour session held 6 weeks prior to scheduled registration. **Activities:** Bands, choral groups, dance, drama, music ensembles, opera, student government, student newspaper, Newman Club, Latter-day Saints, Baptist Student Union, united campus ministries, international club, InterCambio club, students with disabilities.

Athletics. **Intramural:** Badminton, basketball, bowling, cross-country, golf, racquetball, sailing, softball, swimming, table tennis, tennis, track and field, volleyball. **Team name:** Vikings.

Student services. Adult student services, career counseling, student employment services, financial aid counseling, on-campus daycare, personal counseling, placement for graduates, veterans' counselor. **Physically disabled:** Services for visually, speech, hearing impaired. **Transfer:** Special adviser for new students. College fairs on campus for students transferring to 4-year colleges.

Contact. Phone: (361) 698-1255 Toll-free number: (800) 652-3357
Fax: (361) 698-1595
Frances Jordan, Assistant Dean of Admissions and Advising/Registrar, Del Mar College, 101 Baldwin Boulevard, Corpus Christi, TX 78404-3897

Eastfield College

Mesquite, Texas
www.efc.dcccd.edu **CB code: 6201**

- Public 2-year community and liberal arts college
- Commuter campus in small city

General. Founded in 1970. Regionally accredited. **Enrollment:** 3,275 full-time, degree-seeking students. **Degrees:** 328 associate awarded. **Location:** One mile from Dallas. **Calendar:** Semester, limited summer session. **Full-time faculty:** 89 total. **Part-time faculty:** 389 total. **Class size:** 83% < 20, 16% 20-39, less than 1% 40-49, less than 1% 50-99, less than 1% >100. **Special facilities:** Automotive diagnostic center.

Student profile.

Out-of-state:	1%	**25 or older:**	45%

Transfer out. **Colleges most students transferred to 2005:** University of Texas-Arlington, University of Texas-Dallas, University of North Texas, Texas A&M-Commerce, Southern Methodist University.

Basis for selection. Open admission. Interview recommended for international students. **Adult students:** Entrance exam policies same as for first-time freshmen.

High school preparation. 22 units recommended. Recommended units include English 4, mathematics 3, social studies 1, history 1, science 2,

Two-Year Colleges

academic electives 5.5. Recommend health education 0.5; speech 0.5; history, geography or science 1.0; technical applications 1.0; history or geography 1.0.

2005-2006 Annual costs. Tuition/fees: $990; $1,800 out-of-district; $2,880 out-of-state. Per-credit charge: $33 in-district; $60 out-of-district; $96 out-of-state. Books/supplies: $400. Personal expenses: $935.

Financial aid. Need-based: Need-based aid available for part-time students. Work study available nights, weekends and for part-time students.

Application procedures. Admission: No deadline. No application fee. Admission notification on a rolling basis. **Financial aid:** Priority date 5/1; no closing date. FAFSA, institutional form required. Applicants notified on a rolling basis starting 4/15.

Academics. Special study options: Cooperative education, distance learning, ESL, honors, independent study. **Credit/placement by examination:** CLEP, IB, institutional tests. 15 credit hours maximum toward associate degree. **Support services:** GED preparation, learning center, pre-admission summer program, remedial instruction, tutoring.

Majors. Business: General, accounting, administrative services, business admin, management information systems, office management, office technology. **Communications technology:** General, desktop publishing, graphic/printing. **Computer sciences:** General, applications programming, computer science, data processing, networking, programming. **Engineering:** Electrical, software. **Engineering technology:** CAD/CADD, electrical. **Family/consumer sciences:** Child development. **Foreign languages:** Sign language interpretation. **Health:** Mental health services, substance abuse counseling. **Legal studies:** Legal secretary. **Liberal arts:** Arts/sciences. **Mechanic/repair:** Auto body, automotive, diesel, heating/ac/refrig, industrial. **Protective services:** Criminal justice. **Public administration:** Social work.

Computing on campus. 152 workstations in library, computer center. Online library available.

Student life. Freshman orientation: Available. Online and on-campus orientations offered. **Policies:** Student code of conduct in effect. Freshmen permitted cars on campus. **Activities:** Bands, choral groups, dance, drama, music ensembles, musical theater, student government, student newspaper, Fellowship of Christian Athletes, Latter-day Saint student association, multicultural club, Vital Signers, piano club, poetry club, automotive club, jazz dance club.

Athletics. NJCAA. **Intercollegiate:** Baseball M, basketball M, golf M, volleyball W. **Intramural:** Archery, basketball M, bowling, golf M, gymnastics, tennis, volleyball. **Team name:** Harvesters.

Student services. Career counseling, student employment services, health services, personal counseling, placement for graduates, veterans' counselor. **Physically disabled:** Services for visually, speech, hearing impaired. **Transfer:** Special adviser for new students. College fairs on campus for students transferring to 4-year colleges.

Contact. E-mail: efc@dcccd.edu
Phone: (972) 860-7100 Fax: (972) 860-8306
Linda Richardson, Dean of Admissions and Testing, Eastfield College, 3737 Motley Drive, Mesquite, TX 75150

El Centro College

Dallas, Texas
www.elcentrocollege.edu **CB code: 6199**

- Public 2-year community college
- Commuter campus in very large city

General. Founded in 1966. Regionally accredited. **Enrollment:** 4,686 degree-seeking undergraduates; 1,459 non-degree-seeking students. **Degrees:** 453 associate awarded. **ROTC:** Army. **Location:** Downtown. **Calendar:** Semester, limited summer session. **Full-time faculty:** 157 total; 39% minority, 64% women. **Part-time faculty:** 262 total; 35% minority, 50% women. **Class size:** 79% < 20, 20% 20-39, less than 1% 40-49, less than 1% 50-99. **Special facilities:** Outdoor amphitheater, art studios, interior design and fashion design studios, allied health laboratories. **Partnerships:** Formal partnerships with regional CISCO training center, many local businesses, and area high schools.

Student profile. Among degree-seeking undergraduates, 45% enrolled in a transfer program, 55% enrolled in a vocational program, 1% already have a bachelor's degree or higher, 707 enrolled as first-time, first-year students, 1,498 transferred in from other institutions.

Part-time:	74%	**Asian American:**	5%
Out-of-state:	1%	**Hispanic American:**	26%
Women:	71%	**International:**	2%
African American:	36%	**25 or older:**	58%

Transfer out. Colleges most students transferred to 2005: University of Texas at Arlington, University of North Texas, University of Texas at Dallas, Southern Methodist University.

Basis for selection. Open admission, but selective for some programs. Specific application requirements for nursing, some allied health, and food and hospitality programs. Interview recommended for international students. **Adult students:** Entrance exam policies same as for first-time freshmen.

2005-2006 Annual costs. Tuition/fees: $990; $1,800 out-of-district; $2,880 out-of-state. Per-credit charge: $33 in-district; $60 out-of-district; $96 out-of-state. Books/supplies: $750. Personal expenses: $600.

Financial aid. Need-based: Need-based aid available for part-time students. **Additional information:** Interview required for financial aid applicants.

Application procedures. Admission: No deadline. No application fee. Application may be submitted online. Admission notification on a rolling basis beginning on or about 6/1. **Financial aid:** Priority date 5/1; no closing date. FAFSA required. Applicants notified on a rolling basis; must reply within 2 week(s) of notification.

Academics. Special study options: Accelerated study, combined bachelor's/graduate degree, cooperative education, cross-registration, distance learning, double major, dual enrollment of high school students, ESL, external degree, honors, internships, liberal arts/career combination, teacher certification program. License preparation in nursing, paramedic, radiology. **Credit/placement by examination:** AP, CLEP, IB, institutional tests. 45 credit hours maximum toward associate degree. **Support services:** GED preparation, learning center, reduced course load, remedial instruction, study skills assistance, tutoring.

Majors. Business: Accounting, business admin, executive assistant, management information systems. **Computer sciences:** Data processing, information systems, programming. **Education:** Teacher assistance. **Health:** Cardiovascular technology, clinical lab technology, medical radiologic technology/radiation therapy, medical records admin, medical records technology, nursing (RN), respiratory therapy technology, sonography. **Legal studies:** Paralegal. **Liberal arts:** Arts/sciences. **Personal/culinary services:** Baking, chef training. **Science technology:** Biological. **Visual/performing arts:** Fashion design, interior design.

Most popular majors. Business/marketing 9%, health sciences 49%, legal studies 11%, liberal arts 22%.

Computing on campus. 832 workstations in library, computer center, student center. Commuter students can connect to campus network. Online course registration, online library, helpline available.

Student life. Freshman orientation: Mandatory. Preregistration for classes offered. **Policies:** Freshmen permitted cars on campus. **Activities:** Choral groups, drama, music ensembles, musical theater, student government, Phi Theta Kappa, organization of Latin American students, El Centro computer society, international college association, Disabled and Realizing Excellence, teacher education preparatory program, Circle-K, association of black college students.

Athletics. Intramural: Basketball, volleyball, weight lifting.

Student services. Adult student services, career counseling, services for economically disadvantaged, student employment services, financial aid counseling, health services, minority student services, personal counseling, placement for graduates, veterans' counselor. **Physically disabled:** Services for visually, hearing impaired. **Transfer:** Special adviser, orientation for new students. Transfer adviser, college fairs on campus for students transferring to 4-year colleges.

Contact. E-mail: sgs5310@dcccd.edu
Phone: (214) 860-2311 Fax: (214) 860-2233
Stevie Stewart, Director of Admissions/Registrar, El Centro College, 801 Main Street, Dallas, TX 75202

El Paso Community College

El Paso, Texas **CB member**
www.epcc.edu **CB code: 6203**

- Public 2-year community college
- Commuter campus in very large city

General. Founded in 1969. Regionally accredited. Multicampus institution. Teaching locations at Fort Bliss, local schools, community centers, satellite centers, and at local businesses. **Enrollment:** 26,000 degree-seeking undergraduates. **Degrees:** 1,705 associate awarded. **ROTC:** Army. **Location:** 240 miles from Albuquerque, New Mexico. **Calendar:** Semester, extensive summer session. **Full-time faculty:** 366 total; 13% have terminal degrees, 50% minority, 50% women. **Part-time faculty:** 1,080 total; 4% have terminal degrees, 61% minority, 47% women. **Special facilities:** Advanced technology center. **Partnerships:** Formal partnerships with local high schools for Tech Prep programs and with hospitals for health programs.

Student profile.

Out-of-state:	6%	**25 or older:**	45%

Transfer out. Colleges most students transferred to 2005: University of Texas at El Paso, New Mexico State University.

Basis for selection. Open admission, but selective for some programs. Certain reading level requirements and GPA for some health occupations programs with selective admission. Nelson-Denny Reading Test and institutional mathematics test required for admission to health programs. Observes TASP requirements.

2005-2006 Annual costs. Tuition/fees: $1,212; $1,686 out-of-state. Per-credit charge: $44 in-state; $73 out-of-state. Per-credit-hour costs listed are for each additional credit-hour beyond one credit-hour for in-state students, and beyond six credit-hours for out-of-state students. Books/supplies: $545. Personal expenses: $1,223.

Financial aid. Need-based: Work study available nights, weekends and for part-time students. **Non-need-based:** Scholarships awarded for academics, athletics.

Application procedures. Admission: No deadline. $10 fee. Admission notification on a rolling basis. **Financial aid:** Priority date 5/1; no closing date. FAFSA, institutional form required. Applicants notified on a rolling basis starting 7/1; must reply within 2 week(s) of notification.

Academics. Special study options: Cooperative education, cross-registration, distance learning, double major, dual enrollment of high school students, ESL, honors, independent study, internships, teacher certification program, weekend college. License preparation in dental hygiene, nursing, physical therapy, radiology. **Credit/placement by examination:** AP, CLEP, IB, institutional tests. 45 credit hours maximum toward associate degree. **Support services:** GED preparation and test center, learning center, remedial instruction, study skills assistance, tutoring, writing center.

Majors. Area/ethnic studies: Women's. **Biology:** General. **Business:** General, accounting, administrative services, business admin, fashion, finance, hospitality/recreation, international, management science, office/clerical, operations, real estate, tourism promotion, tourism/travel. **Communications:** General, journalism. **Communications technology:** General. **Computer sciences:** General, computer science, information systems, programming, systems analysis. **Education:** Elementary, physical, secondary, special, technology/industrial arts. **Engineering:** General. **Engineering technology:** Drafting, electrical. **English:** Speech/rhetoric. **Family/consumer sciences:** Child care, family studies, institutional food production. **Foreign languages:** General, sign language interpretation. **Health:** Clinical lab technology, dental assistant, dental hygiene, dietetics, medical assistant, medical radiologic technology/radiation therapy, medical records technology, mental health services, nursing (RN), optician, physical therapy assistant, predentistry, premedicine, prepharmacy, preveterinary, respiratory therapy technology, substance abuse counseling, surgical technology. **History:** General. **Legal studies:** Court reporting, paralegal. **Liberal arts:** Arts/sciences. **Math:** General. **Mechanic/repair:** Electronics/electrical, heating/ac/refrig. **Parks/recreation:** Health/fitness. **Personal/culinary services:** Culinary arts. **Physical sciences:** Chemistry, geology, physics. **Protective services:** Corrections, criminal justice, fire safety technology. **Psychology:** General. **Social sciences:** General, political science, sociology. **Visual/performing arts:** Art, cinematography, commercial photography, commercial/advertising art, dramatic, fashion design, interior design, photography.

Computing on campus. 2,000 workstations in library, computer center.

Student life. Freshman orientation: Mandatory. **Activities:** Jazz band, choral groups, dance, drama, film society, literary magazine, music ensembles, radio station, student government, student newspaper, TV station, Phi Theta Kappa, African-American coalition, art student society, architecture club, social science club.

Athletics. NJCAA. **Intercollegiate:** Baseball M, softball W. **Intramural:** Basketball, bowling, cross-country, soccer, softball, table tennis, tennis, track and field, volleyball, weight lifting. **Team name:** Tejanos/Tejanas.

Student services. Career counseling, student employment services, health services, personal counseling, placement for graduates, veterans' counselor, women's services. **Physically disabled:** Services for visually, speech, hearing impaired. **Transfer:** Special adviser, orientation for new students. Transfer adviser, college fairs on campus for students transferring to 4-year colleges.

Contact. Phone: (915) 831-2580 Fax: (915) 831-2161
Daryle Hendry, Director of Admissions, El Paso Community College, Box 20500, El Paso, TX 79998

Everest College: Arlington

Arlington, Texas
www.everest-college.com

- For-profit 2-year business and technical college
- Commuter campus

General. Accredited by ACICS. **Enrollment:** 387 full-time, degree-seeking students. **Degrees:** 55 associate awarded. **Calendar:** Differs by program.

Basis for selection. High school record important.

Application procedures. Admission: No deadline. No application fee.

Academics. Credit/placement by examination: CLEP.

Contact. E-mail: bbassham@cci.edu
Phone: (817) 652-7790 Toll-free number: (888) 741-4270
Fax: (817) 649-6033
Brian Bassham, Director of Admissions, Everest College: Arlington, 2801 East Division Street, Suite 250, Arlington, TX 76011

Everest College: Dallas

Dallas, Texas
www.everest-college.com

- For-profit 2-year business and technical college
- Commuter campus

General. Accredited by ACICS. **Enrollment:** 673 full-time, degree-seeking students. **Degrees:** 103 associate awarded. **Calendar:** Differs by program.

Basis for selection. High school record important.

Application procedures. Admission: No deadline. No application fee.

Academics. Credit/placement by examination: CLEP.

Contact. E-mail: zbelyea@cci.edu
Phone: (214) 234-4850 Toll-free number: (888) 741-4270
Fax: (214) 696-6208
Zane Belyea, Director of Admissions, Everest College: Dallas, 6060 North Central Expressway, Suite 101, Dallas, TX 75206

Frank Phillips College

Borger, Texas
www.fpctx.edu **CB code: 6222**

- Public 2-year community and junior college
- Commuter campus in large town

General. Founded in 1948. Regionally accredited. Guaranteed transfer program. Contract training provided on site or at on-campus location for Occupational Safety and Health Administration mandated certification. **Enrollment:** 803 degree-seeking undergraduates; 472 non-degree-seeking students. **Degrees:** 105 associate awarded. **Location:** 60 miles from Amarillo. **Calendar:** Semester, extensive summer session. **Full-time faculty:** 100 total; 2% have terminal degrees. **Part-time faculty:** 100 total; 1% have terminal degrees. **Class size:** 31% < 20, 68% 20-39, 1% 40-49.

Student profile. Among degree-seeking undergraduates, 62% enrolled in a transfer program, 35% enrolled in a vocational program, 5% already have a bachelor's degree or higher, 105 enrolled as first-time, first-year students, 1,276 transferred in from other institutions.

Part-time:	27%	**Hispanic American:**	18%
Out-of-state:	4%	**International:**	2%
Women:	60%	**25 or older:**	32%
African American:	3%	**Live on campus:**	20%

Two-Year Colleges

Transfer out. **Colleges most students transferred to 2005:** West Texas A&M University, Texas A&M University.

Basis for selection. Open admission. Texas Success Initiative guidelines followed. SAT/ACT, COMPASS, ASSET, TAKS, or ACCUPLACER may be used in lieu of THEA. Veterans receive preferential admission. **Adult students:** Entrance exam policies same as for first-time freshmen. **Home-schooled:** Transcript of courses and grades required.

2005-2006 Annual costs. Tuition/fees: $1,710; $2,280 out-of-district; $2,490 out-of-state. Per-credit charge: $57 in-district; $76 out-of-district; $83 out-of-state. Room/board: $3,100. Books/supplies: $605. Personal expenses: $985.

Financial aid. **Need-based:** Need-based aid available for part-time students. Work study available nights, weekends and for part-time students. **Non-need-based:** Scholarships awarded for academics, athletics, music/drama, state residency. **Additional information:** Some Texas fire department and police department personnel, active duty military personnel, children of military missing in action may qualify for reduced or waived tuition. Out-of-state tuition waived for students living in Oklahoma counties adjacent to Texas.

Application procedures. **Admission:** No deadline. No application fee. Application may be submitted online. Admission notification on a rolling basis. **Financial aid:** FAFSA, institutional form required. Applicants notified on a rolling basis; must reply within 2 week(s) of notification.

Academics. **Special study options:** Cooperative education, distance learning, dual enrollment of high school students, internships, liberal arts/career combination. License preparation in nursing. **Credit/placement by examination:** AP, CLEP, IB, institutional tests. 24 credit hours maximum toward associate degree. **Support services:** GED preparation and test center, learning center, pre-admission summer program, reduced course load, remedial instruction, study skills assistance, tutoring, writing center.

Majors. **Agriculture:** Equestrian studies, farm/ranch, range science. **Biology:** General. **Business:** General, accounting, administrative services, business admin. **Computer sciences:** General. **Construction:** Pipefitting, power transmission. **Education:** General, elementary, secondary. **Engineering technology:** Manufacturing. **Health:** Medical secretary. **History:** General. **Legal studies:** Legal secretary. **Liberal arts:** Arts/sciences. **Math:** General. **Philosophy/religion:** Philosophy. **Physical sciences:** Chemistry, physics. **Psychology:** General. **Social sciences:** General, political science, sociology.

Computing on campus. 59 workstations in dormitories, library, student center. Dormitories wired for high-speed internet access.

Student life. **Freshman orientation:** Mandatory. Preregistration for classes offered. Session available at start of and during semester. **Policies:** Freshmen permitted cars on campus. **Housing:** Single-sex dorms, apartments, substance-free housing available. $135 fully refundable deposit, deadline 8/22. **Activities:** Choral groups, drama, music ensembles, student government, rodeo club, agriculture club, Phi Theta Kappa, cosmetology club, licensed vocational nursing club, Circle K, business club, art club, computer club, Future Educators Association.

Athletics. NJCAA. **Intercollegiate:** Baseball M, basketball, softball W, volleyball W. **Intramural:** Basketball, bowling, cheerleading, racquetball, softball, table tennis, tennis, volleyball. **Team name:** Plainsmen.

Student services. Adult student services, alcohol/substance abuse counseling, career counseling, services for economically disadvantaged, student employment services, financial aid counseling, personal counseling, placement for graduates, veterans' counselor. **Transfer:** Special adviser, orientation, re-entry adviser, pre-admission transcript evaluation for new students. Transfer adviser, college fairs on campus for students transferring to 4-year colleges.

Contact. E-mail: braper@fpc.cc.tx.us
Phone: (806) 457-4200 ext. 740 Fax: (806) 457-4225
Beth Raper, Director of Enrollment Management, Frank Phillips College, Box 5118, Borger, TX 79008-5118

Galveston College

Galveston, Texas
www.gc.edu **CB code: 6255**

- Public 2-year community college
- Commuter campus in small city

General. Founded in 1967. Regionally accredited. **Enrollment:** 2,230 degree-seeking undergraduates. **Degrees:** 159 associate awarded. **Location:** 50 miles from Houston. **Calendar:** Semester, limited summer session. **Full-time faculty:** 55 total; 27% minority, 51% women. **Part-time faculty:** 90 total; 29% minority, 69% women. **Class size:** 75% < 20, 25% 20-39, less than 1% >100. **Special facilities:** Center for health related technology. **Partnerships:** Formal partnership with UTMB in health career profession, Ball High School in the Tech Prep and dual credit programs.

Student profile. Among degree-seeking undergraduates, 60% enrolled in a transfer program, 40% enrolled in a vocational program, 300 enrolled as first-time, first-year students, 455 transferred in from other institutions.

Part-time:	62%	**Asian American:**	3%
Out-of-state:	4%	**Hispanic American:**	24%
Women:	65%	**International:**	1%
African American:	19%	**25 or older:**	44%

Transfer out. **Colleges most students transferred to 2005:** University of Houston-Clear Lake.

Basis for selection. Open admission, but selective for some programs. Health occupations majors have special admission requirements.

2005-2006 Annual costs. Tuition/fees: $1,414; $2,744 out-of-state. Per-credit charge: $30 in-state; $60 out-of-state. Books/supplies: $876. Personal expenses: $1,380.

Financial aid. All financial aid based on need. Need-based aid available for part-time students. Work study available for part-time students.

Application procedures. **Admission:** No deadline. No application fee. Application must be submitted on paper. Admission notification on a rolling basis. **Financial aid:** Priority date 6/9; no closing date. FAFSA required. Applicants notified on a rolling basis starting 6/1.

Academics. **Special study options:** Cooperative education, distance learning, dual enrollment of high school students, ESL, honors, independent study, internships, teacher certification program, weekend college. License preparation in nursing, paramedic. **Credit/placement by examination:** CLEP. 24 credit hours maximum toward associate degree. **Support services:** GED preparation, learning center, remedial instruction, tutoring.

Majors. **Biology:** General, marine. **Business:** Accounting, administrative services, business admin, entrepreneurial studies, marketing, office/clerical. **Computer sciences:** General, computer science, information systems, programming. **Education:** Elementary, physical. **Engineering:** General. **English:** Speech/rhetoric. **Family/consumer sciences:** Family studies. **Foreign languages:** Spanish. **Health:** EMT paramedic, health care admin, medical radiologic technology/radiation therapy, medical records technology, medical secretary, nuclear medical technology, nursing (RN), predentistry, premedicine, preveterinary. **History:** General. **Interdisciplinary:** Biological/physical sciences. **Legal studies:** Prelaw. **Liberal arts:** Arts/sciences. **Math:** General. **Personal/culinary services:** Culinary arts. **Physical sciences:** Chemistry, geology, physics. **Protective services:** Criminal justice, fire safety technology. **Psychology:** General. **Public administration:** Social work. **Social sciences:** Anthropology, economics, geography, political science, sociology. **Visual/performing arts:** Art, dramatic.

Most popular majors. Business/marketing 6%, health sciences 62%, liberal arts 23%.

Computing on campus. 170 workstations in library, computer center.

Student life. **Freshman orientation:** Mandatory. **Policies:** Freshmen permitted cars on campus. **Housing:** Special housing for scholarship athletes. **Activities:** Choral groups, drama, music ensembles, student government, student newspaper, student activities council, journalism club, African American club, Campus Crusade for Christ, Hispanic student organization, single parents organization, environmental awareness club, Phi Theta Kappa, nuclear medicine club, student nurses association.

Athletics. NJCAA. **Intercollegiate:** Baseball M, softball W, volleyball W. **Intramural:** Bowling, golf, tennis. **Team name:** Whitecaps.

Student services. Career counseling, student employment services, on-campus daycare, personal counseling, placement for graduates, veterans' counselor. **Physically disabled:** Services for visually, speech, hearing impaired. **Transfer:** Special adviser, orientation for new students. Transfer adviser, college fairs on campus for students transferring to 4-year colleges.

Contact. E-mail: blowery@gc.edu
Phone: (409) 944-1230 Fax: (409) 944-1501
Brian Lowery, Director of Admissions/Registrar, Galveston College, 4015 Avenue Q, Galveston, TX 77550

Grayson County College

Denison, Texas
www.grayson.edu **CB code: 6254**

- Public 2-year community and technical college
- Commuter campus in large town

General. Founded in 1963. Regionally accredited. **Enrollment:** 2,000 full-time, degree-seeking students. **Degrees:** 421 associate awarded. **Location:** 7 miles from Sherman, 75 miles from Dallas. **Calendar:** Semester, limited summer session. **Full-time faculty:** 81 total. **Part-time faculty:** 167 total. **Special facilities:** Vineyard.

Student profile.

Out-of-state:	2%	**Live on campus:**	6%

Basis for selection. Open admission, but selective for some programs. Special requirements for nursing, radiology, medical lab tech, vocational nursing certificate, EMT/paramedic programs. Observes TASP requirements. **Homeschooled:** Transcript of courses and grades required.

2005-2006 Annual costs. Tuition/fees: $1,260; $1,470 out-of-district; $2,940 out-of-state. Per-credit charge: $42 in-district; $49 out-of-district; $98 out-of-state. Room/board: $3,284. Books/supplies: $504. Personal expenses: $1,192.

Financial aid. Need-based: Need-based aid available for part-time students. **Additional information:** Short term loans available.

Application procedures. Admission: No deadline. No application fee. Admission notification on a rolling basis. **Financial aid:** No deadline. FAFSA required. Applicants notified on a rolling basis; must reply within 5 week(s) of notification.

Academics. Special study options: Combined bachelor's/graduate degree, distance learning, dual enrollment of high school students, ESL, honors, internships. Bachelor's degree programs available on campus. License preparation in nursing, paramedic, radiology. **Credit/placement by examination:** AP, CLEP, institutional tests. 32 credit hours maximum toward associate degree. THEA required of all freshman for placement and counseling. **Support services:** GED preparation and test center, learning center, pre-admission summer program, reduced course load, remedial instruction, study skills assistance, tutoring.

Majors. Biology: General. **Business:** General, accounting, administrative services, office management, office technology, office/clerical. **Computer sciences:** General, programming. **Education:** General, elementary, secondary. **Engineering:** General. **Engineering technology:** Drafting, electrical. **English:** Speech/rhetoric. **Health:** Clinical lab science, EMT paramedic, nursing (RN), predentistry, premedicine, prepharmacy, substance abuse counseling. **Liberal arts:** Arts/sciences. **Math:** General. **Mechanic/repair:** Auto body, electronics/electrical, heating/ac/refrig, industrial. **Physical sciences:** Chemistry, geology, physics. **Protective services:** Law enforcement admin, police science. **Psychology:** General. **Social sciences:** Sociology. **Visual/performing arts:** Art, commercial/advertising art, dramatic.

Computing on campus. Dormitories wired for high-speed internet access. Online course registration, wireless network available.

Student life. Freshman orientation: Available. Preregistration for classes offered. Web-based program. Dates vary. **Policies:** Freshmen permitted cars on campus. **Housing:** Single-sex dorms, substance-free housing available. **Activities:** Jazz band, choral groups, drama, music ensembles, student government, student newspaper.

Athletics. NJCAA. **Intercollegiate:** Baseball M, basketball, softball W. **Intramural:** Baseball M, basketball, softball W. **Team name:** Vikings.

Student services. Adult student services, career counseling, services for economically disadvantaged, financial aid counseling, personal counseling, veterans' counselor. **Transfer:** Special adviser, orientation for new students. College fairs on campus for students transferring to 4-year colleges.

Contact. Phone: (903) 465-8604 Fax: (903) 463-8733
David Petrash, Associate Vice President for Admissions and Records, Grayson County College, 6101 Grayson Drive, Denison, TX 75020

Hallmark Institute of Aeronautics

San Antonio, Texas
www.hallmarkinstitute.com **CB code: 3166**

- For-profit 2-year technical college
- Commuter campus in very large city
- Interview required

General. Accredited by ACCSCT. Located at San Antonio International Airport. **Enrollment:** 233 degree-seeking undergraduates. **Degrees:** 124 associate awarded. **Calendar:** Continuous, extensive summer session. **Full-time faculty:** 8 total; 25% minority, 12% women.

Student profile. Among degree-seeking undergraduates, 100% enrolled in a vocational program, 1% already have a bachelor's degree or higher, 67 enrolled as first-time, first-year students.

Out-of-state:	3%	**Asian American:**	3%
Women:	7%	**Hispanic American:**	58%
African American:	7%	**25 or older:**	49%

Transfer out. Colleges most students transferred to 2005: Texas State Technical College, Palo Alto College.

Basis for selection. Aviation entrance test and interview required. **Adult students:** Entrance exam policies same as for first-time freshmen. **Homeschooled:** Transcript of courses and grades required.

2005-2006 Annual costs. Tuition for combined associate program in airframe technology or powerplant technology: $21,915. Tuition for diploma programs ranges from $12,181 to $17,384. Costs include books, equipment and supplies. Required fees: $200. Registration fee: $100. Course fees vary. International students pay additional 8%.

Application procedures. Admission: No deadline. $100 fee. Admission notification on a rolling basis. **Financial aid:** No deadline. FAFSA required. Applicants notified on a rolling basis.

Academics. Special study options: Accelerated study, honors, liberal arts/career combination. License preparation in aviation. **Credit/placement by examination:** AP, CLEP. 49 credit hours maximum toward associate degree. **Support services:** Tutoring.

Majors. Mechanic/repair: Aircraft, aircraft powerplant, avionics.

Computing on campus. Online library available.

Student life. Freshman orientation: Mandatory. **Policies:** Freshmen permitted cars on campus.

Student services. Career counseling, student employment services, financial aid counseling, placement for graduates. **Transfer:** Special adviser, orientation, pre-admission transcript evaluation for new students.

Contact. E-mail: slava.ross@hallmarkinstitute.com
Phone: (210) 826-1000 Toll-free number: (888) 656-9300
Fax: (210) 826-3707
Sonia Ross, Director of Aviation Admissions, Hallmark Institute of Aeronautics, 8901 Wetmore Road, San Antonio, TX 78230

Hallmark Institute of Technology

San Antonio, Texas
www.hallmarkinstitute.com **CB code: 2307**

- For-profit 2-year business and technical college
- Commuter campus in very large city
- Interview required

General. Founded in 1969. Accredited by ACCSCT. Additional campus focusing on aeronautics (known as Hallmark Institute of Aeronautics) located on property of San Antonio Airport. **Enrollment:** 538 degree-seeking undergraduates. **Degrees:** 275 associate awarded. **Location:** 5 miles from San Antonio, 80 miles from Austin. **Calendar:** Continuous, extensive summer session. **Full-time faculty:** 11 total; 18% have terminal degrees, 91% minority, 36% women. **Part-time faculty:** 31 total; 16% minority, 26% women.

Student profile. Among degree-seeking undergraduates, 100% enrolled in a vocational program, 1% already have a bachelor's degree or higher, 117 enrolled as first-time, first-year students.

Women:	43%	**Hispanic American:**	62%
African American:	15%	**25 or older:**	57%
Asian American:	1%		

Basis for selection. Standardized test scores, interview important. High school diploma or GED required. **Adult students:** Entrance exam policies same as for first-time freshmen. **Homeschooled:** Transcript of courses and grades required.

2005-2006 Annual costs. Per-credit charge: $16. Costs for associate programs range from $14,830 to $23,850; additional registration fee $100 for all programs.

Application procedures. Admission: No deadline. $100 fee. Admission notification on a rolling basis. **Financial aid:** No deadline. FAFSA required. Applicants notified on a rolling basis.

Two-Year Colleges

Academics. **Special study options:** Accelerated study. License preparation in aviation. **Credit/placement by examination:** AP, CLEP. 36 credit hours maximum toward associate degree. **Support services:** Tutoring.

Majors. **Business:** Office technology. **Computer sciences:** Networking. **Engineering technology:** Electrical. **Health:** Medical assistant.

Most popular majors. Business/marketing 29%, computer/information sciences 25%, engineering/engineering technologies 28%, health sciences 17%.

Computing on campus. 193 workstations in library, computer center. Online library, wireless network available.

Student life. **Freshman orientation:** Mandatory.

Student services. Career counseling, student employment services, financial aid counseling, placement for graduates. **Transfer:** Special adviser, orientation, pre-admission transcript evaluation for new students.

Contact. E-mail: sross@hallmarkinstitute.com
Phone: (210) 690-9000 Toll-free number: (800) 880-6600
Fax: (210) 697-8225
Sonia Ross, Vice President of Admissions, Hallmark Institute of Technology, 10401 IH 10 West, San Antonio, TX 78230-1737

Hill College

Hillsboro, Texas
www.hillcollege.edu **CB code: 6285**

- Public 2-year community and junior college
- Commuter campus in small town

General. Founded in 1923. Regionally accredited. **Enrollment:** 3,016 degree-seeking undergraduates. **Degrees:** 192 associate awarded. **Location:** 64 miles from Dallas. **Calendar:** Semester, limited summer session. **Full-time faculty:** 70 total. **Part-time faculty:** 84 total. **Special facilities:** History complex including gun museum and Civil War research center.

Student profile. Among degree-seeking undergraduates, 1% already have a bachelor's degree or higher, 1,192 enrolled as first-time, first-year students.

Part-time:	55%	**Hispanic American:**	11%
Out-of-state:	1%	**Native American:**	1%
Women:	61%	**International:**	2%
African American:	6%	**Live on campus:**	14%
Asian American:	1%		

Transfer out. **Colleges most students transferred to 2005:** Tarleton State University, Tarrant County Junior College, University of Texas at Arlington.

Basis for selection. Open admission, but selective for some programs. Special requirements for nursing program. Observes TASP guidelines. THEA Test or Approved State Alternative Test required for academic students unless exempted by state. **Adult students:** Entrance exam policies same as for first-time freshmen. **Homeschooled:** Transcript of courses and grades required.

2005-2006 Annual costs. Tuition/fees: $1,310; $1,550 out-of-district; $1,950 out-of-state. Per-credit charge: $43 in-district; $51 out-of-district; $51 out-of-state. Room/board: $3,190. Books/supplies: $2,000. Personal expenses: $1,440.

2004-2005 Financial aid. **Need-based:** 97% of total undergraduate aid awarded as scholarships/grants, 3% as loans/jobs. Need-based aid available for part-time students. Work study available for part-time students. **Non-need-based:** Scholarships awarded for academics, athletics, music/drama.

Application procedures. **Admission:** No deadline. No application fee. Application must be submitted on paper. Admission notification on a rolling basis. **Financial aid:** Priority date 8/1; no closing date. FAFSA, institutional form required. Applicants notified on a rolling basis.

Academics. **Special study options:** Combined bachelor's/graduate degree, cooperative education, distance learning, dual enrollment of high school students, honors, independent study, internships, liberal arts/career combination. Bachelor's degree programs available on campus. **Credit/placement by examination:** AP, CLEP. 24 credit hours maximum toward associate degree. **Support services:** GED test center, learning center, reduced course load, remedial instruction, study skills assistance, tutoring.

Majors. **Agriculture:** Business. **Biology:** General, botany, zoology. **Business:** Administrative services, business admin, office management, office technology, office/clerical, real estate. **Communications:** General, journalism. **Computer sciences:** General, applications programming, computer science, data processing, programming. **Education:** General. **Engineering:** General. **Engineering technology:** Drafting, electrical, robotics. **Family/consumer sciences:** Institutional food production. **Foreign languages:** General. **Health:** Licensed practical nurse. **Interdisciplinary:** Biological/physical sciences. **Legal studies:** Prelaw. **Liberal arts:** Arts/sciences. **Math:** General. **Mechanic/repair:** Auto body, heating/ac/refrig. **Parks/recreation:** Health/fitness. **Physical sciences:** Chemistry, geology, physics. **Protective services:** Criminal justice, fire services admin, law enforcement admin, police science, security services. **Psychology:** General. **Visual/performing arts:** General, art, commercial/advertising art.

Most popular majors. Business/marketing 11%, education 14%, liberal arts 43%, security/protective services 8%.

Computing on campus. 65 workstations in library, computer center. Online library, helpline available.

Student life. **Freshman orientation:** Mandatory. Preregistration for classes offered. **Policies:** Freshmen permitted cars on campus. **Housing:** Single-sex dorms, substance-free housing available. $50 nonrefundable deposit. International students must live in dormitories. **Activities:** Bands, choral groups, drama, film society, music ensembles, student government, Circle K, Young Democrats, Young Republicans, Baptist Student Union, student council.

Athletics. NJCAA. **Intercollegiate:** Baseball M, basketball, soccer W, softball W, volleyball W. **Intramural:** Volleyball.

Student services. Adult student services, career counseling, services for economically disadvantaged, student employment services, financial aid counseling, personal counseling, placement for graduates, veterans' counselor. **Physically disabled:** Services for visually, speech, hearing impaired. **Transfer:** Special adviser for new students. Transfer adviser, college fairs on campus for students transferring to 4-year colleges.

Contact. Phone: (254) 582-2555 Fax: (254) 582-7591
Diane Harvey, Director of Admissions, Hill College, Box 619, Hillsboro, TX 76645

Houston Community College System

Houston, Texas
www.hccs.edu **CB code: 0929**

- Public 2-year community college
- Commuter campus in very large city

General. Founded in 1971. Regionally accredited. Multicampus system. Students may attend campus of choice. College system manages cable television channel with production facilities. **Enrollment:** 39,516 undergraduates. **Degrees:** 1,923 associate awarded. **ROTC:** Army. **Calendar:** Semester, extensive summer session. **Full-time faculty:** 814 total; 40% minority, 50% women. **Part-time faculty:** 2,391 total; 49% minority, 47% women. **Partnerships:** Formal partnerships with local high schools for tech-prep and school-to-work programs; contract training agreements with industry.

Student profile. 1,835 transferred in from other institutions.

Transfer out. **Colleges most students transferred to 2005:** University of Houston-Central, University of Texas-Austin, Texas A&M College Station, University of Houston-Downtown.

Basis for selection. Open admission, but selective for some programs. High school transcript, assessment, personal interview required for admission to some health programs. According to Texas state law, students must take TASP (Texas Academic Skills Program) test or TASP alternative. Some students may qualify for TASP exemptions. International students must demonstrate English proficiency by taking TASP (or accepted alternative) and CELSA. Interview required for health careers. **Adult students:** Entrance exam policies same as for first-time freshmen.

2005-2006 Annual costs. Tuition/fees: $1,470; $3,090 out-of-district; $3,690 out-of-state. Per-credit charge: $49 in-district; $103 out-of-district; $123 out-of-state.

Financial aid. **Need-based:** Need-based aid available for part-time students. Work study available nights and weekends.

Application procedures. **Admission:** No deadline. No application fee. Application may be submitted online. **Financial aid:** Priority date 8/15; no closing date. FAFSA required. Applicants notified on a rolling basis starting 6/1; must reply within 2 week(s) of notification.

Academics. **Special study options:** Cooperative education, distance learning, dual enrollment of high school students, ESL, honors, independent study, internships, study abroad, weekend college. Alternative teacher certification program. License preparation in aviation, dental hygiene, nursing, occupational therapy, paramedic, physical therapy, radiology, real estate. **Credit/placement by examination:** AP, CLEP, institutional tests. 15 credit hours maximum toward associate degree. **Support services:** GED preparation and test center, learning center, remedial instruction, tutoring.

Majors. Agriculture: Horticulture. **Business:** Accounting, administrative services, banking/financial services, business admin, communications, fashion, hotel/motel admin, international, logistics, marketing, operations, real estate, tourism/travel. **Communications technology:** Graphic/printing, radio/tv. **Computer sciences:** General, programming. **Engineering technology:** Computer, construction, drafting, electrical, industrial, water quality. **Family/consumer sciences:** Child care. **Foreign languages:** Sign language interpretation. **Health:** Clinical lab technology, EMT paramedic, histologic assistant, medical radiologic technology/radiation therapy, medical records technology, medical secretary, mental health services, nuclear medical technology, nursing (RN), occupational therapy assistant, physical therapy assistant, respiratory therapy technology. **Legal studies:** Court reporting, paralegal. **Mechanic/repair:** Automotive. **Parks/recreation:** Health/fitness. **Personal/culinary services:** Cosmetic. **Protective services:** Fire safety technology, police science. **Science technology:** Biological, chemical. **Social sciences:** Cartography. **Visual/performing arts:** Commercial photography, commercial/advertising art, fashion design, interior design, music management, music performance, music theory/composition.

Most popular majors. Business/marketing 6%, health sciences 14%, liberal arts 68%.

Computing on campus. 4,121 workstations in library, computer center. Online course registration, helpline available.

Student life. Freshman orientation: Mandatory. Various locations. **Activities:** Drama, literary magazine, student government, student newspaper, TV station, international student association, Vietnamese student association, United Student Council, Black Student Union, Association of Latin American Students, Phi Theta Kappa.

Athletics. Intramural: Football (tackle) M.

Student services. Alcohol/substance abuse counseling, career counseling, services for economically disadvantaged, student employment services, financial aid counseling, minority student services, on-campus daycare, personal counseling, placement for graduates, veterans' counselor, women's services. **Physically disabled:** Services for visually, speech, hearing impaired. **Transfer:** Orientation for new students. College fairs on campus for students transferring to 4-year colleges.

Contact. Phone: (713) 718-8500 Fax: (713) 718-2111
Mary Lemburg, Registrar, Houston Community College System, 3100 Main, Houston, TX 77266-7517

Howard College
Big Spring, Texas
www.howardcollege.edu **CB code: 6277**

- Public 2-year community college
- Commuter campus in large town

General. Founded in 1945. Regionally accredited. **Enrollment:** 2,663 degree-seeking undergraduates; 122 non-degree-seeking students. **Degrees:** 240 associate awarded. **Location:** 105 miles from Lubbock, 40 miles from Midland. **Calendar:** Semester, limited summer session. **Full-time faculty:** 118 total; 6% have terminal degrees, 11% minority, 48% women. **Part-time faculty:** 89 total; 8% minority, 63% women. **Special facilities:** Rodeo arena, arts center.

Student profile. Among degree-seeking undergraduates, 37% enrolled in a transfer program, 61% enrolled in a vocational program, 1% already have a bachelor's degree or higher, 444 enrolled as first-time, first-year students.

Part-time:	68%	**25 or older:**	35%
Out-of-state:	2%	**Live on campus:**	8%
Women:	62%		

Transfer out. Colleges most students transferred to 2005: Texas Tech University, Angelo State University, Tarleton State University, University of Texas-Permian Basin, Texas A&M University.

Basis for selection. Open admission, but selective for some programs. Special requirements for health, cosmetology programs. Interview required for dental hygiene, degree and licensed vocational nursing, cosmetology programs. **Adult students:** Entrance exam policies same as for first-time freshmen.

2005-2006 Annual costs. Tuition/fees: $1,312; $1,672 out-of-district; $2,312 out-of-state. Room/board: $3,140. Books/supplies: $500. Personal expenses: $1,330.

Financial aid. Need-based: Need-based aid available for part-time students. Work study available for part-time students. **Non-need-based:** Scholarships awarded for academics, athletics, leadership, music/drama.

Application procedures. Admission: No deadline. No application fee. Admission notification on a rolling basis. **Financial aid:** Priority date 4/1; no closing date. FAFSA, institutional form required. Applicants notified on a rolling basis starting 7/15; must reply within 2 week(s) of notification.

Academics. Special study options: Cooperative education, cross-registration, distance learning, dual enrollment of high school students, ESL, liberal arts/career combination, weekend college. License preparation in dental hygiene, nursing, paramedic. **Credit/placement by examination:** CLEP, institutional tests. 18 credit hours maximum toward associate degree. **Support services:** GED preparation and test center, learning center, pre-admission summer program, reduced course load, remedial instruction, tutoring.

Majors. Agriculture: General, business. **Biology:** General. **Business:** General, accounting, office/clerical. **Communications:** Journalism. **Computer sciences:** General. **Education:** General. **Foreign languages:** General, sign language interpretation. **Health:** Athletic training, dental hygiene, dental lab technology, EMT ambulance attendant, medical assistant, medical records admin, medical records technology, nursing (RN), physical therapy assistant, predentistry, premedicine, respiratory therapy technology, substance abuse counseling. **Legal studies:** Paralegal. **Liberal arts:** Arts/sciences. **Math:** General. **Parks/recreation:** Health/fitness. **Physical sciences:** Chemistry, physics. **Psychology:** General. **Social sciences:** General. **Visual/performing arts:** General, art, dramatic.

Computing on campus. 100 workstations in dormitories, library, computer center. Dormitories wired for high-speed internet access and linked to campus network. Online library available.

Student life. Freshman orientation: Available. Preregistration for classes offered. **Policies:** Freshmen permitted cars on campus. **Housing:** Single-sex dorms available. **Activities:** Bands, choral groups, dance, drama, music ensembles, musical theater, student government, Phi Theta Kappa.

Athletics. NJCAA. **Intercollegiate:** Baseball M, basketball, cheerleading, rodeo, softball W. **Intramural:** Basketball, bowling, golf, handball, racquetball, softball, tennis, volleyball. **Team name:** Hawks.

Student services. Adult student services, career counseling, services for economically disadvantaged, student employment services, financial aid counseling, health services, on-campus daycare, personal counseling, placement for graduates, veterans' counselor. **Physically disabled:** Services for hearing impaired. **Transfer:** Special adviser for new students. Transfer adviser, college fairs on campus for students transferring to 4-year colleges.

Contact. Phone: (432) 264-5000 Fax: (432) 264-5604
Donna Merrick, Registrar, Howard College, 1001 Birdwell Lane, Big Spring, TX 79720

ITT Technical Institute: Arlington
Arlington, Texas
www.itt-tech.edu **CB code: 3572**

- For-profit 2-year technical college
- Commuter campus in large city

General. Founded in 1982. Accredited by ACICS. **Location:** 11 miles from Fort Worth, 18 miles from Dallas. **Calendar:** Quarter.

Annual costs/financial aid. Tuition varies by program, $260-$368 per credit hour.

Contact. Phone: (817) 794-5100
Director of Recruitment, 551 Ryan Plaza Drive, Arlington, TX 76011

ITT Technical Institute: Austin
Austin, Texas
www.itt-tech.edu **CB code: 2692**

- For-profit 2-year technical college
- Commuter campus in large city

General. Accredited by ACICS. **Calendar:** Quarter.

Annual costs/financial aid. Tuition varies by program, $260-$368 per credit hour.

Contact. Phone: (512) 467-6800
Director of Recruitment, 6330 Highway 290 East, Austin, TX 78723

ITT Technical Institute: Houston
Houston, Texas
www.itt-tech.edu **CB code: 3573**

- For-profit 2-year technical college
- Commuter campus in very large city

General. Founded in 1983. Accredited by ACICS. **Calendar:** Quarter.

Annual costs/financial aid. Tuition varies by program, $260-$368 per credit hour.

Contact. Phone: (713) 952-2294
Director of Recruitment, 2950 South Gessner, Houston, TX 77063-3751

ITT Technical Institute: Houston North
Houston, Texas
www.itt-tech.edu **CB code: 2712**

- For-profit 2-year technical college
- Commuter campus in very large city

General. Accredited by ACICS. **Calendar:** Quarter.

Annual costs/financial aid. Tuition varies by program, $260-$368 per credit hour.

Contact. Phone: (281) 873-0512
Director of Recruitment, 15621 Blue Ash Drive, Houston, TX 77090-5818

ITT Technical Institute: Houston South
Houston, Texas
www.itt-tech.edu **CB code: 2715**

- For-profit 2-year technical college
- Commuter campus in very large city

General. Accredited by ACICS. **Calendar:** Quarter.

Annual costs/financial aid. Tuition varies by program, $260-$368 per credit hour.

Contact. Phone: (281) 486-2630
Director of Recruitment, 2222 Bay Area Boulevard, Houston, TX 77058

ITT Technical Institute: Richardson
Richardson, Texas
www.itt-tech.edu **CB code: 2747**

- For-profit 2-year technical college
- Commuter campus in small city

General. Accredited by ACICS. **Location:** 12 miles from Dallas. **Calendar:** Quarter.

Annual costs/financial aid. Tuition varies by program, $260-$368 per credit hour.

Contact. Phone: (972) 690-9100
Director of Recruitment, 2101 Waterview Parkway, Richardson, TX 75080

ITT Technical Institute: San Antonio
San Antonio, Texas
www.itt-tech.edu **CB code: 2328**

- For-profit 2-year technical college
- Commuter campus in very large city

General. Founded in 1988. Accredited by ACICS. **Location:** 200 miles from Houston, 75 miles from Austin. **Calendar:** Quarter.

Annual costs/financial aid. Tuition varies by program, $260-$368 per credit hour.

Contact. Phone: (210) 694-4612
Director of Recruitment, 5700 Northwest Parkway, San Antonio, TX 78249

Jacksonville College
Jacksonville, Texas
www.jacksonville-college.edu **CB code: 6317**

- Private 2-year junior and liberal arts college affiliated with Baptist faith
- Commuter campus in large town

General. Founded in 1899. Regionally accredited. Affiliated with Baptist Missionary Association of Texas. **Enrollment:** 216 degree-seeking undergraduates. **Degrees:** 59 associate awarded. **Location:** 120 miles from Dallas, 25 miles from Tyler. **Calendar:** Semester, limited summer session. **Full-time faculty:** 11 total. **Part-time faculty:** 14 total.

Student profile.

Out-of-state:	5%	**Live on campus:**	41%
25 or older:	16%		

Transfer out. Colleges most students transferred to 2005: University of Texas at Tyler, Stephen F. Austin State University, Dallas Baptist University, East Texas Baptist University.

Basis for selection. Open admission. Interview recommended. **Adult students:** Entrance exam policies same as for first-time freshmen. **Home-schooled:** Must take ACT or SAT.

2006-2007 Annual costs. Tuition/fees (projected): $5,846. Per-credit charge: $175. Room/board: $2,628. Books/supplies: $800. Personal expenses: $1,135.

2004-2005 Financial aid. Need-based: 97% of total undergraduate aid awarded as scholarships/grants, 3% as loans/jobs. **Non-need-based:** Scholarships awarded for academics, athletics, music/drama, religious affiliation, state residency.

Application procedures. Admission: Priority date 8/15; no deadline. $15 fee. Application may be submitted online. Admission notification on a rolling basis beginning on or about 1/15. **Financial aid:** Priority date 8/1; no closing date. FAFSA required. Applicants notified on a rolling basis.

Academics. Special study options: Dual enrollment of high school students. **Credit/placement by examination:** CLEP, institutional tests. **Support services:** Reduced course load, remedial instruction, tutoring.

Majors. Liberal arts: Arts/sciences.

Computing on campus. 30 workstations in library, computer center.

Student life. Freshman orientation: Available. Preregistration for classes offered. **Policies:** Freshmen permitted cars on campus. **Housing:** Single-sex dorms, apartments available. $80 deposit. **Activities:** Concert band, choral groups, drama, music ensembles, student government, ministerial alliance, mission band.

Athletics. NJCAA. **Intercollegiate:** Basketball, volleyball W. **Intramural:** Basketball, softball, table tennis, tennis, volleyball W. **Team name:** Jaguars.

Student services. Career counseling, health services, personal counseling. **Transfer:** Special adviser, orientation for new students. Transfer adviser, college fairs on campus for students transferring to 4-year colleges.

Contact. E-mail: admissions@jacksonville-college.edu
Phone: (903) 586-2518 Toll-free number: (800) 256-8522
Fax: (903) 586-0743
Melissa Walles, Director of Admissions, Jacksonville College, 105 B.J. Albritton Drive, Jacksonville, TX 75766-4759

Kilgore College
Kilgore, Texas
www.kilgore.edu **CB code: 6341**

- Public 2-year community college
- Commuter campus in large town

General. Founded in 1935. Regionally accredited. **Enrollment:** 4,752 degree-seeking undergraduates. **Degrees:** 485 associate awarded. **Location:** 120

miles from Dallas, 60 miles from Shreveport, Louisiana. **Calendar:** Semester, extensive summer session. **Full-time faculty:** 133 total. **Part-time faculty:** 116 total. **Class size:** 39% < 20, 59% 20-39, 2% 40-49, less than 1% 50-99. **Special facilities:** Experimental farm, oil museum.

Student profile.

Out-of-state:	4%	**Live on campus:**	10%
25 or older:	31%		

Transfer out. **Colleges most students transferred to 2005:** University of Texas at Tyler, University of North Texas, Stephen F. Austin State University, Texas A&M University, University of Texas at Austin.

Basis for selection. Open admission, but selective for some programs. For health occupation programs and some public service programs, standardized test scores, secondary school record, essay used as admissions criteria.

2005-2006 Annual costs. Tuition/fees: $1,050; $2,190 out-of-district; $3,030 out-of-state. Per-credit charge: $35 in-district; $73 out-of-district; $101 out-of-state. Room/board: $3,630. Books/supplies: $1,000. Personal expenses: $1,200.

2004-2005 Financial aid. **Need-based:** 95% of total undergraduate aid awarded as scholarships/grants, 5% as loans/jobs. Need-based aid available for part-time students. Work study available for part-time students. **Non-need-based:** Scholarships awarded for academics, alumni affiliation, art, athletics, job skills, leadership, music/drama, state residency. **Additional information:** State of Texas grants and loans available for honor graduates with unmet needs and for non-traditional students.

Application procedures. **Admission:** Priority date 8/15; no deadline. No application fee. Application may be submitted online. Admission notification on a rolling basis. **Financial aid:** Priority date 6/1, closing date 7/15. FAFSA, institutional form required. Applicants notified on a rolling basis starting 3/1; must reply within 2 week(s) of notification.

Academics. **Special study options:** Cooperative education, distance learning, dual enrollment of high school students, ESL, internships. License preparation in nursing. **Credit/placement by examination:** AP, CLEP, institutional tests. 14 credit hours maximum toward associate degree. **Support services:** GED preparation and test center, learning center, pre-admission summer program, reduced course load, remedial instruction, study skills assistance, tutoring, writing center.

Majors. **Agriculture:** General. **Biology:** General. **Business:** General, accounting, business admin, e-commerce, executive assistant, management information systems, operations, real estate. **Communications:** General, journalism. **Computer sciences:** General, programming, systems analysis. **Education:** General, art, biology, chemistry, health, health occupations, history, social science. **Engineering:** General, chemical, civil. **Engineering technology:** Civil, drafting, electrical, metallurgical, occupational safety. **Family/consumer sciences:** Child care. **Foreign languages:** French, German, Spanish. **Health:** Clinical lab technology, EMT paramedic, medical assistant, medical radiologic technology/radiation therapy, nursing (RN), physical therapy assistant, surgical technology. **History:** General. **Legal studies:** Court reporting, legal secretary, paralegal, prelaw. **Liberal arts:** Arts/sciences. **Math:** General. **Mechanic/repair:** Auto body, automotive, diesel, electronics/electrical. **Parks/recreation:** Health/fitness. **Physical sciences:** Chemistry, physics. **Production:** Machine tool. **Protective services:** Criminal justice, law enforcement admin, police science. **Psychology:** General. **Social sciences:** Sociology. **Visual/performing arts:** Art, commercial photography, commercial/advertising art, dance, dramatic.

Computing on campus. 350 workstations in library, computer center, student center. Online course registration available.

Student life. **Freshman orientation:** Mandatory. Preregistration for classes offered. **Policies:** Freshmen permitted cars on campus. **Housing:** Single-sex dorms available. $100 deposit, deadline 8/15. **Activities:** Bands, choral groups, dance, drama, music ensembles, musical theater, radio station, student government, student newspaper, TV station, church organizations, rodeo club, physical therapy club.

Athletics. NJCAA. **Intercollegiate:** Basketball, football (tackle) M. **Intramural:** Badminton, bowling, handball, racquetball, softball, swimming, tennis, volleyball. **Team name:** Rangers.

Student services. Career counseling, student employment services, health services, on-campus daycare, personal counseling, placement for graduates, veterans' counselor. **Physically disabled:** Services for visually, speech, hearing impaired. **Transfer:** Pre-admission transcript evaluation for new students. College fairs on campus for students transferring to 4-year colleges.

Contact. Phone: (903) 983-8209 Fax: (903) 983-8607
Bill Gibbs, Director of Admissions, Kilgore College, 1100 Broadway, Kilgore, TX 75662-3299

Lamar State College at Orange

Orange, Texas
www.lsco.edu **CB code: 1694**

- Public 2-year junior and liberal arts college
- Commuter campus in small city

General. Regionally accredited. **Enrollment:** 1,000 full-time, degree-seeking students. **Degrees:** 105 associate awarded. **Location:** 92 miles from Houston. **Calendar:** Semester, limited summer session. **Full-time faculty:** 48 total; 15% have terminal degrees, 12% minority, 71% women. **Part-time faculty:** 57 total; 12% have terminal degrees, 9% minority, 63% women. **Partnerships:** Formal partnership with CISCO.

Student profile.

Out-of-state:	9%	**25 or older:**	35%

Transfer out. **Colleges most students transferred to 2005:** Lamar University, Texas A&M-College Station, Sam Houston State University, Lamar State College-Port Arthur.

Basis for selection. Open admission, but selective for some programs. Nursing program selective; high school record and test scores may be evaluated for admission. Interview required for students without high school diploma or GED. Purpose of interview to determine if applicant can benefit from available educational programs. **Adult students:** Entrance exam policies same as for first-time freshmen.

High school preparation. 12 units recommended. Recommended units include English 4, mathematics 3, history 2 and science 3.

2005-2006 Annual costs. Tuition/fees: $3,070; $11,350 out-of-state. Per-credit charge: $76 in-state; $352 out-of-state. Books/supplies: $560. Personal expenses: $1,562.

2004-2005 Financial aid. All financial aid based on need. 98% of total undergraduate aid awarded as scholarships/grants, 2% as loans/jobs. Need-based aid available for part-time students. Work study available for part-time students.

Application procedures. **Admission:** No deadline. No application fee. Admission notification on a rolling basis. **Financial aid:** Priority date 4/1; no closing date. FAFSA, institutional form required. Applicants notified on a rolling basis starting 5/15; must reply within 2 week(s) of notification.

Academics. **Special study options:** Distance learning, dual enrollment of high school students, internships, liberal arts/career combination, teacher certification program. License preparation in nursing, paramedic. **Credit/placement by examination:** CLEP. 15 credit hours maximum toward associate degree. **Support services:** GED test center, learning center, remedial instruction, study skills assistance, tutoring.

Majors. **Business:** Accounting technology, administrative services, business admin. **Computer sciences:** General. **Engineering technology:** Environmental. **Health:** Clinical lab technology, EMT paramedic, medical secretary, nursing (RN). **Liberal arts:** Arts/sciences.

Most popular majors. Business/marketing 8%, computer/information sciences 9%, health sciences 28%, liberal arts 52%.

Computing on campus. 150 workstations in library, computer center, student center. Commuter students can connect to campus network. Online library available.

Student life. **Freshman orientation:** Available. Preregistration for classes offered. **Activities:** Student government.

Athletics. **Intramural:** Basketball, racquetball, volleyball.

Student services. Career counseling, financial aid counseling, placement for graduates, veterans' counselor. **Physically disabled:** Services for visually, hearing impaired. **Transfer:** Special adviser, orientation for new students.

Contact. Phone: (409) 882-3364 Fax: (409) 882-3055
Kerry Olson, Director of Admissions and Financial Aid, Lamar State College at Orange, 410 West Front Street, Orange, TX 77630

Lamar State College at Port Arthur

Port Arthur, Texas
www.lamarpa.edu **CB code: 6589**

- Public 2-year community and technical college
- Commuter campus in small city

General. Regionally accredited. **Enrollment:** 1,150 full-time, degree-seeking students. **Degrees:** 204 associate awarded. **Location:** 90 miles from Houston. **Calendar:** Semester, limited summer session. **Full-time faculty:** 68 total. **Part-time faculty:** 60 total. **Partnerships:** Formal partnerships with Microsoft and Novell (authorized training center).

Student profile.

Out-of-state:	1%	**25 or older:**	40%

Transfer out. Colleges most students transferred to 2005: Lamar University.

Basis for selection. Open admission, but selective for some programs. Special requirements for nursing programs only.

2005-2006 Annual costs. Tuition/fees: $3,100; $11,380 out-of-state. Per-credit charge: $76 in-state; $352 out-of-state. Books/supplies: $643. Personal expenses: $1,597.

Financial aid. All financial aid based on need. Need-based aid available for part-time students. Work study available nights, weekends and for part-time students.

Application procedures. Admission: No deadline. No application fee. Application may be submitted online. Admission notification on a rolling basis. **Financial aid:** Priority date 4/1; no closing date. FAFSA, institutional form required. Applicants notified on a rolling basis starting 4/15; must reply within 2 week(s) of notification.

Academics. Special study options: Cooperative education, cross-registration, distance learning, double major, dual enrollment of high school students, ESL, external degree, honors, independent study, internships, liberal arts/career combination, weekend college. License preparation in nursing. **Credit/placement by examination:** CLEP, institutional tests. SAT used for math placement if submitted. **Support services:** GED test center, learning center, pre-admission summer program, reduced course load, remedial instruction, study skills assistance, tutoring.

Majors. Business: Accounting, administrative services, business admin. **Computer sciences:** General. **Engineering technology:** Electrical, instrumentation. **Family/consumer sciences:** General, child care. **Health:** Medical secretary, nursing (RN), substance abuse counseling, surgical technology. **Legal studies:** Legal secretary. **Mechanic/repair:** Automotive, heating/ac/refrig. **Personal/culinary services:** Cosmetic. **Protective services:** Criminal justice.

Computing on campus. 79 workstations in library, computer center, student center. Online course registration, online library available.

Student life. Freshman orientation: Available. Preregistration for classes offered. Held 1 day in July and 1 in August. **Activities:** Choral groups, drama, musical theater, student government, student newspaper, association of family and consumer sciences, Baptist Student Ministry, criminal justice association, Epsilon Delta Phi honor society, legal assistant student school organization, historical society, Phi Theta Kappa academic honor society.

Athletics. Team name: Seahawks.

Student services. Adult student services, career counseling, services for economically disadvantaged, student employment services, financial aid counseling, on-campus daycare, personal counseling, placement for graduates, veterans' counselor. **Physically disabled:** Services for visually, speech, hearing impaired. **Transfer:** Special adviser, orientation, pre-admission transcript evaluation for new students. College fairs on campus for students transferring to 4-year colleges.

Contact. E-mail: connie.nicholas@lamarpa.edu
Phone: (409) 984-6168 Toll-free number: (800) 477-5872 ext. 6168
Fax: (409) 984-6025
Connie Nicholas, Registrar, Lamar State College at Port Arthur, Box 310, Port Arthur, TX 77641-0310

Laredo Community College

Laredo, Texas
www.laredo.edu

CB member
CB code: 6362

- Public 2-year community college
- Commuter campus in large city

General. Founded in 1946. Regionally accredited. Two-campus institution. **Enrollment:** 8,147 degree-seeking undergraduates; 151 non-degree-seeking students. **Degrees:** 794 associate awarded. **ROTC:** Army. **Location:** 150 miles from San Antonio, 140 miles from Corpus Christi. **Calendar:** Semester, extensive summer session. **Full-time faculty:** 211 total; 73% minority, 38% women. **Part-time faculty:** 159 total; 80% minority, 55% women. **Special facilities:** Museums, Abraham Kazen papers, special collections relating to regional history.

Student profile. Among degree-seeking undergraduates, 53% enrolled in a transfer program, 47% enrolled in a vocational program, 1% already have a bachelor's degree or higher, 1,318 enrolled as first-time, first-year students, 151 transferred in from other institutions.

Part-time:	61%	**25 or older:**	33%
Out-of-state:	4%	**Live on campus:**	2%
Women:	58%		

Transfer out. Colleges most students transferred to 2005: Texas A&M International University, University of Texas at San Antonio.

Basis for selection. Open admission, but selective for some programs. Special admissions requirements for nursing and allied health programs.

2005-2006 Annual costs. Tuition/fees: $1,626; $2,586 out-of-district; $3,546 out-of-state. Per-credit charge: $32 in-district; $64 out-of-district; $96 out-of-state. Room only: $2,200. Books/supplies: $700. Personal expenses: $1,238.

2005-2006 Financial aid. Need-based: 91% of total undergraduate aid awarded as scholarships/grants, 9% as loans/jobs.

Application procedures. Admission: No deadline. No application fee. Admission notification on a rolling basis. **Financial aid:** Priority date 5/1; no closing date. FAFSA, institutional form required. Applicants notified on a rolling basis.

Academics. Mandatory assessment program provides effective educational services for students. **Special study options:** Accelerated study, cooperative education, cross-registration, distance learning, dual enrollment of high school students, ESL, exchange student, honors, liberal arts/career combination, teacher certification program, weekend college. License preparation in nursing, occupational therapy, paramedic, physical therapy, radiology, real estate. **Credit/placement by examination:** AP, CLEP, institutional tests. 30 credit hours maximum toward associate degree. **Support services:** GED preparation and test center, learning center, remedial instruction, tutoring.

Majors. Agriculture: General. **Biology:** General, bacteriology, botany, marine, zoology. **Business:** General, accounting, administrative services, fashion, finance, marketing, office management, office technology, office/clerical, real estate, sales/distribution. **Communications:** General, broadcast journalism. **Computer sciences:** General, computer science, information systems, programming. **Construction:** Power transmission. **Education:** General, agricultural, art, bilingual, biology, business, chemistry, computer, early childhood, elementary, English, family/consumer sciences, foreign languages, health, history, mathematics, music, physical, physics, reading, Spanish, special, speech. **Engineering:** General, aerospace, agricultural, architectural, electrical, petroleum. **Engineering technology:** Civil. **Family/consumer sciences:** General, child care. **Foreign languages:** General, Spanish. **Health:** Clinical lab technology, EMT paramedic, medical assistant, medical radiologic technology/radiation therapy, medical secretary, mental health services, nursing (RN), occupational health, occupational therapy assistant, physical therapy assistant, predentistry, premedicine, prepharmacy, preveterinary. **History:** General. **Interdisciplinary:** Math/computer science. **Liberal arts:** Arts/sciences. **Math:** General. **Mechanic/repair:** Electronics/electrical. **Philosophy/religion:** Philosophy. **Physical sciences:** Chemistry, geology, physics. **Protective services:** Criminal justice, fire safety technology. **Psychology:** General. **Public administration:** Human services, social work. **Social sciences:** General, economics, political science, sociology. **Visual/performing arts:** Art, dramatic.

Most popular majors. Business/marketing 14%, education 16%, health sciences 8%, liberal arts 31%, security/protective services 8%.

Computing on campus. 1,200 workstations in library, computer center. Online course registration, online library, repair service available.

Student life. Freshman orientation: Available. Preregistration for classes offered. **Policies:** Freshmen permitted cars on campus. **Housing:** Coed dorms available. $100 deposit. Pets allowed in dorm rooms. **Activities:** Bands, choral groups, dance, drama, literary magazine, music ensembles, musical theater, opera, student government, student newspaper, symphony orchestra.

Athletics. NJCAA. **Intercollegiate:** Baseball M, tennis, volleyball W. **Intramural:** Baseball M, basketball, bowling, football (tackle) M, golf, handball, racquetball, softball, tennis, volleyball. **Team name:** Palominos.

Student services. Alcohol/substance abuse counseling, campus ministries, career counseling, services for economically disadvantaged, student employment services, financial aid counseling, health services, on-campus daycare, personal counseling, placement for graduates, veterans' counselor. **Physically disabled:** Services for visually, speech, hearing impaired. **Transfer:** Special adviser for new students. Transfer adviser, college fairs on campus for students transferring to 4-year colleges.

Contact. E-mail: admissions@laredo.edu
Phone: (956) 721-5117 Fax: (956) 721-5493
Olga Rubio, Director of Admissions and Records, Laredo Community College, West End Washington Street, Laredo, TX 78040-4395

Lee College

Baytown, Texas
www.lee.edu
CB member
CB code: 6363

- Public 2-year community college
- Commuter campus in small city

General. Founded in 1934. Regionally accredited. **Enrollment:** 2,394 degree-seeking undergraduates; 2,277 non-degree-seeking students. **Degrees:** 330 associate awarded. **Location:** 25 miles from Houston. **Calendar:** Semester, limited summer session. **Full-time faculty:** 160 total; 14% have terminal degrees, 12% minority, 46% women. **Part-time faculty:** 200 total; 2% have terminal degrees, 12% minority, 43% women.

Student profile. Among degree-seeking undergraduates, 20% enrolled in a transfer program, 25% enrolled in a vocational program, 1% already have a bachelor's degree or higher, 250 enrolled as first-time, first-year students.

Part-time:	59%	**Asian American:**	1%
Out-of-state:	1%	**Hispanic American:**	24%
Women:	65%	**International:**	2%
African American:	18%		

Basis for selection. Open admission, but selective for some programs. Special requirements for allied health programs. TASP guidelines.

2005-2006 Annual costs. Tuition/fees: $1,294; $2,044 out-of-district; $3,094 out-of-state. Per-credit charge: $25 in-district; $50 out-of-district; $85 out-of-state. Books/supplies: $600. Personal expenses: $1,248.

Financial aid. Need-based: Need-based aid available for part-time students. Work study available for part-time students. **Non-need-based:** Scholarships awarded for academics, art, athletics, job skills, music/drama.

Application procedures. Admission: No deadline. No application fee. Admission notification on a rolling basis. **Financial aid:** Priority date 4/1; no closing date. FAFSA required. Applicants notified on a rolling basis starting 6/1.

Academics. Special study options: Cooperative education, distance learning, dual enrollment of high school students, ESL, honors, independent study, internships, weekend college. **Credit/placement by examination:** CLEP, institutional tests. 30 credit hours maximum toward associate degree. **Support services:** GED preparation and test center, learning center, remedial instruction, tutoring.

Majors. Business: Accounting, administrative services, business admin, office/clerical. **Communications technology:** Graphic/printing. **Computer sciences:** General, data processing, information systems, programming. **Construction:** Pipefitting. **Engineering technology:** Drafting, electrical. **English:** English lit, technical writing. **Foreign languages:** General. **Health:** EMT paramedic, medical records technology, substance abuse counseling. **Interdisciplinary:** Natural sciences. **Legal studies:** Paralegal. **Liberal arts:** Arts/sciences. **Math:** General. **Mechanic/repair:** Electronics/electrical, heating/ac/refrig. **Parks/recreation:** Health/fitness. **Physical sciences:** General. **Protective services:** Police science. **Visual/performing arts:** Dramatic.

Computing on campus. 500 workstations in library, computer center, student center. Online course registration, wireless network available.

Student life. Freshman orientation: Available. Preregistration for classes offered. **Policies:** Freshmen permitted cars on campus. **Activities:** Bands, choral groups, drama, literary magazine, music ensembles, student government, Baptist Student Union, awareness club, Phi Theta Kappa, Texas nursing students association, environmental science club, cosmetology club, digital information society, student honors council.

Athletics. NJCAA. **Intercollegiate:** Basketball M, tennis W, volleyball W. **Intramural:** Basketball, bowling, football (non-tackle), softball, table tennis, volleyball. **Team name:** Rebels.

Student services. Career counseling, student employment services, financial aid counseling, personal counseling, placement for graduates, veterans' counselor. **Physically disabled:** Services for hearing impaired. **Transfer:** Special adviser for new students. Transfer adviser for students transferring to 4-year colleges.

Contact. E-mail: admissions@lee.edu
Phone: (281) 425-6393 Fax: (281) 425-6831
Becki Griffith, Registrar, Lee College, Box 818, Baytown, TX 77522

Lon Morris College

Jacksonville, Texas
www.lonmorris.edu
CB code: 6369

- Private 2-year junior and liberal arts college affiliated with United Methodist Church
- Residential campus in large town
- SAT or ACT (ACT writing optional) required

General. Founded in 1873. Regionally accredited. **Enrollment:** 396 degree-seeking undergraduates. **Degrees:** 88 associate awarded. **ROTC:** Army, Navy, Air Force. **Location:** 100 miles from Dallas, 25 miles from Tyler. **Calendar:** Semester, limited summer session. **Full-time faculty:** 35 total; 57% have terminal degrees, 6% minority, 57% women. **Part-time faculty:** 10 total; 60% have terminal degrees, 10% minority, 50% women. **Class size:** 39% < 20, 58% 20-39, 3% 40-49. **Special facilities:** Chapel, learning enrichment center.

Student profile.

Out-of-state:	7%	**Live on campus:**	76%

Transfer out. Colleges most students transferred to 2005: Stephen F. Austin State University, University of Texas at Tyler, Schreiner University, Southwestern University.

Basis for selection. School achievement record, minimum GPA of 2.0, recommendation, ACT/SAT scores important. Audition required for choral, drama; interview recommended for academically weak; portfolio recommended for art. **Adult students:** Entrance exam policies same as for first-time freshmen. **Homeschooled:** Transcript of courses and grades required. **Learning Disabled:** Students with learning disabilities SAT/ACT exempt.

High school preparation. 9 units recommended. Recommended units include English 4, social studies 2, science 2 and foreign language 1.

2005-2006 Annual costs. Tuition/fees: $9,400. Room/board: $5,600. Books/supplies: $450. Personal expenses: $1,500.

2005-2006 Financial aid. Need-based: 71% of total undergraduate aid awarded as scholarships/grants, 29% as loans/jobs. Need-based aid available for part-time students. **Non-need-based:** Scholarships awarded for academics, athletics.

Application procedures. Admission: No deadline. $35 fee, may be waived for applicants with need. Application may be submitted online. Admission notification on a rolling basis. **Financial aid:** Priority date 5/1; no closing date. FAFSA, institutional form required. Applicants notified on a rolling basis starting 4/1; must reply within 3 week(s) of notification.

Academics. Special study options: Dual enrollment of high school students, ESL, independent study. **Credit/placement by examination:** CLEP, IB, SAT, ACT, institutional tests. 15 credit hours maximum toward associate degree. **Support services:** Learning center, pre-admission summer program, reduced course load, remedial instruction, study skills assistance, tutoring, writing center.

Majors. Biology: General. **Business:** General, accounting. **Computer sciences:** Computer science. **Education:** General. **English:** Speech/rhetoric. **Foreign languages:** Spanish. **Health:** Predentistry, premedicine, prenursing, prepharmacy, preveterinary. **History:** General. **Legal studies:** Prelaw. **Liberal arts:** Arts/sciences. **Math:** General. **Philosophy/religion:** Philosophy, religion. **Physical sciences:** Astronomy, chemistry, physics. **Protective services:** Criminal justice. **Psychology:** General. **Social sciences:** General, economics, political science, sociology. **Visual/performing arts:** General, art, art history/conservation, dramatic, music history, music performance, music theory/composition, piano/organ, studio arts, theater design, theater history, voice/opera.

Computing on campus. 32 workstations in library, computer center. Dormitories wired for high-speed internet access and linked to campus network. Online library, student web hosting, wireless network available.

Student life. Freshman orientation: Mandatory. Preregistration for classes offered. Held the week before classes begin. Students have opportunity to pay bills and move into dorms. **Policies:** Freshmen permitted cars on campus. **Housing:** Single-sex dorms available. $100 deposit. **Activities:** Bands, choral groups, dance, drama, literary magazine, music ensembles, musical theater, ecology club, poetry and literary group, midnight club, Christian service organization, Disciples on Campus, Christian worship group, international club, student senate, LMC Chamber, student activity association.

Athletics. NJCAA. **Intercollegiate:** Baseball M, basketball, golf, soccer, softball W, volleyball W. **Intramural:** Baseball M, basketball, football (non-tackle), soccer, softball, swimming, table tennis, tennis, volleyball. **Team name:** Bearcats.

Student services. Campus ministries, career counseling, student employment services, financial aid counseling, health services, personal counseling. **Physically disabled:** Services for visually, speech, hearing impaired. **Learning disabled:** Comprehensive services available. **Transfer:** Special adviser, pre-admission transcript evaluation for new students. Transfer adviser, college fairs on campus for students transferring to 4-year colleges.

Contact. Phone: (903) 589-4005 Fax: (903) 589-4006
Pam Horton, Director of Admissions, Lon Morris College, 800 College Avenue, Jacksonville, TX 75766

McLennan Community College

Waco, Texas
www.mclennan.edu
CB member
CB code: 6429

- Public 2-year community and junior college
- Commuter campus in small city

General. Founded in 1965. Regionally accredited. **Enrollment:** 3,250 full-time, degree-seeking students. **Degrees:** 492 associate awarded. **ROTC:** Air Force. **Location:** 100 miles from Dallas and Austin. **Calendar:** Semester, extensive summer session. **Full-time faculty:** 325 total. **Part-time faculty:** 100 total.

Basis for selection. Open admission, but selective for some programs. Admission to health careers programs is selective. Institution observes TASP guidelines in testing for placement.

2005-2006 Annual costs. Tuition/fees: $1,860; $2,220 out-of-district; $3,660 out-of-state. Per-credit charge: $53 in-district; $65 out-of-district; $113 out-of-state. Books/supplies: $725. Personal expenses: $1,596.

Financial aid. Non-need-based: Scholarships awarded for athletics.

Application procedures. Admission: No deadline. No application fee. Admission notification on a rolling basis. **Financial aid:** Priority date 6/1; no closing date. FAFSA required. Applicants notified on a rolling basis starting 5/1.

Academics. Special study options: Distance learning, dual enrollment of high school students, honors, internships, study abroad. **Credit/placement by examination:** CLEP, institutional tests. 24 credit hours maximum toward associate degree. **Support services:** Learning center, reduced course load, remedial instruction, tutoring.

Majors. Business: General, accounting, office technology, real estate. **Communications:** General. **Computer sciences:** General, data processing, programming. **Family/consumer sciences:** Child care. **Foreign languages:** Sign language interpretation. **Health:** Clinical lab technology, EMT paramedic, medical radiologic technology/radiation therapy, medical records technology, medical secretary, mental health services, respiratory therapy technology, substance abuse counseling. **Interdisciplinary:** Gerontology. **Legal studies:** Legal secretary, paralegal. **Protective services:** Law enforcement admin.

Computing on campus. 425 workstations in library, computer center, student center.

Student life. Freshman orientation: Available. **Activities:** Bands, choral groups, dance, drama, music ensembles, musical theater, student government, student newspaper.

Athletics. NJCAA. **Intercollegiate:** Baseball M, basketball, golf M, tennis W. **Intramural:** Baseball M, basketball, gymnastics M, softball W, track and field.

Student services. Adult student services, career counseling, student employment services, health services, on-campus daycare, personal counseling, placement for graduates, veterans' counselor. **Physically disabled:** Services for visually, hearing impaired. **Transfer:** Special adviser, orientation for new students. Transfer adviser, college fairs on campus for students transferring to 4-year colleges.

Contact. Phone: (254) 299-8628 Fax: (254) 299-8694
Vivian Jefferson, Director of Admissions and Recruitment, McLennan Community College, 1400 College Drive, Waco, TX 76708

Midland College

Midland, Texas
www.midland.edu
CB code: 6459

- Public 2-year community college
- Commuter campus in small city
- Interview required

General. Founded in 1969. Regionally accredited. **Enrollment:** 4,585 degree-seeking undergraduates. **Degrees:** 432 associate awarded. **Location:** 300 miles from El Paso, 300 miles from Dallas. **Calendar:** Semester, extensive summer session. **Full-time faculty:** 128 total. **Part-time faculty:** 150 total. **Class size:** 29% < 20, 71% 20-39.

Student profile.

Out-of-state:	1%	**Live on campus:**	2%
25 or older:	60%		

Transfer out. Colleges most students transferred to 2005: University of Texas of the Permian Basin, Texas A&M University, Angelo State University, West Texas A&M University, Texas Tech University.

Basis for selection. Open admission, but selective for some programs. Special requirements for allied health science programs. Observes TASP requirements. **Adult students:** Entrance exam policies same as for first-time freshmen.

2005-2006 Annual costs. Tuition/fees: $1,350; $1,710 out-of-district; $2,580 out-of-state. Per-credit charge: $37 in-district; $49 out-of-district; $78 out-of-state. Additional $48 charge per credit hour for baccalaureate program. Room/board: $3,520. Books/supplies: $666. Personal expenses: $1,450.

2005-2006 Financial aid. Need-based: 12% of total undergraduate aid awarded as scholarships/grants, 88% as loans/jobs. Need-based aid available for part-time students. Work study available for part-time students. **Non-need-based:** Scholarships awarded for academics, athletics, minority status, music/drama, state residency.

Application procedures. Admission: Priority date 9/1; no deadline. No application fee. Application may be submitted online. Admission notification on a rolling basis. **Financial aid:** Closing date 6/1. FAFSA required. Applicants notified on a rolling basis starting 5/15; must reply within 2 week(s) of notification.

Academics. Special study options: Cooperative education, cross-registration, distance learning, dual enrollment of high school students, ESL, honors, internships, liberal arts/career combination, Washington semester. License preparation in aviation, nursing, paramedic. **Credit/placement by examination:** CLEP, institutional tests. 12 credit hours maximum toward associate degree. **Support services:** GED preparation and test center, learning center, reduced course load, remedial instruction, study skills assistance, tutoring, writing center.

Majors. Biology: General. **Business:** General, accounting, administrative services, business admin, entrepreneurial studies, management information systems, management science, managerial economics, office technology, office/clerical. **Communications:** General, broadcast journalism, journalism. **Communications technology:** Graphic/printing. **Computer sciences:** General, computer graphics, data processing, information systems, programming. **Conservation:** Environmental science. **Education:** Physical, teacher assistance. **Engineering:** Petroleum. **Engineering technology:** Drafting, electrical. **English:** Speech/rhetoric. **Family/consumer sciences:** Child care. **Foreign languages:** General, French, Spanish. **Health:** EMT ambulance attendant, EMT paramedic, medical radiologic technology/radiation therapy, medical records technology, nursing (RN), predentistry, premedicine, prepharmacy, respiratory therapy technology, substance abuse counseling, veterinary technology/assistant. **History:** General. **Legal studies:** Legal secretary, paralegal, pre-law. **Math:** General. **Mechanic/repair:** Automotive, electronics/electrical, heating/ac/refrig. **Parks/recreation:** Exercise sciences. **Physical sciences:** Chemistry, geology, physics. **Production:** Welding. **Protective services:** Fire safety technology, firefighting, law enforcement admin, police science. **Psychology:** General. **Public administration:** Social work. **Social sciences:** General, economics, political science, sociology. **Transportation:** Airline/commercial pilot. **Visual/performing arts:** Art, dramatic, music performance.

Computing on campus. 274 workstations in library, computer center, student center. Dormitories wired for high-speed internet access and linked

to campus network. Online course registration, repair service, wireless network available.

Student life. Freshman orientation: Available. Preregistration for classes offered. 3-hour session held 5 times throughout year. **Policies:** Freshmen permitted cars on campus. **Housing:** Coed dorms, single-sex dorms, apartments available. $100 deposit, deadline 7/1. **Activities:** Bands, choral groups, drama, literary magazine, music ensembles, student government, student newspaper, several religious groups, ethnic and service clubs, clubs related to majors.

Athletics. NJCAA. **Intercollegiate:** Basketball, golf M, softball W. **Intramural:** Basketball, bowling, football (non-tackle), soccer M, table tennis, tennis, volleyball. **Team name:** Chaparrals.

Student services. Career counseling, student employment services, on-campus daycare, personal counseling, placement for graduates, veterans' counselor. **Physically disabled:** Services for visually, speech, hearing impaired. **Transfer:** Special adviser, orientation for new students. Transfer center, transfer adviser, college fairs on campus for students transferring to 4-year colleges.

Contact. E-mail: rhaines@midland.edu
Phone: (432) 685-4502 Fax: (432) 685-4623
Trey Wetendorf, Admissions Director, Midland College, 3600 North Garfield, Midland, TX 79705

Mountain View College

Dallas, Texas
www.mvc.dcccd.edu **CB code: 6438**

- Public 2-year community college
- Commuter campus in very large city

General. Founded in 1970. Regionally accredited. College campus designated as Urban Wildlife Sanctuary by the Humane Society of the United States. **Enrollment:** 3,976 degree-seeking undergraduates. **Degrees:** 349 associate awarded. **ROTC:** Army. **Location:** 8 miles from downtown. **Calendar:** Semester, extensive summer session. **Full-time faculty:** 75 total. **Part-time faculty:** 120 total. **Partnerships:** Formal partnerships with many local businesses and local offices of national/international corporations.

Student profile.

Out-of-state:	1%	**25 or older:**	38%

Transfer out. Colleges most students transferred to 2005: University of Texas at Arlington, University of North Texas, Texas A&M University.

Basis for selection. Open admission. High school students accepted if principal recommends enrollment. Observes TASP guidelines. **Adult students:** Entrance exam policies same as for first-time freshmen.

2005-2006 Annual costs. Tuition/fees: $990; $1,800 out-of-district; $2,880 out-of-state. Per-credit charge: $33 in-district; $60 out-of-district; $96 out-of-state.

2005-2006 Financial aid. Need-based: 98% of total undergraduate aid awarded as scholarships/grants, 2% as loans/jobs. Need-based aid available for part-time students. Work study available nights and weekends. **Non-need-based:** Scholarships awarded for academics.

Application procedures. Admission: No deadline. No application fee. Application may be submitted online. Admission notification on a rolling basis. **Financial aid:** Priority date 5/1; no closing date. FAFSA, institutional form required. Applicants notified on a rolling basis starting 6/1.

Academics. Special study options: Accelerated study, cooperative education, distance learning, double major, dual enrollment of high school students, ESL, honors, independent study, liberal arts/career combination, study abroad, teacher certification program, weekend college. License preparation in aviation. **Credit/placement by examination:** CLEP, institutional tests. 45 credit hours maximum toward associate degree. Test scores or local assessment must show ability to enroll in college level classes. **Support services:** GED preparation and test center, learning center, reduced course load, remedial instruction, study skills assistance, tutoring, writing center.

Majors. Business: General, accounting, business admin, e-commerce, executive assistant. **Computer sciences:** Computer science, data processing, LAN/WAN management, networking, programming, web page design. **Education:** Early childhood, kindergarten/preschool, middle. **Engineering technology:** Computer, drafting, electrical. **Health:** Medical records technology. **Interdisciplinary:** Natural sciences. **Liberal arts:** Arts/sciences. **Math:** General. **Production:** Welding. **Protective services:** Criminal justice. **Science technology:** Biological. **Transportation:** Air traffic control, airline/commercial pilot, aviation management. **Visual/performing arts:** Studio arts.

Computing on campus. 700 workstations in library, computer center, student center. Commuter students can connect to campus network. Online course registration, online library, helpline available.

Student life. Freshman orientation: Available. Preregistration for classes offered. **Policies:** Freshmen permitted cars on campus. **Activities:** Concert band, choral groups, dance, drama, music ensembles, musical theater, student government, LULAC, black student club, international student organization.

Athletics. NJCAA. **Intercollegiate:** Basketball, soccer, softball W, volleyball W. **Intramural:** Basketball, soccer, tennis, volleyball. **Team name:** Lions.

Student services. Adult student services, career counseling, services for economically disadvantaged, student employment services, financial aid counseling, health services, minority student services, personal counseling, placement for graduates, veterans' counselor, women's services. **Physically disabled:** Services for visually, speech, hearing impaired. **Transfer:** Special adviser, orientation for new students. Transfer adviser, college fairs on campus for students transferring to 4-year colleges.

Contact. E-mail: GMH9782@dcccd.edu
Phone: (214) 860-8600 Fax: (214) 860-8570
Linda Osagie, Director of Admissions, Mountain View College, 4849 West Illinois Avenue, Dallas, TX 75211-6599

MTI College of Business and Technology

Houston, Texas
www.mti-tex.com **CB code: 2376**

- For-profit 2-year business and technical college
- Commuter campus in very large city
- Interview required

General. Founded in 1980. Accredited by ACCSCT. **Enrollment:** 390 degree-seeking undergraduates. **Degrees:** 190 associate awarded. **Location:** 10 miles from downtown. **Calendar:** Semester, limited summer session. **Full-time faculty:** 75 total. **Part-time faculty:** 25 total.

Basis for selection. Entrance examination and interview most important. Institutional entrance exam administered. **Adult students:** Entrance exam policies same as for first-time freshmen.

2005-2006 Annual costs. Tuition varies by program from $7,400 to $22,500.

Application procedures. Admission: No deadline. No application fee. Admission notification on a rolling basis. **Financial aid:** FAFSA required.

Academics. Special study options: Cooperative education, ESL. **Credit/placement by examination:** CLEP. **Support services:** Tutoring.

Majors. Business: Accounting, administrative services, business admin.

Computing on campus. 6 workstations in library.

Student life. Freshman orientation: Mandatory.

Student services. Career counseling, financial aid counseling, placement for graduates.

Contact. E-mail: info@mti.edu
Phone: (713) 974-7181 Toll-free number: (800) 344-1990
Fax: (713) 974-2090
David Wood, Director of Admissions, MTI College of Business and Technology, 7277 Regency Square Boulevard, Houston, TX 77036

MTI College of Business and Technology

Houston, Texas
www.mti.edu **CB code: 3063**

- For-profit 2-year business and technical college
- Commuter campus in small town
- Interview required

General. Founded in 1980. Accredited by ACCSCT. **Enrollment:** 136 degree-seeking undergraduates; 16 non-degree-seeking students. **Degrees:** 105 associate awarded. **Location:** 25 miles from downtown. **Calendar:** Semester.

Full-time faculty: 13 total. **Part-time faculty:** 7 total. **Partnerships:** Formal partnerships with 16 major high school independent districts.

Student profile. Among degree-seeking undergraduates, 100% enrolled in a vocational program.

Women:	53%	**Hispanic American:**	44%
African American:	13%	**Native American:**	1%
Asian American:	1%	**25 or older:**	45%

Basis for selection. Standardized test score and interview most important. Applicants for degree programs must have high school diploma, or recognized equivalency certificate (GED), or evidence of successful completion of at least 2 years study from an accredited college or university towards a bachelor's degree. Applicants for certificate programs may have a high school diploma, equivalency certificate (GED), or prove ability-to-benefit by obtaining a satisfactory score on the Ability to Benefit Examination (ATB), which is provided on campus. Students must be beyond the age of compulsory education. **Adult students:** Entrance exam policies same as for first-time freshmen.

2006-2007 Annual costs. Tuition/fees (projected): $9,000. Tuition and fees vary by program.

Application procedures. Admission: No deadline. No application fee. Admission notification on a rolling basis.

Academics. Special study options: ESL. **Credit/placement by examination:** AP, CLEP. **Support services:** Tutoring.

Majors. Business: Administrative services. **Engineering technology:** Computer systems.

Computing on campus. 6 workstations in library.

Student life. Freshman orientation: Mandatory.

Student services. Career counseling, financial aid counseling, placement for graduates.

Contact. E-mail: info@mti.edu
Phone: (281) 333-3363 Toll-free number: (888) 532-7675
Fax: (281) 333-4118
Raoul Navarro, Admissions Manager, MTI College of Business and Technology, 1275 Space Park Drive, Houston, TX 77058

Navarro College
Corsicana, Texas
www.nav.cc.tx.us **CB code: 6465**

- Public 2-year community college
- Commuter campus in large town

General. Founded in 1946. Regionally accredited. **Enrollment:** 6,512 degree-seeking undergraduates. **Degrees:** 465 associate awarded. **Location:** 50 miles from Dallas. **Calendar:** Semester, limited summer session. **Full-time faculty:** 116 total. **Part-time faculty:** 274 total. **Special facilities:** Arts, science and technology center; IMAX theater.

Student profile.

Out-of-state:	7%	**Live on campus:**	15%

Basis for selection. Open admission, but selective for some programs. Special requirements for nursing and art programs. Portfolio required for art.

2005-2006 Annual costs. Tuition/fees: $1,210; $1,840 out-of-district; $2,450 out-of-state. Per-credit charge: $115 in-district; $136 out-of-district; $729 out-of-state. Room/board: $3,854. Books/supplies: $846. Personal expenses: $920.

2004-2005 Financial aid. Need-based: 61% of total undergraduate aid awarded as scholarships/grants, 39% as loans/jobs.

Application procedures. Admission: No deadline. No application fee. Admission notification on a rolling basis. **Financial aid:** Priority date 6/1; no closing date. FAFSA required. Applicants notified on a rolling basis starting 7/1; must reply within 2 week(s) of notification.

Academics. Special study options: Distance learning, dual enrollment of high school students, ESL, honors, independent study, internships, liberal arts/career combination. License preparation in paramedic. **Credit/placement by examination:** CLEP, institutional tests. 30 credit hours maximum toward associate degree. CLEP credit awarded only after successful completion of 12 credit hours in residence. **Support services:** GED preparation and test center, learning center, reduced course load, remedial instruction, tutoring.

Majors. Agriculture: Business, farm/ranch. **Biology:** General. **Business:** General, accounting, administrative services, business admin, management information systems, office technology, real estate, taxation. **Communications:** General, broadcast journalism, journalism. **Communications technology:** Graphic/printing. **Computer sciences:** General. **Education:** General, elementary, physical, secondary. **Engineering:** General. **Engineering technology:** Drafting. **English:** Speech/rhetoric. **Family/consumer sciences:** Child care, clothing/textiles. **Foreign languages:** Linguistics. **Health:** EMT paramedic, licensed practical nurse, medical radiologic technology/radiation therapy, predentistry, premedicine, prepharmacy, preveterinary. **Interdisciplinary:** Biological/physical sciences. **Liberal arts:** Arts/sciences. **Math:** General. **Physical sciences:** Chemistry, physics. **Protective services:** Criminal justice, fire safety technology, police science. **Psychology:** General. **Social sciences:** General. **Transportation:** Aviation. **Visual/performing arts:** Art, commercial/advertising art, dramatic, music performance, voice/opera.

Student life. Policies: Freshmen permitted cars on campus. **Housing:** Single-sex dorms, apartments available. $100 deposit. **Activities:** Bands, choral groups, drama, music ensembles, student government, TV station, religious organizations, honorary and special interest clubs.

Athletics. NJCAA. **Intercollegiate:** Baseball M, basketball, football (tackle) M, golf, tennis. **Intramural:** Softball. **Team name:** Bulldogs.

Student services. Career counseling, student employment services, personal counseling, placement for graduates, veterans' counselor. **Transfer:** Pre-admission transcript evaluation for new students. Transfer adviser, college fairs on campus for students transferring to 4-year colleges.

Contact. E-mail: lbarn@nav.cc.tx.us
Phone: (903) 874-6501 Fax: (903) 875-7353
Judy Cutting, Registrar, Navarro College, 3200 West Seventh Avenue, Corsicana, TX 75110

North Central Texas College
Gainesville, Texas
www.nctc.edu **CB code: 6245**

- Public 2-year community college
- Commuter campus in large town

General. Founded in 1924. Regionally accredited. **Enrollment:** 7,009 degree-seeking undergraduates. **Degrees:** 787 associate awarded. **Location:** 70 miles from Dallas. **Calendar:** Semester, extensive summer session. **Full-time faculty:** 90 total. **Part-time faculty:** 185 total. **Special facilities:** Planetarium, experimental farm, cattle center, horse arena.

Student profile.

Out-of-state:	9%	**Live on campus:**	3%
25 or older:	40%		

Basis for selection. Open admission, but selective for some programs. Special requirements for some health professions programs. Observes TASP guidelines.

High school preparation. 16 units recommended. Recommended units include English 4, mathematics 2, social studies 2 and science 2.

2005-2006 Annual costs. Tuition/fees: $1,260; $2,040 out-of-district; $3,000 out-of-state. Per-credit charge: $33 in-district; $59 out-of-district; $91 out-of-state. Room/board: $3,350. Books/supplies: $1,050. Personal expenses: $1,300.

Financial aid. All financial aid based on need. Need-based aid available for part-time students. Work study available nights and for part-time students.

Application procedures. Admission: No deadline. No application fee. Admission notification on a rolling basis. High school transcript, proof of state residency, pre-TASP placement required for certain courses of study. **Financial aid:** Priority date 5/1; no closing date. FAFSA required. Applicants notified on a rolling basis starting 6/1; must reply within 4 week(s) of notification.

Academics. Special study options: Cross-registration, distance learning, dual enrollment of high school students. **Credit/placement by examination:** AP, CLEP, institutional tests. 18 credit hours maximum toward associate degree. **Support services:** Learning center, remedial instruction, tutoring.

Majors. Agriculture: Equestrian studies, farm/ranch. **Business:** General, administrative services, office technology, office/clerical. **Computer sciences:** General, data processing. **Engineering technology:** Drafting, electrical. **Health:** EMT paramedic, nursing (RN), occupational health, occupational therapy assistant. **Interdisciplinary:** Biological/physical sciences. **Legal studies:** Legal secretary, paralegal. **Mechanic/repair:** Diesel. **Protective services:** Criminal justice, police science. **Social sciences:** Criminology. **Visual/performing arts:** Commercial photography.

Computing on campus. 60 workstations in dormitories, library, computer center, student center. Dormitories linked to campus network. Commuter students can connect to campus network. Online course registration, online library, helpline available.

Student life. Freshman orientation: Mandatory. One-day program throughout summer and when classes commence. **Housing:** Coed dorms, special housing for disabled available. $150 deposit. **Activities:** Choral groups, drama, literary magazine, music ensembles, student government, Baptist Student Union, Future Farmers of America, honor society, Catholic campus community, nursing student association, criminal justice club, Methodist student organization, computer club.

Athletics. NJCAA. **Intercollegiate:** Baseball M, rodeo, tennis W, volleyball W. **Intramural:** Badminton, basketball, bowling, golf, racquetball, softball, table tennis, tennis, track and field, volleyball. **Team name:** Lions.

Student services. Adult student services, career counseling, student employment services, personal counseling, veterans' counselor, women's services. **Transfer:** Special adviser for new students. Transfer adviser for students transferring to 4-year colleges.

Contact. E-mail: admissions@nctc.edu
Phone: (940) 668-4222 ext. 222 Fax: (940) 668-6049
Michelle Winters, Director of Admissions, North Central Texas College, 1525 West California, Gainesville, TX 76240

North Harris Montgomery Community College District

The Woodlands, Texas
www.nhmccd.edu **CB code: 6508**

- Public 2-year community college
- Commuter campus in large city

General. Founded in 1972. Regionally accredited. North Harris Montgomery Community College District includes: Kingwood College, Tomball College, North Harris College, Montgomery College, Cy-Fair College. Each college has a full-service campus. **Enrollment:** 35,921 degree-seeking undergraduates; 3,107 non-degree-seeking students. **Degrees:** 1,880 associate awarded. **Location:** 40 miles from Houston. **Calendar:** Semester, extensive summer session. **Full-time faculty:** 630 total. **Part-time faculty:** 1,345 total. **Class size:** 46% < 20, 53% 20-39, less than 1% 40-49, less than 1% 50-99, less than 1% >100.

Student profile. Among degree-seeking undergraduates, 79% enrolled in a transfer program, 21% enrolled in a vocational program, 3% already have a bachelor's degree or higher, 6,284 enrolled as first-time, first-year students.

Part-time:	73%	**Asian American:**	6%
Out-of-state:	1%	**Hispanic American:**	20%
Women:	61%	**International:**	3%
African American:	12%	**25 or older:**	33%

Transfer out. Colleges most students transferred to 2005: University of Houston, Sam Houston State University, Texas A&M-College Station, University of Texas-Austin.

Basis for selection. Open admission, but selective for some programs. Admission screening for nursing, respiratory therapy, occupational therapy, physical therapist assistant program, veterinary tech, diagnostic medical imagery, cosmetology. Placement testing required in reading, writing, and mathematics. **Adult students:** Entrance exam policies same as for first-time freshmen.

2006-2007 Annual costs. Tuition/fees (projected): $1,224; $2,424 out-of-district; $2,874 out-of-state. Per-credit charge: $52 in-district; $92 out-of-district; $220 out-of-state. Books/supplies: $600. Personal expenses: $1,600.

2004-2005 Financial aid. Need-based: 82% of total undergraduate aid awarded as scholarships/grants, 18% as loans/jobs. Need-based aid available for part-time students. Work study available nights and weekends. **Non-need-based:** Scholarships awarded for academics.

Application procedures. Admission: No deadline. No application fee. Application may be submitted online. Admission notification on a rolling basis. **Financial aid:** Priority date 4/1; no closing date. FAFSA, institutional form required. Applicants notified on a rolling basis starting 7/1.

Academics. Special study options: Combined bachelor's/graduate degree, cooperative education, distance learning, dual enrollment of high school students, ESL, honors, independent study, internships, liberal arts/career combination, study abroad, teacher certification program, weekend college. Bachelor's degree programs available on campus. License preparation in dental hygiene, nursing, occupational therapy, paramedic, physical therapy, radiology. **Credit/placement by examination:** AP, CLEP, institutional tests. 18 credit hours maximum toward associate degree. **Support services:** GED preparation and test center, learning center, pre-admission summer program, reduced course load, remedial instruction, study skills assistance, tutoring, writing center.

Majors. Architecture: Technology. **Biology:** Biotechnology. **Business:** General, accounting, administrative services, business admin, marketing, office technology. **Communications technology:** Graphic/printing. **Computer sciences:** General, information systems. **Education:** Kindergarten/preschool, middle, social science. **Engineering technology:** Electrical, industrial. **Family/consumer sciences:** Child care, child development. **Foreign languages:** Sign language interpretation. **Health:** EMT paramedic, medical radiologic technology/radiation therapy, medical records technology, medical secretary, mental health services, nursing (RN), occupational therapy assistant, pharmacy assistant, physical therapy assistant, respiratory therapy technology, sonography, veterinary technology/assistant. **Legal studies:** Legal secretary, paralegal. **Liberal arts:** Arts/sciences. **Mechanic/repair:** Aircraft, automotive, heating/ac/refrig. **Personal/culinary services:** Cosmetic, cosmetology. **Production:** Welding. **Protective services:** Criminal justice, firefighting. **Public administration:** Human services. **Science technology:** Biological. **Social sciences:** Cartography. **Visual/performing arts:** Interior design.

Most popular majors. Health sciences 16%, liberal arts 68%.

Computing on campus. 500 workstations in library, computer center, student center. Commuter students can connect to campus network. Online course registration, online library, helpline, wireless network available.

Student life. Freshman orientation: Mandatory. Preregistration for classes offered. Available on campus and online. **Policies:** Freshmen permitted cars on campus. **Activities:** Bands, choral groups, dance, drama, literary magazine, music ensembles, musical theater, radio station, student government, student newspaper, symphony orchestra, TV station, Phi Theta Kappa, honors student association, student nurses association, international student association, African American society, Latin American student association, Asian student association, Campus Crusade for Christ, Muslim student organization, Show of Hands (deaf students).

Athletics. Intercollegiate: Baseball M. **Intramural:** Badminton, basketball, bowling, golf, racquetball, soccer, softball, table tennis, tennis, volleyball.

Student services. Adult student services, career counseling, services for economically disadvantaged, student employment services, financial aid counseling, minority student services, on-campus daycare, personal counseling, placement for graduates, veterans' counselor. **Physically disabled:** Services for visually, speech, hearing impaired. **Transfer:** Special adviser, orientation for new students. Transfer adviser, college fairs on campus for students transferring to 4-year colleges.

Contact. Phone: (832) 813-6500
Mary Shafer, Associate Vice Chancellor, Student Information Services, North Harris Montgomery Community College District, 5000 Research Forest Drive, The Woodlands, TX 77381-4356

North Lake College

Irving, Texas **CB member**
www.northlakecollege.edu **CB code: 6519**

- Public 2-year community college
- Commuter campus in small city

General. Founded in 1977. Regionally accredited. **Enrollment:** 7,000 degree-seeking undergraduates. **Degrees:** 320 associate awarded. **Location:** 15 miles from Dallas. **Calendar:** Semester, limited summer session. **Full-time faculty:** 98 total; 15% have terminal degrees, 31% minority, 39% women. **Part-time faculty:** 439 total; 1% have terminal degrees, 22% minority, 44% women. **Class size:** 59% < 20, 36% 20-39, 3% 40-49, less than 1% 50-99, less than 1% >100.

Student profile.

Out-of-state:	4%	**25 or older:**	40%

Transfer out. Colleges most students transferred to 2005: University of Texas at Arlington.

Basis for selection. Open admission. **Adult students:** Entrance exam policies same as for first-time freshmen. **Homeschooled:** Must take placement test.

2005-2006 Annual costs. Tuition/fees: $990; $1,800 out-of-district; $2,880 out-of-state. Per-credit charge: $33 in-district; $60 out-of-district; $96 out-of-state. Books/supplies: $600.

Financial aid. Need-based: Need-based aid available for part-time students.

Application procedures. Admission: No deadline. No application fee. Application may be submitted online. Admission notification on a rolling basis. **Financial aid:** Priority date 5/1; no closing date. FAFSA required. Applicants notified on a rolling basis.

Academics. Special study options: Accelerated study, cross-registration, distance learning, dual enrollment of high school students, ESL, internships, liberal arts/career combination, study abroad. License preparation in nursing, real estate. **Credit/placement by examination:** AP, CLEP. 15 credit hours maximum toward associate degree. **Support services:** GED preparation and test center, learning center, remedial instruction, study skills assistance, tutoring, writing center.

Majors. Business: Accounting, administrative services, business admin, management science, office management, office technology, real estate. **Computer sciences:** General. **Construction:** Carpentry, power transmission. **Education:** Kindergarten/preschool, music, teacher assistance. **Engineering technology:** Electrical. **Liberal arts:** Arts/sciences. **Math:** General. **Visual/performing arts:** Cinematography.

Computing on campus. 1,100 workstations in library, computer center. Online library available.

Student life. Freshman orientation: Mandatory. Preregistration for classes offered. **Policies:** Freshmen permitted cars on campus. **Activities:** Jazz band, choral groups, dance, drama, literary magazine, music ensembles, musical theater, student government, student newspaper, Association of Black Collegians, environmental club, Christians on Campus, international club, Phi Theta Kappa, Single Parents Association, Estamos Unidos, South Asian student organization, student ambassadors, anime club.

Athletics. NJCAA. **Intercollegiate:** Baseball M, basketball M, volleyball W. **Intramural:** Soccer. **Team name:** Blazers.

Student services. Alcohol/substance abuse counseling, career counseling, services for economically disadvantaged, student employment services, financial aid counseling, health services, minority student services, personal counseling, placement for graduates, veterans' counselor. **Physically disabled:** Services for visually, hearing impaired. **Transfer:** Special adviser for new students. Transfer adviser, college fairs on campus for students transferring to 4-year colleges.

Contact. Phone: (972) 273-3183 Fax: (972) 273-3112
Stephen Twenge, Director of Admissions and Registration, North Lake College, 5001 North MacArthur Boulevard, Irving, TX 75038-3899

Northeast Texas Community College

Mount Pleasant, Texas
www.ntcc.edu **CB code: 6531**

- Public 2-year community college
- Commuter campus in large town

General. Founded in 1984. Regionally accredited. **Enrollment:** 1,275 full-time, degree-seeking students. **Degrees:** 243 associate awarded. **Location:** 60 miles from Texarkana, 118 miles from Dallas. **Calendar:** Semester, extensive summer session. **Full-time faculty:** 55 total. **Part-time faculty:** 85 total. **Class size:** 64% < 20, 35% 20-39, less than 1% 40-49.

Student profile.

Out-of-state:	1%	**Live on campus:**	4%
25 or older:	35%		

Basis for selection. Open admission, but selective for some programs. Special requirements for nursing, EMS, cosmetology, some criminal justice programs. Observes all TASP guidelines. **Adult students:** Entrance exam policies same as for first-time freshmen.

High school preparation. 19 units recommended. Recommended units include English 4, mathematics 2, social studies 4, science 2 and foreign language 3. 0.5 fine arts recommended.

2005-2006 Annual costs. Tuition/fees: $1,740; $2,520 out-of-district; $3,780 out-of-state. Per-credit charge: $27 in-district; $53 out-of-district; $95 out-of-state. Room/board: $3,260. Books/supplies: $600. Personal expenses: $1,477.

Financial aid. Need-based: Need-based aid available for part-time students. **Non-need-based:** Scholarships awarded for academics, art, athletics, job skills, music/drama, state residency.

Application procedures. Admission: No deadline. No application fee. Admission notification on a rolling basis. **Financial aid:** Priority date 6/1; no closing date. FAFSA, institutional form required. Applicants notified on a rolling basis starting 6/1.

Academics. Special study options: Cooperative education, distance learning, dual enrollment of high school students, ESL, liberal arts/career combination. Bachelor's degree programs available on campus. License preparation in dental hygiene, nursing, paramedic, real estate. **Credit/placement by examination:** CLEP. 15 credit hours maximum toward associate degree. **Support services:** GED preparation and test center, learning center, remedial instruction, study skills assistance, tutoring, writing center.

Majors. Agriculture: General. **Biology:** General. **Business:** Accounting, administrative services, banking/financial services, business admin, real estate. **Communications:** Journalism. **Computer sciences:** General, programming. **Education:** General. **Engineering:** Physics. **English:** Speech/rhetoric. **Foreign languages:** Spanish. **Health:** Dental hygiene, medical secretary, nursing (RN), premedicine. **History:** General. **Legal studies:** Legal secretary. **Liberal arts:** Arts/sciences. **Math:** General. **Mechanic/repair:** Diesel. **Parks/recreation:** Health/fitness. **Personal/culinary services:** Cosmetic. **Physical sciences:** Chemistry. **Protective services:** Police science. **Psychology:** General. **Social sciences:** Political science, sociology. **Visual/performing arts:** Art, dramatic.

Computing on campus. 150 workstations in dormitories, library, computer center.

Student life. Freshman orientation: Mandatory. Preregistration for classes offered. Online program. **Policies:** Freshmen permitted cars on campus. **Housing:** Single-sex dorms available. **Activities:** Jazz band, choral groups, drama, literary magazine, music ensembles, student government, student newspaper, student coordinating board, Baptist Student Union, student nurses, Phi Theta Kappa, computer club, career opportunities in protective services.

Athletics. NJCAA. **Intercollegiate:** Baseball M, softball W. **Intramural:** Basketball M, softball, tennis, volleyball. **Team name:** Eagles.

Student services. Career counseling, services for economically disadvantaged, student employment services, financial aid counseling, personal counseling, placement for graduates, veterans' counselor. **Transfer:** Special adviser, orientation, pre-admission transcript evaluation for new students. Transfer center, college fairs on campus for students transferring to 4-year colleges.

Contact. E-mail: skeys@ntcc.edu
Phone: (903) 572-1911 ext. 263 Toll-free number: (800) 870-0142 ext. 263
Fax: (903) 572-6712
Sherry Keys, Director of Admissions and Recruitment, Northeast Texas Community College, Box 1307, Mount Pleasant, TX 75456-1307

Northwest Vista College

San Antonio, Texas
www.accd.edu/nvc **CB code: 6517**

- Public 2-year community college
- Commuter campus in very large city

General. Regionally accredited. **Enrollment:** 9,162 degree-seeking undergraduates. **Degrees:** 391 associate awarded. **Location:** 16 miles from downtown. **Calendar:** Semester, extensive summer session. **Full-time faculty:** 83 total; 42% women. **Part-time faculty:** 414 total; 53% women.

Student profile. Among degree-seeking undergraduates, 1,376 enrolled as first-time, first-year students.

Part-time:	63%	**Women:**	58%
Out-of-state:	1%	**25 or older:**	22%

Transfer out. Colleges most students transferred to 2005: University of Texas at San Antonio, Texas State University, Palo Alto College, San Antonio College, St. Philips College.

Basis for selection. Open admission. All students required to comply with Texas Academic Skills Program, which includes assessment, placement, remediation if necessary. **Adult students:** Entrance exam policies same as for first-time freshmen. **Homeschooled:** Transcript of courses and grades required.

High school preparation. 22 units recommended. Recommended units include English 4, mathematics 3, social studies 5, history 1, science 3, foreign language 2 and academic electives 3.

2006-2007 Annual costs. Tuition/fees (projected): $1,472; $2,672 out-of-district; $5,072 out-of-state.

Financial aid. Need-based: Need-based aid available for part-time students. Work study available nights, weekends and for part-time students. **Non-need-based:** Scholarships awarded for academics, leadership.

Application procedures. Admission: Priority date 4/23; deadline 8/20. No application fee. Application may be submitted online. **Financial aid:** Priority date 4/1; no closing date. FAFSA required. Applicants notified on a rolling basis starting 5/15; must reply within 2 week(s) of notification.

Academics. Special study options: Cross-registration, distance learning, dual enrollment of high school students, ESL, liberal arts/career combination, weekend college. **Credit/placement by examination:** CLEP, institutional tests. 32 credit hours maximum toward associate degree. **Support services:** Learning center, remedial instruction, study skills assistance, tutoring.

Majors. Biology: General. **Business:** Business admin. **Communications:** General, journalism, media studies. **Communications technology:** General. **Computer sciences:** General, computer science, networking, programming. **Education:** General. **English:** Speech/rhetoric. **Foreign languages:** General. **Health:** Health services. **History:** General. **Interdisciplinary:** Behavioral sciences. **Legal studies:** Prelaw. **Liberal arts:** Arts/sciences. **Math:** General. **Parks/recreation:** Exercise sciences, health/fitness. **Physical sciences:** Chemistry. **Psychology:** General. **Public administration:** Social work. **Science technology:** Biological. **Social sciences:** General, economics, political science, sociology.

Computing on campus. 600 workstations in library, computer center, student center. Commuter students can connect to campus network. Online course registration, online library, helpline available.

Student life. Freshman orientation: Mandatory, $75 fee. Preregistration for classes offered. **Policies:** Freshmen permitted cars on campus. **Activities:** Dance, film society, student government.

Athletics. Team name: Wildcats.

Student services. Career counseling, student employment services, financial aid counseling, personal counseling, placement for graduates, veterans' counselor. **Physically disabled:** Services for visually, speech, hearing impaired. **Learning disabled:** Comprehensive services available. **Transfer:** Special adviser, orientation, pre-admission transcript evaluation for new students. Transfer center, transfer adviser, college fairs on campus for students transferring to 4-year colleges.

Contact. E-mail: nvcinfo@accd.edu
Phone: (210) 348-2020 Fax: (210) 348-2024
Jill Weston, Director of Enrollment Services, Northwest Vista College, 3535 North Ellison Drive, San Antonio, TX 78251-4217

Odessa College

Odessa, Texas
www.odessa.edu **CB code: 6540**

- Public 2-year community college
- Commuter campus in small city

General. Founded in 1946. Regionally accredited. Extension centers in Pecos, Monahans, Andrews, Crane, Kermit, McCamey, and Seminole. **Enrollment:** 4,790 degree-seeking undergraduates. **Degrees:** 348 associate awarded. **Location:** 140 miles from Lubbock, 290 miles from El Paso. **Calendar:** Semester, extensive summer session. **Full-time faculty:** 119 total. **Part-time faculty:** 146 total. **Special facilities:** Theater, college-owned and operated NPR radio stations.

Student profile. Among degree-seeking undergraduates, 60% enrolled in a transfer program, 40% enrolled in a vocational program, 1,130 enrolled as first-time, first-year students.

Part-time:	61%	**25 or older:**	34%
Out-of-state:	1%	**Live on campus:**	4%
Women:	61%		

Basis for selection. Open admission, but selective for some programs. Allied health programs require successful completion of placement exams, supporting applications, and interviews. Requirements for other selective programs vary. **Adult students:** Entrance exam policies same as for first-time freshmen. **Homeschooled:** Transcript of courses and grades required.

2006-2007 Annual costs. Tuition/fees (projected): $1,440; $1,740 out-of-district; $2,190 out-of-state. Room/board: $4,770. Books/supplies: $1,000. Personal expenses: $1,071.

2004-2005 Financial aid. Need-based: 88% of total undergraduate aid awarded as scholarships/grants, 12% as loans/jobs. Need-based aid available for part-time students. Work study available nights and for part-time students. **Non-need-based:** Scholarships awarded for academics, athletics, music/drama.

Application procedures. Admission: No deadline. No application fee. Application may be submitted online. Admission notification on a rolling basis. **Financial aid:** Priority date 5/1; no closing date. FAFSA required. Applicants notified on a rolling basis starting 6/15.

Academics. Special study options: Cooperative education, cross-registration, distance learning, dual enrollment of high school students, independent study, internships, liberal arts/career combination. License preparation in nursing, paramedic, physical therapy, radiology. **Credit/placement by examination:** AP, CLEP, institutional tests. 15 credit hours maximum toward associate degree. **Support services:** GED preparation and test center, learning center, reduced course load, remedial instruction, study skills assistance, tutoring, writing center.

Majors. Biology: General. **Business:** General, administrative services, business admin. **Communications:** Radio/tv. **Computer sciences:** Computer science, information systems, programming. **Construction:** Carpentry, maintenance. **Education:** General, teacher assistance. **Engineering technology:** Drafting, occupational safety, petroleum. **Family/consumer sciences:** Child care. **Foreign languages:** General. **Health:** Clinical lab science, EMT paramedic, medical radiologic technology/radiation therapy, medical secretary, nursing (RN), physical therapy assistant, respiratory therapy technology, substance abuse counseling, surgical technology. **Legal studies:** Legal secretary, paralegal. **Liberal arts:** Arts/sciences. **Math:** General. **Mechanic/repair:** Automotive, diesel, electronics/electrical, heating/ac/refrig. **Personal/culinary services:** Chef training, cosmetic. **Physical sciences:** Chemistry, geology. **Production:** Machine tool, welding. **Protective services:** Fire safety technology, firefighting, police science. **Psychology:** General. **Social sciences:** General. **Visual/performing arts:** Art, commercial photography.

Computing on campus. 775 workstations in dormitories, library, computer center, student center. Dormitories wired for high-speed internet access and linked to campus network. Commuter students can connect to campus network. Online course registration, online library, student web hosting available.

Student life. Freshman orientation: Available. Preregistration for classes offered. **Policies:** Freshmen permitted cars on campus. **Housing:** Apartments available. **Activities:** Bands, choral groups, music ensembles, radio station, student government, Baptist Student Union, Black Organization of Successful Students, Student Alliance of Latinos Succeeding Academically, Changing Attitudes Helping Others Overcome the Situation.

Athletics. NJCAA. **Intercollegiate:** Baseball M, basketball, golf M, rodeo, softball W. **Intramural:** Racquetball, softball, table tennis, tennis, volleyball. **Team name:** Wranglers.

Student services. Campus ministries, career counseling, student employment services, financial aid counseling, on-campus daycare, personal counseling, placement for graduates, veterans' counselor. **Physically disabled:** Services for visually, hearing impaired. **Transfer:** Special adviser, orientation, pre-admission transcript evaluation for new students. Transfer adviser, college fairs on campus for students transferring to 4-year colleges.

Contact. E-mail: ngarcia@odessa.edu
Phone: (432) 335-6432 Fax: (432) 335-6824
Norma Garcia, Assistant Director of Admissions, Odessa College, 201 West University, Odessa, TX 79764-7127

Palo Alto College

San Antonio, Texas
www.accd.edu

CB member
CB code: 3730

- Public 2-year community college
- Commuter campus in very large city

General. Founded in 1987. Regionally accredited. **Enrollment:** 8,199 degree-seeking undergraduates. **Degrees:** 474 associate awarded. **Calendar:** Semester, limited summer session. **Full-time faculty:** 117 total. **Part-time faculty:** 323 total. **Special facilities:** FAA aviation education resource center.

Student profile.

Out-of-state:	2%	**25 or older:**	35%

Transfer out. Colleges most students transferred to 2005: University of Texas at San Antonio, St. Mary's University, Our Lady of the Lake University, University of the Incarnate Word.

Basis for selection. Open admission. SLEP used for placement of non-native speakers.

2005-2006 Annual costs. Tuition/fees: $1,472; $2,672 out-of-district; $5,072 out-of-state. Books/supplies: $500.

2004-2005 Financial aid. All financial aid based on need. Need-based aid available for part-time students.

Application procedures. Admission: No deadline. No application fee. Application may be submitted online. Admission notification on a rolling basis. **Financial aid:** Priority date 3/31, closing date 6/1. FAFSA required. Applicants notified on a rolling basis starting 5/31.

Academics. Special study options: Cooperative education, distance learning, dual enrollment of high school students, ESL, honors, internships, liberal arts/career combination, weekend college. Bachelor's degree programs available on campus. License preparation in aviation. **Credit/placement by examination:** CLEP, institutional tests. 32 credit hours maximum toward associate degree. **Support services:** GED preparation, learning center, remedial instruction, study skills assistance, tutoring.

Majors. Agriculture: Agribusiness operations, animal sciences, horticultural science, landscaping, ornamental horticulture, turf management. **Area/ethnic studies:** Hispanic-American/Latino/Chicano, Latin American. **Biology:** General. **Business:** Accounting, administrative services, banking/financial services, business admin, entrepreneurial studies, fashion, logistics, office management, office technology. **Communications:** General, advertising, journalism. **Computer sciences:** General, computer science, information systems, programming. **Conservation:** Environmental science. **Education:** General. **Engineering:** General, environmental. **Engineering technology:** Environmental. **Family/consumer sciences:** Food/nutrition. **Foreign languages:** General. **Health:** Health services, nursing assistant. **History:** General. **Interdisciplinary:** Biological/physical sciences. **Liberal arts:** Arts/sciences. **Math:** General. **Parks/recreation:** Exercise sciences. **Philosophy/religion:** Philosophy. **Physical sciences:** General, chemistry, physics. **Protective services:** Law enforcement admin. **Psychology:** General. **Public administration:** Social work. **Social sciences:** Anthropology, economics, political science, sociology. **Transportation:** Aviation. **Visual/performing arts:** Art, studio arts.

Computing on campus. Commuter students can connect to campus network. Online course registration, online library, wireless network available.

Student life. Freshman orientation: Mandatory. **Activities:** Jazz band, choral groups, dance, drama, music ensembles, student government, student newspaper, Catholic campus ministries, international club, veterinary technician association, Phi Theta Kappa.

Athletics. NJCAA. **Intercollegiate:** Cross-country, diving, swimming. **Intramural:** Weight lifting. **Team name:** Palominos.

Student services. Adult student services, career counseling, services for economically disadvantaged, student employment services, financial aid counseling, health services, on-campus daycare, personal counseling, veterans' counselor. **Physically disabled:** Services for visually, speech, hearing impaired. **Learning disabled:** Comprehensive services available. **Transfer:** Special adviser, orientation for new students. Transfer center, transfer adviser, college fairs on campus for students transferring to 4-year colleges.

Contact. Phone: (210) 921-5270 Fax: (210) 921-5005
Rachel Montejano, Director of Enrollment Management, Palo Alto College, 1400 West Villaret, San Antonio, TX 78224

Panola College

Carthage, Texas
www.panola.edu

CB code: 6572

- Public 2-year community and junior college
- Commuter campus in small town

General. Founded in 1947. Regionally accredited. Off-campus sites in Marshall and Center. **Enrollment:** 1,906 degree-seeking undergraduates; 21 non-degree-seeking students. **Degrees:** 180 associate awarded. **Location:** 40 miles from Shreveport, Louisiana, 160 miles from Dallas. **Calendar:** Semester, limited summer session. **Full-time faculty:** 57 total; 10% have terminal degrees, 7% minority, 58% women. **Part-time faculty:** 47 total; 4% have terminal degrees, 4% minority, 45% women. **Class size:** 60% < 20, 37% 20-39, 2% 40-49, 1% 50-99.

Student profile. Among degree-seeking undergraduates, 18% enrolled in a transfer program, 82% enrolled in a vocational program, 1% already have a bachelor's degree or higher, 360 enrolled as first-time, first-year students, 165 transferred in from other institutions.

Part-time:	51%	**Native American:**	1%
Women:	66%	**International:**	1%
African American:	17%	**25 or older:**	17%
Asian American:	1%	**Live on campus:**	10%
Hispanic American:	4%		

Transfer out. 20% of students enrolled in the transfer program go on to 4-year colleges. **Colleges most students transferred to 2005:** Stephen F. Austin State University, University of Texas at Tyler, Texas A&M Commerce, East Texas Baptist University.

Basis for selection. Open admission, but selective for some programs. Institution observes Texas Success Initiative guidelines. Departmental admission required prior to registration for some occupational/vocational programs of study. Early admissions for dual credit, tech prep. Interview required for some health program applicants. Auditions required for some fine arts scholarships. **Adult students:** Entrance exam policies same as for first-time freshmen.

High school preparation. College-preparatory program recommended. Recommended units include English 4, mathematics 3, social studies 4, science 3, foreign language 2, academic electives 5.5.

2005-2006 Annual costs. Tuition/fees: $1,350; $2,040 out-of-district; $2,430 out-of-state. Room/board: $3,300. Books/supplies: $1,400. Personal expenses: $2,870.

2004-2005 Financial aid. Need-based: Average need met was 85%. Average scholarship/grant was $1,000. 98% of total undergraduate aid awarded as scholarships/grants, 2% as loans/jobs. Need-based aid available for part-time students. Work study available nights, weekends and for part-time students. **Non-need-based:** Scholarships awarded for academics, alumni affiliation, art, athletics, leadership, music/drama.

Application procedures. Admission: No deadline. No application fee. Application may be submitted online. **Financial aid:** Priority date 6/5; no closing date. FAFSA, institutional form required. Applicants notified on a rolling basis starting 6/1.

Academics. Special study options: Distance learning, dual enrollment of high school students, liberal arts/career combination. License preparation in nursing, occupational therapy. **Credit/placement by examination:** AP, CLEP. 12 credit hours maximum toward associate degree. **Support services:** GED preparation and test center, learning center, remedial instruction, study skills assistance, tutoring.

Majors. Business: General, administrative services, management information systems. **Computer sciences:** General. **Education:** General. **Engineering technology:** Industrial. **Health:** Medical records technology, nursing (RN), occupational therapy assistant. **Liberal arts:** Arts/sciences.

Most popular majors. Health sciences 22%, liberal arts 73%.

Computing on campus. 376 workstations in dormitories, library, computer center, student center. Dormitories wired for high-speed internet access and linked to campus network. Commuter students can connect to campus network. Online course registration, online library, helpline, repair service, wireless network available.

Student life. Freshman orientation: Available, $84 fee. Preregistration for classes offered. **Policies:** Freshmen permitted cars on campus. **Housing:**

Coed dorms, single-sex dorms, apartments, substance-free housing available. $150 partly refundable deposit, deadline 7/15. **Activities:** Bands, choral groups, drama, literary magazine, music ensembles, musical theater, student government, student newspaper, Baptist student ministry, Catholic student ministry, Young Republicans, Excel Club, forensics club, chemistry club, Phi Theta Kappa, computer club, nursing club, biology club, Circle K.

Athletics. NJCAA. **Intercollegiate:** Baseball M, basketball, rodeo, volleyball W. **Intramural:** Basketball, football (non-tackle), racquetball, softball, volleyball. **Team name:** Ponies and Fillies.

Student services. Alcohol/substance abuse counseling, career counseling, services for economically disadvantaged, financial aid counseling, personal counseling, veterans' counselor. **Physically disabled:** Services for visually, speech, hearing impaired. **Transfer:** Special adviser for new students. College fairs on campus for students transferring to 4-year colleges.

Contact. E-mail: bsimpson@panola.edu
Phone: (903) 693-2038 Fax: (903) 693-2031
Barbara Simpson, Registrar/Director of Admissions, Panola College, 1109 West Panola Street, Carthage, TX 75633

Paris Junior College
Paris, Texas
www.paris.cc.tx.us **CB code: 6573**

- Public 2-year community and junior college
- Large town

General. Founded in 1924. Regionally accredited. Jewelry technology and watchmaking and repair school available. **Enrollment:** 4,071 degree-seeking undergraduates; 266 non-degree-seeking students. **Degrees:** 384 associate awarded. **Location:** 110 miles from Dallas. **Calendar:** Semester, limited summer session. **Full-time faculty:** 105 total. **Part-time faculty:** 95 total. **Special facilities:** Regional archives, collection of historical documents and artifacts of region, biological field laboratory with nature trails.

Student profile. Among degree-seeking undergraduates, 76% enrolled in a transfer program, 24% enrolled in a vocational program, 1,457 enrolled as first-time, first-year students.

Part-time:	56%	**Hispanic American:**	6%
Out-of-state:	13%	**Native American:**	2%
Women:	61%	**25 or older:**	40%
African American:	11%	**Live on campus:**	12%
Asian American:	1%		

Transfer out. 85% of students enrolled in the transfer program go on to 4-year colleges.

Basis for selection. Open admission, but selective for some programs. Special admission to nursing program; interview required.

2006-2007 Annual costs. Tuition/fees (projected): $1,320; $2,025 out-of-district; $3,200 out-of-state. Room/board: $3,500. Books/supplies: $500.

Financial aid. Need-based: Need-based aid available for part-time students. **Non-need-based:** Scholarships awarded for athletics, music/drama.

Application procedures. Admission: No deadline. No application fee. Admission notification on a rolling basis. **Financial aid:** Priority date 6/1; no closing date. FAFSA required. Applicants notified on a rolling basis starting 6/1.

Academics. Special study options: Accelerated study, cross-registration, dual enrollment of high school students. **Credit/placement by examination:** CLEP, institutional tests. **Support services:** GED preparation and test center, learning center, reduced course load, remedial instruction, tutoring.

Majors. Biology: General. **Business:** General, accounting, administrative services, business admin, office management, office technology, real estate. **Communications:** Journalism. **Computer sciences:** Data processing. **Construction:** Carpentry. **Education:** General. **Engineering technology:** Drafting, electrical. **Foreign languages:** General, French, German, Spanish. **Health:** Licensed practical nurse, medical records technology, predentistry, premedicine, prepharmacy, preveterinary. **History:** General. **Legal studies:** Prelaw. **Liberal arts:** Arts/sciences. **Math:** General. **Mechanic/repair:** Heating/ac/refrig, watch/jewelry. **Physical sciences:** Chemistry, physics. **Production:** Welding. **Psychology:** General. **Social sciences:** Political science, sociology. **Visual/performing arts:** Dramatic, metal/jewelry, studio arts.

Student life. Freshman orientation: Available. Preregistration for classes offered. **Housing:** Single-sex dorms, apartments available. **Activities:** Choral groups, drama, music ensembles, radio station, student government, student newspaper, Baptist Student Union, Afro-American club, honorary business fraternity, honorary scholastic fraternity, United Campus Ministry.

Athletics. NJCAA. **Intercollegiate:** Baseball M, basketball, golf M, softball W. **Intramural:** Basketball M, bowling, football (non-tackle) M. **Team name:** Dragons.

Student services. Career counseling, services for economically disadvantaged, student employment services, financial aid counseling, health services, personal counseling, placement for graduates, veterans' counselor.

Contact. Phone: (903) 785-7661 Fax: (903) 784-9370
Shelia Reese, Director of Admissions, Paris Junior College, 2400 Clarksville Street, Paris, TX 75460

Ranger College
Ranger, Texas
www.ranger.cc.tx.us **CB code: 6608**

- Public 2-year junior college
- Small town

General. Founded in 1926. Regionally accredited. **Enrollment:** 910 degree-seeking undergraduates. **Degrees:** 38 associate awarded. **Location:** 85 miles from Fort Worth. **Calendar:** Semester, limited summer session. **Full-time faculty:** 22 total. **Part-time faculty:** 24 total.

Basis for selection. Open admission, but selective for some programs. Observes TASP guidelines. Selective admissions to vocational nursing program.

2005-2006 Annual costs. Tuition/fees: $1,480; $1,600 out-of-district; $1,780 out-of-state. Per-credit charge: $37 in-district; $41 out-of-district; $47 out-of-state. Room/board: $3,050. Books/supplies: $450. Personal expenses: $810.

Application procedures. Admission: No deadline. No application fee. Admission notification on a rolling basis beginning on or about 8/1. **Financial aid:** FAFSA, institutional form required. Applicants notified on a rolling basis; must reply within 2 week(s) of notification.

Academics. Special study options: Dual enrollment of high school students, honors. 2-2 programs in education, business administration, computer systems, and information sciences with Tarleton State University. **Credit/placement by examination:** CLEP, institutional tests. 12 credit hours maximum toward associate degree. **Support services:** GED test center, learning center, reduced course load, remedial instruction.

Majors. Business: Administrative services. **Computer sciences:** General. **Liberal arts:** Arts/sciences. **Mechanic/repair:** Automotive. **Production:** Welding.

Computing on campus. 30 workstations in computer center.

Student life. Freshman orientation: Mandatory. **Policies:** Freshmen permitted cars on campus. **Housing:** Single-sex dorms available. **Activities:** Bands, dance, music ensembles, student government, student newspaper.

Athletics. NJCAA. **Intercollegiate:** Baseball M, basketball, football (tackle) M, softball W, track and field. **Intramural:** Basketball, softball. **Team name:** Ranger Rangers.

Student services. Career counseling, student employment services, health services, personal counseling, placement for graduates, veterans' counselor. **Transfer:** Special adviser for new students. Transfer adviser for students transferring to 4-year colleges.

Contact. Phone: (254) 647-3234 ext. 115 Fax: (254) 647-1656
Tammy Adams, Director of Admissions, Ranger College, College Circle, Ranger, TX 76470

Remington College: Dallas
Garland, Texas
www.educationamerica.com **CB code: 3232**

- For-profit 2-year junior and technical college
- Small city

General. Accredited by ACICS. **Enrollment:** 870 degree-seeking undergraduates. **Degrees:** 75 associate awarded. **Calendar:** Continuous. **Full-time faculty:** 15 total. **Part-time faculty:** 20 total.

Basis for selection. Open admission, but selective for some programs.

2005-2006 Annual costs. Tuition for full 24-month associate programs: $30,480 for most programs. Tuition for 8-month diploma program in medical assisting and pharmacy technician: $11,280. Registration fee $50. Personal expenses: $3,360.

Application procedures. Admission: No deadline. $50 fee.

Academics. Credit/placement by examination: CLEP.

Majors. Business: Business admin.

Contact. E-mail: swhisenhunt@edamerica.com
Phone: (972) 686-7878
Remington College: Dallas, 1800 Eastgate Drive, Garland, TX 75041

Remington College: Fort Worth

Fort Worth, Texas
www.remingtoncollege.edu **CB code: 3151**

- For-profit 2-year branch campus and technical college
- Large city
- Interview required

General. Accredited by ACCSCT. **Enrollment:** 1,660 degree-seeking undergraduates. **Degrees:** 109 associate awarded. **Location:** 7 miles from downtown. **Calendar:** Differs by program, extensive summer session. **Full-time faculty:** 40 total. **Part-time faculty:** 5 total.

Basis for selection. Open admission. ASSET test required of applicants to associate degree programs; Wonderlic required of applicants to diploma programs. Institution observes Texas Success Initiative guidelines.

2005-2006 Annual costs. Tuition for full 18-month associate degree programs $30,480; diploma programs $11,280.

Application procedures. Admission: No deadline. $50 fee. Application must be submitted on paper. Admission notification on a rolling basis.

Academics. Credit/placement by examination: CLEP.

Majors. Computer sciences: Networking. **Engineering technology:** Electrical.

Contact. E-mail: donald.devito@remingtoncollege.edu
Phone: (817) 451-0017 Toll-free number: (800) 336-6668
Fax: (817) 496-1257
Donald DeVito, Director of Admissions, Remington College: Fort Worth, 300 East Loop 820, Fort Worth, TX 76112

Remington College: Houston

Houston, Texas
www.remingtoncollege.edu **CB code: 3152**

- For-profit 2-year technical college
- Commuter campus in very large city

General. Accredited by ACCSCT. **Enrollment:** 507 undergraduates. **Degrees:** 20 associate awarded. **Calendar:** Quarter. **Full-time faculty:** 27 total. **Part-time faculty:** 7 total.

Basis for selection. Open admission. ASSET used as admissions exams for degree programs.

2005-2006 Annual costs. Cost of tuition, books, tools and lab fees for all full associate programs (24 months): $30,480. Allied Health diploma program (8 months): $11,280. Registration fee $50. Personal expenses: $1,764.

Financial aid. Need-based: Need-based aid available for part-time students. Work study available nights. **Non-need-based:** Scholarships awarded for state residency.

Application procedures. Admission: No deadline. $50 fee. Application must be submitted on paper. Admission notification on a rolling basis. **Financial aid:** No deadline. FAFSA, institutional form required. Applicants notified on a rolling basis.

Academics. Special study options: Internships. **Credit/placement by examination:** CLEP. **Support services:** Tutoring.

Majors. Computer sciences: General, applications programming, networking, programming, systems analysis. **Engineering:** Electrical, software.

Computing on campus. 200 workstations in library, computer center. Online library, helpline, repair service available.

Student life. Policies: Freshmen permitted cars on campus.

Student services. Adult student services, career counseling, student employment services, financial aid counseling. **Transfer:** Orientation, pre-admission transcript evaluation for new students.

Contact. Phone: (281) 899-1240 Fax: (281) 597-8466
Kevin Wilkerson, Director of Recruitment, Remington College: Houston, 3110 Hayes Road Suite 380, Houston, TX 77082

Richland College

Dallas, Texas **CB member**
www.rlc.dcccd.edu **CB code: 6607**

- Public 2-year community college
- Commuter campus in very large city

General. Founded in 1972. Regionally accredited. **Enrollment:** 4,650 full-time, degree-seeking students. **Degrees:** 736 associate awarded. **Location:** 15 miles from downtown. **Calendar:** Semester, extensive summer session. **Full-time faculty:** 139 total. **Part-time faculty:** 635 total. **Special facilities:** Planetarium, laser light theater, art galleries, horticulture demonstration garden, meditation labyrinth.

Basis for selection. Open admission. Students required by legislative mandate to take TASP test or alternative assessment before enrolling in college-level courses. **Homeschooled:** Require completed application, concurrent enrollment permission form, student information profile sheet, student health history form, authorization to release test scores, official home school transcripts.

2005-2006 Annual costs. Tuition/fees: $990; $1,800 out-of-district; $2,880 out-of-state. Per-credit charge: $33 in-district; $60 out-of-district; $96 out-of-state. Books/supplies: $350. Personal expenses: $935.

Financial aid. Need-based: Need-based aid available for part-time students. Work study available nights and for part-time students. **Non-need-based:** Scholarships awarded for art, leadership, music/drama.

Application procedures. Admission: No deadline. No application fee. Application may be submitted online. Admission notification on a rolling basis. **Financial aid:** Priority date 5/2; no closing date. FAFSA required. Applicants notified on a rolling basis starting 6/1; must reply within 2 week(s) of notification.

Academics. Special study options: Cooperative education, cross-registration, distance learning, dual enrollment of high school students, ESL, honors, independent study, internships, study abroad, teacher certification program, weekend college. License preparation in real estate. **Credit/placement by examination:** AP, CLEP, institutional tests. 45 credit hours maximum toward associate degree. **Support services:** GED preparation, learning center, remedial instruction, study skills assistance, tutoring.

Majors. Agriculture: Horticultural science, horticulture. **Business:** Accounting, administrative services, business admin, entrepreneurial studies, management information systems, real estate, tourism/travel. **Communications technology:** General. **Computer sciences:** General, applications programming. **Education:** Bilingual, teacher assistance. **Engineering technology:** Electrical, manufacturing. **Health:** Insurance coding, medical informatics, medical records technology. **Legal studies:** Legal secretary. **Liberal arts:** Arts/sciences.

Most popular majors. Business/marketing 28%, liberal arts 55%.

Computing on campus. 210 workstations in computer center. Commuter students can connect to campus network. Online course registration, online library available.

Student life. Freshman orientation: Available. Orientation sessions held in Assessment Center prior to students taking state-mandated assessments for placement. **Policies:** Freshmen permitted cars on campus. **Activities:** Bands, choral groups, dance, drama, music ensembles, musical theater, student government, student newspaper, Spanish heritage association, arts club, Educators of America, Baptist student ministries, Sierra Student Coalition, German film club.

Athletics. NJCAA. **Intercollegiate:** Baseball M, basketball M, soccer, volleyball W. **Intramural:** Basketball, bowling, cross-country, football (non-tackle), golf, soccer, softball, tennis, volleyball. **Team name:** Thunder Ducks.

Student services. Adult student services, career counseling, services for economically disadvantaged, student employment services, financial aid counseling, health services, personal counseling, placement for graduates, veterans' counselor, women's services. **Physically disabled:** Services for visually, speech, hearing impaired. **Transfer:** Special adviser, orientation for new students. Transfer adviser, college fairs on campus for students transferring to 4-year colleges.

Contact. Phone: (972) 238-6106 Fax: (972) 238-6346
Oscar Lopez, Registrar and Director of Admissions, Richland College, 12800 Abrams Road, Dallas, TX 75243-2199

St. Philip's College

San Antonio, Texas — **CB member**
www.accd.edu/spc — **CB code: 6642**

- Public 2-year community college
- Commuter campus in very large city

General. Founded in 1898. Regionally accredited. Some courses held at off-campus sites throughout San Antonio. **Enrollment:** 9,792 degree-seeking undergraduates. **Degrees:** 622 associate awarded. **ROTC:** Army. **Location:** 1 mile from downtown. **Calendar:** Semester, extensive summer session. **Full-time faculty:** 216 total; 9% have terminal degrees, 44% minority, 41% women. **Part-time faculty:** 371 total; 6% have terminal degrees, 44% minority, 41% women. **Class size:** 55% < 20, 43% 20-39, 1% 40-49, less than 1% 50-99. **Special facilities:** Restaurant on campus run by hospitality students, human patient simulator for nursing and allied health students. **Partnerships:** Formal partnerships with Boeing and Dee Howard for aircraft technology training.

Student profile. Among degree-seeking undergraduates, 52% enrolled in a transfer program, 48% enrolled in a vocational program, 1,915 enrolled as first-time, first-year students, 1,125 transferred in from other institutions.

Part-time:	57%	**Women:**	58%
Out-of-state:	1%	**25 or older:**	48%

Transfer out. Colleges most students transferred to 2005: University of Texas at San Antonio, Southwest Texas State University.

Basis for selection. Open admission. PTASP or ACCUPLACER may be taken at entry in lieu of TASP, SAT, or ACT scores for placement. **Adult students:** Students age 65 and older do not have to test if they are auditing classes. **Homeschooled:** Transcript of courses and grades required.

2005-2006 Annual costs. Tuition/fees: $1,472; $2,672 out-of-district; $5,072 out-of-state. Books/supplies: $900. Personal expenses: $2,185.

2004-2005 Financial aid. All financial aid based on need. 68% of total undergraduate aid awarded as scholarships/grants, 32% as loans/jobs. Need-based aid available for part-time students. Work study available nights, weekends and for part-time students.

Application procedures. Admission: No deadline. No application fee. Application may be submitted online. **Financial aid:** Priority date 3/1; no closing date. FAFSA required. Applicants notified on a rolling basis starting 7/15.

Academics. Special study options: Accelerated study, cooperative education, cross-registration, distance learning, double major, dual enrollment of high school students, ESL, honors, internships, weekend college. License preparation offered on campus for dietetic technology and massage therapy. License preparation in aviation, nursing, occupational therapy, physical therapy, radiology. **Credit/placement by examination:** AP, CLEP, institutional tests. 32 credit hours maximum toward associate degree. **Support services:** GED preparation and test center, learning center, pre-admission summer program, reduced course load, remedial instruction, study skills assistance, tutoring, writing center.

Majors. Architecture: Interior. **Biology:** General, biomedical sciences. **Business:** Accounting, accounting technology, administrative services, business admin, construction management, hospitality admin, tourism/travel. **Communications technology:** General. **Computer sciences:** Data entry, data processing, information systems, LAN/WAN management, programming, webmaster. **Construction:** Carpentry, electrician, maintenance. **Education:** General, teacher assistance. **Engineering:** General. **Engineering technology:** Biomedical, computer hardware, construction, drafting, electrical, heat/ac/refrig, instrumentation. **English:** Composition, speech/rhetoric. **Family/consumer sciences:** Child care, institutional food production. **Foreign languages:** General, Spanish. **Health:** Clinical lab technology, medical radiologic technology/radiation therapy, medical records admin, medical records technology, medical secretary, nursing (RN), occupational therapy assistant, physical therapy assistant, predentistry, premedicine, prenursing, respiratory therapy technology. **History:** General. **Legal studies:** Legal secretary, paralegal, prelaw. **Liberal arts:** Arts/sciences. **Math:** General. **Mechanic/repair:** Aircraft, aircraft powerplant, auto body, automotive, communications systems, diesel, electronics/electrical, heating/ac/refrig. **Parks/recreation:** Health/fitness. **Personal/culinary services:** Chef training, culinary arts, restaurant/catering. **Philosophy/religion:** Philosophy. **Physical sciences:** Chemistry, geology. **Production:** Machine tool, welding. **Protective services:** Law enforcement admin. **Psychology:** General. **Public administration:** Social work. **Social sciences:** Economics, political science, sociology, urban studies. **Visual/performing arts:** Art, dramatic, studio arts.

Most popular majors. Business/marketing 8%, engineering/engineering technologies 11%, health sciences 28%, liberal arts 19%, personal/culinary services 6%, trade and industry 14%.

Computing on campus. 1,000 workstations in library, computer center. Commuter students can connect to campus network. Online course registration, online library, helpline, repair service available.

Student life. Freshman orientation: Available. Preregistration for classes offered. **Policies:** Freshmen permitted cars on campus. **Activities:** Jazz band, choral groups, dance, drama, literary magazine, music ensembles, musical theater, student government, student newspaper, Phi Theta Kappa, Black Educational Network, Los Unidos, MECHA, Native American club, campus ministry.

Athletics. Intramural: Basketball, softball, swimming, table tennis, tennis, volleyball, weight lifting. **Team name:** Tigers.

Student services. Adult student services, campus ministries, career counseling, services for economically disadvantaged, student employment services, financial aid counseling, health services, on-campus daycare, personal counseling, placement for graduates, veterans' counselor, women's services. **Physically disabled:** Services for visually, hearing impaired. **Transfer:** Special adviser for new students. Transfer center, transfer adviser, college fairs on campus for students transferring to 4-year colleges.

Contact. E-mail: angarza@accd.edu
Phone: (210) 531-4831 Fax: (210) 531-4836
Burton Crow, Dean of Enrollment Management, St. Philip's College, 1801 Martin Luther King Drive, San Antonio, TX 78203

San Antonio College

San Antonio, Texas — **CB member**
www.accd.edu/sac — **CB code: 6645**

- Public 2-year community college
- Commuter campus in very large city

General. Founded in 1925. Regionally accredited. **Enrollment:** 20,565 degree-seeking undergraduates. **Degrees:** 932 associate awarded. **ROTC:** Army, Air Force. **Location:** Downtown. **Calendar:** Semester, extensive summer session. **Full-time faculty:** 415 total. **Part-time faculty:** 605 total. **Special facilities:** Planetarium.

Transfer out. Colleges most students transferred to 2005: University of Texas at San Antonio.

Basis for selection. Open admission, but selective for some programs. Nursing requires 2.5 GPA, satisfactory completion of human anatomy/physiology and ethics. Mortuary science program requires admissions interview, proof of complete hepatitis B vacination series (or submit a waiver/declination form), and counseling card. Dental assisting requires complete dental assisting technology program application, proof of advisement, formal admission to college, and counseling card. **Adult students:** Entrance exam policies same as for first-time freshmen. Texas Higher Education Assessment required. **Homeschooled:** Transcript of courses and grades, state high school equivalency certificate required. Present notarized record of high school equivalent work completed and date of succesful completion. Work should be consistent with Texas Education Agency (TEA) minimums for high school completion. Agree to limitations or conditions of admissions established by institution.

2005-2006 Annual costs. Tuition/fees: $1,472; $2,672 out-of-district; $5,072 out-of-state. Books/supplies: $900. Personal expenses: $1,648.

Financial aid. Need-based: Work study available nights, weekends and for part-time students. **Additional information:** Leveraging Educational Assistance Partnership (LEAP), public student incentive grant, towards excellence access and success grants (Texas and Texas II grants) available.

Application procedures. **Admission:** Closing date 8/25. No application fee. Application must be submitted online. Admission notification on a rolling basis. Nursing applicants must apply by January 15. **Financial aid:** Priority date 3/1; no closing date. Applicants notified by 7/1.

Academics. **Special study options:** Cooperative education, cross-registration, distance learning, double major, dual enrollment of high school students, ESL, honors, internships, liberal arts/career combination, study abroad, weekend college. Internet courses, premedical/predental program, alternative teacher certification program, basic skills enrichment program, distance education through Virtual College of Texas, teaching academy program. License preparation in dental hygiene, nursing, paramedic, real estate. **Credit/placement by examination:** CLEP, institutional tests. 32 credit hours maximum toward associate degree. Student must earn 6 credits at college before credit by examination may be posted on transcript. No credit by examination may be earned for course already completed in classroom. **Support services:** GED preparation and test center, learning center, reduced course load, remedial instruction, study skills assistance, tutoring.

Majors. **Business:** General, accounting, accounting technology, administrative services, banking/financial services, business admin, office management, operations, real estate. **Communications:** Journalism, radio/tv. **Computer sciences:** General, LAN/WAN management, programming, security, system admin. **Education:** Multi-level teacher, teacher assistance. **Engineering:** General. **Engineering technology:** General, architectural, CAD/CADD, civil, electrical, mechanical drafting, occupational safety, telecommunications. **English:** Speech/rhetoric. **Family/consumer sciences:** Aging, child care. **Foreign languages:** Sign language interpretation. **Health:** Dental assistant, EMT paramedic, medical assistant, mental health services, nursing (RN), substance abuse counseling. **Interdisciplinary:** Global studies. **Legal studies:** Court reporting, legal secretary, paralegal. **Liberal arts:** Arts/sciences. **Math:** General. **Personal/culinary services:** Mortuary science. **Protective services:** Corrections, criminal justice, fire safety technology, fire services admin. **Psychology:** General. **Public administration:** General. **Social sciences:** General. **Visual/performing arts:** Commercial/advertising art, dramatic, graphic design, photography, studio arts.

Computing on campus. 325 workstations in library, computer center, student center. Online course registration, online library, helpline, wireless network available.

Student life. **Freshman orientation:** Mandatory. **Policies:** Freshmen permitted cars on campus. **Housing:** Special program places students in homes of elderly residents who have spare rooms and need assistance. **Activities:** Bands, choral groups, dance, drama, film society, literary magazine, music ensembles, musical theater, radio station, student government, student newspaper, symphony orchestra, TV station, Baptist Student Center, Catholic Student Center, Methodist Student Center, Church of Christ Student Center, Black Student Alliance, United Mexican-American Students, College Republicans, Young Democrats, Young Socialist Alliance.

Athletics. **Intramural:** Basketball, cross-country, fencing, golf, racquetball, soccer, softball, swimming, tennis, volleyball, water polo. **Team name:** Rangers.

Student services. Adult student services, alcohol/substance abuse counseling, campus ministries, career counseling, services for economically disadvantaged, student employment services, financial aid counseling, health services, on-campus daycare, personal counseling, placement for graduates, veterans' counselor, women's services. **Physically disabled:** Services for visually, speech, hearing impaired. **Transfer:** Special adviser, orientation, pre-admission transcript evaluation for new students. Transfer center, transfer adviser, college fairs on campus for students transferring to 4-year colleges.

Contact. E-mail: sacar@accd.edu
Phone: (210) 733-2583 Toll-free number: (800) 944-7575
Fax: (210) 733-2579
Rosemarie Hoopes, Director of Admissions and Records, San Antonio College, 1300 San Pedro Avenue, San Antonio, TX 78212-4299

San Jacinto College: Central Campus

Pasadena, Texas
www.sjcd.edu **CB code: 6694**

- Public 2-year community college
- Small city

General. Founded in 1960. Regionally accredited. San Jacinto College has three campuses and multiple extension centers. **Enrollment:** 7,800 degree-seeking undergraduates. **Degrees:** 800 associate awarded. **Location:** 20 miles from Houston. **Calendar:** Semester, extensive summer session. **Full-time faculty:** 230 total. **Part-time faculty:** 285 total. **Special facilities:** Learning center.

Basis for selection. Open admission, but selective for some programs. Special requirements for health science program. In some selective programs, specific courses taken successfully within San Jacinto district may obviate need for qualifying SAT/ACT scores. SAT or ACT score used for nursing, medical laboratory technology, radiography, and respiratory programs. Interview recommended for nursing program.

2005-2006 Annual costs. Tuition/fees: $1,160; $1,910 out-of-district; $2,510 out-of-state. Per-credit charge: $30 in-district; $55 out-of-district; $75 out-of-state. Books/supplies: $830. Personal expenses: $1,908.

Application procedures. **Admission:** No deadline. No application fee. Admission notification on a rolling basis. **Financial aid:** Priority date 6/1; no closing date. FAFSA, institutional form required. Applicants notified on a rolling basis.

Academics. **Special study options:** Cooperative education, cross-registration, distance learning, honors, internships, weekend college. License preparation in aviation, nursing, paramedic, real estate. **Credit/placement by examination:** CLEP. 12 credit hours maximum toward associate degree. **Support services:** Remedial instruction.

Majors. **Business:** General, administrative services, fashion, hospitality/recreation, management information systems, office technology, real estate. **Communications technology:** Graphic/printing. **Engineering technology:** Drafting. **Family/consumer sciences:** Institutional food production. **Health:** Clinical lab science, medical assistant, medical radiologic technology/radiation therapy, nursing (RN), respiratory therapy technology. **Protective services:** Fire safety technology, police science. **Theology:** Bible. **Visual/performing arts:** Commercial/advertising art.

Student life. **Freshman orientation:** Available. **Policies:** Freshmen permitted cars on campus. **Activities:** Jazz band, choral groups, dance, drama, literary magazine, music ensembles, musical theater, student government, student newspaper.

Athletics. NJCAA. **Intercollegiate:** Basketball M, tennis, track and field, volleyball W. **Team name:** Ravens.

Student services. Career counseling, student employment services, personal counseling, placement for graduates. **Transfer:** Special adviser for new students. Transfer adviser, college fairs on campus for students transferring to 4-year colleges.

Contact. Phone: (281) 476-1816 Fax: (281) 478-2720
Del Long, Associate Dean of Admissions, San Jacinto College: Central Campus, 8060 Spencer Highway, Pasadena, TX 77505-5999

San Jacinto College: North

Houston, Texas
www.sjcd.edu **CB code: 6729**

- Public 2-year community and technical college
- Commuter campus in very large city

General. Founded in 1974. Regionally accredited. **Enrollment:** 5,536 degree-seeking undergraduates. **Degrees:** 258 associate awarded. **ROTC:** Army. **Location:** 15 miles from downtown. **Calendar:** Semester, limited summer session. **Full-time faculty:** 91 total. **Part-time faculty:** 141 total. **Special facilities:** Nature preserve.

Student profile.

Out-of-state:	1%	**25 or older:**	37%

Transfer out. **Colleges most students transferred to 2005:** University of Houston, University of Houston Clear Lake.

Basis for selection. Open admission, but selective for some programs. Psychological Services Bureau test required of nursing applicants. Interview required for nursing program. **Adult students:** Entrance exam policies same as for first-time freshmen.

2006-2007 Annual costs. Tuition/fees (projected): $1,480; $2,280 out-of-district; $2,920 out-of-state. Books/supplies: $1,500.

2005-2006 Financial aid. All financial aid based on need. 67% of total undergraduate aid awarded as scholarships/grants, 33% as loans/jobs. Need-based aid available for part-time students. Work study available nights, weekends and for part-time students.

Application procedures. **Admission:** No deadline. No application fee. Application must be submitted online. Admission notification on a rolling basis. **Financial aid:** Priority date 6/1; no closing date. FAFSA, institutional form required. Applicants notified on a rolling basis starting 8/1; must reply within 2 week(s) of notification.

Academics. Special study options: Accelerated study, cross-registration, distance learning, dual enrollment of high school students, ESL, honors, internships, weekend college. License preparation in nursing, paramedic, real estate. **Credit/placement by examination:** AP, CLEP, institutional tests. 16 credit hours maximum toward associate degree. Freshman College Composition CLEP subject examination must be accompanied by essay. **Support services:** GED preparation and test center, learning center, remedial instruction, study skills assistance, tutoring.

Majors. Biology: General. **Business:** Accounting, administrative services, business admin, international, management information systems, office management, office technology, office/clerical, real estate. **Communications:** Journalism. **Computer sciences:** General, data processing, programming. **Construction:** Maintenance, power transmission. **Education:** Bilingual, early childhood, elementary, reading, special. **Engineering technology:** Construction, drafting, electrical. **English:** Speech/rhetoric. **Family/consumer sciences:** Child care, family studies, institutional food production. **Foreign languages:** General, Spanish. **Health:** EMT paramedic, medical records technology. **History:** General. **Legal studies:** Paralegal. **Liberal arts:** Arts/sciences. **Math:** General. **Mechanic/repair:** Auto body, diesel, electronics/electrical, heating/ac/refrig. **Personal/culinary services:** Cosmetic, culinary arts. **Physical sciences:** Chemistry, geology, physics. **Protective services:** Criminal justice, police science. **Psychology:** General. **Social sciences:** General, sociology. **Visual/performing arts:** Art, dramatic.

Computing on campus. 400 workstations in library, computer center. Online course registration, helpline, repair service, wireless network available.

Student life. Freshman orientation: Available. Preregistration for classes offered. 4-hour sessions scheduled several times prior to beginning of semester. **Policies:** Freshmen permitted cars on campus. **Activities:** Bands, choral groups, literary magazine, music ensembles, musical theater, student newspaper, Baptist student union, Friends of Young Children, Webb historical society, Hispanic heritage club, Rotaract, computer science association, Phi Theta Kappa.

Athletics. NJCAA. **Intercollegiate:** Baseball M, basketball W. **Intramural:** Badminton, basketball, racquetball, softball, swimming, tennis, volleyball, weight lifting. **Team name:** Gators.

Student services. Career counseling, student employment services, financial aid counseling, on-campus daycare, personal counseling, veterans' counselor, women's services. **Physically disabled:** Services for visually, speech, hearing impaired. **Transfer:** Special adviser, orientation for new students. Transfer adviser, college fairs on campus for students transferring to 4-year colleges.

Contact. E-mail: wanda.simpson@sjcd.edu
Phone: (281) 998-6150 Fax: (281) 459-7125
Wanda Simpson, Director of Enrollment Services, San Jacinto College: North, 5800 Uvalde Road, Houston, TX 77049

South Plains College

Levelland, Texas
www.southplainscollege.edu **CB code: 6695**

- Public 2-year community and junior college
- Commuter campus in large town

General. Founded in 1957. Regionally accredited. Continuing education and workforce development programs available. **Enrollment:** 9,069 degree-seeking undergraduates. **Degrees:** 814 associate awarded. **Location:** 30 miles from Lubbock. **Calendar:** Semester, extensive summer session. **Full-time faculty:** 220 total. **Part-time faculty:** 110 total. **Special facilities:** Audio/video recording studio seating 300 for live, televised music performances.

Student profile. Among degree-seeking undergraduates, 37% enrolled in a transfer program, 63% enrolled in a vocational program, 3,169 enrolled as first-time, first-year students.

Part-time:	61%	**Hispanic American:**	25%
Out-of-state:	3%	**Native American:**	1%
Women:	54%	**International:**	1%
African American:	4%	**25 or older:**	21%
Asian American:	1%	**Live on campus:**	10%

Transfer out. 60% of students enrolled in the transfer program go on to 4-year colleges. **Colleges most students transferred to 2005:** Texas Tech University, San Angelo State University, West Texas A&M University, Eastern New Mexico State University.

Basis for selection. Open admission, but selective for some programs. Special requirements for allied health, cosmetology, law enforcement academy programs. State law requires TASP exam before student may enroll in college-level course work. Interview required for health care.

2005-2006 Annual costs. Tuition/fees: $1,712; $2,372 out-of-district; $2,852 out-of-state. Room/board: $3,100. Books/supplies: $580. Personal expenses: $1,100.

Financial aid. Need-based: Need-based aid available for part-time students. **Non-need-based:** Scholarships awarded for academics, athletics.

Application procedures. Admission: No deadline. No application fee. Admission notification on a rolling basis. **Financial aid:** Priority date 6/1; no closing date. FAFSA required. Applicants notified on a rolling basis starting 6/30; must reply within 2 week(s) of notification.

Academics. Special study options: Distance learning, dual enrollment of high school students, internships. License preparation in nursing, occupational therapy, paramedic, physical therapy, radiology, real estate. **Credit/placement by examination:** AP, CLEP, institutional tests. 15 credit hours maximum toward associate degree. **Support services:** GED preparation, learning center, remedial instruction, study skills assistance, tutoring.

Majors. Agriculture: Business. **Biology:** General, zoology. **Business:** Accounting, administrative services, business admin, fashion, office management, real estate. **Communications:** General, broadcast journalism, journalism. **Communications technology:** Graphic/printing. **Computer sciences:** General, computer science, data processing. **Construction:** Power transmission. **Education:** General. **Engineering:** General. **Engineering technology:** Drafting. **Family/consumer sciences:** General, child care. **Foreign languages:** French, Spanish. **Health:** Athletic training, EMT paramedic, health services, medical radiologic technology/radiation therapy, medical records technology, medical secretary, nursing (RN), predentistry, premedicine, prenursing, preop/surgical nursing, prepharmacy, preveterinary, respiratory therapy technology. **History:** General. **Interdisciplinary:** Behavioral sciences. **Legal studies:** Legal secretary, paralegal. **Liberal arts:** Arts/sciences. **Math:** General. **Mechanic/repair:** Auto body, automotive, diesel, electronics/electrical, heating/ac/refrig. **Parks/recreation:** Health/fitness. **Physical sciences:** Chemistry, geology, physics. **Protective services:** Fire safety technology, firefighting, law enforcement admin. **Psychology:** General. **Public administration:** Human services. **Social sciences:** Criminology, political science, sociology. **Visual/performing arts:** Cinematography, commercial/advertising art, design, dramatic.

Computing on campus. 2,000 workstations in library, computer center, student center. Dormitories linked to campus network. Commuter students can connect to campus network. Online course registration, online library, wireless network available.

Student life. Freshman orientation: Mandatory. Preregistration for classes offered. **Policies:** Freshmen permitted cars on campus. **Housing:** Single-sex dorms, special housing for disabled, apartments available. $100 deposit. **Activities:** Bands, choral groups, dance, drama, literary magazine, music ensembles, musical theater, radio station, student government, student newspaper, TV station.

Athletics. NJCAA. **Intercollegiate:** Basketball, cheerleading, cross-country, rodeo, track and field. **Intramural:** Basketball, racquetball, softball, table tennis, volleyball. **Team name:** Texans/ Lady Texans.

Student services. Career counseling, student employment services, financial aid counseling, health services, minority student services, personal counseling, placement for graduates, veterans' counselor. **Physically disabled:** Services for visually, hearing impaired. **Transfer:** Special adviser, orientation for new students. Transfer adviser, college fairs on campus for students transferring to 4-year colleges.

Contact. E-mail: arangel@southplainscollege.edu
Phone: (806) 894-9611 ext. 2373 Fax: (806) 897-3167
Andrea Rangel, Dean of Admissions and Records, South Plains College, 1401 College Avenue, Levelland, TX 79336

South Texas College

McAllen, Texas
www.southtexascollege.edu **CB code: 6654**

- Public 2-year community and technical college
- Commuter campus in small city

General. Regionally accredited. **Enrollment:** 17,138 degree-seeking undergraduates. **Degrees:** 1,024 associate awarded. **Calendar:** Semester, extensive summer session. **Full-time faculty:** 800 total; 73% minority, 50% women. **Part-time faculty:** 686 total; 76% minority, 48% women.

Basis for selection. Open admission, but selective for some programs. Special requirements for nursing program. **Adult students:** Entrance exam policies same as for first-time freshmen. **Homeschooled:** Transcript of courses and grades required.

2005-2006 Annual costs. Tuition/fees: $1,940; $2,453 out-of-district; $6,230 out-of-state.

2005-2006 Financial aid. All financial aid based on need. 98% of total undergraduate aid awarded as scholarships/grants, 2% as loans/jobs. Need-based aid available for part-time students. Work study available nights, weekends and for part-time students.

Application procedures. Admission: No deadline. No application fee. Application must be submitted on paper. **Financial aid:** Priority date 3/1; no closing date. FAFSA required. Applicants notified on a rolling basis starting 4/15.

Academics. Special study options: Cooperative education, distance learning, dual enrollment of high school students, ESL, weekend college. Bachelor's degree programs available on campus. **Credit/placement by examination:** CLEP, institutional tests. **Support services:** Learning center, remedial instruction, study skills assistance, tutoring, writing center.

Majors. Architecture: Technology. **Biology:** General. **Business:** Accounting, banking/financial services, business admin, marketing, office management. **Computer sciences:** General, computer science, database management, networking, security, web page design, webmaster. **Education:** Early childhood, elementary, middle, secondary. **Engineering:** General. **Engineering technology:** Drafting. **English:** English lit. **Family/consumer sciences:** Child development. **Health:** EMT paramedic, medical records technology, nursing assistant, occupational therapy assistant, office assistant, pharmacy assistant, physical therapy assistant, radiologic technology/medical imaging. **History:** General. **Interdisciplinary:** Intercultural. **Legal studies:** Legal secretary, paralegal. **Liberal arts:** Arts/sciences. **Math:** General. **Mechanic/repair:** Automotive, diesel, heating/ac/refrig. **Personal/culinary services:** General, restaurant/catering. **Philosophy/religion:** Philosophy. **Physical sciences:** Chemistry, physics. **Production:** General. **Protective services:** Law enforcement admin. **Public administration:** Human services. **Social sciences:** General, political science. **Visual/performing arts:** General, studio arts.

Computing on campus. Online course registration available.

Student life. Freshman orientation: Mandatory. Preregistration for classes offered. **Policies:** Freshmen permitted cars on campus. **Activities:** Drama, student government.

Athletics. Intramural: Basketball, football (non-tackle), football (tackle), softball, volleyball. **Team name:** Jaguars.

Student services. Career counseling, student employment services, financial aid counseling, personal counseling, placement for graduates, veterans' counselor. **Physically disabled:** Services for visually, speech, hearing impaired. **Learning disabled:** Comprehensive services available. **Transfer:** Special adviser, orientation for new students. Transfer center, transfer adviser, college fairs on campus for students transferring to 4-year colleges.

Contact. Phone: (956) 618-8311
Matthew Hebbard, Director of Admissions and Registrar, South Texas College, 3201 West Pecan Boulevard, McAllen, TX 78502

Southwest Institute of Technology

Austin, Texas
www.switaustin.com **CB code: 2471**

- For-profit 2-year technical college
- Commuter campus in large city

General. Accredited by ACCSCT. **Calendar:** Quarter.

Annual costs/financial aid. Costs shown above are for electronics technology associate degree program. Digital electronics technician: $17,069 tuition, $100 required fees, $1526 books and supplies including components students use to build own computer. Books/supplies: $1,329. Need-based financial aid available for full-time students.

Contact. Phone: (512) 892-2640
Admissions Coordinator, 5424 Highway 290 West, Suite 200, Austin, TX 78735

Southwest Texas Junior College

Uvalde, Texas
www.swtjc.cc.tx.us **CB code: 6666**

- Public 2-year community and junior college
- Commuter campus in large town

General. Founded in 1946. Regionally accredited. **Enrollment:** 2,250 full-time, degree-seeking students. **Degrees:** 435 associate awarded. **Location:** 80 miles from San Antonio, 70 miles from Del Rio. **Calendar:** Semester, limited summer session. **Full-time faculty:** 104 total. **Part-time faculty:** 102 total.

Student profile.

Out-of-state:	10%	**Live on campus:**	9%

Basis for selection. Open admission.

2005-2006 Annual costs. Tuition/fees: $1,439; $2,092 out-of-district; $2,369 out-of-state. Per-credit charge: $29 in-district; $51 out-of-district; $60 out-of-state. Additional fees for off-campus classes may apply. Room/board: $2,320. Books/supplies: $900. Personal expenses: $745.

Financial aid. Need-based: Need-based aid available for part-time students.

Application procedures. Admission: No deadline. No application fee. Admission notification on a rolling basis. **Financial aid:** Priority date 6/15; no closing date. FAFSA required. Applicants notified on a rolling basis starting 5/1; must reply within 2 week(s) of notification.

Academics. Special study options: Dual enrollment of high school students. License preparation in aviation, nursing. **Credit/placement by examination:** CLEP. TASP required of all students for placement and counseling. **Support services:** GED preparation and test center, learning center, remedial instruction, study skills assistance, tutoring, writing center.

Majors. Agriculture: General, agribusiness operations, business, farm/ranch. **Business:** Administrative services, management information systems, office technology. **Computer sciences:** General, data processing. **Education:** General. **Health:** Licensed practical nurse, nursing (RN). **Liberal arts:** Arts/sciences.

Computing on campus. 150 workstations in dormitories, library, computer center. Dormitories wired for high-speed internet access and linked to campus network. Commuter students can connect to campus network. Online library, helpline available.

Student life. Freshman orientation: Mandatory. Preregistration for classes offered. **Policies:** Freshmen permitted cars on campus. **Housing:** Coed dorms, single-sex dorms available. **Activities:** Drama, literary magazine, radio station, student government, student newspaper.

Athletics. Intercollegiate: Rodeo. **Intramural:** Baseball M, basketball, golf, racquetball, softball, swimming, tennis, volleyball.

Student services. Adult student services, campus ministries, career counseling, services for economically disadvantaged, student employment services, financial aid counseling, health services, minority student services, on-campus daycare, personal counseling, placement for graduates, veterans' counselor. **Physically disabled:** Services for visually, hearing impaired. **Transfer:** Special adviser, orientation, pre-admission transcript evaluation for new students. Transfer adviser, college fairs on campus for students transferring to 4-year colleges.

Contact. E-mail: luana.rodriguez@swtjc.cc.tx.us
Phone: (830) 278-4401 Fax: (830) 591-7396
Joe Barker, Dean of Admissions/Student Services, Southwest Texas Junior College, Garner Field Road, Uvalde, TX 78801

Tarrant County College

Fort Worth, Texas
www.tccd.edu **CB code: 6834**

- Public 2-year community college
- Commuter campus in very large city

General. Founded in 1965. Regionally accredited. 4 campuses. **Enrollment:** 11,800 full-time, degree-seeking students. **Degrees:** 1,870 associate awarded. **ROTC:** Army, Air Force. **Location:** 30 miles from Dallas. **Calendar:** Semester, extensive summer session. **Full-time faculty:** 440 total. **Part-time faculty:** 880 total.

Student profile.

Out-of-state:	1%	**25 or older:**	45%

Transfer out. **Colleges most students transferred to 2005:** University of Texas at Arlington, University of North Texas, Texas Woman's University, Texas Tech University, Southwest Texas State University.

Basis for selection. Open admission, but selective for some programs. Special requirements for nursing and allied health programs, honors program, and certain automotive programs; must submit separate application and meet highly selective admission criteria. Placement testing required of all first-time college students and for those entering certain English, math, and reading-based courses. Interview and essay may be required for selective admission programs. **Adult students:** Entrance exam policies same as for first-time freshmen.

2006-2007 Annual costs. Tuition/fees (projected): $1,500; $1,900 out-of-district; $4,500 out-of-state. Books/supplies: $1,100. Personal expenses: $1,500.

2004-2005 Financial aid. **Need-based:** 78% of total undergraduate aid awarded as scholarships/grants, 22% as loans/jobs. **Non-need-based:** Scholarships awarded for academics.

Application procedures. **Admission:** No deadline. No application fee. Application must be submitted on paper. Admission notification on a rolling basis. Applicants 18 years of age or older without high school diploma may be admitted on individual basis. **Financial aid:** Priority date 4/15; no closing date. FAFSA, institutional form required. Applicants notified on a rolling basis starting 3/1; must reply within 2 week(s) of notification.

Academics. Core curriculum guaranteed to transfer to any Texas public university. **Special study options:** Distance learning, double major, dual enrollment of high school students, ESL, honors, liberal arts/career combination. Limited Saturday classes available. License preparation in aviation, dental hygiene, nursing, paramedic, physical therapy, radiology, real estate. **Credit/placement by examination:** AP, CLEP, institutional tests. 18 credit hours maximum toward associate degree. **Support services:** GED preparation and test center, learning center, reduced course load, remedial instruction, study skills assistance, tutoring, writing center.

Majors. **Agriculture:** Horticulture. **Business:** General, accounting, administrative services, business admin, entrepreneurial studies, fashion, hospitality admin, operations, real estate, sales/distribution, tourism/travel. **Communications technology:** General, graphic/printing. **Computer sciences:** General, programming. **Engineering technology:** Architectural, drafting, electrical. **Family/consumer sciences:** Child care, institutional food production. **Foreign languages:** Sign language interpretation. **Health:** Dental hygiene, EMT paramedic, medical radiologic technology/radiation therapy, medical records technology, mental health services, nursing (RN), physical therapy assistant, respiratory therapy technology. **Legal studies:** Paralegal. **Mechanic/repair:** Aircraft, auto body, automotive, electronics/electrical, heating/ac/refrig. **Protective services:** Criminal justice, fire safety technology, firefighting, police science. **Public administration:** General.

Computing on campus. 3,000 workstations in library, computer center, student center. Commuter students can connect to campus network. Online course registration, online library available.

Student life. **Freshman orientation:** Available. Preregistration for classes offered. 1-2 hours, held intermittently. **Policies:** Freshmen permitted cars on campus. **Activities:** Bands, choral groups, dance, drama, music ensembles, student government, student newspaper.

Athletics. **Intramural:** Basketball M, table tennis.

Student services. Career counseling, services for economically disadvantaged, student employment services, financial aid counseling, health services, personal counseling, placement for graduates. **Physically disabled:** Services for visually, speech, hearing impaired. **Transfer:** College fairs on campus for students transferring to 4-year colleges.

Contact. E-mail: antonia.kilpatrick@tccd.edu
Phone: (817) 515-8223 Fax: (817) 515-5278
Cathie Jackson, Director of Admissions and Records, Tarrant County College, 1500 Houston Street, Fort Worth, TX 76102

Temple College
Temple, Texas
www.templejc.edu **CB code: 6818**

- Public 2-year community college
- Commuter campus in small city

General. Founded in 1926. Regionally accredited. **Enrollment:** 3,720 degree-seeking undergraduates; 177 non-degree-seeking students. **Degrees:** 283 associate awarded. **Location:** 65 miles from Austin. **Calendar:** Semester, limited summer session. **Full-time faculty:** 85 total; 20% have terminal degrees, 9% minority, 58% women. **Part-time faculty:** 139 total; 14% have terminal degrees, 9% minority, 54% women. **Class size:** 56% < 20, 35% 20-39, 8% 40-49, 1% 50-99. **Special facilities:** Health sciences simulation center. **Partnerships:** Formal partnerships with area high schools for tech prep programs.

Student profile. Among degree-seeking undergraduates, 71% enrolled in a transfer program, 29% enrolled in a vocational program, 1% already have a bachelor's degree or higher, 649 enrolled as first-time, first-year students.

Part-time:	64%	**Hispanic American:**	15%
Out-of-state:	1%	**Native American:**	1%
Women:	66%	**25 or older:**	32%
African American:	14%	**Live on campus:**	3%
Asian American:	2%		

Transfer out. 48% of students enrolled in the transfer program go on to 4-year colleges. **Colleges most students transferred to 2005:** Texas A&M University, Texas State University, University of Texas at Austin, Tarleton State University, University of Mary Hardin-Baylor.

Basis for selection. Open admission, but selective for some programs. Limited enrollment in allied health programs; interview required. **Adult students:** Entrance exam policies same as for first-time freshmen.

High school preparation. 23 units recommended. Recommended units include English 4, mathematics 3, social studies 2, history 2, science 3, foreign language 2 and academic electives 7.

2006-2007 Annual costs. Tuition/fees (projected): $1,860; $2,850 out-of-district; $4,500 out-of-state. Per-credit charge: $62 in-district; $95 out-of-district; $150 out-of-state. Books/supplies: $1,200. Personal expenses: $1,407.

Financial aid. All financial aid based on need. Need-based aid available for part-time students. Work study available nights and for part-time students.

Application procedures. **Admission:** No deadline. No application fee. Application must be submitted on paper. Admission notification on a rolling basis. **Financial aid:** Priority date 6/1; no closing date. FAFSA required. Applicants notified on a rolling basis starting 5/1; must reply within 4 week(s) of notification.

Academics. **Special study options:** Accelerated study, cooperative education, distance learning, dual enrollment of high school students, honors, internships. License preparation in dental hygiene, nursing, paramedic. **Credit/placement by examination:** AP, CLEP, IB, institutional tests. 32 credit hours maximum toward associate degree. Last 16 hours or total 32 hours earned in residence may not be earned by credit by examination. **Support services:** GED preparation, learning center, remedial instruction, study skills assistance, tutoring, writing center.

Majors. **Biology:** General. **Business:** General, office management. **Computer sciences:** General, data entry, LAN/WAN management, programming, system admin, webmaster. **Education:** Elementary, teacher assistance. **Engineering technology:** Drafting. **Family/consumer sciences:** Child care. **Health:** Clinical lab technology, dental hygiene, EMT paramedic, nursing (RN), respiratory therapy technology. **Liberal arts:** Arts/sciences. **Mechanic/repair:** Computer, electronics/electrical. **Protective services:** Criminal justice, police science. **Public administration:** Social work. **Social sciences:** Cartography. **Visual/performing arts:** Art.

Most popular majors. Business/marketing 11%, computer/information sciences 6%, education 9%, health sciences 28%, liberal arts 34%.

Computing on campus. 100 workstations in library, computer center. Dormitories wired for high-speed internet access. Commuter students can connect to campus network. Online library available.

Student life. **Freshman orientation:** Available. Preregistration for classes offered. Held prior to fall semester; 4 hours over 2 days. **Policies:** Freshmen permitted cars on campus. **Housing:** Apartments available. Privately run student apartments on campus. **Activities:** Bands, choral groups, dance, drama, literary magazine, music ensembles, musical theater, student government, symphony orchestra, Baptist Student Ministries, black American cultural club, society of Latin American cultures, College Republicans, Young Democrats, literary club.

Athletics. NJCAA. **Intercollegiate:** Baseball M, basketball, softball W, tennis, volleyball W. **Intramural:** Basketball, bowling, football (non-tackle), golf, racquetball, soccer, softball, swimming, table tennis, tennis, volleyball. **Team name:** Leopards.

Student services. Adult student services, career counseling, services for economically disadvantaged, student employment services, financial aid counseling, personal counseling, placement for graduates, veterans' counselor. **Physically disabled:** Services for visually, hearing impaired. **Learning disabled:** Comprehensive services available. **Transfer:** Special adviser, preadmission transcript evaluation for new students. Transfer adviser for students transferring to 4-year colleges.

Contact. Phone: (254) 298-8300 Toll-free number: (800) 460-4636
Fax: (254) 298-8288
Paul Foutz, Director of Admission and Records, Temple College, 2600 South First Street, Temple, TX 76504-7435

Texarkana College

Texarkana, Texas
www.texarkanacollege.edu **CB code: 6819**

- Public 2-year community college
- Commuter campus in small city

General. Founded in 1927. Regionally accredited. **Enrollment:** 4,122 degree-seeking undergraduates. **Degrees:** 187 associate awarded. **Location:** 80 miles from Shreveport, Louisiana, 180 miles from Dallas. **Calendar:** Semester, limited summer session. **Full-time faculty:** 88 total; 9% have terminal degrees, 7% minority, 58% women. **Part-time faculty:** 94 total; 2% have terminal degrees, 7% minority, 58% women. **Special facilities:** 365-acre farm.

Student profile.

Out-of-state:	30%	**Live on campus:**	3%
25 or older:	38%		

Transfer out. Colleges most students transferred to 2005: Texas A&M at Texarkana, Southern Arkansas University.

Basis for selection. Open admission. Interview recommended for nursing program.

2005-2006 Annual costs. Tuition/fees: $960; $1,470 out-of-district; $1,970 out-of-state. Per-credit charge: $29 in-district; $46 out-of-district; $63 out-of-state. Arkansas and Oklahoma residents pay out-of-district rates. Books/supplies: $750. Personal expenses: $1,200.

Financial aid. Need-based: Need-based aid available for part-time students. Work study available nights, weekends and for part-time students. **Non-need-based:** Scholarships awarded for academics, athletics.

Application procedures. Admission: No deadline. No application fee. Admission notification on a rolling basis. **Financial aid:** Priority date 6/1; no closing date. FAFSA, institutional form required. Applicants notified on a rolling basis starting 3/1.

Academics. Special study options: Cooperative education, cross-registration, distance learning, dual enrollment of high school students, internships, liberal arts/career combination. License preparation in nursing, paramedic, real estate. **Credit/placement by examination:** CLEP. 14 credit hours maximum toward associate degree. **Support services:** GED test center, learning center, remedial instruction, tutoring.

Majors. Agriculture: General. **Biology:** General. **Business:** General, administrative services, business admin, marketing. **Communications:** Journalism. **Computer sciences:** General. **Engineering:** General. **Engineering technology:** Drafting, electrical. **Family/consumer sciences:** Child development. **Foreign languages:** General. **Health:** EMT paramedic, nursing (RN), substance abuse counseling. **History:** General. **Liberal arts:** Humanities. **Math:** General. **Physical sciences:** Chemistry, physics. **Protective services:** Criminal justice, law enforcement admin. **Social sciences:** General, political science. **Visual/performing arts:** Art, dramatic.

Most popular majors. Business/marketing 11%, health sciences 32%, liberal arts 31%.

Computing on campus. 500 workstations in library, computer center.

Student life. Freshman orientation: Available. **Policies:** Freshmen permitted cars on campus. **Activities:** Concert band, choral groups, drama, literary magazine, musical theater, radio station, student government, student newspaper.

Athletics. NJCAA. **Intercollegiate:** Baseball M, softball W. **Intramural:** Archery, badminton, basketball, bowling, handball, racquetball, sailing, skin diving, swimming, tennis, volleyball. **Team name:** Bulldogs.

Student services. Career counseling, student employment services, personal counseling, veterans' counselor. **Transfer:** Special adviser, orientation for new students.

Contact. E-mail: admissions@texarkanacollege.edu
Phone: (903) 832-5565 ext. 3358 Fax: (903) 832-5030
Van Miller, Director of Admissions and Registrar, Texarkana College, 2500 North Robison Road, Texarkana, TX 75599

Texas Southmost College

Brownsville, Texas
www.utb.edu **CB code: 6825**

- Public 2-year community college
- Commuter campus in small city

General. Founded in 1926. Regionally accredited. **Enrollment:** 5,525 full-time, degree-seeking students. **Degrees:** 801 associate awarded. **Location:** 160 miles from Corpus Christi. **Calendar:** Semester, extensive summer session. **Full-time faculty:** 285 total. **Part-time faculty:** 271 total.

Basis for selection. Open admission, but selective for some programs. For some allied health programs, entrance examination may be required.

2005-2006 Annual costs. Tuition/fees: $3,325; $3,895 out-of-district; $12,175 out-of-state. Per-credit charge: $31 in-district; $50 out-of-district; $326 out-of-state. Books/supplies: $824. Personal expenses: $1,348.

Application procedures. Admission: No deadline. No application fee. Admission notification on a rolling basis. **Financial aid:** Priority date 4/1, closing date 6/1. FAFSA required. Applicants notified on a rolling basis starting 7/1; must reply by 8/1.

Academics. Special study options: Cooperative education, cross-registration, dual enrollment of high school students, honors. **Credit/placement by examination:** AP, CLEP, institutional tests. 38 credit hours maximum toward associate degree. **Support services:** Remedial instruction, tutoring.

Majors. Business: General, accounting, business admin, hospitality admin, office management, office technology, sales/distribution. **Computer sciences:** General. **Engineering technology:** Drafting, electrical. **Family/consumer sciences:** Child care. **Health:** Clinical lab science, EMT paramedic, medical radiologic technology/radiation therapy, nursing (RN), respiratory therapy technology, substance abuse counseling. **Legal studies:** Legal secretary. **Liberal arts:** Arts/sciences. **Protective services:** Corrections, law enforcement admin, police science.

Student life. Freshman orientation: Mandatory, $15 fee. **Activities:** Bands, choral groups, dance, drama, music ensembles, student government, student newspaper, symphony orchestra.

Athletics. NJCAA. **Intercollegiate:** Badminton, baseball M, volleyball W. **Intramural:** Archery, basketball, bowling, golf, gymnastics, handball, sailing, soccer M, softball, table tennis, tennis, volleyball.

Student services. Career counseling, student employment services, health services, on-campus daycare, personal counseling, placement for graduates, veterans' counselor.

Contact. Phone: (956) 544-8254 Fax: (956) 544-8832
Rene Villarreal, Director of Enrollment, Registrar, Texas Southmost College, 80 Fort Brown, Brownsville, TX 78520

Texas State Technical College: Harlingen

Harlingen, Texas
www.harlingen.tstc.edu **CB code: 6843**

- Public 2-year technical college
- Commuter campus in small city

General. Founded in 1969. Regionally accredited. **Enrollment:** 1,600 degree-seeking undergraduates. **Degrees:** 288 associate awarded. **Location:** 25 miles from Brownsville, 30 miles from South Padre Island. **Calendar:** Semester, extensive summer session. **Full-time faculty:** 162 total. **Part-time faculty:** 48 total. **Class size:** 46% < 20, 48% 20-39, 3% 40-49, 2% 50-99. **Special facilities:** State-of-the-art computer labs including digital imaging technology, semi-conductor technology training center.

Student profile.

Out-of-state:	1%	**Live on campus:**	12%
25 or older:	35%		

Transfer out. Colleges most students transferred to 2005: University of Texas at Brownsville, University of Texas-Pan American, University of Texas-San Antonio, South Texas Community College, Texas Southmost College.

Basis for selection. Open admission, but selective for some programs. Competitive admissions for dental assisting, surgical technology, dental hygiene, and health information technology programs. Associate degree candidates required to take state-mandated Texas Academic Skills Program. Results used only for placement. SAT/ACT scores may be substituted.

2005-2006 Annual costs. Tuition/fees: $2,330; $5,450 out-of-state. Per-credit charge: $58 in-state; $162 out-of-state. Room/board: $2,538. Books/supplies: $900. Personal expenses: $1,380.

2005-2006 Financial aid. Need-based: 83% of total undergraduate aid awarded as scholarships/grants, 17% as loans/jobs. Need-based aid available for part-time students.

Application procedures. Admission: No deadline. No application fee. Application must be submitted on paper. Admission notification on a rolling basis. **Financial aid:** Closing date 4/13. FAFSA, institutional form required. Applicants notified on a rolling basis starting 6/30; must reply within 2 week(s) of notification.

Academics. Special study options: Cooperative education, distance learning, dual enrollment of high school students, ESL, independent study, internships, liberal arts/career combination, teacher certification program, weekend college. License preparation in aviation, dental hygiene, paramedic. **Credit/placement by examination:** AP, CLEP, institutional tests. **Support services:** GED preparation and test center, learning center, remedial instruction, study skills assistance, tutoring.

Majors. Agriculture: Business technology. **Business:** Administrative services. **Computer sciences:** Information technology, programming. **Education:** Teacher assistance. **Engineering technology:** Biomedical, computer systems, construction, drafting, electrical, electromechanical, telecommunications. **Health:** Dental hygiene, dental lab technology, EMT paramedic, medical assistant, medical records technology, surgical technology. **Legal studies:** Legal secretary. **Mechanic/repair:** Aircraft, auto body, heating/ac/refrig. **Personal/culinary services:** Institutional food service. **Production:** Tool and die. **Science technology:** Chemical. **Visual/performing arts:** Commercial/advertising art.

Computing on campus. Online library available.

Student life. Freshman orientation: Mandatory. Preregistration for classes offered. **Policies:** Freshmen permitted cars on campus. **Housing:** Guaranteed on-campus for all undergraduates. Coed dorms, special housing for disabled, apartments, substance-free housing available. $100 deposit. **Activities:** Dance, literary magazine, student government, student newspaper, Baptist Student Union, Hispanic club.

Athletics. Intramural: Baseball, basketball, football (tackle), racquetball, soccer, softball, table tennis, tennis, track and field, volleyball, weight lifting.

Student services. Alcohol/substance abuse counseling, career counseling, student employment services, financial aid counseling, health services, on-campus daycare, personal counseling, placement for graduates, veterans' counselor, women's services. **Physically disabled:** Services for visually, speech, hearing impaired. **Transfer:** Special adviser, orientation for new students. Transfer adviser, college fairs on campus for students transferring to 4-year colleges.

Contact. E-mail: blanca.guerra@harlingen.tstc.edu
Phone: (956) 364-4320 Toll-free number: (800) 852-8784
Fax: (956) 364-5117
Blanca Guerra, Director of Admissions and Records, Texas State Technical College: Harlingen, 1902 North Loop 499, Harlingen, TX 78550-3697

Texas State Technical College: Marshall

Marshall, Texas
www.marshall.tstc.edu **CB code: 6328**

- Public 2-year technical college
- Large town

General. Regionally accredited. **Enrollment:** 485 degree-seeking undergraduates. **Degrees:** 145 associate awarded. **Location:** 150 miles from Dallas, 230 miles from Houston. **Calendar:** Semester, extensive summer session. **Full-time faculty:** 36 total. **Part-time faculty:** 10 total.

Basis for selection. Open admission. Admission tests used only for placement.

2005-2006 Annual costs. Tuition/fees: $2,330; $5,450 out-of-state. Per-credit charge: $58 in-state; $162 out-of-state. Room only: $2,390.

Application procedures. Admission: No deadline. No application fee. Admission notification on a rolling basis. **Financial aid:** Priority date 6/1; no closing date. FAFSA required.

Academics. Credit/placement by examination: CLEP.

Majors. Business: E-commerce. **Communications technology:** General. **Computer sciences:** A.i./robotics, LAN/WAN management, networking. **Engineering technology:** Industrial, telecommunications. **Health:** Environmental health.

Student life. Freshman orientation: Mandatory. **Activities:** Student newspaper.

Contact. Phone: (903) 935-1010
Susan Carter, Director of Admissions, Texas State Technical College: Marshall, 2400 East End Boulevard South, Marshall, TX 75672

Texas State Technical College: Waco

Waco, Texas
www.waco.tstc.edu **CB code: 6328**

- Public 2-year technical college
- Residential campus in small city

General. Founded in 1965. Regionally accredited. **Enrollment:** 4,431 degree-seeking undergraduates; 317 non-degree-seeking students. **Degrees:** 686 associate awarded. **Location:** 90 miles from Dallas and Austin. **Calendar:** Semester, extensive summer session. **Full-time faculty:** 232 total; 4% have terminal degrees, 11% minority, 23% women. **Part-time faculty:** 18 total; 11% have terminal degrees, 11% minority, 11% women. **Special facilities:** Advanced manufacturing center, 8,600-foot runway at TSTC-Waco airport, institutionally owned and operated 18-hole golf course.

Student profile. Among degree-seeking undergraduates, 100% enrolled in a vocational program, 1,840 enrolled as first-time, first-year students.

Part-time:	30%	**Women:**	22%

Basis for selection. Open admission. International students must have an I-20 and provide other required documentation to be admitted. All others must provide proof of high school graduation or GED. Students without high school diploma or GED may be admitted on individual approval and must be tested prior to admission and interview with counseling and testing staff. Accuplacer or THEA test required prior to enrollment; used for placement purposes only. Interview recommended for students without high school diploma or GED. **Adult students:** SAT/ACT scores not required. **Home-schooled:** Transcript of courses and grades required.

2005-2006 Annual costs. Tuition/fees: $2,333; $5,453 out-of-state. Per-credit charge: $58 in-state; $162 out-of-state. Room/board: $3,990. Books/supplies: $751. Personal expenses: $1,899.

2005-2006 Financial aid. All financial aid based on need. 57% of total undergraduate aid awarded as scholarships/grants, 43% as loans/jobs. Need-based aid available for part-time students. Work study available for part-time students.

Application procedures. Admission: Closing date 8/29 (receipt date). No application fee. Application may be submitted online. Admission notification on a rolling basis. **Financial aid:** Priority date 6/1; no closing date. FAFSA required. Applicants notified on a rolling basis starting 5/15.

Academics. Special study options: Cooperative education, cross-registration, distance learning, dual enrollment of high school students, liberal arts/career combination. License preparation in aviation. **Credit/placement by examination:** AP, CLEP, IB, institutional tests. 18 credit hours maximum toward associate degree. 25% of total hours for degree is maximum number of credit awarded for prior work and/or life experiences. **Support services:** GED test center, learning center, remedial instruction, study skills assistance, tutoring.

Majors. Agriculture: Turf management. **Business:** Operations. **Communications technology:** General, graphic/printing. **Computer sciences:** General, computer science, data processing, information systems, programming.

Construction: Maintenance, power transmission. **Engineering technology:** Drafting, electrical. **Family/consumer sciences:** Institutional food production. **Health:** Clinical lab science. **Mechanic/repair:** General, aircraft, auto body, automotive, avionics, diesel, electronics/electrical, heating/ac/refrig, industrial. **Physical sciences:** General. **Transportation:** Aviation. **Visual/performing arts:** Cinematography, commercial/advertising art.

Computing on campus. 1,000 workstations in library, computer center, student center. Dormitories wired for high-speed internet access and linked to campus network. Commuter students can connect to campus network. Helpline, student web hosting, wireless network available.

Student life. Freshman orientation: Mandatory. Preregistration for classes offered. Held prior to semester. **Policies:** Freshmen permitted cars on campus. **Housing:** Coed dorms, single-sex dorms, special housing for disabled, apartments, substance-free housing available. $150 deposit. Duplexes and houses available to married students or students with families. **Activities:** Student government, student newspaper.

Athletics. Intramural: Basketball, football (non-tackle), golf, racquetball, softball, volleyball.

Student services. Adult student services, career counseling, student employment services, financial aid counseling, health services, on-campus daycare, personal counseling, placement for graduates, veterans' counselor, women's services. **Physically disabled:** Services for visually, speech, hearing impaired. **Transfer:** Special adviser, orientation, pre-admission transcript evaluation for new students. Transfer adviser for students transferring to 4-year colleges.

Contact. Phone: (254) 867-2361 Toll-free number: (800) 792-8784
Fax: (254) 867-2250
Dawn Khoury, Director of Admissions and Records, Texas State Technical College: Waco, 3801 Campus Drive, Waco, TX 76705

Texas State Technical College: West Texas

Sweetwater, Texas
www.westtexas.tstc.edu **CB code: 3137**

- Public 2-year technical college
- Commuter campus in large town

General. Founded in 1970. Regionally accredited. **Enrollment:** 1,385 degree-seeking undergraduates; 292 non-degree-seeking students. **Degrees:** 189 associate awarded. **Location:** 50 miles from Abilene. **Calendar:** Semester, limited summer session. **Full-time faculty:** 106 total. **Part-time faculty:** 19 total. **Special facilities:** Robotics lab, Cisco Academy, Microsoft Academy.

Student profile. Among degree-seeking undergraduates, 100% enrolled in a vocational program, 418 enrolled as first-time, first-year students.

Part-time:	39%	**Hispanic American:**	24%
Out-of-state:	1%	**International:**	1%
Women:	45%	**25 or older:**	40%
African American:	8%	**Live on campus:**	14%
Asian American:	1%		

Basis for selection. Open admission, but selective for some programs. Special admissions to nursing program; base score on placement test considered. Standardized test scores, if submitted, may be used in placement and counseling. SAT and ACT scores, if high enough, may exempt an applicant from THEA testing requirements. **Adult students:** Entrance exam policies same as for first-time freshmen.

2005-2006 Annual costs. Tuition/fees: $2,330; $5,450 out-of-state. Per-credit charge: $58 in-state; $162 out-of-state. Room/board: $3,450. Books/supplies: $1,100. Personal expenses: $650.

2004-2005 Financial aid. Need-based: 42% of total undergraduate aid awarded as scholarships/grants, 58% as loans/jobs. Need-based aid available for part-time students. Work study available nights, weekends and for part-time students. **Non-need-based:** Scholarships awarded for academics, leadership.

Application procedures. Admission: Priority date 8/1; no deadline. No application fee. Application may be submitted online. Admission notification on a rolling basis. **Financial aid:** Priority date 5/1; no closing date. FAFSA, institutional form required. Applicants notified on a rolling basis starting 7/1; must reply by 8/20.

Academics. Special study options: Cooperative education, distance learning, dual enrollment of high school students, internships, liberal arts/career combination. 1-1 and 1-1-2 electronics technology programs with numerous area institutions. License preparation in aviation, nursing, paramedic. **Credit/placement by examination:** AP, CLEP, institutional tests. Varies per program and individual student. **Support services:** GED test center, learning center, reduced course load, remedial instruction, study skills assistance, tutoring.

Majors. Business: Management information systems. **Communications technology:** General. **Computer sciences:** Networking, programming, web page design. **Conservation:** Environmental science. **Engineering technology:** Construction, drafting, electrical, robotics. **Health:** EMT paramedic, medical records technology. **Mechanic/repair:** Aircraft, automotive, diesel. **Personal/culinary services:** Chef training. **Production:** Machine tool. **Science technology:** Biological. **Transportation:** Airline/commercial pilot. **Visual/performing arts:** Design.

Most popular majors. Communication technologies 16%, computer/information sciences 51%, health sciences 12%, trade and industry 12%.

Computing on campus. 50 workstations in library, student center. Dormitories wired for high-speed internet access. Commuter students can connect to campus network. Online library, helpline, wireless network available.

Student life. Freshman orientation: Mandatory, $15 fee. Preregistration for classes offered. Held day before start of classes. **Policies:** Freshmen permitted cars on campus. **Housing:** Coed dorms, special housing for disabled, apartments, substance-free housing available. $150 partly refundable deposit. Pets allowed in dorm rooms. **Activities:** Student government, student newspaper, Mexican American club, Baptist Student Union, technical students association, data processing management association, Business Professionals of America, society of manufacturing engineers, Vocational Industrial Clubs of America.

Athletics. Intramural: Basketball, bowling, golf, softball, swimming, table tennis, tennis, volleyball W.

Student services. Career counseling, services for economically disadvantaged, student employment services, financial aid counseling, health services, personal counseling, placement for graduates, veterans' counselor, women's services. **Physically disabled:** Services for hearing impaired. **Transfer:** Special adviser, orientation for new students. Transfer adviser, college fairs on campus for students transferring to 4-year colleges.

Contact. E-mail: maria.aguirre@tstc.edu
Phone: (325) 235-7300 Toll-free number: (800) 592-8784
Fax: (325) 235-7416
Maria Aguirre-Acuna, Coordinator of New Student Admissions, Texas State Technical College: West Texas, 300 College Drive, Sweetwater, TX 79556

Trinity Valley Community College

Athens, Texas
www.tvcc.edu **CB code: 6271**

- Public 2-year community college
- Commuter campus in large town

General. Founded in 1946. Regionally accredited. 3 extension centers in state. **Enrollment:** 5,825 degree-seeking undergraduates. **Degrees:** 530 associate awarded. **Location:** 70 miles from Dallas. **Calendar:** Semester, limited summer session. **Full-time faculty:** 124 total. **Part-time faculty:** 80 total. **Special facilities:** 2 operating ranches with more than 500 acres.

Student profile. Among degree-seeking undergraduates, 52% enrolled in a transfer program, 48% enrolled in a vocational program.

Out-of-state:	3%	**Live on campus:**	10%

Basis for selection. Open admission, but selective for some programs. Special requirements for nursing program. Institution observes all TASP requirements.

2005-2006 Annual costs. Tuition/fees: $1,050; $1,650 out-of-district; $2,400 out-of-state. Per-credit charge: $20 in-district; $40 out-of-district; $65 out-of-state. Room/board: $3,400. Books/supplies: $435. Personal expenses: $980.

Financial aid. Need-based: Need-based aid available for part-time students. Work study available nights and weekends. **Non-need-based:** Scholarships awarded for academics, athletics.

Application procedures. Admission: No deadline. No application fee. Admission notification on a rolling basis. **Financial aid:** Priority date 7/1; no closing date. FAFSA, institutional form required. Applicants notified on a rolling basis starting 7/1; must reply within 2 week(s) of notification.

Academics. Special study options: Distance learning, dual enrollment of high school students, honors, internships, liberal arts/career combination, weekend college. **Credit/placement by examination:** CLEP. 18 credit hours maximum toward associate degree. **Support services:** GED preparation and test center, learning center, remedial instruction, tutoring.

Majors. Agriculture: Business, farm/ranch, horticulture. **Biology:** General. **Business:** Accounting, administrative services, business admin, office technology. **Communications:** General, journalism. **Computer sciences:** General, computer graphics, data processing, programming. **Education:** General, early childhood, elementary, middle. **Engineering:** General, polymer. **Engineering technology:** Drafting. **English:** Speech/rhetoric. **Family/consumer sciences:** Child care. **Foreign languages:** Spanish. **Health:** Nursing (RN), predentistry, premedicine, prenursing, prepharmacy, preveterinary. **Legal studies:** Legal secretary, paralegal, prelaw. **Liberal arts:** Arts/sciences. **Math:** General. **Parks/recreation:** Health/fitness. **Physical sciences:** Chemistry, physics. **Protective services:** Firefighting, law enforcement admin. **Psychology:** General. **Social sciences:** General, sociology. **Visual/performing arts:** General, art, dramatic.

Student life. Freshman orientation: Available, $20 fee. **Housing:** Single-sex dorms available. **Activities:** Bands, choral groups, dance, drama, music ensembles, student government, student newspaper, Baptist Student Union, United Campus Ministry, nontraditional student organization, Phi Beta Kappa, international student organization, criminal justice fraternity.

Athletics. NJCAA. **Intercollegiate:** Basketball, football (tackle) M. **Intramural:** Basketball, bowling, handball M, racquetball, soccer M, softball, table tennis, tennis, volleyball. **Team name:** Cardinals.

Student services. Career counseling, student employment services, personal counseling, placement for graduates, veterans' counselor. **Physically disabled:** Services for speech impaired. **Transfer:** Special adviser, preadmission transcript evaluation for new students. Transfer adviser, college fairs on campus for students transferring to 4-year colleges.

Contact. Phone: (903) 675-6357 Fax: (903) 675-6209
Audrey Hawkins, Director of School Relations, Trinity Valley Community College, 100 Cardinal Drive, Athens, TX 75751

Tyler Junior College

Tyler, Texas
www.tjc.edu **CB code: 6833**

- Public 2-year junior college
- Commuter campus in small city

General. Founded in 1926. Regionally accredited. **Enrollment:** 8,500 full-time, degree-seeking students. **Degrees:** 955 associate awarded. **Location:** 85 miles from Dallas; 85 miles from Shreveport, Louisiana. **Calendar:** Semester, extensive summer session. **Full-time faculty:** 245 total. **Part-time faculty:** 210 total. **Class size:** 48% < 20, 46% 20-39, 4% 40-49, 1% 50-99, less than 1% >100. **Special facilities:** Planetarium, conservatory.

Student profile. Among full-time, degree-seeking students, 680 transferred in from other institutions.

Out-of-state:	2%	**Live on campus:**	1%
25 or older:	28%		

Transfer out. Colleges most students transferred to 2005: Stephen F. Austin State University, Texas A&M University, University of Texas at Tyler.

Basis for selection. Open admission, but selective for some programs. Admission to allied health programs based on test scores. High school units mandated by state law may vary by program. Texas Higher Education Assessment (THEA) required by Texas law for all incoming students. Interview required for some allied health programs, recommended for others. **Homeschooled:** Must complete equivalent of accepted high school diploma.

2005-2006 Annual costs. Tuition/fees: $1,520; $2,480 out-of-district; $2,780 out-of-state. Per-credit charge: $20 in-district; $52 out-of-district; $62 out-of-state. Room/board: $4,000. Books/supplies: $600. Personal expenses: $1,312.

Financial aid. Need-based: Need-based aid available for part-time students. Work study available for part-time students. **Non-need-based:** Scholarships awarded for academics, alumni affiliation, art, athletics, leadership, music/drama.

Application procedures. Admission: No deadline. No application fee. Admission notification on a rolling basis. **Financial aid:** Priority date 6/1; no closing date. FAFSA, institutional form required. Applicants notified on a rolling basis starting 3/1; must reply within 2 week(s) of notification.

Academics. Special study options: Accelerated study, cooperative education, cross-registration, distance learning, dual enrollment of high school students, ESL, honors, internships, liberal arts/career combination, weekend college. License preparation in dental hygiene, nursing, paramedic, radiology, real estate. **Credit/placement by examination:** AP, CLEP, IB, institutional tests. **Support services:** GED preparation and test center, learning center, remedial instruction, study skills assistance, tutoring.

Honors college/program. SAT 1070 (exclusive of Writing), minimum 500 Math and Verbal; ACT 23, minimum 19 in each area.

Majors. Agriculture: General, farm/ranch. **Biology:** General. **Business:** General, accounting technology, administrative services, business admin, managerial economics, marketing, office management. **Communications:** Journalism. **Communications technology:** Graphic/printing. **Computer sciences:** General, applications programming, information systems, web page design. **Construction:** Electrician, maintenance. **Education:** General. **Engineering:** General. **Engineering technology:** Civil drafting, drafting, electrical, surveying. **English:** Speech/rhetoric. **Family/consumer sciences:** General, child care. **Foreign languages:** General, French, sign language interpretation, Spanish. **Health:** Clinical lab assistant, dental hygiene, EMT ambulance attendant, EMT paramedic, medical radiologic technology/radiation therapy, medical records technology, medical secretary, nursing (RN), office admin, ophthalmic lab technology, predentistry, premedicine, prenursing, prepharmacy, preveterinary, radiologic technology/medical imaging, respiratory therapy technology, sonography, substance abuse counseling, surgical technology. **History:** General. **Interdisciplinary:** Natural sciences. **Legal studies:** Legal secretary, paralegal, prelaw. **Liberal arts:** Arts/sciences. **Math:** General. **Mechanic/repair:** Automotive, heating/ac/refrig. **Parks/recreation:** Exercise sciences, health/fitness. **Physical sciences:** Chemistry, geology, physics. **Protective services:** Criminal justice, fire safety technology, police science. **Psychology:** General. **Public administration:** Human services. **Social sciences:** General, sociology. **Visual/performing arts:** General, art, commercial/advertising art, dance, dramatic, interior design, music performance, studio arts.

Computing on campus. 95 workstations in library, computer center, student center. Dormitories wired for high-speed internet access. Commuter students can connect to campus network. Online course registration, online library, helpline, repair service, student web hosting, wireless network available.

Student life. Freshman orientation: Mandatory, $50 fee. Preregistration for classes offered. 2-day orientation program in summer. **Policies:** Freshmen permitted cars on campus. **Housing:** Single-sex dorms available. $200 deposit. **Activities:** Bands, choral groups, dance, drama, literary magazine, music ensembles, musical theater, student government, student newspaper, symphony orchestra, TV station, Bible chairs, international student association, Phi Theta Kappa.

Athletics. NAIA, NJCAA. **Intercollegiate:** Baseball M, basketball, cheerleading, football (tackle) M, golf, soccer M, tennis, volleyball W. **Intramural:** Badminton, basketball, football (tackle) M, handball, racquetball, softball, table tennis, tennis, volleyball M. **Team name:** Apaches.

Student services. Adult student services, alcohol/substance abuse counseling, campus ministries, career counseling, services for economically disadvantaged, student employment services, financial aid counseling, health services, personal counseling, placement for graduates, veterans' counselor, women's services. **Physically disabled:** Services for visually, speech, hearing impaired. **Transfer:** Special adviser for new students. College fairs on campus for students transferring to 4-year colleges.

Contact. E-mail: admissions@tjc.edu
Phone: (903) 510-2523 Toll-free number: (800) 687-5680 ext. 2523
Fax: (903) 510-2161
Joel Renaud, Director of Admissions, Tyler Junior College, Box 9020, Tyler, TX 75711-9020

Universal Technical Institute

Houston, Texas
www.uticorp.com **CB code: 2503**

- For-profit 2-year technical college
- Large city
- Interview required

General. Accredited by ACCSCT. **Enrollment:** 1,850 degree-seeking undergraduates. **Calendar:** 3-week sections. **Full-time faculty:** 200 total.

Basis for selection. Open admission. GED not accepted.

Application procedures. **Admission:** No deadline. $100 fee.

Academics. **Credit/placement by examination:** CLEP.

Student life. **Freshman orientation:** Mandatory.

Student services. Career counseling, student employment services, health services, personal counseling, placement for graduates, veterans' counselor.

Contact. Phone: (281) 443-6262 Fax: (281) 443-0616
Wayne Bates, Admission Director, Universal Technical Institute, 721 Lockhaven Drive, Houston, TX 77073

Vernon College

Vernon, Texas
www.vernoncollege.edu **CB code: 6913**

- Public 2-year community and junior college
- Commuter campus in large town

General. Founded in 1970. Regionally accredited. **Enrollment:** 2,803 degree-seeking undergraduates. **Degrees:** 158 associate awarded. **Location:** 50 miles from Wichita Falls. **Calendar:** Semester, limited summer session. **Full-time faculty:** 55 total. **Part-time faculty:** 70 total.

Student profile.

Out-of-state:	5%	**Live on campus:**	6%
25 or older:	49%		

Basis for selection. Open admission, but selective for some programs. Additional requirements for nursing and cosmetology applicants.

2005-2006 Annual costs. Tuition/fees: $1,380; $1,995 out-of-district; $3,120 out-of-state. Per-credit charge: $46 in-district; $67 out-of-district; $104 out-of-state. Room/board: $3,036. Books/supplies: $800. Personal expenses: $1,082.

2004-2005 Financial aid. All financial aid based on need. 82% of total undergraduate aid awarded as scholarships/grants, 18% as loans/jobs. Need-based aid available for part-time students. Work study available nights, weekends and for part-time students.

Application procedures. **Admission:** No deadline. $10 fee. Application may be submitted online. Admission notification on a rolling basis. **Financial aid:** Priority date 7/1; no closing date. FAFSA required. Applicants notified on a rolling basis starting 4/1.

Academics. **Special study options:** Cooperative education, distance learning, dual enrollment of high school students, internships. License preparation in nursing. **Credit/placement by examination:** CLEP, institutional tests. 45 credit hours maximum toward associate degree. **Support services:** GED test center, learning center, reduced course load, remedial instruction, study skills assistance, tutoring, writing center.

Majors. **Agriculture:** Farm/ranch. **Business:** General, accounting, administrative services, human resources, marketing, office technology. **Computer sciences:** Data processing. **Engineering technology:** Drafting. **Health:** Nursing (RN). **Legal studies:** Paralegal. **Liberal arts:** Arts/sciences. **Mechanic/repair:** Electronics/electrical. **Protective services:** Criminal justice.

Most popular majors. Business/marketing 10%, computer/information sciences 10%, health sciences 30%, liberal arts 40%.

Computing on campus. 60 workstations in library, computer center.

Student life. **Policies:** Freshmen permitted cars on campus. **Housing:** Coed dorms, single-sex dorms available. **Activities:** Choral groups, drama, music ensembles, musical theater, student government.

Athletics. NJCAA. **Intercollegiate:** Baseball M, rodeo, softball W, volleyball W. **Intramural:** Archery, badminton, baseball M, basketball, golf, handball, racquetball, softball, swimming, table tennis, tennis, track and field, volleyball. **Team name:** Chaparral.

Student services. Career counseling, student employment services, health services, personal counseling, placement for graduates, veterans' counselor. **Physically disabled:** Services for visually, speech, hearing impaired. **Transfer:** Special adviser for new students. Transfer adviser for students transferring to 4-year colleges.

Contact. E-mail: sdavenport@vernoncollege.edu
Phone: (940) 552-6291 Fax: (940) 553-1753
Joe Hite, Dean of Admissions and Financial Aid/Registrar, Vernon College, 4400 College Drive, Vernon, TX 76384

Victoria College

Victoria, Texas
www.victoriacollege.edu **CB code: 6915**

- Public 2-year community college
- Commuter campus in small city

General. Founded in 1925. Regionally accredited. **Enrollment:** 3,981 degree-seeking undergraduates. **Degrees:** 278 associate awarded. **Location:** 125 miles from Houston and Austin. **Calendar:** Semester, limited summer session. **Full-time faculty:** 80 total. **Part-time faculty:** 40 total. **Special facilities:** Coastal bend museum.

Student profile. Among degree-seeking undergraduates, 623 enrolled as first-time, first-year students.

Part-time:	62%	**Asian American:**	1%
Women:	66%	**Hispanic American:**	32%
African American:	5%		

Basis for selection. Open admission, but selective for some programs. Special requirements for allied health programs; interview required. THEA required. **Adult students:** Entrance exam policies same as for first-time freshmen.

High school preparation. 24 units recommended. Recommended units include English 4, mathematics 3, social studies 2.5, history 1, science 3, foreign language 2, academic electives 3.5. 0.5 economics, 1 fine arts, 0.5 speech, 1 technical applications recommended.

2005-2006 Annual costs. Tuition/fees: $1,260; $1,740 out-of-district; $2,040 out-of-state. Per-credit charge: $29 in-district; $45 out-of-district; $55 out-of-state. Books/supplies: $550. Personal expenses: $1,098.

Financial aid. **Need-based:** Work study available for part-time students. **Non-need-based:** Scholarships awarded for academics, art, minority status, music/drama.

Application procedures. **Admission:** No deadline. No application fee. Application may be submitted online. Admission notification on a rolling basis beginning on or about 7/1. **Financial aid:** Priority date 4/15; no closing date. FAFSA, institutional form required. Applicants notified on a rolling basis.

Academics. **Special study options:** Distance learning, dual enrollment of high school students. 2+2 plans with University of Texas-San Antonio, University of Houston-Victoria, Texas A&M-Corpus Christi, University of Texas-Brownsville. **Credit/placement by examination:** AP, CLEP, IB, institutional tests. **Support services:** GED preparation and test center, learning center, remedial instruction, tutoring.

Majors. **Business:** Administrative services, business admin. **Computer sciences:** General, information systems, networking, programming, system admin, web page design, webmaster. **Engineering technology:** Electrical, instrumentation. **Health:** Clinical lab technology, EMT paramedic, nursing (RN), respiratory therapy technology. **Legal studies:** Paralegal. **Liberal arts:** Arts/sciences.

Most popular majors. Business/marketing 9%, computer/information sciences 6%, engineering/engineering technologies 9%, health sciences 37%, liberal arts 34%.

Computing on campus. Online library, helpline available.

Student life. **Freshman orientation:** Mandatory, $20 fee. Summer 1-day orientation sessions; online orientation also available. **Policies:** Freshmen permitted cars on campus. **Activities:** Bands, choral groups, drama, literary magazine, music ensembles, student government, campus ministry.

Athletics. **Intramural:** Basketball, bowling, golf, swimming, tennis, volleyball, weight lifting.

Student services. Career counseling, services for economically disadvantaged, student employment services, financial aid counseling, personal counseling, veterans' counselor. **Physically disabled:** Services for visually impaired. **Transfer:** Special adviser for new students. College fairs on campus for students transferring to 4-year colleges.

Contact. E-mail: registrar@victoriacollege.edu
Phone: (361) 572-6408 Fax: (361) 582-2525
LaVern Dentler, Registrar, Victoria College, 2200 East Red River, Victoria, TX 77901

Virginia College at Austin
Austin, Texas
www.vc.edu/austin

- For-profit 2-year business and technical college
- Commuter campus

General. Accredited by ACICS. **Calendar:** Continuous.

Contact. Phone: (512) 371-3500
Director of Admissions, 6301 East Highway 290, Austin, TX 78723

Wade College
Dallas, Texas
www.wadecollege.com **CB code: 1537**

- For-profit 2-year junior college
- Residential campus in very large city

General. Founded in 1965. Regionally accredited. Regional apparel markets held on campus throughout year. **Enrollment:** 230 degree-seeking undergraduates. **Degrees:** 100 associate awarded. **Location:** 2 miles from downtown. **Calendar:** Trimester, extensive summer session. **Full-time faculty:** 7 total. **Part-time faculty:** 6 total. **Class size:** 77% < 20, 23% 20-39.

Student profile.

Out-of-state:	40%	**Live on campus:**	51%
25 or older:	28%		

Transfer out. Colleges most students transferred to 2005: University of North Texas, University of Texas at Arlington, Dallas Baptist University, Southwest Texas State University.

Basis for selection. Open admission. Interview recommended.

2005-2006 Annual costs. Tuition/fees: $10,410. Room only: $3,360.

Financial aid. All financial aid based on need. Need-based aid available for part-time students. Work study available nights, weekends and for part-time students.

Application procedures. Admission: No deadline. No application fee. Application may be submitted online. Admission notification on a rolling basis beginning on or about 1/31. **Financial aid:** No deadline. FAFSA required. Applicants notified on a rolling basis; must reply within 4 week(s) of notification.

Academics. All students attend 4 consecutive trimesters to complete associate degree in 16 months. New students may enter at beginning of any trimester. **Special study options:** Accelerated study, cooperative education, double major, internships, study abroad. **Credit/placement by examination:** CLEP, IB. **Support services:** Learning center, reduced course load, remedial instruction, study skills assistance, tutoring.

Majors. Business: Fashion, sales/distribution. **Computer sciences:** Computer graphics. **Family/consumer sciences:** Clothing/textiles. **Visual/performing arts:** Design, fashion design, interior design.

Most popular majors. Business/marketing 45%, visual/performing arts 55%.

Computing on campus. 50 workstations in library, computer center. Online library available.

Student life. Freshman orientation: Mandatory. **Policies:** Freshmen permitted cars on campus. **Housing:** Guaranteed on-campus for all undergraduates. Apartments available. $200 deposit, deadline 9/1. **Activities:** Drama, student government, student newspaper.

Student services. Adult student services, career counseling, student employment services, health services, personal counseling, placement for graduates, veterans' counselor. **Transfer:** Special adviser, orientation, re-entry adviser, pre-admission transcript evaluation for new students. Transfer adviser for students transferring to 4-year colleges.

Contact. E-mail: admissions@wadecollege.com
Phone: (800) 624-4850 Toll-free number: (800) 624-4850
Fax: (214) 637-0827
Tracey Taylor, Director of Admissions, Wade College, Box 586343, Dallas, TX 75258

Weatherford College
Weatherford, Texas
www.wc.edu **CB code: 6931**

- Public 2-year community college
- Commuter campus in large town

General. Founded in 1869. Regionally accredited. Off-campus courses held at education center in Mineral Wells and Decatur, and high schools in Aledo, Bridgeport, Granbury, Decatur, Jacksboro, Springtown, and Azle Community; semiconductor program. **Enrollment:** 4,552 undergraduates. **Degrees:** 326 associate awarded. **ROTC:** Air Force. **Location:** 25 miles from Fort Worth. **Calendar:** Semester, extensive summer session. **Full-time faculty:** 90 total. **Part-time faculty:** 105 total. **Special facilities:** 300-acre college farm. **Partnerships:** Formal partnerships with tech prep program and dual credit articulation agreements.

Student profile. 69% enrolled in a transfer program, 31% enrolled in a vocational program, 2% already have a bachelor's degree or higher.

Out-of-state:	3%	**Live on campus:**	5%
25 or older:	50%		

Transfer out. Colleges most students transferred to 2005: Tarleton State University, University of North Texas, University of Texas at Arlington, Texas Tech University.

Basis for selection. Open admission, but selective for some programs. Nursing school requires entrance examination. Texas Academic Skills Program (TASP) required of all students unless TASP-exempt.

2005-2006 Annual costs. Tuition/fees: $1,440; $1,950 out-of-district; $3,150 out-of-state. Per-credit charge: $48 in-district; $65 out-of-district; $105 out-of-state. Room/board: $6,715. Books/supplies: $580. Personal expenses: $1,116.

Financial aid. All financial aid based on need. Work study available nights, weekends and for part-time students.

Application procedures. Admission: No deadline. No application fee. Admission notification on a rolling basis. **Financial aid:** Priority date 7/3; no closing date. FAFSA required. Applicants notified on a rolling basis; must reply within 2 week(s) of notification.

Academics. Special study options: Cooperative education, distance learning, dual enrollment of high school students, ESL, honors, internships, liberal arts/career combination, teacher certification program, weekend college. License preparation in nursing. **Credit/placement by examination:** AP, CLEP, institutional tests. 30 credit hours maximum toward associate degree. Credit earned by examination does not reduce resident requirement of 15 semester hours of class completed at college. **Support services:** GED preparation and test center, learning center, remedial instruction, study skills assistance, tutoring.

Majors. Agriculture: Business, equestrian studies, farm/ranch. **Business:** General, accounting, administrative services, human resources, marketing, office/clerical, operations. **Communications:** General. **Computer sciences:** General, data processing, programming. **Engineering technology:** Electrical. **English:** Speech/rhetoric. **Family/consumer sciences:** Child care. **Health:** EMT paramedic, respiratory therapy technology. **Liberal arts:** Arts/sciences. **Personal/culinary services:** Cosmetic. **Protective services:** Corrections, police science. **Social sciences:** Sociology.

Computing on campus. 300 workstations in library, computer center. Dormitories linked to campus network.

Student life. Freshman orientation: Available, $45 fee. Two-day program held twice a summer; limited to 350 students per session. **Policies:** Freshmen permitted cars on campus. **Housing:** Coed dorms, single-sex dorms, special housing for disabled, substance-free housing available. $100 deposit, deadline 8/15. **Activities:** Jazz band, choral groups, dance, drama, music ensembles, musical theater, student government, black awareness student organization, Hispanic student organization, Baptist student union, international student organization, Wesleyan foundation, Baptist student ministries, A Better Life Through Education, disabled club.

Athletics. NJCAA. **Intercollegiate:** Baseball M, basketball, rodeo, tennis W. **Intramural:** Basketball, softball, tennis, volleyball. **Team name:** Coyotes.

Student services. Adult student services, career counseling, student employment services, personal counseling, placement for graduates, veterans' counselor. **Physically disabled:** Services for visually, speech, hearing impaired. **Transfer:** Special adviser, orientation, pre-admission transcript evaluation for new students. Transfer adviser, college fairs on campus for students transferring to 4-year colleges.

Contact. Phone: (817) 598-6241 Toll-free number: (800) 287-5471
Fax: (817) 598-6205
Ralph Willingham, Dean of Admissions, Weatherford College, 225 College Park Drive, Weatherford, TX 76086

Western Technical College
El Paso, Texas
www.wtc-ep.edu **CB code: 2941**

- For-profit 2-year technical college
- Commuter campus in very large city

General. Accredited by ACCSCT. Two campuses: main campus downtown, branch campus in NE section. **Enrollment:** 435 degree-seeking undergraduates. **Degrees:** 216 associate awarded. **Calendar:** Continuous. **Full-time faculty:** 64 total. **Part-time faculty:** 32 total.

Basis for selection. Open admission, but selective for some programs. Some programs require CPAT or other entrance requirements.

2005-2006 Annual costs. Tuition varies by program. Automotive: $18,150; refrigeration: $18,150; welding: $10,257; computer: $22,230; electronics: $18,525; medical assisting: $8,640; massage therapy: $3,600; health information: $11,115. Registration fee $100.

Financial aid. All financial aid based on need. Need-based aid available for part-time students.

Application procedures. Admission: No deadline. No application fee. **Financial aid:** No deadline. FAFSA required. Applicants notified on a rolling basis.

Academics. Credit/placement by examination: CLEP. **Support services:** GED preparation, remedial instruction, tutoring.

Majors. Mechanic/repair: General.

Computing on campus. 200 workstations in library, computer center, student center. Online library, wireless network available.

Contact. Phone: (915) 532-3737
Bill Terrell, Director of Admissions, Western Technical College, 1000 Texas Avenue, El Paso, TX 79901

Western Technical Institute: Diana Drive
El Paso, Texas
www.wtc-ep.edu

- For-profit 2-year technical college
- Very large city
- Interview required

General. Accredited by ACCSCT. **Enrollment:** 744 degree-seeking undergraduates. **Degrees:** 563 associate awarded. **Calendar:** Continuous. **Full-time faculty:** 55 total. **Part-time faculty:** 10 total.

Student profile. Among degree-seeking undergraduates, 100% enrolled in a vocational program.

Basis for selection. Open admission, but selective for some programs. Assessment test and various minimum scores required for following programs: medical assisting, health technology, computer technology, electronics technology, automotive technology, refrigeration technology, combination welding.

2005-2006 Annual costs. Tuition varies by program. Automotive: $18,150; refrigeration: $18,150; welding: $10,257; computer: $22,230; electronics: $18,525; medical assisting: $8,640; massage therapy: $3,600; health information: $11,115.

Application procedures. Admission: No deadline. No application fee.

Academics. Credit/placement by examination: AP, CLEP.

Majors. Mechanic/repair: Automotive, heating/ac/refrig.

Contact. Phone: (915) 566-9621 Toll-free number: (800) 522-2072
Bill Terrell, Director of Admissions, Western Technical Institute: Diana Drive, 9451 Diana Drive, El Paso, TX 79924

Western Texas College
Snyder, Texas
www.wtc.edu **CB code: 6951**

- Public 2-year community and junior college
- Commuter campus in large town

General. Founded in 1969. Regionally accredited. **Enrollment:** 462 full-time, degree-seeking students. **Degrees:** 129 associate awarded. **Location:** 80 miles from Lubbock. **Calendar:** Semester, extensive summer session. **Full-time faculty:** 28 total; 14% have terminal degrees, 4% minority, 36% women. **Part-time faculty:** 51 total; 4% have terminal degrees, 53% women. **Class size:** 80% < 20, 18% 20-39, 1% 40-49, less than 1% 50-99.

Student profile. Among full-time, degree-seeking students, 60% enrolled in a transfer program, 30% enrolled in a vocational program.

Out-of-state:	2%	**Live on campus:**	15%
25 or older:	32%		

Transfer out. Colleges most students transferred to 2005: Texas Tech University, Angelo State University, University of Texas, Texas A&M University.

Basis for selection. Open admission, but selective for some programs. Special requirements for nursing program. Institutional placement tests may be submitted in place of SAT/ACT. Interview recommended. **Adult students:** Entrance exam policies same as for first-time freshmen.

2006-2007 Annual costs. Tuition/fees (projected): $1,530; $1,680 out-of-district; $1,830 out-of-state. Per-credit charge: $36 in-district; $41 out-of-district; $46 out-of-state. Room/board: $3,900. Books/supplies: $500. Personal expenses: $900.

2004-2005 Financial aid. Need-based: Average need met was 53%. Average scholarship/grant was $2,000. 95% of total undergraduate aid awarded as scholarships/grants, 5% as loans/jobs. Need-based aid available for part-time students. Work study available nights and weekends. **Non-need-based:** Scholarships awarded for academics, art, athletics, leadership, music/drama, state residency.

Application procedures. Admission: No deadline. No application fee. Application must be submitted on paper. Admission notification on a rolling basis beginning on or about 11/5. **Financial aid:** Priority date 7/1; no closing date. FAFSA, institutional form required. Applicants notified on a rolling basis starting 5/1; must reply within 2 week(s) of notification.

Academics. Special study options: Distance learning, dual enrollment of high school students, honors, independent study, internships. License preparation in nursing, paramedic. **Credit/placement by examination:** CLEP, institutional tests. 12 credit hours maximum toward associate degree. **Support services:** GED preparation and test center, learning center, pre-admission summer program, reduced course load, remedial instruction, tutoring.

Majors. Agriculture: Animal sciences, greenhouse operations, horticulture, landscaping, nursery operations, ornamental horticulture, turf management. **Biology:** General. **Business:** General, accounting, administrative services, business admin. **Communications:** Journalism. **Computer sciences:** General, computer science, data processing, LAN/WAN management, programming. **Education:** General, early childhood. **Engineering:** General. **English:** English lit. **Foreign languages:** General. **Health:** EMT paramedic, predentistry, premedicine, prenursing, prepharmacy, preveterinary. **History:** General. **Legal studies:** Prelaw. **Liberal arts:** Arts/sciences. **Math:** General. **Parks/recreation:** Facilities management, health/fitness. **Philosophy/religion:** Philosophy. **Physical sciences:** Chemistry, geology, physics. **Production:** Welding. **Protective services:** Corrections, law enforcement admin, police science. **Psychology:** General. **Social sciences:** General, economics, geography, international relations, political science, sociology. **Visual/performing arts:** Art, ceramics, dramatic, drawing, metal/jewelry, painting, photography, sculpture.

Most popular majors. Agriculture 10%, business/marketing 16%, computer/information sciences 15%, family/consumer sciences 6%, liberal arts 9%, social sciences 25%.

Computing on campus. 70 workstations in dormitories, library, computer center, student center. Dormitories wired for high-speed internet access and linked to campus network. Online library available.

Student life. **Freshman orientation:** Available. Preregistration for classes offered. **Policies:** Freshmen permitted cars on campus. **Housing:** Guaranteed on-campus for all undergraduates. Single-sex dorms, apartments available. $50 deposit. **Activities:** Drama, literary magazine, musical theater, student government, TV station, Baptist Student Union, Phi Theta Kappa.

Athletics. NJCAA. **Intercollegiate:** Baseball M, cheerleading M, cross-country, rodeo, softball W, volleyball W. **Intramural:** Basketball, bowling, diving, golf, handball, racquetball, softball, swimming, volleyball, weight lifting. **Team name:** Westerners.

Student services. Adult student services, alcohol/substance abuse counseling, career counseling, services for economically disadvantaged, student employment services, financial aid counseling, personal counseling, placement for graduates, veterans' counselor. **Transfer:** Special adviser, orientation, pre-admission transcript evaluation for new students. Transfer adviser, college fairs on campus for students transferring to 4-year colleges.

Contact. E-mail: vrowland@wtc.edu
Phone: (325) 573-8511 ext. 372 Toll-free number: (888) 468-6982
Fax: (325) 573-9321
Jim Clifton, Dean of Student Services, Western Texas College, 6200 College Avenue, Snyder, TX 79549

Westwood College: Dallas
Dallas, Texas
www.westwoodcollege.com

- For-profit 2-year technical college
- Commuter campus in very large city
- SAT or ACT (ACT writing optional), interview required

General. Accredited by ACICS. **Enrollment:** 344 degree-seeking undergraduates; 228 non-degree-seeking students. **Degrees:** 145 associate awarded. **Calendar:** Continuous, extensive summer session.

Student profile. Among degree-seeking undergraduates, 100% enrolled in a vocational program, 1% already have a bachelor's degree or higher, 307 enrolled as first-time, first-year students.

Women:	67%	**25 or older:**	33%

Transfer out. 5% of students enrolled in the transfer program go on to 4-year colleges.

Basis for selection. Proof of high school degree and ACT, SAT, ACCUPLACER, or Wonderlic scores most important. ACCUPLACER or Wonderlic tests may be submitted in place of SAT/ACT. **Adult students:** Entrance exam policies same as for first-time freshmen. **Homeschooled:** Transcript of courses and grades required. **Learning Disabled:** Disclose disabilities so accommodations can be provided.

Application procedures. **Admission:** No deadline. $100 fee. Application may be submitted online.

Academics. **Special study options:** Accelerated study. **Credit/placement by examination:** CLEP, SAT, ACT. **Support services:** Learning center, reduced course load, remedial instruction, tutoring.

Computing on campus. 15 workstations in library.

Student life. **Freshman orientation:** Available. Preregistration for classes offered. Usually held the Saturday before classes start; lasts 2.5 to 3 hours.

Student services. Adult student services, career counseling, student employment services, financial aid counseling, placement for graduates. **Transfer:** Orientation, re-entry adviser for new students. Transfer adviser for students transferring to 4-year colleges.

Contact. Phone: (214) 570-0100
Eric Southwell, Director of Admissions, Westwood College: Dallas, 8390 LBJ Freeway, Dallas, TX 75243

Westwood College: Ft. Worth
Fort Worth, Texas

- For-profit 2-year health science and technical college
- Commuter campus

General. Accredited by ACICS. **Enrollment:** 425 full-time, degree-seeking students. **Degrees:** 144 associate awarded. **Calendar:** Continuous. **Part-time faculty:** 10 total.

Basis for selection. Personal career assessment, application/evaluation, and entrance assessment required.

Application procedures. **Admission:** No deadline. $25 fee.

Academics. **Credit/placement by examination:** CLEP.

Majors. **Computer sciences:** Networking. **Engineering technology:** Architectural drafting.

Contact. Phone: (817) 547-9600 Toll-free number: (866) 533-9998
Fax: (817) 547-9602
Westwood College: Ft. Worth, 4232 North Freeway, Fort Worth, TX 76137

Westwood College: Houston South
Houston, Texas
www.westwood.edu/

- For-profit 2-year health science and technical college
- Very large city

General. Accredited by ACCSCT. **Calendar:** Continuous.

Contact. Phone: (866) 340-3677
7322 Southwest Freeway, Houston, TX 77074

Wharton County Junior College
Wharton, Texas
www.wcjc.edu **CB code: 6939**

- Public 2-year junior college
- Commuter campus in small town

General. Founded in 1946. Regionally accredited. **Enrollment:** 6,029 degree-seeking undergraduates. **Degrees:** 356 associate awarded. **Location:** 60 miles from Houston. **Calendar:** Semester, limited summer session. **Full-time faculty:** 136 total; 19% have terminal degrees, 15% minority, 59% women. **Part-time faculty:** 121 total; 12% have terminal degrees, 14% minority, 56% women.

Student profile. Among degree-seeking undergraduates, 73% enrolled in a transfer program, 27% enrolled in a vocational program, 1% already have a bachelor's degree or higher, 1,404 enrolled as first-time, first-year students, 406 transferred in from other institutions.

Part-time:	56%	**Hispanic American:**	24%
Out-of-state:	3%	**International:**	4%
Women:	58%	**25 or older:**	20%
African American:	9%	**Live on campus:**	3%
Asian American:	4%		

Transfer out. 80% of students enrolled in the transfer program go on to 4-year colleges. **Colleges most students transferred to 2005:** Texas A&M University, University of Houston, Sam Houston State University, Southwest Texas State University, University of Texas.

Basis for selection. Open admission, but selective for some programs. Test scores and school achievement record important factors for admission into nursing, dental hygiene, physical therapy, and radiology programs. Audition required for music scholarship applicants. **Adult students:** Entrance exam policies same as for first-time freshmen.

High school preparation. Recommended units include English 4, mathematics 3, science 3 and foreign language 2.

2006-2007 Annual costs. Tuition/fees (projected): $1,620; $2,700 out-of-district; $3,660 out-of-state. Per-credit charge: $54 in-district; $90 out-of-district; $122 out-of-state. Room/board: $2,600. Books/supplies: $700. Personal expenses: $1,520.

Financial aid. **Need-based:** Need-based aid available for part-time students. **Non-need-based:** Scholarships awarded for academics, athletics.

Application procedures. **Admission:** Priority date 7/1; no deadline. $10 fee. Application must be submitted on paper. Admission notification on a rolling basis beginning on or about 2/1. **Financial aid:** Priority date 6/1; no closing date. FAFSA required. Applicants notified on a rolling basis starting 8/1; must reply by 8/15.

Academics. **Special study options:** Cooperative education, cross-registration, distance learning, dual enrollment of high school students, internships, teacher certification program. License preparation in dental hygiene, nursing, paramedic, physical therapy, radiology. **Credit/placement**

by examination: AP, CLEP, institutional tests. 16 credit hours maximum toward associate degree. **Support services:** GED preparation and test center, learning center, remedial instruction.

Majors. Agriculture: General, farm/ranch. **Biology:** General. **Business:** Business admin. **Computer sciences:** Data entry, data processing, LAN/WAN management, programming. **Education:** Early childhood, elementary. **Engineering:** General. **Engineering technology:** Drafting, electrical. **Family/consumer sciences:** Child development. **Foreign languages:** Spanish. **Health:** Clinical lab technology, dental hygiene, medical radiologic technology/radiation therapy, medical records technology, mental health services, nursing (RN), physical therapy assistant. **History:** General. **Liberal arts:** Arts/sciences. **Math:** General. **Physical sciences:** Chemistry, physics. **Protective services:** Law enforcement admin. **Psychology:** General. **Social sciences:** Criminology, sociology. **Visual/performing arts:** Art, dramatic.

Most popular majors. Business/marketing 8%, health sciences 22%, liberal arts 43%.

Computing on campus. 500 workstations in library, computer center, student center. Online course registration, online library available.

Student life. Freshman orientation: Available. Preregistration for classes offered. **Policies:** Freshmen permitted cars on campus. **Housing:** Single-sex dorms available. $100 fully refundable deposit, deadline 7/1. **Activities:** Bands, choral groups, dance, drama, music ensembles, musical theater, student government.

Athletics. NJCAA. **Intercollegiate:** Baseball M, rodeo, volleyball W. **Team name:** Pioneers.

Student services. Career counseling, personal counseling, placement for graduates. **Physically disabled:** Services for visually, speech, hearing impaired. **Transfer:** Special adviser for new students. Transfer adviser, college fairs on campus for students transferring to 4-year colleges.

Contact. Phone: (979) 532-4560 ext. 6303 Toll-free number: (800) 561-9252 Fax: (979) 532-6494
Albert Barnes, Director of Admissions/Registrar, Wharton County Junior College, 911 Boling Highway, Wharton, TX 77488-0080

Utah

Careers Unlimited
Orem, Utah
www.ucdh.edu/

- For-profit 2-year health science college
- Commuter campus in large city

General. Accredited by ACCSCT. **Calendar:** Semester.

Contact. Phone: (801) 226-1081
1176 South 1480 West, Orem, UT 84058

College of Eastern Utah
Price, Utah
www.ceu.edu/ **CB code: 4040**

- Public 2-year community college
- Commuter campus in small town

General. Founded in 1938. Regionally accredited. **Enrollment:** 1,811 degree-seeking undergraduates. **Degrees:** 323 associate awarded. **Location:** 65 miles from Provo, 125 miles from Salt Lake City. **Calendar:** Semester, limited summer session. **Full-time faculty:** 71 total. **Part-time faculty:** 103 total. **Class size:** 69% < 20, 26% 20-39, 4% 40-49, 1% 50-99, less than 1% >100. **Special facilities:** Observatory, prehistoric museum.

Student profile.

Out-of-state:	6%	**Live on campus:**	15%
25 or older:	26%		

Basis for selection. Open admission, but selective for some programs. Admission to nursing program based on test scores and prerequisites.

2005-2006 Annual costs. Tuition/fees: $1,980; $7,121 out-of-state. Room/board: $3,268. Books/supplies: $750. Personal expenses: $1,179.

Financial aid. Need-based: Need-based aid available for part-time students. Work study available nights and weekends. **Non-need-based:** Scholarships awarded for academics, art, athletics, leadership, minority status, music/drama, religious affiliation, state residency.

Application procedures. Admission: Priority date 3/1; no deadline. $25 fee. Admission notification on a rolling basis. **Financial aid:** Priority date 2/1; no closing date. FAFSA, institutional form required. Applicants notified on a rolling basis starting 3/15; must reply within 2 week(s) of notification.

Academics. Special study options: Cooperative education, distance learning, double major, dual enrollment of high school students, ESL. **Credit/placement by examination:** AP, CLEP, institutional tests. 32 credit hours maximum toward associate degree. **Support services:** GED preparation and test center, learning center, remedial instruction, study skills assistance, tutoring, writing center.

Majors. Business: Administrative services, business admin. **Computer sciences:** Computer graphics, systems analysis. **Construction:** Carpentry. **Education:** Early childhood. **Family/consumer sciences:** Child care. **Liberal arts:** Arts/sciences. **Mechanic/repair:** Diesel. **Personal/culinary services:** Cosmetic.

Computing on campus. 150 workstations in dormitories, library, computer center, student center. Dormitories linked to campus network. Commuter students can connect to campus network. Online course registration, online library, helpline available.

Student life. Freshman orientation: Mandatory, $10 fee. Preregistration for classes offered. **Policies:** Freshmen permitted cars on campus. **Housing:** Coed dorms, single-sex dorms available. $100 deposit. **Activities:** Bands, choral groups, dance, drama, literary magazine, music ensembles, musical theater, radio station, student government, student newspaper, religious clubs, Catholic Newman Club, theater club, Native American club, recreation club, leadership club, PBL (business) club.

Athletics. NJCAA. **Intercollegiate:** Baseball M, basketball, golf M, volleyball W. **Intramural:** Basketball M, racquetball, tennis. **Team name:** Eagles.

Student services. Adult student services, alcohol/substance abuse counseling, career counseling, services for economically disadvantaged, student employment services, financial aid counseling, health services, personal counseling, placement for graduates, veterans' counselor, women's services. **Physically disabled:** Services for visually, speech, hearing impaired. **Transfer:** Special adviser, orientation for new students. Transfer adviser for students transferring to 4-year colleges.

Contact. E-mail: jan.young@ceu.edu
Phone: (435) 613-5226 Fax: (435) 613-5814
Todd Olsen, Director of Admissions and Scholarships, College of Eastern Utah, 451 East 400 North, Price, UT 84501

Dixie State College of Utah
St. George, Utah
www.dixie.edu **CB code: 4283**

- Public 2-year community and technical college
- Commuter campus in small city
- SAT or ACT (ACT writing optional) required

General. Founded in 1911. Regionally accredited. Bachelor's and master's degree course work from Utah's 4-year universities presented over distance-learning media and on-campus instruction. Four-year programs in business, computer tech, education and nursing offered on campus. **Enrollment:** 5,082 degree-seeking undergraduates. **Degrees:** 94 bachelor's, 846 associate awarded. **Location:** 300 miles from Salt Lake City, 120 miles from Las Vegas. **Calendar:** Semester, extensive summer session. **Full-time faculty:** 99 total. **Part-time faculty:** 235 total. **Class size:** 48% < 20, 40% 20-39, 5% 40-49, 5% 50-99, less than 1% >100.

Student profile. Among degree-seeking undergraduates, 1,489 enrolled as first-time, first-year students.

Part-time:	34%	**Hispanic American:**	3%
Out-of-state:	14%	**Native American:**	2%
Women:	50%	**International:**	1%
African American:	1%	**25 or older:**	21%
Asian American:	2%		

Transfer out. Colleges most students transferred to 2005: University of Utah, Utah State, BYU, Weber State University, Southern Utah University.

Basis for selection. Open admission, but selective for some programs. Some health occupation programs require prerequisites before admission into program. Those applying for bachelor's degree programs must have received associate degree. Some courses use test score combined with HS GPA as prerequisite. CPT (computerized placement test) or COMPASS may be taken in lieu of ACT/SAT. **Adult students:** Entrance exam policies same as for first-time freshmen. If English not primary language, TOEFL required. **Homeschooled:** Letter from parent certifying that student has completed the equivalent of a high school diploma will meet high school diploma requirement.

High school preparation. 16 units recommended. Recommended units include English 4, mathematics 3, history 3, science 3 (laboratory 1) and foreign language 2. One computer literacy unit recommended.

2005-2006 Annual costs. Tuition/fees: $1,984; $7,390 out-of-state. Room/board: $2,780. Books/supplies: $700. Personal expenses: $3,232.

2005-2006 Financial aid. Need-based: 55% of total undergraduate aid awarded as scholarships/grants, 45% as loans/jobs. Work study available nights, weekends and for part-time students. **Non-need-based:** Scholarships awarded for academics, alumni affiliation, art, athletics, leadership, minority status, music/drama.

Application procedures. Admission: No deadline. $35 fee. Application may be submitted online. Admission notification on a rolling basis. **Financial aid:** Priority date 4/1; no closing date. FAFSA required. Applicants notified on a rolling basis starting 5/1; must reply within 2 week(s) of notification.

Academics. Special study options: Cooperative education, distance learning, dual enrollment of high school students, ESL, honors, liberal arts/career combination. Bachelor's degree programs available on campus. License preparation in dental hygiene, nursing, paramedic. **Credit/placement by examination:** AP, CLEP, SAT, ACT, institutional tests. 32 credit hours maximum toward associate degree. **Support services:** GED preparation and test center, learning center, remedial instruction, study skills assistance, tutoring, writing center.

Majors. **Biology:** General, ecology, genetics. **Business:** General, accounting, business admin, office/clerical, retailing, travel services. **Communications:** General, broadcast journalism, journalism. **Communications technology:** General, graphic/printing. **Computer sciences:** Computer graphics, computer science, data processing. **Conservation:** General, environmental science, forestry, management/policy, wildlife. **Education:** Early childhood, elementary, physical, secondary. **Engineering:** General. **Family/consumer sciences:** Child care, food/nutrition. **Foreign languages:** Translation. **Health:** Dental hygiene, EMT paramedic, nursing (RN). **History:** General. **Legal studies:** Prelaw. **Math:** General. **Mechanic/repair:** Automotive, diesel. **Philosophy/religion:** Philosophy. **Physical sciences:** Chemistry, geology, physics. **Protective services:** Criminal justice. **Psychology:** General. **Public administration:** Social work. **Social sciences:** Economics, political science, sociology. **Visual/performing arts:** Art, art history/conservation, ceramics, dance, dramatic, drawing, painting, photography, printmaking, sculpture.

Most popular majors. Biological/life sciences 7%, business/marketing 16%, education 8%, health sciences 12%, liberal arts 34%.

Computing on campus. 375 workstations in dormitories, library, computer center, student center. Dormitories wired for high-speed internet access and linked to campus network. Commuter students can connect to campus network. Online course registration, online library, helpline, repair service available.

Student life. **Freshman orientation:** Mandatory. Preregistration for classes offered. **Policies:** Freshmen permitted cars on campus. **Housing:** Coed dorms, single-sex dorms, apartments, substance-free housing available. $100 deposit. **Activities:** Bands, choral groups, dance, drama, literary magazine, music ensembles, musical theater, radio station, student government, student newspaper, symphony orchestra, TV station, international club, religious groups, Native American club, rodeo club, polynesian club, College Democrats, College Republicans, Diversity Club, A.C.M Club, A.D.A Club.

Athletics. NJCAA. **Intercollegiate:** Baseball M, basketball, football (tackle) M, golf M, rodeo, soccer W, softball W, volleyball W. **Intramural:** Basketball, football (non-tackle) M, golf, soccer, softball, tennis, volleyball. **Team name:** Rebels.

Student services. Adult student services, alcohol/substance abuse counseling, campus ministries, career counseling, services for economically disadvantaged, student employment services, financial aid counseling, health services, minority student services, personal counseling, placement for graduates, veterans' counselor. **Physically disabled:** Services for visually, speech, hearing impaired. **Transfer:** Special adviser, orientation, re-entry adviser for new students. Transfer adviser, college fairs on campus for students transferring to 4-year colleges.

Contact. E-mail: admit@dixie.edu
Phone: (435) 652-7702 Toll-free number: (888) 462-3494
Fax: (435) 656-4005
David Roos, Director of Admissions and Records, Dixie State College of Utah, 225 South 700 East, St. George, UT 84770-3876

Everest College: Salt Lake City

West Valley City, Utah
www.cci.edu **CB code: 5341**

- For-profit 2-year business and junior college
- Commuter campus in small city
- Interview required

General. Founded in 1981. Accredited by ACICS. **Enrollment:** 700 undergraduates. **Degrees:** 161 associate awarded. **Location:** 5 miles from Salt Lake City. **Calendar:** Quarter, extensive summer session. **Full-time faculty:** 5 total. **Part-time faculty:** 30 total. **Class size:** 74% < 20, 25% 20-39, 1% 40-49.

Basis for selection. CPAT test required for all applicants. ACT may be substituted for CPAT.

2005-2006 Annual costs. Tuition/fees: $12,675. Per-credit charge: $280. Books/supplies: $1,800. Personal expenses: $1,552.

Financial aid. **Need-based:** Need-based aid available for part-time students. Work study available nights and for part-time students. **Non-need-based:** Scholarships awarded for academics.

Application procedures. **Admission:** No deadline. $50 fee. Admission notification on a rolling basis. **Financial aid:** No deadline. FAFSA, institutional form required. Applicants notified on a rolling basis.

Academics. **Special study options:** Internships. **Credit/placement by examination:** CLEP, institutional tests. 16 credit hours maximum toward associate degree. **Support services:** Learning center, reduced course load, remedial instruction, tutoring.

Majors. **Business:** Accounting, administrative services, business admin, office management, tourism/travel. **Computer sciences:** Applications programming, programming. **Health:** Medical assistant. **Legal studies:** Legal secretary, paralegal.

Most popular majors. Business/marketing 53%, computer/information sciences 11%, health sciences 16%, legal studies 20%.

Computing on campus. 65 workstations in library, computer center.

Student life. **Activities:** Student government, student newspaper, data processing management association, Legal Assistant of Utah, tutoring club.

Student services. Adult student services, career counseling, student employment services, financial aid counseling, placement for graduates, veterans' counselor. **Transfer:** Special adviser, orientation for new students.

Contact. Phone: (801) 485-0221 Fax: (801) 485-0057
John Rios, Admissions Director, Everest College: Salt Lake City, 3280 W 3500 S, West Valley City, UT 84119-2668

LDS Business College

Salt Lake City, Utah
www.ldsbc.edu **CB code: 4412**

- Private 2-year business and junior college affiliated with Church of Jesus Christ of Latter-day Saints
- Commuter campus in small city
- Interview required

General. Founded in 1886. Regionally accredited. **Enrollment:** 1,252 degree-seeking undergraduates. **Degrees:** 311 associate awarded. **Calendar:** Semester, limited summer session. **Full-time faculty:** 20 total. **Part-time faculty:** 81 total. **Class size:** 37% < 20, 53% 20-39, 8% 40-49, 3% 50-99.

Student profile.

Out-of-state:	50%	**Live on campus:**	12%
25 or older:	23%		

Transfer out. **Colleges most students transferred to 2005:** Brigham Young University, University of Utah.

Basis for selection. Open admission. Nonnative English speakers must submit minimum TOEFL test scores of 173 or paper test scores of 500. Color board required for placement in interior design program. SAT/ACT recommended for counseling, used as pre-test and placement in English or math. **Adult students:** Students who have not taken ACT or SAT must take COMPASS for placement in English and math. **Homeschooled:** Students must submit transcript or GED if not from accredited home school program. Students qualify for admission after reaching age 17. **Learning Disabled:** Must submit documentation under ADA.

2006-2007 Annual costs. Tuition/fees: $2,540. Per-credit charge: $105. Students who are not members of The Church of Jesus Christ of Latter-day Saints pay tuition of $3,720 per academic year, $155 per-credit-hour. Room only: $2,236. Books/supplies: $850. Personal expenses: $1,400.

2004-2005 Financial aid. **Need-based:** 2% of total undergraduate aid awarded as scholarships/grants, 98% as loans/jobs. Need-based aid available for part-time students. **Non-need-based:** Scholarships awarded for academics, leadership.

Application procedures. **Admission:** No deadline. $30 fee. Application may be submitted online. Admission notification on a rolling basis. **Financial aid:** Priority date 7/1; no closing date. FAFSA required. Applicants notified on a rolling basis starting 3/1; must reply within 3 week(s) of notification.

Academics. **Special study options:** Cooperative education, dual enrollment of high school students, internships. **Credit/placement by examination:** AP, CLEP, IB, institutional tests. 30 credit hours maximum toward associate degree. **Support services:** Reduced course load, study skills assistance, tutoring.

Majors. **Business:** General, accounting, administrative services, business admin, executive assistant, office management. **Computer sciences:** Information technology, webmaster. **Health:** Medical records admin, medical secretary, office admin, office assistant. **Legal studies:** Legal secretary. **Visual/performing arts:** Interior design.

Most popular majors. Business/marketing 9%, liberal arts 32%.

Computing on campus. 350 workstations in dormitories, library, computer center. Dormitories linked to campus network. Helpline available.

Student life. Freshman orientation: Available. Half-day session held Friday before start of classes. **Policies:** Religious observance required. Freshmen permitted cars on campus. **Housing:** Single-sex dorms available. $100 deposit. All on-campus housing facilities include kitchens. **Activities:** Choral groups, student government, student newspaper, Latter-Day Saint Student Association, alumni association, international students association, Institute Men's Association, Institute Women's Association, Students in Free Enterprise (SIFE), Service-Learning Council.

Student services. Career counseling, student employment services, financial aid counseling, health services, personal counseling, placement for graduates. **Transfer:** Special adviser, orientation for new students. Transfer adviser, college fairs on campus for students transferring to 4-year colleges.

Contact. E-mail: admissions@ldsbc.edu
Phone: (801) 524-8145 Toll-free number: (800) 999-5767
Fax: (801) 524-1900
Renae Richards, Director of Enrollment Management, LDS Business College, 411 East South Temple, Salt Lake City, UT 84111-1392

Provo College

Provo, Utah
www.provocollege.edu — **CB code: 3021**

- For-profit 2-year junior college
- Small city

General. Accredited by ACCSCT. **Enrollment:** 700 degree-seeking undergraduates. **Degrees:** 149 associate awarded. **Calendar:** Quarter. **Full-time faculty:** 60 total.

Basis for selection. Open admission.

2005-2006 Annual costs. Books/supplies: $600. Personal expenses: $2,088.

Academics. Credit/placement by examination: CLEP.

Majors. Business: Accounting, administrative services, business admin, hospitality/recreation. **Computer sciences:** General, programming. **Health:** Dental assistant, medical secretary, physical therapy assistant. **Visual/performing arts:** General, commercial/advertising art.

Contact. Phone: (801) 375-1861 Toll-free number: (800) 748-4834
Fax: (801) 375-9728
Ryan Wright, Director of Admissions, Provo College, 1450 West 820 North, Provo, UT 84601

Salt Lake Community College

Salt Lake City, Utah — **CB member**
www.slcc.edu — **CB code: 4864**

- Public 2-year community and technical college
- Commuter campus in very large city

General. Founded in 1948. Regionally accredited. 5 campus locations, 9 teaching centers. **Enrollment:** 22,527 degree-seeking undergraduates; 1,584 non-degree-seeking students. **Degrees:** 2,786 associate awarded. **ROTC:** Army, Air Force. **Location:** 5 miles from downtown Salt Lake City. **Calendar:** Semester, extensive summer session. **Full-time faculty:** 335 total. **Part-time faculty:** 1,085 total. **Class size:** 54% < 20, 43% 20-39, 2% 40-49, less than 1% 50-99.

Student profile. Among degree-seeking undergraduates, 62% enrolled in a transfer program, 38% enrolled in a vocational program, 8% already have a bachelor's degree or higher, 3,694 enrolled as first-time, first-year students.

Part-time:	65%	**Women:**	50%
Out-of-state:	5%	**25 or older:**	37%

Transfer out. Colleges most students transferred to 2005: University of Utah, Utah State University, Weber State University, Westminster College.

Basis for selection. Open admission, but selective for some programs. Admission for health science and flight technology programs based on testing, and for health sciences based on school records and prerequisite courses. **Adult students:** Entrance exam policies same as for first-time freshmen.

High school preparation. Biological science recommended for health science programs. Algebra recommended for preengineering and electronics.

2005-2006 Annual costs. Tuition/fees: $2,312; $7,232 out-of-state. Books/supplies: $1,580. Personal expenses: $1,510.

2004-2005 Financial aid. Need-based: 60% of total undergraduate aid awarded as scholarships/grants, 40% as loans/jobs. Need-based aid available for part-time students. Work study available nights, weekends and for part-time students. **Non-need-based:** Scholarships awarded for academics, alumni affiliation, art, athletics, leadership, minority status, music/drama.

Application procedures. Admission: No deadline. $35 fee. Application may be submitted online. Admission notification on a rolling basis. **Financial aid:** Priority date 5/1; no closing date. FAFSA, institutional form required. Applicants notified on a rolling basis starting 5/1; must reply within 4 week(s) of notification.

Academics. Special study options: Cooperative education, distance learning, double major, dual enrollment of high school students, ESL, internships, study abroad, weekend college. Bachelor's degree programs available on campus. License preparation in aviation, dental hygiene, nursing. **Credit/placement by examination:** AP, CLEP, IB, institutional tests. 50 credit hours maximum toward associate degree. **Support services:** GED preparation and test center, learning center, pre-admission summer program, reduced course load, remedial instruction, study skills assistance, tutoring, writing center.

Majors. Agriculture: Landscaping. **Biology:** General. **Business:** General, accounting technology, business admin, entrepreneurial studies, finance, logistics, marketing, restaurant/food services. **Communications:** General, digital media. **Communications technology:** Animation/special effects, photo/film/video, radio/tv. **Computer sciences:** General, computer science. **Construction:** Carpentry, concrete, electrician, maintenance, pipefitting, plumbing, site management. **Education:** Early childhood special. **Engineering:** Electrical, manufacturing, materials, mechanical. **Engineering technology:** Architectural drafting, civil drafting, computer, computer systems, drafting, environmental, instrumentation, manufacturing, mechanical, surveying, telecommunications. **English:** English lit. **Family/consumer sciences:** Family studies. **Foreign languages:** Sign language interpretation. **Health:** Clinical lab technology, dental hygiene, medical radiologic technology/radiation therapy, nursing (RN), occupational therapy assistant, physical therapy assistant, surgical technology. **History:** General. **Interdisciplinary:** Global studies. **Legal studies:** Paralegal. **Liberal arts:** Humanities. **Mechanic/repair:** Auto body, automotive, avionics, diesel, electronics/electrical, heating/ac/refrig, heavy equipment, industrial. **Parks/recreation:** Sports admin. **Personal/culinary services:** Chef training, cosmetic. **Physical sciences:** Chemistry, geology, physics. **Production:** Cabinetmaking/millwright, ironworking, machine tool, sheet metal, welding. **Protective services:** Criminal justice. **Psychology:** General. **Public administration:** Social work. **Science technology:** Biological, chemical, radiologic. **Social sciences:** Economics, geography, political science, sociology. **Transportation:** Airline/commercial pilot. **Visual/performing arts:** Design, photography, theater design.

Most popular majors. Business/marketing 12%, health sciences 12%, liberal arts 49%.

Computing on campus. 2,400 workstations in library, computer center, student center. Commuter students can connect to campus network. Online course registration, helpline, wireless network available.

Student life. Freshman orientation: Available, $3 fee. Preregistration for classes offered. One-day program. **Activities:** Jazz band, choral groups, dance, drama, literary magazine, music ensembles, musical theater, radio station, student government, student newspaper, TV station, Circle-K, Latter-Day Saints student association, Hispanos Unidos, African-American student association, American Indian club, Asian club, Polynesian club, American Sign Language club, professional societies.

Athletics. NJCAA. **Intercollegiate:** Baseball M, basketball, softball W, volleyball W. **Team name:** Bruins.

Student services. Alcohol/substance abuse counseling, career counseling, services for economically disadvantaged, student employment services, financial aid counseling, health services, minority student services, on-campus daycare, personal counseling, placement for graduates, veterans' counselor. **Physically disabled:** Services for visually, speech, hearing impaired. **Transfer:** Special adviser for new students. Transfer center, transfer adviser, college fairs on campus for students transferring to 4-year colleges.

Contact. E-mail: evans.loren@slcc.edu
Phone: (801) 957-4298 Fax: (801) 957-4961
Eric Weber, Dean of Student Enrollment Services, Salt Lake Community College, 4600 South Redwood Road, Salt Lake City, UT 84130-0808

Snow College
Ephraim, Utah
www.snow.edu **CB code: 4727**

- Public 2-year community and junior college
- Commuter campus in small town

General. Founded in 1888. Regionally accredited. **Enrollment:** 3,333 undergraduates. **Degrees:** 683 associate awarded. **Location:** 120 miles from Salt Lake City, 70 miles from Provo. **Calendar:** Semester, limited summer session. **Full-time faculty:** 119 total. **Part-time faculty:** 372 total. **Class size:** 48% < 20, 2% 20-39, less than 1% 50-99, 49% >100.

Student profile.

Out-of-state:	2%	**Live on campus:**	10%
25 or older:	14%		

Basis for selection. Open admission. Auditions for Fine Arts. **Adult students:** Entrance exam policies same as for first-time freshmen.

2005-2006 Annual costs. Tuition/fees: $1,996; $7,204 out-of-state. Room/board: $3,000. Books/supplies: $530. Personal expenses: $900.

Financial aid. Need-based: Work study available for part-time students. **Non-need-based:** Scholarships awarded for academics, athletics, state residency.

Application procedures. Admission: Priority date 6/1; no deadline. $30 fee. Application may be submitted online. Admission notification on a rolling basis beginning on or about 12/1. Applications received after May 15 will be on a space-available basis. **Financial aid:** Priority date 3/1, closing date 7/15. FAFSA, institutional form required. Applicants notified on a rolling basis starting 8/1; must reply within 1 week(s) of notification.

Academics. Special study options: Cooperative education, distance learning, dual enrollment of high school students, ESL, honors, independent study. **Credit/placement by examination:** AP, CLEP, institutional tests. 45 credit hours maximum toward associate degree. **Support services:** GED test center, learning center, reduced course load, remedial instruction, study skills assistance, tutoring, writing center.

Majors. Agriculture: Agribusiness operations, animal sciences, business, farm/ranch, food science, poultry. **Biology:** General, bacteriology, botany, pharmacology, physiology, zoology. **Business:** General, accounting, business admin, managerial economics. **Communications:** Journalism. **Computer sciences:** General, computer science, information systems. **Conservation:** General, forestry, management/policy, wildlife. **Construction:** General. **Education:** General, business, early childhood, elementary, ESL, family/consumer sciences, health, physical, secondary, special. **Engineering:** General, chemical. **Engineering technology:** Drafting. **English:** Composition. **Family/consumer sciences:** General, child care, clothing/textiles, family/community services, food/nutrition. **Foreign languages:** General, French, Japanese, Spanish. **Health:** Clinical lab science, EMT paramedic, licensed practical nurse, predentistry, premedicine, prenursing, prepharmacy, preveterinary, veterinary technology/assistant. **History:** General. **Interdisciplinary:** Biological/physical sciences, natural sciences. **Legal studies:** Prelaw. **Math:** General, statistics. **Mechanic/repair:** General. **Parks/recreation:** General, health/fitness. **Personal/culinary services:** Barbering, chef training, cosmetic, cosmetology, culinary arts. **Philosophy/religion:** Philosophy. **Physical sciences:** Astronomy, chemistry, geochemistry, geology, geophysics, physics. **Protective services:** Law enforcement admin. **Psychology:** General. **Public administration:** Social work. **Social sciences:** General, anthropology, economics, geography, political science, sociology. **Visual/performing arts:** General, art, dance.

Most popular majors. Business/marketing 13%, education 13%, health sciences 14%, liberal arts 26%.

Computing on campus. 235 workstations in library, computer center, student center. Dormitories wired for high-speed internet access. Helpline available.

Student life. Freshman orientation: Mandatory. Preregistration for classes offered. **Policies:** Freshmen permitted cars on campus. **Housing:** Coed dorms, single-sex dorms, apartments available. **Activities:** Bands, choral groups, dance, drama, literary magazine, music ensembles, musical theater, radio station, student government, student newspaper, symphony orchestra, Latter-Day Saints Student Association, Associated Women Students, Associated Men Students, Badgers Against Alcohol & Drugs, Polynesian Club, ski club, Spanish Club, international club.

Athletics. NJCAA. **Intercollegiate:** Baseball M, basketball, football (tackle) M, softball W, volleyball W. **Intramural:** Basketball, golf, racquetball, soccer, softball, tennis, volleyball. **Team name:** Badgers.

Student services. Adult student services, alcohol/substance abuse counseling, career counseling, financial aid counseling, on-campus daycare, personal counseling, veterans' counselor. **Physically disabled:** Services for visually, hearing impaired. **Learning disabled:** Comprehensive services available. **Transfer:** Special adviser, orientation, pre-admission transcript evaluation for new students. Transfer adviser, college fairs on campus for students transferring to 4-year colleges.

Contact. E-mail: hsrelations@snow.edu
Phone: (435) 283-7150 Fax: (435) 283-6879
Katie Larsen, Director of Admissions and Records, Snow College, 150 East College Avenue, Ephraim, UT 84627

Stevens-Henager College: Murray
Salt Lake City, Utah
www.stevenshenager.edu

- For-profit 2-year business college
- Large town

General. Accredited by ACCSCT. **Enrollment:** 400 degree-seeking undergraduates. **Degrees:** 64 bachelor's, 90 associate awarded. **Calendar:** Continuous. **Full-time faculty:** 9 total. **Part-time faculty:** 20 total.

2005-2006 Financial aid. Need-based: 99% of total undergraduate aid awarded as scholarships/grants, 1% as loans/jobs. **Additional information:** Financial aid application must be completed prior to enrollment.

Application procedures. Admission: No deadline. No application fee.

Academics. Credit/placement by examination: CLEP.

Contact. Phone: (800) 622-2640
Jennifer Polanalski, Admissions Director, Stevens-Henager College: Murray, 838 West Vine Street, Salt Lake City, UT 84123

Utah Career College
West Jordan, Utah
www.utahcollege.edu **CB code: 2892**

- For-profit 2-year technical college
- Commuter campus in small city
- Interview required

General. Accredited by ACCSCT. **Enrollment:** 505 degree-seeking undergraduates; 64 non-degree-seeking students. **Degrees:** 94 associate awarded. **Location:** 8 miles from Salt Lake City. **Calendar:** Quarter, extensive summer session. **Full-time faculty:** 15 total. **Part-time faculty:** 40 total.

Student profile. Among degree-seeking undergraduates, 100% enrolled in a vocational program, 3% already have a bachelor's degree or higher, 97 enrolled as first-time, first-year students.

Part-time:	74%	**Hispanic American:**	6%
Women:	79%	**Native American:**	1%
Asian American:	1%	**25 or older:**	53%

Transfer out. Colleges most students transferred to 2005: Salt Lake Community College.

Basis for selection. Open admission. **Adult students:** Entrance exam policies same as for first-time freshmen. **Homeschooled:** GED certificate and documentation required.

2005-2006 Annual costs. Books and fees range from $300 to $400 per quarter.

2004-2005 Financial aid. All financial aid based on need. 30% of total undergraduate aid awarded as scholarships/grants, 70% as loans/jobs. Need-based aid available for part-time students.

Application procedures. Admission: No deadline. No application fee. Application must be submitted on paper. Admission notification on a rolling basis. **Financial aid:** No deadline. FAFSA, institutional form required. Applicants notified on a rolling basis starting 7/1; must reply within 2 week(s) of notification.

Academics. Special study options: Distance learning, honors, liberal arts/career combination. **Credit/placement by examination:** AP, CLEP. Credits for prior work experience and examination may not exceed 75% of total credits required to complete student's program. **Support services:** Reduced course load, study skills assistance, tutoring.

Majors. Business: Business admin. **Computer sciences:** Computer graphics. **Health:** Athletic training, licensed practical nurse, massage therapy, medical assistant, pharmacy assistant, veterinary technology/assistant. **Legal studies:** Paralegal. **Parks/recreation:** Exercise sciences, sports admin.

Most popular majors. Computer/information sciences 18%, health sciences 65%, parks/recreation 12%.

Computing on campus. 90 workstations in library, computer center.

Student life. Freshman orientation: Mandatory. Preregistration for classes offered. **Policies:** Drug and alcohol free campus. Freshmen permitted cars on campus.

Student services. Career counseling, student employment services, financial aid counseling, placement for graduates, veterans' counselor. **Transfer:** Special adviser, orientation, re-entry adviser, pre-admission transcript evaluation for new students.

Contact. E-mail: admissions@utahcollege.edu
Phone: (801) 304-4224 Toll-free number: (866) 304-4224
Fax: (801) 304-4229
Denice Dunker, Director of Admissions, Utah Career College, 1902 West 7800 South, West Jordan, UT 84088

Vermont

Community College of Vermont
Waterbury, Vermont
www.ccv.edu **CB code: 3286**

- Public 2-year community college
- Commuter campus in small town

General. Founded in 1970. Regionally accredited. Courses offered in 12 locations statewide and online. **Enrollment:** 3,909 degree-seeking undergraduates. **Degrees:** 426 associate awarded. **Calendar:** Semester, limited summer session. **Part-time faculty:** 600 total.

Transfer out. Colleges most students transferred to 2005: University of Vermont, Johnson State College.

Basis for selection. Open admission. Skill assessments administered by the college are required for placement purposes. International students must provide TOEFL score. Recommendation required if applicant has neither high school diploma nor GED.

2005-2006 Annual costs. Tuition/fees: $4,990; $9,880 out-of-state. Per-credit charge: $163 in-state; $326 out-of-state. New England Board of Higher Education rate for students from other New England states: 150% of Vermont resident tuition. Available to degree candidates in academic areas not offered by educational institutions in their home states. Books/supplies: $600.

Financial aid. All financial aid based on need. Need-based aid available for part-time students. Work study available nights.

Application procedures. Admission: No deadline. No application fee. Application may be submitted online. Admission notification on a rolling basis. **Financial aid:** No deadline. FAFSA, institutional form required. Applicants notified on a rolling basis starting 9/1; must reply within 3 week(s) of notification.

Academics. Special study options: Cooperative education, cross-registration, distance learning, double major, dual enrollment of high school students, ESL, external degree, independent study, internships, liberal arts/career combination, student-designed major, study abroad, weekend college. **Credit/placement by examination:** AP, CLEP, institutional tests. 50 credit hours maximum toward associate degree. **Support services:** Learning center, reduced course load, remedial instruction, study skills assistance, tutoring, writing center.

Majors. Business: General. **Education:** General. **Health:** Health services. **Liberal arts:** Arts/sciences. **Mechanic/repair:** General.

Most popular majors. Business/marketing 22%, education 6%, liberal arts 58%, public administration/social services 7%.

Computing on campus. 300 workstations in library, computer center. Online course registration, online library available.

Student life. Freshman orientation: Available. Preregistration for classes offered. **Activities:** Choral groups, student government.

Student services. Adult student services, career counseling, student employment services, financial aid counseling, placement for graduates, veterans' counselor. **Physically disabled:** Services for visually, speech, hearing impaired. **Transfer:** Special adviser, orientation for new students. Transfer adviser for students transferring to 4-year colleges.

Contact. Phone: (802) 241-3535 Toll-free number: (800) 228-6686
Fax: (802) 254-3473
Susan Henry, Admissions Director, Community College of Vermont, 103 South Main Street, Waterbury, VT 05676-0120

Landmark College
Putney, Vermont
www.landmark.edu **CB code: 0081**

- Private 2-year liberal arts college
- Residential campus in small town
- Application essay, interview required

General. Founded in 1983. Regionally accredited. College is exclusively for bright students with dyslexia, attention disorders, or specific learning disabilities. We also offer professional development workshops and consultancies. **Enrollment:** 371 degree-seeking undergraduates. **Degrees:** 71 associate awarded. **Location:** 8 miles from Brattleboro, 23 miles from Keene, New Hampshire. **Calendar:** Semester, limited summer session. **Full-time faculty:** 95 total; 10% have terminal degrees, 1% minority, 59% women. **Part-time faculty:** 2 total; 50% have terminal degrees, 50% minority, 100% women. **Class size:** 99% < 20, less than 1% 20-39. **Special facilities:** Fine arts building, ropes course.

Student profile. Among degree-seeking undergraduates, 100% enrolled in a transfer program, 120 enrolled as first-time, first-year students, 55 transferred in from other institutions.

Part-time:	37%	**Hispanic American:**	2%
Out-of-state:	92%	**International:**	3%
Women:	25%	**25 or older:**	6%
African American:	5%	**Live on campus:**	96%
Asian American:	3%		

Transfer out. 76% of students enrolled in the transfer program go on to 4-year colleges. **Colleges most students transferred to 2005:** American University, University of Denver, University of Vermont, Marlboro College, College of Charleston.

Basis for selection. Successful applicants are highly motivated, have average-to-superior intellectual ability and diagnosis of dyslexia, attentional disorder (ADHD), or specific learning disability. WAIS III or Woodcock Johnson Cognitive assessment required. Nelson-Denny reading scores required. **Adult students:** Entrance exam policies same as for first-time freshmen.

2006-2007 Annual costs. Tuition/fees: $39,270. Notebook computer and software required. Cost through school $1,850. Room/board: $7,200. Books/supplies: $1,000. Personal expenses: $2,500.

2005-2006 Financial aid. All financial aid based on need. 61% of total undergraduate aid awarded as scholarships/grants, 39% as loans/jobs. Need-based aid available for part-time students. Work study available nights, weekends and for part-time students. **Additional information:** Students encouraged to apply to their state departments of vocational rehabilitation for additional financial assistance.

Application procedures. Admission: Priority date 5/15; no deadline. $75 fee, may be waived for applicants with need. Application must be submitted on paper. Admission notification on a rolling basis beginning on or about 12/1. **Financial aid:** Priority date 3/30; no closing date. FAFSA, institutional form required. Applicants notified on a rolling basis starting 4/30; must reply within 2 week(s) of notification.

Academics. Special study options: Internships, study abroad. **Credit/placement by examination:** AP, CLEP, institutional tests. **Support services:** Learning center, pre-admission summer program, reduced course load, remedial instruction, study skills assistance, writing center.

Majors. Business: Business admin. **Liberal arts:** Arts/sciences.

Computing on campus. PC or laptop required. 50 workstations in dormitories, library, student center. Dormitories wired for high-speed internet access and linked to campus network. Commuter students can connect to campus network. Online library, helpline, repair service, wireless network available.

Student life. Freshman orientation: Mandatory. **Policies:** Alcohol not permitted on campus. Freshmen permitted cars on campus. **Housing:** Guaranteed on-campus for all undergraduates. Coed dorms, special housing for disabled, substance-free housing available. All new students must live on campus. Others may petition to live off-campus. **Activities:** Jazz band, choral groups, dance, drama, literary magazine, music ensembles, student government, community service club, international students organization, Phi Theta Kappa honor society, cultural diversity club, charity garden club.

Athletics. Intercollegiate: Baseball M, basketball, cross-country, soccer, softball W. **Intramural:** Basketball, volleyball. **Team name:** Landsharks.

Student services. Adult student services, alcohol/substance abuse counseling, career counseling, financial aid counseling, health services, on-campus daycare, personal counseling, placement for graduates, women's services. **Learning disabled:** Comprehensive services available. **Transfer:** Special adviser, orientation for new students. Transfer center, transfer adviser, college fairs on campus for students transferring to 4-year colleges.

Contact. E-mail: admissions@landmark.edu
Phone: (802) 387-6718 Fax: (802) 387-6868
Dale Herold, Vice President for Enrollment Management, Landmark College, River Road South, Putney, VT 05346

New England Culinary Institute
Montpelier, Vermont
www.neci.edu **CB code: 3405**

- For-profit 2-year culinary school
- Residential campus in large town
- Application essay, interview required

General. Founded in 1980. Accredited by ACCSCT. Branch campuses in Essex Junction and Tortola, Virgin Islands. **Enrollment:** 525 undergraduates. **Degrees:** 25 bachelor's, 144 associate awarded. **Location:** 39 miles from Burlington. **Calendar:** Differs by program. **Full-time faculty:** 70 total. **Part-time faculty:** 15 total. **Special facilities:** Gourmet restaurant, bakeshop, cafeteria, catering business, American cuisine restaurant. **Partnerships:** Formal partnerships with The Council of Independent Restaurants of America.

Basis for selection. High school achievement record, essay or personal statement, interview, and letter of recommendation. Advanced placement standing available to students through school testing. **Adult students:** Entrance exam policies same as for first-time freshmen.

High school preparation. Transcript must demonstrate proficiency in English and mathematics. Foreign language and culinary arts training highly desirable.

2005-2006 Annual costs. Tuition/fees: $24,050. Costs will vary with program. Room/board: $6,415.

Financial aid. Need-based: Work study available nights and weekends.

Application procedures. Admission: No deadline. No application fee. Application may be submitted online. Admission notification on a rolling basis. **Financial aid:** No deadline. FAFSA required. Applicants notified on a rolling basis.

Academics. Special study options: Accelerated study, internships. Bachelor's degree programs available on campus. **Credit/placement by examination:** AP, CLEP, IB. **Support services:** Learning center, study skills assistance, tutoring.

Majors. Personal/culinary services: Chef training, culinary arts.

Computing on campus. 20 workstations in library, computer center. Dormitories wired for high-speed internet access.

Student life. Freshman orientation: Mandatory. Orientation and registration held 2-3 days prior to first day of classes. **Policies:** Freshmen permitted cars on campus. **Housing:** Coed dorms, single-sex dorms, apartments available. **Activities:** Student newspaper.

Student services. Student employment services, financial aid counseling, placement for graduates.

Contact. E-mail: admissions@neci.edu
Phone: (802) 223-6324 Toll-free number: (877) 223-6324
Fax: (802) 225-3280
Dawn Hayward, Director of Admissions, New England Culinary Institute, 250 Main Street, Montpelier, VT 05602

New England Culinary Institute: Essex Junction
Essex Junction, Vermont
www.neci.edu **CB code: 3100**

- For-profit 2-year culinary school and business college
- Small city

General. Accredited by ACCSCT. **Location:** 8 miles from Burlington. **Calendar:** Quarter.

Annual costs/financial aid. Tuition/fees (2005-2006): $24,050. Room/board: $6,415. Books/supplies: $1,000. Need-based financial aid available for full-time students.

Contact. Phone: (802) 872-3400
Admissions Director, 5 Franklin Street, Essex Junction, VT 05452

Virginia

Advanced Technology Institute
Virginia Beach, Virginia
www.auto.edu

- For-profit 2-year technical college
- Large city

General. Accredited by ACCSCT. **Calendar:** Continuous.

Annual costs/financial aid. Total program cost varies by program: $8,000 - $19,000.

Contact. Phone: (757) 490-1241
5700 Southern Boulevard, Virginia Beach, VA 23462

Blue Ridge Community College
Weyers Cave, Virginia
www.brcc.edu **CB code: 5083**

- Public 2-year community college
- Commuter campus in rural community

General. Founded in 1965. Regionally accredited. **Enrollment:** 3,527 degree-seeking undergraduates; 276 non-degree-seeking students. **Degrees:** 418 associate awarded. **Location:** 12 miles from Harrisonburg, 15 miles from Staunton. **Calendar:** Semester, limited summer session. **Full-time faculty:** 50 total. **Part-time faculty:** 120 total. **Special facilities:** Arboretum. **Partnerships:** Tech Prep Consortium.

Student profile. Among degree-seeking undergraduates, 52% enrolled in a transfer program, 37% enrolled in a vocational program, 820 enrolled as first-time, first-year students, 554 transferred in from other institutions.

Part-time:	60%	**Women:**	58%
Out-of-state:	2%	**25 or older:**	36%

Transfer out. 54% of students enrolled in the transfer program go on to 4-year colleges. **Colleges most students transferred to 2005:** James Madison University, Mary Baldwin College, Old Dominion University, Eastern Mennonite University, Bridgewater College.

Basis for selection. Open admission, but selective for some programs. Special requirements for veterinary assistant technology and nursing programs; interview required.

High school preparation. 8 units recommended. Recommended units include English 4, mathematics 2, social studies 1 and science 1.

2005-2006 Annual costs. Tuition/fees: $2,185; $6,565 out-of-state. Per-credit charge: $68 in-state; $214 out-of-state. Books/supplies: $600. Personal expenses: $900.

Financial aid. Need-based: Need-based aid available for part-time students. **Non-need-based:** Scholarships awarded for academics, job skills, leadership, minority status.

Application procedures. Admission: No deadline. No application fee. Application may be submitted online. Admission notification on a rolling basis. Closing date for veterinary assistant technology is January 1. Nursing clinical component application deadline is January 31. **Financial aid:** Priority date 5/1; no closing date. FAFSA, institutional form required. Applicants notified on a rolling basis starting 5/30; must reply within 2 week(s) of notification.

Academics. Special study options: Accelerated study, cross-registration, distance learning, double major, dual enrollment of high school students, ESL, honors, independent study, internships, study abroad. Bachelor's degree programs available on campus. License preparation in nursing. **Credit/placement by examination:** AP, CLEP, institutional tests. Credit cannot duplicate earned course credits, nor courses audited or failed. **Support services:** Learning center, remedial instruction, tutoring.

Majors. Agriculture: Animal sciences. **Business:** Accounting, administrative services, business admin. **Computer sciences:** General, information systems, programming, systems analysis. **Engineering technology:** Electrical. **Health:** Health services, nursing (RN), veterinary technology/assistant. **Liberal arts:** Arts/sciences. **Public administration:** Human services.

Computing on campus. 285 workstations in library, computer center. Online course registration, online library available.

Student life. Freshman orientation: Mandatory. Preregistration for classes offered. **Activities:** Student government, Phi Theta Kappa, Christian Fellowship, special interest groups.

Athletics. Intramural: Basketball M.

Student services. Career counseling, student employment services, financial aid counseling, minority student services, personal counseling, placement for graduates, veterans' counselor, women's services. **Physically disabled:** Services for visually, speech, hearing impaired. **Transfer:** Special adviser, orientation for new students. Transfer adviser, college fairs on campus for students transferring to 4-year colleges.

Contact. Phone: (540) 234-9261 ext. 2287 Toll-free number: (888) 750-2722 ext. 2287 Fax: (540) 453-2437
Robert Clemmer, Coordinator of Admissions and Records Officer, Blue Ridge Community College, Box 80, Weyers Cave, VA 24486-9989

Bryant & Stratton College: Richmond
Richmond, Virginia
www.bryantstratton.edu **CB code: 4762**

- For-profit 2-year business college
- Small city

General. Accredited by ACICS. **Calendar:** Continuous.

Annual costs/financial aid. Tuition/fees (2005-2006): $11,820. Books/supplies: $738. Personal expenses: $1,384.

Contact. Phone: (804) 745-2444
Director of Admissions, 8141 Hull Street Road, Richmond, VA 23235

Bryant & Stratton College: Virginia Beach
Virginia Beach, Virginia
www.bryantstratton.edu **CB code: 4761**

- For-profit 2-year business and junior college
- Commuter campus in large city
- Interview required

General. Founded in 1952. Candidate for regional accreditation; also accredited by ACICS. **Enrollment:** 435 degree-seeking undergraduates; 16 non-degree-seeking students. **Degrees:** 26 bachelor's, 73 associate awarded. **Location:** 10 miles from Norfolk. **Calendar:** Semester, extensive summer session. **Full-time faculty:** 11 total; 36% have terminal degrees, 46% minority, 36% women. **Part-time faculty:** 37 total; 19% have terminal degrees, 43% minority, 54% women. **Class size:** 85% < 20, 15% 20-39.

Student profile. Among degree-seeking undergraduates, 141 enrolled as first-time, first-year students.

Part-time:	48%	**Hispanic American:**	4%
Women:	80%	**Native American:**	1%
African American:	66%	**25 or older:**	59%
Asian American:	3%		

Transfer out. Colleges most students transferred to 2005: Tidewater Community College, Strayer University, University of Phoenix.

Basis for selection. Open admission. Test scores, personal interview most important. TOEFL used for non-native English speakers. **Adult students:** Entrance exam policies same as for first-time freshmen.

High school preparation. Recommended units include English 4, mathematics 2, social studies 3, science 2, foreign language 2 and academic electives 1.

2006-2007 Annual costs. Tuition/fees (projected): $11,820. Per-credit charge: $394. Technology fee $100 per semester. Books/supplies: $1,300. Personal expenses: $1,560.

Financial aid. Need-based: Need-based aid available for part-time students. Work study available nights and for part-time students.

Application procedures. Admission: No deadline. $25 fee, may be waived for applicants with need. Application may be submitted online. Admission notification on a rolling basis. **Financial aid:** No deadline. FAFSA required. Applicants notified on a rolling basis.

Academics. Free tutoring and extensive academic advising are available. Portfolio projects in all classes. **Special study options:** Cooperative education, double major, independent study, internships, liberal arts/career combination, weekend college. Bachelor's degree programs available on campus. **Credit/placement by examination:** AP, CLEP, institutional tests. 30 credit hours maximum toward associate degree, 60 toward bachelor's. **Support services:** Learning center, reduced course load, remedial instruction, study skills assistance, tutoring.

Majors. Business: Accounting, administrative services, business admin. **Computer sciences:** General. **Health:** Medical assistant. **Legal studies:** General.

Most popular majors. Business/marketing 53%, computer/information sciences 17%, health sciences 10%, legal studies 17%.

Computing on campus. 100 workstations in library, computer center.

Student life. Freshman orientation: Mandatory. Preregistration for classes offered. Held week classes start, 2 to 3 hours. **Policies:** Freshmen permitted cars on campus. **Activities:** Student government, student newspaper, Alpha Beta Gamma, Phi Beta Lambda, law society, medical club, computer club, Society for the Advancement of Management.

Student services. Adult student services, career counseling, student employment services, on-campus daycare, personal counseling, placement for graduates, veterans' counselor. **Transfer:** Special adviser, orientation, pre-admission transcript evaluation for new students.

Contact. E-mail: gesmith@bryantstratton.edu
Phone: (757) 499-7900 Fax: (757) 499-9977
Greg Smith, Director of Admissions, Bryant & Stratton College: Virginia Beach, 301 Centre Pointe Drive, Virginia Beach, VA 23462-4417

Central Virginia Community College

Lynchburg, Virginia — CB member
www.cv.cc.va.us — CB code: 5141

- Public 2-year community college
- Commuter campus in small city

General. Founded in 1966. Regionally accredited. **Enrollment:** 2,535 degree-seeking undergraduates. **Degrees:** 306 associate awarded. **Location:** 120 miles from Richmond. **Calendar:** Semester, limited summer session. **Full-time faculty:** 55 total. **Part-time faculty:** 170 total.

Transfer out. Colleges most students transferred to 2005: Lynchburg College, Virginia Polytechnic Institute and State University, Longwood College, Old Dominion University.

Basis for selection. Open admission, but selective for some programs. Allied health program applicants must have 2 interviews with program head and meet specific criteria. Only 15 applicants accepted in each program each year. Interview required for health program.

2005-2006 Annual costs. Tuition/fees: $2,166; $6,546 out-of-state. Per-credit charge: $68 in-state; $214 out-of-state. Books/supplies: $600. Personal expenses: $1,550.

Financial aid. Need-based: Work study available for part-time students. **Non-need-based:** Scholarships awarded for academics, alumni affiliation. **Additional information:** Payment plan available.

Application procedures. Admission: Priority date 9/5; no deadline. No application fee. Admission notification on a rolling basis. **Financial aid:** Priority date 3/15; no closing date. FAFSA required. Applicants notified on a rolling basis starting 5/1; must reply within 2 week(s) of notification.

Academics. GPA of 2.0 required to graduate. System-wide core curriculum to ensure ease of transfer. **Special study options:** Cooperative education, distance learning, dual enrollment of high school students, independent study, internships. Bachelor's degree programs available on campus. **Credit/placement by examination:** AP, CLEP, IB, institutional tests. 45 credit hours maximum toward associate degree. **Support services:** Learning center, reduced course load, remedial instruction, study skills assistance, tutoring.

Majors. Business: General, accounting, administrative services, business admin, finance, management information systems. **Computer sciences:** Information systems. **Education:** General. **Engineering technology:** Architectural, civil, electrical. **Health:** Clinical lab technology, physics/radiologic health. **Liberal arts:** Arts/sciences. **Protective services:** Law enforcement admin. **Visual/performing arts:** Commercial/advertising art.

Computing on campus. 230 workstations in library, computer center. Commuter students can connect to campus network. Online library available.

Student life. Freshman orientation: Mandatory, $65 fee. **Activities:** Drama, literary magazine, student government, student newspaper, Black Student Union, art club, honor society, Students Together For Environmental Protection, data processing management association, Spanish club, medical lab club, respiratory club, radiology club.

Athletics. Intramural: Softball, volleyball.

Student services. Career counseling, student employment services, financial aid counseling, personal counseling, placement for graduates, veterans' counselor. **Physically disabled:** Services for visually, speech, hearing impaired. **Transfer:** Special adviser for new students. Transfer adviser, college fairs on campus for students transferring to 4-year colleges.

Contact. Phone: (434) 832-7633 Toll-free number: (800) 562-3060
Fax: (434) 832-7793
Geoffrey Hicks, Chief Academic Officer, Central Virginia Community College, 3506 Wards Road, Lynchburg, VA 24502-2498

Dabney S. Lancaster Community College

Clifton Forge, Virginia
www.dslcc.edu — CB code: 5139

- Public 2-year community college
- Commuter campus in small town

General. Founded in 1967. Regionally accredited. **Enrollment:** 1,311 undergraduates. **Degrees:** 57 associate awarded. **Location:** 55 miles from Roanoke. **Calendar:** Semester, extensive summer session. **Full-time faculty:** 20 total. **Part-time faculty:** 90 total. **Special facilities:** Modern sawmill.

Basis for selection. Open admission, but selective for some programs. Special requirements for nursing program. High school diploma or GED required of applicants under 18. Interview requried for nursing program.

High school preparation. Course recommendations vary according to planned curriculum.

2005-2006 Annual costs. Tuition/fees: $2,157; $6,537 out-of-state. Per-credit charge: $68 in-state; $214 out-of-state. Books/supplies: $580. Personal expenses: $1,680.

Financial aid. Need-based: Need-based aid available for part-time students.

Application procedures. Admission: No deadline. No application fee. Application may be submitted online. Admission notification on a rolling basis beginning on or about 2/1. **Financial aid:** Priority date 3/15; no closing date. FAFSA, institutional form required. Applicants notified on a rolling basis starting 4/15; must reply within 2 week(s) of notification.

Academics. Special study options: Cooperative education, distance learning, double major, dual enrollment of high school students, independent study, internships. **Credit/placement by examination:** CLEP, institutional tests. **Support services:** Learning center, pre-admission summer program, reduced course load, remedial instruction, study skills assistance, tutoring, writing center.

Majors. Business: Administrative services, business admin, communications, office management, office/clerical. **Communications technology:** Graphic/printing. **Computer sciences:** General. **Conservation:** Forestry. **Engineering technology:** Electrical. **Liberal arts:** Arts/sciences. **Protective services:** Criminal justice, police science.

Most popular majors. Business/marketing 30%, health sciences 18%, liberal arts 26%, natural resources/environmental science 15%, security/protective services 6%.

Computing on campus. 60 workstations in library, computer center. Helpline, wireless network available.

Student life. Freshman orientation: Mandatory. Preregistration for classes offered. **Activities:** Choral groups, drama, literary magazine, student government, student newspaper, various social, religious and service clubs available.

Athletics. Intramural: Basketball, softball, volleyball.

Student services. Career counseling, student employment services, personal counseling, placement for graduates, veterans' counselor. **Physically disabled:** Services for visually, speech, hearing impaired. **Transfer:** Special adviser, orientation for new students. Transfer adviser, college fairs on campus for students transferring to 4-year colleges.

Contact. Phone: (540) 863-2815 Fax: (540) 863-2915
Mary Wilson, Director of Student Services, Dabney S. Lancaster Community College, Box 1000, Clifton Forge, VA 24422

Danville Community College

Danville, Virginia
www.dcc.vccs.edu **CB code: 5163**

- Public 2-year community college
- Commuter campus in small city

General. Founded in 1967. Regionally accredited. **Enrollment:** 2,355 degree-seeking undergraduates. **Degrees:** 250 associate awarded. **Location:** 45 miles from Greensboro, North Carolina. **Calendar:** Semester, limited summer session. **Full-time faculty:** 147 total. **Part-time faculty:** 164 total. **Class size:** 71% < 20, 28% 20-39, 1% 50-99.

Student profile.

Out-of-state:	2%	25 or older:	52%

Transfer out. Colleges most students transferred to 2005: Averett University, Virginia Polytechnic Institute, Radford University.

Basis for selection. Open admission, but selective for some programs. Special requirements for nursing program.

High school preparation. Recommended units include English 4 and mathematics 1.

2005-2006 Annual costs. Tuition/fees: $2,185; $6,565 out-of-state. Per-credit charge: $68 in-state; $214 out-of-state. Books/supplies: $700. Personal expenses: $1,328.

2004-2005 Financial aid. All financial aid based on need. Need-based aid available for part-time students. Work study available for part-time students.

Application procedures. Admission: Priority date 8/20; no deadline. No application fee. Admission notification on a rolling basis beginning on or about 1/15. **Financial aid:** Priority date 6/1; no closing date. FAFSA required. Applicants notified on a rolling basis starting 5/1; must reply within 2 week(s) of notification.

Academics. System-wide core curriculum to ensure ease of transfer. **Special study options:** Accelerated study, cooperative education, distance learning, double major, dual enrollment of high school students, honors, independent study, internships. Bachelor's degree programs available on campus. License preparation in dental hygiene, nursing, real estate. **Credit/placement by examination:** AP, CLEP, institutional tests. **Support services:** GED preparation and test center, learning center, pre-admission summer program, reduced course load, remedial instruction, study skills assistance, tutoring.

Majors. Business: General, accounting, administrative services, business admin, executive assistant, receptionist. **Communications technology:** Graphic/printing. **Computer sciences:** General, computer science, programming. **Engineering:** General. **Engineering technology:** Drafting, manufacturing. **Family/consumer sciences:** Child development. **Health:** Dental hygiene, medical secretary, office assistant, respiratory therapy assistant. **Interdisciplinary:** Biological/physical sciences, science/society. **Liberal arts:** Arts/sciences, humanities. **Mechanic/repair:** Heating/ac/refrig. **Protective services:** Law enforcement admin.

Most popular majors. Business/marketing 40%, education 15%, liberal arts 33%, security/protective services 11%.

Computing on campus. 425 workstations in library, computer center. Online course registration, online library available.

Student life. Freshman orientation: Mandatory. Preregistration for classes offered. Two 1-day summer sessions to choose from. **Policies:** Freshmen permitted cars on campus. **Activities:** Choral groups, student government, African-American culture club, Christian Students Fellowship, graphics club, International Association of Administrative Professionals, Phi Theta Kappa, National Vocational-Technical Honor Society, gospel club, Lambda Alpha Epsilon (criminal justice).

Athletics. Team name: Knights.

Student services. Adult student services, campus ministries, career counseling, student employment services, financial aid counseling, on-campus daycare, personal counseling, placement for graduates, veterans' counselor, women's services. **Physically disabled:** Services for visually, speech, hearing impaired. **Transfer:** Special adviser, orientation for new students. College fairs on campus for students transferring to 4-year colleges.

Contact. E-mail: ethornton@dcc.vccs.edu
Phone: (434) 797-8467 Toll-free number: (800) 560-4291
Fax: (434) 797-8541
Peter Castiglione, Director of Student Development & Enrollment Management, Danville Community College, 1008 South Main Street, Danville, VA 24541

Eastern Shore Community College

Melfa, Virginia
www.es.vccs.edu **CB code: 5844**

- Public 2-year community college
- Commuter campus in rural community

General. Founded in 1971. Regionally accredited. **Enrollment:** 576 degree-seeking undergraduates. **Degrees:** 55 associate awarded. **Location:** 70 miles from Norfolk. **Calendar:** Semester, limited summer session. **Full-time faculty:** 20 total. **Part-time faculty:** 55 total.

Basis for selection. Open admission. **Adult students:** Entrance exam policies same as for first-time freshmen.

High school preparation. 18 units recommended. Recommended units include English 4, mathematics 3, social studies 2 and science 2.

2005-2006 Annual costs. Tuition/fees: $2,166; $6,546 out-of-state. Per-credit charge: $68 in-state; $214 out-of-state. Books/supplies: $500. Personal expenses: $1,196.

Financial aid. Need-based: Need-based aid available for part-time students.

Application procedures. Admission: No deadline. No application fee. Application may be submitted online. Admission notification on a rolling basis. **Financial aid:** Priority date 5/1; no closing date. FAFSA required. Applicants notified on a rolling basis starting 6/1; must reply within 2 week(s) of notification.

Academics. Special study options: Cross-registration, distance learning, dual enrollment of high school students, ESL. Bachelor's degree programs available on campus. License preparation in real estate. **Credit/placement by examination:** AP, CLEP, institutional tests. 30 credit hours maximum toward associate degree. Students who do not achieve minimum scores on institutional placement tests must enroll in developmental courses. **Support services:** GED preparation and test center, learning center, reduced course load, remedial instruction, study skills assistance, tutoring.

Majors. Business: Business admin, office/clerical. **Computer sciences:** General. **Education:** General, science. **Engineering:** Electrical. **Liberal arts:** Arts/sciences. **Mechanic/repair:** Electronics/electrical.

Computing on campus. 53 workstations in library, computer center. Online course registration, helpline, wireless network available.

Student life. Freshman orientation: Available. Preregistration for classes offered. **Policies:** Freshmen permitted cars on campus. **Activities:** Student government, Phi Theta Kappa, Phi Beta Lambda.

Student services. Career counseling, student employment services, financial aid counseling, health services, personal counseling, placement for graduates, veterans' counselor. **Physically disabled:** Services for visually, hearing impaired. **Transfer:** Special adviser, orientation for new students. Transfer adviser for students transferring to 4-year colleges.

Contact. E-mail: fwilson@es.vccs.edu
Phone: (757) 789-1737 Fax: (757) 789-1737
Ronald May, Vice President Academic and Student Services, Eastern Shore Community College, 29300 Lankford Highway, Melfa, VA 23410-9755

ECPI Technical College

Richmond, Virginia
www.ecpi.edu **CB code: 3145**

- For-profit 2-year technical college
- Small city

General. Accredited by ACCSCT. **Calendar:** Continuous.

Annual costs/financial aid. Required fee is for books. Personal expenses: $2,072.

Contact. Phone: (804) 359-3535
Director of Admissions, 800 Moorefield Park Drive, Richmond, VA 23236

ECPI Technical College: Roanoke

Roanoke, Virginia
www.ecpitech.edu **CB code: 3147**

- For-profit 2-year technical college
- Commuter campus in small city

General. Accredited by ACCSCT. **Calendar:** Continuous.

Annual costs/financial aid. Personal expenses: $2,072. Need-based financial aid available to full-time and part-time students.

Contact. Phone: (540) 563-8080
Director, 5234 Airport Road, Roanoke, VA 24012

Germanna Community College

Locust Grove, Virginia
www.gcc.vccs.edu **CB code: 5276**

- Public 2-year community college
- Commuter campus in rural community

General. Founded in 1969. Regionally accredited. Off-campus sites in high schools; 18 dual enrollment programs with local school districts. **Enrollment:** 5,019 undergraduates. **Degrees:** 364 associate awarded. **Location:** 15 miles from Culpeper, 18 miles from Fredericksburg. **Calendar:** Semester, limited summer session. **Full-time faculty:** 50 total; 54% women. **Part-time faculty:** 261 total; 59% women. **Class size:** 41% < 20, 59% 20-39. **Special facilities:** Art exhibits, local history collection.

Student profile. 42% enrolled in a transfer program, 26% enrolled in a vocational program.

Out-of-state:	1%	**25 or older:**	30%

Transfer out. 57% of students enrolled in the transfer program go on to 4-year colleges. **Colleges most students transferred to 2005:** Mary Washington College, Old Dominion University, Radford University, Virginia Commonwealth University, James Madison University.

Basis for selection. Open admission, but selective for some programs. Special requirements for nursing program with local applicants given preference. **Adult students:** SAT/ACT scores not required. SAT scores, GCC placement tests, or proof of college transcripts required. **Homeschooled:** Transcript of courses and grades required. Provide current copy of signed home school agreement between appropriate school system and authorizing parent or guardian. Provide written recommendation from home school teacher or tutor.

2005-2006 Annual costs. Tuition/fees: $2,173; $6,567 out-of-state. Per-credit charge: $68 in-state; $214 out-of-state. Books/supplies: $800. Personal expenses: $2,400.

2004-2005 Financial aid. Need-based: 91% of total undergraduate aid awarded as scholarships/grants, 9% as loans/jobs. Need-based aid available for part-time students. Work study available for part-time students. **Non-need-based:** Scholarships awarded for academics.

Application procedures. Admission: No deadline. No application fee. Application may be submitted online. Admission notification on a rolling basis. Nursing program applications must be completed by February 1. **Financial aid:** Priority date 4/1; no closing date. FAFSA required. Applicants notified on a rolling basis starting 5/15; must reply within 2 week(s) of notification.

Academics. Systemwide core curriculum to ensure ease of transfer. **Special study options:** Accelerated study, cross-registration, distance learning, double major, dual enrollment of high school students, ESL, independent study, internships, liberal arts/career combination, weekend college. Bachelor's degree programs available on campus. License preparation in dental hygiene, nursing. **Credit/placement by examination:** AP, CLEP, institutional tests. 8 credit hours maximum toward associate degree. **Support services:** GED test center, pre-admission summer program, reduced course load, remedial instruction, study skills assistance, tutoring.

Majors. Biology: General. **Business:** General, business admin. **Computer sciences:** General. **Education:** General. **Health:** Dental hygiene, nursing (RN). **Liberal arts:** Arts/sciences. **Physical sciences:** General.

Most popular majors. Biological/life sciences 10%, business/marketing 17%, computer/information sciences 9%, education 9%, health sciences 15%, liberal arts 37%.

Computing on campus. 90 workstations in library, computer center. Online course registration, online library, wireless network available.

Student life. Freshman orientation: Mandatory. Preregistration for classes offered. **Policies:** Freshmen permitted cars on campus. **Activities:** Student government, student newspaper, Black studies, student Christian associations.

Athletics. Team name: Grizzly Bears.

Student services. Career counseling, student employment services, financial aid counseling, personal counseling, placement for graduates, veterans' counselor. **Physically disabled:** Services for visually, hearing impaired. **Transfer:** Special adviser, orientation for new students. Transfer adviser, college fairs on campus for students transferring to 4-year colleges.

Contact. Phone: (540) 727-3030 Fax: (540) 727-3389
Rita Dunston, Registrar, Germanna Community College, 2130 Germanna Highway, Locust Grove, VA 22508-2102

J. Sargeant Reynolds Community College

Richmond, Virginia
www.reynolds.edu **CB code: 5676**

- Public 2-year community college
- Commuter campus in very large city

General. Founded in 1972. Regionally accredited. **Enrollment:** 7,621 degree-seeking undergraduates. **Degrees:** 727 associate awarded. **ROTC:** Army. **Location:** Downtown. **Calendar:** Semester, extensive summer session. **Full-time faculty:** 135 total. **Part-time faculty:** 450 total. **Special facilities:** Hospitality development center, distance education center. **Partnerships:** Formal partnerships with local medical facilities, Microsoft, IBM, Heilig Meyers, Richmond-Times Dispatch, Henrico Industrial Authority, Henrico County.

Student profile. Among degree-seeking undergraduates, 26% enrolled in a transfer program, 40% enrolled in a vocational program.

Out-of-state:	1%	**25 or older:**	57%

Transfer out. Colleges most students transferred to 2005: Virginia Commonwealth University, Old Dominion University.

Basis for selection. Open admission, but selective for some programs. Special requirements for nursing, health technology, engineering, legal assisting programs; interview recommended. **Adult students:** Entrance exam policies same as for first-time freshmen.

High school preparation. College preparatory units recommended for applicants to college transfer programs. Recommended units vary per program of study and include up to 4 English, 4 mathematics, 2 lab science, 2 foreign language, 2 social studies.

2005-2006 Annual costs. Tuition/fees: $2,269; $6,649 out-of-state. Per-credit charge: $68 in-state; $214 out-of-state. Books/supplies: $1,000. Personal expenses: $900.

Financial aid. Need-based: Need-based aid available for part-time students. Work study available nights, weekends and for part-time students. **Non-need-based:** Scholarships awarded for academics.

Application procedures. Admission: No deadline. No application fee. Application may be submitted online. Admission notification on a rolling basis beginning on or about 1/15. **Financial aid:** Priority date 6/30; no closing date. FAFSA required. Applicants notified on a rolling basis starting 7/15; must reply within 2 week(s) of notification.

Academics. Special study options: Cooperative education, distance learning, double major, dual enrollment of high school students, ESL, independent study, internships, weekend college. License preparation in dental hygiene, nursing, paramedic, real estate. **Credit/placement by examination:** AP, CLEP, IB, institutional tests. 53 credit hours maximum toward associate degree. Essay required for composition and literature subject exams (CLEP). **Support services:** Learning center, pre-admission summer program, reduced course load, remedial instruction, study skills assistance, tutoring, writing center.

Majors. Agriculture: Horticulture, landscaping, ornamental horticulture, turf management. **Business:** General, accounting, administrative services, business admin, fashion, hospitality admin, marketing. **Computer sciences:** General, computer science, data processing, information systems, programming. **Education:** Early childhood. **Engineering:** General. **Engineering technology:** Architectural, civil, electrical. **Family/consumer sciences:** Child care, institutional food production. **Health:** Clinical lab technology, dental lab technology, nursing (RN), occupational therapy assistant, optician, respiratory therapy technology. **Interdisciplinary:** Biological/physical sciences, natural sciences. **Legal studies:** Paralegal. **Liberal arts:** Arts/sciences. **Mechanic/repair:** Automotive. **Personal/culinary services:** Culinary arts. **Protective services:** Criminal justice, firefighting. **Public administration:** Community org/advocacy. **Social sciences:** General.

Computing on campus. 1,100 workstations in library, computer center, student center. Commuter students can connect to campus network. Online course registration, helpline, repair service available.

Student life. Freshman orientation: Available, $42 fee. **Activities:** Music ensembles, student government, TV station, Phi Theta Kappa, Student nurses association, SGA, Phi Beta Lambda, NAACP, African American Achievement Alliance, Young Republicans, Baptist student union.

Student services. Career counseling, student employment services, financial aid counseling, personal counseling, veterans' counselor. **Physically disabled:** Services for visually, speech, hearing impaired. **Transfer:** Special adviser, orientation for new students. Transfer adviser, college fairs on campus for students transferring to 4-year colleges.

Contact. E-mail: kpettis-walden@reynolds.edu
Phone: (804) 523-5029 Fax: (804) 371-3650
Karen Pettis-Walden, Director of Admissions and Records, J. Sargeant Reynolds Community College, Admissions and Records, Richmond, VA 23285-5622

John Tyler Community College

Chester, Virginia
www.jtcc.edu
CB member
CB code: 5342

- Public 2-year community college
- Commuter campus in small city

General. Founded in 1965. Regionally accredited. **Enrollment:** 3,681 degree-seeking undergraduates. **Degrees:** 148 associate awarded. **ROTC:** Army. **Location:** 16 miles from Richmond. **Calendar:** Semester, extensive summer session. **Full-time faculty:** 66 total. **Part-time faculty:** 253 total. **Partnerships:** Formal partnership with Virgina Power.

Student profile.

Out-of-state:	2%	25 or older:	43%

Basis for selection. Open admission, but selective for some programs. Special requirements for nursing, funeral services and police science programs.

High school preparation. Biology and/or chemistry required for allied health programs.

2005-2006 Annual costs. Tuition/fees: $2,171; $6,551 out-of-state. Per-credit charge: $68 in-state; $214 out-of-state.

2004-2005 Financial aid. Need-based: 76% of total undergraduate aid awarded as scholarships/grants, 24% as loans/jobs. Need-based aid available for part-time students. Work study available nights, weekends and for part-time students. **Non-need-based:** Scholarships awarded for academics, state residency.

Application procedures. Admission: Priority date 8/1; no deadline. No application fee. Admission notification on a rolling basis. High school students may attend with written approval of school principal. **Financial aid:** Priority date 5/15, closing date 7/15. FAFSA required. Applicants notified on a rolling basis starting 6/20.

Academics. Students seeking associate degree must complete 25% of core courses at college. **Special study options:** Cooperative education, distance learning, dual enrollment of high school students, internships, weekend college. 2-2 transfer programs in various engineering technology disciplines and business education; 1-3 transfer certificate in art. License preparation in nursing. **Credit/placement by examination:** AP, CLEP, IB, institutional tests. **Support services:** Learning center, remedial instruction, study skills assistance, tutoring.

Majors. Business: General, administrative services. **Computer sciences:** General, programming, systems analysis. **Education:** Teacher assistance. **Engineering:** Architectural, civil, electrical, environmental, mechanical. **Engineering technology:** Architectural, electrical, manufacturing, mechanical. **Family/consumer sciences:** Child care. **Health:** Nursing (RN). **Liberal arts:** Arts/sciences. **Personal/culinary services:** Mortuary science. **Public administration:** Human services. **Visual/performing arts:** Studio arts.

Most popular majors. Business/marketing 11%, education 6%, engineering/engineering technologies 15%, health sciences 22%, liberal arts 34%, personal/culinary services 8%.

Computing on campus. 165 workstations in library, student center. Commuter students can connect to campus network. Online course registration, online library available.

Student life. Freshman orientation: Mandatory. Preregistration for classes offered. **Policies:** Freshmen permitted cars on campus. **Activities:** Drama, literary magazine, student government, student newspaper, student nurses association, data processing club, human services organization, business honor society, funeral services student organization, biology club, art club.

Student services. Adult student services, alcohol/substance abuse counseling, career counseling, financial aid counseling, personal counseling, veterans' counselor. **Physically disabled:** Services for visually, speech, hearing impaired. **Transfer:** Special adviser for new students. Transfer adviser, college fairs on campus for students transferring to 4-year colleges.

Contact. E-mail: AdmissionsandRecords@jtcc.edu
Phone: (804) 706-5220 Toll-free number: (800) 552-3490
Fax: (804) 796-4362
Joy James, Coordinator of Admission, John Tyler Community College, 13101 Jefferson Davis Highway, Chester, VA 23831-5316

Lord Fairfax Community College

Middletown, Virginia
www.lfcc.edu
CB member
CB code: 5381

- Public 2-year community college
- Commuter campus in rural community

General. Founded in 1969. Regionally accredited. Students can enroll at Fauquier Campus in Warrenton. **Enrollment:** 5,490 undergraduates. **Degrees:** 458 associate awarded. **Location:** 12 miles from Winchester, 70 miles from Washington, DC. **Calendar:** Semester, limited summer session. **Full-time faculty:** 58 total. **Part-time faculty:** 120 total.

Student profile. 36% enrolled in a transfer program, 21% enrolled in a vocational program.

Transfer out. Colleges most students transferred to 2005: Shenandoah University; Old Dominion University.

Basis for selection. Open admission. **Adult students:** Entrance exam policies same as for first-time freshmen.

2005-2006 Annual costs. Tuition/fees: $2,171; $6,551 out-of-state. Per-credit charge: $68 in-state; $214 out-of-state. Books/supplies: $800. Personal expenses: $1,312.

Financial aid. All financial aid based on need. Need-based aid available for part-time students.

Application procedures. Admission: No deadline. No application fee. Application may be submitted online. Admission notification on a rolling basis. **Financial aid:** Priority date 5/1; no closing date. FAFSA required. Applicants notified on a rolling basis starting 6/1.

Academics. System-wide core curriculum to ensure ease of transfer. **Special study options:** Cooperative education, distance learning, double major, dual enrollment of high school students, ESL, honors, independent study. Bachelor's degree programs available on campus. License preparation in dental hygiene, nursing. **Credit/placement by examination:** AP, CLEP, institutional tests. 32 credit hours maximum toward associate degree. 50% of hours needed for degree may be earned by examination. **Support services:** Learning center, reduced course load, remedial instruction, tutoring.

Majors. Agriculture: Business, horticulture. **Business:** General, accounting, administrative services, business admin, management information systems, office management. **Communications:** General. **Computer sciences:** General, programming. **Conservation:** Management/policy. **Education:** General. **Engineering technology:** Civil, electrical. **Health:** Dental hygiene, nursing (RN), prepharmacy. **Interdisciplinary:** Biological/physical sciences. **Liberal arts:** Arts/sciences.

Most popular majors. Business/marketing 22%, computer/information sciences 7%, education 12%, health sciences 13%, liberal arts 35%.

Computing on campus. 650 workstations in library, computer center, student center. Online course registration, online library, wireless network available.

Student life. Freshman orientation: Available. Preregistration for classes offered. **Policies:** Freshmen permitted cars on campus. **Activities:** Drama, musical theater, student government, special interest and program-related organizations, ambassador's club, honor society, business fraternity.

Athletics. Intercollegiate: Soccer. **Team name:** Cannons.

Student services. Adult student services, career counseling, services for economically disadvantaged, student employment services, financial aid counseling, personal counseling, placement for graduates, veterans' counselor, women's services. **Physically disabled:** Services for visually, speech, hearing impaired. **Transfer:** Special adviser, orientation for new students. Transfer center, transfer adviser, college fairs on campus for students transferring to 4-year colleges.

Contact. E-mail: admissions@lfcc.edu
Phone: (540) 868-7107 Toll-free number: (800) 906-5322
Fax: (540) 868-7005
Barbara Ratcliff, Director of Enrollment Management, Lord Fairfax Community College, 173 Skirmisher Lane, Middletown, VA 22645

Miller-Motte Technical College: Lynchburg

Lynchburg, Virginia
www.miller-motte.com

- For-profit 2-year technical college
- Commuter campus in small city
- Interview required

General. Enrollment: 215 degree-seeking undergraduates. **Degrees:** 77 associate awarded. **Location:** 60 miles from Charlottesville, 180 miles from Richmond. **Calendar:** Quarter. **Full-time faculty:** 5 total; 20% minority, 60% women. **Part-time faculty:** 31 total; 6% have terminal degrees, 3% minority, 84% women. **Special facilities:** College-operated massage therapy clinic, aesthetics clinic.

Student profile. Among degree-seeking undergraduates, 100% enrolled in a vocational program, 10% already have a bachelor's degree or higher.

Basis for selection. Open admission. Students must have either a high school diploma or GED. All applicants are required to complete the admissions process before acceptance as a student. **Adult students:** Entrance exam policies same as for first-time freshmen.

Financial aid. All financial aid based on need. Need-based aid available for part-time students. Work study available nights and for part-time students.

Application procedures. Admission: No deadline. $35 fee. Application must be submitted on paper. Admission notification on a rolling basis. **Financial aid:** No deadline. FAFSA required. Applicants notified on a rolling basis.

Academics. Special study options: Cooperative education, dual enrollment of high school students. **Credit/placement by examination:** AP, CLEP, institutional tests. Students are encouraged to test out of introductory classes if they feel they have the necessary experience. There is a $100 nonrefundable examination fee. Students are not encouraged to test out of advanced classes leading to the associate degree. **Support services:** Learning center, tutoring.

Majors. Business: Management science. **Computer sciences:** General. **Health:** Massage therapy, medical assistant, office assistant, pharmacy assistant, surgical technology.

Computing on campus. 75 workstations in library, computer center.

Student life. Freshman orientation: Available. Preregistration for classes offered.

Student services. Student employment services, financial aid counseling.

Contact. Phone: (434) 239-5222 Toll-free number: (877) 333-6622
Fax: (434) 239-1069
Miller-Motte Technical College: Lynchburg, 1011 Creekside Lane, Lynchburg, VA 24502

Mountain Empire Community College

Big Stone Gap, Virginia
www.me.vccs.edu **CB code: 5451**

- Public 2-year community college
- Commuter campus in small town

General. Founded in 1970. Regionally accredited. **Enrollment:** 1,743 degree-seeking undergraduates; 1,211 non-degree-seeking students. **Degrees:** 187 associate awarded. **Location:** 40 miles from Bristol. **Calendar:** Semester, limited summer session. **Full-time faculty:** 50 total. **Part-time faculty:** 80 total.

Student profile. Among degree-seeking undergraduates, 42% enrolled in a transfer program, 55% enrolled in a vocational program, 1,135 enrolled as first-time, first-year students, 108 transferred in from other institutions. Of all enrolled students, 1% already have a bachelor's degree or higher.

Part-time:	42%	**Women:**	66%
Out-of-state:	4%	**25 or older:**	40%

Transfer out. 90% of students enrolled in the transfer program go on to 4-year colleges. **Colleges most students transferred to 2005:** University of Virginia's College at Wise, Radford University, Virginia Polytechnic Institute and State University, East Tennessee State University.

Basis for selection. Open admission, but selective for some programs. Nursing students must meet admission test score, plus biology, chemistry and algebra I required. Respiratory therapy students must meet admission test score, plus algebra I and biology required. High school diploma or GED required for practical nursing, nursing and respiratory care programs. **Adult students:** Entrance exam policies same as for first-time freshmen.

High school preparation. Recommended units include English 4, mathematics 1 and social studies 2. 1 algebra, 1 biology, 1 chemistry required for nursing program; 1 algebra, 1 biology required for respiratory care program.

2005-2006 Annual costs. Tuition/fees: $2,211; $6,591 out-of-state. Per-credit charge: $68 in-state; $214 out-of-state. Books/supplies: $860.

2004-2005 Financial aid. Need-based: 98% of total undergraduate aid awarded as scholarships/grants, 2% as loans/jobs. Need-based aid available for part-time students. Work study available for part-time students. **Non-need-based:** Scholarships awarded for academics, state residency. **Additional information:** The college does not participate in loan programs. All financial aid is in form of grants, scholarships, or work study.

Application procedures. Admission: No deadline. No application fee. Application may be submitted online. Admission notification on a rolling basis beginning on or about 1/1. **Financial aid:** Priority date 5/1; no closing date. FAFSA required. Applicants notified on a rolling basis starting 1/1.

Academics. System-wide core curriculum to ensure ease of transfer. **Special study options:** Accelerated study, distance learning, double major, dual enrollment of high school students, independent study, internships, liberal arts/career combination, student-designed major. Bachelor's degree programs available on campus. **Credit/placement by examination:** AP, CLEP, IB, institutional tests. 16 credit hours maximum toward associate degree. Maximum 25% of credits awarded for work and/or life experience. **Support services:** Learning center, pre-admission summer program, reduced course load, remedial instruction, tutoring.

Majors. Agriculture: Soil science. **Biology:** General. **Business:** General, accounting, business admin, office management, office/clerical. **Computer sciences:** General, information systems, information technology, networking, word processing. **Conservation:** General, environmental science, forestry. **Education:** General. **Engineering:** Electrical, manufacturing. **Engineering technology:** CAD/CADD, computer hardware, electrical, manufacturing. **Health:** EMT paramedic, medical secretary, medical transcription, nursing (RN), predentistry, premedicine, prepharmacy, preveterinary, respiratory therapy technology. **Legal studies:** Legal secretary, paralegal, prelaw. **Liberal arts:** Arts/sciences. **Math:** General. **Mechanic/repair:** Electronics/electrical. **Protective services:** Corrections, criminal justice, law enforcement admin. **Public administration:** Social work.

Most popular majors. Business/marketing 17%, computer/information sciences 16%, education 12%, health sciences 10%, legal studies 6%, liberal arts 26%.

Computing on campus. 400 workstations in library, computer center.

Student life. Freshman orientation: Mandatory. Preregistration for classes offered. **Policies:** Freshmen permitted cars on campus. **Activities:** Drama, student government, service, business, nursing organizations available.

Athletics. Intramural: Archery, badminton, basketball, bowling, softball, table tennis, tennis, volleyball.

Student services. Career counseling, student employment services, financial aid counseling, health services, personal counseling, placement for graduates, veterans' counselor. **Transfer:** Special adviser, orientation, preadmission transcript evaluation for new students. Transfer adviser for students transferring to 4-year colleges.

Contact. E-mail: pcarroll@me.vccs.edu
Phone: (276) 523-2400 Fax: (276) 523-8297
Perry Carroll, Director of Enrollment Services, Mountain Empire Community College, 3441 Mountain Empire Road, Big Stone Gap, VA 24219

National College of Business & Technology: Bluefield

Bluefield, Virginia
www.ncbt.edu **CB code: 3246**

- For-profit 2-year business college
- Commuter campus in small city

General. Accredited by ACICS. **Enrollment:** 170 degree-seeking undergraduates. **Degrees:** 45 associate awarded. **Calendar:** Quarter. **Full-time faculty:** 1 total. **Part-time faculty:** 24 total.

Basis for selection. Open admission. Interview recommended.

2006-2007 Annual costs. Tuition/fees: $8,976. Per-credit charge: $187. Books/supplies: $1,200.

Financial aid. All financial aid based on need. Need-based aid available for part-time students.

Application procedures. Admission: No deadline. $30 fee, may be waived for applicants with need. Application may be submitted online. Admission notification on a rolling basis. **Financial aid:** No deadline. FAFSA required. Applicants notified on a rolling basis starting 9/1.

Academics. Special study options: Double major, internships, liberal arts/career combination. **Credit/placement by examination:** CLEP, institutional tests. **Support services:** Tutoring.

Majors. Business: Accounting, administrative services, business admin, office management. **Computer sciences:** Computer science. **Health:** Medical assistant.

Computing on campus. 35 workstations in computer center.

Student life. Freshman orientation: Mandatory. Preregistration for classes offered.

Student services. Career counseling, personal counseling. **Transfer:** Special adviser, orientation for new students.

Contact. E-mail: tharris@ncbt.edu
Phone: (540) 326-3621 Fax: (276) 650-2516
Larry Steele, Vice President of Admissions, National College of Business & Technology: Bluefield, 100 Logan Street, Bluefield, VA 24605

National College of Business & Technology: Charlottesville

Charlottesville, Virginia
www.ncbt.edu **CB code: 3248**

- For-profit 2-year business college
- Commuter campus in small city
- Interview required

General. Accredited by ACICS. **Enrollment:** 126 degree-seeking undergraduates. **Degrees:** 36 associate awarded. **Calendar:** Quarter, limited summer session. **Full-time faculty:** 7 total. **Part-time faculty:** 19 total.

Basis for selection. Open admission.

2006-2007 Annual costs. Tuition/fees: $8,976. Books/supplies: $1,200.

Financial aid. All financial aid based on need. Need-based aid available for part-time students.

Application procedures. Admission: No deadline. $30 fee, may be waived for applicants with need. Application may be submitted online. Admission notification on a rolling basis. **Financial aid:** No deadline. FAFSA required. Applicants notified on a rolling basis.

Academics. Special study options: Double major, internships, liberal arts/career combination. **Credit/placement by examination:** CLEP, institutional tests. **Support services:** Tutoring.

Majors. Business: Accounting, administrative services, business admin. **Computer sciences:** Computer science. **Health:** Medical assistant.

Computing on campus. 35 workstations in library, computer center.

Student life. Freshman orientation: Mandatory. Preregistration for classes offered.

Student services. Transfer: Special adviser, orientation for new students.

Contact. Phone: (804) 295-0136 Toll-free number: (800) 664-1886
Fax: (804) 979-8061
Larry Steele, Vice President of Admissions, National College of Business & Technology: Charlottesville, 1819 Emmet Street, Charlottesville, VA 22901

National College of Business & Technology: Danville

Danville, Virginia
www.ncbt.edu **CB code: 3249**

- For-profit 2-year branch campus and business college
- Commuter campus in small city

General. Accredited by ACICS. **Enrollment:** 262 degree-seeking undergraduates. **Degrees:** 43 associate awarded. **Calendar:** Quarter, limited summer session. **Full-time faculty:** 5 total. **Part-time faculty:** 31 total.

Basis for selection. Open admission. Interview recommended.

2006-2007 Annual costs. Tuition/fees: $8,976. Per-credit charge: $187. Books/supplies: $1,200.

Financial aid. All financial aid based on need. Need-based aid available for part-time students.

Application procedures. Admission: No deadline. $30 fee, may be waived for applicants with need. Application may be submitted online. Admission notification on a rolling basis. **Financial aid:** No deadline. FAFSA required. Applicants notified on a rolling basis starting 9/1.

Academics. Special study options: Double major, internships. **Credit/placement by examination:** CLEP, institutional tests. **Support services:** Tutoring.

Majors. Business: Accounting, administrative services, business admin. **Computer sciences:** Computer science. **Health:** Medical assistant.

Computing on campus. 35 workstations in library, computer center.

Student life. Freshman orientation: Mandatory. Preregistration for classes offered.

Student services. Career counseling, student employment services, personal counseling, placement for graduates. **Transfer:** Special adviser, orientation for new students.

Contact. E-mail: market@educorp.edu
Phone: (804) 793-6822
Larry Steele, Director of Admissions, National College of Business & Technology: Danville, PO Box 6400, Roanoke, VA 24017

National College of Business & Technology: Harrisonburg

Harrisonburg, Virginia
www.ncbt.edu **CB code: 3173**

- For-profit 2-year business college
- Commuter campus in large town

General. Accredited by ACICS. **Enrollment:** 234 degree-seeking undergraduates. **Degrees:** 31 associate awarded. **Calendar:** Quarter, limited summer session. **Full-time faculty:** 7 total. **Part-time faculty:** 12 total.

Basis for selection. Open admission. Interview recommended.

2006-2007 Annual costs. Tuition/fees: $8,976. Per-credit charge: $187. Books/supplies: $1,200.

Financial aid. All financial aid based on need. Need-based aid available for part-time students.

Application procedures. Admission: No deadline. $30 fee, may be waived for applicants with need. Application may be submitted online. Admission notification on a rolling basis. **Financial aid:** No deadline. FAFSA required. Applicants notified on a rolling basis starting 9/1.

Academics. Special study options: Double major, internships. **Credit/placement by examination:** CLEP, institutional tests. **Support services:** Tutoring.

Majors. Business: Accounting, administrative services, business admin, office management. **Computer sciences:** Computer science. **Health:** Medical assistant.

Computing on campus. 35 workstations in library, computer center.

Student life. Freshman orientation: Mandatory.

Student services. Career counseling, personal counseling. **Transfer:** Special adviser, orientation for new students.

Contact. E-mail: market@educorp.edu
Phone: (540) 432-0943 Fax: (540) 432-1133
Larry Steele, Director of Admissions, National College of Business & Technology: Harrisonburg, PO Box 6400, Roanoke, VA 24017

National College of Business & Technology: Lynchburg

Lynchburg, Virginia
www.ncbt.edu **CB code: 3172**

- For-profit 2-year business college
- Commuter campus in small city

General. Accredited by ACICS. **Enrollment:** 283 degree-seeking undergraduates. **Degrees:** 76 associate awarded. **Calendar:** Quarter, limited summer session. **Full-time faculty:** 1 total. **Part-time faculty:** 34 total.

Basis for selection. Open admission. Interview recommended.

2006-2007 Annual costs. Tuition/fees: $8,976. Per-credit charge: $187. Books/supplies: $1,200.

Financial aid. All financial aid based on need. Need-based aid available for part-time students.

Application procedures. Admission: No deadline. $30 fee, may be waived for applicants with need. Application may be submitted online. Admission notification on a rolling basis. **Financial aid:** No deadline. FAFSA required. Applicants notified on a rolling basis starting 9/1.

Academics. Special study options: Double major, internships. **Credit/placement by examination:** CLEP, institutional tests. **Support services:** Tutoring.

Majors. Business: Accounting, administrative services, business admin. **Computer sciences:** General, computer science. **Health:** Medical assistant.

Computing on campus. 35 workstations in library, computer center.

Student life. Freshman orientation: Mandatory. Preregistration for classes offered.

Student services. Career counseling, student employment services, financial aid counseling, personal counseling, placement for graduates, veterans' counselor. **Transfer:** Special adviser, orientation for new students.

Contact. E-mail: market@educorp.edu
Phone: (804) 239-3500 Toll-free number: (800) 664-1886
Larry Steele, Vice President of Admissions, National College of Business & Technology: Lynchburg, PO Box 6400, Roanoke, VA 24017

National College of Business & Technology: Martinsville

Martinsville, Virginia
www.ncbt.edu **CB code: 3171**

- Private 2-year business and junior college
- Commuter campus in small city

General. Accredited by ACICS. **Enrollment:** 277 degree-seeking undergraduates. **Degrees:** 56 associate awarded. **Calendar:** Quarter, limited summer session. **Full-time faculty:** 5 total. **Part-time faculty:** 27 total.

Basis for selection. Open admission.

2006-2007 Annual costs. Tuition/fees: $8,976. Per-credit charge: $187. Books/supplies: $1,200.

Financial aid. All financial aid based on need. Need-based aid available for part-time students.

Application procedures. Admission: No deadline. $30 fee, may be waived for applicants with need. Application may be submitted online. Admission notification on a rolling basis. **Financial aid:** No deadline. FAFSA required. Applicants notified on a rolling basis.

Academics. Special study options: Double major, internships. **Credit/placement by examination:** CLEP, institutional tests. **Support services:** Tutoring.

Majors. Business: Accounting, administrative services, business admin. **Computer sciences:** Computer science.

Computing on campus. 35 workstations in library, computer center.

Student life. Freshman orientation: Mandatory. Preregistration for classes offered.

Student services. Career counseling, student employment services, personal counseling. **Transfer:** Special adviser, orientation for new students.

Contact. Phone: (540) 632-5621
Larry Steele, Admissions Vice President, National College of Business & Technology: Martinsville, PO Box 6400, Roanoke, VA 24017

National College of Business & Technology: Tri Cities/Bristol

Roanoke, Virginia
www.ncbt.edu **CB code: 3247**

- For-profit 2-year business college
- Commuter campus in large town

General. Accredited by ACICS. **Calendar:** Quarter.

Annual costs/financial aid. Tuition/fees (2005-2006): $8,544. Books/supplies: $1,200. Need-based financial aid available to full-time and part-time students.

Contact. Phone: (276) 669-5333
Director of Admissions, 300 A Piedmont Avenue, Bristol, VA 24201

New River Community College

Dublin, Virginia
www.nr.edu **CB code: 5513**

- Public 2-year community college
- Commuter campus in rural community

General. Founded in 1966. Regionally accredited. **Enrollment:** 2,105 degree-seeking undergraduates. **Degrees:** 319 associate awarded. **ROTC:** Navy. **Location:** 50 miles from Roanoke. **Calendar:** Semester, limited summer

Two-Year Colleges

session. **Full-time faculty:** 55 total. **Part-time faculty:** 136 total. **Class size:** 57% < 20, 36% 20-39, 5% 40-49, 1% 50-99, less than 1% >100.

Transfer out. Colleges most students transferred to 2005: Radford University, Virginia Tech, Old Dominion University.

Basis for selection. Open admission. Interview required for nursing program.

2005-2006 Annual costs. Tuition/fees: $2,170; $6,550 out-of-state. Per-credit charge: $68 in-state; $214 out-of-state. Books/supplies: $700. Personal expenses: $1,200.

2004-2005 Financial aid. Need-based: 69% of total undergraduate aid awarded as scholarships/grants, 31% as loans/jobs. Need-based aid available for part-time students.

Application procedures. Admission: No deadline. No application fee. Admission notification on a rolling basis. **Financial aid:** Priority date 4/15; no closing date. FAFSA, institutional form required. Applicants notified on a rolling basis starting 6/1.

Academics. Special study options: Cooperative education, distance learning, dual enrollment of high school students, teacher certification program. License preparation in real estate. **Credit/placement by examination:** AP, CLEP, institutional tests. **Support services:** GED preparation and test center, learning center, remedial instruction, study skills assistance, tutoring, writing center.

Majors. Business: Accounting, administrative services, business admin, logistics, office technology. **Computer sciences:** General, computer graphics, networking, programming. **Education:** General, early childhood. **Engineering:** General, computer. **Engineering technology:** Architectural, drafting, electrical, instrumentation. **Health:** Medical secretary. **Interdisciplinary:** Biological/physical sciences, gerontology. **Legal studies:** Legal secretary, paralegal. **Liberal arts:** Arts/sciences. **Mechanic/repair:** Automotive. **Production:** Machine shop technology. **Protective services:** Forensics, law enforcement admin. **Public administration:** Human services.

Most popular majors. Business/marketing 44%, engineering/engineering technologies 16%, health sciences 11%, liberal arts 24%.

Computing on campus. Commuter students can connect to campus network. Online course registration, repair service available.

Student life. Freshman orientation: Available. **Activities:** Concert band, choral groups, literary magazine, music ensembles, TV station, Black Student Union, Phi Beta Lambda, Phi Theta Kappa.

Athletics. Intramural: Basketball, soccer, softball, table tennis, tennis, volleyball. **Team name:** Knights.

Student services. Career counseling, student employment services, on-campus daycare, personal counseling, placement for graduates, veterans' counselor. **Physically disabled:** Services for visually, hearing impaired. **Learning disabled:** Comprehensive services available. **Transfer:** Special adviser, orientation for new students. Transfer adviser, college fairs on campus for students transferring to 4-year colleges.

Contact. E-mail: nrtaylm@nr.edu
Phone: (540) 674-3603 Toll-free number: (866) 462-6722
Fax: (540) 674-3644
Margaret Taylor, Coordinator of Admissions and Records, New River Community College, Drawer 1127, Dublin, VA 24084

Northern Virginia Community College

Annandale, Virginia
www.nv.cc.va.us

CB member
CB code: 5515

- Public 2-year community college
- Commuter campus in small city

General. Founded in 1965. Regionally accredited. 5 campuses in Alexandria, Annandale, Loudoun County, Manassas, Woodbridge. **Enrollment:** 10,500 full-time, degree-seeking students. **Degrees:** 2,699 associate awarded. **Location:** 12 miles from Washington, DC. **Calendar:** Semester, limited summer session. **Full-time faculty:** 550 total. **Part-time faculty:** 1,020 total.

Transfer out. Colleges most students transferred to 2005: George Mason University.

Basis for selection. Open admission, but selective for some programs. Admission to health and veterinary technology programs based on academic prerequisites, placement tests, and space availability. Interview recommended for allied health, animal science, dental hygiene, nursing programs.

2005-2006 Annual costs. Tuition/fees: $2,146; $6,526 out-of-state. Per-credit charge: $68 in-state; $214 out-of-state. Books/supplies: $550. Personal expenses: $1,920.

Financial aid. Non-need-based: Scholarships awarded for academics, athletics, state residency.

Application procedures. Admission: No deadline. No application fee. Admission notification on a rolling basis. **Financial aid:** Priority date 3/1; no closing date. FAFSA, institutional form required. Applicants notified on a rolling basis starting 5/15; must reply within 2 week(s) of notification.

Academics. Systemwide core curriculum to ensure ease of transfer. **Special study options:** Cooperative education, distance learning, double major, dual enrollment of high school students, ESL, honors, independent study, internships, liberal arts/career combination, student-designed major, study abroad, weekend college. Old Dominion University Teletechnet degree programs. **Credit/placement by examination:** AP, CLEP, IB, institutional tests. Maximum of 75% of credit hours required for program may be awarded through CLEP. 25% of requirements must be completed at institution. **Support services:** Learning center, reduced course load, remedial instruction, tutoring, writing center.

Majors. Agriculture: Horticultural science. **Business:** Accounting, business admin, international, management information systems, office management, purchasing, real estate, tourism/travel. **Communications:** General. **Computer sciences:** General, computer science, programming. **Education:** Art, early childhood. **Engineering:** Civil. **Engineering technology:** Architectural, civil, drafting, electrical. **Family/consumer sciences:** Institutional food production. **Health:** Clinical lab assistant, clinical lab technology, dental hygiene, EMT paramedic, medical radiologic technology/radiation therapy, medical records technology, physical therapy assistant, respiratory therapy technology, substance abuse counseling, veterinary technology/assistant. **Interdisciplinary:** Biological/physical sciences, biopsychology, gerontology. **Legal studies:** Paralegal. **Liberal arts:** Arts/sciences. **Math:** General. **Mechanic/repair:** Aircraft, automotive, electronics/electrical, heating/ac/refrig. **Parks/recreation:** Facilities management. **Protective services:** Fire safety technology, fire services admin, law enforcement admin, security services. **Psychology:** General. **Public administration:** Human services. **Transportation:** Aviation. **Visual/performing arts:** Commercial photography, commercial/advertising art, interior design, photography, studio arts.

Computing on campus. 2,000 workstations in library, computer center.

Student life. Activities: Bands, choral groups, dance, drama, music ensembles, musical theater, student government, student newspaper, symphony orchestra, TV station, honor societies, African American student organizations, religious groups, Korean and Vietnamese student organizations, data processing management club, art association, physical therapist assistants club, Omega Engineering Students, international student council.

Athletics. Intramural: Basketball, football (tackle), soccer, volleyball.

Student services. Career counseling, veterans' counselor. **Physically disabled:** Services for visually, hearing impaired. **Transfer:** Special adviser for new students. Transfer adviser, college fairs on campus for students transferring to 4-year colleges.

Contact. Phone: (703) 323-3000
Northern Virginia Community College, 4001 Wakefield Chapel Road, Annandale, VA 22003-3796

Parks College: Arlington

Arlington, Virginia

- For-profit 2-year branch campus and business college
- Large city
- Interview required

General. Accredited by ACICS. Parks College is part of the Corinthian College system. **Enrollment:** 644 degree-seeking undergraduates. **Degrees:** 85 associate awarded. **Calendar:** Quarter.

Student profile. Among degree-seeking undergraduates, 100% enrolled in a vocational program.

Basis for selection. Adult students: SAT/ACT scores not required.

Application procedures. Admission: No deadline. $25 fee. Application may be submitted online. Admission notification on a rolling basis.

Academics. Credit/placement by examination: CLEP.

Majors. Business: General. **Legal studies:** Paralegal. **Protective services:** Criminal justice, law enforcement admin, police science.

Contact. E-mail: elubin@cci.edu
Phone: (703) 248-8887 Toll-free number: (888) 741-4270
Mr. Ed Lubin, Director of Admissions, Parks College: Arlington, 801 North Quincy Street, Arlington, VA 22207

Parks College: Tysons Corner

McLean, Virginia
www.parks-college.com

- For-profit 2-year branch campus college
- Large city

General. Accredited by ACICS. Branch campus of Blair College (Colorado Springs, CO). **Enrollment:** 301 degree-seeking undergraduates. **Calendar:** Quarter. **Full-time faculty:** 3 total. **Part-time faculty:** 11 total.

Academics. Credit/placement by examination: CLEP.

Contact. E-mail: dbrent@cci.edu
Phone: (703) 288-3131 Toll-free number: (888) 741-4270
Fax: (703) 288-3757
Deborah Brent, Director of Admissions, Parks College: Tysons Corner, 1430 Spring Hill Road, Suite 200, McLean, VA 22102

Patrick Henry Community College

Martinsville, Virginia
www.ph.vccs.edu **CB code: 5549**

- Public 2-year community college
- Commuter campus in large town

General. Founded in 1962. Regionally accredited. **Enrollment:** 3,229 degree-seeking undergraduates. **Degrees:** 327 associate awarded. **Location:** 50 miles from Roanoke, 50 miles from Greensboro, North Carolina. **Calendar:** Semester, limited summer session. **Full-time faculty:** 46 total. **Part-time faculty:** 122 total. **Special facilities:** Southern history collection, Virginia literature collection, fine arts theater.

Student profile.

Out-of-state:	1%	**25 or older:**	50%

Basis for selection. Open admission. High school diploma or GED required for some programs.

2005-2006 Annual costs. Tuition/fees: $2,151; $6,531 out-of-state. Per-credit charge: $68 in-state; $214 out-of-state. Books/supplies: $500. Personal expenses: $840.

Financial aid. Need-based: Need-based aid available for part-time students.

Application procedures. Admission: Priority date 8/1; no deadline. No application fee. Admission notification on a rolling basis beginning on or about 2/1. Deadline for nursing applicants 03/01. **Financial aid:** Priority date 6/1; no closing date. FAFSA required. Applicants notified on a rolling basis starting 6/15.

Academics. System-wide core curriculum to ensure ease of transfer. **Special study options:** Cooperative education, distance learning, double major, dual enrollment of high school students, independent study, internships, teacher certification program, weekend college. Bachelor's degree programs available on campus. License preparation in nursing. **Credit/placement by examination:** CLEP, institutional tests. 12 credit hours maximum toward associate degree. **Support services:** Learning center, pre-admission summer program, reduced course load, remedial instruction, study skills assistance, tutoring, writing center.

Majors. Business: Accounting, business admin. **Computer sciences:** General, programming. **Engineering technology:** Drafting. **Legal studies:** Paralegal. **Liberal arts:** Arts/sciences.

Computing on campus. 500 workstations in library, computer center. Commuter students can connect to campus network. Online library, helpline, repair service available.

Student life. Activities: Choral groups, drama, musical theater, student government, student newspaper, TV station, Black student association, Phi Theta Kappa, campus awareness network, nurses association.

Athletics. Intercollegiate: Baseball M, basketball M, soccer M, softball M. **Intramural:** Basketball, football (tackle) M, soccer, softball, table tennis, tennis, volleyball. **Team name:** Patriots.

Student services. Adult student services, career counseling, student employment services, personal counseling, placement for graduates, veterans' counselor. **Physically disabled:** Services for visually, speech, hearing impaired. **Transfer:** Special adviser for new students. Transfer adviser, college fairs on campus for students transferring to 4-year colleges.

Contact. E-mail: gvalentine@ph.vccs.edu
Phone: (276) 656-0325 Toll-free number: (800) 232-7997
Fax: (276) 656-0352
Graham Valentine, Admissions Counselor, Patrick Henry Community College, Box 5311, Martinsville, VA 24115-5311

Paul D. Camp Community College

Franklin, Virginia
www.pc.vccs.edu **CB code: 5557**

- Public 2-year community college
- Commuter campus in small town

General. Founded in 1970. Regionally accredited. Campuses in Franklin and Suffolk, site in Smithsfield. **Enrollment:** 793 degree-seeking undergraduates. **Degrees:** 105 associate awarded. **Location:** 50 miles from Norfolk. **Calendar:** Semester, limited summer session. **Full-time faculty:** 25 total. **Part-time faculty:** 60 total. **Class size:** 87% < 20, 11% 20-39, 2% 40-49.

Transfer out. Colleges most students transferred to 2005: Old Dominion University, Christopher Newport University, Norfolk State University.

Basis for selection. Open admission, but selective for some programs. Limited enrollment to nursing programs. **Adult students:** Entrance exam policies same as for first-time freshmen. **Homeschooled:** Student must provide to the Admissions and Records Office a current copy of a signed home school agreement between the appropriate school system and the authorizing parent or guardian. See home school student enrollment section in college catalog.

High school preparation. Recommended units include English 4, mathematics 2, social studies 2, history 2, science 2 (laboratory 2) and foreign language 1.

2005-2006 Annual costs. Tuition/fees: $2,121; $6,501 out-of-state. Per-credit charge: $68 in-state; $214 out-of-state. Books/supplies: $500. Personal expenses: $900.

Financial aid. Need-based: Need-based aid available for part-time students. Work study available nights and for part-time students.

Application procedures. Admission: Priority date 8/1; no deadline. No application fee. Application may be submitted online. Admission notification on a rolling basis. **Financial aid:** Priority date 6/1; no closing date. FAFSA required. Applicants notified on a rolling basis starting 8/1; must reply within 2 week(s) of notification.

Academics. Special study options: Cross-registration, distance learning, dual enrollment of high school students, honors, independent study, internships. License preparation in nursing, real estate. **Credit/placement by examination:** AP, CLEP, institutional tests. 52 credit hours maximum toward associate degree. **Support services:** Learning center, pre-admission summer program, reduced course load, remedial instruction, study skills assistance, tutoring.

Majors. Business: Administrative services, business admin, office management. **Computer sciences:** General. **Education:** General. **Engineering technology:** Drafting, electrical. **Health:** Nursing (RN). **Interdisciplinary:** Biological/physical sciences. **Mechanic/repair:** Electronics/electrical. **Protective services:** Police science.

Most popular majors. Business/marketing 22%, computer/information sciences 13%, interdisciplinary studies 6%, liberal arts 37%, security/protective services 18%.

Computing on campus. 100 workstations in library, computer center. Online course registration, online library available.

Student life. Freshman orientation: Mandatory. Preregistration for classes offered. **Policies:** Freshmen permitted cars on campus. **Activities:** Student government, student newspaper, honor societies, Circle K.

Athletics. Intramural: Volleyball.

Student services. Career counseling, student employment services, personal counseling, placement for graduates, veterans' counselor. **Transfer:** Special adviser, orientation, pre-admission transcript evaluation for new students. College fairs on campus for students transferring to 4-year colleges.

Contact. Phone: (757) 569-6700 Fax: (757) 569-6795
Monette Williams, Director of Student Development Services, Paul D. Camp Community College, 100 North College Drive, Franklin, VA 23851-0737

Piedmont Virginia Community College

Charlottesville, Virginia
www.pvcc.edu
CB member
CB code: 5561

- Public 2-year community college
- Commuter campus in large town

General. Founded in 1969. Regionally accredited. **Enrollment:** 2,806 degree-seeking undergraduates; 1,358 non-degree-seeking students. **Degrees:** 287 associate awarded. **ROTC:** Army, Air Force. **Location:** 70 miles from Richmond. **Calendar:** Semester, limited summer session. **Full-time faculty:** 55 total; 44% have terminal degrees, 9% minority, 56% women. **Part-time faculty:** 157 total; 8% minority, 51% women. **Class size:** 58% < 20, 39% 20-39, 2% 40-49, less than 1% 50-99. **Partnerships:** With local businesses, including nursing/retirement home and hospitals.

Student profile. Among degree-seeking undergraduates, 69% enrolled in a transfer program, 31% enrolled in a vocational program, 6% already have a bachelor's degree or higher, 630 enrolled as first-time, first-year students.

Part-time:	66%	**Asian American:**	2%
Out-of-state:	5%	**Hispanic American:**	2%
Women:	61%	**International:**	2%
African American:	15%	**25 or older:**	38%

Transfer out. 60% of students enrolled in the transfer program go on to 4-year colleges. **Colleges most students transferred to 2005:** University of Virginia, James Madison University, Virginia Commonwealth University, Old Dominion University, Mary Baldwin College.

Basis for selection. Open admission, but selective for some programs. Special requirements for nursing program; interview recommended. **Adult students:** Entrance exam policies same as for first-time freshmen. **Home-schooled:** Students must meet with Dean of Student Services prior to enrolling.

2005-2006 Annual costs. Tuition/fees: $2,199; $6,579 out-of-state. Per-credit charge: $68 in-state; $214 out-of-state. Books/supplies: $950. Personal expenses: $1,908.

2004-2005 Financial aid. All financial aid based on need. 96% of total undergraduate aid awarded as scholarships/grants, 4% as loans/jobs. Need-based aid available for part-time students. Work study available nights and for part-time students.

Application procedures. Admission: No deadline. No application fee. Application may be submitted online. Admission notification on a rolling basis. Accepted applicants to nursing program must reply within 10 days. **Financial aid:** Priority date 3/31; no closing date. FAFSA, institutional form required. Applicants notified on a rolling basis starting 5/1.

Academics. System-wide core curriculum to ensure ease of transfer. **Special study options:** Accelerated study, cooperative education, distance learning, dual enrollment of high school students, ESL, honors, independent study, internships, weekend college. License preparation in aviation, nursing, paramedic, real estate. **Credit/placement by examination:** AP, CLEP, institutional tests. **Support services:** Learning center, reduced course load, remedial instruction, study skills assistance, tutoring.

Majors. Biology: Biotechnology. **Business:** General, administrative services, business admin, management information systems. **Computer sciences:** Applications programming, LAN/WAN management, programming, web page design. **Construction:** Carpentry, electrician, masonry, plumbing. **Education:** General. **Engineering technology:** General, electrical, manufacturing, mechanical. **Health:** EMT paramedic, licensed practical nurse. **Interdisciplinary:** Biological/physical sciences. **Liberal arts:** Arts/sciences. **Physical sciences:** General. **Protective services:** Police science. **Science technology:** Biological. **Visual/performing arts:** General.

Most popular majors. Business/marketing 29%, health sciences 23%, interdisciplinary studies 8%, liberal arts 24%, security/protective services 6%.

Computing on campus. 339 workstations in library, computer center. Online course registration, online library, helpline, wireless network available.

Student life. Policies: Freshmen permitted cars on campus. **Activities:** Choral groups, dance, drama, student government, student newspaper, Black student alliance, Phi Theta Kappa, Christian Fellowship Organization, Ambassadors club, international club, engineering club, Masquers club, Chem Club.

Athletics. Intramural: Basketball, bowling, football (non-tackle), golf, lacrosse, soccer, softball, tennis, volleyball, weight lifting.

Student services. Adult student services, career counseling, services for economically disadvantaged, student employment services, financial aid counseling, personal counseling, placement for graduates, veterans' counselor. **Physically disabled:** Services for visually, speech, hearing impaired. **Transfer:** Special adviser, orientation for new students. Transfer adviser, college fairs on campus for students transferring to 4-year colleges.

Contact. E-mail: admissions@pvcc.edu
Phone: (434) 961-5404 Fax: (434) 961-5425
Tracey Templeton, Registrar, Piedmont Virginia Community College, 501 College Drive, Charlottesville, VA 22902-7589

Rappahannock Community College

Glenns, Virginia
www.rcc.vccs.edu
CB code: 5590

- Public 2-year community college
- Commuter campus in rural community

General. Founded in 1970. Regionally accredited. **Enrollment:** 2,870 undergraduates. **Degrees:** 133 associate awarded. **Location:** 12 miles from West Point. **Calendar:** Semester, limited summer session. **Full-time faculty:** 30 total. **Part-time faculty:** 100 total.

Basis for selection. Open admission. In-house test used for assessment purposes.

2005-2006 Annual costs. Tuition/fees: $2,151; $6,531 out-of-state. Per-credit charge: $68 in-state; $214 out-of-state. Books/supplies: $690. Personal expenses: $1,500.

Financial aid. Need-based: Need-based aid available for part-time students.

Application procedures. Admission: No application fee. Admission notification on a rolling basis. **Financial aid:** Priority date 5/15; no closing date. FAFSA, institutional form required. Applicants notified on a rolling basis starting 6/30.

Academics. Special study options: Cooperative education, cross-registration, distance learning, double major, dual enrollment of high school students, independent study, internships, liberal arts/career combination. Bachelor's degree programs available on campus. License preparation in nursing. **Credit/placement by examination:** AP, CLEP, institutional tests. **Support services:** Learning center, reduced course load, remedial instruction, study skills assistance, tutoring.

Majors. Business: Accounting, accounting/business management, business admin. **Computer sciences:** Information systems. **Education:** General. **Engineering technology:** General, electrical, electromechanical. **Health:** Nursing (RN). **Liberal arts:** Arts/sciences. **Protective services:** Criminal justice.

Computing on campus. 48 workstations in library, computer center. Online course registration, online library available.

Student life. Freshman orientation: Mandatory. Preregistration for classes offered. **Activities:** Student government, Phi Theta Kappa Honors Society.

Athletics. Intramural: Baseball M, bowling, table tennis, tennis, volleyball.

Student services. Adult student services, career counseling, services for economically disadvantaged, student employment services, financial aid counseling, personal counseling, placement for graduates, veterans' counselor. **Physically disabled:** Services for visually, speech, hearing impaired. **Transfer:** Special adviser, orientation for new students. Transfer adviser, college fairs on campus for students transferring to 4-year colleges.

Contact. Phone: (804) 758-6700 Fax: (804) 758-3852
Willnet Willis, Admissions and Student Records Officer, Rappahannock Community College, 12745 College Drive, Glenns, VA 23149

Richard Bland College

Petersburg, Virginia **CB member**
www.rbc.edu **CB code: 5574**

- Public 2-year junior and liberal arts college
- Commuter campus in small city
- Application essay required

General. Founded in 1960. Regionally accredited. Prepares students to transfer with junior status to a wide variety of public and private institutions located in Virginia. Affiliated with The College of William and Mary. **Enrollment:** 1,105 degree-seeking undergraduates; 332 non-degree-seeking students. **Degrees:** 214 associate awarded. **ROTC:** Army. **Location:** 25 miles from Richmond. **Calendar:** Semester, limited summer session. **Full-time faculty:** 35 total. **Part-time faculty:** 25 total. **Class size:** 46% < 20, 46% 20-39, 6% 40-49, 3% 50-99. **Special facilities:** Nature trail, Civil War sites.

Student profile. Among degree-seeking undergraduates, 401 enrolled as first-time, first-year students, 91 transferred in from other institutions.

Part-time:	28%	**Asian American:**	2%
Out-of-state:	2%	**Hispanic American:**	2%
Women:	65%	**Native American:**	1%
African American:	19%	**25 or older:**	15%

Transfer out. 50% of students enrolled in the transfer program go on to 4-year colleges. **Colleges most students transferred to 2005:** Virginia Commonwealth University, College of William and Mary, James Madison University, Longwood University, Virginia Tech University, Virginia State University.

Basis for selection. Academic record most important; test scores, essay also important; recommendations, extracurricular activities, interview considered. SAT or ACT recommended. All students must take COMPASS placement test. Interview recommended depending on GPA. **Adult students:** Entrance exam policies same as for first-time freshmen. **Homeschooled:** GED required. **Learning Disabled:** Students eligible for ADA must meet with coordinator for Counseling and Diversity Programs to request services.

High school preparation. 13 units required. Required units include English 4, mathematics 3, history 2, science 2 and foreign language 2.

2005-2006 Annual costs. Tuition/fees: $2,514; $9,772 out-of-state. Per-credit charge: $91 in-state; $398 out-of-state. Books/supplies: $700. Personal expenses: $1,500.

2004-2005 Financial aid. Need-based: 44 full-time freshmen applied for aid; 38 were judged to have need; 38 of these received aid. Average need met was 50%. Average scholarship/grant was $728. 98% of total undergraduate aid awarded as scholarships/grants, 2% as loans/jobs. Need-based aid available for part-time students. Work study available for part-time students. **Non-need-based:** Awarded to 183 full-time undergraduates, including 11 freshmen. Scholarships awarded for academics, state residency.

Application procedures. Admission: Priority date 5/15; deadline 8/15. $20 fee, may be waived for applicants with need. Admission notification on a rolling basis beginning on or about 2/1. **Financial aid:** Priority date 5/1; no closing date. FAFSA, institutional form required. Applicants notified by 6/1; must reply within 2 week(s) of notification.

Academics. Special study options: Dual enrollment of high school students. Educational trips abroad during spring break and summer session for academic credit, as a junior college, we provide the general education curriculum necessary to prepare students to transfer as juniors to 4-year programs. Bachelor's degree programs available on campus. **Credit/placement by examination:** AP, CLEP, institutional tests. 24 credit hours maximum toward associate degree. **Support services:** Remedial instruction, tutoring, writing center.

Majors. Business: General. **Liberal arts:** Arts/sciences. **Physical sciences:** General.

Computing on campus. 75 workstations in library, computer center. Commuter students can connect to campus network. Online course registration, online library available.

Student life. Freshman orientation: Available. Preregistration for classes offered. One-day program. **Policies:** Campus-wide honor code observed. Freshmen permitted cars on campus. **Activities:** Choral groups, dance, drama, literary magazine, music ensembles, student government, student newspaper, International Unity, Christian Ministries, Spanish club, Gay Lesbian Bisexual Transgender Alliance, Student Ambassadors, wellness club.

Athletics. Intramural: Basketball, cheerleading W, golf, softball, tennis, volleyball.

Student services. Career counseling, financial aid counseling. **Physically disabled:** Services for visually, speech, hearing impaired. **Transfer:** Pre-admission transcript evaluation for new students. Transfer adviser, college fairs on campus for students transferring to 4-year colleges.

Contact. E-mail: admit@rbc.edu
Phone: (804) 862-6249 Fax: (804) 862-6490
Randy Dean, Director of Admissions and Student Activities, Richard Bland College, 11301 Johnson Road, Petersburg, VA 23805

Southside Virginia Community College

Alberta, Virginia
www.sv.vccs.edu **CB code: 5660**

- Public 2-year community college
- Commuter campus in rural community
- Interview required

General. Founded in 1970. Regionally accredited. Additional campuses at John H. Daniel Campus, Keysville, VA; Campus Without Walls, Emporia, VA. **Enrollment:** 2,390 degree-seeking undergraduates; 2,473 non-degree-seeking students. **Degrees:** 329 associate awarded. **ROTC:** Army. **Location:** 70 miles from Richmond. **Calendar:** Semester, limited summer session. **Full-time faculty:** 75 total; 13% have terminal degrees, 16% minority, 51% women. **Part-time faculty:** 204 total; 4% have terminal degrees, 20% minority, 70% women. **Special facilities:** Nature trail, fitness trail. **Partnerships:** Workforce development programs, tech prep program with high schools.

Student profile. Among degree-seeking undergraduates, 25% enrolled in a transfer program, 75% enrolled in a vocational program, 366 enrolled as first-time, first-year students.

Part-time:	55%	**Asian American:**	1%
Out-of-state:	1%	**Hispanic American:**	1%
Women:	74%	**25 or older:**	46%
African American:	43%		

Transfer out. 90% of students enrolled in the transfer program go on to 4-year colleges. **Colleges most students transferred to 2005:** Longwood University, Old Dominion University, Saint Paul's College, Virginia Commonwealth University.

Basis for selection. Open admission, but selective for some programs. National League for Nursing Pre-Admissions Examination required for nursing applicants. Psychological Services Bureau Revised Aptitude for Practical Nursing Examination required for practical nursing applicants. **Adult students:** Entrance exam policies same as for first-time freshmen. **Homeschooled:** If not enrolled in program leading to a completion credential, student should obtain GED.

2005-2006 Annual costs. Tuition/fees: $2,181; $6,561 out-of-state. Per-credit charge: $68 in-state; $214 out-of-state. Books/supplies: $1,040. Personal expenses: $1,922.

2005-2006 Financial aid. Need-based: 97% of total undergraduate aid awarded as scholarships/grants, 3% as loans/jobs. Need-based aid available for part-time students. Work study available nights and for part-time students. **Non-need-based:** Scholarships awarded for academics.

Application procedures. Admission: No deadline. No application fee. Application may be submitted online. Admission notification on a rolling basis. **Financial aid:** Priority date 6/1, closing date 8/1. FAFSA required. Applicants notified on a rolling basis starting 6/15.

Academics. Systemwide core curriculum to ensure ease of transfer. **Special study options:** Cross-registration, distance learning, dual enrollment of high school students, honors, internships, study abroad. Cooperative programs in respiratory therapy with J. Sargeant Reynolds Community College; medical laboratory program with Central Virginia Community College. Bachelor's degree programs available on campus. License preparation in nursing. **Credit/placement by examination:** AP, CLEP, institutional tests. 45 credit hours maximum toward associate degree. **Support services:** GED preparation and test center, reduced course load, remedial instruction, study skills assistance, tutoring.

Majors. Business: Administrative services, business admin, management science. **Computer sciences:** General. **Education:** General. **Engineering technology:** Drafting, electrical. **Health:** Clinical lab technology, nursing (RN), respiratory therapy technology. **Interdisciplinary:** Biological/physical sciences. **Liberal arts:** Arts/sciences. **Protective services:** Police science. **Public administration:** Human services.

Most popular majors. Business/marketing 22%, health sciences 28%, liberal arts 39%, security/protective services 8%.

Computing on campus. 200 workstations in library, computer center.

Student life. Freshman orientation: Mandatory, $73 fee. Preregistration for classes offered. **Policies:** Freshmen permitted cars on campus. **Activities:** Choral groups, drama, music ensembles, student government, Phi Theta Kappa, Criminal Justice Organization, Phi Beta Lambda, Lambda Alpha Epsilon, Alpha Delta Omega.

Athletics. Intramural: Basketball, softball, table tennis, tennis, volleyball.

Student services. Career counseling, financial aid counseling, personal counseling, veterans' counselor. **Transfer:** Special adviser, orientation, pre-admission transcript evaluation for new students. College fairs on campus for students transferring to 4-year colleges.

Contact. E-mail: Rhina.Jones@sv.vccs.edu
Phone: (434) 949-1000 Fax: (434) 949-7863
Ronald Mattox, Dean of Admissions, Records and Institutional Research, Southside Virginia Community College, 109 Campus Drive, Alberta, VA 23821

Southwest Virginia Community College

Richlands, Virginia
www.sw.edu **CB code: 5659**

- Public 2-year community college
- Commuter campus in small town

General. Founded in 1967. Regionally accredited. **Enrollment:** 3,446 degree-seeking undergraduates. **Degrees:** 348 associate awarded. **Location:** 45 miles from Bluefield and Bristol. **Calendar:** Semester, extensive summer session. **Full-time faculty:** 75 total. **Part-time faculty:** 210 total. **Class size:** 79% < 20, 18% 20-39, less than 1% 40-49, 2% 50-99.

Student profile. Among degree-seeking undergraduates, 28% enrolled in a transfer program, 73% enrolled in a vocational program, 1% already have a bachelor's degree or higher.

Part-time:	56%	**African American:**	2%
Out-of-state:	2%	**25 or older:**	55%
Women:	59%		

Transfer out. 33% of students enrolled in the transfer program go on to 4-year colleges. **Colleges most students transferred to 2005:** Virginia Tech, Radford University, University of Virginia at Wise, East Tennessee State University.

Basis for selection. Open admission, but selective for some programs. Special requirements for engineering and health programs. Interview required for full-time.

High school preparation. Subject and unit requirements vary with degree programs.

2005-2006 Annual costs. Tuition/fees: $2,166; $6,546 out-of-state. Per-credit charge: $68 in-state; $214 out-of-state. Books/supplies: $650. Personal expenses: $1,250.

Financial aid. All financial aid based on need.

Application procedures. Admission: No deadline. No application fee. Admission notification on a rolling basis. Applicants for nursing and allied health programs must apply by January 15 and reply within 2 weeks of acceptance. No deferred admission for these programs. **Financial aid:** Priority date 5/30; no closing date. FAFSA, institutional form required. Applicants notified on a rolling basis starting 7/1.

Academics. Special study options: Accelerated study, cooperative education, distance learning, double major, dual enrollment of high school students, honors, independent study, internships. **Credit/placement by examination:** AP, CLEP. **Support services:** Learning center, pre-admission summer program, reduced course load, remedial instruction, study skills assistance, tutoring, writing center.

Majors. Business: General, accounting, administrative services, business admin, managerial economics. **Computer sciences:** General. **Conservation:** Environmental studies. **Education:** General, early childhood. **Engineering:** General, electrical. **Health:** EMT paramedic, health services, medical radiologic technology/radiation therapy, medical secretary, nursing (RN), radiologic technology/medical imaging, respiratory therapy assistant. **Liberal arts:** Arts/sciences. **Protective services:** Corrections, police science. **Public administration:** Human services.

Most popular majors. Business/marketing 11%, computer/information sciences 6%, education 23%, health sciences 19%, liberal arts 28%.

Computing on campus. 150 workstations in library, computer center. Commuter students can connect to campus network. Online course registration, online library available.

Student life. Freshman orientation: Mandatory, $68 fee. **Activities:** Jazz band, choral groups, literary magazine, student government, student newspaper, Intervoice Club, Black Student Union, Phi Theta Kappa, Lion's Club, International Friends, Phi Beta Lambda, Lambda Alpha Epsilon, Helping Minds, Campus Crusade for Christ.

Athletics. Intercollegiate: Baseball M, basketball M, cheerleading M, golf M. **Intramural:** Baseball M, basketball M, bowling, racquetball, rugby M, softball, tennis, volleyball, weight lifting. **Team name:** Eagles.

Student services. Career counseling, student employment services, financial aid counseling, health services, personal counseling, placement for graduates, veterans' counselor. **Physically disabled:** Services for visually, hearing impaired. **Transfer:** Special adviser, orientation for new students. Transfer adviser, college fairs on campus for students transferring to 4-year colleges.

Contact. E-mail: admissions@sw.edu
Phone: (276) 964-2555 Toll-free number: (800) 822-7822
Fax: (276) 964-7716
Jim Farris, Director of Admissions and Counseling, Southwest Virginia Community College, 369 College Road, Richlands, VA 24641-1101

TESST College of Technology: Alexandria

Alexandria, Virginia
www.tesst.com

- For-profit 2-year technical college
- Small city

General. Accredited by ACCSCT. **Calendar:** Semester.

Annual costs/financial aid. Medical, IT, and Criminal Justice programs range from $5,000 to $12,000 per year.

Contact. Phone: (703) 354-1005
Executive Director, 6315 Bren Mar Drive, Alexandria, VA 22312

Thomas Nelson Community College

Hampton, Virginia
www.tncc.edu **CB code: 5793**

- Public 2-year community college
- Commuter campus in small city

General. Founded in 1967. Regionally accredited. **Enrollment:** 6,498 degree-seeking undergraduates; 2,097 non-degree-seeking students. **Degrees:** 640 associate awarded. **ROTC:** Army. **Location:** 20 miles from Norfolk, 35 miles from Virginia Beach. **Calendar:** Semester, extensive summer session. **Full-time faculty:** 92 total; 56% women. **Part-time faculty:** 395 total; 47% women.

Student profile. Among degree-seeking undergraduates, 1,211 enrolled as first-time, first-year students.

Part-time:	62%	**Women:**	62%

Transfer out. Colleges most students transferred to 2005: Christopher Newport University, Old Dominion University, Norfolk State University, Hampton University.

Basis for selection. Open admission, but selective for some programs. Special requiremenst for nursing program. **Homeschooled:** Must be 18 or have GED.

High school preparation. Nursing program requires specific high school units.

2005-2006 Annual costs. Tuition/fees: $2,142; $6,522 out-of-state. Per-credit charge: $68 in-state; $214 out-of-state. Books/supplies: $1,600. Personal expenses: $794.

Financial aid. Need-based: Need-based aid available for part-time students. Work study available nights and for part-time students.

Application procedures. **Admission:** No deadline. No application fee. Application may be submitted online. Admission notification on a rolling basis. **Financial aid:** Priority date 5/1; no closing date. FAFSA required. Applicants notified on a rolling basis starting 6/1; must reply within 2 week(s) of notification.

Academics. System-wide core curriculum to ensure ease of transfer, 2-2 program available. **Special study options:** Accelerated study, cooperative education, cross-registration, distance learning, dual enrollment of high school students, ESL, honors, independent study, internships, weekend college. License preparation in nursing. **Credit/placement by examination:** AP, CLEP, institutional tests. SAT Critical Reading or ACT English tests may be substituted for institutional placement examinations if scores high enough. **Support services:** Learning center, remedial instruction, study skills assistance, tutoring, writing center.

Majors. **Business:** Accounting, business admin, management science, office management. **Computer sciences:** General, computer graphics, computer science, information systems, networking, programming. **Education:** Early childhood. **Engineering:** General, electrical. **Engineering technology:** CAD/CADD, electrical. **Health:** Optician. **Interdisciplinary:** Natural sciences. **Liberal arts:** Arts/sciences. **Mechanic/repair:** Automotive. **Protective services:** Fire services admin, law enforcement admin. **Public administration:** General, human services, social work. **Social sciences:** General. **Visual/performing arts:** Commercial/advertising art, photography, studio arts.

Computing on campus. Online library available.

Student life. **Freshman orientation:** Available. **Policies:** Freshmen permitted cars on campus. **Activities:** Choral groups, dance, drama, literary magazine, student government, student newspaper, Baptist student union, disabled students concerns union, human resources club, black student alliance, Phi Theta Kappa.

Athletics. **Intramural:** Basketball. **Team name:** Gators.

Student services. Career counseling, student employment services, financial aid counseling, personal counseling, placement for graduates, veterans' counselor. **Physically disabled:** Services for visually, speech, hearing impaired. **Transfer:** Special adviser, orientation for new students. Transfer center, transfer adviser, college fairs on campus for students transferring to 4-year colleges.

Contact. E-mail: Admissions@tncc.edu
Phone: (757) 825-2800 Fax: (757) 825-2763
Vicki Richmond, Associate Vice President for Enrollment Services, Thomas Nelson Community College, Box 9407, Hampton, VA 23670

Tidewater Community College

Norfolk, Virginia **CB member**
www.tcc.vccs.edu **CB code: 5226**

- Public 2-year community college
- Commuter campus in large city

General. Founded in 1968. Regionally accredited. Multi-location institution with campuses at Portsmouth, Virginia Beach, Chesapeake, and Norfolk. **Enrollment:** 12,196 degree-seeking undergraduates. **Degrees:** 1,731 associate awarded. **Calendar:** Semester, extensive summer session. **Full-time faculty:** 233 total; 11% minority, 48% women. **Part-time faculty:** 830 total. **Special facilities:** Visual arts center, observatory.

Student profile. Among degree-seeking undergraduates, 54% enrolled in a transfer program, 21% enrolled in a vocational program, 1,631 transferred in from other institutions.

Out-of-state:	10%	**25 or older:**	53%

Transfer out. 49% of students enrolled in the transfer program go on to 4-year colleges. **Colleges most students transferred to 2005:** Old Dominion University, Norfolk State University, Virginia Wesleyan College, Christopher Newport University.

Basis for selection. Open admission, but selective for some programs. Special requirements for health science programs. ACT required for placement for students enrolling in English or mathematics courses. Interview required for medical technologies and other limited enrollment programs. **Adult students:** Entrance exam policies same as for first-time freshmen. **Homeschooled:** Transcript of courses and grades, letter of recommendation (nonparent) required.

2005-2006 Annual costs. Tuition/fees: $2,281; $6,661 out-of-state. Per-credit charge: $68 in-state; $214 out-of-state. Books/supplies: $1,200. Personal expenses: $710.

Financial aid. All financial aid based on need. Need-based aid available for part-time students.

Application procedures. **Admission:** No deadline. No application fee. Application may be submitted online. Admission notification on a rolling basis. **Financial aid:** Priority date 4/1; no closing date. FAFSA required. Applicants notified on a rolling basis starting 4/1.

Academics. System-wide core curriculum to ensure ease of transfer. **Special study options:** Cooperative education, cross-registration, distance learning, double major, dual enrollment of high school students, ESL, honors, independent study, internships, study abroad, weekend college. Member Virginia Tidewater Consortium of Higher Education. License preparation in real estate. **Credit/placement by examination:** AP, CLEP, institutional tests. **Support services:** GED preparation and test center, learning center, reduced course load, remedial instruction, study skills assistance, tutoring, writing center.

Majors. **Agriculture:** Business technology, horticulture. **Business:** Accounting, administrative services, banking/financial services, business admin, hospitality admin, real estate, sales/distribution. **Computer sciences:** General, networking, systems analysis. **Conservation:** Environmental studies. **Education:** General, early childhood, teacher assistance. **Engineering:** General, industrial. **Engineering technology:** CAD/CADD, civil, drafting, electromechanical, occupational safety, quality control. **Foreign languages:** American Sign Language. **Health:** EMT paramedic, medical radiologic technology/radiation therapy, medical records technology, nursing (RN), occupational therapy assistant, physical therapy assistant, respiratory therapy technology. **Interdisciplinary:** Biological/physical sciences. **Legal studies:** Paralegal. **Liberal arts:** Arts/sciences. **Mechanic/repair:** Automotive, industrial. **Parks/recreation:** General, facilities management. **Personal/culinary services:** Culinary arts. **Production:** Welding. **Protective services:** Firefighting. **Public administration:** General. **Transportation:** Truck/bus/commercial vehicle. **Visual/performing arts:** Commercial/advertising art, graphic design, interior design, multimedia, photography, studio arts.

Most popular majors. Biological/life sciences 10%, business/marketing 18%, computer/information sciences 8%, education 7%, health sciences 13%, liberal arts 19%, social sciences 6%.

Computing on campus. Commuter students can connect to campus network. Online course registration available.

Student life. **Freshman orientation:** Available. **Activities:** Choral groups, drama, music ensembles, student government, student newspaper, honorary societies, black student alliance, Inter-Varsity Christian Fellowship, student nurses association.

Athletics. **Intercollegiate:** Soccer M. **Intramural:** Baseball M, basketball, bowling, golf, skiing, softball, table tennis, tennis, volleyball. **Team name:** Storm.

Student services. Adult student services, career counseling, student employment services, financial aid counseling, personal counseling, placement for graduates, veterans' counselor, women's services. **Physically disabled:** Services for visually, speech, hearing impaired. **Transfer:** Special adviser, orientation for new students. Transfer adviser, college fairs on campus for students transferring to 4-year colleges.

Contact. E-mail: tcc@tcc.vccs.edu
Phone: (757) 822-1100 Fax: (757) 822-1247
Michael Summers, Vice President for Academic and Student Affairs, Tidewater Community College, 7000 College Drive/Portsmouth Campus, Portsmouth, VA 23703

Tidewater Tech

Virginia Beach, Virginia
www.tidetech.com

- For-profit 2-year technical college

General. Accredited by ACCSCT. **Enrollment:** 570 degree-seeking undergraduates. **Degrees:** 146 associate awarded. **Calendar:** Modules begin every 5 weeks. **Full-time faculty:** 10 total. **Part-time faculty:** 20 total.

Basis for selection. Open admission, but selective for some programs.

2005-2006 Annual costs. Annual tuition varies from $18,000 to $18,200, depending on program.

Application procedures. **Admission:** No deadline. $25 fee.

Academics. **Credit/placement by examination:** CLEP.

Majors. **Business:** General. **Legal studies:** Paralegal.

Contact. E-mail: directorttv@tidetech.com
Phone: (757) 340-2121 Fax: (757) 340-9704
Jonathan Jarman, Director of Admissions, Tidewater Tech, 2697 Dean Drive, Suite 100, Virginia Beach, VA 23452

Tidewater Tech: Norfolk
Norfolk, Virginia
www.tidewatertech.edu/tidewater-tech-norfolk.asp

- Private 2-year branch campus and technical college
- Large city

General. Accredited by ACCSCT. **Calendar:** Continuous.

Contact. Phone: (757) 853-2121
7020 North Military Highway, Norfolk, VA 23518-4202

Virginia Highlands Community College
Abingdon, Virginia
www.vhcc.edu **CB code: 5927**

- Public 2-year community college
- Commuter campus in small town

General. Founded in 1967. Regionally accredited. **Enrollment:** 1,667 degree-seeking undergraduates. **Degrees:** 198 associate awarded. **Location:** 120 miles from Roanoke. **Calendar:** Semester, extensive summer session. **Full-time faculty:** 48 total; 10% have terminal degrees, 4% minority, 58% women. **Part-time faculty:** 116 total; 8% have terminal degrees, less than 1% minority, 46% women. **Special facilities:** Greenhouse.

Student profile.

Out-of-state:	11%	**25 or older:**	36%

Transfer out. Colleges most students transferred to 2005: ETSU, VA Tech, Radford, ODU and UVA@Wise.

Basis for selection. Open admission, but selective for some programs. Paramedic, nursing, radiography, physical therapy, dental hygiene, and medical laboratory technology programs have special requirements. COMPASS required for placement. **Learning Disabled:** Developmental courses are to be taken by students who test below set standards on the COMPASS and/or ASSET test.

High school preparation. College-preparatory program recommended. 12 units recommended. Recommended units include English 4, mathematics 2, social studies 4, science 1 (laboratory 1).

2005-2006 Annual costs. Tuition/fees: $2,143; $6,523 out-of-state. Per-credit charge: $68 in-state; $214 out-of-state. Books/supplies: $750. Personal expenses: $1,272.

2004-2005 Financial aid. Need-based: 89% of total undergraduate aid awarded as scholarships/grants, 11% as loans/jobs. Work study available for part-time students.

Application procedures. Admission: No deadline. No application fee. Application may be submitted online. Admission notification on a rolling basis. **Financial aid:** No deadline. FAFSA, institutional form required. Applicants notified on a rolling basis starting 5/1.

Academics. Special study options: Cooperative education, distance learning, double major, dual enrollment of high school students, independent study, internships, liberal arts/career combination. License preparation in nursing, paramedic, real estate. **Credit/placement by examination:** AP, CLEP, institutional tests. 45 credit hours maximum toward associate degree. **Support services:** Learning center, pre-admission summer program, reduced course load, remedial instruction, tutoring.

Majors. Agriculture: Farm/ranch. **Business:** Accounting, administrative services, business admin, office management. **Computer sciences:** General, data processing. **Education:** General, drama/dance. **Engineering technology:** Drafting, electrical. **Health:** Clinical lab assistant, dental hygiene, medical radiologic technology/radiation therapy, nursing (RN), physical therapy assistant. **Interdisciplinary:** Biological/physical sciences. **Legal studies:** Legal secretary. **Liberal arts:** Arts/sciences. **Protective services:** Police science. **Public administration:** Social work.

Computing on campus. 230 workstations in library, computer center, student center. Online course registration, wireless network available.

Student life. Freshman orientation: Mandatory, $68 fee. Preregistration for classes offered. **Policies:** Freshmen permitted cars on campus. **Activities:** Choral groups, drama, music ensembles, musical theater, student government, student newspaper, IMPACT Club, law enforcement club, Roteract Club, College Republicans, College Democrats, angler's club, VATNP (Nursing) Club, National Honors Society, Christian Club.

Athletics. Intramural: Basketball.

Student services. Career counseling, services for economically disadvantaged, student employment services, financial aid counseling, personal counseling, placement for graduates, veterans' counselor. **Physically disabled:** Services for visually, speech, hearing impaired. **Transfer:** Special adviser for new students. Transfer adviser, college fairs on campus for students transferring to 4-year colleges.

Contact. E-mail: dbarrett@vhcc.edu
Phone: (276) 739-2460 Fax: (276) 739-2591
David Matlock, Director of Admissions, Records and Financial Aid, Virginia Highlands Community College, PO Box 828, Abingdon, VA 24212-0828

Virginia Western Community College
Roanoke, Virginia
www.virginiawestern.edu **CB code: 5868**

- Public 2-year community college
- Commuter campus in small city

General. Founded in 1966. Regionally accredited. **Enrollment:** 8,244 undergraduates. **Degrees:** 505 associate awarded. **ROTC:** Army. **Location:** 3 miles from downtown. **Calendar:** Semester, extensive summer session. **Full-time faculty:** 89 total. **Part-time faculty:** 279 total. **Special facilities:** Arboretum.

Transfer out. Colleges most students transferred to 2005: Virginia Tech, Radford University, Old Dominion University, Roanoke College, Hollins University.

Basis for selection. Open admission, but selective for some programs. Special requirements for health programs. Interview required for health technologies. **Adult students:** SAT/ACT scores not required.

2005-2006 Annual costs. Tuition/fees: $2,168; $6,548 out-of-state. Per-credit charge: $68 in-state; $214 out-of-state. Books/supplies: $550. Personal expenses: $1,200.

Financial aid. Need-based: Need-based aid available for part-time students. **Non-need-based:** Scholarships awarded for academics, state residency.

Application procedures. Admission: No deadline. No application fee. Admission notification on a rolling basis. **Financial aid:** No deadline. FAFSA required. Applicants notified on a rolling basis starting 4/1.

Academics. Special study options: Cooperative education, distance learning, dual enrollment of high school students, external degree, honors, independent study, internships, liberal arts/career combination, study abroad, weekend college. Bachelor's degree programs available on campus. License preparation in dental hygiene, nursing, radiology, real estate. **Credit/placement by examination:** AP, CLEP, IB, institutional tests. **Support services:** Learning center, pre-admission summer program, reduced course load, remedial instruction, study skills assistance, tutoring, writing center.

Majors. Agriculture: Horticultural science, horticulture, landscaping. **Business:** General, accounting, administrative services, banking/financial services, business admin, management information systems, office technology, real estate. **Communications technology:** General. **Computer sciences:** General, computer science. **Education:** General, early childhood, social science. **Engineering:** General. **Engineering technology:** Architectural, civil, electrical. **Family/consumer sciences:** Child care. **Health:** Dental hygiene, health services, medical radiologic technology/radiation therapy, medical secretary, mental health services, nursing (RN). **Interdisciplinary:** Biological/physical sciences, natural sciences. **Legal studies:** Legal secretary, paralegal. **Liberal arts:** Arts/sciences. **Mechanic/repair:** General, heating/ac/refrig. **Protective services:** Criminal justice, police science. **Public administration:** Human services. **Social sciences:** General. **Visual/performing arts:** Commercial/advertising art, studio arts.

Computing on campus. 100 workstations in library, computer center. Online course registration, helpline, wireless network available.

Student life. Freshman orientation: Mandatory. Preregistration for classes offered. **Policies:** Freshmen permitted cars on campus. **Activities:** Choral groups, drama, student government, student newspaper, Minority Student

Alliance, Christian Fellowship,Student Government Association, Professional Organizations.

Athletics. Intramural: Baseball M, basketball, cheerleading W.

Student services. Adult student services, alcohol/substance abuse counseling, career counseling, services for economically disadvantaged, student employment services, financial aid counseling, minority student services, personal counseling, placement for graduates, veterans' counselor. **Physically disabled:** Services for visually, speech, hearing impaired. **Learning disabled:** Comprehensive services available. **Transfer:** Special adviser, orientation for new students. Transfer center, transfer adviser, college fairs on campus for students transferring to 4-year colleges.

Contact. E-mail: mpatterson@vw.vccs.edu
Phone: (540) 857-7231 Fax: (540) 857-6102
Meg Patterson, Admissions and Records Coordinator/Registrar, Virginia Western Community College, Box 14007, Roanoke, VA 24038

Wytheville Community College

Wytheville, Virginia
www.wcc.vccs.edu **CB code: 5917**

- Public 2-year community college
- Commuter campus in small town

General. Founded in 1962. Regionally accredited. **Enrollment:** 723 degree-seeking undergraduates. **Degrees:** 269 associate awarded. **Location:** 74 miles from Roanoke. **Calendar:** Semester, limited summer session. **Full-time faculty:** 40 total. **Part-time faculty:** 100 total.

Basis for selection. Open admission, but selective for some programs. Limited admissions to allied health programs. High school transcripts required of all allied health applicants. Interview required for allied health, police science. **Adult students:** Entrance exam policies same as for first-time freshmen. **Homeschooled:** Statement describing homeschool structure and mission required.

2005-2006 Annual costs. Tuition/fees: $2,151; $6,531 out-of-state. Per-credit charge: $68 in-state; $214 out-of-state. Books/supplies: $700. Personal expenses: $200.

Financial aid. All financial aid based on need. Need-based aid available for part-time students.

Application procedures. Admission: No deadline. No application fee. Admission notification on a rolling basis. **Financial aid:** Priority date 4/1; no closing date. FAFSA, institutional form required. Applicants notified on a rolling basis starting 5/1; must reply within 4 week(s) of notification.

Academics. Special study options: Distance learning, dual enrollment of high school students, honors, independent study, internships. **Credit/placement by examination:** AP, CLEP, institutional tests. **Support services:** Remedial instruction, tutoring.

Majors. Business: Accounting, administrative services, business admin, managerial economics. **Computer sciences:** Information systems. **Construction:** Electrician, plumbing. **Education:** General. **Engineering:** Computer. **Engineering technology:** Drafting, electrical. **Family/consumer sciences:** Child care. **Health:** Clinical lab technology, dental hygiene. **Interdisciplinary:** Biological/physical sciences. **Liberal arts:** Arts/sciences. **Protective services:** Police science.

Most popular majors. Business/marketing 20%, computer/information sciences 6%, education 11%, health sciences 39%, liberal arts 11%, security/protective services 6%.

Computing on campus. 133 workstations in library, computer center, student center.

Student life. Activities: Concert band, drama, student government, student newspaper.

Athletics. Intramural: Basketball, softball, table tennis, tennis, volleyball.

Student services. Career counseling, student employment services, personal counseling, placement for graduates, veterans' counselor. **Physically disabled:** Services for visually, hearing impaired. **Transfer:** Special adviser for new students. College fairs on campus for students transferring to 4-year colleges.

Contact. E-mail: wcdixxs@wc.cc.va.us
Phone: (276) 223-4700 Toll-free number: (800) 468-1195
Fax: (276) 223-4860
Sherry Dix, Registrar, Wytheville Community College, 1000 East Main Street, Wytheville, VA 24382

Two-Year Colleges

Washington

Bates Technical College

Tacoma, Washington
www.bates.ctc.edu/
CB code: 4152

- Public 2-year technical college
- Small city

General. **Enrollment:** 3,000 undergraduates. **Degrees:** 150 associate awarded. **Calendar:** Quarter. **Full-time faculty:** 130 total.

Basis for selection. COMPASS required for admission.

Application procedures. **Admission:** No deadline. No application fee.

Academics. **Credit/placement by examination:** CLEP.

Majors. **Business:** Accounting technology. **Computer sciences:** Information technology, programming. **Health:** Dental lab technology, licensed practical nurse. **Mechanic/repair:** General, heavy equipment. **Protective services:** Fire safety technology, fire services admin.

Contact. E-mail: registration@bates.ctc.edu
Phone: (253) 680-7002
Bates Technical College, 1101 South Yakima Avenue, Tacoma, WA 98405

Bellevue Community College

Bellevue, Washington
www.bcc.ctc.edu
CB code: 4029

- Public 2-year community college
- Commuter campus in small city

General. Founded in 1965. Regionally accredited. **Enrollment:** 4,631 degree-seeking undergraduates; 8,419 non-degree-seeking students. **Degrees:** 1,539 associate awarded. **Location:** 12 miles from Seattle. **Calendar:** Quarter, limited summer session. **Full-time faculty:** 145 total; 14% have terminal degrees, 14% minority, 51% women. **Part-time faculty:** 361 total; 9% have terminal degrees, 7% minority, 53% women. **Special facilities:** Planetarium, National Workforce Center for Emerging Technologies, greenhouses, observatory, scanning electron microscope.

Student profile. Among degree-seeking undergraduates, 47% enrolled in a transfer program, 30% enrolled in a vocational program, 15% already have a bachelor's degree or higher, 176 enrolled as first-time, first-year students.

Part-time:	52%	**Asian American:**	12%
Out-of-state:	6%	**Hispanic American:**	1%
Women:	57%	**Native American:**	1%
African American:	4%	**International:**	3%

Transfer out. **Colleges most students transferred to 2005:** University of Washington, Washington State University, Central Washington University, Seattle University, Western Washington University.

Basis for selection. Open admission, but selective for some programs. Interview, essay, 2 letters of recommendation, transcripts required of applicants to allied health programs, including radiologic technology, diagnostic ultrasound, radiation therapy. **Adult students:** Entrance exam policies same as for first-time freshmen. **Homeschooled:** Must be at least 18 years old. **Learning Disabled:** Through Disability Support Services Office, student may request reasonable classroom accommodations. Student must provide documentation from appropriate professional.

High school preparation. Allied health programs have special requirements.

2005-2006 Annual costs. Tuition/fees: $2,655; $7,863 out-of-state. Per-credit charge: $79 in-state; $251 out-of-state. Books/supplies: $750. Personal expenses: $1,968.

2004-2005 Financial aid. **Need-based:** 76% of total undergraduate aid awarded as scholarships/grants, 24% as loans/jobs. Need-based aid available for part-time students. Work study available nights, weekends and for part-time students. **Non-need-based:** Scholarships awarded for academics, athletics.

Application procedures. **Admission:** No deadline. $25 fee. Application may be submitted online. Admission notification on a rolling basis. **Financial aid:** Priority date 4/15; no closing date. FAFSA, institutional form required. Applicants notified on a rolling basis starting 8/1.

Academics. **Special study options:** Distance learning, dual enrollment of high school students, ESL, honors, independent study, internships, study abroad. Bachelor's degree programs available on campus. **Credit/placement by examination:** AP, CLEP, institutional tests. 15 credit hours maximum toward associate degree. **Support services:** GED preparation and test center, learning center, remedial instruction, tutoring, writing center.

Majors. **Business:** Accounting, accounting technology, administrative services, business admin, marketing, office management, real estate. **Computer sciences:** General, computer graphics, database management, networking, programming, security, web page design. **Education:** Early childhood. **Health:** Medical radiologic technology/radiation therapy, nuclear medical technology, nursing (RN), sonography. **Liberal arts:** Arts/sciences. **Parks/recreation:** General. **Protective services:** Fire safety technology, fire services admin, firefighting, law enforcement admin. **Visual/performing arts:** Interior design.

Most popular majors. Business/marketing 12%, computer/information sciences 8%, health sciences 8%, liberal arts 64%.

Computing on campus. 244 workstations in library, computer center. Commuter students can connect to campus network. Online course registration, online library, helpline, student web hosting, wireless network available.

Student life. **Freshman orientation:** Available. Quarterly, prior to the start of the term. **Policies:** Freshmen permitted cars on campus. **Activities:** Jazz band, choral groups, dance, drama, literary magazine, music ensembles, musical theater, radio station, student government, student newspaper, TV station.

Athletics. NAIA, NJCAA. **Intercollegiate:** Baseball M, basketball, cross-country, golf M, soccer, softball W, tennis, track and field, volleyball W. **Intramural:** Badminton, basketball, racquetball, soccer W, softball W, table tennis, tennis, volleyball. **Team name:** Bulldogs.

Student services. Career counseling, services for economically disadvantaged, student employment services, financial aid counseling, health services, minority student services, on-campus daycare, personal counseling, placement for graduates, veterans' counselor, women's services. **Physically disabled:** Services for visually, speech, hearing impaired. **Transfer:** Orientation for new students. Transfer center, transfer adviser, college fairs on campus for students transferring to 4-year colleges.

Contact. E-mail: admissions@bcc.ctc.edu
Phone: (425) 564-2222 Fax: (425) 564-4065
Morenika Jacobs, Director, Enrollment Services, Bellevue Community College, 3000 Landerholm Circle SE, Bellevue, WA 98007-6484

Bellingham Technical College

Bellingham, Washington
www.btc.ctc.edu
CB code: 3499

- Public 2-year technical college
- Commuter campus in small city

General. Regionally accredited. **Enrollment:** 1,829 full-time, degree-seeking students. **Degrees:** 242 associate awarded. **Location:** 90 miles from Seattle. **Calendar:** Quarter, limited summer session. **Full-time faculty:** 48 total. **Part-time faculty:** 117 total. **Class size:** 84% < 20, 15% 20-39, less than 1% 40-49, less than 1% 50-99.

Student profile.

Out-of-state:	1%	**25 or older:**	52%

Basis for selection. Open admission.

2005-2006 Annual costs. Tuition/fees: $2,835. Books/supplies: $2,029. Personal expenses: $3,250.

Financial aid. All financial aid based on need. Need-based aid available for part-time students. Work study available for part-time students.

Application procedures. **Admission:** No deadline. $33 fee. Admission notification on a rolling basis. **Financial aid:** Priority date 4/30; no closing date. FAFSA required. Applicants notified on a rolling basis starting 7/1; must reply within 2 week(s) of notification.

Academics. Special study options: License preparation in nursing, paramedic, real estate. **Credit/placement by examination:** CLEP, institutional tests. **Support services:** GED preparation and test center, learning center, remedial instruction, study skills assistance, tutoring.

Majors. Business: General, accounting, office management, operations. **Computer sciences:** General, information systems. **Conservation:** Fisheries. **Construction:** Electrician, maintenance. **Engineering technology:** Civil, electrical, surveying. **Health:** EMT paramedic, surgical technology. **Legal studies:** Legal secretary. **Mechanic/repair:** General, auto body, automotive, diesel, electronics/electrical, heating/ac/refrig, industrial. **Personal/culinary services:** Culinary arts.

Computing on campus. 14 workstations in library. Online course registration, online library available.

Student life. Activities: Student government.

Student services. Adult student services, career counseling, services for economically disadvantaged, financial aid counseling, minority student services, veterans' counselor. **Physically disabled:** Services for visually, speech, hearing impaired. **Transfer:** Special adviser, orientation, pre-admission transcript evaluation for new students.

Contact. Phone: (360) 715-8356
David Klafke, Dean of Student Services, Bellingham Technical College, 3028 Lindbergh Avenue, Bellingham, WA 98225

Big Bend Community College
Moses Lake, Washington
www.bigbend.edu **CB code: 4024**

- Public 2-year community college
- Commuter campus in large town

General. Founded in 1962. Regionally accredited. **Enrollment:** 1,170 degree-seeking undergraduates. **Degrees:** 350 associate awarded. **Location:** 107 miles from Spokane, 170 miles from Seattle. **Calendar:** Quarter, limited summer session. **Full-time faculty:** 56 total; 9% have terminal degrees, 5% minority, 39% women. **Part-time faculty:** 72 total; 3% have terminal degrees, 26% minority, 57% women. **Partnerships:** Formal partnership with high schools for Tech Prep programs.

Student profile. Among degree-seeking undergraduates, 60% enrolled in a transfer program, 40% enrolled in a vocational program, 1% already have a bachelor's degree or higher, 121 transferred in from other institutions.

Out-of-state:	5%	**Native American:**	1%
African American:	1%	**25 or older:**	47%
Asian American:	1%	**Live on campus:**	5%
Hispanic American:	19%		

Transfer out. Colleges most students transferred to 2005: Central Washington University, Eastern Washington University, Washington State University.

Basis for selection. Open admission, but selective for some programs. Special admission criteria for aviation and nursing programs. **Adult students:** Entrance exam policies same as for first-time freshmen.

2005-2006 Annual costs. Tuition/fees: $2,871; $3,351 out-of-state. Per-credit charge: $75 in-state; $89 out-of-state. Room/board: $5,160. Books/supplies: $984. Personal expenses: $1,560.

2004-2005 Financial aid. All financial aid based on need. 72% of total undergraduate aid awarded as scholarships/grants, 28% as loans/jobs. Need-based aid available for part-time students. Work study available nights, weekends and for part-time students.

Application procedures. Admission: No deadline. $30 fee. Application may be submitted online. Admission notification on a rolling basis. **Financial aid:** Priority date 4/15; no closing date. FAFSA, institutional form required. Applicants notified on a rolling basis starting 5/15; must reply within 2 week(s) of notification.

Academics. Special study options: Cooperative education, distance learning, dual enrollment of high school students, liberal arts/career combination. Bachelor's degree programs available on campus. License preparation in aviation, nursing. **Credit/placement by examination:** AP, CLEP, institutional tests. 45 credit hours maximum toward associate degree. **Support services:** GED preparation and test center, learning center, reduced course load, remedial instruction, study skills assistance, tutoring, writing center.

Majors. Agriculture: Production. **Business:** Accounting technology, office management. **Computer sciences:** General, programming. **Construction:** Electrician. **Education:** Teacher assistance. **Engineering technology:** Civil. **Health:** Nursing (RN), office admin. **Liberal arts:** Arts/sciences. **Mechanic/repair:** Aircraft, automotive, industrial. **Physical sciences:** General. **Production:** Welding. **Transportation:** Airline/commercial pilot.

Most popular majors. Health sciences 7%, liberal arts 75%, trade and industry 9%.

Computing on campus. 421 workstations in dormitories, library, computer center, student center. Dormitories wired for high-speed internet access and linked to campus network. Online course registration, student web hosting, wireless network available.

Student life. Freshman orientation: Available. Preregistration for classes offered. Half-day fall orientations held throughout the summer. **Policies:** Freshmen permitted cars on campus. **Housing:** Coed dorms, substance-free housing available. $200 fully refundable deposit. **Activities:** Choral groups, music ensembles, student government.

Athletics. Intercollegiate: Baseball M, basketball, softball W, volleyball W. **Team name:** Vikings.

Student services. Career counseling, student employment services, financial aid counseling, minority student services, on-campus daycare, personal counseling, placement for graduates, veterans' counselor. **Physically disabled:** Services for visually, hearing impaired. **Transfer:** Special adviser, orientation for new students. Transfer adviser, college fairs on campus for students transferring to 4-year colleges.

Contact. E-mail: admissions@bigbend.edu
Phone: (509) 793-2061 Toll-free number: (877) 745-1212
Fax: (509) 762-6243
Candy Lacher, Dean of Enrollment Services, Big Bend Community College, 7662 Chanute Street, Moses Lake, WA 98837-3299

Cascadia Community College
Bothell, Washington
www.cascadia.ctc.edu/ **CB code: 2859**

- Public 2-year community college
- Large town

General. Enrollment: 1,950 undergraduates. **Degrees:** 261 associate awarded. **Calendar:** Quarter.

Basis for selection. COMPASS required for admission.

Application procedures. Admission: No deadline. No application fee.

Academics. Credit/placement by examination: CLEP.

Majors. Biology: General. **Computer sciences:** General. **Conservation:** Environmental science. **Physical sciences:** Atmospheric physics, chemistry, climatology, geology, physics.

Contact. E-mail: admissions@cascadia.ctc.edu
Phone: (425) 352-8860
Cascadia Community College, 18345 Campus Way NE, Bothell, WA 98011

Centralia College
Centralia, Washington
www.centralia.edu **CB code: 4045**

- Public 2-year community college
- Commuter campus in large town

General. Founded in 1925. Regionally accredited. **Enrollment:** 3,278 degree-seeking undergraduates; 551 non-degree-seeking students. **Degrees:** 309 associate awarded. **Location:** 90 miles from Seattle, 90 miles from Portland, Oregon. **Calendar:** Quarter, limited summer session. **Full-time faculty:** 58 total; 19% have terminal degrees, 5% minority, 52% women. **Part-time faculty:** 176 total; 2% have terminal degrees, 2% minority, 43% women. **Class size:** 50% < 20, 43% 20-39, 5% 40-49, 2% 50-99.

Student profile. Among degree-seeking undergraduates, 41% enrolled in a transfer program, 29% enrolled in a vocational program, 1% already have a bachelor's degree or higher, 106 transferred in from other institutions.

Part-time:	65%	**Asian American:**	2%
Out-of-state:	1%	**Hispanic American:**	12%
Women:	52%	**Native American:**	2%
African American:	1%	**25 or older:**	55%

Transfer out. 83% of students enrolled in the transfer program go on to 4-year colleges. **Colleges most students transferred to 2005:** Western Washington University, Washington State University, The Evergreen State College, Saint Martin's College, Central Washington University.

Basis for selection. Open admission, but selective for some programs. Special requirements for nursing program, includes prerequisites and grade point average criteria. **Adult students:** Entrance exam policies same as for first-time freshmen.

High school preparation. 16 units recommended. Recommended units include English 4, mathematics 3, social studies 2, history 1, science 2 (laboratory 1), foreign language 2 and academic electives 1.

2005-2006 Annual costs. Tuition/fees: $2,702; $3,167 out-of-state. Per-credit charge: $72 in-state; $244 out-of-state. Books/supplies: $924. Personal expenses: $1,524.

2004-2005 Financial aid. **Need-based:** 92% of total undergraduate aid awarded as scholarships/grants, 8% as loans/jobs. Need-based aid available for part-time students. **Non-need-based:** Scholarships awarded for academics, alumni affiliation, art, leadership, minority status, music/drama.

Application procedures. **Admission:** Priority date 9/1; no deadline. No application fee. Application may be submitted online. Admission notification on a rolling basis beginning on or about 12/1. **Financial aid:** Priority date 5/1; no closing date. FAFSA, institutional form required. Applicants notified by 7/1; Applicants notified on a rolling basis starting 7/10; must reply within 2 week(s) of notification.

Academics. **Special study options:** Cooperative education, cross-registration, distance learning, double major, dual enrollment of high school students, ESL, honors, independent study, internships, liberal arts/career combination, student-designed major, study abroad, weekend college. Bachelor's degree programs available on campus. License preparation in nursing, paramedic, real estate. **Credit/placement by examination:** AP, CLEP, IB, institutional tests. 45 credit hours maximum toward associate degree. **Support services:** GED preparation and test center, learning center, reduced course load, remedial instruction, study skills assistance, tutoring, writing center.

Majors. **Biology:** General, botany, zoology. **Business:** General, accounting, business admin, marketing, office technology, office/clerical, receptionist, sales/distribution. **Communications:** Broadcast journalism, journalism, radio/tv. **Communications technology:** Graphics, radio/tv. **Computer sciences:** General, computer science, data processing, information systems, LAN/WAN management, networking, programming. **Conservation:** Environmental studies, forestry. **Education:** General, early childhood. **Engineering:** General, civil. **Engineering technology:** Civil, civil drafting, drafting, electrical, surveying. **Family/consumer sciences:** Child care. **Foreign languages:** General, French, German, Spanish. **Health:** Athletic training, medical records technology, medical secretary, nursing (RN), office assistant, predentistry, premedicine, prenursing, prepharmacy, preveterinary, receptionist. **History:** General. **Interdisciplinary:** Biological/physical sciences. **Legal studies:** Legal secretary, prelaw. **Liberal arts:** Arts/sciences. **Math:** General. **Mechanic/repair:** Diesel, electronics/electrical. **Parks/recreation:** Exercise sciences, health/fitness. **Physical sciences:** General, chemistry, geology, physics, planetary. **Production:** Welding. **Protective services:** Criminal justice, law enforcement admin, police science. **Psychology:** General. **Social sciences:** General, anthropology, economics, sociology. **Visual/performing arts:** General, art, commercial/advertising art, dramatic, graphic design, music theory/composition, studio arts.

Most popular majors. Health sciences 9%, liberal arts 80%.

Computing on campus. 150 workstations in library, computer center, student center. Online course registration, online library, helpline, wireless network available.

Student life. **Freshman orientation:** Available, $20 fee. Preregistration for classes offered. Held 2 days prior to fall quarter. **Policies:** Freshmen permitted cars on campus. **Activities:** Bands, choral groups, drama, literary magazine, music ensembles, musical theater, radio station, student government, student newspaper, symphony orchestra, TV station, honors club, international student club, Rotaract.

Athletics. NJCAA. **Intercollegiate:** Baseball M, basketball, golf W, softball W, volleyball W. **Team name:** Trailblazers.

Student services. Adult student services, career counseling, services for economically disadvantaged, student employment services, financial aid counseling, minority student services, on-campus daycare, personal counseling, placement for graduates, veterans' counselor. **Physically disabled:** Services for visually, speech, hearing impaired. **Transfer:** Special adviser, orientation, re-entry adviser, pre-admission transcript evaluation for new students. Transfer center, transfer adviser, college fairs on campus for students transferring to 4-year colleges.

Contact. E-mail: admissions@centralia.edu
Phone: (360) 736-9391 ext. 221 Fax: (360) 330-7503
Scott Copeland, Director of Enrollment Services, Centralia College, 600 West Locust, Centralia, WA 98531

Clark College

Vancouver, Washington
www.clark.edu **CB code: 4055**

- Public 2-year community college
- Commuter campus in small city

General. Founded in 1933. Regionally accredited. **Enrollment:** 5,750 degree-seeking undergraduates; 635 non-degree-seeking students. **Degrees:** 1,002 associate awarded. **ROTC:** Army, Air Force. **Location:** 8 miles from Portland, Oregon. **Calendar:** Quarter, extensive summer session. **Full-time faculty:** 195 total; 15% have terminal degrees. **Part-time faculty:** 380 total; 7% have terminal degrees. **Class size:** 38% < 20, 55% 20-39, 7% 40-49, less than 1% 50-99, less than 1% >100. **Special facilities:** Environmental education center, arboretum. **Partnerships:** Formal partnerships with Toyota T-10 and Cisco; industry partnerships to train students in specific equipment use.

Student profile. Among degree-seeking undergraduates, 51% enrolled in a transfer program, 20% enrolled in a vocational program, 62% already have a bachelor's degree or higher, 1,114 enrolled as first-time, first-year students.

Part-time:	45%	**Asian American:**	5%
Out-of-state:	4%	**Hispanic American:**	4%
Women:	59%	**Native American:**	1%
African American:	2%	**25 or older:**	35%

Transfer out. **Colleges most students transferred to 2005:** Washington State University-Vancouver, Portland State University, Washington State University-Pullman, Western Washington University, University of Washington.

Basis for selection. Open admission, but selective for some programs. ASSET required for placement in math and English. Interview required for dental hygiene, nursing, and pharmacy technician applicants. **Adult students:** Entrance exam policies same as for first-time freshmen.

2005-2006 Annual costs. Tuition/fees: $2,704; $7,912 out-of-state. Per-credit charge: $72 in-state; $244 out-of-state. Books/supplies: $750. Personal expenses: $1,968.

2004-2005 Financial aid. **Need-based:** 70% of total undergraduate aid awarded as scholarships/grants, 30% as loans/jobs. Need-based aid available for part-time students. Work study available nights, weekends and for part-time students. **Non-need-based:** Scholarships awarded for academics, alumni affiliation, art, athletics, job skills, leadership, minority status, music/drama, religious affiliation, ROTC, state residency.

Application procedures. **Admission:** Priority date 8/3; no deadline. No application fee. Application must be submitted on paper. Admission notification on a rolling basis. **Financial aid:** Priority date 5/1; no closing date. FAFSA, institutional form required. Applicants notified on a rolling basis starting 5/1; must reply within 2 week(s) of notification.

Academics. **Special study options:** Cooperative education, cross-registration, distance learning, dual enrollment of high school students, ESL, honors, independent study, internships, liberal arts/career combination, study abroad. Bachelor's degree programs available on campus. License preparation in dental hygiene, nursing. **Credit/placement by examination:** AP, CLEP, IB, institutional tests. 30 credit hours maximum toward associate degree. **Support services:** GED preparation and test center, learning center, reduced course load, remedial instruction, study skills assistance, tutoring, writing center.

Majors. **Agriculture:** Horticulture, landscaping. **Business:** Accounting technology, business admin, executive assistant, human resources, office technology, retailing, selling. **Computer sciences:** Data entry, networking, programming, webmaster. **Education:** Early childhood. **Engineering technology:** Construction, electrical, manufacturing, telecommunications. **Health:** Dental hygiene, EMT paramedic, medical assistant, medical secretary, nursing

(RN), substance abuse counseling. **Legal studies:** Legal secretary, paralegal. **Liberal arts:** Arts/sciences. **Mechanic/repair:** Automotive, diesel. **Parks/recreation:** Sports admin. **Personal/culinary services:** Baking, chef training. **Production:** Machine tool, welding.

Most popular majors. Business/marketing 13%, health sciences 13%, liberal arts 60%.

Computing on campus. 750 workstations in library, computer center, student center. Online course registration, online library, helpline available.

Student life. Freshman orientation: Available. Preregistration for classes offered. Sessions held during quarterly registration period. Online orientation option available. **Policies:** Freshmen permitted cars on campus. **Activities:** Bands, choral groups, dance, drama, literary magazine, music ensembles, musical theater, student government, student newspaper, symphony orchestra, Clark Anime & Japanese Cultural Club, Latter-day Saints Student Association, Students for Political Action Now, Future Teachers Club, Multicultural Students United, Amigos de Clark College, Alpha Sigma Phi, Addiction Counseling Educaiton Students, Northwest Collegiate Ministries, Young Democrats.

Athletics. Intercollegiate: Basketball, cross-country, soccer, track and field, volleyball W. **Intramural:** Basketball, fencing, football (non-tackle), soccer, softball, table tennis, volleyball. **Team name:** Penguins.

Student services. Adult student services, alcohol/substance abuse counseling, career counseling, services for economically disadvantaged, student employment services, financial aid counseling, health services, legal services, minority student services, on-campus daycare, personal counseling, placement for graduates, veterans' counselor, women's services. **Physically disabled:** Services for visually, speech, hearing impaired. **Transfer:** Special adviser, orientation for new students. Transfer adviser, college fairs on campus for students transferring to 4-year colleges.

Contact. E-mail: admissionrequest@clark.edu
Phone: (360) 992-2107 Fax: (360) 992-2867
Sheryl Anderson, Director of Admissions, Clark College, 1800 East McLoughlin Boulevard, Vancouver, WA 98663-3598

Clover Park Technical College

Lakewood, Washington
www.cptc.edu **CB code: 3971**

- Public 2-year technical college
- Commuter campus in small city

General. Regionally accredited. **Enrollment:** 1,685 degree-seeking undergraduates. **Degrees:** 299 associate awarded. **Location:** 10 miles from Tacoma, 40 miles from Seattle. **Calendar:** Quarter, extensive summer session. **Full-time faculty:** 111 total; 12% minority, 52% women. **Part-time faculty:** 188 total; 16% minority, 58% women. **Class size:** 70% < 20, 27% 20-39, 2% 40-49, 1% 50-99.

Basis for selection. Open admission, but selective for some programs. Some programs have test score minimums and/or course prerequisite requirements. Placement tests used that are not listed above. **Adult students:** Entrance exam policies same as for first-time freshmen.

2005-2006 Annual costs. Tuition/fees: $3,108; $3,108 out-of-state. Tuition Costs and fees vary by program; From $3,022 to $3,455 per academic year. Books/supplies: $900. Personal expenses: $1,440.

2004-2005 Financial aid. All financial aid based on need. 72% of total undergraduate aid awarded as scholarships/grants, 28% as loans/jobs. Need-based aid available for part-time students. Work study available nights and weekends.

Application procedures. Admission: No deadline. $50 fee. Application may be submitted online. Admission notification on a rolling basis. **Financial aid:** Priority date 6/15, closing date 8/25. FAFSA, institutional form required. Applicants notified on a rolling basis.

Academics. Special study options: Cooperative education, distance learning, dual enrollment of high school students, ESL, internships. License preparation in aviation, nursing. **Credit/placement by examination:** CLEP, institutional tests. 15 credit hours maximum toward associate degree. 25 percent of total approved hours may be awarded for prior work and/or life experience. **Support services:** GED preparation and test center, tutoring.

Majors. Agriculture: Landscaping. **Business:** Accounting technology, marketing, office management. **Communications technology:** Graphic/printing, radio/tv. **Computer sciences:** LAN/WAN management, networking, programming, security, web page design. **Education:** Early childhood, teacher assistance. **Engineering technology:** Architectural, environmental, mechanical. **Health:** Clinical lab assistant, health services, massage therapy. **Legal studies:** Legal secretary. **Mechanic/repair:** Aircraft powerplant, automotive, avionics, business machine, heating/ac/refrig, heavy equipment. **Production:** Machine tool. **Transportation:** Airline/commercial pilot. **Visual/performing arts:** Interior design.

Most popular majors. Business/marketing 10%, computer/information sciences 19%, education 8%, engineering/engineering technologies 14%, health sciences 18%, trade and industry 20%, visual/performing arts 6%.

Computing on campus. 94 workstations in library. Online library available.

Student life. Freshman orientation: Available. **Policies:** Freshmen permitted cars on campus. **Activities:** Student government.

Student services. Adult student services, career counseling, services for economically disadvantaged, student employment services, financial aid counseling, minority student services, on-campus daycare, veterans' counselor. **Physically disabled:** Services for visually, speech, hearing impaired.

Contact. E-mail: judy.richardson@cptc.edu
Phone: (253) 589-5678 Fax: (253) 589-5852
Judy Richardson, Registrar, Clover Park Technical College, 4500 Steilacoom Boulevard SW, Lakewood, WA 98499-4098

Columbia Basin College

Pasco, Washington
www.cbc2.org **CB code: 4077**

- Public 2-year community college
- Commuter campus in small city

General. Founded in 1955. Regionally accredited. Branch campus in Richland serves Benton County residents. **Enrollment:** 6,438 degree-seeking undergraduates. **Degrees:** 58 associate awarded. **Location:** 130 miles from Spokane, 200 miles from Seattle. **Calendar:** Quarter, limited summer session. **Full-time faculty:** 116 total. **Part-time faculty:** 225 total.

Student profile.

Out-of-state:	1%	**25 or older:**	58%

Transfer out. Colleges most students transferred to 2005: Washington State University (WSU).

Basis for selection. Open admission, but selective for some programs. Special requirements for nursing and dental hygiene programs. Applicants who are not graduates of regional accredited high school or have a GED must submit Washington Pre-College Test, SAT, or ACT scores.

High school preparation. 11 units recommended. Recommended units include English 3, mathematics 2, social studies 3, science 2 and foreign language 1.

2005-2006 Annual costs. Tuition/fees: $2,614; $3,195 out-of-state. Per-credit charge: $93 in-state; $126 out-of-state. Books/supplies: $618. Personal expenses: $1,644.

2004-2005 Financial aid. Need-based: 78% of total undergraduate aid awarded as scholarships/grants, 22% as loans/jobs. Need-based aid available for part-time students. Work study available nights, weekends and for part-time students. **Non-need-based:** Scholarships awarded for academics, athletics, state residency.

Application procedures. Admission: No deadline. $26 fee, may be waived for applicants with need. Application may be submitted online. Admission notification on a rolling basis. **Financial aid:** Priority date 4/1; no closing date. FAFSA, institutional form required. Applicants notified on a rolling basis starting 6/15; must reply within 2 week(s) of notification.

Academics. Special study options: Cross-registration, distance learning, dual enrollment of high school students, ESL, internships, liberal arts/career combination, weekend college. License preparation in dental hygiene, nursing, paramedic. **Credit/placement by examination:** CLEP, IB, institutional tests. 30 credit hours maximum toward associate degree. **Support services:** GED preparation and test center, learning center, reduced course load, remedial instruction, study skills assistance, tutoring, writing center.

Majors. Agriculture: Agribusiness operations, business. **Business:** Accounting, administrative services, management information systems, office management, purchasing, sales/distribution. **Computer sciences:** General, computer science, data processing, programming. **Construction:** Carpentry. **Education:** General, early childhood. **Engineering technology:** Electrical. **Family/consumer sciences:** Child care. **Health:** Clinical lab technology, dental hygiene, EMT paramedic, licensed practical nurse, medical records admin, medical transcription. **Interdisciplinary:** Biological/physical sciences, math/computer science. **Legal studies:** Paralegal. **Liberal arts:** Arts/sciences. **Mechanic/repair:** Auto body, automotive, diesel. **Physical sciences:** General. **Protective services:** Firefighting, law enforcement admin, police science. **Public administration:** Human services. **Visual/performing arts:** General, commercial/advertising art.

Most popular majors. Health sciences 7%, liberal arts 77%.

Computing on campus. 680 workstations in library, computer center. Online course registration available.

Student life. **Freshman orientation:** Mandatory. **Activities:** Bands, choral groups, drama, music ensembles, musical theater, student government, student newspaper.

Athletics. NJCAA. **Intercollegiate:** Baseball M, basketball, golf, soccer, softball W, volleyball W. **Intramural:** Basketball, bowling, soccer M, softball, volleyball. **Team name:** Hawks.

Student services. Adult student services, career counseling, student employment services, minority student services, personal counseling, placement for graduates, veterans' counselor, women's services. **Physically disabled:** Services for visually, speech, hearing impaired. **Learning disabled:** Comprehensive services available. **Transfer:** Special adviser, orientation for new students. Transfer adviser, college fairs on campus for students transferring to 4-year colleges.

Contact. E-mail: dkorstad@cbc2.org
Phone: (509) 547-0511 Fax: (509) 546-0401
Patricia Campbell, Director of Admissions and Registration, Columbia Basin College, 2600 North 20th Avenue, Pasco, WA 99301

Edmonds Community College

Lynnwood, Washington
www.edcc.edu
CB member
CB code: 4307

- Public 2-year community college
- Commuter campus in small city

General. Founded in 1967. Regionally accredited. **Enrollment:** 7,600 undergraduates. **Degrees:** 865 associate awarded. **Location:** 15 miles from Seattle. **Calendar:** Quarter, limited summer session. **Full-time faculty:** 140 total; 24% have terminal degrees, 15% minority, 55% women. **Part-time faculty:** 275 total; 9% minority, 58% women. **Special facilities:** Center for Business and Employment Development, golf course.

Transfer out. **Colleges most students transferred to 2005:** University of Washington, Central Washington University, Western Washington University, Washington State University.

Basis for selection. Open admission. ASSET required for all students for placement. Interview recommended for international studies, travel tourism majors; audition required for music performance majors. **Learning Disabled:** SSD is available to provide appropriate accommodation.

2005-2006 Annual costs. Tuition/fees: $2,652; $7,860 out-of-state. Per-credit charge: $72 in-state; $244 out-of-state. Books/supplies: $690. Personal expenses: $1,824.

Financial aid. **Need-based:** Need-based aid available for part-time students. Work study available nights and for part-time students. **Non-need-based:** Scholarships awarded for athletics.

Application procedures. **Admission:** No deadline. $15 fee, may be waived for applicants with need. Application may be submitted online. Admission notification on a rolling basis. TOEFL optional for students whose first language is not English. **Financial aid:** Priority date 5/1; no closing date. FAFSA, institutional form required. Applicants notified on a rolling basis starting 6/1; must reply within 4 week(s) of notification.

Academics. **Special study options:** Cooperative education, cross-registration, distance learning, dual enrollment of high school students, ESL, exchange student, honors, independent study, internships, study abroad, weekend college. **Credit/placement by examination:** CLEP, institutional tests. 15 credit hours maximum toward associate degree. Edmonds Community College catalog has detailed explanation under Policy, Procedure and Records. **Support services:** GED preparation and test center, learning center, remedial instruction, tutoring, writing center.

Majors. **Agriculture:** Business technology, landscaping, nursery operations. **Business:** Accounting, accounting technology, business admin, fashion, human resources, international, marketing, office management, tourism promotion, travel services. **Communications technology:** General. **Computer sciences:** General, data processing, programming. **Education:** General. **Engineering technology:** General, computer systems, construction, electrical. **Family/consumer sciences:** Child care. **Health:** Community health services, health aide, health services, medical secretary, mental health services, substance abuse counseling, vocational rehab counseling. **Interdisciplinary:** Gerontology. **Legal studies:** General, legal secretary, paralegal. **Liberal arts:** Arts/sciences. **Mechanic/repair:** General. **Personal/culinary services:** Chef training, culinary arts. **Physical sciences:** General. **Production:** Welding. **Protective services:** Fire safety technology, fire services admin. **Public administration:** Human services. **Science technology:** Chemical.

Computing on campus. 1,129 workstations in library, computer center. Commuter students can connect to campus network. Online course registration available.

Student life. **Freshman orientation:** Available. Students receive brief orientation prior to placement test. **Policies:** Freshmen permitted cars on campus. **Housing:** Host families available for international students. **Activities:** Jazz band, choral groups, dance, drama, literary magazine, music ensembles, student government, student newspaper, Phi Theta Kappa, international club, Design and Invention Club, I-Hope Club, DESI Club, Baptist Collegiate Ministry, Black Student Association, American Indian Student Association, Gay and Lesbian Alliance, Digital Production Club.

Athletics. **Intercollegiate:** Baseball M, basketball, golf, soccer, softball W, volleyball W. **Intramural:** Basketball M, bowling, golf, table tennis, volleyball. **Team name:** Tritons.

Student services. Adult student services, career counseling, student employment services, financial aid counseling, minority student services, on-campus daycare, personal counseling, placement for graduates, women's services. **Physically disabled:** Services for visually, speech, hearing impaired. **Transfer:** Special adviser, orientation for new students. Transfer center, transfer adviser, college fairs on campus for students transferring to 4-year colleges.

Contact. E-mail: admiss@edcc.edu
Phone: (425) 640-1459 Fax: (425) 640-1159
Sharon Bench, Director of Entry & Recruiting Services, Edmonds Community College, 20000 68th Avenue West, Lynnwood, WA 98036-5912

Everest College: Vancouver

Vancouver, Washington
www.everest-college.com

- For-profit 2-year business college
- Large city

General. Accredited by ACICS. **Calendar:** Quarter.

Contact. Phone: (360) 254-3282
Admissions Director, 120 N.E. 136th Avenue, Suite 130, Vancouver, WA 98684

Everett Community College

Everett, Washington
www.everettcc.edu
CB code: 4303

- Public 2-year community college
- Commuter campus in small city

General. Founded in 1941. Regionally accredited. Offers direct-transfer associate degrees that assure full transfer to most Washington and Oregon universities. **Enrollment:** 2,746 degree-seeking undergraduates; 2,989 non-degree-seeking students. **Degrees:** 825 associate awarded. **Location:** 30 miles from Seattle. **Calendar:** Quarter, limited summer session. **Full-time faculty:** 134 total; 53% have terminal degrees, 12% minority, 54% women. **Part-time faculty:** 252 total. **Class size:** 48% < 20, 49% 20-39, 3% 40-49, less than 1% 50-99. **Partnerships:** Formal partnership with Boeing.

Student profile. Among degree-seeking undergraduates, 59% enrolled in a transfer program, 41% enrolled in a vocational program, 3% already have

a bachelor's degree or higher, 393 enrolled as first-time, first-year students, 76 transferred in from other institutions.

Part-time:	45%	**Hispanic American:**	5%
Out-of-state:	5%	**Native American:**	2%
Women:	65%	**International:**	1%
African American:	2%	**25 or older:**	41%
Asian American:	5%		

Transfer out. 57% of students enrolled in the transfer program go on to 4-year colleges. **Colleges most students transferred to 2005:** Western Washington University, University of Washington, Central Washington University, Washington State University.

Basis for selection. Open admission, but selective for some programs. Special requirements for nursing, fire science, and criminal justice. Interview recommended for nursing. **Adult students:** Entrance exam policies same as for first-time freshmen.

High school preparation. 16 units recommended. Recommended units include English 4, mathematics 3, social studies 3, history 2, science 2 and foreign language 2.

2005-2006 Annual costs. Tuition/fees: $2,550; $7,758 out-of-state. Per-credit charge: $72 in-state; $244 out-of-state. Books/supplies: $750. Personal expenses: $1,968.

2004-2005 Financial aid. All financial aid based on need. 71 full-time freshmen applied for aid; 59 were judged to have need; 59 of these received aid. Average need met was 19%. Average scholarship/grant was $2,026; average loan $1,103. 74% of total undergraduate aid awarded as scholarships/grants, 26% as loans/jobs. Need-based aid available for part-time students. Work study available nights, weekends and for part-time students.

Application procedures. Admission: No deadline. No application fee. Application may be submitted online. Admission notification on a rolling basis. **Financial aid:** Priority date 5/2; no closing date. FAFSA, institutional form required. Applicants notified on a rolling basis starting 6/15; must reply within 4 week(s) of notification.

Academics. Transfer degrees for specific majors at designated universities can be designed by the student and faculty advisor. **Special study options:** Cooperative education, distance learning, dual enrollment of high school students, ESL, independent study, internships, study abroad. Bachelor's degree programs available on campus. License preparation in aviation, nursing, paramedic. **Credit/placement by examination:** AP, CLEP, IB, institutional tests. 45 credit hours maximum toward associate degree. **Support services:** GED preparation and test center, learning center, reduced course load, remedial instruction, study skills assistance, tutoring, writing center.

Majors. Agriculture: Animal sciences. **Area/ethnic studies:** Asian. **Biology:** General. **Business:** General, accounting, administrative services, business admin, management information systems, office/clerical. **Communications:** General, advertising, journalism. **Computer sciences:** General, computer graphics, computer science, information systems, networking, programming, webmaster. **Conservation:** General, environmental science. **Education:** General, early childhood. **Engineering:** General. **Engineering technology:** General, CAD/CADD, manufacturing. **English:** American lit, British lit, composition, creative writing, speech/rhetoric, technical writing. **Foreign languages:** General, comparative lit, French, German, Japanese, Russian, Spanish. **Health:** Dental hygiene, medical assistant, nursing (RN), predentistry, premedicine, prepharmacy, preveterinary. **History:** General. **Interdisciplinary:** Natural sciences. **Legal studies:** Prelaw. **Liberal arts:** Arts/sciences. **Math:** General. **Mechanic/repair:** Aircraft powerplant. **Personal/culinary services:** Cosmetology. **Philosophy/religion:** Philosophy. **Physical sciences:** Astronomy, atmospheric science, chemistry, geology, oceanography, physics. **Protective services:** Corrections, firefighting, law enforcement admin. **Psychology:** General. **Public administration:** Human services. **Social sciences:** General, anthropology, economics, geography, political science, sociology. **Visual/performing arts:** General, art, commercial/advertising art, dramatic, music performance, photography, studio arts.

Most popular majors. Business/marketing 13%, computer/information sciences 6%, health sciences 12%, liberal arts 56%.

Computing on campus. 850 workstations in library, computer center. Online course registration available.

Student life. Freshman orientation: Mandatory. Preregistration for classes offered. One day program of placement testing, orientation and advising sessions. **Housing:** Housing in private homes available for foreign students. **Activities:** Choral groups, drama, literary magazine, music ensembles, musical theater, student government, student newspaper, 25 student clubs.

Athletics. Intercollegiate: Baseball M, basketball, cross-country, soccer, softball W, volleyball W. **Intramural:** Basketball, bowling, golf, soccer, softball, tennis, volleyball, weight lifting. **Team name:** Trojans.

Student services. Adult student services, career counseling, services for economically disadvantaged, student employment services, financial aid counseling, minority student services, on-campus daycare, personal counseling, placement for graduates, veterans' counselor, women's services. **Physically disabled:** Services for visually, speech, hearing impaired. **Transfer:** Special adviser, orientation for new students. Transfer adviser, college fairs on campus for students transferring to 4-year colleges.

Contact. E-mail: admissions@everettcc.edu
Phone: (425) 388-9219 Fax: (425) 388-9173
Linda Baca, Admissions Manager, Everett Community College, 2000 Tower Street, Everett, WA 98201-1352

Grays Harbor College

Aberdeen, Washington
www.ghc.edu **CB code: 4332**

- Public 2-year community college
- Commuter campus in large town

General. Founded in 1930. Regionally accredited. **Enrollment:** 858 degree-seeking undergraduates; 1,501 non-degree-seeking students. **Degrees:** 258 associate awarded. **Location:** 100 miles from Seattle. **Calendar:** Quarter, limited summer session. **Full-time faculty:** 59 total; 2% minority, 37% women. **Part-time faculty:** 96 total; 2% minority, 55% women. **Class size:** 84% < 20, 15% 20-39, 1% 40-49, less than 1% 50-99. **Special facilities:** 4-acre lake linked to Grays Harbor estuary and fish hatcheries; 440 seat theater. **Partnerships:** Formal partnerships with local businesses for internships and short-term training.

Student profile. Among degree-seeking undergraduates, 39% enrolled in a transfer program, 61% enrolled in a vocational program, 3% already have a bachelor's degree or higher, 110 enrolled as first-time, first-year students, 60 transferred in from other institutions.

Part-time:	33%	**Women:**	57%
Out-of-state:	1%		

Transfer out. Colleges most students transferred to 2005: Evergreen State College, Washington State University, University of Washington, Western Washington University, Central Washington University.

Basis for selection. Open admission, but selective for some programs. High School diploma or GED required of applicants under 18 years of age. Selective admission to nursing program. **Adult students:** Entrance exam policies same as for first-time freshmen.

2005-2006 Annual costs. Tuition/fees: $2,622; $7,830 out-of-state. Per-credit charge: $72 in-state; $244 out-of-state. Books/supplies: $750. Personal expenses: $1,932.

2004-2005 Financial aid. Need-based: 81% of total undergraduate aid awarded as scholarships/grants, 19% as loans/jobs. Need-based aid available for part-time students. Work study available nights and for part-time students. **Non-need-based:** Scholarships awarded for academics, art, athletics, music/drama.

Application procedures. Admission: Priority date 9/1; no deadline. No application fee. Application may be submitted online. Admission notification on a rolling basis. **Financial aid:** Priority date 5/1; no closing date. FAFSA, institutional form required. Applicants notified on a rolling basis starting 5/15.

Academics. Special study options: Accelerated study, cooperative education, distance learning, double major, dual enrollment of high school students, ESL, independent study, internships. Bachelor's degree programs available on campus. License preparation in nursing. **Credit/placement by examination:** AP, CLEP, institutional tests. 45 credit hours maximum toward associate degree. **Support services:** GED preparation and test center, learning center, reduced course load, remedial instruction, study skills assistance, tutoring, writing center.

Majors. Business: Accounting technology, business admin, office management. **Computer sciences:** Data processing. **Conservation:** General, wildlife. **Construction:** Carpentry. **Education:** Teacher assistance. **Health:** Nursing (RN). **Liberal arts:** Arts/sciences. **Mechanic/repair:** Automotive, diesel. **Production:** Welding. **Protective services:** Police science. **Public administration:** Human services.

Most popular majors. Health sciences 14%, liberal arts 71%.

Computing on campus. 286 workstations in library, computer center, student center. Online course registration, online library, helpline, repair service, student web hosting available.

Student life. **Freshman orientation:** Mandatory. Preregistration for classes offered. Offered online or face to face. **Policies:** Freshmen permitted cars on campus. **Activities:** Bands, choral groups, drama, music ensembles, musical theater, student government, student newspaper, symphony orchestra, Native American Student Association, the Tyee Honorary Service Club, Human Services Student Association, AGAPE Christian ministry, Foreign Language and Culture, Student Nurses Association.

Athletics. **Intercollegiate:** Baseball M, basketball, golf, softball W, volleyball W. **Team name:** Chokers.

Student services. Career counseling, student employment services, financial aid counseling, on-campus daycare, personal counseling, placement for graduates, veterans' counselor. **Physically disabled:** Services for visually, speech, hearing impaired. **Transfer:** Special adviser, orientation, preadmission transcript evaluation for new students. Transfer adviser, college fairs on campus for students transferring to 4-year colleges.

Contact. E-mail: bdell@ghc.edu
Phone: (360) 538-4026 Toll-free number: (800) 562-4830
Fax: (360) 538-4293
Nancy DeVerse, Associate Dean for Student Services/Registrar, Grays Harbor College, 1620 Edward P Smith Drive, Aberdeen, WA 98520

Green River Community College

Auburn, Washington
www.greenriver.edu **CB code: 4337**

- Public 2-year community college
- Commuter campus in large town

General. Founded in 1965. Regionally accredited. **Enrollment:** 4,220 degree-seeking undergraduates. **Degrees:** 909 associate awarded. **Location:** 35 miles from Seattle. **Calendar:** Quarter, limited summer session. **Full-time faculty:** 125 total. **Part-time faculty:** 251 total.

Basis for selection. Open admission, but selective for some programs. Special requirements for health occupation programs. Interview required for occupational therapy.

2005-2006 Annual costs. Tuition/fees: $2,743; $3,139 out-of-state. Per-credit charge: $72 in-state; $85 out-of-state. Books/supplies: $939. Personal expenses: $1,170.

Financial aid. All financial aid based on need. Need-based aid available for part-time students.

Application procedures. **Admission:** No deadline. No application fee. Application may be submitted online. Admission notification on a rolling basis. **Financial aid:** Priority date 4/15; no closing date. FAFSA, institutional form required. Applicants notified on a rolling basis starting 6/30; must reply within 2 week(s) of notification.

Academics. **Special study options:** Cooperative education, cross-registration, distance learning, dual enrollment of high school students, ESL, independent study, internships, study abroad. **Credit/placement by examination:** AP, CLEP, institutional tests. **Support services:** GED preparation and test center, learning center, reduced course load, remedial instruction, tutoring.

Majors. **Business:** Accounting, marketing, office technology, office/clerical, real estate. **Computer sciences:** Information systems. **Conservation:** Forest resources. **Construction:** Carpentry. **Education:** Early childhood. **Engineering technology:** Drafting, electrical, hazardous materials. **Health:** Medical secretary, occupational therapy assistant, physical therapy assistant. **Legal studies:** Court reporting, legal secretary. **Liberal arts:** Arts/sciences. **Mechanic/repair:** Auto body. **Protective services:** Police science. **Transportation:** General, aviation. **Visual/performing arts:** General.

Computing on campus. 130 workstations in library, computer center.

Student life. **Freshman orientation:** Available. **Housing:** Apartments available. **Activities:** Jazz band, choral groups, dance, drama, music ensembles, radio station, student government, student newspaper, Asian Student Union, Black Student Union, Native American Student Association, Los Latinos Unidos, Phi Theta Kappa, Teachers of Tomorrow, Skills USA, forestry club, court reporting club, American Society of Mechanical Engineers.

Athletics. NJCAA. **Intercollegiate:** Baseball M, basketball, golf, soccer, softball W, tennis, volleyball W. **Intramural:** Badminton, baseball M, basketball, soccer, softball, tennis, volleyball. **Team name:** Gators.

Student services. Career counseling, services for economically disadvantaged, student employment services, financial aid counseling, health services, minority student services, on-campus daycare, personal counseling, placement for graduates, veterans' counselor, women's services. **Physically disabled:** Services for visually, hearing impaired. **Transfer:** Special adviser, orientation for new students. Transfer center, transfer adviser, college fairs on campus for students transferring to 4-year colleges.

Contact. Phone: (253) 833-9111 ext. 2500 Fax: (253) 288-3454
Denise Bennatts, Registrar, Green River Community College, 12401 South East 320th Street, Auburn, WA 98092

Highline Community College

Des Moines, Washington
www.highline.ctc.edu **CB code: 4348**

- Public 2-year community college
- Commuter campus in large town

General. Founded in 1961. Regionally accredited. **Enrollment:** 5,610 undergraduates. **Degrees:** 911 associate awarded. **ROTC:** Army, Air Force. **Location:** 18 miles from Seattle. **Calendar:** Quarter, limited summer session. **Full-time faculty:** 140 total; 19% minority, 56% women. **Part-time faculty:** 216 total.

Basis for selection. Open admission, but selective for some programs. School achievement record considered for health programs. College and work experience also considered for nursing.

High school preparation. Health occupation programs require chemistry and algebra.

2005-2006 Annual costs. Tuition/fees: $2,520; $7,728 out-of-state. Per-credit charge: $72 in-state; $244 out-of-state. Books/supplies: $618. Personal expenses: $1,644.

Financial aid. **Need-based:** Need-based aid available for part-time students.

Application procedures. **Admission:** No deadline. No application fee. Admission notification on a rolling basis. **Financial aid:** Priority date 4/4; no closing date. FAFSA required. Applicants notified on a rolling basis starting 6/1.

Academics. **Special study options:** Accelerated study, cooperative education, cross-registration, distance learning, double major, dual enrollment of high school students, ESL, honors, independent study, internships, student-designed major. **Credit/placement by examination:** CLEP, institutional tests. **Support services:** GED preparation and test center, learning center, preadmission summer program, reduced course load, remedial instruction, tutoring.

Majors. **Business:** General, accounting, administrative services, business admin, fashion, hospitality/recreation, international, office/clerical, sales/distribution, tourism/travel. **Communications:** General, journalism. **Computer sciences:** General. **Education:** General, teacher assistance. **Engineering:** General. **Engineering technology:** Drafting, manufacturing. **Family/consumer sciences:** General, child care, food/nutrition. **Foreign languages:** General, French, German, linguistics. **Health:** Dental assistant, health care admin, medical assistant, medical transcription, nursing (RN), respiratory therapy technology. **History:** General. **Legal studies:** General, paralegal, prelaw. **Liberal arts:** Arts/sciences, library assistant. **Math:** General. **Parks/recreation:** Health/fitness. **Physical sciences:** Astronomy, geology. **Psychology:** General. **Public administration:** Human services. **Social sciences:** General, anthropology, economics, geography, sociology. **Transportation:** General, aviation. **Visual/performing arts:** General, art, commercial/advertising art, dramatic, multimedia.

Most popular majors. Business/marketing 6%, computer/information sciences 6%, health sciences 9%, liberal arts 66%.

Computing on campus. 100 workstations in library, computer center, student center.

Student life. **Activities:** Bands, choral groups, drama, literary magazine, music ensembles, student government, student newspaper, TV station, Indian and international student clubs, political forum, paralegal and arts societies, respiratory care club, academic honor society, campus crusade for Christ.

Athletics. NJCAA. **Intercollegiate:** Basketball, cross-country, soccer, softball W, track and field, volleyball W, wrestling M.

Student services. Adult student services, career counseling, student employment services, health services, minority student services, on-campus daycare, personal counseling, placement for graduates, veterans' counselor, women's services. **Physically disabled:** Services for visually, speech, hearing impaired. **Transfer:** Special adviser, orientation for new students. Transfer adviser, college fairs on campus for students transferring to 4-year colleges.

Contact. E-mail: dfaison@hcc.ctc.edu
Phone: (206) 878-3710 ext. 3361 Fax: (206) 870-3782
Debbie Faison, Assistant Registrar, Highline Community College, 2400 South 240th Street, Des Moines, WA 98198-9800

Lake Washington Technical College
Kirkland, Washington
www.lwtc.ctc.edu **CB code: 1453**

- Public 2-year technical college
- Commuter campus in large town

General. Founded in 1949. Regionally accredited. **Enrollment:** 3,600 undergraduates. **Degrees:** 11 associate awarded. **Location:** 10 miles from Seattle. **Calendar:** Quarter, extensive summer session. **Full-time faculty:** 54 total; 15% minority, 46% women. **Part-time faculty:** 166 total; 5% minority, 51% women. **Class size:** 3% < 20, 97% 20-39. **Partnerships:** High Tech Center at local high school.

Basis for selection. Open admission, but selective for some programs. Limited admissions for dental hygiene; special requirements for other allied health programs and hospitality programs.

2005-2006 Annual costs. Tuition fees vary by program. Books/supplies: $720. Personal expenses: $1,896.

Financial aid. Need-based: Need-based aid available for part-time students. Work study available for part-time students.

Application procedures. Admission: No application fee. Application may be submitted online. Admission notification on a rolling basis. **Financial aid:** Priority date 4/15; no closing date. FAFSA, institutional form required. Applicants notified on a rolling basis.

Academics. Special study options: Cooperative education, distance learning, dual enrollment of high school students, ESL, internships, liberal arts/career combination, weekend college. License preparation in dental hygiene, nursing, real estate. **Credit/placement by examination:** CLEP. 15 credit hours maximum toward associate degree. **Support services:** GED preparation and test center, learning center, reduced course load, remedial instruction, study skills assistance, tutoring, writing center.

Majors. Agriculture: Horticulture. **Business:** Accounting, administrative services, hospitality/recreation. **Computer sciences:** Data processing. **Engineering technology:** Architectural, drafting, electrical. **Family/consumer sciences:** Child care. **Health:** Dental assistant, dental hygiene, licensed practical nurse, medical assistant. **Legal studies:** Legal secretary, paralegal. **Mechanic/repair:** Auto body, automotive, diesel. **Personal/culinary services:** Culinary arts.

Computing on campus. 1,200 workstations in library, computer center.

Student life. Freshman orientation: Available. **Activities:** Student government, John 3:16 Club, Chinese club, single parent program/displaced homemakers, Welfare-to-Work, wellness group.

Student services. Adult student services, career counseling, student employment services, on-campus daycare, placement for graduates. **Physically disabled:** Services for visually, speech, hearing impaired. **Transfer:** Special adviser, orientation, pre-admission transcript evaluation for new students. Transfer adviser for students transferring to 4-year colleges.

Contact. E-mail: admissions@lwtc.edu
Phone: (425) 739-8104 Fax: (425) 739-8110
David Minger, Director of Admissions and Registration, Lake Washington Technical College, 11605 132nd Avenue, NE, Kirkland, WA 98034

Lower Columbia College
Longview, Washington
www.lcc.ctc.edu **CB code: 4402**

- Public 2-year community college
- Commuter campus in small city

General. Founded in 1934. Regionally accredited. **Enrollment:** 1,592 degree-seeking undergraduates; 1,631 non-degree-seeking students. **Degrees:** 415 associate awarded. **Location:** 50 miles from Portland, Oregon, 120 miles from Seattle. **Calendar:** Quarter, limited summer session. **Full-time faculty:** 85 total. **Part-time faculty:** 80 total. **Class size:** 73% < 20, 25% 20-39, less than 1% 40-49, less than 1% 50-99, less than 1% >100.

Student profile. Among degree-seeking undergraduates, 25% enrolled in a transfer program, 44% enrolled in a vocational program, 4% already have a bachelor's degree or higher, 332 enrolled as first-time, first-year students.

Part-time:	30%	**Asian American:**	2%
Out-of-state:	2%	**Hispanic American:**	3%
Women:	62%	**Native American:**	1%
African American:	1%	**25 or older:**	50%

Transfer out. 16% of students enrolled in the transfer program go on to 4-year colleges. **Colleges most students transferred to 2005:** Washington State University-Vancouver, Washington State University-Pullman, Central Washington University, Eastern Washington University, Western Washington University.

Basis for selection. Open admission, but selective for some programs. Special requirements for nursing program and medical assistant program. Early application advisable because of enrollment caps.

2005-2006 Annual costs. Tuition/fees: $2,645; $3,226 out-of-state. Per-credit charge: $78 in-state; $100 out-of-state. Books/supplies: $975. Personal expenses: $1,950.

2004-2005 Financial aid. All financial aid based on need. 74% of total undergraduate aid awarded as scholarships/grants, 26% as loans/jobs. Work study available for part-time students.

Application procedures. Admission: No deadline. $13 fee. Admission notification on a rolling basis. **Financial aid:** Priority date 5/1; no closing date. Institutional form, CSS PROFILE required. Applicants notified on a rolling basis starting 4/21; must reply within 2 week(s) of notification.

Academics. Special study options: Cooperative education, cross-registration, distance learning, dual enrollment of high school students, ESL, honors, independent study, liberal arts/career combination, student-designed major, study abroad. Bachelor's degree programs available on campus. **Credit/placement by examination:** AP, CLEP, institutional tests. **Support services:** GED preparation and test center, learning center, remedial instruction, study skills assistance, tutoring.

Majors. Business: Accounting, accounting technology, administrative services, business admin, office technology, office/clerical. **Computer sciences:** General, computer science, data entry, data processing, networking, programming. **Education:** Teacher assistance. **Engineering:** General, chemical. **Engineering technology:** Electrical. **Family/consumer sciences:** Child development. **Health:** Licensed practical nurse, medical assistant, medical secretary, nursing (RN), nursing assistant, substance abuse counseling. **Legal studies:** Legal secretary, paralegal. **Liberal arts:** Arts/sciences. **Mechanic/repair:** Auto body, automotive, diesel, electronics/electrical, heavy equipment, industrial, industrial electronics. **Production:** Welding. **Protective services:** Law enforcement admin.

Most popular majors. Liberal arts 53%, trade and industry 47%.

Computing on campus. 150 workstations in library, computer center, student center. Online course registration, online library, helpline, wireless network available.

Student life. Freshman orientation: Available. **Policies:** Freshmen permitted cars on campus. **Housing:** Apartments normally available in local community. **Activities:** Bands, choral groups, drama, literary magazine, music ensembles, musical theater, student government, student newspaper, multicultural students club, international students, theater club, student nurses organization, services and relations club, campus entertainment, diesel mechanics club, Phi Theta Kappa.

Athletics. NJCAA. **Intercollegiate:** Baseball M, basketball, cross-country, golf, soccer W, softball W, volleyball W. **Team name:** Red Devils.

Student services. Adult student services, career counseling, services for economically disadvantaged, student employment services, financial aid counseling, on-campus daycare, personal counseling, placement for graduates, veterans' counselor. **Physically disabled:** Services for visually, hearing impaired. **Transfer:** Special adviser, orientation for new students. Transfer center, transfer adviser, college fairs on campus for students transferring to 4-year colleges.

Contact. E-mail: entry@lcc.ctc.edu
Phone: (360) 442-2311 Fax: (360) 442-2379
Lynn Lawrence, Registrar, Lower Columbia College, 1600 Maple Street, Longview, WA 98632-0310

North Seattle Community College
Seattle, Washington
www.northseattle.edu **CB code: 4554**

- Public 2-year community college
- Commuter campus in very large city

General. Founded in 1970. Regionally accredited. Associate degree programs available via distance learning. College's Watchmaking Institute one of only 3 certified programs in country. **Enrollment:** 2,993 degree-seeking undergraduates; 2,966 non-degree-seeking students. **Degrees:** 554 associate awarded. **Location:** 8 miles from downtown. **Calendar:** Quarter, limited summer session. **Full-time faculty:** 101 total; 8% have terminal degrees, 29% minority, 54% women. **Part-time faculty:** 182 total; 1% have terminal degrees, 12% minority, 65% women. **Class size:** 47% < 20, 52% 20-39, 1% 40-49, less than 1% 50-99. **Special facilities:** Wetlands, wellness center, observatory.

Student profile. Among degree-seeking undergraduates, 64% enrolled in a transfer program, 36% enrolled in a vocational program, 14% already have a bachelor's degree or higher, 1,074 enrolled as first-time, first-year students, 545 transferred in from other institutions.

Part-time:	36%	**Asian American:**	16%
Out-of-state:	4%	**Hispanic American:**	6%
Women:	55%	**Native American:**	2%
African American:	8%	**25 or older:**	54%

Transfer out. Colleges most students transferred to 2005: University of Washington.

Basis for selection. Open admission. Applicants with deficient English or Math skills are required to take remedial courses to qualify for college level work. Test scores required in English and mathematics for placement only.

2005-2006 Annual costs. Tuition/fees: $2,552; $7,760 out-of-state. Per-credit charge: $72 in-state; $244 out-of-state. Books/supplies: $924. Personal expenses: $1,524.

2004-2005 Financial aid. Need-based: 89% of total undergraduate aid awarded as scholarships/grants, 11% as loans/jobs. Need-based aid available for part-time students. Work study available nights, weekends and for part-time students.

Application procedures. Admission: No deadline. No application fee. Admission notification on a rolling basis. **Financial aid:** Priority date 4/30, closing date 8/31. FAFSA, institutional form required. Applicants notified on a rolling basis starting 8/1; must reply within 2 week(s) of notification.

Academics. Distance learning opportunities. **Special study options:** Cooperative education, cross-registration, distance learning, dual enrollment of high school students, ESL, independent study, internships, liberal arts/career combination, study abroad. License preparation in nursing, radiology, real estate. **Credit/placement by examination:** AP, CLEP, IB, institutional tests. 45 credit hours maximum toward associate degree. **Support services:** GED preparation and test center, learning center, reduced course load, remedial instruction, study skills assistance, tutoring, writing center.

Majors. Business: General, administrative services, office technology, office/clerical, real estate. **Communications technology:** General. **Computer sciences:** General, computer science, data processing, information systems, LAN/WAN management, programming, systems analysis, webmaster. **Education:** General, early childhood. **Engineering:** Software. **Engineering technology:** Architectural drafting, biomedical, CAD/CADD, computer hardware, drafting, electrical. **Family/consumer sciences:** Child care. **Health:** Licensed practical nurse, medical assistant, nursing (RN), office assistant, pharmacy assistant, radiologic technology/medical imaging. **Mechanic/repair:** Electronics/electrical, watch/jewelry. **Visual/performing arts:** General, art, dramatic, studio arts.

Most popular majors. Business/marketing 14%, engineering/engineering technologies 8%, liberal arts 60%.

Computing on campus. 2,000 workstations in library, computer center, student center. Commuter students can connect to campus network. Online course registration, online library, helpline, repair service, student web hosting, wireless network available.

Student life. Freshman orientation: Available. Preregistration for classes offered. Students can select from in-person or on-line orientations. **Activities:** Bands, choral groups, drama, literary magazine, music ensembles, student government, student newspaper, TV station, Phi Theta Kappa, Black student union, Indonesian Community Club, Vietnamese student association, art group, international club, student leadership, Muslim student association, biomed club, Glof club.

Athletics. Intercollegiate: Basketball. **Intramural:** Basketball. **Team name:** Storm.

Student services. Adult student services, career counseling, services for economically disadvantaged, student employment services, financial aid counseling, minority student services, on-campus daycare, personal counseling, placement for graduates, veterans' counselor, women's services. **Physically disabled:** Services for visually, speech, hearing impaired. **Transfer:** Special adviser, orientation for new students. Transfer adviser, college fairs on campus for students transferring to 4-year colleges.

Contact. E-mail: NSCCRegistration@sccd.ctc.edu
Phone: (206) 527-3663 Fax: (206) 527-3671
Abts Betsy, Registrar / Director of Amdissions, North Seattle Community College, 9600 College Way North, Seattle, WA 98103

Northwest Aviation College
Auburn, Washington
www.afsnac.com **CB code: 3115**

- Private 2-year technical college
- Large town

General. Accredited by ACCSCT. Designated as 14 CFR Part 141 flight school, INS approved for issuance of I-20 for M1 and F1 visa. VA approved. **Enrollment:** 21 degree-seeking undergraduates; 22 non-degree-seeking students. **Degrees:** 3 associate awarded. **Location:** 7 miles from Seattle. **Calendar:** Quarter, extensive summer session.

Student profile. Among degree-seeking undergraduates, 100% enrolled in a vocational program.

Part-time:	38%	**Hispanic American:**	5%
Women:	29%		

Basis for selection. Open admission.

2005-2006 Annual costs. Program cost $45,006; includes tuition, books, materials, aircraft rental.

Application procedures. Admission: No deadline. No application fee. Application must be submitted on paper. Admission notification on a rolling basis.

Academics. Special study options: License preparation in aviation. **Credit/placement by examination:** CLEP.

Majors. Mechanic/repair: Avionics. **Transportation:** Airline/commercial pilot.

Contact. E-mail: spratt@afsnac.com
Phone: (253) 854-4960 Fax: (253) 931-0768
Shawn Pratt, Asst. Dir. of Education, Northwest Aviation College, 506 23rd St NE, Auburn, WA 98002

Northwest Indian College
Bellingham, Washington
www.nwic.edu **CB code: 3973**

- Private 2-year community college
- Small city

General. Regionally accredited. **Calendar:** Quarter.

Contact. Phone: (360) 676-2772
2522 Kwina Road, Bellingham, WA 98226-9217

Northwest School of Wooden Boatbuilding
Port Hadlock, Washington
www.nwboatschool.org **CB code: 3116**

- Private 1-year technical and maritime college
- Commuter campus in large town

General. Accredited by ACCSCT. Institution teaches traditional and contemporary wooden boatbuilding, including woodworking, drafting, lofting, repair and restoration, and yacht interiors. Supplemental courses are available in sailmaking, blacksmithing, rigging, boat design, and systems and wiring. **Enrollment:** 32 degree-seeking undergraduates. **Degrees:** 20 associate awarded. **Calendar:** Quarter, limited summer session. **Full-time faculty:** 6 total. **Special facilities:** Campus located on the Puget Sound. Classes take place in boathouses over the water.

Student profile.

Out-of-state:	80%	**Asian American:**	3%
Women:	9%	**25 or older:**	75%

Basis for selection. Open admission.

2005-2006 Annual costs. Twelve month programs offered for traditional large craft construction, traditional small craft construction, and contemporary wooden boat building at a cost of $14,300. Estimated cost of tools $1075. Books/supplies: $1,000.

Application procedures. Admission: No deadline. $100 fee. Application must be submitted on paper. Admission notification on a rolling basis.

Academics. Credit/placement by examination: AP, CLEP.

Majors. Mechanic/repair: Marine.

Computing on campus. 1 workstations in library.

Student life. Freshman orientation: Mandatory. **Policies:** Freshmen permitted cars on campus.

Contact. E-mail: Info@nwboatschool.org
Phone: (360) 385-4948 Fax: (360) 385-5089
Northwest School of Wooden Boatbuilding, 42 North Water Street, Port Hadlock, WA 98339

Olympic College
Bremerton, Washington
www.olympic.edu **CB code: 4583**

- Public 2-year community and liberal arts college
- Commuter campus in large town

General. Founded in 1946. Regionally accredited. Campuses at Shelton and Poulsbo. Classes also offered off-campus at Bangor Naval Base and some local high schools. **Enrollment:** 3,371 degree-seeking undergraduates; 3,084 non-degree-seeking students. **Degrees:** 964 associate awarded. **Location:** 30 miles from Seattle, 35 miles from Tacoma. **Calendar:** Quarter, extensive summer session. **Full-time faculty:** 100 total. **Part-time faculty:** 200 total. **Partnerships:** Formal partnerships with Puget Sound Naval Shipyard, Running Start (high schools), West Sound Technical (cosmetology), Service Corps of Retired Executives, the NW Women's Business Center, and Kitsap Regional Library.

Student profile. Among degree-seeking undergraduates, 71% enrolled in a transfer program, 29% enrolled in a vocational program, 679 enrolled as first-time, first-year students.

Part-time:	46%	**Asian American:**	8%
Out-of-state:	1%	**Hispanic American:**	5%
Women:	57%	**Native American:**	1%
African American:	3%	**25 or older:**	48%

Transfer out. Colleges most students transferred to 2005: University of Washington, Central Washington University, Washington State University, Western Washington University.

Basis for selection. Open admission, but selective for some programs. Admissions to registered nursing, licensed practical nursing, and medical office assistant programs. Based on number of requirements including prerequisites, academic GPA, and test scores. English and math placement assessment is administered to degree/certificate-seeking applicants or for those who wish to enroll in English or math classes. Nursing and health occupation programs require students to attend a pre-application orientation. **Adult students:** SAT/ACT scores not required. **Homeschooled:** Transcript of courses and grades required.

2005-2006 Annual costs. Tuition/fees: $2,625; $4,034 out-of-state. Per-credit charge: $72 in-state; $116 out-of-state. Books/supplies: $600. Personal expenses: $1,197.

2005-2006 Financial aid. Need-based: 67% of total undergraduate aid awarded as scholarships/grants, 33% as loans/jobs. Need-based aid available for part-time students. Work study available nights and for part-time students. **Non-need-based:** Scholarships awarded for academics, state residency.

Application procedures. Admission: No deadline. No application fee. Application may be submitted online. Admission notification on a rolling basis. **Financial aid:** Priority date 3/1; no closing date. FAFSA, institutional form required. Applicants notified on a rolling basis starting 6/1; must reply within 2 week(s) of notification.

Academics. Special study options: Combined bachelor's/graduate degree, cooperative education, cross-registration, distance learning, dual enrollment of high school students, ESL, independent study, internships, liberal arts/career combination, study abroad. 2-2 program with Old Dominion University permits completion of bachelor degree on premises at Olympic College, programs with Western Washington University and St. Martin's College. Running Start Program available for high school juniors/seniors with 2.5 GPA. Special articulation for professional/technical programs to transfer to Evergreen State College, Old Dominion, University of Washington-Tacoma in Business Management. Bachelor's degree programs available on campus. License preparation in nursing. **Credit/placement by examination:** AP, CLEP, IB, institutional tests. Credit awarded for credit by exam, experiential credit, or CLEP varies by degree program. **Support services:** GED preparation and test center, learning center, remedial instruction, study skills assistance, tutoring, writing center.

Majors. Business: General, accounting technology, administrative services, business admin. **Communications:** General. **Communications technology:** Animation/special effects. **Computer sciences:** Computer science, networking, programming, security. **Construction:** Electrician, plumbing. **Education:** General, early childhood. **Engineering:** General. **Engineering technology:** Drafting, electrical, industrial. **Health:** Licensed practical nurse, medical assistant, nursing (RN). **Legal studies:** Legal secretary. **Liberal arts:** Arts/sciences. **Mechanic/repair:** Automotive, marine. **Personal/culinary services:** Barbering, chef training, cosmetic. **Physical sciences:** Chemistry, geology, physics. **Production:** Welding. **Protective services:** Fire services admin, firefighting, police science. **Social sciences:** Anthropology, political science, sociology. **Visual/performing arts:** General, art.

Computing on campus. 650 workstations in library, computer center, student center. Commuter students can connect to campus network. Online course registration, online library, helpline, student web hosting available.

Student life. Freshman orientation: Available. Preregistration for classes offered. In person or online. In person orientation takes place before advising. **Policies:** Student code of conduct. Freshmen permitted cars on campus. **Housing:** Apartments available in surrounding areas for out-of-region students. **Activities:** Bands, choral groups, drama, music ensembles, musical theater, opera, student government, student newspaper, symphony orchestra, Phi Theta Kappa.

Athletics. NJCAA. **Intercollegiate:** Baseball M, basketball, golf, soccer, softball W, volleyball W, weight lifting. **Intramural:** Golf, soccer, weight lifting. **Team name:** Rangers.

Student services. Adult student services, career counseling, services for economically disadvantaged, student employment services, financial aid counseling, minority student services, on-campus daycare, personal counseling, placement for graduates, veterans' counselor, women's services. **Physically disabled:** Services for visually, speech, hearing impaired. **Transfer:** Special adviser, orientation, re-entry adviser for new students. Transfer adviser, college fairs on campus for students transferring to 4-year colleges.

Contact. E-mail: prospect@olympic.edu
Phone: (360) 475-7479 Toll-free number: (800) 259-6718 ext. 7479
Fax: (360) 475-7202
Gerraldine Stamm, Director, Admissions and Outreach, Olympic College, 1600 Chester Avenue, Bremerton, WA 98337-1699

Peninsula College
Port Angeles, Washington
www.pc.ctc.edu **CB code: 4615**

- Public 2-year community college
- Commuter campus in large town

General. Founded in 1961. Regionally accredited. **Enrollment:** 1,070 degree-seeking undergraduates; 3,062 non-degree-seeking students. **Degrees:** 209 associate awarded. **Location:** 75 miles from Seattle. **Calendar:** Quarter, limited summer session. **Full-time faculty:** 70 total; 27% have terminal degrees, 13% minority, 37% women. **Part-time faculty:** 233 total; 6% minority, 58% women. **Class size:** 76% < 20, 22% 20-39, 1% 40-49, less than 1% 50-99. **Special facilities:** Marine laboratory.

Student profile. Among degree-seeking undergraduates, 53% enrolled in a transfer program, 44% enrolled in a vocational program, 3% already have a bachelor's degree or higher, 164 enrolled as first-time, first-year students.

Part-time:	33%	**Hispanic American:**	4%
Out-of-state:	1%	**Native American:**	4%
Women:	57%	**International:**	2%
African American:	1%	**25 or older:**	63%
Asian American:	3%		

Transfer out. 49% of students enrolled in the transfer program go on to 4-year colleges.

Basis for selection. Open admission, but selective for some programs. Special requirements for nursing program. Admission to college does not guarantee admission to all courses or vocational education programs. Additional applications may be necessary. ASSET required for full-time applicants for placement only.

2005-2006 Annual costs. Tuition/fees: $2,532; $3,008 out-of-state. Per-credit charge: $75 in-state; $88 out-of-state. Books/supplies: $850. Personal expenses: $3,543.

Financial aid. Need-based: Need-based aid available for part-time students. **Non-need-based:** Scholarships awarded for academics, athletics, job skills.

Application procedures. Admission: No deadline. No application fee. Application may be submitted online. Admission notification on a rolling basis. **Financial aid:** Priority date 4/1; no closing date. FAFSA, institutional form required. Applicants notified on a rolling basis starting 6/1; must reply within 2 week(s) of notification.

Academics. Special study options: Distance learning, double major, ESL, honors, internships, liberal arts/career combination, study abroad. License preparation in dental hygiene, nursing. **Credit/placement by examination:** AP, CLEP, institutional tests. 10 credit hours maximum toward associate degree. Must complete minimum 30 quarter hours of credit in residency with 2.75 GPA. **Support services:** GED preparation and test center, learning center, reduced course load, remedial instruction, study skills assistance, tutoring, writing center.

Majors. Business: Accounting, accounting technology, administrative services, business admin, marketing, office management. **Communications:** Journalism. **Computer sciences:** General, applications programming, data processing, networking, vendor certification, web page design. **Conservation:** Fisheries. **Education:** Early childhood. **Engineering technology:** Surveying. **Family/consumer sciences:** Child care. **Health:** Medical assistant, medical secretary, nursing (RN), substance abuse counseling. **Liberal arts:** Arts/sciences. **Mechanic/repair:** Automotive, diesel, electronics/electrical. **Protective services:** Corrections, law enforcement admin.

Most popular majors. Business/marketing 7%, computer/information sciences 6%, health sciences 12%, liberal arts 67%.

Computing on campus. 38 workstations in library, computer center, student center. Online course registration, online library available.

Student life. Freshman orientation: Mandatory. Preregistration for classes offered. **Policies:** Freshmen permitted cars on campus. **Activities:** Jazz band, choral groups, dance, drama, literary magazine, music ensembles, student government, student newspaper, symphony orchestra, Christian Collegiate Fellowship, Communications Careers Club, Native American Nations, Phi Theta Kappa, Phi Beta Lambda, IT club, Basketball Club, German Club.

Athletics. Intercollegiate: Basketball, soccer M, softball W. **Intramural:** Basketball, bowling, soccer, softball, tennis. **Team name:** Pirates.

Student services. Adult student services, career counseling, services for economically disadvantaged, student employment services, financial aid counseling, on-campus daycare, personal counseling, placement for graduates, veterans' counselor. **Physically disabled:** Services for visually, hearing impaired. **Transfer:** Special adviser, orientation, pre-admission transcript evaluation for new students. Transfer adviser, college fairs on campus for students transferring to 4-year colleges.

Contact. E-mail: admissions@pcadmin.ctc.edu
Phone: (360) 452-9277 Toll-free number: (877) 452-9277
Fax: (360) 417-6581
Cindy Lauderback, Enrollment Service Manager, Peninsula College, 1502 East Lauridsen Boulevard, Port Angeles, WA 98362

Pierce College

Lakewood, Washington
www.pierce.ctc.edu **CB code: 4103**

- Public 2-year community college
- Commuter campus in small city

General. Founded in 1967. Regionally accredited. Two colleges in Puyallup and Lakewood and education centers at Fort Lewis, McChord, McNeil Island, Cedar Creek, Western State Hospital and Rainier School. Extensive distance learning. **Enrollment:** 4,639 degree-seeking undergraduates. **Degrees:** 1,441 associate awarded. **ROTC:** Army. **Location:** 10 miles from downtown. **Calendar:** Quarter, limited summer session. **Full-time faculty:** 133 total; 19% have terminal degrees, 16% minority, 51% women. **Part-time faculty:** 337 total; 9% minority, 60% women. **Class size:** 82% < 20, 17% 20-39, 1% 40-49, less than 1% 50-99. **Special facilities:** Bird refuge, international house (video conferencing center for international/cross-cultural communications). **Partnerships:** Formal partnership with the Institute of Real Estate Management (IREM).

Student profile. Among degree-seeking undergraduates, 1,131 enrolled as first-time, first-year students.

Part-time:	47%	**Women:**	59%
Out-of-state:	1%	**25 or older:**	48%

Transfer out. Colleges most students transferred to 2005: University of Washington (Seattle), University of Washington (Tacoma), Western Washington University, Central Washington University.

Basis for selection. Open admission, but selective for some programs. Admissions to dental hygiene and veterinary technology programs based on college course work, high school GPA, and/or related work experience. Running Start students must test at college level in English prior to admission. Students required to take ASSET or COMPASS placement tests to register for math, English, or reading courses. **Learning Disabled:** Accomodations for placement testing.

High school preparation. Algebra, biology, and chemistry required of veterinary technology applicants. Dental hygiene applicants have special mathematics/science requirements.

2005-2006 Annual costs. Tuition/fees: $2,454; $2,907 out-of-state. Per-credit charge: $72 in-state; $86 out-of-state. Books/supplies: $894. Personal expenses: $1,476.

Financial aid. Need-based: Need-based aid available for part-time students. Work study available for part-time students. **Non-need-based:** Scholarships awarded for academics, athletics, music/drama.

Application procedures. Admission: No deadline. No application fee. Application may be submitted online. Admission notification on a rolling basis. March 1 closing date for veterinary technology applications, February 1 for dental hygiene. High school students admitted early through Running Start Program. Must test at college level prior to admission. **Financial aid:** Priority date 4/15; no closing date. FAFSA, institutional form required. Applicants notified on a rolling basis starting 4/15.

Academics. Special study options: Cooperative education, cross-registration, distance learning, double major, dual enrollment of high school students, ESL, independent study, internships, student-designed major, study abroad, weekend college. License preparation in dental hygiene, nursing, real estate. **Credit/placement by examination:** AP, CLEP, institutional tests. 65 credit hours maximum toward associate degree. Credit by exam does not count toward degree residency requirement. **Support services:** GED preparation and test center, learning center, pre-admission summer program, reduced course load, remedial instruction, study skills assistance, tutoring, writing center.

Majors. Agriculture: Animal sciences, landscaping. **Business:** General, accounting, administrative services, business admin, office management, office/clerical. **Computer sciences:** Data processing, programming. **Construction:** Site management. **Education:** Business, early childhood, teacher assistance. **Engineering technology:** Electrical. **Family/consumer sciences:** Child care. **Health:** Clinical lab assistant, dental hygiene, medical secretary, mental health services, substance abuse counseling, veterinary technology/assistant. **Legal studies:** Legal secretary, paralegal. **Liberal arts:** Arts/sciences. **Protective services:** Criminal justice, fire safety technology. **Visual/performing arts:** Commercial/advertising art.

Computing on campus. 600 workstations in library, computer center. Online course registration, helpline, wireless network available.

Student life. Freshman orientation: Available. 2-hour orientation offered quarterly and throughout summer. **Activities:** Bands, choral groups, drama, literary magazine, music ensembles, musical theater, student government, student newspaper, ethnic and foreign student associations, religious organizations, special interest clubs, Phi Theta Kappa, Barrier Breakers (disabled students).

Athletics. Intercollegiate: Baseball M, basketball, soccer M, softball W, volleyball W. **Intramural:** Cheerleading. **Team name:** Raiders.

Student services. Adult student services, career counseling, services for economically disadvantaged, student employment services, financial aid counseling, minority student services, personal counseling, veterans' counselor, women's services. **Physically disabled:** Services for visually, speech, hearing impaired. **Transfer:** Special adviser, orientation for new students. Transfer center, transfer adviser, college fairs on campus for students transferring to 4-year colleges.

Contact. E-mail: cburbank@pierce.ctc.edu
Phone: (253) 964-6501 Fax: (253) 964-6764
Cynthia Torres-Jiminez, Registrar, Pierce College, 9401 Farwest Drive SW, Lakewood, WA 98498-1999

Renton Technical College

Renton, Washington
www.RTC.edu **CB code: 0790**

- Public 2-year technical college
- Commuter campus in large town

General. Founded in 1942. Regionally accredited. **Enrollment:** 1,290 undergraduates. **Degrees:** 190 associate awarded. **Location:** 10 miles from Seattle. **Calendar:** Quarter, extensive summer session. **Full-time faculty:** 80 total. **Part-time faculty:** 150 total.

Student profile. 79% enrolled in a vocational program.

Basis for selection. Open admission. ACT, ASSET and SLEP scores required for all applicants for placement purposes. Interview recommended. **Adult students:** Students must complete on-campus assessment upon arrival.

2005-2006 Annual costs. Tuition/fees: $2,866; $2,866 out-of-state. Books/supplies: $690. Personal expenses: $1,825.

Financial aid. All financial aid based on need. Need-based aid available for part-time students.

Application procedures. Admission: No deadline. $25 fee, may be waived for applicants with need. Application must be submitted on paper. Admission notification on a rolling basis. **Financial aid:** No deadline. FAFSA, institutional form required. Applicants notified on a rolling basis.

Academics. Many programs have co-op component. **Special study options:** Cooperative education, distance learning, dual enrollment of high school students, ESL, external degree, internships, liberal arts/career combination, student-designed major. License preparation in nursing. **Credit/placement by examination:** CLEP. 30 credit hours maximum toward associate degree. **Support services:** GED preparation and test center, learning center, remedial instruction, study skills assistance, tutoring.

Majors. Business: Accounting, administrative services, office management, office/clerical. **Computer sciences:** Applications programming, computer science, networking, programming. **Construction:** Carpentry. **Education:** Business, early childhood, health, teacher assistance, trade/industrial, voc/tech. **Engineering:** Electrical. **Engineering technology:** Drafting, electrical, surveying. **Health:** Dental assistant, insurance coding, licensed practical nurse, massage therapy, medical assistant, medical records admin, medical records technology, medical secretary, pharmacy assistant, surgical technology. **Legal studies:** Paralegal. **Mechanic/repair:** Auto body, automotive, electronics/electrical, heating/ac/refrig, industrial, musical instruments. **Personal/culinary services:** Culinary arts. **Production:** Machine shop technology.

Computing on campus. 150 workstations in library, computer center, student center. Online library available.

Student life. Freshman orientation: Available. **Activities:** Student newspaper.

Student services. Career counseling, student employment services, financial aid counseling, on-campus daycare, personal counseling, placement for graduates. **Physically disabled:** Services for visually, speech, hearing impaired. **Transfer:** Special adviser, orientation for new students. Transfer adviser for students transferring to 4-year colleges.

Contact. E-mail: cdanielson@rtc.edu
Phone: (425) 235-5840 Fax: (425) 235-7832
John Pozega, VP Student Services, Renton Technical College, 3000 Northeast Fourth Street, Renton, WA 98056-4195

Seattle Central Community College

Seattle, Washington
www.seattlecentral.org **CB code: 4741**

- Public 2-year community college
- Commuter campus in very large city

General. Founded in 1966. Regionally accredited. **Enrollment:** 5,830 degree-seeking undergraduates. **Degrees:** 1,150 associate awarded. **Calendar:** Quarter, limited summer session. **Full-time faculty:** 157 total. **Part-time faculty:** 426 total.

Basis for selection. Open admission, but selective for some programs. Limited admission to health sciences and vocational programs. Essay, interview recommended for all; audition recommended for music; portfolio required for art, photography.

2005-2006 Annual costs. Tuition/fees: $2,666; $7,874 out-of-state. Per-credit charge: $71 in-state; $243 out-of-state. Books/supplies: $720. Personal expenses: $1,896.

2004-2005 Financial aid. All financial aid based on need. Need-based aid available for part-time students. Work study available nights, weekends and for part-time students. **Additional information:** Currently enrolled international students can apply for institutional scholarship in second year of study.

Application procedures. Admission: No deadline. No application fee. Admission notification on a rolling basis. **Financial aid:** Priority date 4/30, closing date 8/6. FAFSA, institutional form required. Applicants notified on a rolling basis; must reply within 2 week(s) of notification.

Academics. Special study options: Cooperative education, distance learning, dual enrollment of high school students, independent study, internships, study abroad. **Credit/placement by examination:** CLEP, institutional tests. **Support services:** GED preparation, learning center, remedial instruction, tutoring.

Majors. Biology: Biotechnology. **Business:** Accounting, administrative services, fashion. **Communications:** General, advertising. **Communications technology:** Graphic/printing, graphics, photo/film/video, printing management. **Computer sciences:** General, applications programming, information technology, programming. **Construction:** Carpentry. **Education:** General. **Engineering technology:** Drafting. **Foreign languages:** Sign language interpretation. **Health:** Mental health services, preop/surgical nursing, respiratory therapy technology. **Liberal arts:** Arts/sciences. **Personal/culinary services:** General, baking, chef training, culinary arts. **Production:** Woodworking. **Public administration:** Human services. **Visual/performing arts:** Commercial photography.

Computing on campus. 190 workstations in library, computer center, student center.

Student life. Freshman orientation: Mandatory. **Activities:** Choral groups, dance, drama, student government, student newspaper, numerous ethnic/minority, socio-political, cultural clubs available.

Athletics. Intramural: Baseball M, basketball, soccer, volleyball.

Student services. Career counseling, student employment services, financial aid counseling, minority student services, on-campus daycare, personal counseling, veterans' counselor, women's services. **Physically disabled:** Services for visually, speech, hearing impaired. **Transfer:** Special adviser, orientation for new students. Transfer adviser, college fairs on campus for students transferring to 4-year colleges.

Contact. E-mail: admiss@sccd.ctc.edu
Phone: (206) 587-5450 Fax: (206) 587-6321
Admissions Director, Seattle Central Community College, 1701 Broadway, Seattle, WA 98122

Shoreline Community College

Shoreline, Washington
www.shoreline.edu **CB code: 4738**

- Public 2-year community college
- Commuter campus in small city

General. Founded in 1964. Regionally accredited. Courses available at Lake Forest Park campus. **Enrollment:** 3,299 degree-seeking undergraduates. **Degrees:** 869 associate awarded. **Location:** 10 miles from Seattle. **Calendar:** Quarter, limited summer session. **Full-time faculty:** 157 total; 15% minority, 57% women. **Part-time faculty:** 237 total; 14% minority, 64% women.

Student profile. Among degree-seeking undergraduates, 37% enrolled in a transfer program, 39% enrolled in a vocational program.

Transfer out. Colleges most students transferred to 2005: University of Washington, Western Washington University.

Basis for selection. Open admission, but selective for some programs. Nursing and dental hygiene programs use competitive admissions process. SAT, ACT, or ASSET required for English and math placement unless student has taken college-level English or math with grades of C or better.

2005-2006 Annual costs. Tuition/fees: $2,364; $4,482 out-of-state. Per-credit charge: $72 in-state; $141 out-of-state. Books/supplies: $894. Personal expenses: $3,516.

Financial aid. Need-based: Work study available nights, weekends and for part-time students. **Additional information:** Tuition and/or fee waiver for students with need on space-available basis.

Application procedures. Admission: No deadline. No application fee. Admission notification on a rolling basis beginning on or about 2/1. **Financial aid:** Priority date 4/1; no closing date. FAFSA, institutional form required. Applicants notified on a rolling basis starting 8/1; must reply within 3 week(s) of notification.

Academics. Special study options: Cooperative education, cross-registration, distance learning, dual enrollment of high school students, ESL, independent study, internships, study abroad. Senior College for senior citizens. **Credit/placement by examination:** CLEP, IB. **Support services:** GED preparation and test center, learning center, remedial instruction, tutoring.

Majors. Biology: Biotechnology. **Business:** Accounting technology, business admin, fashion, international, logistics, marketing, sales/distribution, small business admin. **Communications:** Broadcast journalism. **Communications technology:** Graphic/printing. **Computer sciences:** General, data processing, database management, networking, web page design. **Education:** Early childhood, special, teacher assistance. **Engineering:** General, civil, mechanical. **Engineering technology:** CAD/CADD, civil, drafting, industrial, manufacturing, mechanical. **Family/consumer sciences:** Food/nutrition. **Health:** Clinical lab assistant, dental hygiene, dietetics, medical records technology, nursing (RN). **Liberal arts:** Arts/sciences. **Mechanic/repair:** Automotive. **Personal/culinary services:** Cosmetic. **Physical sciences:** General, oceanography. **Production:** Machine tool. **Protective services:** Law enforcement admin. **Science technology:** Biological. **Visual/performing arts:** Cinematography, commercial/advertising art, design, music management, music performance, photography, theater design.

Most popular majors. Health sciences 18%, liberal arts 57%.

Computing on campus. 450 workstations in library, computer center. Commuter students can connect to campus network. Online library, helpline, wireless network available.

Student life. Freshman orientation: Mandatory. Preregistration for classes offered. Two to three hours, prior to each quarter. **Policies:** Freshmen permitted cars on campus. **Activities:** Bands, choral groups, drama, literary magazine, music ensembles, musical theater, opera, student government, student newspaper, International club, Black Student Union, arts and entertainment board, women's club, Cambodian club, Vietnamese club, DEC, Phi Theta Kappa, Student Body Association.

Athletics. NJCAA. **Intercollegiate:** Baseball M, basketball, soccer, softball W, tennis, volleyball W. **Intramural:** Basketball, bowling, diving, fencing, racquetball, skiing, soccer, softball W, swimming, tennis, volleyball. **Team name:** Dolphins.

Student services. Adult student services, career counseling, student employment services, financial aid counseling, minority student services, on-campus daycare, personal counseling, placement for graduates, veterans' counselor, women's services. **Physically disabled:** Services for visually, hearing impaired. **Transfer:** Special adviser, orientation for new students. Transfer adviser, college fairs on campus for students transferring to 4-year colleges.

Contact. E-mail: sccadmis@ctc.edu
Phone: (206) 546-4621 Fax: (206) 546-5835
Chris Melton, Assistant Registrar, Shoreline Community College, 16101 Greenwood Avenue North, Seattle, WA 98133

Skagit Valley College

Mount Vernon, Washington
www.skagit.edu **CB code: 4699**

- Public 2-year community college
- Commuter campus in large town

General. Founded in 1926. Regionally accredited. 2 campuses: Mount Vernon (main campus) and Oak Harbor on Whidbey Island. **Enrollment:** 2,400 full-time, degree-seeking students. **Degrees:** 660 associate awarded. **Location:** 60 miles from Seattle; 90 miles from Vancouver, British Columbia. **Calendar:** Quarter, extensive summer session. **Full-time faculty:** 125 total. **Part-time faculty:** 120 total. **Partnerships:** Contract programs with Washington businesses, Tech Prep, College in the High School.

Student profile.

Out-of-state:	4%	**Live on campus:**	2%
25 or older:	56%		

Transfer out. Colleges most students transferred to 2005: Everett Community College, Whatcom Community College, Western Washington University, Edmonds Community College, University of Washington.

Basis for selection. Open admission. High school diploma required for some programs. ASSET or COMPASS required for degree seeking students or for those wishing to enroll in English and mathematics. **Adult students:** Entrance exam policies same as for first-time freshmen.

2005-2006 Annual costs. Tuition/fees: $2,580; $2,991 out-of-state. Per-credit charge: $75 in-state; $92 out-of-state. Books/supplies: $645. Personal expenses: $1,650.

Financial aid. All financial aid based on need. Need-based aid available for part-time students. Work study available nights, weekends and for part-time students.

Application procedures. Admission: No deadline. No application fee. Application may be submitted online. Admission notification on a rolling basis. **Financial aid:** Priority date 3/1; no closing date. FAFSA, institutional form required. Applicants notified on a rolling basis starting 7/1; must reply within 2 week(s) of notification.

Academics. Special study options: Cooperative education, cross-registration, distance learning, dual enrollment of high school students, ESL, external degree, honors, independent study, internships, study abroad, weekend college. License preparation in nursing. **Credit/placement by examination:** CLEP, IB, institutional tests. 15 credit hours maximum toward associate degree. **Support services:** GED preparation and test center, learning center, pre-admission summer program, reduced course load, remedial instruction, study skills assistance, tutoring, writing center.

Majors. Agriculture: Business, dairy, horticulture. **Business:** Accounting, administrative services, business admin, hospitality/recreation. **Communications:** General. **Computer sciences:** General, applications programming, information systems, programming. **Conservation:** General. **Education:** Early childhood. **Engineering:** Electrical. **Engineering technology:** Electrical. **Health:** Licensed practical nurse, nursing (RN), prenursing. **Legal studies:** Paralegal. **Liberal arts:** Arts/sciences. **Mechanic/repair:** Automotive, diesel, electronics/electrical. **Personal/culinary services:** Culinary arts. **Protective services:** Firefighting. **Public administration:** Human services. **Visual/performing arts:** Commercial/advertising art.

Most popular majors. Business/marketing 7%, computer/information sciences 7%, liberal arts 68%.

Computing on campus. 250 workstations in library, computer center. Commuter students can connect to campus network. Online course registration, helpline, repair service, student web hosting available.

Student life. Freshman orientation: Available. Preregistration for classes offered. Orientation/registration/testing before start of each quarter. Evening and day orientation at beginning of each quarter. **Policies:** Freshmen permitted cars on campus. **Housing:** Apartments available. $180 deposit. **Activities:** Bands, choral groups, dance, drama, literary magazine, music ensembles, musical theater, radio station, student government, student newspaper, symphony orchestra, Calling All Color, nurses club, firefighters club, Campus Christian Fellowship, sailing club, Delta Epsilon Chi, ski club, horticultural club, Phi Theta Kappa, international club.

Athletics. Intercollegiate: Baseball M, basketball, golf, soccer, softball W, tennis, volleyball W. **Intramural:** Badminton, baseball M, basketball, bowling, golf, sailing, soccer, softball, tennis, volleyball. **Team name:** Cardinals.

Student services. Adult student services, career counseling, services for economically disadvantaged, student employment services, financial aid counseling, health services, minority student services, on-campus daycare, personal counseling, placement for graduates, veterans' counselor, women's services. **Physically disabled:** Services for visually, speech, hearing impaired. **Transfer:** Special adviser, orientation, re-entry adviser, pre-admission transcript evaluation for new students. Transfer center, transfer adviser, college fairs on campus for students transferring to 4-year colleges.

Contact. E-mail: admissions@skagit.edu
Phone: (360) 416-7697 Toll-free number: (877) 385-5360
Fax: (360) 416-7890
Karen Ackelson, Recruitment and Admissions, Skagit Valley College, 2405 East College Way, Mount Vernon, WA 98273

South Puget Sound Community College

Olympia, Washington
www.spscc.ctc.edu **CB code: 4578**

- Public 2-year community and junior college
- Commuter campus in small city

General. Founded in 1962. Regionally accredited. **Enrollment:** 5,044 degree-seeking undergraduates. **Degrees:** 656 associate awarded. **ROTC:** Air Force. **Location:** 60 miles from Seattle. **Calendar:** Quarter, limited summer session. **Full-time faculty:** 95 total. **Part-time faculty:** 175 total.

Student profile.

Out-of-state:	5%	**25 or older:**	45%

Transfer out. Colleges most students transferred to 2005: The Evergreen State College, University of Washington, Washington State University, Western Washington State University.

Basis for selection. Open admission, but selective for some programs. Special requirements for nursing, dental assisting, fire protection.

2005-2006 Annual costs. Tuition/fees: $2,435; $2,824 out-of-state. Per-credit charge: $72 in-state; $85 out-of-state. Books/supplies: $720. Personal expenses: $1,896.

Financial aid. Need-based: Need-based aid available for part-time students. **Non-need-based:** Scholarships awarded for academics, athletics.

Application procedures. Admission: Priority date 5/19; no deadline. No application fee. Admission notification on a rolling basis beginning on or about 12/1. Early applicants register in mid-July for fall quarter. **Financial aid:** Priority date 5/1; no closing date. FAFSA, institutional form required. Applicants notified on a rolling basis starting 7/10; must reply within 2 week(s) of notification.

Academics. Special study options: Cooperative education, cross-registration, distance learning, dual enrollment of high school students, ESL, independent study, internships, study abroad, weekend college. License preparation in nursing. **Credit/placement by examination:** AP, CLEP, institutional tests. 45 credit hours maximum toward associate degree. **Support services:** GED preparation and test center, learning center, remedial instruction, tutoring.

Majors. Agriculture: Horticulture, ornamental horticulture. **Business:** General, accounting, administrative services, hospitality admin, office/clerical. **Computer sciences:** Applications programming, data processing, information systems. **Education:** Early childhood. **Engineering technology:** Drafting, electrical. **Health:** Dental assistant, medical assistant, medical secretary, medical transcription. **Legal studies:** Legal secretary, paralegal. **Liberal arts:** Arts/sciences. **Personal/culinary services:** Culinary arts. **Protective services:** Fire services admin, firefighting.

Computing on campus. 450 workstations in library, computer center. Commuter students can connect to campus network. Online course registration available.

Student life. Freshman orientation: Available. **Activities:** Choral groups, drama, literary magazine, student government, student newspaper.

Athletics. NJCAA. **Intercollegiate:** Basketball, soccer M, softball W. **Intramural:** Baseball M, basketball, handball, racquetball, softball, volleyball.

Student services. Career counseling, student employment services, financial aid counseling, minority student services, on-campus daycare, personal counseling, placement for graduates, veterans' counselor. **Physically disabled:** Services for visually, speech, hearing impaired. **Transfer:** Special adviser, orientation for new students. Transfer adviser, college fairs on campus for students transferring to 4-year colleges.

Contact. E-mail: enrollmentservices@spscc.ctc.edu
Phone: (360) 754-7711 ext. 5241 Fax: (360) 596-5907
Kathy Lundeen, Director of Admissions and Outreach Services, South Puget Sound Community College, 2011 Mottman Road Southwest, Olympia, WA 98512-6218

South Seattle Community College

Seattle, Washington
www.southseattle.edu **CB code: 4759**

- Public 2-year community college
- Commuter campus in very large city

General. Founded in 1969. Regionally accredited. **Enrollment:** 1,829 degree-seeking undergraduates; 6,604 non-degree-seeking students. **Degrees:** 400 associate awarded. **Location:** 10 miles from downtown. **Calendar:** Quarter, limited summer session. **Full-time faculty:** 76 total. **Part-time faculty:** 237 total. **Special facilities:** College operated bakery, arboretum; Chinese Garden under development.

Student profile. Among degree-seeking undergraduates, 17% enrolled in a transfer program, 51% enrolled in a vocational program, 11% already have a bachelor's degree or higher.

Part-time:	56%	**25 or older:**	66%
Women:	59%		

Transfer out. Colleges most students transferred to 2005: University of Washington.

Basis for selection. Open admission. COMPASS, CELSA tests used for placement and counseling. **Adult students:** Entrance exam policies same as for first-time freshmen. **Learning Disabled:** Referred to Educational Support Services Office.

High school preparation. Accept students for ABG, GED, high-school and college-level work.

2005-2006 Annual costs. Tuition/fees: $2,552; $7,760 out-of-state. Per-credit charge: $72 in-state; $244 out-of-state. Books/supplies: $894. Personal expenses: $1,476.

2005-2006 Financial aid. Need-based: 92% of total undergraduate aid awarded as scholarships/grants, 8% as loans/jobs. Need-based aid available for part-time students. Work study available for part-time students. **Non-need-based:** Scholarships awarded for academics, state residency.

Application procedures. Admission: No deadline. No application fee. Application may be submitted online. Admission notification on a rolling basis. **Financial aid:** No deadline. FAFSA, institutional form required. Applicants notified on a rolling basis starting 7/1.

Academics. Special study options: Cross-registration, distance learning, dual enrollment of high school students, ESL, independent study, internships, study abroad, teacher certification program. Concurrent enrollment agreements with other colleges in vicinity. License preparation in aviation, nursing. **Credit/placement by examination:** CLEP, IB, institutional tests. Credit awarded for CLEP applies only to electives category of Associate of Arts degree. **Support services:** GED preparation and test center, learning center, remedial instruction, study skills assistance, tutoring, writing center.

Majors. Agriculture: Landscaping, nursery operations, ornamental horticulture. **Architecture:** Landscape. **Area/ethnic studies:** Asian. **Business:** General, accounting, administrative services, hospitality admin, office management, office technology, restaurant/food services. **Computer sciences:** General, computer graphics, information systems, LAN/WAN management, programming, web page design. **Construction:** Electrician. **Education:** Trade/industrial. **Engineering:** General, software. **Engineering technology:** Civil, drafting. **Liberal arts:** Arts/sciences. **Mechanic/repair:** Aircraft, aircraft powerplant, auto body, automotive, avionics. **Personal/culinary services:** Baking, chef training, cosmetic, culinary arts, food prep, restaurant/catering. **Production:** Welding.

Computing on campus. 700 workstations in library, computer center, student center. Commuter students can connect to campus network. Online course registration, online library, helpline, wireless network available.

Student life. Freshman orientation: Available. Preregistration for classes offered. **Policies:** Enrollment in 10 or more credits and 2.0 cumulative GPA required to serve as student government representative. Freshmen permitted cars on campus. **Activities:** Choral groups, literary magazine, student government, student newspaper, Vietnamese Student club, 3 Trio Grant Program, United Student Association, international student club, Afro American Club, Cambodian Club, Gay Straight alliance, engineering club, Aviation Technician Association.

Athletics. Intramural: Baseball, basketball, soccer.

Student services. Adult student services, career counseling, services for economically disadvantaged, student employment services, financial aid counseling, minority student services, on-campus daycare, placement for graduates, veterans' counselor, women's services. **Physically disabled:** Services for visually, speech, hearing impaired. **Transfer:** Special adviser, orientation, pre-admission transcript evaluation for new students. Transfer center, transfer adviser, college fairs on campus for students transferring to 4-year colleges.

Contact. E-mail: rrimando@sccd.ctc.edu
Phone: (206) 786-7943 Toll-free number: (206) 764-6691
Fax: (206) 764-7947
Rosinette Rimando, Director of Admissions, South Seattle Community College, 6000 16th Avenue Southwest, Seattle, WA 98106-1499

Spokane Community College

Spokane, Washington
www.scc.spokane.edu **CB code: 4739**

- Public 2-year community college
- Commuter campus in small city

General. Founded in 1963. Regionally accredited. **Enrollment:** 6,152 degree-seeking undergraduates. **Degrees:** 1,100 associate awarded. **ROTC:** Army, Navy, Air Force. **Location:** 2 miles from downtown. **Calendar:** Quarter, limited summer session. **Full-time faculty:** 200 total. **Part-time faculty:** 190 total. **Special facilities:** Nursery, floral shop, automotive repair service center, cosmetology center.

Student profile. Among degree-seeking undergraduates, 31% enrolled in a transfer program, 51% enrolled in a vocational program, 4% already have a bachelor's degree or higher, 2,011 enrolled as first-time, first-year students.

Part-time:	15%	**Women:**	58%
Out-of-state:	4%	**25 or older:**	54%

Transfer out. Colleges most students transferred to 2005: Eastern Washington University, Washington State University.

Basis for selection. Open admission, but selective for some programs. Some programs require prerequisites or have special selection procedures. Admission to college does not guarantee acceptance in every program. ASSET used for placement. **Homeschooled:** If under 18, must be deemed able to benefit from curricular offerings of college. Required to take ASSET or COMPASS tests and must place at college level.

2005-2006 Annual costs. Tuition/fees: $2,546; $7,754 out-of-state. Per-credit charge: $72 in-state; $244 out-of-state. Books/supplies: $780. Personal expenses: $3,012.

2004-2005 Financial aid. Need-based: 97% of total undergraduate aid awarded as scholarships/grants, 3% as loans/jobs. **Non-need-based:** Scholarships awarded for athletics.

Application procedures. Admission: No deadline. $15 fee, may be waived for applicants with need. Admission notification on a rolling basis beginning on or about 1/1. **Financial aid:** No deadline. FAFSA, institutional form required. Applicants notified on a rolling basis; must reply within 2 week(s) of notification.

Academics. Special study options: Cooperative education, cross-registration, distance learning, dual enrollment of high school students, ESL, independent study, internships, student-designed major, study abroad. License preparation in nursing, paramedic. **Credit/placement by examination:** AP, CLEP, institutional tests. 60 credit hours maximum toward associate degree. **Support services:** Learning center, reduced course load, remedial instruction, study skills assistance, tutoring, writing center.

Majors. Agriculture: Business, greenhouse operations, horticulture, nursery operations, soil science, turf management. **Business:** General, accounting, administrative services, banking/financial services, business admin, management information systems, marketing, office management, office technology, office/clerical, selling, vehicle parts marketing. **Computer sciences:** Applications programming, data processing, information systems. **Conservation:** Forest resources, forestry, water/wetlands/marine, wildlife. **Construction:** Carpentry, power transmission. **Engineering technology:** Architectural, civil, construction, electrical, hydraulics, robotics. **Health:** Cardiovascular technology, clinical lab technology, dental assistant, EMT paramedic, medical secretary, optician, pharmacy assistant, recreational therapy, respiratory therapy technology, surgical technology, ward clerk. **Legal studies:** Legal secretary, paralegal, prelaw. **Liberal arts:** Arts/sciences. **Mechanic/repair:** Aircraft, auto body, diesel, electronics/electrical, heating/ac/refrig, industrial. **Parks/recreation:** Facilities management. **Personal/culinary services:** Cosmetic, culinary arts. **Protective services:** Corrections, fire services admin, law enforcement admin, police science, security services.

Most popular majors. Engineering/engineering technologies 11%, health sciences 25%, liberal arts 33%, trade and industry 14%.

Computing on campus. 913 workstations in library, computer center, student center. Online course registration available.

Student life. Freshman orientation: Available. Preregistration for classes offered. **Policies:** Freshmen permitted cars on campus. **Activities:** Drama, literary magazine, student government, student newspaper.

Athletics. Intercollegiate: Baseball M, basketball, cross-country, golf, soccer, softball W, tennis, track and field, volleyball W. **Team name:** Big Foot.

Student services. Adult student services, career counseling, services for economically disadvantaged, student employment services, financial aid counseling, minority student services, on-campus daycare, personal counseling, placement for graduates, veterans' counselor. **Physically disabled:** Services for visually, speech, hearing impaired. **Transfer:** Orientation for new students. College fairs on campus for students transferring to 4-year colleges.

Contact. Phone: (509) 533-8860 Toll-free number: (800) 248-5644
Fax: (509) 533-8860
Doug Jones, Dean of Student Services for Enrollment Services, Spokane Community College, 1810 North Greene Street, Spokane, WA 99217-5399

Spokane Falls Community College

Spokane, Washington
www.spokanefalls.edu **CB code: 4752**

- Public 2-year community college
- Commuter campus in small city
- Interview required

General. Founded in 1967. Regionally accredited. 60-foot Foucault pendulum. **Enrollment:** 5,528 degree-seeking undergraduates. **Degrees:** 985 associate awarded. **ROTC:** Army. **Location:** 4 miles from downtown. **Calendar:** Quarter, limited summer session. **Full-time faculty:** 161 total; 11% minority, 58% women. **Part-time faculty:** 412 total; 3% minority, 46% women. **Special facilities:** Theater, performing arts center, art gallery.

Student profile. Among degree-seeking undergraduates, 68% enrolled in a transfer program, 22% enrolled in a vocational program, 3% already have a bachelor's degree or higher, 1,828 enrolled as first-time, first-year students.

Part-time:	28%	**Women:**	57%

Transfer out. Colleges most students transferred to 2005: Spokane Community Colleges, Big Bend Community College.

Basis for selection. Open admission, but selective for some programs. Some programs require prerequisites or have special selection procedures. Admission to college does not guarantee acceptance to every program. ASSET test required for placement.

2005-2006 Annual costs. Tuition/fees: $2,576; $7,784 out-of-state. Per-credit charge: $72 in-state; $244 out-of-state. Books/supplies: $780. Personal expenses: $3,012.

Financial aid. All financial aid based on need. Need-based aid available for part-time students.

Application procedures. Admission: No deadline. $15 fee. Application may be submitted online. Admission notification on a rolling basis. **Financial aid:** Priority date 4/1; no closing date. FAFSA, institutional form required. Applicants notified on a rolling basis starting 5/15; must reply within 2 week(s) of notification.

Academics. Special study options: Cooperative education, cross-registration, distance learning, dual enrollment of high school students, ESL, honors, independent study, internships, study abroad, weekend college. License preparation in aviation, physical therapy. **Credit/placement by examination:** AP, CLEP, institutional tests. 60 credit hours maximum toward associate degree. **Support services:** GED preparation and test center, learning center, remedial instruction, study skills assistance, tutoring, writing center.

Majors. Architecture: Interior. **Business:** General, accounting, administrative services, banking/financial services, business admin, fashion, international, management information systems, marketing, office management, office/clerical, tourism/travel. **Communications:** Journalism. **Communications**

technology: General. **Computer sciences:** General, computer graphics, computer science, information systems, web page design. **Education:** General, early childhood, special, teacher assistance. **Engineering:** General. **Engineering technology:** Architectural, drafting, electrical. **Foreign languages:** General, sign language interpretation. **Health:** Athletic training, clinical lab technology, health services, medical assistant, medical records technology, nursing (RN), occupational therapy assistant, orthotics/prosthetics, physical therapy assistant, prenursing, substance abuse counseling, vocational rehab counseling. **Legal studies:** Paralegal. **Liberal arts:** Arts/sciences. **Math:** General. **Mechanic/repair:** Automotive. **Parks/recreation:** Sports admin. **Protective services:** Firefighting, law enforcement admin. **Transportation:** General. **Visual/performing arts:** Commercial photography, commercial/advertising art, interior design.

Most popular majors. Business/marketing 8%, health sciences 8%, liberal arts 75%.

Computing on campus. 400 workstations in library, computer center.

Student life. Freshman orientation: Mandatory. Preregistration for classes offered. **Policies:** Student conduct code. Freshmen permitted cars on campus. **Activities:** Bands, choral groups, drama, literary magazine, music ensembles, opera, student government, student newspaper, symphony orchestra.

Athletics. Intercollegiate: Baseball M, basketball, cross-country, golf, soccer, softball W, tennis, track and field. **Intramural:** Basketball, soccer, table tennis, tennis, volleyball.

Student services. Adult student services, career counseling, services for economically disadvantaged, student employment services, financial aid counseling, health services, minority student services, on-campus daycare, personal counseling, placement for graduates, veterans' counselor, women's services. **Physically disabled:** Services for visually, hearing impaired. **Transfer:** Special adviser, orientation for new students. Transfer adviser, college fairs on campus for students transferring to 4-year colleges.

Contact. Phone: (509) 533-3305 Toll-free number: (888) 509-7944
Fax: (509) 533-3237
Carol Green, Vice President of Student Services, Spokane Falls Community College, 3410 West Fort George Wright Drive, Spokane, WA 99224

Tacoma Community College
Tacoma, Washington
www.tacoma.ctc.edu **CB code: 4826**

- Public 2-year community college
- Commuter campus in small city

General. Founded in 1965. Regionally accredited. Programs offered at Tacoma Campus, at Tacoma Mall, Gig Harbor. **Enrollment:** 6,480 undergraduates. **Degrees:** 849 associate awarded. **Location:** 30 miles from Seattle, 30 miles from Olympia. **Calendar:** Quarter, limited summer session. **Full-time faculty:** 110 total. **Part-time faculty:** 210 total. **Class size:** 59% < 20, 39% 20-39, less than 1% 40-49, 2% 50-99.

Student profile.

Out-of-state:	1%	**25 or older:**	49%

Transfer out. Colleges most students transferred to 2005: University of Washington.

Basis for selection. Open admission.

2005-2006 Annual costs. Tuition/fees: $2,610; $2,999 out-of-state. Per-credit charge: $75 in-state; $88 out-of-state. Books/supplies: $642.

Financial aid. All financial aid based on need. Need-based aid available for part-time students. Work study available nights, weekends and for part-time students.

Application procedures. Admission: No deadline. No application fee. Application may be submitted online. Admission notification on a rolling basis. **Financial aid:** Priority date 3/26; no closing date. FAFSA, institutional form required. Applicants notified on a rolling basis starting 7/20; must reply within 4 week(s) of notification.

Academics. Special study options: Distance learning, dual enrollment of high school students, internships. Concurrent enrollment with nearby community colleges. License preparation in nursing, paramedic. **Credit/placement by examination:** CLEP, institutional tests. 45 credit hours maximum toward associate degree. **Support services:** GED preparation, learning center, reduced course load, remedial instruction, study skills assistance, tutoring.

Majors. Computer sciences: General. **Education:** Teacher assistance. **Health:** EMT paramedic. **Liberal arts:** Arts/sciences. **Protective services:** Corrections.

Computing on campus. 185 workstations in library, computer center. Online course registration available.

Student life. Freshman orientation: Available. **Policies:** Freshmen permitted cars on campus. **Housing:** Homestay Program available for international students. **Activities:** Choral groups, drama, literary magazine, music ensembles, musical theater, student government, student newspaper.

Athletics. Intercollegiate: Baseball M, basketball, golf, volleyball W. **Intramural:** Basketball, football (tackle) M, golf, soccer, volleyball.

Student services. Career counseling, student employment services, minority student services, on-campus daycare, personal counseling, veterans' counselor. **Physically disabled:** Services for visually, speech, hearing impaired. **Transfer:** Special adviser, orientation for new students. Transfer adviser, college fairs on campus for students transferring to 4-year colleges.

Contact. E-mail: ahayward@tcc.tacoma.ctc.edu
Phone: (253) 566-5001 Fax: (253) 566-6011
Barbara Kavalier, Associate Vice President, Tacoma Community College, 6501 South 19th Street, Tacoma, WA 98466-9971

Walla Walla Community College
Walla Walla, Washington
www.wwcc.edu **CB code: 4963**

- Public 2-year community and technical college
- Commuter campus in large town

General. Founded in 1967. Regionally accredited. Academic and vocational courses offered at educational center at Clarkston, Washington. **Enrollment:** 2,255 degree-seeking undergraduates; 3,208 non-degree-seeking students. **Degrees:** 519 associate awarded. **Location:** 158 miles from Spokane, 262 miles from Seattle. **Calendar:** Quarter, limited summer session. **Full-time faculty:** 127 total; 19% have terminal degrees, 9% minority, 40% women. **Part-time faculty:** 230 total; 10% minority, 59% women. **Class size:** 67% < 20, 30% 20-39, less than 1% 40-49, 2% 50-99. **Special facilities:** Enology, viticulture, culinary and John Deere facilities. **Partnerships:** Formal partnerships with John Deere & Company training center, Cisco Corporation.

Student profile. Among degree-seeking undergraduates, 60% enrolled in a transfer program, 55% enrolled in a vocational program, 5% already have a bachelor's degree or higher, 584 enrolled as first-time, first-year students, 527 transferred in from other institutions.

Part-time:	32%	**Asian American:**	2%
Out-of-state:	32%	**Hispanic American:**	17%
Women:	54%	**Native American:**	2%
African American:	2%	**25 or older:**	26%

Transfer out. Colleges most students transferred to 2005: Eastern Washington University, Washington State University, Central Washington University, Walla Walla College, Western Washington University.

Basis for selection. Open admission, but selective for some programs. Special requirements for health science and vocational programs. TOEFL score of 500 or higher needed to demonstrate English proficiency. COMPASS or ASSET placement tests used for English, reading, math. **Learning Disabled:** Flexible procedures; early registration.

2005-2006 Annual costs. Tuition/fees: $2,595; $3,176 out-of-state. Per-credit charge: $79. Books/supplies: $900. Personal expenses: $1,800.

2004-2005 Financial aid. Need-based: 69% of total undergraduate aid awarded as scholarships/grants, 31% as loans/jobs. Need-based aid available for part-time students. Work study available nights and for part-time students. **Non-need-based:** Scholarships awarded for academics, athletics, music/drama.

Application procedures. Admission: No deadline. No application fee. Application may be submitted online. Admission notification on a rolling basis. **Financial aid:** Priority date 3/1; no closing date. FAFSA, institutional form required. Applicants notified on a rolling basis starting 6/1; must reply within 2 week(s) of notification.

Academics. Special study options: Cooperative education, distance learning, dual enrollment of high school students, ESL, external degree, honors, independent study, internships, liberal arts/career combination. Bachelor's degree programs available on campus. License preparation in nursing, paramedic, real estate. **Credit/placement by examination:** AP, CLEP, institutional tests. 45 credit hours maximum toward associate degree. **Support**

services: GED preparation and test center, learning center, pre-admission summer program, reduced course load, remedial instruction, study skills assistance, tutoring, writing center.

Majors. Agriculture: Business, equipment technology, mechanization, production, turf management. **Business:** Accounting technology, banking/financial services, business admin, executive assistant, retailing. **Communications technology:** Desktop publishing. **Computer sciences:** Data entry, data processing, information systems, web page design, webmaster. **Construction:** Carpentry. **Education:** Early childhood, teacher assistance. **Engineering technology:** Civil. **Health:** Medical secretary, nursing (RN). **Legal studies:** Legal secretary. **Liberal arts:** Arts/sciences. **Mechanic/repair:** General, auto body, automotive, computer, heating/ac/refrig. **Parks/recreation:** Facilities management. **Personal/culinary services:** Chef training, cosmetic, cosmetology. **Production:** Welding. **Protective services:** Corrections, criminal justice, firefighting.

Most popular majors. Agriculture 22%, business/marketing 8%, health sciences 44%, trade and industry 14%.

Computing on campus. 350 workstations in library, computer center, student center. Commuter students can connect to campus network. Online course registration, online library, helpline, repair service, student web hosting, wireless network available.

Student life. Freshman orientation: Available. **Policies:** Freshmen permitted cars on campus. **Activities:** Jazz band, choral groups, dance, drama, music ensembles, musical theater, student government, student newspaper, Warriors for Christ, ecology club, international student organization.

Athletics. NJCAA. **Intercollegiate:** Baseball M, basketball, cheerleading W, golf, rodeo, soccer, softball W, volleyball W. **Intramural:** Basketball, golf, racquetball, softball, volleyball. **Team name:** Warriors.

Student services. Adult student services, career counseling, services for economically disadvantaged, student employment services, financial aid counseling, minority student services, on-campus daycare, personal counseling, placement for graduates, veterans' counselor, women's services. **Physically disabled:** Services for visually, speech, hearing impaired. **Transfer:** Special adviser, orientation, re-entry adviser, pre-admission transcript evaluation for new students. Transfer center, transfer adviser, college fairs on campus for students transferring to 4-year colleges.

Contact. E-mail: admissions@mail.ww.cc.wa.us
Phone: (509) 527-4283 Toll-free number: (877) 992-9292
Fax: (509) 527-3661
Sally Wagoner, Director of Admissions and Registrar, Walla Walla Community College, 500 Tausick Way, Walla Walla, WA 99362-9270

Wenatchee Valley College

Wenatchee, Washington
www.wvc.edu **CB code: 4942**

- Public 2-year community college
- Commuter campus in small city

General. Founded in 1939. Regionally accredited. Branch facilities for 4-year universities. **Enrollment:** 2,670 degree-seeking undergraduates. **Degrees:** 510 associate awarded. **Location:** 145 miles from Seattle, 170 miles from Spokane. **Calendar:** Quarter, limited summer session. **Full-time faculty:** 70 total; 81% have terminal degrees, 6% minority, 46% women. **Part-time faculty:** 174 total; 51% have terminal degrees, 5% minority, 58% women. **Class size:** 45% < 20, 51% 20-39, 3% 40-49, 1% 50-99. **Special facilities:** Teaching orchard.

Student profile.

Out-of-state:	2%	**25 or older:**	53%

Transfer out. Colleges most students transferred to 2005: Central Washington University, Washington State University, Eastern Washington University, University of Washington, Western Washington University.

Basis for selection. Open admission, but selective for some programs. Allied health applicants must submit supplemental application form that details work completed in specific program prerequisites. **Homeschooled:** Applicants must be affiliated with their local school district. **Learning Disabled:** Students with learning disabilities are encouraged to meet with our Special Populations Coordinator.

2005-2006 Annual costs. Tuition/fees: $2,571; $2,960 out-of-state. Per-credit charge: $72 in-state; $85 out-of-state. Books/supplies: $678. Personal expenses: $714.

2004-2005 Financial aid. Need-based: 60% of total undergraduate aid awarded as scholarships/grants, 40% as loans/jobs. Need-based aid available for part-time students. Work study available for part-time students. **Non-need-based:** Scholarships awarded for academics, athletics, leadership.

Application procedures. Admission: Priority date 9/1; no deadline. No application fee. Application may be submitted online. Admission notification on a rolling basis beginning on or about 12/1. **Financial aid:** Closing date 3/1. FAFSA required. Applicants notified by 7/2; must reply within 3 week(s) of notification.

Academics. Special study options: Accelerated study, cooperative education, cross-registration, distance learning, double major, dual enrollment of high school students, ESL, independent study, internships, student-designed major. Bachelor's degree programs available on campus. License preparation in nursing, paramedic, radiology. **Credit/placement by examination:** AP, CLEP, institutional tests. 15 credit hours maximum toward associate degree. At least 15 credits must be completed in residence before credits earned by examination will be applied. **Support services:** GED preparation and test center, learning center, remedial instruction, study skills assistance, tutoring, writing center.

Majors. Agriculture: Production, products processing. **Business:** Accounting technology, business admin, office management. **Computer sciences:** Networking. **Education:** Early childhood. **Engineering technology:** Manufacturing. **Foreign languages:** Sign language interpretation. **Health:** Clinical lab assistant, nursing (RN), radiologic technology/medical imaging, sonography, substance abuse counseling. **Liberal arts:** Arts/sciences. **Mechanic/repair:** Automotive, heating/ac/refrig, industrial electronics. **Protective services:** Firefighting.

Most popular majors. Health sciences 21%, liberal arts 68%.

Computing on campus. 75 workstations in library, computer center, student center. Commuter students can connect to campus network. Online course registration, online library, helpline, student web hosting available.

Student life. Freshman orientation: Available. **Policies:** Freshmen permitted cars on campus. **Activities:** Jazz band, choral groups, drama, literary magazine, music ensembles, musical theater, student government, student newspaper, professional associations, Inter-Varsity Fellowship.

Athletics. Intercollegiate: Baseball M, basketball, soccer, softball W. **Intramural:** Basketball, bowling, football (non-tackle), soccer, softball, table tennis, tennis, volleyball. **Team name:** Knights.

Student services. Adult student services, career counseling, services for economically disadvantaged, student employment services, financial aid counseling, minority student services, on-campus daycare, personal counseling, veterans' counselor. **Physically disabled:** Services for visually, speech, hearing impaired. **Learning disabled:** Comprehensive services available. **Transfer:** Special adviser, orientation, pre-admission transcript evaluation for new students. Transfer adviser, college fairs on campus for students transferring to 4-year colleges.

Contact. Phone: (509) 682-6834 Fax: (509) 682-6801
William Maxwell, Director of Enrollment Services, Wenatchee Valley College, 1300 Fifth Street, Wenatchee, WA 98801-1799

Whatcom Community College

Bellingham, Washington
www.whatcom.ctc.edu **CB code: 1275**

- Public 2-year community college
- Commuter campus in small city

General. Founded in 1970. Regionally accredited. **Enrollment:** 2,959 degree-seeking undergraduates. **Degrees:** 735 associate awarded. **Location:** 90 miles from Seattle, 60 miles from Vancouver, Canada. **Calendar:** Quarter, limited summer session. **Full-time faculty:** 54 total; 33% have terminal degrees, 13% minority, 52% women. **Part-time faculty:** 169 total; 6% minority, 60% women. **Class size:** 18% < 20, 77% 20-39, less than 1% 40-49, 4% 50-99.

Transfer out. Colleges most students transferred to 2005: Western Washington University, University of Washington, Washington State University, Central Washington University, Eastern Washington University.

Basis for selection. Open admission.

High school preparation. College-preparatory program recommended. Recommended units include English 4, mathematics 4, social studies 3, science 2 (laboratory 1), foreign language 3 and academic electives 1. One Fine Arts.

Two-Year Colleges

2005-2006 Annual costs. Tuition/fees: $2,484; $7,692 out-of-state. Per-credit charge: $73 in-state; $245 out-of-state. Books/supplies: $924. Personal expenses: $1,692.

2004-2005 Financial aid. Need-based: 71% of total undergraduate aid awarded as scholarships/grants, 29% as loans/jobs. Need-based aid available for part-time students. Work study available nights and for part-time students. **Non-need-based:** Scholarships awarded for academics, athletics, state residency.

Application procedures. Admission: Priority date 6/23; no deadline. No application fee. Application may be submitted online. Admission notification on a rolling basis. **Financial aid:** No deadline. FAFSA, institutional form required. Applicants notified on a rolling basis starting 7/1; must reply within 3 week(s) of notification.

Academics. Special study options: Cooperative education, cross-registration, distance learning, dual enrollment of high school students, ESL, honors, independent study, internships, student-designed major, study abroad. License preparation in nursing. **Credit/placement by examination:** AP, CLEP, institutional tests. 15 credit hours maximum toward associate degree. **Support services:** GED preparation and test center, learning center, reduced course load, remedial instruction, study skills assistance, tutoring, writing center.

Majors. Business: General, accounting. **Computer sciences:** Computer science, data processing, systems analysis. **Education:** General, early childhood, teacher assistance. **Health:** Massage therapy, medical assistant, medical secretary, nursing (RN), physical therapy assistant. **Legal studies:** Paralegal. **Liberal arts:** Arts/sciences. **Protective services:** Police science. **Visual/performing arts:** Commercial/advertising art.

Most popular majors. Liberal arts 87%.

Computing on campus. 294 workstations in library, computer center, student center. Online course registration, online library available.

Student life. Freshman orientation: Available. **Policies:** Freshmen permitted cars on campus. **Activities:** Jazz band, choral groups, drama, film society, student government, student newspaper, Phi Theta Kappa, Anime Anonymous, Deaf Students Fellowship, health & wellness club, international friendship club, snow club, Gay/Straight Alliance (GSA), multicultural club.

Athletics. Intercollegiate: Basketball, soccer M, volleyball W. **Intramural:** Badminton, basketball, soccer, tennis, volleyball. **Team name:** Orcas.

Student services. Adult student services, alcohol/substance abuse counseling, career counseling, student employment services, financial aid counseling, on-campus daycare, personal counseling, veterans' counselor. **Physically disabled:** Services for visually, speech, hearing impaired. **Learning disabled:** Comprehensive services available. **Transfer:** Special adviser, orientation, re-entry adviser for new students. Transfer center, transfer adviser, college fairs on campus for students transferring to 4-year colleges.

Contact. E-mail: admit@whatcom.ctc.edu
Phone: (360) 676-2170 ext. 3214 Fax: (360) 676-2171
Janelle Miner, Registrar, Whatcom Community College, 237 West Kellogg Road, Bellingham, WA 98226

Yakima Valley Community College

Yakima, Washington
www.yvcc.edu **CB code: 4993**

- Public 2-year community college
- Commuter campus in small city

General. Founded in 1928. Regionally accredited. Additional campus in Grandview. **Enrollment:** 6,225 undergraduates. **Degrees:** 470 associate awarded. **Location:** 150 miles from Seattle. **Calendar:** Quarter, extensive summer session. **Full-time faculty:** 110 total. **Part-time faculty:** 181 total. **Special facilities:** Larson Art Gallery.

Student profile. 6,225 enrolled as first-time, first-year students.

Out-of-state:	10%	**Live on campus:**	2%
25 or older:	49%		

Transfer out. Colleges most students transferred to 2005: Central Washington University, Washington State University.

Basis for selection. Open admission, but selective for some programs. Special requirements for allied health programs. ACT/ASSET required for placement and advising of degree seeking students and for math/English placement. Previous college/university transcripts showing successful completion of English and math courses may replace ASSET. Essay required for radiologic technology. **Adult students:** Entrance exam policies same as for first-time freshmen.

2005-2006 Annual costs. Tuition/fees: $2,550; $2,939 out-of-state. Per-credit charge: $72 in-state; $85 out-of-state. Books/supplies: $720. Personal expenses: $1,575.

2004-2005 Financial aid. Need-based: 74% of total undergraduate aid awarded as scholarships/grants, 26% as loans/jobs. Need-based aid available for part-time students. Work study available for part-time students. **Non-need-based:** Scholarships awarded for academics, athletics, music/drama.

Application procedures. Admission: Priority date 5/26; no deadline. $20 fee. Application may be submitted online. Admission notification on a rolling basis. **Financial aid:** Priority date 5/1; no closing date. FAFSA, institutional form required. Applicants notified on a rolling basis starting 8/1; must reply within 2 week(s) of notification.

Academics. Special study options: Combined bachelor's/graduate degree, cooperative education, distance learning, dual enrollment of high school students, ESL, internships, liberal arts/career combination, weekend college. Bachelor's degree programs available on campus. License preparation in dental hygiene, nursing, radiology. **Credit/placement by examination:** AP, CLEP, IB, institutional tests. 45 credit hours maximum toward associate degree. **Support services:** GED preparation and test center, learning center, remedial instruction, study skills assistance, tutoring, writing center.

Majors. Agriculture: General, business, food processing, supplies. **Business:** General, accounting, administrative services, business admin, e-commerce, entrepreneurial studies, marketing. **Communications technology:** General. **Computer sciences:** General, data processing, information systems, networking. **Education:** General, early childhood. **Engineering:** General. **Family/consumer sciences:** Child care. **Health:** Dental hygiene, medical assistant, medical radiologic technology/radiation therapy, medical secretary, nursing (RN), veterinary technology/assistant. **Liberal arts:** Arts/sciences. **Protective services:** Criminal justice, fire services admin, firefighting. **Visual/performing arts:** Design.

Most popular majors. Business/marketing 6%, computer/information sciences 6%, health sciences 15%, liberal arts 56%.

Computing on campus. 600 workstations in dormitories, library, computer center, student center. Dormitories wired for high-speed internet access. Online course registration, helpline, wireless network available.

Student life. Freshman orientation: Available. Preregistration for classes offered. **Policies:** Freshmen permitted cars on campus. **Housing:** Coed dorms, substance-free housing available. $200 fully refundable deposit. **Activities:** Bands, choral groups, drama, music ensembles, musical theater, student government, student newspaper, Mecha, Ebony, Veterans, Tiin Ma, International Club, Phi Theta Kappa, Action, Auto, Allied Health clubs, Playmasters/Drama.

Athletics. NJCAA. **Intercollegiate:** Baseball M, basketball, softball W, volleyball W, wrestling M. **Intramural:** Basketball. **Team name:** Yaks.

Student services. Career counseling, services for economically disadvantaged, financial aid counseling, health services, minority student services, on-campus daycare, personal counseling, veterans' counselor, women's services. **Physically disabled:** Services for visually, speech, hearing impaired. **Transfer:** Special adviser, orientation for new students. Transfer adviser, college fairs on campus for students transferring to 4-year colleges.

Contact. E-mail: admis@yvcc.edu
Phone: (509) 574-4712 Fax: (509) 574-4649
Denise Anderson, Coordinator of Enrollment Services, Yakima Valley Community College, PO Box 22520, Yakima, WA 98907-2520

West Virginia

Corinthian Schools: National Institute of Technology

Cross Lanes, West Virginia
www.cci.edu **CB code: 1579**

- For-profit 2-year technical college
- Commuter campus in large town
- Interview required

General. Founded in 1968. Accredited by ACCSCT. **Enrollment:** 400 undergraduates. **Degrees:** 46 associate awarded. **ROTC:** Navy. **Location:** 12 miles from Charleston. **Calendar:** Quarter, limited summer session. **Full-time faculty:** 13 total. **Part-time faculty:** 8 total.

Basis for selection. Open admission, but selective for some programs. Limited admission to networking program. Qualifying score required on entrance exam. Interview required for counseling purposes. **Adult students:** Entrance exam policies same as for first-time freshmen.

2005-2006 Annual costs. Electronics program $24,150. Medical Assistant $11,130. Massage Therapy program $11,663. Homeland Security Specialist program $10,920. Pharmacy Technician program $11,506.

Financial aid. Non-need-based: Scholarships awarded for academics, art.

Application procedures. Admission: No deadline. No application fee. Admission notification on a rolling basis. **Financial aid:** No deadline. FAFSA required. Applicants notified on a rolling basis.

Academics. Special study options: Cooperative education. **Credit/placement by examination:** CLEP.

Majors. Engineering technology: Electrical. **Health:** Medical assistant.

Student life. Freshman orientation: Available. Preregistration for classes offered. **Activities:** Choral groups, TV station.

Student services. Student employment services, placement for graduates.

Contact. Phone: (304) 776-6290 Fax: (304) 776-6262
Karen Wilkerson, Director of Admission, Corinthian Schools: National Institute of Technology, 5514 Big Tyler Road, Cross Lanes, WV 25313

Eastern West Virginia Community and Technical College

Moorefield, West Virginia
www.eastern.wvnet.edu **CB code: 3837**

- Public 2-year community and technical college
- Commuter campus in rural community

General. Regionally accredited. **Enrollment:** 255 degree-seeking undergraduates; 627 non-degree-seeking students. **Degrees:** 17 associate awarded. **Location:** 55 miles from Winchester, Virginia. **Calendar:** Semester, limited summer session. **Part-time faculty:** 36 total. **Partnerships:** Formal partnership with all schools in our district for a program called EDGE (Earn a Degree Graduate Early).

Student profile. Among degree-seeking undergraduates, 76 enrolled as first-time, first-year students.

Part-time:	71%	**25 or older:**	27%
Women:	71%		

Transfer out. Colleges most students transferred to 2005: Shepherd College, West Virginia University, Potomac State College.

Basis for selection. Open admission. Degree-seeking students required to take ACCUPLACER. **Adult students:** Entrance exam policies same as for first-time freshmen. **Homeschooled:** Applicants advised to take GED.

2005-2006 Annual costs. Tuition/fees: $1,634; $6,824 out-of-state. Per-credit charge: $68 in-state; $284 out-of-state. Books/supplies: $1,200. Personal expenses: $1,000.

2005-2006 Financial aid. Need-based: 88% of total undergraduate aid awarded as scholarships/grants, 12% as loans/jobs. Need-based aid available for part-time students.

Application procedures. Admission: No deadline. No application fee. Admission notification on a rolling basis. **Financial aid:** Priority date 6/1; no closing date. FAFSA, institutional form required. Applicants notified on a rolling basis; must reply within 2 week(s) of notification.

Academics. Special study options: Distance learning, dual enrollment of high school students, external degree, internships, student-designed major. License preparation in nursing. **Credit/placement by examination:** AP, CLEP, institutional tests. **Support services:** GED preparation, reduced course load, remedial instruction, study skills assistance, tutoring.

Majors. Business: Administrative services, business admin. **Computer sciences:** Information systems. **Liberal arts:** Arts/sciences. **Mechanic/repair:** Industrial.

Computing on campus. Online library available.

Student life. Freshman orientation: Available. Preregistration for classes offered. General orientation program is 3 hours long. Second program required for students taking online courses.

Student services. Adult student services, career counseling, services for economically disadvantaged, financial aid counseling, veterans' counselor. **Physically disabled:** Services for visually, hearing impaired. **Transfer:** Special adviser, orientation for new students. College fairs on campus for students transferring to 4-year colleges.

Contact. E-mail: ask@eastern.wvnet.edu
Phone: (304) 434-8000 Toll-free number: (877) 982-2322
Fax: (304) 434-7002
Sharon Bungard, Dean of Learner Support Services, Eastern West Virginia Community and Technical College, 1929 State Road 55, Moorefield, WV 26836

Huntington Junior College

Huntington, West Virginia
www.huntingtonjuniorcollege.edu **CB code: 7310**

- For-profit 2-year junior college
- Commuter campus in small city

General. Founded in 1936. Regionally accredited. **Enrollment:** 767 degree-seeking undergraduates. **Degrees:** 175 associate awarded. **Location:** 45 miles from Charleston. **Calendar:** Quarter, extensive summer session. **Full-time faculty:** 25 total. **Part-time faculty:** 8 total.

Student profile. Among degree-seeking undergraduates, 199 enrolled as first-time, first-year students.

Part-time:	20%	**African American:**	13%
Women:	80%	**Asian American:**	1%

Basis for selection. Open admission. Interview recommended.

2005-2006 Annual costs. Tuition/fees: $6,150. Tuition includes books.

Application procedures. Admission: No deadline. No application fee. Application may be submitted online. Admission notification on a rolling basis. **Financial aid:** No deadline. Applicants notified on a rolling basis.

Academics. Special study options: Double major, internships. **Credit/placement by examination:** CLEP, institutional tests. **Support services:** Learning center, reduced course load, remedial instruction, study skills assistance, tutoring.

Majors. Business: General, accounting, administrative services. **Computer sciences:** General, database management, programming, web page design. **Foreign languages:** Classics. **Health:** Dental assistant, insurance coding, medical assistant. **Legal studies:** Court reporting, legal secretary.

Student life. Freshman orientation: Mandatory. 3 hour program held during the first day of class. **Activities:** Student government.

Student services. Career counseling, student employment services, financial aid counseling, personal counseling, placement for graduates. **Transfer:** Special adviser for new students.

Contact. E-mail: admissions@huntingtonjuniorcollege.edu
Phone: (304) 697-7550 Toll-free number: (800) 344-4522
Fax: (304) 697-7554
James Garrett, Director of Marketing and Education Services, Huntington Junior College, 900 Fifth Avenue, Huntington, WV 25701

Mountain State College
Parkersburg, West Virginia
www.mountainstate.org **CB code: 2389**

- For-profit 2-year business and technical college
- Commuter campus in large town
- Interview required

General. Founded in 1888. Accredited by ACICS. **Enrollment:** 238 degree-seeking undergraduates. **Degrees:** 30 associate awarded. **Location:** 81 miles from Charleston. **Calendar:** Quarter. **Full-time faculty:** 7 total. **Part-time faculty:** 4 total. **Special facilities:** Legal resource center, dependency resource center.

Basis for selection. Open admission. CPAT required for placement.

2005-2006 Annual costs. Tuition/fees: $7,165. Books/supplies: $600.

Application procedures. Admission: No deadline. No application fee. Admission notification on a rolling basis. **Financial aid:** No deadline. FAFSA required. Applicants notified on a rolling basis.

Academics. Special study options: Accelerated study, cooperative education, double major, internships. **Credit/placement by examination:** CLEP. **Support services:** Tutoring.

Majors. Business: Accounting, administrative services, hospitality/recreation, tourism promotion, tourism/travel. **Computer sciences:** General, applications programming. **Health:** Health services, medical assistant, medical transcription, mental health services, substance abuse counseling. **Legal studies:** Legal secretary, paralegal.

Most popular majors. Business/marketing 16%, computer/information sciences 22%, health sciences 51%, legal studies 11%.

Computing on campus. 25 workstations in library, computer center.

Student life. Freshman orientation: Mandatory. Week prior to the beginning of each quarter. **Activities:** Student government.

Student services. Career counseling, student employment services, personal counseling, placement for graduates.

Contact. E-mail: adm@mountainstate.org
Phone: (304) 485-5487 Toll-free number: (800) 841-0201
Fax: (304) 485-3524
Linda Craig, Director of Student Services, Mountain State College, Spring at 16th Street, Parkersburg, WV 26101-3993

New River Community and Technical College
Beckley, West Virginia
ww.nrctc.edu

- Public 2-year community and technical college
- Large town

General. Regionally accredited. **Calendar:** Semester.

Annual costs/financial aid. Tuition/fees (projected): $2,624.

Contact. Phone: (304) 647-6565
101 Church St., Lewisburg, WV 24901

Potomac State College of West Virginia University
Keyser, West Virginia
www.potomacstatecollege.edu **CB code: 5539**

- Public 2-year branch campus and junior college
- Commuter campus in small town

General. Founded in 1901. Regionally accredited. **Enrollment:** 1,279 degree-seeking undergraduates. **Degrees:** 146 associate awarded. **Location:** 90 miles from Morgantown, 150 miles from Baltimore. **Calendar:** Semester, limited summer session. **Full-time faculty:** 33 total. **Part-time faculty:** 78 total. **Special facilities:** 2 fully operational farms.

Transfer out. Colleges most students transferred to 2005: West Virginia University, Fairmont State College, Frostburg State University.

Basis for selection. Open admission. English ACT score used in conjunction with high school GPA to place students in either college-level or remedial composition courses. Scores also used for math placement. Audition recommended for music applicants and for scholarship consideration. **Adult students:** SAT/ACT scores not required if out of high school 5 year(s) or more.

2005-2006 Annual costs. Tuition/fees: $2,328; $7,872 out-of-state. Per-credit charge: $98 in-state; $329 out-of-state. Room/board: $4,914. Books/supplies: $750.

2004-2005 Financial aid. Need-based: 96% of total undergraduate aid awarded as scholarships/grants, 4% as loans/jobs. Need-based aid available for part-time students. Work study available nights and weekends. **Non-need-based:** Scholarships awarded for academics, athletics, leadership.

Application procedures. Admission: No deadline. No application fee. Application may be submitted online. Admission notification on a rolling basis beginning on or about 9/15. **Financial aid:** Priority date 3/1; no closing date. FAFSA required. Applicants notified on a rolling basis starting 4/1; must reply within 2 week(s) of notification.

Academics. Special study options: Distance learning, double major, dual enrollment of high school students, honors, internships, study abroad. Bachelor's degree programs available on campus. **Credit/placement by examination:** AP, CLEP, institutional tests. 30 credit hours maximum toward associate degree. **Support services:** Learning center, reduced course load, remedial instruction, tutoring.

Majors. Agriculture: General, agronomy, animal sciences, horticultural science. **Biology:** General. **Business:** General, accounting, administrative services, business admin, entrepreneurial studies, management information systems, managerial economics. **Communications:** Journalism. **Computer sciences:** General, applications programming, data processing, information technology, programming. **Conservation:** General, forest management, forest resources, forest technology, forestry, wildlife, wood science. **Education:** General, elementary, music, physical, secondary. **Engineering:** General, civil, electrical, mechanical. **Engineering technology:** Electrical. **Foreign languages:** French, Spanish. **Health:** Medical records technology, medical secretary, predentistry, premedicine, prepharmacy, preveterinary. **History:** General. **Legal studies:** Prelaw. **Liberal arts:** Arts/sciences. **Math:** General. **Parks/recreation:** Facilities management. **Personal/culinary services:** General. **Physical sciences:** Chemistry, geology, physics. **Protective services:** Correctional facilities, criminal justice, law enforcement admin. **Psychology:** General. **Public administration:** Social work. **Social sciences:** Economics, political science, sociology.

Most popular majors. Business/marketing 27%, education 14%, liberal arts 24%.

Computing on campus. 100 workstations in library, computer center, student center. Dormitories wired for high-speed internet access. Helpline, repair service available.

Student life. Freshman orientation: Mandatory. Preregistration for classes offered. **Policies:** Freshmen permitted cars on campus. **Housing:** Coed dorms, single-sex dorms available. $150 deposit, deadline 8/23. **Activities:** Bands, choral groups, drama, music ensembles, student government, student newspaper, agriculture and forestry club, Circle K, equestrian club, campus and community ministries, criminal justice club, engineering club, PAWS (Peer Advocates), life sciences club.

Athletics. NJCAA. **Intercollegiate:** Baseball M, basketball, golf, soccer, softball W, volleyball W. **Intramural:** Basketball. **Team name:** Catamounts.

Student services. Adult student services, career counseling, services for economically disadvantaged, student employment services, financial aid counseling, health services, minority student services, on-campus daycare, personal counseling, placement for graduates, veterans' counselor, women's services. **Physically disabled:** Services for visually, hearing impaired. **Transfer:** Special adviser, orientation, pre-admission transcript evaluation for new students. Transfer adviser, college fairs on campus for students transferring to 4-year colleges.

Contact. E-mail: go2psc@mail.wvu.edu
Phone: (304) 788-6820 Toll-free number: (800) 262-7332
Fax: (304) 788-6939
Beth Little, Director of Enrollment Services, Potomac State College of West Virginia University, One Grand Central Park, Suite 2090, Keyser, WV 26726

Two-Year Colleges

Southern West Virginia Community and Technical College

Mount Gay, West Virginia **CB member**
www.southern.wvnet.edu **CB code: 0770**

- Public 2-year community college
- Commuter campus in small town

General. Founded in 1971. Regionally accredited. Additional campuses in Williamson, Saulsville and Madison. **Enrollment:** 1,379 degree-seeking undergraduates. **Degrees:** 338 associate awarded. **Location:** 60 miles from Charleston. **Calendar:** Semester, limited summer session. **Full-time faculty:** 61 total. **Part-time faculty:** 115 total.

Transfer out. Colleges most students transferred to 2005: Marshall University, West Virginia University, West Virginia State University, Mountain State University.

Basis for selection. Open admission, but selective for some programs. Limited admissions to Nursing, Medical Laboratory, Radiologic Technology, Dental Hygiene, Paramedic Science, and Surgical Technology programs. Nursing and medical laboratory program applicants require minimum ACT score of 21. Interview recommended.

2005-2006 Annual costs. Tuition/fees: $1,634; $6,824 out-of-state. Per-credit charge: $68 in-state; $284 out-of-state. Books/supplies: $450. Personal expenses: $900.

Financial aid. Need-based: Need-based aid available for part-time students.

Application procedures. Admission: No deadline. No application fee. Application may be submitted online. Admission notification on a rolling basis. **Financial aid:** No deadline. FAFSA required. Applicants notified on a rolling basis.

Academics. Special study options: Distance learning, dual enrollment of high school students, independent study, internships, teacher certification program. Bachelor's degree programs available on campus. **Credit/placement by examination:** AP, CLEP, institutional tests. 32 credit hours maximum toward associate degree. **Support services:** GED preparation, learning center, reduced course load, remedial instruction, tutoring.

Majors. Business: General, accounting, administrative services, business admin, entrepreneurial studies, hospitality admin, marketing, small business admin. **Communications technology:** General. **Computer sciences:** General, information technology. **Engineering technology:** Drafting, electrical, environmental. **Health:** Clinical lab technology, health services, medical radiologic technology/radiation therapy, nursing (RN). **Liberal arts:** Arts/sciences. **Protective services:** Forensics.

Most popular majors. Business/marketing 15%, computer/information sciences 10%, health sciences 40%, liberal arts 35%.

Computing on campus. 7 workstations in library. Online course registration, online library, helpline available.

Student life. Activities: Drama, musical theater, student government, special interest clubs.

Student services. Career counseling, student employment services, on-campus daycare, personal counseling, placement for graduates, veterans' counselor. **Physically disabled:** Services for visually, speech, hearing impaired. **Transfer:** Special adviser for new students. Transfer adviser, college fairs on campus for students transferring to 4-year colleges.

Contact. Phone: (304) 792-7160 ext. 121 Fax: (304) 792-7056
Roy Simmons, Admissions Director, Southern West Virginia Community and Technical College, PO Box 2900, Mount Gay, WV 25637

Valley College of Technology

Martinsburg, West Virginia
www.vct.edu **CB code: 3176**

- For-profit 2-year business and technical college
- Commuter campus in small city
- Interview required

General. Accredited by ACICS. **Enrollment:** 17 degree-seeking undergraduates. **Degrees:** 22 associate awarded. **Location:** 20 miles from Winchester, Virginia. **Calendar:** Semester, extensive summer session. **Full-time faculty:** 3 total; 33% minority, 33% women. **Part-time faculty:** 1 total. **Class size:** 100% < 20.

Student profile. Among degree-seeking undergraduates, 14 enrolled as first-time, first-year students.

Women:	94%	**Hispanic American:**	6%
African American:	41%	**25 or older:**	53%

Transfer out. Colleges most students transferred to 2005: Mountain State University, Shepherd University.

Basis for selection. Admission based primarily on high school record, standardized test scores, and interview. If no SAT or ACT scores available, institutional test administered. **Adult students:** Entrance exam policies same as for first-time freshmen.

2006-2007 Annual costs. Tuition/fees (projected): $7,300. Per-credit charge: $225. Tuition varies according to program. Books/supplies: $750. Personal expenses: $2,496.

2004-2005 Financial aid. Need-based: 55% of total undergraduate aid awarded as scholarships/grants, 45% as loans/jobs. Need-based aid available for part-time students.

Application procedures. Admission: No deadline. No application fee. Application must be submitted on paper. Admission notification on a rolling basis. **Financial aid:** No deadline. FAFSA, institutional form required. Applicants notified on a rolling basis.

Academics. Credit/placement by examination: CLEP. 29 credit hours maximum toward associate degree. **Support services:** Remedial instruction, study skills assistance.

Majors. Business: General, business admin, small business admin.

Computing on campus. 42 workstations in computer center.

Student life. Freshman orientation: Available. Orientation held during first week of classes.

Student services. Career counseling, student employment services, financial aid counseling, placement for graduates. **Transfer:** Special adviser, orientation, pre-admission transcript evaluation for new students. College fairs on campus for students transferring to 4-year colleges.

Contact. E-mail: martinsburg@vct.edu
Phone: (304) 263-0979 Fax: (304) 263-2413
Ellen Carte, Admissions Director, Valley College of Technology, 287 Aikens Center, Martinsburg, WV 25401

West Virginia Business College

Wheeling, West Virginia
www.wvbusinesscollege.com **CB code: 2546**

- For-profit 2-year business college
- Commuter campus in small city

General. Accredited by ACICS. **Enrollment:** 65 undergraduates. **Degrees:** 20 associate awarded. **Calendar:** Semester. **Part-time faculty:** 13 total; 15% have terminal degrees, 62% women.

Transfer out. Colleges most students transferred to 2005: West Virginia Northern Community College, Belmont Technical College.

Basis for selection. Open admission, but selective for some programs. **Adult students:** Entrance exam policies same as for first-time freshmen.

2005-2006 Annual costs. Tuition/fees: $7,752.

Application procedures. Admission: $75 fee.

Academics. Credit/placement by examination: CLEP. **Support services:** Reduced course load, tutoring.

Majors. Business: Accounting, administrative services, business admin. **Health:** Medical secretary. **Legal studies:** Legal secretary, paralegal.

Most popular majors. Business/marketing 11%, health sciences 11%, legal studies 78%.

Computing on campus. 16 workstations in computer center.

Student life. **Freshman orientation:** Mandatory.

Student services. Financial aid counseling, personal counseling, placement for graduates.

Contact. Phone: (304) 232-0361
West Virginia Business College, 1052 Main Street, Wheeling, WV 26003

West Virginia Business College

Nutter Fort, West Virginia
www.wvbusinesscollege.com **CB code: 2546**

- For-profit 2-year business college
- Large town
- Interview required

General. Accredited by ACICS. **Enrollment:** 65 degree-seeking undergraduates. **Degrees:** 8 associate awarded. **Location:** 35 miles from Morgantown. **Calendar:** Quarter. **Part-time faculty:** 8 total.

Basis for selection. Open admission. **Homeschooled:** State high school equivalency certificate required.

2005-2006 Annual costs. Tuition/fees: $8,400. Associate degree program costs $15,000 for entire 2-year program. Books/supplies: $475.

Application procedures. **Admission:** No deadline. $75 fee. Application must be submitted on paper.

Academics. **Credit/placement by examination:** CLEP.

Majors. **Business:** Administrative services, business admin. **Legal studies:** Paralegal.

Contact. Phone: (304) 624-7695 Toll-free number: (304) 624-7695
Gary Gorby, General Manager, West Virginia Business College, 116 Pennsylvania Avenue, Nutter Fort, WV 26301

West Virginia Junior College

Morgantown, West Virginia
www.wvjc.edu **CB code: 3179**

- For-profit 2-year junior college
- Large town

General. Accredited by ACICS. **Calendar:** Quarter.

Annual costs/financial aid. Cost of books/supplies included in tuition/fees. Personal expenses: $2,529. Need-based financial aid available to full-time and part-time students.

Contact. Phone: (304) 296-8282
148 Willey Street, Morgantown, WV 26505

West Virginia Junior College: Charleston

Charleston, West Virginia
www.wvjc.com **CB code: 3180**

- For-profit 2-year junior and technical college
- Commuter campus in small city

General. **Calendar:** Quarter.

Annual costs/financial aid. Tuition/fees (2005-2006): $9,375. Need-based financial aid available to full-time and part-time students.

Contact. Phone: (304) 345-2820
Associate Director, 1000 Virginia Street East, Charleston, WV 25301

West Virginia Northern Community College

Wheeling, West Virginia
www.northern.wvnet.edu **CB code: 0674**

- Public 2-year community college
- Commuter campus in large town

General. Founded in 1972. Regionally accredited. Additional campuses in New Martinsville and Weirton. **Enrollment:** 2,148 degree-seeking undergraduates; 694 non-degree-seeking students. **Degrees:** 254 associate awarded. **Location:** 50 miles from Pittsburgh. **Calendar:** Semester, limited summer session. **Full-time faculty:** 55 total; 14% have terminal degrees, 4% minority, 64% women. **Part-time faculty:** 122 total; 3% have terminal degrees, 2% minority, 45% women.

Student profile. Among degree-seeking undergraduates, 415 enrolled as first-time, first-year students.

Part-time:	36%	**African American:**	4%
Women:	72%		

Transfer out. **Colleges most students transferred to 2005:** West Liberty State College, Wheeling Jesuit University, West Virginia University, Bethany College, Ohio Eastern University.

Basis for selection. Open admission, but selective for some programs. Special requirements for health programs. Students who graduated from high school or took GED more than 5 years ago not required to take ACT.

High school preparation. Strong science and math background recommended for health science applicants.

2005-2006 Annual costs. Tuition/fees: $1,752; $5,592 out-of-state. Per-credit charge: $73 in-state; $233 out-of-state. Books/supplies: $600. Personal expenses: $1,153.

Financial aid. **Need-based:** Need-based aid available for part-time students.

Application procedures. **Admission:** No deadline. No application fee. Application must be submitted online. Admission notification on a rolling basis. Health science applicants must apply by January 10; late applicants evaluated after June 30 if space available. **Financial aid:** Priority date 3/15; no closing date. FAFSA, institutional form required. Applicants notified on a rolling basis starting 3/10.

Academics. **Special study options:** Accelerated study, distance learning, double major, dual enrollment of high school students, independent study, internships, liberal arts/career combination. 2+2 in education, criminal justice, human services with Franciscan University of Steubenville. 2+2 in social work with West Virginia University. 2+2 in criminal justice with West Liberty State College. License preparation in nursing. **Credit/placement by examination:** AP, CLEP, institutional tests. 45 credit hours maximum toward associate degree. **Support services:** Learning center, pre-admission summer program, reduced course load, remedial instruction, study skills assistance, tutoring.

Majors. **Business:** General, accounting, administrative services, business admin, hospitality admin. **Computer sciences:** Data processing, information systems. **Family/consumer sciences:** Child care. **Health:** Medical radiologic technology/radiation therapy, nursing (RN), respiratory therapy technology, surgical technology. **Liberal arts:** Arts/sciences. **Mechanic/repair:** Electronics/electrical, heating/ac/refrig. **Personal/culinary services:** Culinary arts. **Public administration:** Human services.

Most popular majors. Business/marketing 20%, health sciences 39%, liberal arts 19%.

Computing on campus. 215 workstations in library, computer center. Commuter students can connect to campus network.

Student life. **Freshman orientation:** Mandatory. Preregistration for classes offered. Orientation held during spring and early fall for about 3.5 to 4 hours. **Policies:** Freshmen permitted cars on campus. **Activities:** Student government, student newspaper, African American/multicultural organization.

Athletics. **Intramural:** Basketball, bowling, football (non-tackle) M, golf, softball, volleyball. **Team name:** Thundering Chickens.

Student services. Career counseling, student employment services, personal counseling, placement for graduates, veterans' counselor. **Physically disabled:** Services for visually, hearing impaired. **Transfer:** Special adviser, orientation for new students. Transfer adviser, college fairs on campus for students transferring to 4-year colleges.

Contact. E-mail: info@northern.wvnet.edu
Phone: (304) 233-5900 ext. 4247 Fax: (304) 233-8187
Janet Fike, Dean of Enrollment Management, West Virginia Northern Community College, 1704 Market Street, Wheeling, WV 26003

Wisconsin

Blackhawk Technical College

Janesville, Wisconsin
www.blackhawk.edu
CB code: 7319

- Public 2-year technical college
- Commuter campus in small city

General. Founded in 1912. Regionally accredited. **Enrollment:** 2,476 degree-seeking undergraduates. **Degrees:** 280 associate awarded. **Location:** 75 miles from Milwaukee and Chicago. **Calendar:** Semester, limited summer session. **Full-time faculty:** 105 total. **Part-time faculty:** 399 total.

Basis for selection. Open admission, but selective for some programs. Applicants to nursing, dental hygiene, radiography, and physical therapist assistant programs must meet additional testing and course requirements. National League for Nursing, Pre-Nursing and Guidance examination required for nursing applicants.

2005-2006 Annual costs. Tuition/fees: $2,536; $15,430 out-of-state. Per-credit charge: $81 in-state; $510 out-of-state. Material fees vary by program; minimum $4 per credit. Books/supplies: $900. Personal expenses: $1,100.

2004-2005 Financial aid. Need-based: 61% of total undergraduate aid awarded as scholarships/grants, 39% as loans/jobs. Need-based aid available for part-time students.

Application procedures. Admission: Priority date 9/1; no deadline. $30 fee. Admission notification on a rolling basis beginning on or about 5/20. **Financial aid:** Priority date 4/1, closing date 6/15. Applicants notified on a rolling basis starting 4/15; must reply within 2 week(s) of notification.

Academics. Special study options: Accelerated study, distance learning, dual enrollment of high school students, ESL, external degree, independent study, internships, student-designed major. Bachelor's degree programs available on campus. **Credit/placement by examination:** CLEP. 30 credit hours maximum toward associate degree. **Support services:** GED preparation and test center, learning center, pre-admission summer program, reduced course load, remedial instruction, study skills assistance, tutoring.

Majors. Business: Accounting, administrative services, office management, office technology, office/clerical, operations. **Computer sciences:** Programming. **Engineering:** Electrical. **Engineering technology:** Drafting, robotics. **Family/consumer sciences:** Institutional food production. **Health:** Dental hygiene, medical radiologic technology/radiation therapy, medical secretary, nursing (RN), physical therapy assistant. **Legal studies:** Legal secretary. **Mechanic/repair:** Diesel, electronics/electrical. **Personal/culinary services:** Culinary arts. **Protective services:** Fire safety technology, police science.

Computing on campus. Online course registration, helpline available.

Student life. Freshman orientation: Available. **Activities:** Student government, student newspaper.

Student services. Alcohol/substance abuse counseling, career counseling, services for economically disadvantaged, student employment services, financial aid counseling, minority student services, on-campus daycare, personal counseling, placement for graduates, veterans' counselor. **Physically disabled:** Services for visually, speech, hearing impaired.

Contact. Phone: (608) 757-7665 Fax: (608) 743-4407
Barbara Erlandson, Student Development Specialist, Blackhawk Technical College, Box 5009, Janesville, WI 53547

Bryant & Stratton College: Milwaukee

Milwaukee, Wisconsin
www.bryantstratton.edu
CB code: 3617

- For-profit 2-year business and junior college
- Commuter campus in very large city
- Application essay, interview required

General. Founded in 1854. Regionally accredited. **Enrollment:** 870 degree-seeking undergraduates. **Degrees:** 10 bachelor's, 103 associate awarded. **Location:** 75 miles from Chicago. **Calendar:** Trimester, extensive summer session. **Full-time faculty:** 10 total. **Part-time faculty:** 40 total. **Class size:** 75% < 20, 25% 20-39.

Student profile. Among degree-seeking undergraduates, 870 enrolled as first-time, first-year students.

Part-time:	25%	**25 or older:**	44%
Women:	90%		

Basis for selection. School achievement record, test scores, interview important. SAT/ACT scores can take place of school's entrance exam. **Adult students:** Entrance exam policies same as for first-time freshmen.

2005-2006 Annual costs. Books/supplies: $750.

Financial aid. All financial aid based on need. Work study available nights.

Application procedures. Admission: No deadline. $25 fee. Admission notification on a rolling basis. **Financial aid:** No deadline. FAFSA required. Applicants notified on a rolling basis; must reply within 2 week(s) of notification.

Academics. Special study options: Distance learning, double major, internships. License preparation on campus provided for Medical Coding and Certified Secretary, and Medical Assisting (exam given on campus). Bachelor's degree programs available on campus. **Credit/placement by examination:** AP, CLEP, institutional tests. 30 credit hours maximum toward associate degree. **Support services:** Reduced course load, remedial instruction, study skills assistance, tutoring.

Majors. Business: General, accounting, administrative services. **Computer sciences:** Information systems, systems analysis. **Health:** Medical assistant, medical secretary. **Legal studies:** Legal secretary.

Most popular majors. Business/marketing 45%, computer/information sciences 31%, health sciences 22%.

Computing on campus. 100 workstations in library, computer center.

Student life. Freshman orientation: Mandatory. Preregistration for classes offered. **Housing:** Nearby dormitories available through St. Catherine's Residence for Women. **Activities:** Student government, student newspaper, Association for Information Technology Professionals, Collegiate Secretaries International, Allied Health Association, Phi Beta Lambda, student board.

Athletics. Team name: Bobcats.

Student services. Career counseling, student employment services, financial aid counseling, personal counseling, placement for graduates, veterans' counselor. **Transfer:** Special adviser, orientation, re-entry adviser, pre-admission transcript evaluation for new students. Transfer adviser for students transferring to 4-year colleges.

Contact. Phone: (414) 276-5200 Fax: (414) 276-3930
Kathryn Cotey, Director of Admissions, Bryant & Stratton College: Milwaukee, 310 West Wisconsin Avenue, Suite 500, Milwaukee, WI 53203

Chippewa Valley Technical College

Eau Claire, Wisconsin
www.cvtc.edu
CB code: 0786

- Public 2-year technical college
- Commuter campus in small city

General. Founded in 1912. Regionally accredited. **Enrollment:** 5,627 degree-seeking undergraduates. **Degrees:** 598 associate awarded. **Location:** 90 miles from Minneapolis-St. Paul. **Calendar:** Semester, limited summer session. **Full-time faculty:** 300 total. **Part-time faculty:** 50 total. **Special facilities:** Health education campus with state-of the art equipment and lab facilites.

Transfer out. Colleges most students transferred to 2005: University of Wisconsin-Stout.

Basis for selection. Open admission, but selective for some programs. Additional testing and course requirements for applicants to nursing, dental hygiene, radiography, surgical technologist, medical assistant and physical therapist assistant programs. Entrance examination required for dental hygienist and nursing applicants. Interview required for alcohol abuse prevention and other drug abuse prevention associate programs, and fire protective service technician program.

High school preparation. Algebra and science requirements for some degree programs.

2005-2006 Annual costs. Tuition/fees: $2,560; $15,454 out-of-state. Per-credit charge: $81 in-state; $510 out-of-state. Additional $4 fee per lecture course. Books/supplies: $853. Personal expenses: $1,370.

Financial aid. Need-based: Need-based aid available for part-time students. Work study available nights, weekends and for part-time students.

Application procedures. Admission: No deadline. $30 fee, may be waived for applicants with need. Application may be submitted online. Admission notification on a rolling basis. **Financial aid:** Priority date 3/15; no closing date. FAFSA required. Applicants notified on a rolling basis starting 6/1; must reply within 2 week(s) of notification.

Academics. Special study options: Distance learning, double major, dual enrollment of high school students, ESL, external degree, independent study, internships, student-designed major. License preparation in dental hygiene, nursing, paramedic, real estate. **Credit/placement by examination:** CLEP, institutional tests. 34 credit hours maximum toward associate degree. 50% of semester hours needed for degree may be earned as credit by examination. **Support services:** GED preparation and test center, learning center, reduced course load, remedial instruction, study skills assistance, tutoring.

Majors. Agriculture: General, agronomy, animal sciences. **Business:** General, accounting, administrative services, hospitality/recreation, logistics, office technology, operations. **Computer sciences:** General, applications programming, programming. **Engineering:** Civil. **Engineering technology:** Civil, drafting, electrical, robotics. **Health:** Clinical lab assistant, clinical lab technology, dental hygiene, medical radiologic technology/radiation therapy, medical records technology, nursing (RN), sonography, substance abuse counseling. **Legal studies:** Paralegal. **Mechanic/repair:** Electronics/electrical, heating/ac/refrig, industrial. **Protective services:** Firefighting, police science.

Most popular majors. Business/marketing 30%, computer/information sciences 13%, health sciences 8%, security/protective services 19%, trade and industry 19%.

Computing on campus. 500 workstations in library, computer center.

Student life. Freshman orientation: Mandatory. **Activities:** Student government, student newspaper.

Athletics. Intramural: Basketball, skiing, softball, table tennis, tennis, volleyball.

Student services. Career counseling, student employment services, on-campus daycare, personal counseling, placement for graduates, veterans' counselor. **Physically disabled:** Services for visually, speech, hearing impaired. **Transfer:** Special adviser, pre-admission transcript evaluation for new students. College fairs on campus for students transferring to 4-year colleges.

Contact. E-mail: tshepardson@cvtc.edu
Phone: (715) 833-6246 Toll-free number: (800) 547-2882
Fax: (715) 833-6470
Timothy Shepardson, Admissions Manager, Chippewa Valley Technical College, 620 West Clairemont Avenue, Eau Claire, WI 54701-6162

College of Menominee Nation

Keshena, Wisconsin
www.menominee.edu **CB code: 3974**

- Private 2-year tribal college
- Commuter campus in rural community

General. Regionally accredited. **Enrollment:** 472 degree-seeking undergraduates. **Degrees:** 44 associate awarded. **Location:** 150 miles from Madison, 35 miles from Green Bay. **Calendar:** Semester, limited summer session. **Full-time faculty:** 15 total; 27% have terminal degrees, 47% minority, 40% women. **Part-time faculty:** 19 total; 5% have terminal degrees, 26% minority, 63% women.

Student profile. Among degree-seeking undergraduates, 80% enrolled in a transfer program, 20% enrolled in a vocational program, 3% already have a bachelor's degree or higher.

Transfer out. Colleges most students transferred to 2005: UW-Green Bay, UW-Oshkosh, Silver Lake College.

Basis for selection. Open admission. ACCUPLACER required of all students for placement. **Adult students:** Entrance exam policies same as for first-time freshmen. SAT/ACT scores not required. **Homeschooled:** Must present state certification of completion of requirements.

2005-2006 Annual costs. Tuition/fees: $5,220. Per-credit charge: $172. Books/supplies: $700.

Financial aid. All financial aid based on need. Need-based aid available for part-time students. Work study available nights.

Application procedures. Admission: Closing date 8/30 (postmark date). No application fee. Admission notification on a rolling basis. Students notified of acceptance as early as possible. **Financial aid:** FAFSA required. Applicants notified on a rolling basis.

Academics. Special study options: Double major, independent study, internships, liberal arts/career combination. **Credit/placement by examination:** AP, CLEP, institutional tests. **Support services:** Reduced course load, remedial instruction, study skills assistance, tutoring.

Majors. Business: Accounting, administrative services, business admin. **Computer sciences:** General. **Conservation:** General. **Education:** Early childhood, kindergarten/preschool. **Family/consumer sciences:** Food/nutrition. **Health:** Prenursing. **Legal studies:** Paralegal. **Liberal arts:** Arts/sciences. **Public administration:** Human services.

Computing on campus. 65 workstations in library, computer center. Commuter students can connect to campus network. Online library, wireless network available.

Student life. Freshman orientation: Mandatory. Preregistration for classes offered. **Policies:** Freshmen permitted cars on campus. **Activities:** Student government, Circle K.

Student services. Adult student services, alcohol/substance abuse counseling, career counseling, services for economically disadvantaged, financial aid counseling, minority student services, personal counseling. **Physically disabled:** Services for visually, speech, hearing impaired. **Transfer:** Special adviser, orientation, pre-admission transcript evaluation for new students. College fairs on campus for students transferring to 4-year colleges.

Contact. E-mail: cynthia@menominee.edu
Phone: (715) 799-5600 ext. 3053 Toll-free number: (800) 567-2344
Fax: (715) 799-4392
Cynthia Norton, Admissions Representative, College of Menominee Nation, N172 STH 47/55, Keshena, WI 54135

Fox Valley Technical College

Appleton, Wisconsin **CB member**
www.fvtc.edu **CB code: 0747**

- Public 2-year technical college
- Commuter campus in small city

General. Founded in 1967. Regionally accredited. **Enrollment:** 5,820 degree-seeking undergraduates; 2,035 non-degree-seeking students. **Degrees:** 737 associate awarded. **Location:** 100 miles from Milwaukee. **Calendar:** Differs by program, limited summer session. **Full-time faculty:** 277 total. **Part-time faculty:** 50 total.

Student profile. Among degree-seeking undergraduates, 1,003 enrolled as first-time, first-year students.

Part-time:	73%	**Women:**	53%
Out-of-state:	5%	**25 or older:**	25%

Basis for selection. Open admission, but selective for some programs. Special requirements for nursing and criminal justice programs. ACT, ACCUPLACER, COMPASS required for placement.

2005-2006 Annual costs. Tuition/fees: $2,792; $15,686 out-of-state. Per-credit charge: $81 in-state; $510 out-of-state. Additional fee of $4 per lecture course. Books/supplies: $600.

Application procedures. Admission: No deadline. $30 fee, may be waived for applicants with need. Admission notification on a rolling basis. **Financial aid:** Priority date 3/1; no closing date. FAFSA required. Applicants notified on a rolling basis.

Academics. Special study options: Accelerated study, distance learning, double major, ESL, internships. **Credit/placement by examination:** CLEP, institutional tests. 45 credit hours maximum toward associate degree. **Support services:** Reduced course load, remedial instruction, tutoring.

Majors. Agriculture: Agribusiness operations, business, horticulture, supplies. **Business:** General, accounting, administrative services, banking/financial services, hospitality admin, hospitality/recreation, human resources, insurance, office technology, restaurant/food services, tourism promotion, training/development. **Communications technology:** Graphic/

printing. **Computer sciences:** Applications programming, data processing, information systems. **Conservation:** General. **Construction:** General. **Engineering technology:** Drafting, electrical, mechanical drafting. **Family/consumer sciences:** Child care, institutional food production. **Health:** Dental hygiene, nursing (RN), occupational therapy assistant, substance abuse counseling. **Legal studies:** Legal secretary, paralegal. **Mechanic/repair:** Aircraft powerplant, automotive, avionics. **Parks/recreation:** Facilities management. **Personal/culinary services:** Baking, chef training, culinary arts. **Protective services:** Criminal justice, fire safety technology, police science, security services. **Public administration:** Human services. **Transportation:** Airline/commercial pilot. **Visual/performing arts:** Interior design.

Most popular majors. Business/marketing 19%, computer/information sciences 20%, family/consumer sciences 12%, health sciences 11%, security/protective services 16%, trade and industry 21%.

Computing on campus. 260 workstations in library, computer center, student center. Online library, helpline, repair service available.

Student life. Activities: Student government, student newspaper, 23 curriculum-related clubs.

Athletics. Intramural: Basketball, bowling, golf, soccer, softball, table tennis, tennis, volleyball.

Student services. Alcohol/substance abuse counseling, career counseling, student employment services, health services, minority student services, on-campus daycare, personal counseling, placement for graduates, veterans' counselor, women's services. **Physically disabled:** Services for visually, speech, hearing impaired.

Contact. Phone: (920) 735-5645 Toll-free number: (800) 735-3882
Fax: (920) 735-2582
Bob Burdick, Registrar, Fox Valley Technical College, 1825 North Bluemound Drive, Appleton, WI 54912-2277

Gateway Technical College

Kenosha, Wisconsin
www.gtc.edu
CB member
CB code: 0761

- Public 2-year technical college
- Commuter campus in small city

General. Founded in 1911. Regionally accredited. Campuses at Burlington, Elkhorn and Racine. **Enrollment:** 5,704 degree-seeking undergraduates; 1,478 non-degree-seeking students. **Degrees:** 597 associate awarded. **Location:** 30 miles from Milwaukee, 60 miles from Chicago. **Calendar:** Semester, limited summer session. **Full-time faculty:** 300 total. **Part-time faculty:** 100 total.

Student profile. Among degree-seeking undergraduates, 1,166 enrolled as first-time, first-year students.

Part-time:	78%	**Women:**	67%
Out-of-state:	3%	**25 or older:**	60%

Basis for selection. Open admission, but selective for some programs. GED or high school diploma required for some programs. Interview recommended.

High school preparation. Chemistry and biology required for nursing program applicants.

2005-2006 Annual costs. Tuition/fees: $2,536; $15,430 out-of-state. Per-credit charge: $81 in-state; $510 out-of-state. Materials fees vary by program; minimum $4 per credit. Personal expenses: $900.

Financial aid. Need-based: Need-based aid available for part-time students. Work study available for part-time students. **Non-need-based:** Scholarships awarded for state residency.

Application procedures. Admission: No deadline. $30 fee. Admission notification on a rolling basis. **Financial aid:** Priority date 7/1; no closing date. FAFSA, institutional form required. Applicants notified on a rolling basis starting 5/1; must reply within 2 week(s) of notification.

Academics. Special study options: Cross-registration, distance learning, dual enrollment of high school students, ESL, independent study, internships. License preparation in aviation, nursing, paramedic, physical therapy, real estate. **Credit/placement by examination:** CLEP, institutional tests. 48 credit hours maximum toward associate degree. Institutional biology and chemistry test required for nursing applicants. **Support services:** GED preparation and test center, learning center, remedial instruction, tutoring.

Majors. Agriculture: Horticultural science, horticulture. **Business:** Administrative services, banking/financial services, hotel/motel admin, logistics, marketing, office technology, operations, sales/distribution. **Communications technology:** General, radio/tv. **Computer sciences:** Applications programming, information technology, networking, programming, systems analysis, webmaster. **Education:** Early childhood. **Engineering technology:** Civil, electrical, electromechanical, heat/ac/refrig, hydraulics, manufacturing, mechanical, quality control, robotics. **English:** Technical writing. **Family/consumer sciences:** Child care, institutional food production. **Foreign languages:** Sign language interpretation. **Health:** Dental hygiene, medical radiologic technology/radiation therapy, medical records technology, nursing (RN), physical therapy assistant, surgical technology. **Legal studies:** Court reporting, legal secretary. **Mechanic/repair:** Heating/ac/refrig. **Personal/culinary services:** Restaurant/catering. **Production:** Machine shop technology. **Protective services:** Firefighting, police science. **Public administration:** Human services. **Transportation:** Airline/commercial pilot, aviation. **Visual/performing arts:** Commercial/advertising art, graphic design, interior design.

Most popular majors. Business/marketing 43%, engineering/engineering technologies 9%, health sciences 21%, security/protective services 11%, visual/performing arts 10%.

Computing on campus. 270 workstations in library, computer center.

Student life. Freshman orientation: Available. **Activities:** Radio station, student government, student newspaper, wide variety of occupationally-oriented and community-related organizations available.

Student services. Adult student services, career counseling, student employment services, health services, on-campus daycare, personal counseling, placement for graduates, veterans' counselor. **Physically disabled:** Services for visually, speech, hearing impaired. **Transfer:** Special adviser, orientation for new students. Transfer adviser, college fairs on campus for students transferring to 4-year colleges.

Contact. E-mail: admissions@gtc.edu
Phone: (262) 564-2912 Fax: (262) 564-2301
Susan Roberts, Director of Admissions, Gateway Technical College, 3520 30th Avenue, Kenosha, WI 53144

Lac Courte Oreilles Ojibwa Community College

Hayward, Wisconsin
www.lco-college.edu
CB code: 7351

- Public 2-year community college
- Commuter campus in small town

General. Regionally accredited. **Calendar:** Semester.

Annual costs/financial aid. Tuition/fees (2005-2006): $3,540; $3,540 out-of-state. Need-based financial aid available for full-time students.

Contact. Phone: (715) 634-4790 ext. 104
13466 West Trepania Road, Hayward, WI 54843

Lakeshore Technical College

Cleveland, Wisconsin
www.gotoltc.edu
CB member
CB code: 0618

- Public 2-year technical college
- Commuter campus in rural community

General. Founded in 1912. Regionally accredited. **Enrollment:** 2,309 degree-seeking undergraduates. **Degrees:** 418 associate awarded. **Location:** 15 miles from Sheboygan, 65 miles from Milwaukee. **Calendar:** Semester, limited summer session. **Full-time faculty:** 103 total. **Part-time faculty:** 300 total. **Partnerships:** Formal partnerships with Tech Prep, School-to-Work programs with all public schools in Manitowoc and Sheboygan counties. Youth apprenticeship placements with 58 employers in these counties.

Student profile.

Out-of-state:	1%	**25 or older:**	55%

Basis for selection. Open admission. All health-related, public safety and child care programs require background checks and physical examinations. International students whose first language is not English must have minimum 550 TOEFL. ASSET, COMPASS, ACCUPLACER are preferred placement exams, but will accept ACT/SAT. **Homeschooled:** State high school equivalency certificate required.

2005-2006 Annual costs. Tuition/fees: $2,548; $15,442 out-of-state. Per-credit charge: $81 in-state; $510 out-of-state. Materials fees vary by program; minimum $4 per course. Books/supplies: $1,000. Personal expenses: $1,625.

Financial aid. All financial aid based on need. Need-based aid available for part-time students. Work study available nights and for part-time students.

Application procedures. Admission: No deadline. $30 fee, may be waived for applicants with need. Application may be submitted online. Admission notification on a rolling basis. **Financial aid:** Priority date 6/1; no closing date. FAFSA, institutional form required. Applicants notified on a rolling basis starting 6/1; must reply within 3 week(s) of notification.

Academics. Special study options: Accelerated study, combined bachelor's/graduate degree, cooperative education, cross-registration, distance learning, double major, dual enrollment of high school students, ESL, honors, independent study, internships, student-designed major, weekend college. License preparation in nursing, paramedic, real estate. **Credit/placement by examination:** AP, CLEP, institutional tests. **Support services:** GED preparation and test center, learning center, pre-admission summer program, reduced course load, remedial instruction, study skills assistance, tutoring.

Majors. Business: Accounting, administrative services, logistics, marketing, office technology, operations. **Computer sciences:** Networking, programming, systems analysis, webmaster. **Education:** Early childhood. **Engineering technology:** Drafting, electrical, electromechanical, hazardous materials, mechanical drafting, quality control. **Health:** Clinical lab technology, EMT paramedic, medical radiologic technology/radiation therapy, medical secretary, nursing (RN). **Legal studies:** Court reporting, paralegal. **Protective services:** Police science. **Science technology:** Nuclear power.

Most popular majors. Business/marketing 55%, computer/information sciences 17%, health sciences 20%.

Computing on campus. 792 workstations in library, computer center. Commuter students can connect to campus network. Online course registration, online library, helpline, wireless network available.

Student life. Freshman orientation: Available. Preregistration for classes offered. **Activities:** Student government, student newspaper.

Athletics. Intramural: Basketball, football (non-tackle), volleyball.

Student services. Adult student services, alcohol/substance abuse counseling, career counseling, services for economically disadvantaged, student employment services, financial aid counseling, health services, minority student services, on-campus daycare, personal counseling, placement for graduates. **Physically disabled:** Services for visually, speech, hearing impaired. **Transfer:** Special adviser, orientation, re-entry adviser, pre-admission transcript evaluation for new students. Transfer adviser, college fairs on campus for students transferring to 4-year colleges.

Contact. E-mail: enroll@gotoltc.edu
Phone: (920) 693-8213 Toll-free number: (888) 468-6582
Fax: (920) 693-3561
Karla Zahn, Director of Admissions, Lakeshore Technical College, 1290 North Avenue, Cleveland, WI 53015-9761

Madison Area Technical College

Madison, Wisconsin
www.madison.tec.wi.us **CB code: 1536**

- Public 2-year community and technical college
- Commuter campus in small city

General. Founded in 1912. Regionally accredited. **Enrollment:** 14,233 degree-seeking undergraduates. **Degrees:** 1,209 associate awarded. **Location:** 75 miles from Milwaukee. **Calendar:** Semester, limited summer session. **Full-time faculty:** 401 total. **Part-time faculty:** 1,084 total. **Special facilities:** Satellite downlink.

Student profile.

Out-of-state:	2%	**25 or older:**	10%

Basis for selection. Open admission, but selective for some programs. School achievement record, class rank, test scores considered for all health occupation programs. SAT or ACT (ACT preferred) required of health occupation applicants only.

High school preparation. High school academic subject requirements for health and technical programs.

2005-2006 Annual costs. Tuition/fees: $2,642; $15,536 out-of-state. Per-credit charge: $81 in-state; $510 out-of-state. Additional fee of $4 per lecture course. Books/supplies: $760. Personal expenses: $1,340.

2004-2005 Financial aid. Need-based: 55% of total undergraduate aid awarded as scholarships/grants, 45% as loans/jobs.

Application procedures. Admission: Priority date 11/20; deadline 7/1. $30 fee, may be waived for applicants with need. Admission notification on a rolling basis. Early application recommended for programs with limited enrollment. **Financial aid:** Priority date 4/15; no closing date. FAFSA required. Applicants notified on a rolling basis starting 4/15.

Academics. Special study options: Accelerated study, cross-registration, distance learning, dual enrollment of high school students, ESL, external degree, internships. License preparation in nursing. **Credit/placement by examination:** CLEP, institutional tests. 32 credit hours maximum toward associate degree. **Support services:** GED preparation, learning center, reduced course load, remedial instruction, study skills assistance, tutoring.

Majors. Agriculture: General, animal sciences, horticulture. **Business:** Accounting, administrative services, business admin, communications, fashion, finance, hospitality admin, hospitality/recreation, insurance, office management, real estate, tourism/travel. **Communications technology:** Graphic/printing. **Computer sciences:** General, programming. **Engineering technology:** Architectural, civil. **Family/consumer sciences:** Child care, food/nutrition. **Health:** Clinical lab technology, dental hygiene, EMT paramedic, medical assistant, medical radiologic technology/radiation therapy, medical records admin, medical secretary, mental health services, nursing (RN), occupational therapy assistant, respiratory therapy technology, veterinary technology/assistant. **Interdisciplinary:** Biological/physical sciences. **Legal studies:** Court reporting. **Liberal arts:** Arts/sciences. **Mechanic/repair:** Electronics/electrical. **Personal/culinary services:** Cosmetic, culinary arts. **Protective services:** Police science. **Science technology:** Biological. **Visual/performing arts:** Commercial photography, commercial/advertising art, design, interior design.

Most popular majors. Business/marketing 28%, computer/information sciences 7%, family/consumer sciences 6%, health sciences 19%, trade and industry 12%, visual/performing arts 7%.

Computing on campus. 470 workstations in library, computer center.

Student life. Freshman orientation: Available. **Policies:** Student life department promotes a variety of cultural diversity and activities and plays an active role in student government activities. **Activities:** Jazz band, choral groups, drama, music ensembles, student government, student newspaper.

Athletics. NJCAA. **Intercollegiate:** Baseball M, basketball, bowling, cross-country M, golf M, softball W, volleyball W, wrestling M. **Intramural:** Basketball, racquetball, soccer, swimming, table tennis, tennis, volleyball.

Student services. Career counseling, student employment services, health services, on-campus daycare, personal counseling, placement for graduates, veterans' counselor. **Physically disabled:** Services for visually, speech, hearing impaired. **Transfer:** Special adviser, orientation for new students. Transfer adviser for students transferring to 4-year colleges.

Contact. Phone: (608) 246-6205 Fax: (608) 258-2329
Maureen Menendez, Admissions Administrator, Madison Area Technical College, 3350 Anderson Street, Madison, WI 53704-2599

Mid-State Technical College

Wisconsin Rapids, Wisconsin **CB member**
www.mstc.edu **CB code: 0635**

- Public 2-year technical college
- Commuter campus in large town

General. Founded in 1967. Regionally accredited. Branch campuses in Marshfield and Stevens Point, outreach center in Adams. **Enrollment:** 7,900 degree-seeking undergraduates. **Degrees:** 452 associate awarded. **Location:** 20 miles from Stevens Point, 115 miles from Madison. **Calendar:** Semester, limited summer session. **Full-time faculty:** 95 total; 12% have terminal degrees, 58% women.

Student profile.

Out-of-state:	1%	**25 or older:**	15%

Basis for selection. Open admission, but selective for some programs. Accuplacer required for placement. ACT, SAT, ASSET scores accepted for placement if submitted. Interview required for select students and most health services programs. **Adult students:** Entrance exam policies same as for first-time freshmen.

High school preparation. Biology, anatomy, physiology, chemistry, medical terminology recommended for health programs. Information processing, general business, business law, economics, accounting recommended for business programs. Geometry, drafting, chemistry, advanced math recommended for technical and industrial programs.

2005-2006 Annual costs. Tuition/fees: $2,536; $15,430 out-of-state. Per-credit charge: $81 in-state; $510 out-of-state. Books/supplies: $986. Personal expenses: $1,500.

2004-2005 Financial aid. Need-based: 59% of total undergraduate aid awarded as scholarships/grants, 41% as loans/jobs. Need-based aid available for part-time students. Work study available nights, weekends and for part-time students. **Non-need-based:** Scholarships awarded for academics, leadership.

Application procedures. Admission: No deadline. $30 fee, may be waived for applicants with need. Application may be submitted online. Admission notification on a rolling basis. **Financial aid:** No deadline. FAFSA required. Applicants notified on a rolling basis starting 5/30; must reply within 2 week(s) of notification.

Academics. Special study options: Accelerated study, cooperative education, distance learning, double major, dual enrollment of high school students, ESL, independent study, internships. License preparation in nursing, paramedic. **Credit/placement by examination:** AP, CLEP, institutional tests. 32 credit hours maximum toward associate degree. **Support services:** GED preparation and test center, learning center, reduced course load, remedial instruction, study skills assistance, tutoring.

Majors. Business: Accounting, administrative services, business admin, human resources, marketing, office management, office/clerical. **Computer sciences:** LAN/WAN management, networking, programming, web page design. **Conservation:** Urban forestry. **Education:** Early childhood. **Engineering technology:** Civil, computer systems, electrical, industrial, instrumentation, manufacturing. **Health:** EMT paramedic, nursing (RN), respiratory therapy assistant, respiratory therapy technology. **Mechanic/repair:** Electronics/electrical. **Protective services:** Corrections, firefighting, police science.

Computing on campus. 600 workstations in library, computer center, student center. Online course registration, online library, helpline available.

Student life. Freshman orientation: Available. **Policies:** Freshmen permitted cars on campus. **Activities:** Student government, student newspaper, association for information technology professionals, civil engineering technology highway technician club, corrections student organization, cosmetology & barbering club, law enforcement organization, student nurses' association, athletic booster club, student society of arboriculture.

Athletics. NJCAA. **Intercollegiate:** Basketball. **Intramural:** Basketball, volleyball. **Team name:** Cougars.

Student services. Adult student services, alcohol/substance abuse counseling, career counseling, services for economically disadvantaged, student employment services, financial aid counseling, minority student services, personal counseling, placement for graduates, veterans' counselor, women's services. **Physically disabled:** Services for visually, speech, hearing impaired. **Learning disabled:** Comprehensive services available. **Transfer:** Special adviser, orientation, pre-admission transcript evaluation for new students. Transfer adviser, college fairs on campus for students transferring to 4-year colleges.

Contact. Phone: (715) 422-5444 Toll-free number: (888) 575-6782
Fax: (715) 422-5440
Jim Barrett, Director of Admissions, Mid-State Technical College, 500 32nd Street North, Wisconsin Rapids, WI 54494

Milwaukee Area Technical College

Milwaukee, Wisconsin — **CB member**
http://matc.edu — **CB code: 1475**

- Public 2-year junior and technical college
- Commuter campus in very large city

General. Founded in 1912. Regionally accredited. Campuses in Milwaukee, Oak Creek, Mequon, and West Allis. **Enrollment:** 14,817 degree-seeking undergraduates; 3,728 non-degree-seeking students. **Degrees:** 1,481 associate awarded. **Location:** 85 miles from Chicago. **Calendar:** Semester, limited summer session. **Full-time faculty:** 594 total; 8% have terminal degrees, 24% minority, 49% women. **Part-time faculty:** 809 total; 4% have terminal degrees, 20% minority, 52% women. **Class size:** 80% < 20, 19% 20-39, less than 1% 40-49, less than 1% 50-99.

Student profile. Among degree-seeking undergraduates, 13% enrolled in a transfer program, 87% enrolled in a vocational program, 10% already have a bachelor's degree or higher, 1,899 enrolled as first-time, first-year students.

Part-time:	63%	**Asian American:**	4%
Out-of-state:	1%	**Hispanic American:**	8%
Women:	60%	**Native American:**	1%
African American:	26%	**25 or older:**	85%

Transfer out. 20% of students enrolled in the transfer program go on to 4-year colleges. **Colleges most students transferred to 2005:** University of Wisconsin-Milwaukee, Waukesha County Technical College, Cardinal Stritch University, Gateway Technical College, Alverno College.

Basis for selection. Open admission, but selective for some programs and for out-of-state students. Special requirements for health programs. ACCUPLACER required for placement. Institutionally administered reading, math, and English examinations required for all applicants if SAT or ACT not taken. **Adult students:** Entrance exam policies same as for first-time freshmen. **Homeschooled:** Must complete ACCUPLACER testing.

High school preparation. Specific subject requirements for some programs.

2005-2006 Annual costs. Tuition/fees: $2,677; $15,571 out-of-state. Per-credit charge: $81 in-state; $510 out-of-state. Material fees vary by program. Books/supplies: $1,000.

2004-2005 Financial aid. Need-based: 716 full-time freshmen applied for aid; 582 were judged to have need; 523 of these received aid. Average need met was 50%. Average scholarship/grant was $3,377; average loan $2,153. 64% of total undergraduate aid awarded as scholarships/grants, 36% as loans/jobs. Need-based aid available for part-time students. Work study available for part-time students. **Non-need-based:** Awarded to 99 full-time undergraduates, including 18 freshmen. Scholarships awarded for academics.

Application procedures. Admission: Closing date 8/19 (postmark date). $30 fee. Application may be submitted online. Admission notification on a rolling basis. **Financial aid:** Priority date 3/15; no closing date. FAFSA required. Applicants notified on a rolling basis starting 4/15.

Academics. Special study options: Accelerated study, cooperative education, distance learning, double major, dual enrollment of high school students, ESL, honors, independent study, internships, liberal arts/career combination, weekend college. Teacher education program with guaranteed admission to University of Wisconsin-Milwaukee. License preparation in aviation, dental hygiene, nursing. **Credit/placement by examination:** AP, CLEP, institutional tests. **Support services:** GED preparation and test center, learning center, reduced course load, remedial instruction, study skills assistance, tutoring, writing center.

Majors. Agriculture: Landscaping. **Business:** Accounting, administrative services, apparel, banking/financial services, business admin, e-commerce, hotel/motel admin, international marketing, logistics, marketing, operations, real estate, tourism/travel. **Communications technology:** Graphic/printing, graphics, radio/tv. **Computer sciences:** Computer graphics, networking, programming, security, systems analysis. **Engineering:** Materials. **Engineering technology:** Architectural, biomedical, civil, computer systems, electrical, heat/ac/refrig, industrial, mechanical drafting, plastics, water quality. **Foreign languages:** Sign language interpretation. **Health:** Anesthesiologist assistant, cardiovascular technology, clinical lab technology, dental hygiene, dietetic technician, electroencephalograph technology, medical radiologic technology/radiation therapy, medical records technology, medical secretary, nursing (RN), occupational therapy assistant, physical therapy assistant, respiratory therapy technology, surgical technology. **Legal studies:** Legal secretary, paralegal. **Liberal arts:** Arts/sciences. **Mechanic/repair:** Automotive. **Personal/culinary services:** Mortuary science, restaurant/catering. **Production:** Welding. **Protective services:** Firefighting, police science. **Science technology:** Chemical. **Visual/performing arts:** Commercial photography, graphic design, interior design, music performance.

Computing on campus. 275 workstations in library, computer center, student center. Online course registration, online library, helpline, wireless network available.

Student life. Freshman orientation: Mandatory. **Policies:** Freshmen permitted cars on campus. **Housing:** Certified housing available at nearby colleges and other facilities. **Activities:** Literary magazine, student government, student newspaper, TV station, student senate, student life committee, african american student club, American Culinary Federation, architectural technology club, Association of Information Technology Professionals, campus bible fellowship, criminal Justice student organization, environmental club, Phi Theta Kappa Honor Society, paralegal association.

Athletics. NJCAA. **Intercollegiate:** Baseball M, basketball M, golf, soccer M, softball W, volleyball W. **Intramural:** Basketball, table tennis, volleyball. **Team name:** Lakestormers.

Student services. Alcohol/substance abuse counseling, career counseling, services for economically disadvantaged, student employment services, financial aid counseling, health services, legal services, minority student services, on-campus daycare, personal counseling, placement for graduates, veterans' counselor, women's services. **Physically disabled:** Services for visually, speech, hearing impaired. **Learning disabled:** Comprehensive services available. **Transfer:** Special adviser, orientation for new students. Transfer center, transfer adviser, college fairs on campus for students transferring to 4-year colleges.

Contact. E-mail: bullockr@matc.edu
Phone: (414) 297-6370 Fax: (414) 297-7800
Robert Bullock, Director, Admissions and Testing, Milwaukee Area Technical College, 700 West State Street, Milwaukee, WI 53233-1443

Moraine Park Technical College
Fond du Lac, Wisconsin
www.morainepark.edu **CB code: 0667**

- Public 2-year technical college
- Commuter campus in large town
- Interview required

General. Founded in 1967. Regionally accredited. Campuses at Beaver Dam and West Bend. **Enrollment:** 4,200 degree-seeking undergraduates. **Degrees:** 489 associate awarded. **Location:** 60 miles from Milwaukee. **Calendar:** Semester, limited summer session. **Full-time faculty:** 145 total. **Part-time faculty:** 200 total.

Basis for selection. Open admission, but selective for some programs. Students without high school diploma may be admitted to certain job-entry preparation programs. ACT required of associate-degree-seeking nursing applicants.

High school preparation. 16 units recommended. Recommended units include English 3, mathematics 2, social studies 2 and science 2.

2005-2006 Annual costs. Tuition/fees: $2,536; $15,430 out-of-state. Per-credit charge: $81 in-state; $510 out-of-state. Additional fee of $4 per lecture course. Books/supplies: $900.

2004-2005 Financial aid. Need-based: 61% of total undergraduate aid awarded as scholarships/grants, 39% as loans/jobs. Need-based aid available for part-time students. Work study available nights, weekends and for part-time students. **Non-need-based:** Scholarships awarded for academics, job skills, leadership, minority status, state residency.

Application procedures. Admission: No deadline. $30 fee, may be waived for applicants with need. Application may be submitted online. Admission notification on a rolling basis. Limited enrollment health care programs have varying application deadlines. **Financial aid:** Priority date 5/1; no closing date. FAFSA, institutional form required. Applicants notified on a rolling basis starting 6/15; must reply within 2 week(s) of notification.

Academics. Special study options: Accelerated study, distance learning, double major, dual enrollment of high school students, ESL, independent study, internships, weekend college. **Credit/placement by examination:** CLEP, institutional tests. 30 credit hours maximum toward associate degree. **Support services:** GED preparation and test center, learning center, preadmission summer program, reduced course load, remedial instruction, tutoring.

Majors. Business: Accounting, administrative services, marketing, office management, office technology, sales/distribution. **Communications:** General. **Communications technology:** Graphic/printing. **Computer sciences:** Applications programming, data processing. **Engineering technology:** Civil, drafting. **Family/consumer sciences:** Child care, family studies. **Health:** Health services, medical records technology, medical secretary, nursing (RN), substance abuse counseling. **Legal studies:** Legal secretary. **Liberal arts:** Arts/sciences. **Mechanic/repair:** Electronics/electrical. **Personal/culinary services:** Culinary arts. **Protective services:** Corrections, police science.

Most popular majors. Business/marketing 11%, engineering/engineering technologies 16%, health sciences 57%, trade and industry 8%.

Student life. Freshman orientation: Mandatory. **Activities:** Student government.

Athletics. Intercollegiate: Golf. **Intramural:** Basketball, bowling, softball, table tennis, volleyball.

Student services. Career counseling, student employment services, health services, on-campus daycare, personal counseling, placement for graduates, veterans' counselor. **Physically disabled:** Services for visually, hearing impaired. **Transfer:** Orientation for new students. College fairs on campus for students transferring to 4-year colleges.

Contact. Phone: (920) 924-3408 Toll-free number: (800) 472-4554
Fax: (920) 924-3421
Sally Ruback, Student Enrollment Partner, Moraine Park Technical College, 235 North National Avenue, Fond du Lac, WI 54935-1940

Nicolet Area Technical College
Rhinelander, Wisconsin
www.nicoletcollege.edu **CB code: 0713**

- Public 2-year community and technical college
- Commuter campus in small town
- Interview required

General. Founded in 1967. Regionally accredited. Lakeland branch campus in Minocqua. **Enrollment:** 988 degree-seeking undergraduates. **Degrees:** 190 associate awarded. **Location:** 240 miles from Milwaukee, 200 miles from Minneapolis-St. Paul. **Calendar:** Semester, limited summer session. **Full-time faculty:** 58 total. **Part-time faculty:** 120 total. **Special facilities:** Theatre, sustainable energy initiative, wind turbine, solar powered day care center, alternative energy demonstration sites.

Student profile.

Out-of-state:	1%	**25 or older:**	55%

Transfer out. Colleges most students transferred to 2005: University of Wisconsin - Stevens Point, University of Wisconsin - Eau Claire, University of Wisconsin - Madison, University of Wisconsin - Oshkosh.

Basis for selection. ACCUPLACER scores determine admission to programs at associate degree and transfer levels. ACT and high school grades used in some cases. Conditional admission to degree programs for students who receive lower ACCUPLACER scores than required by programs. Refresher course must be taken. ACT recommended. **Adult students:** Entrance exam policies same as for first-time freshmen. **Homeschooled:** Federal Ability To Benefit criteria is used for non-high school grads.

High school preparation. Recommended units include English 4, mathematics 3, social studies 3 and science 3.

2005-2006 Annual costs. Tuition/fees: $2,513; $15,407 out-of-state. Per-credit charge: $81 in-state; $510 out-of-state. Material fees vary by program; minimum $4 per course. Books/supplies: $760. Personal expenses: $1,249.

2004-2005 Financial aid. Need-based: 78% of total undergraduate aid awarded as scholarships/grants, 22% as loans/jobs.

Application procedures. Admission: Priority date 8/1; no deadline. $30 fee. Application may be submitted online. Admission notification on a rolling basis beginning on or about 1/31. **Financial aid:** Priority date 4/15; no closing date. FAFSA, institutional form required. Applicants notified on a rolling basis starting 6/1; must reply within 2 week(s) of notification.

Academics. Special study options: Accelerated study, distance learning, double major, dual enrollment of high school students, ESL, independent study, internships, liberal arts/career combination, student-designed major. License preparation in real estate. **Credit/placement by examination:** AP, CLEP, institutional tests. 44 credit hours maximum toward associate degree. **Support services:** GED preparation and test center, learning center, reduced course load, remedial instruction, study skills assistance, tutoring.

Majors. Business: Accounting, administrative services, business admin. **Computer sciences:** General, programming. **Education:** Early childhood. **Engineering technology:** Surveying. **Family/consumer sciences:** Child care. **Health:** Medical assistant, nursing (RN), radiologic technology/medical imaging, surgical technology. **Liberal arts:** Arts/sciences. **Mechanic/repair:** Automotive, small engine. **Personal/culinary services:** Culinary arts. **Production:** Welding. **Protective services:** Criminal justice, police science. **Visual/performing arts:** Graphic design.

Most popular majors. Business/marketing 29%, computer/information sciences 11%, health sciences 21%, liberal arts 10%, security/protective services 13%, trade and industry 13%.

Computing on campus. 80 workstations in library, computer center. Commuter students can connect to campus network. Online course registration, online library, helpline, wireless network available.

Student life. Freshman orientation: Mandatory. Held 2 days before start of classes for a full day. **Policies:** Freshmen permitted cars on campus. **Activities:** Choral groups, drama, musical theater, student government, student newspaper, Business Professionals of America, Phi Theta Kappa.

Athletics. NJCAA. **Intercollegiate:** Cross-country. **Intramural:** Basketball, bowling, football (non-tackle), racquetball, skiing, volleyball.

Student services. Alcohol/substance abuse counseling, career counseling, services for economically disadvantaged, student employment services, financial aid counseling, minority student services, on-campus daycare, personal counseling, placement for graduates, veterans' counselor, women's services. **Physically disabled:** Services for visually, speech, hearing impaired. **Transfer:** Special adviser, orientation, pre-admission transcript evaluation for new students. Transfer center, transfer adviser, college fairs on campus for students transferring to 4-year colleges.

Contact. E-mail: inquire@nicoletcollege.edu
Phone: (715) 365-4451 Toll-free number: (800) 544-3039
Fax: (715) 365-4901
Susan Kordula, Director of Enrollment Management, Nicolet Area Technical College, Box 518, Rhinelander, WI 54501

Northcentral Technical College

Wausau, Wisconsin
www.ntc.edu **CB code: 0735**

- Public 2-year community and technical college
- Commuter campus in small city

General. Founded in 1911. Regionally accredited. Regional campuses located in Antigo, Medford, Phillips, Wittenberg and Spencer. Public Safety Training facility in Merrill. **Enrollment:** 4,955 undergraduates. **Degrees:** 498 associate awarded. **Location:** 200 miles from Milwaukee and Minneapolis-St. Paul, 150 miles from Madison. **Calendar:** Semester, limited summer session. **Full-time faculty:** 152 total. **Part-time faculty:** 9 total. **Special facilities:** Health and science center.

Student profile.

Out-of-state:	1%	**Live on campus:**	2%
25 or older:	40%		

Basis for selection. Open admission, but selective for some programs. Special requirements for radiography, nursing, dental hygiene, surgical technician programs. Portfolio required for health occupations. **Homeschooled:** Transcript of courses and grades required.

High school preparation. 3 units each of mathematics and science required for the following programs: radiography, nursing, dental hygiene. Mathematics emphasis for technical programs, chemistry for nursing.

2005-2006 Annual costs. Tuition/fees: $2,561; $15,455 out-of-state. Per-credit charge: $81 in-state; $510 out-of-state. Materials fees vary by program; minimum $4 per course. Books/supplies: $1,000. Personal expenses: $1,100.

2004-2005 Financial aid. Need-based: 61% of total undergraduate aid awarded as scholarships/grants, 39% as loans/jobs. Need-based aid available for part-time students.

Application procedures. Admission: No deadline. $35 fee. Application may be submitted online. Admission notification on a rolling basis beginning on or about 10/15. **Financial aid:** Priority date 4/1; no closing date. FAFSA required. Applicants notified on a rolling basis starting 6/15; must reply within 2 week(s) of notification.

Academics. Special study options: Accelerated study, distance learning, double major, ESL, internships, student-designed major. Bachelor's degree programs available on campus. **Credit/placement by examination:** CLEP, institutional tests. 24 credit hours maximum toward associate degree. **Support services:** GED preparation and test center, learning center, pre-admission summer program, reduced course load, remedial instruction, tutoring, writing center.

Majors. Business: Accounting, administrative services, entrepreneurial studies, office technology, operations. **Communications technology:** Graphic/printing. **Computer sciences:** Programming, systems analysis. **Engineering technology:** Drafting, electrical. **Foreign languages:** Sign language interpretation. **Health:** Dental hygiene, medical radiologic technology/radiation therapy, medical secretary, nursing (RN), surgical technology. **Legal studies:** Legal secretary. **Mechanic/repair:** Auto body, automotive. **Protective services:** Police science.

Most popular majors. Architecture 6%, business/marketing 39%, health sciences 23%, security/protective services 7%, trade and industry 17%.

Computing on campus. 1,200 workstations in library, computer center. Helpline, repair service available.

Student life. Freshman orientation: Mandatory. **Policies:** Freshmen permitted cars on campus. **Housing:** Coed dorms available. **Activities:** Radio station, student government, student newspaper, Campus Crusade for Christ, international student club, multicultural student club.

Athletics. Intramural: Basketball, racquetball, softball, volleyball.

Student services. Adult student services, career counseling, student employment services, health services, personal counseling, placement for graduates. **Physically disabled:** Services for visually, hearing impaired. **Transfer:** Orientation, pre-admission transcript evaluation for new students.

Contact. E-mail: jansedin@ntc.edu
Phone: (715) 675-3331 ext. 4482 Toll-free number: (888) 682-7144
Fax: (715) 675-0629
Kris Janse, Admissions, Northcentral Technical College, 1000 West Campus Drive, Wausau, WI 54401

Northeast Wisconsin Technical College

Green Bay, Wisconsin
www.nwtc.edu **CB code: 4190**

- Public 2-year community and technical college
- Commuter campus in small city

General. Founded in 1913. Regionally accredited. **Enrollment:** 5,450 degree-seeking undergraduates; 5,415 non-degree-seeking students. **Degrees:** 767 associate awarded. **Location:** 129 miles from Milwaukee, 150 miles from Madison. **Calendar:** Semester, limited summer session. **Full-time faculty:** 241 total. **Part-time faculty:** 709 total.

Student profile.

Part-time:	53%	**25 or older:**	15%
Women:	59%		

Transfer out. Colleges most students transferred to 2005: University of Wisconsin-Green Bay, University of Wisconsin-Oshkosh.

Basis for selection. Open admission, but selective for some programs. Special requirements for health programs. ACCUPLACER required unless applicant has minimum ACT, SAT, ASSET, or COMPASS score or previously earned bachelor's or associate degree from Wisconsin technical college. **Adult students:** Entrance exam policies same as for first-time freshmen. **Homeschooled:** State high school equivalency certificate required.

2005-2006 Annual costs. Tuition/fees: $2,538; $15,432 out-of-state. Per-credit charge: $81 in-state; $510 out-of-state. Additional fee of $4 per lecture course. Books/supplies: $972. Personal expenses: $1,674.

2004-2005 Financial aid. Need-based: 59% of total undergraduate aid awarded as scholarships/grants, 41% as loans/jobs. Need-based aid available for part-time students. Work study available nights and for part-time students.

Application procedures. Admission: No deadline. $30 fee, may be waived for applicants with need. Application may be submitted online. Admission notification on a rolling basis. **Financial aid:** Priority date 4/1; no closing date. FAFSA required. Applicants notified on a rolling basis starting 5/1; must reply within 2 week(s) of notification.

Academics. Special study options: Accelerated study, distance learning, double major, ESL, internships, liberal arts/career combination. License preparation in dental hygiene, nursing, paramedic, physical therapy, radiology, real estate. **Credit/placement by examination:** AP, CLEP, institutional tests. 48 credit hours maximum toward associate degree. **Support services:** GED preparation and test center, learning center, reduced course load, remedial instruction, study skills assistance, tutoring.

Majors. Agriculture: Business, farm/ranch, food science. **Business:** General, accounting, administrative services, business admin, fashion, hospitality/recreation, logistics, office management, office technology, sales/distribution, tourism/travel. **Computer sciences:** General, data processing, networking, programming. **Engineering:** Civil. **Engineering technology:** Architectural, civil, drafting, electrical, industrial management. **Health:** Dental hygiene, health care admin, medical records admin, medical secretary, nursing (RN), physical therapy assistant, respiratory therapy technology. **Legal studies:** Paralegal. **Mechanic/repair:** Heating/ac/refrig, industrial. **Protective services:** Fire safety technology, police science. **Transportation:** General.

Most popular majors. Business/marketing 27%, computer/information sciences 7%, engineering/engineering technologies 14%, health sciences 27%, security/protective services 11%, trade and industry 7%.

Computing on campus. Online course registration, online library, helpline, wireless network available.

Student life. Freshman orientation: Mandatory. 2-hour program in conjunction with registration. **Activities:** Student government, student newspaper.

Athletics. Intramural: Basketball, volleyball.

Student services. Adult student services, alcohol/substance abuse counseling, career counseling, services for economically disadvantaged, student employment services, health services, minority student services, personal counseling, placement for graduates, veterans' counselor. **Physically disabled:** Services for visually, speech, hearing impaired. **Transfer:** Special adviser, orientation, re-entry adviser for new students.

Contact. Phone: (920) 498-5444 Toll-free
number: (800) 422-6982 ext. 5444 Fax: (920) 498-6882
Heather Hill, Director of Program Enrollment, Northeast Wisconsin Technical College, 2740 West Mason Street, Green Bay, WI 54307-9042

Southwest Wisconsin Technical College

Fennimore, Wisconsin
www.swtc.edu **CB code: 0900**

- Public 2-year technical college
- Commuter campus in rural community
- Interview required

General. Founded in 1967. Regionally accredited. **Enrollment:** 1,450 degree-seeking undergraduates. **Degrees:** 183 associate awarded. **Location:** 75 miles from Madison; 38 miles from Dubuque, Iowa. **Calendar:** Semester, limited summer session. **Full-time faculty:** 85 total.

Student profile.

Out-of-state:	1%	**Live on campus:**	1%
25 or older:	71%		

Basis for selection. Open admission. Interview and Test of Adult Basic Education required for admission. Secondary school record not considered. Students may have admissions requirements based on admission test scores. Psychological Services Bureau Test required for nursing RN applicants, C-NET test required for LPN applicants.

2005-2006 Annual costs. Tuition/fees: $2,487; $15,381 out-of-state. Per-credit charge: $81 in-state; $510 out-of-state. Materials fees vary by program; minimum $4.00 per course. Books/supplies: $760. Personal expenses: $1,248.

Financial aid. Need-based: Work study available nights and for part-time students.

Application procedures. Admission: No deadline. $30 fee. Admission notification on a rolling basis beginning on or about 9/1. Students notified of admission before July 1 must pay tuition deposit of $100 by July 1; students applying after that date must pay deposit as part of application process. **Financial aid:** Priority date 4/15; no closing date. FAFSA, institutional form required. Applicants notified on a rolling basis starting 5/15; must reply within 4 week(s) of notification.

Academics. Special study options: Distance learning, double major, dual enrollment of high school students, ESL, internships. **Credit/placement by examination:** CLEP, institutional tests. **Support services:** GED preparation and test center, learning center, pre-admission summer program, reduced course load, remedial instruction, tutoring, writing center.

Majors. Agriculture: Agribusiness operations, business. **Business:** Accounting, administrative services. **Computer sciences:** Networking, programming, systems analysis. **Education:** Teacher assistance. **Engineering technology:** Drafting, electrical. **Family/consumer sciences:** Child care, institutional food production. **Health:** Nursing (RN). **Legal studies:** Legal secretary. **Mechanic/repair:** Electronics/electrical. **Personal/culinary services:** Culinary arts. **Public administration:** Human services.

Computing on campus. 250 workstations in library, computer center.

Student life. Freshman orientation: Mandatory. Held about 3 weeks before classes start. **Housing:** Special housing for disabled, apartments available. $200 deposit, deadline 5/1. **Activities:** Student government, student newspaper, Marketing and Management Association, Business Professionals of America, Vocational and Industrial Clubs of America, Professional Food Preparers, Health Occupations Students of America, National Student Nursing Association, post-secondary agricultural students, cross-cultural communications club; exercise area and student activity area available evenings for resident students.

Athletics. Intramural: Basketball, softball, volleyball.

Student services. Alcohol/substance abuse counseling, career counseling, student employment services, financial aid counseling, health services, minority student services, on-campus daycare, personal counseling, placement for graduates, women's services. **Physically disabled:** Services for visually, hearing impaired. **Transfer:** Special adviser, orientation for new students. Transfer adviser for students transferring to 4-year colleges.

Contact. E-mail: studentservices@swtc.edu
Phone: (608) 822-3262 ext. 2354 Toll-free
number: (800) 362-3322 ext. 2354 Fax: (608) 822-6019
Kathy Kreul, Admissions Specialist, Southwest Wisconsin Technical College, 1800 Bronson Boulevard, Fennimore, WI 53809

University of Wisconsin-Baraboo/Sauk County

Baraboo, Wisconsin
www.baraboo.uwc.edu **CB code: 1996**

- Public 2-year branch campus and liberal arts college
- Commuter campus in large town
- SAT or ACT (ACT writing optional) required

General. Founded in 1968. Regionally accredited. **Enrollment:** 485 degree-seeking undergraduates. **Degrees:** 75 associate awarded. **Location:** 46 miles from Madison. **Calendar:** Semester, limited summer session. **Full-time faculty:** 15 total; 87% have terminal degrees, 7% minority, 33% women. **Part-time faculty:** 33 total; 3% minority, 52% women. **Class size:** 57% < 20, 42% 20-39, less than 1% 40-49.

Student profile. Among degree-seeking undergraduates, 100% enrolled in a transfer program, 1% already have a bachelor's degree or higher, 34 transferred in from other institutions.

Transfer out. Colleges most students transferred to 2005: University of Wisconsin-Madison, University of Wisconsin-LaCrosse, University of Wisconsin-Stevens Point, University of Wisconsin-Whitewater, University of Wisconsin-Platteville.

Basis for selection. Secondary school courses, rank in upper 75% of high school graduating class, ACT or SAT test scores most important. Students in bottom 25% of graduating class may be admitted based on individual record and circumstances. Students not admitted may be deferred and admitted following semester. Special attention given to returning adult, homeschooled, learning disabled, and minority students. TOEFL test required for non-native speakers of English. Interview required for those with borderline academic records and class rank and recommended for others with special circumstances. **Adult students:** SAT/ACT scores not required if applicant over 21. University of Wisconsin Placement Test required of all students not having had college credit English and/or mathematics courses. **Homeschooled:** Transcript of courses and grades, interview required. Interview, portfolio of curriculum, method of assessment, work samples and experiences recommended. **Learning Disabled:** Interview recommended, professional testing required to create program to accommodate special needs.

High school preparation. 17 units required. Required and recommended units include English 4, mathematics 3-4, social studies 3, science 3 (laboratory 3-4), foreign language 2 and academic electives 4. Mathematics must be college preparatory. Sciences must include lab exposure/experience.

2005-2006 Annual costs. Tuition/fees: $4,292; $12,992 out-of-state. Per-credit charge: $166 in-state; $528 out-of-state. Minnesota reciprocity tuition: $3,576 full-time, $149 per-credit-hour. Books/supplies: $680. Personal expenses: $2,660.

Financial aid. All financial aid based on need. Need-based aid available for part-time students. Work study available nights and for part-time students.

Application procedures. Admission: Priority date 6/1; deadline 8/31 (receipt date). $35 fee, may be waived for applicants with need. Application may be submitted online. Admission notification on a rolling basis beginning on or about 9/15. **Financial aid:** Priority date 4/15; no closing date. FAFSA, institutional form required. Applicants notified on a rolling basis starting 4/15; must reply within 3 week(s) of notification.

Academics. Required courses for associate degree available evenings over 4-year period. Bachelor's degree available on campus through University of Wisconsin Milwaukee. **Special study options:** Cross-registration, distance learning, dual enrollment of high school students, external degree, honors, independent study, internships, liberal arts/career combination, study abroad. Bachelor's degree programs available on campus. **Credit/placement by examination:** AP, CLEP, IB, institutional tests. **Support services:** Learning center, reduced course load, remedial instruction, study skills assistance, tutoring, writing center.

Majors. Liberal arts: Arts/sciences.

Computing on campus. 50 workstations in library, computer center, student center. Commuter students can connect to campus network. Online course registration, online library, wireless network available.

Student life. Freshman orientation: Mandatory, $200 fee. Preregistration for classes offered. Orientation in 3 parts over summer. **Policies:** Students participate actively in campus governance and committee work with faculty and staff. Freshmen permitted cars on campus. **Housing:** Privately owned apartments adjacent to campus. **Activities:** Bands, choral groups, drama, literary magazine, music ensembles, student government, student newspaper, Campus Crusade for Christ, Phi Theta Kappa, Wellness Alliance, business club, Native American club, Cine club, UWB Ambassadors, green club, art club, Future Educators.

Athletics. NJCAA. **Intercollegiate:** Basketball M, soccer, tennis, volleyball W. **Intramural:** Basketball, cross-country, racquetball, softball, volleyball. **Team name:** Fighting Spirits.

Student services. Adult student services, alcohol/substance abuse counseling, career counseling, financial aid counseling, minority student services, personal counseling, veterans' counselor. **Physically disabled:** Services for visually, speech, hearing impaired. **Transfer:** Special adviser, orientation, pre-admission transcript evaluation for new students. Transfer adviser, college fairs on campus for students transferring to 4-year colleges.

Contact. E-mail: apply@wisconsin.edu
Phone: (608) 356-8351 ext. 245 Fax: (608) 356-0752
Thomas Martin, Assistant Dean for Student Services, University of Wisconsin-Baraboo/Sauk County, 1006 Connie Road, Baraboo, WI 53913-1098

University of Wisconsin-Barron County

Rice Lake, Wisconsin
www.barron.uwc.edu **CB code: 1772**

- Public 2-year branch campus and junior college
- Commuter campus in small town

General. Founded in 1966. Regionally accredited. **Location:** 80 miles from Minneapolis-St. Paul, 50 miles from Eau Claire. **Calendar:** Semester.

Annual costs/financial aid. Tuition/fees (2005-2006): $4,230; $12,930 out-of-state. Minnesota reciprocity tuition: $3,576 full-time, $149 per-credit-hour. Books/supplies: $150. Need-based financial aid available to full-time and part-time students.

Contact. Phone: (715) 234-8024
Director of Student Services, 1800 College Drive, Rice Lake, WI 54868

University of Wisconsin-Fond du Lac

Fond du Lac, Wisconsin
www.fdl.wwc.edu **CB code: 1942**

- Public 2-year branch campus college
- Commuter campus in large town
- SAT or ACT (ACT writing optional) required

General. Founded in 1968. Regionally accredited. **Enrollment:** 765 degree-seeking undergraduates. **Degrees:** 109 associate awarded. **Location:** 70 miles from Milwaukee. **Calendar:** Semester, limited summer session. **Full-time faculty:** 25 total. **Part-time faculty:** 20 total. **Special facilities:** Nature preserve, arboretum.

Student profile.

Out-of-state:	1%	**25 or older:**	30%

Basis for selection. Rank in upper 75% of high school graduating class ensures admission. Students in bottom 25% of graduating class will be placed on waiting list. Students not admitted for specific semester applied for will be admitted at later date. Students with GED automatically placed on waiting list. Applicants ranking in bottom quarter of class restricted to fewer credits on admission, required to participate in summer school program/projects. Interview required for students in lowest 25% of high school. **Adult students:** SAT/ACT scores not required if applicant over 21.

High school preparation. 17 units required. Required units include English 4, mathematics 3, social studies 3 and science 3. 4 additional academic units required.

2005-2006 Annual costs. Tuition/fees: $4,230; $12,930 out-of-state. Per-credit charge: $166 in-state; $528 out-of-state. Minnesota reciprocity tuition: $3,576 full-time, $149 per-credit-hour. Books/supplies: $455. Personal expenses: $810.

Financial aid. Need-based: Need-based aid available for part-time students.

Application procedures. Admission: Priority date 6/30; no deadline. $35 fee, may be waived for applicants with need. Admission notification on a rolling basis. **Financial aid:** Priority date 4/15; no closing date. FAFSA, institutional form required. Applicants notified on a rolling basis starting 6/1; must reply within 2 week(s) of notification.

Academics. Academic advising required of all students carrying 10 or more credits. **Special study options:** Cross-registration, distance learning, dual enrollment of high school students, honors, independent study. **Credit/placement by examination:** AP, CLEP, institutional tests. 18 credit hours maximum toward associate degree. **Support services:** Learning center, pre-admission summer program, reduced course load, remedial instruction, tutoring.

Majors. Liberal arts: Arts/sciences.

Computing on campus. 40 workstations in library, computer center.

Student life. Freshman orientation: Mandatory, $10 fee. **Housing:** Student housing available at nearby Marian College. **Activities:** Bands, choral groups, drama, literary magazine, music ensembles, musical theater, radio station, student government, student newspaper.

Athletics. NJCAA. **Intercollegiate:** Baseball M, basketball, golf, soccer, tennis, volleyball W. **Intramural:** Basketball M, bowling, table tennis, volleyball. **Team name:** Falcons.

Student services. Career counseling, personal counseling, veterans' counselor. **Physically disabled:** Services for visually, speech, hearing impaired. **Transfer:** Special adviser, orientation for new students. Transfer adviser for students transferring to 4-year colleges.

Contact. Phone: (920) 929-3606 Fax: (920) 929-3626
Linda Reiss, Assistant Campus Dean for Student Affairs, University of Wisconsin-Fond du Lac, 400 University Drive, Fond du Lac, WI 54935-2998

University of Wisconsin-Fox Valley

Menasha, Wisconsin
www.uwfoxvalley.uwc.edu **CB code: 1889**

- Public 2-year liberal arts college
- Commuter campus in small city

General. Founded in 1933. Regionally accredited. **Location:** 90 miles from Milwaukee. **Calendar:** Semester.

Annual costs/financial aid. Tuition/fees (2005-2006): $4,193; $12,893 out-of-state. Minnesota reciprocity tuition: $3,576 full-time, $149 per-credit-hour. Books/supplies: $455. Personal expenses: $810. Need-based financial aid available to full-time and part-time students.

Contact. Phone: (920) 832-2620
Assistant Campus Dean for Student Services, 1478 Midway Road, Menasha, WI 54952-2850

University of Wisconsin-Manitowoc

Manitowoc, Wisconsin
www.manitowoc.uwc.edu **CB code: 1890**

- Public 2-year branch campus and liberal arts college
- Commuter campus in large town

General. Founded in 1933. Regionally accredited. **Location:** 45 miles from Green Bay. **Calendar:** Semester.

Annual costs/financial aid. Tuition/fees (2005-2006): $4,184; $12,884 out-of-state. Minnesota reciprocity tuition: $3,576 full-time, $149 per-credit-hour. Books/supplies: $515. Personal expenses: $990.

Contact. Phone: (920) 683-4707
Associate Director, 705 Viebahn Street, Manitowoc, WI 54220-6699

University of Wisconsin-Marathon County

Wausau, Wisconsin
www.uwmc.uwc.edu **CB code: 1995**

- Public 2-year branch campus college
- Commuter campus in large town
- SAT or ACT (ACT writing optional) required

General. Founded in 1933. Regionally accredited. Guaranteed transfer program to University of Wisconsin 4-year schools. **Enrollment:** 1,200 full-time, degree-seeking students. **Degrees:** 90 associate awarded. **Location:** 180 miles from Milwaukee, 180 miles from Minneapolis-St. Paul. **Calendar:** Semester, limited summer session. **Full-time faculty:** 35 total. **Part-time faculty:** 38 total. **Special facilities:** Planetarium, hiking and cross-country ski trails, indoor skating and curling rinks.

Student profile.

Out-of-state:	3%	**Live on campus:**	12%
25 or older:	28%		

Basis for selection. Rank in upper 75 percent of high school graduating class ensures admission. Students in bottom 25 percent and those with GED admitted on basis of interview. **Adult students:** SAT/ACT scores not required if applicant over 21. **Learning Disabled:** Must provide official documentation for review of accommodations 90 days in advance.

High school preparation. 17 units required. Required and recommended units include English 4, mathematics 3-4, social studies 3-4, science 3-4 and foreign language 4. Math units must be algebra, geometry or other courses leading to calculus.

2005-2006 Annual costs. Tuition/fees: $4,197; $12,897 out-of-state. Per-credit charge: $166 in-state; $528 out-of-state. Minnesota reciprocity tuition: $3,576 full-time, $149 per-credit-hour. Books/supplies: $700. Personal expenses: $810.

Financial aid. All financial aid based on need. Need-based aid available for part-time students. Work study available nights and for part-time students.

Application procedures. Admission: Priority date 8/1; no deadline. $35 fee, may be waived for applicants with need. Application may be submitted online. Admission notification on a rolling basis. **Financial aid:** Priority date 4/15; no closing date. FAFSA, institutional form required. Applicants notified on a rolling basis starting 6/1; must reply within 3 week(s) of notification.

Academics. Special study options: Cross-registration, dual enrollment of high school students, honors, independent study, internships, liberal arts/career combination, study abroad. Bachelor's degree programs available on campus. **Credit/placement by examination:** AP, CLEP, IB, institutional tests. 18 credit hours maximum toward associate degree. **Support services:** Learning center, pre-admission summer program, reduced course load, remedial instruction, study skills assistance, tutoring, writing center.

Majors. Liberal arts: Arts/sciences.

Computing on campus. 92 workstations in dormitories, library, computer center. Dormitories wired for high-speed internet access and linked to campus network. Online library, helpline available.

Student life. Freshman orientation: Available, $15 fee. Preregistration for classes offered. 1-day program held week before start of fall classes. **Policies:** Zero tolerance alcohol and drug policy in residence hall. **Housing:** Coed dorms available. $100 deposit. **Activities:** Bands, choral groups, drama, literary magazine, music ensembles, musical theater, student government, student newspaper, symphony orchestra, Christian Fellowship, business club, computer club, drama club, international relations club, biology club, gay lesbian bisexual student association.

Athletics. NJCAA. **Intercollegiate:** Basketball, golf, soccer, tennis, volleyball W. **Intramural:** Archery, badminton, basketball, bowling, fencing, golf, handball, racquetball, skiing, skin diving, softball, swimming, table tennis, tennis, volleyball. **Team name:** Huskies.

Student services. Adult student services, career counseling, student employment services, personal counseling, veterans' counselor. **Physically disabled:** Services for visually, hearing impaired. **Transfer:** Special adviser for new students. Transfer adviser, college fairs on campus for students transferring to 4-year colleges.

Contact. E-mail: uwmc@uwe.edu
Phone: (715) 261-6241 Fax: (715) 261-6331
Nolan Beck, Director of Student Services, University of Wisconsin-Marathon County, 518 South Seventh Avenue, Wausau, WI 54401-5396

University of Wisconsin-Marinette

Marinette, Wisconsin
www.marinette.uwc.edu **CB code: 1891**

- Public 2-year branch campus and liberal arts college
- Commuter campus in large town
- SAT or ACT (ACT writing optional), application essay required

General. Founded in 1946. Regionally accredited. **Enrollment:** 364 degree-seeking undergraduates; 148 non-degree-seeking students. **Degrees:** 89 associate awarded. **Location:** 50 miles from Green Bay, 170 miles from Milwaukee. **Calendar:** Semester, limited summer session. **Full-time faculty:** 17 total; 71% have terminal degrees, 35% women. **Part-time faculty:** 17 total; 18% have terminal degrees, 59% women. **Class size:** 59% < 20, 36% 20-39, 5% 50-99.

Student profile. Among degree-seeking undergraduates, 1% already have a bachelor's degree or higher, 284 enrolled as first-time, first-year students.

Part-time:	24%	**Women:**	56%
Out-of-state:	23%	**25 or older:**	26%

Transfer out. Colleges most students transferred to 2005: UW-Green Bay, UW-Oshkosh, UW-Stevens Point, UW-Madison, Northern Michigan University.

Basis for selection. Class rank, GPA, courses, ACT scores, and involvement. Applicants not meeting minimum standards may be accepted but required to take reduced course load and/or noncredit courses to remedy deficiencies. **Adult students:** SAT/ACT scores not required if applicant over 21.

High school preparation. 17 units required. Required units include English 4, mathematics 3, social studies 3 and science 3. 4 electives of computer science, business, foreign language and/or fine arts required.

2005-2006 Annual costs. Tuition/fees: $4,177; $12,877 out-of-state. Per-credit charge: $166 in-state; $528 out-of-state. Minnesota reciprocity tuition: $3,576 full-time, $149 per-credit-hour. Books/supplies: $600.

Financial aid. All financial aid based on need. Need-based aid available for part-time students. Work study available nights and for part-time students.

Application procedures. Admission: Priority date 7/1; no deadline. $35 fee, may be waived for applicants with need. Application may be submitted online. Admission notification on a rolling basis. Students may be conditionally admitted prior to receipt of ACT scores, but may not register for classes until scores are received. **Financial aid:** Priority date 4/1; no closing date. FAFSA required. Applicants notified on a rolling basis.

Academics. Special study options: Cross-registration, distance learning, dual enrollment of high school students, ESL, independent study, internships, study abroad. Bachelor's degree programs available on campus. **Credit/placement by examination:** AP, CLEP, institutional tests. **Support services:** Reduced course load, remedial instruction, study skills assistance, tutoring.

Majors. Area/ethnic studies: Women's. **Liberal arts:** Arts/sciences.

Computing on campus. 80 workstations in library, computer center, student center. Online course registration, online library, wireless network available.

Student life. Freshman orientation: Mandatory, $50 fee. **Policies:** Freshmen permitted cars on campus. **Activities:** Choral groups, drama, literary magazine, music ensembles, musical theater, student government, student newspaper, Phi Theta Kappa.

Athletics. NJCAA. **Intercollegiate:** Basketball, volleyball W. **Intramural:** Basketball, bowling, football (non-tackle), skiing, table tennis, volleyball. **Team name:** Buccaneers.

Student services. Adult student services, career counseling, services for economically disadvantaged, student employment services, financial aid counseling, minority student services, personal counseling, veterans' counselor. **Physically disabled:** Services for visually, speech, hearing impaired. **Transfer:** Special adviser, orientation for new students. Transfer adviser, college fairs on campus for students transferring to 4-year colleges.

Contact. E-mail: ssinfo@uwc.edu
Phone: (715) 735-4301 Fax: (715) 735-4304
Cynthia Bailey, Assistant Campus Dean for Student Services, University of Wisconsin-Marinette, 750 West Bay Shore Street, Marinette, WI 54143

University of Wisconsin-Marshfield/Wood County

Marshfield, Wisconsin
www.marshfield.uwc.edu **CB code: 1997**

- Public 2-year branch campus college
- Commuter campus in large town
- SAT or ACT (ACT writing optional) required

General. Founded in 1964. Regionally accredited. Two-year transfer program prepares students for any four-year program in Wisconsin system. **Enrollment:** 650 degree-seeking undergraduates. **Degrees:** 65 associate awarded. **Location:** 138 miles from Madison. **Calendar:** Semester, limited summer session. **Full-time faculty:** 16 total. **Part-time faculty:** 25 total. **Class size:** 30% < 20, 67% 20-39, 1% 40-49, 2% 50-99.

Student profile.

Out-of-state:	1%	**25 or older:**	28%

Transfer out. Colleges most students transferred to 2005: University of Wisconsin Steven's Point, University of Wisconsin-Eau Claire, University of Wisconsin Madison.

Basis for selection. Rank in top 75% of high school class and 17 specified high school academic units ensure admission. Students in bottom 25% and/or with missing units may be placed on waiting list. Students not admitted for specific semester applied for may be admitted later. Placement tests required in math and English. **Adult students:** SAT/ACT scores not required if applicant over 21 or out of high school 3 years or more.

High school preparation. 17 units required. Required and recommended units include English 4, mathematics 3-4, social studies 3, science 3-4 and academic electives 4.

2005-2006 Annual costs. Tuition/fees: $4,207; $12,907 out-of-state. Per-credit charge: $166 in-state; $528 out-of-state. Minnesota reciprocity tuition: $3,576 full-time, $149 per-credit-hour. Books/supplies: $500. Personal expenses: $1,022.

Financial aid. All financial aid based on need. Need-based aid available for part-time students. Work study available nights, weekends and for part-time students.

Application procedures. Admission: No deadline. $35 fee. Application may be submitted online. Admission notification on a rolling basis. **Financial aid:** Priority date 4/15; no closing date. FAFSA required. Applicants notified on a rolling basis starting 5/15; must reply within 3 week(s) of notification.

Academics. Special study options: Cross-registration, distance learning, dual enrollment of high school students, independent study, internships, study abroad. **Credit/placement by examination:** AP, CLEP, institutional tests. **Support services:** Pre-admission summer program, reduced course load, remedial instruction, study skills assistance, tutoring.

Majors. Liberal arts: Arts/sciences.

Computing on campus. 40 workstations in library, computer center, student center. Commuter students can connect to campus network. Online course registration available.

Student life. Freshman orientation: Mandatory, $55 fee. Preregistration for classes offered. One day in January and late August. **Policies:** Freshmen permitted cars on campus. **Activities:** Bands, choral groups, drama, literary magazine, music ensembles, musical theater, student government, student newspaper, symphony orchestra, Inter-Varsity Christian Fellowship, business club, nursing associaton, program board, honor fraternity, student education association.

Athletics. NJCAA. **Intercollegiate:** Basketball, golf, tennis, volleyball W. **Intramural:** Basketball, bowling, football (tackle) M, soccer, softball, tennis, volleyball. **Team name:** Marauders.

Student services. Adult student services, alcohol/substance abuse counseling, career counseling, student employment services, financial aid counseling, personal counseling, veterans' counselor. **Physically disabled:** Services for visually, speech, hearing impaired. **Transfer:** Special adviser, orientation for new students. Transfer adviser, college fairs on campus for students transferring to 4-year colleges.

Contact. E-mail: msfadmit@uwc.edu
Phone: (715) 389-6500 Fax: (715) 384-1718
Jeff Meece, Director of Student Services, University of Wisconsin-Marshfield/Wood County, 2000 West Fifth Street, Marshfield, WI 54449

University of Wisconsin-Richland

Richland Center, Wisconsin
http://richland.uwc.edu **CB code: 1662**

- Public 2-year liberal arts college
- Commuter campus in small town
- SAT or ACT (ACT writing optional) required

General. Founded in 1967. Regionally accredited. **Enrollment:** 464 degree-seeking undergraduates. **Degrees:** 72 associate awarded. **Location:** 60 miles from Madison. **Calendar:** Semester, limited summer session. **Full-time faculty:** 15 total. **Part-time faculty:** 15 total. **Class size:** 57% < 20, 43% 20-39.

Student profile. Among degree-seeking undergraduates, 100% enrolled in a transfer program.

Out-of-state:	1%	**Live on campus:**	40%
25 or older:	22%		

Transfer out. 95% of students enrolled in the transfer program go on to 4-year colleges. **Colleges most students transferred to 2005:** University of Wisconsin-LaCrosse, University of Wisconsin-Platteville, University of Wisconsin-Madison, University of Wisconsin-Eau Claire, University of Wisconsin-Whitewater.

Basis for selection. Rank in upper 75% of high school graduating class ensures admission. Students in bottom 25% of graduating class may be admitted on a discretionary category basis. Students not admitted for specific semester applied for will be admitted at later date. Test scores for matriculating students must be received prior to enrollment. Interview required for applicants in bottom quarter of class; recommended for all others. **Adult students:** SAT/ACT scores not required if applicant over 21. **Homeschooled:** 19 ACT composite required.

High school preparation. 17 units required. Required units include English 4, mathematics 3, social studies 3, science 3 and academic electives 4. 4 of the required units may be in foreign language, fine arts, computer science or other academic areas.

2005-2006 Annual costs. Tuition/fees: $4,249; $12,949 out-of-state. Per-credit charge: $166 in-state; $528 out-of-state. Minnesota Reciprocity tuition: $3,576 full-time, $149 per-credit-hour. Books/supplies: $515. Personal expenses: $990.

Financial aid. All financial aid based on need. Need-based aid available for part-time students. Work study available nights, weekends and for part-time students.

Application procedures. Admission: $35 fee, may be waived for applicants with need. Application may be submitted online. Admission notification on a rolling basis. **Financial aid:** Priority date 4/15; no closing date. FAFSA required. Applicants notified on a rolling basis starting 5/15; must reply within 3 week(s) of notification.

Academics. Associate of arts and science degree accepted throughout University of Wisconsin System as transfer tool; satisfies general education requirements of any system campus. The OWL (Online Writing Lab) is available to students at all times. **Special study options:** Cross-registration, distance learning, dual enrollment of high school students, independent study, study abroad, teacher certification program. Field Ecology study program in Belize. Bachelor's degree programs available on campus. **Credit/placement by examination:** AP, CLEP, IB, institutional tests. **Support services:** Reduced course load, remedial instruction, study skills assistance, tutoring, writing center.

Majors. Liberal arts: Arts/sciences.

Computing on campus. 60 workstations in dormitories, library, computer center. Dormitories wired for high-speed internet access and linked to campus network. Commuter students can connect to campus network. Online library available.

Student life. Freshman orientation: Mandatory, $25 fee. Preregistration for classes offered. Orientation held during the first week of fall classes. **Policies:** Freshmen permitted cars on campus. **Housing:** Coed dorms, apartments available. $200 deposit. **Activities:** Concert band, choral groups, drama, literary magazine, music ensembles, musical theater, student government, student newspaper, Educators of the Future, Student Wisconsin Education Association, international club, student senate.

Athletics. Intercollegiate: Basketball, soccer, volleyball W. **Intramural:** Badminton, basketball, football (non-tackle), racquetball, softball, swimming, table tennis, tennis, volleyball, water polo. **Team name:** Roadrunners.

Student services. Adult student services, alcohol/substance abuse counseling, career counseling, student employment services, financial aid counseling, personal counseling. **Transfer:** Special adviser, orientation for new students. Transfer adviser, college fairs on campus for students transferring to 4-year colleges.

Contact. E-mail: rlninfo@uwc.edu
Phone: (608) 647-8422 ext. 3 Fax: (608) 647-2275
John Poole, Director of Student Services, University of Wisconsin-Richland, 1200 Highway 14 West, Richland Center, WI 53581

University of Wisconsin-Rock County

Janesville, Wisconsin
www.rock.uwc.edu **CB code: 1998**

- Public 2-year branch campus and liberal arts college
- Commuter campus in small city

General. Founded in 1966. Regionally accredited. **Enrollment:** 616 degree-seeking undergraduates; 274 non-degree-seeking students. **Degrees:** 70 associate awarded. **Location:** 40 miles from Madison. **Calendar:** Semester, limited summer session. **Full-time faculty:** 30 total. **Part-time faculty:** 15 total. **Class size:** 51% < 20, 46% 20-39, 2% 40-49, less than 1% 50-99.

Student profile. Among degree-seeking undergraduates, 100% enrolled in a transfer program, 274 enrolled as first-time, first-year students.

Out-of-state:	1%	**25 or older:**	31%
Women:	54%		

Transfer out. Colleges most students transferred to 2005: University of Wisconsin-Whitewater, University of Wisconsin-Madison.

Basis for selection. Rank in upper 75% of high school graduating class ensures admission. Students in bottom 25% of graduating class and those with GED admitted under special conditions. SAT or ACT recommended. SAT or ACT scores used for students with GED or in bottom quarter of high school graduating class. ACT always considered. Essays considered. **Adult students:** SAT/ACT scores not required if applicant over 21. **Home-schooled:** Transcript of courses and grades required.

High school preparation. 17 units recommended. Recommended units include English 4, mathematics 3, social studies 3, science 3 and academic electives 4.

2005-2006 Annual costs. Tuition/fees: $4,228; $12,928 out-of-state. Per-credit charge: $166 in-state; $528 out-of-state. Minnesota reciprocity tuition: $3,576 full-time, $149 per-credit-hour. Books/supplies: $500. Personal expenses: $810.

Financial aid. All financial aid based on need. Need-based aid available for part-time students. Work study available nights, weekends and for part-time students.

Application procedures. Admission: No deadline. $35 fee. Application may be submitted online. Admission notification on a rolling basis. **Financial aid:** Priority date 4/15; no closing date. FAFSA, institutional form required. Applicants notified on a rolling basis starting 6/1; must reply within 3 week(s) of notification.

Academics. Special study options: Cross-registration, distance learning, dual enrollment of high school students, independent study, study abroad, weekend college. Bachelor's degree programs available on campus. **Credit/placement by examination:** AP, CLEP, institutional tests. **Support services:** Learning center, reduced course load, remedial instruction, study skills assistance, tutoring, writing center.

Majors. Liberal arts: Arts/sciences.

Computing on campus. 50 workstations in library, computer center. Commuter students can connect to campus network.

Student life. Freshman orientation: Mandatory, $30 fee. 3 hours long, held monthly: May, June, July, August. **Policies:** Freshmen permitted cars on campus. **Activities:** Bands, choral groups, dance, drama, literary magazine, music ensembles, student government, student newspaper, symphony orchestra, SGA, MSU, GLBSA, Future Educators, adult student organization.

Athletics. NJCAA. **Intercollegiate:** Soccer, tennis, volleyball W. **Intramural:** Badminton, basketball, soccer, softball, tennis, volleyball. **Team name:** Rattlers.

Student services. Adult student services, alcohol/substance abuse counseling, career counseling, services for economically disadvantaged, student employment services, financial aid counseling, minority student services, personal counseling, veterans' counselor. **Physically disabled:** Services for visually, hearing impaired. **Transfer:** Special adviser, orientation, re-entry adviser for new students. Transfer adviser, college fairs on campus for students transferring to 4-year colleges.

Contact. E-mail: rckinfo@uwc.edu
Phone: (608) 758-6523 Fax: (608) 758-6579
Cynthia Calvin, Director of Student Services, University of Wisconsin-Rock County, 2909 Kellogg Avenue, Janesville, WI 53546-5699

University of Wisconsin-Sheboygan

Sheboygan, Wisconsin
www.sheboygan.uwc.edu **CB code: 1994**

- Public 2-year community and junior college
- Commuter campus in small city

General. Founded in 1933. Regionally accredited. **Location:** 60 miles from Milwaukee, 50 miles from Green Bay. **Calendar:** Semester.

Annual costs/financial aid. Tuition/fees (2005-2006): $4,225; $12,925 out-of-state. Minnesota reciprocity tuition: $3,576 full-time, $149 per-credit-hour. Books/supplies: $470. Personal expenses: $900.

Contact. Phone: (920) 459-6633
Assistant Campus Dean - Student Services, One University Drive, Sheboygan, WI 53081

University of Wisconsin-Washington County

West Bend, Wisconsin
http://washington.uwc.edu **CB code: 1993**

- Public 2-year branch campus and liberal arts college
- Commuter campus in large town

General. Founded in 1968. Regionally accredited. **Location:** 70 miles from Madison, 35 miles from Milwaukee. **Calendar:** Semester.

Annual costs/financial aid. Tuition/fees (2005-2006): $4,220; $12,920 out-of-state. Minnesota reciprocity tuition: $3,576 full-time, $149 per-credit-hour. Books/supplies: $552. Personal expenses: $930. Need-based financial aid available to full-time and part-time students.

Contact. Phone: (262) 335-5201
Dean of Student Services, 400 University Drive, West Bend, WI 53095

University of Wisconsin-Waukesha

Waukesha, Wisconsin
http://waukesha.uwc.edu **CB code: 1999**

- Public 2-year branch campus and junior college
- Commuter campus in small city
- SAT or ACT (ACT writing optional) required

General. Founded in 1966. Regionally accredited. **Enrollment:** 2,064 degree-seeking undergraduates. **Degrees:** 138 associate awarded. **Location:** 17 miles from Milwaukee. **Calendar:** Semester, limited summer session. **Full-time faculty:** 37 total. **Part-time faculty:** 56 total. **Class size:** 29% < 20, 61% 20-39, 9% 40-49, less than 1% 50-99. **Special facilities:** 98-acre environmental studies field station.

Student profile.

Out-of-state:	5%	**25 or older:**	18%

Transfer out. Colleges most students transferred to 2005: University of Wisconsin-Milwaukee, University of Wisconsin-Whitewater, University of Wisconsin-Madison.

Basis for selection. Rank in top 75 percent of high school class ensures admission. Students in bottom 25 percent and those with GED considered for admission based on interview; if ACT score 19 or higher admission granted. Interview recommended for applicants in bottom 35 percent of class. **Adult students:** SAT/ACT scores not required if applicant over 21.

High school preparation. 17 units required. Required and recommended units include English 4, mathematics 3, social studies 3, science 3, foreign language 2 and academic electives 4.

2005-2006 Annual costs. Tuition/fees: $4,206; $12,906 out-of-state. Per-credit charge: $166 in-state; $528 out-of-state. Minnesota reciprocity tuition: $3,576 full-time, $149 per-credit-hour. Books/supplies: $500. Personal expenses: $1,000.

2004-2005 Financial aid. Need-based: 58% of total undergraduate aid awarded as scholarships/grants, 42% as loans/jobs. Need-based aid available for part-time students. Work study available nights, weekends and for part-time students. **Non-need-based:** Scholarships awarded for academics, leadership, minority status, music/drama.

Application procedures. Admission: Priority date 4/1; no deadline. $35 fee, may be waived for applicants with need. Application may be submitted online. Admission notification on a rolling basis beginning on or about 8/1. **Financial aid:** Priority date 4/15; no closing date. FAFSA required. Applicants notified on a rolling basis starting 5/15; must reply within 3 week(s) of notification.

Academics. Special study options: Cross-registration, distance learning, dual enrollment of high school students, honors, independent study, study abroad. Bachelor's degree programs available on campus. **Credit/placement by examination:** AP, CLEP, institutional tests. CLEP general exams must be taken before 16 degree credits completed. **Support services:** Learning center, pre-admission summer program, reduced course load, remedial instruction, study skills assistance, tutoring, writing center.

Majors. Liberal arts: Arts/sciences.

Computing on campus. 90 workstations in library, computer center, student center.

Student life. Freshman orientation: Mandatory, $100 fee. Held periodically throughout the summer and fall semester. **Activities:** Bands, choral groups, drama, literary magazine, music ensembles, musical theater, radio station, student government, student newspaper, multicultural student alliance, ecology club, philosophy club, Phi Theta Kappa honor society.

Athletics. NJCAA. **Intercollegiate:** Basketball, golf, soccer, tennis, volleyball W. **Intramural:** Basketball, fencing, racquetball, skiing, table tennis, volleyball M. **Team name:** Cougars.

Student services. Adult student services, career counseling, financial aid counseling, on-campus daycare, personal counseling, veterans' counselor. **Physically disabled:** Services for visually, speech, hearing impaired. **Transfer:** Special adviser, orientation for new students. Transfer adviser, college fairs on campus for students transferring to 4-year colleges.

Contact. E-mail: lturner@uwc.edu
Phone: (262) 521-5210 Fax: (262) 521-5530
Becky Gill, Director of Admissions, University of Wisconsin-Waukesha, 1500 University Drive, Waukesha, WI 53188

Waukesha County Technical College

Pewaukee, Wisconsin
www.wctc.edu **CB code: 0724**

- Public 2-year technical college
- Commuter campus in large town

General. Founded in 1923. Regionally accredited. **Enrollment:** 6,393 degree-seeking undergraduates. **Degrees:** 488 associate awarded. **Location:** 17 miles from Milwaukee. **Calendar:** Semester, limited summer session. **Full-time faculty:** 175 total. **Part-time faculty:** 700 total.

Student profile.

Out-of-state:	1%	**25 or older:**	51%

Basis for selection. Open admission, but selective for some programs. Limited admission to health occupation programs: ASSET, COMPASS scores very important; secondary school record considered. Interview required for health occupations programs.

High school preparation. Applicants to electronics programs must have algebra and geometry. Applicants to nursing program must have algebra and chemistry.

2005-2006 Annual costs. Tuition/fees: $2,561; $15,455 out-of-state. Per-credit charge: $81 in-state; $510 out-of-state. Additional fee of $4 per lecture course. Books/supplies: $838. Personal expenses: $1,290.

Financial aid. Need-based: Work study available nights. **Non-need-based:** Scholarships awarded for academics.

Application procedures. Admission: No deadline. $30 fee. Admission notification on a rolling basis. **Financial aid:** Priority date 3/31; no closing date. FAFSA, institutional form required. Applicants notified on a rolling basis.

Academics. Special study options: Accelerated study, cooperative education, distance learning, double major, dual enrollment of high school students, ESL, independent study, internships, student-designed major, study abroad. License preparation in dental hygiene, nursing, real estate. **Credit/placement by examination:** CLEP, institutional tests. SAT or ACT considered for placement. **Support services:** GED preparation and test center, learning center, reduced course load, remedial instruction, study skills assistance, tutoring, writing center.

Majors. Business: Accounting, financial planning, hospitality admin, international, management information systems, marketing, real estate. **Communications technology:** Graphic/printing. **Computer sciences:** General. **Engineering:** Mechanical, mechanics. **Engineering technology:** Architectural, drafting. **Family/consumer sciences:** Child care. **Health:** Dental hygiene, nursing (RN), substance abuse counseling, surgical technology. **Mechanic/repair:** Automotive, electronics/electrical. **Personal/culinary services:** Culinary arts. **Protective services:** Police science. **Public administration:** Human services. **Visual/performing arts:** Fashion design, interior design.

Most popular majors. Business/marketing 10%, computer/information sciences 28%, health sciences 27%, security/protective services 7%, trade and industry 26%.

Computing on campus. Online course registration, online library, wireless network available.

Student life. Freshman orientation: Available. Preregistration for classes offered. **Activities:** Student government, student newspaper.

Athletics. NJCAA. **Intercollegiate:** Baseball M, basketball, golf, volleyball W. **Team name:** Waukesha Owls.

Student services. Adult student services, alcohol/substance abuse counseling, career counseling, services for economically disadvantaged, student employment services, financial aid counseling, health services, minority student services, on-campus daycare, personal counseling, placement for graduates, veterans' counselor, women's services. **Physically disabled:** Services for visually, speech, hearing impaired. **Transfer:** Special adviser, pre-admission transcript evaluation for new students. College fairs on campus for students transferring to 4-year colleges.

Contact. Phone: (262) 691-5275 Fax: (262) 691-5593
Leslie Frederick, Admissions Director, Waukesha County Technical College, 800 Main Street, Pewaukee, WI 53072

Western Wisconsin Technical College

La Crosse, Wisconsin
www.wwtc.edu **CB code: 1087**

- Public 2-year community and technical college
- Residential campus in small city

General. Founded in 1912. Regionally accredited. **Enrollment:** 4,069 degree-seeking undergraduates; 681 non-degree-seeking students. **Degrees:** 581 associate awarded. **Location:** 200 miles from Milwaukee, 150 miles from Minneapolis-St. Paul. **Calendar:** Semester, limited summer session. **Full-time faculty:** 200 total; 3% have terminal degrees, 51% women. **Class size:** 100% < 20.

Student profile. Among degree-seeking undergraduates, 100% enrolled in a vocational program, 5% already have a bachelor's degree or higher, 907 enrolled as first-time, first-year students, 59 transferred in from other institutions.

Part-time:	56%	**Women:**	57%

Basis for selection. Open admission, but selective for some programs. Standardized test scores required for admission into selected health programs. COMPASS required if ACT scores not available. Tests must be taken for admission but no minimum score is necessary. Interviews recommended for placement, portfolios recommended for commercial art applicants for placement. **Adult students:** Entrance exam policies same as for first-time freshmen.

High school preparation. Recommended units include English 3, mathematics 2, social studies 3 and science 2.

2005-2006 Annual costs. Tuition/fees: $2,586; $15,480 out-of-state. Per-credit charge: $81 in-state; $510 out-of-state. Materials fees vary by program; minimum $4 per course. Books/supplies: $866. Personal expenses: $2,312.

2004-2005 Financial aid. Need-based: 53% of total undergraduate aid awarded as scholarships/grants, 47% as loans/jobs. Need-based aid available for part-time students. Work study available nights, weekends and for part-time students.

Application procedures. Admission: No deadline. $30 fee, may be waived for applicants with need. Application may be submitted online. Admission notification on a rolling basis. **Financial aid:** Priority date 3/1; no closing date. FAFSA, institutional form required. Applicants notified on a rolling basis starting 4/1.

Academics. Special study options: Accelerated study, cooperative education, distance learning, double major, ESL, independent study, internships, liberal arts/career combination, student-designed major, weekend college. License preparation in dental hygiene, nursing, occupational therapy, paramedic, physical therapy, radiology, real estate. **Credit/placement by examination:** AP, CLEP, institutional tests. 45 credit hours maximum toward associate degree. **Support services:** GED preparation and test center, learning center, reduced course load, remedial instruction, study skills assistance, tutoring, writing center.

Majors. Agriculture: Business technology. **Architecture:** Technology. **Business:** Accounting, administrative services, business admin, finance, human resources, operations, sales/distribution. **Communications:** Media studies. **Communications technology:** General, desktop publishing. **Computer sciences:** Applications programming, data entry, data processing, LAN/WAN management, networking. **Education:** Teacher assistance. **Engineering technology:** Biomedical, electrical, electromechanical, heat/ac/refrig, mechanical, mechanical drafting. **Family/consumer sciences:** Child care. **Health:** Clinical lab technology, dental hygiene, electroencephalograph technology, medical radiologic technology/radiation therapy, medical records technology, nursing (RN), occupational therapy assistant, physical therapy assistant, respiratory therapy technology. **Legal studies:** Paralegal. **Mechanic/repair:** Automotive, diesel. **Personal/culinary services:** Restaurant/catering. **Production:** Machine shop technology, tool and die. **Protective services:** Fire safety technology, police science. **Public administration:** Community org/advocacy. **Visual/performing arts:** Design, graphic design, industrial design, interior design, music.

Most popular majors. Business/marketing 26%, computer/information sciences 13%, engineering/engineering technologies 6%, family/consumer sciences 14%, health sciences 19%.

Computing on campus. 145 workstations in dormitories, library, computer center. Dormitories wired for high-speed internet access and linked to campus network. Commuter students can connect to campus network. Online course registration, online library, helpline, repair service available.

Student life. Freshman orientation: Available. Preregistration for classes offered. General school orientation held in August. **Policies:** Freshmen permitted cars on campus. **Housing:** Coed dorms available. **Activities:** Student government, student newspaper, TV station, multicultural club, Campus Crusade for Christ.

Athletics. NJCAA. **Intercollegiate:** Baseball M, basketball, volleyball W. **Intramural:** Basketball, volleyball. **Team name:** Cavaliers.

Student services. Adult student services, alcohol/substance abuse counseling, career counseling, services for economically disadvantaged, student employment services, financial aid counseling, health services, minority student services, on-campus daycare, personal counseling, placement for graduates, veterans' counselor, women's services. **Physically disabled:** Services for visually, speech, hearing impaired. **Transfer:** Special adviser, orientation, pre-admission transcript evaluation for new students.

Contact. E-mail: wellsj@wwtc.edu
Phone: (608) 785-9158 Toll-free number: (800) 322-9982
Fax: (608) 785-9148
Jayne Wells, Admissions, Registration and Records, Western Wisconsin Technical College, PO Box 908, La Crosse, WI 54602-0908

Wisconsin Indianhead Technical College

Shell Lake, Wisconsin
www.witc.edu **CB code: 1580**

- Public 2-year technical college
- Commuter campus in rural community
- Interview required

General. Founded in 1972. Regionally accredited. 4 campuses covering 11 county area. **Enrollment:** 2,969 degree-seeking undergraduates; 564 non-degree-seeking students. **Degrees:** 347 associate awarded. **Calendar:** Semester, limited summer session. **Full-time faculty:** 145 total. **Part-time faculty:** 850 total.

Student profile. Among degree-seeking undergraduates, 1,041 enrolled as first-time, first-year students.

Part-time:	48%	**Women:**	60%
Out-of-state:	5%	**25 or older:**	26%

Transfer out. Colleges most students transferred to 2005: University of Wisconsin.

Basis for selection. Scores on ASSET or COMPASS important. Interview required. Prior work experience, secondary school record considered. Required ASSET scores: 44 for nursing program, 39 for other associate degree programs, 36 for technical diplomas. SAT or ACT can be used in lieu of ASSET assessment. **Adult students:** Entrance exam policies same as for first-time freshmen. **Homeschooled:** Must pass ability to benefit assessment.

2005-2006 Annual costs. Tuition/fees: $2,573; $15,467 out-of-state. Per-credit charge: $81 in-state; $510 out-of-state. Materials fees vary by program; minimum $4 per course. Additional fees vary by campus among college's four campuses. Books/supplies: $808. Personal expenses: $1,128.

2004-2005 Financial aid. Need-based: 52% of total undergraduate aid awarded as scholarships/grants, 48% as loans/jobs. Need-based aid available for part-time students. Work study available nights, weekends and for part-time students. **Non-need-based:** Scholarships awarded for state residency.

Application procedures. Admission: No deadline. $30 fee. Admission notification on a rolling basis. **Financial aid:** FAFSA required. Applicants notified on a rolling basis.

Academics. Special study options: Accelerated study, distance learning, double major, internships. **Credit/placement by examination:** AP, CLEP, institutional tests. **Support services:** GED preparation and test center, learning center, pre-admission summer program, reduced course load, remedial instruction, tutoring.

Majors. Business: Accounting, administrative services, finance, marketing, retailing. **Computer sciences:** General, networking, web page design. **Education:** Early childhood. **Engineering technology:** Architectural, computer systems, manufacturing, mechanical drafting. **Health:** Medical secretary, nursing (RN), occupational therapy assistant. **Mechanic/repair:** Communications systems, computer. **Protective services:** Corrections, police science.

Computing on campus. PC or laptop required. 1,900 workstations in library, computer center, student center. Online course registration, online library, helpline, wireless network available.

Two-Year Colleges

Student life. Freshman orientation: Available. Preregistration for classes offered. **Policies:** Freshmen permitted cars on campus. **Activities:** Student government, student newspaper, technical student organizations, vocational student organizations.

Athletics. Intramural: Basketball, bowling, boxing M, skiing, softball, volleyball.

Student services. Adult student services, career counseling, services for economically disadvantaged, student employment services, financial aid counseling, health services, minority student services, on-campus daycare, personal counseling, placement for graduates, veterans' counselor, women's services. **Transfer:** Special adviser, orientation for new students. College fairs on campus for students transferring to 4-year colleges.

Contact. Phone: (715) 468-2815 ext. 2280 Toll-free number: (800) 243-9482 Fax: (715) 468-2819
Mimi Crandall, Dean, Student Services and Marketing, Wisconsin Indianhead Technical College, 505 Pine Ridge Drive, Shell Lake, WI 54871

Wyoming

Casper College
Casper, Wyoming
www.caspercollege.edu **CB code: 4043**

- Public 2-year community college
- Commuter campus in small city

General. Founded in 1945. Regionally accredited. **Enrollment:** 2,792 degree-seeking undergraduates; 1,356 non-degree-seeking students. **Degrees:** 537 associate awarded. **Location:** 280 miles from Denver. **Calendar:** Semester, limited summer session. **Full-time faculty:** 153 total; 21% have terminal degrees, 4% minority, 46% women. **Part-time faculty:** 99 total; 7% have terminal degrees, 4% minority, 46% women. **Class size:** 74% < 20, 23% 20-39, 1% 40-49, 1% 50-99. **Special facilities:** Wildlife museum, geological museum, family resource center.

Student profile. Among degree-seeking undergraduates, 58% enrolled in a transfer program, 42% enrolled in a vocational program, 5% already have a bachelor's degree or higher, 668 enrolled as first-time, first-year students, 268 transferred in from other institutions.

Part-time:	34%	**Native American:**	1%
Out-of-state:	7%	**International:**	1%
Women:	64%	**25 or older:**	44%
African American:	1%	**Live on campus:**	10%
Hispanic American:	3%		

Transfer out. 40% of students enrolled in the transfer program go on to 4-year colleges. **Colleges most students transferred to 2005:** University of Wyoming, University of North Dakota, Colorado State University, Montana State University, Black Hills State University.

Basis for selection. Open admission, but selective for some programs and for out-of-state students. 2.0 GPA required for out-of-state applicants. Selective admission for nursing, respiratory therapy, radiology; requirements vary by program. Audition recommended for music, theater, athletics and forensics; portfolio recommended for art. **Adult students:** Entrance exam policies same as for first-time freshmen. **Homeschooled:** Home-school program must be accredited and recognized by state department of education as being equivalent to high school diploma.

2005-2006 Annual costs. Tuition/fees: $1,536; $4,296 out-of-state. Per-credit charge: $57 in-state; $172 out-of-state. Western Undergraduate Exchange students pay $96 per credit-hour and $2136 per year for full-time students. Room/board: $3,460. Books/supplies: $888. Personal expenses: $2,250.

Financial aid. Need-based: Need-based aid available for part-time students. Work study available nights, weekends and for part-time students. **Non-need-based:** Scholarships awarded for academics, art, athletics, leadership, music/drama, state residency.

Application procedures. Admission: Priority date 8/1; deadline 8/15 (postmark date). No application fee. Application may be submitted online. Admission notification on a rolling basis. **Financial aid:** Priority date 3/15; no closing date. FAFSA required. Applicants notified on a rolling basis starting 4/1.

Academics. Special study options: Cooperative education, cross-registration, distance learning, dual enrollment of high school students, independent study, internships. Bachelor's degree programs available on campus. License preparation in nursing, radiology. **Credit/placement by examination:** AP, CLEP, IB, institutional tests. 30 credit hours maximum toward associate degree. **Support services:** GED preparation and test center, learning center, remedial instruction, study skills assistance, tutoring, writing center.

Majors. Agriculture: General, animal sciences, business. **Area/ethnic studies:** Women's. **Biology:** General. **Business:** Accounting, accounting technology, business admin, construction management, hospitality admin, management information systems, office technology, retailing. **Communications:** General. **Computer sciences:** Networking, programming, vendor certification. **Conservation:** Environmental science, wildlife. **Construction:** General. **Education:** General, early childhood, music, physical, teacher assistance, technology/industrial arts. **Engineering:** General. **Engineering technology:** Drafting, electrical, manufacturing, water quality. **English:** English lit. **Foreign languages:** General. **Health:** Clinical lab technology, medical transcription, nursing (RN), occupational therapy assistant, pharmacy assistant, predentistry, premedicine, prepharmacy, preveterinary, radiologic technology/medical imaging, respiratory therapy technology, substance abuse counseling. **History:** General. **Legal studies:** Paralegal, prelaw. **Liberal arts:** Arts/sciences. **Math:** General. **Mechanic/repair:** Automotive, diesel. **Physical sciences:** Chemistry, geology, physics. **Production:** Machine tool, welding. **Protective services:** Criminal justice, firefighting, forensics. **Psychology:** General. **Public administration:** Social work. **Social sciences:** Anthropology, economics, international relations, political science, sociology. **Transportation:** Airline/commercial pilot. **Visual/performing arts:** Art, commercial/advertising art, dance, dramatic, music performance, photography, studio arts.

Most popular majors. Business/marketing 7%, education 13%, health sciences 19%, liberal arts 14%, security/protective services 8%, visual/performing arts 6%.

Computing on campus. 120 workstations in library, computer center. Dormitories linked to campus network. Wireless network available.

Student life. Freshman orientation: Mandatory. Preregistration for classes offered. One-day program, held 4 times in summer. **Policies:** Freshmen permitted cars on campus. **Housing:** Coed dorms, apartments, substance-free housing available. $100 fully refundable deposit. **Activities:** Bands, choral groups, dance, drama, literary magazine, music ensembles, musical theater, student government, student newspaper, united campus ministry, Latter-day Saints student association, Baptist student union, Phi Theta Kappa, Phi Rho Pi, student nurses association, Students in Free Enterprise, AG club, student activities board, Bakkai.

Athletics. NJCAA. **Intercollegiate:** Basketball, cheerleading, rodeo, volleyball W. **Intramural:** Basketball, bowling, football (non-tackle), golf, racquetball, soccer, softball, table tennis, tennis, volleyball. **Team name:** Thunderbirds.

Student services. Adult student services, alcohol/substance abuse counseling, career counseling, student employment services, financial aid counseling, health services, on-campus daycare, personal counseling, placement for graduates, veterans' counselor. **Physically disabled:** Services for visually, speech, hearing impaired. **Transfer:** Special adviser, orientation for new students. Transfer adviser, college fairs on campus for students transferring to 4-year colleges.

Contact. E-mail: kauzqui@caspercollege.edu
Phone: (307) 268-2458 Toll-free number: (800) 442-2963
Fax: (307) 268-2611
Kirstie Auzqui, Senior Admissions Representative, Casper College, 125 College Drive, Casper, WY 82601

Central Wyoming College
Riverton, Wyoming
www.cwc.edu **CB code: 4115**

- Public 2-year community college
- Commuter campus in large town

General. Founded in 1966. Regionally accredited. **Enrollment:** 1,027 degree-seeking undergraduates; 610 non-degree-seeking students. **Degrees:** 160 associate awarded. **Location:** 120 miles from Casper, 240 miles from Billings, Montana. **Calendar:** Semester, limited summer session. **Full-time faculty:** 41 total; 71% have terminal degrees, 5% minority, 58% women. **Part-time faculty:** 123 total; 40% have terminal degrees, 10% minority, 50% women. **Class size:** 88% < 20, 11% 20-39, less than 1% 50-99. **Special facilities:** Rodeo arena, fine arts center, Microsoft training laboratory, Cisco training laboratory, Native American artifacts, Sinks Canyon center. **Partnerships:** Formal partnerships with Microsoft, Cisco (training labs, software), and the National Outdoor Leadership School.

Student profile. Among degree-seeking undergraduates, 64% enrolled in a transfer program, 36% enrolled in a vocational program, 1% already have a bachelor's degree or higher, 242 enrolled as first-time, first-year students, 64 transferred in from other institutions.

Part-time:	37%	**Native American:**	19%
Out-of-state:	4%	**International:**	2%
Women:	69%	**25 or older:**	30%
Hispanic American:	4%	**Live on campus:**	9%

Transfer out. Colleges most students transferred to 2005: University of Wyoming, Colorado State University, Montana State University, University of Utah.

Basis for selection. Open admission, but selective for some programs. Special admission to nursing program; minimum GPA and test scores required. COMPASS placement tests required for all first-time students who have not taken ACT or SAT. Certain music courses require audition. **Adult students:** Entrance exam policies same as for first-time freshmen.

2005-2006 Annual costs. Tuition/fees: $1,872; $4,632 out-of-state. Per-credit charge: $57 in-state; $172 out-of-state. Students from Western Undergraduate Exchange states pay $2,136 in tuition per year. Room/board: $2,880. Books/supplies: $800.

2004-2005 Financial aid. **Need-based:** 179 full-time freshmen applied for aid; 83 were judged to have need; 83 of these received aid. 71% of total undergraduate aid awarded as scholarships/grants, 29% as loans/jobs. Need-based aid available for part-time students. Work study available nights, weekends and for part-time students. **Non-need-based:** Awarded to 261 full-time undergraduates, including 66 freshmen. Scholarships awarded for academics, alumni affiliation, art, athletics, leadership, minority status, music/drama, state residency.

Application procedures. **Admission:** No deadline. No application fee. Application may be submitted online. Admission notification on a rolling basis beginning on or about 1/1. **Financial aid:** Priority date 4/15; no closing date. FAFSA, institutional form required. Applicants notified on a rolling basis starting 5/1; must reply within 2 week(s) of notification.

Academics. **Special study options:** Cooperative education, distance learning, dual enrollment of high school students, ESL, honors, independent study, student-designed major. License preparation in nursing. **Credit/placement by examination:** AP, CLEP, institutional tests. 32 credit hours maximum toward associate degree. Some DANTES and APE exams accepted. **Support services:** GED preparation and test center, learning center, remedial instruction, tutoring, writing center.

Majors. **Agriculture:** Business, equestrian studies, range science. **Area/ethnic studies:** Native American. **Biology:** General. **Business:** Accounting, accounting technology, business admin, management information systems. **Communications technology:** Radio/tv. **Computer sciences:** Computer graphics, computer science, web page design. **Conservation:** Environmental science. **Education:** Elementary, secondary, teacher assistance. **Engineering technology:** Computer systems. **English:** English lit. **Family/consumer sciences:** Child care. **Health:** Nursing (RN), surgical technology. **Legal studies:** Prelaw. **Mechanic/repair:** Automotive. **Parks/recreation:** Facilities management. **Physical sciences:** General. **Production:** Welding. **Protective services:** Law enforcement admin. **Psychology:** General. **Public administration:** Human services. **Social sciences:** General. **Visual/performing arts:** Acting, art, theater design.

Most popular majors. Business/marketing 16%, education 6%, health sciences 16%, liberal arts 24%, security/protective services 6%, visual/performing arts 6%.

Computing on campus. 300 workstations in dormitories, library, computer center, student center. Dormitories wired for high-speed internet access and linked to campus network. Commuter students can connect to campus network. Online course registration, online library, wireless network available.

Student life. **Freshman orientation:** Mandatory. Preregistration for classes offered. **Policies:** Freshmen permitted cars on campus. **Housing:** Coed dorms, apartments available. $100 fully refundable deposit, deadline 5/1. **Activities:** Jazz band, choral groups, dance, drama, music ensembles, musical theater, radio station, student government, student newspaper, TV station, United Tribes (American Indian) club, multicultural club, social science club, veterans club, Vida Nueva (Hispanic) club, law and justice club, science club, Phi Theta Kappa, American Indian Science and Engineering Society.

Athletics. **Intercollegiate:** Rodeo. **Intramural:** Badminton, basketball, football (non-tackle), skiing, soccer, softball, swimming, table tennis, tennis, volleyball, weight lifting. **Team name:** Rustlers.

Student services. Alcohol/substance abuse counseling, career counseling, services for economically disadvantaged, student employment services, financial aid counseling, personal counseling, placement for graduates, veterans' counselor. **Physically disabled:** Services for visually, hearing impaired. **Transfer:** Special adviser, orientation for new students. Transfer adviser, college fairs on campus for students transferring to 4-year colleges.

Contact. E-mail: admit@cwc.edu
Phone: (307) 855-2119 Toll-free number: (800) 865-0193
Fax: (307) 855-2093
Tami Shultz, Admissions Officer, Central Wyoming College, 2660 Peck Avenue, Riverton, WY 82501

Eastern Wyoming College

Torrington, Wyoming
ewc.wy.edu **CB code: 4700**

- Public 2-year community college
- Commuter campus in small town

General. Founded in 1948. Regionally accredited. **Enrollment:** 608 degree-seeking undergraduates; 801 non-degree-seeking students. **Degrees:** 105 associate awarded. **Location:** 190 miles from Denver. **Calendar:** Semester, limited summer session. **Full-time faculty:** 38 total; 21% have terminal degrees, 37% women. **Part-time faculty:** 64 total; 61% women. **Class size:** 90% <20, 10% 20-39, less than 1% 50-99. **Special facilities:** Fitness/wellness center.

Student profile. Among degree-seeking undergraduates, 46% enrolled in a transfer program, 50% enrolled in a vocational program, 168 enrolled as first-time, first-year students.

Part-time:	30%	**Hispanic American:**	7%
Out-of-state:	26%	**Native American:**	1%
Women:	67%	**International:**	1%
African American:	1%	**25 or older:**	32%

Transfer out. **Colleges most students transferred to 2005:** University of Wyoming, Chadron State College.

Basis for selection. Open admission. **Homeschooled:** Transcript of courses and grades required. ACT recommended but not required. Signed statement that student was homeschooled required for financial aid.

2005-2006 Annual costs. Tuition/fees: $1,848; $4,608 out-of-state. Per-credit charge: $57 in-state; $172 out-of-state. Students from Western Undergraduate Exchange pay $2,136 tuition plus fees per year; $89 per-credit-hour. Room/board: $3,204. Books/supplies: $900. Personal expenses: $1,118.

Financial aid. **Need-based:** Need-based aid available for part-time students. Work study available nights, weekends and for part-time students. **Non-need-based:** Scholarships awarded for academics, art, athletics, leadership, music/drama. **Additional information:** Installment payment plan on room and board contracts offered.

Application procedures. **Admission:** No deadline. No application fee. Application may be submitted online. Admission notification on a rolling basis. **Financial aid:** Priority date 3/15; no closing date. FAFSA, institutional form required. Applicants notified on a rolling basis starting 1/1.

Academics. **Special study options:** Cross-registration, distance learning, dual enrollment of high school students, ESL, independent study, internships. License preparation on campus for welding and joining, veterinary technology, and cosmetology. Bachelor's degree programs available on campus. **Credit/placement by examination:** AP, CLEP, IB, institutional tests. 16 credit hours maximum toward associate degree. **Support services:** GED preparation and test center, learning center, reduced course load, remedial instruction, study skills assistance, tutoring.

Majors. **Agriculture:** General, agribusiness operations, animal sciences, economics, farm/ranch, range science. **Biology:** General, environmental. **Business:** Accounting, administrative services, business admin, management information systems, office management. **Communications:** General. **Conservation:** Wildlife. **Education:** Agricultural, business, elementary, mathematics, music, physical, secondary. **English:** English lit. **Foreign languages:** General. **Health:** Predentistry, premedicine, prepharmacy, preveterinary, veterinary technology/assistant. **History:** General. **Liberal arts:** Arts/sciences. **Math:** General, statistics. **Personal/culinary services:** Cosmetic. **Production:** Welding. **Protective services:** Criminal justice, police science. **Psychology:** General. **Social sciences:** Economics, political science, sociology. **Visual/performing arts:** Art.

Most popular majors. Business/marketing 8%, education 9%, health sciences 14%, liberal arts 33%, personal/culinary services 8%, security/protective services 6%, trade and industry 16%.

Computing on campus. 82 workstations in dormitories, computer center, student center. Dormitories wired for high-speed internet access.

Student life. **Freshman orientation:** Available. Preregistration for classes offered. Held in fall 1 day prior to first day of classes. **Policies:** Freshmen permitted cars on campus. **Housing:** Coed dorms, substance-free housing available. $100 nonrefundable deposit. **Activities:** Choral groups, musical theater, student government, student newspaper, campus ministry.

Athletics. NJCAA. **Intercollegiate:** Basketball M, golf M, rodeo, volleyball W. **Intramural:** Badminton, basketball, bowling, football (non-tackle)

M, handball, racquetball, rodeo, softball, table tennis, tennis, volleyball. **Team name:** Lancers.

Student services. Adult student services, alcohol/substance abuse counseling, campus ministries, career counseling, student employment services, financial aid counseling, personal counseling, placement for graduates, veterans' counselor. **Physically disabled:** Services for visually, speech, hearing impaired. **Transfer:** Special adviser, orientation, re-entry adviser, preadmission transcript evaluation for new students. Transfer adviser, college fairs on campus for students transferring to 4-year colleges.

Contact. E-mail: mcotant@ewc.wy.edu
Phone: (307) 532-8230 Toll-free number: (800) 658-3195
Fax: (307) 532-8222
Marilyn Cotant, Dean of Students, Eastern Wyoming College, 3200 West C Street, Torrington, WY 82240

Laramie County Community College

Cheyenne, Wyoming
www.lccc.wy.edu **CB code: 0360**

- Public 2-year community college
- Small city

General. Founded in 1968. Regionally accredited. Additional campus in Laramie. **Enrollment:** 2,884 degree-seeking undergraduates. **Degrees:** 349 associate awarded. **ROTC:** Air Force. **Location:** 4 miles from downtown, 100 miles from Denver. **Calendar:** Semester, limited summer session. **Full-time faculty:** 90 total. **Part-time faculty:** 187 total. **Special facilities:** Bureau of Land Management Park, indoor arena, networking laboratory.

Student profile.

Out-of-state:	8%	**Live on campus:**	2%

Basis for selection. Open admission, but selective for some programs. Special requirements for nursing, radiography, equine studies, dental hygiene programs. Interview required for equine studies. **Adult students:** Entrance exam policies same as for first-time freshmen.

2005-2006 Annual costs. Tuition/fees: $1,884; $4,644 out-of-state. Per-credit charge: $57 in-state; $172 out-of-state. Students from Western Undergraduate Exchange schools and Nebraska residents pay $2064 in tuition and fees per year; $86 per credit hour. Room/board: $4,872. Books/supplies: $720.

2004-2005 Financial aid. Need-based: Need-based aid available for part-time students.

Application procedures. Admission: No deadline. $20 fee. Application may be submitted online. Admission notification on a rolling basis. Nursing, radiology, and dental hygiene applications must be received by February 1. **Financial aid:** Priority date 4/1; no closing date. FAFSA, institutional form required. Applicants notified on a rolling basis starting 6/1; must reply within 2 week(s) of notification.

Academics. Special study options: Cooperative education, distance learning, dual enrollment of high school students, internships. **Credit/placement by examination:** CLEP, institutional tests. 15 credit hours maximum toward associate degree. **Support services:** Learning center, remedial instruction, tutoring.

Majors. Agriculture: General, agribusiness operations, business, business technology, equestrian studies, farm/ranch. **Biology:** General, wildlife. **Business:** General, accounting, administrative services, business admin, office technology. **Communications:** General, journalism, media studies. **Computer sciences:** General, computer science, information systems, information technology, LAN/WAN management, programming, web page design, webmaster. **Education:** General, elementary, physical, sales/marketing, secondary. **Engineering:** General. **Engineering technology:** General. **English:** Speech/rhetoric. **Health:** Dental hygiene, medical radiologic technology/radiation therapy, nursing (RN), predentistry, premedicine, prepharmacy, preveterinary, surgical technology. **History:** General. **Interdisciplinary:** Biological/physical sciences. **Legal studies:** Paralegal, prelaw. **Liberal arts:** Arts/sciences. **Math:** General. **Mechanic/repair:** Auto body. **Physical sciences:** Chemistry. **Protective services:** Police science. **Psychology:** General. **Social sciences:** General, anthropology, economics, political science, sociology. **Visual/performing arts:** Commercial/advertising art, dramatic, studio arts.

Student life. Freshman orientation: Available. Preregistration for classes offered. **Policies:** Freshmen permitted cars on campus. **Housing:** Coed dorms available. $100 deposit. **Activities:** Bands, choral groups, drama, literary magazine, music ensembles, musical theater, student government, student newspaper, TV station.

Athletics. NJCAA. **Intercollegiate:** Basketball M, rodeo, soccer, volleyball W. **Intramural:** Fencing, soccer. **Team name:** Golden Eagles.

Student services. Adult student services, alcohol/substance abuse counseling, career counseling, services for economically disadvantaged, student employment services, financial aid counseling, on-campus daycare, personal counseling, placement for graduates, veterans' counselor. **Physically disabled:** Services for visually, speech, hearing impaired. **Transfer:** Special adviser for new students. College fairs on campus for students transferring to 4-year colleges.

Contact. E-mail: LearnMore@lccc.wy.edu
Phone: (307) 778-1357 Toll-free number: (800) 522-2993 ext. 1357
Fax: (307) 778-1350
Jenny Hargett, Director of Admissions, Laramie County Community College, 1400 East College Drive, Cheyenne, WY 82007

Northwest College

Powell, Wyoming
www.northwestcollege.edu **CB code: 4542**

- Public 2-year community college
- Residential campus in small town

General. Founded in 1946. Regionally accredited. **Enrollment:** 1,513 degree-seeking undergraduates; 133 non-degree-seeking students. **Degrees:** 299 associate awarded. **Location:** 90 miles from Billings, Montana. **Calendar:** Semester, limited summer session. **Full-time faculty:** 85 total. **Part-time faculty:** 65 total. **Class size:** 85% < 20, 15% 20-39, less than 1% 40-49.

Student profile. Among degree-seeking undergraduates, 69% enrolled in a transfer program, 29% enrolled in a vocational program, 440 enrolled as first-time, first-year students.

Part-time:	26%	**Hispanic American:**	5%
Out-of-state:	26%	**Native American:**	1%
Women:	62%	**25 or older:**	24%
African American:	1%	**Live on campus:**	40%
Asian American:	2%		

Transfer out. Colleges most students transferred to 2005: University of Wyoming, Montana State University-Bozeman, Montana State University-Billings.

Basis for selection. Open admission, but selective for some programs and for out-of-state students. Admissions for out-of-state applicants based on high school GPA and test scores. Nursing, photography, and equestrian training programs require extra applications and qualifications. SAT or ACT required of out-of-state students. **Adult students:** Entrance exam policies same as for first-time freshmen. **Learning Disabled:** Individuals must identify needs in order to to procure services.

High school preparation. Recommended units include English 4, mathematics 2, social studies 2 and science 1.

2005-2006 Annual costs. Tuition/fees: $1,880; $4,640 out-of-state. Per-credit charge: $57 in-state; $172 out-of-state. Students from Western Undergraduate Exchange schools pay $2,064 tuition; $86 per-credit-hour; $512 required fees. Room/board: $3,376. Books/supplies: $700. Personal expenses: $1,285.

Financial aid. Need-based: Work study available nights and for part-time students. **Non-need-based:** Scholarships awarded for academics, athletics. **Additional information:** Interview, essay recommended for scholarships.

Application procedures. Admission: No deadline. No application fee. Admission notification on a rolling basis. **Financial aid:** Priority date 5/1; no closing date. FAFSA, institutional form required. Applicants notified on a rolling basis starting 5/1; must reply within 2 week(s) of notification.

Academics. Special study options: Accelerated study, cooperative education, distance learning, double major, dual enrollment of high school students, honors, independent study, internships, liberal arts/career combination, study abroad, teacher certification program. Bachelor's degree programs available on campus. License preparation in nursing. **Credit/placement by examination:** CLEP, institutional tests. 16 credit hours maximum toward associate degree. Placement tests in mathematics and English required for all first-time freshmen. **Support services:** GED preparation and test center, learning center, reduced course load, remedial instruction, study skills assistance, tutoring.

Majors. Agriculture: General, animal sciences, business, equestrian studies, range science, soil science. **Biology:** General. **Business:** General, administrative services, business admin, management information systems, managerial economics, office management, tourism promotion. **Communications:**

General, journalism. **Communications technology:** Graphic/printing. **Computer sciences:** General, information systems. **Conservation:** Forestry, management/policy, wildlife. **Education:** General, agricultural, early childhood, elementary, secondary, special. **Engineering:** General. **Engineering technology:** Drafting. **Foreign languages:** General. **Health:** Predentistry, premedicine, prepharmacy, preveterinary. **History:** General. **Interdisciplinary:** Biological/physical sciences. **Legal studies:** Prelaw. **Liberal arts:** Arts/sciences. **Math:** General. **Parks/recreation:** Facilities management. **Physical sciences:** Chemistry, physics. **Psychology:** General. **Social sciences:** General, political science, sociology. **Visual/performing arts:** Commercial photography, commercial/advertising art, design, photography.

Computing on campus. 134 workstations in dormitories, library, computer center, student center. Commuter students can connect to campus network.

Student life. **Freshman orientation:** Available, $35 fee. Preregistration for classes offered. Held once in June, July, and August. **Policies:** Freshmen permitted cars on campus. **Housing:** Coed dorms, single-sex dorms, apartments available. $100 deposit. Theme houses available. **Activities:** Bands, choral groups, dance, drama, literary magazine, music ensembles, musical theater, student government, student newspaper, symphony orchestra, Northwest Trail Blazers, civic service organization.

Athletics. NJCAA. **Intercollegiate:** Basketball, volleyball W, wrestling M. **Intramural:** Archery, badminton, baseball M, basketball, cross-country, field hockey W, golf, handball, racquetball, rifle M, sailing, skiing, soccer, softball, squash, swimming, table tennis, tennis, volleyball, wrestling M. **Team name:** Trappers.

Student services. Adult student services, alcohol/substance abuse counseling, campus ministries, career counseling, student employment services, financial aid counseling, health services, minority student services, on-campus daycare, personal counseling, placement for graduates, veterans' counselor. **Physically disabled:** Services for visually, speech, hearing impaired. **Transfer:** Special adviser, orientation, pre-admission transcript evaluation for new students. Transfer adviser, college fairs on campus for students transferring to 4-year colleges.

Contact. E-mail: admissions@northwestcollege.edu
Phone: (307) 754-6101 Toll-free number: (800) 560-4692
Fax: (307) 754-6244
Brad Hammond, Registrar, Northwest College, 231 West 6th Street, Powell, WY 82435

Sheridan College

Sheridan, Wyoming
www.sheridan.edu **CB code: 4536**

- Public 2-year community college
- Commuter campus in large town

General. Founded in 1948. Regionally accredited. **Enrollment:** 1,556 degree-seeking undergraduates; 1,239 non-degree-seeking students. **Degrees:** 197 associate awarded. **Location:** 130 miles from Casper, 130 miles from Billings, Montana. **Calendar:** Semester, limited summer session. **Full-time faculty:** 76 total; 16% have terminal degrees, 4% minority, 62% women. **Part-time faculty:** 93 total; 3% have terminal degrees, 56% women. **Class size:** 70% < 20, 30% 20-39, less than 1% 40-49. **Special facilities:** Geological museum, federal depository for government publications, observatory.

Student profile. Among degree-seeking undergraduates, 39% enrolled in a transfer program, 18% enrolled in a vocational program, 330 enrolled as first-time, first-year students, 102 transferred in from other institutions.

Part-time:	36%	**Hispanic American:**	2%
Out-of-state:	9%	**Native American:**	2%
Women:	66%	**25 or older:**	35%
African American:	1%	**Live on campus:**	7%
Asian American:	1%		

Transfer out. **Colleges most students transferred to 2005:** University of Wyoming, Chadron State College, Black Hills State University, Montana State University.

Basis for selection. Open admission, but selective for some programs. Special admissions for nursing, dental hygiene, massage therapy; requirements vary by program. **Adult students:** Entrance exam policies same as for first-time freshmen.

High school preparation. One chemistry required of dental hygiene applicants.

2005-2006 Annual costs. Tuition/fees: $1,891; $4,651 out-of-state. Per-credit charge: $57 in-state; $172 out-of-state. Room/board: $3,840. Books/supplies: $750. Personal expenses: $1,800.

2004-2005 Financial aid. **Need-based:** 67% of total undergraduate aid awarded as scholarships/grants, 33% as loans/jobs. Need-based aid available for part-time students. Work study available nights, weekends and for part-time students. **Non-need-based:** Scholarships awarded for academics, athletics.

Application procedures. **Admission:** No deadline. No application fee. Application may be submitted online. Admission notification on a rolling basis. **Financial aid:** Priority date 3/1; no closing date. FAFSA, institutional form required. Applicants notified on a rolling basis; must reply within 3 week(s) of notification.

Academics. **Special study options:** Cooperative education, distance learning, double major, dual enrollment of high school students, ESL, independent study, internships, liberal arts/career combination. Bachelor's degree programs available on campus. License preparation in dental hygiene, nursing. **Credit/placement by examination:** AP, CLEP, institutional tests. 18 credit hours maximum toward associate degree. **Support services:** GED preparation and test center, learning center, reduced course load, remedial instruction, study skills assistance, tutoring, writing center.

Majors. **Agriculture:** General, animal sciences, business, farm/ranch, horticulture. **Biology:** General, microbiology, zoology. **Business:** General, accounting, administrative services, banking/financial services, business admin, office management. **Communications:** General. **Computer sciences:** General. **Education:** General, elementary, secondary. **Engineering:** General. **Engineering technology:** General, drafting, surveying. **English:** English lit. **Foreign languages:** General, Spanish. **Health:** Dental hygiene, nursing (RN), prenursing. **History:** General. **Interdisciplinary:** Biological/physical sciences. **Legal studies:** Legal secretary. **Liberal arts:** Arts/sciences, humanities. **Math:** General. **Mechanic/repair:** Diesel. **Parks/recreation:** Health/fitness. **Personal/culinary services:** General, culinary arts. **Physical sciences:** General. **Production:** Machine tool, welding. **Protective services:** Police science. **Psychology:** General. **Public administration:** Social work. **Social sciences:** General, political science, sociology. **Visual/performing arts:** Art.

Most popular majors. Business/marketing 16%, education 7%, health sciences 21%, interdisciplinary studies 6%, liberal arts 18%, trade and industry 9%.

Computing on campus. 200 workstations in dormitories, library, student center. Dormitories wired for high-speed internet access and linked to campus network. Commuter students can connect to campus network. Online course registration, online library, helpline, student web hosting, wireless network available.

Student life. **Freshman orientation:** Mandatory. Preregistration for classes offered. Session lasts approximately 2 hours. **Policies:** Freshmen permitted cars on campus. **Housing:** Coed dorms, single-sex dorms, special housing for disabled, apartments available. $60 deposit. Apartments available for single parents. **Activities:** Bands, choral groups, drama, music ensembles, student government, student newspaper, adult nontraditional students club, art club, nursing clubs, dental auxiliary, multidiversity club.

Athletics. NJCAA. **Intercollegiate:** Basketball, rodeo, volleyball W. **Intramural:** Basketball, bowling, soccer, softball, tennis, volleyball. **Team name:** Generals.

Student services. Adult student services, career counseling, student employment services, financial aid counseling, health services, placement for graduates. **Physically disabled:** Services for visually, speech, hearing impaired. **Transfer:** Special adviser, orientation, pre-admission transcript evaluation for new students. Transfer adviser, college fairs on campus for students transferring to 4-year colleges.

Contact. E-mail: admissions@sheridan.edu
Phone: (307) 674-6446 ext. 2002 Toll-free number: (800) 913-9139
Fax: (307) 674-7205
Zane Garstad, Director of Admissions, Sheridan College, PO Box 1500, Sheridan, WY 82801-1500

Western Wyoming Community College

Rock Springs, Wyoming
www.wwcc.wy.edu **CB code: 4957**

- Public 2-year community college
- Commuter campus in large town

General. Founded in 1959. Regionally accredited. **Enrollment:** 1,789 degree-seeking undergraduates; 649 non-degree-seeking students. **Degrees:** 322 associate awarded. **Location:** 180 miles from Salt Lake City. **Calendar:** Semester, limited summer session. **Full-time faculty:** 69 total; 17% have terminal degrees, 1% minority, 56% women. **Part-time faculty:** 100 total; 10% have terminal degrees. **Class size:** 82% < 20, 18% 20-39. **Special facilities:** Dinosaur museum, natural history museum, wildlife exhibit.

Student profile. Among degree-seeking undergraduates, 75% enrolled in a transfer program, 25% enrolled in a vocational program, 1% already have a bachelor's degree or higher, 306 enrolled as first-time, first-year students, 90 transferred in from other institutions.

Part-time:	42%	**25 or older:**	47%
Out-of-state:	7%	**Live on campus:**	30%
Women:	64%		

Transfer out. Colleges most students transferred to 2005: University of Wyoming, Utah State University, Idaho State University.

Basis for selection. Open admission, but selective for some programs. Admissions to nursing program based on academic performance, pre-entrance exam and prerequisite course completion. **Adult students:** Entrance exam policies same as for first-time freshmen. **Homeschooled:** If home school is not through an accredited institution, student needs to obtain GED.

High school preparation. Recommended units include English 4, mathematics 3, social studies 2, science 3 (laboratory 1) and foreign language 2.

2005-2006 Annual costs. Tuition/fees: $1,658; $4,418 out-of-state. Per-credit charge: $57 in-state; $172 out-of-state. Room/board: $3,517. Books/supplies: $700.

2004-2005 Financial aid. Need-based: 220 full-time freshmen applied for aid; 186 were judged to have need; 186 of these received aid. Average loan was $2,234. 57% of total undergraduate aid awarded as scholarships/grants, 43% as loans/jobs. Need-based aid available for part-time students. Work study available for part-time students. **Non-need-based:** Scholarships awarded for academics, art, athletics, music/drama, state residency.

Application procedures. Admission: No deadline. No application fee. Application may be submitted online. Admission notification on a rolling basis. **Financial aid:** Priority date 4/1; no closing date. FAFSA required. Applicants notified on a rolling basis starting 3/15; must reply within 2 week(s) of notification.

Academics. Special study options: Cooperative education, distance learning, dual enrollment of high school students, ESL, external degree, honors, independent study, internships. Bachelor's degree programs available on campus. License preparation in nursing. **Credit/placement by examination:** AP, CLEP, IB, institutional tests. 40 credit hours maximum toward associate degree. **Support services:** GED preparation and test center, learning center, remedial instruction, study skills assistance, tutoring.

Honors college/program. Competitive program, open to 20 students a year. Students participate in challenging courses and travel to cultural and educational events at the expense of the institution.

Majors. Biology: General, ecology, wildlife. **Business:** Accounting, administrative services, business admin, marketing, office technology. **Communications:** General, journalism. **Computer sciences:** General, computer science, data processing, information systems. **Conservation:** General, environmental studies, water/wetlands/marine, wildlife. **Education:** General, early childhood, elementary, multi-level teacher, secondary, special. **Engineering:** General, electrical. **Engineering technology:** General, instrumentation, mining. **English:** English lit. **Family/consumer sciences:** General. **Foreign languages:** Spanish. **Health:** Licensed practical nurse, medical assistant, medical secretary, predentistry, premedicine, prenursing, prepharmacy, preveterinary. **History:** General. **Legal studies:** Legal secretary, prelaw. **Math:** General. **Mechanic/repair:** Automotive, diesel, electronics/electrical, heavy equipment, industrial, industrial electronics. **Parks/recreation:** General, exercise sciences. **Physical sciences:** Chemistry, geology. **Production:** Welding. **Protective services:** Law enforcement admin. **Psychology:** General. **Public administration:** Social work. **Social sciences:** General, anthropology, archaeology, criminology, economics, geography, international relations, political science, sociology. **Visual/performing arts:** General, art, ceramics, dance, dramatic, photography, studio arts, theater design.

Most popular majors. Business/marketing 9%, education 9%, health sciences 14%, liberal arts 22%, visual/performing arts 17%.

Computing on campus. 240 workstations in dormitories, library, computer center, student center. Dormitories wired for high-speed internet access and linked to campus network. Commuter students can connect to campus network. Online course registration, online library, helpline, wireless network available.

Student life. Freshman orientation: Mandatory. Preregistration for classes offered. Program for students and parents. **Policies:** Freshmen permitted cars on campus. **Housing:** Coed dorms, special housing for disabled, apartments available. $150 partly refundable deposit. **Activities:** Bands, choral groups, dance, drama, music ensembles, musical theater, student government, student newspaper, Phi Theta Kappa, outdoor club, ambassadors, Students Without Borders.

Athletics. NJCAA. **Intercollegiate:** Basketball, cheerleading, volleyball W, wrestling M. **Intramural:** Basketball, football (non-tackle), soccer, softball, table tennis, tennis, volleyball. **Team name:** Spartans.

Student services. Adult student services, alcohol/substance abuse counseling, career counseling, student employment services, financial aid counseling, on-campus daycare, personal counseling, placement for graduates, veterans' counselor. **Physically disabled:** Services for visually, hearing impaired. **Transfer:** Special adviser, pre-admission transcript evaluation for new students. Transfer adviser, college fairs on campus for students transferring to 4-year colleges.

Contact. E-mail: lwatkins@wwcc.wy.edu
Phone: (307) 382-1648 Toll-free number: (800) 226-1181
Fax: (307) 382-1636
Laurie Watkins, Director of Admissions, Western Wyoming Community College, Box 428, Rock Springs, WY 82902-0428

Wyoming Technical Institute

Laramie, Wyoming
www.wyotech.com **CB code: 7141**

- For-profit 2-year technical college
- Large town
- Interview required

General. Founded in 1966. Accredited by ACCSCT. **Enrollment:** 2,290 degree-seeking undergraduates. **Degrees:** 845 associate awarded. **Location:** 50 miles from Cheyenne, 70 miles from Ft. Collins, Colorado. **Calendar:** Differs by program. **Full-time faculty:** 130 total. **Part-time faculty:** 1 total.

Basis for selection. Open admission.

2005-2006 Annual costs. Tuition ranges from $23,300 to $31,000 depending on program. Books and tools loaned at no additional charge except for $100 refundable tool deposit. Room rent in institutional housing $275 per month.

Financial aid. All financial aid based on need.

Application procedures. Admission: No deadline. $100 fee. Admission notification on a rolling basis. **Financial aid:** No deadline. FAFSA required. Applicants notified on a rolling basis.

Academics. Special study options: Double major. **Credit/placement by examination:** CLEP.

Majors. Mechanic/repair: Auto body, automotive, diesel.

Student life. Freshman orientation: Mandatory. **Housing:** Guaranteed on-campus for all undergraduates. Coed dorms, special housing for disabled, apartments available. $50 deposit.

Athletics. Intramural: Basketball M, bowling M, softball M, volleyball M.

Student services. Career counseling, student employment services, personal counseling, placement for graduates. **Physically disabled:** Services for visually, hearing impaired.

Contact. E-mail: admissions@wyotech.com
Phone: (307) 742-3776 Toll-free number: (800) 521-7158
Fax: (307) 742-4852
Glenn Halsey, Director of Admissions, Wyoming Technical Institute, 4373 North Third Street, Laramie, WY 82072

Two-Year Colleges

American Samoa

American Samoa Community College

Pago Pago, American Samoa
www.ascc.as/ **CB code: 0020**

- Public 2-year community college
- Large town

General. Founded in 1970. Regionally accredited. **Location:** 9 miles from downtown. **Calendar:** Semester.

Annual costs/financial aid. Tuition/fees (2005-2006): $1,410; $1,860 out-of-state. Books/supplies: $800. Personal expenses: $900.

Contact. Phone: (684) 699-8867
Admissions Officer, Box 2609, Pago Pago, AS 96799-2609

Guam

Guam Community College

Barrigada, Guam **CB member**
www.guamcc.net **CB code: 2302**

- Public 2-year community and technical college
- Commuter campus in small city

General. Founded in 1977. Regionally accredited. Multi-cultural U.S. territory with island setting. **Enrollment:** 1,547 undergraduates. **Degrees:** 94 associate awarded. **ROTC:** Army. **Location:** 1,500 miles from Manila, Philippines, 3,600 miles from Honolulu. **Calendar:** Semester, limited summer session. **Full-time faculty:** 78 total. **Part-time faculty:** 42 total. **Class size:** 49% < 20, 51% 20-39. **Special facilities:** Pacific Collection, including 400 books (many rare and out of print) about Guam, Micronesia, and the Pacific.

Student profile.

Out-of-state:	4%	25 or older:	35%

Transfer out. Colleges most students transferred to 2005: University of Guam.

Basis for selection. Open admission. **Adult students:** Entrance exam policies same as for first-time freshmen. **Homeschooled:** Official high school transcript required.

High school preparation. Recommended units include English 4, mathematics 3, social studies 3, science 2 and academic electives 9.

2005-2006 Annual costs. Tuition/fees: $1,720; $2,470 out-of-state. Per-credit charge: $50 in-state; $75 out-of-state. Books/supplies: $800. Personal expenses: $2,250.

Financial aid. Additional information: Tuition assistance available for students in nontraditional courses.

Application procedures. Admission: No deadline. No application fee. Application must be submitted on paper. Admission notification on a rolling basis. **Financial aid:** Priority date 5/1; no closing date. FAFSA, institutional form required. Applicants notified on a rolling basis starting 8/28; must reply within 2 week(s) of notification.

Academics. Special study options: Cooperative education, cross-registration, double major, dual enrollment of high school students, independent study, internships. **Credit/placement by examination:** AP, CLEP, institutional tests. 48 credit hours maximum toward associate degree. **Support services:** GED preparation and test center, learning center, remedial instruction, study skills assistance, tutoring.

Majors. Business: Accounting, office management, office technology, sales/distribution, tourism/travel. **Computer sciences:** Computer science. **Education:** Early childhood, teacher assistance. **Family/consumer sciences:** Institutional food production. **Health:** Medical assistant. **Liberal arts:** Arts/sciences. **Mechanic/repair:** Automotive. **Personal/culinary services:** Chef training. **Protective services:** Law enforcement admin. **Visual/performing arts:** Graphic design.

Computing on campus. 79 workstations in library, computer center, student center. Online library, repair service available.

Student life. Freshman orientation: Available. Held 1 week before start of semester. **Policies:** Freshmen permitted cars on campus. **Activities:** Student government, Habitat for Humanity, Health Occupational Students of America, Phi Theta Kappa, Postsecondary Tourism Association.

Student services. Adult student services, alcohol/substance abuse counseling, career counseling, services for economically disadvantaged, student employment services, financial aid counseling, health services, personal counseling, placement for graduates, veterans' counselor. **Physically disabled:** Services for visually, speech, hearing impaired. **Transfer:** Special adviser, orientation, re-entry adviser for new students.

Contact. E-mail: pclymer@guamcc.edu
Phone: (671) 735-5531 Fax: (671) 734-5238
Virginia Tudela, Registrar, Guam Community College, PO Box 23069 GMF, Barrigada, GU 96921

Northern Mariana Islands

Northern Marianas College

Saipan, Northern Mariana Islands
www.nmcnet.edu **CB code: 0781**

- Public 2-year community and liberal arts college
- Commuter campus in large town

General. Founded in 1981. Regionally accredited. **Location:** 150 miles from Guam, 3000 miles from Hawaii. **Calendar:** Semester.

Annual costs/financial aid. Personal expenses: $775.

Contact. Phone: (670) 234-3690 ext. 1528, 1539
P.O. Box 501250, Saipan, MP 96950

Marshall Islands

College of the Marshall Islands

Majuro, Marshall Islands
www.cmiedu.net **CB code: 7142**

- Public 2-year community and junior college
- Commuter campus in large town

General. Regionally accredited. Marine science center in Arrak is operated by the College of the Marshall Islands. **Enrollment:** 599 degree-seeking undergraduates; 5 non-degree-seeking students. **Degrees:** 80 associate awarded. **Location:** 2,280 miles from Honolulu. **Calendar:** Semester, limited summer session. **Full-time faculty:** 25 total. **Part-time faculty:** 10 total. **Special facilities:** Nuclear institute.

Student profile. Among degree-seeking undergraduates, 145 enrolled as first-time, first-year students.

Women:	47%	**Asian American:**	100%

Basis for selection. Minimum 2.0 high school GPA or 35 score on GED required. Applicants who do not meet minimum requirements may be admitted into Developmental Studies program.

2005-2006 Annual costs. Books/supplies: $600.

Application procedures. Admission: Closing date 7/15. $5 fee. Admission notification on a rolling basis. **Financial aid:** Priority date 7/1; no closing date. FAFSA required. Applicants notified on a rolling basis.

Academics. Special study options: Distance learning, double major, ESL, independent study, internships, teacher certification program. **Credit/placement by examination:** CLEP. **Support services:** Learning center, remedial instruction, study skills assistance, tutoring, writing center.

Majors. Business: Business admin. **Education:** Elementary. **Liberal arts:** Arts/sciences. **Mechanic/repair:** General, automotive.

Most popular majors. Business/marketing 24%, education 27%, health sciences 20%, liberal arts 25%.

Student life. Housing: Single-sex dorms available. **Activities:** Student government, student newspaper.

Student services. Health services, personal counseling. **Transfer:** Special adviser, orientation for new students. Transfer center, transfer adviser for students transferring to 4-year colleges.

Contact. E-mail: cmi@ntamar.com
Phone: (692) 625-6895 Fax: (692) 625-7203
Rosita Capelle, Director of Admissions and Records, College of the Marshall Islands, Box 1258, Majuro, MH 96960

Micronesia

College of Micronesia-FSM

Kolonia Pohnpei, Micronesia
www.comfsm.fm **CB code: 0115**

- Public 2-year community and liberal arts college
- Commuter campus in small city

General. Founded in 1963. Regionally accredited. **Location:** 1 mile east of Kolonia. **Calendar:** Semester.

Annual costs/financial aid. Tuition/fees (2005-2006): $2,750. Room/board: $3,087. Books/supplies: $530.

Contact. Phone: (691) 320-2480 ext. 150
Coordinator, PO Box 159, Kolonia, FM 96941

Palau

Palau Community College

Koror, Palau
www.palau.edu/ **CB code: 7329**

- Public 2-year community and technical college
- Commuter campus in small city

General. Founded in 1969. Regionally accredited. **Enrollment:** 618 degree-seeking undergraduates; 29 non-degree-seeking students. **Degrees:** 66 associate awarded. **Location:** 800 miles from Guam, 600 miles from Manila. **Calendar:** Semester, limited summer session. **Full-time faculty:** 28 total; 4% have terminal degrees, 18% minority, 43% women. **Part-time faculty:** 14 total; 7% have terminal degrees, 21% minority, 50% women. **Class size:** 68% < 20, 32% 20-39.

Student profile. Among degree-seeking undergraduates, 106 enrolled as first-time, first-year students, 4 transferred in from other institutions.

Part-time:	30%	**Asian American:**	98%
Women:	57%	**International:**	2%

Basis for selection. Open admission, but selective for some programs. To enter the associate of applied science degree program, a student must be a high school graduate with cumulative grade point average of 2.0 or possess a GED certificate; associate of science and associate of arts degree programs require a TOEFL score of 500 or better in addition to the above requirements; exceptions are degree programs in education and liberal arts, which require 2.5 cumulatve GPA.

2006-2007 Annual costs. Tuition/fees (projected): $2,560. Per-credit charge: $70. Room/board: $2,352. Books/supplies: $300. Personal expenses: $800.

2005-2006 Financial aid. All financial aid based on need. 99 full-time freshmen applied for aid; 99 were judged to have need; 99 of these received aid. Need-based aid available for part-time students. Work study available nights, weekends and for part-time students.

Application procedures. Admission: Closing date 8/29. $10 fee. Application must be submitted on paper. Admission notification on a rolling basis beginning on or about 4/30. **Financial aid:** Priority date 4/1; no closing date. FAFSA, institutional form required. Applicants notified on a rolling basis starting 5/1.

Academics. Special study options: Double major, dual enrollment of high school students, internships. **Credit/placement by examination:** CLEP, institutional tests. **Support services:** Learning center, remedial instruction, study skills assistance, tutoring.

Majors. Agriculture: Plant breeding. **Business:** Administrative services, hospitality admin. **Conservation:** Environmental studies. **Construction:** Electrician, maintenance. **Education:** Early childhood, elementary, special. **Engineering:** Electrical, mechanics. **Engineering technology:** Construction, electrical. **Liberal arts:** Arts/sciences, library science. **Mechanic/repair:** General, electronics/electrical, heating/ac/refrig. **Protective services:** Police science.

Computing on campus. 60 workstations in library, computer center, student center.

Student life. Freshman orientation: Mandatory. Week-long program held prior to first week of classes each term designed to familiarize students with facility, programs, and services; includes administration of placement tests, academic advising, and registration. **Policies:** Possession, consumption, and storage of alcoholic beverages and illegal drugs are prohibited. Freshmen permitted cars on campus. **Housing:** Coed dorms, single-sex dorms available. **Activities:** Student government, Yapese, Chuukese, Kosrean, Pohnpeians, Palauans, and Marshallese ethnic clubs, Pacific writers club, agriculture science majors club.

Athletics. Intramural: Basketball M, softball, swimming, table tennis, volleyball, weight lifting M, wrestling M.

Student services. Alcohol/substance abuse counseling, career counseling, student employment services, financial aid counseling, health services, on-campus daycare, personal counseling, placement for graduates. **Physically disabled:** Services for visually impaired. **Transfer:** Pre-admission transcript evaluation for new students.

Contact. E-mail: dahliapcc@palaunet.com
Phone: (680) 488-2470 Fax: (680) 488-4468
Dahlia Katosang, Director of Admissions & Financial Aid, Palau Community College, PO Box 9, Koror, PW 96940

Bermuda

Bermuda College
Paget, PG BX, Bermuda
www.college.bm
CB code: 2581

- Public 2-year community college
- Commuter campus in small city

General. Calendar: Semester.

Annual costs/financial aid. Tuition and fees are 3,280 BMD per year. Additional required fees for international students. Books/supplies: $400.

Contact. Phone: (441) 239-4048
PO Box PG 297, Paget, PG BX, BM

Canada

Humber College
Etobicoke, Canada
www.humberc.on.ca
CB code: 2168

- Public 2-year liberal arts and technical college
- Very large city

General. Enrollment: 1,500 degree-seeking undergraduates. **Degrees:** 85 bachelor's, 5,800 associate awarded. **Location:** 10 miles from downtown Toronto. **Calendar:** Semester. **Full-time faculty:** 490 total. **Part-time faculty:** 1,000 total.

Basis for selection. Open admission, but selective for some programs. GED not accepted.

2005-2006 Annual costs. Costs reported in Canadian dollars. Tuition and fees vary by degree type and program. Typical annual tuition for a postsecondary degree is $2,452 for Canadians; for non-Canadians $11,098; room and board $6,300 on average, but depends on accommodations.

Application procedures. Admission: Closing date 2/1. Students must apply through Ontario College application center. Application fee $30 Canadian.

Academics. Credit/placement by examination: CLEP.

Majors. Business: General. **Computer sciences:** General, computer graphics, information technology, LAN/WAN management, networking, programming, security, system admin, web page design, webmaster. **Protective services:** Police science, security management. **Public administration:** Social work. **Visual/performing arts:** Acting, commercial photography, commercial/advertising art, design, dramatic, drawing, fashion design, graphic design, illustration, industrial design, interior design, music performance, photography, play/screenwriting, theater design.

Contact. Phone: (416) 675-3111 Fax: (416) 675-2427
John Mason, Registrar, Humber College, 205 Humber College Boulevard, Etobicoke, CN M9W 5-7

Early decision and early action table

The following table lists early decision and early action policies at 441 colleges, which are listed alphabetically by state or country. Colleges were asked to supply the deadline for student applications and the date by which the college will notify the applicant of a decision to admit, deny admission, or defer the application to the regular admission cycle. If a college offers two early decision cycles, both sets of dates are listed.

Some colleges support both a binding early decision plan and a nonbinding early action plan and report dates for both. Colleges with binding early decision plans were asked to give the number of students who applied for early decision and the number of those applicants admitted to the fall 2005 freshman class.

Tables and Indexes

Institution	Early Applicants		Early Decision		Early Action	
	Number applied	Number admitted	Apply by	Notified by	Apply by	Notified by
Alabama						
Auburn University			11/1			
Birmingham-Southern College					12/1	12/15
Judson College						
University of Mobile					11/1	11/15
Alaska						
Alaska Pacific University			12/1	12/15		
Arizona						
Embry-Riddle Aeronautical University: Prescott Campus			12/1	12/31		
Prescott College			12/1	12/15		
Arkansas						
Ouachita Baptist University					12/1	12/8
University of Arkansas					11/15	12/15
California						
Azusa Pacific University					12/1	1/15
Biola University					12/1	1/15
California Baptist University					11/19	12/20
California Institute of Technology					11/1	12/31
California Lutheran University					11/15	12/15
California Polytechnic State University: San Luis Obispo	2077	753	10/31	12/15		
California State University: Sacramento					11/30	
California State University: Stanislaus					10/1	
Chapman University	1517	922			11/30	1/15

Institution	Early Applicants: Number applied	Early Applicants: Number admitted	Early Decision: Apply by	Early Decision: Notified by	Early Action: Apply by	Early Action: Notified by
Claremont McKenna College	276	76	11/15 1/2	12/15 2/15		
Harvey Mudd College			11/15	12/15		
Master's College					11/15	12/22
Menlo College					12/1	12/15
Mills College	107	96			11/15	12/20
Mount St. Mary's College					12/1	1/1
Notre Dame de Namur University					12/1	1/1
Occidental College	111	47	11/15	12/15		
Pitzer College					11/15	1/1
Point Loma Nazarene University					12/1	1/15
Pomona College	402	114	11/1 12/28	12/15 2/15		
Santa Clara University	1664	1087			11/1	12/23
Scripps College	97	49	11/1 1/1	12/15 2/15		
Soka University of America			10/15	12/1		
St. Mary's College of California					11/30	1/15
Stanford University					11/1	12/15
University of Judaism			11/15	12/15		
University of San Diego	1996	1120			11/15	1/31
University of San Francisco	1264	899			11/15	1/16
University of the Pacific					11/15	1/15
Vanguard University of Southern California	459	368			12/1	1/15
Westmont College	1056	815			11/1	12/20
Whittier College					12/1	12/30
Colorado						
Boulder College of Massage Therapy						
Colorado College			11/15	12/20	11/15	1/15
University of Denver	2038	1145			11/1	1/15
Connecticut						
Connecticut College			11/15 1/1	12/15 2/15		
Fairfield University					11/15	12/15
Mitchell College			11/15	12/15		
Post University					11/1	12/1
Sacred Heart University	259	166	10/1 12/1	10/15 12/15		
St. Joseph College					11/15	12/15
Trinity College	382	244	11/15 1/1	12/15 2/15		
United States Coast Guard Academy	581	172			11/1	12/15
University of Connecticut	8281	5313			12/1	1/1
University of Hartford					11/15	12/1
Wesleyan University			11/15 1/1	12/15 2/15		
Yale University					11/1	12/15
Delaware						
University of Delaware	1374	596	11/1	12/15		
Wesley College			11/1	12/1		

Tables and Indexes

Institution	Early Applicants		Early Decision		Early Action	
	Number applied	Number admitted	Apply by	Notified by	Apply by	Notified by
District of Columbia						
American University	418	251	11/15	12/31		
Catholic University of America					11/15	12/15
George Washington University	1603	925	12/1 1/15	12/15 2/1		
Georgetown University	3863	977			11/1	12/15
Howard University			11/1	12/24	11/1	12/15
Trinity University					12/1	1/1
Florida						
Beacon College			12/5	1/6	12/5	1/6
Embry-Riddle Aeronautical University			12/1	12/31		
Flagler College	658	370	12/1 1/15	12/15 2/1		
Florida Southern College	43	42	12/1	12/15		
Jacksonville University					12/1	12/15
Palm Beach Atlantic University					12/1	12/15
Rollins College	287	188	11/15 1/15	12/15 2/1		
Stetson University	44	38	11/1	11/15		
University of Florida			10/1	12/1		
University of Miami	600	300	11/1	12/15	11/1	2/1
University of North Florida					11/15	12/2
Georgia						
Agnes Scott College	78	13	11/15	12/15		
Emory University	1026	533	11/1 1/1	12/15 2/1		
Georgia College and State University	760	480			11/1	12/1
Georgia Southwestern State University			12/15	1/15		
Mercer University	1435	1247			11/1	11/15
Oglethorpe University					12/1	1/1
Oxford College of Emory University					11/15	1/15
Spelman College	1132	661	11/1	12/15	11/15	12/31
University of Georgia	5705	4557			10/15	12/15
Wesleyan College			11/15 1/15	12/15 2/15		
Idaho						
Albertson College of Idaho					11/15	12/31
Northwest Nazarene University					12/15	1/15
Illinois						
DePaul University					11/15	1/1
Kendall College						
Knox College	724	678			12/1	12/31
Lake Forest College	862	667	12/1	12/20	12/1	1/15
Moody Bible Institute			12/1	1/15	12/1	1/15
Northwestern University	1079	524	11/1	12/15		
Principia College	20	20			11/15	12/1
University of Chicago	2459	1189			11/1	12/15
Westwood College of Technology: O'Hare						

Institution	Early Applicants: Number applied	Early Applicants: Number admitted	Early Decision: Apply by	Early Decision: Notified by	Early Action: Apply by	Early Action: Notified by
Wheaton College					11/1	12/31
Indiana						
Butler University	4783	3463			12/1	12/20
DePauw University			11/1	1/5	12/1	2/15
Earlham College	699	583	12/1	12/15	1/1	2/1
Hanover College					12/1	12/20
Saint Mary's College	102	87	11/15	12/15		
Taylor University					12/1	12/20
University of Evansville	1500	1172			12/1	12/15
University of Notre Dame	2719	1383			11/1	12/20
Valparaiso University	1615	1448			11/1	12/1
Wabash College	59	40	11/15	12/15	12/15	1/15
Iowa						
Coe College					12/10	1/20
Cornell College					12/1	2/1
Grinnell College	144	101	11/20	12/20		
Hamilton College						
Kansas						
Sterling College	100	40			11/15	12/15
Tabor College						
Kentucky						
Bellarmine University					10/15	12/1
Centre College	765	601			12/1	1/15
Transylvania University	941	718			12/1	1/15
Louisiana						
Centenary College of Louisiana	174	112	12/1	12/15	1/15	1/15
Dillard University					12/1	12/30
Tulane University			11/1	12/15	11/1	12/15
Xavier University of Louisiana					1/15	2/15
Maine						
Bates College	466	215	11/15 1/1	12/20 2/15		
Bowdoin College	621	183	11/15 1/1	12/31 2/15		
Colby College	425	220	11/15 1/1	12/15 2/1		
College of the Atlantic	45	33	12/1 1/10	12/15 1/25		
Husson College					12/15	12/31
Maine Maritime Academy			12/20	1/1		
St. Joseph's College					11/15	12/15
Thomas College	236	156			12/15	12/31
University of Maine					12/15	1/15
University of Maine at Farmington	485	362			12/1	1/15
University of Maine at Machias					12/15	12/31
Maryland						
Baltimore International College	33	2			12/15	2/15
Frostburg State University						
Goucher College	1046	697			12/15	2/15

Institution	Early Applicants: Number applied	Early Applicants: Number admitted	Early Decision: Apply by	Early Decision: Notified by	Early Action: Apply by	Early Action: Notified by
Hood College	232	171			12/1	12/15
Johns Hopkins University	723	379	11/15	12/15		
Maryland Institute College of Art			11/15	12/15	1/15	1/30
McDaniel College					12/1	1/15
Mount St. Mary's University	272	250			12/1	12/15
Salisbury University					12/1	1/15
St. Mary's College of Maryland	264	136	12/1 1/15	1/1 2/15		
University of Maryland: Baltimore County					11/1	12/15
University of Maryland: College Park	18233	9651			12/1	2/15
University of Maryland: Eastern Shore					11/15	12/1
Washington College			11/15	12/15	12/1	12/20
Massachusetts						
Amherst College	364	127	11/15	12/15		
Assumption College	58	52	11/15	12/15		
Babson College			11/15	12/15	11/15	1/1
Bay Path College					12/15	1/2
Bentley College	1757	1039	11/15	12/22	12/1	1/30
Berklee College of Music					11/1	1/31
Boston College	5510	2035			11/1	12/25
Boston University	705	391	11/1 1/1	12/15 2/15		
Brandeis University	331	171	11/15	12/15		
Bridgewater State College					11/15	12/15
Clark University	99	85	11/15	12/15		
College of the Holy Cross	297	205	12/15	1/15		
Curry College	91	25	12/1	12/15		
Emerson College	1210	596			11/1	12/15
Emmanuel College	3	3	11/1	12/1		
Framingham State College	125	108			11/15	12/15
Gibbs College						
Gordon College	613	569	11/15	12/15	12/1	1/1
Hampshire College	69	53	11/15	12/15	12/1	1/15
Harvard College	4214	892			11/1	12/15
Hebrew College						
Massachusetts College of Art			12/1	12/20		
Massachusetts College of Liberal Arts					12/1	12/15
Massachusetts Institute of Technology	2796	383			11/1	12/15
Massachusetts Maritime Academy					11/1	12/15
Merrimack College	750	520			11/30	12/15
Mount Holyoke College	252	131	11/15 1/1	1/1 2/1		
Newbury College					12/1	1/1
Northeastern University					11/15	12/31
Simmons College	1277	816			12/1	1/20
Smith College	216	164	11/15 1/2	12/15 2/2		
Springfield College	158	64	12/1	2/1		
St. John's Seminary College						

Institution	Early Applicants: Number applied	Early Applicants: Number admitted	Early Decision: Apply by	Early Decision: Notified by	Early Action: Apply by	Early Action: Notified by
Stonehill College	77	51	11/1	12/15	11/1	1/1
Suffolk University	470	450			11/15	12/1
Tufts University	1286	460	11/15 1/1	12/15 2/1		
University of Massachusetts Amherst					11/1	12/15
University of Massachusetts Dartmouth	78	63	11/15	12/15		
Wellesley College	247	117	11/1	12/15		
Wheaton College	237	196	11/15 1/15	12/15 2/15		
Wheelock College	41	41	12/1	1/1		
Williams College	535	211	11/10	12/15		
Worcester Polytechnic Institute	918	865			11/15	12/15
Michigan						
Albion College					12/1	1/1
Cleary University						
Kalamazoo College	14	11	11/15	12/1	12/1	12/20
Olivet College					12/1	1/15
Minnesota						
Bethel University	1270	1006			12/1	1/15
Carleton College	411	209	11/15 1/15	12/15 2/15		
Hamline University					12/1	12/15
Macalester College	247	115	11/15 1/3	12/15 2/7		
St. Olaf College	1832	1666	11/15	12/6	12/15	2/1
University of Minnesota: Morris					12/1	12/15
Mississippi						
Millsaps College	486	437			12/1	12/15
Mississippi College	190	184	12/1	12/15		
Missouri						
Lester L. Cox College of Nursing and Health Sciences			11/1	12/1		
Truman State University	3577	2511			11/15	12/15
Washington University in St. Louis			11/15	12/15		
Nebraska						
Nebraska Wesleyan University	170	163	11/15	12/15		
New Hampshire						
Colby-Sawyer College					12/15	12/15
Dartmouth College	1180	397	11/1	12/15		
Magdalen College						
Rivier College					11/15	12/1
Southern New Hampshire University					11/15	12/15
St. Anselm College	96	72	11/15	12/1		
University of New Hampshire	3667	2926			12/1	1/15
New Jersey						
Bloomfield College	803	247			1/7	1/21
Caldwell College					1/1	1/15
Drew University	178	91	12/1 1/15	12/24 2/15		

Institution	Early Applicants		Early Decision		Early Action	
	Number applied	Number admitted	Apply by	Notified by	Apply by	Notified by
Georgian Court University					11/15	12/30
Monmouth University	2481	1796	12/1	1/1	12/15	1/15
Princeton University	2039	593	11/1	12/15		
Ramapo College of New Jersey					11/15	12/15
Richard Stockton College of New Jersey					2/1	2/15
Rider University	1220	528			11/15	12/15
Stevens Institute of Technology	237	167	11/15 1/15	12/15 2/15		
The College of New Jersey	556	200	11/15	12/15		
New Mexico						
College of Santa Fe			11/15	12/15		
New York						
Adelphi University	1086	441			12/1	12/31
Albany College of Pharmacy			11/1			
Alfred University	55	38	12/1	12/15		
Bard College	345	143			11/1	1/1
Barnard College	412	170	11/15	12/15		
City University of New York: Baruch College	12	3	12/13	1/7		
Clarkson University	155	139	12/1 1/15	12/30 2/1		
Colgate University	638	312	11/15 1/15	12/15 2/15		
College of Mount St. Vincent	34	30			11/1	12/1
College of New Rochelle			11/1	12/15		
Columbia University: Columbia College	1299	446	11/1	12/15		
Columbia University: Fu Foundation School of Engineering and Applied Science	193	132	11/1	12/15		
Concordia College					11/15	12/15
Cooper Union for the Advancement of Science and Art	450	60	12/1	12/22		
Cornell University	2570	1067	11/1	12/11		
Elmira College			11/15 1/15	12/15 1/31		
Eugene Lang College The New School for Liberal Arts			11/15	12/15		
Fashion Institute of Technology	1080	532			11/15	1/31
Five Towns College			12/15	1/15		
Fordham University					11/1	12/25
Hamilton College	455	252	11/15	1/1		
Hartwick College	112	101	1/1	1/15		
Hobart and William Smith Colleges			11/15 1/1	12/15 2/1		
Hofstra University	6855	3578			11/15	12/15
Iona College	661	479			12/1	12/21
Ithaca College	207	153	11/1	12/15		
King's College	98	81			11/15	12/15
Le Moyne College	51	47	12/1	12/15		
Manhattan College			11/15	12/15		
Manhattanville College			12/1	12/31		
Marist College	2137	1464	11/15	12/15	12/1	1/15

Tables and Indexes

Institution	Early Applicants		Early Decision		Early Action	
	Number applied	Number admitted	Apply by	Notified by	Apply by	Notified by
Molloy College					12/1	1/15
Nazareth College of Rochester	30	20	11/15	12/15	12/15	1/15
New York University	3275	1529	11/1	12/15		
Niagara University	1327	609			10/1	12/1
North Country Community College			11/15	12/15		
Pace University	486	365			11/30	1/1
Pratt Institute					11/15	1/10
Rensselaer Polytechnic Institute	158	134	11/15	12/31		
Rochester Institute of Technology	956	697	12/1	1/15		
Russell Sage College			12/1	12/15		
Sage College of Albany			12/1	12/15		
Sarah Lawrence College	233	125	11/15 1/1	12/15 2/15		
School of Visual Arts	200	140	12/1	1/1		
Siena College	2300	1671	12/1	12/15	12/1	1/1
Skidmore College	394	259	11/15 1/15	12/15 2/15		
St. John Fisher College	115	48	12/1	12/15		
St. Lawrence University	212	169	11/15 1/15	12/15 2/15		
St. Thomas Aquinas College			12/15			
State University of New York College at Buffalo	41	28	11/15	12/15		
State University of New York College at Cortland			11/15	12/15		
State University of New York College at Fredonia	87	52	11/1	12/1		
State University of New York College at Geneseo	281	165	11/15	12/15		
State University of New York College at Old Westbury			11/1	12/15		
State University of New York College at Oneonta	1845	1156			11/15	12/15
State University of New York College at Plattsburgh			11/15	12/15		
State University of New York College of Environmental Science and Forestry	130	124			12/1	1/2
State University of New York Maritime College			12/1	12/15		
State University of New York at Albany					11/15	1/1
State University of New York at Binghamton	4199	2367			11/15	12/22
State University of New York at Buffalo	528	329	11/1	12/15		
State University of New York at New Paltz					11/15	1/1
State University of New York at Oswego	110	73	11/15	12/15		
State University of New York at Purchase			11/1	12/5		
State University of New York at Stony Brook					11/15	1/1
Syracuse University	750	567	11/15	12/31		
Union College	271	199	11/15 1/15	12/15 2/1		
United States Merchant Marine Academy			11/1	12/15		

Institution	Early Applicants		Early Decision		Early Action	
	Number applied	Number admitted	Apply by	Notified by	Apply by	Notified by
University of Rochester	536	251	11/1	12/15		
Vassar College	592	250	11/15 1/1	12/15 2/1		
Wagner College						
Webb Institute	34	13	10/15	12/15		
Wells College	166	138	12/15	1/15	12/15	2/1
North Carolina						
Art Institute of Charlotte						
Carolinas College of Health Sciences			12/6	1/6		
Davidson College	441	217	11/15 1/2	12/15 2/1		
Duke University	1482	470	11/1	12/15		
Elon University	4573	2229	11/1	12/7	11/10	12/20
Greensboro College					12/15	1/15
Guilford College	1849	1275			1/15	2/15
High Point University					11/1	11/15
Meredith College	100	60	10/15	11/1		
North Carolina State University	9123	4839			11/1	1/31
Piedmont Baptist College			11/1	12/1	11/1	12/1
University of North Carolina at Asheville					11/27	1/8
University of North Carolina at Chapel Hill	9043	4172			11/1	1/31
University of North Carolina at Charlotte					10/15	12/1
University of North Carolina at Wilmington					11/1	1/20
Wake Forest University	727	382	11/15	12/15		
Warren Wilson College			11/15	12/1		
Ohio						
Antioch College					1/1	2/1
Case Western Reserve University	1910	1557			11/1	1/1
College of Wooster	75	70	12/1 1/15	12/15 2/1		
Denison University	201	164	11/1 1/15	12/1 2/1		
Kenyon College	570	364	12/1 1/15	12/15 2/1		
Miami University: Oxford Campus			11/1	12/15	12/1	2/1
Oberlin College	309	234	11/15 1/2	12/20 2/1		
Ohio Wesleyan University	702	656	12/1	12/30	12/15	1/15
School of Advertising Art						
University of Akron	5821	3850			11/15	12/1
Ursuline College	99	88			11/15	2/15
Wittenberg University	1273	1184	11/15	12/1	1/15	2/15
Xavier University	3057	2418			12/1	1/15
Youngstown State University	2283	1856			2/15	2/20
Oregon						
Eastern Oregon University					12/1	1/15
Lewis & Clark College					11/15	1/15
Linfield College	388	377			11/15	1/15
Oregon State University					11/1	12/15

Institution	Early Applicants		Early Decision		Early Action	
	Number applied	Number admitted	Apply by	Notified by	Apply by	Notified by
Reed College	204	135	11/15 1/2	12/15 2/1		
University of Oregon					11/1	12/15
Willamette University	589	520			12/1	1/15
Pennsylvania						
Allegheny College	98	68	11/15	12/15		
Arcadia University			10/15	12/1		
Bloomsburg University of Pennsylvania	405	303	11/15	12/1		
Bryn Mawr College	141	94	11/15 1/1	12/15 2/1		
Bucknell University	671	387	11/15 1/1	12/15 2/1		
Carlow University	217	126			9/30	10/30
Carnegie Mellon University	429	249	11/15 12/15	12/15 1/15		
Chestnut Hill College			12/1	12/15		
Dickinson College	1659	968	11/15 1/15	12/15 2/15	12/1	1/31
Duquesne University	1212	816	11/1	12/15	12/1	1/15
Franklin & Marshall College	373	287	11/15 1/15	12/15 2/15		
Gettysburg College	330	249	11/15 1/15	12/15 2/15		
Grove City College	632	320	11/15	12/15		
Haverford College	208	104	11/15	12/15		
Juniata College	82	74	11/1	12/30	12/1	1/30
La Salle University					11/15	12/15
Lafayette College						
Lehigh University	819	485	11/15 1/15	12/15 2/15		
Moravian College	195	141	1/15	12/15		
Muhlenberg College						
St. Joseph's University			11/15	12/15	11/15	1/15
Susquehanna University	181	136	11/15 1/1	12/1 1/15		
Swarthmore College			11/15 1/2	12/15 2/15		
University of Pennsylvania			11/1	12/15		
University of Scranton	2013	1750			11/15	12/15
Ursinus College			1/15	2/1	12/1	12/15
Villanova University	3325	1835			11/1	12/20
Washington and Jefferson College	3654	1561	12/1	12/15	1/15	2/15
Puerto Rico						
Inter American University of Puerto Rico: Fajardo Campus						
University of Puerto Rico: Aguadilla		180			1/15	1/30
University of Puerto Rico: Arecibo						
University of Puerto Rico: Humacao						
University of Puerto Rico: Mayaguez					1/30	2/15
Rhode Island						
Brown University	2046	571	11/1	12/15		
Bryant University	126	96	11/15	12/15		
Providence College	1717	1061			11/1	1/1

Institution	Early Applicants: Number applied	Early Applicants: Number admitted	Early Decision: Apply by	Early Decision: Notified by	Early Action: Apply by	Early Action: Notified by
Rhode Island School of Design					12/15	1/31
Roger Williams University	236	213	12/1	12/15		
Salve Regina University	680	503			11/1	12/15
University of Rhode Island					12/15	1/15
South Carolina						
College of Charleston					11/1	12/15
Converse College			11/15	12/1	12/1	12/15
Furman University	572	395	11/15	12/15		
Medical University of South Carolina						
Presbyterian College						
The Citadel						
Wofford College	450	370	11/15	12/1		
Tennessee						
Fisk University					12/1	12/31
Lipscomb University					11/15	12/15
Maryville College	224	184	11/15	12/1		
Rhodes College			11/1 1/1	12/1 2/1		
University of Tennessee: Knoxville					11/1	12/15
University of the South	157	128	11/15	12/15		
Vanderbilt University	1121	535	11/1 1/3	12/15 2/15		
Texas						
Austin College	25	21	12/1	1/10		
Austin Graduate School of Theology						
Hardin-Simmons University					12/9	1/15
Rice University	3552	1032	11/1	12/15	12/1	2/10
Southern Methodist University					11/1	12/31
Southwestern University	74	58	11/1	12/1		
Texas Christian University					11/15	1/1
Trinity University	57	30	11/1	12/15	11/1	12/15
University of Dallas					12/1	1/15
Vermont						
Bennington College	54	29	11/15 1/1	12/15 2/15		
Lyndon State College					11/1	12/1
Marlboro College			11/15	12/15	1/15	2/1
Middlebury College	754	261	11/15 12/15	12/15 2/15		
Norwich University			11/15	12/31		
St. Michael's College	1373	1190			11/1	1/1
Sterling College					12/15	1/15
University of Vermont					11/1	12/15
Virginia						
Christendom College	95	76			12/1	12/15
College of William and Mary			11/1	12/1		
Emory & Henry College			11/1	12/15		
George Mason University					11/1	12/15
Hampden-Sydney College	102	70	11/15	12/15	1/15	2/15
Hampton University					12/1	12/15

Institution	Early Applicants: Number applied	Early Applicants: Number admitted	Early Decision: Apply by	Early Decision: Notified by	Early Action: Apply by	Early Action: Notified by
Hollins University			11/15	12/15		
James Madison University	4731	2533			11/1	1/15
Longwood University	883	780			12/1	1/15
Lynchburg College	186	103	11/15	12/15		
Mary Baldwin College			11/15	12/1		
Old Dominion University	3440	1832			12/15	1/15
Radford University					12/15	1/9
Randolph-Macon College	47	37	12/1	1/1	12/1	1/1
Randolph-Macon Woman's College	25	21	11/15	12/15		
Roanoke College						
Sweet Briar College	71	65	12/1	12/15		
University of Richmond	275	150	11/15 1/15	12/15 2/15		
University of Virginia	2300	977	11/1	12/1		
University of Virginia's College at Wise					12/1	12/15
Virginia Military Institute	273	166	11/15	12/15		
Virginia Polytechnic Institute and State University	2037	1134	11/1	12/15		
Washington and Lee University	333	173	11/15 1/3	12/22 2/1		
Washington						
Gonzaga University					11/15	1/15
Seattle Pacific University					11/15	1/6
University of Puget Sound	145	132	11/15 12/15	12/15 1/15		
Whitman College	197	140	11/15 1/1	12/15 1/23		
Whitworth College					12/1	12/20
West Virginia						
Shepherd University					11/15	12/15
Wisconsin						
Beloit College					12/15	1/15
Lawrence University	466	378	11/15	12/1	12/1	1/15
St. Norbert College			12/1	12/15		
Canada						
Acadia University						
Simon Fraser University						
Lebanon						
American University of Beirut					11/30	1/31
Switzerland						
Franklin College: Switzerland	151	137			12/1	1/15

Wait list table

Students who are wait listed have met a college's admission requirements, but will only be offered a place in the freshman class if space becomes available. The table that follows shows wait list outcomes for students who applied for admission to the freshman class of 2005-2006 at 283 colleges, which are listed alphabetically by state.

Institution	Total applied	Number placed on wait list	Number accepting place on wait list	Number on wait list admitted
Alabama				
Tuskegee University	2037	0		
Arkansas				
Hendrix College	1086	10	2	0
California				
Azusa Pacific University	3127	383	184	56
California Institute of Technology	2760	379	247	0
California Institute of the Arts	2979	63	39	3
Chapman University	3862	264	33	27
Claremont McKenna College	3734	562	162	24
Deep Springs College	140	4	4	3
Harvey Mudd College	1899			0
Pepperdine University	7307	834	359	31
Pitzer College	3251	704	541	0
Santa Clara University	8904	1856	505	351
Scripps College	1836	428	181	1
Sonoma State University	10597	0		
St. Mary's College of California	3381	115	70	40
Thomas Aquinas College	196	57	54	37
University of Redlands	3395	25	25	3
University of San Diego	7862	548	180	4
University of the Pacific	5869	130	85	60
Westmont College	1813	249	83	69
Colorado				
Colorado College	4089	770	304	11
University of Colorado at Boulder	17111			3
University of Denver	4038	123	64	14
Connecticut				
Connecticut College	4183	1061	403	80
Eastern Connecticut State University	3066	150	100	50
Fairfield University	6895	918	458	64
Quinnipiac University	11397	1800	980	180
Trinity College	5744	1259	367	49
University of Connecticut	18608	3287	1272	325
Wesleyan University	6879	1200	600	90
Delaware				
University of Delaware	21617	3176	1248	142

Institution	Total applied	Number placed on wait list	Number accepting place on wait list	Number on wait list admitted
District of Columbia				
George Washington University	19406	2082	634	97
Georgetown University	15285	1832	1100	65
University of the District of Columbia	2026	753	726	489
Florida				
Eckerd College	2740	130	42	42
Flagler College		439	211	31
Florida State University	22450	300	0	0
New College of Florida	684	32	31	0
Rollins College	2958	350	175	40
University of Central Florida	20265	400	380	0
Georgia				
Agnes Scott College	1526	51	13	2
Emory University	12011	1500	800	25
Georgia Institute of Technology	9172	426	208	102
Mercer University	3108	20	20	10
North Georgia College & State University	2081	64	29	29
University of Georgia	12326	493	13	13
Illinois				
Bradley University	4218	118	60	9
Illinois State University	10414	476	456	31
Illinois Wesleyan University	2770	430	55	44
Knox College	1771	69	29	11
Lake Forest College	2195	46	27	22
Northwestern University	16221	1272	735	12
University of Chicago	9011	1545	758	42
University of Illinois at Urbana-Champaign	18987	503	319	0
University of Illinois: Springfield	493	21	19	14
Indiana				
Hanover College	1680	54	51	38
St. Mary-of-the-Woods College	268	268	163	80
University of Indianapolis	2884	15	15	8
University of Notre Dame	11317	787	521	98
Wabash College	1358	71	58	1
Iowa				
Allen College	51	14	14	0
Cornell College	1653	65	65	11
Grinnell College	3121	598	225	30
Northeast Iowa Community College	1161	285	285	285
St. Luke's College	226	18	18	6
University of Iowa	13241	149	149	142
Kansas				
University of Kansas		202	202	141
Kentucky				
Alice Lloyd College	1014	42	42	30
Asbury College	797	0		
Centre College	1989	112	33	10

Institution	Total applied	Number placed on wait list	Number accepting place on wait list	Number on wait list admitted
Louisiana				
Nicholls State University	2339	2339	1566	1566
Maine				
Colby College	3874	624	320	1
College of the Atlantic	284	3	1	1
Husson College	677	0		
New England School of Communications	310	21	18	3
University of Maine	5702	68	30	26
University of New England	2055	17	17	2
Maryland				
Goucher College	2976	266	61	11
Johns Hopkins University	11274	2085	1025	4
Loyola College in Maryland	10391	1682	763	484
McDaniel College	2256	49	25	10
St. Mary's College of Maryland	2200	213	72	6
Towson University	11746	2718	2718	921
United States Naval Academy	11259	100	70	15
University of Maryland: Baltimore County	5229	100	100	25
University of Maryland: College Park	22428	3208	3103	2032
Massachusetts				
Amherst College	6273	1162	506	0
Art Institute of Boston at Lesley University	1351	10	6	3
Assumption College	3357	415	136	55
Bentley College	5802	923	411	5
Boston College	23823	5000	2000	225
Boston University	31431	3551	1824	9
Brandeis University	7343	964	408	74
Bristol Community College		105	105	40
Clark University	4463	122	31	8
College of the Holy Cross	4744	713	274	29
Curry College	2975	25	20	5
Emerson College	5008	1033	440	0
Endicott College	3081	407	147	2
Hampshire College	2243	313	259	0
Harvard College	22796			23
Lesley University	1351	18	6	3
Massachusetts College of Art	1210	58	57	22
Massachusetts College of Pharmacy and Health Sciences	1200	122	47	42
Massachusetts Institute of Technology	10440	469	401	0
Merrimack College	3413	406	189	130
Mount Holyoke College	2924	334	188	0
Northeastern University	25467	5406	2079	0
Simmons College	2303	17	13	1
Smith College	3408		196	120
Stonehill College	4848	660	364	183
Suffolk University	6229	223	223	177
University of Massachusetts Amherst	20205	329	222	86
Wellesley College	4347	886	431	45
Wentworth Institute of Technology	3040	2	2	0

Institution	Total applied	Number placed on wait list	Number accepting place on wait list	Number on wait list admitted
Wheaton College	3697	736	229	2
Williams College	5822	1123	744	23
Michigan				
Grand Valley State University	13255	364	364	57
Hope College	2674	331	169	58
Kalamazoo College	1669	31	31	14
Michigan State University	21844	945	50	42
Minnesota				
Bethel University	1636	25	24	0
Carleton College	5036	1430	310	0
College of St. Benedict	1472	40	35	15
Dakota County Technical College	2651	386	350	350
Hamline University	1806	25	25	10
Macalester College	4317	263	139	18
St. John's University	1167	0		
St. Olaf College	2991	88	72	17
University of St. Thomas	4189	0		
Missouri				
College of the Ozarks	2385	270	270	0
Metro Business College: Jefferson City	55	16	14	4
Washington University in St. Louis	21515			144
Nebraska				
Creighton University	3435	85	75	10
Metropolitan Community College				550
New Hampshire				
Dartmouth College	12756	1200	700	16
Rivier College	1132	26	26	8
St. Anselm College	3258	363	302	150
New Jersey				
Drew University	3802	405	358	144
New Jersey Institute of Technology	2562	21	11	11
Ramapo College of New Jersey	4507	299	44	31
Richard Stockton College of New Jersey	3448	400	345	62
Rowan University	7303	200	85	50
Seton Hall University	4982	899	653	633
Stevens Institute of Technology	2418	269	251	27
The College of New Jersey	7300	502	426	133
New York				
Bard College	4142	311	105	0
Barnard College	4431	1046	664	11
Clarkson University	2405	16	1	1
Cochran School of Nursing-St. John's Riverside Hospital		25	25	16
Colgate University	8008	1159	503	34
Columbia University: Columbia College	15793	2006	796	54
Columbia University: Fu Foundation School of Engineering and Applied Science	2332	161	98	8
Columbia University: School of General Studies	254	2	2	0

Institution	Total applied	Number placed on wait list	Number accepting place on wait list	Number on wait list admitted
Cooper Union for the Advancement of Science and Art	2301	45	39	2
Cornell University	24452	2643	1544	209
Daemen College	1609	269	269	71
Elmira College	1966	73	69	9
Hamilton College	4189	680	184	0
Hofstra University	15981	1649	677	227
Iona College	4802	179	128	78
Juilliard School	2523	45	43	11
King's College	348	10	7	4
Le Moyne College	2946	91	50	23
Mannes College The New School for Music	371	15	6	6
Maria College	258	35	35	10
Marist College	7077	500	400	60
Mohawk Valley Community College	3445	6	6	6
Nazareth College of Rochester	1972	84	26	26
Phillips Beth Israel School of Nursing	50	20	18	5
Pratt Institute	3794	165	120	15
Rochester Institute of Technology	9384	150	125	25
Sarah Lawrence College	2634	500	221	0
School of Visual Arts	2130	10	10	2
Siena College	4326	388	203	53
Skidmore College	6055	1273	391	19
St. Lawrence University	2989	227	166	25
State University of New York College at Geneseo	10448	957	957	14
State University of New York College at Oneonta	10900	224	198	5
State University of New York College at Potsdam	3423	64	64	27
State University of New York College of Environmental Science and Forestry	921	33	33	12
State University of New York at Albany	16725	304	119	0
State University of New York at Binghamton	21658	2711	826	9
State University of New York at Buffalo	18391	785	372	372
Syracuse University	16260	1224	525	0
Union College	4230	759	208	26
University of Rochester	11272	1091	333	29
Utica College	2497	88	18	11
Vassar College	6314	961	430	36
Wagner College	2858	112	73	3
North Carolina				
Elon University	9065	2251	1302	24
Guilford College	2492	115	0	0
University of North Carolina at Chapel Hill	18414	1689	1585	7
University of North Carolina at Wilmington	8820	1000	464	103
Ohio				
College of Wooster	2542	147	31	6
Denison University	5144	391	134	0
Kenyon College	3929	948	322	7
Mercy College of Northwest Ohio	297	18	18	17
Oberlin College	6587	891	640	33

Institution	Total applied	Number placed on wait list	Number accepting place on wait list	Number on wait list admitted
Ohio State University: Columbus Campus	17566	404	134	0
Ohio Wesleyan University	2929	20	18	1
University of Dayton	8675	296	69	4
Xavier University	5468	599	130	47
Oklahoma				
University of Oklahoma	7388	950	950	544
University of Tulsa	2687	272	272	95
Oregon				
Lewis & Clark College	4196	567	170	43
Linfield College	2131	15	15	0
Reed College	2646	775	775	15
University of Portland	3026	145	145	102
Willamette University	2790	182	132	23
Pennsylvania				
Allegheny College	3540	352	352	32
Bloomsburg University of Pennsylvania	8237	71	71	0
Bryn Mawr College	1938	385	209	16
Bucknell University	8306	2375	860	101
Cabrini College	2535	50	50	15
Dickinson College	4784	278	278	20
Drexel University	12093	891	478	379
Franklin & Marshall College	4227	1255	1028	25
Gettysburg College	5097			51
Grove City College	2077	944	246	32
Haverford College	3112	610	169	28
Hussian School of Art	101	0		
Juniata College	1745	72	60	2
Lafayette College	5728	1643	650	67
Lebanon Valley College	2006	15	15	10
Lehigh University	10501	1984	752	0
Manor College		10	10	0
Millersville University of Pennsylvania	6413	905	403	7
Moravian College	1890			17
Muhlenberg College	4217	1539	465	41
Pennsylvania College of Technology	2793	1030	1030	377
Slippery Rock University of Pennsylvania	4360	1541	895	376
St. Joseph's University	9021	2932	1227	0
Susquehanna University	2217	89	9	7
Swarthmore College	4085	959	358	18
University of Pennsylvania	18824	1296	584	35
University of Pittsburgh	18153	226	64	24
University of Scranton	6343	963	491	128
University of the Arts	2283	49	30	12
University of the Sciences in Philadelphia	2897	222	219	0
Ursinus College	1776	26	26	0
Villanova University	10394	2831	1525	116
Washington and Jefferson College	4477	157	64	17
West Chester University of Pennsylvania	11013	850	307	30
Rhode Island				
Bryant University	4214	664	310	78

Institution	Total applied	Number placed on wait list	Number accepting place on wait list	Number on wait list admitted
Providence College	8237	1647	720	355
Roger Williams University	6658	174	71	1
Salve Regina University	4555	498	498	24
South Carolina				
College of Charleston	8217	244	106	17
Furman University	4007	699	140	3
Wofford College	1871	134	26	7
Tennessee				
Rhodes College	3695	188	0	81
University of the South	2027	203	95	2
Vanderbilt University	11663	1361	541	50
Texas				
Southern Methodist University	6981	715	423	76
Southwestern University	1760	88	24	17
St. Edward's University	2217	258	258	49
Texas Christian University	8155	583	284	148
Texas Lutheran University	1147	0		
Trinity University	3864	210	55	0
Vermont				
Bennington College	723	16	14	4
Middlebury College	5254	950	579	38
St. Michael's College	2924	265	130	0
University of Vermont	13015	924	396	1
Vermont Technical College	742	125	125	20
Virginia				
Christendom College	249	15	12	0
College of William and Mary	10610	1812	859	113
Hollins University	686	10	5	2
James Madison University	16388	1179	653	4
Randolph-Macon College	1727	49	18	9
Roanoke College	3016	172	42	3
Shenandoah University	1479	5	2	0
University of Mary Washington	4635	601	248	102
University of Richmond	5778	1092	569	267
University of Virginia	15657	3247	1848	83
Virginia Military Institute	1811	68	46	31
Virginia Polytechnic Institute and State University	17681	1150	625	0
Washington and Lee University	3950	912	382	97
Washington				
Gonzaga University	4328	462	252	58
Seattle University	4339	440	440	3
University of Puget Sound	4711	359	81	54
Western Washington University	8645	227	116	3
Whitman College	2544	343	144	47
Whitworth College	2062	126	126	126
Wisconsin				
Bellin College of Nursing	75	2	2	2
Beloit College	2054	99	31	7

Institution	Total applied	Number placed on wait list	Number accepting place on wait list	Number on wait list admitted
Lawrence University	2060	60	41	2
Marquette University	10348	1516	522	334
University of Wisconsin-Eau Claire	7134	103	91	54
University of Wisconsin-Green Bay	3350	211	211	25
University of Wisconsin-La Crosse	6347	385	385	330
Western Wisconsin Technical College		149	149	149

Indexes

College type

Liberal arts colleges

Four-year

Westminster College
Wilson College
York College of Pennsylvania

Puerto Rico
Caribbean University
Inter American University of Puerto Rico
  Aguadilla Campus
  Arecibo Campus
Universidad Adventista de las Antillas
Universidad del Este
Universidad Metropolitana
University of Puerto Rico
  Aguadilla
  Cayey University College
  Humacao
University of the Sacred Heart

Rhode Island
Brown University
Bryant University
Providence College
Rhode Island College
Roger Williams University
Salve Regina University

South Carolina
Allen University
Anderson University
Benedict College
Charleston Southern University
Claflin University
Coker College
College of Charleston
Columbia College
Converse College
Erskine College
Francis Marion University
Furman University
Lander University
Limestone College
Morris College
Newberry College
North Greenville College
Presbyterian College
Southern Wesleyan University
University of South Carolina
  Aiken
  Beaufort
Voorhees College
Wofford College

South Dakota
Augustana College
Black Hills State University
Dakota Wesleyan University
Mount Marty College
Northern State University
Oglala Lakota College
Sinte Gleska University
University of Sioux Falls

Tennessee
Aquinas College
Austin Peay State University
Bethel College
Bryan College
Carson-Newman College
Crichton College
Cumberland University
Fisk University
Freed-Hardeman University
King College
Lambuth University
Lane College
Lee University
LeMoyne-Owen College
Lincoln Memorial University
Lipscomb University
Martin Methodist College
Maryville College
Milligan College
Rhodes College
South College
Southern Adventist University
Tennessee Wesleyan College
Trevecca Nazarene University
Tusculum College
Union University
Williamson Christian College

Texas
Austin College
College of Saint Thomas More
Concordia University at Austin
East Texas Baptist University
Houston Baptist University
Howard Payne University
Huston-Tillotson College
Jarvis Christian College
Lubbock Christian University
McMurry University
Midwestern State University
Paul Quinn College
St. Edward's University
Schreiner University
Southwestern Adventist University
Southwestern Christian College
Southwestern University
Texas College
Texas Lutheran University
Trinity University
University of Dallas
University of North Texas
University of St. Thomas
University of the Incarnate Word
Wayland Baptist University
Wiley College

Utah
Stevens-Henager College
Westminster College

Vermont
Bennington College
Burlington College
Castleton State College
Champlain College
College of St. Joseph in Vermont
Goddard College
Green Mountain College
Johnson State College
Lyndon State College
Marlboro College
Middlebury College
St. Michael's College
Southern Vermont College
Sterling College

Virginia
Averett University
Bluefield College
Bridgewater College
Christendom College
Christopher Newport University
Eastern Mennonite University
Emory & Henry College
Ferrum College
Hampden-Sydney College
Hollins University
Lynchburg College
Mary Baldwin College
Randolph-Macon College
Randolph-Macon Woman's College
Roanoke College
St. Paul's College
Southern Virginia University
Sweet Briar College
University of Mary Washington
University of Richmond
University of Virginia's College at Wise
Virginia Intermont College
Virginia Military Institute
Virginia Union University
Virginia Wesleyan College
Washington and Lee University

Washington
Antioch University Seattle
Evergreen State College
Gonzaga University
Henry Cogswell College
Heritage University
Northwest University
Saint Martin's University
Trinity Lutheran College
University of Puget Sound
Walla Walla College
Whitman College
Whitworth College

West Virginia
Alderson-Broaddus College
American Public University
Bethany College
Davis and Elkins College
Fairmont State University
Glenville State College
Ohio Valley University
Salem International University
University of Charleston
West Liberty State College
West Virginia State University
West Virginia Wesleyan College
Wheeling Jesuit University

Wisconsin
Alverno College
Beloit College
Cardinal Stritch University
Carroll College
Carthage College
Concordia University Wisconsin
Edgewood College
Lakeland College
Lawrence University
Marian College of Fond du Lac
Mount Mary College
Northland College
Ripon College
St. Norbert College
Silver Lake College
University of Wisconsin
  Green Bay
  Superior
Viterbo University
Wisconsin Lutheran College

France
American University of Paris

Switzerland
Franklin College: Switzerland

United Kingdom
Richmond, The American International University in London

Two-year

Alabama
Calhoun Community College

Arkansas
Arkansas State University: Newport

California
Deep Springs College
Feather River College
Marymount College

Colorado
Colorado Mountain College
  Alpine Campus
  Spring Valley Campus
  Timberline Campus

Georgia
Andrew College
Georgia Highlands College
Georgia Perimeter College
Oxford College of Emory University
Waycross College
Young Harris College

Hawaii
Hawaii Tokai International College
TransPacific Hawaii College

Illinois
Springfield College in Illinois

Indiana
Ancilla College

Kansas
Donnelly College

Massachusetts
Dean College
Fisher College

Michigan
Montcalm Community College

Missouri
Cottey College
Crowder College

Nebraska
Southeast Community College
  Beatrice Campus

New Jersey
Assumption College for Sisters

New York
State University of New York
  College of Technology at Alfred
Villa Maria College of Buffalo

Ohio
Chatfield College

Pennsylvania
University of Pittsburgh
  Titusville

Puerto Rico
Colegio de las Ciencias Artes y Television

South Carolina
Spartanburg Methodist College

Tennessee
Hiwassee College

Texas
Alvin Community College
Eastfield College
Jacksonville College
Lamar State College at Orange
Lon Morris College

Vermont
Landmark College

Virginia
Richard Bland College

Washington
Olympic College

Wisconsin
University of Wisconsin
  Baraboo/Sauk County
  Fox Valley
  Manitowoc
  Marinette
  Richland
  Rock County
  Washington County

Northern Mariana Islands
Northern Marianas College

Micronesia
College of Micronesia-FSM

Canada
Humber College

Upper-division colleges

Alabama
Athens State University
United States Sports Academy

Arizona
International Import-Export

California
Alliant International University
Antioch Southern California
  Antioch University Los Angeles
  Antioch University Santa Barbara
California Institute of Integral Studies
Dominican School of Philosophy and Theology
International Technological University
Loma Linda University
Monterey Institute of International Studies
Pacific Oaks College
Samuel Merritt College

Colorado
Jones International University

Georgia
Medical College of Georgia

Hawaii
University of Hawaii
  West Oahu

Illinois
Governors State University
Lakeview College of Nursing
Rosalind Franklin University of Medicine and Science
Rush University
Saint Anthony College of Nursing
St. Francis Medical Center College of Nursing
St. John's College
West Suburban College of Nursing

Kansas
University of Kansas Medical Center

Louisiana
Louisiana State University Health Sciences Center

Maryland
University of Baltimore
University of Maryland
  Baltimore

Michigan
Walsh College of Accountancy and Business Administration

Minnesota
Walden University

Mississippi
University of Mississippi Medical Center

Missouri
St. Luke's College

Nebraska
University of Nebraska
  Medical Center

New Jersey
University of Medicine and Dentistry of New Jersey
  School of Health Related Professions

New York
Columbia University
  School of Nursing
State University of New York
  Downstate Medical Center
  Upstate Medical University

North Dakota
Medcenter One College of Nursing

Oregon
Oregon Health & Science University

Pennsylvania
Thomas Jefferson University: College of Health Professions

Puerto Rico
Carlos Albizu University: San Juan

South Carolina
Medical University of South Carolina

Tennessee
University of Tennessee Health Science Center

Texas
Amberton University
Austin Graduate School of Theology
Texas A&M University
  Baylor College of Dentistry
  Texarkana
University of Houston
  Clear Lake
  Victoria
University of Texas
  Health Science Center at Houston
  Health Science Center at San Antonio
  Medical Branch at Galveston
  Southwestern Medical Center at Dallas

Virginia
Catholic Distance University

Washington
Antioch University Seattle
Bastyr University

Agricultural and technical colleges

Four-year

Alabama Agricultural and Mechanical University, AL
Alcorn State University, MS
American Sentinel University, AL
Art Institute
  of Colorado, CO
  of Phoenix, AZ
  of Pittsburgh, PA
Art Institute of Fort Lauderdale, FL
Art Institute of Seattle, WA
Baker College
  of Auburn Hills, MI
  of Clinton Township, MI
  of Flint, MI
  of Jackson, MI
  of Muskegon, MI
  of Owosso, MI
  of Port Huron, MI
Bluefield State College, WV
Boise State University, ID
Briarcliffe College, NY
Brown College, MN
Central Pennsylvania College, PA
Charter College, AK
City College, FL
City University of New York
  New York City College of Technology, NY
Clayton State University, GA
Coleman College, CA
College America: Colorado Springs, CO
College America: Fort Collins, CO
College of Court Reporting, IN
Collins College, AZ
Colorado Technical University, CO
Columbia College, PR
Columbia College: Hollywood, CA
Dalton State College, GA
Daniel Webster College, NH
Design Institute of San Diego, CA
DeVry Institute of Technology
  New York, NY
ECPI College of Technology, VA
ECPI Technical College
  Glen Allen, VA
Electronic Data Processing College of Puerto Rico, PR
Gibbs College, VA
Globe Institute of Technology, NY
Hamilton College, IA
Hamilton College
  Cedar Falls, IA
  Mason City, IA
Hamilton Technical College, IA
Herzing College, LA
Herzing College, AL
Herzing College, GA
Herzing College, WI
Herzing College, FL
Hickey College, MO
Institute of Computer Technology, CA
International Academy of Design and Technology: Chicago, IL
International Academy of Design and Technology: Detroit, MI
International Academy of Design and Technology: Henderson, NV
International Academy of Design and Technology: Orlando, FL
International Academy of Design and Technology: Schaumburg, IL
International Academy of Design and Technology: Tampa, FL
ITT Technical Institute
  Albuquerque, NM
  Anaheim, CA
  Arnold, MO
  Birmingham, AL
  Boise, ID
  Burr Ridge, IL
  Earth City, MO
  Everett, WA
  Fort Wayne, IN
  Ft. Lauderdale, FL
  Green Bay, WI
  Greenfield, WI
  Greenville, SC
  Henderson, NV
  Indianapolis, IN
  Jacksonville, FL
  Knoxville, TN
  Lathrop, CA
  Little Rock, AR
  Louisville, KY
  Matteson, IL
  Memphis, TN
  Miami, FL
  Mount Prospect, IL
  Murray, UT
  Nashville, TN
  Norfolk, VA
  Omaha, NE
  Oxnard, CA
  Portland, OR
  Rancho Cordova, CA
  Richmond, VA
  St. Rose, LA
  San Bernardino, CA
  San Diego, CA
  Seattle, WA
  Spokane, WA
  Sylmar, CA
  Tampa, FL
  Thornton, CO
  Torrance, CA
  Tucson, AZ
  West Covina, CA
ITT Technical Institute: Chantilly, VA
ITT Technical Institute: Duluth, GA
ITT Technical Institute: Lake Mary, FL
ITT Technical Institute: Springfield, VA
ITT Technical Institute: Tempe, AZ
Kansas City College of Legal Studies, MO
Kansas State University, KS
Lewis-Clark State College, ID
Louisiana State University and Agricultural and Mechanical College, LA
Maine Maritime Academy, ME
Metropolitan College of Court Reporting, AZ
Miller-Motte Technical College, NC
Minnesota School of Business, MN
Missouri Technical School, MO
Montana State University
  Billings, MT
Montana Tech of the University of Montana, MT
Mt. Sierra College, CA
National American University
  Rapid City, SD
National Education Center
  Spartan School of Aeronautics, OK
Neumont University, UT
New England Institute of Art, MA
New England Institute of Technology, RI
North Carolina Agricultural and Technical State University, NC
Oklahoma Panhandle State University, OK
Peirce College, PA
Pennsylvania College of Technology, PA
Pioneer Pacific College, OR
Platt College
  Ontario, CA
  San Diego, CA
Potomac College, DC
Ranken Technical College, MO
Remington College
  Jacksonville, FL
Remington College: Largo, FL
Remington College: Tampa, FL
Robert Morris College: Chicago, IL
Silicon Valley College
  Western Career College: Emeryville, CA
Southern California Institute of Architecture, CA
Southwest Minnesota State University, MN
State University of New York
  Farmingdale, NY
Sterling College, VT
Stevens-Henager College of Business, UT
Tucson Design College, AZ
University of Advancing Technology, AZ
University of Arkansas
  Monticello, AR
University of Puerto Rico
  Aguadilla, PR
  Bayamon University College, PR
  Mayaguez, PR
  Utuado, PR
Utah Valley State College, UT
Vaughn College of Aeronautics and Technology, NY
Vermont Technical College, VT
Virginia College, AL
Virginia College at Huntsville, AL
Wentworth Institute of Technology, MA
West Virginia University Institute of Technology, WV
Westwood College, CA
Westwood College - Atlanta Midtown, GA
Westwood College - Chicago Loop, IL
Westwood College - DuPage, IL
Westwood College of Technology, CO
Westwood College of Technology
  Inland Empire, CA
  O'Hare, IL
  River Oaks, IL
  South, CO
Westwood College: Long Beach, CA
Williamson Free School of Mechanical Trades, PA
Woodbury College, VT
World College, VA

Two-year

Abraham Baldwin Agricultural College, GA
Academy College, MN
Academy of Court Reporting, OH
Advanced Technology Institute, VA
Aiken Technical College, SC
Albany Technical College, GA
Albuquerque Technical-Vocational Institute, NM
Alexandria Technical College, MN
Allied Medical and Technical Institute, PA
Anoka Technical College, MN
Antonelli College, OH
Antonelli College
  Hattiesburg, MS
  Jackson, MS
Arizona Automotive Institute, AZ
Arkansas State University
  Mountain Home, AR
Art Institute
  of New York City, NY
Asheville-Buncombe Technical Community College, NC
Asnuntuck Community College, CT
Athens Technical College, GA
ATI Career Training Center, TX
ATI Career Training Center, FL
  Ft. Lauderdale, FL
ATI College of Health, FL
Atlanta Technical College, GA
ATS Institute of Technology, OH
Augusta Technical Institute, GA
Austin Business College, TX
Aviation Institute of Maintenance: Indianapolis, IN
Bainbridge College, GA
Bates Technical College, WA
Baton Rouge School of Computers, LA
Bel-Rea Institute of Animal Technology, CO
Bellingham Technical College, WA
Belmont Technical College, OH
Benjamin Franklin Institute of Technology, MA
Berean Institute, PA
Berks Technical Institute, PA
Big Sandy Community and Technical College, KY
Black River Technical College, AR
Blackhawk Technical College, WI
Bluegrass Community and Technical College, KY
Bolivar Technical College, MO
Bradford School, OH
Bradley Academy for the Visual Arts, PA
Bramson ORT College, NY
Branson Technical College, MO
Brooks College, CA
Brooks College: Sunnyvale, CA
Brown Mackie College: Atlanta, GA
Brown Mackie College: Louisville, KY
Brown Mackie College: South Bend, IN
Bryant & Stratton College: Cleveland, OH
Business Institute of Pennsylvania, PA
Caldwell Community College and Technical Institute, NC
California Design College, CA
Cambria-Rowe Business College: Indiana, PA
Cambridge College, CO
Camelot College, LA
Capital Community College, CT
Career College of Northern Nevada, NV
CEI College
  Maric College: Panorama City, CA
Central Carolina Technical College, SC
Central Community College, NE
Central Florida College, FL
Central Georgia Technical College, GA
Central Lakes College, MN
Central Maine Community College, ME
Central Ohio Technical College, OH
Central Texas College, TX
Century Community and Technical College, MN
Chattahoochee Technical College, GA
Chattanooga State Technical Community College, TN
CHI Institute: Broomall, PA
CHI Institute: Southampton, PA
Chippewa Valley Technical College, WI
Cincinnati State Technical and Community College, OH
Cleveland Institute of Electronics, OH
Clover Park Technical College, WA
Colegio de las Ciencias Artes y Television, PR
Coleman College
  San Marcos, CA
College of Business and Technology: Flagler, FL
College of Oceaneering, CA
College of the Mainland, TX
College of the Sequoias, CA
CollegeAmerica-Denver, CO
Colorado School of Trades, CO
Columbus State Community College, OH
Columbus Technical College, GA
Commonwealth Technical Institute, PA
Community College of the Air Force, AL
Corinthian Schools: National Institute of Technology, WV
Court Reporting Institute of Dallas, TX
Court Reporting Institute of Houston, TX
Cowley County Community College, KS
Creative Center, NE
Crownpoint Institute of Technology, NM
Dakota County Technical College, MN

Daytona Beach Community College, FL
Dean Institute of Technology, PA
DeKalb Technical College, GA
Delaware Technical and Community College
- Owens Campus, DE
- Stanton/Wilmington Campus, DE
- Terry Campus, DE

Delta College of Arts & Technology, LA
Delta School of Business & Technology, LA
Denmark Technical College, SC
Denver Automotive & Diesel College, CO
Dixie State College of Utah, UT
Dodge City Community College, KS
DuBois Business College, PA
Dunwoody College of Technology, MN
Durham Technical Community College, NC
Eastern Idaho Technical College, ID
Eastern Maine Community College, ME
Eastern West Virginia Community and Technical College, WV
ECPI Technical College, VA
ECPI Technical College, NC
ECPI Technical College: Roanoke, VA
Electronic Computer Programming College, TN
Elizabethtown Community and Technical College, KY
Elmira Business Institute, NY
Elmira Business Institute: Vestal, NY
Erie Institute of Technology, PA
ETI Technical College of Niles, OH
Everest College, AZ
Everest College: Arlington, TX
Everest College: Dallas, TX
Fayetteville Technical Community College, NC
Florence-Darlington Technical College, SC
Florida Career College: Hialeah, FL
Florida Career College: Miami, FL
Florida Career College: Pembroke Pines, FL
Florida Career College: West Palm Beach, FL
Florida Technical College, FL
Florida Technical College
- Deland, FL
- Jacksonville, FL

Forsyth Technical Community College, NC
Fountainhead College of Technology, TN
Fox College, IL
Fox Valley Technical College, WI
Full Sail Real World Education, FL
Fullerton College, CA
Gallipolis Career College, OH
Gateway Community College, AZ
Gateway Technical College, WI
George C. Wallace State Community College
- Selma, AL

Grayson County College, TX
Greenville Technical College, SC
Gretna Career College, LA
Griffin Technical College, GA
Guam Community College, GU
Gulf Coast College, FL
Gupton Jones College of Funeral Service, GA
Gwinnett Technical College, GA
Hallmark Institute of Aeronautics, TX
Hallmark Institute of Technology, TX
Hamilton College: Omaha, NE
Hawkeye Community College, IA
Haywood Community College, NC
Heald College
- Fresno, CA
- Hayward, CA
- Honolulu, HI
- Rancho Cordova, CA

Helena College of Technology of the University of Montana, MT
Hennepin Technical College, MN
Heritage Institute: Jacksonville, FL
Herzing College
- Minneapolis Drafting School Division of , MN

Hibbing Community College, MN
High-Tech Institute, CA
High-Tech Institute, TN
High-Tech Institute, FL
High-Tech Institute, MO
High-Tech Institute, NV
High-Tech Institute, MN
High-Tech Institute, AZ
High-Tech Institute: Atlanta, GA
Hocking Technical College, OH
Hondros College, OH
Horry-Georgetown Technical College, SC
Huertas Junior College, PR
Humber College, CN
Hussian School of Art, PA
Institute of Design and Construction, NY
IntelliTec College, CO
IntelliTec College: Grand Junction, CO
International Academy of Design and Technology: Pittsburgh, PA
International College of Broadcasting, OH
International Junior College of Business and Technology, PR
Iowa Western Community College, IA
Island Drafting and Technical Institute, NY
ITI Technical College, LA
ITT Technical Institute
- Albany, NY
- Arlington, TX
- Austin, TX
- Bensalem, PA
- Dayton, OH
- Getzville, NY
- Grand Rapids, MI
- Houston, TX
- Houston North, TX
- Houston South, TX
- Liverpool, NY
- Mechanicsburg, PA
- Monroeville, PA
- Norwood, OH
- Norwood, MA
- Pittsburgh, PA
- Richardson, TX
- San Antonio, TX
- Strongsville, OH
- Troy, MI
- Woburn, MA
- Youngstown, OH

ITT Technical Institute: Eden Prairie, MN
J. F. Drake State Technical College, AL
James A. Rhodes State College, OH
Jefferson College, MO
Jefferson Community College, KY
Jefferson Community College, OH
JNA Institute of Culinary Arts, PA
Johnson College, PA
Johnston Community College, NC
Keiser College, FL
Kennebec Valley Community College, ME
Key College, FL
King's College, NC
Lake Area Technical Institute, SD
Lake Superior College, MN
Lake Washington Technical College, WA
Lakeshore Technical College, WI
Lamar State College at Port Arthur, TX
Lamson College, AZ
Laurel Business Institute, PA
Le Cordon Bleu College of Culinary Arts, GA
Le Cordon Bleu College of Culinary Arts, MN
Lehigh Valley College, PA
Lincoln Technical Institute, PA
Lincoln Technical Institute, IN
Lincoln Technical Institute: Philadelphia, PA
Linn State Technical College, MO
Long Technical College, AZ
Los Angeles Trade and Technical College, CA
Louisville Technical Institute, KY
Luna Community College, NM
Madison Area Technical College, WI
Manhattan Area Technical College, KS
Maric College
- Vista, CA

Maric College: Sacramento, CA
Marion Technical College, OH
Martin Community College, NC
Maysville Community College, KY
McCann School of Business
- Pottsville, PA
- Sunbury, PA

McDowell Technical Community College, NC
Mesabi Range Community and Technical College, MN
Mesalands Community College, NM
Metropolitan Career Center, PA
Metropolitan Career Center Computer Technology Institute, PA
Metropolitan Community College, NE
Mid-Plains Community College Area, NE
Mid-State Technical College, WI
Middle Georgia Technical College, GA
Midlands Technical College, SC
Miller-Motte Technical College, SC
Miller-Motte Technical College: Chattanooga, TN
Miller-Motte Technical College: Lynchburg, VA
Milwaukee Area Technical College, WI
Minneapolis Business College, MN
Minneapolis Community and Technical College, MN
Minnesota State College - Southeast Technical, MN
Minnesota State Community and Technical College - Fergus Falls, MN
Minnesota West Community and Technical College: Worthington Campus, MN
Missouri College, MO
Mitchell Technical Institute, SD
Montana State University
- College of Technology-Great Falls, MT

Moraine Park Technical College, WI
Morrison Institute of Technology, IL
Mountain State College, WV
MTI College, CA
MTI College of Business and Technology, TX
MTI College of Business and Technology, TX
Nashville Auto-Diesel College, TN
Nashville State Community College, TN
National College of Business & Technology
- Tennessee, TN

National College of Business & Technology: Bayamon, PR
National College of Business & Technology: Dayton, OH
National College of Business & Technology: Knoxville, TN
National Institute of Technology, CA
National Institute of Technology, OH
Naugatuck Valley Community College, CT
Nebraska College of Technical Agriculture, NE
New Castle School of Trades, PA
New England Institute of Technology, FL
New Hampshire Community Technical College
- Berlin, NH
- Claremont, NH
- Manchester, NH
- Nashua, NH
- Stratham, NH

New Hampshire Technical Institute, NH
New Mexico Junior College, NM
New River Community and Technical College, WV
New York Career Institute, NY
Nicolet Area Technical College, WI
North Arkansas College, AR
North Central Industrial Technical Education Center, PA
North Central Kansas Technical College, KS
North Central State College, OH
North Dakota State College of Science, ND
North Metro Technical College, GA
Northcentral Technical College, WI
Northeast State Technical Community College, TN
Northeast Wisconsin Technical College, WI
Northeastern Technical College, SC
Northern Maine Community College, ME
Northland Community & Technical College, MN
Northwest Aviation College, WA
Northwest School of Wooden Boatbuilding, WA
Northwest State Community College, OH
Northwest Technical College, MN
Northwest Technical Institute, MN
Northwest-Shoals Community College, AL
Northwestern Business College, IL
Northwestern College, CA
Northwestern Connecticut Community College, CT
Northwestern Technical College, GA
Norwalk Community College, CT
Nossi College of Art, TN
Nunez Community College, LA
Ohio Institute of Photography and Technology, OH
Ohio State University
- Agricultural Technical Institute, OH

Ohio Technical College, OH
Ohio Valley College of Technology, OH
Oklahoma State University
- Oklahoma City, OK
- Okmulgee, OK

Orangeburg-Calhoun Technical College, SC
Orleans Technical Institute - Center City Campus, PA
Ouachita Technical College, AR
Ozarka College, AR
Ozarks Technical Community College, MO
Paducah Technical College, KY
Palau Community College, PW
Parks College: Aurora, CO
Pellissippi State Technical Community College, TN
Penn Commercial Business and Technical School, PA
Pennco Tech, PA
Pennsylvania Institute of Culinary Arts, PA
Pennsylvania Institute of Technology, PA
Pennsylvania School of Business, PA
Piedmont Technical College, SC
Pima Community College, AZ
Pine Technical College, MN
Pinnacle Career Institute: Kansas City, MO
Pioneer Pacific College: Springfield, OR
Pitt Community College, NC
Pittsburgh Institute of Aeronautics, PA
Pittsburgh Institute of Mortuary Science, PA
Pittsburgh Technical Institute, PA
Platt College
- Aurora, CO
- Los Angeles, CA
- Newport Beach, CA

Pratt Community College, KS
Prince Institute of Professional Studies, AL
Puerto Rico Tech Junior College, PR
Pulaski Technical College, AR
Quinebaug Valley Community College, CT
Rainy River Community College, MN
Ramirez College of Business and Technology, PR
Randolph Community College, NC
Refrigeration School, AZ
Remington College
- Baton Rouge, LA
- Cleveland, OH
- Colorado Springs, CO
- Dallas, TX
- Fort Worth, TX
- Houston, TX
- Little Rock, AR
- Memphis, TN
- Mobile, AL
- New Orleans, LA
- Tempe, AZ

Tables and Indexes

Remington College: Cleveland West, OH
Renton Technical College, WA
RETS Tech Center, OH
Ridgewater College, MN
Riverland Community College, MN
Robeson Community College, NC
Rochester Community and Technical College, MN
Rockford Business College, IL
Rosedale Technical Institute, PA
Rowan-Cabarrus Community College, NC
Sage College, CA
St. Cloud Technical College, MN
St. Paul College, MN
Salt Lake Community College, UT
San Jacinto College
  North, TX
Sanford-Brown College
  Colorado Technical University: North Kansas City, MO
  Hazelwood, MO
  St. Charles, MO
Savannah Technical College, GA
Sawyer College, IN
Sawyer College: Merrillville, IN
School of Advertising Art, OH
Schuylkill Institute of Business & Technology, PA
Scottsdale Culinary Institute, AZ
Shelton State Community College, AL
Silicon Valley College, CA
Silicon Valley College
  Western Career College: San Jose, CA
Sisseton Wahpeton College, SD
Somerset Community College, KY
South Central College, MN
South College, NC
South Florida Community College, FL
South Hills School of Business & Technology, PA
South Hills School of Business & Technology, PA
South Texas College, TX
Southeast Arkansas College, AR
Southeast Community College
  Milford Campus, NE
Southeast Technical Institute, SD
Southeastern Business College: Lancaster, OH
Southeastern Technical College, GA
Southern Arkansas University Tech, AR
Southern Maine Community College, ME
Southern Union State Community College, AL
Southwest Georgia Technical College, GA
Southwest Institute of Technology, TX
Southwest Tennessee Community College, TN
Southwest Wisconsin Technical College, WI
Southwestern College of Business
  Southwestern College: Franklin, OH
Southwestern Indian Polytechnic Institute, NM
Spartanburg Technical College, SC
Spencerian College: Lexington, KY
Springfield Technical Community College, MA
Stark State College of Technology, OH
State University of New York
  College of Agriculture and Technology at Cobleskill, NY
  College of Agriculture and Technology at Morrisville, NY
  College of Technology at Alfred, NY
  College of Technology at Canton, NY
  College of Technology at Delhi, NY
Stautzenberger College, OH
Stenotype Institute: Orlando, FL
Stevens-Henager College: Boise, ID
Taylor Business Institute, NY
Technical Career Institutes, NY
Technical College of the Lowcountry, SC
Technology Education College, OH
Terra State Community College, OH
TESST College of Technology
  Baltimore, MD
  Beltsville, MD
TESST College of Technology: Alexandria, VA
TESST College of Technology: Towson, MD
Texas County Technical Institute, MO
Texas State Technical College
  Harlingen, TX
  Waco, TX
  West Texas, TX
Texas State Technical College: Marshall, TX
Thaddeus Stevens College of Technology, PA
Thompson Institute, PA
Thompson Institute
  Philadelphia, PA
Three Rivers Community College, CT
Tidewater Tech, VA
Tidewater Tech: Norfolk, VA
Trenholm State Technical College, AL
Tri-County Technical College, SC
Triangle Tech
  DuBois, PA
  Erie, PA
  Greensburg, PA
  Pittsburgh, PA
Triangle Tech: Sunbury, PA
Trident Technical College, SC
Truckee Meadows Community College, NV
Tulsa Welding School, OK
United Tribes Technical College, ND
Universal Technical Institute, TX
Universal Technical Institute, AZ
University College of San Juan, PR
University of Arkansas
  Community College at Hope, AR
University of Hawaii
  Honolulu Community College, HI
University of Northwestern Ohio, OH
Utah Career College, UT
Valley College of Technology, WV
Vatterott College, OK
Vatterott College, MO
Vatterott College, IA
Vatterott College
  Tulsa, OK
Vatterott College: Cleveland, OH
Vatterott College: Kansas City, MO
Vatterott College: Memphis, TN
Vatterott College: O'Fallon, MO
Vatterott College: St. Joseph, MO
Vatterott College: Spring Valley, NE
Vatterott College: Springfield, MO
Vatterott College: Sunset Hills, MO
Vermilion Community College, MN
Vet Tech Institute, PA
Vincennes University, IN
Virginia College at Austin, TX
Virginia College at Mobile, AL
Virginia College at Pensacola, FL
Virginia College Technical, AL
Wake Technical Community College, NC
Walla Walla Community College, WA
Washington County Community College, ME
Waukesha County Technical College, WI
West Georgia Technical College, GA
West Virginia Junior College: Charleston, WV
Western Career College, CA
Western Career College
  Pleasant Hill, CA
  San Leandro, CA
Western Career College: Walnut Creek, CA
Western Dakota Technical Institute, SD
Western School of Health and Business Careers, PA
Western Technical College, TX
Western Technical Institute: Diana Drive, TX
Western Wisconsin Technical College, WI
Westwood College of Aviation Technology, CO
Westwood College of Technology
  Westwood College: Los Angeles, CA
Westwood College: Dallas, TX
Westwood College: Ft. Worth, TX
Westwood College: Houston South, TX
Williamsburg Technical College, SC
Wilson Technical Community College, NC
Wisconsin Indianhead Technical College, WI
Wyoming Technical Institute, WY
WyoTech Institute: Fremont, CA
York County Community College, ME
York Technical College, SC
York Technical Institute, PA
Youngstown College of Massotherapy, OH
Zane State College, OH

Arts/music colleges

Four-year

Academy of Art University, CA
American Academy of Art, IL
American Conservatory of Music, IN
Art Academy of Cincinnati, OH
Art Center College of Design, CA
Art Center Design College, AZ
Art Institute
  of Atlanta, GA
  of California: Orange County, CA
  of California: San Diego, CA
  of Charlotte, NC
  of Colorado, CO
  of Dallas, TX
  of Houston, TX
  of Las Vegas, NV
  of Philadelphia, PA
  of Phoenix, AZ
  of Pittsburgh, PA
  of Washington, VA
Art Institute of Boston at Lesley University, MA
Art Institute of California: San Francisco, CA
Art Institute of Fort Lauderdale, FL
Art Institute of Portland, OR
Art Institute of Seattle, WA
Art Institutes International
  Minnesota, MN
Atlantic College, PR
Berklee College of Music, MA
Boston Conservatory, MA
Brooks Institute of Photography, CA
Brooks Institute of Photography: Ventura, CA
California College of the Arts, CA
California Institute of the Arts, CA
Chester College of New England, NH
Cleveland Institute of Art, OH
Cleveland Institute of Music, OH
Cogswell Polytechnical College, CA
College for Creative Studies, MI
College of Visual Arts, MN
Collins College, AZ
Columbia College Chicago, IL
Columbia College: Hollywood, CA
Columbus College of Art and Design, OH
Conservatory of Music of Puerto Rico, PR
Converse College, SC
Cooper Union for the Advancement of Science and Art, NY
Corcoran College of Art and Design, DC
Cornish College of the Arts, WA
Curtis Institute of Music, PA
DePauw University, IN
DigiPen Institute of Technology, WA
Eastman School of Music of the University of Rochester, NY
Escuela de Artes Plasticas de Puerto Rico, PR
Fashion Institute of Technology, NY
Five Towns College, NY
Harrington College of Design, IL
Illinois Institute of Art-Chicago, IL
Illinois Institute of Art-Schaumburg, IL
Institute of American Indian Arts, NM
International Academy of Design and Technology: Chicago, IL
International Academy of Design and Technology: Detroit, MI
International Academy of Design and Technology: Henderson, NV
International Academy of Design and Technology: Nashville, TN
International Academy of Design and Technology: Schaumburg, IL
International Academy of Design and Technology: Tampa, FL
Johns Hopkins University: Peabody Conservatory of Music, MD
Juilliard School, NY
Kansas City Art Institute, MO
Kendall College of Art and Design of Ferris State University, MI
Laguna College of Art and Design, CA
Lawrence University, WI
Lyme Academy College of Fine Arts, CT
Maine College of Art, ME
Manhattan School of Music, NY
Mannes College The New School for Music, NY
Maryland Institute College of Art, MD
Massachusetts College of Art, MA
Memphis College of Art, TN
Miami International University of Art and Design, FL
Milwaukee Institute of Art & Design, WI
Minneapolis College of Art and Design, MN
Montserrat College of Art, MA
Moore College of Art and Design, PA
New England Conservatory of Music, MA
New England Institute of Art, MA
New York School of Interior Design, NY
NewSchool of Architecture & Design, CA
Northwest College of Art, WA
O'More College of Design, TN
Oberlin College, OH
Otis College of Art and Design, CA
Pacific Northwest College of Art, OR
Paier College of Art, CT
Parsons The New School for Design, NY
Pennsylvania College of Art and Design, PA
Platt College
  San Diego, CA
Pratt Institute, NY
Rhode Island School of Design, RI
Ringling School of Art and Design, FL
Rocky Mountain College of Art & Design, CO
San Francisco Art Institute, CA
San Francisco Conservatory of Music, CA
Savannah College of Art and Design, GA
School of the Art Institute of Chicago, IL
School of the Museum of Fine Arts, MA
School of Visual Arts, NY
Southern California Institute of Architecture, CA
University of the Arts, PA
VanderCook College of Music, IL
Westminster Choir College of Rider University, NJ

Two-year

American Academy of Dramatic Arts, NY
American Academy of Dramatic Arts: West, CA
Antonelli College, OH

Bible colleges

Four-year

Two-year

Business colleges

Four-year

Two-year

Tables and Indexes

Brown Mackie College: Atlanta, GA
Brown Mackie College: Cincinnati, OH
Brown Mackie College: Fort Wayne, IN
Brown Mackie College: Hopkinsville, KY
Brown Mackie College: Merrillville, IN
Brown Mackie College: Miami, FL
Brown Mackie College: North Canton, OH
Bryant & Stratton Business Institute
Bryant & Stratton College: Albany, NY
Bryant & Stratton College: Buffalo, NY
Bryant & Stratton College: Lackawanna, NY
Bryant & Stratton College: Rochester, NY
Bryant & Stratton College: Syracuse, NY
Bryant & Stratton College: Williamsville, NY
Bryant & Stratton College
Parma, OH
Richmond, VA
Willoughby Hills, OH
Bryant & Stratton College: Henrietta, NY
Bryant & Stratton College: Milwaukee, WI
Bryant & Stratton College: Syracuse North, NY
Bryant & Stratton College: Virginia Beach, VA
Business Informatics Center, NY
Business Institute of Pennsylvania, PA
Business Institute of Pennsylvania
Meadville, PA
Cambria-Rowe Business College, PA
Cambria-Rowe Business College: Indiana, PA
Career College of Northern Nevada, NV
Career Colleges of Chicago, IL
City College
Gainesville, FL
Miami, FL
College of Office Technology, IL
College of Westchester, NY
Columbia College
Columbia Centro Universitario, PR
Concorde Career College, MO
Consolidated School of Business
Lancaster, PA
York, PA
Daymar College, KY
Daymar College
Louisville, KY
Delta School of Business & Technology, LA
Douglas Education Center, PA
Draughons Junior College: Clarksville, TN
Draughons Junior College: Nashville, TN
DuBois Business College, PA
DuBois Business College
Huntingdon, PA
Oil City, PA
Duff's Business Institute, PA
Duluth Business University, MN
Elmira Business Institute, NY
Elmira Business Institute: Vestal, NY
Empire College, CA
Erie Business Center, PA
Everest College, AZ
Everest College: Arlington, TX
Everest College: Dallas, TX
Everest College: Portland, OR
Everest College: Salt Lake City, UT
Everest College: Vancouver, WA
Fashion Careers College, CA
Fashion Institute of Design and Merchandising, CA
Fashion Institute of Design and Merchandising
San Diego, CA
San Francisco, CA
Florida Career College: Miami, FL
Florida Career College: Pembroke Pines, FL
Florida Technical College
Auburndale, FL
Gallipolis Career College, OH
Gibbs College, NJ
Gibbs College, CT
Hagerstown Business College, MD
Hallmark Institute of Technology, TX
Hamilton College: Lincoln, NE
Hamilton College: Omaha, NE
Hawaii Business College, HI
Heald College
Concord, CA
Fresno, CA
Honolulu, HI
Roseville, CA
Salinas, CA
San Francisco, CA
San Jose, CA
Stockton, CA
Heritage College, NV
Herzing College
Orlando, FL
Hondros College, OH
Humacao Community College, PR
ICM School of Business & Medical Careers, PA
ICPR Junior College, PR
Indiana Business College, IN
Indiana Business College
Anderson, IN
Columbus, IN
Evansville, IN
Fort Wayne, IN
Lafayette, IN
Marion, IN
Muncie, IN
Terre Haute, IN
Institute of Business & Medical Careers, CO
Interboro Institute, NY
International Academy of Design and Technology: Pittsburgh, PA
International Business College: Indianapolis, IN
International College of Hospitality Management, CT
International Institute of the Americas
Phoenix, AZ
International Junior College of Business and Technology, PR
Jamestown Business College, NY
Katharine Gibbs School
New York, NY
Keiser Career College: Pembroke Pines, FL
Keiser Career College: Port St. Lucie, FL
Keiser Career College: West Palm Beach, FL
Key College, FL
Lansdale School of Business, PA
Las Vegas College, NV
Laurel Business Institute, PA
LDS Business College, UT
Lehigh Valley College, PA
Lewis College of Business, MI
Long Island Business Institute, NY
Long Island Business Institute: Flushing, NY
Maric College, CA
Maric College: Anaheim, CA
Maric College: Sacramento, CA
McCann School of Business: Hazleton, PA
Metro Business College, MO
Metro Business College
Jefferson City, MO
Rolla, MO
Mildred Elley, NY
Miller-Motte Technical College, TN
Minneapolis Business College, MN
Minnesota School of Business: Brooklyn Center, MN
Mountain State College, WV
MTI College, CA
MTI College of Business and Technology, TX
MTI College of Business and Technology, TX
National College of Business & Technology
Bluefield, VA
Charlottesville, VA
Danville, VA
Danville, KY
Florence, KY
Harrisonburg, VA
Lexington, KY
Louisville, KY
Lynchburg, VA
Martinsville, VA
Pikeville, KY
Richmond, KY
Tennessee, TN
Tri Cities/Bristol, VA
National College of Business & Technology: Arecibo, PR
National College of Business & Technology: Bayamon, PR
National College of Business & Technology: Dayton, OH
National College of Business & Technology: Knoxville, TN
National College of Business & Technology: Rio Grande, PR
New England Culinary Institute
Essex Junction, VT
Newport Business Institute, PA
Newport Business Institute, PA
Ohio Business College, OH
Ohio Business College: Sandusky, OH
Ohio Valley College of Technology, OH
Olean Business Institute, NY
Parks College: Arlington, VA
Patricia Stevens College, MO
Penn Commercial Business and Technical School, PA
PJA School, PA
Platt College
Cerritos, CA
Plaza College, NY
Professional Careers Institute, IN
Ramirez College of Business and Technology, PR
Rasmussen College
Eagan, MN
Mankato, MN
Minnetonka, MN
Remington College
Memphis, TN
Rochester Business Institute, NY
Rockford Business College, IL
Sanford-Brown College, MO
Sanford-Brown College
Hazelwood, MO
St. Charles, MO
Santa Barbara Business College, CA
Santa Barbara Business College
Bakersfield, CA
Santa Maria, CA
Santa Barbara Business College: Ventura, CA
Sawyer College, IN
South Coast College, CA
South Hills School of Business & Technology, PA
Southeastern Business College, OH
Southeastern Business College: Jackson, OH
Southeastern Business College: Lancaster, OH
Southeastern Business College: New Boston, OH
Southern Ohio College
Brown Mackie College: North Kentucky, KY
Southwestern College of Business
Southwestern College: Tri-County, OH
Southwestern College: Vine Street Campus, OH
Southwestern College: Dayton, OH
Spencerian College, KY
Stautzenberger College, OH
Stautzenberger College: Strongsville, OH
Stenotype Institute: Jacksonville, FL
Stevens-Henager College
Murray, UT
Stevens-Henager College: Boise, ID
Taylor Business Institute, NY
Taylor Business Institute, IL
Tri-State Business Institute, PA
Trumbull Business College, OH
Universal Technology College of Puerto Rico, PR
University of Northwestern Ohio, OH
Utica School of Commerce, NY
Utica School of Commerce: Canastota, NY
Utica School of Commerce: Oneonta, NY
Valley College of Technology, WV
Virginia College at Austin, TX
Virginia College Gulf Coast, MS
Virginia Marti College of Art and Design, OH
West Tennessee Business College, TN
West Virginia Business College, WV
West Virginia Business College, WV
West Virginia Career Institute, PA
Western School of Health and Business Careers
Monroeville, PA
Yorktowne Business Institute, PA

Culinary schools

Four-year

Art Institute
of California: Orange County, CA
of Las Vegas, NV
of Washington, VA
Art Institutes International
Minnesota, MN
Baltimore International College, MD
Culinary Institute of America, NY
Kendall College, IL
Restaurant School, PA
Sullivan University, KY

Two-year

Art Institute
of New York City, NY
California Culinary Academy, CA
California School of Culinary Arts, CA
Cooking & Hospitality Institute of Chicago, IL
International College of Hospitality Management, CT
Le Cordon Bleu College of Culinary Arts, NV
Mitchell Technical Institute, SD
New England Culinary Institute, VT
New England Culinary Institute
Essex Junction, VT
Orlando Culinary Academy, FL
Pennsylvania Institute of Culinary Arts, PA
Southwestern Oregon Community College, OR
Western Culinary Institute, OR

Engineering colleges

Four-year

Bradley University, IL
California National University for Advanced Studies, CA
Capitol College, MD
Cogswell Polytechnical College, CA
Colorado School of Mines, CO
Columbia University
Fu Foundation School of Engineering and Applied Science, NY
Cooper Union for the Advancement of Science and Art, NY
DigiPen Institute of Technology, WA
Franklin W. Olin College of Engineering, MA
Harvey Mudd College, CA
Henry Cogswell College, WA
Illinois Institute of Technology, IL
Indiana Institute of Technology, IN
Instituto Tecnologico y de Estudios Superiores de Occidente, MX
Inter American University of Puerto Rico
Bayamon Campus, PR
International Technological University, CA
Kettering University, MI
Lafayette College, PA
Maine Maritime Academy, ME
Manhattan College, NY
Missouri Technical School, MO
Montana Tech of the University of Montana, MT
Neumont University, UT
New Mexico Institute of Mining and Technology, NM
Northwestern Polytechnic University, CA
Oregon Institute of Technology, OR
Rose-Hulman Institute of Technology, IN
South Dakota School of Mines and Technology, SD
Southern California Institute of Technology, CA
Southern Polytechnic State University, GA
Stevens Institute of Technology, NJ
Union College, NY
United States Coast Guard Academy, CT

United States Merchant Marine Academy, NY
United States Military Academy, NY
Universidad del Valle de Guatemala, GT
Universidad Politecnica de Puerto Rico, PR
University of Management and Technology, VA
University of Missouri
Rolla, MO
University of Pittsburgh
Johnstown, PA
University of Puerto Rico
Mayaguez, PR
Vaughn College of Aeronautics and Technology, NY
Vermont Technical College, VT
Wentworth Institute of Technology, MA
West Virginia University Institute of Technology, WV

Maritime colleges

Four-year
California Maritime Academy, CA
Maine Maritime Academy, ME
Massachusetts Maritime Academy, MA
State University of New York
Maritime College, NY
Webb Institute, NY

Two-year
College of Oceaneering, CA
Northwest School of Wooden Boatbuilding, WA

Military colleges

Four-year
American Military University, WV
The Citadel, SC
Massachusetts Maritime Academy, MA
Norwich University, VT
United States Air Force Academy, CO
United States Coast Guard Academy, CT
United States Merchant Marine Academy, NY
United States Military Academy, NY
United States Naval Academy, MD
Virginia Military Institute, VA

Two-year
Georgia Military College, GA
Marion Military Institute, AL
New Mexico Military Institute
Junior College, NM
Valley Forge Military College, PA
Wentworth Military Junior College, MO

Nursing and health science colleges

Four-year
Albany College of Pharmacy, NY
Allen College, IA
Aquinas College, TN
Arizona Institute of Business and Technology
International Institute of the Americas: Mesa, AZ
Baker College
of Cadillac, MI
Baptist College of Health Sciences, TN
Bastyr University, WA
Beckfield College, KY
Bellin College of Nursing, WI
Blessing-Reiman College of Nursing, IL
Cabarrus College of Health Sciences, NC
California College: San Diego, CA
Charles R. Drew University of Medicine and Science, CA
Clarkson College, NE
College of New Rochelle, NY
College of Saint Mary, NE
Columbia College of Nursing, WI
Columbia University
School of Nursing, NY
Curry College, MA
D'Youville College, NY
Davenport University, MI
Deaconess College of Nursing, MO
Dominican College of Blauvelt, NY
Dominican University of California, CA
ECPI College of Technology, VA
Electronic Data Processing College: San Sebastian, PR
Florida Hospital College of Health Sciences, FL
Globe College, MN
Gwynedd-Mercy College, PA
Husson College, ME
Independence University, CA
International Institute of the Americas, NM
International Institute of the Americas
Tucson, AZ
International Institute of the Americas: West Valley, AZ
Ithaca College, NY
Jefferson College of Health Sciences, VA
Jewish Hospital College of Nursing and Allied Health, MO
Jones College: Miami, FL
Lakeview College of Nursing, IL
Lester L. Cox College of Nursing and Health Sciences, MO
Lincoln University, CA
Loma Linda University, CA
Louisiana State University Health Sciences Center, LA
Macon State College, GA
Massachusetts College of Pharmacy and Health Sciences, MA
Medcenter One College of Nursing, ND
MedCentral College of Nursing, OH
Medical College of Georgia, GA
Medical University of South Carolina, SC
Mercy College of Health Sciences, IA
Mercy College of Northwest Ohio, OH
Mount Carmel College of Nursing, OH
Mountain State University, WV
National University of Health Sciences, IL
Nebraska Methodist College of Nursing and Allied Health, NE
New York Institute of Technology, NY
Oregon Institute of Technology, OR
Our Lady of the Lake College, LA
Presentation College, SD
Research College of Nursing, MO
Rosalind Franklin University of Medicine and Science, IL
St. Anselm College, NH
Saint Anthony College of Nursing, IL
St. Catharine College, KY
St. Francis Medical Center College of Nursing, IL
St. John's College, IL
St. Luke's College, MO
Samuel Merritt College, CA
South University, GA
South University, AL
South University, SC
South University: West Palm Beach Campus, FL
Springfield College, MA
State University of New York
Downstate Medical Center, NY
Institute of Technology at Utica/Rome, NY
Upstate Medical University, NY
Tennessee Wesleyan College, TN
Texas A&M University
Baylor College of Dentistry, TX
Thomas Jefferson University: College of Health Professions, PA
Trinity College of Nursing and Health Sciences, IL
University of Arkansas
for Medical Sciences, AR
University of Kansas Medical Center, KS
University of Maryland
Baltimore, MD
University of Medicine and Dentistry of New Jersey
School of Health Related Professions, NJ
School of Nursing, NJ
University of Mississippi Medical Center, MS
University of Nebraska
Medical Center, NE
University of Tennessee Health Science Center, TN
University of Texas
Health Science Center at Houston, TX
Health Science Center at San Antonio, TX
Medical Branch at Galveston, TX
Southwestern Medical Center at Dallas, TX
University of the Sciences in Philadelphia, PA
West Coast University, CA
West Suburban College of Nursing, IL
Westwood College of Technology
O'Hare, IL
Winston-Salem State University, NC

Two-year
Academy of Medical Arts and Business, PA
Angley College, FL
Antonelli College
Hattiesburg, MS
ATI College of Health, FL
Bidwell Training Center, PA
Bolivar Technical College, MO
Boulder College of Massage Therapy, CO
Branson Technical College, MO
Brown Mackie College: Atlanta, GA
Brown Mackie College: Cincinnati, OH
Brown Mackie College: Miami, FL
Bryman School, AZ
Camelot College, LA
Careers Unlimited, UT
Carolinas College of Health Sciences, NC
Central Maine Medical Center School of Nursing, ME
Centro de Estudios Multidisciplinarios, PR
City College
Gainesville, FL
Miami, FL
Cochran School of Nursing-St. John's Riverside Hospital, NY
College of Business and Technology: Kendall, FL
Colorado School of Healing Arts, CO
Concorde Career College, CA
Concorde Career College, MO
Concorde Career College, CO
EduTek College, OH
Florida College of Natural Health
Bradenton, FL
Maitland, FL
Good Samaritan College of Nursing and Health Science, OH
Goodwin College, CT
Hawaii Business College, HI
Helene Fuld College of Nursing, NY
Heritage College, NV
Heritage College, CO
Herzing College
Orlando, FL
High-Tech Institute, FL
Huntington College of Health Sciences, TN
ICM School of Business & Medical Careers, PA
Indiana Business College, IN
Indiana Business College
Anderson, IN
Columbus, IN
Evansville, IN
Fort Wayne, IN
Lafayette, IN
Marion, IN
Medical, IN
Muncie, IN
Terre Haute, IN
Institute of Business & Medical Careers, CO
International Institute of the Americas
Phoenix, AZ
Jefferson Davis Community College, AL
Keiser Career College: Pembroke Pines, FL
Keiser Career College: Port St. Lucie, FL
Keiser Career College: West Palm Beach, FL
Kettering College of Medical Arts, OH
Laboure College, MA
Lakeland Academy Division of Herzing College, MN
Las Vegas College, NV
Long Island College Hospital School of Nursing, NY
Maric College, CA
Metro Business College
Jefferson City, MO
Miller-Motte Technical College, TN
Myotherapy Institute, NE
National College of Business & Technology: Rio Grande, PR
National Institute of Technology, CA
National Institute of Technology, OH
Ohio College of Massotherapy, OH
Phillips Beth Israel School of Nursing, NY
Platt College
Tulsa, OK
Ponce Paramedical College, PR
Professional Careers Institute, IN
St. Elizabeth College of Nursing, NY
St. Joseph's College of Nursing, NY
St. Luke's College, IA
St. Vincent Catholic Medical Centers, NY
St. Vincent's College, CT
Sanford-Brown College, MO
Sanford-Brown College
Colorado Technical University: North Kansas City, MO
Sanford-Brown Institute: Tampa, FL
Silicon Valley College, CA
South College, NC
Southeast Missouri Hospital College of Nursing and Health Sciences, MO
Southern Ohio College
Brown Mackie College: North Kentucky, KY
Southwestern College of Business
Southwestern College: Franklin, OH
Southwestern College: Tri-County, OH
Southwestern College: Vine Street Campus, OH
Southwestern College: Florence, KY
Spencerian College, KY
Stautzenberger College: Strongsville, OH
Swedish Institute, NY
Texas County Technical Institute, MO
Thompson Institute, PA
Thompson Institute
Philadelphia, PA
Ultrasound Diagnostic School
Sanford-Brown Institute: Jacksonville, FL
Universal Technology College of Puerto Rico, PR
Vatterott College, IA
Vet Tech Institute, PA
Virginia College Gulf Coast, MS
Wallace State Community College at Hanceville, AL
West Tennessee Business College, TN
Western Career College, CA
Western Career College
Pleasant Hill, CA
San Leandro, CA
Western College of Southern California, OK
Western School of Health and Business Careers
Monroeville, PA
Westwood College: Ft. Worth, TX
Westwood College: Houston South, TX
Yorktowne Business Institute, PA
Youngstown College of Massotherapy, OH

Schools of mortuary science

Four-year
Cincinnati College of Mortuary Science, OH

Two-year

American Academy McAllister Institute of Funeral Service, NY
Commonwealth Institute of Funeral Service, TX
Dallas Institute of Funeral Service, TX
John A. Gupton College, TN
Mid-America College of Funeral Service, IN

Seminary/rabbinical colleges

Four-year

Austin Graduate School of Theology, TX
Baptist Bible College, MO
Baptist Bible College of Pennsylvania, PA
Baptist Missionary Association Theological Seminary, TX
Beis Medrash Heichal Dovid, NY
Beth Hamedrash Shaarei Yosher Institute, NY
Beth Hatalmud Rabbinical College, NY
Beth Medrash Govoha, NJ
Calvary Bible College and Theological Seminary, MO
Central Yeshiva Tomchei Tmimim-Lubavitch, NY
Clear Creek Baptist Bible College, KY
Conception Seminary College, MO
Criswell College, TX
Darkei Noam Rabbinical College, NY
Divine Word College, IA
Dominican School of Philosophy and Theology, CA
Earlham College, IN
Erskine College, SC
Faith Baptist Bible College and Theological Seminary, IA
George Fox University, OR
Global University, MO
Hebrew College, MA
Hebrew Theological College, IL
Hellenic College/Holy Cross, MA
Holy Apostles College and Seminary, CT
Holy Trinity Orthodox Seminary, NY
Jewish Theological Seminary of America, NY
Kehilath Yakov Rabbinical Seminary, NY
King's College and Seminary, CA
Liberty University, VA
Lincoln Christian College and Seminary, IL
Machzikei Hadath Rabbinical College, NY
Master's College, CA
Mesivta Torah Vodaath Seminary, NY
Mirrer Yeshiva Central Institute, NY
Mount Angel Seminary, OR
Multnomah Bible College, OR
Ner Israel Rabbinical College, MD
New Orleans Baptist Theological Seminary: Leavell College, LA
Ohr Somayach Tanenbaum Education Center, NY
Piedmont Baptist College, NC
Pontifical College Josephinum, OH
Rabbi Jacob Joseph School, NJ
Rabbinical Academy Mesivta Rabbi Chaim Berlin, NY
Rabbinical College Beth Shraga, NY
Rabbinical College Bobover Yeshiva B'nei Zion, NY
Rabbinical College Ch'san Sofer of New York, NY
Rabbinical College of America, NJ
Rabbinical College of Long Island, NY
Rabbinical College of Ohr Shimon Yisroel, NY
Rabbinical College of Telshe, OH
Rabbinical Seminary Adas Yereim, NY
Rabbinical Seminary of America, NY
Sacred Heart Major Seminary, MI
St. Charles Borromeo Seminary - Overbrook, PA
St. John Vianney College Seminary, FL
St. John's Seminary College, MA
St. Joseph Seminary College, LA
Shor Yoshuv Rabbinical College, NY
South Florida Bible College and Theological Seminary, FL
Southeastern Baptist Theological Seminary, NC
Southern Christian University, AL
Talmudic College of Florida, FL
Talmudical Academy of New Jersey, NJ
Talmudical Institute of Upstate New York, NY
Talmudical Seminary Oholei Torah, NY
Talmudical Yeshiva of Philadelphia, PA
Telshe Yeshiva-Chicago, IL
Torah Teminah Talmudical Seminary, NY
Trinity College of the Bible and Theological Seminary, IN
U.T.A. Mesivta-Kiryas Jocl, NY
United Talmudical Seminary, NY
University of Dubuque, IA
Washington Bible College, MD
Yeshiva and Kolel Bais Medrash Elyon, NY
Yeshiva and Kollel Harbotzas Torah, NY
Yeshiva Beth Yehuda-Yeshiva Gedolah of Greater Detroit, MI
Yeshiva College of the Nations Capital, MD
Yeshiva D'Monsey Rabbinical College, NY
Yeshiva Derech Chaim, NY
Yeshiva Gedolah Imrei Yosef D'Spinka, NY
Yeshiva Gedolah Rabbinical College, FL
Yeshiva Gedolah Zichron Moshe, NY
Yeshiva Karlin Stolin, NY
Yeshiva Mikdash Melech, NY
Yeshiva of Nitra, NY
Yeshiva of the Telshe Alumni, NY
Yeshiva Ohr Elchonon Chabad/West Coast Talmudical Seminary, CA
Yeshiva Shaar Hatorah, NY
Yeshiva Shaarei Torah of Rockland, NY
Yeshiva Toras Chaim Talmudical Seminary, CO
Yeshivas Novominsk, NY
Yeshivath Beth Moshe, PA
Yeshivath Viznitz, NY

Two-year

Queen of the Holy Rosary College, CA
Salvation Army Crestmont College, CA

Teacher's colleges

Four-year

American Indian College of the Assemblies of God, AZ
Athens State University, AL
Austin College, TX
Baltimore Hebrew University, MD
Baptist College of Florida, FL
Black Hills State University, SD
Bridgewater State College, MA
California State University Monterey Bay, CA
Canisius College, NY
Chadron State College, NE
College of St. Joseph in Vermont, VT
College of Saint Rose, NY
College of the Southwest, NM
Concordia University, IL
Concordia University, MI
Concordia University, NE
D'Youville College, NY
Eastern Illinois University, IL
Emporia State University, KS
Fairmont State University, WV
Fitchburg State College, MA
Florida Christian College, FL
Fort Valley State University, GA
Framingham State College, MA
Frostburg State University, MD
Glenville State College, WV
Great Basin College, NV
Harris-Stowe State University, MO
Heritage University, WA
Howard Payne University, TX
Jarvis Christian College, TX
Keene State College, NH
Lander University, SC
Langston University, OK
Laura and Alvin Siegal College of Judaic Studies, OH
Lesley University, MA
Lock Haven University of Pennsylvania, PA
Lyndon State College, VT
Manhattanville College, NY
Mayville State University, ND
National-Louis University, IL
New England College, NH
Northern New Mexico College, NM
Northwestern Oklahoma State University, OK
Pacific Oaks College, CA
Peru State College, NE
Piedmont College, GA
Plymouth State University, NH
Rabbinical College of Long Island, NY
Rabbinical College of Telshe, OH
Reinhardt College, GA
St. Joseph's College, NY
Sheldon Jackson College, AK
Si Tanka Huron University, SD
Southeastern College of the Assemblies of God, FL
Southeastern Oklahoma State University, OK
State University of New York
- College at Buffalo, NY
- College at Cortland, NY
- College at Plattsburgh, NY
- College at Potsdam, NY

Tennessee Wesleyan College, TN
University of Maine Farmington, ME
University of Montana: Western, MT
Valley City State University, ND
VanderCook College of Music, IL
Wayne State College, NE
West Virginia State University, WV
Western Oregon University, OR
Westfield State College, MA
Wheelock College, MA
Worcester State College, MA
York College, NE

Special characteristics

Colleges for men

Four-year
Beth Medrash Govoha, NJ
Conception Seminary College, MO
Divine Word College, IA
Hampden-Sydney College, VA
Holy Trinity Orthodox Seminary, NY
Machzikei Hadath Rabbinical College, NY
Morehouse College, GA
Mount Angel Seminary, OR
Ner Israel Rabbinical College, MD
Pontifical College Josephinum, OH
Rabbinical Academy Mesivta Rabbi Chaim Berlin, NY
Rabbinical College of America, NJ
Rabbinical College of Long Island, NY
Rabbinical College of Telshe, OH
St. Charles Borromeo Seminary - Overbrook, PA
St. John Vianney College Seminary, FL
St. John's Seminary College, MA
St. John's University, MN
St. Joseph Seminary College, LA
Talmudical Yeshiva of Philadelphia, PA
Telshe Yeshiva-Chicago, IL
Wabash College, IN
Williamson Free School of Mechanical Trades, PA
Yeshiva and Kolel Bais Medrash Elyon, NY
Yeshiva Beth Yehuda-Yeshiva Gedolah of Greater Detroit, MI
Yeshiva College of the Nations Capital, MD
Yeshiva D'Monsey Rabbinical College, NY
Yeshiva Derech Chaim, NY
Yeshiva Gedolah Imrei Yosef D'Spinka, NY
Yeshiva Gedolah Rabbinical College, FL
Yeshiva Mikdash Melech, NY
Yeshivath Beth Moshe, PA

Two-year
Deep Springs College, CA

Colleges for women

Four-year
Agnes Scott College, GA
Alverno College, WI
Barnard College, NY
Bay Path College, MA
Bennett College, NC
Brenau University, GA
Bryn Mawr College, PA
Carlow University, PA
Cedar Crest College, PA
Chatham College, PA
College of New Rochelle, NY
College of Notre Dame of Maryland, MD
College of St. Benedict, MN
College of St. Catherine, MN
College of St. Elizabeth, NJ
College of Saint Mary, NE
Columbia College, SC
Converse College, SC
Georgian Court University, NJ
Hollins University, VA
Judson College, AL
Lexington College, IL
Mary Baldwin College, VA
Meredith College, NC
Midway College, KY
Mills College, CA
Moore College of Art and Design, PA
Mount Holyoke College, MA
Mount Mary College, WI
Mount St. Mary's College, CA
Peace College, NC
Pine Manor College, MA
Randolph-Macon Woman's College, VA
Regis College, MA
Rosemont College, PA
Russell Sage College, NY
St. Joseph College, CT
Saint Mary's College, IN
St. Mary-of-the-Woods College, IN
Salem College, NC
Scripps College, CA
Simmons College, MA
Smith College, MA
Spelman College, GA
Stephens College, MO
Sweet Briar College, VA
Trinity University, DC
Ursuline College, OH
Wellesley College, MA
Wesleyan College, GA
Wilson College, PA

Two-year
Assumption College for Sisters, NJ
Cottey College, MO

Affiliated with a religion

African Methodist Episcopal Church

Four-year
Allen University, SC
Edward Waters College, FL
Paul Quinn College, TX

African Methodist Episcopal Zion Church

Four-year
Livingstone College, NC

American Baptist Churches in the USA

Four-year
Alderson-Broaddus College, WV
Arkansas Baptist College, AR
Bacone College, OK
Benedict College, SC
Eastern University, PA
Florida Memorial University, FL
Franklin College, IN
Judson College, IL
Keuka College, NY
Linfield College, OR
Ottawa University, KS
University of Sioux Falls, SD

Assemblies of God

Four-year
American Indian College of the Assemblies of God, AZ
Bethany University, CA
Central Bible College, MO
Evangel University, MO
Global University, MO
North Central University, MN
Northwest University, WA
Southeastern College of the Assemblies of God, FL
Southwestern Assemblies of God University, TX
Trinity Bible College, ND
Valley Forge Christian College, PA
Vanguard University of Southern California, CA
Zion Bible Institute, RI

Baptist faith

Four-year
American Baptist College of ABT Seminary, TN
Arlington Baptist College, TX
Baptist Bible College of Pennsylvania, PA
Baptist Missionary Association Theological Seminary, TX
Baylor University, TX
Belmont University, TN
Campbellsville University, KY
Cedarville University, OH
Central Baptist College, AR
Corban College, OR
Cornerstone University, MI
Dallas Baptist University, TX
East Texas Baptist University, TX
Hardin-Simmons University, TX
Howard Payne University, TX
Judson College, AL
Liberty University, VA
Maranatha Baptist Bible College, WI
Mars Hill College, NC
Mercer University, GA
Morris College, SC
Piedmont Baptist College, NC
Shaw University, NC
Southwestern College, AZ
Tennessee Temple University, TN
University of Mary Hardin-Baylor, TX
University of the Cumberlands, KY
Virginia Intermont College, VA
Virginia Union University, VA
William Carey College, MS
William Jewell College, MO
Wingate University, NC

Two-year
Jacksonville College, TX

Baptist General Conference

Four-year
Bethel University, MN

Brethren Church

Four-year
Ashland University, OH
Emmaus Bible College, IA
Grace College and Seminary, IN

Christian and Missionary Alliance

Four-year
Crown College, MN
Nyack College, NY
Simpson University, CA
Toccoa Falls College, GA

Christian Church

Four-year
Atlanta Christian College, GA
Bethesda Christian University, CA
Central Christian College of the Bible, MO
Crossroads College, MN
Johnson Bible College, TN
Lincoln Christian College and Seminary, IL
Manhattan Christian College, KS
St. Louis Christian College, MO

Christian Church (Disciples of Christ)

Four-year
Barton College, NC
Bethany College, WV
Chapman University, CA
Columbia College, MO
Culver-Stockton College, MO
Eureka College, IL
Hiram College, OH
Jarvis Christian College, TX
Lynchburg College, VA
Midway College, KY
Northwest Christian College, OR
Texas Christian University, TX
Transylvania University, KY
William Woods University, MO

Christian Methodist Episcopal Church

Four-year
Miles College, AL
Texas College, TX

Christian Reformed Church

Four-year
Calvin College, MI
Dordt College, IA

Church of Christ

Four-year
Abilene Christian University, TX
Austin Graduate School of Theology, TX
Faulkner University, AL
Freed-Hardeman University, TN
Harding University, AR
Heritage Christian University, AL
Lipscomb University, TN
Lubbock Christian University, TX
Magnolia Bible College, MS
Ohio Valley University, WV
Oklahoma Christian University, OK
Pepperdine University, CA
Roanoke Bible College, NC
Rochester College, MI
Southern Christian University, AL
Southwestern Christian College, TX
York College, NE

Two-year
Crowley's Ridge College, AR

Church of God

Four-year
Anderson University, IN
Lee University, TN
Mid-America Christian University, OK
University of Findlay, OH
Warner Pacific College, OR
Warner Southern College, FL

Church of Jesus Christ of Latter-day Saints

Four-year
Brigham Young University, UT
Brigham Young University-Hawaii, HI
Brigham Young University-Idaho, ID

Two-year
LDS Business College, UT

Church of the Brethren

Four-year
Bridgewater College, VA
Elizabethtown College, PA
Juniata College, PA
Manchester College, IN
McPherson College, KS

Church of the Nazarene

Four-year
Eastern Nazarene College, MA
MidAmerica Nazarene University, KS
Mount Vernon Nazarene University, OH
Nazarene Bible College, CO
Northwest Nazarene University, ID
Olivet Nazarene University, IL
Point Loma Nazarene University, CA
Southern Nazarene University, OK
Trevecca Nazarene University, TN

Episcopal Church

Four-year
Bard College, NY
Clarkson College, NE
St. Augustine College, IL
St. Augustine's College, NC
St. Luke's College, MO
St. Paul's College, VA
University of the South, TN
Voorhees College, SC

Evangelical Covenant Church of America

Four-year
North Park University, IL

Evangelical Free Church of America

Four-year
Trinity International University, IL

Evangelical Lutheran Church in America

Four-year
Augsburg College, MN
Augustana College, IL
Augustana College, SD
Bethany College, KS
California Lutheran University, CA
Capital University, OH
Carthage College, WI
Concordia College: Moorhead, MN
Dana College, NE
Finlandia University, MI
Grand View College, IA
Gustavus Adolphus College, MN
Lenoir-Rhyne College, NC
Luther College, IA
Midland Lutheran College, NE
Muhlenberg College, PA
Newberry College, SC
Pacific Lutheran University, WA
Roanoke College, VA
St. Olaf College, MN
Susquehanna University, PA
Texas Lutheran University, TX
Thiel College, PA
Waldorf College, IA

Wartburg College, IA
Wittenberg University, OH

Evangelical Lutheran Synod

Four-year

Bethany Lutheran College, MN

Free Methodist Church of North America

Four-year

Central Christian College of Kansas, KS
Greenville College, IL
Roberts Wesleyan College, NY
Seattle Pacific University, WA
Spring Arbor University, MI

Free Will Baptists

Four-year

Free Will Baptist Bible College, TN
Mount Olive College, NC

General Association of Regular Baptist Churches

Four-year

Faith Baptist Bible College and Theological Seminary, IA

Interdenominational tradition

Four-year

Asbury College, KY
Azusa Pacific University, CA
Biola University, CA
Bryan College, TN
Ecclesia College, AR
God's Bible School and College, OH
Grace University, NE
Heritage University, WA
Hobe Sound Bible College, FL
John Brown University, AR
John Wesley College, NC
Messiah College, PA
Moody Bible Institute, IL
Multnomah Bible College, OR
Oak Hills Christian College, MN
Patten University, CA
Regent University, VA
Southeastern Bible College, AL
Taylor University, IN
Trinity College of Florida, FL
Vennard College, IA
Westmont College, CA
William Jessup University, CA
Williamson Christian College, TN

Jewish faith

Four-year

Beth Medrash Govoha, NJ
Gratz College, PA
Hebrew College, MA
Jewish Theological Seminary of America, NY
Laura and Alvin Siegal College of Judaic Studies, OH
Machzikei Hadath Rabbinical College, NY
Michigan Jewish Institute, MI
Ner Israel Rabbinical College, MD
Rabbinical Academy Mesivta Rabbi Chaim Berlin, NY
Rabbinical College of America, NJ
Rabbinical College of Long Island, NY
Rabbinical College of Telshe, OH
Talmudical Yeshiva of Philadelphia, PA
Telshe Yeshiva-Chicago, IL
University of Judaism, CA
Yeshiva and Kolel Bais Medrash Elyon, NY
Yeshiva Beth Yehuda-Yeshiva Gedolah of Greater Detroit, MI
Yeshiva College of the Nations Capital, MD
Yeshiva D'Monsey Rabbinical College, NY
Yeshiva Derech Chaim, NY
Yeshiva Gedolah Imrei Yosef D'Spinka, NY
Yeshiva Gedolah Rabbinical College, FL
Yeshiva Mikdash Melech, NY
Yeshivath Beth Moshe, PA

Two-year

Bramson ORT College, NY

Lutheran Church - Missouri Synod

Four-year

Concordia College, NY
Concordia College, AL
Concordia University, IL
Concordia University, CA
Concordia University, MI
Concordia University, NE
Concordia University, OR
Concordia University at Austin, TX
Concordia University Wisconsin, WI
Concordia University: St. Paul, MN

Lutheran Church in America

Four-year

Wagner College, NY

Mennonite Brethren Church

Four-year

Fresno Pacific University, CA
Tabor College, KS

Mennonite Church

Four-year

Bethel College, KS
Bluffton University, OH
Eastern Mennonite University, VA
Goshen College, IN

Two-year

Hesston College, KS
Rosedale Bible College, OH

Missionary Church

Four-year

Bethel College, IN

Moravian Church in America

Four-year

Moravian College, PA
Salem College, NC

Nondenominational tradition

Four-year

Alaska Bible College, AK
Amberton University, TX
Appalachian Bible College, WV
Boise Bible College, ID
Calvary Bible College and Theological Seminary, MO
Clearwater Christian College, FL
Colorado Christian University, CO
Crichton College, TN
Dallas Christian College, TX
Davis College, NY
Friends University, KS
Gordon College, MA
Inter American University of Puerto Rico
Fajardo Campus, PR
King's College, NY
King's College and Seminary, CA
Lancaster Bible College, PA
LeTourneau University, TX
Northwestern College, MN
Occidental College, CA
Oral Roberts University, OK
Ozark Christian College, MO
Palm Beach Atlantic University, FL
Puget Sound Christian College, WA
San Diego Christian College, CA
Washington Bible College, MD
Wheaton College, IL
Williamson Free School of Mechanical Trades, PA

Pentecostal Holiness Church

Four-year

Emmanuel College, GA
Southwestern Christian University, OK

Presbyterian Church (USA)

Four-year

Agnes Scott College, GA
Alma College, MI
Arcadia University, PA
Austin College, TX
Belhaven College, MS
Bethel College, TN
Blackburn College, IL
Bloomfield College, NJ
Buena Vista University, IA
Carroll College, WI
Centre College, KY
Coe College, IA
College of the Ozarks, MO
Davidson College, NC
Davis and Elkins College, WV
Eckerd College, FL
Grove City College, PA
Hampden-Sydney College, VA
Hanover College, IN
Hastings College, NE
Jamestown College, ND
King College, TN
Lafayette College, PA
Lake Forest College, IL
Lees-McRae College, NC
Lindenwood University, MO
Lyon College, AR
Macalester College, MN
Mary Baldwin College, VA
Maryville College, TN
Millikin University, IL
Missouri Valley College, MO
Monmouth College, IL
Montreat College, NC
Muskingum College, OH
Peace College, NC
Pikeville College, KY
Presbyterian College, SC
Queens University of Charlotte, NC
Rhodes College, TN
St. Andrews Presbyterian College, NC
Schreiner University, TX
Sheldon Jackson College, AK
Sterling College, KS
Stillman College, AL
Trinity University, TX
Tusculum College, TN
University of Dubuque, IA
University of the Ozarks, AR
University of Tulsa, OK
Warren Wilson College, NC
Waynesburg College, PA
Westminster College, MO
Westminster College, PA
Whitworth College, WA
Wilson College, PA

Reformed Church in America

Four-year

Central College, IA
Hope College, MI
Northwestern College, IA

Reformed Presbyterian Church of North America

Four-year

Geneva College, PA

Roman Catholic Church

Four-year

Albertus Magnus College, CT
Alvernia College, PA
Alverno College, WI
Anna Maria College, MA
Aquinas College, MI
Aquinas College, TN
Ashford University, IA
Assumption College, MA
Avila University, MO
Barry University, FL
Bayamon Central University, PR
Bellarmine University, KY
Belmont Abbey College, NC
Benedictine College, KS
Benedictine University, IL
Boston College, MA
Brescia University, KY
Briar Cliff University, IA
Cabrini College, PA
Caldwell College, NJ
Calumet College of St. Joseph, IN
Canisius College, NY
Cardinal Stritch University, WI
Carlow University, PA
Carroll College, MT
Catholic University of America, DC
Chaminade University of Honolulu, HI
Chestnut Hill College, PA
Christendom College, VA
Christian Brothers University, TN
Clarke College, IA
College Misericordia, PA
College of Mount St. Joseph, OH
College of Mount St. Vincent, NY
College of New Rochelle, NY
College of Notre Dame of Maryland, MD
College of St. Benedict, MN
College of St. Catherine, MN
College of St. Elizabeth, NJ
College of St. Joseph in Vermont, VT
College of Saint Mary, NE
College of Saint Rose, NY
College of St. Scholastica, MN
College of Saint Thomas More, TX
College of the Holy Cross, MA
Conception Seminary College, MO
Creighton University, NE
DePaul University, IL
DeSales University, PA
Divine Word College, IA
Dominican College of Blauvelt, NY
Dominican School of Philosophy and Theology, CA
Dominican University, IL
Dominican University of California, CA
Duquesne University, PA
Edgewood College, WI
Elms College, MA
Emmanuel College, MA
Fairfield University, CT
Felician College, NJ
Fontbonne University, MO
Fordham University, NY
Franciscan University of Steubenville, OH
Gannon University, PA
Georgetown University, DC
Georgian Court University, NJ
Gonzaga University, WA
Gwynedd-Mercy College, PA
Hilbert College, NY
Holy Apostles College and Seminary, CT
Holy Cross College, IN
Holy Family University, PA
Holy Names University, CA
Immaculata University, PA
Iona College, NY
John Carroll University, OH
King's College, PA
La Roche College, PA
La Salle University, PA
Le Moyne College, NY
Lewis University, IL
Lexington College, IL
Loras College, IA
Lourdes College, OH
Loyola College in Maryland, MD
Loyola Marymount University, CA
Loyola University New Orleans, LA
Loyola University of Chicago, IL
Madonna University, MI
Magdalen College, NH
Manhattan College, NY
Marian College, IN
Marian College of Fond du Lac, WI
Marquette University, WI
Marygrove College, MI
Marylhurst University, OR
Marymount University, VA
Marywood University, PA
Mercy College of Health Sciences, IA
Mercy College of Northwest Ohio, OH
Mercyhurst College, PA
Merrimack College, MA
Molloy College, NY
Mount Aloysius College, PA
Mount Angel Seminary, OR
Mount Marty College, SD
Mount Mary College, WI
Mount Mercy College, IA
Mount St. Mary's College, CA
Mount St. Mary's University, MD
Neumann College, PA
Newman University, KS
Niagara University, NY
Notre Dame de Namur University, CA
Ohio Dominican University, OH
Our Lady of Holy Cross College, LA
Our Lady of the Lake College, LA
Our Lady of the Lake University of San Antonio, TX
Pontifical Catholic University of Puerto Rico, PR
Pontifical College Josephinum, OH
Presentation College, SD

Providence College, RI
Quincy University, IL
Regis College, MA
Regis University, CO
Research College of Nursing, MO
Rivier College, NH
Rockhurst University, MO
Rosemont College, PA
Sacred Heart Major Seminary, MI
Sacred Heart University, CT
St. Ambrose University, IA
St. Anselm College, NH
Saint Anthony College of Nursing, IL
St. Bonaventure University, NY
St. Catharine College, KY
St. Charles Borromeo Seminary - Overbrook, PA
St. Edward's University, TX
St. Francis College, NY
St. Francis Medical Center College of Nursing, IL
St. Francis University, PA
St. Gregory's University, OK
St. John Fisher College, NY
St. John Vianney College Seminary, FL
St. John's Seminary College, MA
St. John's University, NY
St. John's University, MN
St. Joseph College, CT
St. Joseph Seminary College, LA
St. Joseph's College, ME
St. Joseph's College, IN
St. Joseph's University, PA
St. Leo University, FL
St. Louis University, MO
Saint Martin's University, WA
Saint Mary's College, IN
St. Mary's College of California, CA
St. Mary's University, TX
St. Mary's University of Minnesota, MN
St. Mary-of-the-Woods College, IN
St. Michael's College, VT
St. Norbert College, WI
St. Peter's College, NJ
St. Thomas University, FL
St. Vincent College, PA
St. Xavier University, IL
Salve Regina University, RI
Santa Clara University, CA
Seattle University, WA
Seton Hall University, NJ
Seton Hill University, PA
Siena College, NY
Siena Heights University, MI
Silver Lake College, WI
Spalding University, KY
Spring Hill College, AL
Stonehill College, MA
Thomas Aquinas College, CA
Thomas More College, KY
Thomas More College of Liberal Arts, NH
Trinity University, DC
Universidad Anahuac, MX
University of Dallas, TX
University of Dayton, OH
University of Detroit Mercy, MI
University of Great Falls, MT
University of Mary, ND
University of Notre Dame, IN
University of Portland, OR
University of St. Francis, IN
University of St. Francis, IL
University of St. Mary, KS
University of St. Thomas, TX
University of St. Thomas, MN
University of San Diego, CA
University of San Francisco, CA
University of Scranton, PA
University of the Incarnate Word, TX
University of the Sacred Heart, PR
Ursuline College, OH
Villanova University, PA
Viterbo University, WI
Walsh University, OH
West Suburban College of Nursing, IL
Wheeling Jesuit University, WV
Xavier University, OH
Xavier University of Louisiana, LA

Two-year

Ancilla College, IN
Assumption College for Sisters, NJ
Chatfield College, OH
Donnelly College, KS
Laboure College, MA
Marian Court College, MA
Marymount College, CA
Queen of the Holy Rosary College, CA
St. Elizabeth College of Nursing, NY
St. Joseph's College of Nursing, NY
St. Vincent Catholic Medical Centers, NY
Springfield College in Illinois, IL
Trocaire College, NY
Villa Maria College of Buffalo, NY

Seventh-day Adventists

Four-year

Andrews University, MI
Atlantic Union College, MA
Columbia Union College, MD
Florida Hospital College of Health Sciences, FL
La Sierra University, CA
Loma Linda University, CA
Oakwood College, AL
Pacific Union College, CA
Southern Adventist University, TN
Southwestern Adventist University, TX
Union College, NE
Universidad Adventista de las Antillas, PR
Walla Walla College, WA

Two-year

Kettering College of Medical Arts, OH

Society of Friends (Quaker)

Four-year

Earlham College, IN
George Fox University, OR
Guilford College, NC
William Penn University, IA
Wilmington College, OH

Southern Baptist Convention

Four-year

Anderson University, SC
Baptist College of Florida, FL
Blue Mountain College, MS
Bluefield College, VA
Brewton-Parker College, GA
California Baptist University, CA
Campbell University, NC
Carson-Newman College, TN
Charleston Southern University, SC
Chowan College, NC
Clear Creek Baptist Bible College, KY
Criswell College, TX
Gardner-Webb University, NC
Georgetown College, KY
Hannibal-LaGrange College, MO
Mid-Continent University, KY
Mississippi College, MS
Missouri Baptist University, MO
New Orleans Baptist Theological Seminary: Leavell College, LA
North Greenville College, SC
Oklahoma Baptist University, OK
Ouachita Baptist University, AR
Samford University, AL
Shorter College, GA
Southwest Baptist University, MO
Truett-McConnell College, GA
Union University, TN
Wayland Baptist University, TX
Williams Baptist College, AR

Ukrainian Catholic Church

Two-year

Manor College, PA

United Brethren in Christ

Four-year

Huntington University, IN

United Church of Christ

Four-year

Catawba College, NC
Deaconess College of Nursing, MO
Defiance College, OH
Doane College, NE
Elmhurst College, IL
Elon University, NC
Fisk University, TN
Heidelberg College, OH
Lakeland College, WI
Northland College, WI
Pacific University, OR
Ripon College, WI
Talladega College, AL

United Methodist Church

Four-year

Adrian College, MI
Albion College, MI
Albright College, PA
Allegheny College, PA
American University, DC
Baker University, KS
Baldwin-Wallace College, OH
Bennett College, NC
Bethune-Cookman College, FL
Birmingham-Southern College, AL
Brevard College, NC
Centenary College, NJ
Centenary College of Louisiana, LA
Central Methodist University, MO
Claflin University, SC
Clark Atlanta University, GA
Columbia College, SC
Cornell College, IA
Dakota Wesleyan University, SD
DePauw University, IN
Drew University, NJ
Duke University, NC
Emory & Henry College, VA
Emory University, GA
Ferrum College, VA
Florida Southern College, FL
Green Mountain College, VT
Greensboro College, NC
Hamline University, MN
Hendrix College, AR
High Point University, NC
Huntingdon College, AL
Illinois Wesleyan University, IL
Iowa Wesleyan College, IA
Kansas Wesleyan University, KS
Kendall College, IL
Kentucky Wesleyan College, KY
LaGrange College, GA
Lambuth University, TN
Lebanon Valley College, PA
Lindsey Wilson College, KY
Lycoming College, PA
MacMurray College, IL
Martin Methodist College, TN
McKendree College, IL
McMurry University, TX
Methodist College, NC
Millsaps College, MS
Morningside College, IA
Mount Union College, OH
Nebraska Methodist College of Nursing and Allied Health, NE
Nebraska Wesleyan University, NE
North Carolina Wesleyan College, NC
North Central College, IL
Ohio Northern University, OH
Ohio Wesleyan University, OH
Oklahoma City University, OK
Otterbein College, OH
Pfeiffer University, NC
Philander Smith College, AR
Randolph-Macon College, VA
Randolph-Macon Woman's College, VA
Reinhardt College, GA
Rust College, MS
Shenandoah University, VA
Simpson College, IA
Southern Methodist University, TX
Southwestern College, KS
Southwestern University, TX
Tennessee Wesleyan College, TN
Texas Wesleyan University, TX
Union College, KY
University of Denver, CO
University of Evansville, IN
University of Indianapolis, IN
Virginia Wesleyan College, VA
Wesley College, DE
Wesleyan College, GA
West Virginia Wesleyan College, WV
Wiley College, TX
Willamette University, OR
Wofford College, SC

Two-year

Andrew College, GA
Hiwassee College, TN
Lon Morris College, TX
Louisburg College, NC
Oxford College of Emory University, GA
Spartanburg Methodist College, SC
Young Harris College, GA

Wesleyan Church

Four-year

Houghton College, NY
Indiana Wesleyan University, IN
Oklahoma Wesleyan University, OK
Southern Wesleyan University, SC

Wisconsin Evangelical Lutheran Synod

Four-year

Martin Luther College, MN
Wisconsin Lutheran College, WI

Historically Black colleges

Four-year

Alabama Agricultural and Mechanical University, AL
Alabama State University, AL
Albany State University, GA
Alcorn State University, MS
Allen University, SC
Arkansas Baptist College, AR
Benedict College, SC
Bennett College, NC
Bluefield State College, WV
Bowie State University, MD
Central State University, OH
Cheyney University of Pennsylvania, PA
Claflin University, SC
Clark Atlanta University, GA
Concordia College, AL
Coppin State University, MD
Delaware State University, DE
Dillard University, LA
Edward Waters College, FL
Elizabeth City State University, NC
Fisk University, TN
Florida Agricultural and Mechanical University, FL
Florida Memorial University, FL
Fort Valley State University, GA
Grambling State University, LA
Hampton University, VA
Harris-Stowe State University, MO
Howard University, DC
Huston-Tillotson College, TX
Jackson State University, MS
Jarvis Christian College, TX
Johnson C. Smith University, NC
Kentucky State University, KY
LeMoyne-Owen College, TN
Lincoln University, PA
Lincoln University, MO
Livingstone College, NC
Miles College, AL
Mississippi Valley State University, MS
Morehouse College, GA
Morgan State University, MD
Morris College, SC
Norfolk State University, VA
North Carolina Agricultural and Technical State University, NC
North Carolina Central University, NC
Oakwood College, AL
Paine College, GA
Paul Quinn College, TX
Philander Smith College, AR
Prairie View A&M University, TX
Rust College, MS
St. Augustine's College, NC
St. Paul's College, VA
Savannah State University, GA
Shaw University, NC
South Carolina State University, SC
Southern University New Orleans, LA
Southern University and Agricultural and Mechanical College, LA
Southwestern Christian College, TX
Spelman College, GA
Stillman College, AL
Talladega College, AL
Tennessee State University, TN
Texas College, TX
Texas Southern University, TX
Tougaloo College, MS
Tuskegee University, AL
University of Arkansas Pine Bluff, AR

University of Maryland
Eastern Shore, MD
University of the District of Columbia, DC
University of the Virgin Islands, VI
Virginia State University, VA
Voorhees College, SC
West Virginia State University, WV
Wiley College, TX
Winston-Salem State University, NC
Xavier University of Louisiana, LA

Two-year

Bishop State Community College, AL
Coahoma Community College, MS
Denmark Technical College, SC
Hinds Community College, MS
J. F. Drake State Technical College, AL
Lawson State Community College, AL
St. Philip's College, TX
Southern University
Shreveport, LA

Hispanic serving colleges

Four-year

Adams State College, CO
American University of Puerto Rico, PR
Atlantic College, PR
Barry University, FL
Bayamon Central University, PR
Boricua College, NY
California State University
Bakersfield, CA
Dominguez Hills, CA
Fresno, CA
Los Angeles, CA
Monterey Bay, CA
Northridge, CA
San Bernardino, CA
Stanislaus, CA
Carlos Albizu University, FL
City University of New York
City College, NY
John Jay College of Criminal Justice, NY
Lehman College, NY
New York City College of Technology, NY
College of Santa Fe, NM
Conservatory of Music of Puerto Rico, PR
Dominican School of Philosophy and Theology, CA
Florida International University, FL
Heritage University, WA
Inter American University of Puerto Rico
Aguadilla Campus, PR
Arecibo Campus, PR
Barranquitas Campus, PR
Bayamon Campus, PR
Fajardo Campus, PR
Guayama Campus, PR
Ponce Campus, PR
San German Campus, PR
Lexington College, IL
Mercy College, NY
Mount Angel Seminary, OR
Mount St. Mary's College, CA
New Jersey City University, NJ
New Mexico State University, NM
Northern New Mexico College, NM
Occidental College, CA
Our Lady of the Lake University of San Antonio, TX
Pontifical Catholic University of Puerto Rico, PR
Robert Morris College: Chicago, IL
St. Augustine College, IL
St. Edward's University, TX
St. John Vianney College Seminary, FL
St. Mary's University, TX
St. Peter's College, NJ
St. Thomas University, FL
San Diego State University, CA
Sul Ross State University, TX
Texas A&M University
Kingsville, TX
Turabo University, PR
Universidad Adventista de las Antillas, PR
Universidad del Este, PR
Universidad Metropolitana, PR
Universidad Politecnica de Puerto Rico, PR
University of Houston
Downtown, TX
University of La Verne, CA
University of Miami, FL
University of New Mexico, NM
University of Puerto Rico
Aguadilla, PR
Arecibo, PR
Bayamon University College, PR
Carolina Regional College, PR
Cayey University College, PR
Humacao, PR
Mayaguez, PR
Ponce, PR
Rio Piedras, PR
Utuado, PR
University of Texas
Brownsville, TX
El Paso, TX
Health Science Center at San Antonio, TX
Pan American, TX
San Antonio, TX
of the Permian Basin, TX
University of the Incarnate Word, TX
University of the Sacred Heart, PR
Vaughn College of Aeronautics and Technology, NY
Western New Mexico University, NM
Whittier College, CA
Woodbury University, CA

Two-year

Albuquerque
Technical-Vocational Institute, NM
Allan Hancock College, CA
Arizona Western College, AZ
Bakersfield College, CA
Central Arizona College, AZ
Cerritos Community College, CA
Chaffey Community College, CA
Citrus College, CA
City Colleges of Chicago
Harry S. Truman College, IL
Malcolm X College, IL
Richard J. Daley College, IL
Wright College, IL
City University of New York
Borough of Manhattan Community College, NY
Bronx Community College, NY
Hostos Community College, NY
LaGuardia Community College, NY
Coastal Bend College, TX
Cochise College, AZ
College of the Desert, CA
College of the Sequoias, CA
Community College of Denver, CO
Del Mar College, TX
Dodge City Community College, KS
Dona Ana Branch Community College of New Mexico State University, NM
East Los Angeles College, CA
Eastern New Mexico University:
Roswell Campus, NM
El Camino College, CA
El Paso Community College, TX
Evergreen Valley College, CA
Fresno City College, CA
Fullerton College, CA
Gavilan Community College, CA
Hartnell College, CA
Heald College
Fresno, CA
Salinas, CA
San Jose, CA
Stockton, CA
Hudson County Community College, NJ
Humacao Community College, PR
Imperial Valley College, CA
Laredo Community College, TX
Long Beach City College, CA
Los Angeles City College, CA
Los Angeles Harbor College, CA
Los Angeles Mission College, CA
Los Angeles Trade and Technical College, CA
Los Angeles Valley College, CA
MacCormac College, IL
Merced College, CA
Miami Dade College, FL
Morton College, IL
Mount San Antonio College, CA
Mountain View College, TX
New Mexico Junior College, NM
New Mexico State University
Carlsbad, NM
Grants, NM
Odessa College, TX
Otero Junior College, CO
Oxnard College, CA
Palo Alto College, TX
Palo Verde College, CA
Pasadena City College, CA
Passaic County Community College, NJ
Phoenix College, AZ
Pima Community College, AZ
Porterville College, CA
Pueblo Community College, CO
Reedley College, CA
Rio Hondo College, CA
Riverside Community College, CA
St. Philip's College, TX
San Antonio College, TX
San Bernardino Valley College, CA
San Jose City College, CA
Santa Ana College, CA
Santa Fe Community College, NM
South Mountain Community College, AZ
South Plains College, TX
Southwest Texas Junior College, TX
Southwestern College, CA
Texas Southmost College, TX
Texas State Technical College
Harlingen, TX
Trinidad State Junior College, CO
University College of San Juan, PR
Ventura College, CA
Victoria College, TX
Waubonsee Community College, IL
West Hills Community College, CA

Tribal colleges

Four-year

Haskell Indian Nations University, KS
Institute of American Indian Arts, NM
Oglala Lakota College, SD
Salish Kootenai College, MT

Two-year

Bay Mills Community College, MI
Blackfeet Community College, MT
Cankdeska Cikana Community College, ND
Chief Dull Knife College, MT
College of Menominee Nation, WI
Dine College, AZ
Fond du Lac Tribal and Community College, MN
Fort Belknap College, MT
Fort Berthold Community College, ND
Fort Peck Community College, MT
Little Big Horn College, MT
Little Priest Tribal College, NE
Nebraska Indian Community College, NE
Sisseton Wahpeton College, SD
Sitting Bull College, ND
Southwestern Indian Polytechnic Institute, NM
Stone Child College, MT
Turtle Mountain Community College, ND

Undergraduate enrollment size

Very small (fewer than 750)

Four-year

Alabama
Andrew Jackson University
Heritage Christian University
Herzing College
Judson College
South University
Southeastern Bible College
Southern Christian University
Talladega College

Alaska
Alaska Pacific University
Charter College

Arizona
American Indian College of the Assemblies of God
Arizona Institute of Business and Technology
International Institute of the Americas: Mesa
Chaparral College
International Institute of the Americas: West Valley
Northcentral University
Southwestern College
Tucson Design College

Arkansas
Ecclesia College
Lyon College
University of the Ozarks
Williams Baptist College

California
Alliant International University
Bethany University
California Institute of Integral Studies
California Maritime Academy
California National University for Advanced Studies
Charles R. Drew University of Medicine and Science
Cogswell Polytechnical College
Coleman College
Columbia College: Hollywood
Design Institute of San Diego
DeVry University
West Hills
Golden Gate University
Holy Names University
LIFE Pacific College
Lincoln University
National Hispanic University
NewSchool of Architecture & Design
Northwestern Polytechnic University
Pacific States University
Platt College
Ontario
San Diego
Samuel Merritt College
San Francisco Art Institute
Thomas Aquinas College
Westwood College: Long Beach
William Jessup University

Colorado
DeVry University
Westminster
DeVry University: Colorado Springs
Naropa University
Nazarene Bible College
Rocky Mountain College of Art & Design
Westwood College of Technology
South

Connecticut
Briarwood College
Holy Apostles College and Seminary
Lyme Academy College of Fine Arts
Mitchell College
Paier College of Art

Delaware
Goldey-Beacom College

District of Columbia
Corcoran College of Art and Design
Potomac College
Southeastern University

Florida
Baptist College of Florida
Beacon College
Clearwater Christian College
Everglades University
Florida College
Jones College
Miami International University of Art and Design
Northwood University
Florida Campus
Remington College: Largo
Remington College: Tampa
St. John Vianney College Seminary
Schiller International University
South University: West Palm Beach Campus
Trinity College of Florida
Universidad FLET
Webber International University
Webster College
Webster College: Holiday

Georgia
Atlanta Christian College
Beulah Heights Bible College
Brenau University
Emmanuel College
Life University
Medical College of Georgia
Thomas University
Truett-McConnell College
Wesleyan College

Illinois
Argosy University
Blackburn College
Blessing-Reiman College of Nursing
Eureka College
Lexington College
Lincoln Christian College and Seminary
MacMurray College
Midstate College
National University of Health Sciences
Principia College
Rosalind Franklin University of Medicine and Science
Rush University
Saint Anthony College of Nursing
St. Francis Medical Center College of Nursing
Shimer College
VanderCook College of Music
West Suburban College of Nursing
Westwood College - Chicago Loop
Westwood College of Technology
O'Hare

Indiana
American Conservatory of Music
College of Court Reporting
DeVry University: Indianapolis
Taylor University: Fort Wayne

Iowa
Allen College
Emmaus Bible College
Faith Baptist Bible College and Theological Seminary
Hamilton College
Cedar Falls
Cedar Rapids
Maharishi University of Management
Mercy College of Health Sciences
Vennard College
Waldorf College

Kansas
Barclay College
Bethany College
Bethel College
Central Christian College of Kansas
Manhattan Christian College
McPherson College
Ottawa University
Sterling College
Tabor College
University of Kansas Medical Center
University of St. Mary

Kentucky
Alice Lloyd College
Beckfield College
Brescia University
Clear Creek Baptist Bible College
Kentucky Mountain Bible College
Kentucky Wesleyan College
St. Catharine College
Union College

Louisiana
Southwest University

Maine
College of the Atlantic
Maine College of Art
New England School of Communications
Thomas College
Unity College
University of Maine
Machias

Maryland
Baltimore International College
Capitol College
DeVry University: Bethesda
Johns Hopkins University: Peabody Conservatory of Music
St. John's College

Massachusetts
Anna Maria College
Atlantic Union College
Boston Architectural Center
Boston Conservatory
Franklin W. Olin College of Engineering
Hebrew College
Hellenic College/Holy Cross
Montserrat College of Art
Pine Manor College
School of the Museum of Fine Arts
Wheelock College

Michigan
Cleary University
Concordia University
Finlandia University
Grace Bible College
Great Lakes Christian College
Marygrove College
Reformed Bible College
Sacred Heart Major Seminary

Minnesota
Bethany Lutheran College
College of Visual Arts
Devry University: Edina
Minneapolis College of Art and Design
Oak Hills Christian College

Mississippi
Blue Mountain College
Magnolia Bible College
Wesley College

Missouri
Baptist Bible College
Calvary Bible College and Theological Seminary
Central Christian College of the Bible
Conception Seminary College
Hickey College
Kansas City Art Institute
Lester L. Cox College of Nursing and Health Sciences
Missouri Technical School
National American University
Kansas City
Research College of Nursing
St. Louis Christian College
St. Luke's College
Stephens College

Montana
University of Great Falls

Nebraska
Clarkson College
Dana College
Grace University
Nebraska Christian College
Nebraska Methodist College of Nursing and Allied Health
York College

Nevada
DeVry University: Las Vegas
International Academy of Design and Technology: Henderson
Morrison University
Sierra Nevada College

New Hampshire
Chester College of New England
Magdalen College
Thomas More College of Liberal Arts

New Jersey
Westminster Choir College of Rider University

New Mexico
College of the Southwest
Institute of American Indian Arts
International Institute of the Americas
Metropolitan College of Court Reporting
St. John's College

New York
Berkeley College
Concordia College
Davis College
Holy Trinity Orthodox Seminary
Juilliard School
King's College
Manhattan School of Music
Mannes College The New School for Music
New York School of Interior Design
State University of New York
Downstate Medical Center
Upstate Medical University
Webb Institute
Wells College
Yeshiva Mikdash Melech

North Carolina
Bennett College
Brevard College
Cabarrus College of Health Sciences
DeVry University: Charlotte
John Wesley College
North Carolina School of the Arts
Peace College
Piedmont Baptist College
Roanoke Bible College
St. Andrews Presbyterian College

North Dakota
Medcenter One College of Nursing
Trinity Bible College

Ohio
Allegheny Wesleyan College
Antioch College
Art Academy of Cincinnati
Cincinnati College of Mortuary Science
Circleville Bible College
Cleveland Institute of Art
Cleveland Institute of Music
Lake Erie College
Laura and Alvin Siegal College of Judaic Studies
MedCentral College of Nursing
Mercy College of Northwest Ohio
Mount Carmel College of Nursing
Pontifical College Josephinum

Oklahoma
Mid-America Christian University
Southwestern Christian University

Oregon
DeVry University: Portland
Eugene Bible College
Mount Angel Seminary
Multnomah Bible College
Northwest Christian College
Oregon Health & Science University
Pacific Northwest College of Art
Pioneer Pacific College
Warner Pacific College

Pennsylvania
Baptist Bible College of Pennsylvania
Bryn Athyn College of the New Church
Chatham College
Curtis Institute of Music
DeVry University
Ft. Washington
Gratz College
Immaculata University
Lancaster Bible College
Moore College of Art and Design
Penn State
Lehigh Valley
Wilkes-Barre
Restaurant School
Rosemont College
St. Charles Borromeo Seminary - Overbrook
Williamson Free School of Mechanical Trades
Wilson College

Puerto Rico
Atlantic College
Conservatory of Music of Puerto Rico

Rhode Island
Zion Bible Institute

South Carolina
- Allen University
- Columbia International University
- Erskine College
- Limestone College
- Medical University of South Carolina
- South University
- Voorhees College

Tennessee
- Free Will Baptist Bible College
- Martin Methodist College
- Memphis College of Art
- Milligan College
- O'More College of Design
- South College
- Williamson Christian College

Texas
- Amberton University
- Arlington Baptist College
- Austin Graduate School of Theology
- Baptist Missionary Association Theological Seminary
- Baptist University of the Americas
- College of Saint Thomas More
- Criswell College
- Dallas Christian College
- DeVry University: Houston
- Huston-Tillotson College
- Jarvis Christian College
- Northwood University: Texas Campus
- Southwestern Christian College
- Texas A&M University
    - Baylor College of Dentistry
- Texas Tech University Health Sciences Center
- University of Texas
    - Health Science Center at Houston
    - Medical Branch at Galveston
    - Southwestern Medical Center at Dallas

Utah
- Neumont University

Vermont
- Bennington College
- College of St. Joseph in Vermont
- Goddard College
- Green Mountain College
- Marlboro College
- Southern Vermont College
- Sterling College
- Woodbury College

Virginia
- Christendom College
- DeVry University
    - Arlington
- ECPI Technical College
    - Glen Allen
- Randolph-Macon Woman's College
- St. Paul's College
- Sweet Briar College
- World College

Washington
- Bastyr University
- Crown College
- DigiPen Institute of Technology
- Henry Cogswell College
- Northwest College of Art
- Trinity Lutheran College

West Virginia
- Alderson-Broaddus College
- Appalachian Bible College
- Davis and Elkins College
- Ohio Valley University
- Salem International University

Wisconsin
- Bellin College of Nursing
- DeVry University: Milwaukee
- Northland College
- Silver Lake College

France
- American University of Paris

Monaco
- International University of Monaco

Switzerland
- Franklin College: Switzerland

Two-year

Alabama
- Prince Institute of Professional Studies
- Remington College
    - Mobile
- Virginia College Technical

Alaska
- Ilisagvik College
- Prince William Sound Community College

Arizona
- Lamson College
- Long Technical College
- Paralegal Institute
- Tohono O'odham Community College

Arkansas
- University of Arkansas
    - Cossatot Community College of the

California
- American Academy of Dramatic Arts: West
- College of Oceaneering
- Deep Springs College
- Empire College
- Fashion Institute of Design and Merchandising
    - San Diego
- Feather River College
- Marymount College
- MTI College
- Queen of the Holy Rosary College
- Salvation Army Crestmont College

Colorado
- Boulder College of Massage Therapy
- CollegeAmerica-Denver
- Colorado Northwestern Community College
- Denver Academy of Court Reporting
- Institute of Business & Medical Careers
- Parks College: Aurora
- Remington College
    - Colorado Springs

Delaware
- Delaware College of Art and Design

Florida
- Angley College
- Central Florida College
- City College: Casselberry
- Florida Career College: Hialeah
- Florida Career College: Miami
- Florida Career College: Pembroke Pines
- Florida Technical College
    - Deland
- Herzing College
    - Orlando
- Southwest Florida College
    - Tampa
- Ultrasound Diagnostic School
    - Sanford-Brown Institute: Jacksonville

Georgia
- Andrew College
- Brown Mackie College: Atlanta
- Gupton Jones College of Funeral Service
- Gwinnett College
- Le Cordon Bleu College of Culinary Arts
- Oxford College of Emory University
- Young Harris College

Hawaii
- Hawaii Tokai International College
- Remington College
    - Honolulu

Idaho
- Eastern Idaho Technical College

Illinois
- College of Office Technology
- Fox College
- Springfield College in Illinois

Indiana
- Brown Mackie College: Michigan City
- Indiana Business College
- Indiana Business College
    - Anderson
    - Columbus
    - Evansville
    - Fort Wayne
    - Lafayette
    - Marion
    - Medical
    - Muncie
    - Terre Haute
- Sawyer College: Merrillville

Iowa
- St. Luke's College

Kansas
- Brown Mackie College
- Donnelly College
- Hesston College
- Manhattan Area Technical College
- Pratt Community College

Kentucky
- Daymar College
- Daymar College
    - Louisville
- Louisville Technical Institute
- Spencerian College: Lexington

Louisiana
- New Orleans School of Urban Missions

Maine
- Andover College
- Beal College
- Central Maine Medical Center School of Nursing

Maryland
- TESST College of Technology: Towson

Massachusetts
- Fisher College
- Laboure College
- Marian Court College
- Urban College of Boston

Michigan
- Bay Mills Community College
- Lewis College of Business
- Saginaw Chippewa Tribal College

Minnesota
- Academy College
- Duluth Business University
- Minneapolis Business College
- Northwest Technical Institute
- Pine Technical College
- Rainy River Community College

Missouri
- Everest College: Springfield
- Metro Business College
    - Jefferson City
- Missouri College
- Patricia Stevens College
- Pinnacle Career Institute: Kansas City
- Vatterott College
- Vatterott College: St. Joseph
- Vatterott College: Springfield

Montana
- Blackfeet Community College
- Chief Dull Knife College
- Dawson Community College
- Fort Belknap College
- Little Big Horn College
- Miles Community College
- Stone Child College

Nebraska
- Creative Center
- Hamilton College: Lincoln
- Little Priest Tribal College
- Nebraska College of Technical Agriculture
- Vatterott College: Spring Valley

Nevada
- Career College of Northern Nevada
- Heritage College
- High-Tech Institute
- Las Vegas College
- Le Cordon Bleu College of Culinary Arts

New Jersey
- Assumption College for Sisters
- Somerset Christian College

New Mexico
- Art Center Design College
- Crownpoint Institute of Technology
- Mesalands Community College
- New Mexico Military Institute Junior College
- New Mexico State University
    - Grants
- Southwestern Indian Polytechnic Institute

New York
- American Academy of Dramatic Arts
- Bramson ORT College
- Bryant & Stratton Business Institute
    - Bryant & Stratton College: Albany
    - Bryant & Stratton College: Rochester
- Bryant & Stratton College: Syracuse North
- Cochran School of Nursing-St. John's Riverside Hospital
- Elmira Business Institute
- Helene Fuld College of Nursing
- Jamestown Business College
- Long Island College Hospital School of Nursing
- Maria College
- Mildred Elley
- New York Career Institute
- Olean Business Institute
- Phillips Beth Israel School of Nursing
- Plaza College
- St. Elizabeth College of Nursing
- St. Joseph's College of Nursing
- Swedish Institute
- Villa Maria College of Buffalo

North Carolina
- Beaufort County Community College
- Martin Community College
- Montgomery Community College

North Dakota
- Aakers College: Fargo
- Fort Berthold Community College
- Lake Region State College
- Minot State University: Bottineau Campus

Ohio
- AEC Southern Ohio College
    - Brown Mackie College: Akron
- Art Institute of Cincinnati
- Bradford School
- Bryant & Stratton College
    - Parma
- College of Art Advertising
- Davis College
- ETI Technical College of Niles
- Gallipolis Career College
- Good Samaritan College of Nursing and Health Science
- Kettering College of Medical Arts
- Ohio College of Massotherapy
- Ohio Institute of Photography and Technology
- Ohio Valley College of Technology
- Remington College
    - Cleveland
- School of Advertising Art
- Southeastern Business College
- Southeastern Business College: Jackson
- Southeastern Business College: New Boston
- Southwestern College of Business
    - Southwestern College: Franklin
    - Southwestern College: Tri-County
    - Southwestern College: Vine Street Campus
- Technology Education College
- Wright State University: Lake Campus

Oklahoma
- Heritage College Hair Design
- Vatterott College
    - Tulsa
- Western College of Southern California

Oregon
- Pioneer Pacific College: Springfield

Pennsylvania
- Academy of Medical Arts and Business
- Allied Medical and Technical Institute
- Antonelli Institute of Art and Photography
- Berean Institute
- Berks Technical Institute
- Bidwell Training Center
- Bradley Academy for the Visual Arts
- Business Institute of Pennsylvania
- Business Institute of Pennsylvania
    - Meadville
- Cambria-Rowe Business College
- Career Training Academy
- Career Training Academy: Monroeville
- CHI Institute: Southampton
- Commonwealth Technical Institute
- Consolidated School of Business
    - Lancaster
    - York

- Dean Institute of Technology
- Douglas Education Center
- DuBois Business College
- Erie Business Center
- Erie Business Center South
- Erie Institute of Technology
- Harcum College
- Hussian School of Art
- International Academy of Design and Technology: Pittsburgh
- Lansdale School of Business
- Lincoln Technical Institute
- Lincoln Technical Institute: Philadelphia
- Manor College
- McCann School of Business
  - Pottsville
- Metropolitan Career Center
- Newport Business Institute
- Newport Business Institute
- North Central Industrial Technical Education Center
- Oakbridge Academy of Arts
- Orleans Technical Institute - Center City Campus
- Pace Institute
- Penn Commercial Business and Technical School
- Penn State
  - Beaver
  - Dubois
  - McKeesport
  - New Kensington
  - Shenango
- Pennco Tech
- Pittsburgh Institute of Aeronautics
- Pittsburgh Institute of Mortuary Science
- Rosedale Technical Institute
- Schuylkill Institute of Business & Technology
- South Hills School of Business & Technology
- Thaddeus Stevens College of Technology
- Thompson Institute
- Thompson Institute
  - Philadelphia
- Triangle Tech
  - DuBois
  - Erie
  - Greensburg
  - Pittsburgh
- University of Pittsburgh
  - Titusville
- Valley Forge Military College
- Vet Tech Institute
- West Virginia Career Institute
- Western School of Health and Business Careers
- Western School of Health and Business Careers
  - Monroeville
- Yorktowne Business Institute

Puerto Rico
- Humacao Community College

South Carolina
- Forrest Junior College
- Miller-Motte Technical College
- Spartanburg Methodist College

South Dakota
- Kilian Community College

Tennessee
- Hiwassee College
- John A. Gupton College
- Nossi College of Art
- Vatterott College: Memphis

Texas
- Austin Business College
- Commonwealth Institute of Funeral Service
- Dallas Institute of Funeral Service
- Everest College: Arlington
- Hallmark Institute of Aeronautics
- Hallmark Institute of Technology
- MTI College of Business and Technology
- MTI College of Business and Technology
- Remington College
  - Houston
- Texas State Technical College: Marshall
- Wade College
- Westwood College: Dallas
- Westwood College: Ft. Worth

Utah
- Everest College: Salt Lake City
- Provo College
- Utah Career College

Vermont
- Landmark College
- New England Culinary Institute

Virginia
- Bryant & Stratton College: Virginia Beach
- Miller-Motte Technical College: Lynchburg

Washington
- Northwest Aviation College
- Northwest School of Wooden Boatbuilding

West Virginia
- Corinthian Schools: National Institute of Technology
- Eastern West Virginia Community and Technical College
- Valley College of Technology
- West Virginia Business College
- West Virginia Business College

Wisconsin
- College of Menominee Nation
- University of Wisconsin
  - Baraboo/Sauk County
  - Marinette
  - Richland
  - Rock County

Wyoming
- Eastern Wyoming College

Marshall Islands
- College of the Marshall Islands

Palau
- Palau Community College

Small (750-1,999)

Four-year

Alabama
- Birmingham-Southern College
- Huntingdon College
- Oakwood College
- Spring Hill College
- University of Mobile
- University of West Alabama
- Virginia College

Alaska
- University of Alaska
  - Southeast

Arizona
- DeVry University
  - Phoenix
- Embry-Riddle Aeronautical University: Prescott Campus
- Prescott College
- University of Advancing Technology

Arkansas
- Hendrix College
- John Brown University
- Ouachita Baptist University

California
- Art Center College of Design
- Art Institute
  - of California: Orange County
  - of California: San Diego
- California College of the Arts
- California Institute of Technology
- California Institute of the Arts
- Claremont McKenna College
- Concordia University
- DeVry University
  - Fremont
  - Long Beach
  - Pomona
- Dominican University of California
- Fresno Pacific University
- Hope International University
- Humphreys College
- La Sierra University
- Master's College
- Menlo College
- Mills College
- Mount St. Mary's College
- Occidental College
- Pacific Union College
- Pitzer College
- Pomona College
- Scripps College
- Simpson University
- University of California: Merced
- University of La Verne
- Vanguard University of Southern California
- Westmont College
- Westwood College of Technology
  - Inland Empire
- Whittier College
- Woodbury University

Colorado
- Colorado Christian University
- Colorado College
- Johnson & Wales University
- Jones International University
- Regis University

Connecticut
- Albertus Magnus College
- Charter Oak State College
- Connecticut College
- Post University
- St. Joseph College
- United States Coast Guard Academy
- University of Bridgeport

Florida
- Chipola College
- DeVry University
  - Miramar
  - Orlando
- Eckerd College
- Edward Waters College
- Florida Hospital College of Health Sciences
- Florida Memorial University
- Florida Metropolitan University
  - Brandon Campus
- Florida Metropolitan University: Jacksonville
- Florida Southern College
- International College
- New College of Florida
- Ringling School of Art and Design
- Rollins College
- St. Leo University
- St. Thomas University
- Warner Southern College

Georgia
- Agnes Scott College
- Bauder College
- Berry College
- Brewton-Parker College
- Covenant College
- DeVry University
  - Alpharetta
  - Decatur
- Fort Valley State University
- LaGrange College
- Oglethorpe University
- Paine College
- Piedmont College
- Reinhardt College
- Shorter College
- South University
- Toccoa Falls College

Hawaii
- Chaminade University of Honolulu
- University of Hawaii
  - West Oahu

Idaho
- Albertson College of Idaho
- Northwest Nazarene University

Illinois
- Aurora University
- DeVry University
  - Addison
  - Tinley Park
- Dominican University
- Greenville College
- Harrington College of Design
- Illinois College
- Judson College
- Kendall College
- Knox College
- Lake Forest College
- Moody Bible Institute
- North Park University
- Quincy University
- Rockford College
- Trinity Christian College
- Trinity International University
- University of St. Francis

Indiana
- Calumet College of St. Joseph
- Earlham College
- Franklin College
- Goshen College
- Grace College and Seminary
- Hanover College
- Huntington University
- Manchester College
- Marian College
- Oakland City University
- Rose-Hulman Institute of Technology
- St. Joseph's College
- Saint Mary's College
- St. Mary-of-the-Woods College
- Taylor University
- Tri-State University
- University of St. Francis
- Wabash College

Iowa
- Briar Cliff University
- Buena Vista University
- Central College
- Clarke College
- Coe College
- Cornell College
- Dordt College
- Graceland University
- Grand View College
- Grinnell College
- Hamilton College
- Iowa Wesleyan College
- Loras College
- Morningside College
- Mount Mercy College
- Northwestern College
- Simpson College
- University of Dubuque
- Wartburg College

Kansas
- Baker University
- Haskell Indian Nations University
- MidAmerica Nazarene University
- Newman University
- Southwestern College

Kentucky
- Asbury College
- Berea College
- Campbellsville University
- Centre College
- Georgetown College
- Kentucky State University
- Lindsey Wilson College
- Mid-Continent University
- Midway College
- Pikeville College
- Thomas More College
- Transylvania University
- University of the Cumberlands

Louisiana
- Centenary College of Louisiana

Maine
- Bates College
- Bowdoin College
- Colby College
- Husson College
- Maine Maritime Academy
- St. Joseph's College
- University of Maine
  - Fort Kent
  - Presque Isle
- University of New England

Maryland
- College of Notre Dame of Maryland
- Columbia Union College
- Goucher College
- Hood College
- Maryland Institute College of Art
- McDaniel College
- Mount St. Mary's University
- St. Mary's College of Maryland
- Sojourner-Douglass College
- University of Maryland
  - Baltimore
- Washington College

Massachusetts
- American International College
- Amherst College
- Art Institute of Boston at Lesley University
- Bay Path College
- Becker College
- Cambridge College
- Eastern Nazarene College
- Elms College
- Gordon College
- Hampshire College
- Lasell College
- Lesley University
- Massachusetts College of Art
- Massachusetts College of Liberal Arts
- Massachusetts College of Pharmacy and Health Sciences
- Massachusetts Maritime Academy
- New England Institute of Art
- Nichols College
- Regis College
- Simmons College
- Wheaton College
- Williams College

Michigan
- Adrian College
- Albion College
- Alma College
- Andrews University
- Aquinas College
- Baker College
  - of Cadillac
  - of Jackson
  - of Port Huron
- College for Creative Studies
- Hillsdale College
- Kalamazoo College

Tables and Indexes

Kendall College of Art and Design of Ferris State University
Northwood University
Siena Heights University
Walsh College of Accountancy and Business Administration

Minnesota

Art Institutes International Minnesota
Brown College
Carleton College
College of St. Benedict
College of St. Scholastica
Concordia University: St. Paul
Crown College
Hamline University
Macalester College
Martin Luther College
Minnesota School of Business
North Central University
Northwestern College
St. John's University
St. Mary's University of Minnesota
University of Minnesota
  Crookston
  Morris
Walden University

Mississippi

Millsaps College
Rust College
Tougaloo College

Missouri

Avila University
Central Methodist University
College of the Ozarks
Columbia College
Culver-Stockton College
DeVry University
  Kansas City
Drury University
Evangel University
Hannibal-LaGrange College
Jewish Hospital College of Nursing and Allied Health
Missouri Baptist University
Missouri Valley College
Ozark Christian College
Ranken Technical College
Rockhurst University
Westminster College
William Jewell College
William Woods University

Montana

Carroll College
Montana Tech of the University of Montana
Rocky Mountain College
Salish Kootenai College
University of Montana: Western

Nebraska

Chadron State College
College of Saint Mary
Concordia University
Doane College
Hastings College
Midland Lutheran College
Nebraska Wesleyan University
Peru State College
Union College
University of Nebraska Medical Center

Nevada

Art Institute
  of Las Vegas

New Hampshire

Colby-Sawyer College
Franklin Pierce College
Granite State College
New England College
Rivier College
St. Anselm College
Southern New Hampshire University
University of New Hampshire at Manchester

New Jersey

Caldwell College
Centenary College
College of St. Elizabeth
DeVry University: North Brunswick
Drew University
Felician College
Georgian Court University
Stevens Institute of Technology

New Mexico

College of Santa Fe
New Mexico Highlands University
New Mexico Institute of Mining and Technology
Western New Mexico University

New York

Albany College of Pharmacy
Alfred University
Bard College
Boricua College
Cazenovia College
College of Mount St. Vincent
College of New Rochelle
Columbia University
  Fu Foundation School of Engineering and Applied Science
  School of General Studies
Cooper Union for the Advancement of Science and Art
D'Youville College
Daemen College
DeVry Institute of Technology
  New York
Dominican College of Blauvelt
Elmira College
Eugene Lang College The New School for Liberal Arts
Five Towns College
Globe Institute of Technology
Hamilton College
Hartwick College
Hilbert College
Hobart and William Smith Colleges
Houghton College
Keuka College
Laboratory Institute of Merchandising
Manhattanville College
Marymount Manhattan College
Medaille College
Paul Smith's College
Polytechnic University
Roberts Wesleyan College
Russell Sage College
Sage College of Albany
St. Thomas Aquinas College
Sarah Lawrence College
State University of New York
  College of Environmental Science and Forestry
  Institute of Technology at Utica/Rome
United States Merchant Marine Academy
Vaughn College of Aeronautics and Technology
Wagner College

North Carolina

Art Institute
  of Charlotte
Barton College
Belmont Abbey College
Catawba College
Chowan College
Davidson College
Greensboro College
Johnson C. Smith University
Livingstone College
Mars Hill College
Meredith College
Miller-Motte Technical College
Montreat College
North Carolina Wesleyan College
Pfeiffer University
Queens University of Charlotte
Salem College
Warren Wilson College
Wingate University

North Dakota

Jamestown College
Mayville State University
Valley City State University

Ohio

Bluffton University
Central State University
Cincinnati Christian University
College of Mount St. Joseph
College of Wooster
Columbus College of Art and Design
Defiance College
Franciscan University of Steubenville
Heidelberg College
Hiram College
Kenyon College
Lourdes College
Malone College
Marietta College
Muskingum College
Ohio State University
  Lima Campus
  Mansfield Campus
  Marion Campus
  Newark Campus
Ohio University
  Chillicothe Campus
  Lancaster Campus
  Zanesville Campus
Ohio Wesleyan University
Tiffin University
Union Institute & University
University of Rio Grande
Urbana University
Ursuline College
Walsh University
Wilmington College
Wittenberg University

Oklahoma

Bacone College
National Education Center
  Spartan School of Aeronautics
Northwestern Oklahoma State University
Oklahoma Baptist University
Oklahoma Christian University
Oklahoma City University
Oklahoma Panhandle State University
St. Gregory's University
Southern Nazarene University
University of Science and Arts of Oklahoma

Oregon

Art Institute of Portland
Concordia University
Corban College
George Fox University
Lewis & Clark College
Linfield College
Marylhurst University
Pacific University
Reed College
Willamette University

Pennsylvania

Alvernia College
Arcadia University
Bryn Mawr College
Cabrini College
Carlow University
Cedar Crest College
Central Pennsylvania College
Chestnut Hill College
Cheyney University of Pennsylvania
College Misericordia
Delaware Valley College
Franklin & Marshall College
Geneva College
Haverford College
Juniata College
Keystone College
King's College
La Roche College
Lebanon Valley College
Lincoln University
Lycoming College
Marywood University
Moravian College
Mount Aloysius College
Peirce College
Penn State
  Harrisburg
  Schuylkill - Capital College
Philadelphia Biblical University
St. Francis University
St. Vincent College
Seton Hill University
Susquehanna University
Swarthmore College
Thiel College
Thomas Jefferson University: College of Health Professions
University of Pittsburgh
  Bradford
  Greensburg
University of the Sciences in Philadelphia
Ursinus College
Valley Forge Christian College
Washington and Jefferson College
Waynesburg College
Westminster College

Puerto Rico

Columbia College
Electronic Data Processing College: San Sebastian
Universidad Adventista de las Antillas
University of Puerto Rico
  Utuado

Rhode Island

Rhode Island School of Design

South Carolina

Anderson University
Claflin University
Columbia College
Converse College
Morris College
Newberry College
North Greenville College
Presbyterian College
Southern Wesleyan University
University of South Carolina
  Beaufort
Wofford College

South Dakota

Augustana College
Dakota State University
Dakota Wesleyan University
Mount Marty College
Northern State University
Presentation College
South Dakota School of Mines and Technology
University of Sioux Falls

Tennessee

Aquinas College
Bethel College
Bryan College
Carson-Newman College
Christian Brothers University
Crichton College
Cumberland University
Fisk University
Freed-Hardeman University
Johnson Bible College
King College
Lambuth University
LeMoyne-Owen College
Lincoln Memorial University
Maryville College
Rhodes College
Tennessee Wesleyan College
Trevecca Nazarene University
University of the South

Texas

Art Institute
  of Dallas
  of Houston
Austin College
Concordia University at Austin
DeVry University
  Irving
East Texas Baptist University
Hardin-Simmons University
Houston Baptist University
Howard Payne University
Lubbock Christian University
McMurry University
Our Lady of the Lake University of San Antonio
Paul Quinn College
Schreiner University
Southwestern Adventist University
Southwestern Assemblies of God University
Southwestern University
Texas A&M University
  Galveston
  Texarkana
Texas College
Texas Lutheran University
Texas Wesleyan University
University of Dallas
University of Houston
  Victoria
University of St. Thomas
Wayland Baptist University
Wiley College

Utah

Stevens-Henager College
Westminster College

Vermont

Castleton State College
Johnson State College
Lyndon State College
St. Michael's College
Vermont Technical College

Virginia

Art Institute
  of Washington
Averett University
Bluefield College
Bridgewater College
Eastern Mennonite University
Emory & Henry College
Ferrum College
Hampden-Sydney College
Hollins University
Jefferson College of Health Sciences
Lynchburg College
Mary Baldwin College
Randolph-Macon College
Regent University
Roanoke College
Shenandoah University
University of Virginia's College at Wise
Virginia Intermont College
Virginia Military Institute
Virginia Union University
Virginia Wesleyan College

Washington and Lee University

Washington
Cornish College of the Arts
DeVry University
Federal Way
Heritage University
Northwest University
Saint Martin's University
Walla Walla College
Whitman College

West Virginia
Bethany College
Glenville State College
University of Charleston
West Virginia Wesleyan College
Wheeling Jesuit University

Wisconsin
Beloit College
Edgewood College
Lawrence University
Maranatha Baptist Bible College
Marian College of Fond du Lac
Mount Mary College
Ripon College
St. Norbert College

Virgin Islands, U.S.
University of the Virgin Islands

United Arab Emirates
American University in Dubai - United Arab Emirates

Two-year

Alabama
J. F. Drake State Technical College
Jefferson Davis Community College
Snead State Community College
Trenholm State Technical College

Arizona
Chandler-Gilbert Community College
Williams Campus
Dine College

Arkansas
Arkansas Northeastern College
Arkansas State University
Mountain Home
East Arkansas Community College
Mid-South Community College
North Arkansas College
Ouachita Technical College
Ozarka College
Southern Arkansas University Tech
University of Arkansas
Community College at Batesville
Community College at Hope
University of Arkansas
Community College at Morrilton

California
California School of Culinary Arts
Fashion Institute of Design and Merchandising
San Francisco
Palo Verde College
WyoTech Institute: Fremont

Colorado
Denver Automotive & Diesel College
Morgan Community College
Trinidad State Junior College

Connecticut
Asnuntuck Community College
Gibbs College
Goodwin College
Middlesex Community College
Northwestern Connecticut Community College
Quinebaug Valley Community College

Florida
Florida Career College: West Palm Beach
Florida Keys Community College
Orlando Culinary Academy
South Florida Community College
Southwest Florida College

Georgia
Atlanta Metropolitan College
Northwestern Technical College
West Georgia Technical College

Hawaii
University of Hawaii
Kauai Community College
Windward Community College

Illinois
Highland Community College
Illinois Eastern Community Colleges
Lincoln Trail College
Olney Central College
John Wood Community College
Northwestern Business College

Indiana
Brown Mackie College: Fort Wayne
Ivy Tech State College
Ivy Tech Community College: Columbus
Ivy Tech Community College: Southeast
Ivy Tech Community College: Whitewater
Lincoln Technical Institute

Iowa
AIB College of Business
Northeast Iowa Community College
Northwest Iowa Community College

Kansas
Colby Community College
Labette Community College
Seward County Community College

Kentucky
Henderson Community College
Spencerian College

Maine
Eastern Maine Community College
Kennebec Valley Community College
Northern Maine Community College

Maryland
Cecil Community College
TESST College of Technology
Baltimore

Massachusetts
Bay State College
Berkshire Community College
Gibbs College
Greenfield Community College

Michigan
Glen Oaks Community College
Gogebic Community College
Kirtland Community College
Montcalm Community College

Minnesota
Alexandria Technical College
Dunwoody College of Technology
Itasca Community College
Mesabi Range Community and Technical College
Minnesota School of Business: Brooklyn Center
Minnesota State College - Southeast Technical
Northwest Technical College

Mississippi
Coahoma Community College
Southwest Mississippi Community College

Missouri
Blue River Community College
Missouri State University: West Plains
North Central Missouri College

Montana
Helena College of Technology of the University of Montana

Nebraska
Mid-Plains Community College Area
Western Nebraska Community College

New Hampshire
McIntosh College
New Hampshire Community Technical College
Nashua

New Jersey
Salem Community College
Warren County Community College

New Mexico
New Mexico State University
Carlsbad

New York
Art Institute
of New York City
College of Westchester
Columbia-Greene Community College
Long Island Business Institute
North Country Community College
Rochester Business Institute
Sullivan County Community College
Taylor Business Institute
Trocaire College

North Carolina
Bladen Community College
Brunswick Community College
Carteret Community College
Cleveland Community College
Edgecombe Community College
James Sprunt Community College
Louisburg College
Mayland Community College
Roanoke-Chowan Community College
Sampson Community College
South Piedmont Community College
Southeastern Community College
Southwestern Community College
Wilson Technical Community College

North Dakota
Williston State College

Ohio
Belmont Technical College
Jefferson Community College
Kent State University
Ashtabula Regional Campus
East Liverpool Regional Campus
Salem Regional Campus
Trumbull Campus
Tuscarawas Campus
Ohio State University
Agricultural Technical Institute
University of Akron: Wayne College
Zane State College

Oklahoma
Connors State College
Northeastern Oklahoma Agricultural and Mechanical College
Redlands Community College
Western Oklahoma State College

Oregon
Blue Mountain Community College
Clatsop Community College
Klamath Community College
Southwestern Oregon Community College
Treasure Valley Community College

Pennsylvania
CHI Institute: Broomall
ICM School of Business & Medical Careers
Lackawanna College
Lehigh Valley College
Penn State
Delaware County
Fayette
Hazleton
Mont Alto
Worthington Scranton
York
Pennsylvania Highlands Community College
Pennsylvania Institute of Culinary Arts
Pittsburgh Technical Institute
Tri-State Business Institute
York Technical Institute

Puerto Rico
University College of San Juan

South Carolina
Northeastern Technical College
Technical College of the Lowcountry
University of South Carolina
Lancaster
Sumter

South Dakota
Mitchell Technical Institute
Western Dakota Technical Institute

Texas
ATI Career Training Center
Clarendon College
Court Reporting Institute of Dallas
Everest College: Dallas
Frank Phillips College
Panola College
Ranger College
Remington College
Dallas
Fort Worth
Texas State Technical College
West Texas
Western Technical Institute: Diana Drive
Western Texas College

Virginia
Dabney S. Lancaster Community College
Eastern Shore Community College
Mountain Empire Community College
Paul D. Camp Community College
Richard Bland College

Washington
Cascadia Community College
Grays Harbor College
Lower Columbia College
Peninsula College
Renton Technical College
South Seattle Community College

West Virginia
Huntington Junior College

Wisconsin
Bryant & Stratton College: Milwaukee
University of Wisconsin
Marathon County

Wyoming
Central Wyoming College
Northwest College
Sheridan College
Western Wyoming Community College

Guam
Guam Community College

Medium to large (2,000-7,499)

Four-year

Alabama
Alabama Agricultural and Mechanical University
Alabama State University
American Sentinel University
Athens State University
Auburn University at Montgomery
Faulkner University
Jacksonville State University
Samford University
Tuskegee University
University of Alabama
Huntsville
University of Montevallo
University of North Alabama

Alaska
University of Alaska
Fairbanks

Arizona
Arizona State University West
Grand Canyon University

Arkansas
Arkansas Tech University
Harding University
Henderson State University
Southern Arkansas University
University of Arkansas
Fort Smith
Monticello
Pine Bluff

California
Academy of Art University
Azusa Pacific University
Biola University
California Baptist University
California Lutheran University
California State University
Bakersfield
Monterey Bay
San Marcos
Stanislaus
Chapman University
Humboldt State University
Loyola Marymount University

National University
Pepperdine University
Point Loma Nazarene University
St. Mary's College of California
Santa Clara University
Sonoma State University
Stanford University
University of Redlands
University of San Diego
University of San Francisco
University of the Pacific

Colorado
Adams State College
Colorado School of Mines
Colorado State University
  Pueblo
Colorado Technical University
Fort Lewis College
Mesa State College
University of Colorado
  Colorado Springs
University of Denver
Western State College of Colorado

Connecticut
Eastern Connecticut State University
Fairfield University
Quinnipiac University
Sacred Heart University
Trinity College
University of Hartford
University of New Haven
Wesleyan University
Western Connecticut State University
Yale University

Delaware
Delaware State University
Wilmington College

District of Columbia
American University
Catholic University of America
Georgetown University
Howard University
University of the District of Columbia

Florida
Art Institute of Fort Lauderdale
Barry University
Bethune-Cookman College
Embry-Riddle Aeronautical University
Flagler College
Florida Gulf Coast University
Florida Institute of Technology
Jacksonville University
Johnson & Wales University
Lynn University
Nova Southeastern University
Palm Beach Atlantic University
Southeastern College of the Assemblies of God
Stetson University
University of Tampa

Georgia
Armstrong Atlantic State University
Augusta State University
Clark Atlanta University
Columbus State University
Dalton State College
Emory University
Georgia College and State University
Georgia Southwestern State University
Macon State College
Mercer University
Morehouse College
North Georgia College & State University
Savannah College of Art and Design
Southern Polytechnic State University
Spelman College

Hawaii
Brigham Young University-Hawaii
Hawaii Pacific University
University of Hawaii
  Hilo

Idaho
Lewis-Clark State College

Illinois
Augustana College
Benedictine University
Bradley University
Chicago State University
DeVry University
  Chicago
Elmhurst College
Governors State University
Illinois Institute of Technology
Illinois Wesleyan University
International Academy of Design and Technology: Chicago
Lewis University
McKendree College
National-Louis University
North Central College
Robert Morris College: Chicago
Roosevelt University
St. Xavier University
School of the Art Institute of Chicago
University of Chicago
University of Illinois
  Springfield
Wheaton College

Indiana
Anderson University
Bethel College
Butler University
DePauw University
Indiana Institute of Technology
Indiana University
  East
  Kokomo
  Northwest
  South Bend
  Southeast
University of Evansville
University of Indianapolis
Valparaiso University

Iowa
Drake University
Luther College
St. Ambrose University

Kansas
Emporia State University
Friends University
Pittsburg State University
Washburn University of Topeka

Kentucky
Bellarmine University
Morehead State University
Sullivan University

Louisiana
Grambling State University
Louisiana State University
  Alexandria
  Shreveport
Nicholls State University
Our Lady of the Lake College

Maine
University of Maine
  Augusta
  Farmington
University of Southern Maine

Maryland
Bowie State University
Coppin State University
Frostburg State University
Johns Hopkins University
Loyola College in Maryland
Morgan State University
Salisbury University
United States Naval Academy
University of Baltimore
University of Maryland
  Eastern Shore
Villa Julie College

Massachusetts
Assumption College
Bentley College
Berklee College of Music
Brandeis University
Bridgewater State College
Clark University
College of the Holy Cross
Curry College
Emerson College
Emmanuel College
Endicott College
Fitchburg State College
Framingham State College
Harvard College
Massachusetts Institute of Technology
Merrimack College
Mount Holyoke College
Salem State College
Smith College
Springfield College
Stonehill College
Suffolk University
Tufts University
University of Massachusetts
  Dartmouth
Wellesley College
Wentworth Institute of Technology
Western New England College
Westfield State College
Worcester Polytechnic Institute
Worcester State College

Michigan
Baker College
  of Auburn Hills
  of Clinton Township
  of Flint
  of Muskegon
  of Owosso
Calvin College
Cornerstone University
Hope College
Kettering University
Lake Superior State University
Lawrence Technological University
Madonna University
Michigan Technological University
Spring Arbor University
University of Detroit Mercy
University of Michigan
  Dearborn
  Flint

Minnesota
Augsburg College
Bemidji State University
Bethel University
College of St. Catherine
Concordia College: Moorhead
Gustavus Adolphus College
Metropolitan State University
Minnesota State University
  Moorhead
St. Olaf College
Southwest Minnesota State University
University of St. Thomas

Mississippi
Alcorn State University
Belhaven College
Delta State University
Jackson State University
Mississippi College
Mississippi Valley State University

Missouri
Fontbonne University
Lincoln University
Lindenwood University
Maryville University of Saint Louis
Missouri Southern State University
Northwest Missouri State University
St. Louis University
Southwest Baptist University
Truman State University
University of Missouri
  Kansas City
  Rolla
Washington University in St. Louis
Webster University

Montana
Montana State University
  Billings

Nebraska
Bellevue University
Creighton University
University of Nebraska
  Kearney
Wayne State College

Nevada
Great Basin College

New Hampshire
Dartmouth College
Keene State College
Plymouth State University

New Jersey
Berkeley College
Bloomfield College
The College of New Jersey
Fairleigh Dickinson University
  College at Florham
  Metropolitan Campus
Monmouth University
New Jersey City University
New Jersey Institute of Technology
Princeton University
Ramapo College of New Jersey
Richard Stockton College of New Jersey
Rider University
Rutgers, The State University of New Jersey
  Camden Regional Campus
  Newark Regional Campus
St. Peter's College
Seton Hall University

New Mexico
Eastern New Mexico University
Northern New Mexico College

New York
Adelphi University
Barnard College
Berkeley College of New York City
Briarcliffe College
Canisius College
City University of New York
  Medgar Evers College
  York College
Clarkson University
Colgate University
College of Saint Rose
Columbia University
  Columbia College
Culinary Institute of America
Dowling College
Fordham University
Iona College
Ithaca College
Le Moyne College
Long Island University
  Brooklyn Campus
  C. W. Post Campus
Manhattan College
Marist College
Mercy College
Molloy College
Monroe College
Mount St. Mary College
Nazareth College of Rochester
New York Institute of Technology
Niagara University
Pace University
Parsons The New School for Design
Pratt Institute
Rensselaer Polytechnic Institute
St. Bonaventure University
St. Francis College
St. John Fisher College
St. Joseph's College
St. Joseph's College: Suffolk Campus
St. Lawrence University
School of Visual Arts
Siena College
Skidmore College
State University of New York
  College at Brockport
  College at Cortland
  College at Fredonia
  College at Geneseo
  College at Old Westbury
  College at Oneonta
  College at Plattsburgh
  College at Potsdam
  Farmingdale
  New Paltz
  Oswego
  Purchase
Union College
United States Military Academy
University of Rochester
Utica College
Vassar College
Yeshiva University

North Carolina
Campbell University
Duke University
Elizabeth City State University
Elon University
Fayetteville State University
Gardner-Webb University
Guilford College
High Point University
Johnson & Wales University
Mount Olive College
North Carolina Central University
University of North Carolina
  Asheville
  Pembroke
Wake Forest University
Western Carolina University
Winston-Salem State University

North Dakota
Dickinson State University
Minot State University
University of Mary

Ohio
Ashland University
Baldwin-Wallace College
Capital University
Case Western Reserve University
Cedarville University
Denison University
DeVry University
  Columbus
Franklin University
John Carroll University

Mount Union College
Mount Vernon Nazarene University
Oberlin College
Ohio Dominican University
Ohio Northern University
Otterbein College
Shawnee State University
University of Dayton
University of Findlay
Xavier University

Oklahoma

Cameron University
East Central University
Rogers State University
Southeastern Oklahoma State University
University of Tulsa

Oregon

Eastern Oregon University
Oregon Institute of Technology
Southern Oregon University
University of Portland
Western Oregon University

Pennsylvania

Albright College
Allegheny College
Art Institute
- Online
- of Philadelphia
- of Pittsburgh

Bucknell University
California University of Pennsylvania
Carnegie Mellon University
Clarion University of Pennsylvania
DeSales University
Dickinson College
Duquesne University
East Stroudsburg University of Pennsylvania
Eastern University
Edinboro University of Pennsylvania
Elizabethtown College
Gannon University
Gettysburg College
Grove City College
Gwynedd-Mercy College
La Salle University
Lafayette College
Lehigh University
Lock Haven University of Pennsylvania
Mansfield University of Pennsylvania
Mercyhurst College
Messiah College
Millersville University of Pennsylvania
Muhlenberg College
Neumann College
Penn State
- Abington
- Altoona
- Berks
- Erie, The Behrend College

Pennsylvania College of Technology
Philadelphia University
Point Park University
Robert Morris University
St. Joseph's University
Shippensburg University of Pennsylvania
Slippery Rock University of Pennsylvania
University of Pittsburgh
- Johnstown

University of Scranton
University of the Arts
Villanova University
Widener University
Wilkes University
York College of Pennsylvania

Puerto Rico

American University of Puerto Rico
Bayamon Central University
Inter American University of Puerto Rico
- Aguadilla Campus
- Barranquitas Campus
- Bayamon Campus
- Fajardo Campus
- Guayama Campus
- Ponce Campus
- San German Campus

Universidad Politecnica de Puerto Rico
University of Puerto Rico
- Aguadilla
- Arecibo
- Bayamon University College
- Carolina Regional College
- Cayey University College
- Humacao
- Ponce

University of the Sacred Heart

Rhode Island

Brown University
Bryant University
New England Institute of Technology
Providence College
Rhode Island College
Roger Williams University
Salve Regina University

South Carolina

Benedict College
Charleston Southern University
The Citadel
Coastal Carolina University
Francis Marion University
Furman University
Lander University
South Carolina State University
University of South Carolina
- Aiken
- Upstate

Winthrop University

South Dakota

University of South Dakota

Tennessee

Belmont University
Lee University
Lipscomb University
Southern Adventist University
Tennessee State University
Tennessee Technological University
Tusculum College
Union University
University of Tennessee
- Chattanooga
- Martin

Vanderbilt University

Texas

Abilene Christian University
Angelo State University
Dallas Baptist University
LeTourneau University
Midwestern State University
Prairie View A&M University
Rice University
St. Edward's University
St. Mary's University
Southern Methodist University
Sul Ross State University
Texas A&M University
- Commerce
- Kingsville

Texas Christian University
Texas Woman's University
Trinity University
University of Houston
- Clear Lake

University of Mary Hardin-Baylor
University of Texas
- Tyler
- of the Permian Basin

University of the Incarnate Word
West Texas A&M University

Utah

Southern Utah University
Western Governors University

Vermont

Champlain College
Middlebury College

Virginia

Christopher Newport University
College of William and Mary
ECPI College of Technology
Hampton University
Longwood University
Marymount University
Norfolk State University
University of Mary Washington
University of Richmond
Virginia State University

Washington

Art Institute of Seattle
Evergreen State College
Gonzaga University
Pacific Lutheran University
Seattle Pacific University
Seattle University
University of Puget Sound
Whitworth College

West Virginia

Mountain State University
Shepherd University
West Liberty State College
West Virginia State University
West Virginia University at Parkersburg

Wisconsin

Alverno College
Carroll College
Carthage College
Concordia University Wisconsin
Milwaukee School of Engineering
University of Wisconsin
- Green Bay
- Parkside
- Platteville
- River Falls
- Stout
- Superior

Guam

University of Guam

Arab Republic of Egypt

American University in Cairo

Guatemala

Universidad del Valle de Guatemala

Lebanon

American University of Beirut

Mexico

Universidad Anahuac

Two-year

Alabama

Central Alabama Community College
Gadsden State Community College
George C. Wallace State Community College
- George C. Wallace Community College at Dothan

James H. Faulkner State Community College
Jefferson State Community College
Lawson State Community College
Northeast Alabama Community College
Northwest-Shoals Community College
Shelton State Community College
Southern Union State Community College

Arizona

Arizona Western College
Central Arizona College
Eastern Arizona College
Estrella Mountain Community College
Glendale Community College
High-Tech Institute
Mohave Community College
Northland Pioneer College
Paradise Valley Community College
South Mountain Community College
Universal Technical Institute
Yavapai College

Arkansas

Arkansas State University
- Beebe

National Park Community College
Northwest Arkansas Community College
Southeast Arkansas College

California

Barstow College
Canada College
Cerro Coso Community College
Chabot College
College of Alameda
College of Marin: Kentfield
College of the Desert
College of the Redwoods
College of the Siskiyous
Columbia College
Contra Costa College
Copper Mountain College
Crafton Hills College
Fashion Institute of Design and Merchandising
Gavilan Community College
Lake Tahoe Community College
Las Positas College
Lassen College
Los Angeles Southwest College
Mendocino College
Merritt College
MiraCosta College
Oxnard College
Porterville College
Reedley College
Santiago Canyon College
Solano Community College
Vista Community College
West Hills Community College

Colorado

Pueblo Community College
Red Rocks Community College

Connecticut

Capital Community College
Gateway Community College
Naugatuck Valley Community College
Norwalk Community College
Three Rivers Community College
Tunxis Community College

Delaware

Delaware Technical and Community College
- Owens Campus
- Stanton/Wilmington Campus
- Terry Campus

Florida

Central Florida Community College
Florida Community College at Jacksonville
Full Sail Real World Education
Gulf Coast Community College
Lake-Sumter Community College
Pasco-Hernando Community College
Polk Community College
St. Johns River Community College

Georgia

Albany Technical College
Athens Technical College
Bainbridge College
Chattahoochee Technical College
Coastal Georgia Community College
Columbus Technical College
DeKalb Technical College
Gainesville State College
Georgia Highlands College
Georgia Military College
Gordon College
Gwinnett Technical College
Middle Georgia College
Middle Georgia Technical College
Savannah Technical College

Hawaii

University of Hawaii
- Honolulu Community College
- Leeward Community College

Idaho

College of Southern Idaho
North Idaho College

Illinois

Black Hawk College
Carl Sandburg College
Heartland Community College
Illinois Eastern Community Colleges
- Wabash Valley College

Kankakee Community College
Kaskaskia College
Kishwaukee College
Lake Land College
Lincoln Land Community College
McHenry County College
Morton College
Prairie State College
Rock Valley College
Sauk Valley Community College
South Suburban College of Cook County
Southeastern Illinois College
Waubonsee Community College

Indiana

Ivy Tech State College
- Ivy Tech Community College: Bloomington
- Ivy Tech Community College: East Central
- Ivy Tech Community College: Kokomo
- Ivy Tech Community College: Lafayette
- Ivy Tech Community College: North Central
- Ivy Tech Community College: Northeast
- Ivy Tech Community College: Northwest
- Ivy Tech Community College: South Central
- Ivy Tech Community College: Southwest
- Ivy Tech Community College: Wabash Valley

Iowa
Hawkeye Community College
Indian Hills Community College
North Iowa Area Community College
Southeastern Community College
North Campus

Kansas
Allen County Community College
Barton County Community College
Butler County Community College
Cloud County Community College
Cowley County Community College
Garden City Community College
Hutchinson Community College
Kansas City Kansas Community College
Neosho County Community College

Kentucky
Ashland Community and Technical College
Big Sandy Community and Technical College
Elizabethtown Community and Technical College
Hazard Community College
Hopkinsville Community College
Madisonville Community College
Somerset Community College
Southeast Kentucky Community and Technical College

Louisiana
Bossier Parish Community College

Maine
Central Maine Community College
Southern Maine Community College

Maryland
Allegany College of Maryland
Baltimore City Community College
Carroll Community College
Frederick Community College
Hagerstown Community College
Harford Community College
Howard Community College
Wor-Wic Community College

Massachusetts
Bristol Community College
Bunker Hill Community College
Cape Cod Community College
Holyoke Community College
Massachusetts Bay Community College
Massasoit Community College
Mount Wachusett Community College
North Shore Community College
Northern Essex Community College
Quincy College
Quinsigamond Community College
Roxbury Community College
Springfield Technical Community College

Michigan
Bay de Noc Community College
Jackson Community College
Kellogg Community College
Mid Michigan Community College
Monroe County Community College
Mott Community College
Muskegon Community College
North Central Michigan College
Northwestern Michigan College
St. Clair County Community College
Southwestern Michigan College

Minnesota
Anoka Technical College
Central Lakes College
Dakota County Technical College
Inver Hills Community College
Lake Superior College
Minnesota State Community and Technical College - Fergus Falls
Minnesota West Community and Technical College: Worthington Campus
North Hennepin Community College
Northland Community & Technical College
Ridgewater College
Riverland Community College
Rochester Community and Technical College
St. Cloud Technical College
St. Paul College

Mississippi
Copiah-Lincoln Community College
Itawamba Community College
Meridian Community College

Missouri
Crowder College
East Central College
Jefferson College
Longview Community College
Maple Woods Community College
Mineral Area College
Moberly Area Community College
Penn Valley Community College
St. Charles Community College
State Fair Community College
Three Rivers Community College

Nebraska
Central Community College
Metropolitan Community College
Northeast Community College

Nevada
Western Nevada Community College

New Hampshire
New Hampshire Community Technical College
Manchester
Stratham
New Hampshire Technical Institute

New Jersey
Atlantic Cape Community College
Burlington County College
Cumberland County College
Gloucester County College
Hudson County Community College
Ocean County College
Raritan Valley Community College
Sussex County Community College

New Mexico
Clovis Community College
Dona Ana Branch Community College of New Mexico State University
Eastern New Mexico University: Roswell Campus
Luna Community College
New Mexico Junior College
San Juan College
Santa Fe Community College

New York
Adirondack Community College
ASA Institute of Business and Computer Technology
Cayuga County Community College
City University of New York
Hostos Community College
Clinton Community College
Erie Community College
City Campus
North Campus
South Campus
Finger Lakes Community College
Genesee Community College
Jamestown Community College
Mohawk Valley Community College
Niagara County Community College
Orange County Community College
Rockland Community College
State University of New York
College of Agriculture and Technology at Cobleskill
College of Agriculture and Technology at Morrisville
College of Technology at Alfred
College of Technology at Canton
College of Technology at Delhi
Tompkins-Cortland Community College

North Carolina
Alamance Community College
Asheville-Buncombe Technical Community College
Blue Ridge Community College
Caldwell Community College and Technical Institute
Catawba Valley Community College
Coastal Carolina Community College
College of the Albemarle
Durham Technical Community College
Gaston College
Johnston Community College
Lenoir Community College
Mitchell Community College
Nash Community College
Pitt Community College
Robeson Community College
Rowan-Cabarrus Community College
Sandhills Community College
Stanly Community College
Surry Community College
Wayne Community College
Wilkes Community College

North Dakota
North Dakota State College of Science

Ohio
Bowling Green State University: Firelands College
Central Ohio Technical College
Cincinnati State Technical and Community College
Clark State Community College
Cleveland Institute of Electronics
Edison State Community College
Hocking Technical College
James A. Rhodes State College
Kent State University
Stark Campus
Marion Technical College
Miami University
Hamilton Campus
Southern State Community College
Stark State College of Technology
University of Cincinnati
Clermont College
University of Northwestern Ohio
Washington State Community College

Oklahoma
Carl Albert State College
Oklahoma State University
Okmulgee

Oregon
Central Oregon Community College
Linn-Benton Community College
Rogue Community College
Umpqua Community College

Pennsylvania
Butler County Community College
Lehigh Carbon Community College
Luzerne County Community College
Reading Area Community College
Westmoreland County Community College

South Carolina
Aiken Technical College
Central Carolina Technical College
Florence-Darlington Technical College
Horry-Georgetown Technical College
Spartanburg Technical College
Tri-County Technical College
York Technical College

South Dakota
Southeast Technical Institute

Tennessee
Chattanooga State Technical Community College
Cleveland State Community College
Columbia State Community College
Dyersburg State Community College
Jackson State Community College
Motlow State Community College
Northeast State Technical Community College
Pellissippi State Technical Community College
Roane State Community College
Volunteer State Community College
Walters State Community College

Texas
Alvin Community College
Angelina College
Brazosport College
Cedar Valley College
Cisco Junior College
Coastal Bend College
College of the Mainland
El Centro College
Galveston College
Grayson County College
Hill College
Howard College
Lamar State College at Orange
Lamar State College at Port Arthur
Lee College
Mountain View College
North Central Texas College
Northeast Texas Community College
Odessa College
Paris Junior College
Southwest Texas Junior College
Temple College
Texas State Technical College
Harlingen
Waco
Trinity Valley Community College
Universal Technical Institute
Vernon College
Victoria College
Weatherford College
Wharton County Junior College

Utah
Dixie State College of Utah
Snow College

Vermont
Community College of Vermont

Virginia
Blue Ridge Community College
Germanna Community College
Lord Fairfax Community College
New River Community College
Piedmont Virginia Community College
Rappahannock Community College
Southside Virginia Community College
Southwest Virginia Community College
Thomas Nelson Community College
Virginia Highlands Community College

Washington
Bates Technical College
Bellevue Community College
Bellingham Technical College
Big Bend Community College
Centralia College
Clark College
Everett Community College
Green River Community College
Highline Community College
Lake Washington Technical College
North Seattle Community College
Olympic College
Pierce College
Skagit Valley College
South Puget Sound Community College
Spokane Community College
Spokane Falls Community College
Tacoma Community College
Walla Walla Community College
Wenatchee Valley College
Whatcom Community College
Yakima Valley Community College

West Virginia
West Virginia Northern Community College

Wisconsin
Chippewa Valley Technical College
Fox Valley Technical College
Gateway Technical College
Northcentral Technical College
Northeast Wisconsin Technical College
Southwest Wisconsin Technical College
Western Wisconsin Technical College
Wisconsin Indianhead Technical College

Wyoming
Casper College

Large (7,500-14,499)

Four-year

Alabama
University of Alabama
  Birmingham
University of South Alabama

Arizona
Northern Arizona University

Arkansas
Arkansas State University
University of Arkansas
University of Central Arkansas

California
California State University
  Chico
  Dominguez Hills
  East Bay
  Los Angeles
  San Bernardino
University of California
  Riverside
  Santa Cruz

Colorado
University of Colorado
  Denver and Health Sciences Center
University of Northern Colorado

Connecticut
Central Connecticut State University
Southern Connecticut State University

District of Columbia
George Washington University

Florida
Embry-Riddle Aeronautical University: Extended Campus
University of Miami
University of North Florida
University of West Florida

Georgia
Georgia Institute of Technology
Georgia Southern University
University of West Georgia
Valdosta State University

Hawaii
University of Hawaii
  Manoa

Idaho
Brigham Young University-Idaho
Idaho State University
University of Idaho

Illinois
Columbia College Chicago
DePaul University
Eastern Illinois University
Loyola University of Chicago
Northeastern Illinois University
Northwestern University
Southern Illinois University
  Edwardsville
Western Illinois University

Indiana
Indiana State University
Indiana University-Purdue University Fort Wayne
Indiana Wesleyan University
Purdue University
  Calumet
University of Notre Dame
University of Southern Indiana

Iowa
University of Northern Iowa

Kansas
Fort Hays State University
Wichita State University

Kentucky
Eastern Kentucky University
Murray State University
Northern Kentucky University
University of Louisville

Louisiana
Northwestern State University
Southeastern Louisiana University
Southern University and Agricultural and Mechanical College
Tulane University
University of Louisiana at Monroe

Maine
University of Maine

Maryland
Towson University
University of Maryland
  Baltimore County

Massachusetts
Boston College
Northeastern University
University of Massachusetts
  Boston
  Lowell

Michigan
Davenport University
Ferris State University
Northern Michigan University
Oakland University
Saginaw Valley State University

Minnesota
Minnesota State University
  Mankato
St. Cloud State University
University of Minnesota
  Duluth

Mississippi
Mississippi State University
University of Mississippi
University of Southern Mississippi

Missouri
Central Missouri State University
Grantham University
Missouri State University
Park University
Southeast Missouri State University
University of Missouri
  St. Louis

Montana
Montana State University
  Bozeman

Nebraska
University of Nebraska
  Omaha

Nevada
University of Nevada
  Reno

New Hampshire
University of New Hampshire

New Jersey
Kean University
Montclair State University
Rowan University
Thomas Edison State College
William Paterson University of New Jersey

New Mexico
New Mexico State University

New York
City University of New York
  Baruch College
  Brooklyn College
  College of Staten Island
  Hunter College
  John Jay College of Criminal Justice
  Lehman College
  New York City College of Technology
  Queens College
Cornell University
Fashion Institute of Technology
Hofstra University
Rochester Institute of Technology
St. John's University
State University of New York
  Albany
  Binghamton
  College at Buffalo
  Empire State College
  Stony Brook
Syracuse University

North Carolina
Appalachian State University
North Carolina Agricultural and Technical State University
University of North Carolina
  Greensboro
  Wilmington

North Dakota
North Dakota State University
University of North Dakota

Ohio
Cleveland State University
Miami University
  Oxford Campus
Wright State University
Youngstown State University

Oklahoma
Northeastern State University
University of Central Oklahoma

Pennsylvania
Bloomsburg University of Pennsylvania
Drexel University
Indiana University of Pennsylvania
Kutztown University of Pennsylvania
University of Pennsylvania
West Chester University of Pennsylvania

Puerto Rico
Turabo University
Universidad del Este
Universidad Metropolitana
University of Puerto Rico
  Mayaguez

Rhode Island
Johnson & Wales University
University of Rhode Island

South Carolina
Clemson University
College of Charleston

South Dakota
South Dakota State University

Tennessee
Austin Peay State University
East Tennessee State University

Texas
Baylor University
Lamar University
Sam Houston State University
Stephen F. Austin State University
Tarleton State University
Texas Southern University
University of Houston
  Downtown
University of Texas
  Brownsville
  Dallas
  Pan American

Utah
Utah State University

Vermont
University of Vermont

Virginia
Liberty University
Old Dominion University
Radford University
University of Virginia

Washington
Eastern Washington University
Western Washington University

West Virginia
Marshall University

Wisconsin
Marquette University
University of Wisconsin
  Eau Claire
  La Crosse
  Oshkosh
  Stevens Point
  Whitewater

Wyoming
University of Wyoming

Two-year

Alabama
Calhoun Community College

Arizona
Phoenix College
Scottsdale Community College

Arkansas
Pulaski Technical College

California
Allan Hancock College
Antelope Valley College
Bakersfield College
Butte College
Cabrillo College
Citrus College
Coastline Community College
College of San Mateo
College of the Sequoias
Cuesta College
Cypress College
Evergreen Valley College
Glendale Community College
Golden West College
Hartnell College
Imperial Valley College
Irvine Valley College
Laney College
Los Angeles Harbor College
Los Angeles Mission College
Los Angeles Trade and Technical College
Los Medanos College
Merced College
Mission College
Moorpark College
Mount San Jacinto College
Napa Valley College
Ohlone College
San Bernardino Valley College
San Diego City College
San Diego Miramar College
San Jose City College
Santa Barbara City College
Shasta College
Skyline College
Southwestern College
Taft College
Ventura College
Victor Valley College
West Los Angeles College
West Valley College
Yuba Community College District

Colorado
Community College of Denver

Florida
Daytona Beach Community College
Edison College
Manatee Community College
Palm Beach Community College
Seminole Community College
Tallahassee Community College

Illinois
College of Lake County
Elgin Community College
Lewis and Clark Community College
Moraine Valley Community College
Parkland College
Triton College
William Rainey Harper College

Indiana
Ivy Tech State College
  Ivy Tech Community College: Central Indiana

Kentucky
Bluegrass Community and Technical College

Maryland
Anne Arundel Community College
College of Southern Maryland
Prince George's Community College

Massachusetts
Middlesex Community College

Michigan
Delta College
Grand Rapids Community College
Henry Ford Community College
Kalamazoo Valley Community College
Lansing Community College
Macomb Community College
Oakland Community College
Schoolcraft College
Wayne County Community College

Minnesota
Century Community and Technical College
Hennepin Technical College
Minneapolis Community and Technical College
Normandale Community College

Mississippi
Mississippi Gulf Coast Community College
  Jefferson Davis Campus

Missouri
Ozarks Technical Community College
St. Louis Community College
  Meramec

Nebraska
Southeast Community College
  Lincoln Campus

Nevada
Truckee Meadows Community College

New Jersey
Bergen Community College
Camden County College
County College of Morris
Essex County College
Mercer County Community College

Union County College

New York
City University of New York
Bronx Community College
LaGuardia Community College
Queensborough Community College
Dutchess Community College
Westchester Community College

North Carolina
Central Piedmont Community College
Fayetteville Technical Community College
Guilford Technical Community College
Wake Technical Community College

Ohio
Cuyahoga Community College
Metropolitan Campus
Lakeland Community College
Owens Community College
Toledo

Oklahoma
Oklahoma City Community College
Rose State College

Oregon
Chemeketa Community College
Clackamas Community College

Pennsylvania
Bucks County Community College
Delaware County Community College
Harrisburg Area Community College
Montgomery County Community College
Northampton County Area Community College

Rhode Island
Community College of Rhode Island

South Carolina
Greenville Technical College
Midlands Technical College
Trident Technical College

Texas
Amarillo College
Blinn College
Brookhaven College
Central Texas College
Del Mar College
Eastfield College
Laredo Community College
McLennan Community College
North Lake College
Northwest Vista College
Palo Alto College
Richland College
St. Philip's College
San Jacinto College
Central Campus
South Plains College
Texas Southmost College
Tyler Junior College

Virginia
J. Sargeant Reynolds Community College
Virginia Western Community College

Washington
Clover Park Technical College
Edmonds Community College
Shoreline Community College

Wisconsin
Milwaukee Area Technical College

Very large (15,000 or more)

Four-year

Alabama
Auburn University
Troy University
University of Alabama

Alaska
University of Alaska
Anchorage

Arizona
Arizona State University
University of Arizona
University of Phoenix

California
California Polytechnic State University: San Luis Obispo
California State Polytechnic University: Pomona
California State University
Fresno
Fullerton
Long Beach
Northridge
Sacramento
San Diego State University
San Francisco State University
San Jose State University
University of California
Berkeley
Davis
Irvine
Los Angeles
San Diego
Santa Barbara
University of Southern California

Colorado
Colorado State University
Metropolitan State College of Denver
University of Colorado
Boulder

Connecticut
University of Connecticut

Delaware
University of Delaware

District of Columbia
Strayer University

Florida
Florida Atlantic University
Florida International University
Florida State University
University of Central Florida
University of Florida
University of South Florida

Georgia
Georgia State University
Kennesaw State University
University of Georgia

Idaho
Boise State University

Illinois
Illinois State University
Northern Illinois University
Southern Illinois University
Carbondale
University of Illinois
Chicago
Urbana-Champaign

Indiana
Ball State University
Indiana University
Bloomington
Indiana University-Purdue University Indianapolis
Purdue University

Iowa
Iowa State University
Kaplan University
University of Iowa

Kansas
Kansas State University
University of Kansas

Kentucky
University of Kentucky
Western Kentucky University

Louisiana
Louisiana State University and Agricultural and Mechanical College
University of Louisiana at Lafayette

Maryland
University of Maryland
College Park
University College

Massachusetts
Boston University
University of Massachusetts
Amherst

Michigan
Central Michigan University
Eastern Michigan University
Grand Valley State University
Michigan State University
University of Michigan
Wayne State University
Western Michigan University

Minnesota
University of Minnesota
Twin Cities

Missouri
University of Missouri
Columbia

Nebraska
University of Nebraska
Lincoln

Nevada
University of Nevada
Las Vegas

New Jersey
Rutgers, The State University of New Jersey
New Brunswick Regional Campus

New Mexico
University of New Mexico

New York
Excelsior College
New York University
State University of New York
Buffalo

North Carolina
East Carolina University
North Carolina State University
University of North Carolina
Chapel Hill
Charlotte

Ohio
Bowling Green State University
Kent State University
Ohio State University
Columbus Campus
Ohio University
University of Akron
University of Cincinnati
University of Toledo

Oklahoma
Oklahoma State University
University of Oklahoma

Oregon
Oregon State University
Portland State University
University of Oregon

Pennsylvania
Penn State
University Park
Temple University
University of Pittsburgh

Puerto Rico
University of Puerto Rico
Rio Piedras

South Carolina
University of South Carolina

Tennessee
Middle Tennessee State University
University of Memphis
University of Tennessee
Knoxville

Texas
Texas A&M University
Texas State University: San Marcos
Texas Tech University
University of Houston
University of North Texas
University of Texas
Arlington
Austin
El Paso
San Antonio

Utah
Brigham Young University
University of Utah
Utah Valley State College
Weber State University

Virginia
George Mason University
James Madison University
Virginia Commonwealth University
Virginia Polytechnic Institute and State University

Washington
University of Washington
Washington State University

West Virginia
West Virginia University

Wisconsin
University of Wisconsin
Madison
Milwaukee

Canada
McGill University
Simon Fraser University
University of Alberta
University of British Columbia
University of Manitoba

Two-year

Arizona
Pima Community College
Rio Salado College

California
American River College
Cerritos Community College
Chaffey Community College
City College of San Francisco
College of the Canyons
De Anza College
Diablo Valley College
East Los Angeles College
El Camino College
Foothill College
Fresno City College
Fullerton College
Grossmont Community College
Long Beach City College
Los Angeles City College
Los Angeles Pierce College
Los Angeles Valley College
Modesto Junior College
Mount San Antonio College
Orange Coast College
Palomar College
Pasadena City College
Rio Hondo College
Riverside Community College
Sacramento City College
Saddleback College
San Diego Mesa College
San Joaquin Delta College
Santa Ana College
Santa Monica College
Santa Rosa Junior College
Sierra College

Florida
Broward Community College
Miami Dade College
St. Petersburg College
Valencia Community College

Georgia
Georgia Perimeter College

Illinois
College of DuPage

Iowa
Des Moines Area Community College
Kirkwood Community College

Kansas
Johnson County Community College

Maryland
Community College of Baltimore County
Montgomery College

New Mexico
Albuquerque Technical-Vocational Institute

New York
Nassau Community College

Ohio
Columbus State Community College
Sinclair Community College

Oklahoma
Tulsa Community College

Pennsylvania
Community College of Philadelphia

Texas
Austin Community College
Collin County Community College District
El Paso Community College
Houston Community College System
North Harris Montgomery Community College District
South Texas College
Tarrant County College

Utah
Salt Lake Community College

Virginia
Northern Virginia Community College
Tidewater Community College

Canada
Humber College

Admission selectivity

Admit under 50% of applicants

Four-year

Alabama
Faulkner University
Talladega College

Alaska
Alaska Pacific University

Arkansas
Arkansas Tech University

California
Art Institute
of California: Orange County
California Institute of Technology
California Institute of the Arts
California Polytechnic State University: San Luis Obispo
California State Polytechnic University: Pomona
California State University
Bakersfield
Dominguez Hills
Sacramento
San Bernardino
San Marcos
Claremont McKenna College
Design Institute of San Diego
Harvey Mudd College
La Sierra University
Mt. Sierra College
Occidental College
Pepperdine University
Pitzer College
Pomona College
San Diego State University
San Francisco Conservatory of Music
Scripps College
Soka University of America
Stanford University
University of California
Berkeley
Los Angeles
San Diego
University of Southern California

Colorado
Colorado College
United States Air Force Academy

Connecticut
Connecticut College
Trinity College
United States Coast Guard Academy
Wesleyan University
Yale University

Delaware
University of Delaware

District of Columbia
George Washington University
Georgetown University
Howard University

Florida
Florida International University
Hobe Sound Bible College
Palm Beach Atlantic University
St. Leo University
Trinity College of Florida
University of Miami

Georgia
Atlanta Christian College
Brenau University
Clark Atlanta University
Clayton State University
Emmanuel College
Emory University
Fort Valley State University
Georgia State University
LaGrange College
Paine College
Spelman College
Truett-McConnell College

Hawaii
Brigham Young University-Hawaii

Idaho
Lewis-Clark State College

Illinois
Chicago State University
Kendall College
Northwestern University
University of Chicago
Westwood College - DuPage

Indiana
University of Notre Dame

Iowa
Grinnell College
William Penn University

Kansas
Central Christian College of Kansas
University of St. Mary

Kentucky
Berea College

Louisiana
Tulane University

Maine
Bates College
Bowdoin College
Colby College

Maryland
Bowie State University
Columbia Union College
Johns Hopkins University
Loyola College in Maryland
Maryland Institute College of Art
Morgan State University
United States Naval Academy
University of Maryland
College Park

Massachusetts
Amherst College
Babson College
Bentley College
Boston College
Boston Conservatory
Brandeis University
College of the Holy Cross
Emerson College
Endicott College
Franklin W. Olin College of Engineering
Harvard College
Massachusetts Institute of Technology
New England Conservatory of Music
New England Institute of Art
Northeastern University
Smith College
Tufts University
Wellesley College
Wheaton College
Williams College

Michigan
Andrews University
Ferris State University
Marygrove College
Siena Heights University

Minnesota
Carleton College
Macalester College

Mississippi
Jackson State University
Rust College

Missouri
College of the Ozarks
Deaconess College of Nursing
Lindenwood University
Northwest Missouri State University
Washington University in St. Louis

Nebraska
Union College

New Hampshire
Chester College of New England
Dartmouth College

New Jersey
Bloomfield College
The College of New Jersey
Princeton University
Ramapo College of New Jersey
Rowan University
Rutgers, The State University of New Jersey
Newark Regional Campus
Stevens Institute of Technology

New Mexico
College of the Southwest
Institute of American Indian Arts

New York
Bard College
Barnard College
City University of New York
Baruch College
Brooklyn College
Hunter College
Lehman College
Queens College
Colgate University
College of New Rochelle
Columbia University
Columbia College
Fu Foundation School of Engineering and Applied Science
School of General Studies
Cooper Union for the Advancement of Science and Art
Cornell University
Eastman School of Music of the University of Rochester
Fashion Institute of Technology
Fordham University
Hamilton College
Juilliard School
Manhattan School of Music
Mannes College The New School for Music
Marist College
Mercy College
New York School of Interior Design
New York University
Parsons The New School for Design
Sage College of Albany
Sarah Lawrence College
Skidmore College
State University of New York
Binghamton
College at Brockport
College at Buffalo
College at Cortland
College at Geneseo
College at Oneonta
Institute of Technology at Utica/Rome
New Paltz
Purchase
Union College
United States Merchant Marine Academy
United States Military Academy
University of Rochester
Vassar College
Webb Institute

North Carolina
Davidson College
Duke University
Elon University
Johnson C. Smith University
North Carolina School of the Arts
Roanoke Bible College
St. Augustine's College
University of North Carolina
Chapel Hill
Wake Forest University

North Dakota
Trinity Bible College

Ohio
Art Academy of Cincinnati
Central State University
Circleville Bible College
Cleveland Institute of Music
Denison University
Kenyon College
Lourdes College
Oberlin College
Otterbein College

Oregon
Eugene Bible College
Reed College

Pennsylvania
Bryn Mawr College
Bucknell University
Carnegie Mellon University
Curtis Institute of Music
Dickinson College
Franklin & Marshall College
Gettysburg College
Grove City College
Haverford College
Lafayette College
Lehigh University
Lincoln University
Muhlenberg College
St. Joseph's University
Slippery Rock University of Pennsylvania
Swarthmore College
University of Pennsylvania
University of the Arts
Washington and Jefferson College
West Chester University of Pennsylvania

Puerto Rico
Inter American University of Puerto Rico
Barranquitas Campus
Bayamon Campus
Fajardo Campus
University of Puerto Rico
Aguadilla
Arecibo
Humacao
Ponce
Rio Piedras
Utuado

Rhode Island
Brown University
Rhode Island School of Design

South Carolina
Claflin University
University of South Carolina
Aiken
Voorhees College

Tennessee
Lincoln Memorial University
Memphis College of Art
O'More College of Design
Rhodes College
Tennessee State University
Vanderbilt University

Texas
Art Institute
of Houston
Dallas Christian College
Paul Quinn College
Rice University
Texas Wesleyan University

Vermont
Middlebury College

Virginia
College of William and Mary
University of Richmond
University of Virginia
Washington and Lee University

Washington
DigiPen Institute of Technology
Whitman College

West Virginia
Davis and Elkins College
West Virginia State University

Wisconsin
Bellin College of Nursing

Two-year

California
American Academy of Dramatic Arts: West
Deep Springs College

Iowa
St. Luke's College

Maine
Central Maine Medical Center School of Nursing

Massachusetts
Laboure College

Mississippi
Holmes Community College

New York
Phillips Beth Israel School of Nursing
St. Joseph's College of Nursing

Ohio
Kettering College of Medical Arts

Texas
Hallmark Institute of Technology

Admit 50 to 75% of applicants

Four-year

Alabama
Alabama State University
Huntingdon College
Samford University
Southeastern Bible College
University of Alabama
University of Mobile
University of Montevallo

Alaska
University of Alaska
Anchorage
Southeast

Arizona
Arizona State University West
Southwestern College

Arkansas
Arkansas State University
Harding University
Henderson State University
John Brown University
Lyon College
Ouachita Baptist University
University of Central Arkansas
Williams Baptist College

California
Art Center College of Design
Azusa Pacific University
Bethany University
California Baptist University
California Lutheran University
California Maritime Academy
California State University
Fresno
Fullerton
Long Beach
Los Angeles
Monterey Bay
Northridge
Stanislaus
Chapman University
Charles R. Drew University of Medicine and Science
Concordia University
Dominican University of California
Fresno Pacific University
Humboldt State University
Laguna College of Art and Design
Loyola Marymount University
Menlo College
Otis College of Art and Design
Point Loma Nazarene University
San Diego Christian College
San Francisco State University
San Jose State University
Santa Clara University
Simpson University
Sonoma State University
University of California
Davis
Irvine
Santa Barbara
University of La Verne
University of Redlands
University of San Diego
University of San Francisco
University of the Pacific
West Coast University
Westmont College
William Jessup University

Colorado
Adams State College
Fort Lewis College
University of Colorado
Denver and Health Sciences Center
Westwood College of Technology South

Connecticut
Central Connecticut State University
Eastern Connecticut State University
Fairfield University
Mitchell College
Post University
Quinnipiac University
Sacred Heart University
St. Joseph College
Southern Connecticut State University
University of Bridgeport
University of Connecticut
University of Hartford
University of New Haven
Western Connecticut State University

Delaware
Delaware State University
Wesley College

District of Columbia
American University
Corcoran College of Art and Design

Florida
Barry University
Beacon College
Bethune-Cookman College
Eckerd College
Florida Agricultural and Mechanical University
Florida Atlantic University
Florida Christian College
Florida College
Florida Southern College
Florida State University
Jacksonville University
Johnson & Wales University
New College of Florida
Northwood University
Florida Campus
Nova Southeastern University
Remington College: Tampa
Rollins College
South University: West Palm Beach Campus
Stetson University
University of Central Florida
University of Florida
University of North Florida
University of South Florida
University of Tampa
University of West Florida
Warner Southern College

Georgia
Agnes Scott College
Augusta State University
Columbus State University
Covenant College
Dalton State College
Georgia College and State University
Georgia Institute of Technology
Georgia Southern University
Georgia Southwestern State University
Kennesaw State University
Morehouse College
North Georgia College & State University
Oglethorpe University
Piedmont College
Savannah College of Art and Design
Shorter College
Southern Polytechnic State University
Toccoa Falls College
University of Georgia
University of West Georgia
Valdosta State University
Wesleyan College

Hawaii
University of Hawaii
Manoa

Idaho
Brigham Young University-Idaho
Northwest Nazarene University

Illinois
Aurora University
Blackburn College
Concordia University
DePaul University
Illinois College
Illinois Institute of Technology
Illinois Wesleyan University
Lake Forest College
Lewis University
Lexington College
MacMurray College
McKendree College
Millikin University
North Central College
North Park University
Northeastern Illinois University
Northern Illinois University
Roosevelt University
St. Xavier University
University of Illinois
Chicago
Springfield
University of St. Francis
VanderCook College of Music
Western Illinois University
Wheaton College

Indiana
Butler University
DePauw University
Earlham College
Grace College and Seminary
Hanover College
Indiana Institute of Technology
Indiana University
Northwest
Indiana University-Purdue University Indianapolis
Manchester College
Rose-Hulman Institute of Technology
St. Mary-of-the-Woods College
Tri-State University
University of St. Francis
Wabash College

Iowa
Allen College
Ashford University
Clarke College
Coe College
Cornell College
Graceland University
Iowa Wesleyan College
Maharishi University of Management
Mercy College of Health Sciences
Vennard College
Waldorf College

Kansas
Baker University
Bethany College
Bethel College
Kansas State University
MidAmerica Nazarene University
Sterling College

Kentucky
Alice Lloyd College
Asbury College
Bellarmine University
Brescia University
Campbellsville University
Centre College
Eastern Kentucky University
Kentucky Christian University
Morehead State University
Murray State University
Thomas More College

Louisiana
Centenary College of Louisiana
Louisiana State University and Agricultural and Mechanical College
Loyola University New Orleans
Nicholls State University
Southern University and Agricultural and Mechanical College
University of New Orleans

Maine
College of the Atlantic
New England School of Communications
Thomas College
University of Maine
Farmington

Maryland
Capitol College
Goucher College
Hood College
Ner Israel Rabbinical College
St. Mary's College of Maryland
Salisbury University
Towson University
University of Maryland
Baltimore County
Eastern Shore
Villa Julie College
Washington Bible College
Washington College

Massachusetts
Art Institute of Boston at Lesley University
Bay Path College
Becker College
Berklee College of Music
Boston University
Clark University
Curry College
Emmanuel College
Fitchburg State College
Framingham State College
Hampshire College
Hebrew College
Lasell College
Lesley University
Massachusetts College of Art
Massachusetts College of Liberal Arts
Massachusetts Maritime Academy
Merrimack College
Mount Holyoke College
Simmons College
Simon's Rock College of Bard
Springfield College
Stonehill College
University of Massachusetts
Boston
Dartmouth
Lowell
Wentworth Institute of Technology
Western New England College
Westfield State College
Worcester State College

Michigan
College for Creative Studies
Grace Bible College
Grand Valley State University
Kalamazoo College
Kettering University
Reformed Bible College
University of Detroit Mercy
University of Michigan
University of Michigan
Dearborn
Wayne State University

Minnesota
Bemidji State University
Concordia University: St. Paul
Crown College
Oak Hills Christian College
St. Olaf College
University of Minnesota
Twin Cities

Mississippi
Alcorn State University
Belhaven College
Blue Mountain College
Mississippi College
Mississippi State University
University of Mississippi
University of Southern Mississippi
Wesley College

Missouri
Avila University
Columbia College
Fontbonne University
Jewish Hospital College of Nursing and Allied Health
Kansas City Art Institute
Maryville University of Saint Louis
Missouri Baptist University
Park University
Research College of Nursing
Rockhurst University
University of Missouri
Kansas City
St. Louis
Webster University
William Jewell College
William Woods University

Montana
Montana State University
Bozeman

Nebraska
College of Saint Mary
Nebraska Methodist College of Nursing and Allied Health

Nevada
Sierra Nevada College

New Hampshire
Franklin Pierce College
Rivier College
St. Anselm College
Southern New Hampshire University
University of New Hampshire

New Jersey
Fairleigh Dickinson University
College at Florham
Metropolitan Campus
Georgian Court University
Kean University
Monmouth University
Montclair State University
New Jersey City University
New Jersey Institute of Technology
Richard Stockton College of New Jersey
Rutgers, The State University of New Jersey
Camden Regional Campus
New Brunswick Regional Campus
St. Peter's College
William Paterson University of New Jersey

New Mexico
College of Santa Fe
Eastern New Mexico University
University of New Mexico

New York
Adelphi University
Albany College of Pharmacy
Berkeley College of New York City
Canisius College
College of Mount St. Vincent
College of Saint Rose
Concordia College
Culinary Institute of America
D'Youville College
Davis College
Elmira College
Eugene Lang College The New School for Liberal Arts
Hobart and William Smith Colleges
Hofstra University
Iona College

King's College
Laboratory Institute of Merchandising
Le Moyne College
Long Island University
Brooklyn Campus
Manhattan College
Manhattanville College
Medaille College
Molloy College
Monroe College
Polytechnic University
Pratt Institute
Rochester Institute of Technology
St. John Fisher College
St. John's University
St. Lawrence University
School of Visual Arts
Siena College
State University of New York
Albany
Buffalo
College at Fredonia
College at Old Westbury
College at Plattsburgh
College at Potsdam
College of Environmental Science and Forestry
Farmingdale
Maritime College
Oswego
Stony Brook
Syracuse University
Wagner College
Wells College
Yeshiva and Kolel Bais Medrash Elyon

North Carolina

Appalachian State University
Barton College
Bennett College
Brevard College
Cabarrus College of Health Sciences
Campbell University
Catawba College
Chowan College
East Carolina University
Gardner-Webb University
Greensboro College
Guilford College
High Point University
John Wesley College
Johnson & Wales University
Lees-McRae College
Mount Olive College
North Carolina State University
Queens University of Charlotte
Salem College
Shaw University
University of North Carolina
Asheville
Greensboro
Wilmington
Western Carolina University

North Dakota

University of North Dakota

Ohio

Antioch College
Bluffton University
Case Western Reserve University
Cleveland Institute of Art
College of Mount St. Joseph
College of Wooster
Columbus College of Art and Design
Defiance College
Heidelberg College
Mercy College of Northwest Ohio
Mount Carmel College of Nursing
Ohio Dominican University
Ohio State University
Columbus Campus
Ohio Wesleyan University
Tiffin University
University of Findlay
Ursuline College
Xavier University

Oklahoma

Bacone College
Oklahoma Baptist University
Oral Roberts University
Southeastern Oklahoma State University
Southwestern Christian University

Oregon

Concordia University
Eastern Oregon University
Lewis & Clark College
Linfield College
Northwest Christian College
Pacific Northwest College of Art
Western Oregon University
Willamette University

Pennsylvania

Albright College
Allegheny College
Bloomsburg University of Pennsylvania
Cabrini College
Carlow University
Cedar Crest College
Chatham College
Chestnut Hill College
Cheyney University of Pennsylvania
East Stroudsburg University of Pennsylvania
Elizabethtown College
Geneva College
Gwynedd-Mercy College
Holy Family University
Indiana University of Pennsylvania
Juniata College
La Roche College
La Salle University
Lancaster Bible College
Mansfield University of Pennsylvania
Messiah College
Millersville University of Pennsylvania
Moravian College
Penn State
Harrisburg
Lehigh Valley
University Park
Philadelphia University
Rosemont College
St. Vincent College
Seton Hill University
Shippensburg University of Pennsylvania
Temple University
University of Pittsburgh
University of the Sciences in Philadelphia
Ursinus College
Valley Forge Christian College
Villanova University
Waynesburg College
Wilson College
York College of Pennsylvania

Puerto Rico

Conservatory of Music of Puerto Rico
Inter American University of Puerto Rico
Ponce Campus
Pontifical Catholic University of Puerto Rico
Turabo University
University of Puerto Rico
Cayey University College
Mayaguez

Rhode Island

Bryant University
Providence College
Rhode Island College
Salve Regina University

South Carolina

Charleston Southern University
Clemson University
Coastal Carolina University
College of Charleston
Columbia International University
Erskine College
Francis Marion University
Furman University
Limestone College
Newberry College
Southern Wesleyan University
University of South Carolina
University of South Carolina Upstate
Wofford College

Tennessee

Belmont University
Bethel College
Christian Brothers University
Cumberland University
Lambuth University
Southern Adventist University
Trevecca Nazarene University
Tusculum College
University of Memphis
University of Tennessee
Knoxville
University of the South

Texas

Abilene Christian University
Austin College
Baylor University
Concordia University at Austin
Dallas Baptist University
Hardin-Simmons University
Houston Baptist University
Howard Payne University
Jarvis Christian College
Lamar University
Lubbock Christian University
Northwood University: Texas Campus
Our Lady of the Lake University of San Antonio
Prairie View A&M University
St. Edward's University
St. Mary's University
Sam Houston State University
Schreiner University
Southern Methodist University
Southwestern Assemblies of God University
Southwestern University
Stephen F. Austin State University
Texas A&M University
Texas A&M University Commerce
Texas Christian University
Texas Lutheran University
Texas Tech University
Texas Woman's University
Trinity University
University of Mary Hardin-Baylor
University of North Texas
University of Texas
Arlington
Austin
Dallas
Wayland Baptist University
West Texas A&M University

Vermont

Bennington College
Champlain College
College of St. Joseph in Vermont
Marlboro College
Norwich University
St. Michael's College
Southern Vermont College
Sterling College
Vermont Technical College

Virginia

Art Institute of Washington
Ferrum College
George Mason University
Hampden-Sydney College
Hampton University
James Madison University
Liberty University
Lynchburg College
Norfolk State University
Old Dominion University
Roanoke College
St. Paul's College
Shenandoah University
University of Mary Washington
Virginia Commonwealth University
Virginia Intermont College
Virginia Military Institute
Virginia Polytechnic Institute and State University
Virginia Union University

Washington

Cornish College of the Arts
Gonzaga University
Heritage University
Saint Martin's University
Seattle University
Trinity Lutheran College
University of Puget Sound
University of Washington
Washington State University
Western Washington University
Whitworth College

West Virginia

Appalachian Bible College
West Virginia University Institute of Technology

Wisconsin

Alverno College
Beloit College
Lakeland College
Lawrence University
Maranatha Baptist Bible College
Marquette University
Milwaukee School of Engineering
Mount Mary College
University of Wisconsin
Eau Claire
Green Bay
La Crosse
Madison
Superior
Whitewater

Virgin Islands, U.S.

University of the Virgin Islands

Arab Republic of Egypt

American University in Cairo

Canada

McGill University
Simon Fraser University
University of British Columbia

France

American University of Paris

Lebanon

American University of Beirut

Switzerland

Franklin College: Switzerland

Two-year

California

Marymount College

Colorado

Bel-Rea Institute of Animal Technology

Georgia

Atlanta Metropolitan College
Georgia Perimeter College
Young Harris College

Massachusetts

Dean College
Fisher College

Minnesota

Dunwoody College of Technology

New York

American Academy of Dramatic Arts
Maria College
St. Elizabeth College of Nursing
State University of New York
College of Agriculture and Technology at Cobleskill
College of Agriculture and Technology at Morrisville
College of Technology at Alfred

Ohio

Good Samaritan College of Nursing and Health Science

Pennsylvania

Antonelli Institute of Art and Photography
Harcum College

South Carolina

University of South Carolina Sumter

Tennessee

Hiwassee College

Texas

Hallmark Institute of Aeronautics

Vermont

Landmark College

Admit over 75% of applicants

Four-year

Alabama

Auburn University
Auburn University at Montgomery
Birmingham-Southern College
Jacksonville State University
Judson College
South University
Spring Hill College
Tuskegee University
University of Alabama
Birmingham
Huntsville
University of North Alabama
University of South Alabama
University of West Alabama

Alaska

University of Alaska
Fairbanks

Arizona

Arizona State University
Embry-Riddle Aeronautical University: Prescott Campus
Northern Arizona University
Prescott College
University of Arizona

Arkansas

Central Baptist College
Hendrix College
Southern Arkansas University
University of Arkansas
University of the Ozarks

California

Biola University
Brooks Institute of Photography
California College of the Arts
California State University
Chico

Cogswell Polytechnical College
Golden Gate University
Holy Names University
Hope International University
King's College and Seminary
LIFE Pacific College
Lincoln University
Master's College
Mills College
Mount St. Mary's College
NewSchool of Architecture & Design
Northwestern Polytechnic University
Notre Dame de Namur University
Platt College
    Ontario
St. Mary's College of California
Southern California Institute of Architecture
Thomas Aquinas College
University of California
    Riverside
    Santa Cruz
University of California: Merced
University of Judaism
Vanguard University of Southern California
Whittier College
Woodbury University

Colorado

Colorado Christian University
Colorado School of Mines
Colorado State University
Johnson & Wales University
Mesa State College
Naropa University
Regis University
Rocky Mountain College of Art & Design
University of Colorado
    Boulder
    Colorado Springs
University of Denver
University of Northern Colorado

Connecticut

Albertus Magnus College
Lyme Academy College of Fine Arts
Paier College of Art

District of Columbia

Catholic University of America
Gallaudet University
Trinity University

Florida

Baptist College of Florida
Clearwater Christian College
Embry-Riddle Aeronautical University
Florida Gulf Coast University
Florida Institute of Technology
Florida Metropolitan University
    Melbourne Campus
Lynn University
Miami International University of Art and Design
St. Thomas University
Yeshiva Gedolah Rabbinical College

Georgia

Albany State University
Armstrong Atlantic State University
Berry College
Brewton-Parker College
Macon State College
Mercer University
Savannah State University

Hawaii

Chaminade University of Honolulu
Hawaii Pacific University

Idaho

Albertson College of Idaho
Boise Bible College
Boise State University
Idaho State University
University of Idaho

Illinois

Augustana College
Benedictine University
Bradley University
Dominican University
Eastern Illinois University
Elmhurst College
Greenville College
Illinois State University
Judson College
Knox College
Lincoln Christian College and Seminary
Loyola University of Chicago
Monmouth College
National-Louis University
Olivet Nazarene University
Principia College
Quincy University
School of the Art Institute of Chicago
Shimer College
Southern Illinois University
    Carbondale
Southern Illinois University
    Edwardsville
Telshe Yeshiva-Chicago
Trinity Christian College
Trinity International University
University of Illinois
    Urbana-Champaign

Indiana

Anderson University
Ball State University
Franklin College
Goshen College
Huntington University
Indiana State University
Indiana University
    Bloomington
    East
    Kokomo
    South Bend
    Southeast
Indiana University-Purdue University Fort Wayne
Indiana Wesleyan University
Marian College
Purdue University
Purdue University
    Calumet
St. Joseph's College
Saint Mary's College
Taylor University
Taylor University: Fort Wayne
University of Evansville
University of Indianapolis
University of Southern Indiana
Valparaiso University

Iowa

Briar Cliff University
Buena Vista University
Central College
Divine Word College
Dordt College
Drake University
Grand View College
Iowa State University
Loras College
Luther College
Morningside College
Mount Mercy College
Northwestern College
St. Ambrose University
Simpson College
University of Dubuque
University of Iowa
University of Northern Iowa
Wartburg College

Kansas

Barclay College
Emporia State University
McPherson College
Pittsburg State University
Tabor College
Wichita State University

Kentucky

Georgetown College
Kentucky Wesleyan College
Lindsey Wilson College
Transylvania University
University of Kentucky
University of Louisville
University of the Cumberlands

Louisiana

Louisiana Tech University
New Orleans Baptist Theological Seminary: Leavell College
Northwestern State University
Southeastern Louisiana University
University of Louisiana at Lafayette
University of Louisiana at Monroe
Xavier University of Louisiana

Maine

Husson College
St. Joseph's College
University of Maine
University of Maine
    Machias
    Presque Isle
University of New England
University of Southern Maine

Maryland

Baltimore International College
College of Notre Dame of Maryland
Frostburg State University
McDaniel College
Mount St. Mary's University
St. John's College

Massachusetts

American International College
Anna Maria College
Assumption College
Bridgewater State College
Elms College
Gordon College
Hellenic College/Holy Cross
Massachusetts College of Pharmacy and Health Sciences
Montserrat College of Art
Mount Ida College
Nichols College
Pine Manor College
Regis College
Salem State College
School of the Museum of Fine Arts
Suffolk University
University of Massachusetts
    Amherst
Wheelock College
Worcester Polytechnic Institute

Michigan

Adrian College
Albion College
Alma College
Aquinas College
Calvin College
Central Michigan University
Concordia University
Cornerstone University
Eastern Michigan University
Finlandia University
Great Lakes Christian College
Hillsdale College
Hope College
Kendall College of Art and Design of Ferris State University
Lake Superior State University
Lawrence Technological University
Madonna University
Michigan State University
Michigan Technological University
Northern Michigan University
Northwood University
Oakland University
Sacred Heart Major Seminary
Saginaw Valley State University
Spring Arbor University
University of Michigan
    Flint
Western Michigan University
Yeshiva Beth Yehuda-Yeshiva Gedolah of Greater Detroit

Minnesota

Augsburg College
Bethany Lutheran College
Bethel University
College of St. Benedict
College of St. Catherine
College of St. Scholastica
Concordia College: Moorhead
Gustavus Adolphus College
Hamline University
Martin Luther College
Metropolitan State University
Minneapolis College of Art and Design
Minnesota State University
    Mankato
North Central University
Northwestern College
St. Cloud State University
St. John's University
St. Mary's University of Minnesota
Southwest Minnesota State University
University of Minnesota
    Crookston
    Duluth
    Morris
University of St. Thomas
Winona State University

Mississippi

Delta State University
Millsaps College
Tougaloo College

Missouri

Central Missouri State University
Culver-Stockton College
Drury University
Evangel University
Missouri Southern State University
Missouri State University
St. Louis University
Southeast Missouri State University
Southwest Baptist University
Stephens College
Truman State University
University of Missouri
    Columbia
Westminster College

Montana

Carroll College
Montana State University
    Billings
Montana Tech of the University of Montana
Rocky Mountain College
University of Great Falls
University of Montana: Missoula

Nebraska

Concordia University
Creighton University
Dana College
Doane College
Grace University
Hastings College
Midland Lutheran College
Nebraska Wesleyan University
University of Nebraska
    Kearney
    Lincoln
    Omaha
York College

Nevada

University of Nevada
    Las Vegas
    Reno

New Hampshire

Colby-Sawyer College
Keene State College
Magdalen College
New England College
Plymouth State University
Thomas More College of Liberal Arts

New Jersey

Berkeley College
Caldwell College
Centenary College
College of St. Elizabeth
Drew University
Felician College
Rabbinical College of America
Rider University
Seton Hall University

New Mexico

New Mexico Institute of Mining and Technology
New Mexico State University
St. John's College

New York

Alfred University
Briarcliffe College
Cazenovia College
City University of New York
    City College
    College of Staten Island
    John Jay College of Criminal Justice
Clarkson University
Daemen College
Dominican College of Blauvelt
Dowling College
Five Towns College
Hartwick College
Hilbert College
Holy Trinity Orthodox Seminary
Houghton College
Ithaca College
Keuka College
Long Island University
    C. W. Post Campus
Machzikei Hadath Rabbinical College
Marymount Manhattan College
Metropolitan College of New York
Mount St. Mary College
Nazareth College of Rochester
New York Institute of Technology
Niagara University
Pace University
Paul Smith's College
Rensselaer Polytechnic Institute
Roberts Wesleyan College
Russell Sage College
St. Bonaventure University
St. Francis College
St. Joseph's College
St. Joseph's College: Suffolk Campus
St. Thomas Aquinas College
State University of New York
    Empire State College
Utica College
Vaughn College of Aeronautics and Technology
Yeshiva Mikdash Melech
Yeshiva University

North Carolina
Belmont Abbey College
Elizabeth City State University
Fayetteville State University
Lenoir-Rhyne College
Livingstone College
Meredith College
Methodist College
North Carolina Agricultural and Technical State University
North Carolina Central University
North Carolina Wesleyan College
Peace College
Pfeiffer University
St. Andrews Presbyterian College
University of North Carolina
  Charlotte
  Pembroke
Warren Wilson College
Wingate University
Winston-Salem State University

North Dakota
Jamestown College
Minot State University
North Dakota State University
University of Mary
Valley City State University

Ohio
Ashland University
Baldwin-Wallace College
Bowling Green State University
Capital University
Cedarville University
Cincinnati Christian University
Franciscan University of Steubenville
God's Bible School and College
Hiram College
John Carroll University
Kent State University
Lake Erie College
Malone College
Marietta College
Mount Union College
Mount Vernon Nazarene University
Muskingum College
Ohio Northern University
Ohio University
Pontifical College Josephinum
Rabbinical College of Telshe
University of Akron
University of Cincinnati
University of Dayton
Walsh University
Wilmington College
Wittenberg University

Oklahoma
Northeastern State University
Northwestern Oklahoma State University
Oklahoma City University
Oklahoma State University
St. Gregory's University
Southwestern Oklahoma State University
University of Oklahoma
University of Science and Arts of Oklahoma
University of Tulsa

Oregon
Corban College
George Fox University
Multnomah Bible College
Oregon Institute of Technology
Oregon State University
Pacific University
Portland State University
Southern Oregon University
University of Oregon
University of Portland

Pennsylvania
Alvernia College
Arcadia University
Baptist Bible College of Pennsylvania
Bryn Athyn College of the New Church
California University of Pennsylvania
Clarion University of Pennsylvania
College Misericordia
Delaware Valley College
DeSales University
Drexel University
Duquesne University
Eastern University
Edinboro University of Pennsylvania
Gannon University
Immaculata University
Keystone College
King's College
Kutztown University of Pennsylvania
Lebanon Valley College
Lock Haven University of Pennsylvania
Lycoming College
Marywood University
Mercyhurst College
Moore College of Art and Design
Mount Aloysius College
Neumann College
Penn State
  Abington
  Altoona
  Berks
  Erie, The Behrend College
  Schuylkill - Capital College
  Wilkes-Barre
Philadelphia Biblical University
Point Park University
Robert Morris University
St. Charles Borromeo Seminary - Overbrook
St. Francis University
Susquehanna University
Thiel College
University of Pittsburgh
  Bradford
  Johnstown
University of Scranton
Westminster College
Widener University
Wilkes University

Puerto Rico
Inter American University of Puerto Rico
  Guayama Campus
Universidad Politecnica de Puerto Rico

Rhode Island
Johnson & Wales University
Roger Williams University
University of Rhode Island

South Carolina
Anderson University
The Citadel
Columbia College
Converse College
Morris College
North Greenville College
Presbyterian College
South Carolina State University

South Dakota
Augustana College
Black Hills State University
Dakota State University
Mount Marty College
Northern State University
Presentation College
South Dakota School of Mines and Technology
South Dakota State University
University of Sioux Falls
University of South Dakota

Tennessee
Austin Peay State University
Carson-Newman College
East Tennessee State University
Fisk University
Freed-Hardeman University
Johnson Bible College
King College
Lipscomb University
Maryville College
Middle Tennessee State University
Milligan College
Tennessee Technological University
Tennessee Wesleyan College
Union University
University of Tennessee
  Chattanooga
  Martin

Texas
Angelo State University
East Texas Baptist University
LeTourneau University
McMurry University
Midwestern State University
Tarleton State University
Texas A&M University
  Galveston
  Kingsville
Texas State University: San Marcos
University of Dallas
University of Houston
University of St. Thomas
University of Texas
  El Paso
  San Antonio
  Tyler
  of the Permian Basin
University of the Incarnate Word

Utah
Brigham Young University
Southern Utah University
University of Utah
Westminster College

Vermont
Castleton State College
Green Mountain College
Johnson State College
Lyndon State College
University of Vermont

Virginia
Averett University
Bridgewater College
Christendom College
Eastern Mennonite University
Emory & Henry College
Hollins University
Longwood University
Mary Baldwin College
Marymount University
Radford University
Randolph-Macon College
Randolph-Macon Woman's College
Sweet Briar College
University of Virginia's College at Wise
Virginia State University
Virginia Wesleyan College

Washington
Central Washington University
Eastern Washington University
Evergreen State College
Henry Cogswell College
Northwest University
Pacific Lutheran University
Seattle Pacific University
Walla Walla College

West Virginia
Alderson-Broaddus College
Bethany College
Glenville State College
Shepherd University
University of Charleston
West Liberty State College
West Virginia University
West Virginia Wesleyan College
Wheeling Jesuit University

Wisconsin
Cardinal Stritch University
Carroll College
Carthage College
Concordia University Wisconsin
Edgewood College
Marian College of Fond du Lac
Northland College
Ripon College
St. Norbert College
Silver Lake College
University of Wisconsin
  Milwaukee
  Oshkosh
  Parkside
  Platteville
  River Falls
  Stevens Point
Viterbo University

Wyoming
University of Wyoming

Mexico
Universidad Anahuac

United Kingdom
Richmond, The American International University in London

Two-year

California
Platt College
  Cerritos
Salvation Army Crestmont College

Florida
Florida Career College: Miami
Florida Career College: Pembroke Pines
Key College

Georgia
Gainesville State College
Gordon College
Middle Georgia College

Illinois
College of Lake County
Springfield College in Illinois

Kentucky
Louisville Technical Institute

Minnesota
Lakeland Academy Division of Herzing College

New Hampshire
New Hampshire Technical Institute

New Jersey
Assumption College for Sisters

New York
ASA Institute of Business and Computer Technology
Bryant & Stratton College: Syracuse North
Jamestown Business College
Rochester Business Institute
State University of New York College of Technology at Canton

North Carolina
Louisburg College

Ohio
Art Institute of Cincinnati
Bradford School
Bryant & Stratton College
  Parma
Davis College
Rosedale Bible College
School of Advertising Art
University of Northwestern Ohio

Pennsylvania
Business Institute of Pennsylvania
Business Institute of Pennsylvania
  Meadville
Hussian School of Art
Penn State
  Beaver
  Delaware County
  Dubois
  Fayette
  Hazleton
  McKeesport
  Mont Alto
  New Kensington
  Shenango
  Worthington Scranton
  York
University of Pittsburgh
  Titusville

Puerto Rico
University College of San Juan

South Carolina
Spartanburg Methodist College

Texas
Everest College: Arlington
Everest College: Dallas
Westwood College: Ft. Worth

Utah
Stevens-Henager College
  Murray

Virginia
Richard Bland College

Wisconsin
University of Wisconsin
  Marinette

Open admission

Four-year

Alabama
American Sentinel University
Andrew Jackson University
Columbia Southern University
Concordia College
Heritage Christian University
Huntsville Bible College
Miles College
Southern Christian University
Virginia College
Virginia College at Huntsville

Alaska
Alaska Bible College
Charter College
Sheldon Jackson College

Arizona
Arizona Institute of Business and Technology
  International Institute of the Americas: Mesa
Collins College
Grand Canyon University
International Institute of the Americas
  Tucson
International Institute of the Americas: West Valley
Tucson Design College
University of Phoenix

Arkansas
Ecclesia College
Philander Smith College
University of Arkansas
Fort Smith
Monticello

California
Academy of Art University
Bethesda Christian University
Coleman College
Columbia College: Hollywood
Humphreys College
Institute of Computer Technology
National University
Pacific States University
Platt College
San Diego
Remington College
San Diego
Silicon Valley College
Western Career College: Emeryville
Southern California Institute of Technology

Colorado
National American University
Denver
Nazarene Bible College

Connecticut
Briarwood College

Delaware
Wilmington College

District of Columbia
Southeastern University
University of the District of Columbia

Florida
Carlos Albizu University
Chipola College
City College
Edward Waters College
Florida Metropolitan University
Tampa College
International Academy of Design and Technology: Orlando
International College
Jones College
Okaloosa-Walton College
Remington College
Jacksonville
Remington College: Largo
Schiller International University
Southeastern College of the Assemblies of God
Universidad FLET
Webster College
Webster College: Holiday

Georgia
Bauder College
Beulah Heights Bible College
Life University
Reinhardt College
Thomas University

Illinois
American Academy of Art
Columbia College Chicago
East-West University
Governors State University
Harrington College of Design
International Academy of Design and Technology: Chicago
Robert Morris College: Chicago
St. Augustine College

Indiana
College of Court Reporting
Oakland City University

Iowa
Faith Baptist Bible College and Theological Seminary
Hamilton College
Cedar Falls
Cedar Rapids
Kaplan University
Upper Iowa University

Kansas
University of Kansas Medical Center
Washburn University of Topeka

Kentucky
Beckfield College
Clear Creek Baptist Bible College
Midway College
Northern Kentucky University
Pikeville College
St. Catharine College
Spalding University
Union College
Western Kentucky University

Louisiana
Grambling State University
Louisiana State University
Alexandria
Our Lady of the Lake College
Southern University
New Orleans
Southwest University

Maine
University of Maine
Augusta
Fort Kent

Maryland
University of Maryland
University College

Massachusetts
Boston Architectural Center
Cambridge College

Michigan
Baker College
of Auburn Hills
of Cadillac
of Clinton Township
of Flint
of Jackson
of Muskegon
of Owosso
of Port Huron
Davenport University
Michigan Jewish Institute
Walsh College of Accountancy and Business Administration

Minnesota
Art Institutes International
Minnesota
Brown College
Globe College
National American University
St. Paul

Mississippi
Magnolia Bible College
University of Mississippi Medical Center
William Carey College

Missouri
Baptist Bible College
Calvary Bible College and Theological Seminary
Global University
Grantham University
Hickey College
Lester L. Cox College of Nursing and Health Sciences
Lincoln University
Missouri Western State University
National American University
Kansas City
Ranken Technical College

Montana
Salish Kootenai College

Nebraska
Bellevue University
Chadron State College
Clarkson College
Peru State College
Wayne State College

Nevada
Art Institute
of Las Vegas
Great Basin College
International Academy of Design and Technology: Henderson
Morrison University

New Jersey
Thomas Edison State College

New Mexico
International Institute of the Americas
National American University
New Mexico Highlands University
Northern New Mexico College
Western New Mexico University

New York
City University of New York
Medgar Evers College
New York City College of Technology
Excelsior College
Globe Institute of Technology

North Carolina
Miller-Motte Technical College

North Dakota
Dickinson State University
Mayville State University

Ohio
Allegheny Wesleyan College
Cincinnati College of Mortuary Science
Cleveland State University
Franklin University
Ohio State University
Lima Campus
Mansfield Campus
Marion Campus
Newark Campus
Ohio University
Chillicothe Campus
Eastern Campus
Lancaster Campus
Southern Campus at Ironton
Zanesville Campus
Shawnee State University
University of Rio Grande
University of Toledo
Wright State University
Youngstown State University

Oklahoma
Cameron University
Metropolitan College
Oklahoma Christian University
Oklahoma Panhandle State University
Rogers State University
Southern Nazarene University

Oregon
Marylhurst University
Pioneer Pacific College
Warner Pacific College

Pennsylvania
Art Institute
of Philadelphia
Central Pennsylvania College
Peirce College
Pennsylvania College of Technology
Restaurant School

Puerto Rico
American University of Puerto Rico
Atlantic College
Bayamon Central University
Columbia College
Universidad Adventista de las Antillas
Universidad del Este

Rhode Island
New England Institute of Technology

South Carolina
Allen University
Benedict College
Lander University
South University

South Dakota
Oglala Lakota College

Tennessee
Free Will Baptist Bible College
Lee University
Martin Methodist College
Williamson Christian College

Texas
Arlington Baptist College
Art Institute
of Dallas
Baptist Missionary Association Theological Seminary
Baptist University of the Americas
College of Biblical Studies-Houston
Southwestern Christian College
Texas College
Texas Southern University
University of Houston
Downtown
University of Texas
Brownsville
Wiley College

Utah
Neumont University
Stevens-Henager College
Stevens-Henager College of Business
Utah Valley State College
Weber State University
Western Governors University

Vermont
Goddard College
Woodbury College

Virginia
National College of Business & Technology
Salem

Washington
City University
Crown College

West Virginia
Marshall University
Mountain State University
West Virginia University at Parkersburg

Wisconsin
Herzing College

Guam
University of Guam

Canada
University of Manitoba

Guatemala
Universidad del Valle de Guatemala

Mexico
Instituto Tecnologico Autonomo de Mexico

Monaco
International University of Monaco

Two-year

Alabama
Alabama Southern Community College
Bevill State Community College
Bishop State Community College
Calhoun Community College
Central Alabama Community College
Chattahoochee Valley Community College
Community College of the Air Force
Enterprise-Ozark Community College
Gadsden State Community College
George C. Wallace State Community College
George C. Wallace Community College at Dothan
Selma
J. F. Drake State Technical College
James H. Faulkner State Community College
Jefferson Davis Community College
Jefferson State Community College
Lawson State Community College
Lurleen B. Wallace Community College
Northeast Alabama Community College
Northwest-Shoals Community College
Prince Institute of Professional Studies
Remington College
Mobile
Shelton State Community College
Snead State Community College
Southern Union State Community College
Trenholm State Technical College
Virginia College Technical
Wallace State Community College at Hanceville

Alaska
Ilisagvik College
Prince William Sound Community College

Arizona
Arizona Western College
Bryman School
Central Arizona College
Chandler-Gilbert Community College
Pecos
Williams Campus
Cochise College
Coconino County Community College
Dine College
Eastern Arizona College
Estrella Mountain Community College
Everest College
Gateway Community College
Glendale Community College
High-Tech Institute
International Institute of the Americas
Phoenix
Lamson College
Long Technical College
Mesa Community College
Mohave Community College
Northland Pioneer College
Paradise Valley Community College
Paralegal Institute
Phoenix College

Pima Community College
Refrigeration School
Rio Salado College
Scottsdale Community College
South Mountain Community College
Tohono O'odham Community College
Universal Technical Institute
Yavapai College

Arkansas

Arkansas Northeastern College
Arkansas State University
  Beebe
  Mountain Home
Arkansas State University: Newport
Crowley's Ridge College
East Arkansas Community College
Mid-South Community College
National Park Community College
North Arkansas College
Northwest Arkansas Community College
Ouachita Technical College
Ozarka College
Phillips Community College of the University of Arkansas
Pulaski Technical College
Rich Mountain Community College
South Arkansas Community College
Southeast Arkansas College
Southern Arkansas University Tech
University of Arkansas
  Community College at Batesville
  Community College at Hope
  Cossatot Community College of the
University of Arkansas Community College at Morrilton

California

Allan Hancock College
American River College
Antelope Valley College
Bakersfield College
Barstow College
Brooks College
Butte College
Cabrillo College
California School of Culinary Arts
Canada College
CEI College
  Maric College: Panorama City
Cerritos Community College
Cerro Coso Community College
Chabot College
Chaffey Community College
Citrus College
City College of San Francisco
Coastline Community College
College of Alameda
College of Marin: Kentfield
College of San Mateo
College of the Canyons
College of the Desert
College of the Redwoods
College of the Sequoias
College of the Siskiyous
Columbia College
Contra Costa College
Copper Mountain College
Cosumnes River College
Crafton Hills College
Cuesta College
Cuyamaca College
Cypress College
De Anza College
Diablo Valley College
East Los Angeles College
El Camino College
Empire College
Evergreen Valley College
Fashion Institute of Design and Merchandising
Fashion Institute of Design and Merchandising
  San Diego
  San Francisco
Feather River College
Foothill College
Fresno City College
Fullerton College
Gavilan Community College
Glendale Community College
Golden West College
Grossmont Community College
Hartnell College
Heald College
  Stockton
Imperial Valley College
Irvine Valley College
Lake Tahoe Community College
Laney College
Las Positas College
Lassen College
Long Beach City College
Los Angeles City College
Los Angeles Harbor College
Los Angeles Mission College
Los Angeles Pierce College
Los Angeles Southwest College
Los Angeles Trade and Technical College
Los Angeles Valley College
Los Medanos College
Maric College: Anaheim
Maric College: Sacramento
Mendocino College
Merced College
Merritt College
MiraCosta College
Mission College
Modesto Junior College
Monterey Peninsula College
Moorpark College
Mount San Antonio College
Mount San Jacinto College
Napa Valley College
Ohlone College
Orange Coast College
Oxnard College
Palo Verde College
Palomar College
Pasadena City College
Porterville College
Reedley College
Rio Hondo College
Riverside Community College
Sacramento City College
Saddleback College
San Bernardino Valley College
San Diego City College
San Diego Mesa College
San Diego Miramar College
San Joaquin Delta College
San Joaquin Valley College Inc.
San Jose City College
Santa Ana College
Santa Barbara City College
Santa Monica College
Santa Rosa Junior College
Santiago Canyon College
Shasta College
Sierra College
Silicon Valley College
  Western Career College: San Jose
Skyline College
Solano Community College
Southwestern College
Taft College
Ventura College
Victor Valley College
Vista Community College
West Hills Community College
West Los Angeles College
West Valley College
Yuba Community College District

Colorado

Aims Community College
Arapahoe Community College
Blair College
Boulder College of Massage Therapy
CollegeAmerica-Denver
Colorado Mountain College
  Alpine Campus
  Spring Valley Campus
  Timberline Campus
Colorado Northwestern Community College
Colorado School of Healing Arts
Colorado School of Trades
Community College of Aurora
Community College of Denver
Denver Automotive & Diesel College
Front Range Community College
Heritage College
Institute of Business & Medical Careers
IntelliTec College: Grand Junction
Morgan Community College
Northeastern Junior College
Otero Junior College
Parks College: Aurora
Pikes Peak Community College
Pueblo Community College
Red Rocks Community College
Remington College
  Colorado Springs
Trinidad State Junior College

Connecticut

Asnuntuck Community College
Capital Community College
Gateway Community College
Goodwin College
Housatonic Community College
Manchester Community College
Middlesex Community College
Naugatuck Valley Community College
Northwestern Connecticut Community College
Norwalk Community College
Quinebaug Valley Community College
Three Rivers Community College
Tunxis Community College

Delaware

Delaware Technical and Community College
  Owens Campus
  Stanton/Wilmington Campus
  Terry Campus

Florida

Brevard Community College
Broward Community College
Central Florida College
Central Florida Community College
Daytona Beach Community College
Edison College
Florida Career College: Hialeah
Florida Career College: West Palm Beach
Florida College of Natural Health
Florida College of Natural Health
  Bradenton
Florida Community College at Jacksonville
Florida Keys Community College
Florida National College
Florida Technical College
  Deland
Full Sail Real World Education
Gulf Coast Community College
Herzing College
  Orlando
Hillsborough Community College
Indian River Community College
Lake City Community College
Lake-Sumter Community College
Manatee Community College
Miami Dade College
New England Institute of Technology
North Florida Community College
Orlando Culinary Academy
Palm Beach Community College
Pasco-Hernando Community College
Pensacola Junior College
Polk Community College
St. Johns River Community College
St. Petersburg College
Santa Fe Community College
Seminole Community College
South Florida Community College
Southwest Florida College
Southwest Florida College
  Tampa
Tallahassee Community College
Valencia Community College

Georgia

Albany Technical College
Athens Technical College
Bainbridge College
Central Georgia Technical College
Chattahoochee Technical College
Coastal Georgia Community College
Columbus Technical College
DeKalb Technical College
Georgia Military College
Gupton Jones College of Funeral Service
Gwinnett College
High-Tech Institute: Atlanta
Le Cordon Bleu College of Culinary Arts
Middle Georgia Technical College
Northwestern Technical College
Savannah Technical College
Southwest Georgia Technical College
West Georgia Technical College

Hawaii

Hawaii Business College
Heald College
  Honolulu
University of Hawaii
  Hawaii Community College
  Honolulu Community College
  Kapiolani Community College
  Kauai Community College
  Leeward Community College
  Maui Community College
  Windward Community College

Idaho

College of Southern Idaho
Eastern Idaho Technical College
North Idaho College

Illinois

Black Hawk College
  East Campus
Carl Sandburg College
City Colleges of Chicago
  Harold Washington College
  Harry S. Truman College
  Kennedy-King College
  Malcolm X College
  Olive-Harvey College
  Richard J. Daley College
  Wright College
College of DuPage
College of Office Technology
Danville Area Community College
Elgin Community College
Fox College
Heartland Community College
Highland Community College
Illinois Central College
Illinois Eastern Community Colleges
  Frontier Community College
  Lincoln Trail College
  Olney Central College
  Wabash Valley College
Illinois Valley Community College
John A. Logan College
John Wood Community College
Joliet Junior College
Kankakee Community College
Kaskaskia College
Kishwaukee College
Lake Land College
Lewis and Clark Community College
Lincoln Land Community College
MacCormac College
McHenry County College
Moraine Valley Community College
Morrison Institute of Technology
Morton College
Oakton Community College
Parkland College
Prairie State College
Rend Lake College
Richland Community College
Rock Valley College
Sauk Valley Community College
South Suburban College of Cook County
Southeastern Illinois College
Southwestern Illinois College
Spoon River College
Taylor Business Institute
Triton College
Waubonsee Community College
William Rainey Harper College

Indiana

Ancilla College
Brown Mackie College: Fort Wayne
Brown Mackie College: Michigan City

Ivy Tech State College
Ivy Tech Community College: Bloomington
Ivy Tech Community College: Central Indiana
Ivy Tech Community College: Columbus
Ivy Tech Community College: East Central
Ivy Tech Community College: Kokomo
Ivy Tech Community College: Lafayette
Ivy Tech Community College: North Central
Ivy Tech Community College: Northeast
Ivy Tech Community College: Northwest
Ivy Tech Community College: South Central
Ivy Tech Community College: Southeast
Ivy Tech Community College: Southwest
Ivy Tech Community College: Wabash Valley
Ivy Tech Community College: Whitewater
Lincoln Technical Institute
Mid-America College of Funeral Service
Vincennes University

Iowa

Clinton Community College
Des Moines Area Community College
Ellsworth Community College
Hawkeye Community College
Indian Hills Community College
Iowa Central Community College
Iowa Lakes Community College
Iowa Western Community College
Kirkwood Community College
Marshalltown Community College
Muscatine Community College
North Iowa Area Community College
Northeast Iowa Community College
Northwest Iowa Community College
Scott Community College
Southeastern Community College
North Campus
Southwestern Community College
Vatterott College
Western Iowa Tech Community College

Kansas

Allen County Community College
Barton County Community College
Brown Mackie College
Butler County Community College
Cloud County Community College
Coffeyville Community College
Colby Community College
Cowley County Community College
Dodge City Community College
Donnelly College
Fort Scott Community College
Garden City Community College
Hesston College
Highland Community College
Hutchinson Community College
Johnson County Community College
Kansas City Kansas Community College
Labette Community College
Manhattan Area Technical College
Neosho County Community College
North Central Kansas Technical College
Pratt Community College
Seward County Community College

Kentucky

Ashland Community and Technical College
Big Sandy Community and Technical College
Bluegrass Community and Technical College
Brown Mackie College: Hopkinsville
Brown Mackie College: Louisville
Daymar College
Daymar College
Louisville
Draughons Junior College
Elizabethtown Community and Technical College
Hazard Community College
Henderson Community College
Hopkinsville Community College
Jefferson Community College
Madisonville Community College
Maysville Community College
National College of Business & Technology
Danville
Florence
Lexington
Louisville
Pikeville
Richmond
Owensboro Community College
Paducah Technical College
Somerset Community College
Southeast Kentucky Community and Technical College
Southern Ohio College
Brown Mackie College: North Kentucky
Southwestern College: Florence
Spencerian College
Spencerian College: Lexington
West Kentucky Community and Technical College

Louisiana

Baton Rouge Community College
Bossier Parish Community College
Delgado Community College
Gretna Career College
ITI Technical College
Nunez Community College
Southern University
Shreveport

Maine

Andover College
Beal College
Central Maine Community College
Eastern Maine Community College
Kennebec Valley Community College
Southern Maine Community College
Washington County Community College
York County Community College

Maryland

Allegany College of Maryland
Anne Arundel Community College
Baltimore City Community College
Carroll Community College
Cecil Community College
Chesapeake College
College of Southern Maryland
Community College of Baltimore County
Frederick Community College
Garrett College
Hagerstown Business College
Hagerstown Community College
Harford Community College
Howard Community College
Montgomery College
Prince George's Community College
TESST College of Technology
Baltimore
TESST College of Technology: Towson
Wor-Wic Community College

Massachusetts

Berkshire Community College
Bristol Community College
Bunker Hill Community College
Cape Cod Community College
Gibbs College
Greenfield Community College
Holyoke Community College
Massachusetts Bay Community College
Massasoit Community College
Middlesex Community College
Mount Wachusett Community College
New England College of Finance
North Shore Community College
Northern Essex Community College
Quincy College
Quinsigamond Community College
Roxbury Community College
Springfield Technical Community College
Urban College of Boston

Michigan

Alpena Community College
Bay de Noc Community College
Bay Mills Community College
Delta College
Glen Oaks Community College
Gogebic Community College
Grand Rapids Community College
Henry Ford Community College
Jackson Community College
Kalamazoo Valley Community College
Kellogg Community College
Kirtland Community College
Lake Michigan College
Lansing Community College
Lewis College of Business
Macomb Community College
Mid Michigan Community College
Monroe County Community College
Montcalm Community College
Mott Community College
Muskegon Community College
North Central Michigan College
Northwestern Michigan College
Oakland Community College
Saginaw Chippewa Tribal College
St. Clair County Community College
Schoolcraft College
Southwestern Michigan College
Washtenaw Community College
Wayne County Community College
West Shore Community College

Minnesota

Academy College
Alexandria Technical College
Anoka Technical College
Anoka-Ramsey Community College
Central Lakes College
Century Community and Technical College
Dakota County Technical College
Fond du Lac Tribal and Community College
Hennepin Technical College
Hibbing Community College
High-Tech Institute
Inver Hills Community College
Itasca Community College
Lake Superior College
Mesabi Range Community and Technical College
Minneapolis Business College
Minneapolis Community and Technical College
Minnesota State College - Southeast Technical
Minnesota State Community and Technical College - Fergus Falls
Minnesota West Community and Technical College: Worthington Campus
Normandale Community College
North Hennepin Community College
Northland Community & Technical College
Northwest Technical College
Pine Technical College
Rainy River Community College
Rasmussen College
Eagan
Mankato
Minnetonka
St. Cloud
Ridgewater College
Riverland Community College
Rochester Community and Technical College
St. Cloud Technical College
St. Paul College
South Central College
Vermilion Community College

Mississippi

Antonelli College
Hattiesburg
Jackson
Coahoma Community College
Copiah-Lincoln Community College
East Central Community College
Hinds Community College
Itawamba Community College
Jones County Junior College
Meridian Community College
Mississippi Delta Community College
Mississippi Gulf Coast Community College
Jefferson Davis Campus
Pearl River Community College
Southwest Mississippi Community College

Missouri

Blue River Community College
Crowder College
East Central College
High-Tech Institute
Jefferson College
Longview Community College
Maple Woods Community College
Metro Business College
Jefferson City
Mineral Area College
Missouri State University: West Plains
Moberly Area Community College
North Central Missouri College
Ozarks Technical Community College
Patricia Stevens College
Penn Valley Community College
Pinnacle Career Institute: Kansas City
St. Charles Community College
St. Louis Community College
Florissant Valley
Meramec
Southeast Missouri Hospital College of Nursing and Health Sciences
State Fair Community College
Three Rivers Community College
Vatterott College: St. Joseph
Vatterott College: Springfield

Montana

Blackfeet Community College
Chief Dull Knife College
Dawson Community College
Flathead Valley Community College
Fort Belknap College
Fort Peck Community College
Helena College of Technology of the University of Montana
Little Big Horn College
Miles Community College
Montana State University
College of Technology-Great Falls
Stone Child College

Nebraska

Central Community College
Hamilton College: Lincoln
Little Priest Tribal College
Metropolitan Community College
Mid-Plains Community College Area
Nebraska College of Technical Agriculture
Nebraska Indian Community College
Northeast Community College
Southeast Community College
Lincoln Campus
Western Nebraska Community College

Nevada

Career College of Northern Nevada
Community College of Southern Nevada
Heritage College
High-Tech Institute
Las Vegas College
Le Cordon Bleu College of Culinary Arts
Truckee Meadows Community College
Western Nevada Community College

New Hampshire

McIntosh College
New Hampshire Community Technical College
Claremont
Manchester
Nashua
Stratham

New Jersey

Atlantic Cape Community College
Bergen Community College
Brookdale Community College
Burlington County College
Camden County College
County College of Morris

Cumberland County College
Essex County College
Gloucester County College
Hudson County Community College
Mercer County Community College
Middlesex County College
Ocean County College
Passaic County Community College
Raritan Valley Community College
Salem Community College
Sussex County Community College
Union County College
Warren County Community College

New Mexico

Albuquerque
  Technical-Vocational Institute
Clovis Community College
Crownpoint Institute of Technology
Dona Ana Branch Community College of New Mexico State University
Eastern New Mexico University: Roswell Campus
Luna Community College
Mesalands Community College
New Mexico Junior College
New Mexico State University
  Alamogordo
  Carlsbad
  Grants
San Juan College
Santa Fe Community College
Southwestern Indian Polytechnic Institute

New York

Adirondack Community College
American Academy McAllister Institute of Funeral Service
Art Institute
  of New York City
Broome Community College
Bryant & Stratton Business Institute
  Bryant & Stratton College: Buffalo
  Bryant & Stratton College: Lackawanna
Business Informatics Center
Cayuga County Community College
City University of New York
  Borough of Manhattan Community College
  Hostos Community College
  Kingsborough Community College
  LaGuardia Community College
  Queensborough Community College
Clinton Community College
Columbia-Greene Community College
Corning Community College
Dutchess Community College
Elmira Business Institute
Erie Community College
  City Campus
  North Campus
  South Campus
Finger Lakes Community College
Fulton-Montgomery Community College
Genesee Community College
Herkimer County Community College
Hudson Valley Community College
Institute of Design and Construction
Interboro Institute
Island Drafting and Technical Institute
Jamestown Community College
Jefferson Community College
Long Island Business Institute
Mildred Elley
Mohawk Valley Community College
Monroe Community College
Nassau Community College
New York Career Institute
Niagara County Community College
North Country Community College
Olean Business Institute
Onondaga Community College
Orange County Community College
Rockland Community College
Schenectady County Community College
State University of New York
  College of Technology at Delhi
Suffolk County Community College
Sullivan County Community College
Taylor Business Institute
Technical Career Institutes
Tompkins-Cortland Community College
Trocaire College
Ulster County Community College
Utica School of Commerce
Villa Maria College of Buffalo
Westchester Community College

North Carolina

Alamance Community College
Asheville-Buncombe Technical Community College
Beaufort County Community College
Bladen Community College
Blue Ridge Community College
Brunswick Community College
Caldwell Community College and Technical Institute
Cape Fear Community College
Carteret Community College
Catawba Valley Community College
Central Carolina Community College
Central Piedmont Community College
Cleveland Community College
Coastal Carolina Community College
College of the Albemarle
Craven Community College
Davidson County Community College
Durham Technical Community College
Edgecombe Community College
Fayetteville Technical Community College
Forsyth Technical Community College
Gaston College
Guilford Technical Community College
Halifax Community College
Haywood Community College
Isothermal Community College
James Sprunt Community College
Johnston Community College
Lenoir Community College
Martin Community College
Mayland Community College
McDowell Technical Community College
Mitchell Community College
Montgomery Community College
Nash Community College
Pamlico Community College
Piedmont Community College
Pitt Community College
Randolph Community College
Richmond Community College
Roanoke-Chowan Community College
Robeson Community College
Rockingham Community College
Rowan-Cabarrus Community College
Sampson Community College
Sandhills Community College
South College
South Piedmont Community College
Southeastern Community College
Southwestern Community College
Stanly Community College
Surry Community College
Tri-County Community College
Vance-Granville Community College
Wake Technical Community College
Wayne Community College
Western Piedmont Community College
Wilkes Community College
Wilson Technical Community College

North Dakota

Aakers College: Fargo
Bismarck State College
Cankdeska Cikana Community College
Fort Berthold Community College
Lake Region State College
Minot State University: Bottineau Campus
North Dakota State College of Science
Sitting Bull College
Turtle Mountain Community College
Williston State College

Ohio

AEC Southern Ohio College
  Brown Mackie College: Akron
Belmont Technical College
Bowling Green State University: Firelands College
Bryant & Stratton College
  Willoughby Hills
Central Ohio Technical College
Chatfield College
Cincinnati State Technical and Community College
Clark State Community College
Cleveland Institute of Electronics
College of Art Advertising
Columbus State Community College
Cuyahoga Community College
  Metropolitan Campus
Edison State Community College
ETI Technical College of Niles
Gallipolis Career College
Hocking Technical College
James A. Rhodes State College
Jefferson Community College
Kent State University
  Ashtabula Regional Campus
  East Liverpool Regional Campus
  Salem Regional Campus
  Stark Campus
  Trumbull Campus
  Tuscarawas Campus
Lakeland Community College
Marion Technical College
Miami University
  Hamilton Campus
National College of Business & Technology: Dayton
Ohio Business College: Sandusky
Ohio College of Massotherapy
Ohio Institute of Photography and Technology
Ohio State University
  Agricultural Technical Institute
Owens Community College
  Toledo
Sinclair Community College
Southeastern Business College
Southeastern Business College: Jackson
Southeastern Business College: Lancaster
Southeastern Business College: New Boston
Southern State Community College
Southwestern College of Business
  Southwestern College: Franklin
  Southwestern College: Tri-County
  Southwestern College: Vine Street Campus
Stark State College of Technology
Stautzenberger College
Technology Education College
Trumbull Business College
University of Akron: Wayne College
University of Cincinnati
  Clermont College
  Raymond Walters College
Washington State Community College
Wright State University: Lake Campus
Zane State College

Oklahoma

Carl Albert State College
Connors State College
Eastern Oklahoma State College
Heritage College Hair Design
Murray State College
Northeastern Oklahoma Agricultural and Mechanical College
Oklahoma City Community College
Oklahoma State University
  Oklahoma City
  Okmulgee
Platt College
  Tulsa
Redlands Community College
Rose State College
Seminole State College
Tulsa Community College
Tulsa Welding School
Vatterott College
Western College of Southern California
Western Oklahoma State College

Oregon

Blue Mountain Community College
Central Oregon Community College
Chemeketa Community College
Clackamas Community College
Clatsop Community College
Klamath Community College
Lane Community College
Linn-Benton Community College
Mount Hood Community College
Pioneer Pacific College: Springfield
Portland Community College
Rogue Community College
Southwestern Oregon Community College
Treasure Valley Community College
Umpqua Community College

Pennsylvania

Berean Institute
Berks Technical Institute
Bradley Academy for the Visual Arts
Bucks County Community College
Butler County Community College
Cambria-Rowe Business College: Indiana
Career Training Academy
Career Training Academy: Monroeville
Commonwealth Technical Institute
Community College of Allegheny County
Community College of Beaver County
Community College of Philadelphia
Consolidated School of Business
  Lancaster
  York
Dean Institute of Technology
Delaware County Community College
DuBois Business College
DuBois Business College
  Huntingdon
  Oil City
Erie Business Center
Erie Business Center South
Erie Institute of Technology
Harrisburg Area Community College
JNA Institute of Culinary Arts
Johnson College
Lackawanna College
Lansdale School of Business
Lehigh Carbon Community College
Lehigh Valley College
Lincoln Technical Institute
Lincoln Technical Institute: Philadelphia
Luzerne County Community College
McCann School of Business
  Pottsville
Metropolitan Career Center
Montgomery County Community College
Newport Business Institute
Newport Business Institute
Northampton County Area Community College
Pace Institute
Penn Commercial Business and Technical School
Pennsylvania Highlands Community College
Pennsylvania Institute of Technology
Pennsylvania School of Business
Pittsburgh Institute of Mortuary Science
Pittsburgh Technical Institute
Reading Area Community College

Rosedale Technical Institute
Schuylkill Institute of Business & Technology
South Hills School of Business & Technology
Thompson Institute
Thompson Institute
 Philadelphia
Tri-State Business Institute
Triangle Tech
 DuBois
 Erie
 Greensburg
 Pittsburgh
West Virginia Career Institute
Western School of Health and Business Careers
Westmoreland County Community College
York Technical Institute
Yorktowne Business Institute

Puerto Rico

Humacao Community College
National College of Business & Technology: Bayamon

Rhode Island

Community College of Rhode Island

South Carolina

Aiken Technical College
Central Carolina Technical College
Denmark Technical College
Florence-Darlington Technical College
Forrest Junior College
Greenville Technical College
Horry-Georgetown Technical College
Midlands Technical College
Northeastern Technical College
Orangeburg-Calhoun Technical College
Piedmont Technical College
Spartanburg Technical College
Technical College of the Lowcountry
Tri-County Technical College
Trident Technical College
University of South Carolina
 Lancaster
Williamsburg Technical College
York Technical College

South Dakota

Kilian Community College
Mitchell Technical Institute
Sisseton Wahpeton College
Southeast Technical Institute
Western Dakota Technical Institute

Tennessee

Chattanooga State Technical Community College
Cleveland State Community College
Columbia State Community College
Dyersburg State Community College
Jackson State Community College
John A. Gupton College
Miller-Motte Technical College
Motlow State Community College
Nashville State Community College
National College of Business & Technology
 Tennessee
National College of Business & Technology: Knoxville
Northeast State Technical Community College
Pellissippi State Technical Community College
Roane State Community College
Southwest Tennessee Community College
Vatterott College: Memphis
Volunteer State Community College
Walters State Community College

Texas

Alvin Community College
Amarillo College
Angelina College
Austin Community College
Blinn College
Brazosport College
Brookhaven College
Cedar Valley College
Central Texas College
Cisco Junior College
Clarendon College
Coastal Bend College
College of the Mainland
Collin County Community College District
Court Reporting Institute of Dallas
Dallas Institute of Funeral Service
Del Mar College
Eastfield College
El Centro College
El Paso Community College
Frank Phillips College
Galveston College
Grayson County College
Hill College
Houston Community College System
Howard College
Jacksonville College
Kilgore College
Lamar State College at Orange
Lamar State College at Port Arthur
Laredo Community College
Lee College
McLennan Community College
Midland College
Mountain View College
Navarro College
North Central Texas College
North Harris Montgomery Community College District
North Lake College
Northeast Texas Community College
Northwest Vista College
Odessa College
Palo Alto College
Panola College
Paris Junior College
Ranger College
Remington College
 Dallas
 Fort Worth
 Houston
Richland College
St. Philip's College
San Antonio College
San Jacinto College
 Central Campus
 North
South Plains College
South Texas College
Southwest Texas Junior College
Tarrant County College
Temple College
Texarkana College
Texas Southmost College
Texas State Technical College
 Harlingen
 Waco
 West Texas
Texas State Technical College: Marshall
Trinity Valley Community College
Tyler Junior College
Universal Technical Institute
Vernon College
Victoria College
Wade College
Weatherford College
Western Technical College
Western Technical Institute: Diana Drive
Western Texas College
Wharton County Junior College

Utah

College of Eastern Utah
Dixie State College of Utah
LDS Business College
Provo College
Salt Lake Community College
Snow College
Utah Career College

Vermont

Community College of Vermont

Virginia

Blue Ridge Community College
Bryant & Stratton College: Virginia Beach
Central Virginia Community College
Dabney S. Lancaster Community College
Danville Community College
Eastern Shore Community College
Germanna Community College
J. Sargeant Reynolds Community College
John Tyler Community College
Lord Fairfax Community College
Miller-Motte Technical College: Lynchburg
Mountain Empire Community College
National College of Business & Technology
 Bluefield
 Charlottesville
 Danville
 Harrisonburg
 Lynchburg
 Martinsville
New River Community College
Northern Virginia Community College
Patrick Henry Community College
Paul D. Camp Community College
Piedmont Virginia Community College
Rappahannock Community College
Southside Virginia Community College
Southwest Virginia Community College
Thomas Nelson Community College
Tidewater Community College
Tidewater Tech
Virginia Highlands Community College
Virginia Western Community College
Wytheville Community College

Washington

Bellevue Community College
Bellingham Technical College
Big Bend Community College
Centralia College
Clark College
Clover Park Technical College
Columbia Basin College
Edmonds Community College
Everett Community College
Grays Harbor College
Green River Community College
Highline Community College
Lake Washington Technical College
Lower Columbia College
North Seattle Community College
Northwest Aviation College
Northwest School of Wooden Boatbuilding
Olympic College
Peninsula College
Pierce College
Renton Technical College
Seattle Central Community College
Shoreline Community College
Skagit Valley College
South Puget Sound Community College
South Seattle Community College
Spokane Community College
Spokane Falls Community College
Tacoma Community College
Walla Walla Community College
Wenatchee Valley College
Whatcom Community College
Yakima Valley Community College

West Virginia

Corinthian Schools: National Institute of Technology
Eastern West Virginia Community and Technical College
Huntington Junior College
Mountain State College
Potomac State College of West Virginia University
Southern West Virginia Community and Technical College
West Virginia Business College
West Virginia Business College
West Virginia Northern Community College

Wisconsin

Blackhawk Technical College
Chippewa Valley Technical College
College of Menominee Nation
Fox Valley Technical College
Gateway Technical College
Lakeshore Technical College
Madison Area Technical College
Mid-State Technical College
Milwaukee Area Technical College
Moraine Park Technical College
Northcentral Technical College
Northeast Wisconsin Technical College
Southwest Wisconsin Technical College
Waukesha County Technical College
Western Wisconsin Technical College

Wyoming

Casper College
Central Wyoming College
Eastern Wyoming College
Laramie County Community College
Northwest College
Sheridan College
Western Wyoming Community College
Wyoming Technical Institute

Guam

Guam Community College

Palau

Palau Community College

Canada

Humber College

Admission/placement policies

No closing date

Four-year

Alabama

American Sentinel University
Andrew Jackson University
Athens State University
Auburn University at Montgomery
Birmingham-Southern College
Columbia Southern University
Faulkner University
Heritage Christian University
Herzing College
Jacksonville State University
Judson College
Oakwood College
Samford University
South University
Southern Christian University
Talladega College
Troy University
University of Alabama
University of Mobile
University of North Alabama
University of West Alabama
Virginia College
Virginia College at Huntsville

Alaska

Charter College
Sheldon Jackson College
University of Alaska
  Southeast

Arizona

American Indian College of the Assemblies of God
Arizona Institute of Business and Technology
  International Institute of the Americas: Mesa
Arizona State University
Arizona State University West
Art Center Design College
Chaparral College
Collins College
DeVry University
  Phoenix
Embry-Riddle Aeronautical University: Prescott Campus
Grand Canyon University
International Institute of the Americas
  Tucson
Metropolitan College of Court Reporting
Northcentral University
Northern Arizona University
Tucson Design College
University of Advancing Technology
University of Phoenix
Western International University

Arkansas

Arkansas Baptist College
Arkansas Tech University
Henderson State University
John Brown University
Lyon College
Ouachita Baptist University
University of Arkansas
  Fort Smith
  Little Rock
  Monticello
  Pine Bluff
University of Central Arkansas
University of the Ozarks
Williams Baptist College

California

Academy of Art University
Alliant International University
Antioch Southern California
  Antioch University Santa Barbara
Art Center College of Design
Art Institute
  of California: Orange County
  of California: San Diego
Art Institute of California: San Francisco
Bethesda Christian University
Brooks Institute of Photography
California Baptist University
California College of the Arts
California Institute of Integral Studies
California Maritime Academy
California State University
  Bakersfield
  Monterey Bay
  San Bernardino
Cogswell Polytechnical College
Coleman College
Columbia College: Hollywood
Concordia University
Design Institute of San Diego
DeVry University
  Fremont
  Long Beach
  Pomona
  West Hills
Dominican School of Philosophy and Theology
Dominican University of California
Golden Gate University
Hope International University
Humphreys College
Institute of Computer Technology
International Technological University
John F. Kennedy University
King's College and Seminary
La Sierra University
Laguna College of Art and Design
Lincoln University
Loma Linda University
Loyola Marymount University
Master's College
Menlo College
Mt. Sierra College
National Hispanic University
National University
NewSchool of Architecture & Design
Notre Dame de Namur University
Otis College of Art and Design
Pacific States University
Pacific Union College
Platt College
  Ontario
  San Diego
Remington College
  San Diego
Samuel Merritt College
San Francisco Art Institute
Silicon Valley College
  Western Career College: Emeryville
Simpson University
Southern California Institute of Technology
Thomas Aquinas College
University of Judaism
University of La Verne
University of San Francisco
University of the Pacific
Vanguard University of Southern California
Westwood College: Long Beach
Whittier College
Woodbury University

Colorado

Adams State College
Art Institute
  of Colorado
Colorado Technical University
DeVry University
  Westminster
DeVry University: Colorado Springs
Johnson & Wales University
Jones International University
Mesa State College
Naropa University
National American University
  Denver
Nazarene Bible College
Rocky Mountain College of Art & Design
Teikyo Loretto Heights University
University of Northern Colorado
Westwood College of Technology
Westwood College of Technology South

Connecticut

Albertus Magnus College
Briarwood College
Charter Oak State College
Eastern Connecticut State University
Holy Apostles College and Seminary
Lyme Academy College of Fine Arts
Mitchell College
Paier College of Art
Post University
Sacred Heart University
St. Joseph College
University of Bridgeport
University of Hartford
University of New Haven
Western Connecticut State University

Delaware

Delaware State University
Wilmington College

District of Columbia

Corcoran College of Art and Design
Gallaudet University
Potomac College
Southeastern University
Strayer University
Trinity University

Florida

Art Institute of Fort Lauderdale
Barry University
Bethune-Cookman College
Carlos Albizu University
Chipola College
City College
DeVry University
  Miramar
  Orlando
Eckerd College
Edward Waters College
Embry-Riddle Aeronautical University
Embry-Riddle Aeronautical University: Extended Campus
Everglades University
Florida Institute of Technology
Florida International University
Florida Memorial University
Florida Metropolitan University
  Brandon Campus
  Melbourne Campus
  Orlando College North
  Orlando College South
  Pinellas
  Pompano Beach
  Tampa College
  Tampa College Lakeland
International Academy of Design and Technology: Orlando
International Academy of Design and Technology: Tampa
International College
Jacksonville University
Johnson & Wales University
Jones College
Lynn University
Miami International University of Art and Design
Northwood University
  Florida Campus
Nova Southeastern University
Okaloosa-Walton College
Palm Beach Atlantic University
Remington College
  Jacksonville
Remington College: Largo
Remington College: Tampa
Ringling School of Art and Design
St. Thomas University
Schiller International University
South University: West Palm Beach Campus
Southeastern College of the Assemblies of God
Stetson University
Universidad FLET
University of South Florida
University of Tampa
Warner Southern College
Webster College
Webster College: Holiday

Georgia

Augusta State University
Bauder College
Beulah Heights Bible College
Brenau University
Brewton-Parker College
Clayton State University
Covenant College
Dalton State College
DeVry University
  Alpharetta
  Decatur
Fort Valley State University
LaGrange College
Oglethorpe University
Reinhardt College
Savannah College of Art and Design
South University
Thomas University

Hawaii

Chaminade University of Honolulu
Hawaii Pacific University

Idaho

Idaho State University
Lewis-Clark State College

Illinois

American Academy of Art
Argosy University
Augustana College
Aurora University
Benedictine University
Blackburn College
Blessing-Reiman College of Nursing
Columbia College Chicago
Concordia University
DePaul University
DeVry University
  Addison
  Chicago
  Tinley Park
Dominican University
East-West University
Eastern Illinois University
Elmhurst College
Harrington College of Design
Illinois Institute of Art-Schaumburg
Illinois Institute of Technology
Illinois Wesleyan University
International Academy of Design and Technology: Chicago
Judson College
Kendall College
Lake Forest College
Lewis University
Lexington College
Lincoln Christian College and Seminary
Loyola University of Chicago
MacMurray College
McKendree College
Midstate College
Millikin University
Monmouth College
National-Louis University
North Central College
Quincy University
Robert Morris College: Chicago
St. Augustine College
St. Xavier University
School of the Art Institute of Chicago
Telshe Yeshiva-Chicago
Trinity Christian College
Trinity International University
University of Illinois
  Springfield
Westwood College - DuPage
Westwood College of Technology O'Hare

Indiana

Ball State University
Butler University
Calumet College of St. Joseph
DeVry University: Indianapolis
Franklin College
Indiana Institute of Technology
Indiana University
  Bloomington
  East
  Kokomo
  Northwest
  South Bend
  Southeast
Indiana University-Purdue University Fort Wayne
International Business College
Manchester College
Martin University
Oakland City University
Purdue University
Purdue University
  Calumet
  North Central Campus
St. Joseph's College
Saint Mary's College
Taylor University
Taylor University: Fort Wayne
University of Indianapolis
University of St. Francis
Wabash College

Iowa

Ashford University
Briar Cliff University
Buena Vista University
Central College
Clarke College
Drake University
Emmaus Bible College
Graceland University
Hamilton College

Tables and Indexes

Hamilton College
Cedar Falls
Cedar Rapids
Hamilton Technical College
Iowa Wesleyan College
Kaplan University
Loras College
Luther College
Morningside College
Northwestern College
St. Ambrose University
Simpson College
University of Dubuque
Upper Iowa University
Vennard College
Waldorf College
Wartburg College
William Penn University

Kansas
Baker University
Benedictine College
Bethel College
Emporia State University
Fort Hays State University
Friends University
Kansas State University
Kansas Wesleyan University
McPherson College
Newman University
Ottawa University
Pittsburg State University
Southwestern College
Tabor College
University of Kansas Medical Center
University of St. Mary
Wichita State University

Kentucky
Alice Lloyd College
Asbury College
Beckfield College
Brescia University
Campbellsville University
Kentucky Christian University
Kentucky Mountain Bible College
Kentucky State University
Kentucky Wesleyan College
Lindsey Wilson College
Mid-Continent University
Midway College
Morehead State University
St. Catharine College
Spalding University
Sullivan University
Union College

Louisiana
Louisiana State University
Alexandria
Louisiana Tech University
Loyola University New Orleans
New Orleans Baptist Theological Seminary: Leavell College
Nicholls State University
Our Lady of Holy Cross College
St. Joseph Seminary College
Southwest University
University of Louisiana at Lafayette
University of Louisiana at Monroe

Maine
Maine College of Art
New England School of Communications
St. Joseph's College
Thomas College
Unity College
University of Maine
University of Maine
Farmington
Fort Kent
Presque Isle
University of Southern Maine

Maryland
Baltimore International College
Bowie State University
Capitol College
College of Notre Dame of Maryland
Columbia Union College
DeVry University: Bethesda
Frostburg State University
Hood College
Morgan State University
Mount St. Mary's University
National Labor College
Ner Israel Rabbinical College
St. John's College
Sojourner-Douglass College
University of Baltimore
University of Maryland
University College
Villa Julie College

Massachusetts
American International College
Anna Maria College
Art Institute of Boston at Lesley University
Bay Path College
Becker College
Boston Architectural Center
Bridgewater State College
Cambridge College
Eastern Nazarene College
Elms College
Fitchburg State College
Gordon College
Hebrew College
Lasell College
Lesley University
Massachusetts College of Liberal Arts
Massachusetts Maritime Academy
Montserrat College of Art
Mount Ida College
New England Conservatory of Music
New England Institute of Art
Newbury College
Nichols College
Pine Manor College
Regis College
Salem State College
School of the Museum of Fine Arts
Suffolk University
University of Massachusetts
Dartmouth
Lowell
Wentworth Institute of Technology
Western New England College
Wheelock College

Michigan
Alma College
Andrews University
Aquinas College
Baker College
of Auburn Hills
of Cadillac
of Clinton Township
of Flint
of Jackson
of Muskegon
of Owosso
of Port Huron
Central Michigan University
Concordia University
Cornerstone University
Davenport University
Eastern Michigan University
Great Lakes Christian College
Hope College
Kendall College of Art and Design of Ferris State University
Kettering University
Lake Superior State University
Lawrence Technological University
Madonna University
Michigan Jewish Institute
Michigan State University
Michigan Technological University
Northern Michigan University
Northwood University
Oakland University
Olivet College
Reformed Bible College
Rochester College
Saginaw Valley State University
Siena Heights University
University of Michigan
Dearborn
Flint
Walsh College of Accountancy and Business Administration
Western Michigan University
Yeshiva Beth Yehuda-Yeshiva Gedolah of Greater Detroit

Minnesota
Art Institutes International Minnesota
Bemidji State University
Brown College
Capella University
College of St. Benedict
College of St. Catherine
College of St. Scholastica
College of Visual Arts
Concordia College: Moorhead
Devry University: Edina
Globe College
Hamline University
Minneapolis College of Art and Design
Minnesota School of Business
National American University
St. Paul
Oak Hills Christian College
Pillsbury Baptist Bible College
St. John's University
St. Olaf College
Southwest Minnesota State University
University of Minnesota
Twin Cities
University of St. Thomas
Walden University

Mississippi
Alcorn State University
Belhaven College
Blue Mountain College
Jackson State University
Magnolia Bible College
Mississippi College
Mississippi State University
Rust College
Tougaloo College
University of Southern Mississippi
William Carey College

Missouri
Avila University
Baptist Bible College
Central Bible College
Central Christian College of the Bible
Central Methodist University
Central Missouri State University
Columbia College
Culver-Stockton College
DeVry University
Kansas City
Global University
Grantham University
Harris-Stowe State University
Hickey College
Kansas City Art Institute
Kansas City College of Legal Studies
Lindenwood University
Missouri Baptist University
Missouri Southern State University
Missouri Technical School
Missouri Valley College
National American University
Kansas City
Northwest Missouri State University
Ranken Technical College
Research College of Nursing
Southeast Missouri State University
Southwest Baptist University
Stephens College
University of Missouri
Columbia
Kansas City
Westminster College
William Woods University

Montana
Montana State University
Billings
Bozeman
Montana Tech of the University of Montana
Rocky Mountain College
Salish Kootenai College
University of Montana: Missoula
University of Montana: Western

Nebraska
Bellevue University
Chadron State College
College of Saint Mary
Dana College
Doane College
Grace University
Hastings College
Midland Lutheran College
Peru State College
Union College
University of Nebraska
Kearney
Wayne State College

Nevada
Art Institute
of Las Vegas
DeVry University: Las Vegas
Great Basin College
International Academy of Design and Technology: Henderson
Morrison University
Sierra Nevada College
University of Nevada
Reno

New Hampshire
Chester College of New England
Colby-Sawyer College
Daniel Webster College
Franklin Pierce College
Granite State College
New England College
Rivier College
St. Anselm College
Southern New Hampshire University
Thomas More College of Liberal Arts

New Jersey
Berkeley College
Caldwell College
Centenary College
DeVry University: North Brunswick
Fairleigh Dickinson University
College at Florham
Metropolitan Campus
Felician College
Rider University
Rutgers, The State University of New Jersey
Camden Regional Campus
New Brunswick Regional Campus
Newark Regional Campus
St. Peter's College
Seton Hall University
Thomas Edison State College
University of Medicine and Dentistry of New Jersey
School of Health Related Professions
School of Nursing
Westminster Choir College of Rider University

New Mexico
College of Santa Fe
College of the Southwest
Eastern New Mexico University
International Institute of the Americas
Metropolitan College of Court Reporting
National American University
New Mexico Highlands University
New Mexico State University
Northern New Mexico College
St. John's College
Western New Mexico University

New York
Adelphi University
Alfred University
Berkeley College
Berkeley College of New York City
Boricua College
Briarcliffe College
Cazenovia College
City University of New York
City College
College of Staten Island
Medgar Evers College
New York City College of Technology
Queens College
York College
College of Mount St. Vincent
College of New Rochelle
Columbia University
School of Nursing
Culinary Institute of America
D'Youville College
Daemen College
Davis College
DeVry Institute of Technology
New York
Dominican College of Blauvelt
Dowling College
Excelsior College
Five Towns College
Globe Institute of Technology
Hofstra University
Houghton College
Keuka College
Laboratory Institute of Merchandising
Le Moyne College
Long Island University
Brooklyn Campus
C. W. Post Campus
Marymount Manhattan College
Medaille College
Mercy College
Metropolitan College of New York
Molloy College
Monroe College
Mount St. Mary College
New York Institute of Technology
New York School of Interior Design
Nyack College
Paul Smith's College

Polytechnic University
Rabbinical Academy Mesivta Rabbi Chaim Berlin
Rabbinical College of Long Island
Rochester Institute of Technology
Russell Sage College
Sage College of Albany
St. Francis College
St. John Fisher College
St. John's University
St. Joseph's College
St. Joseph's College: Suffolk Campus
St. Thomas Aquinas College
School of Visual Arts
State University of New York
- Binghamton
- Buffalo
- College at Brockport
- College at Buffalo
- College at Cortland
- College at Fredonia
- College at Old Westbury
- College at Oneonta
- College at Potsdam
- College of Environmental Science and Forestry
- Empire State College
- Farmingdale
- Institute of Technology at Utica/Rome
- Maritime College
- Oswego
- Stony Brook
- Upstate Medical University

Touro College
Utica College
Vaughn College of Aeronautics and Technology
Yeshiva and Kolel Bais Medrash Elyon
Yeshiva Derech Chaim
Yeshiva Mikdash Melech
Yeshiva University

North Carolina

Appalachian State University
Art Institute
- of Charlotte

Barton College
Bennett College
Brevard College
Cabarrus College of Health Sciences
Catawba College
Chowan College
DeVry University: Charlotte
Gardner-Webb University
Greensboro College
Johnson & Wales University
Johnson C. Smith University
Lees-McRae College
Mars Hill College
Meredith College
Methodist College
Miller-Motte Technical College
Montreat College
Mount Olive College
North Carolina Agricultural and Technical State University
North Carolina School of the Arts
North Carolina Wesleyan College
Peace College
Pfeiffer University
Piedmont Baptist College
Queens University of Charlotte
Roanoke Bible College
St. Andrews Presbyterian College
Salem College
University of North Carolina
- Pembroke

Wingate University
Winston-Salem Bible College

North Dakota

Dickinson State University
Jamestown College
Mayville State University
Medcenter One College of Nursing
Minot State University
Trinity Bible College
University of Mary
Valley City State University

Ohio

Allegheny Wesleyan College
Antioch College
Ashland University
Baldwin-Wallace College
Capital University
Cedarville University
Central State University
Cincinnati College of Mortuary Science
Cleveland Institute of Art
Columbus College of Art and Design
David N. Myers University
Defiance College
DeVry University
- Columbus

Franklin University
God's Bible School and College
Lake Erie College
Laura and Alvin Siegal College of Judaic Studies
Lourdes College
Mercy College of Northwest Ohio
Mount Carmel College of Nursing
Mount Union College
Ohio Dominican University
Ohio University
- Chillicothe Campus
- Eastern Campus
- Lancaster Campus
- Southern Campus at Ironton
- Zanesville Campus

Otterbein College
Pontifical College Josephinum
Shawnee State University
Tiffin University
Union Institute & University
University of Dayton
University of Rio Grande
University of Toledo
Urbana University
Ursuline College
Wilmington College
Wright State University

Oklahoma

Bacone College
Cameron University
East Central University
Metropolitan College
Metropolitan College
Mid-America Christian University
National Education Center
- Spartan School of Aeronautics

Northwestern Oklahoma State University
Oklahoma Christian University
Oklahoma Panhandle State University
Oklahoma State University
Oklahoma Wesleyan University
Oral Roberts University
Rogers State University
St. Gregory's University
Southeastern Oklahoma State University
Southwestern Oklahoma State University
University of Central Oklahoma
University of Tulsa

Oregon

Art Institute of Portland
DeVry University: Portland
Marylhurst University
Northwest Christian College
Oregon State University
Pacific Northwest College of Art
Pacific University
Pioneer Pacific College
Portland State University
Southern Oregon University
Warner Pacific College
Western Oregon University

Pennsylvania

Albright College
Alvernia College
Arcadia University
Art Institute
- of Philadelphia
- of Pittsburgh

Bloomsburg University of Pennsylvania
Cabrini College
California University of Pennsylvania
Cedar Crest College
Central Pennsylvania College
Chestnut Hill College
Cheyney University of Pennsylvania
Clarion University of Pennsylvania
College Misericordia
Delaware Valley College
DeVry University
- Ft. Washington

Eastern University
Edinboro University of Pennsylvania
Elizabethtown College
Gannon University
Geneva College
Gratz College
Holy Family University
Indiana University of Pennsylvania
King's College
Kutztown University of Pennsylvania
La Roche College
La Salle University
Lancaster Bible College
Lebanon Valley College
Lincoln University
Lock Haven University of Pennsylvania
Mansfield University of Pennsylvania
Marywood University
Mercyhurst College
Messiah College
Millersville University of Pennsylvania
Mount Aloysius College
Neumann College
Peirce College
Penn State
- Abington
- Altoona
- Berks
- Erie, The Behrend College
- Harrisburg
- Lehigh Valley
- Schuylkill - Capital College
- University Park
- Wilkes-Barre

Philadelphia Biblical University
Philadelphia University
Point Park University
Restaurant School
Rosemont College
St. Francis University
Shippensburg University of Pennsylvania
Slippery Rock University of Pennsylvania
Talmudical Yeshiva of Philadelphia
Thomas Jefferson University: College of Health Professions
University of Pittsburgh
University of Pittsburgh
- Bradford
- Johnstown

University of Scranton
University of the Arts
University of the Sciences in Philadelphia
Waynesburg College
West Chester University of Pennsylvania
Widener University
Wilkes University
Wilson College
Yeshivath Beth Moshe
York College of Pennsylvania

Puerto Rico

American University of Puerto Rico
Atlantic College
Columbia College
Electronic Data Processing College: San Sebastian
Inter American University of Puerto Rico
- Barranquitas Campus
- Guayama Campus

Turabo University
Universidad Adventista de las Antillas
Universidad del Este
University of Puerto Rico
- Utuado

Rhode Island

Johnson & Wales University
New England Institute of Technology
Roger Williams University
Salve Regina University
University of Rhode Island
Zion Bible Institute

South Carolina

Benedict College
Charleston Southern University
The Citadel
Coker College
Columbia College
Columbia International University
Erskine College
Francis Marion University
Lander University
Morris College
Newberry College
Presbyterian College
South University
University of South Carolina
- Beaufort
- Upstate

Voorhees College
Winthrop University

South Dakota

Dakota State University
Northern State University
Oglala Lakota College
South Dakota School of Mines and Technology
South Dakota State University
University of Sioux Falls
University of South Dakota

Tennessee

Aquinas College
Bethel College
Crichton College
Cumberland University
East Tennessee State University
Free Will Baptist Bible College
Freed-Hardeman University
King College
Lambuth University
Lincoln Memorial University
Lipscomb University
Memphis College of Art
Rhodes College
South College
Tennessee Wesleyan College
Trevecca Nazarene University
Tusculum College
University of Tennessee
- Chattanooga

Williamson Christian College

Texas

Amberton University
Arlington Baptist College
Art Institute
- of Dallas
- of Houston

Austin Graduate School of Theology
Baptist Missionary Association Theological Seminary
Baylor University
College of Biblical Studies-Houston
College of Saint Thomas More
Criswell College
Dallas Baptist University
DeVry University
- Irving

DeVry University: Houston
Hardin-Simmons University
Houston Baptist University
Howard Payne University
Jarvis Christian College
Northwood University: Texas Campus
Paul Quinn College
St. Mary's University
Southwestern Assemblies of God University
Stephen F. Austin State University
Sul Ross State University
Texas A&M University
- Galveston
- Kingsville
- Texarkana

Texas College
Texas Wesleyan University
University of Houston
- Victoria

University of Mary Hardin-Baylor
University of St. Thomas
University of Texas
- Arlington
- Southwestern Medical Center at Dallas
- Tyler

University of the Incarnate Word
Wayland Baptist University
West Texas A&M University
Wiley College

Utah

Neumont University
Stevens-Henager College
Stevens-Henager College of Business
Utah State University

Vermont

Castleton State College
College of St. Joseph in Vermont
Goddard College
Green Mountain College
Johnson State College
Lyndon State College
Norwich University
Southern Vermont College
Sterling College
Vermont Technical College
Woodbury College

Virginia

Art Institute
- of Washington

Bridgewater College
Christendom College
DeVry University
- Arlington

Eastern Mennonite University
ECPI College of Technology
ECPI Technical College
- Glen Allen

Emory & Henry College
Hollins University
Jefferson College of Health Sciences
Liberty University
Longwood University
Lynchburg College
Mary Baldwin College
Marymount University
Potomac College
Randolph-Macon Woman's College
St. Paul's College
Virginia Intermont College
Virginia Union University
Virginia Wesleyan College
World College

Washington

Art Institute of Seattle
Bastyr University
City University
Crown College
DeVry University
  Federal Way
DigiPen Institute of Technology
Evergreen State College
Henry Cogswell College
Heritage University
Pacific Lutheran University
Saint Martin's University
Seattle University
Walla Walla College
Washington State University

West Virginia

Alderson-Broaddus College
Appalachian Bible College
Bethany College
Bluefield State College
Concord University
Davis and Elkins College
Glenville State College
Marshall University
Mountain State University
Salem International University
Shepherd University
University of Charleston
West Liberty State College
West Virginia State University
West Virginia University at Parkersburg
Wheeling Jesuit University

Wisconsin

Bellin College of Nursing
Cardinal Stritch University
Carroll College
Carthage College
Columbia College of Nursing
DeVry University: Milwaukee
Herzing College
Lakeland College
Maranatha Baptist Bible College
Marian College of Fond du Lac
Milwaukee School of Engineering
Mount Mary College
Northland College
Ripon College
St. Norbert College
Silver Lake College
University of Wisconsin
  Eau Claire
  Green Bay
  La Crosse
  Oshkosh
  Platteville
  River Falls
  Stevens Point
  Stout
  Superior
  Whitewater
Viterbo University
Wisconsin Lutheran College

Canada

Acadia University

Mexico

Instituto Tecnologico Autonomo de Mexico

United Kingdom

Richmond, The American International University in London

Two-year

Alabama

Alabama Southern Community College
Bevill State Community College
Bishop State Community College
Calhoun Community College
Chattahoochee Valley Community College
Community College of the Air Force
Enterprise-Ozark Community College
Gadsden State Community College
George C. Wallace State Community College
  George C. Wallace Community College at Dothan
  Selma
J. F. Drake State Technical College
James H. Faulkner State Community College
Jefferson Davis Community College
Jefferson State Community College
Lawson State Community College
Lurleen B. Wallace Community College
Northeast Alabama Community College
Northwest-Shoals Community College
Prince Institute of Professional Studies
Remington College
  Mobile
Shelton State Community College
Southern Union State Community College
Trenholm State Technical College
Virginia College Technical
Wallace State Community College at Hanceville

Alaska

Ilisagvik College
Prince William Sound Community College

Arizona

Arizona Western College
Bryman School
Central Arizona College
Chandler-Gilbert Community College
  Pecos
  Williams Campus
Cochise College
Coconino County Community College
Dine College
Eastern Arizona College
Everest College
Gateway Community College
Glendale Community College
High-Tech Institute
International Institute of the Americas
  Phoenix
Lamson College
Long Technical College
Mesa Community College
Mohave Community College
Northland Pioneer College
Paradise Valley Community College
Paralegal Institute
Phoenix College
Pima Community College
Refrigeration School
Rio Salado College
Scottsdale Community College
South Mountain Community College
Universal Technical Institute
Yavapai College

Arkansas

Arkansas Northeastern College
Arkansas State University
  Beebe
Black River Technical College
Crowley's Ridge College
East Arkansas Community College
Mid-South Community College
National Park Community College
North Arkansas College
Northwest Arkansas Community College
Ouachita Technical College
Ozarka College
Phillips Community College of the University of Arkansas
Pulaski Technical College
Remington College
  Little Rock
Rich Mountain Community College
South Arkansas Community College
Southeast Arkansas College
University of Arkansas
  Community College at Batesville
  Community College at Hope
  Cossatot Community College of the
University of Arkansas
  Community College at Morrilton

California

Allan Hancock College
American Academy of Dramatic Arts: West
American River College
Antelope Valley College
Art Institute
  of California: Los Angeles
Bakersfield College
Barstow College
Brooks College
Butte College
Cabrillo College
California Culinary Academy
California School of Culinary Arts
Canada College
CEI College
  Maric College: Panorama City
Cerritos Community College
Cerro Coso Community College
Chabot College
Chaffey Community College
Citrus College
City College of San Francisco
Coastline Community College
College of Alameda
College of Marin: Kentfield
College of Oceaneering
College of San Mateo
College of the Canyons
College of the Redwoods
College of the Sequoias
College of the Siskiyous
Columbia College
Concorde Career College
Contra Costa College
Copper Mountain College
Cosumnes River College
Crafton Hills College
Cuesta College
De Anza College
Diablo Valley College
El Camino College
Empire College
Evergreen Valley College
Fashion Careers College
Fashion Institute of Design and Merchandising
Fashion Institute of Design and Merchandising
  San Diego
  San Francisco
Feather River College
Foothill College
Fresno City College
Fullerton College
Gavilan Community College
Glendale Community College
Golden West College
Grossmont Community College
Hartnell College
Heald College
  Concord
  Fresno
  Hayward
  Rancho Cordova
  Roseville
  Salinas
  San Francisco
  San Jose
  Stockton
Imperial Valley College
Irvine Valley College
Lake Tahoe Community College
Laney College
Las Positas College
Long Beach City College
Los Angeles Harbor College
Los Angeles Mission College
Los Angeles Southwest College
Los Angeles Trade and Technical College
Los Angeles Valley College
Los Medanos College
Maric College
  Vista
Maric College: Anaheim
Maric College: Sacramento
Marymount College
Mendocino College
Merced College
Merritt College
MiraCosta College
Mission College
Modesto Junior College
Monterey Peninsula College
Moorpark College
Mount San Antonio College
MTI College
Napa Valley College
National Institute of Technology
Northwestern College
Ohlone College
Orange Coast College
Oxnard College
Palo Verde College
Platt College
  Cerritos
  Los Angeles
  Newport Beach
Porterville College
Professional Golfers Career College
Reedley College
Rio Hondo College
Riverside Community College
Sacramento City College
Saddleback College
Sage College
Salvation Army Crestmont College
San Bernardino Valley College
San Diego City College
San Diego Mesa College
San Diego Miramar College
San Joaquin Delta College
San Joaquin Valley College Inc.
San Jose City College
Santa Ana College
Santa Barbara Business College
  Bakersfield
  Santa Maria
Santa Barbara Business College: Ventura
Santa Monica College
Santa Rosa Junior College
Shasta College
Sierra College
Silicon Valley College
  Western Career College: San Jose
Solano Community College
Southwestern College
Taft College
Ventura College
Victor Valley College
Vista Community College
West Hills Community College
West Los Angeles College
West Valley College
Western Career College
  Pleasant Hill
  San Leandro
Western Career College: Walnut Creek
Westwood College of Technology
  Westwood College: Los Angeles
Yuba Community College District

Colorado

Aims Community College
Arapahoe Community College
Bel-Rea Institute of Animal Technology
Blair College
Boulder College of Massage Therapy
Cambridge College
CollegeAmerica-Denver
Colorado Mountain College
  Alpine Campus
  Timberline Campus
Colorado Northwestern Community College
Colorado School of Healing Arts
Colorado School of Trades
Community College of Aurora
Community College of Denver
Concorde Career College
Denver Academy of Court Reporting
Denver Automotive & Diesel College
Front Range Community College
Heritage College
Institute of Business & Medical Careers
IntelliTec College: Grand Junction
Morgan Community College
Northeastern Junior College
Otero Junior College
Parks College
Parks College: Aurora
Pikes Peak Community College
Pueblo Community College
Red Rocks Community College
Remington College
  Colorado Springs
Trinidad State Junior College

Connecticut

Asnuntuck Community College
Capital Community College
Gibbs College
Goodwin College
Housatonic Community College
International College of Hospitality Management
Manchester Community College

Naugatuck Valley Community College
Northwestern Connecticut Community College
Norwalk Community College
Quinebaug Valley Community College
Three Rivers Community College
Tunxis Community College

Delaware

Delaware Technical and Community College
Owens Campus
Stanton/Wilmington Campus
Terry Campus

Florida

Brevard Community College
Broward Community College
Central Florida College
Central Florida Community College
City College
Miami
City College: Casselberry
Daytona Beach Community College
Florida Career College: Hialeah
Florida Career College: Miami
Florida Career College: Pembroke Pines
Florida Career College: West Palm Beach
Florida College of Natural Health
Florida College of Natural Health
Bradenton
Maitland
Miami
Florida Community College at Jacksonville
Florida Keys Community College
Florida National College
Florida Technical College
Deland
Full Sail Real World Education
Gulf Coast Community College
Herzing College
Orlando
Hillsborough Community College
Indian River Community College
Key College
Lake City Community College
Lake-Sumter Community College
Manatee Community College
Miami Dade College
New England Institute of Technology
North Florida Community College
Orlando Culinary Academy
Pasco-Hernando Community College
Pensacola Junior College
Polk Community College
St. Johns River Community College
St. Petersburg College
Santa Fe Community College
South Florida Community College
Southwest Florida College
Southwest Florida College
Tampa
Ultrasound Diagnostic School
Sanford-Brown Institute: Jacksonville

Georgia

Abraham Baldwin Agricultural College
Athens Technical College
Chattahoochee Technical College
Darton College
East Georgia College
Georgia Highlands College
Gordon College
Griffin Technical College
Gupton Jones College of Funeral Service
Gwinnett College
Le Cordon Bleu College of Culinary Arts
Middle Georgia College
Middle Georgia Technical College
Northwestern Technical College
Oxford College of Emory University
Savannah Technical College
Southwest Georgia Technical College
Waycross College
West Georgia Technical College
Young Harris College

Hawaii

Hawaii Business College
Heald College
Honolulu
Remington College
Honolulu
University of Hawaii
Honolulu Community College
Kauai Community College
Maui Community College
Windward Community College

Idaho

College of Southern Idaho

Illinois

Black Hawk College
East Campus
Career Colleges of Chicago
Carl Sandburg College
City Colleges of Chicago
Harold Washington College
Harry S. Truman College
Kennedy-King College
Malcolm X College
Olive-Harvey College
Richard J. Daley College
Wright College
College of DuPage
College of Lake County
College of Office Technology
Danville Area Community College
Elgin Community College
Fox College
Heartland Community College
Highland Community College
Illinois Central College
Illinois Eastern Community Colleges
Frontier Community College
Lincoln Trail College
Olney Central College
Wabash Valley College
Illinois Valley Community College
John A. Logan College
John Wood Community College
Joliet Junior College
Kankakee Community College
Kaskaskia College
Kishwaukee College
Lake Land College
Lewis and Clark Community College
Lincoln Land Community College
MacCormac College
McHenry County College
Moraine Valley Community College
Morrison Institute of Technology
Morton College
Northwestern Business College
Oakton Community College
Parkland College
Prairie State College
Rend Lake College
Richland Community College
Rock Valley College
Rockford Business College
Sauk Valley Community College
South Suburban College of Cook County
Southeastern Illinois College
Southwestern Illinois College
Spoon River College
Springfield College in Illinois
Taylor Business Institute
Triton College
Waubonsee Community College
William Rainey Harper College

Indiana

Ancilla College
Brown Mackie College: Fort Wayne
Brown Mackie College: Michigan City
Indiana Business College
Indiana Business College
Anderson
Columbus
Evansville
Fort Wayne
Lafayette
Marion
Medical
Muncie
Terre Haute
International Business College: Indianapolis
Ivy Tech State College
Ivy Tech Community College: Bloomington
Ivy Tech Community College: Central Indiana
Ivy Tech Community College: Columbus
Ivy Tech Community College: East Central
Ivy Tech Community College: Kokomo
Ivy Tech Community College: Lafayette
Ivy Tech Community College: North Central
Ivy Tech Community College: Northeast
Ivy Tech Community College: Northwest
Ivy Tech Community College: South Central
Ivy Tech Community College: Southeast
Ivy Tech Community College: Southwest
Ivy Tech Community College: Wabash Valley
Ivy Tech Community College: Whitewater
Lincoln Technical Institute
Mid-America College of Funeral Service
Professional Careers Institute
Sawyer College
Sawyer College: Merrillville

Iowa

AIB College of Business
Clinton Community College
Des Moines Area Community College
Ellsworth Community College
Hawkeye Community College
Indian Hills Community College
Iowa Central Community College
Iowa Lakes Community College
Iowa Western Community College
Kirkwood Community College
Marshalltown Community College
Muscatine Community College
North Iowa Area Community College
Northeast Iowa Community College
Northwest Iowa Community College
Scott Community College
Southeastern Community College
North Campus
Southwestern Community College
Vatterott College
Western Iowa Tech Community College

Kansas

Allen County Community College
Barton County Community College
Brown Mackie College
Butler County Community College
Cloud County Community College
Coffeyville Community College
Colby Community College
Cowley County Community College
Dodge City Community College
Donnelly College
Fort Scott Community College
Garden City Community College
Hesston College
Highland Community College
Hutchinson Community College
Johnson County Community College
Kansas City Kansas Community College
Labette Community College
Manhattan Area Technical College
Neosho County Community College
North Central Kansas Technical College
Pratt Community College
Seward County Community College

Kentucky

Ashland Community and Technical College
Big Sandy Community and Technical College
Brown Mackie College: Hopkinsville
Brown Mackie College: Louisville
Daymar College
Daymar College
Louisville
Draughons Junior College
Elizabethtown Community and Technical College
Hazard Community College
Henderson Community College
Hopkinsville Community College
Jefferson Community College
Louisville Technical Institute
Madisonville Community College
Maysville Community College
National College of Business & Technology
Danville
Florence
Lexington
Louisville
Pikeville
Richmond
Owensboro Community College
Paducah Technical College
Somerset Community College
Southeast Kentucky Community and Technical College
Southern Ohio College
Brown Mackie College: North Kentucky
Southwestern College: Florence
Spencerian College
Spencerian College: Lexington
West Kentucky Community and Technical College

Louisiana

Baton Rouge Community College
Delgado Community College
Gretna Career College
ITI Technical College
Nunez Community College
Remington College
Lafayette
New Orleans
Southern University
Shreveport

Maine

Andover College
Beal College
Central Maine Community College
Eastern Maine Community College
Kennebec Valley Community College
Northern Maine Community College
Southern Maine Community College
York County Community College

Maryland

Allegany College of Maryland
Anne Arundel Community College
Baltimore City Community College
Carroll Community College
Cecil Community College
Chesapeake College
College of Southern Maryland
Community College of Baltimore County
Frederick Community College
Garrett College
Hagerstown Business College
Hagerstown Community College
Harford Community College
Howard Community College
Montgomery College
Prince George's Community College
TESST College of Technology
Baltimore
TESST College of Technology: Towson
Wor-Wic Community College

Massachusetts

Bay State College
Benjamin Franklin Institute of Technology
Berkshire Community College
Bristol Community College
Cape Cod Community College
Dean College
Fisher College
Gibbs College
Greenfield Community College
Holyoke Community College
Laboure College
Marian Court College
Massachusetts Bay Community College
Massasoit Community College
Middlesex Community College
Mount Wachusett Community College
New England College of Finance
North Shore Community College
Northern Essex Community College
Quincy College
Quinsigamond Community College
Roxbury Community College

Springfield Technical Community College
Urban College of Boston

Michigan

Alpena Community College
Delta College
Glen Oaks Community College
Gogebic Community College
Henry Ford Community College
Jackson Community College
Kalamazoo Valley Community College
Kellogg Community College
Kirtland Community College
Lake Michigan College
Lansing Community College
Lewis College of Business
Macomb Community College
Mid Michigan Community College
Monroe County Community College
Montcalm Community College
Mott Community College
Muskegon Community College
North Central Michigan College
Northwestern Michigan College
Oakland Community College
Saginaw Chippewa Tribal College
Schoolcraft College
Southwestern Michigan College
Washtenaw Community College
Wayne County Community College
West Shore Community College

Minnesota

Academy College
Alexandria Technical College
Anoka-Ramsey Community College
Central Lakes College
Century Community and Technical College
Dakota County Technical College
Duluth Business University
Dunwoody College of Technology
Fond du Lac Tribal and Community College
Hennepin Technical College
Hibbing Community College
High-Tech Institute
Inver Hills Community College
Lakeland Academy Division of Herzing College
Mesabi Range Community and Technical College
Minneapolis Business College
Minneapolis Community and Technical College
Minnesota School of Business: Brooklyn Center
Minnesota State College - Southeast Technical
Minnesota State Community and Technical College - Fergus Falls
Minnesota West Community and Technical College: Worthington Campus
Normandale Community College
North Hennepin Community College
Northland Community & Technical College
Northwest Technical College
Northwest Technical Institute
Pine Technical College
Rainy River Community College
Rasmussen College
- Eagan
- Mankato
- Minnetonka
- St. Cloud

Ridgewater College
Rochester Community and Technical College
St. Cloud Technical College
St. Paul College
South Central College
Vermilion Community College

Mississippi

Antonelli College
- Jackson

Coahoma Community College
Copiah-Lincoln Community College
East Central Community College
Holmes Community College
Itawamba Community College
Jones County Junior College
Mississippi Delta Community College
Mississippi Gulf Coast Community College
- Jefferson Davis Campus

Pearl River Community College
Southwest Mississippi Community College

Missouri

Blue River Community College
Cottey College
Crowder College
East Central College
Everest College: Springfield
Jefferson College
Longview Community College
Maple Woods Community College
Metro Business College
- Jefferson City

Mineral Area College
Missouri College
Moberly Area Community College
North Central Missouri College
Ozarks Technical Community College
Patricia Stevens College
Penn Valley Community College
Pinnacle Career Institute: Kansas City
St. Charles Community College
St. Louis Community College
- Florissant Valley
- Meramec

State Fair Community College
Three Rivers Community College
Vatterott College
Vatterott College: St. Joseph
Vatterott College: Springfield

Montana

Blackfeet Community College
Chief Dull Knife College
Dawson Community College
Flathead Valley Community College
Fort Belknap College
Helena College of Technology of the University of Montana
Little Big Horn College
Miles Community College
Montana State University
- College of Technology-Great Falls

Stone Child College

Nebraska

Central Community College
Creative Center
Hamilton College: Lincoln
Little Priest Tribal College
Metropolitan Community College
Mid-Plains Community College Area
Nebraska Indian Community College
Northeast Community College
Southeast Community College
- Lincoln Campus

Western Nebraska Community College

Nevada

Career College of Northern Nevada
Community College of Southern Nevada
Heritage College
High-Tech Institute
Las Vegas College
Le Cordon Bleu College of Culinary Arts
Truckee Meadows Community College
Western Nevada Community College

New Hampshire

McIntosh College
New Hampshire Community Technical College
- Berlin
- Claremont
- Manchester
- Nashua
- Stratham

New Hampshire Technical Institute

New Jersey

Assumption College for Sisters
Bergen Community College
Brookdale Community College
Burlington County College
Camden County College
County College of Morris
Cumberland County College
Essex County College
Gloucester County College
Hudson County Community College
Mercer County Community College
Middlesex County College
Ocean County College
Passaic County Community College
Raritan Valley Community College
Salem Community College
Somerset Christian College
Sussex County Community College
Union County College
Warren County Community College

New Mexico

Albuquerque Technical-Vocational Institute
Art Center Design College
Clovis Community College
Crownpoint Institute of Technology
Dona Ana Branch Community College of New Mexico State University
Eastern New Mexico University: Roswell Campus
Luna Community College
Mesalands Community College
New Mexico Junior College
New Mexico Military Institute Junior College
New Mexico State University
- Alamogordo
- Carlsbad

San Juan College
Santa Fe Community College

New York

American Academy of Dramatic Arts
Art Institute
- of New York City

ASA Institute of Business and Computer Technology
Bramson ORT College
Broome Community College
Bryant & Stratton Business Institute
- Bryant & Stratton College: Albany
- Bryant & Stratton College: Buffalo
- Bryant & Stratton College: Lackawanna
- Bryant & Stratton College: Rochester
- Bryant & Stratton College: Syracuse

Bryant & Stratton College: Henrietta
Business Informatics Center
Cayuga County Community College
City University of New York
- Borough of Manhattan Community College
- LaGuardia Community College
- Queensborough Community College

Clinton Community College
Cochran School of Nursing-St. John's Riverside Hospital
College of Westchester
Columbia-Greene Community College
Corning Community College
Dutchess Community College
Elmira Business Institute
Erie Community College
- City Campus
- North Campus
- South Campus

Finger Lakes Community College
Fulton-Montgomery Community College
Genesee Community College
Helene Fuld College of Nursing
Herkimer County Community College
Hudson Valley Community College
Institute of Design and Construction
Interboro Institute
Island Drafting and Technical Institute
Jamestown Business College
Jamestown Community College
Jefferson Community College
Katharine Gibbs School
- New York

Long Island Business Institute
Mildred Elley
Mohawk Valley Community College
Monroe Community College
New York Career Institute
Olean Business Institute
Orange County Community College
Plaza College
Rochester Business Institute
Rockland Community College
St. Joseph's College of Nursing
Schenectady County Community College
State University of New York
- College of Agriculture and Technology at Cobleskill
- College of Agriculture and Technology at Morrisville
- College of Technology at Alfred
- College of Technology at Canton
- College of Technology at Delhi

Suffolk County Community College
Sullivan County Community College
Swedish Institute
Taylor Business Institute
Tompkins-Cortland Community Gollege
Trocaire College
Ulster County Community College
Utica School of Commerce
Villa Maria College of Buffalo
Westchester Community College
Wood Tobe-Coburn School

North Carolina

Alamance Community College
Asheville-Buncombe Technical Community College
Beaufort County Community College
Bladen Community College
Blue Ridge Community College
Brunswick Community College
Caldwell Community College and Technical Institute
Cape Fear Community College
Carolinas College of Health Sciences
Carteret Community College
Catawba Valley Community College
Central Carolina Community College
Central Piedmont Community College
Cleveland Community College
Coastal Carolina Community College
College of the Albemarle
Craven Community College
Davidson County Community College
Durham Technical Community College
Edgecombe Community College
Fayetteville Technical Community College
Forsyth Technical Community College
Gaston College
Guilford Technical Community College
Halifax Community College
Haywood Community College
Isothermal Community College
James Sprunt Community College
Johnston Community College
King's College
Lenoir Community College
Louisburg College
Martin Community College
Mayland Community College
McDowell Technical Community College
Mitchell Community College
Montgomery Community College
Nash Community College
Pamlico Community College
Piedmont Community College
Pitt Community College
Randolph Community College
Richmond Community College
Roanoke-Chowan Community College
Rockingham Community College
Rowan-Cabarrus Community College
Sampson Community College
Sandhills Community College
South College
South Piedmont Community College
Southeastern Community College
Southwestern Community College
Stanly Community College
Surry Community College
Tri-County Community College

Vance-Granville Community College
Wake Technical Community College
Wayne Community College
Western Piedmont Community College
Wilkes Community College
Wilson Technical Community College

North Dakota

Aakers College: Fargo
Bismarck State College
Fort Berthold Community College
Lake Region State College
Minot State University: Bottineau Campus
North Dakota State College of Science
Sitting Bull College
Turtle Mountain Community College
Williston State College

Ohio

AEC Southern Ohio College
- Brown Mackie College: Akron

Belmont Technical College
Bradford School
Bryant & Stratton College
- Parma

Bryant & Stratton College: Cleveland
Central Ohio Technical College
Chatfield College
Cincinnati State Technical and Community College
Clark State Community College
Cleveland Institute of Electronics
College of Art Advertising
Columbus State Community College
Cuyahoga Community College
- Metropolitan Campus

Edison State Community College
ETI Technical College of Niles
Gallipolis Career College
Good Samaritan College of Nursing and Health Science
Hocking Technical College
International College of Broadcasting
James A. Rhodes State College
Jefferson Community College
Kent State University
- Ashtabula Regional Campus
- East Liverpool Regional Campus
- Salem Regional Campus
- Stark Campus
- Trumbull Campus
- Tuscarawas Campus

Kettering College of Medical Arts
Lakeland Community College
Marion Technical College
Miami University
- Hamilton Campus

National College of Business & Technology: Dayton
Ohio Business College: Sandusky
Ohio College of Massotherapy
Ohio Institute of Photography and Technology
Ohio Valley College of Technology
Owens Community College
- Toledo

Remington College
- Cleveland

Rosedale Bible College
School of Advertising Art
Sinclair Community College
Southeastern Business College: New Boston
Southern State Community College
Southwestern College of Business
- Southwestern College: Franklin
- Southwestern College: Tri-County
- Southwestern College: Vine Street Campus

Stark State College of Technology
Stautzenberger College
Technology Education College
Trumbull Business College
University of Akron: Wayne College
University of Cincinnati
- Clermont College
- Raymond Walters College

University of Northwestern Ohio
Washington State Community College
Wright State University: Lake Campus
Zane State College

Oklahoma

Carl Albert State College
Connors State College
Eastern Oklahoma State College
Heritage College Hair Design
Murray State College
Northeastern Oklahoma Agricultural and Mechanical College
Oklahoma City Community College
Oklahoma State University
- Oklahoma City
- Okmulgee

Platt College
- Tulsa

Redlands Community College
Seminole State College
Tulsa Community College
Tulsa Welding School
Vatterott College
Vatterott College
- Tulsa

Western College of Southern California
Western Oklahoma State College

Oregon

Blue Mountain Community College
Central Oregon Community College
Chemeketa Community College
Clackamas Community College
Clatsop Community College
Everest College: Portland
Klamath Community College
Lane Community College
Mount Hood Community College
Pioneer Pacific College: Springfield
Portland Community College
Rogue Community College
Southwestern Oregon Community College
Treasure Valley Community College
Umpqua Community College

Pennsylvania

Academy of Medical Arts and Business
Allied Medical and Technical Institute
Antonelli Institute of Art and Photography
Berean Institute
Berks Technical Institute
Bidwell Training Center
Bradley Academy for the Visual Arts
Business Institute of Pennsylvania
Business Institute of Pennsylvania
- Meadville

Butler County Community College
Cambria-Rowe Business College
Cambria-Rowe Business College: Indiana
Career Training Academy
Career Training Academy: Monroeville
CHI Institute: Broomall
CHI Institute: Southampton
Commonwealth Technical Institute
Community College of Allegheny County
Community College of Beaver County
Community College of Philadelphia
Consolidated School of Business
- Lancaster
- York

Dean Institute of Technology
Delaware County Community College
DuBois Business College
DuBois Business College
- Huntingdon
- Oil City

Duff's Business Institute
Erie Business Center
Erie Institute of Technology
Harcum College
Harrisburg Area Community College
Hussian School of Art
ICM School of Business & Medical Careers
International Academy of Design and Technology: Pittsburgh
JNA Institute of Culinary Arts
Johnson College
Lackawanna College
Lansdale School of Business
Laurel Business Institute
Lehigh Carbon Community College
Lehigh Valley College
Lincoln Technical Institute
Luzerne County Community College
McCann School of Business
- Pottsville

Metropolitan Career Center
Montgomery County Community College
New Castle School of Trades
Newport Business Institute
Newport Business Institute
North Central Industrial Technical Education Center
Northampton County Area Community College
Oakbridge Academy of Arts
Orleans Technical Institute - Center City Campus
Pace Institute
Penn State
- Beaver
- Delaware County
- Dubois
- Fayette
- Hazleton
- McKeesport
- Mont Alto
- New Kensington
- Shenango
- Worthington Scranton
- York

Pennco Tech
Pennsylvania Highlands Community College
Pennsylvania Institute of Culinary Arts
Pennsylvania Institute of Technology
Pennsylvania School of Business
Pittsburgh Institute of Aeronautics
Pittsburgh Institute of Mortuary Science
Pittsburgh Technical Institute
PJA School
Reading Area Community College
Rosedale Technical Institute
Schuylkill Institute of Business & Technology
South Hills School of Business & Technology
Thompson Institute
- Philadelphia

Tri-State Business Institute
Triangle Tech
- DuBois
- Erie
- Greensburg
- Pittsburgh

University of Pittsburgh
- Titusville

Vet Tech Institute
West Virginia Career Institute
Western School of Health and Business Careers
Western School of Health and Business Careers
- Monroeville

Westmoreland County Community College
York Technical Institute
Yorktowne Business Institute

Puerto Rico

Humacao Community College
National College of Business & Technology: Arecibo
National College of Business & Technology: Bayamon

Rhode Island

Community College of Rhode Island

South Carolina

Aiken Technical College
Central Carolina Technical College
Denmark Technical College
Forrest Junior College
Greenville Technical College
Horry-Georgetown Technical College
Midlands Technical College
Miller-Motte Technical College
Orangeburg-Calhoun Technical College
Piedmont Technical College
Spartanburg Methodist College
Spartanburg Technical College
Technical College of the Lowcountry
Tri-County Technical College
University of South Carolina
- Lancaster
- Salkehatchie Regional Campus
- Sumter
- Union

Williamsburg Technical College
York Technical College

South Dakota

Kilian Community College
Lake Area Technical Institute
Mitchell Technical Institute
Southeast Technical Institute

Tennessee

Chattanooga State Technical Community College
Cleveland State Community College
Columbia State Community College
Dyersburg State Community College
Hiwassee College
Jackson State Community College
John A. Gupton College
Miller-Motte Technical College
Nashville State Community College
National College of Business & Technology
- Tennessee

National College of Business & Technology: Knoxville
Northeast State Technical Community College
Nossi College of Art
Roane State Community College
Southwest Tennessee Community College
Vatterott College: Memphis
Walters State Community College

Texas

Alvin Community College
Amarillo College
Angelina College
ATI Career Training Center
Austin Business College
Austin Community College
Blinn College
Brazosport College
Brookhaven College
Cedar Valley College
Central Texas College
Cisco Junior College
Clarendon College
Coastal Bend College
College of the Mainland
Collin County Community College District
Commonwealth Institute of Funeral Service
Court Reporting Institute of Dallas
Dallas Institute of Funeral Service
Del Mar College
Eastfield College
El Centro College
El Paso Community College
Everest College: Arlington
Everest College: Dallas
Frank Phillips College
Galveston College
Grayson County College
Hallmark Institute of Aeronautics
Hallmark Institute of Technology
Hill College
Houston Community College System
Howard College
Jacksonville College
Kilgore College
Lamar State College at Orange
Lamar State College at Port Arthur
Laredo Community College
Lee College
Lon Morris College
McLennan Community College
Midland College
Mountain View College
MTI College of Business and Technology
MTI College of Business and Technology
Navarro College
North Central Texas College
North Harris Montgomery Community College District
North Lake College
Northeast Texas Community College
Odessa College
Palo Alto College
Panola College
Paris Junior College
Ranger College

Remington College
  Dallas
  Fort Worth
  Houston
Richland College
St. Philip's College
San Jacinto College
  Central Campus
  North
South Plains College
South Texas College
Southwest Texas Junior College
Tarrant County College
Temple College
Texarkana College
Texas Southmost College
Texas State Technical College
  Harlingen
  West Texas
Texas State Technical College: Marshall
Trinity Valley Community College
Tyler Junior College
Universal Technical Institute
Vernon College
Victoria College
Wade College
Weatherford College
Western Technical College
Western Technical Institute: Diana Drive
Western Texas College
Westwood College: Dallas
Westwood College: Ft. Worth
Wharton County Junior College

Utah
College of Eastern Utah
Dixie State College of Utah
Everest College: Salt Lake City
LDS Business College
Salt Lake Community College
Snow College
Stevens-Henager College
  Murray
Utah Career College

Vermont
Community College of Vermont
Landmark College
New England Culinary Institute

Virginia
Blue Ridge Community College
Bryant & Stratton College: Virginia Beach
Central Virginia Community College
Dabney S. Lancaster Community College
Danville Community College
Eastern Shore Community College
Germanna Community College
J. Sargeant Reynolds Community College
John Tyler Community College
Lord Fairfax Community College
Miller-Motte Technical College: Lynchburg
Mountain Empire Community College
National College of Business & Technology
  Bluefield
  Charlottesville
  Danville
  Harrisonburg
  Lynchburg
  Martinsville
New River Community College
Northern Virginia Community College
Parks College: Arlington
Patrick Henry Community College
Paul D. Camp Community College
Piedmont Virginia Community College
Southside Virginia Community College
Southwest Virginia Community College
Thomas Nelson Community College
Tidewater Community College
Tidewater Tech
Virginia Highlands Community College
Virginia Western Community College
Wytheville Community College

Washington
Bates Technical College
Bellevue Community College
Bellingham Technical College
Big Bend Community College
Cascadia Community College
Centralia College
Clark College
Clover Park Technical College
Columbia Basin College
Edmonds Community College
Everett Community College
Grays Harbor College
Green River Community College
Highline Community College
Lower Columbia College
North Seattle Community College
Northwest Aviation College
Northwest School of Wooden Boatbuilding
Olympic College
Peninsula College
Pierce College
Renton Technical College
Seattle Central Community College
Shoreline Community College
Skagit Valley College
South Puget Sound Community College
South Seattle Community College
Spokane Community College
Spokane Falls Community College
Tacoma Community College
Walla Walla Community College
Wenatchee Valley College
Whatcom Community College
Yakima Valley Community College

West Virginia
Corinthian Schools: National Institute of Technology
Eastern West Virginia Community and Technical College
Huntington Junior College
Mountain State College
Potomac State College of West Virginia University
Southern West Virginia Community and Technical College
Valley College of Technology
West Virginia Business College
West Virginia Northern Community College

Wisconsin
Blackhawk Technical College
Bryant & Stratton College: Milwaukee
Chippewa Valley Technical College
Fox Valley Technical College
Gateway Technical College
Lakeshore Technical College
Mid-State Technical College
Moraine Park Technical College
Nicolet Area Technical College
Northcentral Technical College
Northeast Wisconsin Technical College
Southwest Wisconsin Technical College
University of Wisconsin
  Fond du Lac
  Marathon County
  Marinette
  Marshfield/Wood County
  Rock County
  Waukesha
Waukesha County Technical College
Western Wisconsin Technical College
Wisconsin Indianhead Technical College

Wyoming
Central Wyoming College
Eastern Wyoming College
Laramie County Community College
Northwest College
Sheridan College
Western Wyoming Community College
Wyoming Technical Institute

Guam
Guam Community College

SAT Subject Tests required for admission

Four-year

Arkansas
Arkansas Tech University*
Henderson State University*

California
California Institute of Technology
Fresno Pacific University*
Harvey Mudd College
Pomona College*
University of California
  Berkeley
  Davis
  Irvine
  Los Angeles
  Riverside
  San Diego
  Santa Barbara
  Santa Cruz
University of California: Merced

Connecticut
Wesleyan University*
Yale University*

Florida
Florida Hospital College of Health Sciences*

Kansas
Newman University*

Louisiana
Southeastern Louisiana University*

Maryland
Salisbury University*

Massachusetts
Amherst College*
Boston College*
Boston University
Franklin W. Olin College of Engineering
Harvard College
Massachusetts Institute of Technology
Tufts University
Williams College

Michigan
Concordia University*
Kendall College of Art and Design of Ferris State University

Minnesota
Augsburg College*
Winona State University*

Nebraska
University of Nebraska*
  Kearney
  Lincoln

New Hampshire
Dartmouth College

New Jersey
Fairleigh Dickinson University*
  College at Florham
  Metropolitan Campus
Princeton University

New York
Barnard College*
City University of New York*
  John Jay College of Criminal Justice
Columbia University
  Columbia College
  Fu Foundation School of Engineering and Applied Science
Cornell University
State University of New York*
  College at Buffalo
Vassar College
Webb Institute

North Carolina
Duke University*
North Carolina Agricultural and Technical State University

Ohio
Bowling Green State University*

Oregon
Corban College*

Pennsylvania
Bryn Mawr College*
Haverford College
Swarthmore College*
University of Pennsylvania*

Puerto Rico
University of Puerto Rico
  Cayey University College
  Ponce

Rhode Island
Brown University*

South Carolina
North Greenville College
Presbyterian College*

South Dakota
University of South Dakota*

Tennessee
Southern Adventist University*

Texas
Rice University
Trinity University*

Vermont
Middlebury College*

Virginia
Washington and Lee University

West Virginia
Alderson-Broaddus College*

Wisconsin
Carroll College*

SAT Subject Tests recommended for admission

Four-year

California
Chapman University
Claremont McKenna College
Dominican University of California
Mills College
Occidental College
Stanford University
University of the Pacific
Westmont College

Delaware
University of Delaware

District of Columbia
American University
Catholic University of America
Georgetown University
Howard University
Trinity University*

Florida
Johnson & Wales University
South University: West Palm Beach Campus*

Georgia
Clark Atlanta University
Emory University
University of Georgia

Illinois
Aurora University*
Northwestern University

Indiana
Indiana University
  Bloomington

Maryland
Johns Hopkins University

Massachusetts
Babson College
Smith College
Worcester Polytechnic Institute*

Michigan
Calvin College
Hillsdale College
Lawrence Technological University
University of Michigan
  Flint

Minnesota
Carleton College

Montana
University of Great Falls

New Hampshire
St. Anselm College

New York
City University of New York
  Queens College
Clarkson University
Dowling College
Fordham University
Hofstra University
New York University
St. Joseph's College: Suffolk Campus
Skidmore College
State University of New York
  Stony Brook
University of Rochester

North Carolina
Davidson College

Ohio
Oberlin College
Wittenberg University

* ACT accepted as an alternative to SAT Subject Tests

Oklahoma
National Education Center
Spartan School of Aeronautics

Oregon
Reed College

Pennsylvania
Cheyney University of Pennsylvania
Immaculata University
Lafayette College
Restaurant School*

Puerto Rico
University of Puerto Rico
Bayamon University College

Rhode Island
Providence College

Tennessee
Lee University
Union University*
Vanderbilt University

Texas
University of Houston

Virginia
George Mason University
Hampden-Sydney College
University of Mary Washington
University of Virginia

West Virginia
University of Charleston

Canada
University of Alberta

Switzerland
Franklin College: Switzerland

Two-year

California
Deep Springs College
Marymount College*
Queen of the Holy Rosary College

New York
St. Elizabeth College of Nursing

* ACT accepted as an alternative to SAT Subject Tests

Colleges that offer ROTC

Air Force ROTC

Four-year

Alabama
Alabama State University
Auburn University
Auburn University at Montgomery
Birmingham-Southern College
Faulkner University
Huntingdon College
Miles College
Samford University
Spring Hill College
Stillman College
Troy University
Tuskegee University
University of Alabama
University of Alabama
 Birmingham
University of Mobile
University of Montevallo
University of South Alabama
University of West Alabama

Alaska
University of Alaska
 Anchorage

Arizona
Arizona State University
DeVry University
 Phoenix
Embry-Riddle Aeronautical University: Prescott Campus
Northern Arizona University
Southwestern College
University of Arizona

Arkansas
John Brown University
University of Arkansas
University of Arkansas
 Fort Smith

California
Biola University
California Baptist University
California Institute of Technology
California Lutheran University
California State Polytechnic University: Pomona
California State University
 Dominguez Hills
 Fresno
 Los Angeles
 Northridge
 Sacramento
 San Bernardino
 San Marcos
Chapman University
Claremont McKenna College
Harvey Mudd College
Holy Names University
King's College and Seminary
Loyola Marymount University
National University
Occidental College
Pepperdine University
Pitzer College
Point Loma Nazarene University
St. Mary's College of California
Samuel Merritt College
San Diego Christian College
San Diego State University
San Francisco State University
San Jose State University
Santa Clara University
Scripps College
Sonoma State University
Stanford University
University of California
 Berkeley
 Davis
 Irvine
 Los Angeles
 Riverside
 San Diego
 Santa Cruz
University of Redlands
University of San Diego
University of San Francisco
University of Southern California
University of the Pacific
Vanguard University of Southern California
Westmont College
Whittier College

Colorado
Colorado Christian University
Colorado School of Mines
Colorado State University
Metropolitan State College of Denver
Regis University
University of Colorado
 Boulder
 Denver and Health Sciences Center
University of Denver
University of Northern Colorado

Connecticut
Central Connecticut State University
Eastern Connecticut State University
Quinnipiac University
Southern Connecticut State University
University of Connecticut
University of Hartford
Wesleyan University
Western Connecticut State University
Yale University

Delaware
Delaware State University
University of Delaware
Wilmington College

District of Columbia
American University
Catholic University of America
George Washington University
Georgetown University
Howard University
University of the District of Columbia

Florida
Barry University
Bethune-Cookman College
Eckerd College
Embry-Riddle Aeronautical University
Florida Agricultural and Mechanical University
Florida Atlantic University
Florida College
Florida International University
Florida Southern College
Florida State University
Lynn University
St. Leo University
University of Central Florida
University of Florida
University of Miami
University of South Florida
University of Tampa
University of West Florida

Georgia
Agnes Scott College
Clark Atlanta University
Clayton State University
Emory University
Georgia Institute of Technology
Georgia State University
Kennesaw State University
Morehouse College
Southern Polytechnic State University
Spelman College
University of Georgia
Valdosta State University

Hawaii
Brigham Young University-Hawaii
Chaminade University of Honolulu
Hawaii Pacific University
University of Hawaii
 Manoa
 West Oahu

Idaho
Lewis-Clark State College
Northwest Nazarene University
University of Idaho

Illinois
Elmhurst College
Governors State University
Illinois Institute of Technology
Lewis University
McKendree College
North Central College
Northeastern Illinois University
Northwestern University
St. Xavier University
Southern Illinois University
 Carbondale
Southern Illinois University
 Edwardsville
University of Chicago
University of Illinois
 Chicago
 Urbana-Champaign
Wheaton College

Indiana
Butler University
DePauw University
Holy Cross College
Indiana State University
Indiana University
 Bloomington
 South Bend
 Southeast
Indiana University-Purdue University Indianapolis
Purdue University
Rose-Hulman Institute of Technology
Saint Mary's College
St. Mary-of-the-Woods College
University of Notre Dame
Valparaiso University

Iowa
Coe College
Drake University
Grand View College
Iowa State University
University of Iowa

Kansas
Baker University
Haskell Indian Nations University
Kansas State University
Manhattan Christian College
MidAmerica Nazarene University
University of Kansas
University of St. Mary
Washburn University of Topeka

Kentucky
Asbury College
Bellarmine University
Centre College
Eastern Kentucky University
Georgetown College
Kentucky State University
Northern Kentucky University
Spalding University
Sullivan University
Thomas More College
Transylvania University
University of Kentucky
University of Louisville
Western Kentucky University

Louisiana
Dillard University
Louisiana State University and Agricultural and Mechanical College
Loyola University New Orleans
Our Lady of Holy Cross College
Our Lady of the Lake College
Southern University
 New Orleans
Southern University and Agricultural and Mechanical College
Tulane University
University of Louisiana at Monroe
University of New Orleans
Xavier University of Louisiana

Maine
University of Maine
 Augusta
University of Southern Maine

Maryland
Bowie State University
Johns Hopkins University
Loyola College in Maryland
Towson University
University of Maryland
 College Park

Massachusetts
American International College
Anna Maria College
Assumption College
Babson College
Bay Path College
Becker College
Boston College
Boston University
Brandeis University
Bridgewater State College
Clark University
College of the Holy Cross
Eastern Nazarene College
Elms College
Endicott College
Fitchburg State College
Gordon College
Harvard College
Massachusetts Institute of Technology
Massachusetts Maritime Academy
Merrimack College
Montserrat College of Art
Mount Holyoke College
Northeastern University
Salem State College
Smith College
Springfield College
Tufts University
University of Massachusetts
 Amherst
 Lowell
Wellesley College
Western New England College
Westfield State College
Worcester Polytechnic Institute
Worcester State College

Michigan
Concordia University
Eastern Michigan University
Finlandia University
Lawrence Technological University
Michigan State University
Michigan Technological University
Oakland University
University of Michigan
University of Michigan
 Dearborn
Wayne State University

Minnesota
Augsburg College
Bethel University
College of St. Catherine
College of St. Scholastica
Concordia College: Moorhead
Concordia University: St. Paul
Hamline University
Macalester College
Minnesota State University
 Moorhead
North Central University
Northwestern College
University of Minnesota
 Crookston
 Duluth
 Twin Cities
University of St. Thomas

Mississippi
Mississippi State University
University of Mississippi
University of Southern Mississippi
William Carey College

Missouri
Central Methodist University
Central Missouri State University
Columbia College
Harris-Stowe State University
Lincoln University
St. Louis University
Southeast Missouri State University
Stephens College
University of Missouri
 Columbia
 Kansas City
 Rolla
 St. Louis
Washington University in St. Louis
Webster University
Westminster College
William Woods University

Montana
Montana State University
 Bozeman

Nebraska
Bellevue University
Clarkson College
College of Saint Mary
Concordia University
Creighton University
Dana College
Doane College
Nebraska Wesleyan University
University of Nebraska
 Lincoln
 Medical Center
 Omaha
York College

Nevada
University of Nevada
 Las Vegas

New Hampshire
Colby-Sawyer College
Daniel Webster College
Franklin Pierce College
Keene State College
New England College
Plymouth State University
Rivier College

St. Anselm College
Southern New Hampshire University
University of New Hampshire
University of New Hampshire at Manchester

New Jersey

The College of New Jersey
Fairleigh Dickinson University
- College at Florham
- Metropolitan Campus

Kean University
Monmouth University
New Jersey Institute of Technology
Princeton University
Ramapo College of New Jersey
Rutgers, The State University of New Jersey
- Camden Regional Campus
- New Brunswick Regional Campus
- Newark Regional Campus

St. Peter's College
Stevens Institute of Technology
William Paterson University of New Jersey

New Mexico

College of Santa Fe
National American University
New Mexico State University
University of New Mexico

New York

Adelphi University
Albany College of Pharmacy
Cazenovia College
Clarkson University
College of Mount St. Vincent
College of Saint Rose
Columbia University
- Columbia College
- Fu Foundation School of Engineering and Applied Science
- School of General Studies

Cornell University
Dowling College
Elmira College
Fordham University
Globe Institute of Technology
Hamilton College
Hartwick College
Iona College
Ithaca College
Le Moyne College
Manhattan College
Molloy College
Nazareth College of Rochester
New York Institute of Technology
Rensselaer Polytechnic Institute
Roberts Wesleyan College
Rochester Institute of Technology
Russell Sage College
Sage College of Albany
St. Francis College
St. John Fisher College
St. Joseph's College: Suffolk Campus
St. Lawrence University
St. Thomas Aquinas College
Siena College
Skidmore College
State University of New York
- Albany
- Binghamton
- College at Brockport
- College at Cortland
- College at Geneseo
- College at Old Westbury
- College at Potsdam
- College of Environmental Science and Forestry
- Farmingdale
- Maritime College
- Stony Brook

Syracuse University
Union College
University of Rochester
Utica College
Vaughn College of Aeronautics and Technology
Wells College

North Carolina

Belmont Abbey College
Bennett College
Davidson College
Duke University
East Carolina University
Elon University
Fayetteville State University
Greensboro College
High Point University
Johnson C. Smith University
Meredith College
Methodist College
North Carolina Agricultural and Technical State University
North Carolina Central University
North Carolina State University
Peace College
Queens University of Charlotte
St. Augustine's College
Shaw University
University of North Carolina
- Chapel Hill
- Charlotte
- Greensboro
- Pembroke

Wingate University

North Dakota

Mayville State University
North Dakota State University
University of North Dakota

Ohio

Ashland University
Baldwin-Wallace College
Bowling Green State University
Capital University
Case Western Reserve University
Cedarville University
Central State University
College of Mount St. Joseph
Heidelberg College
Kent State University
Lourdes College
Malone College
Miami University
- Oxford Campus

Mount Union College
Ohio Northern University
Ohio State University
- Columbus Campus
- Lima Campus
- Mansfield Campus
- Marion Campus
- Newark Campus

Ohio University
Ohio University
- Lancaster Campus

Ohio Wesleyan University
Otterbein College
University of Akron
University of Cincinnati
University of Dayton
University of Findlay
University of Toledo
Wittenberg University
Wright State University
Xavier University
Youngstown State University

Oklahoma

Oklahoma Baptist University
Oklahoma Christian University
Oklahoma City University
Oklahoma State University
Oklahoma Wesleyan University
Oral Roberts University
Rogers State University
St. Gregory's University
Southern Nazarene University
University of Oklahoma
University of Tulsa

Oregon

Concordia University
Corban College
George Fox University
Linfield College
Oregon State University
Pacific University
Portland State University
University of Portland
Warner Pacific College
Western Oregon University
Willamette University

Pennsylvania

Bloomsburg University of Pennsylvania
Bryn Mawr College
Carlow University
Carnegie Mellon University
Chatham College
College Misericordia
Drexel University
Duquesne University
East Stroudsburg University of Pennsylvania
Eastern University
Keystone College
King's College
La Roche College
La Salle University
Marywood University
Penn State
- Abington
- Altoona
- University Park
- Wilkes-Barre

Philadelphia Biblical University
Point Park University
Robert Morris University
Rosemont College
St. Francis University
St. Joseph's University
St. Vincent College
Swarthmore College
Temple University
Thomas Jefferson University: College of Health Professions
University of Pennsylvania
University of Pittsburgh
University of Pittsburgh
- Greensburg

University of Scranton
University of the Sciences in Philadelphia
Villanova University
Washington and Jefferson College
West Chester University of Pennsylvania
Widener University
Wilkes University

Puerto Rico

Bayamon Central University
Inter American University of Puerto Rico
- Bayamon Campus
- Fajardo Campus
- San German Campus

Pontifical Catholic University of Puerto Rico
Universidad Metropolitana
Universidad Politecnica de Puerto Rico
University of Puerto Rico
- Carolina Regional College
- Mayaguez
- Rio Piedras

South Carolina

Anderson University
Benedict College
Charleston Southern University
The Citadel
Clemson University
College of Charleston
South Carolina State University
Southern Wesleyan University
University of South Carolina

South Dakota

Dakota State University
South Dakota State University

Tennessee

Carson-Newman College
Christian Brothers University
Free Will Baptist Bible College
LeMoyne-Owen College
Lipscomb University
Rhodes College
Tennessee State University
Tennessee Technological University
University of Memphis
University of Tennessee
- Knoxville

Vanderbilt University

Texas

Angelo State University
Baylor University
Concordia University at Austin
Dallas Baptist University
Huston-Tillotson College
McMurry University
Midwestern State University
Our Lady of the Lake University of San Antonio
Rice University
St. Edward's University
St. Mary's University
Southern Methodist University
Texas A&M University
Texas Christian University
Texas Lutheran University
Texas State University: San Marcos
Texas Tech University
Texas Wesleyan University
Texas Woman's University
Trinity University
University of Dallas
University of Houston
University of Mary Hardin-Baylor
University of North Texas
University of Texas
- Arlington
- Austin
- Dallas
- El Paso
- Pan American
- San Antonio

University of the Incarnate Word
Wayland Baptist University

Utah

Brigham Young University
University of Utah
Utah State University
Utah Valley State College
Weber State University
Westminster College

Vermont

Lyndon State College
Norwich University
St. Michael's College

Virginia

George Mason University
James Madison University
Liberty University
Mary Baldwin College
University of Virginia
Virginia Military Institute
Virginia Polytechnic Institute and State University

Washington

Central Washington University
Seattle Pacific University
Seattle University
University of Washington
Washington State University

West Virginia

Shepherd University
West Virginia University

Wisconsin

Alverno College
Carroll College
Carthage College
Maranatha Baptist Bible College
Marquette University
Milwaukee School of Engineering
University of Wisconsin
- Madison
- Milwaukee
- Superior
- Whitewater

Wisconsin Lutheran College

Wyoming

University of Wyoming

Two-year

Alabama

Bishop State Community College
Enterprise-Ozark Community College
Jefferson State Community College
Marion Military Institute
Shelton State Community College

Arizona

Chandler-Gilbert Community College
- Williams Campus

Coconino County Community College
Estrella Mountain Community College
Gateway Community College
Mesa Community College
Phoenix College
Pima Community College
Yavapai College

Arkansas

Northwest Arkansas Community College

California

Antelope Valley College
Chabot College
College of San Mateo
College of the Sequoias
Cuyamaca College
De Anza College
Foothill College
Fresno City College
Irvine Valley College
Los Angeles City College
Los Angeles Mission College
Mission College
Mount San Antonio College
Mount San Jacinto College
Ohlone College
Riverside Community College
Sacramento City College
San Diego City College
Solano Community College
Ventura College
West Valley College

Colorado

Aims Community College
Arapahoe Community College
Front Range Community College

Connecticut

Capital Community College
Tunxis Community College

Florida

Broward Community College
Daytona Beach Community College
Hillsborough Community College
Miami Dade College

Santa Fe Community College
Tallahassee Community College

Hawaii
University of Hawaii
- Honolulu Community College
- Leeward Community College

Illinois
John A. Logan College
Lincoln Land Community College
Parkland College
Southwestern Illinois College

Indiana
Vincennes University

Iowa
Hawkeye Community College
Iowa Western Community College

Louisiana
Delgado Community College

Maryland
Prince George's Community College

Massachusetts
Holyoke Community College
Middlesex Community College
Quinsigamond Community College

Michigan
Lansing Community College

Minnesota
Anoka-Ramsey Community College
Inver Hills Community College
Normandale Community College
North Hennepin Community College

Mississippi
Jones County Junior College

Missouri
St. Louis Community College
- Meramec

New Jersey
Brookdale Community College
Raritan Valley Community College
Union County College

New Mexico
Albuquerque Technical-Vocational Institute
Dona Ana Branch Community College of New Mexico State University
New Mexico State University
- Alamogordo

New York
Corning Community College
Hudson Valley Community College
Maria College
Monroe Community College
Onondaga Community College
Schenectady County Community College
State University of New York
- College of Technology at Canton

North Carolina
Guilford Technical Community College

Ohio
Columbus State Community College
Cuyahoga Community College
- Metropolitan Campus

Hocking Technical College
Kent State University
- Ashtabula Regional Campus
- East Liverpool Regional Campus
- Salem Regional Campus
- Stark Campus
- Trumbull Campus
- Tuscarawas Campus

Miami University
- Hamilton Campus

Owens Community College
- Toledo

Sinclair Community College
University of Akron: Wayne College
University of Cincinnati
- Raymond Walters College

Oklahoma
Northeastern Oklahoma Agricultural and Mechanical College
Rose State College

Oregon
Clackamas Community College
Linn-Benton Community College

Pennsylvania
Lackawanna College
Luzerne County Community College
Penn State
- Delaware County
- Hazleton
- Worthington Scranton

Valley Forge Military College

South Carolina
Midlands Technical College
Tri-County Technical College
University of South Carolina
- Salkehatchie Regional Campus

Tennessee
Roane State Community College
Southwest Tennessee Community College

Texas
Austin Community College
Lon Morris College
McLennan Community College
San Antonio College
Tarrant County College
Weatherford College

Utah
Salt Lake Community College

Virginia
Piedmont Virginia Community College

Washington
Clark College
Highline Community College
South Puget Sound Community College
Spokane Community College

Wyoming
Laramie County Community College

Army ROTC

Four-year

Alabama
Alabama Agricultural and Mechanical University
Alabama State University
Auburn University
Auburn University at Montgomery
Birmingham-Southern College
Faulkner University
Huntingdon College
Jacksonville State University
Judson College
Miles College
Samford University
Spring Hill College
Stillman College
Talladega College
Troy University
Tuskegee University
University of Alabama
University of Alabama
- Birmingham
- Huntsville

University of Mobile
University of Montevallo
University of North Alabama
University of South Alabama

Alaska
University of Alaska
- Fairbanks

Arizona
Arizona State University
Embry-Riddle Aeronautical University: Prescott Campus
Grand Canyon University
Northern Arizona University
University of Arizona

Arkansas
Arkansas State University
Arkansas Tech University
Central Baptist College
Harding University
Henderson State University
Hendrix College
John Brown University
Ouachita Baptist University
Philander Smith College
University of Arkansas
University of Arkansas
- Little Rock
- Monticello
- Pine Bluff

University of Central Arkansas
Williams Baptist College

California
Azusa Pacific University
Biola University
California Baptist University
California Institute of Technology
California Lutheran University
California Polytechnic State University: San Luis Obispo
California State Polytechnic University: Pomona
California State University
- Dominguez Hills
- Fresno
- Fullerton
- Long Beach
- Los Angeles
- Northridge
- Sacramento
- San Bernardino
- San Marcos

Chapman University
Claremont McKenna College
Harvey Mudd College
Holy Names University
King's College and Seminary
Loyola Marymount University
Menlo College
National Hispanic University
National University
Occidental College
Pepperdine University
Pitzer College
Point Loma Nazarene University
St. Mary's College of California
Samuel Merritt College
San Diego Christian College
San Diego State University
San Francisco State University
San Jose State University
Santa Clara University
Scripps College
Sonoma State University
Stanford University
University of California
- Berkeley
- Davis
- Irvine
- Los Angeles
- Riverside
- San Diego
- Santa Barbara
- Santa Cruz

University of La Verne
University of Redlands
University of San Diego
University of San Francisco
University of Southern California
Westmont College
Whittier College

Colorado
Colorado Christian University
Colorado College
Colorado School of Mines
Colorado State University
Colorado State University
- Pueblo

Colorado Technical University
Metropolitan State College of Denver
Regis University
University of Colorado
- Boulder
- Colorado Springs
- Denver and Health Sciences Center

University of Denver
University of Northern Colorado

Connecticut
Central Connecticut State University
Eastern Connecticut State University
Fairfield University
Post University
Quinnipiac University
Sacred Heart University
Southern Connecticut State University
Trinity College
University of Bridgeport
University of Connecticut
University of Hartford
Western Connecticut State University
Yale University

Delaware
Delaware State University
University of Delaware
Wesley College
Wilmington College

District of Columbia
American University
Catholic University of America
George Washington University
Georgetown University
Howard University
Trinity University
University of the District of Columbia

Florida
Barry University
Bethune-Cookman College
Clearwater Christian College
Eckerd College
Edward Waters College
Embry-Riddle Aeronautical University
Florida Agricultural and Mechanical University
Florida Atlantic University
Florida College
Florida Institute of Technology
Florida International University
Florida Memorial University
Florida Southern College
Florida State University
Okaloosa-Walton College
St. Leo University
Southeastern College of the Assemblies of God
Stetson University
University of Central Florida
University of Florida
University of Miami
University of South Florida
University of Tampa
University of West Florida

Georgia
Agnes Scott College
Albany State University
Armstrong Atlantic State University
Augusta State University
Clark Atlanta University
Clayton State University
Columbus State University
Emory University
Fort Valley State University
Georgia College and State University
Georgia Institute of Technology
Georgia Southern University
Georgia State University
Kennesaw State University
Mercer University
Morehouse College
North Georgia College & State University
Paine College
Savannah State University
Southern Polytechnic State University
Spelman College
University of Georgia
University of West Georgia

Hawaii
Brigham Young University-Hawaii
Chaminade University of Honolulu
Hawaii Pacific University
University of Hawaii
- Manoa
- West Oahu

Idaho
Albertson College of Idaho
Boise State University
Brigham Young University-Idaho
Idaho State University
Lewis-Clark State College
Northwest Nazarene University
University of Idaho

Illinois
Aurora University
Benedictine University
Bradley University
Chicago State University
DePaul University
Eastern Illinois University
Elmhurst College
Governors State University
Illinois Institute of Technology
Illinois State University
Illinois Wesleyan University
Lewis University
Loyola University of Chicago
McKendree College
Monmouth College
North Central College
Northeastern Illinois University
Northern Illinois University
Northwestern University
Olivet Nazarene University
Robert Morris College: Chicago
Rockford College
Southern Illinois University
- Carbondale

Southern Illinois University
Edwardsville
University of Chicago
University of Illinois
Chicago
Urbana-Champaign
Western Illinois University
Wheaton College

Indiana
Ball State University
Butler University
DePauw University
Franklin College
Holy Cross College
Indiana State University
Indiana University
Bloomington
Northwest
South Bend
Southeast
Indiana University-Purdue University Indianapolis
Indiana Wesleyan University
Marian College
Purdue University
Purdue University
Calumet
Rose-Hulman Institute of Technology
Saint Mary's College
St. Mary-of-the-Woods College
University of Indianapolis
University of Notre Dame
University of Southern Indiana
Wabash College

Iowa
Allen College
Clarke College
Coe College
Drake University
Grand View College
Iowa State University
Loras College
University of Dubuque
University of Iowa
University of Northern Iowa

Kansas
Baker University
Benedictine College
Kansas State University
Manhattan Christian College
MidAmerica Nazarene University
Pittsburg State University
University of Kansas
University of St. Mary
Washburn University of Topeka

Kentucky
Asbury College
Bellarmine University
Centre College
Eastern Kentucky University
Georgetown College
Kentucky State University
Midway College
Morehead State University
Murray State University
Northern Kentucky University
Spalding University
Thomas More College
Transylvania University
Union College
University of Kentucky
University of Louisville
University of the Cumberlands
Western Kentucky University

Louisiana
Dillard University
Grambling State University
Louisiana State University
Alexandria
Shreveport
Louisiana State University and Agricultural and Mechanical College
Louisiana Tech University
Loyola University New Orleans
Northwestern State University
Our Lady of Holy Cross College
Southeastern Louisiana University
Southern University
New Orleans
Southern University and Agricultural and Mechanical College
Tulane University
University of Louisiana at Lafayette
University of Louisiana at Monroe
University of New Orleans
Xavier University of Louisiana

Maine
Colby College
Husson College
New England School of Communications
St. Joseph's College
Unity College
University of Maine
University of Maine
Augusta
University of New England
University of Southern Maine

Maryland
Bowie State University
Capitol College
College of Notre Dame of Maryland
Coppin State University
Goucher College
Johns Hopkins University
Loyola College in Maryland
Maryland Institute College of Art
McDaniel College
Morgan State University
Mount St. Mary's University
Salisbury University
Towson University
University of Baltimore
University of Maryland
Baltimore County
College Park
Villa Julie College

Massachusetts
American International College
Assumption College
Babson College
Bay Path College
Becker College
Bentley College
Boston College
Boston University
Brandeis University
Bridgewater State College
Clark University
College of the Holy Cross
Curry College
Eastern Nazarene College
Elms College
Emmanuel College
Endicott College
Framingham State College
Gordon College
Hampshire College
Harvard College
Massachusetts Institute of Technology
Massachusetts Maritime Academy
Mount Holyoke College
Nichols College
Northeastern University
Regis College
St. John's Seminary College
Simmons College
Smith College
Springfield College
Stonehill College
Suffolk University
Tufts University
University of Massachusetts
Amherst
Dartmouth
Wellesley College
Wentworth Institute of Technology
Western New England College
Westfield State College
Wheaton College
Worcester Polytechnic Institute
Worcester State College

Michigan
Alma College
Calvin College
Central Michigan University
Concordia University
Eastern Michigan University
Ferris State University
Finlandia University
Grace Bible College
Hope College
Kalamazoo College
Lawrence Technological University
Michigan State University
Michigan Technological University
Northern Michigan University
Spring Arbor University
University of Michigan
University of Michigan
Dearborn
Western Michigan University

Minnesota
Augsburg College
Bethany Lutheran College
Bethel University
College of St. Benedict
Concordia College: Moorhead
Concordia University: St. Paul
Gustavus Adolphus College
Minnesota State University
Mankato
Moorhead
North Central University
Northwestern College
St. Cloud State University
St. John's University
St. Mary's University of Minnesota
University of Minnesota
Twin Cities
University of St. Thomas
Winona State University

Mississippi
Alcorn State University
Jackson State University
Millsaps College
Mississippi College
Mississippi State University
Mississippi Valley State University
Tougaloo College
University of Mississippi
University of Southern Mississippi
William Carey College

Missouri
Avila University
Central Methodist University
Central Missouri State University
College of the Ozarks
Columbia College
Drury University
Evangel University
Harris-Stowe State University
Lincoln University
Lindenwood University
Maryville University of Saint Louis
Missouri Baptist University
Missouri State University
Missouri Valley College
Missouri Western State University
Northwest Missouri State University
Park University
Research College of Nursing
Rockhurst University
St. Louis University
Southwest Baptist University
Stephens College
Truman State University
University of Missouri
Columbia
Kansas City
Rolla
St. Louis
Washington University in St. Louis
Webster University
Westminster College
William Woods University

Montana
Carroll College
Montana State University
Bozeman
Montana Tech of the University of Montana
University of Montana: Missoula

Nebraska
Bellevue University
Chadron State College
Clarkson College
College of Saint Mary
Concordia University
Creighton University
Dana College
Doane College
Nebraska Methodist College of Nursing and Allied Health
Nebraska Wesleyan University
University of Nebraska
Lincoln
Medical Center
Omaha
Wayne State College
York College

Nevada
Sierra Nevada College
University of Nevada
Las Vegas
Reno

New Hampshire
Colby-Sawyer College
Daniel Webster College
Dartmouth College
Franklin Pierce College
Granite State College
New England College
Plymouth State University
St. Anselm College
Southern New Hampshire University
University of New Hampshire
University of New Hampshire at Manchester

New Jersey
Bloomfield College
Caldwell College
The College of New Jersey
Fairleigh Dickinson University
College at Florham
Metropolitan Campus
Kean University
New Jersey Institute of Technology
Princeton University
Rider University
Rowan University
Rutgers, The State University of New Jersey
Camden Regional Campus
New Brunswick Regional Campus
Newark Regional Campus
St. Peter's College
Seton Hall University
Stevens Institute of Technology

New Mexico
New Mexico State University
University of New Mexico

New York
Adelphi University
Albany College of Pharmacy
Alfred University
Canisius College
Cazenovia College
City University of New York
Baruch College
Lehman College
Queens College
Clarkson University
Colgate University
College of New Rochelle
College of Saint Rose
Columbia University
Columbia College
Fu Foundation School of Engineering and Applied Science
School of General Studies
Cornell University
D'Youville College
Daemen College
Elmira College
Fordham University
Globe Institute of Technology
Hamilton College
Hartwick College
Hilbert College
Hofstra University
Houghton College
Iona College
Ithaca College
Le Moyne College
Long Island University
Brooklyn Campus
C. W. Post Campus
Manhattan College
Marist College
Medaille College
Molloy College
Monroe College
Nazareth College of Rochester
New York Institute of Technology
Niagara University
Pace University
Polytechnic University
Rensselaer Polytechnic Institute
Roberts Wesleyan College
Rochester Institute of Technology
Russell Sage College
Sage College of Albany
St. Bonaventure University
St. Francis College
St. John Fisher College
St. John's University
St. Joseph's College: Suffolk Campus
St. Lawrence University
Siena College
Skidmore College
State University of New York
Albany
Buffalo
College at Brockport
College at Buffalo
College at Cortland
College at Geneseo
College at Old Westbury
College at Potsdam
College of Environmental Science and Forestry
Farmingdale
Institute of Technology at Utica/Rome
Maritime College
Oswego
Stony Brook
Syracuse University
Union College
University of Rochester

Utica College
Vaughn College of Aeronautics and Technology

North Carolina

Appalachian State University
Belmont Abbey College
Bennett College
Campbell University
Catawba College
Davidson College
Duke University
East Carolina University
Elizabeth City State University
Elon University
Fayetteville State University
Gardner-Webb University
Greensboro College
High Point University
Johnson C. Smith University
Lees-McRae College
Lenoir-Rhyne College
Livingstone College
Meredith College
Methodist College
North Carolina Agricultural and Technical State University
North Carolina Central University
North Carolina State University
Peace College
Pfeiffer University
Queens University of Charlotte
St. Augustine's College
Shaw University
University of North Carolina
- Chapel Hill
- Charlotte
- Greensboro
- Pembroke

Wake Forest University
Wingate University
Winston-Salem State University

North Dakota

Mayville State University
North Dakota State University
University of North Dakota

Ohio

Bowling Green State University
Capital University
Case Western Reserve University
Cedarville University
Central State University
Cleveland Institute of Art
Cleveland State University
College of Mount St. Joseph
Denison University
DeVry University
- Columbus

Franklin University
Heidelberg College
John Carroll University
Kent State University
Lourdes College
Malone College
Miami University
- Oxford Campus

Mount Union College
Ohio Dominican University
Ohio Northern University
Ohio State University
- Columbus Campus
- Lima Campus
- Mansfield Campus
- Marion Campus
- Newark Campus

Ohio University
Ohio University
- Lancaster Campus

Ohio Wesleyan University
Otterbein College
Tiffin University
University of Akron
University of Cincinnati
University of Dayton
University of Findlay
University of Rio Grande
University of Toledo
Ursuline College
Wittenberg University
Wright State University
Xavier University
Youngstown State University

Oklahoma

Cameron University
Northeastern State University
Oklahoma Christian University
Oklahoma City University
Oklahoma State University
St. Gregory's University
Southern Nazarene University
University of Central Oklahoma
University of Oklahoma

Oregon

Corban College
Northwest Christian College
Oregon Institute of Technology
Oregon State University
Pacific University
Portland State University
University of Oregon
University of Portland
Warner Pacific College
Western Oregon University

Pennsylvania

Alvernia College
Arcadia University
Bloomsburg University of Pennsylvania
Bucknell University
Cabrini College
California University of Pennsylvania
Carlow University
Carnegie Mellon University
Cedar Crest College
Chatham College
Cheyney University of Pennsylvania
Clarion University of Pennsylvania
College Misericordia
DeSales University
Dickinson College
Drexel University
Duquesne University
East Stroudsburg University of Pennsylvania
Eastern University
Edinboro University of Pennsylvania
Gannon University
Geneva College
Gettysburg College
Grove City College
Immaculata University
Indiana University of Pennsylvania
Keystone College
King's College
Kutztown University of Pennsylvania
La Roche College
La Salle University
Lafayette College
Lebanon Valley College
Lehigh University
Lincoln University
Lock Haven University of Pennsylvania
Lycoming College
Marywood University
Mercyhurst College
Millersville University of Pennsylvania
Moravian College
Muhlenberg College
Neumann College
Penn State
- Abington
- Altoona
- Erie, The Behrend College
- Harrisburg
- Lehigh Valley
- University Park
- Wilkes-Barre

Pennsylvania College of Technology
Point Park University
Robert Morris University
Rosemont College
St. Francis University
St. Joseph's University
Seton Hill University
Shippensburg University of Pennsylvania
Slippery Rock University of Pennsylvania
Susquehanna University
Swarthmore College
Temple University
University of Pennsylvania
University of Pittsburgh
University of Pittsburgh
- Bradford
- Greensburg

University of Scranton
University of the Sciences in Philadelphia
Villanova University
Washington and Jefferson College
Waynesburg College
West Chester University of Pennsylvania
Westminster College
Widener University
Wilkes University
Wilson College
York College of Pennsylvania

Puerto Rico

American University of Puerto Rico
Bayamon Central University
Inter American University of Puerto Rico
- Aguadilla Campus
- Bayamon Campus
- Guayama Campus
- San German Campus

Pontifical Catholic University of Puerto Rico
Turabo University
Universidad del Este
Universidad Metropolitana
Universidad Politecnica de Puerto Rico
University of Puerto Rico
- Aguadilla
- Arecibo
- Bayamon University College
- Carolina Regional College
- Cayey University College
- Humacao
- Mayaguez
- Ponce
- Rio Piedras
- Utuado

Rhode Island

Brown University
Bryant University
Johnson & Wales University
Providence College
Rhode Island College
Roger Williams University
Salve Regina University
University of Rhode Island

South Carolina

Allen University
Anderson University
Benedict College
The Citadel
Claflin University
Clemson University
Columbia College
Converse College
Furman University
Lander University
Limestone College
Morris College
Newberry College
North Greenville College
Presbyterian College
South Carolina State University
Southern Wesleyan University
University of South Carolina
University of South Carolina
- Upstate

Voorhees College
Wofford College

South Dakota

Black Hills State University
Dakota State University
Mount Marty College
South Dakota School of Mines and Technology
South Dakota State University
University of South Dakota

Tennessee

Austin Peay State University
Belmont University
Carson-Newman College
Christian Brothers University
Cumberland University
East Tennessee State University
Fisk University
Free Will Baptist Bible College
LeMoyne-Owen College
Lipscomb University
Middle Tennessee State University
Milligan College
Rhodes College
Tennessee Technological University
Trevecca Nazarene University
University of Memphis
University of Tennessee
- Knoxville
- Martin

Vanderbilt University

Texas

Concordia University at Austin
Dallas Baptist University
Houston Baptist University
Huston-Tillotson College
Our Lady of the Lake University of San Antonio
Prairie View A&M University
Rice University
St. Edward's University
St. Mary's University
Sam Houston State University
Southern Methodist University
Southwestern Assemblies of God University
Stephen F. Austin State University
Tarleton State University
Texas A&M University
Texas A&M University
- Kingsville

Texas Christian University
Texas Lutheran University
Texas Southern University
Texas State University: San Marcos
Texas Tech University
Texas Wesleyan University
Texas Woman's University
University of Dallas
University of Houston
University of Houston
- Downtown

University of North Texas
University of St. Thomas
University of Texas
- Arlington
- Austin
- Dallas
- El Paso
- Pan American
- San Antonio

University of the Incarnate Word
Wayland Baptist University

Utah

Brigham Young University
Southern Utah University
University of Utah
Utah State University
Utah Valley State College
Weber State University
Westminster College

Vermont

Castleton State College
Champlain College
Johnson State College
Middlebury College
Norwich University
St. Michael's College
University of Vermont
Vermont Technical College

Virginia

Christopher Newport University
College of William and Mary
George Mason University
Hampden-Sydney College
Hampton University
James Madison University
Liberty University
Longwood University
Mary Baldwin College
Marymount University
Norfolk State University
Old Dominion University
Radford University
Randolph-Macon College
St. Paul's College
University of Richmond
University of Virginia
Virginia Military Institute
Virginia Polytechnic Institute and State University
Virginia State University
Virginia Union University
Virginia Wesleyan College
Washington and Lee University

Washington

Central Washington University
Eastern Washington University
Gonzaga University
Northwest University
Pacific Lutheran University
Saint Martin's University
Seattle Pacific University
Seattle University
University of Puget Sound
University of Washington
Washington State University
Whitworth College

West Virginia

Marshall University
University of Charleston
West Virginia State University
West Virginia University
West Virginia University Institute of Technology

Wisconsin

Alverno College
Bellin College of Nursing
Carroll College
Carthage College
Marian College of Fond du Lac
Marquette University
Milwaukee School of Engineering
Ripon College
St. Norbert College

- University of Wisconsin
  - Green Bay
  - La Crosse
  - Madison
  - Milwaukee
  - Oshkosh
  - Parkside
  - River Falls
  - Stevens Point
  - Whitewater
- Viterbo University
- Wisconsin Lutheran College

Wyoming
- University of Wyoming

Guam
- University of Guam

Virgin Islands, U.S.
- University of the Virgin Islands

Two-year

Alabama
- Bishop State Community College
- Chattahoochee Valley Community College
- Gadsden State Community College
- Jefferson State Community College
- Marion Military Institute
- Northwest-Shoals Community College
- Shelton State Community College

Arizona
- Central Arizona College
- Chandler-Gilbert Community College
  - Williams Campus
- Coconino County Community College
- Gateway Community College
- Mesa Community College
- Paradise Valley Community College
- Phoenix College
- Pima Community College
- Yavapai College

Arkansas
- Northwest Arkansas Community College
- Ouachita Technical College

California
- Chabot College
- College of San Mateo
- Cuyamaca College
- De Anza College
- Diablo Valley College
- El Camino College
- Foothill College
- Fresno City College
- Los Angeles City College
- Los Angeles Mission College
- Mount San Jacinto College
- Riverside Community College
- Sacramento City College
- San Diego City College
- West Valley College

Colorado
- Arapahoe Community College
- Community College of Denver
- Front Range Community College
- Red Rocks Community College

Connecticut
- Capital Community College
- Tunxis Community College

Florida
- Broward Community College
- Daytona Beach Community College
- Hillsborough Community College
- Miami Dade College
- Pasco-Hernando Community College
- Pensacola Junior College
- Polk Community College
- Santa Fe Community College
- Tallahassee Community College
- Valencia Community College

Georgia
- Darton College
- Georgia Military College

Hawaii
- University of Hawaii
  - Honolulu Community College
  - Leeward Community College
  - Windward Community College

Illinois
- Carl Sandburg College
- John A. Logan College
- Kishwaukee College
- Lewis and Clark Community College
- Lincoln Land Community College
- Parkland College
- Spoon River College
- Waubonsee Community College

Indiana
- Vincennes University

Iowa
- Hawkeye Community College
- Iowa Western Community College

Kentucky
- Jefferson Community College

Louisiana
- Delgado Community College

Maryland
- Allegany College of Maryland
- Prince George's Community College

Massachusetts
- Holyoke Community College
- Quinsigamond Community College
- Roxbury Community College

Michigan
- Lansing Community College
- Washtenaw Community College

Minnesota
- Anoka-Ramsey Community College
- Century Community and Technical College
- Lake Superior College
- Normandale Community College

Mississippi
- Hinds Community College

Missouri
- St. Louis Community College
  - Florissant Valley
  - Meramec

Nevada
- Community College of Southern Nevada
- Truckee Meadows Community College

New Jersey
- Brookdale Community College
- Middlesex County College
- Raritan Valley Community College

New Mexico
- Albuquerque Technical-Vocational Institute
- Dona Ana Branch Community College of New Mexico State University
- New Mexico Military Institute Junior College

New York
- Corning Community College
- Erie Community College
  - City Campus
  - North Campus
  - South Campus
- Finger Lakes Community College
- Herkimer County Community College
- Hudson Valley Community College
- Maria College
- Mohawk Valley Community College
- Monroe Community College
- Nassau Community College
- Niagara County Community College
- Onondaga Community College
- Orange County Community College
- State University of New York
  - College of Agriculture and Technology at Morrisville
  - College of Technology at Alfred
  - College of Technology at Canton

North Carolina
- College of the Albemarle
- Guilford Technical Community College
- Pitt Community College

Ohio
- Cincinnati State Technical and Community College
- Columbus State Community College
- Hocking Technical College
- Kent State University
  - Ashtabula Regional Campus
  - East Liverpool Regional Campus
  - Salem Regional Campus
  - Stark Campus
  - Trumbull Campus
  - Tuscarawas Campus
- Owens Community College
  - Toledo
- Sinclair Community College
- University of Akron: Wayne College
- University of Cincinnati
  - Clermont College
  - Raymond Walters College

Oklahoma
- Rose State College

Oregon
- Linn-Benton Community College

Pennsylvania
- Community College of Philadelphia
- Harrisburg Area Community College
- Lackawanna College
- Lehigh Carbon Community College
- Penn State
  - Delaware County
  - Hazleton
  - Mont Alto
- Valley Forge Military College

Rhode Island
- Community College of Rhode Island

South Carolina
- Denmark Technical College
- Midlands Technical College
- Orangeburg-Calhoun Technical College
- Spartanburg Methodist College
- Tri-County Technical College
- University of South Carolina
  - Lancaster
  - Salkehatchie Regional Campus
  - Sumter

Tennessee
- Jackson State Community College
- Pellissippi State Technical Community College
- Roane State Community College
- Southwest Tennessee Community College
- Walters State Community College

Texas
- Angelina College
- Austin Community College
- Cedar Valley College
- Central Texas College
- Del Mar College
- El Centro College
- El Paso Community College
- Houston Community College System
- Laredo Community College
- Lon Morris College
- Mountain View College
- St. Philip's College
- San Antonio College
- San Jacinto College
  - North
- Tarrant County College

Utah
- Salt Lake Community College

Virginia
- J. Sargeant Reynolds Community College
- John Tyler Community College
- Piedmont Virginia Community College
- Richard Bland College
- Southside Virginia Community College
- Thomas Nelson Community College
- Virginia Western Community College

Washington
- Clark College
- Highline Community College
- Pierce College
- Spokane Community College
- Spokane Falls Community College

Guam
- Guam Community College

Naval ROTC

Four-year

Alabama
- Alabama Agricultural and Mechanical University
- Auburn University
- Miles College
- Stillman College

Arizona
- Southwestern College
- University of Arizona

California
- California Maritime Academy
- California State University
  - San Marcos
- King's College and Seminary
- Loyola Marymount University
- National Hispanic University
- National University
- Point Loma Nazarene University
- Samuel Merritt College
- San Diego State University
- San Francisco State University
- Sonoma State University
- Stanford University
- University of California
  - Berkeley
  - Davis
  - Los Angeles
  - San Diego
  - Santa Cruz
- University of Redlands
- University of San Diego
- University of Southern California
- Whittier College

Colorado
- Regis University
- University of Colorado
  - Boulder

Connecticut
- Post University

District of Columbia
- Catholic University of America
- George Washington University
- Georgetown University
- University of the District of Columbia

Florida
- Embry-Riddle Aeronautical University
- Florida Agricultural and Mechanical University
- Florida State University
- Jacksonville University
- University of Florida
- University of North Florida
- University of South Florida
- University of Tampa

Georgia
- Armstrong Atlantic State University
- Clark Atlanta University
- Clayton State University
- Emory University
- Georgia Institute of Technology
- Georgia State University
- Morehouse College
- Savannah State University
- Southern Polytechnic State University
- Spelman College

Idaho
- Lewis-Clark State College
- University of Idaho

Illinois
- Illinois Institute of Technology
- Loyola University of Chicago
- Northwestern University
- University of Illinois
  - Chicago
  - Urbana-Champaign

Indiana
- Indiana University
  - South Bend
- Indiana University-Purdue University Indianapolis
- Purdue University
- Saint Mary's College
- University of Notre Dame

Iowa
- Iowa State University

Kansas
- University of Kansas
- Washburn University of Topeka

Louisiana
- Dillard University

Tables and Indexes

Louisiana State University and
Agricultural and Mechanical
College
Louisiana Tech University
Loyola University New Orleans
Our Lady of Holy Cross College
Southern University
New Orleans
Southern University and
Agricultural and Mechanical
College
Tulane University
University of New Orleans
Xavier University of Louisiana

Maine
Husson College
Maine Maritime Academy
University of Maine
University of Maine
Augusta

Maryland
University of Maryland
College Park

Massachusetts
Babson College
Becker College
Boston College
Boston University
Clark University
College of the Holy Cross
Harvard College
Massachusetts Institute of
Technology
Massachusetts Maritime Academy
Northeastern University
Tufts University
Worcester Polytechnic Institute
Worcester State College

Michigan
Eastern Michigan University
Finlandia University
Lawrence Technological
University
University of Michigan
University of Michigan
Dearborn

Minnesota
Augsburg College
Concordia University: St. Paul
Macalester College
University of Minnesota
Twin Cities
University of St. Thomas

Mississippi
Tougaloo College
University of Mississippi

Missouri
Columbia College
Lincoln University
Stephens College
University of Missouri
Columbia
Rolla
Westminster College
William Woods University

Nebraska
University of Nebraska
Lincoln
York College

New Mexico
National American University
University of New Mexico

New York
Albany College of Pharmacy
City University of New York
Queens College
College of Saint Rose
Columbia University
Columbia College
Fu Foundation School of
Engineering and Applied
Science
Cornell University
Eastman School of Music of the
University of Rochester
Fordham University
Globe Institute of Technology
Molloy College
Rensselaer Polytechnic Institute
Rochester Institute of Technology
Russell Sage College
State University of New York
College at Brockport
Maritime College
Union College
University of Rochester

North Carolina
Belmont Abbey College
Duke University
North Carolina State University
Peace College
University of North Carolina
Chapel Hill

Ohio
Cleveland State University
Miami University
Oxford Campus
Ohio State University
Columbus Campus
Lima Campus
Mansfield Campus
Marion Campus
Newark Campus
Ohio University
Lancaster Campus

Oklahoma
Oklahoma Wesleyan University
University of Oklahoma

Oregon
Oregon State University
Warner Pacific College
Western Oregon University

Pennsylvania
Carlow University
Carnegie Mellon University
Chatham College
Drexel University
Duquesne University
Penn State
University Park
St. Francis University
St. Joseph's University
Swarthmore College
Temple University
Thomas Jefferson University:
College of Health Professions
University of Pennsylvania
University of Pittsburgh
Villanova University
Widener University

Puerto Rico
Inter American University of
Puerto Rico
Bayamon Campus
Ponce Campus
Universidad Metropolitana

South Carolina
The Citadel
University of South Carolina

Tennessee
Belmont University
Christian Brothers University
Fisk University
University of Memphis
Vanderbilt University

Texas
Houston Baptist University
Huston-Tillotson College
Prairie View A&M University
Rice University
Texas A&M University
Texas A&M University
Galveston
University of Houston
University of Texas
Austin

Utah
University of Utah
Weber State University
Westminster College

Vermont
Norwich University

Virginia
Hampton University
Mary Baldwin College
Norfolk State University
Old Dominion University
University of Virginia
Virginia Military Institute
Virginia Polytechnic Institute and
State University

Washington
Seattle Pacific University
Seattle University
University of Washington
Washington State University

Wisconsin
Marquette University
Milwaukee School of Engineering
University of Wisconsin
Madison
Wisconsin Lutheran College

Two-year

Arizona
Gateway Community College
Mesa Community College
Pima Community College

California
Contra Costa College
Diablo Valley College
Foothill College
Fullerton College
Los Angeles City College
Mission College
Riverside Community College
Sacramento City College

Connecticut
Capital Community College
Tunxis Community College

Florida
Florida Community College at
Jacksonville
Pasco-Hernando Community
College
Santa Fe Community College
Tallahassee Community College

Hawaii
University of Hawaii
Hawaii Community College

Illinois
Lincoln Land Community College
Parkland College

Iowa
Hawkeye Community College

Minnesota
Anoka-Ramsey Community
College
Lake Superior College
Normandale Community College

New Mexico
Albuquerque
Technical-Vocational Institute

New York
Corning Community College
Katharine Gibbs School
New York
Maria College
Monroe Community College

North Carolina
Guilford Technical Community
College

Ohio
Cuyahoga Community College
Metropolitan Campus
Miami University
Hamilton Campus
University of Cincinnati
Raymond Walters College

South Carolina
Midlands Technical College
University of South Carolina
Salkehatchie Regional
Campus

Texas
Lon Morris College

Virginia
New River Community College

Washington
Spokane Community College

West Virginia
Corinthian Schools: National
Institute of Technology

Colleges with NCAA sports

Baseball Division I

Alabama
Alabama Agricultural and Mechanical University M
Alabama State University M
Auburn University M
Birmingham-Southern College M
Jacksonville State University M
Samford University M
Troy University M
University of Alabama M
University of Alabama
  Birmingham M
University of South Alabama M

Arizona
Arizona State University M
University of Arizona M

Arkansas
Arkansas State University M
University of Arkansas M
University of Arkansas
  Little Rock M
  Pine Bluff M

California
California Polytechnic State University: San Luis Obispo M
California State University
  Fresno M
  Fullerton M
  Long Beach M
  Northridge M
  Sacramento M
Loyola Marymount University M
Pepperdine University M
St. Mary's College of California M
San Diego State University M
San Jose State University M
Santa Clara University M
Stanford University M
University of California
  Berkeley M
  Irvine M
  Los Angeles M
  Riverside M
  Santa Barbara M
University of San Diego M
University of San Francisco M
University of Southern California M
University of the Pacific M

Colorado
United States Air Force Academy M

Connecticut
Central Connecticut State University M
Fairfield University M
Quinnipiac University M
Sacred Heart University M
University of Connecticut M
University of Hartford M
Yale University M

Delaware
Delaware State University M
University of Delaware M

District of Columbia
George Washington University M
Georgetown University M

Florida
Bethune-Cookman College M
Florida Agricultural and Mechanical University M
Florida Atlantic University M
Florida International University M
Florida State University M
Jacksonville University M
Stetson University M
University of Central Florida M
University of Florida M
University of Miami M
University of South Florida M

Georgia
Georgia Institute of Technology M
Georgia Southern University M
Georgia State University M
Mercer University M
Savannah State University M
University of Georgia M

Hawaii
University of Hawaii
  Hilo M
  Manoa M

Illinois
Bradley University M
Chicago State University M
Eastern Illinois University M
Northern Illinois University M
Northwestern University M
Southern Illinois University
  Carbondale M
University of Illinois
  Chicago M
  Urbana-Champaign M

Indiana
Ball State University M
Butler University M
Indiana State University M
Indiana University
  Bloomington M
Indiana University-Purdue University Fort Wayne M
Purdue University M
University of Evansville M
University of Notre Dame M
Valparaiso University M

Iowa
University of Iowa M
University of Northern Iowa M

Kansas
Kansas State University M
University of Kansas M
Wichita State University M

Kentucky
Eastern Kentucky University M
Morehead State University M
Murray State University M
University of Kentucky M
University of Louisville M
Western Kentucky University M

Louisiana
Centenary College of Louisiana M
Grambling State University M
Louisiana State University and Agricultural and Mechanical College M
Louisiana Tech University M
Nicholls State University M
Northwestern State University M
Southeastern Louisiana University M
Southern University and Agricultural and Mechanical College M
Tulane University M
University of Louisiana at Lafayette M
University of Louisiana at Monroe M
University of New Orleans M

Maine
University of Maine M

Maryland
Coppin State University M
Mount St. Mary's University M
Towson University M
United States Naval Academy M
University of Maryland
  Baltimore County M
  College Park M
  Eastern Shore M

Massachusetts
Boston College M
College of the Holy Cross M
Harvard College M
Northeastern University M
University of Massachusetts
  Amherst M

Michigan
Central Michigan University M
Eastern Michigan University M
Michigan State University M
Oakland University M
University of Michigan M
Western Michigan University M

Minnesota
University of Minnesota
  Twin Cities M

Mississippi
Alcorn State University M
Jackson State University M
Mississippi State University M
Mississippi Valley State University M
University of Mississippi M
University of Southern Mississippi M

Missouri
Missouri State University M
St. Louis University M
Southeast Missouri State University M
University of Missouri
  Columbia M

Nebraska
Creighton University M
University of Nebraska
  Lincoln M

Nevada
University of Nevada
  Las Vegas M
  Reno M

New Hampshire
Dartmouth College M

New Jersey
Fairleigh Dickinson University
  Metropolitan Campus M
Monmouth University M
Princeton University M
Rider University M
Rutgers, The State University of New Jersey
  New Brunswick Regional Campus M
St. Peter's College M
Seton Hall University M

New Mexico
New Mexico State University M
University of New Mexico M

New York
Canisius College M
Columbia University
  Columbia College M
Cornell University M
Fordham University M
Hofstra University M
Iona College M
Le Moyne College M
Long Island University
  Brooklyn Campus M
Manhattan College M
Marist College M
New York Institute of Technology M
Niagara University M
Pace University M
St. Bonaventure University M
St. Francis College M
St. John's University M
Siena College M
State University of New York
  Albany M
  Binghamton M
  Buffalo M
United States Military Academy M
Wagner College M

North Carolina
Appalachian State University M
Campbell University M
Davidson College M
Duke University M
East Carolina University M
Elon University M
Gardner-Webb University M
High Point University M
North Carolina Agricultural and Technical State University M
North Carolina State University M
University of North Carolina
  Asheville M
  Chapel Hill M
  Charlotte M
  Greensboro M
  Wilmington M
Wake Forest University M
Western Carolina University M

Ohio
Bowling Green State University M
Cleveland State University M
Kent State University M
Miami University
  Oxford Campus M
Ohio State University
  Columbus Campus M
Ohio University M
University of Akron M
University of Cincinnati M
University of Dayton M
University of Toledo M
Wright State University M
Xavier University M
Youngstown State University M

Oklahoma
Oklahoma State University M
Oral Roberts University M
University of Oklahoma M

Oregon
Oregon State University M
University of Portland M

Pennsylvania
Bucknell University M
Duquesne University M
La Salle University M
Lafayette College M
Lehigh University M
Penn State
  University Park M
St. Joseph's University M
Temple University M
University of Pennsylvania M
University of Pittsburgh M
Villanova University M

Rhode Island
Brown University M
University of Rhode Island M

South Carolina
Charleston Southern University M
The Citadel M
Clemson University M
Coastal Carolina University M
College of Charleston M
Furman University M
University of South Carolina M
Winthrop University M
Wofford College M

Tennessee
Austin Peay State University M
Belmont University M
East Tennessee State University M
Lipscomb University M
Middle Tennessee State University M
Tennessee Technological University M
University of Memphis M
University of Tennessee
  Knoxville M
  Martin M
Vanderbilt University M

Texas
Baylor University M
Dallas Baptist University M
Lamar University M
Prairie View A&M University M
Rice University M
Sam Houston State University M
Stephen F. Austin State University M
Texas A&M University M
Texas Christian University M
Texas Southern University M
Texas State University: San Marcos M
Texas Tech University M
University of Houston M
University of Texas
  Arlington M
  Austin M
  Pan American M
  San Antonio M

Utah
Brigham Young University M
Southern Utah University M
University of Utah M
Utah Valley State College M

Vermont
University of Vermont M

Virginia
College of William and Mary M
George Mason University M
James Madison University M
Liberty University M
Norfolk State University M
Old Dominion University M
Radford University M
University of Richmond M
University of Virginia M
Virginia Commonwealth University M
Virginia Military Institute M
Virginia Polytechnic Institute and State University M

Washington
Gonzaga University M
University of Washington M
Washington State University M

West Virginia
Marshall University M
West Virginia University M

Wisconsin
University of Wisconsin
  Milwaukee M

Baseball Division II

Alabama
Miles College M
Stillman College M
Tuskegee University M
University of Alabama
Huntsville M
University of Montevallo M
University of North Alabama M
University of West Alabama M

Arizona
Grand Canyon University M

Arkansas
Arkansas Tech University M
Harding University M
Henderson State University M
Ouachita Baptist University M
Southern Arkansas University M
University of Arkansas
Monticello M
University of Central Arkansas M

California
California State Polytechnic
University: Pomona M
California State University
Chico M
Dominguez Hills M
Los Angeles M
Monterey Bay M
San Bernardino M
Stanislaus M
San Francisco State University M
Sonoma State University M
University of California
Davis M
San Diego M

Colorado
Colorado Christian University M
Colorado School of Mines M
Colorado State University
Pueblo M
Mesa State College M
Metropolitan State College of
Denver M
Regis University M
University of Northern Colorado
M

Connecticut
Post University M
Southern Connecticut State
University M
University of Bridgeport M
University of New Haven M

Delaware
Wilmington College M

Florida
Barry University M
Eckerd College M
Florida Gulf Coast University M
Florida Institute of Technology M
Florida Southern College M
Lynn University M
Nova Southeastern University M
Palm Beach Atlantic University M
Rollins College M
St. Leo University M
University of North Florida M
University of Tampa M
University of West Florida M

Georgia
Albany State University M
Armstrong Atlantic State
University M
Augusta State University M
Clark Atlanta University M
Columbus State University M
Georgia College and State
University M
Kennesaw State University M
Morehouse College M
North Georgia College & State
University M
Paine College M
University of West Georgia M
Valdosta State University M

Hawaii
Hawaii Pacific University M

Idaho
Northwest Nazarene University M

Illinois
Lewis University M
Quincy University M
Southern Illinois University
Edwardsville M

Indiana
Oakland City University M
St. Joseph's College M
University of Indianapolis M
University of Southern Indiana M

Iowa
Upper Iowa University M

Kansas
Emporia State University M
Fort Hays State University M
Pittsburg State University M
Washburn University of Topeka
M

Kentucky
Bellarmine University M
Kentucky State University M
Kentucky Wesleyan College M
Northern Kentucky University M

Maryland
Columbia Union College M

Massachusetts
American International College M
Assumption College M
Bentley College M
Merrimack College M
Stonehill College M
University of Massachusetts
Lowell M

Michigan
Grand Valley State University M
Hillsdale College M
Northwood University M
Saginaw Valley State University
M
Wayne State University M

Minnesota
Bemidji State University M
Concordia University: St. Paul M
Minnesota State University
Mankato M
St. Cloud State University M
Southwest Minnesota State
University M
University of Minnesota
Crookston M
Duluth M
Morris M
Winona State University M

Mississippi
Delta State University M

Missouri
Central Missouri State University
M
Lincoln University M
Missouri Southern State
University M
Missouri Western State University
M
Northwest Missouri State
University M
Rockhurst University M
Southwest Baptist University M
Truman State University M
University of Missouri
Rolla M
St. Louis M

Montana
Montana State University
Billings M

Nebraska
University of Nebraska
Kearney M
Omaha M
Wayne State College M

New Hampshire
Franklin Pierce College M
St. Anselm College M
Southern New Hampshire
University M

New Jersey
Bloomfield College M
Caldwell College M
Felician College M
New Jersey Institute of
Technology M

New Mexico
Eastern New Mexico University
M
New Mexico Highlands
University M

New York
Adelphi University M
City University of New York
Queens College M
College of Saint Rose M
Concordia College M
Dominican College of Blauvelt M
Dowling College M
Long Island University
C. W. Post Campus M
Mercy College M
Molloy College M
Nyack College M
St. Thomas Aquinas College M

North Carolina
Barton College M
Belmont Abbey College M
Catawba College M
Elizabeth City State University M
Lenoir-Rhyne College M
Mars Hill College M
Mount Olive College M
Pfeiffer University M
St. Andrews Presbyterian College
M
St. Augustine's College M
Shaw University M
University of North Carolina
Pembroke M
Wingate University M

North Dakota
North Dakota State University M
University of North Dakota M

Ohio
Ashland University M
Tiffin University M
University of Findlay M

Oklahoma
Cameron University M
East Central University M
Northeastern State University M
Oklahoma Panhandle State
University M
Southeastern Oklahoma State
University M
Southwestern Oklahoma State
University M
University of Central Oklahoma
M

Oregon
Western Oregon University M

Pennsylvania
Bloomsburg University of
Pennsylvania M
California University of
Pennsylvania M
Clarion University of
Pennsylvania M
East Stroudsburg University of
Pennsylvania M
Gannon University M
Indiana University of
Pennsylvania M
Kutztown University of
Pennsylvania M
Lock Haven University of
Pennsylvania M
Mansfield University of
Pennsylvania M
Mercyhurst College M
Millersville University of
Pennsylvania M
Philadelphia University M
Shippensburg University of
Pennsylvania M
Slippery Rock University of
Pennsylvania M
University of Pittsburgh
Johnstown M
University of the Sciences in
Philadelphia M
West Chester University of
Pennsylvania M

Puerto Rico
University of Puerto Rico
Bayamon University College
M
Cayey University College M
Mayaguez M

Rhode Island
Bryant University M

South Carolina
Anderson University M
Benedict College M
Claflin University M
Coker College M
Erskine College M
Francis Marion University M
Lander University M
Limestone College M
Newberry College M
North Greenville College M
Presbyterian College M
University of South Carolina
Aiken M
Upstate M

South Dakota
Augustana College M
Northern State University M
South Dakota State University M

Tennessee
Carson-Newman College M
Christian Brothers University M
LeMoyne-Owen College M
Lincoln Memorial University M
Tusculum College M

Texas
Abilene Christian University M
Angelo State University M
St. Edward's University M
St. Mary's University M
Tarleton State University M
Texas A&M University
Kingsville M
University of the Incarnate Word
M
West Texas A&M University M

Vermont
St. Michael's College M

Virginia
Longwood University M
St. Paul's College M
Virginia State University M

Washington
Central Washington University M
Saint Martin's University M

West Virginia
Alderson-Broaddus College M
Bluefield State College M
Concord University M
Davis and Elkins College M
Ohio Valley University M
Salem International University M
Shepherd University M
University of Charleston M
West Liberty State College M
West Virginia State University M
West Virginia University Institute
of Technology M
West Virginia Wesleyan College
M
Wheeling Jesuit University M

Wisconsin
University of Wisconsin
Parkside M

Baseball Division III

Alabama
Huntingdon College M

Arkansas
Hendrix College M
University of the Ozarks M

California
California Institute of Technology
M
California Lutheran University M
California State University
East Bay M
Chapman University M
Claremont McKenna College M
Menlo College M
Occidental College M
Pitzer College M
Pomona College M
University of La Verne M
University of Redlands M
Whittier College M

Connecticut
Albertus Magnus College M
Eastern Connecticut State
University M
Mitchell College M
Trinity College M
United States Coast Guard
Academy M
Wesleyan University M
Western Connecticut State
University M

Delaware
Wesley College M

District of Columbia
Catholic University of America M
Gallaudet University M

Georgia
Emory University M
LaGrange College M
Oglethorpe University M
Piedmont College M

Illinois
Augustana College M
Aurora University M
Benedictine University M
Blackburn College M
Concordia University M
Dominican University M
Elmhurst College M
Eureka College M
Greenville College M
Illinois College M
Illinois Wesleyan University M
Knox College M
MacMurray College M

Tables and Indexes

- Millikin University M
- Monmouth College M
- North Central College M
- North Park University M
- Principia College M
- Rockford College M
- University of Chicago M
- Wheaton College M

Indiana

- Anderson University M
- DePauw University M
- Earlham College M
- Franklin College M
- Hanover College M
- Manchester College M
- Rose-Hulman Institute of Technology M
- Tri-State University M
- Wabash College M

Iowa

- Buena Vista University M
- Central College M
- Clarke College M
- Coe College M
- Cornell College M
- Grinnell College M
- Loras College M
- Luther College M
- Simpson College M
- University of Dubuque M
- Wartburg College M

Kentucky

- Centre College M
- Thomas More College M
- Transylvania University M

Maine

- Bates College M
- Bowdoin College M
- Colby College M
- Husson College M
- St. Joseph's College M
- Thomas College M
- University of Maine
  - Farmington M
  - Presque Isle M
- University of Southern Maine M

Maryland

- Frostburg State University M
- Johns Hopkins University M
- McDaniel College M
- St. Mary's College of Maryland M
- Salisbury University M
- Villa Julie College M
- Washington College M

Massachusetts

- Amherst College M
- Anna Maria College M
- Babson College M
- Becker College M
- Brandeis University M
- Bridgewater State College M
- Clark University M
- Curry College M
- Eastern Nazarene College M
- Elms College M
- Endicott College M
- Fitchburg State College M
- Framingham State College M
- Gordon College M
- Massachusetts College of Liberal Arts M
- Massachusetts Institute of Technology M
- Massachusetts Maritime Academy M
- Nichols College M
- Salem State College M
- Springfield College M
- Suffolk University M
- Tufts University M
- University of Massachusetts
  - Boston M
  - Dartmouth M
- Wentworth Institute of Technology M
- Western New England College M
- Westfield State College M
- Wheaton College M
- Williams College M
- Worcester Polytechnic Institute M
- Worcester State College M

Michigan

- Adrian College M
- Albion College M
- Alma College M
- Calvin College M
- Finlandia University M
- Hope College M
- Kalamazoo College M
- Olivet College M

Minnesota

- Augsburg College M
- Bethany Lutheran College M
- Bethel University M
- Carleton College M
- College of St. Scholastica M
- Concordia College: Moorhead M
- Crown College M
- Gustavus Adolphus College M
- Hamline University M
- Macalester College M
- Martin Luther College M
- North Central University M
- Northwestern College M
- St. John's University M
- St. Mary's University of Minnesota M
- St. Olaf College M
- University of St. Thomas M

Mississippi

- Millsaps College M
- Mississippi College M
- Rust College M

Missouri

- Fontbonne University M
- Maryville University of Saint Louis M
- Washington University in St. Louis M
- Webster University M
- Westminster College M

Nebraska

- Nebraska Wesleyan University M

New Hampshire

- Colby-Sawyer College M
- Daniel Webster College M
- Keene State College M
- New England College M
- Plymouth State University M
- Rivier College M

New Jersey

- Centenary College M
- The College of New Jersey M
- Drew University M
- Fairleigh Dickinson University
  - College at Florham M
- Kean University M
- Montclair State University M
- New Jersey City University M
- Ramapo College of New Jersey M
- Richard Stockton College of New Jersey M
- Rowan University M
- Rutgers, The State University of New Jersey
  - Camden Regional Campus M
  - Newark Regional Campus M
- Stevens Institute of Technology M
- William Paterson University of New Jersey M

New York

- Cazenovia College M
- City University of New York
  - Baruch College M
  - City College M
  - College of Staten Island M
  - John Jay College of Criminal Justice M
  - Lehman College M
- Clarkson University M
- College of Mount St. Vincent M
- D'Youville College M
- Hamilton College M
- Hartwick College M
- Hilbert College M
- Ithaca College M
- Keuka College M
- Manhattanville College M
- Medaille College M
- Mount St. Mary College M
- Polytechnic University M
- Rensselaer Polytechnic Institute M
- Rochester Institute of Technology M
- St. John Fisher College M
- St. Joseph's College: Suffolk Campus M
- St. Lawrence University M
- Skidmore College M
- State University of New York
  - College at Brockport M
  - College at Cortland M
  - College at Fredonia M
  - College at Old Westbury M
  - College at Oneonta M
  - College at Plattsburgh M
  - Farmingdale M
  - Institute of Technology at Utica/Rome M
  - Maritime College M
  - New Paltz M
  - Oswego M
  - Purchase M
- Union College M
- United States Merchant Marine Academy M
- University of Rochester M
- Utica College M
- Vassar College M
- Yeshiva University M

North Carolina

- Chowan College M
- Greensboro College M
- Guilford College M
- Methodist College M
- North Carolina Wesleyan College M

Ohio

- Baldwin-Wallace College M
- Bluffton University M
- Capital University M
- Case Western Reserve University M
- College of Mount St. Joseph M
- College of Wooster M
- Defiance College M
- Denison University M
- Heidelberg College M
- Hiram College M
- John Carroll University M
- Kenyon College M
- Lake Erie College M
- Marietta College M
- Mount Union College M
- Muskingum College M
- Oberlin College M
- Ohio Northern University M
- Ohio Wesleyan University M
- Otterbein College M
- Wilmington College M
- Wittenberg University M

Oregon

- George Fox University M
- Lewis & Clark College M
- Linfield College M
- Pacific University M
- Willamette University M

Pennsylvania

- Albright College M
- Allegheny College M
- Alvernia College M
- Arcadia University M
- Baptist Bible College of Pennsylvania M
- College Misericordia M
- Delaware Valley College M
- DeSales University M
- Dickinson College M
- Eastern University M
- Elizabethtown College M
- Franklin & Marshall College M
- Gettysburg College M
- Grove City College M
- Gwynedd-Mercy College M
- Haverford College M
- Juniata College M
- Keystone College M
- King's College M
- La Roche College M
- Lebanon Valley College M
- Lincoln University M
- Marywood University M
- Messiah College M
- Moravian College M
- Mount Aloysius College M
- Muhlenberg College M
- Neumann College M
- Penn State
  - Altoona M
  - Berks M
  - Erie, The Behrend College M
- Philadelphia Biblical University M
- Susquehanna University M
- Swarthmore College M
- Thiel College M
- University of Pittsburgh
  - Bradford M
  - Greensburg M
- University of Scranton M
- Ursinus College M
- Washington and Jefferson College M
- Waynesburg College M
- Westminster College M
- Widener University M
- Wilkes University M
- York College of Pennsylvania M

Rhode Island

- Johnson & Wales University M
- Rhode Island College M
- Roger Williams University M
- Salve Regina University M

South Dakota

- Presentation College M

Tennessee

- Fisk University M
- Maryville College M
- Rhodes College M
- University of the South M

Texas

- Austin College M
- Concordia University at Austin M
- East Texas Baptist University M
- Hardin-Simmons University M
- Howard Payne University M
- LeTourneau University M
- McMurry University M
- Schreiner University M
- Southwestern University M
- Sul Ross State University M
- Texas Lutheran University M
- Trinity University M
- University of Dallas M
- University of Mary Hardin-Baylor M
- University of Texas
  - Dallas M
  - Tyler M

Vermont

- Castleton State College M
- Middlebury College M
- Norwich University M
- Southern Vermont College M

Virginia

- Averett University M
- Bridgewater College M
- Christopher Newport University M
- Eastern Mennonite University M
- Emory & Henry College M
- Ferrum College M
- Hampden-Sydney College M
- Lynchburg College M
- Randolph-Macon College M
- Roanoke College M
- Shenandoah University M
- University of Mary Washington M
- Virginia Wesleyan College M
- Washington and Lee University M

Washington

- Pacific Lutheran University M
- University of Puget Sound M
- Whitman College M
- Whitworth College M

West Virginia

- Bethany College M

Wisconsin

- Beloit College M
- Carroll College M
- Carthage College M
- Concordia University Wisconsin M
- Edgewood College M
- Lakeland College M
- Lawrence University M
- Maranatha Baptist Bible College M
- Marian College of Fond du Lac M
- Milwaukee School of Engineering M
- Northland College M
- Ripon College M
- St. Norbert College M
- University of Wisconsin
  - La Crosse M
  - Oshkosh M
  - Platteville M
  - Stevens Point M
  - Stout M
  - Superior M
  - Whitewater M
- Wisconsin Lutheran College M

Basketball Division I

Alabama

- Alabama Agricultural and Mechanical University
- Alabama State University
- Auburn University
- Birmingham-Southern College
- Jacksonville State University
- Samford University
- Troy University
- University of Alabama
- University of Alabama
  - Birmingham
- University of South Alabama

Arizona

- Arizona State University
- Northern Arizona University
- University of Arizona

Arkansas

- Arkansas State University
- University of Arkansas

University of Arkansas
Little Rock
Pine Bluff

California
California Polytechnic State University: San Luis Obispo
California State University
Fresno
Fullerton
Long Beach
Northridge
Sacramento
Loyola Marymount University
Pepperdine University
St. Mary's College of California
San Diego State University
San Jose State University
Santa Clara University
Stanford University
University of California
Berkeley
Irvine
Los Angeles
Riverside
Santa Barbara
University of San Diego
University of San Francisco
University of Southern California
University of the Pacific

Colorado
Colorado State University
United States Air Force Academy
University of Colorado
Boulder
University of Denver

Connecticut
Central Connecticut State University
Fairfield University
Quinnipiac University
Sacred Heart University
University of Connecticut
University of Hartford
Yale University

Delaware
Delaware State University
University of Delaware

District of Columbia
American University
George Washington University
Georgetown University
Howard University

Florida
Bethune-Cookman College
Florida Agricultural and Mechanical University
Florida Atlantic University
Florida International University
Florida State University
Jacksonville University
Stetson University
University of Central Florida
University of Florida
University of Miami
University of South Florida

Georgia
Georgia Institute of Technology
Georgia Southern University
Georgia State University
Mercer University
Savannah State University
University of Georgia

Hawaii
University of Hawaii
Manoa

Idaho
Boise State University
Idaho State University
University of Idaho

Illinois
Bradley University
Chicago State University
DePaul University
Eastern Illinois University
Illinois State University
Loyola University of Chicago
Northern Illinois University
Northwestern University
Southern Illinois University
Carbondale
University of Illinois
Chicago
Urbana-Champaign
Western Illinois University

Indiana
Ball State University
Butler University
Indiana State University
Indiana University
Bloomington
Indiana University-Purdue University Fort Wayne
Indiana University-Purdue University Indianapolis
Purdue University
University of Evansville
University of Notre Dame
Valparaiso University

Iowa
Drake University
Iowa State University
University of Iowa
University of Northern Iowa

Kansas
Kansas State University
University of Kansas
Wichita State University

Kentucky
Eastern Kentucky University
Morehead State University
Murray State University
University of Kentucky
University of Louisville
Western Kentucky University

Louisiana
Centenary College of Louisiana
Grambling State University
Louisiana State University and Agricultural and Mechanical College
Louisiana Tech University
Nicholls State University
Northwestern State University
Southeastern Louisiana University
Southern University and Agricultural and Mechanical College
Tulane University
University of Louisiana at Lafayette
University of Louisiana at Monroe
University of New Orleans

Maine
University of Maine

Maryland
Coppin State University
Loyola College in Maryland
Morgan State University
Mount St. Mary's University
Towson University
United States Naval Academy
University of Maryland
Baltimore County
College Park
Eastern Shore

Massachusetts
Boston College
Boston University
College of the Holy Cross
Harvard College
Northeastern University
University of Massachusetts
Amherst

Michigan
Central Michigan University
Eastern Michigan University
Michigan State University
Oakland University
University of Detroit Mercy
University of Michigan
Western Michigan University

Minnesota
University of Minnesota
Twin Cities

Mississippi
Alcorn State University
Jackson State University
Mississippi State University
Mississippi Valley State University
University of Mississippi
University of Southern Mississippi

Missouri
Missouri State University
St. Louis University
Southeast Missouri State University
University of Missouri
Columbia
Kansas City

Montana
Montana State University
Bozeman
University of Montana: Missoula

Nebraska
Creighton University
University of Nebraska
Lincoln

Nevada
University of Nevada
Las Vegas
Reno

New Hampshire
Dartmouth College
University of New Hampshire

New Jersey
Fairleigh Dickinson University
Metropolitan Campus
Monmouth University
Princeton University
Rider University
Rutgers, The State University of New Jersey
New Brunswick Regional Campus
St. Peter's College
Seton Hall University

New Mexico
New Mexico State University
University of New Mexico

New York
Barnard College W
Canisius College
Colgate University
Columbia University
Columbia College M
Cornell University
Fordham University
Hofstra University
Iona College
Long Island University
Brooklyn Campus
Manhattan College
Marist College
Niagara University
St. Bonaventure University
St. Francis College
St. John's University
Siena College
State University of New York
Albany
Binghamton
Buffalo
Stony Brook
Syracuse University
United States Military Academy
Wagner College

North Carolina
Appalachian State University
Campbell University
Davidson College
Duke University
East Carolina University
Elon University
Gardner-Webb University
High Point University
North Carolina Agricultural and Technical State University
North Carolina State University
University of North Carolina
Asheville
Chapel Hill
Charlotte
Greensboro
Wilmington
Wake Forest University
Western Carolina University

Ohio
Bowling Green State University
Cleveland State University
Kent State University
Miami University
Oxford Campus
Ohio State University
Columbus Campus
Ohio University
University of Akron
University of Cincinnati
University of Dayton
University of Toledo
Wright State University
Xavier University
Youngstown State University

Oklahoma
Oklahoma State University
Oral Roberts University
University of Oklahoma
University of Tulsa

Oregon
Oregon State University
Portland State University
University of Oregon
University of Portland

Pennsylvania
Bucknell University
Drexel University
Duquesne University
La Salle University
Lafayette College
Lehigh University
Penn State
University Park
Robert Morris University
St. Francis University
St. Joseph's University
Temple University
University of Pennsylvania
University of Pittsburgh
Villanova University

Rhode Island
Brown University
Providence College
University of Rhode Island

South Carolina
Charleston Southern University
The Citadel M
Clemson University
Coastal Carolina University
College of Charleston
Furman University
South Carolina State University
University of South Carolina
Winthrop University
Wofford College

Tennessee
Austin Peay State University
Belmont University
East Tennessee State University
Lipscomb University
Middle Tennessee State University
Tennessee State University
Tennessee Technological University
University of Memphis
University of Tennessee
Chattanooga
Knoxville
Martin
Vanderbilt University

Texas
Baylor University
Lamar University
Prairie View A&M University
Rice University
Sam Houston State University
Southern Methodist University
Stephen F. Austin State University
Texas A&M University
Texas Christian University
Texas Southern University
Texas State University: San Marcos
Texas Tech University
University of Houston
University of North Texas
University of Texas
Arlington
Austin
El Paso
Pan American
San Antonio

Utah
Brigham Young University
Southern Utah University
University of Utah
Utah State University
Utah Valley State College
Weber State University

Vermont
University of Vermont

Virginia
College of William and Mary
George Mason University
Hampton University
James Madison University
Liberty University
Norfolk State University
Old Dominion University
Radford University
University of Richmond
University of Virginia
Virginia Commonwealth University
Virginia Military Institute M
Virginia Polytechnic Institute and State University

Washington
Eastern Washington University
Gonzaga University
University of Washington
Washington State University

West Virginia
Marshall University
West Virginia University

Wisconsin
Marquette University
University of Wisconsin
Green Bay
Madison
Milwaukee

Wyoming
University of Wyoming

Basketball Division II

Alabama
Miles College
Stillman College
Tuskegee University
University of Alabama
Huntsville
University of Montevallo
University of North Alabama
University of West Alabama

Alaska
University of Alaska
Anchorage
Fairbanks

Arizona
Grand Canyon University

Arkansas
Arkansas Tech University
Harding University
Henderson State University
Ouachita Baptist University
Southern Arkansas University
University of Arkansas
Monticello
University of Central Arkansas

California
California State Polytechnic University: Pomona
California State University
Bakersfield
Chico
Dominguez Hills
Los Angeles
Monterey Bay
San Bernardino
Stanislaus
Humboldt State University
Notre Dame de Namur University
San Francisco State University
Sonoma State University
University of California
Davis
San Diego

Colorado
Adams State College
Colorado Christian University
Colorado School of Mines
Colorado State University
Pueblo
Fort Lewis College
Mesa State College
Metropolitan State College of Denver
Regis University
University of Colorado
Colorado Springs
University of Northern Colorado
Western State College of Colorado

Connecticut
Post University
Southern Connecticut State University
University of Bridgeport
University of New Haven

Delaware
Goldey-Beacom College
Wilmington College

District of Columbia
University of the District of Columbia

Florida
Barry University
Eckerd College
Florida Gulf Coast University
Florida Institute of Technology
Florida Southern College
Lynn University
Nova Southeastern University
Palm Beach Atlantic University
Rollins College
St. Leo University
University of North Florida
University of Tampa
University of West Florida

Georgia
Albany State University
Armstrong Atlantic State University
Augusta State University
Clark Atlanta University
Clayton State University
Columbus State University
Fort Valley State University
Georgia College and State University
Kennesaw State University
Morehouse College M
North Georgia College & State University
Paine College
University of West Georgia
Valdosta State University

Hawaii
Brigham Young University-Hawaii M
Chaminade University of Honolulu M
Hawaii Pacific University M
University of Hawaii
Hilo M

Idaho
Northwest Nazarene University

Illinois
Lewis University
Quincy University
Southern Illinois University
Edwardsville

Indiana
Oakland City University
St. Joseph's College
University of Indianapolis
University of Southern Indiana

Iowa
Upper Iowa University

Kansas
Emporia State University
Fort Hays State University
Pittsburg State University
Washburn University of Topeka

Kentucky
Bellarmine University
Kentucky State University
Kentucky Wesleyan College
Northern Kentucky University

Maryland
Bowie State University
Columbia Union College

Massachusetts
American International College
Assumption College
Bentley College
Merrimack College
Stonehill College
University of Massachusetts
Lowell

Michigan
Ferris State University
Grand Valley State University
Hillsdale College
Lake Superior State University
Michigan Technological University
Northern Michigan University
Northwood University
Saginaw Valley State University
Wayne State University

Minnesota
Bemidji State University
Concordia University: St. Paul
Minnesota State University
Mankato
Moorhead
St. Cloud State University
Southwest Minnesota State University
University of Minnesota
Crookston
Duluth
Morris
Winona State University

Mississippi
Delta State University

Missouri
Central Missouri State University
Drury University
Lincoln University
Missouri Southern State University
Missouri Western State University
Northwest Missouri State University
Rockhurst University
Southwest Baptist University
Truman State University
University of Missouri
Rolla
St. Louis

Montana
Montana State University
Billings

Nebraska
Chadron State College
University of Nebraska
Kearney
Omaha
Wayne State College

New Hampshire
Franklin Pierce College
St. Anselm College
Southern New Hampshire University

New Jersey
Bloomfield College
Caldwell College
Felician College
Georgian Court University W
New Jersey Institute of Technology

New Mexico
Eastern New Mexico University
New Mexico Highlands University
Western New Mexico University

New York
Adelphi University
City University of New York
Queens College
College of Saint Rose
Concordia College
Dominican College of Blauvelt
Dowling College
Le Moyne College
Long Island University
C. W. Post Campus
Mercy College
Molloy College
New York Institute of Technology
Nyack College
Pace University
St. Thomas Aquinas College

North Carolina
Barton College
Belmont Abbey College
Catawba College
Elizabeth City State University
Fayetteville State University
Johnson C. Smith University
Lees-McRae College
Lenoir-Rhyne College
Livingstone College
Mars Hill College
Mount Olive College
North Carolina Central University
Pfeiffer University
Queens University of Charlotte
St. Andrews Presbyterian College
St. Augustine's College
Shaw University
University of North Carolina
Pembroke
Wingate University
Winston-Salem State University

North Dakota
North Dakota State University
University of Mary W
University of North Dakota

Ohio
Ashland University
Central State University
Tiffin University
University of Findlay

Oklahoma
Cameron University
East Central University
Northeastern State University
Oklahoma Panhandle State University
Southeastern Oklahoma State University
Southwestern Oklahoma State University
University of Central Oklahoma

Oregon
Western Oregon University

Pennsylvania
Bloomsburg University of Pennsylvania
California University of Pennsylvania
Cheyney University of Pennsylvania
Clarion University of Pennsylvania
East Stroudsburg University of Pennsylvania
Edinboro University of Pennsylvania
Gannon University
Holy Family University
Indiana University of Pennsylvania
Kutztown University of Pennsylvania
Lock Haven University of Pennsylvania
Mansfield University of Pennsylvania
Mercyhurst College
Millersville University of Pennsylvania
Mount Aloysius College M
Philadelphia University
Shippensburg University of Pennsylvania
Slippery Rock University of Pennsylvania
University of Pittsburgh
Johnstown
University of the Sciences in Philadelphia
West Chester University of Pennsylvania

Puerto Rico
University of Puerto Rico
Bayamon University College
Cayey University College
Mayaguez
Rio Piedras

Rhode Island
Bryant University

South Carolina
Anderson University
Benedict College
Claflin University
Coker College
Converse College W
Erskine College
Francis Marion University
Lander University
Limestone College
Newberry College
North Greenville College
Presbyterian College
University of South Carolina
Aiken
Upstate

South Dakota
Augustana College
Northern State University
South Dakota State University
University of South Dakota

Tennessee
Carson-Newman College
Christian Brothers University
LeMoyne-Owen College
Lincoln Memorial University
Tusculum College

Texas
Abilene Christian University
Angelo State University
Midwestern State University
St. Edward's University
St. Mary's University
Tarleton State University
Texas A&M University
Commerce
Kingsville
Texas Woman's University W
University of the Incarnate Word
West Texas A&M University

Vermont
Green Mountain College
St. Michael's College

Virginia
Longwood University
St. Paul's College
Virginia State University
Virginia Union University

Washington
Central Washington University
Saint Martin's University
Seattle Pacific University
Seattle University
Western Washington University

West Virginia
Alderson-Broaddus College
Bluefield State College
Concord University
Davis and Elkins College
Glenville State College
Ohio Valley University
Salem International University
Shepherd University
University of Charleston
West Liberty State College
West Virginia State University
West Virginia University Institute of Technology
West Virginia Wesleyan College
Wheeling Jesuit University

Wisconsin
University of Wisconsin
Parkside

Basketball Division III

Alabama
Huntingdon College

Arkansas
Hendrix College
University of the Ozarks

California
California Institute of Technology
California Lutheran University
California State University
  East Bay
Chapman University
Claremont McKenna College
Menlo College
Occidental College
Pitzer College
Pomona College
University of California
  Santa Cruz
University of La Verne
University of Redlands
Whittier College

Colorado
Colorado College

Connecticut
Albertus Magnus College
Connecticut College
Eastern Connecticut State University
Mitchell College
St. Joseph College W
Trinity College
United States Coast Guard Academy
Wesleyan University
Western Connecticut State University

Delaware
Wesley College

District of Columbia
Catholic University of America
Gallaudet University
Trinity University W

Georgia
Agnes Scott College W
Emory University
LaGrange College
Oglethorpe University
Piedmont College
Spelman College W
Wesleyan College W

Illinois
Augustana College
Aurora University
Benedictine University
Blackburn College
Concordia University
Dominican University
Elmhurst College
Eureka College
Greenville College
Illinois College
Illinois Wesleyan University
Knox College
Lake Forest College
MacMurray College
Millikin University
Monmouth College
North Central College
North Park University
Principia College
Rockford College
University of Chicago
Wheaton College

Indiana
Anderson University
DePauw University
Earlham College
Franklin College
Hanover College
Manchester College
Rose-Hulman Institute of Technology
Saint Mary's College W
Tri-State University
Wabash College M

Iowa
Buena Vista University
Central College
Clarke College
Coe College
Cornell College
Grinnell College
Loras College
Luther College
Simpson College
University of Dubuque
Wartburg College

Kentucky
Centre College
Thomas More College
Transylvania University

Maine
Bates College
Bowdoin College
Colby College
Husson College
Maine Maritime Academy
St. Joseph's College
Thomas College
University of Maine
  Farmington
  Presque Isle
University of New England
University of Southern Maine

Maryland
College of Notre Dame of Maryland W
Frostburg State University
Goucher College
Hood College
Johns Hopkins University
McDaniel College
St. Mary's College of Maryland
Salisbury University
Villa Julie College
Washington College

Massachusetts
Amherst College
Anna Maria College
Babson College
Bay Path College W
Becker College
Brandeis University
Bridgewater State College
Clark University
Curry College
Eastern Nazarene College
Elms College
Emerson College
Emmanuel College
Endicott College
Fitchburg State College
Framingham State College
Gordon College
Lasell College
Lesley University
Massachusetts College of Liberal Arts
Massachusetts Institute of Technology
Mount Holyoke College W
Mount Ida College
Newbury College
Nichols College
Pine Manor College W
Regis College W
Salem State College
Simmons College W
Smith College W
Springfield College
Suffolk University
Tufts University
University of Massachusetts
  Boston
  Dartmouth
Wellesley College W
Wentworth Institute of Technology
Western New England College
Westfield State College
Wheaton College
Wheelock College W
Williams College
Worcester Polytechnic Institute
Worcester State College

Michigan
Adrian College
Albion College
Alma College
Calvin College
Finlandia University
Hope College
Kalamazoo College
Olivet College

Minnesota
Augsburg College
Bethany Lutheran College
Bethel University
Carleton College
College of St. Benedict W
College of St. Catherine W
College of St. Scholastica
Concordia College: Moorhead
Crown College
Gustavus Adolphus College
Hamline University
Macalester College
Martin Luther College
North Central University
Northwestern College
St. John's University M
St. Mary's University of Minnesota
St. Olaf College
University of St. Thomas

Mississippi
Millsaps College
Mississippi College
Rust College

Missouri
Baptist Bible College W
Fontbonne University
Maryville University of Saint Louis
Washington University in St. Louis
Webster University
Westminster College

Nebraska
Nebraska Wesleyan University

New Hampshire
Colby-Sawyer College
Daniel Webster College
Keene State College
New England College
Plymouth State University
Rivier College

New Jersey
Centenary College
The College of New Jersey
College of St. Elizabeth W
Drew University
Fairleigh Dickinson University
  College at Florham
Kean University
Montclair State University
New Jersey City University
Ramapo College of New Jersey
Richard Stockton College of New Jersey
Rowan University
Rutgers, The State University of New Jersey
  Camden Regional Campus
  Newark Regional Campus
Stevens Institute of Technology
William Paterson University of New Jersey

New York
Alfred University
Bard College
Cazenovia College
City University of New York
  Baruch College
  Brooklyn College
  City College
  College of Staten Island
  Hunter College
  John Jay College of Criminal Justice
  Lehman College
  Medgar Evers College
  New York City College of Technology
  York College
Clarkson University
College of Mount St. Vincent
College of New Rochelle W
D'Youville College
Elmira College
Hamilton College
Hartwick College
Hilbert College
Hobart and William Smith Colleges
Ithaca College
Keuka College
Manhattanville College
Medaille College
Mount St. Mary College
Nazareth College of Rochester
New York University
Polytechnic University
Rensselaer Polytechnic Institute
Rochester Institute of Technology
Russell Sage College W
St. John Fisher College
St. Joseph's College: Suffolk Campus
St. Lawrence University
Skidmore College
State University of New York
  College at Brockport
  College at Buffalo
  College at Cortland
  College at Fredonia
  College at Geneseo
  College at Old Westbury
  College at Oneonta
  College at Plattsburgh
  College at Potsdam
  Farmingdale
  Institute of Technology at Utica/Rome
  Maritime College
  New Paltz
  Oswego
  Purchase
Union College
United States Merchant Marine Academy
University of Rochester
Utica College
Vassar College
Yeshiva University M

North Carolina
Bennett College W
Chowan College
Greensboro College
Guilford College
Meredith College W
Methodist College
North Carolina Wesleyan College
Peace College W
Salem College W

Ohio
Baldwin-Wallace College
Bluffton University
Capital University
Case Western Reserve University
College of Mount St. Joseph
College of Wooster
Defiance College
Denison University
Heidelberg College
Hiram College
John Carroll University
Kenyon College
Lake Erie College
Marietta College
Mount Union College
Muskingum College
Oberlin College
Ohio Northern University
Ohio Wesleyan University
Otterbein College
Wilmington College
Wittenberg University

Oregon
George Fox University
Lewis & Clark College
Linfield College
Pacific University
Willamette University

Pennsylvania
Albright College
Allegheny College
Alvernia College
Arcadia University
Baptist Bible College of Pennsylvania M
Bryn Mawr College W
Cabrini College
Carnegie Mellon University
Cedar Crest College W
Chatham College W
Chestnut Hill College
College Misericordia
Delaware Valley College
DeSales University
Dickinson College
Eastern University
Elizabethtown College
Franklin & Marshall College
Gettysburg College
Grove City College
Gwynedd-Mercy College
Haverford College
Immaculata University
Juniata College
Keystone College
King's College
La Roche College
Lebanon Valley College
Lincoln University
Lycoming College
Marywood University
Messiah College
Moravian College
Mount Aloysius College W
Muhlenberg College
Neumann College
Penn State
  Altoona
  Berks
  Erie, The Behrend College
Philadelphia Biblical University
Rosemont College W
Susquehanna University
Swarthmore College
Thiel College
University of Pittsburgh
  Bradford
  Greensburg
University of Scranton
Ursinus College
Washington and Jefferson College
Waynesburg College
Westminster College
Widener University
Wilkes University
Wilson College W
York College of Pennsylvania

Rhode Island
Johnson & Wales University
Rhode Island College
Roger Williams University
Salve Regina University

South Dakota
Presentation College

Tennessee
Fisk University
Maryville College
Rhodes College
University of the South

Texas
Austin College
Concordia University at Austin
East Texas Baptist University
Hardin-Simmons University
Howard Payne University
LeTourneau University
McMurry University
Schreiner University
Southwestern University
Sul Ross State University
Texas Lutheran University
Trinity University
University of Dallas
University of Mary Hardin-Baylor
University of Texas
Dallas
Tyler

Vermont
Castleton State College
Johnson State College
Middlebury College
Norwich University
Southern Vermont College

Virginia
Averett University
Bridgewater College
Christopher Newport University
Eastern Mennonite University
Emory & Henry College
Ferrum College
Hampden-Sydney College M
Hollins University W
Lynchburg College
Mary Baldwin College W
Marymount University
Randolph-Macon College
Randolph-Macon Woman's College W
Roanoke College
Shenandoah University
University of Mary Washington
Virginia Wesleyan College
Washington and Lee University

Washington
Pacific Lutheran University
University of Puget Sound
Whitman College
Whitworth College

West Virginia
Bethany College

Wisconsin
Alverno College W
Beloit College
Carroll College
Carthage College
Concordia University Wisconsin
Edgewood College
Lakeland College
Lawrence University
Maranatha Baptist Bible College
Marian College of Fond du Lac
Milwaukee School of Engineering
Mount Mary College W
Northland College
Ripon College
St. Norbert College
University of Wisconsin
Eau Claire
La Crosse
Oshkosh
Platteville
River Falls
Stevens Point
Stout
Superior
Whitewater
Wisconsin Lutheran College

Cross-country Division I

Alabama
Alabama Agricultural and Mechanical University
Alabama State University
Auburn University
Birmingham-Southern College
Jacksonville State University
Samford University
Troy University
University of Alabama
University of Alabama
Birmingham W
University of South Alabama

Arizona
Arizona State University
Northern Arizona University
University of Arizona

Arkansas
Arkansas State University
University of Arkansas
University of Arkansas
Little Rock
Monticello M
Pine Bluff

California
California Polytechnic State University: San Luis Obispo
California State University
Fresno W
Fullerton
Long Beach
Northridge
Sacramento
Loyola Marymount University
Notre Dame de Namur University M
Pepperdine University
St. Mary's College of California
San Diego State University W
San Jose State University
Santa Clara University
Stanford University
University of California
Berkeley
Irvine
Los Angeles
Riverside
Santa Barbara
University of San Diego
University of San Francisco
University of Southern California W
University of the Pacific W

Colorado
Colorado Christian University M
Colorado State University
Metropolitan State College of Denver M
United States Air Force Academy
University of Colorado
Boulder

Connecticut
Central Connecticut State University
Fairfield University
Quinnipiac University
Sacred Heart University
University of Connecticut
University of Hartford
Yale University

Delaware
Delaware State University
University of Delaware

District of Columbia
American University
George Washington University
Georgetown University
Howard University

Florida
Bethune-Cookman College
Florida Agricultural and Mechanical University
Florida Atlantic University
Florida International University
Florida State University
Jacksonville University
Stetson University
University of Central Florida
University of Florida
University of Miami
University of South Florida
University of Tampa M

Georgia
Georgia Institute of Technology
Georgia Southern University W
Georgia State University
Mercer University
North Georgia College & State University M
Savannah State University
University of Georgia

Hawaii
University of Hawaii
Manoa W

Idaho
Boise State University
Idaho State University
University of Idaho

Illinois
Bradley University
Chicago State University
DePaul University
Eastern Illinois University
Illinois State University
Loyola University of Chicago
Northern Illinois University W
Northwestern University W
Southern Illinois University
Carbondale
University of Illinois
Chicago
Urbana-Champaign
Western Illinois University

Indiana
Ball State University W
Butler University
Indiana State University
Indiana University
Bloomington
Indiana University-Purdue University Fort Wayne
Indiana University-Purdue University Indianapolis
Purdue University
University of Evansville
University of Notre Dame
Valparaiso University

Iowa
Drake University
Iowa State University
University of Iowa
University of Northern Iowa

Kansas
Kansas State University
University of Kansas
Wichita State University

Kentucky
Eastern Kentucky University
Morehead State University
Murray State University
University of Kentucky
University of Louisville
Western Kentucky University

Louisiana
Centenary College of Louisiana
Grambling State University
Louisiana State University and Agricultural and Mechanical College
Louisiana Tech University
Nicholls State University
Northwestern State University
Southeastern Louisiana University
Southern University and Agricultural and Mechanical College
Tulane University W
University of Louisiana at Lafayette
University of Louisiana at Monroe
University of New Orleans

Maine
University of Maine

Maryland
Coppin State University
Loyola College in Maryland
Morgan State University
Mount St. Mary's University
Towson University W
United States Naval Academy
University of Maryland
Baltimore County
College Park
Eastern Shore

Massachusetts
Boston College
Boston University
College of the Holy Cross
Harvard College W
Northeastern University
University of Massachusetts
Amherst

Michigan
Central Michigan University
Eastern Michigan University
Michigan State University
Oakland University
University of Detroit Mercy
University of Michigan
Western Michigan University W

Minnesota
University of Minnesota
Twin Cities

Mississippi
Alcorn State University
Jackson State University
Mississippi State University
Mississippi Valley State University
University of Mississippi
University of Southern Mississippi W

Missouri
Missouri State University
St. Louis University
Southeast Missouri State University
University of Missouri
Columbia
Kansas City

Montana
Montana State University
Bozeman
University of Montana: Missoula

Nebraska
Creighton University
University of Nebraska
Lincoln

Nevada
University of Nevada
Las Vegas W
Reno W

New Hampshire
Dartmouth College
University of New Hampshire

New Jersey
Fairleigh Dickinson University
Metropolitan Campus
Monmouth University
Princeton University
Rider University
Rutgers, The State University of New Jersey
New Brunswick Regional Campus
St. Peter's College
Seton Hall University

New Mexico
New Mexico State University
University of New Mexico
Western New Mexico University M

New York
Barnard College W
Canisius College
Colgate University
Columbia University
Columbia College M
Cornell University
Fordham University
Hofstra University
Iona College
Long Island University
Brooklyn Campus
Manhattan College
Marist College
Niagara University
St. Bonaventure University
St. Francis College
St. John's University W
Siena College
State University of New York
Albany
Binghamton
Buffalo
Stony Brook W
Syracuse University
United States Military Academy
Wagner College

North Carolina
Appalachian State University
Campbell University
Davidson College
Duke University
East Carolina University
Elon University
Gardner-Webb University
High Point University
North Carolina Agricultural and Technical State University
North Carolina State University
University of North Carolina
Asheville
Chapel Hill
Charlotte
Greensboro
Wilmington
Wake Forest University
Western Carolina University

Ohio
Bowling Green State University
Cleveland State University W
Kent State University
Miami University
Oxford Campus

Ohio State University
Columbus Campus
Ohio University
University of Akron
University of Cincinnati
University of Dayton
University of Toledo
Wright State University
Xavier University
Youngstown State University

Oklahoma
Cameron University M
Oklahoma State University
Oral Roberts University
University of Oklahoma
University of Tulsa

Oregon
Oregon State University W
Portland State University
University of Oregon
University of Portland

Pennsylvania
Bucknell University
Duquesne University
La Salle University
Lafayette College
Lehigh University
Penn State
University Park
Philadelphia University M
Robert Morris University
St. Francis University
St. Joseph's University
Temple University
University of Pennsylvania
University of Pittsburgh
Villanova University

Rhode Island
Brown University
Providence College
University of Rhode Island

South Carolina
Charleston Southern University
The Citadel
Clemson University
Coastal Carolina University
College of Charleston
Furman University
South Carolina State University
University of South Carolina W
Winthrop University
Wofford College

Tennessee
Austin Peay State University
Belmont University
East Tennessee State University
Lipscomb University
Middle Tennessee State University
Tennessee State University
Tennessee Technological University
University of Memphis
University of Tennessee
Chattanooga
Knoxville
Martin
Vanderbilt University

Texas
Baylor University
Lamar University
Prairie View A&M University
Rice University
Sam Houston State University
Southern Methodist University W
Stephen F. Austin State University
Texas A&M University
Texas Christian University
Texas Southern University
Texas State University: San Marcos
Texas Tech University
University of Houston
University of North Texas
University of Texas
Arlington
Austin
El Paso
Pan American
San Antonio

Utah
Brigham Young University
Southern Utah University
University of Utah W
Utah State University
Utah Valley State College
Weber State University

Vermont
University of Vermont

Virginia
College of William and Mary
George Mason University
Hampton University
James Madison University
Liberty University
Norfolk State University
Radford University
University of Richmond
University of Virginia
Virginia Commonwealth University
Virginia Military Institute
Virginia Polytechnic Institute and State University

Washington
Eastern Washington University
Gonzaga University
University of Washington
Washington State University

West Virginia
Marshall University
West Virginia University W

Wisconsin
Marquette University
University of Wisconsin
Green Bay
Madison
Milwaukee

Wyoming
University of Wyoming

Cross-country Division II

Alabama
Miles College
Stillman College
Tuskegee University
University of Alabama
Huntsville
University of Montevallo W
University of North Alabama
University of West Alabama

Alaska
University of Alaska
Anchorage
Fairbanks

Arkansas
Arkansas Tech University W
Harding University
Henderson State University W
Ouachita Baptist University W
Southern Arkansas University
University of Arkansas
Monticello W
University of Central Arkansas

California
California State Polytechnic University: Pomona
California State University
Bakersfield W
Chico
Dominguez Hills W
Los Angeles W
Monterey Bay
San Bernardino W
Stanislaus
Humboldt State University
Notre Dame de Namur University W
San Francisco State University
Sonoma State University W
University of California
Davis
San Diego

Colorado
Adams State College
Colorado Christian University W
Colorado School of Mines
Colorado State University
Pueblo W
Fort Lewis College
Mesa State College W
Metropolitan State College of Denver W
Regis University
University of Colorado
Colorado Springs
University of Northern Colorado W
Western State College of Colorado

Connecticut
Mitchell College M
Post University
Southern Connecticut State University
University of Bridgeport
University of New Haven

Delaware
Goldey-Beacom College
Wilmington College

District of Columbia
University of the District of Columbia

Florida
Florida Gulf Coast University
Florida Institute of Technology
Florida Southern College
Nova Southeastern University
Palm Beach Atlantic University
Rollins College
St. Leo University
University of North Florida
University of Tampa W
University of West Florida

Georgia
Albany State University
Augusta State University W
Clark Atlanta University
Clayton State University
Columbus State University
Fort Valley State University
Georgia College and State University
Kennesaw State University
Morehouse College M
North Georgia College & State University W
Paine College
University of West Georgia W
Valdosta State University

Hawaii
Brigham Young University-Hawaii
Chaminade University of Honolulu
Hawaii Pacific University
University of Hawaii
Hilo

Idaho
Northwest Nazarene University

Illinois
Lewis University
Southern Illinois University
Edwardsville

Indiana
Oakland City University
St. Joseph's College
University of Indianapolis
University of Southern Indiana

Kansas
Emporia State University
Fort Hays State University
Pittsburg State University

Kentucky
Bellarmine University
Kentucky State University
Northern Kentucky University

Maryland
Bowie State University
Columbia Union College

Massachusetts
Assumption College
Bentley College
Merrimack College
Stonehill College
University of Massachusetts
Lowell

Michigan
Ferris State University
Grand Valley State University
Hillsdale College
Lake Superior State University
Michigan Technological University
Northern Michigan University W
Northwood University
Saginaw Valley State University
Wayne State University

Minnesota
Bemidji State University W
Concordia University: St. Paul
Minnesota State University
Mankato
Moorhead
North Central University M
St. Cloud State University
University of Minnesota
Duluth
Morris W
Winona State University

Mississippi
Delta State University W

Missouri
Central Missouri State University
Drury University
Lincoln University W
Missouri Southern State University
Northwest Missouri State University
Southwest Baptist University
Truman State University
University of Missouri
Rolla

Montana
Montana State University
Billings

Nebraska
University of Nebraska
Kearney
Omaha W
Wayne State College

New Hampshire
Franklin Pierce College
St. Anselm College
Southern New Hampshire University

New Jersey
Bloomfield College
Caldwell College W
Felician College
Georgian Court University W
New Jersey Institute of Technology

New Mexico
Eastern New Mexico University
New Mexico Highlands University
Western New Mexico University W

New York
Adelphi University
College of Saint Rose
Concordia College
Dominican College of Blauvelt
Dowling College W
Le Moyne College
Long Island University
C. W. Post Campus
Mercy College
Molloy College
New York Institute of Technology
Nyack College
Pace University
St. Thomas Aquinas College
State University of New York
Purchase M
Wells College M

North Carolina
Barton College
Belmont Abbey College
Catawba College
Elizabeth City State University
Fayetteville State University
Johnson C. Smith University
Lees-McRae College
Lenoir-Rhyne College
Livingstone College
Mars Hill College
Mount Olive College
North Carolina Central University
Pfeiffer University
Queens University of Charlotte
St. Andrews Presbyterian College
St. Augustine's College
Shaw University
University of North Carolina
Pembroke
Wingate University
Winston-Salem State University

North Dakota
North Dakota State University
University of Mary W
University of North Dakota

Ohio
Ashland University
Central State University
Tiffin University
University of Findlay

Oklahoma
East Central University
Oklahoma Panhandle State University
Southeastern Oklahoma State University W
Southwestern Oklahoma State University W
University of Central Oklahoma W

Oregon
Western Oregon University

Pennsylvania
Bloomsburg University of Pennsylvania
California University of Pennsylvania

Cheyney University of Pennsylvania
Clarion University of Pennsylvania
East Stroudsburg University of Pennsylvania
Eastern University M
Edinboro University of Pennsylvania
Gannon University
Holy Family University
Indiana University of Pennsylvania
Kutztown University of Pennsylvania
Lock Haven University of Pennsylvania
Mansfield University of Pennsylvania
Mercyhurst College
Millersville University of Pennsylvania
Mount Aloysius College M
Philadelphia University W
Shippensburg University of Pennsylvania
Slippery Rock University of Pennsylvania
University of Pittsburgh
Johnstown W
University of the Sciences in Philadelphia
West Chester University of Pennsylvania

Puerto Rico
University of Puerto Rico
Bayamon University College
Cayey University College
Mayaguez
Rio Piedras

Rhode Island
Bryant University
Salve Regina University M

South Carolina
Anderson University
Benedict College
Claflin University
Coker College
Converse College W
Erskine College
Francis Marion University
Lander University W
Limestone College
Newberry College
North Greenville College
Presbyterian College
University of South Carolina
Aiken W

South Dakota
Augustana College
Northern State University
South Dakota State University
University of South Dakota

Tennessee
Carson-Newman College
Christian Brothers University
LeMoyne-Owen College
Lincoln Memorial University
Tusculum College

Texas
Abilene Christian University
Angelo State University
Dallas Baptist University
Midwestern State University W
St. Edward's University
St. Mary's University W
Tarleton State University
Texas A&M University
Commerce
Kingsville
University of the Incarnate Word
West Texas A&M University

Vermont
Green Mountain College
St. Michael's College

Virginia
Longwood University
St. Paul's College
Virginia State University
Virginia Union University

Washington
Central Washington University
Saint Martin's University
Seattle Pacific University
Seattle University
Western Washington University

West Virginia
Alderson-Broaddus College
Bluefield State College
Concord University
Davis and Elkins College
Glenville State College
Ohio Valley University
Salem International University M
University of Charleston
West Liberty State College
West Virginia Wesleyan College
Wheeling Jesuit University

Wisconsin
University of Wisconsin
Parkside

Cross-country Division III

Arkansas
Hendrix College
University of the Ozarks

California
California Institute of Technology
California Lutheran University
California State University
East Bay
Chapman University
Claremont McKenna College
Harvey Mudd College M
Menlo College
Mills College W
Occidental College
Pitzer College
Pomona College
University of California
Santa Cruz W
University of La Verne
University of Redlands
Whittier College

Colorado
Colorado College

Connecticut
Albertus Magnus College
Connecticut College
Eastern Connecticut State University
Mitchell College W
St. Joseph College W
Trinity College
United States Coast Guard Academy
Wesleyan University

Delaware
Wesley College

District of Columbia
Catholic University of America

Georgia
Agnes Scott College W
Emory University
LaGrange College
Oglethorpe University
Piedmont College
Spelman College W

Illinois
Augustana College
Aurora University
Benedictine University
Blackburn College
Concordia University
Dominican University
Elmhurst College
Greenville College
Illinois College
Illinois Wesleyan University
Knox College
Lake Forest College
MacMurray College
Millikin University
Monmouth College
North Central College
North Park University
Principia College
Rockford College
University of Chicago
Wheaton College

Indiana
Anderson University
DePauw University
Earlham College
Franklin College
Hanover College
Manchester College
Rose-Hulman Institute of Technology
Saint Mary's College W
Tri-State University
Wabash College M

Iowa
Buena Vista University
Central College
Clarke College
Coe College
Cornell College
Grinnell College
Loras College
Luther College
Simpson College
University of Dubuque
Wartburg College

Kentucky
Centre College
Thomas More College
Transylvania University

Maine
Bates College
Bowdoin College
Colby College
Maine Maritime Academy
St. Joseph's College
University of Maine
Farmington
Presque Isle
University of New England
University of Southern Maine

Maryland
Frostburg State University
Goucher College
Hood College
Johns Hopkins University
McDaniel College
Salisbury University
Villa Julie College

Massachusetts
Amherst College
Anna Maria College M
Babson College
Bay Path College W
Becker College M
Brandeis University
Bridgewater State College
Clark University
Curry College W
Eastern Nazarene College
Elms College
Emerson College
Emmanuel College
Endicott College
Fitchburg State College
Framingham State College
Gordon College
Lasell College
Massachusetts College of Liberal Arts
Massachusetts Institute of Technology
Massachusetts Maritime Academy
Mount Holyoke College W
Mount Ida College W
Newbury College
Pine Manor College W
Regis College W
Salem State College
Smith College W
Springfield College
Suffolk University
Tufts University
University of Massachusetts
Boston
Dartmouth
Wellesley College W
Western New England College
Westfield State College
Wheaton College
Williams College
Worcester Polytechnic Institute
Worcester State College

Michigan
Adrian College
Albion College
Alma College
Calvin College
Finlandia University
Hope College
Kalamazoo College
Olivet College

Minnesota
Augsburg College
Bethel University
Carleton College
College of St. Benedict W
College of St. Catherine W
College of St. Scholastica
Concordia College: Moorhead
Crown College
Gustavus Adolphus College
Hamline University
Macalester College
Martin Luther College
North Central University W
Northwestern College
St. John's University M
St. Mary's University of Minnesota
St. Olaf College
University of St. Thomas

Mississippi
Millsaps College
Mississippi College
Rust College

Missouri
Fontbonne University W
Maryville University of Saint Louis
Washington University in St. Louis
Webster University W
Westminster College W

Nebraska
Nebraska Wesleyan University

New Hampshire
Daniel Webster College
Keene State College
New England College
Rivier College

New Jersey
Centenary College
The College of New Jersey
Drew University
Fairleigh Dickinson University
College at Florham
Kean University
Montclair State University M
New Jersey City University
Ramapo College of New Jersey
Richard Stockton College of New Jersey
Rowan University
Rutgers, The State University of New Jersey
Camden Regional Campus
Stevens Institute of Technology
William Paterson University of New Jersey

New York
Alfred University
Bard College
Cazenovia College
City University of New York
Baruch College W
Brooklyn College
Hunter College
John Jay College of Criminal Justice
Lehman College
Medgar Evers College
New York City College of Technology
York College
Clarkson University
College of Mount St. Vincent
College of New Rochelle W
D'Youville College W
Hamilton College
Hartwick College
Hilbert College
Hobart and William Smith Colleges
Ithaca College
Keuka College
Medaille College W
Nazareth College of Rochester
New York University
Polytechnic University
Rensselaer Polytechnic Institute
Rochester Institute of Technology
St. Joseph's College W
St. Joseph's College: Suffolk Campus M
St. Lawrence University
State University of New York
College at Brockport
College at Buffalo
College at Cortland
College at Fredonia
College at Geneseo
College at Old Westbury
College at Oneonta
College at Plattsburgh
College at Potsdam
Farmingdale
Institute of Technology at Utica/Rome
Maritime College
New Paltz
Oswego
Union College
United States Merchant Marine Academy
University of Rochester
Vassar College
Wells College W
Yeshiva University M

North Carolina
Chowan College W
Greensboro College
Guilford College
Methodist College
Peace College W
Salem College W

Ohio
Baldwin-Wallace College
Bluffton University
Capital University

Case Western Reserve University
College of Mount St. Joseph
College of Wooster
Defiance College
Denison University
Heidelberg College
Hiram College
John Carroll University
Kenyon College
Lake Erie College
Marietta College
Mount Union College
Muskingum College
Oberlin College
Ohio Northern University
Ohio Wesleyan University
Otterbein College
Wilmington College
Wittenberg University

Oregon
George Fox University
Lewis & Clark College
Linfield College
Pacific University
Willamette University

Pennsylvania
Albright College
Allegheny College
Alvernia College
Arcadia University
Baptist Bible College of
Pennsylvania
Bryn Mawr College W
Cabrini College
Carnegie Mellon University
Cedar Crest College W
Chestnut Hill College
College Misericordia
Delaware Valley College
DeSales University
Dickinson College
Elizabethtown College
Franklin & Marshall College
Gettysburg College
Grove City College
Gwynedd-Mercy College
Haverford College
Immaculata University W
Juniata College
Keystone College
King's College
La Roche College
Lebanon Valley College
Lincoln University
Lycoming College
Marywood University
Messiah College
Moravian College
Mount Aloysius College W
Muhlenberg College
Penn State
Altoona
Berks
Erie, The Behrend College
Susquehanna University
Swarthmore College
Thiel College
University of Pittsburgh
Bradford
Greensburg
University of Scranton
Ursinus College
Washington and Jefferson College
Waynesburg College
Westminster College M
Widener University
York College of Pennsylvania

Rhode Island
Johnson & Wales University
Rhode Island College
Roger Williams University
Salve Regina University W

South Dakota
Presentation College

Tennessee
Fisk University
Maryville College
Rhodes College
University of the South

Texas
Concordia University at Austin
East Texas Baptist University
LeTourneau University
McMurry University
Southwestern University
Sul Ross State University
Texas Lutheran University W
Trinity University
University of Dallas
University of Texas
Dallas
Tyler

Vermont
Castleton State College
Johnson State College
Middlebury College
Norwich University
Southern Vermont College

Virginia
Averett University
Bridgewater College
Christopher Newport University
Eastern Mennonite University M
Emory & Henry College
Ferrum College
Hampden-Sydney College M
Lynchburg College
Mary Baldwin College W
Marymount University
Roanoke College
Shenandoah University
University of Mary Washington
Virginia Wesleyan College
Washington and Lee University

Washington
Pacific Lutheran University
University of Puget Sound
Whitman College
Whitworth College

West Virginia
Bethany College

Wisconsin
Alverno College W
Beloit College
Carroll College
Carthage College
Concordia University Wisconsin
Edgewood College
Lakeland College
Lawrence University
Maranatha Baptist Bible College
Milwaukee School of Engineering
Northland College
Ripon College
St. Norbert College
University of Wisconsin
Eau Claire
La Crosse
Oshkosh
Platteville
River Falls
Stevens Point
Stout
Superior
Whitewater
Wisconsin Lutheran College

Fencing Division I

California
California State University
Fullerton
Stanford University

Colorado
United States Air Force Academy

Connecticut
Sacred Heart University
Yale University

Illinois
Northwestern University W

Indiana
University of Notre Dame

Massachusetts
Boston College
Harvard College

Michigan
University of Detroit Mercy

New Jersey
Fairleigh Dickinson University
Metropolitan Campus W
Princeton University
Rutgers, The State University of
New Jersey
New Brunswick Regional
Campus

New York
Barnard College W
Columbia University
Columbia College M
Cornell University W
St. John's University

North Carolina
Duke University
University of North Carolina
Chapel Hill

Ohio
Cleveland State University
Ohio State University
Columbus Campus

Pennsylvania
Lafayette College
Penn State
University Park
Temple University W
University of Pennsylvania

Rhode Island
Brown University

Virginia
James Madison University W

Fencing Division II

California
University of California
San Diego

Michigan
Wayne State University

New Jersey
New Jersey Institute of
Technology

New York
City University of New York
Queens College W

Fencing Division III

California
California Institute of Technology

Maryland
Johns Hopkins University

Massachusetts
Brandeis University
Massachusetts Institute of
Technology
Tufts University W
Wellesley College W

New Jersey
Drew University
Stevens Institute of Technology

New York
City University of New York
City College W
Hunter College
New York University
Vassar College
Yeshiva University M

Pennsylvania
Haverford College

Wisconsin
Lawrence University

Field hockey Division I

California
Stanford University W
University of California
Berkeley W
University of the Pacific W

Connecticut
Fairfield University W
Quinnipiac University W
Sacred Heart University W
University of Connecticut W
Yale University W

Delaware
University of Delaware W

District of Columbia
American University W
Georgetown University W

Illinois
Northwestern University W

Indiana
Ball State University W
Indiana University
Bloomington W

Iowa
University of Iowa W

Kentucky
University of Louisville W

Maine
University of Maine W

Maryland
Towson University W
University of Maryland
Baltimore County W
College Park W

Massachusetts
Boston College W
Boston University W
College of the Holy Cross W
Harvard College W
Northeastern University W
University of Massachusetts
Amherst W

Michigan
Central Michigan University W
Michigan State University W
University of Michigan W

Missouri
Missouri State University W
St. Louis University W

New Hampshire
Dartmouth College W
University of New Hampshire W

New Jersey
Monmouth University W
Princeton University W
Rider University W
Rutgers, The State University of
New Jersey
New Brunswick Regional
Campus W

New York
Barnard College W
Colgate University W
Cornell University W
Hofstra University W
Siena College W
State University of New York
Albany W
Syracuse University W

North Carolina
Appalachian State University W
Davidson College W
Duke University W
University of North Carolina
Chapel Hill W
Wake Forest University W

Ohio
Kent State University W
Miami University
Oxford Campus W
Ohio State University
Columbus Campus W
Ohio University W

Pennsylvania
Bucknell University W
Drexel University W
La Salle University W
Lafayette College W
Lehigh University W
Penn State
University Park W
Robert Morris University W
St. Francis University W
St. Joseph's University W
Temple University W
University of Pennsylvania W
Villanova University W
West Chester University of
Pennsylvania W

Rhode Island
Brown University W
Providence College W
University of Rhode Island W

Vermont
University of Vermont W

Virginia
College of William and Mary W
James Madison University W
Old Dominion University W
Radford University W
University of Richmond W
University of Virginia W
Virginia Commonwealth
University W

Field hockey Division II

Connecticut
Southern Connecticut State
University W

Kentucky
Bellarmine University W

Massachusetts
American International College
W
Assumption College W
Bentley College W
Merrimack College W
Stonehill College W
University of Massachusetts
Lowell W

New Hampshire
Franklin Pierce College W
St. Anselm College W

New York
Long Island University
C. W. Post Campus W

North Carolina
Catawba College W

Pennsylvania
Bloomsburg University of Pennsylvania W
East Stroudsburg University of Pennsylvania W
Indiana University of Pennsylvania W
Kutztown University of Pennsylvania W
Lock Haven University of Pennsylvania W
Mansfield University of Pennsylvania W
Mercyhurst College W
Millersville University of Pennsylvania W
Philadelphia University W
Shippensburg University of Pennsylvania W
Slippery Rock University of Pennsylvania W

Rhode Island
Bryant University W

Vermont
St. Michael's College W

Virginia
Longwood University W

Field hockey Division III

Connecticut
Connecticut College W
Eastern Connecticut State University W
Trinity College W
Wesleyan University W
Western Connecticut State University W

Delaware
Wesley College W

District of Columbia
Catholic University of America W

Indiana
DePauw University W
Earlham College W

Kentucky
Centre College W
Transylvania University W

Maine
Bates College W
Bowdoin College W
Colby College W
Husson College W
St. Joseph's College W
Thomas College W
University of Maine Farmington W
University of New England W
University of Southern Maine W

Maryland
College of Notre Dame of Maryland W
Frostburg State University W
Goucher College W
Hood College W
Johns Hopkins University W
McDaniel College W
St. Mary's College of Maryland W
Salisbury University W
Villa Julie College W
Washington College W

Massachusetts
Amherst College W
Anna Maria College W
Babson College W
Becker College W
Bridgewater State College W
Clark University W
Elms College W
Endicott College W
Fitchburg State College W
Framingham State College W
Gordon College W
Lasell College W
Massachusetts Institute of Technology W
Mount Holyoke College W
Nichols College W
Regis College W
Salem State College W
Simmons College W
Smith College W
Springfield College W
Tufts University W
University of Massachusetts Dartmouth W
Wellesley College W
Western New England College W
Westfield State College W
Wheaton College W
Wheelock College W
Williams College W
Worcester Polytechnic Institute W
Worcester State College W

New Hampshire
Keene State College W
New England College W
Plymouth State University W

New Jersey
The College of New Jersey W
Drew University W
Fairleigh Dickinson University College at Florham W
Kean University W
Montclair State University W
Ramapo College of New Jersey W
Richard Stockton College of New Jersey W
Rowan University W
Stevens Institute of Technology W
William Paterson University of New Jersey W

New York
Elmira College W
Hamilton College W
Hartwick College W
Hobart and William Smith Colleges W
Ithaca College W
Manhattanville College W
Nazareth College of Rochester W
Rensselaer Polytechnic Institute W
St. Lawrence University W
Skidmore College W
State University of New York
College at Brockport W
College at Cortland W
College at Geneseo W
College at Oneonta W
New Paltz W
Oswego W
Union College W
University of Rochester W
Utica College W
Vassar College W
Wells College W

Ohio
College of Wooster W
Denison University W
Kenyon College W
Oberlin College W
Ohio Wesleyan University W
Wittenberg University W

Pennsylvania
Albright College W
Alvernia College W
Arcadia University W
Bryn Mawr College W
Cabrini College W
Cedar Crest College W
College Misericordia W
Delaware Valley College W
DeSales University W
Dickinson College W
Eastern University W
Elizabethtown College W
Franklin & Marshall College W
Gettysburg College W
Gwynedd-Mercy College W
Haverford College W
Immaculata University W
Juniata College W
King's College W
Lebanon Valley College W
Marywood University W
Messiah College W
Moravian College W
Muhlenberg College W
Neumann College W
Philadelphia Biblical University W
Rosemont College W
Susquehanna University W
Swarthmore College W
University of Scranton W
Ursinus College W
Washington and Jefferson College W
Widener University W
Wilkes University W
Wilson College W
York College of Pennsylvania W

Rhode Island
Salve Regina University W

Tennessee
Rhodes College W
University of the South W

Vermont
Castleton State College W
Middlebury College W

Virginia
Bridgewater College W
Christopher Newport University W
Eastern Mennonite University W
Hollins University W
Lynchburg College W
Mary Baldwin College W
Randolph-Macon College W
Randolph-Macon Woman's College W
Roanoke College W
Shenandoah University W
Sweet Briar College W
University of Mary Washington W
Virginia Wesleyan College W
Washington and Lee University W

Football (tackle) Division IA

Alabama
Auburn University M
Troy University M
University of Alabama M
University of Alabama Birmingham M

Arizona
Arizona State University M
University of Arizona M

Arkansas
Arkansas State University M
University of Arkansas M

California
California State University Fresno M
San Diego State University M
San Jose State University M
Stanford University M
University of California
Berkeley M
Los Angeles M
University of Southern California M

Colorado
Colorado State University M
United States Air Force Academy M
University of Colorado Boulder M

Connecticut
University of Connecticut M

Florida
Florida State University M
University of Central Florida M
University of Florida M
University of Miami M
University of South Florida M

Georgia
Georgia Institute of Technology M
University of Georgia M

Hawaii
University of Hawaii Manoa M

Idaho
Boise State University M
University of Idaho M

Illinois
Northern Illinois University M
Northwestern University M
University of Illinois Urbana-Champaign M

Indiana
Ball State University M
Indiana University Bloomington M
Purdue University M
University of Notre Dame M

Iowa
Iowa State University M
University of Iowa M

Kansas
Kansas State University M
University of Kansas M

Kentucky
University of Kentucky M
University of Louisville M

Louisiana
Louisiana State University and Agricultural and Mechanical College M
Louisiana Tech University M
Tulane University M
University of Louisiana at Lafayette M
University of Louisiana at Monroe M

Maryland
United States Naval Academy M
University of Maryland College Park M

Massachusetts
Boston College M

Michigan
Central Michigan University M
Eastern Michigan University M
Michigan State University M
University of Michigan M
Western Michigan University M

Minnesota
University of Minnesota Twin Cities M

Mississippi
Mississippi State University M
University of Mississippi M
University of Southern Mississippi M

Missouri
University of Missouri Columbia M

Nebraska
University of Nebraska Lincoln M

Nevada
University of Nevada
Las Vegas M
Reno M

New Jersey
Rutgers, The State University of New Jersey
New Brunswick Regional Campus M

New Mexico
New Mexico State University M
University of New Mexico M

New York
State University of New York Buffalo M
Syracuse University M
United States Military Academy M

North Carolina
Duke University M
East Carolina University M
North Carolina State University M
University of North Carolina Chapel Hill M
Wake Forest University M

Ohio
Bowling Green State University M
Kent State University M
Miami University Oxford Campus M
Ohio State University Columbus Campus M
Ohio University M
University of Akron M
University of Cincinnati M
University of Toledo M

Oklahoma
Oklahoma State University M
University of Oklahoma M
University of Tulsa M

Oregon
Oregon State University M
University of Oregon M

Pennsylvania
Penn State University Park M
Temple University M
University of Pittsburgh M

South Carolina
Clemson University M
University of South Carolina M

Tennessee
Middle Tennessee State University M
University of Memphis M
University of Tennessee Knoxville M
Vanderbilt University M

Texas
Baylor University M
Rice University M

Southern Methodist University M
Texas A&M University M
Texas Christian University M
Texas Tech University M
University of Houston M
University of North Texas M
University of Texas
Austin M
El Paso M

Utah
Brigham Young University M
University of Utah M
Utah State University M

Virginia
University of Virginia M
Virginia Polytechnic Institute and State University M

Washington
University of Washington M
Washington State University M

West Virginia
Marshall University M
West Virginia University M

Wisconsin
University of Wisconsin
Madison M

Wyoming
University of Wyoming M

Football (tackle) Division IAA

Alabama
Alabama Agricultural and Mechanical University M
Alabama State University M
Jacksonville State University M
Samford University M

Arizona
Northern Arizona University M

Arkansas
University of Arkansas
Pine Bluff M

California
California Polytechnic State University: San Luis Obispo M
California State University
Sacramento M
St. Mary's College of California M
University of San Diego M

Connecticut
Central Connecticut State University M
Sacred Heart University M
Yale University M

Delaware
Delaware State University M
University of Delaware M

District of Columbia
Georgetown University M
Howard University M

Florida
Bethune-Cookman College M
Florida Agricultural and Mechanical University M
Florida Atlantic University M
Florida International University M
Jacksonville University M

Georgia
Georgia Southern University M
Savannah State University M

Idaho
Idaho State University M

Illinois
Eastern Illinois University M
Illinois State University M
Southern Illinois University
Carbondale M
Western Illinois University M

Indiana
Butler University M
Indiana State University M
Valparaiso University M

Iowa
Drake University M
University of Northern Iowa M

Kentucky
Eastern Kentucky University M
Morehead State University M
Murray State University M
Western Kentucky University M

Louisiana
Grambling State University M
Nicholls State University M
Northwestern State University M
Southeastern Louisiana University M
Southern University and Agricultural and Mechanical College M

Maine
University of Maine M

Maryland
Morgan State University M
Towson University M

Massachusetts
College of the Holy Cross M
Northeastern University M
University of Massachusetts
Amherst M

Mississippi
Alcorn State University M
Jackson State University M
Mississippi Valley State University M

Missouri
Missouri State University M
Southeast Missouri State University M

Montana
Montana State University
Bozeman M
University of Montana: Missoula M

New Hampshire
Dartmouth College M
University of New Hampshire M

New Jersey
Monmouth University M
Princeton University M
St. Peter's College M

New York
Colgate University M
Cornell University M
Fordham University M
Hofstra University M
Iona College M
Marist College M
State University of New York
Albany M
Stony Brook M
Wagner College M

North Carolina
Appalachian State University M
Davidson College M
Elon University M
Gardner-Webb University M
North Carolina Agricultural and Technical State University M
Western Carolina University M

Ohio
University of Dayton M
Youngstown State University M

Oregon
Portland State University M

Pennsylvania
Bucknell University M
Duquesne University M
La Salle University M
Lafayette College M
Lehigh University M
Robert Morris University M
St. Francis University M
University of Pennsylvania M
Villanova University M

Rhode Island
Brown University M
University of Rhode Island M

South Carolina
Charleston Southern University M
The Citadel M
Coastal Carolina University M
Furman University M
South Carolina State University M
Wofford College M

Tennessee
Austin Peay State University M
Tennessee State University M
Tennessee Technological University M
University of Tennessee
Chattanooga M
Martin M

Texas
Prairie View A&M University M
Sam Houston State University M
Stephen F. Austin State University M
Texas Southern University M
Texas State University: San Marcos M

Utah
Southern Utah University M
Weber State University M

Virginia
College of William and Mary M
Hampton University M
James Madison University M
Liberty University M
Norfolk State University M
University of Richmond M
Virginia Military Institute M

Washington
Eastern Washington University M

Football (tackle) Division II

Alabama
Miles College M
Stillman College M
Tuskegee University M
University of North Alabama M
University of West Alabama M

Arkansas
Arkansas Tech University M
Harding University M
Henderson State University M
Ouachita Baptist University M
Southern Arkansas University M
University of Arkansas
Monticello M
University of Central Arkansas M

California
Humboldt State University M
University of California
Davis M

Colorado
Adams State College M
Colorado School of Mines M
Fort Lewis College M
Mesa State College M
University of Northern Colorado M
Western State College of Colorado M

Connecticut
Southern Connecticut State University M

Georgia
Albany State University M
Clark Atlanta University M
Fort Valley State University M
Morehouse College M
University of West Georgia M
Valdosta State University M

Illinois
Quincy University M

Indiana
St. Joseph's College M
University of Indianapolis M

Iowa
Upper Iowa University M

Kansas
Emporia State University M
Fort Hays State University M
Pittsburg State University M
Washburn University of Topeka M

Kentucky
Kentucky State University M
Kentucky Wesleyan College M

Maryland
Bowie State University M

Massachusetts
American International College M
Assumption College M
Bentley College M
Merrimack College M
Stonehill College M

Michigan
Ferris State University M
Grand Valley State University M
Hillsdale College M
Michigan Technological University M
Northern Michigan University M
Northwood University M
Saginaw Valley State University M
Wayne State University M

Minnesota
Bemidji State University M
Concordia University: St. Paul M
Minnesota State University
Mankato M
Moorhead M
St. Cloud State University M
Southwest Minnesota State University M
University of Minnesota
Crookston M
Duluth M
Morris M
Winona State University M

Mississippi
Delta State University M

Missouri
Central Missouri State University M
Lincoln University M
Missouri Southern State University M
Missouri Western State University M
Northwest Missouri State University M
Southwest Baptist University M
Truman State University M
University of Missouri
Rolla M

Nebraska
Chadron State College M
University of Nebraska
Kearney M
Omaha M
Wayne State College M

New Hampshire
St. Anselm College M

New Mexico
Eastern New Mexico University M
New Mexico Highlands University M
Western New Mexico University M

New York
Long Island University
C. W. Post Campus M
Pace University M

North Carolina
Catawba College M
Elizabeth City State University M
Fayetteville State University M
Johnson C. Smith University M
Lenoir-Rhyne College M
Livingstone College M
Mars Hill College M
North Carolina Central University M
St. Augustine's College M
Shaw University M
Wingate University M
Winston-Salem State University M

North Dakota
North Dakota State University M
University of North Dakota M

Ohio
Ashland University M
Central State University M
Tiffin University M
University of Findlay M

Oklahoma
East Central University M
Northeastern State University M
Oklahoma Panhandle State University M
Southeastern Oklahoma State University M
Southwestern Oklahoma State University M
University of Central Oklahoma M

Oregon
Western Oregon University M

Pennsylvania
Bloomsburg University of Pennsylvania M
California University of Pennsylvania M
Cheyney University of Pennsylvania M
Clarion University of Pennsylvania M
East Stroudsburg University of Pennsylvania M
Edinboro University of Pennsylvania M
Gannon University M
Indiana University of Pennsylvania M
Kutztown University of Pennsylvania M

Lock Haven University of Pennsylvania M
Mansfield University of Pennsylvania M
Mercyhurst College M
Millersville University of Pennsylvania M
Shippensburg University of Pennsylvania M
Slippery Rock University of Pennsylvania M
West Chester University of Pennsylvania M

Rhode Island
Bryant University M

South Carolina
Benedict College M
Newberry College M
North Greenville College M
Presbyterian College M

South Dakota
Augustana College M
Northern State University M
South Dakota State University M
University of South Dakota M

Tennessee
Carson-Newman College M
Tusculum College M

Texas
Abilene Christian University M
Angelo State University M
Midwestern State University M
Tarleton State University M
Texas A&M University
Commerce M
Kingsville M
West Texas A&M University M

Virginia
St. Paul's College M
Virginia State University M
Virginia Union University M

Washington
Central Washington University M
Western Washington University M

West Virginia
Concord University M
Glenville State College M
Shepherd University M
University of Charleston M
West Liberty State College M
West Virginia State University M
West Virginia University Institute of Technology M
West Virginia Wesleyan College M

Football (tackle) Division III

Alabama
Huntingdon College M

California
California Lutheran University M
Chapman University M
Claremont McKenna College M
Menlo College M
Occidental College M
Pitzer College M
Pomona College M
University of La Verne M
University of Redlands M
Whittier College M

Colorado
Colorado College M

Connecticut
Trinity College M
United States Coast Guard Academy M
Wesleyan University M
Western Connecticut State University M

Delaware
Wesley College M

District of Columbia
Catholic University of America M

Illinois
Augustana College M
Aurora University M
Benedictine University M
Blackburn College M
Concordia University M
Elmhurst College M
Eureka College M
Greenville College M
Illinois College M
Illinois Wesleyan University M
Knox College M
Lake Forest College M
MacMurray College M
Millikin University M
Monmouth College M
North Central College M
North Park University M
Principia College M
Rockford College M
University of Chicago M
Wheaton College M

Indiana
Anderson University M
DePauw University M
Earlham College M
Franklin College M
Hanover College M
Manchester College M
Rose-Hulman Institute of Technology M
Tri-State University M
Wabash College M

Iowa
Buena Vista University M
Central College M
Coe College M
Cornell College M
Grinnell College M
Loras College M
Luther College M
Simpson College M
University of Dubuque M
Wartburg College M

Kentucky
Centre College M
Thomas More College M

Maine
Bates College M
Bowdoin College M
Colby College M
Husson College M
Maine Maritime Academy M

Maryland
Frostburg State University M
Johns Hopkins University M
McDaniel College M
Salisbury University M

Massachusetts
Amherst College M
Becker College M
Bridgewater State College M
Curry College M
Endicott College M
Fitchburg State College M
Framingham State College M
Massachusetts Institute of Technology M
Massachusetts Maritime Academy M
Mount Ida College M
Nichols College M
Springfield College M
Tufts University M
University of Massachusetts Dartmouth M
Western New England College M
Westfield State College M
Williams College M
Worcester Polytechnic Institute M
Worcester State College M

Michigan
Adrian College M
Albion College M
Alma College M
Hope College M
Kalamazoo College M
Olivet College M

Minnesota
Augsburg College M
Bethel University M
Carleton College M
Concordia College: Moorhead M
Crown College M
Gustavus Adolphus College M
Hamline University M
Macalester College M
Martin Luther College M
Northwestern College M
St. John's University M
St. Olaf College M
University of St. Thomas M

Mississippi
Millsaps College M
Mississippi College M

Missouri
Washington University in St. Louis M
Westminster College M

Nebraska
Nebraska Wesleyan University M

New Hampshire
Plymouth State University M

New Jersey
The College of New Jersey M
Fairleigh Dickinson University Metropolitan Campus M
Kean University M
Montclair State University M
Rowan University M
William Paterson University of New Jersey M

New York
Alfred University M
Hamilton College M
Hartwick College M
Hobart and William Smith Colleges M
Ithaca College M
Rensselaer Polytechnic Institute M
St. John Fisher College M
St. Lawrence University M
State University of New York
College at Brockport M
College at Buffalo M
College at Cortland M
Union College M
United States Merchant Marine Academy M
University of Rochester M
Utica College M

North Carolina
Chowan College M
Greensboro College M
Guilford College M
Methodist College M
North Carolina Wesleyan College M

Ohio
Baldwin-Wallace College M
Bluffton University M
Capital University M
Case Western Reserve University M
College of Mount St. Joseph M
College of Wooster M
Defiance College M
Denison University M
Heidelberg College M
Hiram College M
John Carroll University M
Kenyon College M
Marietta College M
Mount Union College M
Muskingum College M
Oberlin College M
Ohio Northern University M
Ohio Wesleyan University M
Otterbein College M
Wilmington College M
Wittenberg University M

Oregon
Lewis & Clark College M
Linfield College M
Willamette University M

Pennsylvania
Albright College M
Allegheny College M
Carnegie Mellon University M
Delaware Valley College M
Dickinson College M
Franklin & Marshall College M
Gettysburg College M
Grove City College M
Juniata College M
King's College M
Lebanon Valley College M
Lycoming College M
Moravian College M
Muhlenberg College M
Susquehanna University M
Thiel College M
Ursinus College M
Washington and Jefferson College M
Waynesburg College M
Westminster College M
Widener University M
Wilkes University M

Rhode Island
Salve Regina University M

Tennessee
Maryville College M
Rhodes College M
University of the South M

Texas
Austin College M
East Texas Baptist University M
Hardin-Simmons University M
Howard Payne University M
McMurry University M
Sul Ross State University M
Texas Lutheran University M
Trinity University M
University of Mary Hardin-Baylor M

Vermont
Middlebury College M
Norwich University M

Virginia
Averett University M
Bridgewater College M
Christopher Newport University M
Emory & Henry College M
Ferrum College M
Hampden-Sydney College M
Randolph-Macon College M
Shenandoah University M
Washington and Lee University M

Washington
Pacific Lutheran University M
University of Puget Sound M
Whitworth College M

West Virginia
Bethany College M

Wisconsin
Beloit College M
Carroll College M
Carthage College M
Concordia University Wisconsin M
Lakeland College M
Lawrence University M
Maranatha Baptist Bible College M
Ripon College M
St. Norbert College M
University of Wisconsin
Eau Claire M
La Crosse M
Oshkosh M
Platteville M
River Falls M
Stevens Point M
Stout M
Whitewater M
Wisconsin Lutheran College M

Golf Division I

Alabama
Alabama Agricultural and Mechanical University
Alabama State University
Auburn University
Birmingham-Southern College
Jacksonville State University
Samford University
Troy University
University of Alabama
University of Alabama Birmingham
University of South Alabama

Arizona
Arizona State University
Northern Arizona University W
University of Arizona

Arkansas
Arkansas State University
University of Arkansas
University of Arkansas
Little Rock
Pine Bluff

California
California Polytechnic State University: San Luis Obispo
California State University
Fresno
Long Beach
Northridge
Sacramento
Loyola Marymount University M
Pepperdine University
St. Mary's College of California M
San Diego State University
San Jose State University
Santa Clara University
Stanford University
University of California
Berkeley
Irvine
Los Angeles
Riverside
Santa Barbara M
University of San Diego M
University of San Francisco
University of Southern California
University of the Pacific M

Colorado
Colorado State University
United States Air Force Academy M
University of Colorado
Boulder

University of Denver

Connecticut
Central Connecticut State University
Fairfield University
Quinnipiac University M
Sacred Heart University
University of Connecticut M
University of Hartford
Yale University

Delaware
University of Delaware M

District of Columbia
American University M
George Washington University M
Georgetown University

Florida
Bethune-Cookman College
Florida Agricultural and Mechanical University M
Florida Atlantic University
Florida International University
Florida State University
Jacksonville University
Stetson University
University of Central Florida
University of Florida
University of Miami W
University of North Florida M
University of South Florida

Georgia
Augusta State University
Georgia Institute of Technology M
Georgia Southern University M
Georgia State University
Mercer University
Savannah State University
University of Georgia

Hawaii
University of Hawaii
Manoa

Idaho
Boise State University
Idaho State University
University of Idaho

Illinois
Bradley University
Chicago State University
DePaul University M
Eastern Illinois University
Illinois State University
Loyola University of Chicago
Northern Illinois University
Northwestern University
Southern Illinois University
Carbondale
University of Illinois
Urbana-Champaign
Western Illinois University

Indiana
Ball State University
Butler University
Indiana State University W
Indiana University
Bloomington
Indiana University-Purdue University Fort Wayne
Indiana University-Purdue University Indianapolis
Purdue University
University of Evansville
University of Notre Dame

Iowa
Drake University M
Iowa State University
University of Iowa
University of Northern Iowa

Kansas
Kansas State University
University of Kansas
Wichita State University

Kentucky
Eastern Kentucky University
Morehead State University M
Murray State University
University of Kentucky
University of Louisville
Western Kentucky University

Louisiana
Centenary College of Louisiana
Grambling State University
Louisiana State University and Agricultural and Mechanical College
Louisiana Tech University M
Nicholls State University
Southeastern Louisiana University M
Southern University and Agricultural and Mechanical College
University of Louisiana at Lafayette M
University of Louisiana at Monroe
University of New Orleans

Maryland
Loyola College in Maryland M
Mount St. Mary's University
Towson University M
United States Naval Academy M
University of Maryland
College Park

Massachusetts
Boston College
Boston University
College of the Holy Cross
Harvard College

Michigan
Eastern Michigan University
Michigan State University
Oakland University
University of Detroit Mercy
University of Michigan
Western Michigan University W

Minnesota
University of Minnesota
Twin Cities

Mississippi
Alcorn State University
Jackson State University
Mississippi State University
Mississippi Valley State University
University of Mississippi
University of Southern Mississippi

Missouri
Missouri State University
St. Louis University M
Southeast Missouri State University M
University of Missouri
Columbia
Kansas City

Montana
Montana State University
Bozeman W
University of Montana: Missoula W

Nebraska
Creighton University
University of Nebraska
Lincoln

Nevada
University of Nevada
Las Vegas
Reno

New Hampshire
Dartmouth College

New Jersey
Fairleigh Dickinson University
Metropolitan Campus M
Monmouth University
Princeton University
Rider University M
Rutgers, The State University of New Jersey
New Brunswick Regional Campus
St. Peter's College M
Seton Hall University M

New Mexico
New Mexico State University
University of New Mexico

New York
Barnard College W
Canisius College M
Colgate University M
Columbia University
Columbia College M
Cornell University M
Fordham University M
Hofstra University
Iona College M
Long Island University
Brooklyn Campus
Manhattan College M
Niagara University M
St. Bonaventure University M
St. John's University
Siena College
State University of New York
Albany W
Binghamton M
United States Military Academy M
Wagner College

North Carolina
Appalachian State University
Campbell University
Davidson College M
Duke University
East Carolina University
Elon University
Gardner-Webb University M
High Point University
North Carolina State University
University of North Carolina
Chapel Hill
Charlotte M
Greensboro
Wilmington
Wake Forest University
Western Carolina University

Ohio
Bowling Green State University
Cleveland State University
Kent State University
Miami University
Oxford Campus M
Ohio State University
Columbus Campus
Ohio University
University of Akron M
University of Cincinnati
University of Dayton
University of Toledo
Wright State University M
Xavier University
Youngstown State University

Oklahoma
Oklahoma State University
Oral Roberts University
University of Oklahoma
University of Tulsa

Oregon
Oregon State University
Portland State University W
University of Oregon
University of Portland

Pennsylvania
Bucknell University
Drexel University M
Duquesne University M
La Salle University M
Lafayette College M
Lehigh University
Penn State
University Park
Robert Morris University
St. Francis University
St. Joseph's University M
Temple University M
University of Pennsylvania
Villanova University M

Rhode Island
Brown University
University of Rhode Island M

South Carolina
Charleston Southern University
The Citadel W
Clemson University M
Coastal Carolina University
College of Charleston
Furman University
South Carolina State University
University of South Carolina
Winthrop University
Wofford College

Tennessee
Austin Peay State University
Belmont University
East Tennessee State University
Lipscomb University
Middle Tennessee State University
Tennessee State University
Tennessee Technological University
University of Memphis
University of Tennessee
Chattanooga M
Knoxville
Martin M
Vanderbilt University

Texas
Baylor University
Lamar University
Prairie View A&M University
Rice University M
Sam Houston State University
Southern Methodist University
Stephen F. Austin State University M
Texas A&M University
Texas Christian University
Texas Southern University
Texas State University: San Marcos
Texas Tech University
University of Houston M
University of North Texas
University of Texas
Arlington M
Austin
El Paso
Pan American
San Antonio

Utah
Brigham Young University
Southern Utah University M
University of Utah M
Utah State University M
Utah Valley State College
Weber State University

Virginia
College of William and Mary
George Mason University M
Hampton University
James Madison University
Liberty University M
Old Dominion University
Radford University
University of Richmond
University of Virginia
Virginia Commonwealth University M
Virginia Polytechnic Institute and State University M

Washington
Eastern Washington University W
Gonzaga University
University of Washington
Washington State University

West Virginia
Marshall University

Wisconsin
Marquette University M
University of Wisconsin
Green Bay M
Madison

Wyoming
University of Wyoming

Golf Division II

Alabama
University of Montevallo
University of North Alabama M

Arizona
Grand Canyon University

Arkansas
Arkansas Tech University
Harding University M
Henderson State University
Ouachita Baptist University M
Southern Arkansas University M
University of Arkansas
Monticello
University of Central Arkansas

California
California State University
Bakersfield M
Chico
Dominguez Hills M
Monterey Bay
San Bernardino M
Stanislaus M
Notre Dame de Namur University
Sonoma State University M
University of California
Davis
San Diego M

Colorado
Adams State College
Colorado Christian University M
Colorado School of Mines M
Colorado State University
Pueblo
Fort Lewis College M
Mesa State College W
Regis University
University of Colorado
Colorado Springs M
University of Northern Colorado

Connecticut
Post University M
University of New Haven M

Delaware
Goldey-Beacom College M
Wilmington College M

Florida
Barry University
Eckerd College M
Florida Gulf Coast University
Florida Institute of Technology
Florida Southern College
Lynn University
Nova Southeastern University
Rollins College

St. Leo University
University of Tampa M
University of West Florida

Georgia

Armstrong Atlantic State University
Clayton State University M
Columbus State University M
Georgia College and State University M
Kennesaw State University
Morehouse College M
Paine College M
University of West Georgia
Valdosta State University M

Hawaii

Brigham Young University-Hawaii
Chaminade University of Honolulu
Hawaii Pacific University
University of Hawaii
Hilo

Idaho

Northwest Nazarene University M

Illinois

Lewis University
Quincy University
Southern Illinois University
Edwardsville W

Indiana

Oakland City University
St. Joseph's College
University of Indianapolis
University of Southern Indiana

Iowa

Upper Iowa University

Kansas

Fort Hays State University
Pittsburg State University M
Washburn University of Topeka M

Kentucky

Bellarmine University
Kentucky State University M
Kentucky Wesleyan College
Northern Kentucky University

Massachusetts

American International College M
Assumption College M
Bentley College M
University of Massachusetts
Lowell M

Michigan

Ferris State University
Grand Valley State University
Northern Michigan University M
Northwood University
Saginaw Valley State University M
Wayne State University M

Minnesota

Bemidji State University
Concordia University: St. Paul
Minnesota State University
Mankato
Moorhead W
St. Cloud State University
Southwest Minnesota State University W
University of Minnesota
Crookston
Morris
Winona State University

Mississippi

Delta State University M

Missouri

Central Missouri State University M
Drury University
Lincoln University M
Missouri Southern State University M
Missouri Western State University
Rockhurst University
Southwest Baptist University M
Truman State University
University of Missouri
St. Louis

Montana

Montana State University
Billings

Nebraska

Chadron State College W
University of Nebraska
Kearney
Omaha W
Wayne State College

New Hampshire

Franklin Pierce College
St. Anselm College M
Southern New Hampshire University M

New Jersey

Caldwell College M
Felician College M

New Mexico

Western New Mexico University

New York

Adelphi University M
City University of New York
Queens College M
College of Saint Rose M
Dominican College of Blauvelt M
Dowling College M
Le Moyne College M
Nyack College M
Pace University
St. Thomas Aquinas College M

North Carolina

Barton College M
Belmont Abbey College
Catawba College
Elizabeth City State University M
Fayetteville State University M
Johnson C. Smith University
Lees-McRae College M
Lenoir-Rhyne College
Mars Hill College
Mount Olive College
North Carolina Central University M
Pfeiffer University
Queens University of Charlotte
St. Andrews Presbyterian College
St. Augustine's College M
Shaw University M
University of North Carolina
Pembroke M
Wingate University
Winston-Salem State University M

North Dakota

North Dakota State University
University of North Dakota

Ohio

Ashland University
Central State University
Tiffin University
University of Findlay

Oklahoma

Cameron University
East Central University M
Northeastern State University
Oklahoma Panhandle State University
Southeastern Oklahoma State University M
Southwestern Oklahoma State University
University of Central Oklahoma

Pennsylvania

California University of Pennsylvania
Clarion University of Pennsylvania M
Gannon University
Holy Family University M
Indiana University of Pennsylvania M
Kutztown University of Pennsylvania W
Mercyhurst College
Millersville University of Pennsylvania M
Philadelphia University M
Slippery Rock University of Pennsylvania M
University of Pittsburgh
Johnstown M
University of the Sciences in Philadelphia M
West Chester University of Pennsylvania

Rhode Island

Bryant University M

South Carolina

Anderson University
Benedict College
Coker College M
Francis Marion University M
Lander University M
Limestone College
Newberry College
North Greenville College M
Presbyterian College
University of South Carolina
Aiken M
Upstate

South Dakota

Augustana College
Northern State University
South Dakota State University
University of South Dakota

Tennessee

Carson-Newman College M
Christian Brothers University
LeMoyne-Owen College M
Lincoln Memorial University
Tusculum College

Texas

Abilene Christian University M
Dallas Baptist University
St. Edward's University
St. Mary's University
Tarleton State University W
Texas A&M University
Commerce
University of the Incarnate Word
West Texas A&M University

Vermont

Green Mountain College M
St. Michael's College M

Virginia

Longwood University
St. Paul's College M
Virginia State University
Virginia Union University M

Washington

Saint Martin's University
Western Washington University

West Virginia

Bluefield State College M
Concord University M
Davis and Elkins College M
Glenville State College
Ohio Valley University M
Salem International University
Shepherd University M
University of Charleston M
West Liberty State College
West Virginia State University
West Virginia University Institute of Technology M
West Virginia Wesleyan College M
Wheeling Jesuit University

Wisconsin

University of Wisconsin
Parkside M

Golf Division III

Alabama

Huntingdon College M

Arkansas

Hendrix College

California

California Institute of Technology M
California Lutheran University M
California State University
East Bay
Chapman University M
Claremont McKenna College M
Harvey Mudd College M
Menlo College M
Occidental College M
Pitzer College M
Pomona College M
University of California
Santa Cruz W
University of La Verne M
University of Redlands M
Whittier College M

Connecticut

Mitchell College M
Trinity College M
Wesleyan University M

Delaware

Wesley College M

Georgia

Emory University M
LaGrange College M
Oglethorpe University
Piedmont College

Illinois

Augustana College
Aurora University
Benedictine University M
Blackburn College M
Elmhurst College
Eureka College M
Illinois College
Illinois Wesleyan University
Knox College
MacMurray College
Millikin University
Monmouth College
North Central College
North Park University
Principia College M
Rockford College M
Wheaton College

Indiana

Anderson University
DePauw University
Franklin College
Hanover College
Manchester College
Rose-Hulman Institute of Technology
Saint Mary's College W
Tri-State University
Wabash College M

Iowa

Buena Vista University
Central College
Clarke College
Coe College
Cornell College
Grinnell College
Loras College
Luther College
Simpson College
University of Dubuque
Wartburg College

Kentucky

Centre College
Thomas More College
Transylvania University

Maine

Bates College
Bowdoin College
Colby College M
Husson College M
Maine Maritime Academy M
St. Joseph's College M
Thomas College M
University of Maine
Farmington M
Presque Isle M
University of New England M
University of Southern Maine

Maryland

Frostburg State University
Hood College
McDaniel College
Villa Julie College

Massachusetts

Amherst College
Anna Maria College M
Babson College M
Becker College M
Brandeis University M
Elms College M
Endicott College M
Massachusetts College of Liberal Arts M
Massachusetts Institute of Technology M
Mount Holyoke College W
Newbury College M
Nichols College M
Salem State College M
Springfield College M
Suffolk University M
Tufts University M
University of Massachusetts
Dartmouth M
Wellesley College W
Wentworth Institute of Technology M
Western New England College M
Williams College
Worcester State College M

Michigan

Adrian College
Albion College
Alma College
Calvin College
Hope College
Kalamazoo College
Olivet College

Minnesota

Augsburg College
Bethany Lutheran College
Bethel University M
Carleton College
College of St. Benedict W
Concordia College: Moorhead
Crown College M
Gustavus Adolphus College
Macalester College
Martin Luther College M
North Central University M
Northwestern College M
St. John's University M
St. Mary's University of Minnesota
St. Olaf College

University of St. Thomas

Mississippi
Millsaps College
Mississippi College

Missouri
Fontbonne University M
Maryville University of Saint Louis
Webster University M
Westminster College

Nebraska
Nebraska Wesleyan University

New Jersey
Centenary College M
The College of New Jersey M
Fairleigh Dickinson University
College at Florham M
Rutgers, The State University of New Jersey
Camden Regional Campus M

New York
Cazenovia College M
Clarkson University M
D'Youville College M
Elmira College
Hamilton College M
Hartwick College M
Hilbert College M
Hobart and William Smith Colleges
Keuka College M
Manhattanville College M
Medaille College
Nazareth College of Rochester
New York University M
Rensselaer Polytechnic Institute M
St. John Fisher College M
St. Joseph's College: Suffolk Campus M
St. Lawrence University
Skidmore College M
State University of New York
College at Cortland W
College at Potsdam M
Farmingdale M
Institute of Technology at Utica/Rome M
Oswego M
United States Merchant Marine Academy M
University of Rochester M
Utica College M
Vassar College W
Yeshiva University M

North Carolina
Chowan College M
Greensboro College M
Guilford College M
Methodist College
North Carolina Wesleyan College M

Ohio
Baldwin-Wallace College
Capital University
College of Mount St. Joseph
College of Wooster M
Denison University M
Heidelberg College M
Hiram College
John Carroll University
Kenyon College M
Lake Erie College M
Mount Union College
Muskingum College
Oberlin College M
Ohio Northern University
Ohio Wesleyan University M
Otterbein College
Wilmington College
Wittenberg University

Oregon
Lewis & Clark College
Linfield College
Pacific University
Willamette University

Pennsylvania
Albright College M
Allegheny College M
Alvernia College M
Arcadia University M
Baptist Bible College of Pennsylvania M
Cabrini College M
Carnegie Mellon University M
Chestnut Hill College
College Misericordia M
Delaware Valley College M
DeSales University M
Dickinson College
Eastern University M
Elizabethtown College M
Franklin & Marshall College
Gettysburg College
Grove City College
Gwynedd-Mercy College M
Immaculata University M
Keystone College M
King's College M
La Roche College M
Lebanon Valley College M
Lycoming College M
Messiah College M
Moravian College M
Mount Aloysius College
Muhlenberg College
Neumann College M
Penn State
Altoona M
Berks M
Erie, The Behrend College
Philadelphia Biblical University M
Susquehanna University
Swarthmore College M
Thiel College
University of Pittsburgh
Bradford
Greensburg
University of Scranton M
Ursinus College
Washington and Jefferson College
Waynesburg College
Westminster College
Widener University M
Wilkes University M
York College of Pennsylvania M

Rhode Island
Johnson & Wales University M
Rhode Island College M

South Dakota
Presentation College

Tennessee
Rhodes College
University of the South

Texas
Concordia University at Austin M
Hardin-Simmons University
LeTourneau University
McMurry University
Schreiner University M
Southwestern University
Texas Lutheran University
Trinity University
University of Dallas M
University of Mary Hardin-Baylor
University of Texas
Dallas
Tyler

Vermont
Castleton State College M
Middlebury College

Virginia
Averett University M
Bridgewater College M
Christopher Newport University M
Emory & Henry College M
Ferrum College M
Hampden-Sydney College M
Hollins University W
Lynchburg College M
Marymount University M
Randolph-Macon College M
Roanoke College M
Shenandoah University M
Virginia Wesleyan College M
Washington and Lee University M

Washington
Pacific Lutheran University
University of Puget Sound
Whitman College
Whitworth College

West Virginia
Bethany College M

Wisconsin
Beloit College
Carroll College
Carthage College
Concordia University Wisconsin
Edgewood College
Lakeland College
Lawrence University M
Marian College of Fond du Lac
Milwaukee School of Engineering
Ripon College
St. Norbert College
University of Wisconsin
Eau Claire
Oshkosh W
Platteville W
River Falls W
Stevens Point W
Whitewater W
Wisconsin Lutheran College

Gymnastics Division I

Alabama
Auburn University W
University of Alabama W

Arizona
Arizona State University W
University of Arizona W

Arkansas
University of Arkansas W

California
California State University
Fullerton W
Sacramento W
San Jose State University W
Stanford University
University of California
Berkeley
Davis W
Los Angeles W

Colorado
United States Air Force Academy
University of Denver W

Connecticut
Yale University W

District of Columbia
George Washington University W

Florida
University of Florida W

Georgia
University of Georgia W

Idaho
Boise State University W

Illinois
Illinois State University W
Northern Illinois University W
University of Illinois
Chicago
Urbana-Champaign

Indiana
Ball State University W

Iowa
Iowa State University W
University of Iowa

Kentucky
University of Kentucky W

Louisiana
Centenary College of Louisiana W
Louisiana State University and Agricultural and Mechanical College W

Maryland
Towson University W
United States Naval Academy M
University of Maryland
College Park W

Michigan
Central Michigan University W
Eastern Michigan University W
Michigan State University W
University of Michigan
Western Michigan University W

Minnesota
University of Minnesota
Twin Cities

Missouri
Southeast Missouri State University W
University of Missouri
Columbia W

Nebraska
University of Nebraska
Lincoln

New Hampshire
University of New Hampshire W

New Jersey
Rutgers, The State University of New Jersey
New Brunswick Regional Campus W

New York
Cornell University W
United States Military Academy M

North Carolina
North Carolina State University W
University of North Carolina
Chapel Hill W

Ohio
Bowling Green State University W
Kent State University W
Ohio State University
Columbus Campus

Oklahoma
University of Oklahoma

Oregon
Oregon State University W

Pennsylvania
Penn State
University Park
Temple University
University of Pennsylvania W
University of Pittsburgh W

Rhode Island
Brown University W
University of Rhode Island W

Utah
Brigham Young University W
Southern Utah University W
University of Utah W
Utah State University W

Virginia
College of William and Mary
James Madison University

Washington
University of Washington W

West Virginia
West Virginia University W

Gymnastics Division II

Connecticut
Southern Connecticut State University W
University of Bridgeport W

Minnesota
Winona State University W

Pennsylvania
West Chester University of Pennsylvania W

Texas
Texas Woman's University W

Washington
Seattle Pacific University W

Gymnastics Division III

Massachusetts
Massachusetts Institute of Technology
Springfield College

Minnesota
Gustavus Adolphus College W
Hamline University W

New York
Ithaca College W
State University of New York
College at Brockport W
College at Cortland W

Pennsylvania
Ursinus College W
Wilson College W

Rhode Island
Rhode Island College W

Wisconsin
University of Wisconsin
Eau Claire W
La Crosse W
Oshkosh W
Stout W
Whitewater W

Ice hockey Division I

Alabama
University of Alabama
Huntsville M

Alaska
University of Alaska
Anchorage M
Fairbanks M

Colorado
Colorado College M
United States Air Force Academy M
University of Denver M

Connecticut
Quinnipiac University M
Sacred Heart University M
University of Connecticut M
Yale University M

Indiana
University of Notre Dame M

Maine
University of Maine M

Massachusetts
American International College M
Bentley College M
Boston College M
Boston University M
College of the Holy Cross M
Harvard College M
Merrimack College M
Northeastern University M
University of Massachusetts
Amherst M
Lowell M

Michigan
Ferris State University M
Lake Superior State University M
Michigan State University M
Michigan Technological University M
Northern Michigan University M
University of Michigan M
Wayne State University M
Western Michigan University M

Minnesota
Bemidji State University M
Minnesota State University
Mankato M
St. Cloud State University M
University of Minnesota
Duluth M
Twin Cities M

Nebraska
University of Nebraska
Omaha M

New Hampshire
Dartmouth College M
University of New Hampshire M

New Jersey
Princeton University M

New York
Canisius College M
Clarkson University M
Colgate University M
Cornell University M
Niagara University M
Rensselaer Polytechnic Institute M
St. Lawrence University M
Union College M
United States Military Academy M

North Dakota
University of North Dakota M

Ohio
Bowling Green State University M
Miami University
Oxford Campus M
Ohio State University
Columbus Campus M

Pennsylvania
Mercyhurst College M
Robert Morris University M

Rhode Island
Brown University M
Providence College M

Vermont
University of Vermont M

Wisconsin
University of Wisconsin
Madison M

Ice hockey Division II

Massachusetts
Assumption College M
Stonehill College M

Minnesota
University of Minnesota
Crookston M

New Hampshire
Franklin Pierce College M
St. Anselm College M
Southern New Hampshire University M

Vermont
St. Michael's College M

Ice hockey Division III

Connecticut
Connecticut College M
Trinity College M
Wesleyan University M

Illinois
Lake Forest College M

Maine
Bowdoin College M
Colby College M
University of Southern Maine M

Massachusetts
Amherst College M
Babson College M
Curry College M
Fitchburg State College M
Framingham State College M
Nichols College M
Salem State College M
Suffolk University M
Tufts University M
University of Massachusetts
Boston M
Dartmouth M
Wentworth Institute of Technology M
Western New England College M
Williams College M
Worcester State College M

Michigan
Finlandia University M

Minnesota
Augsburg College M
Bethel University M
College of St. Scholastica M
Concordia College: Moorhead M
Gustavus Adolphus College M
Hamline University M
St. John's University M
St. Mary's University of Minnesota M
St. Olaf College M
University of St. Thomas M

New Hampshire
New England College M
Plymouth State University M

New York
Elmira College M
Hamilton College M
Hobart and William Smith Colleges M
Manhattanville College M
Rochester Institute of Technology M
Skidmore College M
State University of New York
Buffalo M
College at Brockport M
College at Cortland M
College at Fredonia M
College at Geneseo M
College at Plattsburgh M
College at Potsdam M
Oswego M
Utica College M

Pennsylvania
Lebanon Valley College M
Neumann College M
University of Scranton M

Rhode Island
Johnson & Wales University M
Salve Regina University M

Vermont
Castleton State College M
Middlebury College M
Norwich University M

Wisconsin
Lawrence University M
Marian College of Fond du Lac M
Milwaukee School of Engineering M
Northland College M
St. Norbert College M
University of Wisconsin
Eau Claire M
River Falls M
Stevens Point M
Stout M
Superior M

Lacrosse Division I

California
St. Mary's College of California W
Stanford University W
University of California
Berkeley W

Colorado
United States Air Force Academy M
University of Denver

Connecticut
Central Connecticut State University W
Fairfield University
Quinnipiac University
Sacred Heart University
University of Connecticut W
University of Hartford M
Yale University

Delaware
University of Delaware
Wilmington College W

District of Columbia
American University W
George Washington University W
Georgetown University
Howard University W

Illinois
Northwestern University W

Indiana
Butler University M
University of Notre Dame

Maryland
Johns Hopkins University
Loyola College in Maryland
Mount St. Mary's University
Towson University
United States Naval Academy M
University of Maryland
Baltimore County
College Park

Massachusetts
Boston College W
Boston University W
College of the Holy Cross
Pine Manor College W
University of Massachusetts
Amherst

New Hampshire
Dartmouth College
University of New Hampshire W

New Jersey
Monmouth University W
Princeton University
Rutgers, The State University of New Jersey
New Brunswick Regional Campus

New York
Barnard College W
Canisius College
Colgate University
Cornell University
Hobart and William Smith Colleges M
Hofstra University
Iona College W
Le Moyne College W
Long Island University
Brooklyn Campus W
Manhattan College
Marist College
Molloy College W
Niagara University W
St. Bonaventure University W
St. John's University M
St. Thomas Aquinas College W
Siena College
State University of New York
Albany
Binghamton
Farmingdale W
Stony Brook
Syracuse University
United States Military Academy M
Wagner College

North Carolina
Belmont Abbey College W
Davidson College W
Duke University
North Carolina Wesleyan College W
University of North Carolina
Chapel Hill

Ohio
Ohio State University
Columbus Campus
Ohio University W

Oregon
University of Oregon W

Pennsylvania
Bucknell University
Drexel University
Duquesne University W
La Salle University W
Lafayette College
Lehigh University
Penn State
University Park
Robert Morris University
St. Francis University W
St. Joseph's University
Temple University W
University of Pennsylvania
Villanova University
York College of Pennsylvania W

Rhode Island
Brown University
Providence College M

South Carolina
Presbyterian College W

Tennessee
Vanderbilt University W

Vermont
University of Vermont

Virginia
College of William and Mary W
George Mason University W
James Madison University W
Old Dominion University W
University of Richmond W
University of Virginia
Virginia Military Institute M
Virginia Polytechnic Institute and State University W

Lacrosse Division II

California
Notre Dame de Namur University M
University of California
Davis W

Colorado
Regis University W

Connecticut
Southern Connecticut State University W
University of New Haven W

Florida
St. Leo University M

Kentucky
Bellarmine University M

Massachusetts
American International College
Assumption College
Bentley College
Merrimack College
Stonehill College W

New Hampshire
Franklin Pierce College
St. Anselm College
Southern New Hampshire University

New York
Adelphi University
Dominican College of Blauvelt M
Dowling College M
Le Moyne College M
Long Island University
C. W. Post Campus
Molloy College M
New York Institute of Technology M
Pace University M

North Carolina
Belmont Abbey College M
Catawba College M
Lees-McRae College
Mars Hill College M
Pfeiffer University
Queens University of Charlotte
St. Andrews Presbyterian College
Wingate University M

Pennsylvania
Bloomsburg University of Pennsylvania W
East Stroudsburg University of Pennsylvania W
Gannon University W
Indiana University of Pennsylvania W
Lock Haven University of Pennsylvania W
Mercyhurst College
Millersville University of Pennsylvania W
Philadelphia University W
Shippensburg University of Pennsylvania W

West Chester University of Pennsylvania W

Rhode Island
Bryant University

South Carolina
Limestone College
Presbyterian College M

Vermont
Green Mountain College M
St. Michael's College

Virginia
Longwood University W

West Virginia
Wheeling Jesuit University M

Lacrosse Division III

California
Claremont McKenna College W
University of Redlands W
Whittier College

Colorado
Colorado College

Connecticut
Connecticut College
Eastern Connecticut State University
Mitchell College M
St. Joseph College W
Trinity College
Wesleyan University
Western Connecticut State University

Delaware
Wesley College

District of Columbia
Catholic University of America
Trinity University W

Maine
Bates College
Bowdoin College
Colby College
Maine Maritime Academy M
Thomas College
University of New England
University of Southern Maine

Maryland
College of Notre Dame of Maryland W
Frostburg State University W
Goucher College
Hood College
McDaniel College
St. Mary's College of Maryland
Salisbury University
Villa Julie College
Washington College

Massachusetts
Amherst College
Babson College
Becker College M
Bridgewater State College W
Clark University M
Curry College
Elms College W
Emerson College
Endicott College
Gordon College
Lasell College
Massachusetts Institute of Technology
Massachusetts Maritime Academy M
Mount Holyoke College W
Mount Ida College M
Nichols College
Regis College W
Smith College W
Springfield College
Tufts University
University of Massachusetts
Boston M
Dartmouth
Wellesley College W
Wentworth Institute of Technology M
Western New England College
Wheaton College
Williams College
Worcester State College W

New Hampshire
Colby-Sawyer College W
Daniel Webster College M
Keene State College
New England College
Plymouth State University

New Jersey
Centenary College
The College of New Jersey W
Drew University
Fairleigh Dickinson University
College at Florham M
Kean University
Montclair State University
Richard Stockton College of New Jersey M
Rowan University W
Stevens Institute of Technology

New York
Alfred University
Cazenovia College
Clarkson University
College of Mount St. Vincent
Elmira College
Hamilton College
Hartwick College
Hobart and William Smith Colleges W
Ithaca College
Keuka College
Manhattanville College
Medaille College
Nazareth College of Rochester
Rensselaer Polytechnic Institute
Rochester Institute of Technology
St. John Fisher College
St. Lawrence University
Skidmore College
State University of New York
Buffalo W
College at Brockport
College at Cortland
College at Fredonia W
College at Geneseo
College at Oneonta
College at Plattsburgh M
College at Potsdam
Farmingdale M
Maritime College M
Oswego
Union College
United States Merchant Marine Academy M
University of Rochester W
Utica College
Vassar College
Wells College W

North Carolina
Greensboro College
Guilford College
Methodist College W

Ohio
College of Wooster
Denison University
Kenyon College
Oberlin College
Ohio Wesleyan University
Wittenberg University

Oregon
Linfield College W

Pennsylvania
Allegheny College W
Alvernia College
Arcadia University W
Bryn Mawr College W
Cabrini College
Cedar Crest College W
Chestnut Hill College W
College Misericordia
DeSales University M
Dickinson College
Eastern University
Elizabethtown College
Franklin & Marshall College
Gettysburg College
Gwynedd-Mercy College W
Haverford College
Immaculata University W
King's College
Lycoming College
Messiah College
Moravian College
Muhlenberg College
Neumann College
Rosemont College W
Susquehanna University
Swarthmore College
University of Scranton
Ursinus College
Washington and Jefferson College M
Widener University
Wilkes University W
York College of Pennsylvania M

Rhode Island
Rhode Island College W
Roger Williams University
Salve Regina University

Texas
University of Dallas W

Vermont
Castleton State College
Johnson State College M
Middlebury College
Norwich University M

Virginia
Averett University W
Bridgewater College W
Christopher Newport University W
Ferrum College W
Hampden-Sydney College M
Hollins University W
Lynchburg College
Marymount University
Randolph-Macon College
Roanoke College
Shenandoah University
Sweet Briar College W
University of Mary Washington
Virginia Wesleyan College
Washington and Lee University

Washington
University of Puget Sound W

Rifle Division I

Alabama
Birmingham-Southern College W
Jacksonville State University M
University of Alabama
Birmingham W

California
University of San Francisco

Colorado
United States Air Force Academy

Georgia
Mercer University M

Kentucky
Morehead State University
Murray State University M
University of Kentucky

Maryland
United States Naval Academy

Mississippi
University of Mississippi W

Missouri
University of Missouri
Kansas City

Nebraska
University of Nebraska
Lincoln W

Nevada
University of Nevada
Reno

New York
United States Military Academy

North Carolina
North Carolina State University

Ohio
Ohio State University
Columbus Campus
University of Akron

South Carolina
The Citadel
Wofford College M

Tennessee
Austin Peay State University W
Tennessee Technological University
University of Memphis
University of Tennessee
Martin W

Texas
Texas Christian University W
University of Texas
El Paso W

Virginia
Virginia Military Institute M

West Virginia
West Virginia University

Rifle Division II

Alaska
University of Alaska
Fairbanks

Rifle Division III

Connecticut
United States Coast Guard Academy M

Indiana
Rose-Hulman Institute of Technology

Massachusetts
Massachusetts Institute of Technology
Massachusetts Maritime Academy W
Wentworth Institute of Technology W

New York
City University of New York
John Jay College of Criminal Justice M
State University of New York
Maritime College

Pennsylvania
University of the Sciences in Philadelphia

Wisconsin
University of Wisconsin
Oshkosh

Rowing (crew) Division I

California
California State University
Sacramento W
Loyola Marymount University W
St. Mary's College of California W
San Diego State University W
Santa Clara University W
Stanford University W
University of California
Berkeley W
Irvine W
Los Angeles W
University of San Diego W
University of Southern California W

Connecticut
Fairfield University W
Sacred Heart University W
University of Connecticut W
Yale University W

Delaware
University of Delaware W

District of Columbia
George Washington University W
Georgetown University W

Florida
Jacksonville University W
Stetson University W
University of Central Florida W
University of Miami W

Indiana
Indiana University
Bloomington W
University of Notre Dame W

Iowa
Drake University W
University of Iowa W

Kansas
Kansas State University W
University of Kansas W

Kentucky
Murray State University W
University of Louisville W

Maryland
Loyola College in Maryland W
United States Naval Academy W

Massachusetts
Boston College W
Boston University W
College of the Holy Cross W
Harvard College W
Massachusetts Institute of Technology W
Northeastern University W
University of Massachusetts
Amherst W

Michigan
Eastern Michigan University W
Michigan State University W
University of Michigan W

Minnesota
University of Minnesota
Twin Cities W

Nebraska
Creighton University W

New Hampshire
Dartmouth College W
University of New Hampshire W

New Jersey
Princeton University W
Rutgers, The State University of New Jersey
New Brunswick Regional Campus W

New York
Barnard College W
Colgate University W
Cornell University W
Fordham University W
Iona College W
Marist College W
State University of New York
Buffalo W
Syracuse University W

North Carolina
Duke University W
University of North Carolina
Chapel Hill W

Ohio
Ohio State University
Columbus Campus W
University of Cincinnati W
University of Dayton W

Oklahoma
University of Tulsa W

Oregon
Oregon State University W

Pennsylvania
Bucknell University W
Drexel University W
Duquesne University W
La Salle University W
Lehigh University W
Robert Morris University W
St. Joseph's University W
Temple University W
University of Pennsylvania W
Villanova University W

Rhode Island
Brown University W
University of Rhode Island W

South Carolina
Clemson University W

Tennessee
University of Tennessee
Knoxville W

Texas
Southern Methodist University W
University of Texas
Austin W

Virginia
George Mason University W
University of Virginia W

Washington
Gonzaga University W
University of Washington W
Washington State University W

West Virginia
West Virginia University W

Wisconsin
University of Wisconsin
Madison W

Rowing (crew) Division II

California
Humboldt State University W
University of California
Davis W
San Diego W

Florida
Barry University W
Florida Institute of Technology W
Nova Southeastern University W
Rollins College W
University of Tampa W

Massachusetts
Assumption College W

New Hampshire
Franklin Pierce College W

New York
Dowling College W

Pennsylvania
Mercyhurst College W

Washington
Seattle Pacific University W
Western Washington University W

West Virginia
University of Charleston W

Rowing (crew) Division III

California
Chapman University W
Mills College W

Connecticut
Connecticut College W
Trinity College W
United States Coast Guard Academy W
Wesleyan University W

Illinois
North Park University W

Maine
Bates College W
Colby College W

Maryland
Johns Hopkins University W
Washington College W

Massachusetts
Clark University W
Lesley University W
Massachusetts Maritime Academy W
Mount Holyoke College W
Simmons College W
Smith College W
Tufts University W
Wellesley College W
Williams College W
Worcester Polytechnic Institute W

New Jersey
Richard Stockton College of New Jersey W
Rutgers, The State University of New Jersey
Camden Regional Campus W

New York
Cazenovia College W
D'Youville College W
Hamilton College W
Hobart and William Smith Colleges W
Ithaca College W
Rochester Institute of Technology W
St. Lawrence University W
Skidmore College W
State University of New York
Maritime College W
Union College W
United States Merchant Marine Academy W
Vassar College W

Ohio
Marietta College W

Oregon
Lewis & Clark College W
Willamette University W

Pennsylvania
Bryn Mawr College W

Virginia
University of Mary Washington W

Washington
Pacific Lutheran University W
University of Puget Sound W

Skiing Division I

Colorado
University of Colorado
Boulder
University of Denver

Idaho
Boise State University W

Maine
Colby College

Massachusetts
Boston College
Harvard College
University of Massachusetts
Amherst

Montana
Montana State University
Bozeman

Nevada
University of Nevada
Reno

New Hampshire
Dartmouth College
University of New Hampshire

New Mexico
University of New Mexico

Rhode Island
Brown University W

Utah
University of Utah

Vermont
University of Vermont

Wisconsin
University of Wisconsin
Green Bay

Skiing Division II

Alaska
University of Alaska
Anchorage
Fairbanks

Colorado
Western State College of Colorado

Michigan
Michigan Technological University
Northern Michigan University

Minnesota
St. Cloud State University W

New Hampshire
St. Anselm College

Vermont
Green Mountain College
St. Michael's College

Skiing Division III

Maine
Bates College
Bowdoin College
University of Maine
Presque Isle

Massachusetts
Babson College
Smith College W
Williams College

Minnesota
College of St. Benedict W
Gustavus Adolphus College
St. John's University M
St. Olaf College

Nebraska
Clarkson College M

New Hampshire
Colby-Sawyer College
Plymouth State University

New York
Clarkson University W
St. Lawrence University

Vermont
Middlebury College

Washington
Whitman College

Soccer Division I

Alabama
Alabama Agricultural and Mechanical University
Alabama State University W
Auburn University W
Birmingham-Southern College
Jacksonville State University W
Samford University W
Troy University W
University of Alabama W
University of Alabama
Birmingham
University of South Alabama W

Arizona
Arizona State University W
Northern Arizona University W
University of Arizona W

Arkansas
Arkansas State University W
University of Arkansas W
University of Arkansas
Little Rock W
Pine Bluff W

California
California Polytechnic State University: San Luis Obispo
California State University
Fresno W
Fullerton
Long Beach W
Northridge
Sacramento
Loyola Marymount University
Pepperdine University W
St. Mary's College of California
San Diego State University
San Jose State University
Santa Clara University
Stanford University
University of California
Berkeley
Irvine
Los Angeles
Riverside
Santa Barbara
University of San Diego
University of San Francisco
University of Southern California W
University of the Pacific W

Colorado
Colorado College W
United States Air Force Academy
University of Colorado
Boulder W
University of Denver

Connecticut
Central Connecticut State University
Fairfield University
Quinnipiac University
Sacred Heart University
University of Connecticut
University of Hartford
Yale University

Delaware
Delaware State University W
University of Delaware

District of Columbia
American University
George Washington University
Georgetown University
Howard University

Florida
Florida Atlantic University
Florida International University
Florida State University W
Jacksonville University
Stetson University
University of Central Florida
University of Florida W
University of Miami W
University of South Florida

Georgia
Georgia Southern University
Georgia State University
Mercer University
University of Georgia W

Hawaii
University of Hawaii
Manoa W

Idaho
Boise State University W
Idaho State University W
University of Idaho W

Illinois
Bradley University M
DePaul University
Eastern Illinois University
Illinois State University W
Loyola University of Chicago
Northern Illinois University
Northwestern University
University of Illinois
Chicago M
Urbana-Champaign W
Western Illinois University

Indiana
Ball State University W
Butler University
Indiana State University W
Indiana University
Bloomington
Indiana University-Purdue University Fort Wayne
Indiana University-Purdue University Indianapolis
Purdue University W
University of Evansville
University of Notre Dame
Valparaiso University

Iowa
Drake University
Iowa State University W
University of Iowa W
University of Northern Iowa W

Kansas
University of Kansas W

Kentucky
Eastern Kentucky University W
Morehead State University W
Murray State University W
University of Kentucky
University of Louisville
Western Kentucky University

Louisiana
Centenary College of Louisiana
Grambling State University W
Louisiana State University and Agricultural and Mechanical College W
Louisiana Tech University W
Nicholls State University W
Northwestern State University W
Southeastern Louisiana University W
Southern University and Agricultural and Mechanical College W
University of Louisiana at Lafayette W
University of Louisiana at Monroe W

Maine
University of Maine

Maryland
Loyola College in Maryland
Mount St. Mary's University
Towson University
United States Naval Academy
University of Maryland
  Baltimore County
  College Park

Massachusetts
Boston College
Boston University
College of the Holy Cross
Harvard College
Northeastern University
University of Massachusetts
  Amherst

Michigan
Central Michigan University W
Eastern Michigan University W
Michigan State University
Oakland University
University of Detroit Mercy
University of Michigan
Western Michigan University

Minnesota
University of Minnesota
  Twin Cities W

Mississippi
Alcorn State University W
Jackson State University W
Mississippi State University W
Mississippi Valley State University W
University of Mississippi W
University of Southern Mississippi W

Missouri
Drury University
Missouri State University
St. Louis University
Southeast Missouri State University W
University of Missouri
  Columbia W
  Kansas City M

Montana
University of Montana: Missoula W

Nebraska
Creighton University
University of Nebraska
  Lincoln W

Nevada
University of Nevada
  Las Vegas
  Reno W

New Hampshire
Dartmouth College
University of New Hampshire

New Jersey
Fairleigh Dickinson University
  Metropolitan Campus
Monmouth University
New Jersey Institute of Technology M
Princeton University
Rider University
Rutgers, The State University of New Jersey
  New Brunswick Regional Campus
St. Peter's College
Seton Hall University

New Mexico
University of New Mexico

New York
Adelphi University M
Barnard College W
Canisius College
Colgate University
Columbia University
  Columbia College M
Cornell University
Fordham University
Hartwick College M
Hofstra University
Iona College
Long Island University
  Brooklyn Campus
Manhattan College
Marist College
Niagara University
St. Bonaventure University
St. Francis College M
St. John's University
Siena College
State University of New York
  Albany
  Binghamton
  Buffalo
  College at Oneonta M
  Stony Brook
Syracuse University
United States Military Academy
Wagner College W

North Carolina
Appalachian State University
Campbell University
Coastal Carolina Community College W
Davidson College
Duke University
East Carolina University
Elon University
Gardner-Webb University
High Point University
North Carolina State University
University of North Carolina
  Asheville
  Chapel Hill
  Charlotte
  Greensboro
  Wilmington
Wake Forest University
Western Carolina University W

Ohio
Bowling Green State University
Cleveland State University
Kent State University W
Miami University
  Oxford Campus W
Ohio State University
  Columbus Campus
Ohio University W
University of Akron
University of Cincinnati
University of Dayton
University of Toledo W
Wright State University
Xavier University
Youngstown State University W

Oklahoma
Oklahoma State University W
Oral Roberts University
University of Oklahoma W
University of Tulsa

Oregon
Oregon State University
Portland State University W
University of Oregon W
University of Portland

Pennsylvania
Bucknell University
Drexel University
Duquesne University
La Salle University
Lafayette College
Lehigh University
Penn State
  University Park
Philadelphia University M
Robert Morris University
St. Francis University
St. Joseph's University
Temple University
University of Pennsylvania
University of Pittsburgh
Villanova University

Rhode Island
Brown University
Providence College
University of Rhode Island

South Carolina
Charleston Southern University W
The Citadel W
Clemson University
Coastal Carolina University M
College of Charleston
Furman University
South Carolina State University W
University of South Carolina
Winthrop University
Wofford College

Tennessee
Austin Peay State University W
Belmont University
East Tennessee State University W
Lipscomb University
Middle Tennessee State University W
Tennessee Technological University W
University of Memphis
University of Tennessee
  Chattanooga W
  Knoxville W
  Martin W
Vanderbilt University

Texas
Baylor University W
Prairie View A&M University W
Rice University W
Sam Houston State University W
Southern Methodist University
Stephen F. Austin State University W
Texas A&M University W
Texas Christian University W
Texas Southern University W
Texas State University: San Marcos W
Texas Tech University W
University of Houston W
University of North Texas W
University of Texas
  Austin W
  El Paso W

Utah
Brigham Young University W
Southern Utah University W
University of Utah W
Utah State University W
Utah Valley State College W
Weber State University W

Vermont
University of Vermont

Virginia
College of William and Mary
George Mason University
James Madison University
Liberty University
Old Dominion University
Radford University
University of Richmond
University of Virginia
Virginia Commonwealth University
Virginia Military Institute
Virginia Polytechnic Institute and State University

Washington
Eastern Washington University W
Gonzaga University
University of Washington
Washington State University W

West Virginia
Marshall University
West Virginia University

Wisconsin
Marquette University
University of Wisconsin
  Green Bay
  Madison
  Milwaukee

Wyoming
University of Wyoming W

Soccer Division II

Alabama
University of Alabama
  Huntsville
University of Montevallo
University of North Alabama W

Arizona
Grand Canyon University

Arkansas
Harding University
Ouachita Baptist University
University of Central Arkansas

California
California State Polytechnic University: Pomona
California State University
  Bakersfield
  Chico
  Dominguez Hills
  Los Angeles
  Monterey Bay
  San Bernardino
  Stanislaus
Humboldt State University
Notre Dame de Namur University
San Francisco State University
Sonoma State University
University of California
  Davis
  San Diego

Colorado
Adams State College W
Colorado Christian University
Colorado School of Mines
Colorado State University
  Pueblo
Fort Lewis College
Mesa State College W
Metropolitan State College of Denver
Regis University
University of Colorado
  Colorado Springs M
University of Northern Colorado W

Connecticut
Post University
Southern Connecticut State University
University of Bridgeport
University of New Haven

Delaware
Goldey-Beacom College
Wilmington College

District of Columbia
University of the District of Columbia

Florida
Barry University
Eckerd College
Florida Institute of Technology
Florida Southern College
Lynn University
Nova Southeastern University
Palm Beach Atlantic University
Rollins College
St. Leo University
University of North Florida
University of Tampa
University of West Florida

Georgia
Clayton State University
Columbus State University W
Georgia College and State University W
Kennesaw State University W
North Georgia College & State University
University of West Georgia W

Idaho
Northwest Nazarene University W

Illinois
Lewis University
Quincy University
Southern Illinois University
  Edwardsville

Indiana
Oakland City University
St. Joseph's College
University of Indianapolis
University of Southern Indiana

Iowa
Upper Iowa University

Kansas
Emporia State University W
Washburn University of Topeka W

Kentucky
Bellarmine University
Kentucky Wesleyan College
Northern Kentucky University

Maryland
Columbia Union College

Massachusetts
American International College
Assumption College
Bentley College

Merrimack College
Stonehill College
University of Massachusetts
Lowell

Michigan

Ferris State University W
Grand Valley State University W
Northern Michigan University W
Northwood University
Saginaw Valley State University

Minnesota

Bemidji State University W
Concordia University: St. Paul W
Minnesota State University
Mankato W
Moorhead W
St. Cloud State University W
Southwest Minnesota State University W
University of Minnesota
Crookston W
Duluth W
Morris W
Winona State University W

Mississippi

Delta State University

Missouri

Central Missouri State University W
Missouri Southern State University
Missouri Western State University W
Northwest Missouri State University W
Rockhurst University
Southwest Baptist University W
Truman State University
University of Missouri
Rolla
St. Louis

Montana

Montana State University
Billings

Nebraska

University of Nebraska
Omaha W
Wayne State College W

New Hampshire

Franklin Pierce College
St. Anselm College
Southern New Hampshire University

New Jersey

Bloomfield College
Caldwell College
Felician College
Georgian Court University W
New Jersey Institute of Technology W

New Mexico

Eastern New Mexico University
New Mexico Highlands University W

New York

Adelphi University W
City University of New York
Queens College W
College of Saint Rose
Concordia College
Dominican College of Blauvelt
Dowling College
Le Moyne College
Long Island University
C. W. Post Campus
Mercy College
Molloy College
New York Institute of Technology
Nyack College
Pace University W
St. Thomas Aquinas College

North Carolina

Barton College
Belmont Abbey College
Catawba College
Lees-McRae College
Lenoir-Rhyne College
Mars Hill College
Mount Olive College
Pfeiffer University
Queens University of Charlotte
St. Andrews Presbyterian College
University of North Carolina
Pembroke
Wingate University

North Dakota

North Dakota State University W
University of Mary W
University of North Dakota W

Ohio

Ashland University
Tiffin University
University of Findlay

Oklahoma

East Central University W
Northeastern State University
Southwestern Oklahoma State University W
University of Central Oklahoma W

Oregon

Western Oregon University W

Pennsylvania

Bloomsburg University of Pennsylvania
California University of Pennsylvania
Clarion University of Pennsylvania W
East Stroudsburg University of Pennsylvania
Edinboro University of Pennsylvania W
Gannon University
Holy Family University
Indiana University of Pennsylvania W
Kutztown University of Pennsylvania
Lock Haven University of Pennsylvania
Mansfield University of Pennsylvania W
Mercyhurst College
Millersville University of Pennsylvania
Philadelphia University W
Shippensburg University of Pennsylvania
Slippery Rock University of Pennsylvania
University of Pittsburgh
Johnstown
West Chester University of Pennsylvania

Puerto Rico

University of Puerto Rico
Mayaguez M
Rio Piedras M

Rhode Island

Bryant University

South Carolina

Anderson University
Coker College
Converse College W
Erskine College
Francis Marion University
Lander University
Limestone College
Newberry College
North Greenville College
Presbyterian College
University of South Carolina
Aiken
Upstate

South Dakota

Augustana College W
Northern State University W
South Dakota State University W
University of South Dakota W

Tennessee

Carson-Newman College
Christian Brothers University
Lincoln Memorial University
Tusculum College

Texas

Angelo State University W
Dallas Baptist University
Midwestern State University
St. Edward's University
St. Mary's University
Texas A&M University
Commerce W
Texas Woman's University W
University of the Incarnate Word
West Texas A&M University

Vermont

Green Mountain College
St. Michael's College

Virginia

Longwood University

Washington

Central Washington University W
Seattle Pacific University
Seattle University
Western Washington University

West Virginia

Alderson-Broaddus College M
Concord University W
Davis and Elkins College
Ohio Valley University
Salem International University
Shepherd University
University of Charleston
West Virginia University Institute of Technology W
West Virginia Wesleyan College
Wheeling Jesuit University

Wisconsin

University of Wisconsin
Parkside

Soccer Division III

Alabama

Huntingdon College

Arkansas

Hendrix College
University of the Ozarks

California

California Institute of Technology M
California Lutheran University
California State University
East Bay
Chapman University
Claremont McKenna College
Harvey Mudd College W
Menlo College
Mills College W
Occidental College
Pitzer College W
Pomona College
University of California
Santa Cruz
University of La Verne
University of Redlands
Whittier College

Colorado

Colorado College M

Connecticut

Albertus Magnus College
Connecticut College
Eastern Connecticut State University
Mitchell College
St. Joseph College W
Trinity College
United States Coast Guard Academy
Wesleyan University
Western Connecticut State University

Delaware

Wesley College

District of Columbia

Catholic University of America
Gallaudet University
Trinity University W

Georgia

Agnes Scott College W
Emory University
LaGrange College
Oglethorpe University
Piedmont College
Spelman College W
Wesleyan College W

Illinois

Augustana College
Aurora University
Benedictine University
Blackburn College
Concordia University
Dominican University
Elmhurst College
Greenville College
Illinois College
Illinois Wesleyan University
Knox College
Lake Forest College
MacMurray College
Millikin University
Monmouth College
North Central College
North Park University
Principia College
Rockford College
University of Chicago
Wheaton College

Indiana

Anderson University
DePauw University
Earlham College
Franklin College
Hanover College
Manchester College
Rose-Hulman Institute of Technology
Saint Mary's College W
Tri-State University
Wabash College M

Iowa

Buena Vista University
Central College
Clarke College
Coe College
Cornell College
Grinnell College
Loras College
Luther College
Simpson College
University of Dubuque
Wartburg College

Kentucky

Centre College
Thomas More College
Transylvania University

Maine

Bates College
Bowdoin College
Colby College
Husson College
Maine Maritime Academy
St. Joseph's College
Thomas College
University of Maine
Farmington
Presque Isle
University of New England
University of Southern Maine

Maryland

College of Notre Dame of Maryland W
Frostburg State University
Goucher College
Hood College
Johns Hopkins University
McDaniel College
St. Mary's College of Maryland
Salisbury University
Villa Julie College
Washington College

Massachusetts

Amherst College
Anna Maria College
Babson College
Bay Path College W
Becker College
Brandeis University
Bridgewater State College
Clark University
Curry College
Eastern Nazarene College
Elms College
Emerson College
Emmanuel College
Endicott College
Fitchburg State College
Framingham State College
Gordon College
Lasell College
Lesley University W
Massachusetts College of Liberal Arts
Massachusetts Institute of Technology
Massachusetts Maritime Academy M
Mount Holyoke College W
Mount Ida College
Newbury College M
Nichols College
Pine Manor College W
Regis College W
Salem State College
Simmons College W
Smith College W
Springfield College
Suffolk University M
Tufts University
University of Massachusetts
Boston
Dartmouth
Wellesley College W
Wentworth Institute of Technology
Western New England College
Westfield State College
Wheaton College
Wheelock College W
Williams College
Worcester Polytechnic Institute
Worcester State College

Michigan

Adrian College
Albion College
Alma College
Calvin College
Finlandia University
Hope College
Kalamazoo College
Olivet College

Minnesota

Augsburg College
Bethel University
Carleton College

College of St. Benedict W
College of St. Catherine W
College of St. Scholastica
Concordia College: Moorhead
Crown College
Gustavus Adolphus College
Hamline University
Macalester College
Martin Luther College
North Central University M
Northwestern College
St. John's University M
St. Mary's University of Minnesota
St. Olaf College
University of St. Thomas

Mississippi
Millsaps College
Mississippi College
Rust College M

Missouri
Baptist Bible College
Fontbonne University
Maryville University of Saint Louis
Washington University in St. Louis
Webster University
Westminster College

Nebraska
Nebraska Wesleyan University

New Hampshire
Colby-Sawyer College
Daniel Webster College
Keene State College
New England College
Plymouth State University
Rivier College

New Jersey
Centenary College
The College of New Jersey
College of St. Elizabeth W
Drew University
Fairleigh Dickinson University
College at Florham
Kean University
Montclair State University
New Jersey City University
Ramapo College of New Jersey
Richard Stockton College of New Jersey
Rowan University
Rutgers, The State University of New Jersey
Camden Regional Campus
Newark Regional Campus
Stevens Institute of Technology
William Paterson University of New Jersey

New York
Alfred University
Bard College
Cazenovia College
City University of New York
Baruch College M
Brooklyn College M
City College
College of Staten Island
Hunter College M
John Jay College of Criminal Justice
Medgar Evers College
New York City College of Technology M
York College M
Clarkson University
College of Mount St. Vincent
D'Youville College
Elmira College
Hamilton College
Hartwick College W
Hilbert College
Hobart and William Smith Colleges
Ithaca College
Keuka College
Manhattanville College
Medaille College
Mount St. Mary College
Nazareth College of Rochester
New York University
Polytechnic University
Rensselaer Polytechnic Institute
Rochester Institute of Technology
Russell Sage College W
St. John Fisher College
St. Joseph's College: Suffolk Campus
St. Lawrence University
Skidmore College
State University of New York
College at Brockport
College at Buffalo
College at Cortland
College at Fredonia
College at Geneseo
College at Old Westbury M
College at Oneonta W
College at Plattsburgh
College at Potsdam
Farmingdale
Institute of Technology at Utica/Rome
Maritime College
New Paltz
Oswego
Purchase W
Union College
United States Merchant Marine Academy M
University of Rochester
Utica College
Vassar College
Wells College W
Yeshiva University M

North Carolina
Chowan College
Greensboro College
Guilford College
Meredith College W
Methodist College
North Carolina Wesleyan College
Peace College W
Salem College W

Ohio
Baldwin-Wallace College
Bluffton University
Capital University
Case Western Reserve University
College of Mount St. Joseph
College of Wooster
Defiance College
Denison University
Heidelberg College
Hiram College
John Carroll University
Kenyon College
Lake Erie College
Marietta College
Mount Union College
Muskingum College
Oberlin College
Ohio Northern University
Ohio Wesleyan University
Otterbein College
Wilmington College
Wittenberg University

Oregon
George Fox University
Lewis & Clark College W
Linfield College
Pacific University
Willamette University

Pennsylvania
Albright College
Allegheny College
Alvernia College
Arcadia University
Bryn Mawr College W
Cabrini College
Carnegie Mellon University
Cedar Crest College W
Chatham College W
Chestnut Hill College
College Misericordia
Delaware Valley College
DeSales University
Dickinson College
Eastern University
Elizabethtown College
Franklin & Marshall College
Gettysburg College
Grove City College
Gwynedd-Mercy College
Haverford College
Immaculata University
Juniata College
Keystone College
King's College
La Roche College
Lebanon Valley College
Lincoln University
Lycoming College
Marywood University
Messiah College
Moravian College
Mount Aloysius College
Muhlenberg College
Neumann College
Penn State
Altoona
Berks
Erie, The Behrend College
Philadelphia Biblical University
Susquehanna University
Swarthmore College
Thiel College
University of Pittsburgh
Bradford
Greensburg
University of Scranton
Ursinus College
Washington and Jefferson College
Waynesburg College
Westminster College
Widener University
Wilkes University
Wilson College W
York College of Pennsylvania

Rhode Island
Johnson & Wales University
Rhode Island College
Roger Williams University
Salve Regina University

South Dakota
Presentation College

Tennessee
Fisk University M
Maryville College
Rhodes College
University of the South

Texas
Austin College
Concordia University at Austin
East Texas Baptist University
Hardin-Simmons University
LeTourneau University
McMurry University
Schreiner University
Southwestern University
Texas Lutheran University
Trinity University
University of Dallas
University of Mary Hardin-Baylor
University of Texas
Dallas
Tyler

Vermont
Castleton State College
Johnson State College
Middlebury College
Norwich University
Southern Vermont College

Virginia
Averett University
Bridgewater College
Christopher Newport University
Eastern Mennonite University
Emory & Henry College
Ferrum College
Hampden-Sydney College M
Hollins University W
Lynchburg College
Mary Baldwin College W
Marymount University
Randolph-Macon College
Randolph-Macon Woman's College W
Roanoke College
Shenandoah University
Sweet Briar College W
University of Mary Washington
Virginia Wesleyan College
Washington and Lee University

Washington
Pacific Lutheran University
University of Puget Sound
Whitman College
Whitworth College

West Virginia
Bethany College

Wisconsin
Alverno College W
Beloit College
Carroll College
Carthage College
Concordia University Wisconsin
Edgewood College
Lakeland College
Lawrence University
Maranatha Baptist Bible College
Marian College of Fond du Lac
Milwaukee School of Engineering
Mount Mary College W
Northland College
Ripon College
St. Norbert College
University of Wisconsin
Eau Claire W
La Crosse W
Oshkosh
Platteville
River Falls W
Stevens Point W
Stout W
Superior
Whitewater
Wisconsin Lutheran College

Softball Division I

Alabama
Alabama Agricultural and Mechanical University W
Alabama State University W
Auburn University W
Birmingham-Southern College W
Jacksonville State University W
Samford University W
Troy University W
University of Alabama W
University of Alabama Birmingham W

Arizona
Arizona State University W
University of Arizona W

Arkansas
University of Arkansas W
University of Arkansas Pine Bluff W

California
California Polytechnic State University: San Luis Obispo W
California State University
Fresno W
Fullerton W
Long Beach W
Northridge W
Sacramento W
Loyola Marymount University W
St. Mary's College of California W
San Diego State University W
San Jose State University W
Santa Clara University W
Stanford University W
University of California
Berkeley W
Los Angeles W
Riverside W
Santa Barbara W
University of San Diego W
University of the Pacific W

Colorado
Colorado State University W

Connecticut
Central Connecticut State University W
Fairfield University W
Quinnipiac University W
Sacred Heart University W
University of Connecticut W
University of Hartford W
Yale University W

Delaware
Delaware State University W
University of Delaware W

District of Columbia
George Washington University W
Georgetown University W
Howard University W

Florida
Bethune-Cookman College W
Florida Agricultural and Mechanical University W
Florida Atlantic University W
Florida International University W
Florida State University W
Jacksonville University W
Stetson University W
University of Central Florida W
University of Florida W
University of South Florida W

Georgia
Georgia Institute of Technology W
Georgia Southern University W
Georgia State University W
Mercer University W
Savannah State University W
University of Georgia W

Hawaii
University of Hawaii Manoa W

Illinois
Bradley University W
DePaul University W
Eastern Illinois University W
Illinois State University W
Loyola University of Chicago W
Northern Illinois University W
Northwestern University W
Southern Illinois University Carbondale W
University of Illinois
Chicago W
Urbana-Champaign W
Western Illinois University W

Indiana
Ball State University W

Butler University W
Indiana State University W
Indiana University
Bloomington W
Indiana University-Purdue University Fort Wayne W
Indiana University-Purdue University Indianapolis W
Purdue University W
University of Evansville W
University of Notre Dame W
Valparaiso University W

Iowa

Drake University W
Iowa State University W
University of Iowa W
University of Northern Iowa W

Kansas

University of Kansas W
Wichita State University W

Kentucky

Eastern Kentucky University W
Morehead State University W
University of Kentucky W
University of Louisville W
Western Kentucky University W

Louisiana

Centenary College of Louisiana W
Grambling State University W
Louisiana State University and Agricultural and Mechanical College W
Louisiana Tech University W
Nicholls State University W
Northwestern State University W
Southeastern Louisiana University W
Southern University and Agricultural and Mechanical College W
University of Louisiana at Lafayette W
University of Louisiana at Monroe W

Maine

University of Maine W

Maryland

Coppin State University W
Morgan State University W
Mount St. Mary's University W
Towson University W
University of Maryland
Baltimore County W
College Park W
Eastern Shore W

Massachusetts

Boston College W
Boston University W
College of the Holy Cross W
Harvard College W
University of Massachusetts
Amherst W

Michigan

Central Michigan University W
Eastern Michigan University W
Michigan State University W
Oakland University W
University of Detroit Mercy W
University of Michigan W
Western Michigan University W

Minnesota

University of Minnesota
Twin Cities W

Mississippi

Alcorn State University W
Jackson State University W
Mississippi State University W
Mississippi Valley State University W
University of Mississippi W
University of Southern Mississippi W

Missouri

Missouri State University W
St. Louis University W
Southeast Missouri State University W
University of Missouri
Columbia W
Kansas City W

Nebraska

Creighton University W
University of Nebraska
Lincoln W

Nevada

University of Nevada
Las Vegas W
Reno W

New Hampshire

Dartmouth College W

New Jersey

Fairleigh Dickinson University
Metropolitan Campus W
Monmouth University W
Princeton University W
Rider University W
Rutgers, The State University of New Jersey
New Brunswick Regional Campus W
St. Peter's College W
Seton Hall University W

New Mexico

New Mexico State University W
University of New Mexico W

New York

Barnard College W
Canisius College W
Colgate University W
Cornell University W
Fordham University W
Hofstra University W
Iona College W
Long Island University
Brooklyn Campus W
Manhattan College W
Marist College W
Niagara University W
St. Bonaventure University W
St. Francis College W
St. John's University W
Siena College W
State University of New York
Albany W
Binghamton W
Buffalo W
Stony Brook W
Syracuse University W
United States Military Academy W
Wagner College W

North Carolina

Appalachian State University W
Campbell University W
East Carolina University W
Elon University W
Gardner-Webb University W
North Carolina Agricultural and Technical State University W
North Carolina State University W
University of North Carolina
Chapel Hill W
Charlotte W
Greensboro W
Wilmington W
Western Carolina University W

Ohio

Bowling Green State University W
Cleveland State University W
Kent State University W
Miami University
Oxford Campus W
Ohio State University
Columbus Campus W
Ohio University W
University of Akron W
University of Dayton W
University of Toledo W
Wright State University W
Youngstown State University W

Oklahoma

Oklahoma State University W
University of Oklahoma W
University of Tulsa W

Oregon

Oregon State University W
Portland State University W
University of Oregon W

Pennsylvania

Bucknell University W
Drexel University W
La Salle University W
Lafayette College W
Lehigh University W
Penn State
University Park W
Robert Morris University W
St. Francis University W
St. Joseph's University W
Temple University W
University of Pennsylvania W
University of Pittsburgh W
Villanova University W

Rhode Island

Brown University W
Providence College W
University of Rhode Island W

South Carolina

Charleston Southern University W
Coastal Carolina University W
College of Charleston W
Furman University W
South Carolina State University W
University of South Carolina W
Winthrop University W

Tennessee

Austin Peay State University W
Belmont University W
East Tennessee State University W
Lipscomb University W
Middle Tennessee State University W
Tennessee State University W
Tennessee Technological University W
University of Tennessee
Chattanooga W
Knoxville W
Martin W

Texas

Baylor University W
Prairie View A&M University W
Sam Houston State University W
Stephen F. Austin State University W
Texas A&M University W
Texas Southern University W
Texas State University: San Marcos W
Texas Tech University W
University of Houston W
University of North Texas W
University of Texas
Arlington W
Austin W
El Paso W
San Antonio W

Utah

Brigham Young University W
Southern Utah University W
University of Utah W
Utah State University W
Utah Valley State College W

Vermont

University of Vermont W

Virginia

George Mason University W
Hampton University W
James Madison University W
Liberty University W
Norfolk State University W
Radford University W
University of Virginia W
Virginia Polytechnic Institute and State University W

Washington

University of Washington W

West Virginia

Marshall University W

Wisconsin

University of Wisconsin
Green Bay W
Madison W

Softball Division II

Alabama

Miles College W
Stillman College W
Tuskegee University W
University of Alabama
Huntsville W
University of North Alabama W
University of West Alabama W

Arizona

Grand Canyon University W

Arkansas

Arkansas Tech University W
Henderson State University W
Ouachita Baptist University W
Southern Arkansas University W
University of Arkansas
Monticello W
University of Central Arkansas W

California

California State University
Bakersfield W
Chico W
Dominguez Hills W
Monterey Bay W
San Bernardino W
Stanislaus W
Humboldt State University W
Notre Dame de Namur University W
San Francisco State University W
Sonoma State University W
University of California
Davis W
San Diego W

Colorado

Adams State College W
Colorado School of Mines W
Colorado State University
Pueblo W
Fort Lewis College W
Mesa State College W
Regis University W
University of Colorado
Colorado Springs W
University of Northern Colorado W

Connecticut

Post University W
Southern Connecticut State University W
University of Bridgeport W
University of New Haven W

Delaware

Goldey-Beacom College W
Wilmington College W

Florida

Barry University W
Eckerd College W
Florida Gulf Coast University W
Florida Institute of Technology W
Florida Southern College W
Lynn University W
Nova Southeastern University W
Palm Beach Atlantic University W
Rollins College W
St. Leo University W
University of North Florida W
University of Tampa W
University of West Florida W

Georgia

Albany State University W
Armstrong Atlantic State University W
Augusta State University W
Clark Atlanta University W
Columbus State University W
Fort Valley State University W
Georgia College and State University W
Kennesaw State University W
North Georgia College & State University W
Paine College W
University of West Georgia W
Valdosta State University W

Hawaii

Brigham Young
University-Hawaii W
Chaminade University of Honolulu W
Hawaii Pacific University W
University of Hawaii
Hilo W

Idaho

Northwest Nazarene University W

Illinois

Lewis University W
Quincy University W
Southern Illinois University
Edwardsville W

Indiana

Oakland City University W
St. Joseph's College W
University of Indianapolis W
University of Southern Indiana W

Iowa

Upper Iowa University W

Kansas

Emporia State University W
Fort Hays State University W
Pittsburg State University W
Washburn University of Topeka W

Kentucky

Bellarmine University W
Kentucky State University W
Kentucky Wesleyan College W
Northern Kentucky University W

Maryland

Bowie State University W
Columbia Union College W

Massachusetts

American International College W
Assumption College W
Bentley College W
Merrimack College W

Tables and Indexes

Stonehill College W
University of Massachusetts
Lowell W

Michigan
Ferris State University W
Grand Valley State University W
Hillsdale College W
Lake Superior State University W
Northwood University W
Saginaw Valley State University W
Wayne State University W

Minnesota
Bemidji State University W
Concordia University: St. Paul W
Minnesota State University
Mankato W
Moorhead W
St. Cloud State University W
Southwest Minnesota State University W
University of Minnesota
Crookston W
Duluth W
Morris W
Winona State University W

Mississippi
Delta State University W

Missouri
Central Missouri State University W
Lincoln University W
Missouri Southern State University W
Missouri Western State University W
Northwest Missouri State University W
Rockhurst University W
Southwest Baptist University W
Truman State University W
University of Missouri
Rolla W
St. Louis W

Montana
Montana State University
Billings W

Nebraska
University of Nebraska
Kearney W
Omaha W
Wayne State College W

New Hampshire
Franklin Pierce College W
St. Anselm College W
Southern New Hampshire University W

New Jersey
Bloomfield College W
Caldwell College W
Felician College W
Georgian Court University W

New Mexico
Eastern New Mexico University W
New Mexico Highlands University W
Western New Mexico University W

New York
Adelphi University W
City University of New York
Queens College W
College of Saint Rose W
Concordia College W
Dominican College of Blauvelt W
Dowling College W
Le Moyne College W
Long Island University
C. W. Post Campus W
Mercy College W
Molloy College W
New York Institute of Technology W
Nyack College W
Pace University W
St. Thomas Aquinas College W

North Carolina
Barton College W
Belmont Abbey College W
Catawba College W
Elizabeth City State University W
Fayetteville State University W
Johnson C. Smith University W
Lees-McRae College W
Lenoir-Rhyne College W
Livingstone College W
Mars Hill College W
Mount Olive College W
North Carolina Central University W
Pfeiffer University W
Queens University of Charlotte W
St. Andrews Presbyterian College W
St. Augustine's College W
Shaw University W
University of North Carolina
Pembroke W
Wingate University W
Winston-Salem State University W

North Dakota
North Dakota State University W
University of Mary W
University of North Dakota W

Ohio
Ashland University W
Tiffin University W
University of Findlay W

Oklahoma
Cameron University W
East Central University W
Northeastern State University W
Oklahoma Panhandle State University W
Southeastern Oklahoma State University W
Southwestern Oklahoma State University W
University of Central Oklahoma W

Oregon
Western Oregon University W

Pennsylvania
Bloomsburg University of Pennsylvania W
California University of Pennsylvania W
Clarion University of Pennsylvania W
East Stroudsburg University of Pennsylvania W
Edinboro University of Pennsylvania W
Gannon University W
Holy Family University W
Indiana University of Pennsylvania W
Kutztown University of Pennsylvania W
Lock Haven University of Pennsylvania W
Mansfield University of Pennsylvania W
Mercyhurst College W
Millersville University of Pennsylvania W
Philadelphia University W
Shippensburg University of Pennsylvania W
Slippery Rock University of Pennsylvania W
University of the Sciences in Philadelphia W
West Chester University of Pennsylvania W

Puerto Rico
University of Puerto Rico
Cayey University College W
Mayaguez W

Rhode Island
Bryant University W

South Carolina
Anderson University W
Benedict College W
Claflin University W
Coker College W
Erskine College W
Francis Marion University W
Lander University W
Limestone College W
Newberry College W
North Greenville College W
Presbyterian College W
University of South Carolina
Aiken W
Upstate W

South Dakota
Augustana College W
Northern State University W
South Dakota State University W
University of South Dakota W

Tennessee
Carson-Newman College W
Christian Brothers University W
LeMoyne-Owen College W
Lincoln Memorial University W
Tusculum College W

Texas
Abilene Christian University W
Angelo State University W
Midwestern State University W
St. Edward's University W
St. Mary's University W
Tarleton State University W
Texas A&M University
Kingsville W
Texas Woman's University W
University of the Incarnate Word W
West Texas A&M University W

Vermont
Green Mountain College W
St. Michael's College W

Virginia
Longwood University W
St. Paul's College W
Virginia State University W
Virginia Union University W

Washington
Central Washington University W
Saint Martin's University W
Seattle University W
Western Washington University W

West Virginia
Alderson-Broaddus College W
Bluefield State College W
Concord University W
Davis and Elkins College W
Glenville State College W
Ohio Valley University W
Salem International University W
Shepherd University W
University of Charleston W
West Liberty State College W
West Virginia State University W
West Virginia University Institute of Technology W
West Virginia Wesleyan College W
Wheeling Jesuit University W

Wisconsin
University of Wisconsin
Parkside W

Softball Division III

Alabama
Huntingdon College W

Arkansas
Hendrix College W
University of the Ozarks W

California
California Lutheran University W
California State University
East Bay W
Chapman University W
Claremont McKenna College W
Menlo College W
Occidental College W
Pitzer College W
Pomona College W
University of La Verne W
University of Redlands W
Whittier College W

Colorado
Colorado College W

Connecticut
Albertus Magnus College W
Eastern Connecticut State University W
Mitchell College W
St. Joseph College W
Trinity College W
United States Coast Guard Academy W
Wesleyan University W
Western Connecticut State University W

Delaware
Wesley College W

District of Columbia
Catholic University of America W
Gallaudet University W
Trinity University W

Georgia
Agnes Scott College W
Emory University W
LaGrange College W
Piedmont College W
Spelman College W
Wesleyan College W

Illinois
Augustana College W
Aurora University W
Benedictine University W
Blackburn College W
Concordia University W
Dominican University W
Elmhurst College W
Eureka College W
Greenville College W
Illinois College W
Illinois Wesleyan University W
Knox College W
Lake Forest College W
MacMurray College W
Millikin University W
Monmouth College W
North Central College W
North Park University W
Rockford College W
University of Chicago W
Wheaton College W

Indiana
Anderson University W
DePauw University W
Franklin College W
Hanover College W
Manchester College W
Rose-Hulman Institute of Technology W
Saint Mary's College W
Tri-State University W

Iowa
Buena Vista University W
Central College W
Clarke College W
Coe College W
Cornell College W
Grinnell College W
Loras College W
Luther College W
Simpson College W
University of Dubuque W
Wartburg College W

Kentucky
Centre College W
Thomas More College W
Transylvania University W

Maine
Bates College W
Bowdoin College W
Colby College W
Husson College W
Maine Maritime Academy W
St. Joseph's College W
Thomas College W
University of Maine
Farmington W
Presque Isle W
University of New England W
University of Southern Maine W

Maryland
Frostburg State University W
Hood College W
McDaniel College W
Salisbury University W
Villa Julie College W
Washington College W

Massachusetts
Amherst College W
Anna Maria College W
Babson College W
Bay Path College W
Becker College W
Brandeis University W
Bridgewater State College W
Clark University W
Curry College W
Eastern Nazarene College W
Elms College W
Emerson College W
Emmanuel College W
Endicott College W
Fitchburg State College W
Framingham State College W
Gordon College W
Lasell College W
Lesley University W
Massachusetts College of Liberal Arts W
Massachusetts Institute of Technology W
Massachusetts Maritime Academy W
Mount Ida College W
Newbury College W
Nichols College W
Pine Manor College W
Regis College W
Salem State College W
Simmons College W
Smith College W
Springfield College W
Suffolk University W
Tufts University W
University of Massachusetts
Boston W
Dartmouth W
Wellesley College W
Wentworth Institute of Technology W
Western New England College W

Westfield State College W
Wheaton College W
Wheelock College W
Williams College W
Worcester Polytechnic Institute W
Worcester State College W

Michigan
Adrian College W
Albion College W
Alma College W
Calvin College W
Finlandia University W
Hope College W
Kalamazoo College W
Olivet College W

Minnesota
Augsburg College W
Bethany Lutheran College W
Bethel University W
Carleton College W
College of St. Benedict W
College of St. Catherine W
College of St. Scholastica W
Concordia College: Moorhead W
Crown College W
Gustavus Adolphus College W
Hamline University W
Macalester College W
Martin Luther College W
North Central University W
Northwestern College W
St. Mary's University of Minnesota W
St. Olaf College W
University of St. Thomas W

Mississippi
Millsaps College W
Mississippi College W
Rust College W

Missouri
Fontbonne University W
Maryville University of Saint Louis W
Washington University in St. Louis W
Webster University W
Westminster College W

Nebraska
Nebraska Wesleyan University W

New Hampshire
Daniel Webster College W
Keene State College W
New England College W
Plymouth State University W
Rivier College W

New Jersey
Centenary College W
The College of New Jersey W
College of St. Elizabeth W
Drew University W
Fairleigh Dickinson University
College at Florham W
Kean University W
Montclair State University W
New Jersey City University W
Ramapo College of New Jersey W
Richard Stockton College of New Jersey W
Rowan University W
Rutgers, The State University of New Jersey
Camden Regional Campus W
Newark Regional Campus W
William Paterson University of New Jersey W

New York
Alfred University W
Cazenovia College W
City University of New York
Baruch College W
Brooklyn College W
College of Staten Island W
Hunter College W
John Jay College of Criminal Justice W
Lehman College W
New York City College of Technology W
York College W
College of Mount St. Vincent W
College of New Rochelle W
D'Youville College W
Elmira College W
Hamilton College W
Hartwick College W
Hilbert College W
Ithaca College W
Keuka College W
Manhattanville College W
Medaille College W
Mount St. Mary College W
Polytechnic University W
Rensselaer Polytechnic Institute W
Rochester Institute of Technology W
Russell Sage College W
St. John Fisher College W
St. Joseph's College: Suffolk Campus W
St. Lawrence University W
Skidmore College W
State University of New York
College at Brockport W
College at Buffalo W
College at Cortland W
College at Fredonia W
College at Geneseo W
College at Old Westbury W
College at Oneonta W
College at Plattsburgh W
College at Potsdam W
Farmingdale W
Institute of Technology at Utica/Rome W
Maritime College W
New Paltz W
Oswego W
Purchase W
Union College W
United States Merchant Marine Academy W
University of Rochester W
Utica College W
Wells College W

North Carolina
Chowan College W
Greensboro College W
Guilford College W
Meredith College W
Methodist College W
North Carolina Wesleyan College W
Peace College W
Salem College W

Ohio
Baldwin-Wallace College W
Bluffton University W
Capital University W
Case Western Reserve University W
College of Mount St. Joseph W
College of Wooster W
Defiance College W
Denison University W
Heidelberg College W
Hiram College W
John Carroll University W
Kenyon College W
Lake Erie College W
Marietta College W
Mount Union College W
Muskingum College W
Oberlin College W
Ohio Northern University W
Ohio Wesleyan University W
Otterbein College W
Wilmington College W
Wittenberg University W

Oregon
George Fox University W
Lewis & Clark College W
Linfield College W
Pacific University W
Willamette University W

Pennsylvania
Albright College W
Allegheny College W
Alvernia College W
Arcadia University W
Baptist Bible College of Pennsylvania W
Cabrini College W
Cedar Crest College W
Chatham College W
Chestnut Hill College W
College Misericordia W
Delaware Valley College W
DeSales University W
Dickinson College W
Eastern University W
Elizabethtown College W
Franklin & Marshall College W
Gettysburg College W
Grove City College W
Gwynedd-Mercy College W
Haverford College W
Immaculata University W
Juniata College W
Keystone College W
King's College W
La Roche College W
Lebanon Valley College W
Lycoming College W
Marywood University W
Messiah College W
Moravian College W
Mount Aloysius College W
Muhlenberg College W
Neumann College W
Penn State
Altoona W
Berks W
Erie, The Behrend College W
Philadelphia Biblical University W
Rosemont College W
Susquehanna University W
Swarthmore College W
Thiel College W
University of Pittsburgh
Bradford W
Greensburg W
University of Scranton W
Ursinus College W
Washington and Jefferson College W
Waynesburg College W
Westminster College W
Widener University W
Wilkes University W
Wilson College W
York College of Pennsylvania W

Rhode Island
Johnson & Wales University W
Rhode Island College W
Roger Williams University W
Salve Regina University W

South Dakota
Presentation College W

Tennessee
Fisk University W
Maryville College W
Rhodes College W
University of the South W

Texas
Concordia University at Austin W
East Texas Baptist University W
Hardin-Simmons University W
Howard Payne University W
LeTourneau University W
Schreiner University W
Sul Ross State University W
Texas Lutheran University W
Trinity University W
University of Dallas W
University of Mary Hardin-Baylor W
University of Texas
Dallas W
Tyler W

Vermont
Castleton State College W
Johnson State College W
Middlebury College W
Norwich University W
Southern Vermont College W

Virginia
Averett University W
Bridgewater College W
Christopher Newport University W
Eastern Mennonite University W
Emory & Henry College W
Ferrum College W
Lynchburg College W
Mary Baldwin College W
Randolph-Macon College W
Randolph-Macon Woman's College W
Roanoke College W
Shenandoah University W
Sweet Briar College W
University of Mary Washington W
Virginia Wesleyan College W

Washington
Pacific Lutheran University W
University of Puget Sound W
Whitworth College W

West Virginia
Bethany College W

Wisconsin
Alverno College W
Beloit College W
Carroll College W
Carthage College W
Concordia University Wisconsin W
Edgewood College W
Lakeland College W
Lawrence University W
Maranatha Baptist Bible College W
Marian College of Fond du Lac W
Milwaukee School of Engineering W
Mount Mary College W
Northland College W
Ripon College W
St. Norbert College W
University of Wisconsin
Eau Claire W
La Crosse W
Oshkosh W
Platteville W
River Falls W
Stevens Point W
Stout W
Superior W
Whitewater W
Wisconsin Lutheran College W

Swimming Division I

Alabama
Auburn University
University of Alabama

Arizona
Arizona State University
Northern Arizona University W
University of Arizona

Arkansas
University of Arkansas W
University of Arkansas
Little Rock W

California
California Polytechnic State University: San Luis Obispo
California State University
Northridge
Loyola Marymount University W
Pepperdine University W
San Diego State University W
San Jose State University W
Stanford University
University of California
Berkeley
Irvine
Los Angeles W
Santa Barbara
University of San Diego W
University of Southern California
University of the Pacific

Colorado
United States Air Force Academy
University of Denver

Connecticut
Central Connecticut State University W
Fairfield University
Sacred Heart University W
University of Connecticut
Yale University

Delaware
University of Delaware

District of Columbia
American University
George Washington University
Georgetown University
Howard University

Florida
Florida Agricultural and Mechanical University
Florida Atlantic University
Florida International University W
Florida State University
University of Florida
University of Miami
University of North Florida W

Georgia
Georgia Institute of Technology
Georgia Southern University W
University of Georgia

Hawaii
University of Hawaii
Manoa

Idaho
University of Idaho W

Illinois
Eastern Illinois University
Illinois State University W
Northwestern University
Southern Illinois University
Carbondale
University of Illinois
Chicago
Urbana-Champaign W
Western Illinois University

Indiana
Ball State University
Butler University
Indiana University
Bloomington

Indiana University-Purdue University Indianapolis
Purdue University
University of Evansville
University of Notre Dame
Valparaiso University

Iowa
Iowa State University W
University of Iowa
University of Northern Iowa W

Kansas
University of Kansas W

Kentucky
University of Kentucky
University of Louisville
Western Kentucky University

Louisiana
Centenary College of Louisiana
Louisiana State University and Agricultural and Mechanical College
University of Louisiana at Monroe
University of New Orleans W

Maine
University of Maine

Maryland
Loyola College in Maryland
Mount St. Mary's University W
Towson University
United States Naval Academy
University of Maryland
Baltimore County
College Park

Massachusetts
Boston College
Boston University
College of the Holy Cross
Harvard College
Northeastern University W
University of Massachusetts
Amherst

Michigan
Eastern Michigan University
Michigan State University
Oakland University
University of Michigan

Minnesota
University of Minnesota
Twin Cities

Missouri
Missouri State University
St. Louis University
University of Missouri
Columbia

Nebraska
University of Nebraska
Lincoln W

Nevada
University of Nevada
Las Vegas
Reno W

New Hampshire
Dartmouth College
University of New Hampshire

New Jersey
Princeton University
Rider University
Rutgers, The State University of New Jersey
New Brunswick Regional Campus
St. Peter's College
Seton Hall University

New Mexico
New Mexico State University W
University of New Mexico W

New York
Barnard College W
Canisius College
Colgate University
Columbia University
Columbia College M
Cornell University
Fordham University
Iona College
Manhattan College W
Marist College
Niagara University
St. Bonaventure University
St. Francis College
Siena College W
State University of New York
Binghamton
Buffalo
Stony Brook
Syracuse University
United States Military Academy
Wagner College W

North Carolina
Campbell University W
Davidson College
Duke University
East Carolina University
Gardner-Webb University W
North Carolina Agricultural and Technical State University W
North Carolina State University
University of North Carolina
Chapel Hill
Wilmington

Ohio
Bowling Green State University W
Cleveland State University
Miami University
Oxford Campus
Ohio State University
Columbus Campus
Ohio University
University of Akron W
University of Cincinnati
University of Toledo W
Wright State University
Xavier University
Youngstown State University W

Oregon
Oregon State University W

Pennsylvania
Bucknell University
Drexel University
Duquesne University
La Salle University
Lafayette College
Lehigh University
Penn State
University Park
St. Francis University W
University of Pennsylvania
University of Pittsburgh
Villanova University

Rhode Island
Brown University
Providence College
University of Rhode Island

South Carolina
Clemson University
College of Charleston
University of South Carolina

Tennessee
University of Tennessee
Knoxville

Texas
Rice University W
Southern Methodist University
Texas A&M University
Texas Christian University
University of Houston W
University of North Texas W
University of Texas
Austin

Utah
Brigham Young University
University of Utah

Vermont
University of Vermont W

Virginia
College of William and Mary
George Mason University
James Madison University
Old Dominion University
Radford University W
University of Richmond W
University of Virginia
Virginia Military Institute
Virginia Polytechnic Institute and State University

Washington
University of Washington
Washington State University W

West Virginia
Marshall University W
West Virginia University

Wisconsin
University of Wisconsin
Green Bay
Madison
Milwaukee

Wyoming
University of Wyoming

Swimming Division II

Alaska
University of Alaska
Fairbanks W

Arkansas
Henderson State University
Ouachita Baptist University

California
California State University
Bakersfield
University of California
Davis
San Diego

Colorado
Colorado School of Mines
Mesa State College W
Metropolitan State College of Denver
University of Northern Colorado W

Connecticut
Southern Connecticut State University
University of Bridgeport W

Florida
Florida Southern College
Rollins College
St. Leo University
University of Tampa

Illinois
Lewis University

Indiana
University of Indianapolis

Massachusetts
Bentley College

Michigan
Grand Valley State University
Hillsdale College W
Northern Michigan University W
Wayne State University

Minnesota
Minnesota State University
Mankato
Moorhead W
St. Cloud State University
University of Minnesota
Morris W

Mississippi
Delta State University

Missouri
Drury University
Truman State University
University of Missouri
Rolla M

Nebraska
University of Nebraska
Kearney W
Omaha W

New Jersey
New Jersey Institute of Technology

New York
Adelphi University
City University of New York
Queens College
College of Saint Rose
Le Moyne College
Long Island University
C. W. Post Campus W
Pace University

North Carolina
Catawba College W
Lenoir-Rhyne College W
Mars Hill College W
Pfeiffer University W
Wingate University

North Dakota
University of North Dakota

Ohio
Ashland University
University of Findlay

Pennsylvania
Bloomsburg University of Pennsylvania
California University of Pennsylvania W
Clarion University of Pennsylvania
East Stroudsburg University of Pennsylvania W
Edinboro University of Pennsylvania
Gannon University
Indiana University of Pennsylvania
Kutztown University of Pennsylvania
Lock Haven University of Pennsylvania W
Mansfield University of Pennsylvania W
Millersville University of Pennsylvania W
Shippensburg University of Pennsylvania
Slippery Rock University of Pennsylvania
West Chester University of Pennsylvania

Puerto Rico
University of Puerto Rico
Bayamon University College
Mayaguez M
Rio Piedras W

Rhode Island
Bryant University

South Carolina
Limestone College W

South Dakota
South Dakota State University
University of South Dakota

Texas
University of the Incarnate Word W

Vermont
St. Michael's College

Washington
Seattle University

West Virginia
West Virginia Wesleyan College
Wheeling Jesuit University

Swimming Division III

Arkansas
Hendrix College

California
California Institute of Technology
California Lutheran University
California State University
East Bay W
Chapman University W
Claremont McKenna College
Mills College W
Occidental College
Pitzer College M
Pomona College
University of California
Santa Cruz
University of La Verne
University of Redlands
Whittier College

Colorado
Colorado College

Connecticut
Albertus Magnus College W
Connecticut College
Eastern Connecticut State University W
St. Joseph College W
Trinity College
United States Coast Guard Academy
Wesleyan University
Western Connecticut State University W

District of Columbia
Catholic University of America
Gallaudet University

Georgia
Agnes Scott College W
Emory University
LaGrange College

Illinois
Augustana College
Benedictine University
Eureka College
Illinois Wesleyan University
Knox College
Lake Forest College
Millikin University
Monmouth College
North Central College
Principia College
University of Chicago
Wheaton College

Indiana
DePauw University
Rose-Hulman Institute of Technology
Saint Mary's College W
Tri-State University M
Wabash College M

Iowa
Coe College
Grinnell College

Loras College
Luther College
Simpson College W

Kentucky

Centre College
Transylvania University

Maine

Bates College
Bowdoin College
Colby College
Husson College W
University of New England W

Maryland

College of Notre Dame of Maryland W
Frostburg State University
Goucher College
Hood College
Johns Hopkins University
McDaniel College
St. Mary's College of Maryland
Salisbury University
Washington College

Massachusetts

Amherst College
Babson College
Brandeis University
Bridgewater State College
Clark University
Elms College
Gordon College
Massachusetts Institute of Technology
Mount Holyoke College W
Regis College W
Salem State College W
Simmons College W
Smith College W
Springfield College
Tufts University
University of Massachusetts
 Dartmouth
Wellesley College W
Western New England College W
Westfield State College W
Wheaton College
Wheelock College W
Williams College
Worcester Polytechnic Institute

Michigan

Albion College
Alma College
Calvin College
Hope College
Kalamazoo College
Olivet College

Minnesota

Augsburg College W
Carleton College
College of St. Benedict W
College of St. Catherine W
Concordia College: Moorhead W
Gustavus Adolphus College
Hamline University
Macalester College
St. John's University M
St. Mary's University of Minnesota
St. Olaf College
University of St. Thomas

Missouri

Washington University in St. Louis
Webster University

New Hampshire

Colby-Sawyer College
Keene State College
Plymouth State University W

New Jersey

The College of New Jersey
College of St. Elizabeth W
Drew University
Fairleigh Dickinson University
 College at Florham W
 Metropolitan Campus M
Montclair State University
Rowan University
Stevens Institute of Technology
William Paterson University of New Jersey

New York

Alfred University
City University of New York
 Baruch College
 College of Staten Island
 Hunter College W
 John Jay College of Criminal Justice W
 Lehman College
 York College
Clarkson University
College of Mount St. Vincent W
College of New Rochelle W
Hamilton College
Hartwick College
Hobart and William Smith Colleges W
Ithaca College
Mount St. Mary College
Nazareth College of Rochester
New York University
Rensselaer Polytechnic Institute
Rochester Institute of Technology
St. Joseph's College W
St. Lawrence University
Skidmore College
State University of New York
 College at Brockport
 College at Buffalo
 College at Cortland
 College at Fredonia
 College at Geneseo
 College at Old Westbury
 College at Oneonta
 College at Potsdam
 Maritime College
 New Paltz
 Oswego
 Purchase W
Union College
United States Merchant Marine Academy
University of Rochester
Utica College
Vassar College
Wells College W

North Carolina

Greensboro College W
Guilford College W
Salem College W

Ohio

Baldwin-Wallace College
Case Western Reserve University
College of Wooster
Denison University
Hiram College
John Carroll University
Kenyon College
Mount Union College
Oberlin College
Ohio Northern University
Ohio Wesleyan University
Wilmington College
Wittenberg University

Oregon

Lewis & Clark College
Linfield College
Pacific University
Willamette University

Pennsylvania

Albright College
Allegheny College
Arcadia University
Bryn Mawr College W
Cabrini College W
Carnegie Mellon University
Chatham College W
College Misericordia
Dickinson College
Elizabethtown College
Franklin & Marshall College
Gettysburg College
Grove City College
Juniata College W
King's College
Lebanon Valley College
Lycoming College
Penn State
 Altoona
 Erie, The Behrend College
Susquehanna University
Swarthmore College
University of Scranton
Ursinus College
Washington and Jefferson College
Westminster College
Widener University
York College of Pennsylvania

Rhode Island

Roger Williams University

Tennessee

Rhodes College
University of the South

Texas

Austin College
McMurry University
Southwestern University
Trinity University

Vermont

Middlebury College
Norwich University

Virginia

Emory & Henry College W
Hollins University W
Mary Baldwin College W
Marymount University
Randolph-Macon College W
Randolph-Macon Woman's College W
Sweet Briar College W
University of Mary Washington
Washington and Lee University

Washington

Pacific Lutheran University
University of Puget Sound
Whitman College
Whitworth College

West Virginia

Bethany College

Wisconsin

Beloit College
Carroll College
Carthage College
Lawrence University
Ripon College
St. Norbert College W
University of Wisconsin
 Eau Claire
 La Crosse
 Oshkosh
 River Falls
 Stevens Point
 Whitewater

Tennis Division I

Alabama

Alabama Agricultural and Mechanical University
Alabama State University
Auburn University
Birmingham-Southern College
Jacksonville State University
Samford University
Troy University
University of Alabama
University of Alabama
 Birmingham
University of South Alabama

Arizona

Arizona State University
Northern Arizona University
University of Arizona

Arkansas

Arkansas State University W
University of Arkansas
University of Arkansas
 Little Rock
 Pine Bluff

California

California Polytechnic State University: San Luis Obispo
California State University
 Fresno
 Fullerton W
 Long Beach W
 Northridge W
 Sacramento
Loyola Marymount University
Pepperdine University
St. Mary's College of California
San Diego State University
San Jose State University W
Santa Clara University
Stanford University
University of California
 Berkeley
 Irvine
 Los Angeles
 Riverside
 Santa Barbara
University of San Diego
University of San Francisco
University of Southern California
University of the Pacific

Colorado

Colorado State University W
United States Air Force Academy
University of Colorado
 Boulder
University of Denver

Connecticut

Fairfield University
Quinnipiac University
Sacred Heart University
University of Connecticut
University of Hartford
Yale University

Delaware

Delaware State University
University of Delaware

District of Columbia

American University
George Washington University
Georgetown University
Howard University

Florida

Bethune-Cookman College
Florida Agricultural and Mechanical University
Florida Atlantic University
Florida International University W
Florida State University
Jacksonville University
Stetson University
University of Central Florida
University of Florida
University of Miami
University of South Florida

Georgia

Georgia Institute of Technology
Georgia Southern University
Georgia State University
Mercer University
Savannah State University
University of Georgia

Hawaii

University of Hawaii
 Manoa

Idaho

Boise State University
Idaho State University
University of Idaho

Illinois

Bradley University
Chicago State University
DePaul University
Eastern Illinois University
Illinois State University
Northern Illinois University
Northwestern University
Southern Illinois University
 Carbondale
University of Illinois
 Chicago
 Urbana-Champaign
Western Illinois University

Indiana

Ball State University
Butler University
Indiana State University
Indiana University
 Bloomington
Indiana University-Purdue University Fort Wayne
Indiana University-Purdue University Indianapolis
Purdue University
University of Evansville W
University of Notre Dame
Valparaiso University

Iowa

Drake University
Iowa State University W
University of Iowa
University of Northern Iowa W

Kansas

Kansas State University W
University of Kansas W
Wichita State University

Kentucky

Eastern Kentucky University
Morehead State University
Murray State University
University of Kentucky
University of Louisville
Western Kentucky University

Louisiana

Centenary College of Louisiana
Grambling State University
Louisiana State University and Agricultural and Mechanical College
Louisiana Tech University W
Nicholls State University
Northwestern State University W
Southeastern Louisiana University
Southern University and Agricultural and Mechanical College
University of Louisiana at Lafayette
University of Louisiana at Monroe W
University of New Orleans

Maryland

Coppin State University
Loyola College in Maryland
Morgan State University
Mount St. Mary's University
Towson University W
United States Naval Academy M
University of Maryland
 Baltimore County
 College Park
 Eastern Shore

Tables and Indexes

Massachusetts
Boston College
Boston University
College of the Holy Cross
Harvard College
University of Massachusetts
  Amherst W

Michigan
Eastern Michigan University W
Michigan State University
Oakland University W
University of Detroit Mercy W
University of Michigan
Western Michigan University

Minnesota
University of Minnesota
  Twin Cities

Mississippi
Alcorn State University
Jackson State University
Mississippi State University
Mississippi Valley State University
University of Mississippi
University of Southern Mississippi

Missouri
Missouri State University
St. Louis University
Southeast Missouri State University W
University of Missouri
  Columbia W
  Kansas City

Montana
Montana State University
  Bozeman
University of Montana: Missoula

Nebraska
Creighton University
University of Nebraska
  Lincoln

Nevada
University of Nevada
  Las Vegas
  Reno

New Hampshire
Dartmouth College
University of New Hampshire

New Jersey
Fairleigh Dickinson University
  Metropolitan Campus
Monmouth University
Princeton University
Rider University
Rutgers, The State University of New Jersey
  New Brunswick Regional Campus
St. Peter's College
Seton Hall University W

New Mexico
New Mexico State University
University of New Mexico

New York
Barnard College W
Colgate University W
Columbia University
  Columbia College M
Cornell University
Fordham University
Hofstra University
Long Island University
  Brooklyn Campus W
Manhattan College
Marist College
Niagara University
St. Bonaventure University
St. Francis College
St. John's University
Siena College
State University of New York
  Albany W
  Binghamton
  Buffalo
  Stony Brook
Syracuse University W
United States Military Academy
Wagner College

North Carolina
Appalachian State University
Campbell University
Davidson College
Duke University
East Carolina University
Elon University
Gardner-Webb University
High Point University
North Carolina Agricultural and Technical State University
North Carolina State University
University of North Carolina
  Asheville
  Chapel Hill
  Charlotte
  Greensboro
  Wilmington
Wake Forest University
Western Carolina University W

Ohio
Bowling Green State University W
Cleveland State University
Miami University
  Oxford Campus W
Ohio State University
  Columbus Campus
University of Akron W
University of Cincinnati W
University of Dayton
University of Toledo
Wright State University
Xavier University
Youngstown State University

Oklahoma
Oklahoma State University
Oral Roberts University
University of Oklahoma
University of Tulsa

Oregon
University of Oregon
University of Portland

Pennsylvania
Bucknell University
Drexel University
Duquesne University
La Salle University
Lafayette College
Lehigh University
Penn State
  University Park
Robert Morris University
St. Francis University
St. Joseph's University
Temple University
University of Pennsylvania
University of Pittsburgh W
Villanova University

Rhode Island
Brown University
Providence College W
University of Rhode Island

South Carolina
Charleston Southern University
The Citadel M
Clemson University
Coastal Carolina University
College of Charleston
Furman University
South Carolina State University
University of South Carolina
Winthrop University
Wofford College

Tennessee
Austin Peay State University
Belmont University
East Tennessee State University
Lipscomb University
Middle Tennessee State University
Tennessee State University
Tennessee Technological University
University of Memphis
University of Tennessee
  Chattanooga
  Knoxville
  Martin
Vanderbilt University

Texas
Baylor University
Lamar University
Prairie View A&M University
Rice University
Sam Houston State University W
Southern Methodist University
Stephen F. Austin State University W
Texas A&M University
Texas Christian University
Texas Southern University
Texas State University: San Marcos W
Texas Tech University
University of Houston W
University of North Texas W
University of Texas
  Arlington
  Austin
  El Paso W
  Pan American
  San Antonio

Utah
Brigham Young University
Southern Utah University W
University of Utah
Utah State University
Weber State University

Virginia
College of William and Mary
George Mason University
Hampton University
James Madison University
Liberty University
Norfolk State University
Old Dominion University
Radford University
University of Richmond
University of Virginia
Virginia Commonwealth University
Virginia Polytechnic Institute and State University

Washington
Eastern Washington University
Gonzaga University
University of Washington
Washington State University W

West Virginia
Marshall University W
West Virginia University W

Wisconsin
Marquette University
University of Wisconsin
  Green Bay
  Madison
  Milwaukee W

Wyoming
University of Wyoming W

Tennis Division II

Alabama
Stillman College
Tuskegee University
University of Alabama
  Huntsville
University of Montevallo W
University of North Alabama
University of West Alabama

Arizona
Grand Canyon University W

Arkansas
Arkansas Tech University W
Harding University
Henderson State University W
Ouachita Baptist University
Southern Arkansas University W
University of Central Arkansas W

California
California State Polytechnic University: Pomona
California State University
  Bakersfield W
  Los Angeles W
  San Bernardino W
Sonoma State University
University of California
  Davis
  San Diego

Colorado
Colorado Christian University
Colorado State University
  Pueblo
Mesa State College
Metropolitan State College of Denver
University of Colorado
  Colorado Springs
University of Northern Colorado

Connecticut
Post University M
University of New Haven W

Delaware
Goldey-Beacom College W

District of Columbia
University of the District of Columbia

Florida
Barry University
Eckerd College
Florida Gulf Coast University
Florida Institute of Technology
Florida Southern College
Lynn University
Nova Southeastern University W
Palm Beach Atlantic University
Rollins College
St. Leo University
University of North Florida
University of Tampa W
University of West Florida

Georgia
Albany State University W
Armstrong Atlantic State University
Augusta State University
Clark Atlanta University W
Clayton State University W
Columbus State University
Fort Valley State University
Georgia College and State University
Kennesaw State University W
Morehouse College M
North Georgia College & State University
Valdosta State University

Hawaii
Brigham Young University-Hawaii
Chaminade University of Honolulu
Hawaii Pacific University
University of Hawaii
  Hilo

Illinois
Lewis University
Quincy University
Southern Illinois University
  Edwardsville

Indiana
Oakland City University
St. Joseph's College
University of Indianapolis
University of Southern Indiana

Iowa
Upper Iowa University M

Kansas
Emporia State University
Fort Hays State University W
Washburn University of Topeka

Kentucky
Bellarmine University
Kentucky State University W
Kentucky Wesleyan College W
Northern Kentucky University

Maryland
Bowie State University W

Massachusetts
American International College
Assumption College
Bentley College
Merrimack College
Stonehill College

Michigan
Ferris State University
Grand Valley State University
Lake Superior State University
Michigan Technological University
Northwood University
Saginaw Valley State University W
Wayne State University

Minnesota
Bemidji State University W
Minnesota State University
  Mankato
  Moorhead W
St. Cloud State University
Southwest Minnesota State University W
University of Minnesota
  Crookston W
  Duluth W
  Morris
Winona State University

Mississippi
Delta State University

Missouri
Drury University
Lincoln University W
Missouri Southern State University W
Missouri Western State University W
Northwest Missouri State University
Rockhurst University
Southwest Baptist University
Truman State University
University of Missouri
  St. Louis

Montana
Montana State University
  Billings

Nebraska
University of Nebraska
Kearney
Omaha W

New Hampshire
Franklin Pierce College
St. Anselm College
Southern New Hampshire University

New Jersey
Bloomfield College M
Caldwell College
Georgian Court University W
New Jersey Institute of Technology

New Mexico
Eastern New Mexico University W
Western New Mexico University

New York
Adelphi University
City University of New York
Queens College
College of Saint Rose W
Concordia College
Dowling College
Le Moyne College
Long Island University
C. W. Post Campus W
Mercy College M
Molloy College W
Pace University
St. Thomas Aquinas College

North Carolina
Barton College
Belmont Abbey College
Catawba College
Elizabeth City State University W
Fayetteville State University W
Johnson C. Smith University
Lees-McRae College
Lenoir-Rhyne College W
Livingstone College W
Mars Hill College
Mount Olive College
North Carolina Central University
Pfeiffer University
Queens University of Charlotte
St. Andrews Presbyterian College
St. Augustine's College
Shaw University
University of North Carolina
Pembroke W
Wingate University
Winston-Salem State University

North Dakota
University of Mary W
University of North Dakota W

Ohio
Ashland University W
Central State University
Tiffin University
University of Findlay

Oklahoma
Cameron University
East Central University
Northeastern State University W
Southeastern Oklahoma State University
University of Central Oklahoma

Pennsylvania
Bloomsburg University of Pennsylvania
California University of Pennsylvania W
Cheyney University of Pennsylvania W
Clarion University of Pennsylvania W
East Stroudsburg University of Pennsylvania
Holy Family University W
Indiana University of Pennsylvania W
Kutztown University of Pennsylvania
Mercyhurst College
Millersville University of Pennsylvania
Philadelphia University
Shippensburg University of Pennsylvania W
Slippery Rock University of Pennsylvania
University of the Sciences in Philadelphia
West Chester University of Pennsylvania

Puerto Rico
University of Puerto Rico
Bayamon University College
Cayey University College
Mayaguez
Rio Piedras M

Rhode Island
Bryant University

South Carolina
Anderson University
Benedict College
Claflin University
Coker College
Converse College W
Erskine College
Francis Marion University
Lander University M
Limestone College
Newberry College
North Greenville College
Presbyterian College
University of South Carolina
Aiken
Upstate

South Dakota
Augustana College
South Dakota State University
University of South Dakota W

Tennessee
Carson-Newman College
Christian Brothers University
LeMoyne-Owen College
Lincoln Memorial University
Tusculum College

Texas
Abilene Christian University
Dallas Baptist University
Midwestern State University
St. Edward's University
St. Mary's University
Tarleton State University W
University of the Incarnate Word

Vermont
Green Mountain College
St. Michael's College

Virginia
Longwood University
St. Paul's College
Virginia State University
Virginia Union University

West Virginia
Bluefield State College
Concord University
Salem International University M
Shepherd University
University of Charleston
West Liberty State College
West Virginia State University
West Virginia University Institute of Technology
West Virginia Wesleyan College

Tennis Division III

Alabama
Huntingdon College

Arkansas
Hendrix College
University of the Ozarks

California
California Institute of Technology
California Lutheran University
Chapman University
Claremont McKenna College
Mills College W
Occidental College
Pitzer College M
Pomona College
University of California
Santa Cruz
University of La Verne
University of Redlands
Whittier College

Colorado
Colorado College

Connecticut
Albertus Magnus College
Connecticut College
Mitchell College
St. Joseph College W
Trinity College
United States Coast Guard Academy M
Wesleyan University
Western Connecticut State University

Delaware
Wesley College

District of Columbia
Catholic University of America
Gallaudet University M
Trinity University W

Georgia
Agnes Scott College W
Emory University
LaGrange College
Oglethorpe University
Piedmont College
Spelman College W
Wesleyan College W

Illinois
Augustana College
Aurora University
Benedictine University W
Blackburn College W
Concordia University
Dominican University
Elmhurst College
Eureka College
Greenville College
Illinois College
Illinois Wesleyan University
Knox College
Lake Forest College
MacMurray College
Millikin University W
Monmouth College
North Central College
Principia College
Rockford College
University of Chicago
Wheaton College

Indiana
Anderson University
DePauw University
Earlham College
Franklin College
Hanover College
Manchester College
Rose-Hulman Institute of Technology
Saint Mary's College W
Tri-State University
Wabash College M

Iowa
Buena Vista University
Central College
Clarke College
Coe College
Cornell College
Grinnell College
Loras College
Luther College
Simpson College
University of Dubuque
Wartburg College

Kentucky
Centre College
Thomas More College
Transylvania University

Maine
Bates College
Bowdoin College
Colby College
Thomas College M
University of Southern Maine

Maryland
College of Notre Dame of Maryland W
Frostburg State University
Goucher College
Hood College
Johns Hopkins University
McDaniel College
St. Mary's College of Maryland
Salisbury University
Villa Julie College
Washington College

Massachusetts
Amherst College
Babson College
Bay Path College W
Becker College
Brandeis University
Bridgewater State College
Clark University
Curry College
Eastern Nazarene College
Emerson College
Emmanuel College W
Endicott College
Gordon College
Massachusetts College of Liberal Arts W
Massachusetts Institute of Technology
Mount Holyoke College W
Newbury College
Nichols College
Pine Manor College W
Regis College W
Salem State College
Simmons College W
Smith College W
Springfield College
Suffolk University
Tufts University
University of Massachusetts
Boston
Dartmouth
Wellesley College W
Wentworth Institute of Technology
Western New England College
Wheaton College
Williams College
Worcester State College W

Michigan
Adrian College
Albion College
Alma College
Calvin College
Hope College
Kalamazoo College
Olivet College W

Minnesota
Bethany Lutheran College
Bethel University
Carleton College
College of St. Benedict W
College of St. Catherine W
College of St. Scholastica
Concordia College: Moorhead
Gustavus Adolphus College
Hamline University
Macalester College
Martin Luther College
Northwestern College M
St. John's University M
St. Mary's University of Minnesota
St. Olaf College
University of St. Thomas

Mississippi
Millsaps College
Mississippi College
Rust College

Missouri
Fontbonne University
Maryville University of Saint Louis
Washington University in St. Louis
Webster University
Westminster College

Nebraska
Nebraska Wesleyan University

New Hampshire
Colby-Sawyer College
Plymouth State University W

New Jersey
The College of New Jersey
College of St. Elizabeth W
Drew University
Fairleigh Dickinson University
College at Florham
Kean University W
Ramapo College of New Jersey
Richard Stockton College of New Jersey W
Rutgers, The State University of New Jersey
Newark Regional Campus
Stevens Institute of Technology
William Paterson University of New Jersey W

New York
Alfred University
Bard College
City University of New York
Baruch College
Brooklyn College
City College
College of Staten Island
Hunter College
John Jay College of Criminal Justice
Lehman College
New York City College of Technology
York College M
Clarkson University
College of Mount St. Vincent
College of New Rochelle W
Elmira College
Hamilton College
Hartwick College
Hobart and William Smith Colleges
Ithaca College
Keuka College
Manhattanville College
Mount St. Mary College
Nazareth College of Rochester
New York University
Polytechnic University
Rensselaer Polytechnic Institute
Rochester Institute of Technology

Tables and Indexes

Russell Sage College W
St. John Fisher College
St. Joseph's College M
St. Joseph's College: Suffolk Campus W
St. Lawrence University
Skidmore College
State University of New York
College at Brockport W
College at Cortland W
College at Fredonia W
College at Geneseo W
College at Oneonta
College at Plattsburgh W
College at Potsdam W
Maritime College M
New Paltz W
Oswego
Purchase
Union College
United States Merchant Marine Academy M
University of Rochester
Utica College
Vassar College
Wells College W
Yeshiva University M

North Carolina
Chowan College M
Greensboro College
Guilford College
Meredith College W
Methodist College
North Carolina Wesleyan College
Peace College W
Salem College W

Ohio
Baldwin-Wallace College
Bluffton University
Capital University
Case Western Reserve University
College of Mount St. Joseph
College of Wooster
Defiance College
Denison University
Heidelberg College
Hiram College
John Carroll University
Kenyon College
Marietta College
Mount Union College
Muskingum College
Oberlin College
Ohio Northern University
Ohio Wesleyan University
Otterbein College
Wilmington College
Wittenberg University

Oregon
George Fox University
Lewis & Clark College
Linfield College
Pacific University
Willamette University

Pennsylvania
Albright College
Allegheny College
Alvernia College
Arcadia University
Baptist Bible College of Pennsylvania W
Bryn Mawr College W
Cabrini College
Carnegie Mellon University
Cedar Crest College W
Chatham College W
Chestnut Hill College
College Misericordia W
DeSales University
Dickinson College
Eastern University
Elizabethtown College
Franklin & Marshall College
Gettysburg College
Grove City College
Gwynedd-Mercy College
Haverford College
Immaculata University
Juniata College
Keystone College
King's College
Lebanon Valley College
Lincoln University
Lycoming College
Marywood University
Messiah College
Moravian College
Muhlenberg College
Neumann College
Penn State
Altoona
Berks
Erie, The Behrend College
Philadelphia Biblical University M
Rosemont College W
Susquehanna University
Swarthmore College
Thiel College
University of Pittsburgh
Greensburg M
University of Scranton
Ursinus College
Washington and Jefferson College
Waynesburg College
Westminster College
Wilkes University
Wilson College W
York College of Pennsylvania

Rhode Island
Johnson & Wales University
Rhode Island College
Roger Williams University
Salve Regina University

Tennessee
Fisk University
Maryville College
Rhodes College
University of the South

Texas
Austin College
Concordia University at Austin
Hardin-Simmons University
Howard Payne University
LeTourneau University
McMurry University
Schreiner University
Southwestern University
Sul Ross State University
Texas Lutheran University
Trinity University
University of Dallas
University of Mary Hardin-Baylor
University of Texas
Dallas
Tyler

Vermont
Castleton State College
Johnson State College
Middlebury College
Norwich University M

Virginia
Averett University
Bridgewater College
Christopher Newport University
Eastern Mennonite University
Emory & Henry College
Ferrum College
Hampden-Sydney College M
Hollins University W
Lynchburg College
Mary Baldwin College W
Randolph-Macon College
Randolph-Macon Woman's College W
Roanoke College
Shenandoah University
Sweet Briar College W
University of Mary Washington
Virginia Wesleyan College
Washington and Lee University

Washington
Pacific Lutheran University
University of Puget Sound
Whitman College
Whitworth College

West Virginia
Bethany College

Wisconsin
Beloit College
Carroll College
Carthage College
Concordia University Wisconsin
Edgewood College W
Lakeland College
Lawrence University
Marian College of Fond du Lac
Milwaukee School of Engineering
Mount Mary College W
Ripon College
St. Norbert College
University of Wisconsin
Eau Claire
La Crosse
Oshkosh
River Falls W
Stevens Point W
Stout W
Whitewater
Wisconsin Lutheran College W

Track, indoor Division I

Alabama
Alabama Agricultural and Mechanical University
Alabama State University
Auburn University
Jacksonville State University W
Samford University
Troy University W
University of Alabama
University of Alabama
Birmingham W
University of South Alabama

Arizona
Arizona State University
Northern Arizona University
University of Arizona

Arkansas
Arkansas State University
University of Arkansas
University of Arkansas
Little Rock
Pine Bluff W

California
California Polytechnic State University: San Luis Obispo W
California State University
Fresno W
Fullerton W
Long Beach
Northridge
Sacramento
San Diego State University W
Stanford University
University of California
Berkeley
Irvine W
Los Angeles
Riverside
University of Southern California

Colorado
Colorado State University
United States Air Force Academy
University of Colorado
Boulder

Connecticut
Central Connecticut State University
Quinnipiac University
Sacred Heart University
University of Connecticut
University of Hartford
Yale University

Delaware
Delaware State University
University of Delaware

District of Columbia
American University
Georgetown University
Howard University

Florida
Bethune-Cookman College
Florida Agricultural and Mechanical University
Florida Atlantic University W
Florida International University
Florida State University
Jacksonville University W
University of Central Florida W
University of Florida
University of Miami
University of South Florida W

Georgia
Georgia Institute of Technology
Georgia Southern University W
Georgia State University
Savannah State University
University of Georgia

Hawaii
University of Hawaii
Manoa W

Idaho
Boise State University
Idaho State University
University of Idaho

Illinois
Bradley University W
Chicago State University
DePaul University
Eastern Illinois University
Illinois State University
Loyola University of Chicago
Northern Illinois University W
Southern Illinois University
Carbondale
University of Illinois
Chicago
Urbana-Champaign
Western Illinois University

Indiana
Ball State University W
Butler University
Indiana State University
Indiana University
Bloomington
Indiana University-Purdue University Fort Wayne W
Purdue University
University of Notre Dame
Valparaiso University

Iowa
Drake University
Iowa State University
University of Iowa
University of Northern Iowa

Kansas
Kansas State University
University of Kansas
Wichita State University

Kentucky
Eastern Kentucky University
Morehead State University
Murray State University
University of Kentucky
University of Louisville
Western Kentucky University

Louisiana
Grambling State University
Louisiana State University and Agricultural and Mechanical College
Louisiana Tech University
Nicholls State University W
Northwestern State University
Southeastern Louisiana University
Southern University and Agricultural and Mechanical College
Tulane University W
University of Louisiana at Lafayette
University of Louisiana at Monroe
University of New Orleans

Maine
University of Maine

Maryland
Coppin State University
Loyola College in Maryland W
Morgan State University
Mount St. Mary's University
Towson University W
United States Naval Academy
University of Maryland
Baltimore County
College Park
Eastern Shore

Massachusetts
Boston College
Boston University
College of the Holy Cross
Harvard College
Northeastern University
University of Massachusetts
Amherst

Michigan
Central Michigan University
Eastern Michigan University
Michigan State University
University of Detroit Mercy
University of Michigan
Western Michigan University W

Minnesota
University of Minnesota
Twin Cities

Mississippi
Alcorn State University
Jackson State University
Mississippi State University W
Mississippi Valley State University
University of Mississippi
University of Southern Mississippi

Missouri
Missouri State University
Southeast Missouri State University
University of Missouri
Columbia
Kansas City

Montana
Montana State University
Bozeman
University of Montana: Missoula

Nebraska
University of Nebraska
Lincoln

Nevada
University of Nevada
Las Vegas W
Reno W

New Hampshire
Dartmouth College

University of New Hampshire

New Jersey
Fairleigh Dickinson University
  Metropolitan Campus
Monmouth University
Princeton University
Rider University
Rutgers, The State University of New Jersey
  New Brunswick Regional Campus
St. Peter's College
Seton Hall University

New Mexico
New Mexico State University W
University of New Mexico

New York
Barnard College W
Colgate University
Columbia University
  Columbia College M
Cornell University
Fordham University
Iona College
Long Island University
  Brooklyn Campus
Manhattan College
Marist College
St. Francis College
St. John's University W
State University of New York
  Albany
  Binghamton
  Buffalo
  Stony Brook
Syracuse University
United States Military Academy
Wagner College

North Carolina
Appalachian State University
Campbell University
Davidson College
Duke University
East Carolina University
Elon University W
Gardner-Webb University
High Point University
North Carolina Agricultural and Technical State University
North Carolina State University
University of North Carolina
  Asheville
  Chapel Hill
  Charlotte
  Wilmington
Wake Forest University
Western Carolina University

Ohio
Bowling Green State University W
Kent State University
Miami University
  Oxford Campus W
Ohio State University
  Columbus Campus
Ohio University
University of Akron
University of Cincinnati W
University of Dayton W
University of Toledo W
Wright State University W
Xavier University
Youngstown State University

Oklahoma
Oklahoma State University
Oral Roberts University
University of Oklahoma
University of Tulsa

Oregon
Portland State University
University of Oregon
University of Portland

Pennsylvania
Bucknell University
Duquesne University W
La Salle University
Lafayette College
Lehigh University
Penn State
  University Park
Robert Morris University
St. Francis University
St. Joseph's University
Temple University
University of Pennsylvania
University of Pittsburgh
Villanova University

Rhode Island
Brown University
Providence College
University of Rhode Island

South Carolina
Charleston Southern University
The Citadel
Clemson University
Coastal Carolina University W
College of Charleston W
Furman University W
South Carolina State University
University of South Carolina
Winthrop University
Wofford College

Tennessee
Austin Peay State University W
Belmont University
East Tennessee State University
Lipscomb University
Middle Tennessee State University
Tennessee State University
Tennessee Technological University W
University of Memphis
University of Tennessee
  Chattanooga
  Knoxville
Vanderbilt University W

Texas
Baylor University
Lamar University
Prairie View A&M University
Rice University
Sam Houston State University
Southern Methodist University W
Stephen F. Austin State University
Texas A&M University
Texas Christian University
Texas Southern University
Texas State University: San Marcos
Texas Tech University
University of Houston
University of North Texas
University of Texas
  Arlington
  Austin
  El Paso
  Pan American
  San Antonio

Utah
Brigham Young University
Southern Utah University
University of Utah W
Utah State University
Utah Valley State College
Weber State University

Vermont
University of Vermont

Virginia
College of William and Mary
George Mason University
Hampton University
James Madison University
Liberty University
Norfolk State University
Radford University
University of Richmond
University of Virginia
Virginia Commonwealth University
Virginia Military Institute
Virginia Polytechnic Institute and State University

Washington
Eastern Washington University
University of Washington
Washington State University

West Virginia
Marshall University W
West Virginia University W

Wisconsin
Marquette University
University of Wisconsin
  Madison
  Milwaukee

Wyoming
University of Wyoming

Track, indoor Division II

Alabama
University of Alabama
  Huntsville

Alaska
University of Alaska
  Anchorage

Arkansas
Harding University

California
California State University
  Bakersfield
  Dominguez Hills W
  Los Angeles W
  Stanislaus
San Francisco State University W
University of California
  Davis

Colorado
Adams State College
Colorado School of Mines
University of Colorado
  Colorado Springs
Western State College of Colorado

Connecticut
Southern Connecticut State University
University of New Haven

Florida
University of North Florida

Georgia
Clayton State University
Kennesaw State University
Morehouse College M

Idaho
Northwest Nazarene University

Illinois
Lewis University
Southern Illinois University
  Edwardsville

Indiana
St. Joseph's College
University of Indianapolis
University of Southern Indiana

Kansas
Emporia State University
Fort Hays State University
Pittsburg State University

Kentucky
Bellarmine University
Kentucky State University
Northern Kentucky University

Maryland
Bowie State University

Massachusetts
Assumption College
Bentley College
Stonehill College
University of Massachusetts
  Lowell

Michigan
Ferris State University
Grand Valley State University
Hillsdale College
Lake Superior State University
Northern Michigan University W
Northwood University
Saginaw Valley State University

Minnesota
Bemidji State University
Concordia University: St. Paul
Minnesota State University
  Mankato
  Moorhead
St. Cloud State University
University of Minnesota
  Duluth
  Morris
Winona State University W

Missouri
Central Missouri State University
Lincoln University
Missouri Southern State University
Northwest Missouri State University
Southwest Baptist University
Truman State University
University of Missouri
  Rolla

Nebraska
Chadron State College
University of Nebraska
  Kearney
  Omaha W
Wayne State College

New York
Long Island University
  C. W. Post Campus
Mercy College
New York Institute of Technology M
St. Thomas Aquinas College

North Carolina
Lees-McRae College
Livingstone College
North Carolina Central University
St. Andrews Presbyterian College M
St. Augustine's College
Shaw University

North Dakota
North Dakota State University
University of North Dakota

Ohio
Ashland University
Central State University
Tiffin University
University of Findlay

Oregon
Western Oregon University

Pennsylvania
Bloomsburg University of Pennsylvania
Cabrini College M
California University of Pennsylvania
Cheyney University of Pennsylvania
Clarion University of Pennsylvania
East Stroudsburg University of Pennsylvania
Edinboro University of Pennsylvania W
Indiana University of Pennsylvania
Kutztown University of Pennsylvania
Lock Haven University of Pennsylvania
Mansfield University of Pennsylvania
Millersville University of Pennsylvania
Shippensburg University of Pennsylvania
Slippery Rock University of Pennsylvania
West Chester University of Pennsylvania

Rhode Island
Bryant University

South Carolina
Anderson University
Claflin University

South Dakota
Augustana College
Northern State University W
South Dakota State University
University of South Dakota

Texas
Abilene Christian University
Dallas Baptist University
Texas A&M University
  Kingsville

Virginia
St. Paul's College
Virginia State University

Washington
Central Washington University
Saint Martin's University
Seattle Pacific University
Seattle University
Western Washington University

West Virginia
Alderson-Broaddus College
Concord University
Wheeling Jesuit University

Wisconsin
University of Wisconsin
  Parkside

Track, indoor Division III

California
California Lutheran University
Occidental College
Pomona College
University of La Verne
University of Redlands

Colorado
Colorado College W

Connecticut
Connecticut College
Eastern Connecticut State University
Trinity College
United States Coast Guard Academy
Wesleyan University

District of Columbia
Catholic University of America
Gallaudet University

Georgia
Emory University

Illinois
Augustana College
Aurora University
Benedictine University
Concordia University
Elmhurst College
Greenville College
Illinois College
Illinois Wesleyan University
Knox College
Millikin University
Monmouth College
North Central College
North Park University
Principia College
Rockford College
University of Chicago
Wheaton College

Indiana
Anderson University
DePauw University
Earlham College
Hanover College
Manchester College
Rose-Hulman Institute of Technology
Tri-State University
Wabash College M

Iowa
Buena Vista University
Central College
Clarke College M
Coe College
Cornell College
Grinnell College
Loras College
Luther College
Simpson College
University of Dubuque
Wartburg College

Maine
Bates College
Bowdoin College
Colby College
University of Southern Maine

Maryland
Frostburg State University
Goucher College
Johns Hopkins University
McDaniel College
Salisbury University
Villa Julie College

Massachusetts
Amherst College
Brandeis University
Bridgewater State College
Emerson College W
Emmanuel College
Fitchburg State College
Gordon College
Massachusetts Institute of Technology
Mount Holyoke College W
Regis College W
Salem State College
Smith College W
Springfield College
Tufts University
University of Massachusetts
  Dartmouth
Wellesley College W
Westfield State College
Wheaton College
Williams College
Worcester Polytechnic Institute
Worcester State College

Michigan
Adrian College
Albion College
Calvin College
Olivet College

Minnesota
Augsburg College
Bethel University
Carleton College
College of St. Benedict W
College of St. Catherine W
College of St. Scholastica
Concordia College: Moorhead
Gustavus Adolphus College
Hamline University
Macalester College
North Central University
St. John's University M
St. Mary's University of Minnesota
St. Olaf College
University of St. Thomas

Mississippi
Mississippi College

Missouri
Maryville University of Saint Louis
Washington University in St. Louis

Nebraska
Nebraska Wesleyan University

New Hampshire
Keene State College

New Jersey
The College of New Jersey
Kean University
Montclair State University
New Jersey City University
Ramapo College of New Jersey
Richard Stockton College of New Jersey
Rowan University
Rutgers, The State University of New Jersey
  Camden Regional Campus
Stevens Institute of Technology
William Paterson University of New Jersey

New York
Alfred University
City University of New York
  City College
  Hunter College
  Lehman College
  Medgar Evers College
  York College
Hamilton College
Hartwick College
Ithaca College
Nazareth College of Rochester
New York University
Rensselaer Polytechnic Institute
Rochester Institute of Technology
St. Joseph's College: Suffolk Campus
St. Lawrence University
State University of New York
  College at Brockport
  College at Buffalo
  College at Cortland
  College at Fredonia
  College at Geneseo
  College at Oneonta
  College at Plattsburgh
  Farmingdale
  Oswego
Union College
United States Merchant Marine Academy
University of Rochester

North Carolina
Methodist College

Ohio
Baldwin-Wallace College
Bluffton University
Capital University
Case Western Reserve University
College of Mount St. Joseph
College of Wooster
Defiance College
Denison University
Heidelberg College
Hiram College
John Carroll University
Kenyon College
Marietta College
Mount Union College
Muskingum College
Oberlin College
Ohio Northern University
Ohio Wesleyan University
Otterbein College
Wilmington College
Wittenberg University

Oregon
Linfield College
Pacific University

Pennsylvania
Albright College
Allegheny College
Baptist Bible College of Pennsylvania
Bryn Mawr College W
Cabrini College W
Carnegie Mellon University
College Misericordia
Delaware Valley College
DeSales University
Dickinson College
Elizabethtown College
Franklin & Marshall College
Gettysburg College
Gwynedd-Mercy College
Haverford College
Juniata College
Lebanon Valley College
Lincoln University
Messiah College
Moravian College
Muhlenberg College
Penn State
  Erie, The Behrend College
Susquehanna University
Swarthmore College
Thiel College
Ursinus College
Washington and Jefferson College
Westminster College
Widener University

Rhode Island
Rhode Island College

Tennessee
Fisk University
Rhodes College
University of the South

Texas
McMurry University
Trinity University W

Vermont
Middlebury College

Virginia
Bridgewater College
Christopher Newport University
Eastern Mennonite University
Lynchburg College
Roanoke College
University of Mary Washington
Virginia Wesleyan College
Washington and Lee University

Washington
Pacific Lutheran University
University of Puget Sound
Whitworth College

West Virginia
Bethany College

Wisconsin
Beloit College
Carroll College
Carthage College
Concordia University Wisconsin
Lawrence University
Milwaukee School of Engineering
Ripon College
St. Norbert College
University of Wisconsin
  Eau Claire
  La Crosse
  Oshkosh
  Platteville
  River Falls
  Stevens Point
  Stout
  Superior
  Whitewater
Wisconsin Lutheran College

Track, outdoor Division I

Alabama
Alabama Agricultural and Mechanical University
Alabama State University
Auburn University
Jacksonville State University
Samford University
Troy University
University of Alabama
University of Alabama
  Birmingham W
University of South Alabama

Arizona
Arizona State University
Northern Arizona University
University of Arizona

Arkansas
Arkansas State University
University of Arkansas
University of Arkansas
  Little Rock
  Pine Bluff W

California
California Polytechnic State University: San Luis Obispo
California State University
  Fresno
  Fullerton
  Long Beach
  Northridge
  Sacramento
Loyola Marymount University
Pepperdine University W
San Diego State University W
Santa Clara University
Stanford University
University of California
  Berkeley
  Irvine
  Los Angeles
  Riverside
  Santa Barbara
University of San Francisco M
University of Southern California

Colorado
Colorado State University
United States Air Force Academy
University of Colorado
  Boulder

Connecticut
Central Connecticut State University
Quinnipiac University
Sacred Heart University
University of Connecticut
University of Hartford
Yale University

Delaware
Delaware State University
University of Delaware

District of Columbia
American University
Georgetown University
Howard University

Florida
Bethune-Cookman College
Florida Agricultural and Mechanical University
Florida Atlantic University W
Florida International University
Florida State University
Jacksonville University W
University of Central Florida W
University of Florida
University of Miami
University of South Florida

Georgia
Georgia Institute of Technology
Georgia Southern University W
Georgia State University
Savannah State University
University of Georgia

Hawaii
University of Hawaii
  Manoa W

Idaho
Boise State University
Idaho State University
University of Idaho

Illinois
Bradley University W
Chicago State University
DePaul University
Eastern Illinois University
Illinois State University
Loyola University of Chicago
Northern Illinois University W
Southern Illinois University
  Carbondale
University of Illinois
  Chicago
  Urbana-Champaign
Western Illinois University

Indiana
Ball State University W
Butler University
Indiana State University
Indiana University
  Bloomington
Indiana University-Purdue University Fort Wayne W
Purdue University
University of Notre Dame
Valparaiso University

Iowa
Drake University
Iowa State University
University of Iowa
University of Northern Iowa

Kansas
Kansas State University
University of Kansas
Wichita State University

Kentucky
Eastern Kentucky University
Morehead State University
Murray State University
University of Kentucky
University of Louisville
Western Kentucky University

Louisiana
Grambling State University
Louisiana State University and Agricultural and Mechanical College
Louisiana Tech University
Nicholls State University W

Tables and Indexes

Northwestern State University
Southeastern Louisiana University
Southern University and Agricultural and Mechanical College
Tulane University
University of Louisiana at Lafayette
University of Louisiana at Monroe
University of New Orleans

Maine
University of Maine

Maryland
Coppin State University
Loyola College in Maryland W
Morgan State University
Mount St. Mary's University
Towson University W
United States Naval Academy
University of Maryland
Baltimore County
College Park
Eastern Shore

Massachusetts
Boston College
Boston University
College of the Holy Cross
Harvard College
Northeastern University
University of Massachusetts
Amherst

Michigan
Central Michigan University
Eastern Michigan University
Michigan State University
Oakland University M
University of Detroit Mercy
University of Michigan
Western Michigan University W

Minnesota
University of Minnesota
Twin Cities

Mississippi
Alcorn State University
Jackson State University
Mississippi State University
Mississippi Valley State University
University of Mississippi
University of Southern Mississippi

Missouri
Missouri State University
Southeast Missouri State University
University of Missouri
Columbia
Kansas City

Montana
Montana State University
Bozeman
University of Montana: Missoula

Nebraska
University of Nebraska
Lincoln

Nevada
University of Nevada
Las Vegas W
Reno W

New Hampshire
Dartmouth College
University of New Hampshire

New Jersey
Fairleigh Dickinson University
Metropolitan Campus
Monmouth University
Princeton University
Rider University
Rutgers, The State University of New Jersey
New Brunswick Regional Campus
St. Peter's College
Seton Hall University

New Mexico
New Mexico State University W
University of New Mexico

New York
Barnard College W
Colgate University
Columbia University
Columbia College M
Cornell University
Fordham University
Iona College
Long Island University
Brooklyn Campus
Manhattan College
Marist College
St. Francis College
St. John's University W
State University of New York
Albany
Binghamton
Buffalo
Stony Brook
Syracuse University
United States Military Academy
Wagner College

North Carolina
Appalachian State University
Campbell University
Davidson College
Duke University
East Carolina University
Elon University W
Gardner-Webb University
High Point University
North Carolina Agricultural and Technical State University
North Carolina State University
University of North Carolina
Asheville
Chapel Hill
Charlotte
Greensboro
Wilmington
Wake Forest University
Western Carolina University

Ohio
Bowling Green State University W
Kent State University
Miami University
Oxford Campus
Ohio State University
Columbus Campus
Ohio University
University of Akron
University of Cincinnati
University of Dayton W
Wright State University W
Xavier University
Youngstown State University

Oklahoma
Oklahoma State University
Oral Roberts University
University of Oklahoma
University of Tulsa

Oregon
Portland State University
University of Oregon
University of Portland

Pennsylvania
Bucknell University
Duquesne University
La Salle University
Lafayette College
Lehigh University
Penn State
University Park
Robert Morris University
St. Francis University
St. Joseph's University
Temple University
University of Pennsylvania
University of Pittsburgh
Villanova University

Rhode Island
Brown University
Providence College
University of Rhode Island

South Carolina
Charleston Southern University
The Citadel
Clemson University
Coastal Carolina University
College of Charleston W
Furman University
South Carolina State University
University of South Carolina
Winthrop University
Wofford College

Tennessee
Austin Peay State University W
Belmont University
East Tennessee State University
Lipscomb University
Middle Tennessee State University
Tennessee State University
Tennessee Technological University W
University of Memphis
University of Tennessee
Chattanooga
Knoxville
Vanderbilt University W

Texas
Baylor University
Lamar University
Prairie View A&M University
Rice University
Sam Houston State University
Southern Methodist University W
Stephen F. Austin State University
Texas A&M University
Texas Christian University
Texas Southern University
Texas State University: San Marcos
Texas Tech University
University of Houston
University of North Texas
University of Texas
Arlington
Austin
El Paso
Pan American
San Antonio

Utah
Brigham Young University
Southern Utah University
University of Utah
Utah State University
Utah Valley State College
Weber State University

Vermont
University of Vermont

Virginia
College of William and Mary
George Mason University
Hampton University
James Madison University
Liberty University
Norfolk State University
Radford University
University of Richmond
University of Virginia
Virginia Commonwealth University
Virginia Military Institute
Virginia Polytechnic Institute and State University

Washington
Eastern Washington University
Gonzaga University
University of Washington
Washington State University

West Virginia
Marshall University W
West Virginia University W

Wisconsin
Marquette University
University of Wisconsin
Madison
Milwaukee

Wyoming
University of Wyoming

Track, outdoor Division II

Alabama
Miles College
Stillman College
Tuskegee University
University of Alabama
Huntsville

Alaska
University of Alaska
Anchorage

Arkansas
Harding University
Southern Arkansas University
University of Central Arkansas W

California
California State Polytechnic University: Pomona
California State University
Bakersfield
Chico
Dominguez Hills W
Los Angeles
Stanislaus
Humboldt State University
San Francisco State University
Sonoma State University W
University of California
Davis
San Diego

Colorado
Adams State College
Colorado School of Mines
Mesa State College W
University of Colorado
Colorado Springs
University of Northern Colorado
Western State College of Colorado

Connecticut
Southern Connecticut State University
University of New Haven

Florida
Florida Southern College
University of North Florida
University of Tampa
University of West Florida

Georgia
Albany State University
Clark Atlanta University
Clayton State University
Fort Valley State University
Kennesaw State University
Morehouse College M
Paine College

Idaho
Northwest Nazarene University

Illinois
Lewis University
Southern Illinois University
Edwardsville

Indiana
St. Joseph's College
University of Indianapolis
University of Southern Indiana

Kansas
Emporia State University
Fort Hays State University
Pittsburg State University

Kentucky
Bellarmine University
Kentucky State University
Northern Kentucky University

Maryland
Bowie State University
Columbia Union College

Massachusetts
Assumption College
Bentley College
Stonehill College
University of Massachusetts
Lowell

Michigan
Ferris State University
Grand Valley State University
Hillsdale College
Lake Superior State University
Michigan Technological University
Northern Michigan University W
Northwood University
Saginaw Valley State University

Minnesota
Bemidji State University
Concordia University: St. Paul
Minnesota State University
Mankato
Moorhead
St. Cloud State University
University of Minnesota
Duluth
Morris
Winona State University W

Missouri
Central Missouri State University
Lincoln University
Missouri Southern State University
Northwest Missouri State University
Southwest Baptist University
Truman State University
University of Missouri
Rolla

Nebraska
Chadron State College
University of Nebraska
Kearney
Omaha W
Wayne State College

New Mexico
Eastern New Mexico University
New Mexico Highlands University W

New York
Long Island University
C. W. Post Campus
Mercy College
New York Institute of Technology M
Pace University
St. Thomas Aquinas College

North Carolina
Johnson C. Smith University
Lees-McRae College
Lenoir-Rhyne College M

Livingstone College
Mars Hill College
North Carolina Central University
Queens University of Charlotte
St. Andrews Presbyterian College
St. Augustine's College
Shaw University
University of North Carolina
Pembroke
Winston-Salem State University

North Dakota

North Dakota State University
University of Mary W
University of North Dakota

Ohio

Ashland University
Central State University
Tiffin University
University of Findlay

Oregon

Western Oregon University

Pennsylvania

Bloomsburg University of Pennsylvania
California University of Pennsylvania
Cheyney University of Pennsylvania
Clarion University of Pennsylvania
East Stroudsburg University of Pennsylvania
Edinboro University of Pennsylvania
Indiana University of Pennsylvania
Kutztown University of Pennsylvania
Lock Haven University of Pennsylvania
Mansfield University of Pennsylvania
Millersville University of Pennsylvania
Shippensburg University of Pennsylvania
Slippery Rock University of Pennsylvania
University of Pittsburgh
Johnstown W
West Chester University of Pennsylvania

Puerto Rico

University of Puerto Rico
Bayamon University College
Cayey University College
Mayaguez
Rio Piedras

Rhode Island

Bryant University

South Carolina

Anderson University
Benedict College
Claflin University
Francis Marion University

South Dakota

Augustana College
Northern State University
South Dakota State University
University of South Dakota

Tennessee

Carson-Newman College

Texas

Abilene Christian University
Angelo State University
Dallas Baptist University
Tarleton State University
Texas A&M University
Commerce
Kingsville
University of the Incarnate Word

Virginia

St. Paul's College
Virginia State University
Virginia Union University

Washington

Central Washington University
Saint Martin's University
Seattle Pacific University
Seattle University
Western Washington University

West Virginia

Alderson-Broaddus College
Concord University
Glenville State College
University of Charleston
West Liberty State College
West Virginia Wesleyan College
Wheeling Jesuit University

Wisconsin

University of Wisconsin
Parkside

Track, outdoor Division III

Arkansas

Hendrix College

California

California Institute of Technology
California Lutheran University
California State University
East Bay
Chapman University W
Claremont McKenna College
Occidental College
Pitzer College M
Pomona College
University of La Verne
University of Redlands
Whittier College

Colorado

Colorado College

Connecticut

Connecticut College
Eastern Connecticut State University
Trinity College
United States Coast Guard Academy
Wesleyan University

District of Columbia

Catholic University of America
Gallaudet University

Georgia

Emory University
Oglethorpe University

Illinois

Augustana College
Aurora University
Benedictine University
Concordia University
Elmhurst College
Eureka College
Greenville College
Illinois College
Illinois Wesleyan University
Knox College
Millikin University
Monmouth College
North Central College
North Park University
Principia College
Rockford College
University of Chicago
Wheaton College

Indiana

Anderson University M
DePauw University
Earlham College
Franklin College
Hanover College
Manchester College
Rose-Hulman Institute of Technology
Tri-State University
Wabash College M

Iowa

Buena Vista University
Central College
Clarke College
Coe College
Cornell College
Grinnell College
Loras College
Luther College
Simpson College
University of Dubuque
Wartburg College

Kentucky

Centre College

Maine

Bates College
Bowdoin College
Colby College
University of Southern Maine

Maryland

Frostburg State University
Goucher College
Johns Hopkins University
McDaniel College
Salisbury University

Massachusetts

Amherst College
Babson College
Brandeis University
Bridgewater State College
Emmanuel College
Fitchburg State College
Gordon College
Massachusetts Institute of Technology
Mount Holyoke College W
Regis College W
Salem State College
Smith College W
Springfield College
Tufts University
University of Massachusetts
Dartmouth
Wellesley College W
Westfield State College
Wheaton College
Williams College
Worcester Polytechnic Institute
Worcester State College

Michigan

Adrian College
Albion College
Alma College
Calvin College
Hope College
Olivet College

Minnesota

Augsburg College
Bethel University
Carleton College
College of St. Benedict W
College of St. Catherine W
College of St. Scholastica
Concordia College: Moorhead
Gustavus Adolphus College
Hamline University
Macalester College
Martin Luther College
North Central University
Northwestern College
St. John's University M
St. Mary's University of Minnesota
St. Olaf College
University of St. Thomas

Mississippi

Mississippi College
Rust College

Missouri

Baptist Bible College W
Maryville University of Saint Louis
Washington University in St. Louis

Nebraska

Nebraska Wesleyan University

New Hampshire

Colby-Sawyer College
Keene State College

New Jersey

The College of New Jersey
Kean University
Montclair State University
New Jersey City University
Ramapo College of New Jersey
Richard Stockton College of New Jersey
Rowan University
Rutgers, The State University of New Jersey
Camden Regional Campus
Stevens Institute of Technology
William Paterson University of New Jersey

New York

Alfred University
City University of New York
City College
Hunter College
Lehman College
Medgar Evers College
York College
College of Mount St. Vincent W
Hamilton College
Hartwick College
Ithaca College
Nazareth College of Rochester
New York University
Rensselaer Polytechnic Institute
Rochester Institute of Technology
St. Joseph's College: Suffolk Campus
St. Lawrence University
State University of New York
College at Brockport
College at Buffalo
College at Cortland
College at Fredonia
College at Geneseo
College at Oneonta
College at Plattsburgh
Farmingdale
Oswego
Union College
United States Merchant Marine Academy
University of Rochester

North Carolina

Methodist College

Ohio

Baldwin-Wallace College
Bluffton University
Capital University
Case Western Reserve University
College of Mount St. Joseph
College of Wooster
Defiance College
Denison University
Heidelberg College
Hiram College
John Carroll University
Kenyon College
Marietta College
Mount Union College
Muskingum College
Oberlin College
Ohio Northern University
Ohio Wesleyan University
Otterbein College
Wilmington College
Wittenberg University

Oregon

George Fox University
Lewis & Clark College
Linfield College
Pacific University
Willamette University

Pennsylvania

Albright College
Allegheny College
Bryn Mawr College W
Cabrini College
Carnegie Mellon University
College Misericordia
Delaware Valley College
DeSales University
Dickinson College
Elizabethtown College
Franklin & Marshall College
Gettysburg College
Grove City College
Gwynedd-Mercy College
Haverford College
Juniata College
Keystone College
Lebanon Valley College
Lincoln University
Messiah College
Moravian College
Muhlenberg College
Penn State
Erie, The Behrend College
Susquehanna University
Swarthmore College
Thiel College
Ursinus College
Washington and Jefferson College
Waynesburg College
Westminster College
Widener University
York College of Pennsylvania

Rhode Island

Rhode Island College
Salve Regina University W

South Carolina

Anderson University W

Tennessee

Fisk University
Rhodes College
University of the South

Texas

Howard Payne University
McMurry University
Southwestern University
Sul Ross State University
Texas Lutheran University W
Trinity University
University of Dallas

Vermont

Middlebury College

Virginia

Bridgewater College
Christopher Newport University
Eastern Mennonite University
Lynchburg College
Roanoke College
University of Mary Washington
Virginia Wesleyan College
Washington and Lee University

Washington

Pacific Lutheran University
University of Puget Sound
Whitworth College

West Virginia

Bethany College

Wisconsin
- Beloit College
- Carroll College
- Carthage College
- Concordia University Wisconsin
- Lakeland College
- Lawrence University
- Milwaukee School of Engineering
- Ripon College
- St. Norbert College
- University of Wisconsin
  - Eau Claire
  - La Crosse
  - Oshkosh
  - Platteville
  - River Falls
  - Stevens Point
  - Stout
  - Superior
  - Whitewater
- Wisconsin Lutheran College

Volleyball Division I

Alabama
- Alabama Agricultural and Mechanical University W
- Alabama State University W
- Auburn University W
- Birmingham-Southern College W
- Jacksonville State University W
- Samford University W
- Troy University W
- University of Alabama W
- University of Alabama
  - Birmingham W
- University of South Alabama W

Arizona
- Arizona State University W
- Northern Arizona University W
- University of Arizona W

Arkansas
- Arkansas State University W
- University of Arkansas W
- University of Arkansas
  - Little Rock W
  - Pine Bluff W

California
- California Polytechnic State University: San Luis Obispo W
- California State University
  - Fresno W
  - Fullerton W
  - Long Beach
  - Northridge
  - Sacramento W
- Loyola Marymount University W
- Pepperdine University
- St. Mary's College of California W
- San Diego State University W
- San Jose State University W
- Santa Clara University W
- Stanford University
- University of California
  - Berkeley W
  - Irvine
  - Los Angeles
  - Riverside W
  - Santa Barbara
- University of San Diego W
- University of San Francisco W
- University of Southern California
- University of the Pacific

Colorado
- Colorado State University W
- United States Air Force Academy W
- University of Colorado
  - Boulder W
- University of Denver W

Connecticut
- Central Connecticut State University W
- Fairfield University W
- Quinnipiac University W
- Sacred Heart University
- University of Connecticut W
- University of Hartford W
- Yale University W

Delaware
- Delaware State University W
- University of Delaware W

District of Columbia
- American University W
- George Washington University W
- Georgetown University W
- Howard University W

Florida
- Bethune-Cookman College W
- Florida Agricultural and Mechanical University W
- Florida Atlantic University W
- Florida International University W
- Florida State University W
- Jacksonville University W
- Stetson University W
- University of Central Florida W
- University of Florida W
- University of Miami W
- University of South Florida W

Georgia
- Georgia Institute of Technology W
- Georgia Southern University W
- Georgia State University W
- Mercer University W
- Savannah State University W
- University of Georgia W

Hawaii
- University of Hawaii
  - Manoa

Idaho
- Boise State University W
- Idaho State University W
- University of Idaho W

Illinois
- Bradley University W
- Chicago State University W
- DePaul University W
- Eastern Illinois University W
- Illinois State University W
- Loyola University of Chicago
- Northern Illinois University W
- Northwestern University W
- Southern Illinois University
  - Carbondale W
- University of Illinois
  - Chicago W
- Western Illinois University W

Indiana
- Ball State University
- Butler University W
- Indiana State University W
- Indiana University
  - Bloomington W
- Indiana University-Purdue University Fort Wayne
- Indiana University-Purdue University Indianapolis W
- Purdue University W
- University of Evansville W
- University of Notre Dame W
- Valparaiso University W

Iowa
- Drake University W
- Iowa State University W
- University of Iowa W
- University of Northern Iowa W

Kansas
- Kansas State University W
- University of Kansas W
- Wichita State University W

Kentucky
- Eastern Kentucky University W
- Morehead State University W
- Murray State University W
- University of Kentucky W
- University of Louisville W
- Western Kentucky University W

Louisiana
- Centenary College of Louisiana W
- Grambling State University W
- Louisiana State University and Agricultural and Mechanical College W
- Louisiana Tech University W
- Nicholls State University W
- Northwestern State University W
- Southeastern Louisiana University W
- Southern University and Agricultural and Mechanical College W
- Tulane University W
- University of Louisiana at Lafayette W
- University of Louisiana at Monroe W
- University of New Orleans W

Maine
- University of Maine W

Maryland
- Coppin State University W
- Loyola College in Maryland W
- Morgan State University W
- Towson University W
- United States Naval Academy W
- University of Maryland
  - Baltimore County W
  - College Park W
  - Eastern Shore W

Massachusetts
- Boston College W
- College of the Holy Cross W
- Harvard College
- Northeastern University W

Michigan
- Central Michigan University W
- Eastern Michigan University W
- Michigan State University W
- Oakland University W
- University of Michigan W
- Western Michigan University W

Minnesota
- University of Minnesota
  - Twin Cities W

Mississippi
- Alcorn State University W
- Jackson State University W
- Mississippi State University W
- Mississippi Valley State University W
- University of Mississippi W
- University of Southern Mississippi W

Missouri
- Missouri State University W
- St. Louis University W
- Southeast Missouri State University W
- University of Missouri
  - Columbia W
  - Kansas City W

Montana
- Montana State University
  - Bozeman W
- University of Montana: Missoula W

Nebraska
- Creighton University W
- University of Nebraska
  - Lincoln W

Nevada
- University of Nevada
  - Las Vegas W
  - Reno W

New Hampshire
- Dartmouth College W
- University of New Hampshire W

New Jersey
- Fairleigh Dickinson University
  - Metropolitan Campus W
- Princeton University
- Rider University W
- Rutgers, The State University of New Jersey
  - New Brunswick Regional Campus W
  - Newark Regional Campus M
- St. Peter's College W
- Seton Hall University W

New Mexico
- New Mexico State University W
- University of New Mexico W

New York
- Barnard College W
- Canisius College W
- Colgate University W
- Cornell University W
- Fordham University W
- Hofstra University W
- Iona College W
- Long Island University
  - Brooklyn Campus W
- Manhattan College W
- Marist College W
- Niagara University W
- St. Francis College W
- St. John's University W
- Siena College W
- State University of New York
  - Albany W
  - Binghamton W
  - Buffalo W
  - Stony Brook W
- Syracuse University W
- United States Military Academy W
- Wagner College W

North Carolina
- Appalachian State University W
- Campbell University W
- Davidson College W
- Duke University W
- East Carolina University W
- Elon University W
- Gardner-Webb University W
- High Point University W
- North Carolina Agricultural and Technical State University W
- North Carolina State University W
- University of North Carolina
  - Asheville W
  - Chapel Hill W
  - Charlotte W
  - Greensboro W
  - Wilmington W
- Wake Forest University W
- Western Carolina University W

Ohio
- Bowling Green State University W
- Cleveland State University W
- Kent State University W
- Miami University
  - Oxford Campus W
- Ohio State University
  - Columbus Campus
- Ohio University W
- University of Akron W
- University of Cincinnati W
- University of Dayton W
- University of Toledo W
- Wright State University W
- Xavier University W
- Youngstown State University W

Oklahoma
- Oral Roberts University W
- University of Oklahoma W
- University of Tulsa W

Oregon
- Oregon State University W
- Portland State University W
- University of Oregon W
- University of Portland W

Pennsylvania
- Bucknell University W
- Duquesne University W
- La Salle University W
- Lafayette College W
- Lehigh University W
- Penn State
  - University Park
- Robert Morris University W
- St. Francis University
- Temple University W
- University of Pennsylvania W
- University of Pittsburgh W
- Villanova University W

Rhode Island
- Brown University W
- Providence College W
- University of Rhode Island W

South Carolina
- Charleston Southern University W
- The Citadel W
- Clemson University W
- Coastal Carolina University W
- College of Charleston W
- Furman University W
- South Carolina State University W
- University of South Carolina W
- Winthrop University W
- Wofford College W

Tennessee
- Austin Peay State University W
- Belmont University W
- East Tennessee State University W
- Lipscomb University W
- Middle Tennessee State University W
- Tennessee State University W
- Tennessee Technological University W
- University of Memphis W
- University of Tennessee
  - Chattanooga W
  - Knoxville W
  - Martin W

Texas
- Baylor University W
- Lamar University W
- Prairie View A&M University W
- Rice University W
- Sam Houston State University W
- Southern Methodist University W
- Stephen F. Austin State University W
- Texas A&M University W
- Texas Christian University W
- Texas Southern University W
- Texas State University: San Marcos W
- Texas Tech University W
- University of Houston W

University of North Texas W
University of Texas
Arlington W
Austin W
El Paso W
Pan American W
San Antonio W

Utah

Brigham Young University
University of Utah W
Utah State University W
Utah Valley State College W
Weber State University W

Virginia

College of William and Mary W
George Mason University
Hampton University W
James Madison University W
Liberty University W
Norfolk State University W
Radford University W
University of Virginia W
Virginia Commonwealth University W
Virginia Polytechnic Institute and State University W

Washington

Eastern Washington University W
Gonzaga University W
University of Washington W
Washington State University W

West Virginia

Marshall University W
West Virginia University W

Wisconsin

Marquette University W
University of Wisconsin
Green Bay W
Madison W
Milwaukee W

Wyoming

University of Wyoming W

Volleyball Division II

Alabama

Miles College W
Stillman College W
Tuskegee University W
University of Alabama
Huntsville W
University of Montevallo W
University of North Alabama W
University of West Alabama W

Alaska

University of Alaska
Anchorage W
Fairbanks W

Arizona

Grand Canyon University W

Arkansas

Arkansas Tech University W
Harding University W
Henderson State University W
Ouachita Baptist University W
Southern Arkansas University W
University of Arkansas
Monticello W
University of Central Arkansas W

California

California State Polytechnic University: Pomona W
California State University
Bakersfield W
Chico W
Dominguez Hills W
Los Angeles W
Monterey Bay W
San Bernardino W
Stanislaus W
Humboldt State University W
Notre Dame de Namur University W
Sonoma State University W
University of California
Davis W
San Diego

Colorado

Adams State College W
Colorado Christian University W
Colorado School of Mines W
Colorado State University
Pueblo W
Fort Lewis College W
Mesa State College W
Metropolitan State College of Denver W
Regis University W
University of Colorado
Colorado Springs W
University of Northern Colorado W
Western State College of Colorado W

Connecticut

Post University W
Southern Connecticut State University W
University of Bridgeport W
University of New Haven

Delaware

Goldey-Beacom College W
Wilmington College W

District of Columbia

University of the District of Columbia W

Florida

Barry University W
Eckerd College W
Florida Gulf Coast University W
Florida Institute of Technology W
Florida Southern College W
Lynn University W
Nova Southeastern University W
Palm Beach Atlantic University W
Rollins College W
St. Leo University W
University of North Florida W
University of Tampa W
University of West Florida W

Georgia

Albany State University W
Armstrong Atlantic State University W
Augusta State University W
Clark Atlanta University W
Fort Valley State University W
Paine College W
University of West Georgia W
Valdosta State University W

Hawaii

Brigham Young University-Hawaii W
Chaminade University of Honolulu W
Hawaii Pacific University W
University of Hawaii
Hilo W

Idaho

Northwest Nazarene University W

Illinois

Lewis University
Quincy University
Southern Illinois University
Edwardsville W

Indiana

Oakland City University W
St. Joseph's College W
University of Indianapolis W
University of Southern Indiana W

Iowa

Upper Iowa University W

Kansas

Emporia State University W
Fort Hays State University W
Pittsburg State University W
Washburn University of Topeka W

Kentucky

Bellarmine University W
Kentucky State University W
Kentucky Wesleyan College W
Northern Kentucky University W

Maryland

Bowie State University W

Massachusetts

American International College W
Assumption College W
Bentley College W
Merrimack College W
Stonehill College W
University of Massachusetts
Lowell W

Michigan

Ferris State University W
Grand Valley State University W
Hillsdale College W
Lake Superior State University W
Michigan Technological University W
Northern Michigan University W
Northwood University W
Saginaw Valley State University W
Wayne State University W

Minnesota

Bemidji State University W
Concordia University: St. Paul W
Minnesota State University
Mankato W
Moorhead W
St. Cloud State University W
Southwest Minnesota State University W
University of Minnesota
Crookston W
Duluth W
Morris W
Winona State University W

Missouri

Central Missouri State University W
Drury University W
Missouri Southern State University W
Missouri Western State University W
Northwest Missouri State University W
Rockhurst University W
Southwest Baptist University W
Truman State University W
University of Missouri
St. Louis W

Montana

Montana State University
Billings W

Nebraska

Chadron State College W
University of Nebraska
Kearney W
Omaha W
Wayne State College W

New Hampshire

Franklin Pierce College W
St. Anselm College W
Southern New Hampshire University W

New Jersey

Bloomfield College W
Felician College W
Georgian Court University W
New Jersey Institute of Technology

New Mexico

Eastern New Mexico University W
New Mexico Highlands University W
Western New Mexico University W

New York

Adelphi University W
City University of New York
Queens College
College of Saint Rose W
Concordia College W
Dominican College of Blauvelt W
Dowling College W
Le Moyne College W
Long Island University
C. W. Post Campus W
Mercy College W
Molloy College W
New York Institute of Technology W
Nyack College W
Pace University W

North Carolina

Barton College W
Belmont Abbey College W
Catawba College W
Elizabeth City State University W
Fayetteville State University W
Johnson C. Smith University W
Lees-McRae College
Lenoir-Rhyne College W
Livingstone College W
Mars Hill College W
Mount Olive College
North Carolina Central University W
Pfeiffer University W
Queens University of Charlotte W
St. Andrews Presbyterian College W
St. Augustine's College W
Shaw University W
University of North Carolina
Pembroke W
Wingate University W
Winston-Salem State University W

North Dakota

North Dakota State University W
University of Mary W
University of North Dakota W

Ohio

Ashland University W
Central State University
Tiffin University W
University of Findlay W

Oklahoma

Cameron University W
Oklahoma Panhandle State University W
Southeastern Oklahoma State University W
University of Central Oklahoma W

Oregon

Western Oregon University W

Pennsylvania

California University of Pennsylvania W
Cheyney University of Pennsylvania W
Clarion University of Pennsylvania W
East Stroudsburg University of Pennsylvania
Edinboro University of Pennsylvania W
Gannon University W
Holy Family University W
Indiana University of Pennsylvania W
Kutztown University of Pennsylvania W
Lock Haven University of Pennsylvania W
Mercyhurst College
Millersville University of Pennsylvania W
Philadelphia University W
Shippensburg University of Pennsylvania W
Slippery Rock University of Pennsylvania W
University of Pittsburgh
Johnstown W
University of the Sciences in Philadelphia W
West Chester University of Pennsylvania W

Puerto Rico

University of Puerto Rico
Bayamon University College
Cayey University College
Mayaguez
Rio Piedras

Rhode Island

Bryant University W

South Carolina

Anderson University W
Benedict College W
Claflin University W
Coker College W
Converse College W
Francis Marion University W
Lander University W
Limestone College W
Newberry College W
North Greenville College W
Presbyterian College W
University of South Carolina
Aiken W
Upstate W

South Dakota

Augustana College W
Northern State University W
South Dakota State University W
University of South Dakota W

Tennessee

Carson-Newman College W
Christian Brothers University W
LeMoyne-Owen College W
Lincoln Memorial University W
Tusculum College W

Texas

Abilene Christian University W
Angelo State University W
Dallas Baptist University W
Midwestern State University W
St. Edward's University W
St. Mary's University W
Tarleton State University W
Texas A&M University
Commerce W
Kingsville W
Texas Woman's University W

University of the Incarnate Word W
West Texas A&M University W

Vermont
Green Mountain College W
St. Michael's College W

Virginia
St. Paul's College W
Virginia State University W
Virginia Union University W

Washington
Central Washington University W
Saint Martin's University W
Seattle Pacific University W
Seattle University W
Western Washington University W

West Virginia
Alderson-Broaddus College W
Bluefield State College W
Concord University W
Davis and Elkins College W
Glenville State College W
Ohio Valley University W
Salem International University W
Shepherd University W
University of Charleston W
West Liberty State College W
West Virginia State University W
West Virginia University Institute of Technology W
West Virginia Wesleyan College W
Wheeling Jesuit University W

Wisconsin
University of Wisconsin
Parkside W

Volleyball Division III

Alabama
Huntingdon College W

Arkansas
Hendrix College W

California
California Institute of Technology W
California Lutheran University W
California State University
East Bay W
Chapman University W
Claremont McKenna College W
Menlo College W
Mills College W
Occidental College W
Pomona College W
University of California
Santa Cruz
University of La Verne W
University of Redlands W
Whittier College W

Colorado
Colorado College W

Connecticut
Albertus Magnus College W
Connecticut College W
Eastern Connecticut State University W
Mitchell College W
St. Joseph College W
Trinity College W
United States Coast Guard Academy W
Wesleyan University W
Western Connecticut State University W

Delaware
Wesley College W

District of Columbia
Catholic University of America W
Gallaudet University W
Trinity University W

Georgia
Agnes Scott College W
Emory University W
LaGrange College W
Oglethorpe University W
Piedmont College W
Spelman College W
Wesleyan College W

Illinois
Augustana College W
Aurora University W
Benedictine University W
Blackburn College W
Concordia University W
Dominican University W
Elmhurst College W
Eureka College W
Greenville College W
Illinois College W
Illinois Wesleyan University W
Knox College W
Lake Forest College W
MacMurray College W
Millikin University W
Monmouth College W
North Central College W
North Park University W
Principia College W
Rockford College W
University of Chicago W
Wheaton College W

Indiana
Anderson University W
DePauw University W
Earlham College W
Franklin College W
Hanover College W
Manchester College W
Rose-Hulman Institute of Technology W
Saint Mary's College W
Tri-State University W

Iowa
Buena Vista University W
Central College W
Clarke College
Coe College W
Cornell College W
Grinnell College W
Loras College W
Luther College W
Simpson College W
University of Dubuque W
Wartburg College W

Kentucky
Centre College W
Thomas More College W
Transylvania University W

Maine
Bates College W
Bowdoin College W
Colby College W
Husson College W
Maine Maritime Academy W
St. Joseph's College W
Thomas College W
University of Maine
Farmington W
Presque Isle W
University of New England W
University of Southern Maine W

Maryland
College of Notre Dame of Maryland W
Frostburg State University W
Goucher College W
Hood College W
Johns Hopkins University W
McDaniel College W
St. Mary's College of Maryland W
Salisbury University W
Villa Julie College
Washington College W

Massachusetts
Amherst College W
Anna Maria College W
Babson College W
Bay Path College W
Becker College W
Brandeis University W
Bridgewater State College W
Clark University W
Eastern Nazarene College W
Elms College
Emerson College W
Emmanuel College
Endicott College
Framingham State College W
Gordon College W
Lasell College
Lesley University
Massachusetts College of Liberal Arts W
Massachusetts Institute of Technology
Massachusetts Maritime Academy W
Mount Holyoke College W
Mount Ida College
Newbury College
Pine Manor College W
Regis College W
Salem State College W
Simmons College W
Smith College W
Springfield College
Suffolk University W
Tufts University W
University of Massachusetts
Boston W
Dartmouth W
Wellesley College W
Wentworth Institute of Technology
Western New England College W
Westfield State College W
Wheaton College W
Williams College W
Worcester Polytechnic Institute W
Worcester State College W

Michigan
Adrian College W
Albion College W
Alma College W
Calvin College W
Finlandia University W
Hope College W
Kalamazoo College W
Olivet College W

Minnesota
Augsburg College W
Bethel University W
Carleton College W
College of St. Benedict W
College of St. Catherine W
College of St. Scholastica W
Concordia College: Moorhead W
Crown College W
Gustavus Adolphus College W
Hamline University W
Macalester College W
Martin Luther College W
North Central University W
Northwestern College W
St. Mary's University of Minnesota W
St. Olaf College W
University of St. Thomas W

Mississippi
Millsaps College W
Mississippi College W
Rust College W

Missouri
Fontbonne University W
Maryville University of Saint Louis W
Washington University in St. Louis W
Webster University W
Westminster College W

Nebraska
Nebraska Wesleyan University W

New Hampshire
Colby-Sawyer College W
Daniel Webster College W
Keene State College W
Plymouth State University W
Rivier College

New Jersey
Centenary College W
College of St. Elizabeth W
Fairleigh Dickinson University
College at Florham W
Kean University W
Montclair State University W
New Jersey City University
Ramapo College of New Jersey
Richard Stockton College of New Jersey W
Rowan University W
Rutgers, The State University of New Jersey
Camden Regional Campus W
Newark Regional Campus W
Stevens Institute of Technology
William Paterson University of New Jersey W

New York
Alfred University W
Bard College
Cazenovia College W
City University of New York
Baruch College
Brooklyn College
City College
College of Staten Island W
Hunter College
John Jay College of Criminal Justice W
Lehman College
Medgar Evers College
New York City College of Technology
York College
Clarkson University W
College of Mount St. Vincent
College of New Rochelle W
D'Youville College
Elmira College W
Hamilton College W
Hartwick College W
Hilbert College
Ithaca College W
Keuka College W
Medaille College
Mount St. Mary College W
Nazareth College of Rochester W
New York University
Polytechnic University
Rochester Institute of Technology W
Russell Sage College W
St. John Fisher College W
St. Joseph's College: Suffolk Campus W
St. Lawrence University W
Skidmore College W
State University of New York
College at Brockport W
College at Buffalo W
College at Cortland W
College at Fredonia W
College at Geneseo W
College at Old Westbury W
College at Oneonta W
College at Plattsburgh W
College at Potsdam W
Farmingdale W
Institute of Technology at Utica/Rome W
Maritime College W
New Paltz
Oswego W
Purchase
Union College W
United States Merchant Marine Academy W
University of Rochester W
Utica College W
Vassar College
Yeshiva University M

North Carolina
Chowan College W
Greensboro College W
Guilford College W
Meredith College W
Methodist College W
North Carolina Wesleyan College W
Peace College W
Salem College W

Ohio
Baldwin-Wallace College W
Bluffton University W
Capital University W
Case Western Reserve University W
College of Mount St. Joseph W
College of Wooster W
Defiance College W
Denison University W
Heidelberg College W
Hiram College W
John Carroll University W
Kenyon College W
Lake Erie College W
Marietta College W
Mount Union College W
Muskingum College W
Oberlin College W
Ohio Northern University W
Ohio Wesleyan University W
Otterbein College W
Wilmington College W
Wittenberg University W

Oregon
George Fox University W
Lewis & Clark College W
Linfield College W
Pacific University W
Willamette University W

Pennsylvania
Albright College W
Allegheny College W
Alvernia College W
Arcadia University W
Baptist Bible College of Pennsylvania
Bryn Mawr College W
Cabrini College W
Carnegie Mellon University W
Cedar Crest College W
Chatham College W
Chestnut Hill College W
College Misericordia W
Delaware Valley College W
DeSales University W
Dickinson College W
Eastern University W
Elizabethtown College W
Franklin & Marshall College W

Gettysburg College W
Grove City College W
Gwynedd-Mercy College W
Haverford College W
Immaculata University W
Juniata College
Keystone College W
King's College W
La Roche College W
Lebanon Valley College W
Lincoln University W
Lycoming College W
Marywood University W
Messiah College W
Moravian College W
Mount Aloysius College W
Muhlenberg College W
Neumann College W
Penn State
Altoona W
Berks W
Erie, The Behrend College W
Philadelphia Biblical University
Rosemont College W
Susquehanna University W
Swarthmore College W
Thiel College W
University of Pittsburgh
Bradford W
Greensburg W
University of Scranton W
Ursinus College W
Washington and Jefferson College W
Waynesburg College W
Westminster College W
Widener University W
Wilkes University W
Wilson College W
York College of Pennsylvania W

Rhode Island
Johnson & Wales University
Rhode Island College W
Roger Williams University W
Salve Regina University W

South Dakota
Presentation College W

Tennessee
Fisk University W
Maryville College W
Rhodes College W
University of the South W

Texas
Austin College W
Concordia University at Austin W
East Texas Baptist University W
Hardin-Simmons University W
Howard Payne University W
LeTourneau University W
McMurry University W
Schreiner University W
Southwestern University W
Sul Ross State University W
Texas Lutheran University W
Trinity University W
University of Dallas W
University of Mary Hardin-Baylor W
University of Texas
Dallas W
Tyler W

Vermont
Castleton State College W
Middlebury College W
Southern Vermont College

Virginia
Averett University W
Bridgewater College W
Christopher Newport University W
Eastern Mennonite University
Emory & Henry College W
Ferrum College W
Hollins University W
Lynchburg College W
Mary Baldwin College W
Marymount University W
Randolph-Macon College W
Randolph-Macon Woman's College W
Roanoke College W
Shenandoah University W
Sweet Briar College W
University of Mary Washington W
Virginia Wesleyan College W
Washington and Lee University W

Washington
Pacific Lutheran University W
University of Puget Sound W
Whitman College W
Whitworth College W

West Virginia
Bethany College W

Wisconsin
Alverno College W
Beloit College W
Carroll College W
Carthage College
Concordia University Wisconsin W
Edgewood College W
Lakeland College W
Lawrence University W
Maranatha Baptist Bible College W
Marian College of Fond du Lac W
Milwaukee School of Engineering
Mount Mary College W
Northland College W
Ripon College W
St. Norbert College W
University of Wisconsin
Eau Claire W
La Crosse W
Oshkosh W
Platteville W
River Falls W
Stevens Point W
Stout W
Superior W
Whitewater W
Wisconsin Lutheran College W

Water polo Division I

California
California State University
Long Beach M
Loyola Marymount University M
Pepperdine University M
Santa Clara University M
Stanford University M
University of California
Berkeley M
Irvine M
Los Angeles M
Santa Barbara M
University of Southern California M
University of the Pacific M

Colorado
United States Air Force Academy M

District of Columbia
George Washington University M

Maryland
United States Naval Academy M

Massachusetts
Harvard College M

New Jersey
Princeton University M

New York
Fordham University M
Iona College M
St. Francis College M

Pennsylvania
Bucknell University M

Rhode Island
Brown University M

Water polo Division II

California
University of California
Davis M
San Diego M

Hawaii
Brigham Young University-Hawaii M
Chaminade University of Honolulu M

New York
City University of New York
Queens College M

Pennsylvania
Gannon University M
Mercyhurst College M
Slippery Rock University of Pennsylvania M

West Virginia
Salem International University M

Water polo Division III

California
California Institute of Technology M
California Lutheran University M
Chapman University M
Claremont McKenna College M
Occidental College M
Pitzer College M
Pomona College M
University of California
Santa Cruz M
University of La Verne M
University of Redlands M
Whittier College M

Connecticut
Connecticut College M

Maryland
Johns Hopkins University M

Massachusetts
Massachusetts Institute of Technology M

Pennsylvania
Penn State
Erie, The Behrend College M
Washington and Jefferson College M

Wisconsin
Carthage College M

Wrestling Division I

Arizona
Arizona State University M

California
California Polytechnic State University: San Luis Obispo M
California State University
Bakersfield M
Fresno M
Fullerton M
Stanford University M
University of California
Davis M

Colorado
United States Air Force Academy M

Connecticut
Sacred Heart University M

Delaware
Delaware State University M

District of Columbia
American University M

Idaho
Boise State University M

Illinois
Eastern Illinois University M
Northern Illinois University M
Northwestern University M
University of Illinois
Urbana-Champaign M

Indiana
Indiana University
Bloomington M
Purdue University M

Iowa
Iowa State University M
University of Iowa M
University of Northern Iowa M

Maryland
United States Naval Academy M
University of Maryland
College Park M

Massachusetts
Boston University M
Harvard College M

Michigan
Central Michigan University M
Eastern Michigan University M
Michigan State University M
University of Michigan M

Minnesota
University of Minnesota
Twin Cities M

Missouri
University of Missouri
Columbia M

Nebraska
University of Nebraska
Lincoln M

New Jersey
Princeton University M
Rider University M
Rutgers, The State University of New Jersey
New Brunswick Regional Campus M

New York
Columbia University
Columbia College M
Cornell University M
Hofstra University M
State University of New York
Binghamton M
Buffalo M
United States Military Academy M
Wagner College M

North Carolina
Appalachian State University M
Campbell University M
Davidson College M
Duke University M
Gardner-Webb University M
North Carolina State University M
University of North Carolina
Chapel Hill M
Greensboro M

Ohio
Cleveland State University M
Kent State University M
Ohio State University
Columbus Campus M
Ohio University M

Oklahoma
Oklahoma State University M
University of Oklahoma M

Oregon
Oregon State University M
Portland State University M
University of Oregon M

Pennsylvania
Bloomsburg University of Pennsylvania M
Bucknell University M
Clarion University of Pennsylvania M
Drexel University M
Duquesne University M
East Stroudsburg University of Pennsylvania M
Edinboro University of Pennsylvania M
Franklin & Marshall College M
Lehigh University M
Lock Haven University of Pennsylvania M
Millersville University of Pennsylvania M
Penn State
University Park M
Slippery Rock University of Pennsylvania M
University of Pennsylvania M
University of Pittsburgh M

Rhode Island
Brown University M

South Carolina
The Citadel M

Tennessee
University of Tennessee
Chattanooga M

Utah
Utah Valley State College M

Virginia
George Mason University M
James Madison University M
Old Dominion University M
University of Virginia M
Virginia Military Institute M
Virginia Polytechnic Institute and State University M

West Virginia
West Virginia University M

Wisconsin
University of Wisconsin
Madison M

Wyoming
University of Wyoming M

Wrestling Division II

California
San Francisco State University M

Colorado
Adams State College M
Colorado School of Mines M
University of Northern Colorado M
Western State College of Colorado M

Illinois
Southern Illinois University
Edwardsville M

Indiana
University of Indianapolis M

Iowa
Upper Iowa University M

Kansas
Fort Hays State University M

Massachusetts
American International College M

Minnesota
Minnesota State University
Mankato M
Moorhead M
St. Cloud State University M
Southwest Minnesota State
University M

Missouri
Central Missouri State University
M
Truman State University M

Nebraska
Chadron State College M
University of Nebraska
Kearney M
Omaha M

New Mexico
New Mexico Highlands
University M

North Carolina
Belmont Abbey College M
University of North Carolina
Pembroke M

North Dakota
North Dakota State University M

Ohio
Ashland University M
University of Findlay M

Oklahoma
University of Central Oklahoma
M

Pennsylvania
Gannon University M
Kutztown University of
Pennsylvania M
Mercyhurst College M
Shippensburg University of
Pennsylvania M
University of Pittsburgh
Johnstown M

Puerto Rico
University of Puerto Rico
Bayamon University College
M
Mayaguez M

South Carolina
Anderson University M
Limestone College M
Newberry College M

South Dakota
Augustana College M
Northern State University M
South Dakota State University M

Tennessee
Carson-Newman College M

West Virginia
West Liberty State College M

Wisconsin
University of Wisconsin
Parkside M

Wrestling Division III

California
Menlo College M

Connecticut
Trinity College M
United States Coast Guard
Academy M
Wesleyan University M

Illinois
Augustana College M
Elmhurst College M
Illinois College M
Knox College M
MacMurray College M
Millikin University M
North Central College M
University of Chicago M
Wheaton College M

Indiana
Manchester College M
Rose-Hulman Institute of
Technology M
Tri-State University M
Wabash College M

Iowa
Buena Vista University M
Central College M
Coe College M
Cornell College M
Loras College M
Luther College M
Simpson College M
University of Dubuque M
Wartburg College M

Maine
University of Southern Maine M

Maryland
Johns Hopkins University M
McDaniel College M

Massachusetts
Bridgewater State College M
Massachusetts Institute of
Technology M
Springfield College M
Western New England College M
Williams College M
Worcester Polytechnic Institute M

Michigan
Olivet College M

Minnesota
Augsburg College M
Concordia College: Moorhead M
St. John's University M
St. Olaf College M

New Hampshire
Plymouth State University M

New Jersey
Centenary College M
The College of New Jersey M
Montclair State University M
Stevens Institute of Technology M

New York
City University of New York
Hunter College M
Ithaca College M
New York University M
Rochester Institute of Technology
M
State University of New York
College at Brockport M
College at Cortland M
College at Oneonta M
Maritime College M
Oswego M
United States Merchant Marine
Academy M
Yeshiva University M

Ohio
Baldwin-Wallace College M
Case Western Reserve University
M
College of Mount St. Joseph M
Heidelberg College M
John Carroll University M
Mount Union College M
Muskingum College M
Ohio Northern University M
Wilmington College M

Oregon
Pacific University M

Pennsylvania
Albright College M
Delaware Valley College M
Elizabethtown College M
Gettysburg College M
King's College M
Lycoming College M
Messiah College M
Muhlenberg College M
Thiel College M
University of Scranton M
Ursinus College M
Washington and Jefferson College
M
Waynesburg College M
Wilkes University M
York College of Pennsylvania M

Rhode Island
Johnson & Wales University M
Rhode Island College M
Roger Williams University M

Vermont
Norwich University M

Virginia
Washington and Lee University M

Wisconsin
Concordia University Wisconsin
M
Lakeland College M
Lawrence University M
Maranatha Baptist Bible College
M
Milwaukee School of Engineering
M
University of Wisconsin
Eau Claire M
La Crosse M
Oshkosh M
Platteville M
Stevens Point M
Whitewater M

Alphabetical Index

Tables and Indexes

Tables and Indexes

Tables and Indexes

Tables and Indexes

Tables and Indexes

Tables and Indexes

Also Available from the College Board

The College Board Book of Majors, 2nd Edition

What's the major for you? Where can you study it? In this book, 180 college professors describe the majors they teach: what you'll study, careers the major can lead to, and how to prepare for the major in high school. Includes listings showing which colleges offer each of 900 majors, and at what degree level.

1,250 pages, paperbound
ISBN 0-87447-765-4
$24.95

The College Board Guide to Getting Financial Aid 2007

This step-by-step guide tells you how to get aid, when to apply, and what kinds of aid to expect from colleges. Includes a planning calendar, tips from college financial aid officers, and indexes showing which colleges offer merit scholarships for your interests.

1,000 pages, paperbound
ISBN 0-87447-766-2
$19.95

The College Board Scholarship Handbook 2007

This no-nonsense guide speeds you straight to scholarships targeted to who you are, where you live, and what you want to study. Includes detailed profiles of more than 2,100 scholarship, internship, and loan programs.

600 pages, paperbound
ISBN 0-87447-767-0
$27.95

The College Application Essay, Revised Edition

by Sarah Myers McGinty

Trying to find a topic for your application essay? Former admissions dean Sarah Myers McGinty shares strategies that will help you stand out from the crowd. Includes critiqued sample essays written by real students, jump starts for writer's block, and a chapter for your parents that explains their role in the process.

160 pages, paperbound
ISBN 0-87447-711-5
$15.95

Campus Visits & College Interviews, 2nd Edition

by Zola Dincin Schneider

Visiting campuses and talking to admissions deans is a great way to learn more about which colleges are right for you. Experienced school counselor Zola Dincin Schneider shows you how to make the most of your visit and make a good impression during interviews. Includes interview tips for the shy.

140 pages, paperbound
ISBN 0-87447-675-5
$12.95

CollegeBoard
connect to college success™

Available wherever books are sold.
Distributed by Holtzbrinck Publishers, Inc.